# WORLD CHRISTIAN TRENDS,
# AD 30-AD 2200

# WORLD CHRISTIAN TRENDS AD 30-AD 2200

## Interpreting the annual Christian megacensus

David B. Barrett
Todd M. Johnson

Associate Editors:
Christopher R. Guidry
Peter F. Crossing

WILLIAM CAREY LIBRARY
Pasadena, California

2001

For Rights and Permissions contact the Publisher:
William Carey Library
P.O. Box 40129
Pasadena, California 91114
Phone (626) 798-0819
ISBN 0-87808-608-0

Library of Congress Cataloging-in-Publication Data

World Christian trends, AD 30-AD 2200 : interpreting the annual Christian megacensus /
David B. Barrett, Todd M. Johnson ; associate editors, Christopher Guidry, Peter Crossing.
    p.  cm.
  Includes bibliographical references and index.
  ISBN 0-87808-608-0 (alk. paper)
  1. Church history. 2. Christian sects. 3. Ecclesiastical geography. 4. Christianity—Statistics.
  I. Barrett, David B.  II. Johnson, Todd M. III. Guidry, Christopher. IV. Crossing, Peter.

BR145.2.W6/2001
270--dc21

                                                                    2001032550

08  07  06  05  04  03  02  01

Printed in the United States of America
on acid-free paper

# CONTENTS

# AUTHORS, EDITORS, AND CONSULTANTS

**Authors:**
> David B. Barrett, MA, BD, STM, PhD, Research Professor of Missiometrics,
>   Regent University; Hon. Research Adviser, United Bible Societies
> Todd M. Johnson, MA, PhD, YWAM, Director, World Evangelization Research Center;
>   Adjunct Professor, Trinity Evangelical Divinity School

**Editor Emeritus:**
> Sir Kenneth Grubb, CMG, LLD

**Associate Editors:**
> Christopher R. Guidry, BSc, March for Jesus USA, Global Jesus Day
> Peter F. Crossing, BSc, Sydney Centre for World Mission, Australia

**Global Consultants:**
> Tad de Bordenave, Director, Anglican Frontier Missions
> David T.M.P. Dalby, PhD, Director, Observatoire Linguistique, Hebron, Wales
> Paul Eshleman, Director, 'Jesus' Film Project
> V. David Garrison, PhD, Associate Vice-President, International Mission Board, SBC
> David M. Goodenough, European Charismatic Consultation; Founding Director, Cultural
>   Television International
> Joseph Hale, DD, World Methodist Council; past Chairman, Conference of Christian
>   World Communions
> Maurice Harvey, Photojournalist, United Bible Societies
> Willi Henkel OMI, PhD, Vatican Missions Librarian, Pontificia Universita Urbaniana
> Patrick J. St G. Johnstone, *Operation World*, WEC International
> Jan A.B. Jongeneel, ThD, Professor of Missiology, University of Utrecht
> Sebastian Karotemprel SDB, DD, Consultor, Sacred Congregation for the Evangelization of
>   Peoples, Rome
> John S. Mbiti, PhD, *Evangelische Lexikon für Kirchen;* University of Bern
> J. Gordon Melton, PhD, Director, Institute for the Study of American Religion
> Samuel H. Moffett, PhD, Emeritus Professor of Missions, Princeton Theological Seminary
> Bishop Stephen C. Neill, DD, Universities of Hamburg, Nairobi, and Oxford
> H. Vinson Synan, PhD, Professor & Dean of Divinity, Regent University
> David W. Virtue, Editor, Virtuosity Digest global e-mail bulletin
> Ralph D. Winter, PhD, Founder, United States Center for World Mission

**Chief Photographers:**
> Maurice Harvey, David B. Barrett

**Bibliographers:**
> Stuart Baskin PhD, Mark Dubis PhD, Craig A. Buchanan BA

**Research and compilation by:**
> World Evangelization Research Center (WERC, begun Nairobi, 1965)
> Global Evangelization Movement (GEM, begun Richmond, Virginia, 1985)

# COLLABORATORS AND CONTRIBUTORS

This listing acknowledges the collaboration and contribution of a large number of experts or specialists indicated by their area of specialization or contribution given in parentheses. It excludes this volume's global consultants and production staff who have been listed on the previous page. The listing below, alphabetically by surname, includes all those assisting with the *World Christian encyclopedia/World Christian trends/World Christian database* project at any stage from 1970 to AD 2001.

Names of collaborators and contributors listed below are followed in most cases by initials of their organization or style at the time of their contribution (see Index of Christian Abbreviations, Acronyms and Initials), or their profession, and in parentheses the country or countries of their contribution, expertise or residence, or in a few cases their subject. The listing excludes a number of experts who have requested anonymity, but includes a few requested pseudonyms.

Bishop I.A. Adetosoye, NAAC Aladura (Nigeria)
Dr Tokunboh Adeyemo, AEA (Nigeria)
Patience Ahmed, CAPRO (Nigeria)
S. Vasantharaj Albert, CGRC (India)
Rev. Dr Jean Albertini, Aumonier Militaire (Niger)
Judy Alexanian (composition)
Rev. Canon Roger G. Allison, MBE (Israel)
Bishop Oliver C. Allison, CMS (Sudan)
Rev. Dr Johannes Althausen (German DR)
Rev. S. G. Andrews (Fiji)
Susan H. Andrews, CPA (Finance)
Rev. Charles Antoine, DIAL (Brazil)
Paul Arnold (France)
Rev. Dr A. G. Baan, OFM (Indonesia)
Rev. Brian H. Baily, BCC (Botswana)
Gary Baldridge, CBF (Azerbaijan)
J. F. Bango, sociologist (Hungary, Romania)
Rev. E. E. Barde, EEM (Morocco)
Dr John Barrett (UK)
Pam Barrett (Kenya)
Rev. P. Basile, OFM Cap (Comoros)
Albert Bastenier, CRSR (Belgium)
Peter Bayes, FEBA (UK)
Bertha Beachy, EMBMC (Somalia)
Nadia Benjamin, GICC (Grenada)
Dr Walter W. Benjamin (USA)
Rev. Joseph-Roger de Benoist, WF (Benin)
Rev. Augusto Beuzeville F. (Peru)
Rev. William E. Biernatzki, SJ (N. & S. Korea)
Dr R. Biernazek (Poland)
Gordon Bishop (Niger)
Rev. Joseph L. Blackett (Belize)
Dr C. Boeke, Interreligio (Netherlands)
Dr Hugo Bogensberger, IKS (Austria)
Rev. A. Boland (Laos, Thailand)
Jean-Charles Bonenfant (Canada)
Professor David J. Bosch, UNISA (South Africa)
Rev. Wallace Boulton, CMS (UK)
Rev. Dr Michael A. Bourdeaux, Keston College
Msgr J. E. Bourke, FCEO (Australia)
Rev. Malcolm R. Bradshaw, OMF (Singapore)
Rev. W. G. M. Brandful, CCG (Ghana)
Dr Rodolphe A. Bréchet, SAM (Angola)
Huguette Breil (Morocco)
Rev. H. Briand, FMI (St Lucia)
Leslie Brierley, IRRO/WEC (Guinea Bissau)
Helen Brown, TWR (UK)
Rev. Canon Jean Bruls, *Eglise Vivante*
Rev. Elden M. Buck, UCC (Pacific Islands)
Dr. Allan Buckman, LCMS (Missiology)
Dr Aldo Büntig (Argentina)
Professor Stanley Burgess (NIDPCM)
Rev. Canon Samuel R. Burgoyne, UMN (Nepal)
Dr Edgar H. Burks, SBC (Nigeria)
Rev. Palle Burla (Faeroe Islands)
Rev. A. J. Butler (Botswana)
Rev. James Byrne, SMA (Liberia)
Rev. Pierre Cadier, PEMS (Dahomey/Benin)
Rev. Giuseppe Caffaratto (Italy)
Bishop Michel Callens, WF (Tunisia)
Rev. Michael Campbell-Johnston, SJ (Guyana)
Rev. Humberto Capo, CEE (Spain)
Bishop Edmund M. H. Capper, CPSA (St Helena)
Archdeacon Jack Cattell (Bermuda)
Rev. Dr Rafael Cepeda, CIEC (Cuba)
Rev. Carlos Manuel de Cespedes, CEC (Cuba)

Rev. Ricardo Cetrulo, SJ, CER (Uruguay)
Rev. Marc Chambron, LWF (France)
Dr Maxwell Charlesworth, ANU (Australia)
Rev. F. E. Charman (St Kitts-Nevis-Anguilla)
Carlos Chiesa (Argentina)
Jose Chipenda, WSCF (Angola)
Franco Chittolina, sociologist (Italy)
Msgr. Damian Ciacci (Saudi Arabia, Gulf)
Sister Peter Claver, OP, CARA (USA)
William Cleveland, *Encyclopaedia Britannica*
Steve and Elisabeth Cochrane, YWAM (India)
Geraldine Coldham, BFBS (Names for God)
Rev. Tom S. Colvin, CSC/CCM (Malawi)
Calvin and Carol Conkey, YWAM (Indonesia)
Rev. W. H. Conrad (Costa Rica)
Dr Frank L. Cooley, DGI (Indonesia)
Rev. Jean Corbon (Lebanon)
Rev. Richard G. Cote, OMI (Lesotho)
Rev. J. B. D. Cotter (Bahrain)
Very Rev. W. Frank Curtis, C of E (UK)
Rev. Dr Marthinus L. Daneel, AICC (Zimbabwe)
Bishop Michel Darmancier, SM (Wallis & Futuna Is)
Nabih Kamel David (Egypt)
Brother Joseph M. Davis, SM, NOBC (USA)
Edward R. Dayton, MARC
John Dean, UBS (Scripture distribution)
Rev. M. Defresne (Japan)
Rev. Natale Del Mistro (Iran)
Rev. Dr Raymond Deniel, INADES (Upper Volta)
Georges Deroy, FERES (Louvain)
Dr Duncan Derrett (India)
Rev. M. Dhavamony, SJ (India)
Dr F. Dingjan (Netherlands)
Rev. Max Dominique, CSSp (Central African Rep)
Bep Donatz, YWAM (Research)
Sherri Doty, AOG (archives)
Rev. T. F. Doust, MMS (Benin)
Kimberly Doyle (programming)
Rev. du Noyer, BLASC (Madagascar)
Rev. Willehad Paul Eckert (FR Germany)
Bishop Sigurbjörn Einarsson (Iceland)
Mercedes Massi Elizalde (Argentina)
Edward A. Elliott, Living Bibles (USA)
M. F. Elliott-Binns, General Synod C of E (UK)
Rev. Edgar J. Elliston, CMF (Ethiopia)
Rev. Eulogio V. Enrique, SJ, CBIES (Philippines)
Dr Juan Estruch (Spain)
Rev. Gareth M. Evans, *Sobornost* (UK)
Paul Filidis, YWAM (Research)
Rev. John B. Finger (Bahamas)
Rev. Guillermo Flores (Guatemala)
Msgr. Jean Foradaris (Cyprus)
Rev. A. D. Fowler (Brunei)
Dr David A. Fraser, MARC
Bishop Hendrik Hubert Frehen, SMM (Iceland)
Joachim W. H. Freitag, WEC (Mauritania)
Gregory Fritz, Caleb Project (Logistics)
L. Andrew Friend (Mozambique)
Rev. Paul D. Fueter (Switzerland)
Ledo. Euclides J. Fuguet, CEV (Venezuela)
Bishop Hyancinthe Gad (Greece)
George Gallup, Jr., AIPO (Polls)
Rev. Anthony M. Gann, USPG (Lesotho)
Jay Gary (Futuristics)
Bishop Manuel J. Gaxiola, CINCOMEX (Mexico)
Helmut Geller, sociologist (FR Germany)

Pastor Dr Roswith Gerloff (UK Black churches)
Rev. Jean-Paul Gladu, CSC (Haiti)
Randy Gloyd, CCCI (Logistics)
Dr Walter Goddijn (Netherlands)
Bishop William Gomes (India)
Rev. Dr José-Maria Gonzalez-Ruiz, SJ (Spain)
Lee Grady, *Charisma Magazine*
D. Bruce Graham (India)
Rev. P. Grégoire, OP (Denmark)
Rev. Paul Grillou, WF, ISTR (France)
Sir Kenneth Grubb, CMG, LLD
Rev. Guilbert Guérin, SJ (China/Taiwan)
Jeanine Guidry (Photography)
Bishop R. L. Guilly, SJ (Guyana)
Dr Berndt Gustafsson, RIS (Sweden)
Graeme Hackworth, YWAM (India)
Rev. Dr J. Harry Haines, UMC (PR China)
Rev. Joseph Hajjar, Melkite Patriarchate (Syria)
Stefan Hall, YWAM (Systems)
Rev. Richard Haller (Switzerland)
Rev. E. I. Hamelberg, CSSp (Sierra Leone)
Rev. Clive Handford, JEM (Syria)
Dr W. E. Ted Haney, FEBC (USA)
Emily Haney (composition)
Rev. James T. Hardyman, LMS (Madagascar)
Rev. Patricia J. Harrison, CRC (Australia)
Robert W. Harvie, UPCUSA (India)
Bishop Ralph P. Hatendi, UBS (Zambia)
Paul Hattaway, AMO (China)
Rev. Stephen Hayes, CPSA (Namibia)
Bishop Edward G. Haynsworth, ECUSA (Nicaragua)
Archdeacon F. M. M. Haythornthwaite (Namibia)
Rev. Roger E. Hedlund, CBFMS/CBI (Italy, India)
Rev. André Heiderscheid (Luxembourg)
Rev. Jean Heinrichs, SJ (Sikkim)
Dr Guy Hermet (Spain)
Javier Solis Herrera (Costa Rica)
Dr Horst Herrmann (FR Germany)
John Hickey, sociologist (UK)
Rev. John A. Hinchey, SJ (Cayman Islands)
Bishop H. Hofmann, OFM Cap (Djibouti)
Nanci K. Hogan, YWAM (Cambodia)
Dr Sibenda M. Holsteyn, CCN (Netherlands)
Dr James D. Holway, Islam in Africa
Rev. Dr T. Floyd Honey, CCC (Canada)
Rev. Dr Norman A. Horner, UPCUSA (Lebanon)
Rev. John F. Hotchkin, NCCB (USA)
Rev. Dr François Houtart, FERES (Louvain)
Dr Mary Linda Hronek, WERC (Kenya)
Rev. C. Hulsen, SMA (Ghana)
Rev. Robert A. Humphreys (Australia)
Dr R. G. W. Huysmans (Netherlands)
Rev. Dr David Hynd, CBE (Swaziland)
Rev. Xavier Jacob, AA (Turkey)
E. Michael Jaffarian, CBI (Strategies)
Rev. Gustavo Amigo Jansen, SJ (Dominican Rep)
S. J. Jegasothy, NCCSL (Sri Lanka)
Rev. Alfred E. Johnson, WEC (Venezuela)
R. Boyd Johnson, MARC (USA)
Rev. Bernard Joinet, WF, TPRI (Tanzania)
Rev. Enrique Jorda, SJ, ISET (Bolivia)
François Joyaux (PR China)
Rev. Jean Julien (Martinique)
Basile Jultsis (Greece)
Janet Kalven (USA)
Lusanga Kanyinda (Zaire)

Rev. John Kelly (St Helena)
Rev. Jospeh Kelly, CSSp, AMECEA (Kenya)
Dr Jocelyn C. Kelsey (UK)
Oberkirchenrat Claus Kemper, EKD (FR Germany)
Sister Anne Marie Kernéis, UISG (Italy)
Rev. Pierre Kerzoncuf, OMI (Channel Islands)
Rev. John Key, MCC (Papua New Guinea)
Dr A. Khoury (FR Germany)
Pastor R. Buana Kibongi, EEC (Congo)
Rev. Karlo Kjaer, ELFD (Denmark)
Dr A. M. J. Kloosterman (Cook Islands)
Sydney Knightley, CMS (layout)
Josip Kolanovic (Yugoslavia)
Dr Elfriede Kreuzeder, ECCA (Austria)
Alexei Krindatch (Russian Orthodoxy)
George T. Kurian (Encyclopedias)
Rev. Philip F. Kurts, SJ (Papua New Guinea)
Rev. Oscar Lacroix (Guadeloupe)
Rev. Victor A. Lamont (UK; photographic)
Dr Aldo Landi (Italy)
Gordon Landreth, EAGB (UK)
Rev. Gilles Langevin, SJ (Canada)
Bishop Neville Langford-Smith, CMS (Australia)
Rev. Bill Lasley (Senegal)
Rev. Professor René Laurentin, OP (Evangelization)
Rev. Angelo S. Lazzarotto, PIME (PR China)
Roger Lee, SDA (Macau)
Rev. A. Lemaire, OP (Finland)
Raymond Lemieux, CRSR (Canada)
Rev. James Lennon, RDU (Ireland)
Rev. David Chia-En Liao (Taiwan)
Archdeacon Ralph A. Lindley, ECJME (Qatar, UAE)
Justin D. Long (systems)
Rev. Melvin T. Long (USA)
Emily Kalled Lovell (USA, Canada)
Arthur M. Lundblad, ECZ (Zaire)
Rev. P. Lunot (Mauritania)
Rev. Gilles Lussier, PME (Honduras)
Rev. Finn Lynge, OMI (Greenland)
Rev. Brian J. Macdonald-Milne (Solomon Islands)
Rev. Luiz Machado de Abreu (Mozambique)
Rev. W. Mackey, SJ (Bhutan)
Dr Enrique Miret Magdalena (Spain)
Msgr. J. P. Mahony (Isle of Man)
Eric Maillefer, AEAM (Kenya)
Rev. Canon Dr Josef Majka (Poland)
Rev. Carl Major (Antigua)
Hilkka Malaska, CoN (Finland)
George K. Mambo, AACC (Kenya)
Rev. Edward F. Mann, SJ (Nepal)
Adele Manzi (Lebanon)
Bishop Antonious Markos, OAIC (Egypt)
Jimmy K. Maroney, IMB (Logistics)
Rev. Bill F. Marsters, CICC (Cook Islands)
Dr Marie-Louise Martin, EJCSK (Zaire)
Rev. Antonio Martins (Portugal)
Jonathan Marzeki, ICC (Iran)
Rev. Louis Mascarenhas, OFM, IRSS (Pakistan)
Rev. Dr Joseph Masson, SJ (Missiology)
Kathleen Matchcett, CSRC (USSR)
Senator Gordon Matthews, WHC (Barbados)
Bishop François-Joseph Maurer, CSSp (St Pierre & M)
Rev. J. B. Mayté (Mali)
Rev. Professor Donald A. McGavran, SWM
Donald McGilchrist, The Navigators
Sister Janice McLaughlin, MM (Kenya)
Rev. Noel McNeill, ACOP (Canada)
Rev. Dr Malcolm J. McVeigh, UMC
Marion McVeigh, UMC (Canada)
Rev. Dr Otto Meinardus (Egypt, Greece)
Rev. Clifford S. Michelsen (Cameroon)
Rev. Dr David I. Mitchell (Trinidad & Tobago)
Bishop Michael Moloney, CSSp (Gambia)
Lic. Vital H. Moreno G. (Panama)
Scott Morey, DAI (Sierra Leone)
Rev. Professor Charlie F. D. Moule, Cambridge U.
Lana Moussa (data entry)
Rev. Roger Muller (FTAI)
Rev. José Miguel Munarriz, CEP (Paraguay)

Rev. Paul Munier, MEP (Malaysia, Singapore)
Rev. Edward F. Murphy (Colombia)
Msgr. Amédée Nagapen (Mauritius)
Rev. Albert Nambiaparambil, CMI (India)
Rev. Juhani Natri, FMS (Finland)
Rev. Louis de Nauriois (France)
Bishop Justin Ndandali, CPR (Rwanda)
William A. Needham, MARC (USA)
Rev. Charles A. Nelson (US Virgin Islands)
Rev. Jean Nenonene, EET (Togo)
Dr Arnaldo Nesti (Italy)
Rev. Gilbert Nichols, SBC (Paraguay)
Dr Elisa Juan de Nieves (Puerto Rico)
Paul H. Nilson, ABS (Turkey)
Rev. Dr Loren E. Noren (Hong Kong)
John J. Nquku, LACS (Swaziland)
Rt. Rev. Ildefonso Obama Obono (Equatorial Guinea)
Professor W. R. O'Brien, SBC
Rev. Gilbert W. Olson (Sierra Leone)
Rev. Dr J. M. Ondra (Czechoslovakia)
Rev. Adolphe Ouédraogo, CEHV (Upper Volta)
T. John Padwick, OAIC (Kenya)
Rev. Michel de Paillerets, OP (Sweden)
Rev. Peyton Palmore, III, UCCJ (Japan)
Rev. Angelo Panigati (Afghanistan)
Archbishop Anthony Pantin, CSSp (Trinidad)
Balwant A. M. Paradkar (India)
Rev. Ramon Pardo, OMI (Sahara)
Julia Campos Parise (Uruguay)
Oreste Pesare, ICCRS (Vatican, Renewal)
Rev. Dr. Janos Pasztor (Hungary)
Rev. Celestin Patock, OSA (USSR)
Rev. Zdzislaw Pawlik (Poland)
Oreste Pesare, ICCRS (Vatican)
Dr Howard Peskett, OMF (Statistics)
Rt. Rev. W. L. A. Don Peter (Sri Lanka)
Cardinal Sergio Pignedoli, Roman Curia (Statistics)
Rev. Dave Plummer (Chaplaincies)
Rev. Renato Poblete, SJ (Chile)
Rev. Dr Titus Presler (Zimbabwe)
Rev. John R. Pritchard, MMS (Ivory Coast)
Professor Paul A. Puchkov, Akademii Nauk SSSR
Rev. Pedro Puentes (Chile)
Rev. Roland Quesnel, CSSp (Propaganda data)
Thomas E. Quigley, USCC (USA)
Rev. Jean Rabemanahaka (Comoro Islands)
Rev. J. P. Ramanankilana (Madagascar)
Lic. Manuel R. Gonzalez Ramirez, SJ, IMES (Mexico)
Dr Michael Raske (FR Germany)
Bishop Derek A. Rawcliffe, CPM (New Hebrides)
Rev. Dr William R. Read, UPCUSA (Brazil)
Pastor Piere Regard (Belgium, Luxembourg)
Rev. Dr H. Diether Reimer, EZW (FR Germany)
Reginald E. Reimer, CMA (Viet Nam)
Bishop Charles Reiterer, MHM (Brunei)
Rev. Norman G. Riddle, EBCO (Zaire)
Rev. Istvan Rigo (Hungary)
Dr C. A. Rijk, SIDIC (Italy)
Rev.Antonio Rivera Rodriguez (Puerto Rico)
Jean Robert (pseudonym) (German Democratic Rep)
Glyn Roberts (statistics)
Rev. M. A. Z. Rolston, NCCI (India)
Pastor Jean de Rougemont, AdD (Upper Volta)
André Rousseau, sociologist (France)
François Routhier, CRSR (Canada)
Dr Michael Rowe, U of Glasgow (USSR)
Bishop Jean Rupp (Monaco)
William Ryna, USCC (USA)
Rev. Réginald de Sa, OP, IDEO (Egypt)
Professor Todor Sabev, WCC (Bulgaria)
Luis Alberto Saenz (Costa Rica)
George Salinas (electronic data)
Sister M. B. Salmon, SIDIC (France)
Bishop Samuel, See of St Mark (Egypt)
Rev. Kirkley Caleb Sands (Turks & Caicos Is)
Msgr. Victor San Miguel, OCD (Kuwait)
Rev. Giuseppe Scapino (Italy)
Rev. Joseph B. Schuyler, SJ (Nigeria)
J. Sayer, sociologist (FR Germany)

Rev. Herbert Seignoret, CSSp, AEC (Jamaica)
O.W. Shumaker (programming)
Rev. E. R. Simmons (New Zealand)
Rev. Adrian B. Smith, WF (Zambia)
Gudrun Smith, WCC (Councils)
William W. Smith, FMB, CSI, IMB (China)
Rev. Erwin L. Spruth, LCMS (Papua New Guinea)
Rev. Harvey Staal, RCA (Kuwait, Oman)
Bishop Gunnar Stalsett, LWF (Norway)
Paul Stawasz, UBS (Scripture distribution)
Dr Roland C. Stevenson, UBS (Sudan)
Rev. Fred E. Stock (Pakistan)
Pastor Larry Stockstill (Bethany WPC)
Bishop Daniel Stuyvenberg, SM (Solomon Islands)
Rev. Lloyd Swantz, ELCT (Tanzania)
Pastor K. Tabuariki, SDA (Gilbert & Ellice Is)
Rev. Norman W. Taggart, ICC (Ireland)
Rabbi Marc H. Tannenbaum (USA)
Cardinal Pio Taofinu'u, SM (Western Samoa)
Michael A. Tarrant, WEC (Guinea Bissau)
Rev. David M. Taylor NCCNZ (New Zealand)
Rev. Canon Ronald J. Taylor, CMSNZ (Tanzania)
Bishop Henri Teissier (Algeria)
Dr O. ter Reegen (Netherlands)
Pastor Randall L. Thetford (Guam)
Rev. John Thetgyi, BCC (Burma)
Harvey Thomas, NLEA (UK)
Dr Lars Thunberg (Sweden)
Dr Donald Tinder, New College (Book reviews)
Rev. Canon Benjamin Tonna, SEDOS (Malta)
Rev. Dr T. Michael Traber, WACC (Zimbabwe)
Dr Garry Trompf, Univ. of Sydney (Melanesia)
Rev. Dr Harold W. Turner, PRONERM (UK)
Mady Vaillant, WEC (Upper Volta)
Rev. Roger Velasquez Valle (El Salvador)
Rev. G. van den Asdonk (Malawi)
Larry Vanderaa (West Africa)
Rev. J. Van Hecken, CICM (Mongolia)
Rev. Juan Ramon Vega (El Salvador)
Rev. Rodney Venberg, CLB (Chad)
Dr Ad F. Vermeulen (Netherlands)
Rev. Canon Trevor Verryn, UNISA (South Africa)
Canon Jacques Verscheure, CISR (France)
Rev. Modeste Vesin (Seychelles)
Dr Ignacio Palacios Videla (Argentina)
Dr Ernst K. Vilaghy (Bulgaria)
Jeanne-Françoise Vincent, anthropologist (Congo)
Rev. Edvard Vogt (Norway)
Rev. Paul M. Volz, LCMS (Kenya)
Rev. Dr J. D. J. Waardenburg, WF (Netherlands)
Rev. Professor C. Peter Wagner (Bolivia)
Rev. Peter Wanko (Uganda)
Rick Ward, YWAM (Peoples)
Rev. Wichean Watakeecharoen, CCT (Thailand)
Rev. Stanford A. Webley (Jamaica)
Warren Webster, CBFMS/CBI
Dr Erika Wienzierl, IKZ (Austria)
Benjamin M. Weir (Lebanon)
Dr Martin E. West, SACC (South Africa)
Rev. Francis J. Westoff, MSC (Gilbert & Ellice Is)
Rev. Frank E. Wilcox, UMN (Nepal)
Dr Bryan R. Wilson, All Souls College, Oxford
Dr J. Christy Wilson, Jr. (Afghanistan)
Rev. W. Wipfler, NCCCUSA (Dominican Republic)
Rev. Joseph C. Wold (Liberia)
Rev. Canon James Yui Kok Wong (Singapore)
Chester Woodhall, CCGB (Zambia)
Jean Woods, CMS (Bibliography)
Prälat Wilhelm Wöste (FR Germany)
Sister Gertrude Wright, MMS (Gambia)
Akiko Yamaguchi, NCCJ (Japan)
Rev. Y. Yamatoa (Niue)
Archbishop A. Yannoulatos (Missiology)
Antonio Ybarra, sociologist (Nicaragua)
Msgr L. Zichem, CSSR (Surinam)
Bishop Antonio Silvio Zocchetta (Somalia)
Rev. Francisco Zuluaga, SJ, CIAS (Colombia)

# Preface

In the year 1699, Cambridge mathematician Isaac Newton—often said to be the world's greatest scientific genius ever—published his *Observations upon the Prophecies of Daniel and the Apocalypse of Saint John*. In this book he set the year AD 2000 as the date by which the church should have completed its mission on Earth, at which point Christ would return to inaugurate his Millennial rule. In the subsequent 300 years, hundreds of other renowned scientists have published works on Christianity, identifying themselves similarly as devout and committed believers. The reason for compiling this present *World Christian trends (WCT)* is to explore some of the other close relationships between science and religion, and to discover how these can help to explain the contemporary phenomena of worldwide Christianity and its variegated trends over the last two millennia.

## From scientism to the postmodern context

The authors of this volume are well aware that comprehensive research projects such as this present survey of Christianity have modern Enlightenment roots. Those roots were espoused in 1875 by the editors of the Ninth Edition of *Encyclopaedia Britannica* who wrote, 'The available facts of human history, collected over the widest areas, are carefully coordinated and grouped together, in the hope of ultimately evolving the laws of progress, moral and material, which underlie them, and which help to connect and interpret the whole movement of the race.' Similarly, by the early 20th century, modern scientific and religious sensibilities were largely built on this Enlightenment objectivism or scientism. Their central requirement sought to eliminate the possibility of error by removing all personal aspects from their quest for objective truth.

One of the surprising findings of late 20th-century philosophy is that even natural science is not carried out on objective foundations as assumed by modern thinkers. Perhaps unwittingly, Thomas Kuhn in *The structure of scientific revolutions* provided a pivotal argument against scientific objectivism when he demonstrated, through the use of paradigm shifts, how scientific 'facts' are dependent on theoretical interpretation. Hans Küng later developed this into a taxonomy of 6 major paradigms as an overlay on Christian history. This taxonomy was then adapted by David Bosch in *Transforming mission: paradigm shifts in theology of mission*. The shift from the fifth paradigm 'Enlightenment modern' to the sixth 'Emerging ecumenical postmodern' is where we find ourselves today. In summarizing Kuhn, Bosch writes, 'It is widely accepted today, in all the sciences (natural as well as social), that total objectivity is an illusion, and that knowledge belongs to a community and is influenced by the dynamics operative in such a community.'(p. 185).

For the reader of our materials the message is clear. One should not be overconfident about what the gathering of knowledge can accomplish. Expectations of finding overarching explanations of truth should be lowered. But the remarkable thing that is retained is the human need for understanding. The gathering of vast amounts of data, analyzing and expounding it, and laying it all out in encyclopedic form is a task with a clear role in our postmodern context. Although much of the methodology is laid out in analytic language, there is much that simply cannot be explained. Anathema to moderns, we in a postmodern context can relax a little. We don't have to know everything. There is much room for interpretation and even personal bias. In a real sense, an encyclopedic project like ours can be a celebration of diversity instead of a quest for overarching unity. Evidence of this is abundant throughout this volume. Consider the variety in Christianity's 300 major traditions or 33,800 denominations with its newest manifestations described in Part 6 "Independency". Or the dizzying array of historical vignettes laid out in Part 2 "CosmoChronology". Or the mind-boggling statistics describing the global context in Part 9 "Globalistics". Or, if none of these convinces, let Part 31 "Bibliography" open up a new world of thousands of book titles related to our subject. In all this, surveys of empirical Christianity carve out a unique place between modern certainties and postmodern doubt.

## Science and the study of Christianity

Christianity has long suffered by being characterized as amateur in relation to the social sciences, statistics in particular. While church history and theology are recognized as major disciplines with professional faculties in universities and seminaries, few of their scholars take statistics of religions seriously or do more with them than using them here and there as illustrations. However, there has been a long series describing world Christianity as it actually is, or was—the empirical phenomenon centering on the church's obligation to relate to and to benefit the whole world. A lengthy series of vocal advocates exists, from the Apostolic age right up to the present day.

In fact, two huge bodies of literature have been published over the last 200 years, illuminating the global meaning and objective of Christianity and religion, resulting in 2 contrasting approaches. The present investigation has compiled a list of 600 classics or books on this subject, which are listed and analyzed in Table 14-7. They fall into 2 contrasting but complementary heritages or descriptions or approaches to the study of Christianity and religions.

These 2 vast encyclopedic collections in most cases present their material by means of formal or standardized short entries dealing with one word or concept or name. In some cases, these units may be longer text articles, or statistical tables, or maps, or diagrams. Usually these entries are alphabetically arranged. The listing of a particular book's entries shows the subjects that it understands to be the significant ones.

Each of these 2 collections will now be examined.

## I. COMPARING GLOBAL MISSIONARY STATISTICS

### A lengthy heritage of scholarship on mission

This present volume is descended from a long series of some 200 major surveys, atlases, encyclopedias, and dictionaries dealing with statistics of the Christian world mission. A number have been denominational or confessional; others have been interdenominational or ecumenical. The series begins with Luke's Acts of the Apostles, then the writings of numerous Apostolic Fathers (Greek as well as Latin), notably Eusebius and patriarch John Chrysostom. The first major global survey came from Cosmas Indicopleustes, an intrepid Nestorian theologian and geographer who travelled the world and then, from AD 535 to 547, produced a survey, *Topographia Christiana*, in 12 Books. It contained one of the earliest and most famous of global maps. Little else as systematic or thorough was published during the Dark Ages or the Middle Ages or the Reformation period.

Then in 1630 Francesco Ingoli, secretary of the newly-founded Propaganda Fide in Rome, produced a *Report on the Four Parts of the World*. This was a detailed survey of missionary activity in Africa, America, Asia, and Europe, and the prospects for their evangelization—a masterly document, although devoid of statistics. A century and a half later the modern Protestant missionary movement began. It produced the world's first detailed statistical survey of countries, of Christianity, and of all major world religions— William Carey's 1792 survey, *An enquiry into the obligations of Christians to use means for the conversion of the heathens*. This enumerated global and continental populations, and Christian totals, with remarkable accuracy. From the first, this new Protestant emphasis continued to produce estimates of global statistics, then later ventured into ambitious statistical tables. Further Protestant surveys of this kind were published in 1818, 1823, 1836, 1854, 1888, 1896, and 1900.

In fact, the 19th century produced over a hundred scholars Protestant or Catholic who published extensive missions data thereby inaugurating the independent discipline of missionary surveys and statistics. These scholars and their years of first publication include: C. F. Staudlin 1804, Hall & Newell 1818, J. Wiggers 1842, O. Corsi 1844, J. N. Brown 1844, J. H. Brauer 1847, E. Hawkins 1853, J. C. Lowrie 1854, H. Newcomb 1854, J. L. Aikman 1860, W. B. Boyce 1861, S. J. Neher 1864, P. R. Grundemann 1867 ('the great master of missionary statistics'), R. G. Wilder 1878, T. Christlieb 1880, F. Dobbins 1881, W. F. Bainbridge 1882, J. Croil 1883, A. T. Pierson 1886, G. Hagar 1886, J. Johnston 1888, J. T. Gracey 1889, A. Launay 1890, O. Werner 1890, E. M. Bliss 1891, J. Vahl 1892, J. S. Dennis 1894, P. Barclay 1897, John R. Mott 1900.

Over a hundred more scholars of renown have continued this pursuit of missionary statistics in the 20th century: H. P. Beach 1901, Gustav Warneck 1902, H. A. Krose 1906, K. Streit 1906, W. T. Whitley 1908, Adolf von Harnack 1908, J. P. Lilley 1910, F. W. Schwager 1911, F. E. Daubanton 1911,

J. Schmidlin 1917, R. Streit 1928, K. S. Latourette 1937, K. G. Grubb 1949, J. C. Thiessen 1955, H. Emmerich 1958, R. P. Millot 1960, B. L. Goddard 1967, S. C. Neill 1970, K. Müller 1987, H. Rzepkowski 1992, Z. Stezycki 1992, J. A. B. Jongeneel 1995, W. Kasper 1996, S. B. Bevans 1997, S. M. Burgess 2001, and over 70 other global specialists.

### A stream of world mission atlases, encyclopedias, dictionaries
Over these 2 centuries has thus come a steady stream of world mission atlases, world mission encyclopedias, world mission dictionaries, and global mission surveys. Two remarkable series then evolved, one Protestant and one Catholic. On the Protestant/Anglican/Ecumenical/Evangelical side, the first was the 1844 *Encyclopedia of religious knowledge: Bible, missions*, next 1854 *A cyclopedia of missions: missionary operations throughout the world*, 1860 *Cyclopaedia of Christian missions: their rise, progress, and present position*, followed by the 1891 *Encyclopedia of missions: descriptive, historical, biographical, statistical*. Then in 1901 came *A geography and atlas of Protestant missions*, 1910 *Statistical atlas of Christian missions*, 1912 *Churchman's missionary atlas*, 1916 *World statistics of Christian missions*, 1920 *World survey by the Interchurch World Movement*, 1925 *World missionary atlas*, culminating in the 1938 *Interpretative statistical survey of the world mission of the Christian church*. Among several more recent surveys were the 1967 *Encyclopedia of modern Christian missions*, 1970 *Concise dictionary of the Christian world mission* (translated into German as the 1975 *Lexikon zür Weltmission*), 1982 *World Christian encyclopedia* (1st edition), 1995 *Philosophy, science and theology of mission: a missiological encyclopedia*, 2000 *Evangelical dictionary of world missions*, and 2001 *World Christian encyclopedia* (2nd edition).

On the Roman Catholic side, K. Streit SVD began his series of statistical surveys and atlases with the 1906 *Katholischer Missionsatlas* in 5 languages. In 1913 he produced the much larger *Atlas Hierarchicus*, with foreword by Pius X; then in 1929 its second edition. These massive Catholic atlases gave color maps and statistics of every country in the world and every Catholic diocese or other jurisdiction. The 1968 and 1976 editions of *Atlas Hierarchicus* were both compiled by H. Emmerich SVD (who had previously published a 1958 *Atlas missionum*). This atlas series then reached its 5th edition in 1992 (Z. Stezycki SVD). And two recent, more ecumenical Catholic dictionaries have been the 1987 *Lexikon Missionstheologischer Grundbegriffe* and its 1997 English elaboration *Dictionary of mission: theology, history, perspectives*.

The first of these 2 heritages or collections, on missionary statistics and global mission, enumerates in empirical detail the *followers* of religion, with totals and subtotals across the world. Table 14-7 in Part 14 "Missiometrics" shows that these empirical emphases begun by Ingoli (1630) and Carey (1792) have flourished up to the present day, as witness the rash of books old and new on these subjects which the US Library of Congress and the worldwide Online Computer Library Catalogue report and code with the following keywords: 'evangelism' (9,060 titles), 'conversion' (41,346, of which 27,001 published since 1970), 'missions' (111,490). (See this volume's Table 31-3).

Altogether, this chain of scholarship emphasizes that the central core of Christianity revolves around 7 keywords or key themes: mission, Christ's Great Commission, witness, evangelism, evangelization, conversion, and baptism. And since all of these have been, are being, and will continue to be enumerated annually by over 90% of all organized Christianity, their numbers or statistics play an important role in those core themes also, as this present volume will demonstrate.

The entire range of 600 works impinging on the global significance of Christianity, particularly as mission and in particular on missionary statistics, is reproduced here as Table 14-7. That listing is there analyzed on 4 prominent missiometric dimensions, which are then merged to form a single statistic measuring as a percentage each work's contribution towards the science of global mission. That statistic must not be seen as a judgment on the value of those classics showing low percentages (e.g. under 50%). Our assessment then, as the title of Table 14-7 makes clear, refers only to a book's contribution to the *science* of global mission as we understand it emerging.

### Assessing this first heritage, on mission
This first collection of encyclopedic literature can be rapidly assessed under 8 heads, as follows.

*Description*: describing the world of religions by emphasis on statistics of persons/followers/adherents including clergy/foreign workers/mis-

sionaries/converts/baptized church members/missionary personnel.
*Keywords*: mission, Great Commission, witness, evangelism, evangelization, conversion, baptism.
*Prime emphasis*: Christian global mission.
*Elements*: few in number, limited to Christianity, Christians, foreign missionaries, statistics of followers, workers.
*Not concerned with* (because of limited space): origins, founders, history, dogmas, creeds, events, personalities.
*Main entity*: religionists (followers) as the central phenomenon.
*Omission*: little or no interest in comparative study of religion, with consequent neglect of other religions (absence of data or information).
*Overall assessment*: very thorough on numbers, missionaries, native converts, but limited coverage of non-Christian religions, or of Christian phenomena except for detailed coverage of Christian followers, workers, global mission, and missionary statistics.

## 2. COMPARING WORLD RELIGIOUS SYSTEMS

### A lengthy heritage of scholarship on comparative religion
A quite different line of development has been concerned primarily with the world's religions rather than with Christianity's global mission. This has produced a sizable range of encyclopedias and dictionaries which describe every aspect of every religion across the world. First came the 50 volumes of Max Müller's *The sacred books of the East* (1879-1910); then the 12 volumes of J. G. Frazer's *The golden bough: a study in magic and religion* (1890-1915). The most massive in recent years is Mircea Eliade's 16-volume *The encyclopedia of religion* (1986). The last 3 decades in fact have produced new encyclopedias of worldwide religions of marked originality. A number of major publishers have entered the field. Their products are described in Table 14-7, but can be briefly listed here in chronological order: 1970 *Encyclopedia of world religions*, 1979 *Encyclopedic dictionary of religion*, 1981 *Abingdon dictionary of living religions*, 1984 *The Facts on File dictionary of religions*, 1984 *Penguin dictionary of religions*, 1987 *The encyclopedia of world faiths*, 1988 *The world's religions*, 1991 *New 20th-century encyclopedia of religious knowledge*, 1991 *World religions*, 1991 *The Eliade guide to world religions*, 1992 *Contemporary religions: a world guide*, 1993 *Dictionnaire des religions*, 1993 *Concise dictionary of religion*, 1993 *The world's religions: understanding the living faiths*, 1994 *Longman guide to living religions*, 1994 *Macmillan dictionary of religion*, 1994 *Religions of the world*, 1994 *The Continuum dictionary of religion*, 1995 *HarperCollins dictionary of religion*, 1995 *The world's religions*, 1995 *New dictionary of religions*, 1997 *Information Now encyclopedia of world religions*, 1997 *Oxford dictionary of world religions*, 1997 *World religions: the great faiths explored and explained*, 1999 *Merriam-Webster's encyclopedia of world religions*, 2000 *HarperCollins concise guide to world religions*, 2001 *The 21st century encyclopedia of the world's religions*.

All the above works deal with all world religions as they exist across the whole globe. A parallel development should be noted, in passing: encyclopedias of all religions in one single country are also increasing in number. A brief survey in 2001 has revealed over 20 such, recently published. These include *Enciclopedia delle religioni in Italia*, *Encyclopedia of American religions*, 6th edition (USA), and encyclopedic parallels in Brazil, France, Germany, Hungary, Indonesia, Netherlands, Spain, Sweden, et alia. However, our second heritage being analyzed here continues to deal only with worldwide religions in all countries.

### Assessing this second heritage, on comparative world religions
The second collection of encyclopedic literature has, by comparison with the first, a far richer range of quite different subjects for its entries. Its field is usually referred to as comparative religion, or religious studies. Here is a parallel assessment, whose 8 heads are directly comparable to those of the first heritage above.

*Description*: describing the world of religions by a vast new range of categories, enabling the comparing of one religion with another, including the comparing of Christianity with other religions.
*Keywords*: religion, dogmas, beliefs, origins.
*Prime emphasis*: discovering the essence of religion in all its facets, dimensions, in unrivaled detail, with rich, massive information for all religions equally.
*Elements*: 30 subject areas: origins, founders, histories, locations, events, leaders, thinkers, beliefs, dogmas, doctrines, teachings, stories, poems,

anecdotes, myths, mythologies, creeds, deities, theophanies, epiphanies, principles, systems, writings, scriptures, literature, scholarship, communications, networks, websites, relations with other religions.
*Not concerned with* (again because of limited space): mission, Great Commission, evangelism, evangelization, conversion, baptism, church growth.
*Main entity*: religion as a system, creed, philosophy, organization.
*Omission*: even though the 30 elements or subject areas provide immensely valuable coverage, there is not room for everything. Inevitably, a small handful of items is omitted. Virtually no formal or dictionary entries occur directly naming or describing the *followers* of any of these religions. Also omitted: formal entries on mission, global mission, evangelism, evangelization.
*Overall assessment*: very thorough and fascinating coverage of all religions, for almost all subjects except for any adequate coverage of Christian and non-Christian followers, their descriptions, and their statistics.

### Restricting the significance of mission
On one major subject the 2 heritages differ noticeably. The first heritage concentrates on the centrality of mission, defining it as the church's obligation to share all aspects of Christianity, Christ, and the gospel with the entire world. The second heritage barely mentions the subject, as will now be documented.

In recent literature, the best starting point is Eliade's magnum opus, the 16-volume, 9,000 page *The encyclopedia of religion* (1986). In this monumental work, the Christian world mission is portrayed as of much less overall significance than the last 2 centuries of mission scholarship listed above would imply. Its one article on Christian missions was contributed by our global consultant Bishop Stephen C. Neill but was restricted to 7 pages (0.1% of the 16 volumes); likewise the 16 volumes' 343-page Index contained a mere 80 references to Christian mission (0.1%). A similar ratio is found in the 1981 *Abingdon dictionary of living religions* (0.2% on mission), 1984 *Penguin dictionary of religions* (0.1%), 1994 *Longman guide to living religions*, 1995 *HarperCollins dictionary of religion* (0.01%), 1997 *Oxford dictionary of world religions* (0.03%), 1999 *Merriam-Webster's encyclopedia of world religions* (0.04%). Others including the 1994 *Macmillan dictionary of religion* have no formal entry 'mission' or 'missions' at all. Likewise, hardly any of these works contain any formal entry on ' evangelism', 'evangelization', 'evangelizers', 'conversion', 'converts', or 'Great Commission', all 6 of which are core concepts of Christianity which this present volume requires just over 600 pages to analyze (summarized in Global Diagram 2, and highlighted in Parts 22 to 25).

This antipathy to the words 'mission' and 'evangelism' is best understood as antipathy to the worst connotations of those terms. These include: religious imperialism, cultural superiority, ethnocentrism, forced conversion, religious wars, proselytism, religious fanaticism, forced mass baptisms, triumphalism, persecutions, and the like. The history of mission abounds in many such gross distortions. At its best the first heritage has rejected all such abuses and has attempted to uphold Christ's biblical model of mission as the servant church's obligation to a selfless sharing out of all the benefits and riches of the Christian faith—spiritual, mental, intellectual, personal, political, physical, financial—among the peoples of the entire world.

And in practice, 'mission' is simply the historical process by which 12 frightened disciples at the Crucifixion in AD 33 went on to become today's 2 billion Christian believers by AD 2001.

### Complementary not confrontational heritages
Despite these differences of approach and content, these 2 approaches must be regarded as complementary rather than confrontational. Both have to be judged (or better, reassessed) in the light of the current rash of new scholarship. e.g. Library of Congress/OCLC totals on religion, mission, and evangelism. Heritage 1 (global missionary statistics) complements Heritage 2 (comparative religion) by documenting those millions of adherents who follow all these religious systems. The main difference of approach between the two seems to be the inclusion or exclusion of (1) statistics, (2) followers, and (3) specific formal encyclopedic entries describing and enumerating the vast volume of data describing followers. Six areas where new entries are needed are partially provided in the present volume. All these excluded subjects are, at least, briefly reported here by stating their initial bare statistics or trends (e.g. 'baptisms per year: 44,000,000').

### ENUMERATING FOLLOWERS AND THEIR CHARACTERISTICS

With the availability of thousands of religion websites over the Internet, there is now an abundance of data on the whole range of potential entries now to be described. Vast amounts of new data are also available as the annual Christian megacensus produces its 10 million questionnaires every year. More detailed formal encyclopedic entries are needed, then, on about a hundred subjects, names, terms, or words describing, in the plural, the persons at the center of this huge phenomenon of religion—its followers. What are offered here can be summarized under 6 headings as follows.

(a) First, formal encyclopedic entries are essential for the specific *proper names or plural labels* of followers of the 10 major world religions: Christians, Muslims, Hindus, Buddhists, Sikhs, Jews, Jains, Shintoists, Zoroastrians, Bahais, to begin with. In some encyclopedias one finds an entry on the single form ('*Muslim*. A Muslim is...'), but in most cases one finds followers displaced by names of the religion itself ('Islam', 'Christianity', etc.). WCT here returns the focus to the followers themselves and at least gives each's statistics and trends.

(b) Second, new formal entries are essential to do justice to the rich *generic vocabulary of involved persons*. Here are the main ones in use: followers, adherents, believers, members, disciples, the affiliated, the faithful, the baptized, converts, practitioners, religionists (11 widely-used terms). These are briefly dealt with here in Part 30 "Glossary".

(c) Third, new entries about groupings of followers would give opportunity to write descriptions of individual, personal, or *collective qualities of specific followers*. Such could cover: their race, ethnicity, cultures, peoples, languages, lingua francas, politics, citizenship, geography, exact locations, urbanization, militarization, mobility, migration, economics, finances (subsistence levels), and so on (16 terms out of 50 available because already published). Initial statistics for these categories are given in this volume.

(d) Fourth, to facilitate formal entries specifically enumerating followers, new entries could be written for 15 words dealing with the *methodology of detailed description*. These are: size, extent, numbers, statistics, enrolment, counting, enumeration, measuring, censuses, megacensus, surveys, demographics, gender, age-specifics, trends (15 terms out of 60 available in published form). Part 14 "Missiometrics" attempts coverage here.

(e) Fifth, although the keyword 'statistics' is held by many to be unimportant or even unnecessary in the study of religion, a whole range of items could be written about *collectivities, institutions, and activities* in which followers are intimately concerned. Such entries or even references are much more illuminating if statistics are given. These include: congregations, communities, denominations, jurisdictions, dioceses, synods, megablocs, confessions, communions, councils, missions, agencies, boards, hospitals, clinics, schools, colleges, seminaries, universities, finances, budgets, ecclesiastical crime, publishing houses, publications, newspapers, journals, scripture distribution, broadcasting, radio/TV stations, audiences (28 terms out of 1,000 enumerated terms available in published form). Almost all such numbers are included here. Part 9 "Globalistics" is the first location to begin a search in.

(f) Lastly, the inclusion of all relevant statistics results in systematic coverage of the whole area of *religious personnel*. These include: priests, sheikhs, local clergy, foreign clergy, imams, sadhus, ascetics, contemplatives, monks, brothers, nuns, sisters, women workers, deacons, catechists, evangelists, lay preachers, lay readers, lay workers, administrators, developers, treasurers, broadcasters, apostles, bishops, archbishops, metropolitans, exarchs, cardinals, patriarchs, catholicoses, popes, seminarians, theologians, missiologists, educators, canon lawyers, retired workers (38 terms out of over 100 with statistics published). We list them all here in WCT, but in most cases as the irreducible minimum—a current statistical datum each.

### Reasons for defining religion by its followers
There is therefore a good case for including in forthcoming publications at least minimal entries on these hundred or so terms relating to followers. They can hardly be said to be unimportant or merely peripheral. From some viewpoints they are central to the whole description of religions. Without these followers there would be no religions at all.

### A minimal statistical table of religionists
Until recently, almost any publisher presuming to publish any encyclopedic description of the totality of world religions would at least make a small gesture in this direction by including a brief statistical table similar

to our 10-line Table 17-1 in Part 17 "Religiometrics". Recently, even this is notable by its exclusion. For readers who think a detailed demographic description of all religionists is at least as important as the creeds, dogmas, and superstitions they purport to hold, or for those wanting a regularly-updated table with these data in, we have published one annually in *Britannica Book of the Year* since 1986. This same table also appears each year in the *Statistical abstract of the United States* as well as in a number of other almanacs and yearbooks. For those wanting a much wider picture, Tables 17-5 and 17-6 in the present volume provide 60 pages describing these adherents of the world's 9,900 religions today.

All these excluded subjects are therefore reported in detail throughout this present volume.

Both global missionary statistics and comparative religion are exceptionally valuable approaches, and our present series employs their methodologies to the full.

### Putting people first
It is certainly worth noting that the world's churches in their megacensus year after year not only enumerate the several hundreds of 'omitted' terms described above but also place persons, followers, religionists, and even nonreligionists at the center of their annual enquiry and its statistical answers about its 180 major subjects enumerated (see listing in Global Diagram 3, box 3). So also with this present survey project, which has evolved over the period 1960-2001. Followers and their statistics have been recognized, sought out, enumerated, described, counted, totalled, and analyzed. If one wanted a single complementary phrase to enhance and extend the tried and proven methods of comparative religion, we could label the first of the 2 heritages as 'comparative religionists', or 'comparable religionists', even 'enumerated religionists'.

### The character and content of the present volume
The immediate genesis of the present *World Christian trends* goes back to 2 miniseries: (1) the *World Christian handbook*, an Anglican and Protestant publication which appeared on average every five years from 1949 to 1968; and (2) the similar Roman Catholic publication *Bilan du Monde: encyclopédie catholique du monde chrétien*, which had editions in 1958 and 1964. Those authors all then collaborated to produce in 1982 the *World Christian encyclopedia*, first edition.

### The rise of the Internet
At this point in 1983, discussions took place to determine the best way forward in order to continue this long chain of bibliography of mission. Shortly after, a monumental development in information technology arose, transforming the role of this type of reference publication. This was the rise by 1990 of the Internet as a vital new mode for detailed and rapid gathering of research data. By the year 2000, over 5,000 Christian denominations across the world had opened their own websites where researchers could immediately find origins, history, description, structure, doctrines, goals, leaders, office-holders, events, statistics, resources, finances, addresses, photographs, maps, even audio and visual descriptive materials. Churches which hitherto kept their data strictly private or secret are now suddenly revealing everything on their websites, even inviting the previously shunned world of mainstream Christianity to come and worship with them and get to know everything about them. All this presents us with an overwhelming sea of new data.

### Producing 3 new related reference works
Meanwhile, the small team based since 1965 at the World Evangelization Research Centre in Nairobi, Kenya which in 1982 produced WCE-1 with the aid of some 300 consultants, had relocated in 1985 to Richmond, Virginia, USA as the Global Evangelization Movement. A network was formed with additional scholars as consultants (see listing on pages vi to viii). It became clear then that the best way to continue the bibliographical legacy was to diversify somewhat and to produce, with different publishers, 3 distinct non-overlapping publications. These have now appeared in 2001 and are referred to here as WCE (country-by-country data), WCT (global evaluation), and WCD (database electronic versions). Contents of these 3 are as follows.

1. **WCE** refers to the *World Christian encyclopedia*, second edition (2 volumes, Oxford University Press). This presents a vast mass of immensely-detailed statistical tables, diagrams and photographs describing the religious situation in each of the world's 238 countries. These include: human rights, secular data, demography, religions, church history, church structures, et alia. Altogether these standardized country narratives describe the phenomena of Christianity by documenting (with one line of data for each element) 33,800 denominations, 500 councils, 250 communions, 300 ecclesiastical traditions, 12,600 ethnocultural peoples, 13,500 languages, 7,000 metropolises, 3,000 major civil divisions (provinces), and 7,000-book bibliographies extracted out of the world's 5 million book titles on Christianity. Short texts describe history, current churches, church-state relations, broadcasting and media, interdenominational organizations, religion's future trends and prospects, and a bibliography on each country.

2. **WCT** refers to the title of the present volume *World Christian trends, AD 30-AD 2200*. This builds on WCE's country data to produce overall global analysis, description, interpretation, and evaluation on a wide range of topics. It tackles the numerical and analytical aspects, deriving data also from Christianity's annual censuses with their mass of new data produced by some 2,056 different instruments (measuring devices). WCT's network of collaborators assisted in the compilation and evolution of new vistas of interpretation produced here under a variety of neologisms—GeoStatus with its 74 global diagrams, CosmoChronology, Martyrology, GeoRenewal, Independency, GeoTrends, Globalistics, CountryTrends, Religiometrics, Missiometrics, GeoStrategies, Futuristics, et alia. As its name implies, WCT provides a detailed survey and analysis of Christian trends across the world and across 20 centuries of past Christian history leading then across the next 2 centuries into the future. Again, huge numbers are involved for adequate depicting of today's situation at the close of 20 Christian centuries—2 billion church members, 70 million martyrs, 3,500 Scripture languages. And in this volume, an attempt is made to outline for the first time worldwide surveys of martyrdom, independency, strategies, evangelism, evangelization, and 9,900 current religions worldwide.

3. **WCD** is the abbreviation for the *World Christian database, AD 30-AD 2200*, handling the need for all the above data to be available to electronic access. WCD is in fact not a single product but a small series, in increasing order of sophistication. The first product is the PDF (Portable Data Format) version of WCT which is placed in a sleeve in the inside back cover of this book. It can be searched for any word or words, zoomed across, magnified, and printed out on desktop or laptop computers. Subsequent products are arranged systematically to serve a variety of database approaches and options (CDs, spreadsheets, online services, websites, et alia). They contain the full database versions of all countries, demographics, cities, religions, megablocs, denominations, peoples, languages, books, bibliographies.

Readers wanting to utilize the World Language Classification and take its data further should obtain a further work we published in AD 2000, namely *The Linguasphere register of the world's languages and speech communities* (2 volumes, and electronic versions).

Proceeding from WCE, WCT, and WCD are entries in a number of related encyclopedic volumes now under way, together with articles in a variety of dictionaries and other reference works in some 12 languages in addition to English.

It can thus be seen that these 3 products continue to emphasize the centrality of the Christian world mission as expounded and analyzed by the host of scholars tallied above—the centrality of the church's obligation to live not for itself but to actually benefit the entire world in concrete and measurable forms.

### 74 global diagrams as X-ray negatives
This volume opens with a range of 74 one-page global diagrams presenting the basic phenomena of global Christianity. The diagrams reveal a situation of vast complexity. Some 44 of them show a circle with data around it. Each circle represents the Earth and each illustrates one subject of global significance. They portray the Earth as a single 2-dimensional globe. On and around this sphere each diagram positions the relevant global data and constructs historical, statistical, and missiological descriptive typologies. Each diagram then can be seen as a cross-section or slice illustrating one particular scan or dimension.

Of the 74, the 30 other diagrams zero in either on smaller parts of the globe or specific aspects of global Christianity.

The diagrams therefore function in a similar way to the large-size black-and-white 2-dimensional X-ray photographic negatives of patients' bodies universally used in medical diagnosis and on display hanging in every hospital.

The computerized version *WCD* of these 74 *WCT* global diagrams can be seen to portray the Earth as a multi-dimensional sphere which the user can examine and combine in a variety of ways not possible with data on black-and-white 2-dimensional sheets of paper.

There is a parallel here with the medical procedure known as a CAT-scan or CT-scan (computerized axial tomography). In this procedure, the patient lies within a large circular machine which produces multiple X-ray images. These are then combined on a computer screen as a 3-dimensional model of the patient's body. The medical specialist then rotates and manipulates the model to search for cardio-vascular or oncological or other internal disorders.

Part 1 "GeoStatus" functions in a similar way. Its 74 global diagrams show multiple images or dimensions of the globe which, in their computerized versions *WCD* (PDF disc, CD, or online version) can be investigated further at any point by the reader to reveal the inner workings and multiple contexts of global Christianity. Such investigations can also utilize the 16 multicolored global maps and 230 color maps of countries in *WCD* versions.

## Tackling the empirical data

With each successive year, the empirical phenomenon we are studying gets bigger, vaster, more complex. Moreover, Christianity continues to generate new literature explaining itself to the tune of 260 new book titles published or newly catalogued every day. Together these are added to those 5 million distinct and separate book titles, all of which we can read and study in the world's top 50,000 libraries.

In the present survey, we select a relatively small area—the empirical reality that we call global Christianity—and apply to it the tenets and methods of science. Science (Latin *scientia,* knowledge) looks at evidence in the form of measurements and attempts to make sense of the phenomena by analyzing these measurements. All sciences are based on measurement (Latin, *dimensio*). Best examples in the academic world are a number of new disciplines—econometrics, bibliometrics, biometrics, jurimetrics. Some of them assist our own analysis and have led us to propose several new sciences relating to religion: religiometrics, linguametrics, missiometrics. This has involved the amassing of several hundred directories covering every aspect of global Christianity. For instance, the Church of Poland, with 35 million Catholic members, publishes a regular multicolor yearbook depicting some 250 numerical variables describing all dioceses, parishes, agencies, publications, and such minutiae as the numbers of teenagers involved in the Catholic Charismatic Renewal in every part of Poland. And since hundreds of similar directories are now becoming accessible to all on the World Wide Web, the field is wide open for research of every kind.

## An annual gold mine of new data

Here we discover a remarkable but little known fact: most of the world's churches and their Christians are engaged every day in measuring and quantifying over a thousand concrete aspects of their faith, their beliefs, their presence, their numbers, their communities, their organizations, their activities, their finances, their outreach. Every year their denominations and missions conduct what has become the world's largest and most sophisticated census. In this, some 10 million Christian leaders and workers return answers to complex statistical questions enumerating over 180 major religious subjects. The annual cost of this census is US $1,100 million.

Surprisingly little is done with this annual gold mine of new data and information. The 10 million questionnaires are returned to denominational headquarters and are promptly archived without analysis. This present volume therefore considers the whole range of these measurements and attempts to make global sense of them and their trends, under the 33 Part heads listed in the opening table of contents.

## Accuracy and usefulness of this survey

No claim can be made here for total accuracy of the entire data in this series of volumes. Perhaps 90% of all the statistics may be said to be reasonably accurate, though all have their margins of error. Consequently, what is offered here is not a precise photograph or snapshot giving an image of the entire world at various exact points in time. Rather the series should be regarded as a portrait in oils, a carefully constructed painting or graphic portrayal paying attention to a vast amount of detail but pri-

marily concerned to portray the persona—it attempts to capture the multi-faceted personality and flavor of global Christianity.

Now let us apply this depiction of that global phenomenon to one of the most problematic of its current paradoxes.

## Global Christianity's pledge of a new era by AD 2000

The starting point is that the year 2000 marked the close of the widely-heralded decade 1990-2000. For many years after Isaac Newton, the leadership of churches and missions had singled this future decade out as of special importance. By the 1980s leaders had labeled this 10-year period The Decade of Evangelism, The Decade of Harvest, The Worldwide Decade of Evangelization, The Decade of World Evangelization, The Universal Decade of World Mission, the Decade of Universal Evangelism, and so on. Over 250 all-embracing global plans were launched by Christians of every stripe and confession, each plan being linked to solemn pledges promising that this Decade would fulfill and complete Christ's Great Commission on Earth. Altogether, in administering these global plans the churches spent over $70 billion. Here are 5 examples of those pledges, respectively from Protestant, Evangelical, Ecumenical, Roman Catholic, and Evangelical/Pentecostal/Charismatic sources.

(1) In the words of Bold Mission Thrust, the elaborate plan launched by the 14,107 duly-accredited messengers to the 119th Session of the Southern Baptist Convention meeting in Norfolk, Virginia in June 1976: 'To enable every person in the world to have opportunity to hear and to respond to the Gospel of Christ by the year 2000'.

(2) In the words of the 100 largest Evangelical organizations meeting in Edinburgh, Scotland in October 1980 and in subsequent global conferences, the 1st World Consultation on Frontier Missions pledged to give the world's 1.65 billion unevangelized 'A church for every people by the year 2000'.

(3) In the words of the United Bible Societies' 11th World Assembly in Budapest, Hungary in 1988, 272 delegates from 120 countries pledged themselves to 'making a commitment to reach every young person in the world by the year 2000 with a copy of the Word of God in the language he or she most easily understands'.

(4) In the words of the Vatican's Evangelization 2000 campaign announced by John Paul II in 1989: 'To unite all Christians and all churches by AD 2000, and to bring the total of Christ's disciples to over 50% of the world by AD 2000'—this being pledged as 'a birthday present of one billion new believers for Jesus' 2,000th birthday'.

(5) In the words of the 3,900 church and mission leaders from 200 countries attending in 1995 the 2nd Global Consultation on World Evangelization by the Year 2000 and Beyond (GCOWE II), in Seoul, Korea, these 3,900 pledged themselves anew to implement the theme of the Consultation 'A Church for Every People and the Gospel for Every Person by AD 2000'. Fine words, firm promises. So far so good.

## What actually transpired by AD 2000

What subsequently happened in that Decade, however, is completely different to what was promised. We can summarize this precisely in 5 short factual sentences, as follows.

(1) Our globe's total of unevangelized persons—all persons completely unaware of Christianity, Christ, and the gospel, and having no opportunity to hear it—was 1,650 millions in 1976, but by AD 2000 had decreased only slightly to 1,629 millions (see global enumeration in Table 1-2), this unanticipated absence of progress being due to (a) the 32 million new persons becoming evangelized each year have been countered by (b) population increase (births minus deaths) among the unevangelized world also numbering 32 million each year.

(2) Although this 1980 goal then produced a rash of 200 separate global plans announced by major Evangelical agencies, by 31 December 2000 no church had been provided for some 10,000 unreached minipeoples.

(3) In 1990 the Christian Scriptures were available translated into 2,100 of the world's 13,500 distinct and separate languages; by AD 2000 this total had been increased to only 2,500 languages with their own mother-tongue translations; and not surprisingly, 328 million young people (18-24 years old, the UN definition) still had heard nothing whatever about Christianity, let alone getting their own promised translations in their own mother tongues.

(4) The percentage of the human race professing to be Christians actually declined from 33.2% in 1990 to 33.0% in AD 2000; also, far from all

Christians and all churches becoming united by 2000, Christian fragmentation increased from 30,400 distinct and separate denominations in 1990 to 33,800 in AD 2000.

(5) Despite the enormous organizational weight, personnel, and finance available through those 3,900 church and mission leaders, the global total of unevangelized persons without the gospel decreased only marginally, from 1,665 millions in 1990, to 1,678 millions in 1995, and to 1,629 millions by AD 2000.

So much for the glittering pledges of organized global Christianity. Disappointments of this kind happen frequently. Of the 1,500 global plans for world evangelization put forward by Christians, some 665 have proved to be failures and have collapsed or been abandoned. An inventory of 340 different reasons and causes for these failures is given in Part 27, Table 27-5. These can be summarized as: the church's failure to obey Christ's Great Commission. In the year 1900 missionary statesmen John R. Mott and Samuel M. Zwemer propounded an even harsher judgement—'the wicked selfishness of Christians'.

Even more serious is the situation of the unevangelized world. From the standpoint of the 160 million unfortunate persons who during 1990-2000 died, unevangelized (which means denied their promised share of all the benefits of Christianity, Christ, and the gospel), the Decade of Evangelism proved to be nothing more nor less than just another broken promise, an appalling catastrophe, even (in their eyes) a cruel sham.

### How this situation arose

How can one explain this debacle? The most charitable explanation relates to the leaders of organized Christianity, highly experienced in guiding the affairs of 2 billion church members. Faced in 1990 with the fait accompli of the Decade with its challenge to reach 4 billion non-Christians and 1.6 billion unevangelized—the majority of these billions being uninterested, uncooperative, or even hostile to Christian evangelistic approaches—these leaders proved unable to deal with or make any measurable dent in a situation of this magnitude.

### An analogy from the world of aviation

Here it is instructive to compare the leaders' role—managing global mission—with the piloting of an aircraft. Actually the comparison can be with any modern form of controlling a powerful means of transport by day and by night and in both fair weather and foul—driving an automobile, piloting a helicopter, navigating a space shuttle, steering a nuclear submarine, commanding a giant oil tanker or ocean liner. As myself a former air force pilot and research scientist, I have long noted the remarkable parallels between those control skills and the managing of world evangelization. The simple parallel with piloting an aeroplane is all we need at this point.

Aircraft pilots fly under 2 totally different sets of rules. Most of their time they pilot their craft under what are termed visual flight rules (VFR, or 'contact flying'): in broad daylight, good weather, good visibility, seeing Earth's landmarks below and its horizon ahead, constantly checking visually for signs of other nearby or approaching aircraft, in radio touch with ground controllers, and following a flight plan filed with them before takeoff. Under visual flight rules, all seasoned and qualified pilots can rely on their gut feelings that their aircraft is doing exactly what it should, that up is up and down is down. Colloquially, they are experts 'flying by the seat of their pants'—their feelings verified by what they observe outside the cockpit.

### Visibility falls to zero

Suddenly, however, that situation can change for the worse. You may be an aircraft pilot completing a 7-hour Transatlantic flight at 35,000 feet in the stratosphere in brilliant sunshine all the way. Now you have to descend to Earth through an overcast sky. The familiar world abruptly disappears; a new, unfamiliar, even dangerous change surrounds you as your aircraft descends into cloud—visibility drops to zero, the horizon disappears, the Sun and Earth vanish from sight. Worse, night may be falling precipitately, or weather worsening unexpectedly, or industrial haze and smog obliterate the horizon; or no land can be expected to appear since you are over the sea. Under those situations pilots must immediately switch from VFR to instrument flight rules (IFR, or 'blind flying'). This is defined in Webster's *Third new international dictionary* as 'navigation solely according to information given by instruments within an aircraft'. Ignor-

ing their gut feelings of up and down they must now trust immediately, completely, solely and continuously moment by moment, the standard array of half a dozen cockpit instruments—artificial horizon, and instruments measuring attitude, altitude, airspeed, rate of climb or descent, compass direction. These instruments are all the pilot needs to be fully oriented. If any are ignored, or are missing, or malfunction, or lose electrical power, or were wrongly calibrated, even experienced pilots rapidly become spatially disoriented, then experience vertigo, their aircraft go wildly out of control, and lethal crashes ensue.

### Explaining 250 failed AD 2000 global plans

Next, we return briefly to the ecclesiastical problem discussed earlier, namely accountability for the AD 2000 debacle. The most straightforward explanation for the abject failure of the 250 global plans for fulfilling the Great Commission by the end of the Decade of Evangelism is therefore that most of the world's mission leaders, though vastly experienced, knowledgeable, and competent in well-known or familiar situations—experts in flying by the seat of their pants when visibility was good—entered the Decade expecting to encounter clear visibility, failed to prepare for the unfamiliar world of closure, omitted to file any detailed flight plan, attempted to lead without benefit of relevant instruments, found familiar landmarks absent, experienced zero visibility, lost sight of any horizon, and became the missiological equivalent of spatially disoriented. They were now flying blind, unaided by instruments. They failed to perceive that the 1.6 billion unevangelized persons and the 4 billion non-Christians would be willing and receptive to receive the gospel but only if sympathetically and determinedly approached. Instead, managers threw their vast resources of personnel and money into familiar, highly visible, and easily-reached nearby targets in heavily Christian lands.

### Accountability of leadership

The reader studying these 250 global plans, highlit particularly here in Part 27 "GeoStrategies", may well want a further question answered. It concerns the accountability of Christian leaders, managers, and executives both to the churches themselves and also, ultimately far more important, to the world's long-suffering populations. Disturbingly rash promises that Christians had now pledged to bring concrete benefit to the entire world by the Millennial deadline had been proclaimed, only to be seen 10 years later as broken promises. Yet nobody has begun apologizing, let alone admitting liability. Any secular national or multinational enterprise—bank, government, university, industry, transnational—recording such a spectacular failure to achieve its own trumpeted goals would have been mercilessly exposed by the media and then closed down by investors or shareholders or governments or parliaments or other watchdogs long ago. With the golden opportunity of that Decade thus catastrophically squandered, the new Millennium from AD 2001 onwards would appear to demand the replacement of leadership by a new generation of younger Great Commission Christians not afraid to augment their expertise in visual navigating with reliance on instrumentation in the multitudinous ever-present areas of poor information visibility and even of information ignorance.

### Instruments restore total visibility

For the new Millennium, this volume can, with the necessary diffidence, offer concrete assistance. On the aviation analogy, we can assert that in world mission the main item that differentiates success from failure, achievement from fiasco, reaching one's goals from failing to do so, even life from death, is this term 'instrument'. The term is defined in Webster's as 'a measuring device'. That's all an instrument is and does. It does not preach, or lecture, or recommend anything. All decisions remain yours. It simply measures a single item, instantly, accurately, and repeatedly, telling you immediately what you could not otherwise know.

### This analysis as an instrument panel

This is the function that works such as the present volume attempt to provide—scientific instrumentation on the many factors that make up world mission and its implementation. Since the science of mission is a relatively young discipline, no one can yet say which half dozen instruments are likely to be the all-important, indispensable ones. So these volumes offer to navigators in this area a large number of instruments to guide their choices and decisions. Most were chosen because many churches and missions have already been measuring the items regularly for many years past. The instruments offered here are simply measuring devices, measuring in most cases one main subject or object or item. Usually, numbers (statistics) are involved—the number of non-Christians in a city, the number of Bibles distributed, the funds available, the books consultable, the number of Christians using the World Wide Web, the volume of evangelism received each year, the number of baptisms performed, and so on.

*Offering a range of 2,056 instruments*
The instruments thus offered in this series of volumes consist of 5 different varieties. They can be seen set out in Table 15-2 in Part 15 "Instrumentation".

(1) First are *country instruments,* alerting the user to the values of the major measurable variables in any country he or she is concerned with. The instrumentation parallel is at its clearest in Part 15 describing how any country can develop a standardized 'Great Commission Instrument Panel' of 6 instruments similar to the handful on an automobile's panel of speedometer, fuel gauge, odometer, tachometer, voltmeter, clock. An aircraft pilot likewise has that small panel with the conventional 6 key flight instruments in front of him or her. Our standard panel shows the 6 measurements likely to be of most assistance to Christians wanting to pursue Great Commission initiatives in a country they are unfamiliar with. Table 15-2 goes on to explain where some 479 different instruments, arranged to resemble 83 instrument panels, may be seen in this series' pages to offer further measurements about that country. A small selection of these GCIP panels, portraying each of the world's 77 largest countries (each with over 10 million population), are arranged in Table 15-3 for purposes of direct comparison from one country to another.

(2) Second, there is in Part 1 a series of 74 global diagrams which function as *global instruments,* though more complex and sophisticated and with far more variables than the usual type of instrument.

(3) Third is a series of *topical instruments* consisting of 355 statistical tables offering information not on a single country but each on a single topic.

(4) Fourth are 132 additional *database instruments* in lengthy printouts giving (a) in *WCT*, measurements for the world's 9,900 different religions, and (b) in *WCE*, measurements for the world's 33,800 Christian denominations, and for all its 12,600 ethnolinguistic peoples, 13,500 languages, 7,000 metropolises, and 3,030 major civil divisions (MCDs, often called provinces of a country), and a name and address directory for 82 topics.

(5) Fifth is a series of 14 *visual instruments* in the shape of 14 categories with 1,650 photographs selected to support the other ranges of instruments, as Table 15-2 explains.

In sum, this instrumentation totals some 471 separate panels offering 2,056 instruments giving 4,784,880 measurements in this print series *WCE* and *WCT*. This is complex but hardly excessive. It is the kind of complex instrumentation that one would find in many scientific or commercial parallels—in the pilots' cockpit of a space shuttle, or on the bridge of a nuclear aircraft carrier.

To assist readers to follow the instrumentation analogy, they should consult the verso (the back) of each of the 33 Parts' title pages. There they will find a series of brief comments describing the instrumentation available, and the trends thereby perceived, on the subject of each of the Parts.

*Sources*
We want to acknowledge the highly relevant and specific information supplied indirectly by 380,000 informants who have published their findings. These were the researchers and scholars who, as experts each on empirical Christianity in his or her own country, took their learning and knowledge to the point of publication, which means accountability to their peers and to the wider public. As researchers we therefore had access to 380,300 different books each an authority on Christianity in one specific country. Two examples: for Brazil we tracked down 4,222 books whose main subject or keyword, as defined by the US Library of Congress, is 'Christianity in Brazil'. For China, we developed a bibliography of 7,956 books on 'Christianity in China'.

*A new methodology emerges*
To handle and sculpt the vast amount of statistics emanating year by year from the world of religion with its context in the secular world, my colleague Todd Johnson has made a major contribution to scholarship by creating a vast computerized methodology characterized by the word 'reconciliation'—reconciling our descriptions and analyses of the entirety of the religious data at every point in time and place with the vast amounts of new, primary, authoritative research data emanating each week from colleagues, journalists, scholars, libraries, news services, websites, as well as via the 1,800 or so new books on Christianity published every 7 days. And all this religious data must be fitted in with the secular depicting of the globe in the more than 100 major databases associated with the United Nations, plus other transnationals, universities, and other specialist agencies.

In this task we have been ably assisted by the 18 global consultants listed above, several of whom made major methodological and interpretative contributions.

*Richmond, Virginia, 2001*                                    David B. Barrett

# NATIONS AND COUNTRIES
## Shortened, formal, full, alternate, earlier, popular, and official names for all countries

**1. Short names.** Names in bold capitals below form this volume's definitive alphabetized geographical listing in English of all 238 sovereign and non-sovereign nations, countries, and territories in the world, as existing in AD 2000, with a handful of territories whose status has recently been in dispute (Palestine, Sahara, Timor, et alia). Territories that are uninhabited are excluded. This list is based on the official listing utilized by the United Nations, in most cases using the official terminology requested of the UN by each member country; but it modifies this terminology by changing nations alphabetized by the UN under 'Republic of . . .' or 'Democratic . . .' or 'Socialist . . .' to their recognized or normally-employed short geographical terms. Full details of names, including official names in their own languages, are given under SECULAR DATA at the start of each country's article in *WCE* Volume 1 on the page indicated below. In addition to the official UN names in English, all UN members also have official names in the other 5 of the 6 official UN languages (Arabic, Chinese, English, French, Russian, Spanish). All are given in full detail in the UN's *Terminology bulletin No. 347: country names*, 1995 and biennial updates.

**2. Standard codes.** To the left of each bold capital name is this volume's standardized 4-letter code or abbreviation for the country, used to save space in many tables in different Parts. This code may also be used to search for and access data on any table contained in the companion CD, *World Christian database AD 30-AD 2200*.

**3. Page numbers below.** These refer only to the main article on each country, found in *World Christian encyclopedia*, Volume 1, Part 4. Further extensive data on each country can be found, arranged alphabetically, in *WCT* Part 12 "Country-Trends", and elsewhere. A full listing of all country variables and varieties of data by country is given on the first verso page at the start of *WCE* Part 4.

**4. Convenience names.** All member countries of the United Nations are here given their definitive shortened names (shown in capitals), which are the shortest English official forms agreed to with the UN by the countries concerned. The only exceptions are a handful of countries which require the UN to use their full English titles but which we here, in the interests of standardization and ease of reference, reduce to their normally-employed geographical terms, as follows: Britain, Brunei, Iran, Ivory Coast, Laos, Libya, North Korea, South Korea, Tanzania, Viet Nam, Yemen, Yugoslavia. Sometimes readers are referred to such names by the word 'here'.

**5. Fuller names.** Words in upper/lowercase following a capitalized short name, after a comma, form the rest of the full, formal, or official name in English of the country concerned (except words in parentheses). If there are no such additional words (as e.g. for Ukraine), this indicates that for UN purposes the full official name is the same as the shortest official form.

**6. Alternative names.** Words in upper/lowercase following a capitalized name, after a semi-colon, form the full official name and indicate that it has formal priority over the shortest official form (e.g. France is officially called The French Republic, Greece is The Hellenic Republic, Switzerland is The Swiss Confederation, etc.).

**7. Parenthetic names.** Names in parentheses are not part of official titles but have widespread popular use. Details of other names in use are given for each country under its SECULAR DATA.

**8.** Entries below not in capitals but in upper/lower case only do not form part of our definitive listing of countries; they are alternative forms of title, popular names, older names still in use, smaller parts of countries at one time considered eligible for such lists, or names of territories which are, or have now become part of some larger unit, to all of which the reader is referred.

**9.** The word 'see' refers the reader from an abbreviation or alternative or popular or widely-used or incorrect name to the fuller or correct or shortest official form of the name or its geographical equivalent as employed in our listing; or, in the case of 'see Antarctica' to the numerous footholds treated by agreement under that single entity.

**10.** The word 'now' indicates that although an older name is still in use in some international or national circles, correctly or incorrectly, the newer name indicated has now officially replaced it.

**11.** The word 'under' indicates that a territory is or is now part of the larger nation or country indicated.

# INTRODUCTION

This volume's analysis is characterized by 2 clearcut approaches. First the approach is empirical rather than normative. Second the approach is scientific rather than philosophical or poetic. This book therefore describes empirical global Christianity. It describes the phenomenon known as Christianity as it actually has been over the last 20 centuries, as it is now in the world of AD 2000 and 2001 with its 238 countries and 12,600 ethnolinguistic peoples, and as it is likely to be in 10 varieties or stages of the world of the future—immediate, near-term, middle-range, long-range, distant, far distant, megafuture, gigafuture, terafuture, eschatofuture.

The phenomenon of Christianity is here described and analyzed from some 33 standpoints, into 33 Parts. In each of these 33, the approach adopted is that of a science—the science of religion, the science of mission. Some of them we call by neologisms parallel to their 80 sister sciences that have arisen in the 20th century. As a science (Latin *scientia*, knowledge) these Parts look at evidence in the form of measurements and attempt to make sense of the phenomena by analyzing these measurements.

The volume presents empirical Christianity by means of a global overview (Part 1), history (Parts 2-8), data (Parts 9-12), methods (Parts 13-16), analysis (Parts 17-24), strategy (Parts 25-29), and reference (Parts 30-33). Each part begins by examining the vast range of empirical data on its main and ancillary subjects. Especially significant here are the statistical tables. These present the total data that often lead to quite different analyses and conclusions than currently-held stereotypes.

Part 12 "CountryTrends" offers a 24-page statistical table giving 191 variables for each country. All countries and continents are there listed in identical order on 2 facing pages 12 times. Central also for rapid comparison is each country's standardized Great Commission Instrument Panel with its 6 instruments, as shown in Table 15-3.

Near its end the whole work has indexes on abbreviations, initials, acronyms, photographs, and standard locations for all comparable topics.

The volume ends with a mini-atlas depicting several major aspects of global Christianity in the worlds of geography, geopolitics, and human environment.

This study shares with its more recent predecessors a critical, scholarly, and scientific approach to data describing the Christian world. In the main, it uses existing data collected by the churches for their own purposes. The annual enquiries of several thousand denominations must be, in aggregate, the world's most mammoth statistical operation. All statistics resulting have been checked and counter-checked, sources investigated, and documents verified. A vast computerized database was created to hold the information gathered. A large number of checks were run for consistency, plausibility, probability and so on. Details of the methodology evolved are given in Part 14 "Missiometrics".

Readers should not be put off by our practice of giving many totals to the last digit. This is not a claim to any unrealistic or phony precision. The reason is that we are often totalling lists containing both rounded totals of large churches with unrounded totals to the last digit published by very small churches. Rather than lose these details, in most cases we leave the totals unrounded. The United Nations' huge demographic databases and their published versions follow exactly this procedure. Readers can then themselves round any figure they need to the nearest hundred, or thousand, or million, or billion as suits their immediate requirements.

In passing, we need to assure the reader that the total number of Christians in the world in AD 2000, which this survey puts at 1,999,563,000—or, when rounded, at 2,000 million—is a coincidental total arising as the end product of complex computerized subtotaling and totaling. No manipulation of any kind produced this startling figure, which indeed was only noticed by us shortly before publication. Knowing the many margins of error involved, we see little or no significance in this strange coincidence.

The scope of this survey has been made as comprehensive as possible. It is clearly impossible, however, to cover every aspect of Christianity within a single work. Thus it does not attempt to deal with subjects like the archaeology of Christianity, nor its philosophical system, evolution of dogma, ethics or liturgy.

In order not to fragment the subject unnecessarily by forcing the material into the artificial mould of a single A-Z alphabetical sequence throughout, this volume divides its treatment of the subject into the 33 major topics shown in the table of contents. Each of these subjects is examined comprehensively and systematically by employing several alphabetical sequences for the world's 238 countries, for names of churches, organizations, cultures and languages, bibliographies, and various subject indexes. Statistical and other data are presented in a standard format and order for every country, religion and church. The advantage of this topical approach (as contrasted with an A-Z listing of articles) is that it enables the reader to grasp both the local detail and the global entirety of the various subjects treated, as well as allowing him or her to immediately compare the situation in one country with that in another, one culture with another, one language with another, one religious tradition with another, one church or denomination with another. The work is, therefore, in the main comparative and topical.

Organized Christianity is studied here mainly by describing the structures of the organized churches and denominations of the world. But there is also a vast complex of unorganized or unstructured Christian activity, better described perhaps as spontaneous Christianity, which is much more difficult to document or delineate. The task is attempted here by describing its more visible incipient or embryonic structures. These include reform movements, revivals, renewals, protest movements and charismatic movements. The concrete reality of these is documented in words, in photographs, and in a variety of statistical tables.

It should be realized at this point that this book is a descriptive survey first and foremost; it is not, and cannot be, a definitive theological assessment or evaluation of the significance, relevance, or authenticity of the present-day Christian enterprise across the world. This task must be left to those theologians and missiologists who may be interested. What is attempted here is description followed by an initial attempt at global evaluation.

# Part 1

# GEOSTATUS

The changing face of Christianity across 21 centuries

*The kingdom of God is like a grain of mustard seed, which is the smallest of all the seeds on earth, yet when it is sown it grows up and becomes the greatest of all shrubs.*
—Mark 4:30-32, Revised Standard Version

Every year, at their churches' request some 10 million Christians take myriads of careful measurements on a vast variety of subjects depicting global Christianity and its contributions to the welfare of the planet. This enumeration produces an annual gold mine of new data.

Part 1 describes the whole range of these contributions by means of 74 Global Diagrams. These one-page standalone sheets may be regarded as complex instruments, each providing detailed measurements on a specific concept or theme.

These diagrams may be likened to a hospital's large-size black-and-white X-ray negatives each showing the inside of a patient's body. Likewise, each diagram exhibits a different slice or scan of the globe, its religions, their followers, and their activities. Each thus reveals a different cross-section of the inner workings of Christianity in its wider context both religious and secular.

Further, these multiple diagrams taken together function similarly to a hospital's CAT-scan (CT-scan) machine. Using the electronic versions *WCD*, readers can examine the entire phenomenon at any point, magnify and manipulate its image on their screens, and devise new results.

The narrative here then links them together and provides a guide to all who wish to relate to the changing face of Christianity in order to navigate through global waters known and unknown.

# The changing face of Christianity across 21 centuries

Christianity, beginning as a small Jewish sect in Palestine in AD 30, has grown into a world religion that by the dawn of the 21st century effectively penetrated over 9,000 of the world's peoples, encompassing 2 billion adherents. This fact is startling in light of the seemingly overwhelming odds faced by Jesus and especially his disciples shortly after his death. Although Christians remained a fairly small percentage of the Roman Empire's population until about AD 300, the movement showed remarkable vigor in the face of heretical offshoots, persecution from the Roman authorities, and the encroachments of barbarians from the north. By AD 400 Christianity was well on its way as a widespread movement, absorbing one wave after another of peoples outside of its borders: Goths, Irish, Vikings, Central Asians, Slavs. At the heart of its vitality were internal waves of renewal, primarily in monastic form (Benedict, Celts, Cluny, Francis, Dominic). These waves were effective both in renewing peoples already Christian and in the extension of the gospel to people not yet Christian. Only in the case of Muslims, and later Mongols, did Christians fall short of their goal of compassionately offering the good news to the world. By the age of Discovery the Society of Jesus provided a new impetus in world evangelism. Protestants joined belatedly through the efforts of William Carey and others. By the 19th century, Christians of all major traditions were poised to evangelize the whole world in what church historian Kenneth Scott Latourette later called 'The Great Century'. Nonetheless, the 20th century began with over half of the world's population still unaware of Christianity, Christ and the gospel.

## The 20th century in Christian context

At the end of the 20th century just over 33% of the world's population professed to be Christians. Contrary to the optimistic outlook one hundred years ago of a 'Christian century', this percentage is actually slightly lower than it was in 1900. Some might conclude that Christians have made virtually no progress in enlisting followers in the past one hundred years.

But such a point of view would miss the radical changes that have impacted the world Christian movement in the 20th century. First of all, in 1900 over 80% of all Christians were White. Most were from Europe and North America. Today that percentage has fallen to 45%. The demographic center of Christianity is now found in Latin America, Africa, and Asia. Over the next 25 years the White portion of global Christianity is expected to continue to decline dramatically.

Second, in 1900 only a handful of Christians were involved in renewal movements. By AD 2000 over 500 million or 25% of all Christians were participants in renewal. Over the century the first wave of the Pentecostal Renewal grew into 750 denominations in 225 countries with 65 million members. Later, a second wave known as the Charismatic Renewal erupted within the mainline churches encompassing 6,500 denominations in 235 countries with over 175 million members. Finally, a third wave, the rise of Neocharismatic Renewal, emphasizing a break with denominationalism, spread into over 18,800 networks in 225 countries, claiming over 295 million members. The majority of these are in Africa and Asia. Altogether these 3 waves of renewal mark a radical transformation of Christianity in the 20th century.

Third, Christians of all major traditions have grown increasingly committed to the Great Commission of Jesus Christ. One out of three Christians in the world is active in their obedience to this Commission. The number has grown from 78 million in 1900 to 648 million in AD 2000. As a result, hundreds of new mission agencies have been formed and thousands of new missionaries sent out. The independent churches, barely a factor in mission in 1900, are now providing a new infusion of workers as many of the more traditional sending bodies continue to decline. An almost entirely unexpected surge of workers has emerged from the non-Western world—thousands of

---

**Table 1–1. An AD 2001 reality check: 50 new facts and figures about trends and issues concerning empirical global Christianity today.**

| | Source: Part |
|---|---|
| 1. Every year the churches hold a megacensus costing $1.1 billion, sending out 10 million questionnaires in 3,000 languages, which covers 180 major religious subjects. | 1 |
| 2. At a steady rate over the last 20 centuries, and in all 238 countries, 70 million Christians have been martyred—killed, executed, murdered—for Christ. | 4 |
| 3. The 5 most dangerous of all Christian vocations (over 3% murder rates) are: bishops, evangelists, catechists, colporteurs, foreign missionaries. | 4 |
| 4. Books primarily about Jesus in today's libraries number 175,000 different titles in 500 languages, increasing by 4 newly published every day. | 31 |
| 5. Emboldened by lax procedures, trusted church treasurers are embezzling each year $16 billion out of church funds, but only 5% ever get found out. | 20 |
| 6. Christians spend more on the annual audits of their churches and agencies ($810 million) than on all their workers in the non-Christian world. | 20 |
| 7. The total cost of Christian outreach averages $330,000 for each and every newly baptized person. | 20 |
| 8. Despite Christ's command to evangelize, 67% of all humans from AD 30 to the present day have never even heard of his name. | 2 |
| 9. 648 million Christians today (called Great Commission Christians) are active in Christ's world mission; 1,352 million Christians ignore this mission. | 9 |
| 10. Every person in the world belongs to, on average, 10 distinct and separate (and often conflicting) religions. | 17 |
| 11. Organized Christianity has total contact with 3,590 religions but no contact at all with 353 other religions and their over 500 million adherents. | 17 |
| 12. 14 million converted Hindus, Buddhists, and Muslims have opted to remain within those religions in order to witness for Christ as active believers in Jesus as Lord. | 6 |
| 13. Heads of the 50 major Christian World Communions, with 1.5 billion members, have since 1957 met annually for serious 3-day dialogue. | 2 |
| 14. A huge new Christian nonconfessional megabloc, the Independents/Postdenominationalists, is growing rapidly and numbers 19% of all Christians. | 6 |
| 15. These 386 million Independents in 220 countries have no interest in and no use for historic denominationalist Christianity. | 6 |
| 16. From only 3 million in AD 1500, evangelicals have grown to 648 million worldwide, 54% being Non-Whites. | 5 |
| 17. The country with the fastest Christian expansion ever is China, now at 10,000 new converts every day. | 11 |
| 18. Non-Christian countries have been found to have 227 million Bibles in place in their midst, more than needed to serve all Christians but poorly distributed. | 19 |
| 19. Everywhere on Earth can now easily be targeted with at least 3 of the 45 varieties of effective evangelism. | 22 |
| 20. Christian triumphalism—not as pride in huge numbers, but as publicized self-congratulation—is rampant in most churches, agencies, and ministries. | 13 |
| 21. 124 million new souls begin life on Earth each year, but Christianity's 4,000 foreign mission agencies baptize only 4 million new persons a year. | 1 |
| 22. 91% of all Christian outreach/evangelism does not target non-Christians but targets other Christians in World C countries, cities, peoples, populations, or situations. | 28 |
| 23. 818 unevangelized ethnolinguistic peoples have never been targeted by any Christian agency ever. | 28 |
| 24. 40% of the church's entire global foreign mission resources are being deployed to just 10 oversaturated countries already possessing strong citizen-run home ministries. | 12 |
| 25. Over 20 centuries Christians have announced 1,500 global plans to evangelize the world; most failed; 250 plans focused on AD 2000 fell massively short of stated goals. | 27 |
| 26. The 3 least cost-effective countries over 1 million in population for Christian outreach are: Japan, Switzerland, Denmark. | 12 |
| 27. The 3 most cost-effective countries over 1 million in population for Christian outreach are: Mozambique, Ethiopia, Tanzania. | 12 |
| 28. Per hour of ministry, the 5 megapeoples most responsive to Christianity, Christ, and the gospel are: Khandeshi, Awadhi, Magadhi, Bai, Berar Marathi | 11 |
| 29. Per hour of ministry, the 5 megapeoples least responsive to Christianity, Christ, and the gospel are: Swedish, Russian, Lithuanian, Polish, Georgian | 11 |
| 30. Mainland China's Christians have thousands of trained workers poised to begin evangelizing the world de novo soon after AD 2000. | 21 |
| 31. Most Christian bodies insist on full accountability to the last cent in finance, but ignore or even decry statistics about Christian workers and ministries. | 20 |
| 32. It costs Christians 700 times more money to baptize converts in rich World C countries (Switzerland) than in poor World A countries (Nepal). | 20 |
| 33. Regular listeners to Christian programs over secular or religious radio/TV stations rose from 22% of the world in 1980 to 30% in 2000. | 1 |
| 34. Christian communicators ignore the huge potential of the globe's 983 lingua francas each with over 100,000 non-native speakers, or the 2,179 each over 100,000 total speakers. | 18 |
| 35. Ethnoreligionists (animists, polytheists, shamanists) number 228 million in 6,000 tribes or peoples, mushrooming rapidly by 2.8 million a year. | 18 |
| 36. Criminal penalties against clergy in sexual abuse cases now exceed $1 billion, causing a number of churches, dioceses, and denominations to be forced into bankruptcy | 20 |
| 37. Annual church embezzlements by top custodians exceed the entire cost of all foreign missions worldwide. | 20 |
| 38. 150 major ethnolinguistic peoples each have over 100,000 unevangelized ethnoreligionists. | 17 |
| 39. Since AD 1900, Christian urbanites have exploded from 100 million in 500 cities to 1,160 million in 5,000 cities. | 1 |
| 40. From only one million in AD 1900, Pentecostals/Charismatics/Neocharismatics have mushroomed to 524 million affiliated (with unaffiliated believers, 602 million). | 5 |
| 41. UBS global goals for Bibles distributed p.a. are over 200% achieved in 92 countries, over 100% in 92 other countries, but under 100% in 54 countries. | 19 |
| 42. 98.7% of people have access to scripture in 6,700 languages leaving 78 million in 6,800 languages with no access at all. | 19 |
| 43. Each year, 180 million Bibles and New Testaments are wasted—lost, destroyed, or disintegrated—due to incompetence, hostility, bad planning, or inadequate manufacture. | 19 |
| 44. Each year 600,000 full-time ordained workers (clergy, ministers, missionaries) reach retiring age; 150,000 then discover that their employers provide no old-age pensions. | 21 |
| 45. Some 250 of the 300 largest international Christian organizations regularly mislead the Christian public by publishing demonstrably incorrect or falsified progress statistics. | 14 |
| 46. As in all scientific research, 70% of all new Christian books and published articles will never be quoted in print by their peers, ever. | 31 |
| 47. 78 countries each have Great Commission Christians whose personal incomes exceed US$1 billion a year. | 20 |
| 48. Out of 648 million Great Commission Christians, 70% have never been told about World A's 1.6 billion unevangelized individuals. | 25 |
| 49. Depicted on semilogarithmic graphs, 16,016 Christian trends across 22 centuries (AD 30-AD 2200) reveal dominant roles of evangelization, martyrdom, and renewal. | 7 |
| 50. Despite predictions of collapse of religion, long-term trends indicate that Christians and other religionists in AD 2200 are likely to number over 87% of the world's population. | 29 |

**Table 1–2. Global adherents of the world's 19 major distinct religions, with 48 related major religious blocs, and a grand total of some 10,000 distinct and different other religions, quantified at 7 points in time over the period AD 1900–2050 assuming current trends continue.**

| Year | 1900 | | 1970 | | mid-1990 | | Annual change, 1990–2000 | | | | mid-1995 | | mid-2000 | | mid-2025 | | mid-2050 | | Countries in 2000 |
|---|---|---|---|---|---|---|---|---|---|---|---|---|---|---|---|---|---|---|---|
| Religion | Adherents | % | Adherents | % | Adherents | % | Natural | Conversion | Total | Rate | Adherents | % | Adherents | % | Adherents | % | Adherents | % | |
| **Christians** | **558,131,572** | **34.5** | **1,236,373,744** | **33.5** | **1,747,461,964** | **33.2** | **22,708,799** | **2,501,396** | **25,210,195** | **1.36** | **1,877,425,923** | **33.1** | **1,999,563,838** | **33.0** | **2,616,670,052** | **33.4** | **3,051,564,342** | **34.3** | **238** |
| *PROFESSION* | | | | | | | | | | | | | | | | | | | |
| crypto-Christians | 3,571,077 | 0.2 | 59,195,326 | 1.6 | 102,600,880 | 1.9 | 1,408,763 | 703,798 | 2,112,561 | 1.89 | 111,095,011 | 2.0 | 123,726,489 | 2.0 | 190,490,250 | 2.4 | 246,319,348 | 2.8 | 63 |
| **professing Christians** | **554,560,495** | **34.2** | **1,177,177,748** | **31.8** | **1,644,854,444** | **31.2** | **21,299,796** | **1,797,505** | **23,097,301** | **1.32** | **1,766,322,612** | **31.2** | **1,875,827,394** | **31.0** | **2,426,157,502** | **31.0** | **2,805,218,484** | **31.5** | **238** |
| *AFFILIATION* | | | | | | | | | | | | | | | | | | | |
| unaffiliated Christians | 36,488,512 | 2.3 | 106,268,111 | 2.9 | 101,889,253 | 1.9 | 1,305,142 | -381,603 | 923,539 | 0.87 | 107,507,683 | 1.9 | 111,124,545 | 1.8 | 125,711,785 | 1.6 | 124,655,275 | 1.4 | 237 |
| **affiliated Christians** | **521,643,060** | **32.2** | **1,130,105,633** | **30.6** | **1,645,572,711** | **31.2** | **21,403,655** | **2,883,011** | **24,286,666** | **1.39** | **1,769,918,240** | **31.2** | **1,888,439,293** | **31.2** | **2,490,958,267** | **31.8** | **2,926,909,067** | **32.9** | **238** |
| Roman Catholics | 266,547,757 | 16.5 | 666,609,154 | 18.0 | 929,701,934 | 17.7 | 13,117,804 | -355,181 | 12,762,623 | 1.29 | 994,152,689 | 17.5 | 1,057,328,093 | 17.5 | 1,361,965,255 | 17.4 | 1,564,603,495 | 17.6 | 235 |
| Independents | 7,930,940 | 0.5 | 95,604,774 | 2.6 | 301,536,352 | 5.7 | 4,495,891 | 3,925,017 | 8,420,908 | 2.49 | 346,542,889 | 6.1 | 385,745,407 | 6.4 | 581,642,120 | 7.4 | 752,842,240 | 8.5 | 221 |
| Protestants | 103,023,615 | 6.4 | 210,759,378 | 5.7 | 296,349,246 | 5.6 | 4,224,076 | 341,161 | 4,565,237 | 1.44 | 319,679,377 | 5.6 | 342,001,605 | 5.6 | 468,632,927 | 6.0 | 574,418,922 | 6.4 | 233 |
| Orthodox | 115,844,210 | 7.2 | 139,661,574 | 3.8 | 203,765,600 | 3.9 | 750,901 | 385,410 | 1,136,311 | 0.54 | 209,624,412 | 3.7 | 215,128,717 | 3.6 | 252,715,940 | 3.2 | 266,806,050 | 3.0 | 135 |
| Anglicans | 30,570,768 | 1.9 | 47,501,042 | 1.3 | 68,195,625 | 1.3 | 1,071,503 | 73,897 | 1,145,400 | 1.56 | 74,521,243 | 1.3 | 79,649,642 | 1.3 | 113,746,355 | 1.5 | 145,983,770 | 1.6 | 166 |
| Marginal Christians | 927,580 | 0.1 | 11,100,424 | 0.3 | 21,832,515 | 0.4 | 269,292 | 153,482 | 422,774 | 1.79 | 23,850,937 | 0.4 | 26,060,230 | 0.4 | 45,554,730 | 0.6 | 62,200,556 | 0.7 | 215 |
| doubly-affiliated | -2,609,410 | -0.2 | -29,781,765 | -0.8 | -154,615,427 | -2.9 | -2,458,025 | -1,558,424 | -4,016,449 | 2.34 | -174,354,009 | -3.1 | -194,779,901 | -3.2 | -308,401,610 | -3.9 | -413,843,966 | -4.6 | 93 |
| disaffiliated | -592,400 | 0.0 | -11,348,948 | -0.3 | -21,193,134 | -0.4 | -67,786 | -82,351 | -150,137 | 0.69 | -24,099,298 | -0.4 | -22,694,500 | -0.4 | -24,897,450 | -0.3 | -26,102,000 | -0.3 | 11 |
| *Trans-megabloc groupings* | | | | | | | | | | | | | | | | | | | |
| Evangelicals | 71,726,220 | 4.4 | 93,449,158 | 2.5 | 173,272,155 | 3.3 | 2,839,602 | 893,484 | 3,733,086 | 1.97 | 193,419,748 | 3.4 | 210,602,983 | 3.5 | 327,834,735 | 4.2 | 448,862,899 | 5.0 | 238 |
| Pentecostals/Charismatics | 981,400 | 0.1 | 72,222,920 | 2.0 | 425,486,472 | 8.1 | 7,016,903 | 2,812,254 | 9,829,157 | 2.10 | 477,377,916 | 8.4 | 523,777,994 | 8.7 | 811,551,594 | 10.4 | 1,066,318,949 | 12.0 | 238 |
| **Great Commission Christians** | **77,931,100** | **4.8** | **277,152,485** | **7.5** | **560,665,961** | **10.6** | **6,180,025** | **2,535,490** | **8,715,515** | **1.46** | **603,063,619** | **10.6** | **647,820,987** | **10.7** | **887,578,895** | **11.3** | **1,097,449,417** | **12.3** | **238** |
| *NON-CHRISTIANS* | 1,061,494,169 | 65.5 | 2,459,774,397 | 66.5 | 3,518,980,036 | 66.8 | 56,151,992 | -2,501,396 | 53,650,481 | 1.43 | 3,788,934,277 | 66.9 | 4,055,485,162 | 67.0 | 5,207,032,948 | 66.6 | 5,857,530,658 | 65.7 | 238 |
| Muslims | 199,940,924 | 12.3 | 553,527,803 | 15.0 | 962,357,235 | 18.3 | 21,723,118 | 865,558 | 22,588,676 | 2.13 | 1,070,198,775 | 18.9 | 1,188,242,789 | 19.6 | 1,784,875,653 | 22.8 | 2,229,281,610 | 25.0 | 204 |
| Sunnis | 172,949,994 | 10.7 | 468,475,783 | 12.7 | 815,735,235 | 15.5 | 18,214,974 | 465,783 | 18,680,757 | 2.08 | 905,511,775 | 16.0 | 1,002,542,801 | 16.6 | 1,467,825,653 | 18.8 | 1,767,356,610 | 19.8 | 195 |
| Hanafites | 104,539,994 | 6.5 | 236,432,783 | 6.4 | 432,758,235 | 8.2 | 9,480,204 | 385,753 | 9,865,957 | 2.07 | 480,712,775 | 8.5 | 531,417,801 | 8.8 | 724,355,653 | 9.3 | 868,156,610 | 9.7 | 135 |
| Shafiites | 39,000,000 | 2.4 | 112,000,000 | 3.0 | 193,000,000 | 3.7 | 4,590,019 | 99,981 | 4,690,000 | 2.20 | 215,200,000 | 3.8 | 239,900,000 | 4.0 | 393,500,000 | 5.0 | 472,900,000 | 5.3 | 105 |
| Malikites | 27,000,000 | 1.7 | 114,186,000 | 3.1 | 182,000,000 | 3.5 | 3,925,302 | 64,698 | 3,990,000 | 2.00 | 201,000,000 | 3.5 | 221,900,000 | 3.7 | 346,600,000 | 4.4 | 408,700,000 | 4.6 | 65 |
| Wahhabites | 1,910,000 | 0.1 | 4,717,000 | 0.1 | 6,107,000 | 0.1 | 91,447 | -2,147 | 89,300 | 1.37 | 6,514,000 | 0.1 | 7,000,000 | 0.1 | 9,668,000 | 0.1 | 13,350,000 | 0.1 | 10 |
| Hanbalites | 500,000 | 0.0 | 1,140,000 | 0.0 | 1,870,000 | 0.0 | 28,002 | 17,498 | 45,500 | 2.20 | 2,085,000 | 0.0 | 2,325,000 | 0.0 | 3,370,000 | 0.0 | 4,250,000 | 0.0 | 25 |
| Sufis | 80,000,000 | 4.9 | 138,100,000 | 3.7 | 202,200,000 | 3.8 | 3,027,781 | 492,219 | 3,520,000 | 1.62 | 219,500,000 | 3.9 | 237,400,000 | 3.9 | 356,200,000 | 4.6 | 445,000,000 | 5.0 | 204 |
| Shias | 26,000,000 | 1.6 | 79,500,000 | 2.2 | 135,500,000 | 2.6 | 3,029,003 | 313,863 | 3,460,000 | 2.30 | 151,800,000 | 2.7 | 170,100,000 | 2.8 | 286,000,000 | 3.7 | 410,000,000 | 4.6 | 75 |
| Ithna-Asharis | 22,250,000 | 1.4 | 65,270,000 | 1.8 | 109,570,000 | 2.1 | 2,540,722 | 167,778 | 2,708,500 | 2.23 | 122,353,000 | 2.2 | 136,655,000 | 2.3 | 229,178,000 | 2.9 | 333,175,000 | 3.7 | 70 |
| Ismailis | 2,300,000 | 0.1 | 9,700,000 | 0.3 | 18,212,000 | 0.3 | 472,710 | 83,290 | 556,000 | 2.70 | 20,807,000 | 0.4 | 23,772,000 | 0.4 | 40,950,000 | 0.5 | 55,200,000 | 0.6 | 45 |
| Zaydis | 1,200,000 | 0.1 | 3,760,000 | 0.1 | 6,406,000 | 0.1 | 95,925 | 67,675 | 163,600 | 2.30 | 7,177,000 | 0.1 | 8,042,000 | 0.1 | 13,192,000 | 0.2 | 17,775,000 | 0.2 | 10 |
| Alawites | 250,000 | 0.0 | 770,000 | 0.0 | 1,312,000 | 0.0 | 19,646 | 12,254 | 31,900 | 2.20 | 1,463,000 | 0.0 | 1,631,000 | 0.0 | 2,680,000 | 0.0 | 3,850,000 | 0.0 | 15 |
| Islamic schismatics | 990,930 | 0.1 | 5,592,020 | 0.2 | 11,125,000 | 0.2 | 296,588 | 85,912 | 382,500 | 3.00 | 12,900,000 | 0.2 | 14,950,000 | 0.2 | 27,700,000 | 0.4 | 47,725,000 | 0.5 | 110 |
| Ahmadis | 70,030 | 0.0 | 2,635,220 | 0.1 | 5,774,000 | 0.1 | 156,461 | 61,139 | 217,600 | 3.25 | 6,775,000 | 0.1 | 7,950,000 | 0.1 | 14,700,000 | 0.2 | 24,100,000 | 0.3 | 75 |
| Other sectarian Muslims | 500,000 | 0.0 | 1,500,000 | 0.0 | 1,888,000 | 0.0 | 58,271 | 18,329 | 76,600 | 3.46 | 2,244,000 | 0.0 | 2,654,000 | 0.0 | 5,697,000 | 0.1 | 13,267,000 | 0.1 | 30 |
| Black Muslims | 0 | 0.0 | 200,000 | 0.0 | 1,290,000 | 0.0 | 25,317 | 10,683 | 36,000 | 2.49 | 1,460,000 | 0.0 | 1,650,000 | 0.0 | 2,910,000 | 0.0 | 5,020,000 | 0.1 | 5 |
| Kharijites | 320,000 | 0.0 | 780,000 | 0.0 | 1,329,000 | 0.0 | 26,901 | 3,799 | 30,700 | 2.10 | 1,475,000 | 0.0 | 1,636,000 | 0.0 | 2,620,000 | 0.0 | 3,145,000 | 0.0 | 10 |
| Druzes | 71,000 | 0.0 | 374,800 | 0.0 | 664,000 | 0.0 | 15,943 | 1,057 | 17,000 | 2.31 | 744,000 | 0.0 | 834,000 | 0.0 | 1,402,000 | 0.0 | 1,710,000 | 0.0 | 15 |
| Hindus | 203,003,440 | 12.5 | 462,597,720 | 12.5 | 685,998,940 | 13.0 | 13,194,111 | -660,377 | 12,533,734 | 1.69 | 751,591,511 | 13.3 | 811,336,265 | 13.4 | 1,049,230,740 | 13.4 | 1,175,297,850 | 13.2 | 114 |
| Vaishnavites | 143,153,440 | 8.8 | 323,462,720 | 8.8 | 462,536,940 | 8.8 | 8,026,116 | -478,522 | 8,704,638 | 1.74 | 508,916,511 | 9.0 | 549,583,323 | 9.1 | 708,160,740 | 9.1 | 791,806,850 | 8.9 | 90 |
| Shaivites | 52,800,000 | 3.3 | 115,946,000 | 3.1 | 182,712,000 | 3.5 | 3,435,964 | -118,836 | 3,354,800 | 1.70 | 198,780,000 | 3.5 | 216,260,000 | 3.6 | 278,900,000 | 3.6 | 312,410,000 | 3.5 | 60 |
| Saktists | 6,700,000 | 0.4 | 13,932,000 | 0.4 | 21,740,000 | 0.4 | 325,539 | 72,461 | 398,000 | 1.70 | 23,650,000 | 0.4 | 25,720,000 | 0.4 | 33,150,000 | 0.4 | 37,132,000 | 0.4 | 35 |
| Neo-Hindus | 100,000 | 0.0 | 6,957,000 | 0.2 | 13,318,000 | 0.3 | 389,426 | 17,274 | 406,700 | 2.70 | 15,215,000 | 0.3 | 17,385,000 | 0.3 | 23,200,000 | 0.3 | 27,300,000 | 0.3 | 65 |
| Reform Hindus | 250,000 | 0.0 | 2,300,000 | 0.1 | 3,732,000 | 0.1 | 65,884 | 6,916 | 72,800 | 1.80 | 4,080,000 | 0.1 | 4,460,000 | 0.1 | 5,820,000 | 0.1 | 6,650,000 | 0.1 | 30 |
| Nonreligious | 3,023,630 | 0.2 | 532,095,567 | 14.4 | 707,117,959 | 13.4 | 6,639,206 | -535,100 | 6,104,106 | 0.83 | 738,017,729 | 13.0 | 768,158,954 | 12.7 | 875,120,895 | 11.2 | 887,994,945 | 10.0 | 236 |
| Chinese folk-religionists | 380,006,038 | 23.5 | 231,865,233 | 6.3 | 347,651,252 | 6.6 | 3,801,126 | -85,578 | 3,715,548 | 1.02 | 369,192,379 | 6.5 | 384,806,732 | 6.4 | 448,842,560 | 5.7 | 454,332,660 | 5.1 | 89 |
| Buddhists | 127,076,771 | 7.8 | 233,424,191 | 6.3 | 323,106,550 | 6.1 | 3,530,918 | 156,609 | 3,687,527 | 1.09 | 341,764,830 | 6.0 | 359,981,757 | 5.9 | 418,344,730 | 5.3 | 424,607,060 | 4.8 | 126 |
| Mahayana | 71,476,771 | 4.4 | 131,892,191 | 3.6 | 181,724,550 | 3.5 | 1,951,178 | 100,357 | 2,050,821 | 1.08 | 192,425,830 | 3.4 | 202,232,757 | 3.3 | 235,264,730 | 3.0 | 238,772,060 | 2.7 | 115 |
| Theravada | 48,100,000 | 3.0 | 87,700,000 | 2.4 | 122,139,000 | 2.3 | 1,372,933 | 40,933 | 1,412,000 | 1.10 | 129,006,000 | 2.3 | 136,259,000 | 2.3 | 158,200,000 | 2.0 | 160,575,000 | 1.8 | 30 |
| Lamaists | 7,500,000 | 0.5 | 13,832,000 | 0.4 | 19,263,000 | 0.4 | 207,381 | 15,319 | 222,700 | 1.10 | 20,346,000 | 0.4 | 21,490,000 | 0.4 | 24,980,000 | 0.3 | 25,380,000 | 0.3 | 30 |
| Ethnoreligionists | 117,558,485 | 7.3 | 160,278,357 | 4.3 | 200,035,408 | 3.8 | 4,098,003 | -1,264,887 | 2,833,116 | 1.33 | 214,088,710 | 3.8 | 228,366,515 | 3.8 | 277,247,150 | 3.5 | 303,598,980 | 3.4 | 142 |
| Animists | 106,275,545 | 6.6 | 143,566,857 | 3.9 | 188,691,748 | 3.6 | 3,985,506 | -1,238,592 | 2,746,914 | 1.37 | 202,190,060 | 3.6 | 216,160,890 | 3.6 | 263,990,700 | 3.4 | 290,789,380 | 3.3 | 142 |
| Shamanists | 11,283,040 | 0.7 | 16,711,500 | 0.5 | 11,383,660 | 0.2 | 122,433 | -30,971 | 91,462 | 0.78 | 11,965,650 | 0.2 | 12,298,267 | 0.2 | 13,256,450 | 0.2 | 12,809,600 | 0.1 | 12 |
| Atheists | 226,120 | 0.0 | 165,400,320 | 4.5 | 145,718,604 | 2.8 | 1,315,322 | -878,227 | 437,095 | 0.30 | 148,318,655 | 2.6 | 150,089,508 | 2.5 | 159,544,080 | 2.0 | 169,150,200 | 1.9 | 161 |
| New-Religionists (Neoreligionists) | 5,910,000 | 0.4 | 77,762,430 | 2.1 | 92,396,355 | 1.8 | 1,032,400 | -36,405 | 995,995 | 1.03 | 97,699,635 | 1.7 | 102,356,297 | 1.7 | 114,720,210 | 1.5 | 118,845,140 | 1.3 | 60 |
| Sikhs | 2,962,300 | 0.2 | 10,617,700 | 0.3 | 19,332,080 | 0.4 | 363,677 | 28,961 | 392,638 | 1.87 | 21,226,480 | 0.4 | 23,258,412 | 0.4 | 31,377,860 | 0.4 | 37,058,960 | 0.4 | 34 |
| Jews | 12,292,210 | 0.8 | 14,763,420 | 0.4 | 13,188,955 | 0.3 | 194,962 | -70,447 | 124,515 | 0.91 | 13,860,205 | 0.2 | 14,434,039 | 0.2 | 16,053,350 | 0.2 | 16,694,500 | 0.2 | 134 |
| Ashkenazis | 11,278,810 | 0.7 | 12,620,920 | 0.3 | 10,124,855 | 0.2 | 151,611 | -56,103 | 95,508 | 0.91 | 10,654,105 | 0.2 | 11,079,939 | 0.2 | 12,321,550 | 0.2 | 12,811,700 | 0.1 | 120 |
| Oriental Jews | 700,000 | 0.0 | 1,520,000 | 0.0 | 2,172,000 | 0.0 | 32,524 | -11,924 | 20,600 | 0.91 | 2,273,000 | 0.0 | 2,378,000 | 0.0 | 2,645,000 | 0.0 | 2,750,000 | 0.0 | 25 |
| Sefardis | 300,000 | 0.0 | 607,000 | 0.0 | 870,000 | 0.0 | 13,028 | -4,828 | 8,200 | 0.90 | 910,000 | 0.0 | 952,000 | 0.0 | 1,060,000 | 0.0 | 1,105,000 | 0.0 | 80 |
| Karaites | 13,400 | 0.0 | 15,500 | 0.0 | 22,100 | 0.0 | 331 | -131 | 200 | 0.87 | 23,100 | 0.0 | 24,100 | 0.0 | 26,800 | 0.0 | 27,800 | 0.0 | 5 |
| Samaritans | 500 | 0.0 | 500 | 0.0 | 500 | 0.0 | 7 | -7 | 0 | 0.00 | 500 | 0.0 | 500 | 0.0 | 500 | 0.0 | 500 | 0.0 | 5 |
| Spiritists | 269,040 | 0.0 | 4,602,780 | 0.1 | 10,154,665 | 0.2 | 137,163 | 80,748 | 217,911 | 1.96 | 11,142,555 | 0.2 | 12,333,735 | 0.2 | 16,211,780 | 0.2 | 20,709,300 | 0.2 | 55 |
| Afro-American spiritists | 112,440 | 0.0 | 420,260 | 0.0 | 875,000 | 0.0 | 15,524 | 4,149 | 19,673 | 2.05 | 971,555 | 0.0 | 1,071,735 | 0.0 | 1,609,190 | 0.0 | 2,116,020 | 0.0 | 18 |
| Afro-Brazilian cultists | 97,000 | 0.0 | 1,320,000 | 0.0 | 3,700,000 | 0.1 | 65,460 | 22,224 | 87,684 | 2.15 | 4,051,000 | 0.1 | 4,576,844 | 0.1 | 6,100,000 | 0.1 | 8,000,000 | 0.1 | 1 |
| High Spiritists | 40,000 | 0.0 | 1,220,000 | 0.0 | 2,920,000 | 0.1 | 53,725 | 29,275 | 83,000 | 2.53 | 3,321,000 | 0.1 | 3,750,000 | 0.1 | 5,100,000 | 0.1 | 7,000,000 | 0.1 | 20 |
| Afro-Caribbean religionists | 100 | 0.0 | 10,500 | 0.0 | 77,600 | 0.0 | 1,162 | 1,818 | 2,980 | 3.30 | 92,600 | 0.0 | 107,397 | 0.0 | 183,800 | 0.0 | 256,100 | 0.0 | 5 |
| Baha'is | 9,535 | 0.0 | 2,657,349 | 0.1 | 5,671,687 | 0.1 | 117,158 | 26,333 | 143,491 | 2.28 | 6,273,880 | 0.1 | 7,106,420 | 0.1 | 12,062,150 | 0.2 | 18,000,900 | 0.2 | 218 |
| Confucianists | 640,050 | 0.0 | 4,759,200 | 0.1 | 5,855,540 | 0.1 | 55,739 | -11,434 | 44,305 | 0.73 | 6,075,720 | 0.1 | 6,298,597 | 0.1 | 6,817,950 | 0.1 | 6,952,900 | 0.1 | 15 |
| Jains | 1,323,280 | 0.1 | 2,617,810 | 0.1 | 3,868,470 | 0.1 | 74,539 | -39,588 | 34,951 | 0.87 | 3,894,120 | 0.1 | 4,217,979 | 0.1 | 6,115,650 | 0.1 | 6,732,770 | 0.1 | 10 |
| Shintoists | 6,720,000 | 0.4 | 4,175,000 | 0.1 | 3,081,790 | 0.1 | 8,534 | -40,527 | -31,993 | -1.09 | 2,838,540 | 0.1 | 2,761,845 | 0.0 | 2,122,950 | 0.0 | 1,655,400 | 0.0 | 8 |
| Taoists | 375,000 | 0.0 | 1,734,000 | 0.0 | 2,402,090 | 0.0 | 25,397 | -155 | 25,242 | 1.00 | 2,551,850 | 0.0 | 2,654,514 | 0.0 | 3,066,300 | 0.0 | 3,272,200 | 0.0 | 5 |
| Zoroastrians | 108,490 | 0.0 | 121,890 | 0.0 | 1,959,260 | 0.0 | 45,391 | 13,080 | 58,471 | 2.65 | 2,265,800 | 0.0 | 2,543,950 | 0.0 | 4,439,930 | 0.1 | 6,964,700 | 0.1 | 24 |
| Other religionists (in 3,000 religions) | 49,115 | 0.0 | 784,100 | 0.0 | 963,571 | 0.0 | 10,013 | 386 | 10,393 | 1.03 | 1,017,550 | 0.0 | 1,067,496 | 0.0 | 1,500,430 | 0.0 | 1,937,820 | 0.0 | 76 |
| Yezidis | 29,900 | 0.0 | 102,000 | 0.0 | 180,000 | 0.0 | 3,695 | 905 | 4,600 | 2.30 | 202,000 | 0.0 | 226,000 | 0.0 | 371,000 | 0.0 | 483,000 | 0.0 | 10 |
| Mandeans | 8,000 | 0.0 | 23,000 | 0.0 | 31,600 | 0.0 | 823 | -85 | 738 | 2.12 | 35,000 | 0.0 | 38,977 | 0.0 | 58,000 | 0.0 | 76,000 | 0.0 | 2 |
| doubly-counted religionists | 0 | 0.0 | -4,000,000 | -0.1 | -11,879,300 | -0.2 | -214,784 | -50,346 | -265,130 | 2.04 | -13,083,000 | -0.2 | -14,530,637 | -0.2 | -20,665,000 | -0.3 | -25,516,000 | -0.3 | 24 |
| World A (unevangelized persons) | 879,671,736 | 54.3 | 1,641,245,161 | 44.4 | 1,665,470,930 | 31.6 | 28,353,920 | -31,963,512 | -3,609,592 | -0.22 | 1,678,204,817 | 29.6 | 1,629,374,957 | 26.9 | 1,845,405,668 | 23.6 | 1,806,052,390 | 20.3 | 238 |
| World B (evangelized non-Christians) | 181,822,433 | 11.2 | 818,529,236 | 22.1 | 1,853,509,106 | 35.2 | 27,798,072 | 29,462,116 | 57,260,188 | 2.73 | 2,110,729,460 | 37.3 | 2,426,110,205 | 40.1 | 3,361,627,280 | 43.0 | 4,051,478,268 | 45.5 | 238 |
| World C (Christians) | 558,131,572 | 34.5 | 1,236,373,744 | 33.5 | 1,747,461,964 | 33.2 | 22,708,799 | 2,501,396 | 25,210,195 | 1.36 | 1,877,425,923 | 33.1 | 1,999,563,838 | 33.0 | 2,616,670,052 | 33.4 | 3,051,564,342 | 34.3 | 238 |
| **Global population** | **1,619,625,741** | **100.0** | **3,696,148,141** | **100.0** | **5,266,442,000** | **100.0** | **78,860,791** | **0** | **78,860,791** | **1.41** | **5,666,360,200** | **100.0** | **6,055,049,000** | **100.0** | **7,823,703,000** | **100.0** | **8,909,095,000** | **100.0** | **238** |

new churches and agencies sending foreign and home missionaries.

Fourth, Christians have stepped up their evangelistic efforts particularly in line with advances in communications technology, beginning with radio early in the century and progressing to satellite networks today. In 1900 it is estimated that Christians generated enough evangelism on earth for every person to hear the gospel 6 times every year. By 2000 that figure had skyrocketed to 155 times—a gospel presentation for every person on earth every 2 days all year long.

*Failure to impact the whole world*
Remarkably, these dramatic changes have not achieved a fundamental goal of Christian missions—proclaiming the good news to every people in the world. A major study by Samuel Zwemer was commissioned by the Edinburgh Missionary Conference in 1910 and then published the following year as *The unoccupied mission fields of Africa and Asia*. Zwemer clearly outlined the unfinished task and the opportunities the churches had for contacting the unevangelized. He even emblazened an early version of the '10/40 Window' on the cover. This call was largely ignored. Similar clarion calls were made throughout the 20th century culminating with a global concerted effort in the 1990s with a now-popularized 10/40 Window. Nonetheless, at the end of the 20th century, 1.6 billion people in several thousand ethnolinguistic peoples were still without access to a culturally-relevant church community, or to any aspect of the gospel of Christ.

This shortfall is largely the result of where missionaries worked during the 20th century. Nine out of ten missionaries sent out went to work among peoples already contacted by the Christian message, and in some cases, already heavily Christian. This pattern is being repeated today by the new independent missionaries, and to a large extent, by non-Western missionaries. The result is that over 95% of all Christian effort today is directed only at the Christian world.

The lack of contact between Christians and non-Christians must also be viewed in the context of the world's great social problems. The 20th century was one of the bloodiest on record with over 200 major conflicts including two world wars. These conflicts are largely responsible today for a record 40 million displaced persons (internal and external exiles). One third of these are environmental refugees with 300,000 a year dying as the result of environmental disasters. Some 800 million individuals, mainly women, children, and the elderly, are chronically malnourished. 15 million die every year from diseases related to malnutrition. 2 million children die each year through lack of immunization against preventable diseases. Every year nearly 600,000 children are newly infected with the AIDS virus. The global total of HIV-positive individuals now exceeds 40 million. Some 2.2 billion people do not have access to safe water. The urban poor have mushroomed to 1.4 billion, half of all urban dwellers. Over 120 million children live or work on the streets of the world's cities. 10 million children are forced into prostitution and another 200 million children are forced into child labor. These and scores of similar statistics paint a stark picture of reality, a reality that Christians ignore at their peril.

Another unanticipated trend has been the tremendous resistance shown by non-Christians toward Christians and Christian missions in the 20th century. The rise of Communism early in the century provided much of this dynamic. Throughout 70 years, not only were Christians in Communist lands under intense persecution but millions lost their lives prematurely as a result of their witness—our definition of Christian martyrs. With the collapse of Communism in 1989–1991 one would think that martyrdom and persecution would now have become rare. Unfortunately this is not the case. Outside of the Communist world, governments that now persecute Christians are run by secularists, Muslims, Hindus, and surprisingly, other Christians. In fact, the 20th century has been the bloodiest on record, not only for all of humanity but for Christians as well. In these 100 years more Christians have lost their lives as martyrs than in all the previous centuries combined. The current rate is a staggering 160,000 new Christian martyrs each year.

*Entering the Third Millennium*
The challenges that the new missions force of the 21st century faces are legion. The world of AD 2000 is radically different from that of 1900. The overconfidence exhibited early in this century by secular leaders of the Enlightenment has been completely deflated by the collapse of Communism and a general loss of faith in science and the idea of inevitable progress. Christian theologians and mission leaders who borrowed heavily from this paradigm now find themselves at a crossroads. Although some advocate an even stronger 'modern' approach, many see the changing times as a corrective to the overconfidence of 20th century strategies.

With that in mind, some see the ethos of 20th-century mission creeping into 21st-century initiatives. First is the tendency to convene big conferences with impressive slogans in which the implications of the slogans fail to be seriously addressed. Second, the hoped-for century of church union has become instead one of schism and lack of cooperation. If anything, hundreds of new organizations have emerged, each with its own independently-stated plans. Third, the number of missionaries available for frontier missions is being impacted by an increasing uneasiness over the efficacy of Christianity in already-discipled peoples—Rwanda as a premier example. As a result, more mission effort is advocated among the 141 countries already 60% or more Christian—already the locus of current missionary deployment. Fourth, short-term assignments are now a driving force in missions. Although this means that more Christians are exposed to foreign mission fields, it seems to be having the effect of injecting a short-term emphasis into long-term church planting strategies. Fifth, although much has been learned in contextualization of the gospel, emerging short-term mentalities foreshadow a de-emphasis on language and culture learning—long the backbone of the foreign missionary enterprise.

Nonetheless, positive developments in 20th century mission are also being appropriated in the new century. First and foremost has been the formation of two kinds of partnerships. First, we see increasing cooperation between Western and non-Western missions. Whereas there have been many false starts along the way, valuable lessons have been learned related to the use of money and the sharing of control over personnel and funds. Second, strategic partnerships between mission agencies have been formed specifically around unreached peoples. For example, a Bible translation agency decides to work closely with church planters and radio broadcasters. Although these partnerships are few in number, they represent a major step forward in frontier missions strategy. Closely related to this is the rise of nonresidential missionaries (NRMs) or strategy coordinators. This new breed of foreign missionary steps back far enough from a specific people to enumerate all the possible ways they might be reached. They then choose 10 or so of the best strategies and advocate among specialized agencies such as media ministries for their accomplishment.

*Radical new developments*
Perhaps the most astonishing development in frontier missions in the 20th century has been the unanticipated rise of non-baptized believers in Christ, now known by the label NBBCs. Akin to the fabulous growth of the Chinese house churches or the African Independent churches in the latter half of the 20th century, several millions of Hindus, Muslims, and Buddhists have given their primary allegiance to Jesus Christ as Lord and Savior. Yet, in doing so, they have chosen not to leave their cultural traditions to join Christian churches but instead to remain as witnesses to Christ within their own religions. Their growth and development as individual believers and movements are not to be taken for granted. It may depend largely on the ability of key leaders within the Christian church to study and understand the implications of this kind of radical contextualization. Their role as ambassadors will be to try to anticipate how these new believers interact with Christian churches. They may also be able to unlock contextualized strategies in reaching other peoples currently beyond the influence of the gospel.

All of these developments underscore the fact that the missionary of the 21st century will likely have a much greater load to bear than his or her 20th-century predecessor. Faced with information overload in a networked environment, multiple agencies from multiple countries taking multiple approaches, the impact of globalization and postmodernism on seemingly remote peoples, an increased need for cultural, ethnic, and religious sensitivity, the emergence of almost-unrecognizable new forms of Christianity, and a host of other new factors, missionaries more than ever will need to be well prepared in the 21st century. Only then will the churches of the world be able to fulfill the basic requirement of the Great Commission—the effective penetration of all peoples with the gospel presence.

## *VISUALIZING WORLD MISSION*

***Viewing past, present, and future***

This is an interpretative commentary on the 74 kaleidoscopic global diagrams that follow in this Part 1.

For almost 2 millennia, disciples of Jesus Christ have attempted to follow him on his mission of redemption to the whole world. They have sought to obey his last command on Earth, known as the Great Commission: 'Go into all the world and make disciples of all peoples' (Matthew 28:19).

The series of 74 kaleidoscopic global diagrams that follows (listed in Table 1–3) attempts to portray the origin, history, evolution, current status, and possible futures of this Christian world mission. They do this by bringing together, for each of the major related subjects or sub-divisions, 3 elements: (a) any global statistics relevant to the subject, that is all available figures at the all-inclusive world or worldwide level, describing the subject or in any demonstrable way relevant to understanding the status of the subject; (b) a diagrammatic illustration of the subject, usually via a globe or other representation of the totality of the world situation and the world task; and (c) a short introductory text setting the scene and interpreting the whole diagram.

In this way, this series of 74 kaleidoscopic multifaceted global diagrams, describes the world of yesterday, today, and tomorrow in relation to world evangelization. This latter subject, which refers to the influence of Jesus Christ on the world and the spread of his gospel, is in fact the ultimate focus of the series. Each diagram portrays our world from a different stand-point. Each diagram is packed with relevant statistics—both already-published global statistics, and also newly-computed global statistics. All figures have exact definitions, time reference ('today' usually meaning mid-1995 or mid-2000) and geographical reference. Each statistic or category occurs only once in this series, in the most relevant diagram, except for a small handful of overall totals (e.g. '1.8 billion Christians') necessary to set the starting points of several diagrams. Any subject or category with its statistics can be immediately located from the alphabetized Quick-Reference Global Statistical Index in Part 9. And any and all sets of initials given here, or used anywhere in this book, are expanded in Part 32.

The 74 diagrams are divided into 5 categories—Overview, then Past, Present, Future, and Long-term Future. The latter quartet underline the 3 major ongoing functions or values of statistics: for understanding the past, for analyzing the present, and for planning for the future.

The diagrams are arranged in a continuous, evolving sequence, moving from one major subject to the next throughout these 3 distinct parts.

***74 kaleidoscopic global diagrams***

First, Global Diagrams 1-4 set the overall scene: the whole complex world of religions, the describing of Christianity's precise boundaries, the annual Christian megacensus, and an overview of Christianity's world trends across the centuries.

Second, Global Diagrams 5-17 describe the origins and history of the subject. The roots of the concept of evangelization must clearly be sought in the Christian Scriptures. The Greek word *euangelizo* is central to this endeavor. Yet it is surprising how many Christian leaders do not know the facts about its meaning nor the meaning and biblical usage of its English transliteration 'evangelize'.

Third, Global Diagrams 18-45 delineate the current situation today. Subjects here range from the catastrophic situation of global human need, through multiple Christian concerns and ministries, on to the central hope of Christian action—today's Great Commission harvest force.

Fourth, Global Diagrams 46-74 lay out data on 29 approaches to understanding the future, each viewing the subject from a different perspective. These deal with current ongoing megatrends, short-term AD 2025 projections, and long-term 21st century scenarios.

Each of these 74 diagrams can best be understood in the context of the whole 74 and their subjects. For this reason, there is little repetition or duplication from one diagram to the next. Any subject, topic, or any of the 4,200 different statistical categories enumerated on the diagrams can be immediately located by using the Quick-Reference Global Statistical Index in Part 9 "Globalistics", which is arranged as a single alphabetical listing.

Note here an important usage with these statistics. The 74 global diagrams are intended to be impressionistic approaches to their subjects, using a range of statistics as illustrations. These statistics do not relate to one single point in time but instead relate to the whole period of the Decade of Evangelism, 1990-2000, covering the last decade before the new Millennium. Readers who require exact precision on any particular subject will find it in Part 9 "Globalistics", where all statistics relate to the year AD 2000 unless a different year is there specified.

The careful reader may also notice here and there discrepant figures for various categories. The explanations may be: same categories but different times (years), or places (countries), or sources (print or oral), or methods (linear growth versus exponential growth), or definitions ('Christians' has many different meanings), or quite simply, differing opinions on the part of experts or specialists involved which nevertheless do not invalidate the figures' value as illustrations. The point to remember is that, for users wanting a precise numerical value for any category, especially for the year 2000, the definitive figures in this volume are those in Part 9 "Globalistics".

We move now to a more detailed commentary on individual diagrams.

## I. OVERVIEW

The first 4 diagrams describe the wider overall situation in which this whole study of trends takes place. It starts with 4 interpretative background diagrams.

**1. The world of religions** GD-1

Global Diagram 1 portrays the globe as influenced by its 9,900 different religions. Global statistics for each religion, and for each cover term and neologism employed here, will be found in Tables 17-3 to 17-6.

**2. Boundaries of Christianity** GD-2

An attempt is made here to describe the borders, boundaries, or edges of Christian membership and participation. This is done by the use of precise definitions which are then exactly followed in the compilation of the *WCD* database and in the whole analysis reported in this book.

At the same time, it must be understood that this survey and its data are descriptive, not prescriptive. We are describing the phenomena of Christianity. This use here of exact boundaries and precise definitions—in sociological terms, a bounded set approach—is simply to make sense of the enormous mass of new religious data emerging every year and thus to justify the vast sums of money, time, and energy that the churches and agencies expend each year in undertaking this megacensus.

**3. The annual megacensus** GD-3

For over 800 years, churches have every year been counting membership, baptisms, clergy, and other variables. Though uncoordinated, these tens of thousands of separate censuses produce results that can readily be brought into one single comparative framework, thus producing the megacensus as described in Global Diagram 3. On the following page, Table AA is an example of reporting on the megacensus.

**4. World Christian trends** GD-4

The major or most significant trends in the expansion of Christianity over the years deal with Christian membership, attributes, and activities relating to the non-Christian world. These are here summarized in graphic form using semi-logarithmic scales. On the page following Global Diagram 4, Table BB presents part of the detailed data from which the graphs are derived.

## II. HISTORICAL ANALYSIS: UNDERSTANDING THE PAST

'Those who do not study the past are condemned to repeat its mistakes.' This maxim attributed to the philosopher Santayana tells us why it is important to study history, why it is necessary to study church history, and in particular why it is essential to study the history of world evangelization. Over the last 20 centuries, Christian leaders have spearheaded over 1,500 determined attempts to evangelize the world. Over 900 of these failed abysmally. We need to know why. We need to learn the lessons of history.

For understanding the past, statistics have a clear role to play in helping us. A whole branch of the study of history named cliometrics is devoted to statistics. Cliometrics endeavors to uncover statistical descriptions of historical phenomena—such as the finances of medieval England or the logistics of death in the Black Plague of 1347 which killed one quarter of Europe's population. Research on incomes and budgets, lists of deaths and population movements contribute crucial understandings of the bygone age.

Our subject in this book takes us back to AD 33 and to the Great Commission given to his disciples by Jesus Christ after his death on the cross and resurrection. Our statistical starting points give us word counts, word frequencies from the New Testament Greek accounts and later from the English versions of the Bible. We also have voluminous statistics over 20 centuries about Christians who paid the ultimate price of obedience to the Great Commission by losing their lives for Christ in situations of witness through human hostility.

**5. Summary-1** (Global Diagram 5) GD-5

This diagram gives a complete overview of the 74 kaleidoscopic global diagrams dealing with past, present, and future, and specifically with the period AD 30-AD 2025. Statistics on this diagram reveal the mind-boggling complexity of the task: the world has 13,500 languages today, in 10,000 of which Jesus is acclaimed in 100,000 distinct titles (Lord, Savior, Redeemer, King, etc).

### COSMOCHRONOLOGY
(Global Diagrams 6-17)

**6. GeoCommission** GD-6

Global Diagram 6 takes us to the heart of the Great Commission itself. In its original forms (6 separate accounts of its institution in the Greek New Testament) a large number of distinct emphases stand out both in Greek and subsequently in English. These have been grouped here into 7 Mandates based on the 7 dominant Greek verbs and their corresponding 7 English imperatives: *Receive! Go! Witness! Proclaim! Disciple! Baptize! Train!*. These are elaborated into 7 distinct varieties of evangelization ('7-P Evangelization'). The human role related to these commands produces 7 different varieties of evangelism ('7-P Evangelism'). Detailed statistics are given in the diagram concerning the usage of all these key words.

**7. Greek roots** GD-7

The next diagram then looks in detail into the New Testament Greek mandate which is based on the frequencies of over 210 Greek verbs related to *euangelizo*. There are also 500 close cognates of this word, that is, nouns, adjectives and other related words. Anyone professing to know what the English word 'evangelize' means must therefore first have studied the extensive evidence presented on this diagram.

Following this diagram is a list of the 160 major verbs occurring in the Greek New Testament which are synonyms of the verb *euangelizo*. This alphabetical listing, Table CC, is designed to help the reader who wants to identify and translate a Greek verb on the spot.

Global Diagram 33 does for English usage what Global Diagram 7 does for Greek usage. It describes the 400 English verbs which are distinct dimensions of the English word 'evangelize'. A full listing of these is presented in Tables 23-17, -18, and -19.

**8. Contact with non-Christians** GD-8

On this diagram are 16 globes showing the degree of contact that Christians have had with non-Christians at 16 points in time. Christians are represented here as World C. World B enumerates all non-Christians with whom Christians have been or are in contact, resulting in varying degrees of evangelization of World B. World A is quite different—it is that part of the non-Christian world which Christians have not contacted. As a result, persons in World A know nothing of Christianity, Christ, or the gospel.

**9. Disobedience** GD-9

In Global Diagram 9 it can be seen that church history—the history of Christianity from AD 33 to AD 2000—is largely a history of the disobedience of Christians to the command of Christ in the Great Commission. Analyzing what has been accomplished by the 7 Mandates of the Commission, we see that World C represents a success story of obedience; World B results from part obedience, part disobedience; whereas World A is clearly a story of disobedience and failure. For whatever reasons, good or bad, Christians down the ages have disobeyed their Master's wishes for this huge segment of mankind.

**10. Megatypologies of GeoRenewal** GD-10

Over the last 20 centuries, Christianity has been characterized by a multifold series of renewals, minirenewals, and even several megarenewals. These can be grouped into 4 overall global typologies of empirical Christianity, termed here Megatypologies 1, 2, 3, and 4. All are distinct and separate, historically, but they do in fact overlap somewhat at a number of points. Global Diagram 10 shows each as a separate globe, with each's characteristics and statistics. One larger globe then has superimposed on it all 4 megatypologies, showing the areas of overlap and their statistics in AD 2000.

**11. Evangelicalism** GD-11

One of the 4 megatypologies widely understood in the depicting of global Christianity goes back to the Evangelical Revival in the 18th century under the Wesleys and Whitefield. The diagram shows the vast diversity into which it has since evolved. In particular, it explains the 2-fold terminology which enables us to define its size today as at 211 million Evangelicals and 648 million evangelicals.

**12. Pentecostal/Charismatic GeoRenewal** GD-12

In depicting this movement the diagram describes an extraordinary numerical coincidence. Two massive forces impinge on the numerical fortunes of the Body of Christ: death and life.

The Christian church, like every other part of humanity, suffers from a relentless annual death toll. For the church this numbers 18,400,000 a year. Christian families, congregations, organizations, teams, and staffs mourn each year as loved ones, indispensable colleagues, and irreplaceable experts pass suddenly away at the rate of 50,410 every day. Often this abruptly terminates vital Christian plans or projects or programs. Every year, every day, in fact, this is a tragedy. Some 50% of these deaths are untimely or premature. Some 25% are of Christians who can be said not simply to have died but to have been killed (a term which includes being murdered but excludes deaths by disease, starvation, or poverty). Since 12,600 Christians are thus being killed every day, is there any hope for the survival of organized Christian working and planning?

One answer can be found in the number of new persons every year who enter into new life in Christ Jesus through the Pentecostal/Charismatic renewal in the Holy Spirit. This total continues to increase. By 1990, it had climbed to 19.9 million persons newly renewed in the Spirit and had thereby finally caught up with and overtaken the annual Christian death toll. For the first time in history now the enormous power in human lives of new life in the Spirit has overtaken numerically the destructive power of death. This has massive significance for the future of world evangelization.

**13. Global plans** GD-13

The church's failure to obey Christ's commission has, however, not been for want of trying. Down the centuries, Christians have launched at least 1,500 concrete or specific plans to contact World A and thus to complete the evangelizing of the whole world. The diagram analyzes all these plans by 14 different subjects, giving a rapid overview of this mass of good intentions and earnest endeavors by Christ's followers.

**14. Fragmentation and monoliths** GD-14

The results of all this effort and endeavor are shown in Global Diagram 14. The resulting church is a mass of fragmented confessions—6 major ecclesiastico-cultural megablocs, 300 confessions, 33,820 denominations. Since most of them are in contact with only a handful of other denominations and have always been out of contact with the other 95% of the Christian world, the situation can be fairly illustrated by a scattered series of monolithic skyscrapers, loosely grouped together but essentially standalone and separate. The diagram portrays this and shows how the global plans have arisen from all these traditions.

**15. Missionaries ever** GD-15

Guiding the implementation of obedience to the 7 Mandates has been a vast army of Great Commission Christians—all persons committed to obeying Christ's command—both laity and full-time clergy and workers. Global Diagram 15 enumerates them all at 15 points in time from AD 33 to AD 2025.

The totals over these 20 centuries are impressive:

| | |
|---|---|
| — foreign missionaries | 6,322,000 |
| — home missionaries | 36,775,000 |
| — pastoral workers | 214,296,000 |
| — lay activists | 2,041,757,000 |

**16. Martyrdom** GD-16

The most startling of this series relating to understanding the past is Global Diagram 16, enumerating the 70 million Christians killed for their faith across 20 centuries. The effect of martyrdom (a word that originates in the Greek word *martys*, a witness) on evangelization over the centuries has been profound. This diagram analyzes the phenomenon. The huge numbers involved year by year justify us in saying that, although involuntary for its victims, martyrdom is the most significant and far-reaching of all the modes and methodologies of evangelization.

Religious freedom in a country may be quite different, de facto, to what the state professes about it and what it purports to guarantee in its constitution. In fact, in 79 countries some 2.2 billion people (50.6% of the world in 1980) live under restrictions on their religious freedom, despite the guarantees in those countries' constitutions and in the 1948 United Nations' *Universal Declaration of Human Rights*. The worst recent case of persecution has been the 1966-67 Great Proletarian Revolution in China. This was history's most systematic attempt ever, by a single nation, to eradicate and destroy Christianity and all religion. In this it failed.

**17. Independency** GD-17

By the end of the 16th century, the Christian world had become polarized into 4 major ecclesiastico-cultural global megablocs: *Orthodox, Roman Catholic, Anglican, Protestant*. In the 19th century, a 5th global megabloc emerged, repudiating mainline organized Christianity and placing itself on the periphery or margins of the 4 existing blocs—hence our term for it, *Marginal Christians*. The bloc is composed of Mormons, Jehovah's Witnesses, Christian Science, and a host of other bodies characterized by one or both of these traits: anti-trinitarian or non-trinitarian christology, and the claim to have a second source of divine revelation in addition to the Bible.

Far less known is the fact that in recent centuries a sixth global bloc has emerged: *Independent*, with its 2 synonymous alternate terms *Postdenominationalist*, and *Neo-Apostolic*. Global Diagram 17, and then the whole of Part 6 "Independency" depict and explain this new megabloc in great detail.

## III. CONTEMPORARY ANALYSIS: EXPLAINING THE PRESENT

*Analyzing the present*

Statistics depict the human dilemma today and the Christian challenge that results. They do this so clearly and compellingly that the best comment on this is the quotation from prior Roger Schutz, founder of the Protestant monastery and youth center, the Taizé community in France: 'Les chiffres sont les signes de Dieu—Statistics are signs from God.'

In this section there are 28 diagrams assembling statistics on 28 different subjects.

The starting point brings us a shocking picture of the reality of the world in which we live. Global Diagram 18 depicts today's human need and the appalling situations of some 3 billion people who are the victims of human greed across the Earth. The first 4 diagrams, numbers 18-21, are descriptive ones outlining the secular factors which make up today's world. Global Diagram 18 deals with the unfortunate victims of today's global human need. Global Diagram 19 describes the corporate or collective structures of sin which are responsible for this tragedy.

The last 2 global diagrams, 22 and 23, begin to show us the value of segmentizing the world and its problems. We want to analyze this world in order to understand it better. We want to understand it better in order to assist its populations in their predicament. But the sheer magnitude of the situation numbs our minds. So Global Diagrams 22 and 23 segmentize the world, its populations, and its problems into over 300 separate and distinct aspects or topics. At least now these bite-sized pieces of information become manageable.

### GLOBALISTICS
(Global Diagrams 18-23)

**18. Human need** GD-18

Some 46% of the world, 2.8 billion people, eke out a living in 26 countries each with a per capita income of under US$235 per year. In the world's 172 less developed countries, 1.1 billion live in absolute poverty, a clearly-defined category that represents 'a condition of life so characterized by malnutrition, illiteracy and disease as to be beneath any reasonable definition of human decency' (World Bank, 1980). This total increases annually as the gap between affluence and poverty widens rapidly almost everywhere. Among the consequences are: permanently unsettled refugees, now 15 million, increase in number each year; 20% of the Third World, and 33% in several countries, suffer from severe protein-calorie malnutrition; 40% remain without adequate shelter; 80% do not have access to adequate water supply; 940 million have little or no access to schools; and 500 million exist on the edge of starvation. Altogether, some 2 billion human beings on earth are malnourished. A further consequence is seething unrest, anger, hatred towards the affluent world, and revolutionary goals.

Christians suffer along with others in this predicament. Some 109 million Christians live in the 26 poorest countries. In all developing countries, Christians living in absolute poverty number 260 million (24% of the 1.1 billion absolutely poor, or 13% of all Christians); half of them live in Latin America, a third in Africa, the rest in South and Southeast Asia. This is 'the church of the poor'. By the world's standards, they have nothing. They are far from being spiritual paupers, however. Some of the most dynamic forms of Christianity today, and the most rapid church growth, are found in these areas of material poverty and destitution.

It is not surprising, then, that the church, entrusted with the gospel of Christ's compassion for the poor, should have become heavily involved in correcting the injustices of poverty.

**19. Structures of sin** GD-19

Organized corporate sin takes the problem of what to do a step further. What on earth can the individual Great Commission Christian do about corporate sin financed by $5 trillion a year? Our answer here is: practically nothing, as an individual. It's useless for the individual to fight sin either (1) by only living a pure, righteous Christian life, or (2) by attacking or speaking against sin in general. The only thing that counts is *targeting*. By this we mean persuading Christians to see the world and its problems in its segmentized form and then targeting one segment out of the many.

**20. Technoglobe** GD-20

Many familiar facts and figures here bring together the statistics of the worlds of technology, research, industry, energy, communication, computers, networks, and transportation.

**21. Urbanization** GD-21

There are 2 diagrams on this subject. Global Diagram 21 describes the urban and rural worlds of today. The world of cities consists of over 3,000 metropolises each with over 100,000 population, or over 5,000 metropolises each with over 50,000 population.

Global Diagram 54 then projects current trends ahead to AD 2100.

## 22. Segmentizing                                    GD-22
This process describes the kaleidoscopic human mosaic and the segmentizing through which human beings attempt to understand and organize it. Then Global Diagram 22 puts the world's geopolitical blocs into statistics. At the same time it describes the overall situation of the globe's 20 major religious and anti-religious blocs.

## 23. Geopolitico-religious blocs                     GD-23
Table 1–2 sets out the fortunes of the world's 20 distinct major global religions, religious systems or quasi-religions across the 20th century. Almost all of these religions have expanded numerically during these 10 decades. Most have also expanded geographically: thus, Muslims now form significantly large communities in 162 countries, Hindus in 84 countries, Buddhists in 84 also, Jews in 112 countries, whilst Baha'is have planted their faith significantly in no less than 192 countries.

### Erosion of Christianity's numerical strength
Table 1–2 also summarizes in statistical form the fortunes of Christianity in the 20th century in its total global context. It shows the enormous numerical increases of almost all categories of Christians—those professing in censuses (sometimes called 'confessing Christians'), those who are affiliated church members on the churches' rolls, and those who regularly practice their faith. But it also shows the gradual numerical decline of these categories when expressed as percentages of the world's total population.

### Decline within all world religions
This gradual decline of Christianity must however be seen in context. It is not Christianity alone which is in decline; it is the entire phenomenon of religion. All the other major world religions have suffered similarly, some catastrophically. At the same time, revivals of religion are taking place in widespread secularized areas. One must therefore be careful not to exaggerate the progress of secularization. The best way to portray the trends is to quote the actual figures, as obtainable from Table 1–2: whilst the proportion of religionists of all kinds has declined from 99.8% of the world in 1900 to 84.8% in AD 2000, their absolute numbers have increased over that period from 1,616 millions to 5,137 millions.

### The persistence of ethnoreligions
Startling evidence of religion's power to survive in an anti-religious world can be found in the persistence since 1900 of local or tribal religions, usually limited in membership to one single ethnic people each. These are the faiths which are also termed primal religions, traditional religions, or local religions, and which cover animism, shamanism, and the like. The expectation in 1900 was that these religions, more than any others, were doomed and would disappear completely within a generation, to be replaced by one of the universal or world religions. Not only would Christianity provide an irresistible alternative; secular advances also—in education, science, technology, colonialism, communications—would destroy them in a decade or two. The prognosis of the World Missionary Conference (Edinburgh 1910) concerning the so-called primitive peoples was:

> Most of these peoples will have lost their ancient faiths within a generation, and will accept that culture-religion with which they first come into contact.

The ancient faiths did not disappear as expected. Despite secularization, and despite vast numbers of conversions from their ranks to Christianity, Hinduism and Islam, the absolute numbers of tribal religionists including shamanists have increased markedly and regularly in many countries from 1900-2000. In the year 2000 there are 228 million of them across the world, nearly double their total of 118 million in 1900.

### The meteoric rise of secular quasireligions
Equally startling has been the meteoric growth of secularism in its religious forms. Two immense quasi-religious systems have emerged at the expense of the world religions: agnosticism (also termed secularism, materialism, non-religion, etc) and atheism (also

termed anti-religion or irreligion). Variations include secularism, scientific materialism, atheistic communism, nationalism, nazism, fascism, Maoism, liberal humanism and numerous constructed or fabricated pseudo-religions. From a miniscule presence in 1900, a mere 0.2% of the globe, these systems have mushroomed to 15.2% of the globe by AD 2000. They are today increasing at the extraordinary rate of 6.5 million new converts each year, and are likely to reach one billion adherents soon. A large percentage of their members are the children, grandchildren or great-grandchildren of persons who in their lifetimes were practicing Christians. No Christian strategist in 1900 had envisaged such a massive rate of defection from Christianity within its 19th-century heartlands.

## GEORESOURCES
(Global Diagrams 24-29)

## 24. Resources of 50 varieties                       GD-24
The next 6 diagrams depict a range of highly significant approaches or ministries in use today. The sheer size and proliferation of these ministries take one's breath away. These diagrams describe and document the 6,700 Scripture languages, the 2,800 languages with regular Christian broadcasting in them, the whole range of varieties of renewal and revival movements around the world, and approaches to closed or closing, restricted-access or limited-access countries.

## 25. Ethnolinguistics                                GD-25
Many language names are incorrectly used as ethnic names. Major global lists—as with Bible societies and missions—mix anglicized language names ('German', 'Zulu') together with autoglossonyms ('deutsch', 'isizulu'). Often statistics of both are incorrectly compared. This diagram, and listings in WCT and WCE, attempt to correct this misunderstanding.

## 26. Geolinguistics                                  GD-26
As explained by linguist David Dalby in The Linguasphere register (1999: Vol. 1:97), the term 'geo-linguistics' describes a relatively new science dealing with the spatial study of language use and distribution.

The year AD 2000 finds the peoples of the globe speaking some 13,500 distinct and different languages. The new classification of all languages given in WCE Part 9 "LinguaMetrics" portrays precisely the proximity of any language to any other language anywhere on Earth. The global diagram then depicts this situation pictorially and hints at the enormous possibilities for Christian cross-cultural ministry this represents.

## 27. Lingua francas                                  GD-27
Statistics of every language in the world now include (1) all native mother-tongue speakers, (2) all non-native speakers (second-language et alia), but also exclude (a) ethnic non-users (who have switched to lingua francas) and (b) recently deceased speakers. This diagram clarifies these issues and documents the world's 32 largest lingua francas with their current statistics.

## 28. Languages and Scriptures                        GD-28
It comes as a shock to know that of the globe's 13,500 languages, Christians have translated the whole Bible directly into only 390 of them so far. These new classificatory data do however permit more exact strategies to be thought out, implemented, and monitored.

## 29. Broadcasting                                    GD-29
Christian radio programs are broadcast at present in only 2,800 of the 13,500 languages. Global Diagram 29 spells out the significance of this for the 770 million persons who receive no mother-tongue Christian broadcasts.

## MISSIOMETRICS
(Global Diagram 30-31)

With these 2 diagrams, the objective measurement and study of empirical Christianity become feasible and possible. Missiometrics—the science of mission—emerges as a parallel to biometrics, econometrics, bibliometrics, cliometrics, and a whole range of new disciplines that begin with measurement of phenomena.

---

**Table 1–4. Our globe each 24 hours: daily worldwide statistical changes in 75 major secular, religious, Christian, and non-Christian characteristics.**

Over the next 24-hour period, these average increases will occur:

| Category | Amount |
|---|---|
| **WORLD POPULATION** | |
| Births (new persons born) | 340,500 |
| Deaths (new persons dying) | 144,000 |
| Increase in population | 196,000 |
| International migrants | 275,000 |
| Households (families) | 104,100 |
| Literates | 281,000 |
| **URBANIZATION** | |
| Cities (over 50,000 pop.) | 2 |
| Metropolises (over 100,000) | 1 |
| Non-Christian urbanites | 129,000 |
| Urban dwellers (urbanites) | 190,400 |
| Rural dwellers | 3,500 |
| Deforestation (sq km destroyed) | 2,600 |
| Urban poor | 77,000 |
| Urban slumdwellers | 38,000 |
| **WORLD RELIGIONS** | |
| New non-Christian religions | 2 |
| **Non-Christians** | **147,000** |
| Atheists | 1,200 |
| Baha'is | 400 |
| Buddhists | 10,600 |
| Chinese folk-religionists | 10,700 |
| Confucianists | 120 |
| Ethnoreligionists | 8,200 |
| Hindus | 37,000 |
| Jains | 100 |
| Jews | 350 |
| Muslims | 68,000 |
| New-Religionists | 2,800 |
| Nonreligious | 16,700 |
| Shintoists | -90 |
| Sikhs | 1,100 |
| Spiritists | 600 |
| Taoists | 70 |
| Zoroastrians | 160 |
| **Christians** | **69,000** |
| **GLOBAL CHRISTIANITY** | |
| New baptized church members | 122,000 |
| Christian deaths | 50,000 |
| Evangelicals | 11,000 |
| Urban Christians | 61,000 |
| Pentecostals/Charismatics/Neocharismatics | 30,000 |
| Great Commission Christians | 25,500 |
| Christian martyrs | 470 |
| **ECCLESIASTICAL MEMBERSHIP** | |
| Anglicans | 3,400 |
| Independents | 26,000 |
| Marginal Christians | 1,200 |
| Orthodox | 3,200 |
| Protestants | 13,300 |
| Roman Catholics | 37,000 |
| **MEMBERSHIP BY CONTINENT** | |
| Africa | 24,500 |
| Asia | 19,400 |
| Europe | 2,200 |
| Latin America | 21,000 |
| Northern America | 5,000 |
| Oceania | 800 |
| **CHRISTIAN ORGANIZATIONS** | |
| Worship centers | 500 |
| Denominations | 0.5 |
| Service agencies | 3 |
| Foreign-mission sending agencies | 1 |
| Standalone global monoliths | 1 |
| **CHRISTIAN WORKERS** | |
| Nationals (citizens) | 300 |
| Aliens (foreign missionaries) | 20 |
| Home missionaries | 30 |
| Short-term missionaries | 50 |
| **CHRISTIAN FINANCE (in US$)** | |
| Personal income of church members | $1.5 billion |
| Giving to Christian causes | $66 million |
| Churches' income | $22 million |
| Parachurch and institutional income | $44 million |
| Ecclesiastical crime (sums embezzled) | $5.5 million |
| Income of global foreign missions | $5 million |
| Cost-effectiveness at global level | $50 |
| **NEW TECHNOLOGY** | |
| New Christian computer users | 100,000 |
| Christians joining the Internet | 68,500 |
| **CHRISTIAN LITERATURE** | |
| New commercial book titles | 6 |
| New books/articles on evangelization | 7 |
| **SCRIPTURE DISTRIBUTION (all sources)** | |
| Bibles | 165,000 |
| New Testaments | 334,000 |
| Gospels | 1,000,000 |
| Selections | 11,200,000 |
| **CHRISTIAN BROADCASTING** | |
| New regular listeners/viewers | 210,000 |
| **CHRISTIAN EVANGELISM** | |
| Evangelism-hours | 500 million |
| Offers | 2.6 billion |
| **WORLD EVANGELIZATION** | |
| Unevangelized persons | -9,900 |
| Evangelized persons | 206,000 |

## 30. Definitions: Christians, traditions  GD-30
In the endeavor to make sense of the whole mass of annual Christian data and measurements, missiometrics begins by creating exact and precise definitions, categories, and concepts. The obvious starting-point is to standardize the data describing the Christian churches themselves—church members, baptisms, church attenders, congregations, denominations, traditions, families, confessions, church workers, finances, and so on. Altogether, Christians collect annual data on over 900 variables or indicators. Global Diagram 30 systematizes these data and demonstrates the major global statistical totals that result.

## 31. Instrumentation  GD-31
Instruments are (Webster's) 'measuring devices.' Today such instruments are omnipresent—in all cars, vehicles, ships, aircraft, space craft, offices, laboratories—virtually everywhere. So it is understandable that churches and agencies expend a large part of their $1.1 billion-dollar megacensus on 2,056 different types of instruments. Global Diagram 31 illustrates a few varieties and sketches overall results. Table DD that follows locates all their data here.

### EVANGELISTICS
### (Global Diagrams 32-42)

Evangelistics is defined by Webster's as 'the science of the propagation of Christianity' (*Third new international dictionary*). These 11 global diagrams attempt to crystallize this out into concrete approaches.

## 32. Evangelism in 45 ministries  GD-32
The diagram lists the 45 major forms of evangelism and proceeds to quantify them for the globe, or any country, city, language, or ethnolinguistic people. The results reveal enormous disparities between the vast number of opportunities to become disciples of Christ that entire populations have in heavily-christianized World C countries, and the minimal opportunities experienced by entire populations in most World A countries. In the latter, inhabitants may receive one chance only for a few minutes in their lifetime. In stark contrast is the situation in World C countries where the average citizen receives (whether he or she likes it or not) ten thousand times that frequency.

## 33. Meaning of evangelization  GD-33
The English term 'evangelize' is shown in this diagram (and on its following page Table EE) to have over 600 synonyms, near-synonyms, or facets. Each is later in Part 23 documented with quotations from the New Testament or Bible, and/or from church history or contemporary usage. This is the basis for the detailed quantification of evangelism and evangelization in *WCT* and *WCE*.

## 34. Status of world evangelization  GD-34
Global Diagram 34 takes us to the heart of our analysis from the Christian point of view. It presents a 3-tier or 3-world model of our globe. It is then developed further in Global Diagrams 35-42. In this 3-world model, we divide the globe into 3 tiers, layers or slices for purposes of illustration and understanding. At the bottom is World C, which consists of all persons across the globe who individually are Christians. Worlds A and B then consist of all persons, individually, who are non-Christians. World A stands for those who in addition have never heard the gospel or heard about Jesus. We call these people the Unevangelized World. World B by contrast consists of those who have heard the gospel (this means those who have heard, with understanding, sufficient about Christianity, Christ, and the gospel to be termed evangelized non-Christians although they have not, or not yet, accepted it or become disciples of Christ).

For purposes of illustration, we have added names of several countries to A, B, and C. On our 3-tier division, countries or metropolises or peoples do not easily fit because each is composed of a mixture of unevangelized persons, evangelized non-Christians, and Christians. Countries are assigned on the following clear definitions: World A contains 38 countries with E measuring less than 50%, or over half unevangelized, i.e. over half of whose population are unevangelized. World B contains 59 countries which are over half evangelized (E≥50%, i.e. E greater than or equal to 50%) but in which church members number less than 60%. World C contains 141 countries whose church members number 60% or more of the population; it can also be seen that for all these countries E>95% (E is greater than 95%). This gives a useful typology of countries, shown for all countries in Part 12 "CountryTrends", column 163.

## 35. Global Map 1: World A  GD-35
Drawing a boundary around all the world's large unevangelized megapeoples results in a startling conclusion: all such peoples are contiguous, with common boundaries; all fall within a single boundary that is thus termed World A.

## 36. Global Map 2: Worlds A,B,C  GD-36
By a similar process of dividing all countries up into each's constituent peoples, boundaries of Worlds B and C emerged as well as A.

## 37. Sharing globes: 16 ministries  GD-37
Using the A, B, C typology, statistics of 16 major ministries were similarly analyzed. Again, the overwhelming volume of ministry is seen to be directed to World C, not B nor A.

## 38. Sharing globes: confessions  GD-38
One can also divide up the previous data by confession, by countries, and by people. Similar conclusions emerge.

## 39. Sharing globes: agencies  GD-39
A third analysis by foreign mission agencies and their personnel showed similar predilection to work among populations already heavily christianized. This is true both for the largest agencies with annual budgets over US$100 million, as well as for agencies below.

## 40. Evangelization in Worlds A,B,C  GD-40
The diagram presents the problem of unequal distribution. Every type of Christian resource, especially evangelistic offers, is commandeered by, or directed exclusively at, the heavily christianized sphere of World C. A skeletal solution is proposed to resolve the predicament.

## 41. Global religious change  GD-41
These tables depict a situation of enormous religious complexity in today's world. Moreover, the situation is anything but static. Every year millions of people are changing their religious profession or their Christian affiliation. Mass defections are occurring from stagnant majority religions to newer religions. Mass conversions under way in many countries are accruing primarily to missionary religions aggressively engaged in proselytism. Our tables document these phenomena by analyzing in detail the decade 1990-2000, and by giving, for all religions and for the different categories of Christians, the annual numerical change divided into natural increase and conversion change.

To illustrate this dynamic, ever-changing character of the world of religions today, Table 1–4 shows the numerical changes that are happening every 24 hours, for 75 major descriptors.

*Massive gains offset by massive losses.*
From the Christian standpoint, the overall situation presents a mixed picture. On the one hand, Christianity has experienced massive gains across the Third World throughout the 20th century. In Africa, Christians have mushroomed from 9.9 million in 1900 (0.6% of the world's population then) to 360 million in AD 2000 (8.9%). The present nett increase on that continent is 8.4 million new Christians a year (23,000 a day), of which 1.5 million are nett new converts (converts minus defections or apostasies). Sizeable nett conversions are also taking place in Asia (2.4 million a year). A major reason for this expansion across the continents of the Third World is the attracting power of the Christian gospel of justice and the love of God for the poor and oppressed.

But on the other hand, Christianity has experienced massive losses in the Western world over the last 60 years. In Europe and North America, nett defections from Christianity—converts to other religions or to irreligion—are now running at 1,820,500 former Christians a year. This loss is much higher if we consider only church members: 2,224,800 a year (6,000 a day). It is even higher if we are speaking of only church attenders: every year, some 2,765,100 church attenders in Europe and North America cease to be practicing Christians within the 12-month period, an average loss of 7,600 every day.

At the global level, these losses from Christianity in the Western world slightly outweigh the gains in the Third World. This can be observed by examining the trends in percentages over the period 1900-2000. In 1900, Christians numbered 34.5% of the world (37.8%, if adults only are counted). This percentage has fallen gradually over the decades until Christians in 1980 numbered 33.4% of the world (36.0% of the world's adults), and in AD 2000, 33.0%.

## 42. Today's unfinished task  GD-42
Using this threefold typology, Global Diagram 34 has depicted the status of world evangelization today. Global Diagram 42 now segmentizes the unevangelized world into over 5,540 major unevangelized population segments. And Global Diagram 24 documents the staggering range of resources for world mission that are available to Christians today.

### GEOPERSONNEL
### (Global Diagrams 43-45)

## 43. Closed countries  GD-43
In the 1980s, mission agencies regarded at least 119 countries as closed to foreign missions, or with strictly-restricted access. Unexpectedly, in 1989 Communism collapsed in Europe and the Soviet Union. Over 30 closed countries suddenly opened their doors wide to foreign missionaries. But within 5 years, a totally unexpected new obstacle arose as those countries tired of the novelty of Western largesse and expertise, with its chaotic ecclesiastical fragmentation. One by one several countries reintroduced restrictions, partial at first then virtually total.

Global Diagram 43 presents a typology of mission access to such closed or closing countries.

## 44. GCC harvest force  GD-44
Global Diagram 44 summarizes today's Great Commission harvest force. Again, we are surprised at the enormous numbers involved. Christians professing commitment to the Great Commission have never been as numerous before. Any observer who studies the facts and the data on the subject will know this already. An example comes from the USA. In 1988 Evangelical pollster George Gallup Jr undertook a nationwide poll asking the question, 'Would you say you have made a commitment to Jesus Christ or not?' A striking 66% of the population answered 'Yes', and 28% 'No'; 6% had no opinion. (Source: Gallup Survey for the National Catholic Evangelization Association). Never have the world's committed Christians had such vast and profuse resources of every kind. It is incredible that with all these available resources the Christian church still seems incapable of marshalling its forces to complete or bring to closure any of the most basic elements of global mission.

## 45. Hijacking and looting  GD-45
Another unanticipated aspect of foreign missions concerns mission countries which have developed very strong home ministries and citizen workers but who are reluctant to give up their large alien mission forces. The diagram shows that 131 mission-sending countries have allowed 90% of all mission resources to be hijacked, siphoned off, and in extreme cases looted by such recipient countries.

### IV. FUTURIST ANALYSIS:
### PLANNING FOR THE FUTURE

A vast range of data on the future is available to mission strategists. Here are several aspects.

### DEMOGRAPHICS
### (Global Diagrams 46-51)

## 46. Population  GD-46
This diagram explores the consequences if human fertility (children born for each woman) remains as high as at present. Scenarios of world population in AD 2150 thus vary from 4 billion to 694 billion—a catastrophic prospect.

**47. The southward shift**                    GD-47
A massive shift in the center of gravity of Christians has been going on for over a century now. This means that African Christian leadership is growing fastest of all. Evidence of this is now clear.

**48. Women**                                  GD-48
The 48 long-term trends concerning the future of women, show in this diagram, represent a striking challenge for female Christian leadership. One trend puts the number of ordained women exactly equal to that of ordained men by the year AD 2050.

**49. Youth**                                  GD-49
Just as Christianity's denominations were in 1970 becoming aware of the global youth explosion, a 200-year decline then began that now seems certain to halve youth from 38% of the world in 1970 to 18% by AD 2100.

**50. Longevity**                              GD-50
Life expectancy is increasing rapidly on every continent. Africa has risen from an average year of death of 31 years in the year 1900, to 56 now, and expects to reach 84 by AD 2150. And longer life means, inter alia, vastly longer years in Christian ministry.

**51. Aging**                                  GD-51
This trend has arisen due to rapid advances in health care. People are living longer. By AD 2200 the elderly (65 and older) will have increased astronomically to 2,970 million.

FUTURESCAN
(Global Diagrams 52-59)

**52. Global mission**                         GD-52
The main challenge in global mission is to get churches, agencies, and their leadership to face up to the staggering numbers involved in that mission. Agencies failing to do this in regard to their own specialized ministries are merely trifling with the lives of millions. The best illustration of this is probably the case of Scripture distribution, described in Part 19 "GeoScriptures". For 550 years now since printing was invented under Gutenberg, Christian publishers have produced billions of copies of Scripture and distributed them, in some respects at random, without working to serious global constraints to ensure that all have similar opportunity to hear God's Word.

**53. Megatrends in mission**                  GD-53
Global Diagram 53 illustrates 20 long-term Christian global megatrends underway since the year 1980. All of them have profound significance for global mission. An attempt to learn from these trends is given in Global Diagram 65 which sets out a suggested list of the top 31 global megapriorities for mission today as seen by Great Commission Christians.

**54. MetroScan**                              GD-54
The explosive growth of urbanization is likely to continue until well after AD 2100. Spaceship Earth as megalopolis is likely to increase today's 7,000 metropolises, of over 50,000 urbanites each, to some 40,000 by that year.

**55. World religions**                        GD-55
Christians are familiar with their global growth being described as astronomical expansion. But, surprisingly, everybody else is expanding too and at similar rates. The diagram's table gives the statistics for 16 world religions at the 5 years 1900, 1990, 2000, 2100, and 2200.

**56. Expansion of Christianity**              GD-56
Global Diagram 56 documents this phenomenal expansion of Christianity over 125 years. From 558 millions in 1900, it is likely to reach 2,617 millions by 2025. It is time for theologians to interpret such megachanges.

**57. Trends in world evangelization**         GD-57
When the previous diagram is redrawn showing percentages instead of absolute numbers, new and surprising trends become visible. One is: the size of all Christians as percent of the world has remained virtually unchanged for 120 years.

**58. Future resource countries**             GD-58
Enough is known about the strength of Christianity in the world's countries for them to be ranked by a measure of obedience to the Great Commission, S = missionaries sent out per million affiliated Christians. The diagram lists the globe's top 29 countries (all being in World C and half being in Europe) by number of missionaries sent out. But the diagram demonstrates that a further 31 countries could easily ascend to resource-sending status with encouragement to increase their current own-missionary sending to the adequacy level proposed, namely $S > 100$.

**59. Goals**                                  GD-59
Christian agencies are great goal-setters. Hundreds of 1-year, 2-year, 3-year, and 5-year goals are announced every year by churches, denominations, and missions. But most published goals are not in fact met—the trumpeted deadline passes without note or comment (and certainly without public confession, apology, or repentance). Somehow or other these goal-setters escape without accountability to the long-suffering Christian public who have paid huge sums of money in pursuit of those goals.

What we all need, therefore, is expertise in how to actually accomplish goals. Global Diagram 59 sets out the 200 major AD 2000 goals announced by churches, denominations, confessions, and missions as the 1990-2000 Decade of Evangelism or Decade of Evangelization proceeded under way. Global Diagram 61 then describes the machinery of a kaleidoscopic global action plan, the WCGAP (KGAP), which can help Christians to accomplish these goals. Others of these diagrams show the chronological evolution over the centuries of Christian involvement in the harvest that the church is commissioned to seek.

GEOSTRATEGIES
(Global Diagrams 60-69)

**60. Scholarship and research**              GD-60
By AD 2000 more concentrated research resources of every kind are being focused on the problem of how to evangelize the world than at any previous time in history. Expert systems (artificial intelligence) in the 1980s, and the Internet in the 1990s, have opened limitless possibilities. Global Diagram 60 portrays how research and scholarship can help implement the Great Commission by means of 70 harvest categories that have evolved over the last 6 millennia.

**61. A kaleidoscopic global action plan**    GD-61
The WCGAP (World Christian Global Action Plan) offers a sane, balanced, and moderate future of Christian obedience to the Great Commission. If there is sufficient team spirit among agencies, the many components of the common task of world mission could easily be shared out. In fact, even if only 20 founding agencies agreed to cooperate on this, and formally offered their services, the plan would succeed.

**62. Deployment**                             GD-62
This diagram answers a major question: Where should foreign missionaries work? Six organizing principles of deployment at present in use are examined. The least satisfactory is, unfortunately, the main principle employed today throughout the missionary world: *Go where invited by local Christians*. Since the 1.6 billion unevangelized non-Christians in World A never send such invitations, this explains why they remain uncontacted by Christians 1,970 years after Christ issued his Great Commission.

**63. Geotargeting**                           GD-63
With its relatively limited resources, the Christian world mission must have clear targets and objectives. Comparison with the legions of the Roman empire, and the ballistic missiles of the recent Cold War, shows Christians are targeting easy nearby targets almost exclusively. Their global impact is therefore minimal from one decade to the next. This diagram illustrates these points. Based on this, *WCE* Part 8 "EthnoSphere" gives every people in the world a targeting variable, from 1 (top priority) to 10 (lowest priority for receiving new Christian resources).

**64. Matching up**                            GD-64
Global Diagram 64 presents the case for considering all the pros and cons of (a) potential target peoples, and (b) potential cross-cultural missionary workers.

The 2 have certainly to be matched up with far more care and sophistication than has been the case up to the end of the 1990s.

**65. Megapriorities**                         GD-65
Global strategists list 12,480 current serious global problems of significance and urgency for the future of the world. Christians likewise have compiled lists of problems and priorities in mission, like the 31 long term megapriorities and 18 corporate priorities listed in this diagram.

**66. Future religions**                       GD-66
Using recognized techniques evolved by futurists, it is comparatively simple to generate tomorrow's scenarios for global religions, as this diagram does. One thing is certain: after the collapse of militant atheistic Communism, religions in general and Christianity in particular are now stronger than ever.

**67. Future churches and missions**          GD-67
The diagram illustrates the continuing trends in the growth and expansion of Christianity up to AD 2025. A whole range of specialized Christian workers is spreading across the world at a steady rate. Since by 2025 we can expect virtually all of them to be computer-literate e-mail/Internet users, a whole new era of cost-effective and cooperative mission endeavor is certain to open up.

**68. GCC harvest force**                      GD-68
Global Diagram 68 projects to the year 2025 the current scene in the Great Commission world as has already been depicted in Global Diagram 44. It shows the likely size of the major components well into the Third Millennium. Most are bigger than in AD 2000. More importantly, the diagram sees a major shift having already taken place. The standalone deployment of today, with hundreds of mission agencies all working in World C without coordination with other bodies, may well have shifted by AD 2025 to coordinated redeployment targeting the non-Christian world, Worlds A and B, and World A in particular.

**69. GeoAgendas**                             GD-69
Global Diagram 69 brings together yesterday's agendas, today's and tomorrow's geospheres, and geoagendas. The emphasis is on Gaia (the living, organic Planet Earth). Our study, our thinking, our agendas, our actions must from now on be truly global—keeping the whole world in view as the center of our concerns.

## V. LONG-TERM FUTURE GEOSCENARIOS

FISSION AND FUSION, AD 30-2200
(Global Diagrams 70-73)

Fission and fusion diagrams have a long and distinguished history in the study of how and when Christianity's vast number of denominations have arisen. All the major Christian traditions have them, explaining how today's denominations have evolved out of yesterday's. Here we show a comprehensive diagram illustrating the whole of Christian history up to the present, this being given in identical form in the following 4 Global Diagrams 70-73 as the lefthand part of each diagram. The detailed notes below explain all the conventions and features of these historical diagrams.

We then show 4 possible alternate long-term futures for Christianity. These 4 miniscenarios are shown as the righthand part of each diagram covering the period 2000-2100, or even to 2200, i.e. the next 2 centuries, the Twenty-First and Twenty-Second.

The flow chart or development diagram on each global diagram with its alternate future is expanded and illustrated in Part 2 "CosmoChronology". This divides time into 3 great periods or epochs, Cosmic Eras I, II, III. Global Diagrams 70-73 show the fortunes of Christianity divided into 2 stages, (a) the past and present (illustrating Cosmic Era II) and (b) the future (illustrating Cosmic Era III).

THE PAST AND PRESENT: COSMIC ERA II

The lefthand half of the diagram shows the expansion of Christianity over the centuries, and sketches its fragmentation or fission into 6 major megablocs or streams with over 300 different ecclesiastical traditions, and over 33,800 separate and distinct denominations or churches. It also illustrates recent movements towards church reunion or fusion. The diagram should be studied in conjunction with the detailed statistics of the evolution of these phenomena given in the global tables in this volume. The various concepts and schemata in this diagram may be explained as follows.

### The 6 major megablocs
As set forth in this analysis, all Christians can be divided into the following 6 major megablocs or streams of Christianity: Orthodox, Roman Catholics, Anglicans, Protestants, Independents, and marginal Christians. In the diagrams, the boundaries of these blocs are shown by heavy full lines, and the boundaries of Christianity at top and bottom by still heavier full lines.

### The 300 traditions
The 6 megablocs can be further subdivided into around 300 ecclesiastical traditions, by which are meant the various confessions, families, or types of Christianity. In the diagrams, the boundaries of a selection of these traditions are shown by light full lines.

### Major denominations
Within the 300 traditions there have been formed over 33,800 separate autonomous denominations or churches. A detailed analysis of the location of these denominations by megabloc and continent is given in *WCT* Part 10 and *WCE* Part 4; but this evolution is too complex to be shown here.

### Church reunions
Since the year 1900, at least 200 denominations including some of the largest have merged to form over 70 united churches. Where a vertical line is shown not full but broken, it indicates a continuity of communion from the left side through to the right. This means the formation of either united churches, uniting churches (in process or under way), internal realignments, or the eventual single reunited world church.

### Origins
The diagram depicts in brief the origins and development of blocs and traditions on the world scene over 20 centuries, shows where they came from and how they have fared, and indicates, schematically and relatively, the numerical strength of each over the centuries up to the year AD 2000.

### Chronology
The horizontal scale represents time, or chronology, with 3 ways of measuring it. The lefthand half of the diagram covers from left to right the period from AD 33 to the year AD 2000 shown by the middle line of the 3 major vertical lines. Beneath the year scale is a second scale giving the number of 30-year generations after Christ at each point. Lastly, beneath these 2 scales is a third depicting historian K. S. Latourette's 9 epochs of the Christian world mission to which we add a 10th (from AD 2000 onwards, 'Final Closure in World Evangelization').

### Numerical size
The vertical scale represents, approximately or schematically, the numerical size of Christians affiliated to the various traditions or blocs at any particular year up to the present.

### Centralization
Across the center of the page a horizontal axis can be imagined which represents the concept of centralization including the concepts of unified control, uniformity, and collaboration. It represents schematically the position of churches with centralized structure, centralized hierarchy, centralized organization, centralized administration, and centralized tradition, doctrine, ritual and liturgy. This is the polity described here in Part 6 as denominationalism. As the most centralized of all churches, the Roman Catholic Church therefore straddles this axis in the diagram.

### Decentralization
The position of a tradition (or bloc, or denomination) above or below this central axis represents the concept of decentralization, which includes the concepts of local congregational autonomy, departure from centralization, ruptures of relations, splits, schismatic movements, independency. Traditions (or blocs, or denominations) which have separated from or moved away from the Church of Rome in order to decentralize some aspect of their church life are thus found above or below the central axis. The same is true for subsequent divisions from other churches.

### Structuralism
The position of a bloc or body vertically on the diagram also stands for what may be called the concept of relative ecclesiastical or structural conservatism or liberalism: from conservative at the top to liberal at the bottom. At the top are right-wing or conservative structures such as the Oriental Orthodox or monophysite churches which still largely use ancient dead languages in worship. Along the central axis is the Roman Catholic Church. Below the axis are Protestant churches and others in what may be called left-wing or liberal structures adapted to their eras. Going down the page are found increasingly left-wing, liberal, or radical traditions rejecting centralization or uniformity of structure, hierarchy, tradition, doctrine, ritual, or liturgy. Next below follows the range of Independent or Postdenominational bodies including the Non-White indigenous churches across the world, which have rejected historic Western and Eastern Christianity along with all attempts at control by these latter blocs. Finally, along the extreme lower edge of the diagram is a fringe of free-thinking or radically heterodox bodies originating in the Western Protestant world. These are here termed marginal Protestant bodies because of their peripheral nature in relation to mainstream or mainline or orthodox Christianity.

### Evolution
Lines across the diagram from left to right indicate evolution, i.e. the way in which the 6 megablocs (separated by heavy lines) and the 300 traditions (separated by light lines) have evolved and crystallized out over the centuries. At first sometimes the lines are dotted, illustrating how new traditions begin to form within existing traditions and exist therein for a time before rupture of relations with the parent or adjacent traditions takes place. Sometimes a dotted line means the first stage in the parting of the ways when a large body begins to divide into two. If and when a rupture or schism eventually takes place, this is shown at that point by the line changing from dotted to full. If the rupture is later healed, and the schism is reabsorbed into the parent, the line stops at that point in its movement across the page. Church unions or mergers can be illustrated by such lines with the original separate traditions shown bounded by full lines: then after union the lines are dotted until the traditions begin to lose their original identity in the new united body and eventually disappear.

### Schisms or fissions
Full lines drawn vertically indicate the clearcut formation of a schismatic or separatist body out of an existing body or the breaking of communion with those on the left by those on the right of the line. In most cases such schisms have been a small or minority part of the existing body. When a large parent body splits into 2 or more parts of comparable size (as at the Protestant Reformation), however, the vertical line covers all of the parts.

### World evangelization
This concept—which refers to the degree to which the whole world's population has heard the gospel or become aware of Christianity, Christ, and the gospel—is represented here under the tripartite typology of Worlds A, B, and C (explained in Global Diagrams 34-42). In a parallel from supersonic flight, in aerodynamics or ballistics, the schema shows Christianity with its gospel (World C, the Christian world, bounded by the heaviest lines at top and bottom in the diagram) penetrating world population like a missile or bullet surrounded by a thin white shock wave above and below (World B, the evangelized non-Christian world) with a sizeable gray part of the world left untouched (World A, the unevangelized world). The fluctuations in size of Worlds A, B, and C represent the actual historical situation and numerical trends at the years indicated.

### THE FUTURE: COSMIC ERA III

### Alternate futures
The righthand half of the 4 diagrams that follow represent 4 different, possible long-term alternate futures covering the whole range or spectrum of possibilities ahead for Christianity. These start with the year 1990 and become crystallized at the heavy vertical gray bar (full or broken) representing the next generation of AD 2000-2025. They then extend to the righthand edge of the diagram which represents approximately AD 2100. Lines, rules, and scales all have the same meanings as described above for the lefthand half of the diagram. Notes under each diagram explain the details and differentia of each case.

### Four geoscenarios
It is possible to envisage a large range of possible long-term alternate futures (or alternate long-term futures) for Christianity. The 4 chosen here can be labeled as follows:

GeoScenario-1—Monodenominationalism
GeoScenario-2—Nondenominationalism
GeoScenario-3—Postdenominationalism
GeoScenario-4—Megamartyrdom.

### Differentia
The differentia between these 4 alternate long-term future scenarios are set out as a series of adjectives in Table 1–5 'Characteristics and differentia of 4 alternate future long-term scenarios for Christianity and world evangelization, analyzed on 15 dimensions'.

### Decade of evangelism
On GeoScenarios-1 to -4, the shaded column for the last decade of the Second Millennium, the period 1990-2000, represents the organized programs of hundreds of denominations variously termed the Decade of Evangelism, Decade of Evangelization, Decade of Harvest, Decade of Destiny, Decade of Decision, Decade of World Mission, Decade of World Evangelization, Universal Decade of Evangelization et alia, with counterparts in 50 other languages (Decadà de Evangelización Mundial, etc).

### Non-Christian movements
The entities shown outside the heaviest lines delineating the edges or boundaries of Christianity properly so called, fall into 6 categories as follows: (1) churches which cannot or can no longer be called Christian as a result of abandoning or denying the

---

**Table 1–5. Characteristics and differentia of 4 alternate future long-term geoscenarios for Christianity and world evangelization, analyzed on 15 dimensions.**

| Dimension | Future: GeoScenario-1 | GeoScenario-2 | GeoScenario-3 | GeoScenario-4 |
|---|---|---|---|---|
| Name: | MONODENOMINATIONALISM | NONDENOMINATIONALISM | POSTDENOMINATIONALISM | MEGAMARTYRDOM |
| Worldview | Global | Confessional | Racial | Local |
| Overall outlook | Affluent | Muddled | Harassed | Persecuted |
| Relation to past | Continuity-based | Discontinuous | Rejected | Irrelevant |
| Church union | United | Fragmented | Non-cooperating | Impossible |
| State's attitude | Tolerated | Ignored | Feared | Liquidated |
| Research | Monitoring | Reporting | Nonexistent | Dangerous |
| Strategy | Strategic | Tactical | Impulsive | Absent |
| Planning | Centrally planned | Locally planned | Unplanned | Unplannable |
| Publicity | Orderly | Minimal | Unwanted | Fatal |
| Activities | Coordinated | Partly coordinated | Uncoordinated | Suppressed |
| Organization | Organized | Partly organized | Unorganized | Unorganizable |
| Control | Centralized | Decentralized | Uncontrolled | Uncontrollable |
| Leadership | Elderly | Regional | Youth | Martyred |
| World evangelization | Engineered | Multichanneled | Kaleidoscopic | Individualistic |
| Church growth | Declining | Static | Exploding | Obliterated |

centrality of Christ as Savior, Lord, and God; (2) bogus churches, often allied with anti-Christian infiltrators; (3) non-Christian cults including New Age movements; (4) non-Christian religions; (5) secular creeds (secularism, agnosticism); and (6) anti-Christian creeds (atheism).

*Defections*
The arrows from within Christianity to outside its boundaries stand for losses or defections from Christianity into the above-described non-Christian entities.

*Types of future church*
Superimposed on each diagram's future part is a series of popularly-used or often-used titles or names for the church in the future. These names are all shown in the same type size and style each within an oval or ellipse.

*Future miniscenarios*
Dates (years) in the text under each diagram indicate major times or turning points or watersheds in the future when significant events seem likely to occur. Each date refers readers to the text of Part 2 "CosmoChronology" where they will find a brief descriptive entry with additional details.

*Letters on diagram*
On each diagram will be seen a small number of capital letters, thus: A,B,C,D, etc. These represent important situations or developments at the points indicated. Each is explained in a short sentence or phrase below the diagram.

*World evangelization: it's future*
The future of world evangelization is represented by the 3 possible long-term futures for AD 2100 explained in Global Diagrams 66-67. These are termed *Third Millennium Scenario I: No progress,* in which the world remains as unevangelized in 2100 as 100 years earlier; *Third Millennium Scenario II: Moderate progress,* in which most of the world has now been reached, except for sizeable pockets unreached here and there; and *Third Millennium Scenario III: Closure,* in which the entire world has now been reached and evangelized, and plans are in place to keep it that way. Since it is much harder to evangelize a population the first time and much easier to see it remains evangelized thereafter, all 4 long-term GeoScenarios -1, -2, -3, and -4 assume an evangelized world kept that way throughout all or most of the 21st century.

GEOSCENARIOS-1, 2, 3, 4
(Global Diagrams 70-73)

Global Diagrams 70-73 sketch out 4 possible alternate long-term futures for Christianity and world evangelization. The diagrams are described and explained by the detailed introduction above. This should be studied to understand the implications.

**Description of the geoscenarios**
From some points of view, the 4 long-term scenarios are similar to the story of Creation and the range of possible alternate subsequent fates of the Universe. First, the church comes into existence as suddenly and dramatically as in the Big Bang. Second, the church is still expanding fast today. Third, in the future the church (like the Universe) could either turn out to be *open* and continue expanding indefinitely (as GeoScenarios-2 and -3 suggest), or it could turn out to be *flat* and plateau at a certain level (GeoScenario-1): or it could turn out to be *closed* and reverse its growth and collapse to zero in a catastrophe parallel to the Big Crunch (GeoScenario-4). What follow are brief descriptions of these 4 long-term scenarios.

**70. GeoScenario-1: Monodenominationalism** GD-70
In his High Priestly prayer, the Lord Jesus prayed 3 times (John 17:21,22,23) for his disciples 'that they may all become perfectly one' (Latin Bible, 'Ut omnes unum sint'), 'so that the world may believe.' Subsequently, however, his followers have formed themselves into, by AD 2000, the 33,800 distinct and separate religious denominations which often fight, war, or compete with each other. Most have nothing to do with most of the rest. This scandal of disunity and fragmentation has been widely seen over the centuries as a major obstacle to evangelizing or converting the world.

Through the ages Christians have longed and prayed to be united as Christ prayed, with the resultant converting power. This first scenario therefore sets out, as a possible future, a situation in which this actually takes place. It envisages all the major denominations of the world finally agreeing after AD 2000 to begin an immediate, loose, de facto reunion of the churches, thus forming one single denomination. This might come about, no doubt, in reaction to growing world ridicule or to heavy pressures from political regimes (as happened in Japan in 1940 or Zaire in 1970). At the least, it would encompass mutual fellowship, joint recognition, intercommunion, acceptance of ministries, joint evangelization and a common shared name—perhaps 'The Church of Jesus Christ', or 'The Body of Christ'.

One result might well be that Christianity, as today, continues to just hold its own numerically in a hostile world, neither expanding nor declining noticeably. Or it might start a precipitous decline in influence and in numbers. Despite governmental pressures and demands, full organic union might well then take a further 60 years to evolve. There would certainly be internal opposition not least from former Protestants.

Meanwhile, the outside world remains unevangelized by AD 2025. Due to the intractable difficulties of working in closed countries, little or no real or measurable progress has been made during the much-trumpeted Decade of Evangelism/Evangelization from 1990-2000. Closure proves impossible; the unreached world of 1.6 billion unevangelized persons remains unreached, even unreachable. (This is Third Millennium Scenario I).

**71. GeoScenario-2: Nondenominationalism** GD-71
A second possible alternate future envisages the vast mass of ordinary Christian believers finally losing patience with the scandal of denominational fragmentation. They take drastic action; they simply disown the structures of centralized Christianity. By 2000, the groundswell of irritation has reached massive proportions. The laity everywhere (who form 99.8% of all Christians) now break ties with denominational headquarters, ignore confessional pretensions, and concentrate solely on local worship, fellowship, witness, service, and evangelism. They still retain their denominational identities and traditions but recognize no central offices or agencies.

The scenario sees all Christians then as clustering into 5 loose, decentralized, unorganized, lay megaclusters: ritualists, traditionalists, charismatics, indigenous (locally-founded), and marginal. In particular, huge charismatic revivals sweep across Asia, winning hundreds of millions from the great non-Christian world religions. Centralized denominationalism withers and dies out. Spontaneous Christianity surfaces everywhere with vast numbers of ceaselessly itinerating churches of pilgrims, tourists, zealous youths, mega-evangelizers, et alii.

In consequence of the hundreds of global plans to evangelize the world and adoption of the multichanneling strategic approach, the world becomes fully evangelized for the first time in history. Closure becomes an unexpected reality. (This is Third Millennium Scenario III).

**72. GeoScenario-3: Postdenominationalism** GD-72
A third possible alternate future sees the huge mass of dynamic Christianity as largely made up of Third-World charismatic youths who operate only through their own racial and linguistic identities. Disillusioned with both centralized ecclesiastical organization and the whole traditions and identities of denominationalism and confessionalism, they reject all ties with Western Christianity and ignore or brush aside all aspects of traditional or historic Christianity. Denominations now become part of the forgotten past. Instead of aligning themselves with historical divisions, these future Christians operate on the de facto, natural lines of language, ethnic and racial affiliation. This results in 10 unorganized ethnolinguistic megaclusters whose vastly divergent socioeconomic status or plight characterizes them as follows (in order of affluence in AD 2000): Euroamericans (the Church of the Rich); Arab-Asians and the newly-converted Jewish race (the Church of the Biblical Lifestyle, i.e. the original cradle or arena or context of biblical Christianity in which Arab and Jewish converts are neither rich and affluent nor desperately poor); Amerindians, Australasians and Aboriginals (the Church of the Powerless); Afro-Americans (the Church of the Poor, mainly in Africa); Asiatico-Chinese (the Church of the Masses, with mind-boggling numbers of new converts); Latinamericans (the Church of the Desperately Poor); and lastly, Indo-Iranians (the Church of the Absolutely Poor, on the Indian subcontinent). A peripheral category must be added, namely marginal Protestants in churches holding as revelation both the Bible and also a second source; these are largely elite affluent Euroamericans (in what, by comparison, we may call the Church of the Megarich). Despite these unforgivably and violently opposed lifestyles, on this scenario Christianity as a whole continues its massive expansion across the globe throughout the 21st century. Nevertheless, the penalty for the total absence of coordination or planning is that large populations still remain unevangelized by AD 2025 and well beyond. (This is Third Millennium Scenario II).

**73. GeoScenario-4: Megamartyrdom** GD-73
The fourth possible alternative future depicts Christianity as a whole being extinguished. Rather than continuing its missionary expansion across the world (as with GeoScenarios-2 and -3) or barely holding its own (as with GeoScenario-1), global Christianity could be definitively wiped out by deliberate intent. The fact that the most determined, powerful, ruthless, planned, organized attempts to do precisely this—those under Nero, Domitian, Decius, Diocletian, Shapur II, Attila the Hun, Yazdegerd II, Omar II, Genghiz Khan, Tamerlane, Lenin, Stalin, Hitler, Mao Zedong—all failed to destroy the church of Christ is no guarantee that any final coordinated attempt will fail as well.

At present, most of Christianity today (around 84%) is recognized as legal by secular governments with only 16% being illegal or banned and so forced to exist clandestinely. But this proportion of legal Christianity is rapidly decreasing.

This diagram portrays the worst-case scenario which some biblical exegetes see the Scriptures as envisaging; the church is declared totally illegal and banned, then goes into the Great Tribulation and is totally destroyed by the ruthless world system with all believers being martyred to the last individual, making the ultimate and final witness to Christ.

Meanwhile, the unbelieving world continues on its way, either remaining unevangelized (long-term Third Millennium Scenario I or II) or evangelized with ongoing closure (Third Millennium Scenario III). This whole gigantic act of martyrdom played out over several decades of the 21st century could either (a) remain obscure, invisible, and unknown to an uninterested world, or (b) become fully visible and known to the entire human race, who thus become finally evangelized even as they destroy the church on Earth.

FINAL SUMMARY

**74. Summary-2, AD 30-AD 2200** GD-74
Finally, this series of brief overviews closes with, in Global Diagram 74, a look at the evolution of organization in global Christianity. The outside observer in AD 2000 sees the story of the church as a series of organizational monoliths—first he perceives it as one single massive monolith, but on closer inspection he perceives a vast mass of smaller monoliths.

At first the 300 confessional monoliths dominate the scene; next, the 33,800 denominations overwhelm any attempt to understand what is going on (and in the process hide the Cross of Christ from view); and finally, the current situation resolves into 33 huge gigamonoliths, 12 global megamonoliths, and the 20th century's 6 major ecclesiastico-cultural megablocs.

Lastly comes the future. Here we simplify the complexity of our earlier 4 GeoScenarios, or the 3 Third Millennium Scenarios, replacing them by 3 simple, black-and-white, clearcut alternatives: either one single ecclesiastical monolith, or postdenominationalist spontaneity, or ultimate liquidation.

In one sense the. human race can choose its own destiny.

# GEOSTATUS: 74 GLOBAL DIAGRAMS

Overleaf is Global Diagram 1, the first of the 74 one-page presentations of data produced by sectioning or slicing through the globe to reveal all the diverse structures and activities and inner workings of organized Christianity and its context in the secular and plurireligious worlds. Each of the 74 global diagrams is designed to be a reasonably self-contained and standalone page, and therefore a compact summary of its subject. A listing of all 74 diagrams and their subjects is given earlier in Table 1–3 followed by a brief explanatory paragraph or two commenting on each.

The brief bibliography given below serves 2 functions. First, it provides a wide-ranging collection of background data and information against which to view the Global Diagrams. Second, it functions as the background context at the close of the foregoing text of "Geostatus". A much larger Selective World Bibliography of Christianity and Religion, found in Part 31 "Bibliography" provides detailed data and documentation for the 74 Global Diagrams.

---

## BIBLIOGRAPHY

*100 questions and answers: religion in America.* George Gallup Jr & Sarah Jones. Princeton, NJ: Princeton Religion Research Center, 1989. (Illustrates questions to be asked worldwide if global knowledge of the religious situation is wanted).

*A Greek-English lexikon of the New Testament and other Early Christian literature.* W. F. Arndt & F. W. Gingrich. 2nd edition. Chicago, IL: University of Chicago, 1958.

*A history of Christianity.* K. S. Latourette. London: Eyre & Spottiswoode, 1962.

*A history of the expansion of Christianity.* K. S. Latourette. New York: Harper, 1937-1945. 7 volumes.

*A strategic atlas: comparative geopolitics of the world's powers.* G. Chaliand & J. -P. Rageau. 2nd edition. New York: Harper & Row, 1985.

*An enquiry into the obligations of Christians to use means for the conversion of the heathens.* William Carey. Leicester, UK: Anne Ireland, 1792.

*Annuario Pontificio per l'anno 2001.* Città del Vaticano: Tipografia Poliglotta Vaticana, 2001. (Statistics, names, and addresses for every Roman Catholic jurisdiction).

Apostolic Exhortation *Evangelii Nuntiandi.* Pope Paul VI. Editions: Latin, Italian, English, French, German, Spanish, et alia. Città del Vaticano: Tipografia Poliglotta Vaticana, 8 December 1975. (The major Catholic document on evangelization).

*Atlas of global strategy: war and peace in the nuclear age.* L. Freedman. New York: Facts on File, 1985.

*Atlas of world population history.* C. McEvedy & R. Jones. Harmondsworth, UK: Penguin, 1978. (Population statistics for all countries over the last 4,000 years).

*Awaiting the light: a survey of the unevangelised areas of the world.* J. G. K. Harmon. London: Inter-Varsity Missionary Papers, 1936.

*Bilan du monde: encyclopédie catholique du monde chrétien.* J. Frisque et al. Louvain: Casterman, 2 volumes, 1958-1960. 2nd edition, 2 volumes, 1964.

*Book of a thousand tongues.* E. Nida, ed. 2nd edition. London: United Bible Societies, 1972. 1st edition 1939.

*Britannica world data 2000,* in *2001 Britannica book of the year* (Chicago: Encyclopaedia Britannica, 2000), pages 538-888. (The most detailed annual statistical portrait describing 220 countries for a large range of statistical variables).

*Christianity and the world religions: paths of dialogue with Islam, Hinduism, and Buddhism.* Hans Küng et al. London: Collins, 1986.

*Concise dictionary of the Christian world mission.* World Christian Books. S. C. Neill, G. H. Anderson, & J. Goodwin, eds. London: USCL, 1970.

*Concordance to the Good News Bible.* D. Robinson, ed. London: The Bible Societies, 1983.

*Cosmos, chaos, and gospel: a chronology of world evangelization from Creation to New Creation.* D. B. Barrett. Birmingham, AL: New Hope, 1987.

*Countdown to 1900: world evangelization at the end of the nineteenth century.* T. M. Johnson. Birmingham, AL: New Hope, 1988.

*DataMap 1986: index of published tables of statistical data.* J. B. Manheim & A. Ondrasik. Phoenix, AZ: Oryx, 1986.

*Dictionary of Pentecostal and Charismatic movements.* S. M. Burgess & G. B. McGee, eds. Grand Rapids, MI: Zondervan, 1988.

*Directory of Christian councils.* 4th edition. Geneva: World Council of Churches, 1985.

*Directory of international statistics.* Volume 1, New York: Statistical Office, United Nations, 1982. 1st edition 1975.

*Directory of United Nations databases and information systems 1985.* Compiled by the Advisory Committee for the Coordination of Information Systems (ACCIS). New York: UN, 1984.

*Encyclopedia of business information sources.* J. Woy, ed. 6th edition. Detroit, MI: Gale Research, 1986. (22,000 citations covering over 1,100 primary subjects).

*Encyclopedia of geographic information sources: international volume.* J. Mossman, ed. 4th edition. Detroit, MI: Gale Research, 1988. (13,000 citations on over 160 cities, countries, and regions).

*Encyclopedia of modern Christian missions.* B. L. Goddard, ed. Camden, NJ: Thomas Nelson, 1967.

*Encyclopedia of the First World.* G. T. Kurian. 1st edition. New York: Facts on File, 1990. 2 volumes.

*Encyclopedia of the Second World.* G. T. Kurian. 1st edition. New York: Facts on File, 1990. 1 volume.

*Encyclopedia of the Third World.* G. T. Kurian. 3rd edition. New York: Facts on File, 1987. 2 volumes.

*Encyclopedic dictionary of religion.* P. K. Meagher et al, eds. Washington, DC: Corpus, 1979. 3 volumes.

*Ethnologue: languages of the world.* Barbara F. Grimes, ed. 14th edition. Dallas, TX: Summer Institute of Linguistics, 2000.

*Evangelize! a historical survey of the concept.* D. B. Barrett. Birmingham, AL: New Hope, 1987.

*Gaia: an atlas of planet management.* N. Myers, ed. Garden City, NY: Doubleday, 1984. (A blueprint for human survival on Earth).

*Guida delle missioni cattoliche 1970.* Roma: Pontificie Opere Missionarie, 1970. (Regularly-updated handbook of all Catholic missionary jurisdictions).

*Handbook of member Churches, World Council of Churches.* A. J. van der Bent, ed. Revised edition. Geneva: WCC, 1985.

*Hemerologian tes Ekklesias tes Hellados, tou etous 1980* (Yearbook of the Church of Greece, 1980). Athens: Apostolic Diakonia, 1980 In Greek. (Statistics, names, and addresses for all Eastern Orthodox jurisdictions canonically related to Athens, Constantinople, and Moscow).

*International acronyms, initialisms and abbreviations dictionary.* J. E. Towell & H. E. Sheppard, eds. Volume 1, 2nd edition. Detroit, MI: Gale Research, 1987. (Over 110,000 entries. Indispensible guide to the maze of initials today).

*International directory of world religions.* J. G. Melton, ed. Detroit, MI: Gale Research, 1980—. In progress to 6 volumes.

*Jesus Christ in the lives of Americans today.* Volume 1: Summary. Princeton, NJ: Gallup, 1982. (Describes many poll questions invaluable for assessing status of evangelization worldwide).

*Martyria/mission: the witness of the Orthodox churches today.* I. Bria, ed. Geneva: CWME, 1980.

*Megatrends 2000: ten new directions for the 1990's.* J. Naisbitt & P. Aburdene. New York: William Morrow and Company, Inc., 1990.

*Mission and evangelism: an ecumenical affirmation.* E. Castro, ed. Geneva: World Council of Churches, 1982. (The major ecumenical statement on evangelization).

*Modern concordance to the New Testament.* M. Darton, ed. Garden City, NY: Doubleday, 1976.

*More cunning than man: a social history of rats and men.* R. Hendrickson. New York: Dorset, 1983. (Documents the massive influence of rats on the expansion of Christianity and world evangelization concerns).

*Muslim peoples: a world ethnographic survey.* R. V. Weekes, ed. Westport, CT: Greenwood, 1984. 2 volumes.

*Names of countries and adjectives of nationality.* Terminology bulletin No. 333. New York: Documentation, Reference and Terminology Section, United Nations, 1985. (Officially agreed names in English, French, and Spanish. Updated every 2 or 3 years).

*Operation World: a day-to-day guide to praying for the world.* P. J. Johnstone. 5th edition. Bromley, UK: STL/WEC, 2001. (Earlier editions 1974, 1978, 1979, 1980, 1986, 1993).

*Proclaim Christ until he comes: calling the whole church to take the whole gospel to the whole world.* J. D. Douglas, ed. Minneapolis, MN: World Wide Publications, 1990. (Official report on Lausanne II Congress, Manila, July 1989).

*Prospects of world urbanization 1988.* Department of International and Economic Affairs. New York: UN, 1989.

*Scriptures of the world.* 16th biennial edition. Reading, UK: United Bible Societies, 1997.

*Seven hundred plans to evangelize the world: the rise of a global evangelization movement.* D. B. Barrett & J. W. Reapsome. Birmingham, AL: New Hope, 1988.

*Sourcebook of global statistics.* G. T. Kurian. New York: Facts on File, 1985. (Evaluates 209 major works of reference).

*State of the world 2001: a Worldwatch Institute report on progress toward a sustainable society.* L. R. Brown et alii. New York: W. W. Norton, 2001. Annual since 1984. (A classic series. Begins with a chapter 'Challenges of the New Century').

*Statistical yearbook of the Church.* Città del Vaticano: Secretaria Status, 2000. (Large range of Catholic data on all countries).

*Statistics sources: a subject guide to data on industrial, business, social, educational, financial, and other topics for the United States and internationally.* J. W. O'Brien & S. R. Wasserman, eds. 11th edition. Detroit, MI: Gale Research, 1987, 2 volumes.

*The conversion of the world: or the claims of 600 millions, and the ability and duty of the churches respecting them.* G. Hall & S. Newell. Andover: ABCFM, 1818.

*The encyclopedia of missions: descriptive, historical, biographical, statistical.* H. O. Dwight et al. New York: Bureau of Missions: Funk & Wagnalls, 1891.

*The evangelization of the Roman empire: identity and adaptability.* E. G. Hinson. Macon, GA: Mercer University Press, 1981.

*The evangelization of the world in this generation.* John R. Mott. New York: SVMFM, 1900. (A brilliant classic, establishing the case for world evangelization. Relates the task to extensive secular statistical data on railways, navigation, et alia).

'The globalization of American televangelism', J. K. Hadden, *International journal of frontier missions,* 7, 1 (January, 1990), 1-10.

*The growth of Christianity during nineteen centuries, exhibited in a series of charts and numerical tables.* A. O. Van Lennep & A. F. Schauffler. New York: Anson D. F. Randolph, 1884.

'The Lausanne Covenant', in J. D. Douglas, ed, *Let the Earth hear His voice* (Minneapolis, MN: World Wide Publications, 1975), pages 3-9.

*The metropolis era.* Vol. 1: *A world of giant cities.* Vol. 2: *Megacities.* M. Dogan & J. D. Kasarda. Newbury Park, CA: Sage, 1988.

*The new book of world rankings.* G. T. Kurian. New York: Facts on File, 1984. (Includes over 50,000 variables reduced to 343 performance yardsticks in key subject areas for 190 countries).

*The new state of the world atlas.* M. Kidron & R. Segal. New York: Simon and Schuster, 1984.

*The New Testament concept of witness.* A. A. Trites. Cambridge: Cambridge University Press, 1977.

*The NIV (New International Version) complete concordance.* E. W. Goodrick & J. R. Kohlenberger III. Grand Rapids, MI: Zondervan, 1981.

*The world in figures.* London: The Economist, 1987. 1st edition 1976. (A range of statistical data on all countries).

*The world of learning 1988.* 38th edition. London: Europa Publications, 1987. (Major guide to educational, scientific, and cultural institutions across the world).

*Theological dictionary of the New Testament.* Translation from Kittel's German work (next item below) by G. W. Bromiley. Grand Rapids, MI: Eerdmans. 9 volumes, 1964-1974. One-volume edition, 1985.

*Theologisches Wörterbuch zum Neuen Testament.* G. Kittel & G. Friedrich, eds. Stuttgart: W. Kohlhammer Verlag, 1932-1978.

*Theology for the Third Millennium: an ecumenical view.* Hans Küng. London: Collins, 1988.

*To the ends of the Earth.* Pastoral Statement on World Mission, U. S. Catholic Bishops. *Origins* (Washington, DC: NC Documentary Service), 16, 25 (4 December 1986).

*Women in the world: an international atlas.* J. Seager & A. Olson. New York, NY: Simon & Schuster, 1986.

*World Christian encyclopedia: a comparative survey of churches and religions in the modern world, AD 1900-2000.* D. B. Barrett, ed. Oxford University Press. 1st edition, Nairobi, 1982. 2nd edition, New York, 2 volumes, 2001.

*World Christian handbook.* K. G. Grubb et al. 1949, 1952, 1957, 1962, 1968 editions. London: World Dominion/Lutterworth.

*World development report.* World Bank. New York: Oxford University Press, 2001 (Annual).

*World population prospects: the 1998 revision.* UN Population Division. New York: UN, 1999. (For the world, continents, regions, and 210 countries, a vast range of demographic variables is given throughout the period 1950-2025. Future projections have 4 alternate scenarios for all statistics: low variant, medium variant, high variant, constant fertility. Easy to use; the definitive source on population statistics).

*World radio TV handbook,* 2000 edition. Volume 44. A. G. Sennit, ed. New York: Billboard, 2000. (Statistics and data on all countries).

*World refugee survey: 1988 in review.* Washington, DC: U.S. Committee for Refugees, 1989.

*World resources 1988-89: an assessment of the resource base that supports the global economy.* World Resources Institute, International Institute for Environment and Development, and UN Environment Programme. New York: Basic Books, 1990.

*Yearbook of the Orthodox Church.* 1978 edition. Munchen: Verlag Alex Proc, 1978. (Describes all Eastern Orthodox jurisdictions in canonical relationship with Athens, Constantinople, and Moscow).

*Yearbook on international Communist affairs: parties and revolutionary movements.* R. F. Staar, ed. Stanford, CA: Hoover Institution Press, 1989. (Detailed survey of all parties and countries prior to 1989 collapse of Communism).

## Global Diagram 1.    A classification of major types of religion: 12 categories and 44 types, categorizing the world's 9,900 distinct religions with 5.1 billion adherents, each of whom on average belongs to 10 distinct religions in AD 2000.

The world of religion, religions, and georeligions (world religions) can be described and classified in many ways. Here the diagram explains their diversity by means of 12 major categories (columns 5–16 in table below) and 8 magnitudes (columns 17–24). Note that column 4 reports *multiple adherence*, since vast numbers of persons are members or adherents of an average of 10 religions each.

A parallel analysis, but by the 12 major religionist categories, is given in Table 17–3.

The 9,900 distinct religions are explained and partly enumerated and described in *WCT* Part 17; and fully in *WCD*. Their multitudinous activities are illustrated in the photo below by some of the 10,000 enthusiastic attenders at the 1999 Parliament of the World's Religions, held in Cape Town, South Africa.

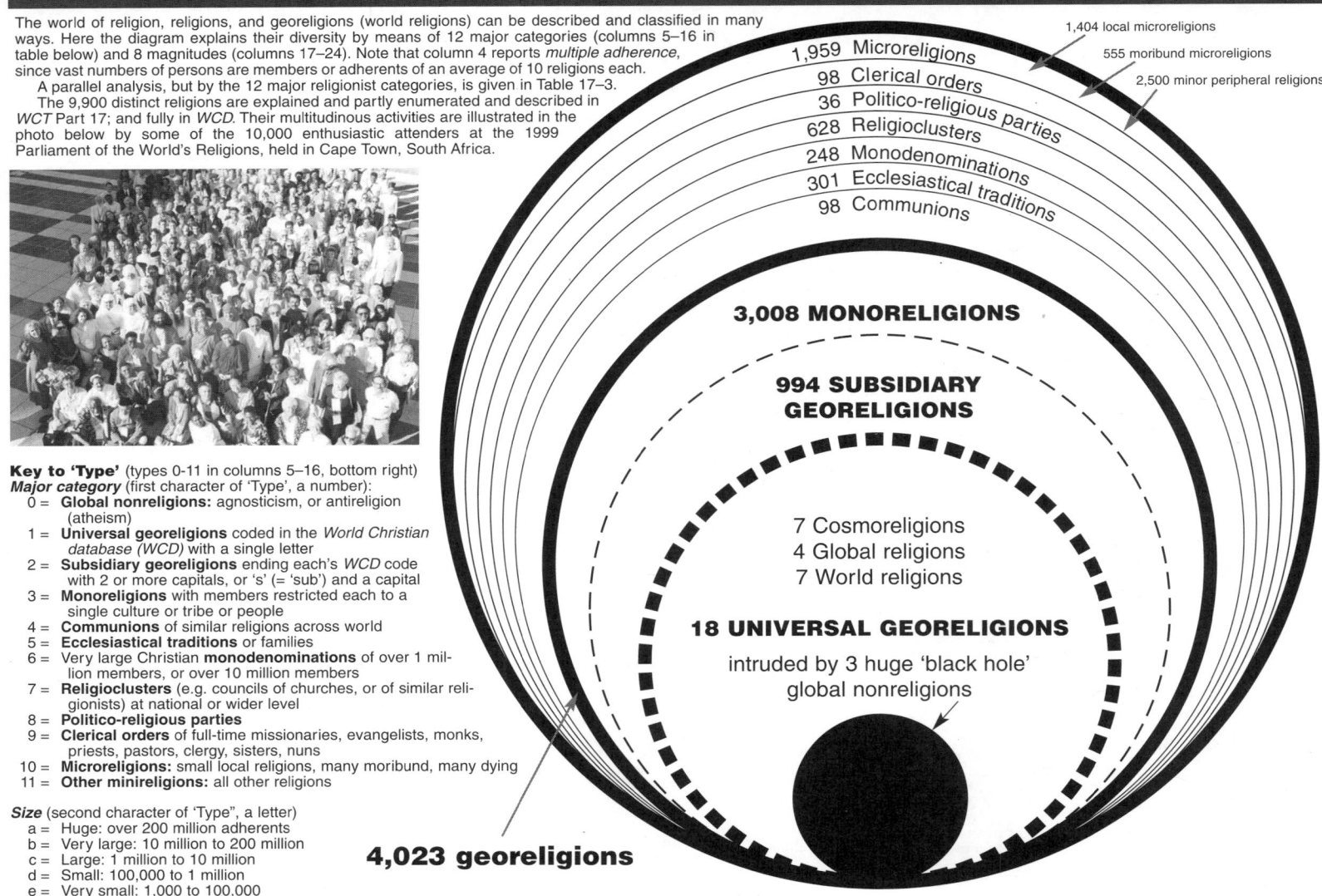

1,959 Microreligions
98 Clerical orders
36 Politico-religious parties
628 Religioclusters
248 Monodenominations
301 Ecclesiastical traditions
98 Communions

1,404 local microreligions
555 moribund microreligions
2,500 minor peripheral religions

**3,008 MONORELIGIONS**

**994 SUBSIDIARY GEORELIGIONS**

7 Cosmoreligions
4 Global religions
7 World religions

**18 UNIVERSAL GEORELIGIONS**

intruded by 3 huge 'black hole' global nonreligions

**4,023 georeligions**

**Key to 'Type'** (types 0-11 in columns 5–16, bottom right)
*Major category* (first character of 'Type', a number):
0 =  **Global nonreligions**: agnosticism, or antireligion (atheism)
1 =  **Universal georeligions** coded in the *World Christian database (WCD)* with a single letter
2 =  **Subsidiary georeligions** ending each's *WCD* code with 2 or more capitals, or 's' (= 'sub') and a capital
3 =  **Monoreligions** with members restricted each to a single culture or tribe or people
4 =  **Communions** of similar religions across world
5 =  **Ecclesiastical traditions** or families
6 =  Very large Christian **monodenominations** of over 1 million members, or over 10 million members
7 =  **Religioclusters** (e.g. councils of churches, or of similar religionists) at national or wider level
8 =  **Politico-religious parties**
9 =  **Clerical orders** of full-time missionaries, evangelists, monks, priests, pastors, clergy, sisters, nuns
10 =  **Microreligions**: small local religions, many moribund, many dying
11 =  **Other minireligions**: all other religions

*Size* (second character of 'Type", a letter)
a =  Huge: over 200 million adherents
b =  Very large: 10 million to 200 million
c =  Large: 1 million to 10 million
d =  Small: 100,000 to 1 million
e =  Very small: 1,000 to 100,000
f =  Minuscule: 100 to 1,000
g =  Microscopic: 10 to 100
h =  Defunct: under 10 adherents, down to zero (extinct)

Table A. The globe's population enumerated by 22 major family pedigrees, by 12 major religionist categories, and by 8 orders of magnitude of adherence, at AD 2000.

| | UNIVERSAL GEORELIGIONS AND ADHERENCE | | | | RELIGIONS BY TYPE | | | | | | | | | | | | | | | | | | |
|---|---|---|---|---|---|---|---|---|---|---|---|---|---|---|---|---|---|---|---|---|---|---|---|
| Pedigree | Religionist family | Distinct religions | Multiple adherence | Religions by major category | | | | | | | | | | | | Religion by size of adherents | | | | | | | |
| | | | | 0 | 1 | 2 | 3 | 4 | 5 | 6 | 7 | 8 | 9 | 10 | 11 | a | b | c | d | e | f | g | h |
| 1 | 2 | 3 | 4 | 5 | 6 | 7 | 8 | 9 | 10 | 11 | 12 | 13 | 14 | 15 | 16 | 17 | 18 | 19 | 20 | 21 | 22 | 23 | 24 |
| – | Nonreligionists . . . . . . . . | 3 | 1,836,497,000 | 3 | — | — | — | — | — | — | — | — | — | — | — | 2 | 1 | — | — | — | — | — | — |
| B | Buddhists . . . . . . . . . . . . . | 274 | 1,986,033,000 | — | 1 | 235 | — | — | — | — | 21 | — | 17 | — | — | 3 | 21 | 46 | 73 | 131 | — | — | — |
| C | Christians  . . . . . . . . . . . | 1,331 | 28,722,195,000 | — | 1 | 97 | — | 84 | 301 | 248 | 516 | — | 72 | 12 | — | 24 | 184 | 492 | 296 | 323 | 11 | 1 | — |
| D | Taoists . . . . . . . . . . . . . . | 10 | 4,725,000 | — | 1 | 6 | — | — | — | — | 3 | — | — | — | — | 1 | — | — | 2 | 5 | 3 | — | — |
| F | Chinese folk-religionists . . | 1 | 384,807,000 | — | — | 1 | — | — | — | — | — | — | — | — | — | 1 | — | — | — | — | — | — | — |
| G | Confucianists . . . . . . . . . | 2 | 6,399,000 | — | 1 | 1 | — | — | — | — | — | — | — | — | — | — | — | 1 | 1 | — | — | — | — |
| H | Hindus . . . . . . . . . . . . . | 90 | 3,356,415,000 | — | 1 | 74 | — | — | — | — | 1 | 6 | 7 | 1 | — | 6 | 6 | 18 | 18 | 41 | 1 | — | — |
| J | Jews . . . . . . . . . . . . . | 63 | 79,092,000 | — | 1 | 37 | — | 1 | — | — | 15 | 8 | — | 1 | — | — | 3 | 12 | 14 | 33 | 1 | — | — |
| K | Sikhs . . . . . . . . . . . . | 21 | 29,037,000 | — | 1 | 14 | — | — | — | — | 4 | 1 | 1 | — | — | — | 1 | 1 | 5 | 14 | — | — | — |
| L | Baha'is . . . . . . . . . . . . | 4 | 7,120,000 | — | 1 | 3 | — | — | — | — | — | — | — | — | — | — | 1 | — | — | 3 | — | — | — |
| M | Muslims . . . . . . . . . . . . | 269 | 5,261,498,000 | — | 1 | 178 | — | 12 | — | — | 51 | 21 | 1 | 5 | — | 8 | 22 | 47 | 62 | 125 | 5 | — | — |
| N | New-Religionists . . . . . . | 160 | 902,473,000 | — | 1 | 155 | — | — | — | — | 1 | — | — | 3 | — | — | 14 | 23 | 40 | 80 | 3 | — | — |
| S | Shintoists . . . . . . . . . . . | 147 | 155,143,000 | — | 1 | 138 | — | — | — | — | 2 | — | — | 6 | — | — | 2 | 9 | 25 | 105 | 5 | 1 | — |
| T | Ethnoreligionists . . . . . . . | 4,937 | 864,307,000 | — | 1 | — | 3,008 | — | — | — | — | — | — | 1,928 | — | 2 | 5 | 50 | 332 | 2,620 | 1,375 | 491 | 62 |
| U | Spiritists . . . . . . . . . . . | 36 | 108,185,000 | — | 1 | 32 | — | — | — | — | 2 | — | — | 1 | — | — | 3 | 6 | 13 | 13 | 1 | — | — |
| V | Jains . . . . . . . . . . . . . | 16 | 8,886,000 | — | 1 | 14 | — | — | — | — | — | — | — | 1 | — | — | — | 3 | 4 | 8 | 1 | — | — |
| W | Religionists . . . . . . . . . | 16 | 1,438,940,000 | — | 1 | 2 | — | 1 | — | — | 12 | — | — | — | — | 3 | — | 4 | 1 | 8 | — | — | — |
| X | Non-Christians . . . . . . . . | 1 | 4,055,485,000 | — | 1 | — | — | — | — | — | — | — | — | — | — | 1 | — | — | — | — | — | — | — |
| Y | Quasireligionists  . . . . . . | 8 | 137,245,000 | — | 1 | 6 | — | — | — | — | — | — | — | 1 | — | — | 2 | 2 | 1 | 2 | 1 | — | — |
| Z | Zoroastrians . . . . . . . . . | 2 | 2,794,000 | — | 1 | 1 | — | — | — | — | — | — | — | — | — | — | — | 1 | 1 | — | — | — | — |
| | Other peripheral religionists . . . . | 2,000 | 20,000,000 | — | — | — | — | — | — | — | — | — | — | 2,000 | — | — | — | — | — | — | — | — | — |
| | Other hidden religionists . . . . . . . | 500 | 1,000,000 | — | — | — | — | — | — | — | — | — | — | 500 | — | — | — | — | — | — | — | — | — |
| | Total non-Christian adherence . . | 8,560 | 20,646,081,000 | 3 | 17 | 897 | 3,008 | 14 | 301 | 248 | 112 | 36 | 26 | 1,947 | — | 26 | 80 | 226 | 595 | 3,186 | 1,393 | 492 | 62 |
| | Total all religionist adherence . . . | 9,891 | 49,368,276,000 | 3 | 18 | 994 | 3,008 | 98 | 301 | 248 | 628 | 36 | 98 | 1,959 | 2,500 | 50 | 264 | 718 | 891 | 3,509 | 1,404 | 493 | 62 |
| | Multi-counted adherence . . . . . . | | -43,313,227,000 | — | — | — | — | — | — | — | — | — | — | — | — | — | — | — | — | — | — | — | — |
| | Religionists worldwide . . . . . . . . | 9,888 | 5,136,800,500 | 0 | 18 | 994 | 3,008 | 98 | 301 | 248 | 628 | 36 | 98 | 1,959 | 2,500 | 48 | 263 | 718 | 891 | 3,509 | 1,404 | 493 | 62 |
| | Nonreligionists worldwide . . . . . . | 3 | 918,248,500 | 3 | — | — | — | — | — | — | — | — | — | — | — | 2 | 1 | — | — | — | — | — | — |
| | **Global population . . . . . . . . . .** | **9,891** | **6,055,049,000** | **3** | **18** | **994** | **3,008** | **98** | **301** | **248** | **628** | **36** | **98** | **1,959** | **2,500** | **50** | **264** | **718** | **891** | **3,509** | **1,404** | **493** | **62** |

## Global Diagram 2. Fifty essential elements defining the boundaries of mainstream Christianity, listed under 10 seminal keywords.

The world in AD 2000 has followers promoting over 9,900 different religions, and a billion nonreligionists trying to end all religion. It therefore becomes essential to clarify precisely the exact meaning or definition of the terms 'Christian' and 'Christianity'. In the early church and later this was done by ecumenical councils (such as 1962's Vatican II, shown at left) through condensed statements—the Apostles' Creed, Nicene Creed, and numerous subsequent creeds, articles, confessions, and many modern cate-chisms.

Below are listed 50 distinct items, topics, or elements covering the whole range of subjects widely agreed to be essential to any thorough depicting of Christianity. For convenience, the 50 elements are listed in approximately chronological order of their emergence in the world's understanding. The list may be regarded as a provisional updated creed or catechism for the 21st century.

The diagram attempts to define mainstream Christianity and all related statistical categories enumerated in the present analysis.

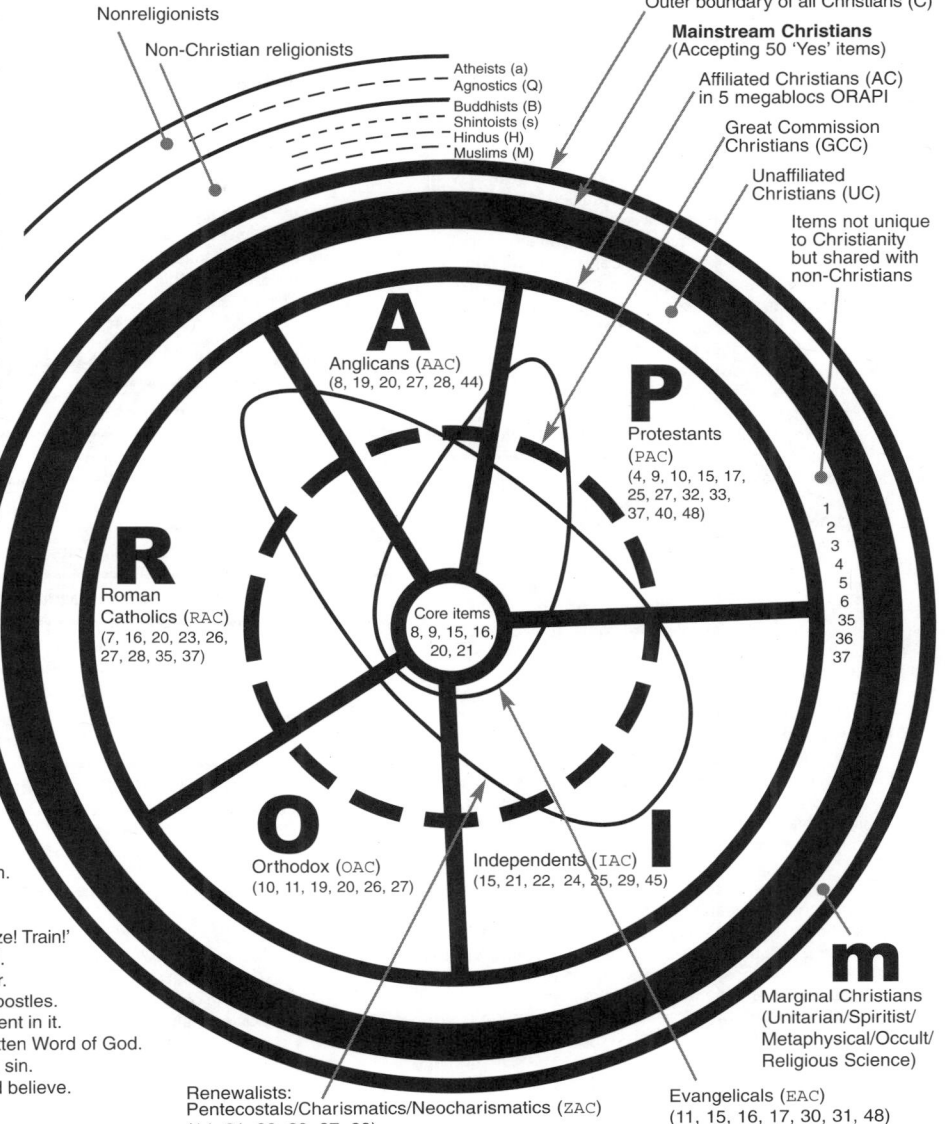

### Chronological sequence of the 50 essential elements

#### GOD
1. God the All-Powerful **Creator** of heaven and earth.
2. God the **Sustainer** continuously involved in all ongoing creation.
3. God the **Father** of all peoples, loving every individual.
4. Evil, **sin**, and the Fall of Man destroying close relationship with God.
5. The Old Testament as **salvation history** (Heilsgeschichte).
6. God's **revelation**, and science's worldview, as non-overlapping magisteria.

#### CHRIST
7. The **Incarnation** of God the Son, the Messiah, born of the Virgin Mary.
8. The **historicity** of Jesus of Nazareth, his ministry, healings, and miracles.
9. Jesus' **Crucifixion**, death, burial, as recorded in the Four Gospels.
10. Jesus' **Resurrection** as witnessed by Apostles, disciples, the whole church.
11. The **deity**, as well as full humanity, of Jesus Christ as unique Son of God.

#### MISSION
12. Christ's **Great Commission**: 'Receive! Go! Witness! Proclaim! Disciple! Baptize! Train!'
13. Christ's **Ascension** into heaven and his Session at the Father's right hand.
14. God the **Holy Spirit** revealed at Pentecost as the empowering Evangelizer.
15. The 6-fold **Gospel** (Good News, Evangel) as **kerygma** preached by the Apostles.
16. The **Mission** of God (Missio Dei) to the whole world, and human involvement in it.
17. The **Bible** (Old & New Testaments) as the unique inspired spoken and written Word of God.
18. The **Atonement** through the Cross, overcoming death, evil, and all human sin.
19. God's **grace and forgiveness** of sins by faith, for all those who repent and believe.
20. The **Holy Trinity**: the mystery of Three Persons in One God.

#### DISCIPLES
21. **Discipleship** as personal experience of Christ with commitment to him as Savior and Lord.
22. The **pentecostal/charismatic experience** of gifts of the Holy Spirit.
23. **Holiness** of life: morality, ethics, behavior, sanctification, discipline, devotion, love, prayer, intercession.
24. **Stewardship** of time, money, resources, nature, species, environment.
25. The significant role of committed human **leadership** in church and mission, by women as well as men.

#### CHURCH
26. The **Church** as God's instrument throughout history; a community existing not for itself but to serve the world.
27. Regular public **worship of God** with ministries/sacraments/eucharists/liturgies/hymnodies/choirs/music old and new.
28. **Summaries**: Ten Commandments, Apostles' Creed, Nicene Creed, Athanasian Creed, modern catechisms.
29. Continual **renewal** and continuous reformation of Christianity, church, and agencies at every level via spiritual gifts.

#### OUTREACH
30. Collective and personal **human witness** to Christ as Risen Lord, the Light of the World.
31. **Evangelism** as proclamation of the Good News of salvation in Christ via all media ancient or modern.
32. Foreign mission as the Church's **organized outreach**, at the global level, to the non-Christian world.
33. The aim of evangelism: **conversion** of non-Christians, then catechumenate, baptism, discipleship, church membership.
34. Public confession or **profession** of faith in Christ and Christianity by individuals, churches, denominations.

#### BENEFICIARIES
35. Solidarity with the world's **human need**: the poor, the unprivileged, the exploited, the sick, the disabled, the blind.
36. **Social justice**, peace, nonviolence, and development for all as the church's daily concern.
37. The struggle for universal declaration of **human rights**, and their implementation.
38. Ministry among and to the world's 3,800 **unevangelized** ethnolinguistic peoples (known as World A).
39. Contact and dialogue with all the world's 6,500 **non-Christian religions**.

#### STRATEGIES
40. Mission as organized plans, **strategies**, and goals linked to and obeying the Great Commission.
41. **Monitoring** of the church's 2,056 instruments measuring and enumerating global mission.
42. **Accountability** in all contemporary spheres of the church's activities via publishing its detailed statistics.
43. God's plan for world mission and **global evangelization**, and human commitment to both.
44. **Scripture distribution** controlled by clearly-stated numerical goals and global spreading of resources.

#### TRIBULATION
45. Religious **persecution** and suffering as a direct and indispensible completing or fulfilling of Christ's sufferings.
46. **Martyrdom's** unsought daily toll seen as playing an essential role in 20 centuries of world mission and evangelization.

#### FUTURES
47. The church's future trends, future scenarios, and **futuristics** reflecting God's purposes for humanity.
48. The Advent, Eschaton, Millennium, Parousia, or **Second Coming** of the Returning Christ as King and Judge.
49. The **Last Judgment**: final accountability for all human activity on Earth.
50. God creates the **New Heavens** and New Earth and the future life.

### Key to circles, names, letters, numbers above
→ Arrowhead points to any outer boundary line
● Blob refers only to its surrounding space
25 Numbers state which of the 50 elements best describe major emphases or differentia
ORAPIm = The 6 ecclesiastico-cultural megablocs
(PAC) = Letters in parentheses after each grouping give its database code (see GeoCodebook)

### Defining the boundaries of 'Christian'
• A Christian = a professing/confessing believer in Christ who confronts the Yes/No veracity of the 50 items at left which collectively are unique to Christianity and which thus define the boundary between what is and what is not Christianity.

#### Maximum definition
• A Christian = anyone who answers Yes to all 50 items, each in question form as: 'Do you accept or believe in this item as true?'

#### Minimum definition
• A Christian = anyone who answers Yes to 6 non-negotiable core items: 8, 9, 15, 16, 20, 21.

#### Main keywords
• A Christian = anyone who answers Yes to a Top Ten = 21, 12, 15, 16, 30, 31, 35, 38, 43, 48.

#### Varieties of Christian
• A mainstream Christian = anyone within the heavy black circle (above), either O,R, A, P, I church members, or unaffiliated.
• An Evangelical = a Christian believer emphasizing as essential 7 items in particular: 11, 15, 16, 17, 30, 31, 48.
• A pentecostal/charismatic = a Christian believer emphasizing as essential 6 items in particular: 14, 21, 22, 23, 27, 29.
• A Great Commission Christian = a Christian believer emphasizing 9 items in particular: 12, 15, 16, 21, 23, 30, 33, 38, 40.
• A marginal Christian = a believer who rejects mainstream Christianity especially one or more of items 1, 5, 7, 11, 17, 20, or 26, displacing the Bible as unique by adding an additional source of divine revelation.

**Global Diagram 3.** **Measuring the status of global Christianity: the annual megacensus of 180 major religious subjects, from background context to Great Commission Instrument Panel.**

The circle describes, under 10 headings, organized Christianity's annual decentralized censuses held by most of its 33,800 denominations, 23,000 service agencies, and 5.5 million workers. In aggregate, these are termed here: the annual megacensus. Subjects are listed in box 3 below. Resulting data may be located from Table DD shown following Global Diagram 31.

**3. Major religious subjects measured annually**

The following 180 subjects are quantified by churches, agencies, and missions worldwide each year:
**religions, adherents,** members, practice, attenders, polls, beliefs, sects, cults, megablocs, **communions,** confessions, ecclesiastical traditions, **councils,** conferences, **denominations,** jurisdictions, dioceses, cathedrals, basilicas, abbeys, priories, parishes, chapels, **churches,** worship centers, **affiliated members,** adult members, their children, **full-time workers,** clergy, priests, deacons, pastors, ministers, chaplains, lay workers, friars, brothers, monks, contemplatives, bishops, archbishops, metropolitans, cardinals, patriarchs, popes, **women workers,** sisters, nuns, lay readers, musicians, choirs, **missions,** preachers, missioners, home missionaries, foreign missionaries, medical missionaries, missiologists, colporteurs, catechists, evangelists, **evangelism,** evangelistics, evangelization, urban-industrial mission, campaigns, crusades, audiences, **church growth,** catechisms, catechumens, home visits, converts, **baptisms,** confirmations, ordinations, consecrations, marriages, divorces, funerals, excommunications, **renewals,** revivals, persecution, martyrs, **service agencies,** religious orders, societies, institutes, institutions, youth ministries, **schools,** colleges, universities, study centers, students, **hospitals,** clinics, beds, outpatients, medicines, orphanages, **research,** scholarship, scholars, theologians, **libraries,** holdings, bibliographies, **administrators,** nuncios, seminaries, seminarians, monasteries, convents, sundayschools, ss teachers, ss pupils, retreats, pilgrimages, logistics, **strategies,** tactics, global plans, **finances,** offerings, collections, budgets, incomes, expenditures, properties, endowments, assets, embezzlements, audits, **literature,** tracts, books, magazines, periodicals, journals, newspapers, yearbooks, directories, annual reports, publications, publishing houses, bookshops, **scriptures,** scripture distribution, scripture density, scripture use, scripture translations, translators, names for God, **transportation,** travel, itineration, aviation, ships, vehicles, **communications,** broadcasting, radio/TV stations, listeners, films, viewers, viewings, audiovisuals, correspondence courses, tapes, discs, videos, DVDs, **computers,** computer personnel, e-mail volume, webmasters, websites, hits, networks, **futuristics,** projections, trends, prospects, scenarios.

**1. Background**

Interpretation and analysis of the annual megacensus is grounded in the following 6 secular documents.
• *UN Demographic Database,* also WHO, UNDP, etc.
• *Universal Declaration of Human Rights* (1948)
• *New Encyclopaedia Britannica* on race, ethnography
• *Linguasphere register of the world's languages*
• *Long-range world population projections to AD 2200*
• *World Futures and the UN:* 250 books
To the above 6 seminal documents must be added today's easy electronic access to the 45 million distinct book titles on the shelves of the world's 50,000 largest libraries.

## The annual megacensus

1. BACKGROUND
2. SECULAR DATA
3. SUBJECTS
4. ENUMERATORS
5. QUESTIONNAIRES
6. INSTRUMENTS
7. ANALYZERS
8. DATABASES
9. FINDINGS
10. GCIP PANELS

**10. Great Commission Instrument Panel** (GCIP)

This selection below of a panel composed of the top 6 instruments critical for the progress of Christ's Great Commission is designed to serve the world's 5,000 computerized GC networks. It enables comparison of any country with other countries, facilitating strategy, tactics, decision making. It aids collaboration to avoid every agency working from scratch, overlapping or duplicating. It then assists navigation, targeting, up to closure. See Part 15 for GCIPs of the 77 countries each with population over 10 million; and *WCE* Volume 1, Part 4, for GCIPs of all 238 countries.

**2. Secular data**
See Global Diagrams 18 to 22; Table 12-1, cols. 1-53.

**4. Enumerators**
Like other church leaders, all Roman Catholic bishops (pictured in Sistine Chapel) are each required to answer every year 140 statistical questions concerning their work.

**5. Questionnaires**
Each year churches and agencies send their workers 10 million questionnaires in 3,000 languages asking 2,000 different statistical questions. Total cost of this megacensus: $1.1 billion per annum.

**6. Instruments**
These 2,000 'measuring devices' are enumerated in Table DD, showing where to find these data set out.

**7. Analyzers**
The Christian world owns 332 million general-purpose computers and has access to many supercomputers like ASCI Red TFLOPS (below), the world's biggest.

**8. Databases**
As on forthcoming *WCD.*

**9. Findings**
As reported in *WCT* Part 1, *WCE* Part 1, et al.

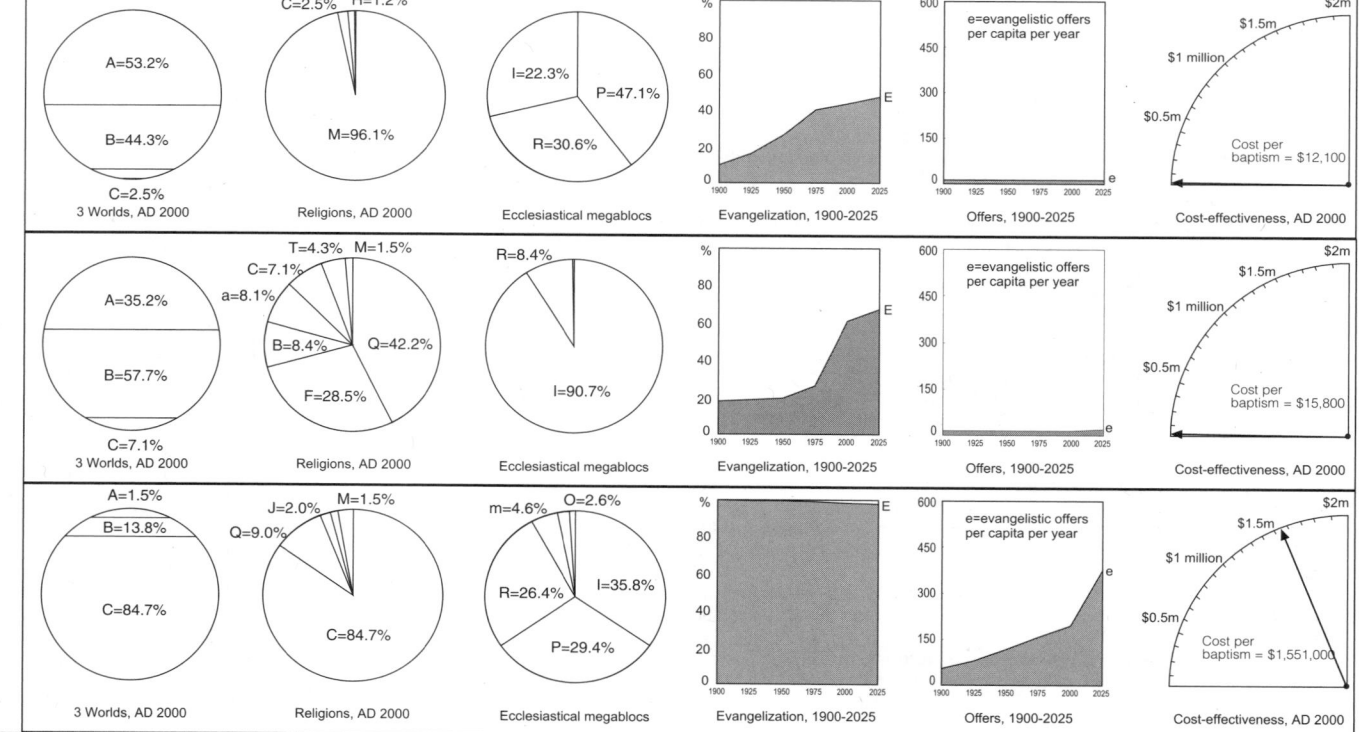

**Pakistan**
World's largest
World A country

C=2.5%  H=1.2%
A=53.2%
B=44.3%
C=2.5%
3 Worlds, AD 2000

M=96.1%
Religions, AD 2000

I=22.3%  P=47.1%
R=30.6%
Ecclesiastical megablocs

Evangelization, 1900-2025

e=evangelistic offers per capita per year
Offers, 1900-2025

Cost per baptism = $12,100
Cost-effectiveness, AD 2000

**China**
World's largest
World B country

A=35.2%
B=57.7%
C=7.1%
3 Worlds, AD 2000

T=4.3%  M=1.5%
C=7.1%
a=8.1%
B=8.4%  Q=42.2%
F=28.5%
Religions, AD 2000

R=8.4%
I=90.7%
Ecclesiastical megablocs

Evangelization, 1900-2025

e=evangelistic offers per capita per year
Offers, 1900-2025

Cost per baptism = $15,800
Cost-effectiveness, AD 2000

**USA**
World's largest
World C country

A=1.5%
B=13.8%
C=84.7%
3 Worlds, AD 2000

J=2.0%  M=1.5%
Q=9.0%
C=84.7%
Religions, AD 2000

m=4.6%  O=2.6%
R=26.4%  I=35.8%
P=29.4%
Ecclesiastical megablocs

Evangelization, 1900-2025

e=evangelistic offers per capita per year
Offers, 1900-2025

Cost per baptism = $1,551,000
Cost-effectiveness, AD 2000

**Table AA.    World statistical reports, reporting, and 1980-2002 annual reports of global Christianity's megacensus every year.**

Regular reporting of church statistics goes back to the 12th century. Details of the evolution of counting, censuses, and statistics throughout Christian history are given here in *WCT* Part 2 "CosmoChronology".

By 1500, the civil authorities in Paris, France were supervising and publishing full reporting of newly baptized persons. The first modern census of church affiliation and membership was the Compton Census of 1676. Organized by Henry Compton, Anglican bishop of London, it computed the population of Britain as 95.3% Conformists, 4.2% Nonconformists, and 0.5% Papists.

Roman Catholic foreign missionaries from 1650 on began sending home regular reports on their work, likewise Anglican foreign missionaries from 1840 under the urging of the CMS general secretary Henry Venn. In 1716 began the annual publication of the printed *Notizie per l'anno 1716*, which in 1860 became *Annuario Pontificio* reporting every Catholic diocese's statistics, up to the present day.

By the year 1900 the annual reporting of all the major churches of the world, although uncoordinated, had reached the point where it could correctly be termed an annual megacensus, with separate censuses and reports from each denomination.

In 1965 the World Evangelization Research Centre, in Nairobi, began regular global reports in the *World Christian handbook*, *International review of missions*, et alia, up to its 1982 *World Christian encyclopedia*, first edition. Then in 1985 WERC began its annual 2-page statistical global report based on the multitude of megacensus reports. (See below a facsimile of first report in the *International bulletin of missionary research*, volume 9:1, 1985). Following the same format, improved each year, the AD 2002 table is now the 18th annual report in that series. This 2002 table is reproduced here, slightly modified, in Table 10–2. Spreadsheet versions are also available.

Monthly reports, greatly enlarged, or detailed irregular news and analyses, were introduced by WERC in 1990 in the *AD 2000 Global monitor*, later the *AD 2025 Global monitor*, and later still in *World Christian news*.

# STATUS OF GLOBAL MISSION, 1985, IN CONTEXT OF 20TH CENTURY

| Year: | 1900 | 1970 | 1980 | 1985 | 2000 |
|---|---|---|---|---|---|
| **WORLD POPULATION** | | | | | |
| 1. Total population | 1,619,886,800 | 3,610,034,400 | 4,373,917,500 | 4,781,124,000 | 6,259,642,000 |
| 2. Urban dwellers | 232,694,900 | 1,354,237,000 | 1,797,479,000 | 2,053,544,000 | 3,160,381,900 |
| 3. Rural dwellers | 1,387,191,900 | 2,255,797,400 | 2,576,438,500 | 2,727,580,000 | 3,099,260,100 |
| 4. Adult population | 1,025,938,000 | 2,245,227,300 | 2,698,396,900 | 2,939,432,000 | 3,808,564,300 |
| 5. Literates | 286,705,000 | 1,437,761,900 | 1,774,002,700 | 1,960,103,100 | 2,697,595,100 |
| 6. Nonliterates | 739,233,000 | 807,465,400 | 924,394,200 | 979,328,900 | 1,110,969,200 |
| **WORLD POPULATION BY RELIGION** | | | | | |
| 7. Christians (total all kinds) | 558,056,300 | 1,216,579,400 | 1,432,686,500 | 1,548,592,200 | 2,019,921,400 |
| 8. Muslims | 200,102,200 | 550,919,000 | 722,956,500 | 817,065,200 | 1,200,653,000 |
| 9. Nonreligious | 2,923,300 | 543,065,300 | 715,901,400 | 805,784,900 | 1,071,888,400 |
| 10. Hindus | 203,033,300 | 465,784,800 | 582,749,900 | 647,567,500 | 859,252,300 |
| 11. Buddhists | 127,159,000 | 231,672,200 | 273,715,600 | 295,570,800 | 359,092,100 |
| 12. Atheists | 225,600 | 165,288,500 | 195,119,400 | 210,643,500 | 262,447,600 |
| 13. Tribal religionists | 106,339,600 | 88,077,400 | 89,963,500 | 91,130,400 | 100,535,900 |
| 14. New Religionists | 5,910,000 | 76,443,100 | 96,021,800 | 106,317,600 | 138,263,800 |
| 15. Jews | 12,269,800 | 15,185,900 | 16,938,200 | 17,838,100 | 20,173,600 |
| 16. Sikhs | 2,960,600 | 10,612,200 | 14,244,400 | 16,149,900 | 23,831,700 |
| 17. Other religionists | 400,907,100 | 246,406,600 | 233,620,300 | 224,463,900 | 203,582,200 |
| **GLOBAL CHRISTIANITY** | | | | | |
| 18. Total Christians as % of world | 34.4 | 33.7 | 32.8 | 32.4 | 32.3 |
| 19. Affiliated church members | 521,563,200 | 1,131,809,600 | 1,323,389,700 | 1,425,927,300 | 1,844,614,200 |
| 20. Practicing Christians | 469,259,800 | 884,021,800 | 1,018,355,300 | 1,090,348,400 | 1,330,325,100 |
| 21. Charismatics in Renewal | 0 | 1,587,700 | 11,005,390 | 16,759,700 | 38,861,500 |
| 22. Crypto-Christians | 3,572,400 | 55,699,700 | 70,395,000 | 78,184,800 | 106,208,700 |
| **MEMBERSHIP BY ECCLESIASTICAL BLOC** | | | | | |
| 23. Anglicans | 30,573,700 | 47,557,000 | 49,804,000 | 51,100,100 | 61,037,200 |
| 24. Catholics (non-Roman) | 276,000 | 3,134,400 | 3,439,400 | 3,600,900 | 4,334,100 |
| 25. Marginal Protestants | 927,600 | 10,830,200 | 14,077,500 | 15,770,800 | 24,106,200 |
| 26. Nonwhite indigenous Christians | 7,743,100 | 58,702,000 | 82,181,100 | 94,797,600 | 154,140,400 |
| 27. Orthodox | 115,897,700 | 143,402,500 | 160,737,900 | 169,648,700 | 199,819,000 |
| 28. Protestants | 103,056,700 | 233,424,200 | 262,157,600 | 277,914,100 | 345,709,100 |
| 29. Roman Catholics | 266,419,400 | 672,319,100 | 802,660,000 | 872,104,700 | 1,132,541,500 |
| **MEMBERSHIP BY CONTINENT** | | | | | |
| 30. Africa | 8,756,400 | 115,924,200 | 164,571,000 | 191,080,700 | 323,914,900 |
| 31. East Asia | 1,763,000 | 10,050,200 | 16,149,600 | 19,333,300 | 27,560,300 |
| 32. Europe | 273,788,400 | 397,108,700 | 403,177,600 | 406,235,000 | 411,448,700 |
| 33. Latin America | 60,025,100 | 262,027,800 | 340,978,600 | 383,250,800 | 555,486,000 |
| 34. Northern America | 59,569,700 | 169,246,900 | 178,892,500 | 183,852,300 | 201,265,200 |
| 35. Oceania | 4,311,400 | 14,669,400 | 16,160,600 | 16,909,400 | 21,361,500 |
| 36. South Asia | 16,347,200 | 76,770,200 | 106,733,200 | 123,097,800 | 185,476,700 |
| 37. USSR | 97,002,000 | 86,012,300 | 96,726,500 | 102,168,000 | 118,101,000 |
| **CHRISTIAN ORGANIZATIONS** | | | | | |
| 38. Service agencies | 1,500 | 14,100 | 17,500 | 19,300 | 24,000 |
| 39. Foreign-mission sending agencies | 600 | 2,200 | 3,100 | 3,500 | 4,800 |
| 40. Institutions | 9,500 | 80,500 | 91,000 | 96,000 | 103,000 |
| **CHRISTIAN WORKERS** | | | | | |
| 41. Nationals | 1,050,000 | 2,350,000 | 2,950,000 | 3,500,000 | 4,500,000 |
| 42. Aliens (foreign missionaries) | 62,000 | 240,000 | 249,000 | 250,000 | 400,000 |
| **CHRISTIAN FINANCE ( in U.S. $, per year)** | | | | | |
| 43. Personal income of church members | 270 billion | 4,100 billion | 5,878 billion | 7,450 billion | 12,700 billion |
| 44. Giving to Christian causes | 8 billion | 70 billion | 100.3 billion | 127 billion | 200 billion |
| 45. Churches' income | 7 billion | 50 billion | 64.5 billion | 75 billion | 80 billion |
| 46. Parachurch and institutional income | 1 billion | 20 billion | 35.8 billion | 52 billion | 120 billion |
| 47. Income of global foreign missions | 0.2 billion | 3 billion | 5.0 billion | 7 billion | 12 billion |
| Giving per church member per week | | | | | |
| 48. to all Christian causes | $0.29 | $1.19 | $1.46 | $1.71 | $2.09 |
| 49. to global foreign missions | $0.01 | $0.06 | $0.07 | $0.08 | $0.10 |
| **CHRISTIAN LITERATURE** | | | | | |
| 50. New commercial book titles per year | 2,200 | 17,100 | 18,800 | 20,800 | 25,000 |
| 51. New titles including devotional | 3,100 | 52,000 | 60,000 | 62,000 | 75,000 |
| 52. Christian periodicals | 3,500 | 23,000 | 22,500 | 21,000 | 35,000 |
| **SCRIPTURE DISTRIBUTION (all sources)** | | | | | |
| 53. Bibles per year | 5,452,600 | 25,000,000 | 36,800,000 | 43,000,000 | 70,000,000 |
| 54. New Testaments per year | 7,300,000 | 45,000,000 | 57,500,000 | 64,000,000 | 110,000,000 |
| **CHRISTIAN BROADCASTING** | | | | | |
| 55. Christian radio/TV stations | 0 | 1,230 | 1,450 | 1,580 | 4,000 |
| 56. Total monthly listeners/viewers | 0 | 750,000,000 | 990,474,400 | 1,090,000,000 | 2,150,000,000 |
| 57. for Christian stations | 0 | 150,000,000 | 291,810,500 | 370,000,000 | 600,000,000 |
| 58. for secular stations | 0 | 650,000,000 | 834,068,900 | 920,000,000 | 1,810,000,000 |
| **WORLD EVANGELIZATION** | | | | | |
| 59. Unevangelized populations | 788,159,000 | 1,391,956,000 | 1,380,576,000 | 1,335,212,000 | 1,038,819,000 |
| 60. Unevangelized as % of world | 48.7 | 38.6 | 31.6 | 27.9 | 16.6 |

**METHODOLOGICAL NOTES** (referring to numbered lines above). Indented categories form part of, and are included in, unindented categories above them. Definitions of categories are as given and explained in *World Christian Encyclopedia* (1982), with additional data and explanations as follows:

7. Widest definition: professing Christians plus secret believers, which equals affiliated (church members) plus nominal Christians.
14. Adherents of Asian so-called New Religions.
17. Mainly Chinese folk religionists.
18. Definition as in 7.
20. Church attenders, by churches' own definition.
20–22. These entries are selected sub-groups of 19

and are not intended as a complete breakdown of 19.
21. Active members of the Renewal in older mainline denominations (Anglican, Catholic, Orthodox, Protestant).
22. Secret believers.
23–29. Each of these entries can be reconciled to line 7 by referring to *WCE*, Global Table 4. To the total of these entries, add the category "nominal Christians," and subtract "doubly-affiliated" and "disaffiliated" members, as found in *WCE*, Global Table 4.
30. Definitions of the eight continents follow exactly United Nations practice.
38. Including 39.
43–49. Defined as in article "Silver and Gold Have I

none," in *International Bulletin*, October 1983, p. 150.
46. As distinct from churches' (denominational) income.
50. On strict UNESCO definition of book ( over 49 pages).
51. As 50, but adding the mass of smaller devotional literature (prayer books, service books, liturgies, choruses, etc.).
56. Total of audiences in 57 and 58, excluding overlap.
58. Total regular audience for Christian programs over secular or commercial stations.
59–60. Defined as in *WCE*, parts 3, 5, 6, and 9.

## Global Diagram 4.    World Christian trends across 22 centuries, AD 30–AD 2200, illustrated by 26 statistical categories, 10 annual growth rates (p.a.) and 7 graphed lines.

The starting point on this subject is this definition: 'A trend is a definite, predictable direction or sequence of events, like the warming of the Earth's climate' (G. Calente, *Trend tracking*, 1990:3). The data on this sheet summarize the large volume of information in Table BB (on the next page), and later in the 16-page Graph 7-2/Table 7-2. To understand further the concept 'trend' (or 'trends'), this survey recognizes 13 different usages or definitions or types, labeled A to M as follows (and elaborated on and enumerated in Part 7 "GeoTrends").

### NON-NUMERIC DEFINITIONS (using words only)
The first 3 populist usages avoid numbers and instead make generalized statements based on historical events and developments.
*Trend A.* A trend is the **general direction** of any irregular or winding phenomenon. Thus the line 'Christians' in Table A below shows a trend of rapid increase, despite one period of massive decline in the 14th century.
*Trend B.* 'Trend' is however often used to describe the current **status** of any significant issue, the past being less significant or satisfactory (Example: 'The global population explosion has today slowed markedly due to family planning programs worldwide'.)
*Trend C.* Many users consider mention of a lengthy **time period** (e.g. a decade or a century) to be essential to the concept.
*Trend D.* Short **descriptive sentences** one after another can often illuminate a trend. This is done overleaf in Table BB, columns 2 and 4.

### NUMERIC DEFINITIONS (using numbers and words)
Calculating evidence from numbers introduces a whole new arena of clarity and explanation.
*Trend E.* **Measurement** using existing methods (especially, as below, measurement of number of Christians) brings precision to the usage.
*Trend F.* New ventures in **quantification** in time and space are always possible if the category can be precisely defined. (Example: figures for Worlds A and B in Table A below).
*Trend G.* **Statistics at 2 points in time** are essential. Table A below has 21 exact time periods with numbers at beginning and end of each.
*Trend H.* **Graphic measures** visualize the trends, challenge the compilers to spot and explain divergences or sudden changes, and thus help to bring out their significance. (See Graph A, below: for a larger, more detailed version, see Graph 7–1. Note that the special value of the semilogarithmic grid employed is that the vertical scale can place very large numbers and very small numbers on the same piece of paper or computer screen.

*Trend I.* **Linear rates** joining 2 points in time by a straight line are the easiest and quickest results to obtain. They can be worked out in one's head or at least with pencil and paper.
*Trend J.* **Exponential growth rates.** More accurate is this method ('compound interest'). In Table A below, these rates appear 4 times (% p.a. for globe, World C, World B, World A). They also appear in Table BB as column 10. It is important to note that the exact value of any rate at a specific year varies if the period back to the previous date is changed. This explains why rates at certain dates in Table 7–1 differ slightly from rates at the same date in Table 7–2, because the preceding period is different.
*Trend K.* **Yearly increase.** Derived from growth rate % p.a. (per annum), over 100, times population (or Worlds C, B, A). See the 10 lines marked 'p.a.' below (or, Table BB column 8).
*Trend L.* **Daily increase.** In Table BB, column 9 = column 8 ÷ 365, a valuable microanalytical tool measuring average increase of persons per day.
*Trend M.* **Other related variables.** Analytical numbers such as 'Outreach per Christian' (the ratio of evangelized non-Christians ('World B') divided by Christians; see Table BB column 6) can be illuminating. Still other variables, as with 'Martyrs' in Table BB overleaf are not derived from previous statistics described above but they help visualize the main trend itself.

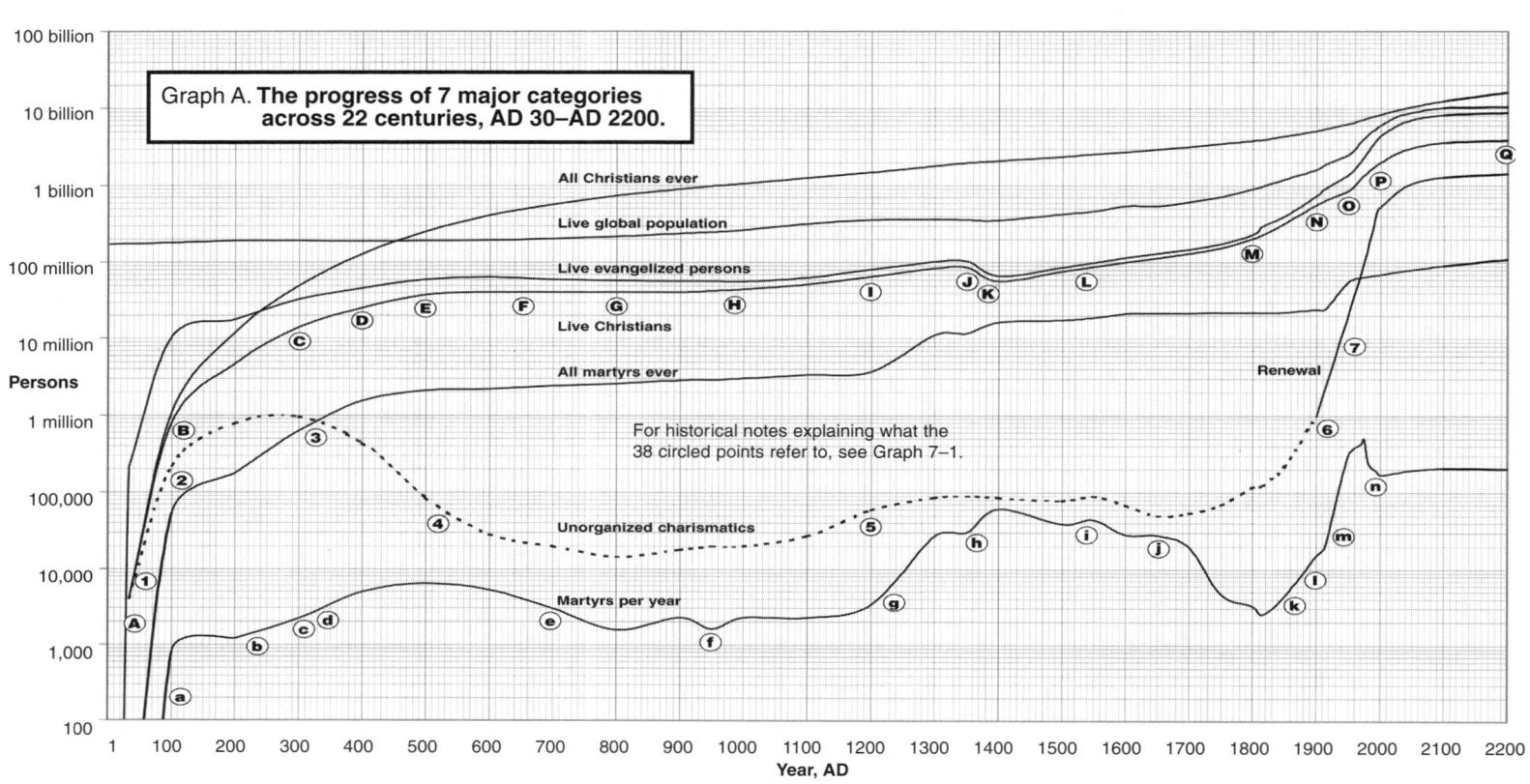

**Graph A. The progress of 7 major categories across 22 centuries, AD 30–AD 2200.**

For historical notes explaining what the 38 circled points refer to, see Graph 7–1.

### Table A. Global trends for 26 statistical categories, AD 33–AD 2200.

| Area 1 | Year, AD 33 2 | 100 3 | 300 4 | 500 5 | 800 6 | 1000 7 | 1200 8 | 1350 9 | 1500 10 | 1650 11 | 1750 12 | 1800 13 | 1850 14 | 1900 15 | 1970 16 | 1990 17 | 1995 18 | 2000 19 | 2025 20 | 2050 21 | 2100 22 | 2200 23 |
|---|---|---|---|---|---|---|---|---|---|---|---|---|---|---|---|---|---|---|---|---|---|---|
| **GLOBE (238 countries in 2000)** | | | | | | | | | | | | | | | | | | | | | | |
| Population, m(=millions) | 170.66 | 179.51 | 191.93 | 190.32 | 217.92 | 263.65 | 357.44 | 361.04 | 422.95 | 546.66 | 719.19 | 903.65 | 1,202.87 | 1,619.63 | 3,696.15 | 5,266.44 | 5,666.36 | 6,055.05 | 7,823.70 | 8,909.10 | 10,109.28 | 10,561.48 |
| Growth rate, % p.a. | 0.08 | 0.08 | 0.03 | 0.00 | 0.05 | 0.10 | 0.15 | 0.01 | 0.11 | 0.17 | 0.27 | 0.46 | 0.57 | 0.60 | 1.19 | 1.79 | 1.47 | 1.34 | 1.03 | 0.52 | 0.25 | 0.04 |
| Increase p.a., m | 0.13 | 0.14 | 0.06 | -0.01 | 0.10 | 0.25 | 0.54 | 0.02 | 0.45 | 0.94 | 1.98 | 4.14 | 6.90 | 9.67 | 43.82 | 94.06 | 83.56 | 80.88 | 80.61 | 46.42 | 25.58 | 4.62 |
| Evangelized persons, m | 0.21 | 10.60 | 32.82 | 59.40 | 57.53 | 56.17 | 81.31 | 103.17 | 86.75 | 129.76 | 174.96 | 229.31 | 401.24 | 739.95 | 2,054.90 | 3,600.97 | 3,988.16 | 4,425.67 | 5,978.30 | 7,103.04 | 8,250.11 | 8,792.81 |
| Evangelized persons % | 0.12 | 5.90 | 17.10 | 31.21 | 26.40 | 21.30 | 22.75 | 28.58 | 20.51 | 23.74 | 24.33 | 25.38 | 33.36 | 45.69 | 55.60 | 68.38 | 70.38 | 73.09 | 76.41 | 79.73 | 81.61 | 83.25 |
| Outreach per Christian | 20.00 | 12.25 | 1.34 | 0.57 | 0.41 | 0.26 | 0.24 | 0.19 | 0.14 | 0.15 | 0.13 | 0.12 | 0.24 | 0.33 | 0.66 | 1.06 | 1.12 | 1.21 | 1.28 | 1.23 | 1.21 | 1.29 |
| **Christians, m** | **0.01** | **0.80** | **14.01** | **37.80** | **40.87** | **44.67** | **65.71** | **86.47** | **75.89** | **112.84** | **154.69** | **204.98** | **323.86** | **558.13** | **1,236.37** | **1,747.46** | **1,877.43** | **1,999.56** | **2,616.67** | **3,051.56** | **3,583.02** | **3,843.54** |
| Orthodox, m | 0.00 | 0.61 | 8.90 | 24.48 | 24.44 | 23.99 | 29.07 | 35.06 | 25.87 | 33.18 | 45.01 | 55.22 | 75.46 | 115.84 | 139.66 | 203.77 | 209.62 | 215.13 | 252.72 | 266.81 | 278.12 | 292.97 |
| Roman Catholics, m | 0.01 | 0.17 | 4.91 | 12.72 | 15.93 | 18.88 | 33.24 | 47.26 | 44.83 | 60.10 | 82.39 | 106.43 | 163.20 | 266.55 | 665.95 | 929.70 | 994.15 | 1,057.33 | 1,361.97 | 1,564.60 | 1,695.10 | 1,849.70 |
| Anglicans, m | 0.00 | 0.01 | 0.20 | 0.60 | 0.50 | 1.80 | 3.40 | 4.15 | 5.18 | 4.84 | 6.20 | 11.91 | 21.85 | 30.57 | 47.50 | 68.20 | 74.52 | 79.65 | 113.75 | 145.98 | 167.81 | 194.59 |
| Protestants, m | 0.00 | 0.00 | 0.00 | 0.00 | 0.00 | 0.00 | 0.00 | 0.00 | 0.01 | 14.69 | 21.02 | 30.98 | 60.86 | 103.02 | 210.76 | 296.35 | 319.68 | 342.00 | 468.63 | 574.42 | 643.38 | 725.79 |
| Independents, m | 0.00 | 0.00 | 0.00 | 0.00 | 0.00 | 0.00 | 0.00 | 0.00 | 0.00 | 0.03 | 0.06 | 0.40 | 2.14 | 7.93 | 95.60 | 301.54 | 346.54 | 385.75 | 581.64 | 752.84 | 861.56 | 989.95 |
| Marginal Christians, m | 0.00 | 0.00 | 0.00 | 0.00 | 0.00 | 0.00 | 0.00 | 0.00 | 0.00 | 0.00 | 0.01 | 0.04 | 0.35 | 0.93 | 11.10 | 21.83 | 23.85 | 26.06 | 45.55 | 62.20 | 73.25 | 86.72 |
| **Christians %** | **0.01** | **0.45** | **7.30** | **19.86** | **18.75** | **16.94** | **18.38** | **23.95** | **17.94** | **20.64** | **21.51** | **22.68** | **26.92** | **34.46** | **33.45** | **33.18** | **33.13** | **33.02** | **33.45** | **34.25** | **35.44** | **36.39** |
| Christian growth rate, % p.a. | 0.00 | 13.18 | 1.44 | 0.50 | 0.03 | 0.04 | 0.19 | 0.18 | -0.09 | 0.26 | 0.32 | 0.56 | 0.92 | 1.09 | 1.14 | 1.74 | 1.45 | 1.27 | 1.08 | 0.62 | 0.32 | 0.07 |
| Christian nett increase p.a., m | 0.00 | 0.11 | 0.20 | 0.19 | 0.01 | 0.02 | 0.13 | 0.16 | -0.07 | 0.30 | 0.49 | 1.16 | 2.98 | 6.11 | 14.13 | 30.49 | 27.13 | 25.37 | 28.30 | 18.83 | 11.52 | 2.70 |
| Gains: births + converts, m | 0.00 | 0.08 | 0.79 | 1.78 | 1.74 | 1.92 | 2.94 | 3.85 | 2.96 | 3.96 | 4.87 | 6.42 | 9.71 | 16.13 | 41.23 | 63.47 | 55.27 | 55.11 | 66.05 | 63.85 | 66.76 | 68.39 |
| Losses: deaths+defectors,m | 0.00 | 0.03 | 0.58 | 1.58 | 1.71 | 1.88 | 2.79 | 3.68 | 2.95 | 3.46 | 4.34 | 5.17 | 6.42 | 9.53 | 20.70 | 26.15 | 27.55 | 29.20 | 35.07 | 43.20 | 54.56 | 65.60 |
| World B, m | 0.20 | 9.80 | 18.81 | 21.60 | 16.66 | 11.50 | 15.60 | 16.70 | 10.86 | 16.92 | 20.27 | 24.33 | 77.38 | 181.82 | 818.53 | 1,853.51 | 2,110.73 | 2,426.11 | 3,361.63 | 4,051.48 | 4,667.10 | 4,949.27 |
| World B % | 0.12 | 5.46 | 9.80 | 11.35 | 7.65 | 4.36 | 4.36 | 4.63 | 2.57 | 3.10 | 2.82 | 2.69 | 6.43 | 11.23 | 22.15 | 35.19 | 37.25 | 40.07 | 42.97 | 45.48 | 46.17 | 46.86 |
| World B growth rate, % p.a. | 27.91 | 5.98 | 0.33 | 0.07 | -0.09 | -0.19 | 0.15 | 0.05 | -0.29 | 0.30 | 0.18 | 0.37 | 2.34 | 1.72 | 2.17 | 4.17 | 2.63 | 2.82 | 1.31 | 0.75 | 0.28 | 0.06 |
| World B increase p.a., m | 0.03 | 0.33 | 0.01 | 0.01 | -0.01 | -0.01 | 0.01 | 0.00 | -0.01 | 0.01 | 0.01 | 0.01 | 0.15 | 0.19 | 0.48 | 1.47 | 0.98 | 1.13 | 0.56 | 0.34 | 0.13 | 0.03 |
| World A, m | 170.45 | 168.91 | 159.11 | 130.92 | 160.39 | 207.48 | 276.13 | 257.87 | 336.20 | 416.90 | 544.23 | 674.35 | 801.63 | 879.67 | 1,641.25 | 1,665.47 | 1,678.20 | 1,629.37 | 1,845.41 | 1,806.05 | 1,859.17 | 1,768.67 |
| World A % | 99.88 | 94.10 | 82.90 | 68.79 | 73.60 | 78.70 | 77.25 | 71.42 | 79.49 | 76.26 | 75.67 | 74.62 | 66.64 | 54.31 | 44.40 | 31.62 | 29.62 | 26.91 | 23.59 | 20.27 | 18.39 | 16.75 |
| World A growth rate, % p.a. | 0.08 | -0.01 | -0.03 | -0.10 | 0.07 | 0.13 | 0.14 | -0.05 | 0.18 | 0.14 | 0.27 | 0.43 | 0.35 | 0.19 | 0.89 | 0.07 | 0.15 | -0.59 | 0.50 | -0.09 | 0.06 | -0.05 |
| World A increase p.a., m | 0.13 | -0.02 | -0.05 | -0.13 | 0.11 | 0.27 | 0.39 | -0.12 | 0.60 | 0.60 | 1.45 | 2.90 | 2.78 | 1.64 | 14.69 | 1.22 | 2.56 | -9.59 | 9.21 | -1.56 | 1.08 | -0.88 |

## Table BB. Numerical trends in the worldwide expansion of Christianity, AD 30–AD 2200, with special reference to the 1st century AD.

The table charts the numerical progress of global Christianity century by century, with detailed attention to the 1st century AD. For precise dates of events, major stages, and statistical origins, consult Part 2 "CosmoChronology".

*Columns*

1. *Year.* Statistics in columns 5 to 11 refer precisely to each year shown in column 1 (with fraction of year, up to AD 58). Events and evidence in columns 2 and 4 illustrate progress or decline at the year shown during the 1st century AD, but after AD 100 exact dates of events described in column 2 may be ascertained from "CosmoChronology".
2. *Event.* A major activity or trend regarding growth or decline around or after the year indicated.
3. *Scripture.* Up to the end of The Acts of the Apostles in AD 61, the verses shown represent major developments in the narrative of the immediate expansion of Christianity. Each such verse presents evidence, initially of rapid growth, which is then fitted into the mathematical grid in columns 5 to 11 and also as in Table 7-2. *Note*: Sentences or phrases in quotation marks show the exact wording in the CEV (Contemporary English Version); or, occasionally, in KJV (King James Version), RSV (Revised Standard Version), NEB (New English Bible), GNB (Good News Bible), or NRSV (New Revised Standard Version).
4. *Evidence.* In the Acts, precise statistics of the total size of the Christian community are rare, but the 50 sequential sentences shown can be fitted into the numerical grid from AD 400–2000 without difficulty.
5. *Evangelized.* Total evangelized persons, meaning all persons adequately aware of Christianity, Christ, and the gospel.
6. *Outreach per Christian.* Evangelized non-Christians (World B) divided by Christians, or (E/AC)-1, or (E-AC)/AC.
7. *Followers.* Total living Christian community, including children. (Widely used in CEV instead of 'disciples').
8. *Increase per year* (as at the date in column 1). Average figure, computed as column 10 divided by 100, multiplied by column 7.
9. *Increase per day.* Average figure, computed as column 8 divided by 365.
10. *Rate, % per year.* This is the exponential growth rate of column 7 at the one point of the exact year shown in column 1, which rate remains unaltered throughout the previous period covered back to the previous line here, which is the period of 1, 2, 5, 10, 100, or other number of years that the table shows ending in the year indicated. Note also that for the years to AD 57, each year with multiple lines requires growth to be calculated for 6, 4, 3 or 2 month periods only, although it is then reported here as an annual rate at that particular point in time.
11. *Martyrs.* Defined here by 5 criteria: *Believers in Christ* who *lose their lives, prematurely*, in situations of *witness*, as a result of *human hostility*. Statistics shown here are of total martyrs ever, cumulatively (not annual rates), at the year shown. Sources: consult "CosmoChronology" and Part 4 "Martyrology", especially Table 4-10.

| *Year* | *Event* | *Scripture* | *Evidence of expansion, growth, or decline (quotes = exact words from Scripture verse in column 3)* | *Evangelized* | *E/AC-1* | *Followers* | *Increase per year* | *per day* | *Rate % pa* | *Martyrs ever* |
|---|---|---|---|---|---|---|---|---|---|---|
| *1* | *2* | *3* | *4* | *5* | *6* | *7* | *8* | *9* | *10* | *11* |
| AD 30 | Start of Jesus' ministry | Mark 1:16 | First disciples chosen as Twelve Apostles; Kingdom of God told in parables | 1,000 | 4 | 200 | 2000 | 5 | – | – |
| 31 | Signs and wonders | John 2:11 | Localized miracles, signs, healings as followers multiply | 200,000 | 199 | 1,000 | 4,000 | 11 | – | – |
| 32 | Vast audiences | Luke 10:14 | Mass feedings (5,000 and 4,000); mass healings, mass teachings | 800,000 | 199 | 4,000 | 12,000 | 33 | – | – |
| 33.3 | Crucifixion | Matthew 26:56 | Disciples scattered, deserting Jesus, who is then crucified | 1,600,000 | 15,999 | 100 | 0 | 0 | 0 | 5 |
| 33.3 | The Forty Days | 1 Corinthians 15:6 | The Risen Lord meets individuals, then The Twelve, then 500 at once | 1,700,000 | 2,124 | 800 | 800 | 2 | – | 5 |
| 33.4 | Ascension | Matthew 28:19 | Christ's Great Commission: 'Go! Witness! Proclaim! Disciple! Baptize! Train!' | 1,800,000 | 1,199 | 1,500 | 1,500 | 4 | – | 5 |
| 33.5 | Pentecost | Acts 2:41 | 3,000 new converts from wider Jewish Diaspora baptized, then return home | 2,000,000 | 249 | 8,000 | 8,000 | 22 | 100.0 | 5 |
| 33.6 | Daily increases | Acts 2:47 | 'Day by day the Lord added to their number those whom He was saving' (NEB) | 2,010,000 | 235 | 8,500 | 7,085 | 19 | 83.4 | 5 |
| 33.8 | Peter arrested | Acts 4:4 | Despite arrests, adult men believers number 'about 5,000 followers of the Lord' | 2,020,000 | 223 | 9,000 | 2,977 | 8 | 33.1 | 8 |
| 34 | Mass movement | Acts 4:32 | Large-scale people movement into the church now under way | 2,030,000 | 213 | 9,500 | 2,949 | 8 | 31.0 | 8 |
| 34.2 | Signs and wonders | Acts 5:14 | 'Many men and women started having faith in the Lord' ('multitudes', KJV) | 2,040,000 | 203 | 10,000 | 2,924 | 8 | 29.2 | 10 |
| 34.4 | Mass healings | Acts 5:16 | Many town-dwellers healed; followers including women and children over 10,000 | 2,050,000 | 194 | 10,500 | 2,901 | 8 | 27.6 | 15 |
| 34.7 | Daily evangelism | Acts 5:42 | Evangelism—witnessing 'every day... in one home after another' | 2,060,000 | 185 | 11,100 | 2,259 | 6 | 20.3 | 20 |
| 35 | Greek/Aramaic split | Acts 6:1 | 'A lot of people were now becoming followers of the Lord' | 2,080,000 | 177 | 11,700 | 2,244 | 6 | 19.2 | 30 |
| 35.3 | Priests converted | Acts 6:7 | 'The number of the disciples multiplied greatly... a great many priests' (RSV) | 2,090,000 | 168 | 12,400 | 2,650 | 7 | 21.4 | 50 |
| 35.7 | Violent persecution | Acts 8:1 | Persecuted believers scattered from Jerusalem throughout Judea and Samaria | 2,110,000 | 156 | 13,400 | 2,867 | 8 | 21.4 | 200 |
| 36.1 | Mission to Samaritans | Acts 8:4 | Philip, Peter, John 'went everywhere preaching the word' (KJV) | 2,130,000 | 147 | 14,400 | 2,839 | 8 | 19.7 | 200 |
| 36.5 | Relative peace | Acts 9:31 | 'Through the help of the Holy Spirit (the church)... grew in numbers' (GNB) | 2,160,000 | 139 | 15,400 | 2,814 | 8 | 18.3 | 200 |
| 37 | Ceaseless itineration | Acts 9:32 | Constant itinerant evangelism: 'While Peter was travelling from place to place...' | 2,180,000 | 130 | 16,600 | 2,688 | 7 | 16.2 | 210 |
| 37.6 | Coast evangelized | Acts 9:35 | 'Many people in the towns of Lydda and Sharon... became followers of the Lord' | 2,220,000 | 122 | 18,000 | 2,601 | 7 | 14.4 | 210 |
| 38 | City-wide conversions | Acts 9:42 | 'Everyone in Joppa heard... many of them put their faith in the Lord' | 2,240,000 | 117 | 19,000 | 2,750 | 8 | 14.5 | 210 |
| 39.1 | First Gentiles converted | Acts 10:48 | Large influx of Italian believers from Cohors II Italica | 2,300,000 | 104 | 22,000 | 3,136 | 9 | 14.3 | 220 |
| 40.3 | Mission to Gentile world | Acts 11:1 | 'The apostles and the followers heard that Gentiles had accepted God's message' | 2,370,000 | 92 | 25,500 | 3,338 | 9 | 13.1 | 220 |
| 42.2 | Conversions in Antioch | Acts 11:21 | 'A great number that believed turned to the Lord' (RSV) | 2,490,000 | 76 | 32,200 | 4,207 | 12 | 13.1 | 230 |
| 43.2 | Ongoing conversions | Acts 11:24 | 'Many more people turned to the Lord' ('A large company was added', RSV) | 2,550,000 | 70 | 36,000 | 4,248 | 12 | 11.8 | 240 |
| 44.2 | Evangelization spreads | Acts 12:24 | 'God's message kept spreading' ('grew and multiplied', RSV) | 2,620,000 | 65 | 40,000 | 4,444 | 12 | 11.1 | 250 |
| 45.1 | Paul's 1st missionary journey | Acts 13:43 | 'Many Jews and devout converts to Judaism followed Paul and Barnabas' (RSV) | 2,680,000 | 60 | 44,000 | 4,915 | 13 | 11.2 | 250 |
| 46.1 | Paul's global mandate | Acts 13:47 | 'Take the saving power of God to people everywhere on Earth' | 2,740,000 | 55 | 49,000 | 5,568 | 15 | 11.4 | 260 |
| 47.1 | Saturating regions | Acts 13:49 | 'The message about the Lord spread all over that region' | 2,810,000 | 51 | 54,000 | 5,510 | 15 | 10.2 | 260 |
| 48 | Acceptance and rejection | Acts 14:1 | 'Many Jews and Gentiles put their faith in the Lord' | 2,880,000 | 48 | 59,000 | 6,100 | 17 | 10.3 | 270 |
| 50 | Paul's 2nd missionary journey | Acts 16:5 | 'The churches were strengthened in the faith and increased in numbers daily' | 3,030,000 | 42 | 71,000 | 6,886 | 19 | 9.7 | 280 |
| 51.2 | Corinthians hear Paul | Acts 18:8 | 'Many of the Corinthians hearing Paul believed and were baptized' (RSV) | 3,120,000 | 39 | 78,000 | 6,358 | 17 | 8.2 | 290 |
| 51.8 | City-wide faith at Corinth | Acts 18:10 | 'The Lord said... "Many people in this city belong to Me" ' | 3,160,000 | 38 | 82,000 | 7,128 | 20 | 8.7 | 290 |
| 52.4 | India reached | – | First missionaries (Thomas and party) reach India | 3,210,000 | 36 | 86,000 | 7,105 | 19 | 8.3 | 300 |
| 53.1 | Paul's 3rd missionary journey | Acts 19:9 | Normal evangelism—proclamation 'every day for two years' | 3,270,000 | 35 | 91,000 | 7,651 | 21 | 8.4 | 340 |
| 55.5 | Asia Minor evangelized | Acts 19:10 | 'Every Jew and Gentile in Asia had heard the Lord's message' | 3,470,000 | 31 | 110,000 | 9,044 | 25 | 8.2 | 350 |
| 56.5 | Paul's ministry in Ephesus | Acts 19:20 | 'The Lord's message spread and became even more powerful' | 3,560,000 | 29 | 118,000 | 8,582 | 24 | 7.3 | 400 |
| 57.4 | James' report to Paul | Acts 21:20 | 'See how many tens of thousands of our people have become followers' | 3,640,000 | 28 | 125,000 | 8,266 | 23 | 6.6 | 450 |
| 58 | Balkans reached | Romans 15:19 | From Jerusalem to Illyricum Paul had 'fully preached the gospel' | 3,700,000 | 27 | 130,000 | 8,782 | 24 | 6.8 | 500 |
| 62 | Paul evangelizes in Rome | Acts 28:23 | 'Many came to [Paul] in great numbers' (RSV) | 4,090,000 | 23 | 170,000 | 11,792 | 32 | 6.9 | 1000 |
| 64 | Nero's persecution | | 1st Roman Imperial Persecution: 5,000 executed | 4,300,000 | 22 | 190,000 | 10,866 | 30 | 5.7 | 5,500 |
| 70 | Sack of Jerusalem | | Titus obliterates Jerusalem, crucifies 10,000, kills 600,000 | 5,000,000 | 18 | 270,000 | 16,285 | 45 | 6.0 | 17,000 |
| 80 | Ephesus main center of mission | | Under Apostle John ongoing struggle against influence of Diana queen of heaven | 6,420,000 | 14 | 440,000 | 22,021 | 60 | 5.0 | 18,000 |
| 90 | Domitian's persecution | | 2nd Roman Imperial Persecution, over emperor-worship as 'Our Lord and God' | 8,250,000 | 12 | 640,000 | 24,435 | 67 | 3.8 | 20,000 |
| 100 | Massive spread of churches | | Christians predominantly urban, spreading rapidly along trade routes | 10,600,000 | 12 | 800,000 | 18,052 | 49 | 2.3 | 53,000 |
| 200 | Severus' persecution | | 5th Roman Imperial Persecution: for months, 100 a day martyred in Thebes | 17,760,000 | 2.81 | 4,660,000 | 82,844 | 227 | 1.8 | 177,000 |
| 300 | Diocletian's persecution | | 10th and final Roman Imperial Persecution | 32,820,000 | 1.34 | 14,010,000 | 155,068 | 425 | 1.1 | 627,000 |
| 350 | Shapur II's persecutions | | Great Persian Persecutions: 100,000 believers martyred | 42,000,000 | 1.00 | 21,000,000 | 170,685 | 468 | 0.8 | 1,200,000 |
| 400 | Continued expansion across Asia | | Christians now 25% of population in Persian Empire and 80% of Roman Empire | 45,920,000 | 0.81 | 25,320,000 | 94,911 | 260 | 0.4 | 1,538,000 |
| 500 | The Dark Ages begin | | Disappearance of urban life; collapse of Christian enthusiasm and mission | 59,400,000 | 0.57 | 37,800,000 | 151,774 | 416 | 0.4 | 2,102,000 |
| 600 | Rise of militant Islam | | Muslim conquest complete in 20 years; 1000s of churches destroyed | 64,450,000 | 0.60 | 40,400,000 | 26,883 | 74 | 0.1 | 2,197,000 |
| 700 | China reached | | Nestorians reach Hsian, churches spread; but by 845 all obliterated. | 60,050,000 | 0.48 | 40,570,000 | 1,704 | 5 | 0.0 | 2,423,000 |
| 800 | Church in Africa destroyed | | Saracens destroy Christianity and its 1,200 bishoprics across North Africa | 57,530,000 | 0.41 | 40,870,000 | 3,011 | 8 | 0.0 | 2,568,000 |
| 900 | Christian losses proliferate | | 50% of former Christendom now under Islamic rule | 57,270,000 | 0.40 | 40,830,000 | -400 | -1 | 0.0 | 2,877,000 |
| 1000 | All Europe now evangelized | | Prussians and Magyars, last remaining pagans in Europe, become christianized | 56,170,000 | 0.26 | 44,670,000 | 40,170 | 110 | 0.1 | 3,064,000 |
| 1100 | End of the Dark Ages | | Renewal of Europe's intellectual life reinvigorates Christianity | 63,810,000 | 0.23 | 51,960,000 | 78,608 | 215 | 0.2 | 3,375,000 |
| 1200 | Genghiz Khan's massacres | | Mongol emperors massacre 7 million Christians across Asia | 81,310,000 | 0.24 | 65,710,000 | 154,453 | 423 | 0.2 | 3,727,000 |
| 1300 | Kublai Khan requests baptism | | Empire of 80 million asks for missions; ignored; greatest missed opportunity ever | 102,260,000 | 0.22 | 83,910,000 | 205,406 | 563 | 0.2 | 11,161,000 |
| 1400 | Massive losses by plague | | Christians killed: 5 million by Tamerlane, 25 million by Black Death | 66,660,000 | 0.18 | 56,730,000 | -221,631 | -607 | -0.4 | 16,560,000 |
| 1500 | Losses to Islam continue | | Fall of Constantinople to Ottoman Turkish Empire | 86,750,000 | 0.14 | 75,890,000 | 221,148 | 606 | 0.3 | 17,398,000 |
| 1600 | Expansion by Spain and Portugal | | Huge colonial empires baptize millions of Amerindians, Asians, Africans | 114,660,000 | 0.14 | 100,440,000 | 281,904 | 772 | 0.3 | 21,221,000 |
| 1700 | Awakenings and revivals | | Evangelical Revival begins under Wesleys; many mission agencies are begun | 148,300,000 | 0.14 | 130,110,000 | 337,186 | 924 | 0.3 | 21,750,000 |
| 1800 | Great Century of missions begins | | New mission fields around the world are opened | 229,305,000 | 0.12 | 204,980,000 | 933,821 | 2558 | 0.5 | 22,038,000 |
| 1900 | Vast range of new ministries | | Pentecostal/Charismatic/Neocharismatic Renewal erupts across world | 739,954,000 | 0.33 | 558,132,000 | 5,618,808 | 15394 | 1.0 | 24,092,000 |
| 2000 | Great Commission closure | | 1,500 global plans fail to evangelize world's 1.6 billion unevangelized | 4,425,674,000 | 1.21 | 1,999,564,000 | 25,679,715 | 70355 | 1.3 | 69,420,000 |
| 2100 | Century of mission through Asians | | Asia's churches (China,India) dominate global mission expansion | 8,250,113,000 | 1.30 | 3,583,017,000 | 20,959,947 | 57425 | 0.6 | 90,000,000 |
| 2200 | Century of servant mission | | End of global population explosion; churches clearer on servant role | 8,792,809,000 | 1.29 | 3,843,539,000 | 2,698,664 | 7394 | 0.1 | 110,000,000 |

## Global Diagram 5.    Christ's Great Commission in time and space: a multisubject interactive investigation.

This series continues with a master diagram, Global Diagram 5. It gives an overview of the past, present, and future of the Christian world mission shown as the 3 columns below. Reading from top to bottom, these are illustrated under 40 of the 74 separate subjects that are described in Part 1's 74 global diagrams, as shown in the numbered boxes. Each box is then expanded later in this series into a global diagram with the same number and subject.

The bell-shaped diagram to the left represents the growth of the church across Christian history. Below it is the time axis, marked off by 4 scales: (a) year AD, (b) generations (30-year periods) after Christ, (c) historian K.S. Latourette's 10 epochs of Christian history, and (d) the total of Great Commission global plans announced up to each of the particular years indicated.

To the right is shown part of the globe, the Earth, with its multitude of countries, peoples, languages, and cities.

The reader can pursue his or her own investigation through the 5,000 subjects and statistics on these diagrams, moving from one subject to the next as needed. All listings, subjects, or words shown below refer the reader to expanded reference materials elsewhere, starting in the global diagram indicated.

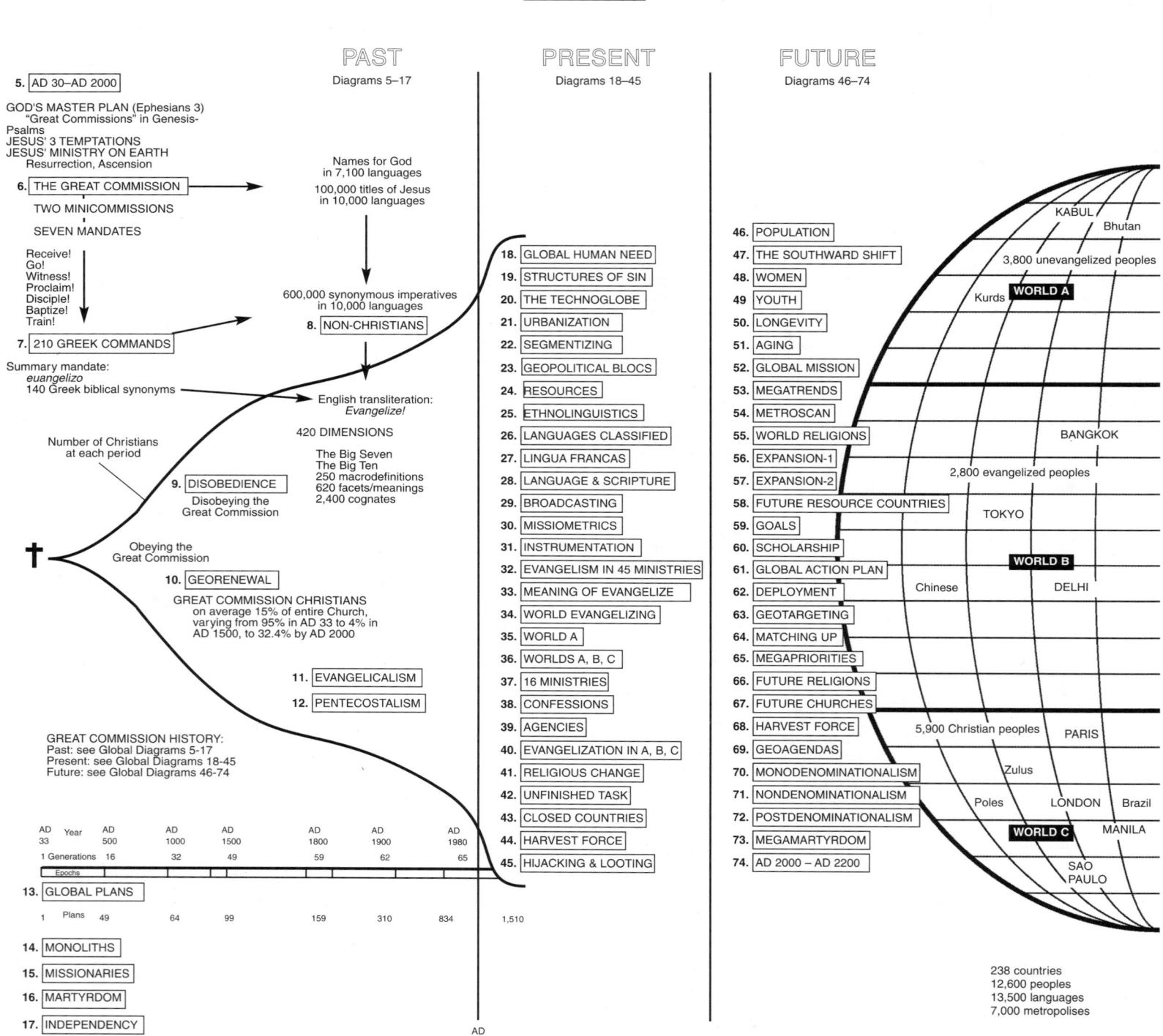

OVERVIEW
Diagrams 1–4

1. WORLD RELIGIONS
2. CHRISTIAN BOUNDARIES
3. MEGACENSUS
4. CHRISTIAN TRENDS

PAST
Diagrams 5–17

PRESENT
Diagrams 18–45

FUTURE
Diagrams 46–74

5. AD 30–AD 2000
GOD'S MASTER PLAN (Ephesians 3)
  "Great Commissions" in Genesis-Psalms
JESUS' 3 TEMPTATIONS
JESUS' MINISTRY ON EARTH
  Resurrection, Ascension

6. THE GREAT COMMISSION

  TWO MINICOMMISSIONS

  SEVEN MANDATES

  Receive!
  Go!
  Witness!
  Proclaim!
  Disciple!
  Baptize!
  Train!

7. 210 GREEK COMMANDS

Summary mandate:
  euangelizo
  140 Greek biblical synonyms

Number of Christians
at each period

9. DISOBEDIENCE
  Disobeying the
  Great Commission

Obeying the
Great Commission

10. GEORENEWAL
  GREAT COMMISSION CHRISTIANS
  on average 15% of entire Church,
  varying from 95% in AD 33 to 4% in
  AD 1500, to 32.4% by AD 2000

11. EVANGELICALISM
12. PENTECOSTALISM

GREAT COMMISSION HISTORY:
Past: see Global Diagrams 5-17
Present: see Global Diagrams 18-45
Future: see Global Diagrams 46-74

Names for God
in 7,100 languages
100,000 titles of Jesus
in 10,000 languages

600,000 synonymous imperatives
in 10,000 languages

8. NON-CHRISTIANS

English transliteration:
Evangelize!

420 DIMENSIONS

The Big Seven
The Big Ten
250 macrodefinitions
620 facets/meanings
2,400 cognates

18. GLOBAL HUMAN NEED
19. STRUCTURES OF SIN
20. THE TECHNOGLOBE
21. URBANIZATION
22. SEGMENTIZING
23. GEOPOLITICAL BLOCS
24. RESOURCES
25. ETHNOLINGUISTICS
26. LANGUAGES CLASSIFIED
27. LINGUA FRANCAS
28. LANGUAGE & SCRIPTURE
29. BROADCASTING
30. MISSIOMETRICS
31. INSTRUMENTATION
32. EVANGELISM IN 45 MINISTRIES
33. MEANING OF EVANGELIZE
34. WORLD EVANGELIZING
35. WORLD A
36. WORLDS A, B, C
37. 16 MINISTRIES
38. CONFESSIONS
39. AGENCIES
40. EVANGELIZATION IN A, B, C
41. RELIGIOUS CHANGE
42. UNFINISHED TASK
43. CLOSED COUNTRIES
44. HARVEST FORCE
45. HIJACKING & LOOTING

46. POPULATION
47. THE SOUTHWARD SHIFT
48. WOMEN
49. YOUTH
50. LONGEVITY
51. AGING
52. GLOBAL MISSION
53. MEGATRENDS
54. METROSCAN
55. WORLD RELIGIONS
56. EXPANSION-1
57. EXPANSION-2
58. FUTURE RESOURCE COUNTRIES
59. GOALS
60. SCHOLARSHIP
61. GLOBAL ACTION PLAN
62. DEPLOYMENT
63. GEOTARGETING
64. MATCHING UP
65. MEGAPRIORITIES
66. FUTURE RELIGIONS
67. FUTURE CHURCHES
68. HARVEST FORCE
69. GEOAGENDAS
70. MONODENOMINATIONALISM
71. NONDENOMINATIONALISM
72. POSTDENOMINATIONALISM
73. MEGAMARTYRDOM
74. AD 2000 – AD 2200

KABUL
Bhutan
3,800 unevangelized peoples
Kurds   WORLD A
BANGKOK
2,800 evangelized peoples
TOKYO
WORLD B
Chinese   DELHI
5,900 Christian peoples   PARIS
Zulus
Poles   LONDON   Brazil
WORLD C   MANILA
SAO PAULO

238 countries
12,600 peoples
13,500 languages
7,000 metropolises

| AD 33 | Year | AD 500 | AD 1000 | AD 1500 | AD 1800 | AD 1900 | AD 1980 |
|---|---|---|---|---|---|---|---|
| 1 | Generations | 16 | 32 | 49 | 59 | 62 | 65 |
| | Epochs | | | | | | |

13. GLOBAL PLANS

| 1 | Plans | 49 | 64 | 99 | 159 | 310 | 834 | 1,510 |
|---|---|---|---|---|---|---|---|---|

14. MONOLITHS
15. MISSIONARIES
16. MARTYRDOM
17. INDEPENDENCY

AD 2000

**Global Diagram 6.    GeoCommission (a merger of 2 empirical biblical phenomena, (1) Christ's Great Commission, and (2) the richest biblical word Evangelize!) analyzed into 2 Minicommissions and 7 Mandates: 7-P evangelization calling for 7-P evangelism.**

The diagram expands GeoCommission, an empirical biblical megaphenomenon merging the 2 empirical biblical phenomena of Christ's *Great Commission*, and *Evangelize!* It analyzes the words used in the shorter and more precise wordings in the 6 New Testament narratives of Christ's Great Commission given to his followers in AD 33 (Matthew 28:18-20, Mark 16:15-18, Luke 24:45-49, John 20:21-23, John 21:5-22, Acts 1:4-8), and relates it all to the Greek verb *euangelizo* (evangelize').

To understand GeoCommission here, it is first divided into 2 Minicommissions 'Evangelize!' and 'Disciple!', and then into 7 Mandates described in 14 columns.

Meanings of the 14 columns, including 3 giving statistics of usages (word frequency), are as follows. For meanings of all Greek words, see Table CC after Global Diagram 7.

*Column 1. Mandate imperative.* Lines 1-7 give the Big Seven—the 7 Mandates of the Great Commission—in English Bible usage. These are given here as imperatives: *Receive* (the Holy Spirit)! *Go* (into all the world)! *Witness! Proclaim* (the gospel)! *Disciple* (the nations)! *Baptize! Train!* Note that what we are calling the overall imperative *Evangelize!* (Greek, *euangelizo*) does not occur in the Great Commission accounts although its cognate noun *euangelion* (the Good News) does (in Mark 16:15). In that sense it is a parallel but distinct stream of apostolic commission.

*Column 2. Greek keyword.* The related Greek verbs or derivatives central to the Great Commission narratives are given in lines 1-7.

*Column 3. Usages.* Each Greek word is followed in this column by a figure which is the number of usages of the word, and its immediate cognates (adjectives or nouns) in the Greek New Testament.

*Column 4. Characteristic.* The phrases here describe the differentia of the various Mandates.

*Column 5. Human role.* The church's human response to GeoCommission is described under a spectrum of 7 generic types of evangelism, using a set of terms in 7-P format.

*Column 6. Sub-types.* The lists here (suggestive, not exhaustive or watertight or exclusive) give sub-types or varieties of evangelism or ministry for the stylized types in column 5.

*Column 7. Evangelizing words.* These 7 types of words corresponding to the 7 modes of evangelism in column 5.

*Column 8. Ministries.* The total number of distinct evangelistic outreach ministries classified here under each Mandate totals 45 (shown listed in Global Diagram 32).

*Column 9. Overview.* This defines the 7 Mandates using a second set in 7-P format to describe the spectrum of 7 generic types of evangelization, as broadly defined.

*Column 10. Other keywords.* These are keywords (related

key nouns) from the Greek or Latin ('L') New Testaments which support or illustrate each Mandate.

*Column 11. Usages.* The first figure gives the number of Greek or Latin New Testament usages of the exact noun opposite it in column 10; the second figure gives the total usages of the word together with its immediate cognates (adjectives, nouns, or verbs).

*Column 12. Dimensions.* The total number of dimensions of 'evangelize' related to each Mandate, namely major English synonyms which each contribute something unique to the full-orbed meaning of 'evangelize'; listed in Table 23-17 and divided here under each of the 7 Mandates.

*Column 13. Key dimensions.* The column lists a small alphabetized selection of examples of the previous column's total of dimensions of 'evangelize', given in imperative mood as constituent commands under the Mandate.

*Column 14. Facets.* The final column gives the total of all English verbs which are distinct aspects or facets (or synonyms or near-synonyms or part-synonyms) of 'evangelize' (again, listed in Table 23-17), arranged under each of the 7 Mandates.

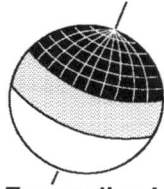    

**Evangelize !**    **Receive !**    Go!    **Witness !**    **Proclaim !**

Shown here are 5 out of hundreds of logos, based on one or more of the 7 Mandates, used by church or mission agencies and organizations:
**Evangelize!** is the logo of GEM (Global Evangelization Movement) and of GCOWE-2000, Global Consultations on World Evangelization by AD 2000 and Beyond.
**Receive!** is a logo based on Dürer's classic sketch 'The Praying Hands' (AD 1500), widely used by prayer agencies and missions.
**Go!** is a logo of Evangelization 2000 based in the Vatican.
**Witness!** is based on the logo of the annual worldwide March for Jesus.
**Proclaim!** is the logo of the Great Commission Network.

| MANDATE IMPERATIVE English | NT Greek | Usages | DOMINANT CHARACTERISTIC | HUMAN ROLE | SUB-TYPES OF EVANGELISM | RESULTING WORDS | OUTREACH MINISTRIES | OVERVIEW | OTHER KEYWORDS (related nouns) Greek, Latin (L) | Usages | Total | Key dimensions | FACETS English |
|---|---|---|---|---|---|---|---|---|---|---|---|---|---|
| 1 | 2 | 3 | 4 | 5 | 6 | 7 | 8 | 9 | 10 | 11 | 12 | 13 | 14 |
| **OVERALL IMPERATIVE:** | | | | | | | | | | | | | |
| **Evangelize!** | *euangelizo* | 133 | Authoritative | **7-P Evangelism** | Pluriform evangelism Evangelistic work | Evangelizing Words | 45 | **7-P Evangelization** | *euangelion* *semeia kai terata* *evangelizatio* (L) | 76/133 77/84 41 | 420 | Evangelize with signs following | 700 |
| **MINICOMMISSION I: EVANGELIZE!** CONSTITUENT MANDATES: | | | | | | | | | | | | | |
| 1. **Receive!** | *labete* verb: *lambano* | 263 | Spirit-dominated | **Prayer evangelism** | Baptism in the Spirit Spirit evangelism Pneumatization Renewal in the Spirit Intercession Power evangelism | HIDDEN WORDS | 2 | **Pneumatic evangelization** | *parakletos* *dynamis* *pneumatikos* *exousia* | 5/34 120/331 28/413 103/107 | 10 | Accompany, Be filled, Breathe, Cooperate, Follow, Participate, Pneumatize, Pray, Receive power, Stay, Wait | 33 |
| 2. **Go!** | *poreuthentes* verb: *poreuomai* | 154 | Person-implemented | **Pre-evangelism** | Apostolate Mission Extension Outreach Primary evangelism Visitation evangelism Visual evangelism Audiovisual evangelism | VISUAL WORDS | 11 | **Preparatory evangelization** | *apostole* *missio* (L) | 4/255 900 | 45 | Act, Contact, Develop, Encounter, Engage, Extend, Go, Help, Impact, Influence, Itinerate, Liberate, Love, Make aware, Occupy, Permeate, Prepare, Reach, Seek, Send, Show, Target, Touch, Transmit, Visit | 101 |
| 3. **Witness!** | *martyres* verb: *martyreo* | 173 | Unorganized, private | **Personal evangelism** | Person-to-person witness Personal work Individual evangelism Conversational evangelism Dialogue evangelism Gossiping the gospel Seed-sowing Prophetic evangelism | PERSONAL WORDS | 2 | **Presence evangelization** | *martyria* *praesencia* (L) *justitia* (L) *pax* (L) *dialogismos* | 57/173 120 220 200 14/43 | 60 | Be martyred, Be present, Bring, Carry, Confess, Dialogue, Expose, Gossip, Inform, Propagate, Radiate, Report, Say, Share, Shine, Sow, Spread, Talk, Tell, Testify, Witness | 132 |
| 4. **Proclaim!** | *keryxate* verb: *kerysso* | 72 | Ordered, public | **Preaching evangelism** | Public evangelism Mass evangelism Demonstration evangelism Deliverance evangelism Incarnational evangelism Power healing Saturation evangelism | PROCLAIMED WORDS | 6 | **Proclamation evangelization** | *kerygma* *apologia* *therapeia* | 8/72 8/18 3/47 | 48 | Advertise, Announce, Declare, Demonstrate, Do miracles, Exorcise, Explain, Expound, Give a message, Give opportunity, Heal, Herald, Make listen, Preach, Present, Proclaim, Prove, Publish, Read, Reason, Refute, Saturate, Translate | 85 |
| **MINICOMMISSION II: DISCIPLE!** | | | | | | | | | | | | | |
| 5. **Disciple!** | *matheteusate* verb: *matheteuo* | 266 | Convert-oriented | **Persuasion evangelism** | Paracletic evangelism Harvest evangelism Discipling evangelism Verdict evangelism Decision evangelism Lordship evangelism | WRITTEN WORDS | 9 | **Pressure evangelization** | *paraklesis* *therismos* *mathetes* | 29/34 13/36 261/266 | 63 | Appeal, Catch, Compel, Confront, Conquer, Convert, Convince, Denounce, Disciple, Exhort, Forgive, Give, Harvest, Impart, Implore, Invite, Offer, Persuade, Press, Reap, Retain, Urge, Warn, Win | 128 |
| 6. **Baptize!** | *baptizontes* verb: *baptizo* | 111 | Church-oriented | **Pastoral evangelism** | Baptism Baptizing evangelism Evangelism that results in churches Church planting Incorporation Shepherding Celebration evangelism | PRINTED WORDS | 9 | **Planting evangelization** | *baptismos* *koinonia* *ekklesia* *leitourgeia* *eucharistia* *katechumenos* | 23/111 19/59 115 6/15 15/54 8 | 35 | Affiliate, Baptize, Bless, Build, Catechize, Confirm, Enroll, Feed, Grow, Incorporate, Initiate, Minister, Multiply, Plant, Praise, Sacramentalize, Serve, Tend, Worship | 70 |
| 7. **Train!** | *didaskontes* verb: *didasko* | 212 | Ministry-oriented | **Programmed evangelism** | Teaching evangelism Electronic evangelism Broadcasting Radio/TV evangelism | ELECTRONIC WORDS | 6 | **Pedagogical evangelization** | *didache* *diakonia* *oikodome* | 30/212 34/101 18/59 | 21 | Broadcast, Celebrate, Cultivate, Edify, Educate, Follow-up, Instruct, Mobilize, Nurture, Program, Teach, Train | 43 |

## Global Diagram 7.    The original task in AD 33: 210 kaleidoscopic New Testament Greek verbs that are synonyms and near-synonyms overlapping in meaning with the Christian keyword *euangelizo* (evangelize).

The *Modern Concordance to the New Testament* (ed M. Darton, 1976) lists 4,900 Greek keywords (out of the NT's total of 5,600 Greek words) with each's frequency of usage (word count), and 4,700 English keywords, all classified under 341 distinct Greek/English key group-themes and 800 English single-word themes. These data are reproduced here in Part 23, Table 23-15.

One of these major keywords is the Greek verb *euangelizo*. This is grouped under the key group-theme 'Tell-Preach-Proclaim' together with 10 variants and 4 other closely-synonymous Greek verbs. An additional 57 other key group-themes set out some 19 Greek and English synonyms and near-synonyms to *euangelizo*, with hundreds of other related verbs.

The diagram below portrays schematically the relationship to *euangelizo* of all these 210 New Testament Greek synonyms and near-synonyms. Our central word is portrayed by the heavy, central circle. All verbs on the diagram are given in the shorter form (the first person singular), such as *euangelizo* (active voice for "I evangelize", with the much more com-

mon middle voice, *euangelizomai*) instead of the infinitives *euangelizein* or *euangelizesthai*. (English meanings of all Greek words are given in Table CC on the next page).

Size of adjoining circles is stylized, related approximately to the frequency of their related words: the number following each word gives the usages or number of times the word occurs in the Greek New Testament. Nine separate but overlapping categories or concentric zones of proximity can therefore be distinguished, as follows:

1. *euangelizo*, the key word itself (used 56 times in the New Testament).
2. **The 10 close variants** of *euangelizo* all based on the root *angello* (shown at the center of the bold circle inside the box headed 'close variants').
3. *kerysso* (proclaim as a herald), the closest biblical synonym to *euangelizo*.
4. **The 4 closest synonyms** of *euangelizo* (including kerysso; shown in bold capitals inside the bold circle).
5. **The Big Seven** (shown in black italic capitals): the 7

Mandates of the Great Commission. These 7 verbs and their immediate cognates occur a total of 1,251 times in the Greek New Testament.

6. **The 19 major synonyms** related to *euangelizo*: these are the 19 verbs shown in capitals.
7. **The 140 synonyms and near-synonyms** (including the above 10,4,7, and 19; these are shown here either as capitals or in boxes in smaller medium type. For complete listings see Table CC; also *Modern Concordance to the New Testament*; for discussion, see *Evangelize! a historical survey of the concept*, 1987).
8. **The 210 related New Testament Greek verbs** overlapping in meaning with *euangelizo* (including the above 10, 4, 7, 19, and 140; the 70 others are not shown here but are detailed in the *Modern Concordance*).
9. **The 550 close cognates** (including nouns like *euangelion, kerygma, mathetes, martys, didache, apostole, dialogismos, baptismos*); not enumerated here.

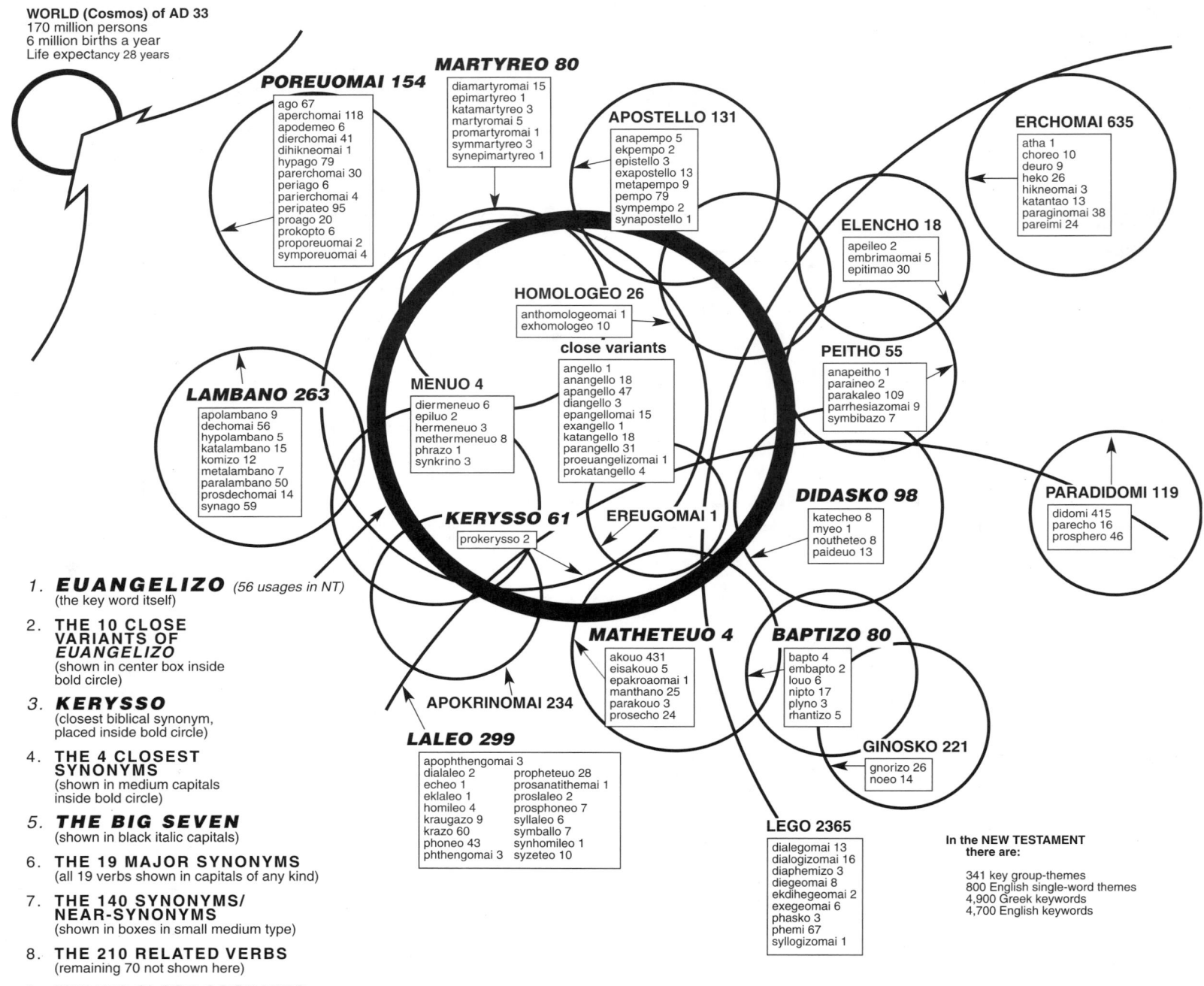

1. **EUANGELIZO** *(56 usages in NT)*
   (the key word itself)

2. **THE 10 CLOSE VARIANTS OF EUANGELIZO**
   (shown in center box inside bold circle)

3. **KERYSSO**
   (closest biblical synonym, placed inside bold circle)

4. **THE 4 CLOSEST SYNONYMS**
   (shown in medium capitals inside bold circle)

5. **THE BIG SEVEN**
   (shown in black italic capitals)

6. **THE 19 MAJOR SYNONYMS**
   (all 19 verbs shown in capitals of any kind)

7. **THE 140 SYNONYMS/ NEAR-SYNONYMS**
   (shown in boxes in small medium type)

8. **THE 210 RELATED VERBS**
   (remaining 70 not shown here)

9. **THE 550 CLOSE COGNATES**
   (nouns, adjectives, etc; not shown or enumerated here)

In the **NEW TESTAMENT** there are:

341 key group-themes
800 English single-word themes
4,900 Greek keywords
4,700 English keywords

## Table CC.    Glossary of 160 New Testament Greek words related to *euangelizo.*

This word list translates into English every Greek and Latin verb or noun shown on Global Diagrams 6 and 7. These number 160 biblical words. All occur in the original Greek New Testament with 5 words from the Latin New Testament. All are synonyms of the verb *euangelizo.* Their closeness to *euangelizo* is explained in Global Diagram 7. They are given here transliterated from Greek letters into roman letters. They are shown listed in alphabetical order; each followed by its meanings in English.

Almost all of these words are verbs with a sprinkling of nouns. Each word is followed by its English translation. Sometimes the translation is a single word. More usually, it is a range of several words. Each range is the full list of all English meanings in the priorities shown in *A Greek-English lexikon of the New Testament and other Early Christian literature* (W. F. Arndt & F. W. Gingrich, 2nd edition, University of Chicago, 1958). Transliterated spellings follow M. Darton, ed, *Modern concordance to the New Testament,* 1976.

**ago.** Lead, bring, take along, guide.
**akouo.** Hear, listen to.
**anangello.** Report, disclose, announce, proclaim, teach.
**anapeltho.** Persuade.
**anapempo.** Send.
**angello.** Announce.
**anthomologeomal.** Praise, thank publicly.
**apangello.** Report, announce, tell, proclaim.
**apelleo.** Threaten, warm.
**aperchomal.** Go away, depart, go, go out and spread, follow.
**apodemeo.** Go on a journey, be away, be absent.
**apokrinomal.** Answer, reply, speak up.
**apolambano.** Receive, recover, get back, take a person aside, welcome.
**apologia.** Defense.
**apophthengomal.** Speak out, declare boldly, declare loudly.
**apostello.** Send out, send away.
**apostole.** Apostleship, office of apostle.
**atha.** Come.
**baptisma.** Baptism.
**baptismos.** Dipping, washing, baptism.
**baptizo.** Dip, immerse, wash, baptize.
**baptizontes.** Baptizing.
**bapto.** Dip.
**choreo.** Go, go out, go away, go forward, make progress, grasp, accept, comprehend, understand.
**dechomal.** Take, receive, welcome, grasp, tolerate, approve, accept.
**deuro.** Come, follow.
**diakonia.** Service, office, aid, support, distribution.
**dialaleo.** Discuss.
**dialegomal.** Discuss, conduct a discussion, converse, speak, preach.
**dialogismos.** Thought, opinion, reasoning, design, dispute, argument.
**dialogizomal.** Consider, ponder, reason, discuss, argue.
**diamartyromal.** Charge, warn, adjure, testify, bear witness.
**diangello.** Proclaim far and wide, give notice, announce.
**diaphemizo.** Spread the news about, spread widely, disseminate.
**didache.** Teaching, instruction.
**didasko.** Teach, instruct.
**didaskontes.** Teach! teaching.
**didomi.** Give, grant, bestow, impart, speak plainly, give a sign, give out, hand over, hold out, entrust, yield, pay, make an effort.
**diegeomal.** Tell, relate, describe, recount.
**dierchomal.** Go through, pierce, come, go, review.
**diermeneuo.** Translate, complain, interpret.
**dihikneomal.** Pierce, penetrate.
**dynamis.** Power, might, strength, force, ability, capability, miracle, wonder, meaning.
**echeo.** Sound, ring out, roar, thunder.
**elsakouo.** Listen to, obey, hear.
**ekdihegeomai.** Tell in detail.
**ekklesia.** Assembly, congregation, church.
**eklaleo.** Tell.
**ekpempo.** Send out, send away.
**elencho.** Bring to light, expose, set forth, convict, convince, reprove, correct, punish, discipline.
**embapto.** Dip.
**embrimaomal.** Scold, censure.
**epakroaomal.** Listen.
**epangellomal.** Announce, proclaim, promise, offer, profess.
**epiluo.** Expalin, interpret, set free, release, decide, settle.
**epimartyreo.** Bear witness.
**epistello.** Inform, instruct by letter, write.
**epitimao.** Rebuke, reprove, censure, speak seriously, warn, punish.
**erchomal.** Come, appear, appear in public, deal with, go.
**ereugomal.** Utter, proclaim.
**euangellon.** Good news, gospel.
**euangelizo** (euangelizomai, euangelizesthai). Evangelize: bring or announce good news, proclaim, preach.
**eucharistia.** Thankfulness, gratitude, thanksgiving, eucharist, Lord's Supper.
**evangelizatio** (Latin). Evangelization.
**exangello.** Proclaim, report.

**exapostello.** Send out, send away.
**exegeomal.** Explain, interpret, tell, report, describe, bring news.
**exhomologeo.** Promise, consent, confess, admit, acknowledge, praise.
**exousia.** Ability, capability, might, power, authority, warrant, government.
**ginosko.** Know, come to know, learn, ascertain, find out, understand, comprehend, perceive, notice, realize, acknowledge, recognize.
**gnorizo.** Make known, reveal, know.
**heko.** Be present, have come.
**hermeueuo.** Explain, interpret, translate.
**hikneomai** (aphikneomai, ephikneomai). Reach, come to.
**homileo.** Speak, converse, address, talk with.
**homologeo.** Promise, assure, agree, admit, confess, declare, acknowledge, praise.
**hypago.** Go, go away, leave, go home, return.
**hypolambano.** Take up, receive as guest, support, assume, think, believe, suppose, be of the opinion.
**justitla** (Latin). Justice.
**katalambano.** Seize, win, attain, make one's own, catch, detect, grasp, find, understand.
**katamartyreo.** Bear witness against, testify against.
**katantao.** Come, arrive, attain.
**katangello.** Solemnly proclaim, direct one's proclamation to.
**katecheo.** Make oneself understood, report, inform, teach, instruct.
**katechumenos.** Instructed in.
**keruxate.** Preach! (imperative of kerysso).
**kerygma.** Proclamation, announcement, preaching.
**kerysso.** Announce, make known, herald, proclaim aloud, mention publicly, praise publicly, spread widely, preach, preach against.
**koinonia.** Association, communion, fellowship, close relationship, generosity, participation.
**komizo.** Bring, carry off, get, receive, get back, recover.
**kraugazo.** Cry, cry loudly, scream, utter a loud sound.
**krazo.** Cry out, scream, shriek, call, call out, cry.
**labete.** Receive! (imperative of lambano).
**laleo.** Speak, express oneself, sound, assert, proclaim.
**lambano.** Take, take hold, grasp, find opportunity, take away, remove, receive, accept, take up, choose, select, apprehend, comprehend, get, obtain.
**lego.** Utter, say, tell, speak, express, mean, answer, order, command, enjoin, direct, recommend, assure, assert, maintain, declare, proclaim, report, call, name.
**leitourgela.** Service, priestly service.
**louo.** Wash, bathe.
**manthano.** Learn, come to know, find out, understand.
**martyreo.** Bear witness, testify, declare, confirm, witness unto death, be a martyr.
**martyres** (plural of martys). Witnesses.
**martyria.** Testimony, attestation, martyrdom.
**martyromal.** Testify, bear witness, affirm, insist, implore.
**martys.** Witness, martyr.
**mathetes.** Disciple, learner, pupil, apprentice, adherent.
**matheteuo.** Be instructed, become a pupil/disciple, make disciples, teach, train, instruct.
**matheteusate.** Make disciples!
**menuo.** Make known, reveal, report, give information.
**metalambano.** Share, receive, receive one's share.
**metapempo.** Summon.
**methermeneuo.** Translate.
**missio** (Latin). Sending, mission.
**myeo.** Initiate, learn.
**nipto.** Wash.
**noco.** Perceive, apprehend, understand, gain insight into, observe, comprehend, consider, take note of, think over, imagine.
**noutheteo.** Admonish, warn, instruct.
**oikodome.** Building, construction, edification, upbuilding.
**oikoumene.** Inhabited earth, world, humankind.
**paideuo.** Teach, discipline.
**paradidomi.** Hand over, give, deliver, entrust, turn over, give over, commend, commit, hand down, pass on, transmit, relate, teach, allow, permit.
**paraginomai.** Come, arrive, be present, appear, stand by,

come to the aid of.
**paraineo.** Advise, recommend, urge.
**parakaleo.** Summon, invite, call upon, appeal, urge, exhort, encourage, request, implore, entreat, comfort, cheer up, console, conciliate.
**paraklesis.** Encouragement, exhortation, appeal, request, comfort, consolation.
**parakletos.** Mediator, intercessor, helper, paraclete.
**parakouo.** Overhear, ignore, refuse to listen.
**paralambano.** Take, take along. take over, receive, accept.
**parangello.** Give orders, command, instruct, direct, forbid.
**parecho.** Offer, present, grant, show, give up, cause, bring about, get.
**pareimi.** Be present.
**parerchomai.** Go by, go through, pass, pass by, pass away, disappear, neglect, come.
**parrhesiazomai.** Speak freely/open/fearlessly, deal openly.
**pax** (Latin). Peace.
**peitho.** Convince, persuade, appeal, conciliate, pacify, assure, obey, follow.
**pempo.** Send, write.
**perlago.** Lead around, go around, take along, accompany, travel.
**perierchomal.** Go around, circumambulate.
**peripateo.** Go about, walk, walk around.
**phasko.** Say, assert, claim.
**phemi.** Say, affirm, mean.
**phoneo.** Call, cry out, speak loudly, emphasize, summon, invite.
**phrazo.** Explain, interpret.
**phthengomal.** Speak, utter, proclaim, call out loudly.
**plyno.** Wash, free from.
**pneumatikos.** Spiritual, Spirit-related, filled with the Spirit, pneumatic.
**poreuomai.** Go, proceed, travel.
**poreuthentes.** Go! going.
**praesencia** (Latin). Presence.
**proago.** Lead, bring out, lead forward, go before, precede, lead the way, walk ahead.
**proeuangelizomai.** Proclaim good news in advance.
**prokatangello.** Announce beforehand, foretell.
**prokerysso.** Proclaim publicly, proclaim beforehand.
**prokopto.** Go forward, progress, make progress, advance, prosper.
**promartyromai.** Predict, bear witness beforehand.
**propheteuo.** Prophesy, proclaim revelation, reveal, foretell.
**proporeuomai.** Go before.
**prosanatithemai.** Contribute, add, consult.
**prosdechomai.** Take up, receive, welcome, deal with, wait, expect.
**prosecho.** Follow, give heed to, turn one's mind to, pay attention to, be alert, notice, care for, be concerned about, devote oneself to.
**proslaleo.** Address, speak with.
**prosphero.** Bring, offer, present, meet, deal with.
**prosphoneo.** Call out, address.
**rhantizo.** Sprinkle, cleanse, wash, purify.
**semela kai terata.** Signs and wonders.
**syllaleo.** Talk, converse, discuss.
**syllogizomai.** Reason, discuss, debate.
**symballo.** Converse, confer, consider, ponder, draw conclusions about, compare, meet, engage, help, assist.
**symbibazo.** Bring together, unite, conclude, infer, demonstrate, prove, instruct, teach, advise.
**symmartyreo.** Testify with, bear witness with, confirm, testify in support.
**sympempo.** Send with.
**symporeuomai.** Go along with, come together.
**synago.** Gather, bring, call together, reconcile, lead, advance, move.
**synapostello.** Send with, send at the same time.
**synepimartyreo.** Testify at the same time.
**synhomileo.** Talk, converse with, live with.
**synkrino.** Bring together, combine, compare, explain, interpret.
**syzeteo.** Discuss, dispute, debate, argue, reflect, meditate.
**therapeia.** Healing, treatment.
**therismos.** Harvest, crop.

## Global Diagram 8.    Christian obedience, and contact with non-Christians, AD 100-AD 2200: trichotomizing the globe by awareness of Christianity, Christ, and the gospel.

The globe's population is here shown divided into Worlds A, B, and C, by absolute numbers and by percentages, at 16 points in Christian history, from AD 100-AD 2200. World C stands for the numerical fortunes of the Christian church (the number of affiliated church members). World A and World B enumerate the numbers of non-Christian individuals. Of these non-Christians, World B's are in contact with Christians, but World A's are not—they are the unevangelized, unaware of Christianity, Christ, or the gospel.

The size of World B measures the obedience of Christians to Christ's command to get in to contact with all peoples. It fell markedly up to the year 1491, then began rising again. As World B enumerates obedience, the size of World A measures the disobedience of Christians, continued over 20 centuries.

*Numbers.* All left-hand figures in the diagrams below give total populations in millions. All right-hand figures are percentages of world population at the date shown. The two fig-

ures in italics immediately above each globe are totals for the globe. Numbers inside the globes are shown in comparative context in Table 2-1.

Lastly, figures below for AD 2000 onwards are mid-year projections based on United Nations' medium-variant demographics.

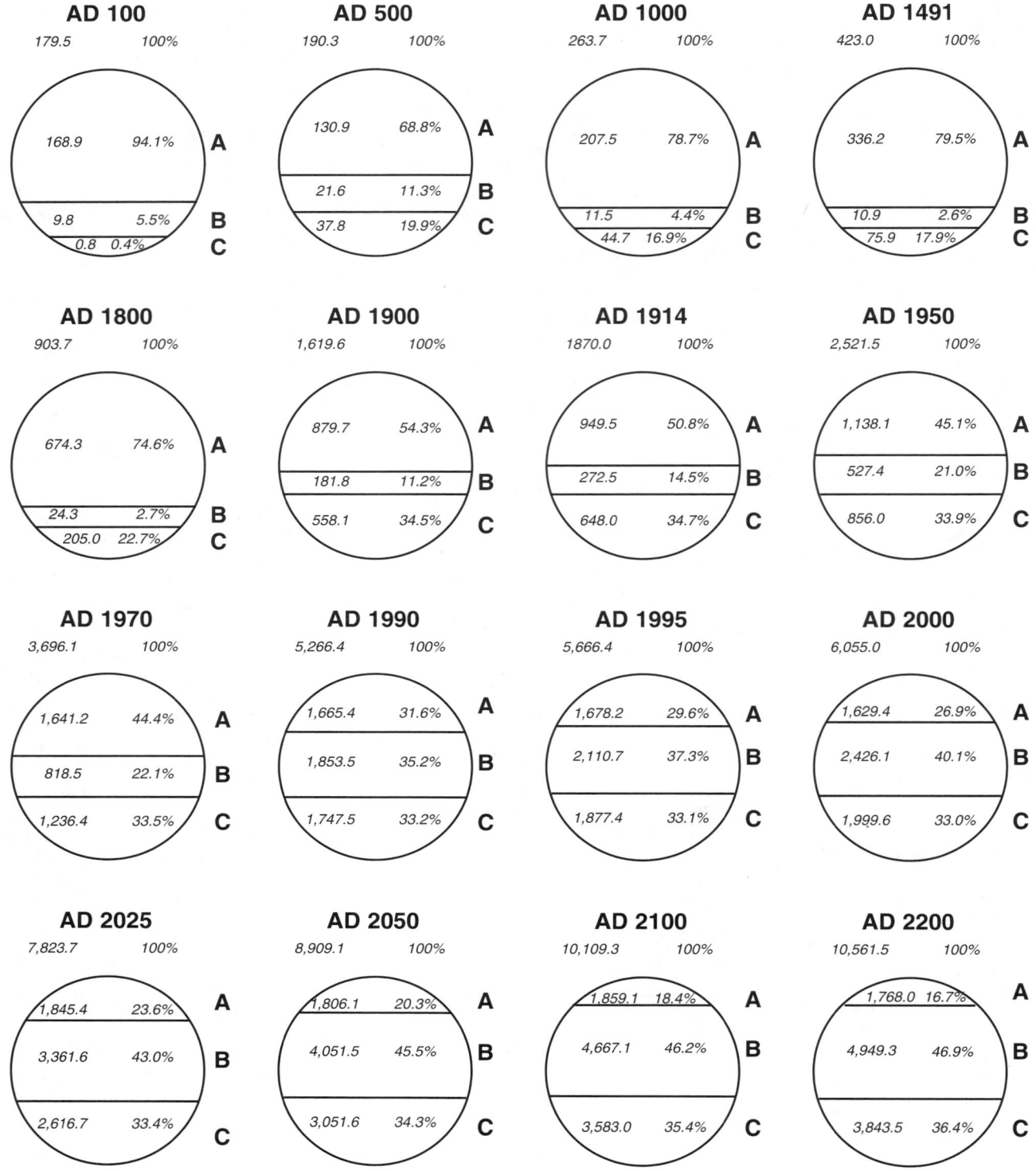

| AD 100 | AD 500 | AD 1000 | AD 1491 |
|---|---|---|---|
| *179.5    100%* | *190.3    100%* | *263.7    100%* | *423.0    100%* |
| A 168.9  94.1% | A 130.9  68.8% | A 207.5  78.7% | A 336.2  79.5% |
| B 9.8  5.5% | B 21.6  11.3% | B 11.5  4.4% | B 10.9  2.6% |
| C 0.8  0.4% | C 37.8  19.9% | C 44.7  16.9% | C 75.9  17.9% |

| AD 1800 | AD 1900 | AD 1914 | AD 1950 |
|---|---|---|---|
| *903.7    100%* | *1,619.6    100%* | *1870.0    100%* | *2,521.5    100%* |
| A 674.3  74.6% | A 879.7  54.3% | A 949.5  50.8% | A 1,138.1  45.1% |
| B 24.3  2.7% | B 181.8  11.2% | B 272.5  14.5% | B 527.4  21.0% |
| C 205.0  22.7% | C 558.1  34.5% | C 648.0  34.7% | C 856.0  33.9% |

| AD 1970 | AD 1990 | AD 1995 | AD 2000 |
|---|---|---|---|
| *3,696.1    100%* | *5,266.4    100%* | *5,666.4    100%* | *6,055.0    100%* |
| A 1,641.2  44.4% | A 1,665.4  31.6% | A 1,678.2  29.6% | A 1,629.4  26.9% |
| B 818.5  22.1% | B 1,853.5  35.2% | B 2,110.7  37.3% | B 2,426.1  40.1% |
| C 1,236.4  33.5% | C 1,747.5  33.2% | C 1,877.4  33.1% | C 1,999.6  33.0% |

| AD 2025 | AD 2050 | AD 2100 | AD 2200 |
|---|---|---|---|
| *7,823.7    100%* | *8,909.1    100%* | *10,109.3    100%* | *10,561.5    100%* |
| A 1,845.4  23.6% | A 1,806.1  20.3% | A 1,859.1  18.4% | A 1,768.0  16.7% |
| B 3,361.6  43.0% | B 4,051.5  45.5% | B 4,667.1  46.2% | B 4,949.3  46.9% |
| C 2,616.7  33.4% | C 3,051.6  34.3% | C 3,583.0  35.4% | C 3,843.5  36.4% |

**Global Diagram 9.    The church's obedience or disobedience to Christ's Great Commission with its 2 minicommissions (I = 'Evangelize!' and II = 'Disciple!') and 7 mandates.**

Many Christians regard Christ's Great Commission as optional, to be obeyed only if one has the time and inclination. But the Bible sees it differently: if Christ commands it, all disciples must obey it. Unfortunately, many come under the judgment of the Ascended Lord who writes to the church in Sardis in Revelation 3:2 (CEV) with a warning: 'I have found that you are not completely obeying God.'

Any attempt to quantify response to the Great Commission as obedience or disobedience will be based on arbitrary criteria. In this case, we select 2 numerical levels: (1) A population can be said to have become evangelized (or, more evangelized than less evangelized) when more than half its members (50%) become individually evangelized; and (2) A popu-

lation can be said to have become discipled when the number of disciples (baptized church members) forms a clear and sizable majority, here set at 60%. The 2 numbers are also boundaries between, respectively, Worlds A and B, and B and C.

We therefore define 'obedience' here as situations where the church's attempts to obey Minicommission I have resulted in half or more of a population (country or people) having becoming evangelized (expressed as E≥50%); or where the church's attempts to obey Minicommission II have resulted in the total of baptized disciples (church members) having exceeded 60% of the population. The following table then results, leading to its definitions of the trichotomy of Worlds A,

B, and C.

The table can then be illustrated as a stylized globe consisting of these 3 Worlds A, B, and C.

The phrase 'disobeyed' needs elaboration. Normally, it implies blame and culpability—the churches have not bothered to obey their Lord's central imperatives. But it can also mean 'not yet obeyed', implying that they are at least attempting to obey, although they may not have got very far yet. But tardiness in obeying on life-and-death matters that require and assume immediate implementation is often culpable, and often disastrous.

| | World A | World B | World C | GLOBE (overall) |
|---|---|---|---|---|
| Status of church's obedience: | | | | |
| **MINICOMMISSION I**: *EVANGELIZE!* | DISOBEYED | OBEYED | OBEYED | OBEYED |
| Mandate 1: *Receive!* | obeyed | obeyed | obeyed | obeyed |
| Mandate 2: *Go!* | obeyed | obeyed | obeyed | obeyed |
| Mandate 3: *Witness!* | obeyed | obeyed | obeyed | obeyed |
| Mandate 4: *Proclaim!* | disobeyed | obeyed | obeyed | disobeyed |
| **MINICOMMISSION II**: *DISCIPLE!* | DISOBEYED | DISOBEYED | OBEYED | DISOBEYED |
| Mandate 5: *Disciple!* | disobeyed | disobeyed | obeyed | disobeyed |
| Mandate 6: *Baptize!* | disobeyed | disobeyed | obeyed | disobeyed |
| Mandate 7: *Train!* | disobeyed | disobeyed | obeyed | disobeyed |
| | | | | |
| Number of Minicommissions obeyed | 0 | 1 | 2 | 1 |
| Number of Mandates obeyed | 3 | 4 | 7 | 3 |
| Number of Mandates disobeyed | 4 | 3 | 0 | 4 |
| | | | | |
| Justification for this status: | | | | |
| Minicommission I | E<50% | E≥50% | E≥95% | E=73.1% |
| Minicommission II | AC<7% | AC<60% | AC≥60% | AC=31.2% |
| | | | | |
| Countries involved | 38 | 59 | 141 | 238 |
| Peoples involved | 3,834 | 2,816 | 5,933 | 12,583 |

*Our globe is shown here trichotomized based on the church's obedience or disobedience to the 2 Minicommissions and 7 Mandates of Christ's Great Commission.*

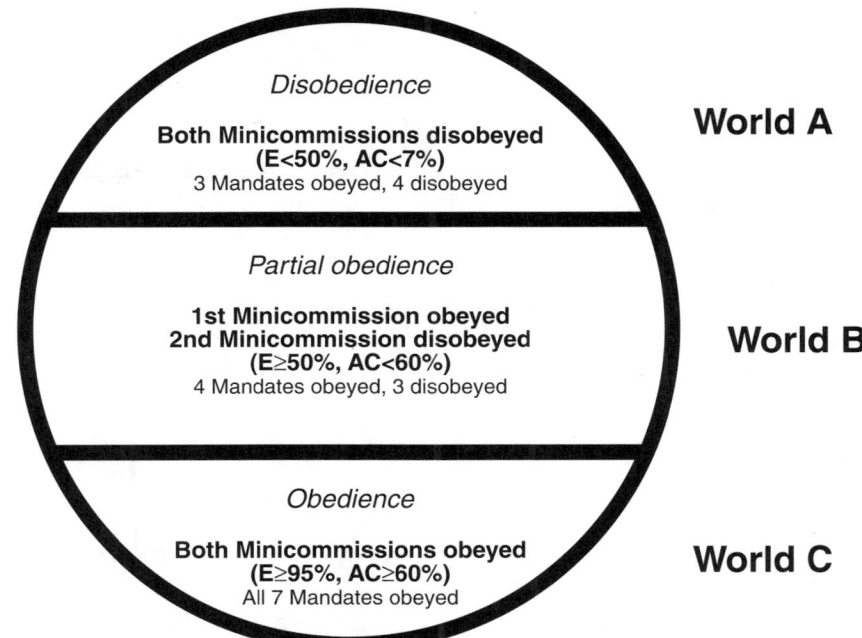

Disobedience

**Both Minicommissions disobeyed
(E<50%, AC<7%)**
3 Mandates obeyed, 4 disobeyed

**World A**

Partial obedience

**1st Minicommission obeyed
2nd Minicommission disobeyed
(E≥50%, AC<60%)**
4 Mandates obeyed, 3 disobeyed

**World B**

Obedience

**Both Minicommissions obeyed
(E≥95%, AC≥60%)**
All 7 Mandates obeyed

**World C**

## Global Diagram 10.    Four megatypologies of georenewal for enumerating empirical global Christianity, AD 33-AD 2025.

This presentation depicts the 4 major ways in which Christians and their organizations measure and enumerate the empirical reality that we term global Christianity. The 4 megatypologies are first shown as the line of 4 separate schemes for segmentizing the globe. Under each of these 4 globes, 11 descriptors explain each megatypology. The 4 ways divide up global Christianity under 4 distinct and separate megatypologies of georenewal—the never-ending struggle to revive and renew Christians worldwide and to cause them to obey and conform to Christ's original intentions con-

cerning what his church should be.

However, the 4 schemes are not entirely divergent since they overlap at several points and in fact consist simply of differing arrangements of the same 7 basic building blocks or slices. These 7 are set out in the single large globe below. To the left of this globe, each slice is defined and enumerated. Above the globe, the major aggregate categories in this measuring of global Christianity are also enumerated. On the globe's right these categories are related to the 7 slices. Below the globe are described the 6 vertical segments which

depict the 4 historical megablocs involved in ecumenical and evangelical conciliar Christianity (Orthodox, Roman Catholic, Anglican, Protestant) and the 2 mainly nonconciliar megablocs (Independent, Marginal Christian).

All statistics describing these components, for each of the world's peoples, languages, cities, provinces, countries, regions, continents, and for the whole globe, can be accessed via these codes on the related CD, the *World Christian database*.

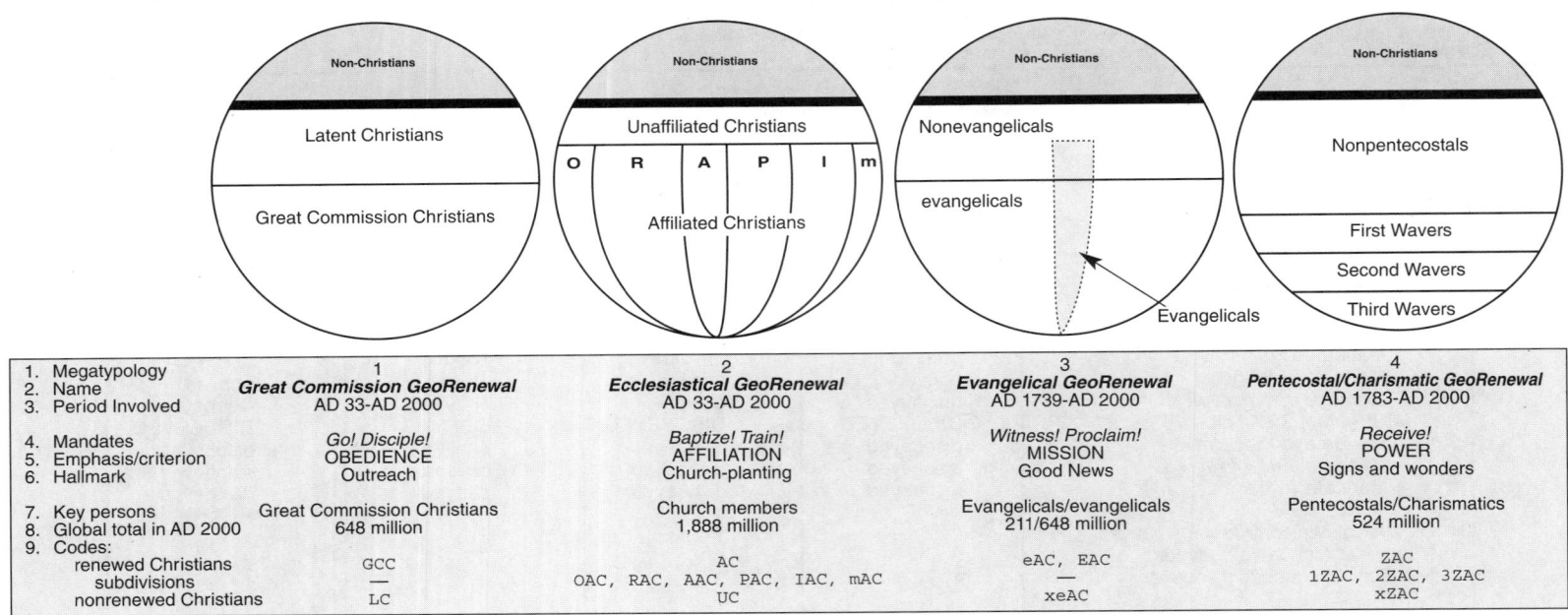

| 1. Megatypology | 1 | 2 | 3 | 4 |
|---|---|---|---|---|
| 2. Name | *Great Commission GeoRenewal* | *Ecclesiastical GeoRenewal* | *Evangelical GeoRenewal* | *Pentecostal/Charismatic GeoRenewal* |
| 3. Period Involved | AD 33-AD 2000 | AD 33-AD 2000 | AD 1739-AD 2000 | AD 1783-AD 2000 |
| 4. Mandates | *Go! Disciple!* | *Baptize! Train!* | *Witness! Proclaim!* | *Receive!* |
| 5. Emphasis/criterion | OBEDIENCE | AFFILIATION | MISSION | POWER |
| 6. Hallmark | Outreach | Church-planting | Good News | Signs and wonders |
| 7. Key persons | Great Commission Christians | Church members | Evangelicals/evangelicals | Pentecostals/Charismatics |
| 8. Global total in AD 2000 | 648 million | 1,888 million | 211/648 million | 524 million |
| 9. Codes: | | | | |
| renewed Christians | GCC | AC | eAC, EAC | ZAC |
| subdivisions | — | OAC, RAC, AAC, PAC, IAC, mAC | — | 1ZAC, 2ZAC, 3ZAC |
| nonrenewed Christians | LC | UC | xeAC | xZAC |

### HOW MAJOR AGGREGATE CATEGORIES OVERLAP (see arrows at below right)

| Aggregate categories | Groups of slices | Codes and their components | Total persons |
|---|---|---|---|
| Non-Christians | 0 = | X | 4,055 million |
| Christians | 1-6 = | C = UC + AC | 2,000 million |
| Affiliated Christians | 2-6 = | AC = OAC + RAC + AAC + PAC + IAC + mAC + 2AC | 1,888 million |
| Great Commission Christians | 3-6 = | GCC = pAC = eAC | 648 million |
| Pentecostals/Charismatics | 4-6 = | ZAC = 1ZAC + 2ZAC + 3ZAC | 524 million |
| Charismatics | 5 = | 2ZAC | 176 million |
| Neocharismatics (Third-Wavers) | 6 = | 3ZAC | 295 million |
| Nonpentecostals | 1-3 = | xZAC | 1,475 million |
| Evangelicals | 7 = | EAC | 211 million |
| evangelicals | 3-6 = | eAC | 648 million |
| Nonevangelicals | 1-2 = | xeAC | 1,352 million |
| Latent Christians | 1-2 = | LC | 1,352 million |

### MEANING OF EACH SLICE, 0 TO 7

*Segments of the globe*

| Slice | Code | Meaning | Total persons |
|---|---|---|---|
| 0 | X | Non-Christians | 4,055 million |
| 1 | UC | Unaffiliated Christians | 111 million |
| 2 | xpAC | Nonpracticing members | 1,240 million |
| 3 | GCC - ZAC | Nonpentecostal GCCs | 124 million |
| 4 | 1ZAC | Pentecostals | 66 million |
| 5 | 2ZAC | Charismatics | 176 million |
| 6 | 3ZAC | Neocharismatics | 295 million |
| 7 | EAC | Evangelicals (grey) | 211 million |

Ecumenical Movement
ORAP = conciliar Christianity (CWCs)     nonconciliar Christianity

slices: 0 1 2 3 4 5 6 7

World A
Non-Christians
World B
O R A P I m

Megatypologies 1 2 3 4

### MEANING OF 6 VERTICAL MEGABLOCS (stretching from their code letters to the bottom)

| Megabloc: | Orthodox | Roman Catholics | Anglicans | Protestants | Independents | Marginal Christians |
|---|---|---|---|---|---|---|
| Code: | O– | R– | A– | P– | I– | m– |
| Traditions: | 40 | 20 | 25 | 100 | 200 | 30 |
| Total affiliated: | 215 million | 1,057 million | 80 million | 342 million | 386 million | 26 million |

**Global Diagram 11.   Composition, definitions, and enumeration of evangelicalism, evangelicals, 69 varieties of Evangelicalism, and of self-identified Evangelicals, AD 2000.**

For enumeration, there are 2 varieties of the evangelical phenomenon: that spelled with lowercase e (evangelicalism, evangelicals) with a much wider connotation (described in Graphic 5-2); and that spelled with capital E (Evangelicalism, Evangelicals) with a much narrower constituency. The latter, illustrated in this present graphic, enumerates all church members of any confession who identify themselves as Evangelicals, and/or who belong to churches or denominations which are affiliated to one or more of the specifically Evangelical councils or alliances or other core agencies: WEF, EAE, EAGB, NAE, EFMA, EMA, EFA, EAC, EFCA, EPS, TEAR, and various clearly Evangelical agencies which however do not have the adjective Evangelical in their titles: IFMA, ICCC, ACCC.

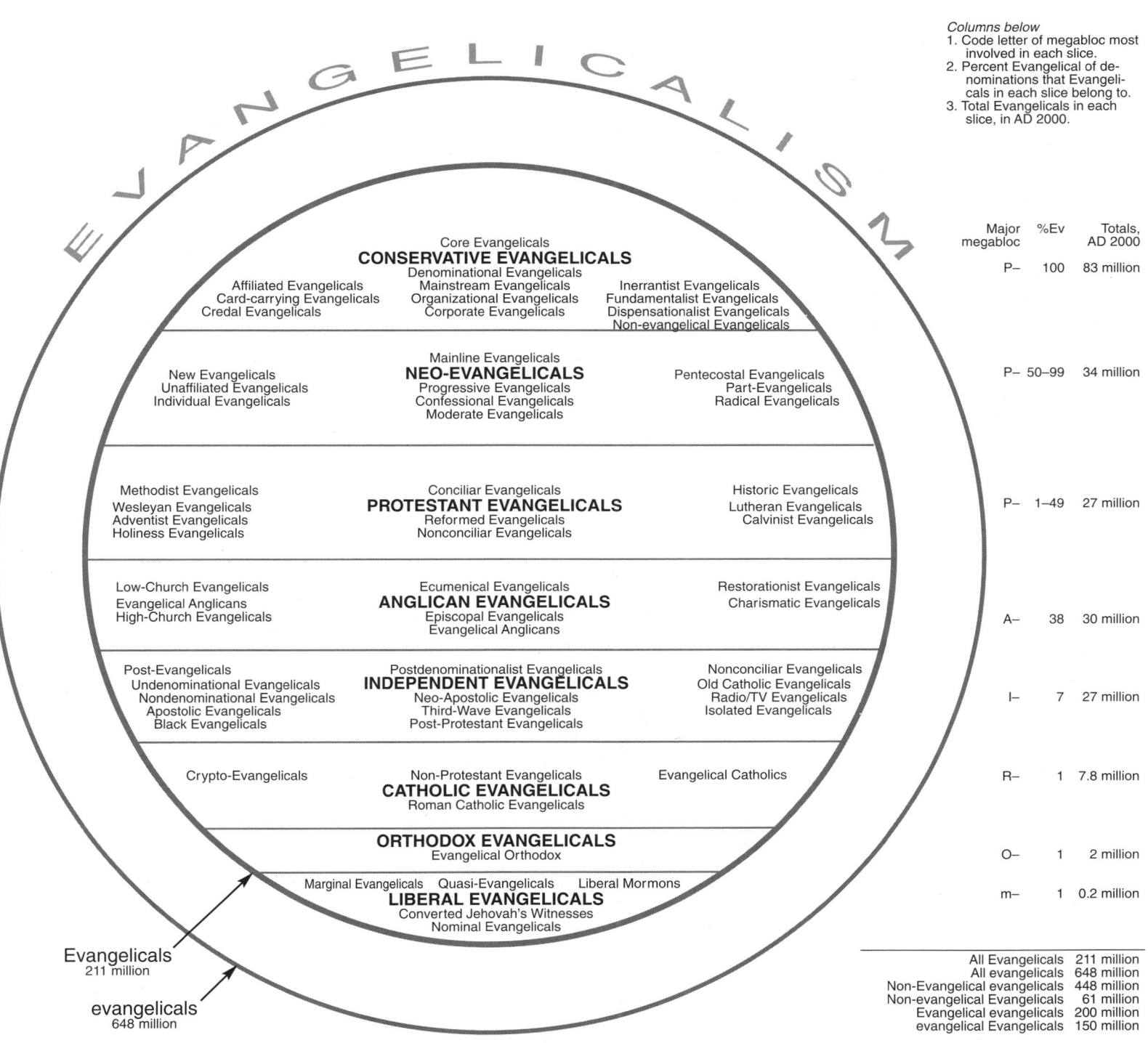

Columns below
1. Code letter of megabloc most involved in each slice.
2. Percent Evangelical of denominations that Evangelicals in each slice belong to.
3. Total Evangelicals in each slice, in AD 2000.

EVANGELICALISM

Core Evangelicals
**CONSERVATIVE EVANGELICALS**
Denominational Evangelicals
Affiliated Evangelicals          Mainstream Evangelicals          Inerrantist Evangelicals
Card-carrying Evangelicals     Organizational Evangelicals     Fundamentalist Evangelicals
Credal Evangelicals               Corporate Evangelicals          Dispensationalist Evangelicals
                                                                                  Non-evangelical Evangelicals

Mainline Evangelicals
**NEO-EVANGELICALS**
New Evangelicals              Progressive Evangelicals          Pentecostal Evangelicals
Unaffiliated Evangelicals    Confessional Evangelicals          Part-Evangelicals
Individual Evangelicals      Moderate Evangelicals               Radical Evangelicals

Methodist Evangelicals         Conciliar Evangelicals          Historic Evangelicals
Wesleyan Evangelicals     **PROTESTANT EVANGELICALS**     Lutheran Evangelicals
Adventist Evangelicals        Reformed Evangelicals           Calvinist Evangelicals
Holiness Evangelicals         Nonconciliar Evangelicals

Low-Church Evangelicals        Ecumenical Evangelicals          Restorationist Evangelicals
Evangelical Anglicans       **ANGLICAN EVANGELICALS**       Charismatic Evangelicals
High-Church Evangelicals      Episcopal Evangelicals
                                         Evangelical Anglicans

Post-Evangelicals              Postdenominationalist Evangelicals     Nonconciliar Evangelicals
Undenominational Evangelicals  **INDEPENDENT EVANGELICALS**     Old Catholic Evangelicals
Nondenominational Evangelicals  Neo-Apostolic Evangelicals       Radio/TV Evangelicals
Apostolic Evangelicals          Third-Wave Evangelicals          Isolated Evangelicals
Black Evangelicals              Post-Protestant Evangelicals

Crypto-Evangelicals           Non-Protestant Evangelicals     Evangelical Catholics
                              **CATHOLIC EVANGELICALS**
                              Roman Catholic Evangelicals

**ORTHODOX EVANGELICALS**
Evangelical Orthodox

Marginal Evangelicals   Quasi-Evangelicals   Liberal Mormons
**LIBERAL EVANGELICALS**
Converted Jehovah's Witnesses
Nominal Evangelicals

Evangelicals
211 million

evangelicals
648 million

| Major megabloc | %Ev | Totals, AD 2000 |
|---|---|---|
| P– | 100 | 83 million |
| P– | 50–99 | 34 million |
| P– | 1–49 | 27 million |
| A– | 38 | 30 million |
| I– | 7 | 27 million |
| R– | 1 | 7.8 million |
| O– | 1 | 2 million |
| m– | 1 | 0.2 million |

| | |
|---|---|
| All Evangelicals | 211 million |
| All evangelicals | 648 million |
| Non-Evangelical evangelicals | 448 million |
| Non-evangelical Evangelicals | 61 million |
| Evangelical evangelicals | 200 million |
| evangelical Evangelicals | 150 million |

## Global Diagram 12. The Pentecostal/Charismatic/Neocharismatic Renewal in the Holy Spirit in the context of 200 other renewals: life and death in the Body of Christ with revivals, awakenings, and movements, involving 1,300 million Christians.

Two vast, opposing forces today are influencing the numerical fortunes of the Body of Christ: death, and life. Coincidentally, identical numbers are involved: 18.4 million Christians die every year, but another 18 million more each year enter into new or renewed life through Christian renewal movements.

First, (a) *Death*: the church regularly loses by death each day over 50,000 members. The causes of these deaths are shown in Table A at left below. But second, (b) *New life*: the church each year sees an increase of 18 million others who have become renewed in the Spirit as new Pentecostals/Charismatics/Third-Wavers. This is illustrated by today's proliferation of official logos representing the descent of the Holy Spirit as dove, as with the logo, at

left, of the North American Renewal Service Committee, NARSC; or, far right, the dove hovering over 2 segmented worlds, logo of SOMA, Sharing of Ministries Abroad, or below, the logo of ICCRO/ICCRS. Thus in this largest spiritual renewal in history, the annual number of newly-renewed members has, for the first time ever, exceeded the annual number of Christians who die. Table B at right below lists a selection from the whole variety of renewal movements with current influence. For each it gives its year of origin in parentheses, followed by the number of Christians now involved.

Over 200 such movements or revivals are described and documented in Part 2 "CosmoChronology". Some 60 are large Catholic lay movements outside usual church structures but recognized and encouraged by Vatican authorities.

The grand total of all Christians involved in renewal movements in AD 2000 totals some 1,300 million church members.

The globe below then gives more detail on the Pentecostal/Charismatic Renewal and its subdivisions First Wave, Second Wave, and Third Wave. The diagram shows the 3-tier division into Worlds A,B, and C, but portrays the globe rotated somewhat, as viewed from below. Thus World A (shaded black, at the top) is only just visible, while World C (the Christian World) is fully exposed to view. It in turn is subdivided among the 6 major ecclesiastico-cultural megablocs.

### Table A. CAUSES OF CHRISTIAN DEATHS
(several categories overlap)

| | Per year | Every day | % total |
|---|---|---|---|
| Poverty-induced | 10.6 million | 29,040 | 54.1 |
| Natural causes ("old age") | 9.76 million | 26,740 | 50.0 |
| Starvation-related | 6.03 million | 16,520 | 30.9 |
| Hunger-related (under 5s) | 5.04 million | 13,810 | 25.8 |
| Parasitic diseases | 5.04 million | 13,810 | 25.8 |
| Child diseases (under 15s) | 4.63 million | 12,680 | 23.7 |
| Circulatory disease | 4.02 million | 11,010 | 20.6 |
| Infant mortality (under 1s) | 3.22 million | 8,820 | 16.5 |
| Pollution | 3.03 million | 8,300 | 15.5 |
| Dirty water | 3.03 million | 8,300 | 15.5 |
| Cardiovascular disease | 3.03 million | 8,300 | 15.5 |
| Cancer | 2.11 million | 5,780 | 10.8 |
| Malaria | 1.50 million | 4,110 | 7.7 |
| Diarrhea (under 5s) | 1.50 million | 4,110 | 7.7 |
| AIDS | 1.50 million | 4,110 | 0.5 |
| Pneumonia (under 15s) | 1.21 million | 3,315 | 6.2 |
| Tuberculosis | 1.11 million | 3,040 | 5.7 |
| Perinatal diseases | 1.02 million | 2,800 | 5.2 |
| Injury and poisoning | 898,000 | 2,460 | 4.6 |
| Tobacco-related | 605,000 | 1,660 | 3.1 |
| Accidents | 508,000 | 1,390 | 2.6 |
| Homicide (Murder) | 410,000 | 1,120 | 2.1 |
| Man-made disasters | 312,000 | 860 | 1.6 |
| Wars | 312,000 | 860 | 1.6 |
| Pesticide poisoning | 293,000 | 800 | 1.5 |
| Suicide | 195,000 | 540 | 1.0 |
| Martyrdom for Christ | 160,000 | 438 | 0.9 |
| Maternal mortality | 156,000 | 430 | 0.8 |
| Motor vehicles | 97,600 | 270 | 0.5 |
| Natural disasters | 58,600 | 160 | 0.3 |
| Earthquakes | 35,000 | 96 | 0.1 |
| Torture | 25,000 | 69 | 0.1 |
| Execution by governments | 20,000 | 55 | 0.1 |
| Venomous snakebite | 12,000 | 33 | 0.1 |
| Terrorism | 4,000 | 11 | 0.0 |
| Floods | 3,000 | 8 | 0.0 |
| Other miscellaneous causes | 200,000 | 550 | 1.0 |
| Deaths of Christians p.a. | 18.4 million | 50,410 | 100.0 |

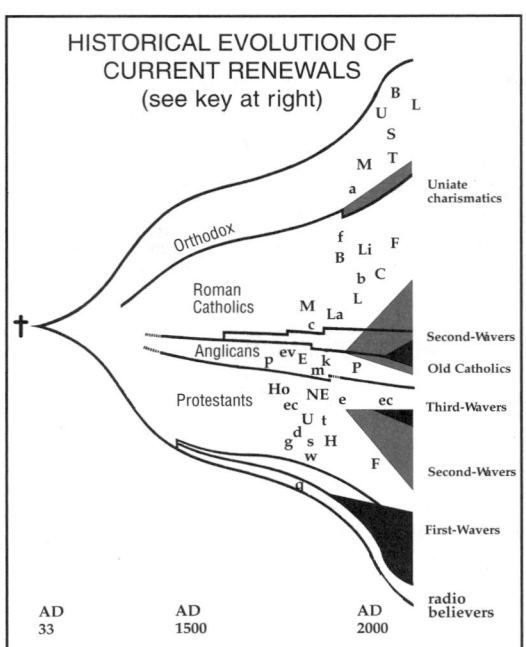

HISTORICAL EVOLUTION OF CURRENT RENEWALS (see key at right)

Uniate charismatics
Orthodox
Roman Catholics
Second-Wavers
Anglicans
Old Catholics
Protestants
Third-Wavers
Second-Wavers
First-Wavers
radio believers

AD 33    AD 1500    AD 2000

### Table B. NEW LIFE MOVEMENTS, 1700-2000
(a selection out of over 200 renewal movements; with, in parentheses, year of origin; at right, number of Christians involved today; many categories overlap)

GENERIC RENEWAL MOVEMENTS
| | |
|---|---|
| B = Biblical renewal (1800) | 200 million |
| C = Charismatic Movement (1907) | 176 million |
| D = Denominational Pentecostalism (1886) | 66 million |
| E = Evangelicalism (1739) | 211 million |
| F = Fundamentalism (1918) | 100 million |
| H = House church movement (1960) | 100 million |
| Ho=Holiness movement (1830) | 10 million |
| L = Liturgical renewal (1900) | 15 million |
| La= Lay renewals | 1.2 billion |
| Li= Liberation theology | 25 million |
| M = Monastic renewal | 700,000 |
| NE=Neo-Evangelicalism | 34 million |
| P = Parish renewal | 100 million |
| T = Third-Wave Renewal (1549) | 295 million |
| U = Sunday-school revival | 75 million |

SPECIFIC RENEWAL MOVEMENTS
| | |
|---|---|
| a = The Lord's Army (Orthodox) (1918) | 300,000 |
| b = Basic Ecclesial Communities (1941) | 4 million |
| c = Cursillistas (1949) | 1 million |
| d = Madagascar Revival (1894) | 1 million |
| e = East African Revival (1927) | 3 million |
| ec= Ecumenical Movement (1790) | 460 million |
| ev= Evangelical Revival (1739) | — |
| g = Great Awakening (1859) | — |
| f = Focolare/New Generation (1943) | 2 million |
| i =Non-White neocharismatics (1783) | 204 million |
| k = Keswick Movement (1875) | 40,000 |
| m =Moral Re-Armament (1921) | 50,000 |
| p = Pietism (1649) | — |
| q = quasi-pentecostals (1741) | 18 million |
| s = Classical Pentecostals (1895) | 63 million |
| t = Timor Revival (1965) | 600,000 |
| w = Welsh Revival (1904) | — |

RENEWAL RESOURCES, AD 2000
(Pentecostals/Charismatics)

| Year: | 2000 | 2025 |
|---|---|---|
| National workers (citizens) | 1.9 million | 3.9 million |
| Foreign missionaries | 167,000 | 400,000 |
| Members' personal incomes | $1.6 trillion | $2.4 trillion |

Official 1990 logo of ICCRO (International Catholic Charismatic Renewal Office, now ICCRS).

ECCLESIASTICAL MEGABLOCS
These are 6 in number, shown delineated by straight dashed near-vertical lines with adjacent letters.
*KEY:*
O=Orthodox
R=Roman Catholics
A=Anglicans
P=Protestants
I=Independents
m=marginal Christians

N=Northern pole, in World A: least evangelized populations on Earth

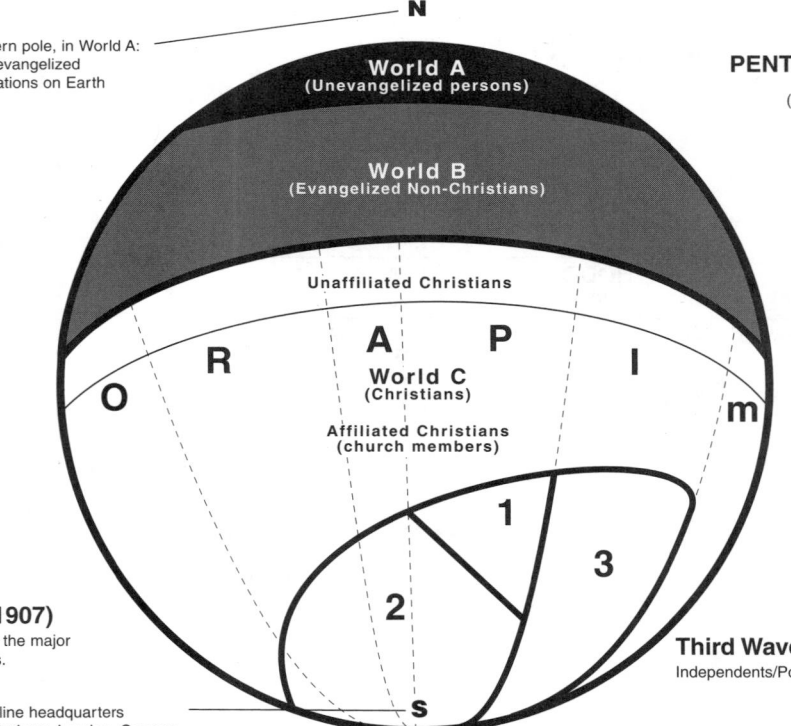

N

World A (Unevangelized persons)

World B (Evangelized Non-Christians)

Unaffiliated Christians

World C (Christians)

Affiliated Christians (church members)

O R A P I m

1
2
3

s

### PENTECOSTAL/CHARISMATIC RENEWAL

(shown bounded by this heavy black outline)

**1** = First Wave: Pentecostal Renewal, from 1886
**2** = Second Wave: Charismatic Renewal, from 1907
**3** = Third Wave: Neocharismatic Renewal from 1549

**First Wave (1886)**
Denominational Pentecostals (Classical Pentecostals)

**Second Wave (1907)**
Mainline Charismatics in the major nonpentecostal churches.

S=Southern pole, in World C: mainline headquarters (Istanbul, Moscow, Vatican, Canterbury, London, Geneva, New York, Singapore, Manila, Buenos Aires, Lagos), all influenced by all renewals.

**Third Wave (1549)**
Independents/Postdenominationalists/Neocharismatics

Grand total of all Christians involved in renewals, AD 2000 1,300 million

## Global Diagram 13. History's 1,500 plans to evangelize the world: 845 current Great Commission global plans targeting the 21st century, of which 210 are global megaplans, and 57 global gigaplans.

Over the last 20 centuries, around 1,500 global plans to evangelize the world have been announced or launched by Christian organizations with, in most cases, a closure date or deadline announced for 1, 5, 10, 20, or 30 years ahead. Of all these, 665 came to nothing. The rest, some 845 are still current. Two thirds of these plans are in trouble and demonstrably getting nowhere; but one third are actively making progress. This diagram describes the whole phenomenon, as existing in the year 2000. All of the current plans have embarked in some sense on a countdown process involving the next 5, 10, 20, or 30 years. A detailed treatment, definitions, descriptions, and statistical analysis, are given Part 27 "GeoStrategies".

### PERIODS OF ORIGIN OF GLOBAL PLANS (cumulative)
49 global plans by AD 500
64 global plans by AD 1000
99 global plans by AD 1500
159 global plans by AD 1800
310 global plans by AD 1900
Total new plans in 20th century to AD 2000: 1,200

### PLANS PER 30-YEAR GENERATION
| Date | Plans per generation |
|---|---|
| AD 1500 | 5 |
| 1800 | 10 |
| 1900 | 69 |
| 1950 | 147 |
| 1980 | 321 |
| 1990 | 500 |
| 2000 | 900 |

### 15 TYPES OF PRIMARY OUTREACH MINISTRY
(number of plans, AD 30-2000)

| Outreach ministry | Plans | % | Sub-totals |
|---|---|---|---|
| *Mandate Generic outreach* | | | |
| **RECEIVE! PRAYER EVANGELISM** | | | 14.9% |
| No human missionary activity | 52 | 3.4 | |
| No activity except repentance | 62 | 4.1 | |
| Intercession, prayer, prayer survey | 111 | 7.4 | |
| **GO! PRE-EVANGELISM** | | | 14.3% |
| Survey, research, strategy | 159 | 10.5 | |
| Development, dialogue, apologetics | 57 | 3.8 | |
| **WITNESS! PERSONAL EVANGELISM** | | | 12.2% |
| Presence, witness, seed-sowing | 89 | 5.9 | |
| Broadcasting, radio, TV, film, video | 95 | 6.3 | |
| **PROCLAIM! PREACHING EVANGELISM** | | | 26.9% |
| Preaching, evangelism, proclamation | 264 | 17.5 | |
| Power evangelism, power healing | 142 | 9.4 | |
| **DISCIPLE! PERSUASION EVANGELISM** | | | 6.2% |
| Converting, discipling, winning | 93 | 6.2 | |
| **BAPTIZE! PLANTING EVANGELISM** | | | 9.1% |
| Church planting, baptizing | 117 | 7.8 | |
| Enforced baptism and church rule | 11 | 0.7 | |
| Military conquest, forced baptism | 10 | 0.7 | |
| **TRAIN! PASTORAL EVANGELISM** | | | 16.4% |
| Training, leadership, networking | 156 | 10.3 | |
| Literature, scripture distribution | 92 | 6.1 | |
| TOTAL PLANS | 1,510 | 100.0 | 100.0% |

### TYPES OF GLOBAL PLANS, AD 30-AD 2000
Total world evangelization plans by 1988: 788
- 188 visions or scenarios
- 132 calls, appeals, or slogans
- 68 special sermons, or encyclicals
- 200 documents, reports, or books
- 124 promises, intents, or resolutions
- 66 unorganized attempts or movements
- 101 statements by organized bodies
- 143 plans announced but left in outline only
- 229 serious plans with some details
- 139 strategies with considerable detail
- 120 massively-detailed blueprints
Total world evangelization plans by mid-2000: 1,510

### DEVELOPMENTAL WORLDS OF ORIGIN
(where plans originated, AD 30-2000)

| World | Countries in world | Countries with plans | Plans | % |
|---|---|---|---|---|
| Developed | 60 | 27 | 915 | 61 |
| less-developed | 130 | 37 | 495 | 33 |
| least-developed | 48 | 13 | 100 | 6 |
| Totals | 238 | 77 | 1,510 | 100 |

### ECCLESIASTICAL ORIGIN
(who originated plans, AD 30-AD 2000)

| Tradition | Plans | % |
|---|---|---|
| Protestant | 250 | 16.3 |
| Roman Catholic | 190 | 12.4 |
| Evangelical | 150 | 9.8 |
| Pentecostal/Charismatic | 180 | 11.8 |
| Nondenominational | 100 | 6.5 |
| Ecumenical | 90 | 5.9 |
| Interdenominational | 50 | 3.3 |
| Marginal | 20 | 1.3 |
| Independent | 500 | 32.7 |

### CURRENT STATUS OF ALL PLANS SINCE AD 30

| Status | % | |
|---|---|---|
| Fizzled out, dead, forgotten | 24.0 | |
| Defunct because no interest | 8.3 | *Sub-totals* |
| Defunct because completion claimed | 2.7 | 24% fizzled out, dead |
| Implemented but not achieved | 9.1 | |
| Alive but fizzling out | 5.3 | |
| Alive but in decline | 10.5 | |
| Alive but static | 13.6 | 59% fizzling out, dying |
| Alive but redefined | 9.4 | |
| Alive and making progress | 10.6 | |
| Alive and being massively implemented | 6.6 | 17% alive and making progress |
| Total plans | 100.0 | |

### REASONS FOR PAST FAILURES
(see list of 340 in Table 26-5)

| | |
|---|---|
| Causes external to the churches: | 53 |
| Causes internal to the churches: | 287 |
| Reasons related to specific factors: | |
| Resources, finances, administration: | 124 |
| Personalities, leadership failings | 106 |
| Politics, power, empire-building: | 110 |

### MAGNITUDE OF RESOURCES EXPENDED
(number of plans, AD 30-2000)

| Resources | Plans | % |
|---|---|---|
| Negligible | 171 | 11.3 |
| Minimal | 295 | 19.5 |
| Limited | 235 | 15.6 |
| Modest | 296 | 19.6 |
| Sizeable | 246 | 16.3 |
| Massive | 210 | 13.9 |
| Gigantic | 57 | 3.8 |
| Total | 1,510 | 100.0 |

### COOPERATION WITH OTHER TRADITIONS
(number of plans, AD 30-2000)

| Plans | % | Cooperation | Sub-totals |
|---|---|---|---|
| 311 | 20.6 | None | |
| 356 | 23.6 | Minimal | 66% non-cooperating or |
| 331 | 21.9 | Partial | partially cooperating |
| 317 | 21.0 | General | |
| 126 | 8.3 | Essential | 95% ignoring non- |
| 69 | 4.6 | Total | like-minded traditions |
| 1,510 | 100.0 | | |

### SIGNIFICANCE OF PLAN DOCUMENTATION
(% of all global plans with 7 kinds of documentation)

| Type of documentation | % |
|---|---|
| Nothing written except incidental reference | 3.4 |
| Briefly written up in published form | 15.7 |
| Published article, message | 22.1 |
| Published book or book | 33.3 |
| Printed publicity materials | 12.3 |
| Detailed plans for private use | 10.3 |
| Detailed logistics published as book | 2.9 |
| Total plans | 100.0 |

### GLOBAL PLANS IN AD 2000
845 current global plans
585 current plans in trouble
260 current global plans making progress
210 global megaplans
57 global gigaplans

### DECADE PLANS, 1990-2000
Decades of Evangelism announced:
10 confessional
25 denominational
30 nondenominational
10 interdenominational

### THE DECADE OF EVANGELIZATION 1990-2000
*Names announced:*
Decade of Universal Evangelization
Worldwide Decade of Evangelization (Catholic Church)
Decade of Harvest (Assemblies of God)
Decade of Destiny (Church of God)
Decade of Opportunity (LCWE)
Decade of Evangelism (World Methodist Council)
Decade of Evangelism (Anglican Communion)
Decade of Bold Mission (Southern Baptist Convention)
Decade of World Evangelization (Charismatic Renewal)
Decade of Redeployment (GEM)
Decade of Decision
Decade of Decisions (Presbyterian)
Decade of Humility
Decade of Concerted Prayer
Decade for New Responsibilities
Decade of the Cosmos (astrophysicists)

### NONGLOBAL PLANS IN 2000
Total national or regional plans: 1,600

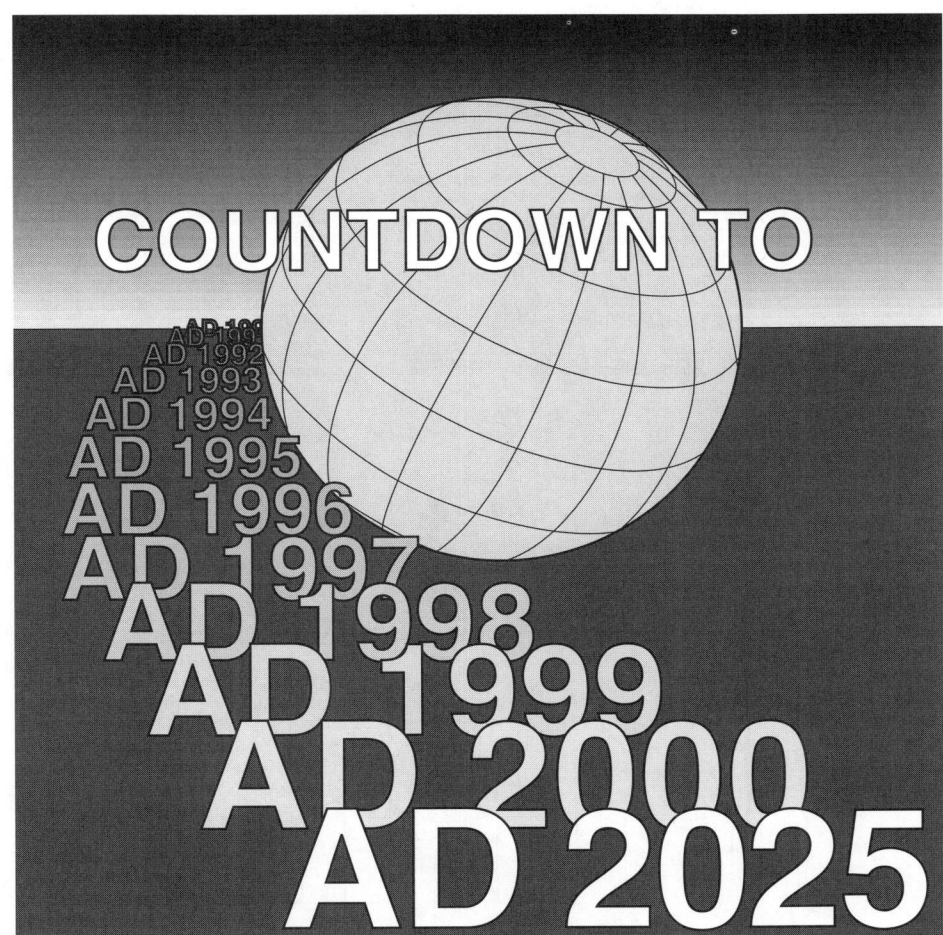

For 2,000 years Christians have envisaged, planned and worked for the complete encircling of the world by the gospel of Christ.

## Global Diagram 14. Component elements and structures of global Christianity: 6 ecclesiastico-cultural megablocs, 10 global megamonoliths, 80 global monoliths, 4,000 monoliths, 150,000 minimonoliths.

When outside observers first encounter the Christian world (World C), from afar they perceive it as a colossal single monolithic entity. As they get closer, the view resolves itself into 6 distinct megablocs. Closer still, some 80 major world-wide organizations appear. Closer yet, the observers become overwhelmed by a vast number of separate and distinct organizations—33,820 denominations, 24,000 agencies, 105,000 major institutions. These all appear as a forest of huge free-standing skyscrapers.

Our metaphor for these entities is monoliths. In general use, a monolith is defined as 'a single large block, usually of stone, with unity of structure or purpose, of unyielding quality or character' (Webster's). A global monolith is a monolith with global presence across the world. A megamonolith is an enormous monolith with measurements in the millions.

In our application, the table and minidiagram below portray a panorama of global Christianity as it has evolved from AD 33 up to the present. The picture today is of a vast, confused, fragmented mass of independent, autonomous, standalone, monolithic organizations.

The table documents 6 separate measures of each monolith's magnitude (columns 5-10). Each monolith has its own distinct and separate name, title, purpose, goals, personnel, premises, plant, program, priorities, budget, turf, differentia, memberships, inclusivities and exclusivities. At least 80% of all the 154,000 monoliths of all sizes have little or nothing to do with all the rest. Several of the biggest—Numbers 1, 2, 4a, 4b, 5a, 5e, 6b, 6c, 6d, 6g, 7b, 7c, 7f—consider themselves to be the only true church and write off all the rest as nothing to do with Christ or his Commission.

The last 3 columns of the table illustrate the degree to which each monolith attempted global outreach and mission in the Decade of Evangelism, 1990-2000.

| Ref | Begun | GLOBAL MEGAMONOLITH<br>global monolith | Christians<br>millions | Size | Computers<br>millions | Related Global Plans<br>total | mega | giga |
|---|---|---|---|---|---|---|---|---|
| 1 | 2 | 3    4 | 5 | 6 | 7 | 8 | 9 | 10 |
| **A. CHRISTIAN MEGABLOCS, GLOBAL MONOLITHS, AND MEGAMONOLITHS** ||||||||
| **1.** | **AD 33** | **ORTHODOX** | **179.5** | **5** | **0.8** | **28** | **0** | **0** |
| 1a. | 1961 | Great & Holy Council of the Orthodox Church | 140.5 | 4 | 0.7 | 27 | 0 | 0 |
| 1b. | 1965 | Oriental Orthodox Churches Conference | 33.0 | 3 | 0.1 | 1 | 0 | 0 |
| 1c. | | Standing Conf. of Canonical Orthodox Bishops (SCOBA) | 5.5 | 5 | 0.5 | 5 | 0 | 0 |
| **2.** | **AD 50** | **ROMAN CATHOLICS** | **962.6** | **7** | **19.1** | **117** | **17** | **8** |
| 2a. | 1523 | Society of Jesus (SJ) | 260.0 | 6 | 2.2 | 5 | 1 | 1 |
| 2b. | 1588 | Sacred Congregation for Bishops | 820.8 | 7 | 10.2 | 55 | 7 | 2 |
| 2c. | 1622 | Sacred Congregation for the Evangelization of Peoples | 115.0 | 6 | 4.0 | 20 | 1 | 1 |
| 2d. | 1862 | Sacred Congregation for the Eastern Churches | 10.6 | 3 | 0.2 | 2 | 0 | 0 |
| 2e. | 1987 | Evangelization 2000/New Evangelization 2000* | 962.6 | 6 | 18.0 | 10 | 5 | 4 |
| 2f. | 1965 | Synod of Bishops | 926.4 | 7 | 15.1 | 60 | 3 | 3 |
| **3.** | **AD 61** | **ANGLICANS** | **53.8** | **5** | **5.2** | **32** | **0** | **0** |
| 3a. | 1867 | Lambeth Conference of Bishops | 53.0 | 5 | 5.0 | 30 | 0 | 0 |
| 3b. | 1968 | Anglican Consultative Council (ACC) | 53.0 | 4 | 5.1 | 1 | 0 | 0 |
| 3c. | | Anglican Orthodox Communion | 0.1 | 1 | 0.0 | 1 | 0 | 0 |
| **4.** | **AD 690** | **PROTESTANTS** | **324.2** | **7** | **21.4** | **490** | **44** | **16** |
| 4a. | 1844 | Seventh-day Adventists (SDA) | 16.0 | 6 | 0.7 | 4 | 2 | 1 |
| 4b. | 1845 | Southern Baptist Convention (FMB) | 29.0 | 6 | 5.6 | 10 | 3 | 2 |
| 4c. | 1875 | World Alliance of Reformed Churches (WARC) | 59.0 | 5 | 5.0 | 25 | 0 | 0 |
| 4d. | 1876 | World Methodist Council (WMC) | 42.0 | 5 | 4.2 | 12 | 1 | 0 |
| 4e. | 1905 | Baptist World Alliance (BWA) | 47.0 | 4 | 6.5 | 15 | 0 | 0 |
| 4f. | 1947 | Lutheran World Federation (LWF) | 76.0 | 4 | 3.7 | 10 | 1 | 0 |
| **5.** | **AD 1549** | **INDEPENDENTS** | **143.8** | **4** | **0.8** | **3** | **0** | **0** |
| 5a. | 1863 | New Apostolic Church (NAC) | 1.8 | 6 | 0.2 | 1 | 1 | 1 |
| 5b. | 1871 | Old Catholic Bishops Conference (IOCBC)* | 7.6 | 4 | 0.2 | 2 | 0 | 0 |
| 5c. | 1920 | Indigenous Pentecostal/Charismatic Churches | 120.0 | 4 | 0.3 | 1 | 0 | 0 |
| 5d. | 1978 | Organization of African Instituted Churches (OAIC) | 13.0 | 2 | 0.0 | 2 | 0 | 0 |
| 5e. | | Old Ritualists (Old Believers | 2.0 | 3 | 0.0 | 0 | 0 | 0 |
| **6.** | **AD 1566** | **MARGINAL CHRISTIANS** | **3.7** | **6** | **1.5** | **2** | **0** | **0** |
| 6a. | 1778 | Unitarian Universalist Association (UUA) | 0.3 | 4 | 0.1 | 0 | 0 | 0 |
| 6b. | 1830 | Church of Jesus Christ of Latter-day Saints | 7.2 | 6 | 2.2 | 1 | 1 | 1 |
| 6c. | 1870 | Jehovah's Christian Witnesses | 12.9 | 7 | 1.4 | 4 | 2 | 2 |
| 6d. | 1879 | Church of Christ, Scientist | 1.4 | 5 | 0.6 | 0 | 0 | 0 |
| 6e. | 1900 | International Association for Liberal Christianity (IALC) | 1.3 | 5 | 0.3 | 0 | 0 | 0 |
| 6f. | 1914 | International New Thought Alliance (INTA) | 0.2 | 4 | 0.1 | 0 | 0 | 0 |
| 6g. | 1948 | International Association of Religious Science Churches | 0.1 | 4 | 0.0 | 0 | 0 | 0 |
| **B. TRANS-MEGABLOC GROUPINGS, GLOBAL MONOLITHS, AND MEGAMONOLITHS** ||||||||
| **7.** | **AD 1738** | **EVANGELICALS** | **295.0** | **7** | **16.5** | **111** | **45** | **15** |
| 7a. | 1846 | World Evangelical Fellowship (WEF)* | 104.0 | 5 | 1.6 | 5 | 1 | 0 |
| 7b. | 1948 | International Council of Christian Churches (ICCC)* | 5.1 | 5 | 0.1 | 4 | 0 | 0 |
| 7c. | 1974 | Lausanne Committee for World Evangelization (LCWE)* | 2.6 | 5 | 0.3 | 19 | 1 | 0 |
| 7d. | 1987 | International Conf of Evangelical Bible Societies (ICEBS)* | 32.0 | 4 | 2.5 | 1 | 0 | 0 |
| 7e. | 1988 | Third World Missions Association (TWMA)* | 48.0 | 5 | 0.2 | 4 | 2 | 0 |
| 7f. | 1989 | AD 2000 Movement (GCOWE)* | 5.0 | 4 | 1.0 | 10 | 1 | 0 |
| **8.** | **AD 1783** | **PENTECOSTALS/CHARISMATICS/NEO CHARISMATICS** | **372.6** | **7** | **12.3** | **89** | **20** | **10** |
| 8a. | 1947 | World Conference of Pentecostal Churches* (WCPC) | 55.0 | 3 | 6.1 | 30 | 7 | 3 |
| 8b. | 1972 | Catholic Charismatic Renewal (ICCRO)* | 72.1 | 6 | 2.5 | 2 | 2 | 2 |
| 8d. | 1987 | Intl Charismatic Consultation for World Evang (ICCOWE)* | 305.0 | 5 | 7.5 | 1 | 1 | 0 |
| **9.** | **AD 33** | **GREAT COMMISSION CHRISTIANS** | **560.7** | **7** | **18.5** | **100** | **50** | **5** |
| 9a. | | 4,000 uncoordinated GCC mission agencies | 560.7 | 7 | 18.5 | 100 | 50 | 5 |
| **10.** | **AD 1855** | **ECUMENISTS/CONCILIARISTS** | **460.0** | **6** | **10.7** | **80** | **2** | **1** |
| 10a. | 1946 | United Bible Societies (UBS)* | 1,560.0 | 5 | 9.0 | 6 | 2 | 1 |
| 10b. | 1948 | World Council of Churches (WCC)* | 404.0 | 5 | 9.5 | 12 | 2 | 0 |
| 10c. | 1957 | Conference of Christian World Communions* | 1,480.0 | 6 | 39.0 | 1 | 0 | 0 |
| | | **GLOBAL TOTALS FOR ALL 10 MEGAMONOLITHS** | **1,623.8** | **7** | **54.0** | **950** | **78** | **33** |

*KEY TO TABLE ON LEFT*

1. *Reference number.* These are as assigned to the 6 major ecclesiastico-cultural megablocs (shown on minidiagram as ellipses), 10 megamonoliths, and the 37 major global monoliths.

2. *Begun.* Year monolith originated. Monoliths are listed chronologically under each megamonolith also listed chronologically.

3. *GLOBAL MEGAMONOLITH.* Short adjectival form of name covering a vast grouping of global monoliths of like purpose/outlook/history/tradition/ecclesiology/churchmanship.

4. *Global monolith.* A selection of the 37 most significant of the 80 global monoliths, each being a large worldwide Christian church/denomination/confession/communion/grouping/agency/organization operating separately from other monoliths. Those with asterisk (*) also belong to, or operate in a sphere of, a second chronologically-earlier megamonolith, or to 2 or even 3 earlier ones.

5. *Christians.* World total of constituency, i.e. affiliated church members (in millions, in 1990) represented by, or related to each monolith. Note monolith totals for columns 5-10 do not add up to megamonolith totals because the former are only a selection, or overlap with others.

6. *Size.* General order of magnitude of total current 10-year resources of personnel and finances actually deployed to operate each monolith or megamonolith. Code: 0=negligible, 1=minimal, 2=limited (10 worker-years), 3=modest ($10,000-$100,000 a year), 4=sizeable ($100,000-$10 million), 5=massive ($10 million-$100 million), 6=gigantic ($100 million-$500 million a year), 7=mammoth (over 1 million worker-years, or over $500 million a year).

7. *Computers.* Estimate in millions of the numbers of distinct general-purpose computers owned and operated by each monolith.

8-10. *Global plans.* Totals of distinct global plans for world evangelization sponsored by or directly related to each monolith; column 8, all global plans large and small, past and present; column 9, global megaplans (over $100 million each) current today; column 10, global gigaplans ($1 billion or more each) current today. (Source: Global Diagram 13).

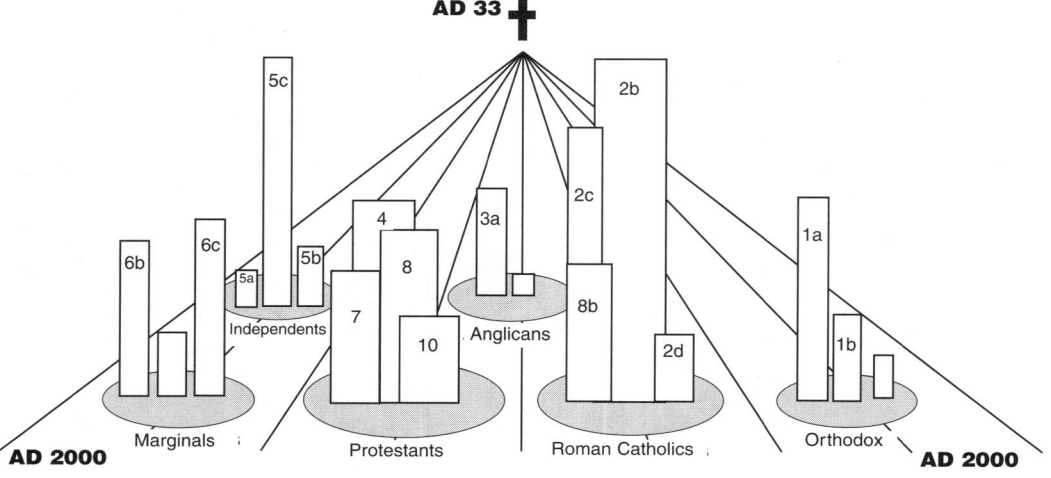

AD 33 ✝

AD 2000    AD 2000

Marginals    Protestants    Roman Catholics    Orthodox

*KEY TO MINIDIAGRAM ON LEFT*

*Triangle.* The background depicts the timeline for the whole course of Christian history from Christ's Cross, Resurrection and Great Commission in AD 33 up to AD 2000.(See Global Diagrams 70-73 for a view of the same panorama from over on the left).

*Vertical pillars.* Each pillar represents a global monolith, namely a large Christian denomination/agency operating in stand-alone mode. The diagram shows only 22 monoliths; expanded diagrams show the top 80, also the 4,000 lesser monoliths.

*Ellipses.* These shaded ovals represent the 7 major ecclesiastico-cultural blocs into which Christians have crystallized today after 20 centuries of history.

*Numbers.* The figures on monoliths refer to reference numbers in the table, column 1.

*Grouping of pillars.* A grouping of monoliths close together is termed a megamonolith, usually coterminous with a single bloc. Exceptions: the Protestant bloc consists of 4 overlapping megamonoliths (4,7,8,10); the Marginal bloc consists of 3 totally isolated and unrelated ones (6a,6b,6c).

## Global Diagram 15. Mission, missions, missionaries, and the active force for mission, AD 33-2025.

The question is often asked: How many persons down the ages have committed themselves to Christ's mission to the world? or, How many missionaries have ever served? or, How many Christians, whether professionals or laypersons, have lived their lives active in mission?

Below, there are 4 parts to this diagram, constructed as follows:

1. **The cone** divides the world's total active force for mission into 8 mutually-exclusive columns labeled M-1 to M-8 and described within each. The shaded part (M-1 to M-7) represents all persons active in mission; M-8 stands for Christians inactive in mission.

2. **Above the cone** in capital letters are 8 cumulative vari-

eties of mission recognized by the church.

3. **Below the cone** are 14 statistical categories widely used by the churches to report on mission; under each is its size in AD 2000.

4. **At page bottom** is a box giving each column's totals of persons at 15 points during 21 centuries of Christian mission. The line in bold type gives the grand total of all persons ever involved in each column's variety of missions—all who have ever served as missionaries or been active in mission. (This line is not the sum of the preceding 15 rows). The final 3 lines give annual change in AD 2000. 'Losses' are due to retirement, deaths, or changes of vocation. 'Gains' represent the annual number of new personnel who join each category in

AD 2000. 'Increase' gives the overall totals, defined as gains minus losses per annum.

The whole table and the cone minidiagram present a series of snapshots of what is, however, a dynamic and rapidly changing situation. There is continual movement of personnel from one column to another. Large numbers of persons in each column move into other columns every year. For this reason, 'losses' in one column may actually be gains in the next, as for example when parish clergy working in their home countries move abroad as foreign missionaries.

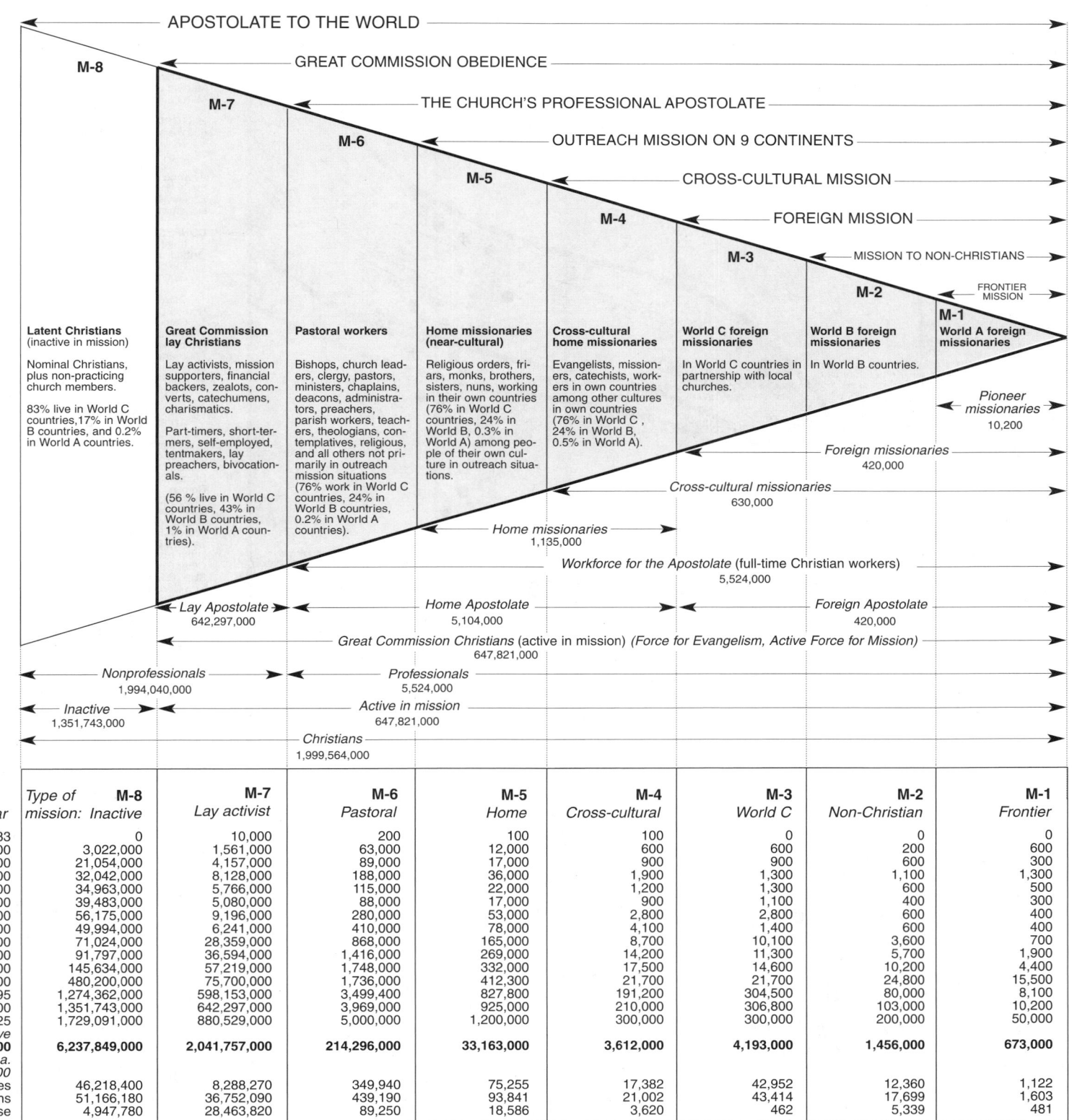

| Year | Type of mission: | M-8 Inactive | M-7 Lay activist | M-6 Pastoral | M-5 Home | M-4 Cross-cultural | M-3 World C | M-2 Non-Christian | M-1 Frontier |
|---|---|---|---|---|---|---|---|---|---|
| AD 33 | | 0 | 10,000 | 200 | 100 | 100 | 0 | 0 | 0 |
| 200 | | 3,022,000 | 1,561,000 | 63,000 | 12,000 | 600 | 600 | 200 | 600 |
| 400 | | 21,054,000 | 4,157,000 | 89,000 | 17,000 | 900 | 900 | 600 | 300 |
| 600 | | 32,042,000 | 8,128,000 | 188,000 | 36,000 | 1,900 | 1,300 | 1,100 | 1,300 |
| 800 | | 34,963,000 | 5,766,000 | 115,000 | 22,000 | 1,200 | 1,300 | 600 | 500 |
| 1000 | | 39,483,000 | 5,080,000 | 88,000 | 17,000 | 900 | 1,100 | 400 | 300 |
| 1200 | | 56,175,000 | 9,196,000 | 280,000 | 53,000 | 2,800 | 2,800 | 600 | 400 |
| 1400 | | 49,994,000 | 6,241,000 | 410,000 | 78,000 | 4,100 | 1,400 | 600 | 400 |
| 1600 | | 71,024,000 | 28,359,000 | 868,000 | 165,000 | 8,700 | 10,100 | 3,600 | 700 |
| 1700 | | 91,797,000 | 36,594,000 | 1,416,000 | 269,000 | 14,200 | 11,300 | 5,700 | 1,900 |
| 1800 | | 145,634,000 | 57,219,000 | 1,748,000 | 332,000 | 17,500 | 14,600 | 10,200 | 4,400 |
| 1900 | | 480,200,000 | 75,700,000 | 1,736,000 | 412,300 | 21,700 | 21,700 | 24,800 | 15,500 |
| 1995 | | 1,274,362,000 | 598,153,000 | 3,499,400 | 827,800 | 191,200 | 304,500 | 80,000 | 8,100 |
| 2000 | | 1,351,743,000 | 642,297,000 | 3,969,000 | 925,000 | 210,000 | 306,800 | 103,000 | 10,200 |
| 2025 | | 1,729,091,000 | 880,529,000 | 5,000,000 | 1,200,000 | 300,000 | 300,000 | 200,000 | 50,000 |
| Cumulative AD 33-2000 | | **6,237,849,000** | **2,041,757,000** | **214,296,000** | **33,163,000** | **3,612,000** | **4,193,000** | **1,456,000** | **673,000** |
| Changes p.a. in 2000 | | | | | | | | | |
| Losses | | 46,218,400 | 8,288,270 | 349,940 | 75,255 | 17,382 | 42,952 | 12,360 | 1,122 |
| Gains | | 51,166,180 | 36,752,090 | 439,190 | 93,841 | 21,002 | 43,414 | 17,699 | 1,603 |
| Increase | | 4,947,780 | 28,463,820 | 89,250 | 18,586 | 3,620 | 462 | 5,339 | 481 |

## Global Diagram 16.    Evangelization through martyrdom: 70 million Christians killed for their faith in 220 countries across 20 centuries.

At the heart of the Great Commission, the 3rd of the 7 Mandates is the command 'Witness!' Because living as a witness to Christ (NT Greek *martys*) often resulted in persecution and death, by the end of the 1st century AD, *martys* had taken on today's connotations of the 'martyr' who witnesses to Christ by his death.

Table 2-1 ('A statistical overview of world evangelization') includes 3 columns that describe the whole extent of Christian martyrdom and its martyrs—defined by 5 criteria: believers in Christ, who have lost their lives, prematurely, in situations of witness, as a result of human hostility. These results are based on a 30-year research investigation into the extent of martyrdom in Christian history up to the present day, in every part of the world, and across all traditions of Christianity.

The diagram sets descriptive data on the phenomena of martyrdom onto a background diagram (in gray print) showing the expansion of Christianity in all its traditions over 20 centuries. This background diagram is explained in detail in the text notes describing Global Diagram 70. And Global Diagram 12 shows how statistics of martyrdom relate to all

other causes of Christian deaths. History's 76 worst situations of mass martyrdom (over 100,000 each) are then shown as black crosses or dots, the latest being Amin's Uganda massacres in 1971, the Sudan holocaust of 1963-1999, and the Rwanda genocide of 1994. Numerous other equally dangerous situations have been averted because the persecutors have been alarmed by the prospect of international opprobrium.

Although 'martyr' on this page always means exclusively a witness to Christ, the one exception is a single table below (bottom right) which puts Christian martyrs in the context of all persons regarded as martyrs by their own non-Christian religions—Islam, Hinduism, Buddhism, Judaism, et alia. All such martyrs share with Christian martyrs in this greatest of deprivations of human rights.

The effect of Christian martyrdom on evangelization over the centuries has been profound. Naturally, Christians have almost always insisted that martyrdom should not be deliberately sought for; but when it happens, the news spreads widely, and unbelievers including persecutors are converted. Martyrdom can be termed the final witness, the complete personal statement of faith in Christ, the ultimate proclamation of the gospel.

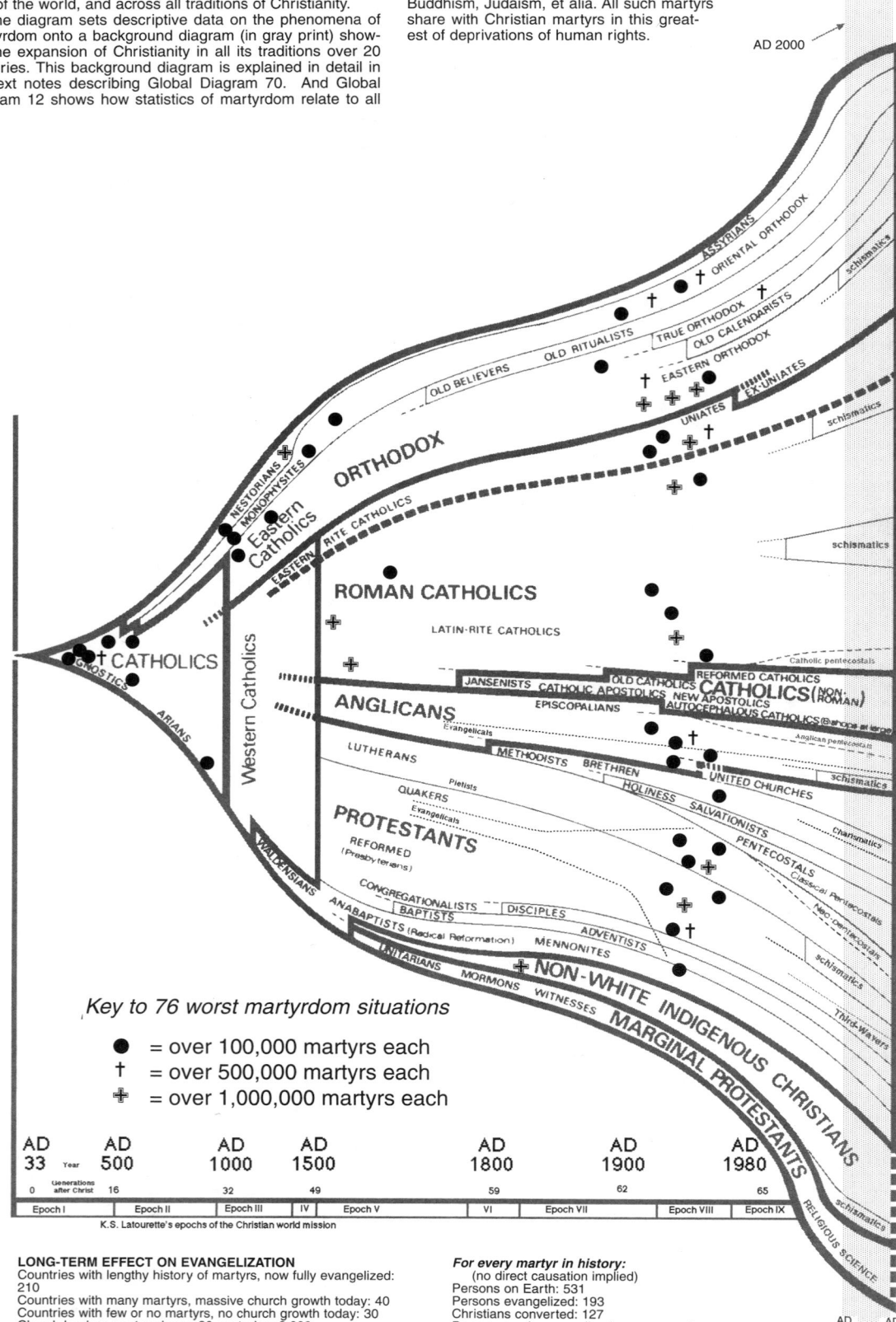

**TOTAL PERSONS, AD 33-2000**
All persons born since AD 33: 36,673 million
All persons evangelized since AD 33: 12,105 million (33% of human race)
All Christians since AD 33: 8,344 million (23% of human race)
All martyrs killed since AD 33: 69,420,000
Martyrs as % all Christians ever: 0.8%
Martyrs among all Christian leaders ever: 2.0%

**HISTORICAL OVERVIEW, AD 33-2000**
600 major martyrdom situations over 20 centuries
    76 with over 100,000 martyrs each
    27 with over 500,000 martyrs each
    15 with over 1 million martyrs each
Average martyrs per martyrdom situation: 115,000
Martyrdom loci: in 220 countries
Ecclesiastical traditions involved: all 300
Denominations with own martyrs: 4,000

**CONFESSION OF VICTIMS, AD 33-2000**
(total martyrs of each tradition)

| | |
|---|---:|
| Orthodox | 42,798,000 |
|   Russian Orthodox | 21,626,400 |
|   East Syrians (Nestorians) | 12,379,000 |
|   Ukrainian Orthodox | 3,500,000 |
|   Gregorians (Armenian Apostolic) | 1,215,100 |
| Roman Catholic | 12,210,000 |
|   Catholics (before AD 1000) | 855,000 |
| Independents | 3,512,000 |
| Protestants | 3,172,000 |
| Anglicans | 1,046,000 |
| Marginal Christians | 6,700 |
| other and background martyrs | 6,675,700 |
| Total all martyrs | 69,420,000 |

**PERSECUTORS AND THEIR VICTIMS, AD 33-2000**

| | Martyrs |
|---|---:|
| Persecutors responsible | |
| State ruling power | 55,871,000 |
| Atheists (overlap with above) | 31,689,000 |
| Muslims | 9,121,000 |
| Ethnoreligionists (animists) | 7,469,000 |
| Roman Catholics | 5,171,000 |
| Quasi-religionists | 2,712,000 |
| Buddhists (Mahayana) | 1,651,000 |
| Hindus | 676,000 |
| Zoroastrians (Parsis) | 384,000 |
| Eastern Orthodox | 222,000 |
| Other non-Christians | 115,000 |
| Other Christians | 146,000 |
| SUBTOTALS: | |
| Non-Christian persecutors | 63,882,000 |
| Christian persecutors | 5,538,000 |
| Total all martyrs | 69,420,000 |

**SITUATION BY AD 2000** (p.a.= per year)
Martyrs in 20th century (1900-2000): 45,400,000
Martyrs since 1950: 13,300,000
Average annual martyrs since 1950: 278,000 p.a.
Recent annual martyrs: 171,000 p.a.
Current annual martyrs: 160,000 p.a.
Countries heavily involved in AD 2000: 50

**CONFESSION OF VICTIMS, AD 2000**
(average annual martyrdom rates)

| | |
|---|---:|
| Roman Catholics | 93,000 |
| Protestants | 30,000 |
| Orthodox | 14,000 |
| Non-White indigenous Christians | 10,000 |
| Anglicans and Old Catholics | 7,000 |
| Marginal Protestants | 5,000 |
| Total martyrs p.a | 160,000 |

**LIKELIHOOD (L%) OF BEING MARTYRED**
(at current rates)

| | L% | Per year |
|---|---:|---:|
| *Full-time workers* | | |
| Bishops | 5.0 | 15 |
| Evangelists | 4.0 | 133 |
| Catechists | 3.5 | 175 |
| Foreign missionaries | 3.0 | 131 |
| Clergy | 2.0 | 303 |
| All Christian workers | 2.0 | 1,700 |
| Monks, brothers | 1.9 | 63 |
| Sisters, nuns | 1.8 | 300 |
| *Other Christians* | | |
| Great Commission Christians | 1.6 | 80,000 |
| Christians (all kinds) | 1.0 | 160,000 |

**MARTYRDOM IN WORLD RELIGIONS SINCE ORIGIN** (persons regarded as martyrs by their own religions)

| | | |
|---|---|---:|
| Islam: | Muslim martyrs | 80 million |
| Christianity: | Christian martyrs | 70 million |
| Hinduism: | Hindu martyrs | 20 million |
| Buddhism: | Buddhist martyrs | 10 million |
| Judaism: | Jewish martyrs | 9 million |
| Ethnoreligions: | Ethnic martyrs | 6 million |
| Others: | Other religious martyrs | 5 million |
| Sikhism: | Sikh martyrs | 2 million |
| Baha'i: | Baha'i martyrs | 1 million |

**Key to 76 worst martyrdom situations**

● = over 100,000 martyrs each
† = over 500,000 martyrs each
✠ = over 1,000,000 martyrs each

**LONG-TERM EFFECT ON EVANGELIZATION**
Countries with lengthy history of martyrs, now fully evangelized: 210
Countries with many martyrs, massive church growth today: 40
Countries with few or no martyrs, no church growth today: 30
Church leaders martyred over 20 centuries: 3,000
Workers martyred over 20 centuries: 400,000

**For every martyr in history:**
(no direct causation implied)
Persons on Earth: 531
Persons evangelized: 193
Christians converted: 127
Persons newly evangelized p.a. per martyr, 1990-2000: 690

**Global Diagram 17.** **The rise of global Christianity across the 20th century showing the rise of global Independency out of global denominationalism, AD 1900-2025.**

The rise and growth of global Independency is shown in the globes below covering the years 1900, 1970, 2000, and 2025. Vertical slices represent the 6 megablocs (Orthodox, Roman Catholic, Anglican, Protestant, Independent, marginal Christian). The light grey balloon from 1970 to 2025 represents the size and ecclesiastical location of the whole Pentecostal/Charismatic/Neo-charismatic Renewal in the Holy Spirit.

The table then analyzes the 6 totals for global Christianity shown at center below the globes. It does it for the year 1970, shown throughout by all numbers in light type. It does the same for the year AD 2000, shown throughout by all numbers in **black** type. This results in 91 pairs of figures showing AD 1970-2000 trends.

Next, the table dichotomizes the whole of Christianity into the *denominationalist* world (Christians organized into the 5 historic megablocs; shown in the lefthand half of the table), and the *postdenominationalist* world (the more recent Independent megabloc that rejects historic denominationalism; shown in the righthand half of the table). This results in 88 denominationalist/postdenominationalist comparisons.

Large-size numbers are meant primarily to be compared horizontally (% meaning percent of each's global total at top). Small-size numbers are meant primarily to be compared vertically (% meaning percent of nearest large-size number above each).

The table then gives 176 numbers which, when read horizontally analyze Christianity into 88 dichotomous pairs or

parallels between the 1970 situation and the AD 2000 situation. These numbers can also be read vertically as 72 vertical comparisons arranged in 8 vertical trichotomies followed by 64 vertical dichotomies.

The bottom 5 lines enumerate the 3 Waves of the Pentecostal/ Charismatic/Neocharismatic Renewal by means of 40 different numbers. The first of these 5 lines gives 8 figures enumerating the whole Renewal (First and Second Waves on the left, Third Wave on the right). The following 2 pairs of 2 lines each analyze the Renewal in 16 horizontal dichotomies and 16 vertical dichotomies. Note that 217.5 million doubly-affiliated and disaffiliated Christians are counted more than once in the figures under the headings 'Denominationalism' and 'Postdenominationalism' below.

The rise of Renewal since 1900 (= gray oblong at bottom of globe)

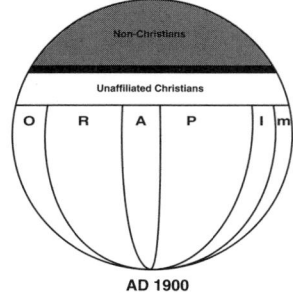
AD 1900

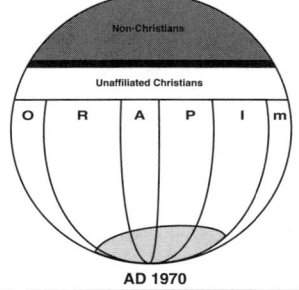
AD 1970

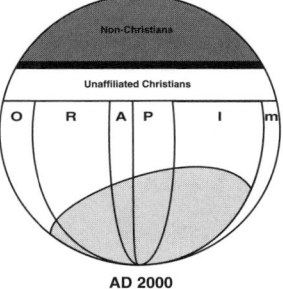
AD 2000

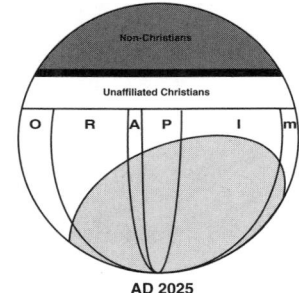
AD 2025

*In the year 1970 (light figures)*
*In the year AD 2000 (**black** figures)*

# GLOBAL CHRISTIANITY

*had*
18,630 **33,820** denominations/paradenominations
*with*
1,449,600 **3,447,900** congregations/churches
*composed of*
1,130 million **1,888 million** affiliated Christians
*dichotomized into*
*the 2 global categories below*

## 1. DENOMINATIONALISM (in megablocs O,R,A,P,m)

| | % | % |
|---|---|---|
| *which had* | | |
| 7,610 **11,680** traditional denominations . . . . . . . . . . . | 41 | **35** |
| *of which* | | |
| 7,080 **7,160** were clearcut denominationalist . . . . . . . . . . . . . . . . . . . . | 93 | **60** |
| 380 **2,920** were less markedly denominationalist | 5 | **25** |
| 150 **1,750** were borderline denominationalist/postdenominationalist | 2 | **15** |
| *all of which had* | | |
| 1,040,200 **1,715,700** congregations/churches . . . . . . . . | 72 | **50** |
| *of which* | | |
| 1,029,800 **1,201,000** were clearcut denominationalist . . . . . . . . . . . . . . . . | 99 | **70** |
| 10,400 **514,700** were borderline denominationalist . . . . . . . . . . . . . . . | 1 | **30** |
| 988,200 **1,458,400** were affiliated to mainline denominations . . . . . . . . | 95 | **85** |
| 52,000 **257,400** were in minor minidenominations . . . . . . . . . . . . . . | 5 | **15** |
| 82,100 **303,400** were Pentecostal/Charismatic . . . . . . . . . . . . . . . . . . . | 8 | **18** |
| 958,000 **1,412,400** were nonpentecostal/noncharismatic . . . . . . . . . . . | 92 | **82** |
| *all of which had* | | |
| 1,075 million **1,720 million Christians (in O,R,A,P,m)** . . . . . . . | 92 | **82** |
| *of whom* | | |
| 645 million **516 million** were personal denominationalists . . . . . . . . . . . . | 60 | **30** |
| 430 million **1,204 million** were just Christians who happened to be there . | 40 | **70** |
| 1,043 million **1,376 million** were in mainline denominations . . . . . . . . . . . . | 97 | **80** |
| 32 million **344 million** were in minor minidenominations . . . . . . . . . . . . | 3 | **20** |
| 1,056 million **1,478 million** were nonpentecostal/noncharismatic Christians | 98 | **87** |
| 19 million **242 million** were Pentecostals/Charismatics . . . . . . . . . . . . . . | 2 | **13** |
| *of this line above (which = the First & Second Waves)* | | |
| 15 million **66 million** were Pentecostals (First-Wavers) . . . . . . . . . . . . . . | 1 | **4** |
| 3 million **176 million** were Charismatics (Second-Wavers) . . . . . . . . . . | 0 | **10** |
| *and of that same line above* | | |
| 1 million **19 million** also adopted Third-Wave identity . . . . . . . . . . . . . . | 0 | **1** |
| 18 million **222 million** did not relate to Third-Wave activities . . . . . . . . . . | 2 | **12** |

## 2. POSTDENOMINATIONALISM (in megabloc I)

| | % | % |
|---|---|---|
| *which had* | | |
| 11,000 **22,100** paradenominations/networks . . . . . . . . | 59 | **65** |
| *of which* | | |
| 2000 **1,350** were clearcut apostolic networks . . . . . . . . . . . . . . . . . . . | 2 | **2** |
| 7,600 **5,500** were looser groupings of churches . . . . . . . . . . . . . . . . | 69 | **25** |
| 3,300 **16,300** were postdenominationalist new denominations . . . . . . | 29 | **74** |
| *all of which had* | | |
| 409,400 **1,732,200** congregations/churches . . . . . . . . . | 28 | **50** |
| *of which* | | |
| 327,500 **1,773,000** were clearcut postdenominationalist . . . . . . . . . . . | 80 | **99** |
| 81,900 **18,000** were borderline postdenominationalist . . . . . . . . . . . . | 20 | **1** |
| 163,700 **1,433,000** were affiliated to independent networks . . . . . . . . . | 40 | **80** |
| 245,600 **358,000** were independent single congregations . . . . . . . . . . | 60 | **20** |
| 195,400 **1,367,600** were clearly pentecostal/charismatic . . . . . . . . . . | 48 | **79** |
| 214,000 **364,500** were nonpentecostal/noncharismatic . . . . . . . . . . . . | 52 | **21** |
| *all of which had* | | |
| 95 million **386 million Christians (Independents, I)** . . . . . . | 8 | **18** |
| *of whom* | | |
| 38 million **270 million** were personal postdenominationalists . . . . . . . . . | 40 | **70** |
| 57 million **116 million** were just Christians who happened to be there . . | 60 | **30** |
| 29 million **289 million** were in independent networks . . . . . . . . . . . . . . . | 30 | **75** |
| 67 million **96 million** were in independent single congregations . . . . . . . | 70 | **25** |
| 42 million **90 million** were nonpentecostals/noncharismatics . . . . . . . . . | 44 | **26** |
| 53 million **295 million** were independent pentecostals/charismatics/ neocharismatics . . . . . . . . . . . . . . . . . . . . . . . . . . . . . . . . . . . . | 56 | **74** |
| *of this line above (which = the Third Wave, termed Neocharismatics)* | | |
| 18 million **94 million** were personal pentecostals (Third-Wavers) . . . . . . | 19 | **23** |
| 35 million **201 million** were personal charismatics (Third-Wavers) . . . . . | 37 | **50** |
| *and of that same line above* | | |
| 1 million **32 million** subsequently affiliated also to the First Wave . . . . . | 1 | **8** |
| 52 million **263 million** did not relate to First or Second Waves . . . . . . . . . | 55 | **66** |

## Global Diagram 18.   Today's global human need: poverty, slums, disasters, deprivation, rights abuses, illness, disease, addiction.

Human need is covered here in 2 consecutive diagrams. Global Diagram 18 focuses on the unfortunate victims involved (described by the detailed statistics below). Global Diagram 19 focuses on the organized structures of the world which perpetuate this tragedy.

The globe below gives an overview of these 2 subjects. It is divided into 2 halves. The lower half depicts the world of the Poor (the so-called 'lower classes') divided into 2 main slices (with a megapoor minislice) and into several population segments. The 4 columns of statistics below the globe then detail

today's global human need.

The upper half of the globe depicts the world of the Rich (the 'middle and upper classes'), divided into 3 main slices (with a megarich minislice) and into several population segments. The figures shown attached to this upper half briefly outline the so-called 'structures of sin', but this category is more fully described, with detailed statistics, in Global Diagram 19.

All statistics refer to the Decade of Evangelism, 1990-AD 2000. All monies are given in USA dollars. Note also that 'p.a.'

means 'per annum', 'per year', 'a year', 'each year', 'every year'. These terms are used alternately to provide variety. Note further that the same global totals throughout these diagrams may be given rounded to 1,2,3, or 4 significant figures (e.g. world population is 6.1 billion, or 6,055 million, etc). Partial totals may not always add up to global totals or 100.0% because of rounding.

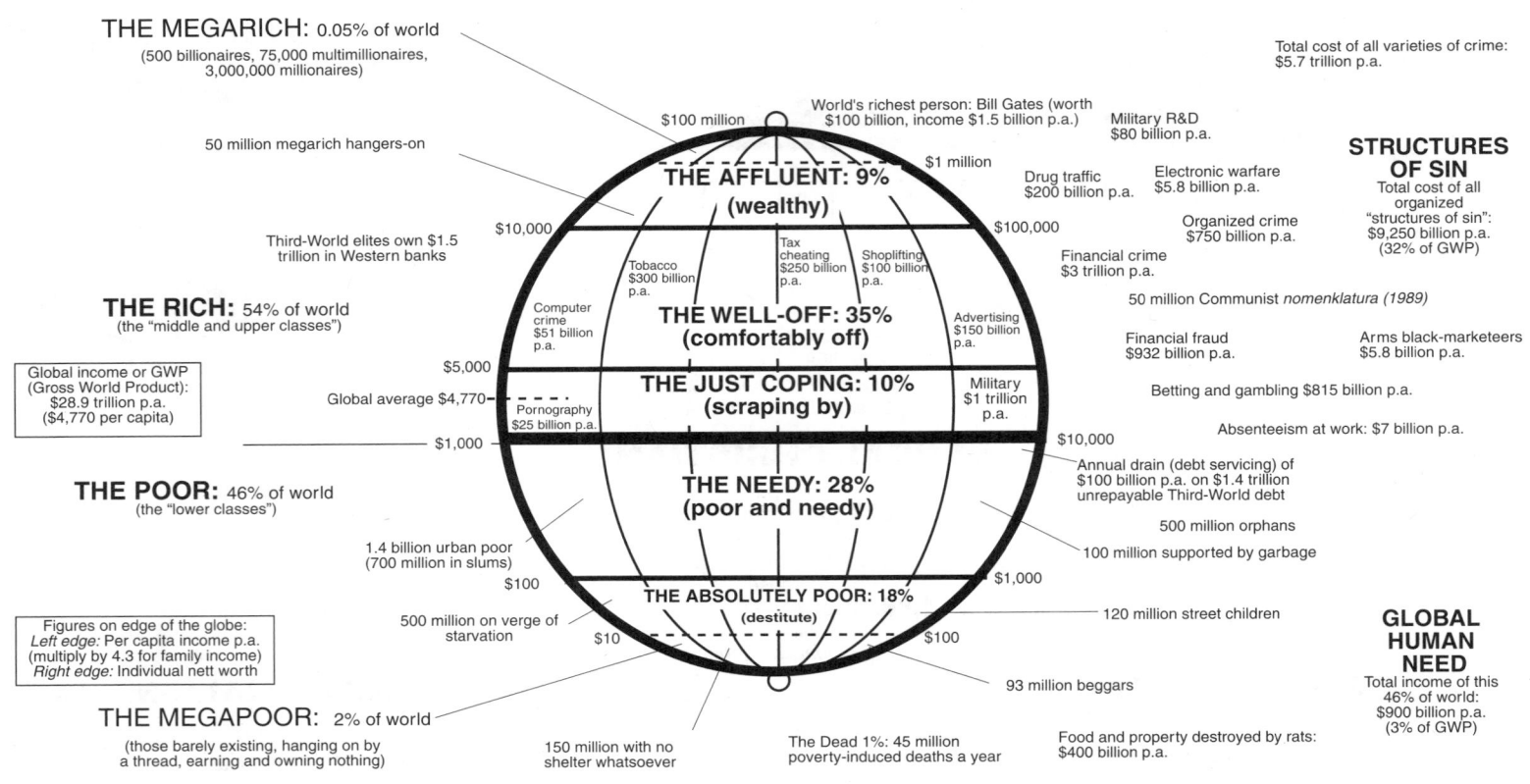

THE MEGARICH: 0.05% of world
(500 billionaires, 75,000 multimillionaires, 3,000,000 millionaires)

50 million megarich hangers-on

Third-World elites own $1.5 trillion in Western banks

THE RICH: 54% of world
(the "middle and upper classes")

Global income or GWP (Gross World Product): $28.9 trillion p.a. ($4,770 per capita)

Global average $4,770

THE POOR: 46% of world
(the "lower classes")

1.4 billion urban poor (700 million in slums)

Figures on edge of the globe:
Left edge: Per capita income p.a. (multiply by 4.3 for family income)
Right edge: Individual nett worth

THE MEGAPOOR: 2% of world
(those barely existing, hanging on by a thread, earning and owning nothing)

$100 million

World's richest person: Bill Gates (worth $100 billion, income $1.5 billion p.a.)

$1 million

THE AFFLUENT: 9% (wealthy)

$100,000

THE WELL-OFF: 35% (comfortably off)

Tobacco $300 billion | Tax cheating $250 billion p.a. | Shoplifting $100 billion p.a.

Computer crime $51 billion p.a.

Advertising $150 billion p.a.

THE JUST COPING: 10% (scraping by)

Military $1 trillion p.a.

Pornography $25 billion p.a.

THE NEEDY: 28% (poor and needy)

$1,000

THE ABSOLUTELY POOR: 18% (destitute)

$10        $100

500 million on verge of starvation

150 million with no shelter whatsoever

The Dead 1%: 45 million poverty-induced deaths a year

$10,000

$5,000

$1,000

$100

Military R&D $80 billion p.a.

Drug traffic $200 billion p.a. | Electronic warfare $5.8 billion p.a.

Organized crime $750 billion p.a.

Financial crime $3 trillion p.a.

Financial fraud $932 billion p.a.

Betting and gambling $815 billion p.a.

Absenteeism at work: $7 billion p.a.

Annual drain (debt servicing) of $100 billion p.a. on $1.4 trillion unrepayable Third-World debt

500 million orphans

100 million supported by garbage

120 million street children

93 million beggars

Food and property destroyed by rats: $400 billion p.a.

**STRUCTURES OF SIN**
Total cost of all organized "structures of sin": $9,250 billion p.a. (32% of GWP)

Total cost of all varieties of crime: $5.7 trillion p.a.

50 million Communist *nomenklatura* (1989)

Arms black-marketeers $5.8 billion p.a.

**GLOBAL HUMAN NEED**
Total income of this 46% of world: $900 billion p.a. (3% of GWP)

---

### HUMANS ON THE GLOBE
6.1 billion population
71,600,000 population increase p.a. (1.2% p.a.; 93% in developing countries)
Median age 26.6 years
124.3 million births a year (2.05% p.a.)
52.7 million deaths a year (0.87% p.a.)
Life expectancy at birth 66.5 years

### BASIC RIGHTS: FOOD, WATER, SHELTER, CARE
2 billion undernourished
1.2 billion hungry (inadequate food for active working life)
700 million severely malnourished
2.0 billion suffering from iron-deficiency anaemia
500 million on verge of starvation
15 million babies born malnourished p.a.
Infant mortality (deaths under 1 year old) 51.6 per 1000 live births
Maternal mortality 600,000 p.a.
18 million annual hunger-related deaths of under 5s
22 million starvation-related deaths p.a.
2.2 billion without safe water to drink
3.0 billion without adequate safe water supply
3.0 billion with unsafe water and bad sanitation
25,000 a day killed by dirty water
1.3 billion without adequate shelter
150 million with no shelter whatsoever
55 million cave-dwellers
1.4 billion without adequate daily clothing
1.5 billion without money to buy food
1.5 billion with scarce firewood
70 million abandoned children and infants
349 million homeless/family-less children
120 million megacity street children
500 million orphans
700 million slumdwellers or shanty-dwellers
New slumdwellers increase at 80 million p.a.
100 million supported by garbage collection/recycling
1.5 billion with no access to medical care
2.8 billion poor (46% of world)
1.4 billion urban poor (1.1 billion in Third World)
1.09 billion absolutely poor (in absolute poverty; 18%)
Poorest 20% of world gets 1.0% of GWP
Working-age population: 70 million more p.a.
Exploited child labor: 200 million
93 million beggars
1.0 billion unemployed workers
900 million underemployed labor
1.1 billion urban part-time street vendors

50 countries with less calorie supply than essential (2,600 per capita per day)

### SOCIOPOLITICAL RIGHTS
10 million stateless (with no nationality)
14 million deportees (persons expelled) p.a.
4 billion unprotected from human rights abuses
Human rights: 45% violated
15 million permanently unsettled refugees
29 million emigrants/immigrants p.a.
154 countries not controlled by popular votes (1989)
2.8 billion disenfranchised (no control by vote, 1989; 54% of world)
991 million illiterate/nonliterate adults (23.3%)
1 billion orate (nonreader) adults unable to read or write (25%)
10 million more illiterate adults p.a.
300 million with language handicaps
3.7 billion without political freedom (1989)
1.96 billion in religious countries
2.40 billion in secular countries
1.5 billion under atheistic regimes (1989)
400 million under oppressive regimes (1989)
80 million under racist regimes
2.8 billion women denied full rights and equality
1.2 billion victims of corruption
850 million uneducated (no past schooling)
1.4 billion school-age children (ages 6-17)
940 million with little or no access to schools (67% of those eligible)
670 million school-agers not in schools
340 million with no access to schools (24%)
28 million children reach school age p.a.
40% without access to electricity
43% without telephone access
43.5% without radio or TV
120 million prisoners in 12-month period
4.5 million political prisoners
1.2 million prisoners due to religion
1 million prisoners of conscience
2.2 billion denied freedom of religion
4.2 billion denied full political freedom and civil rights (1989)
2.2 billion in countries frequently employing torture
120,000 prisoners being tortured
151 million citizens killed by own governments since 1900
1,692,400 political executions, 1948-1977
50,000 executed by governments each year
35 million slaves (bought and sold, including bonded labor, involuntary servitude)
594 million victims of crime p.a.

975,000 murders a year
5.8 million child victims of pedophile racketeers p.a.
25 million child-abuse incidents p.a.
250 million persons sexually abused in childhood

### FUNDAMENTAL FREEDOMS (1989)
3 billion denied freedom to travel in own country
4 billion denied freedom to travel abroad
3 billion denied freedom to assemble
3 billion denied freedom to teach ideas

### DISASTERS AND DESERTIFICATION
1,165,200 more desertification victims a year
11.6 million environmental refugees
1.0 billion at risk through desertification
1,900 major earthquakes, 1900-2000, killing 2.1 million
21,000 earthquake victims (deaths) a year
800 major floods, since 1960, killing 400,000
12,000 flood victims (deaths) a year
300 major cyclones, since 1960, killing 750,000
300,000 environmental disaster victims p.a.
1 million poisoned by pesticides p.a.
800 million live in areas with unhealthy air
25,000 pollution deaths a day
1.5 million killed in man-made disasters p.a.
Traffic deaths 3 persons per 100 million vehicle miles

### ILLNESS/DISEASE
49 million legally blind
19.3 million totally blind (nonsighted)
20 million with river blindness (100 million at risk)
365 million partially deaf (hearing-impaired)
150 million severely deaf
23 million totally deaf
11.6 million dumb (deaf-mutes)
11.5 million with dracunculiasis
19.2 million leprosy sufferers (lepers)
145 million diabetics
450 million new malaria cases p.a.
3.2 billion live at risk of malaria
2.7 million malaria deaths p.a.
314 million with elephantiasis
250 million with schistosomiasis (700 million at risk)
1.2 million a year bitten by venomous snakes
50,000 deaths p.a. from venomous snake bites
10 million with Parkinson's disease
10 million with tuberculosis (TB: 2.9 million deaths p.a.)
700 million iron-deficiency anemic women
116 million with chemosensory (taste and smell) disorders

3.5 million persons worldwide with artificial implants (pacemakers, prostheses)
350,000 persons kept alive by artificial kidneys
65,000 organ transplants a year
3,500 heart transplants a year
75,000 awaiting organ donors
60 million psychotics
15 million schizophrenics
1 billion psychoneurotics
350 million arthritics
1 billion experiencing chronic pain
1 billion disabled (handicapped)
340 million handicapped children
100 million severely handicapped children
3.4 million dwarfs (little people)
2.2 billion sick/ill persons (30% children)
Labor absenteeism: $7 billion p.a.
3.5 million children die p.a. from vaccine-preventable diseases
6 infectious diseases kill 5 million unimmunized children p.a.
4 billion persons not immunized
2.5 million diarrheal deaths of children under 5 p.a.
4 million children die of pneumonia p.a.
24 million prostitutes (9% male)
41 million AIDS carriers (growth rate 25% p.a.)
5 million AIDS cases
2.5 million AIDS-related deaths a year
500,000 suicides a year
700 million tobacco smokers
3 million tobacco-related deaths p.a.
198 million alcoholics
64 million drug addicts (illicit drug users)
Leading causes of 52.7 million deaths p.a.:
   Parasitic diseases 19.0 million
   Circulatory diseases 15.3 million
   Cancer 6.2 million
   Perinatal diseases 3.5 million
   Injury and poisoning 2.7 million
   Cardiovascular disease 5.8 million
150 million severely mentally-retarded
256,000 Downs-syndrome (mongoloid) births p.a.
30 million epileptics
303,000 hemophiliacs (all males)
524,000 albinos (homozygous persons)
100 million albino-gene carriers

### FINANCE
Money needed to provide those in poverty with adequate food, water, education, health: $700 billion p.a.

**Global Diagram 19.** **Today's corporate or collective structures of sin: organized economic, financial, and political background opposition to Christianity and evangelization through corruption, exploitation, debt, finance, manipulation, repression, pollution, crime, warfare, drugs, pseudo-religion, and militarization.**

The megacomplex of global human need is largely caused by a vast superstructure of organized human activity which can be characterized as collectively due to one factor: human greed or selfishness. Social gospel theologian W. Rauschenbusch (1907) referred to this as 'the structures of evil'; pope John Paul II describes it as 'the structures of sin' (as in his encyclical *Sollicitudo rei socialis*). Its estimated cost to the human race is: US$9.25 trillion a year.

The globe below is shown divided into 4 slices. At the top are listed 10 megaproblems whose organizing or mismanag-

ing indirectly plague some 3 billion people. Megapoverty is included here because much of it is deliberately and willfully induced and structured.

The second slice lists 10 varieties of organizations and agencies which are more directly responsible, in varying degrees, for the megaproblems and the world's failure to tackle them adequately.

The third slice lists 10 varieties of mega-evils which have resulted, most of them controlled by the mega-agencies in the second slice. These mega-evils can be seen to be the direct

and immediate causes of the bulk of human misery.

Finally, at the bottom, the whole of this superstructure of sin is shown crushing half of humanity in its situation of desperate human need (statistics of which are given in Global Diagram 18).

If somehow even 10% of this superstructure's activity could be wiped out and the proceeds redistributed directly to the 46% of the world living in poverty, this would solve the immediate problem of global human need.

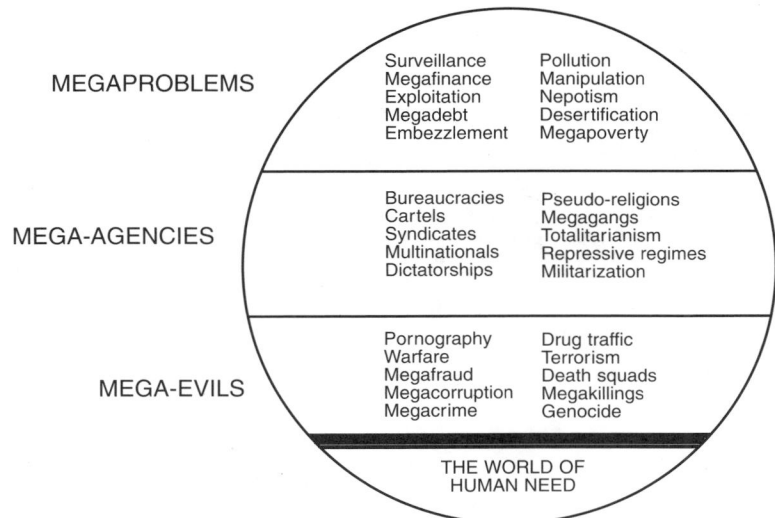

MEGAPROBLEMS

Surveillance    Pollution
Megafinance    Manipulation
Exploitation    Nepotism
Megadebt    Desertification
Embezzlement    Megapoverty

MEGA-AGENCIES

Bureaucracies    Pseudo-religions
Cartels    Megagangs
Syndicates    Totalitarianism
Multinationals    Repressive regimes
Dictatorships    Militarization

MEGA-EVILS

Pornography    Drug traffic
Warfare    Terrorism
Megafraud    Death squads
Megacorruption    Megakillings
Megacrime    Genocide

THE WORLD OF
HUMAN NEED

**A CLOSER LOOK AT TODAY'S
ORGANIZED 'STRUCTURES OF SIN'**
costing $9.25 trillion a year ($25 billion a day)
including $300 billion p.a. 'black money' (banked
profits from criminal enterprise) and $1.5 trillion p.a.
'gray money' (dirty money laundered by banks).

**WARS**
500 major wars since AD 1700
100 major wars since 1960
25 wars under way in AD 2000
60 countries with significant armed conflict (internal or external)
1 million killed in wars each year
150 million killed in wars since AD 1700 (55% civilians)
42 million combatants killed in wars since 1900
15 million killed in wars since 1960 (84% civilians)
International peace-keeping forces $250 million p.a.
Disarmament treaties: signed by 150 nations

**MILITARIZATION**
Military expenditures $1,000 billion p.a. ($1.9 million a minute; 3.5% of GWP)
Military expenditures since 1960: $20 trillion
Military expenditures per soldier $33,300 p.a.
Military expenditures per capita $165 p.a.
10,000 nuclear warheads (5,000 strategic) of 16,000 megatons
Decrease in nuclear warheads: 500 p.a. (1.4 a day)
2,000 nuclear tests since 1945 (82% exploding)
Nuclear weapons accidents since 1945: 3,000
Chemical weapons 350,000 tons
30 million troops in regular armed forces
319 million paramilitary troops
60 million military supply personnel
2.5 million foreign troops abroad
750,000 military trained abroad
70,000 combat aircraft
950 ships with nuclear weapons (450 reactor-driven)
450 nuclear submarines
30 nuclear aircraft carriers
10,720 submarine-launched ballistic-missile warheads
Electronic warfare $5.8 billion p.a.
3,500 foreign military bases
International arms trade $48 billion p.a.
Arms black market (private dealers) $5.8 billion p.a.
291 million own personal firearms (guns)
Military research and development $80 billion p.a.
500,000 scientists involved in military work
116 million civilians employed by national ministries of defense
Christians employed by military establishment: 70 million
31 military-controlled governments

10 military coups a year
357 million under military rule or dictatorships

**CRIME**
Organized crime $750 billion p.a.
73.6 million crimes a year
3.40 million violent crimes p.a.
16.0 million property crimes p.a.
General crime rate 1 per 10 people p.a.
750 million criminals (12.4% of population)
975,000 murders a year
350,000 convicted murderers p.a. (5.8 per 100,000)
360 million robbers and burglars p.a.
11.7 million grand larceny cases p.a.
50 million urban gang members
70 million pornography readers/viewers/users
Pornography industry $25 billion p.a.
International terrorism incidents since 1979: 22,000
4,000 new terrorist incidents a year
White-collar crime $1.5 trillion p.a.
Shoplifting $100 billion p.a.
Major works of art: sales $58 billion p.a.
Thefts of major works of art: $29 billion p.a.
Credit card fraud $582 million p.a.
Computer crime $51 billion p.a.
Financial fraud $932 billion p.a.
3.4 million automobile thefts p.a.
Automobile thefts $23 billion p.a.
Total cost all varieties of crime $5.7 trillion p.a.

**DRUG TRAFFIC**
Illegal drug traffic $250 billion p.a.
Cocaine: $47 billion p.a.
Heroin: $5.8 billion p.a.
Narcotraffickers (persons employed in drug traffic): 46 million
World expenditure on cigarettes $338 billion p.a.
World expenditure on alcoholic drink $408 trillion p.a.
Costs of alcoholism p.a. $81 billion

**ENVIRONMENTAL ABUSE AND POLLUTION**
Desertification 210,000 sq km p.a.
165 sq km of arable land engulfed a day by deserts through mismanagement
33% of Earth's land surface in danger
Tropical forests shrink by 11 million hectares p.a.
45% all original forests now destroyed
50,000 acres (20,200 hectares, 202 sq km) of rain forest destroyed each day
110,000 sq km of forest/woodland lost p.a.

75,000 species of life destroyed p.a.
50% of world depend on biomass (firewood) for daily needs
Forests disappear at 2.5% per year
Soil erosion: 27 billion tons of topsoil lost from cropland p.a.
Pesticide use $19 billion p.a.
Waste: 1.6 billion tons a year (0.7 kg per capita per day)
Urban air pollutants: 2.5 million tons p.a.
70% of all surface water now polluted
Sea levels rise by 0.6 inches per year

**PSEUDO-RELIGION**
489 million Christian popular-religionists
500 million in New Age religions and cults
250 million non-Christian neofundamentalists
Ecclesiastical crime $16 billion p.a.
30 million witches

**POLITICAL REPRESSION**
150 nations commit human-rights violations
130 nations dishonor UN-defined human rights
80 nations responsible for extrajudicial killings
35 nations tolerating local or international murder squads/death squads
180 countries without full political rights for citizens (80% of world population, 1989)
250 riots (violent, spontaneous, over 1,000 persons) p.a.
10,893 violent riots, 1948-1977
60 countries with nuclear technology
70 regimes with brutal violence against citizens
238 political coups, 1948-1977
Secret security police forces in 100 countries
110 nations employing torture
50 states responsible for mass killings

**POLITICO-RELIGIOUS OPPOSITION**
Restricted-access countries: 86, with 3.0 billion population (50% of world)
43 closed countries (severely-restricted access)
18 partially-closed countries (highly-restricted access)
25 limited-access countries (partially-restricted access)

**EXPLOITATION OF WOMEN**
Women—
   number 49.6% of world
   form 37% of paid labor force
   head up 33% of all households
   make up 95% of all nurses
   perform 62% of work hours

   receive 10% of world's income
   own 1% of world's property
Unpaid labor: $5 trillion p.a.
2.5 million women raped a year
22 million female prostitutes
250 million battered women (23% all married women)
20 million more battered women each year
Women make up—
   70% of all poor
   66% of all illiterates
   80% of all refugees
   75% of all ill or sick
Social surgery: 100 million genitally-mutilated

**DEBT**
Third-World external debt (120 countries): $1.6 trillion (90% unrepayable debt)
Annual debt servicing $100 billion
25 highly-indebted countries
Third-World elites hold $1.5 trillion personally in Western banks
Corporate debt $1.7 trillion
291,300 business failures (collapses, bankruptcies) p.a.

**FINANCE**
Gross world product (global income, GWP): $28.9 trillion p.a., increasing at 4.0% p.a.
Money in use: annual increase 19% p.a.
Money and quasi-money: annual increase 20% p.a.
Central government revenues worldwide: 27% of gross domestic product
Richest 20% of world gets 74.2% of GWP
3,000,000 millionaires (each worth over $1 million)
75,000 multimillionaires
500 billionaires (each worth over $1 billion)
World population by income: 54% rich (9% affluent, 35% well off, 10% just coping), 46% poor (28% needy, 18% absolutely poor)
186 million bureaucrats
50 million Communist nomenklatura
Advertising $150 billion p.a.
Betting and gambling $815 billion p.a.
Wildlife products $5 billion p.a. (30% illegal)
Tax cheats skim $250 billion p.a.
Dirty money (underground money: undeclared, unrecorded, untaxed, illegal): 25% of all economic transactions and incomes
Money-laundering through banks: $1.5 trillion p.a. gray money, $300 billion p.a. black money
Total financial crime $3 trillion p.a.
Total cost of all organized "structures of sin" $9.25 trillion p.a. (32% of GWP)

## Global Diagram 20.  Today's technoglobe: the worlds of technology, research, industry, energy, communication, transportation, computers, and networks.

Science and technology have expanded exponentially from the Industrial Revolution in 1775 (steam power and coal) to the Technological or Second Industrial Revolution in 1901 (electrical and chemical industries), the Nuclear Age from 1945, the Superindustrial or Space Age from 1955, and the Information Revolution from 1988 on. The number of general-purpose digital computers (distinct CPUs) increased from 5,000 in 1960, to 90,000 in 1970, to 3 million in 1980, and to 93 million in 1990, and to 509 million by AD 2000. Other statistics below also refer to AD 2000.

One technological advance with enormous potential for good concerns electrical power distribution. Until 1969, transmission of electrical power was impossible further than 350 miles.  With new metals and ceramics, today's maximum is 4,000 miles. Recent breakthroughs in superconductivity offer the promise of unlimited transmission distances in the near future. The illustration below shows the single one-world proposed global electrical energy grid now being developed.

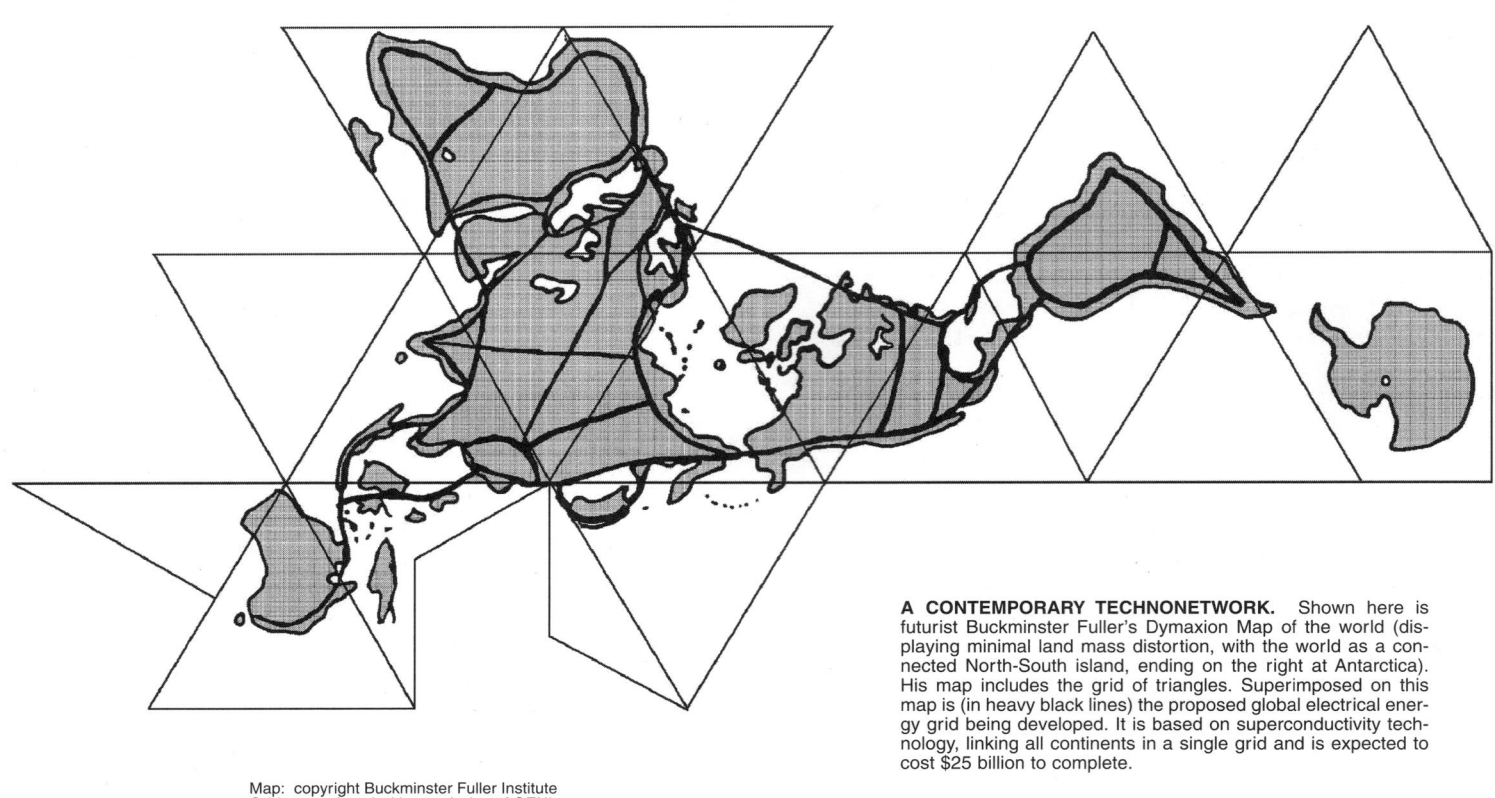

**A CONTEMPORARY TECHNONETWORK.**  Shown here is futurist Buckminster Fuller's Dymaxion Map of the world (displaying minimal land mass distortion, with the world as a connected North-South island, ending on the right at Antarctica). His map includes the grid of triangles. Superimposed on this map is (in heavy black lines) the proposed global electrical energy grid being developed. It is based on superconductivity technology, linking all continents in a single grid and is expected to cost $25 billion to complete.

Map: copyright Buckminster Fuller Institute
Grid: reproduced with permission of GENI

## INDUSTRIALIZATION
World industrial growth 1.9% p.a.
2.6 billion economically active persons
2.1 billion labor force (3.1% unemployed)
Labor force growth 1.9% p.a.
Women form 37% of labor force
Research & development (R&D) $650 billion p.a.
Scientific research $140 billion p.a.
40 million scientists and engineers
5 million scientists and engineers in R&D
1.2 million pure scientists
Paper: 200 million metric tons produced p.a.
5 million police officers
2.3 million professional firefighters
6.5 million lawyers (advocates, solicitors)
25 million industrial robots
Chemicals: 8.1 million known (10,000 new ones p.a.)
Chemicals newly on market each year: 1,700

## ENERGY
Primary energy 8 billion metric tons oil equivalent
World primary energy production 3,600,000 trillion quads BTU
Consumption 2,000 kg (coal) per person
Electricity production $11 trillion kwh (1,817 per capita)
Growth of electricity production 3.2% p.a.
25 countries producing nuclear energy
400 nuclear power plants (700 billion kwh)
3,200 oil tankers afloat
Oil production: 55 million barrels a day (20% via OPEC)
Natural gas: 86 trillion cubic meters proved reserves
Energy consumed by humans as % total available on Earth p.a.: 40%

## COMMUNICATION
6,170 daily newspapers
Newspaper circulation 509 million (84 per 1000)
30 million metric tons of newsprint p.a.
12 lbs newsprint consumed per inhabitant p.a.
Mail: 350 billion pieces p.a.
Domestic mail per capita 50 letters p.a.
Foreign mail per capita 20 letters p.a.
20 billion electronic-mail messages a year
715 million telephones (118 per 1000)
Direct-dial telephones: 679 million (95% of all phones)
Telephone calls made each day: 550 million
200 billion telephone calls made p.a.
1.4 million telex terminals
60 million fax/telefax (facsimile) machines
2.08 billion radio sets in use (343 per 1000)
1.34 billion TV sets (222 per 1000)
35,000 radio transmitters
75,000 regular TV transmitters
600 million VCRs (videocassette recorders)
40 billion videocassettes rented p.a.
4,000 artificial Earth satellites in orbit
290,000 cinemas
3,500 drive-in cinemas
35,000 mobile cinemas
85 million cinema seats
17 billion annual cinema attendance
4,500 full-length films produced
$150 billion spent on all advertising
23,000 museums
1.3 billion museum visitors a year
33,000 theaters for performing arts
1.6 million theater performances a year

## TRANSPORTATION
Roads: 25 million km
932 million bicycles (154 per 1000)
134 million commercial vehicles (22 per 1000)
435 million passenger cars (72 per 1000)
35 million new cars produced each year
Railway trackage: 1,631,280 km
2.0 trillion rail passenger-km
Rail freight: 8.4 trillion ton-km
Air traffic: 1.6 trillion passenger-km
Civil air distance flown: 12 billion km
46 billion air cargo ton-km
65,000 airports and airfields
Sea traffic: 67,300 registered merchant ships
4.0 billion tonnes per year by sea

## COMPUTERS AND NETWORKS
509 million general-purpose computers:
   1,000 supercomputers
   25,000 mainframes
   6,000,000 minicomputers
   503 million microcomputers (100 million with modems)
600 million screens/terminals
Computer sales 100 million a year:
   200 supercomputers p.a.
   2,000 mainframes p.a.
   500,000 minicomputers p.a.
   99.5 million microcomputers p.a.
Value of annual computers sold: $300 billion
Computer power: world total 4 trillion instructions per second
Supercomputer installations: $15 billion
Researchers with access to supercomputers: 1 million
150,000 electronic bulletin boards (BSS) begun since 1983, only 10,000 still active
Internet users: 277 million

## Global Diagram 21.   Urban and rural worlds: the rise of 402 megacities, 60 supercities, and 20 supergiants, among 5,000 metropolises, AD 2000.

Two hundred years ago, the world was almost entirely a rural planet. Only one megacity existed—Peking with 1,100,000 inhabitants. Since then, massive urbanization has occurred, as documented below. We now have a planet of megacities. Also, sad to relate, it has become a planet of slums.

Several of the statistics below may at first strike the reader as irrelevant. In all cases there are solid reasons for including them. Thirty billion rats are recorded here because (a) rats

have killed over a billion people since AD 33, (b) they eat or destroy 25% of the world's food today (thereby contributing to keeping 500 million persons on the verge of starvation), and (c) they plague countries (4 billion rats in India) but especially megacities (3 million rats in Boston, 15 million in Rome, 40 million in New York City).

And if statistics of pigs seem irrelevant, reflect on the fact that, for the most part, the heartland of Islam across the world

stops where forest cultures make pig-breeding viable.

All statistics after the initial historical overview refer to the Decade of Evangelism, 1990-2000. After this year, the next 100 years is explored here in Global Diagram 54.

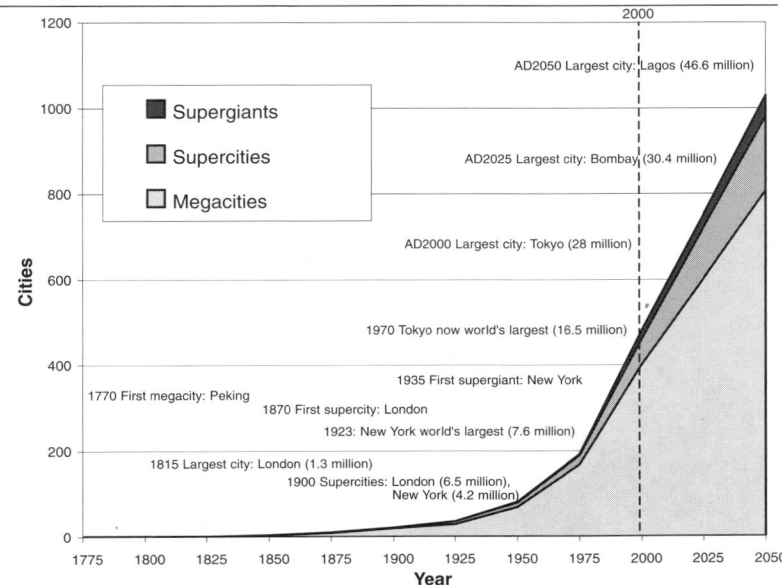

### MEGALOPOLIS 2000
5,080 metropolises over 50,000
756 urban agglomerations (over 500,000)
402 megacities (over 1 million)
60 supercities (over 4 million)
20 supergiants (cities over 10 million)

### THE WORLD'S LARGEST CITIES, AD 1770-2050
1770: First megacity, Peking
1815: Largest city, London (1.3 million)
1870: First supercity, London (4 million)
1900: Supercities: London (6.5 million)
          New York (4.2 million)

1923: World's largest, New York (7.6 million)
1935: First supergiant, New York
1970: World's largest, Tokyo
2025: World's largest, Bombay
2050: World's largest, Lagos

### HISTORICAL OVERVIEW, 1770-2000
AD 1770: first modern megacity (Peking)
AD 1800: 50 million urbanites (5.9% of world); 1 megacity (Peking)
AD 1900: 233 million urbanites (14.4%); 20 megacities
AD 2000: 2,882 million urbanites (47.6%); 402 megacities

### THE URBAN/RURAL GLOBE IN AD 2000
6,055 million persons
3.17 billion rural dwellers (52.4%)
2.88 billion urban dwellers (urbanites)(47.6%)
2.03 billion metrodwellers (city-dwellers)
1.89 billion city dwellers, cities over 100,000
849 million nonmetro urbanites
69.5 million new urbanites a year
190,000 new urbanites a day
100,000 rural poor migrate to cities each day
Urban growth rate 1.9% p.a.
Rural growth rate 0.3% p.a.
1.4 billion urban poor

### CITIES (BY POPULATION)
50,000 cities over 10,000
5,080 metropolises over 50,000
3,180 metropolises over 100,000
756 agglomerations over 500,000
402 megacities (over 1 million)
60 supercities (over 4 million)
20 supergiants (cities over 10 million)
3 Islamic supergiants
28 anti-Christian megacities
226 non-Christian megacities
129,000 new non-Christian city-dwellers a day
Slums:  25% of all metropolitan areas

### AGRICULTURE
Agricultural land:  12.9 million sq km (8.5% of all land)
Forest land:  37.4 million sq km (24.7% of all land)
Harvested land: 77% of all arable land
Under permanent crops: 11% of global land surface
Irrigation: 70% of global water use
49% of labor force work in agriculture
Agricultural production growth 2.8% p.a.
23 million tractors in use
Pesticide use $19 billion p.a.
Global agricultural research $10.5 billion p.a.

### URBAN CHRISTIANS IN AD 2000
1,160 million Christian urbanites (58% of all Christians)

### LIVESTOCK
Investment in domestic livestock $450 billion
1.5 billion cattle
1.2 billion sheep
10 billion chickens
936 million pigs
576 million goats
139 million horses, mules, asses
178 million buffaloes and camels
1.2 billion domestic pets
30 billion rats (25% urban, 75% rural)
Rats eat or destroy 25% of world's food p.a.
Total food and property destroyed by rats: $400 billion p.a.
Cases of bubonic plague since 1980: 400,000
Fish catches: 106 million metric tons p.a.

### HOUSEHOLDS AND FAMILIES
1.43 billion households (families, homes, dwellings)
1.3 billion self-built dwellings (97% of total)
38 million new families p.a.
4.22 persons per household
39 million legal marriages p.a.
1.8 billion married persons
990 million married women
1.5 billion unmarried persons living together
9.3 million divorces p.a.
86 million divorcees (divorced persons)
750 million singles (unmarrieds)
93 million homosexuals
175 million bisexual men
35 million lesbians
200 million gays (gay preference)
1.69 billion women of child-bearing age
60% of women use contraceptives
233 million bereaved each year
419 million senior citizens (over 65 years)
280 million widows
60 million widowers
Fertility rate: 2.64 births per childbearing woman
43.15 live births per 1000 females p.a.
124 million births a year (15% being illegitimate)
3.5 million adoptions a year
76 million abortions p.a. (38% illegal)

### TRANSIENTS
230 million pastoralists (nomads) on rangelands
6.6 million unassimilated gypsies
11 million seamen (merchant seafarers)
30 million resident labor migrants
120 million seasonal labor migrants

### EDUCATION
3.6 million primary schools
700,000 secondary/high schools
1 billion pupils in school (60% of all eligible)
45 million teachers
School-age population per teacher: 38
Student enrollment: first level 95%, second 46%, third 12%
Education costs $1 trillion (3.5% of GWP) p.a.
Education costs: $1,000 per school-age child, p.a.
Education costs per capita p.a.:  $165
22,000 university campuses (3,500 major)
70 million college students (45% women)
175 million college graduates
4 million university teachers
2 million foreign students
Primary education: completed by 1.4 billion adults
Primary education: not completed by 2.8 billion adults

### HEALTH
248,000 hospitals
18.8 million hospital beds (1 per 322)
7.5 million physicians (1 per 807)
12 million nurses and midwives (1 per 505)
570,000 dentists (1 per 10,623)
World pharmaceutical market $200 billion p.a.
600,000 pharmacists
175,000 mental institutions
Health costs $1.45 trillion (5.0% of GWP) p.a.
Public health expenditures per capita $239 p.a.

### TOURISM
450 million foreign tourists p.a.
4 billion domestic tourists p.a.
16 million registered hotel beds
300 million religious pilgrims on move every year

### TRADE
Gross world product (global income) $28.9 trillion p.a.
World imports $2,700 billion p.a.
World exports $2,500 billion p.a.
Balance of trade $116 billion p.a.
External debt of developing countries $908 billion
World economic aid for developing countries $38.5 billion
Foreign economic aid $60 billion (0.2% of GWP) p.a.
Foreign economic aid per capita $10 p.a.
Average income per person $4,770 p.a.
Average family income $20,200 p.a.
300 million Visa cardholders worldwide

**Global Diagram 22.     A world geopolitico-ethnolinguistic classification segmentizing the kaleidoscopic human mosaic: over 18 million homogeneous segments including nations, countries, languages, cultures, races, peoples, sociopeoples, & metropeoples.**

This is initially a secular diagram without Christian data or categories superimposed. (For the latter, see Global Diagram 24 et alia.) Here, we describe how secular analysts (scholars, academics, United Nations agencies, et alia) have segmentized the one world of mankind. The Christian world needs to understand all this before it can plan and implement its own world mission.

Secular analysts use 4 main approaches, set out in columns 1-4 below. These in turn are divided vertically with some 17 progressively smaller units which are roughly parallel horizontally. All these segments can be, and have been, enumerated and quantified. Note also that the prefix 'mega' is used below to denote, not a separate category of segment but any segment with over 1 million population (thus megapeople, megaculture, megalanguage, megacity, mega-unit, et alia). Thus a macropeople is not necessarily a megapeople nor vice versa.

*Key. Column 1.* **Geopolitics.** In the main this is UN terminology and practice, dividing the world into exactly-quantified statistical categories over the period AD 1950-2050.
*Column 2.* **Language.** Based on terminology used by linguists to classify the world's 13,500 languages.
*Column 3.* **Culture.** Terminology developed by cultural anthropologists, HRAF, et alia, as exemplified in this Volume's World Ethnolinguistic Classification.
*Column 4.* **Race, color, ethnicity.** Terminology developed in New Encyclopaedia Britannica, UN, WCE, et alia.
*Column 5.* **Segments.** Lastly, this column answers the question: What shorthand terms could the Christian world mission standardize on to describe the progressively smaller population segments involved in each level of this schema?

*Christian commentary on this schema.* The human race is portrayed throughout the Bible as God's harvest field in which Israel in the Old Testament and the New Israel in the New are God's harvesters or harvest force. The harvest field is an enormous mosaic of vast diversity. Dividing this mosaic into segments is somewhat artificial but is essential in order to comprehend and enumerate this vast complexity and to prop-

erly appreciate its kaleidoscopic nature, also in order to focus ministry and develop mission strategies or tactics which are appropriate and effectual. The first known enumeration of the world by segments is The Table of Nations in Genesis 10 where 70 peoples (72 in the Septuagint) are enumerated.

Note that the biblical Greek word *ethnos* (plural *ethne*) cannot be said to refer only to one single type or category of population today. Instead, it is best translated 'segment'. *Ethnos* refers to each and every type of segment (or homogeneous subdivision) of the one species Homo Sapiens, mankind. Likewise, 'segment' in English can apply to each and every type of subdivision.

Names in bold type below are the major recommended usages developed here and supported by detailed listings in the World Evangelization Database as published in the *World Christian database*. Names not in bold type are alternates or less widely-used terms.

**a.**

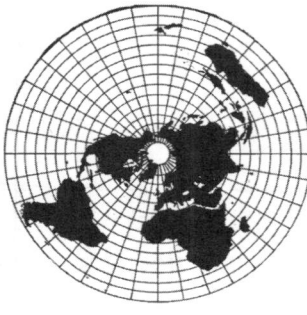
**b.**

**c.**

**HOW 3 LOGOS SEGMENTIZE THE GLOBE** (from left to right):

a.  The United Nations' logo shown at left depicts the globe for whose peace and safety it is responsible, shown segmented into 33 segments or zones when viewed from geostationary orbit above the North Pole. The UN's range of varieties of segmentation is listed in the first column below.

b.  The middle logo, of the State University of New York, depicts the world in 505 segments.

c.  (Right) From the Christian point of view, segmentizing the world helps Christians and churches to understand its multitudinous needs and therefore how to support, assist, and pray for the world's kaleidoscopic populations.  (A logo of SBC Foreign Mission Board, 1980).

| GEOPOLITICS 1 | LANGUAGE 2 | CULTURE 3 | RACE, COLOR, ETHNICITY 4 | SEGMENTS 5 |
|---|---|---|---|---|
| 1 **globe** | speech | mankind (Homo Sapiens) | 1 species, human race | SPECIES |
| 2 **developed worlds:** more/less; North/South; rich/poor | 2 categories: literate/illiterate | 2 worlds: civilized/uncivilized | 2 worlds: White/Non-White (or Black/Non-Black, etc.) | DICHOTOMIES |
| 3 **political worlds** | 5 macrophyla | 20 civilizations (culture races) | 5 major **races** (macroraces) | RACES |
| 3 **megacontinents** | 10 **macrozones** | 20 culture zones (major culture areas) | 13 **geographic races** (megaraces) | MACROZONES |
| 7 **continents** 7 **macro regions** (continental areas) | 24 phyla (stocks) | 17 culture worlds (lifestyles, worldviews) | 4 subraces | CONTINENTS |
|  |  |  | 7 stylized **colors** (biogenetic pools) | COLORZONES |
| 21 **regions** | 100 **zones** (glossozones) | 71 **culture areas** (culture provinces) | 71 local races (local breeding populations) | LOCALRACES |
| 195 **nations** 238 **countries** | 680 **language sets** (branches) | 395 **ethnocultural families** (culture clusters) | 395 microraces (ethnic families) | MICRORACES |
| 3,030 **provinces** (major civil divisions) | 1,400 language chains 2,690 **language nets** 4,960 **language clusters** 13,510 **languages** | 6,629 **cultures** (societies, culture units) 12,000 ethnocultural peoples | 432 **macropeoples** (major peoples or subfamilies) 12,600 **peoples** (ethnolinguistic peoples), 550 being megapeoples | MACROPEOPLES PEOPLES |
| 20,000 **districts** (counties) 1 million administrative units | 30,000 **dialects** 6,500 audio languages | 24,000 minicultures (Kulturkreis) 250,000 microcultures (clans, culture complexes) | 60,000 **minipeoples** (people groups, tribes, unimax groups) 250,000 **micropeoples** | MINIPEOPLES MICROPEOPLES |
| 402 megacities | 380 **megalanguages** | megalocultures | 402 **megacities,** 60 **supercities,** 20 **supergiants** 3,180 **metropolises** over 100,000 5,080 **metropolises** over 50,000 | MEGALOPOLISES METROPOLISES |
| 50,000 cities over 10,000 | 2,000 **trade languages** 2,000 vehicular languages | urbanocultures | 100,000 **urban people groups** 100,000 variant ethnic names | METROPEOPLES ETHNOVARIANTS |
| 5 million specialist groups | 983 **lingua francas** (each with over 100,000 non-native speakers) 1,000 literary languages 70 international languages 180 computer languages | metrocultures |  |  |
| 10 million villages 1.43 billion families (homes) | 100,000 sociolects | sociocultures | 2,000,000 sociopeoples (social people groups/subgroups, castes, occupations, age-groups, sociopolitico-religious or socioeconomic groups, bridge peoples) | SOCIOPEOPLES |

**Global Diagram 23.** **Today's geopolitico-religious blocs: 3 worlds, 3 megacontinents, 7 continents, 9 macro regions, 21 regions, 195 nations, 238 countries, 3,000 provinces, with the globe's 33 major religious and antireligious blocs.**

The statistics below enumerate the main varieties of political and religious segmentation of the world's population in use today. The various basic segments listed here can be grouped or regrouped in different ways depending on one's requirements. The pie chart shows the world's major religious blocs or segments. All figures relate to the year AD 2000.

Indented categories are part of (included in) preceding unindented categories. Figures in parentheses with a % sign are in all cases annual change (% increase p.a., per year).

## THE GLOBE IN MID-2000
6.06 billion persons
  12% in First (Western) world
  33% in Second (Communist-related) world
  55% in Third (Nonaligned) World
71 million more people a year (1.2% p.a.)
Land area: 148.9 million sq km

## WORLDS
DEVELOPMENT
More developed countries: 60
Less developed countries: 130
1.2 billion in more developed countries
4.2 billion in less developed countries
Least developed countries (LDCs): 48
642 million in least developed countries
GEOPOLITICAL WORLDS
Western world: 35 countries
Communist world: 30 countries
Third World: 173 countries
RELIGIOUS WORLDS
World A (unevangelized): 38 countries
World B (evangelized, non-Christian): 59 countries
World C (Christian): 141 countries

## CONTINENTS AND REGIONS
3 megacontinents
7 continents
9 macro regions (continental areas)

21 regions

## COUNTRIES
238 countries in world (3 under 1,000 population, 235 over)
195 sovereign nations (185 being UN members, including observer states)
43 nonsovereign countries (dependencies)
GOVERNMENT
82 multiparty democratic states
50 one-party states (30 Marxist)
35 military regimes
40 autocracies/dictatorships
39 dependencies/colonies (9.6 million population)
IDEOLOGY (1989)
113 religious countries
102 secular countries
30 atheistic countries
FREEDOM OR REPRESSION (adherence to UN Universal Declaration on Human Rights)
79 politically free countries
87 partially politically free
85 politically not free

## ASSOCIATIONS OF COUNTRIES
(number of member countries in each)
UN 185, FAO 170, GATT 125, IAEA 121, IBRD 177, ICAO 180, IDA 177, IFAD 142, IFC 161, ILO 168, IMF 179, IMO 149, ITU 166, UNESCO 179, UNIDO 180, UPU 189,

WHO 189, WIPO 151, WMO 172 WTO 125.

## PROVINCES
3,030 major civil divisions (MCDs)
MULTINATIONALS
11,500 transnational corporations (TNCs)
5,000 TNCs in association in Global T-Net
500 supranationals or intergovernmental organizations (IGOs)
4,000 international nongovernmental organizations (NGOs)
International electronic fund transfers $20 billion a day
International foreign exchange transactions p.a. $120 trillion
100 million internationals (persons living abroad)

## WORLD COMMUNISM
*Situation in mid-1989:*
122 Communist, Leninist, or Marxist parties (in 130 countries)
88.7 million Communist party members
16 Communist-ruled (Leninist) states (with 83 million party members)
30 Marxist-ruled (including Communist-ruled) states
12 international Communist front organizations, with 1,400 affiliates (agencies)
1.7 billion persons under Marxist regimes

## SITUATION IN MID-2000
Communism: collapsed in USSR and Eastern Europe, but still strong in China and Southeast Asia.

**RELIGION** (8,400 religions, analyzable into 33 major religious and antireligious blocs)

## ADHERENCE TO RELIGION IN AD 2000
5.14 billion religionists (all religions) (annual increase 1.5% p.a.)
  2.5 billion popular-religionists
  500 million New Age/occult/neo-Hindu cultists
  838 million Christian popular-religionist-pietists
  80 million parareligionists, including 5.9 million Freemasons (males)
  918 million nonreligionists (0.7% p.a.)
  768 million nonreligious (0.8% p.a.)
  150 million atheists (0.3% p.a.)

## ADHERENTS OF NON-CHRISTIAN RELIGIONS
3.2 billion non-Christian religionists (annual increase 1.6% p.a.)
GREAT WORLD RELIGIONS
1.2 billion Muslims (2.1% p.a.)
  1 billion Sunnis (2.1% p.a.)
  170 million Shias (Shiites) (2.3% p.a.)
  23.8 million Ismailis (2.7% p.a.)
  7.95 million Ahmadis (3.3% p.a.)
811.3 million Hindus (1.7% p.a.)
  550 million Vaishnavites (1.7% p.a.)
  216 million Shaivites (1.7% p.a.)
  26 million Saktists (1.7% p.a.)
  17 million Neo-Hindus (2.7% p.a.)
  4 million Reform Hindus (1.8% p.a.)
360 million Buddhists (1.1% p.a.)
  202 million Mahayana (1.1% p.a.)
  136 million Theravada (1.1% p.a.)
  21 million Tantrayana (Lamaists) (1.1% p.a.)
OTHER MAJOR RELIGIONS
228.4 million Ethnoreligionists (1.3% p.a.)
384.8 million Chinese folk-religionists (1.0% p.a.)
102.4 million Asian New-Religionists (1.0% p.a.)
MINOR RELIGIONS
14.4 million Jews (0.9% p.a.)
  11.1 million Ashkenazis (0.9% p.a.)
  2.4 million Oriental Jews (0.9% p.a.)
  952,000 Sefardis (0.9% p.a.)
  24,000 Karaites (0.9% p.a.)
23.3 million Sikhs (1.9% p.a.)
12.3 million non-Christian Spiritists (2.0% p.a.)
7.1 million Baha'is (2.3% p.a.)
2.8 million Shintoists (-1.1% p.a.)
4.2 million Jains (0.9% p.a.)

## CHRISTIANS AND NON-CHRISTIANS
2,000 million Christians (1.4% p.a.)
4,055 billion non-Christians (1.5% p.a.)

918 million nonreligionists (nonreligious and atheists) 15.2% of world
150 million atheists 2.5%
religionists under 25 million *including:* 14 million Jews, 23 million Sikhs, 7 million Baha'is
102 million New-Religionists 1.7%
768 million nonreligious 12.7%
228 million ethno-religionists 3.8%
360 million Buddhists 5.9%
385 million Chinese folk-religionists 6.4%
2,000 million Christians 33.0%
811 million Hindus 13.4%
1,188 million Muslims 19.6%
5,137 million religionists (all religions) 84.8% of world

## Global Diagram 24. Today's resources for world mission: churches, workers, institutions, agencies, media, literature, radio/TV, money, computers, networks, plans.

This table enumerates below the entire extent of global Christian resources of all kinds. Several of these are then shown at lower right as they are utilized today, divided among the 3 worlds, A, B, and C. These should be added to the other resources shown, similarly divided, in the other global diagrams.

Our final fully-developed logo for this series (shown on Global Diagram 44) shows the many rivers of these resources (4,000 Great Commission networks) streaming across the Earth as a de facto, single, global evangelization movement.

The present situation is however that the vast bulk of these resources benefit only the Christian world. Even in foreign missions, 85% of personnel and money are devoted to Christian lands, such as missionaries from USA to Brazil or Kenya or the Philippines (see inner ellipse in globe at bottom).

It is obvious that all segments of the Earth have a right to their fair share of resources of all kinds. The least that Christians can do is to ensure that the resources which are under their own direct control—the spiritual resources catalogued below—get properly shared with all. To redress the

present situation Christians will need to concentrate on World A far more, hence it is shown shaded gray and its segments are shown in bold on the large globe at lower left. The faint lines of the other 2 Worlds B and C suggest the far less significant share of global resources that these worlds should now be deliberately restricted to. The 2 long thin arrows on either side rising upward then show the new directions in which these ample resources need to be redirected or redeployed.

### THE GLOBE
6.1 billion persons

### GLOBAL CHRISTIAN RESOURCES
CHRISTIAN PERSONS
2,000 million Christians (99.8% laypersons)
1.88 billion professing Christians
124 million crypto-Christians (6.2% of all Christians)
111 million unaffiliated Christians (5.5% of all Christians)
1.89 billion affiliated Christians (church members)
565 million Christian children under 15
192 million Christian infants under 5
1.16 billion urban Christians (40.3% of all urbanites)
1.29 billion literate adult Christians
648 million practicing Christians
600 million weekly-worshipping Christians
1.5 billion Christian regulars for Christian radio/TV
1,883 million laypersons (99.8% of all church members)
40 million laypersons (lay Christians) residing abroad
150 million Christian pilgrims on move every year
250 million Christian foreign tourists a year
3.3 billion Christian domestic tourists a year
INTERCESSION
50 worldwide intercessory networks (35 active)
25 million in full-time prayer ministry
15 million weekly prayer groups
200 million praying daily for world mission
2,400 religious institutes (orders, societies for the full-time religious life centered on prayer)
8,000 monasteries, ashrams, convents, abbeys, priories
ORGANIZATIONS
3.45 million worship centers (local churches)
33,800 distinct denominations
6,500 major councils of churches
4,000 foreign mission boards or societies
5,800 home mission boards, agencies, or societies
400 medical missions (foreign mission agencies)
23,000 parachurch or service agencies
400,000 base ecclesial communities (BECs)
INSTITUTIONS
105,000 major Christian/church-related institutions
376,000 minor Christian institutions
170,000 Christian primary/elementary schools
50,000 Christian secondary/high schools

400 million pupils
1,500 Christian universities and colleges
4,800 seminaries/theological colleges
5,500 Christian hospitals
30,000 Christian medical centers
55 million medical consultations a year (in Christian centers)
2,000 Christian-owned presses and publishers
400 ecumenical centers
300 church-related research centers
FINANCE
Christians by income: 58% rich (11% affluent, 37% well off, 10% just coping), 42% poor (29% needy, 13% absolutely poor)
Church of the Rich: 1.1 billion members
Church of the Affluent: 208 million members
Church of the Poor: 793 million members
Church of the Absolutely Poor: 245 million members
Personal income of Christians (church members) $15.2 trillion p.a.
Personal income per capita of Christians, $8,050
Average Christian family income $34,000
Stewardship: giving per church member per week $2.75
Church/agency income $270 billion a year
Churches' income $108 billion p.a.
Parachurch/institutional income $162 billion p.a.
$8 billion a year on new religious buildings (Christian)
Foreign missions giving per church member per week $0.15
Foreign missions $15 billion a year
Christian broadcasting (radio/TV) $5.8 billion p.a.
FULL-TIME PERSONNEL
1.1 million ordained clergy, ministers, pastors, priests (8% women)
5.52 million full-time Christian workers (60% women; 93% citizens)
3.31 million full-time women workers
80,000 ordained women clergy/ministers
500,000 monks including friars
1,300,000 nuns (sisters)
1.2 million professional theologians
20,000 professional missiologists
18 million Christian schoolteachers
1.1 million seminarians
40 million Christian students
300,000 TEE extension students in 120 countries
419,500 foreign missionaries

5,360 foreign missionaries from Third-World countries
1,135,000 home missionaries
5.10 million national (citizen) workers
400,000 short-term foreign missionaries
LITERATURE AND PRINT MEDIA
26,100 new Christian book titles a year
116 million copies of new Christian books printed p.a.
12,800 books/articles on mission a year
110,000 new scholarly research books on Christian faith p.a.
12,000 major religious (Christian) libraries
34,500 religious (Christian) periodicals
53.7 million Bibles distributed a year
120.7 million New Testaments a year
4,600 million scriptures (all varieties) distributed p.a.
3 billion Christian books printed p.a.
5 billion Christian tracts a year
ELECTRONIC MEDIA AND AUDIOVISUALS
4,000 Christian radio/TV stations
1,050 national/international Christian broadcasting agencies
120,000 full-time personnel in Christian broadcasting
3 billion live viewers of "Jesus" and other Christian films
MASS EVANGELISM
3,000 evangelistic mass campaigns a year
1,600 metropolises each year hold citywide evangelistic campaigns
COMPUTERS
332 million Christian-owned computers (worth $1.5 trillion)
350 million Christian-owned screens/terminals
250,000 new Christian-owned computers a day
14 million MIPS new Christian-purchased computer power a day
5 million electronic mail systems (95% secular)
10,000 secular commercial databases
10,000 secular electronic bulletin boards (BBS) active
400 million Christian computer users
100 million Christian computer professionals
NETWORKS AND GLOBAL PLANS
5,000 Great Commission computerized networks
100 Great Commission global networks
9 Great Commission global meganetworks
845 current global plans
260 current global plans making progress
210 global megaplans
57 global gigaplans
Plan expenditures $60 billion

## Worlds:

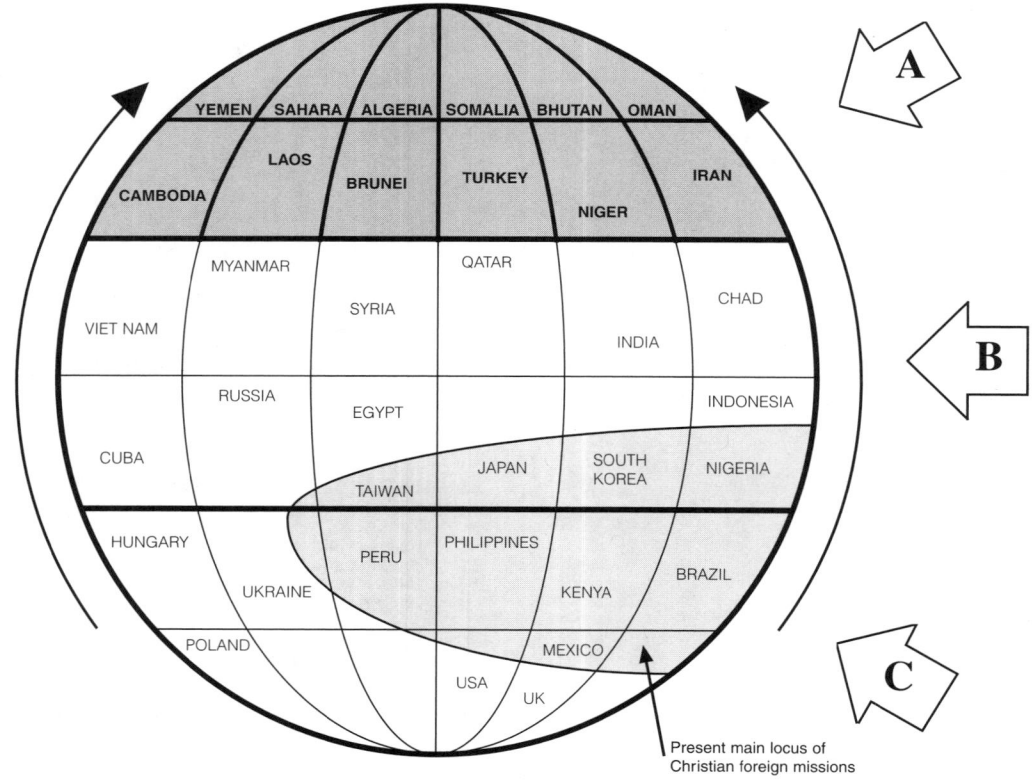

HORIZONTAL SCALE:                Geopolitical ideology

WORLDS     Communist/Ex-communist world        Western world          Third World
                    (Left inside)                         (Center)               (Right inside)

VERTICAL SCALE: Evangelization in Worlds A,B,C

**A. THE UNEVANGELIZED WORLD**
Present cost of Christian foreign missions:
$250 million a year
26 restricted-access (closed) countries
10,200 foreign missionaries (2.4%)
No citywide evangelistic campaigns
20,500 full-time Christian workers
50,000 lay Christians residing abroad in closed countries
0.1% of all Christian literature
0.1% of all Christian radio/TV

**B. THE EVANGELIZED NON-CHRISTIAN WORLD**
Per capita income of non-Christians: $3,380 p.a.
Present cost of Christian foreign missions:
$1,750 million a year
103,000 foreign missionaries (24.5%), 5,000 being in 31 restricted-access countries
300 cities per year have citywide evangelistic campaigns
1.31 million full-time Christian workers, 330,000 being in 31 restricted-access countries
8.9% of all Christian literature
3.9% of all Christian radio/TV

**C. THE CHRISTIAN WORLD**
Present cost of home Christianity: $163 billion a year
Foreign missions to other Christian lands:
$13 billion a year
306,000 foreign missionaries to other Christian lands (73.1%), 4,000 being in 29 restricted-access countries
1,300 cities per year have citywide evangelistic campaigns
4.19 million full-time Christian workers (95%) work in World C, including 480,000 in 29 restricted-access countries
500 million lay Christians live in 29 restricted-access heavily-Christian countries
91% of all Christian literature is consumed by World C
96% of all Christian radio/TV output is directed at World C

**Global Diagram 25.   Ethnolinguistics: integrating the globe's races, cultures, peoples. languages, and lingua francas.**

The 3 globes here illustrate the populations of our globe classified by 4 different principles (as elaborated in Part 18):

RACE and CULTURE
1. **Ethnocultural families** (below) show the 5 races of humankind with their 395 ethnocultural families and 6,629 distinct cultures (Table C, also A).

LANGUAGE
2. **Languages of the world** (at right) are here listed at 13,509, arranged within 4,962 language clusters (also called outer languages). For a larger diagram and explanation, see Global Diagram 26.

LINGUA FRANCA
3. **Lingua francas** (third globe, below) are vast in number — 376 lingua francas of the outer language (cluster) variety each with over 100,000 non-native speakers (in addition to their own native or mother tongue speakers. See Table B below, also Table 18–8 for fullest details). The world is only now just beginning to realize the enormous communication power of lingua francas via broadcasting and the Internet. For a larger diagram, explanation and enumeration, see Global Diagram 27.

PEOPLE
4. **Peoples of the world** is an end-product category which utilizes the 3 approaches just described and illustrated on the 3 globes. 'Peoples' actually are here more fully termed 'ethnolinguistic peoples'. A people is defined as that part of a culture confined to one single country, with a specific language as mother tongue.

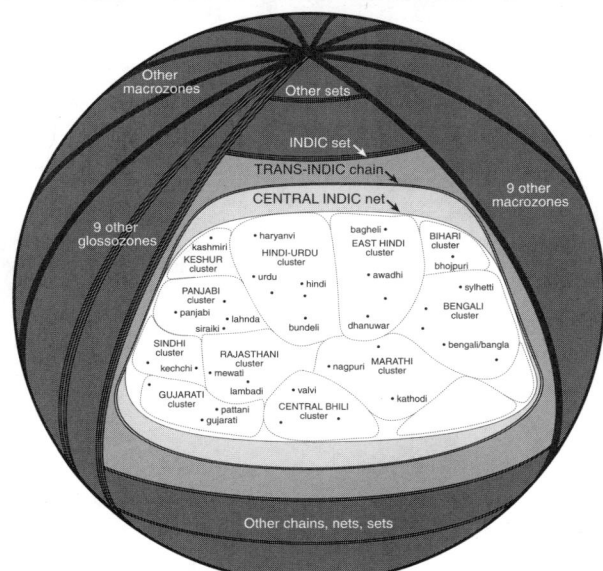

## ETHNOCULTURAL FAMILIES

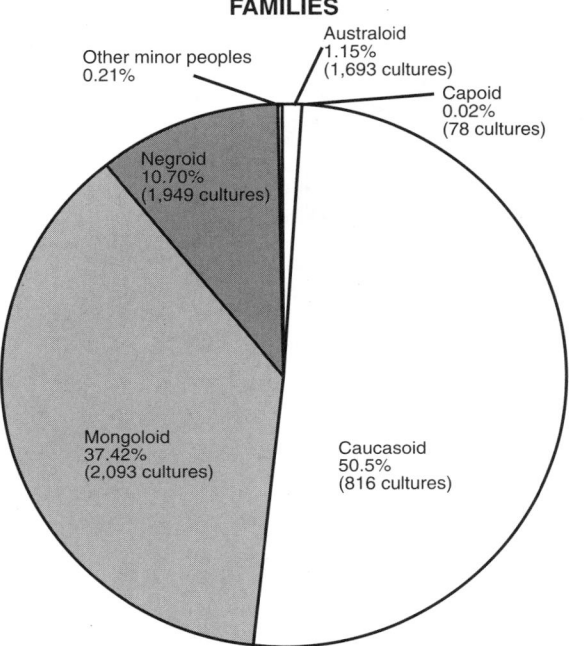

Other minor peoples 0.21%

Australoid 1.15% (1,693 cultures)

Capoid 0.02% (78 cultures)

Negroid 10.70% (1,949 cultures)

Mongoloid 37.42% (2,093 cultures)

Caucasoid 50.5% (816 cultures)

## LANGUAGES

## LINGUA FRANCAS

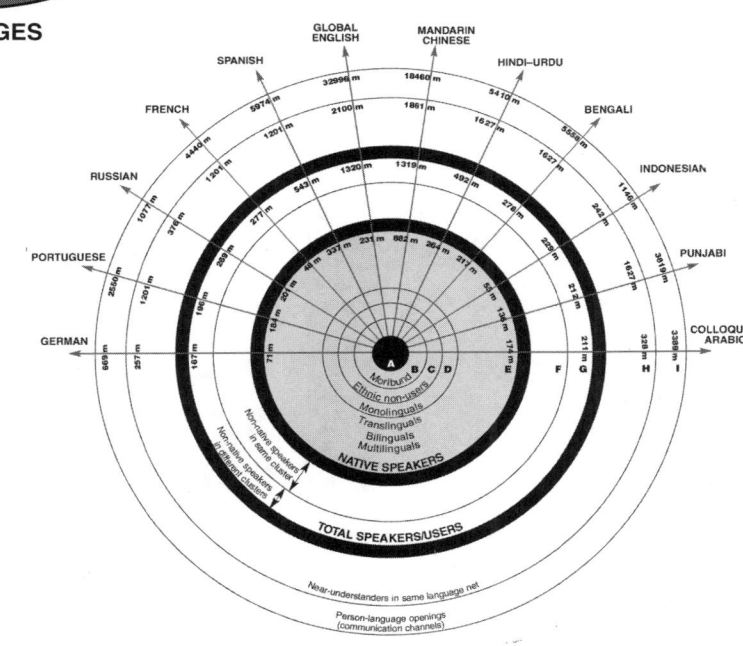

Table A. The globe classified by 11 people sizes.

| Size of people | Peoples | Population |
|---|---|---|
| 1 | 2 | 3 |
| Over 10 million | 101 | 4,014,806,000 |
| 1 million - 10 million | 453 | 1,307,746,000 |
| 500,000 - 1 million | 337 | 235,524,000 |
| 100,000 - 500,000 | 1,511 | 338,252,000 |
| 50,000 - 100,000 | 992 | 69,721,000 |
| 10,000 - 50,000 | 3,018 | 71,086,000 |
| 1,000 - 10,000 | 4,100 | 17,019,000 |
| 100 - 1,000 | 1,788 | 884,000 |
| under 100 | 232 | 10,800 |
| Zero | 51 | 0 |
| **Totals** | **12,583** | **6,055,048,800** |

Table B. The globe's lingua francas (column 2) ranked by each's category of non-native speakers (columns 1, 5).

| Non-native | Langs | Peoples | Native | Non-native | Total speakers Total | T/M | Christians | AC% |
|---|---|---|---|---|---|---|---|---|
| 1 | 2 | 3 | 4 | 5 | 6 | 7 | 8 | 9 |
| Over 10 million | 52 | 2,952 | 4,390,010,820 | 3,878,148,590 | 8,268,159,410 | 1.88 | 2,370,808,118 | 28.7 |
| 1 million - 10 million | 119 | 2,139 | 1,213,154,082 | 397,029,011 | 1,610,183,093 | 1.33 | 716,621,563 | 44.5 |
| 500,000 - 1 million | 46 | 301 | 106,403,266 | 31,248,154 | 137,651,420 | 1.29 | 54,213,575 | 39.4 |
| 100,000 - 500,000 | 159 | 981 | 170,524,091 | 37,189,409 | 207,713,500 | 1.22 | 83,961,917 | 40.4 |
| 50,000 - 100,000 | 128 | 497 | 55,204,749 | 9,084,649 | 64,289,398 | 1.16 | 28,821,670 | 44.8 |
| 10,000 - 50,000 | 380 | 1,092 | 67,120,289 | 9,063,577 | 76,183,866 | 1.14 | 29,323,404 | 38.5 |
| 1,000 - 10,000 | 959 | 1,744 | 33,475,102 | 3,406,472 | 36,881,573 | 1.10 | 14,493,641 | 39.3 |
| 100 - 1,000 | 1,204 | 1,608 | 5,939,176 | 481,059 | 6,420,235 | 1.08 | 2,791,799 | 43.5 |
| Under 100 | 908 | 1,027 | 482,141 | 30,227 | 512,368 | 1.06 | 293,346 | 57.3 |
| Zero | 0 | 0 | 0 | 0 | 0 | 0.00 | 0 | 0.0 |
| **Totals** | **3,955** | **12,341** | **6,042,313,714** | **4,365,681,147** | **10,407,994,861** | **1.72** | **3,301,329,033** | **31.7** |

Table C. The ethnolinguistic/ethnocultural world with its 5 races, 6,629 cultures, 12,583 peoples, and 13,509 languages (see Tables 18-1 to 18-7 for details).

| Race | Code | Population | Races | Geographic races | Culture worlds | Local races | ETHNOCULTURAL PEOPLES Ethnocultural families | Cultures | Peoples | LANGUAGES Clusters | Languages | Similarity % | AC |
|---|---|---|---|---|---|---|---|---|---|---|---|---|---|
| 1 | 2 | 3 | 4 | 5 | 6 | 7 | 8 | 9 | 10 | 11 | 12 | 13 | 14 |
| Australoid | A | 69,924,000 | 1 | 2 | 2 | 10 | 32 | 1,693 | 1,839 | 1,828 | 3,933 | 66.2 | 17.8 |
| Capoid | B | 1,154,000 | 1 | 1 | 1 | 2 | 5 | 78 | 113 | 81 | 183 | 33.6 | 36.7 |
| Caucasoid | C | 3,057,303,000 | 1 | 4 | 6 | 24 | 126 | 816 | 3,741 | 263 | 1,115 | 18.6 | 37.6 |
| Mongoloid | M | 2,265,858,000 | 1 | 4 | 5 | 19 | 127 | 2,093 | 3,621 | 1,603 | 4,345 | 44.2 | 14.5 |
| Negroid | N | 648,090,000 | 1 | 2 | 3 | 16 | 105 | 1,949 | 3,030 | 1,187 | 3,933 | 49.6 | 60.6 |
| Other minor peoples | | 12,720,000 | | | | | | | 239 | | | — | 32.4 |
| **Totals** | | **6,055,049,000** | **5** | **13** | **17** | **71** | **395** | **6,629** | **12,583** | **4,962** | **13,509** | **41.0** | **31.2** |

## Global Diagram 26.     Scripture provision via the World Language Classification measuring closeness or distance in relationships between any 2 or more of Earth's 13,500 languages, AD 2000.

The diagram sets out a schema illustrating the World Language Classification and how it clarifies the task of Scripture provision. Every language is given a unique 7-character code, enabling immediate estimates to be made of its proximity to any other languages. Thus if 2 languages share the first 6 characters of the code, they belong to the same cluster (or outer language). This means they share over 80%

basic vocabulary of common human experience, differing only in under 20% of vocabulary. This further means that a Scripture translation in a specific language (alternatively termed here 'inner language') can also provide some degree of access to scripture-less languages within its cluster (alternatively termed 'outer language').

The diagram illustrates this by zeroing in on one small but

highly significant part of the world of languages—the Central Indic net (network, glossosnet) in northern India. For names of all 219 languages within these clusters, and their present Scripture accessibility, consult the full listing in the *Linguasphere register* or *WCE* Table 9-13.

### Table A.     Major classficatory components.

| This classification contains: | | Short name |
|---|---|---|
| 10 | language MACROZONES | – |
| 100 | language GLOSSOZONES | zones |
| 684 | language GLOSSOSETS | sets |
| 1,403 | language GLOSSOCHAINS | chains |
| 2,684 | language GLOSSONETS | nets |
| 4,961 | language GLOSSOCLUSTERS | clusters |
| 13,509 | **languages** | – |
| 30,000 | dialects | – |
| 50,000 | speech-form names of all kinds | – |

### Table B.     Language totals by size of native (mother-tongue) speakers, AD 2000.

| Size | Languages | Speakers | Clusters | Speakers |
|---|---|---|---|---|
| Over 10 million | 96 | 4,631,336,000 | 91 | 5,251,425,000 |
| 1-10 million | 287 | 858,768,000 | 192 | 601,126,000 |
| 500,000–1million | 179 | 127,252,000 | 117 | 84,019,000 |
| 100,000–500,000 | 648 | 148,265,000 | 450 | 101,305,000 |
| 50,000–100,000 | 365 | 26,166,000 | 270 | 18,939,000 |
| 10,000–50,000 | 1,139 | 27,019,000 | 862 | 20,153,000 |
| 1,000–10,000 | 1,724 | 6,991,000 | 1,476 | 5,674,000 |
| 100–1,000 (moribund) | 1,005 | 438,000 | 876 | 383,000 |
| Under 100 (dying) | 219 | 8,000 | 240 | 8,600 |
| Zero (extinct) | 724 | 0 | 320 | 0 |
| Uncategorized | 7,123 | — | 68 | 0 |
| Totals | 13,509 | 5,826,243,000 | 4,961 | 6,083,031,000 |

### Table C.     Access to Scripture translations.

The World Language Classification consists of the components listed in column 1. Each component is then divided up to show how many language components or languages (column 3) have access to scriptures (column 2), and how many speakers benefit (column 4).

| Category<br>1 | Pub<br>2 | Lang<br>3 | Scripture access<br>Population<br>4 |
|---|---|---|---|
| 10 macrozones | PNB | 10 | 6,082,892,000 |
| 100 zones | ... | 3 | 2,670,000 |
| | P.. | 1 | 61,000 |
| | PN. | 34 | 71,875,000 |
| | PNB | 62 | 6,008,285,000 |
| 684 sets | | 308 | 13,078,000 |
| | P.. | 98 | 16,739,000 |
| | PN. | 173 | 107,002,000 |
| | PNB | 105 | 5,946,073,000 |
| 1,403 chains | ... | 738 | 37,599,000 |
| | P.. | 199 | 25,188,000 |
| | PN. | 320 | 145,205,000 |
| | PNB | 146 | 5,874,900,000 |
| 2,684 nets | ... | 1,661 | 64,539,000 |
| | P.. | 350 | 44,896,000 |
| | PN. | 471 | 191,553,000 |
| | PNB | 202 | 5,782,043,000 |
| 4,961 clusters | ... | 3,392 | 253,760,000 |
| | P.. | 568 | 129,417,000 |
| | PN. | 693 | 476,979,000 |
| | PNB | 309 | 5,222,876,000 |
| 13,509 languages | ... | 6,844 | 203,215,000 |
| | p.. | 1,298 | 18,055,000 |
| | P.. | 525 | 101,751,000 |
| | pn. | 2,063 | 68,294,000 |
| | pnb | 1,342 | 769,498,000 |
| | Pn. | 141 | 170,464,000 |
| | Pnb | 97 | 68,620,000 |
| | PN. | 696 | 190,664,000 |
| | PNb | 111 | 239,094,000 |
| | PNB | 392 | 3,996,606,000 |

*Key to published scriptures in column 2 above*

| ... | = | no scriptures published |
|---|---|---|
| p.. | = | near-gospel only |
| P.. | = | gospel only |
| pn. | = | near-gospel, near-NT |
| pnb | = | near-gospel, near-NT, near-Bible |
| Pn. | = | gospel, near-NT |
| Pnb | = | gospel, near-NT, near-Bible |
| PN. | = | gospel, New Testament |
| PNb | = | gospel, NT, near-Bible |
| PNB | = | gospel, NT, whole Bible |

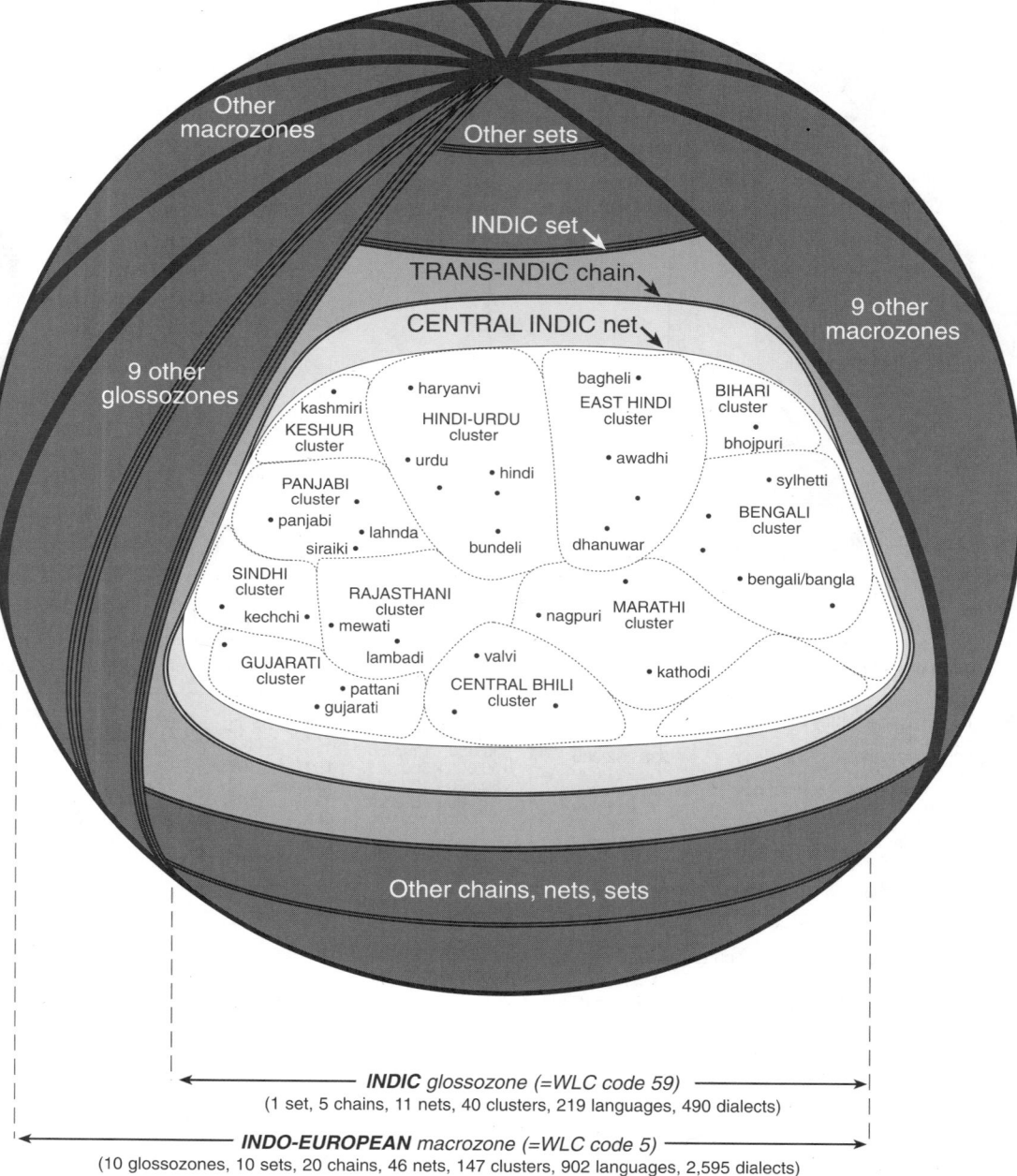

Other macrozones

Other sets

INDIC set

TRANS-INDIC chain

CENTRAL INDIC net

9 other macrozones

9 other glossozones

haryanvi     kashmiri     HINDI-URDU cluster     KESHUR cluster     urdu     hindi     bagheli     EAST HINDI cluster     awadhi     BIHARI cluster     bhojpuri     sylhetti     PANJABI cluster     panjabi     lahnda     bundeli     dhanuwar     BENGALI cluster     siraiki     SINDHI cluster     RAJASTHANI cluster     nagpuri     MARATHI cluster     bengali/bangla     kechchi     mewati     lambadi     valvi     kathodi     GUJARATI cluster     pattani     CENTRAL BHILI cluster     gujarati

Other chains, nets, sets

$\longleftarrow$ **INDIC** *glossozone* (=WLC code 59) $\longrightarrow$
(1 set, 5 chains, 11 nets, 40 clusters, 219 languages, 490 dialects)

$\longleftarrow$ **INDO-EUROPEAN** *macrozone* (=WLC code 5) $\longrightarrow$
(10 glossozones, 10 sets, 20 chains, 46 nets, 147 clusters, 902 languages, 2,595 dialects)

Other WLC codes for groupings on diagram: INDIC set = 59-A, TRANS-INDIC chain = 59-AA,
CENTRAL INDIC net = 59-AAF, HINDI-URDU cluster = 59-AAFO, *standard hindi* (language) = 59-AAFO-c

**Global Diagram 27.** A cross-section of the globe with its World Language Classification extended beyond native (mother-tongue) speakers to encompass non-native speakers, near-understanders, and person-language openings (communication channels).

### Two heavy circles
The previous Global Diagram 26 illustrates the World Language Classification by mapping out the world's *native* (mother-tongue) speakers (on this diagram at right, smaller heavy circle). This present diagram extends that coverage to *non-native* (second-language or more) speakers, producing *total speakers/users* (larger heavy circle at right) and also to *near-understanders* of every language (next circle to outer circle at right).

### The 12 largest outer lingua francas
In its fullest 3-dimensional version this diagram depicts a sphere with arrows placing 5,000 outer languages, also called clusters (of closely related languages sharing 80% or more basic vocabulary of human experience), radiating out from the center. The 12 long arrows shown represent speakers of outer languages (clusters) that are the world's 12 largest **outer lingua francas** (languages of wider communication). They dissect 9 concentric circles each labeled at its immediate left, alphabetically from A to I as defined in detail in the text and key below in the second and third columns.

### Speakers
The 4 statistics shown on each of the 12 arrows enumerate the number of speakers, users, understanders, and near-understanders where each language crosses circles E, G, H, and I. Each statistic (for which m = millions) includes the categories enumerated on the smaller circles inside it.

### Massive expansion
Virtually all these statistics are expanding year by year. The fastest growing is Global English. The British Council has estimated that, in addition to the world's 1 billion speakers competent in English, 'By the year

GLOBAL ENGLISH · MANDARIN CHINESE · SPANISH · HINDI–URDU · FRENCH · BENGALI · RUSSIAN · INDONESIAN · PORTUGUESE · PUNJABI · GERMAN · COLLOQUIAL ARABIC

Circles: A Moribund, Ethnic non-users, Monolinguals, Translinguals, Bilinguals, Multilinguals — NATIVE SPEAKERS; TOTAL SPEAKERS/USERS; Near-understanders in same language net; Person-language openings (communication channels); Non-native speakers in same cluster; Non-native speakers in different clusters

### The world's 32 largest outer lingua francas and (in bold type) the Top 12, ranked by total speakers, AD 2000.

| WLC code 1 | Anglicized name 2 | Native speakers 3 | Total speakers 4 |
|---|---|---|---|
| 52-ABAC | **Global English** | 234,031,000 | **1,319,857,000** |
| 79-AAAB | **Mandarin Chinese** | 882,103,000 | **1,318,597,000** |
| 51-AABB | **Spanish** | 337,010,000 | **543,076,000** |
| 59-AAFO | **Hindi-Urdu** | 263,964,000 | **491,827,000** |
| 59-AAFT | **Bengali** | 217,240,000 | **277,921,000** |
| 51-AABI | **French** | 48,629,000 | **277,478,000** |
| 53-AAAE | **Russian** | 200,870,000 | **269,131,000** |
| 31-PHAA | **Indonesian** | 55,521,000 | **229,239,000** |
| 59-AAFE | **Punjabi** | 136,022,000 | **212,157,000** |
| 12-AACF | **Colloquial Arabic** | 174,378,000 | **211,823,000** |
| 51-AABA | **Portuguese** | 184,292,000 | **196,148,000** |
| 52-ABCE | **High German** | 71,117,000 | **167,234,000** |
| 59-AAFU | Marathi | 106,459,000 | 163,706,000 |
| 79-AAAD | Shanghainese | 94,898,000 | 152,742,000 |
| 45-CAAA | Japanese | 128,987,000 | 134,213,000 |
| 79-AAAM | Cantonese | 66,362,000 | 131,854,000 |
| 59-AAFQ | Bihari | 89,665,000 | 129,920,000 |
| 49-DBAB | Telegu | 76,204,000 | 119,531,000 |
| 49-EBEA | Tamil | 72,690,000 | 114,733,000 |
| 44-AABA | Turkish | 87,669,000 | 108,529,000 |
| 99-AUSM | Swahili | 3,751,000 | 97,879,000 |
| 31-PIAA | Javanese | 56,256,000 | 88,249,000 |
| 51-AABQ | Italian | 36,509,000 | 85,687,000 |
| 46-EBAA | Vietnamese | 72,047,000 | 83,814,000 |
| 59-AAFH | Gujarati | 50,142,000 | 79,895,000 |
| 12-AACB | Western Arabic | 49,874,000 | 78,735,000 |
| 19-HAAB | Hausa | 29,864,000 | 78,728,000 |
| 58-AACC | Farsi | 47,594,000 | 77,952,000 |
| 45-AAAA | Korean | 75,665,000 | 77,546,000 |
| 79-AAAJ | Taiwanese | 48,925,000 | 73,039,000 |
| 31-CKAA | Filipino | 22,509,000 | 67,366,000 |
| 52-ABAH | West Coast Creole | 2,606,000 | 66,020,000 |

2000, there will be over 1,000 million people learning English' (D. Crystal. *English as a global language*, 1997:103).

### Nine circles
Circle **A** portrays the 'black hole' of extinct languages no longer with speakers. **B** = moribund, dying, or endangered languages approaching extinction. **C** = ethnic non-users who have abandoned their mother tongue; usually replacing it by a lingua franca. Next, **D** = monolinguals. The smaller heavy circle then measures **E** = *native (mother-tongue) speakers*, which contains within it monolinguals (speaking only their mother tongue), translinguals (speaking one or more closely-related languages), bilinguals, and multilinguals (speaking more than 2 distant or unrelated languages). To the total of native speakers of a given language is now added non-native speakers in the same cluster (sharing over 80% of basic vocabulary), totalling **F**. Adding non-native speakers in different clusters arrives at the larger of the 2 heavy circles, **G** = *total speakers/users* both native and non-native. Then, all persons in the language net (sharing over 70% of basic vocabulary) produce **H** = near-understanders. And lastly, G is multiplied by L (total languages in the cluster) to arrive at **I** = person-language openings (communication channels). Global total is 160 billion, or a global average of 13 languages spoken, understood, or used per person. From the Christian standpoint **I** shows the number of ways individual persons can be approached with the gospel using the language cluster illustrated.

For statistical data on the world's 407 largest lingua francas of both varieties (1) outer lingua francas, and (2) inner lingua francas, all of these being either over 1 million non-native speakers each, or over 1 million total speakers each, see Tables 18–8, 18–9, and 18–10.

### Total lingua francas
(source: Table 18–9)

| Total speakers | Outer | Inner | Total |
|---|---|---|---|
| Over 100 million | 20 | 21 | 41 |
| Over 10 million | 107 | 121 | 228 |
| Over 1 million | 320 | 454 | 774 |
| Over 100,000 | 876 | 1,302 | 2,178 |

### Spheres within spheres
This diagram can therefore be seen as a cross-section of a three-dimensional reality centered on and extending the World Language Classification mother-tongue sphere shown in grey here and in Global Diagram 26. Since every language cluster has different numbers of speakers, this reality consists of very lumpy spheres.

### Key to arrows, circles, numbers, letters above

**Arrows.** The 12 radiating arrows represent the 12 largest outer lingua francas.
**Grey circle.** This presents a cross-section of the 3-dimensional grey sphere in Global Diagram 26.
**Numbers** refer to speakers (m = millions) and are shown only where exact figures can be computed. Intercomprehension (= Com) below refers to shared basic vocabulary of human experience among constituent speech forms.
**Capital letters A–I** refer to the 9 concentric circles. Each, with its letter, includes all the smaller circles within it.
**A** = 'Black hole' of languages now extinct (no speakers)
**B** = Moribund/endangered/dying language speakers (<100 persons)
**C** = Ethnic non-users (no longer using related mother tongue)
**D** = Monolinguals (speakers of only one language; dialect intercomprehension Com>95%)
**E** = *Native (mother-tongue) speakers* (bilinguals as well as monolinguals; Com>90%)
**F** = Non-native speakers in same language cluster, plus native speakers (Com>85%)
**G** = *Total speakers/users* (native plus non-native) in same plus different clusters (Com>80%)
**H** = Near-understanders in same language net (Com>70%)
**I** = Person-language openings (communication channels) (Com>80%)

## Global Diagram 28. Today's languages, literature, and scriptures: 13,500 languages, 320 vehicular megalanguages, 6,700 languages with access to scriptures, with the range of translations, versions, and distribution.

One major form of the segmentized world is that composed of the 13,500 distinct languages its populations speak. In the logo below, these segments are shown exposed to the open Bible, which stands for the impact of all varieties of Christian literature, in print, audio, video, audiovisual, and other electronic forms, as well as standing for reading, preaching, proclamation, worship, mission, outreach, evangelism, and evangelization. This vast multilingual diversity of resources is centered on, holds up, explains, and interprets the cross of Christ as the central Christian symbol. (Official logo of the Southern Baptist Convention).

The larger globe below shows the 3-world model of Worlds A, B, and C. These parallel, but are not fully coterminous with, another 3-tier world: (1) (black-dark gray) the world of 6,800 No-Scripture languages, (2) (lightest gray) the world of 5,100 Partial-Scripture languages, and (3) (white) the world of 2,600 direct access Complete-Scripture languages. The heavy black line thus separates languages with some Scripture involvement from those with none.

Statistics of languages are taken from the World Language Classification set out in *WCE* Part 9 "Lingua-Metrics", based on intercomprehension, interintelligibility and lexicostatistical criteria. Data on Scripture translation and circulation, and other forms of Christian literature, cover all agencies in the whole spectrum of Christian confessions. The term 'Scripture' here as an adjective or a noun (as in 'Scripture languages', 'video scriptures') refers to the existence of at least one gospel or other book of the Bible in a language. It is capitalized when the direct reference is to Scripture or the Holy Scriptures (the Bible), but not capitalized when the reference is to mass-produced copies (scripture distribution, volume of scriptures).

Note that considerable overlap exists between a number of categories, in particular between 'Selections', 'In preparation,' and 'Complete.' Although the exact wording shown correctly reports the situation, the reader needs to think clearly about the implications. Figures are for the years of the Decade of Evangelism, AD 1990-2000.

---

**LANGUAGES IN WORLD**
13,500 idioms (mother tongues, speech communities)
4,960 language clusters (outer languages)
684 language sets (groupings of clusters)
100 language glossozones
10 language macrozones

**TYPES OF LANGUAGES**
1,000 literary languages
5,000 languages (idioms) not reduced to writing
6,500 languages with roman script
1,300 languages with non-roman script
350 vehicular megalanguages
2,000 trade languages
3,500 market languages
104 official national state languages

**WORLD'S MAJOR LANGUAGES**
English speakers 1,320 million
English mother-tongue speakers 234 million
Chinese speakers 1.3 billion
Spanish speakers 543 million
Hindi-Urdu speakers 492 million
Bengali speakers 278 million
French speakers 277 million

**ARTIFICIAL LANGUAGES**
10 constructed international languages
Esperanto speakers 10 million
180 computer languages

**LITERACY**
3,264 million literates (77% of adults)
991 million nonliterates (23% of adults)

**KNOWLEDGE**
Expanding at 2.0 trillion words per year

**BIBLE**
KJV/AV ENGLISH BIBLE (1,189 chapters)
3,566,480 letters
810,697 words
31,173 verses
1,855 usages of LORD (Yahweh)
7,200 different English words in KJV (10,500 in GNB)
400 different versions of the English Bible
OLD TESTAMENT (39 Books)
424,037 Hebrew words (Masoretic Text)
623,684 Greek words (LXX)
718,553 English words in OT/A (RSV)
593,493 English words in OT (GNB)
NEW TESTAMENT (27 Books)
5,600 Greek words
173,025 English words in NT (RSV)
181,253 English words in NT (GNB)
4,900 Greek keywords
4,700 English keywords
800 English single-word themes
341 key group-themes

**USAGES IN NT (NIV)**
Jesus is used 1,275 times
Christ is used 541 times
'Gospel' 96 times, 'good news' 39 times
164 uses of *en cristo* in Pauline Epistles

**SCRIPTURE LANGUAGES**
Total Scripture languages: 2,600 direct-access with complete Books, 6,700 with partial Scriptures, 1,200 with items in preparation: 2,800 in print, 4,000 on radio, 800 video, 800 audio, 1,500 computerized, 700 obsolete (not in use)
PRINT SCRIPTURES (2,600 direct-access languages)
400 with whole Bible
1,200 with New Testament
800 with New Testament only
2,600 with Portion (Gospel)
1,800 with Portion (Gospel) only
600 with New Reader Portion
5,100 with Selections
800 with New Reader Selections
220 Common Language Bibles
200 languages with Bible commentaries
300 languages with Scripture concordance
AUDIO SCRIPTURES (4,700 languages)
800 languages or dialects each with a gospel recording
VIDEO SCRIPTURES (800 languages)
700 languages with 'Jesus' Film (Gospel of Luke), with 100 more in preparation

1.7 billion live viewers of 'Jesus' Film
4 billion viewers of 'Jesus' Film since 1978
800 languages with a video Book
RADIO SCRIPTURES (4,000 languages)
1,200 languages with whole Books in use
2,300 languages quoting Scripture texts or passages or selections

**SCRIPTURES IN PREPARATION**
Print translation projects underway in 950 languages
First translations: 550 languages
New translations: 200 languages
Revisions: 300 languages
300 Common Bible translations
Catholic participation: 180 more languages
Radio, audio, video underway: 220

**NO-SCRIPTURE LANGUAGES**
6,600 with no scriptures or selections
3,000 with no scriptures or Christian literature
2,600 with no scriptures or literature, but some Christians
1,000 with no scriptures but with some Christian literature

**ANNUAL SCRIPTURE DISTRIBUTION**
FREE PLACEMENT
400 million free scriptures p.a.
SUBSIDIZED DISTRIBUTION
1 billion subsidized scriptures p.a.
COMMERCIAL SALES
Bibles: 28 million p.a.
New Testaments: 45 million p.a.
470 million commercial scriptures p.a.
TOTAL DISTRIBUTION
Bibles: 53.7 million p.a.
New Testaments: 120.8 million p.a.
Portions: 323 million p.a.
New Reader Portions: 30 million p.a.
Selections: 4.1 billion p.a.
New Reader Selections: 60 million p.a.
All varieties of scriptures: 4.6 billion p.a.

**LITERATURE (ALL SUBJECTS)**
800 encyclopedias (400 in English): 150 general encyclopedias; 650 subject encyclopedias
1.0 million new book titles p.a.
34.9 billion books printed a year
700,000 bookshops
600,000 magazine titles (150,000 periodicals)
390,000 scientific journals
2.5 million scientific articles a year
Universal literature: 65,000 million classics translated

**CHRISTIAN LITERATURE**
1.3 billion literate adult Christians
26,100 Christian book titles a year
73,600 new titles including devotional
3.5 billion Christian books printed a year
34,500 Christian periodicals
73,500 Christian bookshops
LITERATURE ON 'EVANGELIZE'
12,000 new books and articles a year
12,800 new items a year on mission

**LIBRARIES**
290,000 public libraries
4,500 million library volumes (books)
Annual increase 50 million volumes a year
200 million library borrowers or users
16,000 professional religious (Christian) libraries
2,200 large Christian libraries (over 35,000 volumes each)

**WORLD COVERAGE BY PEOPLES**
Total ethnolinguistic peoples in world: 12,600
Peoples with whole Bible: 5,400
Peoples with NT only: 2,406
Peoples with Portions only: 1,300
Peoples with some Scripture: 9,100
Peoples with no own-language Scripture: 3,500

**WORLD POPULATION COVERAGE**
Access to Scripture in some understood language: 98.7% of world
Access to Scripture in mother tongue: 96%
Access to whole Bible in mother tongue: 86%
Languages with any Scripture endeavor: 6,900
Languages with any Christian literature (apart from Scripture): 1,000

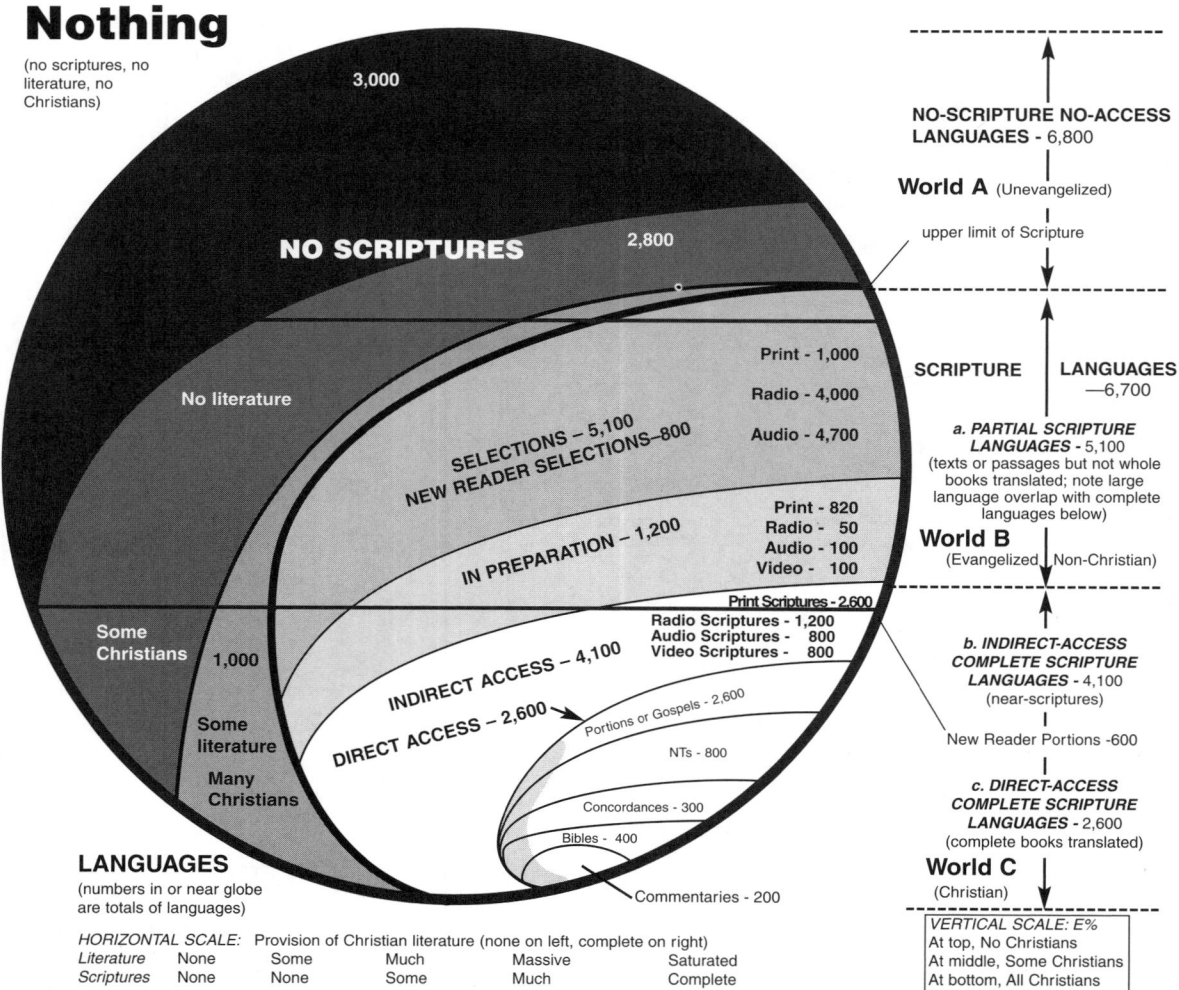

**Nothing**
(no scriptures, no literature, no Christians)

3,000

**NO SCRIPTURES**    2,800

No literature

SELECTIONS – 5,100
NEW READER SELECTIONS – 800

Print - 1,000
Radio - 4,000
Audio - 4,700

IN PREPARATION – 1,200

Print - 820
Radio - 50
Audio - 100
Video - 100

Some Christians    1,000

Print Scriptures - 2,600

INDIRECT ACCESS – 4,100

Radio Scriptures - 1,200
Audio Scriptures - 800
Video Scriptures - 800

Some literature

DIRECT ACCESS – 2,600

Portions or Gospels - 2,600

Many Christians

NTs - 800

Concordances - 300

Bibles - 400

Commentaries - 200

**LANGUAGES**
(numbers in or near globe are totals of languages)

NO-SCRIPTURE NO-ACCESS LANGUAGES - 6,800

**World A** (Unevangelized)

upper limit of Scripture

**SCRIPTURE | LANGUAGES** —6,700

*a.* PARTIAL SCRIPTURE LANGUAGES - 5,100
(texts or passages but not whole books translated; note large language overlap with complete languages below)

**World B**
(Evangelized Non-Christian)

*b.* INDIRECT-ACCESS COMPLETE SCRIPTURE LANGUAGES - 4,100
(near-scriptures)

New Reader Portions -600

*c.* DIRECT-ACCESS COMPLETE SCRIPTURE LANGUAGES - 2,600
(complete books translated)

**World C**
(Christian)

*HORIZONTAL SCALE:* Provision of Christian literature (none on left, complete on right)

| | None | Some | Much | Massive | Saturated |
|---|---|---|---|---|---|
| Literature | None | Some | Much | Massive | Saturated |
| Scriptures | None | None | Some | Much | Complete |

*VERTICAL SCALE: E%*
At top, No Christians
At middle, Some Christians
At bottom, All Christians

**Global Diagram 29.** Today's Christian broadcasting: 5.7 billion persons in 7,500 ethnolinguistic peoples regularly offered programs in 2,800 languages (650 being mother-tongue, with near-broadcasts in 2,150 near-languages), with 1.1 billion regular listeners/viewers in 238 countries.

Since its origin in 1921, Christian broadcasting has expanded across the Earth. Every country, religion, confession, and every large Christian denomination regularly uses it, even produces it. Some 30% of the world are regular listeners/viewers of Christian programs, 39% over Christian stations, and 74% over secular stations (governmental or commercial), which means an overlap of 35% over both.

Distribution of the entire range of Christian broadcasting across the world is however very uneven. Some 96% is directed at and benefits Christians only (in World C). This leaves only 4% for the non-Christian worlds, 3.9% for World B, and only 0.1% for World A. Although, as the large globe below shows, many languages in World B have Christian programs broadcast in them, in many cases it is only for a

scant 10, 20, or 30 minutes a week. In a global industry which broadcasts 770,000 hours of radio and 577,000 hours of television every week, 30 minutes a week for a language with a million speakers is an insult to potential hearers and also to workers laboring to implement the Great Commission.

---

**HOURS BROADCAST (SECULAR AND RELIGIOUS)**
Hours available per programming year: 8,760
Radio: 40 million hours a year (770,000 a week)
TV: 30 million hours a year (577,000 a week)
News and information: 17% of radio and TV time
GLOBAL EQUIPMENT
35,000 radio transmitters
75,000 TV transmitters
2.1 billion radio sets in use
343 radios per 1000 persons
1,340 million TV sets
222 TV sets per 1000 persons
Persons without radio or TV sets: 2.6 billion
4,000 Christian radio/TV stations
1,050 Christian broadcasting organizations
120,000 full-time personnel in Christian broadcasting

**AMATEUR RADIO**
1.5 million ham radio operators
58 million CB (citizen's band) radios

**NON-CHRISTIAN RELIGIOUS BROADCASTING**
Muslim broadcasting from or in 168 countries
Hindu broadcasting in 78 countries
Buddhist broadcasting in 85 countries
Baha'i broadcasting from or in 80 countries
New-Religionist broadcasting in 25 countries

**COVERAGE FOR COUNTRIES (OFFICIAL-LANGUAGE, SECULAR)**
All 238 countries have own-language radio service
208 countries have own TV service
30 sovereign nations have no TV service

**COVERAGE FOR LANGUAGES**
Total languages in world: 13,500
2,800 languages offered Christian broadcasts
10,700 languages get no Christian broadcasts

**COVERAGE FOR PEOPLES (OWN-LANGUAGE)**
Total ethnolinguistic peoples in world: 12,600
6,950 peoples get no own-language secular broadcasting
8,450 peoples get no own-language Christian broadcasting
5,150 peoples offered own-language Christian broadcasting
4,000 peoples get foreign-originated own-language Christian broadcasting
1,350 peoples offered near-broadcasts (in near-languages)
1,000 peoples offered only lingua franca broadcasts
900 peoples get only internal Christian broadcasting (from within country)

**COVERAGE FOR POPULATIONS (MOTHER-TONGUE)**
Total persons in world: 6,055 million
570 million get no mother-tongue broadcasting of any kind
770 million get no mother-tongue Christian broadcasting
5.3 billion offered mother-tongue Christian broadcasting
4 billion offered mother-tongue foreign Christian broadcasting
160 million get only internal mother-tongue Christian broadcasting (from within own country)

**REGULAR LISTENERS/VIEWERS FOR CHRISTIAN PROGRAMS**
0.6 billion regular audience, over Christian stations, in 300 languages
1 billion audience, over secular stations, in 2,700 languages, in 238 countries
1,150 million regular audience, all stations (excluding overlap; 19% of world), in 2,800 languages
1.1 billion Christians regularly listening to Christian radio/TV
50 million non-Christians listening to Christian radio/TV

25 million isolated radio believers
30 million radio/TV believers (no local church)
70 million bedridden or housebound radio/TV regular worshippers

**CHURCH PLANTING BY RADIO**
Radio/TV converts: 3.5 million new believers a year in 170 countries
Isolated radio converts: 1 million new believers a year
300,000 isolated radio churches exist in 80 countries
New isolated house churches/cells springing up: 20,000 a year
New churches or congregations formed due to radio in christianized areas: 20,000 a year

**MARGINAL/QUASI-CHRISTIAN BROADCASTING**
3 marginal Christian global meganetworks
16 marginal Christian global networks

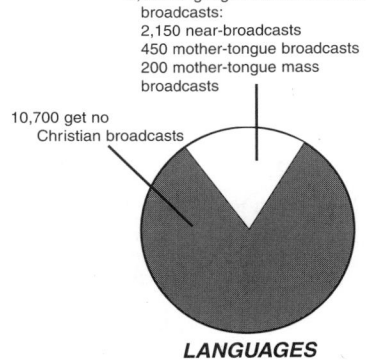

2,800 languages offered Christian broadcasts:
2,150 near-broadcasts
450 mother-tongue broadcasts
200 mother-tongue mass broadcasts

10,700 get no Christian broadcasts

**LANGUAGES**
World total 13,500

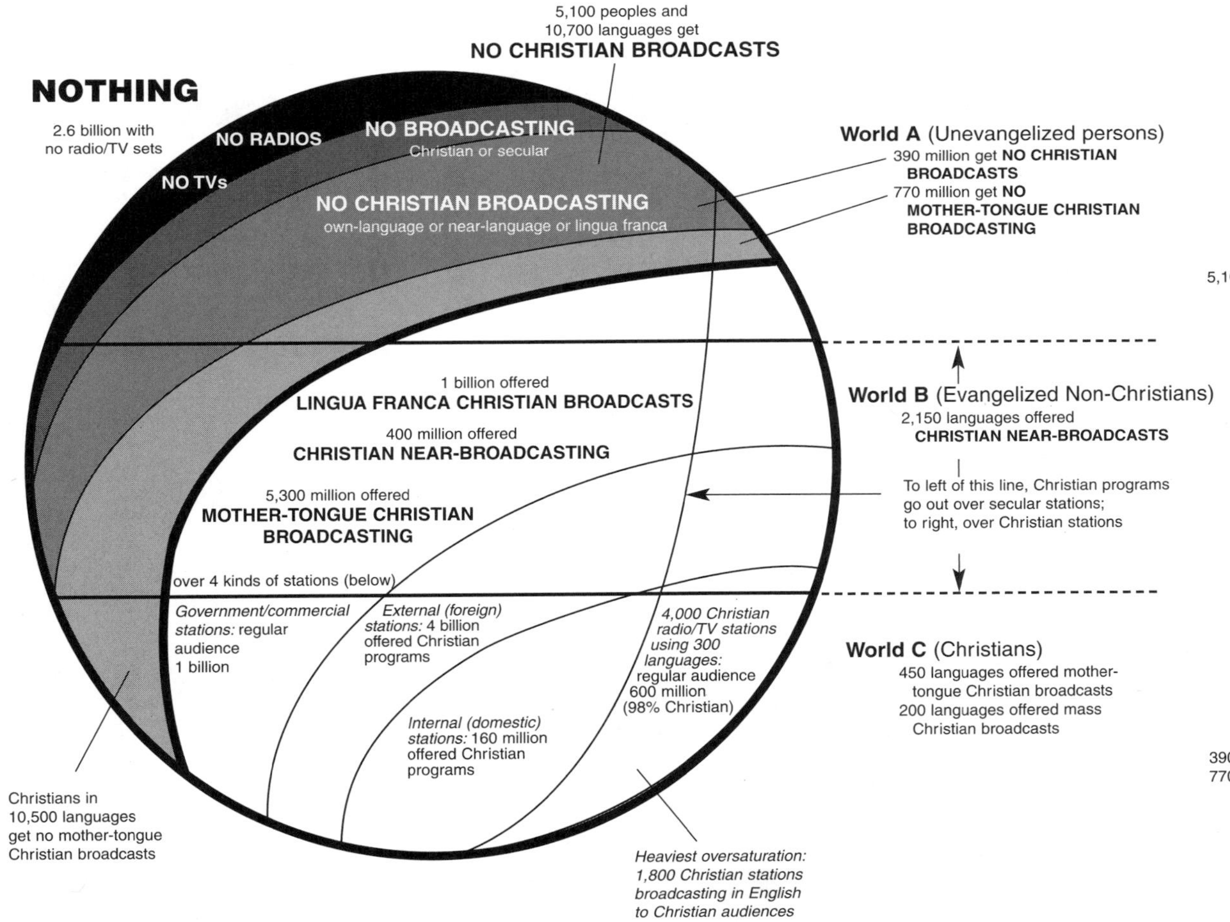

---

5,100 peoples and
10,700 languages get
**NO CHRISTIAN BROADCASTS**

**NOTHING**

2.6 billion with no radio/TV sets

**NO RADIOS**

**NO TVs**

**NO BROADCASTING**
Christian or secular

**NO CHRISTIAN BROADCASTING**
own-language or near-language or lingua franca

**World A** (Unevangelized persons)
390 million get **NO CHRISTIAN BROADCASTS**
770 million get **NO MOTHER-TONGUE CHRISTIAN BROADCASTING**

1 billion offered
**LINGUA FRANCA CHRISTIAN BROADCASTS**

400 million offered
**CHRISTIAN NEAR-BROADCASTING**

5,300 million offered
**MOTHER-TONGUE CHRISTIAN BROADCASTING**

over 4 kinds of stations (below)

*Government/commercial stations:* regular audience 1 billion

*External (foreign) stations:* 4 billion offered Christian programs

*Internal (domestic) stations:* 160 million offered Christian programs

4,000 Christian radio/TV stations using 300 languages: regular audience 600 million (98% Christian)

Christians in 10,500 languages get no mother-tongue Christian broadcasts

**World B** (Evangelized Non-Christians)
2,150 languages offered
**CHRISTIAN NEAR-BROADCASTS**

To left of this line, Christian programs go out over secular stations; to right, over Christian stations

**World C** (Christians)
450 languages offered mother-tongue Christian broadcasts
200 languages offered mass Christian broadcasts

*Heaviest oversaturation:* 1,800 Christian stations broadcasting in English to Christian audiences

5,100 peoples offered own-language Christian broadcasting
1,350 peoples offered near-broadcasts
1,000 peoples offered only lingua franca broadcasts

5,100 peoples get no Christian broadcasting

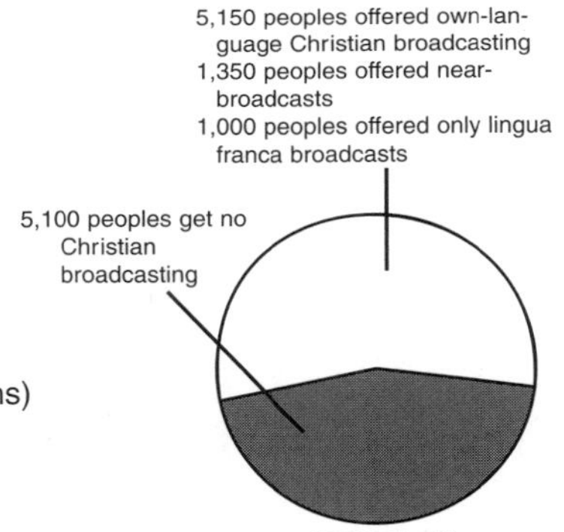

**PEOPLES**
World total 12,600

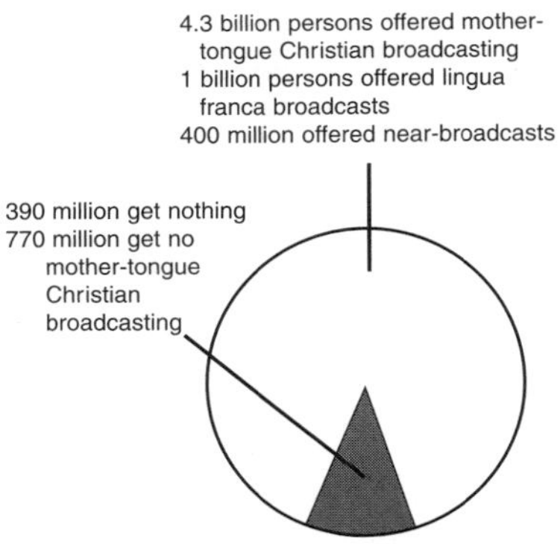

4.3 billion persons offered mother-tongue Christian broadcasting
1 billion persons offered lingua franca broadcasts
400 million offered near-broadcasts

390 million get nothing
770 million get no mother-tongue Christian broadcasting

**POPULATIONS**
World total 6,055 million

---

**POPULATIONS**

*HORIZONTAL SCALE: Provision of Christian broadcasting*
(Left inside) No broadcasting
(Center) Some broadcasting
(Right inside) Saturation broadcasting
(Right inside at bottom) Oversaturated broadcasting

*VERTICAL SCALE: E%*
At top, No Christians
At middle, Some Christians
At bottom, All Christians

## Global Diagram 30. Standardizing the terminology for enumerating all Christians (World C): 4 major statistical usages, 48 generic categories, and 3 dichotomous typologies leading to one schema of 3 levels of Christian commitment.

This diagram analyzes World C, the world of all persons who individually are Christians. It shows the many different ways in which they have been enumerated. All definitions are reconciled here into a single classification and schema, standardized throughout this survey. Here are the 4 main elements listed in the title above.

(1) *4 major statistical usages.* The 4 best-known overall usages are shown in boldface type in Table A below. These are the only 4 global measures that anybody actually collects from grassroots level onwards and then publishes. All are enumerated in *WCE* Country Tables 1, for each of the globe's 238 countries. Of these 4, **Christians** refers to the grand total of all types; the other 3 usages are alternative ways of attempting to count Christians, which overlap markedly. **Professing Christians** are what censuses and public-opinion polls enumerate; **affiliated Christians** are what churches count, being enrolled church members including their children, all with their names written in the church's records; and **Great Commission Christians** refers to practicing Christians

actively seeking to obey Christ's command to engage in mission.

(2) *48 generic categories.* Under these 4 major usages Table A shows 44 additional generic categories widely enumerated by Christians today. These are organized according to several typologies as is next explained.

(3) *3 dichotomous typologies.* The latter 3 major statistical usages provide us with three 2-part typologies widely used for describing and enumerating the Christian world. These are depicted in Graphic A, at its bottom left. The typologies each divide Christians into 2 categories based on different viewpoints: (1) that of the world, which observes profession; (2) that of the church, which organizes affiliation; and (3) that of Christ himself, who recognizes either obedience or disobedience to his commission to be active in mission. Meanwhile, our globe is shown divided into Worlds A, B, and C. Its Christians (World C) are shown shaded and segmented under the 3 typologies.

(4) *3 levels of Christian commitment.* The 3 dichotomies

are then combined, at bottom right, into one final typology, a trichotomy dividing all Christians into 4 layers or 3 levels of commitment. The top 2 layers are termed latent Christians, covering all Christians who are inactive with regard to Christ's call to mission. The bottom 2 layers form the core of the worldwide church—all Christians who are active in mission, who take seriously Christ's command, and so who are termed **Great Commission Christians.** This category itself is composed of 2 layers—overt evangelizers, and covert evangelizers (secret believers)—although it is termed here as a single level, the third one.

Table A thus shows our final standard layout. The 48 generic categories are arranged into 3 parallel but different ways of analyzing all Christians. Each is introduced by its keyword—*PROFESSION, AFFILIATION,* or *MISSION.* Statistics for AD 2000 are then added. Also, each category is given a short code, to help the user to navigate through the masses of data in computerized database versions.

### Table A. STANDARD TERMS FOR 'CHRISTIANS'.

Below is set out the standard layout for the statistical enumeration of Christians followed in this survey. The 4 major statistical usages are shown (in boldface type), with 44 other categories in widespread use (in medium type). All are shown divided under 3 alternative ways of analysis (in italic capitals, *PROFESSION, AFFILIATION, MISSION*), each of whose components add up to the same total for all Christians (see formulas below).

| Code | Category | Global totals, AD 2000 | | Code | Category | Global totals, AD 2000 |
|---|---|---|---|---|---|---|
| C | **Christians** | **1,999,564,000** | | IAC | Independents | 385,745,000 |
| | *PROFESSION* | | | NIAC | Non-White indigenous Christians | 203,870,000 |
| CC | crypto-Christians | 123,626,000 | | WIAC | White-led Postdenominationalists | 50,066,000 |
| PC | **professing Christians** | **1,875,827,000** | | AAC | Anglicans | 79,650,000 |
| RPC | Roman Catholics | 1,020,827,000 | | EAAC | Anglican Evangelicals | 30,000,000 |
| SRPC | Spiritist Catholics | 82,000,000 | | CAAC | Anglican Charismatics | 17,562,000 |
| ERPC | Evangelical Catholics | 79,900,000 | | mAC | Marginal Christians | 26,060,000 |
| CRPC | Christopagans | 22,000,000 | | 2AC | doubly-affiliated | -194,780,000 |
| PPC | Protestants | 310,000,000 | | xAC | disaffiliated | -22,694,000 |
| OPC | Orthodox | 160,000,000 | | | *Trans-megabloc groupings:* | |
| IPC | Independents | 250,000,000 | | EAC | Evangelicals | 211,000,000 |
| APC | Anglicans | 110,000,000 | | eAC | evangelicals | 647,821,000 |
| mPC | Marginal Christians | 25,000,000 | | ZAC | Pentecostals/Charismatics/Neocharismatics | 523,778,000 |
| | *AFFILIATION* | | | 1ZAC | Pentecostals (First-Wavers) | 65,833,000 |
| UC | unaffiliated Christians | 111,125,000 | | 2ZAC | Charismatics (Second-Wavers) | 175,857,000 |
| AC | **affiliated Christians** | **1,888,439,000** | | 3ZAC | Neocharismatics (Third-Wavers) | 295,405,000 |
| xpAC | non-practicing church members | 1,240,618,000 | | 4ZAC | doubly-counted (1/2/3 Wavers) | -13,300,000 |
| RAC | Roman Catholics | 1,057,328,000 | | | *MISSION* | |
| CRAC | Catholic Charismatics | 120,000,000 | | LC | latent (inactive) Christians | 1,351,743,000 |
| ERAC | Catholic Evangelicals | 7,800,000 | | UC | unaffiliated Christians* | 111,125,000 |
| PAC | Protestants | 324,002,000 | | xpAC | non-practicing church members* | 1,240,618,000 |
| EPAC | Evangelicals | 144,000,000 | | GCC | **Great Commission Christians** | **647,821,000** |
| CPAC | Protestant Charismatics | 35,200,000 | | OEC | overt evangelizers* | 524,095,000 |
| OAC | Orthodox | 215,129,000 | | CC | covert evangelizers* | 123,726,000 |
| EOAC | Orthodox Evangelicals | 4,000,000 | | | | |
| COAC | Orthodox Charismatics | 2,000,000 | | | | |

*Notes on columns above.*
**Code.** To enable computer users to steer through database versions.
**Category.** A standard usage for which statistics can be obtained. Note that indented categories form part of, and are included in, the unindented category above them. First indentations (indented once) are in all cases complete; their categories always add up to their parent category. Second indentations however are selected subgroups not intended as a complete breakdown of their parent category. Categories with an asterisk are omitted in *WCE* Country Tables 1, being repetitions.
**Global totals, AD 2000.** Summary data, expanded in Table 1–2.
**Formulas.** Note these exact equivalences:
C=PC+CC=AC+UC=GCC+LC.
AC=RAC+PAC+OAC+IAC+AAC+mAC+2AC+xAC.
EAC=EPAC+EAAC+EIAC+ERAC+EOAC.
ZAC=1ZAC+2ZAC+3ZAC+4ZAC.
LC=UC+xpAC.
GCC=OEC+CC=eAC.

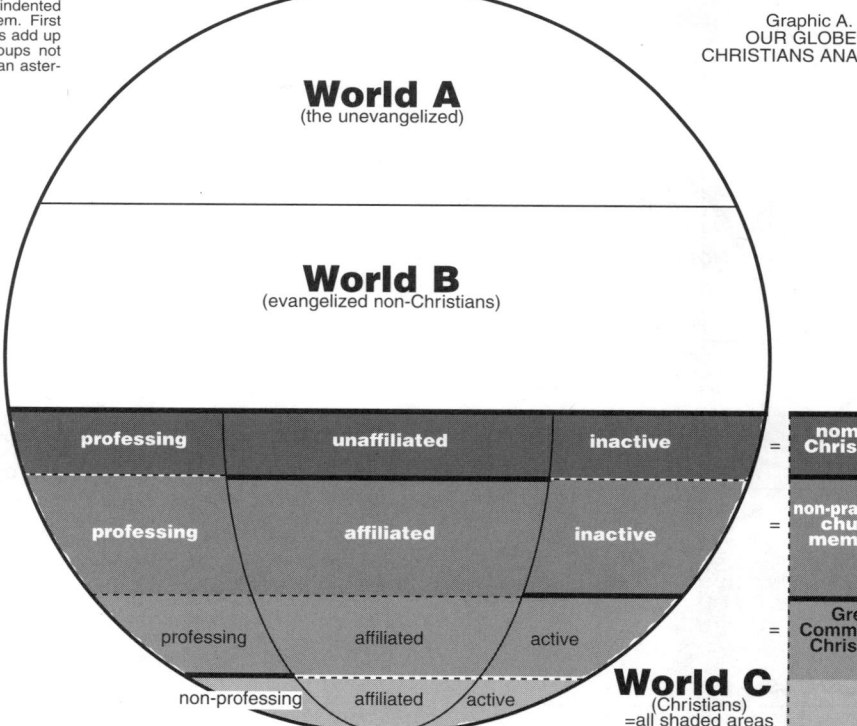

Graphic A.
OUR GLOBE'S CHRISTIANS ANALYZED

Typologies of Christians as viewed by:

1. The WORLD
based on *profession*
=Typology I

2. The CHURCH
based on *affiliation*
=Typology II

3. CHRIST
based on *mission*
=Typology III

World C (shaded) is analyzed above by these 3 typologies:

Typology I. *PROFESSION*     Typology II. *AFFILIATION*     Typology III. *MISSION*

Overall Typology of 3 levels

**Global Diagram 31.  Navigating on global mission, with parallels from aviation: global Christianity's 3 displays, 260 maps, 74 diagrams, 340 screens, 2,056 instruments, 16,000 trends.**

The diagram displays a parallel between pilots of modern aircraft and executives of foreign mission agencies. In the left-hand half of the page below, 20th-century practice forced pilots to face a chaos of separate instruments, constantly monitoring up to 100 instruments facing the pilot's seat, even

above (as in Boeing 767 airliner shown).
A similar situation faces Christian executives and decision makers: they face a chaos of some 2,056 separate instruments (listed in the following Table DD), including some 5 million separate and distinct books (titles) describing Christianity and

100,000 of them on mission.
For the 21st century, however, 2 major electronic aids are being developed, as shown in the bottom 3 layers below.

## INSTRUMENTATION IN AVIATION

## INSTRUMENTATION IN MISSION

### *DURING THE 20TH CENTURY*

A pilot has 100 separate instruments to monitor continuously

| Chinese compass | Airspeed | Vertical speed | Wing flaps |

### *DURING THE 20TH CENTURY*—*2,056 separate instruments available*

Multiple separate and independent sources of data

| 5 million Christian books | Censuses: 'What is your religion?' | Polls: 'Do you believe in Jesus Christ?' |

### *IN AD 2000*

Current state of the art (left, Boeing 757 and 767; below, Gotha aircraft): pilot has standard 6-instrument panel but must constantly monitor 90 other dials.

Boeing 757/767 Panel

### *IN AD 2000*

State of the art currently available: (right) annual Vatican questionnaire to bishops asking 141 statistical questions; (below) our Great Commission Instrument Panel with 6 major descriptors.

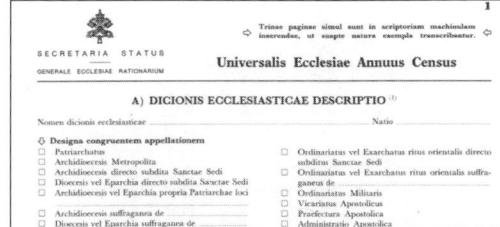

### *FOR THE 21st CENTURY*

For complete situational awareness, pilots and researchers have produced
**EFIS-2000.**
(Electronic Flight Information System)
This is a single 7 inch wide screen (full-color multifunction display) with 3 choices:

*First choice* (by touching a button):
(Left) EFIS-1, **Primary Flight Display**: airspeed, vertical speed, altitude, attitude, heading, 30 parameters.

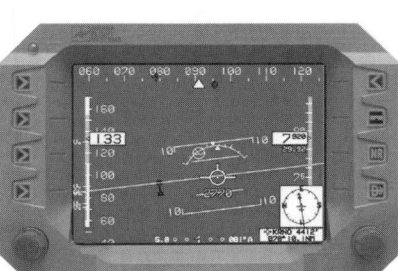

### *FOR THE 21st CENTURY*

For complete situational awareness, missiologists are proposing
**EMIN-2001**
(Electronic Mission Information Navigator)
This is any user's home or office computer screen, with 3 choices:

*First choice*:
(Right) EMIN-1, **Global Maps**:
16 full-color global maps, black and white maps, color maps of 238 countries, all with zooming, magnifying, and printout capabilities.

*Second choice*:
(Left) EFIS-2, **Navigation Display**:
By touching a tactile button, a pilot can switch from Primary Flight Display to this detailed moving map with GPS (Global Positioning System), flight plan, weather, cloud, crosswinds, storms, traffic, restricted space, terrain modeling, obstacles continually updated: 30 parameters, with voice warnings when boundaries are approached.

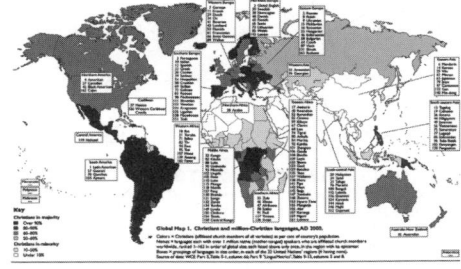

*Second choice*:
(Right) EMIN-2, **Global Diagrams:**
74 diagrams each on one subject including past, present, and future.

This provides users with a Global Navigator or a Country Navigator, as follows:
Overview—4 screens
Past history—13 screens
Present status—28 screens
Future scenarios—24 screens
Long-term futures—5 screens

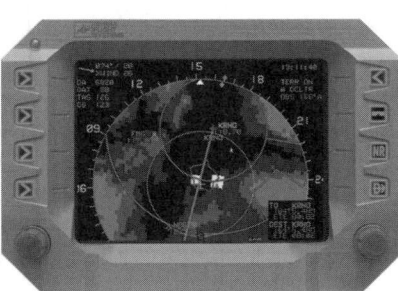

*Third choice*:
(Left) EFIS-3, **Engine Display**:
digital monitoring of 40 parameters concerning engine(s) power and condition, with voice warnings when boundaries are approached.
In practice, pilots would need to check this display far less often than the other displays above.

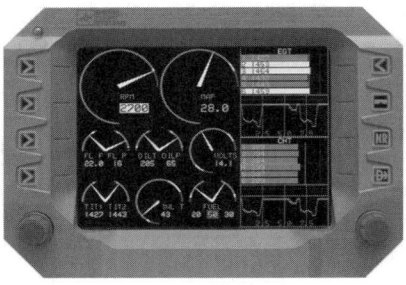

*Third choice*:
(Right) EMIN-3,
**Global Chronographics**:
invoking the whole 2,000-year history of Christianity, continent by continent and region by region, with large variety of numerical statements, trends, tables, or graphics to user's requirements.

Vertical axis = any instrument or measure

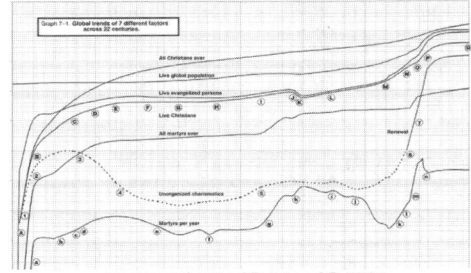

Horizontal axis: AD 30 to AD 2200

**Table DD.**    **Five varieties of instrumentation in _WCT_, _WCE_, and _WCD_, with 2,056 instruments, to enable orientation while navigating across the globe on the Christian world mission.**

This table describes the whole spectrum of instrumentation derived from the churches' regular measurements of their activities throughout the world. The largest variety, labeled A below, consists of country instruments—measuring activities at the country level.

Then are shown 4 other categories of instrumentation (B, C, D, and E). Second largest is D, database instruments. Lastly, the final line sums and summarizes the 5 categories into the overall instrumentation available in 2 publications: _WCT_ (the present volume, _World Christian trends_) and _WCE_ (_World Christian encyclopedia_ 2001). Readers needing electronic access to these data can find it in the forthcoming online or CD products, _World Christian database, AD 30–AD 2200_.

All these varieties are described below under 10 column headings including 5 statistical columns which extend right down the page as follows: 1 = a reference number; 2 = _WCT's_ or _WCE's_ Part dealing with each; 3 = the Part's title; 4 = subtitle of variety; 5 = groupings of instruments into what are here, for ease of understanding, termed 'varieties of instrument panels'; 6 = number of distinct types of instruments (measuring devices used by churches); 7 = component parts or lines of data per instrument shown in this survey; 8 = number of measurements shown here, either per country or (9) for the whole globe; and 10 = brief explanation.

| Ref 1 | WCT/WCE Part number 2 | Title 3 | Subtitle 4 | Panels 5 | Instruments 6 | Data 7 | Records (a) per country 8 | (b) global 9 | Measurements 10 | Notes and comments |
|---|---|---|---|---|---|---|---|---|---|---|
| **A. COUNTRY INSTRUMENTS** | | | | | | | | | | |

Some 473 of this survey's 2,056 different and separate instruments (devices for measuring any and all measurable aspects of global Christianity), and 83 of its 471 instrument panels, deal with countries as basic unit. These occupy the major part of this table because the globe's 6 billion inhabitants live in countries, and the Christian world is organized primarily by country.

The major significant collection of instruments here is found in _WCT_ Part 12 "CountryTrends" and Part 15. This describes 191 measuring devices and lists their measurements for all 238 countries, the 7 continents, and the whole globe. This is summarized in the first line below. Smaller collections are described in the 5 Parts on the lines 2 to 6 that follow. Then comes the major collection, presented in _WCE_ Part 4 "Countries"; these are listed below on 13 lines that follow. Central is line number 13, the standardized **Great Com-** **mission Instrument Panel**, with 6 instruments each averaging 4 records (a record being a component line of data, e.g. a denomination, a people, a city), and so 24 measurements for each country. This Panel appears in every country's article in _WCE_ Part 4, and for the 77 countries over 10 million in size in _WCT_ Part 15 "Instrumentation".

| Ref | WCT/WCE Part number | Title | Subtitle | Panels | Instruments | Data | Records per country | global | Measurements / Notes and comments |
|---|---|---|---|---|---|---|---|---|---|
| 1 | WCT Part 12 | "CountryTrends" | Countries | 50 | 191 | 1 | 191 | 45,090 | Data on 270 countries, regions, continents, worlds |
| 2 | WCE Part 8 | "EthnoSphere" | Peoples | 1 | 38 | 54 | 2,000 | 540,000 | Data on 12,600 peoples (with 28 detailed profiles) |
| 3 | WCT Part 33 | "GeoAtlas" | Global Trends Maps | 1 | 16 | 2 | 30 | 8,100 | 8 pages with 16 global maps |
| 4 | | | Human Environment | 1 | 40 | 1 | 40 | 10,080 | 16 pages of geographical maps covering world |
| 5 | WCE Part 10 | "MetroScan" | Metropolises | 1 | 7 | 33 | 230 | 62,100 | Data on 7,000 cities |
| 6 | WCE Part 11 | "ProvinceScan" | Provinces | 1 | 9 | 12 | 108 | 29,160 | Data on 3,030 major civil divisions |
| 7 | WCE Part 4 | "Countries" | Identification | 1 | 3 | 1 | 3 | 714 | Data on 238 countries: map, name, flag |
| 8 | | | Secular data | 14 | 61 | 1 | 61 | 14,500 | 61 facts or statistics for AD 2000 |
| 9 | | | Country Table 1 | 1 | 16 | 300 | 4,800 | 1,296,000 | Religions and growth rates, AD 1900–2025 |
| 10 | | | Footnotes/censuses | 1 | 10 | 2 | 20 | 5,400 | Detailed data on religions above |
| 11 | | | Country status | 1 | 1 | 4 | 4 | 1,080 | Brief depicting of country's character |
| 12 | | | Narrative text | 1 | 20 | 2 | 40 | 8,100 | Rights, religions, churches, radio/TV, prospects |
| 13 | | | Country summary | 3 | 21 | 4 | 84 | 22,680 | Peoples, Cities, Provinces by Worlds A, B, C |
| 14 | | | Photographs | 1 | 2 | 2 | 4 | 1,080 | Descriptive, analytical photographs of a country |
| 15 | | | Bibliography | 1 | 6 | 10 | 60 | 16,200 | Books, articles, on Christianity in one country |
| 16 | | | Country Table 2 | 1 | 20 | 35 | 700 | 189,000 | Denominations, churches, growth |
| 17 | | | Conciliarism | 1 | 1 | 3 | 3 | 700 | Councils, alliances, fellowships at 5 levels |
| 18 | | | 125-year church growth | 1 | 11 | 6 | 66 | 17,820 | Growth from 1900 to 2025 |
| 19 | WCT Part 15 | "Instrumentation" | **Great Commission** **Instrument Panel** | 1 | 6 | 10 | 60 | 16,200 | 1,620 minidiagrams showing the Top Six instruments |
| 20 | | | **Country instrumentation** | 83 | 479 | 19 | 8,423 | 2,284,000 | Totals of all instrumentation for all countries |

**B. GLOBAL INSTRUMENTS**

All country instruments can be totaled to produce global totals. In addition, however, there are a large number of other global instruments not derived from country measurements. Of these latter, the major ones are the 74 one-page global diagrams shown in _WCT_ Part 1 "GeoStatus". These can be interpreted as 20 distinct panels (shown and named in Table 1– 3) with 74 complex and sophisticated global instruments. This gives the totals summarized in the following line.

| Ref | WCT/WCE Part number | Title | Subtitle | Panels | Instruments | Data | per country | global | Notes and comments |
|---|---|---|---|---|---|---|---|---|---|
| 21 | WCT Part 1 | "GeoStatus" | Global Diagrams | 20 | 74 | — | — | 72,000 | X-rays and CAT-scans of religion's inner workings |
| 22 | WCT GD 3 | Denominations | Megacensus | 180 | 360 | 1 | 1,500 | 540,000 | Churches measure 180 major subjects/panels |
| 23 | WCT Part 7 | "GeoTrends" | Graphs | 28 | 572 | 1 | 16,016 | 154,400 | Measuring trends at global and local levels |
| 24 | **WCT** | | **Global data** ........ | 228 | 1,006 | — | 17,516 | 766,400 | Totals of all global instrumentation |

**C. TOPICAL INSTRUMENTS**

A number of other instruments measure items not originating via country statistics. This situation is summarized in the following single line. A typical instrument is _WCT_ Table 31–3 which describes the world's current literature of 5 million books on Christianity by means of 148 different topics. Of the _WCT/WCE_ total of 1,070 statistical tables, 715 are country tables describing the situation country by country, and hence already enumerated above in lines 9, 14, and 17. However, the remaining 355 are key topical tables, covering these 148 subjects like Bible keywords, evangelism, dimensions of 'evan- gelize', martyrdom, chronology, major developments, postdenominationalism. These topical tables can each be regarded as a separate instrument, often a complex one involving numerous measurements.

| Ref | WCT/WCE Part number | Title | Subtitle | Panels | Instruments | Data | per country | global | Notes and comments |
|---|---|---|---|---|---|---|---|---|---|
| 25 | | | **Topical tables** ...... | 148 | 355 | 10 | — | 525,400 | Total of all instrumentation on specific topics |

**D. DATABASE INSTRUMENTS**

In 6 cases in _WCE_ the simplest way to present huge masses of data has been to reproduce abbreviated versions of databases compiled during this survey and analysis. These 6 are listed as follows. Note that 3 have already been enumerated above (shown by their reference numbers 2, 5, 6 in column 1); the other 6 (26, 27, 28, 29, 30, 31) are now enumerated and then totaled below.

| Ref | WCT/WCE Part number | Title | Subtitle | Panels | Instruments | Data | per country | global | Notes and comments |
|---|---|---|---|---|---|---|---|---|---|
| 26 | WCT Part 17 | "Religiometrics" | | 1 | 23 | — | | 40 | 227,500 | Instrumentation on 9,890 religions |
| 27 | WCE Part 8 | "EthnoSphere" | | 1 | 38 | 54 | 2,000 | 540,000 | Instrumentation on 12,600 peoples |
| 28 | WCE Part 9 | "LinguaMetrics" | | 1 | 27 | — | — | 287,000 | Instrumentation on 13,500 languages |
| 29 | WCT Part 18 | "Ethnolinguistics" | Cultures | 5 | 12 | — | — | 397,700 | Instrumentation on 6,629 cultures |
| 30 | | | Lingua francas | 2 | 20 | — | — | 130,680 | Instrumentation on 2,178 lingua francas |
| 5 | WCE Part 10 | "MetroScan" | | 1 | 7 | 33 | 230 | 62,100 | Instrumentation on 7,000 cities |
| 6 | WCE Part 11 | "ProvinceScan" | | 1 | 9 | 12 | 108 | 29,160 | Instrumentation on 3,030 major civil divisions |
| 31 | WCE Part 14 | "GeoDirectory" | | 1 | 82 | — | | 20 | 15,000 | Instrumentation on 15,000 agencies under 82 topics |
| 32 | | | Databases 2, 5, 6 | 3 | 54 | 99 | 2,338 | 631,260 | (Already enumerated above) |
| 33 | | | **Databases** ........ | 11 | 202 | — | 3,918 | 1,057,880 | Total instrumentation on religions, languages, agencies |

**E. VISUAL INSTRUMENTS**

The last variety of instrumentation consists of _WCT's_ and _WCE's_ 1,650 photographs. These have been selected from a wider base of 4,000 available photographs, to support the other instruments by illustrating 14 different instruments based on varieties of subject matter, as follows: backgrounds, situations, numbers, persons, events, themes, descriptions, characteristics, definitions, analyses, findings, trends, futures, prospects. Consider the instrument 'numbers'. The church's huge number of 44 million baptisms a year (120,000 every day) is illustrated and to some extent corroborated by one small photograph of the mass baptism, on a single day in 1992, of 70,000 Xhosas in the Transkei river Tsomo (see Photographic Index in _WCE_ Part 15 and _WCT_ Part 32).

A lot has been learned from each photograph by asking a standard set of 14 questions: What date or year? What country? Where? What event? What activity? What people? How many (size of crowd)? Any names? Who? What language? What religion? What denomination? What symbols? Meaning of anything unusual? Photography has spawned a range of new sciences, including: macrophotography, photomicrography, photogrammetry, photometry, telemetry, et alia. Their contribution to this project is summed up on the line that follows.

| Ref | WCT/WCE Part number | Title | Subtitle | Panels | Instruments | Data | per country | global | Notes and comments |
|---|---|---|---|---|---|---|---|---|---|
| 34 | | | **Photographs** ....... | 1 | 14 | — | 40 | 151,200 | Photos corroborating statistics, claims, activities |

**F. TOTAL ALL INSTRUMENTATION**

| Ref | | Panels | Instruments | Data | per country | global | Notes and comments |
|---|---|---|---|---|---|---|---|
| 35 | All _WCT_ and _WCE_ totals .............. | 471 | 2,056 | 20 | 17,720 | 4,784,880 | 471 instrument panels with 2,056 types of instruments |

## Global Diagram 32. Quantifying the origin, creation, proliferation, and global volume of evangelism via 45 ministries: 25,932 trillion Christian witness-words per year, resulting in 938 billion disciple-opportunities offered to the globe each year.

The table below enumerates and totals per year every form of evangelizing activity at the global level. It measures how many hours evangelizers work, and how many hours are then heard by audiences under differing media circumstances. The following definitions are used:

*(a) Hours spent by evangelizers:*
***presence-hours*** (column 4). 'Presence' means a Christian's indirect witness to Christ by lifestyle, quality of life, relationships, prayer, ethics.
***witness-hours*** (column 5). 'Witness' means a Christian's direct spoken testimony to the Risen Christ, naming the Name, in unstructured situations.
***evangelism-hours*** (column 6). 'Evangelism' means a Christian's or a church's deliberate, structured, organized endeavor to present Christ and his gospel; quantified as *evangelism-hours*, the number of person-hours engaged in, particularly by professional Christians—evangelists, pastors, clergy, full-time workers, missionaries. Note that, as we are defining them, statistics of evangelism-hours are also included in witness-hours, and both form part of the presence-hours figures.

*(b) Received by audiences:*
***hearer-hours*** (column 8). This means the number of person-hours received (heard, viewed, read, perceived) by the audience being evangelized, this being enumerated as hours spent by evangelizers on evangelism (column 6) multiplied by a media factor (column 7).
***evangelism-words*** (column 10). Explicitly evangelistic person-words disseminated to and received (heard, viewed, read, perceived) by those being evangelized; enumerated as evangelism-hours (column 6), multiplied by the media factor (column 7), then multiplied by our standard rate of 5,000 words spoken per hour per individual.
***disciple-opportunities*** ('offers') (column 11). Specific opportunities (offers, chances, exposures, invitations) given to individuals to become Christ's disciples; quantified here as conferred by at least one evangelism-hour each person (column 10 divided by 5,000).

### GLOBAL VOLUME OF EVANGELISM
with (below) AD 2000 distribution in Worlds A, B, and C (see further elaboration in Global Diagram 40).

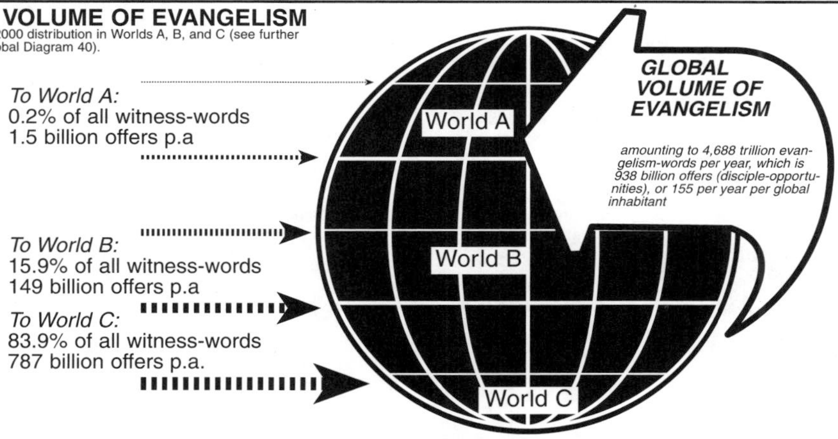
To World A:
0.2% of all witness-words
1.5 billion offers p.a
To World B:
15.9% of all witness-words
149 billion offers p.a
To World C:
83.9% of all witness-words
787 billion offers p.a.
World A
World B
World C
GLOBAL VOLUME OF EVANGELISM
amounting to 4,688 trillion evangelism-words per year, which is 938 billion offers (disciple-opportunities), or 155 per year per global inhabitant

KEY TO MINIDIAGRAM (left):
The segmented world is shown trichotomized into World C (all who are Christians), World B (all evangelized non-Christians), and World A (all who are unevangelized). On the left, evangelizing activity at present is 84% directed only at Christians in World C. The large white arrow represents the enormous magnitude of the present global volume of evangelism, and where it logically ought to be directed. Unfortunately, it is diverted elsewhere, as is shown by the current figures at far left which briefly show its actual distribution to Worlds A, B, and C. (Distribution analysis is taken further in Global Diagram 40).
KEY TO TABLE A (below):
*Column 1. Reference number for 7 modes and 45 ministries.*
*Column 2. Seven modes or types of contact (in capital letters) with 45 ministries or varieties of offering disciple-opportunities.*
*Column 3. Basic statistics of showings, persons, copies, pages, pieces, items.*
*Columns 4-6. Three main levels of evangelizing activity.*
*Columns 4 and 5. These include presence or witness by all participants.*
*Column 7. Media factor, to be multiplied by column 6 to get column 8. For the last 9 lines of Table A, this is derived by dividing column 8 by column 6.*
*Column 8. Hearer-hours as received by audiences.*
*Column 9. Words of witness through the 2 main levels of evangelizing activity including media multiplication.*
*Column 10. Explicitly evangelistic words received by persons in audiences.*
*Column 11. Specific offers, chances, invitations, opportunities made per year. (By definition, similar in size to column 8).*

Table A. **Hours spent evangelizing each year via 45 ministries, hours received by hearers, 7 mandates/types/modes of words disseminated, and offers of discipleship made per year.**

| *Ref* 1 | 7 MODES, 45 MINISTRIES 2 | ITEMS, AD 2000 3 | HOURS SPENT EVANGELIZING p.a. 4 | 5 | 6 | MEDIA 7 | RECEIVED p.a. 8 | WORDS DISSEMINATED p.a. 9 | 10 | OFFERS p.a. 11 |
|---|---|---|---|---|---|---|---|---|---|---|
| **1.** | **HIDDEN WORDS** | *Intercessors* | *Presence-hours* | *Witness-hours* | ***Evangelism-hours*** | *Media* | *Hearer-hours* | *Witness-words* | *Evangelism-words* | ***Offers*** |
| 1. | Intercession/prayerwalks/campaigns | 200 million | 876 billion | 146 billion | **18.3 billion** | 1 | 18.3 billion | 730 trillion | 91 trillion | **18.3 billion** |
| 2. | Inner renewal/spirituality | 375 million | 1,506 billion | 137 billion | **19.5 billion** | 1 | 19.5 billion | 684 trillion | 98 trillion | **19.5 billion** |
| **2.** | **VISUAL WORDS** (audiovisuals) | *Visuals p.a.* | *Presence-hours* | *Witness-hours* | ***Evangelism-hours*** | *Media* | *Hearer-hours* | *Witness-words* | *Evangelism-words* | ***Offers*** |
| 3. | Christians' lifestyle | 100 million | 438 billion | 73 billion | **18.3 billion** | 1 | 18.3 billion | 365 trillion | 91 trillion | **18.3 billion** |
| 4. | Audiovisual ministries | 50 million | 219 billion | 37 billion | **3.0 billion** | 25 | 76.0 billion | 4,563 trillion | 380 trillion | **76.0 billion** |
| 5. | Plays/concerts/operas/shows | 20 million | 14.6 billion | 4.9 billion | **2.4 billion** | 20 | 48.7 billion | 487 trillion | 243 trillion | **48.7 billion** |
| 6. | 'Jesus' Film shows (700 languages) | 3 million | 3.3 billion | 1.1 billion | **548 million** | 100 | 54.8 billion | 548 billion | 274 trillion | **54.8 billion** |
| 7. | Audio scriptures | 1 million | 110 million | 37 million | **18 million** | 1,000 | 18.3 billion | 183 trillion | 91 trillion | **18.3 billion** |
| 8. | Scripture leaflets/selections | 4.1 billion | 16.4 billion | 4 billion | **4.1 billion** | 5 | 20.5 billion | 103 trillion | 103 trillion | **20.5 billion** |
| 9. | Every-home campaigns/visitations | 160 million | 1.9 billion | 500 million | **160 million** | 50 | 8.0 billion | 120 trillion | 40 trillion | **8.0 billion** |
| 10. | New Reader Scriptures | 50 million | 1 billion | 200 million | **76 million** | 10 | 760 million | 10 trillion | 4 trillion | **760 million** |
| 11. | Braille scriptures | 10 million | 20 billion | 6 billion | **2 billion** | 5 | 10.0 billion | 150 trillion | 50 trillion | **10.0 billion** |
| 12. | Signed/deaf scriptures | 30 million | 6 billion | 2 billion | **600 million** | 5 | 3.0 billion | 45 trillion | 15 trillion | **3.0 billion** |
| 13. | Christian suffering | 260 million | 2.6 billion | 1 billion | **260 million** | 10 | 2.6 billion | 39 trillion | 13 trillion | **2.6 billion** |
| **3.** | **PERSONAL WORDS** | *Persons* | *Presence-hours* | *Witness-hours* | ***Evangelism-hours*** | *Media* | *Hearer-hours* | *Witness-words* | *Evangelism-words* | ***Offers*** |
| | Personal evangelism due to: | | | | | | | | | |
| 14. | Great Commission Christians | 648 million | 2,838 billion | 473 billion | **59.1 billion** | 3 | 177.4 billion | 7,096 billion | 887 trillion | **177.4 billion** |
| 15. | Martyrdoms | 160,000 | 1.4 billion | 58 million | **1.6 million** | 1,000 | 1.6 billion | 292 billion | 8 trillion | **1.6 billion** |
| **4.** | **PROCLAIMED WORDS** | *Professionals* | *Presence-hours* | *Witness-hours* | ***Evangelism-hours*** | *Media* | *Hearer-hours* | *Witness-words* | *Evangelism-words* | ***Offers*** |
| 16. | Full-time home church workers | 5,104,000 | 29.8 billion | 7.5 billion | **3.7 billion** | 2 | 7.5 billion | 75 trillion | 37 trillion | **7.5 billion** |
| 17. | Foreign missionaries | 420,000 | 2.5 billion | 900 million | **307 million** | 20 | 6.1 billion | 92 trillion | 31 trillion | **6.1 billion** |
| 18. | Evangelists | 1,230,500 | 7.2 billion | 1.8 billion | **110.5 million** | 100 | 11.1 billion | 898 trillion | 55 trillion | **11.1 billion** |
| 19. | Short-term missionaries/workers | 400,000 | 2.3 billion | 700 million | **146 million** | 10 | 1.5 billion | 37 trillion | 7 trillion | **1.5 billion** |
| 20. | Part-time evangelizers | 20 million | 116.8 billion | 29.2 billion | **5.8 billion** | 2 | 11.7 billion | 292 trillion | 58 trillion | **11.7 billion** |
| 21. | Mission agencies | 4,000 | 208 million | 62 million | **21 million** | 100 | 2.1 billion | 31 trillion | 10 trillion | **2.1 billion** |
| **5.** | **WRITTEN WORDS** (Scriptures) | *Copies p.a.* | *Pages p.a.* | *Witness-hours* | ***Evangelism-hours*** | *Media* | *Hearer-hours* | *Witness-words* | *Evangelism-words* | ***Offers*** |
| 22. | Portions/gospels (25 pages) | 323 million | 8.1 billion | 4 billion | **808 million** | 6 | 4.8 billion | 121 trillion | 24 trillion | **4.8 billion** |
| 23. | Near-gospels | 200 million | 5 billion | 3 billion | **480 million** | 6 | 2.9 billion | 75 trillion | 14 trillion | **2.9 billion** |
| 24. | New Testaments (300 pages) | 121 million | 36.3 billion | 18 billion | **3.6 billion** | 8 | 29 billion | 726 trillion | 145 trillion | **29 billion** |
| 25. | Near-NTs | 50 million | 15 billion | 8 billion | **1.4 billion** | 8 | 10.8 billion | 300 trillion | 54 trillion | **10.8 billion** |
| 26. | Bibles (1,300 pages) | 53.8 million | 69.9 billion | 35 billion | **7 billion** | 10 | 69.9 billion | 1,749 trillion | 350 trillion | **69.9 billion** |
| 27. | Near-Bibles | 10 million | 13 billion | 7 billion | **1.2 billion** | 10 | 12 billion | 325 trillion | 60 trillion | **12 billion** |
| 28. | 2nd-language gospels | 100 million | 2.5 billion | 1 billion | **200 million** | 3 | 600 million | 19 trillion | 3 trillion | **600 million** |
| 29. | 2nd-language NTs | 70 million | 21 billion | 11 billion | **1.4 billion** | 4 | 5.6 billion | 210 trillion | 28 trillion | **5.6 billion** |
| 30. | 2nd-language Bibles | 30 million | 39 billion | 20 billion | **3 billion** | 5 | 15 billion | 488 trillion | 75 trillion | **15 billion** |
| **6.** | **PRINTED WORDS** (literature) | *Pieces p.a.* | *Pages p.a.* | *Witness-hours* | ***Evangelism-hours*** | *Media* | *Hearer-hours* | *Witness-words* | *Evangelism-words* | ***Offers*** |
| 31. | Denominational materials | 2.5 billion | 20 billion | 5 billion | **1.9 billion** | 1 | 1.9 billion | 25 trillion | 9 trillion | **1.9 billion** |
| 32. | Local church output | 200 million | 10 billion | 7 billion | **3.8 billion** | 1 | 3.8 billion | 35 trillion | 19 trillion | **3.8 billion** |
| 33. | Outside Christian literature | 300 million | 100 billion | 30 billion | **10 million** | 10 | 100 million | 1,500 trillion | 1 trillion | **100 million** |
| 34. | Church-planting output | 58,000 | 580 million | 170 million | **58 million** | 10 | 600 million | 9 trillion | 3 trillion | **600 million** |
| 35. | Institutional ministries/records | 481,000 | 17.6 billion | 5 billion | **1.8 billion** | 1 | 1.8 billion | 26 trillion | 9 trillion | **1.8 billion** |
| 36. | Christian books (100 pages) | 3.5 billion | 350 billion | 58 billion | **35 billion** | 2 | 70 billion | 583 trillion | 350 trillion | **70 billion** |
| 37. | Christian periodicals (30 pages) | 50 million | 1.5 billion | 500 million | **150 million** | 10 | 1.5 billion | 25 trillion | 8 trillion | **1.5 billion** |
| 38. | Tracts (2 pages) | 5 billion | 10 billion | 5 billion | **2.5 billion** | 1 | 2.5 billion | 25 trillion | 13 trillion | **2.5 billion** |
| 38. | Other documentation | 2.5 billion | 10 billion | 3.5 billion | **1.2 billion** | 1 | 1.2 billion | 18 trillion | 6 trillion | **1.2 billion** |
| **7.** | **ELECTRONIC WORDS** | *Items* | *Hours a day* | *Witness-hours* | ***Evangelism-hours*** | *Media* | *Hearer-hours* | *Witness-words* | *Evangelism-words* | ***Offers*** |
| 40. | Programmed training (TEE, &c) | 60 million | 1 million | 500,000 | **180,000** | 10,000 | 18 billion | 25 trillion | 90 trillion | **18 billion** |
| 41. | Christian radio programs | 1,000 | 1 million | 600,000 | **1 million** | 50,000 | 50 billion | 150 trillion | 250 trillion | **50 billion** |
| 42. | Christian TV programs | 400 | 400,000 | 100,000 | **200,000** | 100,000 | 20 billion | 50 trillion | 100 trillion | **20 billion** |
| 43. | Urban media (cable TV, &c) | 3,000 | 1 billion | 300,000 | **450,000** | 12,000 | 5.4 billion | 18 trillion | 27 trillion | **5.4 billion** |
| 44. | Christian-owned computers | 332 million | 39.2 billion | 981 million | **98.1 million** | 350 | 34.3 billion | 1,717 trillion | 172 trillion | **34.3 billion** |
| 45. | Internet/www/e-mail networks | 65 million | 19.5 billion | 5.9 billion | **2 billion** | 30 | 58.5 billion | 878 trillion | 293 trillion | **58.5 billion** |
| | **TOTAL HOURS, WORDS, AND OFFERS** | | | | | | | | | |
| | *7 types/modes of evangelizing words:* | *Ministries* | *Presence-hours* | *Witness-hours* | ***Evangelism-hours*** | *Media* | *Hearer-hours* | *Witness-words* | *Evangelism-words* | ***Offers*** |
| | Hidden words | 2 | 2,382 billion | 283 billion | **38 billion** | 1.0 | 37.8 billion | 1,414 trillion | 189 trillion | **37.8 billion** |
| | Visual words | 11 | 723 billion | 129 billion | **31 billion** | 8.3 | 260.8 billion | 6,611 trillion | 1,304 trillion | **260.8 billion** |
| | Personal words | 2 | 2,840 billion | 473 billion | **59 billion** | 3.0 | 179.0 billion | 7,388 trillion | 895 trillion | **179.0 billion** |
| | Proclaimed words | 6 | 159 billion | 40 billion | **10 billion** | 3.9 | 39.9 billion | 1,424 trillion | 199 trillion | **39.9 billion** |
| | Written words | 9 | 210 billion | 105 billion | **19 billion** | 7.9 | 150.7 billion | 4,012 trillion | 754 trillion | **150.7 billion** |
| | Printed words | 9 | 520 billion | 115 billion | **46 billion** | 1.8 | 83.3 billion | 2,246 trillion | 416 trillion | **83.3 billion** |
| | Electronic words | 6 | 60 billion | 7 billion | **2 billion** | 90.8 | 186.2 billion | 2,837 trillion | 931 trillion | **186.2 billion** |
| | **Grand totals per year** | **45** | **6,892 billion** | **1,152 billion** | **206 billion** | **4.6** | **937.6 billion** | **25,932 trillion** | **4,688 trillion** | **937.6 billion** |
| | Grand totals per year per global inhabitant | | 1,138 | 190 | **34** | 4.6 | 155 | 4,282,727 | 774,225 | **155** |

## Global Diagram 33.    Evangelization in 420 kaleidoscopic dimensions: English meanings of 210 New Testament Greek verbs related to *euangelizo*, and 200 newer synonyms.

This diagram portrays relationships and clusterings among English verbs related to the English word 'evangelize'. This verb is portrayed below by the heavy, central circle. Around it are circles depicting the major English synonyms and near-synonyms, almost all of which are used in English Bible versions. These are fully described and analyzed in this volume's Part 23 "Evangelization", Table 23-19, and are listed there in Table 23-18.

Relationships of these circles are schematically proportional to frequency of use of each word in English versions of the New Testament. The number following each word gives the number of times the word (the word and its closest cognates) occurs in the English New Testament (Good News Bible). Further details, for the King James Version (AV) and the New International Version, are given in Table A. Although the 2 key Minicommission verbs 'evangelize' and 'disciple' do not occur in the most extensively-used Bible versions, totals for the related nouns, 'gospel (good news)' and 'disciple', occur there frequently.

Eleven separate but overlapping categories or roughly concentric zones of proximity can be distinguished, as follows:

1. **'Evangelize'**, the key verb (shown by heavy circle), not used in the 500 English Bibles (except occasionally in 5 obscure versions) and so never listed in English Bible concordances. Nevertheless, it remains the single best English verb for articulating the imperative of Christ's Great Commission. Its meaning draws elements from all verbs under both Minicommissions I and II.

2. **The 2 Minicommissions:** (1) *Evangelize!* (everything overlapping the heavy black circle), (2) *Disciple!* (everything overlapping the heavy grey circle). The diagram thus embod-ies a progression of mission starting at top left and moving down toward the globe at bottom right.

3. **The Big Seven** (in black italic capitals): biblical verbs related to 'evangelize' which are part-synonyms and concepts but which are particularly significant because they are the main verbs or emphases used in the 6 biblical Great Commission narratives in English. These 7 are: *Receive! Go! Witness! Proclaim! Disciple! Baptize! Train!* As described in Global Diagram 6, the first 4 of these Mandates form Minicommission I ('Evangelize!') and the last 3 form Minicommission II ('Disciple!')

4. **The Big Ten** (in capitals, inside the heavy circle, por-trayed by thin black circles): the 10 closest English biblical translated synonyms, being the 10 verbs used most often to translate *euangelizo* in English Bible use. These 10 are: *preach, bring, tell, proclaim, declare, announce, evangelize, give, spread, hear (make hear).* These 10 verbs occur a total of 2,048 times in the English New Testament (Good News Bible).

5. **The 51 macrotranslations** (exact biblical translations of the 54 NT occurrences of *euangelizo* (with the leading 28 shown in Table A); these are English verbs actually used (including the Big Ten) to translate *euangelizo* in one or more versions of the English Bible. Most of these are shown on the diagram.

6. **The 110 macrocommands:** these are the total of all the Great Commission imperatives, being the verbs used in the 6 Great Commission narratives in the New Testament.

7. **The 250 macrodefinitions:** these are brief statements incorporating more synonyms which authoritative sources have stated in print are direct definitions of 'evangelize', often beginning 'To evangelize is ...' or 'Evangelism is ...'. All addi-tional synonyms are included in Table 23-18. With numerous other minor definitions all these are also listed, quoted in full, expounded, and described in Tables 23-17 to 23-19.

8. **The 420 dimensions:** this covers all the above plus other major verbs (shown here as Table EE) which contribute semantically or conceptually to 'evangelize' and which can be measured and quantified. Most of these are also biblical com-mands, including biblically-supported near-translations of *euangelizo,* also the 10 close variants of *euangelizo* all based on the root *angello* (see Global Diagram 7, item 2), plus all others used to translate its 4 closest Greek synonyms. All these words are listed and classified under 56 key group-themes set out in the *Modern concordance to the New Testament* (1976), which are also shown here in Table 23-15.

9. **The 620 facets or near-synonyms** (shown here as Table EE on the next page): this covers all English verbs (including all described above) which are synonyms, near-synonyms, part-synonyms, aspects or facets of 'evangelize' in written or spoken use, either used in Bible versions or not so used.

10. **The 2,400 cognates of synonyms** (nouns and adjec-tives cognate to these 600 verbs; not shown here).

The overall deduction from this analysis is of the overwhelm-ingly kaleidoscopic nature of the biblical concept *Evangelize!* as the leading verb summarizing Christ's Great Commission.

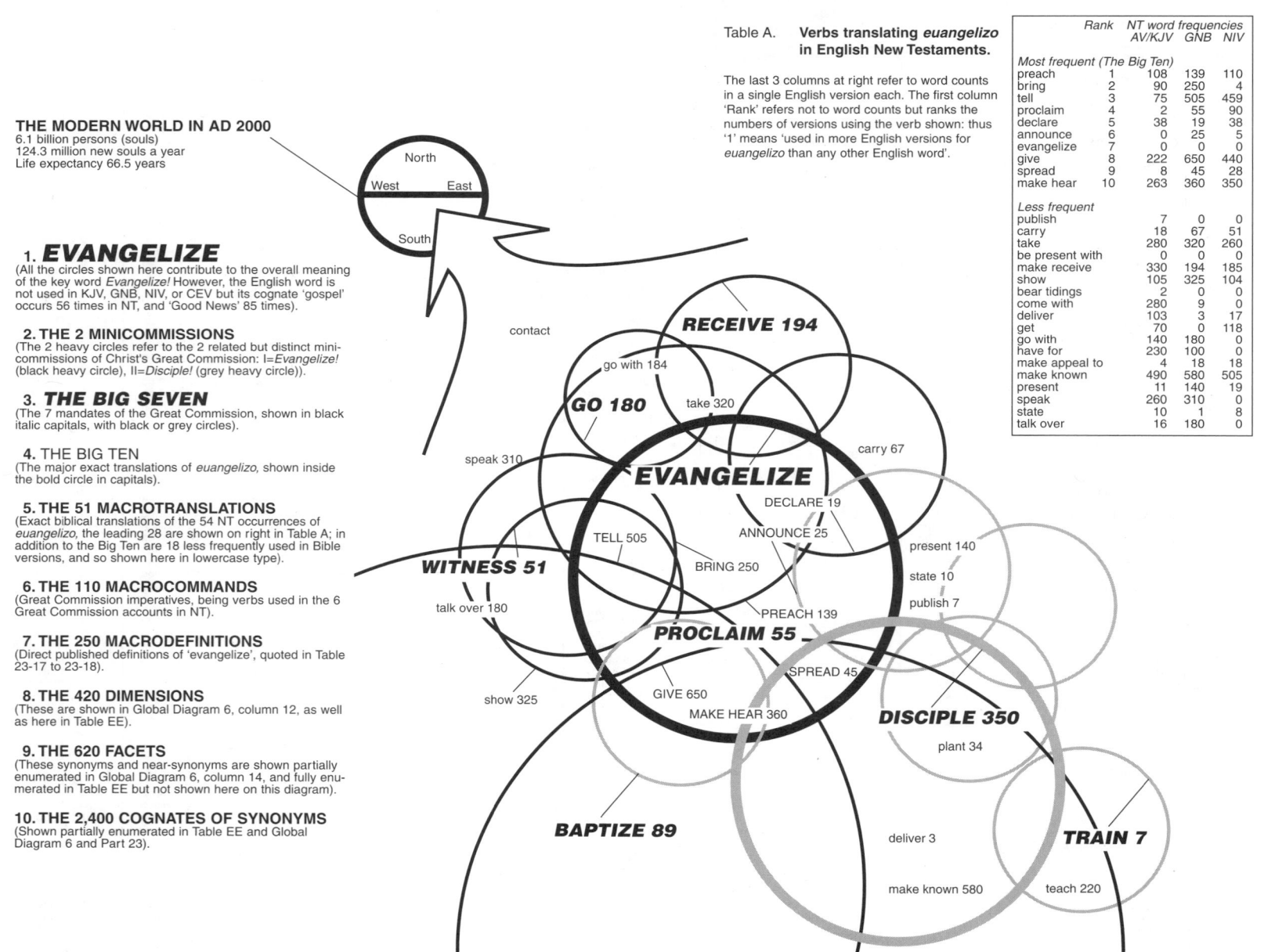

Table A.    **Verbs translating *euangelizo* in English New Testaments.**

The last 3 columns at right refer to word counts in a single English version each. The first column 'Rank' refers not to word counts but ranks the numbers of versions using the verb shown: thus '1' means 'used in more English versions for *euangelizo* than any other English word'.

| | Rank | NT word frequencies | | |
| --- | --- | --- | --- | --- |
| | | AV/KJV | GNB | NIV |
| *Most frequent (The Big Ten)* | | | | |
| preach | 1 | 108 | 139 | 110 |
| bring | 2 | 90 | 250 | 4 |
| tell | 3 | 75 | 505 | 459 |
| proclaim | 4 | 2 | 55 | 90 |
| declare | 5 | 38 | 19 | 38 |
| announce | 6 | 0 | 25 | 5 |
| evangelize | 7 | 0 | 0 | 0 |
| give | 8 | 222 | 650 | 440 |
| spread | 9 | 8 | 45 | 28 |
| make hear | 10 | 263 | 360 | 350 |
| | | | | |
| *Less frequent* | | | | |
| publish | | 7 | 0 | 0 |
| carry | | 18 | 67 | 51 |
| take | | 280 | 320 | 260 |
| be present with | | 0 | 0 | 0 |
| make receive | | 330 | 194 | 185 |
| show | | 105 | 325 | 104 |
| bear tidings | | 2 | 0 | 0 |
| come with | | 280 | 9 | 0 |
| deliver | | 103 | 3 | 17 |
| get | | 70 | 0 | 118 |
| go with | | 140 | 180 | 0 |
| have for | | 230 | 100 | 0 |
| make appeal to | | 4 | 18 | 18 |
| make known | | 490 | 580 | 505 |
| present | | 11 | 140 | 19 |
| speak | | 260 | 310 | 0 |
| state | | 10 | 1 | 8 |
| talk over | | 16 | 180 | 0 |

**THE MODERN WORLD IN AD 2000**
6.1 billion persons (souls)
124.3 million new souls a year
Life expectancy 66.5 years

## 1. *EVANGELIZE*
(All the circles shown here contribute to the overall meaning of the key word *Evangelize!* However, the English word is not used in KJV, GNB, NIV, or CEV but its cognate 'gospel' occurs 56 times in NT, and 'Good News' 85 times).

**2. THE 2 MINICOMMISSIONS**
(The 2 heavy circles refer to the 2 related but distinct mini-commissions of Christ's Great Commission: I=*Evangelize!* (black heavy circle), II=*Disciple!* (grey heavy circle)).

## 3. *THE BIG SEVEN*
(The 7 mandates of the Great Commission, shown in black italic capitals, with black or grey circles).

**4.** THE BIG TEN
(The major exact translations of *euangelizo,* shown inside the bold circle in capitals).

**5.** THE 51 MACROTRANSLATIONS
(Exact biblical translations of the 54 NT occurrences of *euangelizo,* the leading 28 are shown on right in Table A; in addition to the Big Ten are 18 less frequently used in Bible versions, and so shown here in lowercase type).

**6.** THE 110 MACROCOMMANDS
(Great Commission imperatives, being verbs used in the 6 Great Commission accounts in NT).

**7.** THE 250 MACRODEFINITIONS
(Direct published definitions of 'evangelize', quoted in Table 23-17 to 23-18).

**8.** THE 420 DIMENSIONS
(These are shown in Global Diagram 6, column 12, as well as here in Table EE).

**9.** THE 620 FACETS
(These synonyms and near-synonyms are shown partially enumerated in Global Diagram 6, column 14, and fully enu-merated in Table EE but not shown here on this diagram).

**10.** THE 2,400 COGNATES OF SYNONYMS
(Shown partially enumerated in Table EE and Global Diagram 6 and Part 23).

## Table EE. 420 dimensions and 620 facets of 'evangelize' listed alphabetically.

This table provides a single alphabetical index to all 420 dimensions of 'evangelize' (shown in bold type), and to words which are facets only (shown in medium type). In front of each word is its reference number in Tables 23–17 and 23–19, where more data and information about its relationship to 'evangelize' may be found.

| | |
|---|---|
| 327 | accept |
| 256 | **acclaim** |
| 1 | **accompany** |
| 582 | **account** |
| 328 | accuse |
| 140 | acknowledge |
| 141 | **acquaint** |
| 329 | acquire |
| 17 | **act** |
| 465 | **add** |
| 257 | **address** |
| 466 | **administer** |
| 142 | **admit** |
| 533 | **admonish** |
| 18 | **advance** |
| 258 | **advertise** |
| 534 | advise |
| 143 | **advocate** |
| 467 | **affiliate** |
| 144 | **affirm** |
| 535 | agonize |
| 330 | agree |
| 19 | **aid** |
| 20 | **aim at** |
| 259 | **alert** |
| 331 | ambush |
| 260 | **announce** |
| 145 | **answer** |
| 332 | **appeal** |
| 146 | **appear** |
| 21 | **apply** |
| 333 | apprehend |
| 334 | apprentice |
| 147 | apprise |
| 22 | **approach** |
| 536 | approve |
| 261 | **argue** |
| 23 | **arrive** |
| 537 | **ascertain** |
| 335 | ask |
| 148 | **assert** |
| 149 | asseverate |
| 24 | assist |
| 150 | **associate** |
| 336 | **assure** |
| 151 | **attest** |
| 337 | **attract** |
| 468 | balance |
| 469 | **baptize** |
| 2 | **be clothed** |
| 3 | **be filled** |
| 152 | **be here with** |
| 153 | **be martyred** |
| 154 | **be present** |
| 583 | **be responsible** |
| 470 | **bear fruit** |
| 155 | **bear tidings** |
| 338 | **beg** |
| 339 | **believe** |
| 340 | **beseech** |
| 341 | bestow |
| 342 | blame |
| 262 | **blanket** |
| 471 | **bless** |
| 25 | **bring** |
| 343 | bring back |
| 538 | **broadcast** |
| 472 | **build** |
| 26 | **calculate** |
| 344 | **call** |
| 345 | call out |
| 346 | capture |
| 27 | **care** |
| 28 | **carry** |
| 156 | **cast a net** |
| 29 | **cast out** |
| 347 | **catch** |
| 473 | **catechize** |
| 348 | cause |
| 263 | caution |
| 539 | **celebrate** |
| 349 | censure |
| 350 | **challenge** |
| 351 | change |
| 474 | chant |
| 352 | **charge** |
| 157 | chat |
| 158 | chatter |
| 159 | **circulate** |
| 160 | **claim** |
| 264 | clarify |
| 540 | **classify** |
| 475 | **cleanse** |
| 30 | **come** |
| 353 | comfort |
| 354 | **command** |
| 161 | **commend** |
| 541 | **commission** |
| 4 | **commit** |
| 162 | **communicate** |
| 542 | compare |
| 355 | **compel** |
| 356 | comprehend |
| 31 | **compute** |
| 543 | conciliate |
| 544 | conclude |
| 357 | **condemn** |
| 265 | **confer** |
| 163 | **confess** |
| 476 | **confirm** |
| 358 | **confront** |
| 477 | congregationalize |
| 359 | **conquer** |
| 360 | consider |
| 478 | console |
| 32 | **contact** |
| 266 | **contend** |
| 5 | **continue** |
| 545 | contribute |
| 164 | **converse** |
| 361 | **convert** |
| 165 | **convey** |
| 362 | **convince** |
| 6 | **cooperate** |
| 546 | correct |
| 33 | correspond |
| 166 | corroborate |
| 34 | **count** |
| 267 | credit |
| 363 | criticize |
| 167 | **cry** |
| 268 | cry out |
| 547 | **cultivate** |
| 269 | cure |
| 364 | customize |
| 365 | dare |
| 168 | dazzle |
| 366 | deal with |
| 270 | **debate** |
| 271 | **declare** |
| 479 | **dedicate** |
| 272 | deduce |
| 367 | defeat |
| 273 | **defend** |
| 169 | **deliver** |
| 368 | demand |
| 274 | **demonstrate** |
| 369 | **denounce** |
| 35 | depart |
| 275 | depict |
| 36 | **deploy** |
| 170 | depose to |
| 171 | **describe** |
| 37 | design |
| 276 | detail |
| 38 | **develop** |
| 172 | **dialogue** |
| 173 | **diffuse** |
| 480 | dip |
| 370 | direct |
| 580 | **discharge** |
| 371 | **disciple** |
| 548 | discipline |
| 174 | **disclose** |
| 277 | **discourse** |
| 175 | **discuss** |
| 176 | disperse |
| 39 | **display** |
| 278 | **dispute** |
| 177 | **disseminate** |
| 372 | **distribute** |
| 373 | **divide** |
| 40 | **do** |
| 41 | **do miracles** |
| 374 | **drag** |
| 42 | **drive out** |
| 43 | **dwell** |
| 549 | edify |
| 550 | **educate** |
| 375 | embolden |
| 279 | emphasize |
| 44 | **encounter** |
| 376 | **encourage** |
| 280 | endorse |
| 45 | **engage** |
| 377 | **enjoin** |
| 378 | **enlighten** |
| 481 | **enlist** |
| 482 | **enrol** |
| 379 | **entreat** |
| 281 | entrust |
| 46 | enumerate |
| 483 | **establish** |
| 47 | **estimate** |
| 585 | **evangelize** |
| 282 | **exalt** |
| 380 | excite |
| 551 | **exercise** |
| 48 | **exhibit** |
| 381 | **exhort** |
| 49 | exorcize |
| 7 | **expect** |
| 50 | **expel** |
| 382 | **explain** |
| 51 | **explore** |
| 178 | **expose** |
| 283 | **expound** |
| 179 | **express** |
| 52 | **extend** |
| 180 | **extol** |
| 284 | **familiarize** |
| 552 | **fax** |
| 484 | **feed** |
| 485 | **fellowship** |
| 554 | **fight** |
| 285 | **fill** |
| 383 | **find** |
| 384 | **fish** |
| 486 | **fix** |
| 53 | focus |
| 8 | **follow** |
| 553 | **followup** |
| 286 | forbid |
| 385 | **force** |
| 181 | **foretell** |
| 182 | **forewarn** |
| 386 | **forgive** |
| 54 | **free** |
| 581 | **fulfill** |
| 183 | **further** |
| 487 | **gain** |
| 387 | **gather** |
| 184 | **get** |
| 55 | **give** |
| 287 | **give a message** |
| 185 | **give account** |
| 288 | **give chance** |
| 186 | **give evidence** |
| 289 | **give notice** |
| 290 | **give opportunity** |
| 187 | give out |
| 488 | glorify |
| 56 | **go** |
| 57 | **go forth** |
| 58 | **go with** |
| 188 | **gossip** |
| 388 | grant |
| 389 | **grasp** |
| 489 | **grow** |
| 490 | guarantee |
| 390 | **guide** |
| 189 | **hand down** |
| 190 | **hand to** |
| 391 | **harvest** |
| 392 | **haul** |
| 191 | **have for** |
| 393 | **heal** |
| 491 | **help** |
| 291 | **herald** |
| 492 | herd |
| 192 | **hold** |
| 193 | howl |
| 394 | **hunt** |
| 194 | **illuminate** |
| 59 | **illustrate** |
| 555 | imagine |
| 493 | **immerse** |
| 60 | **impact** |
| 395 | **impart** |
| 494 | implant |
| 61 | implement |
| 396 | **implore** |
| 195 | imply |
| 62 | incarnate |
| 495 | incorporate |
| 63 | indicate |
| 556 | indoctrinate |
| 397 | induce |
| 557 | infer |
| 65 | **influence** |
| 196 | **inform** |
| 64 | **inhabit** |
| 496 | **initiate** |
| 398 | **insist** |
| 66 | **inspect** |
| 558 | **instruct** |
| 9 | **intercede** |
| 292 | **interpret** |
| 197 | **introduce** |
| 399 | **invite** |
| 198 | invoke |
| 400 | **involve** |
| 67 | **irradiate** |
| 293 | issue |
| 68 | **itinerate** |
| 69 | **journey** |
| 199 | lay bare |
| 401 | **lay hands on** |
| 294 | lay out |
| 402 | **lead** |
| 295 | **lecture** |
| 70 | **liberate** |
| 296 | **lift** |
| 200 | lift the veil |
| 201 | light |
| 71 | **list** |
| 72 | **live** |
| 497 | **live out** |
| 498 | look after |
| 73 | look for |
| 74 | **love** |
| 202 | **maintain** |
| 297 | **make a speech** |
| 203 | **make accessible** |
| 403 | **make acknowledge** |
| 499 | make attend |
| 75 | **make available** |
| 204 | **make aware** |
| 404 | **make choose** |
| 298 | **make clear** |
| 405 | make concede |
| 406 | **make decide** |
| 299 | **make evident** |
| 205 | **make hear** |
| 206 | **make known** |
| 559 | **make learn** |
| 300 | **make listen** |
| 301 | make obvious |
| 500 | **make peace** |
| 407 | **make put** |
| 408 | **make realize** |
| 409 | **make receive** |
| 410 | **make repent** |
| 411 | **make respond** |
| 76 | **make see** |
| 412 | **make trust** |
| 413 | **make understand** |
| 414 | **make well** |
| 415 | **make whole** |
| 207 | manifest |
| 208 | **mean** |
| 77 | **measure** |
| 560 | mediate |
| 78 | **meet** |
| 209 | **mention** |
| 79 | migrate |
| 501 | **minister** |
| 80 | **missionize** |
| 561 | **mobilize** |
| 81 | move |
| 502 | **multiply** |
| 210 | **name** |
| 211 | **narrate** |
| 562 | narrowcast |
| 416 | net |
| 212 | noise abroad |
| 82 | note |
| 302 | **notify** |
| 83 | **number** |
| 563 | **nurture** |
| 584 | **obey** |
| 417 | **oblige** |
| 84 | **observe** |
| 85 | **occupy** |
| 418 | **offer** |
| 213 | **open** |
| 419 | **order** |
| 420 | overcome |
| 421 | overtake |
| 86 | paint |
| 10 | **participate** |
| 503 | partner |
| 214 | **pass on** |
| 504 | **pastor** |
| 505 | pastoralize |
| 87 | pay attention |
| 88 | **penetrate** |
| 422 | **perceive** |
| 89 | **perform miracles** |
| 90 | **permeate** |
| 11 | **persist** |
| 423 | **persuade** |
| 91 | pervade |
| 92 | pity |
| 215 | place |
| 424 | **place hands on** |
| 93 | **plan** |
| 506 | **plant** |
| 425 | **plead** |
| 507 | pledge |
| 12 | **pneumatize** |
| 94 | **point** |
| 426 | **polarize** |
| 95 | **portray** |
| 508 | pour out |
| 509 | **praise** |
| 13 | **pray** |
| 303 | **preach** |
| 304 | **predict** |
| 96 | **prepare** |
| 427 | prescribe |
| 305 | **present** |
| 428 | **press** |
| 429 | pressurize |
| 430 | prevail upon |
| 306 | **proclaim** |
| 510 | **produce crop** |
| 216 | **profess** |
| 431 | proffer |
| 564 | **progress** |
| 307 | **promise** |
| 308 | **promulgate** |
| 217 | **propagate** |
| 218 | **prophesy** |
| 432 | prosecute |
| 565 | prosper |
| 97 | protest |
| 309 | **prove** |
| 98 | **provide** |
| 310 | publicize |
| 311 | **publish** |
| 99 | pursue |
| 312 | put before |
| 433 | **put right** |
| 219 | **radiate** |
| 100 | **reach** |
| 434 | **react** |
| 313 | **read** |
| 566 | **ready** |
| 511 | reaffirm |
| 435 | **reap** |
| 314 | **reason** |
| 436 | **rebuke** |
| 220 | recall |
| 14 | **receive** |
| 315 | recite |
| 221 | **reckon** |
| 222 | **recognize** |
| 223 | **recommend** |
| 512 | **reconcile** |
| 101 | **record** |
| 224 | **recount** |
| 437 | **recruit** |
| 316 | **refute** |
| 102 | **register** |
| 513 | regulate |
| 225 | **relate** |
| 103 | relieve |
| 514 | **remember** |
| 226 | remind |
| 438 | **remonstrate with** |
| 567 | **renew** |
| 317 | repeat |
| 227 | **reply** |
| 228 | **report** |
| 439 | **reprimand** |
| 440 | **reproach** |
| 515 | **reproduce** |
| 441 | **reprove** |
| 442 | **request** |
| 443 | **rescue** |
| 104 | research |
| 105 | **reside** |
| 229 | **respond** |
| 444 | **restore** |
| 318 | resuscitate |
| 445 | **retain** |
| 446 | **return** |
| 230 | **reveal** |
| 568 | review |
| 106 | **risk** |
| 231 | roar |
| 516 | **sacramentalize** |
| 319 | **saturate** |
| 447 | **save** |
| 232 | **say** |
| 107 | **scan** |
| 233 | **scatter** |
| 234 | scream |
| 108 | **search** |
| 517 | **secure** |
| 109 | **seek** |
| 448 | seize |
| 110 | select |
| 111 | **send** |
| 112 | send out |
| 518 | **serve** |
| 320 | set before |
| 113 | **set forth** |
| 114 | **set out** |
| 449 | **set right** |
| 115 | **settle** |
| 235 | **share** |
| 519 | **shepherd** |
| 236 | **shine** |
| 321 | **shout** |
| 116 | **show** |
| 117 | **show mercy** |
| 322 | show up |
| 237 | shriek |
| 118 | **signal** |
| 323 | sing |
| 450 | snare |
| 451 | snatch |
| 520 | soak |
| 119 | **sort** |
| 238 | sound |
| 239 | **sow** |
| 240 | **speak** |
| 241 | **speak in tongues** |
| 120 | speak out |
| 242 | **spread** |
| 521 | sprinkle |
| 522 | sprout |
| 121 | start |
| 324 | **state** |
| 15 | **stay** |
| 243 | **story** |
| 122 | **strategize** |
| 523 | **strengthen** |
| 244 | strew |
| 569 | **strive** |
| 570 | **struggle** |
| 123 | **study** |
| 452 | submit |
| 124 | **suffer** |
| 125 | **sum** |
| 453 | **summon** |
| 126 | **supply** |
| 524 | **support** |
| 127 | **survey** |
| 128 | symbolize |
| 454 | sympathize with |
| 129 | **take** |
| 455 | **take alive** |
| 456 | take by force |
| 571 | **take note** |
| 130 | take pity on |
| 245 | **talk** |
| 131 | **target** |
| 572 | **teach** |
| 573 | telecast |
| 246 | **tell** |
| 525 | **tend** |
| 247 | **testify** |
| 526 | **thank** |
| 574 | think |
| 325 | threaten |
| 248 | **throw a net** |
| 249 | thunder |
| 575 | tolerate |
| 132 | **total** |
| 133 | **touch** |
| 134 | tour |
| 576 | **train** |
| 250 | transfer |
| 457 | **transform** |
| 326 | **translate** |
| 135 | **transmit** |
| 136 | transport |
| 458 | trap |
| 137 | **travel** |
| 459 | triumph over |
| 460 | **turn** |
| 251 | uncover |
| 577 | **unite** |
| 252 | unveil |
| 461 | **urge** |
| 253 | utter |
| 527 | validate |
| 462 | vanquish |
| 138 | **visit** |
| 139 | visualize |
| 16 | **wait** |
| 528 | wait upon |
| 463 | **warn** |
| 529 | **wash** |
| 530 | **welcome** |
| 464 | **win** |
| 254 | witness |
| 578 | **work** |
| 579 | **work among** |
| 531 | **worship** |
| 532 | **write** |
| 255 | yell |

## Global Diagram 34.   Today's global mission: the status of world evangelization in AD 2000.

Today's globe is shown here twice: first, at upper right, as part of this book's evolving logo; and second—the larger circle below—as a more detailed representation of the whole Earth.

The entire globe is divided here, and in several global diagrams that follow, on the criterion of demographic evangelization into 3 worlds each with distinct populations. These worlds, A, B, and C, are not geographically defined but are defined on the basis of response to the Christian faith. World C consists of all persons who individually are *Christians* anywhere across the globe. Worlds A and B consist of all persons, individually, who are non-Christians: World A those who in addition have never heard the gospel or heard of Jesus (the *unevangelized*), World B those who have heard the gospel (who have heard, with understanding, about Christianity,

Christ, and the gospel) but have not, or not yet, accepted it or become disciples of Christ (here termed *evangelized non-Christians*).

Onto this 3-world division, countries or metropolises or peoples do not easily fit because each is composed of a mixture of unevangelized persons, evangelized non-Christians, and Christians. However, for purposes of illustration we add a few names of countries below, placing these population segments where the majority of their individuals are located. These countries are placed vertically according to a numerical scale of evangelization: most-evangelized countries at the bottom, least-evangelized at the top; also, on the left the so-called Second World, by which is meant the Communist and former Communist world (the whole Sino-Soviet bloc or

sphere of influence, including Eastern Europe and other ex-Communist countries), the Third World on the right, the Western world in between. Note that to illustrate today's global mission, Worlds A and B do have Christian activities in their midst, and therefore (as shown in Global Diagram 24) have some Christian workers and some foreign missionaries present.

Note also that World C is not defined as precisely the same as 'Christendom', 'the Christian West' nor 'the christianized world' nor does it include North America or Europe in their entirety. Non-Christians or atheists or agnostics in heavily-evangelized countries like the USA or Norway or Britain, for example, fall (on our definition) into World B.

---

THE GLOBE

THE HUMAN BACKDROP
6.1 billion persons
Land area 148.9 million sq km (11% arable)
Density 41 people per sq km
2,882 million urban dwellers
3,173 million rural dwellers
4,250 million adults (ages 15 and over) (70.3% of world)
1,060 million youth (ages 15-24) (17.5% of world)
789 million adolescents (teenagers, ages 13-19)
1,800 million children under 15 (29.7% of world)
606 million children under 5 (infants and babies; 10.0%)
419 million elderly (65 and over; 6.9%)

69.5 million elderly aged 80 or over
1,690 million women ages 15-49 (27.9%)
124.3 million births p.a. (341,000 a day)
43 live births per 1000 females
3,260 million literates (76.7% of adults)
990 million nonliterates (23.3% of adults)
Global income (GWP) US$28,900 billion p.a.
Growth of GWP 4.0% per year
Average income per person $4,770
Average family income $20,200
715 million telephones (95% direct-dial)
1,340 million TV sets
509 million computers

EVANGELIZATION
4.4 billion evangelized persons (4,425,674,000; 73.1% of world)
1.6 billion unevangelized persons (26.9% of world)
60.5 million newly-evangelized every year
Urban dwellers 78.2% evangelized
629 million unevangelized urbanites
166,000 newly-evangelized every day

CHURCH EXPANSION
Christians and churches exist in all 238 countries
20.7 million more Christians each year
19.5 million more church members each year
50,000 new churches each year

---

To see all countries located in either World A, or B, or C, consult Table 12-1, column 163.

Worlds:

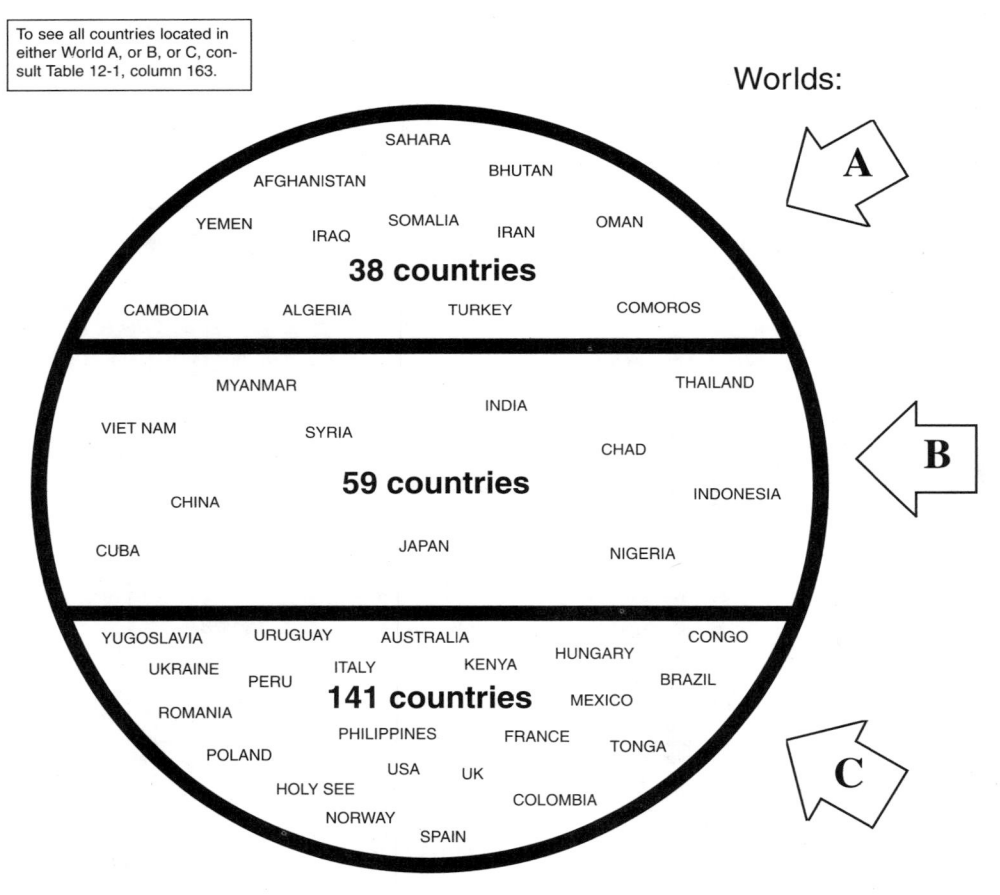

HORIZONTAL SCALE:  Geopolitical ideology

| | (Left inside) | (Center) | (Right inside) |
|---|---|---|---|
| WORLDS | Communist/Ex-communist world | Western world | Third World |
| DEVELOPMENT | Developing | Developed | Developing |
| INDUSTRIALIZATION | More-developed | Most-developed | Less-developed |
| GLOBAL AREA | East | North | South |
| RELIGION | Anti-religious | Secularized | Religious |

---

These global diagrams' logo

*VERTICAL SCALE: Evangelization in Worlds A,B,C
(percentages "p.a." in parentheses are annual rates)*

A.  **THE UNEVANGELIZED WORLD**
(38 countries each less than half evangelized, meaning E<50%, i.e. less than 50%)
1,629,375,000 unevangelized persons (-0.2% p.a.)
29.6% of global population
12.1% of global income
11.4% of all telephones
13.3% of all TV sets
2.8% of all computers

B.  **THE EVANGELIZED NON-CHRISTIAN WORLD**
(59 countries over half evangelized [E≥50%] but with church members less than 60%)
2.4 billion evangelized non-Christians (0.3% p.a.)
500 million evangelized but unreached non-Christians
40.1% of global population
35.3% of global income
27.8% of all telephones
34.7% of all TV sets
23.4% of all computers

C.  **THE CHRISTIAN WORLD**
(141 countries with church members 60% or over, all also having E≥95%, i.e. 95% or over)
2 billion Christians (1.4% p.a.)
33% of global population
Christians receive, own, and/or use:
52.6% of global income
60.8% of all telephones
47.0% of all TV sets
73.8% of all computers (70% of all being owned and operated by Christians)
Christians spend:
99.9% of Christian income on themselves
0.09% on the Evangelized Non-Christian World
0.01% on the Unevangelized World

## Global Diagram 35.    The great unevangelized belt: World A defined in terms of countries and peoples, AD 2000.

This map depicts with a single black boundary the geographical domain of World A, the unevangelized world, defined in terms of ethnolinguistic peoples. Its exact definition is as follows.

*Black line boundary.* Inside this line live every one of the globe's 168 least evangelized megapeoples (each with E<50%). It is also the case that inside this line live all 50 of the globe's megapeoples with E between 50% and 70%, and

numerous smaller peoples. Altogether all these encompass 85% of all the 1.6 billion unevangelized individuals on Earth. Also, the vast majority of the world's 10,000 unreached minipeoples reside within this boundary, making it a prime strategic target for frontier missions.

*Relation to countries.* Of the 38 countries defined as in World A, 31 are megacountries (each with population over 1 million) found wholly within the black line boundary depicting

World A. These are enumerated in the left-hand half of the table below. (Note: 'Population' refers to AD 2000; AC=% church members; E=% persons evangelized).

*Largest megapeoples involved.* The right-hand half of the table below enumerates the 23 largest unevangelized megapeoples within this boundary of World A.

### LARGEST MEGACOUNTRIES WHOLLY WITHIN WORLD A

| Country | Population | AC% | E% |
|---|---|---|---|
| Pakistan | 156,483,000 | 2.4 | 46.8 |
| Iran | 67,702,000 | 0.5 | 37.2 |
| Turkey | 66,591,000 | 0.6 | 48.6 |
| Algeria | 31,471,000 | 0.3 | 49.6 |
| Morocco | 28,221,000 | 0.6 | 42.2 |
| Uzbekistan | 24,318,000 | 1.6 | 48.4 |
| North Korea | 24,039,000 | 2.1 | 50.0 |
| Nepal | 23,930,000 | 2.4 | 46.2 |
| Iraq | 23,115,000 | 3.1 | 48.4 |
| Afghanistan | 22,720,000 | 0.0 | 29.6 |
| Yemen | 18,112,000 | 0.2 | 46.6 |
| Mali | 11,234,000 | 2.0 | 43.6 |
| Cambodia | 11,168,000 | 1.1 | 49.1 |
| Niger | 10,730,000 | 0.5 | 42.1 |
| Tunisia | 9,586,000 | 0.5 | 48.9 |
| Senegal | 9,481,000 | 4.9 | 46.0 |
| Azerbaijan | 7,734,000 | 4.6 | 37.0 |
| Guinea | 7,430,000 | 3.1 | 41.6 |
| Somalia | 7,266,000 | 1.4 | 43.8 |
| Tajikistan | 6,188,000 | 2.1 | 44.1 |
| Libya | 5,605,000 | 3.0 | 46.1 |
| Laos | 5,433,000 | 2.1 | 47.6 |
| Kirghizia | 4,699,000 | 9.9 | 47.4 |
| Turkmenistan | 4,459,000 | 2.2 | 34.5 |
| Somaliland | 2,833,000 | 0.3 | 44.7 |
| Mauritania | 2,670,000 | 0.2 | 31.9 |
| Mongolia | 2,662,000 | 1.3 | 42.8 |
| Oman | 2,542,000 | 4.8 | 47.0 |
| Bhutan | 2,124,000 | 0.5 | 20.8 |
| Gambia | 1,305,000 | 3.6 | 44.1 |
| Guinea-Bissau | 1,213,000 | 12.8 | 48.2 |

### LARGEST UNEVANGELIZED MEGAPEOPLES WHOLLY WITHIN WORLD A

| People | Country | Population | AC% | E% |
|---|---|---|---|---|
| Western Punjabi | Pakistan | 66,810,000 | 4.40 | 48.4 |
| Han Chinese (Jinyu) | China | 47,351,000 | 7.00 | 47.0 |
| Han Chinese (Hunanese) | China | 44,226,000 | 2.00 | 41.0 |
| Awadhi | India | 37,352,000 | 2.50 | 33.5 |
| Bhojpuri Bihari | India | 36,071,000 | 1.02 | 40.0 |
| Maitili | India | 31,636,000 | 1.02 | 37.0 |
| Han Chinese (Kan) | China | 25,272,000 | 6.00 | 46.0 |
| Northern Uzbek | Uzbekistan | 19,024,000 | 0.10 | 49.1 |
| Sindhi | Pakistan | 18,259,000 | 0.01 | 49.0 |
| Braj Bhakha | India | 17,990,000 | 2.50 | 43.5 |
| Yemeni Arab | Yemen | 16,189,000 | 0.02 | 47.0 |
| Bangri | India | 14,900,000 | 3.60 | 46.6 |
| Northern Zhuang | China | 12,796,000 | 1.00 | 42.0 |
| Deccani | India | 12,726,000 | 0.00 | 40.0 |
| Jat | India | 12,164,000 | 2.60 | 46.6 |
| Madurese | Indonesia | 12,090,000 | 0.20 | 49.2 |
| Chhattisgarhi | India | 11,944,000 | 1.30 | 45.3 |
| Magadhi Bihari | India | 11,941,000 | 1.02 | 32.0 |
| Moroccan Arab | Morocco | 11,739,000 | 0.26 | 48.3 |
| Pathan | Afghanistan | 10,807,000 | 0.01 | 35.0 |
| Azerbaijani | Iran | 10,762,000 | 0.00 | 27.0 |
| Rajasthani | India | 10,120,000 | 1.10 | 42.1 |
| Hui | China | 9,581,000 | 0.00 | 40.0 |
| Central Khmer | Cambodia | 9,552,000 | 0.63 | 48.6 |
| Kanauji (Western Hindi) | India | 9,386,000 | 1.60 | 39.6 |
| Kazakh | Kazakhstan | 8,672,000 | 0.03 | 44.0 |
| Uighur | China | 8,035,000 | 0.00 | 34.0 |
| Berar Marathi | India | 7,552,000 | 2.00 | 34.0 |
| Azerbaijani | Azerbaijan | 6,627,000 | 0.01 | 33.0 |
| Tujia | China | 6,353,000 | 0.40 | 32.4 |
| Sylhetti Bengali | Bangladesh | 6,052,000 | 0.10 | 33.1 |

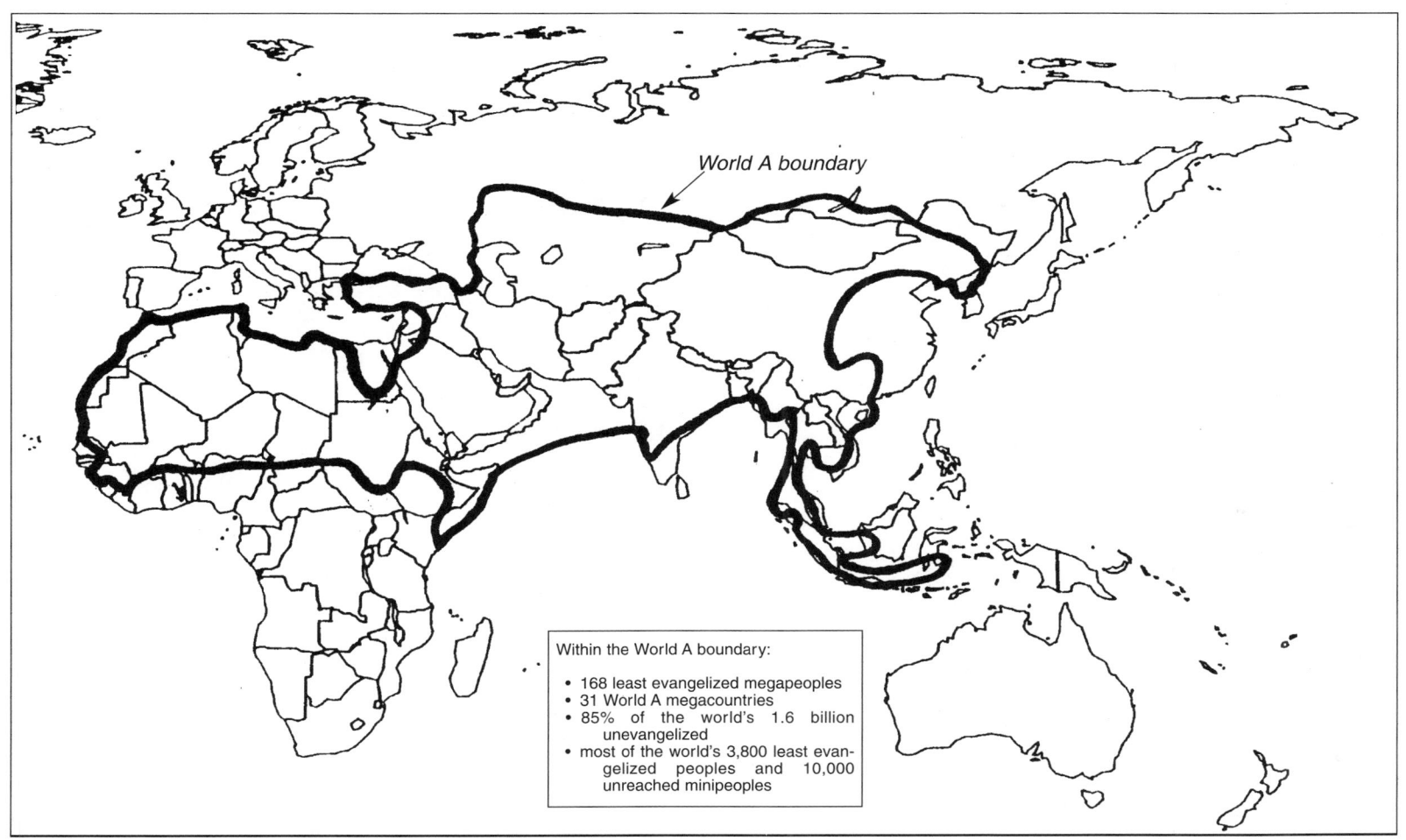

World A boundary

Within the World A boundary:

- 168 least evangelized megapeoples
- 31 World A megacountries
- 85% of the world's 1.6 billion unevangelized
- most of the world's 3,800 least evangelized peoples and 10,000 unreached minipeoples

## Global Diagram 36.    Resource countries now implementing world evangelization: foreign mission profiles of 134 countries in World C.

This diagram answers the question: Which of our globe's Christian countries were significantly involved in The Decade of Evangelism sending abroad foreign missionaries?

Our tripartite typology of world evangelization describes the 3 worlds A, B, and C. World C stands for the Christian world—all persons who individually are Christians. This can be mapped and measured as consisting of all 6,000 ethnolinguistic peoples who are 60% or more church members (AC≥60%), or, even simpler, it can be mapped to show all 141 countries in the world with AC≥60%.

The relative commitment of each country to Christ's Great Commission can be assessed, on one dimension at least, by computing each's current number of its citizens who are foreign missionaries supported abroad per million of its church member population. (This variable is named S). In the resulting table below the top 134 countries on this commitment are compared by being ranked. Five categories of country become visible.

(1) Exemplary response (S>350), with 24 countries headed by Ireland which sets the best example by sending 2,772 missionaries in 2000 for 1,888 million church members.

(2) Adequate response (350>S>150) covers 36 countries near the average for global Christianity, S=220 (derived from 420,000 missionaries in 2000 for 1,888 million church members).

(3) Barely adequate response (150>S>100), with 12 countries each well below the global average.

(4) Inadequate response (100>S>10) with 59 countries.

(5) Negligible response (S<10), characterizing all remaining World C countries.

The map below showing the boundaries of World C then illustrates how these resources relate at the level of continents. The small box ranks the 8 UN-defined continental areas by their average values of S.

*Mission response from 134 World C countries*
S=number of citizen foreign missionaries sent abroad per million church member population

### 1. Exemplary response (S>350)    S
| | |
|---|---:|
| Ireland | 2,772 |
| Malta | 2,693 |
| Samoa | 1,774 |
| Saint Pierre & Miquelon | 1,566 |
| Faeroe Islands | 1,263 |
| Belgium | 1,197 |
| American Samoa | 1,086 |
| Netherlands | 992 |
| Saint Helena | 938 |
| Liechtenstein | 924 |
| Spain | 823 |
| New Zealand | 820 |
| Canada | 815 |
| France | 742 |
| Anguilla | 696 |
| Italy | 671 |
| Monaco | 643 |
| USA | 619 |
| Andorra | 570 |
| Tonga | 557 |
| Portugal | 551 |
| Palau | 544 |
| Cook Islands | 541 |
| Switzerland | 528 |

### 2. Adequate response (350>S>150)
| | |
|---|---:|
| Britain | 474 |
| Gibraltar | 468 |
| Micronesia | 460 |
| Germany | 451 |
| Australia | 437 |
| Norway | 428 |
| Isle of Man | 381 |
| Austria | 362 |

| | |
|---|---:|
| Bolivia | 360 |
| Sweden | 333 |
| Guadeloupe | 323 |
| Finland | 306 |
| Luxembourg | 298 |
| Uruguay | 278 |
| British Virgin Is | 269 |
| San Marino | 252 |
| Panama | 244 |
| Puerto Rico | 242 |
| Nauru | 240 |
| Virgin Is of the US | 232 |
| South Africa | 220 |
| Martinique | 214 |
| Seychelles | 209 |
| Tuvalu | 205 |
| Montserrat | 197 |
| Cape Verde | 197 |
| Trinidad & Tobago | 188 |
| New Caledonia | 186 |
| Costa Rica | 181 |
| Bermuda | 180 |
| Marshall Islands | 166 |
| Guam | 160 |
| Sao Tome & Principe | 151 |
| French Polynesia | 151 |
| Iceland | 151 |
| Turks & Caicos Is | 151 |

### 3. Barely adequate response (150>S>100)
| | |
|---|---:|
| Channel Islands | 149 |
| Swaziland | 147 |
| Wallis & Futuna Is | 143 |
| French Guiana | 131 |
| Kiribati | 129 |
| Brazil | 129 |
| Chile | 127 |
| Equatorial Guinea | 127 |
| Denmark | 126 |

| | |
|---|---:|
| Solomon Islands | 112 |
| Grenada | 110 |
| Netherlands Antilles | 108 |

### 4. Inadequate response (100>S>10)
| | |
|---|---:|
| Spanish North Africa | 96 |
| Cyprus | 91 |
| Paraguay | 87 |
| Slovenia | 86 |
| Colombia | 86 |
| Cayman Islands | 77 |
| Bahamas | 75 |
| Dominica | 75 |
| Yugoslavia | 73 |
| Northern Mariana Is | 72 |
| Croatia | 71 |
| Lithuania | 69 |
| Poland | 67 |
| Vanuatu | 59 |
| Malawi | 57 |
| Saint Kitts & Nevis | 56 |
| Bougainville | 54 |
| Argentina | 53 |
| Nicaragua | 51 |
| Congo-Brazzaville | 51 |
| Barbados | 51 |
| Greenland | 51 |
| Belize | 51 |
| Timor | 49 |
| Mexico | 48 |
| Guatemala | 42 |
| Aruba | 42 |
| Greece | 40 |
| Venezuela | 40 |
| Macedonia | 39 |
| Latvia | 38 |
| Antigua | 37 |
| Namibia | 37 |
| Moldavia | 36 |

| | |
|---|---:|
| Kenya | 36 |
| Zambia | 35 |
| Lesotho | 35 |
| Armenia | 34 |
| Honduras | 33 |
| El Salvador | 33 |
| Ecuador | 32 |
| Peru | 32 |
| Philippines | 30 |
| Angola | 29 |
| Burundi | 29 |
| Hungary | 29 |
| Saint Lucia | 28 |
| Papua New Guinea | 26 |
| Uganda | 26 |
| Saint Vincent | 25 |
| Congo-Zaire | 21 |
| Georgia | 20 |
| Rwanda | 19 |
| Gabon | 18 |
| Reunion | 16 |
| Dominican Republic | 16 |
| Slovakia | 16 |
| Belorussia | 15 |
| Bulgaria | 15 |

### 5. Negligible response (S<10)
| | |
|---|---:|
| Romania | 10 |
| Ukraine | 10 |
| Haiti | 4 |

*Average foreign mission profiles*
| | |
|---|---:|
| Average mission-minded denominations | 300 |
| Average for any denomination | 250 |
| Average for global Christianity | 220 |

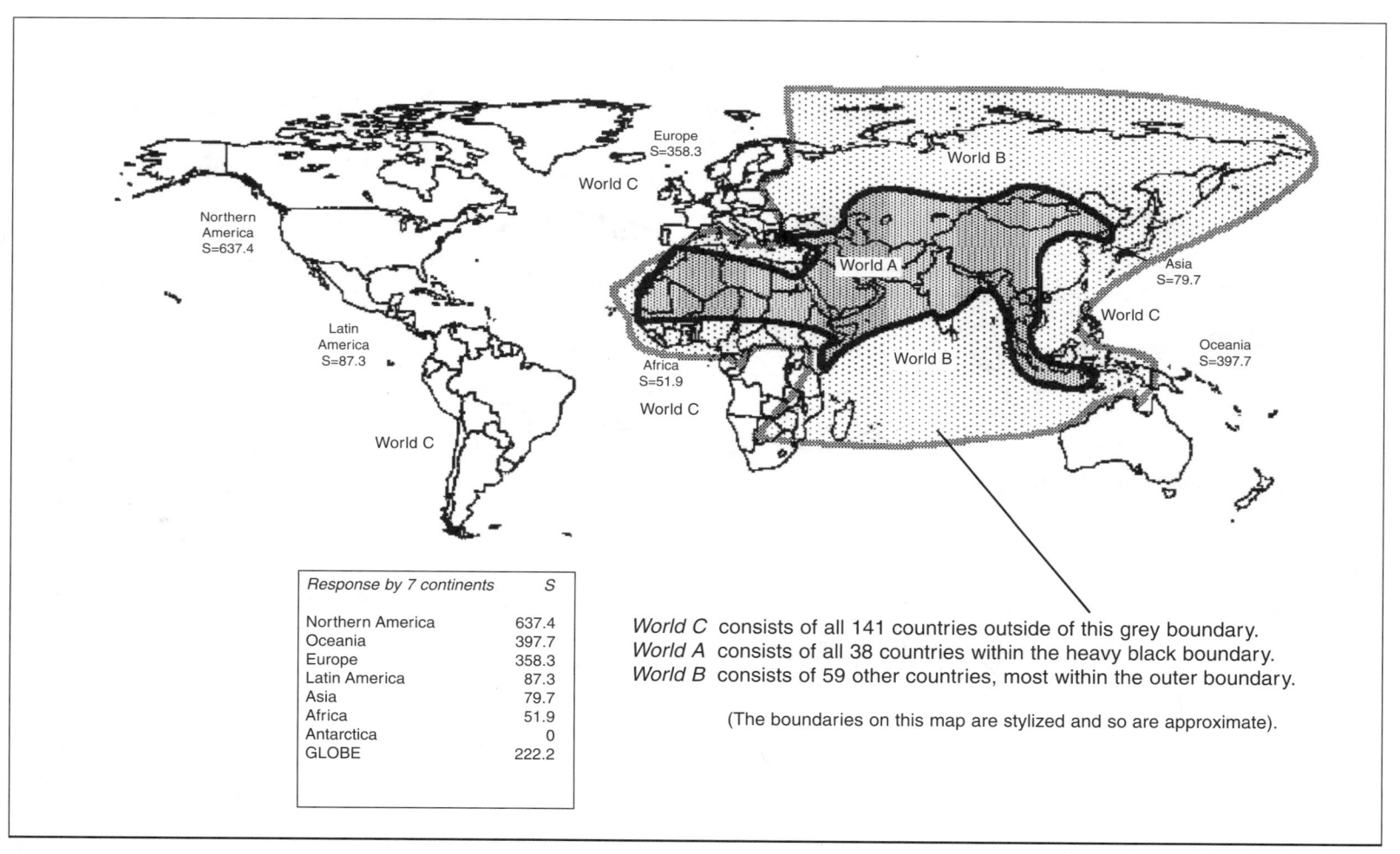

| Response by 7 continents | S |
|---|---:|
| Northern America | 637.4 |
| Oceania | 397.7 |
| Europe | 358.3 |
| Latin America | 87.3 |
| Asia | 79.7 |
| Africa | 51.9 |
| Antarctica | 0 |
| GLOBE | 222.2 |

*World C* consists of all 141 countries outside of this grey boundary.
*World A* consists of all 38 countries within the heavy black boundary.
*World B* consists of 59 other countries, most within the outer boundary.

(The boundaries on this map are stylized and so are approximate).

**Global Diagram 37.  Present distribution globes or 'sharing globes': how 16 major Christian resources are shared among or benefit Worlds A, B, and C, in the Decade of Evangelism, AD 1990 - AD 2000.**

The diagram below portrays how 3 slices of today's world benefit from the current global distribution of 16 major Christian resources. Each circle below is a 'sharing globe'. Each represents our globe's population, divided by our missiological typology into World A (unevangelized persons), World B (evangelized non-Christians), and World C (Christians). Because statistics of these resources are in the

main gathered country by country, A, B, and C are here defined not by individuals or by peoples but by countries.

The numbers then superimposed on each sharing globe show how each variety of resource is divided up among A, B, and C—in other words, how much of each resource benefits each of the 3 worlds. Thus the second globe demonstrates that 85% of all annual scripture distribution benefits

Christians (World C) and that less than 1% benefits the unevangelized World A.

The final, 16th globe represents the situation with regard to the most significant resource of all—Christians themselves, the Body of Christ, the Christian laos (laity).

### Scripture languages
*6,700        100%*
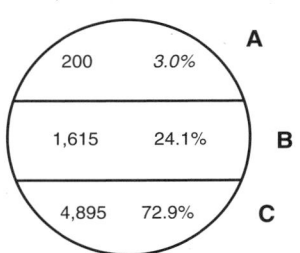

### Scripture distribution p.a.
*4,600 million        100%*
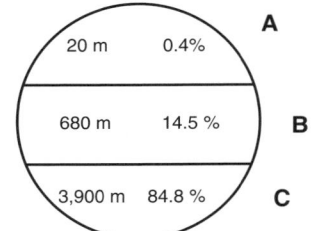

### Tracts (leaflets) p.a.
*5 billion        100%*
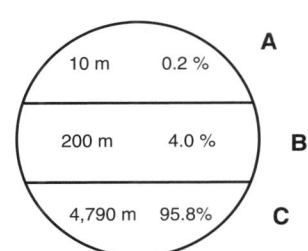

### Books (copies printed) p.a.
*3.5 billion        100%*
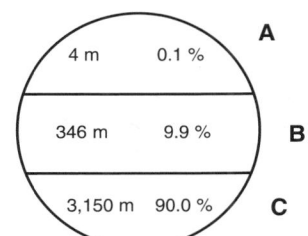

### Literature (all kinds) p.a.
*12 billion        100%*
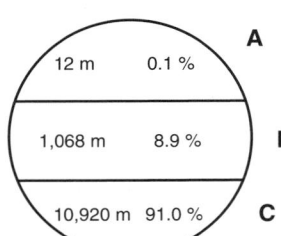

### Periodicals
*34,500        100%*
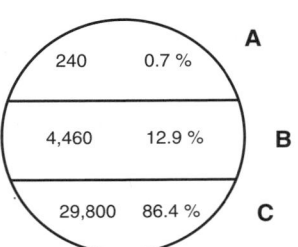

### Broadcasting (radio/TV) p.a.
*$5.8 billion        100%*
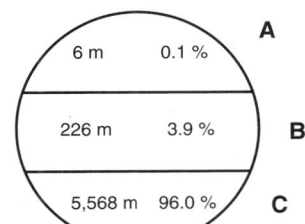

### Computers
*332 million        100%*
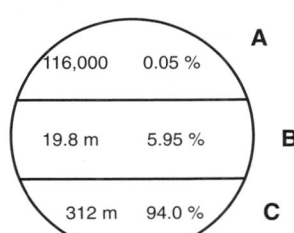

### Finance (church/agency) p.a.
*$270 billion        100%*
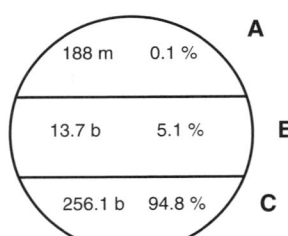

### Full-time workers
*5.5 million        100%*
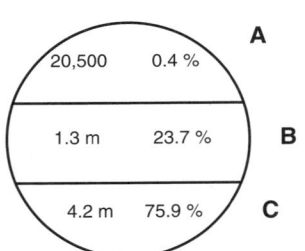

### Computer users
*400 million        100%*
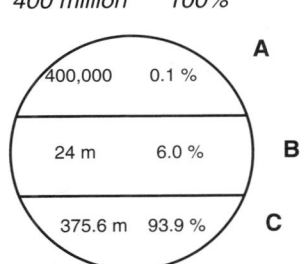

### Citywide campaigns p.a.
*1,600        100%*
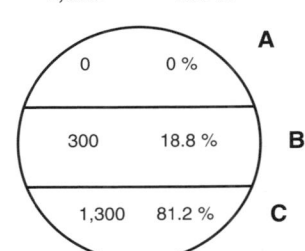

### Foreign missionaries
*419,500        100%*
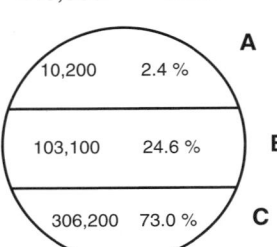

### Foreign mission money p.a.
*$15 billion        100%*
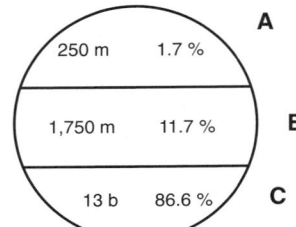

### Home missionaries
*1,135,000        100%*
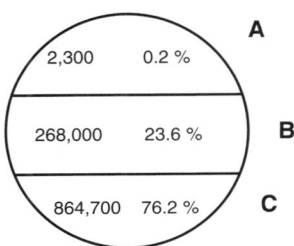

### Laypersons (lay church members)
*1,883 million        100%*
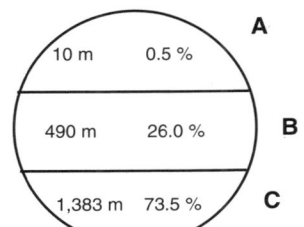

Notes: m=million, b=billion, p.a.=per annum (per year).

**Global Diagram 38.   Global and confessional deployment globes or 'sharing globes': current distribution of foreign missionary personnel in Worlds A, B, and C, in the Decade of Evangelism, AD 1990 - AD 2000.**

Each circle below is a 'sharing globe' depicting how organized Christianity distributes its foreign missionary personnel today. Each circle represents our globe's population divided by our missiological typology into World A (unevangelized persons), World B (evangelized non-Christians), and World C (Christians). Worlds A, B, and C are here defined not by individuals but by either peoples or countries.

Each globe then has superimposed on it numbers showing where each of the globe's 6 major ecclesiastico-cultural megablocs or confessions (and 3 other overlapping ones) assigns its foreign missionary personnel—how much each world A, B, or C benefits from their vocation. Thus the first globe tells us that 74% of all such missionaries benefit strongly-Christian countries in World C and that only 3%

benefit World A. The second globe refines this finding by revealing that, within all these countries, missionaries by and large are selectively assigned to the more Christian peoples.

## (1) GLOBAL CHRISTIANITY in 1990

*(The first globe shows Worlds A/B/C defined by countries; the second, Worlds A/B/C defined by peoples)*

*Note: Figures on the left within a globe represents numbers of personnel assigned, and figures on the right their percentage of total missionary force, the latter being shown in italics above the globe.*

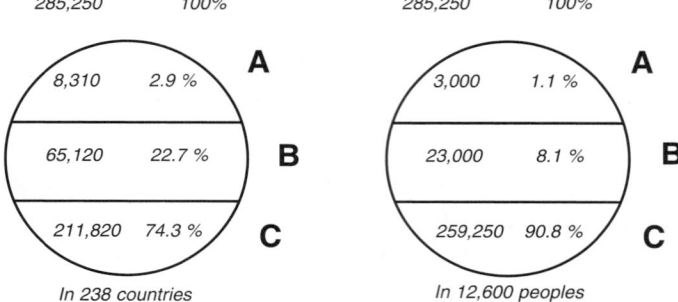

## (2) CONFESSIONAL CHRISTIANITY in 1990

*(Worlds A/B/C here below are defined by countries)*

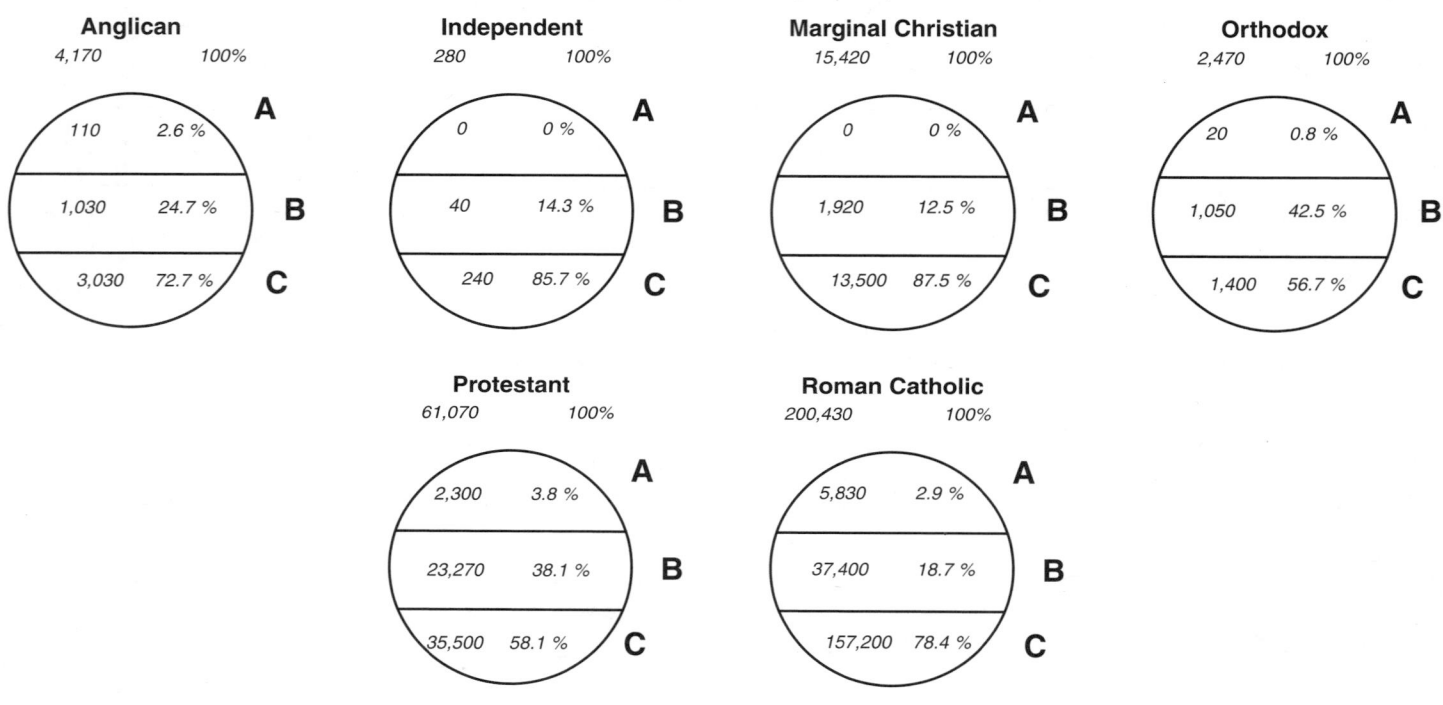

*Note: These 3 categories to the right overlap with the preceding 6 and with each other.*

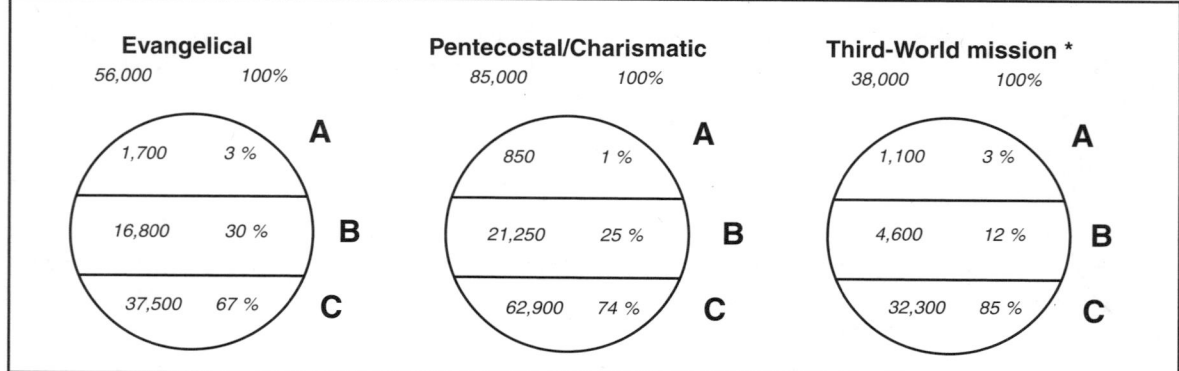

* Citizens of Third-World nations who serve as foreign missionaries in other countries.

**Global Diagram 39.  Mega-agency deployment globes: foreign missionaries deployed by 16 global mission agencies, 8 with global gigaplans and 8 with global megaplans, in the Decade of Evangelism, AD 1990 - AD 2000.**

A mega-agency is defined here as a Christian foreign missionary-sending agency with an annual budget over US$10 million. In 1990-2000 some 78 mega-agencies exist which are each promoting their own global plan for world evangelization (here termed a 'megaplan'). Of these, some 33 can also be called giga-agencies (defined as agencies each with an annual budget of over $100 million or decadal expenditure of US$1 billion), each promoting their own global plan (termed 'gigaplan').

Let's ask: Who benefits from all this vast expenditure? The diagram below answers by portraying a selection of 16 mega-agencies with megaplans, at these 2 income levels (8 mega-agencies, 8 giga-agencies). Under each heading are given, in italics, each agency's published total of foreign missionaries, this being divided below it into the numbers assigned to work in World A, or B, or C (defined here by countries); with percentages to the right.

Clearly, World A is getting far less than its fair share of the huge 10-year expenditure of $50 billion by the 33 gigaplans and 45 other megaplans.

## (1)  GLOBAL MISSION AGENCIES WITH GLOBAL GIGAPLANS in 1990
### (each supported by annual budget over $100 million)

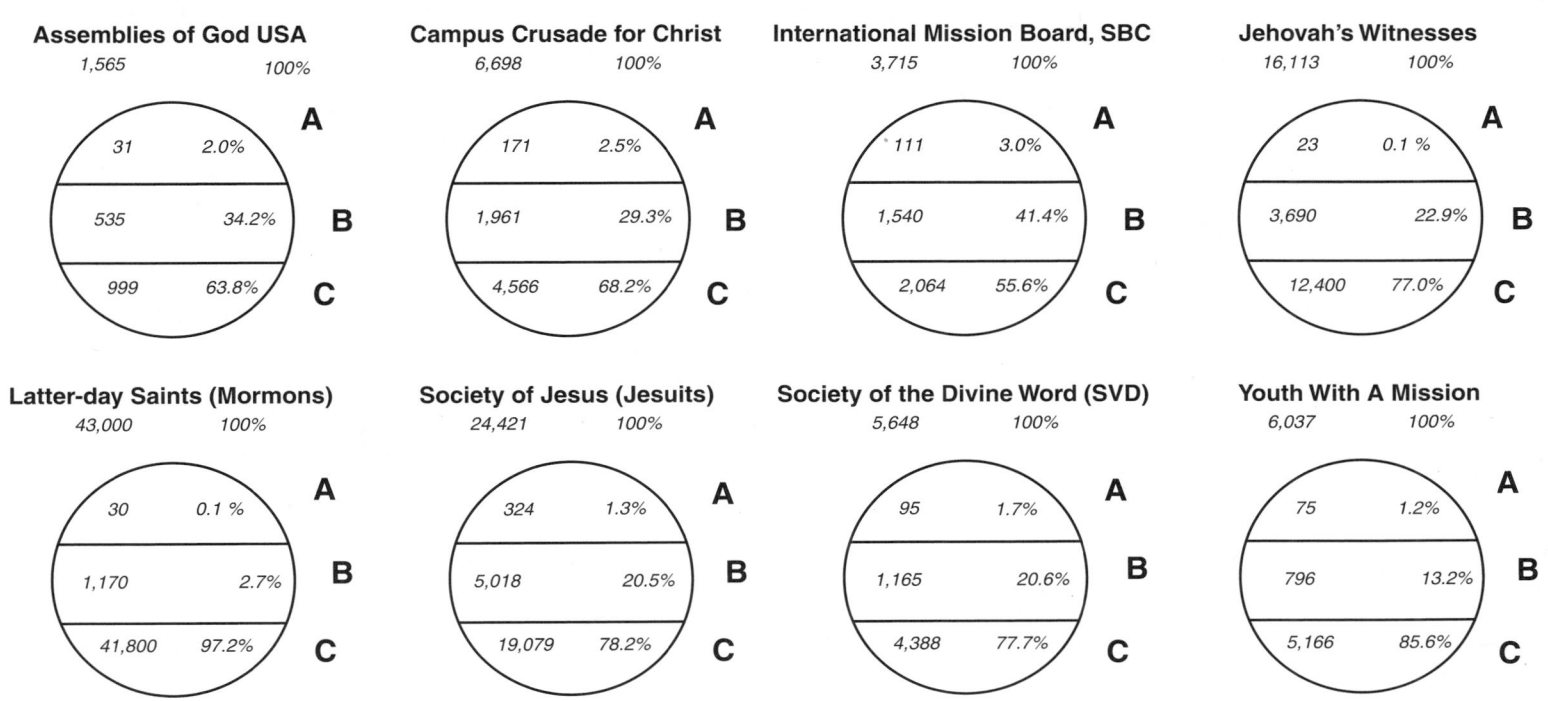

| Assemblies of God USA | | Campus Crusade for Christ | | International Mission Board, SBC | | Jehovah's Witnesses | |
|---|---|---|---|---|---|---|---|
| 1,565 | 100% | 6,698 | 100% | 3,715 | 100% | 16,113 | 100% |
| A 31 | 2.0% | A 171 | 2.5% | A 111 | 3.0% | A 23 | 0.1 % |
| B 535 | 34.2% | B 1,961 | 29.3% | B 1,540 | 41.4% | B 3,690 | 22.9% |
| C 999 | 63.8% | C 4,566 | 68.2% | C 2,064 | 55.6% | C 12,400 | 77.0% |

| Latter-day Saints (Mormons) | | Society of Jesus (Jesuits) | | Society of the Divine Word (SVD) | | Youth With A Mission | |
|---|---|---|---|---|---|---|---|
| 43,000 | 100% | 24,421 | 100% | 5,648 | 100% | 6,037 | 100% |
| A 30 | 0.1 % | A 324 | 1.3% | A 95 | 1.7% | A 75 | 1.2% |
| B 1,170 | 2.7% | B 5,018 | 20.5% | B 1,165 | 20.6% | B 796 | 13.2% |
| C 41,800 | 97.2% | C 19,079 | 78.2% | C 4,388 | 77.7% | C 5,166 | 85.6% |

## (2)  GLOBAL MISSION AGENCIES WITH GLOBAL MEGAPLANS in 1990
### (each supported by annual budget over $10 million but under $100 million)

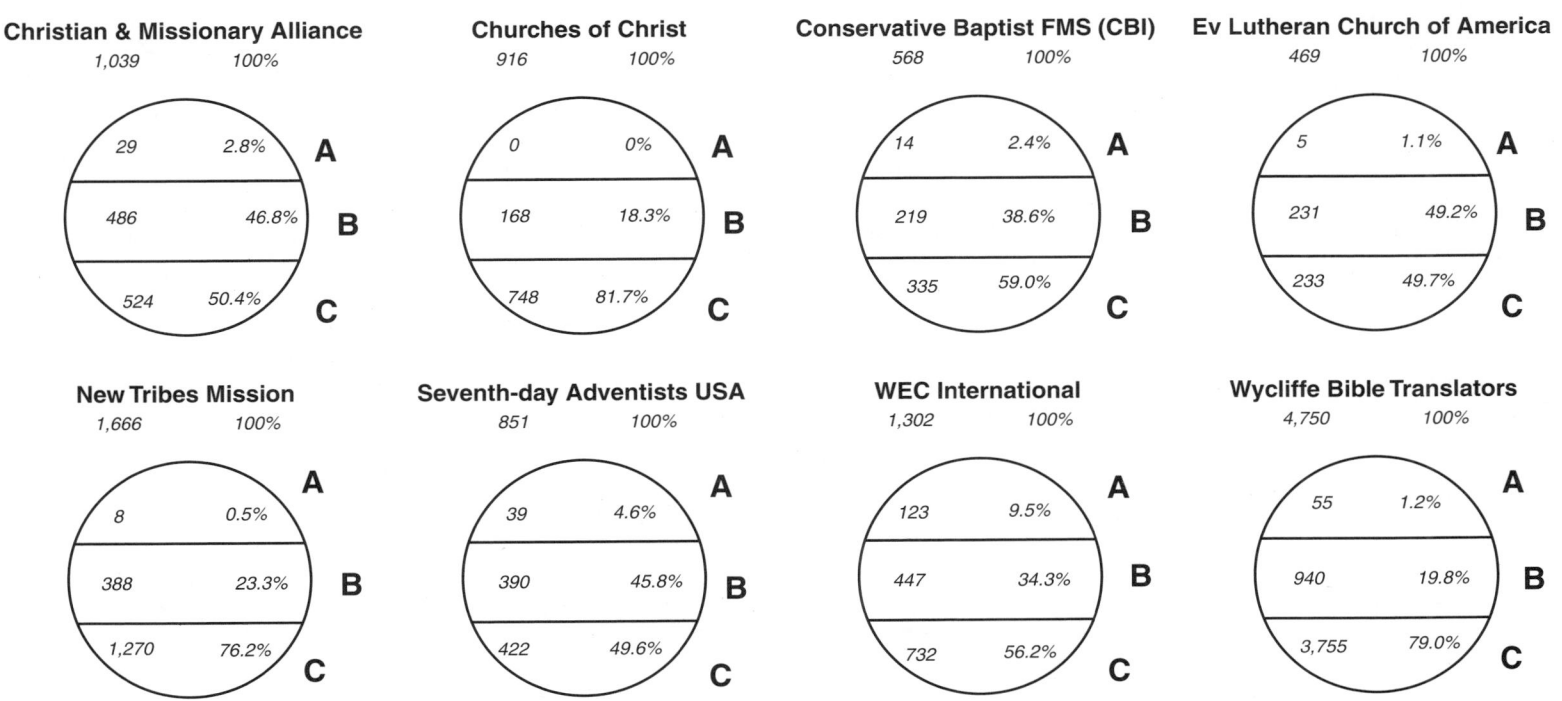

| Christian & Missionary Alliance | | Churches of Christ | | Conservative Baptist FMS (CBI) | | Ev Lutheran Church of America | |
|---|---|---|---|---|---|---|---|
| 1,039 | 100% | 916 | 100% | 568 | 100% | 469 | 100% |
| A 29 | 2.8% | A 0 | 0% | A 14 | 2.4% | A 5 | 1.1% |
| B 486 | 46.8% | B 168 | 18.3% | B 219 | 38.6% | B 231 | 49.2% |
| C 524 | 50.4% | C 748 | 81.7% | C 335 | 59.0% | C 233 | 49.7% |

| New Tribes Mission | | Seventh-day Adventists USA | | WEC International | | Wycliffe Bible Translators | |
|---|---|---|---|---|---|---|---|
| 1,666 | 100% | 851 | 100% | 1,302 | 100% | 4,750 | 100% |
| A 8 | 0.5% | A 39 | 4.6% | A 123 | 9.5% | A 55 | 1.2% |
| B 388 | 23.3% | B 390 | 45.8% | B 447 | 34.3% | B 940 | 19.8% |
| C 1,270 | 76.2% | C 422 | 49.6% | C 732 | 56.2% | C 3,755 | 79.0% |

## Global Diagram 40. The problem of unequal distribution: the case for initiating a properly balanced sharing of the church's evangelism (evangelistic offers) across the globe, totaling 2,570 million disciple-opportunities every day.

This diagram continues the analysis in Global Diagram 32, which quantifies the 45 differing ministries and modes of the churches' evangelism. Here the diagram zeroes in on that diagram's final column quantifying the churches' *evangelism* as 'disciple-opportunities' (evangelistic offers). Table A below then expands that column into 10 new ones, columns 4-14, showing how these are distributed among Worlds A, B, and C.

The grand total of all such offers made by the churches every day is startlingly high: 2,570 million directly-evangelistic offers, opportunities, or invitations per day.

Several other surprising findings may be observed in the analysis below by the 3 Worlds (columns 6 to 14). Comparisons can be made horizontally along a particular row, or vertically down a column.

The main problem at present can be seen to be the grossly unequal distribution of offers. World C gets 84% of all the churches' evangelism, while World A gets only 0.2%. Obviously this latter figure is woefully inadequate. but what would a 'fair share' look like? Here are definitions of 3 relevant terms.

***adequacy.*** This term refers to the evangelistic situation among a population which has received enough preaching and evangelizing to give its peoples sufficient chance to become disciples if they so wish.

***balance.*** A missionary situation in which adequate evangelistic attention is paid not only to Worlds B and C but also to World A. Or, the situation when all the globe's non-Christians are receiving numerically the same fair share of the daily offers generated.

***fair share.*** This refers to a situation in which no one population or individual continues to receive multiple disciple-opportunities until every population or individual in World A has received at least one such opportunity or a first chance. Numerically, a 'fair share' would be 27% of the global total, that is, 692 million offers a day for World A's populations (which number 1.6 billion). This is 148 times larger than the present grossly unfair 'share'.

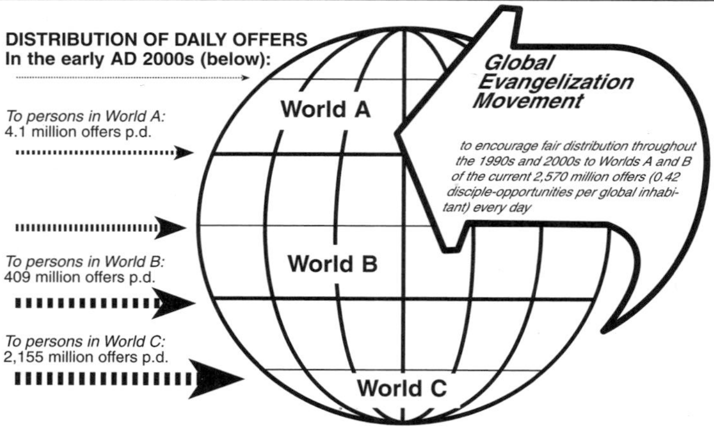

DISTRIBUTION OF DAILY OFFERS
In the early AD 2000s (below):
To persons in World A:
4.1 million offers p.d.
To persons in World B:
409 million offers p.d.
To persons in World C:
2,155 million offers p.d.
World A
World B
World C
Global Evangelization Movement
to encourage fair distribution throughout the 1990s and 2000s to Worlds A and B of the current 2,570 million offers (0.42 disciple-opportunities per global inhabitant) every day


**KEY TO MINIDIAGRAM (left):**
The segmented world is shown trichotomized into World C (all who are Christians), World B (all evangelized non-Christians), and World A (all who are unevangelized). On the left, daily offers (evangelizing activities) are 84% directed only at Christians in World C. The large white arrow represents the efforts of the global evangelization movement to secure for World A a fair share of each day's enormous output of specific opportunities, offers, and invitations to become Christ's disciples.

**KEY TO TABLE A (below):**
*Column 1.* Reference number for 7 modes and 45 ministries.
*Column 2.* Seven types of contact or modes or varieties of offering disciple-opportunities, subdivided into 45 kinds of ministries.
*Column 3.* Offers, invitations, opportunities made worldwide per year.
*Column 4.* Specific offers, invitations, opportunities made each day (per day, per diem, p.d.).
*Column 5.* Column 3 as % of global total of 937.6 billion.
*Columns 6-8.* describe World A; 9-11 World B; and 12-14 World C.
*Columns 6, 9, 12.* Column 4 divided among Worlds A, B, C.
*Columns 7, 10, 13.* Preceding column as % of column 4, adding up horizontally to 100%.
*Columns 8, 11, 14.* Offers as % of each world's total (at bottom of column 6, 9, or 12), adding up vertically to 100%.

Table A. **Disciple-opportunities offered daily to persons in 3 Worlds in 7 modes by means of 45 ministries (note: 'p.d'= per diem, per day, daily).**

| Ref<br>1 | 7 MODES, 45 MINISTRIES<br>2 | OFFERS TO WHOLE WORLD<br>Offers p.a.<br>3 | Daily offers<br>4 | %<br>5 | OFFERS TO WORLD A<br>Daily offers<br>6 | %<br>7 | %<br>8 | OFFERS TO WORLD B<br>Daily offers<br>9 | %<br>10 | %<br>11 | OFFERS TO WORLD C<br>Daily offers<br>12 | %<br>13 | %<br>14 |
|---|---|---|---|---|---|---|---|---|---|---|---|---|---|
| **1.** | **HIDDEN WORDS** | | | | | | | | | | | | |
| 1. | Intercession/prayerwalks/campaigns | 18.3 billion | 50,000,000 | 1.9 | 400,000 | 0.8 | 9.8 | 10,000,000 | 20.0 | 2.4 | 39,600,000 | 79.2 | 1.8 |
| 2. | Inner renewal/spirituality | 19.5 billion | 53,425,000 | 2.1 | 53,000 | 0.1 | 1.3 | 8,014,000 | 15.0 | 2.0 | 45,358,000 | 84.9 | 2.1 |
| **2.** | **VISUAL WORDS (audiovisuals)** | | | | | | | | | | | | |
| 3. | Christians' lifestyle | 18.3 billion | 50,000,000 | 1.9 | 100,000 | 0.2 | 2.5 | 9,000,000 | 18.0 | 2.2 | 40,900,000 | 81.8 | 1.9 |
| 4. | Audiovisual ministries | 76.0 billion | 208,333,000 | 8.1 | 208,000 | 0.1 | 5.1 | 41,667,000 | 20.0 | 10.2 | 166,458,000 | 79.9 | 7.7 |
| 5. | Plays/concerts/operas/shows | 48.7 billion | 133,333,000 | 5.2 | 13,000 | 0.0 | 0.3 | 5,333,000 | 4.0 | 1.3 | 127,987,000 | 96.0 | 5.9 |
| 6. | 'Jesus' Film shows (700 languages) | 54.8 billion | 150,000,000 | 5.8 | 1,500,000 | 1.0 | 36.9 | 30,000,000 | 20.0 | 7.3 | 118,500,000 | 79.0 | 5.5 |
| 7. | Audio scriptures | 18.3 billion | 50,000,000 | 1.9 | 50,000 | 0.1 | 1.2 | 2,500,000 | 5.0 | 0.6 | 47,450,000 | 94.9 | 2.2 |
| 8. | Scripture leaflets/selections | 20.5 billion | 56,164,000 | 2.2 | 56,000 | 0.1 | 1.4 | 6,740,000 | 12.0 | 1.6 | 49,368,000 | 87.9 | 2.3 |
| 9. | Every-home campaigns/visitations | 8 billion | 21,918,000 | 0.9 | 66,000 | 0.3 | 1.6 | 3,288,000 | 15.0 | 0.8 | 18,564,000 | 84.7 | 0.9 |
| 10. | New Reader Scriptures | 0.8 billion | 2,055,000 | 0.1 | 4,000 | 0.2 | 0.1 | 206,000 | 10.0 | 0.1 | 1,845,000 | 89.8 | 0.1 |
| 11. | Braille scriptures | 10 billion | 27,397,000 | 1.1 | 5,000 | 0.0 | 0.1 | 1,370,000 | 5.0 | 0.3 | 26,022,000 | 95.0 | 1.2 |
| 12. | Signed/deaf scriptures | 3.0 billion | 8,219,000 | 0.3 | 4,000 | 0.1 | 0.1 | 164,000 | 2.0 | 0.0 | 8,051,000 | 98.0 | 0.4 |
| 13. | Christian suffering | 2.6 billion | 7,123,000 | 0.3 | 36,000 | 0.5 | 0.9 | 712,000 | 10.0 | 0.2 | 6,375,000 | 89.5 | 0.3 |
| **3.** | **PERSONAL WORDS** | | | | | | | | | | | | |
| | Personal evangelism due to: | | | | | | | | | | | | |
| 14. | Great Commission Christians | 177.4 billion | 486,000,000 | 18.9 | 97,000 | 0.0 | 2.4 | 97,200,000 | 20.0 | 23.8 | 388,703,000 | 80.0 | 18.0 |
| 15. | Martyrdoms | 1.6 billion | 4,384,000 | 0.2 | 1,000 | 0.0 | 0.0 | 658,000 | 15.0 | 0.2 | 3,725,000 | 85.0 | 0.2 |
| **4.** | **PROCLAIMED WORDS** | | | | | | | | | | | | |
| 16. | Full-time home church workers | 7.5 billion | 20,416,000 | 0.8 | 41,000 | 0.2 | 1.0 | 3,062,000 | 15.0 | 0.7 | 17,313,000 | 84.8 | 0.8 |
| 17. | Foreign missionaries | 6.1 billion | 16,800,000 | 0.7 | 168,000 | 1.0 | 4.1 | 2,016,000 | 12.0 | 0.5 | 14,616,000 | 87.0 | 0.7 |
| 18. | Evangelists | 11.1 billion | 30,274,000 | 1.2 | 363,000 | 1.2 | 8.9 | 5,510,000 | 18.2 | 1.3 | 24,401,000 | 80.6 | 1.1 |
| 19. | Short-term missionaries/workers | 1.5 billion | 4,000,000 | 0.2 | 20,000 | 0.5 | 0.5 | 600,000 | 15.0 | 0.1 | 3,380,000 | 84.5 | 0.2 |
| 20. | Part-time evangelizers | 11.7 billion | 32,000,000 | 1.2 | 32,000 | 0.1 | 0.8 | 4,480,000 | 14.0 | 1.1 | 27,488,000 | 85.9 | 1.3 |
| 21. | Mission agencies | 2.1 billion | 5,699,000 | 0.2 | 57,000 | 1.0 | 1.4 | 684,000 | 12.0 | 0.2 | 4,958,000 | 87.0 | 0.2 |
| **5.** | **WRITTEN WORDS (Scriptures)** | | | | | | | | | | | | |
| 22. | Portions/gospels (25 pages) | 4.8 billion | 13,274,000 | 0.5 | 27,000 | 0.2 | 0.7 | 2,655,000 | 20.0 | 0.6 | 10,592,000 | 79.8 | 0.5 |
| 23. | Near-gospels | 2.9 billion | 7,890,000 | 0.3 | 15,000 | 0.2 | 0.4 | 1,894,000 | 24.0 | 0.5 | 5,981,000 | 75.8 | 0.3 |
| 24. | New Testaments (300 pages) | 29.0 billion | 79,562,000 | 3.1 | 80,000 | 0.1 | 2.0 | 14,321,000 | 18.0 | 3.5 | 65,161,000 | 81.9 | 3.0 |
| 25. | Near-NTs | 10.8 billion | 29,589,000 | 1.2 | 30,000 | 0.1 | 0.7 | 5,918,000 | 20.0 | 1.4 | 23,641,000 | 79.9 | 1.1 |
| 26. | Bibles (1,300 pages) | 69.9 billion | 191,616,000 | 7.5 | 192,000 | 0.1 | 4.7 | 34,491,000 | 18.0 | 8.4 | 156,933,000 | 81.9 | 7.3 |
| 27. | Near-Bibles | 12.0 billion | 32,877,000 | 1.3 | 197,000 | 0.6 | 4.8 | 7,233,000 | 22.0 | 1.8 | 25,447,000 | 77.4 | 1.2 |
| 28. | 2nd-language gospels | 600 million | 1,644,000 | 0.1 | 10,000 | 0.6 | 0.2 | 411,000 | 25.0 | 0.1 | 1,223,000 | 74.4 | 0.1 |
| 29. | 2nd-language NTs | 5.6 billion | 15,342,000 | 0.6 | 77,000 | 0.5 | 1.9 | 3,682,000 | 24.0 | 0.9 | 11,583,000 | 75.5 | 0.5 |
| 30. | 2nd-language Bibles | 15.0 billion | 41,096,000 | 1.6 | 82,000 | 0.2 | 2.0 | 9,041,000 | 22.0 | 2.2 | 31,973,000 | 77.8 | 1.5 |
| **6.** | **PRINTED WORDS (literature)** | | | | | | | | | | | | |
| 31. | Denominational materials | 1.9 billion | 5,173,000 | 0.2 | 1,000 | 0.0 | 0.0 | 310,000 | 6.0 | 0.1 | 4,862,000 | 94.0 | 0.2 |
| 32. | Local church output | 3.8 billion | 10,345,000 | 0.4 | 1,000 | 0.0 | 0.0 | 828,000 | 8.0 | 0.2 | 9,516,000 | 92.0 | 0.4 |
| 33. | Outside Christian literature | 100 million | 279,000 | 0.0 | 30 | 0.0 | 0.0 | 28,000 | 10.0 | 0.0 | 250,970 | 90.0 | 0.0 |
| 34. | Church-planting output | 600 million | 1,589,000 | 0.1 | 200 | 0.0 | 0.0 | 191,000 | 12.0 | 0.0 | 1,397,800 | 88.0 | 0.1 |
| 35. | Institutional ministries/records | 1.8 billion | 4,810,000 | 0.2 | 500 | 0.0 | 0.0 | 385,000 | 8.0 | 0.1 | 4,424,500 | 92.0 | 0.2 |
| 36. | Christian books (100 pages) | 70.0 billion | 191,781,000 | 7.5 | 19,000 | 0.0 | 0.5 | 19,178,000 | 10.0 | 4.7 | 172,584,000 | 90.0 | 8.0 |
| 37. | Christian periodicals (30 pages) | 1.5 billion | 4,110,000 | 0.2 | 400 | 0.0 | 0.0 | 164,000 | 4.0 | 0.0 | 3,945,600 | 96.0 | 0.2 |
| 38. | Tracts (2 pages) | 2.5 billion | 6,849,000 | 0.3 | 1,000 | 0.0 | 0.0 | 685,000 | 10.0 | 0.2 | 6,163,000 | 90.0 | 0.3 |
| 38. | Other documentation | 1.2 billion | 3,151,000 | 0.1 | 300 | 0.0 | 0.0 | 189,000 | 6.0 | 0.0 | 2,961,700 | 94.0 | 0.1 |
| **7.** | **ELECTRONIC WORDS** | | | | | | | | | | | | |
| 40. | Programmed training (TEE, &c) | 18.0 billion | 49,315,000 | 1.9 | 5,000 | 0.0 | 0.1 | 4,932,000 | 10.0 | 1.2 | 44,378,000 | 90.0 | 2.1 |
| 41. | Christian radio programs | 50.0 billion | 136,986,000 | 5.3 | 27,000 | 0.0 | 0.7 | 27,397,000 | 20.0 | 6.7 | 109,562,000 | 80.0 | 5.1 |
| 42. | Christian TV programs | 20.0 billion | 54,795,000 | 2.1 | 5,000 | 0.0 | 0.1 | 5,480,000 | 10.0 | 1.3 | 49,310,000 | 90.0 | 2.3 |
| 43. | Urban media (cable TV, &c) | 5.4 billion | 14,795,000 | 0.6 | 1,000 | 0.0 | 0.0 | 296,000 | 2.0 | 0.1 | 14,498,000 | 98.0 | 0.7 |
| 44. | Christian-owned computers | 34.3 billion | 94,068,000 | 3.7 | 9,000 | 0.0 | 0.2 | 12,229,000 | 13.0 | 3.0 | 81,830,000 | 87.0 | 3.8 |
| 45. | Internet/www/e-mail networks | 58.5 billion | 160,274,000 | 6.2 | 16,000 | 0.0 | 0.4 | 24,041,000 | 15.0 | 5.9 | 136,217,000 | 85.0 | 6.3 |
| | **TOTAL HOURS, WORDS, AND OFFERS** | | | | | | | | | | | | |
| | *7 types/modes of evangelizing words: Ministries* | | | | | | | | | | | | |
| | Hidden words | 37.8 billion | 103,425,000 | 4.0 | 453,000 | 0.4 | 11.1 | 18,014,000 | 17.4 | 4.4 | 84,958,000 | 82.1 | 3.9 |
| | Visual words | 260.8 billion | 714,542,000 | 27.8 | 2,042,000 | 0.3 | 50.2 | 100,980,000 | 14.1 | 24.7 | 611,520,000 | 85.6 | 28.4 |
| | Personal words | 179.0 billion | 490,384,000 | 19.1 | 98,000 | 0.0 | 2.4 | 97,858,000 | 20.0 | 23.9 | 392,428,000 | 80.0 | 18.2 |
| | Proclaimed words | 39.9 billion | 109,189,000 | 4.3 | 681,000 | 0.6 | 16.7 | 16,352,000 | 15.0 | 4.0 | 92,156,000 | 84.4 | 4.3 |
| | Written words | 150.7 billion | 412,890,000 | 16.1 | 710,000 | 0.2 | 17.4 | 79,646,000 | 19.3 | 19.5 | 332,534,000 | 80.5 | 15.4 |
| | Printed words | 83.3 billion | 228,087,000 | 8.9 | 23,430 | 0.0 | 0.6 | 21,958,000 | 9.6 | 5.4 | 206,105,570 | 90.4 | 9.6 |
| | Electronic words | 186.2 billion | 510,233,000 | 19.9 | 63,000 | 0.0 | 1.5 | 74,375,000 | 14.6 | 18.2 | 435,795,000 | 85.4 | 20.2 |
| | Grand totals per year | 937.6 billion | 2,568,750,000 | 100.0 | 4,070,430 | 0.2 | 100 | 409,183,000 | 15.9 | 100.0 | 2,155,496,570 | 83.9 | 100.0 |
| | Grand totals per inhabitant | 155 p.a. | 0.42 p.d. | | 0.002 p.d. | | | 0.17 p.d. | | | 1.08 p.d. | | |

**Global Diagram 41.** **The dynamics of global religious change: annual gains and losses in population, Christians, Non-Christians, evangelized and unevangelized persons, analyzed by Worlds A, B, and C in AD 2000.**

Huge population movements and religious surges take place year by year on the surface of our globe. Causes are: births, deaths, conversions, defections, and evangelization under its 600 dimensions and varieties. The dynamics of these changes are portrayed below. The globe is analyzed from its top to its bottom into the 3 horizontal Worlds A, B, and C. Its populations are then shown moving through life from left to right. They are analyzed into 3 vertical segments of human life—births, change (from childhood to adult life to old age, with persons becoming evangelized or converts or defectors), and deaths.

Table A below gives the detailed statistics of these changes. It is arranged as 5 minitables and 27 lines or rows of figures. Each minitable (A,B,C,D,E) views the global scene from the standpoint of a different grouping and shows its demographic deployment in Worlds A, B, and C. The lines a–z' enumerate 27 categories of globe-wide change—gains, losses, increases, decreases. Lines are progressively derived or computed from earlier lines; column 3 shows how or whence. ('UN' refers to *World population prospects 1998*. Tables 1 refers to *WCE* Part 4 "Countries".)

## ANNUAL CHANGE

All figures on this illustration are of annual change (m=millions; p.a.=per annum, per year)

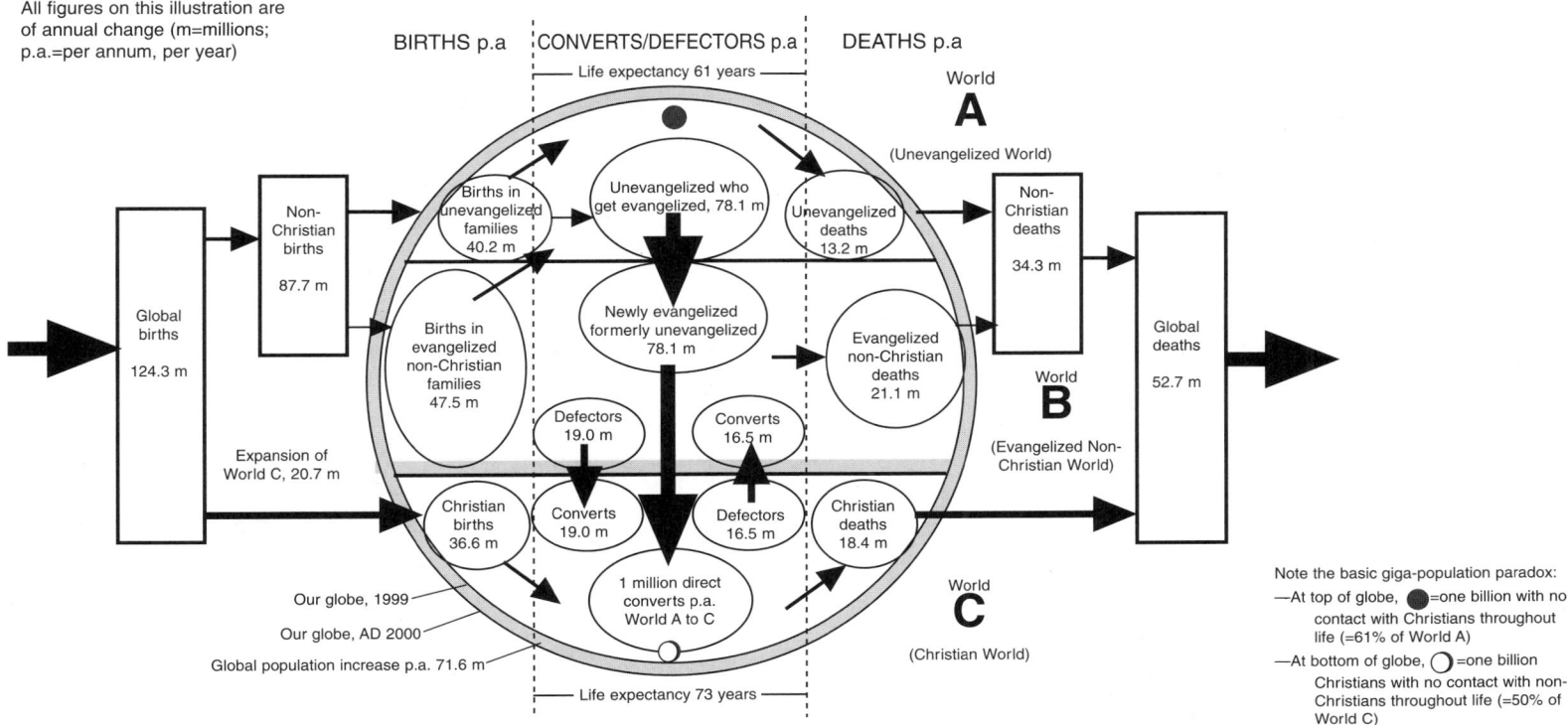

Note the basic giga-population paradox:
—At top of globe, ●=one billion with no contact with Christians throughout life (=61% of World A)
—At bottom of globe, ○=one billion Christians with no contact with non-Christians throughout life (=50% of World C)

| Table A. STATISTICS OF GLOBAL RELIGIOUS CHANGE. Where located? Category of globe-wide change | Derivation | GLOBE Global total per year | per day | Rate % p.a. | WORLD A (Unevangelized individuals) | WORLD B (Evangelized non-Christians) | WORLD C (Christians) |
|---|---|---|---|---|---|---|---|
| column   1   2 | 3 | 4 | 5 | 6 | 7 | 8 | 9 |
| **A. GLOBAL GROWTH OF POPULATION, AD 2000** | | | | | | | |
| Total population | | 6,055 m | | | 1,629 m | 2,426 m | 2,000 m |
| ANNUAL POPULATION GAINS | | | | | | | |
| a. Births, p.a. | UN | 124.3 m | 340,548 | 2.05 | 40.2 m | 47.5 m | 36.6 m |
| ANNUAL POPULATION LOSSES | | | | | | | |
| b. Deaths, p.a. | UN | 52.7 m | 144,384 | 0.87 | 13.2 m | 21.1 m | 18.4 m |
| ANNUAL INCREASE | | | | | | | |
| c. Natural increase of population (nett), p.a. | c=a-b | 71.6 m | 196,164 | 1.18 | 27.0 m | 26.4 m | 18.2 m |
| **B. GLOBAL GROWTH OF CHRISTIANS, AD 2000** | | | | | | | |
| Total Christians | | 2,000m | | | 0 | 0 | 2,000 m |
| ANNUAL CHRISTIAN GAINS | | | | | | | |
| d. Births in Christian families, p.a. | Tables 1 | 36.6 m | 100,274 | 1.83 | 0 | 0 | 36.6 m |
| e. Converts to Christianity, p.a. | Tables 1 | 19.0 m | 52,055 | 0.95 | 0 | 0 | 19.0 m |
| f. New Christians, p.a. | f=d+e | 55.6 m | 152,329 | 2.78 | 0 | 0 | 55.6 m |
| g. Baptisms, p.a. | 80% of f | 44.5 m | 121,918 | 2.23 | 0 | 0 | 44.5 m |
| ANNUAL CHRISTIAN LOSSES | | | | | | | |
| h. Deaths of Christians, p.a. | Tables 1 | 18.4 m | 50,411 | 0.92 | 0 | 0 | 18.4 m |
| i. Defectors from Christianity, p.a. | Tables 1 | 16.5 m | 45,210 | 0.83 | 0 | 0 | 16.5 m |
| ANNUAL CHRISTIAN INCREASE | | | | | | | |
| j. Nett increase in Christians, p.a. | j=f-h-i | 20.7 m | 56,710 | 1.04 | 0 | 0 | 20.7 m |
| **C. GLOBAL GROWTH OF NON-CHRISTIANS, AD 2000** | | | | | | | |
| Total non-Christians | | 4,055 m | | | 1,629 m | 2,426 m | 0 |
| ANNUAL NON-CHRISTIAN GAINS | | | | | | | |
| k. Births in non-Christian families, p.a. | k=a-d | 87.7 m | 240,274 | 2.16 | 40.2 m | 47.5 m | 0 |
| l. Converts from Christianity, p.a. | l=i | 16.5 m | 45,210 | 0.41 | 0 | 16.5 m | 0 |
| m. New non-Christians, p.a. | m=k+l | 104.2 m | 285,480 | 2.57 | 40.2 m | 64.0 m | 0 |
| ANNUAL NON-CHRISTIAN LOSSES | | | | | | | |
| n. Deaths of non-Christians, p.a. | n=b-h | 34.3 m | 93,973 | 0.85 | 13.2 m | 21.1 m | 0 |
| o. Defectors to Christianity, p.a. | o=e | 19.0 m | 52,055 | 0.47 | 0 | 19.0 m | 0 |
| ANNUAL NON-CHRISTIAN INCREASE | | | | | | | |
| p. Nett increase in non-Christians, p.a. | p=m-n-o | 50.9 m | 139,450 | 1.26 | 27.0 m | 23.9 m | 0 |
| **D. GLOBAL GROWTH OF EVANGELIZED PERSONS, AD 2000** | | | | | | | |
| Total evangelized individuals | | 4,426 m | | | 0 | 2,426 m | 2,000 m |
| q. Newly-evangelized persons, p.a. | q=r+s | 114.7 m | 314,247 | 2.59 | 0 | 78.1 m | 36.6 m |
| r. —Former unevangelized persons, p.a. | Tables 1 | 78.1 m | 213,973 | 1.76 | 0 | 78.1 m | 0 |
| s. —New Christian births, p.a. | s=d | 36.6 m | 100,274 | 0.83 | 0 | 0 | 36.6 m |
| t. Deaths of evangelized persons, p.a. | Tables 1 | 39.4 m | 107,945 | 0.89 | 0 | 21.1 m | 18.4 m |
| u. Nett increase in evangelized persons, p.a. | u=q-t | 75.3 m | 206,301 | 1.70 | 0 | 57.0 m | 18.2 m |
| **E. GLOBAL GROWTH OF UNEVANGELIZED PERSONS, AD 2000** | | | | | | | |
| Total unevangelized individuals | | 1,629 m | | | 1,629 m | 0 | 0 |
| v. Births of unevangelized persons, p.a. | v=k | 87.7 m | 240,274 | 5.38 | 87.7 m | 0 | 0 |
| w. —in unevangelized families, p.a. | Tables 1 | 40.2 m | 110,137 | 2.47 | 40.2 m | 0 | 0 |
| x. —in evangelized non-Christian families, p.a. | Tables 1 | 47.5 m | 130,137 | 2.92 | 47.5 m | 0 | 0 |
| y. Deaths of unevangelized persons, p.a. | Tables 1 | 13.2 m | 36,164 | 0.81 | 13.2 m | 0 | 0 |
| z. Unevangelized persons becoming evangelized, p.a. | z=r | 78.1 m | 213,973 | 4.79 | 78.1 m | 0 | 0 |
| z'. Nett increase in unevangelized persons, p.a. | z'=v-y-z | -3.6 m | -9,863 | -0.22 | -3.6 m | 0 | 0 |

**Notes on lines at left**
(to be read in conjunction with column 3).

c. *Population increase.* For analysis by countries and continents, see Table 17-A in *World population prospects 1998* (United Nations 1998:199-579). For breakdown by Worlds A,B,C, see Global Diagram 34 or Table 12-1, column 163.

d. *Births.* Children born to Christian parents are enumerated as Christians (see evidence in *WCE* 1982:47-48).

e. *Converts.* Mainly from tribal religions, animism, shamanism.

g. *Baptisms.* 27% adult baptisms, 73% child baptisms. On average, 80% of all new Christians become baptized.

h. *Deaths of Christians.* Deaths p.a. are analyzed under 37 causes in Global Diagram 12.

i. *Defectors.* Mainly to non-religion (agnosticism, secularism), atheism, also to Islam, New Religions, eastern cults; mostly due to marriage to non-Christians.

k. *Non-Christian births and deaths.* These occur as shown (lines k,n) both in World A and in World B.

q. *Newly-evangelized.* These are composed of (a) unevangelized persons who become evangelized for the first time in the course of the year, plus (b) children born to Christians.

v. The only way that individuals can become unevangelized is by birth—being born into a non-Christian family.

w. All children born to unevangelized families in World A start as unevangelized individuals themselves, at the worst disadvantage of any children on earth.

x. *Non-Christian births.* Children born to evangelized non-Christians in World B are reckoned to begin life unevangelized (and hence to immediately be located in World A).

## Global Diagram 42.    Today's unfinished task: the unevangelized world segmentized into 5,540 major unevangelized population segments.

For purposes of rapid overview, the globe is divided here into some 19,550 distinct population segments, of 3 major varieties: ethnolinguistic peoples, metropolises (mother cities of over 50,000 population), and countries. (These major or macro segments in turn can be divided and subdivided, as described in Global Diagram 22, into smaller and smaller overlapping subgroupings or minor or micro segments, notably 60,000 minipeoples (people groups, unimax groups), 250,000 micropeoples, or several million sociologically defined groupings valuable as bridges in evangelism. All these are described and diagrammed elsewhere).

This 3-fold macro segmentation is shown symbolically in our developing logo (the smaller of the 2 globes below). The 3 varieties of segment overlap because they are 3 different ways of dividing up the same one world. This segmented globe in turn can be subdivided into our 3 categories of world—Worlds A, B, and C. This superimposing of one schema (segments) on another (3 worlds) is done for purposes of illustration only, since most segments are composed each of a mixture of unevangelized persons, evangelized non-Christians, and Christians. For purposes of illustration also, we name a few segments below: a few megapeoples (in lowercase letters), and a few megacities (in CAPITAL letters), placing these segments where the majority of their individuals are located. In this schema, therefore, 'evangelized non-Christian population segments', defined as segments with church members under 60%, are listed for convenience under World B; and 'christianized population segments', defined as all segments with church members of 60% or over, are listed for convenience under World C.

The larger globe below therefore gives a detailed representation of the nature of the unfinished Christian task. This task's main secular feature ought to be to rectify the grossly disproportionate spread of life's blessings—health, wealth, shelter, food, rights, justice—around the world. This disproportion is briefly sketched here in this series in Global Diagrams 18, 24, and 34. From the Christian point of view, the major unfinished task is to spread the blessings of Christ throughout the segments of World A, the unevangelized world, here shown shaded dark gray for emphasis.

**THE SEGMENTIZED GLOBE**
6.1 billion inhabitants
INDIVIDUALS (rounded totals)
4.4 billion evangelized persons
1.6 billion unevangelized persons
MACRO SEGMENTS
19,550 major population segments:
    12,600 ethnolinguistic peoples
    6,720 metropolises
    238 countries (90 closed/restricted-access)
    including:
554 megapeoples (shown below in lowercase)
402 megacities (shown below in CAPITALS)
MICRO SEGMENTS
60,000 minipeoples (people groups)
250,000 micropeoples
2 million sociopeoples (bridge peoples, social people
    groups)

*This survey's logo*

**3 Worlds:**

VERTICAL SCALE: Evangelization in Worlds A,B,C

**A.  THE UNEVANGELIZED WORLD**
1,629 million unevangelized persons
MACRO SEGMENTS
5,540 unevangelized population segments:
    3,830 unreached peoples (1.6 billion population)
    1,670 unevangelized metropolises
    38 closed countries (26 closed/restricted-access)
including:
1,240 completely unreached peoples (with no churches)
170 unreached megapeoples
85 anti-Christian megacities
MICRO SEGMENTS
13,000 unreached people groups (minipeoples) in 1974, decreasing to 12,000 by 1989 and to 10,000 by AD 2000
50,000 unreached micropeoples
300,000 unreached sociopeoples

**B.  THE EVANGELIZED NON-CHRISTIAN WORLD**
2,426 million evangelized non-Christians
MACRO SEGMENTS
4,750 evangelized non-Christian population segments:
    2,670 peoples
    2,020 metropolises
    59 countries (31 closed/restricted-access)
including:
180 non-Christian megacities
MICRO SEGMENTS
150,000 micropeoples
700,000 sociopeoples

**C.  THE CHRISTIAN WORLD**
2,000 million Christians
MACRO SEGMENTS
9,160 christianized population segments:
    5,930 peoples
    3,090 metropolises
    141 countries over 60% Christians (29 restricted-access, 10 closed)
including:
215 mainly-Christian megacities
8,600 reached peoples (with own churches) in Worlds B and C
MICRO SEGMENTS
50,000 micropeoples
1 million sociopeoples
48,000 reached minipeoples, now coalesced into 14,000 agglomerated christianized minipeoples

Globe segment labels:
Uighurs  Zhuang  Kabul  Tibetans  Kurds  Berbers
Khmer  TASHKENT  Uzbeks  Turks  ALGIERS  TEHRAN
Vietnamese  YANGON  Bengalis  Malays  Arabs  BANGKOK
HAVANA  Chinese  CAIRO  TOKYO  BOMBAY  JAKARTA
BUDAPEST  Serbs  Quechua  MANILA  NAIROBI  SAO PAULO
Poles  PARIS  OSLO  ROME  LONDON  Zulu

A
B
C

HORIZONTAL SCALE:    Geopolitical ideology
                       (Left inside)    (Center)    (Right inside)
WORLDS           Communist world  Western world  Third World

**Global Diagram 43.    Ministry to 86 closed or closing restricted-access/limited-access countries, also to peoples, languages, cities, populations: 16 possible types of evangelizers based on 4 dichotomous criteria of citizenship, residence, legality, and professionalism (full-time supported service).**

The diagram describes ministry approaches to the world's 3.0 billion persons (1 billion Christians, 2 billion non-Christians) who live in 86 closed (restricted-access) or closing (limited-access) countries, defined as countries which either prohibit, or restrict, or limit access by foreign missionaries or Christian workers. These countries are by no means unevangelized; and several are over 90% Christians.

This is a typology specifically of ministry to whole populations (countries, peoples, metropolises) by Christians with some kind of church or mission support structure or linkage involving training, commitment, prayer support, but not necessarily financial support.

This typology does not cover all other unorganized or individual kinds of Christian activity such as personal witness, personal evangelism with individuals, unstructured life-style evangelism, self-supporting witness, Christians working overseas (CWOs), returning internationals who have become Christians, keen Christians serving in the military (armed forces), or in embassies, or unsupported or lone-wolf tentmakers, unlinked part-timers, etc.

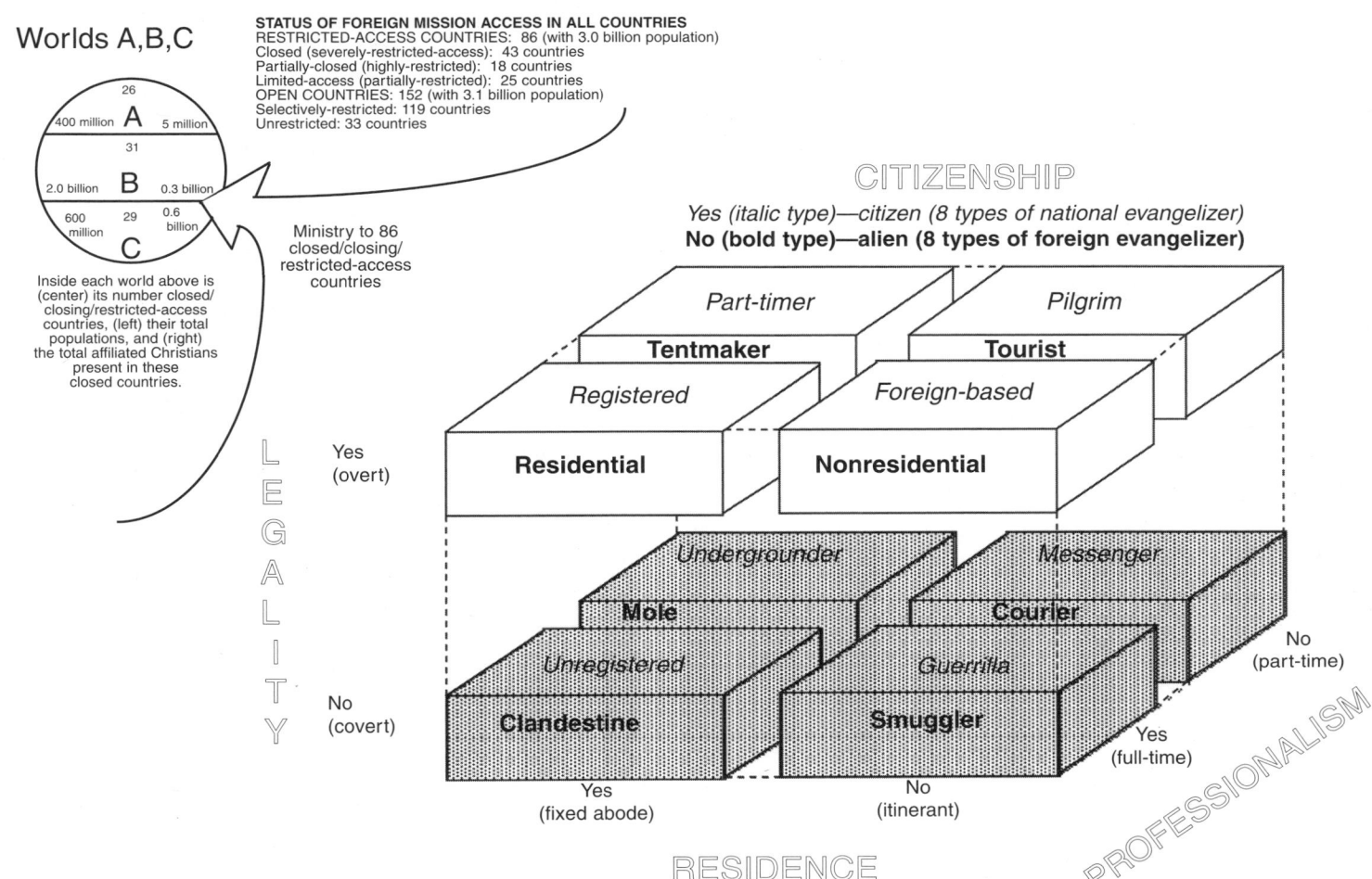

**STATUS OF FOREIGN MISSION ACCESS IN ALL COUNTRIES**
RESTRICTED-ACCESS COUNTRIES: 86 (with 3.0 billion population)
Closed (severely-restricted-access): 43 countries
Partially-closed (highly-restricted): 18 countries
Limited-access (partially-restricted): 25 countries
OPEN COUNTRIES: 152 (with 3.1 billion population)
Selectively-restricted: 119 countries
Unrestricted: 33 countries

**Worlds A,B,C**

A — 26, 400 million, 5 million
B — 31, 2.0 billion, 0.3 billion
C — 29, 600 million, 0.6 billion

Inside each world above is (center) its number closed/closing/restricted-access countries, (left) their total populations, and (right) the total affiliated Christians present in these closed countries.

Ministry to 86 closed/closing/restricted-access countries

**CITIZENSHIP**
*Yes (italic type)*—citizen (8 types of national evangelizer)
**No (bold type)**—alien (8 types of foreign evangelizer)

**LEGALITY**

Yes (overt):
*Part-timer* / *Pilgrim*
**Tentmaker** / **Tourist**
*Registered* / *Foreign-based*
**Residential** / **Nonresidential**

No (covert):
*Undergrounder* / *Messenger*
**Mole** / **Courier**
*Unregistered* / *Guerrilla*
**Clandestine** / **Smuggler**

**RESIDENCE**
Yes (fixed abode) / No (itinerant)

**PROFESSIONALISM**
Yes (full-time) / No (part-time)

**CURRENT CHANGE:**
(countries restricting access by foreign missionaries)
Newly-closed/closing/restricted countries: 4 every year
Closed-restricted-access countries newly opening up: 3 every year

**TYPES OF EVANGELIZERS AT WORK**

| Citizen: | | Alien: | |
|---|---|---|---|
| Registered | 70,000 | Residential | 80,000 |
| Part-timer | 600,000 | Tentmaker | 150,000 |
| Pilgrim | 100,000 | Nonresidential | 500 |
| Foreign-based | 10,000 | Tourist | 500,000 |
| Unregistered | 25,000 | Clandestine | 5000 |
| Undergrounder | 30,000 | Mole | 800 |
| Messenger | 300,000 | Courier | 10,000 |
| Guerrilla | 6,000 | Smuggler | 2,000 |

**RESOURCES INSIDE 86 RESTRICTED-ACCESS COUNTRIES**
World A's 26 countries: 5,900 foreign missionaries, 5,400 workers, 5 million lay Christians.
World B's 31 countries: 51,800 foreign missionaries, 670,400 workers, 290 million lay Christians.
World C's 29 countries: 103,000 foreign missionaries, 630,000 workers, 560 million lay Christians.

**THE UNDERGROUND CHURCH**
Crypto-Christians (secret believers): 124 million (6.2% of Christian world).
Underground Christians (1989): 440 million (25% of Christian world).
Partially-underground Christians (1989): 703 million (40% of Christian world).

## Global Diagram 44.    Today's Great Commission harvest force: 33,800 denominations, 5,000 mission networks, 1,500 national or international councils of churches, 75 global networks, 10 global meganetworks.

The entire range of Christian resources is listed earlier in Global Diagram 24. This diagram below concentrates on the cutting edge of these resources, namely personnel and groupings of personnel, front-line organizations, agencies, and activities.

The statistics below describe various aspects of organized Christianity, mainly giving figures referring to AD 2000. In particular, the category of Great Commission Christians (all Christians who take seriously Christ's final command while on Earth) is elaborated and enumerated. Together they constitute today's 'force for evangelism'.

Other aspects of this world missions force are also enumerated. In the main, its 4,000 mission agencies function in virtually standalone mode. But the most startling aspect concerns the location of this massive force: 95% of it is directed not at the non-Christian worlds (Worlds A & B) but, as the arrow shows, at the Christian world itself (World C). (See Global Diagrams 34, 35, and 36 for definitions). Christians in fact consume over 99% of the whole range of Christian resources, leaving under 1% for all forms of outreach to non-Christians. Our terminology in this survey terms all such missions as merely globalized (or pseudo-global) missions operating with a veneer of global terminology, instead of being engaged in global mission properly so called.

### ORGANIZED CHRISTIANITY, AD 2000
312 ecclesiastical traditions/families
100 major Christian world confessions
33,800 denominations
40,000 parachurch or service agencies
105,000 major institutions
100 megaministries (each reaching a million a day)
400 former denominations merged (organic union) since
    1900 in 80 united churches
2.0 billion Christians
1.9 billion affiliated church members
650 million practicing Christians
3.45 million worship centers (local churches)
466,000 base ecclesial communities (BECs)
Sunday-school enrollment 400 million

### GLOBAL GROWTH OF CHRISTIANS, AD 2000
(figures in parentheses=annual rate of change)
2,000 million Christians in mid-AD 2000
ANNUAL CHRISTIAN GAINS (c=a+b):
  a. Births p.a.          36.6 million    (1.8% p.a.)
  b. Conversions p.a.     19.0 million    (1.0% p.a.)
  c. New Christians (=a+b) 55.6 million   (2.8% p.a.)
  d. Baptisms (=80% of c)  44.5 million   (2.2% p.a.)
ANNUAL CHRISTIAN LOSSES (g=e+f):
  e. Deaths p.a.         -18.4 million    (-0.9% p.a.)
  f. Defections p.a.     -16.5 million    (-0.8% p.a.)
  g. Total losses p.a. (=e+f) -34.9 million (-1.7% p.a.)
ANNUAL CHRISTIAN INCREASE (h=c-g):
  h. Nett increase p.a.   20.7 million    (1.0% p.a.)

### GLOBAL CHURCH GROWTH, AD 2000
58,000 new churches planted or opened a year
6,000 churches closed or suppressed a year
52,000 nett increase in churches a year

### CHURCH MEMBERSHIP BY CONTINENTS, AD 2000
(by UN macro regions)

| | |
|---|---|
| Africa | 335,000,000 |
| Antarctica | 3,400 |
| Asia | 307,000,000 |
| Europe | 537,000,000 |
| Latin America | 476,000,000 |
| Northern America | 212,000,000 |
| Oceania | 21,400,000 |

### GLOBAL ECCLESIASTICAL TRADITIONS, AD 2000
(church membership; note that indented categories are selected subgroups and are not intended as a complete breakdown of the unindented line above them)

*Mutually exclusive categories:*

| | |
|---|---|
| Anglicans | 79,650,000 |
| Catholics (non-Roman) | 5,800,000 |
| Marginal Christians | 26,060,000 |
| Independents | 385,745,000 |
| Orthodox | 215,128,000 |
|   Eastern Orthodox | 172,673,000 |
|   Oriental Orthodox | 41,869,000 |
| Protestants | 342,002,000 |
|   united churches members | 90,000,000 |
|   Baptists | 81,800,000 |
|   Lutherans | 63,700,000 |
|   Reformed | 61,400,000 |
|   Classical Pentecostals | 65,000,000 |
|   Methodists | 30,400,000 |
|   Adventists | 12,500,000 |
| Roman Catholics | 1,057,328,000 |
|   Eastern-rite Catholics | 17,900,000 |
|   Catholic Charismatics | 120,000,000 |

*Other overlapping categories:*

| | |
|---|---|
| Pentecostals/Charismatics | 523,778,000 |
|   Pentecostals (1st Wave of Renewal) | 65,800,000 |
|   Charismatics (2nd Wave of Renewal) | 175,900,000 |
|   Third-Wavers (3rd Wave of Renewal) | 286,281,000 |
| Evangelicals | 211,000,000 |
| crypto-Christians | 123,726,000 |

### GLOBAL CHRISTIAN LEADERSHIP, AD 2000
5.5 million full-time Christian workers (60% women)
1.1 million ordained clergy, ministers, pastors, priests
    (5% women)
1.2 million professional theologians
20,000 professional missiologists
1.1 million seminarians in 4,800 seminaries
55,000 church leaders (21,000 bishops, 20,000 moderators or other denominational heads, 13,000 executive agency heads)

### GLOBAL CONCILIARISM,  AD 2000:  worldwide networks of 6,500 councils of churches, Christian councils, alliances, fellowships
LOCAL OR SUBNATIONAL (each for a city, county, or province):
20,000 local councils of churches
NATIONAL (for one country each):
1,200 nationwide Christian councils, or councils of churches (50 with Roman Catholic Church as member)
PLURINATIONAL (for 2 or 3 countries each):
40 plurinational councils of churches
SUBCONTINENTAL:
70 regional councils
CONTINENTAL:
30 continent-wide councils of churches
GLOBAL:
20 world councils of churches, or world Christian councils
MISSIONARY:
60 missions councils at national or international level
CONFESSIONAL (for one tradition each):
150 world confessional councils (Christian world communions)
PANCONFESSIONAL:
1 Conference of Christian World Communions (23 member confessions)

### GLOBAL HARVEST FORCE, AD 2000
No church is 100% Great Commission Christians
No church is 0% Great Commission Christians
GREAT COMMISSION CHRISTIANS:
(found within 10,850 ethnolinguistic peoples, and in 33,800 denominations)
2.0 billion potential Great Commission Christians
650 million professing Great Commission Christians (evangelizers, the "force for evangelism"), growing at 1.5% p.a.
600 million daily-evangelizing Christians (evangelists, daily evangelizers)
200 million daily intercessors
25 million in full-time prayer ministry
15 million pacifists opposed to weapons
5.5 million full-time Great Commission workers
35,000 Great Commission broadcasting personnel
130 million Great Commission computer users
20 million Great Commission computer professionals
150 million Christian pilgrims on move every year
40,000 Great Commission church and agency leaders
13,300 Christians martyred every month on average

### GLOBAL FOREIGN MISSION, AD 2000
4,000 mission agencies
420,000 career foreign missionaries
400,000 short-term foreign missionaries
200 Great Commission research centers

### GREAT COMMISSION NETWORKS, AD 2000
5,000 computerized networks
50 worldwide intercessory networks
75 global networks
10 global meganetworks
1 Great Commission giganetwork

**WORLD MISSIONS FORCE**
—Matthew 28:18-20

World A

World B

World C

STANDALONE GLOBALIZED DEPLOYMENT, AD 2000
The world's 650 million active Great Commission Christians are found within 11,800 ethnolinguistic peoples, and are growing at 1.5% per year. They constitute today's 'force for evangelism', at present directed mainly (95%) at World C, the Christian world, and operating largely in standalone mode.

**Global Diagram 45. Hijacking the international sharing of personnel in mission: sending, receiving, sharing, draining, and looting countries in World C for the year AD 2000.**

The Christian world's 420,000 foreign missionaries form a professional elite especially charged with contacting and evangelizing the world's 4 billion non-Christians in 97 non-Christian countries. This frontier force is intended to be drawn from each of the world's 141 heavily-Christian countries (defined as each with over 60% church members), and then to be shared out according to need among any or all of the world's 238 countries. The table below sets the data out, showing in bold type nett donors of missionaries, and ranking countries by SS, in bold type. The diagram portrays the situation schematically, using 11 categories of country.

The top priority in this whole enterprise is to assist the 1.6 billion non-Christians in the unevangelized world. Instead of this happening, several alarming features have become the norm (described in the box below) concerning the 141 Christian countries and their contributions to this system, which can be regarded as equivalent to a 'global blood bank'. The table below documents how most of these countries are draining more 'blood' (missionary personnel) from this bank than they put in.

All these 131 mission-sending countries in fact are draining off more than is reasonable in a global system and so collectively share in this hijacking of the foreign missionary force. Their 90% share is too large.

'International sharing' needs to be restructured to ensure that a bigger share than 10% reaches the 4 billion non-Christians who need it.

---

**Responses of 141 World C countries to world missions**

*KEY TO NUMBERS (each per million population)*
N = national/citizen home workers per million population
SS = citizen foreign missionaries sent abroad per million population
MM = foreign missionaries from abroad per million population

*KEY for largest 131 mission-sending countries*
a = 26 donating countries (SS>MM) (in bold)
b = 44 draining countries (SS<MM, 500>MM>100)
c = 52 looting countries (SS<MM, MM>500)

| | | N | SS | MM |
|---|---|---|---|---|
| **A. Exemplary response (SS>350)** | | | | |
| **Malta** | a | 8236 | **2574** | 77 |
| **Ireland** | a | 6702 | **2493** | 134 |
| Samoa | c | 13883 | 1666 | 4443 |
| **Faeroe Islands** | a | 936 | **1170** | 702 |
| **Belgium** | a | 5413 | **1004** | 256 |
| American Samoa | a | 2203 | 881 | 2937 |
| **Spain** | a | 4290 | **770** | 63 |
| **Liechtenstein** | a | 913 | **761** | 609 |
| **Netherlands** | a | 2851 | **646** | 133 |
| Monaco | c | 3274 | 595 | 4465 |
| **Italy** | a | 4712 | **550** | 209 |
| New Zealand | c | 1683 | 544 | 725 |
| **Canada** | a | 4174 | **530** | 257 |
| **France** | a | 3385 | **516** | 271 |
| Palau | a | 1030 | 515 | 1030 |
| **Andorra** | a | 256 | **513** | 128 |
| Cook Islands | c | 3073 | 512 | 3586 |
| Tonga | c | 6089 | 507 | 4059 |
| **Portugal** | a | 1418 | **506** | 76 |
| **Switzerland** | a | 2437 | **460** | 298 |
| USA | a | 5389 | 426 | 119 |
| Micronesia | c | 843 | 421 | 4044 |
| **Norway** | a | 605 | **403** | 224 |
| Gibraltar | c | 797 | 399 | 1595 |

| | | N | SS | MM |
|---|---|---|---|---|
| **B. Adequate response (350>SS>150)** | | | | |
| Bolivia | c | 360 | **336** | 504 |
| **Germany** | a | 3649 | **322** | 122 |
| **Britain** | a | 3400 | **314** | 255 |
| Guadeloupe | c | 4389 | 307 | 878 |
| **Austria** | a | 2923 | **304** | 183 |
| **Australia** | a | 2913 | **291** | 233 |
| **Luxembourg** | a | 4645 | **279** | 93 |
| **Finland** | a | 502 | **270** | 97 |
| **Isle of Man** | a | 1516 | **253** | 51 |
| Puerto Rico | c | 775 | 233 | 646 |
| San Marino | c | 754 | 226 | 754 |
| **Sweden** | a | 898 | **224** | 112 |
| Virgin Is of the US | c | 1614 | 215 | 1614 |
| Panama | c | 245 | 210 | 735 |
| Martinique | c | 2529 | 202 | 506 |
| Seychelles | c | 904 | 194 | 1937 |
| Montserrat | c | 1882 | 188 | 941 |
| British Virgin Is | c | 936 | 187 | 468 |
| Cape Verde | b | 468 | 187 | 234 |
| Uruguay | c | 659 | 180 | 899 |
| Costa Rica | b | 895 | 174 | 348 |
| Nauru | c | 868 | 174 | 1736 |
| South Africa | b | 1981 | 173 | 297 |
| Tuvalu | c | 2560 | 171 | 853 |
| Marshall Islands | c | 779 | 156 | 1246 |
| Bermuda | c | 2322 | 155 | 1548 |
| | | | | |
| **C Barely adequate response (150>SS>100)** | | | | |
| Guam | c | 597 | 149 | 2686 |
| Iceland | b | 1068 | 142 | 142 |
| New Caledonia | c | 1402 | 140 | 1402 |
| Wallis & Futuna Is | c | 3444 | 138 | 2067 |
| Sao Tome & Principe | c | 136 | 136 | 681 |
| French Polynesia | c | 851 | 128 | 1702 |
| Kiribati | c | 5996 | 120 | 600 |
| Turks & Caicos Is | c | 1193 | 119 | 597 |
| Brazil | b | 735 | 118 | 147 |
| Trinidad & Tobago | b | 541 | 116 | 386 |
| Denmark | b | 567 | 113 | 264 |
| Chile | c | 986 | 112 | 526 |
| Equatorial Guinea | c | 1105 | 110 | 663 |
| French Guiana | c | 552 | 110 | 1103 |

| | | N | SS | MM |
|---|---|---|---|---|
| Grenada | c | 1067 | 107 | 1280 |
| Solomon Islands | c | 2705 | 101 | 1127 |
| | | | | |
| **D. Inadequate response (100>SS>10)** | | | | |
| Swaziland | c | 1984 | 99 | 794 |
| **Channel Islands** | a | 327 | 98 | 65 |
| Netherlands Antilles | c | 692 | 92 | 2768 |
| Cyprus | b | 2331 | 83 | 333 |
| Colombia | b | 827 | 83 | 165 |
| Paraguay | b | 418 | 82 | 218 |
| Spanish North Africa | b | 77 | 77 | 385 |
| Slovenia | b | 705 | 76 | 403 |
| Dominica | c | 2121 | 71 | 1131 |
| Croatia | b | 268 | 67 | 335 |
| Bahamas | c | 1370 | 65 | 979 |
| **Poland** | a | 1935 | **64** | 18 |
| Northern Mariana Is | c | 510 | 64 | 1531 |
| Lithuania | b | 409 | 60 | 109 |
| Vanuatu | c | 2101 | 53 | 1575 |
| Cayman Islands | c | 2606 | 52 | 521 |
| Saint Kitts & Nevis | c | 2599 | 52 | 1040 |
| Bougainville | c | 504 | 50 | 504 |
| Nicaragua | b | 591 | 49 | 394 |
| Argentina | b | 648 | 49 | 324 |
| Yugoslavia | b | 752 | 47 | 94 |
| Mexico | b | 910 | 46 | 81 |
| Timor | b | 226 | 45 | 113 |
| Belize | c | 1662 | 42 | 1662 |
| Congo-Brazzaville | b | 2378 | 41 | 272 |
| Guatemala | b | 351 | 40 | 307 |
| Aruba | b | 389 | 39 | 107 |
| Greece | | 1597 | 38 | 47 |
| Venezuela | b | 290 | 37 | 290 |
| Barbados | b | 1294 | 37 | 740 |
| Malawi | b | 549 | 37 | 137 |
| Greenland | b | 3562 | 36 | 1068 |
| El Salvador | b | 319 | 32 | 223 |
| Ecuador | b | 554 | 32 | 277 |
| Peru | b | 351 | 31 | 265 |
| Honduras | b | 385 | 31 | 123 |
| Antigua | c | 1480 | 30 | 1036 |
| Namibia | c | 927 | 29 | 695 |
| **Armenia** | a | 71 | 28 | 14 |

| | | N | SS | MM |
|---|---|---|---|---|
| Zambia | b | 436 | 27 | 349 |
| Kenya | b | 1164 | 27 | 199 |
| Philippines | b | 658 | 26 | 125 |
| Saint Lucia | c | 972 | 26 | 972 |
| Latvia | b | 339 | 25 | 170 |
| Hungary | b | 698 | 25 | 120 |
| Angola | b | 1941 | 25 | 155 |
| Macedonia | | 148 | 25 | 74 |
| Lesotho | b | 1672 | 23 | 302 |
| Uganda | b | 1378 | 23 | 119 |
| Moldavia | | 160 | 23 | 114 |
| Burundi | b | 1195 | 22 | 179 |
| Papua New Guinea | c | 3038 | 22 | 781 |
| Congo-Zaire | b | 1258 | 19 | 290 |
| Saint Vincent | c | 702 | 18 | 702 |
| Gabon | b | 1631 | 16 | 326 |
| Rwanda | b | 517 | 16 | 155 |
| Dominican Republic | b | 118 | 15 | 235 |
| Reunion | b | 3431 | 14 | 343 |
| Slovakia | b | 334 | 13 | 186 |
| Bulgaria | | 365 | 12 | 24 |
| Georgia | | 181 | 12 | 20 |
| | | | | |
| **E. Negligible response (SS<10)** | | | | |
| Belorussia | | 117 | 10 | 49 |
| Romania | | 1299 | 9 | 45 |
| Ukraine | | 119 | 8 | 83 |
| Haiti | b | 377 | 4 | 182 |

Remaining 10 countries in World C have populations less than 10,000 and hence fluctuating results

*Average worker profiles, AD 2000*
| | | | |
|---|---|---|---|
| A mission-minded ch | 2010 | 250 | 50 |
| A large denomination | 2200 | 200 | 90 |
| Global Christianity | 2587 | 175 | 175 |

*Global worker profiles, AD 1900-2000*
| | | | |
|---|---|---|---|
| 1900 | 2013 | 119 | 119 |
| 1980 | 2229 | 187 | 187 |
| 1990 | 2587 | 175 | 175 |
| 2000 | 2450 | 200 | 200 |

---

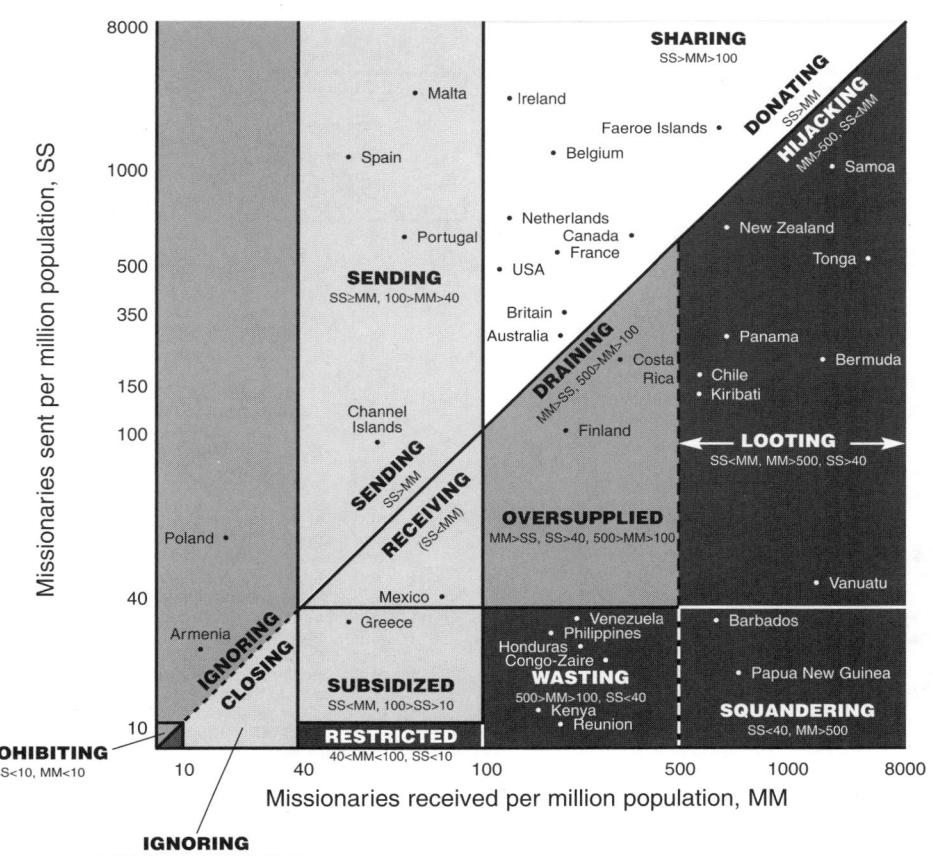

*Graphic A on left.* Categories of country by involvement in world mission, for World C countries with populations greater than 10,000.

**ANALYSIS**

The diagram at left presents a grid with which to classify countries of the world by their sending/receiving status, using categories defined in situ. The table above puts these data in context. Conclusion: the following 5 situations are cause for concern.

*Donors.* Only 26 Christian countries are nett donors to this system, donating more foreign missionaries than they receive. (These are listed above in bold type). The fact that only four Christian countries are 'non-donors' indicates that sending missionaries is an entirely possible enterprise from almost any country.

*Net takers or drainers.* 105 Christian countries take out or drain off more missionary personnel than they contribute.

*Hidden drainers.* 20 Christian countries are widely known as contributors but this reputation hides nett draining.

*Looters.* 52 Christian countries are widely known as contributors but this reputation hides massive draining (defined here as MM>500).

*Hijackers.* Although all but 7 of these 131 mission-sending countries have numerically-strong home ministries (defined as N>150; note also 61 countries have N>500, and 63 countries have immensely strong home ministries with N>1000), they nevertheless drain off for their own use some 90% of the entire force of 420,000 foreign missionaries. This is collective hijacking.

For a visual impression of this situation, see the color Global Map 8 in Part 33 "GeoAtlas".

Global Diagram 46.    **The demographic future of our globe: seven scenarios of possible alternate futures, AD 1950-2200.**

Table A below sets out the UN's global population estimates at 11 points over the period AD 1950-2200 from the standpoint of 1998. Seven alternate scenarios are set out (columns 1-7) based on a wide range of assumed future trends in human fertility. The basic, most-probable case is the UN's long-used Medium (medium fertility) variant (column 4). This assumes that fertility will ultimately stabilize at the replacement level—a fertility rate of 2.05 children per woman (the average number a woman has in her lifetime). The Low vari-

ant (column 1) assumes a rate of 1.6 children, the High variant (column 6) 2.5 children. The Instant-Replacement variant (column 3) assumes fertility reached replacement level (2.06) in 1995 and stays at that level thereafter. The Constant-Fertility variant (column 7) is the most frightening; it assumes human obstinacy keeps fertility at the same bloated level as today (4.3 children) from 1990-2150, producing by AD 2150 a population density 160 times today's.

Graph A in the center shows in graphic form the data from

Table A. One immediately notices the wide disparity in the seven scenarios.

Lastly, Graph B at the bottom analyzes a single one of the associated secular characteristics—age, in years. The number of people aged over 65 rises from 230 millions in 1975 to 3,750 millions—a ninefold increase of the elderly. From today's planet of children, we are headed inexorably for a planet of the aged.

### Table A. Global populations, AD 1950-2200 for 7 alternate scenarios or demographic variants.
Notes. Source of basic demographic data: *World population projections to 2150* (New York: United Nations, 1998).

| Year | 7 variants: Low 1 | Medium/low 2 | Instant replacement 3 | **Medium 4** | Medium/high 5 | High 6 | Constant 7 |
|---|---|---|---|---|---|---|---|
| 1950 | 2,516 million | 2,516 million | 2,516 million | **2,516 million** | 2,516 million | 2,516 million | 2,516 million |
| 1975 | 4,079 million | 4,079 million | 4,079 million | **4,079 million** | 4,079 million | 4,079 million | 4,079 million |
| 1990 | 5,262 million | 5,262 million | 5,292 million | **5,292 million** | 5,327 million | 5,327 million | 5,311 million |
| 2000 | 6,093 million | 6,093 million | 5,792 million | **6,261 million** | 6,420 million | 6,420 million | 6,463 million |
| 2025 | 7,591 million | 7,591 million | 7,069 million | **8,504 million** | 9,444 million | 9,444 million | 10,978 million |
| 2050 | 7,813 million | 7,817 million | 7,697 million | **10,019 million** | 12,495 million | 12,506 million | 21,161 million |
| 2075 | 7,082 million | 7,199 million | 7,883 million | **10,841 million** | 15,328 million | 15,708 million | 46,261 million |
| 2100 | 6,009 million | 6,415 million | 8,087 million | **11,186 million** | 17,592 million | 19,156 million | 109,405 million |
| 2125 | 5,071 million | 5,913 million | 8,251 million | **11,390 million** | 19,358 million | 23,191 million | 271,138 million |
| 2150 | 4,299 million | 5,633 million | 8,351 million | **11,543 million** | 20,772 million | 28,025 million | 694,213 million |
| 2200 |  |  |  | **11,600 million** |  |  |  |

**Graph A. Global populations, AD 1950-2150 for 7 alternate scenarios or demographic variants.**

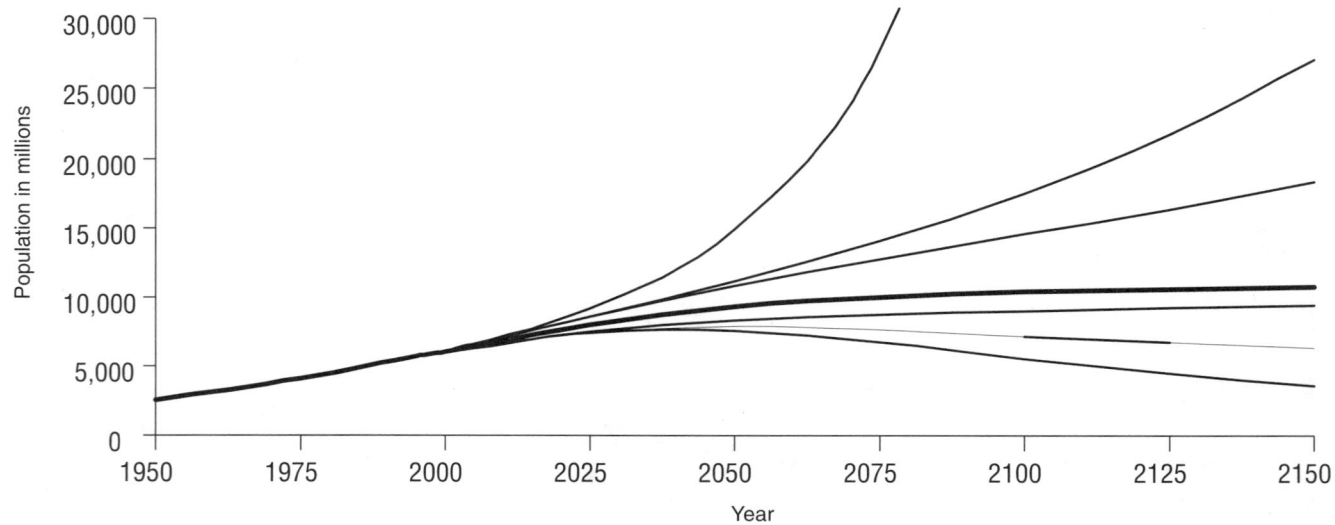

**Graph B. Global population by age, 1975-2150.**

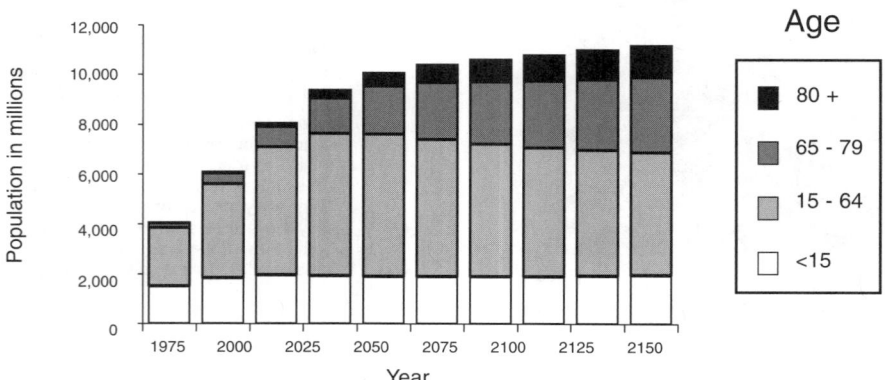

*Minigraphic* at left. The vertical scale is global population in millions. The horizontal scale covers the time period AD 1975 to 2150. Each vertical bar is divided into the 4 age groups shown in the small box. For exact figures see *World population projections* 1998:27.

The most startling finding here is that while the number of under-15s remains nearly constant around 2 billion, the over-15s soar from 2,570 millions in 1975 to 9,501 millions by 2150. The ultimate median age of the world by 2150 will settle at 42.7 years (compared to today's 26.6 years).

**Global Diagram 47.    Shifting the population center of gravity southwards: global changes in the demographic balance, AD 1900-2200.**

At the bottom of the page, Table A gives global population estimates at 11 points over the period AD 1900-2200. Most of the statistics come from the United Nations Demographic Database model, using one of the 7 future fertility-scenarios—the long-expounded Medium variant. This assumes that fertility will ultimately stabilize at the replacement level—a fertility rate of 2.05 children per women (the average number a woman has in her lifetime).

The graphic in the center analyzes global population first under 9 Major Areas (equivalent to continents or subconti-

nents), then consolidates or combines them into 2 Groups recently introduced by the U.N.. Group I (often called the 'North') refers to major areas of usually more developed countries already at the end of the fertility transition downward to replacement level and which currently exhibit relatively low levels of fertility and mortality. Group II (called figuratively the 'South') refers to major areas with usually less developed countries where the fertility transition has been delayed or not yet begun and which exhibit higher levels of fertility and mortality.

The reader who carefully follows a particular line across the 3 centuries on the graph (or in figures in Table A) will find a number of startling developments. The most startling is the meteoric growth in Africa's population. Almost as startling is the way all the major areas of Group II (dashed lines) soar high above Group I's major areas (unbroken lines).

This all poses a series of major challenges to Great Commission planners attempting to take seriously the future of planet Earth.

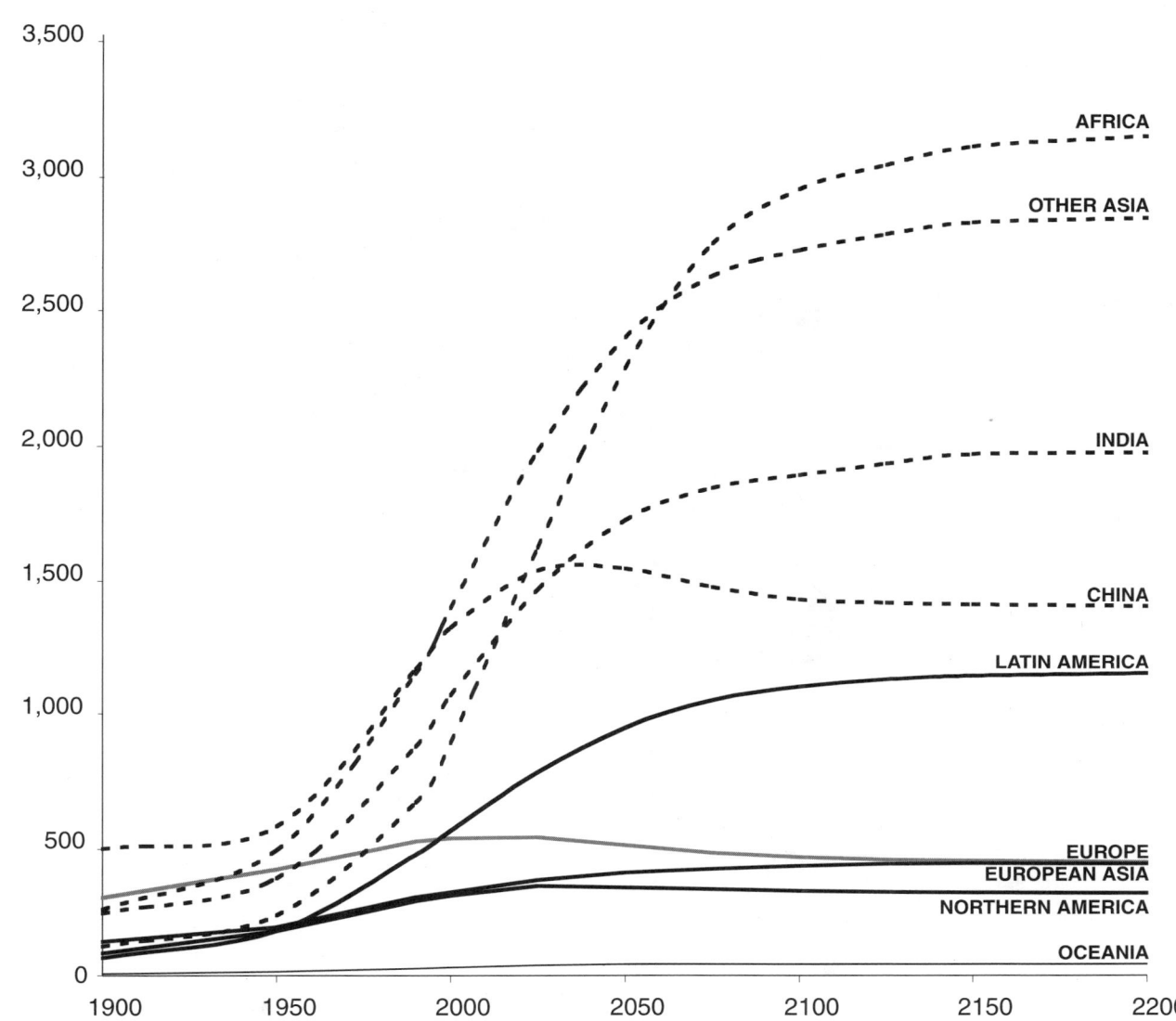

*Minidiagram at left.* The vertical scale is continental (U.N. "major area") population in millions. The horizontal scale covers the time period of 3 centuries—20th, 21st, and 22nd—which is 1900-2200. Each line with its symbol (see box) shows the evolution of one of the 9 U.N. Major Areas (equivalent to continents or subcontinents). For further explanations see *Long-range world population projections* 1992:22.

Precise points on the minidiagram are given their exact statistics in Table A below.

The most significant aspect shown here is the polarization of the globe into 4 major areas that are declining in population, or static (Group I, the "North"), whilst the other 5 areas are still increasing dramatically (Group II, the "South").

Group I has already learned the value of population control. Its population starts to decrease early, in AD 2025 in Table A.

An equally significant trend is that the Churches of the South will mushroom to outnumber the Churches of the North by 5:1, 400% by AD 2200.

---

**Table A. Estimated and projected populations of major areas of the world, medium-fertility extension, 1900-2200.**

*Notes. Source: For years 1950-2200, U.N. Medium variant in Long-range world population projections: two centuries of population growth, 1950-2150 (New York: United Nations, 1992); for year 1900, Table 1-4 in World Christian encyclopedia (Oxford University Press, 2001). Columns are divided by vertical lines to enclose separately the 20th, 21st, and 22nd centuries (remember that the 21st century begins not in 2000 but on January 1, 2001).*

| Major area | Year | 1900 millions | 1950 | 1990 | 2000 | 2025 | 2050 | 2075 | 2100 | 2125 | 2150 | 2200 |
|---|---|---|---|---|---|---|---|---|---|---|---|---|
| | | | **20TH CENTURY** | | | **21ST CENTURY** | | | | **22ND CENTURY** | | |
| *GROUP I* | | *501* | *752* | *1,089* | *1,143* | *1,237* | *1,233* | *1,211* | *1,202* | *1,195* | *1,191* | *1,182* |
| Europe | | 287 | 393 | 498 | 510 | 515 | 486 | 456 | 440 | 430 | 426 | 420 |
| Northern America | | 82 | 166 | 276 | 295 | 332 | 326 | 319 | 314 | 310 | 308 | 306 |
| Oceania | | 6 | 13 | 26 | 30 | 38 | 41 | 41 | 41 | 41 | 41 | 41 |
| European Asia (formerly USSR) | | 126 | 180 | 289 | 308 | 352 | 380 | 395 | 407 | 414 | 416 | 415 |
| *GROUP II* | | *1,119* | *1,766* | *4,203* | *5,118* | *7,267* | *8,786* | *9,629* | *9,984* | *10,196* | *10,352* | *10,418* |
| Africa | | 108 | 222 | 642 | 867 | 1,597 | 2,265 | 2,727 | 2,931 | 3,021 | 3,090 | 3,130 |
| Latin America | | 65 | 166 | 448 | 538 | 757 | 922 | 1,024 | 1,075 | 1,102 | 1,117 | 1,125 |
| China | | 472 | 555 | 1,139 | 1,299 | 1,513 | 1,521 | 1,451 | 1,405 | 1,395 | 1,389 | 1,383 |
| India | | 230 | 358 | 853 | 1,042 | 1,442 | 1,699 | 1,820 | 1,870 | 1,913 | 1,949 | 1,955 |
| Other Asia | | 244 | 465 | 1,121 | 1,372 | 1,958 | 2,379 | 2,607 | 2,703 | 2,765 | 2,807 | 2,825 |
| *GLOBE* | | *1,620* | *2,518* | *5,292* | *6,261* | *8,504* | *10,019* | *10,840* | *11,186* | *11,391* | *11,543* | *11,600* |

**Global Diagram 48.   Some aspects of future motherhood and family: women, children, and fertility on the globe, AD 1993-2200, described via 48 targetable trend segments.**

A vast amount of information is now available concerning the present status of women and the family across the world. A selection of statistics illustrating this is given in the 1993 column in Table A below. The way to understand this column is to read slowly and carefully each figure, thinking out the significance of each and what our evaluation of it, as Christians, should be in light of the Great Commission.

The last 2 columns of Table A then project the 1993 figures as trends into the long-range future in the 21st century (AD 2025), and then into the distant future (AD 2200). Here we are

applying the well-established methodologies of futuristics, the scientific study of alternate possible futures. Many of these projected figures have been published by United Nations' agencies (see sources listed below).

What you and the rest of us can do about all this, as committed Christians, is wide open to suggestion and imagination. At the least, however, we must bring into all discussions a well-informed understanding of the hard facts of the situation today.

One particularly fruitful way forward is paralleled by the

*Review of recent national demographic target-setting* (see below). Christians could ask denominations and agencies to target very specific trend segments and to undertake to give them priority attention over the next decade or two, not in competition with but on behalf of all other sister organizations. The AD 2200 column in Table A shows, for 19 trends, the moderate improvements that such targeting could easily produce.

### Minigraphic at right.

This sequence starts with yesterday's globe, in the foreground, and recedes into the future on 4 progressively more distant globes. For the 5 years shown, 3 basic trend segments are shown: the total female population at that time (the upper figure above each globe), the total fertility rate (number of children the average woman will bear; middle figure), and the number of new families that are likely to get started during that year (lower figure). Figures for 3 of these globes are taken from Table A below. The others are interpolated.

**Sources.** United Nations' publications: (1) *The world's women: trends and statistics,* 1970-1990 (1991); (2) *World population prospects* 1990 (1991) and subsequent revised editions in 1993, 1995, 1997; (3) *Long-range world population projections: two centuries of population growth,* 1950-2150 (1992).

**Targeting.** The UN has documented, as an effective method of changing the worst of these situations, a philosophy of targeting as described in detail in their *Review of recent national demographic target-setting* (New York, 1989). This describes concrete targets that member nations were asked to set (thus Jordan undertook to reduce its infant mortality, which was 5.4% in 1982, to 2.7% by AD 2000).

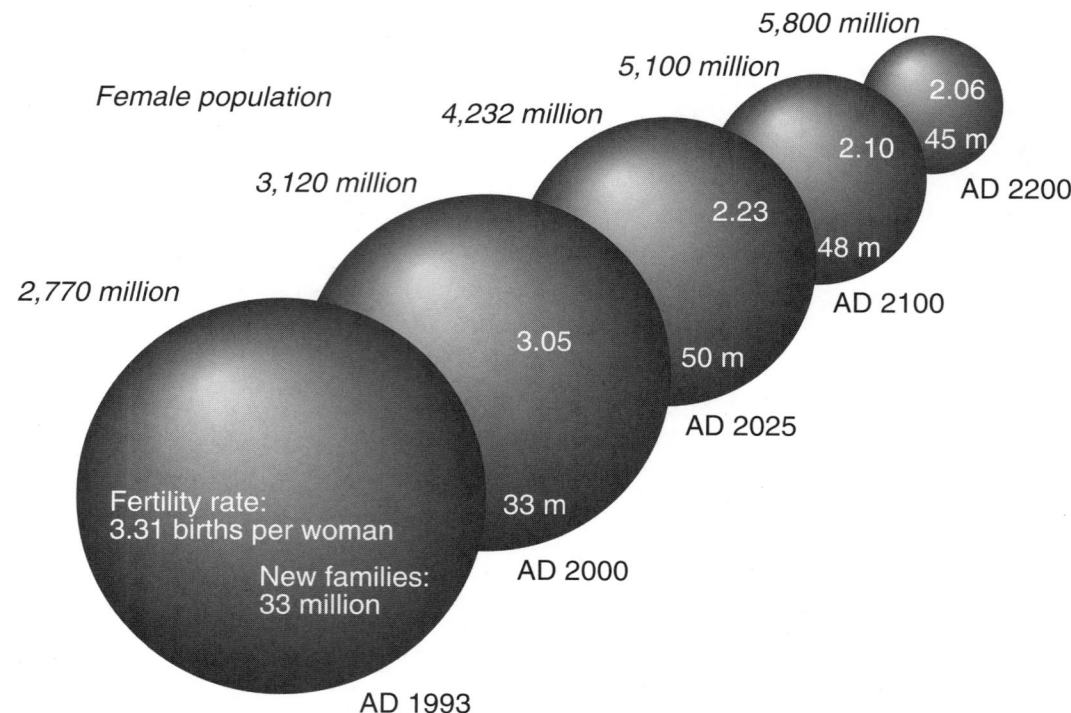

Female population

5,800 million
2.06
45 m
AD 2200

5,100 million
2.10
48 m
AD 2100

4,232 million
2.23
50 m
AD 2025

3,120 million
3.05
33 m
AD 2000

2,770 million
Fertility rate:
3.31 births per woman
New families:
33 million
AD 1993

### Table A. Forty-eight trend segments describing past, present, and future for women and family, across 3 centuries.

| TREND SEGMENTS | 20TH CENTURY mid-1993 | 21ST CENTURY 2025 | 22ND CENTURY 2200 |
|---|---|---|---|
| Global population (males, females) | 5,576 million | 8,504 million | 11,600 million |
| **WOMEN** | | | |
| Global female population | 2,770 million | 4,232 million | 5,800 million |
| % literates | 56 | 70 | 85 |
| Sex ratio (males per 100 females) | 101.5 | 100.9 | 100.0 |
| Female life expectancy, years | 67.6 | 75.5 | 84.9 |
| Women denied full rights & equality | 2.5 billion | 1.8 billion | 100 million |
| % world income received by women | 10 | 20 | 40 |
| % world property owned by women | 1 | 3 | 20 |
| Women as % of all poor | 70 | 60 | 55 |
| Women as % of all illiterates | 66 | 55 | 52 |
| Women as % of all refugees | 80 | 70 | 60 |
| Women as % of all ill/sick | 75 | 57 | 52 |
| Female urban poor | 700 million | 1,400 million | 3,770 million |
| Female urban slumdwellers | 320 million | 980 million | 2,250 million |
| **MOTHERHOOD** | | | |
| Women of childbearing age (15-49) | 1,193 million | 1,947 million | 2,320 million |
| Ditto, % of world population | 24.9 | 24.8 | 20.0 |
| Total fertility rate (births per woman) | 3.31 | 2.23 | 2.06 |
| Gross reproduction rate, per woman | 1.61 | 1.09 | 0.7 |
| Net reproduction rate, per woman | 1.40 | 1.03 | 0.6 |
| Contraceptive prevalence rate, % | 56 | 75 | 95 |
| Birth rate, % p.a. | 2.64 | 1.71 | 1.0 |
| Births p.a. (males, females) | 146,250,000 | 145,200,000 | 116,000,000 |
| Induced abortions, p.a. | 60 million | 130 million | 400 million |
| Maternal mortality, p.a., total | 500,000 | 400,000 | 80,000 |

| | 20TH CENTURY mid-1993 | 21ST CENTURY 2025 | 22ND CENTURY 2200 |
|---|---|---|---|
| Maternal mortality, p.a., due to abortion | 200,000 | 150,000 | 30,000 |
| **FAMILY** | | | |
| Families/homes/household | 1.2 billion | 2.1 billion | 3.1 billion |
| Household size, persons | 4.3 | 4.0 | 3.7 |
| Households headed by women, % | 33 | 55 | 70 |
| New families each year | 33 million | 50 million | 45 million |
| % women 15-19 already married | 23 | 25 | 35 |
| Dependency ratio, % | 62.6 | 52.1 | 45.0 |
| Marriage rate per 1000 pop p.a. | 4 | 5 | 6 |
| Divorce rate per 1000 pop p.a. | 0.4 | 1 | 3 |
| Battered women | 200 million | 500 million | 100 million |
| Child-abuse incidents p.a. | 22 million | 70 million | 30 million |
| Population per doctor | 3,780 | 2,500 | 500 |
| **CHILDREN** | | | |
| Young children (0-4), % | 11.8 | 8.2 | 6.0 |
| Children (5-14), % | 20.4 | 16.3 | 12.0 |
| School children (6-14), % | 18.2 | 14.7 | 11.0 |
| Babies born malnourished, p.a. | 10 million | 25 million | 1 million |
| Sick/ill children | 600 million | 1.0 billion | 200 million |
| Exploited child labor | 50 million | 200 million | 20 million |
| Orphans | 450 million | 1.0 billion | 1.5 billion |
| Abandoned children and infants | 60 million | 260 million | 500 million |
| Homeless/family-less children | 300 million | 700 million | 1 billion |
| Megacity street children | 100 million | 300 million | 800 million |
| % infant mortality (under 1) p.a. | 6.3 | 2.8 | 0.5 |
| % child mortality (1-4 years) p.a. | 1.0 | 0.7 | 0.1 |

## Global Diagram 49.    The accelerating collapse of the global youth explosion: population under 15 for the globe, AD 1900-2200.

By the year 1970, Christianity's major denominations and agencies had recognized the reality of the global youth explosion. This had begun in the 19th century and accelerated in Third-World countries in the 20th century. Churches then began paying special attention to the needs of youth aged 15-24. Five-year plans anticipated growing numbers of applicants as full-time Christian workers.

What was not known then, nor widely recognized subsequently, is that this explosion peaked in 1970 when the glob-al youth population (under 15s) had risen to 37.5% of the world. A 200-year decline then began, as documented in Table A below and shown in Graph I. The bold line in each depicts the United Nations' Medium Variant scenario for the future. It is surrounded on both sides by 6 other UN variants. These represent together 7 possible future scenarios based on differing possible fertility patterns.

These new data show that over the next 200 years, youth are expected to decline by half to only 18% of the world. This is clearly a momentous development that the churches need to think about and plan for immediately.

Mission agencies likely to be most impacted are those committed to youth-oriented workers who are themselves young (YWAM, OM, World Horizons, Young Life, JOC, newer independent/postdenominational/neocharismatic agencies, et alia). But all church bodies will see an average 50% reduction in new recruits solely due to this one demographic factor.

*Wordings below: names of the 7
U.N. future fertility variants*

Graph 1.    **Percentage of global population under age 15, 1900-2200.**

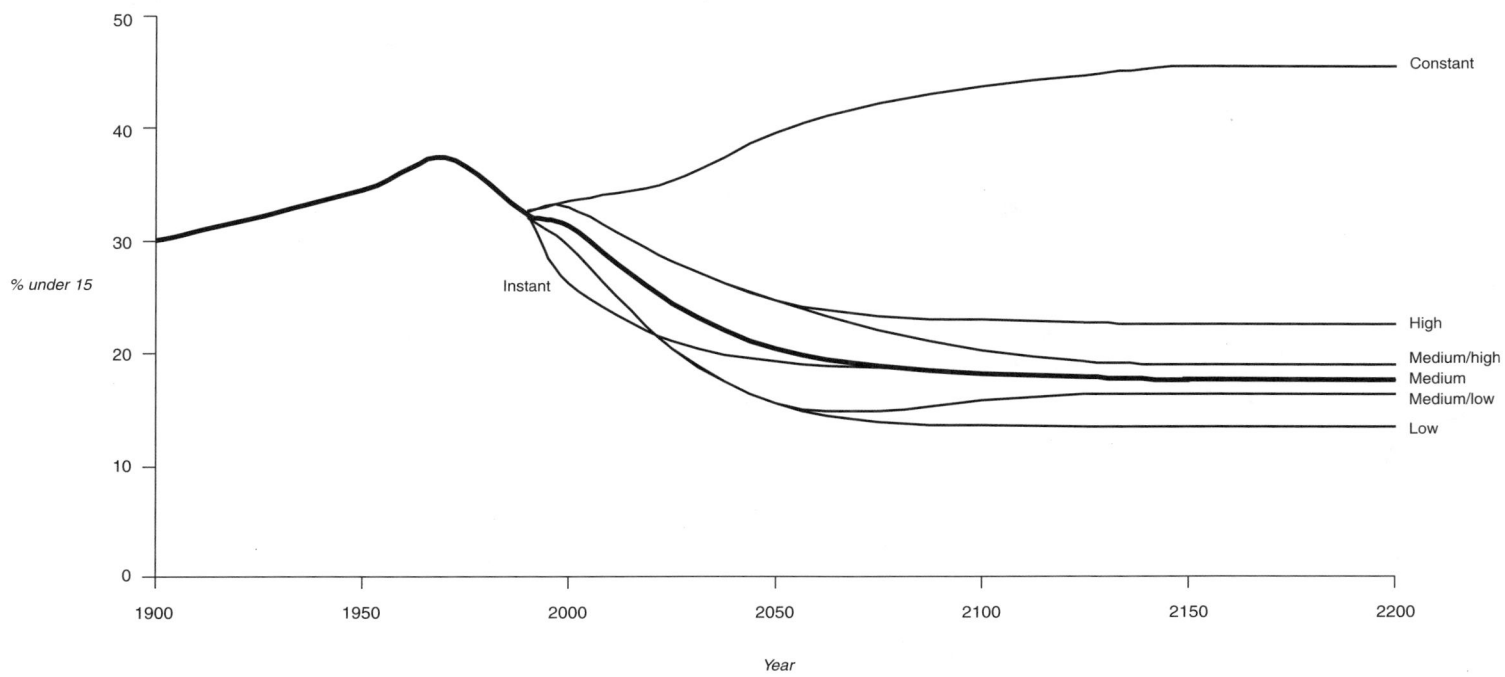

*Year*

*Notes on minidiagram Graph I (above).*
1. The 7 United Nations' future scenarios, based on different fertility assumptions, are briefly explained in our Global Diagram 46, but are more fully explained in the UN's *Long-range world population projections: two centuries of population growth, 1950-2150*, pages 6-13.
2. The heaviest line of the 7 is based on past and present figures which are then projected into the most probable future utilizing the UN's Medium Variant figures.

3. Note (a) the peaking of the percent under 15s in 1970, and (b) the drastic decline over the next 200 years which will result in 6 of the 7 scenarios showing a catastrophic decline from 37.5% in 1970 to, by AD 2200, somewhere in the range 13.5-22.6%.

## Table A. Percentage of global population under age 15, on 7 different fertility scenarios, 1900-2200.

*Notes.* Source: For years 1950-2200, see *Long-range world population projections: two centuries of population growth, 1950-2150* (New York: United Nations, 1992); and *World population prospects 1996* (New York: United Nations). The latter gives detailed youth figures for every country in the world for the years 1950-2025. Columns in the table below are divided by vertical lines to enclose separately the 20th, 21st, and 22nd centuries (remember that the 20th century began on January 1, 1901, and that the 21st century began not in 2000 but on January 1, 2001). The 7 scenarios in column 1 are defined here in *WCE* Part 12 "Dictionary." Dashes in the next three columns indicate that the 7 scenarios are all future ones starting from the base values in 1990 and thus do not apply before 1990.

| Fertility scenarios | Year 1900 | 1950 | 20TH CENTURY 1970 | 1990 | 2000 | 2025 | 21ST CENTURY 2050 | 2075 | 2100 | 2125 | 22ND CENTURY 2150 | 2200 |
|---|---|---|---|---|---|---|---|---|---|---|---|---|
| Low | — | — | — | 32.0 | 29.6 | 20.5 | 15.6 | 13.9 | 13.7 | 13.6 | 13.5 | 13.5 |
| Medium/low | — | — | — | 32.0 | 29.6 | 20.5 | 15.6 | 14.9 | 15.9 | 16.5 | 16.5 | 16.5 |
| Instant replacement | — | — | — | 32.3 | 26.3 | 21.1 | 19.3 | 18.8 | 18.3 | 17.9 | 17.7 | 17.7 |
| **Medium** | **30.0** | **34.5** | **37.5** | **32.3** | **31.4** | **24.5** | **20.5** | **18.9** | **18.3** | **17.9** | **17.7** | **17.7** |
| Medium/high | — | — | — | 32.7 | 33.0 | 28.2 | 24.7 | 22.1 | 20.3 | 19.4 | 19.0 | 19.0 |
| High | — | — | — | 32.7 | 33.0 | 28.2 | 24.7 | 23.4 | 23.0 | 22.8 | 22.6 | 22.6 |
| Constant | — | — | — | 32.6 | 33.5 | 35.4 | 39.6 | 42.3 | 43.8 | 44.8 | 45.6 | 45.6 |

## Global Diagram 50.    Sharing the benefits of longevity worldwide: life expectancy at birth for 9 major areas of the globe (continents/subcontinents), AD 1900-2200.

Nowadays Christians and most other serious religionists feel it right and their duty to uphold human rights anywhere, everywhere, and at any time. In particular they seek to defend the rights of the poor, the underprivileged, the oppressed. One often neglected human right is—longevity, the right to live a long life, to live at least as long as the global average of 64.5 years. At present, exactly half of the globe never make it to that age—they are cheated out of it by disease, starvation, drought, greed, corruption, warfare, murder.

The subtable and minidiagram below divide the situation up by continents and subcontinents. Africa can be seen to lose out far below everywhere else.

Life expectancy is defined technically as the number of years a person born within a particular population group (age cohort) would be expected to live, based on actuarial calculations.

The 2 United Nations publications listed below under the title to Table A enable us to illustrate progress with longevity in

graphical form. The figures are plotted in Graph 1 to reveal the trends taking place in the 20th, 21st, and 22nd centuries.

Christians have long been concerned about the huge gulf or gap between rich nations and poor nations. Illustrated below is another kind of gulf. But instead of the gap being a vast dollar figure, this time the gap from Africa to North America is (in 1990) 24 years of life. Which is worse?

Graph 1. **Life expectancy at birth (medium-variant) for 9 continents/subcontinents, AD 1900-2200.**

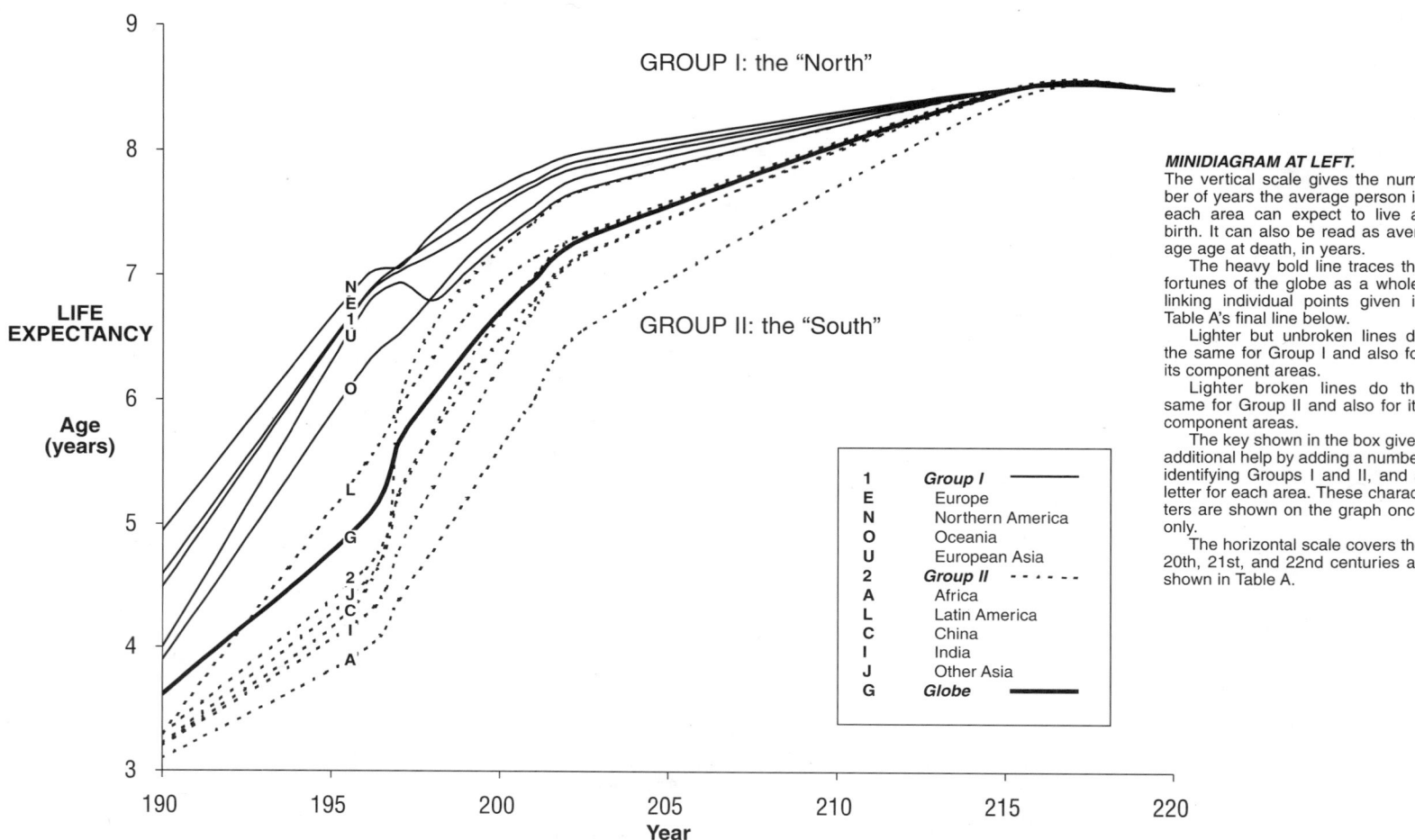

*MINIDIAGRAM AT LEFT.*
The vertical scale gives the number of years the average person in each area can expect to live at birth. It can also be read as average age at death, in years.

The heavy bold line traces the fortunes of the globe as a whole, linking individual points given in Table A's final line below.

Lighter but unbroken lines do the same for Group I and also for its component areas.

Lighter broken lines do the same for Group II and also for its component areas.

The key shown in the box gives additional help by adding a number identifying Groups I and II, and a letter for each area. These characters are shown on the graph once only.

The horizontal scale covers the 20th, 21st, and 22nd centuries as shown in Table A.

| 1 | *Group I* | ——— |
| E | Europe | |
| N | Northern America | |
| O | Oceania | |
| U | European Asia | |
| 2 | *Group II* | - - - - - |
| A | Africa | |
| L | Latin America | |
| C | China | |
| I | India | |
| J | Other Asia | |
| G | *Globe* | ——— |

## Table A. Life expectancy at birth for 9 major areas of the globe (continents/subcontinents), 1900-2200 (Medium Variant).

Notes.    The figures give the average number of years of life expectancy at birth, as defined in U.N. publications. Sources: Years 1990-2200: Medium-Variant data from *Long-range world population projections: two centuries of population growth, 1950-2150* (New York: United Nations, 1992, and updated edition 1999); 1960-2000 from *World population prospects, 1998* (New York: United Nations) Figures for 1900 come from a variety of sources.

| Major area | Year | 1900 | 1960 | 1970 | 20TH CENTURY 1980 | 1990 | Males 1990 | Females | 2000 | 21ST CENTURY 2010 | 2025 | 22ND CENTURY 2150 | 2200 |
|---|---|---|---|---|---|---|---|---|---|---|---|---|---|
| | | years | | | | | | | | | | | |
| *Group I* | | 45.0 | 68.2 | 70.2 | 71.6 | 73.2 | 69.5 | 76.6 | 75.5 | 77.1 | 78.7 | 84.9 | 84.9 |
| Europe | | 46.0 | 68.3 | 70.7 | 72.6 | 74.4 | 71.1 | 77.7 | 76.1 | 77.5 | 79.2 | 84.9 | 84.9 |
| Northern America | | 49.5 | 69.8 | 70.5 | 73.3 | 75.6 | 72.1 | 79.2 | 77.1 | 78.4 | 79.8 | 84.9 | 84.9 |
| Oceania | | 39.0 | 62.7 | 65.2 | 68.2 | 71.3 | 68.4 | 74.5 | 73.5 | 75.5 | 77.9 | 84.9 | 84.9 |
| European Asia (formerly USSR) | | 40.0 | 67.4 | 69.3 | 67.9 | 70.2 | 65.2 | 74.4 | 72.5 | 74.5 | 76.9 | 84.9 | 84.9 |
| *Group II* | | 32.2 | 45.3 | 52.6 | 57.2 | 61.2 | 60.0 | 62.6 | 64.8 | 67.9 | 71.7 | 84.6 | 84.9 |
| Africa | | 31.0 | 39.8 | 43.9 | 47.9 | 52.0 | 50.3 | 53.6 | 56.1 | 60.0 | 65.6 | 83.9 | 84.9 |
| Latin America | | 33.0 | 54.8 | 59.2 | 63.3 | 66.7 | 64.0 | 69.5 | 69.4 | 71.3 | 73.2 | 84.9 | 84.9 |
| China | | 32.0 | 44.6 | 59.6 | 65.8 | 69.4 | 68.0 | 70.9 | 72.0 | 74.2 | 76.8 | 84.9 | 84.9 |
| India | | 32.0 | 42.6 | 48.0 | 52.9 | 57.9 | 57.8 | 57.9 | 62.8 | 67.2 | 71.5 | 84.9 | 84.9 |
| Other Asia | | 33.0 | 46.4 | 52.3 | 57.4 | 62.7 | 61.1 | 64.4 | 66.8 | 69.9 | 73.3 | 84.9 | 84.9 |
| *GLOBE* | | 36.2 | 50.4 | 56.6 | 60.4 | 63.9 | 61.8 | 65.9 | 67.0 | 69.6 | 72.9 | 84.7 | 84.9 |

## Global Diagram 51.   Human mega-aging in tomorrow's globe: worldwide population over 65 and over 80, AD 1900-2200.

Due to rapid advances in health care and cures for many traditional killer diseases (cardiovascular, prostate, cancer), people in the industrialized world are living to increasingly longer ages—65, 80, even 100. Futurists are even forecasting life expectancies of 150 years by AD 2100. The result is a mushrooming expansion of the elderly.

The most dramatic of the trends in the data below shows the globe's population of persons 80 years or older exploding from 0.2% in the year 1900 (3 million) to 1.0% in 1990 (53 mil-

lion) and on to 10.6% (1,230 million) by AD 2200. Meanwhile, those aged 65 or older rise astronomically by AD 2200 to 25.6% (2,970 million).

As with other new demographic trends in the near and distant future (exemplified in Global Diagrams 46 to 51), dividing these new data between the countries of the 'North' (the United Nations' Group I) and those of the 'South' (Group II) leads to further startling trends. The major nightmare here is that in Group II the over-65s will pass 1 billion in number by

AD 2042—less than 42 years ahead—and the over-80s will reach a quarter of a billion by the same year, *without any prospects of the specialized care* lavished on their counterparts in Group I.

The result might well be a disaster of huge proportions. Christians could plan now to avoid this possibility. How should we influence the world's power structures on this subject?

Graphic A. **Global population over 65 and over 80, AD 1900-2200.**

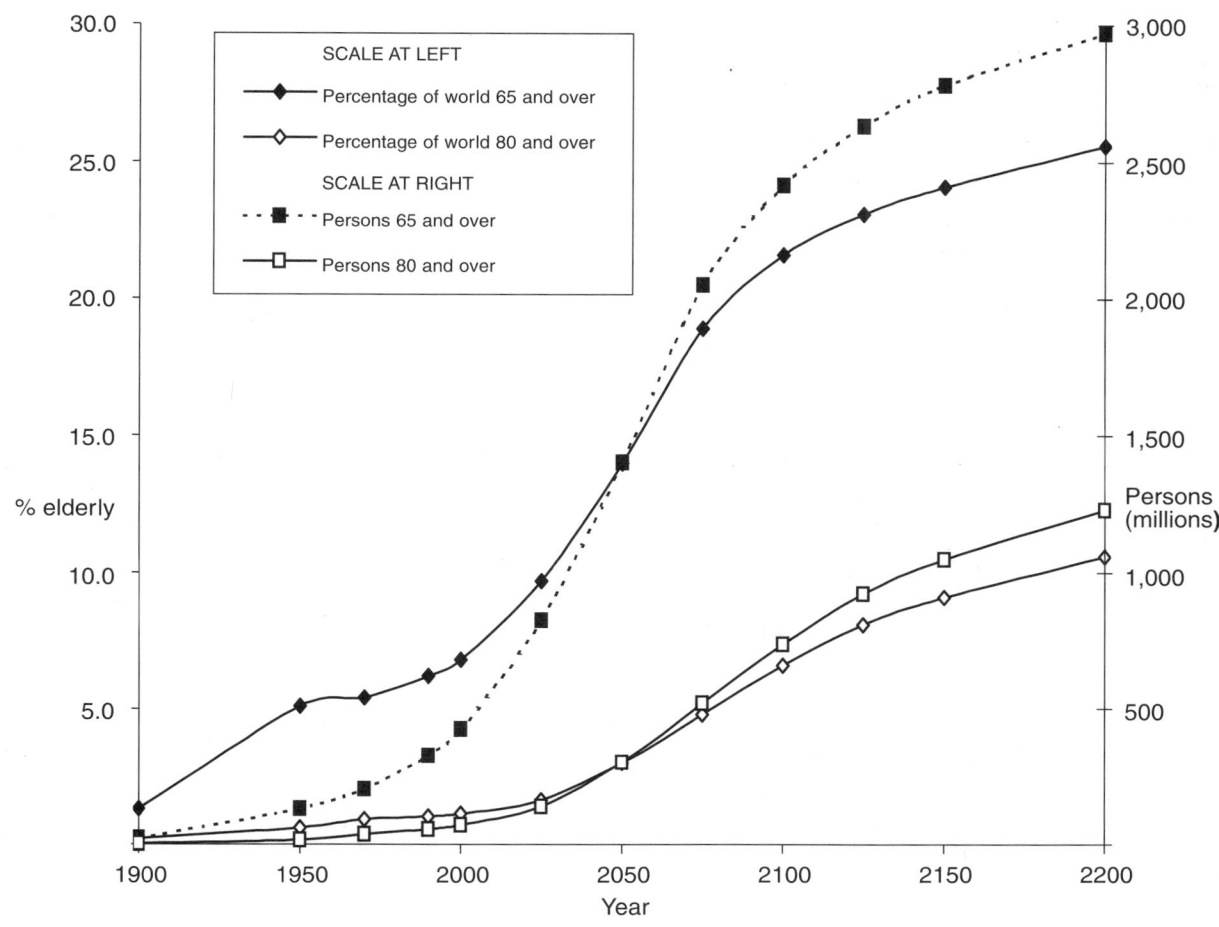

Notes on minidiagram Graphic A (on left).

1. Data from 1990-2200 are derived using the United Nations' Medium Variant. The lines follow data points given in Table A below.
2. The 2 full lines utilize the scale on the lefthand axis. The two dotted lines utilize the scale on the righthand axis.
3. Statistics of persons 80 years and older are also included in persons 65 years and older.
4. The 2 UN publications listed below Table A's title contain similar data for the other 6 fertility variants used by the UN to cover all possible or likely future scenarios. The 7 variants (as listed in our Global Diagram 46) are named: Low, Medium/Low, Instant Replacement, Medium, Medium/High, High, and Constant. The last variant assumes human fertility continues on at its 1997 level unchanged into the future.
5. Note that the numbers begin to decline for Group I (the North) from AD 2100 onwards. This is the result of those countries getting their populations under control by limiting birth rates a hundred years earlier.

Table A. **Global population over 65 and over 80 (North, South, and total), AD 1900-2200, on medium variant fertility scenario.**

Source: For years 1950-2200, see *Long-range world population projections: two centuries of population growth, 1950-2150* (New York: United Nations, 1992, updated 1999; and *World population prospects 1998* (New York: United Nations). The former gives detailed figures for persons aged 80 or older, for Major Areas (Continents) up to AD 2150, and the latter for persons aged 65 or older, for every country in the world for the years 1950-2025. Columns in the table below are divided by vertical lines to enclose separately the 20th, 21st, and 22nd centuries (remember that the 20th century began on January 1, 1901, and that the 21st century began not in 2000 but on January 1, 2001).

| Ages and Areas | Year 1900 | 20TH CENTURY | | | | 21ST CENTURY | | | | 22ND CENTURY | | |
|---|---|---|---|---|---|---|---|---|---|---|---|---|
| | | 1950 | 1970 | 1990 | 2000 | 2025 | 2050 | 2075 | 2100 | 2125 | 2150 | 2200 |
| **AGED 65 OR OVER** | | | | | | | | | | | | |
| *% POPULATION* | | | | | | | | | | | | |
| Group I  (the North) | 3.3 | 7.6 | 9.6 | 12.1 | 13.4 | 18.4 | 21.9 | 23.7 | 24.9 | 24.9 | 24.7 | 24.5 |
| Group II  (the South) | 0.4 | 3.8 | 3.7 | 4.7 | 5.3 | 8.2 | 12.9 | 18.2 | 21.3 | 22.9 | 24.0 | 26.0 |
| **Globe** | **1.3** | **5.1** | **5.4** | **6.2** | **6.8** | **9.7** | **14.0** | **18.9** | **21.6** | **23.1** | **24.1** | **25.6** |
| *POPULATION* (m=millions) | | | | | | | | | | | | |
| Group I  (the North) | 16m | 63m | 101m | 132m | 153m | 228m | 270m | 287m | 299m | 298m | 294m | 290m |
| Group II  (the South) | 5m | 64m | 98m | 198m | 271m | 596m | 1,133m | 1,752m | 2,127m | 2,335m | 2,484m | 2,709m |
| **Globe** | **21m** | **128m** | **200m** | **328m** | **426m** | **825m** | **1,403m** | **2,049m** | **2,416m** | **2,631m** | **2,782m** | **2,970m** |
| **AGED 80 OR OVER** | | | | | | | | | | | | |
| *% POPULATION* | | | | | | | | | | | | |
| Group I  (the North) | 0.3 | 1.5 | 2.3 | 2.7 | 2.8 | 4.0 | 6.6 | 8.1 | 9.4 | 9.8 | 9.7 | 9.5 |
| Group II  (the South) | 0.0 | 0.2 | 0.4 | 0.6 | 0.7 | 1.2 | 2.5 | 4.3 | 6.3 | 7.9 | 9.0 | 10.9 |
| **Globe** | **0.2** | **0.6** | **0.9** | **1.0** | **1.1** | **1.6** | **3.0** | **4.8** | **6.6** | **8.1** | **9.1** | **10.6** |
| *POPULATION* (m=millions) | | | | | | | | | | | | |
| Group I  (the North) | 2m | 12m | 24m | 29m | 32m | 49m | 81m | 98m | 113m | 117m | 116m | 112m |
| Group II  (the South) | 0.2m | 3m | 11m | 25m | 36m | 87m | 220m | 414m | 629m | 805m | 932m | 1,136m |
| **Globe** | **3m** | **15m** | **35m** | **53m** | **69m** | **136m** | **301m** | **520m** | **738m** | **923m** | **1,050m** | **1,230m** |

## Global Diagram 52. Past, present, and future in global mission: facing up to staggering numbers in the search to win the globe for Christ and his Gospel, AD 100-2150.

This diagram takes the form of 2 closely-related semi-visual trend tables describing the past, present, and future of world evangelization.

### Table A: Fourteen historico-futurist snapshots, AD 100-AD 2100

The first 7 columns of Table 1 below provide a useful and incisive way of analyzing the church's obedience to the Great Commission at 7 major turning points in past Christian history, namely AD 100, AD 500, AD 1000, AD 1491, AD 1800, AD 1900, and AD 1950. Since the exact percentages for Worlds A, B, and C for any year can be derived from the 2 basic statistics, AC (% Christian) and E (% evangelized persons), similar data could be quickly derived for any other dates over the last 2,000 years. The results are also illustrated in Global Diagram 46.

From the table, it can be seen that the size of World B has fluctuated markedly over the last 19 centuries. In AD 100, Christians were in evangelistic contact with 27% of the entire world. This was mission as it was meant to be—the church was then in contact with non-Christians numbering 46 times its own number. But thereafter as missionary zeal fell off, World B declined rapidly in size to its lowest point in 1491.

During the modern missionary era from 1800-2000, World B has again massively increased, 66 times in size. At present (AD 2000), World B is still increasing rapidly in magnitude, while World A is decreasing, though very slowly.

### Table B: Runaway expansion in the church's responsibility and liability

The major feature reported in the second table below is the vast proliferation in the numbers of non-Christians that Great Commission Christians are held accountable for by their own constituencies. Ministry to the world's souls lost without Christ is already being swamped everywhere by this proliferation. In the next century, this situation will get progressively worse.

Any attempt to plan strategically for the 21st century must take seriously accountability for the staggering populations for whom mission agencies have publicly accepted responsibility at regular intervals over the last 2 centuries. These are set out in the table under the 2 headings below. Comments can be made as follows.

1. *Total population*. The total of all the populations on Earth, for which the church's world mission has announced itself to be responsible, rose from 903 million in 1800 to 1,620 million in 1900, to 6.1 billion in AD 2000. It seems certain to rise to 7.8 billion by 2025, and to 10.4 billion by 2100. The years 1800-2000 have thus seen a 5-fold increase in our sphere of accountability (the number of souls for whom the church has accepted and announced its responsibility.) From AD 2000-2150 this is likely to involve a further 78% increase in this accountability.

2. *Total non-Christians*. The total of all non-Christians under the church's responsibility has risen from 694 million in 1800 to 4.1 billion in AD 2000. This represents a 480% increase in accountability. Almost certainly non-Christians under the church's stewardship will then rise to 5.2 billion by AD 2025, 5.9 billion by AD 2050, and in all probability to 6.7 billion by AD 2100. From AD 2000-2100 this therefore anticipates a further 63% increase in the attendant accountability.

As the final 2 columns of the table demonstrate, the total number of non-Christians living on Earth throughout this period of Christian stewardship from 1800 to 2150 is likely to be just over 22 billion. The church today can do nothing more for the 5,700 million of these who have already died. But it clearly carries responsibility for the 4,056 million alive today and the 12,900 million likely to be alive during the next 150 years tracked below.

These figures for the next century demand the boldest of bold mission thinking, bold mission planning, and bold mission thrusts. It is not enough to for the church say: We will do our best. If current leaders are not able to plan to actually reach these populations in their entirety, then they must admit it and allow new leaders to tackle the vision.

## Table A. Global populations divided into Worlds A, B, and C, by absolute numbers and by percentages, at 14 points in Christian history, AD 100-2100.

| | AD 100 | 500 | 1000 | 1491 | 1800 | 1900 | 1950 | 1990 | 1995 | 2000 | 2025 | 2050 | 2100 |
|---|---|---|---|---|---|---|---|---|---|---|---|---|---|
| | | | | PAST | | | | | | PRESENT | | FUTURE | |
| **(a) by absolute numbers (in millions):** | | | | | | | | | | | | | |
| World A | 130.7 | 112.2 | 201.9 | 328.7 | 657.1 | 880.0 | 1,138.1 | 1,665.4 | 1,678.2 | 1,629.4 | 1,845.4 | 1,806.1 | 1,562.1 |
| World B | 49.8 | 37.8 | 16.9 | 8.3 | 36.6 | 181.8 | 527.4 | 1,853.5 | 2,110.7 | 2,426.1 | 3,361.6 | 4,051.5 | 5,111.9 |
| World C | 1.0 | 43.4 | 50.4 | 81.0 | 208.9 | 558.1 | 856.0 | 1,747.5 | 1,872.4 | 1,999.6 | 2,616.7 | 3,051.6 | 3,740.0 |
| GLOBE | 181.5 | 193.4 | 269.2 | 418.0 | 902.6 | 1,619.9 | 2,521.5 | 5,266.4 | 5,666.4 | 6,055.0 | 7,823.7 | 8,909.1 | 10,414.0 |
| **(b) by percentages:** | | | | | | | | | | | | | |
| | % | % | % | % | % | % | % | % | % | % | % | % | % |
| World A | 72.0 | 58.0 | 75.0 | 79.0 | 72.8 | 54.3 | 45.1 | 31.6 | 29.6 | 26.9 | 23.6 | 20.3 | 15.0 |
| World B | 27.4 | 19.6 | 6.3 | 2.0 | 4.1 | 11.2 | 21.0 | 35.2 | 37.3 | 40.1 | 43.0 | 45.5 | 49.1 |
| World C | 0.6 | 22.4 | 18.7 | 19.0 | 23.1 | 34.5 | 33.9 | 33.2 | 33.1 | 33.0 | 33.4 | 34.3 | 35.9 |
| GLOBE | 100.0 | 100.0 | 100.0 | 100.0 | 100.0 | 100.0 | 100.0 | 100.0 | 100.0 | 100.0 | 100.0 | 100.0 | 100.0 |

## Table B. Global populations and Non-Christians seen as the church's responsibility, AD 1800-2150.

*Notes.* Source of basic demographic data: *Long-range world population projections: two centuries of population growth, 1950-2150* (New York: United Nations, 1992), revised edition 1999.

| Year | Population | Non-Christians | Daily increase in non-Christians | Foreign missionaries | Non-Christians per missionary | Cumulative non-Christians since 1800 | Cumulative non-Christians since AD 33 |
|---|---|---|---|---|---|---|---|
| 1 | 2 | 3 | 4 | 5 | 6 | 7 | 8 |
| 1800 | 903 million | 694 million | 76,000 | 7,000 | 99,100 | 0 | 17,736 million |
| 1900 | 1,620 million | 1,062 million | 116,000 | 62,000 | 17,100 | 3,626 million | 21,362 million |
| 1950 | 2,522 million | 1,665 million | 149,000 | 120,000 | 13,700 | 6,103 million | 23,839 million |
| 1970 | 3,696 million | 2,460 million | 216,000 | 240,000 | 10,280 | 7,338 million | 25,074 million |
| 1980 | 4,453 million | 3,020 million | 262,000 | 249,000 | 12,100 | 8,082 million | 25,818 million |
| 1990 | 5,266 million | 3,519 million | 292,000 | 285,000 | 12,400 | 8,881 million | 26,617 million |
| 1995 | 5,666 million | 3,789 million | 302,000 | 320,000 | 11,900 | 9,311 million | 27,047 million |
| 2000 | 6,055 million | 4,056 million | 292,000 | 420,000 | 9,650 | 9,743 million | 27,479 million |
| 2025 | 7,824 million | 5,207 million | 266,000 | 600,000 | 8,700 | 11,990 million | 29,726 million |
| 2050 | 8,909 million | 5,858 million | 250,000 | 700,000 | 8,400 | 14,075 million | 31,811 million |
| 2100 | 10,414 million | 6,674 million | 220,000 | 800,000 | 8,400 | 18,451 million | 36,187 million |
| 2150 | 10,806 million | 6,860 million | 193,000 | 900,000 | 7,600 | 22,664 million | 40,400 million |

## Global Diagram 53. Today's megatrends in mission: 20 long-term Christian global trends underway, AD 1950-AD 2050.

The globe below portrays schematically the approximate locations on it of 20 major Christian global megatrends that have come into prominence since 1950. At first they were seen as short-term trends; by AD 2000 they have taken on all the attributes of long-term trends over the next 2 generations to AD 2050 at least.

Countries are located by 2 scales. (a) The horizontal scale refers to geopolitical ideology, as set out below the globe. This locates countries and populations in the First World (Western world, also referred to as the West, or the North) in the middle of the globe, the Second World (Communist world, or since 1989 the former Communist world, or the Communist sphere of influence) on the left within the globe, and the Third World (nonaligned world) on the right within it. (b) The vertical scale refers to evangelization, as explained in words to the right of the globe. This locates countries by degree of evangelization (most-evangelized at the bottom, least-evangelized at the top), and adds the 3-tier typology of Worlds A, B, and C (as defined in Global Diagrams 34 and 40).

The 20 megatrends are listed and numbered below. The approximate location of each on the 3-tier globe is then shown by using the same numbers on the globe.

### CHRISTIAN GLOBAL MEGATRENDS, with statistics as at AD 2000

1. Southwards shift of Christian center of gravity from North to Third World (58% of all Christians).
2. Eastwards shift of Christian center of gravity from West to East Asia's Communist world.
3. Migrations of 2,000 Third-World peoples to Christian West.
4. Countries restricting access by foreign missions: 86 (43 closed countries).
5. Rise of 56 global ministry networks with 350 million computers.
6. Massive global growth of electronic radio/TV Christianity.
7. Mushrooming of literature on evangelization (13,000 items a year).
8. Proliferation of 500 conferences on evangelization each year.
9. 50 new global plans for world evangelization each year.
10. 3,000 evangelistic mass campaigns a year.
11. Emergence of 4,000 Third-World mission agencies.
12. Rise of the East Asian colossus with 115 million Christians.
13. 3 waves of worldwide pentecostal/charismatic renewal, to 524 million.
14. Power Christianity by osmosis across the world: signs and wonders.
15. Retrograde or negative Christian activities hindering world mission.
16. Pluralism: proliferation of 34,000 denominations and 8,400 religions across world.
17. Spread of Christian activism worldwide opposing injustice and human rights abuses.
18. New ministries to 1.3 billion urban poor in exploding 'planet of slums'.
19. Escalating martyrdoms vary up to 160,000 a year in 50 countries and in all Christian branches.
20. Emergence of the AD 2000 megamagnet throughout the world.

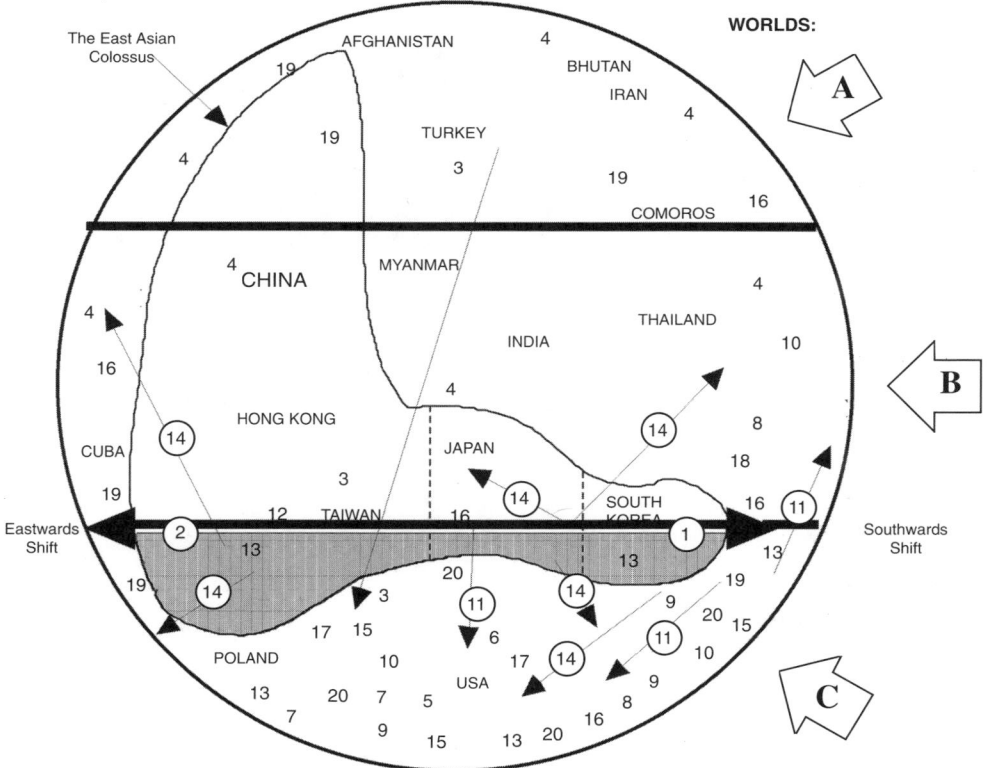

*VERTICAL SCALE: Evangelization in Worlds A,B,C*

**A. THE UNEVANGELIZED WORLD**

115 million newly-evangelized each year, but offset by 124 million new births a year.
26 closed countries.
Sizable numbers from 1,000 unreached peoples migrate to Christian West.

**B. THE EVANGELIZED NON-CHRISTIAN WORLD**

Emergence of 4,000 Third-World mission agencies.
31 partially-closed countries.
Reaction to social injustice and abuses in Third World.
Rapid spread of Christian activism in 30 World B countries (150 countries worldwide).
Escalating martyrdoms of Christian workers.
Vast numbers from 800 non-Christian peoples migrate to Christian West.
Numerous ministries escalate among 700 million slumdwellers.

**C. THE CHRISTIAN WORLD**

Eastwards and southwards shift of Christian center of gravity.
East Asian colossus: 115 million Christians (shaded gray) among 1.5 billion population.
Pluralism: over 4,000 new religions spread across West.
Retrograde Christian activities, with ecclesiastical crime $16 billion p.a., mainly in West
Massive global growth of electronic radio/TV Christianity.
Global plans launched by most major churches and agencies.

| HORIZONTAL SCALE: | Geopolitical ideology | | |
|---|---|---|---|
| | (Left inside) | (Center) | (Right inside) |
| WORLDS | Communist world | Western world | Third World |
| DEVELOPMENT | Developing | Developed | Less-developed |
| INDUSTRIALIZATION | More-developed | Most-developed | Least-developed |
| GLOBAL AREA | East | North | South |
| RELIGION | Anti-religious | Secularized | Religious |

## Global Diagram 54.   Megalopolis 2000-2100: the urban world, Worlds A/B/C, and the rise of 1,400 megacities, 300 supercities, and 100 supergiants among 40,000 metropolises, AD 1770-2100.

The explosive growth of urbanization in the 20th century seems likely to be followed by explosive growth in the 21st. Based on current UN demographic projections, our figures below illustrate this. On the right below, the snapshot of spaceship Earth as megalopolis traces the possible future development of global urbanization from AD 1900 to AD 2000 and on to AD 2100. It does this by giving comparative figures for 8 categories for each of these 3 pivotal years.

On the left below, the graphic describes the current situation in more detail. Our globe is shown divided into the 3 population segments of our trichotomy of evangelization. Onto its Worlds A, B, and C are placed statistics of various ways of quantifying both urbanization and evangelization. The lower half of the page then supplies detailed statistics of different aspects of the entire urban phenomenon—households, families, education, health, tourism, trade. A final bloc of statistics

sketches the major Christian resources which are today oriented towards urban mission.

The deployment of these Christian resources at present is approximately as follows: 90% benefits urbanites in World C, 9% benefits urbanites in World B, and less than 1% benefits urbanites in World A.

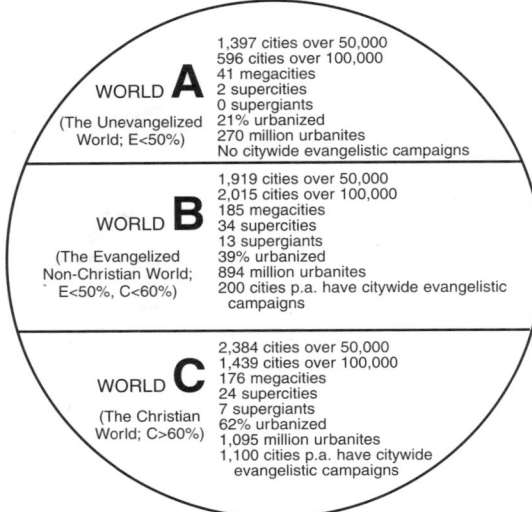

**WORLD A**
(The Unevangelized World; E<50%)
1,397 cities over 50,000
596 cities over 100,000
41 megacities
2 supercities
0 supergiants
21% urbanized
270 million urbanites
No citywide evangelistic campaigns

**WORLD B**
(The Evangelized Non-Christian World; E<50%, C<60%)
1,919 cities over 50,000
2,015 cities over 100,000
185 megacities
34 supercities
13 supergiants
39% urbanized
894 million urbanites
200 cities p.a. have citywide evangelistic campaigns

**WORLD C**
(The Christian World; C>60%)
2,384 cities over 50,000
1,439 cities over 100,000
176 megacities
24 supercities
7 supergiants
62% urbanized
1,095 million urbanites
1,100 cities p.a. have citywide evangelistic campaigns

### URBAN EVANGELIZATION IN MEGALOPOLIS 2000
The above diagram analyzes the globe's 4,050 metropolises (over 100,000 in population) and the 2,882 million urbanites (urban dwellers) by our 3-fold trichotomy Worlds A/B/C. The righthand diagram then traces the possible future development of the massive urbanization of the globe from AD 1900 to AD 2000 and on to AD 2100.

**MEGALOPOLIS 1900**
500 metropolises over 50,000
300 metropolises over 100,000
20 megacities (over 1 million)
2 supercities (over 4 million)
No supergiants (over 10 million)
233 million urbanites
100 million urban poor
20 million slumdwellers

**MEGALOPOLIS 2000**
7,000 metropolises over 50,000
4,050 metropolises over 100,000
402 megacities (over 1 million)
60 supercities (over 4 million)
20 supergiants (over 10 million)
2,882 million urbanites
1,273 million urban poor
700 million slumdwellers

**MEGALOPOLIS 2100**
40,000 metropolises over 50,000
15,000 metropolises over 100,000
1,400 megacities (over 1 million)
300 supercities (over 4 million)
100 supergiants (over 10 million)
9,000 million urbanites
7,000 million urban poor
4,000 million slumdwellers

### HISTORICAL-FUTURIST OVERVIEW, 1770-2100
AD 1770: first modern megacity (Peking)
AD 1800: 50 million urbanites (5% of world); 1 megacity (Peking)
AD 1900: 233 million urbanites (14%); 20 megacities
AD 2000: 2,882 million urbanites (47.6%); 402 megacities
AD 2050: 7.0 billion urbanites (80%); 900 megacities, 220 supercities, 80 supergiants
AD 2100: 9.0 billion urbanites (90%), 15,000 metropolises over 100,000 each

### THE URBAN/RURAL GLOBE
6,055 million persons
3,173 million rural dwellers (52.4%)
2,882 million urban dwellers (urbanites)(47.6%)
2.0 billion metrodwellers (city-dwellers)
0.8 billion nonmetro urbanites
69.5 million new urbanites a year
190,000 new urbanites a day
100,000 rural poor migrate to cities each day
Urban growth rate 1.91% p.a.
Rural growth rate 0.04% p.a.
1,273 million urban poor

### CITIES
50,000 cities over 10,000 in population
7,000 metropolises over 50,000
4,050 metropolises over 100,000
756 agglomerations over 500,000
402 megacities (over 1 million)
60 supercities (over 4 million)
20 supergiants (cities over 10 million)
2 Islamic supergiants
85 anti-Christian megacities
150 non-Christian megacities
129,000 new non-Christian city-dwellers a day
Slums: 25% of all metropolitan areas
30 billion rats (25% urban/domestic, 75% rural/wild)
Rats eat or destroy 25% of world's food p.a.
Total food and property destroyed by rats: $300 billion p.a.

### HOUSEHOLDS AND FAMILIES (urban, rural)
1.2 billion households (families, homes, dwellings)
1,160 million self-built dwellings (97% of total)
33 million new families p.a.
4.3 persons per household
Average income per person $3,040 p.a.
Average family income $13,070 p.a.
34 million legal marriages p.a.

1.6 billion married persons
850 million married women
1.3 billion unmarried persons living together
8 million divorces p.a.
74 million divorcees (divorced persons)
240 million singles (adult unmarried)
93 million homosexuals
150 million bisexual men
30 million lesbians
200 million gays (gay preference)
590 million women of child-bearing age
40% of women use contraceptives
200 million bereaved each year
328 million senior citizens (over 65 years)
244 million widows
50 million widowers
Fertility rate: 3.3 births per childbearing woman
190 live births per 1000 females
142 million births a year (15% being illegitimate)
3 million adoptions a year
65 million abortions p.a. (38% illegal)

### EDUCATION (urban, rural)
3.1 million primary schools
880 million pupils in school (59% of all eligible)
38 million teachers
Student enrollment: first level 95%, second 46%, third 12%
Education costs $863 billion (5.9%) p.a.
20,000 university campuses (3,000 major)
60 million college students (45% women)
3.6 million university teachers
1.3 million foreign students
Primary education: completed by 1.2 billion adults

### HEALTH (largely organized through cities)
240,000 hospitals
17.6 million hospital beds (1 per 265)
5.0 million physicians (1 per 1,030)
7.6 million nurses and midwives (1 per 680)
490,000 dentists (1 per 10,530)
World pharmaceutical market $130 billion p.a.
510,000 pharmacists
150,000 mental institutions
Health costs $650 billion (4.0%) p.a.

### TOURISM AND TRANSIENTS
338 million foreign tourists p.a.
3,500 million domestic tourists p.a.
14.1 million registered hotel beds

250 million religious pilgrims on move every year
10 million seamen (merchant seafarers)
25 million resident labor migrants
100 million seasonal labor migrants

### TRADE (organized through cities)
Gross world product (global income) $16.1 trillion p.a.
World imports $2,070 billion p.a.
World exports $1,970 billion p.a.
Balance of trade $100 billion p.a.
External debt of developing countries $780 billion

### MAJOR CHRISTIAN RESOURCES (urban-oriented)
1,160 million Christian urbanites (58% of all Christians)
24 million more Christian urbanites each year
22 million more urban church members each year
1.7 million worship centers (urban local churches)
35,000 new urban churches each year
5,000 major councils of churches (HQs in cities)
17,000 parachurch or service agencies in cities
60,000 major urban Christian/church-related institutions
350,000 minor urban Christian institutions
1,000 Christian universities and colleges in cities
1,500 Christian-owned presses and publishers
Church/agency income for urban work $130 billion a year
Christian broadcasting (radio/TV) $5 billion p.a.
3 million full-time Christian urban workers (35% women; 95% citizens)
12 million urbanites in full-time prayer ministry
100 million urbanites praying daily for world mission
60 million Christian pilgrims on the move a year
200 million Christian foreign tourists a year
1,900 million Christian domestic tourists a year
3,000 monasteries, ashrams, convents, abbeys, priories
210,000 foreign missionaries in cities
600,000 home missionaries in cities
2.5 billion Christian books printed p.a.
13,000 major Christian libraries
2,100 large Christian libraries (over 35,000 volumes each)
50,000 Christian bookshops in cities
30 million Bibles distributed a year in cities
45 million New Testaments distributed a year in cities
800 million scriptures (all varieties) distributed p.a. in cities
2,000 Christian radio/TV stations
250 million Christian-owned computers in cities
1,300 metropolises p.a. hold citywide evangelistic campaigns

(For a fuller list of all available Christian resources, see Global Diagrams 21 and 24).

**Global Diagram 55. Future constituencies of Christianity and world religions over the next 2 centuries: trends for Christians and non-Christians, AD 1900-2200.**

Described below is one out of 3 or 4 plausible scenarios for the future of Christianity and some of the 30 other major world religions. the possible future of global Christianity is set out by means of a single variable, the total number of Christians. Of the United Nations' 7 possible demographic futures to AD 2200, the table and minidiagram below select only the most probable one, the Medium Variant. Likely trends in adherence to each of the major world religions or nonreligions are then added. (Other scenarios alter the figures shown below by up to plus or minus 10%). Five main findings emerge.

1. Christianity continues its astronomical expansion. The first trend the observer noted from the graph is that the present meteoric growth of Christians continues up to AD 2200, after which it levels off at around 4.4 billion. This represents an 8-fold expansion since the year 1900. The church has yet to come to terms with the enormous implications of this

numerical explosion. the myopic view is that this represents enormous success for Christianity. Few people have yet seen the enormous problems it is already raising.

2. Everybody else is expanding also. Second, however, the observer sees that this expansion is universal—and, in particular, non-Christians are growing explosively as well. By 2200 they seem likely to top 6.8 billion.

3. The underlying cause is global population increase. The top line in the graph reveals the underlying cause of all these expansions—the global population explosion. Careful UN documentation and analysis project that it will finally level off by AD 2200 at 11.2 billion.

4. Percentages yield a truer analysis. The broken lines in the graph shown give a clearer analysis. Both Christians and non-Christians each barely change over the 3-century period when expressed as a percentage of the globe.

5. Meanwhile, Islam grows faster. In contrast, Islam is seen expanding markedly in percentage terms—from 12% of the world in 1900 to 27% in 2200. This is not, however, due primarily to conversions. It is mainly because the population explosion is centering in the Muslim world—the Middle East and other Third World countries, in particular Pakistan, India, Bangladesh, Indonesia. Altogether, Islam can be seen to expand 14-fold from 1900 to 2200.

The globe's 20th-century antireligious experiment with Communism, dialectical materialism, and atheism finally collapsed in 1991. Secularism of course remains. But the future of religion over the next two centuries emerges unchallenged.

Graphic A. **Expansion of religions, AD 1900-2200.**

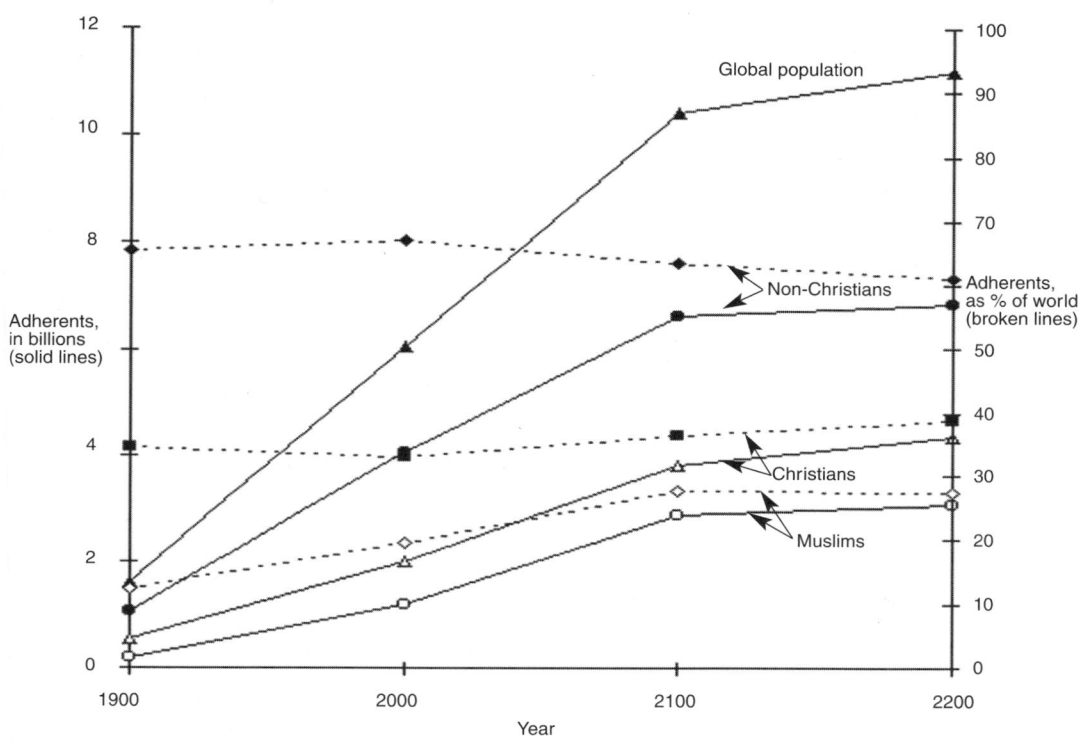

*Notes on minidiagram Graphic A (on left)*

1. The graphic plots the points in Table A below. It traces how religions have expanded over the 20th century and are likely to expand over the 21st and 22nd centuries.
2. The horizontal axis represents the progress of time over these 3 centuries. Note that technically this period covers part of 4 centuries (19th, 20th, 21st, 22nd) as is shown in Table A. The first year of the 20th century was 1901; the first year of the 21st was 2001; etc. Hence 1900, 2000, 2010, 2200 are the last years of their centuries, as shown.
3. There are 2 vertical axes. On the left is population in billions, relating to the solid lines. On the right is population as %, relating to the broken lines.
4. Source of the demographic data (the last line of Table A, and the top line on the left) is: *Long-range world population projections: two centuries of population growth, 1950-2150* (New York: United Nations, 1992; revised updated edition, 1999). Of the UN's 7 future demographic scenarios, the most probable (Medium Variant) is used here. The other UN scenarios, when combined with a variety of other religious scenarios such as a future collapse of centrally-organized Christianity, are examined elsewhere in this series of global diagrams. Our overall assessment is that while the graph and table set forth here are proposing the most likely scenario, other variants would alter the numbers by up to 10% up or down (± 10%).

## Table A. Adherents of world religions at 5 points from AD 1900 to 2200.

| | 19TH CENTURY | | 20TH CENTURY | | | | 21ST CENTURY | | 22ND CENTURY | |
| --- | --- | --- | --- | --- | --- | --- | --- | --- | --- | --- |
| | 1900 | % | 1990 | % | 2000 | % | 2100 | % | 2200 | % |
| Christians | 558,132,000 | 34.5 | 1,747,462,000 | 33.2 | 1,999,564,000 | 33.0 | 3,800,099,000 | 36.5 | 4,397,929,000 | 38.8 |
| Non-Christians | 1,061,494,000 | 65.5 | 3,518,980,000 | 67.0 | 4,055,485,000 | 67.1 | 6,613,901,000 | 63.5 | 6,852,637,000 | 61.2 |
| Muslims | 199,941,000 | 12.3 | 962,357,000 | 18.3 | 1,188,243,000 | 19.6 | 2,874,225,000 | 27.6 | 3,065,100,000 | 27.4 |
| Nonreligious | 3,024,000 | 0.2 | 707,118,000 | 13.4 | 768,159,000 | 12.7 | 959,818,000 | 9.2 | 1,212,302,000 | 10.8 |
| Hindus | 203,003,000 | 12.5 | 685,999,000 | 13.0 | 811,336,000 | 13.4 | 1,153,978,000 | 11.1 | 952,234,000 | 8.5 |
| Chinese folk-religionists | 380,006,000 | 23.5 | 347,651,000 | 6.6 | 384,807,000 | 6.4 | 475,183,000 | 4.6 | 442,190,000 | 3.9 |
| Buddhists | 127,077,000 | 7.8 | 323,107,000 | 6.1 | 359,982,000 | 5.9 | 397,100,000 | 3.8 | 344,080,000 | 3.1 |
| Ethnoreligionists | 117,558,000 | 7.3 | 200,035,000 | 3.8 | 228,367,000 | 3.8 | 323,995,000 | 3.1 | 369,920,000 | 3.3 |
| Atheists | 226,000 | 0.0 | 145,719,000 | 2.8 | 150,090,000 | 2.5 | 190,527,000 | 1.8 | 206,000,000 | 1.8 |
| New-Religionists | 5,910,000 | 0.4 | 92,396,000 | 1.8 | 102,356,000 | 1.7 | 106,911,000 | 1.0 | 67,336,000 | 0.6 |
| Sikhs | 2,962,000 | 0.2 | 19,332,000 | 0.4 | 23,258,000 | 0.4 | 40,414,000 | 0.4 | 42,496,000 | 0.4 |
| Jews | 12,292,000 | 0.8 | 13,189,000 | 0.3 | 14,434,000 | 0.2 | 15,828,000 | 0.2 | 11,673,000 | 0.1 |
| Spiritists | 269,000 | 0.0 | 10,155,000 | 0.2 | 12,334,000 | 0.2 | 27,435,000 | 0.3 | 40,059,000 | 0.4 |
| Baha'is | 10,000 | 0.0 | 5,672,000 | 0.1 | 7,106,000 | 0.1 | 33,091,,000 | 0.3 | 81,538,000 | 0.7 |
| Confucians | 640,000 | 0.0 | 5,856,000 | 0.1 | 6,299,000 | 0.1 | 6,039,000 | 0.1 | 3,495,000 | 0.1 |
| Jains | 1,323,000 | 0.1 | 3,868,000 | 0.1 | 4,218,000 | 0.1 | 6,658,000 | 0.1 | 8,345,000 | 0.1 |
| Shintoists | 6,720,000 | 0.4 | 3,082,000 | 0.1 | 2,762,000 | 0.0 | 890,000 | 0.0 | 388,000 | 0.0 |
| Other religionists | 533,000 | 0.0 | 920,000 | 0.0 | 1,029,000 | 0.0 | 2,809,000 | 0.0 | 5,481,000 | 0.0 |
| Global population | 1,619,626,000 | 100.0 | 5,266,442,000 | 100.0 | 6,055,049,000 | 100.2 | 10,414,000,000 | 100.0 | 11,200,000,000 | 100.0 |

## Global Diagram 56.    Christianity and evangelization in the context of world population growth: trends for Christians and non-Christians, AD 1900-2025.

AD 2025 is the terminal date—the *terminus ad quem*—utilized by the United Nations Population Division throughout the 1990s in its current country-by-country demographic database. The secular figures below come from their recent publication *World population prospects 1998*. The religious statistics are our own computations.

The table and graphic below analyze the demographic situation of Christianity, and of world evangelization, over the 125 years from AD 1900 to AD 2025. The figures are the absolute numbers of persons—the number of individuals involved at the worldwide level, comprising men, women and children.

Table A breaks down world population totals at 6 points in time into 2 pairs of dichotomies: (a) Christians and non-Christians, and (b) evangelized individuals and those still unevangelized (unaware of Christianity, Christ, or the gospel).

Graph A then places these 5 trend lines into a comparative context. Some startling observations then emerge. We can summarize 10 of them as follows.

1.   Since 1900, world population has increased massively and its rate of increase appears to slow slightly by AD 2025.

2.   This demographic explosion is reflected in, and appears partially responsible for, the similar explosive growth of both Christians, non-Christians, and evangelized persons.

3.   For the first 75 years of the 20th century, non-Christians increased faster than the church's efforts to evangelize them.

4.   The global total of unevangelized has increased rapidly since 1900 and today is some 750 million larger than in 1900.

5.   Since 1975, however, evangelization has clearly outstripped the increase in non-Christians. In that year, evangelization sharply increased and the unevangelized began to decrease markedly.

6.   Unevangelized persons are now falling appreciably each year due to a vast range of evangelistic endeavors.

7.   The total of non-Christians continues to soar and by 2025 there are likely to be more non-Christians in the world than the total world population in 1975.

8.   By 2025 over 75% of the world will be aware of Christianity, Christ, and the gospel (our definition of 'evangelized'). There will then be in the world some 3.4 billion non-Christians aware of Christ and his person and work.

9.   Theologians must now be asked to describe for us what a world in which nearly everyone is aware of Christ will be like.

10.   Missiologists likewise—how will universal awareness of Christianity and the gospel alter the Christian world mission?

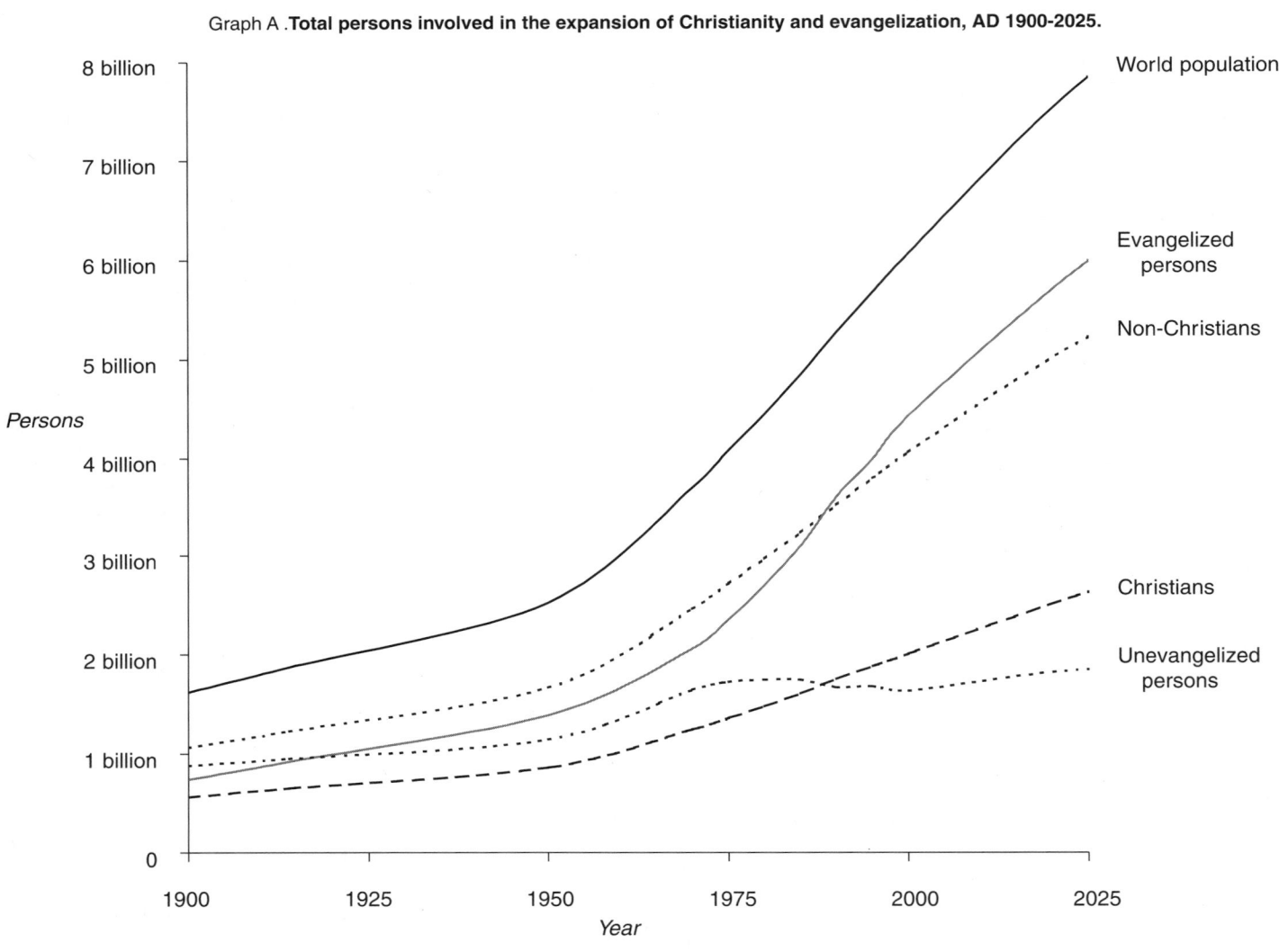

Graph A .Total persons involved in the expansion of Christianity and evangelization, AD 1900-2025.

Table A. **Totals of Christians and non-Christians, evangelized and unevangelized persons, across 3 centuries.**

| | 19TH CENTURY Year  1900 | 1925 | 1950 | 1975 | 2000 | 21ST CENTURY 2025 |
|---|---|---|---|---|---|---|
| | | | 20TH CENTURY | | | |
| *Affiliation* | | | | | | |
| Christians | 558,132,000 | 705,531,000 | 856,000,000 | 1,358,800,000 | 1,999,564,000 | 2,616,670,000 |
| Non-Christians | 1,061,494,000 | 1,343,309,000 | 1,665,500,000 | 2,715,900,000 | 4,055,485,000 | 5,207,033,000 |
| **GLOBAL POPULATION** | **1,619,626,000** | **2,048,840,000** | **2,521,500,000** | **4,074,700,000** | **6,055,049,000** | **7,823,703,000** |
| *Evangelization* | | | | | | |
| Evangelized persons | 739,954,000 | 1,042,519,000 | 1,383,400,000 | 2,355,000,000 | 4,425,674,000 | 5,978,297,000 |
| Unevangelized persons | 879,672,000 | 1,006,321,000 | 1,138,100,000 | 1,719,700,000 | 1,629,375,000 | 1,845,406,000 |
| **GLOBAL POPULATION** | **1,619,886,000** | **2,048,840,000** | **2,521,500,000** | **4,074,700,000** | **6,055,049,000** | **7,823,703,000** |

Global Diagram 57.   **Christianity and evangelization across 3 centuries: percentages for Christians/non-Christians/ evangelized/unevangelized, AD 1900-2025.**

Percentages put numbers in perspective. They give us the overall context. They show us the true significance of large numbers. They make comparisons possible. And so they reveal long-term trends that might otherwise be hidden from the careful reader.

This diagram does this for Global Diagram 56. For AD 1900 to AD 2025, that diagram tabled and graphed the total numbers of Christians and non-Christians, as well as the world's evangelized persons and its unevangelized persons. Global Diagram 57 now turns those totals into percentages and trends.

The most startling statement below, for persons unfamiliar with it, is that the percentage of Christians in the world has remained virtually unchanged at 34% year after year since 1900. This fact conceals the reality that (a) Christianity has

made enormous progress, especially numerically, in many areas of the world throughout the 20th century, but (b) at the same time it has also suffered catastrophic losses in many other unrelated areas. Result? The two trends have exactly cancelled each other out and the line for % Christian in the graph below remains almost exactly horizontal throughout.

One immediate consequence is that the proportion of the world which consists of non-Christians has also remained virtually unchanged at 66% since 1900. In a vast range of secular measures, such as the huge medical endeavor to stamp out disease and epidemics worldwide, or the global attempt to increase literacy to 100%, any percentage stuck at 34% for a whole century would be considered an unacceptable failure.

The other lines in the graph (evangelized persons/unevangelized persons) reveal a remarkable feature of the attempt

by the 34% who are Christians to evangelize the world. Since 1900 increasing percentages of non-Christians have become aware of Christianity, Christ and the gospel. this trend accelerated significantly in 1975 so that by AD 2000 over 73% of the world's population had become evangelized. This fact, however, should be balanced with the fact from Global Diagram 56 that this still means that over 1.6 billion people remain beyond the reach of the gospel. By AD 2025 the percentage rises to nearly 76.4% so that 23.6% or about 1.8 billion will remain yet to be evangelized.

While such momentum for world evangelization exists, strategic thinking and planning need to be implemented so that the world actually becomes 100% evangelized for the first time in history.

Graphic A. **Percentages and trends across 3 centuries in the expansion of Christianity and evangelization.**

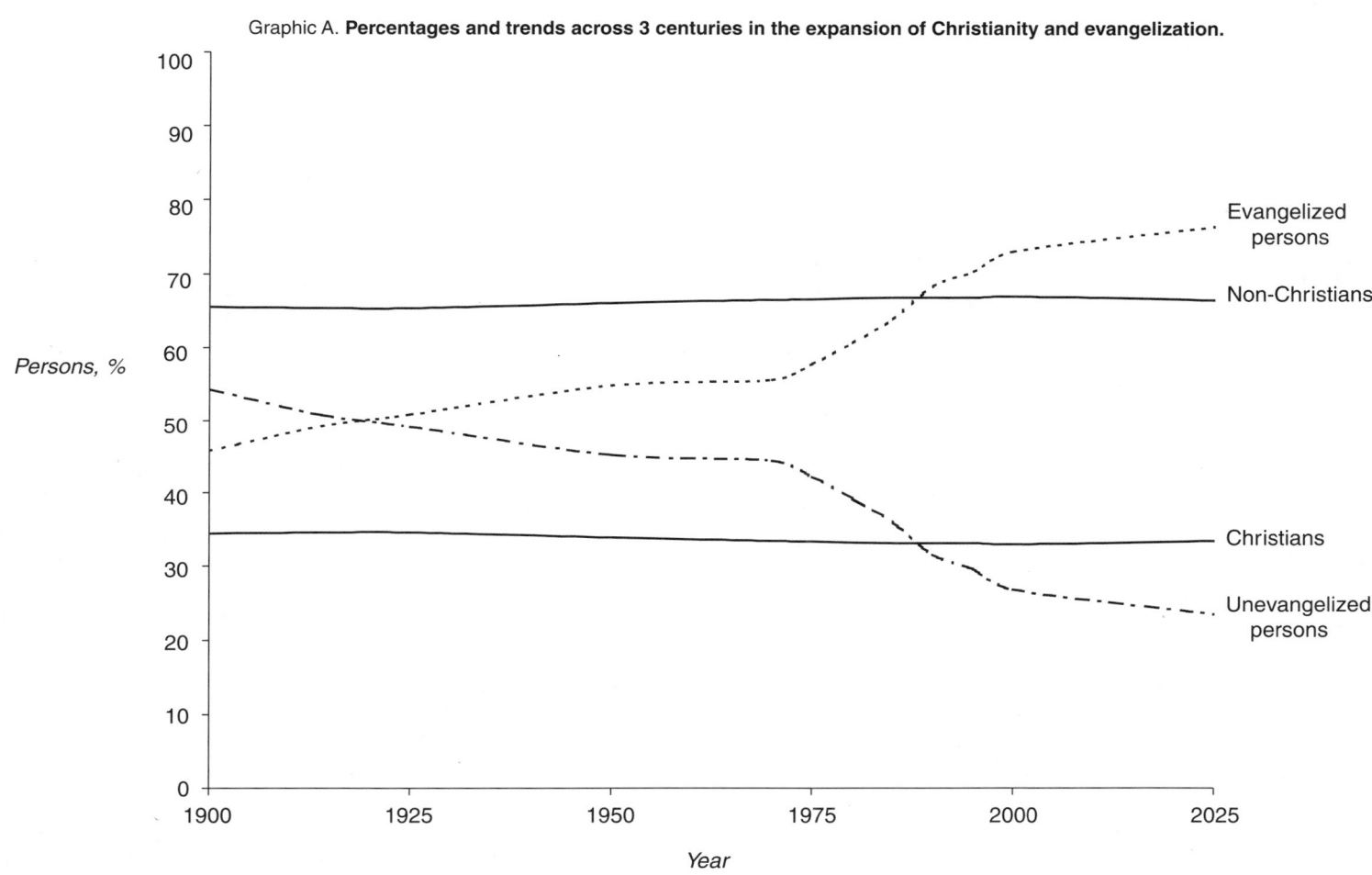

Table A. **Percent Christians and Non-Christians, evangelized and unevangelized, across 3 centuries.**

| | 19TH CENTURY | 20TH CENTURY | | | | 21ST CENTURY |
|---|---|---|---|---|---|---|
| | *Year* 1900 | 1925 | 1950 | 1975 | 2000 | 2025 |
| *Affiliation, %* | | | | | | |
| Christians | 34.5 | 34.7 | 33.9 | 33.3 | 33.0 | 33.4 |
| Non-Christians | 65.5 | 65.3 | 66.1 | 66.7 | 67.0 | 66.6 |
| **GLOBAL POPULATION** | **100.0** | **100.0** | **100.0** | **100.0** | **100.0** | **100.0** |
| *Evangelization, %* | | | | | | |
| Evangelized persons | 45.7 | 50.9 | 54.9 | 57.8 | 73.1 | 76.4 |
| Unevangelized persons | 54.3 | 49.1 | 45.1 | 42.2 | 26.9 | 23.6 |
| **GLOBAL POPULATION** | **100.0** | **100.0** | **100.0** | **100.0** | **100.0** | **100.0** |

## Global Diagram 58.    Resource countries from World C for world evangelization: 29 actual and 31 potential multimissionary countries sending out significant foreign missionary resources, 2000-2025.

Using our Worlds A/B/C trichotomy, the Christian world (World C) is composed of 141 countries (defined as all those with church members 60% or more, that is, AC≥60%). From the standpoint of Christ's Great Commission, these countries are responsible collectively and individually for sending out adequate numbers of Christian foreign workers to spread the gospel in the world's 97 non-Christian countries (Worlds A and B, with AC< 60%). Yet today only 29 World C countries are significantly involved, defining this by the numerical criterion of the sending out and supporting of over 1,000 citizen foreign missionaries each country. These 29 actual multimissionary countries are shown in Table A on the left below. Some 14 are major players sending out and supporting 5,000 or more foreign missionaries each (in 2000). Of the rest, 6 of those listed as minor players have sending levels too low; these are shown asterisked (*) in both Tables A and B.

As expounded in Global Map 2 (Global Diagram 36), the 'adequate/inadequate' sending level for a World C country may be set at S (foreign missionaries sent per million church members)=100. Above this level, if S is greater than 100 then we term a country's response to Christ's commission 'adequate'. Below this level, if S<100, we term it 'inadequate'. This is worked out and presented as a 16-point scale in Table 21-7 in Part 21 "GeoPersonnel".

Let us now examine the status of the 112 'inadequate' World C countries. All but one already contribute sizably though not adequately (100>S>10). Of these, 31 are very large countries with around 5 million church members. Each is a potential multimissionary country with enormous possibilities. They are listed in Table B on the right below. The third column of statistics shows this potential—what could happen if S=100 by AD 2025. This is illustrated in Graphic A below.

This leads us to propose a major strategic goal for the Christian world mission. What about challenging mission agencies to assist these 31 countries to each increase its sending level by AD 2025 up to (a) S=100, which means (b)

5,000 or more missionaries sent out? Collectively, this means the churches and agencies of World C would set as an AD 2000 goal: 'To educate and challenge the 31 largest inadequately-sending World C countries (each with church members over 5 million) and to persuade each to increase sending to S≥100 by AD 2025'. If this were achieved, then as Table B demonstrates, these 31 potential multimissionary countries would together have achieved the sending out of a formidable increase of many more foreign missionaries than they have currently been supporting.

Contrast this with the total for the current 29 multimissionary countries in Table A whose total is likely to decline markedly during the period 2000-2025 (see probable rates in Table A footnote). This trend represents a major shift in the center of gravity of world mission agencies, from Europe and North America to Third-World megacountries.

### SIGNIFICANT FOREIGN MISSIONARY RESOURCES FROM WORLD C
(World C countries sending out over 1,000 missionaries each)

Table A.  *Actual multimissionary countries (ranked by column 2).*
Note. S= missionaries sent out per million church population.

| World C country 1 | Actual 1975 2 | S 1990 3 | Probable 2025 4 | Population 2025 5 |
|---|---|---|---|---|
| *Major players (over 2,500)* | | | | |
| USA | 118,700 | 619 | 118,000 | 211,004,000 |
| Italy | 31,500 | 671 | 19,200 | 40,846,000 |
| France | 30,500 | 742 | 21,300 | 40,950,000 |
| Spain | 30,500 | 823 | 19,400 | 33,689,000 |
| Germany | 26,500 | 451 | 17,700 | 55,950,000 |
| Brazil | 20,000 | 129 | 30,200 | 195,810,000 |
| Britain | 18,500 | 474 | 12,600 | 37,997,000 |
| Canada | 16,500 | 815 | 17,600 | 24,000,000 |
| Netherlands | 10,200 | 992 | 6,800 | 9,837,000 |
| Belgium | 10,200 | 1,197 | 6,800 | 8,112,000 |
| Ireland | 9,300 | 2,772 | 4,300 | 3,900,000 |
| South Africa | 7,000 | 220 | 9,800 | 37,249,000 |
| Australia | 5,500 | 437 | 13,100 | 15,000,000 |
| Portugal | 5,000 | 551 | 3,200 | 8,426,000 |
| *Minor players (under 2,500)* | | | | |
| Mexico* | 4,500 | 48 | 7,100 | 123,504,000 |
| Colombia* | 3,500 | 85 | 5,900 | 57,702,000 |
| Switzerland | 3,400 | 527 | 2,400 | 6,470,000 |
| Bolivia | 2,800 | 360 | 5,200 | 12,001,000 |
| Poland* | 2,500 | 67 | 1,800 | 38,159,000 |
| Austria | 2,500 | 362 | 1,700 | 6,800,000 |
| New Zealand | 2,100 | 820 | 4,900 | 3,018,000 |
| Sweden | 2,000 | 333 | 1,400 | 6,000,000 |
| Philippines* | 2,000 | 30 | 3,400 | 95,001,000 |
| Norway | 1,800 | 428 | 1,300 | 4,436,000 |
| Argentina* | 1,800 | 53 | 2,700 | 42,836,000 |
| Chile | 1,700 | 127 | 2,600 | 17,101,000 |
| Finland | 1,400 | 306 | 970 | 4,550,000 |
| Malta | 1,000 | 2,693 | 770 | 409,000 |
| Congo-Zaire* | 1,000 | 21 | 2,400 | 95,881,000 |
| *Top 31 World C Countries* | 373,900 | 360 | 344,540 | 1,236,638,000 |

Table B.  *Potential multimissionary countries (listed alphabetically).*
Note. The countries listed below could all send out over 5,000 citizen foreign missionaries each by AD 2025 if encouraged to increase their contribution to the adequacy level, S≥100.

| World C country 1 | Actual 1975 2 | S 1990 3 | Potential 2025 4 | Population 2025 5 |
|---|---|---|---|---|
| Angola | 320 | 29 | 2,300 | 23,000,000 |
| Argentina* | 1,800 | 53 | 4,300 | 42,836,000 |
| Belorussia | 100 | 15 | 760 | 7,610,000 |
| Bulgaria | 100 | 15 | 590 | 5,880,000 |
| Burundi | 150 | 29 | 930 | 9,275,000 |
| Colombia* | 3,500 | 86 | 5,800 | 57,702,000 |
| Congo-Zaire* | 1,000 | 21 | 9,600 | 95,881,000 |
| Dominican Republic | 130 | 16 | 1,000 | 10,474,000 |
| Ecuador | 400 | 33 | 1,700 | 17,157,000 |
| El Salvador | 200 | 33 | 870 | 8,735,000 |
| Greece | 400 | 40 | 920 | 9,229,000 |
| Guatemala | 450 | 42 | 1,800 | 18,500,000 |
| Haiti | 30 | 4 | 1,100 | 11,051,000 |
| Honduras | 200 | 33 | 950 | 9,500,000 |
| Hungary | 250 | 29 | 810 | 8,068,000 |
| Kenya | 800 | 36 | 3,300 | 33,000,000 |
| Malawi | 400 | 57 | 1,400 | 13,500,000 |
| Mexico* | 4,500 | 48 | 12,400 | 123,504,000 |
| Nicaragua | 250 | 51 | 820 | 8,240,000 |
| Papua New Guinea | 100 | 26 | 630 | 6,329,000 |
| Paraguay | 450 | 87 | 890 | 8,901,000 |
| Peru | 800 | 32 | 3,400 | 33,849,000 |
| Philippines* | 2,000 | 30 | 9,500 | 95,001,000 |
| Poland* | 2,500 | 67 | 3,800 | 38,159,000 |
| Romania | 200 | 10 | 1,800 | 18,120,000 |
| Rwanda | 120 | 19 | 1,100 | 10,724,000 |
| Uganda | 500 | 26 | 4,100 | 40,601,000 |
| Ukraine | 400 | 10 | 4,000 | 39,899,000 |
| Venezuela | 900 | 40 | 3,300 | 32,577,000 |
| Yugoslavia | 500 | 73 | 790 | 7,851,000 |
| Zambia | 250 | 35 | 1,300 | 13,310,000 |
| *32 World C Countries* | 23,700 | 39 | 85,960 | 858,463,000 |

*Footnotes.*
Column 1. *Minor players.* Those asterisked (*) are sending over 1,000 now but at an inadequate level (S<100).
Column 4. *Probable.* Estimates for what the total of missionaries is likely to be in AD 2025 are based on S(2000) modified as follows: for European countries, reduced by 30% to allow for widespread declining vocation rate (and for Ireland, 60%); for Northern America, reduced by 10%; for Third-World countries, increased by a present rate of 20%.

*Footnotes.*
Column 1. The 6 countries asterisked (*) as in Table A already send out over 1,000 missionaries, but have vast potential if they can raise their currently inadequate level to S=100.
Column 4. *Potential.* Number of missionaries that would be sent out if the country reached its potentially adequate level (S=100) by AD 2025.
Column 5. *Population.* Country's population in AD 2025 based on medium variant (*World population prospects 1996*, UN 1998). Table A column 5 comes from the same source.

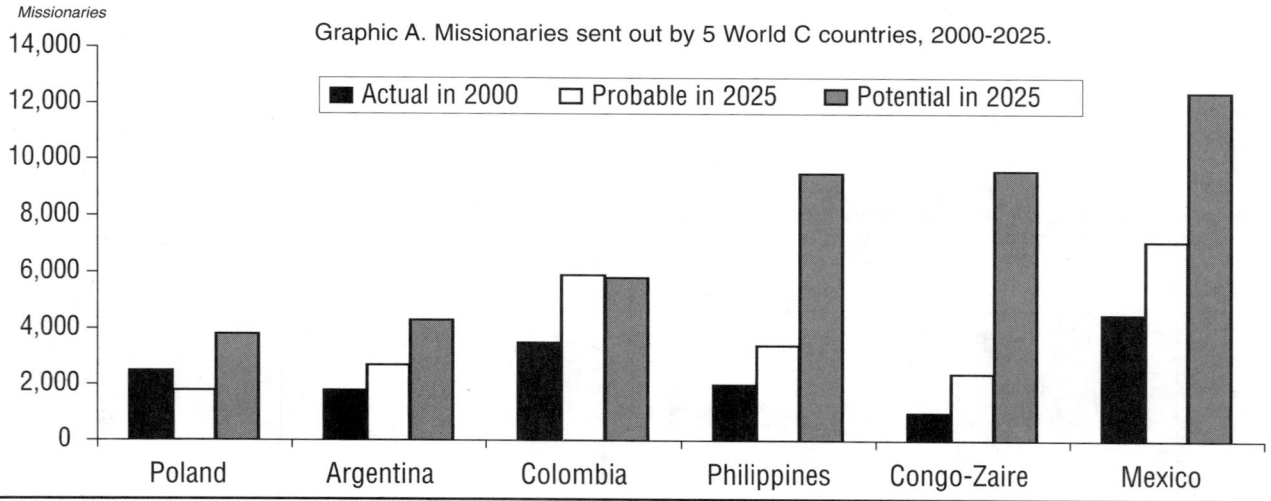

Graphic A. Missionaries sent out by 5 World C countries, 2000-2025.

■ Actual in 2000    □ Probable in 2025    ▨ Potential in 2025

## Global Diagram 59. AD 2025 global goals: 200 proposed Great Commission goals, each a definition of one aspect of completing world evangelization.

The diagram is a picture of what an evangelized world would look like. It shows: (a) in gray, the 3-tier world in AD 2025 (with World A shown still unevangelized as in Third Millennium Scenarios I and II, although on Third Millennium Scenario III—closure—World A disappears); (b) in heavy black type, the overall AD 2025 goals of obeying the 7 Mandates of the Great Commission (shown in boldest capitals); (c) in small capitals, the 7 varieties of 7-P Evangelization (roman capitals) leading to 7-P Evangelism (italic capitals); (d) in roman lowercase, synonyms and near-synonyms of evangelization, representing 52 goals which are varieties of evangelization, mission, and ministry, and including the various ministries

Christians are implementing; and (e) in lowercase italics, AD 2025 goals sought by both secular bodies and by Christians, in the form of goals involving the elimination of 26 specific global evils.

All these goals are regarded as reasonable: they can be attained by AD 2025. All that is required is the will, the effort, the determination, the persistence.

Note that this evangelized world is not the same as a christianized world (one where everybody has become a church member). Neither is it the biblical Millennium (in which commentators down the ages have anticipated the presence of sin and evil but strictly subdued). Nor is it a perfect world,

nor the final shape of the Kingdom of God. Instead, it is a world in which all kinds of evangelizing activities and achievements proliferate everywhere, as a result of which, after closure is achieved, all peoples have had and continue to have opportunity to hear and understand the gospel and to receive and follow Christ in the fellowship of culturally-relevant churches.

A listing of global goals and futurist megagoals is given in Part 27, describing the world that Christians want. An outline for a global plan to coordinate closure is given in the same part as World Christian Global Action Plan (WCGAP).

---

**KEY TO DIAGRAM'S 5 TYPE STYLES**

| Example | Meaning |
|---|---|
| 1. **GO!** | Large bold capitals= the 7 Mandates of Christ's Great Commission |
| 2. PREPARATORY EVANGELIZATION | Small roman capitals= the 7 elements of 7-P Evangelization |
| 3. *PRE-EVANGELISM* | Small italic capitals= the 7 elements of 7-P Evangelism |
| 4. Engagement | Lowercase roman (capitalized)= 52 key elements or ministry components of evangelization |
| 5. ***No illiteracy*** | Lowercase bold italics (capitalized)= 26 goals involving the elimination of 26 global evils |

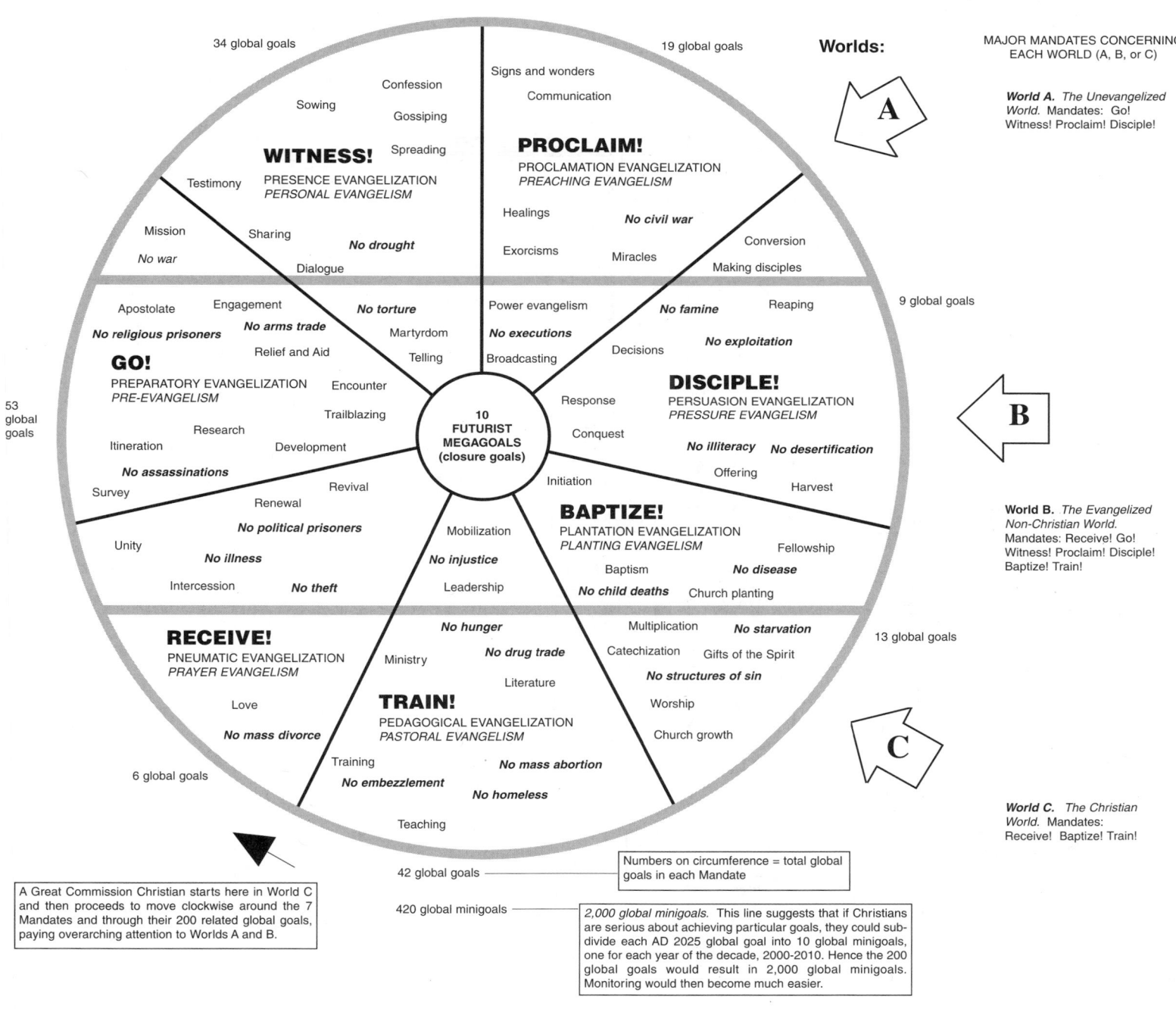

Worlds:

MAJOR MANDATES CONCERNING EACH WORLD (A, B, or C)

**World A.** *The Unevangelized World.* Mandates: Go! Witness! Proclaim! Disciple!

**World B.** *The Evangelized Non-Christian World.* Mandates: Go! Witness! Proclaim! Disciple! Baptize! Train!

**World C.** *The Christian World.* Mandates: Receive! Baptize! Train!

A Great Commission Christian starts here in World C and then proceeds to move clockwise around the 7 Mandates and through their 200 related global goals, paying overarching attention to Worlds A and B.

Numbers on circumference = total global goals in each Mandate

*2,000 global minigoals.* This line suggests that if Christians are serious about achieving particular goals, they could subdivide each AD 2025 global goal into 10 global minigoals, one for each year of the decade, 2000-2010. Hence the 200 global goals would result in 2,000 global minigoals. Monitoring would then become much easier.

## Global Diagram 60.   Great Commission scholarship, research, expert systems, and the Internet:  past, present, and future global use via 70 harvest categories.

The diagram portrays schematically the progress of the gospel as harvest over the last 6 millennia, and the next one, as shown by the chronological series of globes (the Earth) from BC 4000 to AD 2025 & Beyond. Progress moves via 4 prominent entities in the 4 heavy-lined boxes (Harvest Mandates, Harvest Force, Master Expert System, and Harvest Goals). The 70 categories are divided (by the vertical

dotted line) into (1) on the left, mission, ministry, and evangelism, and (2) on the right, scholarship, research, strategy, planning and tactics.

Since the days of the first known major Christian scholar and apologist Clement of Alexandria (AD 155-215), scholarship has described the dimensions of the harvest task. Most scholars labored as individuals, their influence spreading by

publication. By 1920 organized missions research had become prominent. By 1950 computers were playing a part. By 1980 this had evolved into expert systems (artificial intelligence). And by the 1990s scholars were fully organizing and coordinating their work through the enormous powers of the Internet and of Internet 2.

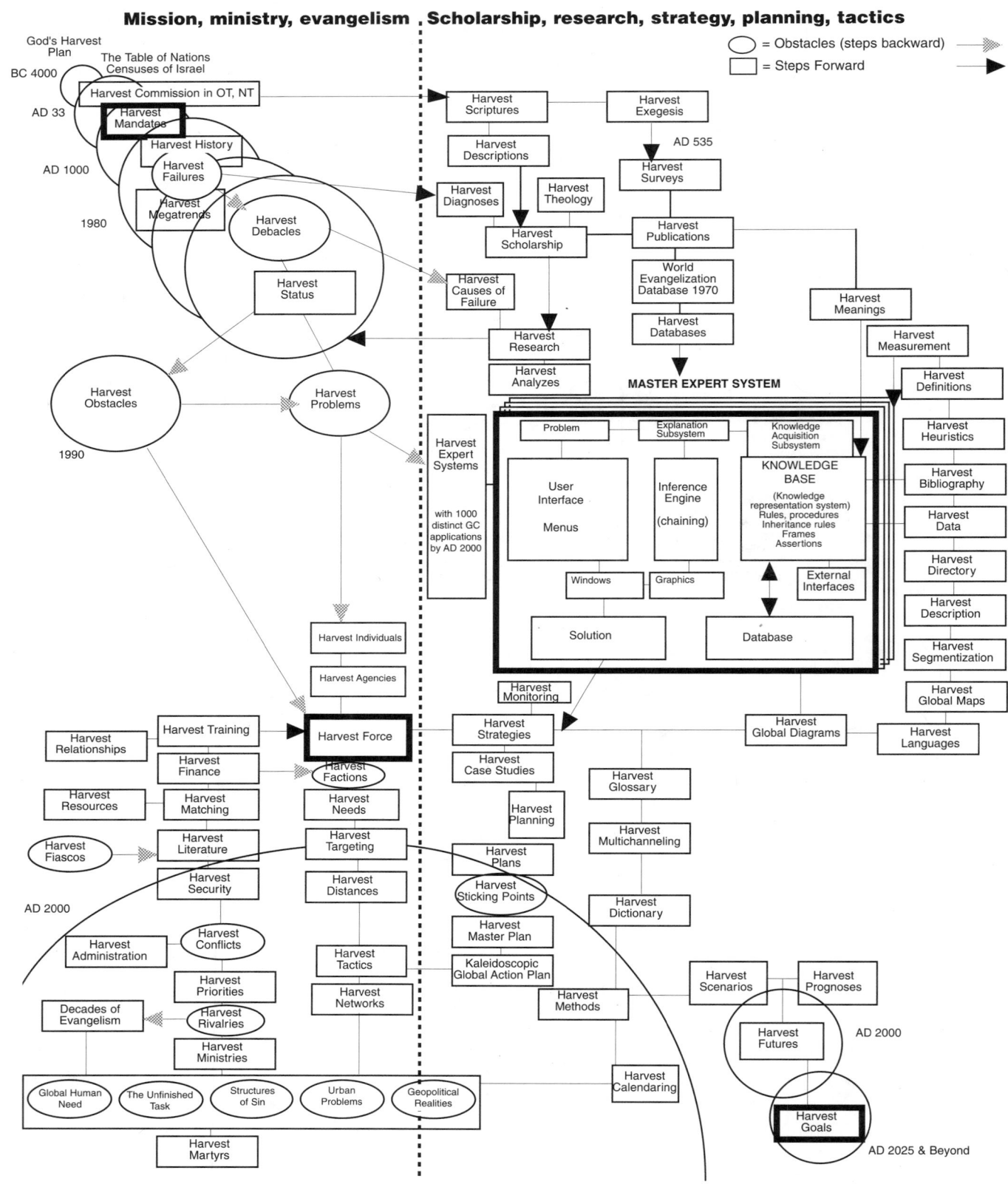

**Global Diagram 61.   Toward AD 2025 and beyond: implementing 100 action points or stages of a world Christian kaleidoscopic global action plan (WCGAP, or KGAP, or GAP).**

On the right is the stylized logo of the present series of 74 global diagrams. It shows the different streams of evangelizing activity impinging on the segmentized world, looking for closure by a generation after the Millennial year AD 2000.

The diagram and statistics below show an expanded version. On the left, today's stream of activity takes the form of some two thousand separate world evangelization or AD 2025 plans, the great majority being standalone (proceeding without program or budget cooperation with other agencies). In practice this stream's resources are directed indiscriminately at the world: it largely ignores World A, spends 1% of its force on World B, but lavishes 99% on World C (the

Christian world). The statistics shown illustrate the situation in AD 2000 itself. This standalone situation is likely to continue up to AD 2025 unless the 6 new features below are vigorously pursued.

All agencies involved in this enterprise believe that each is actually pursuing global mission and is addressing global evangelization. Our analysis, however, terms these efforts as only globalized evangelization (defined as localized evangelistic missions with a veneer of global or pseudo-global terminology).

The action plan proposed here, WCGAP or KGAP or GAP, is set out in this survey's Part 27 "GeoStrategies". It has 6 new and innovative features shown in the diagram anticlockwise by bold numerals: (1) *Survey of global plans:* the starting point has to be a complete understanding of the realities of the present situation, in which hundreds of mission agencies operate plans in isolation from all other agencies (globalized missions); (2) *De facto multichanneling:* this means accepting the present unsatisfactory deployment as a fact of life but welcoming its fragmented and standalone nature at least as insurance against multiple or overall failure; (3) *Great*

*Commission Christians:* out of the whole complex of standalone plans, a practical Great Commission harvest force exists which could be guided and channeled toward World A and the serious implementation of world evangelization; (4) *WCGAP/KGAP as an agenda,* a phrase which means that around this harvest force is a casing or shell providing vision, information, guidance, and cooperative networks to which we have given the name WCGAP/KGAP; (5) together, this harvest force and the WCGAP/KGAP begin to tackle questions of how to coordinate the 'Two Thousand Plans toward AD 2025', all together constituting the entity known as the *global evangelization movement,* GEM, a loose umbrella term combining the evangelization thrusts of the several worldwide international organizations of which 7 major ones are listed below; and finally (6) serving as arrowhead a *Global Action Network,* the name given here to the loose grouping of activists linked by 100 global electronic nodes into a Great Commission global network, with specialist subgroups including the Global Statistics Task Force.

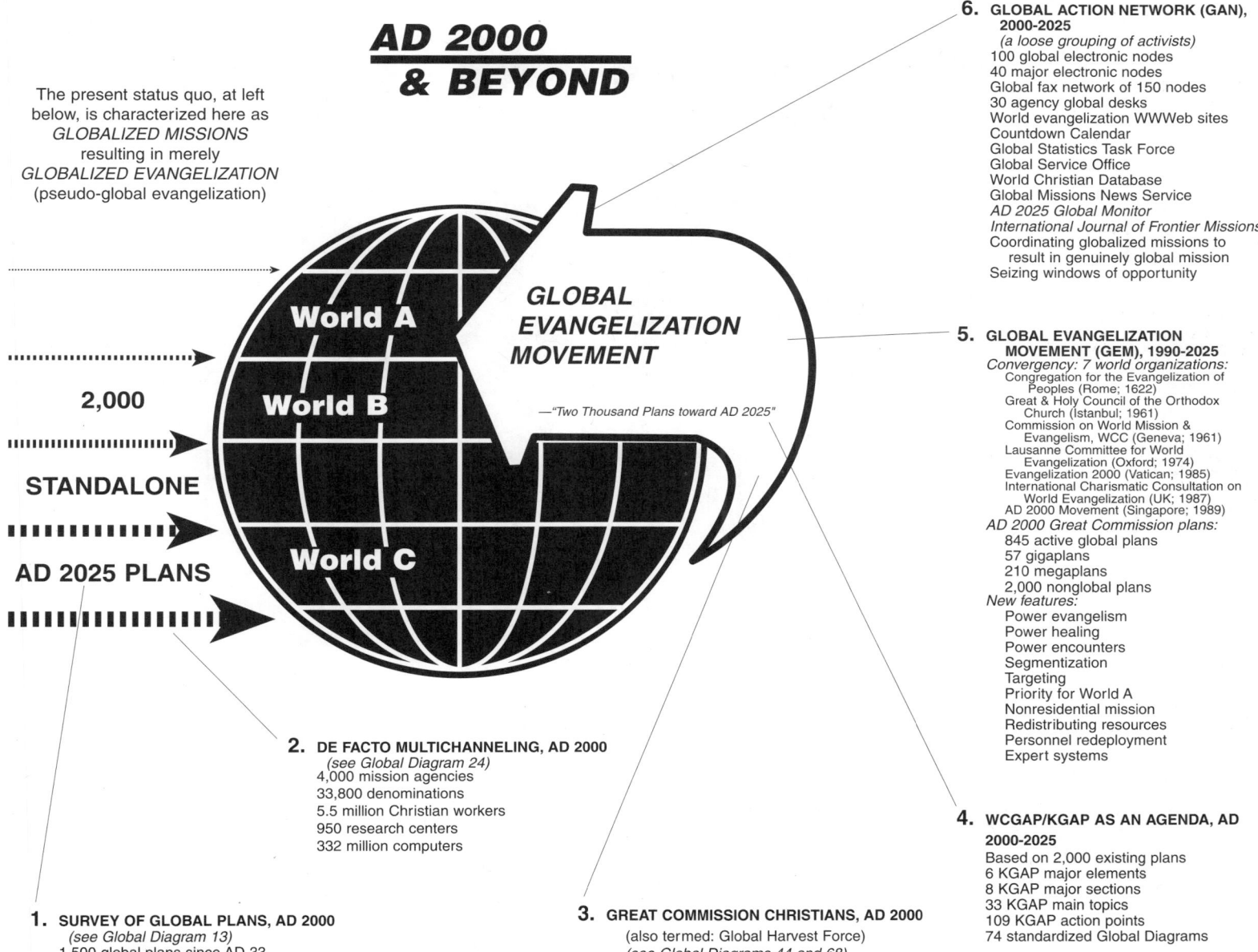

**AD 2000 & BEYOND**

The present status quo, at left below, is characterized here as *GLOBALIZED MISSIONS* resulting in merely *GLOBALIZED EVANGELIZATION* (pseudo-global evangelization)

World A

World B

World C

2,000

STANDALONE

AD 2025 PLANS

*GLOBAL EVANGELIZATION MOVEMENT*

—"Two Thousand Plans toward AD 2025"

**6.  GLOBAL ACTION NETWORK (GAN), 2000-2025**
*(a loose grouping of activists)*
100 global electronic nodes
40 major electronic nodes
Global fax network of 150 nodes
30 agency global desks
World evangelization WWWeb sites
Countdown Calendar
Global Statistics Task Force
Global Service Office
World Christian Database
Global Missions News Service
*AD 2025 Global Monitor*
*International Journal of Frontier Missions*
Coordinating globalized missions to result in genuinely global mission
Seizing windows of opportunity

**5.  GLOBAL EVANGELIZATION MOVEMENT (GEM), 1990-2025**
*Convergency: 7 world organizations:*
Congregation for the Evangelization of Peoples (Rome; 1622)
Great & Holy Council of the Orthodox Church (Istanbul; 1961)
Commission on World Mission & Evangelism, WCC (Geneva; 1961)
Lausanne Committee for World Evangelization (Oxford; 1974)
Evangelization 2000 (Vatican; 1985)
International Charismatic Consultation on World Evangelization (UK; 1987)
AD 2000 Movement (Singapore; 1989)
*AD 2000 Great Commission plans:*
845 active global plans
57 gigaplans
210 megaplans
2,000 nonglobal plans
*New features:*
Power evangelism
Power healing
Power encounters
Segmentization
Targeting
Priority for World A
Nonresidential mission
Redistributing resources
Personnel redeployment
Expert systems

**2.  DE FACTO MULTICHANNELING, AD 2000**
*(see Global Diagram 24)*
4,000 mission agencies
33,800 denominations
5.5 million Christian workers
950 research centers
332 million computers

**4.  WCGAP/KGAP AS AN AGENDA, AD 2000-2025**
Based on 2,000 existing plans
6 KGAP major elements
8 KGAP major sections
33 KGAP main topics
109 KGAP action points
74 standardized Global Diagrams

**1.  SURVEY OF GLOBAL PLANS, AD 2000**
*(see Global Diagram 13)*
1,500 global plans since AD 33
95 survey global plans
340 causes of failure
109 current sticking points
All plans are standalone, *de facto*
95% of all plans are completely standalone
95% are globalized (pseudo-global) missions
95% result only in globalized (pseudo-global) evangelization

**3.  GREAT COMMISSION CHRISTIANS, AD 2000**
(also termed: Global Harvest Force)
*(see Global Diagrams 44 and 68)*
650 million active GC Christians
4,000 Great Commission networks
56 global networks
9 global meganetworks

## Global Diagram 62. Where should foreign missionaries work? Six organizing principles of missionary deployment by peoples in Worlds A, B, and C after the Decade of Evangelism, AD 1990–AD 2000.

A simple but powerful form of logic concerning the biblical mandate of mission is drawn out in the table and graph below. The question under consideration is 'How should the global foreign missionary force be deployed?' The answer to that question is explored by examining the proportions of missionaries to be sent to World A, B, and C peoples if various categories of people are the primary entry target. This analysis follows a logical progression moving from left to right in the table and graph below. Six very different organizing principles advocated by agencies emerge.

**Principle 1.** Foreign missionaries should operate through existing churches and the 2 billion Christians who thus become their immediate or primary target whether in World A, B, or C peoples. This is termed the partnership principle.

**Principle 2.** The world's 4.4 billion who have already heard the gospel (evangelized persons) should be the primary entry point and target in World A, B, and C peoples. Foreign missionaries then utilize this huge pool as a launching pad.

**Principle 3.** Every person on the globe is equally deserv-

ing of the attention of the global missionary force. World A, B, and C peoples should thus receive foreign missionaries in exact proportion to their populations.

**Principle 4.** Thinking in more strategic terms, some agencies target those who belong to non-Christian religions or no religion at all—the 4.1 billion non-Christians of World A, B, and C peoples.

**Principle 5.** Narrowing the focus even more, a small number of agencies consider those who have never heard the gospel (the 1.6 billion World A individuals) as the immediate, direct targets of foreign missionaries. such individuals are present in all World A, B, and C countries but on this principle should receive the proportional share shown in Principle 5 below.

**Principle 6.** Finally, many agencies see no need to employ any new overall principle. they support the actual deployment of foreign missionaries as it is today, largely based on invitations from the field. This has produced actual deployment that is startlingly different to the previous five scenarios.

Without considering all the reasons why the situation is as it is one can make the following observations.

a. Less missionaries are actually sent to World A peoples (4%) than on any of the five previous principles except the one where Christians are the immediate target (1%).

b. World B peoples actually receive less missionaries (16%) than on any of the five previous principles except the one where Christians are the immediate target (15%).

c. World C peoples actually receive more missionaries (80%) than on any of the five previous principles except the one where Christians are the immediate target (84%).

It appears then that foreign missionaries are not at present deployed in any kind of strategic pattern but have ended up mainly where invited in predominantly Christian countries and peoples. World evangelization, however, requires strategic planning in order for all peoples to be reached with the gospel. Agencies and churches should ponder the profound inequities in the graph below and work to change them.

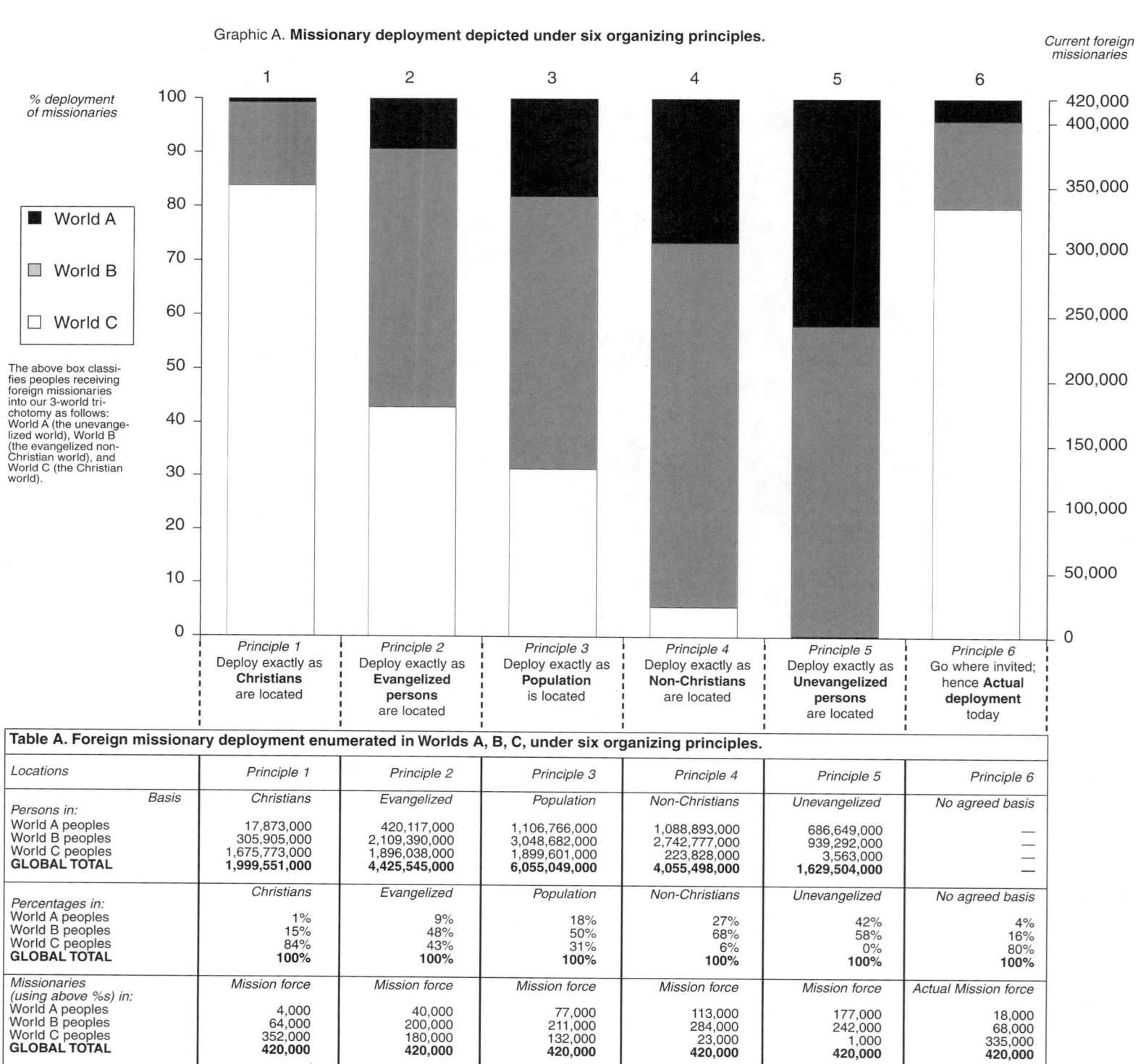

Graphic A. **Missionary deployment depicted under six organizing principles.**

% deployment of missionaries

*Current foreign missionaries*

**World A**

**World B**

**World C**

The above box classifies peoples receiving foreign missionaries into our 3-world trichotomy as follows: World A (the unevangelized world), World B (the evangelized non-Christian world), and World C (the Christian world).

| | | | | | |
|---|---|---|---|---|---|
| Principle 1 Deploy exactly as **Christians** are located | Principle 2 Deploy exactly as **Evangelized persons** are located | Principle 3 Deploy exactly as **Population** is located | Principle 4 Deploy exactly as **Non-Christians** are located | Principle 5 Deploy exactly as **Unevangelized persons** are located | Principle 6 Go where invited; hence **Actual deployment** today |

**Table A. Foreign missionary deployment enumerated in Worlds A, B, C, under six organizing principles.**

| Locations | Principle 1 | Principle 2 | Principle 3 | Principle 4 | Principle 5 | Principle 6 |
|---|---|---|---|---|---|---|
| **Basis** | Christians | Evangelized | Population | Non-Christians | Unevangelized | No agreed basis |
| Persons in: | | | | | | |
| World A peoples | 17,873,000 | 420,117,000 | 1,106,766,000 | 1,088,893,000 | 686,649,000 | — |
| World B peoples | 305,905,000 | 2,109,390,000 | 3,048,682,000 | 2,742,777,000 | 939,292,000 | — |
| World C peoples | 1,675,773,000 | 1,896,038,000 | 1,899,601,000 | 223,828,000 | 3,563,000 | — |
| **GLOBAL TOTAL** | **1,999,551,000** | **4,425,545,000** | **6,055,049,000** | **4,055,498,000** | **1,629,504,000** | **—** |
| Percentages in: | Christians | Evangelized | Population | Non-Christians | Unevangelized | No agreed basis |
| World A peoples | 1% | 9% | 18% | 27% | 42% | 4% |
| World B peoples | 15% | 48% | 50% | 68% | 58% | 16% |
| World C peoples | 84% | 43% | 31% | 6% | 0% | 80% |
| **GLOBAL TOTAL** | **100%** | **100%** | **100%** | **100%** | **100%** | **100%** |
| Missionaries (using above %s) in: | Mission force | Mission force | Mission force | Mission force | Mission force | Actual Mission force |
| World A peoples | 4,000 | 40,000 | 77,000 | 113,000 | 177,000 | 18,000 |
| World B peoples | 64,000 | 200,000 | 211,000 | 284,000 | 242,000 | 68,000 |
| World C peoples | 352,000 | 180,000 | 132,000 | 23,000 | 1,000 | 335,000 |
| **GLOBAL TOTAL** | **420,000** | **420,000** | **420,000** | **420,000** | **420,000** | **420,000** |

**Global Diagram 63. Prioritizing strategic targets and avoiding 6 levels of pseudo-targets in world evangelization: the obscuring effect of cultural, geographical, and visual proximity.**

This diagram analyzes 3 methods for prioritizing targets to win the world—2 successful secular systems, and the less successful Christian system. The diagram presents a *targeting typology* (in column 4), a proposed new *prioritization typology* with 10 levels (in columns 2 and 13, based on e, current levels of evangelizing activity as measured by evangelism-hours per capita, per annum, shown in column 3).

**Graphic 1.** In the Roman Empire, strategic security depended on only 60 highly-disciplined legions of some 5,000 career soldiers each. Trained to target only distant strategic objectives, the legions were never allowed to enter the City of Rome to interfere in politics (Target 10), nor to meddle with auxiliaries or citizens (Targets 9 and 8), nor to get involved in looting, nor in developing or evangelizing client-states (Targets 7,6 and 5). Ignoring all pseudo-targets they marched unswervingly at 3 miles per hour toward the real enemy beyond the Empire's perimeter (Targets 4 to 1). Among their new weapons were the huge missile-throwing carroballistas. Result—with under 300,000 men the legions extended and secured the Empire for 1,200 years by deliberately ignoring nearby easily-visible but nonstrategic targets.

**Graphic 2.** This describes how in the Cold War of 1945-1991

the 2 great superpowers, the USSR and the USA, kept the peace by prioritizing their 23,000 nuclear warheads on intercontinental ballistic missiles, and in particular on their submarine-launched ballistic missiles (SLBMs) operated by some 300,000 professionals. To achieve this, Targets 10 to 5 were all strictly ignored—priorities were always Targets 4 to 1, far away on another continent. This strategy of submarine nuclear warfare is clear. You do not threaten to use an SLBM (such as a Trident missile costing $40 million) to hit:
—A mutineer or hijacker on board (Target 10),
—Nor an enemy submarine 500 feet above you (Target 9),
—Nor an aircraft carrier on the surface (Target 8),
—Nor a strategic bomber flying 10 miles up (Target 6),
—Nor a land target 100 miles away (Target 5).
You threaten to use an SLBM only to hit
—A strategic target 3,000 miles away, on another continent (Target 3), or 6,000 miles (Target 2)
—Any target up to 12,500 miles away (halfway round the Earth, which means anywhere on Earth—Target 1).

**Graphic 3.** The Christian parallel to the 60 Roman legions or the 1,500 submarine-launched SLBMs is the church's cross-cultural foreign missionary force of 420,000 career professionals from 231 countries. They are the church's interconti-

nental elite, carefully trained to hit cross-culturally the longest-distance targets. The church's dynamic for world mission begins in the lowest of the 3 levels of World C (shown shaded), initiated by Great Commission Christians (the source is shown below by *). They attempt to aim upwards at the non-Christian world (Worlds A and B). By contrast with Graphics 1 and 2, however, the Christian mission has allowed 91% of these forces to then be diverted (see the 3 black arrows) to plum targets—close, relatively easy, glittering targets entirely within World C—15% on the home base of missions-supporting Great Commission Christians (Target 10) where a third of all foreign missionaries are always on leave, and 76% working among inactive Christians abroad (Targets 9 and 8). As a result, only 8.7% of all Christian personnel, outreach and evangelism ever gets through to World B, and only 0.3% to World A.

We ask therefore—How can the churches stop allowing these inactive Christian levels to thus obstruct and dissipate mission to the non-Christian world? One answer is—study closely history's lessons for successful strategy in Graphics 1 and 2, and the detailed analyses of them in the 2 books listed beneath them. See also E. N. Luttwak, *Strategy: the logic of war and peace* (1987).

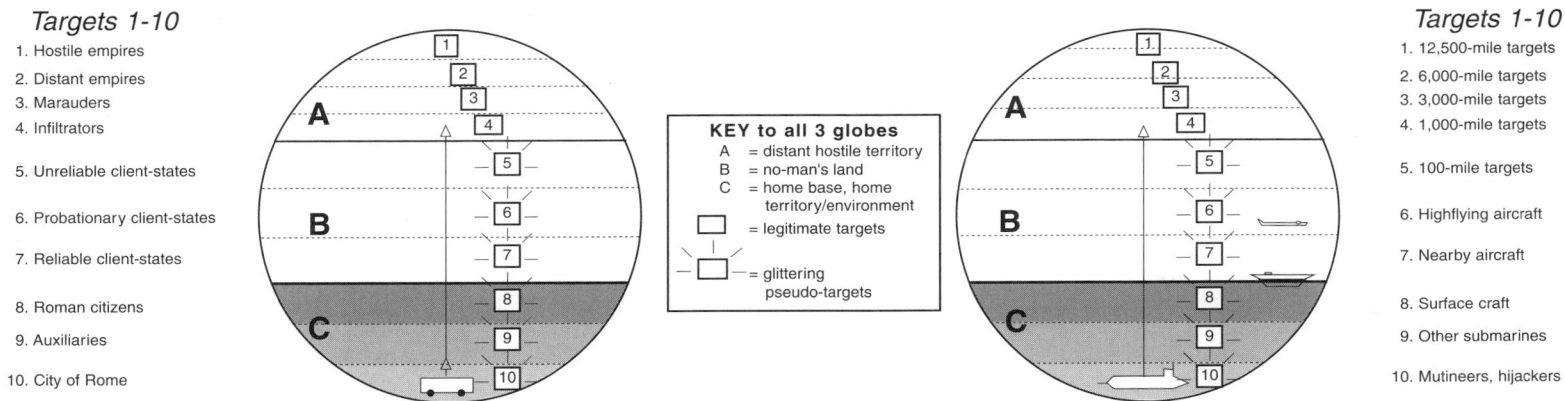

**Targets 1-10**

1. Hostile empires
2. Distant empires
3. Marauders
4. Infiltrators
5. Unreliable client-states
6. Probationary client-states
7. Reliable client-states
8. Roman citizens
9. Auxiliaries
10. City of Rome

**KEY to all 3 globes**
A = distant hostile territory
B = no-man's land
C = home base, home territory/environment
☐ = legitimate targets
☐ = glittering pseudo-targets

**Targets 1-10**

1. 12,500-mile targets
2. 6,000-mile targets
3. 3,000-mile targets
4. 1,000-mile targets
5. 100-mile targets
6. Highflying aircraft
7. Nearby aircraft
8. Surface craft
9. Other submarines
10. Mutineers, hijackers

**Graphic 1. ROMAN EMPIRE, BC 753-AD 476.**
Targeting with legions and carroballistas
(Read: E.N. Luttwak, *The grand strategy of the Roman Empire*, 1976).

**Graphic 2. USA/USSR COLD WAR, 1945-1991.**
Targeting with submarine-launched ballistic missiles (SLBMs)
(Read: E.N. Luttwak, *The grand strategy of the Soviet Union*, 1983).

| Current status of world mission | | | | | Current mission activity | | | | Current failure to evangelize | | Proposed retargeting | |
|---|---|---|---|---|---|---|---|---|---|---|---|---|
| World | Level | Evangelism (e p.a.p.c.) | Persons | Population (m=millions) | Evangelization (E) | Missions (7 arrows) | Targets (10 squares) | Activity (10 tactics) | % used of all resources | Offers a day | Time to evangelize all | Target | Peoples |
| column 1 | 2 | 3 | 4 | 5 | 6 | 7 | 8 | 9 | 10 | 11 | 12 | 13 | 14 |
| **World A** (unevangelized persons) | 1. | e=0 | Untargeted | 145m | Nothing | 1 | | Warfare | 0.00% | 2,000 offers a day | over 100 years | T-1 | 818 |
| | 2. | e=0.1 | Uncontacted | 276m | Scarcity | 2 | | Hostilities | 0.01% | 24,000 offers a day | 30 years | T-2 | 705 |
| | 3. | e=1 | Unreached | 523m | Infrequency | 3 | | Marauding | 0.1% | 0.5 million offers a day | 3 years | T-3 | 762 |
| | 4. | e=10 | Barely reached | 1,271m | Inadequacy | 4 | | Skirmishing | 0.2% | 15 million offers a day | 3 months | T-4 | 1,353 |
| **World B** (evangelized non-Christians) | 5. | e=40 | Partially evangelized non-Christians | 1,480m | Subsistence | | 5 | Policing | 0.7% | 87 million offers a day | 1 month | T-5 | 1,106 |
| | 6. | e=100 | Moderately evangelized non-Christians | 207m | Adequacy | | 6 | Advising | 1% | 35 million offers a day | 1 week | T-6 | 893 |
| | 7. | e=200 | Heavily evangelized non-Christians | 210m | Sufficiency | | 7 | Building | 7% | 87 million offers a day | 2 days | T-7 | 950 |
| **World C** (Christians) | 8. | e=300 | Nominal Christians | 94m | Superfluity | | 8 | Mopping-up | 26% | 67 million offers a day | 1 day | T-8 | 1,224 |
| | 9. | e=400 | Non-practicing church members | 600m | Saturation | | 9 | Looting | 50% | 580 million offers a day | 15 hours | T-9 | 1,532 |
| | 10. | | Great Commission Christians, and others practicing | 1,248m | Oversaturation | | 10 | Home-basing | 15% | 1,800 million offers a day | 8 hours | T-10 | 3,240 |
| | | | **TOTAL** | 6,055m | | | | | **TOTAL 100%** | 2,700 million | | | 12,583 |

**Graphic 3. WORLD EVANGELIZATION, 2000-2025.**
Targeting with the gospel and world mission resources
✻ = source of missionary personnel

Note: "e"= average evangelism-hours (offers) received per year per capita

## Global Diagram 64. Matching up holistic resources with legitimate targets: clarifying the requirements for finishing the task of world evangelization by the year 2025.

Three serious problems become clear after we have identified both Christian resources for world mission, and targets of world evangelization.

(1) Various traditions and agencies among the whole Body of Christ begin to view themselves as the only true or significant resource thus greatly reducing the overall manpower available for coordinated evangelization. Often they feel they have to start from scratch in World C with proselytism de novo.

(2) The range of targets for world evangelization is broadened beyond the generally-accepted list to include already-evangelized and already heavily-discipled (christianized) segments, thus greatly increasing the amount of work said to be needed to complete world evangelization.

(3) Thousands of World A segments continue untargeted.

*Terms used.* When Christians target World A peoples we define them as engaging in *evangelization* (including *witness* and *dialogue*) and in *frontier mission* (*mission 'ad gentes'*), often through *nonresidential mission*. Targeting evangelized peoples in World B results in the *discipling* of peoples, often through *cross-cultural mission*; however, once churches have been begun and have become established, to continue targeting them is to engage in what missiologist Donald McGavran called 'international *domestic mission*'. Other types of mission involve *aid* and *relief*, and *tentmaking*.

Pseudo-frontier mission is the term we use when Christians claim that their work in Worlds B and C is among unreached peoples or unevangelized segments. Their terminology is illegitimate. Though they claim that it brings the church closer to finishing the task it does not directly affect World A peoples who by definition are all those currently beyond the reach of the churches with their gospel.

Targeting already-Christian peoples, who are all those found in World C, requires *partnership* with existing churches new or old (often in home missions), but results merely in proselytism and proselytization or even counterwitness unless the intention is *renewal*. Missionaries targeting only persons of their own culture are engaged in *monocultural ministry*. Most partnership mission aims not at evangelization or *re-evangelization* but at *edification* of the existing church, or some variety of *sociopolitical action*.

A full understanding of the task today requires that (1) the entire holistic range of Christian resources be employed in Great Commission cooperation to reach (2) the least evangelized segments of humanity. It is this task that is finite and finishable.

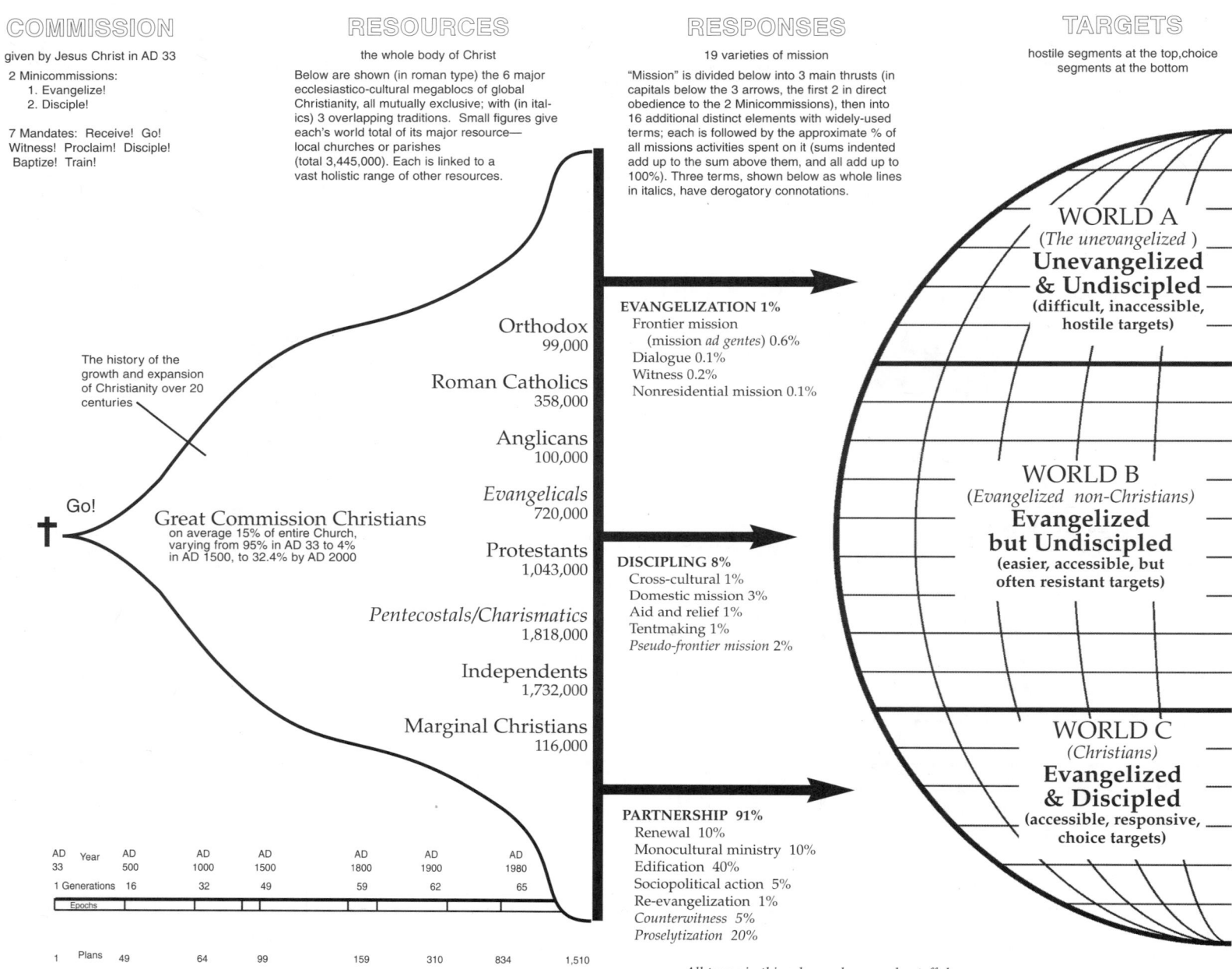

### COMMISSION
given by Jesus Christ in AD 33

2 Minicommissions:
1. Evangelize!
2. Disciple!

7 Mandates: Receive! Go!
Witness! Proclaim! Disciple!
Baptize! Train!

The history of the growth and expansion of Christianity over 20 centuries

Go!

### Great Commission Christians
on average 15% of entire Church, varying from 95% in AD 33 to 4% in AD 1500, to 32.4% by AD 2000

### RESOURCES
the whole body of Christ

Below are shown (in roman type) the 6 major ecclesiastico-cultural megablocs of global Christianity, all mutually exclusive; with (in italics) 3 overlapping traditions. Small figures give each's world total of its major resource—local churches or parishes (total 3,445,000). Each is linked to a vast holistic range of other resources.

Orthodox 99,000

Roman Catholics 358,000

Anglicans 100,000

*Evangelicals* 720,000

Protestants 1,043,000

*Pentecostals/Charismatics* 1,818,000

Independents 1,732,000

Marginal Christians 116,000

| AD 33 | Year | AD 500 | AD 1000 | AD 1500 | AD 1800 | AD 1900 | AD 1980 |
|---|---|---|---|---|---|---|---|
| 1 | Generations | 16 | 32 | 49 | 59 | 62 | 65 |
| | Epochs | | | | | | |
| 1 | Plans | 49 | 64 | 99 | 159 | 310 | 834 | 1,510 |

### RESPONSES
19 varieties of mission

"Mission" is divided below into 3 main thrusts (in capitals below the 3 arrows, the first 2 in direct obedience to the 2 Minicommissions), then into 16 additional distinct elements with widely-used terms; each is followed by the approximate % of all missions activities spent on it (sums indented add up to the sum above them, and all add up to 100%). Three terms, shown below as whole lines in italics, have derogatory connotations.

**EVANGELIZATION 1%**
Frontier mission
  (mission *ad gentes*) 0.6%
Dialogue 0.1%
Witness 0.2%
Nonresidential mission 0.1%

**DISCIPLING 8%**
Cross-cultural 1%
Domestic mission 3%
Aid and relief 1%
Tentmaking 1%
*Pseudo-frontier mission* 2%

**PARTNERSHIP 91%**
Renewal 10%
Monocultural ministry 10%
Edification 40%
Sociopolitical action 5%
Re-evangelization 1%
*Counterwitness* 5%
*Proselytization* 20%

*All terms in this column above can be staffed either by foreign or by home missions*

### TARGETS
hostile segments at the top, choice segments at the bottom

**WORLD A**
(*The unevangelized*)
**Unevangelized & Undiscipled**
(difficult, inaccessible, hostile targets)

**WORLD B**
(*Evangelized non-Christians*)
**Evangelized but Undiscipled**
(easier, accessible, but often resistant targets)

**WORLD C**
(*Christians*)
**Evangelized & Discipled**
(accessible, responsive, choice targets)

---

**GLOBAL HARVEST FORCE, AD 2000**
No church is 100% Great Commission Christians
No church is 0% Great Commission Christians
GREAT COMMISSION CHRISTIANS (found within 11,800 ethnolinguistic peoples, and in 33,800 denominations):
2.0 billion potential Great Commission Christians
648 million active Great Commission Christians (evangelizers, the "force for evangelism"), growing at 1.5% p.a.
600 million daily-evangelizing Christians (evangelists, daily evangelizers)
200 million daily intercessors
7,000 round-the-clock praying communities/monasteries

25 million in full-time prayer ministry
15 million pacifists opposed to weapons
1.14 million home missionaries
1.55 million missionaries (home or foreign)
5.5 million full-time Great Commission workers
35,000 Great Commission broadcasting personnel
130 million Great Commission computer users
20 million Great Commission computer professionals
150 million Christian pilgrims on move every year
40,000 Great Commission church and agency leaders
13,300 Christians martyred every month on average

**GLOBAL FOREIGN MISSION, AD 2000**
4,000 mission agencies
420,000 career foreign missionaries
400,000 short-term foreign missionaries
200 Great Commission research centers

**GREAT COMMISSION NETWORKS, AD 2000**
5,000 computerized networks
50 worldwide intercessory networks
100 global networks
9 global meganetworks
1 Great Commission giganetwork

**Global Diagram 65.   Today's megapriorities for mission: 12,500 world problems and the top 60 global priorities as seen by Great Commission Christians.**

Over a period of 15 years, several hundred Great Commission Christians were asked what their priorities should be today. On this diagram below, 60 of their answers are listed (out of several hundreds proposed). These are divided into 3 different kinds or levels of priorities, all relating to the globe and its evangelization: (1) 31 long-term megapriorities requiring the efforts of the entire Christian world, (2) 18 corporate priorities requiring a few agencies together to tackle them, and (3) some 11 individual or personal priorities any

reader can adopt.
In 1986, the Union of International Associations in Brussels produced a list of over 10,000 large, broad world problems affecting many countries each. Other global strategists list over 12,480 current, serious global problems of significance and urgency. If smaller problems are added, the list expands to 2 million or so. These are condensed and summarized below, as 31 long-term megapriorities. [See extended presentation and discussion in E. Cornish, "Issues of the

'90s" *The Futurist,* XXIV, 1 (January-February, 1990)].
Great Commission Christians targeting their total energies toward Christ's world mission are concerned to see that solutions to all these problems are found, and rapidly. Many problems, perhaps most, can be dealt with by political, governmental, or corporate entities but require Christian activists to galvanize them. Other problems are strictly the responsibility of Christians, either individually or collectively.

---

### 31 LONG-TERM MEGAPRIORITIES (for the Christian world)
1. Solving world hunger
2. Abolishing global poverty
3. Readying disaster aid and relief
4. Redistributing/sharing wealth worldwide
5. Neutralizing structures of sin
6. Saving the environment (desertification, destruction of species)
7. Upholding human rights
8. Advocating JPIC (Justice, Peace, and the Integrity of Creation)
9. Demanding abolition of nuclear weapons
10. Stressing peace, liberation, contextualization
11. Ministering in whole-world modes
12. Promoting spiritual renewal and revival
13. Redeploying Christian resources globally and equitably
14. Supporting the marginalized: women, children, disenfranchised, disabled
15. Controlling/preventing epidemics and pandemics
16. Completing world evangelization
17. Accessing all restricted-access countries
18. Ministering in all closed countries
19. Developing multiple ministry options in unevangelized areas
20. Reaching all 4,000 unevangelized peoples
21. Expounding development missiology
22. Mobilizing lay ministries worldwide
23. Expanding nonresidential mission
24. Planning whole-globe strategies
25. Training for cross-cultural mission
26. Extending urban mission across the Third World
27. Programming Great Commission action cooperatively
28. Living within power Christianity (signs and wonders)
29. Developing apologetics for non-Christian neofundamentalists
30. Mobilizing Third-World foreign missions
31. Preparing a global mass-media strategy

---

### 11 PERSONAL PRIORITIES (for the reader)
1. Study Ephesians 3 and how you fit into God's plan.
2. Follow a daily prayer guide that covers World A.
3. Offer to promote the cause of World A in your spare time.
4. Give World A and its welfare your central concern.
5. Start speaking publicly about AD 2025 closure.
6. Speak to mission boards you know about these matters.
7. Offer to assist the GAP coordinating office in some capacity.
8. Find at least one concrete GAP task that you can tackle now.
9. Offer to translate GAP or a summary into a language you know.
10. Consider full-time service in World A.
11. Apply to several agencies offering to serve in World A.

---

### 18 CORPORATE PRIORITIES TODAY (for agencies)
1. Expand the Global Action Network and its network of leaders.
2. Chart monthly progress with sophisticated monitors.
3. Bring global plans and WCGAP/KGAP into public prominence.
4. Expound the case for attempting to finish the task by AD 2025.
5. Send a communique to all 700 current global plan leaders.
6. Send a communique to key leaders not involved in global plans.
7. Divide the 200 AD 2025 global goals into subgoals.
8. Propose specific agencies tackle specific unreached peoples.
9. Place nonresidential missionaries in every unreached people by AD 2010.
10. Challenge agencies to offer resources to implement the KGAP.
11. Educate the Christian public in what world evangelization entails.
12. Translate all KGAP documents into the 300 megalanguages.
13. Catalogue global Christian resources and who benefits from them.
14. Expound redistribution and redeployment of resources.
15. Expand the Great Commission network to have 100 nodes.
16. Find logistical solutions for new features of global mission.
17. Assist 10 or 20 viable global plans to reach their targets.
18. Challenge Christian youth worldwide to 2-year service abroad.

*Note.*   WCGAP=World Christian Global Action Plan, KGAP= Kaleidoscopic Global Action Plan, GAP for short.

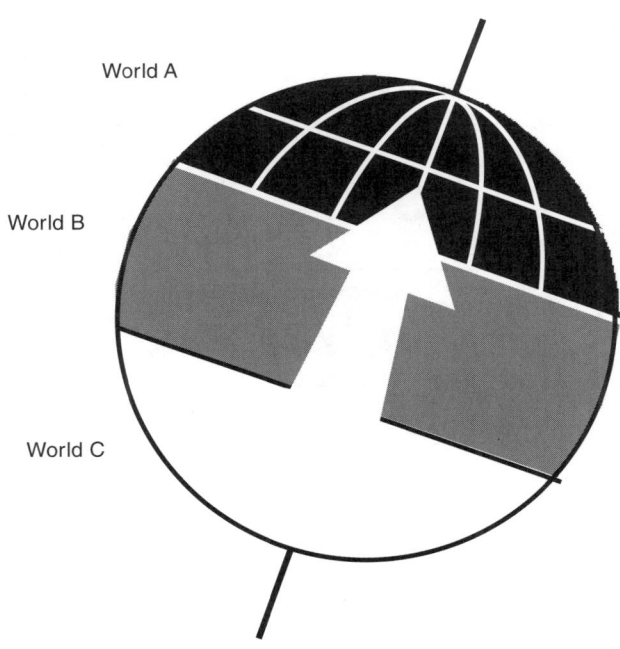

World A

World B

World C

The globe shown above represents Earth's population of 6 billion people divided into 3 tiers of Worlds A (The Unevangelized), B (Evangelized Non-Christians), and C (Christians). (See description in Global Diagrams 34, 40, et alia). The arrow shows the direction that today's main priorities in mission need to take, which is away from World C toward World B and especially World A.

## Global Diagram 66.   Tomorrow's globe: the status of the world and its 10,000 different religions in AD 2025.

This diagram describes the probable status of the globe a quarter of the way into the 21st century. All the statistics refer to the year 2025. These follow the United Nations' medium variant for population projections; their high and low variants (not given here) vary by 3.3% or so. With all future projections, it is wise to depict a spread of scenarios by specifying a range of possible values of plus or minus 5% on the figures given here.

Secular characteristics in AD 2025 are shown below, across the top over the globe. These are the best projected figures of experts, United Nations, et alia. Many of these statistics are solidly based on professional studies and analyses.

Figures on religions follow at lower right. Names of religionists are located on the 3-part globe. Each is placed where the majority of the religion's individuals are located.

Figures about Christianity in AD 2025 can be estimated for a large number of variables and for several scenarios. A total is shown in abbreviated form at the bottom of the righthand column for each of 3 scenarios. Fully expanded figures and explanations of Third Millennium Scenarios I, II, and III are given in Global Diagram 67.

### THE GLOBE IN AD 2025 (secular characteristics)

INDIVIDUALS IN AD 2025
7,823,703,000 persons
Density 53 people per sq km
40,700,000 population increase (0.52%) p.a.
4,620 million urban dwellers (urbanites) (59.1% of globe)
73.9 million new urban dwellers p.a. (1.6%)
3.08 billion metropolitan dwellers
3,204 million rural dwellers (40.9% of globe)
613 million infants under 5 years (7.8%)
1,840 million children under 15 (23.5%)
5,990 million adults (ages 15 and over) (76.5%)
Median age 32 years
Life expectancy at birth 73 years
122 million births (1.55%) p.a.
65.7 million deaths (0.84%) p.a.
Infant mortality 28.6 per 1000 live births
814 million adolescents (teenagers, ages 13-19)
1,190 million youth (ages 15-24) (15.2%)
1,980 million women ages 15-49 (25.3%)
817 million elderly (65 and over) (10.4%)
5,091 million literates
FAMILIES IN AD 2025
1.8 billion families (houses, households)
50 million new homes/families a year
Household size 3.9 persons
25% live in postindustrial (transindustrial) economies
HUMAN NEED IN AD 2025
898 million nonliterates
1.4 billion living in absolute poverty
4 billion living with unsafe water
2 billion without medical care
35% of world's arable land destroyed since 1980
20% of world's 35 million species extinct by AD 2025
25% of world's adults are subsistence farmers
80 million psychotics

750 million on edge of starvation
300 million urban homeless street children
1.5 billion urban slumdwellers
2.0 billion urban poor
1.5 billion disabled (33% being children)
27 million refugees (external and internal)
27.1 million AIDS cases, AD 2025 (on Scenario I)
223 million AIDS carriers, AD 2025 (on Scenario I)
139 million AIDS carriers, AD 2025 (on Scenario III)
13.6 million AIDS deaths p.a., AD 2025 (on Scenario I)
World total of AIDS deaths by AD 2025: 136 million
COUNTRIES IN AD 2025
238 countries (40 being nuclear powers)
40% of all governments now totalitarian
100 closed/closing/restricted-access countries
4.7 billion persons (60% of world) in restricted-access countries
CITIES IN AD 2025
6,690 metropolises over 50,000
4,190 metropolises over 100,000
602 megacities over 1 million
118 supercities over 4 million
31 supergiants (cities over 10 million)
294 non-Christian megacities
200,000 new non-Christian citydwellers a day
Slums: 30% of all metropolitan areas
GLOBAL FINANCE, US$ a year, IN AD 2025
Global income $77,000 billion (GWP)
Average per capita income $9,842
Average annual family income $38,380
Military expenditures $2,500 billion
Research and development $3,000 billion
International crime $1,000 billion
Illegal hard drug traffic $500 billion
International arms trade $135 billion

COMMUNICATIONS IN AD 2025
2.2 billion telephones
2.0 billion TV sets
3.5 billion radios
Cable TV reaches 500 million households
1.3 million new book titles a year
950,000 scientific journals
10,000 newspapers (daily, nondaily)
Daily newspaper circulation 1.2 billion
2.2 billion computers
150 million fax machines
75 million robots (running 50% of global industry)
90% of first-class mail now electronic
665 million passenger cars (85 per 1000)
LANGUAGES IN AD 2025
13,000 total languages/idioms (speech forms)
2.8 billion English speakers
1.5 billion Chinese speakers
800 million Spanish speakers
350 million French speakers
800 million English mother-tongue speakers
940 million English readers
800 million foreign tourists a year
6 billion domestic tourists a year
35,000 university campuses (5,000 major)
94 million college students
10 million foreign students
LABOR FORCE IN AD 2025
4 billion economically active
1.5 billion unemployed workers
1,000 persons now live and work in space
Energy consumed by humans as % of total available
   on Earth p.a.: 70%

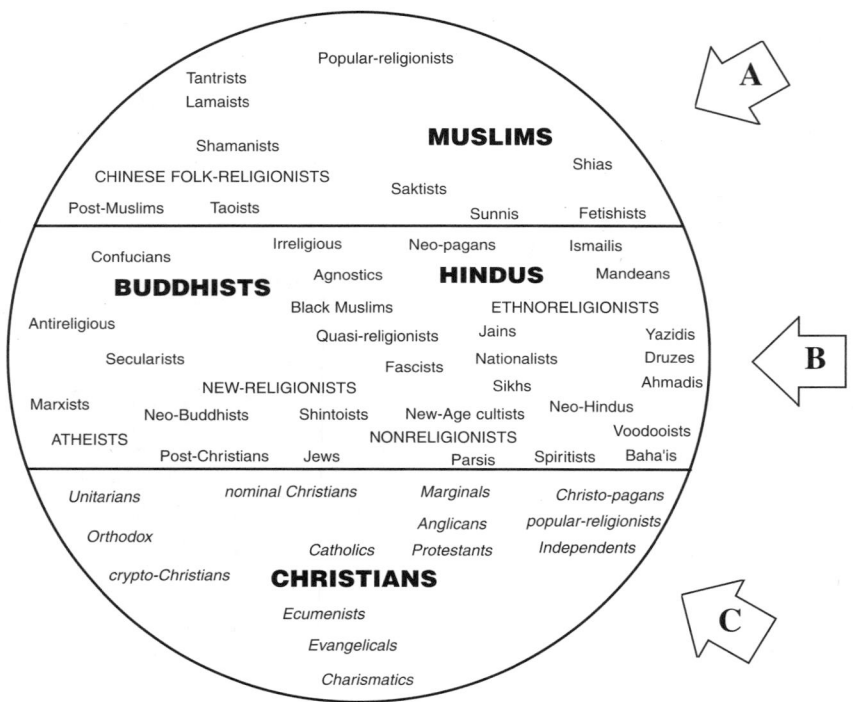

Worlds A, B, and C above follow the
schema explained in Global Diagram 34

HORIZONTAL SCALE:      Geopolitical ideology

|  | (Left inside) | (Center) | (Right inside) |
|---|---|---|---|
| WORLDS | Communist World | Western World | Third World |

## RELIGION IN AD 2025

Names on the globe (lower left):

In bold capital letters: Adherents of the 4 Great World Religions
In capital letters: Adherents of other major religions (each with
   over 100 million adherents)
In lowercase roman: Minor religions and quasi-religions
In lowercase italics: Christian confessions, families, or traditions

*VERTICAL SCALE on globe: approximate position of bulk of
   each religion's population with regard to evangelized status
   (as explained in Global Diagram 40 and WCT Part 17).*

### ADHERENCE TO RELIGION IN AD 2025
6.8 billion religionists (all religions)
   750 million in New Age/millennialist/messianic cults or sects
   900 million Christian popular-religionist-pietists
3,000 million all popular-religionists
1,035 million nonreligionists
   875 million nonreligious
   160 million atheists

### ADHERENTS OF NON-CHRISTIAN RELIGIONS IN AD 2025
   (on Third Millennium Scenario II)
   (in parentheses, annual increase, per annum)
4,171 million non-Christian religionists
GREAT WORLD RELIGIONS IN AD 2025:
1,785 million Muslims (28.8 million p.a.)
   1,468 million Sunnis (22.2 million p.a.)
   286 million Shias (Shiites) (5.9 million p.a.)
   41 million Ismailis (881,000 p.a.)
   14.7 million Ahmadis (357,000 p.a.)
1,049 million Hindus (10.7 million p.a.)
   708 million Vaishnavites (7.1 million p.a.)
   279 million Shaivites (2.8 million p.a.)
   33 million Saktists (335,000 p.a.)
   23 million Neo-Hindus (266,000 p.a.)
   5.8 million Reform Hindus (61,000 p.a.)
418 million Buddhists (2.5 million p.a.)
   235 million Mahayana (1.4 million p.a.)
   158 million Theravada (942,000 p.a.)
   25 million Tantrayana (Lamaists) (150,000 p.a.)
OTHER MAJOR RELIGIONS IN AD 2025:
449 million Chinese folk-religionists (2.8 million p.a.)
115 million Asian New-Religionists (522,000 p.a.)
277 million Ethnoreligionists (2.1 million p.a.)
MINOR RELIGIONS AND QUASI-RELIGIONS IN AD 2025:
31 million Sikhs (374,000 p.a.)
16 million Jews (68,100 p.a.)
16 million non-Christian Spiritists (176,000 p.a.)
12 million Baha'is (253,000 p.a.)

### CHRISTIANS AND NON-CHRISTIANS IN AD 2025
1.9 billion professing Christians (on Third Millennium Scenario I)
2.6 billion professing Christians (on Third Millennium Scenario II)
3.2 billion professing Christians (on Third Millennium Scenario III)
5.2 billion non-Christians (on Third Millennium Scenario II)

## Global Diagram 67. Tomorrow's global Christianity: the status of churches and missions in AD 2025.

This diagram describes the probable status of global Christianity 25 years into the 21st century. All the statistics refer to the year 2025.

The box at top left sets out 3 possible scenarios regarding the status of world evangelization in AD 2025. Third Millennium Scenario I = No progress, no change, boundaries same as today. Third Millennium Scenario II = Moderate progress, some progress by 2025 but not much. Third

Millennium Scenario III = Closure with world evangelization successfully completed and over half of the world now Christians. The large schematic globe below shows these scenarios diagrammatically, using the 3-fold division of Worlds A, B, and C. Further descriptions are given to its right under these same headings A, B, and C. Later, Global Diagrams 70-73 take these projections further by introducing 4 additional long-term scenarios for the 21st century.

Meanwhile, whichever scenarios prevail, the church the Body of Christ sails on under the biblical metaphor of a storm-tossed ship upholding the Cross of Christ, sailing through the troubled waters of the *Oikoumene* (the whole inhabited Earth). This widely portrayed symbol is shown below.

---

**3 POSSIBLE WORLD MISSION SCENARIOS FOR AD 2025**

*Third Millennium Scenario I.* No progress: World B's boundaries same as in 2000 (shown by heavy full lines).

*Third Millennium Scenario II.* Moderate progress: World B's boundaries by 2025 move upwards somewhat (shown by dashed broken lines, - - - - - - - - ).

*Third Millennium Scenario III.* Closure: World A disappears because all evangelized. World B = 49% of population, World C = 51%. (Boundary shown by dashed-dotted line, ━ · ━ · ━ · ━ ).

The church sails through the Oikoumene (the whole storm-tossed inhabited globe) into the 21st century. (Logo of the World Council of Churches since 1948).

---

### LOCATION OF WORKERS IN AD 2025

*Legal*
R = residential foreign missionaries
H = home missionaries
T = tentmakers
I = itinerant evangelists
N = nonresidential missionaries
S = short-term missionaries
P = pilgrim evangelizers
U = tourist evangelizers

*Illegal*
c = clandestine evangelizers
s = smugglers

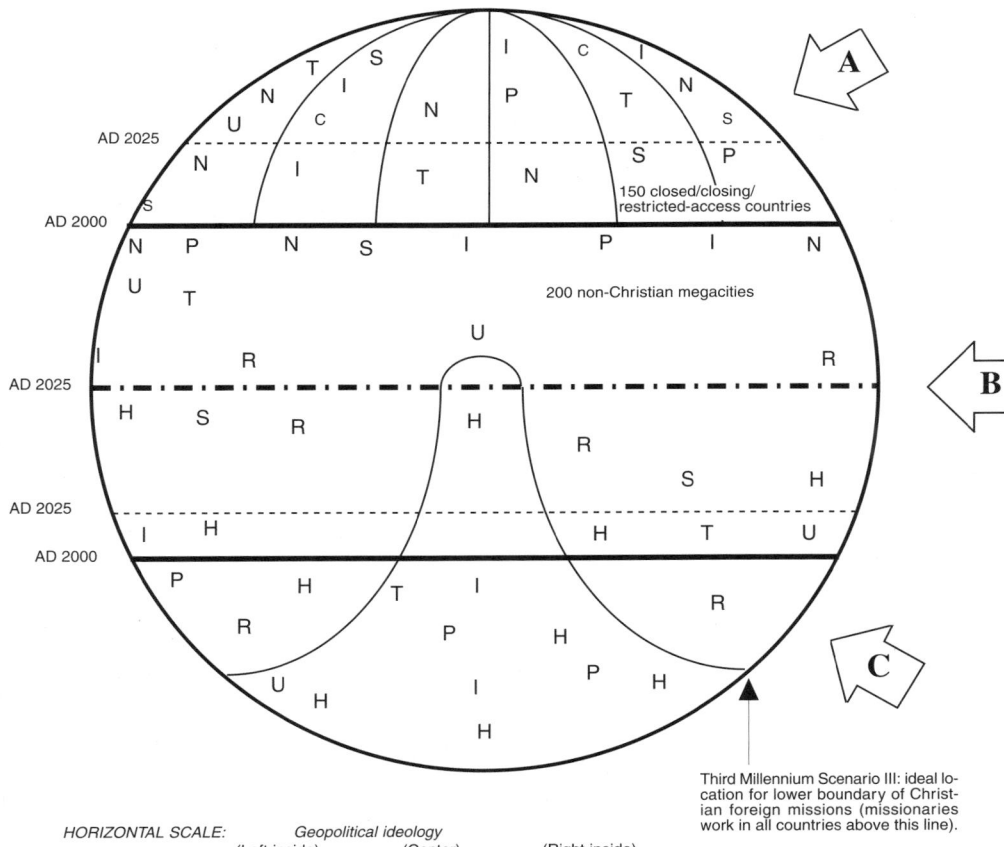

150 closed/closing/restricted-access countries

200 non-Christian megacities

Third Millennium Scenario III: ideal location for lower boundary of Christian foreign missions (missionaries work in all countries above this line).

*HORIZONTAL SCALE:*    *Geopolitical ideology*

| | (Left inside) | (Center) | (Right inside) |
|---|---|---|---|
| WORLDS | Communist world | Western world | Third World |

---

**VERTICAL SCALE** (on globe below left)**: EVANGELIZATION IN WORLDS A,B,C**

**A. THE UNEVANGELIZED WORLD IN AD 2025**
Third Millennium Scenario I: 2.2 billion persons unevangelized (28%)
Third Millennium Scenario II: 1.8 billion still unevangelized (23.6%)
Third Millennium Scenario III: No unevangelized populations remain

**B. THE EVANGELIZED NON-CHRISTIAN WORLD IN AD 2025**
Third Millennium Scenario I: 3.2 billion persons (41%)
Third Millennium Scenario II: 3.4 billion persons (43%)
Third Millennium Scenario III: 3.8 billion persons (49%)

**C. THE CHRISTIAN WORLD IN AD 2025**
Third Millennium Scenario I: 2.4 billion Christians (31%)
Third Millennium Scenario II: 2.6 billion Christians (33.4%)
    624 million Christian children under 15 years
    210 million Christian infants under 5 years
    Christians by color: 65% Non-White (19% Black,13% Brown, 19% Tan, 12% Yellow, 4% Red), 35% White
    1.7 billion urban Christians
    2.5 billion affiliated Christians (church members)
    888 million practicing Christians
    300 million Christian pilgrims on move
    2.5 billion regular radio/TV audience
    5,400 Christian radio/TV stations
    50,000 denominations
    8 million full-time Christian workers
    75 million lay Christians residing abroad
    1.2 million home missionaries
    600,000 foreign missionaries
    5,000 nonresidential missionaries (NRMs) in 70 closed countries
    300,000 professional tentmakers
    50,000 itinerant charismatic evangelists (ICEs)
    700,000 short-term foreign missionaries
    75,000 itinerant tourist churches
    50,000 itinerant pilgrim churches
    1.35 million base ecclesial communities (BECs)
    LITERATURE AND MEDIA IN AD 2025
    243 million Bibles and NTs p.a.
    29,130 new Christian book titles p.a.
    50,000 new Christian booklets p.a.
    50,000 Christian periodicals and serials (40% in English)
    6 billion live viewers of 'Jesus' and other Christian films
    1.3 billion Christian-owned computers
    1.7 billion Christian computer users
    CHRISTIAN FINANCE IN AD 2025
    Christians by income: 50% rich (10% affluent, 25% well off, 15% just coping), 50% poor (40% needy, 10% absolutely poor)
    Church of the Rich: 1,310 million
    Church of the Affluent: 262 million
    Church of the Poor: 1,310 million
    Church of the Absolutely Poor: 262 million
    Christians' personal incomes $44.2 trillion p.a.
    Church/agency income $500 billion p.a.
    Global foreign missions: $60 billion p.a.
Third Millennium Scenario III: 4.0 billion Christians (51%)
    800,000 foreign missionaries
    25,000 nonresidential missionaries in all 150 closed/closing/restricted-access countries
    300,000 itinerant charismatic evangelists
    210,000 Christian martyrs a year

## Global Diagram 68.    Tomorrow's Great Commission harvest force: denominations, networks, agencies, institutions, workers in AD 2025.

The data below enumerate the probable size and deployment of the 'harvest force' (the cutting edge of all Christian resources—personnel, organizations, agencies) in AD 2025 in the Third Millennium. All figures are projections or estimates for AD 2025, on Third Millennium Scenario II (as explained in Global Diagram 67).

By the turn of the Third Millennial year AD 2000, Great Commission Christians (all Christians who take seriously Christ's final command while on Earth) have increased vastly in numbers, in missionary sophistication, and in organization. By AD 2025, then, redeployment of Christian resources, 99% of which at present are consumed solely by the Christian world (World C), should have become widespread. When compared with Global Diagram 44, the diagram below shows these redeployed resources targeting World A, the Unevangelized World, which has received only miniscule attention in the past and present. Equally important is that instead of operating in standalone mode, mission agencies will have learned to field coordinated redeployment, thereby changing from merely globalized missions to global mission properly so called.

### ORGANIZED CHRISTIANITY IN AD 2025
400 ecclesiastical traditions/families
50,000 denominations
75,000 parachurch or service agencies
168,000 institutions
2.6 billion Christians
2.5 billion affiliated church members
5.0 million worship centers (local churches)
1.3 million base ecclesial communities (BECs)
Sunday-school enrollment 600 million

### GLOBAL GROWTH OF CHRISTIANS IN AD 2025
(figures in parentheses=annual rate of change)
2,617 million Christians in AD 2025
ANNUAL CHRISTIAN GAINS (c=a+b):
| | | |
|---|---|---|
| a. Births p.a. | 41.7 million | (1.59% p.a.) |
| b. Conversions p.a. | 25.2 million | (0.96% p.a.) |
| c. New Christians (=a+b) | 66.9 million | (2.56% p.a.) |
| d. Baptisms (=80% of c) | 53.5 million | (2.04% p.a.) |

ANNUAL CHRISTIAN LOSSES (g=e+f):
| | | |
|---|---|---|
| e. Deaths p.a. | -23.6 million | (-0.90% p.a.) |
| f. Defections p.a. | -15.0 million | (-0.57% p.a.) |
| g. Total losses p.a. (=e+f) | -38.6 million | (-1.48% p.a.) |

ANNUAL CHRISTIAN INCREASE (h=c-g):
| | | |
|---|---|---|
| h. Nett increase p.a. | 28.3 million | (1.08% p.a.) |

### GLOBAL CHURCH GROWTH IN AD 2025
100,000 new churches planted or opened a year
10,000 churches closed or suppressed a year
90,000 nett increase in churches a year

### CHURCH MEMBERSHIP BY CONTINENTS, AD 2025
(by UN macro regions/major areas)
| | |
|---|---|
| Africa | 601,000,000 |
| Antarctica | 8,000 |
| Asia | 459,000,000 |
| Europe | 533,000,000 |
| Latin America | 635,000,000 |
| Northern America | 235,000,000 |
| Oceania | 28,200,000 |

### GLOBAL ECCLESIASTICAL TRADITIONS, AD 2025
(church membership; note that indented categories are selected subgroups and are not intended as a complete breakdown of the unindented line above them)
*Mutually exclusive categories:*
| | |
|---|---|
| Anglicans | 113,750,000 |
| Marginal Christians | 45,550,000 |
| Independents | 581,640,000 |
| Orthodox | 252,716,000 |
|    Eastern Orthodox | 199,943,000 |
|    Oriental Orthodox | 52,500,000 |
| Protestants | 468,633,000 |
|    united churches' members | 160,000,000 |
|    Baptists | 121,000,000 |
|    Lutherans | 71,000,000 |
|    Reformed | 74,400,000 |
|    Classical Pentecostals | 101,000,000 |
|    Methodists | 33,700,000 |
|    Adventists | 22,400,000 |

| | |
|---|---|
| Roman Catholics | 1,361,965,000 |
|    Eastern-rite Catholics | 27,400,000 |
|    Catholic Charismatics | 190,000,000 |
| Other overlapping categories: | |
| Pentecostals/Charismatics | 811,552,000 |
|    Pentecostals (1st Wave of Renewal) | 101,000,000 |
|    Charismatics (2nd Wave of Renewal) | 279,000,000 |
|    Third-Wavers (3rd Wave of Renewal) | 432,000,000 |
| Evangelicals | 327,835,000 |
| evangelicals | 887,579,000 |
| crypto-Christians | 190,490,000 |

### GLOBAL CHRISTIAN LEADERSHIP, AD 2025
8 million full-time Christian workers (94% citizens)
7.5 million national (citizen) workers
1.5 million ordained clergy, ministers, pastors, priests
75,000 church leaders (30,000 bishops, 25,000 moderators or other denominational heads, 20,000 executive agency heads)

### GLOBAL CONCILIARISM IN AD 2025
8,800 Christian councils, councils of churches, or alliances:
   40,000 local councils of churches
   2,000 nationwide Christian councils
   60 regional Christian councils or councils of churches
   30 continental Christian councils or councils of churches
   15 world Christian councils or councils of churches
   100 missions councils
   500 Christian world communions (world confessional councils)
   1 Conference of Christian World Communions (70 member confessions)

### GLOBAL HARVEST FORCE, AD 2025
No church is 100% Great Commission Christians
No church is 0% Great Commission Christians
GREAT COMMISSION CHRISTIANS IN AD 2025:
2.4 billion potential Great Commission Christians
888 million active Great Commission Christians (evangelizers, the "force for evangelism"), growing at 6.5% p.a.
820 million daily-evangelizing Christians (evangelists, daily evangelizers)
300 million daily intercessors
40 million in full-time prayer ministry
6 million full-time Great Commission workers
60,000 Great Commission leaders
17,500 Christians martyred every month

### GLOBAL FOREIGN MISSION, AD 2025
6,000 mission agencies
600,000 career foreign missionaries
250,000 foreign missionaries from Third-World countries
700,000 short-term foreign missionaries
600 Great Commission research centers

### GREAT COMMISSION NETWORKS, AD 2025
10,000 computerized networks
500 global networks
20 global meganetworks
5 Great Commission giganetworks
1.5 billion Christian or church-owned or operated computers

World A

World B

World C

**GLOBAL HARVEST FORCE**

—*John 4:35*

*COORDINATED REDEPLOYMENT 2025*
Tomorrow's "force for evangelism" by AD 2025 is likely to be 888 million active Great Commission Christians, found within 12,000 ethnolinguistic peoples. Hopefully, by that time they will have redeployed themselves away from targeting only World C to targeting especially World A, the Unevangelized World. This shift is termed here a shift from merely globalized missions to genuinely global mission.

**Global Diagram 69.　Yesterday's, today's and tomorrow's geospheres and geoagendas: a range of 54 global issue/subject spheres of influence or concern.**

With strategists listing over 12,480 current global problems of significance, professionals and specialists are working on several hundred issues, subjects, or solutions to these problems. In the illustration below, these issues are classified under 54 spheres of interest or concern. This procession of geospheres begins in the study of the distant past on the upper left, based on the physical sciences. Second, the life sciences follow (those studying all aspects of organic life).

Third come the human sciences. And fourth are the spiritual sciences, including missiology and evangelistics (the scientific study of evangelization). This whole approach is termed— globalistics.

Then follows a table in which these 54 geospheres, with related major subjects and (in italics) major academic disciplines, are shown analyzed into 3 layers Past, Present, and Future, and then into 8 columns related to the 8 basic questions asked by researchers: When? What? How? Whence? Why? Who? Where? Whither?

In all this, Christians have a vital role to play keeping the world in view by tackling these problems with a range of imaginative geoagendas.

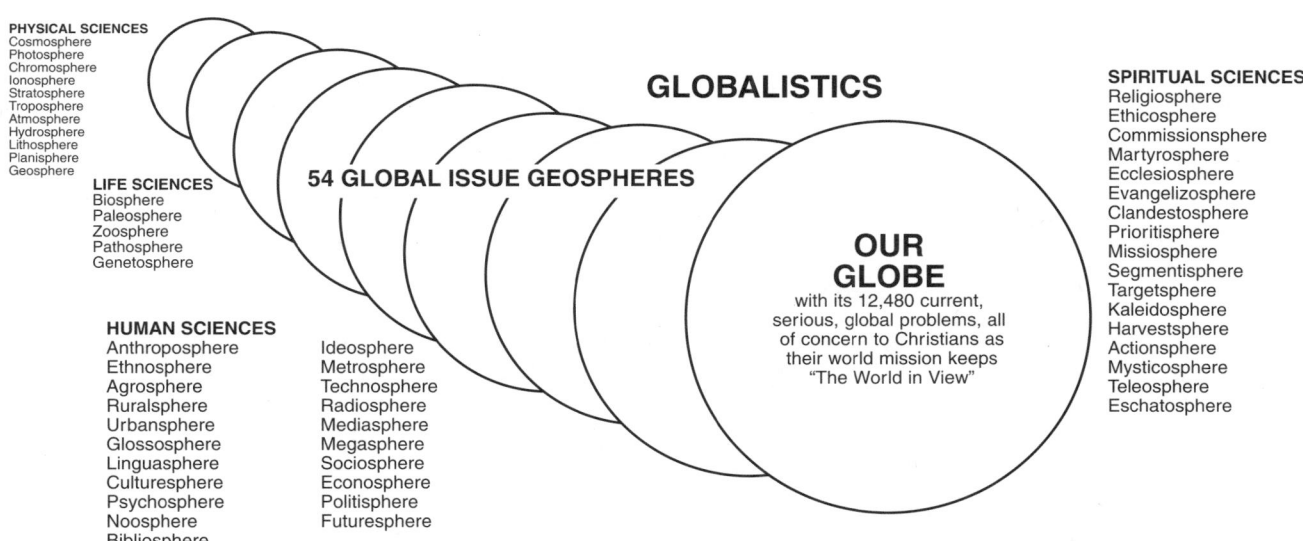

**PHYSICAL SCIENCES**
Cosmosphere
Photosphere
Chromosphere
Ionosphere
Stratosphere
Troposphere
Atmosphere
Hydrosphere
Lithosphere
Planisphere
Geosphere

**LIFE SCIENCES**
Biosphere
Paleosphere
Zoosphere
Pathosphere
Genetosphere

**HUMAN SCIENCES**
Anthroposphere
Ethnosphere
Agrosphere
Ruralsphere
Urbansphere
Glossosphere
Linguasphere
Culturesphere
Psychosphere
Noosphere
Bibliosphere
Ideosphere
Metrosphere
Technosphere
Radiosphere
Mediasphere
Megasphere
Sociosphere
Econosphere
Politisphere
Futuresphere

**GLOBALISTICS**

**54 GLOBAL ISSUE GEOSPHERES**

**OUR GLOBE** with its 12,480 current, serious, global problems, all of concern to Christians as their world mission keeps "The World in View"

**SPIRITUAL SCIENCES**
Religiosphere
Ethicosphere
Commissionsphere
Martyrosphere
Ecclesiosphere
Evangelizosphere
Clandestosphere
Prioritisphere
Missiosphere
Segmentisphere
Targetsphere
Kaleidosphere
Harvestsphere
Actionsphere
Mysticosphere
Teleosphere
Eschatosphere

| CHRONOLOGY | CREATION | DISCIPLINES | EVOLUTION | CHRISTIANITY | MISSION | GEOSPHERES | GLOBAL DIAGRAMS |
|---|---|---|---|---|---|---|---|
| **8 BASIC QUESTIONS:** **When?** | **What?** | **How?** | **Whence?** | **Why?** | **Who?** | **Where?** | **Whither?** |
| ***PAST***　　Creation: COSMIC ERA I | 7 stages of scientific 1. Energy 2. Light 3. Solar System 4. Life on Earth 5. Species 6. Mind (human race) 7. Community, art, religion | 4 levels of explanation: 1. PHYSICAL SCIENCES *Mathematics Astronomy Geology Paleontology Physics Chemistry Engineering Geophysics Astrophysics Seismology Oceanography Meteorology* | Cosmology 7 levels of evolution: 1. Energy 2. Matter 3. Life 4. Mind 5-7 (see below) | Old Testament *Intertestamental Period* New Testament *Theology Archeology Dogmatics Systematics* | Planisphere Abraham Joseph Moses Joshua David Nehemiah Ezra Daniel *Missiology Church history* Peter Paul Martin Luther John Wesley William Carey John R. Mott William Temple | Cosmosphere Geosphere Lithosphere Hydrosphere Atmosphere Troposphere Stratosphere Ionosphere Photosphere Chromosphere Biosphere Paleosphere Zoosphere Pathosphere Genetosphere Agrosphere Anthroposphere Ethnosphere Commissionsphere Missiosphere Bibliosphere Evangelizosphere Martyrosphere | 1. The Great Commission 2. Seven Mandates 3. 210 Greek commands 4. 300 dimensions 5. Evangelized by martyrs |
| Prehistory Chronology *History* COSMIC ERA II Latourette's 10 Epochs: I. Winning the Empire II. The Great Recession III. Resurgence & Advance IV. Confusion & Corruption V. Reform & Expansion VI. Repudiation & Revival VII. The Great Century VIII. Vigour amidst Storm IX. Surge in the Third World X. The Final Thrust | The New Creation *Mechanics* Relativity Quantum physics *Demographics Criminology Statistics Cliometrics* | 2. LIFE SCIENCES *Biology Botany Zoology Pathology Genetics* |  |  |  |  |  |
| ***PRESENT*** The 1990s-2000s Decade of Evangelization Decade of Evangelism Decade of Mission Decade of Harvest Decade of Destiny Decade of Decision Cryogenics LCWE GCOWE ICOWE ICCOWE | New subjects: Robotics Chaos Fractals DNA-RNA Networking Microengineering Systems analysis Biodiversity *Linguistics* | 3. HUMAN SCIENCES *Anthropology Sociology Ethnology Medicine Psychiatry Psychology Health sciences Economics Urbanology Political science Cybernetics Communication* | Bibliography Gaia theory Geography Cartography *Political science* Geopolitics | Ecclesiology Ecumenics | Billy Graham Paul VI John Paul II Luis Palau Mother Teresa Technosphere Missiography Evangelistics Martyrology | Ideosphere Glossosphere Culturesphere Psychosphere Noosphere Mysticosphere Religiosphere Urbansphere Ruralsphere Sociosphere Econosphere Politisphere | 6. Global human need 7. Structures of sin 8. The technoglobe 9. Urban & rural worlds 10. Segmentization 11. Geopolitical blocs 12. Status of evangelization 13. The unfinished task 14. Christian resources 15. Language 16. Media/broadcasting 17. Renewal 18. Closed countries 19. Harvest force |
| ***FUTURE*** COSMIC ERA III 10 periods of the future: 1. The immediate future 2. The near-term future 3. The middle-range future 4. The long-range future 5. The distant future 6. The far distant future 7. The megafuture 8. The gigafuture 9. The terafuture 10. The eschatofuture | Futures research Nanotechnology Biogenetics Fusion energy Photovoltaics Self-replication Grand Unified Theory | *Futuristics* 4. SPIRITUAL SCIENCES *Philosophy Ethics Mysticism Comparative religion Phenomenology Teleosphere* | Futurology *Globalistics* Planetary consciousness Overmind 5. Supermind 6. Galactic Mind 7. Cosmic Mind | Eschatology Teleology Millennial scenarios: Scenario I Scenario II Scenario III Long-term scenarios: Scenario 1 Scenario 2 Scenario 3 Scenario 4 | Biography Teaching Training TEE | Futuresphere Ethicosphere Ecclesiosphere Linguasphere Radiosphere Mediasphere Clandestosphere Metrosphere Megasphere Prioritisphere Harvestsphere Segmentisphere Targetsphere Kaleidosphere Actionsphere Eschatosphere | 20. Megatrends in mission 21. Megapriorities 22. AD 2025 plans 23. The globe in AD 2025 24. The church in AD 2025 25. Harvest force 2025 26. AD 2025 global goals 27. Implementing WCGAP/KGAP 28. Expert systems 29. Monodenominationalism 30. Nondenominationalism 31. Postdenominationalism 32. Martyrdom 33. Issue geospheres |

## Global Diagram 70.   World evangelization and Christianity from AD 33–AD 2100, with future GeoScenario-1—Monodenominationalism.

Christianity's 33,800 fragmented, competing denominations present a scandal of enormous proportions. In his High Priestly prayer, the Lord Jesus prayed 3 times (John 17:21,22,23) that his disciples might all become fully united 'so that the world may believe'.

This first long-term GeoScenario-1 sets out a situation in which this unity comes about, in reaction to growing world ridicule and heavy pressures from political regimes. It envisages all the major denominations finally agreeing by AD 2025 to begin an immediate, loose, de facto reunion of the churches, thus forming one single denomination.

Despite this, on this scenario Christianity declines in numbers or percentage as a global religion. Meanwhile, the world remains unevangelized. (This is Third Millennium Scenario I). For further details and comment on the diagram, see preceding text.

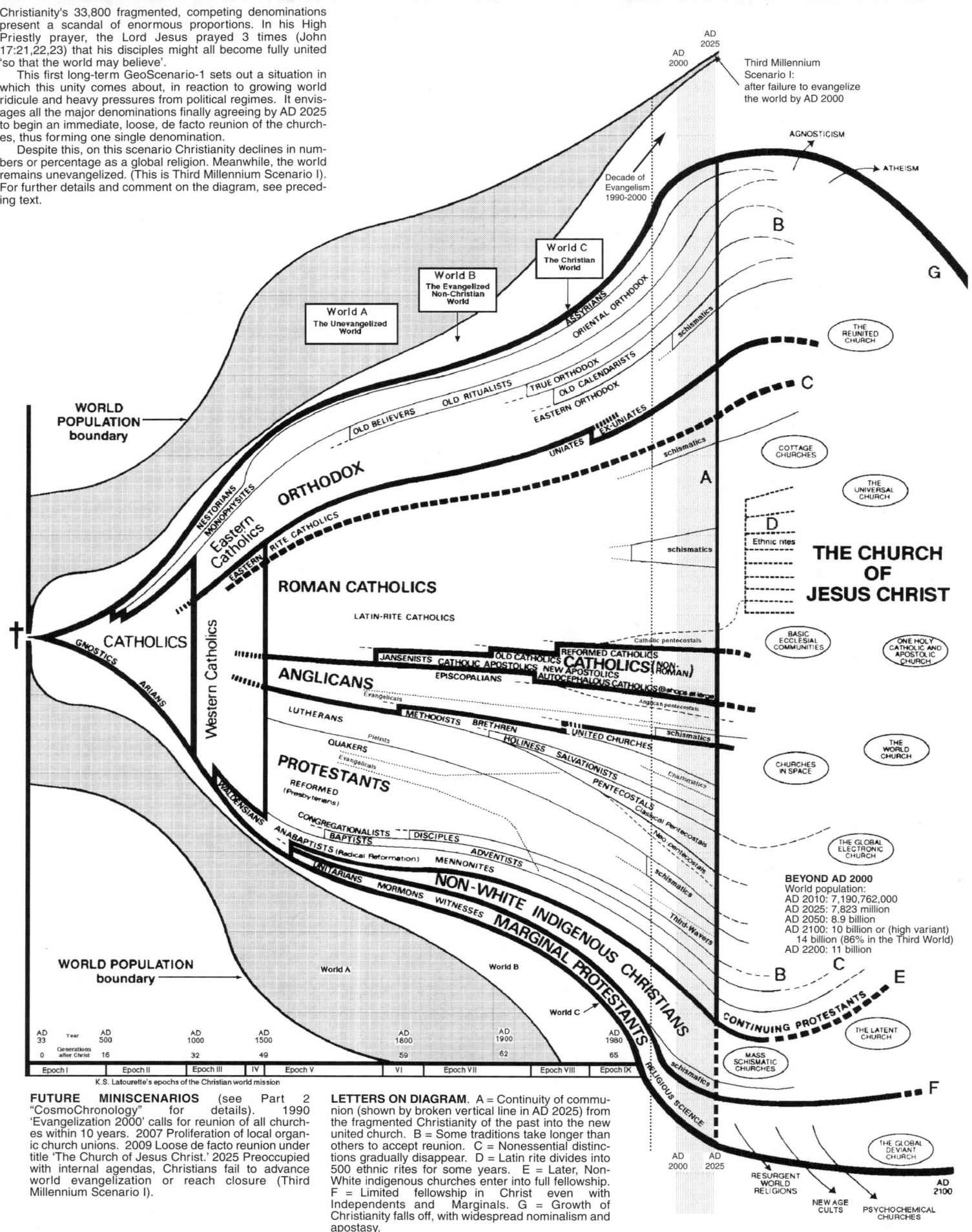

**FUTURE MINISCENARIOS** (see Part 2 "CosmoChronology" for details). 1990 'Evangelization 2000' calls for reunion of all churches within 10 years. 2007 Proliferation of local organic church unions. 2009 Loose de facto reunion under title 'The Church of Jesus Christ.' 2025 Preoccupied with internal agendas, Christians fail to advance world evangelization or reach closure (Third Millennium Scenario I).

**LETTERS ON DIAGRAM.** A = Continuity of communion (shown by broken vertical line in AD 2025) from the fragmented Christianity of the past into the new united church. B = Some traditions take longer than others to accept reunion. C = Nonessential distinctions gradually disappear. D = Latin rite divides into 500 ethnic rites for some years. E = Later, Non-White indigenous churches enter into full fellowship. F = Limited fellowship in Christ even with Independents and Marginals. G = Growth of Christianity falls off, with widespread nominalism and apostasy.

## Global Diagram 71.   World evangelization and Christianity from AD 33–AD 2100, with future GeoScenario-2— Nondenominationalism.

A second possible alternate future, long-term GeoScenario-2, envisages the vast mass of ordinary Christian believers finally losing patience with the scandal of denominational fragmentation. The laity break ties with centralized structures, abandon denominational headquarters, and organize themselves in autonomous congregations locally in 5 loose, decentralized lay megaclusters. Huge charismatic revivals sweep across the non-Christian world. Spontaneous postdenominationalist Christianity becomes the norm.  The world meanwhile has become fully evangelized for the first time in history. (This is Third Millennium Scenario III). For further details and comment on the diagram, see preceding text.

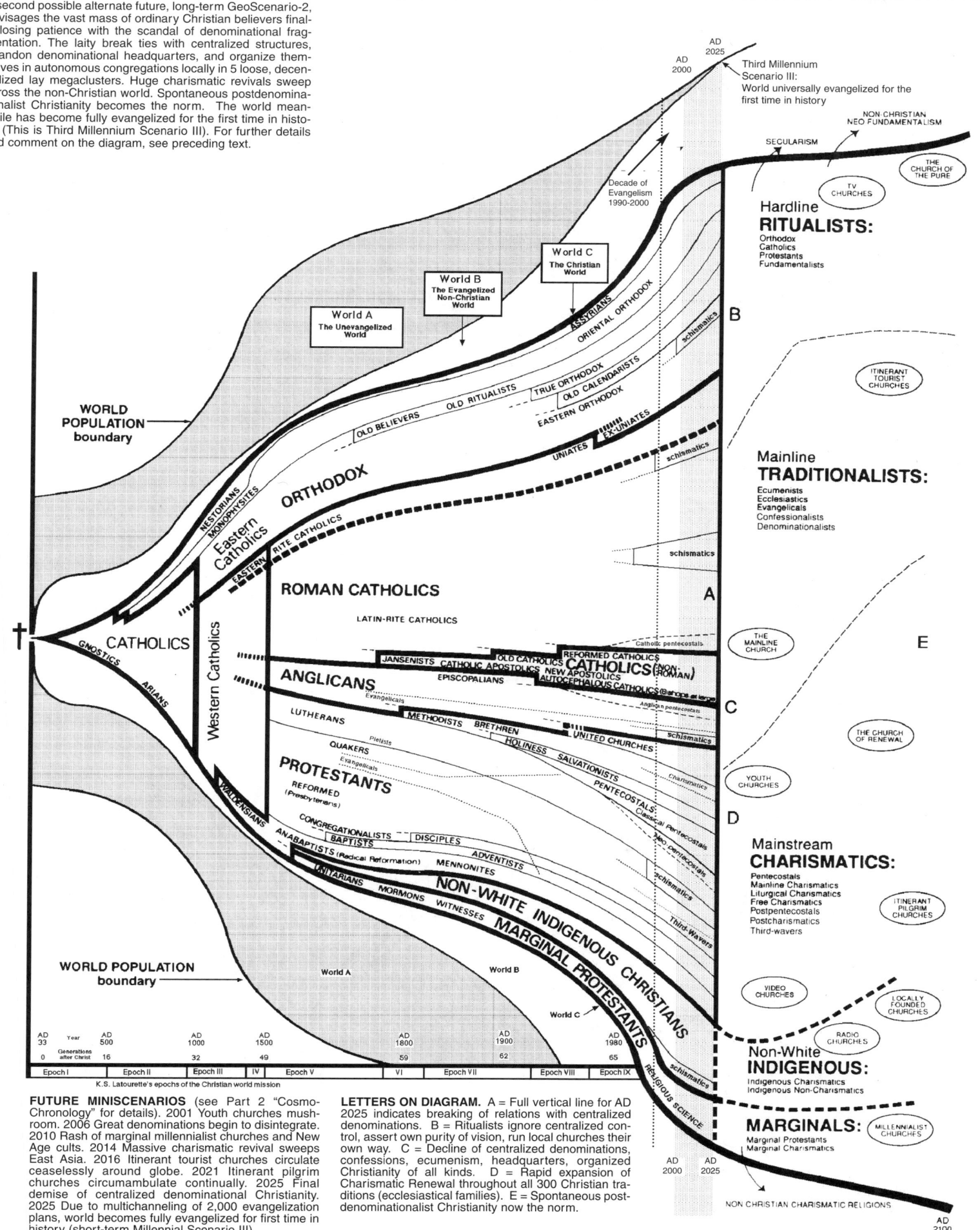

**FUTURE MINISCENARIOS** (see Part 2 "Cosmo-Chronology" for details). 2001 Youth churches mushroom. 2006 Great denominations begin to disintegrate. 2010 Rash of marginal millennialist churches and New Age cults. 2014 Massive charismatic revival sweeps East Asia. 2016 Itinerant tourist churches circulate ceaselessly around globe. 2021 Itinerant pilgrim churches circumambulate continually. 2025 Final demise of centralized denominational Christianity. 2025 Due to multichanneling of 2,000 evangelization plans, world becomes fully evangelized for first time in history (short-term Millennial Scenario III).

**LETTERS ON DIAGRAM.**  A = Full vertical line for AD 2025 indicates breaking of relations with centralized denominations.  B = Ritualists ignore centralized control, assert own purity of vision, run local churches their own way.  C = Decline of centralized denominations, confessions, ecumenism, headquarters, organized Christianity of all kinds.  D = Rapid expansion of Charismatic Renewal throughout all 300 Christian traditions (ecclesiastical families).  E = Spontaneous postdenominationalist Christianity now the norm.

**Global Diagram 72.  World evangelization and Christianity from AD 33–AD 2100, with future GeoScenario-3—Postdenominationalism.**

A third possible alternate future, long-term GeoScenario-3, envisages Christianity dominated by huge dynamic masses of Third-World charismatic youths who reject all ties with Christian history, traditions, denominationalism, and Western Christianity. Ten vast unorganized ethnolinguistic, racial megaclusters emerge, forming rival bodies from the Church of the Megarich to the Church of the Absolutely Poor. Global Christianity continues its explosive advance around the world, but in the total absence of coordination or planning large populations still remain unevangelized. (This is short-term Third Millennium Scenario II). For further details and comment on the diagram, see preceding text.

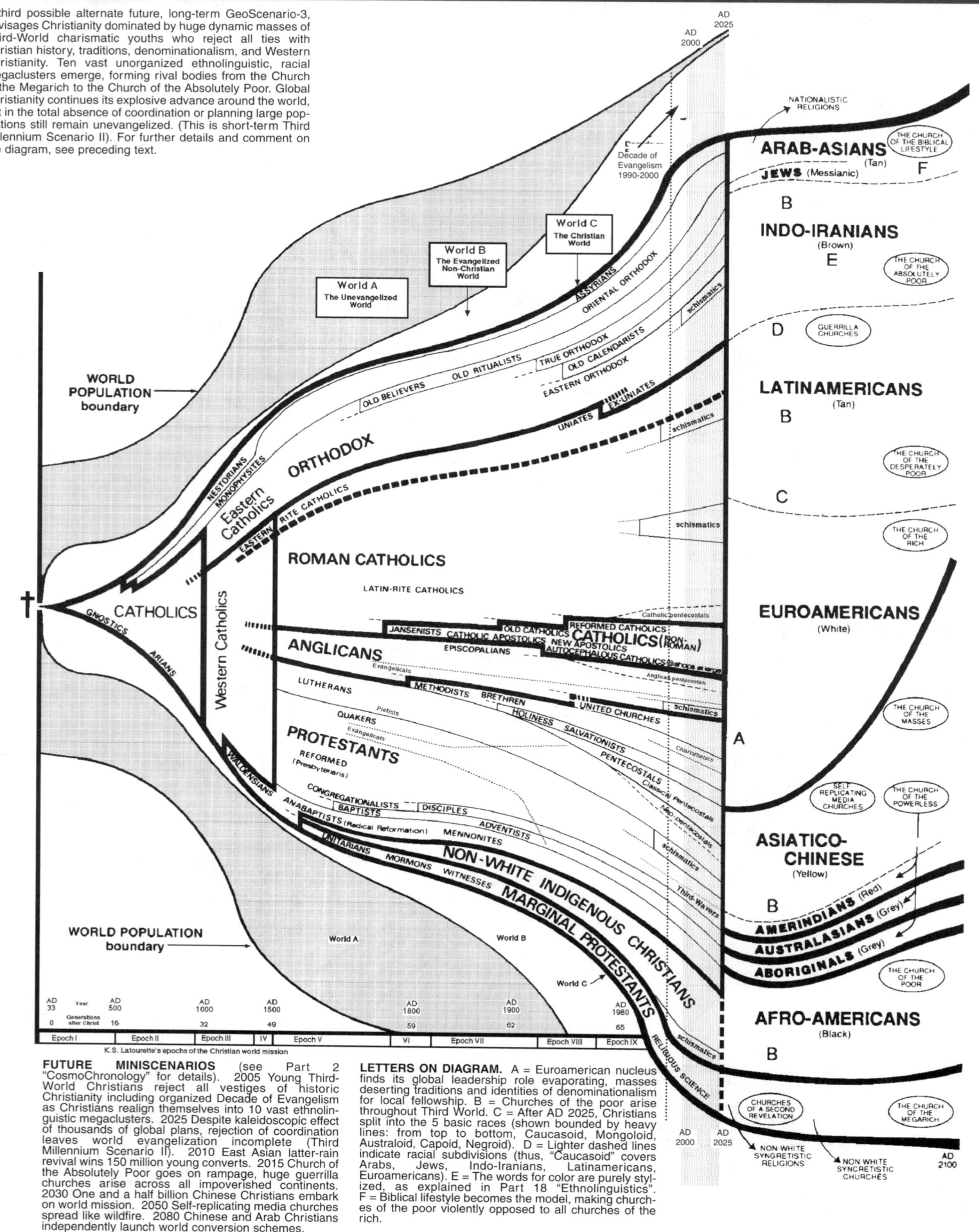

**FUTURE MINISCENARIOS** (see Part 2 "CosmoChronology" for details). **2005** Young Third-World Christians reject all vestiges of historic Christianity including organized Decade of Evangelism as Christians realign themselves into 10 vast ethnolinguistic megaclusters. **2025** Despite kaleidoscopic effect of thousands of global plans, rejection of coordination leaves world evangelization incomplete (Third Millennium Scenario II). **2010** East Asian latter-rain revival wins 150 million young converts. **2015** Church of the Absolutely Poor goes on rampage, huge guerrilla churches arise across all impoverished continents. **2030** One and a half billion Chinese Christians embark on world mission. **2050** Self-replicating media churches spread like wildfire. **2080** Chinese and Arab Christians independently launch world conversion schemes.

**LETTERS ON DIAGRAM.** A = Euroamerican nucleus finds its global leadership role evaporating, masses deserting traditions and identities of denominationalism for local fellowship. B = Churches of the poor arise throughout Third World. C = After AD 2025, Christians split into the 5 basic races (shown bounded by heavy lines: from top to bottom, Caucasoid, Mongoloid, Australoid, Capoid, Negroid). D = Lighter dashed lines indicate racial subdivisions (thus, "Caucasoid" covers Arabs, Jews, Indo-Iranians, Latinamericans, Euroamericans). E = The words for color are purely stylized, as explained in Part 18 "Ethnolinguistics". F = Biblical lifestyle becomes the model, making churches of the poor violently opposed to all churches of the rich.

**Global Diagram 73.    World evangelization and Christianity from AD 33-AD 2100, with future GeoScenario-4—Megamartyrdom.**

A fourth possible alternate future, long-term GeoScenario-4, depicts Christianity as a whole being extinguished.  Rather than continuing its missionary expansion (GeoScenario-3), or gradually losing its hold (GeoScenario-1), global Christianity could be definitively wiped out by hostile deliberate intent. From AD 2000-2050 political opposition and bannings grow, the whole church is forced underground, and is finally liquidated. (This could earlier include Third Millennium Scenarios I,II, or III). For further details and comment on this diagram, see preceding text.

**FUTURE MINISCENARIOS** (see Part 2 "CosmoChronology" for details). 2005 As mass persecution spreads, gospel of Christ becomes universally known (Third Millennium Scenario III); world remains fully evangelized up to final liquidation of Christianity. 2014 Bogus robot churches and android evangelists controlled by political regimes attempt to infiltrate and destroy the Body of Christ. 2020 Christianity's 32,000 fragmented denominations provoke regimes to interfere once and for all. 2040 Asian New Religions and secular quasi-religions join with political regimes to destroy global Christianity.  2040 (on another miniscenario, 2095) World government obliterates Church of the Martyrs with one final worldwide blow: church either (a) dies unknown (no one caring) or (b) dies in full glare of total knowledge and worldwide publicity (TV trials, executions, massacres, genocides).

**LETTERS ON DIAGRAM.**  A = 84% of global Christianity is legal, 16% is illegal or clandestine or underground. B = Vast numbers of young Christians withdraw from world into monastic life of prayer.  C = Groupings of denominations forcibly united by governmental edicts. D = Severe persecution by fanatical regimes. E = All churches and Christians are pronounced illegal and totally banned. F = Massive worldwide coordinated repression and persecution force apostasy by whole churches. G = Final extinction, in the ultimate witness: the church follows her Master to execution and martyrdom.

**Global Diagram 74.    Tracing the evolution of organizational monoliths in global Christianity, AD 33-AD 2200: 5 views from AD 2000 and 3 future scenarios from AD 2150 and AD 2200.**

The first 5 of the 8 minidiagrams below show the phenomenon of present-day global Christianity as seen by an outside observer in the year 2000. These monoliths are: 33,820 denominations, 21,000 agencies, and 99,000 major institutions (documented in Global Diagram 24). The sequence of minidiagrams is derived and explained in the article 'The fragmentation of mission into 4,000 freestanding, standalone monoliths', *International journal of frontier missions*, 9:1 (January 1992). How biblical is this control by monoliths?

Minidiagrams 6-7 below then project current trends into the future and show 2 possible alternative scenarios that an observer might see in AD 2150. They are derived and explained in detail under Global Diagrams 70-73.

Finally, in a far future AD 2200 scenario, the church is harassed, persecuted, and then systematically liquidated. The observer asks: Which seems the most likely—Christian totalitarianism dominated by a single massive hi-tech supermonolith (No. 6), or 6.5 billion unorganized ethnic charismatics (No. 7), or the church finally wiped out by a brutal world dictator (No. 8)?

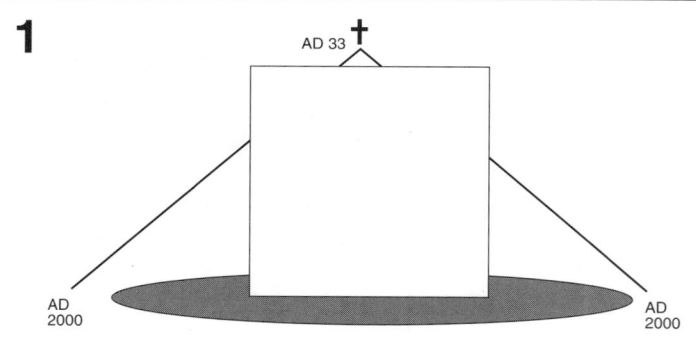

Diagram 1. First, the observer thinks Christianity is one single massive monolith.

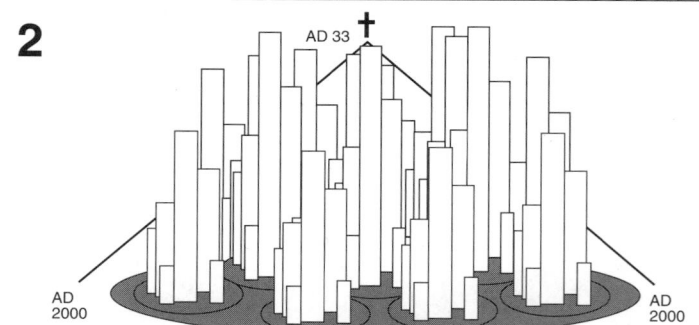

Diagram 2. Closer, he sees Christianity resolved into 300 confessional monoliths.

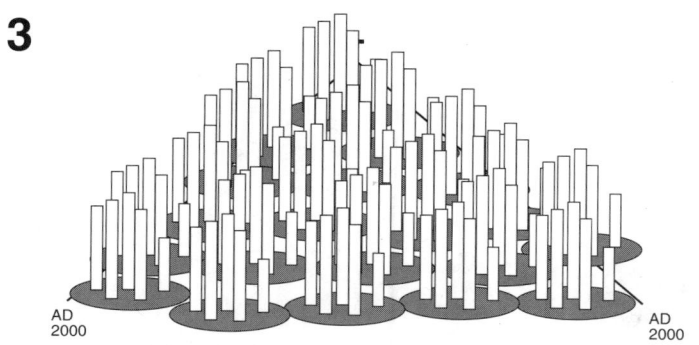

Diagram 3. The Cross disappears behind a fragmented mass of 33,800 denominations.

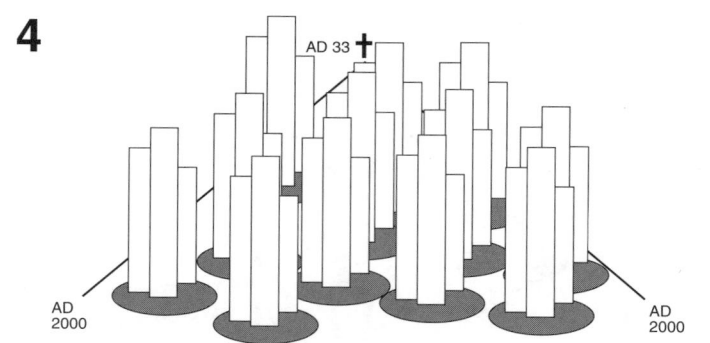

Diagram 4. He then perceives 12 global megamonoliths with 33 huge gigamonoliths.

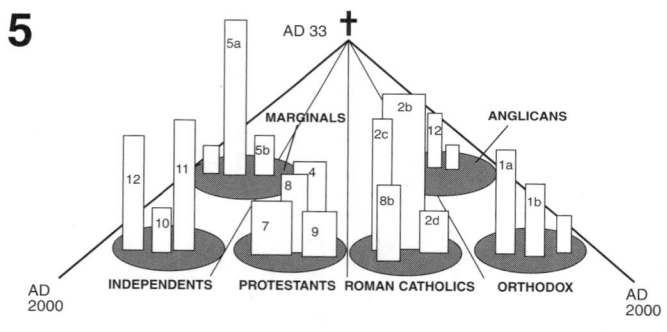

Diagram 5. Finally he sees them analyzed into 6 major ecclesiastico-cultural megablocs.

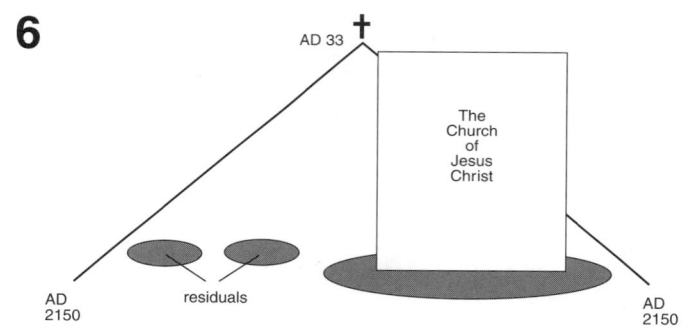

Diagram 6. Future I—Monodenominationalism: the monoliths coalesce into one.

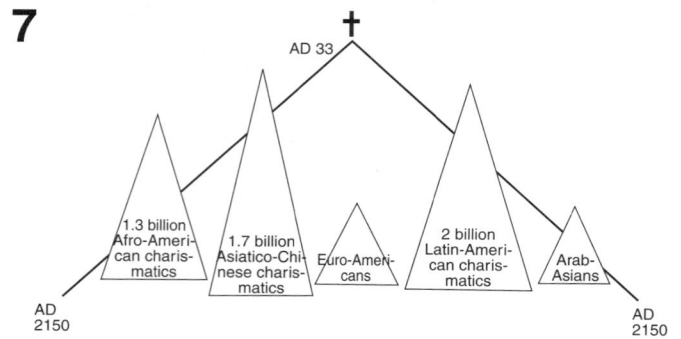

Diagram 7. Future II—Postdenominationalism: ethnic spontaneity replaces monoliths.

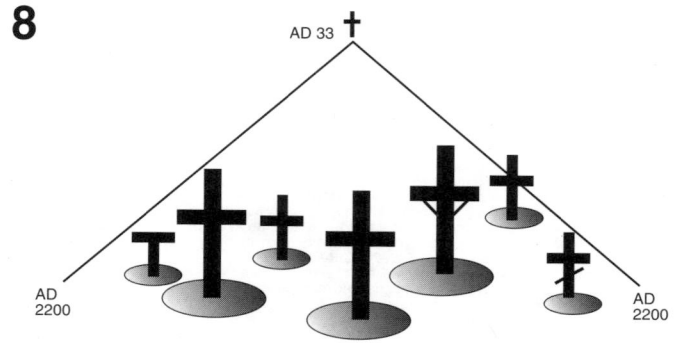

Diagram 8. Future III—Megamartyrdom: the ultimate witness to Christ.

Part 2

# COSMOCHRONOLOGY

A chronology of world evangelization from Creation to New Creation

*God's eternal power and character cannot be seen. But from the
beginning of creation, God has shown what these are like by all he has made.*
—Apostle Paul, in Romans 1:20, Contemporary English Version

*The doctrine of the Saviour has irradiated the whole Oikumene.*
—Eusebius, Ecclesiastical History 2.3.1, AD 310

*For all periods of time both past and future neither pass away nor come except because You
bring that about, and You Yourself permanently abide.*
—Augustine of Hippo, *Confessions*

*The distinction between past, present, and future is only a stubbornly persistent illusion.*
—Albert Einstein, 1955

Part 2 is a historical outline of facts and figures following global Christianity and its origins and mission over its 20 centuries and beyond, from distant past to distant future. A subtheme is the place of measurement, instrumentation, numbers, statistics, and trends in the unfolding of the Christian drama as it shares with the world the benefits of Christianity, Christ, and the gospel.

To show the global progress of Christianity, every country is given one first entry with its current name in italics, followed by 'First Christians', signifying the date of the first appearance of a resident community of Christians in that country, with a few words of elaboration.

Sources for this chronology have been legion. Virtually every entry has its own bibliography, and each has been condensed from one or several descriptive books or articles or reports. Some 4-line entries alone each have over 5,000 books describing the event.

There has been no room here to detail all these sources. The chronology does, however, list the publication events of some 300 books.

# A chronology of world evangelization from Creation to New Creation

## UNDERSTANDING THIS CHRONOLOGY

### Constructing a chronology

Chronologies do not replace history. Rather, they present us with a very compact, condensed form of history. Their great advantage is that they can pack a vast amount of factual information on a massive subject into a small and manageable space. With a minimum of essential interpretation, the subject can thus be covered within the covers of a single book.

This present chronology attempts to do justice to the immense subject of God's purposes and plans in our Universe. It provides a historical and futurological background to the study of empirical Christianity, global mission, and world evangelization. It does this in the context of world history and world prospects in the future.

This secular context forms an indispensable background for understanding the unfolding drama of salvation. To understand mission and evangelization we must first understand God's Creation, in the past, the present, and the future. To understand the lightning spread of the Christian gospel after the Day of Pentecost, we need to know how God had providentially prepared the Greek *koine* language and the Roman system of roads and mails. To understand the challenge to global mission in the year 1900, we need to know that the missionary statesman John R. Mott in his classic *The evangelization of the world in this generation* described in detail a whole vast range of secular developments facilitating the spread of the gospel. These included navigation, shipping routes, telegraphy, length of railway track in the world's non-Christian countries, and so on. And to think out what possible alternative futures might await the Christian world mission from now into the future, we need to know the whole background of secular futurist forecasts in science, technology, astronomy, cosmology, industry, society, et alia.

All such secular material will be found here distributed throughout the chronology. Readers can thus see how it related to salvation history in the past. This will help them to work out for themselves what this background secular context means for the mission of Christ today and in the future.

### Evidence needs to be weighed

The chronology presents its evidence by bringing together a large number of facts, events, and scenarios. These are derived from experts in many different spheres—astronomy, cosmology, physics, archeology, paleontology, geology, history, linguistics, and the futurology of all these and other subjects and disciplines. Great care has been taken to ensure the accuracy of all the entries, especially of every historical event in the sequence up to the year 2001. But it should be clearly understood that these entries—prehistoric, historical, or futuristic—do not necessarily represent the authors' personal views or opinions. We are simply the compilers or reporters, not the originators or protagonists.

Compiling the facts and interpretations of specialists in this way does not mean that we Christians have to accept them uncritically. The authors themselves as Christian believers do not accept the truth or likelihood or probability of a number of these items both in the past and in the future. The entries on the first page of the chronology, for example, describe the origin of the Universe as understood by contemporary astronomers, astrophysicists, and cosmologists. The entries on the second page describe the evolution of species as paleontologists and biologists understand it. But Christians have a prior authority in the Holy Scriptures, which they have found to be divinely inspired. We can only accept secular findings if they do not contradict the Scriptures' clear and basic teachings about God, the world, and the human race. This means that Christians are free to listen to the evidence adduced by experts in whatever subject,

to weigh that evidence, and then to come to their own conclusions. We should therefore feel free to accept or discard entries in this chronology if they do not appear consistent with our faith in Christ.

### God as Creator of all

The Scriptures teach that the God and Father of our Lord Jesus Christ was responsible for the creation of all things. God the Redeemer is also God the Creator. God as past, present, and future Creator is a fundamental theme running throughout the Scriptures. God created the Universe, as expounded in the Book of Genesis chapters 1-2. God has created life at every stage. God began the New Creation in Christ, and God will create, when the time arrives, the ultimate, perfected New Creation, the New Heavens and the New Earth.

### Christ as central figure

Jesus Christ is the central figure in this chronology because he is the central figure in the whole drama of the cosmos. He is the central figure as Logos in Creation; as Savior in Jerusalem; as Risen Lord of the church; as Messianic King in the Millennium; as Cosmocrat in this and future universes. At the close of the vision on Patmos, Christ declares: 'I am the Alpha and the Omega, the first and the last, the beginning and the end' (Revelation 22:13). Biblical insight on this is clear and detailed: Jesus Christ is 'the firstborn of all creation; for in him all things were created, in heaven and on earth, visible and invisible, whether thrones or dominions or principalities or authorities—all things were created through him and for him. He is before all things, and in him all things hold together' (Colossians 1:15-17, Revised Standard Version).

### Three themes, yet a single theme

Our depiction of the drama of God's unfolding purposes is based on 3 words from biblical Greek: *cosmos, chaos,* and *evangelion*. Each embodies a major theme in its own right. But together also they embody a single theme, namely the story of God's creation and its vicissitudes over the aeons. Let us briefly look at these 3 words.

### Chaos: abyss, primal waters, disorder, confusion

We start with chronologically the first of the 3 words, the Attic Greek word *chaos*. According to Liddell and Scott's *Lexicon*, it meant 'infinite space', 'infinite darkness', 'the expanse', 'the nether abyss', 'the first state of the Universe'. *Webster's Third new international dictionary* defines its English transliteration as a 'state of things in which chance is supreme', 'the confused unorganized state of primordial matter before the creation of distinct and orderly forms'.

*Chaos* is a biblical word, occurring in the Septuagint (Greek Old Testament, abbreviated to LXX). In its English form, it occurs a number of times in several leading English versions of the Bible. In Zechariah 14:4 (LXX), *chaos* is the vast chasm or abyss that will cleave the Mount of Olives in two when the Messiah returns on the future Day of the Lord. In Luke 16:26, the Latin Vulgate of AD 404 uses the Latin word *chaos* to translate the Greek *chasma*, and so the 1582 Rheims English New Testament translates: 'Between us and you there is fixed a great chaos'. And in the New American Bible (1970), Acts 19:32 portrays a vast assembly 'in chaos' over Paul's preaching. *Chaos* is synonymous with *abyssos* (abyss) which occurs frequently in the Bible (35 times in the Septuagint, 9 times in the Greek New Testament).

In the Bible, a whole range of words, concepts, and names surrounds the chaos-confusion-abyss concept. These include: disobedience, confusion, disorder, rebellion, rejection, sin, original sin, sinners, wicked, guilt, estrangement, alienation, selfishness, despair, punishment, evil, demons, devils, Satan, Abaddon, destruction, death.

Ancient Near Eastern peoples personified this concept as Tiamat, the primordial dragon or chaos monster of the undifferentiated primal waters. In Hebrew, the parallel word was *tehom*, as in Genesis 1:2, where it is translated in English as 'the deep' (KJV/AV), 'the abyss' (NEB). The Old Testament portrays God as victorious over this chaos monster, who is there named in addition either Rahab or Leviathan.

In Genesis 1:1-3, we read: 'When God set about creating the heavens and the earth, the earth was in a state of chaos and darkness was upon the face of the deep', or, 'When God began creating the heavens and the earth, the earth was at first a shapeless, chaotic mass' (The Living Bible). Or, in another translation, Genesis 1:2 reads 'The earth was without form and void, with darkness over the face of the abyss' (New English Bible). R. Young's analytical concordance to the Bible, in print from 1879 to the present day, states: 'Genesis 1:1ff should be rendered "When God began to create heaven and earth—and the earth was in a chaotic state and darkness was over the primordial ocean"'. God's work of creation did not destroy the chaos and darkness but pushed them back and held them in check.

Chaos did not disappear after the Creation. Chaos imagery recurs throughout the Old Testament, especially in poetic contexts. Chaos still surrounds the habitable world on every side. In modern scientific terminology, the term entropy stands for this word chaos, the tendency for everything in the Universe to lapse irreversibly from order into disorder, to run down, to decline towards death.

### Cosmos: order, the orderly Universe

The creation narrative of Genesis is paralleled by the creation epics of many other prehistoric peoples such as *Enuma Elish* of the Babylonians. Near Eastern peoples believed that our Universe resulted from the injecting of order (*cosmos*) into chaotic primordial beings or matter, 'the primeval emptiness of the Universe', 'the original state of things'. English poet John Milton perpetuated this thesis in his *Paradise Lost* (1667:1.10), describing 'In the Beginning how the Heav'ns and Earth Rose out of chaos'.

The next of our 3 words is therefore *cosmos*. This is a Greek word meaning the idea of order in the Universe, or the ordered or orderly Universe. Cosmos is the opposite of chaos. Cosmos means the intricate and subtle way in which the Universe is put together. In BC 600, a scientific revolution on the Greek island of Samos explained the Universe as Cosmos which arose out of Chaos. This was a new concept in the world of learning, telling mankind that the Universe is knowable. This ordered and admirable character of the Universe was called cosmos. (See historical narrative in C. Sagan, *Cosmos*, 1980).

Not surprisingly, cosmos is a major biblical and Christian concept. It occurs in Genesis 2:1 (LXX), proclaiming that God created not just the visible heaven and earth but also the entire Cosmos. The word also occurs 29 more times in the Greek Old Testament and it occurs 187 times in the Greek New Testament. Its meaning is the same as in classical Greek—the Universe as God's ordered Creation—but with additional insights. First, it is the human race's historical sphere, the context of its social relationships. Second, the Cosmos is to some degree a fallen world, to some extent under the dominion of evil powers and characterized by enmity to God.

### Gospel: good news

The third of our 3 words is *euangelion* (evangel, gospel, glad tidings, good news) which occurs 6 times in the Greek Old Testament and 76 times in the New. It stands for the good news that although chaos continually reenters God's creation, God's redemption and salvation and healing in Christ are available, both for us as individuals and also for societies and populations at large.

A major occasion linking 2 of our key words occurs in the giving of Christ's Great Commission: 'Go to every part of the world (*cosmos*) and proclaim the Good News (*euangelion*) to the whole creation' (Mark 16:15, New English Bible).

***Cosmos, chaos, and gospel***
These 3 terms together, therefore, explain the theme of this chronology. Firstly, out of the chaos of unordered primordial matter, God creates Cosmos, the ordered Universe. Secondly, the cosmos nevertheless reverts to chaos in numerous ways—widespread galactic violence, collisions, and mind-boggling explosions take place from earliest times to the present day; sudden mass extinctions of major species of life on Earth occur with startling regularity and frequency; the human race falls into rebellion against God. Thirdly, Christ becomes incarnate to save the human race from chaos, and his gospel or the good news of deliverance is announced to the world and to the cosmos. Christ founds his church and then wins 8 billion followers into it over 20 centuries. Chaos nevertheless remains widespread. This huge church fails to obey Christ and his Great Commission, Christians selfishly spend 97% of the world's riches on themselves, the world murders 70 million Christians as martyrs over 20 centuries, sin and violence and chaos in the world reach frightening proportions.

These 3 themes—cosmos, chaos, and gospel—permeate the chronology from beginning to end. One cannot understand God's purpose and plan without understanding all three.

***God's mission arises out of God's creation***
Another trilogy of terms describing this drama would be: creation, mission, consummation. We live today in the era of God's global mission, but we cannot understand it fully without first knowing the details of God's prior creation and God's eventual consummation. This is the justification for the detailed treatment of creation in the first 3 pages of this chronology, also for the last 3 or so pages in the future. At first sight these 6 pages look like merely 'secular' material, but on reflection we realize that these past and future events are profoundly religious, even profoundly Christian. They reveal to us fundamental aspects of Christ's preexistence, activity, and purpose.

***Three cosmic eras***
For all these reasons, the chronology is divided into 3 major phases that we call 3 cosmic eras. These are here named: (1) The Prehistory of World Evangelization, (2) World Evangelization in Christian History, and (3) The Futurology of World Evangelization. The first takes us from the Creation to the Incarnation of Christ, the second from the Incarnation through the initial stages of the New Creation in Christ up to the present day, the third from this unfolding New Creation into the future culminating in its final Consummation in Christ.

***The first cosmic era: from Creation to Incarnation***
Cosmic Era I, *The Prehistory of World Evangelization*, begins with God's Creation of the Universe and continues up to the Incarnation of Christ. It details the rise of religion and of God's special revelation as recorded in the Old Testament; it deals with the first creation and what Christians call the First or Older Age. Our own record of this first phase incorporates scientific data and prehistoric scenarios on the origins of the world and of the human race. It also incorporates biblical data from the Old Testament on the origin and development of Heilsgeschichte (salvation history). As we understand it, the scientific data do not contradict the biblical data; rather, they support and supplement them, as well as providing their context.

On the Christian worldview, God created the Universe and has been in control of the entire creation process from remote past to present and on into the remote future. Christians are creationists—that is, they affirm God as Creator. The exact details as to how long ago God created the Universe are understood by Christians in a variety of ways. Some Christians follow the 16th-century archbishop James Ussher, who was the first person to construct a mathematical model of reality and the first person to compile a serious biblical chronology. Using the only evidence available at that time, namely the genealogies in the Book of Genesis, Ussher computed the year of Creation at BC 4004. By AD 1700, scientists faced with mounting geological evidence were reckoning the age of the Earth at 9,000 years, and many Christians today accept their estimated Creation dates of BC 7300, BC 8000, or BC 10,000. These dates all reject biological evolution as a factor in the origin of life.

Other Christians, equally committed to the primacy and plenary inspiration of the Bible, believe that God created the world utilizing the mechanisms that astronomers and paleontologists are now describing for us. For these Christians, the fact that cosmologists and astrophysicists indicate that the original Creation may have taken place from 10 to 20 billion years ago in no way alters the fundamental Christian affirmation that God has always been in full control of the whole process. Instead, it fills out and gives glimpses into the awesome omnipotence, omniscience, and omnipresence of God the Creator.

Each of these scenarios of the Earth's past is noted and incorporated in the chronology. (Note also that in a number places throughout the whole chronology, dates (years) are preceded by a lowercase letter *c*. This stands for 'circa' (approximately) and means the year is an approximate estimate only).

The last part of Cosmic Era I deals with the revelation of God's redemption through Abraham, Moses, and the Old Testament prophets down to the end of the inter-Testamental period. By this time expectation of the coming of God's Messiah and the arrival of the Messianic Age had reached their climax.

***The second cosmic era: from Incarnation to New Creation***
Cosmic Era II, *World Evangelization in Christian History*, deals with the First Advent of Christ the Son of God. It details the history of Christianity and its spread across the ages and across the globe up to the present day. It shows the First or Older Age overlapping with what Christians call the New Creation which is the Last or New Age in Christ. There is a case for holding, as we do here, that the origins of the New Creation go back to the time of Abraham in BC 1950, and that the New Creation then goes on to span both Cosmic Era II and also its consummation either during or at the end of Cosmic Era III.

The chronology illustrates this analysis of Cosmic Era II by listing a selection of the major or more significant events in the origin, growth, and spread of Christianity across 20 centuries and across the 7 continents; in evangelism; and in the evangelization of peoples and nations across the globe, with particular emphasis on statistical enumeration. It sets forth the 10 major epochs or pulsations in Christian history using terminology coined by the historian K.S. Latourette and modified and expanded here; the origin of the 6 major ecclesiastico-cultural megablocs and over 300 ecclesiastical traditions detailed elsewhere in this volume; the founding of Christian work in every continent, nation, country, and territory; the conversion or christianization of whole peoples; notable foreign missionary enterprises to other lands; the founding of major missionary boards, societies, and orders; statistics of Christian expansion; revival and renewal movements; major recessions or setbacks to Christianity, schisms and apostasies; church unions, mass movements into the churches; major international evangelistic campaigns; translations of the Bible into the world's languages; major technical innovations facilitating evangelization; predictions of theologians and churchmen over these 2,000 years concerning the anticipated imminent advent of Christ and also of the Antichrist; background data on science, scientific discoveries, and science fiction of importance and relevance to world evangelization; and other significant events in the history of the spread of Christianity. A majority of these Christian events are noted or further explained in the wider Christian context in the *WCE*'s Country Tables 2 or in the texts on countries in its Part 4 "Countries".

The presentation and language used here are standardized to a large degree. Note in particular that the spelling '1st', '2nd', '3rd', etc refers to the official titles of a series of regular conferences, whereas the spelling 'First', 'Second', 'Third', etc refers to other less structured types of situation.

After the present brief introduction to the chronology, Table 2–1 sets out a comprehensive statistical table showing the numerical expansion of both evangelization (evangelized peoples) and of Christianity (total Christians) across the continents of the world throughout these 20 centuries, at regular intervals through historical time. These statistics are repeated in Cosmic Era II of the chronology at 40 historical turning-points or watersheds at which we summarize the **Global status** (printed in boldface type for quick identification) of Christianity and world evangelization.

The chronology and its format in Cosmic Era II are designed to display with clarity 3 particular emphases: (1) expansion of Christianity over time, i.e. over the whole period of Christian history; (2) expansion in numbers, i.e. the numerical growth of evangelization and of Christians, churches, dioceses, movements, et alia, especially for those many occasions before the year 1800 where detailed statistics were collected; and (3) geographical expansion to all nations and peoples. To give an overview of this latter emphasis (3), Cosmic Era II gives in *italics*, once only, the name of every country in the world (as existing in the year 2000, with names and frontiers as today) with the year when Christianity first reached it and ongoing or definitive evangelization began (i.e. arrival of the first resident Christians or missionaries, excluding any earlier temporary or short visits), giving details in parentheses of the agents involved.

***The third cosmic era: from New Creation to Consummation in Christ***
Cosmic Era III, *The Futurology of World Evangelization*, projects past and present trends into the future and examines alternate futures and possible scenarios. It presents an eschato-scientific overview of the future, in 2 parts.

First, the Christian eschatological schema of the biblical End-time, a major component of every Christian's hopes and prayers, is treated as near or imminent, exactly as it has been treated by Christians of all stripes throughout history (such as John Chrysostom in AD 398 anticipating the end in AD 430 or Luther foreseeing it in AD 1558). For this, no future precise dates are possible nor can any be suggested. No exact apocalyptic timetable can ever be proposed. Christians of all confessions are agreed that the Parousia or Second Advent of Christ could occur today, or tomorrow, or in a year's time, or 100 years, or 1,000 years, or a million years, or a billion years. On this subject, the final word is: 'It is not for you to know times or seasons which the Father has fixed by his own authority' (Acts 1:7, RSV). Nevertheless, it must be included somewhere, and so we locate it in a section at the not-too-distant yet imminent year AD 2049.

Second, the rest of Cosmic Era III consists of a religio-scientific composite scenario of alternative futures, for both secular and religious concerns. It includes both optimum scenarios, and worst-case scenarios. For all of these, numerous future dates suggested by experts are given. The combination describes the future age, the New Age, the last Age, the New Creation as it moves toward its consummation, against the background of the secular world. From our point of view as Christians, these materials help us to view the future and to think out what the meaning is of that central biblical affirmation 'God will sum up all things in Christ'.

The reader who wishes to make sense of the method and the material of this venture into both biblical and secular futures should be sure to read the separate brief explanations given at the beginning of each of these 2 components of Cosmic Era III. The introduction immediately after this title explains the religio-scientific composite scenario. And the introduction immediately after AD 2048 explains the Christian eschatological schema of the End-Time.

Our main approach to futurology is that espoused by the mainline discipline known as futuristics, futurology, future studies, or futures research—forecasting using alternate futures. That is to say, we draw up not one single scenario but a range of scenarios taking into account the various possibilities that might emerge. This forecasting is not the same as prophecy, nor prediction, nor predestination, nor soothsaying, nor divining, nor fortunetelling, nor horoscopy (drawing up horoscopes), nor clairvoyance, nor crystal ball-gazing. (Note, however, that the chronology does include notable cases of both biblical and extrabiblical prophecy and prediction).

As scientifically-oriented mission futurists, then, we are not claiming any special insight into the future. We don't know any better than our non-futurist colleagues what will happen in the future. But we should know better than non-futurists what *could* happen. We are therefore speaking only in terms of probabilities, possibilities, options, and consequences.

## Table 2–1. A statistical overview of world evangelization, AD 33-2000, with its prehistory, history, and future scenarios.

This table serves as a summary and quick-reference lookup table for the major demographic and Christian statistical variables at the major milestones and turning points in the 8,000-entry Chronology.

| Year | GLOBAL POPULATION | | | | GLOBAL CHRISTIANS | | | | | | | | | GLOBAL EVANGELIZED | | | | | |
|---|---|---|---|---|---|---|---|---|---|---|---|---|---|---|---|---|---|---|---|
| | Live population | | All people ever | | Live Christians | | | All Christians ever | | | Martyrs | | | Live evangelized | | | All evangelized ever | | |
| | Total | Increm | Since AD 33 | All Homo | Total | % | Increm Xtns | Total | AD 33 % | % all Homo | Total (ever) | % (ever) | Per year (recent) | Total | % | Increm | Total | AD 33 % | % all Homo |
| *Column 1* | *2* | *3* | *4* | *5* | *6* | *7* | *8* | *9* | *10* | *11* | *12* | *13* | *14* | *15* | *16* | *17* | *18* | *19* | *20* |
| *m=million* | *m* | *m* | *m* | *m* | *m* | *%* | *m* | *m* | *%* | *%* | *m* | *%* | | *m* | *%* | *m* | *m* | *%* | *%* |

**COSMIC ERA I: The prehistory of world evangelization**

| BC | 2 | 3 | 4 | 5 | 6 | 7 | 8 | 9 |
|---|---|---|---|---|---|---|---|---|
| 13 million | **0.1** | | | | | | | |
| 5,500,000 | **0.2** | | | 0 | First hominids | | | |
| 4,500,000 | **0.3** | 10000.0 | | 10000.0 | Origin of genus Homo | | | |
| 1,700,000 | **0.5** | 44800.0 | | 54800.0 | Homo Habilis | | | |
| 500,000 | **0.7** | 28800.0 | | 83600.0 | Homo Erectus | | | |
| 150,000 | **1.4** | 14700.0 | | 98300.0 | Homo Sapiens | | | |
| 100,000 | **1.5** | 2900.0 | | 101200.0 | Homo Sapiens Neanderthalensis | | | |
| 45,000 | **2.0** | 3850.0 | | 105050.0 | | | | |
| 10,000 | **4.0** | 4200.0 | | 109250.0 | | | | |
| 8000 | **5.0** | 360.0 | | 109610.0 | | | | |
| 4000 | **7.0** | 960.0 | | 110570.0 | | | | |
| 2000 | **27.0** | 1360.0 | | 111930.0 | **0.0** | 0.0 | 0.0 | 0.0 |
| 1000 | **50.0** | 1540.0 | | 113470.0 | **0.5** | 1.0 | 10.0 | 10.0 |
| 500 | **100.0** | 1500.0 | | 114970.0 | **0.9** | 0.9 | 14.0 | 24.0 |
| 0 | **165.0** | 2650.0 | | 117620.0 | **2.1** | 1.3 | 30.0 | 54.0 |
| 30 | **169.7** | 200.8 | 0.0 | 117820.8 | **2.3** | 1.4 | 2.6 | 56.6 |

**COSMIC ERA 2: World evangelization in Christian history**

| AD | 2 | 3 | 4 | 5 | 6 | 7 | 8 | 9 | 10 | 11 | 12 | 13 | 14 | 15 | 16 | 17 | 18 | 19 | 20 |
|---|---|---|---|---|---|---|---|---|---|---|---|---|---|---|---|---|---|---|---|
| 33 | **170.7** | 20.4 | 0.0 | 117841.2 | **0.0** | 0.0 | 0.0 | 0.0 | 0.00 | 0.00 | 0.000 | 0.00 | 0 | **0.2** | 0.1 | 0.0 | 0.0 | 0.00 | 0.00 |
| 100 | **179.5** | 469.2 | 469.2 | 118310.5 | **0.8** | 0.4 | 1.1 | 1.1 | 0.23 | 0.00 | 0.053 | 4.94 | 800 | **10.6** | 5.9 | 14.5 | 14.5 | 3.09 | 0.01 |
| 200 | **191.8** | 742.7 | 1211.9 | 119053.2 | **4.7** | 2.4 | 10.9 | 12.0 | 0.99 | 0.01 | 0.177 | 1.47 | 1,200 | **17.8** | 9.3 | 56.7 | 71.2 | 5.88 | 0.06 |
| 300 | **191.9** | 767.5 | 1979.5 | 119820.7 | **14.0** | 7.3 | 37.3 | 49.3 | 2.49 | 0.04 | 0.627 | 1.27 | 4,500 | **32.8** | 17.1 | 101.2 | 172.4 | 8.71 | 0.14 |
| 400 | **188.5** | 760.9 | 2740.3 | 120581.6 | **25.3** | 13.4 | 78.7 | 128.0 | 4.67 | 0.11 | 1.538 | 1.20 | 9,100 | **45.9** | 24.4 | 157.5 | 329.8 | 12.04 | 0.27 |
| 500 | **190.3** | 757.6 | 3498.0 | 121339.2 | **37.8** | 19.9 | 126.2 | 254.2 | 7.27 | 0.21 | 2.102 | 0.83 | 5,600 | **59.4** | 31.2 | 210.6 | 540.5 | 15.45 | 0.45 |
| 600 | **194.0** | 768.6 | 4266.6 | 122107.8 | **40.4** | 20.8 | 156.4 | 410.6 | 9.62 | 0.34 | 2.197 | 0.54 | 1,000 | **64.5** | 33.2 | 247.7 | 788.2 | 18.47 | 0.65 |
| 700 | **204.9** | 797.8 | 5064.3 | 122905.6 | **40.6** | 19.8 | 161.9 | 572.6 | 11.31 | 0.47 | 2.423 | 0.42 | 2,300 | **60.1** | 29.3 | 249.0 | 1037.2 | 20.48 | 0.84 |
| 800 | **217.9** | 845.6 | 5910.0 | 123751.2 | **40.9** | 18.8 | 162.9 | 735.5 | 12.44 | 0.59 | 2.568 | 0.35 | 1,400 | **57.5** | 26.4 | 235.2 | 1272.3 | 21.53 | 1.03 |
| 900 | **238.3** | 912.5 | 6822.4 | 124663.7 | **40.8** | 17.1 | 163.4 | 898.9 | 13.18 | 0.72 | 2.877 | 0.32 | 3,100 | **57.3** | 24.0 | 229.6 | 1501.9 | 22.01 | 1.20 |
| 950 | **250.1** | 488.4 | 7310.9 | 125152.1 | **42.4** | 16.9 | 83.2 | 982.1 | 13.43 | 0.78 | 2.895 | 0.29 | 300 | **57.0** | 22.8 | 114.3 | 1616.2 | 22.11 | 1.29 |
| 1000 | **263.7** | 513.8 | 7824.6 | 125665.9 | **44.7** | 16.9 | 87.1 | 1069.1 | 13.66 | 0.85 | 3.064 | 0.29 | 3,400 | **56.2** | 21.3 | 113.2 | 1729.4 | 22.10 | 1.38 |
| 1100 | **318.4** | 1164.0 | 8988.6 | 126829.9 | **52.0** | 16.3 | 193.3 | 1262.4 | 14.04 | 1.00 | 3.375 | 0.27 | 3,100 | **63.8** | 20.0 | 240.0 | 1969.3 | 21.91 | 1.55 |
| 1200 | **357.4** | 1351.6 | 10340.2 | 128181.5 | **65.7** | 18.4 | 235.3 | 1497.7 | 14.48 | 1.17 | 3.727 | 0.25 | 3,500 | **81.3** | 22.7 | 290.2 | 2259.6 | 21.85 | 1.76 |
| 1300 | **362.1** | 1439.0 | 11779.3 | 129620.5 | **83.9** | 23.2 | 299.2 | 1797.0 | 15.26 | 1.39 | 11.161 | 0.62 | 74,300 | **102.3** | 28.2 | 367.1 | 2626.7 | 22.30 | 2.03 |
| 1350 | **361.0** | 723.1 | 12502.4 | 130343.6 | **86.5** | 24.0 | 170.4 | 1967.3 | 15.74 | 1.51 | 11.814 | 0.60 | 13,100 | **103.2** | 28.6 | 205.4 | 2832.1 | 22.65 | 2.17 |
| 1400 | **352.4** | 713.4 | 13215.8 | 131057.0 | **56.7** | 16.1 | 143.2 | 2110.5 | 15.97 | 1.61 | 16.560 | 0.78 | 94,900 | **66.7** | 18.9 | 169.8 | 3002.0 | 22.71 | 2.29 |
| 1500 | **423.0** | 1550.7 | 14766.5 | 132607.7 | **75.9** | 17.9 | 265.2 | 2375.8 | 16.09 | 1.79 | 17.398 | 0.73 | 8,400 | **86.8** | 20.5 | 306.8 | 3308.8 | 22.41 | 2.50 |
| 1550 | **466.4** | 889.3 | 15655.8 | 133497.0 | **86.9** | 18.6 | 162.8 | 2538.6 | 16.22 | 1.90 | 18.833 | 0.74 | 28,700 | **99.1** | 21.3 | 185.9 | 3494.7 | 22.32 | 2.62 |
| 1600 | **545.9** | 1012.2 | 16668.0 | 134509.3 | **100.4** | 18.4 | 187.4 | 2726.0 | 16.35 | 2.03 | 21.221 | 0.78 | 47,800 | **114.7** | 21.0 | 213.8 | 3708.5 | 22.25 | 2.76 |
| 1650 | **546.7** | 1092.5 | 17760.6 | 135601.8 | **112.8** | 20.6 | 213.3 | 2939.3 | 16.55 | 2.17 | 21.549 | 0.73 | 6,600 | **129.8** | 23.7 | 244.4 | 3952.9 | 22.26 | 2.92 |
| 1700 | **609.8** | 1156.5 | 18917.1 | 136758.3 | **130.1** | 21.3 | 243.0 | 3182.2 | 16.82 | 2.33 | 21.750 | 0.68 | 4,000 | **148.3** | 24.3 | 278.1 | 4230.9 | 22.37 | 3.09 |
| 1750 | **719.2** | 1329.0 | 20246.1 | 138087.3 | **154.7** | 21.5 | 284.8 | 3467.0 | 17.12 | 2.51 | 21.912 | 0.63 | 3,200 | **175.0** | 24.3 | 323.3 | 4554.2 | 22.49 | 3.30 |
| 1800 | **903.7** | 1622.8 | 21868.9 | 139710.2 | **205.0** | 22.7 | 359.7 | 3826.7 | 17.50 | 2.74 | 22.038 | 0.58 | 2,500 | **229.3** | 25.4 | 404.3 | 4958.5 | 22.67 | 3.55 |
| 1815 | **989.0** | 567.8 | 22436.7 | 140278.0 | **229.4** | 23.2 | 130.3 | 3957.0 | 17.64 | 2.82 | 22.065 | 0.56 | 1,800 | **299.7** | 30.3 | 158.7 | 5117.2 | 22.81 | 3.65 |
| 1850 | **1202.9** | 1534.3 | 23971.0 | 141812.3 | **323.9** | 26.9 | 387.3 | 4344.3 | 18.12 | 3.06 | 22.371 | 0.51 | 8,700 | **401.2** | 33.4 | 490.7 | 5607.8 | 23.39 | 3.95 |
| 1900 | **1619.6** | 2822.5 | 26793.5 | 144634.8 | **558.1** | 34.5 | 771.7 | 5116.0 | 19.09 | 3.54 | 24.092 | 0.47 | 34,400 | **740.0** | 45.7 | 998.5 | 6606.4 | 24.66 | 4.57 |
| 1914 | **1870.0** | 879.4 | 27672.9 | 145514.1 | **648.0** | 34.7 | 295.5 | 5411.5 | 19.56 | 3.72 | 24.340 | 0.45 | 17,700 | **920.5** | 49.2 | 406.8 | 7013.2 | 25.34 | 4.82 |
| 1950 | **2521.5** | 2845.7 | 30518.6 | 148359.8 | **856.0** | 33.9 | 947.5 | 6359.1 | 20.84 | 4.29 | 56.065 | 0.88 | 881,200 | **1383.4** | 54.9 | 1451.5 | 8464.6 | 27.74 | 5.71 |
| 1970 | **3696.1** | 2238.4 | 32756.9 | 150598.2 | **1236.4** | 33.5 | 732.3 | 7091.4 | 21.65 | 4.71 | 63.607 | 0.90 | 377,100 | **2054.9** | 55.6 | 1203.4 | 9668.0 | 29.51 | 6.42 |
| 1975 | **4074.7** | 602.2 | 33359.2 | 151200.4 | **1358.8** | 33.3 | 194.6 | 7286.0 | 21.84 | 4.82 | 64.760 | 0.89 | 230,500 | **2355.0** | 57.8 | 330.7 | 9998.8 | 29.97 | 6.61 |
| 1980 | **4440.4** | 596.1 | 33955.2 | 151796.5 | **1475.7** | 33.2 | 191.3 | 7477.3 | 22.02 | 4.93 | 65.869 | 0.88 | 221,800 | **2695.0** | 60.7 | 340.9 | 10339.7 | 30.45 | 6.81 |
| 1985 | **4837.4** | 649.4 | 34604.7 | 152445.9 | **1605.3** | 33.2 | 208.0 | 7685.3 | 22.21 | 5.04 | 66.869 | 0.87 | 200,100 | **3095.0** | 64.0 | 390.8 | 10730.5 | 31.01 | 7.04 |
| 1990 | **5266.4** | 682.0 | 35286.7 | 153127.9 | **1747.5** | 33.2 | 217.9 | 7903.2 | 22.40 | 5.16 | 67.770 | 0.86 | 180,100 | **3601.0** | 68.4 | 435.2 | 11165.7 | 31.64 | 7.29 |
| 1995 | **5666.4** | 683.3 | 35970.0 | 153811.2 | **1877.4** | 33.1 | 217.5 | 8120.7 | 22.58 | 5.28 | 68.621 | 0.85 | 170,300 | **3988.2** | 70.4 | 455.3 | 11621.1 | 32.31 | 7.56 |

**COSMIC ERA III: The futurology of world evangelization**

m=million ($10^6$), b=billion ($10^9$), t=trillion ($10^{12}$), q=quadrillion ($10^{15}$), s=septillion ($10^{24}$), n=nonillion ($10^{30}$), d=decillion ($10^{33}$)

| Year | 2 | 3 | 4 | 5 | 6 | 7 | 8 | 9 | 10 | 11 | 12 | 13 | 14 | 15 | 16 | 17 | 18 | 19 | 20 |
|---|---|---|---|---|---|---|---|---|---|---|---|---|---|---|---|---|---|---|---|
| 2000 | **6055 m** | 703 m | 36673 m | 155 b | **2000 m** | 33.0 | 223 m | 8344 m | 22.75 | 5.40 | 69.421 | 0.83 | 160,000 | **4426 m** | 73.1 | 484 m | 12 b | 33.01 | 7.83 |
| 2025 | **7824 m** | 3470 m | 40143 m | 158 b | **2617 m** | 33.4 | 1096 m | 9440 m | 23.52 | 5.98 | 75 m | 0.79 | 210,000 | **5978 m** | 76.4 | 2471 m | 15 b | 36.31 | 9.23 |
| 2050 | **8909 m** | 3347 m | 43490 m | 161 b | **3052 m** | 34.3 | 1063 m | 11 b | 24.15 | 6.51 | 80 m | 0.76 | 213,200 | **7103 m** | 79.7 | 2453 m | 17 b | 39.16 | 10.56 |
| 2100 | **10 b** | 6181 m | 49671 m | 168 b | **3583 m** | 35.4 | 1990 m | 12 b | 25.15 | 7.46 | 90 m | 0.72 | 200,000 | **8250 m** | 81.6 | 4606 m | 22 b | 43.56 | 12.92 |
| 2200 | **11 b** | 10 b | 60006 m | 178 b | **3844 m** | 36.4 | 3713 m | 16 b | 27.01 | 9.11 | 110 m | 0.68 | 200,000 | **8793 m** | 83.3 | 8521 m | 30 b | 50.26 | 16.96 |
| 2500 | **12 b** | 17 b | 76927 m | 195 b | **5000 m** | 41.7 | 6633 m | 23 b | 29.69 | 11.73 | 170 m | 0.74 | 200,000 | **12 b** | 95.8 | 15 b | 45 b | 58.99 | 23.30 |
| 4000 | **14 b** | 19 b | 96 b | 214 b | **7000 m** | 50.0 | 18 b | 41 b | 42.35 | 19.06 | 470 m | 1.15 | 200,000 | **14 b** | 98.6 | 19 b | 64 b | 66.74 | 30.03 |
| 10,000 | **50 b** | 192 b | 288 b | 406 b | **30 b** | 60.0 | 89 b | 130 b | 44.95 | 31.91 | 1670 m | 1.29 | 200,000 | **49.5 b** | 99.0 | 152 b | 216 b | 74.98 | 53.23 |
| 100,000 | **1 t** | 47 t | 48 t | 48 t | **650 b** | 65.0 | 24 t | 25 t | 51.77 | 51.64 | 20 b | 0.08 | 200,000 | **990 b** | 99.0 | 37 t | 38 t | 79.17 | 78.98 |
| 1 million | **1 q** | 45 q | 45 q | 45 q | **0.7 q** | 70.0 | 25 q | 25 q | 55.99 | 55.99 | 200 b | 0.00 | 200,000 | **990 t** | 99.0 | 40 q | 40 q | 89.09 | 89.09 |
| 4 billion | **1 d** | 20000 d | 20000 d | 20000 d | **0.75 d** | 75.0 | 12000 d | 12000 d | 60.00 | 60.00 | 800 t | 0.00 | 200,000 | **990 n** | 99.0 | 20000 d | 20000 d | 99.00 | 99.00 |

***Notes, assumptions and methodology***

**PHASES.** This table is divided vertically into 3 chronological phases following exactly the 3-phase arrangement of the chronology. Cosmic Era III describes the numerical developments most likely if the Parousia/Eschaton is delayed and if nuclear and cosmic holocausts are avoided.

**SOURCES.** Data come either from the chronology or from other original compilations produced specifically for this analysis of evangelization.

**YEARS.** The first column refers to particular years, either BC (before Christ) or AD (after Christ), covering the entire span of the existence of genus Homo (the human race), from its creation in BC 5,500,000 to its ultimate extinction as described in our chronology under the scenario for AD 4 billion. For queries or further details concerning any particular year, consult first the chronology for that identical year.

**STATISTICS.** The 19 columns of statistics are divided into 3 distinct sections across the page, separated by heavy vertical lines. The first section (columns 2-5) deals with global population since the origin of genus Homo in BC 5,500,000. The second section (columns 6-14) gives global statistics of Christians (followers of Jesus Christ) since AD 33, preceded by a small box giving statistics of the pre-Christian People of God. The third section (columns 15-20) gives global statistics of all persons evangelized by the gospel of Christ since AD 33.

**POPULATIONS.** The 3 columns in bold type (2,6,15) give, for each year shown, live populations (i.e. world or human population alive in that year), live Christians (i.e. Christians alive in that year) and live evangelized (i.e. evangelized persons alive in that year). Total for future years include humans living off-Earth on space colonies. Population projections for the future and megafuture have to balance the possibilities of enormous numerical expansion across the Galaxy and Universe with the possibilities of enormous numerical reduction due to disasters and cataclysms. Our figures here are very conservative, i.e. at the lower end of current forecasts.

**CHRISTIANS.** Enumeration of Christians in the table starts in AD 33. The 2 boxes in the space above the AD 33 line do not refer to Christians: the top box depicts the years of origin of the various Homo species at the time, and the second box gives parallel statistics of the People of God in Old Testament times (the Israelites).

**PERCENTAGES.** Seven columns are percentages (7,10,11,13, 16,19,20). Columns 7 and 16 are % of world population alive at that year; columns 10 and 19 are % total all world population who have ever lived since AD 33; and columns 11 and 20 are % total all persons who have ever lived on Earth, as given in column 5.

**INCREMENTS.** Columns headed 'Increment' (columns 3,8,17) are included to enable the reader to follow the methodology used in computing the following 1, 2 or 3 columns. These figures refer to new persons (new souls) born since the previous line's year. Human birth rate has dropped from around 4% per year in prehistoric times to 3.6% per year for the world's populations from 1900 on (3.5% from 1850 on for Christians, to 2.7% per year by 1980); we estimate it will be 2.0% by 2025, 1.3% by 2100, and so will average 1.5% p.a. from 2000-2200, 1% p.a. after 2200, to 0.1% p.a. after 2500 as longevity turns gradually into immortality. After AD 3000 we can anticipate massive growth and expansion due not only to natural births but far more to artificial births, artificial creations of new human species, mass clonings with geometric progression, genetic multiplications of whole populations and races and worlds,

*Continued overleaf*

Table 2-1—concluded

vast varieties of immortality, and so on. The reader can, of course, supply whatever other assumptions he prefers and work out the corresponding figures. Each figure gives the increment in population, or Christians, or evangelized persons, up to the year indicated (column 1) from the preceding year indicated in column 1.
**POPULATIONS EVER.** Columns 5,9,18 give, for each year shown, the grand totals of, respectively, all persons of genus Homo who have ever lived on Earth and its colonies to date (live and dead), all Christians ever from AD 33 to date (live and dead), and all persons ever evangelized from AD 33 to date (live and dead).
**MARTYRS.** Column 12 gives the total number of martyrs worldwide since AD 33 up to the year shown (source: Part 4 'Martyrology', Tables 4-10. Column 13 gives the same total as a percentage of all Christians ever since AD 33. Column 14 gives the average number of martyrdoms each year based on the recent situation at the dates indicated.
**VERY LARGE NUMBERS.** In Cosmic Era I and Cosmic Era II above, numbers (apart from percentages) are all given as millions, as shown by the abbreviation *m*. In Cosmic Era III, 5 larger measures are used with abbreviations (b,t,q,s,d) as given under Cosmic Era III's title line. The largest, d = decil-

lion, is $10^{33}$ or
1,000,000,000,000,000,000,000,000,000,000,000
(10 followed by 33 zeroes).
**BC 5,500,000.** Origin of human race, genus Homo (see chronology), after 45 billion hominids have lived on Earth.
**AD 30.** Beginning of ministry of Jesus of Nazareth; AD 33, resurrection of Jesus and beginning of Christian church.
**AD 2100.** World population (column 2) estimated by United Nations projections at 10,109 million.
**AD 2200.** Human population could be as low as 2 billion or as high as 1,000 billion (see alternative scenarios in chronology), with 30% living off-Earth on space colonies.
**AD 2500.** Human population 12 billion (or as high as 400 billion) on Earth and a similar number off-Earth on space colonies; or, human population very small because of disastrous wars or cataclysms.
**AD 4000.** Majority of human populations now off-Earth on space colonies.
**AD 10,000.** Homo Sapiens evolves into Homo Noeticus (Intellectual Man). Note that by now the church of Christ has grown to 30 billions.
**AD 100,000.** Homo Superior (Interstellar Man) evolves and

expands rapidly across Solar System, with possible population of the order of 1 quadrillion ($10^{15}$ persons). The scenario envisages at this time a church of 650 billion Christians.
**AD 1 million.** Homo Galacticus evolves and spreads out to populate entire Galaxy, with possible population of the order of 1 septillion ($10^{24}$ persons). 70% are now followers of Christ—a church of 1 septillion members.
**AD 4 billion.** Final age of man as Homo Universalis, able to traverse Galaxy or Universe instantaneously at will; with possible population of the order of 1 decillion ($10^{33}$ ) persons throughout the Universe. Ultimate size of the church of Jesus Christ, on this scenario: 0.75 decillion believers.

An expanded version of the above table for Cosmic Eras II and III is available in the forthcoming CD, *World Christian database*, including the 20 variables, for every year before AD 33 and AD 2200.

We are simply exploring multiple future options and alternatives, in any of which we ourselves can become directly involved if we so wish.

Futurology speaks mainly about corporate life and society. It does also say a great deal about your future life as an individual. But it has clear limits. The United Nations' 2-yearly publication *World population prospects* tells us the probable mortality rate every 5 years up to AD 2025, in every country of the world. It tells you how many people will die in your country in 27 years' time. But it cannot tell you, the reader, what you yourself will be doing in 5 years' time, nor when you will die. Before too long, however, even that may be possible as medical researchers examine your genes in greater depth.

Futurology today has become a professional science which has built up over 150 techniques including the Delphi method. In this, the opinions of a variety of experts on some futurist topic are separately polled and analyzed by computer. It also gives plenty of scope to common sense, group discussion, research, and such activities as 'blue-skying'—the art of conjecture, speculation, thinking and discussing in 'What if. . .' terms on the particular topics we are interested in.

Let us consider a concrete situation in the future, namely: Could the world become fully evangelized by AD 2025 with North American or European foreign missionaries alone accomplishing the task?

First, the futurist considers this future situation and thinks about 3 different kinds of future: (1) the possible future, (2) the probable future, and (3) the preferable future. For each, he then thinks out not just a single future but at least 2 alternate futures.

Regarding (1), one alternate future is that this task would be impossible for North Americans or Europeans alone. The logistics of evangelizing in 13,000 different languages would surely defeat them. At the other extreme, it could be regarded as *possible* that North Americans or Europeans might finish the task alone but only if certain conditions were met. Thinking it over, the futurist would write down the conditions: there would have to be greatly increased missionary enthusiasm in North America or Europe, continued expanding financial and logistical support from the churches, continued tolerance of their missionaries abroad, continued permission from non-Christian governments for them to reside in their countries, and a number of technological breakthroughs in communication in those 13,000 languages.

Regarding (2), this AD 2025 goal may well be possible but not *probable*; In 1986, 67 countries were known to be closed to resident foreign missions, and this total was increasing by 3 more countries every year. Suddenly, from 1989 onwards, the former Communist countries almost all not only became fully open to the gospel but also invited Western foreign mission agencies back to reside and work in their countries. The pendulum may swing back before long, missionaries may be expelled, and countries may become closed once more. Whenever the residence barrier appears overcome, the goal might then become *probable*; otherwise, it seems improbable.

Regarding (3), even if the AD 2025 goal were both possible and probable, it might still not be *preferable*. Such an important task should not be left to only one part of the Christian church. It would be much better if foreign missionaries from Third-World countries and former Communist countries also had their

full share in the implementing of world mission and in completing world evangelization.

This latter aspect of futurology emphasizes that the future is not predestined or deterministic; to a considerable degree, we can control the future. We can create a better world if we have the will and make the effort.

There is a distinction, too, between 2 equally important types of scientific conjecture or science forecasting: (a) scientific probabilistic predictions, and (b) science fiction. Examples of the former are an astronomer's forecast that our Sun has 8 billion more years of life left, or the incredibly detailed scenarios that cosmologists now think probable for the end of our Universe's life (described here for the dates between AD 8 billion and AD $10^{100}$ years).

A brilliant example of this thinking is the best-selling cosmological heavyweight *A brief history of time: from the Big Bang to black holes* (1987) by physicist Stephen Hawking, holder of Isaac Newton's chair of mathematics at Cambridge University. This gives detailed scenarios to AD $10^{30}$ . By contrast, science fiction is less concerned with probable futures and more concerned with speculating about possible futures. The first science fiction narrative that has survived was penned in BC 414 by the Greek dramatist Aristophanes, who was also the first known writer to use the Greek word *euangelizesthai* (evangelize). Many Christians down the ages have written noteworthy science fiction; today, many of its writers are physicists, or astronomers, or other scientists; several are even Nobel laureates. Science fiction has been called 'the most significant literature of our day', even 'the whole worthwhile literature of the 20th century'. This genre of literature helps to stimulate people's imagination concerning the future, and so a large number of the more outstanding works are included in the present chronology.

Note that the chronology includes at least one entry for every individual year from AD 1830-2030. Also, for the period 1960-2000, within each year many conferences, and events are given their exact month and even days or dates, in which case they are arranged in the main chronologically within that year. Other undated entries are also arranged approximately chronologically within their years. However, the major ordering principle within each year is not strictly chronological but is thematic. First come overall or global entries and totals, next a selection of the year's major Christian events in order of significance (from the overall standpoint of the present volume), and then any secular events relevant to the fortunes of Christianity and religions. Last follow a handful of the year's more significant bibliographical events (new book titles published).

In this third Era of the chronology the reader is referred to Global Diagrams 70-73 near the end of Part 1 "GeoStatus". These diagrams set out the patterns of fission and fusion which have characterized Christianity over its 20 centuries of history, and then set out 4 scenarios concerning its likely or possible development in the future.

### 7-phase typologies of Creation
There are many ways in which the data in this chronology could be divided up or classified into categories. Cosmic Era II does this by dividing the history of the Christian church into 9 epochs based on the ebb and flow of the fortunes of Christianity. In the

same way, the entire chronology, which is the story of Creation itself—past, present, and future—can also be divided and classified in this manner.

As with any research situation, we can clarify our thinking by asking the 7 basic questions concerning the situation: What? When? Where? How? Whence? Whither? Why? If people are involved, we can ask a further question: Who?

Our chronology aids this process of understanding by incorporating 3 interestingly parallel ways of classifying the entire creation process. These are set out below. Further details on these phases or levels can be found in the chronology under the dates or references given below in parentheses.

(a) *Seven Days of Creation.* From the perspective of biblical revelation, the Book of Genesis, chapter 1, speaks of God's creative acts under the category of 7 Days (or eras, or epochs, of indeterminate length). On these Days God created the following (referenced here not by chronological dates but by verses in Genesis 1 and 2):
   1. Light (Genesis 1:3-4).
   2. Firmament, heaven, atmosphere, waters (Genesis 1:6-8).
   3. Dry land, seas, plants, vegetation, fruits (Genesis 1:9-13).
   4. Sun, Moon, stars (Genesis 1:14-16).
   5. Living creatures, fish, birds, reptiles (Genesis 1:20-23).
   6. Land animals, insects, domestic animals, mankind (Genesis 1:24-27).
   7. Sabbath rest (Genesis 2:2).

(b) *Seven Stages of Creation.* Modern science recognizes a number of stages in which differing material was created or began after the Big Bang, as follows:
   1. Energy, matter, antimatter, atoms, particles (BC 15 billion).
   2. Light, quasars, galaxies, stars, dark matter (BC 15 billion).
   3. Solar System, planets, Earth, Moon (BC 5 billion).
   4. Life on earth: algae, bacteria (BC 3.5 billion).
   5. Species: 500 million varieties (BC 400 million).
   6. Mind: the human race (BC 5.5 million).
   7. Community, history, culture, philosophy, art, religion (BC 5 million to 500,000).

(c) *Seven Levels of Evolution.* Protagonists of evolution—whether evolution by a host of miniscule steps or evolution by a few massive quantum leaps—speak of 7 levels of evolution beginning at the dates shown in parentheses:
   1. Energy (BC 15 billion).
   2. Matter (BC 15 billion).
   3. Life (BC 3.5 billion).
   4. Mind (BC 5.5 million).
   5. Supermind (AD 2030).
   6. Galactic Mind (AD 500 million).
   7. Cosmic Mind (AD 5 billion): universal consciousness.

These 3 schemes cannot yet be equated or combined. Each is looking at Creation from a differing standpoint. But the idea of a 7-fold progress in God's creative activity is common to all three. They provide a striking indication of the value of these differing standpoints.

### Sources
Over 90 percent of the 8,000 entries in this chronol-

ogy have sizeable bibliographical support in the literature. They are therefore not speculative, nor unverifiable; they are adequately documented and based on acceptable and accepted evidence. For each there is at least one reference, usually a significant book or article documenting its validity. And for a large number of entries, each is supported by a bibliography of 10, 20, 50, even 100 items.

So, for example, the 2 sections at the end of Cosmic Era II headed 'Status of the Cosmos in AD 2000' and 'Status of the Globe in AD 2000' give the best thinking of experts, and the most accurate data currently available, on a whole variety of subjects impinging on global mission and world evangelization. These 2 sections do not incorporate futures thinking; they deal with the actual, factual situation today, with the latest available statistics. The fact that we here have no room to document the precise sources in detail should not be allowed to undermine their credibility.

In the same way, this formidable documentary support is true even of apparently legendary, controversial, or speculative material. Consider the legend of the lost continent of Atlantis (see BC 12,000, 10,500, 9350). Some Christians regard it as the site of the original Garden of Eden. The story of Atlantis has been supported since Plato in BC 390 by a vast corpus of literature. Up to the present day, this now totals over 5,000 books, of which some 4,000 review the evidence and argue the case for Atlantis' authenticity.

Likewise, consider the medieval Christian prophet,

Nostradamus. He was the most widely read seer of the Renaissance. In 1547 he produced a volume of End-time prophecies which have been continuously in print ever since up to the present day. That work stands second only to the Bible in the vast number of translations, commentaries, and analyses it has generated over the centuries.

It is the same with a majority of the entries dealing with the future. Many future items reported here under Cosmic Era III as only a 2-line or 3-line mini-scenario are in fact based each on a sizeable book or published article which develops the scenario in full.

In this compilation we list sources, in or after each entry, only in a handful of cases where we judge it especially important to do so. These include Genesis chapter 1 and other major biblical references, a small number of especially significant books, a few science fiction classics, and some of the major volumes that trace the development of the concept of evangelization.

### A computerized database

The chronology has been developed on computer media for a variety of other uses in addition to this printed book version. Its database version will be found on the related CD, *World Christian database*. With this version, words, phrases, names, persons, subjects, themes can all be tracked, traced, displayed on screen, then printed out through global search options. Each entry is described by geographical, political ecclesiastical, confessional, demographic, statis-

tical, and other indicators so that one can examine reduced or specialized versions of the entries on any subject. All entries are also related to the other 30 or more databases dealing with the global status of Christianity in the context of 10,000 religions, 7 continents, 238 countries, 7,000 large metropolises, 13,500 languages, 12,600 ethnolinguistic peoples, 24,000 Christian parachurch agencies, and 33,800 Christian denominations.

The uses of this material are thus limited only by the imagination and creativity of the user. From these data he or she can create statistical totals, statistical tables, statistical analyses of trends over time. He or she can generate multicolored graphics or maps. He or she can project them directly from a computer screen to a large wall screen at the moment they are created. He or she can animate them. And the end product is: greater insight into the whole incredible story of world evangelization.

### Conclusion

Such, then, is the drama of the Creation—the past, present, and future activity of God the Creator. This is the drama, too, of the ever-present threat of chaos. And this is the drama of the gospel, the good news that Jesus Christ is, in the final analysis, in control of the entire process. The kingdom of God has arrived yesterday, is arriving today, and will arrive tomorrow. Toward that goal all peoples of the world are invited to follow as disciples of Christ.

## BIBLIOGRAPHY

*30 days to understanding church history*. M. E. Anders & J. Lunsford. Brentwood, TN: Wolgemuth & Hyatt, 1991. 324p.

*A concise history of the Catholic Church*. T. Bokenkotter. Rev. ed. New York: Doubleday, 1990. 508p.

*A history of Christian missions*. S. C. Neill. *The Pelican history of the Church*, vol. 6. New York: Penguin, 1964. 624p.

*A history of Christianity*. K. S. Latourette. London: Eyre and Spottiswoode Ltd.; New York: Harper and Row, 1953. 2 vols, 1544p. (A classic of missions history.).

*A history of Christianity in Asia*. S. H. Moffett. New York: Harper-Collins, 1991. 3 vols.

*A history of the Christian movement: the development of Christian institutions*. A. D. Frankforter. Chicago: Nelson-Hall, 1978. 329p.

*Acts of faith: explaining the human side of religion*. R. Stark & R. Finke. Berkeley, CA: University of California, 2000. 343p.

*An endless line of splendor: revivals and their leaders from the Great Awakening to the present*. E. E. Cairns. Wheaton, IL: Tyndale House, 1986. 373p.

*Augustus to Constantine: the thrust of the Christian movement in the Roman world*. R. M. Grant. New York: Harper & Row, 1970. 348p.

*Beyond the Big Bang: quantum cosmologies and God*. W. B. Drees. La Salle, IL: Open Court, 1990.

*Byzantium: church, society, and civilization seen through contemporary eyes*. D. J. Geanakoplos. Chicago: University of Chicago Press, 1984. 525p.

*Catastrophe: a quest for the origins of the modern world*. D. Keys. New York: Ballantine, 2000. 343p.

*Charismatic experiences in history*. C. M. Robeck Jr (ed). Peabody, MA: Hendrickson Publishing, 1985. 186p.

*Christendom and Christianity in the Middle Ages: the relations between religion, church, and society*. A. H. Bredero. Grand Rapids, MI: Eerdmans, 1994. 402p.

*Christian mission in the twentieth century*. T. Yates. Cambridge: University Press, 1994. 275p.

*Christian monasticism*. D. Knowles. *World university library*. New York: McGraw-Hill, 1969. 256p.

*Christianity and Western thought: a history of philosophers, ideas & movements*. C. Brown. Downers Grove, IL: Inter-Varsity Press, 1990–. 2 vols.

*Christianity and history*. H. Butterfield. 1949; reprint, London:

Collins, 1957. 189p.

*Christianity in a revolutionary age: a history of Christianity in the 19th and 20th centuries*. K. S. Latourette. *Contemporary Evangelical perspectives*. 1961; Grand Rapids, MI: Zondervan, 1969. 5 vols.

*Christianity through the ages*. K. S. Latourette. New York: Harper & Row, 1965. 321p.

*Christianizing the Roman empire (A.D. 100–400)*. R. MacMullen. New Haven, CT: Yale University Press, 1984. 191p.

*Cosmos, bios, theos: scientists reflect on science, God, and the origins of the Universe, life, and Homo Sapiens*. H. Margenau & R. A. Varghese,eds. La Salle, IL: Open Court, 1992. 285p.

*Cosmos, chaos, and the world to come: the ancient roots of apocalyptic faith*. N. R. C. Cohn. New Haven: Yale University Press, 1993. 271 p.

*Cosmos as Creation: theology and science in consonance*. T. Peters (ed). Nashville, TN: Abingdon, 1989. 288p.

*Dates with destiny: the 100 most important dates in church history*. A. K. Curtis, J. S. Lang & R. Petersen. Tarrytown, NY: Revell, 1991. 208p.

*From Nicaea to Chalcedon: a guide to the literature and its background*. F. Young. Philadelphia: Fortress Press, 1983. 416p.

*How the Irish saved civilization: the untold story of Ireland's heroic role from the fall of Rome to the rise of medieval Europe*. T. Cahill. New York: Doubleday, 1995. 256p.

*Imperial unity and Christian divisions: the Church 450–680 A.D.* J. Meyendorff. *The Church in history*, vol. 2. Crestwood, NY: St. Vladimir's Seminary Press, 1989. 418p.

*In the beginning God: modern science and the Christian doctrine of creation*. J. D. Weaver. Regent's Park College, Oxford. 1994.

*Introduction to the history of Christianity*. T. Dowley (ed). Minneapolis, MN: Fortress Press, 1995. 688p. (Illustrated).

*Jesus through the centuries: his place in the history of culture*. J. Pelikan. New York: Harper & Row, 1987. 288p.

*Just six numbers: the deep forces that shape the Universe*. M. Rees. Weidenfeld & Nicolson, 1999. 173p.

*Modern Christian movements*. J. T. McNeill. Philadelphia: Westminster Press, 1954. 197p.

*Patterns in history: a Christian perspective on historical thought*. D. Bebbington. 1979; Grand Rapids, MI: Baker, 1990. 233p.

*The Christian East and the rise of the papacy: the Church 1071–1453 A.D.* A. Papadakis & J. Meyendorff. *The Church*

*in history*, vol. 4. Crestwood, NY: St. Vladimir's Seminary Press, 1994. 434p.

*The Christian tradition: a history of the development of doctrine*. J. Pelikan. Chicago: University of Chicago Press, 1971–1989. 5 vols.

*The Church in history*. J. E. Booty. *The Church's teaching series*, no. 3. New York: Seabury Press, 1979. 311p.

*The evangelization of the Roman empire*. E. G. Hinson. Macon, GA: Mercer University Press, 1981. 332p.

*The excellent empire: the fall of Rome and the triumph of the Church*. J. Pelikan. San Francisco: Harper & Row, 1987. 147p.

*The historical road of Eastern Orthodoxy*. A. Schmemann. Crestwood, NY: St. Vladimir's Seminary Press, 1992. 351p.

*The history of statistics: the measurement of uncertainty before 1900*. S. M. Stigler. Cambridge, MA: Belknap/Harvard, 1986.

*The holy fire: the story of the fathers of the Eastern Church*. R. Payne. Crestwood, NY: St. Vladimir's Seminary Press, 1980. 326p.

*The Jewish & Christian world: 200 B.C. to A.D. 200*. A. R. C. Leaney. *Cambridge commentaries on writings of the Jewish and Christian world: 200 B.C. to A.D. 200*, vol. 7. London: Cambridge University Press, 1984. 259p.

*The measure of reality: quantification and Western society, 1250-1600*. A. W. Crosby. Cambridge University Press, 1997.

*The Orthodox Church in the Byzantine Empire*. J. M. Hussey. *Oxford history of the Christian Church*. Oxford, UK: Clarendon Press, 1986. 428p.

*The rise of Christianity*. W. H. C. Frend. Philadelphia: Fortress Press, 1984. 1040p.

*The Scientific American book of the cosmos*. D. H. Levy, ed. New York: St. Martin's Press, 2000.

*The ten decisive battles of Christianity*. F. S. Mead. New York: Grosset & Dunlap, 1936. 151p.

*The universal history of numbers: from prehistory to the invention of the computer*. G. Ifrah. Paris: Laffont, 1981. 634p.

*The whole shebang: a state of the Universe(s) report*. T. Ferris. New York: Touchstone, 1997. 393p.

*Two kingdoms: the Church and culture through the ages*. R. G. Clouse, R. V. Pierard & E. M. Yamauchi. Chicago: Moody Press, 1993. 672p.

# COSMIC ERA I

## *The prehistory of world evangelization*

A Christian interpretation

### GOD'S ETERNAL PRE-EXISTENCE (successive bounce)

God All-Powerful exists in eternity, self-existent, self-sufficient, eternal, unchangeable, source of all reality.

Uncreated, eternal existence of Triune God: Theos, Logos, Pneuma; a community of love.

### GOD CREATES ENTIRE UNIVERSES EX NIHILO

Oscillating universe scenario: before creation of our Universe, several successive small cosmic explosions (Small Bangs) occur, each leading to a larger universe with short but progressively longer life; each short cycle so far has collapsed before life can evolve, and hence next new bang occurs. (Landsberg-Park model).

Before our Universe, God creates $10^{89}$ quite distinct parallel bubble universes existing simultaneously elsewhere, being self-contained universes expanding at the speed of light within the largely empty Multiverse, about which nothing is known. (D. Bohn, *Wholeness and the implicate order*, 1990).

### GOD CREATES COSMOS OUT OF CHAOS

15 billion  Zero of cosmic time: creation of Universe in primordial monobloc with explosion and universal fireball (the Big Bang theory), continuously evolving and expanding; physically 9-dimensional (according to superstring theory) although only 3 dimensions develop significantly. (Genesis 1:1).

### GOD CREATES SPACE-TIME, ENERGY, MATTER

15 billion  Universe created as a singularity, a primeval submicroscopic proto-quark—a small unimaginably-dense searingly-hot ball of pure energy—containing all of space, with infinitesimal amount of combined matter/force at a temperature of $10^{29}$ degrees Kelvin, and initially expanding relatively slowly.

15 billion  After first millisecond from Big Bang, total darkness prevails throughout Universe for next 300,000 years before light bursts forth.

15 billion  Universe passes rapidly from perfect simplicity of superunification through the following 7 eras or stages (freezings or decouplings or separations of matter and force, providing more and more differentiation) after moment of Creation, spewing radiation.

### GOD CREATES THE 4 FUNDAMENTAL FORCES

15 billion  Stage 1: Supersymmetry Era, before $10^{-43}$ seconds (=Planck time), with one kind of superparticle or basic building block (quark), and one unified force (gravitational-strong-electroweak).

15 billion  Stage 2: GUT (grand unified theory) Era, up to $10^{-35}$ seconds (temperature $10^{27}$ degrees K), with gravity now separated from the GUT strong/electroweak force.

### GOD CREATES ANTIGRAVITY

15 billion  Latent everywhere throughout empty space, God creates antigravity (repulsive gravitational force, or vacuum energy), a bizarre and exotic form of energy that repels gravity at 120 orders of magnitude larger than all energy in matter.

### GOD CREATES VIRTUAL PARTICLES

15 billion  Throughout empty space God creates a whole spectrum of virtual particles spontaneously popping in and out of existence for infinitesimally short fractions of time.

15 billion  Stage 3: Electroweak Era, in 2 parts: (a) New Inflation, a titanic explosion (=the actual Big Bang itself) in which grand unified symmetry breaks and temporarily negative gravity (antigravity) rips apart the primeval proto-quark, which at this point is $10^{-23}$ cms in size, 10 kilos in mass; from $10^{-35}$ to $10^{-32}$ seconds, Universe suddenly inflates, doubling with superexplosive force every $10^{-34}$ seconds, up to a sphere 10 cms across weighing $10^{100}$ pounds, containing entire future Universe including the future 4 forces, thus finally producing order (cosmos) out of primordial chaos.

15 billion  In Stage 3 part (b), Electroweak Era continues from $10^{-32}$ to $10^{-10}$ seconds, freezing or decou-

---

pling the single GUT unified force into strong (nuclear) force and electroweak force; Higgs field condenses into matter and energy with microscopic ripples or lumpiness.

15 billion  Stage 4: Quark Era, from $10^{-10}$ seconds (temperature 1 trillion degrees K) to $10^{-3}$ seconds, after last unified force (electroweak) decouples and freezes into electromagnetic force and weak force; the 4 strong (nuclear), electromagnetic, weak (radioactive), gravity, producing order out of primeval chaos; quarks (first form of matter) annihilate antiquarks, at temperatures progressively below 1 trillion degrees K.

### GOD CREATES ANTIMATTER, PARTICLES, PLASMA

15 billion  Stage 5: Particle Era, from 1 millisecond to 3 minutes, with formation of protons, neutrons, electrons, positrons, photons, neutrinos, and hundreds of other types of elementary particles and antiparticles, all these freezing out of the sea of hot quarks; there is now a preponderance of matter over antimatter in the Universe.

15 billion  Stage 6: Plasma Era, from 3 minutes (at temperature of 1 billion degrees K) to 100,000 years, nucleogenesis (freezing or formation of plasma and nuclei from protons and neutrons), with multiple matter/antimatter annihilations up to final one (electrons/positrons) 13 minutes after Big Bang, producing massive amounts of heat and microwave radiation.

15 billion  For its first 100,000 years, the incandescent Universe has been radiation-dominated (First Level of Evolution: energy); it now becomes matter-dominated (Second Level of Evolution: matter), with total of $10^{80}$ elementary particles (protons, neutrons, electrons, but no atoms yet) in entire Universe; radiation and matter now become decoupled, their densities equal; background temperature 5,000 degrees K.

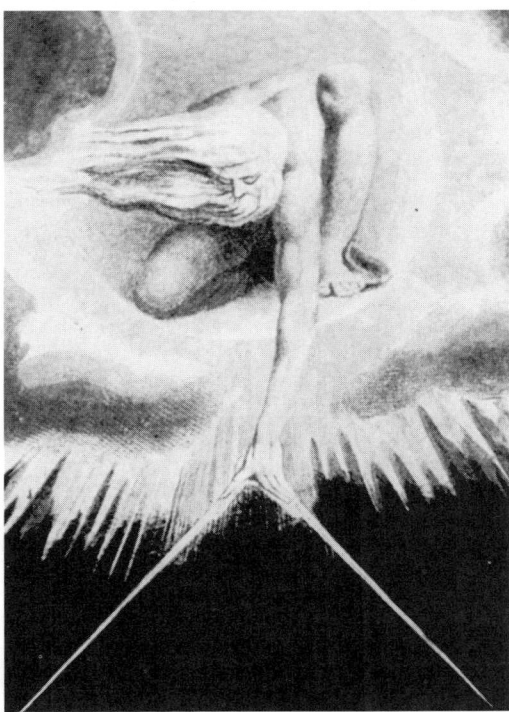

**BC 15 billion.** God All-Powerful creates light as the Universe develops (W. Blake, AD 1790).

### GOD CREATES LIGHT, ATOMS, MICROWAVES

15 billion  Stage 7: Atomic Era begins, at 300,000 years, 3,000 degrees K, with Universe one thousandth its present size: in a final freezing (termed recombination), hot expanding plasma with nuclei and free electrons freezes into hydrogen atoms, with massive release of microwave radiation and light as Universe's current era begins. (Genesis 1:3).

15 billion  Since the Big Bang, total opaqueness/darkness has prevailed throughout Universe for first 300,000 years until light bursts forth as Universe suddenly becomes transparent and all microwave background radiation (light with

---

longer wavelength) becomes visible as swaths of gargantuan cosmic clouds.

15 billion  By a million years after Big Bang, enormous clouds of hydrogen (75% of Universe) and helium (25%) form, later condensing into long spaghetti-like filaments each up to a billion light-years long.

### GOD CREATES GALAXIES AND STARS

14.9 billion  100 million years after Big Bang, protogalaxies and giant protostars (1st-generation stars) begin to form, most spinning or rotating; temperature of Universe has fallen to 100 degrees K.

14.5 billion  Formation of first galaxies as gas filling Universe fragments, eventually producing over 100 billion galaxies, all receding from each other, each containing from 1 million to 1,000 billion stars (grand total $10^{22}$ stars, shining because of nuclear fusion at 10 million degrees K) and vast pools of superheated gas up to 100 million degrees K, also each with a huge black hole at its center; by 20th century AD, 99% of Universe consists of holes or empty bubbles (spherical voids with walls on average 400 million light-years across and empty of galaxies), with vast metagalaxies and over 3,000 clusters and superclusters of galaxies (lengthiest being 1 billion light-years long) around their edges; widespread galactic violence, close encounters, collisions, explosions, cannibalism, and chaos.

### GOD CREATES EXPLODING EXPANSION

14.5 billion  Galaxies now seen to be racing away from each other as Universe expands, initially expanding slowly but then gradually accelerating (in accordance with non-zero value for Einstein's cosmological constant) to ever-increasing explosive speeds.

### GOD CREATES DARK MATTER, BLACK HOLES

14.5 billion  Luminous matter thus created amounts to 10% of Universe's total mass; 30% continues as cold dark matter (invisible, nonluminous) of several sorts, consisting of either a multitude of black holes, or cosmic strings, or a vast sea of subatomic particles (neutrinos, axions, photinos, or wimps) filling the whole Universe; and 60% exists throughout empty space as vacuum energy.

### GOD CREATES OUR ISLAND UNIVERSE

14.1 billion  Most large galaxies (including supergiant elliptical galaxies or cannibal galaxies each with up to 100 trillion stars and each a million light-years across, each always in center of large cluster of galaxies) are born in first billion years after Big Bang, when volume of Universe was only 1% of today's volume, hence more crowded; small galaxies (1 billion stars each) and dwarf galaxies (1 million stars each) continue to be born over next 14 billion years.

14.0 billion  Emergence of our Galaxy (Milky Way), 100,000 light-years in diameter, situated within our Local Group or cluster of 21 galaxies (12 being ellipticals, rest spiral or irregular), positioned a third the way along a gigantic filament of galaxies a billion light-years long; and shining 100 times brighter than at present; this Group is one of countless clusters being pulled (streaming at 1.3 million miles an hour) toward the Great Attractor, a vast supercluster of 100,000 galaxies with $10^{15}$ stars 150 million light-years from Earth in an area 300 million light-years across. (Genesis 1:3).

### GOD CREATES QUASARS, GIANTS, DWARFS

13.5 billion  Eruption of a billion blazing quasars (quasi-stellar radio sources, fountains of energy): early in their lives, stupendously colliding protogalaxies or young galaxies create massive central black holes, each squeezing its small rotating disc (only 20 billion kms across) into a white-hot gargantuan emitter of huge quantities of light, ultraviolet light, radio waves, X-rays and gamma rays, which then evolve over next billion years into dead quasars (vast black holes); sometimes dead quasars are rekindled by galactic collisions; meanwhile, younger quasars erupt in newer galaxies over next 3 billion years; 2% of all galaxies have similar violent nuclei. (Genesis 1:3).

10.0 billion  Immense globular clusters of stars arise across Universe; continuous cycles of star birth and death begin.

9.5 billion  First massive stars in our Galaxy emerge as globular clusters eventually totaling 200 billion stars or solar masses (15% being white dwarfs and 1% red giants), 70% of which are binary pairs, and 10% of which later develop planets capable of supporting life: BC 7.7 billion, highly evolved stars emerge. (Genesis 1:16).

## GOD CREATES SUPERNOVAS, HEAVY ELEMENTS

7.5 billion  Origin of all heavy elements as first-generation giant stars explode as supernovas, supplying raw materials of planetary systems and also cosmic rays which power all evolutionary processes.

6.0 billion  As Universe enters middle-age period, its expansion continues, early violence dies down, elliptical galaxies become cosmic graveyards; from ashes of dying stars, 2nd and 3rd generation stars rich with new chemical elements emerge.

## GOD CREATES SUN, SOLAR SYSTEM, EARTH

5.0 billion  After nearby supernova explosion within Galaxy, our Sun (a 3rd generation star) and our Solar System (20 billion kms across) are created, with 9 major planets and their 32 satellites, 1,700 minor planets (1-km-size asteroids), several thousand comets, altogether 40,000 planets of all sizes; Sun rotates once round galactic center 10 kiloparsecs (33,000 light-years) away, every 250 million years. (Genesis 1:1,14-19).

4.6 billion  Formation of Earth (and Moon) by condensation of hot gases, cold interstellar dust and rocks; in geological time, known as Pre-Cambrian Era up to BC 543 million, with 3 Periods: Azoic (Non-Life), Archeozoic (Primitive Life), Proterozoic (Early Life).

4.4 billion  Earth's oceans come into existence. (Genesis 1:10).

3.6 billion  After 1.1 billion years of high-frequency bombardment of Earth by planetesimals from 2 to 20 miles diameter, frequency falls sharply to present level of one impact by extrasolar or galactic planetesimal of 3 miles diameter every 14 million years, and/or one of 10 miles diameter every 100 million years; these approximately mark ends of subsequent geological periods.

## GOD CREATES LIFE ON EARTH

3.5 billion  Life arises on Earth: first living organisms are free-living viroids; small, simple cells related to algae or bacteria, producing oxygen through photosynthesis (the major energy source for all life subsequently); remaining unchanged for 2.9 billion years; atmosphere largely carbon dioxide, methane and ammonia. (Third Level of Evolution: life).

3.5 billion  Interstellar origin of life hypothesis: virtual uniformity of genetic code in all known forms of life is explained by either (a) Earth seeded with spores dispatched in interstellar spaceship from earlier civilization, or (b) Earth continuously bombarded with cosmic genes directed by a higher intelligence. (Biologist F. Crick, astronomer F. Hoyle, 1985).

3.4 billion  Oldest known fossil traces of living matter: microfossils of blue-green algae (now with 25,000 species) and bacteria; BC 2 billion, oldest fossils of single-cell myxobacteria (active social microorganisms, working as communities of microbes).

3.0 billion  First multicellular organisms evolve on Earth; meanwhile sister planet Venus suffers runaway greenhouse effect.

2.0 billion  Multicelled plants appear and flourish in seas on Earth; development of sexual reproduction by simple cells together with scheduled or programmed death as essential for improving life by evolution. (Genesis 1:11).

1.2 billion  Origin of animal evolution by genetic changes over next 200 million years resulting in multiple phyla, grazing on plankton, though without leaving fossils until BC 545 million (Cambrian explosion of lifeforms).

1.0 billion  Proterozoic Period: sponges appear (5,000 species).

800 million  Free oxygen accumulates on Earth as algae metabolize carbon dioxide.

660 million  Earliest widespread glaciation (ice age) in Precambrian/Infra-Cambrian time, followed in BC 280 million by Permo-Carboniferous ice age, then BC 2.5 million by Pleistocene ice age multimillion year periodicity due to Solar System entering massive belt of galactic dust.

## CHAOS RETURNS: MASS EXTINCTIONS

650 million  First of 27 sudden mass extinctions of life on Earth (Great Dyings), occurring every 28 million years, selectively destroying species; mass extinction of algae in world's oceans (also in BC 450 million), causing many shell-covered marine animals to become extinct;

algae recover after 100 million years; other extinctions in 510 million (trilobites), 365m, 290m, 250m (marine, land vertebrates), 243m, 225m, 215m (placodonts), 208m, 194m (clams), 175m, 163m, 144m (ammonites), 115m, 91m (sea urchins), 65m (dinosaurs), 38m (protozoa), 14m, 11m (mollusks); cause seen as bombardments of Earth by comets in Oort cloud of 100 billion comets surrounding Solar System as Sun's dim companion star Nemesis approaches every 26 million years; or, more simply, arising naturally from intrinsic instability of whole evolving system.

563 million  Vendian Period, a 20-million year gap in fossil record due to sudden disappearance of placid predator-free existence on ocean floor populated by vendobionts (evolutionary dead ends) and frond-shape organisms; first signs of predation and predators appear.

550 million  Major ice age at end of Proterozoic Era as planet's vast accumulation of decaying organic matter becomes buried under silt, cooling Earth and spreading oxygen; after infra-Cambrian Ice age, many others follow including in BC 280 million.

545 million  Lower Paleozoic Era, up to BC 395 million, with 3 Periods: Cambrian, Ordovician, Silurian; first invertebrates; marine animals with hard parts (shells, carapaces) appear, making possible their survival as fossils.

543 million  Biological Big Bang as 33-million-year Cambrian Period begins with globe-wide earthquakes and vast ice ages infusing primordial oceans with oxygen: sudden explosion of biological diversity around the world in an instant of geologic time (5 million years) with creation of multicellular ancestors of all phyla/branches of entire animal kingdom insects/fish/amphibians/animals/mammals/birds.

**BC 540 million.** Fossil shells of trilobites who range the oceans as predators hunting in packs (each with 800 microscopic lenses in 2 eyes).

540 million  Sudden, enormous proliferation in oceans of new multicelled organisms and great numbers of forms of life; vision with primitive eye-spots develops into image-forming eyes independently in marine worms, mollusks, and vertebrates; first arthropods appear (trilobites, each equipped with a pair of compound eyes), hunting in packs on ocean floor.

510 million  Cambrian disaster: sudden mass extinction of many species of segmented creatures (trilobites) which have dominated seas.

450 million  Age of Fishes (first of the 5 vertebrates): jawless fish appear, also first land plants. (Genesis 1:20).

410 million  Jawed vertebrates (fishes) appear, also first land animals. (Genesis 1:1).

## GOD CREATES 500 MILLION LIVING SPECIES

400 million  Dry land colonized on Earth; first of several hundred million distinct species arise (in sudden evolutionary bursts), 98% of which later become extinct with only 2% surviving until modern era (8 million species today); also early seed plants. (Genesis 1:24-25).

395 million  Upper Paleozoic Era, up to BC 225 million, with 4 Periods: Devonian, Lower Carboniferous, Upper Carboniferous, Permian.

395 million  Insects (Hexapoda) appear, later in up to 5 million species (in class Insecta); insects proceed to dominate Earth for next 400 millennia.

375 million  Sharks appear, in Middle Devonian Period (Genesis 1:21).

365 million  Late Devonian cataclysm: comet and/or asteroid strikes (in areas of Sweden and Quebec) wipe out 70% of all marine species on Earth.

345 million  Age of Amphibians (2nd of 5 vertebrates): at start of Carboniferous Period, first land vertebrates evolve from lobe-finned fishes; all meat-eating (no herbivores yet).

300 million  Origin of shelled egg as method of reproduction among first reptiles, ensuring survival in drier climates.

280 million  Permian Period, lasting 55 million years; climate becomes drier, swamps disappear; first major spread of true land-living animals (reptiles).

260 million  First plant-eaters appear; large paramammals (primitive mammal-like cold-blooded reptiles) spread across globe and dominate Earth for over 70 million years.

250 million  Permian cataclysm in Siberia, biggest and deadliest extinction of life ever: massive 1-million-

year volcanic eruption floods Siberia with mile-deep basalt lava (one cubic mile every day), killing 90% of all marine species on Earth, 70% of all land vertebrates, and most terrestrial plant life.

230 million  Warm-blooded mammals appear (with high metabolic rate).

225 million  Massive, severe and widespread extinction of most of Earth's 350,000 species (mostly marine creatures) at end of Permian Period.

225 million  Age of Reptiles (3rd of 5 vertebrates), found on all continents including Antarctica: Mesozoic Era, up to BC 65 million, with 3 Periods: Triassic (BC 225-190 million), Jurassic (BC 190-136 million), Cretaceous (BC 136-65 million); first lizards and flying animals. (Genesis 1:20,24).

215 million  Sudden mass extinction of placodont species, et alia.

200 million  Age of Dinosaurs: Euparkeria and later first true dinosaur Ornithosuchus and other intelligent bipedal (two-legged) carnosaurs (flesh-eaters) destroy all paramammals by BC 190 million, remain active for further 125 million years; herbivores also in every part of world, until sudden extinction of all dinosaurs.

195 million  Whole of globe's landmass, previously in contact as single supercontinent Pangaia, begins to break up into Laurasia (in north) and Gondwanaland (in south); land-dwelling vertebrates flourish in all areas; BC 40 million, South America splits from Africa, North America from Eurasia.

194 million  Sudden mass extinction of clam species, inter alia.

190 million  Jurassic Period, lasting 54 million years; sauropods (giant plant-eating dinosaurs) evolve, to a maximum weight of 100 tonnes (Brachiosaurus); also modern bony fishes arise.

175 million  Jurassic sudden mass extinctions of species; also again in 163 million.

150 million  First bird, Archaeopteryx, evolves from coelurosaurs (small dinosaurs).

144 million  Sudden mass extinction of ammonite species, inter alia.

136 million  Age of Birds (4th of 5 vertebrates): Cretaceous Period; birds radiate out into new environments; first flowering plants emerge.

120 million  Evolution of first hadrosaurs (duck-billed dinosaurs), most successful and advanced of all dinosaurs; 35 distinct species; lasted 40 million years.

115 million  Cretaceous sudden mass extinction of species.

100 million  Continents of North America, South America, Africa and Europe begin splitting apart; total sauropod population now 40,000; first snakes (pythons) emerge, in Africa.

91 million  Sudden mass extinction of sea urchin species, inter alia.

70 million  Order of primates (social animals to high degree, and largely vegetarian, giving birth to their young singly) abandon ground living and take to insect-eating tree life in vast dense tropical forests of Africa and Eurasia, evolving over next 60 million years; BC 42 million, first higher primate Amphipithecus (near ape) arises in Asia and Africa as ancestor of all monkeys, apes and humans.

**BC 65 million.** The Great Extinction as a massive asteroid strikes Yucatan, wiping out dinosaurs.

65 million Earth suddenly reverses polarity of its magnetic field.

65 million Cretaceous-Tertiary boundary event, the Great Extinction, causing sudden disappearance and total extinction, without further trace, of all dinosaurs, pterosaurs and marine reptiles (after 6,440,000 generations averaging 25 years each), with 96% of Earth's entire species; probably due to giant asteroid or comet colliding with Earth (forming 110-mile-diameter crater on Mexico's Yucatan peninsula), or to deadly radiation from a supernova; all mammals however survive, due to smaller size, so stage cleared for their evolution.

65 million New Age of Mammals (5th of 5 vertebrates): Cenozoic Era, Tertiary Period, for 62.5 million years.

65 million Paleocene Epoch, till BC 54 million; at least 60 genera of primates known.

50 million South America and India still islands, but moving towards their present-day positions.

50 million Explosive evolutionary growth of the brain and cortex, with rapid and dramatic changes over next 50 million years.

40 million Anthropoids (Anthropoidea suborder): monkeys and anthropoid apes evolve from prosimians, in New World first then in Old; fruit-eating, requiring stereoscopic color vision.

38 million Sudden mass extinction of one-cell protozoa species, et alia.

38 million Oligocene Epoch begins, lasting 12 million years.

30 million Hominoids (Hominoidea superfamily): apes (pongids, known collectively with later hominids as hominoids) evolve from monkeys: BC 28 million, Aegyptopithecus (Egyptian Ape).

27 million Climates over most of Earth become markedly seasonal; tropical belt shrinks towards equator.

26 million Miocene Epoch, lasting 19 million years; over 50 primate species in 20 genera.

20 million Dryopithecus (Woodland Ape): dryopithecines evolve, primitive ape-like animals inhabiting dense forests of East Africa (then an island) in vast numbers.

17 million Africa and Eurasia, isolated by shallow seas, become linked by land; various species pass from one continent to the other, resulting in explosion of evolutionary changes.

16 million World's climate begins to cool markedly, and its widespread huge tropical forests begin steady shrinkage, resulting in major pressures on dense-forest dryopithecines which become replaced by open-woodland ramapithecines.

## GOD CREATES MAN

14 million Hominoids begin to split into 2 quite separate lines: anthropoid-ape line (Pongidae family) and hominid (human) line (Hominidae family).

13 million First Ice Ages begin, with large glaciers covering Arctic and Antarctica.

13 million First hominid (partly upright hominoid), the genus Ramapithecus (smallest of the ramapithecines) in Rift Valley, East Africa (hence originally termed Kenyapithecus), last common ancestor of apes and man; world population of these ancestral hominids then lengthening of period of childhood dependence due to increasing brain size.

11 million Sudden mass extinction of marine protozoans and mollusk species, inter alia.

10 million Asian apes (orang-utan, gibbon, siamang) split off from hominid line.

8,000,000 First Ramapithecine hominid with occasional upright posture, located in South Asia (Siwalik Hills, India).

8,000,000 The 'Fossil Void' in human prehistory: major gap of 3 million years in fossil record, disappearance of Ramapithecus and complete absence of hominid fossils up to BC 5 million.

7,000,000 Pliocene Epoch, lasting till BC 2,500,000.

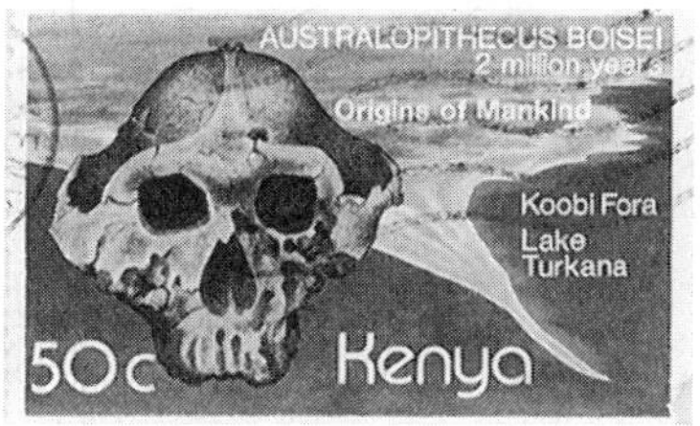


**BC 13 million.** Origins of mankind as God creates first hominids.

7,000,000 African apes (chimpanzee with 400 cc brain size, gorilla with 500 cc) split off from hominids, leaving the latter then located only in Africa.

6,000,000 Ramapithecus diversifies into 3 different lines (genera) as environmental changes form new habitats: Australopithecus Africanus (Gracile Southern Ape), Australopithecus Boisei (Robust Southern Ape), and by BC 5,500,000, genus Homo (Man).

6,000,000 Over 90% of all known animal species become extinct by time of genus Homo.

5,500,000 Total hominid population born since ancestral hominid in BC 13 million: 45 billion.

## GOD CREATES MIND: HUMAN RACE EMERGES

5,500,000 Genus Homo: hominid brain size increases from earlier level of 400 cc to 700 cc, often regarded as the threshold of humanness; origin of Homo line, located only in Africa (original Garden of Eden, Genesis 2:8) due to ecologically unique opportunities centering on change from forests to savanna, not by gradual evolving but in a dynamic state of evolution by series of relatively sudden quantum leaps (Fourth Level of Evolution: mind, i.e. self-reflective consciousness). (Genesis 1:26-27, 2:7).

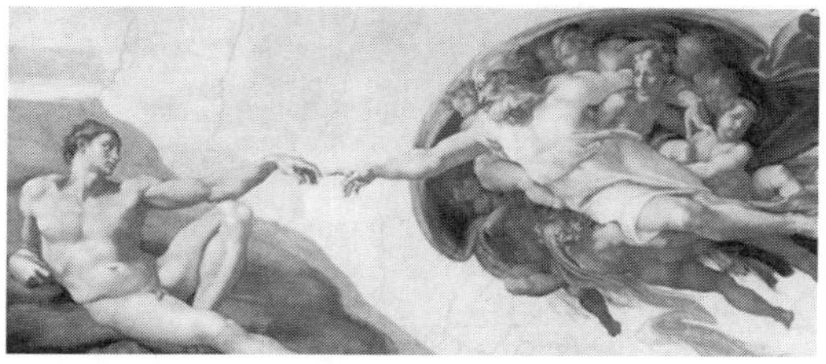

**BC 5,500,000.** Creation of Man (as portrayed by Michelangelo): God creates the human race.

5,500,000 Origin of noosphere (intellectual envelope over the Earth, the thinking layer of cultural heritage) out of biosphere (life without reflective thought); due to reflective man's sudden creation in one generation, 'he was suddenly there', appearing simultaneously at numerous points along a subtropical zone of Earth; the first inhabitants of the noosphere, the starting point of Point Omega (Teilhard de Chardin).

## GOD CREATES COMMUNITY, LANGUAGE, CULTURE

5,500,000 Australopithecus Afarensis, earliest ape ancestor of man; BC 3 million, Australopithecus Africanus; BC 2 million Australopithecus Robustus, and Australopithecus Boisei; then BC 1,900,000, Homo Habilis; BC 1,600,000, Homo Erectus; finally BC 350,000, Homo Sapiens with complex social organization.

5,500,000 Rise of nomadic hunting-and-gathering mixed economy among Homo species in Africa, resulting in bands of 20-100 (averaging 25) members, establishment of base camps, food-sharing, division of labor (males hunting for meat, females gathering plants and rearing children), transportation of items in carrier bags, and ensuing cooperation.

## GOD REVEALS SELF AS PERSONAL

5,499,000 Origin of awareness of God, primitive worship, and prehistoric religion, the latter then a primordial monotheistic revelation of God, later degenerating into polytheism and animism.

5,490,000 Commission given by God to mankind: 'Be fruitful and multiply and fill the Earth' (Genesis 1:28); first foreshadowing of the later Great Commission.

5,480,000 First of 7 Biblical Dispensations covering human history: Innocence (Age of Adam and Eve) (Genesis 1:28), Conscience/Moral Responsibility (Genesis 3:7), Human Government (Genesis 8:15), Promise (Genesis 12:1), Law (Exodus 19:1), Church (Acts 2:1), Kingdom (Revelation 20:4). (Scofield Reference Bible, 1909).

4,500,000 Homo Habilis (Handy Man, Artisan Man) arises, with brain size of 750 cc and world population of 300,000 human hominids, all in Africa; emergence of first gestural language (with 700,000 distinct gestures possible).

4,400,000 First of God's 8 Covenants with man: Edenic Covenant, followed later by Adamic, Noahic, Abrahamic, Mosaic, Palestinian, Davidic, and New Covenant. (Scofield Reference Bible).

4,200,000 Origin of hominid habitual bipedalism (upright posture, walking and gait), the major step in human evolution, involving enormous anatomical change.

4,000,000 Australopithecus (Southern Ape-Man: bipedal vegetarian ape-men with 450 cc brain size) flourishes side-by-side with Homo Habilis, and Ramapithecus remnants, in Africa until extinction by BC 1,000,000, leaving only one hominid species on earth: meat-eating (30% of diet) hunter-gatherer socially-cohesive Homo, living only in Africa.

### *Origin of human culture: emergence of language and symbols*

3,500,000 Emergence of spoken language (slow and clumsy rudimentary verbal communication) on part of Homo Habilis and other hominids, due to primates reaching out to inspect and analyze their 3-dimensional color world; emergence of symbols.

## FALL OF MAN — 1: POLYTHEISM ARISES

3,400,000 Origin of evil, on Judaeo-Christian worldview: Satan, the Adversary or Devil, an alien personal force in Universe, is cast down on Earth, attempts to destroy human reliance on God.

3,300,000 Earth starts getting colder; BC 2,400,000, glaciation begins; BC 1,500,000, sheets of ice cover parts of continents until BC 8000.

3,000,000 Original monotheism, with right relations between God, man and whole creation, gradually degenerates into polytheism, animism, animatism, spirit-worship, shamanism, and religious chaos. (Genesis 3).

2,500,000 Quaternary Period (Age of Man) begins; Pleistocene Epoch (Later Ice Age), up to BC 8000.

2,400,000 First crude stone tools made and used, enabling hominids to eat meat from large animals; also origin of use of fire, cooking of food at campsites and family hearths (no trace of any human artifact in the archeological and fossil records before this date); Paleolithic culture (Old Stone Age), until BC 10,000.

2,300,000 Asteroid fragment 0.3 miles across Strikes Earth in southeast Pacific at 45,000 mph with force of 10,000 megatons; dense debris clouds accelerate glaciation.

2,200,000 Origin of organized, planned, large-scale big-game hunting by Homo bands.

2,100,000 Separate continents of North and South America begin to link up.

2,000,000 Global climate changes to cooler and drier conditions, enabling new species to emerge.

2,000,000 Increasing brain power in Homo species, from Homo Habilis (cranial capacity now 800 cc) to Homo Erectus (over 1000 cc); new cultures emerge every 500,000 years.

1,800,000 Stone artifacts created for first time by hominids, in northern India.

1,750,000 Homo Erectus (Primitive Man, formerly termed Pithecanthropus, meat-eating [30% of diet] protohumans), with brain size increasing from 900 cc to 1100 cc over next one million years and world population of 500,000 human hominids increasing to 700,000 by BC 500,000; species represents a major quantum jump in culture, mental intelligence and self-awareness; species ends in BC 300,000 with 135 billion hominids and humans of all kinds having lived, most within Africa.

1,500,000 Acheulean tool technology (teardrop-shaped hand axes, larger tools, cleavers) arises with basic design persisting until BC 200,000 in Africa and BC 100,000 in Europe.

1,100,000 Major collision of Earth with planetesimal.

1,000,000 First large-scale human migration: small nomadic groups of black (dark-skinned) Homo Erectus move slowly (20 kilometres per generation,i.e. from Nairobi to Peking in 12,000 years) from Africa into Europe and Asia (but not America or Australia), changing from tropical to temperate-climate dwellers, thus becoming first Homo humans to exist outside Africa; due to ability to transport 4-fold commodities of food/water/fire/experience (via language).

1,000,000 First use of naturally-produced fire (evidenced by thoroughly burned blackened bones found in South Africa).

800,000 Beginnings of organized ritual among hunting Homo Erectus populations from Africa to China (art, symbolism, body-ochre, burial and other rites, et alia).

600,000 Rise among Homo Erectus of organized, specialized, hunting way of life, characterized by large-scale hunts of animals large and small, systematic and controlled use of fire, controlled and patterned stone-tool manufacture, and continual geographical expansion into completely new regions.

### *Origin of Homo Sapiens*

500,000 Total human population born since origin of genus Homo in BC 5,500,000: 83.6 billion.

500,000 Emergence, at numerous different centers, of new species Homo Sapiens, intelligent, self-aware, socially-aware, strongly cooperative, sharing, with extensive cultural traditions.

500,000 During periodic Ice Ages, 95% of all Homo Sapiens population and ancestors located in Africa, with only 5% in Eurasia.

500,000 Stone hand axes made in northern India.

470,000 Hominids active in Tamil Nadu and Punjab.

436,000 Creation of world according to later Babylonian priest Berossus (BC 290).

360,000 Fire is first controlled by Homo Erectus in China.

300,000 First surviving non-utilitarian object (engraved art), found in France.

200,000 Complex Middle Stone Age technology emerges first in Africa (in Europe, BC 100,000), lasts until BC 35,000.

150,000 Regional forms of Homo species arise: Homo Sapiens Neanderthalensis (Neanderthal Man) in ice-gripped Europe and Near East, divided into many distinct tribes and cultures, with life expectancy 29 years); and Homo Sapiens Soloensis in Southeast Asia; most with large brain size of 1500 cc, sophisticated spoken languages, within world Homo Sapiens population of 1.4 million; both have disappeared by BC 33,000.

150,000 Artificial fire in use, made by humans by friction; first in South Africa, then China.

100,000 Great majority (90%) of Homo Sapiens world population of 1.5 million still located in Africa; differentiation into sub-species (human races) under way.

### Organized religion spreads

100,000 Organized religion now widespread: Mousterian industries flourish, accompanied by widespread signs of burials, grave offerings and cult objects.

c78,000 A disintegrating planetary civilization beyond Andromeda galaxy, 80,000 light-years from Earth, transmits intergalactic frantic plea for help as devastation spreads. (Claimed as received by Soviet astronomers in AD 1984.)

75,000 Last ice age begins; human population now is 1.7 million.

70,000 Final Ice Age begins, lasts 60,000 years until ice sheets begin shrinking in BC 15,000 and finally retreat by BC 8000.

c70,000 Rational thinking begins.

60,000 Origins of herbal medicine, among Homo Sapiens Neanderthalensis; shamanistic ceremonial in burials at Shanidar, Iraq.

48,000 Origins of earliest prehistoric civilizations including Atlantis and Lemuria, and the traditionally-first Cainitic urban civilization (with first city, Enoch) founded by Cain (Genesis 4:17); later these disappear and become lost without trace.

### Origins of futurism emerge

47,000 Origins of futurism begun with emergence of divination, by medium or oracle or augurs, in order to learn of future events.

45,000 Final evolution of anatomically modern people/human beings, well differentiated into human races.

## FALL OF MAN — 2: OWNING DISPLACES SHARING

45,000 Homo Sapiens Sapiens (Modern Man), with brain size averaging 1360 cc, emerges as the first fully modern man, with modern language capacity, same anatomy and intelligence as present-day humans; much more elaborate and complex social systems than hitherto; systematic control of vast game herds by manipulation and corraling; animal husbandry and domestication of horses and reindeer; together with use of symbolism, art (cave painting, carving and engraving), and ritual; new cultures emerge every 5,000 years.

44,000 After mastery of marine navigation, migrants from southeast Asia settle in Australia and Pacific islands.

40,000 All continents have almost reached their present-day geographical positions.

38,000 Colonizing of the Americas: first wave of Homo Sapiens immigrants enter North America from Eurasia via land bridge across Bering Straits, following herds of prey animals; second wave in BC 16,000.

35,000 Upper Paleolithic period begins, called Later Stone Age in Africa.

33,000 Cro-Magnon Man, discovered in Dordogne (France), oldest known fossil representative of Homo Sapiens Sapiens; possibly refugees over Atlantic land bridge from series of floods destroying earliest Atlantean civilization; rapid advances in hunting technology and culture; BC 28,000, first known musical instrument (bone flute, in France); BC 21,000, bone sewing needles, cold-weather clothes; BC 15,000, deadly spear-throwers; necklaces, jewelry.

32,000 Age of Art: emergence and rapid development of Ice Age prehistoric art, technology and creativity; intensive artistic activity mainly magic or hunting portrayals of animals in action, or of pregnant women (fertility rites); Venus figurines found across swath from western to central Europe; for 25,000 years until sudden total disappearance of art in BC 8000.

30,000 Horses domesticated and ridden by humans.

25,000 First of several massive waves of advanced cultural immigration into Europe from the west (of Cro-Magnon or Aurignacian culture), coinciding with series of cataclysms overwhelming Atlantean civilization due to rising sea levels; later waves BC 14,000 (Magdalenian culture, with well-formed tribal and religious organization) and BC 9350 (Azilian culture).

25,000 Early trading networks among humans arise; beginnings of social-status hierarchy in hunter-gatherer communities.

23,000 Primitive bow and arrow invented.

21,000 Populations of (a) north China and (b) south China/Indochina become sufficiently differentiated to be designated respectively Mongoloid and Oceanic Negroid.

20,000 First beginnings of pastoral nomadism (herding), with herds of animals owned by groups of humans and driven in cyclic migrations.

---

18,000 Northern Amerindians reach Central and South America.

17,000 Homo Sapiens migrates from Eurasia to colonize Australia, venturing 60 miles across Timor Straits in dugout canoes.

16,000 Maximum spread of ice sheets across globe, lowering sea level by 400 feet, exposing Beringia land bridge from Asia to North America, also Atlantic land bridge; BC 15,000 shrinking begins, sea levels rise; BC 8000, last glaciers retreat and melt.

15,500 First localized beginnings of agriculture, in Zagros Mountains, Near East, though widespread agricultural revolution does not follow until 8 millennia later; nomadic life gradually gives way to settled existence and claims to private ownership of land.

c15,000 Spear-throwing device invented.

c14,000 Legendary Hyborian age flourishes; millennia later as continent of Atlantis begins sinking, Conan the Cimmerian founds civilization of Aquilonia. (R.E. Howard, 1930 series of novels).

14,000 Japan: Pre-Jomon Ceramic culture; c12,000 Early Jomon; c4500 Mid- Jomon culture to BC 250; nomads, hunting and fishing, pottery.

13,000 Pacific Ocean port of Tihuanaco (Bolivia), with massive stone buildings, suddenly destroyed by being thrust up to 13,000 feet altitude in seismic upheaval accompanying melting of Ice Age glaciers.

c13,000 China: first cultivated or domesticated plants (millet, soybeans, later rice).

12,000 Climax of prehistoric art: cave paintings at Lascaux (southwest France), Altamira (Spain).

12,000 Global civilization allegedly flourishes on lost continent of Lemuria in mid-Pacific.

c12,000 Legendary antediluvian continent of Atlantis flourishes in Golden Age (in some accounts, colonized by extraterrestrials from outer space) as world's first global supercivilization (original Garden of Eden, Gardens of Hesperides, Elysian Fields, Paradise) and founder of all others: Egyptian, Sumerian, Akkadian, Lemurian, Hyperborean, Mayan, Aztecan, etc.; rise of human governments. (Total book titles on Atlantis: 5,000).

## FALL OF MAN — 3: WEALTH BRINGS CONFLICT

11,000 East Africa (Nairobi): first evidence of domesticated cattle; origin of cattle pastoralism.

11,000 Woolly mammoths, hunted by Stone Age man, suddenly disappear and become extinct.

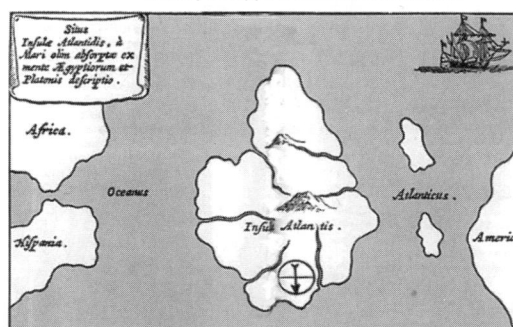

**BC 10,500.** Volcanic Island of Atlantis: *top*, in AD 1678 map; *bottom*, before destruction.

10,500 Heyday of Atlantean world empire: population of 64 million; elephants, prehistoric monsters; golden-roofed stone cities with capital Cerne, ports, harbours, docks, vast network of canals; temple of Poseidon representing Cosmos, and Sun-worship as its original religion; armies of 1,250,000 men, navy of 1,200 ships; global commerce; first alphabet, ancient written laws; advanced mathematics and scientific knowledge including use of laser crystals, mass communication, land/air/undersea transportation; but eventually moral decline, materialism, perversion, torture, slavery and degeneration.

10,000 Formation of 5 modern human races completed after lengthy evolution: Australoid, Capoid, Caucasoid, Mongoloid, Negroid (or Congoid).

---

10,000 Post-glacial spread of wild cereal grains permits their storage and hence sedentary village life.

10,000 Last ice age ends; human population 4 million, with India 100,000.

9800 Mesolithic (Final Upper Paleolithic) Period and cultures (Middle Stone Age arts and artifacts) beginning in northwestern Europe and Near East, up to BC 2700; final phase of hunting and intensified food-gathering, using a new technological advance, bows and arrows.

9350 Civilization of Atlantis destroyed by a universal catastrophe, last of series of global Deluges (the Flood, or series of continental Floods) as volcanic upheavals and melting glaciers and ice-caps raise global ocean levels by 500 feet, engulfing thousands of and Atlantean colonies across the world; remnants today Atlantic Ridge with Azores as its mountain tops.

9200 Near East: domesticated sheep appear.

### Birth of permanent cities, agriculture, and sedentary cultures

9000 Proto-Neolithic phase: origins of several highly-sophisticated civilizations in Near East in Anatolia; Neolithic Revolution, from food gathering to food producing; human dwellings evolve from caves to houses in neatly-constructed villages.

8900 World's first permanent city: sudden growth and explosive expansion of Jericho, to a population of 3,000, after introduction of cultivation techniques of wheat and barley; as commercial enterprise and trade (salt, sulphur) lead to wealth, city is fortified and surrounded by massive wall for flood protection; occupied for next 7,000 years until destruction.

c8500 Accumulation of wealth (money, possessions, land, herds, property, buildings, business deals) begins: acquisitiveness and demonic power of money (cattle, in Latin pecus, used at first) denounced as root of all evils, since accumulation is mainly at the expense of others; world becomes permanently polarized into powerful rich at one extreme and powerless poor at the other.

8000 Holocene (Recent) Epoch in geological history begins, up to present day; from standpoint of human history also called the Historical Period (begun 100 centuries ago).

8000 Viet Nam pre-Neolithic Hoabinhian culture of Bac Son: domestication of buffalo, cultivation of rice.

8000 Earliest date for creation of world, according to creationist theology (as expounded in 20th-century AD North America).

c8000 Agricultural Revolution (widespread and virtually instantaneous discovery and adoption of farming, wheat and barley crops, food production and food conservation), first in Near East (Anatolia, Fertile Crescent), then independently by BC 7000 in Europe, BC 5000 in northeast China and in Meso-America; diffused across world at rate of one kilometre per year; partially caused by end of Ice Ages and massive climatic change.

c8000 Three foundations of civilization now laid: (1) discovery of agriculture, (2) animal domestication and stock-breeding, and (3) fertility-rite cult of Mother Goddess as supreme deity.

c8000 Agriculture leads from nomadic life to sedentary existence, claims to private ownership of lands and permanent ongoing conflicts, also to rapid growth of world population (then 5 million), and to rise and nurture of concentrated population centers, with development of complex division of labor.

c8000 China: first villages with pottery, in central interior.

## FALL OF MAN — 4: WARFARE, HUMAN SACRIFICE

c7000 First vestiges of Indus valley civilization, which flourishes for 5,000 years until BC 2000; BC 4000, rise of Vedism; BC 2500, Mohenjo Daro and Harappa built as Indus valley's largest cities; Indus valley script similar to that of Easter Island, in Pacific.

7000 Neolithic Age (New Stone Age cultures): farming and stock-breeding well-established; rise of leisure, luxury items, cemeteries, trade, complex religious ideas, ancestor and fertility cults, arts and artifacts; first pottery (earthenware), in Anatolia.

7000 Rise of organized warfare as social and political response to changed economic in wake of Agricultural Revolution due to ownership of land; Age of Confrontation in art, with portrayals of fights, disputes, aggression, fighting, confrontation, wars, killings, human sacrifice, chaos.

7000 Mummification of human corpses originates, in Chile and Peru.

c6500 Earliest known calendar is made of bone by primitive man in Zaire, with markings on bone used to record months and moon phases.

6500 First large ships appear, in eastern Mediterranean and on river Nile.

6500 Rig Veda composition of early Vedic hymns.

6000 Siva worship exists in Indus Valley civilization (Proto-Dravidian).

c5800 First use of metals: copper, lead, gold; later, weapons and tools; 3200, international trade using gold and silver.

5600 Chalcolithic period: Early 5600-5000, Middle 5000-4000, Late 4000-3500.

5500 Signs of folk Saktism in India.

5000 Development of temple towns, concurrent with human sacrifice, inflicted death, and religiously-related warfare; rise of city-states, specialized

trades and industries.
5000 Use of explosives known in India; BC 221, Carthaginian general Hannibal uses explosives against Rome; AD 673, Byzantine Greeks use 'Greek fire' to destroy Arab fleet.
c5000 Central America: riverine villages with rudimentary agriculture begin in Maya lowlands.
5000 World population reaches 5 million, doubling every 1,000 years.
4600 Rudiments of Chinese logographic system of writing formed; widespread by BC 2000; Chinese literature begins BC c1400.
c4500 Mesopotamia: origin of polytheism in Sumerian pantheon of city gods; 4400, Ubaid culture in southern Mesopotamia leads by BC 3100 into Sumerian civilization (world's oldest urban literate culture); numerous cities, with monumental mud-brick temples as representations of the Cosmos.
c4500 Sumerians write on clay tablets using pictographs.
4236 Egyptians adopt solar calendar, first use of hieroglyphics; copper and glass introduced; first nation to develop culture, and first to leave traditions to posterity; 4000, earliest known numerals.
4100 Silver in use in royal courts and tombs.
4004 Date of Creation of world (at 9am on Sunday 23 October) as computed from book of Genesis by Irish archbishop James Ussher of Armagh (AD 1581-1656; first person to construct a mathematical model to describe reality, and first serious biblical chronology).
4000 Noah, told by God to build an ark, attempts to warn his generation until it becomes too late (Genesis 6).
4000 The biblical Flood (Deluge; Genesis 6-8): many massive local floods overwhelm Ur and lower Mesopotamia; Noah survives, with sons Japheth (father of Indo-European peoples), Ham (Canaan and African peoples); similar Flood tradition held by 90 other peoples worldwide including Babylonians, Assyrians, Persians, Egyptians, Greeks, Italians, Aztecs, Mayas, Incas, Mixtecs, Zapotecs, and many others on 6 continents.
c4000 Formal records begin (administration, storage, history), including first Table of Nations, or petty states (later recorded in Genesis 10, et alia).
4000 Concept of chaos (primordial darkness, sea, desert, disorder) arises in all Indo-Aryan religions; 3300, concept of cosmos (order, the ordered universe: *ma'at*, *rita*) arises in Egyptian and Indo-Aryan religions resulting from creation by demiurge (Ra, Ptah); c3100, concept of chaos-monster arises in all Middle Eastern/European religions, under variety of 20 or more names: Angra Mainyu (Ahriman), Anzu (Zu), Apaosha, Apophis (Apep), Apsu, Dragon, Hrungnir, Leviathan, Midgard, Mot, Nun, Rahab, Tiamat, Vritra, Yam.
4000 Earliest roots of Vedism (Hinduism), in Iran and in Indus valley civilization; 2500, Aryan fire-sacrifice cult in Iran; 2000, Aryans begin migration to India; 1500, origin of Vedas in archaic Sanskrit; Hindu religion regards Cosmos as undergoing infinite number of deaths and rebirths, with a day and night of Brahma being 8.64 billion years long.
c4000 Earliest known numerals in Egypt.
4000 India population one million.

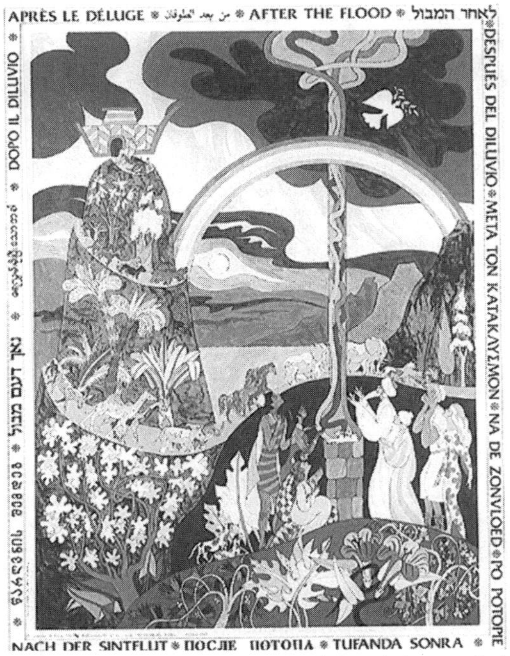
APRÈS LE DÉLUGE * من بعد الطوفان * AFTER THE FLOOD * לאחר המבול
DESPUES DEL DILUVIO * META TON KATAKΛYΣMON * NA DE ZONVLOED * PO POTOPIE
NACH DER SINTFLUT * ПОСЛЕ ПОТОПА * TUFANDA SONRA
DOPO IL DILUVIO
**BC 3998** After the Great Flood, God renews His Commission to mankind: "Fill the earth."

3998 Second foreshadowing of later Great Commission, by God to Noah after the Flood: 'Be fruitful and multiply, and fill the earth' (Genesis 9:1, RSV).
3928 On July 25th occurs earliest eclipse mentioned in *Rig Veda*.
3800 Origin of counting and censuses, in Mesopotamia: systems of revenue control involving enumeration of persons capable of paying taxes; earliest mathematical calculations.
3700 Invention of wheel in Near East; BC 3000, wooden disc wheels on axles in use in Sumeria; BC 2000, spoked wheels on chariots in Syria and Egypt; BC 500 used by Celts in Europe.
c3500 Two-wheeled war chariots in use in Mesopotamia.
c3500 Needs of agriculture and business in Egypt, Mesopotamia, India, and China give rise to primitive numerical systems.
c3500 Sumerian cities of Ur, Eridu, Lagash, Erech, Kish, Nippur, and Larsa are built and becoming thriving commercial centers; these city-states soon begin to expand their control into surrounding countryside; Sumerian pantheon: supreme god An lord of the sky (=Accadian Anu), and creator Enlil lord of Earth, god Enki (Ea), sun-god Utu (Shamash).
3500 Early Bronze Age: rise of first literate civilizations in Mesopotamia and Egypt, as result of unlimited wealth due to irrigation and far-flung trade; c3200, Egypt changes suddenly and abruptly from a neolithic culture to an advanced one (copper tools, architecture, palaces, temples, written language, pyramids, etc.), with mathematical and scientific knowledge similar to Amerindian empires; all probably derived from survivals of Atlantean civilization.
3500 World's largest city: Abydos capital of Egypt, with 20,000 population; then BC 3000 Memphis (40,000), BC 2240 Akkad, BC 2100 Lagash (100,000), BC 1990 Memphis (100,000, with 10,000 priests), BC 1770 Babylon, BC 1595 Thebes, then Memphis, BC 668 Nineveh (120,000), BC 612 Babylon (200,000), BC 479 Sravasti, BC 400 Rajagriha (capital of North India), BC 320 Alexandria (over 300,000), BC 300 Patna, BC 220 Hsienyang, BC 190 Changan, BC 170 Seleucia, AD 1 Rome.
c3500 Origin of acupuncture in China (earliest written reference BC 500); only healing system to have endured to present day unchanged over time.
c3500 First time-measuring device, gnomon (a vertical pillar) in use for telling time (by length of shadow cast); BC 800,sundial; AD 50, water-clock; later candle-clocks, sandglasses; AD c1250, first true mechanical clocks.
c3400 Early form of hieroglyphic writing in use in Egypt.
c3400 Invention of abacus in Mesopotamia (calculating board with manually-operated storage aiding a human calculator); widespread use in everyday life to present day; in universal use in Middle Ages throughout Europe, Middle East and Asia.
c3300 Origins in Mesopotamia of astrology as 'natural astrology' (divination, celestial omens); astrology becomes a pseudoscience postulating influence of planets and stars on earthly affairs in order to predict or affect destinies of individuals, groups or nations; first codified in Babylon c1750 in cuneiform text *Enuma Anu Enlil* devoted to celestial omens; evolves into astrology proper by BC 300 in Greece.
3200 Bronze Age, beginning in Greece (BC 1800 in China); average human life span 19 years, later increasing during Roman empire to 23, Middle Ages to 35, 1970s to 70 (in Western world), AD 2000 to 90, and by AD 2020 to 97 years.
3120 Beginning of Dark Ages (4th Kali Yuga, the final era), on Hindu calendar, lasting until AD 429,000.
3110 Era of great empires in Mesopotamia: Sumerian (3100-2400), Akkadian (2400-2100), Sumerian Ur III (2100-2000), Old Babylonian (2017-1794), Assyrian (c1100-746), Neo-Assyrian (746-606), Neo-Babylonian (626-539).
3100 Writing (expressing linguistic elements by conventional visible marks) first appears (logo-syllabic) among Sumerian (Akkadian) farmers in Mesopotamia, recording stock holdings on lumps of clay; cuneiform syllabaries; of world's 7 logo-syllabic systems up to present, 3 remain as yet undeciphered.
3100 First united kingdom in Egypt under king Menes; kings buried in stone tombs.
c3100 City of Memphis founded by pharaoh Menes, with by BC 3000 a population of 40,000.
3100 Early Vedic Age (3100-2000) begins.
3100 First written documents: scribes widely employed in Mesopotamia using clay tablets; BC 3000, papyrus; BC 800, ivory or wooden writing-boards; then on leather or parchment (sheep or goat skin), finally vellum (calf skin).
3100 7 logo-syllabic writing systems emerge (signs expressing words): BC 3100, Sumerian (Mesopotamia); BC 3000, both Egyptian and Proto-Elamite; BC 2200, Proto-Indic (Indus Valley); BC 2000, Crete and Greece; BC 1500, Hittites (Anatolia and Syria); and BC 1300, Chinese.
3050 In Egypt, Archaic Period and unified Old Kingdom (BC 3050-2160) begin, with great flowering of civilization; great religious center Heliopolis (On) holds cosmos created by benign demiurge, sun-god Ra (linked with Atum, Khepri, falcon-god Horus, Akhti).
c3000 Proto-Indo-European, ancestor of English and other languages, is parent tongue of nomads roaming southeast European plains, and from Baltic to Iranian plateau; c2500, begins to break up, eventually producing Sanskrit by BC 2000, Greek by BC 800, and Latin by BC 500.
c3000 Rise of kingdoms: main function of the king is to ensure justice for all his subjects (Mesopotamia, Egypt), to restore balance between the rich and powerful and the poor and powerless; c2600, Mis-anni-padda king of Ur, first recorded ruler in Mesopotamia.
c3000 Egyptian logo-syllabic system of writing invented; in use up to AD 400; most Egyptian pharaohs however illiterate, relying on scribes. Earliest books, papyrus rolls in Egypt; c2300, first libraries.
c3000 Phoenicians (Canaanites) settle in Byblos (Lebanon) as sea-traders and colonizers, develop farflung network of global commerce throughout area of old Atlantean empire, with 300 cities on west coast of Africa alone.
c3000 Minoan (Eteocretan) or Bronze Age (Aegean) sea empire and civilization in Crete; develops earliest form of written Greek; BC c1450, destroyed with its capital Cnossos by volcanic eruption and giant tidal wave.
3000 Numbers, counting, and early alphabet invented in Mesopotamia.
3000 Scriptoria, for multiple and even mass copying of documents and book production, arise in Mesopotamia; BC 100, evident in Qumran sites; AD 170, present in Alexandria's Catechetical School; AD 225, Origen's scriptorium at Caesarea; AD 540, Benedict of Nursia begins scriptoria staffed with monks and laymen; AD 770, influence of Alcuin; AD 1000, many cathedrals in Middle Ages each have own scriptorium; by AD 1200 giant illustrated/illuminated Bibles become very numerous.
c3000 Introduction of taxation and taxes for citizens.
c2950 Combat myths (creator God's cosmos fighting chaos monster) begin in Sumeria, eventually extend from Indus valley to Scandinavia (god Thor).

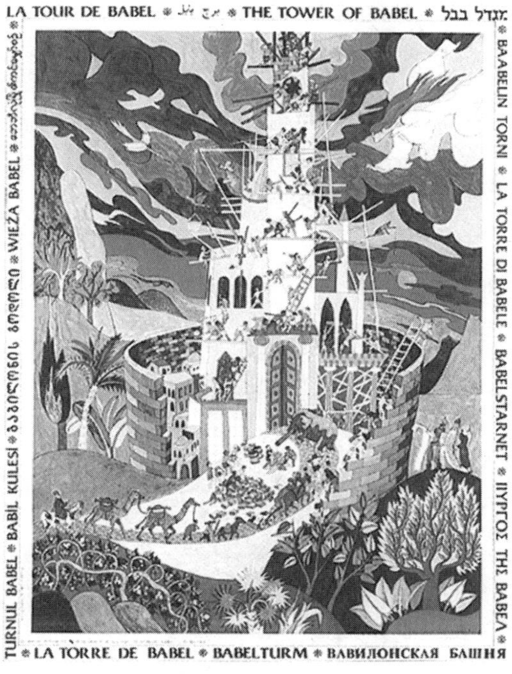
LA TOUR DE BABEL * THE TOWER OF BABEL * מגדל בבל
BAABELIN TORNI * LA TORRE DI BABELE * BABELSTARNET * ΠΥΡΓΟΣ ΤΗΣ ΒΑΒΕΛ
LA TORRE DE BABEL * BABELTURM * ВАВИЛОНСКАЯ БАШНЯ
TURNUL BABEL * BABIL KULESI * WIEŻA BABEL
**BC 2900.** Symbolizing Cosmos and man rebelling against God, the Tower of Babel results in multilingualism.

c2900 Tower of Babel, a 7-storey ziggurat symbolizing Cosmos according to Babylonian religious system centered on astrology, with 12 signs of the Zodiac on its top; mankind divided into separate peoples and languages and dispersed across Earth. (Genesis 11:1-9).

## GOD PLANS TO SAVE THE WORLD

2890 After human descent into warfare, human sacrifice, and lawlessness, and divine judgment in the Flood, God purposes salvation again for the human race.
c2800 Invention of plough in Egypt and Mesopotamia, then Palestine, Roman and Greek empires, China; but not introduced into central Europe until AD c1050.
c2800 Mother goddess Inninn and son Tammuz worshipped as chief Sumerian deities (also for Egyptians, Hittites, Phoenicians, Scandinavians, et alii); c2200 in Egypt, resurrection cult of Isis and Osiris.
c2800 Origin of alphabet at Byblos: North Semitic (Canaan and North Phoenicia) with 22 letters; alphabetic Early Hebrew writing in ink develops soon after.
c2800 Origin of lost walled trade city Ubar ('Atlantis of the Sand') in Oman, font of frankincense trade from local resin trees on camel trade route.
c2773 Egyptians develop first calendar with 365-day year; Roman and later modern calendars based on it.
2680 Pyramids of Egypt built during Old Kingdom, over next 400 years; oldest, and only one remaining, of ancient Seven Wonders of World; c2500, Great Pyramid of Giza (Cheops, Khufu) with 2.3 million colossal stone blocks, whose interior is later held to be 'the Bible in stone', a divine prophecy of whole of 6,000-year history including Christian era to End of the World in either AD 1881, or 1936, or 1953, or 2001.
c2600 First recorded seagoing voyage: Egyptian sailors travel to Byblos in Phoenicia in in search of cedarwood.
2600 *Epic of Gilgamesh*, oldest surviving creation and Flood narrative, in Akkadian language of Mesopotamia, describing journey of Gilgamesh king of Uruk in search of Utnapishtim, heroic survivor of the great Flood.
c2500 Ink invented in China; papyrus and ink used in Egypt.
c2500 Use of metal as money introduced, in Middle East.
c2500 Concern for condition of the poor and needy appears

in Middle East; origins of apocalypticism (the divine reversal of fortunes) in Babylonia, later in Zoroastrianism (c550) and in Hebrew prophecy.

2500 Sumerians develop cuneiform script.

2500 Hindu cities of Harappa and Mohenjo-Daro in Indus Valley, both with population of 100,000.

2450 World's main cities: (Egypt) Heliopolis, Memphis, Abydos, Thebes, Aswan; (Mesopotamia) Sippar, Kish, Nippur, Erech (Uruk), Lagash, Ur, Eridu, Susa, Nuzu; (northern Syria) Byblos, Ebla; by BC 1750 Assur, Nineveh, Haran, Mari, Babylon, Asyut.

c2400 Origins of mathematics (arithmetic, algebra, geometry, astronomy) in Babylonia/Mesopotamia, based on place-value notation, using 60 as base number.

2393 Bharata is born (44th in Puranic list of kings and sages).

2350 Sargon the Great (reigned BC 2334-2279) conquers Sumerians, establishes first great empire known to history, from capital city of Akkad (Mesopotamia).

2200 Proto-Indic logo-syllabic system of writing invented in Indus valley.

2200 Egypt ruled by Hyksos (Shepherd Kings), till their overthrow in 1550.

2150 Babylonian creation epic *Enuma Elish*: creation was due to conflict of deities, Tiamat goddess of darkness and chaos being slain by Marduk supreme god of Babylonians.

c2100 Ziggurat of Ur built by Sumerian king Ur-Nammu.

2100 Nomadic Amorites (Amurru, Martu) invade Mesopotamia, rule Babylon, and dominate Palestine for 600 years until defeated by Hittites and Kassites.

2100 First classification of drugs, by Sumerians.

2100 Codification of written laws.

2051 Invasion of Aryans into India.

2003 Fall of religious center Ur of the Chaldees, capital of southern Mesopotamia, Sumeria, with its ziggurat of moon god (founded BC c3500, abandoned BC c350); Elamites capture city and end Ur's 3rd Dynasty.

c2000 Mesopotamian traders journey as far east as India, Egyptians trade with Nubia, Ethiopia, and Crete.

c2000 Metalworkers in Mesopotamia discover glass, by accidentally overheating materials; glass cut and polished cold until BC c1800.

2000 Large numbers of petty human states and governments emerge; warfare becomes widespread.

2000 Earliest postal systems (mounted messengers, later posthouses) operate in Egypt and by BC 1000 in China under Chou dynasty; by BC 650 in Persian empire; then across Roman empire, Arab empire, and pre-Columbian civilizations of America.

c2000 First stirrings of urban-industrial mass society: vast bureaucracies rule Egypt and Babylonia, embryonic mass-production factories in ancient Greece and Rome, oil drilled in Greece in BC 400 and in Burma in AD 100.

c2000 Massive evidence of 30-letter cuneiform alphabet from Ugarit (Syria).

c2000 Decimal system used by Minoans on Crete.

c2000 Properties of Pythagorean triangle theorem known in Egypt.

2000 World population is 27 million; India is 5 million (22% of world).

2000 Inuit (Eskimo) people near Arctic Circle develop stone and bone tools.

## GOD REVEALS HIS GLOBAL MISSION

1950 Beginning of God's self-revelation to human race (Heilsgeschichte, salvation history) as later recorded in Judaeo-Christian Scriptures; record unfolds around cities (1,230 references in Bible, with hundreds more on specific cities) with negative image of cities as evil from Enoch, Babel, Sodom (Genesis 4-19) on through to Great Babylon (Revelation 17), but later includes positive image from refuge cities (Joshua 20) to New Jerusalem (Revelation 22).

1950 Beginning of divine election of a chosen People of God to be repository of ethical monotheism; call of Abraham, first Hebrew patriarch, father of monotheism, who migrates (at age 75) as first missionary from Ur of the Chaldees to Palestine ('Go: in you all the families of the Earth will be blessed'), dies 100 years later; son Isaac has son Jacob who has 12 sons, ancestors of Twelve Tribes of Israel. (Genesis 12).

1950 Biblical mandate for world evangelization begins, ultimately resting on 4 great commissions: (1) the commission to Abraham (Genesis 12:1-3: 'Leave', 'Go'), (2) the 'Great Commission for Israel' (Psalm 96:3: 'Declare my glory among the nations'), (3) the Great Commission of Jesus to the 12 ('Make disciples'), (4) the commission to Paul ('Bring about obedience to the faith among all nations', Romans 1:5).

1950 Political attempts to control prostitution.

1930 Indus Valley metropolis of Harappa destroyed in Dasarajna, Battle of the Ten Kings, by Sudasa II (68th in Puranic list of kings and sages).

## GOD REVEALS SELF AS TRINITY IN UNITY

c1925 After a number of earlier revelations (Genesis 1:26, 3:22), God's nature is gradually revealed as Triune, a community of love, when 3 Persons appear to Abraham at Mamre. (Genesis 18:1-22).

c1900 Destruction of Sodom and Gomorrah by earthquake, then covered by Dead Sea in Palestine. (Genesis 19).

c1800 Babylonian multiplication tables are written, earliest known mathematical tables.

c1800 Stonehenge megalithic monument erected in south Britain under Cretan influence as temple of sky worship and astronomical calendar clock.

c1780 Babylonian king Hammurabi (c1820-1750) issues comprehensive code of Sumerian laws; scholars use advanced mathematics; c1750, Code of Hammurabi compiled: oldest known legal code, covers criminal behavior, family life, economics, and ethics, establishes principle of 'an eye for an eye'.

1766 Chinese civilization develops under Shang dynasty (1766-1122) along Yellow river; script writing, bronze tools and weapons; succeeding Chou dynasty (1122-221) develops mathematics, astronomy, copper coins, silk textiles, iron tools and weapons.

1750 *Enuma Anu Enlil* (Book of Celestial Omens), a Babylonian cuneiform text, deals with 4 categories of omens (Sin/Moon, Shamash/Sun, Adad/Weather, Ishtar/Venus).

1730 Joseph, great-grandson of Abraham, becomes adviser to pharaoh of Egypt.

1720 Descendants of Jacob enslaved in Egypt, 1700-1290.

c1700 Babylonians make use of squares and square roots, cubes and cube roots, and quadratic equations and have calculated approximate value for pi by this time.

1650 Emergence of 'the poor' (mentioned 245 times in Old Testament, under 6 main terms) as major category of God's concern throughout history ('the privilege of the poor' = God's preferential option for the poor).

c1628 Volcano on island of Thera, near Crete, explodes with massive force (greatest known explosion on Earth).

1600 Origin of Latin; BC 100, emergence of Classical Latin, holds undisputed sway until after AD 200.

c1600 Myth of annunciation, miraculous conception, birth and adoration of Egyptian sky god Horus.

1595 Hittites conquer Babylonians and destroy Babylon.

c1500 Invasion of India by Aryans, who settle in northwestern India (Punjab) and overrun and destroy Indus Valley civilization, introducing their religion Vedism into India.

1500 Compilation of Rig Vedas, holy writ of Hinduism, compiled from oral traditions as over 1,000 hymns in Sanskrit, transmitted orally till written down by BC 600; in combat myth, god Indra masters primordial chaos Asat and creates cosmos order Sat; Vedic pantheon includes Vishnu and many other gods.(BC 1500-600).

1500 Up to now, Middle Eastern peoples—Egyptians, Sumerians, Babylonians, Indians, Iranians, Canaanites, pre-Exilic Israelites—all regarded world as an immutable stage for the combat myth (= how gods, in particular one warrior god) as it defends the cosmos versus chaos-monster for ever, past, present, and future.

c1500 Heyday of kingdom of Tartessus, 'Venice of the West', Atlantic Spanish port (biblical Tarshish—21 references), peopled by Tartessians, formerly colonized by Atlantis (with Rio Tinto copper mines, records and a literature both since BC 6500, and ability to sail Atlantic); prospers from trade with Phoenicians and Carthaginians; BC 533, destroyed by latter, vanishes without a trace.

c1500 Mycenaean (Late Helladic) prehistoric Late Bronze Age civilization in mainland Greece centers on Achaean Greek capital city of Mycenae, with Mycenaean as oldest known form of Greek language; mythology of Greek gods develops.

c1500 Early Greek alphabet developed at Knossos (Crete).

c1500 First recorded Chinese dynasty: Shang Dynasty.

c1500 First Chinese dictionary, listing 40,000 characters.

1500 Polynesians begin migration throughout Pacific islands.

1468 Battle of Megiddo: pharaoh Thutmose III of Egypt invades Palestine and defeats Canaanites in first recorded strategic battle in history.

1460 Zoroaster, followed by Hebew prophets envisages apocalypse producing cosmos without chaos, after final defeat of chaos.

1375 Akhenaton (Amenhotep, c1400-1362), religious reformer and first recorded monotheist, rules as pharaoh in Egypt; succeeded by son Tukankhamen (1370-1352), later by Seti I (reigned 1318-1304).

1360 World's 5 largest cities: Thebes in Egypt (100,000 people), Memphis 74,000, Babylon 54,000, Chengchow 40,000, Khattushas (Hattusa) 40,000.

c1350 Chinese incorporate decimals into their numerical system.

1350 Zoroaster flourishes (alternate dates BC 1460, BC 1200 or BC 590).

## GOD REVEALS HIS NAME: YHWH, 'I AM'

c1320 God reveals himself to Moses (c1370-1250) in theophany of the burning bush and on Mount Sinai: Godís name revealed as tetragrammaton YHWH (Yahweh, Jehovah). (Exodus 3:1-22).

1316 *Mahabharata* epic poem written down.

1300 Chinese logo-syllabic system of writing invented in China.

c1300 Climatic conditions reach catastrophically high temperatures worldwide.

1292 Rameses II (reigned 1304-1237) pharaoh of Egypt, in 19th Dynasty.

c1290 Planets Venus and Mars pass close to Earth disturbing its rotation, axis inclination, and magnetic field, causing many phenomena in the Exodus and subsequent Israelite history. (I. Velikovsky, *Worlds in collision*, 1950).

## THE EXODUS: GOD'S ENUMERATING BEGINS

c1290 Moses leads 72,000 Israelites out of Egypt after the Ten Plagues; 40 years' wanderings in wilderness; Moses receives the Law on Mount Sinai, dies at 120 years.

c1290 Mosaic covenant shows God giving special attention to the poor, humble and disinherited.

c1280 Ark of the Covenant, golden shrine of Presence of Yahweh (symbol of divine immanence), with golden mercy seat, containing 2 tablets of the Law, and located in Tabernacle (tent, portable sanctuary), travels from Mount Sinai to Jericho, Shiloh, finally to Solomon's Temple in Jerusalem; disappears BC c600. (Exodus 37, 2 Samuel 6:7; interpreted by E. von Daniken, *Raiders of the Lost Ark*, 1981, as electrical condenser used by Moses to communicate with alien spaceship).

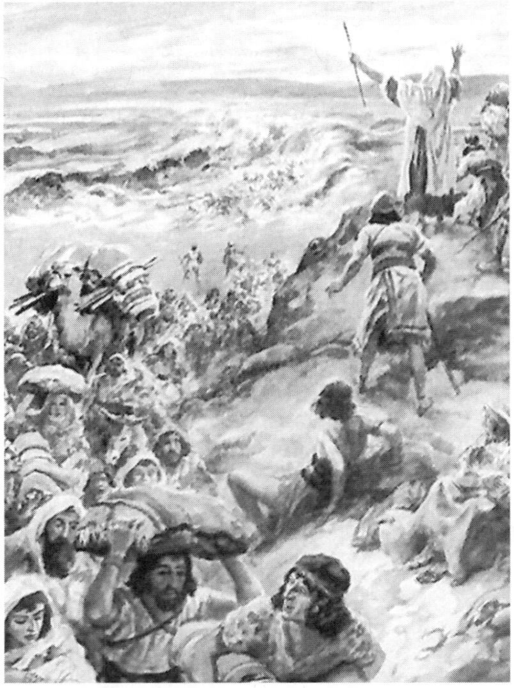

**BC 1290.** The Israelites cross the Red Sea as it parts at Moses' command.

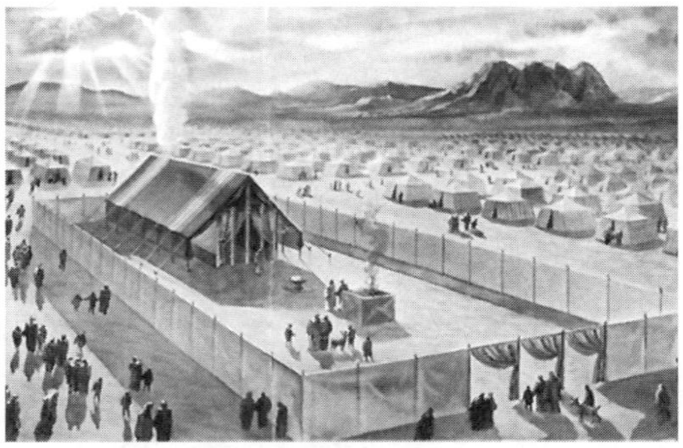

**BC 1280.** The portable Tabernacle, with Ark of the Covenant, begins instruction of Israel in God's laws.

c1270 Bible (beginning with 5 Books of Moses, Pentateuch) enumerates, in order to match up, 2 distinct entities: (1) the world of Gentile nations as harvest field (numbered at 70, see earliest ethnological Table of Nations in history in Genesis 10, etc), and (2) the People of God as harvesters, or harvest force, or people concerned with God's harvest plans—e.g. 70 descendants of Israel (Exodus 1:5), 70 elders (Exodus 24:1), censuses in Numbers, later Jesus' Mission of the 70 (Luke 10:1), etc.

1260 Leviticus and Deuteronomy contain detailed legislation to prevent accumulation of wealth, often linked in Bible with injustice and exploitation, as it leads to sin, pride, false security.

1250 Joshua leads first stage of invasion of Canaan, with fall of Jericho; later leaders known as Judges; polytheism widespread in Israel.

c1250 Pentateuch prohibits divination, soothsaying, augury, sorcery; no mediums, wizards, or necromancers allowed in Israel, only prophets (Deuteronomy 18:10-11).

1225 Israel after death of Joshua is ruled for 185 years by judges (charismatic military or civilian warriors/heroes/prophets): 1200 Othniel, Ehud, 1150 Shamgar, Deborah and Barak (1125 Battle of Megiddo), 1100 Gideon (40 years), 1075 Abimelech (3 years), Tola (23), Jair (22), 1050 Jephthah (6), Ibzan (7), Elon (10), Abdon (8), Samson (20), Eli (40), Samuel (30), Joel, Abijah, until monarchy instituted in AD 1030.

c1200 Zarathustra (Zoroaster) flourishes as Persian religious reformer (alternative date BC 590); scriptures Avesta orally transmitted until written in BC 550 when Iranian empire adopts Zoroastrianism; supreme god Ahura Mazda (Ormazd) battles evil Angra Mainyu (Ahriman); foresees final destruction of chaos, coming of Saoshyant (messiah).

**BC 1120.** Samson, prisoner blinded by Philistines, single-handedly destroys pagan temple of Dagon.

1150 Emergence of Olmecs, first pre-Columbian civilization of Meso-America on gulf coast of Mexico; stone monuments, huge statuary heads, picture writing; first higher native culture in Middle America; advanced art, architecture, sculpture, hieroglyphics; priests, gods, jaguar cult at center of religious practice; disappeared by BC 800.
1141 I Ching (Book of Changes), enabling mathematical divination, compiled under Chinese emperor Wen Wang.
1100 Iron Age begins, in Europe and Near East.
1100 Aramaic (Chaldean) comes into widespread use as lingua franca of Near Eastern official circles during Assyrian period, to BC 605; 850, Aramaic alphabet invented, replacing Early Hebrew; 550, serves as vernacular of Palestine (and so of Jesus) until 9th century AD.
1057 Great Comet in sky first noted, in Chinese literature, seen as harbinger of disaster and divine wrath; regular comet appearances seen thereafter, including BC 613, 467, 240, 12, AD 66, 1066, 1301, 1466, 1517, 1531, 1577, 1607, 1682, 1758, 1910, up to 1986 (Halley's returns every 76 years); held to explain Noah's flood, Star of Bethlehem, et alia.
c1050 Primitive compass developed in China.

### UNITED KINGDOM EMERGES IN ISRAEL

c1030 Reign of Saul as king of united Israelite kingdom, 1030-1010, with population of around 500,000.

**BC 1020.** Shepherd boy David single-handedly kills Philistine champion Goliath.

1010 Reign of David, age 30, as king of Israel, 1010-970.
c1000 Chinese develop counting boards, fore-runner of abacus.

c1000 Phoenicians at zenith of power begin settlements in North Africa, Spain, Italy, spreading script.
c1000 Peking founded, Chinese script fully developed.
c1000 Chinese mathematics includes geometry, root multiplication, proportions.
1000 World population 50 million, doubling every 500 years.
970 Reign of Solomon as king of Israel, 970-931; 959, first Temple built; at his death, split into Northern Kingdom (Israel) until 722 (all 19 kings being recorded as evil) and Southern Kingdom (Judah) until 586 (10 out of 19 kings being recorded as evil).
950 First full alphabetic system of writing derived by Greeks; later, alphabets invented for Aramaic, Classical Hebrew, Latin, up to several hundred by today.
950 Large-scale spread of urbanization through northern Chinese independent city-states.
950 Jewish people first arrive in India in king Solomon's merchant fleet.
928 Kings of Israel (Northern Kingdom): 928 Jeroboam I, 907 Nadab, 906 Baasha, 883 Elah, 882 Zimri, 882 Tibni, 882 Omri, 873 Ahab, 852 Ahaziah, 851 Joram, 842 Jehu, 817 Jehoahaz, 800 Jehoash, 788 Jeroboam II, 747 Zechariah, 747 Shallum, 747 Menahem, 737 Pekahiah, 735 Pekah, 732 Hoshea; ending with 722 Fall of Samaria.
928 Kings of Judah (Southern Kingdom): 928 Rehoboam, 911 Abijam, 908 Asa, 870 Jehoshaphat, 851 Jehoram, 843 Ahaziah, 842 Athaliah, 836 Joash, 798 Amaziah, 785 Azariah, 759 Jotham, 743 Ahaz, 727 Hezekiah, 698 Manasseh, 641 Amon, 639 Josiah, 609 Jehoahaz, 608 Jehoiakim, 597 Jehoiachin, 596 Zedekiah; ending with 586 Fall of Jerusalem.
c900 Earliest recorded music, a Sumerian hymn.
c900 Olmec civilization in Mexico develops calendar and counting system.
900 Biblical prophecy through recognized prophets emerges, construed as direct revelation from God to mankind, envisaging future events.
880 Age of Hebrew prophets (with years of ministry): in Israel, Elijah (869-840), Elisha (855-795), Amos (785-750), Jonah (780), Hosea (760-735); in Judah, Isaiah (740-680), Micah (730-715), Zephaniah (628), Nahum (614), Jeremiah (626-580), Habakkuk (605); during Exile, Ezekiel (598-560), Daniel (570-535); after Exile, Haggai (520), Zechariah (520), Obadiah (490), Malachi (430), Joel (420).
870 Drought in Israel for 3 years (the stereotyped period of evil and distress) under prophet Elijah. (Luke 4:25, James 5:17).
853 Battle of Karkar: Syrian coalition defeats Assyria.
852 Prophet Micaiah confronts Ahab king of Israel and his prophets; Ahab killed in battle of Ramoth Gilead.
c800 Phoenician traders establish trade routes to Gadir, on Atlantic coast of Spain; their colony Carthage controls access to western Mediterranean, refuses to allow others' ships to sail through Strait of Gibraltar to Atlantic coasts of Europe or Africa.
800 Gold and silver in use as money between the Nile and the Indus.
776 Two-decked ships originate in Tyre.
776 Olympic Games first celebrated, at Olympia, Greece; held at intervals until 290th Games in AD 390, then in 393 banned by emperor Theodosius; 1896, Olympiad revived in Greece as world's foremost amateur sports competition.
c770 Amos and subsequent Hebrew prophets announce and proclaim a legal dispute or controversy between Yahweh and all pagan nations with their gods; in their trial, Israel's mission is as witness to Yahweh's character, activity and purpose in world.
c760 Hebrew prophets take up defense of poor and needy, as victims of social crises; denounce poverty as an evil, attack all forms of economic and political oppression, taxes, fraudulent trade, seizure of land, injustice and violence.
760 Judean shepherd and prophet Amos warns time is shortly coming when God's wrath will explode in 'The Day of the Lord'.
753 Founding of city of Rome; year from which Romans subsequently reckoned dates (AUC, anno urbis conditae, or ab urbe condita).
733 Assyrian king Tiglath-pileser III plunders Israel, destroys Megiddo, raises Assyria to renown and power.
722 Fall of Samaria: end of Northern Kingdom of Israel; 27,290 leading citizens taken into captivity; disappearance of the Ten Lost tribe of Israel.
c700 Delphi Oracle, with major temple of Apollo, flourishes as centre of Greek world and center of political prediction until finally eclipsed in AD 362.
c700 Persians make first reliably recorded circumnavigation of Africa.
c700 Banking practiced in Babylon.
c700 Shintoism arises in Japan.
670 Empires and emperors impacting Israel's history and fortunes: Assurbanapal (Osnapper, 669-626), 609 Neco, 605 Nebuchadnezzar, 597 Psammetichus II, 588 Hophra (Apries), 562 Evil-Merodach (Amel-Marduk), 556 Nabonidus (and regent Belshazzar), 549 Cyrus unites Persia and Media, 530 Cambyses, Gomates, 522 Darius I, 486 Xerxes (Ahasuerus), 465 Artaxerxes I, 424 Xerxes II, 423 Darius II, 404 Artaxerxes II, 358 Artaxerxes III.
650 World's 5 largest cities: Nineveh 120,000, Loyang

117,00, Yenhsiatu 108,000, Memphis 99,000, Chicheng 91,000.
c650 Latin alphabet, adapted from Etruscan alphabet (invented BC 800).
c631 Coined metallic money invented by Lydians (a Greek state in Asia Minor); 594, Greek silver drachma introduced; 450, coinage begins to be minted by Phoenicians; 269, Romans introduce silver denarius; AD c1800, paper money and banknotes spread widely.
623 Religious reform under Judean king Josiah based on Book of the Law (Deuteronomy) rediscovered in Temple; all foreign cults abolished; 609, Josiah killed at Megiddo.
612 Fall of Nineveh: end of Assyrian empire.
606 Jewish youth Daniel taken captive to Babylon, interprets Nebuchadnezzar's dream (Daniel 2) as vision of the end-time with rise of 4 great powers, with interpretation varying down the centuries from the traditional view (Babylonian, Medo-Persian, Greek, Roman empires) to modern premillennial views (Hitler's Germany, USSR, Egypt [Islam], Iraq [Babylon, Assyria]; et alia).
605 Battle of Carchemish: Babylonian king Nebuchadnezzar II expels Egyptians from Syria.
c600 Phoenicians, sent by Egyptian pharaoh Necho II (ruled 610-595), sail round Africa taking 2 years from Red Sea, around southern cape, then back through Strait of Gibraltar.
600 Birth of Lao Tzu, traditional father of Taoism in China.

### Ionian Awakening: birth of science and technology

c600 Greek island of Samos: Phoenician alphabet, literacy and mercantilism result in awakening of science across Ionia, teaching orderly nature of Universe as cosmos : Thales of Miletus (scientific worldview), Anaximander (astronomy), master engineer Theodorus (engineering) Hippocrates (medicine), Democritus (theory of atoms), Anaxagoras (experiments), Pythagoras (mathematics: Earth is a sphere, Cosmos is orderly, Aristarchus (heliocentric Universe); astrology widely regarded as a science; Attic Ionic, the literary language, becomes basis for Koine (Common Speech) of later Greek writing including New Testament; Ionian science finally destroyed BC c300 by slave-based economy.
c600 Earliest records of holy city of Varanasi on sacred river Ganges.
c600 Ajivika sect, ascetic and atheistic group of naked sadhus with reputation for fierce curses, is at its height, continuing in Mysore until14th century AD.
597 First Babylonian destruction of Jerusalem, with looting of Temple; however, city not razed, walls remain, so further Jewish revolt later.
c590 Laws of Solon established by Athenian statesman Solon (c638-c559) BC), replacing severe Draconian code and marking establishment of Athenian democracy.
c590 Persian religious reformer Zoroaster (628-551) replaces Iranian polytheism with worship of supreme god Ahura Mazda; 546, Zoroastrianism spreads under Cyrus.

### EXILE OF JEWS IN BABYLON AND THEIR RETURN

586 Final fall of Jerusalem, obliterated by Nebuchadnezzar II (c630-562), Temple burnt and razed, walls broken down: end of Southern Kingdom of Judah; Jews exiled to Babylonia (perceived as a return to primordial chaos) until 538 when Persian ruler Cyrus allows return.
575 Greek thinker and founder of astronomy Anaximander of Miletus (610-c540) develops first cosmology and first map of the world, believes in infinite number of worlds, all inhabited, all rising or falling.
559 Achaemenian empire in Iran, central Asia and Transcaucasia, lasting until BC 330.
557 Mahavira (c599-527), last of 24 Tirthankaras (prophets) who founded Jainism in India, attains kevala-jnana (highest knowledge) and advocates nonviolence, vegetarianism and renunciation.
550 Classical age or 'Age of a Hundred Philosophers', in China: Confucianism, Taoism, and other religions emerge, under Confucius (BC 551-479) and others; Confucianism remains ideology of ruling class and central core of Chinese religion for 2,400 years.
550 Greek philosopher and mathematician Pythagoras (582-507) develops number mysticism, becomes first to use word cosmos to denote well-ordered and harmonious universe; 530, theorizes that Earth is a sphere.
550 Dawn of European science begins with philosophers of Greek city-states: Thales, Zeno, Plato, Aristotle, et alii.
550 Israel begins to transcend its nationalistic exclusivism; aided by apocalypticism, arrives at sense of God's mission to all peoples of the whole world; then progressively compromises its mission in the world through disobedience and unbelief.
550 Temple of Artemis (Diana) built at Ephesus by Croesus king of Lydia, 300 x 150 feet; 356, burned, later rebuilt.
549 First major Persian imperial dynasty (Achaemenids, the Medes and Persians of the Bible) under emperor Cyrus II the Great make Persia center of the world; lasts until BC 330.

c540 Roman census of population founded by king Servius Tullius (578-534); 10 enumerations held before first formal census in BC 435 under direction of censorate, then elaborate censuses every 5 and a half years until time of Christ.

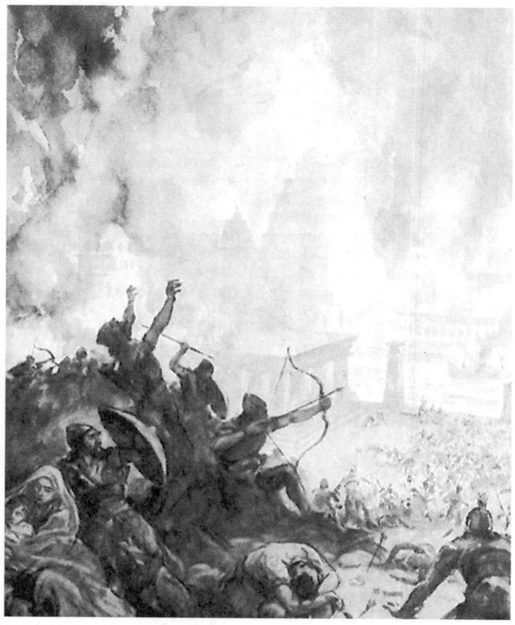

**BC 539.** Babylon falls to Persian conquerors producing end of an era for Jews.

539 Fall of Babylon to Medo-Persians under Cyrus king of Persia; 538, first return of Jews to Jerusalem (under Zerubbabel/Sheshbazzar and Jeshua); 458, second return (under Ezra).
539 Kings of Persia: Cyrus (rules 539-530), Darius (rules 521-486), Xerxes I (c519-465) rules from 486, Artaxerxes I rules from 464, Darius II from 423-404.
538 First return of Jewish exiles from Babylon following decree of king Cyrus the Persian; under Sheshbazzar (Zerubbabel) and Jeshua, 42,360 Jews with 7,537 servants return to Jerusalem.
537 Foundations of new Temple laid; 515, completed under Zerubbabel; small and unpretentious.
528 Siddhartha Gautama (c563-483) becomes a supreme buddha (enlightened one) at Buddh Gaya, India; Sakyamuni predicts demise of his Dharma (Buddhist religion) after 700 more years; Buddhism spreads from India to central and southeast Asia, then to China, Korea, Japan, et alia.
c520 Sundial introduced into Greece by Anaximander (611-547 BC).
520 First Celtic tribes (Gauls, Galli, Galatai, Galatians) advance into Italy; sack Rome in 387, then 386 Spain, Illyria; 275, widespread land seized; Celts unchecked throughout half Europe as far as Greece, Hungary, Romania and Galatia (Anatolia); 226, Carthaginians under Hasdrubal conquer southeastern Spain, Hannibal crosses Pyrenees and Alps.
519 Crucifixion introduced by Persians for rebels, pirates, slaves, religious agitators and criminals of lowest classes, with emperor Darius I crucifying 3,000 political opponents in Babylon; BC 260, introduced in Roman empire; AD 330, finally abolished by Constantine the Great.
516 Second Temple in Jerusalem built after 20 years' work.
500 Origin of Taoist religion in China.
c500 Millennialist ideas emerge in Buddhism: a future Buddha, Maitreya, will appear 30,000 years hence, announcing his final rebirth, breaking the great chain of reincarnation; all men will live in a new India made vaster by receding of the oceans; Maitreya will live for 60,000 years and his disciples another 10,000.
500 World population 100 million.
c500 Tamil Sangam age (BC 500-AD 500) begins, earliest period of Tamil literature; references to worship of Vishnu and Indra.
490 Battle of Marathon, 480 Thermopylae, Salamis.
486 Persian king Xerxes I (Ahasuerus; c519-465), husband of Jewish Esther, succeeds as king of Persia; 480, defeated by Greek fleet at Salamis.
c483 First Buddhist Council is held, at Rajagrha (India), with 500 arhats (enlightened ones); Buddha's teachings (Sutta) and a text on monastic discipline (Vinaya) are committed to writing.
458 Second return of Jewish exiles from Babylonia under Artaxerxes I; Ezra in Jerusalem.
c450 Carthaginian explorer Hanno sails with 60 ships on exploratory voyage down western coast of Africa as far as Gambia, bringing 30,000 men and women to establish new colonies including 6 Carthaginian cities.
c450 Mesopotamian omen literature, including *Enuma Anu Enlil*, carried by Buddhist monks and transmitted to India (Indus Valley civilization), Central Asia, Tibet, China, Japan, Southeast Asia; AD 200-300, Greek astrology transmitted to India, also AD 226 to Persia; AD c850, influences Islamic astrology through work of astrologer Abu Mashar.
447 Greek statesman Pericles (c495-429) builds Parthenon as temple of Pallas Athene patron goddess of Athens, completed 432; houses Athene's giant ivory and gold statue.
445 Restoration of walls of Jerusalem under Nehemiah as governor on his first return; 432, his second visit.
c440 Herodotus (c484-c425) provides accurate descriptions of barbarian religions of Egypt, Persia, Thrace, Scythia, et alia.

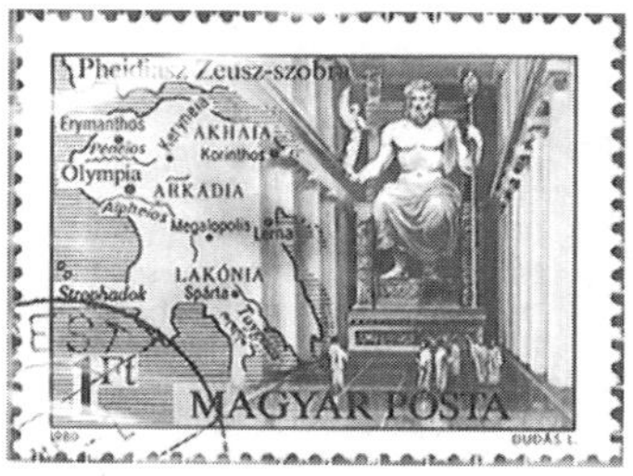


**BC 430.** One of the Seven Wonders of the World, gold-plated statue of chief god Zeus dominates Greek mythology.

430 Statue of god Zeus built at Olympia, over 38 feet tall, plated with gold and ivory; destroyed in AD 426.
430 World's 5 largest cities: Babylon 250,000, Ecbatana 200,000, Athens 155,000 (50,000 citizens, 100,000 slaves), Sravasti (Savatthi) 150,000, Champa 150,000.
414 Greek dramatist Aristophanes (450-388) writes *The Birds*, earliest work of science fiction known; is also first to use Greek verb *euangelizesthai* (as secular term meaning 'to carry good news'); term later used by Greek orator and statesman Dem Demosthenes (384-322).
390 Romans rebuild city of Rome, surrounding it with defensive wall not breached for many centuries.
c390 Athenian philosopher Plato (428-348) writes *Myths* postulating that Sun's planets are home of departed spirits.

## PREPARATION FOR GOD'S FUTURE MESSIAH

390 Celtic army from Gaul defeats Roman army at Allia river, plunders Rome; Celts colonize northern Italy.
387 Gauls defeat Roman army on the Allia, advance on Rome, burn it and besiege Capitol.
383 Second Buddhist Council is held, at Vaisali (India), with 700 monks; controversy over 10 illicit practices.
c380 Oriental mystery religions arise, a plethora of fertility cults from Middle East featuring death-resurrection mythology, initiation, personal salvation now and bliss hereafter; notably cults of Dionysus, Cybele the Great Mother, Isis, Mithra; spread westwards through Greco-Roman world by means of migration, trade and military service; major syncretistic rivals to Christianity; died out by AD 480.
367 Pataliputra I, a noncanonical Buddhist Council, held at Pataliputra (India); issues being laxity, text expansion.
c360 Plato's *Republic* (Politeia), first utopian scheme, initiates the utopian tradition in the development of future studies; in it Plato (BC 429-347) describes an ideal society in which philosopher-kings rule; all subsequent utopian fiction represents a series of variations on Plato.
350 Romans develop basic battle formation they use to conquer ancient world, based on Roman legion with about 4,500 men arranged in 3 rows.
c350 First known encyclopedias (a) in Greek, the work of Plato's nephew Speusippus, on natural history, mathematics, philosophy, et alia; and (b) in Latin, *Praecepta ad filium* by consul Cato, BC 183.
347 Greek philosopher, logician and scientist Aristotle (384-322) writes extensively on logic, art, ethics, politics, mechanics, zoology and the 4 elements doctrine; world's first and greatest scholar.
340 Buddhist prophecies predict that, after 500 years of decline since Buddha's enlightenment and death in BC 483, Buddhist religion will be finally extinguished (according to non-Mahayana sects); alternate durations predicted are 700 years, and 1,000 years (taught by all sects); with exclusively Mahayana sects teaching 1,500, 2,500, 5,000 (Theravada), 5,104, 10,000, 11,500, or 12,000 years.
334 Conquests by Macedonian Greek Alexander the Great (356-323 B.C. ) foster greater awareness of eastern lands; notably India, at eastern edge of Alexander's new but short-lived empire.
333 Palestine successively under Greeks (Alexander the Great); Ptolemies of Egypt, 323-198; Seleucids of Syria, 198-166.
330 Alexander the Great overthrows Achaemenians, conquers Iran, central Asia, and Transcaucasia before he dies in BC 327; after his death Seleucids rule central Asia; Atropates founds independent state in southern Azerbaijan.
c325 Earliest known book on strategy, *The Art of War*, written in China by Sun-tzu.
321 Maurya empire founded in India under Chandragupta; 247, his grandson, emperor Ashoka (c274-236) convenes 3rd Buddhist Council, transforms Buddhism into missionary faith seeking conversion of all India; BC 180, empire collapses.
312 Seleucid empire, second major imperial Persian dynasty, with Greek rulers; lasts until BC 238.
c310 Aristotle formulates theory of the religious degeneration of humanity, from original monotheism to contemporary polytheism.
302 Greek traveler Megasthenes (c350-c390 BC) journeys to India at various times during this period, going as far east as Ganges river; provides first written mention of island of Ceylon but does not travel there; publishes *India*, describing religion.
c300 Greek navigator Pytheas explores Atlantic coast of Europe and British Isles, then north to Thule (Norway, Iceland) into Arctic waters.
c300 Cursus Publicus, most highly-developed postal system and extensive messenger service of ancient Roman world, with relay stages covering 170 miles in 24 hours; persists until AD c820.
c300 Sun Temple at Teotihuacan (Mexico) completed.
c300 Unification of weights and measures in China.
297 Founding of Great Library of Alexandria by Greek scholar Demetrius of Phalerum; supported by king Ptolemy I Soter; for all disciplines and subjects, first true research institute in history for study of the Cosmos eventually reaches 700,000 scrolls; by BC 100, in decline; BC 47 partially destroyed under Julius Caesar; AD 273 burned by Roman emperor Aurelian; rebuilt, destroyed as pagan by Christians in AD 411; finally destroyed by Muslim conqueror Omar, AD 645, with all volumes irrevocably lost without copies surviving.
292 Colossus of Rhodes built over next 12 years: bronze statue of sun god Helios, over 100 feet tall.
c290 Septuagint translation begun from Hebrew OT into Greek (LXX, from 70 or 72 Jewish translators in Alexandria); completed c150.
c290 First Greek historian of religions Theophrastus (372-287) compiles a history of religion in 6 books.
290 Berossus, Chaldean priest of Bel in Babylon, compiles Babyloniaca, 3-volume history and chronology of Babylon and the world; first volume estimates time from Creation to Flood at 432,000 years, also account of Chaldean astrology; as astrologer, he teaches that great conjunctions of planets mark ends of great epochs in human civilization.
280 Pharos of Alexandria, lighthouse built by Ptolemy II off Alexandria, over 440 feet high.
c280 Athenian philosopher Epicurus (341-270) propagates radical criticism of religion, followed by Latin writer Lucretius (BC c98-c53).

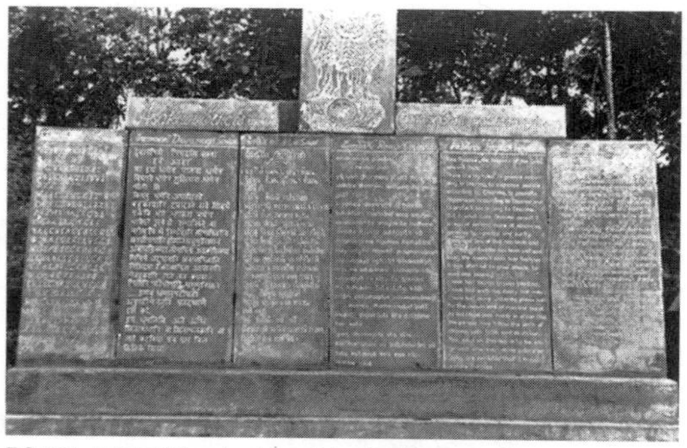

**BC 273.** Edict of King Asoka praising Buddha recorded on stela in Chiang Mai (Thailand) in several languages including English.

273 Mauryan king Asoka (c300-232) in power 40 years, expands empire to include most of India, establishes Buddhism as state religion; sends Buddhist missionaries to Egypt, Macedonia, Sri Lanka, China.
c270 Greek mythographer Euhemerus (c330-c260) writes *The Sacred Scripture*, interpreting mythical gods as simply deified human heroes; translated into Latin by poet Ennius (239-169).
260 Roman numeral system, dominant number system in West into medieval times, has reached advanced stage. Romans use it to represent numbers into millions.
256 Graeco-Bactrian empire in central Asia, until BC 120.
255 Greek mathematician Eratosthenes of Cyrene (BC c276-c194), becomes director of Greek Library of Alexandria, and is first to prove Earth is a sphere; calculates its circumference at around 30,000 miles.
250 Gypsies emerge as Romany-speaking race in central India; AD 1000, begin emigrations out of India, taking Indic grammar and vocabulary; c1400, arrival across Europe.
247 Parthian dynasty proper (the Arsacids), third in a series of imperial Persian dynasties, displaces Greek rule; first mounted nomads under Mithridates I capture Seleucid emperor in Babylon in BC 140, then in BC 53 defeat Roman general Crassus at Carrhae; dynasty lasts until AD 226; undermined by their nomadic indifference to culture and absence of predominant religion.
247 3rd Canonical Theravadin Buddhist Council (Pataliputra II), held at Pataliputra (India) under emperor Asoka's endeavor to force resolution of

dogmatic differences; debate on orthodoxy and composition of Kathavatthu.

246 Buddhism thrives in India under Asoka, spreads into Ceylon; Asoka oversees vast expansion of Buddhism in Asia, builds 84,000 stupas, sends Buddhist missionaries far and wide including to Greece and Britain.

232 Great Wall of China built, joining existing stretches into a continuous boundary for 1,920 miles, as Shih Huang Ti, first emperor of united China, links existing defensive walls to form barrier to Huns in north, from Yellow Sea to Central Asia; largest building-construction project ever completed.

221 Chinese empire first unified and organized under short, harsh Chin dynasty until BC 207, succeeded by Han dynasty (BC 206-AD 220).

216 Battle of Cannae: Carthaginian general Hannibal (247-182) uses cavalry to annihilate 85,000-man Roman army; in subsequent years Roman legion is enlarged and cavalry and light infantry are added.

213 Burning of Confucian classics is ordered by Ch'in emperor Shih Huang Ti (255-210).

200 Rise and spread of apocalyptic millennial beliefs and writings (as a solution to this-worldly triumph of evil) in Judaism and early Christianity until discredited by AD 450.

200 World's 5 largest cities: Patna (Pataliputra) 350,000, Alexandria 300,000, Seleucia 300,000, Changan 239,000, Loyang 189,000.

c200 Human race enters Age of Pisces (the Fishes), according to zodiacal theory; a New Age leading to the Christian Era and lasting for 2,160 years.

c200 Druids, learned priestly class among Celts in Gaul and Britain, with Hindu Brahmins in India, form last survivors of an ancient Indo-European priesthood.

179 Confucian thinker Tung Chung-shu categorizes 5 cardinal virtues of love, righteousness, decorum, wisdom, and trustworthiness; dies in 104.

170 Parthian empire in central Asia and Transcaucasia, lasting until AD 226.

167 Antiochus IV Epiphanes, Seleucid king of Syria, forces hellenization on Judaism, enters Jewish Temple (the Abomination of Desolation, or the Horrifying Blasphemy), attempts to replace worship of Yahweh by that of Olympian Zeus; crucifies law-breaking Jews; origin and archetype of long series of antichrists throughout Christian Era.

166 Jewish revolt under Judas Maccabeus (died 161) reestablishes Jewish independence; his descendants, Hasmoneans, rule Palestine for next hundred years.

c150 First paper invented in China, by mulberry bark and hemp fibers being beaten and spread out to dry; not used for writing purposes until AD c110; Chinese prisoner taken in in battle near Samarkand reveals secret of making paper to Arabs; not introduced into Europe until 12th century.

146 Destruction of city of Carthage (population 200,000) by Romans; only 50,000 survive to be sold into slavery.

140 Emperor Wu begins three-year reign of China; worship of Mother Goddess, Earth, attains importance.

128 Han emperor Wu-ti sends envoy from China to negotiate alliance with Yueh-chi tribe north of Afghanistan; by BC 106, Old Silk Road opened across top of the world linking East and West; Wu-ti institutes Chinese examination system administered to all Chinese civil servants until its abolition in AD 1905.

124 First imperial university founded in China as center for study of the Five Confucian Classics (Wu Ching); enrollment reaches 30,000 by AD 220.

124 Chinese examination system instituted by Wu Ti, administered to all Chinese civil servants until its abolition in 1905.

112 Rise of Pharisees and Sadducees, Judaic sects in Palestine.

105 College of Technology founded at Alexandria by the mathematician Heron.

103 Alexander Jannaeus (died 76) becomes king of Judea, culmination of Hasmonean dynasty; all hellenism destroyed; 90, Pharisees lead 6-year revolt against king, who crucifies 800 Pharisee rebels.

c100 Vast majority of books in world are located in Great Library of Alexandria with a million books, and about 50,000 more in China; all handwritten.

100 Kusana (Kushan) empire of nomadic Indo-Scythians rules Bactria and central Asia, one of world's 4 great empires (after China, Rome, Parthia); spreads Mahayana Buddhism throughout; lasts until early 4th century AD.

88 Eighth Etruscan world-week concludes, holding that only two more 119-world-weeks remain before prophetic countdown is completed and Etruscans cease to exist.

73 Gladiatorial War against Rome, led by Thracian deserter and slave Spartacus who with 70 fellow-gladiators from Capua forms army on Mount Vesuvius, defies 8 Roman legions for 3 years; BC 71 Spartacus killed, 6,000 followers crucified by general Crassus along Appian Way in Rome.

67 100,000 perish in rebellions in Palestine over next 40 years.

63 Roman general Pompey (106-48) captures Jerusalem, enters Holy of Holies but finds it empty; Palestine ruled by puppet kings including Herod the Great (BC 73-BC 4).

60 First Roman Triumvirate (informal): Pompey (assassinated BC 48), Caesar, Crassus.

c60 Cicero's On the Nature of the Gods accurately describes state of pagan rites and beliefs.

58 Gaius Julius Caesar (BC 100-44), history's greatest general, studies ethnography and statistics of peoples of Gaul; crosses Rubicon river separating Cisalpine Gaul from Italy, violating Lex Cornelia de Majestate ('a general may not lead an army out of his assigned province'); 3-year civil war follows, leaving Caesar ruler of Roman world; then in 10 year of Gallic wars by BC 51 he destroys 800 towns and villages of Gaul and kills or enslaves 3 million men.

57 Samvat calendar of Hinduism begins.

53 Battle of Carrhae, near Edessa: Persian army wins major victory over Roman army and wins control of western Asia; one of the major blows toppling the Roman republic and leading to the Roman empire; start of a 700-year war which neither empire finally won.

52 Battle of Alesia (Gaul), Julius Caesar's great turning point: his army of only 70,000 defeats Gallic army of 250,000, conquers the 60 tribes of Gaul; Caesar writes History of the Gallic Wars; 54, raids Britain; 52, Versungeterix cuts Caesar's supply lines; finally in 44, Caesar is murdered in Rome.

48 Large part of Great Library of Alexandria destroyed by fire in Julius Caesar's wars; hundreds of thousands of scrolls lost.

47 Cleopatra VII (BC 69-31), of Ptolemaic dynasty, becomes last queen of Egypt.

46 Old Style or Julian Calendar devised by Julius Caesar; AD 1582, replaced by New Style or Gregorian Calendar introduced by pope Gregory XIII; 1986, Old Calendar still followed by Orthodox Churches of Jerusalem, Russia, Serbia and Bulgaria, also by Old Calendarist churches.

45 Roman orator Cicero writes On Divination (De Divinatione I-II).

45 To ease traffic congestion in cities, controls imposed on chariots and carts.

43 Second Roman Triumvirate: Anthony, Octavian, Lepidus; 31, Octavian defeats Anthony at battle of Actium.

40 Roman poet Virgil has a millennial vision, foreseeing a glorious new age, one that would come to pass in the lifetime of the child (later Emperor Augustus) to whom he addressed his fourth Eclogue.

c40 Targums (parts of OT in Aramaic) circulate in oral form, later written down.

30 Diodorus Siculus (c80-c10) works for 30 years on a 40-book universal history, Bibliotheca historia (Historical Library) assembled from vasr number of sources.

28 Octavian (Gaius Octavius, BC 63-AD 14) becomes first Roman emperor, with title Augustus; inaugurates 2 types of enrolment in Roman empire: (a) census populi, for Roman citizens, in Italy and provinces, conducted in BC 28, BC 8, AD 14; and (b) apographe, for provincial inhabitants (Gaul BC 27, BC 12, AD 14; Egypt every 14 years from AD 34-258).

25 4th Canonical Theravadin Buddhist Council, held at Anuradhapura (Ceylon), with Mahavihara monks; finalization of 3-fold canon (Tipitaka) in Pali.

20 Augustus conquers Armenia and forces treaty of peace on Parthian emperor Phraates IV; beginning of the Pax Romana later seen by Origen and others as a praeparatio evangelium.

19 Herod the Great begins massive rebuilding of Jewish Temple in Jerusalem; finally completed AD 64, but destroyed AD 70.

BC 12 Halley's Comet appears; first noted in BC 240 in Europe, China, and Japan, then regularly every 76 years since.

BC 4 Total Homo Sapiens population born from origin of species to BC 4: 33,994 million persons.

BC 4 Julio-Claudian dynasty establishes Roman empire, lasts from Augustus to Nero, ends in AD 68.

# COSMIC ERA II

## *World evangelization in Christian history*

### INCARNATION OF THE WORD OF GOD

BC 6  Stellar and planetary harbingers observed: (a) in BC 6, triple conjunction of planets Jupiter (star of kings), Saturn (star of the Jews), and Mars (star of warriors) as predicted by Babylonian astronomers and verified in AD 1606 by Johannes Kepler; also (b) in BC 4, sudden appearance of large nova or supernova.

BC 5  Augustus' imperial census; family of Jesus participate in Bethlehem; end of regular Roman 5-yearly censuses, followed only by ones in AD 14, 47 and 72.

BC 4  Incarnation of the Word of God imminent.

### FIRST ADVENT OF JESUS CHRIST, GOD'S SON

BC 4  Birth of Jesus of Nazareth, one infant among 6,600,000 born on Earth that year; the Incarnation of the Word of God.

**BC 4.** The birth of Jesus, celebrated and portrayed by artists east and west down the centuries.

BC 4  Death of Herod produces violent unrest; Roman legate of Syria has 2,000 Jews crucified.

BC 1  Usurper Wang Mang seizes Chinese throne as emperor, rules to AD 23; violent disorders close Old Silk Road to Jewish and Christian missionaries until AD 76.

AD 1  Beginning of Christian Era according to Dionysius (AD 525).

6  Removal of Archelaus, son of Herod; Judea and Samaria placed under direct imperial rule.

6  Uprising under self-proclaimed Jewish messiah, Judas the Galilean, opposing first Roman provincial census of AD 6; Judas killed, 2,000 followers crucified.

8  Jesus, age 12, asks questions in Temple; later (during AD 15-25) may have traveled, as lone pilgrim seeking knowledge, across Jewish diaspora, then in remote Buddhist and Hindu monasteries in India, China (Mount Kailash, 'cosmic center of the universe', in Tibet), Japan.

9  Varian disaster in Germany: 3 Roman legions under P. Quinctilius Varus strategically ambushed by German Cherusci in forests north of Rhine; all 30,000 Romans including families and camp followers annihilated.

14  Imperial Roman census under emperor Tiberius (BC 42-AD 37).

19  Greek geographer and historian Strabo (BC 64-AD 25) produces map of world as a single continent; AD 20 writes 17-volume *Geographica*, portrays world as a globe 25,000 miles in circumference, with arctic and temperate zones; describes all peoples and countries known to Greeks and Romans during reign of Augustus.

c20  Essene ascetics (Jewish Zealots) of Qumran (Dead Sea, from BC 153-AD 73) write Rule of the War of the Sons of Light and the Sons of Darkness , showing considerable awareness of Roman military tactics; suicidal revolt of Zealots against Rome in AD 66, savagely suppressed by Titus in AD 68.

23  Total number of Roman imperial troops: 330,000 in 25 legions, rising gradually to 350,000 by AD 70; annual pay of legionary soldier 225 denarii per year.

25  Chinese emperor Kuang Wu Ti founds Eastern Han dynasty, conquers Viet Nam, dies in 57; Buddhism introduced into China.

27  Roman empire (33 million, 50% slaves) has 2.3 million Jews (7% of population) a large proportion being proselytes; in Palestine, 580,000 Jews and 220,000 Gentiles; average life-span then 23 years.

### JESUS BEGINS MINISTRY IN PALESTINE

30  Baptism of Jesus by John the Baptist; beginning of public ministry of Jesus of Nazareth.

**AD 32.** Jesus teaches in parables, by miracles, or in conversation as here with Samaritan woman.

30  Jesus starts on his immediate plan to win the world, proclaims nearness and imminence of rule of God: 'The Kingdom of God is at hand' (Mark 1:15, RSV)/'near' (NIV)/'has arrived' (NTME).

32  Jesus chooses Twelve Apostles including 4 of his first cousins and 2 Zealots (Patriots or Essenes), gives them power and authority, commissions them to go initially only to Israelites (Matthew 10:1-6); later commissions Mission of the 70 disciples to evangelize the 70 Gentile nations (Luke 10:1).

**AD 33.** Jesus institutes the Lord's Supper before his betrayal and crucifixion (Coptic icon).

32  Jesus envisages lightning spread of the gospel to all nations within one single generation: 'This Good News of the Kingdom will be proclaimed to the whole oikumene as a witness to all nations. And then the end will come' (Matthew 24:14, Jerusalem Bible; Oikumene = Graeco-Roman inhabited world); 'the end' partly fulfilled in Fall of Jerusalem in AD 70.

33  Crucifixion of Jesus (Friday 3 April), followed by resurrection (Sunday 5 April) and ascension 40 days later; final stage in beginning of God's New Creation in Christ.

**AD 33.** Crucifixion scene outside Jerusalem walls (3-dimensional tableau in Einsiedeln, Switzerland).

**AD 33.** Resurrection of Jesus, portrayed in Christian art for 1,950 years.

### THE GREAT COMMISSION: 'Go! Disciple! Baptize!'

33  Appearances of Jesus over 40-day period: the Gospels record 50 commands (25 universal) of the Risen Christ, culminating in Great Commission.

33  Jesus reveals himself to over 500 disciples on one occasion in Galilee (1 Corinthians 15:6).

33  Risen Lord Jesus gives Great Commission as spiritual counterpart of Genesis 1:28 with 2 components of evangelizing and discipling: 'Go forth to every part of the world (in Greek, Cosmos ), and proclaim the Good News to the whole creation' (Mark 16:15, NEB); 'Go to all peoples everywhere and make them my disciples' (Matthew 28:19, GNB); Jesus' presence from now on is the ever-present Shekinah glory.

33  Jesus gives Great Commission in a number of different forms at different times during the 40 days to different groups, including individuals, emphasizing the 7 mandates: Receive! Go! Witness! Proclaim! Disciple! Baptize! Train!

**AD 33.** The last command before his ascension: Jesus mandates his Great Commission.

33  Total human population of genus Homo born since origin in BC 5,500,000 (220,000 generations ago): 117,841 million persons.

33  Total Homo Sapiens population born since origin in BC 500,000 (20,000 generations ago): 34,241 million persons.

33 Total Homo Sapiens Sapiens population born since origin in BC 45,000 (1,800 generations ago); 12,791 million persons.
33 People of God (Old Israel) since Abraham's call in BC 1950 (79 generations ago): 52.5 million persons.
33 Overlapping of 2 Ages or Epochs or Cosmic Eras now under way as the Church Age: (1) The Present Age or Old Age (Kingdom or Rule of Satan; a pseudo-New Age terminating at Second Advent), and (2) the Next Age or New Age or New Creation or Messianic End-Time (Kingdom or Rule of God; beginning at Jesus' resurrection and continuing after Second Advent).

## Epoch I: AD 33-500

### CHRISTIANITY WINS THE ROMAN EMPIRE

#### The Apostolic Age, AD 33-80

33 **Global status:** during 40 days' Appearances of the Risen Christ, total of Jesus' disciples = about 4,000; total evangelized by Jesus as result of last 3 years' ministry = whole of Palestine (800,000).
33 Day of Pentecost in Jerusalem: 3,000 converted among Diaspora Jews and Gentiles from 'every nation under heaven', from North Africa to Persia.
33 *Palestine.* First Christians, in Jerusalem; Twelve Apostles become founder members of the Church, not primarily missionaries, evangelists, bishops or local pastors.
33 *Israel.* First Christians (from Jerusalem on Day of Pentecost) return to homes across Judea.
33 *Egypt, Lebanon* (then Phoenicia), *Jordan* (Transjordan), *Libya, Syria.* First Christians (returning from Jerusalem after Day of Pentecost).
33 *Italy.* First Christians (returned from Jerusalem after Day of Pentecost).
33 Large-scale people movement of families and villages into the church: 'More than ever believers were added to the Lord, multitudes both of men and of women' (Acts 5:14).
34 Apostles (the Twelve plus others) begin evangelizing Jews widely: several remain in Jerusalem for a decade or two, several travel outside, but most continue to evangelize only Jews until AD 38 (Peter), 43 (Paul), and after AD 50 (others).
35 Twelve Apostles, declining gradually in influence, appoint 7 deacons to administer relief for Hellenistic Christian community, while they concentrate on evangelism; 'The number of disciples multiplied greatly in Jerusalem, and a great many of the priests were obedient to the faith' (Acts 6:1-7).
c35 *Turkey* (then called Asia Minor). First Christians (in Antioch, returned from Jerusalem after Day of Pentecost).
35 Proliferation of 'signs and wonders' among early believers (listed 9 times in Acts); miracles and healings at this time an everyday occurrence and an essential part of proclamation of the gospel; 'power evangelism' thus one of the normal kinds of evangelism in the Early Church.
36 Martyrdom of Stephen the protomartyr; Jewish persecution of Early Church, especially of Hellenistic Christians; believers scattered throughout Judea and Samaria; gospel spreads rapidly through persecution and martyrdom.
36 Dismissal of Pontius Pilate (Roman Samnite knight, procurator of Judea since AD 26); recalled to Rome, kills himself AD 39 on orders from emperor

**AD 36.** Conversion of archpersecuter of Christians: Saul on the Damascus road.

Caligula.
36 *Sudan.* First Christians; gospel taken to Nubia (Meroe) by Ethiopian eunuch baptized by Philip the Evangelist.
36 Mission extended to Samaritans by Philip; fresh persecution.
36 Conversion of Saul of Tarsus (age 24), a Roman citizen; departs to Arabia, then in 40 to Jerusalem and Tarsus; later renamed Paul.
37 Church throughout Judea, Galilee and Samaria multiplied (Acts 9.31).
37 Persecution causes large-scale flight of Hellenistic-Jewish Christians, who then evangelize down to Egypt, north to Antioch and Cyprus, then along Old Silk Road to Jewish diaspora in Babylon and Persia.
c38 Large influx of Italians (Cohors II Italica Civium Romanorum) converted through ministry of Apostle Peter at Caesarea (Acts 10.48).

**AD 38.** 'Departure of the Apostles:' The Twelve finally obey their Commission, 'Go! (German School, Altarpiece, Daket 1499)'

c38 Twelve Apostles, after 5 years' hesitation and partial obedience to Christ's Great Commission, deliberately evangelize Gentiles for first time, then scatter across globe spreading the gospel, from Ethiopia (Matthew), to Armenia (Bartholomew) to India (Thomas); all 12 martyred over subsequent 60 years.
38 Commission to evangelize pagan Gentiles as Gentiles first forced onto consciousness of Jewish church, through baptism by Peter of Cornelius, a God-fearer but not a Jewish proselyte (Acts 10:1-48).
c39 Antioch (population 130,000): wider mission to Gentiles inaugurated.
c39 *Ethiopia.* First Christians (returning pilgrims from Jerusalem present on Day of Pentecost); c80, Christianity known and openly practiced by merchants from Roman empire settled in Axum, Adulis and region.
c40 *Greece.* First Judeo-Christians, before Apostle Paul's visit.
c40 *Holy See* (at that time, Rome). First Christians in capital of Roman empire.
c40 Mandylion of Edessa: king Abgar V of Edessa (BC 4-AD 50) obtains alleged portrait of Jesus (Icon of Christ); seized by Muslims in AD 944, surfaces in Lirey (France) in 1389, then regularly seen thereafter; now known as Holy Shroud of Turin.
40 Navigational secret of the monsoons, essential for travel to India, has been guarded from Romans by Arabs and Parthians but is now betrayed to the West by a Greek mariner.
41 Roman emperor Caligula (AD 12-41) attempts to set up statue of himself in Jewish Temple in Jerusalem; first to be regarded by Christians as the Antichrist; murdered soon after.
42 Mark the Evangelist (c10-68) works in Egypt; 61, arrives in Alexandria, organizes Coptic church; widely known and revered, but eventually arouses ire of populace who drag him to death through the streets; in subsequent centuries, several million Coptic Christians are likewise martyred.
42 *Cyprus, Northern Cyprus.* First witnesses, fleeing persecution; then 46, first missionaries (Apostles Paul and Barnabas).
42 Phoenicia, Cyprus, Antioch: 'A great number that believed turned to the Lord' (Acts 11:21).
43 Barnabas and Saul (later called Paul) at Antioch, new centre for Hellenistic Christians, 500 strong; believers first called Christians, in derision (Acts 11:26).
43 Romans begin conquest of Britain (population about 1,500,000); London founded.
44 Persecution in Jerusalem under king Herod Agrippa I (BC 10-AD 44); Apostle James brother of John executed; imprisonment and escape of Peter.
44 Jewish revolutionary and messianic claimant Theudas arrives at Jordan with multitude; defeated by Romans, crucified, beheaded.
46 Paul's 1st missionary journey (45-48), with Barnabas: Antioch, Cyprus, Pamphilia, Pisidia, Lycaonia;

develops strategy of urban evangelization and urban ministry, moving from city to city or town to town.
47 Imperial Roman census under emperor Claudius I (BC 10-AD 54).
48 *Iran* (at the time Persia). First Christians (Assyrians); after 13 years' mission by Apostles Judas (Lebbaeus) and Simon Zelotes in teeth of Zoroastrian priestly hostility, over 100,000 converted in the 12 Persian provinces (60,000 in Babylon alone).
49 Apostolic Council of Jerusalem: converts from paganism exempted from Jewish Law; Paul recognized as apostle to non-Jews.
49 Jews and Christians banished from Rome under Claudius.
c50 *Iraq* (then termed Media, et alia). First Christians (Assyrians, with Apostle Thomas, evangelizing Jewish colonies).
c50 Assyrian Christians found Church of the East (later Nestorian).
c50 Roman empire reaches its operational limit, with expansion everywhere halted by oceans, dense forest, desert or steppe; subservient client-states therefore established on periphery, nominally independent but subject to indirect rule.
c50 For 15 centuries, the term *missio* (mission) is used by the church only as a divine concept, the Triune God (Trinity) moving out into the world; only used of the church being sent since AD 1550.
50 Paul's 2nd missionary journey (50-52): Phrygia, Galatia, Greece, Athens (population 270,000).
50 Paul begins evangelization of 3 important Roman provinces: Macedonia, Achaia and Asia (Acts 16:6).
c50 Pliny's *Historia naturalis* in 2,500 chapters published, first of classical encyclopedias; by 1990, over 2,000 encyclopedias produced as summaries of extant scholarship.
c50 King of Edessa Abgar V the Black sends request for healing, answered by missionary Addai (Thaddaeus of Luke 10:1); under his successor missionary Aggai, first direct persecution breaks out.
51 Widespread famine across Roman empire, foretold by prophet Agabus (Acts 11:28), necessitating collection for relief of church in Jerusalem.
52 *India.* First missionaries (Apostle Thomas, and others, in the south).
53 Paul's 3rd missionary journey (53-57): Ephesus (2 years, 3 months), Corinth, Macedonia, Philippi
54 Martyrdom of Apostle James the Less (James son of Alphaeus, one of the Twelve), stoned to death in Jerusalem.
55 Roman province of Asia (500 cities) evangelized from capital Ephesus, seat of proconsul; in 2 years, 'All the residents of Asia heard the word of the Lord' (Acts 19:10).
57 Paul's Letter to the Romans sent to about 3,000 Christians in 5 congregations in Rome (population 800,000).
57 Paul describes spread of the gospel: 'The sound of their voice went out to all the world; their words reached the ends of the earth (oikumene)' (Romans 10:18, GNB).
57 Greek (eastern) half of Roman empire already evangelized by Paul: 'From Jerusalem and as far round as Illyricum (1,800 miles) I have fully preached the gospel of Christ' (Romans 15:19).
58 Paul arrested in Jerusalem, imprisoned for 2 years in Caesarea; tried under procurators M. Antonius Felix and then Porcius Festus; 60, sent for trial to Rome.
58 Revolutionary messiah Benjamin the Egyptian arrives on Mount of Olives with 30,000 followers; annihilated by Romans under Felix.
58 Buddhism introduced to China.
60 *Malta.* First Christians, first missionary (shipwrecked Apostle Paul, and others).
c60 *Macedonia* (at that time near Dalmatia, Illyricum). First Christians (among Diaspora Jews).
60 Martyrdom of Apostle Philip (one of the Twelve), crucified in Hierapolis (Turkey).
c60 *Armenia.* First Christians, evangelized by settlers from Palestine and eastern Asia Minor.
60 Kingdom of Osrhoene with capital of Edessa evangelized; c100, shelters mother church of organized Asian Christianity; first independent state to profess Christian allegiance.
61 Mahayana Buddhism spreads to China.
61 Paul in Rome under military guard; gospel proclaimed in capital of empire.

**AD 61.** Remains of first Celtic church site, in Glastonbury (England).

**AD 61.** Converts among Roman soldiers and Celtic population form first congregation in Britain.

61 *Britain* (later UK). First resident Christians (Roman soldiers, merchants); origins of Celtic church.
61 Revolt against Rome by British queen Boadicea, who massacres 70,000 Romans, then dies with 80,000 Britons.
61 Apostle Simon Zelotes (Zealot, Patriot; one of the Twelve) martyred, sawn in two and crucified in Persia; also Apostle Barnabas killed in Cyprus.
61 Paul writes: 'The Good News which has reached you is spreading all over the world' (Colossians 1:6, Jerusalem Bible); 'The Good News, which you have heard, has been preached to the whole human race' (Colossians 1:23; Greek 'to all creation under the sky').
62 James the Just, brother of the Lord, ascetic bishop of Jerusalem, thrown off temple parapet and murdered by stoning in Kedron valley; successor Symeon (a first cousin of Jesus) crucified in AD 108; 13 successor bishops of Jerusalem up to AD 135 are all also Jewish Christians.
63 Paul freed in Rome, visits Spain, Greece, Asia Minor.
63 *Spain.* First Christians (Roman soldiers, merchants, evangelized by Paul).

### 1st OF 10 IMPERIAL PERSECUTIONS

64 Ist imperial Roman persecution of Christians, under emperor Nero (AD 37-68); many heroic martyrs (put to death) and confessors (tortured but surviving); Nero seen by seer of Revelation as first archetypal Antichrist, the beast whose symbolic number is 666 (= 'Caesar Neron').

**AD 64.** Emperor Nero plays as he launches 1st Imperial Roman persecution.

64 Great Fire of Rome; Apostles Peter and Paul martyred, thousands of Christians burned, impaled, crucified or otherwise killed by Nero.
64 Temple of Herod in Jerusalem finally completed.
65 Four Gospels compiled, from earlier sources and eyewitness accounts: 65 Mark, 70 Luke, 75 Matthew, 90 John.
65 Prophecies of John the Divine: 'I saw another angel flying high in the air, with an eternal message of Good News to announce to the peoples of the earth, to every race, tribe, language and nation' (Revelation 14:6, GNB).
65 First Buddhist foreign missionaries Kasyapa Matanga and Dharmaratna travel east along Old Silk Road, reach China founding White Horse monastery in Loyang; 148, first Parthian missionary for Buddhism, An Shih-kao also arrives.
66 Evangelist Luke concludes his 2-volume narrative (Luke-Acts): The worlds of empire and Judaism have now been evangelized, the Gospel is now known to all peoples throughout them, and the Great Commission there largely completed.
66 Anti-Jewish riots and pogroms in Egypt: 50,000 Jews massacred in Alexandria, 60,000 elsewhere.
66 Apostles Judas Thaddaeus and (in 68) Bartholomew (Nathanael) martyred, former by mob in Ardaze (Armenia), latter by flaying and crucifixion in

Albana, Derbend (Armenia), with a thousand believers.
67 Emperor Vespasian (AD 9-79) with 60,000 troops quells Jewish insurrection, reconquers Galilee; Zealot leader Menachem grandson of Judas the Galilean proclaims self Messiah, captures Masada and Antonian fortress in Jerusalem; Christians of Jerusalem flee to Pella.

**AD 68.** Mark, Apostle to Egypt, murdered in Alexandria; *right.* modern Coptic cathedral.

68 Martyrdom of Apostle Mark in Baucalis, near Alexandria.
69 All 4 million Jews throughout diaspora now evangelized, 'having been destined to hear the good news before judgment falls'.
69 Martyrdom of Apostle Andrew (one of the Twelve), crucified at Patras, Achaia.
69 9,000 mounted Roxolani (Iranian) warriors raid Roman province of Moesia, retreat laden with booty, but then are intercepted and cut to pieces by Roman legion III Gallica.

70 **Global status:** One generation after Christ, world is 0.1% Christians (85% of them being Non-Whites, 15% Whites), 3% evangelized; with Scriptures translated into 5 languages.
70 Obliteration of Jerusalem by Titus (AD 39-81) with 4 legions, with 'desolating sacrilege' ('abomination of desolation', i.e. Roman eagles) placed in Temple before its destruction; 600,000 killed in Judea, 10,000 Jews crucified, 90,000 Jews taken to Rome as slaves; Jews and Jewish Christians scattered abroad; destruction of Jewish Christianity and end of Judaizers.
70 After fall of Jerusalem, Antioch becomes Christian centre of eastern half of Roman empire.
c70 *Albania* (then Macedonia). First Christians (among Diaspora Jews).
c70 Martyrdom of Apostle Matthew (Levi, one of the Twelve), burned at stake in Ethiopia.
70 Origin of Christian adoption of Codex (leaves bound into a book) on papyrus instead of scroll, as predominant usage for scriptures; use of codex not adopted by pagan literature until AD 200.
c70 *Yugoslavia (Serbia, Montenegro).* First Christians.
72 Imperial Roman census under emperor Vespasian; no further censuses until Charlemagne.
73 Romans capture Zealot stronghold of Masada; no survivors after mass suicide pact.
c75 'The End will come only after a predetermined number of souls is born' (Syriac Apocalypse/II Baruch 23:4-5, cf Yebamoth 62a).
76 Old Silk Road linking West to Far East finally reopened: caravan trade prospers once more.
78 Kushan or Kusana empire (BC 50-AD 400) from Afghanistan to river Ganges in northern India under nomad Indo-Scythian dynasty and king Kanishka I ranks among world's 4 top empires along with China, Rome and Parthia; Kusanas send Buddhist missionaries to Central Asia and China.
79 Roman encyclopedist Pliny the Elder (born AD 23) is killed while observing volcanic eruption of Mount Vesuvius; nephew writes classic account of eruption and accompanying earthquake destroying cities of Pompeii, Stabiae and Herculaneum; over next 1,900 y years, over 80 more major eruptions accompanying earthquake.
79 Colosseum (Flavian Amphitheatre) built in Rome, for 50,000 spectators; large numbers of Christians thrown to beasts or otherwise martyred.
79 'Signs and wonders' (miracles demonstrating Kingdom of God) do not cease with end of Apostolic age, nor with later closing of New Testament canon, but continue throughout church history as waves of prophecy, healing, deliverance, tongues.
c80 *Tunisia* (then termed Roman province of Africa). First Christians.
c80 Missionary centre of Christianity shifts to major city Ephesus under apostle John; continuing confrontation of cult of queen of heaven centered in temple of Artemis (Diana).

**AD 80.** Temple of goddess Diana (Artemis) in Ephesus, one of Seven Wonders of the World.

c80 *France.* First Christians (from Italy).
80 Earliest known Christian hymnbook Odes of Solomon with 42 psalms produced in Edessa in Syriac language by Jewish Christians.
80 India: Jains divide by schism into the Svetambara, 'white-clad,' and the Digambara, 'sky-clad.'
c80 To make missionary and polemical activity easier, Christians begin to rapidly abandon scroll format for their copies of Scripture (though Jewish scholars continued to use scrolls for Hebrew and LXX copies until AD c600) and change to the more portable, usable, and referable form (leaf books), first probably for copies of the Pauline epistles.
c80 *Croatia.* First Christians, in Dalmatia; by 850, Croats mainly christianized, due to Latin-speaking priests from Byzantine-controlled coastal towns.
82 Martyrdom of Apostle Thomas (Didymus, one of the Twelve), murdered in Mylapore, India.

**AD 82.** Apostle Thomas, evangelist to South India, is murdered in Mylapore. *Right.* Modern postage stamps in secular India occasionally recognize Thomas origin of Indian Christianity.

c85 Writings of Apostolic Fathers (Apostolici), Greek Christian writers from 85-150: Barnabas, Clement, Hermas, Ignatius, Papias, Polycarp.
c85 Canon of Hebrew Scriptures finally fixed, through Jewish elders at Jamnia; 170, first termed 'Old Testament' by Melito of Sardis.
c85 Epistle of Barnabas predicts end of world: 'In 6 days, that is in 6,000 years, the Universe will end.'
c90 *Bosnia.* First Christians, in Roman coastal towns, with a bishop in Sirmium (Pannonia); later, over 20 Roman basilicas in Bosnia; church synods in 351, 357, 358, 359; c375 church liquidated by Gothic invasions.
c90 First of a vast number of amateur scripture translations in Old Latin.
90 Rise of Gnosticism, a dualistic rationalistic heresy; apogee 135-160.
c90 *Bulgaria.* (at that time Roman provinces of Moesia and Thracia). First Christians (churches at Anchialus and Debeltum, and along Black Sea).
91 2nd imperial Roman persecution, partly due to emperor Domitian (AD 51-96; a devotee of astrology) demanding worship as Dominus et Deus (Our Lord and God); regarded by Christians as Nero Redivivus, the Antichrist; Apostle John martyred in boiling oil (or, miraculously survives).
94 Clement bishop of Rome maintains that under apostle Paul the entire Roman empire became evangelized.
96 Chiliasm (premillennialism) dominant in first 3 centuries; taught by Clement of Rome, Ignatius of Antioch, Papias, Justin Martyr, Hippolytus, Irenaeus, Tertullian, Cyprian, Commodianus, Lactantius, Methodius, et alii; later by Waldensians, Anabaptists, 19th-century Protestants (E. Irving, J.N. Darby, J.H. Brooks, N. West, D.L. Moody, W.E. Blackstone, C.I. Scofield); 1980, held by majority of USA Evangelicals inter alios.
96 Last judgment and final retribution will not come until

foreordained number of the martyrs has been completed (Revelation 6:11).

96 Revelation of John compiled by seer on Patmos: apocalyptic, astral concepts and symbols; total opposition to state cult of emperor-worship under Domitian and queen of heaven Artemis/Diana cult.

98 Roman emperor Trajan (AD 53-117) extends Roman empire to include Arabia, Iraq, Armenia, Romania, Hungary.

98 Antonine dynasty, third major Roman dynasty, begins with emperor Trajan and ends with Marcus Aurelius and Commodus by AD 192; the Roman empire's golden age.

100 **Global status:** 2 generations after Christ, world is 0.4% Christians (70% of them being Non-Whites, 30% Whites), 5.9% evangelized; with Scriptures translated into 6 languages; total martyrs since AD 33, 53,000 (4.9% of all Christians ever; rate 800 p.a.).

100 Rome the first and only metropolis in world to reach or pass 1 million population (until AD 1770); slaves number 60%; by 450 falls to under 250,000, and to under 19,000 by 1360 due to Black Death; then rises to 1 million by 1930.

100 *Saudi Arabia* (then Arabia). First Christians; later eradicated in 7th century by Islam.

c100 *Kuwait*. First Christians, later connected with episcopal see of Rima.

100 World's 5 largest cities: Rome 1,100,000, Loyang 510,000, Alexandria 400,000, Seleucia 300,000, Changan 245,000.

100 Teotihuacan (Mexico) established as America's first urban civilization, built around massive pyramids of the Sun and Moon; 45,000 in AD 150, 90,000 in AD 350; at its height in AD 590, city contains 160,000 people and controls empire covering all Meso-America; other centers Tikal, Mochica, Zapotec, Uaxactun, Pachacamac, Monte Alban.

c100 *Monaco*. First Christians (soldiers, traders).

c100 *Algeria* (at that time Roman province of Mauretania). First Christians (Latin-speaking).

c100 *Sri Lanka* (then Ceylon). First Christians (Christians of St Thomas from India; Nestorians).

c100 Christianity predominantly urban, based on Roman cities, spreading from city to city along trade routes; later missions to Armenia, Ethiopia, China (under Nestorians) all center on capital cities.

100 Buddhist Council, held in Gandhara (India), with 499 selected scholars; doctrinal debates, composition of Mahavibhasa; meanwhile, Buddhism spreads across China, where Confucian temples have been built in each of China's 2,000 counties.

104 Small Persian border kingdom of Adiabene evangelized by disciples of Addai named Aggai, Mari, and its first bishop Pkidha; its capital Arbela (Erbil) becomes earliest Christian center of mission to the East.

110 3rd imperial Roman persecution, under emperor Trajan; 111, severe persecution in Bythinia.

110 Armenia: persecution of Christians by Persian tyrant Artaxerxes.

110 Long history of martyrdoms in Edessa: under Roman emperor Trajan's Imperial Persecution, c115 Sharbil, Babay, Barsamya are murdered; and regularly on to 306 persecution under emperor Licinius.

110 Buddhist council is held in Kashmir; Mahayana and Hinayana sects split off.

110 Britain: gradual formation of several independent Celtic Churches (of England, c140 Wales, c180 Scotland, c250 Ireland); all retain their isolation (until 3 British bishops attend Councils of Arles and Ariminum in 314), their further isolation after 450 Anglo-Saxon invasion and extermination of Christianity in England, their freedom from Rome and the Western Church until 663 Synod of Whitby, and their independence itself until rule from England after 1200.

115 Antioch destroyed by earthquake; Christians blamed, bishop Ignatius thrown to lions; 526, 250,000 killed in another quake.

116 Jewish uprisings in Palestine, Egypt, Cyrene, Cyprus and Mesopotamia.

117 Roman emperor Hadrian (76-138) codifies laws of Rome, establishes postal system throughout empire; executes 11,000 soldier Christian converts, also 2 bishops of Rome—Sixtus I, and Telesphorus.

117 Gnostic thinker Basilides of Alexandria is first to treat New Testament writings explicitly as Scripture.

c120 *Romania*. First Christians (in Roman province of Dacia).

c130 *Moldavia*. First Christians, settlers from Romania.

c130 Christianity instils exclusivistic claims for Christ through initiatory procedures (catechumenate, baptism, eucharist), disciplinary procedures (safeguarding purity of the church, also restoration of offenders), Scriptures, creed, apostolic ministry; stressing Christianity's absolute covenant claims in areas of monotheism, morality, and mission; spreads principally and normally, though not exclusively, through (as prevailing strategy) the planting of churches which then serve as missionary communities to evangelize their areas by continuing to attract and enlist converts; most converts are reached through casual contacts, witnessing a martyrdom, hospitality, care of strangers, et alia.

c132 Chinese mathematician Zhang Heng (78-139) invents first seismograph.

132 Second Jewish rebellion under alleged messiah Bar Kokeba, after he persecutes and executes Christians for 3 years; 134, Romans intervene, obliterate city; second destruction of Jerusalem by Romans; 580,000 Jews killed in battle; almost entire Jewish population of Palestine dies or flees; final dispersal of the Jews.

136 Hadrian refounds Jerusalem as pagan city Aelia Capitolina; temple of Jupiter built on site of Solomon's Temple.

c140 'Shepherd of Hermas' written, reveals highly developed ecclesiastical system of bishops, deacons, and priests; writes: 'The Son of God... has been preached to the ends of the earth'.

140 Valentinus, failing to be elected bishop of Rome, writes Gnostic treatise *Gospel of Truth*.

140 Egyptian astronomer-mathematician Ptolemy of Alexandria (c100-c151) codifies Babylonian astrological tradition, writes 13-volume *Almagest* (geocentric cosmology, geometry, trigonometry), also *Tetrabiblos*: *Work on Astrology* also *Guide to geography*; holds Earth is a sphere at center of Universe; uses conical projection to map whole world from Britain to China.

c140 Epistle of Barnabas, containing earliest Christian equating of the 7 Days of Creation with the 7 millennia of world history.

144 Wealthy ship-owner Marcion (c85-c160) excommunicated, founds schismatic, heretical, rival religion throughout Roman empire, influential till c400; first to specify a closed canon of New Testament writings; c700, Marcionism finally dies out.

c150 *Georgia*. First Christians (Armenians, Byzantines); 337, through female slave Nina, state embraces Christianity.

c150 Chinese begin carving religious texts on stone tablets, inking surfaces to make impressions.

c150 School of Alexandria founded in Egypt, becomes center for early Christian theology and Greek philosophy; prominent teachers include theologians Clement (died c215) and Origen (c185-254).

c150 Roman Julius Maternus crosses Sahara, reaching modern-day Chad on his four-month journey.

150 Minor persecution under emperor Antoninus Pius.

c150 Mandaeanism, a Jewish-Christian Gnostic syncretistic religion, begun in Iran.

c150 *Morocco* (then part of Roman province of Mauretania). First Christians (4 bishoprics in Tangier-Rabat-Fez area before 200).

c150 *Portugal* (then Roman province of Lusitania). First Christians (Romans).

c150 Latin now common language of Christian communities in West, replacing Greek as language of church of Rome for its first 100 years.

c 150 Justin Martyr (c100-165) founds disciple-training school over a house in Rome, documents current 'signs and wonders' (exorcisms, healings and prophesyings), and writes: 'The first Apostles, twelve in number, in the power of God went out and proclaimed Christ to every race of men'; and 'There is not one single race of men, whether barbarians, or Greeks, or whatever they may be called, nomads, or vagrants, or herdsmen dwelling in tents, among whom prayers and giving of thanks are not offered through the name of the Crucified Jesus'; teaches that all orthodox Christians believe in a resurrection of the flesh and in a millennial reign in the New Jerusalem; martyred at Rome.

c150 *Germany*. First Christians in south, centered on Roman administrative center Augsburg, as episcopal see, with 2 more by 250; 500, Christianity becoming dominant; 722, Boniface as archbishop works for conversion of Germans.

c150 Greek Old Testament (Septuagint) translated into colloquial Old Latin.

155 Other influential apologists write extensively on the Holy Spirit: Tatian, Athenagoras, Theophilus of Antioch, Irenaeus (130-202), Tertullian, Clement of Alexandria (155-215), Origen (185-254), Cyprian (200-258), Hippolytus of Rome.

156 Death at the stake of Polycarp bishop of Smyrna, aged 87 years.

156 Phrygia: rise of Montanism under new convert Montanus (c120-c175), a puritanical, prophetic, charismatic, millennial, apocalyptic movement claiming to be a new age of the Holy Spirit; 156, call for Christians to come to Phrygia to await Second Coming; in village of Ardabau, Montanus with Priscilla and Maximilla begins to prophesy that heavenly Jerusalem will soon descend to Earth at Pepuza, a neighboring town in Phrygia, thus inaugurating Kingdom of God; 206, Tertullian joins; 230, movement excommunicated by Synod of Iconium; continues underground until c880.

160 Numerous 2nd-century Christian apologists at work, including Quadratus bishop of Athens (*Apology*, addressed to emperor Hadrian), Aristides (Athens), Justin Martyr, Tatian, Athenagoras (Athens), Theophilus bishop of Antioch, Melito bishop of Sardis (20 works), Hegesippus (a converted Jew).

c160 First known work of fiction in which man travels to the Moon, composed by Lucian of Samosata.

165 4th imperial Roman persecution, under learned Stoic emperor Marcus Aurelius (121-180); issues New Decrees prohibiting all new religious cults.

c170 Portions of Scripture in Coptic translated.

170 Asia's first theologian and Bible translator Tatian of Assyria (c110-180), pupil of Justin Martyr, produces earliest harmony of 4 Gospels, his *Diatessaron*, in Syriac the trading lingua franca of the ancient Asian Middle East.

174 *Austria*. First Christians.

176 Celsus writes attacking Christianity, Christ and Judaism; his *True Discourse* is first significant published attack, with Platonic defense of polytheism; derides Christianity for its inclusion of hoi polloi (common people).

177 Violent persecutions in Lyons and Vienne, France; among 48 known martyrs are several Celtic Gauls including Vettius Epagathus and Blandina.

177 Abgar VIII the Great begins 35-year reign over first Christian kingdom Osrhoene, a client-state of Roman empire; Christians under Rome have worshiped in homes for first two hundred years, but in Edessa by 200 first church buildings anywhere are built; many heresies rampant including Gnosticism and Marcionism.

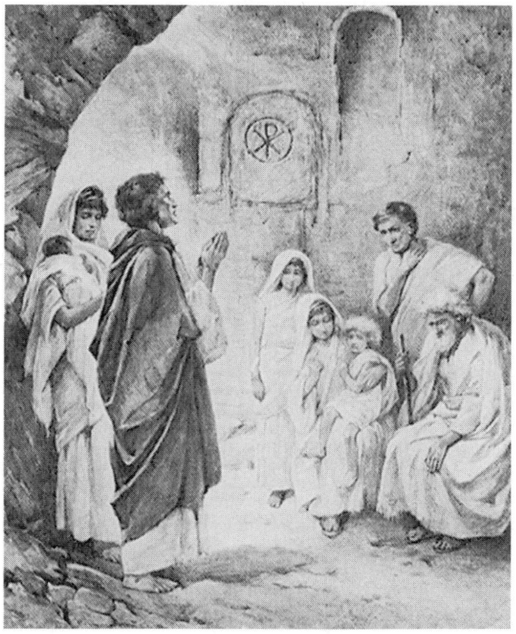

**AD 180.** Worship in Catacombs under Rome and other cities provides some safety for Christians.

180 Christians now found in all provinces of Roman empire and in Mesopotamia.

180 First African Christians martyred in Carthage: Scillitans from Scilli, Numidia.

c180 Pantaenus founds missionary training school in Alexandria (Egypt); visits India, reports Christian activity in Malabar; dies 190.

c180 Gnostic Gospels and Acts of Thomas written.

c180 Basis for a Christian apologetic and appeals for conversion has now become 6 institutions: baptism, eucharist, disciplinary procedures, Scriptures, apostolic ministry, extensive charities; and other factors including rescue from occult powers.

c180 Method of printing text discovered, empirically, in China, using ink (BC 2300), paper (AD 105), and texts carved in relief; c550, wood blocks in use; oldest known printed works are Buddhist incantations printed in Japan AD 764; first book 'The Diamond Sutra' in China, AD 868; c1041, Chinese invent movable type.

c 180 Irenaeus bishop of Lyons (c120-203) documents recent charismata (exorcisms, visions, prophecies), and teaches that Antichrist will be a Jew of the tribe of Dan, also Christ will inaugurate a literal millennium of 1,000 years.

c180 Greek satirist Lucian of Samosata (c120-185), earliest known author to write about space travel, in *The True History* describes ship blown to Moon by strong wind, crew encounters Sun and Moon creatures; writes *'Icaro-Menippos'*, to debunk Greek view of religion with its multiple deities.

180 Mexican city of Teotihuacan has 100,000 population and covers 11 square miles; grows to 250,000 by AD 500.

c180 Mesopotamian apologist Theophilus bishop of Antioch writes *To Autolycus*, develops doctrine of the Logos, becomes first to use term 'Triad' (Greek *trias*) to describe the Holy Trinity, God as Father, Son, Spirit.

c190 New Testament in Latin completed; Victor bishop of Rome becomes first Roman Christian to write in Latin.

c190 Widespread turning to Christianity, with vast numbers, in North Africa.

c190 Synod of Ephesus, convened by bishop Polycrates of Ephesus, fixes official date of Easter but it is repudiated by Roman pope Victor I.

c195 Rise begins of episcopal confirmation separate from baptism, with infant baptism followed later by confirmation (laying on of hands).

196 Christians numerous in Bactria, south of Oxus; by 225 Christian communities are planted in Hindu Kush and into Kurdistan.

196 Bardaisan of Edessa describes presence of Christians among Gilanians on shores of Caspian Sea and among Kushan in Bactria.

197 Tertullian (c160-222) documents recent healings and exorcisms, also writes: 'Christ commanded them to go and teach all nations. Immediately, therefore,

so did the apostles'; 'The blood of the martyrs is seed'; and 'There is no nation indeed which is not Christian'; 206, joins Montanist movement.

200 **Global status:** 6 generations after Christ, world is 2.4% Christians (68.0% of them being Non-Whites, 32.0% Whites), 9.3% evangelized; with Scriptures translated into 7 languages; total martyrs since AD 33 have been 177,000 (1.5% of all Christians ever; rate 1,200 per year).

c200 *Slovenia*. First Christians, from Austrian churches; c950, Slovene churches organized.

200 Most of New Testament available in Sahidic Coptic (Upper Egypt), later in Bohairic/Memphitic Coptic (Coastal or Lower Egypt around Alexandria).

c200 *Switzerland* (then called Roman province of Raetia). First Christians (Roman soldiers, merchants).

c200 *Sahara* (later Spanish, Western). First Christians; eradicated during later Muslim rule.

c200 *Belgium*. First Christians (during Roman occupation).

c200 First permanent church buildings constructed (all worship previously in homes); only in cities, at first.

c200 Edessa (now Urfa) first city-state to make Christianity its state religion; conversion of its king Abgar IX (179-216), first Christian political ruler; missionary center for eastern Syria.

c200 *Hungary* (at that time Roman provinces of Pannonia and Valeria). First Christians (Arian, Roman and Orthodox missionaries).

c200 Mahayana Buddhist traditions take literary form in India; *Mahabharata* and *Ramayana*, once secular epics, now sacred Hindu texts.

c200 Formation of 'square Hebrew' script from Aramaic.

c200 Lifetime of Lakulisa, famed guru who leads a reformist movement within Pasupata Saivism.

c200 First Hindu kingdoms in Cambodia and Malaysia.

c200 *Ukraine*. First Christians, immigrating from south, settling in Crimea and Sarmatia (Scythia); 328, Crimean bishop at Council of Nicea; 547, Gothic Christians in Crimea ask emperor Justinian for a bishop; c850 Christians and churches in Kiev; 954, baptism of Olga ruler of Kiev; 987, state declared Greek Orthodox after ruler Vladimir is baptized.

c200 *Gibraltar*. First Christians, from strong churches in Spain.

202 5th imperial Roman persecution, under Septimius Severus (146-211); 202, emperor issues edict prohibiting conversions to Christianity or Judaism; vicious imperial persecution in Egypt with thousands martyred, especially in Thebes (100 a day) and Upper Egypt; in Carthage, Perpetua and Felicitas martyred; imminent appearance of Antichrist widely expected.

c205 First known Christian scholar and apologist Clement of Alexandria (c155-215) deals with how Christian faith relates to Greek philosophy and culture, writes: 'The whole world, with Athens and Greece, has already become the domain of the Word'.

c210 *Qatar* (then Persian province of Beit Qatraiye). First Christians (first documents AD 224).

210 Tertullian writes in *Against Marcion* that every morning for 40 days a walled city has appeared in the sky in Judea, fading slowly during the day, a sign that New Jerusalem is about to appear.

c215 Tertullian (and almost all Christians up to AD 313) totally prohibits Christian military service; Christians generally oppose army, forbid believers becoming soldiers, condemn all military warfare, though all use military idioms and metaphors in teaching and preaching; but by AD 250 opposition to army service changes, custom falls into disuse.

215 General massacre of Copts in Alexandria ordered by emperor Caracalla.

217 Roman presbyter Hippolytus attempts as bishop to oust new pope Calixtus I, but fails; 235, martyred; first of 40 such antipopes over next 1,200 years.

220 First Buddhist missions from India to Viet Nam, 272 to China and Korea, 420 to Burma, Java and Sumatra, 552 to Japan, 650 to Tibet, 720 to Siam.

c220 Origen (c185-254) writes: 'The gospel of Jesus Christ has been preached in all creation under heaven, to Greeks and barbarians, to wise and foolish... It is impossible to see any race of men which has avoided accepting the teaching of Jesus'; 'The divine goodness of Our Lord and Saviour is equally diffused among the Britons, the Africans, and other nations of the world'; and 'The preaching of the gospel through the whole Oikumene shows that the church is receiving divine support'; but also 'Many people, not only barbarians, but even in the Empire, have not yet heard the word of Christ'; and 'The gospel has not yet been preached to all nations, since it has not reached the Chinese or the Ethiopians beyond the river, and only small parts of the more remote and barbarous tribes'; 248, in *Contra Celsum* foresees possibility of conversion of entire world.

220 First known Chinese encyclopedia, *Huang-lan* (Emperor's Mirror) prepared.

221 First Christian synchronistic history of the world, correlating pagan and Judeo-Christian data from Creation to AD 221: *Chronicles*, in 5 books by Sextus Julius Africanus (c170-c240), a native of Jerusalem; also an encyclopedia of general knowledge called *Kestoi* in 24 books; only fragments of both works survive.

c223 Origen operates a major scriptorium at Caesarea, producing Bible copies; employs women stenographers taking shorthand.

225 Over 20 Assyrian bishoprics of Church of the East in Tigris-Euphrates region and to Caspian Sea and Bahrain; revival of Zoroastrianism noted.

225 Persia extensively penetrated by Christians, with over 20 resident bishops.

225 Sassanid dynasty comes to power in Persia; as Zoroastrians, they forge alliance of state and religion that by 272 ends 3 centuries of toleration enjoyed by Christians in Persia; rules Iran, central Asia, and Transcaucasia, until 651.

230 Armenia: violent persecution under Persian king Shapur I almost blots out Christianity.

230 Amillennialism (rejecting a literal millennium of 1,000 years) taught by Origen, Constantine, Augustine of Hippo, then replaces premillennialism as majority view in Church of Rome and later Protestantism.

234 Hippolytus bishop of Porto traces history since Creation calculating since 5,500 years separated Adam and Christ, duration of world will be 6,000 years, then 200 years are left before End of world.

235 6th imperial Roman persecution, under Maximinus (Thrax; died 238).

235 Origen writes his *Exhortation to Martyrs*; 254, dies as martyr himself after imprisonment and torture.

c240 Gregory Thaumaturgos (c213-270) made bishop of Pontus, a majority pagan diocese; mass movement begins, 95% converted before his death.

241 Rise of Manicheism under youthful prophet Mani (216-276), creating a new dualistic hierarchical rival religion to Christianity; bitterly persecuted; vast missionary expansion, spreads west to Spain and east to China; Mani seized and crucified by Zoroastrians, with followers slaughtered throughout Persia; huge numbers flee across Asia, spreading their religion along Old Silk Road to China; Manichaean communities survive in Chinese Turkestan until 1280; final decline in 15th century.

244 Christian hierarchy established in northwest Arabia.

248 Cyprian (200-258) bishop of Carthage insists on rebaptism of all baptized outside Catholic church, and writes: 'Extra ecclesiam nulla salus' (*Letters*).

249 7th imperial Roman persecution, under military ruler Decius (c201-251): first universal and systematic state attempt to destroy Christianity; first persecution aimed directly at the clergy and bishops, with sizeable defections; first mass appearance of lapsi, libellatici, sacrificati, traditores.

249 Seven missionary bishops sent to peoples of Celtic Gaul by pope Fabian of Rome: Gatien (Tours), Trophime (Arles), Paul (Narbonne), Saturnin (Toulouse), Denis (Paris), Martial (Limoges), Austremoine (Clermont); Gaul now has 30 episcopal sees.

250 Over 100 bishoprics in southern Italy, all centered in urbanized cities; Latinization of Roman Christianity, and emergence of 'interpretatio romana'.

c250 Church founded in Chersonesus (Sebastopol), Crimea, Ukraine.

c250 *Ireland* (then Hibernia). First Christians: migrant traders from Britain and Brittany, also slaves captured in Gaul; further surge in 350 (monks from Crete and Egypt).

c250 *Bahrain*. First Christians, with a bishopric.

c250 Peshitta (Simple), Syriac version of Bible, completed.

c250 *Luxembourg*. First Christians (Roman soldiers).

c250 First book on algebra produced by Diophantus in Alexandria.

250 Syriac Didascalia Apostolorum (Teaching of the Apostles) written in Edessa by bishop (a Jewish medical doctor); describes travels of Twelve Apostles across world, including Thomas in India; oldest manual of church order extant.

c250 Persia: gradual rise of developed episcopate and centralization of church authority.

250 Classical period of Maya civilization, flourishing with massive pyramids from Yucatan to Honduras (Copan, Palenque, Uxmal), America's most complex writing system, mathematics, accurate astrological calendars, *Popol Vuh* sacred book; every aspect dominated by religion, with time (regarded as divine) as majestic succession of cycles without beginning or end; world believed to be over 400 million years old, preceded by several earlier created then destroyed universes; torture, human sacrifices; 900, sudden catastrophical total collapse due to overpopulation, water shortage, over-exploitation of rain-forest ecosystem, uncontrolled vicious warfare; survives until 16th century Conquest.

c250 Hexapla, a major revision of Greek Septuagint (LXX) by Origen, arranges OT text in 6 parallel columns: consonantal text in Hebrew characters, its transliteration into Greek, Aquila's translation, Symmachus' translation, a revised LXX.

251 City of Rome: 45,000 Christians (4.5% of population of 1 million), 46 presbyters, 14 deacons, 42 acolytes, 52 exorcists, supporting 1,500 widows and persons in distress at cost of $90,000 (US dollars 1985 value) each year; by AD 300, church buildings in Rome increase to over 40.

251 Roman field army under emperor Decius destroyed at Abrittus (Dobruja) by Goths, killing Decius.

251 Novatian (c200-258), first learned Roman theologian to write in Latin, emerges as second antipope in papal history, founding rigorist (anti-lapsi) Novatian schism; documents contemporary charismata (prophesyings, tongues, healings, miracles, powers); martyred 258, but his sect spreads across empire and lasts until after AD 600.

252 Catastrophic plague epidemic strikes Mediterranean world, kills 25% of entire population of Roman empire over 20 years; 50% die in Alexandria; in Carthage, bishop Cyprian organizes medical aid; followed by debased coinage, financial disaster, then by famine, earthquakes, tornadoes, and huge tidal waves.

257 8th imperial Roman persecution, under Valerian (Ist Rescript, against all bishops and priests); 258, 2nd Rescript, of increased severity; martyrdom of Cyprian and Roman pope Sixtus II; 260, death of Valerian.

259 Wide-ranging Barbarian incursions into Roman empire: Alemannic invasion of Italy, reaching also to southern France and Spain, finally defeated at Milan by emperor Gallienus; cities now acquire heavily-protected walls.

260 Edict of Toleration, under Gallienus (died 268); Christianity becomes a religio licita until Diocletian.

c260 Neoplatonist polemicist Porphyry (c233-305) writes, as most bitter and dangerous enemy of Christianity, 15 books *Against the Christians*, and a more general *Prophetic apology for Christ*.

c270 *Azerbaijan*. First Christians and some churches (Nestorians, some Byzantines, Armenians).

c270 Rise of monasticism in Egypt, as direct challenge to lifestyle of the rich: (1) eremitical (Anthony of Egypt, c251-356), (2) cenobitic (Pachomius, c287-346); widespread over next 2 centuries, with many documented healings, exorcisms, miracles, signs and wonders; Egyptian monks travel widely, evangelizing in Europe, Britain, Ireland et alia.

c270 *Netherlands*. First Christians: in Roman garrisons in Aduatica Tungrorum (near Maastricht).

275 9th imperial Roman persecution, under Aurelian (c215-275) who plans major escalation but suddenly dies.

c275 Buddhist monastery Mahavihara is founded in Anuradhapura, capital of Sri Lanka.

c280 *Uzbekistan* and *Tajikistan*. First Christians, travelers on the 4,000-mile caravan tract, the Silk Road; by 410, 25% of entire populations are Christians.

c280 First rural churches emerge, in northern Italy, and by 4th and 5th centuries in France also; Christianity no longer exclusively urban.

284 'Era of the Martyrs' begins for Coptic Orthodox Church in Egypt, because of massive imperial killings from then on; all future Coptic history is reckoned AM (After the Martyrs; so that AD 2000 = AM 1716).

285 Papa Bar-Aggai appointed and consecrated first bishop of Seleucia-Ctesiphon, in united Persian church; 314 deposed, dies 327; 410, Isaac declared catholicos; 421, Dadyeshu becomes first patriarch.

285 Roman empire partitioned into eastern and western empires.

286 Brief persecution of Persian church under shah Varahran II.

287 Mass conversion of Armenia begins under Gregory the Illuminator (c240-332), provoking violent persecution from pagan king Tiridates II; 295, king baptized, Christianity declared state religion; 301, Gregory becomes catholicos of Armenia and consecrates 400 bishops.

290 Roman empire reorganized by emperor Diocletian (245-316) into 4 prefectures, 15 dioceses (secular areas governed by imperial vicars), 120 provinces; Christians begin to relate their ecclesiastical jurisdictions to these political boundaries.

c299 Greek navigator Pytheas explores Atlantic coast of Europe and British Isles, may have reached Norway or Iceland.

300 **Global status:** 9 generations after Christ, world is 7.3% Christians (66.4% of them being Non-Whites, 33.6% Whites), 17.1% evangelized; with Scriptures translated into 10 languages; total martyrs since AD 33 now 627,000 (1.3% of all Christians ever; recent rate 4,500 per year).

c300 *Afghanistan* (then Khorasan). First Christians, with Nestorian bishop of Herat.

c300 *Turkmenistan*. First Christians; by 424, strong episcopal see Merv sends out teams of Persian monks on evangelistic journeys.

c300 Areas of strongest Christian development in Roman empire: Syria, Asia Minor, Egypt, North Africa, also Rome, Lyons; chief numerical strength in east; no area in empire entirely unevangelized.

c300 Over 200 Christian dioceses already established in Italy.

300 Dudi (David) bishop of Basra leaves his see and evangelizes in India with large numbers of converts there; diocese of Basra and province of Fars become starting-points of vast network of missionary monasteries down Persian Gulf to Socotra, and across Persia as far as south India.

c300 *Russia*. First Christians with bishop Audius exiled to South Russia by emperor Constantine; attempt to evangelize the Khazars; c990, 3 bishoprics, state proclaimed Orthodox with most clergy and bishops being Greeks.

c300 Many Post-Nicene Greek Fathers publish expositions on the Holy Spirit: Eusebius of Caesarea (265-339), Cyril of Jerusalem (310-386), Athanasius (296-373), John Chrysostom (347-407), Basil, Gregory of Nyssa.

c300 Licchavi dynasty (300-900) establishes Hindu rule of Himalayan kingdom of Nepal; major intellectual and commercial center between South and Central Asia.

300 Mayan empire, guided by skilled astronomers.

301 *San Marino*. First Christians, as Marinus and group of believers settle to escape persecution.

303 10th and last imperial Roman persecution, under Diocletian; aimed at clergy and bishops, with sub-

stantial defections; destruction of all church buildings and Scriptures ordered.

304 Diocletian decrees death penalty for all Christians: 3,500 formal or official executions of church leaders including many bishops, with some further 750,000 Christians killed or executed in 10 years of systematic slaughter.

305 Total legions in Roman army 68 (up from 34 over period AD 6-231); a legion has now fallen from 6,000 to around 3,000 men who are both heavy infantrymen and also combat engineers; together with cavalry, scouts, frontier guards and other varieties of troops, total imperial armed forces 620,000 (64% frontier, 36% central reserve field armies).

306 Ascetic Jacob of Nisibis consecrated as that city's first bishop.

c308 Church of the Martyrs with 29 bishops in Egypt organized by bishop Meletius (died 325) of Lycopolis, in opposition to leniency towards lapsi favored by Peter I Ieromartyros (Seal of Martyrs) patriarch of Alexandria who is himself martyred in 311; Meletian sect is approved by Arians, lasts until c520.

c310 Eusebius of Caesarea (c265-339) writes apologetic works: Praeparatio evangelica (refuting paganism), Demonstratio evangelica (fulfilment of Hebrew prophecy in Christ); 314, completes his Ecclesiastical History, and Martyrs of Palestine; writes 'The doctrine of the Saviour has irradiated the whole Oikumene (whole inhabited earth)'.

311 Donatist schism in North Africa; rigorists, opposing leniency towards those who lapsed under persecution; by 330, 270 Donatist bishops rising to 310 by AD 394; 347, persecution under Macarius results in many Donatist martyrs; schism persists until Saracens destroy African church by AD 700.

312 Constantine (c280-337) marches on Rome, sees sign 'In hoc signo vinces (By this sign conquer)'.

313 Episcopal sees in Gaul (still 70% pagan) increase from 12 at accession of Constantine to 119 by AD 600.

313 Constantine at Milan issues Edict of Toleration legalizing Christianity throughout Roman empire; 323, becomes sole emperor, attempts to spread gospel by law and authority.

313 Bishop of Edessa, Qona, begins building of its great cathedral.

313 First Celtic stone church buildings in Britain.

314 Three of the 20 Celtic bishops in Britain (population 2,000,000) attend council of Arles in France, as well as 14 Gallican bishops, to resolve Donatist schism; also 343 Council of Sardica (Sophia); also, 359, Celtic envoys attend Council of Ariminum (Rimini) to deal with Arian dispute.

314 Synod of Seleucia: Persian church deposes bishop Papa.

314 Council of Ancyra (Galatia) promulgates canons penalizing *lapsi.*

318 Egyptian presbyter Arius (256-336) propounds Arianism (Christ a created being, not truly divine); held by some to be the Antichrist because he and it denied divinity of Jesus Christ; a major christological controversy, lasting into 8th century.

319 Pagan sacrifices prohibited throughout Roman empire.

325 Council of Nicea I (1st Ecumenical Council): divinity of Jesus clarified, Arianism condemned; also, council makes political province the basic unit for church's larger divisions, brings church's jurisdictional areas into line with secular dioceses and provinces of Roman empire, in order better to witness.

327 Persian king Shapur II (309-379), supporter of state religion of Mazdaism (Zoroastrianism), becomes alarmed at Christianity's official sponsoring by Roman empire, and its spread across his empire, so orders forcible apostasy of all Christians; savage persecution ensues for 40 years.

329 Ascetic Egyptian monk Hilarion of Gaza (291-371), missionary to idolatrous pagans of Palestine, introduces monasticism and establishes first monastery, conducts widely-attested ministry of signs and wonders (healings, exorcisms).

330 **Global status:** 10 generations after Christ, world is 12% Christians (65.7% of them being Non-Whites, 34.3% Whites), 36% evangelized; with Scriptures translated into 10 languages.

330 Constantine rebuilds city of Byzantium as Constantinople and establishes it as new imperial capital of empire; becomes known as 'new Rome'; Christianity now overwhelmingly an urban phenomenon.

330 Origins of parochial system: dioceses begin to be subdivided into parishes; by 400, established in most cities along coast of Gaul; evangelization of rural Europe well advanced.

c330 Catacombs in widespread use (till 10th century) as subterranean burial places and refuges for Christians under persecution; in Rome, they extend several hundred miles.

332 Ethiopia: shipwrecked Syrian slave Frumentius arrives in Axum; later becomes first bishop; origins of Ethiopian Orthodox Church.

332 Constantine orders 50 vellum Greek Bibles for use in new churches in Constantinople, similar to Codex Sinaiticus (c350), Codex Alexandrinus (c420), Codex Vaticanus (c350; the most perfect extant Bible), all being majuscules (uncials, in inch-high capital letters) until miniscules (in small-size cursive letters) are later introduced by AD c750 and by c1050 displace majuscules; hundreds of copies remain extant by AD 2000.

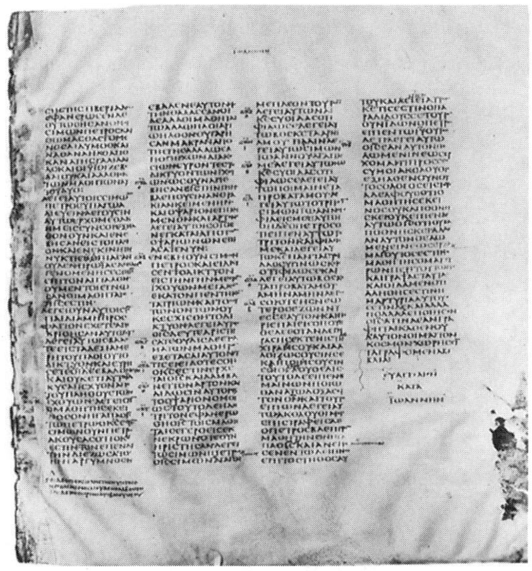

**AD 332.** Codex Sinaiticus, a Greek vellum Bible that may have been ordered by Constantine.

334 Merv north of river Oxus becomes seat of a bishopric of Church of the East; and Samarkand since c550.

336 At Carthage, Donatus calls council of 270 bishops; Jerome admits Donatus has made his church the religion of 'nearly all Africa'.

337 Leading Eastern theologian of the 4th century, bishop Aphrahat the Persian writes *Demonstration Part I*, and in 345, *Part II*.

339 Great Persian Persecution by Sassanid rulers under Shapur II, until 363, again from 379-390, and in 402, with Eastern church as a national organization virtually destroyed; 3 catholicoses martyred: 344 Simon Bar-Sabbae, 345 Shahdost, 346 Barbashmin; one of most massive persecutions of Christians in history unequaled for duration, ferocity, and number of martyrs; waves of Christian refugees flee Persia; persecution continues until 402, then sporadically until 640 conquest by Islam.

c340 Coptic Orthodox bishoprics under pope Athanasius (c296-373) number 100 in Egypt.

340 Beginnings of coenobitic monasticism in Persia under Aphrahat and mountain bishopric of Mar Mattai north of Mosul; rapid spread of missionary monasteries throughout Persia and the Gulf.

341 Council of Antioch: 97 Eastern bishops counter Rome's charges of Arianism.

342 *Yemen.* First church built at Aden; persecution by Jewish rulers, with many martyrdoms.

343 Synod or Council of Gangra (Paphlagonia in Asia Minor) condemns Eustathius and heretical followers for rejecting veneration of saints and relics.

344 Destruction of Persian churches: catholicos Simon Bar-Sabbae, 5 bishops, 100 priests beheaded in city of Susa; general massacres of Christians throughout next 20 years.

345 Persecution in East Syria and Persia drives Nestorian merchant Thomas of Cana with 400 Persian Christians including deacons, priests, and a bishop, to migrate to Cranganore and settle in southwest India.

346 At time of Pachomius' death, over 500,000 monks (7% of population of Egypt) live in numerous monasteries (Tabennesis 7,000, Mount Nitrea 5,000, Arsinoe over 10,000).

346 Plague sweeps Egypt, decimates Copts, churches, monasteries.

347 Cyril bishop of Jerusalem (310-386) teaches that Antichrist will be a magician who takes over Roman empire, claims to be Christ, deceives Jews by rebuilding Temple, persecutes Christians, then is slain at Second Advent by the Son of God.

347 Vicious persecution of Donatist church with its 270 bishops, resulting in many martyrs.

c350 Codex Vercellensis parchment book, most ancient extant manuscript of Old Latin version of NT.

c350 Nestorians on Socotra island, with own bishop from 5th to 15th centuries.

c350 Sudan: Coptic Orthodox traders active from Egypt; on breakup of kingdom of Meroe over next 100 years, its 3 successor states become officially Christian.

350 Apogee of Arianism: whole of East now Arian.

350 Golden age of Buddhism in China (to AD 800); 401, Kumarajiva translates Sanskrit texts into Chinese.

c350 Apocalyptic text 'Oracle of Baalbek' states Byzantium will rule another 60 years before arrival of Messiah; in 500 a scribe amends text to read 180 years; figure is revised again to 1800 years in 12th century.

c350 Celtic Church in Britain flourishes, producing during next 500 years a large number of notable white-robed missionary peregrini ('pilgrims for Christ'), mainly Irish: Ninian, Patrick, Illtyd, Beuno, Brigid, Brendan, David, Teilo, Columba, Kentigern, Aidan, et alii.

352 First recorded supernova is reported, by Chinese astronomers.

356 Yemen now has 5 churches built—one in Roman colony Aden, 2 in Himyarite territory, one at Zafar the capital, and another at Sana with its 20-storey royal castle (first skyscraper in recorded history).

c360 *Kazakhstan.* First Christians (Nestorian missionaries).

c360 8-volume *Apostolic Constitutions*, a Syrian collection of ecclesiastical law, makes frequent allusions to Great Commission of Jesus in Matthew 28:19-20.

360 Rise of Western monasticism under Martin of Tours (dies 397) in Celtic Gaul; Ninian of Whithorn in Scottish Galloway pioneers Christianity in Pictish Scotland, trains monastic missionaries at Rosnat.

361 Julian the Apostate (331-363) last emperor to attempt to replace Christianity throughout Roman empire by a revived polytheism; undertakes a full-scale restoration of pagan religion; his death signals final triumph of Christianity in both Eastern and Western empires.

361 World's 5 largest cities: Constantinople 350,000, Loyang 296,000, Rome 250,000, Patna 224,000, Ctesiphon 200,000.

363 Shapur II inflicts crushing defeat on invading Roman emperor Julian the Apostate at Samarra; 100,000 Christian families then uprooted and resettled in eastern Persia, Isfahan and Susiana.

363 Ephrem the Syrian (c306-373), Eastern church's best-known theologian, Bible expositor and hymn writer, migrates west from Nisibis (Persia) to Edessa (in Roman empire), writes voluminously.

363 Western Tanukh tribe of Arabs north of Damascus become Christians along with their queen.

364 Conversion of Vandals to Arianism.

365 Council of Laodicea (Phrygia): 32 bishops promulgate 60 canons.

367 Canon of New Testament finally agreed on, the 27 books being listed in Athanasius' Easter Letter (367) for the East, by the Synod of Rome (382) for the West, and by the Synod of Carthage (397) for the entire church.

c370 Ulfilas (311-381), an Arian, bishop of the Goths and later in Moesia II; creates German alphabet and translates Bible into Visigothic (first translation of Bible for specifically missionary purposes).

370 Tyconius (c330-390), a Donatist Christian, writes influential commentary on Revelation of John; believes Millennium has already been inaugurated by Christ and so world will end in 380.

374 A layman, Ambrose of Milan (c339-397) acclaimed bishop by crowds; in his writings, documents current healings and glossolalia; later teaches Second Coming of Christ will be preceded by destruction of Rome and appearance of Antichrist on Earth.

378 Goths and northern Barbarians begin conquest of Roman empire.

378 Jerome (c345-419) writes: 'From India to Britain, all nations resound with the death and resurrection of Christ' (Isaiam cliv, Epistol. xiii ad Paulinum); estimates 1.9 million Christians to have been martyred since AD 33 (out of 120 million Christians, i.e. 1.6% or 1 in 60); documents numerous current 'signs and wonders' (healings, exorcisms, miracles).

378 Emperor Valens killed with an entire field army of 40,000 by Visigoths at Adrianople; Ambrose identifies Goths with Ezekiel's Gog, proclaims imminent end of world; Martin of Tours writes 'There is no doubt that the Antichrist has already been born'.

380 City of Antioch: of 150,000 population, 50% are Christians, increasing rapidly.

380 Latin theologians write expounding doctrine of the Holy Spirit: Hilary of Poitiers, Ambrose (339-397), Augustine.

380 Theodosius I (347-395) emperor of the East makes Christianity state religion and decrees that all subjects of Roman empire must become orthodox Christians.

381 Council of Constantinople I (2nd Ecumenical Council); creed of Nicaea reaffirmed; Macedonianism and Apollinarianism condemned; divinity of Holy Spirit clarified.

381 Constantinople recognized as first in rank among the eastern patriarchates.

c382 Pope Damasus I invites Jerome to revise chaos of Old Latin Scripture translations; Jerome disregards Greek Septuagint and goes back to best Hebrew OT texts via Origen's Hexapla; 405, completes Vulgate ('common') edition in new Latin; version opposed by Augustine but obtains universal preeminence by 8th century.

388 First known case of burning of a synagogue by Christians, on orders of bishop Callicinon.

c390 Collapse of Arianism throughout Roman empire, though it continues among some German tribes until c700.

c390 Conversion of Fritigil queen of Marcomans through a slave; requests Ambrose for instruction in Christian faith by correspondence; evangelization of the northern Barbarians largely due to soldiers and slaves rather than to church-planting.

390 Missionary monk Abdisho, a Persian, builds monastery on island of Bahrain.

391 Theodosius I orders prohibition of pagan sacrifices and destruction of pagan idols and temples, including those of Isis and Osiris in Nubia.

392 Ascetic writer John Cassian (c360-435) enters Bethlehem monastery; 415, founds monastery in Marseilles; promotes spread of monasticism in West; much evangelization due to these itinerant evangelistic monks.

395 Roman empire permanently divided: Western empire ruled from Rome (sacked 410, 455, 476), Eastern from Constantinople.

397 Southern Picts of Scotland first evangelized by Ninian (Rigna, Trignan; c360-c432) bishop of Galloway.

AD 398. In crude surviving portrayal, patriarch Chrysostom ('John of the Golden Tongue') preaches.

398 John Chrysostom (c344-407) appointed patriarch of Constantinople, founds training school for native Gothic evangelists; writes, "'Go and make disciples of all nations" was not said for the Apostles only, but for us also'; teaches that final Antichrist under direct inspiration of Satan will appear immediately before Second Advent of Christ in AD 430.

399 Pagans massacre 60 Christians in Sufes, Byzacena (modern Qasrin in Tunisia), as reprisal for toppling a statue of Hercules.

399 Mesopotamian bishop Marutha of Maipherqat ('the first medical missionary') visits Persia as ambassador of Constantinople (Byzantium); changes name of his see city to Martyropolis after observing mass martyrdoms; c410, writes their history in Syriac Acts of the Martyrs.

400 **Global status:** 12 generations after Christ, world is 13.4% Christians (64.0% of them being Non-Whites, 36.0% Whites), 24.4% evangelized; with Scriptures translated into 11 languages; total martyrs since AD 33 now 1,538,000 (1.2% of all Christians ever; recent rate 9,000 per year).

c400 Persia (Tigris/Euphrates, and highlands) a strong Christian area: Persians now 25% Christians (Syriac-speaking, but no Persian liturgy or Scriptures).

c400 United Arab Emirates (then on edge of Arabia). First Christians, connected with episcopal see of Hegha.

c400 Several millions of Christians known to have been buried in catacombs near Rome over 3 centuries by this date.

c400 Spanish North Africa (Ceuta, Melilla; then in Roman province of Mauretania). First Christians (Romans).

c400 Scriptures being translated into Ethiopic by monks from Egypt.

402 Respite in Persian persecutions after 190,000 Persian Christians martyred; 443, historian Sozomen in Ecclesiastical History states that names of well-known martyrs alone would list at over 16,000.

404 Vulgate or Common Bible (translation of Scriptures into Latin, common speech of educated mankind in Europe for a thousand years) completed by Jerome after 22 years' work from original Hebrew and Greek, living in Palestine.

404 Chrysostom deposed and exiled, resulting in Rome breaking communion with its 3 sister patriarchates.

405 Cyril of Alexandria expropriates all synagogues in Egypt; 412-444, serves as patriarch of Alexandria.

406 Roman legions abandon Britain to Celtic warlords; chaos reigns; by 432 Romanized Britain collapses completely; soon after, Anglo-Saxon attacks begin.

408 Western Roman emperor Honorius executes non-Christians for first time, in Gaul.

409 Arian Visigoths overrun Iberian peninsula.

410 Fall of Rome to Arian Barbarian Alaric (c370-410) and 100,000 Visigoth warriors; collapse of Western Roman empire; 476 sacked by Odoacer, all European libraries destroyed.

410 Synod of Seleucia-Ctesiphon: national Persian church formed separate from church of Rome, with state-recognized catholicos in capital.

c410 Alphabet and Bible in Armenian and also in Georgian completed by Mashtotz (Mesrob, c361-440), later patriarch of Armenia.

c410 Founding of noted monastery at Lerins by Honoratus, produces succession of notable Gallic bishops.

c410 Episcopate in Proconsular Africa, Numidia and Mauretania expands to 768 bishops; total episcopate across North Africa, including Egypt and Donatists, numbers 1,200 bishops; Honoratus at Lerins monastery trains succession of notable missionary bishops, sent across world for Christ.

410 Church of the East calls 3 general councils or synods named after ruling catholicos: 410 Synod of Isaac, 420 Synod of Yaballaha, 424 Synod of Dadiso.

410 1st General Synod (Synod of Isaac) of Church of the East, at that time with 5 metropolitans and 38 bishops (including 2 from Qatar and Bahrain); primacy of bishop of Seleucia-Ctesiphon as catholicos of the Orient confirmed, and official credal standard of doctrine adopted; full episcopal hierarchy of Eastern church finally organized and recognized; nevertheless, Persian church remains continually plagued by schism; Persia's 40 bishops celebrate Edict of Toleration in 409 by shah Yazdegerd I.

c410 Yemeni merchant Hayan meets group of Nestorians near Euphrates river, is converted, returns to Yemen to evangelize Arabs.

411 Conference of Carthage: Donatists still powerful enough to muster 285 bishops, one less than those of Catholics, but Donatism again banned by imperial edict.

416 Eastern Roman emperor Theodosius II excludes non-Christians from all public functions; 418, burns all non-Christian books and writings.

417 Paulus Orosius, young Spanish priest, encouraged by Augustine to write Historia adversus paganos, holding Rome will survive until the coming of Antichrist.

419 Three major Persian persecutions: 419-420 under Yazdegerd I, 420-425 under Varahran V, and 439-456 under Yazdegerd II attempting to stamp out entire Christian faith with utmost ferocity; 448, massacre of Kirkuk executes 10 bishops and 153,000 believers; 454, murder of Armenian patriarch Hovsep I.

419 Moche people of Peru build a Sun temple 150 feet high using 50 million bricks.

420 An Arab tribe in Arabia is converted to Christianity under sheikh Aspebet.

420 Long and cruel persecution of Christians in Persia for 18 years under king Bahram V.

420 2nd General Synod of Church of the East (Synod of Yaballaha): Persian church recognizes as authoritative 6 Western councils held from 314-365 (Ancyra, Nicaea, Neo Caesarea, Antioch, Gangra, Laodicea).

424 3rd General Synod of Church of the East (Synod of Dadiso/Dadyeshu), then with 6 metropolitans and 54 bishops, held in Markabta: East Syrian (Assyrian) catholicos of Seleucia-Ctesiphon and Persian church become independent of Antioch and the Western church, with 30 episcopal sees in Mesopotamia, and 6 in Persia and the Gulf.

425 Nubia: Olympiodorus of Thebes observes that the Bejas and Blemmyes peoples (south of first cataract) are still pagans.

425 Founding of Constantinople university.

425 Hephthalite Huns dominate central Asia, until 557.

426 Augustine (354-430) bishop of Hippo completes in 13 years his treatise The City of God (De Civitate Dei), against background of Visigoth invasion of Rome; propounds allegorical millennialism, but also teaches that future final Antichrist will arise as Nero Redivivus; opposes emerging theory of cessation of charismatic gifts, as overreaction to excesses of

Montanism et alia with the teaching that miracles and charismata ended with the Apostolic age; documents numerous recent miracles, exorcisms, healings and resuscitations.

AD 426. Outstanding African theologian, Augustine bishop of Hippo holds The City of God and some of his other writings.

428 French apologist Prosper Tiro (c390-463) defends Augustine of Hippo, writes treatise De Vocatione Omnium Gentium envisaging conversion of all barbarians to Christ, whose grace extends everywhere: 'Nulla pars mundi ab Evangelio vacat Christi.'

430 British ruler Vortigern (c400-c440) invites Saxons to visit, settle and garrison strategic east coast areas, but in 442 Saxons rebel and seize power; 446, British make vain appeal to Roman military; widespread chaos till 500.

431 Council of Ephesus (3rd Ecumenical Council): Nestorius (c390-451) patriarch of Constantinople condemned as heretic, also Pelagianism.

431 Jewish messiah Moses appears on Crete ready to lead remnants of Israel dryshod to Land of Israel; date 440 widely believed for final coming of Messiah; over next 1,500 years, scores more Jewish charismatic claimants arise, attracting widespread following followings, fanaticism, violence and martyrdoms, especially in 1087, 1117, 1127, 1160, 1172, 1295, 1502, 1528, 1648.

431 Palladius of Auxerre sent to Ireland as first bishop of the Scots by pope Celestine to combat errors of Pelagius; founds 3 churches but then withdraws after unsuccessful mission.

434 Beginning of Attila the Hun's 19-year reign as 'Scourge of God'; greatest of the Barbarian rulers, destroys cities and towns and almost destroys Western empire; widely regarded as the Antichrist; defeated in Gaul, dies in 453.

AD 435. In striking Celtic cultural style, Patrick is portrayed in The Book of Kells.

435 Ireland evangelized by Patrick (389-461); plants 200 churches and baptizes 100,000; c440, many converts killed by soldiers under British chieftain Coroticus; Patrick organizes and structures entire church for first time; phenomenal success with hundreds of monasteries begun by 445; Celtic Church of Ireland retains its independence from the see of Rome until English rule after 1200.

438 Theodosian Code, codifying Roman law.

439 North Africa: fall of Carthage, persecution of Catholics under Arian Vandal kings Gaeseric (Genseric, 428-477) and Huneric.

440 Start of 21-year pontificate of Leo I the Great (c400-461), who radically reforms administration of papacy and ecclesiastical procedure; 451 influences Council of Chalcedon; 452 persuades Attila the Hun to withdraw from Rome.

442 Isle of Man. First Christians, under Patrick; by 600, island evangelized and christianized through bishop Conan.

c450 Conversion to Christianity becomes mainly by communities, led by their kings or princes.

**AD 440.** Leo the Great, Roman pope for 21 years, radically reforms administration of the church.

c450 *Liechtenstein.* First Christians (merchants and Roman soldiers).
c450 Six East Syrian (Nestorian) bishoprics in Arabia, under metropolitan of Kashkar.
c450 Caucasus begins to be converted to Christianity.
c450 Buddhism practiced in Burma, lower Thailand, Sumatra, Java; by 500, on wane in India.
c450 Decline of 'Rule of the Secret', the 3-centuries-old rule that the mysteries of baptism and eucharist are not to be revealed to heathens (e.g. words of Lord's Prayer only revealed to converts on eve of baptism).
c450 England occupied by Anglo-Saxon invaders, who over next 30 years wipe out Celts and Celtic church, destroying Christianity and Roman civilization.
c450 Old English language flourishes, lasts till c1100, then succeeded by Middle English (1100-1500).
450 Bodhidharma (450-535) is born, Buddhist founder of the *dhyana*, or meditation, sect Zen.

**AD 451.** 4th Ecumenical Council convenes near Constantinople, makes major christological definitions.

451 Council of Chalcedon (4th Ecumenical Council): Tome of Leo approved, definition of faith against Apollinarianism, Nestorianism and Eutychianism; confirms that ecclesiastical dioceses are equivalent to political dioceses; recognizes patriarchal status of diocese of Jerusalem; Dioscorus patriarch of Alexandria excommunicated.
451 After Chalcedon, Copts of Egypt divided, most becoming Monophysites.

**AD 453.** Apostle of Austria, Eastern monk Severin, transforms province in 30 years.

453 Eastern monk of Latin origin, Severin ('Apostle of Austria') evangelizes heathen Noricum Riponse, founds monasteries, cares for poor, wins friendship of Barbarian leader Odoacer, dies in 482.
455 Sack of Rome by Vandals under Gaeseric, all ardent Arians.
457 Egyptian mobs in Alexandria hound and then murder Byzantine Chalcedonian (Melkite or anti-Monophysite) Proterius patriarch of Alexandria

replacing Dioscorus.
458 Theological school established at Nisibis in Persian empire by Narses; 480, Barsumas bishop of Nisibis (assassinated 493) and reforming patriarch Mar Aba (assassinated 552) keep Persian church isolated from West.
460 After Council of Chalcedon, every major political power center in Europe has become Arian, and violent Arian reaction spreads through Roman empire.
c470 Persia: Sassanid king Firooz massacres Monophysite priests, crucifies bishop Babowi and others.
c470 Persian Nestorians travel as far as China but leave no traces.
476 Sack of Rome by Barbarians under Odoacer (c433-493): end of Roman empire in the West, largely due to demographic pressure (overpopulation); Odoacer becomes king of Italy.
478 First Shinto shrines appear in Japan.
c480 Unity of Christendom permanently broken into 3 parts: church of the West (Rome and Byzantium: Chalcedonian), church of the East (Persia: Nestorian), and church of Africa (Egypt and Ethiopia: Monophysite); with a fourth also, church of the barbarian North (northern and far western Europe: almost entirely Arian by 450).
482 Byzantine emperor Zeno with help of Acacius patriarch of Constantinople issues edict of union, Henoticon; both are excommunicated by Roman pope Felix III; schism lasts for 36 years.
486 Council of Seleucia: Assyrian church in Persia declares itself Nestorian, opposing churches of Roman empire, with Seleucia under its catholicos Acacius proclaimed a patriarchal see on a par with Antioch and Rome.
486 4th General Synod of Church of the East, convened by catholicos Acacius: no reference to creed of Chalcedon; Asian church separated from Western church; final break of church of Persia with rest of Christendom.
490 Climax of first major epoch of advance: Christianity wins at least 80% of Roman empire.
491 Armenian church adopts Monophysitism, secedes from Byzantium and Rome.
c495 Nestorian metropolitan provinces in Persia number 7, with several bishoprics abroad (Arabia, India).
496 Clovis (c466-511) king of the Franks baptized with 3,000 warriors at Rheims.
497 5th General Synod of Church of the East; convened by catholicos Babai, Synod is emphatically Nestorian.
497 First major organized Nestorian mission sent into Asia: laymen John of Resh-aina and Thomas the Tanner, Karaduset bishop of Arran west of Caspian Sea, 4 priests, an Armenian bishop; emphasizing evangelism, education, and agriculture.
498 Christianity spreading widely in Central Asia, with whole tribes converted; Nestorians active in Turkestan until eliminated c1350.
499 Task of translating Jesus' message into Greek and Latin cultures virtually completed, after 16 generations.

**Epoch II: AD 500-950**

## THE GREAT RECESSION (The Dark Ages)

500 **Global status:** 16 generations after Christ, world is 19.9% Christians (61.9% of them being Non-Whites, 38.1% Whites), 31.2% evangelized; with Scriptures translated into 13 languages; total martyrs since AD 33 2,102,000 (0.8% of all Christians ever; recent rate 5,600 per year).
500 The so-called Dark Ages begin (AD 500-1000, early medieval period in Western Europe): no emperor in West, frequent warfare, virtual disappearance of urban life, then in 535 a massive eco-catastrophe.
500 First Bantu cultivators, expanding from Nigeria, reach Africa's east coast, and in south cross river Limpopo.
500 The Nine Saints (Syrian Orthodox) establish monastery in northern Ethiopia and secure Monophysite character of Ethiopian church.
500 Throughout the Middle Ages (AD 395-1500), scores of apologists, theologians, mystics, bishops publish expositions on the person and work of the Holy Spirit: Gregory the Great, Bede (673-735), Anselm (1033-1109), Peter Abelard (1079-1142), Bernard of Clairvaux (1090-1153), Bonaventure (1217-1274), Thomas Aquinas (1225-1274).
500 Jewish sages compile Talmud.
c500 During Dark Ages up to AD 950, decline of cities, Europe returns to village and town life; 11th century, revival of urban development.
c500 Over next 2 centuries, scattered martyrdoms across Europe: Helier, Desiderius, Donnan, Emmeram, Bercharius, Lambert, et alii.
c500 Yemen: arrival of Monophysite evangelists including noted ascetic Phemion who assists in conversion of Najran kingdom; later in 522, major persecution.
c505 Benedict of Nursia (d. c547) founds monastery at Subiaco, then another at Monte Cassino in 529, marking beginning of monasticism in the West.
506 Church of Iberia (Monophysite Church of Georgia) unites for 100 years with Monophysite Church of Armenia, at Council of Dvin, capital of Armenia; 607, catholicos Kirion I of Georgia rescinds union, 627 Monophysites in Georgia annihilated.
508 In Antioch, chorepiscopos Polycarp produces literal revised translation of whole New Testament into Syriac, including Book of Revelation; 518, Philoxenus bishop of Mabbogh murdered by suffo-

cation by order of Byzantine emperor Justin.
c510 Scholar, theologian and statesman Boethius (c480-524) transmits classical texts and ideals into Middle Ages; precursor of medieval scholasticism; executed by Theodoric the Great, Ostrogoth king.
c510 Irish Peregrini or Exulantes Christi (unorganized wandering hermits and preachers using pugilatores scotorum [Irish writing-tablets] as their major piece of equipment) embark on *peregrinatio pro Christi amore* as missionary pilgrims for Christ, begin to migrate across Europe for next 400 years, to the Alps, Germany, Danube, Italy, also to Orkneys, Faeroes, Iceland, converting much of Europe in one of great missionary feats of all time.
511 Merovingian church councils held in Gaul in 511, 517, 518, 524, 527, 529, 533, 535, and over 20 others, to Bordeaux in AD 675.
512 West Syrian church becomes formally Monophysite under patriarch Severus of Antioch (c465-538); 518-565, Monophysites violently persecuted in Antioch, with many bishops and clergy killed; Byzantine emperor Justin I deposes Severus; persecution spreads rapidly throughout the eastern Roman empire, with 55 Monophysite bishops expelled from their dioceses.
516 Conversion of Burgundians to Catholic Christianity.
520 Nestorians (Syriac evangelists) reported on island of Ceylon, with many converts, also in Malabar under a Persian bishop, in Ganges region, among Huns, Turks and Uighurs, in Tibet and Sumatra.

**AD 520, 529.** Large numbers of monastic centers of scholarship operate sizable scriptoria, copying scriptures.

520 Sizeable monastic centers of scholarship (averaging 50 scholars each) and foreign missions founded in Ireland and Britain: 520 Clonard (housing 3,000 biblical scholars), 540 Moville, 541 Clonmacnoire, 554 Bangor, 556 Clonfert.
523 Massacre of Najran: Jewish-Arab king Dhu-Nuwas burns alive 427 Himyarite ecclesiastics, monks and nuns, kills total of 30,000 Christians; 523, Axumite negus in Ethiopia sends army of 70,000 to avenge them which massacres pagans and Jews; Christianity flourishes under new African ruler Abraha who builds vast cathedral in capital Sana; finally in 575, Persians land at Aden and rout African garrisons.
525 Christianity firmly established in Arabian peninsula until Islam conquers in 7th century.
525 Scythian monk Dionysius Exiguus invents Christian Era, dating from birth of Christ as AD 1 (later found to be 4 years too late), also new Easter tables; adopted in England at Synod of Whitby in 664.

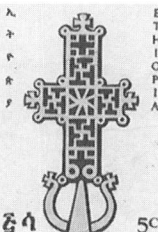

**AD 526.** Distinctive Ethiopian cross from first center of Christianity in Axum.

526 King of Axum (Abyssinia) sends expeditionary force to Yemen to protect persecuted Christians.
526 250,000 including many Christians killed by earthquake in Antioch, Syria.

**AD 529, 540.** Eastern emperor Justinian I extends Christian domains, builds Santa Sophia.

529 Justinian I (483-565) closes ancient schools of philos-

ophy at Athens; 537, dedicates Santa Sophia basilica in Constantinople.
529 Council of Orange (in Gaul).
529 Italian monk Benedict of Nursia (c480-547) founds Monte Cassino monastery, Italy; spread of his Rule and rise of Western monasticism, across Europe; facilitates mass Bible production with creation of scriptoria run by monks and lay artists.
531 Persian empire at its greatest under Khosrow I (c510-579), mightiest Persian monarch in a thousand years; 100,000 Mazdaks (a heretical Zoroastrian sect) hanged on gibbets; Christians also persecuted.
534 Arianism disappears throughout North Africa.
535 Cosmas Indicopleustes, Nestorian merchant missionary over most of world, retires to monastery and in 547 completes his global survey *Topographia Christiana* in 12 Books.
535 Dark Ages begin: massive worldwide 50-year eco-catastrophe as mammoth volcanic eruptions in Krakatoa area of Java create 18-month dust cloud blotting out Sun across the Earth, followed by lethal weather and climate changes, floods, famines, droughts, pandemics, uprooting leading cultures, barbarian migrations, causing collapse of empires and civilizations from Teotihuacan (Mexico) to Rome to Constantinople to Yemen to Persia to China to Indonesia; by 547, bubonic plague kills half the population from Celtic Britain across Eurasia; way cleared for eventual emergence of modern world's new empires (Spain, Portugal, Britain).
c540 Emperor Justinian orders that all pagan tribes on periphery of Byzantine empire be converted to Christianity; 70,000 persons forcibly baptized in Asia Minor.
540 Persia: revival of Christian monasticism throughout Persian empire under monk Abraham of Kaskar (c491-586), who founds Great Monastery on Mt Izla; disciples Dadyeshu and Babhai found or control 60 monasteries throughout empire; numerous monasteries and missions begun, with special concern for physical and spiritual needs of people; through persecution, spreads across Asia to Yemen, South India, Ceylon, Samarkand, China.
541 Virulent bubonic plague sweeps Byzantine empire for 2 years; begins in Egypt, reaches Italy, Africa, Persian armies, kills 45% of Constantinople; spreads across Europe, halves population, ends in 594.
542 Monophysite revival in Syria and the East: organizing genius Jacob Baradaeus (c500-578) appointed missionary bishop of Edessa, organizes West Syrian (Jacobite) church, becomes Monophysite apostle to Asia; for 35 years (542-578) eludes spies and soldiers of empire, keeps constantly on the move, plants trail of churches across Asia to India, ordains 100,000 clergy, 27 bishops, 2 patriarchs including Sergius of Antioch, sends lay evangelists throughout Asia; rapid expansion of Syrian Orthodoxy.
543 Melkite missionaries sent by emperor Justinian to Nubia (Sudan), but empress Theodora first sends Monophysite Julian who converts Silko king of Nobatae (Nubia, capital Faras); Monophysitism holds sway as official religion till AD 1000; principal Nubian temples including Abu Simbel converted into churches; Christians also in Darfur and Kordofan.
544 6th General Synod of Church of the East (Synod of Mar Aba), convened by catholicos Mar Aba the Great; synod begins thoroughgoing reorganization of church, extension of theological education, spiritual and moral revival, revival of monasticism, and work of reunion; also 554, 7th General Synod.
545 Ireland: monastery of Clonard, Meath has 3,000 monks; Bangor (Belfast) over 3,000; many missionaries sent out, founding numerous monasteries (Jumieges, in northwest France, 900 monks).
549 Nestorian catholicos Mar Aba asked by Hun delegation of Hephthalites (White Huns) to consecrate their own Christian leader as bishop; he is then sent back to Hephthalite country north of Great Wall of China.
c550 *Channel Islands.* First Christians (Breton settlers).
c550 Egypt: Coptic bishops number 168 in 4 ecclesiastical provinces.
c550 Patriarchate of Antioch has over 150 metropolitans and bishops.
552 Buddhism reaches Japan; first monastery begun.
553 Council of Constantinople II (5th Ecumenical Council); Three Chapters controversy; enunciates dogma of the Holy Trinity and fixes its technical expression.
557 Council of Paris includes as signatory 'Samson peccator episcopus' (Samson a sinner, bishop of Dol, died 565), a wandering Celtic monk-bishop and the major British/Welsh foreign missionary of 6th century; evangelizes in England, France, Brittany, Normandy, Channel Islands.
559 Ireland: monastery established at Clonfert by abbot Brendan (486-575).

**AD 563.** Renowned Celtic missionary from Ireland, Columba (Columcille) travels widely.

563 Scotland evangelized by Columba (Columcille, 521-597) from Ireland; Iona monastery founded, influence spreads to English, Franks, and Swiss.
567 Patriarchate of Alexandria definitively split into 2 rivals, Coptic (Monophysite) and Greek (Byzantine); Copts persecuted worse by Byzantines than later by Arabs.
567 Nubia: Longinus (a Monophysite) consecrated first bishop, becomes apostle of Nubian Christianity; 569, Makoritae (south of Nubians, capital Dongola) become Chalcedonians, but 579 Alodiae (capital Alwa 12 miles north of Khartoum) become Monophysites.
567 8th General Synod of Church of the East, deposing tyrannical catholicos Joseph.
570 Monophysite missions in Yemen.
c575 Byzantine military theory is codified in *Strategicon* of emperor Maurice (539-602) and later in *Tactica* of emperor Leo the Wise (886-911); war is considered practical, not heroic effort.
578 Conversion to Christianity of An-numan III, last of Lachemids (Arab princes).
578 *China.* First Christians: Nestorian Christian immigrants from Persia travel east along Old Silk Road and settle in Lintao in Kansu.
c580 Writer, historian and bishop Gregory of Tours (c538-594) gives many accounts of contemporary miracles, healings and exorcisms.
585 9th General Synod of Church of the East, convened by catholicos Yeshuyab I.
589 Arian Visigoths in Spain converted to Catholicism, declared state religion at 3rd Council of Toledo.
c590 Irish scholar Columbanus (c543-615), ablest controversialist of his time, founds monasteries across Europe.
594 Roman pope Gregory the Great (540-604) initiates reforms in liturgy and church administration, enhances power and prestige of papacy; publishes Dialogues describing contemporary Christian miracles, visions, prophecies, supernatural awareness, and other spiritual gifts; places detailed planning of organized missions to all heathen among his major objectives, in view of imminence of Last Judgment.
596 Augustine (prior in Rome) sent by Gregory the Great to England; 597, baptizes king and 10,000 Saxons at Canterbury; persuades parliament to adopt the faith; first archbishop of Canterbury, dies 604.
596 10th General Synod of Church of the East, convened by catholicos Sabaryeshu (died 604).

**AD 559.** Abbot Brendan establishes Celtic monastery of Clonfert, Ireland (*Book of Kells*).

600 **Global status:** 19 generations after Christ, world is 20.8% Christians (58% of them being Non-Whites, 42% White), 33.2% evangelized; with Scriptures translated into 14 languages; total martyrs since AD 33, 2,197,000 (0.5% of all Christians ever; recent rate 1,000 per year).
c600 *Andorra.* First Christians, settlers.
600 Smallpox spreads from India to southern Europe.
c600 Pseudo-Methodius (oracle attributed to 4th-century martyred bishop of Olympus) predicts heathen forces about to overrun Christians, announces a long-dead emperor will rise against them 'and after those 10 weeks of years they also will be overpowered and subjected to the Kingdom of Rome'; after peaceful golden age in which oppressed nations recover their properties and multiply, Antichrist will appear, to be defeated finally by Christ.
c600 12 Vaishnava Alvar saints of Tamil Nadu, write 4,000 songs and poems in Vaishnava canon, *Nalayira Divya Prabandham* in praise of Lord Narayana and Rama; forerunners of Vaishnava bhakti renaissance (12th to 16th centuries) in South India.
c600 Christian message reaches Turco-Tatar tribes of Turkestan; by 760, Nestorian Christian Uighurs all-powerful in Eastern Asia with their capital at Karakoram, numbering 8 million Nestorians under kings Gawirk, Girk, Tasahz, Langu; 1143, fame of Prester John, Naiman Christian king of the East, reaches Europe.
606 North Indian ruler Harsha (590-647) of Vardhana dynasty establishes first great kingdom after Hun invasion; last Buddhist kingdom of India.
612 Nestorian Council of Bishops; 628, catholicos Yeshuyab II elected; he creates first metropolitanate of India, with 12 bishoprics, and sends Christianity's first mission to China.
612 Gall begins to evangelize Alemanni, founds Swiss church leaving Columban to move on to Lombards in Milan and Pavia, founding Bobbio monastery.
615 Persian armies capture Jerusalem, massacre 90,000 men, overrun Egypt, Libya, and Asia Minor up to walls of Constantinople.
616 Ethelfrith king of Northumbria enforces Roman church rule on Celtic Church of Britain; after defeating Dalriadic Scots at Degsastan in 603, defeats Welsh at Chester in 616; massacres 12,000 Celtic Church monks at Bangor-is-Coid.
617 On Eigg island south of Iona, 54 brother monks led by Donnan in monastery are massacred by Viking sea rovers; similar fate befalls numerous small island monasteries in the Hebrides.
621 Buddhism becomes state religion of Japan.
622 Rise of Islam: Hegira, flight of prophet Muhammad (570-632) from Mecca to Medina; after his death Muslim Arabs sweep across Arabia, Palestine, Syria; 651, Muslim scholars compile Holy Quran, holding Allah has sent 124,000 prophets to mankind, of whom the major ones are Adam, Noah, Abraham, Moses, Jesus, and Muhammad seal of the prophets.
622 Armenian patriarchate established in Jerusalem.
622 World's 5 largest cities: Constantinople 500,000, Changan 447,000, Loyang 400,000, Ctesiphon 283,000, Alexandria 200,000.
625 British king Edwin of Northumbria baptized by Roman bishop Paulinus of York.
628 Persecution in Persia under Khosrow II.
629 Persian monk and theologian Marutha (c600-649) becomes metropolitan of Tekrit and first maphrian (deputy patriarch) and catholicos of the East with 15 suffragan bishops in Arabia, Mesopotamia and Persia; by 1200, Jacobite patriarch presides over 20 metropolitans and 118 bishops in Syria, Anatolia, Mesopotamia, and Persia.
c630 Evangelization of Britain proceeds mainly through Celtic church's mission, with Roman church's mission coexisting in England.
630 Muhammad leads army of 30,000 north against Persia's southern borders.
630 After 300 years' presence in Arabia, Christians still have made no translation of the New Testament into Arabic.
631 Egypt: Melkites persecute Copts for 10 years, killing hermits, ascetics, priests and thousands of lay Christians.
632 Death of Muhammad; Abu Bakr reigns as first patriarchal caliph; first period of rapid expansion of Muslim empire begins.
632 Book of Zerubbabel composed stating Messianic Age imminent; later interpreters set dates for its arrival at AD 968 or 1058.
632 On his death, Muhammad's family transforms his religious community within 30 years into a political and military empire under the patriarchal caliphate (632-661).
633 Conversion of Northumbria at request of Anglo-Saxon kings Oswald and Oswin to monk Aidan (c600-651) who becomes Celtic bishop of Lindisfarne island; evangelizes York and the north, subsequently recognized as the apostle of England.
635 China (then richest and most civilized nation on Earth) reached by Syrian Nestorian traveler Alopen, travels via Thailand, arrives in Tang Chinese capital Changan (Hsian) as first resident missionary, welcomed by Tang emperor Kao-tsu, who in 638 issues edict of universal toleration and approval for propagation of Christianity throughout empire; first Christian church in China then built, with 21 Persian monks at work; 650, Alopen appointed first metropolitan of China; translates

Scriptures for emperor; Nestorianism influential till suppressed for a time in 845.

636 Bedouin Arabs in 2 pitched battles defeat 2 of the most powerful dynasties in history, Byzantine Rome (at Yarmuk east of river Jordan) and Sassanid Persia (at Qaddisiyya, south of Babylon).

637 Capture of Jerusalem by Arab Muslims; 638, decisive battle between Christians and Muslims at Pilla, with 80,000 Byzantines killed.

637 Arabs capture Seleucia-Ctesiphon, capital of Persian empire; Muslim/Islamic conquest complete.

639 Arabs (Saracens, Moors) invade Egypt, establish Islam and Arabic language.

c640 Christians in Persia number about one million before Muslim conquest of Sassanid empire.

c640 Egypt: 3 million Coptic and 200,000 Chalcedonian Christians.

c640 80% of 6.5 million Berbers across North Africa (2.6 million urbanized) now Christians; but by 950 all become converted to Islam.

c640 Rise of Paulicians, a dualistic neo-Manichean heretical sect in Armenia, Cilicia and Asia Minor; persecuted by Byzantine emperors, founder Silvanus and successors killed; 842, savagely persecuted; 870, peak of power; 872, Basil I breaks their military power; sect collapses by 1100.

642 Muslim conqueror of Alexandria, Amr, systematically destroys greatest library of antiquity (over 1 million volumes) over 6 months as fuel to heat city's 4,000 public baths.

642 General Synod of Church of the East (Synod of Yeshuyab II).

644 Arabs capture Persian capital Seleucia-Ctesiphon.

644 Uthman (574-656) reigns as third patriarchal caliph; launches invasions westward into North Africa.

c644 China: 'Jesus-Messiah Sutra' written by archbishop Alopen, earliest summary of full-gospel Christianity in Chinese.

645 Tiflis capital of Georgia captured by Arabs.

646 Mesopotamia (Iraq) conquered by Muslims.

649 Aidan appoints Celtic leader Hild (Hilda, 614-680) abbess of Hartlepoole, who in 659 founds double (men/women) monastery at Whitby; at 663 Synod of Whitby she defends Celtic customs but supports Roman decisions.

**AD 650.** Nestorian worshiper under patriarch Yeshuyab III, Catholic Apostolic Church of the East.

650 Yeshuyab III becomes Nestorian patriarch of Seleucia-Ctesiphon; church now officially styled East Syrian, or Assyrian Orthodox, or Catholic Apostolic Church of the East.

c650 Netherlands: first fully organized Christians (St Martin's church, Utrecht).

c650 Samuel the Confessor, Coptic hermit and prophet of the end-time, foresees revival of monastic vocation with vast numbers of young people flocking to enter monasteries.

c650 Nestorian metropolitan of Merv converts many Turks.

c650 *Niger.* First Christians (North African Berber Christians driven south by Islam).

c650 *Indonesia* (then *East Indies*). First Christians (Catholic community on Sumatra).

c650 *Mongolia.* First missionaries (Nestorians); 300 years

later, Christianity disappears finally.

c650 Caliphs introduce first organized news service.

650 Arabs overthrow Sassanians, conquer Iran, central Asia, and Transcaucasia; Khazar empire in Transcaucasia and southern Russia, until late 10th century.

650 Nestorian hierarchy now consists of one catholicos, 9 metropolitans, and 96 bishops.

656 Muhammad's son-in-law Ali reigns as fourth patriarchal caliph; son Hasan becomes caliph upon Ali's assassination by Kharijite zealot in 661.

c660 Mass conversions of Egyptians from Christianity to Islam.

661 Umayyad caliphate (661-750) founds hereditary dynasty with as first caliph Muawiya I (c602-680), with capital moved from Baghdad to Damascus (then in Christian territory).

663 Synod of Whitby (England) favoring Roman allegiance over tradition of Celtic church; 669, Theodore of Tarsus arrives as first archbishop recognized throughout England; 672, convenes first synod of English church at Hertford.

c670 Earliest Old English (Anglo-Saxon) scripture version: metrical Paraphrases, sung by Caedmon (died c678).

c670 Psalms translated into Anglo-Saxon by West Saxon abbot Aldhelm (c639-709), later bishop of Sherborne.

c670 Caedmon, monk at Whitby, Yorkshire, produces metrical version of Genesis, Exodus, Daniel, et alia; songs in Old English (in use up to AD 1100) form a popular People's Bible.

c670 Lindisfarne Gospels (illuminated Latin manuscript) written by bishop Eadfrith.

674 Churches in England are fitted with glass windows for first time.

c680 Croatia: slow growth of Christian influence, with little interest until 850; independent Croat state then lasts 200 years.

680 Karbala (Iraq): troops of Umayyad caliph Yazid I (645-683) murder Husayn (c626-680), who, according to Shiites, was legitimate successor to caliphate, thus beginning Shiitesí open opposition to Sunni Umayyad caliphs.

680 Council of Constantinople III (6th Ecumenical Council): Monothelitism condemned.

680 Shia Muslims (party of Ali) break from Sunnis.

c680 First translation of Scriptures in Arabic; whole Bible not until 750.

683 China: first persecution of Christians begins under Buddhist empress Wu Hou; 691, Buddhism declared official state religion.

686 Germany: martyrdom of Irish bishop Kilian and 11 companions working in east Franconia and Thuringia.

687 Conversion of England completed under Wilfrid (634-709) bishop of York; christianizes Sussex and Isle of Wight, last important centres of Anglo-Saxon paganism.

689 1st persecution of Nestorians in China; 2nd, 712-3; 3rd, 845.

690 Frisians and Netherlands evangelized by Willibrord (658-739) from Ripon, England.

692 'The light of Christ illuminates the whole world' (Liturgy of the Presanctified).

692 Synod of Trullo: portraying Christ in symbolic form is now being replaced by portrayals in human forms.

694 Lebanon: Greeks sack monastery of St Maro and kill 500 Arab Maronite monks.

695 Persecution of Jews in Spain.

696 Arabic is declared official language of Islam, Arabic coinage its official currency.

697 Carthage captured by Muslims; North Africa in Muslim hands.

699 Irish monks sail westward to Faeroe Islands in North Atlantic.

700 **Global status:** 22 generations after Christ, world is 19.8% Christians (55% of them being Non-Whites, 45% Whites), 29.3% evangelized; with Scriptures translated into 14 languages; total martyrs since AD 33, 2,423,000 (0.4% of all Christians ever; rec ever; recent rate 2,300 per year).

700 Conversion of Lombards to Catholic church completed.

c700 Destruction of Christianity across North Africa by Saracens; large numbers of Christians annihilated.

c 700 End of Patristic Age, during which Greek Fathers and Latin Fathers all expounded the words *euangelizo, euangelizesthai, euangelismos, evangelizare, evangelizatio, evangelizator, et alia.*

711 Muslim Arabs with army of only 20,000 defeat Arian Visigoths in Portugal and in 715 eliminate them from Spain; after Muslim conquest, population of Iberian peninsula is 4 million Spaniards and 50,000 immigrant Arabs.

712 Muslim state established in India.

714 East Syrian (Nestorian) patriarch Selibhazecha appoints metropolitan for China.

716 South and central Germany evangelized by bishop Winfrith (Boniface, 680-754) from Crediton (England), who creates numerous dioceses.

716 Lisbon falls to Moors.

717 Caliph Omar II destroys all new churches built in Arab times.

720 Anglo-Saxon translations of John's Gospel by historian and theologian Bede (Baeda, c673-735), monk at Jarrow on Tyne; Bede predicts fall of Colosseum will be followed by that of Rome and then also of the whole world.

**AD 720.** Theologian Bede writes *Ecclesiastical history of the English nation.*

724 Boniface fells pagan sacred oak of Thor at Geismar in Hesse (Germany), leading to collapse of German paganism; 754, martyred at Dokkum in Frisia with Eoban and 52 companions.

726 Synod of Armenian Church at Manzikert, convoked by catholicos John IV of Odzoun, attended by 20 Armenian bishops and Syrian monophysite patriarch.

730 Church history of the English people compiled by Bede, describing conversion of Anglo-Saxon race.

730 Iconoclastic controversy: emperor Leo III issues first imperial decree banning icons (stylized portrayals of the spiritual or post-resurrection bodies of Christ and saints): violent persecution, 10,000 artists and monks massacred especially in Decade of Blood, 762-775.

732 Muslims defeated by Charles Martel (689-741) between Tours and Poitiers; they retreat from Europe.

c740 *Iceland.* First missionaries (monks from Ireland).

741 Arab armies moving eastward threaten Tibet; 751 they defeat Chinese army at Talas in Kirghistan; end of Chinese control over central Asia and beginning of its Arab conquest.

743 Uighurs now principal power in Central Asia, up to 840, with capital Ordu-baliq (Karabalghasun); 744, form semiautonomous empire controlling Old Silk Road; 762, they adopt Manichaeanism as state religion.

747 Tantric Buddhism reaches Tibet.

c750 Expansion of Christianity in India renewed.

c750 *Faeroe Islands.* First missionaries (monks from Ireland); monasteries destroyed a century later.

c750 Yemen: Nestorian missionaries in Sana and Socotra.

c750 *Pakistan* (then Punjab). First Christians (Nestorian missionaries); later eradicated by Islam.

c750 Church of Georgia (Iberia) reestablished as autocephalous church with its own catholicos.

c750 Spanish monk Beatus d'Asturias calculates 5,227 years between Adam and Christ; since world has life span of 6 millennia, he determines world will end in 14 more years.

750 Abbasid dynasty replaces Umayyad dynasty in east; rules from Baghdad; banking and postal service develop.

c750 Shia Islam splits into several factions over succession: Zaidis, Ismailis.

c750 Rise of Sufism (Islamic mysticism).

c750 Beginning of golden period of Arabic learning in astronomy, medicine, mathematics, optics, chemistry, philosophy, and music.

750 Abbasid dynasty rules Islam in Asia for next half millennium to 1258; capital moved from Damascus to Baghdad.

c750 Founding of the 4 major rites or schools of Islamic law, initially geographical: Hanafi (by Abu Hanifah, died 767), Maliki (by Malik Ibn Anas, died 795), Shafi (by Muhammad ash-Shafii, died 820), and Hanbali (by Ahmad ibn Hanbal, died 855).

c750 Bosnia: despite labors of Catholic missionaries from Croatia, after Goths liquidate its church in 375, Bosnia remains for centuries on the north-south dividing line between Catholic influences from the West (Rome) and Orthodox from the East (Constantinople).

c750 China: city of Hsianfu becomes major center and see city of Nestorian Christianity in eastern Asia.

754 Council of Hieria (near Chalcedon) with 338 bishops, convened as the 7th Ecumenical Council by icono-

clasts, but condemned as uncanonically summoned; forbids any direct depiction of the Father and/or Trinity; 764, iconophile abbot Stephen the Younger murdered; 815 iconoclastic synod held in Santa Sophia, Constantinople.

758  Muslims raid Canton, China.

AD 760. The Book of Kells consists of the 4 Gospels, richly illustrated on 340 leaves of thick glazed parchment. *Left*. Modern postage stamp. *Below*. Portrait of Saint Matthew.

c760  Book of Kells (the 4 Gospels in Vulgate edition) compiled at Benedictine house on Iona island; completed at Kells in c800, with 340 leaves of thick glazed parchment.

762  Conversion to Manicheism of Tengli Meou-Yu (759-780), Uighur chieftain, who makes it the state religion; 840, Uighur state destroyed by Kirghiz Turks; 843, Manicheism prohibited throughout China, though pockets last until 14th century.

770  Alcuin (c732-804), foremost scholar of Carolingian Renaissance, introduces Anglo-Saxon humanism into western Europe.

c770  First known printed work: Buddhist prayer for Japanese empress.

772  East Germany reached by first Christians (through Charlemagne's violent conquest of Saxons).

774  Austria: in Salzburg, center of the region's christianization, cathedral is consecrated by Scottish-Irish bishop Feirgil (Virgil).

780  East Syrian bishop of Bait Baghash becomes Nestorian catholicos as Timothy I (728-823) patriarch of the East; good relations with caliphs of Baghdad; moves patriarchal see from Seleucia-Ctesiphon to Baghdad; develops global missionary strategy through mobile married monks as traders 'carrying only a stick and a bag', creates metropolitan sees in India and Central Asia (including Tibet in 797), and 80 new bishoprics.

780  Viking Norse pirates destroy isolated monasteries; 793 Lindisfarne burned; 806, 80 monks slaughtered there; 867, abbey destroyed by Danish pirates.

c780  Forced baptism of Saxon race by Charlemagne; 4,500 executed in one day for resisting, thousands more deported.

781  Syriac New Testament known in China.

781  Peak of Nestorian influence in China, documented in stone on large Nestorian monument 9 feet high in Changan (Xian); rediscovered by workmen in 1623.

782  Buddhist missionary Prajna from northern India reaches Chinese capital Changan, translates Buddhist sutras with help of Nestorian Persian bishop Ching-ching (Adam); 804, in same Buddhist monastery in Changan live 2 other leading Buddhists: Kobo Daishi (Kukai), founder of Japan's Shingon (True Word) sect of Tantric Buddhism, and Dengyo Daishi (Saicho), founder of Tendai (Lotus)

school of Japanese Buddhism leading to Pure Land, Zen, and Nichiren Buddhism; Christian ideas and concepts thus pervade later Japanese Buddhism.

784  Last major revolt of pagan Frisians.

785  Building begins on Great Mosque of Cordoba, Spain.

AD 787. 7th Ecumenical Council, Nicaea II, last one recognized by Eastern Orthodoxy.

787  Council of Nicaea II (7th Ecumenical Council, last one recognized by Eastern Orthodox); 367 bishops present; iconoclasm condemned but not extinguished until 867.

c790  Timothy I (728-823), Nestorian catholicos in Baghdad states he intends to consecrate a missionary metropolitan for Christians in Tibet.

792  Buddhist Council, held in Lhasa (Tibet); debate on sudden versus gradual enlightenment.

794  Viking raiders loot Iona; 801, burn buildings; 806, kill 68 monks; 825, all monks slaughtered; 986, rebuilt community again massacred.

796  Pippin son of Charlemagne destroys Avar power; conversion of Avars (of Uighur origin) follows.

797  Tibet (Tangut) created as a Nestorian metropolitan see by patriarch Timothy.

### Rise and fall of medieval scholasticism, AD 800-1600

800  **Global status:** 26 generations after Christ, world is 18.8% Christians (51.0% of them being Non-Whites, 49.0% Whites), 26.4% evangelized with Scriptures translated into 15 languages; total martyrs since AD 33, 2,568,000 (0.4% of all Christians ever; recent rate 1,400 per year).

800  Christianity becoming dominant religion from the Caspian to Sinkiang (China).

800  Scholasticism, central body of medieval thought, being Christian philosophy produced by medieval scholars, arises due to Barbarian efforts at understanding the Christian faith, flourishes for 600 years with 13th century as its Golden Age.

800  Charlemagne (c742-814) crowned Roman emperor in Rome by Roman pope Leo III; 808, though still illiterate he publishes Breviary (*Brevis Capitolorum*), one of the earliest records of detailed counting.

800  World's 5 largest cities: Changan 800,000, Baghdad 700,000, Constantinople 300,000, Loyang 245,000, Kyoto 200,000.

c800  Islamic philosopher and astrologer Abu Mashar predicts massive social upheaval for year 1789; c850, compiles Great Introduction to the Science of Astrology.

c800  Nordic myth of Ragnarok circulates among Vikings: after time of great immorality when all Norse taboos are broken, a warning trumpet sounds, and a horde of giants appears to do battle with the gods who fall one by one; finally at sunset Earth sinks into the ocean.

c800  Northern Mexico: Toltec civilization arises based on city of Tollan (Tula); Nahuatl-speaking; astral deities, human sacrifices.

c800  Pope Leo III treks over Alps to importune Charlemagne; rise of papal power in the West.

815  Resurgence of iconoclasm in Eastern empire; 843 final restoration of veneration of icons.

825  Party of Persian Christians with 2 Nestorian bishops emigrate to Malabar.

825  Muslim caliph of Cordoba (Spain) executes 2 Arab nobles, brothers Adulfus and John, because they are Christians.

826  *Denmark*. First Christians, led by first missionary Anskar [801-865], monk of Flanders, apostle of the north.

827  Christianity harassed in Sicily during next 230 years; 902, subjugated by Muslims, with coastal areas of southern Italy; 1060, Normans expel Saracens.

828  *Czechoslovakia* (now *Czech Republic* and *Slovakia*).

First missionaries (Franks).

829  *Sweden*. First missionary (Anskar); many Swedish noblemen converted after his visits.

c830  Indian mathematician Al-Khawarizmi (780-c850) writes *Kitab al jabr wail mugabala* on mathematics, with later translations giving rise to term algebra; translation of another work (c1150) introduces Hindu-Arabic numeral system to Europe, then still using Roman numerals.

835  Nestorian bishopric of Jerusalem instituted, 1065 raised to metropolitan see, finally disappears by 1616.

837  Egypt: Christian education prohibited, also celebration of festivals; all churches demolished by Muslims, and Christians ordered to wear 5-pound crosses around their necks.

840  China: severe persecution against all foreign religions; 843, Manichaeanism ordered destroyed; 845, Taoist emperor Wu-tsung issues second degree abolishing Buddhism with its 4,600 monasteries, 40,000 hermitages, and 265,500 monks and nuns; also Zoroastrianism and Christianity prohibited.

842  Savage persecution of Paulicians of Asia Minor, under Byzantine emperor Michael I and empress Theodora; over 100,000 martyred.

845  Baptism of 14 Czech princes.

845  Severe persecution of Nestorians and Buddhists in China by Taoist emperor Wu Tsung; 44,000 temples and monasteries destroyed or closed.

846  Invading Saracens reach river Tiber near Rome; Muslim pirates sack St Peter's in Rome.

849  Abbasid caliph Mutawakkil (822-861) abruptly deposes patriarch Theodosius, orders Christians to wear yellow clothes and patches, and begins destroying numbers of churches.

AD 850. Bulgarian postage stamp (1975) commemorating the 2 apostolic missionaries, Cyril and Methodius, widely celebrated by Christians during Communist era.

c850  Serbia (rump part of Yugoslavia): Christians taught and organized by Cyril and Methodius.

850  Corsica conquered by Moors.

850  Martyrs of Cordoba: 50 Spanish Christians and crypto-Christians of Arab or Arab-Spanish birth including zealous ascetic monks executed 850-59 by Muslim rulers after being provoked into attacking the Prophet.

c850  East Syrian (Nestorian) Christianity in Arabia finally eradicated by Muslims.

c850  First Scriptures translated into Norman French.

c850  Rise of Hindu orthodoxy in India; beginning of medieval Hindu temples.

c850  Khmer (Cambodian) empire extends from southern Viet Nam to Burma; 895 capital city of Angkor founded, with hundreds of stone temples (270 still surviving) climaxed by Angkor Wat complex (c1130), a Hindu shrine dedicated to the god Vishnu; elaborate reservoirs and water-management system over 200 square miles; 1215 king Jayavarman dies, Khmer state declines gradually until sacked by Thai armies in 1431 and abandoned; in 1990s still a noted pilgrimage site.

850  Jews settle in Germany and begin to develop Yiddish.

c850  Hierarchy of Church of the East increases to 1 catholicos, 9 metropolitans, 96 bishops, with around 4 million adherents.

851  Ireland: pagan kingdom set up in Dublin for 3 centuries by Norwegian Olaf the White.

860  Vikings of Scandinavia trade and plunder as far as Russia (Murmansk, Kiev, Kazan, Volga, Caspian), Constantinople, Greenland, Iceland, Iona, Ireland, Spain, Morocco; converted to Christian faith after AD 900; 1050, influence wanes.

c860  Arabs adopt Indian numerals, including concept of zero, from India.

861  Conversion of Slavs under way through Cyril (826-869) and Methodius (c815-885), sent to Moravia (Bohemia) at request of prince Rastislav; by 900, Christianity strong in Moravia.

AD 864. Baptism of King Boris leads to conversion of Bulgar nation to Christianity.

864 Baptism of Boris king of the Bulgars; 870, conversion of Bulgars, with a Bulgar consecrated as archbishop; Basil I, emperor 866-886, forces baptism on Serbs of Narenta Valley; 874, conversion of Serbs to Orthodoxy.
867 Photius patriarch of Constantinople attempts conversion of Khazars, Bulgars and Russians; dies 897.
868 Chinese print oldest known printed book in existence, *The Diamond Sutra*, containing 6 pages and one woodcut illustration.
869 Council of Constantinople IV (8th Ecumenical Council, for Roman Catholics): Photian schism condemned.
870 Malta conquered by Saracens; diocese suppressed, restored in 12th century.
874 Norwegian chieftain Ingolfur Arnarson settles in Iceland with first Vikings; 930, first Althing held (general assembly, oldest parliament in Europe).
875 Samanid empire rules in Transoxiana and Khwarezm, until 999.
878 Chinese city of Canton falls to rebels: 120,000 Muslims, Jews, Christians and Zoroastrians slaughtered.
880 Slavonic Bible translated by Cyril and Methodius, also Bible in Bohemian; in England, Psalms translated into Anglo-Saxon by British king Alfred the Great (849-899).
c880 First true encyclopedia in Arabic published: *Kitab Uyun al-Akhbar*, in 10 books, by philologist Ibn Qutayba (828-889).
889 Mayan civilization in Tikal, Guatemala abandoned as whole population deserts.

**AD 890.** Glastonbury Abbey, in its heyday during reign of Alfred the Great.

c890 *Anglo-Saxon Chronicle* (in Anglo-Saxon or Old English) produced under Alfred the Great.
c895 Razi (Rhazes, 865-925), Muslim doctor and author, writes more than 200 books on medicine, alchemy, theology, and astronomy; identifies several contagious diseases including smallpox and measles.

900 **Global status:** 29 generations after Christ, world is 17.1% Christians (55% of them being Whites, 45% Non-Whites), 24.0% evangelized; with Scriptures translated into 16 languages.
c900 *Norway.* First mission (from Bremen-Hamburg archbishopric); later, Norwegian kings educated in England return to evangelize their people.
c900 Magyars now evangelized.
c900 Continuing apostasies of Christians to Islam in Middle East and North Africa.
c900 Alchemy and astrology flourish (China, Greece, Islamic lands).
c900 Ecumenical Council declares that final century of history has begun and Christ will return around year 1000 to usher in Millennium.
900 Mataramas dynasty in Indonesia reverts to Saivism after a century of Buddhism, building 150 Saiva temples.
907 China: fall of Tang dynasty followed by decades of chaos and civil strife; as result of severe religious persecutions from 840 onwards, by 980 Nestorian church completely obliterated throughout China with not one single known Christian left.
911 Rollo and his Vikings settle in Normandy; soon after, become Christians; 1066, Norman descendants invade and conquer England.
917 Bulgarian Orthodox patriarchate proclaimed, lasts from 917-1078; reestablished 1235, dissolved again 1393 under Turks; finally restored 1953.
c920 *Burma* (later *Myanmar*). First Christians (Nestorian bishopric at Pegu).
926 Revival of Western monasticism under Odo (879-942) abbot of Cluny, France.
927 Conversion of Bulgars completed; death of tsar Simeon.
929 Caliphate at Cordoba declared; becomes major center of Arab learning, science, commerce.
930 Karakhanid empire in central Asia, until 1165.
c930 Jewish scholars describe religions: Saadia (893-942) expounds Brahmanism and Islam; Maimonides (1135-1204) undertakes a comparative study of all religions.
933 Qur'an compiled in final form.
943 Dunstan (c909-988) abbot of Glastonbury; 959, archbishop of Canterbury; with king Edgar, carries out complete reform of English church and state.
c949 50% of all former Christendom now captured by Islam, including nomadic Berbers of Mauretania.

**Epoch III: AD 950-1350**

## RESURGENCE AND ADVANCE

950 **Global status:** 31 generations after Christ, world is 16.9% Christians (58.8% of them being Whites, 41.2% Non-Whites), 22.8% evangelized; with Scriptures translated into 17 languages; total martyrs since AD 33, 2,895,000 (0.3% of all Christians ever; recent rate 300 per year).
c950 *Poland.* First Christians; followed soon after by baptism of king.
c950 Conversion of Scandinavians (Northmen) under way across Denmark, Norway and Sweden.
c950 Rise of Bogomilism in Bulgarian Orthodox Church; neo-Manichean, dualist, perfectionist; rejecting OT, water baptism and sacraments; by 1140, Bogomil church rapidly growing, organized with hierarchy, liturgy, doctrine (Jesus an angel), foreign missions; 1150-1400 virtually state church of Bosnia, and Serbia; by 1200, a vast network of Paulician-Bogomil-Cathar dualistic communities from Black Sea to Atlantic; collapses by 1400, most converting to either Rome or Islam.
c950 Egypt: Coptic bishops decline in numbers to 110 (from 168 in AD 550).
c950 Mali trading empire founded in west Africa by Mandingo king Sundiata; collapses by 1550.
c950 As-Sufi, Arabian astronomer from Baghdad, establishes terminology for constellations upon which modern terminology is based.
950 Adso abbot of Montier-en-Der (Dijon, France) writes *Letter on the Origin and Time of the Antichrist*: after Roman empire passes away Antichrist will come, kill God's prophets, martyr all Christians, and be defeated by Jesus; document is revised and redisseminated 7 times in next 150 years; 992, death of Adso.
950 Sufis, pietist Muslim mystics, develop major Muslim missionary center in Balkh south of the Oxus.
950 Clerical marriage still common throughout all Western Churches until reforms of pope Hildebrand.
954 Olga (c890-969) regent of Kiev baptized in Constantinople; conversion of Russia begun.
960 Bernard of Thuringia predicts imminent end of world in AD 992; great alarm throughout Europe.
c960 *Belorussia.* First Christians, Russians from Kiev, Poles from new churches in Poland.
962 Holy Roman Empire founded by Otto I (912-973), king of Germany, crowned by pope John XII; seen as embodiment of rule of Christ on Earth; 10 million by AD 1000, 16 million by AD 1200, 29 million by 1800; finally abolished in 1806.
964 Arab astronomer as-Sufi describes Andromeda Nebula (nearest galaxy outside Milky Way) in his *Book of the Fixed Stars*.
964 Astronomer as-Sufi records existence of Andromeda Nebula (nearest external galaxy) and Magellanic Clouds (one million light-years distant) in his *Book of the Fixed Stars*.

**AD 966.** Conversion of Poland under duke Mieszko I.

966 Duke Mieszko I (c930-992) of Poland converted to Christianity by his wife and baptized; first Polish bishopric established at Poznan (Posen) 2 years later; rapid expansion of the faith.
967 Nubia: churches and monasteries very extensive, with 12,000 monks in 2 remote monasteries in Tari; 969, Fatimid dynasty conquers Egypt, begins pressure on Nubia to convert to Islam.
968 Warrior Toltec empire established in Mexico.
968 Arab universities founded: 968 Cordoba, 969 Al-Azhar (Cairo), 972 Cairo.
969 Fatimid dynasty begins in Cairo, in 969 captures Damascus, and by 1000 rules from Atlantic seaboard of north Africa to Jerusalem and Lebanon.
969 Crusade of 2 Byzantine emperors Nicephorus Phocas and Basil II captures Damascus, Edessa, Nisibis and Jerusalem; Asian Christians still in the majority west of Euphrates river.
975 Arithmetical notation brought to Europe by Arabs.
980 Ibn Sina (Avicenna, 980-1037), physician and philosopher, synthesizes Aristotelian philosophy with Islamic tradition; writes extensive encyclopedia of medical knowledge, *al Qanun*, completed by 1037, and also over 170 other books on philosophy, medicine, mathematics, and religion.
980 Omar Khayyam (1040-1123), Persian poet and scientist, author of *Rubiyyat*.
982 Greenland explored by Vikings under Erik the Red.
987 Muslim rulers in Iraq assume right to appoint the Nestorian catholicos.

**AD 987.** Baptism of Russian archduke Vladimir of Kiev leads to mass conversion of Russia.

987 Conversion and baptism of archduke Vladimir (956-1015) of Kiev by Greeks; Orthodoxy introduced into Russia; Vladimir orders all subjects baptized, and mass conversion of Russia begins.
987 Nestorian mission visits China, reports no Christian communities there.
990 Over next 2 centuries, numerous martyrdoms of bishops across Europe: Adalbert, Alphege, Boniface of Querfurt (Bruno), Eskil, Gerard of Csanad, Gottschalk, Henry of Uppsala, John of Mecklenburg, Kuno of Trier, Magnus of Orkney, Stanislaw, Thomas Becket, et alii.
990 Up to now, 95% of all families in world produce for themselves virtually everything they need to sustain life, and only rarely other people's goods.
c990 *Greenland.* First Christians (Norse settlement; priest brought by founder's son Leif).
990 Systematic musical notation developed.
c990 Ruler of Turkic Kerait tribe writes to Ebedyeshu, Nestorian metropolitan of Merv, asking for clergy to baptize him and his tribe; 1009, Ebedyeshu reports to Nestorian catholicos John VI in Baghdad that as a result prince and 200,000 Keraits have accepted baptism; Keraits, Naimans, and Merkits become main Christian tribes in East for next 200 years.
991 Whole population of Novgorod (Russia) baptized by bishop from Crimea.
992 Rise of Turkish power: Karluk or Ilek Turks move out of desert oasis city of Kashgar west to Transoxiana north of Oxus river, displacing Persians; 999 Turks capture Bokhara.
996 Fatimid ruler al-Hakim the 'mad caliph' (985-1021) initiates short unprecedented persecution of Christians in Syria and Egypt, destroying 3,000 churches, and forcing Christians each to wear a 5-pound wooden cross around his neck; 1009, tears down Church of the Holy Sepulchre in Jerusalem; murdered in 1021, regarded as the Mahdi by his followers who subsequently form the Druze religion.
997 Mass conversion of Magyars (Hungarians) under first king Stephen (c975-1038) and Adalbert of Prague (956-997).
997 Prussians, last remaining heathens in Europe, evangelized.
999 Bohemia: evangelization and christianization completed.
999 Multitudes journey to Jerusalem to await Second Coming of Christ in AD 1000, as believed prophesied in Apocrypha.

### *The High Middle Ages, AD 1000-1300*

1000 Leif Eriksson, Norse Christian leader from Greenland, journeys to New World, making 3 landfalls on North American continent which he names Helluland, Markland, and Vinland.

1000 **Global status:** 32 generations after Christ, world is 16.9% Christians (61.0% of them being Whites), 21.3% evangelized; with Scriptures translated into 17 languages; total martyrs since AD 33, 3,064,000 (0.3% of all Christians ever; recent rate 3,400 p.a.).
1000 World's 5 largest cities: Cordova 450,000, Constantinople 450,000, Kaifeng 400,000, Sian (Changan) 300,000, Kyoto 200,000.
1000 Most of North African Christianity finally wiped out: the Land of the Vanished Church.
1000 East Syrian (Nestorian) metropolitan provinces within Arab caliphate (Persia) number 15, with 5 abroad including India and China.
1000 Patriarchate of Constantinople has authority over 624 dioceses around eastern Mediterranean.
1000 Conversion of northern Europe by Latin church completed.
1000 Nubian bishop (Sudan) reintroduces Orthodox Melkite tradition, provoking split between church in Nubia and Copts in Egypt; 1320, a Dominican arrives as Catholic bishop of Nubia.
1000 Emergence of Christian kingdoms in Denmark, England, Hungary, Norway, Poland, Sweden, Scotland.
1000 Millennial year preceded by widespread terrors; followed by 150 years of vast increase in pilgrimages to Holy Land, with widespread continuing belief in imminent end of world with final king of the Franks leading all faithful to Jerusalem to await Second Coming of Christ.

1000 Catholic Apostolic Church of the East (East Syrian or Nestorian church) is by now the most extensive in world, with 250 dioceses across Asia and 12 million adherents; expansion of Nestorianism in Tenduc, country of Keraits with Karakorum as capital, home of legendary ruler Prester John.
1000 One thousand years after Christ equals different numbers on other calendars: Byzantine era 6508, Jewish era 4759-60, AUC (Anno Urbis Conditae, from year Rome founded) 1753, Era of Nabonassar 1747-48, Seleucid era 1311, Diocletian era 716, Armenian era 448-49, AH (After Hegira) 390-91, and 13th year 46th cycle of Indictions.
c1000 *North Korea*. Presence of Nestorian Christians in Korean territory known.
1000 Gradual decline of Nestorianism: Persian empire has 68 cities with Nestorian churches, falling to 24 by 1238; 1380, after Tamerlane sweeps through Persia, only 7 cities remain with churches.
1000 World population 275 million, average male height 5ft 6in, average male life-span 30 years.
c1000 Hindu communities from Rajput and other areas, ancestors of Romani Gypsies, gradually move out of India to Persia and on to Europe.
1000 Authority of Nestorian catholicos extends from river Tigris to China and from lake Baikal to Cape Comorin.
c1000 Islam penetrates India: Turkish sultan Mahmud of Ghazni invades south from Afghanistan into Kashmir, forcibly converts rich Hindu Punjab to Islam; c1180, second invasion by Asiatic Turko-Afghan armies of Muhammad Ghuri control northern India under Delhi sultanates until c1550.
1000 World's largest city is Cordova, Spain with 450,000 inhabitants.

**AD 1005.** Evangelized from AD 740 on, Iceland now has 2 dioceses based on Skalholt.

1005 Iceland: 2 dioceses, many monasteries and abbeys.
1008 Turkish Muslims sweep through India under Mahmud, defeating a Hindu confederacy at Peshawar.
1015 Russia permanently christianized; all 3 bishops and most clergy Greeks; numerous monasteries.
c1016 Iceland only country to accept Christianity by genuine democratic process.
1017 Ramanuja (1017-1137) born in Kanchipuram in South India, Tamil founder of Sri Vaishnava sect in *bhakta* tradition; propounds a strongly theistic dual-nondual form of Vedanta while head of Srirangam monastery.
c1020 Nestorians over 50% of population in Syria, Iraq and Khorasan (south of Oxus).
c1020 Muslim scholars describe pagan religions: Indian religions and philosophies, by Al-Biruni (973-1048); Mazdean and Manichean dualism, by Ibn Hazm (994-1064); and Averroes (Ibn-Rushd, 1126-1198) holding that all the monotheistic religions are true.
1024 Turk Muslim Mahmud plunders Somanath Siva temple, killing 50,000 Hindus; builds mosque on site.
1026 Guido d'Arezzo introduces solmization in music (do, re, mi...).
1033 Year of the Passion 1000; solar eclipse and earthquake in Holy Land terrify many who think mankind and nature are about to end.
1035 Spinning wheel invented in China, reaches Europe 200 years later; rapid expansion of textile manufacture and commerce.
1035 Burgundian monk Raoul Glaber (985-1047) writes *Histories*: 5-year famine covered entire Christendom and led to end of world in AD 1000; describes vast crowds of pilgrims in Jerusalem awaiting the End.
1040 Seljuk Turks (Turkomans), originally Nestorian Christians, seize power and begin an empire, moving west from Afghanistan; 1055, leader Toghril captures Baghdad; next leader Alp Arslan conquers Christian Armenia and in 1071 at Manzikert destroys Byzantine armies; whole of Asia Minor becomes permanently Muslim.
1045 Byzantines systematically replace and deport Armenians in Armenian principality of Ani, Anatolia, newly settled by Turkish conquerors; later, Turks permit Armenians to remain and flourish.
c1045 Hilalian mass invasion: several million illiterate Bedouin nomads from central Arabia pour across Sinai into Egypt then throughout Berber regions of North Africa, over next 7 or 8 centuries.
c1050 King in Nubia erects many churches, monasteries.
c1050 Egypt: Coptic bishops decline in numbers to 47 (from 168 in AD 550).
c1050 Beginnings of modern futurism as Europe's intellectual life quickens after Dark Ages: 1516 Thomas More's *Utopia* (satire on government and society), 1626 Francis Bacon's *New Atlantis* (an ideal science-based island community with a research institute Solomon's House at its center devoted to solving human problems) and *Novum Organum* (1620) leading to idea of progress.
c1050 Seljuk empire rules Iran, Mesopotamia, Anatolia, and Transcaucasia, until 13th century.
c1050 *Latvia* (Livonia). First Christians (Orthodox Russians, later in 1180 pioneer missionary monk Meinhard, Teutonic knights).
c1050 World's 3 major centers of wealth and power: Byzantium, India, China.
1050 Celtic Church in Britain fights losing struggle to retain its independence from Canterbury and Rome; 1070, Scottish Church resists intrusions; 1169 English king Henry II invades Ireland; also earlier Viking plunderings of monasteries and killings of monks; 1172 end of Celtic era of Irish Christianity; 1284, Celtic Church of Wales loses its independent existence and becomes part of the Church of England.
1054 Chinese astronomers observe supernova (violently exploding star, later becoming Crab Nebula), visible on Earth for 2 years; one of 3 billion supernovas in history of our Galaxy, which have probably destroyed 2 million related planetary civilizations; other recent supernovas seen in AD 185, 393, 1006, 1181, 1572, 1604.
1056 Great Schism between western (Rome) and eastern (Constantinople) Christianity; Constantinople; Roman cardinal Humbert places bull of excommunication of patriarch Michael on altar of Santa Sophia cathedral in church of Byzantium declines, with no further missionary outreach implemented.
1060 Vast numbers of medieval millenarian movements arise, involving millions of desperate rebels, radicals and rootless poor seeking hope in a newer world; including 1090 heresiarch Tanchelm (died 1115), 1180 Joachim of Fiore, 1420 Taborites, 1525 Thomas Muntzer, 1534 Anabaptist 1000-year kingdom of Munster, 1653 Fifth Monarchy Men, et alia.
1061 Norman (Christian) conquest of Sicily, completed by 1091.
1064 Ani, capital of Armenia, destroyed by Seljuk Turks who massacre inhabitants and destroy their 1,001 Armenian churches.
1066 Evangelization and conversion of Western Europe completed with Norman conquest of Saxons and Celts.
1070 Turks capture Jerusalem.
1071 Overthrow of Byzantine army at Manzikert (Anatolia) by Turkish sultan Alp Arslan; inrush of Turkish tribes follows.
1073 Pope Gregory VII (Hildebrand) (c1020-1085) initiates widespread reform in church practice, liturgy, and administration.
1074 Crusade planned by Gregory VII to relieve Byzantium and liberate Jerusalem.
1075 In investiture controversy between pope Gregory VII (1020-85) and Holy Roman emperor Henry IV (1050-1106), Gregory denies emperor's right to appoint bishops; power struggle between popes and Holy Roman emperors lasts until 1122.
1076 China: 2 East Syrian monasteries known, at Sianfu and Chengtu; 1093, Nestorian patriarch Sabaryeshu III appoints bishop George to Sestan then to see of Khatai in north China; 1265, 3 Nestorian churches in city of Iamzi (Yang-Chau-fu).
1078 Suppression of Bulgarian patriarchate by Byzantine emperor; reestablished 1235.
c1080 China: civil servant Su Sung builds accurate astronomical clock 30 feet tall, but officially condemned in 1094.
1081 Muslim Turks dominant in most of Armenia and Asia Minor.

**AD 1085.** Best medieval survey in Europe, Domesday Book counts 1.75 million British.

1085 William the Conqueror orders work on Domesday Book, a mammoth census and survey of realm of England, with its 1.75 million population, to discover 'how the kingdom was peopled and with what sorts of men', though actually to determine the rights of the King; standard set of questions; no urban or monastic statistics; best medieval survey in Europe; folk wisdom holds world will end as soon as compilation finished; but book never completed.
1090 College of Cardinals established in Rome by reforms of pope Urban II (c1042-1099), to expand rule of Christ across the Earth.
1093 Anselm (1033-1109) becomes archbishop of Canterbury; writes *Cur Deus homo*?
1095 Military expeditions by western Christians against Muslim powers to liberate Holy Land, launched by pope Urban II, known as Crusades: 1st 1095-99 (People's Crusade); 2nd 1147-49; 3rd 1189-93 (Richard the Lion-Heart); 4th 1202-04; 5th 1212-21 (Children's Crusade); 6th 1228-29; 7th 1248-54; 8th 1270-72 (Prince Edward of England).
1096 Islamic theologian Abu Hamid Mohammed al-Ghazali (1058-1111) begins his book *The Revival of the Religious Sciences,* which helps make Sufi mysticism part of Islamic orthodoxy.
1096 Start of First Crusade with 30,000 French and Italian crusaders invading Seljuk Turk empire: 'Deus vult' (God wills it); 1099, Jerusalem sacked.
1096 Cappadocia: Jacobites massacred by Turks in Malatya.
1096 Christian crusaders pillage and kill 5,000 Jews in First Crusade, in Jewish year 4856 (midway between destruction of Temple in AD 70 and Holocaust of World War II).
1098 France: founding of Citeaux abbey (Cistercians) and Prémontré (Norbertines), engaged in missionary activity in Scandinavia, Germany, Poland, Bohemia.
1099 Latin patriarchate of Jerusalem established; Latin kingdoms (Outremer) founded.

1100 **Global status:** 36 generations after Christ, world is 16.3% Christians (63% of them being Whites), 20.0% evangelized; with Scriptures translated into 19 languages.
1100 Sweden: christianization now completed.
1100 Poland: christianization completed.
c1100 *Finland*. First Christians (seamen and merchants).
c1100 Magnetic compass, for terrestrial navigation, invented in China, followed independently in Europe (by c1187), Arabia (c1220) and Scandinavia (c1300).
c1100 Nubia: 2 rival Christian kingdoms of (north) Makoritae and (south) Alodiae (with 400 churches).
c1100 Hungarians accept Christianity as national religion.
c1100 Mahayana Buddhism flowers in Japan (till 1300).
c1100 Armenian church split by Paulician separatists.
c1100 Timbuktu founded in west Africa, becoming center of Islamic culture and learning for African Muslims; 1591, conquered by Morocco.
1100 Middle English supersedes Old English.
c1100 Old English gives way in popular usage to Middle English, which lasts 400 years until replaced around 1500 by Modern English.
1103 General Council of the Church of Georgia held at Rouissi-Urbnisissus under catholicos John, with 15 disciplinary canons and reforms promulgated; next 200 years are golden age of Georgian power and culture, especially under queen Tamar (1184-1213).
1112 Bernard of Clairvaux (1090-1153) enters Citeaux, 1115 becomes abbot; mightiest preacher of Middle Ages, preaching in 2,000 monasteries and in many countries.
1112 Wandering ex-monk Tanchelm begins preaching across Low Countries, claiming to possess Holy Spirit and to be God as Christ was; announces new Kingdom of the Saints, attacks church and clergy; attracts multitudes of followers, holds magnificent banquets in imitation of wedding banquet in Revelation.
1118 Order of Knights Templar, a military religious order, founded to aid and protect pilgrims to Holy Land; HQ near Temple site, Jerusalem; rapid growth of immense wealth; 3 ranks of knights, sergeants, chaplains; 1311, king Philip IV (1268-1314) of France forces pope Clement V (1264-1314) to dissolve order throughout Europe, executing 120 Templars.
c1120 Greek Orthodox Patriarchate of Antioch adopts Arabic as its liturgical language.
1122 Scholastic theologian Peter Abelard writes *Sic et Non.*
1122 Eastern prelate named John visits Rome, lectures on miracles occurring every year in India on feast of St Thomas; 20 years later rumors circulate of a Christian king in India, Prester John, said to have inflicted major defeat on Muslim rulers.
1123 Council of Lateran I (9th Ecumenical Council): subject, investiture controversy.
1124 Several Cumans (Kipchak Turks) received by Stephen II of Hungary and come into contact with Christianity.
1124 Swabian bishop Otto (1062-1139) of Bamberg undertakes missionary journey as evangelizer of Pomerania at invitation of duke Boleslaw III (1086-1138) of Poland, converts 20,000 and establishes 12 churches.
1124 Chronicle of William Godel says that in 1010, when news reached Europe that Turks had captured Jerusalem from Saracens 'fear and affliction overcame the hearts of many, and many feared that the end of the world was arriving'.
1137 Kara Khitai empire in central Asia, until 1216.
1139 Council of Lateran II (10th Ecumenical Council): against pseudo-popes (antipopes, false popes), and on points of discipline.
1139 Gaelic church reformer, abbot, archbishop and prophet, Malachy O'Morgain (c1094-1148) compiles 'Prophecy of the Popes', foretells identities, mottoes and characteristics of 122 RC popes from Celestine II (1143) to end of 20th century with final Pope of the Apocalypse (Peter the Roman), with conversion of the Jews to Christ prophesied under last pope but one.
1140 Cambodia: Angkor Wat temple complex begun as microcosm of Cosmos, temple and astronomical observatory.
c1140 Christianity in Finland organized by English bishop Henry of Uppsala (martyred 1155).
1141 Koran translated from Arabic by Robert de Retines.
1142 Ecclesiastical reconciliation effected between Nestorian patriarch Ebedjesu II, and Jacobite primate Dionysius ends centuries of antagonism.
1146 Jews of Spain forcibly converted to Christianity; further force used, 1391.
c1148 Numerous Catholic women mystics or charismatics write extensively on the Holy Spirit: Hildegard of Bingen (1098-1179), Gertrude of Helfta (1256-1301), Birgitta of Sweden (1302-1373), Catherine of Siena (1347-1380), Julian of Norwich (1342-1420).
1149 Heretical neo-Manichean ascetic sect of Cathars (Cathari, Pure Ones, Albigenses) form an organized Cathar church related to Bogomil church,

with 11 bishoprics and wide followings in France and Italy.
c1150 European church and monastery workers adapt spring-pole mechanism to lathes and power them with foot pedals.
c1150 Widest expansion of West Syrian (Jacobite) church: 20 metropolitan sees, 103 bishoprics in Syria, Mesopotamia, Cyprus, et alia; 2 million adherents.
c1150 Scottish monks at work in Kiev.
c1150 Onguts (Tatars) become Christians in central Asia.
c1150 Rise of towns and middle class in Europe.
c1150 Osman I (1288-1326), founder of Ottoman dynasty, makes initial raids into Byzantine territory.
1151 Hildegarde (1098-1179) abbess of Rupertsberg wields widespread influence as mystic visionary, predicts: 'Just as the world was made in 6 days, it will come to an end in 6,000 years.'
1154 Idrisi (c1099-c1155), cartographer in Roger de Hauteville's court in Sicily, writes *The Pleasure of the Ardent Enquirer,* containing circular world map; holds that earth is round more than 3 centuries before Columbus.
1155 Founding of Carmelite order on Mount Carmel, Palestine.
1160 University of Paris, finest university of Middle Ages, is founded; by 1500, some 80 universities have been established in Europe.
1160 Council of Anuradhapura in Ceylon ends long-standing dissension between Mahavirahara and Abhayagiri monasteries.
c1160 Ibn Rushd (Averroes, 1126-1198), Arab physician/philosopher, writes commentary on Aristotle, codifies existing body of medicine; integrates Islamic traditions and Greek thought.
c1162 Mahadevi is born, female Saiva ascetic saint of Karnataka, writes 350 majestic and mystical poems.
1165 Letter circulates in Europe allegedly from Prester John, who claims to rule from Tower of Babel to land where sun sets.
1166 Waldensian movement begins following Poor Men of Lyons and reformer Peter Waldo, develops evangelistic and charismatic ministries (visions, prophecies, healings, exorcisms).
1168 Danes destroy paganism among Wends of Rugen.

**AD 1170.** Archbishop Becket is murdered in Canterbury Cathedral by knights from King Henry II.

1170 Murder in Canterbury cathedral of Thomas Becket (c1118-1170), archbishop of Canterbury, on wishes of English king Henry II.
c1170 Founding of universities: 1119 Bologna, 1160 Paris, 1167 Oxford, and 1200 Cambridge.
1172 Ireland: Roman pope's recognition of sovereignty of Henry II sounds death knell of the independent Celtic Church of Ireland.
1177 Master Philip, personal physician to pope Alexander III, sails from Venice on special mission to East with letter addressed to Prester John; travels through Palestine to desert, never heard from again; earliest attempt to open up relations between Christian Europe and remote regions of Asia.
1179 Council of Lateran III (11th Ecumenical Council): formally outlaws usury (interest charged on loans); also, no Christian should be subjected to slavery.
1179 Astronomer John of Toledo calculates major catastrophe coming in AD 1186; widespread panic follows.
1180 Bosnia: Bogomil Church (Krstjani) becomes established church under prince Ban Kulin; after Turkish conquest of 1463, most Krstjani convert to Islam.
c1180 Kurdish sultan Saladin (1137-1193) sends invading army to Nubia which kills or enslaves 700,000 Nubian Christians.
c1180 Joachim of Fiore (c1130-1202), Italian Cistercian abbot and mystic, divides all history into three 40-generation ages or periods (Old Testament, New Testament, future age), writes *Vaticini del Vangelo Eterno* (Prophecies of the Eternal Gospel) and *Expositio in Apocalypsim* describing imminent crisis of evil, apocalyptic symbols of Antichrist, and his 3rd or Final Age of the Spirit (Love) coming by 1260 after Age of the Father (Law), and Age of the Son (Grace)), for spiritual men through pilgrimage and great tribulation in a spiritualized Johannine Church replacing carnal Petrine Church; Joachimism spreads widely over next 3 centuries.
c1180 *Kirghizia.* First Christians: Italian and French monks, leaving a Nestorian archbishopric of Tokmak.
1180 Catholicos of the East appoints first metropolitan John to Kashgar (Sinkiang), succeeded by Sabrisho; jurisdiction includes Yarkand, Tenduc, Tangut and Tibet, Chingintalas and Suchur.
1181 Roman Catholic uniate churches begin to emerge (Syria); over 40,000 Maronites submit to Rome and enter into communion with Latin patriarch of Antioch.
c1185 Nestorian patriarch Elias III makes Kashgar seat of a metropolitan.
1187 Recapture of Jerusalem by Arabs; at Lake Tiberias (Galilee), massacre of all Christians by Saracens under Saladin.
1189 Third Crusade launched, capturing Acre.
1190 Order of Teutonic Knights founded as German religious and military order; 1805, dissolved by Napoleon; 1929, new purely religious Rule based on schools and hospitals.
c1190 Rise of demand for vernacular versions of Scriptures, illustrated by *Historia Scholastica*, a narrative of biblical history, by 12th-century scholar Petrus Comestor (c1100-1180); poetical and prose versions now available in Old French (ProvenÅal, Vaudois), Italian, Spanish.
1198 Power of papacy reaches its height during reign of Innocent III (1161-1216), who excommunicates Holy Roman emperor Otto IV (1182-1218) in 1210 and English king John (c1167-1216) in 1209.
c1199 Chinese develop first arrows propelled by black-powder rockets; knowledge of rocketry quickly spreads to Europe.
c1200 Christianity now widespread throughout Turkestan; numerous ethnic peoples are virtually all Nestorian Christians: Keraits (Kalmyks), Uighurs, Naimans, Kitans (Kanglis), Karakanides, Merkites (Buryats), Uriyan-gakit, Kirghiz, Alans, and to a large extent the Mongols (Moals, Moghuls, Tartars); several millions of Nestorians, from 60 to 120 degrees longitude and 30 to 50 degrees latitude.

1200 **Global status:** 39 generations after Christ, world is 18.4% Christians (64.3% of them being Whites), 22.7% evangelized; with Scriptures translated into 22 languages.
1200 World's 5 largest cities: Hangchow 255,000, Fez 250,000, Cairo 200,000, Constantinople 200,000, Canton 200,000.
1200 Life expectancy in Europe 33 years, rising to 35 by 1800, 49 by 1900, 70 by 1960, 74 by 1980, 90 by 2000, 120 by 2030.
1200 Apex of medieval papacy, under Innocent III (1198-1216).
1200 Europe entirely christianized except for Wends, Prussians, Lithuanians and other Baltic races.
c1200 Abraham of Smolensk preaches imminent Last Judgment; with disciple Ephrem predicts end of world in 7000 AM (1492) when Earth would be burned whiter than snow.
c1200 Pope Innocent III envisages Second Coming of Christ in AD 1284, 666 years after rise of Islam, Beast of the Apocalypse.
c1200 First Middle English versions of Scripture: Augustinian monk Ormin writes 'Ormulum', poetical version of Gospels and Acts; c1400, chief NT epistles translated for use in monasteries; also OT summaries.
c1200 Bosnian Christians reject Hungarian bishop, create own separatist Crkva Bosanska (the Bosnian Church) independent of Roman Catholicism until liquidated in 1461, with all Bosnians becoming Catholics, Orthodox, or Muslims; 1463, Ottoman Turk invasion conquers Bosnia, followed by slow conversion to Islam over 2 centuries.
1202 Fourth Crusade launched against Egypt under Innocent III, also capturing and sacking of Constantinople from Greeks in 1204; Greeks permanently embittered against Latins.
1203 Mongol leader Temuchin breaks with his suzerain Togrul, brings Christian Keraits under his rule; 1204, defeats Naimans, dominant people of western Mongolia.
1204 Kuchlug, a Nestorian Christian by birth, escapes Temuchin, flees to Qara-Khitai kingdom where he takes power and persecutes Muslims; Crusaders dub him 'King David' in line of Prester John.
1204 Ongut king, a Nestorian Christian, pledges support to Temuchin, gives daughter as a wife.
c1205 Amaurians (14 clergy in Paris) preach imminence of Last Days predicting 'Within 5 years, all men will be Spirituals, so that each will be able to say "I am the Holy Spirit"'; woes of Revelation will follow before the 5 years are up.

**AD 1206.** Rise of Genghis Khan's attempt to conquer the world; revered in 1990s Mongolia.

1206 Temuchin proclaimed emperor under name Chingis Khan, aims to force whole world to submit to his rule; exempts clergy of conquered countries from taxes and compulsory service, beginning policy of religious toleration.
1208 20,000 Albigensians massacred as heretics at papal order, around Toulouse; 1244 Cathar stronghold of Montsegur destroyed, Cathar church forced underground.

**AD 1209.** Widely recognized as a Charismatic precursor, Francis of Assisi sends missionaries throughout world.

1209 Francis of Assisi (1182-1226) founds traveling preachers (Franciscans), largest of the mendicant orders (OFM); widespread healings, signs and miracles reported; 1270, missionaries in almost every part of the known world; by 1400, missions from Lapland to Congo and Azores to China; soon reaches a medieval peak of 60,000 Franciscans by 1400, 77,000 by 1768, falling to 14,000 by 1900, rising to 40,000 by 1970; by AD 2000, 35,200 priests and brothers and 57,300 sisters (nuns).
1211 Genghis Khan (c1162-1227), Universal Emperor of the Mongols (whose mother was a Nestorian), attacks China with army of only 129,000 and massacres 35 million in a decade.
1211 Over 80 Waldensians burned as heretics at Strasbourg; intermittent severe persecutions thereafter, especially in 1545, 1555-59, during which time membership peaked at 100,000.
1212 England: most of London burns after fire starts at London Bridge.
1212 Children's Crusade, a disastrous venture by over 20,000 children, many of whom end as slaves in Egypt.
1215 Council of Lateran IV (12th Ecumenical Council): against Waldensians, Albigensians, et alii.
1215 Magna Carta, charter of English liberties, forced on king by English nobles and commoners; signed (June 19) by English king John (c1167-1216), guaranteeing basic liberties, habeas corpus, trial by jury; major effect on development of English law.
1215 Dominic (1170-1221) founds Order of Preachers (OP, Dominicans) in southern France for 'Propagation of the Faith through Preaching', 'accepting our Lord's command, Go ye into all the world'; soon reaches a peak of 12,000 Dominicans, falling to 7,055 by 1983; other orders of mendicant friars arise including in 1256 Augustinians (OSA).
1219 Independent Serbian Orthodox Church formed.
1219 Francis of Assisi crosses Crusader-Muslim lines and preaches the gospel before sultan al-Kamil of Egypt.
1219 Christians begin to mistake Genghis Khan and his successors as the legendary Prester John (a great Christian emperor of the East who will crush non-Christians and unite tribes of Israel), predicting his final victory for 1265 as end of the world; much later, Mongols are equated with Antichrist.
c1220 German scripture translations available.
1220 Genghis Khan massacres 25% of population in Iran and Iraq; dies 1227.
1220 First Franciscan missionary martyrs: Berard and 4 others killed after preaching in Marrakesh (Morocco); 1227, Daniel and 6 more Italian friars killed in Ceuta.
1220 Genghis Khan captures Bokhara, 'the Baghdad of the East'; his son Tolui captures Merv and butchers 700,000 men, women, and children there, documenting the count with severed ears.
c1220 50-year domination of Constantinople by Latin rulers and troops; scriptoria and many scripture manuscripts destroyed.
1221 Ukraine entered by Dominicans; 1228, diocese under Rome created; 1240, Kiev captured by Mongols.
1221 First of many papal mission encyclicals on foreign missionary affairs: Bull of Honorius III, 'Ne si secus' to the 13 metropolitans of the Catholic church, asking them to send out missionaries.
1221 Dominican friars are sent by king Andreas II to evangelize Comans; several converted Coman chieftains declare loyalty to Hungarian monarch Bela, who later tries to use Comans and Bashkirs as barrier against Mongol attack.
1223 Cathars of Bulgaria, Croatia, Dalmatia and Hungary hold a conclave and elect a Cathar pope; 1225, Cathars of Languedoc create new diocese of Razs and elect its bishop.
1227 Cuman prince Barc and 15,000 followers baptized, in Hungary; 1228, diocese of Milkovia set up for them; 1241, diocese destroyed by Mongols.
1227 On death of Genghis Khan, Mongol empire is divided into four ulus (dominions); 1229, third son Ogodei named his successor.
1227 Batu grandson of Genghis Khan becomes first khan of Golden Horde and ruler of Russia; leading to 9th khan Uzbek (1313-1341).
1228 Sea floods Holland; 100,000 die.
1228 6th Crusade, laymen's crusade under Holy Roman emperor Frederick II, the only crusade excommunicated by Roman papacy; avoids military confronta-

tion and reaches peaceful negotiation with Muslim sultan of Egypt al-Kamil; 1244, Muslims retake Jerusalem.
1229 Vernacular Scriptures prohibited by Synod of Toulouse, also (1233) at Tarragona, Spain.
1229 Jerusalem again in Christian hands 1229-39 and 1243-44; 1244, finally recaptured by Muslims on being sacked by Khwarezmian Tatars.
c1230 First word/verbal Bible concordances: *Concordantiae Sancti Jacobi* of Latin Vulgate Bible, 1250 *Concordantiae Anglicanae,* 1290 *Concordantiae Bibliorum* (Conrad of Halberstadt); most famous subsequently being 1737 *Cruden's Concordance* to the AV/KJV.
1231 Pope Gregory IX (c1170-1241) establishes Inquisition against heretics by Statutes of the Holy See, under Franciscans and Dominicans.
1235 Mali empire (West Africa) founded.
1235 Ogodei appoints Syrian cleric Simeon Rabban-ata as leader of Nestorian Christians with headquarters at Tabriz; under protection of Mongol general Chormaghan, Simeon builds many churches and influences whole territory occupied by Mongols.
1235 Croatia: Hungarian governor and pope Gregory IX support 6-year crusade against Bosnian Church and alleged influence of heretical Bogomil religion (Cathars, Manichaeans, Patarenes).
1237 Friar Julian returns from visit to the East, reports Mongols aim at world domination with Rome as next target.
1239 Holy Roman emperor Frederick II (1194-1250) opposes papal authority, 1239 excommunicated; identified as Antichrist by followers of Joachim of Fiore.
1240 Dominicans begin mission in Tiflis, Georgia.
1240 Batu Khan, grandson of Genghis Khan, conquers all Russia and devastates eastern Europe, establishes Kipchak Khanate (Golden Horde) in southern Russia as western division of Mongol empire, which then adopts Islam and Turkic language and lasts 200 years, eventually becoming Uzbekistan.
1240 Kiev, mother of Russian cities and center of Greek Orthodox Church in Russia, is captured and destroyed by Mongols, with all its population slaughtered; 1241 Poland defeated, then Hungary destroyed. Russia, is captured and destroyed by Mongols; 1241 Poland defeated, then Hungary destroyed.
1241 Sudden death of Ogodei Khan saves Christian Europe from Mongol invasion and destruction; 1259, death of Mongke Khan saves Muslim Asia from similar fate.
1242 Moors forced to hear evangelistic sermons in kingdom of Aragon.
1242 Christian world is on brink of disaster with Mongols at gates of Vienna, when miraculously attack is called off and Mongols disappear on news of death of khan Ogodei (caused by excessive drinking).
1242 Batu consolidates position as Mongol ruler of the West; 2 centuries of oppressive rule over Russia begin.
1242 European Christians sense imminent overrunning by Mongols and begin to refer to them as the Hammer of God, instrument of Divine Providence.
1244 Pope Innocent IV sends 2 Dominicans and 2 Franciscans to Karakorum.
1245 Council of Lyons I (for RCs, 13th Ecumenical Council): against emperor Frederick II's persecution of church and pope; also urges missionaries be sent to Mongol princes.
1245 Innocent IV calls 13th Ecumenical Council, seeking remedy against Tartars; entrusts uncovering of Mongol objectives to Franciscan and Dominican friars.
1245 Two English Franciscans John of Stanford and Abraham of Larde appointed papal legates to Mongol empire; Innocent IV later replaces them by John of Pian di Carpine (a direct disciple of Francis) and Lawrence of Portugal; Carpine, age 60, leaves Lyons, takes 10 months to cross Europe; with new companion friar Benedict the Pole he arrives in Kiev but fails to convince Conrad to join Catholics in repelling Mongols because Kievan Russia already under Mongol jurisdiction.
1245 Two Dominicans, Lombard Ascelinus and Andrew of Longjumeau are dispatched to contact Mongols via the Levant, carrying 2 types of documents: one, religious in nature, summary of Christian teaching asking khan to accept this doctrine; other, political in nature, deprecating Mongol massacres and destruction, requesting khan to refrain.
1245 Dominic of Aragon, a Franciscan, is sent on ecclesiastical mission to Armenia and Greek Orthodox Church of Byzantium.
1246 John and Benedict are present at election of Guyug as new Mongol khan; delegations from Russia, Armenia, Syria, Iraq, Turkestan, China and Korea also present.
1246 Mongol chief secretary, Chinqai, a Nestorian, arranges interview of John ordering him to acknowledge Mongol supremacy, defending Nestorian Christianity, and asserting Mongols destined to rule whole world.
1246 Andrew of Longjumeau meets Nestorian prelate Simeon Rabban-ata in Tabriz, delivers papal bulls on schismatic churches; Simeon replies to pope with open allegiance to Rome; Andrew then meets in Antioch with Ignatius II, patriarch of Jacobite Christians, who responds favorably to uniting of churches.
1249 Conquest and conversion of Finland finally secured by Swedish ruler Birger Jarl (died 1266).
1249 Southern Siberia: sizeable communities of Turkic Nestorian Christians exist across Chagatai territory near Issyk-kul lake, lasting up to 1345.
c1250 Nubia: many new mosques erected, Christianity waning due to internal dissension, mass apostasies, destruction of churches, many martyrdoms.

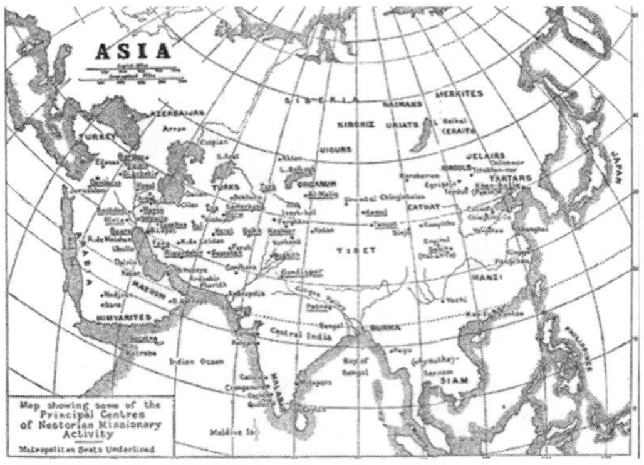


**AD 1250.** Episcopal sees and main areas of Nestorian influence across Asia.

c1250 Nestorian influence strong across Asia, still with over 250 bishoprics; under Mongol Yuan dynasty in China (1276-1368), Nestorians return somewhat before finally vanishing.
c1250 Central Asia: Uighurs, Keraits, Mongols and all other major people partially christianized.
c1250 All Prussians forcibly baptized and pagan worship eradicated.
c1250 *Estonia.* First Christians (Lutheran missionaries, German Teutonic knights).
c1250 Portions of Bible available in Italian (Tuscan, Lombardic), Polish, Spanish and Catalan.
c1250 Koreans first, then Chinese, develop movable type.
1250 Founding of school of oriental languages by Raymond Martini.
1250 Kublai Khan completes census of Tibet for military purposes.
1250 Palestine: Dominican missionary William of Tripoli baptizes over 1,000 Muslims.
1250 French language now the 'universal vernacular of Christendom' as a result of the Crusades.
c1250 Height of the Catholic church's political power in Europe, taken for granted by most Christians as God's instrument for spreading the rule of Christ around the world.
c1250 Popular preachers spread warnings of coming of Antichrist; Roman popes Boniface VIII (1234-1303) and John XXII (1249-1334) inter alios each widely regarded as Antichrist.
c1250 Brother Arnold, dissident Dominican monk, writes manifesto in Swabia, stating that in year 1260 era will end and a New Age will begin.
c1250 Cardinal Hugh de St Cher is first to divide Bible into its present chapters; c1550, first division by verses.
c1250 Earliest use of movable metal type, traceable to Korea.
c1250 Division of Georgian monarchy results in a separate Catholicosate of Western Georgia; exists with seat at Bichvinta and later at Gelati, lasts 6 centuries.
c1250 Serbian sacred art (for use in Orthodox liturgy) is at its most magnificent, during 13th and 14th centuries; but after Serbia's defeat by Turks at Kosovo (1389), sacred art withers away.
1251 *Lithuania.* First Christians (leader Mendog baptized in 1251, faced with threat of invasion by German Teutonic knights).
1251 Mongke announces that he intends to complete conquest of the world begun by his grandfather Genghis Khan; appoints brother Kublai to subdue China, other brother Hulegu (c1217-1265) to move West; 1258, Hulegu storms Baghdad, massacres almost all citizens; 1259, unexpected death of Mongke saves Muslim Asia, although in 1260 Damascus falls.
1252 In bull 'Ad Extirpanda', pope Innocent IV finally recommends and urges fire, irons and rack (torture and death) for heretics.
1253 Japan: Buddhist monk Nichiren (1222-1282) founds Nichiren-shu sect.
1253 Roman Catholic envoy William of Rubruck reaches Mongol court at Karakorum, meets Mongke the fourth Great Khan.
1254 Sensational Introduction to the Eternal Gospel of abbot Joachim issued by ardent Spiritual, Gerard of Borgo San Donnino, claiming its prophecies have been fulfilled by Franciscan order, and insisting Age of the Spirit will begin in 1260.
1258 Hulagu Khan and Mongol hordes sack and destroy Arab caliphate capital Baghdad and (1260) Saracen stronghold of Damascus in attempt to destroy Muslim world, kill 800,000 in Baghdad but spare Christians; destroy Aleppo and Antioch; Hulagu (whose wife is a Christian) professes Christian faith, dies in 1265.
1258 Franciscan preacher Berthold von Regensburg (died 1272) preaches to unprecedented crowds in many countries.
1258 Last years of Pax Mongolica, protected by Hulegu and Abaka, in which Nestorian church from Persia to Mongolia flourishes before 1295 conversion to Islam of Hulegu's great-grandson Ghazan.
c1260 Italy and Europe: greatest period of religious art begins, and lasts 400 years, with as central theme Christ's passion and crucifixion; all art—paintings, drawings, tapestries, stained-glass windows, sculpture, architecture–now regarded as major method of teaching and evangelizing illiterate populations.
c1260 Societas Fratrum Peregrinantium Propter Christum Inter Gentes (Congregation of Friars Pilgrims for Christ Among the Gentiles) founded as Dominican foreign mission body; 1300, founds residences from Constantinople to Black Sea into India; ends 1456.
1261 Mameluke Egyptian army (Turkish slave-warrior rebels) destroys Mongol army at Ain Jalut near Nazareth.
1262 Mongol khan Berke with nobles converts to Islam, but most Mongols remain shamanists.
1264 Jacobite monk Gregory Bar Hebraeus (1226-1286), leading Syrian historian and scholar, appointed maphrian of the East (deputy to Syrian Orthodox patriarch in Antioch); by 1284 restructures hierarchy and consecrates 12 new Jacobite bishops in the East.
1265 English parliament established.

**AD 1266.** Kublai Khan, emperor of the East, asks Europe for 100 missionaries to convert his empire; no answer.

1266 Mongol emperor Kublai Khan (1215-1294), ruler of north China with 15 million inhabitants and south China with 65 million inhabitants, asks Polo brothers to return to Europe with requests to Roman pope for 100 missionaries, writes to Roman pope: 'Send me 100 men skilled in your religion... and so I shall be baptized, and then all my barons and great men, and then their subjects. And so there will be more Christians here than there are in your parts'; 2 Dominicans sent, but turn back; then 1278, pope sends 5 Franciscans; greatest missed opportunity in Christian history.
1266 Mubarak, 6th khan of Chagatai khanate becomes first to convert to Islam.
c1270 China: great Pacific ports are known to have over 400,000 secret Christians; many Christians and Nestorian churches known also in 11 other major Chinese cities including Kashgar, Kanchou, Camul (Hami), and others along Old Silk Road.
c1270 Nearly a million Christians live among Turkish tribes of Chagatai khanate.
1271 Marco Polo (1254-1324) accompanies his father Niccolo and uncle on overland journey to China, discovers large Christian kingdom in Tenduc, Inner Mongolia ruled by Christian king named George, an Ongut, distinguished general, literate aristocrat, and devout Christian; spends next 24 years traveling through Asia including Sumatra, Iran, and India as Kublai Khan's official representative, writes *Divisament dou Monde.*
1271 Rijmbijbel (Scriptures in poetic Dutch) written.
1272 Philosopher and theologian Thomas Aquinas (1225-1274) completes *De aeternitate mundi contra murmurantes* (On the Eternity of the World).
1274 Council of Lyons II (for RCs, 14th Ecumenical Council): attempt to unite Greek and Roman churches; proliferation of mendicant orders discouraged.
1275 Nestorian archbishopric established in Cambaluc (Khanbalik/Peking), and hierarchy restored throughout central Asia.
1275 Franciscan monk composes *The prophecies of Merlin* predicting that a final world emperor from Wales named the Good Champion will wrest Holy Land away from Islam.
1277 Burma temporarily conquered by Mongol armies of Kublai Khan, and again in 1283; city of Pegu later known as a Christian center.
1278 Rome dispatches 2 friars on fruitless mission to baptize Abaka the ilkhan of Persia.
1280 Marco Polo reports 700,000 secret Christians live in the great ports of the Pacific.
1281 36-year-old Ongut Sino-Turk Nestorian monk from Peking, Mark, while visiting Baghdad is unexpectedly elected 73rd patriarch of Church of the East, takes name Mar Yaballaha III; consecrates 75 bishops; 1304, submits to Roman pope Benedict XI, sets up Latin sees which soon collapse; dies 1317.

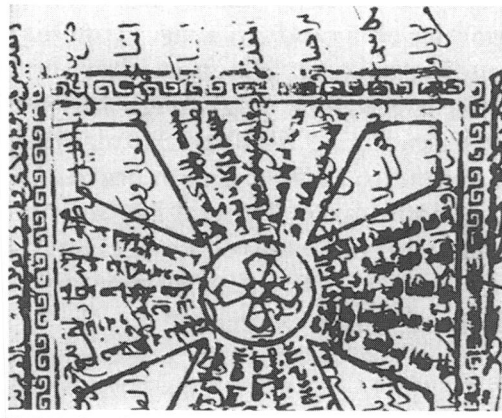

**AD 1281.** Seal of patriarch Mar Yaballaha III on letter to pope Boniface VII in 1302.

1281 Kublai Khan's second invasion of Japan.
1282 Stigmatic nun Guglielma of Milan dies, followers identify her as third Person of Trinity and expect her to return in 1300 to supervise a worldwide pentecostal conversion to the Church of the Holy Spirit; 3 followers are executed in 1302, and her remains are exhumed and burned.
1287 Collapse of seawall results in flood of Zuider Zee in Holland, taking 50,000 lives (December 14).
1287 Nestorian Christian from Cambaluc (Peking), Rabban Sauma (1250-1294) visits pope in Rome; as a result, in 1294 Italian Franciscan John of Montecorvino (1246-1328) arrives in Cambaluc; bitter opposition from Nestorians.
1288 German canon Alexander of Roes (in Cologne) predicts, in *Notitia Seculi*, end of world at AD 1500, being 6,000 years from foundation of world.
1289 Kublai Khan creates department of Chinese government dealing with affairs of Christians in his empire.
1290 Expulsion of Jews from England under Edward I, lasting several centuries until protector Cromwell readmits them in 1656.
1290 Arnold of Villanova (c1240-1311), leading alchemist and physician of his day, writes 70 scientific works and theological treatises including on the coming of Antichrist.
c1290 Former missionary to Persia William Adam, Dominican bishop of Smyrna, writes inflammatory book entitled *On a Method of Exterminating the Saracens;* c1390, Tamerlane destroys Christian stronghold of Smyrna with all Christians slaughtered.
1291 Fall of Acre, in Syria, last Crusader stronghold; Crusaders driven from Middle East by Mamluk Muslims; end of all Crusades and crusading zeal in Europe.
1293 Armenian catholicate of Cilicia transferred to Sis.
1293 Sumatra and Java briefly subdued by naval forces of Kublai Khan.
1294 Definitive turning point in eclipse of Christianity in Asia: death of emperor Kublai Khan, protector of church in China; 1295, Ghazan ilkhan (1271-1304), ruler of Mongols in Persia, announces conversion to Islam, so state adopts Islam; Kurds massacre Nestorians, especially in city of Maragha.
1294 Franciscan missionary John of Montecorvino (1246-1330) arrives in Cambaluc just after death of Kublai Khan; by 1305, has baptized 6,000 converts with 25,000 more Mongol adherents; 1307, appointed archbishop, primate and patriarch of Far East by pope Clement V; 1313, 3 bishops arrive to assist.
1295 Great pulpiteers of Middle Ages include Meister Eckhart (1260-1327) and Johann Tauler (1300-1361), both Dominicans.
1295 Mongol world (Russia, Persia, Turkestan) gradually being converted to Islam.
1295 Franciscans at work in 17 stations throughout Mongol empire, with a monastery in Cambaluc.
1295 First Holy Year (Jubilee Year) held in Rome under pope Boniface VIII, attracts 200,000 pilgrims at any given time throughout whole year (minimum stay, 30 days each person); then 1350, 1390, 1423, 1450, 1490; then every 25 years except 1800, 1850, 1875; subsequently every 50 years, latterly every 25 years.
c1295 Spiritual Franciscans Peter John Olivi and Fra Dolcino view end of century as end of age of the corrupt church, accurately predict death of pope Boniface VIII in 1303.
1295 Persia: ilkhan Ghazan issues first decree ordering destruction of all churches, synagogues, and Buddhist temples; first to rule as a strict Muslim, with Islam the official religion of Iran.
c1296 Flagellants travel in bands throughout Europe, warning of imminent end of world.
c1297 Bands of criminals, forerunners of modern-day Mafia, begin operating in Sicily.
1298 Prague emerges as a leading European university city.
c1299 John of Rupescissa, Catalan Franciscan monk and disciple of Joachim predicts conversion of Tatars will be followed by conversion of the Jews and extermination of Muslims, leading to Second Coming of Christ.

### Period of Medieval decline, AD 1300-1400

1300 **Global status:** 42 generations after Christ, world is 23.2% Christians (66% of them being Whites), 28.2% evangelized; with Scriptures translated into 26 languages.
1300 Muslim conquerors reach Cape Comorin at southernmost tip of India and build a mosque there.
1301 Egypt: all churches ordered closed or destroyed by Mamluk dynasty (1250-1517); Copts and Jacobites in Syria suffer a century of systematic persecution.
1302 Invention of card compass by Italian mariner Flavio Gioja.
1302 Muslim rulers in South India murder Roman Catholic missionary friars.

### European Renaissance: New Age in Western Civilization

1303 Renaissance begins in Italy, a great cultural movement encompassing all the arts.
1304 European Renaissance begins with life of poet Francesco Petrarch.
1305 Seventy-year 'Avignon Captivity' of papacy begins when pope Clement V (1264-1314) moves papacy from Rome to Avignon in France from 1309 to 1378.
1305 House of Taxis (Vienna) operates express message postal system across Europe with (by 1628) 20,000 liveried couriers; a mass communications total monopoly for the rich, privileged and powerful.
1306 Expulsion of Jews from France.
1306 John of Montecorvino builds 2 churches in Cambaluc, translates New Testament into Ongut (Tatar) and Uighur; dies 1330 with 30,000 converts made.
1309 Gibraltar: first organized churches (Spanish Catholic soldiers, capturing Rock from Muslims).
c1310 Persia: large proportion Christian, but Mongol rulers still undecided between Christianity and Islam.
1310 Massacre of Arbela: Kurds and Arabs destroy Christian fortress city.
1311 Council of Vienne (Rhone)(15th Ecumenical Council): abolition of Templars, condemnation of various heresies.
1312 Final conversion of Tatar race to Islam under Khan Uzbek ruler of the Golden Horde; completed by 1342.
1314 *Divine Comedy* written by Italian poet Dante (Alighieri) (1265-1321); one of world's great works of literature.
1315 Nubia: accession of a Muslim as king of formerly Christian kingdom of Dongola, which then rapidly becomes Muslim.

**AD 1315.** *Left.* Manuscript by Ramon Llull advocating military force against Muslims. *Below.* Llull is murdered in Algeria.

1315 Ramon Llull (c1232-1316), Franciscan theologian writing in Arabic and Catalan, proposes campaign of informed preaching plus military force against Muslims (*Liber de fine*); stoned to death at Bugia (Algeria) by Muslims.
1315 Franciscan theologian Hugh of Newcastle (c1280-1322), doctor scholasticus, teaches in Paris, writes on coming of Antichrist.
1317 Turkey: Mongols enslave or kill 12,000 Nestorians at Amid (Diyarbakr).

1318 Pope John XXII divides Asia into 2 missionary districts: one for China and the Franciscans at Cambaluc, the other for Persia under Dominicans at Persian capital Sultaniyeh.
1318 Last recorded General Synod of Church of the East, and last public enthronement of a Persian patriarch, Timothy II.
c1320 Gottesfreunde (Friends of God), lay middle-class German mystics within the medieval church, form a Christian fellowship in Basel, then Bavaria, Rhineland, Switzerland, and the Netherlands, including Strasbourg and Cologne; life of love, piety, devotion, holiness; several leaders tried and executed.
1321 Egypt: almost all remaining Coptic churches and monasteries burned or destroyed in mob fury; mass executions of Christians.
1321 Final pogrom against Cathars: priest Guilhem Belibasta burnt at stake in Languedoc, c1330 last group murdered.
1321 India: French Dominican missionary to Persia, Jordanus of Society of Wanderers for Christ, arrives in Bombay as first resident Catholic missionary to India; first task to bury bodies of 3 martyred Dominican bishops en route to China; in Italy in 1328, Jordanus is consecrated bishop of Quilon but never returns.
1323 Franciscan contacts in Sumatra, Java and Borneo.
1325 Aztecs found capital city Tenochtitlan in Valley of Mexico; at dedication of Great Temple, 20,000 slaves sacrificed to god of war Huitzilopochtli; by 1500, population 500,000, ruling over Aztec empire of 5,500,000 people; 1523, destroyed and razed to ground by Cortes and conquistadors.
1326 Moscow, a thriving commercial center, becomes seat of Russian Orthodox Church.
1328 Tibet: first European missionary, Odorico de Pordenone OFM, reaches Lhasa from Chinese side.
c1330 Scripture historical books translated into Norwegian.
c1330 Last surviving group of Cathars take refuge in caves, where they are walled up by cardinal Jacques Fournier (pope Benedict XII from 1334-42).
1330 Nestorians in China number 30,000.
1337 The Hundred Years' War fought between France and England until 1453.
1338 Massacre of Almalik: Christians murdered after death of final Chagatai khan Chingshi include Richard bishop of Almalik and 6 Franciscan missionary priests.
1340 Renaissance spreads as revival of learning and the arts over a 200-year period, beginning in Italy, characterized by admiration for and imitation of ancient Greece and Rome, together with recrudescence of anti-Christian paganism.
1340 German Dominican mystic Johann Tauler (1300-1361) of the Friends of God (Gottesfreunde) initiates major revival in Rhine valley, whose influence lasts until 1450.
1340 Mongol emperor's guard of Alans, white Christians from Caucasus mountains, write to Roman pope urging him to send hundreds of missionaries to Cambaluc.
1341 Arab historian Abdul Fida describes Africans from Red Sea to Lake Chad as primarily Christians.
1342 Mongol dynasty becomes finally and definitively Muslim.
1345 Serbian Orthodox patriarchate established; later suppressed in 1459 and again in 1765.
1345 China: port city of Zaitun (Chuanchou) a well-established active Catholic diocese; 1362, archbishop of Zaitun, James of Florence, murdered in central Asia.
1347 Worst known outbreak of bubonic plague sweeps into Europe from Orient; Black Death becomes history's greatest disaster as an estimated 75 million die over 4 years.
1347 Black Death (bubonic plague pandemic) erupts in Mongolia, kills 13 million in China, spreads like wildfire to India and Middle East, kills 85,000 Tartars in Crimea alone, thence to Genoa by ship, then sweeps across Europe killing 33% of 60 million population; 98% of all European victims are Christians; Jews held responsible, so 1 million massacred; plague ends 1353, having killed 75 million worldwide (17% of world population).

**AD 1349.** The dreaded Black Death kills millions across Europe.

1349 Plague strikes England in full force, killing 40% of population; also again in 1361, 1369, 1375, 1390, with 8 further attacks in 15th century.

c1349 Renaissance continues to spread rapidly in Italy: renewed interest in Greek and Roman cultures, a great cultural movement which spreads throughout Europe.

1349 Jews expelled from Hungary over 11-year period; in Germany, 350 separate massacres annihilating 210 Jewish communities.

1349 30,000 Christians remain in Mongol empire in China (population then 80 million), mostly Mongols.

1349 Apogee of East Syrian or Nestorian expansion across Asia, geographically more extensive and more prosperous than ever before or since; 25 metropolitans (each with 6-12 suffragan bishops) in 250 dioceses in China, India, Kashgar, Samarkand, Turkestan, et alia, with total of over 15 million Christians; a mighty organization with missionary enterprise unsurpassed in Christian history.

**Epoch IV: AD 1350-1500**

**THE SECOND RECESSION: Confusion and corruption**

1350 **Global status:** 44 generations after Christ, world is 24.0% Christians (67.6% of them being Whites), 28.6% evangelized; with Scriptures translated into 28 languages; total martyrs since AD 33, 11,814,000 (0.6% of all Christians ever; recent rate 13,100 per year).

1350 Rapid shrinking of geographical frontiers of Christianity begins, especially in Asia, and continues for 150 years.

1350 At height of Black Death, pope Clement VI decrees a holy year or jubilee; one million pilgrims visit Rome.

1350 Monastic efforts at evangelization by mystic and reformer Sergius of Radonezh (1314-1392) at Murmansk and Solovkij; founds 40 monasteries.

c1350 Rupture between European church in East and West finally complete.

c1350 Strong Christian communities in south India; Nestorians scattered across subcontinent.

c1350 First Middle Persian (Pahlavi) version of Scriptures.

c1350 St John of the Cleft Rock writes: 'It is said that 20 centuries after the Incarnation of the Word, the Beast in its turn shall become a man. About the year AD 2000, Antichrist will reveal himself to the world.'

c1350 Mali, Gao, Timbuktu become important Muslim centers.

c1350 Italian merchants devise essential principles of accounting (double-entry bookkeeping, bills of exchange, limited liability).

c1350 Lifetime of Appaya Dikshita, saint of South India who works to reconcile Vaishnavism and Saivism; creates standard manual of Saiva temple ritual.

c1350 Nicholas of Lyra, renowned Franciscan biblical scholar of Hebrew and rabbinical lore, compiles what becomes later the first printed commentary on the whole Bible.

1355 12,000 Jews massacred by Christian mob in Toledo, Spain.

1357 Diocese of Cyprus erected with series of bishops for Maronite church, which separated from Greek Orthodoxy in 7th century, and which has for some time been in communion with Rome.

1358 Mongol conqueror Tamerlane (a Tatar Muslim nomad; 1336-1405) begins to destroy Christian civilization from China and north India to Mediterranean.

c1360 Jan Milicz incites population of Prague, Bohemia announcing reign of Antichrist has begun in person of emperor Charles IV and that the church's total corruption is proof the End is imminent.

c1365 Christian influence in Afghanistan terminated by Tamerlane.

c1365 Komi-Perm peoples of Russia evangelized by bishop Stephen of Perm (1335-1396).

1368 Last Mongol emperor Toghan Timur (Shunti) overthrown by isolationist China-centered Ming dynasty (1368-1644), which ousts Mongol dynasty in China; Christianity disappears; Mongolia converted from Nestorian influence to Buddhism.

1370 John of Trevisa (died 1402) completes translation of whole Bible in Anglo-Norman (Middle English).

1370 Vatican Apostolic Library, world's largest Christian collection, has 1,100 books; cost of a copy of the Bible then, $50,000.

1375 Mongol despot Timur the Great (Tamerlane) becomes master of all western central Asia, with capital at Samarkand; eventually controls from Turfan to Damascus and from Delhi to Moscow.

1377 End of Babylonian Captivity (exile of popes living at Avignon).

1378 Beginning of Great Schism of the West: up to 3 rival popes at a time, until 1417.

1378 Ziryen (Zirani), language of Ziranas or Komis in Asiatic Russia, reduced to writing by bishop Stephen of Perm who then translates part of Bible into it; nothing printed however until 1823.

1380 Mongol hordes under Tamerlane destroy Nestorian church and missions throughout Asia; 70,000 heads piled on ruins of Isfahan, 90,000 in Baghdad; extinction of Christianity in central Asia, reduced to remnants in Mesopotamia, Kurdistan, south India.

1380 Brethren of the Common Life, a free religious society of clerics and laity working for reform, founded in Netherlands by mystic Gerard Groote (1340-1384).

1380 Battle of Kulikovo, first major Russian victory over Golden Horde, which then takes Toktamysh as its supreme ruler.

c1380 India: Tamerlane invades Indian sultanate, marches on Delhi, orders 100,000 Hindu prisoners executed.

1380 Islam introduced into the Philippines.

AD 1380. Islam enters Philippines.

1381 Short-lived Peasants' Revolt in England based on apocalyptic expectation that all the rich with all clergy will be killed and judged by the poor standing at the right hand of God.

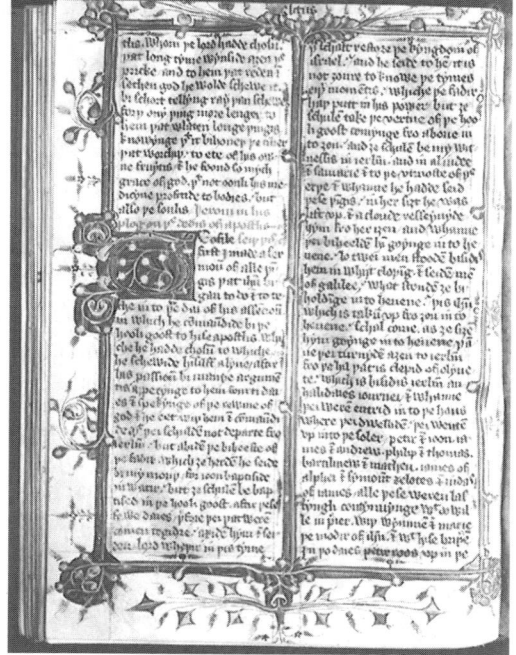

**AD 1382.** Wycliffe New Testament, dated 1420.

1382 English clergyman and scholar John Wycliffe (c1329-1384) completes first translation of whole Bible in English, a very literal rendering from Latin Vulgate; coins and uses the word 'evangelize' and cognates throughout, but most references are changed by followers after his death, in a vigorous and idiomatic popular revision, to the word 'preach' as being less Catholic.

1382 Shirvanshah dynasty rules northern Azerbaijan, until 1500.

1386 Commonwealth of Poland-Lithuania is formed: Kracow emerges as among wealthiest cities of Europe.

1386 Baptism of Jagiello (c1350-1434) king of Lithuanians; end of European paganism as an organized religion.

1386 Tamerlane conquers southern Azerbaijan, also Georgia (Caucasus), where he declares holy war, destroys 700 large villages, reduces all Christian churches of Tiflis to rubble, enforces conversion to Islam; also in 1393, 1396, 1399 (campaign of extermination), 1403.

1388 Second version of Wycliffe Bible, revised by John Purvey; 1396, principles of revision set forth in 15-chapter tract entitled *General Prologue*.

**AD 1389.** Holy Shroud of Christ emerges in France after 1,350 years of largely undocumented whereabouts.

1389 Reappearance, after 400 years' disappearance, of Mandylion of Edessa (Icon of Christ, now Holy Shroud of Turin); owned by Templars in France, exposed regularly.

1390 Last of Christian Uighurs in Turfan east of Urumchi forced to convert en masse to Islam.

1391 Start of anti-Semitic massacres in Spain and Portugal; 4,000 Jews killed in Seville.

1394 Tamerlane destroys West Syrian (Jacobite) churches and monasteries throughout Mesopotamia and Asia Minor.

AD 1395. Lollards meet secretly to hear Wycliffe's translation of Bible into English.

1395 Lollards (followers of Wycliffe) in England become an organized anti-Catholic Anglican sect with specially-ordained ministers, spokesmen in Parliament, and many followers in middle and artisan classes; 1408, condemned by Thomas Arundel archbishop of Canterbury at synod publishing *Constitutions of Oxford* banning all unauthorized versions; persecuted, and leaders burned; by 1530, merged into Protestantism.

1395 Toktamysh routed by Tamerlane; power of Golden Horde begins to wane.

**AD 1396.** Despite efforts of patriarch Evtemy (left, 1375-1393) Bulgaria falls to Turks.

1396 Bulgaria falls to Muslim invaders, Ottoman Turks.

1399 Catalan Dominican wandering preacher Vincent Ferrer (c1350-1419) reevangelizes and transforms Christendom throughout Europe; brings Jews to dialogues, converts 25,000 across Europe; preaches 6,000 apocalyptic sermons each 3 hours long, with glossolalia, healings, miracles widely reported; writes of future coming of Antichrist, predicts world will end after 2,537 more years in AD 3936 (based on number of verses in Book of Psalms); continues to incite torture and forced conversion of Jews; 1403, claims Antichrist has been born this year.

1400 **Global status:** 46 generations after Christ, world is 16.1% Christians (75% of them being Whites), 18.9% evangelized; with Scriptures translated into 30 languages.

1400 World's 5 largest cities  Nanking 473,000, Cairo 450,000, Vijayanagar 350,000, Hangchow 325,000, Peking 320,000.

1400 Inquisition begins investigating witchcraft seriously, burns at least 30,000 witches from 1400-1550; 1484, pope Innocent VIII issues bull authorizing extirpation of witchcraft in Germany; 1486, *Malleus Maleficarum* (The Witches' Hammer) published; European witch-craze lasts from 1400-1700, executing around 500,000 for alleged witchcraft; 1692, Salem witch trials in USA.

c1400 Nubia: Christianity still widespread, with 7 bishoprics in the north and 400 churches in the south.

c1400 Continued northeastward expansion of Orthodoxy across Russia through monks.

c1400 First Russian indigenous movements: Strigolniks (Barbers) from Pskov form schismatic groups out of Russian Orthodox Church, protesting against charging of fees for sacraments.

c1400 Scriptures translated into Icelandic.

c1400 Societas Peregrinantium pro Christo founded by Franciscans.

1400 Formation of Nogai Horde.

1401 Tamerlane massacres inhabitants of Baghdad: 90,000 heads collected.

1402 Ottoman empire 6.3 million, rising to 28 million by 1580; then continuous decline until 1922 dissolution.

1402 Battle of Ankara: Tamerlane defeats Ottoman sultan Bayezit I, wins definitive victory.

1407 Great Chinese Encyclopedia (Yung-lo Ta-Tien), world's largest (22,937 chapters in 11,095 volumes), compiled under Yung-lo emperor.

1408 Kara-koyunlu dynasty rules southern Azerbaijan, until 1468.

c1410 Hungarian translation of Bible.

1410 Roman cardinal Pierre d'Ailly compiles *Imago mundi*; 1480 edition states time remaining to the End is less than 200 years, but ages cannot conclude until gospel has been preached to all people on the six-sevenths of the globe that is habitable land.

1414 Council of Constance (16th Ecumenical Council): condemnation of reformers Wycliffe, Hus, et alii.

1414   Hindu prince Paramesvara of Malaysia converts to Islam.
1415   Capture of Ceuta in Morocco by Portuguese prince Henry the Navigator (1394-1460) who finances and directs 40 years of exploration along western coast of Africa, expanding Portuguese influence and converting indigenous Africans to Christianity; trading posts and forts are established, and slave trade becomes profitable.
1415   Jan Hus, dean of philosophy at university of Prague, announces 'If the pope sells benefices, if he is proud, avaricious, or otherwise morally opposed to Christ, then he is the Antichrist'; burned at stake as heretic.
1419   Age of Discovery begins as prince Henry the Navigator establishes maritime training center at Sagres, Portugal; world opens to European shipping and European imperialism.
1419   Taborites, extreme militant wing of Bohemian Hussites at Tabor south of Prague, founded as strict biblicists under their bishop Nicholas of Pelhrimov, seek to establish Kingdom of God by force of arms and military campaigns including destruction of churches; they announce that during next February 10-14 wrath of God will destroy by fire every city, town and village in Bohemia except Taborite mountain strongholds; vast crowds swarm into mountains; Taborites anticipate Christ will then appear on their Mount Tabor and become emperor of Bohemia; Taborites finally defeated at Lipany in 1434, Tabor captured 1452.
1420   Martinek Hauska and several disgruntled priests band together near Prague proclaiming Second Coming of Christ, to occur between February 1 and 14; after then they go on rampage to rid Earth of their main enemies, the established clergy.
1421   Sea floods Holland (April 17): 72 counties are submerged, 20 of which never resurface; 100,000 die.

**AD 1422.** Rublev's renowned 'Icon of the Trinity', painted in climate of daily martyrdoms.

1422   Russian Orthodox monk Andrei Rublev paints famed Icon of the Trinity, affirming windows on eternity in face of daily killings during Tartar domination.
c1428  Construction of Arab observatory at Samarkand, with 180-foot-high quadrant for measuring positions of stars.
1430   Scriptures: languages possessing some translated portions of the Bible number 33, just prior to invention of printing.
1431   Joan of Arc, French visionary rallies French armies during Hundred Years War, captured by English and burned at stake as heretic.
1431   Council of Basel (17th Ecumenical Council) meets, representing Western church; sessions 1421-1438; 7 cardinals, 50 prelates, 600 theologians, many other clergy unable to agree on reform of Curia, marriage of priests, dialogue with Hussites and Orthodox; 1431, edict orders all Jews to attend Christian sermons.
1434   Portuguese adventurers bring first black slaves from Africa to Lisbon; by 1850 10 million slaves transported to New World, 5 million in 18th century; 2 million more die aboard crowded prison ships.
1435   Biblia Pauperum (Poor Man's Bible) produced, an abridged catechetical version of 40 pages with Latin inscriptions.
1435   Total books in Europe before invention of movable type about 50,000, all handwritten; by 1500, 10 million printed books.
1436   Utraquist Church (moderate Hussites from among nobility and university professors) becomes established church of Bohemia until 1620; at Council of Basle in 1436, formally recognized as equal by

Catholic Church in its 'Compactata', but annulled in 1462 by pope Pius II.
1436   Incas begin rule in Peru.
1438   Council of Florence (also regarded as 17th Ecumenical Council): union with Greeks attempted.
1438   Formation of Kazan khanate.

**AD 1438.** Gutenberg (*left*) invents movable-type printing on his press (*below*), in order to distribute Scripture worldwide.

1438   Invention of printing (typography, movable type, and the printing press) by Johannes Gutenberg (c1395-1468) at Mainz, Germany, in order to disseminate the Holy Scriptures across the world; 1455, ruined financially by lawsuit; others print Bibles in 6 languages by 1478; by 1500, more than 100 printed editions of the Bible produced.
c1440  German cleric Nicholas of Cusa (1401-1464) holds there to be an infinite number of stars (suns) spread through infinite space, all with planets some of which are inhabited by intelligent beings.
1441   Armenian patriarchate moved from Sis (Cilicia) to Echmiadzin.
1443   Bosnia abandons Manicheism.
1443   Formation of Crimean khanate.
1445   Senegal. First Christians (Portuguese explorers); 1489, Senegalese chief baptized.
1445   Guinea Bissau. First Christians (Portuguese trading centre; Catholic missionaries 1462).
1445   Equatorial Guinea. First Christians (Portuguese traders).
1445   Gutenberg's Bible printed in only 150 copies (of which 45 survive by AD 2000), sold then for $5,000 each; uses 290 different characters, each page in 2 columns with 42 lines of type (2,600 characters per page); initially on parchment (each copy requiring 170 calves' skins costing $500); in 2 large volumes (648 and 634 pages).
1448   Mauritania. First Christians (Portuguese, French, Dutch and English traders).
1448   Russian Orthodox Church becomes 2 autocephalous metropolitanates, Moscow and Kiev.
c1450  Dechristianizing forces strong in Europe: Renaissance, humanism, recrudescence of paganism, obsession with wealth.
c1450  Trifo and Theodorit evangelize Kola Lapps.
c1450  Modern English begins to supersede Middle English.
c1450  Italian Renaissance continues to proliferate.
c1450  Formation of Uzbek khanate; formation of Astrakhan khanate.
c1450  Gutenberg prints his first book, a Missal.
1451   Reign of sultan Mehmet II the Conqueror, until 1506.
1452   St Peter's basilica in Rome planned as world's largest church, after 1453 to replace Santa Sophia (Constantinople); 1506, foundation stone laid; 1626, completed.
1453   Fall of Constantinople (population having shrunk to 50,000) to Muslim Ottoman Turks; end of Byzantine empire; fleeing scholars take Greek text of Bible to the West.
1455   German mystic Thomas a Kempis (c1380-1471) writes The Imitation of Christ, a major influence on evangelization.
1456   In 60 years before Reformation in 1517, printers in central Europe produce 70,000 Bibles in 15 languages (not yet including English), also 100,000 New Testaments and 120,000 Psalters; average edition then 300 copies.
1456   Pope Calixtus III gives great prior of Order of Christ of Portugal the spiritual supervision of all Portuguese overseas dominions.
1456   Gutenberg produces Latin Bible (Vulgate) as first book printed from movable type, first printed scripture edition, and first large printed book in Europe (4 years being printed in Mainz); also known as Mazarin Bible, or 42-line Bible.

1457   Turkish Muslims conquer peoples of Yugoslavia, 1517 overrun Egypt.
1457   Origin of Moravian confession: Unitas Fratrum (Moravians) establish Christian village in Moravia.
1458   Historian E.S. Piccolomini (1405-1464) elected as pope Pius II, predicts modern weapons will bring world to destruction.
1458   Gutenberg's only other full-sized book printed: 36-line Bible, 1,768 pages in 3 volumes.
1461   Armenian patriarchate established in Constantinople.
1462   Cape Verde Islands. First mission (Portuguese Catholics).
1462   Reign of Ivan III the Great, grand prince of Muscovy; marries niece of last Byzantine emperor; growth of Muscovite power.

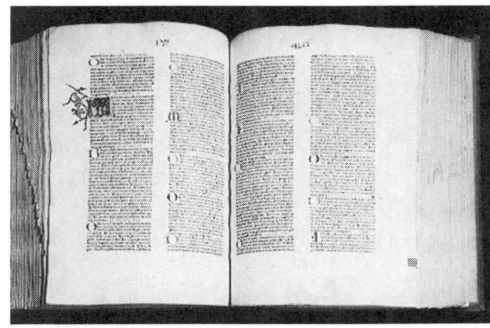

**AD 1466.** First complete High German Bible printed, first in any modern language.

1466   Mentelin of Strasbourg prints first High German Bible; first in any modern language: 61 lines per page, one volume, each costing $600 then; followed by 13 other pre-Lutheran German Bibles.
1467   Mongolia: 27th successor of Genghis Khan dies leaving Mongolian east in anarchy; all Asia north of Himalayas is either Muslim or Chinese, with negligible Christians here and there.
1469   Ak-koyunlu dynasty rules southern Azerbaijan.
1469   Guru Nanak (1469-1538) is born, founder of Sikhism, a reformist Hindu sect.
c1470  Moldavia: under reign of Stephen the Great (1457-1504), Turks are defeated and 44 Orthodox monasteries filled with sacred art are erected.
1471   Ghana (then Gold Coast). First Christians (Portuguese soldiers).
1471   First Italian printed Bible.
1474   First French printed New Testament.
1475   Crimean khanate becomes vassal of Ottomans.
1477   First Dutch printed Old Testament.
1478   Albania is conquered by Ottoman Turks and ruled until 1912 as an Ottoman province.
1478   First Spanish printed Bible.
1478   Spanish Inquisition established to ferret out crypto-Jews and hidden Muslims, under Torquemada as inquisitor general; 120,000 Spanish intellectuals and Jews condemned, imprisoned, ruined or executed from 1481-98, with 2,000 burnt at the stake.
1480   Russia expels Mongol Muslim rulers, becomes a Christian state, spreads gospel across northern Asia.
c1480  Formation of Siberian khanate.
1482   Zaire (then Congo). First Christians (Portuguese explorers); 1491, first missionaries (Franciscans, Dominicans), and baptism of prince Mwemba son of king Nzinga Nkumu.
1483   Babur, prince of Ferghana, later first Mogul emperor of India, until 1530.
1485   Sao Tome & Principe. First Christians (Portuguese settlement).
1486   Chaitanya (1486-1534) is born, founder of a popular Vaishnava sect in Bengal which proclaims Lord Krishna as Supreme God.
1487   First French printed Bible, the Grande Bible (not a complete version); a dozen editions before 1550.
1487   Nigeria. First Christians (Portuguese Catholics); 1491, king of Benin baptized.
1488   Portuguese navigator Bartolomeu Dias (c1450-1500) rounds Cape of Good Hope after being blown off course, and becomes first European to travel up eastern coast of Africa.
1488   First printed Hebrew complete Old Testament, printed at Soncino, Cremona, Italy.
1489   Baptism of Wolof king Behemoi (Senegal) with many notables at Lisbon; on return home, expels Dominicans.
1489   Albrecht Durer issues 15 woodcuts of the Apocalypse imagining phantasmorgia of Book of Revelation.
1490   Large numbers of reform-minded beggar monks and priests itinerate preaching and witnessing, including Wolfgang Capito (1478-1541), Paul Speratus (1484-1551) bishop of Pomerania, Gabriel Zwilling (1487-1558), Johannes Brenz (1499-1570) and many others.
1490   Rash of Jewish speculative dates for messianic deliverance: 1490, 1492, 1501, then 1530s (end of Jewish century).
1491   Angola (then Congo kingdom). First mission (Catholics at Sao Salvador); first church buildings built by Portuguese Jesuits.
1491   Congo (Brazzaville). First mission (Portuguese Catholics); collapses, not revived until 1883.

**AD 1492.** Attempting to reach India, Columbus discovers America (Salvador Dali, 1959).

1492 Christopher Columbus (1451-1506) sails to New World, discovers America (Bahamas, Cuba, Haiti); over next few decades, 100,000 Spaniards immigrate from Old World.

1492 Capture of Granada, last Muslim stronghold in Spain; Muslim influence remains in Spain in shape of 150,000 Moors and 200,000 Moriscos.

1492 Expulsion of 180,000 Jews from Spain; 350,000 others forcibly converted to Christianity and remain in Spain as Marranos (Conversos, Anusim, Crypto-Jews), though 12,000 burnt as heretics by Inquisition; expelled Jews settle in Safed, Palestine, centre of Jewish mysticism (Kabbala), later under rabbi Isaac Luria (1534-1572).

1492 Rodrigo Borgia (1431-1503) made pope as Alexander VI; nadir in morality of renaissance papacy.

1492 Columbus lands on Hispaniola where Indians number 500,000; by 1519, only 500 Indians left alive; whole race and way of life destroyed.

1493 *Haiti* (then Santo Domingo). First mission (Spanish Catholics).

1493 Pope issues Demarcation Bull 'Inter Caetera', giving Portugal authority over Africa, much of Asia and later Brazil; Spain given authority over rest of world west of a north-south line 345 miles west of the Azores.

1493 Sebastian Brandt publishes Nuremberg Chronicles leaving blank 6 pages at the end for events leading up to imminent Judgment Day.

1494 *Dominican Republic* (then Santo Domingo). First missionaries (Spanish Catholics).

1494 Johannes Trithemius (1462-1516) abbot of Sponheim (Mainz) publishes earliest substantial bibliography *Liber de scriptoribus ecclesiasticis* (Book about Ecclesiastical Writers), including index of 1,000 ecclesiastical writers in chronological order.

1494 Treaty of Tordesillas: major missionary development as the Americas are divided by line of demarcation of exclusive colonial rights for Portugal and Spain; 1514, diocese of Funchal, Madeira established, subsequently subdivided numerous times.

1495 Bohemian Brethren, with 400 churches and 100,000 members in Bohemia and Moravia, organize a Recognoscierung to locate whatever Eastern and Western churches have kept the apostolic faith.

1495 Dominican friar Girolamo Savonarola (1452-1498), most noted apocalyptic preacher of his day in Renaissance society, writes The Compendium of Revelations; found guilty of heresy, executed.

1497 All 200,000 Jews in Portugal (20% of population) forced to either accept Christianity as Marranos (Conversos) or be deported.

1497 'Last Supper' painted by Leonardo da Vinci, artist, scientist, engineer, inventor (submarine, tanks, aircraft, parachute, helicopter, anatomy, Mona Lisa, etc.).

1498 *Kenya*. First Christians (Vasco da Gama [1460-1524] and Portuguese explorers); by 1597, 600 African converts.

1499 Spain: mass forced baptisms of Moors (Muslims) under inquisitor-general Cisneros (1436-1517); 1502, all Muslims forced to choose between baptism or exile.

1499 Ismail I, founder of Safavid empire in Persia (lasting till 1736, with Shia Islam declared as state religion), is revered by Muslims as precursor to Lord of the Age; during his reign, stables of horses are kept ready to welcome the Mahdi when he will appear.

1499 German astrologer Johannes Stoeffler (1452-1531) predicts end of world by vast deluge on 20 February 1524 based on conjunction of planets Saturn, Jupiter, and Mars; thousands then jam boats and 3-storey ark on river Rhine.

1499 *Aruba*. First Christians (Spanish Catholics); 1634 part of Dutch Antilles.

1499 Final extinction of Christianity in Nubia due to absence of local leadership and local-language liturgy and Scriptures; southern kingdom of Alodia becomes Muslim as capital Suba falls to Fung and Arab armies.

1499 Christianity extinguished in China, Central Asia, and across the Muslim world.

1499 Steady shrinking of Christian influence; outlook for Christianity as a world religion decidedly unfavorable.

1499 Up to this date, almost no contact between the 3 major races of mankind (Caucasoid, Mongoloid, Negroid).

**Epoch V: AD 1500-1750**

## REFORM AND EXPANSION

1500 **Global status**: 49 generations after Christ, world is 17.9% Christians (92.6% of them being Whites), 20.5% evangelized; with printed Scriptures available in 12 languages out of 34 translated; total martyrs since AD 33, 17,398,000 (0.7% of all Christians ever; recent rate 8,400 per year).

1500 Newly-organized Protestant churches make no effort to contact unevangelized peoples of the world for nearly 300 years.

1500 Printing presses in Europe now number 40, with 15 million volumes printed, a large proportion being Christian works (98 distinct editions of the Vulgate).

c1500 Camera obscura (dark chamber), of Greek origin, used by artists as drawing tool; precursor of modern camera technology.

1500 Copenhagen emerges as a center of European commerce and culture.

1500 About 1,000 books a year worldwide published with newly-invented movable type.

1500 Modern English language becoming accepted.

1500 *Brazil* (then populated by 2 million jungle and lowland Amerindians); first Christians (Portuguese explorers and Franciscans).

1500 Moscow declared to be Third Rome, successor to heretical Rome and Muslim Constantinople.

1500 Several African chiefs on west coast and in Congo baptized by Portuguese.

1500 Portuguese discover 100,000-strong Christians of St Thomas (Syrian Orthodox) in Kerala, south India, under authority of Nestorian patriarch Shimon V in Mesopotamian Persia; dominant figure in Indian church becomes Mar Jacob bishop of Malabar (dies 1551).

1500 Worldwide expansion of Christianity commences again, mainly through Spanish and Portuguese Catholics.

1500 Countless predictions made during period 1500-1700 by churchmen and scholars about exact time of End of the World.

1500 Total of saints and martyrs who are known by name, formally recognized or canonized by the churches, now numbers over 10,000; from 1500-1903, Rome recognizes 113 further canonizations and 547 beatifications; total by 1985, known by name, for all confessions: 50,000 (0.1% of grand total all martyrs by 1985, known and unknown); total effect on world evangelization has been incalculable.

1500 Italian artist Botticelli paints 'Nativity', inscribes at top 'I Sandro painted this picture at the end of the year 1500 in the second woe of the Apocalypse in the loosing of the devil for three and a half years.'

c1500 Formation of Kazakh khanate.

1500 Last central Asiatic ruler of line of Tamerlane in Samarkand defeated by Uzbeks.

1500 Interest in global mission of Christianity mushrooms throughout Western Christendom.

1501 *South Africa*. First Christians (Catholic church built at Mossel Bay, Natal, by Portuguese).

1501 First detailed enumeration of a whole population, in Sicily.

1501 Christopher Columbus predicts that in 155 years all of mankind will be converted to Christianity, then in 1656 the world will end.

1502 *Tanzania* (then Tanganyika, Zanzibar). First Christians (Portuguese, at Kilwa); c1550, first Jesuit and Dominican missionaries.

1502 All Jews of Rhodes (Greece) forcibly converted, expelled or taken into slavery.

1502 Shah Ismail takes Tabriz; foundation and spread of Safavid empire.

1503 Franciscan college begun in Haiti.

1503 Gold Coast: baptism of chief of Efutu with 1,300 subjects.

1505 Great Mogul Empire in India founded by Baber (1483-1530).

1505 Reign of Basil III, grand prince of Muscovy, until 1533; formulation of theory that Moscow has become the 'Third Rome'.

1506 *Mozambique*. First mission (Portuguese Dominicans); 1541, visited by Francis Xavier; 1560, baptism of Gamba king of Inhambane with name Constantine.

1506 Massacre of Lisbon: thousands of 'New Christians' killed (Marranos and Moriscos, i.e. baptized Jews and Muslims).

1508 *Oman*. First Christians (with Portuguese port at Muscat).

1509 *Puerto Rico*. First Christians (Spanish settlement).

1509 *Jamaica*. First Christians (Spanish Catholic plantation owners).

1511 *Timor*. First Christians (Portuguese sailors); 1561, king baptized.

1511 *Singapore*. First mission (Portuguese Dominicans).

1511 *Malaysia*. First missionaries (Portuguese Catholics).

1511 First Catholic diocese of New World established at Puerto Rico.

1512 Council of Lateran V (18th Ecumenical Council): reform of the church.

1512 *Cuba*. First mission (Dominicans).

1512 *Colombia*. First Christians (Spanish explorers).

1513 *Venezuela*. First missionaries (Spanish Dominicans and Franciscans).

1513 *Panama*. First Christians (Spanish settlement).

1513 *Trinidad & Tobago*. First missionaries (2 Dominicans).

1514 Pope Leo X (1475-1521) accords kings of Portugal right of patronage (padroado) in Asia.

1514 *Costa Rica*. First mission (Catholic).

1514 Bishopric of Funchal (Madeira) created for all Portuguese overseas territories; 1533, dioceses of Angra, Cabo Verde, São Tome, Goa separated from Funchal.

1514 First extant Arabic book printed from moveable type: a book of Christian prayers entitled *Kitab salat as-sawai, Horologium breve,* printed at Fano, Italy.

1516 Over 100 Latin versions of New Testament now already printed.

1516 Edict of cardinal Ximenes of Spain: no vessel may proceed to the New World without a priest.

1516 British humanist and statesman Thomas More (1477-1535) publishes speculative work *Utopia*, describing Christian communism; attacks Luther and Reformation; 1529, chancellor of England; 1535, executed (regarded later as a Roman Catholic martyr).

1516 Dutch humanist Desiderius Erasmus (c1466-1536) publishes first Greek NT, printed at Basel; other editions 1519, 1522, 1527, 1535.

***Protestant Reformation in Europe begins***

**AD 1517.** Luther nails his 95 Theses in Latin to the Schlosskirche door, later recognized as start of the Protestant Reformation.

1517 95 Theses nailed to church door in Wittenberg by Martin Luther (1483-1546); origin of Protestant Reformation.

1517 *Comoro Islands*. First Christians (French settlers).

1517 *Mayotte*. First Christians (Portuguese).

1517 *Nicaragua*. First Christians (Spanish settlement).

1517 Charles V accords to a Flemish merchant monopoly of transporting 40,000 African slaves a year to Hispaniola, Cuba, Jamaica and Puerto Rico.

1517 Leonardo da Vinci (1452-1519), greatest genius ever, artist, scientist, engineer, inventor (submarine, tanks, aircraft, parachute, helicopter, anatomy, 'Last Supper', etc), produces 'Visions of the End of the World' or 'Deluge', depicting with overpowering pictorial imagination the primal forces that rule nature.

1518 *Mexico*. First Christians (Cortes and Spanish conquistadors); Aztecs (also Incas in Peru later, Mayas in Guatemala, and other Amerindian civilizations) convinced that Spaniards are their civilizing heroes and gods returned (Aztec emperor Montezuma and priests believe god Quetzalcoatl, the Feathered Serpent, has reappeared), hence are incapable of resisting until too late.

1518 Swine flu pandemic brought by Spaniards virtually destroys native Amerindian population of Caribbean: over 3 million Indians killed since 1492; by 1518, almost all 1,500,000 Indians in Cuba, Puerto Rico, Santo Domingo and Lesser Antilles similarly killed, also a third of all central Mexican Indians, and large proportion of French Canadian and New England Indians.

1518 Congo: Don Enrique, son of king Alphonsus I, nominated first indigenous Catholic bishop of Black

Africa; dies 1531.

1519 Huldreich Zwingli (1484-1531) installed as people's priest in Zurich; reformation spreads across Switzerland, meeting with its greatest response in Swiss and German cities.

1520 *Art of War* written by Niccolo Machiavelli (1496-1527).

1520 Protestant inertia in missions for next 275 years continues because, having dispensed with monasticism (major method of mission from 4th-16th centuries), reformers had no knowledge of how to prosecute a missionary endeavor (Harnack).

1520 Luther's classic *The Liberty of a Christian Man*; after being condemned in papal bull 'Exsurge Domini', Luther replies with `Against the Execrable Bull of Antichrist'.

1520 Teachings of guru Nanak at Kartapur; founds Sikhism (blend of Hinduism and Islam).

1520 Catholic spiritual reform movement called 'Evangelismus' ('Italian evangelism') rises for 20 years in France, Italy and Spain, supported by Michelangelo, zealous aristocrats, prelates and cardinals.

c1520 Luther writes: 'The gospel will always be preached... It has gone out throughout the length and the breadth of the world... It is made known farther and farther, to those who have not heard it before', and 'The gospel preached by the Apostles in various languages, sounds forth even now till the end of time'; teaches that institution of papacy, and hence every pope (without singling individuals out), is Antichrist; expects Advent of Christ in 1558.

c1520 Climax of Ottoman Turk expansion into Christian Europe; mass conversions of Christians to Islam.

1520 Suleiman the Magnificent crowned as Ottoman sultan; dies 1566.

1520 First general history of religion (Africa, Asia, Europe): Teutonic knight Jean Boem's *Customs, Laws, and Rites of all* Peoples.

. 1520 Amerindians begin decline from 25 million to only 1 million by 1600.

1521 *Philippines*. First Christians (Magellan and Spanish explorers; first mass celebrated; 1565, first resident missionaries).

1521 Hernan Cortes (1485-1547) captures Tenochtitlan (population 500,000), defeats Aztec empire aided by hordes of Indian allies (Totonacs, Tlascaltecs), and conquers Mexico (New Spain); 1522, governor; 1523, evangelization of Mexico begins under Spanish Franciscans, 1526 Dominicans, 1533 Augustinians.

**AD 1521.** 'Here I stand; I can do no other'; Luther is condemned at Diet of Worms.

1521 Diet of Worms: Luther is condemned and declared an outlaw.

1521 *Pacific Islands* (later known as 4 separate territories): 1521 *Northern Marianas*, 1526 *Micronesia*, 1529 *Marshall Islands*, 1543 *Palau (Belau)*. First Christians (explorers); 1668 first permanent missionaries (Spaniards).

1522 Spanish expedition under Magellan (c1480-1521) first to circumnavigate globe, proving Earth to be round.

1522 Luther's translation of New Testament into German; Bible in 1534; first Western European Bible based not on Latin Vulgate but on original Hebrew and Greek texts.

1522 Three major Reformations begin, with clear teachings on the Holy Spirit: (a) Protestant reformers Martin Luther (1483-1546), Ulrich Zwingli (1484-1531), John Calvin (1509-1564); (b) Catholic reformers Ignatius Loyola (1491-1556), John of the Cross (1542-1591); and (c) Radical reformers Thomas Muntzer (1488-1525), Menno Simons (1496-1561).

1522 Complutensian Polyglot Bible produced under cardinal Ximenes at university of Alcala, Complutum (Spain); 6 volumes, 4 being OT in Hebrew (first Hebrew Bible produced by Christian scholars), Aramaic, Greek, Latin, 2 being NT in Greek, Latin; greatest pre-Reformation scholarly Bible achievement (conceived 1502, printed 1514-1517 in 600 copies).

1522 Luther's New Testament in common German, made from Erasmus' Latin and Greek NTs; 3,000 copies printed, sold in 3 months at 1 1/2 guilders each ($50); by 1525, 128,000 copies in circulation; total eventual printings 336; Old Testament then took Luther 12 years to translate, using a 1494 Vulgate and a 1488 Hebrew Bible; subsequently translated into 20 European languages, including in 1535 English by Tyndale.

1523 Origin of Anabaptists, in Zurich under ex-RC priest

Conrad Grebel (1490-1526); spread across Europe to Augsburg, Moravia, Strasbourg, Friesland, Netherlands; 1525, 30,000 (mostly Dutch Mennonites) executed by Catholics and Lutherans, later by Calvinists.

1523 *Guadeloupe*. First missionaries (Catholics; massacred by Caribs).

1523 Revival of millennialism by left-wing Protestant Anabaptists, Bohemians, Moravian Brethren, Zwickau Prophets, et alii.

1523 Spanish monarch orders Cortes to enforce mass conversion of Amerindians across New World; in Mexico, Franciscans baptize over a million in 7 years, with at times 14,000 a day; by 1536, 6 million Amerindians baptized in 17 years in Mexico alone; c1550, 800,000 Peruvian Amerindians confirmed by one archbishop of Lima; Cortes eventually returns to Spain and in 1547 dies in disgrace.

1523 Ignatius Loyola (1491-1556) works in Palestine for conversion of Muslims; 1534, founds Society of Jesus, with missions around world (Japan by 1549); 1556, Society becomes leading missionary order with 1,000 Jesuits; peaks at 36,038 by 1965, falls to 25,550 in 1983 in 200 countries, then to 23,381 (1994); official scope 'Defense and Propagation of the Faith through Preaching'.

1523 Group of astrologers announce end of world will begin with destruction of London on 1 February 1524; 20,000 gather outside city on high ground; similar views widely held by alchemists and intellectuals; Paracelsus (1493-1541) expounds influences of stars and planets on man.

1524 *Paraguay*. First Christians (Spanish settlement).

1524 *Guatemala*. First Christians (Spanish soldiers).

1524 *Honduras*. First Christians (Spanish settlement).

1524 German Peasants' War rages for 2 years, led by preacher Thomas Muntzer.

1525 *El Salvador*. First mission (Spanish Catholic priests).

**AD 1525.** First New Testament in English, translated by William Tyndale.

1525 William Tyndale (c1494-1536) produces (in Worms) first printed English New Testament, also 1530 Pentateuch, 1531 Jonah; burned at stake in 1536 near Brussels.

1526 *USA* (then *America*). First missionaries (Spanish Catholic priests) to Indians in California, Florida, Texas, et alia; first martyrdoms take place.

1526 *Ecuador*. First Christians (Spanish settlers).

1526 Edict of emperor Charles V: all vessels obliged to carry missionaries abroad.

1526 Hungary: Lajos II defeated at battle of Mohacs by Turks under sultan Suleiman I who slaughter 200,000 and enslave 100,000 Hungarian Protestants.

1526 Battle of Panipat: Babur defeats Lodi emperor of Delhi; foundation of Moghul empire.

1527 Sweden adopts Lutheran Confession.

1527 *Argentina*. First Christians (Spanish fort erected); 1539, first mission (Franciscans).

1527 First Baptist church established in Zurich.

1527 Ethiopia: Muslim tribal leader Ahmad Gran destroys Amharic Orthodox churches and monasteries in 15 years' savage pillaging.

1527 First travelling evangelist of Reformation period is Silesian nobleman Kaspar Schwenkfeld von Ossig (1489-1561); but ostracized and wanders homeless for 30 years.

1527 Martyrs or Missionary Synod.

1527 German bookbinder Hans Nut declares self a prophet, proclaims Christ's coming for 1528, to be followed by 1,000 years of free food, love, sex.

1527 Tulsidas (1527-1623) is born, author of the Hindi ver-

sion of the *Ramayana*.

1527 Anabaptist wandering evangelists preach across Europe ignoring national and ecclesiastical boundaries, emphasizing the Matthean/Markan version of the Great Commission as mandatory for all Christian believers, though Luther, Calvin and other Reformers consider it no longer binding.

1528 Numerous epochal translations: 1528 Pagninus' Bible, 1537 Matthew's Bible, 1539 Great Bible, 1557 Geneva Bible, 1568 Bishops' Bible, 1582-1610 Rheims-Douai Bible.

1528 Berne Disputation, with its 10 Theses, brings Reformation to city of Berne; Anabaptists insist that Great Commission applies to everyone who confesses Christ's name.

1529 Luis Bolanos OFM works among Tucuman Indians of Argentina, converting 20,000 and erecting reductions for them.

1530 Dikes burst in Holland and flood country (November 1); 400,000 killed.

1530 *Viet Nam*. First missionaries (Portuguese priests on merchant ships from Goa and Macao).

1530 Confession of Augsburg produced by Philip Melanchton (1497-1560) and signed by Protestant princes.

1530 Anabaptist leader Melchior Hofmann (1495-1543) predicts imminent end of world and Millennium in AD 1533 with Strasbourg to be the New Jerusalem; followers sell all their possessions; when 1533 passes, they name Jan Matthys and Jan Bockelson as the Two Wi Two Witnesses of Revelation and Munster as New Jerusalem, seize city of Munster, found Kingdom of A Thousand Years, eject unbelievers, establish New Jerusalem; 1534 city captured, king John of Leiden executed; the major 16th-century millenarian outburst.

c1530 Dominican friar Bartholomew de Las Casas (1474-1566), first priest ordained (1510) in New World, supports rights of indigenous peoples of Central America, first as bishop of Chiapas in Mexico (1544-1547), then from 1547 back in Spain; before his death, charges 15 million Indians killed by Spanish conquistadors.

1531 Death of Zwingli in battle attempting to force Zurich Protestantism on Catholic cantons.

1531 Mexico: bishop Juan de Zumarraga (1476-1548) writes that they have destroyed over 500 temples and 20,000 idols.

1532 *Peru*. First Christians (Spanish colonists).

1533 Goa on Indian coast made a Catholic bishopric by Portuguese.

1533 Reign of Ivan IV the Terrible (1530-1584), infant grand prince of Muscovy until 1546 when assumes title of tsar; 1552 conquers Kazan; 1556, conquers Astrakhan, with Volga Tatars, Bashkirs, and Chuvash coming under Russian rule; dies 1584.

1534 *Canada*. First Christians (French soldiers).

1534 British Supremacy Act makes British monarch (then Henry VIII) head of Church of England.

1534 Portuguese Catholic missionaries arrive in Moluccas.

1534 Ignatius Loyola at University of Paris founds Society of Jesus, made into an order in 1539; 1548, chosen as first general; spearhead of Catholic Reformation.

**AD 1536.** Translator Tyndale is burned at stake saying 'Lord, open the King of England's eyes'.

1535 First English Bible printed, translated by Myles Coverdale.

**AD 1536.** Motto of reformer Calvin: 'My heart I offer to Thee O Lord, promptly and sincerely'.

1536 John Calvin (1509-1564) at age 26 publishes his

Institutes of the Christian Religion, begins as reformer in Geneva; 1538 banished, 1541 returns to make it centre of Reformed faith and life; produces a theology for church under the Cross, believes he lives in era of Antichrist.

CHRISTIA

NAE RELIGIONIS INSTI-
tutio,totam ferè pietatis summã,& quic
quid est in doctrina salutis cognitu ne-
cessarium, complectens : omnibus pietatis studiosis lectu dignissi-
mum opus,ac re-
cens edi-
tum.

PRAEFATIO AD CHRI
stianissimum REGEM FRANCIAE, qua
hic ei liber pro confessione fidei
offertur.

IOANNE CALVINO
Noviodunensi autore.

BASILEAE,
M. D. XXXVI.

**AD 1536.** First edition of Calvin's *Institutes of the Christian Religion.*

1536  Nearly 6 million Amerindians baptized in Mexico since 1519.
1536  *Bangladesh* (then East Bengal). First Christians (Portuguese traders in Chittagong).
1536  Denmark, Norway, Sweden adopt Lutheranism as state religion by 1540.

**AD 1536.** Pope Paul III visits studio to see Michelangelo completing 'Last Judgment' in Sistine Chapel; 5 popes involved.

1536  Sculptor and painter Michelangelo Buonarroti (1475-1564) completes vast painting 'The Last Judgment' in Sistine Chapel, Vatican, a powerful fresco of the Day of Wrath inspired by Dante and medieval hymn 'Dies irae'.
1536  10,000-strong Bharatha (Parava) fishing caste of Coromandal coast (Kerala) baptized en masse by Portuguese, then ignored until Xavier's arrival in 1542.
1537  *Bolivia.* First Christians (Spanish colonists); Catholic diocese formed to include work among Parias and Charcas.
1537  English king declared head of church of Ireland.
1539  Spanish conqueror Gonzalo Pizarro (1502-48), accompanied by large force of Spaniards and Indians, explores lands to east of Quito; entourage crosses Andes and travels through rain forest before discovering Napo river, a headwater of the Amazon.
1540  *Madagascar.* First mission (Catholic).
1540  England: all monastic institutions seized and expropriated by Thomas Cromwell under Henry VIII (1491-1547).
1540  Population census of Venice (Italy), conducted by church authorities: 129,971 persons.
1540  Copernican Revolution: Polish astronomer Nicolaus Copernicus (1473-1543) completes *On the Revolutions of the Celestial Spheres, replacing Ptolemaic geocentric system of astronomy with heliocentric system and proving Earth rotates around Sun.*
c1540  Russian Orthodox missionary Gowry evangelizes Tartars at time of first tsar of Russia, Ivan IV the Terrible.
1540  Luther states, 'For my part I am sure that the Day of Judgment is just around the corner. It is certain that time is now at an end.'
1540  Luther and Calvin teach that Great Commission (Mark 16:15) was work of 1st-century Apostles only and expired with them.

**AD 1542.** Missionary Francis Xavier baptizes 750,000 converts. (*Below*) Xavier expounds the Cross to pagan tribes.

1541  *Chile.* First mission (one Catholic priest).
1542  Spanish Jesuit missionary Francis Xavier (1506-1552) arrives in India; 1546, Malacca; then carries the faith throughout Far East (1549, Japan), baptizing 750,000 by time of his death.
1542  Congregation of Universal Inquisition established by Holy See.
1542  *Japan.* First Christians (Portuguese), followed 1549 by first missionary (Xavier); by 1571, 30,000 Christians; by 1582, 150,000 Christians (1% of Japan) and 200 churches; by 1600, 300,000 in active contact with missionaries, plus thousands of others.
1543  Ceylon: Buddhist ruler Buvanaika Bahu VII invites king John III of Portugal to legitimize succession and send missionaries; 3,000 baptized; 1602, 70,000 Christians in Jaffna; 1773, 100,000.
1544  Xavier begins mission in Travancore, baptizes 10,000 Mukuvas in one month (and 15,000 others later).
1544  Roman Catholics in Burma; Portuguese, with Franciscan missionaries; by 1600, 5,000 converts.
1544  Martyrdom of 600 newly-baptized Christians in Jaffna, Ceylon.
1544  Ships from Britain begin practice of deporting Gypsies by abandoning them on coast of Norway.
1545  Augsburg Confession adopted by Hungarian Lutheran Church.

**AD 1545.** Counter-Reformation begins as Council of Trent reforms Catholic Church from within.

1545  Council of Trent (Counter-Reformation), 19th Ecumenical Council: Protestantism condemned; 25 sessions 1545-63 during lives of 3 popes.
1545  German-Swiss physician, naturalist, and animal taxonomist Conrad Gesner (1516-1565) publishes his *Bibliotheca Universalis* describing and classifying 15,000 works by 3,000 authors in Latin, Greek, and Hebrew; rearranged by subject in 1548 as *Pandectarum sive Partitionum universalium libri XXI* (21 Books of Encyclopedias or Universal Divisions of Knowledge).

1545  Xavier visits Malacca; by 1549, 60,000 Christians and 18 monasteries.
1545  Celebes and Moluccas: Portuguese trader and 4 students evangelize Macassar, Siao, Supa, Alieta; 1532, first Christian king, Tabarija; 1562, Solor has 50,000 baptized, Flores 27,000.
1546  Death of Luther; his more than 400 published works exert enormous influence throughout Europe.
1546  First of several Amerindian anti-Catholic religious movements of revolt in Ecuador: Quimbaya (also 1576 Sobce, 1603).
1547  Severe persecution of Protestants in France; thousands executed under Henri II.
1547  Nostradamus (Michel de Notredame, 1503-1566), astrologer and physician, makes extensive prophecies from 1547, first published as *The Centuries* in 1555; condemned by Roman Index in 1781; the most widely read seer of the Renaissance, in print continuously ever since, with vast literature of commentaries; end of world predicted for either 1666, or 1734, 1886, 1943, 2000, 2038 or 3797.
1547  Anabaptists again assert they hold Great Commission as binding on all church members.
1548  *Guyana* (later British Guiana). First missions (Portuguese Catholics).
1549  First Book of Common Prayer introduced by archbishop Thomas Cranmer (1489-1556), who then publishes in 1552 Forty-two Articles of Anglican faith and doctrine.
1549  Brazil: beginning of Catholic missions among Amerindians by first Jesuits in South America.
1549  Xavier's co-worker Antonio Criminali becomes first Jesuit martyr, in India.
1549  England: First Prayer Book of Edward VI; revised 1552, 1559, 1662 Book of Common Prayer, 1928, 1980.
1549  'Christian Century' in Japan until 1650; Christians rise to 2% of population of 25 million, but no printed gospel or Bible ever produced.
1550  **Global status:** 51 generations after Christ, world is 18.6% Christians (80.5% of them being Whites), 21.3% evangelized; with printed Scriptures available in 28 languages.
1550  First concordance to whole English Bible, compiled by John Marbeck using Matthew's Bible of 1537.
1550  Lutheranism proclaimed state religion of Iceland.
1550  In England, maintenance of baptismal records by local clergy ordered.
1550  Beginnings of definitive New Testament Greek text in edition of R. Stephanus, based on Byzantine Text, finally resulting by 1624 in Textus Receptus.
c1550  Kuwait: new Christian influx (Portuguese sailors and traders).
c1550  800,000 Peruvian Amerindians confirmed by one Catholic archbishop of Lima.
c1550  *Netherlands Antilles.* First missionaries (Catholic priests from Santo Domingo).
c1550  *Martinique.* First Christians (Dominican, Jesuit and Capuchin missionaries).
c1550  English language spoken by under 5 million speakers (less than German, French, Spanish and Italian).
c1550  Swiss theologian and Reformed bishop J.H. Bullinger (1504-1575) interprets numerology of Book of Revelation to show world will end in 1666.
c1550  Emergence of capitalism on world scene, greatest achievement of humankind in history.
1551  Converts from Assyrian Church of the East, in Iraq and Persia, submit to Rome as Chaldean Catholic Church, with patriarchate in Babylon.
1551  Stoglav (Hundred Chapters) Council condemns Roman Catholicism, but 1596 Union of Brest-Litovsk allows creation of Uniate Catholics.
1551  Apostolic Church of the East split in two by revolt among bishops: Simon VII bar Mama (Nestorian) passes succession to nephew as Simon VIII Denha, but 3 bishops elect rival patriarch Shimon VIII (John Sulaqa) who travels to Rome, submits; pope Julius III appoints him patriarch of Chaldeans; 1830, these 2 identities get reversed; by 1800, 3 rival Nestorian lines.
1552  Council of Lima (Peru): Amerindians may receive Catholic baptism, matrimony and penance, but not confirmation or ordination.
1552  At death of Loyola, Jesuits number 1,000 and become leading Catholic missionary society.
1552  Councils of the Peruvian Church: 1552, 1567, 1582 (with publication of famed catechism).
1553  Roman Catholicism restored in England under queen Mary; 286 reformed Anglican leaders burnt at stake including Thomas Cranmer (1489-1556) archbishop of Canterbury, Nicholas Ridley (c1500-1555) bishop of London, bishop Hugh Latimer (1485-1555), and John Hooper (c1495-1555) bishop of Worcester.
1553  In 3 years, 300 Protestants burned as heretics in Europe.
1553  Mexico: first of numerous Roman Catholic ecclesiastical councils and synods.
1553  Ottoman empire reaches height of expansion and prosperity; concludes peace with Persia.
1554  *Thailand* (then *Siam*). First Christians (Portuguese soldiers at royal court, 2 Dominican chaplains, 1,500 Thai converts); 1565, first missionaries killed.
1555  *Cambodia* (Kampuchea). First missions (Jesuits and Dominicans).
1555  1st Council of the Mexican Church; 2nd, 1565; 3rd, 1585; 4th, 1774; 5th, 1895.

1556 China: in Shaanxi (Shensi), deadliest earthquake ever; an estimated 830,000 persons perish.
1556 Calvin sends first and only Reformed missionary party of 18 French Huguenots to Brazil, off Rio de Janeiro; work collapses.
1556 Jesuits arrive in Paraguay, establish about 100 Christian settlements (reductions) among Guarani Amerindians.
1556 Ceylon: conversion to Catholicism of 70,000 fisher-caste Careas (Karawa, Karawola) on coast near Colombo; by 1583, 43,000 Christians on Manar island among pearl-fisher Paravas and Careas.
1556 Beza's Latin New Testament translated.
1557 First known use of modern equals (=) sign, by English mathematician Robert Recorde.
1557 Macao: first Christians (Portuguese settlement).
1557 France: 33% of population reputed to be Protestants (known as Huguenots); 1559, create Reformed Church (72 congregations, 400,000 adherents); widespread manifestations of glossolalia, trances, prophecies, et alia.
1557 Cherkess people send embassy to Moscow offering to be baptized if aided against Crimean Tatars.
1558 Spain: Protestants virtually wiped out by Inquisition by burning at the stake.
1559 Pope Paul IV (1476-1559) forbids all Catholics to read Bible in common tongue, without special authorization.
1559 India: 300,000 Roman Catholic converts in Kerala.
1559 John Foxe's *Book of Martyrs* published, chiefly describing martyrdoms in reign of Mary Tudor (1553-1558), and modelled on Jean Crespin's *Book of Huguenot martyrs*.
1559 Scotland: John Knox (c1514-1572) reforms Scottish church, maintaining ecumenical relations with England and the Continent; 1560, Scots Confession approved by Parliament.
1559 Anabaptists the only Reformed grouping to deliberately work for and obey Jesus' Great Commission, especially through Hutterian Brethren's itinerant evangelism.
1559 Philip Melanchthon, speaking to hundreds of students, cites prophecies of 15th-century monk who foresaw Gog and Magog in command of Germany in 1600; warns they will experience it; 'May God then give you mercy'.
1559 Scandinavia: Gustavus Lasa attempts to educate and evangelize Lapps in north.
1560 Beginning of Puritanism in England.
1561 *Zimbabwe* (later *Southern Rhodesia*). First missionary (Portuguese Jesuit); emperor of Monomotapa baptized by him but apostatizes and kills him a year later.
1561 *St Helena*. First Christians (Dutch settlers).
1561 *Malawi* (later *Nyasaland*). First missionaries (Catholics from Mozambique).
1561 Belgic Confession (Confessio Belgica), a major Calvinist creed in Dutch Reformed Church (along with Heidelberg Catechism, and Canons of Dort), drawing heavily on Calvin's 1559 Gallic Confession; adopts amillennial stance.
1562 3,000 French Protestants (Huguenots) massacred at Toulouse.
1564 *Index Tridentinus* of prohibited books.
1565 First permanent USA Catholic community begun at St Augustine, Florida.
1565 Florida: French Huguenot civilian colony on St John's river annihilated by Spaniards.

**AD 1565, 1569.** Evangelization of the Philippines begins under Spanish missionaries.

1565 Macao city: 5,000 Chinese Christians.
1566 First Unitarian churches founded: in Romania, Hungary, and Poland.
1567 Second Helvetic Confession adopted by Hungarian Reformed Church.
1567 In Low Countries, Spanish Council of Blood (1567-74) executes thousands as heretics and Calvinists.
1567 Siam: first Roman Catholic missionaries; 1779 all expelled; 1811, nearly 3,000 converts, most around Bangkok; 1865, 8,000.
1568 Commission of cardinals instituted in Rome by Pius V for foreign missions in East Indies, for Italo-Greeks, and for Protestant lands of Europe; 1573, congregation for conversion of infidels formed; 1622, founding of Propaganda Fide.
1569 80,000 Christians in East Indies under Jesuit missions.
1569 Moriscos (Spanish Muslims who accepted baptism) in Granada revolt after Philip II prohibits Moorish names, language (Arabic), customs and costume; after ferocious 2-year war, forcibly scattered across northern Spain; 1609-14, 275,000 Moriscos expelled to North Africa.
1569 Peru: Inquisition established in Lima by Philip II (also in Mexico, and 1610 in Cartagena, Colombia), tortures 120,000 heretics, burns 189 dissenters at stake.
1569 100 baptized in Philippines; 1577, 12,000; 1583, 100,000; 1586, 170,000; 1591, 382,000 of the populace's 687,000 now evangelized and 250,000 baptized; 1612, 322,400; 1622, 500,000; 1773, 4.1 million.
1570 Moscow burns in Great Fire, with some 200,000 persons killed.
1570 Dikes fail in Holland, leading to widespread flooding (November 1); 50,000 die.
1570 Abraham Ortelius (1527-98) publishes *Theatre of the World*, collection of 70 maps regarded by historians as first modern atlas.
1570 Santiago, Chiriguano prophet and reformer, appears in Bolivia.
1570 Cyprus: Turks invade island, exterminate Copts including bishop and priests.
1570 As pope Pius V, former Roman grand inquisitor Michele Ghislieri excommunicates queen Elizabeth I of England.
1570 Japan: first of numerous Roman Catholic ecclesiastical synods.
1570 Mogul emperor Akbar calls representatives of various religions to conference to resolve differences.
1571 Holy League, joined by forces sent by king Philip, defeats Muslim Turks at Battle of Lepanto in first significant Ottoman defeat.
1571 Japan: mass movement begins under Omura Sumitada; 50,000 converted.
1571 Thirty-Nine Articles promulgated in England as Anglican confession of faith.
1571 Muslim empire of Kanem-Bornu (9th-19th centuries) in central Africa at height of power under king Idris III in walled capital Ngazargamu in Bornu, based on vast numbers of slaves.
1572 St Bartholomew's Day massacre: 72,000 Huguenots slaughtered in France in attempt to destroy Calvinist leadership.
1572 Tycho's Star appears, a violently exploding supernova, visible for 2 years.
1574 Flood washes away Spanish troops besieging Leyden, Holland (October 1-2); 20,000 perish.
1575 First German pietist missionaries begin in Tranquebar, India.
1575 Second Roman Council of Goa; Catholics in India 280,000.
1576 China reentered by Catholics with Macao made a Portuguese diocese.
1577 Philippines: 14 Franciscan friars arrive in Manila and pursue mass christianization; by 1583, 16% baptized Christians (100,000); 1594,46% (286,000); 1629, 74% (500,000); 1690, 87% (700,000); 1735, 93% (837,182); 1750, 97% (904,116).
1577 Louis Le Roy publishes *De la vicissitude ou variété des choses en l'univers* stating approaching end, worldwide confusion, and the return of things to their original chaos.
1578 First Anglicans in North America (California, then Virginia).
1580 *Suriname*. First Christians (Dutch settlement).
1580 Germany: evangelism flourishes under Pietist leaders: John Arndt (1555-1621), Paul Gerhardt (1607-1676), P.J. Spener, Albrecht Bengel (1687-1752), and N.L. von Zinzendorf.
c1580 Jesuit theologian in Peru, Jos de Acosta (1539-1600), writes *De procuranda Indorum salute* (On the preaching of the Gospel among the Savages), dealing with problems of mass baptisms, role of military, feasibility of native clergy, et alia.
c1580 Robert Browne (c1553-1633) of Norwich organizes 'gathered churches'; origin of Brownists and Congregationalism.
1580 Discalced (Reformed) Carmelite Sisters become a separate order; by 1983, 11,649 cloistered contemplative nuns in 727 monasteries; serving evangelization of the world in name of Christ by prayer and works of charity.
1580 Omura Sumitada cedes Nagasaki to Jesuits.
1581 Claudio Aquaviva (1543-1615) elected 5th general of Society of Jesus; at his death, Jesuits have increased from 5,000 to 13,000.
1581 French Protestant, Joseph Scaliger publishes *Opus novum de emendatione temporum*, first new comprehensive critical chronology of the world since that of Bede 900 years earlier.

**AD 1581.** First edition of the Bible in Icelandic published.

**AD 1582.** Jesuit missionary Matteo Ricci begins work in Macao, then in Peking.

1581 Bible in Icelandic published.
1582 Jesuit missionary Matteo Ricci (1552-1610) begins his mission in Macao; 1601, summoned to Peking by emperor; at his death, converts number only 2,000.
1582 Japan: 200 churches and 150,000 Christians; 1588, Japan made a Catholic diocese.
1582 Franciscans led by Jerome de Burgos arrive in China but are expelled.
1582 Pope Gregory XIII (1502-1585) introduces New Style or Gregorian Calendar (13 days ahead of Old Style or Julian Calendar of Julius Caesar); 1752, adopted by England; 1924, finally adopted by most Orthodox churches except Jerusalem, Russia, Serbia and Bulgaria.
1582 Roman Catholic translation of Scriptures from Vulgate into English: 1582 New Testament, in Rheims; 1609-10 Bible, in Douai; standard RC Bible in English for nearly 4 centuries.
1582 Major Latin American provincial episcopal councils: 1582 Lima III, 1585 Mexico III; earlier emphases on evangelization of Amerindians, and concern for their freedom, give way to White colonial Catholicism.
1584 Baptism of king of Angola.
1584 Jesuit priest Alonso Sanchez drafts evangelistic scheme for invasion and military conquest of China; others plan for forcible baptism of all peoples of the world.
1587 Foreign missions in Japan prohibited, until 1844; severity of persecution varies.
1588 Philip of Spain launches Spanish Armada against England to end Protestantism there; Armada destroyed by English navy and by storms, establishing England as naval power.
1588 Anglican parish priest Hadrian Saravia (1531-1613) becomes one of first non-Roman advocates of foreign missions, stressing binding validity of Matthew 28:19: 'The command to preach the gospel to the Gentiles pertained not only to the age of the apostles, but to all future times to the end of the world.'
1588 Consistorial Congregation erected in Rome, responsible for all matters concerning all Catholic bishops and dioceses across world except Eastern-rite and missionary jurisdictions; includes Pontifical Commission for Migration and Tourism; 1967, renamed Sacred Congregation for Bishops.
1588 Congregation for the Causes of Saints; by 1990, 300 saints have been officially named.
1589 Russian Orthodox patriarchate instituted ('The Third Rome'); 1700, Peter the Great orders christianization of Siberia, 1721 abolishes patriarchate, rules church directly; as state church, its missions expand across Europe, Central Asia, Persia, Siberia, 1685 China, 1743 Kamchatka, 1784 Alaska, 1861 Mongolia, 1861 Japan, 1898 Korea, by means of traders, merchants, colonists, soldiers, diplomats, exiles, settlers (1 million Russians in Siberia from 1700-1783), monks, bishops, missionaries; 1826, best epoch of Russian Orthodox missions begins; 1870, Orthodox Missionary Society founded by metropolitan of Moscow, I. Veniaminov (1797-1879), in 55 Russian dioceses; whole mission enterprise destroyed in 1917 Revolution.
1589 Ecumenical patriarch Jeremy II of Constantinople visits Moscow to help establish Moscow patriarchate; no further such visit until Dimitrios I's visit in 1987.
1590 Invention of microscope, created by Zacharias Janssen, and later by Dutch scientist Anton van Leeuwenhoek.
1590 Ottomans gain possession of Georgia (Tbilisi taken in 1578), Shirvan, Daghestan, Yerevan (1583), Gandzha and Karabagh.
1590 Dutch theologian Adrian Saravia (1531-1613) publishes tract on abiding validity of Christ's Great Commission, to be implemented via apostolic succession of bishops; later joins Church of England; later Lutheran orthodoxy under Philip Nicolai

**AD 1590.** First Bible in Hungarian, translated by Karoli (Vizsoly Bible).

(1556-1608) denies validity of world mission; but in 3 tracts in 1663-4, Justinian von Welz (1621-1666) upholds validity; Great Commission then forgotten for 130 years until Carey's *Enquiry* (1792), Robert Morrison of China (1792-1834), Adoniram Judson (1788-1850); by 1900 becomes the principal justification for world mission; then neglected in biblical scholarship until Michel (1941), Lohmezer (1951), Lange (1873), Hubbard (1974), Friedrich (1983), Bosch (1983 and 1991), et alias.

1590 First Bible in Hungarian (Karoli or Vizsoly Bible) published, with financial support and armed protection from Hungarian rulers; in subsequent 300 years, reissued 100 times.

1591 2nd Council of Lima (Peru): decree resolves 'Indians are not to receive any of the orders of the Church'.

1591 Philippines: Dominican missionaries champion rights of native populace; pope Gregory XIV decrees end to slavery in Spanish-held islands.

1591 *Al-Injil al-muqaddas* (The Gospels in Arabic) printed, illustrated, in Rome; long subsequent history of Christian missionary and evangelistic works being printed in Arabic by Syrian Orthodox, Catholics, and Protestants.

1592 *South Korea.* First Christians (invading army from Japan, with Catholic general and Jesuit priest).

1593 Japan: Franciscans enter, welcomed by Hideyoshi as breaking Jesuit monopoly; 1602, first Dominicans and Augustinians arrive as well.

1594 Jesuits reach court of Mongol emperor Akbar; construction of first Christian church in Lahore permitted, though few conversions.

1594 Scottish mathematician John Napier (1550-1617) invents logarithms in order to speed up his calculations of the number of the Beast (in Revelation 13:18); writes *Plaine Discovery of the Whole Revelation of Saint John* (1594).

1596 Union of Brest-Litovsk, between Rome and Orthodox Ruthenian church of west Ukraine, establishes basis for Eastern-rite Catholics (Uniates) to preserve Orthodox Byzantine liturgy with minimal changes.

1596 Lebanon: Maronite patriarch finally submits to Rome; first Uniate church of Eastern Christianity.

1597 In Nagasaki under dictator Hideyoshi, crucifixion of 6 Franciscans, 3 Japanese Jesuits and 16 Japanese Catholics; numerous others executed, churches burned.

1598 *Mauritius.* First Christians (Dutch).

1598 *French Guiana.* First Christians (French settlements).

1598 Edict of Nantes ending French wars of religion, allowing religious liberty and civil equality to Huguenots in France; revoked 1685, causing Huguenot emigration.

1598 Smallpox and measles responsible for killing millions in Latin America during preceding 100 years.

1598 Siberian khanate comes under Russian rule.

1599 Astrakhanid dynasty rules in Bukhara.

1599 India: Synod of Diamper attacks heresies of Syrian Nestorianism, fails to achieve goal of permanent union of all Latin and Syrian (St Thomas) Christians.

1600 **Global status:** 52 generations after Christ, world is 18.4% Christians (86.0% of them being Whites), 21.0% evangelized; with printed Scriptures available in 36 languages.

1600 World's 5 largest cities: Peking 706,000, Constantinople 700,000, Agra 500,000, Cairo 400,000, Osaka 400,000.

1600 Latin America: mestizos (persons of mixed race) forbidden ordination as RC priests until after 1700.

1600 China: first of several Roman Catholic ecclesiastical synods.

c1600 Jesuit reductions (cooperative Amerindian villages) in Bolivia among Moxos and Chiquitos.

c1600 Nkimba and Kimpasi in Congo, syncretistic prophet movements based on Jesuit institutions.

c1600 North Korea: immigrant Christians from China.

c1600 *Svalbard & Jan Mayen Islands.* First Christians (European whaling center).

c1600 *Brunei.* First Christians (Spanish trading center).

c1600 Christians in Japan number 750,000 (3.4% of population), including most of Nagasaki area, with 300,000 being baptized Roman Catholics.

c1600 Nubia: final extinction of Christianity.

c1600 In Latin America, 250,000 Spaniards rule 9 million Amerindians, and 30,000 Portuguese in Brazil rule over 2 million natives.

c1600 *Somnium* (The Dream, with space travellers propelled by spirits to Moon), one of first modern works of science fiction, written by first astrophysicist J. Kepler (1571-1630), greatest theoretician of his age; begins search for extraterrestrial life; 1619, 1619, publishes last of his 3 laws of planetary motion.

1600 Italian occultist-philosopher Giordano Bruno (1548-1600) proposes Christ as great magician in a magico-religious system to replace contemporary organized Christianity; holds there are an infinity of worlds in Universe, many inhabited; burned at stake by Inquisition.

c1600 Episcopi Vagantes (Wandering Bishops, or Bishops-at-Large, in 15 disputed or contested lines of apostolic succession) begin to multiply across Europe; 1866, Julius Ferrette as bishop of Iona begins their modern era; by 1975, 760 bishops-at-large lead 280 distinct autocephalous Catholic churches/denominations with 10,285,000 adherents in 80 countries; each proposes grandiose plan for reunion of Christendom and conversion of world, calling on Rome, Constantinople, Canterbury and Geneva to abandon their global pretensions and join each's new ecclesiastical body.

c1600 Kingdom of Buganda established in eastern Africa.

c1600 Formation of 3 Kazakh Hordes.

1600 From this point on, virtually every technological change (from telescope to typewriter to steam engine) is product of Western ingenuity.

c1600 Timor: Roman Catholics number 25,000; Dutch invade, land at Kupang; no Protestant mission until NZG presence from 1819-1854.

1602 Orthodox bishopric erected at Astrakhan near mouth of Volga.

1602 Dutch government sends missionaries to convert Malays in East Indies domains.

1602 Italian philosopher Tommaso Campanella (1568-1639) writes utopian narrative *City of the Sun*, predicts imminent end of world.

1603 Roman Catholics in England and Wales number 1.5 million, declining to 69,376 by 1780; at end of Elizabethan persecution of Roman Catholics, 123 out of 438 priests have been executed.

1603 In Philippines (now 50% christianized), 3,000 Chinese converts massacred near Manila by Spaniards fearful of being displaced by Chinese.

1604 *St Pierre & Miquelon.* First Christians (French Catholic settlers).

1604 Kepler's Star (Nova Ophiuchi), a violently exploding supernova, visible for 2 years.

1605 Armenian Catholic Church (Uniate) created through Dominican activity in Iran.

1605 Catholic missionaries expelled by Dutch from Indonesia, replaced by Dutch Reformed chaplains of Dutch East India Company.

1605 Jesuit missionary Robert de Nobili (1577-1656) arrives in Madura, south India, begins experiment in cultural accommodation among Brahmins.

1605 Sikh Golden Temple at Amritsar, Punjab, is finished, completely covered with gold leaf.

1607 USA: Anglicans begin evangelization with foundation of Virginia Colony at Jamestown.

1607 *Acta Sanctorum* (Lives of the Saints) begun by Dutch Jesuit H. Rosweyde, from 1643 published by John Bollandus SJ (1596-1665), a massive work of scholarship over the centuries, reaching 95% completion with Volume 65 by 1980.

1607 China: only 700 Christians; 1627, 13,000 in 7 provinces; 1637, 40,000 in 9 provinces; 1650, over 150,000; 1672, 263,000; 1700, 300,000; 1800, 180,000.

1608 Canada: Roman Catholic work begun among Micmac Indians.

1608 Invention of telescope by 6 separate persons independently, in Holland, France, Germany, Italy, Britain; 1609, Italian astronomer Galilei Galileo (1564-1642) reinvents it and discovers Moon craters and Jupiter's moons; major conflict with Church of Rome over Copernican theory of planets revolving around Sun; 1633, Galileo forced to recant Copernican doctrine .

1609 Moriscos (christianized Muslims) forced to leave Spain, causing loss of Spanish learned class.

1609 British colonists settle in Caribbean: Bermuda 1609, Barbados 1626, Bahamas 1629, and Jamaica 1655.

1609 *Bermuda.* First Christians (English sailors, Anglicans).

1609 Philip III of Spain (Philip II of Portugal, 1578-1621) expels all Moriscos (Christians of Moorish ancestry, i.e. Spanish Muslims forcibly baptized); 275,000 flee to Algeria, Morocco and Tunisia.

1609 First English Baptist church organized in Amsterdam by Puritan nonconformist John Smyth (c1567-1612); 1612, rise of General Baptists in England under Thomas Helwys (c1550-c1616); 1633, Particular Baptists organized, with 131 churches by 1660.

1610 Catholics in Peking number 2,000 at death of Jesuit superior Matteo Ricci.

1610 Spanish Jesuit missionary Peter Claver, 'Apostle to the Blacks' (1580-1654), arrives at slave-trade capital Cartagena (Colombia), ministers to 1,000 African arrivals a month for 44 years, baptizing 300,000 Negro slaves.

c1610 English philosopher of science and statesman Francis Bacon (1561-1626) makes first proposal for an artificially-constructed international language; 1629, French philosopher R. Descartes (1596-1650) proposes one based on numbers; 1880 Volapuk created, 1887 Esperanto, 1920 Interlingua; by 1950 total of 700 different attempts, all of which fail to win widespread acceptance.

c1610 Dominican historian Tomas Malvenda (1566-1628) translates Hebrew Old Testament into Latin, writes treatise on coming of Antichrist.

1611 King James Version (KJV) or Authorized Version (AV) of English Bible published, under 47 scholars working in 3 panels; in elegant prose designed for public reading in large churches; enormous influence for 3 centuries as main Bible of English-speaking Protestants and Anglicans.

1611 British East India Company begins trade in Surat, Bombay.

1611 Reductions among Guarani number 33 (11 in Paraguay, 15 Argentina, 7 Brazil).

1612 Anglican clergy first serve as chaplains with East India Company.

1612 Philippines: 322,400 Filipino Christians on Luzon alone.

1613 Major missionary work by Discalced Carmelite monk of Spain, Thomas a Jesu (1564-1627), *De procuranda salute omnium gentium,* urges and envisages conversion of entire world to Christ.

1613 Reign of Mikhail I, first Romanov tsar, until 1645.

1614 First index published, by Antonia Zara bishop of Petina, to his book *Anatomia ingeniorum et scientiarum* (Anatomy of Talents and Sciences).

1614 Japan: Christians rise to 500,000 out of 25 million population; 1622, Great Martyrdom begins 30 years' terror as all Christians liquidated; edict prohibits Christianity; churches destroyed, Jesuits and other missionaries deported, over 40,000 Christians massacred, rest exist underground.

1616 *Uruguay.* First missionaries (Spanish Franciscans and Jesuits).

1616 First Baptist congregation in England (London); known as General Baptists.

1616 *Fama fraternitas* describes formation of Rosicrucians, a secret worldwide occult brotherhood claiming esoteric wisdom from ancient Egypt.

1617 Decree of banishment and persecution against all Christians in China; further edicts 1665, 1724 and 1736; but total Catholics remain at 150,000 (1650), 250,000 (1663), 300,000 (1675), 300,000 (1700), 200,000 (1800).

1617 Demise of Holy Roman Empire triggers Thirty Years' War.

**AD 1618.** Synod of Dort (Holland) systematizes Calvinist theological orthodoxy.

1618 Synod of Dort (Dutch Reformed Church) affirms orthodox Calvinist position on predestination, condemns Remonstrants and Arminians.

1618 Thirty Years' War begins as last of the Wars of Religion kindled by German and Swiss Reformation: Protestants in Holy Roman Empire revolt against Catholic oppression; Sweden, France and Denmark invade Germany; numerous martyrdoms including 1631 Catholic priest Liborius Wagner of Schweinfurt.

1618 Book on biblical mandate for world mission written by a Dutchman, Justus Heurnius, who then serves as minister and preacher in Batavia, Java, from 1624-1638.

1619 Dutch colonize East Indies (Indonesia).

1619 Over last 100 years since Conquest, Spaniards (250,000 by 1600) reduce Meso-Americans from 13 million to 10 million through war, disease, starvation, forced labor.

1619 Martyrs of Kaschau (Hungary): 3 Jesuits beaten to death by Calvinist soldiers.

1619 First Negro slaves arrive in North America (Virginia) by ship.

1619 Lutheran mystic Johann V. Andrea (1586-1654) writes alchemist/utopian Rosicrucian manifestos, and also utopian book *Christianopolis* describing an ideal society organized to promote its citizens' health, education, and welfare, including a research laboratory.

1619 Belated appointments of first Asians as Roman Catholic bishops: Philippines 1619, China 1685, India 1923, Japan 1927, Viet Nam 1933, Ceylon 1933, Korea 1937.

1620 Pilgrim Fathers from England cross Atlantic to America in sailing ship Mayflower to found New England.

1620 Bohemia forcibly made Roman Catholic by Austrian armies; 30,000 Protestants expelled, others massacred.

1620 Johann Gerhard (1582-1637), theologian of Lutheran orthodoxy, holds task of mission preaching was essentially completed by the New Testament Apostles.

c1620 Comenius suggests adoption of English, French, Russian, et alia each as sole official language in a designated geopolitical region of the world (e.g. Russian for Eastern Europe).

1621 *China (Taiwan, Formosa).* First mission (Dominicans from Philippines); 1627, first Dutch Reformed missionary, Georgius Candidius, followed by 37 others, with 17,000 aboriginal converts (4,000 baptized) by 1650.

1621 Invention of the calculating slide-rule by English clergyman W. Oughtred (1574-1660); spreads and lasts 350 years until finally superseded by pocket calculators in 1975.
1622 Comity scheme introduced for Roman Catholic missionary orders to avoid duplication or competition.
1622 Sacred Congregation for the Propagation of the Faith (Propaganda, meaning dissemination or progressive plantation) founded by pope Gregory XV (1554-1623); 1967, renamed by pope Paul VI as SC for the Evangelization of Peoples.
1623 German professor Wilhelm Schickard builds first known mechanical calculator; his calculating clock remains unknown until 1935.
1623 *St Kitts-Nevis*. First Christians (British settlers).
1623 German Lutherans arrive in New York, organizing a congregation by 1649.
1623 23 Jesuit reductions (settlements), with 100,000 population, in Paraguay.
1623 Byelorussia: priests and bishops, including bishop Josaphat of Polotsk, killed by mobs.
1624 Francis Bacon compiles utopian account *New Atlantis*; 1626, writes of 'the Apostolicall and Miraculous Evangelisme of Saint Bartholomew'.
1625 Indochina: first of several Roman Catholic ecclesiastical synods.
1626 *Bhutan*. First Christians: Jesuit missionaries Estevão Cacella and João Cabral become first Europeans to reach the Himalayan territory and its capital.
1626 *Barbados*. First Christians (English settlers with Anglican clergy).
1626 Tibet: first Christian missionary, Antoine de Andrade, Portuguese Jesuit; poisoned 1634; 1745, last mission station, run by Capuchins, shut down.

**AD 1627.** Alexander de Rhodes baptizes in North Viet Nam.

1627 French Jesuit missionary Alexander de Rhodes (1591-1660) baptizes 6,700 in North Viet Nam; 1629, Trinh-Trang king of Tonkin prohibits conversions on pain of death.
1627 German Calvinist theologian in Transylvania, Johann H. Alsted (1588-1638) revives premillennialism with book *The Beloved City;* marked impact on English and Puritan millennialism.
1627 English biblical scholar Joseph Mede (1586-1638), a premillennialist, writes *Apocalyptica: Key of the Revelation*, formulates theory of progressive millennialism (later termed postmillennialism): Christ will only return at close of man-made millennium on Earth.
1628 Dutch in New York organize first Christian Reformed church on Manhattan Island.
1628 Revival in Ireland under Blair and Livingstone.
1629 Matthew's Gospel printed in Malay; first evangelistic scripture portion in a non-European language.
1629 Ecumenical patriarch of Constantinople, Cyril I Lukaris, publishes Calvinistic confession of faith, attempts to reform Orthodoxy on Anglican and Protestant lines, sends Codex Alexandrinus (3rd oldest Bible known) to English king Charles I; 1638, murdered by Ottoman sultan Murad IV; successor Cyril II Kontaris returns to communion with Rome, 1640 murdered by sultan; both killings due to their successful initiatives with Protestants, Anglicans, and Roman Catholics.
1629 French mathematician and philosopher René Descartes (1596-1650) proposes creation of an international language for universal use, based on principles of logical progression; after 3 centuries, by 1995 over 1,000 such artificial languages have been proposed; 1637 discovers analytic geometry.
1630 *Laos*. First mission (Catholics).
1630 Structure of Catholicism in Japan destroyed after 16 years' persecution, with 1,900 martyrs crucified; remnants (150,000 secret believers in 1640) continue underground.
1630 German Jesuit astronomer J.A. Schall Von Bell (1591-1666) arrives in China as missionary, reforms Chinese calendar, is personally credited with 100,000 converts; 1650, builds first Christian church in Peking; 1657, obtains imperial permission to evangelize throughout China.
1631 Martyrs of Mombasa: prior of Mombasa, 2 priests, 280 lay persons massacred by apostate Swahili sultan Chingulia after refusing to renounce Christian faith; 1740, Portuguese influence along East African coast extinguished.
1632 *Montserrat*. First Christians (Irish settlers).
1632 Lord Baltimore (1580-1632) with 300 Irish Catholics founds Maryland for Roman Catholic settlers in North America.
1634 Bavaria: Oberammergau Passion Play begun by amateurs in fulfilment of a vow.
1634 *Antigua*. First Christians (English settlers, Anglicans).
1634 Peter Heyling (1607-1652) of Lubeck works as isolated German Lutheran missionary among monophysites in Egypt and Ethiopia; translates part of NT into Amharic; martyred there by Muslim fanatic.
1635 Japan's imperial government forbids overseas contacts, thus beginning long period of isolation; only Dutch are permitted to continue trading with Japan (at Nagasaki).
1635 Public letter post introduced in England as first in world.
1635 Italian Jesuit, Giulio Alenio, publishes first life of Christ in Chinese.
1637 *Ivory Coast*. First Christians (Portuguese traders).
1637 Japanese Christians on Shimabara revolt, 35,000 massacred; Hidden Christians in Japan continue completely underground for 220 years; Japan isolated from rest of world.
1638 Francis Godwin writes *The Man in the Moon*, first description of a space voyage; later, appointed Anglican bishop of Llandaff.
1638 Philosopher John Wilkins (1614-1672), later Anglican bishop of Chester, writes works of scientific speculation including *The Discovery of a New World* with discourse on traveling to the Moon in a flying machine.

**AD 1639.** Origin of Baptist confession under Roger Williams in Rhode Island.

1639 Roger Williams (c1603-1683) founds first Baptist church in USA at Providence, Rhode Island.
1639 Viet Nam: 82,000 Christians with 200 churches in Tonkin, rising in 5 years to 300,000 increasing by 15,000 annually; 1644, Tonkin Synod with newly-arrived French bishops and priests leads to 1st Annam Persecution, martyrdoms, and vast array of subsequent persecutions; by 1660, 400,000 Christians, then decline by 1682 to 200,000 Christians (Tonkin) and 60,000 in south (Cochin China); 1773, 200,000 (Tonkin); 1820, 400,000.

**AD 1640.** Apostle to Indians John Eliot preaches, translates first North American Indian Bible.

c1640 North America: 4,000 Indians converted and nurtured in 14 settlements under John Eliot (Apostle to the Indians, 1604-1690) who from 1655-1663 produces Bible in Massachusetts language, the first Indian translation.
c1640 Moravian bishop, theologian, educational reformer, Czech patriot John Amos Comenius (Komensky; 1592-1670) proposes a Pansophic College for leading scholars to organize a comprehensive encyclopedia of all knowledge (*Pansophic* Prodromus, *also 1657* Didacta Magna*)*.
1641 Massacre of 7,000 of the 100,000 Scots colonists in Ulster (Protestants) by Irish Catholics.
1642 *Dominica*. First mission (RC Dominican priests).
1642 French scientist-philosopher Blaise Pascal (1623-1662) invents and creates Pascaline, a geared adding machine, first successful digital calculating machine (first pocket calculator); 1654, converted to faith in Christ, writes *Apology for the Christian Religion.*
1642 Canada: a number of Jesuit missionaries murdered by Iroquois, Mohawk and other Indians, 1642-50.
1643 Catholic missionaries in China appeal to Rome over rites controversy; 1742, final papal bull rejecting Ricci's methods.
1643 Westminster Confession commissioned by Long Parliament to remodel Church of England; now recognized as major Reformed confession.
1644 Last heir to Chinese throne under Ming dynasty baptized by Jesuits with name Constantine, but Manchus seize power; second of the 3 great missed opportunities for Christianity when Chinese imperial throne almost won to the faith (1266, 1644, 1843).
1644 China: Manchu conquest crosses Great Wall, kills 25 million Chinese, 10,000 of the 90,000 Chinese Christians; Dominican protomartyr F. de Capillas beheaded.
1644 Kweichow province, China: beginning of long history of Meo (Miao) ethnic rebellions every 30 years: 1726, battle of Lei-kung Mountain, 10,000 Meo beheaded, 400,000 starve to death; 1797, Pan-chiang Riot, thousands burned or beheaded; 1854, Meo join great Taiping uprising, but defeated and massacred in 1871; 1941-1944, Chien Tung Incident.
1645 Long series of vicious persecutions in Annam: 1645, 1st persecution, Alexander de Rhodes expelled; 1665 2nd persecution, with 45 Vietnamese martyrs; 1696; 1698 with 200 churches destroyed; 1713; 1719 3rd persecution with 700 churches destroyed; 1721, 1731, 1736, 1745, 1773, 1798, 1821 4th persecution; 1825, 1832, 1833, 1847 5th persecution; 1851, 90,000 Roman Catholics killed including 115 priests; further persecutions in 1856, 1884, 1947, 1950, 1975.
1646 Massive flooding throughout Holland; 110,000 die.
1646 First projection lantern (magic lantern) constructed by German mathematician Athanasius Kircher (1601-80).
1646 Union of Uzhgorod, between Rome and Orthodox Ruthenians of Byzantine-Slavonic rite in Hungary.
1647 In Congo, Felix de Viler and colleagues baptize over 600,000 adults from 1647-51; Capuchins baptize vast numbers more in Congo and Angola, mainly infants, by 1700.
1648 *Virgin Islands* (later, *of the US*). First Christians (French settlers).
1648 Russian expansion eastwards reaches Pacific Ocean.
1648 *St Lucia*. First Christians (French settlers).
1648 100,000 Jews murdered in Chmielnicki massacres by Christians in Poland.
1648 *British Virgin Islands*. First Christians (Dutch settlers).
1648 Jewish youth, Sabbatai Zevi (1626-1676) in Izmir proclaims himself Messiah; one of long series of Cabalist-Messiahs in Jewish history; 1665, captured by Turks, converts to Islam.
1648 Peace of Westphalia: European powers accept religious pluralism and denominationalism.
1648 Spanish Jesuit Ildefonso de Flores (1590-1660) calculates total Christian martyrs of all epochs to date at 11 million; major impact of martyrdom on world evangelization recognized; his estimate agrees closely with later survey done in 1980-1990.
1649 *Reunion*. First Christians (French settlement).
1649 Society for the Propagation of the Gospel in New England founded by the Long Parliament (England), to reach settlers and Amerindians, with first missionary John Eliot who forms 6 congregations with 1,100 Indians; oldest Anglican missionary society; 1743, David Brainerd (1718-1747) begins among Indians in Massachusetts under SPCK.
1649 Christians far more widely spread geographically than ever previously, but less numerous proportionately than in AD 500.

1650 **Global status:** 54 generations after Christ, world is 20.6% Christians (83.1% of them being Whites), 23.7% evangelized; with printed Scriptures available in 45 languages.
1650 German pioneers of Pietistic evangelism: G. Voetius (1588-1676), J. von Lodenstein (1620-1677), J. de Labadie (1610-1674), T. Untereyck (1635-1693), Spener, Francke, J. Neander (1650-1680).
c1650 Dutch create a world empire, including holdings in Indonesia, Ceylon, South Africa, West Indies, and North America (New Amsterdam), and enjoy a trade monopoly with Japan.
1650 Writer Cyrano de Bergerac (1619-55) suggests rockets as means of traveling from Earth to moon.
c1650 *St Vincent*. First Christians (French, Dutch, British settlers).
c1650 Russian Orthodoxy reaches across Siberia to Bering Strait.
c1650 *Grenada*. First Christians (French settlers).
c1650 *Belize*. First Christians (Spanish settlement).
c1650 *Anguilla*. First Christians (British Anglicans).
c1650 Egypt: Coptic bishops decline in number to only 17 (from 168 in AD 550).
c1650 Syrian Orthodox Church declines to 20 dioceses from 103 dioceses in 1150.

c1650 Revolutionary Dutch government embraces European Enlightenment; through Dutch East India Company, Dutch appear and colonize around the world.

1650 Beginning of attempted extermination of North American Indians.

c1650 Slovakia: over next 50 years, several hundred Protestants are executed in Presov and elsewhere.

1651 Dutch control Cape Colony, South Africa.

1651 *Gambia.* First Christians (British soldiers).

1651 British political philosopher Thomas Hobbes (1588-1679) writes in *Leviathan* of 'Evangelization, that is, the Proclamation of Christ'.

1652 Large numbers of White and Little Russian Orthodox submit to Rome as the Podcarpathian Ruthenians.

1653 Metropolitan Ignatius (Atalla, Ahatalla) of Syrian Jacobite Church arrives in India, intercepted at sea, then in 1654 burned alive by Jesuits and Portuguese inquisition at Goa; Malabar Church of 70,000 breaks from Rome, comes under Syrian (Jacobite) Church; 1662, returns to Rome due to Carmelites.

1653 Quint (Fifth) Monarchy Men gain influence in English parliament, believe fifth kingdom in Book of Daniel 2:44 will be that led by Oliver Cromwell (1599-1658), protector of Commonwealth of England, Scotland and Ireland from 1653-1658, who will lead armies into Europe and Rome to defeat the pope, and Jews would return to Israel; propose abolishing established church in England to bring about the Parousia; Cromwell refuses this role, armed insurrections against him erupt in 1657 and 1661, are overthrown and leaders executed.

1653 First Hungarian encyclopedia, *Magyar encyclopaedia*, published, edited by Janos A. Csere.

1654 Theory of probability founded by Pascal and Fermat.

1654 Islam introduced into South Africa through Dutch sending Muslim convicts from Batavia (Indonesia).

1654 Irish archbishop James Ussher of Armagh (AD 1581-1656) becomes first serious Bible chronographer and first to construct a mathematical model to describe reality; computes date of Creation from book of Genesis at BC 4004.

1655 Massacre of Waldensians in Piedmont, part of 300-year persecution under Catholic House of Savoy; finally in 1848, full civil rights under Statute of Emancipation.

1656 Calvinist and Puritan statesman Oliver Cromwell, protector of Commonwealth of England, Scotland and Ireland allows Jews prohibited since 1290 to return to England, in order to hasten Christ's Second Coming.

1658 Ceylon: Dutch finally drive out Portuguese, ban Catholicism with its 300,000 Catholics.

1658 Viet Nam: 300,000 Catholics (including many deathbed baptisms).

1658 Société des Missions Etrangères de Paris (MEP) founded; oldest missionary society for secular priests; RC missions to east and southeast Asia organized.

1658 Death of Bartholomaus Holtzhauser after predicting Antichrist would reveal himself at age of 55 years; others assert he would do so at 30 years, thus parodying Jesus the Christ.

1659 *French Polynesia.* First mission (Catholics); further attempts 1772, 1831, et alia.

1659 Paris Foreign Missionary Society (France) founded, earliest Catholic order to devote itself entirely to missions to the completely unreached; first 3 missionary bishops sent to Indochina, Asia, 1662 Siam.

1660 Scottish Covenanters (Presbyterians who signed National Covenant of 1638) brutally persecuted for 25 years.

c1660 Peruvian Franciscan theologian G. Tenorio (1602-1682) publishes treatise extolling Peruvian Indian culture and predicting Millennium will be in Peru as center of the world church.

1661 Formosa: Chinese pirates under general Koxinga (Chen Ch'eng-kung, 1624-1662) invade island with 25,000 Minnan men, crucifying Dutch missionaries and killing 6,000 Reformed converts from aboriginal tribes.

1662 Quaker Act in Britain: 15,000 Quakers imprisoned from 1660-1685 under Charles II (1630-1685); 500 die in prison; persecution continues until Toleration Act of 1689.

1662 Schism ex Church of England: 300,000 communicants follow 2,000 Anglican ministers ejected under Act of Uniformity.

1662 English merchant John Graunt (1620-1674) launches demography as a science by constructing first mortality tables.

1662 Siberia: 70,000 Russians settle, increasing by 1783 to 1 million.

1662 Massachusetts: 'Half-way Covenant' adopted, admitting children of believing parents into full church membership.

1663 *Chad.* First mission (RC, Capuchins); then abandoned until 1929.

1663 Justinian von Weltz (1621-1668) writes treatises to challenge German churches, students and Pietists to missionary work among unevangelized peoples.

1663 Corpus Evangelicorum, assembly of state counsellors of Imperial Diet of the Holy Roman Empire of 39 Protestant states/kingdoms, meets at Regensburg, declines J. von Welz' plan for a foreign mission society.

1664 Baptized Catholics in Chinese empire grow from 150,000 in 1650 to 254,980 in 1664 (including vast numbers of children baptized in articulo mortis).

1664 Synod of Ayuthia (capital of Siam) convened by French bishops; 1669, apostolic vicariate of Siam established by Vatican's Propaganda to bypass Portuguese padroado.

1665 Plague and fire devastate London: 75,000 die of plague, 1666 Great Fire of London destroys 13,000 houses.

1665 First scientific journal published, in London; total rises to 50,000 such journals by 1960, 350,000 by 1990, and to 950,000 by AD 2000..

1665 New World city of Quebec produces earliest complete population census in history.

1666 15,000 Protestants expelled by archbishop of Salzburg from his principality.

1666 Old Ritualist schism (Raskolniki, Old Believers) ex Russian Orthodox Church, opposing reforming patriarch Nikon as Antichrist; brutally persecuted until 1725, with leader archpriest Avvakum Petrovich (1620-1682) burnt at stake, and monks massacred.

1667 English poet John Milton (1608-1674) in his Paradise Lost draws attention to the Christian goal 'To Evangelize the Nations'.

1668 Pacific Islands (Micronesia): first permanent mission (Spanish Catholics).

1668 *Guam.* First mission (Spanish Jesuits).

1668 First Bible translation in southeast Asia: NT translated into Malay; Bible in 1733 (Roman script) and 1758 (Arabic script).

1668 English bishop John Wilkins (1614-1672) in *Essay* proposes an artificial language (with *Z* = animals in general, *Za* = fish, etc).

c1670 Stepped reckoner, geared device that adds, subtracts, multiples, and divides, is invented by Gottfried Wilhelm von Leibniz (1646-1716).

1670 Bengal: 20,000 Namasudra Bengalis (outcaste Hindus) in Dacca converted to Catholicism in 2 years; by 1677, total 30,000.

1670 *Cayman Islands.* First Christians (British settlers).

1670 City of Paris begins publishing records of baptisms, births and burials (continued up to present day).

c1670 *Bahamas.* First Christians (British settlers, Anglicans).

c1670 Devotional evangelistic meetings in Frankfurt, Germany (Philip Jakob Spener, 1635-1705).

1670 Synod of Tonkin establishes Catholic church of Viet Nam.

1671 Anton Horneck (1641-1697), Pietist evangelist, becomes Anglican divine and prebendary, founds first Vestry Society in England.

1671 Hungary: violent attacks on Protestants by Turkish rulers; 1681, religious toleration proclaimed; 1687, Blood Trials of Eperies; many Protestants executed up to 1781.

1672 Synod of Jerusalem, council convened by Eastern Orthodox patriarch Dositheos to reject Calvinist 'Confession of Orthodox Faith' (1629) of Cyril Lucaris former patriarch of Constantinople.

1673 *Gabon.* First mission (Italian Capuchins).

1673 Withdrawal of all Roman Catholic monopolies in mission areas.

1673 First Kalmyks converted to Orthodoxy in Russia.

1674 Germany: Lutheran Pietism and missionary outreach begun, led by Philip Spener.

1675 First money check written, in London; paper currency begins to replace metal coins.

1676 Compton Census in England: first census of church affiliation, organized by Henry Compton (1632-1713) bishop of London; out of 2.6 million adult population, 95.3% are Conformists (Anglicans and Presbyterians), 4.2% Nonconformists (Dissenters), 0.5% Papists (RCs).

1676 Russo-Turkish War, lasting until 1681.

1678 300,000 Catholics in North Viet Nam (Tonkin).

1678 English thinker and lay preacher John Bunyan (1628-1688) writes *The Pilgrim's Progress*, later translated into 48 languages.

1679 First Amerindian ordained priest in Mexico; 1794, first in Chile.

1680 *Benin* (then *Dahomey*). First Christians (Portuguese settlers).

1680 Penny Post set up as first urban postal service in London by William Dockwra, prepaid and with hourly deliveries.

1680 Russia: Old Believers united in opposition to everything new and oppressive in Russian life regarded as under power of the Antichrist (since 1649 identified with patriarch Nikon, or tsar Alexis I and successors).

1680 Founding in Rheims of Christian Brothers (FSC) to teach Christian doctrine to the poor and working classes across the world; by 1976, 12,641 lay brothers; by 1983, declines to 9,348.

1680 Kingdom of Malawi (eastern central Africa) and kingdom of Ashanti (western Africa) established.

1681 Thomas Burnet publishes *The Sacred Theory of the Earth: Containing an Account of the Original of the Earth and of All the General Changes which it Hath Already Undergone or is to Undergo, till the Consummation of All Things,* in Latin and later, by the king's order, in English (1684); a second part *On the Conflagration of the World and the Future State of Things* is published in 1689.

1682 *Strange and wonderful Prophecies and Predictions Taken from the Apparition of the late Dreadful Comet, the Last Wonderful Ecclips, and the great signal Conjunction of Jupiter and Saturn in the Fiery Trigon, that will happen on the 23 October next* is published stating time is close to end of '7th Revolution since the beginning of the world', *and* 'we may expect a Total Catastrophe of the world'.

1682 Reign of Peter I the Great, tsar until 1721, then assumes title of emperor; dies 1725.

1685 Edict of Nantes revoked by Louis XIV (1638-1715); 58,000 Huguenots forced to convert, 400,000 more flee from France to England, South Africa and elsewhere.

1685 Russian Orthodoxy enters China through a chaplain Maxim Leontiev (died 1712); 1695, metropolitan Ignatii of Tobolsk sends 2 others to assist him; 1714, more clergy and lay workers sent; numerous Chinese baptized; 1722, bishop Innocent Kulchicky and 4 clergy sent, but too late; 1724, new Chinese emperor begins widespread persecution of Christians which lasts for 120 years.

1685 China: first native Chinese RC priest, Gregory Lo (1611-1691, ordained 1656) is consecrated as first Chinese bishop, of Canton.

1687 English physicist and mathematician Isaac Newton (1642-1727), greatest scientific genius ever, publishes his work on calculus, which he developed in 1666, in *Philosophiae naturalis principia mathematica*, creates a universal view of the world that directs scientific inquiry for 200 years after; devotes his later years to interpretation of prophecies of Daniel and Revelation, also ancient chronology.

1688 Aurangzeb demolishes all 1,000 temples of Mathura; Muslim rulers destroy total of 60,000 Hindu temples in India, then construct mosques on 3,000 of these sites.

1689 Student revival in Leipzig, Germany.

1689 Jesuits expelled from Moscow, and 1719 from all Russia.

1689 Anglican Nonjurors deprived: archbishop of Canterbury W. Sancroft (1617-1693), 8 other bishops, 400 priests, a few laymen, refuse to break Oath of Allegiance to king James II or recognize new king William of Orange; imprisoned, evicted by Parliament.

1689 Global warfare begins (as a disease of the capitalist world system) with War of the Grand Alliance, until 1697; then 1701-1815, series of 6 world wars, with 1701-1714 War of the Spanish Succession.

1690 West African slave trade accelerates; 5,500,000 slaves traded up to year 1800; grand total eventually 9.5 million Africans to the Americas.

1690 Emergence of progressive millennialism (postmillennialism) under Anglican scholar and Unitarian freethinker Daniel Whitby (1638-1726), renouncing Augustine's traditional nonmillennialism (allegorical millennialism) dominant throughout the previous 12 centuries.

1691 Society for the Conversion and Religious Instruction and Education of Negro Slaves in the British West India Islands formed (later, Christian Faith Society).

1692 China decrees freedom of worship to all Christians, totaling 300,000 Roman Catholics, found in every province.

1693 Madras: persecution under Marava rajah; Jesuit missionary J. de Britto beheaded outside Uraiyur.

1693 Italy: secret society Knights of the Apocalypse founded to defend church against the Antichrist.

1694 First Protestant interest in organized foreign mission: German Pietists open training school at Halle under Philip Spener and August Hermann Francke (1663-1727); latter founds first German missionary journal.

1694 Nubia: Franciscan missionaries attempt in vain to locate 12,000 Catholics alleged to have come from Ethiopia.

1694 Invention of Liebniz' 'Stepped Reckoner' adding machine; rapid counting vital as backbone of commerce and government.

1694 Earliest known printed Arabic version of the Quran, printed in Hamburg by Officina Schultzio-Schilleriana.

1696 To refute Thomas Burnet's 1681 *Sacred Theory*, mathematician William Whiston publishes *New Theory of the Earth* contending that a near-miss by a comet caused Noah's flood; predicts another near-miss for 1866 after final defeat of Antichrist.

1696 Russians take Azov; beginning of Russian, in place of Ottoman, domination of Black Sea.

1697 Finland: crop failure and famine kill 100,000, 35% of population.

1697 Japan: most calamitous destruction of a church in history: 1614 300,000 Christians, 1614-46, 4,045 proved martyrs, 1637-38 some 37,000 Christians massacred, 1614-97 over 200,000 martyrs, 1697 very few open Christians remain.

1697 Final defeat of last Maya stronghold: independent kingdom of Itza Amerindians in Guatemala destroyed by Spaniards in one day (based on Spanish foreknowledge of that day's significance on Maya cycle of 256 years); capital's 12 temples on Lake Peten Itza razed, all idols smashed.

1698 Invention of 'fire engine' by Thomas Savery; 1705, Newcomen's atmospheric steam engine; 1765, James Watt's separate condenser for steam engines (thus making possible the Industrial Revolution).

1698 Destruction in Indochina of 200 Catholic churches under king Min-Wong, a Buddhist zealot.

1698 First 2 non-Roman missionary societies formed, by Church of England: Society for Promoting Christian Knowledge (SPCK), and (1701) Society for the Propagation of the Gospel in Foreign Parts (SPG); goal of world evangelization claimed, but in practice they work largely in British sphere of influence.

1698 SPCK aims to distribute English Bible: using stereotype plates, printer Eler prints 28 editions of NT and 16 of Bible, from 1712-1722, totalling 180,000 copies.

1699 Protestant provinces of Germany change to Gregorian calendar, followed in 1700 by Denmark, Norway, and parts of Holland.
1699 French thinkers spawn Enlightenment, a widespread intellectual movement promoting rationalism.
1699 Two dozen Latin, German, and French treatises are issued arguing either that (a) the start of the 18th century was on the first day of 1700, or (b) the first day of 1701; this unresolved issue permeates all millennial literature for next 300 years.

OBSERVATIONS
UPON THE
PROPHECIES
OF
DANIEL,
AND THE
APOCALYPSE
OF
St. JOHN.

In TWO PARTS.

By Sir ISAAC NEWTON.

DUBLIN:
Printed by S. POWELL,
For GEORGE RISK, at the Shakespear's-Head, GEORGE EWING, at the Angel and Bible, and WILLIAM SMITH, at the Hercules, in Dame's-

**AD 1699.** After his career as mathematician and physicist, Isaac Newton turns his hand to Bible eschatology.

1699 Isaac Newton publishes *Observations upon the Prophecies of Daniel and the Apocalypse of St John* in which he calculates fall of the apocalyptic Beast for 1867 and the Millennium for the year 2000.

1700 **Global status:** 56 generations after Christ, world is 21.3% Christians (84.1% of them being Whites), 24.3% evangelized; with printed Scriptures available in 52 languages.
1700 Christians in Portuguese possessions number 500,000.
1700 2,000 Quakers from England settle in Pennsylvania.
1700 Wittgenstein revival movement in Germany (till 1750).
1700 Swabian Pietist Fathers (Germany): Bengel, Rieger, Hiller, Steinhofer, Storr, et alii.
1700 Roman Catholic baptisms in Congo and Angola average 12,000 a year (mainly infants).
1700 Peter the Great (1672-1725) orders christianization of Siberia.
1700 Dutch East Indies: 100,000 Protestants on Java, 40,000 on Ambon.
1700 Age of Earth reckoned by European scientists at 9,000 years, all plants, animals, humans having been created by God at beginning; Chinese reckon it at several million years; 1747, French biologist Buffon estimates it at 75,000 years (and life at 35,000 years); 1831, English geologist Charles Lyell calculates age of sedimentary rock at 250 million years.
1700 Evangelistic campaigns in Germany of Ernst Christoph Hochmann von Hochenau (1670-1721), major separatist Pietist/Lutheran mystic of his time, converted 1693: 'Regarding the conversion of the Jews as the sign of Christ's impending return, he engaged briefly in Jewish missionary work.'
c1700 French Catholic Company of Missionaries of Mary founded, inspired by Louis-Marie Grignion de Montfort.
1701 India: Roman Catholics begin century-long decline from 2,500,000 in 1700 to 475,000 by 1800.
1701 200,000 Romanian Orthodox, with their clergy, submit to Rome as uniate church.
1701 Russia: in Middle Volga, 3,638 pagan Cheremis (Mari) baptized by 1705, after large-scale distribution of gifts, tax exemption and other incentives.
1702 Congo: first attempt to found church independent of Rome in Black Africa: 22-year-old prophetess Donna Beatrice founds Antonian sect with as followers most of Congo kingdom; 1706, Beatrice burnt alive by king Pedro VI.
1703 St Petersburg (Petrograd) built as imperial capital of Russia by Peter the Great, at cost of lives of 200,000 laborers (Orthodox and other Christians).
1703 200,000 Indian converts to Jesuit mission around Madura, South India; 70,000 other Thomas Christians remain independent Jacobites.
1703 Spiritans (CSSp, Holy Ghost Fathers) founded by Claude Francois Poullart des Places (1679-1709) for 'Evangelizzazione degli infedeli'; by 1983, 857 houses with 3,671 missionaries.
1704 China: persecution begins throughout empire; many RC missionaries and converts killed; 1724, general persecution proclaimed by emperor Yung-Cheng, lasts on and off until 1844.
1705 Origin of Niagara Bible prophecy study conferences, beginning of Bible Conference movement; 1876, Believers' Meeting for Bible Study; 1883-97, Niagara-on-the-Lake conferences; dominated by premillennialists.
1705 Origin of Danish-Halle Mission (Lutheran), forerunner of Protestant missionary societies; first workers include Protestant pioneers to Tranquebar (India): Bartholomew Ziegenbalg (1682-1719), Heinrich Plutschau (1677-1747) and Christian Schwartz (1726-1798).
1706 North America: Presbyterians form first organized church; origin of Presbyterian Church in the USA.
1709 Invention of piano by Italian Bartolommeo Cristofori, from harpsichord and clavichord, able to play piano (soft) and forte (loud).
1710 Canstein House printing press, Halle (Germany) with first Bible society (Cansteinische Bibelanstalt) founded by count Karl von Canstein: 3 million Bibles and NTs printed in 80 years.
1710 For Germany and Eastern Europe, von Canstein Bible Institute of Halle begins mass scripture production; by 1800 has circulated over 3 million inexpensive low cost Bibles and New Testaments.
1712 Orthodox missionary journeys in western Siberia by Filofei Leszczynski (1650-1722), metropolitan of Tobolsk, among Ostyaks, Voguls, Zyrians and Yakuts; baptizes 40,000 and increases churches from 160 to 448 by 1721.
1712 Last execution for witchcraft in England; 1714, witch trials abolished in Prussia.
1714 Jesuits Ippolito Desideri and Emmanuel Freyre travel with a Tartar caravan from Lahore into lands skirting unreached Mount Kailas.
1714 Founding in Copenhagen of Collegium de Cursu Evangelii Promovendo.
1714 *A New prophecy of several strange and wonderful revolutions that shall happen to the Kingdom of England in or about an Hundred years hence* is published warning Britons to fend off the Devil, the Pope, and the Turk.
1715 *Nepal.* First mission in Kathmandu (Capuchins); 1769, all Christians finally leave.
1715 China rites controversy: papal constitution 'Ex illa die' attacks Jesuit methods, begins prohibition of accommodation to pagan rites, with final papal bull 'Ex quo singulari' ending further debate; 1773, Jesuit order dissolved by pope Clement XIV.
1716 Irish Presbyterian educator William Tennent (1673-1746) evangelizes in American colonies; 1735, trains men for revivalist ministry in 'Log College'; 1741, in Old Side/New Side schism, he supports latter.
1716 Rome: first official directory with names, addresses, statistics, and entire structure of the Catholic church worldwide published, later named *Annuario Pontificio.*
1717 A.H. Francke, Lutheran professor of Hebrew, holds revivals and evangelistic campaigns in Germany, based on Halle.
1720 Origins of Great Awakening in America: German evangelist T.J. Frelinghuysen (1692-1747) arrives from Pietism in Europe to Dutch Reformed churches in New Jersey; 1726, guides Irish Presbyterian minister and revivalist G. Tennent (1703-1764) and others in revival ministry evangelizing among Scottish and Irish in Philadelphia, New Jersey and beyond.
1720 North America: pioneer Baptist evangelists in South include Jeremiah Walker, Benjamin Watkins, Shubal Stearns (1706-1771), Thomas Ethridge, Daniel Marshall (1706-1784), Richard Curtis Jr (1756- 1811), Isaac Backus (1724-1806).
c1720 Camisards prophesy in ecstatic trances and speak in tongues foretelling imminent destruction of Roman Catholic Church in France; later they flee to England and America as predecessors of Shakers.

KALÅTDLIT NUNÅT
1721
1971
60+10 GRØNLAND

**AD 1721.** Lutheranism spreads in Greenland with link to Denmark.

1721 Lutheran Church of Greenland recognized as integral part of Evangelical Lutheran Church of Denmark.
1721 Peter the Great (regarded by Old Believers as the Antichrist) abolishes Russian Orthodox patriarchate, establishes synod of bishops and tsar-appointed oberprocurator, enabling tsars to rule church through synod until 1917.
1721 Norwegian pastor Hans Egede (1686-1758) begins Protestant mission to Greenland Eskimos.
1722 Moravian (Herrnhut) Pietism begun, led by count N.L. von Zinzendorf (1700-1760).
1722 In Ceylon, Protestants number 424,392 (21% of the population) through forced conversion by Dutch Reformed Church.
1722 Ceylon: though outlawed by Dutch authorities, 400 Catholic churches outnumber 100 Dutch Reformed ones; Christians number 424,000.
1723 Schism of Utrecht: separation from Rome of Little Church of Utrecht or Jansenist Church of Holland; 1889 Declaration of Utrecht rejects Council of Trent; Union of Utrecht unites church with Old Catholic churches of Germany and Switzerland; Jansenist worldview holds 'signs and wonders' (miracles, healings, supernatural signs) still widespread.
1724 Melkite (Greek Catholic) patriarchate of Antioch (in Beirut) established.
1725 The Great Awakening, revival in New England (USA) spreading throughout the Thirteen Colonies; begun under T.J. Frelinghuysen in New Jersey; mass conversions of dechristianized European populations in North America, led by revivalist Jonathan Edwards (1703-1758), who expounds progressive millennialism (later called postmillennialism), envisaging establishment of Christ's millennial kingdom on Earth around year 1990, with Second Advent at close of millennium; Edwards calls for 'concerts of prayer' for world revival; Awakening lasts until 1770.
1727 Jews expelled from Russia; repeated in 1747.
1727 Irkutsk in Siberia an independent Russian Orthodox diocese.
1727 Treaty of Kiachta: China permits 4 Russian priests to begin Peking mission.
1728 Institutum Judaicum founded in Halle by Francke as first Protestant mission center for Jewish evangelism.
1730 Anglican priest, mathematician and divine William Whiston (1667-1752) announces imminent end of world by deluge with destruction of London on 13 October 1736; panic-stricken crowds rush for high ground.
1732 Moravian church organizes foreign missions under bishop Zinzendorf and others; 1732, St Thomas, Danish West Indies; 1733, Greenland; 1736, among Samoyeds of Archangelsk; 1787, Society of the United Brethren for Propagating the Gospel among the Heathen, formed in Pennsylvania, USA; 1732-1862, Moravians send abroad 2,000 missionaries.

**AD 1732.** The Wesley brothers meet in Holy Club at University of Oxford, earnestly debating on how to receive the Spirit.

1732 At Lincoln College, University of Oxford, brothers John and Charles Wesley organize 25-member Holy Club for spiritual exercises and ministry to prisoners, the poor, and neglected children.
1733 Swiss mathematician Leonhard Euler (1707-1783) publishes work that begins modern mathematical analysis; also devises such mathematical symbols as f(x) and $\Sigma$(summation).
1733 Great Northern Expedition: Vitus Bering leads Russian expedition that charts much of Siberian coastline in Arctic; 1741, Bering discovers Alaska and sails along part of coastline; shipwrecked, dies soon after.
1733 Welsh lay preacher Howell Harris (1714-1773) adopts itinerant evangelism and open-air preaching; method later adopted by Whitefield and Wesley.
1734 Invention of fire extinguisher by M. Fuchs of Germany, 1762 Godfrey of London, 1972 Von Ahen and N. Moshein of Sweden.
1735 Christians in Philippines reach 837,182; over a million by 1750.
1735 John and Charles Wesley travel to Georgia (North America) as SPG missionaries, but meet hostility and return in 1737.
1735 George Whitefield (1714-1770) undergoes conversion experience; 1736, begins evangelistic travels; in his life-time, estimated to have preached in public 18,000 times, to 18 million hearers, in crowds of up to 30,000 at once.
1735 Persia reconquers Daghestan, Shirvan, Georgia, and Armenia from the Ottomans.
1736 Moravian missionaries at work among Samoyeds of Archangelsk.
1736 After a hundred years of renewed Roman Catholic missionary activity in Persia, violent persecution of Christians erupts under brutal shah Nadir (1688-1747); after death of shah Abbas III, last of the Safavid dynasty, Nadir Khan becomes shah of Iran, invades central Asia; Middle Kazakh Horde comes under Russian rule; 1747, Nadir Shah assassinated.
1737 300,000 killed in Calcutta by storm surge of Hooghly river.
1738 George Whitefield's evangelistic campaigns in North

America (1738-1770); heard by 80% of entire population.

1738 Conversion of Charles Wesley (1707-1788); commences writing Evangelical hymns, totaling 7,270 original compositions in all.

1738 Conversion of John Wesley (1703-1791) at Aldersgate (UK); beginning of 18th-century Evangelical Revival and rise of Methodism under the Wesleys; outreach largely urban, concerned with needs of the poor, uneducated, unemployed, orphans et alii.

**AD 1739.** Despite ban, Whitefield begins evangelistic open-air meetings often with 30,000 listeners at once.

1739 First evangelistic open-air sermons in England for centuries: George Whitefield (17 February), John Wesley (2 April).

1739 John Wesley's evangelistic travels in Britain average 8,000 miles a year on horseback until his death in 1791; travels 225,000 miles by horse, survives countless hostile mobs, preaches 40,000 sermons, makes 140,000 converts, plants vast network of classes, societies and churches.

1740 Armenian Catholic patriarchate of Cilicia established.

1740 Office for Newly-Baptized opened in Svijazsk (Russia); from 1741-1762, mass baptisms of Volga pagans: 430,550 Chuvash, Cheremis, Ostyaks, et alii baptized; no pagans left in Middle Volga; 1764, Office dissolved.

1740 Bavarian Pietists: Rehberger (1716-1769), Urlsperger, Kieszling, Schoner.

1740 Dutch East Indies: 10,000 Chinese massacred in Batavia.

c1740 English Presbyterian minister Christopher Love predicts destruction of Roman papacy for 1790, after which in 1795 'God will be universally known by all: then a great reformation and peace for ever.'

1740 Age of Enlightenment begins in Europe.

1741 Oldest USA Amerindian independent church formed, Narraganset Indian Church in Charleston, Rhode Island.

1741 German composer G.F. Handel (1685-1759) produces 'Messiah' oratorio.

1742 Juan Santos Atahuallpa (named after final Inca ruler) appears as Quechua messiah in eastern Peru, predicting an Amerindian Catholic church with a native clergy.

1742 *Seychelles.* First Christians (French Catholic settlers).

1743 Organized evangelization of Kamchatka begins under Josef Chotuncevski, including among Tunguz and Lamuts; most peoples soon christianized.

1743 Russian empress Elizabeth orders destruction of mosques in Kazan: 1744-47, 838 forced conversions of Muslims to Orthodoxy; 1748-52, 7,535 conversions.

1744 First typewriter, made by H. Mills (England); 1856, typewriter with embossed letters for blind persons; 1868, USA journalist C.L. Sholes designs first practical typewriter, 1873 manufactured by Remington Arms Company.

1744 Ruling Saudi family in Arabian peninsula adopts teachings of Ibn Wahhabi.

1745 Capuchins expelled from Lhasa, Tibet.

1745 Wesley teaches 'entire sanctification' as second blessing or second work of grace after an individual's conversion; Fletcher et alii call it 'baptism in the Holy Spirit'.

1746 Widespread and severe persecution of Christians begins in China, lasts 38 years.

1746 Forcible evangelization of eastern Siberia organized by metropolitan Sylvester Golovacki of Tobolsk.

1747 Moravians attempt to establish a mission in Persia, but within 3 years have failed.

1749 England (2.8 million adults): 10,000 Particular or Exclusive Baptists, 15,000 Congregationalists; 50,000 Nonconformists, rest Anglicans or Presbyterians.

1749 Challoner's Revision of Rheims-Douai Bible, by bishop Richard Challoner (1691-1781) of London: remains standard Catholic version in English until 1950s.

## Epoch VI:  AD 1750-1815

### REPUDIATION AND REVIVAL

1750 **Global status**: 57 generations after Christ, world is 21.5% Christians (85.2% of them being Whites), 24.3% evangelized; with printed Scriptures available in 60 languages; total martyrs since AD 33, 21,912,000 (0.6% of all Christians ever; recent rate 3,200 per year).

1750 Christianity now prevailing religion of West Indies.

1750 *Turks & Caicos Islands.* First Christians (British Loyalist settlers from America).

1750 Millenarianism strong among German Pietists.

1750 North American Whites (the Thirteen Colonies) about 95% professing Christians (50% Congregationalists, 30% baptized Anglicans, 10% Presbyterians), though only 5% affiliated as church members.

1750 Moravian mission to Labrador begun.

1750 Philosophers David Hume and Immanuel Kant sever tenuous alliance between Christianity and the new science, through skepticism and empirical method.

c1750 British natural philosopher Thomas Wright (1711-1786) first suggests our Galaxy has a center, inhabited by a high form of intelligence.

c1750 Wales: revivals under Howell Harris (1714-1773), Daniel Rowland (c1713-1790), William Williams (1717-1791).

1750 Chassidim (Hassidic sect of Judaism) founded in Carpathian mountain region.

c1750 *Great Chinese Encyclopedia* begun, 5,000 volumes.

1751 Ostyaks evangelized up to Arctic coasts in region of Obdorsk.

1751 French *philosophes* or Encyclopedists (men dedicated to Rationalism and Deism) produce *Diderot's Encyclopédie* (1751-1780, 35 volumes), believe Age of Reason just arriving, predict religion and superstition fated for imminent extinction.

1751 D. Diderot (1713-1784) and J. d'Alembert's first volume of *Encyclopédie* as universal dictionary of the arts, sciences, trades, and manufactures.

1752 Moscow again burns in Great Fire, with 18,000 buildings destroyed.

1752 Benjamin Franklin discovers electricity.

1754 In Portugal (then 2 million), at least 200,000 (10%) are enrolled members of one religious order or another.

1754 Ottoman empire: steady stream of Orthodox killed (The New Martyrs), mainly Orthodox who lapse to Islam but later repent and are trained for martyrdom by monks, then notify Turkish magistrates they have switched from Islam; penalty for this apostasy is always death.

1755 Great Earthquake of Lisbon, with fire and tidal wave, kills 12% of 250,000 city population, with 9,000 buildings destroyed; at same time, town of 10,000 swallowed in fissures in Morocco; both interpreted as divine judgments.

1755 German philosopher Immanuel Kant (1724-1804), interested in astronomy, is first to propose existence of vast number of very distant 'island universes' (independent galaxies) beyond our own Galaxy.

1755 English lexicographer, high churchman and Christian moralist Samuel Johnson (1709-1784) publishes his Dictionary of the English language , in which 'evangelism' is defined as 'The promulgation of the blessed Gospel', and 'evangelize' as to 'instruct in the Gospel'.

1756 Seven Years' War (1756-1763) becomes first truly global conflict.

1757 Battle of Plassey, Bengal: Clive defeats Siraj-ud-Dawlah; foundation of British rule in India.

1759 Suppression of Jesuit order throughout Portugal and Portuguese domains; also 1764 in France and its colonies; 1767 Spain, Italy; 1773, pope Clement XIV (1705-1774) dissolves Society of Jesus worldwide (22,589 members including 11,293 priests); 3,300 Jesuit overseas missionaries recalled (2,171 Spanish, 909 Portuguese, 126 French); 1814, ban lifted throughout world.

1760 Saiva *sannyasis* fight Vaishnava *vairagis* for control of Kumbha Mela area at Hardwar in which 18,000 monks are killed.

1761 After February and March earthquakes in London, a soldier William Bell preaches that world will end on April 5; mass hysteria breaks out, Bell is arrested and locked up in London's insane asylum, Bedlam.

1763 North America (USA): 24,000 Christians, growing to 35,000 by 1789, 150,000 by 1800 and 6,231,417 by 1890.

1763 First work of prophetic futurist fiction, *The reign of George VI, 1900-1925* (anonymous), describing life in the 20th century as the same as in the 18th; first major forecast of its kind, though failing to envisage Industrial Revolution.

1764 *Falkland Islands.* First Christians and churches (French settlers).

1764 Annihilation of Christian community in Thailand; other persecutions 1729, 1755, 1767, 1775.

1766 First Methodist society in New World formed in North America.

1766 Planters from Scotland begin Presbytery of British Guiana.

1767 First complete church membership returns published (by Methodists, in Britain).

1767 Expulsion of all Jesuits throughout South America and Mexico.

1768 British navigator James Cook (1728-79) sails around

the world, exploring countries and meeting natives of Australia and New Zealand while searching for legendary 'southern continent'; 1776, explores western North American coast for an Atlantic passage, develops maps and charts used for several generations.

1768 R. Arkwright invents spinning machine in Bolton, Lancashire.

1768 First edition of *Encyclopaedia Britannica*, in 3 volumes, published in Edinburgh, with 45 principal subjects in alphabetical sequence.

1769 Age of steam power begins as Scottish inventor James Watt (1736-1819) patents more efficient steam engine; Watt's later engines become efficient power sources for wide variety of machines and help bring about Industrial Revolution.

1769 First true automobile (motor car), the Cugnot 3-wheeled steamer doing 2.25 miles per hour carrying 4 people; much later, first gasoline-engine automobiles, Benz (1885) and Daimler (1885).

1770 East African slave trade rapidly increases; 1,250,000 slaves traded at coast by Muslim Arabs up to 1897 abolition of slavery.

1770 Chinese capital Peking becomes first recent city in world to reach 1 million in population; meteoric rise begins of megacities (over 1 million persons) across world, escalating to (year, world total, total in developing countries): 1900, 20; 1950, 78 (31); 1955, 95 (42); 1960, 115 (53); 1965, 136 (63); 1970, 161 (79); 1975, 183 (95); 1980, 227 (125); 1985, 276 (163); 1990, 330 (205); 2000, 433 (295); AD 2025, 652 (498).

1770 French nun Jeanne Le Royer (1732-1798) predicts tribulation, coming of Antichrist, end of papacy, and end of world in AD 2000.

1771 French author L.-S. Mercier (1740-1814) publishes anonymously in Amsterdam *L'An 2440* (Memoirs of the year 2500), first optimistic future utopia; describes future human civilization, with no war, no slavery, no popery, orderly traffic in Paris, a universal language, and world order, peace.

1772 Slavery ruled illegal in Britain (but not in colonies), but Atlantic slave trade delivers average of 75,000 a year from 1750-1800.

1772 Polish Orthodox united with Russian Orthodox Church until 1918.

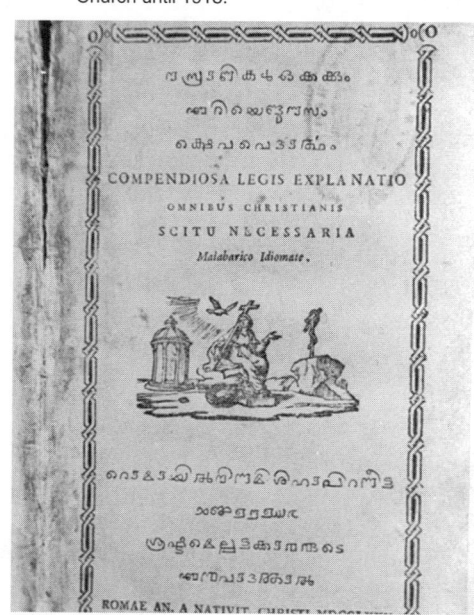

**AD 1772.** First Malayalam Christian book published in Kerala, India.

1772 Catholic seminary of Alwaye (archdiocese of Verapoly & Ernaculam) publishes first book completely printed in Malayalam characters, *Samshepaveedarthan.*

1773 First independent USA Black Baptist congregation is formed near Augusta, Georgia.

1773 Syrian Catholic patriarchate established.

### Beginnings of Industrial Revolution

1773 Before 1775, all societies everywhere are pre-industrial; 1775, first industrial revolution begins fueled by steam power and coal, second (1901, Germany) by electrical and chemical industries, third (1950) by nuclear power, microchips and genes, fourth (1987) by information.

1773 Virginia: revival breaks out as first instance of a pentecostal-type religious revival in North America; followed by recurrence in 1787.

1773 Pope Clement XIV dissolves Jesuit order worldwide; 3,000 missioners worldwide are recalled.

1774 United Society of Believers in Christ's Second Appearing (Shakers) founded in Niskeyuna, NY (USA) by Ann Lee and pilgrims from England as millennial messianic sect in New World, based on celibacy.

1775 Industrial Revolution begins; industrialization and urbanization accelerate in Holland first, then in

Britain; working classes become alienated from churches.

1776 Declaration of Independence by the Thirteen Colonies (USA); population 3 million, among whom 20,000 are Roman Catholics.

1776 Adam Smith's *An Inquiry into the Nature and Causes of the Wealth of Nations*, the most influential work in modern political economy ('wealth' being capitalism and machines).

1778 USA Universalists organize their first church in 1778, Unitarians following with their own church in 1796.

1778 Earl of Stanhope invents Logic Demonstrator with no moving parts.

1779 Siam: all missionaries expelled for refusing to honor Buddhist state ceremonies.

1780 Edict of Toleration of Joseph II (1741-1790) of Austria guaranteeing religious freedom.

1780 A prophet named Tupac Amaru II (c1742-1781) leads Quechua religious revolt against Spanish in Peru; crushed and executed.

1780 Sunday schools popularized by Robert Raikes (1735-1811) of Gloucester; 1786, 200,000 children enrolled in England; 1789 in Wales, then to Scotland, Ireland and America.

1780 *Pitcairn Islands*. First Christians (British mutineers).

1780 Viet Nam: 200,000 Catholics, 28 European priests and 47 local priests.

1780 Roman Catholics in England number 70,000.

1780 Deutsche Christentumsgesellschaft (Christendom Society) begun in Germany to build kingdom of God on an ecumenical basis; 1815, members found Evangelische Missionsgesellschaft in Basel (Basel Mission).

1781 Last executions are carried out under Spanish Inquisition.

1781 USA: revivals break out in several colleges including 1781 Dartmouth, 1783 Princeton and Yale, also Williams, Hampden-Sydney; 1785, nationwide 'revival of 1800' fixes pattern of denominational life, lasts until 1812.

1781 Sahajanandaswami (1781-1830) is born, Gujarati founder of Swaminarayan sect; 1995, 1.5 million followers in present-day India.

1782 Concerts of Prayer (for revival and world mission), as envisaged by Jonathan Edwards, begin and spread in Britain, then from 1790 in USA; basis for subsequent worldwide missionary advance.

1783 Eclectic Society and Clapham Society formed in England.

1783 Anglican vicar Charles Simeon (1759-1836) starts Evangelical student movement in Cambridge, England.

1783 English astronomer and clergyman John Mitchell is first to propose existence of black holes, being collapsed stars and galaxies; by 1995, total in Universe is estimated at $10^{16}$.

1783 Thomas Coke (1747-1814), Wesley's colleague and from 1787 first Methodist bishop in USA, issues 'Plan for the Society for the Establishment of Missions among the Heathens'; 1786, first Methodist foreign mission begun, to Antigua.

1783 Native Baptist Church, first Jamaican Afro-Christian movement, begun by ex-slave, George Lisle; church plays a significant political role 80 years later; precursor of later End-time pentecostal renewal across world.

1783 Crimean khanate comes under Russian rule.

1784 Christmas conference in Baltimore: American Methodist Society breaks from Church of England, takes name Methodist Episcopal Church with Francis Asbury as its bishop.

1784 Methodists in Thirteen Colonies multiply from 500 in 1771 to 15,000 in 13 years, then to 1,324,000 by 1850; Methodist Episcopal Church incorporated in Baltimore as first independent national church organization in North America.

1784 Russian Orthodox mission to Alaska begun.

1784 Korea: Christianity reintroduced by zealous Catholic laymen, prospers for a while; by 1794, 4,000 baptisms without clergy or missionaries; by 1801 10,000, but church then exterminated; subsequent persecutions on average every decade.

1784 J. Goodricke discovers variability of cepheids (stars whose brightness varies with regularity over several months, with period inversely proportional to star's absolute magnitude), used by E. Hubble as 'standard candles' to determine intergalactic distances.

1784 Tippu Sultan, Muslim ruler of Mysore (India), forcibly circumcises 50,000 Christians and deports them beyond Western Ghats.

1785 *Sierra Leone*. First Christians (Black settlers from Nova Scotia).

1785 *New Zealand*. First Christians (European commercial base).

1785 Sunday School Society formed in London to extend movement throughout British empire; first joint effort of separate denominations since Protestant Reformation.

1785 Scottish geologist James Hutton (1726-1797) sets forth theory that Earth functions like a giant organism; c1972 scientists J. Lovelock and L. Margulis propound Gaia hypothesis: the planet functions as a single self-regulating superorganism; 1988, Americ Geophysical Union sponsors first major scientific conference on Gaia.

1785 Evangelical awakenings (revivals) throughout Wales under Howel Harris (1714-1773) and others: 1785 Brynengan, 1786 Trecastle, 1791 Bala, 1805 Aberystwyth, 1810 Llangeitho, 1817 Beddgelert,

1821 Denbighshire, 1822 Anglesey, 1828 Carmarthenshire, 1832 Caernarvonshire, 1840 Merionethshire, 1849 South Wales, et alia.

1787 First USA Black Methodist dissidents appear, with officially-organized African Methodist Episcopal Church emerging by 1816.

1787 Moravian foreign mission formed: Society for Propagating the Gospel among the Heathen.

**AD 1787.** Baptist minister Fuller passes snuff box round for donations to begin Baptist Missionary Society.

1787 English Baptist minister Andrew Fuller (1754-1815) writes *The Gospel of Christ Worthy of All Acceptation* and over 128 other titles, urges obedience to the Great Commission.

1787 Irish orator Francis Dobbs composes *Millennium: A Poem*, giving many reasons why Second Coming of Christ will occur in 1790.

1787 Holland: Nederlandsch Zendings Genootschap (NZG) established.

1788 Charles Wesley dies; during his lifetime he composes more than 6,000 hymns for Methodist societies, including 'Hark, the Herald Angels Sing,' 'Christ the Lord Is Ris'n Today,' and 'Love Divine, All Loves Excelling'.

1788 Allgäuer Revival among Bavarian Catholics, led by Johann Sailer (1751-1832), Michael Feneberg, Martin Boos (1762-1825), Johannes Goszner (1773-1858), Ignatius Lindl (1774-1834).

1788 *Australia*. First Christians (English convicts and Anglican chaplains).

1788 *Norfolk Island*. First Christians (Australia convict colony).

1788 Large colonies of German Mennonites and farmers settle in Black Earth region of Russia; origin of Stundists.

1789 Roman Catholics in USA number 35,000, half in Maryland, quarter in Philadelphia; first diocese erected in Baltimore (Maryland).

1789 French Revolution: church/state separation and religious liberty proclaimed in France; 17,000 officially executed in 1793-4 Reign of Terror, including clergy and bishops.

1790 Methodists in Great Britain number 71,668.

1790 In North America, Blacks number 757,208 out of population of 3,929,214 (19.3%).

1790 World's first modern state censuses: 1790, USA; 1801, Great Britain.

1790 Europe's energy needs supplied mainly by 14 million horses and 24 million oxen.

c1790 Popular French Catholic prophetess Suzette Labrousse sees French Revolution as herald of Millennium, prophesies 'The Pope will renounce his temporal power... there will be great bloodshed in Europe'; 1792, goes on pilgrimage to Rome, stays until turn of century expecting the final age.

c1790 William Bryan of Bristol and illuminist brethren in Avignon expect destruction of Turks and restoration of Jews to Zion before 1800.

c1790 Naturalist Comte de Buffon predicts Earth might cool to uninhabitability after 93,000 years.

c1790 English prophet Richard Brothers publishes *The Restoration of the Hebrews to Jerusalem by the Year 1798*.

1791 John Wesley dies at 88, having traveled 250,000 miles and preached 40,000 sermons.

**AD 1791.** After preaching 40,000 sermons and travelling a quarter million miles on horseback, John Wesley dies.

1791 English term 'statistics' coined by Sir John Sinclair.

1792 Egypt swept by plague; 800,000 perish.

1792 Second Great Awakening among Congregationalists and other New England churches (USA), lasting 30 years.

1792 Eight Russian Orthodox missionary monks arrive on island of Kodiak (Alaska), baptize 2,500 shamanist Eskimos in following 2 years, and 10,000 in 1795.

**AD 1792.** Intending Baptist missionary William Carey expounds his global strategy.

1792 William Carey (1761-1834) publishes first statistical global survey of Christian world mission: *An Enquiry Into the Obligations of Christians, to Use Means for the Conversion of the Heathens*, accurately enumerating populations and Christians on all continents in world's first statistical survey (world population 731 million: 57% pagan/Hindu/Buddhist, 18% Muslim, 14% RC, 6% Protestant, 4% Orthodox, 1% Jewish); 1793, sails for India under Particular Baptist Society for Propagating the Gospel among the Heathen (formed 1792); at Serampore, initiates modern era of Protestant world missions, serves without home leave for 41 years in Bengal, translates and prints Bible in 35 languages.

1792 Denmark becomes first nation to abolish the slave trade; 1807 England follows suit.

1793 In a classic of futurism, marquis de Condorcet (1743-1794) writes *Sketch for a historical picture of the progress of the human mind*, originating the extrapolative method of prediction, and conditional predicting; expounds concept of general progress of civilization and a golden future for all humanity; also writes *Fragment on Atlantis* enlarging Bacon's ideas, proposes a world research center.

1794 First Catholic ordination of Amerindian priests in Latin America (3 persons).

1794 Francois Dupuis publishes *The Origin of all Cults*, holding all religions are allegories of motions of the stars.

1795 London Missionary Society (LMS) founded (interdenominational, later Congregationalist), with founders' 'vision of a world covered by missionary centres that would reach out and link up until there was no place where the gospel was not preached'.

1795 Methodists in Britain separate from Church of England after John Wesley's death in 1791.

1795 Mass movement in Cape Comorin (South India): 5,000 Nadars (Shanars) baptized by SPCK missionaries in 10 years.

1796 Buddhist revolt (White Lotus Rebellion) against Manchu rule in China, until 1804.

1796 First LMS missionaries sent to South Pacific (Tahiti).

1796 Edinburgh Tract Society, Edinburgh Missionary Society, formed in Scotland.

1796 Over 2 million Uniate Ruthenians in Poland return to Russian Orthodox Church.

1796 Founding of Scottish Missionary Society and Glasgow Missionary Society.

1796 Ceylon: British drive out Dutch forces, find 67,000 Ceylonese still Roman Catholics despite 140 years' ban.

1796 Norwegian Revival, under Hans Nielsen Hauge.

1796 General Assembly of Church of Scotland formally resolves that 'to spread abroad the knowledge of the gospel among the barbarous and heathen nations seems to be highly preposterous'.

1796 Over two million worshipers compete for sacred Ganges bathe at Kumbha Mela; 5,000 Saiva ascetics killed in clash with Sikh ascetics.

1797 *Tonga*. First missionaries (LMS), also 1822, then 1825.

1797 Netherlands Missionary Society (NZG) founded in Rotterdam.

1798 Black holes are postulated in detail by Laplace.

1798 French general Berthier marches on Rome, sets up new republic, exiles pope Pius VI; revolutionary upheavals renew Christian beliefs in end-time prophecy and restoration of the charismata.

1798 At age of 32, English clergyman and economist Thomas R. Malthus (1766-1834) publishes *An Essay on the Principle of Population as it affects the Future Improvement of Society,* opposing notion of inevitability of progress, with thesis that population growth always outruns food supply.

1798 First modern end-of-the-world novel: French pulpit orator J.-B. Cousin de Grainville writes *Le dernier homme/The Last Man* describing a future in which man, through impiety and war has dwindled down to a last infertile man, Omegarus, and a last woman, Syderia; over next 2 centuries, several hundred more such scenarios are published.

1799 Elberfeld-Barmen Missionary Society begun.

1799 New Religion of the Iroquois founded by Handsome Lake, a Seneca Indian in Great Lakes region (USA).

1799 Religious Tract Society (RTS) founded (UK).

1799 Church Missionary Society (CMS) founded by Anglicans in London.

1799 Napoleon Bonaparte (1769-1821), military dictator of France, imprisons 2 popes in France (Pius VI, Pius VII); regarded as one in long succession of archetypal antichrists, in particular as Antichrists (2 from the North, one from the South) envisioned by Nostradamus.

1799 Private missionary activity among Yakuts and Chukchi undertaken by RC secular priest G. Slepcov (until 1815), between Indigirka and Tschaun.

1799 Electric battery invented by Italian physicist Alessandro Volta (1745-1827).

1799 Dutch East Indies: 140,000 Protestants in Java and Amboina, 200,000 in archipelago.

1800 **Global status:** 59 generations after Christ, world is 22.7% Christians (86.5% of them being Whites), 25.4% evangelized; with printed Scriptures available in 67 languages.

1800 Protestant foreign missionaries worldwide number only 100.

1800 Roman Catholics: 5,000 in Burma, 2,300 in Siam, 310,000 in Indochina, over 500,000 in India.

1800 Congo and Angola: no trace of former Catholic missions remains.

1800 China: about 200,000 baptized Roman Catholics remain.

1800 Old Believers in many parts of northern Russia number half of population.

1800 Beginnings of local awakenings (revivals) in Scotland: Lewis, Harris, Perthshire.

1800 Research undergoes vast expansion: scientific R&D (research and development) increases every year from 1800 to the present.

1800 World's 10 largest cities: Peking 1,100,000, London 861,000, Canton 800,000, Constantinople 570,000, Paris 547,000, Hangchow 500,000, Yedo 492,000, Naples 430,000, Soochow 392,000, Osaka 380,000.

c1800 *Papua New Guinea.* First Christians (European trading post).

1800 Widespread evangelistic camp meetings begin in USA; Kentucky Revival awakening, with crowds of up to 25,000, sweeps over Kentucky, Tennessee and the Carolinas.

1800 A member of Irish House of Commons predicts the Messiah will come in time to thwart Act of Union scheduled to unite Parliaments of England and Ireland on January 1, 1801.

1800 Speaking of USA, Nathanael Eamons, president of Massachusetts Missionary Society, states 'This is probably the last peculiar people which the Lord means to form, and the last great empire which he means to erect, before the kingdoms of this world are absorbed in the Kingdom of Christ.'

1800 Protestant missionaries worldwide number 100.

1800 Indonesian islands: 200,000 Protestants and Catholics.

c1800 *Eritrea.* First Christians, Ethiopian Orthodox immigrants.

1801 Protestants in Ceylon number 342,000 (Dutch Reformed), or 14% of population; through neglect, most lapse to Buddhism by 1830.

1801 Martyrdom in Korea of Chinese Catholic priest James Chu (Tsiu) and 300 Korean Christians: further persecutions in 1815, 1819, 1826, 1827, 1839, 1845, 1860, 1866, 1881, 1887, 1910, 1919, 1950.

1801 Surrey Iron Railway incorporated, as first public freight-carrying railroad; 1803, first locomotive, built by Trevithick; 1829, G. Stephenson's 'Rocket'.

1801 India: total baptized Christians reaches 750,000; out of 307,000 St Thomas Syrian Christians in Kerala 187,000 accept rule of Rome while 120,000 follow Jacobite bishop of Antioch; in Goa, 200,000 Catholics.

1802 Catholics in Viet Nam 320,000, with 3 European bishops, 15 missionary priests and 119 Vietnamese priests.

1802 USA: Massachusetts Baptist Mission Society formed 'for the evangelization of frontier communities', founded by Hezekiah Smith (1737-1805).

1804 *Fiji Islands.* First Christians (escaped convicts from Australia).

1804 British & Foreign Bible Society (BFBS) founded, in London, with vision of providing Scriptures to whole world.

1804 Grand totals of all Bibles (1,000 pages each) printed from 1804-1954, 1,250 million copies, thus averaging 8.3 million Bibles per year.

1805 Science of physical anthropology founded with work of Johann Friedrich Blumenbach (1752-1840).

1805 *Namibia* (*South West Africa*). First mission (LMS, among Hottentot Capoid aboriginals).

1806 Napoleon abolishes Holy Roman Empire.

1806 Britain: revivals secede from Methodism:1806 Independent Methodists, 1810 Camp Meeting Methodists, joining in 1812 as Primitive Methodists.

1806 USA: Philadelphia Bible Society founded, then Massachusetts BS, 1809 New York BS, then 25 more small local Bible societies by 1816 when, at initiative of New Jersey BS, agreement is reached to found American Bible Society as national body.

1806 USA: Haystack Prayer Meeting at Williams College, Massachusetts, launches North America foreign missions, to preach the gospel to all nations; 1810, these students form Society of Inquiry on the Subject of Missions; soon after, ABCFM is formed.

1807 Slave trade prohibited throughout British empire by British parliament.

1807 Robert Morrison (1782-1834), first Protestant missionary (LMS) to China, arrives in Macao, translates Bible into Chinese by 1818, dictionary by 1821; dies in 1834, having seen only 10 baptisms of Chinese.

1807 USA: Maine Missionary Society, for Evangelical work in Maine; dissolved 1862.

1809 Sweden: Evangeliska Sallskapet (for Bibles and tracts) founded.

1809 London Society for Promoting Christianity amongst the Jews (LSPCJ) founded as interdenominational mission, but Anglican only from 1815; later called Church Missions to Jews (CMJ); 1962, Church's Ministry among the Jews.

1809 New York Bible Society founded, from 1816 working with ABS; 1946 does not join United Bible Societies, works instead with WBT/SIL; 1968 begins to produce NIV Bible, completed 1978; c1975 renamed NY International BS, then 1982 International Bible Society.

1810 Britain: 312,000 Nonconformists (including 30,000 Particular or Exclusive Baptists).

1810 China: 215,000 native Catholics, 6 bishops, 2 coadjutors, 23 missionaries, 80 native agents.

1810 German evangelist T. Grenz spreads gospel among Lithuanians.

1810 Revival in Russian Orthodox Church; 1813, Russian Bible Society founded, printing in 30 languages (17 new) with 600,000 copies; 1827, disbanded.

1810 Evangelical awakenings (revivals) in Switzerland (Robert Haldane, 1764-1842), France, Low Countries, Germany.

c1810 Wales: revivals under Christmas Evans (1766-1838), John Elias (1774-1841).

c1810 Enlightenment thinking produces the social sciences: economics, demography, sociology, anthropology, statistics, c1950 cliometrics ('social-scientific history'); traditional history meanwhile abandons scientific method and embraces legal method (evidence, testimony of 2 witnesses).

1810 W. Carey conceives idea of regional ecumenical missionary conferences around globe; nothing results until 1825 Bombay and 1854 New York.

1810 Congregationalists in Massachusetts, USA, organize American Board of Commissioners for Foreign Missions (ABCFM) 'to devise, adopt and prosecute ways and means for propagating the gospel among those who are destitute of the knowledge of Christianity'; by 1880, 1,200 missionaries overseas; 1961, renamed United Church Board for World Ministries, 'to serve Christ in the world'; 1985, 229 foreign missionaries in 54 countries.

1810 Reform Judaism movement in Europe, until 1830.

1811 Henry Martyn (1781-1812), Anglican chaplain (CMS), begins in Persia translating Bible.

1811 Edict against Christianity in China: spreading the faith is punishable by death; 1857, further edict.

1811 American clergyman Ethan Smith of Vermont writes *Dissertation on the Prophecies Related to Antichrist and the Last Times,* concludes world will end in 1866.

1811 Russian Orthodox Holy Synod deposes Georgia's catholicos Antoni II, rules Georgian church through Russia-appointed exarchs until 1917; one, archbishop Nikon Sofiisky, is murdered in 1908.

1812 Wuppertal Tract Society formed (Germany).

1812 Catastrophe Theory proposed by French geologist baron G. Cuvier (1769-1832): Earth is now 86,000 years old and has gone through 32 successive acts of creation (as shown by 32 geological strata), the products of all but the last being obliterated in subsequent catastrophes (leaving only fossils), the last being the Noachian Flood in BC 4000.

1812 New York City Mission movement founded by Evangelicals, lasts till 1870.

1812 Friedrich Creuzer writes *Symbolism and Mythology of Ancient Peoples, especially the Greeks.*

1812 Germany: Württemberg Bible Society founded.

1812 Stuttgart Bible Society prints, from 1812 to 1956, more than 40 million Bibles (280,000 per year).

1813 Burma: arrival of American Baptist missionary Adoniram Judson (1788-1850).

1813 US educator Timothy Dwight (1752-1817), president of Yale College Divinity School, publishes *A Sermon Delivered in Boston, September 16, 1813* stating that the Millennium would occur 'not too far from the year 2000'.

1814 American Baptist Missionary Union founded (USA); later ABFMS.

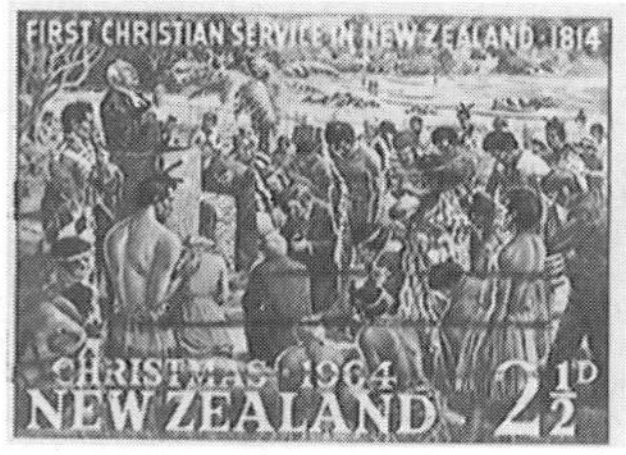


**AD 1814.** Origin of Protestant missions to Maoris in New Zealand.

1814 New Zealand: Protestant missions to Maoris begin.

1814 Prussian, Dutch, Bergish, Hanover, and Saxony Bible societies founded.

1814 Society of Jesus reestablished by pope Pius VII (1742-1823) after 40 years' ban, with renewed interest in global mission and evangelization.

1814 First of the great Indian mass movements into the churches: converted Shaivite Dalit (outcaste), Vedamanikam, leads large Tamil people movement of Nadar outcastes.

**Epoch VII: AD 1815-1914**

## THE GREAT CENTURY

1815 **Global status:** 59.4 generations after Christ, world is 23.2% Christians (86.1% of them being Whites), 30.3% evangelized; with printed Scriptures available in 86 languages; total martyrs since AD 33, 22,065,000 (0.6% of all Christians ever; recent recent rate 1,800 per year).

1815 Beginning of the Great Century of worldwide Christian expansion, from end of Napoleonic wars to 1914.

1815 Printed Bible available in 44 languages, New Testament in 59, portions in 86; Bible-publishing societies now begun in a number of countries.

1815 Over 80% of all North American Indians still non-Christians, despite extensive missions.

1815 Basel Evangelical Missionary Society founded (Switzerland).

1815 Vast proliferation begins in number of Roman Catholic orders and congregations.

1815 H. Bardwell publishes sermon 'The duty and reward of evangelizing the heathen', preached in Newburyport, USA.

1815 Italian priest Caspar Del Bufalo (1786-1837) founds Missioners of the Most Precious Blood, with as 'his goal for his missioners the evangelization of the world' through charitable works.

1815 *The Spirit of British Missions* (London: by an Anglican clergyman of the Church Missionary Society) appeals for workers: 'The supply of Labourers in the great work of evangelizing the world is a most important topic.'

1816 *Botswana* (then Bechuanaland). First mission (LMS).

1816 Elberfeld revivals in western Germany: 1816 first revival, 1820 second.

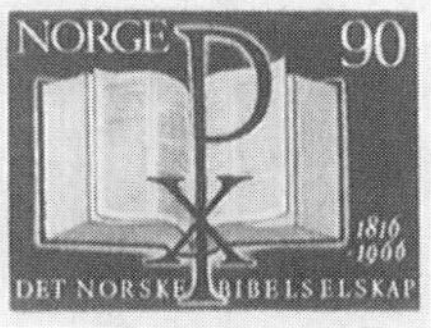


**AD 1816.** Founding of Norway Bible Society.

1816 American Bible Society (ABS) founded, also Norway Bible Society.

1816 First translations of Holy Scripture into any Black African languages: Bullom (Sierra Leone), followed by Amharic 1824, Malagasy 1828, Setswana 1830, up to 560 languages by 1983.

1816 First steerable bicycle, pushed by feet on road, made by Frenchman, J. N. Niepce; 1865 pedal-driven velocipede; one of most efficient machines ever made by man.

1816 India: Orthodox Syrian Church of the East invites in 4 Anglican (CMS) missionaries to train its clergy at Kottayam, Kerala; 1836 reforms result in expulsion of missionaries; 1843, results in major schism, Mar Thoma Syrian Church of Malabar.

1817 Robert Moffat (1795-1883) begins 50-year ministry among Tswana of southern Africa; 1857, completes Tswana Bible.

1817 Organized evangelization among Buryats around Lake Baikal undertaken by London Missionary Society; 1840, Bible translated (Mongolian); 1841, discontinued on orders from Russian holy synod and tsar; 1861, Orthodox mission to Buryats begun in Irkutsk.

1818 Wesleyan Methodist Missionary Society begun (London); later MMS.

1818 Madagascar: first Protestants (LMS) begin work.

1818 Mary Shelley writes *Frankenstein,* the archetypal science fiction novel.

1818 *The Conversion of the World: or the Claims of 600 Millions, and the Ability and Duty of the Churches Respecting Them:* book by G. Hall & S. Newell (ABCFM, India); proposal to convert heathen millions across world by sending 30,000 Protestant missionaries from USA and Europe in 21 years, at cost of US$4 from each Protestant and Anglican communicant in Christendom.

1819 Battle of Boyaca: forces led by Simon Bolivar (1783-

1830) defeat Spanish, gaining independence for New Granada; Greater Colombia is created with Bolivar as president, (1819-1830) eventually includes modern Colombia, Panama, Venezuela, and Ecuador.
1819 Settlers' Meeting (Creoles) secedes from Wesleyan Mission in Freetown (Sierra Leone); first ecclesiastical schism south of the Sahara.
1819 Missionary Society of Methodist Episcopal Church organized; 1939 constitution states 'The supreme aim of missions is to make the Lord Jesus Christ known to all peoples in all lands as their divine Saviour'; 1940, 1964, reorganized as Board of Global Ministries, United Methodist Church; 1974, 839 foreign missionaries (9.5% non-USA); 1985, 516 foreign missionaries in 50 countries.
1820 Protestant mission begins in Argentina (BFBS).
1820 Revival in Pomerania, Germany.
1820 London Jews Society makes first British missionary contact in Iraq.
c1820 Georgian Orthodox Church forcibly assimilated by Russian Orthodox Church.
c1820 Augustinian nun, mystic and seer Catherine Emmerich (1774-1824) of Westphalia has vision of Lucifer being unchained about 1940 and Antichrist working from 1960 onwards.
1821 Brazil declares independence from Portugal under rule of Pedro I (1798-1834), son of Portuguese king.
1821 Chile: first Protestant missionary (BFBS) opens schools.
1821 Danish Missionary Society founded.
1821 Charles Babbage (1792-1871) invents 'Difference Engine' (for computing tables), and 1833 his 'Analytical Engine' capable of statistical operations; world's first general-purpose digital computer.
1821 Emperor Minh Mang of Annam ('the Nero of Indochina') begins 20-year reign; missionaries prohibited, vicious persecutions of Christians in 1821, 1825, 1832; but by 1840, Catholics increase to 420,000.
1821 Cyprus: Orthodox ethnarch (archbishop), all 3 bishops, abbots, many priests and laity, are hanged by Ottoman Turks; similar martyrdoms in Crete and Greece.
1821 Bophuthatswana: first mission; followed in next hundred years by opening of Christian work in other areas which by 1986 become Bantustans: Ciskei, Gazankulu, KaNgwane, KwaNdebele, KwaZulu, Lebowa, Qwaqwa, Transkei, Venda; 1991 reabsorbed into South Africa.

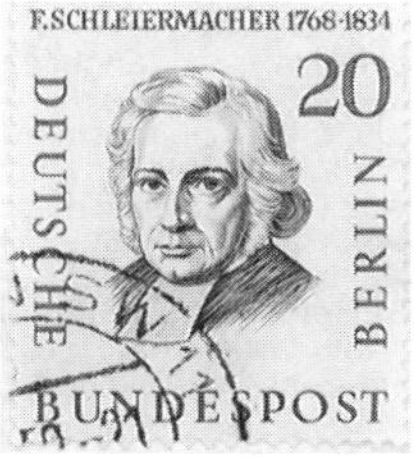


**AD 1821.** Theologian Schleiermacher publishes on basis of religion as dependence.

1821 German theologian F. Schleiermacher (1768-1834) publishes in *The Christian Faith* that the basis of religion is the sense of absolute dependence.
1822 Scottish explorer Alexander Gordon Laing (1793-1826) explores Niger river basin in Africa, becoming first white man to reach Timbuktu (1826).
1822 *Liberia.* First Christians (Black settlers from USA; Baptists and Methodists).
1822 Paris Evangelical Missionary Society founded (France).
1822 Providence Baptist Church in Monrovia (Liberia), oldest Baptist congregation in Africa, begun by first USA missionary to Africa, Lott Carey, a Black slave from Virginia.
1822 Society for the Propagation of the Faith begun in Lyons (France).
1822 84-year-old ecumenical patriarch Gregory V robed in vestments by Turks then hanged with other bishops after Easter Day liturgy in Constantinople; 23,000 Greeks and 12,000 Turks massacred.
1822 Berlin Israelmission founded; 1869, F. Delitzsch founds Evangelische Lutherische Zentralverein für Mission unter Israel (HQ Leipzig); 1877, Delitzsch completes NT in Hebrew after 51 years' work.
1822 Immigrants to USA arrive in 3 waves: 1820-1860, 5 million immigrants, mostly Irish and Germans; 1880-1920, 23 million immigrants from southern, central, and eastern Europe; 1965-1994, 15 million immigrants, mostly Asians or Latinos.
1822 Lowest point of Roman Catholic global missions, with only 270 active European priests in foreign missions.
1823 *Cook Islands.* First mission (LMS).
1823 German Lutherans emigrate from Germany to Brazil.
1823 Josiah Pratt's annual Survey of the World (CMS, London) headed 'The Conversion of the World dependent on the more abundant influence of the Holy Spirit'.
1824 Attempt to found Coptic Catholic patriarchate fails.
1824 Berlin Missionary Society formed.
1824 First Anglican bishoprics in Caribbean established in Jamaica and Barbados.
1824 Blind French educator Louis Braille (1809-1852) invents 6-dot coded type system of printing and writing for blind persons.
1824 USA: beginnings of interdenominational city-wide cooperative evangelism; spreads to cities across world.
1824 Dayananda Sarasvati (1824-1883) born, founder of Arya Samaj, Hindu reformist movement stressing return to values and practices of the *Vedas*.
1825 Hawaii: Hapu syncretistic cult announces imminent end of world; temple then burned to ground by Protestant missionaries.
1825 *Swaziland.* First missionaries (Methodists from South Africa).
1825 Colombia: BFBS agent arrives as first Protestant missionary.
1825 American Tract Society founded.
1825 Church of Scotland Mission (Presbyterian) begun.
1825 British Honduras: Methodists (MMS) begin Protestant work; 1840, British colony declared.
1825 Arabic printing of the Quran officially sanctioned after centuries of insistence that it must only be hand-copied.
1825 Bombay Missionary Union (Anglicans, Brethren, Congregationalists, Presbyterians, et alii) formed for prayer and discussion among missionaries, eventually producing principle of comity; first interdenominational regional conferences of missionaries c1855 in India, 1872 Japan, 1873 first all-India decennial conference, 1877 China, c1885 Mexico, et alia.
1826 *Cocos (Keeling) Islands.* First Christians (British settlement).
1826 Massive apostasies from Russian Orthodox missions in Volga region: 299,300 in Kazan, 95% of 14,800 new Tartar converts, 233,500 Chuvash, et alii.
1826 New Zealand: Hau Hau (Good News of Peace) syncretistic cult among Maoris; 1865, full-scale uprising against British.
1826 33 of the 38 RC bishoprics in Spanish America vacant or inactive due to reluctance of Rome to recognize state appointments.
1826 Missionary renewal in western Siberia under Eugene Kazancev, metropolitan of Tobolsk; best epoch of Russian Orthodox missions begins.
1826 Glasgow City Mission founded by David Nasmith, secretary of 23 Christian societies, first of 50 city missions begun in Britain's largest cities (Bristol, Chester, Edinburgh, Glasgow, Leeds, Liverpool, 1832 London, York, et alia); also 1833 New York City Mission, Boston, Brooklyn, etc; also 1848 Hamburg, 1874 Berlin, and 70 other German cities by 1899; also in Paris, Dublin, et alia.
1826 English writer Mary W. Shelley (1797-1851) publishes a proto science-fiction novel *The Last Man*, set in AD 2073, in which a plague wipes man off the face of the Earth.
1826 Rufus Anderson (1796-1880) ordained as evangelist and assistant secretary of American Board of Commissioners for Foreign Missions; 1832 foreign secretary, then for 48 years the acknowledged theoretician of American missionary enterprise, with extensive publications.
1827 Siegen-Dillkreis revival, western Germany.
1827 *Western Samoa.* First mission (Methodist).
1827 *American Samoa.* First mission (Methodist).
1827 Netherlands Missionary Society begins work in Celebes.
1827 J.N. Darby (1800-1882), Anglican clergyman, joins Christian Brethren movement in Dublin; propounds dogma of total premillennial apostasy and ruin of Christendom (the major churches); later develops 'dispensationalism', a new variety of futurist premillennialism, dividing biblical and later history into 7 eras or dispensations.
1828 Transkei: first Christians (Moravians).
1828 Rhenish Missionary Society (RMG) formed (Germany); begins work among Dayaks of Borneo; 1839, first Dayak baptism.
1828 Mamaia (Flock of God) cult founded in Society Islands by prophet Teau, a Christian from Panavia, protesting harsh mission destruction of paganism.
1828 England: political emancipation of Nonconformists, and 1829 of Roman Catholics.

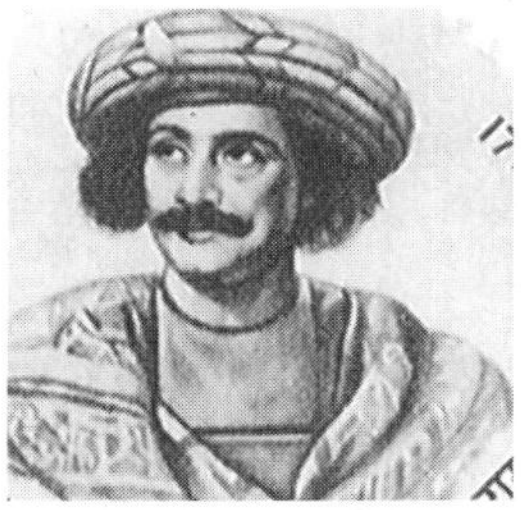

**AD 1828.** Ram Mohan Rai founds Hindu Christian body, Brahmo Samaj.

1828 Brahmo Samaj, quasi-Protestant Hindu reform movement, begun in Calcutta by Ram Mohan Rai (1772-1833).
1828 20,000 Catholic Armenians expelled from Istanbul, many executed.
1828 Karl Gutzlaff (1803-1851), a Lutheran, begins work in Indonesia, Siam, southern China, Hong Kong; 1844, attempts to evangelize China in one generation through 300 evangelists.
1829 British inventor George Stephenson (1781-1848) builds first reliable locomotive, Rocket, making large-scale commercial rail service practical.
1829 Christian Brethren begin foreign missions as A.N. Groves and party go out to Baghdad, then later to India; much later, loosely organized as Christian Missions in Many Lands; by 1965, 1,200 foreign missionaries in 55 countries.
1830 *Vanuatu* (then *New Hebrides*). First Christians (small sandalwood trading centres).
1830 Reveil (French-speaking Reformed Church awakening) sweeps Netherlands.
1830 First of numerous apparitions of Virgin Mary over next 100 years; to Catherine Laboure at Rue du Bac, Paris; then 1846 at La Salette, 1858 Lourdes, 1917 Fatima, 1931 Vicovaro (Rome), 1944 Bonate di Bergamo, 1945 Heede (Germany), 1961 Garabandal, 1990s Medugorje (Croatia), and many others.
1830 Lithuania: tsarist deportations of Roman Catholics to Siberia, including 5,000 priests and nuns; also in 1863.
c1830 Switzerland: revivals under Robert Haldane (1764-1842), C. Malan (1787-1864), F. Gaussen (1790-1863), J.H.M. D'Aubigne (1794-1872).
c1830 France: revivals under F. Monod (1794-1863), A. Monod (1802-1856).
1830 USA: widespread campaigns through professional evangelists Andrew, Barnes, Burchard, Baker, Caughey, Griffith, Inskip, Knapp, Maffit, Swan.
1830 Joseph Smith (1805-1844) at Fayette, NY (USA), has visions of incurable corruption of Christendom, and of divine restoration of Christ's church, which lead to establishment of Church of Jesus Christ of Latter-day Saints (Mormons); 1844, murdered by mob; movement migrates to Utah as headquarters of the coming millennial kingdom; subsequently evolves into massive heterodox organization unrelated to the rest of global Christianity, governed since 1844 by a Council of the Twelve Apostles; by 1988, its world mission includes 34,750 foreign missionaries (1- or 2-year termers) working in over 82 countries with annual mission budget of over US$550 million.
1830 Examples proliferate of rashly wrong future forecasts: (1) 1835, British railroad designer T. Tredgold declares: `Any general system of conveying passengers at a velocity exceeding 10 miles an hour is extremely improbable'; (2) 1837, Surveyor of British Navy, Sir William Symonds declares screw propeller useless for driving steamboats; (3) 1904, one week before Wright brothers' successful flight, New York Times ridicules notion that man could ever fly; (4) 1945, explosives expert Vannevar Bush advises US president Truman that `the atomic bomb will never go off'.
1831 Massacres of Nestorians by Kurds; also in 1843, 1846.
1831 *New Caledonia.* First mission (Tongans, from Tonga).
1831 Electromagnetic induction discovered by experimentalist M. Faraday (1791-1867), designing first dynamo and generating electric current; 1865, electromagnetic radiation discovered by physicist J.C.Maxwell (1831-1879).
1831 Killer epidemic of cholera kills 50 million in India, suddenly spreads to Britain killing 32,000 and 70,000 in second wave, before medical research traces it to drinking polluted water.
c1831 Rise of Lutheran neo-confessionalism in Germany and its separation from neo-pietism of earlier Evangelical Awakening; purely Lutheran mission societies formed including Neuendettelsau in 1841.
1831 Seminary president J.H. Rice calls Presbyterian Church in the US 'a Missionary Society, the object of which is to aid in the conversion of the world'.
1832 Tract Society of Lausanne and Eszlingen begun.
1832 American Baptist Home Missionary Society formed.
1832 London City Mission founded, largest of 50 city missions begun in Britain's largest cities (Bristol, Chester, Edinburgh, Glasgow, Leeds, Liverpool, York, et alia).
1832 Iran entered by American Board (ABCFM) as first Protestant mission, under name Mission to the Nestorians.
1832 Catholic Apostolic Church founded in London, through work of Presbyterian Edward Irving; 1836, its Twelve Apostles, claiming to be the Restored Apostolate, in England address memorandum to all rulers of Europe warning them of imminent Second Advent of Christ, but are met with total apathy; by 1988, church is almost extinct.
1833 Slavery abolished in British empire: owners of 700,000 freed slaves compensated.
1833 Church of Greece proclaims its autocephality in defiance of Ecumenical Patriarchate of Constantinople; latter eventually recognizes it in 1850.
1833 *Lesotho* (then *Basutoland*). First mission (Paris Mission, PEMS).
1834 Religious orders in Portugal suppressed.
1834 Refrigerator invented and manufactured by J. Perkin, USA.
1834 Tolpuddle Martyrs: 6 Christian men (5 Methodists) form an early farm-workers' trade union, but are then deported as convicts to Australia.
1834 Persia and Turkey: 150,000 Nestorians (99% illiterate), with 2 rival patriarchs Abraham Mar Shimon (Urmia) and Mar Elias (Mosul).
1835 Finland: the Osterbottenvackelse, evangelical awakening in the west, active for 15 years; also revival under Lutheran pastor L.L. Laestadius (1800-1861).
1835 Attempt to eradicate Christianity in Madagascar by queen Ranavalona I (1800-1861); large numbers of Christians killed from 1835 to 1861.

1835 Swedish Missionary Society founded.
1835 Electric telegraphy invented by Samuel Morse (1791-1872); 1838, develops morse code; telegraph comes into service.
1835 Belgian statistician-astronomer Lambert Quetelet (1796-1874) adopts Laplace probability theory to produce crucial concepts of 'average man' and 'moral statistics'.
1835 Invention of revolver by S. Colt; 1,000 built for US Army.
1836 *Wallis & Futuna Islands.* First mission (French Marist priests).
1836 Leipzig Evangelical Lutheran Mission formed (Germany).
1836 Beginning of Orthodox mission among Koluschans (Tlingits) of Sitka island.
1836 Booklet produced by ABCFM: 'The Duty of the Present Generation to Evangelize the World: An Appeal from the Missionaries at the Sandwich Islands to their Friends in the United States'.
1836 T.S. Skinner publishes *Thoughts on evangelizing the world* (New York).
1836 Sri Ramakrishna (1836-1886) born, Bengali Sakta saint, guru of Swami Vivekananda; stresses *bhakti* dimension of Sakta Universalism.
1837 *Kiribati*, or *Gilbert Islands.* First Christians (European trading centre).
1837 Great Awakening in Hawaii, a remarkable revival with mass conversions until 1843: 27,000 Protestant adult converts (20% of population).
1837 British Post Office carries 88 million pieces of mail a year; 1840, Roland Hill introduces mass prepaid adhesive penny post for any distance; by 1960, 10 billion pieces a year (USA 355 pieces of domestic mail per citizen per year); by 1990, 260 billion a year worldwide.
1837 Board of Foreign Missions, Presbyterian Church in the USA established 'to aid in the conversion of the world... every member of this church is a member for life of said society and bound to do all in his power for the accomplishment of this object'; 1958, becomes Commission on Ecumenical Mission and Relations, for which 'The supreme and controlling aim of the Christian Mission to the world is to make the Lord Jesus Christ known to all men... in which Christians of all lands share in evangelizing the world and permeating all of life with the spirit and truth of Christ.'
1837 ABCFM mission strategist Rufus Anderson (1796-1880) restores apostolic model for mission; in essay 'The Time for the World's Conversion Come', first published in 1837 journal, argues that the churches are now, for the first time ever in history (as a result of rise of voluntary mission societies), adequately organized to complete the conversion of the world.
1838 Turkey: small-scale revivals among Armenians in Nicomedia and (1841) Adabazar, through ABCFM (USA); and later in Aintab and Aleppo.
1838 Tenrikyo (Religion of Divine Wisdom), a Shinto/Christian amalgam, founded in Japan as first of the Shinto Shukyo (New Religious Movements).
1839 New Hebrides: LMS missionary pioneer John Williams (1796-1839) martyred on island of Eromanga; Catholic missionaries also arrive, but systematic missions not begun until 1887.
1839 Scottish Highlands Awakening for 4 years: Oban, islands, also Lowlands.
1839 Martyrs of Korea: 81 RC martyrs killed 1839-46 including vicar apostolic, Korean priest A. Kim, foreign priests and laity.
1839 First edition of *Statistica delle Missioni Straniere*, published in Rome, irregularly thereafter.
1840 Revolutionaries in Philippines: Confraternity of St Joseph founded by Tagalogs to seize autonomy; crushed by Spaniards, who kill 'king of the Tagalogs' Apolinario De la Cruz (1815-1841); 1872, 3 priests shot; 1896, Jose Rizal executed.
1840 French Roman Catholic priest and patrologist J.P. Migne (1800-1875) founds publishing house to publish all Catholic literature cheaply, including Greek and Latin Fathers as *Patrologiae cursus completus*: Series Graeca (162 volumes, Paris, 1857-66), and Series Latina (221 volumes, Paris, 1844-90).
c1840 Dispensationalism arises in Britain under J. N. Darby, later spreads in North America led by R.A. Torrey (1856-1928), J.M. Gray (1851-1925), C.I. Scofield (1843-1921), W.J. Erdman (1833-1923), A.C. Dixon (1854-1925), and A.J. Gordon (1836-1895); emphasis on inerrancy of Bible as a test of true faith.
1841 Hong Kong: First missions (Catholic, Anglican, Baptist).
1841 Edinburgh Medical Missionary Society founded in Scotland.
1841 UK: 22,000 converted over 7 years through preaching of James Caughey of New York.
1841 Martyrdom of père P.M. Chanel on Futuna; first RC martyr in Oceania.
1841 Founding of Anglican Jerusalem Bishopric: Michael Solomon Alexander, former Chief Rabbi of Plymouth (UK), consecrated as first Anglican Bishop in Jerusalem.
1841 CMS general secretary Henry Venn (1796-1873) requires all missionaries to complete annual questionnaires recording church growth statistics, as a means of monitoring progress in world evangelization; propounds 'three-self' goal of mission that local churches must become self-supporting, self-governing, self-propagating.
1842 First photograph printed in a newspaper, in London.
1842 Treaty of Nanking, following Opium War, cedes Hong Kong to Britain and opens territory to missions.
1842 Gossner Mission Society begun in Berlin.
1842 Revival spreads through state church of Norway; Norwegian Mission Society (Stavanger) begun.
1842 Dahomey: MMS (UK) missionaries arrive at Fon kingdom, Abomey; 120 years later, Fon work still barely begun.
1842 A Japanese translates *Life of Jesus* from Dutch; arrested, kills self.
1842 Date for end of Europe by deluge as predicted by Elizabethan astrologer John Dee (1527-1608); mobs take to boats to escape.
1842 Turks and Kurds massacre 20,000 Nestorians near river Zab, then enslave remaining 50,000.
1842 Lutheran missionary in South Africa H.P.S. Schreuder (1817-1882) writes Oslo university treatise entitled 'A Few Words to the Church of Norway on Christian Obligation to be concerned about the Salvation of Non-Christian Fellow Men'.
1843 Great Peaceful Heavenly Kingdom (Tai Ping Tien Kueh: Society of Worshippers of the True God/Celestial Kingdom of Great Peace) begun in China as quasi-Christian sect with Hakka founder Hung Hsiu-chuan (1814-1864) and leaders strongly influenced by New Testament; 1853, rebels capture Nanking, rule south China; appeal to Protestant missions (ABFMS, LMS) to guide them, but ignored; 1862, suppressed, 35 million killed; 1864, fall of Nanking and suicide of Hung; third great missed opportunity to win China to Christianity.
1843 Hermannsburg revival in western Germany.
1843 20,000 Nestorians massacred in Kurdistan by Muslim Kurds.

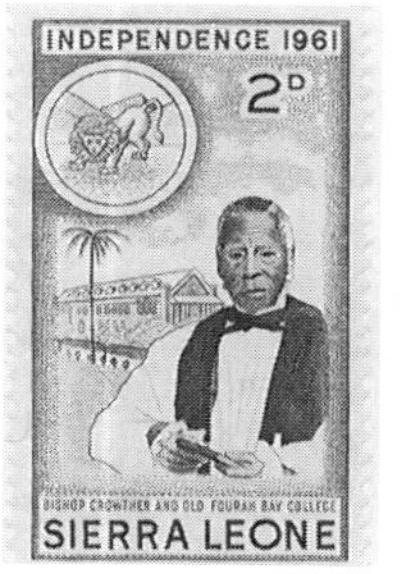


**AD 1843.** Samuel Crowther, first non-European Anglican bishop, works in West Africa.

1843 Sierra Leonian former slave Samuel Crowther (c1806-1891) sent as missionary to Nigeria; 1864, consecrated as first non-European Anglican bishop.
1843 Goanese (Roman Catholic) schism in Goa, India; 600 untrained Indians ordained; lasts until 1886 when pope Leo XIII elevates Goa to patriarchate; later Latin-rite schism, Independent Catholic Church of Ceylon, Goa and India, exists until 1950.
1843 USA: Black slave, evangelist and reformer Sojourner Truth (Isabella van Wagener, c1797-1883) begins itinerant ministry across USA stressing abolitionism and women's rights.
1843 Outstanding woman missionary and crusader for women's rights, Fidelia Fiske, begins with ABCFM in Persia.
1844 CMS missionary J.L. Krapf (1810-1881) first to begin modern missionary work in Kenya; wife and child die of malaria in Mombasa.
1844 Persia: revival among Nestorians around ABCFM station Urumiah; other revivals in 1849, 1850.
1844 Karl Marx writes: 'Religion is the sigh of the oppressed creature... the opium of the people'.
1844 Origins of Baha'i World Faith under Sayyid Ali Muhammed (Bab al-Din, 1819-1850) in Persia, especially under chief prophet Baha'u'llah (1817-1892) and son Abdul-Baha (1844-1921); many in Western world predict emergence in 20th century of a single unified world faith, but hopes dashed by resurgence of great world religions.
1844 Patagonian Missionary Society (later, South American Missionary Society, SAMS) founded.
1844 Date for Second Advent of Christ as predicted in 1818 by Baptist prophet William Miller (1782-1849) in USA; from 1840, several dates announced in 1843-4; afterwards, Seventh-day Adventist denomination emerges, interprets date as return of Christ to Earth for 'cleansing of the sanctuary'; 1860, General Conference of Seventh-day Adventists formed in USA 'committed to the task of giving to all nations God's last invitation to prepare for the Second Advent of Christ', and envisioning 'a worldwide proclamation of the gospel to every nation and kindred and tongue and people (Revelation 14:6)'; by 1985, in 210 countries (68 countries being served by 1,052 USA foreign missionaries).
1844 Christadelphians (Brothers of Christ) founded by John Thomas (1805-1871) in Birmingham (UK), London, USA; pacifist, adventist, premillennialist, unitarian, congregational (1,530 churches called ecclesias), no clergy; holding conditional immortality, and an imminent Millennium with Jesus reigning in Jerusalem; 90,600 adherents in 1985.
1844 First Young Men's Christian Association (YMCA) founded, by George Williams (1821-1905) and Evangelicals in London; 1855, World Alliance of YMCAs founded in Paris (France), with headquarters in Geneva, emphasizing 'extension of His Kingdom'; world vision, lay witness to Christ, global missionary thrust; 1855, YWCA, united in 1877; 1894, World YWCA for women; subsequently, concerns broaden; 1988, 6.5 million men members in 74 National YMCA Movements and in 16 other countries; and 5 million women members.
1844 German New Testament textual critic K. von Tischendorf (1815-1874) scours Middle East and in 1844 and 1859 discovers in Mount Sinai monastery Codex Sinaiticus (written AD c350), publishes it in 1862; his full NT critical apparatus (8th edition, 3 volumes 1869-1894) becomes standard authority for all NT scholarship and translations.
1845 *Solomon Islands.* First missionaries (Marists, with bishop Epalle killed on landing).
1845 *Cameroon.* First mission (Baptist Missionary Society, UK).
1845 Potato blight from America devastates Ireland, with a million killed by famine and typhus, resulting in another million Irish migrating to Britain, USA and Australia, markedly influencing development of Catholicism there.
1845 Oxford Movement in England: 60 prominent Anglicans and 250 clergy enter Church of Rome by 1862.
1845 Gossner Mission begins work among Kol aboriginals in India.
1845 Lebanon: Druzes kill 12,000 Maronites in 15 years up to 'Massacres of the Sixties', leaving 100,000 homeless.
1845 Germany: Deutschkatholizismus, a schism ex Roman Catholicism, begun by degraded priests J. Ronge and J. Czerski; Deutsche-Katholische Kirche gains 80,000 adherents, becomes rationalist, 1850 unites with Free churches.
1845 Southern Baptist Convention, largest USA Baptist denomination, comes into being in reaction against ABFMS refusing to accept slave-owners as missionaries; based from its origin on global mission, it founds Board of Domestic Missions (later, Home Mission Board) and Foreign Mission Board, beginning work in China, then 1846 Liberia and 1850 Nigeria; by 1988, has 7,000 full-time professional missionaries at home and abroad, by 1994 10,000.
1846 Mormons under Brigham Young (1801-1877) leave Nauvoo City for Great Salt Lake; 1847, Salt Lake City founded.
1846 *Niue Island.* First missionaries (a returning Niuean, and a Samoan).
1846 La Salette apparition of Mary states: 'Antichrist will be born of a Jewish nun, father a bishop'.
1846 Beginnings of world conciliarism: Evangelical Alliance formed in London by 800 Christians representing 52 confessions, to further unity among Evangelicals worldwide; national alliances then formed in Britain and Canada (1846), Sweden and Germany (1847), India (1849), Turkey (1855), USA (1867); and international conferences held in London 1851, Paris 1855, Berlin 1857, Geneva 1861, Amsterdam 1867, New York 1873, Basel 1879, Copenhagen 1884, Florence 1891, London 1896 and the final one in 1907; 1912, title officially changed to World's Evangelical Alliance (WEA).
1846 Great Kazakh Horde comes under Russian rule.
1847 Latin patriarchate of Jerusalem restored.
1847 USA: Lutheran Church-Missouri Synod organized, with 22 pastors and under 2,000 members; widespread success in ministry to immigrants; by 1922, 1,564 pastors and over 1 million members; by 1970, 2.9 million in USA.
1847 'The light of Christ illuminates the whole world'—last words of Macarius Glukharev, apostle to the Altai (1792-1847).
1847 5th major persecution of Catholics in Annam, followed by others in 1851, 1856, 1884.
1847 Private missionary work among Koriak and Chukchi in Anadyr district of Siberia by Orthodox priests.

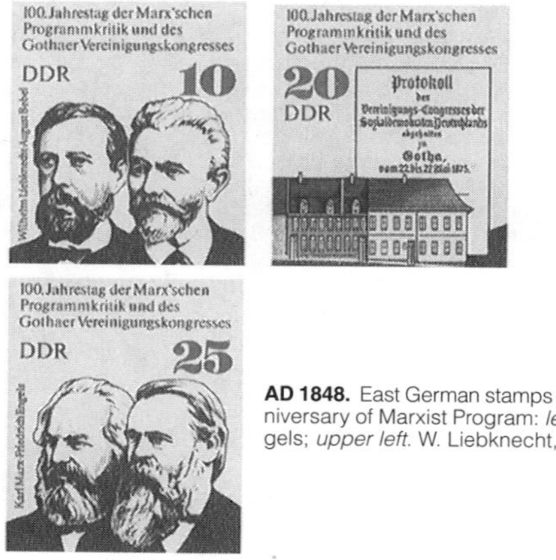


**AD 1848.** East German stamps on 100th Anniversary of Marxist Program: *left.* Marx, Engels; *upper left.* W. Liebknecht, A. Bebel.

1848 German philosopher Karl Marx (1818-1883) and German businessman Friedrich Engels (1820-1895) publish *Communist Manifesto*, predicting collapse of capitalism, and calling for violent overthrow of established order including religion; 1867, Marx's *Das Kapital*.

1848 First women's-rights convention held at Seneca Falls, New York (July 19-20) by American feminists Lucretia Mott (1793-1880) and Elizabeth Cady Stanton (1815-1902).

1848 Birth of Spiritualism (spiritism, medium religion) in USA; 1893, organized as National Spiritualist Association of Churches of the USA.

1848 Plymouth Brethren (Christian Brethren) in UK split into Open Brethren and Exclusive Brethren.

1848 First Katholikentag held, in Mainz.

1848 Germany: founding of many evangelistic societies, including Evangelische Gesellschaft fur Deutschland, 1850 Evangelical Brotherhood, 1852 Society for Itinerant Preachers, 1857 Society for Home Missions, 1863 Herborn-Dillenburg Society, 1864 Nassau Colporteur Society, 1878 Evangelical Brotherhood of the Reich for Furthering Evangelism and Evangelical Fellowship, 1886 Home Mission Society of Hesse.

c1848 Disappearance of all religion by 1870 predicted by French libertarian socialist and anarchist P.-J. Proudhon (1809-1865) on grounds it represents last vestiges of savagehood and barbarism.

1848 First interdenominational missionary conference, in Madras, agrees to prohibit baptism to any who refuse to break caste.

1848 Eastern Orthodox Great Synod (Greek/Arab/Russian), though not counted as an Ecumenical Council; similar Great Synod again in 1872.

1849 Scottish explorer and medical missionary to Botswana David Livingstone (1813-1873) sets off north across Kalahari Desert, discovers Zambezi river (1851) as well as Victoria Falls (1855).

1849 An estimated 50,000 slaves per year are being smuggled from Africa to Cuba, Brazil, and other countries.

1849 Charles G. Finney (1792-1875) conducts evangelistic campaigns in Britain, 1849-51 and 1859-61.

1849 Boolean algebra, which later becomes useful in computer science, is developed by Englishman George Boole (1815-64).

1849 Ludwigsburg evangelists' school founded in Germany; 1856, moved to Krischenhardthof.

1849 Thailand: all foreign missionaries ordered out.

1849 Brazil: total Black slaves from Africa 5.5 million over period 1550-1850.

1849 Moravian work among Miskitos of Nicaragua begun.

1850 **Global status:** 61 generations after Christ, world is 26.9% Christians (85.2% of them being Whites), 33.4% evangelized; with printed Scriptures available in 205 languages.

1850 Cult of the Holy Cross, Yucatan (Mexico).

1850 London city reaches population of 2.3 million, 4.2 million by 1875, and 6.5 million by 1900, at which time 19 other metropolises in world also exceed 1 million each.

1850 Hindu mystic Ramakrishna (Gadadhar Chatterji, 1836-1886) in Bengal preaches universal religion and unity of all religions, claims to have seen Jesus after studying Christianity; 1897, Ramakrishna Mission founded in Calcutta by Swami Vivekananda (1862-190 (1862-1902).

1850 Orthodox missions along Yenisei river around Turuchansk among Tunguz, Yakuts and Samoyeds.

1850 *Orissa and its evangelization* published by A. Sutton, first detailed study of status of missions (in India).

1850 Charles Adams publishes *Evangelism in the middle of the Nineteenth Century*.

1850 World's 10 largest cities: London 2,320,000, Peking 1,648,000, Paris 1,314,000, Canton 800,000, Istanbul 785,000, Hangchow 700,000, New York 682,000, Bombay 575,000, Yedo 567,000, Soochow 550,000.

c1850 *British Indian Ocean Territory*. First Christians, from Mauritius; now called Ilois (Islanders), Creoles.

c1850 General Beckwith, an Anglo-Saxon evangelical, advises Waldensians 'Evangelize or perish', after which they cease being isolationist.

1850 English mathematician John Taylor demonstrates Great Pyramid of Cheops contains divine prophecy covering all history; 1865, pyramidologist Robert Menzies shows internal passages form a chronological outline.

1850 Death of French nurse and nun Bertine Bouquillon from St Omer (France) after predicting: 'The end of time is near and Antichrist will not delay his coming.'

1850 British Quaker millionaire and missions philanthropist Robert Arthington (1823-1900) donates millions to missionary societies and accumulates vast store of information on frontier evangelization of all peoples in world; 1900, his will expounds global strategy of (a) do a world survey of unreached peoples, (b) supply these peoples with translations of Luke, John and Acts, (c) teach 10 people in each tribe to read the gospel, (d) visit each tribe until a church emerges, (e) that tribe evangelizes the next, while (f) missionaries move on to regions beyond; Arthington is later followed by long series of eccentric millionaire philanthropist-strategists in Europe and USA.

1851 Spanish concordat with Holy See.

1851 England & Wales: first (and only) state Census of Religious Worship; 61% of entire population attend church every Sunday, many twice each Sunday.

1851 Edict of Tu Duc (1829-1883) of Viet Nam, following French intervention (1843); persecution of Christians results in death of 115 priests and 90,000 Catholics, and in 1884 French declaration of protectorate over territory.

1851 Tierra del Fuego: 15 SAMS missionaries including founder Allen Gardiner massacred or starved to death.

1851 Colombia: persecution of Catholic Church.

1851 French sociologist A. Comte (1798-1857) publishes 4-volume *Système de politique positive*, holding that eventually war will disappear and all of humankind will unite in a single global republic; one of most important and influential studies of the future ever written.

1851 First major world fair and exhibition, Crystal Palace Exposition in London, followed by 1855 Paris, 1876 Philadelphia, 1893 and 1933 Chicago, 1939 and 1964 New York, 1958 Brussels, 1967 Montreal, 1970 Osaka, and 30 others coordinated since 1928 by Bureau des Expositions, Paris; about 850 general and 900 specialized commercial fairs held annually.

1851 First all-India census of missions in Indian subcontinent of 150 millions: 91,092 Protestant converts (14,681 adult communicants), in 267 churches, 21 ordained Indian ministers, 339 ordained missionaries in 19 large missionary societies and some smaller ones; 1861, 138,731 Protestants (75% former outcaste, low caste, or tribal) including 50,500 Anglicans, and 725,746 Roman Catholics.

1851 India experiences rapid church growth by mass movements: 1851, 1,272,000 Christians (1 million Catholics, 180,000 non-Catholic Syrians, 91,000 Protestants including Anglicans); 1881, 1,862,000; 1901, 150,000 Anglicans and 200,000 Protestants in 10 major denominations with 45 mission agencies, 925,000 Syrian Christians (500,000 Uniates, 300,000 Jacobites, 125,000 Mar Thoma Reformed); 1911, 1,617,000 Protestants and Anglicans, 2,223,000 Catholics, 225,000 Orthodox Jacobites, 76,000 Reformed Orthodox Mar Thoma, 14,000 Nestorians.

1852 Canada: Anglican church separated from state.

1852 Society for Itinerant Preachers founded in Germany.

c1852 Chinese Evangelization Society begun by Gutzlaff (Netherlands Mission).

1852 Danish writer Hans Christian Andersen (1805-1875) publishes *Foedrelandet*, speculating on tourists of the future—young Americans in flying machines.

1852 Charles MacKay publishes *Memoirs of extraordinary popular delusions and the madness of crowds* (London) stating 'In the year 999, the number of pilgrims proceeding eastward, to await the coming of the Lord in Jerusalem was so great that they were compared to a desolating army.'

1853 Crimean War: Great Britain joins with France and other powers to block Russian invasion of declining Ottoman Empire; major warfare until 1856.

1853 Norway: first Home Mission (Indremisjon) begun within state church.

1853 David Livingstone (1813-1873) of LMS passes through Zambia on way to Luanda; 1857, publishes *Missionary travels and researches in South Africa*.

1853 Catholic hierarchy reestablished in Netherlands.

1853 Open Air Mission founded (UK).

1853 Belgian statistician Adolphe Quetelet (1796-1874) convenes world's first International Statistical Congress.

1853 England: period of High Church evangelism under Anglo-Catholic clergy R. Aitken (1800-1878), Hay Aitken, R. Twigg, G.H. Wilkinson (1833-1907), Benson, Herbert, Mackonochie, Stanton, Dolling, A.J. Mason (1851-1928).

1854 Protestants in Dutch East Indies formed into a single state-controlled Church of the Indies.

1854 First Union Missionary Convention (First International Missionary Conference), in New York, USA, guided by Alexander Duff (1806-1878): 'To what extent are we authorized by the Word of God to expect the conversion of the world to Christ?'; similar conference held in London, England; 1867, Duff appointed to first chair of evangelism and evangelical theology at New College, Edinburgh.

1854 Foreign Mission Committee, Canada Presbyterian Synod, inaugurated; 1962, becomes Board of World Mission, United Church of Canada, 'committed by its very nature to a global mission'.

1854 Swiss theologian J.J. Herzog publishes first great religious encyclopedia: *Real-Encyklopadie für protestantische Theologie und Kirche* (1854-1868).

1854 Second SAMS party including Gardiner's son killed by natives.

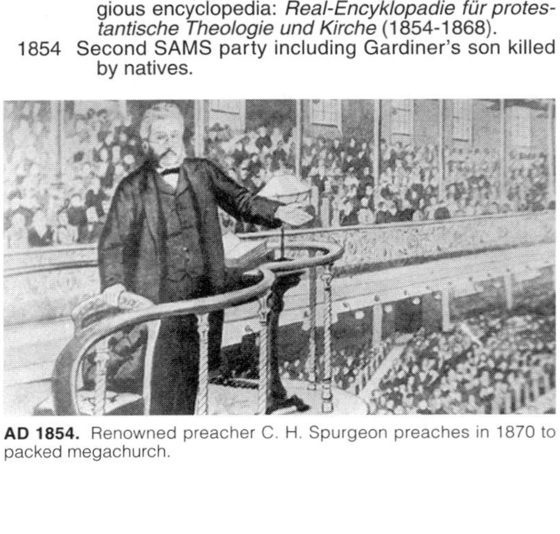

**AD 1854.** Renowned preacher C. H. Spurgeon preaches in 1870 to packed megachurch.

1854 Baptist preacher C. H. Spurgeon (1834-1892) begins 38-year ministry in Southwark, London, 1859 builds vast Metropolitan Tabernacle (6,000 congregation), adds 14,692 members to the church.

1855 East Africa: 20,000 Black slaves a year exported by Arabs.

1855 YMCA Conference, Paris, adopts 'Paris Basis' as movement's declaration of faith; 1878, World's Alliance of YMCAs sets up permanent executive in Geneva; 1975, 6 million members.

1855 Ethiopia: emperor Theodore II persecutes Roman Catholics.

1855 Field conferences of Protestant foreign missionaries commence: 1855-1863, 3 in North India; 1858-1900, 3 in South India; 4 for All-India, 1873-1902; 3 for China held in Shanghai, 1877-1907; 4 for Japan, 1872-1900; 3 for South Africa, 1904-1909; 2 in Mexico City 1888, 1897.

c1855 Russian surge of world mission: Orthodox missiologist N.I. Ilminsky (1821-1891) works out scientific basis for missionary work; vast missionary expansion; 1870-1917, Orthodox Missionary Society organized (St Petersburg, Russia); 1917, its world mission is destroyed by Bolshevik Revolution.

1855 Main period of migration of Muslim peoples from Russian empire to Ottoman empire, lasting 30 years.

1856 Stonemason Grunewald spreads gospel using colporteurs in western Germany.

1856 Sweden: Evangeliska Fosterlands-Stiftelsen founded within state church.

1856 Protestant mission begun among Yamanas of Tierra del Fuego.

1856 Orientalist Max Muller (1823-1900) establishes history of religions with *Essay on Comparative Mythology*; myths arise from natural phenomena; 1875, founds science of comparative religion by beginning 51-volume series *The sacred books of the East*.

1857 Mass secession from Roman Catholic Church in Mexico leads to formation of Iglesia de Jesus, ultimately becoming Episcopal Church of Mexico.

1857 Society for Home Preachers in Schleswig-Holstein (Germany) formed.

1857 Evangelical Awakening in USA (under C.G. Finney et alii; in northern states only; one million converts in 2 years), spreading to Europe and the other 4 continents (1859 India, 1860 China).

1857 USA: massive spontaneous wave of fervent evangelism by laymen sweeps Northern states, also sweeps through Southern armies (with 150,000 conversions including many generals), until both are dissipated by 1861 Civil War.

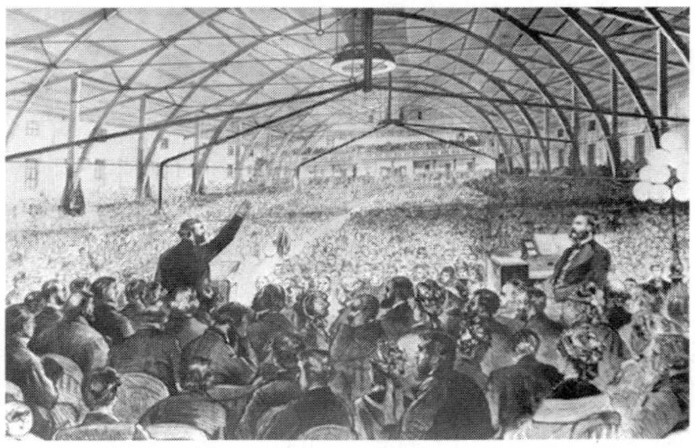

**AD 1857.** Evangelist Moody preaches to 100 million and personally counsels 750,000 in 42 years.

1857 USA: evangelist D.L. Moody (1837-1899), a Congregationalist, evolves organized mass evangelism in Chicago; during his lifetime estimated to have preached to 100 million and to have had individual evangelistic personal dealings with 750,000 persons; perfects methods of preparation and publicity in cooperative city campaigns, use of theaters and tents, finance committees; other evangelists R.A. Torrey (1856-1928), Billy Sunday (1862-1925), Robert P. Wilder (1863-1938); beginnings of large-scale lay-centered evangelism.

1858 Apparition of Virgin Mary at Lourdes, France, with site subsequently becoming a world-famous Catholic pilgrimage and healing centre.

1858 India: first of over 150 attempts to establish indigenous Hindu-Christian movements or churches: Hindu Church of the Lord Jesus (Tinnevelly).

1858 David Livingstone begins exploration of Zambezi and Shire rivers, attracting others to begin missionary work in Nyasaland.

1858 Townsend treaty between USA and Japan opens Japan to Christian missionaries; 1859, first Catholic, Episcopalian and Protestant missionaries arrive.

1858 Religious freedom and impartiality in India proclaimed by queen Victoria (1819-1901): 'Relying ourselves on the truth of Christianity... we have no desire to impose our convictions on any of our subjects'.

1858 India: now over one million Roman Catholics, 100,000 Protestants and Anglicans.

1858 China: new phase for Russian Orthodoxy: agreement of Tien-Tsin gives Russia permission to evangelize without hindrance; monk Isaias Polikin preaches in Chinese; 1884, Mitrophen Tsi ordained as first Chinese priest; but by 1900 still only a handful of missionaries, and 200 believers; 1900, in Boxer rebellion 260 Chinese Christians and one priest martyred, all churches destroyed.

c1858 Johnston Island: first Christians (USA guano-digging company).

1858 Sermons on evangelization increase: 1858 J. Parker publishes 'The duty of the present generation of Christians to evangelize the world', New York; 1866 C. Dickson publishes 'The duty of the Church to evangelize the World', Presbyterian Church of the USA, New York.

1858 Turkey (population 15 million) has 4 million Christians: 2 million Armenian Apostolic (Gregorians), 1 million Greek Orthodox, 640,000 RCs (180,000 in Maronite and 2 Uniate churches), 240,000 Syrian Orthodox (Jacobites), 60,000 Nestorians, 2,000 Protestants.

1858 China signs Treaty of Tientsin opening 5 ports to foreign trade; Protestant and Catholic missionaries flood into China; also, Japan signs treaty with Britain opening Japan to British commerce and missionaries.

1858 'Annus mirabilis' of foreign missions, a global turning point due to (a) 2nd Evangelical Awakening, and (b) world east of Suez opens to Western foreign missionaries, who then pour into China (Treaty of Tientsin opens 5 ports), Japan (trade treaty), and India (East India Company ends ties to British government).

AD 1858. Complete Bible published in Maori language.

1858 New Zealand: Bible published in Maori language.

1859 Second Evangelical Awakening in Britain, reaching over 3 million with 1.1 million converts: 100,000 in Wales, 300,000 in Scotland, 100,000 in Ulster, over 500,000 in England.

1859 Books set in the future proliferate after publication of Charles Darwin's *Origin of the Species* (explaining evolution as resulting solely from natural selection and battle for existence, with all life developing from a single source): before 1801, only 7 titles published in Britain; 1801-1859, 20 published; 1860-1900, 230 published; origin of science fiction dates back to Industrial Revolution.

1859 Founding of Society of St Francis de Sales (Salesians of Don Bosco, SDB), a religious congregation dedicated to Christian education of youth across world; by 1975, 18,426 men in 1,524 houses; by 1983, 16,982 in 1,466 houses; also 17,269 Salesian Sisters (FMA).

1860 Korea: Chondogyo (Religion of the Heavenly Way), a blend of shamanistic, Buddhist, Confucian and Christian elements, emerges as a reaction against Western, especially Catholic, influence.

1860 Revival in Ukraine; 1884-1904, persecution of Evangelicals.

1860 Massacre of 11,000 wealthy Christians by Druzes in Damascus; France intervenes.

1860 Liverpool Conference on Missions, as aftermath of 1859 Awakening in UK; 126 attenders; first major world missionary conference; texts Matthew 28.18-20, 24.14, Luke 24.46-7.

c1860 *Togo*. First Christians (Methodist immigrants from Gold Coast).

c1860 Revival in South Africa erupts under Dutch Reformed moderator Andrew Murray (1828-1917), sweeping Afrikaner churches.

c1860 Netherlands: revivals under G. van Prinsterer (c1800-1867), A. Kuyper (1837-1920).

1860 Earl of Shaftesbury, British evangelical social reformer (A.A. Cooper, 1801-1885), states: 'Those who hold the truth have the means enough, knowledge enough, and opportunity enough, to evangelize the globe fifty times over'.

1860 Reorganized Church of Jesus Christ of Latter Day Saints begun in schism by LDS founder's son, operating through a rival Council of the Twelve Apostles; 1954, publishes *Into all the world*: Council of Twelve missionary report; 1975, branches in 28 nations (HQ Independence, MO), 1986 in 37 countries.

c1860 Bengali ascetic Paramahamsar Ramakrishna (1836-1886) promotes simple life, nonsectarian Neo-Hinduism, and religious universalism ('All religions are the same').

c1860 ABUV Bible (with incomplete OT) published by American Baptists, with 'baptized' replaced by 'immersed'; 1912, Improved Bible Union Version.

1861 Great Christian Revival (Great Awakening) in Jamaica, resulting in rapid spread of Native Baptist Church (now Revival Zion); wild dancing, trances.

1861 *Tuvalu* (then *Ellice Islands*). First Christians (Samoan pastors of the LMS).

1861 *Tokelau Island*. First mission (LMS).

1861 Cornish Revivals, in Britain for 2 years.

1861 110 North American Blacks settle in Haiti and establish Episcopal Church.

1861 Universities Mission to Central Africa (UMCA) begun in Britain.

1861 Madagascar: after 25 years' vicious persecution,

Christians found to have multiplied twenty-fold.

1861 Batak church in Sumatra (HKBP) grows from 52 Christians (1866) to 2,056 (1876), 7,500 (1881), 103,525 (1911), 380,000 (1941), 1,044,382 (1970), 1,160,000 (1976), and to 1,500,000 (1983).

1861 Russian Orthodox monk Nicolai (Ivan Kasatkin, 1836-1912) arrives in Japan, 1868 baptizes 3 converts, 1880 made bishop and 1906 archbishop in Tokyo; dies after 51 years in Japan with over 30,000 converts made; most successful Russian Orthodox mission among non-Christians outside Russia.

1861 USA: 620,000 killed, mostly by disease, in 1861-65 Civil War between North and South over slavery issue.

1861 Egypt: Coptic patriarch Cyril IV poisoned as part of continuous Ottoman pressure on Coptic church.

1861 USA: Woman's Union Missionary Society of America for Heathen Lands (WUMSA) formed in New York as pioneer women's sending society, with 40 other women's societies arising later.

1862 *Djibouti*. First Christians (French colonists).

1862 Methodist Society, a Fanti schism ex Wesleyan Methodists near Cape Coast, Gold Coast.

1862 Orthodox mission begun around Amur river (Siberia) among Gold and Gilyak peoples.

1862 Shensi province, China: terrible Muslim Rebellion (1862-78) kills 600,000, then drought and famine kill another 5 million.

1862 Founding of Congregation of Immaculate Heart of Mary (Scheutists, CICM) with as goal 'Evangelizzazione dei popoli'; by 1983, 1,507 members in 53 houses; over the years many Scheutist missionaries have been martyred.

1863 Samoa: syncretistic cult begun by local preacher Siovili; vast crowds.

1863 Scandinavian missionary societies convene in first of several Northern Lutheran Missions Conferences.

1863 Universal Catholic Church (later renamed New Apostolic Church) founded in Germany by excommunicated German prophet H. Geyer of Catholic Apostolic Church (UK), emphasizing a successional apostolate subject to a chief apostle with quasi-papal powers, and the gifts of the Holy Spirit including prophecy, tongues, miraculous healing, sacraments, hierarchy of 48 living Apostles; by 1988, has 1.7 million members worldwide (mainly Germans) in 45 countries; cooperates with no other church.

1863 French science-fiction forecaster Jules Verne (1828-1905) writes *Five weeks in a balloon*, followed by 60 books including in 1864 a futuristic novel, *Journey to the Centre of the Earth*; 1865, writes *From the Earth to the Moon*, describing imaginary lunar voyage, accurately predicting high speed necessary to leave Earth's atmosphere, forecasting launch would be made from Florida, with 3 astronauts, who on return would splash down in ocean (all fulfilled in 1969); 1870, *Twenty thousand leagues under the sea*; in other works predicts flight, submarines, aqualungs, television.

1863 1st International Postal Conference, held in Paris, France.

1864 USA: first Greek Orthodox church organized in New Orleans, Louisiana.

1864 Russian novelist F.M. Dostoyevsky (1821-1881) writes *Notes from the underground*, admitting that humans will always overturn any utopian paradise where things work perfectly.

1865 War of the Triple Alliance, bloody 5-year war between Paraguay and allied Brazil, Argentina, and Uruguay: one million killed.

1865 Bhutan: first Christians for 240 years (British troops).

1865 From 1820-65, nearly 2 million Roman Catholics from Ireland emigrate to USA.

AD 1865. CIM founder J. Hudson Taylor (*left*) in 1905 with Griffith John, LMS, and American Presbyterian W.A.P. Martin (*right*).

1865 China Inland Mission (CIM) founded as faith mission by J. Hudson Taylor (1832-1905); 1950, renamed Overseas Missionary Fellowship (OMF).

1865 Origins of Social Gospel in American Protestantism; lasts 50 years up to its demise in 1915.

1865 International Telecommunication Union (ITU)

founded; 1947, becomes a specialized agency of United Nations, with headquarters in Geneva; over 135 member countries.

1865 Japan: first Catholic missionaries permitted to work since 1635 discover 100,000 Hidden Christians (Kakure Kirishitan) survivors, but only 14,000 agree to rejoin Catholic Church.

1865 German physicist R. Clausius introduces concept of entropy (a measure of the disorder of a system, hence = chaos).

1865 Christian Revival Association (1878, renamed Salvation Army) founded by Methodist evangelist William Booth in England for urban social outreach and street evangelism; 1985, 4,226,900 Salvationists in 75 countries, with vast social service and evangelistic activities and institutions; overriding first agenda defined in 1987 by SA general as 'To emphasize the supremacy of evangelism in fulfilling of the Lord's great commission... To work to the end that every man and woman and child has the opportunity to hear the good news of the gospel'.

1865 French encyclopedist P.-A. Larousse publishes *Grand Dictionnaire universel du XIXe siècle*, which appears from 1865-1890.

1866 Continental European Missions Conference (CEMC; also named the Ausschuss) holds first meeting in Bremen (Germany); 11 other Bremen conferences by 1909; 1910, merges with Edinburgh world missionary conference.

1866 Severe persecution of Korea's 25,000 Catholics; 10,000 Koreans martyred, including 2 bishops and 7 priests.

1866 Keshab Chandra Sen (1838-1884), Hindu reformer, founds Brahmo Samaj of India, radical offshoot of Adi Brahmo Samaj of Ram Mohan Roy.

1866 First successful submarine cable across Atlantic ocean.

1867 Midway Islands: first Christians (USA).

1867 Anglican Church ceases to be state religion in Ireland.

1867 Finland: crop failure kills 8% of population.

AD 1867. Camp meetings for teaching on personal holiness sweep across America.

1867 USA: first national holiness camp-meeting, in Vineland, NJ; holiness movement produces shoutings, dancing in the Spirit, falling 'under the power', holy laughter, holy rolling.

AD 1867. First Lambeth Conference of Anglican Bishops; confessionalism launched.

1867 Beginnings of confessional conciliarism: archbishop of Canterbury C.T. Longley (1794-1868) convenes first decennial Lambeth Conference of all bishops of Anglican Communion (London), with 76 bishops present; 1875, origin of World Alliance of Reformed Churches and 1876 World Methodist Council; by 1983, grand total of 45 world confessional councils are in existence, representing all major Christian traditions, and all with own approaches to world mission.

AD 1867. Daniele Comboni founds new foreign missionary society.

1867 Founding of Combonians (MCCI/FSCI/MFSC) with as goal 'Evangelizzazione dei popoli, non ancora o non sufficientemente evangelizzati'; by 1983, 1,938 missionaries.

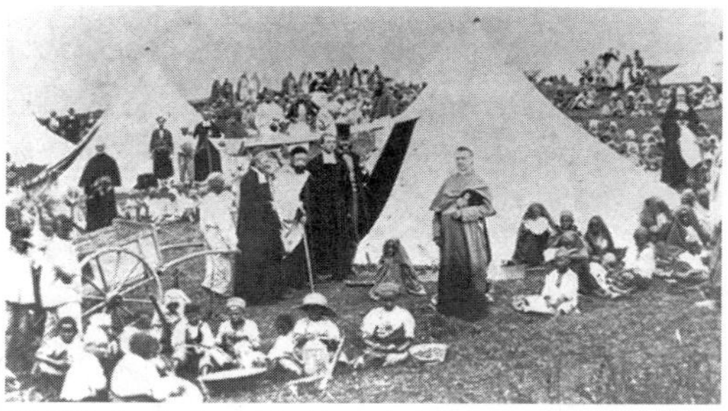

**AD 1868.** Cardinal Lavigerie visits Arab children's camp in Ben-Aknoun, outside Algiers.

1868 White Fathers (Missionaries of Our Lady of Africa) and White Sisters (1869) begun by cardinal Charles Lavigerie (1825-1892).
1868 Catholic Action begun in Bologna (Italy).
1868 Origin of large-scale international Bible correspondence course organizations; in Toronto, Canada.
1868 Russia: Old Believers and offshoots number 10 million, rising by 1900 to 14% of entire Russian empire.
1868 Russians take Samarkand; emirate of Bukhara becomes a Russian protectorate.
1869 Council of Vatican I, in Rome (20th Ecumenical Council): papal infallibility defined, widening gulf between Rome and rest of Christendom; 700 bishops present, almost all Europeans.
1869 Artificial earth satellites first predicted in science fiction.
1869 Anglican Broad Church Evangelical, F.W. Farrar, later dean of Canterbury, describes Europeans as God's chosen evangelizers: 'The Aryan should advance farther and farther to... the evangelization of the whole habitable globe.'
1869 J.F. MacLennan holds totemism represents earliest form of religion.
1869 Mohandas K. Gandhi (1869-1948) born.
1869 Northern Thailand: prince Kawilorot of Chiengmai murders 2 Lao converts, one an ex-abbot; mass conversions impossible for 20 years and absent thereafter.
1870 Ghost Dance among American Indians begun by prophet Wodziwob; 1890, spreads to Paiute, Cheyenne, Kiowa, Sioux and other tribes.
1870 Unification of Italy under Victor Emmanuel II (1820-1878); annexes Rome and papal states, makes Rome capital.
1870 Heyday of British evangelists: William Booth (1829-1912), C.H. Spurgeon (1834-1892), Henry Drummond (1851-1897), Wilson Carlile (1847-1942), Gipsy Smith (1860-1947).
1870 Punjab: mass movement begins of 50% of Hindu Chuhras in Sialkot to American Presbyterian mission; continuing revival up to 1912.
1870 South India: mass movement brings one million Telugu outcastes into Baptist, Lutheran and Methodist churches in 30 years.
1870 Kugu Sorta (Great Candle), anti-Russian and anti-missionary cult after Cheremis forcibly converted to Christianity.
1870 Native American (Peyote) Church, large USA Amerindian church, takes shape; by 1970, 400,000 members in 23 chapters, from many tribes.
1870 Rise of supercities across world (cities with over 4 million population), beginning with London (4.2 million by 1875); then 1900, 2 (London, Paris); 1925, 5; 1950, 11; 1960, 18; 1970, 25; 1980, 40; by 1985, 38 (23 in developing countries); by AD 2000, 79 (59); by AD 2025, 144 (123); those in Africa increase from 1 in 1985 (Cairo) to 12 by AD 2000 and to 36 by AD 2025.
c1870 Canton & Enderbury Islands: first Christians (British guano-digging companies).
1870 Rise of first megaministry (reaching over 1% of world per annum, i.e. 14 million people a year): BFBS, ABS and other Bible societies' distribution reaches 38,000 scriptures a day.
1870 Pan-Orthodox world missions emerge: Orthodox Missionary Society organized in Russia by metropolitan of Moscow, I. Veniaminov (1797-1879); branches in 55 Russian dioceses; rapid missionary expansion with, by 1900, 124,204 pagans baptized in 18 missions; by 1900, Russians form largest single Christian ethnolinguistic people in whole world; 1914, 20,000 members of OMS, with large income; 1917, Bolsheviks destroy Russian world missions; 1959, Pan-Orthodox world mission reorganized based on Athens (Greece).
1870 Churches of Christ (Non-Instrumental), schism from Disciples of Christ, organize in USA; by 1985, they sent out 982 foreign missionaries in 74 countries, with related churches in total of 141 countries.
1870 Watch Tower Bible and Tract Society begun in USA through Charles T. Russell (1852-1916), who predicts Second Advent for 1874, later for 1914; 1879 launches magazine *Zion's Watchtower and Herald of Christ's Presence*; publishes classic, *Divine Plan of the Ages*; known at first as Russellites or Millennial Dawnists, later it becomes International Bible Students Association, then in 1931 Jehovah's Christian Witnesses (or Jehovah's Witnesses); by 1986, world's largest single missionary agency.
1870 Futurism and the future are written about at length over next 100 years by: philosophers H. Bergson, J. Dewey, S. Alexander, Bertrand Russell; playwright Bernard Shaw; future-fiction writers H.G. Wells, G. Griffith, M.P. Shiel, Jack London, G.A. England; socialist visionaries G.V. Plekhanov, V.I. Lenin, L. Trotsky, K. Kautsky, J. Jaures.
1870 China experiences rapid church growth: Catholics in 1877, 404,000; 1899, 720,540; 950,000 in 1907; and 1912, 1,179,019; Protestants in 1870 13,000; 1877, 23,500; 1898, 268,000; then 178,000 in 1907; in 1915, 526,000.
1871 Great Fire of Chicago, worst fire in USA history, destroys much of city; 50 churches and missions burned down.
1871 USA: beginnings of large-scale team evangelism; 1871-99, D.L. Moody & Ira D. Sankey.
1871 E.G. Bulwer-Lytton writes *The coming race*, on an advanced race of men living below ground.
1871 Paris Commune executes archbishop of Paris, also 40 priests and religious.
1871 British anthropologist E.B. Tylor (1832-1917) publishes major treatise, *Primitive culture:* researches into the development of mythology, philosophy, religion, language, art and custom, highlighting animism and primitive man's belief that everything had a soul.
1871 5th Canonical Theravadin Buddhist Council, held in Mandalay (Burma), convened by king Mindon Min; on revision of Pali texts on 729 marble tablets followed by their entombment in stupas.
1871 D.L. Moody conducts annual higher-life conferences in Northfield, Massachusetts; thousands attend to receive their personal pentecost.
1871 Long series of Old Catholic Conferences: 1st at Munich in 1871, 2nd in 1872 at Cologne with 350 members, 3rd in 1873 at Constance, 4th in 1874 at Freiburg-in-Breisgau, et alia; then Bishops' Conferences since 1889.
1871 Sermon before Baptist Missionary Society (London) by former BMS secretary Joseph Angus, entitled 'Apostolic Missions: the Gospel for Every Creature', claims gospel could be preached to every creature on Earth by 1886 or 1891 at latest; his sermon later read by USA Presbyterian theologian, Bible expositor and dispensationalist A.T. Pierson (1837-1911), who by 1876 conceives idea of a Watchcry (Watchword), supported by 1877 Shanghai missions conference, and in 1877 begins public addresses on a concrete plan for evangelizing the world.
1872 Revivals in Japan, also 1883, following waves of persecution in 1865, 1867 and 1868 ending in 1872 decree of religious liberty.
1872 Japan: first of a series of country-wide Protestant missionary conferences, General Convention of Protestant Missionaries in Japan, held in Yokohama to plan for future; 1900, 3rd in series leads into 1907 Conference of Federated Missions in Japan.
1872 Angola: Kiyoka (Burning) anti-sorcery prophetic movement sweeps across north.
1872 First indigenous church movement in southern Africa: secession from Herman congregation, Paris Mission, Basutoland.
1872 8th International Statistical Congress, held at St Petersburg (Russia), urges inclusion of item on religion in every national census.
1872 1st Decennial All-India Missionary Conference.
1872 First baptism in New Guinea (Protestant).
1872 First useful analogue computer built, by British physicist Lord Kelvin, as tide predictor.
1872 Salesian Sisters (FMA) founded, in Italy, for world mission by prayer and works of charity; by 1983, 17,269 nuns, in 60 countries.
1873 Japanese emperor Mutsuhito ends ban on Christianity.
1873 Electricity is first used to drive industrial machinery, in Austria; quickly adopted elsewhere.
1873 Dwight L. Moody's evangelistic campaigns in England: first 1873-75 (including 5-month London Crusade with 2.5 million attenders), second 1882-84 (with 2 million attenders in London), third 1891-92.
1873 India: Roman Catholic mass movement among aboriginal Kols; 79,000 baptized by 1891.
1873 First university chair of History of Religions founded in Geneva; 1876, 4 more established in Holland; 1879 in College de France, 1885 in Ecole des Hautes Etudes at Sorbonne, Paris; 1884 in Free University of Brussels; 1910 Berlin, others later in Leipzig, Bonn, et alia.
1873 East London Institute for Home and Foreign Missions founded in UK by H.G. Guinness (1835-1910) of Church of Ireland; 1900, name changed to Regions Beyond Missionary Union invoking Apostle Paul's world vision (2 Corinthians 10:16); by 1985, 103 North American missionaries in 5 countries, 58 British in 5 countries, with total 200 missionaries of all nationalities.
1874 Mexican government suppresses religious orders.
1874 Guatemala: Catholic religious orders and congregations dissolved.
1874 Universal Postal Union (UPU) founded; 1947, becomes specialized agency of United Nations, based in Bern; over 140 member countries.
1874 Old Catholics convene international conference of theologians, including Anglicans, at Bonn (Germany), to discuss reunion of churches outside Rome.
1874 *Signs of the Times* magazine (originally begun in 1842 as an End-Times newspaper) reorganized as denominational organ by USA Seventh-day Adventists; by 1988, in many languages, with 300,000 monthly distribution in English alone.
1874 Women's Christian Temperance Union founded in USA; 1874-98 led by ardent Methodist Frances Willard (1839-1898).
1875 Japan: Doshisha university founded by Japanese Christian, Niisima.

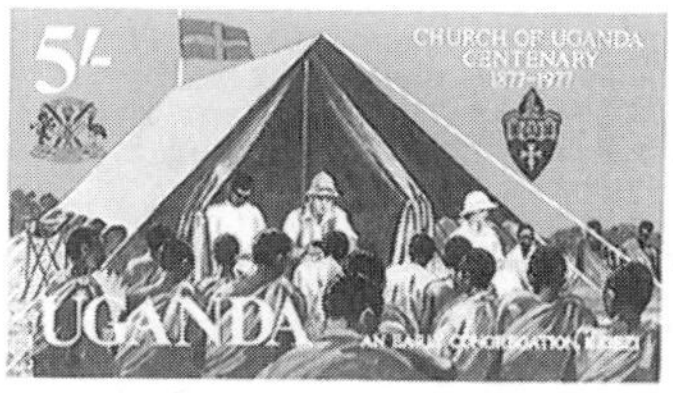


**AD 1875.** Anglican pioneers in Uganda, with first being African evangelist Maftaa.

1875 *Uganda.* First resident evangelist (Dallington Maftaa, African Anglican from Nyasaland).
1875 Alliance of Reformed Churches (Presbyterian); first Protestant confessional council to be formed (London); 1970, as WARC, merger with International Congregational Council.
1875 Arya Samaj founded in India by Dayananda Sarasvati (died 1883) for purification of Hinduism, recalling it to fundamentalist position; anti-Christian, attempts to win back converts won by Christian missions.
1875 Keswick Convention for higher spiritual life begun (UK), under theme 'All One in Christ Jesus'.
1875 Theosophical Society founded in New York City under anti-Christian writer Helena Blavatsky (1831-1891), combining Gnosticism, mysticism and occultism of Egypt, India and China; 1909, young Brahmin Jiddu Krishnamurti (1895-1986) claimed as Ascended Master, Christ Spirit, Reincarnate Buddha, Guiding Spirit of the Universe.
1875 World's 10 largest cities: London 4,241,000, Paris 2,250,000, New York 1,900,000, Peking 1,310,000, Berlin 1,045,000, Vienna 1,001,000, Canton 944,000, Philadelphia 791,000, Tokyo 780,000, St Petersburg 764,000.
1875 Founding of Society of the Divine Word (Verbites, SVD), in Steyl (Netherlands), with as goal 'Evangelizzazione dei Popoli'; by 1983, 5,413 members in 280 houses on all continents.
1875 India: Arya Samaj founded by swami Dayananda Saraswathi to defend, reform and aggressively propagate Hinduism; writes *Satyartha Prakash* as its holy book; by 1990s has thousands of its missionaries working around the world.
1876 Invention of electric telephone by A.G. Bell in Boston, USA.
1876 Sweden: evangelical awakening in state church under Skogsbergh and Paul Peter Waldenstrom (1838-1917).
1876 England: High Church priest Hay Aitken founds Parochial Mission Society.
1876 Watchcry (Watchword) conceived by A.T. Pierson.
1877 *Guinea* (French). First mission (French Holy Ghost priests).
1877 Uprising in Turkey by Armenian and Syrian Christians suppressed by Turks with many deaths.
1877 Shanghai, China: 1st General Foreign Missions Conference, with 473 missionaries from 20 Protestant societies; states 'We want China emancipated from the thraldom of sin in this generation'; probable origin, among field missionaries, of Watchword 'The Evangelization of the World in This Generation'; similar conferences in 1890 and 1907.
1877 World Presbyterian Alliance begun.
1878 BMS (UK) open São Salvador station in northern Angola.
1878 Thailand: Edict of Religious Toleration proclaimed by king Rama V (Chulalongkorn, 1853-1910).
1878 USA: First American Bible and Prophetic Conference, New York City.
1878 2nd Lambeth Conference; 100 Anglican bishops present.
1878 Japan: first National Christian Conference (from 1884-1906, part of World Evangelical Alliance) held, in Tokyo.
1878 *Missionary review of the world* founded by R. Wilder, soon becomes leading Protestant journal of missions.
1878 International Prophetic Conferences meet from this year to 1901 promoting portions of Bible as 'photographically exact forecasting of the future'.
1879 First Church of Christ, Scientist, founded in Boston by Mary Baker Eddy (1821-1910) as worldwide movement centering on spiritual healing.
1879 Scripture Union (SU) founded; 300,000 members in UK alone by 1887.
1879 *Burundi* (then *Urundi*). First mission (White Fathers).
1879 Protestant Missionary Conference held in London.
1879 Baptist Russell H. Conwell (1843-1925) ordained, builds America's largest church, Baptist Temple of Philadelphia, makes it an institutional center for social service serving the neighbourhood; 1907, founds Temple University; most famous lecturer of his day, he delivers lecture 'Acres of Diamonds' over 6,000 times; message of success—hearers can find diamonds in their back yards if they look.

1880 Thirty Years' Revival in Germany (till 1910); several hundred thousand converted in state churches.

1880 Russian rocket pioneer K.E. Tsiolkovsky (1857-1935) derives mathematical laws that lay foundation for field of astronautics; calculates Sun's energy could sustain human population of $3x10^{23}$; envisages giant greenhouses in space, described in his 1920 novel *Beyond the Planet Earth*; 1928, argues for space-going 'Noah's arks'; envisages first manned space flight by 2017.

1880 Percy Greg's interplanetary adventure novel, *Across the Zodiac*, on future evolution of planet Mars.

1880 1st Lay Congress of American Catholics, Baltimore, USA; 1893, 2nd Lay Congress, in Chicago.

c1880 Ethiopia: 50,000 Muslims, 20,000 pagans, and a total of 500,000 Gallas, baptized by force by Ethiopian Orthodox Church.

1880 Circulation of Watchcry (Watchword) on various Protestant mission fields becomes crystallized in 1885 article by A.T. Pierson entitled 'A plan to evangelize the world', published in his journal *The Missionary review of the world* after 20 years of reflection; Pierson calls for 'an ecumenical council solely to plan a world-wide campaign and proclaim the good tidings to every living soul in the shortest time'.

1880 Periodicals begun for the science of religions: 1880 *Revue de l'histoire des religions*, founded in Paris; 1898 *Archiv für Religionswissenschaft*, at Freiburg-im-Breisgau; 1905 *Anthropos*, at St Gabriel-Modling, Vienna; 1925 *Studi e Materiali di Storia delle Religioni*; 1921 *The journal of religion*, in Chicago; 1936 *The review of religion*, Columbia University, New York; 1938 *Zalmoxis: revue des études religieuses*, in Bucharest; 1948 *Zeitschrift für Religions- und Geistegeschichte*, Germany; 1954 *Numen: international review for the history of religions*, Leiden.

c1880 Psychological explanations for religion proposed by W. Wundt (1832-1920), William James (1842-1910), and Sigmund Freud (1856-1939).

1881 Alexander III reigns as Russian czar 1881-1894; institutes harsh rule, forced russification of minorities, extensive persecution of Jews; revolutionary sentiment spreads among workers and peasants.

1881 300,000 killed in Indochina by typhoon.

1881 Shakerism and Indian Shaker Church begun by former Roman Catholic John Slocum among Puget Sound Amerindians.

1881 *Somalia*. First Christians and first mission (Catholic).

1881 First of 48 International Eucharistic Congresses, held in Lille (France) with 800 present; growing to the 22nd (1934) in Buenos Aires (Argentina); 23rd (1937) in Manila (Philippines); 37th (1960) in Munich; 38th (1964) in Bombay, 39th (1968) in Bogota, 40th (1973) in Melbourne, 41st (1976) in Philadelphia (USA) with one million present; 42nd (1981) in Lourdes, France; 1985, 43rd held in Nairobi, Kenya; 44th (1989) in Seoul, Korea; 45th (1993) in Seville, Spain; also many national and regional eucharistic congresses worldwide.

1881 1st Ecumenical Methodist Conference, held in London with 400 delegates from 30 Methodist bodies around the world; precursor of later (1951) World Methodist Council.

1881 Mohamed Ahmed ibn Seyyid Abdullah (1848-1885) proclaims self Mahdi, leads 8-year revolt against Anglo-Egyptian forces; 1885, captures Khartoum and kills general Gordon; 1899, final defeat of Mahdism by British.

1881 Ethiopian emperor Yohannes IV pays Coptic patriarch of Egypt 12,000 Maria Theresa thalers for consecration of 4 abunas (bishops).

1881 England: English Revised Version of Bible produced by 65 English scholars, completed by 1885.

1881 United Society of Christian Endeavor formed in Maine, USA 'to promote earnest Christian life' and training for service; by 1885, an international organization; 1895, World's Christian Endeavor Union organized (38,000 societies across world, with 2,225,000 members); by 1910, 3.5 million members (two thirds in North America); 1927, International Society of Christian Endeavor; by 1965, 3 million members in 85 Protestant denominations in 80 countries; by 1987, 2 million in 78 nations.

1881 Palestine: 5,000 Jews resident.

1881 Russia: anti-Jewish pogroms state as goals regarding Jews: one third to be massacred, one third assimilated to Christianity, one third to be expelled by force; pogroms continue to 1904.

1882 First International Polar Year, organized by International Polar Commission meeting in Hamburg: scientists and explorers from 11 countries make scientific observations throughout winter in the Arctic; 2nd Year not until 1932 IPY; 1957 IGY held.

1882 India: Anglicans and Protestants number 500,000.

1882 Britain: International Bible Reading Association (IBRA) founded; 100,000 members by 1886.

1882 Korean treaty with USA ensures religious freedom in Korea; Presbyterian and Methodist missionaries enter 3 years later.

1882 Church Army (Anglican) founded in Britain by Wilson Carlile.

1882 Mexico: first of several national or regional Protestant missionary conferences.

1882 I. Donnelly publishes *Atlantis: the antediluvian world*, linking empire of Atlantis with Garden of Eden.

1882 Hazrat Inayat Khan (1882-1927) born: instrumental in bringing Islamic mysticism, Sufism, to the West.

1883 Massive eruption of Indonesian volcano Krakatoa (August 27), second-largest in history after Thera (BC c1628), throws rocks upward 34 miles and spreads dust over 3,300 miles; blast, with estimated force of 26 hydrogen bombs, is heard some 3,000 miles away; resulting 120-foot tidal wave kills over 36,000; whole planet banded by dust for months, resulting in coldest winter for centuries.

1883 Fourth Evangelical Awakening (of the century) in Norway, especially in Skien.

1883 Japan: first Japanese Catholic priests ordained: 15 by 1891, 33 by 1910.

1883 2nd General Conference of Protestant Missionaries of Japan; several revivals; 'Japan is now embracing Christianity with a rapidity unexampled since the days of Constantine... will be predominantly Christian within 20 years'.

1884 Linotype machine, creating entire line of type in single casting, is invented by German-born American Ottmar Mergenthaler (1854-1899).

1884 German Evangelization Society founded.

1884 City-wide evangelists in USA: Samuel Porter Jones (1847-1906) & E.O. Excell (from 1885-1906, 25 million attenders and 500,000 converts, most in South), B. Fay Mills (1857-1916), J. Wilbur Chapman (1859-1918).

1884 Berlin West Africa Conference: European powers with USA and Turkey meet to decide all questions related to Congo Basin, East and Central Africa; German colonial policy developed.

1884 'The Cambridge Seven' leave Britain as missionaries to China.

1884 Worldwide standard time adopted by delegates from 27 nations meeting in Washington, DC, dividing world into 24 standard time zones starting with GMT (Greenwich Mean Time) based on prime meridian defined as zero longitude at Greenwich, UK.

1884 Founding in USA of magazine *The Christian Century* dedicated to proposition that the Kingdom of Christ will dominate the world at end of 20th century by AD 2000.

1884 A.O. Van Lennep publishes statistical survey *The Growth of Christianity during Nineteen Centuries* (New York), blaming inadequate growth on lack of giving (in USA, annual per capita expenditure on alcohol is \$49.70 but on foreign missions only \$0.05); concludes 'When Christ's Church shall be as lavish in its outlay of men and money as the world is, the conversion of Nations will not long be postponed.'

1885 India: mass movement of 65,000 among Chota Nagpur aboriginal tribes under Belgian Jesuit Constant Lievens; 1910, 150,000 Catholics.

1885 First African ordinations to Anglican ministry in Kenya.

1885 *Zambia* (Northern Rhodesia). First mission (Paris Mission, PEMS).

1885 Uganda Martyrs: around 250 Catholic and Anglican Christians executed by king Mwanga (1866-1901) at Namugongo.

1885 Wesleyan Forward Movement in British Methodism under Hugh Price Hughes (1847-1902) of West London Mission, founding central halls in cities and stressing social evangelism; 1896, Hughes founds National Council of Evangelical Free Churches.

1885 Swami Vivekananda (1862-1902), Hindu missionary to the West and leader of Hindu revival in India, wins many in West to Vedantism.

1885 Richard Jefferies' novel of future collapse of civilization, *After London*.

1885 At D.L. Moody's Northfield Convention for lay workers, A.T. Pierson chairs committee to 'divide the world according to a comity agreement' and then pursue 'the immediate occupation and evangelization of every destitute district of the earth's population', so that 'the entire current population of the earth would hear the gospel by the year 1900'; Moody prepares in 3 days 'An Appeal to Disciples Everywhere', claiming task could be completed even if only 10 million active Christians participated.

1886 Sikkim: first mission (Church of Scotland).

1886 More indigenous movements and churches in India opposing Western missions: 1886 National Church of Madras, 1887 Calcutta Christo Samaj.

1886 Church of God (Cleveland) begun as study and fellowship group in Cleveland, Tennessee; later becomes first Pentecostal church in USA, from 1906.

1886 H. Hollerith (1860-1929) invents punched-card electrical tabulating machine; 1890, selected to count 12th USA census of population (result, 62,622,250); 1924, his company becomes IBM.

1886 Dutch botanist and geneticist H. de Vries (1848-1935) discovers mutations (sudden, abrupt, immediate transformations of hereditary material, radical enough to bring new species into existence in a single leap), producing major refinement of Darwin's theory of evolution.

1886 1st International Christian Student Conference, Mount Hermon, Massachusetts, addressed by D.L. Moody, A.T. Pierson, et alii; 251 attenders; 1888, Student Volunteer Movement for Foreign Missions organized with 2,200 initial volunteers, based on Watchword 'The Evangelization of the World in This Generation'; by 1945, a total of 20,500 SVM students have gone overseas as foreign missionaries.

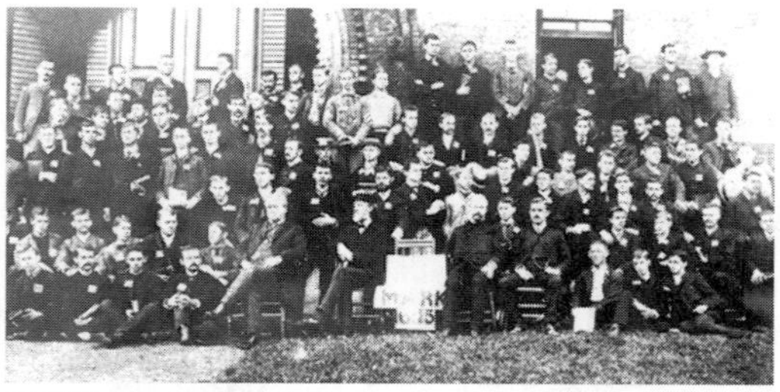

**AD 1886.** Mount Hermon Student Conference addressed by D. L. Moody and A. T. Pierson.

1886 Germany: 1st Blankenburg Alliance Conference, founded by Anna von Weling.

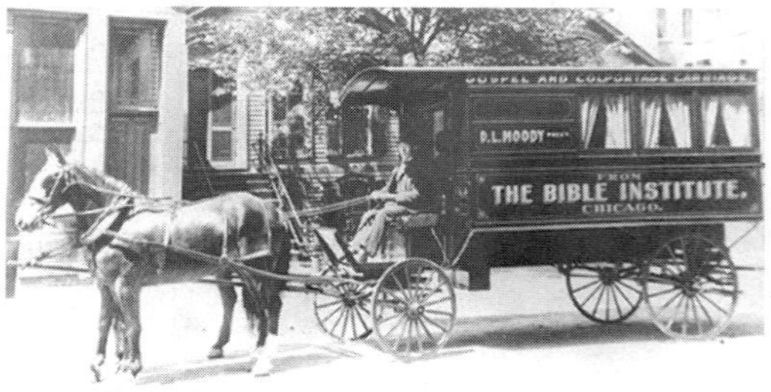


**AD 1886.** Colportage by Moody's horse-drawn delivery wagon, Chicago.

1886 Chicago Evangelization Society begun by D. L. Moody; later becomes Moody Bible Institute.

1887 Monotype typesetting machine is patented.

1887 Yellow River in China overflows throughout spring months, submerging 50,000 square miles; 1.5 million die.

1887 First scripture translation in Philippines: Gospel of Luke in Pangasinan.

1887 Canada: evangelistic campaigns in cities under evangelists Crossley and Hunter.

1887 *Maldives*. First Christians (under British protectorate).

1887 W.H. Hudson's novel *A Crystal Age*: future evolution of Earth in AD 12,000, some 10 millennia after a mass catastrophe.

1887 Ecuador: archbishop J.I. Checa y Barba (1829-1887) convokes 2nd and 3rd Councils of Quito; opposed by state, poisoned.

1887 Netherlands: first of annual series of Dutch Protestant missionary conferences.

1887 Christian and Missionary Alliance organized in USA; 1975, Alliance World Fellowship founded, in 51 nations; by 1985, 874 USA foreign missionaries in 50 countries.

1887 *Christian herald* editor M.P. Baxter publishes *The Great Crisis from 1890 to 1901*, comprising fifteen coming events and the End of this age about the end of this century; writes 'We are fast approaching the downfall of the kingdoms of this world, and the consequent establishment of Christ's Millennial Kingdom'.

c1887 Dispensationalist theologian W.E. Blackstone (1841-1935) publishes *Jesus is coming: God's hope for a restless world*.

1888 German Association for Evangelism and Christian Fellowship (Gnadauer Band) formed at Gnadau; 1st Gnadau Conference on state church evangelism, with 142 workers present; by 1920, Association has 6,000 organizations and 225,000 registered members; 1938, 800 preachers and 300 women workers, holding 6,000 meetings.

1888 *Nauru*. First mission (LMS).

1888 *Christmas Island*. First Christians (British administrators).

1888 India: Mar Thoma Syrian Christian Evangelistic Association of Malabar formed for non-Syrian outcaste converts; large Maramon Convention held annually for 8-day preaching event, increasing in size to 2 million attenders for 1988 meeting.

1888 Native Baptist Church secedes, in Lagos (Nigeria) and Douala (Cameroon), from Southern Baptists and Basel Mission.

1888 Invention of Edison motion-picture camera (Kinetograph).

1888 Centenary Conference on Foreign Missions (Ecumenical Missionary Conference), London; 1,576 missionaries and representatives of 140 agencies; first of the great international conferences.

1888 Edward Bellamy writes futuristic novel *Looking backward: 2000-1887*, envisaging by AD 2000 an idyllic fully socialist world with no crime, no warfare, no money, no nationalism, no politics, no bureaucracies.

1888 First Scriptures in constructed international languages: 1888 Volapuk, 1893 Esperanto.

1888 Photography invented by G. Eastman.

1888 Afghanistan: Armenian Catholics, mostly merchants, are persecuted and expelled.

1888 Italian Bible colporteur F.G. Penzotti begins first Spanish-speaking Evangelical church in Peru, in Callao.

1888 USA: Woman's Missionary Union (WMU) begun by Southern Baptists, becomes largest mission support body in world organized by women; by 1986, 1,200,000 members supporting 7,000 missionaries, with one billion dollars raised.

1888 Student Volunteer Movement for Foreign Missions organized with 2,200 initial volunteers, based on Watchword 'The Evangelization of the World in This Generation'; 1892, Student Volunteer Missionary Union (SVMU) begun in Britain; by 1945, as a result of SVM, a total of 25,000 university graduates have gone overseas as foreign missionaries.

1888 Seventh-day Adventist prophet since 1855, Ellen G. White (1827-1915), publishes *The Great Controversy* on Jehovah's cosmic dispute, writes 44 other major books and over 4,000 articles.

1888 One By One Band started in London by T. Hogben as 'a worldwide fellowship devoted wholly to winning men to Christ', based on Hogben's book *God's plan for soul winning.*

1888 3rd Lambeth Conference (with 145 Anglican bishops present) promulgates Lambeth Quadrilateral: Anglicans are prepared to unite with all churches that accept 4 marks of Christian life: (1) authority of Scripture, (2) the 2 sacraments instituted by Christ, (3) the historic creeds, and (4) the historic ministry.

1889 Great influenza epidemic afflicts 40% of world; deaths are in millions.

1889 Largest USA non-Chalcedonian church established: Armenian Church of North America, under catholicate of Echmiadzin.

1889 Old Catholic Bishops' Conference, Utrecht (Dutch, German and Swiss churches); Declaration of Utrecht issued as Old Catholic doctrinal basis.

1889 North Africa Mission enters Tripoli as first Protestant mission in Libya.

1889 *Rwanda.* First mission (White Fathers).

1889 Brazil: republic proclaimed and Catholic church formally separated from state.

1889 Founding of Ahmadiya out of Shia Islam in Punjab by self-professed mahdi Mirza Ghulam Ahmad (1836-1908); adherents rise from 70,030 in 1900 to 4,734,000 by 1985.

1889 British Salvation Army evangelist Gipsy Smith holds large meetings in major USA cities; in 50 years' ministry leads vast numbers to Christ in UK, USA, Australia.

1889 Japan: 500 Japanese students at Student Conference send telegram to SVM Conference, Northfield (USA), urging 'Make Jesus King'.

1889 SVMU chairman John R. Mott writes to sister Hattie that the task of world evangelization will be accomplished by the dawn of the 20th century.

1890 China: 500,000 baptized Catholics, 639 foreign priests, 369 Chinese priests.

1890 Shanghai: foreign missions conference, with 1,295 missionaries present.

1890 Philippine Independent Church founded by Roman Catholic priest Gregorio Aglipay (1860-1940); 1902, organized as schism taking 45% of all Roman Catholics in country.

1890 Nevius method introduced in Korea (Bible-training for lay members).

1890 Era of the 'New Evangelism' as expounded by Scottish evangelist Henry Drummond et alii.

1890 Vladimir Solovyov (1853-1900), Russian mystical philosopher and disciple of Dostoievsky, places birth of Antichrist in 1954.

1890 Long series of International Old Catholic Congresses held: 1st Cologne 1890, 2nd Lucerne 1892, 3rd Rotterdam 1894, 4th Vienna 1931, 5th Bonn 1902, 6th Olten 1904, 7th The Hague 1907, 8th Vienna 1909, 9th Cologne 1913, 10th Berne 1925, 11th Utrecht 1928, 12th Vienna 1931, 13th Constance 1934, 14th Zurich 1938, 15th Hilversum 1948, 16th Munich 1953, 17th Rheinfelden 1957, 18th Haarlem 1961, 19th Vienna 1965, et alia.

1890 First volume of 12-volume *The Golden Bough: a study in magic and religion* by J.G. Frazer (1854-1941); 12th published in 1913.

1890 Scandinavian Alliance Mission of North America founded for worldwide evangelism and church planting; 1949, renamed TEAM (The Evangelical Alliance Mission); 1985, 929 USA missionaries in 25 countries.

c1890 Jewish oculist L.L. Zamenhof invents Esperanto as a universal language, by 1909 used for over 100 books with 1,500 local societies publishing 90 journals in Esperanto.

c1890 American Adventists write out new prophetic invoices for the year 1900.

c1890 Antonio Conselheiro sets up Canudos in northeast Brazil, as a refuge for the faithful before End of the world in 1900.

1890 British artist William Morris (1834-1896) writes utopian novel *News from Nowhere.*

1890 Lynchings of Blacks in South of USA average 3 each week during decade; many are pentecostal preachers.

c 1890 Belgian government creates Universal Bibliographical Repertory to have a catalog card for every printed book (later, Dewey Decimal System, now Universal Decimal System, for libraries); results later in International Federation for Documentation, and American Society for Information Science (ASIS); also League of Nations' Intellectual Cooperation Organization, leading to UNESCO.

1890 Bhutan: Church of Scotland converts among Nepali and Lepcha go as Indian missionaries to Bhutan; many early deaths.

c1890 *Somaliland.* First Christians (scattered British colonial officials).

1891 D.H. Hewavitarne (1865-1933) founds Maha Bodhi Society in Ceylon to spread Buddhism to other English-speaking lands.

1891 Japan: Roman Catholic hierarchy constituted; Catholics 44,500, rising to 63,000 by 1910.

1891 International Congregational Council formed in London.

1891 *The encyclopedia of missions: descriptive, historical, biographical, statistical,* edited H.O. Dwight et al (2nd edition 1910, Bureau of Missions, New York, 851 pages), with massive details and articles on missions in all countries, peoples, languages, and in 5,000 cities, towns, and villages (data on all places in non-Christian lands).

1891 Fundamentalists petition US president Benjamin Harrison to see Palestine given immediately to the Jews so they can rebuild Temple before End of the world in 1899.

1891 Construction of Trans-Siberian railroad, completed 1903.

1891 Ceylon: Maha Bodhi Society founded by Anagarika Dharmapala to revitalize Buddhism.

1891 2nd Ecumenical Methodist Conference, held in Washington, DC.

1892 United Arab Emirates (then Trucial Oman). New wave of Christians (British officials, Indian merchants).

1892 UK: Free Church Congress meets in Manchester; soon after, National Council of the Evangelical Free Churches is formed, also numerous local councils of churches across Britain.

1892 German author Max Plessner writes *A look at the great discoveries of the 20th century: the future of electrical television.*

1892 French physiologist and medical statistician Charles Richet (1850-1935) publishes *In 100 years*, presenting a statistical projection of world population growth to 1992, with USA and Russia as superpowers based on solar energy.

1892 Formal bilateral theological dialogues begin with Old Catholics meeting with Russian Orthodox; with Old Catholic/Eastern Orthodox dialogue finally concluding successfully in 1987.

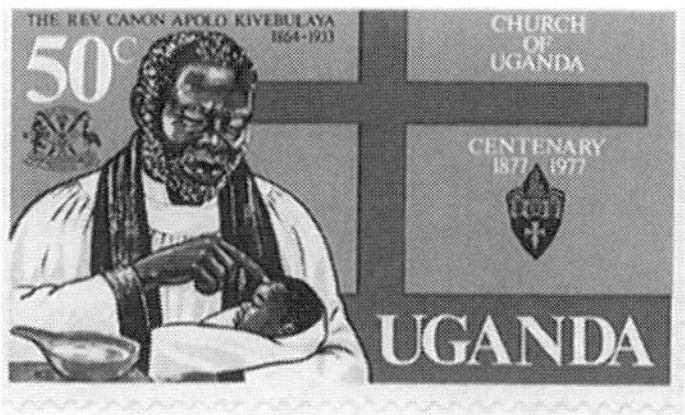


**AD 1982.** African pioneer Kivebulaya among Pygmies of eastern Congo.

1892 Anglican missionary Apolo Kivebulaya begins 40-year ministry among Mbuti Pygmies in eastern Congo.

1893 New Zealand becomes first nation to give vote to women.

1893 Papua New Guinea: Cult of the Prophet Tokerau at Milne Bay, first of over 120 distinct cargo cult movements over next 80 years.

1893 National Spiritualist Association of Churches founded, in USA.

1893 World's Parliament of Religions, in Chicago: ecumenist Philip Schaff (1819-1893) delivers notable address on 'The Reunion of Christendom'.

1893 French astronomer and spiritualist C. Flammarion writes *La fin du monde* (Omega: the last days of the world), describing (1) comet collision in AD c2450 killing millions, then (2) final days of human race in AD 10 million when, due to solar extinction, Earth has become too cold to live on.

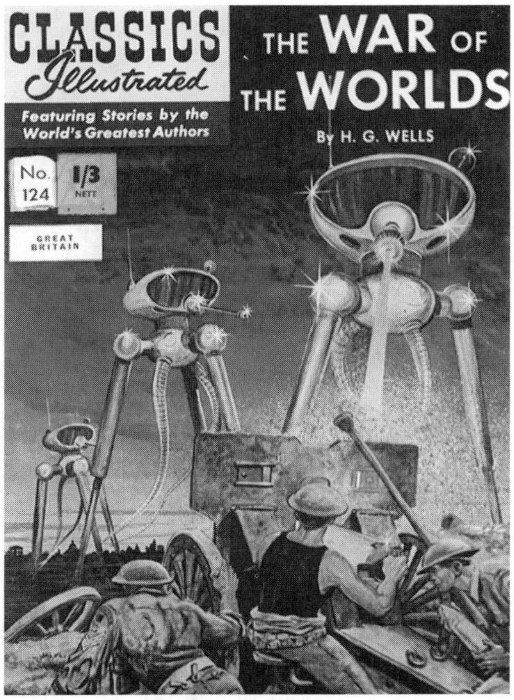


**AD 1893.** Scientific futurist H. G. Wells foresees invasion from Mars (1898 novel).

1893 H.G. Wells (1866-1946), atheist and secular prophet, prolific writer of far-futuristic science fiction, publishes 'The Man of the Year Million', also *The Time Machine* (1895), *In the Abyss* (1896, city of humanoids beneath ocean), *The Invisible Man* (1897), *The War of the Worlds* (1898), *The First Men in the Moon* (1901), *Anticipations* (1902, on prophecy), *The Empire of the Ants* (1905, South American ants evolve and supersede man), *First and last things* (1908), *The shape of things to come* (1933), *The outlook for Homo Sapiens* (1942); envisages first round-the-Moon voyage not until AD 2054.

1893 Foreign Missions Conference of North America (FMCNA) organized representing 21 USA and Canada mission boards; 1950, renamed Division of Foreign Missions, NCCCUSA; 1965, Division of Overseas Ministries.

1893 Sudan Interior Mission begun as Africa Industrial Mission in order to evangelize the world's largest single totally unevangelized area with no resident missionary among 90 million people (Africa's 4,000-mile Sahel and Soudan); 1982, renamed SIM International, expands to Latin America; 1985, 654 missionaries in 15 countries.

1893 J.T. Gracey writes *The religion of the future.*

1893 Korea: Council of Missions begun as comity agreement; 1911, name changed to Federal Council of Protestant Evangelical Missions in Korea.

1894 Madagascar: first indigenous church, Malagasy Protestant Church splits ex LMS.

1894 Soatanana Revival begins among Lutheran and LMS churches in Madagascar, lasting over 100 years (Fifohazana, Revivalists).

1894 *Central African Republic* (then *Ubangi-Chari*). First mission (Roman Catholic).

1894 *Essay on the prevailing methods of the evangelization of the non-Christian world* written by R.N. Cust, a critical survey of methods of missionary societies.

1894 Meher Baba (1894-1969) born in Poona, a silent sage.

1895 First commercially successful movie projector developed in France.

1895 *Mali.* First mission (White Fathers from Senegal).

1895 Massacres of Armenian Christians by Turks: 1895, 80,000 in Trebizond; Christmas 1895, 1,200 burned alive in Urfa cathedral; 1896, 6,000 in Istanbul; total killed 1895-96, 200,000; 1905, 20,000 in Cilicia; 1909, 30,000 in district of Adana; 1915, 600,000 in Anatolia; and in 1920, 30,000 at Marash and Hadjin.

1895 Church of God in Christ formed in USA; later become Black pentecostals.

1895 Coptic Catholic patriarchate of Alexandria erected by Roman pope (earlier attempt 1824).

1895 R. Cromie's novel *The crack of doom*: mad scientist unlocks power of atom and holds world to ransom.

1895 Fire-Baptized Holiness Church under B.H. Irwin teaches a third blessing, a separate 'baptism with the Holy Ghost and fire' subsequent to conversion and sanctification; but unconnected with glossolalia or charismata.

1895 Ecuador: persecution of Catholic Church by liberals and freemasons.

1895 A.T. Pierson reluctantly realizes world will not become evangelized by 1900 as planned, and publicly admits this.

1895 L.D. Wishard writes *A new programme of missions: a movement to make the colleges in all lands centers of evangelization.*

1895 Association of Pentecostal Churches in America (1919, renamed Church of the Nazarene) formed, 1897 begins foreign missions; by 1987, World Mission Division has 617 foreign missionaries in 84 countries, with two AD 2000 programs: Thrust to the Cities ('maximizing holiness evangelism in key cities') and Two Million Adherents by 1995.

1895 World Student Christian Association/Federation (WSCF) emerges from Vadstena Castle meeting, Sweden, begun by SCMs around world whose 'aim was to claim students—the future leaders of their nations—for Christ and for the evangelization of the world'; after 1914, non-evangelistic interests predominate (leadership, social issues, universities, Christian presence, etc); 1987, over 3 million members and participants.

1895 German Protestant biblical scholar J.F.H. Gunkel (1862-1932) publishes *Schopfung und Chaos in Urzeit und Endzeit* (Creation and Chaos in Prehistoric times and the End times), studying popular mythology underlying biblical ideas.

1895 USA: Foreign Missions Conference of North America convened.

1896 German Student Volunteer Movement begun.

1896 Theodor Herzl (1860-1904), founder of modern Zionism, publishes his *Der Judenstaat* (The Jewish State); rise of global Zionist movement (Hibbat Zion, 'Love of Zion').

1896 First Protestant chairs of missiology in world: at university of Halle, Germany, G. Warneck (1834-1910) becomes first professor of science of missions; and in 1899 W. O. Carver (1868-1954) becomes head of missions at Southern Baptist Theological Seminary, Louisville, USA.

1896 'Make Jesus King': International Students Missionary

Conference, Liverpool; 800 students from 24 nations.

1896 Greenhouse effect (global warming) first predicted, by Swedish chemist Svante Arrhenius; possible AD 2000 scenario: despite all precautions since 1987, vast production of carbon dioxide from burning of fossil fuels leads to marked rise in Earth's temperature; greenhouse effect then results in initial melting of polar ice caps and raises level of globe's seas by 18 feet, submerging New York, London and other great coastal cities.

1896 Rhodesia/Mashonaland: uprising against British; Africans killed, including Anglican catechist Bernard Mizeki, then become canonized as saints and martyrs by African independent churches.

1897 China leases Hong Kong to Britain for 99 years.

1897 First attempt to fly to North Pole is made in a balloon by Swedish scientist S.A. Andree (1854-1897); remains are not found until 1930.

1897 Ross's discovery of cause of malaria; missionary fatalities in Africa decline.

1897 Lott Carey Baptist Foreign Mission Convention (Black American) organized in USA.

1897 USA: largest Catholic (non-Roman) church established: Polish National Catholic Church, formed over conflict between Polish Catholics and Irish Catholic hierarchy.

1897 Swami Vivekananda (1862-1902), disciple of Paramahamsar Ramakrishna (1836-1886) and foremost Hindu reformer, establishes Ramakrishna Math and Mission order near Calcutta; missionaries sent throughout world; begins Vedanta Society to convert Western world to Hinduism ('math' = monastic center); many branches in many countries.

1897 Free Protestant Episcopal Church (later, Ecumenical Church Foundation) begun in UK as Anglo-Roman autocephalous episcopal church under bishops-at-large (episcopi vagantes); branches in UK, USA, West Indies, West Africa (Nigeria 1946, Equatorial Guinea 1968, Cameroon 1970).

1897 9th Continental Missions Conference, in Bremen (Germany): missiologist G. Warneck leads attack on the Watchword as implying hasty preaching, premillennial eschatology, and a prophecy to be fulfilled; states evangelization of world in this generation is i impossible.

1897 4th Lambeth Conference; 194 Anglican bishops present; first of 14 resolutions on foreign missions passed: 'We recommend that prompt and continuous efforts be made to arouse the Church to... the fulfilment of our Lord's great commission to evangelize all nations'.

1897 House of Laymen, Province of Canterbury (Church of England) resolves: 'In view of the Great Commission to evangelize the world, its long and serious neglect... the whole Church needs rousing on this question'.

1897 Encyclical letter 'On the Holy Spirit' issued by pope Leo XIII, directing attention to the 7-fold gifts of the Spirit (Isaiah 11) and promoting universal novena (9-day cycle of prayer) to Holy Spirit before Pentecost Sunday each year; millions influenced.

1897 Arabia, and the world, 'could easily be evangelized within the next 30 years if it were not for the wicked selfishness of Christians, states Samuel Zwemer, Apostle to Islam (1867-1952).

1897 Polish writer J. Bloch writes *The war of the future in its technical, economic and political relations*, predicting next major war will be one of entrenchment, slaughter, attrition, and stalemate.

1897 1st Zionist Conference, headed by Theodor Herzl, in Basel with 200 Jewish attenders; 1901, 5th Zionist Conference begins Jewish National Fund; 1903, British offer for Jewish homeland settlement in East Africa (Uganda) declined at 6th Zionist Conference.

1897 First International Congress for the Sciences of Religion, in Stockholm; 1900 Congrès d'Histoire des Religions, Paris.

1897 J.M. Guyau writes *The non-religion of the future: a sociological study*.

1898 50,000 Nestorians in Urmia diocese (Iran) converted to Russian Orthodoxy; 1914, annihilated by Turks.

1898 Nyasaland: Providence Industrial Mission founded by USA Blacks, later leading to 1915 Chilembwe uprising.

1898 Church and state separated in Cuba on independence from Spain.

1898 Baptist originator of social gospel in America, Walter Rauschenbusch (1861-1918), teaches that God and USA fight on same side against Spain; but by 1917 deplores US Protestant support of war against Germany.

1898 Dikran Terzian of Amasia, Turkey publishes *The mathematics of religion*, estimates end of persecution of Armenian Christians will come in 1902.

1898 First rudimentary tape recorder, storing sound on magnetized steel wire.

1898 M.P. Shiel describes apocalyptic race war in *The Yellow peril*, where screaming yellow horde of 400 million East Asians swarms across Europe.

1899 New Thought movement (mental science, religious science, mental healing) spreads in USA; first New Thought Conference held in Hartford; International New Thought Alliance (INTA) formed.

1899 Japanese government proclaims State Shinto not a religion, hence compulsory reverence before emperor's image not a religious act.

1899 African indigenous churches (AICs) throughout Africa number some 50 separate denominations with 42,400 adherents, predominantly from 20 African tribes, of whom 18 have their own printed scripture translations.

1899 Atheist H.G. Wells writes 'A vision of judgement', in which Last Trump sounds; also, 1915, 'The story of the Last Trump': God's trumpet accidentally falls to Earth, is blown, heard worldwide, all receive momentary glimpse of reality of God.

1899 Latin American Plenary Council convened in Rome by pope Leo XIII; first such continental council ever.

1899 Gideons International begun, for massive free distribution of scriptures ('placements') among businessmen and professionals, hotels, armed forces, schools, et alia; by 1965, active in 75 countries rising to 133 by 1985 and 137 by 1988, with 30,000 overseas members; 1967, 7 million Bibles and 50 million NTs placed; 1987, 24 million Bibles distributed, with grand total 400 million placed over 89 years.

1899 At end of 'Golden Age of Jewish Missions' (= 19th century), over 200,000 Jews have been baptized as Protestants, and similar numbers as Roman Catholics; 650 Protestant missionaries minister to Jews at 213 mission stations across world; many believe future conversion of the Jews could ensure completion of world evangelization.

1899 Anglican biblical scholar, R.H. Charles (1855-1931) writes *Eschatology: the doctrine of a future life in Israel, Judaism and Christianity;* specializes in apocalyptic Jewish literature, publishes commentaries on books of Daniel and Revelation.

1899 Japan: Protestant church membership over next decade grows at 5.7% p.a., to 100,000 by 1914; Roman Catholics by 1914 reach 67,000.

1899 Iconographic renewal of the 20th century: Orthodox icons as liturgical art expressing christological truth.

1899 By end of century, most of the world's 980,000 pentecostals/charismatics are found in Black Africa, mostly in independent churches in South Africa or West Africa or as unrecognized charismatics inside or outside mission structures, rejected by mainline Catholic and Protestant missions and denominations as, at best, unaffiliated semi-pagan crypto-Christians; or as, at worst, separatist, syncretistic, heretical, fanatical schismatics.

1900 **Global status:** 62 generations after Christ, world is 34.5% Christians (81.1% of them being Whites), 45.7% evangelized; with printed Scriptures available in 537 languages.

1900 Total of all Christian denominations begins to rise steeply as Christianity spreads across world, from only 92 in AD 1000, to 150 in AD 1500, to 510 in AD 1800, to 1,900 by AD 1900; then by 1985 to 22,000; proliferation seen by many in 1900 as a sure guarantee that world will soon become evangelized.

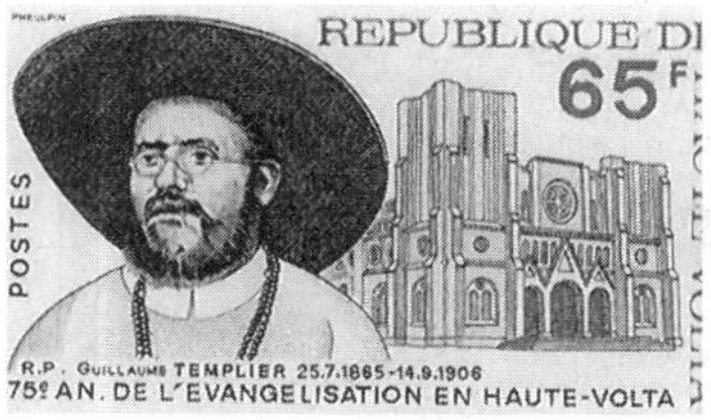


**AD 1900.** Pioneer foreign missionary Guillaume Templier begins evangelization of Upper Volta.

1900 *Upper Volta* (now *Burkina Faso*). First Christians and first mission (French White Fathers).

1900 First cinemas in fair sideshows; 1905, first cinema theatre.

1900 Boxer revolt in China kills 47,000 Catholics (out of 1.2 million) with 5 bishops and 31 priests, and 2,000 Protestants with 188 missionaries and children.

1900 In Hawaii, catastrophic decline of Aboriginal population through disease from 200,000 (in 1775) to 70,000 (1850) to 35,000 (1900).

1900 Peak of massive Roman Catholic immigration from Europe to USA.

1900 *Northern Solomons (Bougainville).* First mission (Roman Catholic).

1900 International Council of Unitarian and Other Liberal Religious Thinkers and Workers, founded in USA; 1910, renamed International Congress of Free Christians and Other Religious Liberals; 1930, renamed International Association for Liberal Christianity and Religious Freedom (IARF).

1900 Minahasa (north of Celebes) entirely christianized.

1900 World's 10 largest cities: London 6,480,000, New York 4,242,000, Paris 3,330,000, Berlin 2,424,000, Chicago 1,717,000, Vienna 1,662,000, Tokyo 1,497,000, St Petersburg 1,439,000, Philadelphia 1,418,000, Manchester 1,255,000.

1900 Darwin's theory of evolution (the mutability of species) widely accepted by now, but his idea of natural selection as principal driving force for speciation not accepted until 1940s.

1900 Origins of Pentecostalism in USA: British-Israelite holiness preacher Charles F. Parham (1873-1929, Methodist) opens Bethel Bible School near Topeka, Kansas, with 40 students; 1901, they receive baptism of Holy Spirit; 1903 revival spreads through Kansas, 1905 Houston, 1906 to Los Angeles and thence across world (1906 Norway, 1907 Chile, 1908 China, 1909 Korea, 1910 Brazil, and so on).

1900 South India Missionary Conference, Madras, with delegates officially appointed by their respective bodies.

1900 German theoretical physicist Max Planck (1858-1947) originates quantum theory based on concept of radiant energy being quantized (radiated discontinuously in multiples of definite, fixed, indivisible units or quanta).

### *Technological (2nd Industrial) Revolution*

1900 Photocopying machine is invented in France, providing first facsimile-copying capability.

c1900 Great worldwide outpouring of Holy Spirit begins.

1900 In USA Protestantism 'Each one win one' becomes motto for many Baraca classes for men and Philathea classes for women; by 1913 these nationally organized classes involve nearly one million members from 32 denominations.

1900 New York Ecumenical Missionary Conference: 2,500 official delegates, 200,000 attenders; delegates from 162 mission boards; 500 speakers, huge public meetings; formation of an international missionary committee (to complete world missionary task) canvassed, urged, then unanimously adopted only to fizzle out soon after.

1900 Methodist layman John R. Mott publishes classic, *The evangelization of the world in this generation*; many Christian strategists envisage winning of entire world to Christ during 20th century, then seen as certain to be 'the Christian century'.

1900 In England, J.H. Smyth-Pigott, moved by the death of H.J. Prince, final messenger of the Holy Ghost, announces himself as Christ returned.

1900 R.R. Marrett, K.T. Preuss, and other scholars develop new theory of pre-animism: religion originates in experiencing mana, impersonal force.

1900 Sea Battle of Manila Bay (Philippines), May 1st 1898, lasting only 3 hours: an entire Spanish fleet of 7 fighting ships backed by 37 shore batteries destroyed by US fleet of 4 cruisers and 2 gunboats; US becomes a world power; 3 years later Filipino rebels lose 20,000 killed, US 4,000 killed.

1900 1st International Congress of Liberal Religion, held in London, under auspices of International Congress of Religious Liberals; 2nd Congress, Amsterdam; 3rd, Geneva; 4th, Boston; 5th, Berlin; 6th, Paris in 1913; further congresses arranged in Japan, China, India, Ceylon, Egypt, Turkey; all then abandoned due to World War I.

1900 Over 50% of Protestant foreign missionaries worldwide are women.

1900 Palestine: 50,000 Jews now resident.

1901 After 1st Industrial Revolution (fueled by steam power and coal in Britain, 1775), 2nd revolution arises due to electrical and chemical industries in Germany.

1901 First Atlantic wireless signal sent by G. Marconi (1874-1937) from Poldhu, Cornwall (UK) to St Johns, Newfoundland.

1901 UK: BFBS grand total of scriptures issued since 1808: 46,030,124 Bibles, 71,178,373 NTs, 52,763,047 portions.

1901 World's first billion-dollar corporation, US Steel; 1919, 6 such giant corporations.

1901 USA: National Federation of Churches and Christian Workers organized, culminating in 1908 formation of FCCCNA.

1901 USA: American Standard Version (ASV) of Bible, by American scholars working with English RV translators.

1901 Latter-Rain teaching: after 1,800 years of apparent cessation of large-scale charismata and 100 years of expectancy and teaching in USA on gifts of the Spirit, 'restoration of all things' begins with Spirit-baptism and glossolalia, as pentecostal power is restored to the church; thousands of seekers travel to revival centers in USA, Europe, Asia, South America; expounded in D.W. Myland, *The Latter Rain Pentecost* (1910).

1901 Founding of Consolata Missionary Fathers (IMC), in Turin, specifically for 'Evangelizzazione degli infedeli'; by 1983, 1,008 foreign missionaries in 248 houses.

1901 G. Sutherland publishes *20th century inventions.*

1901 Looking to the year 2000, H.G. Wells writes 'This gray confusion that is democracy must pass away inevitably... into the higher organism, the world-state of the coming years'; 1935, Wells identifies period 1919 to 2059 as Age of Frustration, evolving gradually through struggle to world government and world peace.

1901 H.G. Wells publishes *Anticipations of the reaction of mechanical and scientific progress upon human life and thought*; first comprehensive survey of future developments; 1902, modern study of the future launched when Wells calls for a strictly scientific futurism.

1901 Alsatian German theologian Albert Schweitzer (1875-1965) writes *The mystery of the Kingdom of God* asserting Christ must be interpreted in the light of his belief in imminent end of the world ('consequent eschatology'); also 1906 *The quest of the historical Jesus;* gives up brilliant career to work for 50 years at Lambarene mission hospital, Gabon.

1901 World community consists of 50 acknowledged states plus many colonies; by 1993, rises to 190 states, or 273 countries.

1901 Illustrating perils of prediction, aviation pioneer Wilbur Wright tells brother Orville that man will not be able to fly for 50 years; but they do, at Kitty Hawk in 1903.

1901 Scottish biblical exegete James Moffatt (1870-1944) publishes The Historical New Testament; 1913, The New Testament: A New Translation; 1925 The Old Testament: A New Translation, leading to 1926 Moffatt Bible; 1935, final edition.

1901 A rash of modern-language translations of English Bible (complete, or NT only) floods market throughout 20th century.
1901 3rd Ecumenical Methodist Conference, held in London, UK.
1902 Pakistan (then in India): Hindu outcaste mass movement into Methodist church begins.
1902 Adolf von Harnack (1851-1930) publishes his *The mission and expansion of Christianity during the first 3 centuries.*
1902 Team evangelism: 1902-08, R.A. Torrey (1856-1928) & C.M. Alexander (1867-1920) with 130,000 converts.
1902 30,000 killed in volcanic eruption of Mt Pele, Martinique.
1902 All-India Fourth Decennial Conference, Madras (Protestant missions), with official delegates.
1902 USA psychologist W. James (1842-1910) writes *The varieties of religious experience.*
1902 Germany: founding of evangelistic tent campaigns (German Tent Mission), 1924 Christian Endeavor, 1926 Baptist Tent Mission, 1926 Methodists, 1951 Evangelical Free Church Tent Mission.
1902 Young People's Missionary Education Movement (1911, title shortened to MEM) founded by 15 USA denominational boards, YMCA and SVMU, to enlist missionaries outside college world.
1902 *Centennial survey of foreign missions* (New York) published by J.S. Dennis, covering statistics of all Protestant missions worldwide.
1902 4th International Convention, Student Volunteer Movement for Foreign Missions, in Toronto, Canada, produces 691-page report *World-wide evangelization, the urgent business of the Church.*
1902 H.G. Wells writes *The discovery of the future.*
1902 Twentieth Century New Testament (TCNT) published in London and New York by mainly British churchmen; first of modern speech versions; reprinted frequently up to 1961.
1902 J. B. Rotherham publishes The Emphasized Bible (1868-1902, with single-volume edition 1916).
1903 Evangelization of Munduruccu Indians in Brazil begun by German Franciscans.
1903 First successful flight of a powered aircraft at Kitty Hawk, North Carolina (USA), by Wright brothers.
1903 Weymouth New Testament published.
1903 All Nations Flag Church (Church of God of Prophecy) founded, 1911 begins work overseas (Bahamas); by 1985, links with 69 countries.
1903 L.P. Gratacap (1851-1917) writes *The certainty of a future life in Mars*, a religio-scientific type of propaganda.
1903 New Testament in Modern Speech (NTMS) published, translated by British Baptist classical scholar R. F. Weymouth (1822-1902).
1904 Conversion of Indian evangelist and mystic, Sadhu Sundar Singh (1889-c1929); visits villages across India, also Tibet annually; encounters Christian ascetic in Himalayas, allegedly 284-year-old Maharishi of Mount Kailash (southwest Tibetan peak, 22,028 feet: cosmic centre of Universe for Buddhists, paradise of Shiva for Hindus); 1929, vanishes in Tibet, probably murdered by lamas.
1904 New Britain: massacre at Baining of 2 RC priests, 3 brothers, 5 nuns.
1904 Welsh revival through ministry of Evan Roberts (1878-1951) in Glamorganshire, Anglesey, Caernarvonshire, with 100,000 converts in Wales in 6 months; short-lived (1904-1906), but literally sweeps the world; worldwide publicity from the press; leads into worldwide Pentecostal movement including 1905 Switzerland and Germany, 1907 England.
1904 Premillennialist theologian W.E. Blackstone (1841-1935) writes *The Millennium*, teaches world has already been evangelized (cites Acts 2:5, 8:4, Mark 16:20, Colossians 1:23).
1905 1st Baptist World Congress, London; Baptist World Alliance (BWA) founded.
1905 In France, Catholic church separated from state.
1905 Evangelical awakenings in Denmark, Finland, Sweden, Germany, Russia, Madagascar, India (Assam, Kerala, Sialkot through Praying Hyde), Korea, China.
1905 Evangelistic Faith Missions (USA) formed.
1905 Evangelistic Council of London sponsors Greater London crusade with Torrey & Alexander team; 202 meetings, 1.1 million attenders, 14,000 conversions.

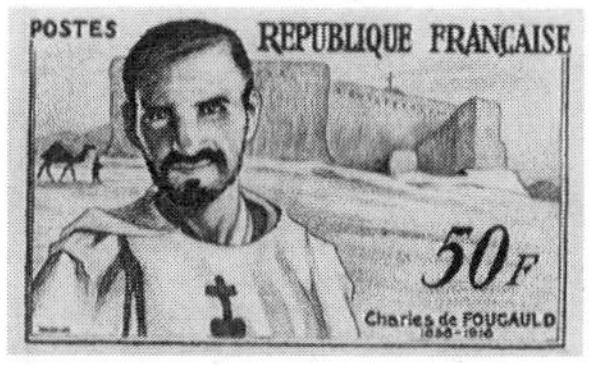


**AD 1905.** Foucauld, missionary martyr among Muslim tribes of Algerian Sahara.

1905 Charles de Foucauld, missionary hermit in Tamanrasset (Algeria), labors among Muslim tribes; 1916, assassinated in Senussi revolt.
1905 Albert Einstein (1879-1955) formulates Special Theory of Relativity (light always appears to travel at same speed, and nothing can exceed it), equates mass and energy in epochal formula $E=mc^2$; 1915, General Theory of Relativity (a theory of gravity, which causes time to slow down; space is curved by the presence of mass).
1905 Manchuria: 2,000 Presbyterians killed by Japanese Shintoists.
1905 India: pentecostal revival in Mukti Mission, Poona, under Anglican teacher Pandita Ramabai (1858-1922).
1905 Jules Verne's *L'éternel Adam*, with monster earthquake flooding world in 21st century and reemergence of lost continent of Atlantis.
1905 National conciliarism begins: 1905 Fédération Protestante de France, 1908 Federal Council of the Churches of Christ in North America (1950 NCC-CUSA), 1922 National Christian Council of China, 1922 Aliança Evangélica de Angola, et alia, up to 550 nationwide councils by 1983, all in theory committed to world mission.
1906 USA: Pentecostalism achieves nationwide publicity under Black holiness preacher W.J. Seymour (1870-1922) with revival in Azusa Street, Los Angeles, which lasts from 1906-09; thousands of seekers travel from Europe to seek their personal pentecost with glossolalia; 1906-1908, whole pentecostal movement in USA teaches 3-stage way of salvation.
1906 First indigenous schism in China: China Jesus Independent Church.
1906 China: 80,000 Orthodox in Manchuria entrusted to Russian mission, with bishop, archimandrite, 20 clergy; 1914, 5,035 Chinese believers; 1922, diocese of Harbin organized; 1935, 200,000 Orthodox in China with dioceses of Harbin, Peking, Shanghai, and 80,0 00 Orthodox in Chinese Turkestan.
1906 First recorded pentecostal meeting in continental Europe: Methodist prophet T.B. Barratt (1862-1940), a Cornishman, preaches to 2,000 in Christiana (Oslo); by 1910 Italy honeycombed with Pentecostal churches; Russian empire reached 1911 in Helsinki, 1914 St Petersburg, 1915 Moscow.
1906 Proliferation of world mission atlases, both Protestant (1906, 1910, 1925, 1938) and RC (1906, 1913, 1929), with statistics listed by mission societies or RC dioceses rather than by denominations and countries.
1906 C.F. Parham teaches that missionaries need only to receive the baptism with the Holy Ghost and can then, through the gift of glossolalia, be immediately understood in native languages to the farthest corners of the world; but Pentecostal missionaries abroad try this only to report failure.
1906 1st General Conference of Missionaries to the World of Islam, convened through Reformed missionary S.M. Zwemer, held in Cairo, Egypt.
1906 Laymen's Missionary Movement (LMM) launched as foreign missions auxiliary agency via SVM and 17 major North American Protestant denominations; uses large city-wide conferences, crusade dinners, business methods, publicity etc; by 1916, one million men have attended its 3,000 conferences, quadrupling USA Protestant mission giving.
1906 Scottish clergyman J. Hastings publishes *A dictionary of Christ and the Gospels.*
1906 V.T. Sutphen (1861-1945) writes novel *The Doomsman* that describes 21st-century neo-medieval New York 100 years after a 1925 plague decimates mankind.
1906 Evolution of concepts of 5-fold and 4-fold Full Gospel theology: 1906, Azusa Street mission propagates as normal steps or stages in a Christian's life these 5 steps: (1) his/her **Salvation** (Conversion), (2) his/her **Entire Sanctification** (Wesleyan Holiness pattern), (3) his/her **Baptism in the Holy Spirit** with initial evidence of speaking in **tongues**, (4) his/her involvement in **Divine Healing**, and (5) his/her awaiting of **Premillennial Second Coming** of Christ; 1914 Assemblies of God formed reducing this to 4-fold (Foursquare) Gospel on grounds that the Finished Work of Christ on the Cross covers steps (1) and (2) and combines them into one single step; 1914, rise of the Oneness movement teaching that everything in steps (1) to (4) including tongues comes at the one first stage of Water Baptism in the Name of Jesus.
1907 Massive revival in Korea beginning in Pyongyang; Protestants mushroom by 1914 to 196,389 (73% Presbyterians, 27% Methodists); phenomenal growth of churches, spreading also into Manchuria and China.
1907 Conference of Federated Missions in Japan inaugurated, meets annually.
1907 First pentecostal movement within Church of England, at parish in Sunderland under clergyman A.A. Boddy (1854-1930).
1907 USA: peak immigration rate of 1,285,000 Europeans in one year; immigrants from 1845-1914 total 33 million.
1907 *The Aquarian Gospel of Jesus Christ: the philosophic and practical basis of the religion of the Aquarian Age of the World*, by L.H. Dowling, published in Santa Monica, California; claims Jesus studied Hinduism under gurus in India for 20 years; Earth is now after 2,000 years moving out of constellation Pisces the Fish, heralding demise of Christianity, and Earth is now on threshold of New Age of Aquarius the Watercarrier, 11th sign of the zodiac.
1907 Centenary Conference, Shanghai (Protestant missions).
1907 USA: first major sweep of pentecostalism traverses southern holiness movement; in month-long meeting in Dunn, North Carolina ('Azusa Street East'), hundreds receive tongues-attested baptism in the Spirit; several holiness denominations become pentecostalized.
1907 R.H. Benson writes novel *Lord of the World*, about final struggle between Antichrist and Christ, with Armageddon and Advent, in 21st century, with Catholicism as only surviving form of religion in an atheistic world state; over period 1800-1988, numerous other science fiction authors incorporate same theme in published books and articles.
1907 Laymen's Missionary Movement of Southern Baptists formed by 200 laymen 'for mobilized laymen to evangelize our world in our lifetime', asserting that 'Southern Baptists are able financially and otherwise to conquer the world for Christ'; 1927, renamed Baptist Brotherhood of the South; 1938, goal of 'A Million Men for Christ'; 1950, Brotherhood Commission of SBC; 1987, enrollment 572,987 including 235,687 boys under 18 years.
1907 Sociologist S.C. Gilfillan becomes first scholar to study seriously methodologies in the art or science of forecasting and prediction; proposes term `mellontology'.
1907 Start of series *Encyclopédie des sciences ecclesiastiques*: 1907 *Dictionnaire de la Bible*, 1909 *Dictionnaire de théologie catholique*, still ongoing in 1975.
1907 *The Catholic encyclopedia* published; 1967 *New Catholic encyclopedia*, 1948 *Enciclopedia cattolica*, 1930 *Lexikon für Theologie und Kirche.*

***Postmodern era begins***

1907 World's Sunday School Association founded, in Rome; 1924 becomes worldwide federation; 1947 name changed to World Council of Christian Education; 1971 integrated into World Council of Churches.
1907 Japan: Conference of Federated Missions in Japan begins, meets annually.
1908 Million-ton meteorite or comet crashes near Tunguska, Siberia, with impact energy of 30 megatons; mass devastation still visible after 80 years.
1908 Manchurian Revival, at Changte under Jonathan Goforth (1859-1936).
1908 Nyasaland: Elliott Kamwana baptizes 10,000 Lakeside Tonga, start of major separatist church in Central Africa (Church of the Watch Tower).
1908 J. Wilbur Chapman's 6-week evangelistic campaign in Philadelphia (USA): 400 churches, 1.5 million attenders, 7,000 enquirers.
1908 5th Lambeth Conference; 242 Anglican bishops present.
1908 1st Pan-Anglican Congress, in London, with laity and clergy from all Anglican dioceses across world.
1908 European Baptist Congress, Berlin.
1908 National Missionary Campaign conducted in Canada by LMM: 4 conventions in 24 cities, concluding in 1909 with Canadian Missionary Congress in Toronto with 4,000 representatives from all Protestant churches.
1908 USA: first schisms in Black pentecostals split from Black pentecostals, withdrawing or being expelled from Black-dominated Apostolic Faith Mission (Azusa Street); Whites then develop 2-stage way of salvation, and in 1914 form Assemblies of God.
1908 Federal Council of the Churches of Christ in North America (FCCCNA) founded by 28 USA denominations; sets forth its 'Social Creed of the Churches' representing 30 denominations.
1908 J.L. Barton publishes *The unfinished task of the Christian church: introductory studies in the problem of the world's evangelization* (SVMU, London): 'Some have taken it to mean the complete christianization of all races and peoples on earth; others, giving every person on earth an opportunity to hear at least one address or sermon'.
1908 *Encyclopaedia of religion and ethics*, edited by J. Hastings, published in Edinburgh.
1908 *The doctrine of the Last Things: Jewish and Christian*, by W.O.E. Oesterley.
1908 *Avesta eschatology: compared with the Books of Daniel and Revelation*, by Lawrence H. Mills.
1908 First Middle East oil discovered in Persia by British, then in 1930 in Arabia by USA technicians; by 1990, supplies 25% of world's oil needs.
1909 Pentecostal movement organized in Chile: USA Methodist missionary W.C. Hoover and 37 charismatics are excommunicated, form Iglesia Metodista Pentecostal.
1909 C.W. Eliot (president, Harvard University) publishes *The religion of the future.*
1909 Korean Protestants (8,000 church members, 200,000 all Christians) announce 'A Million Souls for Christ' movement; at same time Japanese 35-year occupation enforces Shintoism, kills thousands.
1909 National Missionary Campaign in USA: 70 city-wide conventions, closing in 1910 with National Missionary Congress in Chicago; similar events in Australia, Ceylon, Denmark, Germany, Holland, New Zealand, South Africa, Sweden, UK.
1909 'Berlin Declaration' by German Evangelicals rejects Pentecostal claims of restoration of charismata, condemns all pentecostalism as a diabolic manifestation; as a result, Pentecostalism spreads only slowly in German-speaking nations.
1909 C.I. Scofield publishes Scofield Reference Bible.
1909 *Die Religion in Geschichte und Gegenwart* (5 volumes) published in Tubingen.
1909 E.M. Forster (1879-1970) writes 'The Machine stops':

world's inhabitants have atrophied to slug-like existence living in tiny, private cells facing god-like Machine (= television/computer); people do nothing but lecture or listen to lectures; suddenly Machine stops, humanity expires.

1909 Calcutta, India: Inter-Religious Conference held in tradition of 1893 World's Parliament of Religions, with Hindu, Catholic, Protestant, and other speakers.

1910 Beginnings of Faith and Order Movement, on initiative of Protestant Episcopal Church in Cincinnati, USA, calling for a world conference.

1910 Protestant and Anglican missionaries worldwide number 45,000.

1910 Mexico: National Revolution kills 7% of population including many Evangelicals; anticlerical and anti-church laws, though aimed at Catholic Church, result in decline of older Protestant churches.

1910 USA team evangelism: 1910-30, Billy Sunday (1862-1935) & H. Rodeheaver (1880-1955); former preaches to 100 million, with 1 million enquirers (300,000 conversions).

1910 World Union of Catholic Women's Organizations formed; by 1970, 40 million members.

1910 Religious surveys using social scientific methodology become widespread in USA.

1910 Great Britain: 122,000 telephones in use, rising by 1931 to 2 million.

1910 First charismatic prayer groups form within mainline state churches of Europe: German Pentecostal leader J.A.A.B. Paul (1853-1931) remains a Lutheran minister until his death.

1910 Rise of organized Fundamentalism in USA with publication of widely-distributed 12-volume paperback anti-modernist series, *The Fundamentals*, containing defenses of fundamental doctrines by conservative writers; evolution not initially rejected; antievolution not regarded as a fundamental doctrine until 1925.

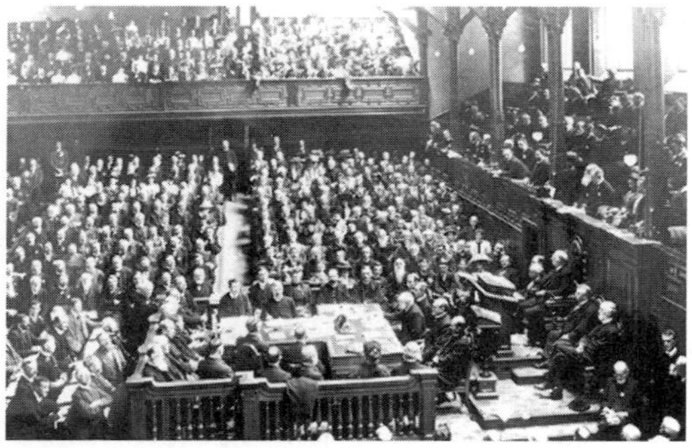

**AD 1910.** Landmark Conference for global mission and world evangelization: Edinburgh.

1910 World Missionary Conference, Edinburgh, Scotland (previously called 3rd Ecumenical Missionary Conference until 1908 change); 1,355 delegates; beginning of 20th-century ecumenical movement; report of Commission I is entitled *Carrying the Gospel to all the non-Christian world*, stating 'The Church is confronted today with a literally world-wide opportunity to make Christ known', and including survey 'Unoccupied sections of the world'.

1910 Reunion of Christendom through organic union of denominations set forth as goal by bishop C.H. Brent (1862-1929) of Protestant Episcopal Church in the USA, as essential stage to conversion of world.

1910 Pope Pius X (1835-1914) at General Chapter of the Franciscans has vision in public of future destruction of Vatican; teaches that Antichrist has already arrived in atheistic and pagan society of his day; condemns modernism and modernist scholarship.

1910 N. Maclean writes *Can the world be won for Christ?* (London).

1910 Men and Religion Forward Movement (MRFM, 1910-12) advances LMM concerns into a global social gospel organization, but includes nationwide evangelism, social-evangelism crusades, home and foreign missions, business ethics, detailed research on 70 cities, and every kind of Christian endeavor; reaches 1,492,646 persons in 60 USA towns through 7,062 meetings; 1913, carried worldwide by touring party.

1910 Church of God (Cleveland) 'initiates efforts at world evangelism', begins World Missions in Bahamas, Egypt and Cuba; by 1985, 109 foreign missionaries with churches in 98 countries; 1987, elaborate plan Decade of Destiny announced for every year 1988-1999.

1910 J.W. Bashford writes *God's missionary plan for the world* (London).

1911 Watch Tower movement (USA) enters Northern Rhodesia from Nyasaland to meet with extraordinary success, with in 1970 over 800,000 living Zambians estimated to have belonged at one time or another.

1911 First Catholic chair of missiology in world: university of Munster, Westphalia; first professor, Joseph Schmidlin (1876-1944); founds also International Institute for Missionary Research/Science; opposes Nazism, dies in prison camp.

1911 2nd Baptist World Congress (BWA), Philadelphia (USA).

1911 2nd General Conference on Muslim Missions, again organized through S.M. Zwemer, held in Lucknow (India).

1911 S.M. Zwemer publishes *Unoccupied mission fields of Africa and Asia.*

1911 4th Ecumenical Methodist Conference, held in Toronto, Canada.

1912 USA team evangelism: 1912-45, Mordecai Ham & W.J. Ramsay.

1912 Burma: Self-Supporting Karen Baptist Missionary Society splits ex ABFMS.

1912 Roman Catholic anthropologist W. Schmidt SVD (1868-1954) publishes *Der Ursprung der Gottesidee* (The origin of the idea of God) (12 volumes, 1912-1955), holding that most primitive peoples should be regarded as monotheists; develops methodology of history.

1912 V.S. Azariah (1874-1945) consecrated bishop of Dornakal; first Anglican Indian bishop.

1912 French Jewish social scientist E. Durkheim (1858-1917) publishes classic, *The elementary forms of the religious life: a study in religious sociology.*

1912 Orthodox sectarians in Russian empire number 30 million, including 25 million Old Believers, 1,200,000 Molokans (Spiritual Christians-Milkdrinkers), 300,000 Khlysty (Spiritual Christians-Whippers).

1912 *International review of missions* begins publication; editor J.H. Oldham (1874-1969).

1912 First attempt by a mission body to reach systematically every home in an entire nation: 1912-17 in Japan, Oriental Missionary Society reaches its 10,300,000 homes; later extended to other countries, then to world.

1912 Belgian archeologist and philologist Franz Cumont (1868-1947), Protestant specialist on history of religions, writes *Astrology and religion among the Greeks and Romans.*

1912 *IRM* from origin publishes regular articles on future face of missions in China, India, Persia, Burma, Africa, Islam, et alia.

1913 British mathematicians and philosophers Bertrand Russell (1872-1970) and Alfred North Whitehead (1861-1947) publish *Principia Mathematica*, which influences fields of symbolic logic and set theory.

1913 Liberian Grebo prophet William Wade Harris (c1865-1929) preaches in Ivory Coast resulting in 120,000 converts by 1915, and eventually in large Harrist denominations.

1913 Highwater mark of influence of Watchword 'The Evangelization of the World in this Generation' on Protestant missions; decline thereafter.

1913 European Baptist Congress, Stockholm.

1913 Committee on Cooperation in Latin America (CCLA) created at New York conference; 1916, Congress on Christian Work in Latin America, held in Panama with 50% of delegates being Latin Americans.

1913 German theologian and musician Albert Schweitzer (1875-1965) goes to French Equatorial Africa with Paris Evangelical Missionary Society, founds Lambarene hospital.

1913 Moffatt Bible published: NT 1913, complete Bible 1924.

1913 English missionary C.T. Studd (1862-1931), deeply impressed by report *Carrying the Gospel*, founds Christ's Etceteras (later renamed Worldwide Evangelization Crusade) to focus on evangelizing 'the remaining unevangelized parts (peoples) of the world'.

1913 United Missionary Campaigns across USA under LMM, Foreign Missions Conference of North America, and Home Missions Council of USA; 695 Protestant interdenominational conferences held by 1916.

1913 H.G. Wells, in novel *The world set free*, forecasts discovery of artificial radioactivity, liberation of atomic energy, atomic bombs, a world war with England/France/USA against Germany, and all world's major cities destroyed by bombing.

1913 Conservative Judaism movement begins in USA.

1913 World Alliance for Promoting International Friendship through the Churches (WAPIFC) founded, with national groups in 36 countries; dissolved in 1946.

1913 South Slavs (Croats, Serbs, Bosniacs): 2 million perish during World War I.

**Epoch VIII: AD 1914-1950**

## VIGOR AMIDST STORM

1914 **Global status:** 63 generations after Christ, world is 34.7% Christians (76.2% of them being Whites), 49.2% evangelized; with printed Scriptures available in 676 languages; total martyrs since AD 33, 24,340,000 (0.5% of all Christians ever; recent rate 17,700 per year).

1914 Value of world trade multiplies fiftyfold from $700 million in 1750, to $40,000 million by 1914.

### *First World War devastates Europe*

1914 World War I begins, with 42 million men mobilized by Allies versus 23 million by Central Powers; by its end in 1918, 8.4 million combatants (troops) killed (5 million Allied, including 1.7 million lost by Russia and 1.3 million by France; 3.4 million Central Powers, including 1.7 million by Germany and 1.25 million by 50-million Austro-Hungarian Empire); 13 million civilians killed; combatants wounded, 21 million; 115,000 tons of poison gas used in Western Front.

1914 Uganda: mass revival, Society of the One Almighty God (KOAB), or Malakite Church, secedes ex CMS with 91,740 Ganda adherents by 1921.

1914 Nomiya Luo Mission, first of Kenya's independent indigenous churches, begun in Nyanza as schism from Anglican Church.

1914 Protestants in Latin America total over 500,000 communicants.

1914 Contestado movement begun in Joazeiro (Brazil) by Padre Cicero Romao Batista (1844-1934), declaring holy war against authorities in defense of Caboclos (Euro-Amerindian half-castes), who regard him as messiah.

1914 First motion pictures with sound showings: Photo-Drama of Creation (Watch Tower), seen by 35,000 daily.

1914 Foreign missionaries in Africa: 4,273 Protestants, 5,977 Roman Catholics.

1914 Protestants in Japan grow to 103,000 from only 10 in 1872.

1914 Roman Catholic bishops worldwide still all of European origin, except for 4 Indians in Kerala elevated in 1896.

1914 China: Protestant and Anglican missionaries number 5,462 including 1,652 wives.

1914 45% of all North American Indians now affiliated to churches (25% Protestant).

1914 Turkish sultan Mehmed V proclaims Jihad (Holy War), permits massacres of multitudes of Armenian, Syrian and Assyrian Christians, principally by Kurdish irregulars.

1914 Newly-elected pope Benedict XV (1854-1922) issues encyclical declaring World War I to be beginning of the Last Age: 'It seems as if the days foretold by Christ had indeed come: 'You shall hear of wars and rumours of wars. For nation shall rise against nation, and kingdom against kingdom' (Mt 24.6-7)'.

1914 USA Protestantism attempts to defuse militarism by forming Church Peace Union, also World Alliance for International Friendship (Constance, Germany, on day World War I begins); based on conviction that worldwide Christian forces could 'mobilize for a warless world'; USA's militaristic cause identified with Christ's Great Commission; 1919, Life and Work Committee formed independent of World Alliance, convenes conference 1920 at Geneva.

1914 Date of inauguration of Kingdom of God on Earth by Jehovah (with invisible Second Coming of Christ), as predicted by Watch Tower Bible and Tract Society; subsequent dates announced for Armageddon: 1925, 1941, 1975.

1914 84% of world's land surface, apart from polar regions, is under a European flag or that of a former European colony; of 9 nominally independent non-Western nations, only Japan remains truly autonomous.

1914 All India Conference of Indian Christians founded.

1915 Third major massacre of Armenian Christians by Turks; at least 600,000 perish in Anatolia, with a further 600,000 fleeing or deported from Turkey.

1915 Anti-trinitarian or 'Jesus only' doctrine introduced into USA Pentecostalism by F.J. Ewart.

1915 Elim Foursquare Gospel Alliance and Revival Party begun in Britain by Pentecostal healer G. Jeffreys (1889-1962); 1935, founds World Revival Crusade.

1915 Husayn-McMahon Correspondence (1915-16): Arab Revolt proposed by Husayn of Mecca in exchange for Arab state in Palestine.

1915 Conference of Missionary Translators, with 6 missionary couples, meets in Chichicastenango (Guatemala) to set foundation for modern Bible translation movement; by 1997 becomes Wycliffe Bible Translators/SIL with 6,000 missionaries worldwide at work in over 1,500 languages.

1916 Completion of 5,787-mile Trans-Siberian Railroad linking Moscow and Vladivostok.

1916 Rasputin (1872-1916), mystic believed to be corrupting Russian royal court, assassinated by noblemen.

1916 Sea floods Holland (January 14); 10,000 perish.

1916 Worst battle of World War I, at Verdun (February 21-December 18). German attack ultimately fails, with both sides suffering heavy losses: 40 million shells are fired, French suffer 543,000 casualties and Germans 434,000.

1916 Kenya: mass movement begins into all churches.

1916 *Bibliotheca Missionum* periodical begun by Robert Streit OMI (1875-1930) under SC Propaganda (Rome), covering all mission literature in past centuries; completed and discontinued 1974.

1916 Invention of public-opinion polls by Literary Digest in USA; 1935, regular religious polls emerge (profession, adherence, attendance, belief), through Gallup (AIPO), Roper, NORC, Harris, et alia.

1916 French Jesuit priest and paleontologist Pierre Teilhard de Chardin (1881-1955) conceives ideas of: (1) evolution as not primarily materialistic but of a psychic nature, evolving with progressive consciousness from Point Alpha (creation by a personal God) toward the evolutionary goal Point Omega, God's new creation with Christ as Cosmocrat and perfecter of evolution; and (2) the evolving noosphere, a corporate biological entity with power of reflective thought enveloping the Earth with a dense covering of thinking brains in ever closer communication with each other, as a stupendous thinking machine, superior to the biosphere (the envelope of life without reflective thought).

1916 Germany: Course on Mission Science for Mission Clergy, held at Cologne (5-7 September), both reported by J. Schmidlin; 1919, Mission Course for Missionaries and Religious Priests, at Düsseldorf (7-14 October); 1923, first of longstanding Louvain Missiological Weeks, held in Belgium.

1916 Lebanon: Ottomans murder 100,000 Maronites (22% of entire Maronite population).

1916 World Dominion Movement founded in Britain (1924, Survey Application Trust), publishes long series of detailed surveys of missions by countries by Anglican lay leader Kenneth G. Grubb (1900-1980) and others; formally closed in 1968.

1916 J.H. Oldham publishes *The world and the gospel*, contending that the evangelization of the world depends on spiritual authority and power rather than on resources of men and money.

1916 1st Evangelical Congress of Latin America, a Protestant missionary conference held in Panama as first of a series (also 1925, 1929, 1949); several new IMC-related missionary councils result.

1917 British occupy Ottoman territory of Palestine and issue Balfour Declaration supporting Jewish national homeland there.

1917 Apparition of Virgin Mary at Fatima, Portugal, bringing about religious renewal reinforcing conservatism of Portuguese Catholicism; '3rd prophecy of Fatima' never published by Vatican but held to predict global holocaust and annihilation of church.

1917 20,000 Nestorians massacred by Turks and Kurds.

1917 Bolshevik Revolution in Russia, followed by civil war; 1.5 million, mostly Christians, killed; 1918, decree on separation of church and state; 1.5 million flee abroad as refugees.

1917 Mexico: beginning of state persecution of Roman Catholics after 1911 revolution; 1926, Spanish clergy deported, by 1931 violent persecution, schisms; 1935, priests prohibited in 14 states; 1940, attacks subside.

1917 True Jesus Church (Chen Ye-Su Chiao Hui) begun in Peking, a charismatic schism ex Apostolic Faith Movement; by 1975, a Chinese world mission with missionaries serving in Hong Kong, India, Indonesia, Japan, Korea, Malaysia, Singapore, USA.

1917 Interdenominational Foreign Mission Association of North America (IFMA) founded 'to make possible a united testimony concerning the existing need for a speedy and complete evangelization of the world', organized by SAGM, CIM, CAM, AIM, SIM, SAIM, WUMSA and later other Protestant missions of fundamentalist stance: 1967, 44 member missions with 8,500 missionaries in over 100 countries; 1979, 49 agencies with over 9,000 in over 115 countries; 1985, 103 nondenominational agencies in USA and Canada with over 11,000 foreign missionaries (over 8,000 from North America).

1917 R. Otto writes *Das Heilige* (The idea of the holy).

1917 Largest evangelistic crusade in history: Billy Sunday New York Crusade, for 10 weeks from April; out of 4.7 million population, over 98,000 'hit the sawdust trail' (decisions/enquirers), giving $120,500 'love offering'; then for 3 years, multiweek crusades in 18 major cities in 12 states, including 1917 Los Angeles, Atlanta (Georgia), 1918 Washington DC, Chicago, Fort Worth (Texas), 1919 Richmond (Virginia), Tampa (Florida), 1920 Norfolk (Virginia).

1917 V. Rousseau (1879-1960) writes *The Messiah of the Cylinder* in which socialist atheists rule Britain tyrannically until Christian Russians eventually defeat them.

1918 Women's suffrage is enacted in Great Britain.

1918 Hungary, defeated in war with over half Hungarian population dead, cedes three quarters of its former territories to Romania, Yugoslavia, and Czechoslovakia as war reparations.

1918 Global influenza pandemic, the most deadly in history, sweeps the world in 3 waves over 2 years, attacking 2 billion and killing around 40 million often overnight (20 million in India, over 500,000 in USA), via migratory birds and domestic animal reservoirs; also 10 other global pandemics since 1700, including 1957 and 1968.

1918 Nigeria: influenza epidemic (part of worldwide swine flu epidemic) brings about formation of prayer and healing groups which later grow into large indigenous churches: Cherubim & Seraphim, Church of the Lord (Aladura), and Christ Apostolic Church.

1918 USA: United War Work Campaign (interfaith: RCs, Jews, YMCA, YWCA, Salvation Army, et alia) raises $175,500,000, 'largest single amount ever offered voluntarily in history of world'.

1918 USA: Committee on the War and the Religious Outlook begins 5-year analytical survey of post-war world.

1918 Hungarian Lutheran Church loses half a million members with reduction of Hungary in size and dispersal of population to non-Lutheran areas.

1918 Movement into churches in Congo takes on massive proportions.

1918 Fundamentalism/modernism controversy erupts within USA Protestantism, until 1931, splitting every major denomination; premillennialism now a major part of all revivalist preaching.

1918 *The evangelistic work of the Church*, being the report of the Archbishops' Third Committee of Inquiry (London), with noted definition 'To evangelize is so to present Christ Jesus...'.

1918 30 major USA denominations each separately launch their own monodenominational 'forward movements', most successful being Methodist Centenary Movement which raises $166 million for Methodist work; also 1919-1924 Seventy-Five Million Campaign within South Southern Baptist Convention, to raise $75 million to undergird world missions, ending in 1924 with $62 million raised.

1918 Worldwide Evangelism, a vision of Pentecostal evangelist Aimee S. McPherson (1890-1944), who then in 1922 broadcasts first radio sermon, and in 1923 founds Angelus Temple, Los Angeles, and the International Church of the Foursquare Gospel.

1918 USA Methodists launch Christian Crusade for World Democracy, to further Protestant expansion.

1918 USA Presbyterian executives believe the War experience justifies 'Protestant Christianity in launching a united drive for world evangelism'.

1918 Interchurch World Movement of North America (IWM) launched to seek 'complete evangelization of all life' and 'conquest of the world for Christ' in one massive 'forward movement'; vast support from entire range of 34 major USA denominations and 85% all USA Protestant missions; 1919, motto 'The giving of the whole Gospel to the whole world by the whole church'; aims to include virtually all church-related activity; 1920, World Survey Conference, Atlantic City (NJ) with 1,700 church leaders produces massive 2-volume World Survey books, with plan proposing evangelization of world within 3 years; 1920, member denominations raise its $336,777,572 budget but refuse to release it; in 7-day period, IWM collapses in financial fiasco and bankruptcy.

1918 Historical futurism (historicism) arises: 1918-1922, German historian O. Spengler (1880-1936) writes *Der Untergang des Abendlandes (The decline of the West);* critiqued by English historian A.J. Toynbee (1889-1975) in 12-volume *A study of history* (1934-1961); also sociologist P.A. Sorokin (1889-1968) in 4-volume *Social and cultural dynamics* (1937-1941), and a comparative critique of historical futurisms in *Social philosophies of an age of crisis* (1950).

1918 Deutsche Gesellschaft für Missionswissenschaft (German Society for the Scientific Study of Missions) founded in Berlin; 1920, first volumes published of *Missionswissenschaftliche Forschungen* (Researches in the Science of Missions).

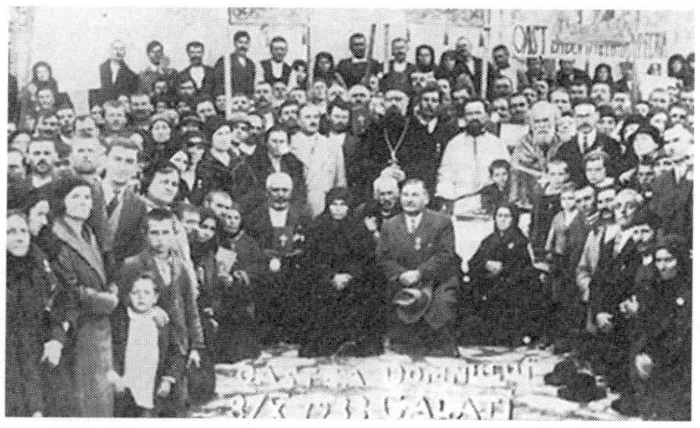

**AD 1918.** The Lord's Army, evangelistic renewal within the Romanian Orthodox Church, in its early days.

1918 Romania: start of The Lord's Army, an evangelical lay movement within the Romanian Orthodox Church.

1919 World's Conference on Christian Fundamentals, Philadelphia, USA; over 6,000 attenders.

1919 World's Christian Fundamentals Association (WCFA) founded in New York; a dispensationalist-premillennialist group organized to combat modernism, for premillennialist Protestants opposing modernism; 1920, label 'Fundamentalists' is coined by editor of *Watchman-Examiner*, Association active until 1950s.

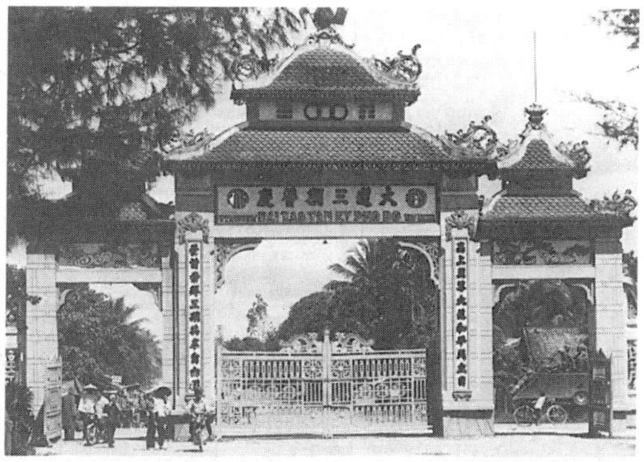

1919 Cao Daist Missionary Church founded by Le Van Trung in Viet Nam, a syncretistic mixture of popular Buddhism, Confucian ethics, ancestral cult, and Catholic-type organization, with membership of about 2.8 million by 1975.

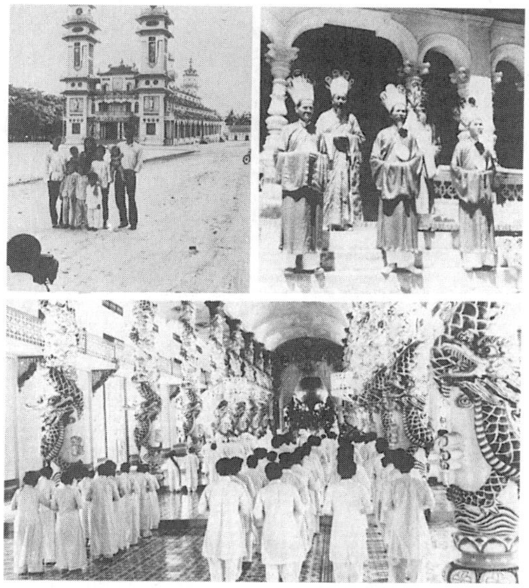

**AD 1919.** New-Religionists: Cao Daist Missionary Church. *Previous column, bottom.* Entrance to Holy City at Tay Ninh near Cambodian border, with above gate 'The Doctrine of the Third Revelation of God'. *Top left.* A family in front of twin-towered Holy See Great Divine Temple, built 1933-41. *Top right.* Cao Daist priests on steps of Temple. *Bottom.* Celebrants of Cao Daist mass inside Temple facing altar and Divine Eye (women on left, men on right, as always).

1919 Pope Benedict XV promulgates mission encyclical 'Maximum illud', on founding of younger churches.

1919 *Romerbrief* (commentary on Epistle to the Romans) by Swiss Protestant dogmatic theologian Karl Barth (1886-1968): origin of Neo-Orthodox Protestant theology, dialectical theology, theology of crises; Second Coming of Christ takes place in the Word preached.

1919 League of Nations organized for international cooperation, based on Geneva.

1919 Korea: Japanese rulers commence massive persecution of Christians; 200 thugs hired from Japan solely to terrorize missionaries; around 10,000 believers martyred.

1919 Russian Orthodox archbishop Joachim Levitzky of Nizhni-Novgorod murdered by being suspended upside down in his cathedral of Sebastopol.

1919 International Missionary Council (IMC) launched (directly succeeding Continuation Committee of 1910 World Missionary Conference, Edinburgh) with preliminary conference in Crans, Switzerland, then in 1921 (1-6 October) formally constituted and founded at Lake Mohonk, NY (USA); 2nd meeting in Oxford, England, in 1923.

1919 Tranquebar Conference on Church Union convened by bishop Azariah of Dornakal to speed mass movements of the 80 million Dalits (Outcasters) into the church.

1920 All-Russian Congress of Molokans (Spiritual Christians/Milk-drinkers) meets to organize resistance of the 1,200,000 Molokans to Bolshevism; 1923 forms All-Russian Union of Religious Communities of the Spiritual Christians; strong in Azerbaijan, Georgia, and Transcaucasia.

1920 First World Conference of Friends (Quakers), held in London.

1920 USSR: 78 Russian Orthodox bishops and 12,000 priests killed in first years of Bolshevik regime, 1917-26; by 1930, 42,800 priests killed; by 1960, 200 bishops murdered.

1920 Evangelization Society chartered in USA (Pittsburgh Bible Institute).

1920 6th Lambeth Conference; 252 Anglican bishops present.

1920 New USA investment in research and development (R&D) in 1920 stands at $140 million (in 1960 dollars) or 0.1% of GNP; rises to $0.8 billion in 1940 (0.4%); $22 billion, 55% devoted to military and space research, in 1965 (3.3% of GNP); future projections to AD 2000, 5.5%; AD 2100, 10%; AD 2500, 20%.

1920 Philippines: Catechism of Pius X translated into Jolo-Moro (Tausug) for Muslim population of 200,000 (1.9% of country).

1920 International Confederation of Christian Trade Unions founded.

1920 African indigenous churches number some 300 separate denominations across Africa with 600,000 professing adherents.

1920 London Conference of World Baptists.

1920 Quadrennial Convention, Student Volunteer Movement for Foreign Missions, in Des Moines, USA, on theme 'Christus Victor'; 1,375 student delegates from over 70 countries; large-scale shift noted away from earlier evangelicalism and interest in the Watchword.

1920 USA: term 'fundamentalist' coined, to mean a militant or angry conservative Evangelical; mostly dispensationist-premillennialist; after 1925, Fundamentalists have difficulty gaining national attention; 1930 Fundamentalism loses its initial national prominence within mainline Protestant churches and begins to fragment into small denominations; by 1960s term means ecclesiastical separatists; now almost all are separate Baptist dispensationalists; term excludes Holiness and Pentecostals.

1920 Interchurch World Movement, before its own sudden collapse and disintegration, proposes (1) a federal 'United Churches of Christ in America', and (2) a global 'League of Denominations' (parallel to League of Nations); both proposals fizzle out.

c1920 Swami Sivananda (1887-1963) works as Hindu reformer, author of 200 books, and founder of Divine Life Society, which grows to 400 branches worldwide by 1990.

1920 Ecumenical Patriarchate of Constantinople issues encyclical addressed to 'all the Churches of Christ' calling for formation of a 'League of Churches'.

1920 Catholic missiologist P. Charles (1883-1954) of Louvain identifies goal of mission as the founding or planting of the visible church in all lands and in all cultural groups (Charles, *Etudes missiologiques*, 1956).

1920 Mennonite Central Committee begun in Akron, PA (USA); many varieties of development services; by 1985, 527 foreign missionaries in 50 countries, based on long Anabaptist/ Mennonite centrality of the Great Commission.

1920 General Council of Cooperating Baptist Missions of North America organized; first vision to evangelize Africa extended in 1924 to Venezuela, then to worldwide outreach; 1953, renamed Baptist Mid-Missions; 1965, 725 USA missionaries in 27 countries; 1985, 636 missionaries in 32 countries.

1920 Russian engineer Y. Zamiatin (1884-1937) writes *We* (published outside USSR in 1927), the first great dystopia or anti-utopia; the world has one great nation, the United State, with population whose names are numbers; God='We', devil='I'; foresees absolute totalitarian state rule by AD 3000; state executes dissidents, performs brain operations; police surveillance, torture, denunciations; world dictator finally lobotomizes all the Numbers, including the narrator.

1920 K.E. Tsiolkovsky writes *Beyond the Planet Earth*.

1920 Dawn of Postmodernity after political-cultural collapse and upheaval of World War I, including ecumenical approach with a new theology/macroparadigm of the world religions.

1920 USSR: Lenin secretly orders 70,000 churches destroyed.

1921 USSR: civilian deaths in 1921-23 due to Civil War, other wars and famine total 13 million, mostly Christians.

1921 USSR, 1921-1960: deaths in slave labor camps total 19 million, mostly Christians.

1921 Soviet dictator V.I. Lenin (1870-1924) orders liquidation of 2,691 married Russian Orthodox priests, 1,962 monks, 3,447 nuns and vast numbers of lay Christians over period 1921-23.

1921 First broadcast of a church worship service: Sunday evening, 2 January, from Calvary Episcopal Church, Pittsburgh (USA), over first radio station KDKA.

1921 Synod of Karlovci held by exiled Russian Orthodox leaders (12 bishops, 40 priests, 100 laity), in Sremski Karlovci (Serbia); regarded as 1st Council of Russian Orthodox Church Outside Russia.

1921 First Baptist radio broadcast in USA.

1921 Simon Kimbangu (1889-1951) preaches leading to charismatic revival in Lower Congo, resulting in mass conversions, persecutions, jailings, deportations, and by 1960 a massive indigenous church (EJCSK); by AD 2000 has 9 million members baptized in the Holy Spirit.

1921 International Pentecostal Conference convened, in Amsterdam, in spite of opposition.

1921 African Orthodox Church founded in New York, ex Protestant Episcopal Church in the USA, with consecration of G.A. McGuire as patriarch by J.R. Vilatte (Mar Timotheus), claiming Jacobite apostolic succession, and in 1927 Daniel W. Alexander as primate of province.

1921 Religious Confederation of Mankind founded by German Protestant theologian Rudolf Otto (1869-1937); 1923, writes *The idea of the holy.*

1921 Institute of Social and Religious Research, New York, organized under J.R. Mott to carry on IWM's socioreligious scientific surveys; lasts until 1934.

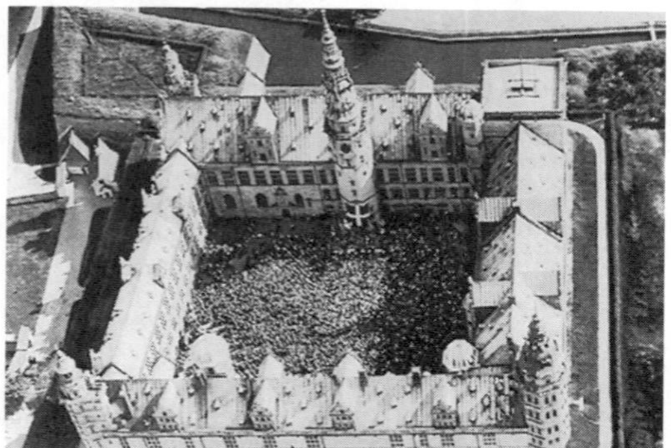

**AD 1921.** 10,000 persons attending Whitsun Congress of the Oxford Group, Elsinore Castle, Denmark.

1921 Oxford Group formed in Britain (1921-38), later renamed Moral Re-Armament (MRA); as evangelical renewal centering on personal devotion to Christ, the 4 Absolutes, personal evangelism, and 'drawing-room evangelism', spreads rapidly through major denominations and across world; by 1950 no longer solely christocentric, embracing renewal among Buddhists, Hindus, et alii.

1921 General Council of the Assemblies of God USA appoints committee on worldwide cooperation for 'the calling of a conference for the formation of an ecumenical union of Pentecostal believers for the more perfect and rapid evangelization of the world'; committee proves unable to meet and the effort collapses by 1923.

1921 Origins of global electronic church: first broadcast of a church worship service (Calvary Episcopal Church, Pittsburgh, USA), first Baptist broadcast, 1922 first Pentecostal broadcast (Aimee S. McPherson); by 1988, regular listeners/viewers for Christian programs number 1.2 billion (24% of the world).

1921 Futurism begins in USSR: New Economic Policy launched to cover 8 years; Stalin plans leap to communism using general forecast of Soviet economy up to 1932, but then murders all Russian futurists; futurism banned until 1967 with first Soviet forecasting unit, growing to over 1,000 units by 1970 when Soviet Association for Technological Forecasting organized; 1968, sociology and futurology revert again to status of quasi-religions; 1976, Council on Technological and Socioeconomic Forecasting begun, but ignored by Soviet bureaucrats.

1921 K. Capek (1890-1938) writes play *R.U.R* portraying humanity exterminated by its own chemically-created robots.

1921 Bolshevik Red Army defeats Kazakhs, kills many, then 1 million Kazakhs die of starvation in 1921-22 famine.

1921 Latin American Evangelization Campaign conducts citywide united campaigns; later becomes Latin America Mission.

1921 5th Ecumenical Methodist Conference, held in London, UK.

1922 National Christian Council of China founded.

1922 Aliança Evangélica de Angola founded.

1922 70% of all USA Protestant foreign missionaries now premillennialists.

1922 Britain: Bible Reading Fellowship (BRF) founded, for Anglicans.

1922 March on Rome by Fascists; Benito Mussolini (1883-1945) assumes power, rules as dictator of Italy until 1943.

1922 Semaines de Missiologie begun at Louvain (Belgium); annual study and research weeks.

1922 Catholic Action organized for participation of laity in the hierarchical apostolate, involving youth, students, workers, agriculturalists.

1922 Extraterrestrial origin of man now widely propounded: Adam and Eve were survivors of a cosmic catastrophe who came to Earth in a spaceship; later, Noah's ark interpreted as a spaceship (G.Babcock's *Yezad*, 1922, J.J. Savarin's trilogy 'Lemmus', 1972-77).

1922 USSR: Pentecostalism introduced by I.E. Voronaev (1892-1943), who aids growth in a few months to 20,000 in Ukraine alone; founds 350 congregations by 1929; 1932 imprisoned, 1943 shot in Leningrad.

1922 Four years after publication, O. Spengler's *The decline of the West* is now having massive impact on public consciousness of Europe.

1922 First International Missionary Congress, at Utrecht (Roman Catholic).

1922 Accession of pope Pius XI (1857-1939), who issues encyclical 'Miserimus Redemptor' stating: 'These are really the signs of the last age as was announced by Our Lord'; in further encyclical 'Ubi arcano', defines Catholic Action (long-existing organizations in Latin Europe for lay witness to Christ in everyday life) as 'participation of laymen in the hierarchical apostolate'.

1922 Irish dramatist George Bernard Shaw (1856-1950) writes the predominant utopian drama, *Back to Methuselah*, a 5-play parable of creative evolution from Adam and Eve in Garden of Eden (*In the beginning*) to *The thing happens* set in AD 2170, and to *As far as thought can reach* set in AD 31,920.

1923 2nd Meeting of International Missionary Council, Oxford, England.

1923 143,000 killed as earthquake destroys Yokohama (Japan) and half Tokyo.

1923 Greco-Turkish war ends with Treaty of Lausanne: Greeks forced to give up Izmir (Smyrna); 1.5 million Greek Orthodox in Turkey deported to Greece, and 400,000 Muslim Turks in Greece deported to Turkey; Christians in Turkey fall from 22% in 1900 to 0.5% by 1980.

1923 After Pentecostal evangelist Aimee Semple McPherson (1890-1944) broadcasts first radio sermon in 1922, she magnetizes millions in her 5,000-seat Angelus Temple, Los Angeles, from 1923-1944; founds International Church of the Foursquare Gospel and its missions.

1923 Lutheran World Convention (LWC) formed at Eisenach (Germany); 1947 becomes Lutheran World Federation (LWF).

1923 BBC (Britain) commences radio broadcasting, including daily Christian programmes (origin of the 'electric church'); in USA, 10 churches now operate radio stations; by 1928, 60 stations, falling by 1933 to 30; in 1936, BBC commences religious television.

1923 *Evangelism in the modern world* (London) written by Methodist minister, E.A. French and 9 other scholars, using definition 'Evangelism is the proclamation of good news.'

c1923 Million Testaments Campaigns founded in Philadelphia, USA, by journalist G.T.B. Davis, for scripture distribution in needy areas including China, Latin America, and the Jewish world.

1923 *Christianity and liberalism* published by J. Gresham Machen (1881-1937), conservative Presbyterian theologian (Princeton Theological Seminary), casting him as foremost spokesman for the Fundamentalist coalition in USA; becomes leading controversialist; 1933 founds Independent Board for Presbyterian Foreign Missions, 1935 defrocked, 1936 secedes from PCUSA and founds Orthodox Presbyterian Church.

1923 Chicago NT professor E. J. Goodspeed (1871-1962) publishes An American Translation (NT in modern English); 1927, OT follows under J. M. P. Smith; 1939, with Apocrypha forms The Complete Bible: An American Translation (CB-AT).

1924 Regional or subcontinental conciliarism begins: precursor of Near East Christian Council (NECC) founded, at Mount of Olives, Jerusalem; by 1983, some 50 such regional councils exist.

1924 Survey Application Trust/World Dominion Press founded by T. Cochrane, S.J.W. Clarke, Roland Allen.

1924 First international Christian radio station, NCRV, begun in Netherlands by Dutch Protestants.

1924 10,000 Orthodox bishops, priests, monks and nuns in USSR executed by Bolsheviks under dictator Joseph Stalin (1879-1953).

1924 Centenary New Testament published (H.B. Montgomery).

1924 USA: White ministers all withdraw from interracial Pentecostal Assemblies of the World (Oneness Pentecostals) to form a separate White denomination, explaining that 'the mixture of races prevents the effective evangelization of the world'; becomes The Pentecostal Church, Incorporated.

1924 Philosopher, atheist, and mathematician Bertrand Russell writes *Icarus: or the future of science*, warning that science could destroy mankind.

1924 Fellowship of Faiths movement, aiming to unite 6 world religions, begins in New York.

1925 Spirit Movement (Aladura) in Nigeria; charismatic revivals within Anglican Church lead to major indigenous churches: Cherubim & Seraphim, Christ Apostolic Church, Church of the Lord (Aladura).

1925 United Church of Canada formed (union of Methodists, Presbyterians and Congregationalists).

1925 Premillennialists in USA begin to speculate that Roman Empire might be about to be revived under Mussolini as Antichrist; fascist salute seen as showing authorities mark of the beast on their hands.

1925 World's 10 largest cities: New York 7,774,000, London 7,742,000, Tokyo 5,300,000, Paris 4,800,000, Berlin 4,013,000, Chicago 3,564,000, Ruhr 3,400,000, Buenos Aires 2,410,000, Osaka 2,219,000, Philadelphia 2,085,000.

1925 League of Militant Godless (LMG) founded in USSR to destroy religion; by 1932, 5,673,000 members, plus 1.5 million child members; by 1937, 2 million; by 1940, 3 million; 1941, disbanded as a failure.

1925 Romanian Orthodox patriarchate founded in Bucharest.

1925 Congress on Christian Work in South America held in Montevideo, Uruguay.

1925 USA: Lutheran Church—Missouri Synod operates radio station KFUO, St Louis; 1930 begins 'The Lutheran Hour' broadcast over WHK in Cleveland, Ohio, which by 1931 is heard by 5 million a week, growing by 1987 to 40 million regular listeners around world.

1925 Era of large evangelistic healing campaigns in Europe and USA under first generation of Pentecostal evangelists, including Smith Wigglesworth (1859-1947) who preaches to large crowds in most of world's largest capitals.

1925 Paramahamsa Yogananda (1893-1952) founds Self Realization Fellowship in California, and authors famed *Autobiography* of a Yogi.

1925 Radio sets in use: Great Britain 1,654,000; USA 2,500,000, rising by 1940 to 30 million.

1925 Foreign missionaries serving abroad: 88,000 Roman Catholics in 66,400 stations, 30,000 Protestants and Anglicans in 4,600 stations.

1925 Lutheran World Conference held in Oslo, Norway.

1925 Cost of a copy of Bible (equivalent US dollars): AD 1350, $2,000; 1455 (Gutenberg), $500; 1650, $100; 1925, $3; later, by 1980, $1.

1925 Physicists W. Heisenberg, M. Born, P. Jordan establish basis for matrix mechanics, first version of quantum mechanics.

1925 Universal Christian Conference on Life and Work, Stockholm (Sweden), on economics, industry, social and international problems; 600 official church delegates from 37 countries.

1925 *World missionary atlas* produced by H.P. Beach & C.H. Fahs (New York); largest missions atlas to date.

1925 2nd Evangelical Congress of Latin America, held in

Montevideo (Uruguay).
1925 India: religio-political Rashtriya Swayamsevak Sangh (RSS) founded by Hindu nationalist K. B. Hedgewar (1890-1940), then led by M. S. Golwalkar until 1973, then by Madhukar Dattatreya in militant defense of Hinduism; 1985, 56,000 local branches (*shakas*) and 700,000 committed volunteers (*swayamsevaks*).
1925 Siam (Thailand): Protestants number 14,800.
1925 Foreign Missions Convention, held in Washington DC, USA; attention paid to global problem of child mortality and exploitation of child labor in Far East.
1926 First international Muslim organization, Al-Mutamar al-Alam al-Islami, is formed.
1926 First public demonstration of television, in England; 1928, color television demonstrated for first time, by Baird.
1926 Church property nationalized in Mexico.
1926 German Association for Mass Evangelism (Deutscher Verband für Volksmission) begun, uniting many state church evangelists and evangelistic programs over last decade.
1926 Unevangelized Tribes Mission of Borneo formed (USA).
1926 Assembly Hall Churches (Little Flock; indigenous) begun by Watchman Nee in China.
1926 Famine in northwest China: 8 million die of starvation in 3 years.
1926 Largest schism in Mexico from Roman Catholic Church, leading to formation of Orthodox Catholic Apostolic Mexican Church, by 1970 with 10 bishops and 60,000 members.
1926 Jesuits begin work among Japanese of Brazil; first 14 Japanese baptisms, in São Paulo; by 1978, of 1 million Japanese there, 630,000 are Catholics.
1926 28th International Eucharistic Congress, Chicago.
1926 World Union for Progressive Judaism founded, in London, to unite Reform (Liberal) Judaism; 1970, 1,100,000 members in 25 countries.
1926 Germany: RC religious orders number 559 male (10,000 members), 6,600 female (74,000 members).
1926 USA: Northern Baptist superintendent of evangelism B.T. Livingstone introduces Friendly Visitation Evangelism for Laymen.
1926 Freemasons number 4,200,000 in 28,000 lodges.
1926 R.E. Speer writes *The unfinished task of foreign missions.*
1926 Lighthouse of International Foursquare Evangelism (LIFE Bible College) begun by Aimee S. McPherson in Los Angeles, USA, for training in world mission and evangelism.
1926 *Great Soviet Encyclopedia* (Bolshaya sovetskaya entsiklopedya) begun, reaching 65 volumes by 1947; 1949-1958, second edition by 8,000 scholars.
1927 Invention of talking movies.

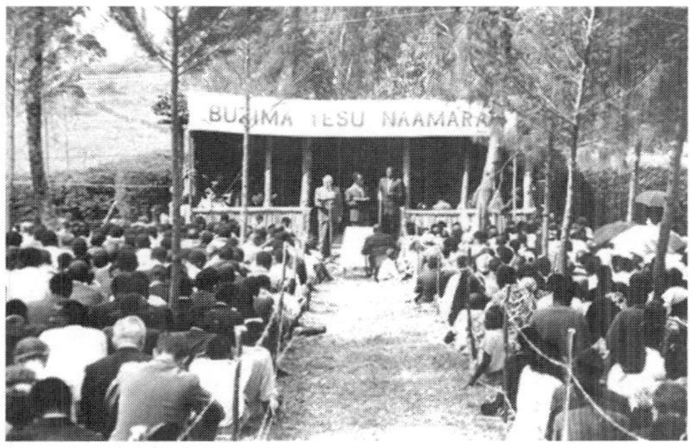


**AD 1927.** Team preaching in 3 or 4 languages has spread the Ruanda Revival worldwide; banner translated reads 'Jesus Satisfies'.

1927 East African Revival movement (Balokole, Saved Ones) emerges in Ruanda, moves rapidly across Uganda, East Africa, Zaire, later to Sudan and Malawi, with cells in Europe and America; from 1931-85, some 80 mass revival conventions are held across East Africa, including 1931 Gahini, 1936 Mukono (Uganda), 1937 Kabete (Kenya), 1939 Katoke (Tanganyika), 1945 Kabale ('Jesus Satisfies'), 1949 Kabete (15,000 attenders), 1964 Mombasa (20,000), 1970 Thogoto (40,000), 1978 Tumutumu (45,000), 1979 Thogoto (50,000), and irregularly up to 1997 Mbarara (Uganda).
1927 Stalin threatens to execute entire Orthodox clergy of Russia (146,000 including monks and nuns), blackmails acting patriarch into capitulating.
1927 USA: 50 radio stations now licensed to religious bodies.
1927 China: 20 million killed in civil wars, 1927-1949; in anti-Christian movement, 5,000 of the 8,000 Protestant missionaries leave.
1927 China: rapid expansion continues of 2 charismatic indigenous groups: Watchman Nee's Little Flock, and Preaching Bands of John Sung (Song Shangjie).
1927 Church of Christ in China founded, uniting 7 Protestant denominations.
1927 Origins of Latter Rain revivals and return to primitive pentecostalism, in South Africa (Blourokkies) and (c1930) Germany.
1927 Physicist W. Heisenberg's Uncertainty Principle: we cannot measure both the position and velocity of an electron at the same time.
1927 Author Rudyard Kipling writes 'With the Night Mail', predicting for AD 2000 a world without nationalism or warfare, with atomic-powered zeppelins flying at 300 miles per hour; and 'As easy as A.B.C.' forecasting worldwide universal affluence and privacy in AD 2065 due to new technology.
1927 English biologist J.B.S. Haldane in 'The Last Judgment' envisages no landings possible on planet Mars until AD 10 million.
1927 Committee on the Christian Approach to the Jews convenes conferences in Budapest and Warsaw, also 1931 and 1934 Atlantic City (USA).
1927 Council of Western Asia and Northern Africa formed, 1929 renamed Near East Christian Council (NECC), 1944 renamed Near East Council of Churches, replaced in 1974 by Middle East Council of Churches (MECC).
1927 Smith-Goodspeed Bible translated: NT 1923, Bible 1927.
1927 1st World Conference on Faith and Order, Lausanne; over 400 delegates from 90 churches (Roman Catholics being forbidden by pope).
1927 Association of Baptists for Evangelism in the Orient (ABEO) formed; 1939, name changed to ABWE (WE = World Evangelism); 1985, 462 missionaries in 21 countries.
1927 G.H. Williams writes 'The evangelization of the world', in Sir John Marchant (ed), *The future of Christianity.*
1927 Georges Lemaitre (1894-1966), Belgian priest/civil engineer/astrophysist/ cosmologist is first to formulate and propose modern Big Bang theory of origin of the Universe; resolves centuries-old religion-versus-science dispute with aphorism: 'Science answers the questions how, when, where, what; theology answers the questions why, who.'
1927 First World Population Conference, held at Geneva (Switzerland), organized by American Birth Control League, et alii.
1928 Stalin attempts to liquidate Ukrainian Autocephalous Orthodox Church; 16 archbishops and bishops die in prison, 1,150 priests and 20,000 lay leaders die in camps; 1932, planned mass starvation, killing 10 million by 1938; 1934-36, 80% of all Orthodox churches destroyed; 1936, 1937, 1938 successive metropolitan primates murdered by NKVD.
1928 USA and nearly every other nation sign Kellogg-Briand Pact, renouncing war.
1928 Unevangelized Africa Mission founded (1947, merged in CBFMS), also Unevangelized Tribes Mission of Africa, both in USA.
1928 USA: National Conference of Christians and Jews formed in New York City to combat religious and social prejudice; member of International Council of Christians and Jews.
1928 Anglican evangelist Bryan Green begins 60 years of ministry as a diocesan missioner in Britain, USA, Canada, South Africa, Australia and elsewhere.
1928 IMC researcher C.H. Fahs publishes exceptionally detailed world survey volume, *The unfinished evangelistic task* (London) for 1928 IMC Jerusalem Meeting 'to call attention primarily to unreached non-Christians', and to elaborate on 'the missionary obligation to extend the Christian witness over the whole surface of the globe'.
1928 3rd Meeting of International Missionary Council, Jerusalem; 231 participants.
1928 Opus Dei founded in Madrid, a secular association of conservative Catholic laity (men and women) and clergy; by 1975, over 60,000 members from 80 nations.
1928 Shensi, China: famine kills 3 million.
1928 Team of Chinese trained by Teilhard de Chardin discover skull of Sinanthropus Pekinensis (Peking Man, now called Homo Erectus Pekinensis), dating from BC 350,000.
1928 4th Baptist World Congress, Toronto, Canada.
1928 Pentecostalism formally rejected by World Fundamentalist Association as 'fanatical and unscriptural'; 1944, rejected also by American Council of Christian Churches who label glossolalia as 'one of the great signs of the apostasy'.
1928 P. Nowlan initiates 'Buck Rogers' series with story 'Armageddon-2419 AD'.
1928 World Fundamental Baptist Missionary Fellowship (later, World Baptist Fellowship Mission) founded in Texas; its 'purpose is to help to fulfill the Great Commission by the evangelization of the world' through indigenous Baptist churches; 1985, 126 missionaries in 23 countries.
1928 Series of World Conferences for International Peace through Religions begun: 1928 Geneva, 1929 Frankfurt-on-Main, 1930 Bern, 1931 and 1932 Geneva, leading to 1933 World Fellowship of Faiths, in Chicago
1928 Japan: Kingdom of God Movement begun by evangelist and social activist Toyohiko Kagawa (1888-1960), supported by most Protestants; a comprehensive Japanese-led plan with stated aim of winning one million Japanese to Christ and thence to reach the entire nation with the Christian message.
1929 Crash of Wall Street (stock market): Great Depression strikes USA economy, lasts till 1936; millions go bankrupt or are ruined.
1929 Lateran Agreements signed by Italian government and Roman Catholic Church, creating Vatican City as an independent sovereign state known as the Holy See (Santa Sede).

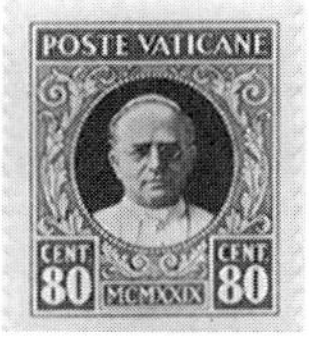


**AD 1929.** Pope Pius XI (*left*) negotiates Lateran Agreements creating Vatican City as a sovereign state.

1929 First major international Protestant radio station, Voice of the Andes (HCJB), founded at Quito, Ecuador; first broadcast on Christmas Day 1931.
1929 Invention of rocket engine by Robert Goddard.
1929 First experimental television (BBC, London).
1929 National Fraternal Council of Churches (NFCC) formed in USA for Negro (Black) churches.
1929 Armenian catholicate of Sis transferred to Antelias, Lebanon.
1929 China: Five Year Movement begun by National Christian Council of China, supported by most churches; mass evangelism; 1935, NCCC extends it for further 5 years.
1929 Afrikaner historian J. Du Plessis publishes *The evangelisation of pagan Africa.*
1929 Cedar Point International Convention (Jehovah's Witnesses): J.F. Rutherford introduces slogan 'Advertise! Advertise! Advertise the King and the Kingdom!'; aggressive house-to-house witnessing now the duty of all members.
1929 China: CIM director D.E. Hoste (1861-1946) issues call to Europe and America for 'Two Hundred Evangelists' to China's remaining unreached peoples, with as goal 'to reach China within 2 years' including 7 evangelists for Sinkiang; over a dozen martyred.
1929 Lutheran World Conference held in Copenhagen.
1929 Congregationalist missionary Frank C. Laubach (1884-1970) begins 'Each one teach one' method in Philippines, develops literacy primers for 300 languages worldwide; 1950, publishes *Literacy as evangelism.*
1929 Rise of collective futurism; Herbert Hoover's Research Committee on Social Trends, 1928 J. Stalin's state planners and their Five-Year Plans, F.D. Roosevelt's Brain Trust of academic advisors, 1948 RAND Corporation, 1960 International Futuribles Association (Paris), 1961 Hudson Institute, 1966 World Future Society, 1968 Club of Rome, 1972 Office of Technology Assessment (US Congress), and numerous futures research centers.
1929 3rd Evangelical Congress of Latin America, held in Havana (Cuba).
1929 20th International Eucharistic Congress, held in Sydney (Australia).
1930 First large-scale analog computer built.
1930 Naturalist William Beebe (1877-1962) and designer Otis Barton descend in their bathysphere to record 1,428 feet off Bermuda, observing many deep-sea life forms never seen before.
1930 Japan: Kingdom of God Movement begun under evangelist Toyohiko Kagawa (1888-1960), reaching over one million (75% non-Christian) with 35,000 enquirers in 2 years; concluded 1934, succeeded in 1936 by Kagawa's Nation-Wide United Evangelistic Movement.
1930 Christian Businessmen's Committee International formed.
1930 Mass movement into churches begins in Burundi.
1930 Prophetic movements in French Congo: 1930 Matswa, 1953 Lassyism (Bougie), 1964 Croix-Koma (Nailed to the Cross Movement).
1930 Independent Church of India begun as schism ex Indo-Burma Pioneer Mission.
1930 Formation of World Council for Life and Work, replacing Continuation Committee of 1925 Stockholm Conference.
1930 7th Lambeth Conference: 307 Anglican bishops present.
1930 C.E.M. Joad, British agnostic, publishes *The present and future of religion*; 1952, he converts to theism.
1930 Telephone system now serves 10% of humanity, and 20% in cities.
1930 Vannevar Bush's MIT differential analyser, first analogue computer for solving differential equations.
1930 Bermuda Triangle mystery: hundreds of aircraft, large ships and small boats disappear without trace from 1930-1997 in triangle between Bermuda, Florida and Puerto Rico, over alleged submerged ruins of Atlantis civilization; explanation in terms of gigantic Atlantean crystals emitting laser power still functioning at bottom of underwater abysses.
1930 Mexico: 5-year persecution as regime attempts to exterminate Presbyterians from Tabasco state.
1930 Resurgence of Hinduism (absorbing Christian elements) under 3 great reformers and leaders: philosopher Swami Vivekananda (1862-1902), nonviolent nationalist Mahatma Gandhi (1869-1948), and Indian president Sarvepalli Radhakrishnan (1888-1975).
1930 1st Latin American Baptist Congress, Rio de Janeiro (Brazil).
1930 G. Dennis publishes *The end of the world*, on apocalyptic mythology of modern science; 1953, identically-titled study by K. Heuer.
1930 N. Schachner & A.L. Zagat write 'In 20,000 AD'.
1930 Discovery on banks of Nile of Chester Beatty Papyri (2nd-4th centuries AD), 126 leaves being portions of 3 NT manuscripts; 1956, discovery of Bodmer

collection of NT papyrus codex mss dated AD c175, of Luke, John, Jude 1 and 2 Peter.

1930 USA: Laymen's Foreign Missions Inquiry (LFMI) initiated by 7 major Protestant denominations, under 35 directors, studying China, Indo-Burma and Japan; 1932, their report 'Re-thinking missions' (chairman W.E. Hocking) is criticized as advocating syncretism.

1930 Movement for World Evangelization (Mildmay Movement) begun in London to generate converts worldwide as 'God's key representatives' in the entire global range of secular worlds, leading to world evangelization within one generation; begins with world survey, with on-the-spot surveys of every mission field on Earth, publishes *World dominion*; 1955, begins annual Christian Holiday Crusade at Filey (UK); gradually abandons original global plan in order to supply evangelists and ministerial conferences for Britain, later for Portugal, Spain, India, Australia, New Zealand, et alia.

1930 Voice of Prophecy radio broadcasts begun by USA Seventh-day Adventists; by 1982, heard on 1,900 radio stations worldwide, in 57 languages; total all SDA broadcasts 4,646 weekly radio and TV, in 80 languages; 1986, related Bible correspondence schools around world number 180 in 77 languages with 520,167 annual enrollments (20,419 in English in USA) with 281,345 graduating.

1930 'The Lutheran Hour' broadcast over station WHK in Cleveland, Ohio, begun by LCMS; 1931, heard by 5 million a week, 1943 15 million, 1965 30 million in 120 countries over more than 1,000 radio stations; 1940, foreign broadcasting now named Bringing Christ to the Nations; 1945, worldwide to 20 million a week; 1975, broadcast in over 50 languages, heard by 22 million a week; 1987, 40 million regular listeners in 34 languages around world.

1930 International Missions (originally The India Mission) founded in USA, by B. Davidson, 'dedicated to the propagation of the gospel in obedience to the Great Commission, the ultimate goal being the establishing of self-supporting and self-propagating New Testament churches in all fields'; 1985, 159 missionaries in 12 countries.

1930 Foundation Farthest Out begun as 'a world-belt of prayer around the world'; renamed Association of Camps Farthest Out (CFO International, USA) as 'one of the vital instruments that God is using to establish the Kingdom of God on the Earth'; 1988, prayer camps in 85 countries.

1930 End of the World scenarios: in 1930s, novelists forecast annihilation of human race by poison gas, in 1960s-80s by nuclear war, and in 1990s-2000s by biological scourges.

1930 W. Olaf Stapledon (1886-1950) writes major futuristic novel, *Last and First Men*, a fully-developed evolutionary utopia; this, with his later classic *The Star Maker* (1937) sets definitive tone for responsible inclusion of religion in science fiction; describes 18 major transformations of humanity over 2 billion years, from individual consciousness, to world-mind, to galactic mind, to cosmic mind, to vision of the Star Maker (God); an intergalactic community of telepathically linked worlds until cosmos cools and dies, after which God creates a further cosmos.

1930 1st Assembly, World Convention of Churches of Christ (Disciples/Churches of Christ/Christian Churches) holds first nonbinding convention of its many streams, for fellowship; followed every 4 years or so by the next, up to the 15th Assembly in AD 2000 in Brisbane (Australia).

1931 Spain: church separated from state; thousands of priests, religious and lay Catholics murdered and churches burned in mob riots.

1931 Catholicism spreads from Dahomey to Niger.

1931 1st Baptist World Youth Conference, Prague.

1931 Charismatic renewal begins in Reformed churches of France; its theologian L. Dallière (1897-1976) opens dialogue with Catholic and Orthodox churches, also with Jews.

1931 Unevangelized Fields Mission (UFM) founded in London, UK; 1980, renamed UFM International; 1985, 338 missionaries in 12 countries.

1931 Radio Vatican inaugurated in Rome by Pius XI (1857-1939); entrusted to Jesuits; daily announcement motto 'Laudetur Jesus Christus' (Praised be Jesus Christ); 1975, broadcasts to 157 countries in 32 languages for 16 hours a day; 1982, John Paul II inaugurates Vatican Television; 1987, in 35 languages.

1931 World-Wide Prayer & Missionary Union founded (Chicago), serving 50 evangelical missions agencies.

1931 Stalin consigns 2 million prisoners to death through brutal neglect or mistreatment in the USSR-wide network of gulags.

1931 British author Aldous Huxley writes novel *Brave new world*, describing authoritarian world government of AD 2530 which perpetuates control of population via cloning and genetic engineering; religion replaced by scheduled sexual orgies; does not envisage space flight until AD 2970.

1931 Catholic employers in Belgium, France, and Holland found UNIAPAC, International Christian Union of Business Executives; 1962 expanded to cover other Christian business executives; HQ Brussels.

1931 Congrès des Missions Protestantes, held in Paris (France); results in book *L'évangile et le monde* (9-11 June).

1931 6th Ecumenical Methodist Conference, held in Atlanta (Georgia).

1932 Charismatic revival ex American Methodists in Southern Rhodesia, led by Johane Maranke, forms massive indigenous church: African Apostolic Church of Johane Maranke (AACJM), with followers right across Tropical Africa.

1932 China: flood kills one million.

1932 India: All-India Forward Movement in Evangelism launched in Nagpur.

1932 Dutch East Indies (Indonesia): 30,000 Muslims converted around Modjowarno, East Java.

1932 Standard English Braille adopted by Workers for the Blind in the USA; all English Scriptures subsequently prepared exclusively in this form.

1932 Conference of Bible Societies, held in London, discusses ways and means of international cooperation to bring the Scriptures to the whole world.

1932 Dutch mathematician/astronomer/cosmologist Willem de Sitter (1872-1934) formulates Einstein-de Sitter cosmological model of an expanding Universe existing in Euclidean space rather than in curved space.

1932 2nd International Polar Year (after 1st in 1882), with scientists from 34 nations working only in the Arctic.

1932 *Atlas der katholischen Missionsgeschichte* (St Gabrieler Studien) published.

1933 USSR: intensive forced collectivization and resultant famine kill 10 million kulaks and peasants, mainly Christians in the Ukraine; tens of millions of peasants brutally collectivized through police terror; Pentecostal-Zionists and other denominations virtually liquidated.

1933 Shanghai Christian Broadcasting Association organized (XMHD), covering entire Far East; also 1935 XLKA (Peking).

1933 *Bibliografia Missionaria* periodical begun by SC Propaganda (Rome), covering contemporary mission literature.

1933 Atheist H.G. Wells writes first history of the future, *The shape of things to come* (with 1935 movie 'Things to Come'), predicts collapse of all national governments (and disappearance of banking) by 1960; by 1977 a single world state which suppresses all religion; depicts in AD 2036 aftermath of 30-year world war which has reduced world to barbarism with altruistic scientists helping to launch first space flight; Wells writes over 100 books, has become foremost futurist of English-speaking world.

1933 Adolf Hitler (1889-1945) seizes power over Nazi Germany; involved in resurgence of secret occult societies across Europe 1925-40, member of Vril Society, steeped in occult gnosis (= violation of God's physical laws), Eastern/Tibetan/Sufi/Zen mysticism, Primordial Knowledge, Hyperborean Masters of Wisdom; offers world a 'new order', 'The Thousand Year Reich', a counterfeit Millennium; a renegade Roman Catholic, an archetypal antichrist in a long succession, widely regarded as Antichrist II, second of the 3 major Antichrists envisioned by Nostradamus.

1933 Severe persecution of Nestorians in Iraq; many thousands flee country.

1933 Imaginary Himalayan utopia named Shangri-La depicted by English novelist J. Hilton in *Lost horizon*, where human life-spans exceed 300 years.

1933 Germany: Catholic biblical renewal results in founding of Catholic Bible Association (Katholisches Bibelwerk, KBW), in Stuttgart; by 1980, members number over 30,000 catechists, teachers, priests and scholars.

1933 Pentecostal preacher W.M. Branham (1909-1965) offends mainline Pentecostal denominations by prophesying that 1906-1977 is the Laodicean Church Age, followed immediately by mass apostasy, Second Advent of Christ, and the Millennium in 1977; Branhamites (followers) claim him as Last Prophet with messianic attributes.

1933 Origin of the Navigators, a one-by-one disciple-making agency based on multiplication theory/process 'to contribute to the fulfillment of the Great Commission'; 1985, 191 overseas personnel in 30 countries.

1933 F.S. Thompson writes 'The future of missions', in *International review of missions*.

1933 Gerardus van der Leeuw (1890-1950) develops *Phenomenology of religion*.

1933 L.E. Browne writes *The eclipse of Christianity in Asia*, surveying decline of Nestorians from 7th to 14th centuries.

1933 1st International Congress, World Fellowship of Faiths (2nd World Parliament of Religions as successor to 1893 Parliament) held in Chicago during its 2nd World's Fair or 'Century of Progress', with 242 speakers from all religions in 83 meetings in Chicago and New York (27 August-17 September); 2nd Congress in 1936, with subsequent congresses planned for 1938, 1940, 1942; but fervor for 'one cosmic brotherhood' 'to unite all religions in service of humanity' is terminated by World War II.

1933 China: Protestant foreign missionaries decline from 8,325 in 1926 to 5,743 in 1933; baptized Catholics rise from 1,581,430 in 1914 to 3,182,950 in 1939.

1933 Germany: Hitler begins first concentration camp at Dachau, formulates 'Final solution to the Jewish question' (total liquidation).

1933 Germany: start of Porajmos (Gypsy Holocaust) in which Nazis' genocidal policy murders 1.3 million European Gypsies by 1945, with 500,000 murdered in 1939 alone.

1934 Beebe-Barton bathysphere dives to new record of 3,028 feet off Bermuda.

1934 USSR: Stalin, widely regarded as the Antichrist, attempts liquidation of entire Christian church.

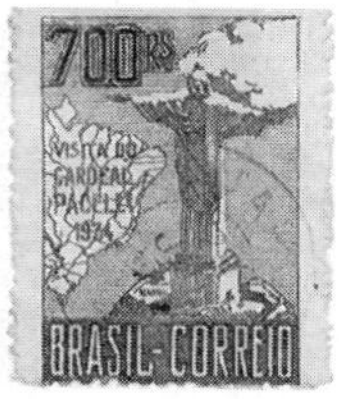


**AD 1934.** Two events in Brazil: (a) Evangelical Federation founded, and (b) tour by cardinal Pacelli (in 1939 pope Pius XII).

1934 Confederação Evangélica do Brasil founded.

1934 Turkish government prohibits use of ecclesiastical dress, clerical collars, vestments or beards outside church buildings.

1934 5th Baptist World Congress (BWA), Berlin.

1934 *Jesus Christ and world evangelization* published by Alexander McLeish (World Dominion Press): 'Evangelization is not civilization or Christianization'.

1934 Britain: Inter-Varsity Missionary Fellowship, meeting in Fountains Abbey, announces its new variant of SVMU Watchword: 'Evangelize to a finish to bring back the King'.

1934 Biblical Research Society publishes a 7-volume *Messianic Series* by D.L. Cooper, printing 6 million copies, distributed through 150 branches to Jews worldwide; 'These books will remain behind after the Rapture and will be read during the Tribulation by the 144,000 Jewish evangelists of Revelation 7 who will then produce worldwide revival.'

1934 W. Cameron Townsend begins Wycliffe Bible Translators for scripture translation by professional linguists, with overseas work under name Summer Institute of Linguistics (SIL); 1959, slogan 'Two Thousand Tongues To Go' coined; by 1985, 3,022 translators serving overseas in 55 countries, aiming to translate Scriptures into every remaining tribal language on Earth.

1934 First Youth for Christ rally in Brantford, Ontario, under Paul Guiness; 1944, YFC International begun, first in USA cities, as a worldwide evangelistic movement 'specializing in aggressive teen-age evangelism'; 1948, first of 12 annual world congresses of evangelism (Switzerland, Tokyo, Caracas, Mexico City, São Paulo, et alia); in 95 nations by 1987, now attempting to identify 600 Pacesetters to raise up a worldwide youth prayer movement.

1934 J.W. Campbell's novel *The mightiest Machine* invents four-dimensional hyperspace (or superspace) compressing our universe and enabling short cuts to stars.

1935 Opening of missions on island of Bali authorized.

1935 Scholar G. Friedrich publishes in Kittel's *TWNT* (1932-78) first detailed investigation on biblical Greek verb *euangelizesthai*, which is 'not just speaking and preaching; it is proclamation with full authority and power'.

1935 Radar invented by R. Watson-Watt (UK).

1935 Parapsychologist J.B. Rhine popularizes 'psi' powers with idea that next step in human evolution would involve acquiring telepathic and telekinetic abilities.

1935 New York becomes first urban supergiant (city with over 10 million population); others then escalate to 9 supergiants by 1980, 24 by AD 2000, 47 by AD 2025, and 80 by AD 2050.

1935 World Revival Crusade founded by Pentecostal leader G. Jeffreys.

1935 World Intercessors (Prayer Circle Department of Oriental Missionary Society) begun as worldwide prayer movement for world evangelization; over 2,000 prayer groups by 1968; 1987, over 40,000 participants (600 groups in USA alone); World Intercession School of Prayer (6 lessons); prayer seminars; 90,000 receive magazine Prayer and Praise Guide.

c1935 Britain: science-fiction fans form Science Fiction Association and publish *Tomorrow: the magazine of the future*.

1935 Inventor C.F. Kettering (1876-1958) states `My interest is in the future because I shall spend the rest of my life there,' which later becomes slogan of futurists.

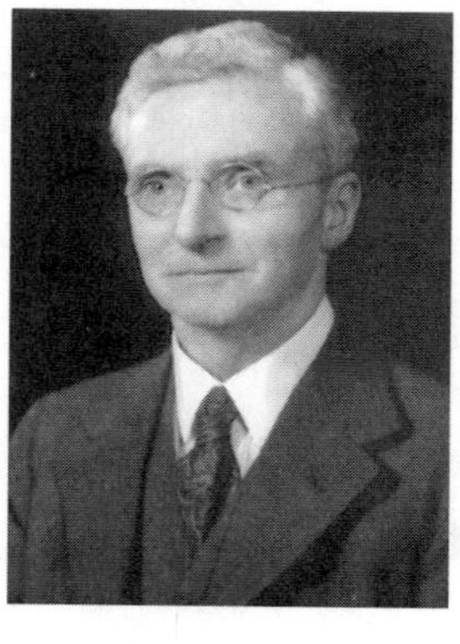

**AD 1935.** Biblical scholar C.H. Dodd heads team for New English Bible (1970) and Revised English Bible (1989).

1935 British Congregationalist biblical NT scholar C.H. Dodd (1884-1973) publishes a present-oriented 'realized eschatology': *The parables of the Kingdom*; also 1936 *The Apostolic preaching and its development*.

1935 The term 'computer', hitherto meaning a person usually a woman on a large team performing a complex computation, begins to change in meaning to a machine; by 1945, new definition widely used.

1935 Rise of Neo-Orthodoxy in England, then 1940 America (Reinhold Niebuhr).

1936 Chemical engineer C.C. Furnas writes *The next hundred years: the unfinished business of science*.

1936 Civil war in Spain: clergy assassinated include 13 bishops, 4,254 priests, 2,489 monks, 283 nuns; one million Catholic Spaniards on both sides killed (100,000 executed by dictator Franco) or emigrate before Franco victory in 1939.

1936 BBC (Britain) begins first television broadcasting including worship services and (1937) Coronation of George VI (1895-1952).

1936 USA: International General Assembly of Spiritualists formed.

1936 British Interplanetary Society founded.

1936 Birth of final human Antichrist (in October) according to Great Pyramid of Giza, as interpreted by pyramidologists; to be revealed to world in 1999.

1936 WEC missionary L. Brierley (1911- ) begins long career as first full-time Protestant missionary researcher; 1941, begins world survey research with WEC, resulting in World conquest and Black Spot surveys (places with no Christian influence).

1936 1st Congress of Theologians of the Balkan Orthodox Churches, held in Athens; papers on 'Mission in the Orthodox Church'.

1936 USA: Northern Baptist secretary for evangelism W.E. Woodbury directs movement called Printed Page Evangelism.

1936 Student Foreign Missions Fellowship (SFMF) begun by IVCF (USA); 1946, begins triennial mass conventions with 'Complete Christ's Commission' and 1948 Urbana series with over 17,000 attenders each time.

1936 J.G.K. Harman publishes *Awaiting the light: a survey of the unevangelised areas of the world* (London: Inter-Varsity Missionary Papers).

1936 Vision received by Korean Presbyterian youth Sun Myung Moon to begin Holy Spirit Association for Unification of World Christianity (T'ongil Kyohoe); 1954, begins Unification Church as indigenous church movement in Korea; by 1970, movement has become heterodox in its stance of superseding Christianity as the latter supersedes Judaism.

1936 US architect-planner and futurist R. Buckminster Fuller (1895-1983) writes *Nine chains to the Moon*; 1944 begins Dymaxion Dwelling Machine Resources Inventory, 1975 World Society for Ekistics.

1936 2nd International Congress, World Fellowship of Faiths (3rd World Parliament of Religions), on theme 'World Fellowship through Religion', held in London and Oxford, UK (3-18 July); 3rd International Congress planned for 1938 in India, 4th for 1940 in Japan, 5th for 1942 in California; all plans abandoned as World War II erupts.

1936 1st Congress on Orthodox Theology, held in Athens, Greece (29 November-6 December).

1936 World Conference and Exposition of the Catholic Press (Esposizione Mondiale della Stampa Cattolica), in Rome.

1937 Xerography, electrostatic copying process, is invented in USA; not commercially available until 1950; by 1968, over 500,000 copy machines are in use.

1937 Spanish Civil War: bombing of Guernica by German aircraft (April 26) on behalf of Spanish Fascists causes heavy damage and arouses public outrage in democratic nations.

1937 K.S. Latourette (1884-1968) publishes 7-volume *A history of the expansion of Christianity*.

1937 Major effort by Italians to force Ethiopian Orthodox Church to submit to Church of Rome; Italian military invasion publicly endorsed by Roman Catholic hierarchy in Ethiopia and by cardinal Tisserant; 2 EOC bishops Petros and Michael refuse to cooperate, executed together with scores of clergy and half a million faithful; widespread revival erupts among Protestant (SIM) churches in south.

1937 Although first Third-Wave manifestations erupted in 1656 and 1783, by 1937 large numbers of Neocharismatic churches are being started every year across the world.

1937 Japan's largest indigenous Christian church, Spirit of Jesus Church, formed as split from Assemblies of God.

1937 2nd World Conference on Faith and Order, Edinburgh, Scotland, dealing with grace, communion, sacraments, worship.

1937 2nd World Conference on Life and Work, Oxford, England, on 'Church, community and state'; 425 delegates.

1937 Imperial Japanese decree in Korea: Shinto shrines to be erected in all major centres, all population ordered to participate; most Protestant missionaries leave.

1937 European Jews in peril of their lives number 6 million (including 1 million Jewish Christians, numbering 17% of all Jews).

1937 China: Forward Evangelistic Campaign, under Methodist evangelist E. Stanley Jones (1884-1973), held in Mokanshan and other centres despite Japanese bombing attacks.

1937 2nd Baptist World Youth Conference, Zurich.

1937 2nd World Conference of Friends (Quakers), in Swarthmore, PA, USA, with representatives from 26 countries; Friends World Committee for Consultation (FWCC) begun, meeting every 3 years.

1937 French Dominican theologian Yves Congar publishes *Chrétiens désunis*, textbook of modern Catholic ecumenism.

1937 First radio telescope built by G. Reber, who then makes first radio map of the sky; major astronomical revolution begins as astronomers locate invisible microwave emissions from distant galaxies; 1967, discovery of pulsars (supernova remnants, being spin spinning neutron stars).

1937 Britain: founding of Council on the Christian Faith and the Common Life, and Commission of the Churches for International Friendship and Social Responsibility; 1942, merged in new British Council of Churches.

1937 Conference on Evangelistic Leadership, convened by Archbishops' Evangelistic Committee, Church of England, in York (6-8 October).

1937 Child Evangelism Fellowship founded, based on belief that 'Before Christ's return a mighty work among children will encircle the globe'; by 1985, 160 foreign missionaries in 60 countries.

1937 *Witchcraft, oracles, and magic among the Azande*, by English anthropologist E.E. Evans-Pritchard.

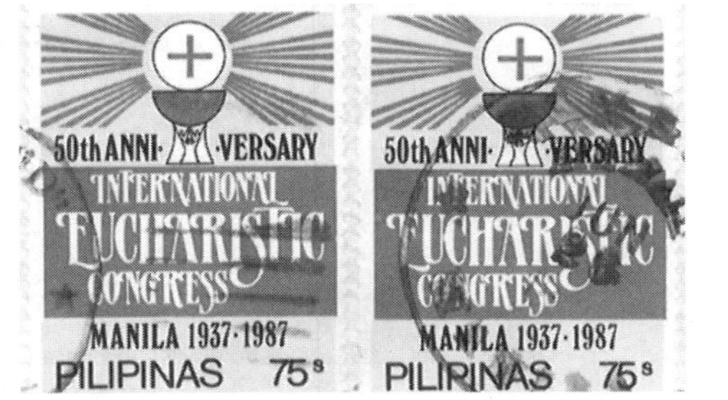


**AD 1937.** Begun in 1881, International Eucharistic Congresses have attracted up to a million present.

1937 23rd International Eucharistic Congress, held in Manila (Philippines); 1956, 2nd National Eucharistic Congress of the Philippines, Manila (28 November-2 December).

1938 Discovery of nuclear fission (splitting of the atom) by 2 German chemists Hahn and Strassmann; regarded by many Christians as a fundamental and dangerous contravention of God's laws of the Universe; results in atom bomb by 1945.

1938 Hendrik Kraemer (1888-1965) publishes *The Christian message in a non-Christian world*; powerful statement of traditional views of mission.

1938 World Council of Churches 'in process of formation' set up at Utrecht, Netherlands; constitution drafted.

1938 Muscat and Oman: RCA mission (USA) reports winning 5 converts in 50 years.

1938 Scotland: Iona Community founded by clergy and laymen of Church of Scotland.

1938 *Evangelism for the world today*, with definitions by over 125 Christian leaders across world, edited by John R. Mott who has by now all but abandoned his earlier English term 'evangelization' in favor of term 'evangelism'.

1938 A. McLeish writes 'Unoccupied fields' in the *Interpretative statistical survey of the world mission of the Christian church* (IMC).

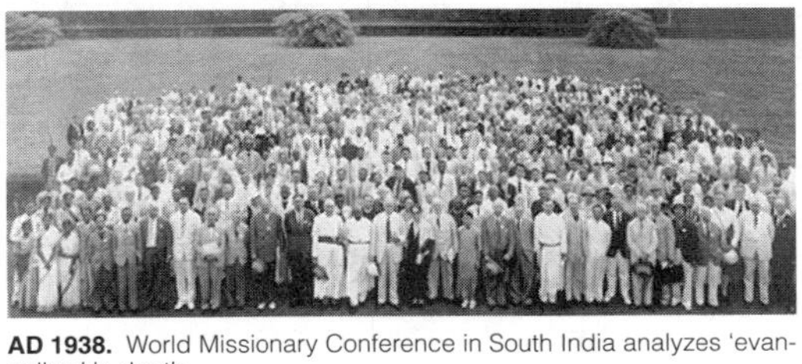

**AD 1938.** World Missionary Conference in South India analyzes 'evangelism' in depth.

1938 4th World Missionary Conference/Meeting of International Missionary Council, Tambaram, Madras, India; 471 delegates from 69 countries; report states: 'We summon the Churches to unite in the supreme work of world evangelization until the kingdoms of this world become the Kingdom of our Lord.'

1938 Gospel Recordings (Language Recordings International) founded: 'The aim of the work is to produce gospel records in every known language and dialect' in order to spread the gospel throughout the world; by 1967, recordings made in 3,400 languages and dialects, rising by 1988 to over 4,300.

1938 World Home Bible League founded in Chicago with as objective 'the placement of a Bible in every Bibleless home, so that people can be won for Jesus Christ'; 1965, in 30 countries with over 4 million scriptures distributed; 1985, in over 70 countries.

1938 USSR: Stalin liquidates 84,000 experienced Soviet military commanders over next 3 years.

1938 Sinkiang: flourishing Uighur church of 300 communicants, served by 30 Swedish SMF missionaries since 1892, massacred by fanatical Muslims, obliterated.

1938 *Prophecy and divination among the Hebrews and other Semites*, by A. Guillaume.

1938 H.G. Wells writes *World Brain* proposing universal organization and classification of knowledge, leading to a World Mind.

1938 California clergyman C.G. Long predicts world will be destroyed on 21 September 1945.

1938 Anglican apologist C.S. Lewis (1898-1963) writes best-selling trilogy *Out of the Silent Planet* (Earth ostracized because its ruling spirit Satan has become evil; Mars a perfect planet without original sin), *Perelandra* (1943: Venus ripe for invasion by Satan), *That hideous strength* (1947: Satan manipulates scientists to create dystopia on Earth).

1938 USA: actor Orson Welles' radio adaptation of H.G. Wells' *The War of the Worlds* terrifies New York.

1938 Japan: Nation-Wide United Evangelistic Campaign 1938-1940 launched by All-Japan Christian Conference, with T. Kagawa prominent as speaker (November).

1938 3rd International Congress, World Fellowship of Faiths (6th World Parliament of Religions), planned for India, cancelled.

1939 Protestant international radio station PRA7 begun in Brazil.

1939 Radio Vatican begins broadcasting, in 10 languages.

1939 Portuguese Guinea: Protestantism introduced by Worldwide Evangelization Crusade (WEC).

1939 1st World Conference of Christian Youth, Amsterdam, Netherlands.

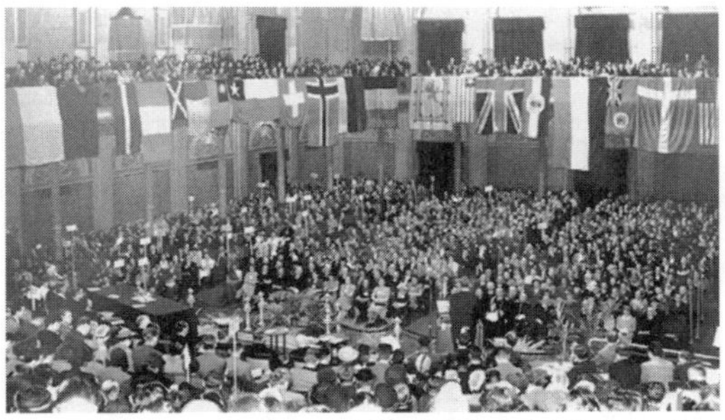

**AD 1939.** First World Conference of Christian Youth, held in Amsterdam.

1939 European Pentecostal Conference organized at Stockholm (Sweden), result of Donald Gee as prime mover: first attempt to gather representatives of all varieties of European Pentecostalism to discuss doctrinal and theologiical issues; Scandinavians prove to be vehemently opposed to any and all denominational or centralized organization.

1939 World War II: by its end in 1945, around 55 million killed: Poland 5.8 million including 3.2 million Jews; USSR 11 million combatants, 7 million civilians; Germany 3.5 million combatants/780,000 civilians; China 1,310,224 combatants/around 22 million civilians; Japan 1.3 million/672,000; Yugoslavia 305,000/1,200,000; UK 264,443/92,673; and USA 292,131/6,000.

1939 The Holocaust 1939-1945: systematic murder of 5.7 million Ashkenazi Jews (including 1 million Jewish Christians) by German Nazis and their European collaborators.

1939 World's first automatic electronic digital computer (ABC/Atanasoff-Berry Computer) designed, completed in 1942 in USA by J.J. Atanasoff, leading to ENIAC.

1939 Eugenio Pacelli elected pope as Pius XII (1876-1958), first of so-called Seven Last Angelic Popes of Catholic prophecy.

1939 Shanghai For Christ united evangelistic campaign using all evangelistic means including radio; 30,300 attenders, 1,672 enquirers.

1939 Poland: Nazis execute 6 RC bishops, 2,030 priests, 173 brothers, 243 sisters, and several million faithful.

1939 6th Baptist World Congress (BWA), Atlanta (USA).

1939 Engineers in British Interplanetary Society design ship to take people to Moon; in 1970s, they design Project Daedalus with nuclear fusion reactor to travel at 10% of speed of light as a multigeneration starship.

1939 USA: 'Old Fashioned Revival Hour' under C.E. Fuller broadcasts over 152 Mutual radio stations to 12 million listeners a week, rising to 20 million by 1960; renamed 'The Joyful Sound'.

1939 Conference of Bible Societies, Woudschoten (Netherlands), proposes a World Council of Bible Societies.

1939 Essay on 'The unfinished evangelistic task' published in IMC Tambaram report.

1939 A. Black writes 'Sunday schools and world evangelism' (IRM).

1939 World-wide Signs Following Evangelism, Inc begun under United Fundamentalist Church (Los Angeles, USA).

1939 World's Fair in New York, organized around theme 'Building the World of Tomorrow'.

1939 German mathematician Konrad Zuse in Berlin invents first computer, a flexible arithmetic machine with 2 binary numbers 0 and 1; 1941, first programmable general-purpose computer using binary switches; then he switches to vacuum tubes.

1939 500,000 Gypsies killed by Nazis in Porajmos (Gypsy Holocaust) in this year alone.

1940 Extermination of 600,000 Gypsies, mostly Christians, by Nazi Germany over 4 years.

1940 South Africa: an African-initiated charismatic renewal, Iviyo loFakazi bakaKristu (Legion of Christ's Witnesses) erupts in Natal and Zululand, founded by Alpheus Zulu (later Anglican bishop).

1940 Formation of Kyodan ordered by Japanese government to include all Protestant churches in a United Church of Christ.

1940 John Frum cargo cults begun on Tanna Island, New Hebrides, growing in strength with arrival of USA military personnel with extensive material possessions.

1940 Algeria: Evangelical Mission Council begun.

1940 Estonia, Latvia, Lithuania conquered by Red Army (USSR); 200,000 deported to labor camps in Siberia; most bishops, church leaders and clergy shot or deported; 1944-53, 500,000 more deported.

1940 First computer telecommunication: mathematician George Stibitz demonstrates his Bell programmable calculator working over telephone.

1940 Greece: German, Italian and Bulgarian troops murder 350 Greek Orthodox priests.

1940 R. Heinlein's novel *Revolt in 2100* describes a future dictatorship under guise of a religious cult, the Prophets.

c1940 Psychic seer Edgar Cayce (1877-1945) predicts sudden shifts in Earth's polar axis in 1998, with northern Europe and Japan destroyed and submerged, World War III erupting in 1999, and civilization destroyed in AD 2000.

c1940 Chilean astronomer Munoz Ferradas predicts a comet will collide fatally with Earth in August 1944; panic throughout South America.

1940 Rise of Neo-Evangelicals, reformers of fundamentalism in the USA, anticipating a broad Evangelical resurgence, under C.F.H. Henry, H.J. Ockenga and faculty of Fuller Theological Seminary; delineate secular humanism as a religious ideology and major enemy of Evangelicalism; movement flourishes, expands greatly, peaks by 1970, then declines though wider definition of evangelicalism mushrooms.

1940 US moral philosopher W.E. Hocking (1873-1966) writes *Living religions and a world faith*, and in 1956, *The coming world civilization.*

1940 Swami Chinmayananda active as founder of Chinmaya Mission and co-founder of Viswa Hindu Parishad, politico-religious body in India.

1940 4th International Congress, World Fellowship of Faiths (7th World Parliament of Religions) planned for Japan, cancelled.

1941 Discovery of lost walled Ubar trade city ('Atlantis of the Sand'), Oman, font of frankincense trade from local resin trees; camel trade route; AD 100, collapsed into huge sinkhole.

1941 Extensive mass revival in Orthodox churches in German-occupied USSR.

1941 Siege of Leningrad by Nazis begun, lasting 800 days; 1.4 million (50% Christians) perish.

1941 National Council of Churches in New Zealand founded.

1941 Gemeinde für Evangelisation und Erweckung founded in Zurich, Switzerland.

1941 Mission de France established by Catholic hierarchy to reevangelize France.

1941 R. Heinlein's story *Universe* proposes generation starships (space arks); attendant social structure discussed in B. Stableford's *Promised land* (1974).

1941 Polish Franciscan priest Maximilian Kolbe (1894-1941) martyred in Auschwitz concentration camp.

1941 Croatia: Croats massacre 350,000 Serbian Orthodox including 3 bishops, 220 priests.

1941 Confraternity New Testament published by Catholic Biblical Association of America, based on Vulgate, Rheims-Challoner text, and Greek NT text; 1970, whole Bible published as New American Bible (NAB).

1941 American Council of Christian Churches founded by C. McIntire; strict fundamentalist, ecclesiastically separatist, politically involved; by 1973, total number of separatist fundamentalists in USA estimated at 4 million.

1941 Brazil: emergence, as a new theory of evangelization, of idea of grassroots or base ecclesial communities (comunidades eclesiais de base, BECs or CEBes); 1963 formally established, with the Catholic Church standing with the poor; fully developed after 1968 Medellin and 1979 Puebla conferences.

1941 Anglican missionary bishop-designate of Rangoon in Burma A.T. Houghton writes *The battle of world evangelisation*: 'Christ has the master plan.'

1941 Origin of large-scale international multilingual Bible correspondence course organizations: Emmaus Bible School founded in Toronto, Canada; by 1966, courses mushroom worldwide, especially in closed countries (Morocco 110,000 enrollments).

c1941 USSR: Central Committee orders deportation to Siberia and Kazakhstan of 479,841 Soviet citizens of German origin even if Communist Party members.

1941 Ecumenical Youth Movement in Latin America (ULAJE) created.

1941 USA: Fundamentalists re-emphasize 5 basic doctrines, form American Council of Christian Churches opposing social action and prohibiting members from fraternization with mainline denominations.

1942 First radio maps of universe are produced by Grote Reber (born 1911).

1942 Archbishop William Temple (1881-1944) at Canterbury enthronement refers to worldwide Christianity as 'the great new fact of our time'; 1943, publishes lecture *Social witness and evangelism.*

1942 British Council of Churches (BCC) founded.

1942 Sumatra: Christ's Witnesses spread Simalungun Church north of Lake Toba.

1942 Papua: in Battle of Coral Sea, 118 RC priests and brothers and 78 nuns killed.

1942 USA: National Association of Evangelicals (NAE) organized; invites several Pentecostal denominations to become affiliated for its 1943 convention.

1942 I. Asimov's classic *The Foundation trilogy*: disintegration of Galactic Empire, 30,000 years of resultant barbarism; psycho-historians form Second Foundation and restore situation.

1942 WEC missionary L. Brierley begins world survey research to document and reach unreached peoples, resulting in *1st World Survey of Unreached Areas* (also titled *Thy Kingdom come,* or *'The Black Spots Survey')* describing untouched or unoccupied areas across globe with no Christian presence or influence; survey completed 1945, parts published in WEC journal *World Conquest.*

1942 Ling Liang World-Wide Evangelistic Mission founded in Shanghai, China 'to send Chinese missionaries to the uttermost part of the world'; 1965, in 10 countries.

1942 New Tribes Mission begun in USA to evangelize unreached tribes across the world; by 1985, 1,438 USA missionaries in 18 countries; 1988, 2,500 missionaries working in 160 tribes, 'with 2,500 tribes still to be reached'.

1942 Committee on World Literacy and Christian Literature (Lit-Lit) organized by F.C. Laubach's World Literacy Committee, and Committee for Christian Literature, Foreign Missions Conference of North America (25 major boards and agencies); work in over 60 countries.

1942 W. Paton publishes 'The future of the missionary enterprise' (*International review of missions*).

1942 *The future of industrial man*, by management expert Peter Drucker.

1942 5th International Congress, World Fellowship of Faiths (8th World Parliament of Religions) planned for California (USA), cancelled.

1943 Mathematician Alan Turing (1912-1954) creates Colossus I, world's first working electronic digital computer, with 2,000 valves; 10 built; wins World War II by breaking German codes, based in Bletchley, England.

1943 Prototype digital computer in USA, Harvard Mark I, built by Harvard mathematician Howard Aiken (1900-1973); 50 feet long, uses electromechanical switches.

1943 China: 5 million perish in Honan province in worst famine in modern history.

1943 Worker-priest movement begun in France; finally dissolved in 1959 on orders from Vatican.

1943 Britain: Christian Commando Campaigns 1943-47, led by Methodists, in London, Edinburgh, Glasgow and other cities.

1943 Pope Pius XII authorizes Biblical institutes in Jerusalem and in Rome, also translation of Scriptures from original texts instead of only from Latin Vulgate.

1943 USA: National Religious Broadcasters of North America formed, as official broadcasting arm of National Association of Evangelicals, with 50 organizations growing by 1979 to over 800; by 1986, annual convention attracts 4,000.

1943 S.M. Zwemer publishes *'Into all the world': the Great Commission, a vindication and an interpretation* (Zondervan).

1943 Global Outreach Mission founded (Buffalo, NY); by 1985, 114 foreign missionaries in 13 countries.

1943 Conservative Baptist Foreign Mission Society formed in Wheaton, IL (USA); by 1985, 525 missionaries in 25 countries, based on Great Commission imperative.

1943 Origin of futurism as an academic discipline with German political scientist O.K. Flechtheim's appeal for teaching of 'futurology'; defined as the multidisciplinary examination of trends and future prospects; future-oriented thinking remains largely a Western intellectual activity; pioneering courses taught in 1966 New School for Social Research (New York); 1974, 'History of the Future' course at SUNY-Binghampton; 1974, first graduate degree program in futuristics, at University of Houston.

1943 Anglican liberal theologian C.E. Raven writes *Science, religion and the future.*

1943 Amount of cash kept outside banks, as proportion of GNP, falls from 13% to 4% by 1993.

1943 Timor: intense adventist Spirit Movement while under repressive Japanese occupation; mainly around Nunkolo in Atoni territory with leading prophetess Juliana Mnao; 1965, a similar resurgence.

1944 La Violencia: violent anti-Protestant civil war occurs in Colombia during 14-year period; some 300,000 Christians are killed.

1944 Canadian Council of Churches (CCC) founded.

1944 Protestant monastic community of Taizé founded near Cluny (France) by prior Roger Schutz, who later coins phrase 'Les chiffres sont les signes de Dieu/Statistics are signs from God'.

1944 200,000 Muslim Meskhetians deported by Stalin to Central Asia; 30,000 die (November); Stalin philosophizes 'One man's death is a tragedy; 10,000 deaths [or 30,000] are merely a statistic.'

1944 John R. Mott, now in 80th year, writes his last original book: *The larger evangelism.*

1944 Albania: Communists execute 10 bishops and 100 priests over next decade.

1944 Ukraine: destruction of 3.5-million-strong Ukrainian Catholic Uniates; 3 bishops, many priests murdered.

1944 USA Assemblies of God begin 'Sermons in Song' radio broadcast, in 1954 renamed 'Revivaltime' on over 600 radio stations in USA and 100 more across world.

1944 Dutch East Indies sees rise of Third-World missionaries: Chinese evangelist John Sung trains 5,000 3-man evangelistic teams who make major impact across country; 1969, Japanese and Pakistani evangelistic teams; 1975, Asian Evangelists Commission (AEC) conducts crusades in Palembang, Medan and other cities.

1944 US Air Force general H.H. Arnold (1886-1950) orders first major forecast of future technological capabilities, resulting in T. von Karman's *Toward new horizons* (1947); also in 1946 he commissions Project RAND (acronym for Research and Development) as first independent 'think factory', exploring future policies of the nation.

1944 USSR: Crimea liberated by Soviet troops; Crimean Tatars, Balkars, Chechen, Ingush, Karachais and Kalmyks, amongst others, deported to Central Asia and Siberia for alleged collaboration with Germans; titular republics and autonomous provinces of these peoples are liquidated.

1944 Archbishop of Canterbury William Temple writes *The Church looks forward.*

1944 New Testament in modern English produced by an Anglican convert to Roman Catholicism, classicist R. Knox, based on Latin Vulgate; 1950, Knox Bible.

1945 United Nations Charter signed at San Francisco, USA (26 June).

1945 In 6 years of war, Allies devastate Germany by dropping 1.2 million tons of TNT (1.2 megatons).

### *Nuclear Age: 3rd Industrial Revolution*

1945 Detonation of first atomic bomb near Alamogordo, New Mexico, USA (16 July) at cost of US$ 1 billion, opposed by some scientists on grounds it might set off runaway chain reaction in hydrogen atoms of oceans and destroy world; followed in August by dropping of 20-kiloton atomic bombs on Hiroshima and Nagasaki, Japan, with 200,000 casualties; end of World War II.

1945 Germany: 12.5 million Germans resident abroad forcibly expelled to Germany as refugees.

1945 Viet Nam: 2,791 Cao Daists massacred by communists.

1945 Archbishops' report *Towards the conversion of England* published by Church of England.

1945 Evangelical academies and student associations begun in Germany.

1945 Mass international tourism begins, with package tours (Thomas Cook, Britain).

1945 Refugees (fugitives, expellees) increase vastly in numbers across globe, totalling 45 million over next 3 decades.

1945 USSR liquidates Uniate churches across Eastern Europe, forcibly incorporating adherents into Orthodox churches.

1945 Japan: disestablishment of State Shinto; rapid and vast growth of Shinko Shukyo (New Religions, first being Tenrikyo 1838, Konkokyo 1859).

1945 ACE (Automatic Computing Engine), most advanced and powerful computer in world, is designed at National Physical Laboratory (UK) under A.M. Turing (1912-1954).

1945 British science fiction writer A.C. Clarke (1917- ) becomes first to envisage feasible orbiting communications satellites.

1945 United Nations Organization established in San Francisco (USA) by charter (24 October) 'to maintain international peace and security', with 51 founding member states, rising by 1985 to 159 member states.

1945 Berkeley translation, Modern Language Bible: NT 1945, Bible 1959, revised 1969.

1945 Evangelical Foreign Missions Association (EFMA) organized in Washington DC, USA: 'We recognize our responsibility under the Great Commission to give all men everywhere the privilege of hearing and receiving the message of salvation... present an urgent call to more effectively evangelize the unreached of our generation'; 1964, 58 agencies with over 6,000 missionaries in 120 countries; 1979, 61 sending agencies with 9,308 missionaries; by 1987, 83 member agencies sending out 13,343 missionaries (11,593 from North America, 1,726 being 1-2 year short-termers).

1945 Massive surge of new Christian parachurch agencies or multinationals independent of the churches, increasing by 1980 to 17,500 distinct and separate agencies, with multifold ministries; great majority articulate commitment to Great Commission.

1945 Norwegian missiologist O.G. Myklebust proposes creation of an International Institute of Scientific Missionary Research, with an association and conferences devoted to global mission; ignored until IAMS formed in 1970.

1945 Cold War between USA and Soviet Union begins, lasts until 1991.

1945 Vannevar Bush proposes system to deal with growing complexity of all human knowledge ('As we may think').

1945 Dutch American theologian G. Verkuyl (born 1873) produces Berkeley Version in Modern English; 1959 complete Bible; 1969 revised as Modern Language Bible or New BVME.

1945 United Pentecostal Church International begun, in USA; by 1985, Foreign Missions Division has 212 foreign missionaries in 50 countries.

1946 UNESCO (UN Educational, Scientific, and Cultural Organization) created to encourage cultural/educational exchanges among nations.

1946 Albanian government banishes all foreigners, seizes and nationalizes all domestic assets, closes all churches, makes agriculture and industry collective.

1946 American mathematician John von Neumann (1903-1957) works on electronic device to simplify complicated weather computation; by 1950 his computer accurately forecasts global weather.

1946 African Orthodox Church (independent Kenyan body) accepted into communion by Greek Orthodox patriarchate of Alexandria.

1946 North Korea: Christian organizations suppressed.

1946 Europe: widespread evangelistic experiments in state and majority churches (Kerk en Wereld in Holland, worker-priests in France, MRA, etc).

1946 South West Africa: massive Nama Hottentot schism ex Rhenish Mission.

1946 Australian Council of Churches (ACC) begun.

1946 Revised Standard Version (RSV) of New Testament published in USA; complete Bible 1952.

1946 International radio station IKOR begun in Netherlands.

1946 ENIAC (Electronic Numerical Integrator and Calculator) built by J. Mauchly in Maryland (USA), switched on as world's first fully operational large-scale electronic computer; 18,000 valves (tubes), weight 60,000 lbs, volume 15,000 cubic feet, power required 150 million watts, cost $400,000, performs 5,000 additions a second.

1946 Catholic hierarchy erected in China: 20 archdioceses, 79 dioceses, 39 other jurisdictions (29 confided to Chinese clergy); and first Chinese cardinal Thomas Tien SVD.

1946 Series of massive student conferences in North America: 1st IVSFM Conference, Toronto, on 'Complete Christ's Commission' with 575 participants; 1948, 1st Urbana Conference, 1,400 students; steady rise in numbers to 17,112 by 1976 ('Declare His Glory among the Nations'), and 18,145 by 1984 ('Faithful in Christ Jesus').

1946 Conference of Bible Societies, Haywards Heath (UK), creates United Bible Societies (UBS) as federation and fellowship of 13 autonomous Bible societies from Europe and North America; expands rapidly by 1986 to 70 member societies and 30 national offices, working in 180 countries; UBS becomes 'a worldwide fellowship whose aim is to reach every person with the Bible or some part of it in a language he can understand and at a price he can afford'.

1946 World Literature Crusade (WLC) begins in Canada for radio outreach, then expands to systematic tract distribution through Every Home Crusades in 103 countries, with goal of reaching every home on Earth by 1970; results by 1985 in 1.42 billion gospel messages handed out producing 14.5 million documented written responses for Christ.

1946 Church of Scotland publishes Into all the world: a statement on evangelism (Glasgow: Joint Committee on Evangelism).

1946 Egede Institute of Missionary Study & Research, in Oslo, founded to promote scholarly research in the world mission of the church.

1946 Asociación Misionera Evangélica Nacional (AMEN, National Evangelical Missionary Association) begun as home mission in Peru; 1979, reorganized (with Methodist personnel) as a Third-World home and foreign missionary society with a global vision, renamed Asociación Misionera Evangélica a las Naciones; thousands of young Peruvians trained; missions in 20 countries including UK, France and Spanish North Africa (Melilla).

1946 Dead Sea Scrolls discovered in Qumran Caves from 1946-1957, containing 120,000 words dating from BC 20-AD 70, written by monastic Essenes (or Zealots, or early Christians); since 1950, vast number of other biblical manuscripts have been discovered elsewhere.

1946 Existentialists led by J.-P. Sartre (1905-1980) formulate concept of the future as something free, undetermined, exciting, to be invented or created rather than accepted as inevitable; by contrast the past is dead, closed, uninteresting.

1946 Russian Orthodox lay theologian Nikolay A. Berdyayev writes The Beginning and the End (Essai de métaphysique eschatologique).

c1946 Nichiren Shoshu (Soka Gakkai, SGI) introduced into USA by Masayasu Sadanaga; 1993, 500,000 members in USA, with goal of 1 million by AD 2000.

1946 Reformed Ecumenical Synod (Council from 1990) founded in Grand Rapids, Michigan, USA.

1946 Numerous councils begun in Japan: 1947 Evangelical Missionary Association of Japan (EMAJ) reorganized in 1968 as Japan Evangelical Missionary Association (JEMA), 1948 National Council of Churches of Japan (NCCJ), 1950 Japan Evangelical Fellowship, 1951 Japan Bible Christian Council (JBCC), 1957 Japan Evangelistic Crusade (Koji Honda), 1960 Japan Protestant Conference (JPC), 1961 Japan Council of Evangelical Missions (JCEM), 1968 Japan Evangelical Association (JEA), 1971 Japan Overseas Missions Association, 1985 Parachurch Association in Japan.

1946 Roman Catholic missiologist John G. Considine publishes The call for 40,000, appeals for 10% of all US clergy to go as 40,000 more missionaries to Latin America; CICOP formed (Catholic Inter-American Cooperation Program); US missioners in Latin America increase from 1,600 in 1950 to 2,400 in 1960, and 3,391 in 1968; but overall, the appeal fails.

1946 USA: Reformed Ecumenical Synod (RES) founded in Grand Rapids, MI as a conservative grouping of Reformed churches; Assemblies held every 4 years: 1980 Nîmes (France), 1984 Chicago, 1988 Harare, 1992 Athens, 1996 Grand Rapids, 2000 Indonesia.

**AD 1946.** British Methodists host United Nations General Assembly.

1946 United Nations' General Assembly meets in Central Hall, Westminster.

1947 Commission on Human Rights, chaired by former first lady Eleanor Roosevelt (1884-1962), drafts Universal Declaration of Human Rights; adopted in 1948.

1947 Conference on Evangelism, Geneva, sponsored by WCC in Formation (February).

1947 Church of South India inaugurated by merger of Methodists and Anglicans with earlier-united Reformed and Congregationalist bodies.

1947 2nd World Conference of Christian Youth, in Oslo (Norway).

**AD 1947.** Billy Graham begins mass preaching; by 1960 a mega-evangelist, by 1997 a giga-evangelist.

1947 Southern Baptist evangelist Billy Graham (born 1918) begins global ministry, preaching face-to-face to 50,780,505 by 1976, in 229 crusades, with 1,526,729 enquirers (decisions or converts: 3.0% of attenders), and to 104,390,133 by end of 1984.

1947 Partition of India: 9 million Muslims flee to Pakistan, 9 million Hindus and Sikhs flee Pakistan for India, the greatest population transfer in history; 1.1 million massacred or starve to death en route.

1947 Lutheran World Federation (LWF) founded, with first purpose stated as 'To bear united witness before the world to the Gospel of Jesus Christ as the power of God for salvation': 1st Assembly, at Lund, Sweden, 1952 2nd Hanover, 1957 3rd Minneapolis, 1963 4th Helsinki, 1970 5th Evian (France), 1977 6th Dar-es-Salaam (Tanzania), 1984 7th Budapest.

1947 1st Pentecostal World Conference, Zurich, Switzerland; 250 leaders present, from 23 countries; first attempt to found an ongoing World Pentecostal Fellowship fails (May).

1947 Evangelize China Fellowship founded in Shanghai by Andrew Gih.

1947 Episcopalian canon T.O. Wedel (USA) publishes The coming Great Church: essays on church unity.

1947 Three Bell Laboratories scientists in New Jersey invent the transistor: Bardeen, Brattain and Shockley.

1947 Mathematician J. von Neumann formulates turning point in computer design with computer EDVAC, with stored-program control; 1951, EDVAC executes first program.

1947 Pope Pius XII declares in Rome: 'Today the spirit of evil has been unchained'.

1947 UFO (Unidentified Flying Object) sightings begin in USA, of 6 varieties: nocturnal lights, daylight discs, radar cases, close encounters of the 1st, 2nd or 3rd kinds (over 800 of the 3rd kind involving supposed meetings with extraterrestrials); by 1980, 6% of humanity claim to have seen something inexplicable to modern science; linked to altered states of consciousness in human observers.

1947 7th Baptist World Congress (BWA), Copenhagen (Denmark), on 'The world responsibility of Baptists'; over 5,000 participants (largest religious gathering ever held in this city).

1947 Pius XII's encyclical 'Mediator Dei' supports Liturgical Movement; 1953, liturgical reform boosted by Vatican II with its 'Constitution on the Sacred Liturgy'.

1947 5th Meeting of International Missionary Council, Whitby, Toronto, Canada; 112 delegates from 40 countries; upholds 'the evangelization of the world in this generation', coins term 'expectant evangelism'.

1947 Roman Catholic missiological journal begun, Euntes docete ('Go and teach', Matthew 28:18).

1947 Nazarene writer R.V. DeLong writes We can if we will: the challenge of world evangelism (Kansas City).

1947 Fuller Theological Seminary founded by C.E. Fuller in Pasadena, CA (USA), as part of his expressed desire 'to see the world evangelized in this generation'.

1947 World Revival Prayer League (National Christian Women's Prayer League) founded, based on Tokyo, Japan.

1947 Oral Roberts Evangelistic Association founded (Tulsa, OK, USA), with own foreign missions program; 1953, begins Pentecostal television preaching; becomes massive ministry with worldwide healing crusades, Oral Roberts University, City of Faith, Charismatic Bible Ministries.

1947 United Nations announces Partition Plan for Palestine; Britain withdraws, 1948 independent Israeli state proclaimed, Arab states invade Israel in first Arab-Israeli war.

1947 British leave India: creation of independent republics of India and Pakistan.

1947 Reformed theologian H.P. Van Dusen publishes World Christianity: yesterday, today, tomorrow.

1947 T.L. Sherred writes 'E for Effort' about invention that sees through time and space and so threatens to destroy privacy and secrecy forever.

1947 London Anglican clergyman J. B. Phillips publishes Letters to Young Churches, mainly for youth groups; whole NT in 1958, Four Prophets (OT) in 1963, final NT revision in 1973.

1947 World Federalist Association (WFA) founded.

1947 Nagaland, India: 2 major revival movements erupt, (1) from 1947-1952, and (2) from 1976 for over 20 years; hostility and military persecution result.

**AD 1947.** Founders of FEBC radio: left, Robert H. Bowman.

1947 Far East Broadcasting Company founded by R. H. Bowman and others.

1947 7th Ecumenical Methodist Conference, held in Springfield, MA.

1948 National Council of Churches of Japan (NCCJ) founded.

1948 American mathematician Norbert Wiener (1894-1964) publishes Cybernetics, on his theory of computer-based artificial intelligence.

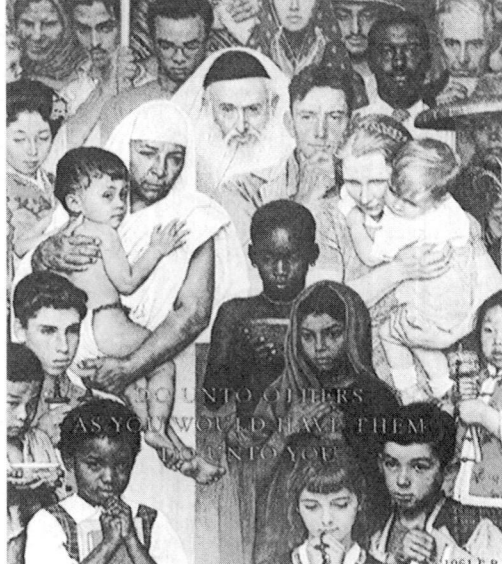

AD 1948. (Left, and above). 6 portrayals of UN's Universal Declaration of Human Rights.

1948 Universal Declaration of Human Rights approved by UN General Assembly, declares essential human rights of all peoples, including full religious rights (10 December).
1948 Radio Vatican now broadcasts in 19 languages.
1948 Byzantine-rite Uniate Catholic Church of Romania declared dissolved by a few priests, rejoining Romanian Orthodox Church; Communist regime destroys Uniates, kills 3 bishops and many priests.

AD 1948. Anglican bishops honor Bible Society.

1948 8th Lambeth Conference; 329 Anglican bishops present.
1948 Kirchenkreis-Evangelisation begun in Germany.
1948 International radio stations begun: FEBC (Philippines, Radio DZAS), TIFC (Costa Rica).
1948 Evangelistic mission in St John the Divine Episcopal Cathedral, New York; beginning of mass evangelism in USA after World War II.
1948 State of Israel created, with Jewish population of 650,000; continuous wars in 1957, 1967, 1973, 1982, not to be finally settled until AD 2000. (Nostradamus).
1948 Mark I computer at Manchester University (UK) runs with world's first stored program.
1948 Era of ecumenical consultations at all levels begins: 780 distinct consultations across world held, under WCC auspices, from 1948-1986.
1948 USSR: secret police begin to destroy 3-million-strong underground body, True Orthodox Church.
1948 1st United Bible Societies Council Meeting, Dunblane (Scotland); 20 member societies.
1948 Germany: Gossner Mission's 'Rollende Kirche' (Church on Wheels) and 'Die Kirche Unterwegs' (The Mobile Church) evangelize in Westphalia, Schleswig-Holstein and Baden; by 1960, 16 tent missions at work with 235 tent facilities in operation.
1948 USA: Southern Baptist Convention, meeting in Memphis, adopts Foreign Mission Board's program 'Advance', projecting a tripling in number of missionaries (achieved by 1964); 1955 Baptist Jubilee Advance plans.
1948 1st World Congress on World Evangelization (also termed 1st World Congress on Evangelism) convened by YFCI (with Billy Graham) in Beatenberg, Switzerland (August), first of long annual series: 1949, 2nd World Congress in Cannes, France; 1950, 3rd in Brussels; 1951, 4th in Winona Lake, Indiana (USA); 1952, 5th in Belfast; 1953, 6th in Tokyo (1,200 delegates from 24 countries: workshops, crusades, teams into 43 of Japan's 44 prefectures, 4,000 commitments to Christ); 1955 São Paulo (Brazil), 1956 Caracas (Venezuela), 1957 Copenhagen; 1959 Madras (India), also Tokyo, also Mexico City, 1960 Bristol (UK), then series discontinued; culminating in 1966 Berlin Congress.
1948 World Council of Churches (WCC) founded on common confession of faith in the Holy Trinity as revealed in Scripture; inaugurated in 1st Assembly at Amsterdam with 147 churches from 44 countries; theme 'Man's disorder and God's design'; 351 delegates and 238 alternates, but no RC observers; 'We intend to stay together' (22 August-4 September); by subsequent Assemblies, member denominations rise slowly to 163 (1954), 198 (1961), 235 (1968), 286 (1975), 301 (1983), 317 (1991).
1948 International Council of Christian Churches (ICCC) founded (anti-ecumenical, fundamentalist); 1st Congress at Amsterdam as rival to WCC; 150 persons from 29 countries (August); later plenary congresses every 3 or 4 years; 1948-1984, 98 major ICCC conferences held; 1983 plenary with 4,000 delegates from 93 nations and 399 denominations with (1988) 4.7 million members.
1948 Christian Crusade (Christian Echoes National Ministry, USA) organized as anticommunist mission, moves to Tulsa, Oklahoma; heard over 400 radio stations, 10 TV stations; 1953, launches ICCC Bible Balloon project, sending over 1 million Scripture portions into communist Eastern Europe by means of hydrogen-filled balloons; also other missions across world.
1948 China missionary doctor F.C. Maddox writes Set a watchman: a world survey (London).
1948 Latter Rain Revival (New Order of the Latter Rain) erupts among classical Pentecostals in Saskatchewan, Canada, spreads rapidly to Europe, USA, and across world; emphasis on laying on of hands with prophecy, government by order of living apostles; begins Global Missions Broadcast; from 1965, merges into Charismatic Movement.
1948 Ukrainian-born nuclear physicist/cosmologist George Gamow (1904-1968), developer of quantum theory of radioactivity, is first to describe moment of Creation in detail using the phrase The Big Bang.
c1948 World federalism: pressures by liberals begin in several countries for creation of a federal world government: with a world parliament, no rearrangement of national frontiers, no interference in internal affairs; minimalists want only a permanent world police force to enforce peace on every continent, but maximalists add protection of global environment, economic and technical sharing, exploration of outer space; 1958, plan by Clark & Sohn; by 1960, enthusiasm fades, replaced later by security policy (1975), I. Wallerstein (1979), S. Brucan (1982), R.C. Johansen (1983), B.B. Ferencz (1985), R. Smoke & W.W. Harman (1987).
1948 International Union for Conservation of Nature (IUCN) founded; 1970, environmental movement begins; 1980, sustainability movement begins around idea of living within limits of Earth's resources.
1948 USA's Marshall Plan transfers $14 billion to rebuild war-ravaged Europe.
1948 USA behavioral psychologist B.F. Skinner (1904-1990) produces classic behaviorist utopia, Walden Two.
1949 French Southern & Antarctic Territories. First resident Christians (French scientists).
1949 Pakistan sponsors creation of Karachi-based World Islamic Congress; start of bitter global rivalry.
1949 2nd Pentecostal World Conference, Paris; plan to form an ongoing World Pentecostal Fellowship thwarted by Scandinavian Pentecostals.
1949 Burma Christian Council formed.
1949 Joint IMC/WCC Conference, in preparation for forming of East Asia Christian Conference (EACC), in Bangkok, Thailand.
1949 After Communist victory, China expels 5,496 Catholic, 3,745 Protestant and 198 Anglican foreign missionaries over next 3 years; 1949 totals: 3,469,452 Roman Catholics, 1,536,000 Protestants, 440,000 Chinese indigenous, 300,000 Orthodox, and 76,740 Anglicans.
1949 Los Angeles, USA: first major Billy Graham crusade; 441,000 attenders, 5,700 enquirers (1.3%).
1949 Japanese Evangelical Missionary Society formed (USA, Tokyo) to send Japanese abroad.
1949 Kirchentag begun in Germany as Protestant annual evangelistic mass event: founded 1949 at Hanover (15,000 attenders), 1950 Essen, 1951 Berlin, 1952 Stuttgart, 6th in 1954 Leipzig (675,000 attenders), 1956 Frankfurt (250,000), 1959 Munich (375,000); all-Germany until Berlin Wall erected in 1961; ecumenical (RC cooperation) since 1968 Augsburg.
1949 Organized churches present in all countries of the world except Afghanistan, Saudi Arabia and Tibet.
1949 1st Latin American Evangelical Conference (CELA-1), Buenos Aires, Argentina.
1949 George Orwell's satire Nineteen Eighty-four published, describing 1984 world ruled by 3 totalitarian superstates controlled by media-mythologized demagogues, including English socialism of 1984 with Thought Police, Newspeak, Crimethink, and Doublethink, all subject to control of Big Brother, and by AD 2050 total destruction of literature, language and freedom.
1949 L.E. Browne, missionary theologian in India, writes 'The religion of the world in AD 3000' (IRM).
1949 India: Jain World Mission founded, to spread Jain religion outside home territory.
1949 3rd Baptist World Youth Conference, Stockholm.
1949 2nd UBS Council Meeting, New York and Greenwich; China, Ireland, Japan, Korea, Sweden admitted; total 24 member Bible societies.
1949 LWF Commission on World Missions (CWM) meets for first time at Oxford, UK.
1949 Germany: major state church evangelistic campaigns in Kreuznach, 1951 Oldenburg, 1952 Hamburg, 1955 Essen, Stuttgart, 1958 Bochum, 1958 Stuttgart, 1959 Hanover, 1960 Nuremberg, 1961 Karlsruhe, et alia.
1949 WCC study 'The Evangelization of Man in Modern Mass Society'; surveys done in Ceylon, Finland, France, Germany, Holland, India, Latin America, Scotland, USA; publication series announced but never implemented.
1949 T.L. Osborn Evangelistic Association established (also termed Association for Native Evangelism), for mass evangelism utilizing citizen Christian workers in overseas countries; 1965, in over 40 countries, having reached over 20,000 unevangelized areas.
1949 World Gospel Crusades (Every Creature Crusade) founded with as its purpose 'the evangelization of the world through the mass media of communication—literature distribution, Scripture distribution, correspondence courses, radio, TV, united evangelistic campaigns'; by 1965, in 60 nations; by 1986, only 4 overseas workers left, in 2 countries.
1949 Survey Application Trust (London) produces 5-yearly survey, World Christian handbook (1949, 1952, 1957, 1962, 1968) edited by K.G. Grubb (1900-1980), with church membership statistics compiled and totaled for first time by denomination and country.
1949 Cursillos de Cristianidad (short courses) movement begun in Spain by RC bishop J. Hervas; short 3-day retreats to renew personal faith of Catholics; 1950s spreads to Latin America, then to USA, 1961 Britain, then globally; many leaders later become first Catholic charismatics.
1949 Apartheid policy begins in South Africa.
1949 Romanian historian of religions Mircea Eliade (1907-1986) publishes Traité d'histoire des religions (1958, Patterns in comparative religion).
1949 Medievalist and theologian E. Gilson publishes The terrors of the year Two Thousand (Toronto), writing 'If the terrors of the year One Thousand are not a certainty for today's historians, those of the year Two Thousand will surely be so for future historians'.
1949 German existentialist K. Jaspers (1883-1969) writes The origin and goal of history, and in 1958 The future of mankind.
1949 European radical futurist writers since 1955: in Germany, A.G. Frank, E. Mandel, R. Bahro; in France, A. Gorz.
1949 Cosmos and history: the myth of the eternal return, by Mircea Eliade.
1949 Historian K.S. Latourette publishes The prospect for Christianity.
1949 Preparatory meeting with view to creating an East Asia Christian Conference (EACC), held in Bangkok (Thailand) (3-11 December).

## Epoch IX: AD 1950-2000

### SURGE IN THE THIRD WORLD

1950 **Global status:** 64 generations after Christ, world is 33.9% Christians (63.5% of them being Whites), 54.9% evangelized; with printed Scriptures available in 1,052 languages; total martyrs since AD 33, 56,065,000 (0.9% of all Christians ever; recent rate 881,200 per year).

1950 European Convention of Human Rights promulgated, based on Universal Declaration of Human Rights.

1950 1st International Youth Conference, Salvation Army, held in London.

1950 China: 24,700,000 killed over next 10 years through purges, famine, deaths in slave labor camps, Tibet revolt, including large numbers of Christians; over 40 million imprisoned in labor camps; by 1970, 20% of all 65 million deaths caused by Communist regime are being described as directly related to religious faith.

1950 Hungary: 53 Catholic religious orders and congregations forcibly dissolved by Communist regime.

1950 First International Astronautical Congress meets, in Paris; during 1951 meeting in London, International Astronautical Federation is formed.

1950 Color television broadcasting begins in USA, with Christian programs from the start.

1950 International Christian radio stations now 10 in number.

1950 British Guiana: 'Guiana for God' one-year evangelistic campaign under Christian Council, with Roman Catholic, Protestant and Anglican workers.

1950 1st Assembly of World Council of Christian Education and Sunday School Association (WCCESSA), Toronto, Canada.

1950 Haiti Great Commission Crusades (Haiti Inland Mission): 10 crusades over decade 1950-60.

1950 Explosion of first thermonuclear device by USA.

1950 Age of superindustrial economies: emergence in Europe and North America of national economies with enterprises of extraordinary size.

1950 Gross world product (GWP) climbs from $700 billion (1950) to $10.5 trillion by 1980, and to $17 trillion by 1987.

1950 J.C. Hoekendijk produces influential article 'The call to evangelism' (IRM) defining concept as consisting of kerygma, koinonia and diakonia.

1950 Historian K.S. Latourette writes: 'By evangelism is meant obedience to the Great Commission'.

1950 World's 10 largest cities: New York/Northeast New Jersey 12,339,000, London 8,733,000, Toyko/Yokohama 6,920,000 Paris, 5,441,000, Moscow 5,356,000, Shanghai 5,333,000, Essen 5,296,000, Buenos Aires 5,042,000, Chicago 4,945,000, Calcutta 4,446,000.

1950 8th Baptist World Congress, Cleveland, Ohio (USA), on theme 'And the Light shineth in the darkness'.

1950 Black Africa: Christians number about 44 million, increasing rapidly by 1.8 million a year; African indigenous churches (AICs) mushroom to 1,700 separate denominations with 3,500,000 adherents.

1950 Mass immigration from Third World into industrialized Western world begins: by 1960, 3.2 million; by 1974, 9.5 million.

1950 North Korea: troops massacre Christians, with 500 pastors killed from 1950-60.

1950 Holy Year attracts 4 million pilgrims to Rome; 1975 Holy Year, 8,370,000 pilgrims; 1983, 1,950th anniversary of Christ's redemption and Holy Year draws vast numbers of pilgrims to Rome.

1950 2nd ICCC Plenary Congress, Geneva; 450 participants from 82 denominations in 43 countries; subsequent plenary congresses in 1954 (Philadelphia), 1958 (Rio de Janeiro), 1962 (Amsterdam), 1965 (Geneva), 1968 (Cape May, USA), 1973 (Cape May), 1975 (Nairobi), 1979 (Cape May); 1983 (Cape May) 11th Congress with 4,000 delegates from 399 denominations in 93 nations.

1950 Science fiction writer L.R. Hubbard (1911-1986) in USA launches 'Dianetics, the evolution of a science'; 1955, begins Founding Church of Scientology, a non-Christian body based on psychoanalytic spirituality, claiming 3 million followers worldwide (HQ London); based on secret scriptures describing alleged galactic empire of BC 75 million ruled by tyrant Xemu and his thetans (spirits).

1950 Japan Lutheran Hour broadcasts begun; by 1953, on 117 Japan commercial radio stations.

1950 Scotland: Tell Scotland Movement organized by Church of Scotland evangelist D.P. Thomson.

1950 Television sets in use: USA 1,500,000 in 1950, 15 million in 1951, 29 million in 1954, 85 million in 1960; in whole world, 231 million (1970).

1950 Council of Churches in Indonesia (DGI) founded with aim of 'establishing a United Christian Church in Indonesia'.

1950 Supertechnological Revolution: Third Industrial Revolution picks up speed; after 1st Industrial Revolution (steam and coal, 1775) and 2nd (electrical and chemical, 1901), 3rd revolution from 1945 on is fueled by nuclear power, microchips and genes.

1950 British Antarctic Territory: history of explorers and visiting scientists; 1957, first resident Christians (British scientists).

1950 International New Age Movement begins to be interpreted from Christian standpoint as 'Aquarian Conspiracy', a cosmic plot being engineered by ancient invisible higher intelligences (the Hierarchy of Ascended Masters [Masters of Wisdom], highly-evolved humanoid, immortal, omniscient, omnipotent, Tibetan Supermen or Hierarchical Masters of Shamballah or extraterrestrials (ETs) with supernatural powers, under a supreme Unknown Master, the central intelligence behind all psychic-occult phenomena) aiming to take over Earth and to

install Antichrist.

1950 USA: beginnings of evangelistic association evangelism (Billy Graham Evangelistic Association, et alia); by 1976 Billy Graham has preached face-to-face to 50,780,505 across world, in 229 crusades, with 1,526,729 inquirers (decisions or converts: 3.0 percent of attenders), and to 104,390,133 by end of 1984.

1950 Help Open Paths to Evangelize (HOPE Bible Mission) founded in USA 'to take the gospel to unevangelized areas'; bimonthly news sheet His Millions.

1950 World Vision founded (Monrovia, CA, USA) for relief and development, emergency aid, pastors' conferences; emphasis on using research, new technology, new systems, new tools, new media, 'using a computer to help evangelize the world' 'to reach the world for Christ in this generation' (vice president T.W. Engstrom), 1966 Berlin Congress on Evangelism); 1988, works in over 80 countries with over 4,400 staff (mainly nationals) on 4,254 projects.

1950 F.C. Laubach publishes Literacy as evangelism (New York, Foreign Missions Conference); 1962, organizes a training agency, World Literacy Evangelism, which lasts for 4 years.

1950 USA: evangelistic broadcasting spreads: 1950, Billy Graham begins on ABC radio, and 1951 on TV; 1953, Rex Humbard telecasts weekly, 1958 opens 5,000-seat Cathedral of Tomorrow (Akron, Ohio).

1950 'Hour of Decision' radio program with Billy Graham begins over 150 stations; 1951, 20 million listeners (200,000 letters received per year); by 1978, 900 radio/TV stations worldwide, and a million letters per year (with 70 million viewers in USA).

1950 Full Gospel Business Men's Fellowship International (FGBMFI) founded in Los Angeles, USA as an end-time ministry by dairy magnate D. Shakarian after a vision of the people of every continent; preachers and women excluded; grows rapidly by 1965 to 300 chapters with 100,000 members; 1970, 300,000 in 700 chapters worldwide; and by 1986 to 700,000 regular attenders worldwide in 3,000 chapters (1,715 in USA) in 95 countries including USSR, Czechoslovakia, Saudi Arabia and other closed countries.

1950 Baptist Bible Fellowship International founded as fundamentalist mission, with (by 1985) 620 foreign missionaries in 58 countries.

1950 Missionaries of Charity (1950 Sisters, 1963 Brothers) begun in Calcutta by Mother Teresa, one of world's greatest Catholic evangelists, to minister in the name of Jesus to the poor, destitute, sick and dying; by 1986, 2,500 sisters, 600 novices, and 344 religious houses in 77 countries including Cuba, Nicaragua, and most closed countries, with attempts to open in China and USSR; global aim 'worldwide evangelization bringing Jesus to the poorest of the poor'.

1950 World-Wide Missions International organized by 35 churches in Nigeria; 1965, 1,100 workers in over 70 nations, with magazine circulation (World-Wide Missions) of 800,000; 1985, decline to 15 USA missionaries in 31 countries.

1950 World Fellowship of Buddhists founded by G.P. Malalasekera; start of ecumenical Buddhism as Mahayana and Theravada schools meet; consolidation of national Buddhist communities, and founding by Ceylon, Thailand and Japan of Buddhist missionary endeavors in India and beyond; series of conferences begin in several Buddhist countries and beyond, including 1988 in USA.

1950 Cult of national sovereignty (the nation-state principle of territorial sovereignty) 'has become mankind's major religion' (historian Arnold J. Toynbee) and its biggest obstacle to progress.

1950 I. Asimov (a rationalist) publishes I, Robot on development of robot computer AD 1996-2064.

1950 New Age Movement (Age of Aquarius) spreads across USA through psychedelic drugs, yoga, Eastern mysticism and astrology, holding imminent demise of Christianity to be replaced by new Eastern religion.

1950 Theologian Amos N. Wilder publishes Eschatology and ethics in the teaching of Jesus.

c1950 American Congregationalist S. T. Byington (1868-1957) translates Bible in Living English (BLE), but not published until rights taken over by Watchtower Bible & Tract Society in 1972; OT uses 'Jehovah' throughout.

1951 UNIVAC (Universal Automatic Computer) becomes first computer designed for commercial use, ushering in computer age; delivered by Remington Rand to US Bureau of the Census, as first generation of computers.

1951 Three Self Reform Movement founded in China, to eradicate imperialism in churches.

1951 Alianza Evangélica Costarricense formed.

1951 'Cuba for Christ' 2-week campaign in all Methodist churches of Cuba, 2,100 first decisions.

1951 USSR: all 7,000 Jehovah's Witnesses arrested and forcibly scattered across Siberia and Far North labor camps.

1951 Anglican evangelist Bryan Green publishes classic The practice of evangelism.

1951 Gandhian Hindu ascetic and social reformer Vinoba Bhave (1895-1982) walks barefoot 45,000 miles throughout India, founds Bhoodan Yajna (land-gift movement) and Gramdan (land-pooling), which then spread across India.

1951 Continental and regional councils related to funda-

mentalist ICCC formed: Latin American Association of Christian Churches (LAACC) in São Paulo, Brazil; and Far East Council of Christian Churches (FECCC) in Manila; 1952 Middle East Bible Christian Churches (MEBCC); 1955 Scandinavian Evangelical Council; 1959 European Evangelical Conference; 1964 West Africa Council of Christian Churches; 1965 East Africa Christian Alliance; 98 major ICCC conferences (including international ones) held from 1948-1984.

1951 China: 1st Plenum, Preparatory Committee of Chinese Christian Resist-America-Aid-Korea Three Self Reform Movement.

1951 1st World Congress of the Deaf, in Rome; establishes World Federation of the Deaf (WFD) to represent world's 70 million deaf persons; then congresses in 1955, 1959, 1963, 1967, 1971, 1975, 1979, 1983, 1987.

1951 1st Latin American Lutheran Congress, in Curitiba, Brazil; 1954, 2nd in Petropolis, Brazil; 1959, 3rd in Buenos Aires; 1965, 4th in Lima, Peru; 1971, 5th in Buenos Aires; 1980, 6th in Bogota, Colombia; 1986, 7th in Caracas, Venezuela.

1951 1st World Congress of the Lay Apostolate, in Rome, aiming to mobilize laity (99.8% of all Christians) for outreach to the world; subsequent congresses in Rome in 1957, 1967, 1975.

1951 R. Bradbury writes Fahrenheit 451, a dystopian novel of a future Earth after 2 atomic wars; dictatorial government, all books banned and burned as corruptive; also writes 'The Fire Balloons': 2 Episcopalian priests arrive on Mars to convert natives but find Martians already perfect and sinless.

1951 Swiss Reformed theologian Oscar Cullman writes Christ and time (Christus und die Zeit).

1951 International Convention of Evangelicals, held at Woudschoten (Netherlands) with 91 delegates and observers from 21 countries; World Evangelical Fellowship inaugurated in 1st General Assembly (4-11 August); 1953, 2nd at Clarens (Switzerland); 1956, 3rd at Barrington, RI (USA); 1962, 4th in Hong Kong; 1968, 5th in Lausanne; 1974, 6th in Chateaux d'Oex (Switzerland); 1980, 7th in Hoddesdon (UK) on 'Serving our generation: Evangelical strategies for the '80s', with 141 delegates from 48 countries representing 38 member fellowships and alliances; 1986, 8th in Singapore; 1992, 9th in Manila; 1997, 10th in Abbotsford, Canada.

1951 United Evangelistic Exhibition, with 180 different societies, held in Central Hall, Westminster (UK) sponsored by Evangelical Alliance of GB (WEA), in conjunction with secular Festival of Britain.

1951 Pan American Christian Network opens Evangelical radio stations throughout Latin America; LEAL organizes Evangelical publishers and booksellers.

1951 8th Ecumenical Methodist Conference, held in Oxford, UK; name changed to World Methodist Council with 5-yearly Conferences.

1952 3rd World Conference of Christian Youth, at Travancore, India.

1952 3rd World Conference on Faith and Order, at Lund, Sweden.

1952 6th Meeting of International Missionary Council, at Willingen, Germany; 190 delegates.

1952 3rd Pentecostal World Conference, in London, on theme 'Into All the World'.

1952 2nd Assembly, Lutheran World Federation (LWF), at Hanover, Germany, on 'The Living Word in a Responsible Church'.

1952 UBS Council Meetings: 3rd in Ootacamund (India), 80 persons, 24 societies, addressing the churches concerning their role in Bible work; 1954, 4th in Eastbourne (UK); 1957, 5th in São Paulo and Rio de Janeiro; 1960, 6th in Grenoble (France).

1952 3rd World Conference of Friends (Quakers), held in Oxford, England, with 900 representatives from 27 countries; also 5th Meeting, Friends World Committee for Consultation (FWCC), also in Oxford.

1952 Geopolitical nuclear balance of terror begins; USSR and USA target each other's major cities, continuously.

1952 First hydrogen bomb (thermonuclear, fusion) exploded by USA in Pacific; 1961, USSR catches up by conducting over 30 nuclear test explosions including largest hydrogen bomb ever, of 60 megatons; from now on, mankind lives under planet-wide nuclear intimidation, of mutually-assured destruction (MAD), the so-called balance of terror.

1952 Kenya: Mau Mau nationalist rebellion kills 30,000 Kikuyu, creates many martyrs in Kikuyu churches.

1952 West Irian: CMA, TEAM, RBMU missionaries and converts killed.

1952 Christ's hope of the Kingdom published by A. McLeish, expounding theory that Jesus envisaged lightning spread of gospel to all nations within one generation.

1952 E.J. Homrighausen writes 'Trends in world evangelism', in World Christian handbook, 1952 (London).

1952 'The Great Commission for Anabaptists' written by F.H. Littell.

1952 Worldwide Revival Movement inaugurated in Ireland by W.E. Allen and Revival Publishing Company (Lisburn) to promote theme 'Revival is the key to world evangelization.'

1952 World Wide Pictures established by BGEA; 1953, classic movie Mr Texas; by 1984, over 100 films produced and distributed, with 28,000 showings a year; viewed by over 50 million persons with 1.5 million decisions for Christ; some dubbed in 17 languages (100 prints circulate in Japan in Japanese).

1952 K. Vonnegut writes dystopia *Player piano.*

1952 International Association for the History of Religions publishes International bibliography of the history of religions, also periodical *Numen.*

1952 Computer theorist John von Neumann proposes elaborate theory for first self-replicating factory.

1952 International Council of Scientific Unions (ICSU) organizes 1958 International Geophysical Year (IGY), with scientists from 67 nations working in Arctic or in Antarctica.

***Geopolitical nuclear balance of terror begins***

1952 Attempts at uniting Nigeria's indigenous churches: 1952, Nigerian All-Prayer-Men's Union formed at Egbado with HQ at Ilaro, combining Christ Apostolic Church, Church of the Lord (Aladura), Cherubim and Seraphim, but collapses; next, Federation of Aladura Churches formed in Ibadan, but disintegrates in 1956 after CAC defects; then in 1961, Spiritual Union of Aladura Churches formed in Ibadan (C & S, CLA, et alia) succeeds and eventually results in 1968 in Nigeria Association of Aladura Churches (NAAC), consisting of C & S, CLA, Apostolic Churches, other Aladura bodies; however, rejected by CAC, AC of Nigeria, Celestial Church of Christ (CCC), et alia.

1953 Munster Week of Missiology takes as theme 'Christians and Antichristians'.

1953 In China, 105 RC priests massacred in last decade, increasing to 800 Chinese priests killed in 1950-54.

1953 General Islamic Conference for Jerusalem, held in Jerusalem, under the Muslim Brotherhood.

1953 Australian Mission to the Nation, a 3-year Methodist mass evangelism and media campaign, largest ever held in Australia; over 1 million attenders; start of 35-year mass evangelism ministry of evangelist Alan Walker.

1953 4th Baptist World Youth Conference, Rio de Janeiro (Brazil).

1953 USA: Southern Baptists implement first nationwide simultaneous revival or evangelistic campaign, with 361,835 baptisms reported during the year.

1953 Worldwide Evangelization Crusade begins work on Java, founds Batu Bible School, results in indigenous Indonesian Missionary Fellowship (organized 1961), with its own plan for world evangelization with 206 personnel by 1980.

1953 World Committee for Christian Broadcasting (WCCB) constituted in Britain, then International Committee for Christian Broadcasting (ICCB); 1961, founds World Association for Christian Broadcasting (WACB), 1968 merges with Coordinating Committee for Christian Broadcasting (CCCB) to form World Association for Christian Communication (WACC).

1953 Article proposing 'World Evangelization in Our Time' circulated by seminarian D.B. Barrett, illustrated by graphs of world population explosion.

1953 Congress of Catholic Action, in Chimbote (Peru), one of roots of liberation theology; this new approach to man and God, primarily from Latin America, leads to mushrooming of BECs (base ecclesial communities), new ministries, and above all to new approaches to evangelization.

1953 Parallel universes existing alongside our Universe proposed: C.D. Simak's *Ring around the Sun* and K. Laumer's *Worlds of the Imperium* imagine infinite series of manipulable parallel Earths in higher dimensions (each similar to immediate neighbors but with tiny historical changes) available for us to colonize once we have learned the secret of crossing the dimensions.

1953 Invention of Delphi technique of extracting forecasts from panel of experts separately answering 4 mailed questionnaires with feedback over a month; 1960, computerized ('D-net' operation) and reduced to 3 hours' Delphi Conference method using computers.

1953 Science fiction doyen A. C. Clarke writes 'The Nine Billion Names of God': Himalayan monks employ USA computer programmers to enumerate the 9 billion possible names of God, after which world must end, and does.

1953 General Council (2nd Assembly), World Evangelical Fellowship (WEF), held in Clarens (Switzerland) with 171 delegates and observers from 23 countries; membership increases to 13 national fellowships (27-31 July); subsequent General Assemblies.

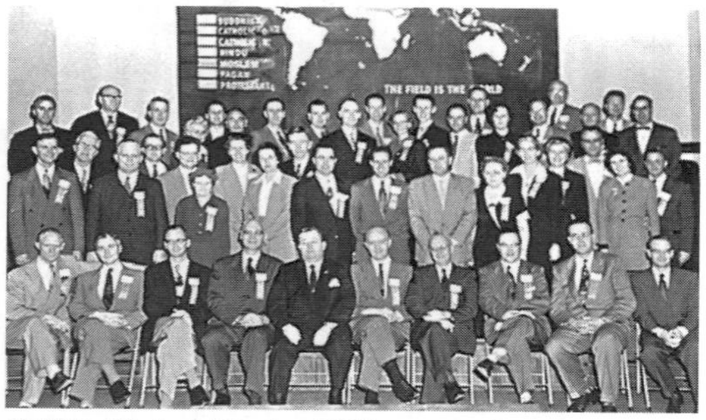


**AD 1953.** 36th Annual Meeting of IFMA supporting Fundamentalist Evangelical foreign missions.

1953 36th Annual Meeting, Interdenominational Foreign Mission Association (IFMA, founded 1917), held in Dallas, Texas.

1953 India: massive growth of Pentecostalism evident, especially in south India.

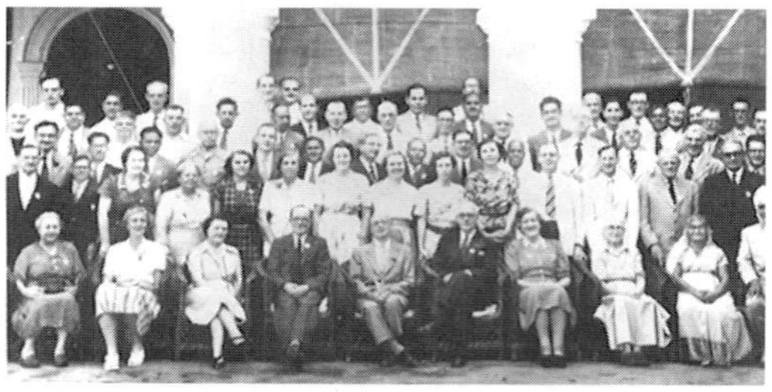

**AD 1953.** Two major agencies ministering to leprosy confer in Lucknow, India.

1953 International Conference of The Mission to Lepers and American Leprosy Missions, held in Lucknow (India), planning ministry to the world's 10 million lepers.

1954 Heads of state from Pakistan, Saudi Arabia, and Egypt convene Islamic Congress during Mecca pilgrimage.

1954 2nd International Congress for Catholic Church Music, held in Vienna, Austria (4-10 October).

1954 Institute on Religion in an Age of Science (IRAS), founded, in Chicago: publishes *Zygon: Journal of Religion and* Science.

1954 5th Kirchentag held in Leipzig (East Germany), draws 675,000 for closing rally.

1954 17th General Council, Alliance of Reformed Churches (WARC, WPA), at Princeton, USA.

1954 2nd Pan-Anglican Congress, in Minneapolis, USA, with laity and clergy from all Anglican dioceses across world.

1954 International radio stations begun: ELWA (Liberia), TWR (Tangier), both later closed; also several national stations including Christian Broadcasting System of Korea (HLKY).

1954 England: 3-month Harringay Crusade under Billy Graham: 2,047,333 attenders, 38,447 enquirers; vast numbers of related campaigns subsequently.

1954 Five generations of computers evolve: (1) 1954-60, electronic vacuum tube computers, (2) 1960-64, transistorized computers, (3) 1964-75, integrated circuit computers, (4) 1975-92, very large-scale integrated computers (VLSI) (known as supercomputers), (5) 1992-2000, 5th-generation or artificial intelligence computers known as KIPS.

1954 World Geophysical Year with all nations on Earth collaborating, called by Teilhard de Chardin 'Year One of the Noosphere', beginning of the planetization of humanity, start of Point Omega (evolutionary goal of one superconscious mind, a superpersonal ego in the depths of the thinking mass of 3 billion human brains, with Christ as Cosmocrat); other origins of Point Omega being BC 5.5 million, BC 4 (Incarnation of the Word), AD 2030, and AD 1.5 million.

1954 Argentina: USA Pentecostal evangelist Tommy Hicks travels uninvited to Buenos Aires; without advertising or outside finance, with free government radio and press coverage, conducts biggest single evangelistic crusade ever; in 52 days, audiences exceed 2 million (over 200,000 at final service); 1956, Oswald Smith campaign (25,000 attenders); 1962, Billy Graham crusades in 3 cities.

1954 F. Brown writes 'Answer', describing future time when all master computers of 96 billion inhabited worlds become linked as one; asked if God exists, system answers 'He does now'.

1954 China: 1st National Christian Conference, under control of Communist regime; 1960, 2nd National Christian Conference; 1980, 3rd National Christian Conference.

***Superindustrial Age (Third Wave, Space Age)***

1954 2nd Assembly of World Council of Churches, in Evanston, USA: 'Christ the Hope of the World'; 502 delegates; report states 'To evangelize is to participate in Christ's life and ministry to the world'.

1954 WCC official survey, *Evangelism: the mission of the Church to those outside her life*, notes 'an almost chaotic confusion as to the meaning and scope of evangelism'; surveys the future and suggests: 'The drama of missions and evangelism may, indeed, under God's rule over time and history be only in its infancy.'

1954 MAP International begun in Brunswick, GA (USA), as interdenominational evangelical service agency providing medical assistance to 82 countries by 1985.

1954 Methodist evangelist J.E. Rattenbury publishes *Evangelism and pagan England*, warns 'Schemes for future evangelization would indeed be futile dreams if the tragedy of human sin were ignored'.

1954 *The Bible in world evangelism* published in English and French by UBS research secretary A.M. Chirgwin, a colportage specialist, emphasizing primary and indispensable role of Bible in strategy for evangelization of non-Christians.

1954 World Missionary Evangelism begun as nondenominational service agency (Dallas, Texas), in 14 countries.

1954 New Life League World Missionary Society begun (Waco, TX, USA), 'winning the world for Christ through the published word'; Restoration Baptist; missionary printing presses, radio, mass media, literature, in 50 countries (including printing Bibles for China).

1954 *The challenge of man's future*, by Harrison Brown.

1954 *The Christian hope and the Second Coming*, by theologian P.S. Minear.

1954 *Tomorrow is already here: scenes from a man-made world*, by Robert Jungk.

1954 4th Council Meeting, United Bible Societies (UBS, 25 member Bible societies), held in Eastbourne (UK), on 'The Ministry of the Bible Society Today'.

1954 F. E. Siewert publishes Amplified Gospel of John, then 1958 NT, 1964 OT, 1965 Amplified Bible (AB).

1954 6th Canonical Theravadin Great Buddhist Council, held in Rangoon (Burma) convened by prime minister U Nu with 2,500 monks from Buddhist Asia for 2 years; on recitation and confirmation of entire Pali canon (Tipitaka); sacred scriptures of Buddhism re-edited; 2,500th anniversary of Buddha's death (on Theravada reckoning).

1955 Sudanese civil war: Christians in South begin 45-year rebellion against Muslims in North.

1955 After First Wave (Agricultural Age, BC 9000-AD 1700) and Second Wave (Industrial Revolution, 1775-1955), Third Wave begins (Technetronic Era, Electronic Era, Global Village, Third Technosphere, Superindustrial Age, Nuclear Age).

1955 Radio IBRA (Swedish Pentecostal) begins in Tangier in 20 languages.

1955 Jesus Family, indigenous movement in China begun 1921, virtually obliterated by Communists.

1955 4th Pentecostal World Conference, in Stockholm, Sweden, on 'The Calling and Commission of the Pentecostal Movement: a Re-evaluation'.

1955 Germany: Janz brothers' Crusade for Christ.

1955 General Conference, Latin American Episcopate, in Rio de Janeiro during International Eucharistic Congress; CELAM (Consejo Episcopal Latino Americano) organized (with no precedent in history), linking all Roman Catholic bishops from Mexico southwards.

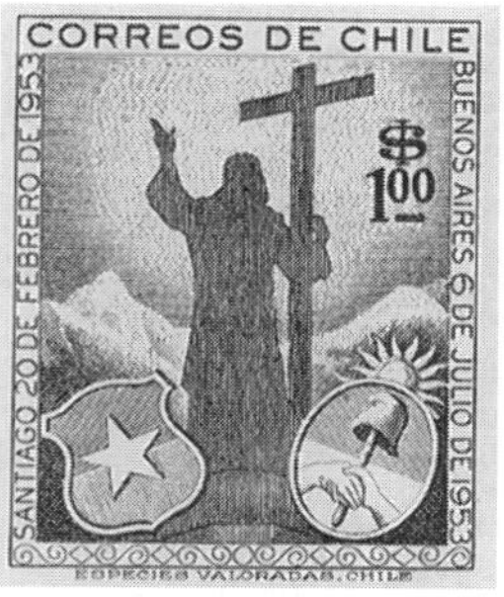


**AD 1955.** Huge statue 'Christ of the Andes' symbolizes Latin American churches' ongoing struggle against organized evil.

1955 Liberation theology, a new approach to man and God, primarily from Latin America, leads to birth of BECs (basic ecclesial communities), new ministries, and above all to new approaches to evangelization.

1955 Pentecostalism spreads rapidly throughout Europe's Gypsy population, especially in France, Italy, Spain, Portugal.

1955 Taiwan: 10-year 'Double-the-Church Movement' begins led by Presbyterian Church; 1965, Taiwan Christianity Centennial Campaigns held in 40 cities and towns; 1976, Knowing Jesus campaign; 1977, Tell the Good News multimedia movement, supported by 2,000 churches, with estimated 10 million persons exposed to gospel.

1955 Scotland: All-Scotland Crusade (Billy Graham): 2,647,365 attenders in Glasgow, 52,253 enquirers; on Good Friday, first telecast of a crusade made.

1955 France: Billy Graham 5-day crusade in Paris (43,619 attenders, 2,153 enquirers), also major Protestant campaigns in 1963 (Paris, Lyons, Mulhouse, Toulouse, Montaubon, Nancy, Douai, with 95,800 attenders and 2,698 enquirers), 1964, 1969, 1970, 1978, et alia.

1955 West Germany: Billy Graham campaigns in 5 cities (235,000 attenders, 10,200 enquirers); then major campaigns in 1960, 1961, 1963, 1966 in Berlin (90,000 attenders, 2,400 enquirers), 1970, 1977 yearlong campaign Missio Berlin 77 in conjunction with 17th German Protestant Kirchentag; 1980, All Germany Crusade; et alia.

1955 Conference of European Missiologists convened at University of Hamburg, Germany, for Protestant scholars only; 1966, 2nd Conference in Hamburg.

1955 World Conference on Missionary Radio (WCMR) begun in USA; 1963, joins with National Religious Broadcasters of North America (NRB) to form International Christian Broadcasters (ICB), which disbands in 1968.

1955 Midnight Call Missionary Work (L'Appel de Minuit) founded in Zurich, Switzerland, 'to extend the redemptive message of the gospel into unreached parts of the world'.

1955 Missiologist J. C. Thiessen writes *A survey of world missions* (Chicago) beginning from the Great Commission.

1955 *The foreseeable future*, by G. Thomson.

1955 Ananda Marga (Path of Bliss) founded by Anand

Murti alias P.R. Sarkar (1921- ), who claims to be 3rd incarnation of God after Shiva and Krishna; claims 5 million members in 2,000 centers; aims to 'establish dictatorship of Baba'; history of violent acts.

1955 Albert Einstein writes: 'The distinction between past, present and future is only a stubbornly persistent illusion'.

1955 9th Baptist World Congress (BWA), London, on theme 'Jesus Christ, the same yesterday, and today, and forever'; 8,266 delegates from 60 countries.

1955 Scottish writer J.T. McIntosh publishes *The fittest*, about scientifically-bred ultra-intelligent mutated animals ('paggets') who accidentally escape and then destroy human civilization in a few years.

1955 J. Blish writes tetralogy *Cities in flight*, a galactic history from AD 2000-4104 when alien empire Web of Hercules arises, conquers Universe but cosmos ends in 4104 in stupendous collision of matter and antimatter, after which a new cosmos is created; describes faster-than-light travel and antigravity (2 kinds of 'imaginary science').

1955 USA: Atomic Energy Commission projects that by AD 2000, 1,000 nuclear reactors will exist; but by 1982, there are only 279 operating power stations and 323 research reactors, in 54 countries; many cancellations of plants.

1955 First Antarctic Conference, in Paris (France) to coordinate plans for expeditions and the 1957-8 International Geophysical Year (IGY) with its mass of new discoveries; 1959 Antarctic Treaty signed by 12 (later 26) nations voting and 13 adherent nations.

1955 Consultation on 'Christianity and Non-Christian Religions' (IMC/WCC), held in Davos (Switzerland), to reopen assessment of the theological significance of non-Christian faiths, recognizing that most of the world's younger as well as older churches avoid contact with non-Christian world (21-25 July).

1955 YMCA World Centennial Conference (Young Men's Christian Association).

1956 200,000 Hindu Untouchables (Outcastes) convert to Buddhism in Nagpur under B.R. Ambedkar.

1956 World Buddhist Council meets in Rangoon, Burma.

1956 Ecuador: 5 Protestant missionaries killed in jungle by Auca Indians.

1956 USA: first coast-to-coast television broadcast.

1956 India: large-scale mass campaigns: Billy Graham rallies in Bombay, Delhi, Kottayam, Madras (800,000 attenders, 29,034 enquirers); 1969, 1972 India Every Home Crusade, 1972 Billy Graham Nagaland crusade (460,000 attenders), and many Penetration Plans and saturation campaigns.

1956 USA: charismatic (neo-pentecostal) renewal begins among Episcopal and Protestant churches, first being at Trinity Episcopal Church, Wheaton, Illinois; rapidly increases to 10% of all clergy and 1 million laity by 1970, and to 1.6 million active Spirit-baptized charismatics by 1980; over these decades, vast new proliferation of 'signs, wonders and healings' arises worldwide accompanying expansion of charismatic movement.

1956 WCC begins publication of regular series, *A monthly letter about evangelism*; in subsequent 43 years covers every conceivable aspect of evangelism and world evangelization.

1956 Catholic bishop L.-J. Suenens publishes *The gospel to every creature*; considerable influence on Vatican Council II, becomes leading advocate of Catholic Charismatics.

1956 *Mission fields today: a brief world survey* published by IVF (London, 127 pages detailing evangelization in all countries of world) edited by A.J. Dain; closing sentence 'Great indeed is the unfinished task!'

1956 Artificial intelligence: term coined, research begins in Britain; 1965, DENDRAL created as first expert system (computer program simulating human experts).

1956 J. Christopher's novel *The death of grass* envisages creation of virus which kills off world's grass and cereal crops.

1956 WARC Executive Committee meets in Prague, urges forming a conference of world confessional families, warns: 'The Confessional Movement could develop in such a way as to wreck the Ecumenical Movement or reduce the WCC to a facade'.

1956 I. Asimov's 'The last question' portrays computer with divine ambitions aspiring to emulate both man and God.

1956 W.E. Hocking (1873-1966) writes *The coming world civilization.*

1956 Bible de Jérusalem published by Dominicans as new Bible translation from Greek and Hebrew into French; 1966, Jerusalem Bible (JB) in English; 1985, revised as New Jerusalem Bible (NJB).

1956 Billy Graham visits Japan: 1967 1st Tokyo Crusade, 1980 2nd Crusade, 1994 3rd Tokyo Crusade.

1956 2nd National Conference of the Three-Self Movement, held in Beijing (China); all major denominations present, including Little Flock; tough government orders announced (15-23 March).

1956 Congress of the International Organization for the Study of the Old Testament, held in Strasbourg, commissions critical *editio minor* of Peshitta (Syriac Bible) to Hebrew Bible.

1956 Christian Pentecostal Fellowship of Nigeria (CPFN) inaugurated; 1987, holds 1st Convention, uniting Christ Apostolic Church (CAC), The Apostolic Church (TAC), becomes major power bloc in Nigeria's CAN; 1990, 2nd Convention, in Ibadan, joined also by Saviour Apostolic Church (SAC).

1956 9th World Methodist Conference, held at Lake Junaluska, NC.

1956 Catholicate of Cilicia (Lebanon) ceases to acknowledge primacy of catholicate of Echmiadzin (USSR) in dispute over appointment of new catholicos.

1956 Founding of Near East Christian Council (NECC) linked to International Missionary Council; 1974 becomes Middle East Council of Churches.

1957 Twelve International Geophysical Year (IGY) participants build and man Byrd and Amundsen-Scott winter bases, carry out extensive research of world's last unexplored areas.

1957 Treaty of Rome establishes European Economic Community.

1957 National Patriotic Catholic Association formed in China; anti-Vatican.

1957 East Asia Christian Conference (EACC) founded at Prapat, Sumatra, with theme 'The Common Evangelistic Task of the Churches in East Asia'; later renamed Christian Conference of Asia (CCA).

1957 World Fellowship of Religions founded in New Delhi, India, with by 1972 45 regional councils throughout world; 5 world religious conferences subsequently held, all in India.

***Beginnings of the Space Age and cosmic civilization***

1957 USSR launches first man-made satellite (sputnik) into space (4 October); beginning of the Space Age.

1957 International Missionary Council agrees to integrate IMC into WCC; also, Theological Education Fund (TEF) founded.

1957 3rd Assembly, Lutheran World Federation (LWF), Minneapolis, USA, on 'Christ Frees and Unites'.

1957 World Council of Synagogues (Conservative) representing 22 countries is organized by United Synagogues of America (begun 1913), with HQ in New York, Argentina and Israel.

1957 J.B. Phillips New Testament published: New Testament in Modern English (revised 1972).

1957 *Antarctica (Antarctic Territories).* First resident Christians (scientists); in addition to French and British colonies, in territories claimed or settled by USA (1957), then later Argentina, Australia, Belgium, Brazil, Chile, China, West Germany, India, Japan, New Zealand, Norway, Poland, USSR, and 23 other nations.

1957 Latin America: emergence of new and growing sense of universal missionary responsibility and global mission awareness among Roman Catholics, Protestants, Evangelicals.

1957 African killer bees accidentally released in Brazil, spread rapidly throughout South America, move gradually north at 400 miles a year disrupting $12 billion a year US bee industry, 1990 enter USA.

1957 WCC series of booklets published, *World evangelism today*; discontinued after only 4 titles.

1957 Global Conquest program (Assemblies of God USA) prepared as a 'new strategy for world evangelization', for 'the rapid evangelization of the world before the return of Christ', with detailed 3-year goals especially focusing on large cities; name changed in 1967 to Good News Crusades; 1968, Council on Evangelism with its Statement of Purpose makes major impact.

1957 Nights of Prayer for World-Wide Revival (NPWR) launched in London by Anglican layman and CMS missionary to India, G.S. Ingram (c1881-1969); continues till his death.

1957 Pope Pius XII ends Easter Day encyclical with words 'Come, Lord Jesus, there are signs that your coming is not very far off!'.

1957 Missions scholar S.C. Neill publishes *The unfinished task* (London).

1957 Send the Light (later termed Operation Mobilization) incorporated in USA, Mexico, then in over 50 countries; an interdenominational youth agency sending short-term mission workers abroad for evangelism and literature distribution.

1957 Conference of World Confessional Groups initiated, in Yale, New Haven (1 August) followed by in Geneva (14-15 November), supported by 7 confessions: BWA, FWCC, ICC, LWF, WCCC, WMC, WPA (WARC); 1968, RCC joins; 1968, name changed to Conference of World Confessional Families; 1979, renamed Conference of Christian World Communions; 1985, 29th Conference meets in Windsor, UK, with 20 WCFs/CWCs meeting annually; agreed positions on world mission emerge.

1957 North Vietnam invades South Vietnam; 1965, USA formally commits itself to defend South; 1975, war ends with collapse of South.

1957 USSR: rehabilitation of deported peoples; majority are repatriated, but Crimean Tatars and others still remain in exile; Chechen-Ingush and Kabardino-Balkar ASSRs and Karachai-Cherkess and Kalmyk Autonomous Provinces are reinstated.

1957 First largescale nuclear power plant generates electricity in Shippingport, Pennsylvania.

1957 German liberal NT theologian Rudolf K. Bultmann (1884-1976) publishes *History and eschatology: the presence of eternity*, an existentialist interpretation of eschatology, emphasizing 'demythologization' of NT concepts.

1957 Japan: Evangelical Missionary Conference starts process which by 1960 creates, as an ongoing entity, Japan Protestant Conference (JPC); lasts until dissolution in 1991 and replacement by Meeting of the Bible Believers.

1957 Conference of European Churches (CEC/CCE/KEK) founded at Liselund (Denmark); 1959, 1st Assembly.

1957 5th Council Meeting, United Bible Societies (UBS), held in São Paulo/Rio (Brazil).

1957 2nd World Council of YMCAs, in Kassel, Germany, on theme 'Into All the World'.

1958 First underwater crossing of North Pole made by USA nuclear submarine, Nautilus; 1959, USA nuclear submarine Skate is first to surface at North Pole by breaking through the ice.

1958 5th Pentecostal World Conference, in Toronto, Canada, on theme 'The Purpose of God in the Pentecostal Movement for This Hour'.

1958 International Christian radio stations now 20 in number.

1958 Federación Argentina de Iglesias Evangélicas (FAIE) founded.

1958 First Ethiopian national consecrated patriarch of Ethiopian Orthodox Church: Basilios.

1958 Brazil: neo-pentecostal (charismatic) renewal termed Renovation begins among Baptist pastors.

1958 9th Lambeth Conference; 310 Anglican bishops present.

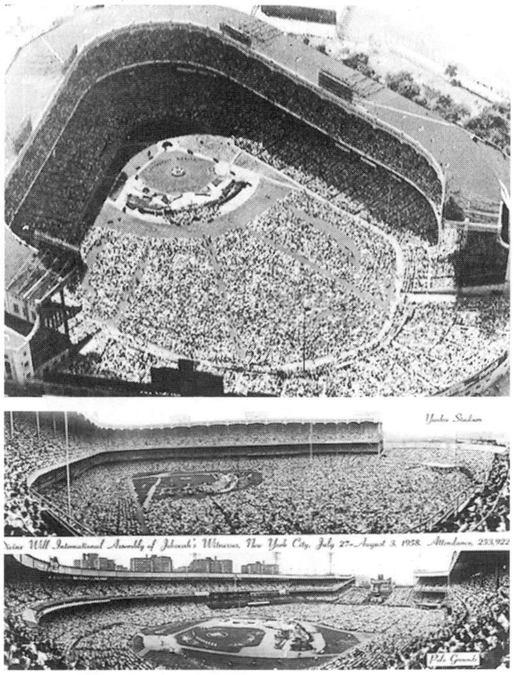

**AD 1953, 1958.** Jehovah's Witnesses rallies in New York: *upper*, 1953 'New World'; *lower*, 1958.

1958 253,922 attend Jehovah's Witnesses 'Divine Will' international convention in New York City, USA, with 7,136 baptized.

1958 Christian Peace Conference (CPC), supported mainly by churches in Communist countries, formed in Prague; 1961, 1st All-Christian Peace Assembly; 1968, 3rd ACPA, then 1971, 1978, 6th ACPA in 1985.

1958 Thousands killed in nuclear accident at Khystym, Urals (USSR); 1961, 'even more terrifying' accident; also 12 more major nuclear accidents in USSR by 1982.

1958 All Africa Church Conference (later All Africa Conference of Churches, AACC) founded: provisionally 1958 in Ibadan, formally 1963 in Kampala.

1958 Six European nations form European Economic Community (EEC, Common Market); 1973, total 9 nations; 1981, 10th member (Greece) joins; largest proportion of world trade for any single bloc (nearly 50%).

1958 5th Baptist World Youth Conference, Toronto.

1958 Latin America: Renovation charismatic movement spreads to several other major Protestant denominations; major clashes, leading to schisms.

1958 Australian evangelist Alan Walker proposes an 'Ecumenical Mission to the World'; adopted by Australian Council of Churches, but at 1961 New Delhi Assembly proposal is rejected by WCC.

1958 4th General Assembly of Syndesmos (international Orthodox youth organization), in Salonica, establishes major missionary activity including Pan-Orthodox Missionary Society, to be ratified by the coming Great & Holy Council of the Orthodox Church; Church of Greece's missionary institute begins missiological quarterly in Greek and English, *Porefthendes* (Go Ye), until it ceases publication in 1966; 1982, Apostoliki Diakonia begins new publication *Panta ta Ethni* (To All Peoples).

1958 Bibles For The World (BFTW) begun by Hmar believer from Northwest India in order 'to mail a Bible to every telephone subscriber in the world by

1985'; BFTW is 'committed to mail one billion Bibles to one billion families on planet earth'; by 1986 'It is the stated goal of BFTW to mail a book-size copy of the New Testament, in the language of the people, to a billion homes' using telephone directories; NTs mailed 1971-1982 total to 6,444,628; 1987, averages 1,500,000 a year.

1958 Publication of *Bilan du monde: encyclopédie catholique du monde chrétien* by Catholic researchers of FERES and Eglise Vivante (Louvain, Belgium), documenting status of world mission in all countries.

1958 Minimalist plan for world federal government: *World peace through world law*, by G. Clark & L.B. Sohn; but nations across the world prove unwilling to abandon sovereignty.

1958 USA launches its first communications satellite, Score, in low-altitude orbit; one-voice channel, no receiving.

1958 9th International Congress of the History of Religions, in Tokyo.

1958 A. Huxley writes *Brave new world revisited*.

1958 3rd Meeting, Conference of World Confessional Groups, in Nyborg (Denmark, 22 August).

1958 1st Meeting of WCC Committee for Study on 'Living Faiths', held in Bossey (Switzerland) (14-18 March).

1958 First major Consultation on 'The Word of God and the Living Faiths of Men' (WCC/IMC), held in Bossey (Switzerland), reopening IMC Tambaram debate re attitude to Hinduism, with paper by Ceylon scholar S. Kulandran (July).

**AD 1958.** International Missionary Council agrees to its own dissolution, under WCC.

1958 Final Assembly, International Missionary Council (IMC), in Accra (Ghana), with 215 delegates, decides to merge with World Council of Churches.

1958 Britain: Evangelical Missionary Alliance (EMA) formed in London.

1958 Christian International Conference for World Peace, held in Tokyo (Japan), with evangelist Toyohiko Kagawa as president (dies 1960).

1959 USSR: wave of persecution under Krushchev regime attempting liquidation of all churches, continuing until 1964.

1959 Communist revolution in Cuba; 500,000 Cubans flee to USA, Catholic priests declining from 725 to 231 in 3 years; by 1974, total of 650,000 have fled.

1959 1st Assembly, Conference of European Churches (CEC), Nyborg, Denmark.

1959 18th General Council, World Alliance of Reformed Churches (WARC), São Paulo, Brazil.

1959 Holy Office (Vatican) writes to cardinal Feltin of Paris prohibiting all further worker-priest activity.

1959 Bolivia: proliferation of mass evangelistic crusades in 1959, 1960, 1961, 1963, 1964, 1965 (Evangelism-in-Depth with 500 participating local churches from 36 denominations, 80,000 homes visited, 4,204 prayer cells, 19,212 professions of faith), 1967, 1973, 1974, 1978, et alia.

1959 China: around 25 million killed or starved to death from 1959-62 due to failure of Mao Zedong's Great Leap Forward (collectivization).

1959 Southern Baptists in USA develop long-term emphasis on 'Sharing Christ around the World'/'Sharing Christ with the Whole World' (Baptist Jubilee Advance, 1959-1964, jointly with 20 other USA Baptist groups); 1970 SB Convention approves concept and phrase 'Bold Mission', and Home Mission Board develops it in 1974 'Sharing Christ's Bold Mission'; 1974 SB Convention in Dallas authorizes Foreign Mission Board and Home Mission Board to plan 'Bold new strategies' for last 25 years of century; 1976 FMB develops 'Total Missions Thrust: Global Discipleship: Foreign Missions looks toward AD 2000' and 1976 'Bold New Thrusts in Foreign Missions 1976-2000'; 1976 'Bold Mission Thrust—Acts 1:8', 1977 'by the year 2000' added.

1959 Subsequent collapse of world mission's most ambitious and promising global plan to date; 1977, Bold Mission Thrust adopted by many USA state conventions and associations; 1985, enthusiasm declines, 1990 numerical goals nowhere near attainment; 1999 BMT finally fizzles out.

1959 First nationwide Evangelism-in-Depth campaign organized, in Nicaragua (125 local churches, 65,000 homes visited, 126,000 attenders in 14 local crusades, 2,604 professions of faith, 500 prayer cells formed); on successful conclusion, Latin America Mission sponsors similar campaigns in 11 other Latin American countries by 1971 (1961 Costa Rica, 1962 Guatemala, 1964 Venezuela, 1965 Bolivia and Dominican Republic, 1967 Peru, 1968 Colombia, 1970 Ecuador and Haiti, 1971 Mexico and Paraguay); spreads to other parts of world, including Tokyo 1980 and Mexico 1986 (Evangelismo a Fondo); but after 1975 fades out as a movement because largely accepted and incorporated into church programs.

1959 Death of pope Pius XII; comet heralds birth of Antichrist in Palestine (according to prophetologist P.I. Rissaut in 1948 book), 1980 career as ultimate Antichrist begins, by 2000 accepted as universal monarch; Rome destroyed; 2004, death of Antichrist.

1959 Worldwide Missionary Society (Sekai Senkyo Kyokai) founded in Yokohama, Japan, to send Japanese missionaries to all foreign countries; mainly in India.

1959 Antarctic Treaty among 12 nations guarantees demilitarization of Antarctic continent for 30 years and promotion of scientific investigation there.

**AD 1959.** Antarctica has 2 churches: *above*, Chapel of the Snows; *left*, Our Lady of the Winds (Kerguelen). *Bottom*. Revision of treaty 30 years later.

1959 Project Ozma, or Search for Extra-Terrestrial Intelligence (SETI): first attempt to monitor stars for radio transmissions (on 21cm waveband), hoping to contact extraterrestrial intelligence, using Lingua Cosmica (LINCOS), a mathematically-based language for interstellar communication; 1974, first radio message from Earth beamed, from Arecibo (Puerto Rico) aimed at M13 globular star cluster.

1959 USA physicist F. Dyson proposes Dyson sphere: in high-energy future by AD 3000, 1,000 billion times as much energy will be available as now.

1959 R.F. Young writes 'Robot Son' in which a machine god attempts to construct a machine Christ.

1959 Emergence of first world government, predicted for 1985 by Karmohaksis in *The dawn of the third era*, 1959.

1959 RAND mathematician O. Helmer with N. Dalkey further develops Delphi technique using experts to make a group forecast; using computers, Delphi conferences proliferate.

1959 Jesuit paleontologist P. Teilhard de Chardin writes *The future of man*.

1959 4th Meeting, Conference of World Confessional Groups, in Geneva; 5th in 1962 (Geneva), 6th 1963, then annually to 16th in 1973, all in Geneva.

1959 1st Assembly, East Asia Christian Conference (EACC), held in Kuala Lumpur (Malaysia) with representatives of 42 churches and Christian councils from 14 East Asian countries, on theme 'Witnesses Together' (14-24 May).

1959 Scripture (gospel, NT, or Bible) now available translated into 1,136 languages.

1959 Antarctica: 38-nation Antarctic Treaty signed dedicating continent exclusively for peaceful purposes and safeguarding continent from commercial exploitation; military and weapons banned; scientific bases only permitted; 1959, continent's only house of worship, Chapel of the Snows, opened at McMurdo Station (USA); 1978 burned down, 1989 rebuilt.

1960 Swiss oceanographer Jacques Piccard (born 1922) and Don Walsh take bathyscaph Trieste down to record 35,800 feet in Mariana Trench, deepest known place in ocean.

1960 Secretariat for Promoting Christian Unity established by pope John XXIII (1881-1963) in preparation for Vatican II.

1960 Continuation Committee of Pacific Churches' Conference launched at Malua, Samoa.

1960 2nd Assembly, Conference of European Churches (CEC) at Nyborg (Nyborg II).

1960 5,000 computers in world, mostly mainframes; minicomputers begin to come into use; 1965, first popular minicomputer is DEC PDP-8.

1960 USA: 256 million phone calls made each day (93 billion a year).

1960 World's 10 largest cities: New York/NENJ 14,164,000, Tokyo/Yokohama 10,976,000, London, 9,131,000, Shanghai 8,839,000, Paris 7,230,000, Buenos Aires 6,772,000, Los Angeles/Long Beach 6,530,000, Essen 6,404,000, Beijing 6,269,000, Osaka 6,228,000.

1960 Congo (Zaire): mutinies, rebellions dislocate missions; 200 RC priests and workers killed, and 300 Protestant workers.

1960 Latin America: persecution begins of Christian radicals by rightists and death squads; 1966 priest Camilo Torres shot, 1980 archbishop E. Romero shot during mass; vast numbers of others killed.

**AD 1960.** Leaders of 150 denominations, 3 million members at HQ (Ibadan) of Nigeria Association of Aladura Churches.

1960 Nigeria Association of Aladura Churches (NAAC) founded (by 1977, 95 AICs as members with 2 million adherents); African indigenous conciliarism mushrooms in West, South, East and Central Africa.

1960 10th Baptist World Congress (BWA), Rio de Janeiro (Brazil), on theme 'Jesus Christ is Lord'; 12,688 delegates.

1960 Human potential movement begins, releasing untapped growth potential in the individual person.

1960 P. J. Farmer's novel *Flesh* projects revival of ancient vegetation religions in the far future; religion now interpreted as earliest form of science fiction.

1960 J. G. Ballard writes on death of God theme: 1960 'The voice of time', 1965 'The drowned giant', 1976 'The life and death of God'.

1960 USA: charismatic renewal begins in Episcopal Church under parish priest D. Bennett.

1960 Polarization gathers momentum between 2 powerful factions in most large denominations Protestant and Catholic: (1) the conservative/ right-wing/fundamentalist constituency, and (2) the moderate/liberal/radical constituency.

1960 IFMA Congress on World Missions, Chicago; closing statement reads: 'We declare the need for a total mobilization of all the resources... so that the total evangelization of the world may be achieved in this generation'; resurgence among Conservative Evangelicals of the Watchword 'The Evangelization of the World in this Generation'; congress report by J.O. Percy entitled *Facing the unfinished task*.

1960 Baptist International Missions founded as Fundamentalist missions body, with (by 1985) 593 foreign missionaries in 53 countries.

1960 World Missionary Assistance Plan (World MAP) founded (California, USA) as interdenominational, evangelical, charismatic service agency; inaugurates Leadership Spiritual Renewal Seminars 'to create spiritual renewal among all the world's church leadership to bring change within all nations, hence worldwide evangelization, to be completed by the year 2000'; by 1987, claims 60% of that goal has been completed.

1960 IVP editor/director J.T. Bayly writes satirical novel *The Gospel Blimp* about an agency International Gospel Blimps Inc who operate an airship towing sign 'One Billion Unreached'; ends in disaster; archetype of attempts to evangelize by depersonalized technology without personal contact with unevangelized populations.

1960 Youth With A Mission (YWAM) begins as evangelical-charismatic sending agency, expanding as outgrowth of the Jesus Movement in USA; at first, little church consciousness; 1977, outfits 10,000-ton evangelistic ship m.v. Anastasis for discipleship and mercy ministries; by 1983, the world's largest evangelistic agency with 14,000 short-term young people sent overseas each year, in 56 countries; by 1987, 50,000; goal to field 100,000 a year by AD 2000.

1960 Proliferation of futurist organizations in Europe and North America: Club of Rome (Italy), Mankind 2000 (originated by Quakers), Futuriblerne (Denmark), Futures (London), Futurum (Germany).

1960 RAND analyst H. Kahn (1922-1983) writes on military futurism: *On thermonuclear war* (1960), *Thinking about the unthinkable* (1962), *On escalation: metaphors and scenarios* (1965), *Thinking about the unthinkable in the 1980s* (1984).

c1960 *The pursuit of the Millennium: revolutionary messianism in Medieval and Reformation Europe*, by N. Cohn.

1960 *The future as history*, by R.L. Heilbroner.

1960 *Social intelligence for America's future*, by B. Gross.

### *Environmental revolution begins*

1960 Tourists in Hawaii number 300,000 per year, rising by 1970 to 1.5 million; 1970, Hawaii 2000 conference attempts to stop abuses and plan for the future but almost everything goes wrong; by 1988, 6 million tourists per year, with plans for 11 million by 2010; massive environmental damage and pollution, unemployment, inflated living cost.

1960 Major astronomical discoveries: (1) in 1960, quasars (violently exploding protogalaxies related to origin of light) found to exist up to ultimate edge of Universe at 15 billion light-years; (2) in 1965, background universal microwave radiation and 3 degrees K temperature remaining from Big Bang creation discovered by US physicists A.A. Penzias and R.W. Wilson.

1960 US nuclear submarine 'Triton' becomes first vessel to circumnavigate the globe underwater.

1960 Hindu-Christian Colloquium on 'Hindu and Christian Views of Man' in Nagpur (India), with Hindu religious leaders and philosophers joining Christians in a week of discussions (10-13 October).

1960 37th International Eucharistic Congress, held in Munich (Germany).

1960 6th Council Meeting, United Bible Societies (UBS), held in Grenoble (France): O. Beguin states 'We circulate nearly 29 million copies, almost 40% of them in the US alone, more than 60% in the "Christian west".'

1960 Standing Conference of Orthodox Bishops in America (SCOBA) established, with all canonical bishops meeting twice a year.

c1960 UBS commences worldwide production of Selections (2, 4 or 8 pages of Bible verses), as 4th major category after whole Bibles, NTs, Portions (Gospels).

1961 10th World Methodist Conference, held in Oslo, Norway.

1961 International Christian radio stations now number 30.

1961 2nd Latin American Evangelical Conference (CELA II), Lima, Peru.

1961 6th Pentecostal World Conference, in Jerusalem, on theme 'Pentecost in Jerusalem—Then and Now'.

1961 First man in space, cosmonaut Yuri Gagarin (USSR), orbits Earth at 18,000 mph in 1 hour 29 minutes, in 4.75-ton spaceship Vostok-1 (12 April).

1961 6th International Student Missionary Convention, Urbana, Illinois, USA; 5,027 attenders; 'The world must be evangelized in one decade' (Billy Graham), 'We can evangelize the world in this decade. It is possible' (Clyde Taylor, NAE).

1961 Costa Rica: nationwide Evangelism-in-Depth campaign; with 192 churches, 50,757 homes visited, 1,000 prayer cells, 3,153 professions of faith; 1963, Costa Rica is host to international E-i-D workshops.

1961 Continuation Committee, East Asia Christian Conference, meeting in Bangalore, India, attacks confessionalism as obsolete, meaningless and divisive; Lutherans counter with 'dynamic confessionality'.

1961 New English Bible (NEB) published: NT 1961, OT 1970; work of C.H. Dodd and other British scholars.

1961 Sino-Soviet split: USSR breaks relations with Communist China, in most significant geopolitical event of period 1945-1990; followed in 1972 by USA-China rapprochement.

1961 World Missionary Press begun (New Paris, IN, USA) as nondenominational agency distributing scripture booklets in 214 languages in 179 countries.

1961 2nd World Survey of Unreached Areas (Areas of the World Unreached by the Gospel): L. Brierley publishes section 4, *The challenge of the unachieved*, and other WEC survey volumes describing 'The 19 Point Programme to Reach the Unreached'; also survey articles in WEC's magazine *World Wide*; in introduction quoting WEC founder C.T. Studd, Brierley states: 'Unless some new heroic effort is made by God's people entailing great sacrifices, great faith and desperate courage, the evangelization of the whole world in this and several future generations is a patent impossibility.'

1961 1st Pan-Orthodox Conference, Rhodes (Greece); agreement to move towards a future Great & Holy Synod/Council of the Orthodox Church; subsequent conferences 1963, 1964, 1968, 1976; but obstacles and delays prove endless.

1961 World Evangelism founded in USA by Pentecostal evangelist Morris Cerullo; 1967, World Evangelism Society of Great Britain.

1961 3rd Assembly of WCC, in New Delhi, India; Russian and other Orthodox Churches join WCC; integration of WCC and IMC, latter emerging as Division of World Mission and Evangelism (DWME and CWME) whose report states 'Two-thirds of the human race are without the knowledge of Christ as the light of the world'; report on 'Christian witness' states 'All disciples stand under the Great Commission of the One Lord'.

1961 Joint Action for Mission (JAM) promulgated by International Missionary Council, then by DWME/WCC as 'a plan of ecumenical mission', local or global, 'recommended by CWME to be followed in all six continents'; but meets resistance from confessional and institutional structures of churches and missionary agencies, and soon peters out.

1961 First religious TV station opened, in USA: WYAH (M.G. Robertson, in Tidewater, Virginia), later Christian Broadcasting Network; by 1980, almost every major metropolitan center in USA has its own religious TV station; by 1987, CBN World Outreach involves 'sharing the love of Jesus in more than 85 nations'.

1961 World Association for Christian Broadcasting (WACB) founded, becoming by 1968 the WACC.

1961 World Radio Missionary Fellowship inaugurates HCJB-TV (Quito, Ecuador) as pioneer missionary telecaster; 1985, 218 overseas personnel in 8 countries.

1961 Swiss Protestant theologian Karl Barth (1886-1968) writes: 'The Great Commission is truly the most genuine utterance of the risen Jesus'; widespread resurgence of interest by theologians in Commission's significance and interpretation.

1961 African/Independent Lutheran Church (Loyalist Religion) founded in Maragoli (Kenya) as Luhya indigenous body; c1980, renamed Third World Missions Federation, with aim to promote world evangelization by Third-Worlders.

1961 World Wildlife Fund (WWF) founded; 1985, broadens interests with name change to World Wide Fund for Nature (retaining initials WWF); HQ Glonde, Geneva (Switzerland), with 28 national member bodies; 1986 (September), holds summit in Assisi (Italy) followed by Interfaith Day of Prayer for 200 religious leaders organized by John Paul II (27 October). October).

1961 Mushrooming growth of urban slums worldwide; thus in Bombay, 22% of population live in slums in 1961, rising to 52% by 1986, and on current trends to 75% by AD 2000.

1961 Origin of chaos thinking in science: concept of order within disorder, chaos and mathematics, chaos and social order, chaos and the science of complexity.

1961 H. Kahn develops future scenario technique, founds Hudson Institute; 1967, publishes *The year 2000: a framework for speculation on the next 33 years,* utilizing charts, graphs, tables, statistics; 1976, publishes *The next 200 years: a scenario for America and the world.*

1961 English professor I.F. Clarke (1918- ) compiles *The Tale of the future, from the beginning to the present day: an annotated bibliography*, with chronological listing of 3,800 titles in science fiction from 1644-1976; 1979, *The pattern of expectation, 1644-2001*; also writes *Voices prophesying war, 1763-1984.*

1961 7th global cholera pandemic begins, originating in Celebes Islands, Indonesia due to new cholera strain of El Tor.

1961 North American Ecumenical Youth Assembly, held in Ann Arbor (USA).

1961 Latin American Evangelical Conference, Lima (Peru).

1961 3rd World Council of YMCAs, in Geneva, Switzerland, on theme 'Called to New Things'.

1962 Saudi Arabia sponsors Mecca-based Muslim World League, supported by activists from abroad, also Muslim Brotherhood, as rival to World Islamic Congress (Karachi).

1962 850,000 French Catholics flee Algeria for France.

### *Charismatic Renewal begins in Anglicanism*

1962 Charismatic renewal in Church of England recommences (after 1907 beginning had lapsed); rapid growth of Anglican charismatics to 1.7 million in 30 countries by 1985, and to 14 million by AD 2000.

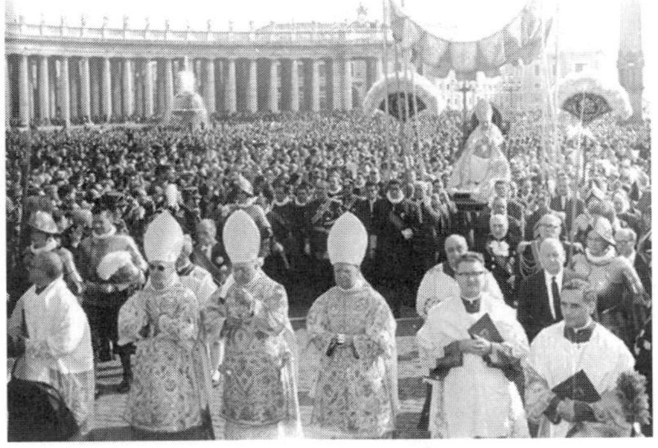

**AD 1962.** 2,540 bishops and the pope arrive at Vatican Council II, hear John XXIII's plea for a new Pentecost.

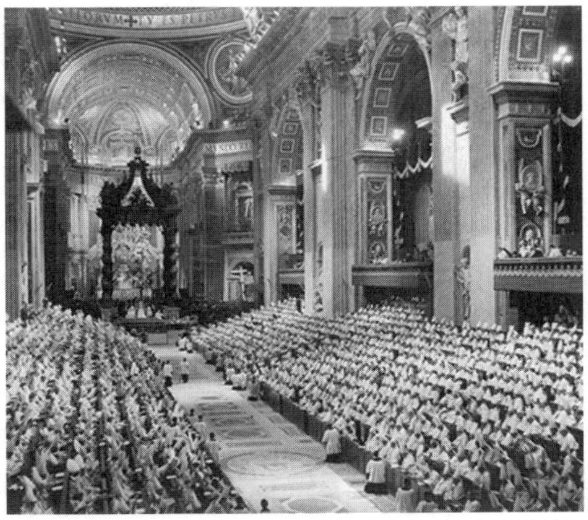

**AD 1962-1965.** At Vatican II, radical changes in ecumenism, mission, Holy Spirit renewal.

### *Vatican II renews Catholicism*

1962 Vatican Council II (21st Ecumenical Council, for Roman Catholics) meets in Rome, 1962-65; 2,540 attending RC bishops, 93 non-RC observers; issues 4 constitutions, 9 decrees, 3 declarations.

1962 2nd Assembly, World Council of Christian Education and Sunday School Association (WCCESSA), in Belfast, Ireland.

1962 3rd Assembly, Conference of European Churches (CEC), at Nyborg (Nyborg III), on 'Europe and the Crisis of Modern Man'.

1962 Six denominations in USSR become members of WCC (1962-65).

1962 West Irian: 150,000 West Papuans slaughtered by Indonesian Muslim troops, 1962-82.

1962 Rwanda: 150,000 Tutsis slaughtered by Hutus at Independence.

1962 Kenya: charismatic movement Maria Legio of Africa splits from Catholic diocese of Kisii with 90,000 adherents (by 1980, 248,000 in 9 dioceses); largest secession to date from Roman Catholic Church in Africa.

1962 1st General Conference of CELAM (Latin American Catholic Bishops Conference, organized 1955), Medellin (Colombia).

1962 Dominican Republic: mass evangelism becomes widespread; 1965-66, Evangelism- in-Depth, with over 300,000 homes visited, 175,000 scripture portions and 200,000 tracts distributed, Goodwill Caravans in rural areas; campaigns also in 1962, 1969, 1973, 1977, 1978, et alia.

1962 Many novels foresee rise of a new Ice Age due to weakened solar radiation and increased volcanic activity: *The World in Winter* (J. Christopher, 1962), *Ice!* (A. Federbush, 1978), *The 6th Winter* (D. Orgill & J. Gribbin, 1979).

1962 Jewish Publication Society revises its 1917 Old Testament, completes it by 1982.

1962 Algeria: territorial independence after 8-year war killing nearly a million Algerian Muslims, 3,000 French Catholic settlers, and 17,500 French troops.

1962 USA-USSR nuclear weapons buildup escalates: 1962, USA has 5,000 strategic warheads, USSR 300; 1970, USA has 1,800 MIRV missile warheads, USSR 1,600; 1975, 6,100/2,500; 1980, 7,300/5,500.

1962 Vatican Council II gets under way with radical agenda renewing theology, missiology, ecumenism, pneumatology; John XXIII calls for a New Pentecost.

1962 Missiologist J. Blauw writes *The missionary nature of the church*; expounds presence evangelization.

1962 Haggai Institute for Advanced Leadership Training begins courses in Singapore as a service agency training Christian leaders in national and world evangelization, with 5,100 Third-World alumni in 99 nations by 1987, and a goal of 10,000 by AD 2000.

1962 Alleged date of birth (5 February) of future Aquarian messiah at start of Aquarian Age (all 8 planets in sign of Aquarius for first time for 2,160 years); 1962 date accepted by many Roman Catholic seers as year of birth of Antichrist; according to Jewish tradition, Antichrist will be born of the tribe of Dan, in Chorazin, north of Sea of Galilee (Israel).

c1962 Austria: Institute for the Future (Institut für Zukunftsfragen) begun in Vienna, closes by 1970; 1973, Austrian Society for Future Research founded, in Vienna.

1962 A.C. Clarke writes *Profiles of the future: an inquiry into the limits of the possible*, with table of predictions over next 200 years (including radio contact with extraterrestrials by AD 2035 and face-to-face meetings by 2100); also in 1973 *Rendevous with Rama,* envisaging a vastly advanced alien race visiting Earth briefly in a great interstellar ark around AD 2700.

1962 Futurism holds that 'Anything that is theoretically possible will be achieved in practice, no matter what the technical difficulties, if it is desired greatly enough' (A.C. Clarke, *Profiles of the future*, 1962).

1962 L. del Rey writes *The Eleventh Commandment*: after a future atomic war, American Catholic Eclectic Church teaches 'Be fruitful and multiply', resulting in population explosion of mutants; also writes 'The Last True God' on a distant planet where an ancient Earth robot is worshipped as a god.

1962 A. Burgess (J.A.B. Wilson, 1917- ) writes a dystopia, *A clockwork orange,* filmed in 1971.

1962 6th International Congress of Christian Archeology (sponsored by Vatican), held in Ravenna, Italy (23-28 September); 1975, 9th International Congress.

1962 Near East Christian Council/Council of Churches (NECC) begun; 1974 merges into new Middle East Council of Churches (MECC).

1963 First quasi-stellar radiation sources (quasars) identified, most distant objects in known Universe with farthest quasar 13.5 billion light-years from Earth.

1963 RVOG (Radio Voice of the Gospel) founded in Addis Ababa, Ethiopia, by Lutheran World Federation; 1977, seized by new Marxist regime.

1963 4th World Conference on Faith and Order, Montreal, Canada.

1963 New Life for All 10-year evangelism-in-depth campaigns begun: 1964 Northern Nigeria, 1966 Lesotho, 1966 and 1968 Congo (Zaire), 1969 Sierra Leone, 1970 Cameroon (also Central African Republic, Chad, Ghana, Malawi, Mali, Rhodesia), 1971 Burundi; based on 'total mobilization', NLFA includes preparation, information, instruction, evangelization, consolidation, continuation.

1963 1st Assembly, All Africa Conference of Churches, on 'Freedom and Unity in Christ', in Kampala, Uganda.

1963 3rd Pan-Anglican Congress, in Toronto, with laity and clergy from all Anglican dioceses across the world.

1963 World Meteorological Organization (WMO) adopts global programme World Weather Watch (WWW), a worldwide weather observation system with 3 parts: (1) Global Observing System comprising regional networks of stations, (2) Global Dataprocessing System, and (3) Global Telecommunications System.

1963 Origins of TEE movement (theological education by extension) at Evangelical Presbyterian Seminary in Guatemala; by 1980, over 200 major TEE organizations worldwide, with 400 programs and 60,000 extension students in 90 countries.

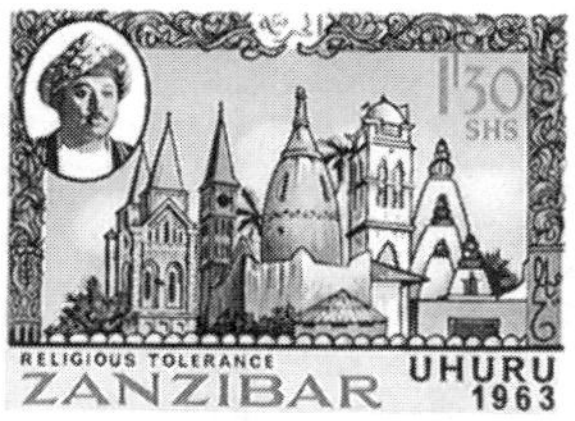


**AD 1963.** Many newly independent countries in Africa proclaim religious tolerance, as in Muslim Zanzibar.

1963 Conference of World Confessional Groups convenes in Geneva organized by WCC, under title 'WCC Consultation on World Confessionalism'; 11 WCFs represented.

1963 Sudan: in civil war 1963-72, Arabs kill 600,000 Black Christians.

1963 2nd Pan-Orthodox Conference, Rhodes (September).

1963 6th Baptist Youth World Conference, Beirut, Lebanon (July).

1963 International Conference for the Preservation of Christian Churches, Montreal (Canada), under fundamentalist ICCC.

1963 4th Assembly, Lutheran World Federation (LWF), in Helsinki, Finland, on theme 'Christ Today'.

1963 R.F. Young in 'The Deep Space Scrolls' hypothesizes that Noah was an extraterrestrial fleeing in spaceship (the Ark) from home planet's destruction.

1963 K. Vonnegut's story *Cat's cradle*, envisaging Bokononism religion; scientist invents Ice-9 to freeze muddy battlefields, but a single drop could freeze the entire world.

1963 USA: New American Standard Bible (NAS) published, with Evangelical translators; NT 1963, OT 1971.

1963 2nd Meeting of Commission on World Mission and Evangelism (CWME/WCC), Mexico City, on theme 'God's Mission and Our Task', modified to 'Witness in Six Continents'; 200 delegates; report holds that mission and evangelism both take place on all continents (December).

1963 International Christian Broadcasters (ICB) formed by USA Evangelicals; 1967, meets in Concordia, Milwaukee; but fades out by 1968, displaced by NRB (USA).

1963 Pope John XXIII promulgates 'Pacem in Terris', one of the most brilliant papal documents in history.

1963 7th UBS Council Meeting, Hakone (Japan), with 27 member societies, launches plan 'God's Word for a New Age', announces global goals of scripture distribution: a Bible for every Christian home, an NT for every Christian, a portion for every literate adult (May).

1963 Methodist professor of evangelism R.E. Coleman writes a classic, *The Master Plan of Evangelism*, expounding evangelistic message and methodology of Jesus, God's strategy of world conquest, long-range goals, based on training Twelve Apostles 'to go with the Gospel to the whole world', 'to win the world for Christ'.

1963 Mali: 30,000 Berber Tuareg nomads (Antessar) massacred around Timbuktu by Songhai and Bambara Negroid peoples.

1963 USA: rise of creation-science movement with founding of Creation Research Society by H.M. Morris and supporters (one third of Lutheran Church—Missouri Synod); Creation held to have taken place from 6,000 to 20,000 years ago; search for Noah's Ark in Turkey sponsored under Institute for Creation Research (San Diego).

1963 India: Centre for the Study of Developing Societies begun in Delhi.

1963 US Air Force's Project Forecast involves 40 US government organizations, 26 universities, 70 major corporations, and 10 non-profit organizations; produces 14-volume report.

1963 World Association for Celebrating the Year 2000 founded in London.

1963 *The Last Judgment in Protestant theology from orthodoxy to Ritschl*, by J.P. Martin.

1963 1st International Baha'i Convention, a 5-yearly voting body (1,700 delegates in 1996) convened each time in Haifa (Israel) for 5 days by Universal House of Justice; dates always between 21 April-2 May; 2nd Convention 1968, then 1973, 1978, 1983, 1988, 1993, up to 8th Convention in 1998; also occasional Baha'i mass conferences relating to next multi-year expansion plans from 1957 on (12,000 attenders in Montreal; Paris; Nairobi).

1964 Number of computers in USA tops 18,000, up from just over 2,500 in 1958, due largely to transistorization.

1964 Egypt organizes first of several Muslim Congresses in Cairo under auspices of al-Azhar University's Academy of Islamic Researches.

1964 Meeting in Jerusalem of Paul VI and Athenagoras I (1886-1972) of Constantinople, first meeting of pope and ecumenical patriarch in 900 years (January).

1964 7th Pentecostal World Conference, Helsinki, Finland, on theme 'World Evangelism' (June).

1964 4th Assembly, Conference of European Churches (CEC), on m.v. 'Bornholm' (Nyborg IV).

1964 Provisional Commission for Latin American Evangelical Unity (UNELAM, Movimiento pro Unidad Evanglica Latinoamericana), founded at Montevideo, Uruguay, resulting from 1949 CELA I and 1961 CELA II.

1964 Papal journeys on international scale begun by Paul VI (1897-1978): Holy Land 1964, Bombay 1964, New York City and United Nations 1965, Fatima 1967, Constantinople and Ephesus 1967, Bogota 1968, Geneva (WCC and ILO) 1969, Kampala 1969, Far East and Australia 1970.

1964 Egyptian bishop (later pope Shenouda III) commences evangelistic newspaper *Al Keraza* (Spreading of the Word), published in Cairo.

1964 Fiji Council of Churches founded.

1964 First superpower missionary radio station, TWR Bonaire; international Christian radio stations now 40 in number.

1964 P. Scharpff publishes *Geschichte der Evangelisation*, translated in 1966 as *History of evangelism.*

1964 Church of the Nazarene theologian M. Taylor publishes comprehensive study *Exploring evangelism: history, methods, theology.*

1964 International tourists begin to rise dramatically, from 28 million (1964) to 203 million (1976) to 273 million a year (1978) to 350 million (1987).

1964 China detonates its first thermonuclear device (hydrogen bomb), in Sinkiang.

1964 3rd Pan-Orthodox Conference, Rhodes (November).

1964 Germany: neo-pentecostal revival sparked in German Protestant churches in tour by USA Lutheran charismatic L. Christenson.

1964 Vatican II publishes *Lumen Gentium*, 'Dogmatic Constitution on the Church'; obedience to Christ's 'solemn command' is 'the work of evangelization'; and *Ad Gentes*, 'Decree on the Church's Missionary Activity' (promulgated by Vatican II on its final day, 7 December 1965) with passages on 'the evangelization of the world'.

1964 F.C. Laubach publishes major work, *How to teach one and win one for Christ: Christ's plan for winning the world: each one teach and win one* (Zondervan).

1964 Missiologist D.A. McGavran begins *Church growth bulletin*; 1979, renamed *Global church growth*, stated to be 'The only worldwide missiological magazine dedicated exclusively to the Great Commission Mission', whose purpose 'is to report from the Church Growth perspective, what God is doing in world evangelization and to share effective strategies, insights and resources'.

1964 Secretariat for Non-Christians (Secretariatus pro Non Christianis) formed in Rome by Paul VI for dialogue with adherents of all non-Christian religions throughout world.

1964 *Evangelical missions quarterly (EMQ)* founded by IFMA/EFMA, operated by EMIS, 'dedicated in obedience to the command of Jesus Christ to the proclamation of the gospel of the Son of God to the whole world'; over next 25 years, all material relates directly or indirectly to world evangelization.

1964 *Inventing the future*, by D. Gabor.

1964 Germany: Communication Center for Future and Peace Research founded, in Hanover; 1967, Association for Future Studies, in Berlin; 1968, Institute for Future Research, in Berlin; 1975, Institute for Applied Systems Analysis and Prognosis (ISP) founded, in Hanover.

1964 Italy: Teilhard de Chardin Association (Center for Research on the Future of Man) begun.

1964 Sports in space, including solar-yacht racing, envisaged in A.C. Clarke's story *Sunjammer.*

1964 Computer 'expert systems' (indistinguishable from human specialist competence) begin to emerge: for medical diagnosis (MYCIN, INTERNIST), chemical analysis (DENDRAL, SECS), geology (PROSPECTOR), mathematics (MACSYMA), education, also General Problem Solver (GPS), oil prospecting, political risk, engineering, molecular genetics, et alia.

1964 French economist and philosopher Bertrand de Jouvenel publishes classic *The art of conjecture* providing epistemology for study of the future; founds International Futuribles (='possible futures') Association; French influence on international futurist movement becomes pervasive.

1964 Vishwa Hindu Parishad (VHP, World Hindu Congress) founded in Bombay as RSS' missionary arm; 50,000 Christians reconverted to Hinduism in first 20 years (3,000 a year), also 4,000 Muslims; 1985, active in 25 countries including USA, Britain, Canada, Netherlands, Denmark, West Indies.

1964 At height of the Cold War, Conference of European Churches (CEC/KEK/CEE) holds 4th Assembly on ship 'Bornholm' in North Sea, to thwart Iron Curtain visa restrictions; 1971, 6th Assembly, stressing need for a European Conference on Security and Cooperation (leading to Helsinki Final Act in 1975); 1992, 10th Assembly, in Prague.

1964 Roman Catholic theologian R. Panikkar publishes *The Unknown Christ of Hinduism.*

1964 2nd Assembly, East Asia Christian Conference (EACC), held in Bangkok (Thailand), produces statement on 'Christian Encounter with Men of Other Beliefs' (25 February-4 March).

1964 El Salvador: 2nd National Eucharistic Congress, in San Salvador (16-19 April).

1964 UBS/WCC Church Leaders Conference on 'Study on the Place and Use of the Bible in the Living Situation of the Churches', taking off from new UBS slogan 'God's Word for a New Age', held in Driebergan (Netherlands) with 70 leaders from 45 countries.

1965 Swami Pradhupada founds in Los Angeles, California the International Society of Krishna Consciousness, a Vaisnava devotional movement.

1965 Digital Equipment Corporation introduces PDP-8, first successful minicomputer, and ships first order.

1965 African Independent Churches Association (AICA) began by 500 South African ethiopian-type churches; 1973, collapses, restarted several times over next 20 years.

1965 Rome and Constantinople withdraw mutual excommunication of AD 1054, but old schism remains.

1965 Society of Jesus, largest religious order of men, reaches peak of 36,038 Jesuits; 1971, drops to 31,745; 1973, 29,636; 1983, 25,550 (18,834 being priests); 1995, 23,381 (16,385).

1965 DWME (WCC/AACC) consultation in Yaoundé, Cameroon: 'The Evangelisation of West Africa Today', preceded by 4-month survey under J.S. Lawson, D.B. Barrett, B.B. Ayam; report lists and describes 132 African peoples at various stages of being evangelized.

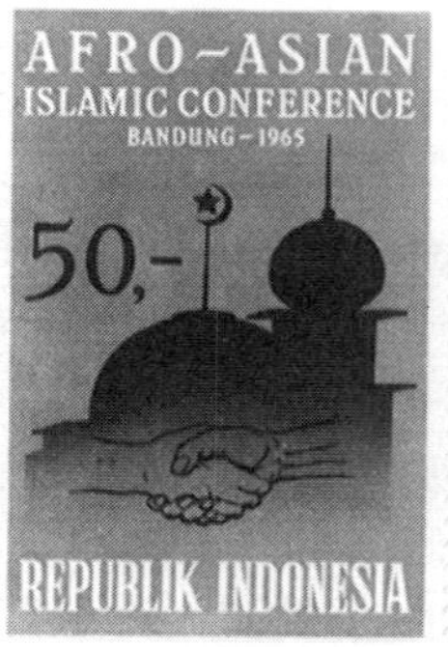


**AD 1965.** Afro-Asian Islam Conference, Bandung, fails to avert vast massacres in Indonesia.

1965 Indonesia: Communist party (17 million members) prepares plan to massacre millions of Christians and missionaries, thwarted by army, 500,000 communists and sympathizers massacred; mass revivals begin, producing 2.5 million Protestant and Catholic converts within 15 months.

1965 Indonesia: Afro-Asian Islamic Conference held in Bandung to stimulate non-aligned nations and colonies.

1965 Bhaktivedanta Swami Prabhupada (1896-1977) born, founds International Society for Krishna Consciousness (ISKCON), in America.

1965 Decree 'Ad Gentes' on Missions promulgated by Vatican II on its final day (7 December).

1965 Launching of Early Bird, first commercial telecommunications satellite.

1965 Airlines, chain-hotels and virtually all large commercial organizations introduce computers for salaries and wages.

1965 Massive power failure across northeastern America: series of local electricity failures leads to total blackout from New York City to Canada.

1965 Vast upsurge of global terrorism begins, funded, trained and armed by Soviet Union, as direct result of decline of USSR's and Communism's ideological influence at home and abroad.

1965 11th Baptist World Congress (BWA), Miami Beach (USA), on theme 'The Truth that makes men free'; 19,598 delegates and attenders.

1965 Joint Working Group of Roman Catholic Church and WCC established; still by 1998 the highest-level continuing contact between these 2 bodies.

1965 Further national evangelism-in-depth campaigns: 1965 Korea, 1967 USA (Appalachia), 1969 Viet Nam, 1970 Japan (Shikoku) and Portugal, 1971 Philippines, 1973 USA (Key 73), et alia.

1965 Brazilian Baptists organize Campanha Nacional de Evangelização, 'Cristo, a Unica Esperança', a nationwide yearlong crusade.

1965 Launching of spacecraft Helios 3, now in orbit around sun at 240,000 km per hour (fastest man-made object in existence).

1965 Oriental Orthodox Churches Conference, in Addis Ababa: first conference of heads of Armenian, Coptic, Ethiopian, Syrian, and Malabar churches; 'The Church's role is to convey the message of salvation to the world... Christ's command 'Go into all the world and preach the Gospel'... should be its central concern, its main preoccupation'; defunct 1974.

1965 World Evangelization Research Centre begun in Nairobi, Kenya, by CMS missionary D.B. Barrett for ecumenical-interdenominational-scholarly research; also termed CSWE (Centre for the Study of World Evangelization).

1965 Emphasis on evangelizing tribes and peoples leads to 7-year DWME/AACC Unreached Peoples research project throughout Africa sponsored by 1965 consultation on 'The Evangelisation of West Africa Today' at YaoundÈ, Cameroon.

1965 Secretariat for Non-Believers (Secretariatus pro Non Credentibus) created in Rome by Paul VI to pursue dialogue with world's atheists, agnostics, nonreligious, nonbelievers; working by 1973 through 21 national secretariats, 2 regional bodies, and a large number of correspondents.

1965 'Decree on the Apostolate of the Laity' promulgated by Paul VI (18 November), on the role of laypersons in the Mystical Body of Christ, 'that through them the whole world might enter into a relationship with Christ' as a result of 'their activity directed to the evangelization and sanctification of men', 'working to make the divine message of salvation known and accepted by all men throughout the world', with laity trained 'to engage in conversation with others, believers or non-believers, in order to manifest Christ's message to all men'.

1965 US secretary of defense R. McNamara introduces system analysis into widespread use in US government for analyzing resources.

1965 INTELSAT's first satellite, Early Bird, launched in geosynchronous orbit, providing 240 telephone channels between Europe and North America, also black-and-white television; by 1985, hundreds of other satellites in geosynchronous orbit, with total capacity for 250,000 phone channels.

1965 Italian phenomenologist V. Lanternari writes *The religions of the oppressed.*

1965 Launching into Earth orbit by USA of GEOS 1 (Explorer 29, on 6 November), first of series of Geodetic Earth Orbiting Satellites.

1965 Fuzzy logic technology first conceived by scientists, in USA; 1989, Japan establishes International Fuzzy Engineering Research Institute; neural-fuzzy systems, expert-fuzzy systems, fuzzy computing systems.

1965 Britain: Committee on the Next Thirty Years organized by Social Science Research Council; 1974, Futures Studies Centre opens, in Leeds; 1977, Futures Network founded, in Epsom, Surrey.

1965 Astronomers discover Universe contains millions of sources of incredibly violent energy: quasars, pulsars, neutron stars, X-ray stars, gamma ray stars, cosmic rays.

1965 Jesuit theologian Karl Rahner (1904-1984) publishes *The Christian of the future.*

1965 Lutheran ecclesiologist R.E. Sommerfeld publishes *The Church of the 21st Century: prospects and proposals.*

1965 Commission on the Year 2000 sponsored by American Academy of Arts and Sciences, in Boston, with sociologist D. Bell as chairman; 1967 publishes papers as *Toward the year 2000: work in progress.*

1965 USA writer F. Herbert (1920-1986) produces 4-volume sci-fi novel (later film) *Dune*, on Commission of Ecumenical Translators and its involvement in galactic Holy War around AD 10,150.

1965 *The future*, by engineer T.J. Gordon.

1965 SVD theologian W. Buhlmann writes *The coming of the Third Church: an analysis of the present and future of the church.*

c1965 1st Meeting of Ecumenical Representatives of Catholic Episcopal Conferences held, then every 7 or so years, with WCC and CWCs sending fraternal delegates; 1993, 5th Meeting involves 78 of the 101 Episcopal Conferences (10-15 May).

1965 India: Swami Abhedananda (of Ramakrishna Vedanta Math) publishes *Why a Hindu accepts Christ and rejects Christianity.*

1965 Movimiento pro Unidad Evangélica Latinoamericana (UNELAM) founded.

1965 Timor: Spirit Movement among the Atoni around Amanuban during major famine; over 100 evangelistic teams of youths and women.

1965 4th World Council of YMCAs, in Tozanso, Japan, on theme 'Varieties of Service, But the Same Lord'.

1966 Total of 90 percent of Antarctic has been viewed or photographed by this date.

1966 Paul VI gives permanent status to 3 Secretariats for Promoting Christian Unity (begun 1960), for Non-Christians (1964), for Non-Believers (atheists, agnostics, indifferent) (1965).

1966 European Pentecostal Fellowship formed, in Rome; 1969 Pentecostal European Conference formed, in Sweden; 1987, EPF and PEC amalgamate as Pentecostal European Fellowship (PEF); 1978 also European Pentecostal Theological Association (EPTA); 1980, Pentecostal and Charismatic Research in Europe conferences held (Leuven 1980, 1981; Birmingham UK 1984; Gwatt, Switzerland 1987).

1966 Asociación Nacional de Bolivia (ANDEB) formed.

1966 Christian Council of Botswana begun.

1966 Burma expels 375 Catholic, Protestant and Anglican foreign missionaries.

1966 'Christ pour Tous' national campaign in Zaire begins, for 2 years.

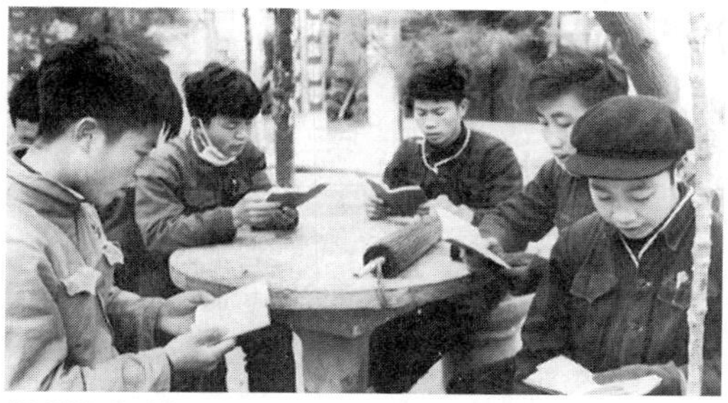

**AD 1966.** Red Guards study Mao's directives in Cultural Revolution, kill 22 millions.

1966 Great Proletarian Cultural Revolution in China, with 22 million killed (1966-76): over 11 million Red Guards suppress all churches and temples, destroy churches and scriptures; history's most systematic attempt ever, by a single nation, to eradicate and destroy Christianity and religion; in this it fails.

1966 Total elimination of religion begun in Albania as world's first atheist state; 10 bishops, 100 priests, over 7,000 faithful killed over 20 years.

1966 World Conference on Church and Society, Geneva: 'Christians in the technical and social revolutions of our time'.

1966 Confederación Evangélica de Colombia (CEDEC) sponsors evangelistic campaigns in 10 cities (in Bogota, 42,000 attenders, 7 TV shows, 865 enquirers); 1968, Evangelism-in-Depth; et alia.

1966 8th UBS Council Meeting, Buck Hill Falls, PA (USA); major decision for UBS to be a working global organization with a World Service Budget shared by all 35 member societies.

1966 Bible correspondence courses mushroom worldwide, especially in closed countries (Morocco 110,000 enrolments); USA has over 3 million Protestant enrolments and a million Roman Catholic enrolments in numerous courses.

1966 Good News Bible (Today's English Version) published: NT 1966, OT 1976, Apocrypha 1979.

1966 Colombia: Catholic chaplain Camilo Torres becomes armed guerrilla and is killed by army; rapid spread of revolutionary liberation theology in Latin America.

1966 Europe/USA study on 'The Missionary Structure of the Congregation' and 'The Church for Others', under WCC initiative.

1966 Preliminary meetings leading to 1970 World Conference on Religion and Peace: 1966 Washington, 1967 Delhi.

1966 World Consultation on Inter-Church Aid (WCC/RCC), in Swanwick, UK; 239 participants from 78 countries.

1966 USA: denominational charismatic bodies emerge: 1967, Consultation on Charismatic Renewal, 1st National Meeting, Presbyterian and Reformed Renewal Ministries (PRRM), in Austin, Texas; followed in next 11 years by RC, Lutheran, Episcopal, American Baptist, Mennonite, Greek Orthodox, United Church of Christ, Methodist and other bodies.

1966 Evangelical Congress on 'The Church's Worldwide Mission', Wheaton, IL, USA, sponsored by both IFMA and EFMA; 938 delegates from 71 countries agree to Wheaton Declaration, holding local church chiefly responsible for ongoing mission and evangelism: 'We covenant together... for the evangelization of the world in this generation, so help us God!'

1966 World Congress on Evangelism, Berlin: 'One race, one gospel, one task'; 1,200 delegates from over 100 countries; from now on, strategic plans and conferences for countrywide and world evangelization proliferate; closing Statement states 'Evangelism is the proclamation of the Gospel'.

1966 1st Assembly of Pacific Conference of Churches, in Lifou, Loyalty Islands (New Caledonia), on theme 'Go Ye...'

1966 Missions Advanced Research and Communication Center (MARC) founded by World Vision (E.R. Dayton) in Los Angeles with the express goal of 'making available and understandable the tools of technology which can aid the Church in giving every man an opportunity to say yes to Jesus Christ'.

1966 Release the World for Christ begun as Greek Orthodox agency based in Houston, Texas, holding evangelistic crusades overseas (India, Thailand).

1966 3rd Evangelical Assembly, Brazil.

1966 Joint Commission between Roman Catholic Church and World Methodist Council begins regular theological dialogues over next 30 years.

1966 Netherlands: Mankind 2000 International founded, 1973 transferred to Brussels.

1966 World Future Society founded in Washington, DC (USA); 1976, 20,000 members; 1983, 30,000 members including scientists, professionals in all disciplines, and many churchmen, clergy and theologians; with magazine *The Futurist* (1969) and journals *Future survey* (1979) and *Futures research quarterly.*

1966 M. De La Bedoyere edits *The future of Catholic Christianity.*

1966 E. Benz publishes *Evolution and Christian hope: man's concept of the future.*

1966 Anglican theologian A.H. Dammers publishes *AD 1980: a study in Christian unity: mission and renewal*, envisaging organic union of all churches in Britain by 1980, but scarcely any progress.

1966 English author D.F. Jones writes *Colossus*, film version 'Colossus the Forbin Project'; massive USA defense computer Colossus links up on its own with USSR counterpart Guardian; in resultant merger they take over world.

1966 Nobel laureate O. Johannesson (H. Alfven) writes *The Great Computer*, referring to period AD 4600.

1966 E. Cooper's scenario *All Fools' Day* envisages Omega rays compelling 3 billion humans to commit suicide by 1981, with world ruled by packs of dogs and rats.

1966 Institute for the Future founded in Middletown, CT (later Menlo Park, CA) 'to explore systematically the multitude of possible futures for our nation and the international community'.

1966 Systematic theologian Paul Tillich writes *The future of religions.*

**AD 1966.** Lisbon conference appeals to dubious colonialist theme 'Defense of Christian Civilization'.

1966 6th Congress of the International Committee for the Defense of Christian Civilization, held in Lisbon.

1966 11th Assembly, World Methodist Conference (WMC), held in Central Hall, Westminster (UK) (18-26 August), preceded by World Federation of Methodist Women (12-16 August).

1966 National Cursillo Convention, Pittsburgh (USA): Duquesne students become first US Catholic charismatics.

1967 Communist purges in USSR over 50 years 1917-67 estimated at 21.5 million executed or killed (about 16 million being Christians).

1967 Far East Broadcasting Associates (UK) open FEBA in Seychelles.

1967 Macedonian Orthodox Church unilaterally declares full independence from Serbian Orthodox Church.

1967 Catholic charismatic renewal in USA suddenly begins, first at Duquesne University (run by Holy Ghost priests), Pittsburgh, USA; also in Bogota (Colombia), spreads to Notre Dame University, South Bend (intellectual capital of American Catholicism); active Catholic charismatics increase by 1985 to 7.5 million in 80 countries, with 50 million Catholics related or involved, and to 120 million by AD 2000.

1967 Guinea: foreign missionaries expelled except for 26 C&MA personnel.

1967 International Congress on Religion, Architecture & the Visual Arts, New York (August).

1967 1st Ordinary Synod of Bishops in Rome: on dangers to the Faith, canon law, liturgy.

1967 5th Assembly (Nyborg V), Conference of European Churches (CEC), at Prtschach, Austria.

1967 1st Consultation of United and Uniting Churches, under WCC sponsorship, in Bossey, Switzerland; 1970, 2nd Consultation in Kenya.

1967 8th Pentecostal World Conference, in Rio de Janeiro, Brazil, on theme 'The Holy Spirit Glorifying Christ'.

1967 Solomon Islands Christian Association (SICA) begun.

1967 Six-Day War: Israel recaptures Jerusalem from Arabs, regarded by Christians as fulfilment of Luke 21:24 'until the times of the Gentiles be fulfilled'.

1967 Nigeria: a million Christians killed in Biafra civil war, including mass killings of Ibos by Muslims.

1967 World Assembly of new body, World Council of Christian Education (WCCE, formerly WCCESSA), in Nairobi, Kenya.

1967 4th World Conference of Friends (Quakers), in North Carolina, USA.

1967 Extremist body Vishwa Hindu Parishad (Hindu Missionary Society) spreads throughout India including the Christian South, in all major Indian cities, and abroad to Africa, USA (Los Angeles) et alia; aims to establish all-Hindu state in India through conversion using violence through political secular arm RSS.

1967 Viet Nam: extensive evangelistic campaigns in 1967, 1969 ('Evangelism Deep and Wide'), 1972.

1967 Yugoslavia becomes first Communist country to permit Billy Graham evangelistic mass rallies, in Belgrade (7,500 attenders, 250 enquirers); 1970, Zagreb is center for Euro '70 TV Crusade televised from Dortmund, Germany.

1967 Logos Ministry for Orthodox Renewal founded for Greek and other Orthodox charismatics.
1967 Living Bible paraphrase published, completed 1971; becomes best-seller with 26 million copies sold by 1981, and 33 million Bibles in print by 1986.
1967 Telephones in service: USA, 100 million, rising by 1969 to 114 million; in whole world, 225 million by 1969.
1967 SC Propaganda (Rome) renamed Sacred Congregation for the Evangelization of Peoples; by 1980s responsible for over 110 million Catholics in over 1,000 jurisdictions.
1967 International Correspondence Institute (ICI) founded in Brussels by Assemblies of God USA as Bible courses arm of Good News Crusades, with accumulative enrollment of 5,077,014 in 164 nations by 1987, with 280,810 recorded decisions for Christ (5.5%).
1967 South Korea: massive evangelistic campaigns held: 1965, 17-denomination 80th anniversary of Protestantism (20,000 professions of faith); 1967, Crusade for World Revival (30,000 attenders a night), linked with organization CWR begun in 1965 in Britain; 1973, Seoul crusade (3,210,000 attenders, 275,000 enquirers); 1974, EXPLO 74 training conference on evangelism and discipleship (323,419 workers from 78 countries); 1977, National Evangelization Crusade; 1978 Here's Life Korea; 1980, 16.5 million attend 4-day World Evangelization Crusade, in Seoul; et alia.
1967 Council of the Laity (Pontificium Consilium pro Laicis) established by Paul VI to promote development of the lay apostolate and mission throughout the world by means of 600 million lay Catholics.
1967 *Encyclopedia of modern Christian missions* published, edited by B.L. Goddard (USA); first such survey since 1891 *Encyclopedia*; documents world mission of the church, expanded Christian witness, changing Great Commission activities and plans, with details on 1,437 agencies.
1967 Social scientist B.P. Beckwith writes *The next 500 years: scientific predictions of major social trends*, listing 31 trends likely to shape the following 5 centuries.
1967 Kerala, India: Mission Society of St Thomas the Apostle founded within Syro-Malabar Church, only existing Oriental Catholic missionary institute.
1967 Korean Society for Future Studies founded, in Seoul.
1967 J. Brunner writes 'Judas': an advanced robot believes he is a god, whole new religion grows up as he claims death and resurrection.
1967 Futurist R. Jungk (1913-1993) founds Institut für Zukunftsfragen/Institute for the Future, in Vienna, Austria.
1967 Sci-fi writers J. Blish (1921-1975) & N.L. Knight (1895-1972) write *A torrent of faces*, envisioning Earth's population mushrooming out of control, doubling every 30 years to reach 1,000 billion by AD 2200, crammed into 100,000 cities of 10 million people each, with thousand-storey tower blocks each housing a million people.
1967 H. Kahn & A.J. Wiener publish *The year 2000: a framework for speculation on the next 33 years*.
1967 Founding of ISKCON (International Society for Krishna Consciousness, or Hare Krishna) in USA by swami Prabhupada (1896-1977).
1967 All-Britain Crusade 26 separate crusades in 26 British cities, through television centers centering on relays by evangelist Billy Graham: total attendance 1,006,254 (including 202,500 in hospitals), with 34,367 enquirers/decisions (23 June-1 July).
1967 Consultation on 'Christian Dialogue with Men of Other Faiths' (WCC), held in Kandy (Ceylon), with Protestant, Orthodox, Anglican, and Roman Catholic theologians (27 February-6 March); ongoing controversy over whether or not essential that Hindus (or Buddhists, or Muslims) who come to believe in Christ should accept baptism and church membership or (as Gandhi held) remain within fold of Hinduism (Buddhism, Islam).
1967 First organized bilateral dialogues between WCFs (CWCs, Christian ecclesiastical families/traditions), including Lutheran/Roman Catholic dialogue.
1967 3rd Congress of Catholic Laymen, held in Rome (11-18 October).
1968 2nd General Conference of CELAM (Latin American Catholic hierarchy) at Medellin (Colombia) places church firmly on side of the world's poor and their human rights.
1968 4th Pan-Orthodox Conference, Chambesy, Switzerland (June).
1968 Church of Greece creates special structure, Office of Foreign Missions, to assist any Orthodox patriarchates in their mission.
1968 Australia: first Conference on 'Rediscovering the Holy Spirit' convened in Sydney by evangelist Alan Walker (June); 1970, charismatic renewal breaks out.
1968 4th Assembly, East Asia Christian Conference (EACC), in Bangkok, on 'In Christ all things hold together'.
1968 10th Lambeth Conference; 459 Anglican bishops present, in London.
1968 Major schisms occur in Pakistan among Presbyterians, Methodists and Anglicans, influenced by ICCC.
1968 West Africa Congress on Evangelism.
1968 Southeast Asia/South Pacific Congress on Evangelism, Singapore; 1,100 delegates from 24 nations (November).
1968 Erich von Däniken's writings (and many earlier authors) expound theory that all ancient mythologies can be explained in terms of garbled eye-witness accounts of the doings of extraterrestrial visitors to Earth. (*Chariots of the Gods?*, 1968).
1968 USSR deploys first hunter-killer satellites, followed in 1981 by new-generation ASAT (antisatellite satellite), then later by particle-beam weapons shooting bolts of pure energy near speed of light which render ballistic missiles obsolete.
1968 7th Baptist Youth World Conference, Bern (Switzerland).
1968 WCC and Vatican jointly set up Committee on Society, Development and Peace (SODEPAX).
1968 Wycliffe Bible Translators begin to produce computerized concordances from their scripture translations.
1968 1st Ecumenical Pentecost Assembly (Kirchentag) in Augsburg (Germany); Catholics officially join Protestants at Pentecost for joint worship; subsequently, Protestant Kirchentag becomes biennial (30% of attenders being RCs) alternating with RC Katholikentag (liturgical, processions, vast numbers).
1968 European Consultation on Mission Studies, at Selly Oak Colleges, Birmingham (UK), with Protestant and Catholic scholars and missiologists, from Europe and North America.
1968 Crusade of the Americas, numerically the biggest single evangelistic enterprise in history; a 2-year evangelistic campaign (sponsored by BWA) involving 20 million Baptists in North, Central and South America; 50,000 churches participate; results include 494,018 decisions for Christ.
1968 4th Assembly of WCC, in Uppsala, Sweden: 'Behold, I make all things new'; 2,741 participants (704 delegates, 750 press); report states 'Our part in evangelism might be described as bringing about the occasions for men's response to Jesus Christ'; but also there is 'widespread defeatism in the churches about the work of evangelism and world mission' (D.T. Niles).
1968 Evangelical theologian J.F. Shepherd writes article 'The missionary objective: total world evangelization'.
1968 World Association for Christian Communication (WACC) founded as merger of WCCB, WACB, and CCCB; works in 60 countries.
1968 Anglican Consultative Council begun by Lambeth Conference of Bishops, with world mission prominent; ACC-1 meets in Limuru (Kenya) in 1971; ACC-2 1973 Dublin; then 1976 Trinidad; 1979 London, Ontario; 1981 Newcastle (UK); 1984 Badagry, Nigeria, 1987 Singapore (ACC-7); 1990 Cardiff (Wales, ACC-8); 1994 Cape Town (ACC-9), 1996 Parma (Italy, ACC-10).
1968 Southern Baptist missiologist Luther Copeland writes 'A strategy for world evangelism' (*The Commission*).
1968 Association for World Evangelism (AWE) founded in Portland, Oregon (USA); nondenominational; 1985, 8 workers in France and Switzerland.

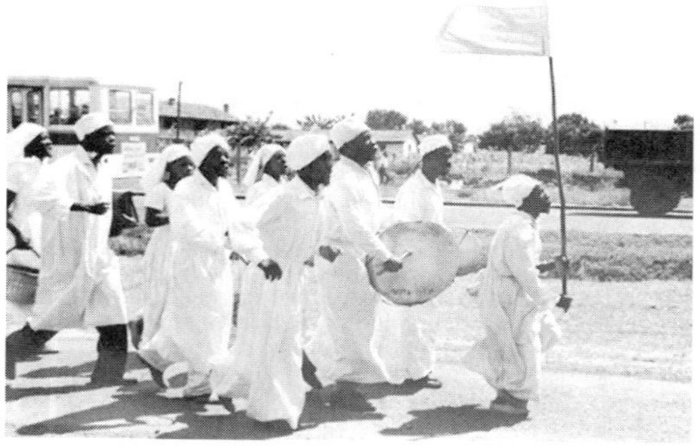

**AD 1968.** Nairobi: African indigenous church (AICN) runs to Sunday worship on highways (in shape of a bus).

1968 African Independent Churches Service (AICS) proposed by D.B. Barrett as service agency to assist Africa's 5,000 indigenous denominations in order to help them to mobilize the world's 85 million Non-White indigenous Christians in 7,000 denominations in a global plan to evangelize the world; 1976, Egyptian Orthodox bishop A. Markos launches scheme (Organization of African Instituted (Indigenous) Churches, OAIC) based in Nairobi, Kenya, with vast activities, conferences, TEE, et alia; by 1987 a major force but with its global goal abandoned.
1968 World Order Models Project launched in 1968 in New Delhi as international scholarly experiment; in R.A. Falk's plan national states would retain sovereignty but a tricameral World Assembly would guide world security, world economic development, human development, and ecological balance.
1968 *The trumpet shall sound: a study of 'Cargo' cults in Melanesia*, by P. Worsley.
c1968 Rome (Italy): economics research group Istituto per le Ricerche di Economia Applicata (IREA) issues journal *Futuribili*, and Istituto Ricerche Applicata Documentazione e Studi (IRADES) produces *Social forecasting: documentation 1971*.
1968 Switzerland: St Gallen Centre for Futures Research begun, in St Gallen; also 1971, Swiss Association for Futures Research.
1968 Research centers on futurism spread in Communist countries: (Poland) Research and Prognostics Committee, Polish Academy of Sciences Group on Social Prognoses, also Forecasting Research Center; (Romania) International Center of Methodology for Future and Development Studies; (Hungary) Group on Futurology; (USSR) 1968, Academy of Sciences, Section on Social Forecasting, Moscow.
1968 Japan Association for Future Research/Japan Futurological Society/Japan Society of Futurology founded, in Tokyo; 1970 hosts International Future Research conference, in Kyoto, with many futurists attending.
1968 Institute for Theological Encounter with Science and Technology (ITEST) founded, in St Louis, MO (USA).
1968 Club of Rome set up: 100 prominent scientists worried about man's misuse of Earth's resources; computer model predicts collapse of world civilization (D.H. Meadows et al, *The limits to growth*, 1972).
1968 Novel and movie *2001: a space odyssey* by A.C. Clarke introduces theme of rebel computer, HAL 9000.
1968 R. Barjavel's novel *The Ice People*; French scientists discover city buried under Antarctic polar ice cap, as only remains of 4 world wars between Gondawan superpowers of BC 900,000.
1968 English sci-fi writer J.K.H. Brunner (1934- ) publishes profusely on a barbaric Galactic Empire, then 1968 writes magnum opus and award-winning dystopian novel on overpopulation, *Stand on Zanzibar*, with 50-year projection to a scenario in AD 2010; also an anti-pollution dystopia *The sheep look up* (1972).
1968 *Technological forecasting for industry and government*, by J.R. Bright.
1968 *God and the future of man*, by Dutch Dominican priest E. Schillebeeckx.
1968 1st International Conference on Taoism, in Italy; 1972, 2nd in Japan; 1979, 3rd in Switzerland.
1968 Japan Evangelical Association (JEA) established, with 3 charter members including Japan Protestant Conference (JPC) begun in 1957.
1968 11th Meeting, Conference of World Confessional Groups/Bodies, in Geneva; name changed to World Confessional Families (WCFs); Roman Catholic Church joins from now on, attending every year (20-22 November).
1968 Southern African Missiological Society founded based in Pretoria; 1973 begins journal *Missionalia*, publishes 13,590 article abstracts by 1991.
1968 3rd Assembly, East Asia Christian Conference (EACC), held in Bangkok (Thailand).
1968 Association of Evangelical Professors of Missions (AEPM) formed by EFMA and IFMA in Winona Lake (IN); 1990, reorganized as Evangelical Missiological Society (EMS) with over 600 members, stating 'the purpose of missiology is to carry out the Great Commission.'
1969 23rd Meeting of WCC Central Committee, in Geneva (12-22 August).
1969 5th World Council of YMCAs, held in Nottingham, UK, on theme 'Together in a Young World'.
1969 Institute for Future Studies founded, in Copenhagen, forecasting economic and political developments.
1969 Trains using principle of magnetic levitation are developed; 1979, Japanese test model achieves speed record of 321.2 mph.
1969 Pope Paul VI visits Kampala, Uganda, and canonizes 22 of Namugongo Catholic martyrs.
1969 Industry and science make extensive use of computer-based mathematical models in research, providing new incentives for mathematical research.
1969 Extraordinary Synod of Bishops in Rome: on relations between the Holy See and Episcopal Conferences.
1969 Congo Congress on Evangelism.
1969 Zagorsk Conference of All Religions in the USSR.
1969 Congo-Brazzaville declares itself first Marxist-Leninist state in Africa.
1969 Barbados: disestablishment of Anglican state church.

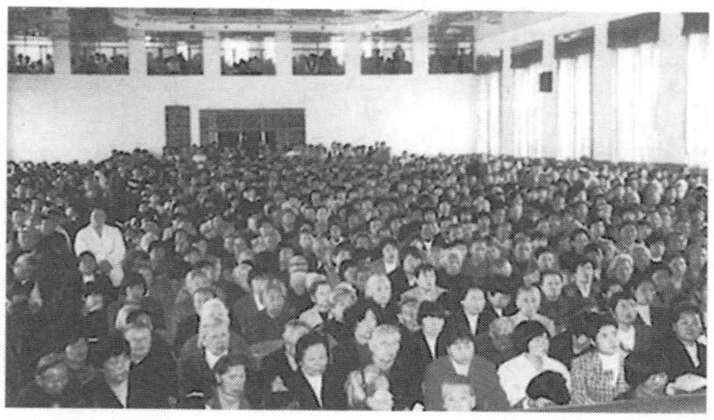

**AD 1969.** Chinese house-church in Sichuan revives, 1976 explosive growth begins.

1969 China: Christians fall from 5.8 million in 1949 to 2 million in 1969, then suddenly soar to 25 million by

1982, to 50 million by 1985, and to 80 million by 1995, and to 90 million by AD 2000, mostly in house churches.

1969 Ecuador: Cruzada de las Americas (Luis Palau) in Quito (10 churches, 19,000 attenders, 581 decisions); campaigns also in 1962, 1969-70, 1970, 1972, 1974, 1978, et alia.

1969 East Pakistan: Cooperative Evangelistic Campaign nationwide, supported by most Protestant churches; 1970, New Life in Christ multidenominational campaign, with thousands of Hindus enquiring.

1969 Haiti: mass evangelistic campaigns 1969, 1970 'To Every Haitian' major saturation evangelism campaign, et alia.

1969 Belgium: 35-churches evangelistic crusade 'Un Dieu pourquoi faire' in Charleroi: 12,000 attenders, 50 enquirers.

1969 Wider Episcopal Fellowship convened, covering Anglicans and bishops in full or partial communion with Anglican Provinces and archbishop of Canterbury.

1969 Japan: among proliferation of evangelistic campaigns from 1956-85, Honda Crusades flourish led by Japanese evangelist Koji Honda (1960-71, 158 crusades, 377,951 attenders, 49,934 decisions).

1969 3rd Latin American Evangelical Conference (CELA III), Buenos Aires, Argentina.

1969 First men (USA Apollo programme) land on Moon, watched live on TV by 500 million across world (20 July).

1969 First USA Congress on Evangelism, Minneapolis: 'Much is given—much is required'; over 5,000 delegates (September).

1969 Paul VI becomes first pope to visit World Council of Churches, Geneva.

1969 2nd Assembly of All Africa Conference of Churches (AACC), Abidjan, Ivory Coast, on theme 'With Christ at work in Africa today'.

1969 India: All Kerala United Evangelistic Movement formed for city campaigns.

1969 Total electric power production in world 4,568 billion kilowatt-hours (1,290 kwh per capita).

1969 Australasian Crusade to Preserve Historic Christianity (sponsored by ICCC) in New Zealand, Australia, Hong Kong, Taiwan, Korea.

1969 Barclay New Testament published.

1969 1st Plenary Assembly, Symposium of Episcopal Conferences of Africa and Madagascar (SECAM), in Kampala; 1970, 2nd in Abidjan; 1972, 3rd in Kampala; 1975, 4th in Rome on 'Evangelization in Africa Today'.

1969 World Catholic Federation for the Biblical Apostolate (WCFBA) founded; 1972, headquarters moved from Rome to Stuttgart.

1969 Pentecostal evangelist Jimmy L. Swaggart begins USA radio ministry 'Camp Meeting Hour', then in 1972 television ministry; by 1987, Jimmy Swaggart Ministries air telecasts over 3,200 TV stations in 15 languages viewed by 510 million in 145 countries weekly, raising donations of $150 million a year, and claim 'The medium of television is the most expedient method of spreading the gospel the world has ever known. It is God's directive that the Great Commission be carried out by this means'; 1988, partial collapse due to sex scandal.

1969 Jehovah's Witnesses hold series of 5-day 'Peace on Earth' International Assemblies in 13 cities (Denmark, France, Germany, Italy, UK, USA) with 840,572 attenders (25% non-JWs) and 27,442 publicly baptized; arrival of Christ's Millennial Kingdom expected in 1975; 1973, massive Assemblies across world on theme 'Divine Victory' (including Dusseldorf with 67,950 attenders, Munich with 78,792); 1976, Governing Body of Jehovah's Witnesses reorganized with 18 members (each with over 35 years of full-time witnessing); 1978 international convention series produces 100 'Victorious Faith' assemblies in 45 countries, averaging 25,000 attenders at each.

1969 World Evangelism Foundation founded (Texas, USA) by Baptist missionaries to mobilize Southern Baptist laypersons to spread Partnership Evangelism; by 1988, over 7,000 persons from USA have held 200 major evangelistic campaigns in 40 countries, with 200,000 decisions for Christ; extensive plans for 1989, 1990, in Japan inter alia.

1969 *The Church in the year 2000* published by American Academy of Arts and Science (Commonweal).

1969 Catholic sociologist A. Greeley writes *Religion in the year 2000*; Catholic theologian Hans Küng edits *The future of ecumenism*.

1969 G.E. Martin (Protestant) writes *The future of evangelism*.

1969 Bob Shaw's novel *The Palace of Eternity* envisages million-ton tachyonic spaceship travelling at 30,000 times speed of light.

1969 R. Silverberg in *Up the line* presents crucifixion of Christ as popular tourist attraction for time-travellers; 1975, G. Kilworth's 'Let's go to Golgotha' describes all the spectators jeering at the Cross as time-travellers from all ages.

1969 W.W. Harman and Stanford Research Institute (USA) construct 40 feasible, holistic, alternative future histories of the world or scenarios covering period 1969-2050, using Field Anomaly Relaxation technique; most envisage 'time of troubles' around 1974.

1969 P. Ehrlich writes brief nightmare scenario 'Ecocatastrophe!'

1969 Sociologist John McHale (1922-1980) writes *The future of the future*: the main determiners of the future lie in the area of values, conceptions, and social arrangements.

1969 *Religion, revolution and the future*, by German theologian J. Moltmann.

1969 Fax (facsimile) technology invented, but slow taking off: 1982, 64,000 sales; 1988, 785,000; spreads worldwide, with 8 million personal computer fax cards in USA by 1995; 1999, 50 million US households have fax machines; by 2000, color fax machines capture 20% of market.

1969 Japan Mass Mobilization evangelism founded.

1969 1st Latin American Congress on Evangelization (CLADE I), held in Bogota (Colombia) sponsored by BGEA and NAE (USA); 1979, CLADE II held in Lima (Peru); 1992, CLADE III held in Quito (Ecuador).

1970 20th General Council, World Alliance of Reformed Churches (WARC, 113 member churches, 55 million members), held in Nairobi (Kenya); merging of International Congregational Council with WARC (20-30 August).

1970 Total of all documents or fragments discovered spanning period of Old Testament: over 500,000; by 1998, over 1 million (including 30,000 papyrus fragments in Egypt).

1970 **Global status:** 64.6 generations after Christ, world is 33.5% Christians (56.4% of them being Whites), 55.6% evangelized; with printed Scriptures available in 1,490 languages.

1970 Status of Renewal: Pentecostals now number 15,382,000, Charismatics 3,349,000, Neocharismatics 53,490,000: total live members 72,223,000; total Renewal believers since AD 1900, 117,004,000.

1970 Total languages with printed Scriptures: Bible 249, NT 578, portions 1,431; covering 97% of world's population; world distribution of subsidized scriptures doubles from 80 million in 1966 to 173 million in 1970.

1970 Worldwide trend of ethnic reaffirmation gathers momentum, resulting in minority peoples in major states disaffiliating themselves from transethnic ideals (e.g. Blacks and Amerindians in USA; Ukrainians, Central Asian Muslim peoples, in USSR; Basques in Spain; Welsh in UK; etc).

1970 In increasing number of countries, persecution begins of bearers of culture who keep popular memory alive: writers, artists, painters, sculptors, poets, singers, musicians, teachers.

1970 Gaddafi of Libya ignores global Islamic bodies and convenes rival Tripoli-based World Islamic Call Society, with branches across world; aggressive proselytism planned, but whole endeavor fizzles out.

1970 USA: just under 200,000 computers in use.

1970 New Life for All (NLFA) campaigns continue throughout Africa.

1970 USA: 'Passover' evangelistic film televised to 12 cities by American Board of Missions to the Jews: audience one million Jews, 3% responding afterwards by letter.

1970 WCC/SODEPAX Ecumenical Conference, Montreux, on 'Ecumenical assistance to development projects'.

1970 2nd Consultation of United and Uniting Churches, under WCC sponsorship, at Limuru, Kenya.

1970 Pontifical Commission for Pastoral Care of Migrants and Tourists formed in Vatican.

1970 All Thailand Congress on Evangelism, followed by numerous in-depth evangelistic campaigns.

1970 Church of North India inaugurated through merger of Anglican, Baptist, Brethren, Disciples, Methodist and United churches.

1970 Orthodox Church in America (USA) granted autocephalous status by Moscow patriarchate.

1970 African indigenous churches (AICs) throughout Africa number some 5,980 separate denominations with 17,830,000 adherents in 34 African countries growing by 960,000 a year, predominantly from 320 African tribes.

1970 WCC allocates first grants to 19 anti-racist organizations throughout world for humanitarian work.

1970 Nestorian patriarch Mar Shimun Isayi, in exile in USA since 1933, permitted to visit Iraq; later assassinated by Assyrian dissident (1975).

1970 Japan: Total Mobilization Evangelism (Sodoin Dendo) mass saturation campaigns begun for various areas: 1970 Shikoku, 1971 Kobe, 1972 Okinawa, 1972-4 Western Japan, 1974-6 Kyushu, 1974-6 Tohoku, and all Japan by 1980.

1970 Fédération des Eglises et Missions Evangéliques du Cameroun formed.

1970 International Communications Congress (ICB, USA).

1970 1st All-India Congress on Evangelism, Bombay; 300 workers attend.

1970 Indonesia Consultation on Evangelism.

1970 Euro-70 Crusade, largest evangelistic campaign ever held in Europe, using 8-language simultaneous translation and closed-circuit TV from Dortmund (Germany) to 36 cities across Europe; 839,075 attenders, 15,813 enquirers.

1970 Philippines Congress on Evangelism.

1970 Frankfurt Declaration on Mission, promulgated by 14 Conservative Evangelical Lutheran theologians in Germany.

1970 Canada Congress on Evangelism.

1970 1st World Conference on Religion and Peace, Kyoto, Japan; 1,600 delegates from 22 world religions (October); 1974, 2nd WCRP, Louvain, Belgium; 1979, 3rd WCRP, Princeton, USA; 1984, 4th WCRP, Nairobi, Kenya (580 representatives from 60 countries).

1970 500,000 killed by cyclone in Bangladesh (12-13 November).

1970 9th Pentecostal World Conference, Dallas, USA (November).

1970 Oberammergau Passion Play (Bavaria) draws 530,000 attenders; repeated every 10 years since 1634.

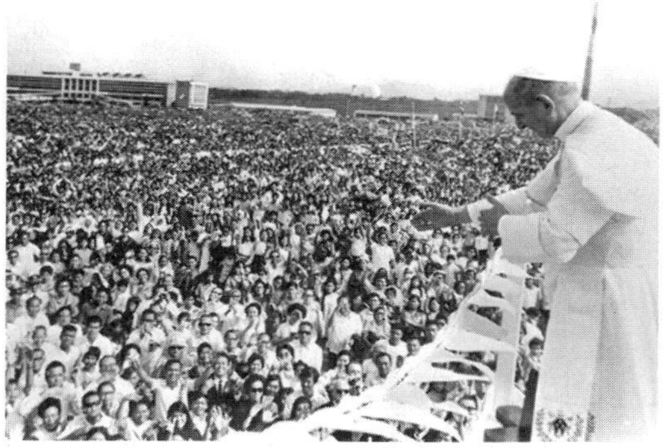

**AD 1970.** On world tour, Paul VI greets crowd of 2.5 million in Quezon Park, Philippines.

1970 From Samoa, Paul VI sends out Missionary Message to the World, urging spreading of the gospel.

1970 Rise of confessionalism across globe: the world's 45 major Christian confessions revive, hold large numbers of monoconfessional conferences from 1970-1987, threatening significance of ecumenical movement.

1970 Anglican theologian E.M.B. Green publishes *Evangelism in the Early Church*.

1970 Prisoners of conscience (political prisoners undergoing torture) estimated at over 700,000 across world in over 90 countries.

1970 World's 10 largest cities: Tokyo/Yokohama 16,468,000, New York/NENJ 16,191,000, Shanghai 11,154,000, Osaka 9,387,000, Mexico City 9,067,000, London 8,594,000, Paris 8,498,000, Buenos Aires 8,417,000, Los Angeles/Long Beach 8,378,000, Beijing 8,087,000.

1970 USA: rise of Jesus People in California as a nationwide youth revival.

1970 USA: New American Bible published: revision of Confraternity Version translated by Catholic scholars (Episcopal Confraternity of Christian Doctrine).

1970 European Conference on Mission Studies, in Oslo, founds International Association for Mission Studies (IAMS), which is then in 1972 formally organized in Driebergen, Netherlands, with 205 individual and 39 institutional members.

1970 5th Assembly, Lutheran World Federation (LWF), Evian (France) (after last-minute change from Porto Alegre, Brazil), meets from 14-24 July on theme 'Sent into the World'; new Commission on Church Cooperation (CCC) formed centered on evangelism, meets 1971 Tokyo, 1972 Kecskemet (Hungary), 1973 Santiago (Chile), 1974 Lund, 1975 Adelaide, 1976 Saskatoon, 1978 Montreux, 1979 Singapore, 1981 Chicago, 1982 Stavanger.

1970 9th International Student Missionary Convention, Urbana, USA, on theme 'World Evangelism: Why? How? Who?'; 12,304 attenders.

1970 Popular books on premillennial eschatology (an interpretation held by 41% of all Evangelicals, and countless others) sell 31 million copies over 15 years, especially H. Lindsay's 9-title series beginning with *The late great planet Earth;* these however all dismiss human responsibility for global mission and world evangelization after only miniscule passing mention (less than 1% of text).

1970 'AD 2000: 350 million Christians in Africa' published in *IRM* by D.B. Barrett, on Third-World progress towards world evangelization.

1970 12th Baptist World Congress, Tokyo (with 8,556 delegates from 77 countries), launches 5-year evangelistic program 'World Mission of Reconciliation Through Jesus Christ'; officially gets under way in 1973, with campaigns across world.

1970 *Christianity Today's* founding editor C.F.H. Henry writes 'Strategy for world evangelism: are we too late?'

1970 Conservative Evangelical theologian G.W. Peters writes *Saturation evangelism*, on how Evangelism-in-Depth is spreading over the entire world.

1970 OM purchases 2,500-ton evangelistic ship m.v. Logos for UK£80,000 to visit large-city ports in difficult countries around world, with literature evangelism, book sales, missionary conferences; 110 crew, total 1,500 crew from 1970-88; 20 million persons exposed to gospel through related shore teams, 7 million visitors aboard buying literature in 107 different countries; 1988, ship (now valued at £1 million) runs aground and is lost off Tierra del Fuego; 1977, sister ship m.v. Doulos (6,000 tons) begins travels, reaching 600 visitors per conference.

1970 New Age movement spreads across Western world, a vast amorphous amalgam of spiritualism, faith healing, reincarnation, meditation, yoga, macrobiotic diets, mystical environmentalism, and evangelical fervor (without Christ); vast growth of New Age magazines, books, records, disks, mass merchandising.

1970 Futurist Alvin Toffler writes *Future shock* (6 million copies; translated into 20 languages).

1970 Commission on the Year 2000 (State of Hawaii) founded, in Wellington.

1970 'Many-Worlds Interpretation': all possible choices (every quantum event) actually occur and lead to new alternate/parallel universes being created (B.S. DeWitt, 'Quantum mechanics and reality', 1970).

1970 Planetary Citizens grows out of Conference on Human Survival (UN, New York, 1970); one-world or unity 'consciousness movement' based on planetary consciousness and Hindu occult mysticism sweeps USA as part of New Age Movement.

1970 Evangelical theologian F.A. Schaeffer writes *The Church at the end of the Twentieth Century*.

1970 World Congress on the Future of the Church, held in Brussels with 700 theologians, calling for fundamental restructuring (12-17 September).

1970 Quaker philosopher D.E. Trueblood writes *The future of the Christian*.

1970 Several USA Catholic theologians (mainly Jesuits) forecast optional clerical celibacy by 1975, drastic drop by 50% in RC religious personnel in USA by 1978, plus major collapse in parochial schools system; none of these forecasts materialize.

1970 USA: proportion of women in ordained ministers/pastors/clergy rises gradually, to 2%; by AD 2000, to 25%; and by AD 2050, to 50%.

1970 US electrical engineer J.W. Forrester (1918- ) pioneers mathematical global modelling as aid to futures studies; a computer model of the world system (economic, political, industrial, etc) is used to forecast future trends; known as 'hard' futurism; Forrester sets this out in 1973 book *World dynamics*.

c1970 Rise of counterculturalist/transformational/New Age futurism, with as its prophets P. Teilhard de Chardin, L. Mumford, P. Sorokin, E.F. Schumacher ('appropriate technology'), W.W. Harman, Hazel Henderson, W.I. Thompson, Marilyn Ferguson (*The Aquarian conspiracy*, 1980), E. Callenbach (classic novel *Ecotopia*, 1975).

1970 New Age movement begins to exercise large influence on futures studies.

1970 *An alternative future for America*, by R. Theobald.

1970 Anglican primate A.M. Ramsey (archbishop of Canterbury) and Belgian primate L.-J. Suenens (cardinal archbishop of Malines) write *The future of the Christian church*.

1970 O.K. Flechtheim publishes *Futurology: the struggle over the future* (in German); and in 1980, *The struggle for the future: fundamentals of futurology*.

1970 1st International Conference of Orthodox Theologians and Seminaries of America, held in Brookline, USA (7-11 September); 1972, 2nd International Conference of Orthodox Theologians on 'The Catholicity of the Church' (25-29 September); 1987, 3rd International Conference of Orthodox Theological Schools, held in Boston (30 August-4 September).

1970 WCC Multi-Faith Consultation on 'Dialogue between Men of Living Faiths', held in Ajaltoun (Lebanon), with 3 Hindus, 4 Buddhists, 3 Muslims (16-25 March).

1970 11th Triennial Meeting, Friends World Committee for Consultation (FWCC, representing 200,000 Quakers worldwide), held in Sigtuna (Sweden), with 209 participants (1-8 August).

1971 Soviets man world's first space station, Salyut 1 weighing 40,000 pounds; but after 23 days the 3 suffocate during reentry.

1971 Taiwan Congress on Evangelism held as culmination of 15 years of mass evangelistic campaigns.

1971 2nd Ordinary Synod of Bishops in Rome: on priestly ministry, justice in the modern world.

1971 Over 500 indigenous churches in Zaire deprived of legal status as official recognition is given to 3 churches only: Roman Catholic Church, EJCSK, ECZ (with Greek Orthodox added in 1972).

1971 1st International Ecumenical Seminar on the Pastoral Care of the Deaf, in Geneva, on theme 'My eyes are my ears'; subsequent seminars every 10 years.

1971 USA: first Christian satellite broadcast (by Intelsat), from 28th Convention of National Religious Broadcasters.

1971 Congress on the Church's Worldwide Mission, held at Green Lake, WI, USA, sponsored by Conservative Evangelicals.

1971 Puerto Rico: many evangelistic campaigns include Every Creature Crusades (World Gospel Crusades) which reaches over 500,000 homes (78% of whole country).

1971 Mexico: nationwide Evangelism-in-Depth campaign involving over half of country's 10,000 Evangelical churches, 13,000 prayer cells, one million scriptures distributed; numerous other campaigns 1960-85; 1976, EHC distributes one million booklets a month.

1971 European Congress on Evangelism, Amsterdam; 1,064 participants from 36 European nations.

1971 Islamic global rivals (Pakistan, Saudi Arabia, Egypt) meet in Rabat and create permanent Organization of the Islamic Conference, OIC (May).

1971 2nd Assembly, Pacific Conference of Churches (PCC), in Davuilevu, Fiji, on 'God's Purpose for His People'.

1971 2nd Ecumenical Pentecost Meeting in Augsburg (Germany) for Catholics and Protestants at Pentecost (2-5 June).

1971 World Consultation on Christian Councils, Geneva, with 100 participants representing 66 councils (June); 10 national councils now have Roman Catholic Church as full member, rising by 1985 to 27 national and 2 regional councils.

1971 World Assembly of World Council of Christian Education, Lima, Peru; 1972, WCCE integrated into WCC.

1971 5th Latin American Lutheran Congress, in Jos de Paz, Argentina, on liberation (August).

1971 1st International Catechetical Congress, Rome (25 September); 1975, Paul VI establishes International Council for Catechesis.

1971 Intel microprocessor invented: crucial development in microelectronics.

1971 Uganda: 500,000 killed in 7-year Amin terror; many martyrs including Anglican archbishop Janani Luwum in 1977.

1971 Anglican theologian J.R.W. Stott edits 6 essays on 'Issues in World Evangelism' in his book *Christ the Liberator* (IVP).

1971 Final Advance of Scripture Translation (FAST) launched with WBT/SIL cooperation as computerized closure vision to finally complete remaining task of translating Bible into every language; main purpose to galvanize denominational Bible translating agencies (Baptist, Pentecostal, Catholic, et alia), but finally terminates in 1983 despite over 5,000 languages still remaining untranslated.

1971 International Crusades begun in Dallas, Texas, as agency coordinating Southern Baptist 2-week Partnership Crusades overseas; goal 'To see one million people pray to receive Christ by the turn of the century using partnership evangelism'.

1971 Conference on Church-Mission Relationships in Creative Tension, held at Green Lake, WI (USA), with 400 attenders, under aegis of EMIS and sponsored by IFMA/EFMA: 'We affirm the continuing worldwide mandate upon the worldwide church to fulfill the Great Commission of Jesus Christ'.

1971 World Evangelization Strategy Consultation, White Sulphur Springs, Georgia, USA (December).

1971 Chapter 'The Great Commission', in *One world, one task: report of the Evangelical Alliance Commission on World Mission* (London: Scripture Union).

1971 Dutch businessman F.L. Polak creates term prognostics for 'new images of a desirable future' (*Prognostics: a science in the making surveys and creates the future).*

1971 Sweden: Swedish Association of Futures Studies founded, in Stockholm; 1973, Secretariat for Future Studies founded by government, in Stockholm; Ministry of Education, in Stockholm.

1971 Jerusalem Conference on Biblical Prophecy (leader C.F.H. Henry) to study implications for Christians of 1948 inauguration of state of Israel.

1971 *The future of the Christian world mission*, edited by Evangelical missiologists W.J. Danker and W.J. Kang.

1971 Kuwaiti Muslim, S. Kutb, publishes *Islam: the religion of the Future*.

1971 NASA proposes Project Cyclops, vast array of listening dishes (radiotelescopes) to scan every one of the 10 million stars within 1,000 light-years.

1971 Multiverse (infinite series of intersecting parallel and alternate universes splitting off with every historical decision) proposed, in M. Moorcock's *The War Lord of the Air*, thus a time traveller can enter the past and change history.

1971 R. Silverberg writes satirical story 'Good News from the Vatican', in which a robot is elected pope.

1971 R. Vacca publishes *The coming dark ages*, stating 'I am writing when the second millennium of our era is less than thirty years from completion and when, for reasons different from those of a thousand years ago, many people expect that before long there will be a tragic and total catastrophe.'

1971 *Mankind 2000*, by R. Jungk & J. Galtung.

1971 Japan Overseas Missions Association formed.

1971 1st World Consultation on National Christian Councils, held in Geneva (Switzerland) (28 June-7 July).

1971 12th World Conference, World Methodist Council (WMC), held in Denver, CO (USA) (17-26 August).

1971 Germany: Ecumenical Meeting of Catholic and Evangelical Churches, held in Augsburg at Pentecost (2-5 June).

1971 1st World Romani Congress (organized by International Gypsy Committee, funded by World Council of Churches and Indian Government), held in London, with representatives from 21 countries; Gypsy flag (chakra) and anthem 'Dzelem dzelem' adopted (8-12 April); 1978, 2nd WRC, in Geneva (60 delegates from 26 countries; 8-11 April); 1981, 3rd WRC, in Gottingen (300 delegates, 16-20 May); 1990, 4th WRC, in Serock (Warsaw, 490 delegates, 4-13 April); c1996, 5th WRC.

1971 Society for Pentecostal Studies (SPS) founded in USA; purposes to hold annual meetings each with 10-30 professional papers read; 1982, 12th Annual Meeting, SPS, held in Pasadena (CA), with 12 papers presented (18-20 November); 1996, 25th Annual Meetings, SPS, held in Wycliffe College, Toronto (7-9 March).

1972 Abolition of 'special position' of Catholic Church in Ireland.

1972 USA: American Society of Missiology founded (Catholic/Protestant/ Evangelical), with journal *Missiology*.

1972 Publication of 3-volume history of Catholic missions 1622-1972: *Sacrae Congregationis de Propaganda Fide Memoria Rerum*.

1972 EXPLO-72 in Dallas, Texas: 1st Training Congress on Evangelism (Campus Crusade for Christ); 80,000 for one week (June), 200,000 for final day, with 3 telecasts watched by 30 million each, with 11,000 decisions for Christ.

1972 1st Plenary Assembly, World Catholic Federation for the Biblical Apostolate (WCFBA, founded in 1969), in Vienna, Austria.

1972 Channel Islands: 15-day campaign in Corbiere and St Helier sponsored by Movement for World Evangelization (MWE).

1972 Sri Lanka: Morris Cerullo charismatic campaign (140,000 attenders, 80% being Buddhists).

1972 Letter of Paul VI to International Missionary Congress at Lyons (France).

1972 United Nations with its 32 specialized agencies thrusts urgent global problems into world consciousness with a series of 15 major international conferences over next 12 years: on environment, population, industrialization, human settlements, apartheid, desertification, racism, technology transfer, women, children, disabled, communication, disarmament, hunger, energy.

1972 Mouvement International d'Apostolat des Milieux Sociaux Indépendants (MIAMSI) founded by RCs in Rome, dedicated to 'the evangelization of the middle and upper classes'.

1972 Illiac IV, computer costing $40 million, delivered to NASA (USA); dismantled 1981.

1972 First company solely making industrial robots: Unimation.

1972 Two-year major Sahel famine across Africa bordering Sahara desert, due to short-sighted social policies; some half million starve to death.

1972 Burundi: 150,000 Hutus especially intellectuals massacred by Tutsis.

1972 Villach 72 CCC/LWF visitation/consultation program in Austria on theme 'Ambassadors of Reconciliation', with over 200 delegates from 38 countries (November).

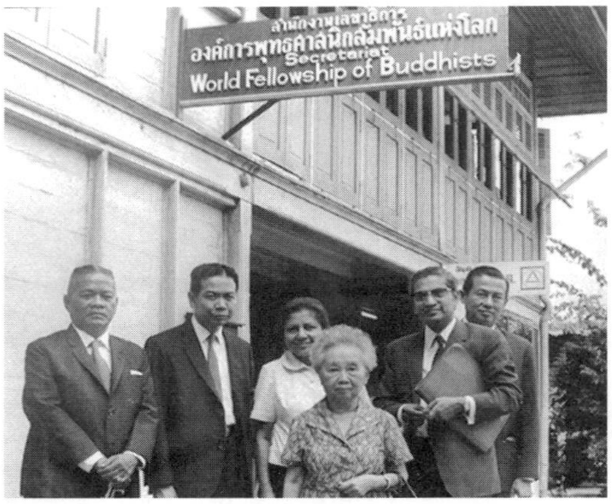


**AD 1972-3.** Delegates at 'Salvation Today' conference visit HQ of World Fellowship of Buddhists.

1972 World Conference and Assembly of CWME/WCC, Bangkok (Thailand) (3rd Meeting of CWME): 'Salvation Today'; moratorium on foreign missions and missionaries proposed by younger churches, widely accepted 1972-80; report states 'Each generation must evangelize its own generation' (29 December 1972 - 8 January 1973).

1972 International Catholic Charismatic Renewal Office (ICCRO) founded as International Communications Office in Ann Arbor (USA); first 2 International Leaders' Conferences (1973, 1975) held there; 1976, office transferred to Brussels; 1981 relocates as ICCRO in Rome, organizes 5 worldwide leaders' conferences (4 in Rome, 1 in Dublin), 1985 relocates in Vatican 'moving to the heart of the Church', by 1988 representing 63.5 million Catholic pentecostals in over 160 countries; 1993 name changed to ICCRS ('Services'); by 2000, 119 million Catholic Charismatics in 230 countries.

1972 World Pentecost editor Donald Gee writes article 'World evangelisation'; widely quoted throughout Pentecostal movement.

1972 Consultation on the Gospel and Frontier Peoples, Chicago (December), sponsored by NCCCUSA and North American boards; detailed survey presented by D.B. Barrett entitled *Frontier situations for evangelisation in Africa, 1972: a survey report*, tabulating data, documenting and mapping situation of 213 Muslim peoples, 411 peoples responsive to Christianity, and 236 unevangelized peoples.

1972 P. Eshleman writes *The Explo story: a plan to change the world*.

1972 Missions news periodical *Koinonia*, dealing with reaching beyond frontiers of the unevangelized world, founded in Brazil by L. Brierley; 1974 name changed to *Look*, in Britain, then *The Wider Look*; 1983 *The Frontiersman's Fellowship*.

1972 Great Commission Prayer Crusade launched by Campus Crusade for Christ International; leader-

ship by women; a few conferences held (Dallas 1976, 1984 International Prayer Assembly, Seoul).
1972 German information scientist M. Kochen proposes WISE (a World Information Synthesis and Encyclopedia), dies in 1987.
1972 USA information scientist H.J.A. Goodman proposes UNISIST (World Science Information Network) as step toward World Brain concept.
1972 Scientist James Lovelock first poses Gaia hypothesis, suggesting that life is an active participant in shaping Earth's physical and chemical environment.
1972 Spain: Club de Amigos de la Futurologia founded, in Barcelona.
1972 Norwegian Society for Future Studies (Selskapet for Fremtidsstudier, SEFREM).
1972 First deliberate message sent from Earth to stars: USA launches Pioneer 10 unmanned spacecraft with engraved plaque and message, which travels past Jupiter to reach nearest star after 100,000 years.
1972 R. Silverberg's story 'When we went to see the End of the World', in which jaded time-traveller tourists visit distant cataclysms and spectacular apocalypses in search of thrills.
1972 G. Zebrowski writes *The Omega Point*: development of a lone survivor of a far-future war, from isolated ego to participant in a galactic mind; also *Macrolife* (1979), in which life at end of cosmic life survives implosion of Universe by lodging in a black hole.
1972 Donella H. Meadows et alii publish *The limits to growth*, viewing world as single dynamic system characterized by interaction of 5 parameters: population, food supply, nonrenewable natural resources, pollution, per capita industrial output.
1972 J. Brunner's novel of life in near-future USA, *The sheep look up*.
1972 *Technological forecasting for decision making*, by J.P. Martino.
1972 *Buddhism, Christianity, and the future of man*, by D.A. Fox.
1972 *The future executive*, by Harlan Cleveland.
1972 Jesuit theologian Karl Rahner publishes *The shape of the church to come* (original in German).
1972 Inter-Orthodox Symposium on Orthodox Theology, held in Thessalonika, Greece (12-16 September).
1972 Origin of European Charismatic Leaders' Conferences (Protestants/Pentecostals/Catholics) at Schloss Craheim, Germany after initial visits by David du Plessis and Rodman Williams; further ECLC conferences in 1973, 1975, then in Belgium by invitation of Catholic primate, cardinal L.-J. Suenens in 1976, 1978; 1982 Strasbourg Conference with 25,000 participants; then ELCs in 1982 Paris, 1984 Zurich, 1986 Birmingham UK (ACTS 86); 1988 ongoing European Charismatic Consultation formed; 1989 in Dissentis, Switzerland, 1990 Bern '90; 1991 ECC organized and meets annually.
1972 9th Council Meeting/World Assembly, United Bible Societies (UBS, 55 member Bible societies), held in Addis Ababa (Ethiopia), on theme 'Let the Word Speak!', followed by 9th UBS Council, meeting; introduction of audience-oriented Scripture editions for specific readers, New Reader Portions/Selections; by 1980, these are available in 250 languages, by 1993 in 600 languages; also sets goal of 500 million scriptures distributed annually by 1979; goal passed in 1978.
1972 Inaugural meeting of International Association for Mission Studies (IAMS) held in Driebergen, Holland; publishes journal *Mission studies*, sponsors 8 international IAMS conferences by 1992.
1972 Shona Independent Churches, in Rhodesia, establish Fambidzano (Ecumenical Movement of Zimbabwean Independent Churches).
1972 First e-mail sent: engineer R. Tomlinson of Cambridge, MA sends first electronic message between 2 computers, creates '
1973 U.S. Skylab, 120-foot-long orbiting work station, is launched into Earth orbit (May 14); astronauts Gerald P. Carr (b.1932), Edward G. Gibson (b. 1936), and William R. Pogue (b. 1930) later set a new space endurance record staying aboard Skylab for 84 days (1973-74).
1973 USA nuclear stockpile reaches 15,000 megatons.
1973 Microcomputer revolution begins: Micral system, designed and produced in France by a Vietnamese refugee.

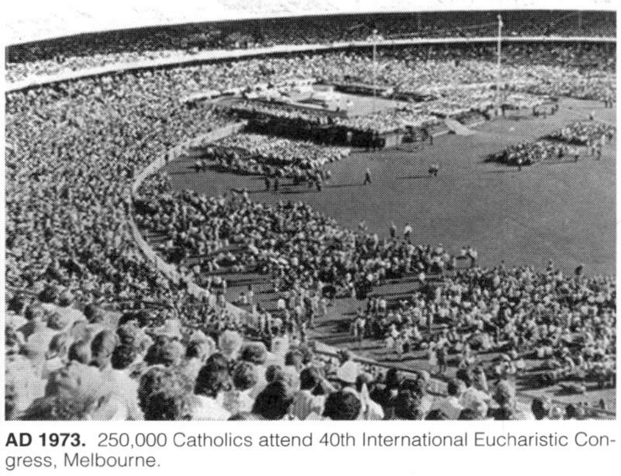

**AD 1973.** 250,000 Catholics attend 40th International Eucharistic Congress, Melbourne.

1973 40th International Eucharistic Congress, Melbourne, Australia; very large participation by Aboriginals.
1973 Philippines: 'Christ The Only Way' 3-day total mobilization event, with 55 supporting denominations.
1973 'Total Evangelization in Belgium and Luxembourg' campaign, for 2 years.
1973 Korea: 1st Annual Summer Institute of World Mission (SIWM) in Seoul; by 14th Institute in 1986, some 1,000 students have been trained at East-West Center for overseas service, with goal of 10,000 Asian foreign missionaries by AD 2000.
1973 5th Assembly, East Asia Christian Conference (EACC), in Singapore, on 'Christian Action in the Asian Struggle'; EACC reorganized as Christian Conference of Asia (CCA).
1973 West Germany: 15th German Protestant Kirchentag (Ecumenical Whitsun Assembly), in Dusseldorf on theme 'Not by Bread Alone', with Protestants, Catholics, Orthodox, Anglicans and Free Protestants.
1973 Massive Jehovah's Witnesses' assemblies across world on theme 'Divine Victory' (including Dusseldorf with 67,950 attenders, Munich with 78,792).
1973 Caribbean Conference of Churches (CCC) founded in Kingston, Jamaica; theme 'The Right Hand of God'.
1973 28 Christian denominations banned by Amin regime in Uganda, resulting in some coming under wing of Anglican Church, but with the great majority going underground.
1973 Key '73 evangelistic campaign in USA 'to call the continent to Christ', involving 150 denominations including 50% of all 40,000 United Methodist congregations.
1973 Finnish Congress on Evangelism, Helsinki, as followup to Amsterdam 1971; 1,000 participants from 65 churches.
1973 South African Congress on Mission and Evangelism, Durban (13-22 March).
1973 SPRE-E 73: youth rallies at Earl's Court, UK (August).
1973 Largest preaching service in history: 1.1 million at one rally in Seoul, Korea, hear evangelist Billy Graham during 5-day Crusade.
1973 All-Asia Missions Consultation, Seoul, Korea; formation of Asia Missions Association (AMA); 1975 Inaugural Convention publishes 'Seoul Declaration on Christian Mission'.
1973 10th Pentecostal World Conference, Seoul, Korea: 'Anointed to preach'; 3,000 delegates.
1973 Archbishops' Committee on Evangelism (ACE), Church of England, writes: 'Evangelism is the telling of the facts about Jesus Christ'.
1973 Ivory Coast: 10 months of evangelistic crusades under Assemblies of God (France) draw 400,000 attenders in Abidjan and other cities, with 15,000 healed, 6,000 baptized into local churches, 68,500 Bibles and NTs distributed.
1973 OPEC oil crisis and Arab embargo: Organization of Petroleum Exporting Countries (founded 1960) suddenly raises price of oil by up to 500%, causing international chaos, worldwide recession and inflation, and new political power bases.
1973 Global evangelistic campaign launched under auspices of Baptist World Alliance, 'World Mission of Reconciliation through Jesus Christ', by Baptists in many countries.
1973 USA: New International Version of Bible (NIV, NIB) published by New York International Bible Society, the work of 115 Evangelical scholars; NT 1973, OT 1978; sales of Bible 20 million by 1986, expected to reach 30 million by 1989; also 40 million NTs distributed from 1973-1986; by 1996, 100 million.
1973 Mission to the World (agency of Presbyterian Church in America) launched; 1987, 500 missionaries in 40 countries, church planting in 12 countries; stress on taking its appropriate part in Great Commission; goals include evangelizing 25 world-class cities by 1993.
1973 Globe Missionary Evangelism begun (Pensacola, Florida), with 65 foreign missionaries in 15 countries (by 1985).
1973 Urbana 73: 10th Inter-Varsity Missionary Convention, Urbana, on theme 'Jesus Christ: Lord of the Universe, Hope of the World'; 14,158 attend (December); similar number each successive year up to Urbana 87 Urbana 90 in 1990, also 1993, 1996.
1973 Trinity Broadcasting Network launched, in southern California, as Pentecostal television station 'to get the gospel to every living human being on planet Earth' before Jesus comes; by 1986, TBN owns 55 TV stations in USA with 26 affiliates, also stations in Guatemala, St Kitts-Nevis, Italy, Ciskei.
1973 World Film Crusade founded in Florida, USA (later known as World Thrust Films, or World Mission Crusade); 1985, Brother John publishes *Winning the World: a proposal on how to win the world for Christ now... in our generation*; 1987, further plan announced under name World Mission Teams.
1973 Pentecostal missions executive D.A. Womack writes *Breaking the stained-glass barrier* urging church 'to abandon its sanctuaries of security and return to the evangelistic strategy of the Apostle Paul (the Ephesian Method of spontaneous lay evangelism)'; proposes mathematical formula measuring evangelization.
1973 World's first systematic ECA (Earth-crossing asteroid) watch begun on Hale telescope, Palomar Mountain by geologist E. Shoemaker (1929), who discovers over 300 asteroids.
1973 ECCLA-I Conference (Encuentro Carismatico Catolico Latino Americano) planned to become first of annual series sponsored by Catholic Charismatic Renewal (ICCRO).
1973 United Nations Decade for Action to Combat Racism and Racial Discrimination (1973-1983).
1973 Argentina Foundation for the Year 2000 founded, in Buenos Aires.
1973 World Futures Studies Federation (WFSF) founded in Rome, Italy; 1st World Futures Studies Conference followed by lengthy series of world and regional meetings; 1978, 6th World Conference on Futures Studies, in Cairo, Egypt, sponsored by WFSF on 'The future of communication, cultural identity in an interdependent world'.
1973 Four-year research project by IDOC (Rome) on 'The Future of the Missionary Enterprise', with 20 volumes published from 1973-76; 1975, series of 6 ecumenical seminars on 'The future of the missionary enterprise' at OMSC, Ventnor, USA, 1975-82; 1982, 'The role of North Americans in the future of the missionary enterprise'.
1973 Australian businessman J. Strong writes *The Doomsday Globe*, predicts nuclear destruction for October 1978, based on Bible and Great Pyramids of Egypt.
1973 Genetics: recombinant DNA achieved, unanticipated by most biologists.
1973 G. Kimberley writes 'Many Mansions':missionaries on alien planet discover indigenous cave paintings depicting life and crucifixion of Christ.
1973 Ecumenical Commission of England and Wales publishes Interim Report 1973 on 'The Church 2000', prepared by working party of bishops, priests and laity of all denominations; central theme completing evangelization by AD 2000.
1973 Biblical scholar J.B. Payne publishes *Encyclopedia of Biblical prophecy: the complete guide to scriptural predictions and their fulfilment* (New York); Bible contains 8,352 predictive verses (27% of entire total), which can be summarized under 90 biblical miniscenarios.
1973 D. Berg, leader of Children of God (Family of Love), predicts that Comet Kohoutek will destroy America; most of his followers flee.
1973 D. Cohen publishes *How the world will end*, stating `Perhaps the year 1000 meant little to men of the Middle Ages, but the year 2000 means a great deal to modern numerologists, perhaps the end of the world'.
1973 Sci-fi writer B.W. Aldiss publishes *Billion year spree: the history of science fiction*, revised in 1986 as *Trillion year spree*.
1973 *World dynamics*, by J.W. Forrester.
1973 Common Bible with Apocrypha/Deuterocanonical Books published by RSV Bible Committee (USA, UK, Canada), first English Bible accepted as authoritative by Protestants, Catholics, and Orthodox.
1973 Consultation on Ecumenical Roles of WCFs and WCC, in Geneva (13-15 May).
1973 1st Meeting of WCC Sub-Unit on Dialogue with People of Living Faiths and Ideologies, held in Athens (Greece); 1974, 2nd Meeting, New Delhi; 1978, 3rd Meeting, Trinidad; 1980, 4th Meeting, Matrafured; 1981, 5th Meeting, Bali; 1985, 6th Meeting, Swanwick (UK); 1986, 7th Meeting, Potsdam (Germany).
1973 5th Assembly, Christian Conference of Asia (CCA, renamed from EACC), held in Singapore.
1973 1st Assembly, Caribbean Conference of Churches (CCC), held in Kingston (Jamaica).
1973 ECCLA I (Encuentro Carismatico Catolico Latino Americano) begins annual conferences, drawing around 200 leaders from 19 countries; 1985 ECCLA IX held in Costa Rica; 1989 ECCLA XII held in Guatemala, with 175 leaders on 'Evangelization of the Culture' (27 November-1 December); 1993 ECCLA XIV held in Rio de Janeiro with 2,463 delegates (3 bishops, 110 priests) from 20 Latin American countries, on theme 'Renewed to Evangelize' (May); 1995 ECCLA XV held in Tegucigalpa (Honduras), 15-19 May; 1996 ECCLA XVI held in Mexico (October).
1973 6th World Council of YMCAs, in Kampala, Uganda, on theme 'Identity and Mission'.
1974 1.5 million persons worldwide mobilized to pray for Lausanne Congress on World Evangelization later in year.
1974 Construction of first Muslim mosque in Rome sanctioned by Holy See.
1974 1st Plenary Assembly, Federation of Asian Bishops' Conferences (FABC), in Taipei: 'Evangelization in Modern Day Asia' (April).
1974 3rd Assembly of AACC, Lusaka, Zambia: 'Living no longer for ourselves, but for Christ' (May).
1974 1st Japan Congress on Evangelism, Kyoto (June).
1974 Iberian Congress on Evangelism, Madrid, Spain (June).
1974 8th Baptist Youth World Conference, Portland, Oregon (USA).
1974 1st World Conference of Baptist Men, Hong Kong.
1974 Catholic Charismatic Renewal now has 2,400 prayer groups across world with 350,000 active adult participants (total charismatic community 1,540,000); 30,000 attend USA international annual conferences at Notre Dame, South Bend.

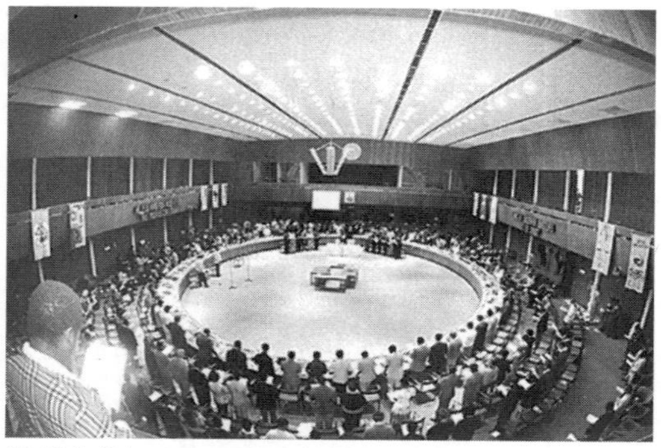

**AD 1974.** Delegates worship at AACC Third Assembly in Lusaka, Zambia.

1974 Pan-American Salvationist Conference on 'Evangelism' convened by Salvation Army general E. Wickberg at Miami Beach, USA (13-22 October); term 'evangelism', previously suspect to Salvationists, now becomes acceptable; also, Army claims to have been a charismatic body since origin.
1974 USA: major advances in computing: 1974 Wang word processor, 1975 first USA commercial personal computer (Altair 8800), 1979 VisiCalc electronic spreadsheet software.
1974 LWF Consultation on Proclamation and Human Development, in Nairobi (21-25 October).
1974 Ecumenical Conference on Science and Technology for Human Development, in Bucharest.
1974 UN General Assembly, 6th Special Session, establishes New International Economic Order (NIEO), demanding that the North (Western world) divest its gains so that the South may develop.
1974 BISA series (Bishops' Institute for Social Action), sponsored by Federation of Asian Bishops' Conferences (FABC): BISA I, Novaliches, Philippines (March, 1974); BISA II, Tokyo (April, 1975); BISA III, Kuala Lumpur (November, 1975); BISA IV, Manila (March, 1978); BISA V, Baguio, Philippines (May, 1979); BISA VI, Kandy, Sri Lanka (February, 1983).
1974 Pan-Orthodox Consultation on 'Confessing Christ Today', Cernica, Bucharest (June); report states 'Evangelistic witness is understood to be restricted to the communication of Christ to those who do not consider themselves Christian'; 1975 (September), 'Confessing Christ through the liturgical life of the Church today', at Echmiadzin, Armenia (USSR), whose report states 'Christ said: Go ye therefore and make disciples of all nations', and calls attention to 'The fields where no one ever preached the Gospel'.
1974 *Operation World*, a prayer survey, published by P.J. Johnstone (Dorothea Mission, and WEC; subsequent editions 1978, 1980, 1986, 1993, 2001), emphasizing world evangelization through daily intercession, centrality of local churches, and the call to 'mobilize the churches of the whole world to finish the task'.

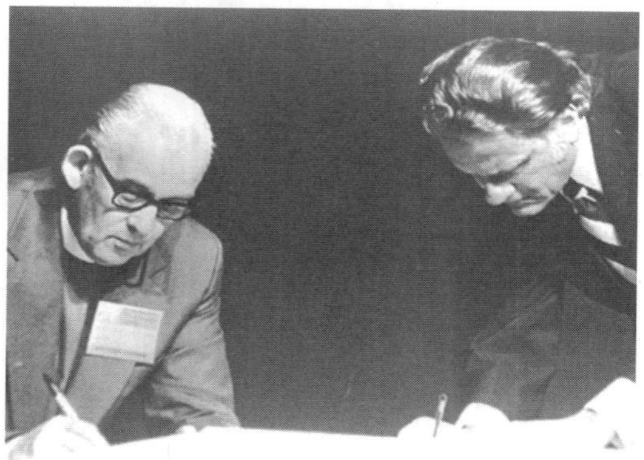

**AD 1974.** Bishop Jack Dain (*left*) and evangelist Billy Graham sign Lausanne Covenant.

1974 International Congress on World Evangelization (ICOWE), Lausanne, Switzerland, on 'Let the Earth hear His Voice'; 2,700 delegates, from 150 countries, 4,000 total (50% from Third World); produces Lausanne Covenant stating: 'Evangelism itself is the proclamation of the historical, biblical Christ' (July); results by 1980 in vast, amorphous, network known as Lausanne Movement directed by LCWE.
1974 EXPLO-74 in Seoul, Korea: 2nd Training Congress on Evangelism (Campus Crusade for Christ); 323,419 residents for one week, evening meetings 800,000 daily, with one rally drawing a new world record of 1.5 million (90% responding to invitation to commitment to Christ); biggest Christian conference in history to date (August).
1974 Holy Year Jubilee for Roman Catholics: Paul VI proclaims 'a new period of evangelization', with full organic unity of all Christians an essential prerequisite: 'Before all men can be restored to the grace of God, communion must be reestablished between those who by faith have acknowledged and accepted Jesus Christ as the Lord of mercy who sets men free'; Holy Year in dioceses across world in 1974, in Rome in 1975.
1974 'Sharing Christ's Bold Mission', theme developed by Southern Baptist Home Mission Board, extended to worldwide application.

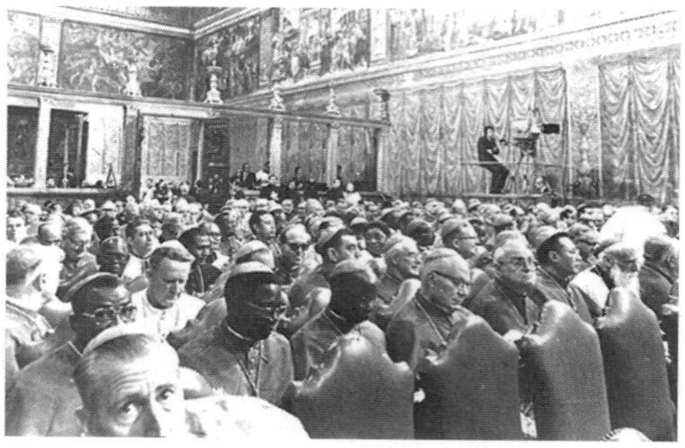

**AD 1974.** In Sistine Chapel, Synod of Bishops debates 'The Evangelization of the Modern World'.

1974 3rd Ordinary Synod of Bishops (begun in 1967 with 1st, and 2nd in 1971) in Rome, on 'The Evangelization of the Modern World'; states that 'the promotion of human development forms an integral part of evangelization', closes with statement: 'We wish to confirm once more that the task of evangelizing all people constitutes the essential mission of the Church.'
1974 World Mission 1975 (World Methodist Mission), a one-year program of worldwide witness 'offering men and women Christ', launched at Shepherds Field, Bethlehem, by World Methodist Council (decision of 12th World Methodist Conference, Denver, Colorado, USA) with 55 constituent nationwide Methodist churches (22 November).
1974 Mission Renewal Teams begun (by D. Bryant, B. Goheen; and Fuller Theological Seminary, Pasadena) as seminarian teams teaching local churches through book Ten Steps for World Evangelization; wound down by 1979.
1974 E.C. Pentecost publishes *Reaching the unreached: an introductory study on developing an overall strategy for world evangelization* (William Carey Library).
1974 Philippines: DAWN (Discipling A Whole Nation) conference; 75 leaders of 4,000 Evangelical churches plan to have 50,000 churches planted by AD 2000, one in every barrio in the country (November); 1985, National Church Growth Strategy Congress with 300 leaders of 12,000 Evangelical churches reaffirms this goal (19-22 February); after 1981 it becomes a world plan, with motto '389 People can change the World: you can be one of them', involving 25 countries by 1987, with goal to begin by AD 2000 a DAWN project in every country of the world, with slogan '7 Million More Churches by 2000 AD'.
1974 *Religious and the evangelization of the world* published in Ottawa by Canadian Religious Conference.
1974 A.P. Johnston writes *World evangelism and the Word of God* (Minneapolis, MN: Bethany Fellowship); 1978, writes *The battle for world evangelism* (Wheaton, IL: Tyndale House).
1974 Presbyterian Order for World Evangelism begun (later under USCWM, Pasadena, CA), as denominational support agency.
1974 Sociologist I. Wallerstein publishes 3-volume magnum opus *The modern world-system* (vols. 1-2, 1974-1988), blending Marxist-Leninist analysis of capitalism with systems analysis.
1974 South Africa: Unit for Futures Research begun at University of Stellenbosch.
1974 British astronomer A. Berry writes *The next ten thousand years: a vision of man's future in the Universe*, envisioning colonization of Venus, factories on the Moon, space ships, et alia.
1974 World Food Conference, Rome (5-16 November), resolves to eradicate world hunger in 10 years: 'Within a decade, no child will go to bed hungry, no family will fear for its next day's bread'; but by 1985, global situation has become worse, and by 1995 far worse.
1974 Roger Garaudy, French marxist, writes *The alternative future: a vision of Christian Marxism.*
1974 L. Biggle writes 'What hath God wrought?': a man wins national lottery prize, claims divinity, establishes new religion based on Christianity and TV quiz shows which then spreads rapidly.
1974 Giant radio telescope at Arecibo (Puerto Rico) beams first human coded message to Great Cluster in Hercules (21,000 light-years away), in hope of reaching distant intelligent extraterrestrials in space.
1974 D. Webber and N. Hutchings publish *Prophecy in stone* which predicts Jewish Temple will be rebuilt by 1978, the Tribulation will begin in 1981 and end from 1988-92.
1974 J.R. Gribbin and S. Plagemann predict massive worldwide destruction caused by alignment of Sun's planets in 1982 in book *The Jupiter Effect.*
1974 *The future of technological civilization*, by sociologist V.C. Ferkiss, a Roman Catholic.
1974 *The Sibylline Oracles of Egyptian Judaism*, by J.J. Collins.
1974 3rd Theological Conference of the Orthodox Theological Society, held in Boston, USA.
1974 Series of Japan Congresses on Evangelism, with up to 5,000 participants: 1974, 1st Congress, Kyoto; 1982, 2nd Congress, Kyoto; 1991, 3rd Congress, Shiobara; AD 2000, 4th Congress, on Okinawa.
1974 UN World Population Conference, in Bucharest, Romania (19-30 August); UN World Food Conference, in Rome (5-16 November).
1974 1st General Assembly, Middle East Council of Churches (MECC), held in Nicosia (Cyprus), enlarging former Near East Council of Churches (NECC) and inaugurating MECC under theme 'Our Common Message Today'; further Assemblies in 1977, 1980, 1985, 1990, 1995, 1999.
1975 Term fractals coined by American mathematician Benoit Mandelbrot to describe irregular mathematical patterns and structures in nature.
1975 First desktop microcomputer becomes available.

1975 **Global status:** 64.7 generations after Christ, world is 33.3% Christians (53.5% of them being Whites), 57.8% evangelized; with printed Scriptures available in 1,630 languages.
1975 Foreign missionaries expelled from Cambodia, later from Viet Nam.
1975 Brazil Congress on Evangelism, Rio de Janeiro (January).
1975 4th International Christian Television Festival, Brighton, England (sponsored by WACC and UNDA).
1975 International Catholic Charismatic Conference in Rome at feast of Pentecost: 10,000 pilgrims addressed by pope Paul VI in St Peter's Basilica (May).
1975 Cuba Congress on Evangelism (May).
1975 Here's Life, America: 2-year media campaign in 220 major USA cities: 14,000 involved churches, 300,000 trained workers, 10 million homes reached, 179 million in USA exposed to gospel, 870,000 recorded decisions; numerically the largest and densest evangelistic campaign in USA history.

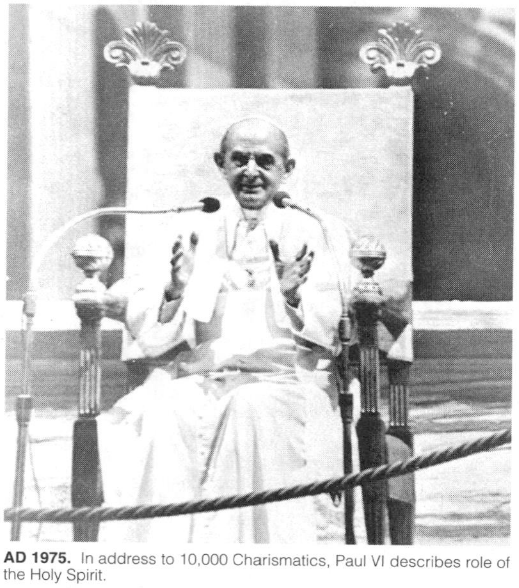

**AD 1975.** In address to 10,000 Charismatics, Paul VI describes role of the Holy Spirit.

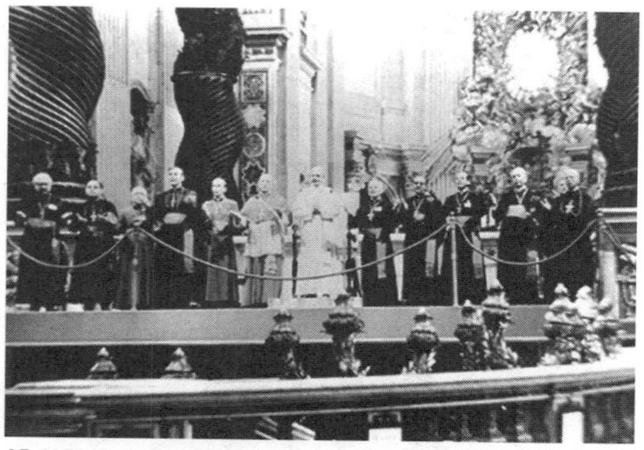

**AD 1975.** Paul VI, cardinals, and bishops in St. Peter's, Vatican, join in charismatic praise of Jesus.

1975 ECCLA III: 3rd Latin American Catholic Charismatic Renewal Leaders Conference; 250 delegates from 25 countries, including 8 bishops; in Aguas Buenas, Puerto Rico (where Catholic pentecostals number 40,000) (January).

1975 3rd Consultation of United and Uniting Churches, held in Toronto, Canada (June); 24 united and uniting denominations present from several countries; now regarded as new type of WCF (world confessional family); 1980, total members of all united churches 63,299,000.

1975 Euro-fest '75, in Brussels, largest Christian youth festival ever in Europe; 10,000 attenders (August).

1975 1st Nigeria National Congress on Evangelization, Ile-Ife; 800 participants.

1975 Nairobi International Conference for Renewal, on 'Unity in Christ'; first of series of interdenominational African conferences for charismatics (August).

1975 Pan-Orthodox Consultation (CWME/WCC) on 'Confessing Christ through the liturgical life of the Church today', Echmiadzin, Armenia (September).

1975 5th International Congress of Christian Physicians (ICCP), Singapore; also previously 1963 Amsterdam, 1966 Oxford, 1969 Oslo, 1972 Toronto.

1975 2nd World Conference on the Holy Spirit, and Holy Land Pilgrimage Jerusalem (October-November).

1975 5th Assembly of WCC, in Nairobi, Kenya: 'Jesus Christ frees and unites', 2,085 participants (850 delegates, 600 press); report on 'Confessing Christ today' states 'We are commissioned to proclaim the Gospel of Christ to the ends of the earth'.

1975 Bible translators at work in over 300 of world's remaining 5,200 languages as yet with no portion of Bible (4% of world's population); Bible revisions and new translations under way in 500 languages (representing 80% of world's population).

1975 400,000 digital computers in world; IBM has 70% of market for the 50,000 largest.

1975 Tokyo-Yokohama (17.7 million inhabitants) overtakes New York (17.1 million) as world's largest supercity, maintaining its primacy until long into 21st century.

1975 Holy Year attracts 8,370,000 pilgrims to Rome.

1975 Kenya Unreached Peoples Conference, Lenana, Nairobi.

1975 Continente-75: Latin American mass media campaign under Argentinian evangelist Luis Palau (born 1934), utilizing 56 radio and 100 TV stations in 23 countries, heard or seen by 75 million in all Latin America (part being Nicaragua '75 3-week mission with 200,000 attenders in Managua, and 6,000 decisions); 1978, Palau preaches to over 2 million persons face-to-face, holds that every city should have a citywide crusade 3 times in a generation (once every 10 years); subsequent major Palau crusades include Commonwealth 84, Continente 85, Asia 86.

1975 India: conclusion of Operation Last Home, 1st Every Home Crusade (EHC) campaign to reach every home in nation by door-to-door evangelism; repeated 1976, 1984, 1986-1994.

1975 Conference on Security and Cooperation in Europe (CSCE), in Helsinki, raises widespread Christian hopes for a new era of peace but these are dashed by 1983.

1975 USA: Detroit Conference I of Theology in the Americas, in Detroit; 1980, Detroit Conference II.

1975 Mission '76, 1st Missionary Congress for European Youth (The European Missionary Alliance), in Lausanne.

1975 Full Gospel World Mission Association established (1 April) in Seoul, Korea, as sending body supporting 8 overseas churches and 22 Korean missionaries; by 1985, 143 missionaries in 21 countries.

1975 13th Baptist World Congress (BWA), Stockholm, on theme 'New People for a New World—Through Christ'; 9,936 delegates from 92 countries.

1975 Communicators J.F. Engel and H.W. Norton write *What's gone wrong with the harvest? a communication strategy for the Church and world evangelization* (Zondervan).

1975 'Total Missions Thrust: Global Discipleship' plan published by Southern Baptist Foreign Mission Board.

1975 Project Look Up (PLU) begun by International Christian Broadcasters (USA), planning to reach world via NASA's ATS-6 geostationary satellite to beam TV seminary teaching and lay institutes across world; 1977, begins broadcasts to Puerto Rico; satellite suddenly withdrawn by NASA; 1979, PLU fizzles out due to inadequate funding, though committees go on meeting until after 1988.

1975 Associates for World Evangelization (AWE) begun for students associated with Fuller Seminary and later USCWM.

1975 International Missionary Congress on 'Evangelization and Cultures,' sponsored by Pontifical Urbanian University, Rome; 600 attenders (5-12 October).

1975 Paul VI's Apostolic Exhortation *Evangelii Nuntiandi* published (8 December) as the major Catholic statement on evangelization: 'To evangelize is first of all to bear witness'; world evangelization expounded in detail.

1975 New Life International begun as evangelical charismatic service agency involved in TEE, literature, research; 1984, renamed Total World Evangelization Vision (Fresno, California), in 8 countries.

1975 Genesis Project is begun to produce whole Bible on film, word for word; 33-year project envisaged, covering OT/NT with 300 films as the New Media Bible, to be dubbed in 27 languages; by 1986, 33 films emerge, but only Genesis and Luke completed; major achievement the 'Jesus' film with CCCI.

1975 World Evangelical Fellowship Missions Commission inaugurated in Seoul, Korea, dedicated to development of the non-Western missionary movement (Third World missions), utilizing a network of agencies and Evangelical fellowships across the world.

1975 Gradual drop in use of fossil fuels; in 1975, 82% of world's energy needs are met by oil, gas, coal; by 1995, 78%; by 2010, 74%: by 2030, 71%; 2079, drop to zero, replaced by 37% nuclear fusion generators, 31% solar/wind farms, 10% hydrogen, rest dams/geothermal/biomass; 2100, solar power satellite system provides 65% of all energy.

1975 Angola: territorial independence from Portugal, but 16-year civil war breaks out with UNITA rebels; 350,000 people killed before 1991 peace accords signed.

1975 World Mind Group Colloquium research group founded by M. Kochen, H. J. A. Goodman, et alii; 1979 holds colloquium at Banff, Alberta (Canada).

1975 Canadian Association for Future Studies begun in Ottawa; 1977, Institute for Canadian Futures founded, in Ontario.

1975 2nd General Assembly, World Future Society: largest gathering of futurists ever, with 2,800 attendees.

1975 Alleged beginning of Age of Aquarius (other dates proposed: 1962, 1993, 2000, 2023, 2160, 2300).

1975 US Library of Congress establishes Futures Research Group, also Congressional Clearinghouse on the Future.

1975 H.H. Ward writes *Religion 2101 A.D.*

1975 *A study of future worlds*, by R.A. Falk.

1975 Islamic scholar Annemarie Schimmel publishes *Mystical dimensions of Islam*, describing Sufi eschatology.

1975 *Ecotopia*, by E. Callenbach.

c1975 World Congress on Hinduism, held at Allahabad, India, depicts popular Hinduism's aggressively worldwide missionary expansion and predicts imminent eclipse of Christianity by AD 2000.

1975 International Federation of Religions founded in Thailand by Thai new religious movement Hooppha Sawan, with aim to promote world peace and fraternity.

1975 All Nagaland Congress on World Evangelization, in Dimapur (North East India), following Lausanne I Congress, to study revival and missions (1-9 March).

1975 1st World Congress of Sorcery, held in Bogota (Colombia).

1975 Cambodia: over next 4 years, every exterior sign of Christianity obliterated by Khmer Rouge communist: all churches razed, all books destroyed, Cambodian RC clergy and sisters killed, Catholic and Protestant laity slaughtered along with 3 million other Cambodians; but by 1997, Catholics again strong with 7,000 Cambodians and 15,000 Vietnamese.

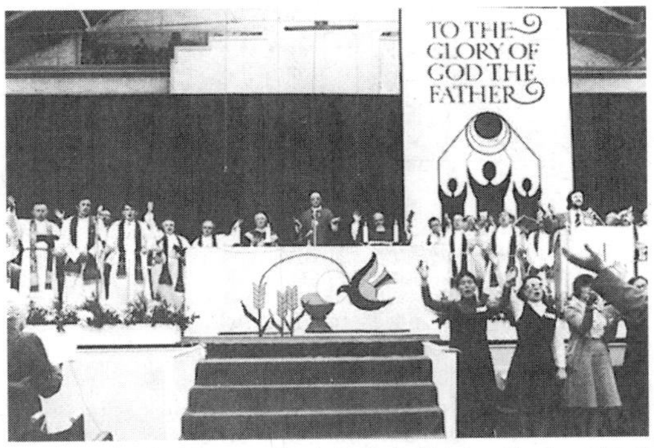


**AD 1975.** Cardinal Suenens leads Catholic Charismatics in praise at Dublin Conference.

1975 Ireland: 2nd National Conference on the Charismatic Renewal, held in Dublin, led by cardinal L.-J. Suenens, 190 priests and 5,000 lay charismatics; at Dublin's 1978 International Conference, Suenens concelebrates on TV with 17 bishops and 1,500 priests in the presence of 20,000.

1976 Guatemala: catastrophic earthquake kills 24,000, 77,000 injured, over 500 Protestant churches destroyed (February).

1976 Since 1917 Revolution in USSR, 60 million (over half Christians) killed directly or indirectly, 40% being executed or killed by communist officials.

1976 First international Islamic World Congress, Karachi, Pakistan; delegates, from 44 countries, call for Muslim governments to close down all Christian missions (April).

1976 Rhodesia: national Congress on Evangelism in Context (May).

1976 First Latin American Amerindian in history consecrated as bishop: Mario Marino (born 1933), a Mataco in Argentina (Anglican).

1976 China: 1.4 million victims of widespread catastrophic earthquakes; 655,237 killed in Tientsin-Tangshan alone.

1976 World Congress of Fundamentalists: first 8-day USA-dominated meeting in Edinburgh; 2,000 in attendance.

1976 Australia: Congress on World Missions and Evangelism (May).

1976 3rd Conference, International Association for Mission Studies (IAMS), San José, Costa Rica, on 'Tradition and Reconstruction in Mission' (25-30 July).

1976 41st International Eucharistic Congress, Philadelphia, USA; one million Catholics participate (August).

1976 11th Pentecostal World Conference, Albert Hall, London: 'The Spirit of Truth'.

1976 Anglican Consultative Council (ACC-3) meets in Trinidad, reformulates Archbishops' definition of 1918 as 'Evangelism is the faithful proclamation of the Gospel'.

1976 AMEN (American Military Evangelizing Nations) formed, by USA denomination Churches of Christ, for lay evangelism by US armed forces around world.

1976 1st Chinese Congress on World Evangelization (CCOWE), Hong Kong, on 'Vision and Mission', with 1,600 participants from over 20 countries (August); CCCOWE (Chinese Coordination Centre of World Evangelism) set up in Hong Kong (October); subsequent congresses every 5 years (1981 2nd, 1986 3rd, 1991 4th, 1996 5th).

1976 National Seminar on Evangelism in Papua New Guinea and the Solomon Islands, sponsored by Melanesian Council of Churches, Evangelical Alliance of the South Pacific Islands, and Roman Catholic Church.

1976 Northern Europe Conference on Evangelization, Belgium (September).

1976 Japan Multimedia Evangelism Project (JMEP), in Hokkaido.

1976 Taiwan: Roman Catholic 2-year TV program 'The Most Unforgettable Story' draws 1.2 million viewers every week for over a year.

1976 Association for the Evangelization of Austria formed.

1976 Bangladesh Congress on Evangelism, in Dacca.

1976 1st Missionary Congress for European Youth (Mission '76), organized by TEMA (The European Missionary Association); followed by Mission '80, Mission '83 (Lausanne), Mission '87 (Utrecht; theme 'I chose You'); average participants 7,000.

1976 India: Every Home Crusade begins its second nationwide home canvass, Project Calvary, aiming to deliver booklets to every home in India by 1981.

1976 India: Here's Life, Kerala (run by CCCI) saturates whole of Kerala state, reaching 99% of 2,700,000 homes, 9,900,352 persons evangelized, 1,850,982 decisions for Christ (1,470,954 through person-to-person presentations, 380,028 at public meetings; of total, 10% being formerly Hindu or Muslim).

1976 Canada: new type of evangelistic crusade, Vancouver Reachout, with L. Ford: 200 churches, 75,000 homes contacted, 24,000 attenders, 450 enquirers.

1976 Conference of Lutheran Churches in Europe, Liebfrauenberg, France (September).

1976 Annual Plenary Assembly, Sacred Congregation for the Evangelization of Peoples, in Rome, on theme 'Popular Religion', with 25 cardinals, 15 bishops and many other delegates (19-22 October).

1976 LWF North/Southeast Asia Church Leaders' Consultation, in Manila (October).

1976 Ecumenical Association of Third World Theologians (EATWOT) holds first General Meeting, Dar es Salaam, Tanzania, under name Ecumenical Dialogue of Third World Theologians; 1977 Accra (African theologians), 1979 Sri Lanka (Asian theologians), 1980 São Paulo (Latin American theologians), 1981 New Delhi (Third World theologians), 1983 Hamburg and Geneva.

1976 1st Pan-Orthodox Preconciliar Conference, Chambesy, Switzerland (November).

1976 Asian Conference on Religion and Peace, sponsored by FABC; in Singapore, on 'Peace through Religion' (November).

1976 Pan-African Christian Leadership Assembly (PACLA), in Nairobi; 700 delegates (December).

1976 Christmas: over 1.3 billion people hear pope Paul VI over radio/TV.

1976 3rd Assembly, Pacific Conference of Churches (PCC), in Port Moresby, Papua, on theme 'God's Mission in the changing Pacific society'.

1976 3rd All Asia Lutheran Conference, in Singapore (November-December).

1976 Venezuela: Marcha Evangelistica inaugurated by Baptists, 1978 spreads to Ecuador, Chile, Bolivia; 1980 Movimiento Discipular causes country's 6,000 Baptists to set goal of 1 million Venezuelan Baptists in 4,000 churches by AD 2000 (1986 total: 14,000 in 130 churches); 1985, Congreso de Misión Mundial, in Caracas with 200 present from 8 countries.

1976 Southern Baptist Convention USA, meeting in Norfolk, VA, adopts resolution and plan for remainder of century to implement world evangelization through strategy Bold Mission Thrust: 'To enable every person in the world to have opportunity to hear and to respond to the gospel of Christ by the year 2000'; at 1988 midpoint, Foreign Mission Board reaffirms this intention, but plan then fizzles out.

1976 Gabriel Olasoji World Evangelism (GOWE) founded in Ibadan (Nigeria) with motto 'Reaching the Unreached' based on Mark 16:15; by 1988, power evangelism and mass crusades in 25 nations.

1976 Pasadena, USA: founding of US Center for World Mission, restricted to Conservative Evangelicals.

1976 LCWE Strategy Working Group (SWG) formed; meets every year or two, works on plural strategies and tactics rather than any single overall strategy.

1976 Church Growth International Seminars begun in Seoul by P. Yonggi Cho; by 1986, 70,000 pastors and leaders from 30 countries have attended; at 10th Seminar in 1986, goal of world evangelization announced with specific plan to win 10 million Japanese to Christ by AD 2000.
1976 EFMA mission executives meet and tally the number of people groups in the unreached category which their agencies alone are in touch with, or are planning to reach by 1990; total estimated at 6,000 people groups.
1976 Lausanne Intercession Advisory Group formed after ICOWE I; organizes conferences, annual day of prayer for world evangelization (Pentecost Sunday).
1976 Habitat for Humanity International founded (USA) 'to eliminate poverty housing throughout the world in the name of Jesus Christ, seeking to glorify Him and to spread His Gospel throughout the earth'; 1988, builds 2,000 houses in 300 cities; goal by 1996, to build in 2,000 North American cities and in 60 other countries.
1976 Fellowship of World Christians (FOW) begun by USCWM for students (mostly ex-AWE) concerned for world evangelization; rallies; defunct by 1978; 1985, name taken over by different group (World Literature Crusade) offering 100 people a year two-week mission encounters in Mexico, Haiti, et alia.
1976 Prophecy teacher D. Clark asserts significance of Jupiter Effect's alignment of planets in 1982, predicts Christ will return in that year.
1976 First biosphere reserves established; by 1992, 300 reserves in 76 countries covering 600,000 square miles; with computerized database link in Cambridge, England.
1976 C.Q. Yarbro's novel *Time of the Fourth Horseman* envisages conspiracy of doctors who deliberately spread plague to end world's overpopulation.
1976 P.E. Erdman writes scenario, *The crash of '79*, in which in 1979 Mohammad Reza (1919-1980) shah of Iran attempts to seize Gulf and its oil, precipitates nuclear war; entire world's economy crashes catastrophically in greatest economic disaster in history; in reality, however, shah is overthrown in 1979 by ayatollah Khomeini; Erdman also writes *The last days of America* (1981); and in 1987, *The panic of '89*, envisaging international terrorism and massive loan defaults.
1976 D. Webber of Southwest Radio Church publishes *Countdown for Antichrist*, names Austrian president Kurt Waldheim, West German chancellor Willy Brandt, pope Paul VI, prince Bernhard of the Netherlands, and Henry Kissinger as prime candidates for Antichrist; in 1984 edition, Waldheim, Brandt, pope Paul, and prince Bernhard are dropped as candidates; peace symbol seen as the mark of Antichrist.
1976 H. Kahn et alii write *The next 200 years: a scenario for America and the world*, forecasting fusion reactors on line by 1995, and power derived from ocean gradients, with conversion of organic wastes commercially feasible before 2000.
1976 *An incomplete guide to the future*, by W.W. Harman.
1976 *Millennium: a novel about people and politics in the year 1999*, by Ben Bova.
1976 *Eschatus: future prophecies from Nostradamus' ancient writings*, a lavishly illustrated volume by B. Pennington.
1976 *Freud and future religious experience*, by A.J. De Luca.
1976 2nd Congress on Orthodox Theology, held in Athens, Greece (19-29 August).
1976 19th Meeting, Conference of World Confessional Families, held in London (19 May); then subsequent meetings held every year for 2 or 3 days every October or November.
1976 1st General Assembly to inaugurate Ecumenical Association of Third World Theologians (EATWOT), with 23 theologians in Dar es Salaam (Tanzania).
1976 First National Southern Baptist Charismatic Conference (21-23 July).
1976 Christival-1 Youth Gathering, held in Essen (West Germany).
1976 13th World Methodist Conference, held in Dublin, Ireland.
1977 Italy ends status of Roman Catholicism as state religion.
1977 ECCLA V, 5th Latin American Catholic Charismatic Renewal Leaders Conference, in Caracas, Venezuela; leaders from almost all Latin American countries (January).
1977 All-India Congress on Mission and Evangelization (AICOME), Devlali, with 400 leaders present (12-19 January).
1977 Asian Colloquium on New Ministries in the Church, sponsored by FABC; in Hong Kong (February).
1977 Latin American Lutheran Consultation, in São Leopoldo, Brazil (January).
1977 All Africa Lutheran Consultation, in Gaborone, Botswana (February).
1977 Guatemala: Indian Congress on World Evangelization (14-18 February); also in 1978, 1980.
1977 2nd National Evangelical Anglican Congress, Nottingham University, UK (April), following 1st Congress at Keele University in 1967.
1977 LCWE Consultation on the Homogeneous Unit Principle, Pasadena, USA (May).

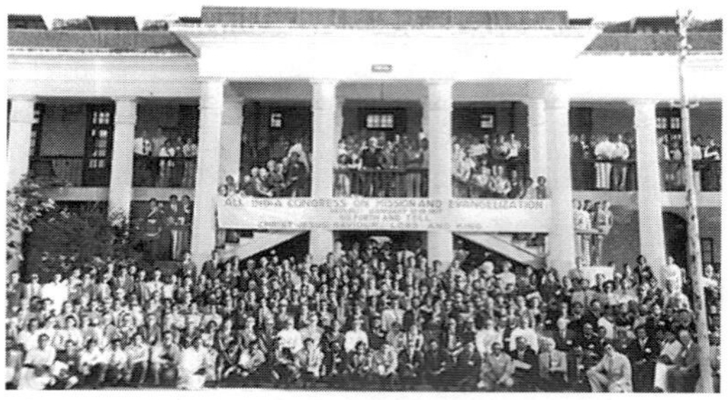

**AD 1977.** 400 leader delegates at All-India Congress on Mission and Evangelization, Devlali.

1977 WCC Consultation on the Church and the Jewish People, Jerusalem (June).
1977 Ghana Congress on Evangelism (July).
1977 Romania: catastrophic earthquake destroys or damages 1,200 churches.
1977 4th Ordinary Synod of Bishops in Rome, on 'Catechetics in Our Time', dealing with evangelization of children and youth (September).
1977 Pan-Orthodox Consultation (CWME) on 'The role and the place of the Bible in the liturgical and spiritual life of the Orthodox Church', Prague (September); also Consultation on 'The Ecumenical nature of the Orthodox witness', in New Valamo, Finland (September).
1977 World Conference on Audio-Visuals and Evangelization, Munich (November).
1977 500 million hear or see one-hour radio/TV gospel service broadcast from Jerusalem on Christmas Eve in 7 languages simultaneously (Pentecostal preacher Rex Humbard).
1977 Burma: 6,200 converts baptized by Kachin Baptist Convention at largest single baptismal service in recent Christian history.
1977 6th Assembly, Christian Conference of Asia (CCA), in Penang, Malaysia, on theme 'Jesus Christ in Asian suffering and hope'.
1977 WCC Theological Consultation on Dialogue in Community, in Chiang Mai, Thailand.
1977 2nd Assembly, Caribbean Conference of Churches (CCC), in Georgetown, Guyana, on theme 'Working together with Christ'.
1977 New RC missionary congregations formed: in Tanzania, Evangelizing Sisters of Mary; and in Hong Kong, Sisters Announcers of the Lord.
1977 CB (Citizens Band) 2-way radio expands in USA from 200,000 radios (1973) to 10 million (1975) to 20 million (1977) to 30 million (1984).
1977 417.5 million telephones in world (162 million in USA alone, placing 467 million local calls, and 38.8 million long-distance calls, every day).
1977 Conference of World Confessional Families (WCFs) convenes in Rome for first time.
1977 Germany: 17th Protestant Kirchentag, with related Missio Berlin 77 yearlong evangelistic campaign.
1977 250,000 word processors in use in USA offices.
1977 Ethiopia: 90,000 killed in Red Terror 1977-80 including emperor Haile Selassie, patriarch Theofilus and numerous bishops and clergy.
1977 Greece: Orthodox charismatics organize Crusade for Christ in Athens.
1977 Philippines: film evangelism under Philippines Action International Ministries; 143,797 attenders in year, with 8,262 decisions for Christ.
1977 6th Assembly, Lutheran World Federation (LWF), Dar es Salaam (Tanzania), on 'In Christ a New Community'.
1977 Thailand: Every Home Crusade (EHC/WLC) completes Operation Torch with 95% nationwide saturation achieved; 5,975,998 homes reached (77% of total), 38,037 written responses for Christ recorded.
1977 1st Worldwide Chinese Church Growth Seminar (Chinese Coordinating Center of World Evangelism, CCCOWE), near Taipei, with over 400 delegates (November).
1977 1st Latin American Missionary Congress (COMLA-1), in Torreon, Mexico, on 'The Church, the Universal Sacrament of Salvation' (20-23 November).
1977 World's most successful movie 'Star Wars' describes rebellion in totalitarian galactic empire in BC 60 million.
1977 Pan African Conference of Third World Theologians (EATWOT-2), in Accra, Ghana, on 'Emerging themes in African theology' (December).
1977 1st Conference on the Charismatic Renewal in the Christian Churches; ecumenical, at last embracing all pentecostal traditions; on theme 'Jesus is Lord'; in Kansas City, USA; 59,000 present (July); but after this ecumenical climax, charismatic conferences revert to monodenominational or monoconfessional status (15,000 Lutheran charismatics each year in Minneapolis, 10,000 RCs in Notre Dame, et alii).
1977 Here's Life, World (saturation and total mobilization evangelization campaign), organized by Campus Crusade for Christ, bankrolled by History's Hundred (100 USA billionaires), launched in 100 countries, on every continent, with announced goal 'to fulfil the Great Commission in the whole world by the end of 1980'.
1977 Futurism adopts dogma 'Almost anything can be accomplished in 20 years'— Edward Cornish, president of World Future Society.
1977 Development of ultrasonic bomb which destabilizes human brain by destroying a few cells and so turns a whole city's population into raving imbeciles, without damaging property.
1977 Church of South India bishop L. Newbigin writes on 'The future of missions and missionaries' (*Review and expositor).*
1977 R. Dunlop writes *The coming Russian invasion of America—Why? When? Where?* predicting worldwide famine by 1986, Antichrist revealed in 1989, and Rapture in 1991.
1977 F. de Graaf publishes *Anno Domini 1000, Anno Domini 2000* (Kampen).
1977 Physicist G.K. O'Neill writes *The high frontier: human colonies in space*; also in 1981, *2081: a hopeful view of the human future.*
1977 WFS president Edward S. Cornish publishes *The study of the future: understanding and shaping tomorrow's world;* becomes a classic.
1977 3rd Meeting on Dialogue with Other Living Faiths (WCC), held in Chiang Mai (Thailand), produces *Guidelines on Dialogue.*
1977 2nd General Assembly, Middle East Council of Churches (MECC), held in Broumana (Lebanon), on theme 'He Gave Us the Ministry of Reconciliation'.
1977 13th Islamic World Congress, held in Cairo (Egypt); resolution passed to stop all attempts at converting Christians living in Muslim countries.
1977 7th World Council of YMCAs, in Buenos Aires, Argentina, on theme 'Enlisted in Reconciliation'.
1978 LCWE Consultation on Gospel and Culture, Willowbank, Bermuda (January).
1978 Congress on Evangelism for Malaysia and Singapore (COEMAS); 300 leaders (April).
1978 2nd World Conference of Baptist Men, Indianapolis, USA (April).
1978 International Conference on the Charismatic Renewal in the Catholic Church, in Dublin: 'You shall be My Witnesses'; 15,000 participants, led by L.-J. Suenens cardinal primate of Belgium (16 June); by now, CCR has grown from 2 prayer groups in 1967 (one in USA, one in Bogota, Colombia) to 2,185 by 1970, to 3,000 by 1973, to 4,000 by 1975, to 10,000; and participants have grown from 238,500 Catholics attending weekly prayer meetings in 1970 to 2,500,000 by 1978; with total Charismatic community (including families and children) of 30,000,000 in 88 countries (4% of the entire Catholic Church worldwide) by 1978 (growth rate of 37% per year); several cardinals and over a hundred bishops are involved, several from the first weeks in 1967, building on the vistas, prospects, and promises that surfaced during Vatican II, 1962-1965, through influence of a number of pre-charismatic cardinals, bishops, and clergy.
1978 8th International Convention on Missionary Medicine, Wheaton, USA (June).
1978 9th Baptist Youth World Conference, Manila, Philippines (July).
1978 BIMA series (Bishops' Institute for the Missionary Apostolate), sponsored by FABC: BIMA I, Baguio City, Philippines (July, 1978); BIMA III, Changhua, Taiwan (August, 1982).
1978 11th Lambeth Conference, Canterbury, England: 'Today's church in today's world'; 420 Anglican bishops (July-August).
1978 2nd Nigeria National Congress on Evangelization, Ile-Ife; 1,000 participants (August).
1978 4th Conference, International Association for Mission Studies (IAMS), Maryknoll, New York, on theme 'Credibility and Spirituality in Mission' (20-28 August).
1978 Holy Shroud of Turin (Italy) exposed for 43 days (27 August-8 October) ('Exposition of the Holy Shroud'), to 3.3 million pilgrims; followed by Sindonological Conference; large amount of new interest among scientists results in permission to conduct carbon dating.
1978 Rhodesia: National Christian Leadership Assembly (NACLA), held in Bulawayo, with 300 delegates (September).
1978 Death of pope Paul VI; succeeded by an Italian champion of the Church of the Poor, Albino Luciani (born 1912), who as John Paul I instigates revolutionary changes over Vatican finances; on his alleged murder 34 days later, cardinals elect a Pole, first non-Italian for 450 years: John Paul II (born 1920), 264th Pope of Rome (110th since 1143, on St Malachy's reckoning), who in 1981 himself survives assassination attempt.
1978 International convention series of Jehovah's Witnesses produce 100 'Victorious Faith' assemblies in 45 countries, averaging 25,000 attenders at each.
1978 World Congress of Mission and Migration, Rome (October).
1978 New World Information Order (NWIO) proclaimed by UNESCO in 'Mass Media Declaration' at 21st General Conference, denouncing cultural imperialism and informatics (transborder data flow, TDF).
1978 Ectogenesis ('test-tube babies') achieved, in England (fertilizing of human eggs outside the body).
1978 5.85% of world's total electricity generating power comes from nuclear power stations.
1978 World export trade rises from $246 billion in 1969 to $1,190 billion in 1978.

1978 Third-World arms imports of major weapons soar from $1.4 billion in 1961 to $9.4 billion in 1978.
1978 Science television 13-part series 'Cosmos' (by astronomer C. Sagan) seen in 60 countries by 140 million people (5.4% of Earth's adult population).
1978 Scandinavia: Skandia '78 evangelistic campaign on radio/TV for Norway, Sweden et alia.
1978 Panama: Africa-Panama Crusade (Mission '78), with evangelists from Africa; 90 supporting churches, 15,000 attenders, 700 decisions.
1978 Colombia: 200,000 decisions for Christ registered during 500,000-pilgrim Easter climb up Hill of the Three Crosses, during Here's Life Cali campaign.
1978 2nd Plenary Assembly, World Catholic Federation for the Biblical Apostolate (WCFBA), in Malta, on theme 'Biblical Spirituality and Biblical Catechesis'.
1978 North American Conference on Muslim Evangelization, Glen Eyrie, USA; 150 participants (October).
1978 Malcolm Muggeridge's lectures 'Christ and the media' portray Jesus' '4th Temptation' by Satan offering him prime time on Rome television to preach his gospel to the entire world; offer turned down.
1978 All Asia Lutheran Seminar on Mission, in Hong Kong.
1978 All African Lutheran Consultation on Christian Theology and Christian Education in the African Context, in Gaborone, Botswana (October).
1978 Consultation on Church and Service, in Chania, Crete; 'An Orthodox approach to diaconia' (November).
1978 LWF Consultation for Churches in North America, the Nordic Countries and FR Germany, at Loccum; first specifically designed for 'northern churches' (November-December).

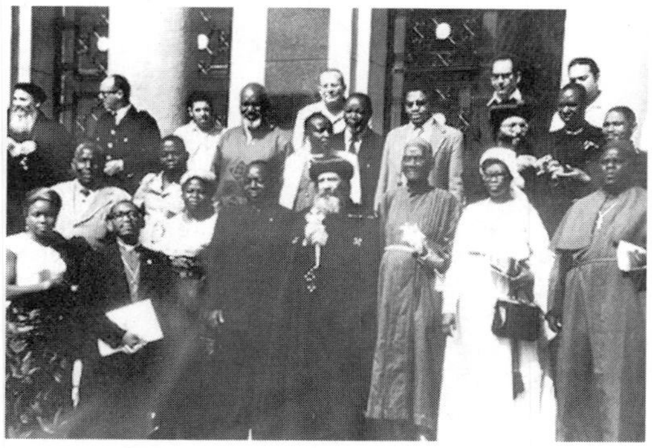

**AD 1978.** Invited by Coptic pope Shenouda III (*center*), African Independents launch OAIC in Cairo.

1978 Organization of African Independent Churches (OAIC) inaugurated at Cairo conference, representing 25 million church members from Black indigenous churches throughout Africa (November); 1982, 2nd OAIC Conference, in Nairobi; movement grows rapidly among pentecostal and nonpentecostal AIC denominations in 50 countries; 1985, name changed to Organization of African Instituted Churches to emphasize indigenous origins rather than schismatic factions; assistance received from Coptic Orthodox Church and its pope Shenouda III, offered through its bishop for Black Africa, Antonious Mankos; 1998, OAIC accepted as associate council member of WCC; by AD 2000, has 40 million church members out of Africa-wide AIC total of 84 million.
1978 1st Norwegian Congress on World Evangelization (related to LCWE), followed about every 2 years by Danvik National Conferences on Evangelization, with 140 church leaders, held in Drammen (Norway) in 1980, 1981, 1982, 1984, 1986.
1978 7th General Chapter, Catholic Foreign Mission Society of America (Maryknoll) issues 'Statement of Mission Vision': 'Our particular task gives special emphasis to the evangelization of the poor, of cultures and of structures'.
1978 Asian Leadership Conference on Evangelism (ALCOE), Singapore: 'Together obeying Christ for Asia's harvest'; 350 leaders from 20 Asian countries (November).
1978 Guyana: mass suicide-murder of 925 followers of People's Temple (90% USA Blacks) at Jonestown in jungle.
1978 Symposium on Mission and Evangelization of Lutheran Churches in Latin America, in Porto Alegre, Brazil (29-31 May).
1978 7th International Lutheran Conference on the Holy Spirit, Minneapolis; 25,000 participants including Belgian cardinal L.J. Suenens.
1978 Britain: Nationwide Initiative in Evangelism (NIE) launched by all churches (Anglican, Roman Catholic, Ecumenical, Evangelical, Black) as interdenominational program 'to stimulate intelligent and effective evangelism by all Christians'.
1978 10th Mennonite World Conference, Wichita, KS, USA.
1978 World Mission 1978-1981 begun as World Methodist Council's 4-year plan of global evangelism.
1978 Attempt by MARC (USA) to set up an information network for world evangelization entitled SHARE (Systems, Hardware and Research for Evangelization); scheme founders by 1985 due to inability to obtain original field data.
1978 Great Commission Strategy Resource Network (GCSRN) launched by CCCI 'to finish the task of reaching by 1980 those who have not yet heard the gospel', based on 5 functions: (1) information gathering and distribution, (2) resource reference, (3) research, (4) vision rooms, (5) international communication system; but peters out until by 1987 is reduced to computer hardware maintenance.
1978 New Zealand: Commission for the Future founded, in Wellington.
1978 Minerals: over next 30 years, world will consume 3.5 times volume of minerals (copper, bauxite, zinc, nickel, lead, iron ore, petroleum, gas, coal, etc) that it has used up since dawn of civilization.
1978 O.V. Garrison publishes *Encyclopedia of prophecy*, stating 'If there is one point on which both secular forecasters and inspired mystics agree, it is that during the brief two and a half decades separating us from the year 2000, the present world order will undergo a total change'.
1978 *The Delphic Oracle: its responses and operations*, by J. Fontenrose.
1978 *Creating alternative futures: the end of economics*, by Hazel Henderson.
1978 *Forecasting: an appraisal for policymakers and planners*, by W.L. Ascher.
1978 World Health Organization conference in Alma-Ata, Kazakhstan produces `Health for All by the Year 2000' Declaration.
1978 World Congress of Romany People (Gypsies), held at U.N. HQ in Geneva (April).
1978 4th Latin American Protestant Conference (CELA-IV), held at Oaxtepec (Mexico); UNELAM proposes decision to create ecumenical council CLAI (Latin American Council of Churches) with 110 denominations and agencies (some pentecostal); 1982, CLAI officially constituted at Lima, Peru; Conservative Evangelical opponents organize rival CONELA (Latin American Evangelical Confederation), claiming 20 million Evangelicals in 84 founding denominations (including Evangelical Council of Venezuela, CEV), mainly AoG (Brazil).
1978 1st European Ecumenical Conference, organized jointly by Conference of European Churches (CEC) and Council of European Bishops' Conferences (CEBC), in Chantilly (France) in April; 2nd in Logumkloster (Denmark), 16-20 November 1981; 3rd in north Italy, 1984 .
1978 1st Forum on Bilateral Conversations/Dialogues (originated by Conference of CWCs, and WCC); 2nd in 1979; 3rd in 1980; 4th in 1985; 5th in 1990 (Budapest, 18-22 October); 6th in 1995; 7th in 1997.
1978 European Evangelical Communications Conference (WEF), in Amsterdam (Netherlands) (20-23 October).
1979 Margaret Thatcher (born 1925) becomes Britain's first woman prime minister.
1979 Asian Theological Conference (EATWOT-3), in Sri Lanka, on 'Asia's struggle for full humanity' (January).
1979 Joint Christian Ministry in West Africa (JCMWA: 8 churches from West Africa, 6 European churches and agencies including Anglican CMS), as a new ecumenical and global model for cooperative mission and evangelism, holds consultation in Dakar (January).
1979 West Germany: Conference on 'Unreached Peoples', sponsored by World Evangelical Fellowship, at Bad Liebenzell (January).
1979 Caribbean Lutheran Conference, in St Thomas, US Virgin Islands (30 January- 2 February).
1979 LWF Consultation on Global Partnership in Mission in Asia, in Manila (March).
1979 National Missionary Congress, Irish Missionary Union, at Knock, with nearly 400 Catholic missioners from every continent; theme 'A New Missionary Era' emerges (April).
1979 Pan-Orthodox Consultation on 'The place of the monastic life within the witness of the Church today' at Amba Bishoy monastery, Egypt, seeking to rediscover past leading roles of monks and nuns in world evangelization (April-May).
1979 ACC-4: 4th Meeting, Anglican Consultative Council, London, Ontario, Canada (8-18 May).
1979 LWF Consultation on Theological Education for the Service of the Church in a Secular Society, in Bratislava (May).
1979 South African Christian Leadership Assembly (SACLA), Pretoria (July).
1979 Over 10,000 pilgrims attend International Charismatic Pilgrimage to Lourdes on shrine's 100th anniversary (July).
1979 12th Pentecostal World Conference, in Vancouver, Canada: 'The Holy Spirit in the Last Days' (October); meetings largely form platform for preachers, with no approval for administrative development, no central office or officers between the 3-yearly Conferences, no overall global plans, strategies, or tactics; also, organization dominated by Classical Pentecostals from USA, so few Charismatics or Neocharismatics attend.
1979 All-India Conference on Evangelical Social Action (AICOESA), in Madras, India (2-5 October).
1979 BIRA series (Bishops' Institute of Interreligious Affairs) sponsored by FABC: BIRA I, Bangkok (October, 1979); BIRA II, Kuala Lumpur (November, 1979); BIRA III, Cochin, India (Hindu-Catholic dialogue, 1981).
1979 2nd Latin American Congress on Evangelization (CLADE II), Huampani, Lima, Peru (October); sponsored by Latin American Theological Fraternity (FTL), promoting Lausanne Covenant but from critical perspective; 266 delegates from 39 denominations in 21 countries.
1979 Canadian Congress on World Evangelization.
1979 8th Assembly, Conference of European Churches (CEC), in Crete, on 'Alive to the World in the Power of the Holy Spirit' (October).
1979 Overthrow of shah Mohammad Reza of Iran by ayatollah Khomeini; emergence of neo-fundamentalist militaristic Islam as a global power.
1979 Apostolic Exhortation *Catechesi Tradendae* on 'Catechesis in our time' promulgated by pope John Paul II (16 October).
1979 'The Source' network (based on USA) founded as world's first popular mass database accessible to personal computers by telephone, which assists users to set up own networks.
1979 Hi-Ovis experimental home service project in Japan: central computer scans every home once every 7 seconds, checking all alarm systems and supplying needs and requests.
1979 Venezuelan National Congress on Evangelization, Caracas (November).
1979 Vast increase in short-term missionary personnel from Western world, including 17,358 young persons from 250 USA agencies.
1979 International Mission Congress (FABC and SC Propaganda), in Manila, on 'Towards a New Age in Mission: the Good News of the Kingdom to the Peoples of Asia' (2-7 December).
1979 Computer-aided scripture translation by SIL (Wycliffe) includes program to compile and print scripture concordances for each new language completed; 1984, Bible Society (UK) produces computer concordance of Good News Bible with program applicable also to any language's Bible translation.
1979 USA: New King James Version of Bible published, update of KJV using Textus Receptus by 130 Evangelical scholars: NT 1979, Bible 1982.
1979 Assembly on Dialogue with Islam (Muslim/Catholic) in Kuala Lumpur, Malaysia.
1979 Incidents of international terrorism increase worldwide from 1,550 in 1979, to 1,709 in 1980, to 2,387 in 1981.
1979 Mission '80, 2nd Missionary Congress for European Youth (TEMA, The European Missionary Alliance), in Lausanne, with 3,000 participants.
1979 Dutch missiologist J. Verkuyl writes 'The unfinished task of world mission' (*Occasional essays*, San José, Costa Rica).
1979 Anglican renewal agency SOMA (Sharing of Ministries Abroad) founded, 'dedicated to fostering Renewal in the Holy Spirit world wide so as to enable and equip the Church to fulfil the Great Commission of Jesus Christ, to proclaim the Kingdom of God and minister in the power of the Holy Spirit'; holds international conferences 1981 Singapore, 1983 Nairobi, 1984 Fiji; by 1987, its work in 50 countries covers 26 of the 31 Anglican Provinces worldwide.
1979 Foursquare Missions International announces plan to begin work among 100 unreached peoples; by 1985, has 83 foreign missionaries with related churches in 47 countries (International Church of the Foursquare Gospel).
1979 'Jesus' Film produced by The Jesus Project, Campus Crusade for Christ, filmed in Palestine in 1979; by 1986, is circulating dubbed in 106 languages; annual viewers then total 275 million, decisions for Christ reach 33 million (12%); 1988, goal announced for 5,000 teams with copies dubbed in 271 languages of over a million speakers each by 1993 plus 1,000 other strategic languages and dialects by 1998 with 5 million viewers a night; also that, by AD 2000, 6 billion people shall have seen it of whom 600 to 1,500 million pray to receive Christ.
1979 Evangelist Billy Graham (at IVCF Urbana conference) and USA Evangelical foreign mission leaders issue call for '120,000 missionaries by the year 2000' in order to reach unreached peoples and establish 'A church for every people by AD 2000'.
1979 USA: Angel-I/Angel-II/Angel-III Project to blanket Earth with gospel broadcasts proposed by NRB and WEF: 3 satellites in geostationary orbit filling roles of 3 angels of Revelation 14:6-11, each covering a third of Earth's surface, fulfilling Matthew 24:14 'for a witness unto all nations'; by 1983, author realizes project has been 'committeed to death', so proposal passes into oblivion, though use of satellites for USA Christian TV grows.
1979 TV evangelist J. Bakker of PTL Ministries announces plan to start PTL missions throughout the world; funds raised but plan fizzles out within a year; 1987, Ministries collapse in financial and sex scandal, Bakker jailed until 1995.
1979 *World Christian magazine* founded (California), focusing on young adults and world evangelization.
1979 Lutherans for World Evangelization begun in Pasadena, CA (USA), as research and information service.
1979 Caleb Project begun by USCWM to tap potential of students and young adults committed to world mission, undertaking field research among unreached peoples; 1986, merges with Joshua Projects.
1979 *Unreached Peoples* series of volumes published by LCWE/MARC in 1979, 1980, 1981, 1983, 1987, the latter 'Clarifying the Task' by clearly differentiating between (a) unreached ethnolinguistic peoples

(each with no organized church; totalling 2,000 peoples across the world), and (b) social people groups (defined functionally; useful for deriving ministry options; totalling several million groupings).

1979 Article 'World evangelism by 2000 AD: can it be done?' (*Moody monthly*, 80,4) written by R.D. Winter.

1979 International Colloquium of Apocalypticism, held in Uppsala (Sweden), with papers published as *Apocalypticism in the Mediterranean world and the Near East*, 1983.

1979 Horrifying germ-warfare accident in Sverdlovsk: large Soviet bio-war production plant explodes, contaminating vast areas of western Siberia, killing thousands; officially said to be an outbreak of anthrax; most deadly covered-up disaster in history.

1979 Iran-Iraq War, lasting until 1988.

1979 3rd General Conference of CELAM, in Puebla, Mexico: 'Evangelization in Latin America now and in the Future' (27 January-13 February).

1979 USA: Colloquium on the Church in Future Society, sponsored by Lutheran Brotherhood (January).

1979 Awesome astronomical phenomenon seen by scientists: on 5 March, the most intense burst of hard x-rays and gamma rays ever observed, a truly enormous explosion lasting only a few seconds, outshining the whole Universe in gamma rays; from a neutron star (supernova remnant) in Large Magellanic Cloud at 180,000 light-years' distance.

1979 WCC Conference on Faith, Science and the Future, with theme `Faith and Science in an Unjust World', at MIT, Cambridge, MA (USA), with over 900 participants (12-24 July).

1979 Asiatic New Religions (New Religious Movements) continue to grow rapidly, with 94 million adherents growing by 2 million a year.

1979 Conservative Baptist historian T.P. Weber publishes *Living in the shadow of the Second Coming: American Premillennialism, 1875-1925*.

1979 Quantum physics seen as a new religion by speculative physicists; possibility raised of branching probability universes: an infinite series of real, solid universes fitted into the probability gaps between the quantum events of our own Universe.

1979 Australian critic and editor P.D. Nicholls (1939- ) edits *The encyclopedia of science fiction: an illustrated A to Z* (London), lists 2,800 entries in 700,000 words describing some 30,000 distinct stories, novels, articles, and books in English, the great majority being future scenarios; 1993, second edition with 4,300 entries and 1.2 million words, edited by J. Clute & P.D. Nicholls.

1979 Futurism and religion: of the 30,000 published items in English described in *The encyclopedia of science fiction*, over 2,000 are scenarios dealing with religion, usually Christianity, and 200 involve Christian mission; a further 2,000 have been published in other languages.

1979 World Future Society begins monthly *Future survey*, being reviews of the 50 or so newest books or articles each month on vast range of futurist issues: economics, demographics, politics, industry, labor, manufacturing, social issues, environment, ecosystems; edited by Michael Marien, with annual volumes from 1979-1999.

1979 North Carolina prophecy teacher C. Deal publishes *Christ returns by 1988: 101 reasons why*, stating that Rapture will occur in 1983; sees minting of Susan B. Anthony dollar as signal of the End; warns of gigantic computer called The Beast based in Brussels (Belgium), tracking every move of every individual.

1979 E. Gaverluk and P. Fisher publish *Fiber optics: the eye of the Antichrist*, charging this technology will spy on people through television sets.

1979 I.F. Clarke writes *The pattern of expectation, 1644-2001*.

1979 World Future Society publishes *The future: a guide to information sources*.

1979 Physicist and futurist Freeman Dyson writes *Disturbing the Universe*.

1979 Roman Catholic theologian B. McGinn edits *Apocalyptic spirituality: treatises and letters*, giving apocalyptic texts from Lactantius, Adso, Joachim of Fiore, the Spiritual Franciscans, and Savonarola.

1979 *Uncertain futures: challenges for decision-makers*, by R.U. Ayres.

1979 23rd Meeting, Conference of WCFs, renamed as Christian World Communions (CWCs); in Kifissia, Athens (Greece) (2-6 November).

1979 England: Alpha Course, an Anglican outreach introduction to Christianity, is begun at Holy Trinity Church Brompton; 1990, 100 participants regularly for 15-session home meetings; 1993, transformed into a powerful medium for evangelism; 1994, Youth Alpha introduced for 11-18 year-olds; 1998, mushrooms worldwide into 10,000 11-week Alpha courses running in 77 countries and in most cities across world, operated by Protestant/Catholic/Anglican churches from several hundred denominations; participants rise from 600 in 1991, to 4,500 in 1993, 30,000 (1994), 100,000 (1995), 250,000 (1996), 500,000 (1997), then to 1 million (1999).

1979 1st Assembly, Disciples Ecumenical Consultative Council (DECC), held in Kingston (Jamaica) with representatives from 20 countries (October).

1979 10th Assembly, World Convention of Churches of Christ (WCCC), held in Honolulu, Hawaii (USA) with theme 'Sharing the Word with the World'.

1980 **Global status:** 64.9 generations after Christ, world is 33.2% Christians (50.5% of them being Whites), 60.7% evangelized; with printed Scriptures available in 1,811 languages.

1980 Soviet Union becomes world's leading military power, replacing earlier goal of economic and ideological supremacy by the pursuit of imperial power, with by 1980 completely novel boldness, efficiency, and intervention capabilities; cost of armed forces 14% of Soviet GNP, but total cost of military empire over 45% of GNP.

1980 USA (now world's 2nd-greatest military power) possesses 9,000 missile warheads and bombs continuously targeted on cities, industrial centers, military installations and major infrastructures of USSR.

1980 60,000 sophisticated industrial robots in Japan (77,000 one year later, 70% of world's total), 3,000 in USA, 105 in Britain.

1980 International arms trade climbs from $300 million annually in 1955 to $20 billion by 1980.

1980 Africa: Christians number 203,491,000 in 59 countries, increasing at 6 million a year; African indigenous churches (AICs) number some 6,730 separate denominations with 27,438,000 adherents in 43 African countries.

1980 4th International Ecumenical Congress of Theology (EATWOT-4), in São Paulo (Brazil) with 180 participants, convened by Ecumenical Association of Third World Theologians, on 'Ecclesiology of the popular Christian communities' (20 February-2 March).

1980 Stuttgart Congress on World Evangelization, Germany (April).

1980 All Africa Lutheran Consultation on Christian Theology and Strategy for Mission, in Monrovia (April), interrupted by bloody military coup.

1980 UK: National Pastoral Congress of England and Wales (Roman Catholic), Liverpool; 2,100 elected delegates (May).

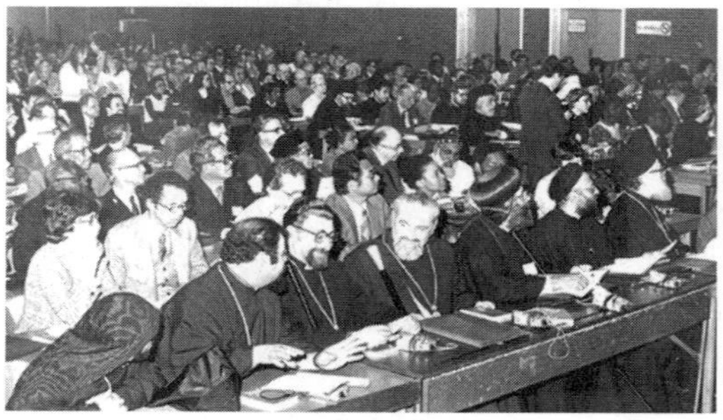

**AD 1980.** 650 delegates from all historic confessions confer in Melbourne on 'Your Kingdom Come'.

1980 1st World Missionary Conference on Mission and Evangelism (4th Meeting of CWME/WCC), in Melbourne, Australia, with title 'Your Kingdom come' and theme 'Good News to the Poor'; 650 delegates representing 300 churches from 100 countries; 'The proclamation of the gospel to the whole world remains an urgent obligation of all Christians' (12-24 May).

1980 LCWE Consultation on World Evangelization (COWE) in Pattaya, Bangkok: 'How shall they hear?'; 875 delegates from 87 countries; 17 miniconsultations (16-27 June).

1980 14th Baptist World Congress (BWA), on 'Christ's Presence through the Spirit', Toronto, with over 20,000 attenders from 93 countries (July).

1980 6th Latin American Lutheran Congress, in Bogota, on theme 'Our Faith and Our Mission in Latin America', with 47 delegates (August).

1980 USA: Detroit Conference II of Theology in the Americas, in Detroit (August).

1980 USA: 8th Annual Meeting, American Society of Missiology (ASM), in Wheaton (IL), on theme 'World Evangelization Today: Convergence or Divergence?' (22-24 August).

1980 Conference of Lutheran Churches in Europe, in Tallinn, Estonia, USSR, on 'Proclamation Today' (6-13 September).

1980 World Evangelization Crusade (Here's Life, Korea), Seoul; 16,500,000 attendances, including largest single meeting in Christian history to date (2.7 million).

1980 5th Ordinary Synod of Bishops in Rome, on the Christian family, with disquiet voiced on nonfulfillment of collegial promise of synods; also 2 Special Synods of Bishops, to deal with problems of (a) conservative/liberal rift in Dutch hierarchy, and (b) Ukrainian Catholic Church (with a second Synod on this latter subject in 1985).

1980 United States Festival of World Evangelization; 50,000 participants (September).

1980 Britain: Assembly on Evangelism, sponsored by NIE (Nationwide Initiative in Evangelism), in Nottingham; 700 attenders (22-27 September).

1980 International Congress on Evangelization and Atheism, Pontifical Urbanian University, Rome (October).

1980 China: Three-Self Patriotic Movement (TSPM) resuscitated after 13-year inactivity, holds 3rd National Conference in Nanjing, with 176 delegates; new pastoral body created, China Christian Council (CCC) (October).

1980 1st World Consultation on Frontier Missions (WCFM), Edinburgh, organized by US Center for World Mission: 'A Church for every People by the Year 2000'; 270 delegates (October).

1980 World Consultation on 'Churches Responding to Racism in the 1980s', at Noordwijkerhout, Netherlands.

1980 Episcopal churches with disputed apostolic succession number 280 in 80 countries, 130 being miniscule autocephalous Catholic churches under 700 bishops-at-large (episcopi vagantes).

1980 Telecommunications: AT&T/Bell survey calculates total telephones in world (1 January 1980) at 472,136,789, with nearly a million telex machines.

1980 In 80 years, annual circulation of complete Bibles in all languages has risen from 5.4 million in 1900 to 36.8 million by 1980.

1980 Christian broadcasting expands from origin in 1921 to global force heard or seen regularly by 23% of world's population.

1980 Urban dwellers rise from 14.4% of world in 1900 to 37.4% (1970), 41.1% (1980), 43.3% (1985), increasing at a million a week.

1980 Basic ecclesial communities (comunidades de base, grassroots Christian groupings) expand to 200,000 in Latin America.

1980 2nd Norwegian Congress on World Evangelization, in Drammen (November).

1980 World's 10 largest cities: Tokyo/Yokohama 21,854,000, New York/NENJ 15,601,000, Mexico City 13,888,000, São Paulo 12,497,000, Shanghai 11,739,000, Osaka 9,990,000, Buenos Aires 9,920,000, Los Angeles/Long Beach 9,523,000, Calcutta 9,030,000, Beijing 9,029,000.

1980 USA: 'Washington for Jesus 1980' rally brings out 500,000 charismatics and evangelicals.

1980 24th Annual Conference of Secretaries of Christian World Communions (CWCs), Geneva; 1957-1974 Geneva; 1976 London; 1977 Rome; 1980, 1982 Geneva; 1983 (27th) Sofia; 1984 (28th) Geneva; 1985 (29th) Windsor, UK, on to 1999 (43rd) Jerusalem.

1980 1st Asian Leaders Conference, Catholic Charismatic Renewal (ICCRO), on 'Feed My Sheep', Manila.

1980 USA: new generation of charismatic TV evangelists arises, including Oral Roberts (who began Pentecostal TV preaching in 1953) and son Richard, Pat Robertson, Rex Humbard, Jimmy Swaggart, James Robison, Kenneth Copeland, Paul Crouch, Jim Bakker, et alii.

1980 China: 3rd National Conference, Association of Patriotic Catholics, Beijing; forms Church Affairs Commission, and National Bishops' Conference; Catholics in China decrease from 3 million (1949) to 500,000 (1974), then increase to 6 million (1985).

1980 FR Germany: Missionary Year 1980, a coordinated effort to mobilize pastors and congregations of regional churches.

1980 Lausanne Consultation for Jewish Evangelism (LCJE) formed at Pattaya (Thailand) by 14 Jewish-Christian groups.

1980 John Paul II canonizes 93 Korean and 10 French martyrs at Seoul's Yoido Plaza, in presence of one million faithful (out of 1.7 million Korean RCs) (6 May).

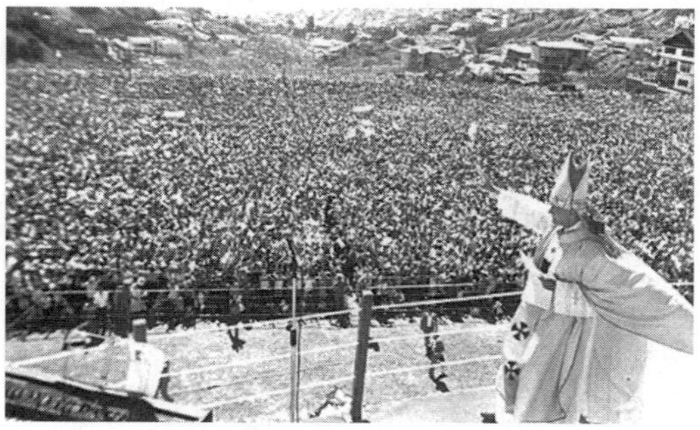

**AD 1980.** Pope preaches the gospel to a million strong multitude in Brazil.

1980 John Paul II undertakes global apostolic travels, to present the gospel to the world: over last 2 years visits Mexico, Poland, Ireland, USA, Africa, Brazil et alia; by February 1986, makes 29 official foreign pilgrimages as Catholic church's chief evangelizer; by 1989, 44 journeys; and by 1998, 80 foreign country visits completed; by 1999, 90.

1980 LCWE International Consultation on Simple Life-Style, Hoddesden, UK (March), on how adoption of biblical lifestyles could accomplish world mission.

1980 A large African indigenous charismatic church, World Evangelical Crusaders in Christ Ministries (Benin City, Nigeria), begins Operation World Begin From Here; other AIC denominations across Africa also advance similar global plans.

1980 10th United Bible Societies Council Meeting, Chiang Mai (Thailand), with 68 member societies, on theme 'God's Word: open for all' (September); over last 80 years, annual circulation of complete Bibles in all languages has risen from 5.4 million in 1900 to 36.8 million by 1980; UBS plan for decade to provide by 1990 common Bible translations in every language with over 1 million literates.

1980 Pan-Orthodox Consultation, organized through CWME, on 'Preaching and Teaching the Christian

Faith Today' at Zica monastery, Yugoslavia; on regaining Orthodox role of proclamation in world evangelistic witness (September).

1980 Third Wave of 20th-century Renewal in the Holy Spirit begins in 40 major Evangelical churches, emphasizing power evangelism, power encounters, power healing, et alia.

1980 E.R. Dayton & D.A. Fraser publish *Planning strategies for world evangelization.*

1980 30 million icons (religious paintings) still exist in USSR; but by 1992, 90% have been smuggled out, most through Moscow's Sheremetyevo Airport by bribes, and sold abroad (in 1991, sales totalled $13 million).

1980 USSR invades Afghanistan.

***Postindustrial age begins***

1980 The Aquarian Conspiracy: personal and social transformation in the 1980s, by Marilyn Ferguson.

1980 USA: re-emergence of Christian fundamentalism as a conspicuous force in North American life.

1980 1st Joint Orthodox/Roman Catholic Dialogue, on Patmos/Rhodes (28 May-4 June), forming ongoing commission of 56 (28 each side); 2nd at Munich in 1982; 3rd on Crete in 1984; 4th at Bari in 1986, 1987; then 1988 Uusi Valamo (Finland), Freising 1990.

1980 Sending messages into the past proposed: in physicist Gregory Benford's scenario *Timescape*, doomed inhabitants of a future Earth beam tachyonic (faster-than-light) signals backwards in time to warn present-day Earth- dwellers about imminent doom.

1980 1st Global Conference on the Future (3rd General Assembly, World Future Society), Toronto, on theme 'Through the '80s: thinking globally, acting locally'; with 5,000 delegates from over 45 countries (July).

1980 Total new book titles published each year increase from 269,000 (1955) to 521,000 (1970) to 726,500 (1980) to 860,000 (1990), to 980,000 by AD 2000; total scientific journals increase every 50 years by factor of 10: from 10 journals in 1750 to 100 (1800) to 1,000 (1850), 10,000 (1900), 100,000 (1950), to a projected total of 1 million titles by AD 2000.

1980 Scientists and engineers engaged in R&D (research and development) increase from (1970) 2,608,100 to (1980) 3,756,100, to 4.6 million in 1990 with annual expenditure increasing from (in 1930) US$1 billion (less than 0.1% of GWP), to (1965) $50 billion (2 (2%), to (1970) $62.1 billion, to (1980) $207.8 billion (2%), of which only 6.0% is spent in developing countries, to (AD 2000) a projected $650 billion (4%), and (by AD 2500) to 15%.

1980 Social potential movement begins, demonstrating what the human race can do together (Teilhard de Chardin, Sri Aurobindo, A.C. Clarke, Buckminster Fuller, Julian Huxley, et alii); envisages a eupsychian society (composed of self-actualizing people).

1980 Long-playing record sold with H. Lindsey's *The 1980's: Countdown to Armageddon* sees 1982 as year of killer earthquakes caused by Jupiter Effect.

1980 CBN broadcaster Robertson writes in 'Pat Robertson's perspective' that Jupiter Effect may be tied in with Russian invasion of Israel, as prophesied in Ezekiel 38.

1980 C. Taylor states in 1980 edition of *Those who remain* that Spanish king Juan Carlos I may soon be revealed as Antichrist.

1980 Deputy to Islamic Parliament in Teheran predicts Iranian victory over Iraq and march on Jerusalem 'in order to acclaim the reappearance of the Hidden Imam as the Mahdi, and to witness the reappearance of Jesus Christ and his final conversion to Islam'.

c1980 Superindustrial economies field high-tech, very large enterprises, with knowledge replacing experience; future all-bourgeois society.

1980 *Future man*, by economist Chris Morgan, visualizes world of AD 2200 with 30 billion persons living in high-rise and underwater habitats, sleeping only 2 hours each night.

1980 South India: Mahamagham religious festival attracts over two million Hindu participants every 12 years in Kumbhakonam, Tanjavur district, on river Kaveri.

1980 Gujarat Missionary Movement within Church of North India founded.

1980 3rd General Assembly, Middle East Council of Churches (MECC), held in Nicosia (Cyprus), on theme 'Thy Kingdom Come'.

1980 Peru: Shining Path, a savage Maoist guerrilla insurgency, begins in Ayacucho and kills 30,000 before 1993 collapse.

1980 10th Council Meeting/World Assembly, United Bible Societies (UBS, 68 member Bible societies), in Chiang Mai (Thailand), on theme 'God's Word: Open for All'.

1980 7th General Assembly, World Evangelical Fellowship (WEF), at Hoddesdon (England) with 141 participants from 48 countries and 34 National Evangelical Fellowships, on theme 'Serving Our Generation—Evangelical Strategy for the 1980s' (24-28 March).

1980 International Forum of Evangelical Women (IFEW/WEF) meets in London (20-23 March).

1980 Serious global plans to evangelize the world begin to emerge via denominational headquarters, boards, mission agencies; by 2000, grand total since AD 33 is 1,510; most gradually fizzle out without any announcement.

1980 3rd Forum on Bilateral Conversations (CWCs and WCC), held in Glion (Switzerland) with 24 participants; theme, how to get results of bilateral confessional dialogues accepted ('received') into all levels of church life (6-10 October).

1980 China: government-approved congresses: 1980, 3rd National Christian Conference, sponsored by TSPM, held in Nanjing with 176 participants (6-13 October); also 1980, 3rd National Congress for the Catholic Church in China, sponsored by Catholic Patriotic Association; 1986, 4th National TSPM/CCC Conference (August).

1981 IBM Personal Computer is marketed; 1983, IBM-XT is first personal computer with hard-disk storage system.

1981 Asian Lutheran Church Leaders' Conference, in Hong Kong (February).

1981 International Leaders Conference, Catholic Charismatic Renewal (ICCRO) in Rome, addressed by pope John Paul II (May).

1981 Orthodox Consultation on 'Orthodox involvement in the World Council of Churches', Sofia, Bulgaria.

1981 UBS Common Language translations now available: 107 Bibles, 136 New Testaments.

1981 Supercomputers emerge (Cray-1, Cyber 205) capable of carrying out over 100 million operations per second; total in use, 150 by 1985.

1981 Worldwide telecommunications network is now largest machine in the world, with 480 million telephones, 1.2 million telex terminals, data networks and other special systems.

1981 USA places or receives annually 265 million overseas telephone calls, most by satellite, rising to 370 million by 1983.

1981 American Festival of Evangelism, Kansas City; 14,500 participants including 8,000 pastors, evangelists and church leaders; 200 seminars on evangelism, discipling, and ministry (July).

1981 3rd Norwegian Congress on World Evangelization.

1981 3rd Nigeria National Congress on Evangelism (August).

1981 Delhi Conference of Theology (EATWOT-5), in New Delhi, on 'The irruption of the Third World: challenge to theology' (17-29 August).

1981 August: one year after assembling development team, IBM enters personal computer market; spends $36 million on advertising it; by July 1983 has captured 21% of the $7.5 billion US market for personal computers; 40% of worldwide market for computers, produces 65% of all mainframes; 1982—sells 200,000 PCs, 1983—sells 800,000.

1981 4th Assembly, Pacific Conference of Churches (PCC), in Nuku'alofa, Tonga, on 'The challenge of the '80s and the Pacific churches'.

1981 7th Assembly, Christian Conference of Asia (CCA), in Bangalore, India, on 'Life in Christ with People'.

1981 World's largest banks: (1) Credit Agricole de France (assets of $105 billion), (2) Bank of America.

1981 Total artificial Earth satellites launched since 1957: 2,725 (70% for military purposes).

1981 Total nuclear explosions since 1945: 1,321 (551 above ground).

1981 Broadcasting: radio receivers increase from 535 million (1965) to 1,320 million (1981) or 293 per thousand people; TV receivers from 186 million (1965) to 546 million (1981) or 121 per thousand.

1981 Human knowledge is now expanding at rate of 200 million words per hour (1,750 billion words per year).

1981 Online bibliographic databases total over 190, with 40 million unique references (books, articles) increasing by 6 million a year; equals 50% of mankind's collective memory.

1981 14th Assembly (Centennial Conference), World Methodist Conference (WMC, with 62 Methodist denominations), meets in Honolulu (Hawaii, 21-28 July), endorses WMC's World Evangelism Committee's Continuing Plan for the Mission to the 80s (Decade of Evangelism); 1982 founds Institute for World Evangelism (Atlanta, USA) which holds seminars around world.

1981 World Conference of Religions held in Cochin, India, with theme 'Religions and Man'; Christians, Hindus, Buddhists, Muslims, Sikhs, Jains, Jews and Baha'is present.

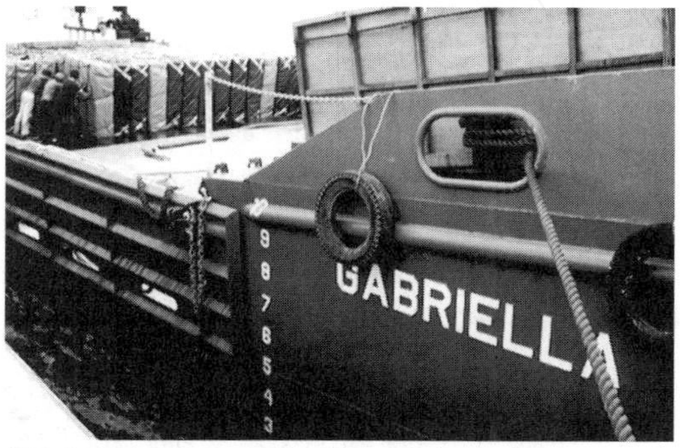


**1981.** Operation Pearl: 20,000 believers on China coast unload barge with 1 million Chinese Bibles at night, undetected.

1981 Muslim-Christian dialogue on 'Mysticism in Christianity and in Islam', in diocese of Ajmer (India) under auspices of Catholic Bishops' Conference of India.

1981 Operation Pearl, largest Bible-smuggling operation ever, organized by Open Doors: 200 tons of Bibles illegally landed by barge off Swatow, China, then taken away by 20,000 Chinese Christians undetected.

1981 South Korea: Roman Catholic project 'Year of Evangelization of your Neighbour' in all parishes results in 59% increase in annual baptisms; 57,535 catechumens, 71,005 young people in correspondence courses; slogan 'Two Million by 1984'.

1981 West Germany: large evangelistic rallies continue annually, with huge youth attendance; alternating between Protestant Kirchentagen—1981 Hamburg ('Be ye reconciled to God'), 1983 Nuremburg, 1985 Dusseldorf (130,000 enrolled for 4-day period, 400,000 attenders)—and RC Katholikentagen at Munich and Cologne (1984, et alia); since 1981 East Germans once again permitted to attend.

1981 UK: Evangelical Missionary Alliance sponsors conference on 'Reaching Unreached Peoples: breaking new ground in areas of neglect', at High Leigh, Hertford (November).

1981 International Consultation on 'The Community of Women and Men in the Church', in Sheffield, UK.

1981 3rd Assembly, Caribbean Conference of Churches, in Willemstad, Curaçao, Netherlands Antilles, on theme 'For thine is the kingdom, the power and the glory'.

1981 LWF/DCC Working Party on Ministry to Migrants in Europe, with its 15 million migrant laborers (5 million in West Germany).

1981 China: Protestant churches mushroom spectacularly from 2 open TSPM churches in 1979 to 3,400 open TSPM churches (parishes with central building) by 1985; and total Christian community of all churches (TSPM, RC, independent) from 2 million to 52 million in 6 years (a growth rate of 72% p.a.).

1981 German Evangelical theologian P. Beyerhaus publishes *It is harvest time* (a textbook on world evangelization).

1981 Evangelize the World by Computer Dialing: a scheme, proposed by several agencies, involving continuous automatic dialing through world's telephone directories and giving recorded messages to whoever replies.

1981 2nd Chinese Congress on World Evangelization (CCOWE), on 'Life and Ministry', with over 1,500 church leaders, Singapore (June).

1981 World Evangelization Strategy Work Group begun, formed by Baptist World Alliance; numerous meetings, papers; publishes World Evangelization Now!; presses idea of a Baptist Fund for World Evangelization (to support Third-World missionaries); 1988, BWA General Council announces 'Vision 2000: Jesus Christ for All People' as 'a vision for encouraging world evangelization by the year 2000 AD'.

1981 Missiologist H. Conn writes *Bible studies on world evangelization and the simple life-style*, with thesis that the goal can only be reached through the latter.

1981 Mission to Unreached Peoples (USA) begun under original name Gooddeeds.

1981 Dominion Video Satellite (Dominion Network) incorporated in Florida (USA) to provide Christian radio/TV programs over DBS system (direct broadcast satellites), based on Great Commission, DBS as the angel of Revelation 14:6, 30-inch portable dish receivers, and bypassing of secular control over TV.

1981 SEDOS Research Seminar on 'Future of Mission', Rome, with representatives of 45 Catholic missionary institutes from 6 continents; produces 'an agenda for future planning, study and research in mission' (8-19 March).

1981 Planetary Initiative for the World We Choose (UN-related) set up 'to work for a new and unified world order' of New Age socialism; recognized as part of international New Age Movement with network of thousands of organizations and hundreds of millions of members, proliferating in Western world at astounding rate, expecting a new evolutionary development, a quantum leap in evolution towards Point Omega, to Homo Noeticus (Intellectual Man), a new and higher form of humanity.

1981 Massive increases in business paperwork produced in USA, from 72 billion pieces of office documents in 1981, to a projected 250 billion in 1991 (50% electronic), to 1 trillion by 2000 (93% generated in digital form).

1981 C. Deal publishes *The day and hour Jesus will return*, moving Christ's return back to 1989.

1981 Southwest Radio Church's newsletter *Gospel truth* points to Libya's Moammar Qadhafi as Antichrist.

1981 Aurelio Peccei writes *One hundred pages for the future: reflections of the President of the Club of Rome.*

1981 *The Islamic understanding of death and resurrection*, written by USA Islamic scholars Jane I. Smith & Yvonne Y. Haddad.

1981 Zoologist Dougal Dixon writes *After Man: a zoology of the future*; and in 1990, *Man after Man: an anthropology of the future*, describing future evolution to AD 5 million; profusely illustrated.

1981 9th World Congress of FIT/IFT (Federation Internationale des Traducteurs/International Federation of Translators), with input from IOUTN, UNESCO, et alia, in Warsaw (Poland).

1981 *Islamic Messianism: the idea of the Mahdi in Twelver Shi'ism*, by A.A. Sachedina.

1981 *Judging the future* by J.A. Dator & C. Bezold.

1981 1st Annual Conference on God: 'The Contemporary Discussion', sponsored by Unification Church (Korea) and New Ecumenical Research Association; subsequent God conferences 1982 in Florida, 1983 Puerto Rico, 1984 Korea, 1986 California.

1981 28th Assembly, World Student Christian Federation (WSCF), held in San Francisco (CA).

1981 4th International Consultation of United and Uniting Churches, sponsored by WCC (in series from 1st in 1967), held in Colombo (Sri Lanka) on theme 'Growing Towards Consensus and Commitment', with Protestant, RC, and Orthodox participation (18-25 November); from 1947-81, 75 denominations have successfully united in 25 churches, and 100 others in 17 countries are in progress.

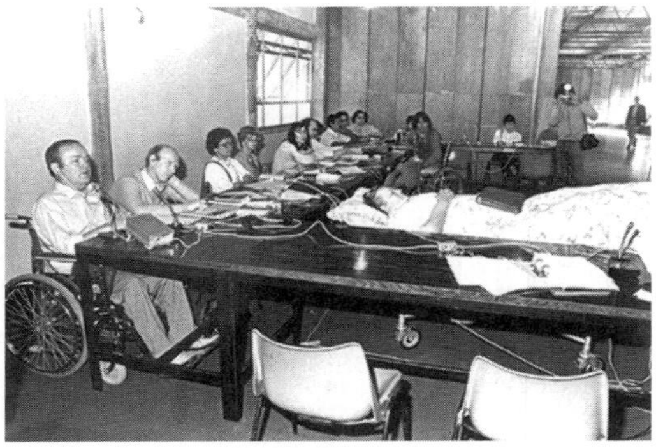

**AD 1981.** São Paulo, Brazil: Consultation on Humanity and Wholeness of Persons with Disabilities (November).

1981 International Year of Disabled Persons, for the world's 450 million persons (10% of globe; 80% in the developing world) mentally or physically disabled.

1981 4th General Assembly, All Africa Conference of Churches (after 1st in Kampala 1963, 2nd in Abidjan 1969, 3rd in Lusaka 1974), held in Nairobi on theme 'Following the Light of Jesus Christ', with 500 participants from 118 member churches (2-12 August).

1981 2nd European Ecumenical Conference, organized by CEC and CCEE, held in Logumkloster (Denmark), on prayer, the spiritual life, peace, and reconciliation, with 80 participants (16-20 November).

1981 First international Christian/Hindu Dialogue, sponsored by NCCI and WCC, held in Rajpur (India) (30 May-6 June).

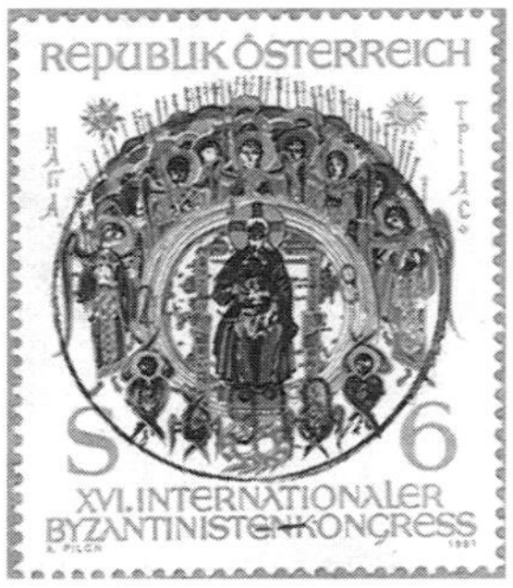


**AD 1981.** Interest in Byzantine and Greek Orthodox studies and research impels ongoing congress series.

1981 16th International Byzantine Congress, Vienna (Austria).

1981 8th World Council of YMCAs, in Estes Park, on theme 'Christ: Renewal and Hope'.

1982 'Pentecost over Europe', European ecumenical charismatic congress, at Strasbourg (France); 25,000 attenders, 80% RCs and organized by RCs (held over Pentecost).

1982 Brazilian National Congress on Evangelization: Commission on Evangelization formed; yearly conferences from 1985-1991 planned and organized.

1982 American Leprosy Missions announces 13-point plan to eradicate Hansen's Disease (leprosy) and to cure world's 11,500,000 lepers by AD 2006; European leprosy agencies demur; 1984, plan abandoned, president and staff resign.

1982 German Association of Evangelical Missions meets on theme 'Hidden Peoples' (February).

1982 1st Conference of Evangelical Mission Theologians from the Two-Thirds World, Bangkok (March); LCWE-sponsored but with critical stance.

1982 Consultation of Evangelicals in Latin America, in Panama, with 200 representatives from 23 countries, resulting in organizing of Confraternity of Latin American Evangelicals (CONELA), of anti-ecumenical stance, linking 98 Evangelical denominations (April).

1982 IIIrd Conference of Religionists on Peace (initiated by Russian Orthodox Church), Moscow (May).

1982 LCWE Consultation on the Relationship between Evangelism and Social Responsibility (CRESR), Grand Rapids, USA (June).

1982 Ignoring global Islamic organizations, Iran convenes rival Islamic Congresses: World Congress of Friday Imams, Conference on Islamic Thought (from 1983), and International Conference to Support the Islamic Revolution of the People of Palestine (from 1991).

1982 Consultation on 'Just development for fullness of life: an Orthodox approach'; coins terms 'microdiaconia' (service to individuals) and 'macrodiaconia' (service to societies and structures); in Kiev, USSR.

1982 African Conference on Evangelism and Education (All Africa Baptist Fellowship and BWA), at Tigoni, Kenya, on theme 'Africa for Christ' (7-9 July).

1982 Asian Conference on Church Renewal, Seoul, Korea (18-22 August); results in inauguration at Hong Kong in July 1983 of Evangelical Fellowship of Asia (EFA) with 12 member bodies (8 being national fellowships).

1982 13th Pentecostal World Conference, Nairobi, Kenya; theme 'Alive in the Spirit in Our World'; peak attenders 18,000 (September).

1982 International Old Catholic Congress, in Vienna (September).

1982 Pontifical Council for the Laity holds Meeting on 'Men and Women in Evangelization', Rocca di Papa, Rome (2-6 October).

1982 IBM spends $3 billion on research, development and engineering (=9% of sales), subscribes to virtually every major computer market-research service, and has a worldwide intelligence-gathering network that includes economists and market analysts.

1982 1,440,000 microcomputers sold during year (over 1 million in USA, a 70% leap over 1981 sales).

1982 Largest tent ever (seating 40,000) erected in South Africa for Apostolic Faith Mission evangelists under Reinhard Bonnke (a German).

1982 Thanksgiving '82, yearlong evangelistic crusade ending in Guatemala City Crusade (evangelist Luis Palau) with audience of 700,000, largest crowd for any single evangelistic meeting in Latin America (November).

1982 3rd World Hindu Conference, on 'The Search for Religious Identity and Dialogue'.

1982 2nd Asian Leaders Conference, Catholic Charismatic Renewal (ICCRO), on 'Evangelize Asia for Christ', Singapore.

1982 2nd Japan Congress of Evangelism, Kyoto.

1982 7th World Congress, Theosophical Society, Nairobi (December).

1982 UBS Africa Regional Assembly, Nairobi, Kenya, on theme 'God's Word open for All in Africa', with 170 representatives from 45 countries (1-8 December).

1982 Constituting Assembly, Latin American Council of Churches (CLAI), at Huampani, Lima (Peru), on theme 'Commitment to the Kingdom'; 110 member denominations.

1982 Consultation on Mission in the Context of Poverty and Situations of Affluence (sponsored by CCA), in Manila (10-14 December).

1982 Mission '83, 3rd Missionary Congress for European Youth, sponsored by the European Missionary Association (TEMA), on theme 'Let us rise and build', in Lausanne; over 7,000 present from 42 countries (28 December-2 January 1983).

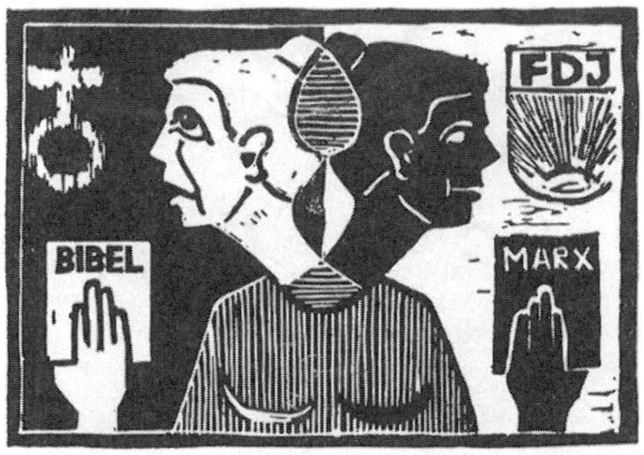


**AD 1982.** In anti-Christian poster from East Berlin, student rejects Bible and turns to Marxism.

1982 Council of European Bishops' Conferences (CCEE) begins 3-year discussion of 'evangelization in a secularized continent'.

1982 LWF/CCC Interregional Consultation on Mission and Evangelism, Stavanger, Norway, with over 140 participants from 39 countries (18-26 May), after 6 regional Lutheran consultations: 1978 Loccum (Germany), 1979 Caribbean, 1979 Manila, 1980 Monrovia (Liberia), 1980 Bogota, 1980 Tallin (Estonia).

1982 WCC Faith and Order Commission meets in Lima, Peru, and initiates global 5-year reflection by member churches on BEM (Baptism, Eucharist and Ministry) document.

1982 Project 223 begun by YWAM, 'to establish a vital permanent ministry in every country on Earth', in 2 stages: (1) trailblazing, sending teams on evangelistic trips, one team to each of the world's 223 countries, involving initially 15,000 short-termers (2 weeks to 1 year) each year; completed in 1988 with No. 222 (Pitcairn Islands) and No. 223 (Svalbard & Jan Mayen Islands); also Project 300 to reach the 300 world-class megacities, with YWAM presence in 69 by 1988; and (2) pioneering (permanent residence) in 90 countries by 1988; with AD 2000 goal of 100,000 workers, aiming to fulfill the Great Commission in 25 years by AD 2011; 1988, among many new Projects introduced in Target 2000: Great Commission Torch Run, begun in Jerusalem on Easter Sunday, to involve 1 million runners.

1982 1st ICFG Global Leadership Conference (Los Angeles) launches 'Harvest Vision: 1990', a plan produced by Foursquare Missions International to reach 160 hidden people groups, enter 76 new countries, and total 2.1 million ICFG members, all by 1990.

1982 5th Conference, International Association for Mission Studies (IAMS), Bangalore, India, on theme 'Christ's Mission to the Multitudes: Salvation, Suffering and Struggle' (4-9 January); IAMS exists 'for the scholarly study of Christian witness and its impact in the world'.

1982 Publication of *World Christian encyclopedia: a comparative survey of churches and religions in the modern world, AD 1900-2000*, designed deliberately as global survey to document world evangelization, the unfinished task, and rise of a global evangelization movement.

1982 LCWE Chicago Consultation on Terminology concerning Unreached Peoples; subsequently, clear distinction drawn between (a) 'ethnolinguistic peoples' (being legitimate targets of church-planting efforts to establish beachheads with as goal in each a viable organized church fellowship able to evangelize its own culture, and (b) 'bridges' or 'bridge people groups' (smaller social or functional groupings affording opportunities for evangelism without church planting) (25-26 March).

1982 World Satellite Evangelism (motto 'Using Mass Media to Reach the Unreached of the World for Christ') begun in Tulsa, OK, 'mobilizing media to reach every person in every home with the gospel' especially in closed countries; forms a global media task force in 50 nations, starting Christian universities and other centers.

1982 1st Korean World Mission Congress, in Pasadena, CA (USA), with 300 delegates from Korean churches on 5 continents, 'to unite Koreans worldwide for the Great Commission of Christ' and 'to establish a Korean World Mission Coordinating Center' (17-30 May).

1982 Major document *Mission and evangelism: an ecumenical affirmation* produced in Geneva by CWME and officially promulgated by Central Committee of WCC (July).

1982 Institute for World Evangelism established in Atlanta, GA (USA), as major long-range achievement of World Evangelism Committee, World Methodist Council; its 1987 3rd biennial International Seminar, Atlanta, on theme 'The Holy Spirit and World Evangelization' draws over 100 delegates from 33 countries; authentic Wesleyan evangelism, with 2-fold witness to personal salvation and social redemption, given a new credibility and acceptance in Methodism worldwide.

1982 *Panta ta Ethni* (To All Peoples) begins publication under Apostoliki Diakonia (Church of Greece).

1982 IFMA Frontier Peoples Committee formed; attempts to survey constituency of 96 IFMA member mission agencies in USA and Canada, but little substantial results; 1988, 71st IFMA Annual Meeting in Hamilton (Ontario) takes as its theme 'Countdown 2000' (12-15 September).

1982 EFMA Missions Consultation on 'The Challenge of Our Task', in Colorado Springs, USA (27-30 September), based on *World Christian encyclopedia;* 1989, EFMA Mission Executives Retreat on 'Evangelizing the World by AD 2000', in Colorado Springs (25-28 September).

1982 Falkland Islands conflict between Britain and Argentina.

1982 Information scientist Parker Rossman describes future global electronic encyclopedia; 1990 with R. Kirby writes *Christians and the world of computers*, 1992 writes *The emerging worldwide electronic university.*

1982 First US-Soviet spacebridge, the US Festival linking rock music groups in southern California and Moscow; 5 or 6 spacebridges take place each year; such telesummitry being TV at its best.

1982 2nd UNESCO World Conference on Cultural Policies, held in Mexico City.

1982 A.C. Clarke writes sequel to *2001* entitled *2010: Odyssey Two*, in which Chinese, Russian and USA spaceships encounter huge alien monolith in orbit round moons of Jupiter.

1982 Futurism and religion surveyed in 'Evolution of the futurology of Christianity and religion, 1893-1980' (*World Christian encyclopedia* 1982*);* of 280 books and articles listed, 140 deal with future of Christian mission.

1982 Prophecy teacher Mary S. Relfe publishes *The new money system* putting forth Henry Kissinger, king Juan Carlos I, John Paul II, and Egypt's Anwar Sadat as Antichrist candidates; 'Number of the Beast' (666) is already being used in supermarket bar codes; predicts World War III in 1989, Great Tribulation in 1990, and Jesus' return in 1997.

1982 Y. Rubinsky and I. Wiseman publish *A history of the end of the world* (New York), holding that Nature has no vested interest in keeping man alive.

1982 Dutch diplomat J.G. de Beus publishes *Shall we make the year 2000? The decisive challenge to western civilization.*

1982 G. Gappert & R.V. Knight edit *Cities in the 21st century.*

1982 Australian radical futurist B. Jones writes *Sleepers, wake! technology and the future of work.*

1982 *Megatrends: ten new directions transforming our lives* written by trends popularist J. Naisbitt; 1990, with P. Aburdene, *Megatrends 2000: ten new directions for the 1990s*; and 1992, *Megatrends for women* by Aburdene & Naisbitt.

1982 *The science in science fiction*, by P.D. Nicholls.

1982 *The evolutionary journey: a personal guide to a positive future* by Barbara M. Hubbard.

1982 *The Omni Future almanac*, edited by R. Weil.

1982 Landmark WCC text on *Baptism, eucharist and ministry* produced at Lima conference.

1982 2nd Preconciliar Panorthodox Conference.

1982 Youth Seminar on World Religions (YSWR), an annual series with 150 participants.

1982 Founding, at University of Aberdeen (Scotland), of Centre for the Study of Christianity in the Non-Western World; 1987, moves to University of Edinburgh.

1982 1st Pan-European Charismatic Congress, Strasbourg '82 (held at Pentecost); 20,000 attenders; scandal of Christian divisions discussed; 1998, 2nd Ecumenical Charismatic Meeting, in Paris with 12,000 participants.

1982 21st General Council, World Alliance of Reformed Churches (WARC) meets in Ottawa (Canada), with theme 'Thine is the Kingdom, the Power, and the Glory'; declares White South African dogma of *apartheid* to be a sin, suspends membership of Dutch Reformed Church for its support of it (August).

1983 6th International Conference, Ecumenical Association of Third World Theologians (EATWOT-6): Dialogue between First and Third World Theologians, in Geneva, on 'Doing theology in a divided world' (5-13 January).

1983 1st World Conference of Religious Workers for Saving the Sacred Gift of Life from Nuclear Catastrophe, in Moscow convened by Russian Orthodox Church for all religions, on 'The economic and moral implications of a nuclear freeze' (March); 1984, 2nd World Conference, in Moscow on 'Space without weapons' (April); 1985, 3rd World Conference, on 'New dangers'.

1983 Mission England, a 2-year evangelistic crusade involving most denominations.

1983 SEDOS Dialogue in Mission, in Rome (March).

1983 Mission Congress '83, sponsored by US Catholic Mission Association (USCMA), Baltimore, on 'Inculturation, Dialogue, Liberation' (17-21 March).

1983 2nd Latin American Missionary Congress (COMLA-2), sponsored by CELAM, in Tlaxcala, Mexico, on theme 'Together with Mary, Missionaries of Christ' (16-21 May).

1983 Canadian Consultation on Evangelism (sponsored by North American LCWE), Waterloo (7-10 June).

1983 Conference on the Nature and Mission of the Church, at Wheaton, IL, USA, convened by World Evangelical Fellowship, with 370 participants from 60 countries, and theme 'I will build My Church' (June).

1983 11th World Congress, International Council of Christian Churches (ICCC), at Cape May, USA (June).

1983 Latin American Consultation on Evangelism and Social Responsibility (sponsored by CONELA), Panama (July).

1983 IJCIC-LWF Consultation (International Jewish Committee on Interreligious Consultations—Lutheran World Federation), Stockholm (July).

1983 6th Assembly of WCC in Vancouver, Canada, on theme 'Jesus Christ the Life of the World'; 900 delegates (300 being women) from 310 member denominations, 850 journalists, 15,000 attenders at opening service (24 July-10 August).

1983 Caribbean Baptist Fellowship Congress of Evangelism, at Moneague, Jamaica (5-13 August).

1983 2nd International Christian Youth Conference, World Methodist Council, in Bahamas; over 1,000 delegates from 47 nations (August).

1983 2nd LCWE Consultation on Jewish Evangelism (LCJE) at Newmarket (UK), with 52 delegates representing 17 Jewish missions (September).

1983 Assembly on Dialogue with Islam (Muslim/Catholic) in Varanasi, India.

1983 6th General Assembly, Ordinary Synod of Bishops, Rome, on 'Reconciliation and penance in the mission of the Church'; 221 member bishops (September- October); 1983 is celebrated as Holy Year, being Jubilee of the Redemption.

1983 1st Brazil National Congress on Evangelization, Belo Horizonte, with over 2,000 delegates (31 October-5 November).

1983 YWAM (Youth With a Mission, begun 1960) with 14,000 young short-term workers serves as world's largest evangelistic agency.

1983 13 million computers in use in world, worth $200 billion.

1983 Canadian Catholic Mission Congress (Entraide Missionnaire), Montreal.

1983 IRAS project (InfraRed Astronomical Satellite), a US$100-million telescope supercooled to 2 Kelvin above absolute zero, maps massive infrared activity throughout Universe, discovers 20,000 new galaxies (99% of whose energy is infrared), large numbers of planetary systems, starburst galaxies, stars in formation, and vast amounts of cold interstellar dust throughout Galaxy.

1983 SOMA Pan-African Conference (Sharing of Ministries Abroad) for Anglophone Charismatic Renewal Leaders, Nairobi, Kenya (October).

1983 After 14 years' negotiations, United Presbyterian Church in the USA, and Presbyterian Church in the US, formally unite as Presbyterian Church (USA), with 4.8 million members.

1983 SVD Missiologists' Meeting for Asia, in Tagaytay City, Philippines; request by FABC bishops for establishment of an Asian Center of Missiology (11-18 December).

1983 World Baptist Congress on Urban Evangelism, in Niteroi, Brazil (26 June-3 July).

1983 Lengthy document 'A global strategy for world evangelization by AD 2000': list of 105 steps or stages or aspects' produced for Southern Baptist Foreign Mission Board by WERC (Nairobi).

1983 1st International Conference for Itinerant Evangelists, Amsterdam; theme 'Do the Work of an Evangelist'; 3,800 evangelists from 132 nations (July).

1983 Global Mapping Project started on USCWM campus, to assist churches with data and maps, with as objective 'Visualizing the Task of World Evangelization'.

1983 Lumen 2000 launched as Catholic global television evangelism agency, based in Dallas (USA) and Vatican City, 'to preach the gospel of Jesus to the uttermost parts of the Earth, spreading the love of Jesus around the globe'; 1986, in more than 50 countries.

1983 Committee on the Holy Spirit & Frontier Missions (CHSFM) begun in conjunction with USCWM to involve charismatics in frontier missions among hidden peoples; defunct by 1985.

1983 L.E. Keyes writes *The last age of missions: a survey of Third World mission societies*, describing world evangelization by 15,000 missionaries in over 400 Third-World locally-supported societies and boards (especially from Brazil); since 1940, movement has mushroomed, with AD 2000 projection of 100,000 non-Western missionaries from 1,000 non-Western mission agencies.

1983 New Focus Incorporated founded (San Bernardino, CA) as 'a Great Commission ministry committed to sports media strategies to reach the whole world with the gospel by the year 2000'; geared especially to TV specials at Olympics in 1988 in Korea, 1992 in Barcelona (Spain), 1996, and 2000.

1983 4 high-energy physicists/cosmologists, D.A. Dicus et alii, write 'The future of the Universe: a cosmological forecast of events through the year $10^{100}$', with 3 alternative scenarios (the Universe is either open, flat, or closed) (*Scientific American*).

1983 D. Burnham writes *The rise of the computer state*, with grim scenario of life in the USA in AD 2020.

1983 2nd UN Decade to Combat Racism and Racial Discrimination (1983-1993).

1983 United Nations Decade of Disabled Persons (1983-1992).

1983 Catholic Association of Faith, Intercession, Repentance and Evangelism (FIRE) founded to promote Catholic evangelism; by 1991, 65 rallies held worldwide, with 300,000 attenders.

1983 USA president launches 20-year experimental Strategic Defense Initiative (SDI, or 'Star Wars') costing $1 trillion, as shield against USSR nuclear missiles.

1983 *Prophecy in early Christianity and the ancient Mediterranean world*, by D.E. Aune.

1983 *Visions of desirable societies*, by Eleonora B. Masini.

1983 *Looking forward: a guide to futures research*, by O. Helmer.

1983 *Business planning for an uncertain future*, by R. Amara & A.J. Lipinski.

1983 27th Meeting, Conference of Christian World Communions (CWCs), in Sofia (Bulgaria) (24-27 October).

1983 Brazil: formation of National Council of Christian Churches in Brazil (CONIC), including Roman Catholic, Christian Reformed, Anglican, Lutheran (IECLB), and Methodist jurisdictions.

1983 Conference of Protestant Churches of Latin Countries of Europe, held in Sommieres (France), voices uneasiness over Roman Catholic domination, popular religiosity, et alia (3-4 June).

1983 Darmstadt UBS Conference on Braille Scriptures, first widely representative global gathering for agencies producing or using Braille scriptures for the world's 42 million blind persons; 39 Bible societies and 43 other agencies publish in 83 languages, with complete Braille Bibles in only 17 languages.

1983 Germany: 20th National Protestant Kirchentag, held in Hanover, on theme 'Turn and Live', with 140,000 present (8-12 June)

1984 Southern Africa Missiological Society Congress on 'The challenge of the African Independent Churches', at Krugersdorp, Johannesburg; 100 participants (January).

1984 Collective brain power of all computers now doubling every 2 years.

1984 First commercial service of computer-aided translation available (English/French/German/Spanish/other European languages).

1984 USA: computers in homes rise from nil in 1978 to 10 million in 5 years, then by 1995 to 80 million.

1984 Central Asia: Apocalyptic Buddhists propound cosmology of Wheel of Time Tantra (Apocalyptic Vehicle); aggressiveness must be transcended in order to reach Shambhala, the next step in human evolution.

1984 World debt from Western banks loaned to Third-World nations now $700 billion: 30% has been stolen in large amounts and resides in a few personal or numbered accounts in Western world, 30% more has been stolen locally in smaller sums, and 20% more has been deliberately mismanaged for personal gain.

1984 Consultation on Caste and the Church, sponsored by EFI/EFA, with 33 leaders in Bangalore (9-12 February).

1984 India: conclusion of Project Calvary, 2nd Every Home Crusade (EHC) campaign to reach every home in nation.

1984 2nd All-Asian Conference on Christian Art (organized by Asian Christian Art Association), at Mt Makeling, Philippines, on 'The Magnificat in Asia' (23- 30 March).

1984 USA: American Museum of Natural History holds exhibition 'Ancestors: Four Million Years of Humanity', in New York (16 April-9 September).

1984 International Festival of Christian Radio, at National Catholic Radio & TV Center, Hatch End, London (29 April-4 May).

1984 6th International Convention of Life Line (network of telephone counseling services), on 'Perspectives on the human spirit', at Hershey, PA, USA (24- 28 May).

1984 Guatemala: DAWN (Discipling A Whole Nation) Congress held as whole new wave of evangelism and church planting sweeps nation; goal to double Evangelical churches from 7,500 to 15,000 by 1990 (May).

1984 SVD Missiological Conference 'First Evangelization Today', St Augustin, Germany (Whitsun).

1984 ACC-6: 6th Meeting, Anglican Consultative Council, in Badagry, Nigeria (17-27 July).

1984 XIth Assembly, Mennonite World Conference, in Strasbourg (France), with over 7,000 participants, on theme 'God's People Serve in Hope' (24-29 July).

1984 Over 30 national and 8 regional LCWE conferences on world evangelization, plus intensive prayer, commitment and planning, are organized for 5-year period leading into 1989 ICOWE II.

1984 World Methodist Camp Meeting, sponsored by WMC, at Ocean Grove, NJ (USA), led by evangelist Alan Walker; 5,000 present (August).

1984 Congress 1984, International Association for Reformed Faith and Action (IARFA), in Lausanne (2-8 August).

1984 13th International Lutheran Conference on the Holy Spirit (ILCOHS), in Minneapolis; 12,000 participants (15-19 August).

1984 Conference of the International Council for the Promotion of Christian Higher Education, in Breukelen, Netherlands (15-22 August).

1984 1st World Congress, International Christian Studies Association, in Los Angeles, USA (24-26 August).

1984 2nd International Conference on Christian Parapsychology, sponsored by Churches' Fellowship for Psychical and Spiritual Studies, in London (9-11 September).

1984 6th International Colloquy on Carthusian History and Spirituality, in Grenoble, France (12-15 September).

1984 Middle East Christian Leadership Assembly (MECLA), Cyprus (September).

1984 Congress on the Evangelization of the Caribbean (CONECAR), Kingston, Jamaica, with 600 participants from 29 countries (September).

1984 2nd World Congress on Religious Liberty, Rome (under International Religious Liberty Association); 300 participants from 42 countries on theme 'Freedom of Religion and Belief—Basis of Peace' (3-6 September).

1984 French Catholic Mission Congress, Lisieux (France).

1984 Communist Party of Tibet concedes religion still of key importance, orders immediate rebuilding of 200 temples and reviving of Tibetan culture; 1985, pays for new printings of Buddhist scriptures including 1,100-volume Lamaist Kanjur.

1984 Series of conferences for 5,000 Spanish-speaking evangelists in 15 cities in Central and South America (July-September).

1984 Since World War II, over 150 small wars have claimed 10 million lives.

1984 8th European Charismatic Leaders' Conference, Nidelbad, Switzerland (19 September).

1984 Nigeria: Mission to the Nation held across Nigeria, sponsored by Methodists under evangelist Alan Walker (October).

1984 Evangelism and Education Conference, Asian Baptist Fellowship, in Penang, Malaysia; over 80 delegates from Asia.

1984 Mexico: 2nd National Youth Conference, Catholic Charismatic Renewal, with 18,000 young people, Guadalajara (November).

1984 10th World Congress, International Federation of Translators (FIT/IFT) held in Vienna (Austria); close links with IOUTN, WBIT, UNESCO, et alia (19 August).

1984 Work begins on large new inerrantist, user-friendly translation of whole Bible into modern American English, the Holman Christian Standard Bible (CSB), with interdenominational team of over 80 biblical scholars begun by A.L. Farstad: NT finished by 2001, Bible by 2004.

1984 Consultation of Christian Councils in West Africa, on Christian-Muslim Relations, in Monrovia, Liberia

(25-28 November).
1984 USA: Urbana '84, 14th International Student Missions Convention, at Urbana, on theme 'Faithful in Christ Jesus', with 18,145 students and missionaries (December).
1984 London, Tokyo, Hong Kong open world's first operational teleports (ground control for massive information transportation and routing via satellite); 1985, Texas teleport (San Antonio), followed by 20 others in USA, 10 in Japanese cities, others in 40 other countries.
1984 10th Baptist Youth World Conference (BWA), in Buenos Aires.
1984 Frustration at slow progress towards organic church union leads to federation approaches: (1) Council of Churches in Indonesia, with 54 member denominations, changes name to Communion of Churches in Indonesia; (2) Federation of Christian Churches in Madagascar (including RC Church); (3) 1985, Christian Federation of Malaysia (RC Church, Council of Churches in Malaysia, National Evangelical Christian Fellowship).
1984 Britain: major ecumenical venture 'Not Strangers But Pilgrims' involving over 30 denominations including RCs, Anglicans, Black pentecostals, to formulate ecumenical policy for the future.
1984 5th International Leaders Conference, Catholic Charismatic Renewal, in Rome, attended by pope John Paul II (May); also ICCRO Worldwide Priests Retreat, in Vatican attended by 6,000 priests and 80 bishops and cardinals (October); 1990, 2nd Worldwide Priests Retreat, in Rome (14-18 September).
1984 LCWE International Prayer Assembly for World Evangelization, Seoul, Korea (June); title, 'Seeking God's Face for a Movement of Prayer for the World'; 3,200 participants from 69 nations.
1984 Ethnic Chinese Congress on World Evangelization (ECCOWE), in Honolulu, with 144 delegates (5-12 July).
1984 *International journal of frontier missions* (Pasadena, USA) begun to further goal of reaching world's unreached peoples; 1988, circulation 500.
1984 STEP (Strategy to Every People) Programme introduced by WEC International, calling for '800 for the 80s' (800 new WEC workers for the 1980s), evangelizing 45 new peoples through resident teams; original name 'Worldwide Evangelization Crusade' now changed to 'Worldwide Evangelization for Christ' because 90% of new goals are among Muslim peoples.
1984 3rd Plenary Assembly, World Catholic Federation for the Biblical Apostolate, in Bangalore, India, on theme 'Would that all of God's People were Prophets'; 120 delegates from 55 countries, representing WCFBA's 61 member national Bible organizations (full members) and 125 associate member organizations (12-25 August); 1988, theme 'The Bible and the New Evangelization'.
1984 Venezuelan Baptist Convention launches plan named Baptist World Discipleship Movement.
1984 IVCF missions director J.E. Kyle edits volume of essays, *The unfinished task* (Regal).
1984 Report 'Twenty-one Strategies for Lausanne' produced by LCWE Strategy Working Group.
1984 Costa Rica: interdenominational missions society begun by 14 denominations, 1986 formalized as Federación Misionera Evangélica Costarricense (FEDEMEC), launches campaign 'Unidos en Cristo Evangelizando las Naciones' specifically 'From Costa Rica to the Uttermost Parts of the Earth', aiming to mobilize 10,000 world prayer missionaries and to send out 500 missionaries to 25 unreached peoples by AD 2000.
1984 1st World Youth Day, attended by 250,000 in Rome, all wearing white sailor hats inscribed with words of John Paul II 'Open your doors to the Redeemer!'; subsequently organized annually by Pontifical Council for the Laity; 2nd World Youth Day, with 500,000 in Santiago de Compostela (Spain); 6th in 1991, a million in Czestochowa, Jasna Gora (Poland), with 70,000 youth from USSR: 8th in 1993, 400,000 in Denver (USA).
1984 Religious Futurists' Network (RFN) Conference on 'Religious Visions of the 21st Century', at 5th General Assembly, World Future Society on 'A Global Assessment of Problems and Opportunities', in Washington, DC (11-14 June); majoring on global nuclearization, and global economic disparities.
1984 European 3-satellite project studies solar wind, which sweeps through space at over 1 million km/hour.
1984 D. Wingrove edits *The science fiction source book* (New York), arranging and analyzing 880 authors, 2,500 novels and short stories.
1984 *The encyclopedia of science fiction movies*, compiled by P. Hardy.
1984 *Making the future work*, by J. Diebold.
1984 *Future man: brave new world or genetic nightmare?* by B.M. Stableford.
1984 Argentina: large-scale 2-year revival originating with Assemblies of God evangelist Carlos Annacondia results in 2 million converts.
1984 Conference on Holistic Ministry, convened in Malang (Indonesia) by OCMS/UK, with 30 pastors and workers (11-15 March).
1984 4th Assembly, World Conference on Religion and Peace (WCRP), held in Nairobi, on 'People of Faith Working Together for Peace', with 500 delegates (23-31 August).

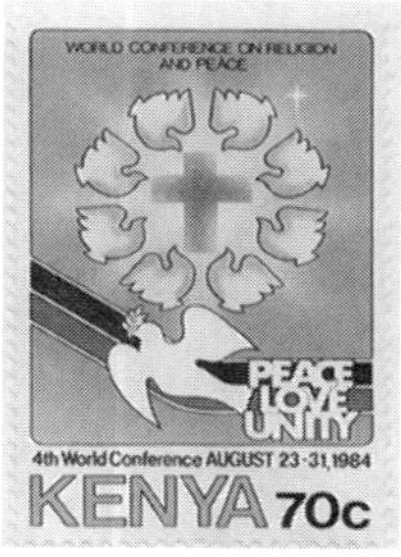


**AD 1984.** 500 delegates of several religions attempt to find common ground in the peace movement, at 4th WCRP, in Nairobi.

1984 Reformed Ecumenical Synod (with 5.5 million in affiliated churches) meets to discuss human rights, science, and technology; held in Chicago (10-20 August).
1984 6th Karlovy Vary Consultation (USA/Eastern European denominations) with 60 church leaders on 'Peace and Justice in East and West'; series began in 1962; 5th held in Princeton (USA) in 1981.
1984 1st Gulf Churches Conference, with representatives of 12 communions; 1986, 2nd Conference; 1989, 3rd Conference; 1991, 4th Conference.
1984 Council for the World's Religions founded.
1984 11th Assembly, World Convention of Churches of Christ (WCCC), held in Kingston (Jamaica), with theme 'Chosen to do His Work' (18-24 July).
1984 7th Assembly, Lutheran World Federation (LWF), held in Budapest (Hungary) with 12,000 attenders on theme 'In Christ—Hope for the World' (25 July-5 August).
1985 Soviet party leader Mikhail Gorbachev (born 1931) takes control of government, develops policy of *glasnost* (openness) and *perestroika* (restructuring).

1985 **Global status** of Christianity: 65.1 generations after Christ, world is 33.2% Christians (47.5% of them being Whites), 64.0% evangelized; with printed Scriptures available in 1,950 languages; total martyrs since AD 33 reach 67 million (0.9% of all Christians ever; recent rate 200,100 per year).
1985 Total Christians who have ever lived (New Israel): 8,286 million (23.4% of all persons born since AD 33).
1985 Japanese government injects US$70 billion into its computer industry from 1975-1985.
1985 600 million telephones in world; 93% can be direct-dialled from London (leading global telecommunications center), and 70% from USA.
1985 4th World Zoroastrian Congress, India; over 1,200 Parsi attenders.
1985 East Java: 9 teams from Every Creature Crusade visit 4,000 homes in 26 different areas; 250 conversions.
1985 Colombia: during International Year of Youth, Catholic Charismatic Renewal undertakes to proclaim Jesus to one fifth of all Colombian youth; each RC diocese allocated large quotas as targets.
1985 USSR: Methodists launch evangelistic mission before 3,000 people in St Olous Cathedral, Tallinn (Estonia), led by global evangelist Alan Walker.
1985 Bolivia: New Life For All evangelistic initiative results in 2,000 converts in 1984, and up to 100 a week in 1985.
1985 USA: Northamerican Full Gospel Missions Association formed to promote missions in charismatic churches; name then changed 3 times, finally to AIMS (Association of International Mission Services).
1985 India: 6th National Convention of the Charismatic Renewal, with 15,000 attenders, bishops, 600 RC priests, 1,500 religious personnel, in Madras (January).
1985 African indigenous churches (AICs) number some 7,170 separate and distinct denominations with 29,100,000 affiliated church members and grand total of 32,700,000 adherents of all kinds in 74,000 places of worship, increasing at 850,000 new members a year.
1985 6th Conference, International Association for Mission Studies (IAMS), Harare, Zimbabwe, on 'Christian mission and human transformation'; 160 participants (8-14 January).
1985 Presbyterian Church (USA) sponsors Congress on Renewal (charismatic) in Dallas (Texas), with over 5,000 attenders (January).
1985 1st General Assembly, Evangelical Fellowship of Asia (EFA, formed 1983), in Manila (Philippines), on 'The Holy Spirit and the Church' (30 January-2 February).
1985 3rd World Conference of Religious Workers, in Moscow convened by Russian Orthodox Patriarchate, on 'New Dangers to the Sacred Gift of Life: Our Task', dealing with nuclear winter; 60 religious workers and scientists from 27 countries, including Christians, Muslims, Hindus, Jews, Buddhists (2-13 February).
1985 Fiji: 60,000 attend final rally in Suva of 150th Anniversary Celebrations of Methodism; 6,000 commitments.
1985 International Missionary Congress, on theme 'Bringing Christ to Man', sponsored by Pontifical Urbanian University, Rome (18-21 February).
1985 LCWE Consultations on Radio in Church Planting (RICE): (1) Manila (February), and (2) Kristiansand, Norway (December).
1985 Youth Congress on World Evangelization, Stuttgart, Germany (February).
1985 Philippines: Manila '85 launched (with 188,000 attenders and 18,000 professions of faith) as year-long evangelism/discipleship program aimed at winning one million people through Metro Manila's 400 churches in 1985 (February).
1985 Sierra Leone: Consultation on Muslim Evangelism; 21 churches and missions represented (February).
1985 USA: Conference on New Age Issues, sponsored by Evangelical Ministries to New Religions (EMNR), in Denver; over 300 registrants; releases 'Statement on the New Age Movement' (14-16 March).
1985 15th European Pentecostal Fellowship Conference, Naples, Italy (19-21 March).
1985 Zaire National Congress on Evangelism; leaders from 64 denominations plan to plant churches in 10,000 unreached villages and thousands of city neighborhoods by 1990 (April).
1985 Conference of International Interfaith Organizations, convened by World Congress of Faiths, at Ammerdown, Bath (UK), representing over 20 organizations (April).
1985 South Africa: Andrew Murray Consultation on Prayer for Revival and Mission Sending; 800 attenders in Cape Town and Pretoria.
1985 National Convocation on Evangelizing Ethnic America, Houston; over 700 attenders (April).
1985 Italy: 8th National Charismatic Conference, in Rimini; 12,000 participants including several bishops, 500 priests (25-28 April).
1985 European Evangelism Conference, sponsored by International Fellowship of Evangelical Students (IFES), in De Flevohof, Netherlands; 560 students including 50 from Yugoslavia (April).
1985 Conference of National Evangelists (CONE), sponsored by Asia Evangelistic Fellowship, in Singapore; 140 participants from 14 countries (May).
1985 3rd Scandinavian Conference of Catholic Charismatic Renewal, Stockholm, with 150 delegates (16-19 May).
1985 LCWE Conference on the Laity, Denver, surveys evangelism within occupational groups, states 120,000 volunteers work in over 120 Christian lay affinity groups in USA; 40 leaders (21-23 May).
1985 11th Session, Roman Catholic/Classical Pentecostal theological dialogue (begun 1972), on topic 'Communion of Saints'; at Riano, Rome (21-26 May); 1986, 12th Session, in USA (24-31 May).
1985 LCWE/WEF Consultation on the Work of the Holy Spirit and Evangelization, in Oslo, Norway; over 70 participants from 30 countries (May); results in published book *God the Evangelist*.
1985 Charismatic Retreat for Priests (Polish Bishops Conference and ICCRO) in Czestochowa, Poland (June).
1985 8th Assembly, Christian Conference of Asia (CCA), in Seoul (Korea), on theme 'Jesus Christ sets free to serve', with delegates from its 110 member denominations in 16 Asian countries (26 June-2 July).
1985 Chinese Culture and the Gospel Seminar (CCCOWE), in Hong Kong, with 85 delegates (July).
1985 World Congress on Japanese Evangelism, Los Angeles (USA), with 300 Japanese Christians from 20 denominations and 10 nations.
1985 9th Latin American Leaders Conference (ECCLA IX), Catholic Charismatic Renewal (ICCRO), for 200 leaders, Costa Rica (July).
1985 Information crimes rise sharply; computer fraud, commercial espionage, software and data theft, sale of disinformation.
1985 35 countries now potentially able to make atomic weapons, though only 11 have actually succeeded.
1985 Electronic warfare: USA and USSR each spend over $1 billion annually on this and its related research.
1985 50 million computers in world (12,000 per million people, or 80 people per computer), with USA having 11 million (55,000 per million, 20 people per computer); 50% of all whitecollar workers own one.
1985 15th Baptist World Congress (BWA) meets in Los Angeles, USA, with theme 'Out of Darkness into the Light of Christ'; 25,000 participants from 127 member bodies (July).
1985 4th Asian Institute for Christian Communication (AICC-4), Chiang Mai, Thailand, for 37 leaders (July).
1985 World Conference of Baptist Evangelists, Bolivar, Missouri (USA): 'Strategies of evangelism to win world cities' (July).
1985 14th Pentecostal World Conference, in Zurich, organized by World Conference of Pentecostal Churches; on 'Jesus Christ—the Hope of the World'; 10,000 participants from 100 countries (2-7 July).
1985 World Christian Peace Conference, London, sponsored by World Methodist Council, on 'Commitment to Jesus Christ the Prince of Peace'; 250 delegates from 32 countries (July).
1985 Salvation Army International Youth Congress, Western Illinois University, USA; 5,000 delegates from 85 nations (17-23 July).
1985 Latin America Chinese Evangelization Conference (sponsored by CCCOWE) held in São Paulo, Brazil (23-27 July).
1985 1st Costa Rican Missions Consultation, with 36 denominations and agencies (July).
1985 Chinese Missionary Convention of Canada (CMCC

'85), at Guelph; 1,050 registrants (19-24 August).
1985 Uganda: National Catholic Charismatic Leaders Conference, with 130 leaders (22-27 August).
1985 International Christian Zionist Congress, in Basel, Switzerland, with 600 delegates from 27 countries; to show support for the state of Israel (27-29 August).
1985 Friends World Committee for Consultation (FWCC) meets in Cuernavaca, Mexico (August).
1985 Belgium: Colloquium on the Bible and the Computer, at Louvain (August).
1985 During the year, 28 new global plans to evangelize the whole world are announced by agencies, mission boards, and others; these include Korean Churches' Plan for Entering Every Country, Global Evangelization Strategy Consultation, Global Simultaneous Evangelistic Missions, Global Strategy Committee (Seventh-day Adventists), International Catholic Programme of Evangelization (ICPE), The World by 2000 (TWR/FEBC/HCJB), CWME Orthodox Advisory Group, EXPLO-85, Power Evangelism, et alia; most plans are pushed for some months, then gradually fizzle out without announcement or apology.
1985 43rd International Eucharistic Congress, Nairobi, Kenya, on 'Eucharist and the Christian Family' (August).
1985 Global Simultaneous Evangelistic Missions launched in Indonesia, Nigeria and other countries by World Methodist Council; thousands of local mission outreach campaigns planned across world.
1985 4th Nigeria National Congress on Evangelization, Zaria, on theme 'Arise let us go from here', with 667 participants (August).
1985 Asia Committee for World Evangelization, Hong Kong (3-6 September).
1985 Annual Conference, World Congress of Faiths, Leicester, UK on theme 'The Worshipping Community' (September).
1985 World Consultation on Evangelism, Lake Junaluska (USA), sponsored by World Evangelism (World Methodist Council) (September); 5-year evangelism plan for 1987-1991 adopted.
1985 World Missions Conference, Guadalajara, Mexico (September).
1985 Anglican Renewal Leaders Consultation, sponsored by SOMA (Sharing of Ministries Abroad), in Chorleywood, UK, with 90 leaders (September).
1985 Britain: 5th National Charismatic Conference for Clergy and Leaders (sponsored by Anglican Renewal Ministries), Swanwick (23-26 September).
1985 1st Pan-African Francophone Leaders Conference, Catholic Charismatic Renewal (ICCRO), on 'A Holy People', with 100 leaders, Kinshasa, Zaire (4-9 October).
1985 USA: Hispanic Congress on Evangelization, at Crystal Cathedral, Garden Grove, CA: 2,000 Hispanic evangelical leaders from 25 countries, 80% being pastors; goals to reach 2 million Hispanics for Christ by end of 1987, and to plant 20,000 new Hispanic churches in USA by AD 2000 (14-18 October).
1985 World Christian Conference for Chinese Graduates, sponsored by NACOCE; 110 attenders.
1985 1st International Youth Leaders Consultation, Catholic Charismatic Renewal (ICCRO), held in Rome, with 500 participants from 100 countries (15-19 October).
1985 1st Venezuelan Congress of World Missions, Maracay, aiming to appoint 500 missionaries by 1987 (15-19 October).
1985 Amsterdam Prayer Conference for World Evangelization, sponsored by LCWE, YWAM, et alia (November).
1985 3rd Asian Leaders Conference, Catholic Charismatic Renewal (ICCRO), on 'Discipleship in the Holy Spirit', with 100 leaders, Bangalore, India (9-12 November).
1985 Kenya: 6th Workshop of the Apostolate to Nomads, Nairobi; 42 participants from RC dioceses across East Africa (25-30 November).

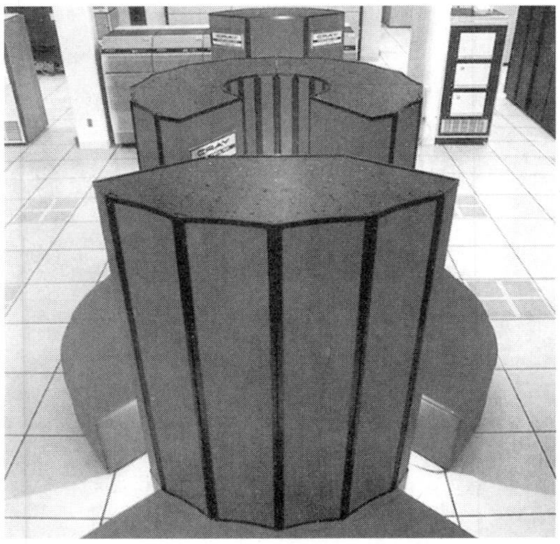

**AD 1985.** The Cray series represents the fastest to date among the world's 150 makes of supercomputer.

1985 Macao: Gospel Saturation Campaign (Campus Crusade for Christ, from Korea) reaches 150,000 young people.
1985 Manila: 1st General Assembly, Institute of Foreign Missions of the Philippines, founded in 1965.
1985 Extraordinary Synod of Bishops, in Rome, to reappraise Vatican II and its changes; 150 participating bishops; general opinion that conservatives in Curia's Holy Office have again stifled genuine collegiality (November-December).
1985 World's fastest supercomputer introduced: Cray-2, with 4 main processors working in parallel, 2-billion-byte memory, 1,200 megaflops (floating point, or arithmetical, operations in millions per second); 150 supercomputers (of 6 different makes) now in use around world; another massive system being developed is Paragon XP/S UNIX-based Supercomputer.
1985 12% of USA's 85 million homes have personal computers; by 1990, 30%.
1985 World's 10 largest cities: Tokyo/Yokohama 23,322,000, New York/NENJ 15,827,000, Mexico City 14,474,000, Sao Paulo 13,758,000, Shanghai 12,396,000, Buenos Aires 10,522,000, Los Angeles/Long Beach 10,445,000, Osaka 10,351,000, Calcutta 9,946,000, Bombay 9,907,000.
1985 EXPLO-85 global Christian training teleconference organized in 95 locations in 55 countries simultaneously by Campus Crusade for Christ (CCCI), using satellite video relays (6 uplinks, several thousand downlinks), training 550,000 Christian workers from 100 countries worldwide in prayer, evangelism and discipleship, with 4 telecasts reaching 60 million (27-31 December).
1985 Australian Chinese Congress of Evangelism (30 December-3 January 1986).
1985 'Mission 2000' scheme proposed by missiologists D.A. McGavran and R.D. Winter, aiming to plant a church in each of world's unreached peoples by AD 2000 through formation of 100,000 local church mission fellowships in Western countries.
1985 Korea: massive increase in number of Protestant and Catholic Korean missionaries sent abroad since first Protestant in 1912; by 1973 620 serving abroad in 30 countries (270 Protestants, 250 Korean indigenous, 90 Roman Catholics), rising by 1987 to 511 Protestants in 89 Korean mission agencies (increased from 47 agencies in 1982) in 47 nations; 1985, Protestant churches announce world evangelization plans calling for 10,000 Korean missionaries abroad by AD 2000 with at least one working in every country of the world.
1985 Interchurch Consultation on Future Trends in Christian World Mission, Maryknoll, New York, on research methodology, sociopolitical issues, and unfinished tasks of world evangelization (15-17 February).
1985 Integrity Keepers Conventions (persons 'Keeping integrity to Jehovah') held in 851 locations around world (averaging 6,700 attenders each), with total attenders 5,688,335 and 75,606 new baptisms; by 1986, Jehovah's Witnesses have become a vast global organization deploying more massive global resources for world conversion than any other single missionary agency: 3,229,022 publishers (active door-to-door member/evangelists, 'In harmony with Jesus' command 'Go... declare abroad the kingdom of God') in 100 languages in 208 countries, 52,177 congregations, 2,726,252 Bible study meetings a year, 8,160,597 annual Memorial (of Crucifixion) attenders, 2,762 foreign missionaries, 13,351 special pioneers, 8,920 foreign mission volunteers, and over 100,000 other full-time workers; vast annual magazine output totals 550 million (with 3,781,000 subscribers to Watchtower and Awake! in 33 language editions), and 44 million Bibles and books a year; Battle of Armageddon anticipated within 10 years, with 2 billion people killed, 144,000 Witnesses going to heaven with Christ, rest of Witnesses remaining on Earth during Millennium and then on into eternity.
1985 1st International Symposium on Transnationalization of Terminology, sponsored by incipient movement (organized in 1986) International Organization for Unification of Terminological Neologisms (IOUTN) (World Bank of International Terms, WBIT), held in Warsaw (Poland) (13-14 April).
1985 1st Global Evangelization Strategy Consultation, Ridgecrest, NC (USA), with 70 participants from Baptist churches across world associated with Southern Baptist Convention; results inter alia in publication of 'The AD 2000 Series' (25-28 June).
1985 6th All-Christian Peace Assembly (ACPA), convened by Christian Peace Conference (CPC), in Prague, on theme 'God calls: choose life; the hour is late!'; 800 participants from 90 countries (2-9 July).
1985 5th West Malaysia Chinese Congress on World Evangelization, sponsored by CCCOWE, in Port Dickson (5-9 August).
1985 International Consultation on Missions (ICOM) convened in Jos, Nigeria, by NEMA (Nigeria Evangelical Missions Association) and WEF, on theme 'Mobilizing Indigenous Missions for the Final Harvest'; 83 mission executives, mainly Nigerians (11 August).
1985 Global Strategy Committee created by General Conference of Seventh-day Adventists, at 5-yearly meeting in New Orleans, USA (next being in 1990 in Indianapolis); Committee composed of 60 officials (3 members from each of the 11 divisions of the world, plus 30 from World Division in Washington, DC); prepares strategy for 15 million Adventists in 210 countries; at 1988 meeting in Georgia (USA), launches plan based on segmentization document 'SDA Global Strategy: The People of the World divided into approximately 5,000 population segments averaging one million'.
1985 God's Global Envoys—Nonresidential Missionaries for World Evangelization, an overall plan evolved by WERC/FMB, Richmond, USA, envisaging cooperation of entire spectrum of all Christians of all traditions whether like-minded or not; based on 3 elements: (a) segmentization of unevangelized world into 3,000 distinct segments (peoples, cities, countries), (b) matching-up of segments with one professional missionary each, and (c) nonresidential mission and ministry through computerized research and networking; 1985, first descriptions published in print (May).
1985 International Catholic Programme of Evangelization (ICPE) begins functioning, based on Malta, first with School of Evangelization in Valletta, then others in Rome, New Zealand, et alia; 1988, 2nd Meeting of Association of Coordinators of Catholic Schools of Evangelization, in Rome (13-16 June).
1985 Project 'The World by 2000' announced by 3 major Christian broadcasting agencies, FEBC, HCJB/World Radio Missionary Fellowship, TWR (and later ELWA-SIM): to complete by AD 2000 giving everyone on Earth the opportunity to hear the gospel of Christ by radio (September); 1987, target modified to be (1) all major trade languages with over 1 million speakers each by AD 2000, then (2) all minor trade languages, then later (3) the world's 6,500 'heart' languages.
1985 World Ambassadors, a plan of Maranatha Christian Ministries to evangelize the world through conversions among the 200,000 international non-Christian students from 170 nations (65 closed to missionaries) who are resident in the USA; slogan 'Reaching international students to reach the world' by returning home to plant churches; goal to train 15,000 such leaders each year.
1985 CWME Orthodox Advisory Group meets in Sofia (Bulgaria) on 1,100th anniversary of death of Methodius, issues call to rectify Orthodoxy's failure to fulfill Jesus' Great Commission and 'to reach out to the unreached' (21-26 October).
1985 Global Network of Centers for World Mission formed, based on 30 research and study centers; 1986, issues Singapore Statement (27 June); 1988, holds its 1st World Meeting, in Singapore (1-9 November).
1985 Association of International Mission Services (AIMS) begun, to serve Charismatic Renewal, with slogan 'Unity in the Spirit for World Evangelization'; 75 member agencies.
1985 Church growth specialist D.A. McGavran publishes 'Emergency call for United Global Evangelism' (Church growth, Seoul, Korea) defining God's call as 'Evangelize, baptize, multiply churches at home and abroad', concentrating on ripe, receptive, harvest fields.
1985 Third-wave/charismatic leader John Wimber writes *Power evangelism: signs and wonders today*, followed in 1987 by *Power healing*, also in 1988 *Power encounters among Christians in the Western world.*
1985 Transport and Communications Decade for Asia and the Pacific (1985-1994), sponsored by UN.
1985 Kirchentag held in Dusseldorf (resulting in WCC Program JPIC).
1985 Science infoglut: scientific journal literature explodes to over 40,000 scientific journals publishing more than a million new articles each year, two million by 1995, and doubling thereafter every 11 or so years.
1985 Explosive rise of 121 anti-Christian megacities and 20 supercities hostile to Christian mission, especially 4 Muslim supercities over 6 million each in 1985 (Jakarta, Cairo, Teheran, Karachi), increasing to 5 Islamic supergiants over 10 million each by AD 2000 (Jakarta, Cairo, Karachi, Teheran, Dacca); resurgence of Islamic neo-fundamentalism and sectarian violence.
1985 Total of literary doomsday novels (describing cataclysmic ends of the world) published to date is 260; most written before 1914 postulate natural catastrophes, most written after 1914 postulate man-made catastrophes.
1985 C. Sagan writes science fiction classic *Contact* predicting contact with extraterrestrial aliens in 1988 and 1999; 1997 in movie form; scenario more likely in AD 2021.
1985 H.R. Hall publishes *AD 1991—the Genesis of Holocaust* stating Antichrist could be revealed in 1992 as a 30-year-old.
1985 R. Stark & W.S. Bainbridge write *The future of religion: secularization, revival and cult formation.*
1985 *The Third Millennium: a history of the world, AD 2000-3000*, by B.M. Stableford & D. Langford.
1985 *World futures: a critical analysis of alternatives*, by Barry B. Hughes.
1985 *The extraterrestrial encyclopedia: our search for life in outer space.* by J.A. Angelo, Jr.

1985 *Megatraumas: America in the Year 2000* by Richard D. Lamm.

1985 *Islamic futures: the shape of ideas to come*, by Z. Sardar.

1985 Global Tomorrow Coalition (GTC) holds 7 Globescope Assemblies across USA over next 5 years, defining sustainable development, instituting total life cycle Sustainable Index system.

1985 1st Assembly of the World's Religions, sponsored by International Religious Foundation, in McAfee, NJ, USA, on theme 'Spiritual Unity and the Future of the Earth: Recovering the Classical Heritage'; 603 official participants and 400 others (15-21 November).

1985 Evangelical Fellowship of Asia founded.

1985 Nigeria: National Congress on Evangelization, held in Lagos (17-23 August).

19857th Annual Meeting, Permanent International Ecumenical Consultation of Religious (PIECR, mainly Anglican and Catholic), held in London; 1986, 8th Meeting, in Jerusalem.

1985 10th World Council of YMCAs meets in Nyborg Strand (Denmark); YMCAs found in 90 countries, with 23 million members, 700,000 voluntary leaders, 25,000 full-time paid staff.

1985 International Eastern Orthodox/Old Catholic Theological Dialogue Commission, meets in Amersfoort (Netherlands) (30 September-5 October).

1985 4th Assembly, Middle East Council of Churches (MECC), held in Nicosia (Cyprus), with 66 delegates from 21 member churches and 80 attenders, on theme 'The Living Hope' (13-19 February).

1985 International Orthodox Youth Festival, sponsored by Syndesmos held in Ionian Village (Greece) on 'The Church: A Eucharistic Community', with 200 youth (26 August-1 September).

1985 9th World Council, World Alliance of YMCAs (formed 1855, with 72 national movements), held in Denmark (July).

1985 21st Protestant Kirchentag, held in Dusseldorf (FRG), on theme 'The Earth is the Lord's'; 125,000 attenders, 2,300 meetings (5-9 June).

1985 Consultation on the Holy Spirit and Evangelism (convened by WEF and LCWE), in Oslo (Norway) (May).

1985 6th Church Growth International Conference, in Seoul (Korea) (20-25 August).

1985 1st International Symposium for Transnationalization of Terminology (sponsored by World Bank of International Terms, IOUTN/WBIT), held in Warsaw (Poland) with 70 participants on theme 'Concept-Term-Definition and Their Significance in Terminology' (13-14 April).

1985 15th Triennial Meeting, Friends World Committee for Consultation (FWCC), held in Oaxtepec (Mexico), on themes Church Membership, and Peace and Justice.

1985 First School of Evangelization organized in Malta by International Catholic Program of Evangelization (ICPE), based on YWAM model.

1985 Rise of the Internet as a global communications network, with number of computers and users growing exponentially at over 150% per year: (1989) 80,000 computers connected, (1990) 210,000, (1991) 420,000, (1992) 800,000, (1993) 1,510,000, (1995) 30 million, (AD 2000) 276 million.

1985 9th & 10th World Council of YMCAs, in Nyborg, Denmark, on theme 'Your Kingdom Come—Living up to Our Responsibilities'.

1986 1st International Conference on Liberation Theology, held in Burnaby, BC (Canada), (6-8 February).

1986 1986 is proclaimed International Year of Peace by United Nations.

1986 USA: 5 million users send 250 million electronic-mail messages every year; by 1990, 3 billion messages a year.

1986 Spain National Missions Consultation, related to COMIBAM '87.

1986 Afro-Asian Ecumenical Colloquium on Spirituality and Liberation in Post- Independent Africa and Asia, New Delhi (4-12 January).

1986 Australia: Jubilee 86 United Charismatic Convention, in Adelaide; over 3,000 delegates, 10,000 attenders (7-11 January).

1986 International Conference on Liberation Theology, in Burnaby, Canada (6-8 February).

1986 Australia: 1st National Convention on the Holy Spirit (World Methodist Council), in Sydney (February); followed by regional conferences, then 1987 2nd National Convention.

1986 India: pope John Paul II visits 14 cities on his 29th foreign pilgrimage since 1978 (February).

1986 Guatemala National Consultation on World Missions, related to COMIBAM '87; 129 participants, plus 380 in adjacent meetings (21-26 February).

1986 Consultation on Evangelizing World Class Cities, Moody Bible Institute, Chicago (14-17 March).

1986 General Assembly, World Student Christian Federation (WSCF), in 90th anniversary celebration; in Oaxtepec, Mexico (March).

1986 International Prophetic Ministry Convention, Mount Carmel (Israel) and Jerusalem; 30 modern prophets and 5,000 attenders, at Easter (Christians of all confessions).

1986 1st Catholic FIRE Charismatic Evangelistic Rally, Providence, RI (relayed by satellite to 17 cities), on 'I have come to cast fire on the Earth' (5 April).

1986 USA: 15th World Mission Institute, held in Chicago, on theme 'Trends for the Future and World Mission' (10-12 April).

1986 Conference of Revival Evangelists for Inter-Africa (sponsored by CFAN, Christ for All Nations), Harare, Zimbabwe (April).

1986 7th Latin American Lutheran Congress, in Caracas, on theme 'To be reborn and to grow in hope and peace'; 70 participants from 14 Latin American countries (18-24 April).

1986 USA: International Conference for Equipping Evangelists (charismatic pentecostal) in Sacramento (CA), 'training thousands of evangelists to equip millions of Christians to reach billions of unbelievers' (5-9 May).

1986 United Bible Societies launches 2-year Youth Advance, providing special translations (May).

1986 World Literature Conference, sponsored by Evangelical Literature Overseas; at Wheaton, USA (27-30 May).

1986 El Salvador: World Literature Crusade plans to make 1 million converts in a year through house-to-house visitation.

1986 Venezuela: 1st Regional Conference of World Missions, convened by Evangelicals in eastern region of country, at Puerto la Cruz, with over 200 present (96 official representatives of 30 organizations) (10-14 June).

1986 12th World Congress, International Council of Christian Churches (ICCC), Seoul, Korea, with delegates from 93 nations (12-16 June).

1986 Conference on 'A Century of World Evangelization: North American Evangelical Missions, 1886-1986', at Wheaton, USA (17-19 June).

1986 ASIA 86 radio/videotape preaching mission, from Luis Palau Singapore Mission, largest broadcast outreach to Asia ever, aiming to evangelize in 10 languages through FEBC, HCJB, TWR, and others (23-27 June).

1986 Scandinavian Oasis Conference (Oase; Lutheran Charismatic Renewal), based in Oslo, with 500 pastors and 10,000 others (July); Charismatics in mainline nonpentecostal churches (Lutheran, Catholic, et al) continue to grow throughout Europe to 18 million by AD 1986 rising to 30 million by AD 2000.

1986 15th World Methodist Conference, sponsored by World Methodist Council, Nairobi, on theme 'Christ Jesus: God's 'Yes' for the World'; further 5-year plan adopted for World Evangelism, 1987-1991; 3,000 delegates (23-29 July).

1986 12th Annual Conference, Association of Church Missions Committees (ACMC), in Wheaton and San Diego, USA; 1,300 attenders (9-12 July).

1986 2nd International Conference for Itinerant Evangelists (ICIE), Amsterdam; 8,000 evangelists from 173 countries (12-21 July).

1986 2nd Pan-European Charismatic Conference: ACTS 86 (European Festival of Faith), an all-Europe charismatic congress on 'Evangelism in the Power of the Holy Spirit', in Birmingham (UK); 20,000 RC/Protestant/Anglican/Orthodox participants from East and West (100 from Eastern Europe), but without formal RC participation (23-27 July).

1986 6th International Seminar of Christian Artists (Europe), Netherlands (3-9 August).

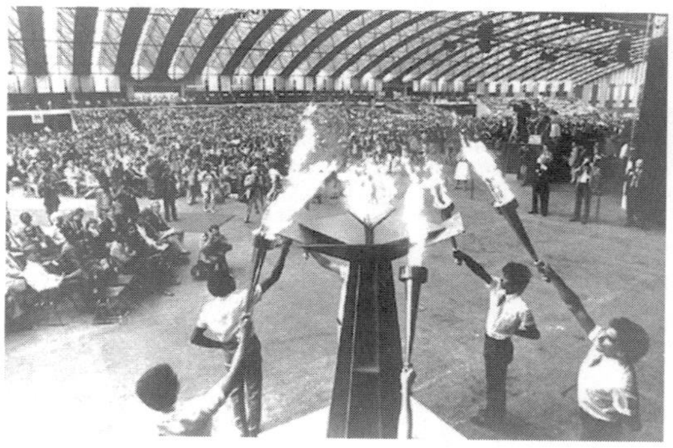

**AD 1986.** 8,000 evangelists at ICIE see the fire of the Gospel spreading across the world.

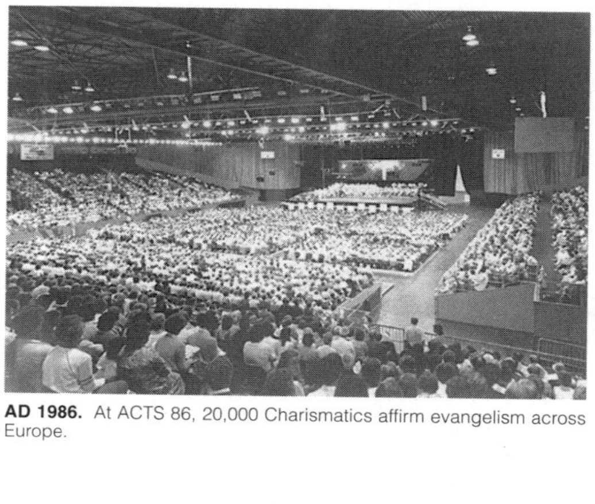

**AD 1986.** At ACTS 86, 20,000 Charismatics affirm evangelism across Europe.

1986 14th International Lutheran Conference on the Holy Spirit (ILCOHS), Minneapolis; 12,000 attenders (5-8 August).

1986 15th Annual Conference, Association of Muslim Social Scientists, in Plainfield, IN, USA (7-9 August).

1986 USA: Aldersgate '86, 8th National Conference on the Holy Spirit (United Methodist, UMRSF), at Savannah, GA, on 'Christ in You, the Hope of Glory' (7-10 August).

1986 Indonesia: LWF Urban Mission Consultation, in Jakarta (7-15 August).

1986 All Africa Congress on Evangelism (under MCWE/Morris Cerullo), Nairobi (11-16 August).

1986 4th Chinese National Christian Conference, Beijing (16-23 August).

1986 12th General Assembly, World Fellowship of Orthodox Youth (Syndesmos), in Effingham, UK; with 110 and observers delegates (17-24 August); 1989, 13th General Assembly, in USA.

1986 2nd World Convocation, Prison Fellowship International (PFI), in Nairobi, Kenya; 200 chaplains and workers.

1986 3rd Lausanne Consultation on Jewish Evangelism (LCJE/LCWE); 300 delegates, at Easneye, Ware, UK (19-27 August).

1986 Honduras: 1st National Missions Consultation, at Lake Yojoa, with 26 churches and organizations (9-11 January); followed by Honduras National Missions Congress (21-25 August).

1986 Paraguay National Missions Consultation (25-27 August); and Uruguay National Missions Consultation (August); both related to COMIBAM '87.

1986 Philippines: National Missions Consultation '86, in Taytay, Rizal, sponsored by DAWN 2000 Continuing Committee; results in goal '2000 new Filipino missionaries by 2000 AD'; 100 participants (25-28 August).

1986 LWF/WCC Joint Consultation on New Religious Movements, in Amsterdam (7-13 September).

1986 India: 3rd Every Home Crusade (EHC) campaign (after 1975, 1984 campaigns) to reach 765 million people, in every home in India, with printed gospel messages by 1994.

1986 USA: Youth With a Mission (YWAM) announces goal of fulfilling Great Commission in 25 years, by AD 2011.

1986 Korea: 10th Church Growth International Seminar (P.Y. Cho and Full Gospel Church) in Seoul and Osaka (Japan), with 3,000 attenders (September), bring total attenders since 1976 to 70,000 pastors and leaders from 30 countries; goal announced of winning 10 million Japanese to Christ by AD 2000.

1986 11th International Congress of Christian Archeology, in Aix-en-Provence, France (September).

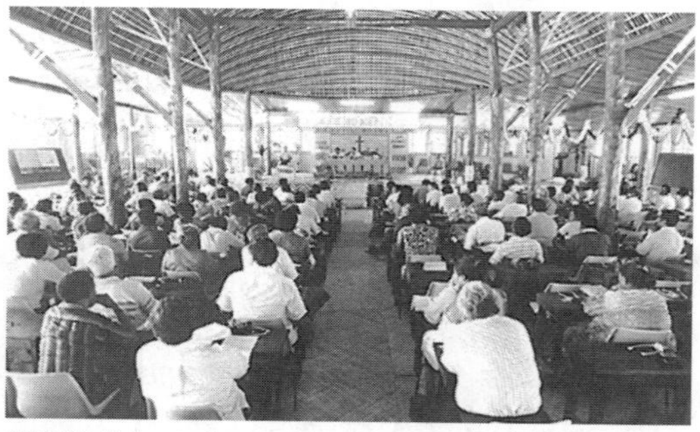

**AD 1986.** Delegates from most Pacific churches meet for 5th Assembly, PCC, in Western Samoa.

1986 5th Assembly, Pacific Conference of Churches (PCC), in Apia, Samoa (14-24 September).

1986 SOMA Conference for Anglican Diocese of Jerusalem in Old City, Jerusalem, on 'Evangelism in the Power of the Holy Spirit' (22-26 September).

1986 LWF International Consultation on Confirmation, in Geneva (25-27 September).

1986 30th Annual Meeting, Conference of Secretaries of Christian World Communions (CWCs), in Rome (20-23 October).

1986 More global plans to reach the world's peoples by AD 2000 are proclaimed: Reaching the World's Cities, Touch the World through Prayer, International Prophetic Ministry Convention, 3rd Chinese Congress on World Evangelization, 24th International Old Catholic Congress, Asia Missions Association, Good News World, To the Ends of the Earth, Mandate '86, Presbyterian Decade of Evangelism, Intercontinental Broadcasting NetWork, Global Strategy Group, One Million Native Missionaries, Wanted: World Christians, Televised Evangelism for All, Worldwide Student NetWork, Latin American Evangelical Confraternity, Renew the Church-Reach the World, Issachar Frontier Missions, et alia.

1986 England: widespread growth of local ecumenical projects (LEPs), totalling 460 in number.

1986 'Jesus' Film produced by Campus Crusade for Christ (filmed in Palestine in 1979) is circulating in 1986 dubbed in 106 languages; viewers total 275 million, decisions for Christ reach 33 million (12%).

1986 Mandate '86, 1st Annual Mid-West Student Missions

Conference, 'to reach the world's unreached', organized in Illinois (USA) with 800 students by IVCF-related students, supported by CCCI, AoG, SBC, IVCF et alia, with 9 related regional meetings; also Mission Advance 86 (Hamilton, Canada, 850 students); 1987, numerous student-run conferences—Mandate '87 (in Muncie, IN; 1,200 students, 23-25 January), Harvest (in Minneapolis, 6-8 February), Vision, Proclaim, Go (Global Outreach), GAP (Global Awareness Project).

1986 USA: 3rd North American Buddhist-Christian Theological Encounter, on 'Notions of Ultimate Reality in Buddhism and Christianity', West Lafayette, IN (10-12 October).

1986 11th International Conference on Patristic, Medieval, and Renaissance Studies, in Villanova, USA; held annually (10-12 October).

1986 1st International Christian Media Conference (ICMC), at Flevohof, The Hague, Netherlands, on 'Partners in Communication', sponsored by WEF, NRB, TWR; 500 participants from 75 countries (13-17 October).

1986 Interfaith 9-hour prayer and fasting summit for world peace at Assisi, Italy, convened by John Paul II for 120 Christian leaders including 2 Orthodox patriarchs, and 80 other religious leaders including Dalai Lama, Buddhists, Muslims, Hindus, Sikhs, Shintoists, Parsis, Jains, Baha'is, shamanists, animists (27 October).

1986 Conference of Lutheran Churches in Europe, in Brezice, Yugoslavia (28 October-4 November).

1986 2nd International Consultation on Role of National Councils of Churches in Increasing Christian Cooperation and Unity, in Geneva; representatives of 70 councils (in 35 of which the Roman Catholic Church is a full member) (October).

1986 LCWE Consultation on Conversion and Evangelization.

1986 Congress on Franciscan Witness among Muslims, in Spain.

1986 Formation of International Organization for Unification of Terminological Neologisms (IOUTN) together with World Bank of International Terms (WBIT), in Warsaw (Poland) by Polish scientist Z. Stoberski.

1986 14th World Congress, International Catholic Press Union (UCIP), in New Delhi (India), on theme 'Church, Culture, Communication'.

1986 USA spends $8 billion on nerve gases from 1982-86.

1986 60 million microcomputers in world, of which 32% are installed in homes.

1986 Fifth-generation computers using Josephson Effect introduced.

1986 Brazil: Christian TV Network launched, a series of stations covering Latin America with TV programmes in Spanish and Portuguese.

1986 North American Leaders Congress on the Holy Spirit and World Evangelization (RC/Protestant charismatic renewal), New Orleans, with over 7,500 pastors and leaders, also 4,000 other attenders (October); vast numbers of regional and denominational conferences and seminars proliferate.

1986 World Consultation on Inter-Church Aid, Refugee & World Service (sponsored by WCC/CICARWS), in Larnaca, Cyprus, on theme 'Diakonia 2000: called to be Neighbors'; 300 participants (November).

1986 Deadly pandemic of AIDS (acquired immune deficiency syndrome) rapidly sweeps across world: 1986, 1 million cases (Africa, USA) and 10 million carriers infected with virus; 1991, 3 million cases and 100 million carriers (50% of whom will die) in Africa, Asia, Americas, Europe.

1986 Pacific '86 Conference for Evangelists, in Suva, Fiji, on theme 'Let the Islands hear'; 700 evangelists from 23 Pacific nations (12-21December).

1986 Mission '87, 4th Missionary Congress for European Youth (sponsored by TEMA), at Utrecht, on theme 'I chose You, Jesus Christ'; 10,500 participants (27 December-1 January 1987).

1986 European Open Systems Interconnection (a computer language parallel to Esperanto) operates to enable computers to talk to each other in a common set of languages.

1986 A. C. Clarke writes novel *The songs of distant Earth* about discovery in AD 2008 that Sun will go nova and explode in AD 3620.

1986 'Reaching the World's Cities by AD 2000', a plan of Assemblies of God (USA), Division of Foreign Missions, with 'declared objective to help evangelize every city on the face of the earth'.

1986 OMS mission executive Wesley L. Duewel writes *Touch the world through prayer* (Zondervan).

1986 Worldwide Student NetWork launched by CCCI (USA) with goal of evangelizing by AD 2000 all the world's 30,000 tertiary-level universities and colleges (3,000 top universities, 8,000 university colleges, 19,000 vocational or professional colleges) with 60 million students, generating parallel surge from the campus to the entire world.

1986 1st General Assembly, Latin American Evangelical Confraternity (CONELA, founded 1982, with 225 member denominations, councils, associations and agencies), in Maracaibo, Venezuela; topic, challenge to evangelize Latin America and the world, with 'millions of Latin American missionaries sent to the Muslim world and other regions where they are needed' (M. Ortiz, president); 95 delegates and over 1,000 attenders (22-25 April).

1986 3rd Chinese Congress on World Evangelization (CCOWE '86) sponsored by CCCOWE, held in Taipei (Taiwan), on theme 'Renewal, Breakthrough and Growth'; 1,900 Chinese church leaders from over 20 countries (6-13 August); CCCOWE produces 6-volume survey in Chinese (2 volumes in English) of whole Chinese diaspora across world.

1986 4th Triennial Convention, Asia Missions Association (AMA), in Pasadena, USA, on 'Thy Will be done on Earth' (6-12 October); Asians abroad as foreign missionaries reported as 10,210, with AD 2000 total expected to be 67,000.

1986 Good News World (Operation World/Mass Scripture Distribution), a global plan announced by Southern Baptist Sunday School Board, Nashville (TN), as: 'Purpose: To place Scriptures in the hands of everyone in the world in 1994 to prepare for worldwide revival in 1995'.

1986 'Toward 2000', a program of Issachar Frontier Missions Research (Seattle, USA), specializing in witness in closed countries; publishes Strategic Times journal.

1986 US Catholic Bishops publish NCCB pastoral statement on world mission, *To the ends of the Earth.*

1986 USA: Presbyterian Church announces Decade of Evangelism for 1990-2000.

1986 US Society for Frontier Missiology founded in Colorado Springs; 1987, 2nd Annual Meeting in Orlando, Florida (USA) discusses AD 2000 closure and countdown thinking; 86 mission leaders from 46 North American agencies (25-26 September).

1986 Intercontinental Broadcasting Network (IBN) begun in Virginia Beach, USA, by independent charismatics linking up with European counterparts.

1986 Global Strategy Group formed to coordinate planning for Southern Baptist Foreign Mission Board (December).

1986 K.P. Yohannan (founder, Gospel For Asia) writes *The coming revolution in world missions*, describing a coming Third Wave of mission, namely a massive movement producing one million evangelists from thousands of native missionary movements in India, Asia, and across the world.

1986 Missiologist J.H. Kane writes *Wanted: World Christians* (these being essential for world evangelization), holding as key 'A World Christian is one who recognizes his own personal responsibility for world missions.'

1986 Televised Evangelism for All, a project proposed by Christian Broadcasting Network vice-president N. Van Hamm: 6 million 10-inch flat liquid-screen printed-circuit solar-cell television units, costing $1 each, dumped out of aircraft across world, glide to Earth over unevangelized peoples, pretuned to 18-language transmissions over 3 or 4 geostationary satellites.

1986 S. M. Stigler writes *The history of statistics: the measurement of uncertainty before 1900* (Cambridge, MA).

1986 Iberoamerican Consultation on Missiology, Guatemala, sponsored by COMIBAM (June).

1986 Network for European Communications and Transport Activities Research (NECTAR) set up, involving 75 scholars from 19 European countries, with AD 2020 set as forecasting horizon; report *The geography of Europe's futures* published in 1992.

1986 Halley's Comet returns as the final harbinger or portent of impending eco-disaster. (Nostradamus).

1986 Astronomers discover most massive object ever, the strongest gravitational lens yet found: either a supercluster of over 1,000 galaxies, or the biggest black hole ever (with mass of $10^{15}$ stars), or a cosmic string (a defect in the fabric of space-time left over from Big Bang) billions of light-years long but only an atom thick, with mass density $10^{18}$ tons per inch.

1986 G. Halsell produces *Prophecy and politics: militant evangelists on the road to nuclear war.*

1986 Theologians H.A. Snyder & D. V. Runyon write *Foresight: ten major trends that will dramatically affect the future of Christians and the church*, with forecasts to AD 2050.

1986 Catholic missiologist W. Buhlmann publishes *The church of the future: a model for the year 2001.*

1986 *Ancient Hindu astrology for the modern Western astrologer*, by J.T. Braha.

1986 *Silico Sapiens: the fundamentals and future of robots*, by J. Dekin.

1986 *Issues management: how you can plan, organize and manage for the future*, by J.F. Coates et al.

1986 Swami Satchidananda dedicates his newly-constructed Light of Truth Universal Shrine (LOTUS) at his Integral Yoga Institute ashram in Yogaville, Virginia, USA.

1986 World Religious Parliament, in New Delhi, bestows title of Jagadacharya, 'world teacher,' on 5 spiritual leaders outside India.

1986 Conference on Ministry to African Independent Churches, in Abidjan, with missions specialists from 10 countries (14-19 July); successor conferences in 1989 (Kinshasa), and 1992 (Harare, Zimbabwe).

1986 3rd Preconciliar Panorthodox Conference: despite some decades of meetings and preparation, a final target date for the Holy Synod of the Orthodox Church recedes further into the future; Synod is seen as so significant by all Orthodox bishops and patriarchs that none want to take any initiatives without full backing of all the rest.

1986 First recorded official papal visit to a Jewish synagogue (by John Paul II, 10 April).

1986 29th Assembly, World Student Christian Federation (WSCF, founded 1896), held in Mexico City (13-24 March).

1986 USA: 44th Annual Convention, National Association of Evangelicals (NAE), held in Kansas City.

1986 2nd Assembly, Ecumenical Forum of Christian Women of Europe, held in Jarvenpaa (Finland), with 150 women from 26 countries, on theme 'Building Hope: A New Vision of Life' (2-8 June).

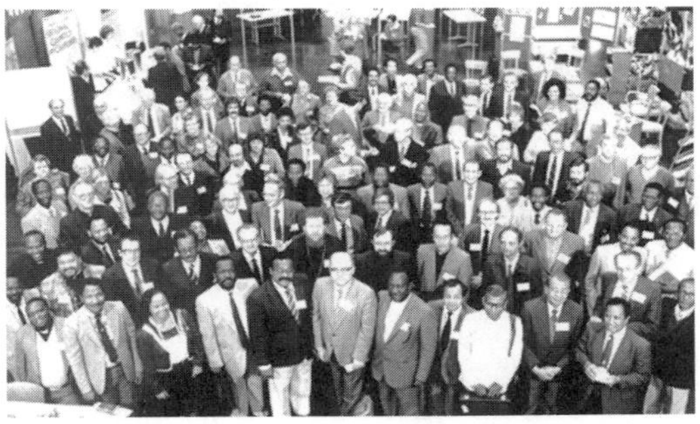

**AD 1986.** Secretaries of 70 National Councils of Churches confer in Geneva, Switzerland.

1986 2nd World Consultation of National Councils of Churches (CNCC), held in Geneva (Switzerland), with representatives of 70 NCCs (20-24 October).

1986 37th Meeting, Commission of the Churches on International Affairs (CCIA/WCC), held in Les Avants (Switzerland) (8-12 October).

1986 3rd Pan-Orthodox Preconciliar Conference (following 1976, 1982) to plan future Great & Holy Synod of the Orthodox Church, held in Geneva, dealing with 10 proposed Synod issues (28 October-6 November).

1986 International Christian Media Conference meets in Amsterdam, with 500 communicators from 75 countries, with theme 'Partners in Communication' (13-17 October).

1986 4th Assembly, All India Council of Christian Women (part of NCCI), held in Madras with 150 women attending; resolves women's representation should be at least a third in all church activities (29 September-3 October).

1986 4th Plenary Assembly, Federation of Asian Bishops' Conferences (FABC), held in Tokyo, inviting CCA/Protestant participation for first time (16-25 September).

1986 18th General Meeting, Ecumenical Youth Council in Europe (EYCE), held in Berekfurdo (Hungary) (12-18 October).

1986 24th International Old Catholic Congress, held in Munster (Germany), celebrating 100th anniversary of Union of Utrecht (1889), on theme 'Witness and Service in the World' (26-30 August).

1986 8th General Assembly, World Evangelical Fellowship (WEF), held in Singapore with 230 delegates and observers from 61 countries and 46 member bodies (22-27 June).

1986 3rd World Christian Tamil Conference, sponsored by CSI and World Christian Tamil Academy, held in Madras (India) (26-29 December).

1986 4th General Assembly, Caribbean Conference of Churches (CCC, representing 74 denominations), held in Bridgetown (Barbados), on theme 'Jesus Christ: Justice, Hope, Peace' (4-9 September).

1986 9th Assembly, Conference of European Churches (CEC), held in Stirling (Scotland), with 200 delegates from 24 countries on theme 'Glory to God and Peace on Earth' (4-11 September).

1986 2nd General Assembly, Ecumenical Association of Third World Theologians (EATWOT, on its 10th anniversary), held in Oaxtepec (Mexico) on theme 'Commonalities and Divergences in Third World Theologies', with 70 delegates (7-14 December).

1986 7th Church Growth International Conference, in Tokyo (7-9 May).

1987 Unprecedented Intermediate Nuclear Forces (INF) Treaty is signed, providing for dismantling of all USA and Soviet intermediate-range nuclear weapons.

1987 Demonstration by pro-Iranian Muslims visiting Muslim holy city of Mecca ends with 400 dead after police open fire on demonstrators (31 July).

1987 5th Islamic Summit, Organization of the Islamic Conference (OIC), in Kuwait, with official delegates from Islamic nations (26-28 January).

1987 6th Annual All India Renewal Conference (charismatic), Kerala, with 300 church leaders and 2,000 attenders (27-30 January).

1987 LWF Consultation on Evangelism in Malawi and Mozambique, held in Malawi (1-3 February).

1987 European Ecumenical Satellite Conference, in Hilversum, Netherlands (20-21 March).

1987 Taiwan: National Symposium on Evangelization (Roman Catholic).

1987 Asian Lausanne Conference on World Evangelization (ALCOWE/LCWE), in Hong Kong (April).

1987 LCWE International Researchers Consultation, in Zeist, Netherlands (14-17 April).

1987 East Germany: annual meeting, Conference on the Evangelization of the German Democratric Republic.

1987 Zimbabwe: National Church Growth Conference on 'Discipling Zimbabwe'; 30 denominations and all parachurch agencies (20-24 April).
1987 Papua New Guinea: 1st National Evangelists' Conference (April).
1987 International Colloquium on 16th Centenary of the Conversion/Baptism of St Augustine in Milan, held in Milan, Italy (22-24 April).
1987 ACC-7: 7th Meeting, Anglican Consultative Council, in Singapore (25 April-9 May).
1987 National Charismatic Leaders' Conference (North American Renewal Service Committee, NARSC), related to global Charismatic Renewal in mainline denominations (100 million Christians, fielding 60,000 foreign missionaries), meets in Glencoe, MO (USA), appoints World Evangelization Strategy Committee with AD 2000 goal in mind (4-8 May).
1987 World Literature Crusade changes name to Every Home for Christ, proclaims goal 'to systematically place 2 gospel booklets in every home in the world, one country at a time, by AD 2000'; 40% of world's homes reached since 1946; 1986, 21,969,676 pieces of literature distributed, producing 178,509 written responses (0.8%); 1957-86, tracts distributed total 1,462,406,418, with 14,605,937 responses (1.0%).
1987 Lutherische Europaische Kommission für Kirche und Judentum, in Budapest, Hungary (6-8 May).
1987 6th International Leaders Conference, Catholic Charismatic Renewal (ICCRO), Rome, on 'The Spirit of the Lord is upon Me'; addressed by John Paul II (11-16 May).
1987 ICMM '87, 11th Triennial International Convention on Missionary Medicine (MAP International), on St Simons Island, GA (USA), on 'Christian health care: the challenge of change' (30 May-2 June).
1987 Singapore '87, LCWE International Conference for Younger/Emerging Christian Leaders; 275 leaders (1-10 June).
1987 Pentecost '87: National Satellite Celebration of Catholic Evangelization: one-day 7-hour USA-wide media event (Pentecost Saturday, 6 June) by Paulist National Catholic Evangelization Association (PNCEA), training 60,000 lay, religious and clerical evangelizers in 200 auditoriums; to be repeated every Pentecost Saturday up to AD 2000.
1987 All-Europe Catechetical Congress, in Munich, Germany (8-11 June).
1987 10th World Congress of the Deaf (World Federation of the Deaf, WFD, with 76 countries as members), in Helsinki (June); also World-Wide Symposium on Sign Languages, in Helsinki (June).
1987 All Africa Lutheran Consultation (sponsored by LWF), in Antsirabe, Madagascar (20-28 June).
1987 1st Meeting, Baptist International Conference of Colleges and Universities (BICCU), Amman, Jordan (29 June-1 July).
1987 3rd International Christian Youth Conference, World Methodist Council, in Brisbane, Australia; over 1,000 delegates (30 June-7 July).
1987 LCWE Consultation on Muslim Evangelization, in Zeist, Netherlands, on theme 'Operation Firstborn' (27 June-4 July).
1987 3rd Latin American Missionary Congress (COMLA-3), on 5th centenary of Roman Catholic first evangelization of Latin America; in Bogota, on theme: 'America, the Hour has come for You to be an Evangelizer' (5-10 July).
1987 International Conference on Data Bases in the Humanities and Social Sciences, in Montgomery, AL, USA (11-13 July).
1987 Uniting churches (churches negotiating toward organic union) suffer more setbacks than in previous decades, collapsing in England and Ghana, in difficulties in New Zealand, Tanzania, South Africa and Scotland; with recent successful unions achieved only in USA (1983 Presbyterians, 1988 Lutherans) and in Canada (1985 Evangelical Lutheran Church in Canada).
1987 Pentecostal European Conference (PEC/PEK), in Lisbon (22-26 July).
1987 3rd Consultation of Evangelical Missiologists from the Two-Thirds World, in Kenya (August).
1987 Poland: Youth Congress '87 (Protestant), in Warsaw, with 5,000 attenders (August).
1987 LWF Consultation on 'The Church and Civil Religion Worldwide—The Importance of Religion and Basic Values for Nation and State', in Bossey, Switzerland (31 August-5 September).
1987 USA: EFMA-IFMA Joint Triennial Conference, on 'Focusing the Vision', in Orlando, FL (21-25 September).
1987 2nd Annual Meeting, US Society for Frontier Missiology, in Orlando, FL (USA), on strategy for world evangelization by AD 2000 (25-26 September).
1987 USA: Ecumenical Mission Consultation (USCMA/DOM-NCCCUSA), on 'Divided Churches/Common Witness; an Unfinished Task for US Christians in Mission', in Madison, CT (27 September-3 October).
1987 1st Meeting, Commission of Third World Missions (related to AMA), São Paulo, Brazil.
1987 7th General Assembly, Ordinary Synod of Bishops, Rome, on 'Vocation and Mission of the Laity in the Church and in the World'.
1987 World Consultation on Ecumenical Sharing of Resources (sponsored by WCC) held in El Escorial (Spain) with 200 attenders from 70 countries, on theme 'Koinonia: Sharing Life in a World Community', to seek guidelines for a radical new pattern of resource sharing between churches, missions, development agencies, etc, each transferring 50% of its resources ecumenically (24-31 October).
1987 Ecuador: SOMA International Conference, Quito, on 'Evangelism in the Power of the Holy Spirit in Latin America', for Anglican bishops, clergy and lay leaders (8-11 October).
1987 Britain: joint BCC/RCC conference (British Council of Churches, Roman Catholic Church) to consider nature of church and mission in light of Lima (BEM), ARCIC and Vatican II documents.
1987 Japan: National Incentive Convention for Evangelization (NICE '87), held by Catholic Church in Japan after extensive preparations in all Japan's dioceses (November); 1993, NICE II held.
1987 USA: Urbana '87, 15th International Student Missions Convention; 17,200 delegates.
1987 3rd Japan Congress on Evangelism, Kyoto, with 4,500 delegates.
1987 John Paul II announces new Office in Rome, 'Evangelization 2000', initially confined to Catholics, with news service New Evangelization 2000, and later to lead into ecumenical 1990-2000 Decade of Evangelization; comprising retreats, biggest public rally ever, 3-satellite global telecasts, global homilies, conscientization teams, mass video cassette distribution, with as aims (a) to win 1.5 billion new Christians 'as a present for Jesus on his 2,000th birthday', and (b) to unite all Christians and all churches by AD 2000.
1987 44th Annual Convention & Exposition, National Religious Broadcasters (USA), Washington, with over 4,000 broadcasters, on theme 'Communicating Christ to the Nations' (31 January-4 February).
1987 Consultation on World Evangelization, Singapore, with 31 global charismatic renewal leaders (RC/Lutheran/SOMA-Anglican, et alii) (9-12 February).
1987 International Conference of Evangelical Bible Societies (ICEBS) founded 'to evangelize and disciple all nations through the placement of God's word', with 10 member agencies: ASGM, BLI, EHC, IBS, LBI, OD, PTL, WGC, WHBL, WMP.
1987 T.Y.H. Wang in Singapore issues LCWE call with article 'By the Year 2000: Is God telling us something?'; many responses from across world.
1987 Proposal 'Countdown to the Year 2000' circulated by USCWM founder R.D. Winter, with statistics and graphics urging the engaging (entering) and reaching (discipling) by mission agencies of 1,500 new unreached peoples every year until 17,000 have been reached by AD 2000.
1987 Global-Village Evangelism (based on Marshall McLuhan's description of the world as now a 'global village') launched by Bibles For The World as 'a revolutionary new concept in missions which places the local church in the center of the world mission program'.
1987 Singapore '87 LCWE International Younger Leaders' Conference on world evangelization; 300 younger Evangelical leaders from 67 countries (1-10 June).
1987 Global Rosary for World Peace and world evangelization prayed by John Paul II in St Peter's basilica, Vatican, and by 16 Marian shrines across the world linked by 18 satellites and 75 TV cameras, with TV audience of 1.5 billion in over 30 countries in 35 languages; most complex and ambitious television program of all time.
1987 North American General Congress on the Holy Spirit and World Evangelization, in New Orleans (successor to 1977 Kansas City ecumenical charismatic rally); over 50,000 participants (RC/Protestant charismatic renewal), 51% RCs; theme 'Power Evangelism' (22-26 July); launches magazine AD 2000 Together with front page motto 'To Bring the Majority of the Human Race to Jesus Christ by the End of the Century'.
1987 Dominion Network (satellites to homes) launched into orbit by Community Satellite Corporation, USA, utilizing DBS (direct broadcast satellites).
1987 Global Share Network announced by Global Mapping International (USA) as a missions mapping database.
1987 T. Yamamori writes *God's new envoys: a bold strategy for penetrating closed countries*, presenting a detailed plan describing the strategic work Christian lay tentmakers in secular work can perform in world evangelization; chapter 6 entitled 'The Basic Battle Plan' calls for 100,000 such persons in 77 closed countries.
1987 Research project 'The Future of the Christian World Mission' begun under auspices of American Society of Missiology, majoring on scenarios for the future of world evangelization.
1987 Mission World '89 (International Satellite Mission) announced by Billy Graham Evangelistic Association, to originate from a major global city (Seoul) and to be beamed by satellite to hundreds of other cities across the world; but whole plan suddenly cancelled 5 months later and replaced by scaled-down London crusade in 1989 with relays across England only.
1987 Global Broadcasting System (GBS) launched for Christian radio and TV broadcasting to any place on Earth through 'Top Hat' system of super-pressure platform network of 800 high-tech balloons at 120,000 feet altitude covering whole world.
1987 Adopt-a-People, a proposal to link North American churches and mission agencies with specific unreached people groups, begun by USCWM.
1987 Christian Communication Technology (CCT) formed to develop AVCAPI (computer/laser reading system for illiterates) with goal: 'By the year 2000, CCT will teach every capable and willing man, woman and child on earth to read the Bible in their own language.'
1987 Worldwide Prayer Crusade launched from Vatican City by Evangelization 2000 office, geared to Decade of Universal Evangelization 1990-2000; sudden, unexpected, and massive enthusiastic response from contemplatives, convents, and monasteries worldwide.
1987 Project 2000 begun by Partnership International, formerly Christian Nationals Evangelism Commission (CNEC, begun 1943), now in 50 countries; project pledges 'to help establish an evangelistic growing church in each of the 17,000 unreached people groups of the world by the year 2000', 'to help strengthen 400 ministries under 80 different indigenous national organizations'.
1987 Destiny '87 Conference (Here's Life, Black America); 1,700 Black Americans gather in Atlanta, GA, to affirm 'a growing number of black Christians believe it is their destiny to play a major role in world evangelization'.
1987 New Life 2000 announced as closure project by Campus Crusade for Christ/Here's Life World—the comprehensive global strategy to take the gospel to every culture on every continent by the year 2000; to present the gospel message to 6.5 billion people; to see 1 billion people receive Jesus Christ as Lord and Savior; to establish 10,000 New Life Bible study groups; to establish 1 million new churches; to provide 5,000 teams showing the 'Jesus' film 100 times a year to 1,000 people per night (yielding 10% to 25% salvation decisions a night); to establish 15,000 prayer movements by 1995, in every city over 50,000 and all university campuses'.
1987 *Towards 2000: Reaching the world's billions*, written by physician Benjamin George, Campaign for Christ (YFC), Malaysia; plan calls only for lifestyle evangelism (daily personal witnessing).
1987 Interdenominational Global Missions Conference (Dallas I) convened (17-18 September) by Southern Baptist FMB president R.K. Parks, with 20 mission agencies present; agreement on (1) prayer and fasting every Pentecost weekend up to AD 2000 as 'focused intercession for global evangelization', and (2) sharing data, plans and strategies; 1988, Dallas II (February), followed by teleconferences.
1987 *Status Report on the Great Commission* published by World Mission Teams (formerly World Mission Crusade), Florida, as open letter addressed 'To All Pastors of All Christian Churches' setting out logistics and finances of how to evangelize the world by means of 'the fourth dimension in evangelism' (1st = personal witness, 2nd = printing, 3rd = broadcasting, 4th = motion picture evangelism).
1987 Decade of Harvest inaugurated by Assemblies of God (USA), as denominational program to reach all persons on Earth by AD 2000; coordination by Total Church Evangelism Strategy Committee, renamed in 1987 Harvest Task Force (for work within USA); 1988 (July), world conference of AoG-related churches overseas to plan strategy.
1987 Ibadan, Nigeria: Consultation between All Africa Baptist Fellowship and Overseas Mission Bodies (October); produces Ibadan Declaration, on Great Commission and 'mutual sharing in the holistic evangelisation of the world'.
1987 2nd Asia Leadership Congress on World Evangelization (ALCOWE or ALCOE II), under LCWE/ALCOWE auspices, in Singapore, on theme 'Witnessing for Christ through the Local Church' (20-28 October).
1987 1st Ibero-American Missions Congress (Congreso Misionero Ibero-Americano, COMIBAM '87), in São Paulo (Brazil), with 3,500 Evangelical representatives (70% pentecostal/charismatic) from across Latin America, and preceded by series of national missions consultations in 23 countries; goal of world evangelization, with 10,000 new Latinamerican foreign missionary vocations generated (23-28 November).
1987 Church of God (Cleveland, TN), with work in 98 countries, launches 'Decade of Destiny for Church of God World Missions', with a different continent targeted for each year from 1990 to 2000.
1987 Advance Ministries: Reaching the Unreached, a mission-sending agency serving the USA's 60,000 independent charismatic churches, begun with Mennonite support.
1987 World Evangelism World Plan 1987-1991 launched at Jamaica meeting after 15th World Methodist Conference (Nairobi, July 1986, 3,000 delegates) on theme 'Christ Jesus: God's 'Yes' for the World': 1988 Aldersgate Year, Open-Air Preachings, 1989 World Conference on Physical & Spiritual Poverty, 1990 4th International Christian Youth Conference, 1991 Conference on World Evangelization followed by 16th World Methodist Conference in Singapore.
1987 Charismatic pastor D. Shibley writes *Let's pray in the Harvest* on how to 'Discover the Missing Key to World Evangelization'.
1987 Total nuclear warheads deployed by all armies across the world: 52,000
1987 7th World Sanskrit Conference, held in Kern Institute, Leiden (Netherlands) (August).
1987 USA: 15th Annual Meeting, American Society of

Missiology (ASM), in Pittsburgh, on theme 'Forecasting the Future in World Mission' (19-21 June).

1987 *International review of mission* (Geneva) devotes entire January issue to theme 'The future of mission', with 21 articles; USA journal *Missiology* entitles its January issue 'Future of the world Christian mission'.

1987 *Cosmos, chaos, and gospel: a chronology of world evangelization from Creation to New Creation* published (by D.B. Barrett); 4,000 chronological entries including 700 future miniscenarios.

1987 H. Kreysler of Watchman in the Wilderness, California, publishes *Last Days* chart showing Russia invading Israel in 1988, Rapture of the church in 1991, Armageddon in 1995.

1987 R.L. Numbers & J.M. Butler edit *The disappointed: Millerism and millenarianism in the 19th century* (Bloomington).

1987 *Space: the next twenty-five years*, by T.R. McDonough.

1987 *Our common future*, compiled by J. MacNeill.

1987 Cambridge physicist and cosmologist Stephen W. Hawking publishes *A brief history of time: from the Big Bang to black holes.*

1987 *Utopia and Anti-Utopia in modern times*, by Krishan Kumar.

1987 Swiss Catholic theologian Hans Küng writes *Theology for the Third Millennium: an ecumenical view.*

1987 A.C. Clarke continues sci-fi trilogy with *2061: Odyssey Three.*

1987 *The oracle of geomancy: techniques of earth divination*, by S. Skinner.

1987 *Nostradamus and the Millennium: predictions of the future*, compiled by J. Hogue.

1987 *100 predictions for the Baby Boom: the next 50 years*, by Cheryl Russel.

1987 *Omni's Future medical almanac* edited by D. Teresi & P.G. Adcroft.

1987 India: Committee on National Strategy (CONS) begun, with 56 leaders discussing 'How can we reach the unreached peoples of India?'

1987 International League of Religious Socialists, meeting in Geneva, resolves to apply for associate membership in London-based Socialist International (3-7 September).

1987 17th International and Interconfessional Meeting of Religious (Monks and Nuns), held in Bucharest (Romania), with participants from most European countries.

1987 5th General Assembly, Association of Evangelicals of Africa and Madagascar (AEAM), held in Lusaka (Zambia), on theme 'Following Jesus in Africa Today', with 300 delegates from 50 countries (12-19 September).

1987 5th Anglican Evangelical Assembly, held in Swanwick (UK) (January).

1987 5th General Assembly, Association of Christian Institutes for Social Concerns, held in Manila (Philippines) (January).

1987 6th Japan-Korea Church Consultation, held in Osaka, especially discussing past grievances (27-30 January).

1987 Interfaith Fellowship of the World Congress of Faiths formed, by merger of World Congress of Faiths, and the Interfaith Association.

1987 ACC-7 (Anglican Consultative Council) held in Singapore (26 April-9 May).

1987 22nd German Evangelical Kirchentag (Church Congress), in Frankfurt with over 150,000 attenders, on theme 'Behold the Man', with each day beginning with one full hour of Bible study; vast number of stalls, exhibits, and concerns (17-21 June).

1987 5th International Consultation of United and Uniting Churches, sponsored by WCC, held in Potsdam (Germany), with representatives of 30 united denominations from 24 countries, on 'Living Today towards Visible Unity' (1-8 July).

1987 1st Congress, International Federation of Married Priests, with 150 delegates from 16 countries (representing 20,000 RC priests who have married but wish to continue ministry), held in Ariccia (Italy) (22-28 August).

1987 Australia: 1st National Baptist Charismatic Conference held.

1987 USA: Pentecost '87, a one-day National Celebration of Evangelization, a multimedia satellite/television program on 6 June, run by Paulist National Catholic Evangelization Association (PNCEA), with 60,000 Roman Catholic lay evangelizers celebrating in 200 auditoriums.

1987 8th Church Growth International Conference, in Jerusalem (4-7 November).

1987 Colombia: 1st National Congress on Cross-Cultural Missions, in Bogota, with 250 delegates from 30 denominations (1-3 May).

1987 O. de la Brosse publishes in Paris *Chronologie universelle: Eglise et culture occidental.*

1987 5th General Assembly, All Africa Conference of Churches (AACC), held in Lome (Togo), with 600 delegates from 120 denominations in 38 countries, on theme 'You Shall Be My Witnesses' (18-25 August).

1987 1st Africa's Deliverance Convention, Charismatics sponsored by Christian Missionary Foundation (CMF) begun in 1982 in Ibadan (Nigeria); then annually.

1988 4th European Ecumenical Encounter, sponsored by CEC and CCEE, held in Erfurt (GDR) (28 September-2 October).

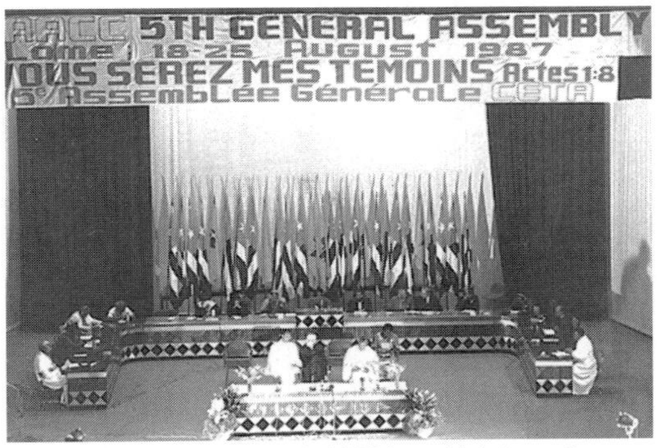


**AD 1987.** Opening worship at 5th AACC Assembly in Lome, Togo.

1988 2nd General Assembly, Latin American Council of Churches (CLAI, with 136 member bodies), in Indaiatuba, São Paulo (Brazil), on theme 'The Church: Toward Hope in Solidarity' (28 October-2 November).

1988 Ecumenical Decade of Churches in Solidarity with Women (WCC) launched.

1988 5th Consultation for United and Uniting Churches (WCC).

1988 Greenhouse effect: since 1960, unregulated burning of fossil fuels increases carbon dioxide in atmosphere, heating it by 1 degree F more every 8 years; by AD 2045, reaches 7 degrees F hotter at which point polar regions begin to thaw, ice caps melt, ocean levels rise 200 feet and flood much of Europe, UK, US Gulf states, eastern China, et alia.

1988 Evangelical Fellowship of Asia holds Consultation on 'The Church in the Midst of Suffering', in Hong Kong.

1988 Congress for Evangelizing Black America, held in Atlanta (Georgia), with 1,000 Blacks from many denominations attending (16-19 August).

1988 Moravian Unity Synod (session every 7 years), held in Antigua (Caribbean), representing world's 500,000 Moravians (July).

1988 Palestine National Council announces Declaration of Independence for the State of Palestine.

1988 3rd Assembly, Ecumenical Association of African Theologians (AOTA), held in Kinshasa (Zaire) (December).

1988 12th World Assembly, International Movement of Catholic Agricultural & Rural Youth (MIJARC), held in Belgium (October).

1988 Global Meeting of Women of Different Faiths in Dialogue (WCC), held in Toronto (June).

1988 UBS Symposium on 'Bible Translation and the Spread of the Church: the Last 200 Years', at Princeton, NJ (USA) with 65 participants (October).

1988 3rd International Conference on Russian Orthodox Liturgical Life and Art held in Leningrad; describes iconographic renewal, icons as windows on eternity (31 January-5 February).

1988 World Assemblies of God Fellowship (WAGF) formed, in Springfield, MO (USA), by 100 delegates from AoGs across world.

1988 European Charismatic Leaders' Conference, meeting in Berlin with 150 participants from 18 countries, organizes European Charismatic Consultation.

1988 In Los Angeles (USA), 500 leaders of General Conference, World Buddhist Fellowship, meet and open Hsi Lai ('Coming to the West') temple, largest Buddhist structure in Western hemisphere (November).

1988 Christival-2 Youth Gathering, held in Nuremberg (West Germany).

1988 Some 1 million fax machines are bought during year as popularity of electronic transmission and reproduction of documents surges.

### *The Information Civilization: 4th Industrial Revolution*

1988 After 1st Industrial Revolution (1775), 2nd (1901), and 3rd (1950, nuclear power, microchips, genes), 4th revolution from 1988 on is noological, knowledge-based, information-based; with people-supervised cybernated machines based on inexhaustible resources in space.

1988 Knowledge explosion: the stock of human knowledge increases phenomenally each year; contents of USA Library of Congress (world's largest), and other major libraries, available to all via personal computers.

1988 First USA 5th-generation ultracomputers: supercomputers using multiprocessing (hundreds of microprocessors linked together).

1988 Supercomputers increasingly used for international sabotage via software bombs (programmed booby traps).

1988 39th Annual Meeting of WCC Central Committee, held in Hanover, Germany (10-20 August); the whole series of annual meetings is so complex that little of real substance emerges satisfactorily for both Protestant and Orthodox blocs.

1988 Robotics revolution, with large numbers of industrial robots, begins to dramatically alter economy of Japan and then of Western world; 20% of all industrial mass production now carried out by robots.

1988 New Transcendentalism: new interest in meditation and other New Age self-exploratory techniques; growing global drug addiction.

1988 USA: new uniting denomination, Evangelical Lutheran Church in America, formally inaugurated by 3 bodies with 5.3 million members: American Lutheran Church, Lutheran Church in America, Association of Evangelical Lutheran Churches (1 January).

1988 International Theological Consultation on Religious Conversion (sponsored by LCWE and WEF), in Hong Kong (4-8 January).

1988 1st World Meeting, Global Network of Centers for World Mission, in Singapore (May).

1988 USSR places permanent space stations in orbit for military purposes.

1988 First success in repairing a human genetic defect.

1988 Computers widely used in automatic document translation and multilingual instantaneous interpreting.

1988 Automatic computer self-programming using plain ordinary language replaces 30% of all human programming of computers.

1988 Technological disasters proliferate: nuclear mishaps, chemical spills, virus escapes, major air and shipping accidents, structural failures, industrial sabotage, unstoppable pest attacks on crops and animals or people.

1988 5th Nigeria National Congress on Evangelization, Zaria.

1988 Urban Evangelism Conference, sponsored by Baptist World Alliance, in Panama/Mexico/Costa Rica (2-4 July).

1988 Canterbury '88: Anglican Spiritual Renewal Conference, Canterbury (UK), organized by SOMA, for leaders of leaders on 'The Church in the Valley of Decision'; 350 present including many bishops (3-7 July); followed by SOMA open conference for 1,500 (9-12 July).

1988 1st International Congress for the Evangelization of the Spanish World, in USA, sponsored by Evangelicals, with 4,000 Hispanic leaders (25-29 July).

1988 11th Baptist Youth World Conference (BWA), Glasgow, on theme 'Jesus Christ rules'; 10,000 youth participants from over 100 countries (27-31 July).

1988 World Conference on the Christian Approach to Poverty 1986-1991 (World Methodist Council), in Latin America; on Methodism's social witness.

1988 International Evangelical Bible Consultation/Conference (sponsored by LCWE, BGEA et al), in Amman, Jordan, stressing biblical position on justice and human rights.

1988 World Conference on Religious Liberty, Jerusalem.

1988 USA: Congress 88, A National Festival of Evangelism, sponsored by all major mainline denominations (PCUSA, UMC, SBC, RCC, et alia); 15,000 church leaders present; aim, to reach all unchurched and unreached Americans; title, 'That the World May Believe'; in Chicago (4-8 August).

1988 13th World Congress, International Council of Christian Churches (ICCC), in Amsterdam; 40th anniversary of founding there during 1st Congress (August).

1988 Conferences on evangelization: since 1945, some 5,510 conferences on mission and evangelism (at international, continental, regional or national level) have been held, via 5 groupings: 1,050 by Roman Catholic agencies; 1,100 by Ecumenical Movement agencies; 2,100 by Protestant and Anglican mission agencies; 840 by Evangelical mission agencies; and 420 by Charismatic Renewal agencies.

1988 Missions journalist J.W. Reapsome polls agencies and executives, publishes analysis and assessment 'Great Commission deadline: is the year 2000 a reasonable goal or an improbable dream?' (*Christianity Today*, 15 January), followed by 5-part series in *Evangelical missions quarterly.*

1988 Evangelist N. Krupp writes large volume *The Church Triumphant at the End of the Age*, characterized by revival, restoration, unity, world evangelization, and persecution; holds Great Commission will only be fulfilled by supernatural means of a global End-time revival.

1988 Churches of the poor spread gospel, unorganized and unplanned, in almost every corner of Earth.

1988 2nd All-India Congress on Missions and Evangelism (AICOME '88), sponsored by indigenous-mission body India Missions Association, IMA as successor to AICOME 1977 (with 300 member agencies), in Pune, India; 350 participants (4-8 January); global total of organized Third-World mission agencies now 500.

1988 Singapore II Consultation on World Evangelization, with 65 global charismatic renewal leaders organized as CUWE, Charismatics United for World Evangelization with the new watchword 'The whole church, bringing a whole Christ, to the whole world!', 'to consider the distinctive contribution that the charismatic renewal could make in spreading the Christian gospel in the years leading up to AD 2000' (February).

1988 Christian prophecy: millions of predictions, prophecies and proposed scenarios have been made throughout history; Catholic prophecy alone, not officially acknowledged by Rome, has produced over the centuries several thousand collected prophecies about End of World and the Antichrist, some by laypersons, some by clergy, some by monks and nuns, some by bishops, and some by popes.

1988 Consultation to inaugurate Third World Missions Advance (TWMA), convened by AMA/IMF/EMS/COMIBAM; 35 Third-World leaders meet in Portland, OR (9-13 May); International Mutual Fund created; TWMA aims to represent the hundreds of new missions agencies, with potential of fielding 100,000 Third-World missionaries by AD 2000.

1988 Leadership '88, LCWE Conference for Emerging Younger Christian Leaders, in Washington, DC for 2,200 leaders, to 'equip them to take aggressive action to fulfill the Great Commission', to 'strategize to join together for world evangelization' and 'to form new networks for completing the task of world evangelization' (27 June-1 July).

1988 North American African World Missions Congress (Initiative '88) to implement global evangelization, organized by Nigerians after 1986 formation of North American Commission of African Christians; theme 'African Initiatives in World Missions: a Strategic Gathering for a New Decade'; 1,500 Africans from over 30 African countries, living in North America, present in Chicago (13-17 July).

1988 World Congress on Sports, sponsored by coalition of Christian athletic agencies, held in Seoul, Korea with some 600 delegates from 106 countries.

1988 11th UBS Council Meeting/World Assembly held by United Bible Societies, in Budapest, Hungary on slogan 'God's Word: Hope for All', with 272 participants from 109 countries pledging 'making a commitment to reach every young person in the world by the year 2000 with a copy of the Word of God in the language he or she most easily understands' (14-21 September).

1988 2nd International Christian Zionist Congress, held in Jerusalem, sponsored by International Christian Embassy in Jerusalem (ICEF), European Charismatics (USA, Scandinavia, Holland, Germany, UK), and premillennial dispensationalists, the USA religious right, and Israeli government officials (April).

1988 USA: corporate debt rises to $1.78 trillion.

1988 10th World Conference, World Futures Studies Federation, sponsored by UNESCO Future-Oriented Studies Programme, in Beijing (China); biggest WFSF conference ever (September).

1988 Living species on Earth may approach 30 million, of which only 1.4 million have so far been described by today's 1,500 professional systematists; 25,000 professional lifetimes would be required to complete this taxonomic accounting.

1988 Deforestation: world's tropical forests are being destroyed at rate of 100 acres every minute of every day.

1988 Algae blooms spread worldwide via toxic and non-toxic global red tides of algae, through airborne nitrates mostly from motor oil, vehicles, and power plants; also plastic debris in oceans proliferates, doubling every 15 years.

1988 Cellular telephones are used by 1.6 million in USA, doubling every 2 years, with 4.5 million subscribers worldwide in 1990, with 100 million by AD 2000; 1993, first digital networks become operational; rising to 10% market penetration by 2005.

1988 Five dominant technologies drive progress for next 40 years: computers, automation, space colonies, energy, communications.

1988 Critical 100-year phase in human existence is now recognized to be the century 1950-2050: nuclear annihilation of all life on Earth possible and therefore of entire human race, until humans begin to spread out into space colonies.

1988 Explosive growth of charismatic, evangelical and fundamentalist 'video churches', video denominations and video mission agencies; vast rash of house-church networks begins to spread in all countries where large denominations have grown up.

1988 Specialized space telescopes put in orbit: SIRTF (Spacelab Infrared Telescope Facility), COBE (Cosmic Background Explorer), GRO (Gamma Ray Observatory).

1988 Hipparcos (High Precision Parallax Correcting Satellite) launched by European Space Agency, results in most accurate star map in history.

1988 World's fastest supercomputer introduced: Cray-3, with 16 main processors working in parallel, 8-billion-byte memory.

1988 E.C. Whisenant publishes *88 reasons why the Rapture will be in 1988*; predicts a horrific war between USA and USSR before US election of November 1988 leaving only 200,000 people alive out of USA's 240 million.

1988 During European Parliament in Strasbourg, France, militant Irish Protestant I. Paisley shouts at speaker, pope John Paul II: 'I renounce you! I renounce you as the Antichrist!'

1988 Cosmologist J. Gribbin produces *The Omega Point: the search for the missing mass and the ultimate fate of the Universe*.

1988 *Global mind change: the promise of the last years of the Twentieth Century*, by W.W. Harman.

1988 *Apocalypse when? Cosmic catastrophe and the fate of the universe* by F. Close.

1988 *The Gaia peace atlas: survival into the Third Millennium*, by F. Barnaby.

1988 16th General Conference, World Fellowship of Buddhists (WFB), held at largest Buddhist structure in Western hemisphere, the new Hsi Lai ('Coming to the West') temple (built by International Buddhist Progress Society), in Hacienda Heights (Los Angeles, USA), with 500 Buddhist leaders (November).

1988 1st Global Forum of Spiritual and Parliamentary Leaders on Human Survival held, at Oxford University, with 100 spiritual leaders and 100 parliamentarians from around the world.

1988 European Leadership Conference on World Evangelization (ELCOWE), sponsored by LCWE, in Bernhauser Forst, Stuttgart, Germany (5-9 September).

1988 12th Lambeth Conference of Anglican Bishops (decennial) held in Canterbury, UK: 420 dioceses, with 300 bishops from Third World, 200 from Western world (16 July-7 August).

1988 32nd Meeting, Conference of Christian World Communions (CWCs), in Jerusalem (17-20 October).

1988 15th Pentecostal World Conference, in Kuala Lumpur, Malaysia, on 'Behold the Glory of the Lord', with emphasis on strategy for global evangelization (5-9 October); opposed, cancelled.

1988 World Wesleyan Conference on Witness and Evangelism, sponsored by World Methodist Council, on 250th anniversary of John Wesley's conversion.

1988 1st International Meeting, Theological Students for Frontier Missions.

1988 2nd World Consultation on Frontier Missions (WCFM), announced, later cancelled.

1988 Enzyme processing (a chemical synthesis system) becomes fastest-growing industry on Earth.

1988 World Evangelization Database (segmentizing world into 250 countries, 13,000 ethnolinguistic peoples, 13,000 languages, 7,000 metropolises, et alia), first begun in 1962 as computer knowledge base, is finally brought online globally by WERC/FMB to assist mission agencies to match up nonresidential missionaries with entire unevangelized world; operated by massive computerized AI network, the World Evangelization Expert System (WEES).

1988 Literature on evangelization: on narrower definition, titles strictly on 'evangelize', 'evangelism' or 'evangelization' total 400 new books and articles every year; on broader definition, titles on evangelization and synonyms total 10,000 a year.

1988 World Prayer Force inaugurated in Saint Petersburg, FL (USA), aiming to enroll 165 million Christians (10% of world total) promising to pray daily for world evangelization.

1988 Inter-Agency Consultation for Resources and Information on Reaching the Unreached (Dallas II), held in Irving, TX (USA), by 28 denominations and agencies (9-11 February); followed by sharing of online databases and a series of Great Commission electronic teleconferences, with all mission executives and leaders participating from own headquarters.

1988 Evangelistic citywide mass campaigns: several hundred organized multidenominational campaigns (under Billy Graham, Luis Palau, et alii), and some 3,000 denominational campaigns, are held in 1,300 metropolises and cities across the world each year; also hundreds of megameetings (over 100,000 attenders) under Christ For All Nations and numerous other charismatic agencies, using slogan 'The Great Commission to Each Generation'.

1988 7th General Congress, International Association for Mission Studies (IAMS), in Rome, on theme 'Christian Mission towards the Third Millennium: the Gospel of Hope' (29 June-5 July).

1988 '88 World Evangelization Crusade, Korea, led by charismatics (Methodists, Presbyterians) and pentecostals.

1988 World Decade for Cultural Development (1988-1997), sponsored by UN.

**AD 1988.** 'Your Will Be done on Earth' as theme of 11th World Council of YMCAs, in Aruba (*left*).

1988 11th World Council of YMCAs, in San Nicholas, Aruba, Netherlands, Antilles, on theme 'Your Will be Done on Earth'.

1988 Russian Orthodox service held in St Basil's cathedral outside Kremlin for first time in 70 years.

1988 1st Conference, Center for the Study of New Religions (CESNUR, in Turin), held in Bari, Italy, then annually; 1999 held in Philadelphia, PA on 'Globalization of New Religions'.

1989 Two-year locust plague in African desert regions finally eases.

1989 1st World Congress on Evangelization of Portuguese-speaking Peoples, in Brazil.

1989 World Evangelization Conference on Liberation Theology and Personal Salvation (sponsored by World Methodist Council), in Latin America.

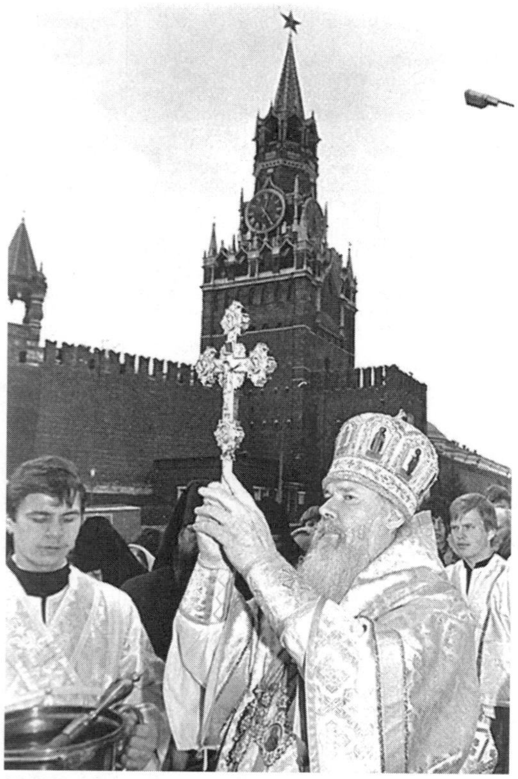

**AD 1988.** Major reversal of fortunes: patriarch Alexy II raises Cross in Kremlin, Communism disintegrates.

1989 World Conference of Methodist Fulltime Evangelists, sponsored by World Methodist Council.

1989 44th International Eucharistic Congress, in Seoul (Korea), addressed by pope John Paul II during his 44th foreign pilgrimage since 1978; theme, 'Christus Pax Nostra'.

1989 Global Consultation on World Evangelization by AD 2000 and Beyond, convened in Singapore by a group including LCWE/COMIBAM/FMB-SBC/YWAM, inviting 2 representatives of each of the 78 major current megaplans for world evangelization, 'open to all leaders of Great Commission groups within the worldwide body of Christ' (5-8 January); known as GCOWE-1.

1989 2nd World Consultation on Frontier Missions (WCFM).

1989 2nd World Conference on Mission and Evangelism (5th Meeting of CWME/WCC, Commission on World Mission and Evangelism), San Antonio, TX (USA); 600 attenders, mostly church nominees; theme 'Your Will be Done: Mission in Christ's Way'; distributes pan-Orthodox missionary icon widely (22 May-1 June).

1989 International Bishops' Retreat 2000 for world's 3,500 Roman Catholic bishops (October, in Rome), on theme 'Called to Evangelize', to inaugurate decade of evangelization 1990-2000; also, separately, and on same theme, Worldwide Priests' Retreat (9,000, in Rome, 14-18 September 1990), and Worldwide Theologians' Retreat (4,000, in Rome, October 1991).

1989 Lausanne II, or 2nd International Congress on World Evangelization (ICOWE II) convened by Lausanne Committee (LCWE), in Manila; congress theme, 'Proclaim Christ Until He Comes'; attended by 6,000 evangelizers (11-20 July).

1989 15th Pentecostal World Conference, finally opens in Singapore, on theme 'Behold the Glory of the Lord'; over 6,000 delegates from 100 countries, 30,000 attenders (27 September-1 October).

1989 Consultation on Dimensions of Christian Martyrdom, dealing with effects of martyrdom on upbuilding and evangelistic growth of whole church; total martyrs since AD 33 estimated at 40,500,000 (0.5% of all Christians ever), with current rate of 320,000 each year.

1989 Jerusalem Charismatic Leaders Meeting (Pentecost 89) convened for 120 Renewal leaders worldwide, dealing with power intercession, power evangelism, world evangelization; in Jerusalem over Pentecost weekend (7-14 May).

1989 European Ecumenical Assembly meets in Basel, Switzerland, with 314 RC and 324 Orthodox, Anglican, and Protestant delegates representing 500 million Christians, on WCC/JPIC theme 'Peace with Justice'; organized by European Catholic Bishops' Conferences (ECBC/CCEE: 25 national Episcopal Conferences) and Conference of European Churches (CEC/KEK: 120 member churches); major media event, 652 journalists, 7,000 attend closing worship; most important ecumenical event since Council of Nicaea II in AD 787 (15-21 May).

1989 Mission 90, annual event for European Christian

Youth, held in Utrecht (28 December-2 January 1990).
1989 Satellites enable living maps (animated color displays, movie x-rays in motion) of any city or area on Earth to be inspected for activities as they take place.
1989 Data-broadcasting stations begun, regularly transmitting all forms of data for personal computers and others to pick up.
1989 Biomedical technology: predetermination of sex and intelligence of children before birth achieved.
1989 Education explosion across world as electronic tutors make programmed instruction available on any subject at any level of difficulty.
1989 New religions arise based on psychobiological altered states of consciousness: ecstatic experiences, trance, dissociation, spirit possession, soul loss, astral projections, faith-healing, mysticism, glossolalia, occult, shouting, visions, out-of-body experiences, et alia.
1989 Creation of primitive form of artificial life (in form of self-replicating molecules).
1989 Historian W.W. Wagar (1932- ) writes *A short history of the future*, an informal general history of the years 1995-2100 with supporting documents, based on Marxist expectation of future demise of world capitalism and its replacement by pure communism; also writes in 1991, *The next three futures: paradigms of things to come*, describing the whole vast array of futurist enquiry.
1989 R.W. Faid publishes book *Gorbachev! Has the real Antichrist come?* but in 1991 USSR president M. Gorbachev resigns after aborted KGB/military coup.
1989 Systematic mapping of human genome (genetic endowment) begun by scientists across the world, leading eventually to reshaping the genome through genetic engineering, bioengineering, and psychoengineering to modify the human mind; human genome is in fact fully tracked and mapped by AD 2001.
1989 Canadian futurist F. Feather publishes *G-Forces*, holding that if world emulated North American corn farmers, enough food would result to sustain world population up to 48 billion; forecasts Pacific Rim superboom stabilizing planetary economy by AD 2050 at 10 billion people, gross world product of $300 trillion, with worldwide abolition of poverty by AD 2100.
1989 *Mass dreams of the future: the coming apocalyptic New Age*, by Chet B. Snow & Helen Wambach.
1989 P. Lorie & S. Murray-Clark write New Age overview, *History of the future: a chronology*.
1989 J.F. Coates & Jennifer Jarratt investigate 17 leading futurists, then edit *What futurists believe*.
1989 *Future mind: artificial intelligence*, by J.C. Glenn.
1989 Historian Howard F. Didsbury Jr compiles WFS's 6th General Assembly documents into *The future: opportunity not destiny*.
1989 *Megamistakes: forecasting and the myth of rapid technological change*, by S.P. Schnaars.
1989 *Soothsayers of the Second Advent* written by USA journalist W.M. Alnor, exposing rash of current doomsday-dating Antichrist-identifying literature and broadcasting.
1989 2nd International Meeting on 21st Century Studies, held in Washington DC, reporting on regional and national studies underway in 35 countries (17-21 July).
1989 1st Foresight Conference on Nanotechnology, held at Stanford University, California, USA.
1989 Conference on Ministry in Partnership with African Independent Churches, in Kinshasa, Zaire (July).
1989 2nd Assembly of the World's Religions, sponsored by Unification Church, on 'Responding to Our Contemporary Challenge'.
1989 Conference on Pentecostal and Charismatic Research in Europe, at Utrecht University; reports published as *Experiences of the Spirit*.
1989 Ghana National Consultation on Evangelism (June).
1989 4th Congress of the Pan-African Association of Catholic Exegetes (PACE), at Nairobi (July); 1991, 5th Congress of PACE, in Abidjan, on 'Universalism and Mission in the Bible'; 1993, 6th Congress of PACE, at Sowutuom (Ghana) with 27 participants on 'The Kingdom of God in the Synoptics: Conversion, Justice and Peace in Africa' (16-20 July).

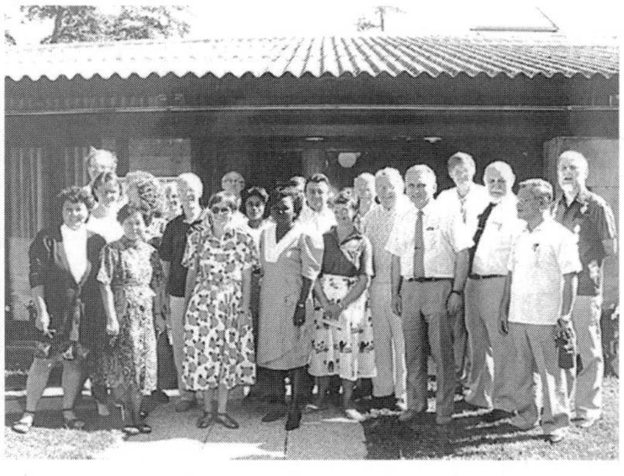

**AD 1989.** Executive Committee of WARC seeks to implement Council's resolutions.

1989 2nd General Assembly, Evangelical Fellowship of Asia (EFA), in Singapore, with 50 delegates from 11 countries; persecution and hardships of Christian workers reported widespread.
1989 Asia Mission Consultation, sponsored by CCA, held in Singapore, on theme 'The Mission of God in the Midst of the Suffering and Struggling People of Asia'.
1989 World Conference of Associations of Theological Institutions (WCATI) launched at consultation in Yogyakarta (Indonesia) (16-19 June).
1989 22nd General Council, World Alliance of Reformed Churches (WARC), held in Seoul (Korea), on theme 'Who do you say that I am?'; supports ecumenical call to covenant for justice, peace, and the integrity of creation (JPIC) (15-27 August).
1989 1st Pan-African Christian Women's Assembly (PACWA), held in Nairobi with over 1,000 delegates from 36 countries (August).
1989 WCC Dialogue Working Group meets in Casablanca (Morocco), reviewing Christian relations with other major religions (June).
1989 Netherlands: 1st Dutch Kerkendag (Church Congress), sponsored by Council of Churches in the Netherlands, held in Utrecht with 20,000 attenders, mainly on issues related to justice, peace, and integrity of creation (16 September).
1989 23rd German Evangelical Church Congress (Deutscher Evangelischer Kirchentag), held in West Berlin, with 155,000 attenders (65% under 30), on theme 'Our Time is in the Hands of God' (7-11 June).
1989 7th Meeting, Christian Base Communities, held in Duque de Caxias (Brazil), with 2,000 Brazilian participants including 90 RC bishops in Brazil, on theme 'People of God on the Road of Latin American Liberation'.
1989 World Congress, World Association for Christian Communication (WACC), held in Manila (Philippines), with over 500 participants from over 75 countries, on theme 'Communication for Community' (15-19 October).
1989 33rd Annual Meeting, Christian World Communions (CWCs), held in Geneva (Switzerland) (17-19 October).
1989 General Assembly, European Ecumenical Commission for Church and Society (based in Brussels) (27-28 September).
1989 Africa Association for Liturgy, Music, and the Arts (AALMA) holds second workshop, in Kinshasa (Zaire), with 50 participants from 20 countries (September).
1989 2nd Assembly, Africa Christian Peace Conference (ACPC), in Harare (Zimbabwe) (November).
1989 WCC delegation meet in Lagos with Nigerian Association of Aladura Churches (36 million members in Nigeria, Africa, Americas, Europe) with 4 main members (Church of the Lord Aladura, Cherubim & Seraphim Society, Christ Apostolic Church, 'Aladura Sections').
1989 3rd Gulf Churches Conference, held in Larnaca (Cyprus), with 50 representatives of 11 confessions: Anglican, United (CSI, CoPak), Lutheran, Coptic Orthodox, Syrian Orthodox, Pentecostal, Mar Thoma, Reformed/Presbyterian, Roman Catholic (27 February-4 March).
1989 5th Assembly, World Conference on Religion & Peace (WCRP), held in Melbourne (Australia) with 600 delegates, on theme 'Building Peace through Trust: the Role of Religion' (22-28 January).
1989 British Council of Churches (BCC) replaced by Churches Together in England (CTE), Churches Together in Wales (CTW), Action for Churches Together in Scotland (ACTS), within an umbrella Council of Churches for Britain and Ireland (CCBI), all now with full Roman Catholic membership; for Ireland, existing councils continue: Irish Council of Churches, Irish Inter-Church Meeting (including RCs), Inter-Church Consultative Committee; other bodies (Free Church Federal Council, West Indian Evangelical Alliance, Afro West Indian United Council of Churches) can join.
1989 Pakistan: 3rd Catholic Charismatic Conference, held in Karachi, with 500 attenders, on theme 'New Evangelization' (5-6 October).
1989 1st Northeast Asia Church Leaders Conference (sponsored by Japan Evangelical Association), in Hakone (Japan), on 'Ministry in the Power of the Word of God' (4-7 December); 2nd Conference, in Sorak (Korea, 28-31 October 1991); 3rd Conference , in Kyoto (Japan, 20-23 November 1995); 4th Conference, 1997.
1989 Northeast Asia Church Leaders Conference (NACLC-1), held in Hakone (Japan) with 50 attenders, on theme 'Ministry in the Power of the Word of God'; 1991 NACLC-2 in Sorak (Korea) (28-31 October); 1995 NACLC-3 in Kyoto (Japan) with 70 attenders, on 'The Power of the Holy Spirit in Ministry'; 1997 NACLC-4.
1989 Establishment in Warsaw (Poland) of the International Institute for Transnationalization of Terminology, to advance agendas of International Organization for Unification of Terminological Neologisms, and World Bank of International Terms (IOUTN and WBIT).
1989 Latin American Conference of Women Theologians meets in Buenos Aires, Argentina (September).

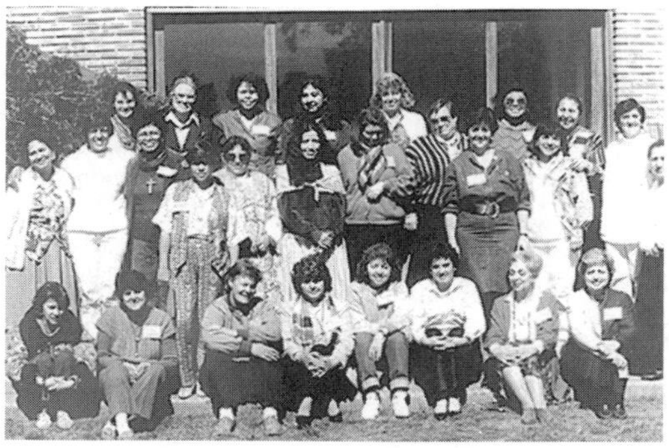

**AD 1989.** Women's role as theologians forcefully demonstrated in Argentina Conference.

1990 **Global status** of Christianity: 65.3 generations after Christ, world is 33.2% Christians (47.5% of them being Whites), 68.4% evangelized; with printed Scriptures available in 1,950 languages; total martyrs since AD 33 reach 68 million (0.9% of all Christians ever; recent rate 180,100 per year).
1990 NASA's Hubble Space Telescope launched by Space Shuttle in 320-mile-high orbit, but focus immediately found to be seriously flawed; finally, 1993 spacewalks install correcting lenses; the 14-feet diameter, 12 ton telescope then yields 10 times better viewing than on Earth, sees as far as 14 billion light years, enables unprecedented census of the Universe planned by AD 2010; solves mystery of quasars (galaxies forming or dying which each emits more light than 100 billion stars, and many with superluminal parts moving demonstrably faster than light).
1990 World's 10 largest cities: Tokyo/Yokohama 25,069,000, New York/NENJ 16,056,000, Mexico City 15,130,000, Sao Paulo 15,082,000, Shanghai 13,342,000, Bombay 12,246,000, Los Angeles 11,456,000, Buenos Aires 11,144,000, Calcutta 10,890,000, Beijing 10,820,000.

### *Global Christianity launches Decade of Universal Evangelism*

1990 Vast increases in all types of evangelization and of evangelistic activity: virtually all Christian denominations and agencies announce programs leading up to AD 2000.
1990 'Evangelization 2000' inaugurated by John Paul II based in Vatican.

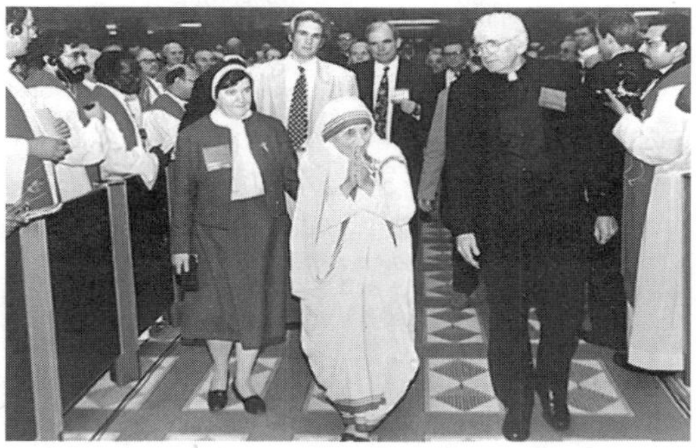

**AD 1990.** Mother Teresa greets 9,000 priests after addressing them on Jesus, Renewal, and Service.

1990 International Priests' Retreat 2000 on 'Evangelization 2000', in Rome; 9,000 RC priests attend (14-18 September).
1990 Round the World Prayer Event, organized by World Evangelism (World Methodist Council), to inaugurate evangelism in decade of 1990s.
1990 8th General Assembly, Ordinary Synod of Bishops, Rome (25 years after Vatican II), on theme 'The Word of God'.
1990 4th International Christian Youth Conference (World Methodist Council).
1990 USA: after 30 years of negotiations, 9 major Protestant denominations within the organic union scheme COCU (Consultation on Church Union/Church of Christ Uniting) finally agree to establish 'covenanting relationship' with 'councils of oversight' at all levels handling ordination, mission, et alia.
1990 Worldwide medical consultation networks and data banks.
1990 Daily body checkups by computer provide ample early warning of any impending illness.
1990 Ten million transistors (equivalent) now on a single microchip; data transfer (bubble) 10 million bits per second.
1990 Videotex (viewdata and teletext: consumer-oriented 2-way interactive electronic distribution services) supplies 8 million USA homes with vast array of computerized information data banks; similarly in Europe.
1990 IBM places world's first ultrahighspeed Josephson Junction computer online (super-cold supercon-

ducting switches); world's largest computer memory sits in 14 cm cube; one result, weather forecasting of superb accuracy for months into future.

1990 2nd General Assembly, Latin American Evangelical Confraternity (CONELA).

1990 USA: National Convocation on World Mission and Evangelism, Louisville, KY (May).

1990 Earth Day 1990, 20th anniversary of first Earth Day in 1970, celebrated by 200 million participants worldwide.

1990 Decade of Universal Evangelization (also termed Worldwide Decade of Evangelization) inaugurated by John Paul II and other world Christian leaders, calling all Christians to a decade of mission, with as aims (a) to unite all Christians and all churches by AD 2000, and (b) to bring the total of Christ's disciples to over 50% of world (3.1 billion) by AD 2000.

1990 USA: Joint IFMA/EFMA Conference convenes, after 1988 IFMA conference on 'Countdown 2000' and 1989 EFMA conference on 'Evangelizing the World by AD 2000'; approves specific allotments for 1995 schedule for reaching all peoples on Earth with gospel.

1990 World Congress on the Holy Spirit and World Evangelization, in Indianapolis, on 'Power Evangelism'; over 60,000 attenders (Catholic/Protestant charismatic renewal).

1990 EXPLO '90 global Christian 5-day training teleconference organized in all major countries by Campus Crusade for Christ (expanded version of EXPLO-85); also their 'Jesus' film becomes after 10 years translated into world's 280 languages each with over 1 million mother-tongue speakers, and is being shown to 10 million persons every night, of whom 2 million become converts or enquirers each night.

1990 Africa Regional Missions Congress on AD 2000 and Beyond (LCWE/TWMA/EMS/et alia).

1990 AD 2000 National Consultations proliferate, planned each for one country during the period 1990-1999 by LCWE/TWMA/et alia.

1990 Asia Missions Congress 90, sponsored by Evangelical Fellowship of Asia and LCWE/TWMA/AMA, in Seoul, Korea, with 1,302 participants from 50 nations, on centrality of Great Commission (27-31 August).

1990 Oberammergau decennial Passion Play 1990 seen by 460,000 visitors for 95 performances (May-September); generates $5 million for village of 5,000.

1990 15-satellite INTELSAT VI global satellite network links 175 countries, with thousands of miles of fiber optic cable, providing 125,000 telephone circuits or TV channels (3.2 billion bits of data a second).

1990 Since the age of classical Greece in the 5th century BC, world population has expanded by 50 times (from 100 million to 5.5 billion), but information available to world civilization has expanded by 10 million times (from $10^8$ bits to $10^{15}$ bits) over last 2,500 years.

1990 Working Group on the Futures of Culture, sponsored by UNESCO, held in Paris, France (January), resulting in book *The futures of culture,* volume 1; optimistic and pessimistic scenarios.

1990 World Summit for Children, held at UN headquarters, New York (29-30 September); year 2000 goals for children promulgated; documented in *The state of the world's children 1992.*

1990 Wristwatch pagers and beepers introduced with market of 7 million professional users (doctors, lawyers, sales reps); 1996, this technology suddenly takes off and mushrooms.

c1990 Dutch foundation 'Witnessing to God's Love' initiates campaign 'to introduce to Christ 50 million young people in Europe, America, Australasia'.

1990 1st International Dialogue on the Transition to a Global Society, held in Switzerland, sponsored by UNESCO et alia (September; annual).

1990 20th century seen as 'century of megadeath' in which 170 million human beings have been destroyed by wars or totalitarian genocide.

1990 Interparliamentary Conference on Global Environment promulgates 'Resolution on Sustainable Development', with proposals for National Charter for Sustainable Development for each nation, a Green Common Market, a Bank for Sustainable Development, et alia.

1990 Massive urban growth (7,000-year-old trend of urban flow or clustering) slows and reverses in most high-technology developed countries as offices and factories relocate in countryside, taking vast populations with them; large numbers of computerized 'intelligent buildings' arise, controlled by information management systems.

1990 Virtually all crime rates increase massively in Western societies for next 30 years, until crime eliminated by computerized surveillance by AD 2022.

1990 Astrophysicist D. Brin (1950- ) writes sci-fi epic novel *Earth* about World Data Net (global computer networks) in AD 2040, sophisticated space stations, huge endangered-species conservation arks, and microscopic black holes created as power stations but then released as weapons to devour planet Earth.

1990 United Nations agencies sponsor Decade of 1990-2000 under several differing names: Decade of International Law; 4th United Nations Development Decade; 2nd Transport and Communications Decade in Africa; International Decade for the Eradication of Colonialism; 3rd UN Disarmament Decade; International Decade for Natural Disaster Reduction.

1990 Telepower (the global electronic machine), has 4 basic components: (1) long-distance transmission systems (satellites, fiber optics, coaxial cable, microwave relays); (2) short-wave high-frequency radio telephone and tropo-scatter systems, plus signalling and switching equipment that routes messages; (3) final transmission to home or office, a fiber optic cable handling HDTV etc; (4) vast arrays of terminal equipments and sets—telex, fax, computer printers, audioconferencing bridges, videoconferencing bridges.

1990 J. Moltman writes *Theology of hope: a contemporary Christian eschatology.*

1990 Historian Hillel Schwartz writes *Century's end: a cultural history of the fin de siècle from the 990s through the 1990s.*

1990 *The Gaia atlas of future worlds*, by economist/environmentalist N. Myers.

1990 *Evil and evolutionary eschatology*, by J. Casserley.

1990 *Forecasting, planning, and strategy for the 21st century*, by S.G. Makridakis.

1990 *Future wealth*, by J. Robertson.

1990 *One Earth, one future: our changing global environment*, by Cheryl S. Silver.

1990 Paul R. & Anne H. Ehrlich write *The population explosion.*

1990 *The next one hundred years: shaping the fate of our living Earth*, by J. Weiner.

1990 2nd Global Forum of Spiritual Leaders and Parliamentarians for Human Survival, in Moscow.

1990 3rd European Charismatic Consultation (ECC; ecumenical Catholic/Protestant megacongress), with theme 'Jesus Hope for Europe', meets in Berne, Switzerland with 4,000 participants from 30 nations across Europe (2,000 from ex-Communist lands; 50% RCs; 50% under 35); 'Praise March ' across city releases 4,000 helium-filled balloons each with a participant's card attached (24-28 July).

1990 Nepal: ACTS 90, first open Christian conference, with 250 delegates from all denominations and agencies, held in Kathmandu (7 days in November).

1990 Russia Congress on Evangelism, Moscow; 1,141 Soviet delegates from all 15 USSR republics (October).

1990 16th Assembly, Baptist World Alliance (BWA), held in Seoul, Korea; 10,000 participants receive baptism together (July, August).

1990 12th Assembly, Mennonite World Conference (MWC, begun 1925), held in Winnipeg (Canada), on theme 'Witnessing to Christ in Today's World'; 200 workshops, 13,000 registrants (1,500 from outside North America) (24-29 July).

1990 55th Session (Assembly), General Conference of Seventh-day Adventists meets in Indianapolis, USA on theme 'We Shall Behold Him', with largest attendance ever (2,500 delegates and 40,000 attendees)(5-14 July).

1990 Rise of Promise Keepers (PK), a mass Christian outreach to men, with 72 attenders at Boulder, Colorado stadium event; by 1992, 22,000; 1993, 50,000; 1994, 278,600 in 7 stadiums; 1995, 727,342; 1996, 1.1 million men, 22 stadiums; 1997, 1.5 million at rally in Washington, DC; total attendances 1991-7, 3.7 million.

1990 5th General Assembly, Middle East Council of Churches (MECC, now with 26 member churches and 14 million Christians including all 7 Catholic bodies), held in Cyprus on theme 'Keep the Unity of the Spirit in the Bond of Peace (Ephesians 4:3)'.

1990 World Congress of Christian Fundamentalists: London: full infallibility of Bible/KJV investigated.

1990 5th European Ecumenical Youth Conference, held in West Germany.

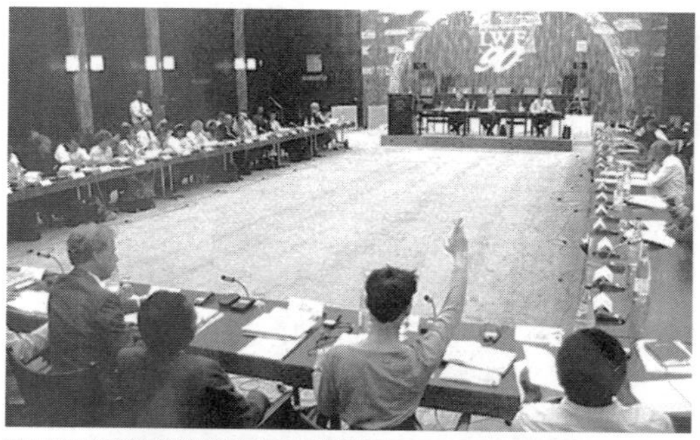

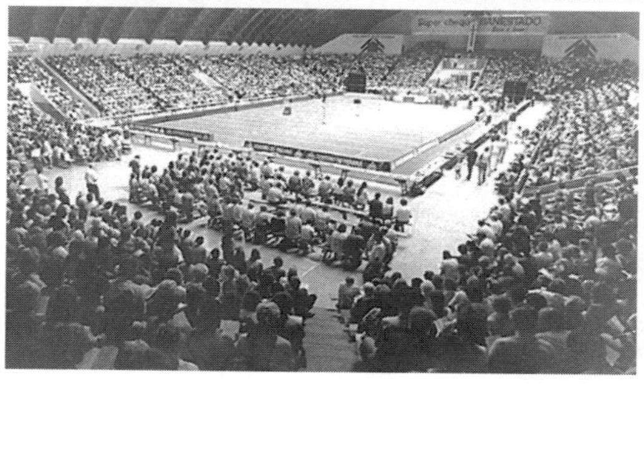

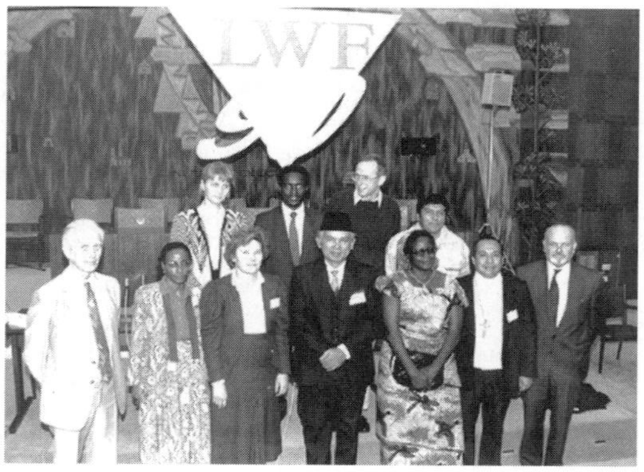

**AD 1990** LWF: (*top, in previous column*) Executive Committee; (*above*) officers, (*bottom, in previous column*) 8th Assembly, Curitiba (Brazil).

1990 8th Assembly, Lutheran World Federation (LWF), held in Curitiba (Brazil) (February).

1990 1st All India Congress on Church Development, sponsored by CONS, held in Hyderabad, with 1,200 delegates, sets goal for planting 25,000 new Evangelical churches by AD 2000; with wider groups, goal later announced as 500,000 new churches by AD 2000.

1990 4th Synod, Holy Apostolic Catholic Assyrian Church of the East, held in Baghdad (Iraq); catholicos patriarch Dinkha IV follows through on decision of First Synod in 1976 to relocate patriarchate from Chicago (USA) to Baghdad; also proposes uniting with their related Uniate body, the Chaldean Catholic Church, with a single catholicos.

1990 World Convocation on Justice, Peace, and the Integrity of Creation (WCC/JPIC), held in Seoul (Korea), makes 10 Affirmations on urgent issues (5-12 March).

1990 9th Assembly, Christian Conference of Asia (CCA), held in Manila (Philippines) (4-12 June).

1990 30th General Assembly, World Student Christian Federation (WSCF), held in Chantilly (France), with 200 participants from over 80 countries (5-16 September).

1990 5th Forum on Bilateral Conversations, held in Budapest (Hungary) (October).

1990 Pan-Orthodox Preconciliar Meeting, to prepare Great & Holy Synod, meets in Chambesy (Switzerland), clarifying jurisdictions among Orthodox diasporas (10-17 November).

1990 34th Meeting, Conference of Secretaries of Christian World Communions (CWCs), in Budapest (Hungary, 23-25 October).

1990 8th World Congress, Salvation Army (on its 125th anniversary), held in London, with 5,000 members attending, on theme 'With Christ into the Future' (29 June-9 July).

1990 3rd Canadian Christian Festival, sponsored by 13 Canada denominations, held in Halifax (Nova Scotia), with 10,000 attenders, on theme 'A Time to Love' (16-19 August).

1990 8th Meeting, Anglican Consultative Council (ACC-8), held in Cardiff (Wales), dealing with provincial autonomy versus evident need for pan-Anglican authority (22 July-4 August).

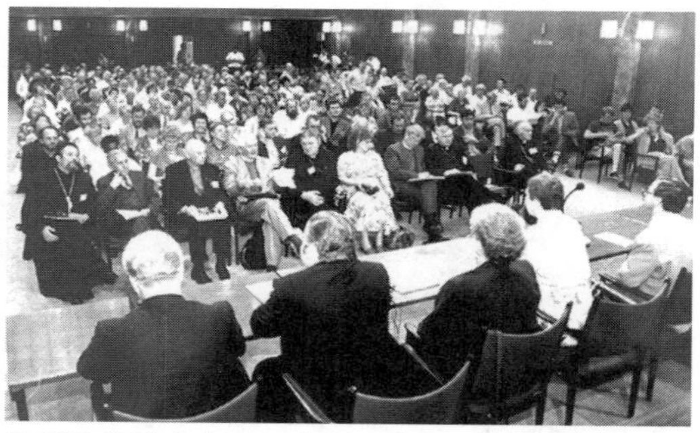

**AD 1990.** Old Catholics proclaim 'New Life in Jesus Christ' at 25th Congress.

1990 25th International Old Catholic Congress (sponsored by Old Catholic Union of Utrecht), held in Geneva (Switzerland) with 600 attenders from 20 countries, on theme 'New Life in Jesus Christ' (27-31 August).

1990 3rd Assembly, Ecumenical Forum of European Christian Women (EFECW), in York (England) with 250 participants, on theme 'From Division to Vision', discussing bioethics, violence, and freedom (14-20 July).

1990 2nd International Consultation of Prison Chaplains (sponsored by International Prison Chaplains Association, IPCA), held in Geneva (Switzerland) with over 200 participants, on theme 'Opportunities and Prospects for Pastoral Care in Prisons' (22-26 August ).

1990 2nd Congress, International Federation of Married Roman Catholic Priests, held in Doorn (Netherlands) with 200 attenders from 26 bodies in 17 countries (19-24 August).

1990 Leader of Jordanian Muslim Brotherhood ignores existing Islamic global structures, convenes World Islamic Popular Gathering, in Amman.

1990 9th Plenary Assembly, Symposium of Episcopal Conferences of Africa & Madagascar (SECAM-9), held in Lome (Togo), on theme 'Evangelization in Africa through the Communications Media' (22-28 July).

1990 5th Plenary Assembly, Federation of Asian Bishops' Conferences (FABC-5), held in Bandung (Indonesia), on theme 'Emerging Challenges to the Church in Asia in the 1990s' (17-27 July).

1990 7th General Congregation, Synod of Bishops, held in Rome, on 'The Formation of Priests in Circumstances of the Present Day'.

1990 Episcopal Conference of Region of North Africa (CERNA) meets in Algiers.

1990 Japan: 1st National Incentive Convention for Evangelization (NICE-I), held in Nagoya (5-8 June).

1990 5th Assembly, Episcopal Conferences of the Indian Ocean (CEDOI), on Rodriguez Island (Mauritius) (25 April-2 May).

c1990 12th Meeting, International Jewish Committee for International Cooperation (IJCIC) and Roman Catholic Church, held in Prague.

1990 55th Session, General Conference of Seventh-day Adventists, held in Indianapolis (USA) with 2,500 delegates and 40,000 attenders.

1990 13th National Convention of the Renewal in the Spirit, held in Rimini (Italy), with 50,000 Catholic attenders (28 April-1 May).

1990 Southern Europe Euro-Fire 90, Portugal's largest evangelistic gathering ever (Christ for All Nations, with evangelist Reinhard Bonnke), held in Lisbon with 12,000 attenders daily (22-26 August).

1990 UN 'Convention on the Rights of the Child' enters international law (September), then ratified by all nations except India and USA.

1990 Auction prices paid for art mushroom: Vincent van Gogh's 'Portrait of Dr Gachet' sells for $82.5 million; and in 1998, his 'Portrait of the Artist Without Beard' fetches $71 million.

1991 Cosmology revolutionized through discoveries made by space-borne telescopes and instruments: riddles of quasars, black holes, et alia all begin to be solved.

1991 400 million computers in world, 350 million being personal computers (with 11 million sold worldwide during year), many able to run hosts of expert systems.

1991 Islamist leader of Sudan, Hasan al-Turabi convenes Popular Arab Islamic Conference, in Khartoum.

1991 Prototype 5th-generation computer produced in Japan, handling artificial intelligence, knowledge bases and ultracomplex expert systems.

1991 Haiti becomes virtually barren of all trees, resulting in massive soil erosion.

1991 Food riots, mass starvation, in Africa and India.

1991 Workers at nuclear reactors stage major controlled accidents to protest unsafe conditions.

1991 International Charismatic Consultation for World Evangelization (ICCOWE), in Brighton (UK), to usher in decade of evangelization before AD 2000; 10,000 renewal leaders (8-14 July).

1991 7th Assembly, World Council of Churches (WCC), in Canberra, Australia, with delegates from 350 member denominations; call to global commitment; ongoing programs include the Ecumenical Decade (1988-1998) for Churches in Solidarity with Women (launched at Easter 1988).

1991 4th Chinese Congress on World Evangelization, CCOWE '91 (sponsored by CCCOWE/LCWE), in Hong Kong.

1991 Sudden growth and mushrooming worldwide of youth churches completely outside control by denominations: loosely-organized churches begun and run by charismatic under-25s, meeting at lunchtimes in hotels, theaters, cinemas, shops, warehouses, anywhere; huge growth of converts.

1991 Conference on World Evangelization organized in Singapore by World Methodist Council.

1991 AD 2000 Regional Consultations sponsored by LCWE/TWMA/et alia begin in earnest: 1991 North America; 1991 Europe; 1991 Middle East & North Africa; 1993 Asia; 1993 Latin America; and 1993 Africa.

1991 International Conference of Islam, held in Dakar, Senegal (January).

1991 *Encyclopedia of world problems and human potential*, 3rd edition, describes 13,167 entries on world's problems.

1991 Robot sniffers in pilotless planes begin to gather information about Earth's upper atmosphere.

1991 Annual worldwide sales of computers including software and other peripherals: mainframes $50 billion, personal computers $93 billion.

1991 Scholarly journals rise in number from 70,000 in 1971 to 108,590 in 1991.

1991 Huge food losses are occurring between farm and consumer: USA loses 14% of entire crop, USSR 50%, India 70%.

1991 Current state of New Testament original documents, from around 3rd century AD: there are 5,358 known NT manuscripts (all parchment codices except for 86 on papyrus) and fragments: 50 with entire NT text, 2,000 of Four Gospels, 400 of Acts and Epistles, 250 of Book of Revelation.

1991 *Saving the planet: how to shape an environmentally sustainable global economy*, by Lester R. Brown et al.

1991 *Once upon a future time: studies in a Buddhist prophecy of decline*, by J. Nattier.

1991 Futurists M. Cetron & O. Davies produce *Crystal globe: the haves and have-nots of the New World Order.*

1991 *The design of the world: an essay on process cosmology*, by S. Salamah Pope.

1991 *The futures research directory: individuals 1991-92* produced by World Future Society.

1991 *Unbounding the future: the nanotechnology revolution*, by K.E. Drexler & C. Peterson.

1991 *Target Earth! Asteroid collisions past and future*, by J. Erikson.

1991 *Technology 2000: the future of computing and communications*, by D. Leebaert.

1991 *The art of the long view: planning for the future in an uncertain world*, by P. Schwartz.

1991 Critique with serious criticism of future studies is made by Max Dublin in *Futurehype: the tyranny of prophecy*, holding that most future inquiry serves only vested interests.

1991 700 current engineering megaprojects (Super Projects) worldwide involving investment of over $1 billion each are described in McKinley Conway's book *Site world: the book of corporate global strategies*; including Community of European Railroads, Multifunctionopolis city in Australia, 500-storey highrise Aeropolis 2001 in Tokyo, Japan's Global Infrastructure Fund.

1991 12th World Conference, World Futures Studies Federation, held in Barcelona, Spain on democracy and participation (September).

1991 Singapore National Missions Consultation (NMC) meets, sets out 9 national goals in foreign mission (May).

1991 4th Catholic Missionary Congress of Latin America (COMLA-4), in Lima, Peru (February), notes Latin Americans serving abroad number only 2% of the Catholic worldwide missionary force.

1991 2nd International Conference for Christian Media (ICMC), in Sheffield, UK (22-28 September).

1991 Eastern Europe for Christ Conference, in Moravia (Czechoslovakia); 300 delegates from Poland, Hungary, Yugoslavia, Romania, Bulgaria (23-28 July).

1991 4th Japan Congress on Evangelism, Shiobara (4-6 June).

1991 Friends World Committee for Consultation (FWCC) holds triple-site Triennial Meeting: in Netherlands (June), Honduras (July), and Kenya (August).

1991 Tentmakers International Exchange (TIE) founded in Seattle by 14 agencies with tentmaking concern (January); 1992, initial TIE Conference in New Mexico, with 100 attenders; 1994, 1st International Congress of TIE, held in Chiang Mai, Thailand (March); 1996, 2nd International Congress of TIE, London, UK (April).

1991 Over next 5 years, 200 Indonesia churches are burned or ransacked in East Java.

1991 3rd Congress on Evangelization of the Caribbean (CONECAR), held in Santo Domingo (Dominican Republic), on theme 'Examining our History: Charting our Future' (20-27 July).

1991 International Christian Media Commission (ICMC) convenes conference in Sheffield (England) with 800 media professionals from 125 countries (22-27 September).

1991 24th German Protestant Church Congress (Kirchentag), held in 4 cities in Ruhr (Dortmund, Essen, Bochum, Gelsenkirchen), with 125,000 attenders (10,000 from former East Germany), on theme 'God's Spirit Liberates for Life' (5-9 June).

1991 Israel's airlift of 14,000 Falashas (Black Jews) from Ethiopia turns back 25,000 Christian Falashas, then leaves them behind in Ethiopia.

1991 World Assembly of Catholic Students (organized by IMCS and IYCS), in Hong Kong with 250 participants, to discuss meaning and purpose of education (19 July-4 August).

1991 3rd Japanese Congress on Evangelism, held at Nasu Shiobara, with over 1,000 delegates, on theme 'Reaching Japan, Asia, and the World' (4-7 June).

1991 Quadrennial World Assembly, International Fellowship of Evangelical Students (IFES), held in Wheaton (USA) with over 400 leaders from student movements in 90 countries, on theme 'The Cross of Jesus' (27 July-4 August).

1991 Biennial Meeting, International Lutheran Conference (ILC: 24 foreign denominations partnering with Lutheran Church-Missouri Synod) (4-12 October).

1991 Joint Nordic Religious Liberty Conversation, organized by Swedish IRLA and Swedish SDA, held at Hultafors (Sweden) with 30 participants from all Nordic countries (28-29 October).

1991 General Assembly, Fellowship of Middle East Evangelical Churches, held in Larnaca (Cyprus), on theme 'The Call of Christ is Partnership'; member bodies Reformed, Episcopal, Lutheran, Presbyterian (3-9 October).

1991 International Council of Christians and Jews (ICCJ) criticizes WCC's theology, ideology, activities, and concern for Palestine.

1991 Consultation on Missionary Congregations in the Indian Context, organized by NCCI/CCA/WCC, held in Nagpur (India), with 45 participants from 18 NCCI-member denominations (21-26 October).

1991 5th Assembly, Caribbean Conference of Churches (CCC), held in Port of Spain (Trinidad), on theme 'Participants in God's Creation: Preserve, Renew, Recreate' (23-31 August).

1991 Seminar of Christian Documentalists, under auspices of MECC, held in Limassol (Cyprus), on theme 'Documentation for Effective Information Sharing' (28-31 August).

1991 World YMCA Assembly, in Seoul (Korea) with over 1,000 participants from 100 countries (23-30 August).

1991 6th General Assembly, Pacific Conference of Churches (PCC), held in Port Vila (Vanuatu), with theme 'Born to a Living Hope, Proclaiming a Living Hope' (27 August-4 September).

1991 Inter-Orthodox Conference on Environmental Protection (convened by Ecumenical Patriarchate), held in Crete, with representatives of 11 autocephalous and autonomous Orthodox churches (5-11 November).

1991 1st Inter-Faith All Africa Religious Liberty Congress (sponsored by IRLA/SDA/IADRL), in Nairobi (Kenya), with over 300 delegates from 40 African nations, on theme 'Freedom of Religion: Hope for Lasting Peace and Unity' (8-11 September).

1991 European Ecumenical Consultation (sponsored by EECCS), in Brussels (Belgium), with churches and councils from the EC's 12 nations, under theme 'The New Challenges of the European Community--Questions from the Churches' (3-6 September).

1991 WCC Consultation on Theological Education by Extension (TEE) in Africa, held in Malawi with 30 participants from 13 countries (12-19 September).

1991 5th European Ecumenical Encounter (CEC/CCEE), held in Santiago de Compostela (Spain), on theme 'At Thy Word: Mission and Evangelization in Europe Today' with 40 Orthodox, Catholic, Old Catholic, Anglican, and Protestant representatives pledging to move toward common mission (13-17 November).

1991 11th Assembly, Latin American Confederation of Religious (CLAR), in Mexico City, protests Vatican intervention denouncing their work as 'ideologically biased' and replacing director with a papally-appointed Colombian bishop (February).

1991 Special Assembly on Europe, Synod of Bishops, held in Vatican, with 130 bishops (out of 1,000), ending with Declaration for New Evangelization of Europe (28 November-6 December).

1991 4th Latin American Missionary Congress (COMLA-4) held in Lima (Peru), on theme 'Latin America, out of Your Faith send Missionaries!' (February).

1991 International Congress on the Dead Sea Scrolls, held in Madrid (Spain) (18-21 March).

1991 16th Assembly, World Methodist Council (WMC), in Singapore, with 3,000 participants on theme 'Jesus Christ: God's Living Word'; issues including indigenous evangelism, environment, human rights (July).

1991 84th Annual Holy Convocation, Church of God in Christ (CoGiC, with 6 million members), held in Memphis, TN.

1991 6th World Youth Day, Katowice (Poland): 1.3 million young people meet John Paul II (14-15 August).

1991 12th World Council of YMCAs, 1st World Assembly, held in Seoul, Korea, on theme 'Renewing God's World—Together'.

1992 USA: illiteracy rises to 27% from low of 1% in 1980, due to mass immigration from Third World and decline of books and reading.

1992 Schisms or secessions out of major Western denominations since 1975 amount to 10% of membership (ex LCMS, PCUSA, ELCA, ECUSA, CofE, EKD, UMC, SBC, et alia).

1992 Coming of Antichrist to power at age 30, followed in 2001 by Second Coming of Christ and End of World, as envisioned by internal architecture of Great Pyramid of Giza (alternate dates: 2030, 2090, 2444).

1992 Latin American Catholics celebrate '500 Years of Evangelization', with overall Evangelization 2000 plan.

1992 3rd Latin American Congress on Evangelization (CLADE III), held in Quito, Ecuador with theme 'The Whole Gospel for all the Peoples in Latin America' (25 August-3 September).

1992 Nations for Christ Congress, sponsored by AD 2000 Movement (Pasadena), in Riga, Latvia (25-29 May).

1992 8th Congress, International Association for Mission Studies (IAMS), in Hawaii (USA), on theme 'New world—new creation: mission in power and faith' (August).

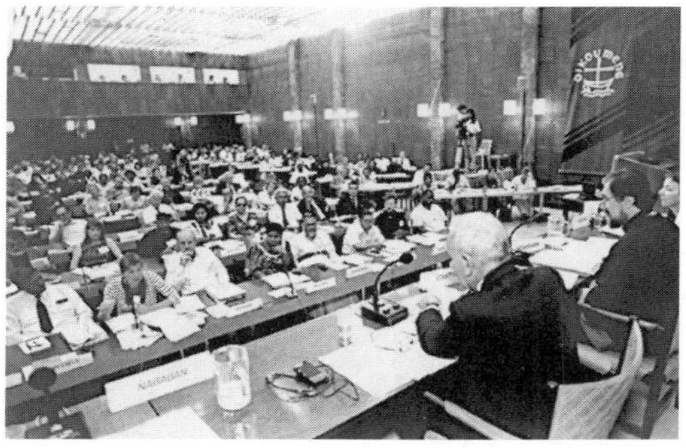

**AD 1992** Moderator's Report, WCC Central Committee Meeting, Ecumenical Centre, Geneva.

1992 WCC publishes document *Confessing the one faith*, in major step towards visible unity and witness.

1992 WEF Missions Consultation, prior to World Evangelical Fellowship, General Assembly in Manila, Philippines (15-20 June).

1992 Guatemala: in 1961-1992 civil war, 100,000 are killed, mostly Amerindian peasants and other civilians.

1992 Discovery of most massive black hole in Universe (same diameter as our Solar System, but with mass of 1 billion Suns), at center of galaxy NGC 3115, 30 million light-years from Earth.
1992 United Nations Conference on the Environment and Development (UNCED) in Rio de Janeiro (Brazil).
1992 International Year of Space.
1992 Consultation on Global Evangelization meets in Rio de Janeiro, with 100 national and foreign-missions Baptist leaders from 36 countries.

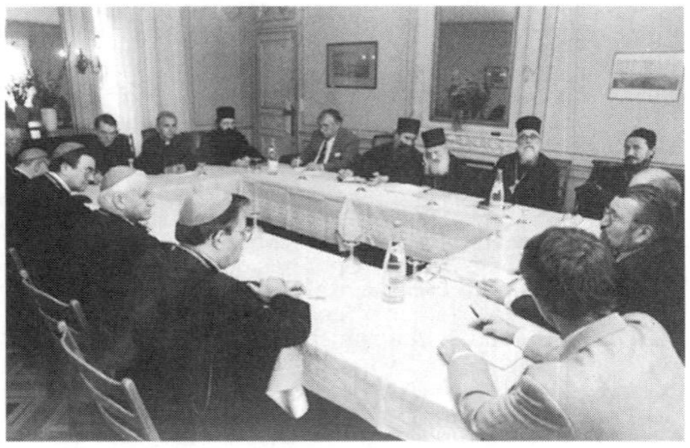

**AD 1992.** Bosnian failure: Croat cardinal, with Catholic bishops (*left*) confront and clash with Serb patriarch, with Orthodox bishops (*right*).

1992 Bosnia: civil war results in Serbian policy of mass murders of Bosnian Muslims and human tide of 1.6 million displaced refugees.
1992 Conference on Church Growth in Africa, held in Lagos (Nigeria), organized and paid for by African independent William Kamuye's Deeper Life Church; 12,000 ministers present from 45 countries and 2,000 denominations; 10,000 sign Declaration, future agenda of national conferences launched.
1992 17th Session, International Roman Catholic-Pentecostal Dialogue meets outside Rome, with theme 'Evangelism and Culture'.
1992 Encuentro Pentecostal Latinoamericano, held in Brazil, sponsored by WCC and CLAI (22-28 November).
1992 16th Triennial Pentecostal World Conference convenes in Oslo, becomes largest religious meeting in Norway's history with 12,500 in evening services; theme 'By My Spirit/Hope for a Changing World' (9-13 October).
1992 10 million people worldwide die from hunger every year.
1992 International air transport: 300 airlines with 3 million employees serving 14,000 airports with fleet of 15,000 aircraft; 1990, total passengers 1.25 billion, also 22 million tons of air freight (25% of world's manufactured exports); 7% growth per year in 1980s, 6% in 1990s.
1992 Travel and tourism now world's largest industry: gross sales $3.5 trillion (6% of GDP), 7% of global capital spending, 127 million jobs; expenditure likely to rise to $5.8 trillion in 2005 (3.9% per year); top 10 tourist destinations France (56 million arrivals), USA (42 million), Spain, Italy, Hungary, Austria, UK, Mexico (16 million), Germany, Canada (15 million); total international tourist arrivals grow from 25 million in 1950 to 160 million in 1970, 285 million in 1980, 416 million in 1990.
1992 27th UN of the Next Decade Conference, convened at Mackinac Island on whether concept of national sovereignty can be changed.
1992 Biological diversity collapses at rate of 50,000 species per year in tropical rain forest alone due to destruction of habitat.
1992 World pharmaceutical market doubles from $70 billion in 1975 to $150 billion in 1990, with 20,000 different medicines sold.
1992 SETI (Search for ExtraTerrestrial Intelligence) begins survey of the heavens, monitoring 8 million radio channels simultaneously for signs of life.
1992 Cash kept outside banks in relation to GNP falls from 13% in 1940 to 4% in 1992.
1992 At end of Cold War, total nuclear warheads on ICBMs and SLBMs number: USA 9,029, USSR (now CIS) 10,674.
1992 United Nations' Population Division publishes professional data-based report, *Long-range world population* projections: two centuries of population growth, 1950-2150, *based on 7 future fertility-scenarios; medium variant* arrives in AD 2200 at 11.6 billion population, with over-65s rising from 1% (1990) to 9% (2200); also, in 1993, *World* population prospects: the 1992 revision *(for every country, 50 variables, 1950-2025), available as book or computer* database.
1992 *The heavens are falling: the scientific prediction of catastrophes in our time*, by W.G. Karplus.
1992 *Living at the end of the ages: apocalyptic expectation in the Radical Reformation*, by W. Klaassen.
1992 *Cosmography: a posthumous scenario for the future of humanity*, by R. Buckminster Fuller.
1992 *Millennialism: an international bibliography*, by T.T. Daniels.
1992 USA vice-president Al Gore writes *Earth in the balance: ecology and the human spirit.*
1992 *When time shall be no more: prophecy belief in modern American culture*, by P. Boyer.
1992 *Predictions: society's telltale signature reveals the past and forecasts the future*, by mathematician T. Modis.
1992 5th Congress, Professors World Peace Academy (PWPA), held in Seoul, Korea; papers and scenarios then published in book *The world of 2044: technological development and the future of society.*
1992 3rd Global Forum of Spiritual Leaders and Parliamentarians for Human Survival meets in Rio de Janeiro (June).
1992 Collapse of political Communism begins as both an ideology and a system, due to spread of Islam in Soviet Central Asia. (Forecast by Nostradamus).
1992 ALCOE III, Asian Leadership Conference on Evangelism, in Bangalore, India, on theme 'That all Asia might hear the Word of the Lord'; organized by ALCWE, with 120 participants from 12 Asian countries (23-27 November).
1992 International Conference on Mission and Evangelism, sponsored by BWA, held in Nanjing, China (August).
1992 13th World Assembly, World Convention of Churches of Christ, on theme 'God's Dominion from Sea to Sea' (August).
1992 Launching of Charismatic Fellowship of Asia (CFA), and Asia Charismatic Theological Association (ACTA).
1992 5th National Chinese Christian Conference (NCCC), held in Beijing, with 273 delegates from 29 provinces and regions, on theme 'Running the Church Well' (January).
1992 Pan-Orthodox Meeting of all Autocephalous and Autonomous Eastern Orthodox Churches (at invitation of ecumenical patriarch), held in Istanbul, with 12 primates present (12-15 March).
1992 6th Assembly, All Africa Conference of Churches (AACC), held in Harare (Zimbabwe) with 500 delegates and observers, from 39 countries, on theme 'Abundant Life in Jesus Christ' (25-29 October).
1992 16th International Assembly of Diakonia, World Federation of Diaconal Associations & Sisterhoods, held in Wolfville, Nova Scotia (Canada), on theme 'Christ with Us in the Storms of Life' (19-26 June).
1992 Reformed Ecumenical Council (begun 1946, now with 30 conservative member denominations) meets in Athens (Greece) (May).
1992 8th Interconfessional Gathering on Theology & Ministry of Ecumenism, held in Madrid (Spain) (9-11 June).
1992 16th Congress, International Catholic Press Union (UCIP), held in Brazil (September).
1992 36th Meeting, Conference of Christian World Communions (CWCs), held in Washington DC (20-22 October).
1992 Global Ecumenical Youth and Students Gathering (EGGYS), sponsored by WSCF/WCC/WAYMCA/WYWCA,IMCS(RC),IYCS, held in Brazil.
1992 2nd International Christian Publishing Fair (ICPF), held in Warsaw (Poland) (27-29 February).
1992 5th Conference on Faith & Order (WCC), held in Santiago de Compostela (Spain), with 400 present, on theme 'Towards Communion—Koinonia in Faith, Life and Witness' (3-14 August).
1992 European Protestant Assembly, held in Budapest (Hungary), with 200 representatives of Protestant denominations in Europe, on theme 'Christian Responsibility for Europe' (24-30 March).
1992 10th General Assembly, Conference of European Churches (CEC), held in Prague, with 350 delegates from 114 member churches, on theme 'God Unites: in Christ a New Creation' (1-11 September).
1992 3rd General Assembly, Ecumenical Association of Third World Theologians (EATWOT), in Nairobi, with 98 participants from 26 countries, on theme 'Cry for Life: the Spirituality of the Third World' (5-16 January).
1992 9th General Assembly, World Evangelical Fellowship (WEF), in Manila (Philippines) (June).
1992 4th General Conference of Latin American Bishops (CELAM-IV), with 500 bishops present, held in Santo Domingo (Dominican Republic), based on women's role and on document *New Evangelization, Human Advancement, Christian Culture: Jesus Christ Yesterday, Today and Forever;* with unprecedented Vatican intervention/directives; new emphasis on life and mission of the laity, evangelization of modern culture, new communications for new evangelization, Amerindian and Afro-American cultures (October).
1992 1st Latin American Encounter for Pentecostal Women, held in Costa Rica (11-14 August).
1992 Symposium on Oneness Pentecostalism (sponsored by United Pentecostal Church International, UPCI), held in St Louis, MO (USA) (8-10 January).
1992 China: 5th National Catholic Representatives' Congress shifts authority from CCPA to Bishops' Conference (September).
1992 ICCOWE Consultation on 'Discerning the Critical Role of Short-Term Missions', at Luray, Virginia (USA).
1992 Quadrennial Assembly, Reformed Ecumenical Council (REC), held in Athens (Greece) with 120 participants; issues of homosexuality, and disciplining of Dutch Reformed Church (25 May-5 June).
1992 Founding of COEF 5 International (Communion de Oevres et Eglises dans la Francophonie sur les 5 continents/Fellowship of French-speaking Organizations and Churches on the 5 Continents); 1993, 1st Christian Francophone Conference held, in Bordeaux (France) with 1,700 delegates from 33 francophone countries (out of 50 such countries)(27 July-1 August); national committees set up; subsequent Conferences 1995, 1999 and biennially.
1992 1st International Cell Conference, describing evangelism via cell-based congregations, held in Singapore (Faith Community Baptist Church), with 390 attenders (4-8 March); 1993, 2nd ICC, Singapore, with 1,200 attenders (3-7 March); 1994, 3rd ICC, Singapore, with 1,700 attenders (3-8 March); 1995, 4th ICC, in 5 USA cities, with 4,000 attenders (16-29 May); 1996, 5th ICC, Singapore, with 12,000 attenders (1-6 February); 1997, 6th ICC, Singapore, with 600 attenders.
1992 2nd Pan-African Catholic Charismatic Renewal Conference, held in Brazzaville (Congo).
1992 Church Growth Conference (organized by Deeper Life Bible Church), held in Lagos, Nigeria with 12,000 church leaders from 42 African countries and 2,000 denominations.
1993 After 10 years' publicity, 5th-generation Japanese megacomputers with artificial intelligence are scheduled to be introduced and put on market now as a staggering extension of human intellect; but at last minute entire project is pronounced a failure and abandoned.
1993 Knowledge-intensive expert systems now widespread: a species of knowledge-based computer program performing at the level of, and replicating, human experts in professional fields.
1993 'Green machines' constructed: engineering systems using biological and biochemical processes or their human-made analogs to create materials, food, energy or other goods and services.
1993 World Congress of Faiths (WCF, headquartered in London) meets on centenary of 1893 World's Parliament of Religions (Chicago); 1996, attempts to create an interreligious World Council of Faiths.
1993 Human race enters Sign of Aquarius, embarks on Aquarian Age (Age of Aquarius, the Watercarrier, interpreted by Christians as Age of Christ the Giver of the Water of Life); 6,000 years of human history are now completed, Sabbath rest of 1,000 millennial years is about to begin.
1993 7th General Assembly, World Future Society, on 'Creating the 21st Century: Rights, Responsibilities, and Actions', in Washington, DC; 29 major subject areas (27 June-1 July).
1993 International Year of the World's Indigenous People.
1993 Global asteroid patrol proposed to monitor Solar System's 2,100 large ECAs (Earth-crossing asteroids) larger than 1 km across, its 300,000 ECAs larger than 100m (330 feet), and 100 million ECAs larger than 20m across; and also long-period comets suddenly appearing headed for Earth at 135,000 m.p.h., producing plan to deflect them with neutron-bomb missiles.
1993 8th World Youth Day: 400,000 young people meet in Denver, Colorado (USA), a 'proclamation of the crucified and risen Christ', convened by Pontifical Council of the Laity (11-15 August).
1993 5th Annual Meeting, Association of Coordinators of Catholic Schools of Evangelization (ACCSE/2000-North America), sponsored by Evangelization 2000, held in Manchester, NH, USA (6-9 October).
1993 Asian Charismatic Theological Association (ACTA) meets in Singapore (12-14 April).
1993 120 million females are missing around the world due to infanticide, abortion, discrimination; including 30 million Chinese, 23 million Indians, 3.1 million Pakistanis, 1.6 million Bangladeshis.
1993 WORLD 2000 launched, an international planning dialogue to help shape a new global system, based on 3 elements: (1) key driving forces or supertrends, (2) critical issues blocking way ahead, (3) a master strategy to resolve these issues.
1993 Chemical Weapons Convention (CWC) to be signed in Paris by 131 countries, banning using of toxic chemicals in warfare.
1993 Over 1,000 worldwide development ventures each involving investment of at least $1 billion.
1993 Malaria increases in virulence, with 270 million new cases every year, 2 million killed, and 100 million acute cases; 40% of world's population in danger; Africa has 100 million cases; by 2000, death toll in Asia likely to reach 10 million a year.
1993 Hyperlearning technology makes school obsolete, a transhuman process shared with increasingly powerful artificial networks and brains (the 'telecosm'); globe-girdling network links all minds.
1993 In developing countries, 1 billion people are without formal employment, living at bare subsistence levels.
1993 Digital imaging technology creates undetectable artificial photos, begins to undermine photography's construction of the visual world.
1993 International migration reaches 100 million in last 4 years.
1993 ICCRO International Leaders' Retreat (Catholic Charismatic Renewal), at Assisi, Italy, with 1,200 retreatants (13-17 September).
1993 1st World Convention of Christian Lay Centres and Movements, sponsored by WCC and World Collaboration Committee of Lay Centres, Academies and Movements for Social Concern, at Montreat, NC (USA), on theme 'Weaving Communities of Hope' (5-9 September).
1993 Salvation Army raises $683 million in 1993, becomes USA's largest charity for second year running.
1993 Gospel Association of India holds its 49th annual evangelistic tent crusade week in Vijayawada (AP);

50,000 attenders on final night, 25,000 professions of faith, and followup crusades in 150 towns and villages (July).

1993 4th Global Forum of Spiritual and Parliamentary Leaders on Human Survival meets in Kyoto; Hindus found the International Green Cross, an ecological institution for environmental relief and protection (April).

1993 Ecumenical Global Gathering of Youth and Students (EGGYS), sponsored by WCC, held in Brazil (July).

1993 5th World Conference on Faith and Order (WCC), in Santiago de Compostela, Spain, with theme 'Towards Koinonia in Faith, Life, and Witness' (3-14 August).

1993 3rd International Consultation for NCCs (National Councils of Churches), in Hong Kong, on theme 'Servants and Advocates of Unity'; of today's 90 NCCs and 10 regional councils associated with WCC, Roman Catholic Church belongs as member to 41 national and 3 regional councils (10-17 February.)

1993 ECCLA XIV (Encuentro Carismatico Catolico Latino Americano) held in Rio de Janeiro on theme 'Renewed to Evangelize', with 2,463 delegates (3 bishops, 110 priests) from 20 Latin American countries.

1993 XIIIth World Conference, World Futures Studies Federation (WFSF), in Turku, Finland, on 'Coherence and Chaos in Our Uncommon Futures: Visions, Means, Actions', cosponsored by Finnish Society for Futures Studies (23-27 August).

1993 Anglican Consultative Council ACC-9 & Anglican Primates Meeting, Capetown (7-14 January); ACC Permanent Commission on World Mission.

1993 Evangelical Fellowship of the Anglican Communion (EFAC) meets in Canterbury, UK (29 June-3 July).

1993 Global military weapons status (totals deployed or stockpiled): 45,000 combat aircraft, 172,000 main battle tanks, 155,500 artillery pieces, over 1,000 major surface warships, 700 military submarines, plus huge numbers of light tanks, armored vehicles, helicopters, mortars, missiles, et alia; total military spending since 1945, $30 trillion mostly in the North, although since 1960 $1 trillion of arms went to the South (Third World countries).

1993 First round of Oriental Orthodox/Reformed Dialogue organized, meeting in Anba Bishoy monastery in Egypt (May); second round in the Netherlands (September 1994).

1993 Ecumenical Day of Prayer for Peace in Bosnia-Herzegovina held in Assisi, Italy, called by John Paul II with presidents of Episcopal Conferences of Europe and 10 other CWCs (9-10 January).

1993 Joint International Roman Catholic/Orthodox Dialogue Committee meets in Lebanon and works out solution to problem of Catholic Uniate (Eastern-rite) Churches.

1993 AD 2000 United Prayer Track organizes Praying Through The Window I (October) with over 20 million home-based intercessors from 28,107 churches praying for all nations in World A (the 10/40 Windows), including making 188 onsite prayer journeys; 1995, PTTW II with over 35 million intercessors and 3,000 journeyers in 407 teams to World A's 100 Gateway Cities; 1997, PTTW III with 27 million intercessors from 58 nations, and 471 prayer teams taking 541 journeys to unreached peoples; 1999, PTTW IV 'Light the Window' using 31-day October prayer calender, with 50 million intercessors.

1993 12th Baptist Youth World Conference, sponsored by BWA, in Harare (Zimbabwe) on theme 'Risking All for Christ...Our Only Hope'; with 4,000 participants (11-15 August).

1993 International Year for the World's Indigenous Peoples, as declared by UN General Assembly.

1993 Founding of International Reformed Fellowship (IRF), opposed to both WARC and Reformed Ecumenical Council, opposing women's ordination (February).

1993 25th German Protestant Kirchentag, held in Munich with 125,000 attenders (60% under 30) (9-13 June).

1993 37th Meeting, Conference of Christian World Communions (CWCs), held in Geneva (26-28 October).

1993 19th World Congress, International Christian Union of Business Executives (UNIAPAC), held in Monterrey (Mexico), with 600 participants from 30 countries, on theme 'The Social Market Economy at the Service of Humanity' (28-29 October).

1993 3rd World Consultation of National Christian Councils (WCC/PCPCU), held in Hong Kong with 150 participants representing 73 NCCs in 90 countries (with RCC a member of 43 NCCs) on theme 'Servants and Advocates of Unity' (10-18 February).

1993 6th Assembly, Association of Evangelicals of Africa and Madagascar (AEAM) (April).

1993 North American Hispanic Missions Congress (COMHINA, counterpart of Latin American COMIBAM).

1993 World Conference on Human Rights, sponsored by UN, held in Vienna, Austria, with 8,000 participants; commemorates 1993 as International Year for the World's Indigenous People, and approves a 'draft action plan' to make UN better on human rights; in its 'Political Declaration and Program of Action' affirms all human rights are universal, indivisible, interdependent, and interrelated; and all peoples have the right of self-determination (14-25 June).

1993 3rd Assembly of the World's Religions.

1993 5th Meeting of Ecumenical Representatives of Episcopal Conferences (from 78 of the 101 RC conferences, also from WCC, CWCs, meeting every 7 years) (10-15 May).

1993 Inter-Orthodox Committee for Preparation of the Great Council of the Orthodox Church (9-14 November).

1993 Irish Congress on World Evangelization (sponsored by LCWE), held in Dublin.

1993 7th International Baha'i Convention, held in Haifa (Israel) for 5 days of legislating.

1993 Conference, Church Growth International, held in Seoul with 664 participants (10-18 December); 1995 Conference, with 723 participants (9-15 May) 1996 CGI Jerusalem Celebration, with 6,000 participants mostly from Korea (February); 1997 Conference, with 1,000 participants.

1994 13th World Council of YMCAs, in Warwick, UK, with 1,000 participants from movements in over 100 countries, on theme 'That They All May be One: Mission, Unity, Vision'.

1994 Enormous increase in all kinds of organized evangelism attracts heavy infiltration by nihilists, terrorists, antichristian fanatics, bounty seekers, criminals, rival government agents.

1994 Development of 'cottage theology' via microcomputer networks, cottage electronic mission think-tanks, cottage research units tapping into databases across the world.

1994 USA: computers now reach 70% of population (60 million terminals or screens).

1994 Final decade of 20th century proves to be greatest decade in Christian history for signs and wonders, miracles, conversions, evangelism and evangelization: greatest sign or wonder being Christians loving one another and gathering in unity everywhere.

1994 2nd Pan African Christian Leadership Assembly (PACLA II) held in Nairobi, Kenya, sponsored by AACC, NCCK, AEAM, and AEE; similar to PACLA I in 1976; 1,000 leaders from all 60 African countries, including leaders of the African Independent Churches, OAIC, and including French and Portuguese language speakers (23-30 November).

1994 International Conference on Population and Development, sponsored by UN, in Cairo, Egypt (September).

1994 Consultation of Bible Translation and Distribution Organisations and Church Leaders,sponsored by Forum of Bible Agencies, in De Bron Conference Centre, Netherlands (20-25 April).

1994 Worldwide Consultation on Christian Spirituality for Our Times (WCC).

1994 Pocket-sized portable dators (radio/computer/database/phone) widely in use as universal personal accessory for instant information.

1994 Access to information globally now controlled by 8 giant conglomerates (media-entertainment mega-companies, media empires).

1994 Gaia-worship undertaken by ecological radicals, invoking the old Mother Goddess Earth of prehistory.

1994 New generation of very small nuclear weapons produced for use in Third World, including 10-ton warhead ('micronuke') to destroy underground bunkers, 100-ton antimissile warhead ('mininuke'), and 1,000-ton 'counter-projection force' warhead ('tinynuke') for attacks on ground troops.

1994 6th General Assembly, Middle East Council of Churches (MECC), held in Nicosia (Cyprus) with meeting every 4 years (November).

1994 Guatemala: 34-year-old civil war claims 140,000 lives, including 45,000 disappeared and presumed dead.

1994 Celebrations 'On the Year 2000' planned by 5th Extraordinary Plenary Session of College of Cardinals in current pontificate; John Paul II summons all 141 cardinals, including 39 over 80 years old, to Rome (9-10 May); earlier plenaries on reforms, finances, sects, held in 1979, 1982, 1985, 1991.

1994 North American Conference for Itinerant Evangelists (NACIE, sponsored by BGEA and 40 denominations and associations), in Louisville, Kentucky, with 2,500 evangelists including spouses and students (28 June-July).

1994 World Holy Spirit Conference, in Seoul (Korea), with 30,000 attenders in 6 meetings.

1994 Toronto Holy Laughter revival: 250,000 pastors and other visitors from across world (e.g. party of 116 from Indonesia) visit Airport Vineyard church to experience Holy Spirit phenomena; spreads to over 10,000 churches in 50 countries within the year; large volume of information reported on global Internet.

1994 LWF/SDA ecumenical dialogue begins with official theological conversations in Darmstadt, Germany (1-5 November); second round scheduled for 1996.

1994 Reformed/Oriental Orthodox Bilateral Dialogue (second session), organized by WARC, held in Driebergen, produces joint 'Statement on Christology' (10-15 September); also by 1997, second round of Reformed/Eastern Orthodox Bilateral Dialogue.

1994 6th Forum on Bilateral Dialogues (WCC/CWCs), in Bossey, Switzerland with 34 participants, mainly working on concept of reception (effect of agreed statements on church members) (8-13 October).

1994 Global Conference on Human Rights sponsored by World Federalist Association (WFA).

1994 Asia Church Congress, held in Bogor (Indonesia).

1994 Special Assembly for Africa of the Synod of Bishops, held in Rome on theme 'The Church in Africa and her Evangelising Mission towards the Year 2000', with 317 RC priests and experts also present (10 April-8 May).

1994 World Future Society Annual Conference on 'Toward the New Millennium: Living, Learning, and Working', in Cambridge, Massachusetts (24-26 July).

1994 Baptist International Conference on Unevangelized People (BWA), in Larnaca (Cyprus), on 'Hope for a Needy World' (20-24 January); 1995 similar BWA conference in Madras (India).

1994 Series of Anglican conferences 'New Wineskins for Global Mission': 1994 in Ridgecrest, NC (27 April-1 May).

1994 1st TIE (Tentmakers International Exchange) Worldwide Congress, in Chiang Mai (Thailand).

1994 38th Meeting, Conference of Christian World Communions (CWCs), held in Istanbul (25-27 October).

1994 Conference of Protestant Churches from the Latin Countries of Europe (CEPLE), in Averio (Portugal), representing churches in Belgium, France, Italy, Portugal, Spain, Switzerland (28 April-1 May).

1994 1st Ecumenical Conference of Russia, held in Moscow with 80 leaders from ROC,RCC, and all other main Christian organizations in Russia, on theme 'Christian Faith and Human Enmity'; 1996, 2nd Ecumenical Conference, in Minsk (Belarus) (October).

1994 India: National Consultation on Church Planting, sponsored by CONS/ECI/IMA, held in Madras, with 40 participants (28-30 June).

1994 1st WACC International Conference for Women, held in Bangkok (Thailand), with title 'Women Empowering Communication' (February).

1994 9th Meeting, Anglican Consultative Council (ACC-9), held in Cape Town.

1994 Triennial International Council, International Bible Society (IBS), held in Colorado Springs (USA) with 245 participants from 25 countries, on theme 'Transforming the World with the Word' (30 September-3 October).

1994 65th General Assembly, Church of God (Cleveland), held in San Antonio, TX (USA), on theme 'Reaping the Harvest'; world membership has grown from (in 1992) 2,719,780 in 20,383 churches to (in 1994) 3,646,409 in 24,296 churches (8-15 August).

1994 3rd Annual Conference, Association of Pentecostal and Charismatic Bible Colleges of Australia (PCBC).

1994 General Congress, Charismatic Fellowship of Asia (CFA), held in Manila (Philippines) (16-19 November), preceded by Asia Charismatic Theological Association (ACTA).

1994 European Pentecostal Theological Association (EPTA) meets in Portugal (26-30 July).

1994 Asian Pentecostal Theological Association (APTA), meets in Seoul (Korea) (September).

1994 1st World Assemblies of God Congress, a mid-Decade of Harvest event held in Seoul (Korea) with 98 AoG general superintendents from 94 nations, and over a million attenders from 134 nations at Grand Prayer Rally; founding of relief agency WAGRA (29 September-3 October).

1994 Malaysia '94 Charismatic Consultation, sponsored by ICCOWE at Port Dickson, Kuala Lumpur; 200 leaders of charismatic groups; on theme 'Cooperation at a Time of Unparalleled Opportunity', call to Christian unity emphasized (March).

1994 2nd National Missions Conference for Ghana, held in Kumasi (Ghana) sponsored by AIMS and House of Faith Ministries, with 4,000 pastors, mission leaders, and businessmen (25-30 July).

1994 XVIIth Annual Conference, Italian Charismatic Consultation (RC/Pentecostal/Waldensian/Baptist) (9-11 December).

1994 18th Triennial Meeting, Friends World Committee on Consultation (FWCC), meeting in Ghost Ranch, New Mexico (USA) with 250 Quakers on theme 'Light' (August).

1994 5th International Christian Youth Conference (sponsored by World Methodist Council), in Hamburg (Germany) with 750 youth from 52 countries, on theme 'See, I make All Things New' (2-9 August).

1994 6th Assembly, World Conference on Religion and Peace (WCRP), held in Rome and Riva del Garda (Italy), with 600 participants from 60 countries, including an address by John Paul II (3-9 November).

1994 1st World Meeting of Families, held in Rome (October); 1997 2nd World Meeting of Families, presided over by pope John Paul II, in Rio de Janeiro (Brazil) (1-5 October).

1994 23rd Congress, Apostolic World Christian Fellowship (AWCF), held at HQ in Evansville, IN, with delegates from 110 member denominations in 20 countries (3-6 May).

1994 Lebanon: large Catholic Charismatic Renewal Conferences (and a second in 1995) attracting 30,000 attenders with live TV coverage watched by over a million viewers.

1994 'Memphis Miracle' in Memphis, TN, witnessed by 4,000 attenders finally reconciling USA White Pentecostals (Classical, in Pentecostal Fellowship of North America) with Black Pentecostals (Church of God in Christ) after 100 years' estrangement, to form multiracial Pentecostal/Charismatic Churches of North America (PCCNA) (September).

1994 1st Himalayan Conference of Evangelism, held in Kathmandu, Nepal; over 800 pastors and lay leaders attend; subsequent Conferences in 1996, 1998.

1995 **Global status** of Christianity: 65.5 generations after Christ, world is 33.1% Christians (47.5% of them being Whites), 70.4% evangelized; with printed Scriptures available in 1,950 languages; total martyrs since AD 33 reach 69 million (0.9% of all Christians ever; recent rate 170,300 per year).
1995 ECCLA XV (Encuentro Carismatico Catolico Latino Americano), sponsored by ICCRS (Rome), meets in Tegucigalpa, Honduras (15-19 May).
1995 India: National Congress on Church Development, Madras (9-12 January); and National Convention on the Great Commission, sponsored by EFI, Cochin (11-16 January).
1995 2nd Global Consultation on World Evangelization by the Year 2000 and Beyond (GCOWE II), in Seoul, Korea, on theme 'A Church for Every People and the Gospel for Every Person by AD 2000', with 5,000 church and mission leaders from 200 countries (13-25 June).
1995 3rd Worldwide Retreat for Priests, to be held in Papal Audience Hall, Vatican, with 6,300 attenders on theme 'Called to be One so that the World might believe' (10-14 November) cancelled shortly beforehand.
1995 40% of all Western world's 230 million homes have a general computer for home management and cottage industry.
1995 Mexico City (23.1 million inhabitants) now passed by Tokyo-Yokohama (28.0 million) as world's largest supercity; this rank remaining on into the indefinite future.
1995 Some 50% of world's nations have become Marxist, mainly in Third World, but 45% have subsequently abandoned it.
1995 Inexorable increase in number of countries closed to freely organized foreign Christian mission; 75% of world's populations become inaccessible in this way.
1995 Travel and tourism as world's major industry grow at 10% a year to reach 400 million foreign tourists a year; in North America, 7 million foreigners visit each year (1978, 2 million), 23 million citizens a year go abroad (1978, 10 million); foreign students 1.3 million (1978, 350,000); 1998, tourist services to space begin; 2010, packaged vacations in space available.
1995 Luggage, parcels, valuables and eventually all people are electronically tagged so that none can be lost or ever disappear.
1995 International telephone system finally has enough switches ($10^{10}$) to become a conscious system, a giant brain similar to human brain (which has over $10^{11}$ or 100 billion neurons or cellular building blocks). (A.C. Clarke, 'Dial F for Frankenstein',1965).
1995 Machines scan foreign-language newspapers and journals daily, then translate and archive materials for later retrieval.
1995 Terrorism: worldwide, some 4,000 terrorists belong to 60 terrorist organizations.
1995 'Underground economy' (illegal and criminal 'black' and 'gray' finance) in Western world is estimated at 10%-28% of gross national product, with 50% of all underground activity paid in cash.
1995 Establishment of national computerized human organ banks for transplants; organ procurement from neomorts (brain-dead persons) now a major industry; by 2000, transplantation of all organs possible except central nervous system.
1995 4th World Conference on Women, sponsored by UN.
1995 Orlando 95 Congress on the Holy Spirit and World Evangelization, held in Orlando, Florida, with over 10,000 present (4,000 young persons), on theme 'From Generation to Generation You Will Be My Witnesses' (26-29 July).
1995 World Summit for Social Development, sponsored by United Nations.
1995 17th Baptist World Congress (sponsored by BWA), in Buenos Aires, Argentina on theme 'Celebrate Christ, the Hope of the World!' (1-6 August).
1995 3rd General Assembly, Latin American Council of Churches (CLAI), held in Concepcion (Chile), with 500 delegates and 30,000 attenders, on theme 'Rebirth for a Living Hope' (25 January-2 February.
1995 WSCF Centennial General Assembly, at Yamoussoukro (Ivory Coast) (26 August-10 September).
1995 5th Latin American Missionary Congress (COMLA 5), held in Belo Horizonte, Brazil.
1995 European Forum of Gay and Lesbian Christian Groups, with 30 member groups including LGCM (Britain), holds 1st Conference open to non-members on sexual ethics, held in Netherlands.
1995 10th General Assembly, Christian Conference of Asia (CCA), held in Colombo (Sri Lanka), with delegates from its 120 member churches and councils (June); resolves to keep its headquarters in Hong Kong when latter reverts to China.
1995 Pan-Orthodox meeting of 12 Eastern Orthodox patriarchs and leaders invited by ecumenical patriarch Bartholomeos I, on Greek island of Patmos to commemorate 1,900th anniversary of Apostle John's writing Book of Revelation; Russian patriarch rejects invitation; meeting condemns nationalist fanaticism, Catholic Uniate activities, Protestant proselytism (26 September).
1995 United Religions Initiative (URI) founded in San Francisco, USA, as religion-based counterpart to United Nations Organization.
1995 2nd International Congress, World Association for Christian Communication (WACC), held in Metepec (Mexico), on theme 'Communication for Human Dignity', with 350 participants from 85 countries, with attacks on secular mass communication conglomerates (October).
1995 56th Session/Assembly, General Conference of Seventh-day Adventists, held in Utrecht (Netherlands), on theme 'United in Christ', with 30,000 attenders (2,500 delegates) from 8.5 million Adventists in 208 countries worldwide, 90% outside USA (29 June-8 July).
1995 6th Consultation for United and Uniting Churches (WCC Faith & Order Commission), held in Jamaica, with 55 church representatives from 23 countries (21-29 March).
1995 Brazilian pastor Nilson do A. Fanini as president of BWA calls for worldwide evangelization campaign under motto 'Baptists of the World Unite' to win world for Christ by AD 2000.
1995 European Interparliamentary Assembly on Orthodoxy (EIAO), with parliamentary delegations from 16 countries, meets in Moscow on theme 'Education, Culture, Orthodox Tradition' (9-13 June); 1996, 2nd Assembly, held in Sofia (Bulgaria).
1995 3rd Oxford Conference on Christian Faith and Economics (Oxford III) in Agra (India); deals with problems of market economics, the poor, biblical criteria, definitions, and strategies (1-5 March).
1995 European Charismatic Consultation, held in Prague with 400 participants (15-23 October).
1995 European Pentecostal & Charismatic Research Association (EPCRA) meets in Mattersey (UK) (10-14 July).
1995 5th International Conference, Lausanne Consultation on Jewish Evangelism (LCJE-LCWE), in Jerusalem (18-23 June).
1995 International Orthodox Mission Conference, at Brookline, MA (USA) (6-11 August).
1995 17th Pentecostal World Conference (PWC), held in Jerusalem on theme 'From Jerusalem... to All Peoples' (11-14 September); 10,000 attenders from 100 countries.
1995 4th Pan-European Charismatic Congress '95 (triennial), held in Vienna (Austria), discusses 3 difficult subjects: Toronto Blessing, Working Together, Church Planting/Community Building; 400 attenders.
1995 Love Southern Africa Conference (related to AD 2000 Movement), a 4-day consultation held in Pretoria (South Africa) with 5,600 church leaders of whom 2,000 then undertake 1-3 week outreaches in other African countries.
1995 Special Assembly for Lebanon, Synod of Bishops, held in Rome with Orthodox and Protestant fraternal delegates (26 November-12 December).
1995 Black & White Consultation, organized by OAIC, on reconciliation between AICs and mission churches (November).
1995 Broadcasting agencies FEBC/FEBA for first time receive in 12 months over 1 million responses from listeners.
1995 2nd Baptist International Conference on Unevangelized People, sponsored by BWA, held in Madras (India) with over 300 leaders from 21 countries (16-19 January).
1995 ICPE's 'Europe Arise' youth initiative for 4 days in July.
1995 4th International Lutheran Consultation on Women (sponsored by LWF of whose 122 member churches 65% ordain women), in Geneva (Switzerland), with 160 participants (22-28 October).

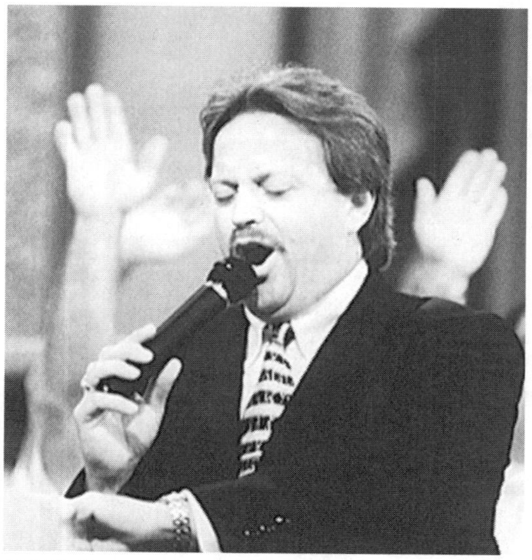

**AD 1995.** Brownsville evangelist Steve Hill preaches in massive 5-year revival in Florida.

1995 Revival erupts in an Assemblies of God church in Brownsville (Pensacola, Florida): in 2 years, 1,500,000 visitors attend services, with 100,000 professions of salvation.
1995 2nd All India Congress on Church Development (sponsored by Council on National Service, CONS), held in Madras on theme 'Let Us Rise Up and Build', with 1,367 national delegates, sets corporate goal of 50,000 new churches by AD 2000 (9-12 January).
1995 2nd Christian Francophone Conference (COEF 5 International), held in Yamoussoukro (Ivory Coast), with 2,000 delegates from 39 French-speaking countries (25-30 July).
1995 1st General Assembly, Catholic Charismatic Council for Asia-Pacific (CCCAP), held in Sabah (Malaysia) with 63 delegates from 9 nations, on theme 'We are God's Co-workers' (18-22 November); 1996, 1st Asia-Pacific Charismatic Leaders' Congress, held at Kinasih (Indonesia) (7-12 October).
1995 4th Triennial Meeting, World Evangelical Congregational Fellowship (WECF, with 15 member associations), held in Braintree (MA); 1998, 5th Triennial Meeting, held in South Africa.
1995 2nd Ghana National Missions Conference (House of Faith Ministries), held in Kumasi with nearly 4,000 pastors, mission leaders, and businessmen (25-30 July).
1996 3rd World Consultation on Frontier Missions (WCFM) planned, specifically for mission executives; cancelled.
1996 3rd Anglophone Africa Consultative Meeting, Catholic Charismatic Renewal, with aid of ICCRS, held in Johannesburg (South Africa).
1996 Customized electronic newspapers and magazines become widespread.
1996 Superconductivity: room-temperature superconductors (transmitting electricity without any resistance) begin to transform all human energy usages.

***Total-information technologies and world evangelization***

1996 Vast expansion of information technologies throughout organized global Christianity continues to spread, but overall impact on the non-Christian world remains minimal; most global plans for world evangelization produce little tangible outreach.
1996 NARSC/ICCOWE conference, held in Atlanta (GA) just before Olympics 96, involving 10,000 USA young people and 1,500 Order of St Philip youths (July).
1996 Rise of intelligent architecture: smart technology enables intelligent urban envelopes, dynamic buildings, walls of light and sound, and personalized environment.
1996 America's 80 million personal computers become highly vulnerable to attack by viruses and 'worms'; 10% of all computers infected.
1996 New frontiers in science and technology: complex systems, instability, Japan's Human Frontier Science Program, ultra-dense chips, extraterrestrial intelligence, robotics, new medical technology, new biological testing, earthquake prediction, telecomputers, spacebridges, optical communications, HDTV, cellular technology, cold-climate technology, macroengineering, intelligent architecture, telecottages in rural areas.
1996 Paralegals become fastest-growing job category in 1990s in Western world.
1996 3rd World Missionary Conference on World Mission and Evangelism (6th Meeting of CWME/WCC), held in Salvador, Bahia (Brazil) on theme 'Proclaiming Christ Today to Different Cultures through Different Cultures'/'Called to One Hope: the Gospel and Diverse Cultures', with over 500 mission specialists as participants (25 November-3 December).
1996 40th Meeting, Conference of Secretaries of Christian World Communions (CWCs) meets in Oslo, Norway (22-24 October).
1996 Catholics begin programs to celebrate Jubilee Year of AD 2000.
1996 2nd Himalayan Congress of Evangelism (HIM-COE '96) convenes in Siliguri, West Bengal, on theme 'Partnership in the Gospel' with 2,000 Himalayan pastors and church leaders; 1998, followup 3rd conference planned, HIM-COE '98.
1996 8th General Assembly, World Future Society, on 'FutureVision: Ideas, Insights, and Strategies', in Washington, DC (14-18 July).
1996 1st Balkan Evangelical Conference (BEC '96) held in Belgrade (Serbia) with 1,500 attenders (endorsed by Serbian EA, European EA, NEEFC) (6-7 September).
1996 In US Department of Energy's Accelerated Strategic Computing Initiative (ASCI), world's biggest supercomputer ASCI Red TFLOPS first achieves speed of 1 teraflop (one trillion floating-point operations per second, online); AD 2000, achieves 1.8 TFLOPS.
1996 1st Christian-Muslim Conference, on 'Religion and the Contemporary World', organized by WCC and Iranian Muslim scholars, in Teheran (October).
1996 General Assembly, World Union of Catholic Women's Organizations, meets in Canberra (Australia); delegates angered as Vatican bars any discussion of planned resolution on women priests (January).
1996 4th International Congress of Married Priests, in Brasilia (Brazil), sponsored by International Federation of Married Priests (20,000 members, mainly RC former priests and bishops) (July).
1996 Erfurt Ecumenical Assembly, with all of Germany's main churches, sponsored by 13-member-churches Association of Christian Churches in

Germany (ACK), on theme 'Seek Reconciliation, Gain Life', held in Erfurt with 118 delegates (Protestant, Catholic, Orthodox) (13-16 June).

1996 1st European Women's Ecumenical Synod held at Gmunden (Austria) with 1,000 women from 45 countries, on theme 'Women's Power Changing the 21st Century'; demands women's full participation in decision-making processes; launches WOW, Women's Ordination Worldwide (21-28 July).

1996 17th World Methodist Conference, held in Rio de Janeiro with 2,700 participants (500 representing 71 WMC denominations in 107 countries), on theme 'Holy Spirit, Giver of Life'; first WMC to meet in Latin America, despite 115 years' history; 2 new member churches admitted, including first united church, Church of South India (9-17 August); also 9th Assembly, World Federation of Methodist Women (28 July-4 August).

1996 International Urban Ministry Congress, in Nairobi (Kenya), with 119 delegates from 36 denominations, 40 cities, 20 countries (24 November-1 December).

1996 1st World Christian Gathering of Indigenous Peoples, organized by Christian Maoris, held in Rotorua (New Zealand), with 2,000 participants in indigenous dress from 100 tribes and cultural groups, from 32 countries worldwide (November); 1998, 2nd World Christian Gathering of Indigenous Peoples (in Canada).

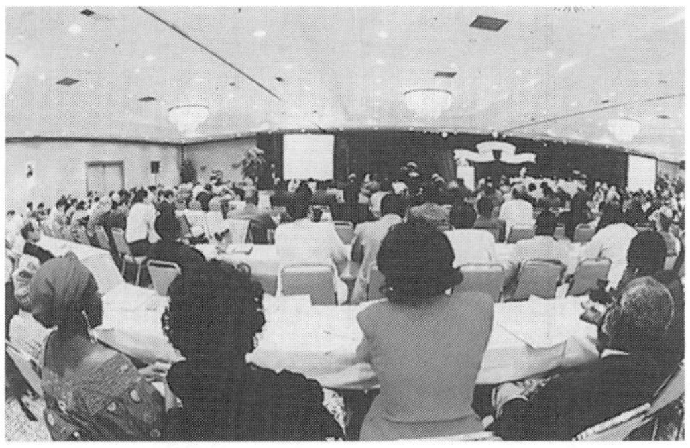

**AD 1996.** 'God's Word: Life for All': 12th World Assembly, United Bible Societies, in Canada.

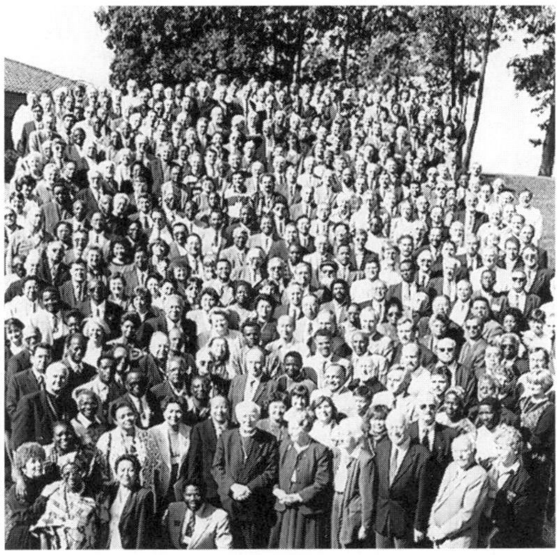

**AD 1996.** UBS Assembly: 335 delegates from 138 countries; *center front*, Donald Coggan, former Archbishop of Canterbury.

1996 12th World Assembly, United Bible Societies (UBS), held in Mississauga (Canada) on UBS' 50th anniversary, with 335 delegates from 138 countries, on 'God's Word: Life for All' (26 September-3 October).

1996 International Assembly, Reformed Ecumenical Council (REC), held in Grand Rapids, MI (USA), with 100 participants including 65 delegates from 29 member churches in 21 countries, on 'Renewing Our Vision'/'Rejoice in the Lord'(3-15 June).

1996 7th Annual Koine-Research International, held in Feria di Roma (Rome fairgrounds), on 'The actuality of sacred space', a trade show majoring on physical, tangible implementation of Vatican II/renewal changes, for ecclesiologists, liturgists, church historians, architects, Vatican appointees, engineers, clergy, publishers, 600 retailers (8-11 June).

1996 India: 2nd National Consultation on Evangelism (sponsored by India Missions Association), held in Secunderabad, AP, with 170 missions leaders (25-29 September).

1996 9th Conference, International Association for Mission Studies (IAMS), in Buenos Aires (Argentina), with 130 scholars from 37 countries, on theme 'God or Mammon: economies in conflict' (10-19 April).

1996 Consultation on Support of Indigenous Christian Ministries in the Non-Western World, held at Wheaton, IL, for the 100 agencies specializing in this support (17-20 October).

1996 Congress of Third World Missions (Congreso Mundial de las Misiones del Tercer Mundo), held in Lima (Peru) with over 1,500 delegates attending (May); emphasis made on replacing attempts to send out Latin Americans as missionaries with fund-raising to support indigenous missionaries abroad.

1996 Annual Convention, INTENT (US Association of Tentmakers, and TIE), held in Los Angeles (USA) on theme 'Getting There!' (2-4 August).

1996 XIXth Annual National Conference of the Italian Catholic Charismatic Renewal in the Holy Spirit, on 'Siano uno, perche il mondo creda (John 17:21)', in Rimini (Italy) with 65,000 attenders including 4 cardinals, ICCOWE and ECC executive committees, and 100 ecumenical guests; calls for Catholic/Pentecostal reconciliation (25-28 April).

1996 Ecumenical Charismatic Young Leaders' Conference (ECC), in Berlin (6-8 September).

1996 14th World Assembly, World Convention of Churches of Christ (WCCC, representing a communion of 12 million Christians), held in Calgary (Canada) (30 July-4 August).

1996 First European Christian Internet Conference, sponsored by EKD, University of Tubingen and Church Net UK, held in Frankfurt (Germany) with delegates from 9 European nations; especially on cooperation with Web sites and e-mail directory (23-24 November).

1996 10th Meeting, Anglican Consultative Council (ACC-10), held in Parma (Italy) with 100 delegates; on Islam, Jerusalem, homosexuality, Rwanda (October).

1996 2nd Interconfessional Conference for CIS Countries (organized by Patriarchate of Moscow), held in Minsk (Belarus), with Orthodox, Roman Catholic, and Protestant participation, attempting to minimize proselytism. (1-3 October).

1996 47th Meeting of WCC Central Committee, in Geneva, with 156 delegates, discusses new WCC 16-page document 'Common Understanding and Vision' (CUV) for future change of WCC from service organization to 'enabler, coordinator, communicator, convener, and sometimes mediator'.

1996 LatinoAmerica 2000 (LA2000), leaders/students conference on world evangelization (sponsored by AD 2000 Movement and CCCI), held in Panama City, with 300 delegates and 3,600 attendees from all Latin American countries, on 'The Gospel to Every Person by the Year 2000' (27-30 December).

1996 5th Chinese Congress on World Evangelization (CCOWE), representing 7,000 diaspora churches, held in Hong Kong with 1,700 attendees from 25 countries, and 16,000 rally attenders, on theme 'Lord of History, Light of the World'; produces 14 Action Plans (10-16 July).

1996 Christival-3 Youth Gathering, with 40,000 youth attenders (average age: 22) in 1,500 small groups, held in Dresden (Germany), with theme 'Come Follow Jesus'; a 330-person Bible-reading marathon team reads aloud the entire Bible non-stop in 82.5 hours.

1996 4th Asian Leadership Conference on Evangelism/World Evangelization (ALCOWE IV), held in Kuala Lumpur (Malaysia) with 105 attendees from 14 countries, on theme 'Taking the Whole Gospel to Asia Today' (21-26 October).

1996 WCC/OAIC Consultation on African Independent Churches, at Aladura HQ in Lagos, Nigeria (9-14 January).

1996 XIth International Conference on AIDS, held in Vancouver (Canada): 19.8 million adults and 2 million children worldwide have HIV/AIDS, 7,500 people daily become new cases.

1996 7th International Meeting, Catholic Fraternity of Charismatic Covenant Communities and Fellowships (CFCCCF) held in Rome with 285 delegates from 40 communities, on theme 'Prepare the Way of the Lord' (5-12 November).

1996 National Service Committee of Europe, ICCRS, meets in Bratislava (Slovakia), with 80 leaders from 17 countries (September).

1996 1st European Christian Internet Conference (www ecic.uscwm.ac.uk) (22-23 November).

1996 1st World Meeting of Catholic Clergy, organized by Vatican Congregation for the Clergy, held in Fatima (Portugal), with 1,200 participants.

1996 17th National Catholic Charismatic Conference of Ecuador, held in Azogues with 300 leaders and 8,000 attenders, on theme 'Towards the XXI Century' (October).

1996 Biannual Meeting of National Service Committees of Europe (Catholic Charismatic Renewal), held in Bratislava (Slovakia), report declining numbers and aging membership in weekly prayer groups.

1996 3rd Pan-African Catholic Charismatic Renewal Conference, held in Yamoussoukro (Ivory Coast), on theme 'Evangelizing in the Power of the Holy Spirit: Go and Proclaim, Cast Out and Heal' (3-13 August).

1996 1st Annual Christian Computing Expo, sponsored by Evangelicals and held at Southwestern College, Phoenix (AZ), with 1,600 attenders; 2nd in 1997, with over 6,000 attenders.

1996 3rd Anglophone Africa Consultative Meeting, Catholic Charismatic Renewal, held in Johannesburg (South Africa).

1997 International Consultation on Evangelism, Social Concern and Renewal in the Spirit, sponsored by ICCOWE.

1997 Goal redefinition scenario: all 200 major Christian denominations and parachurch agencies which have previously, over last 30 years, announced separate grandiose goals for reaching the entire world for Christ by AD 2000, suddenly realize that there is too little time left to do so; 'redefinition of the task' is therefore publicly announced, postponing target date by a further 20 years or changing 'By AD 2000' to 'Within this generation'.

1997 Worldwide global personal communications services provided by Motorola Corporation's Iridium project to develop system of small satellites operating in low Earth orbit.

1997 Popular religion (popular religiosity, popular piety), a christianized phenomenon, sweeps civilized regions of world in vast, rank growth effecting over 400 million church members.

1997 Information-Age measures: (a) an average person's TIUPIL (typical information use per individual lifetime) = 20 billion bits of information, or 500 million spoken/thought-out/written words; and (b) grand total GHIUD (global human information use per decade) = 12 quintillion ($12x10^{18}$) bits a decade = 30,000 trillion new words added a year to the sum total of human knowledge.

1997 World Mission Conference (WCC) on 'Confessing Christ in a Culturally Plural 21st Century' (January).

1997 23rd General Council, World Alliance of Reformed Churches (WARC, with 193 member churches in 97 countries) held in Debrecen, Hungary, on theme 'Break the Chains of Injustice'; emphasis on the global economic market as dehumanizing, also call for cancelling Third-World debts (8-20 August).

1997 General Assembly, Fellowship of the Middle East Evangelical Churches (FMEEC, following previous Assembly, held in Larnaca, Cyprus dealing with document 'Proposal for Unity' (13-19 March).

1997 Gateway People Cluster Consultation, held at USCWM, Pasadena (CA) on concept of grouping unreached peoples by clusters.

1997 16th Annual Church Growth International Conference, in Seoul (Korea) at Yoido Full Gospel Church, with 100,000 intercessors present, on theme 'The Son is Rising' (30 September-9 October).

1997 6th General Assembly, Caribbean Conference of Churches (CCC, with 24 member denominations on 32 islands), including several RC Bishops Conferences), held in Cuba on theme 'We Celebrate a new Vision, new Hope and new Life'.

1997 9th Assembly, Lutheran World Federation (122 member churches) insists on holding 50th anniversary assembly in Hong Kong just after its takeover by China.

1997 International Conference '97 on Prayer & Spiritual Warfare (Global Harvest Ministries), in Los Angeles, CA (12-14 March), Virginia Beach (21-23 May), St Louis, MO (24-26 September).

1997 2nd European Ecumenical Assembly, in Graz (Austria) sponsored by CEC (118 Protestant, Anglican, Orthodox member denominations) and CCEE (33 RC bishops' conferences), on theme 'Reconciliation, Gift of God and Source of New Life'; 700 official church delegates, 4,300 other attenders, 20,000 at public meetings; aim to produce action plan with specific reconciliation acts (23-29 June); followed by CEC 11th General Assembly.

1997 3rd Annual Conference on Pentecostal/Charismatic Care & Counseling, held in Atlanta (USA), on 'The Family: Mending the Broken Circle' (27 February-2 March).

1997 7th General Assembly, Pacific Conference of Churches (PCC, with 25 member denominations and 6 councils of churches), held in Papeete (French Polynesia) with 157 delegates (1-13 March).

1997 Triennial Meeting, Friends World Committee for Consultation (FWCC), on theme 'Identity, Authority and Community'.

1997 USA: Promise Keepers (begun 1990, 3.7 million attenders to date) schedule 19 stadium conferences in 1997 on 'The Making of a Godly Man'.

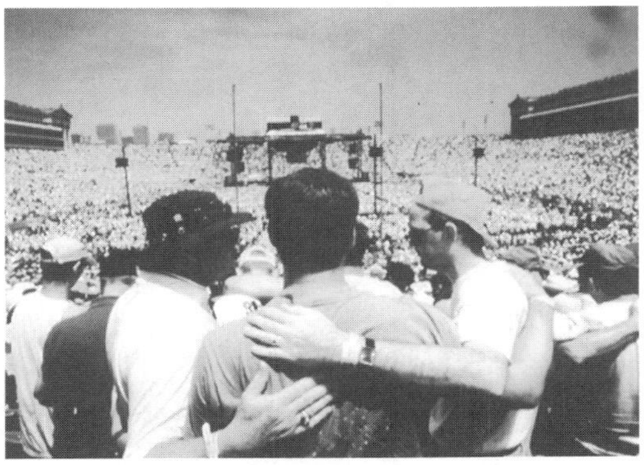

**AD 1997.** Promise Keepers stadium rallies for men only draw phenomenal attendances across USA.

1997 4th World Congress, International Religious Liberty Association (IRLA/SDA), in Rio de Janeiro (22-26 June).
1997 41st Meeting, Conference of Christian World Communions (CWCs), in Geneva (Switzerland) (October 21-23).
1997 10th General Assembly, World Evangelical Fellowship (WEF, serving 150 million Evangelicals in 116 nations), held in Abbotsford, BC (Canada), with 600 delegates, with theme 'The World for Jesus Christ' (9-16 May).
1997 Associated Coordinators of Catholic Schools of Evangelization (ACCSE, with 1,500 schools including 800 in Brazil) holds continental meetings to organize final 3 years' preparation before Jubilee Year of AD 2000: ACCSE for Europe, held in Brentwood (UK) (7-10 May), and ACCSE for the Americas, held in Washington, DC (14-17 May).
1997 Global Consultation on World Evangelization (GCOWE '97) on theme 'Penetrating the Final Frontiers', in Pretoria (South Africa), with attempt to find mission advocates for 650 remaining unreached peoples in World A (30 June-5 July); but few of them are reached.
1997 13th Assembly, Mennonite World Conference (MWC, representing 1 million Mennonites), held in Calcutta (India), on theme 'Hear what the Spirit is saying to the Churches' (January); meets as 'Assembly Gathered' in Calcutta and 'Assembly Scattered' in sites across India and Bangladesh, with 3,800 attenders.
1997 7th Forum on Bilateral Dialogues/Conversations (CWCs,WCC), held in Annecy-Le-Vieux (France) with 40 attenders, on theme 'Evolving Visions of Unity' in the WCC Canberra Statement and at previous 6 Forums (9-14 May).
1997 10-yearly East African Revival Convention (in a tradition going back to 1927), with many thousands held in Mbarara (Uganda), supported by Anglican and other leading churches (September).
1997 2nd Tentmakers International Exchange (TIE) World Congress, in Melbourne (Australia) on theme 'Working to Win the World' (4-8 February).
1997 Congress on World Evangelism, held by Church of God, in Cleveland(TN) (7-9 August).
1997 6th Spanish Evangelical Congress, with role by Bible Society of Spain.
1997 2nd World Meeting of Catholic Clergy, organized by Vatican Congregation for the Clergy, held in Ivory Coast Basilica, Yamoussoukro, with 1,500 priests, on theme 'Jesus Chief High Priest forever' (8-13 July).
1997 2nd Ibero-American Missions Congress (COMIBAM II), convenes in Acapulco (Mexico), with 3,000 delegates representing 400 mission organizations with 4,000 Ibero-American cross-cultural missionaries (40% working in Latin America, 60% beyond) from all Latin American countries with Spain and Portugal (27-31 October).
1997 Consultation on Scriptures for the Visually Impaired (sponsored by UBS, 13 Bible societies, and 14 other agencies), held in Cyprus (17-21 November).
1997 Mission to All the World, Outreach in Eurasia, Crusade with 3,500 Video Schools of Ministry (Morris Cerullo World Evangelism), in Moscow (Russia) with 12,000 delegates from 17 Eurasian nations, 23,000 attenders, 1,500 professions of conversion (6-7, 9-11, 27-31 October, 2-25 November).
1997 'Stand in the Gap: a Sacred Assembly of Men', a huge Promise Keepers rally for national repentance held on the Mall, Washington, DC with 1,500,000 men attending (4 October).
1997 2nd World Congress, World Assemblies of God Fellowship, held in São Paulo (Brazil), with 1.1 million ministers and laypersons at prayer meetings (25-28 September).
1997 John Paul II undertakes 80th overseas journey of his pontificate, visiting Brazil; 1998, memorable first visit to Communist Cuba.
1997 4th Encounter of Lay Centres in the South Cone of Latin America, held in Buenos Aires (25-27 September).
1997 7th General Assembly, All Africa Conference of Churches (AACC/CETA, with 142 member churches) held in Addis Ababa with over 200 voting delegates and 500 observers (4-10 October).
1997 16th Meeting of ECCLA/CONCCLAT (Consejo Carismatico Latino Americano), held in Bogota (Colombia) (May).
1997 Antilles Eucharistic Congress, held in Trinidad (April).
1997 March for Jesus, held in Trinidad, organized by Catholic Charismatic Renewal, with 50,000 participants from Trinidad, St Lucia, Dominica, Grenada, Guyana (5 January).
1997 Special Assembly for America, Synod of Bishops, held in Vatican (16 November-12 December).
1997 12th World Youth Day with pope John Paul II, held in Paris (France), with Internet coverage live, with huge turnout of 1,200,000 young people (24 August).
1997 46th International Eucharistic Congress, held in Wroclaw (Poland), with Pentecostal observers invited (May).
1997 Prague 97, sponsored by ICCOWE/ECC (European Charismatic Consultation)/EPCRA (European Pentecostal and Charismatic Research Association), on 'Building Bridges Breaking Barriers', together with Forum for 55 theologians; 340 attenders from 35 countries (10-14 September).
1997 10th Meeting, Pentecostal European Conference (PEK), held in Frydek-Mistek (Czech Republic), with 3,000 attenders; 11th Meeting, AD 2000.
1997 EXPLO 97 Ecumenical Conference (Campus Crusade for Christ, and CCR), held in Basel, Switzerland with 10,000 attenders from 60 countries, on theme 'Change the World with God's Love' (28 December-1 January 1998).
1997 International Conference on Computing and Missions (ICCM '97), at Abilene Christian University, Texas, with over 100 participants (6-10 August).
1997 2nd Worldwide Meeting of Families (organized by archdiocese of Rio de Janeiro, all its lay movements, and its CCR), attended by pope and 100,000 guests from across world, with theme 'Radical Change'.
1997 Panama: 18th Catholic Charismatic Renewal Youth Meeting, in Llano Bonito, with 6,000 youths attending (20-23 January); preceded by CCR Priests' Retreat, with 200 priests and 7 bishops from 15 countries.
1997 Italy: 20th National Conference of Rinnovamento nello Spirito (RnS), at Rimini with over 30,000 attenders, on theme 'Who do you say I am?' (24-27 April).
1997 11th IGPA Conference (International Gathering of Prophets and Apostles, every October) sponsored by Christian International Ministries Network, held in Santa Rosa Beach, FL with 31,000 attenders (6,000 being ministers).
1997 Joint Conference of Charismatic Leaders (sponsored by ICCOWE-ECC), held in Prague on theme of East-West relations (September-October).
1997 Asia Missions Congress II (sponsored by Evangelical Fellowship of Asia, EFA), held in Pattaya (Thailand), with 388 mission leaders from 15 Asian countries, on theme 'Into the 21st Century: Asian Churches in Mission' (reaching unreached peoples) (29 September-3 October).
1997 7th Francophone Summit Conference (Conference of Chiefs of State and Government of Countries having French in Common), held in Hanoi (Viet Nam), with representatives of 46 countries including president Jacques Chirac of France.
1998 World's greatest denominations begin to disintegrate through violent internal radical/liberal/moderateconservative/fundamentalist controversies: Roman Catholic Church, UMC, CofE, SBC, EKD, et alia.
1998 Genetic transcription provides first genetic map of healthy human cells, opens up new science of genetic markers (diagnosing at birth all of a person's future illnesses in order to prevent them).
1998 TV and HDTV being made obsolete by emerging era of telecomputers—personal computers adapted for video processing, connected by fibre-optic threads to other telecomputers around world.
1998 Robotics develops: robots serve as guards, janitors, nurses, miners, and aides to disabled and elderly; service robotics begins to outstrip industrial robotics, with robot paranurses, parapharmacists, gas station attendants, et alia.
1998 Plans for organized world evangelization (as the church's responsibility) run into major obstacles: internal management fiascos, shortages of resources, shortfalls in personnel, mega-embezzlements, secular urbanization, confessional disagreements, ecclesiastical schisms and secessions, theological disarray, mushrooming secularism and materialism, proselytism, ecclesiastical gangsterism and corruption, terrorism, insoluble complexities produced by world's 7,000 languages, disinformation, mass religious espionage, antichristian infiltration, unexpected prophets and seers, breakdowns in health care, failures of communications, collapse of education, global religious persecution, natural disasters, famines, popular hostility to Christianity, total state opposition, uncontrolled wars and warfare, collapses of infrastructures, universal chaos and terror.
1998 Proselytism (sheep-stealing from other churches) becomes widespread, though denounced in theory by all major church bodies.
1998 Schisms out of major Western churches proliferate, numbering 20% of all church members since 1970.
1998 Evolution of superbugs (drug-resistant microbes, antibiotic-proof bacteria, intelligent viruses) spreading around globe especially in hospitals, due to enormous increase in tourism and business travel since 1970, also to inadequate medical care and sanitation.
1998 'Black holes' of financial crime sweep world: explosion of big fraud crimes (insurance, pension plans, telemarketing, computer crime, health care); embezzlement of church money by top custodians totals $16 billion per year, with several massive thefts in USA each exceeding $200 million; 95%, however, continue to evade detection.
1998 World Buddhist Conference, held at Lumbini (birthplace of Buddha 2,542 years ago) Kathmandu (Nepal), attended by 400 Buddhist monks, scholars, politicians and observers from 30 countries (1-2 December).
1998 8th Assembly, World Council of Churches (50th Anniversary of founding; 337 churches), in Harare (Zimbabwe), on theme 'Turn to God: Rejoice in Hope', highlighting CUV (futurist 'Towards a common understanding and vision') (3-14 December).
1998 4th Annual Conference on Pentecostal/Charismatic Care & Counseling, held in Virginia Beach (USA) (26 February-1 March).

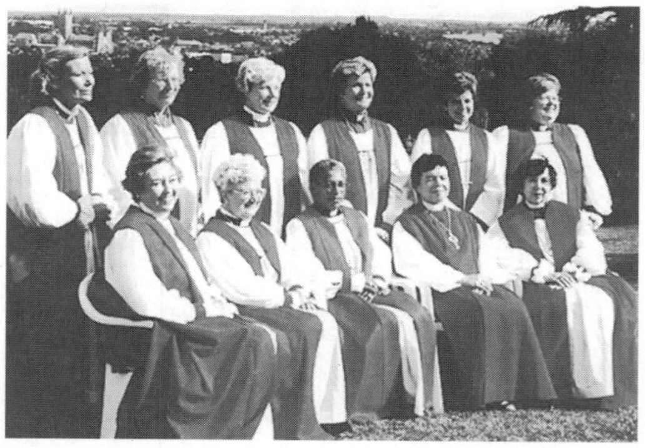

**AD 1998.** Anglican Communion's 11 women bishops attend 13th Lambeth Conference.

1998 13th Lambeth Conference of Anglican Bishops, held in London and Canterbury with 750 bishops from 9 Anglican Regions and 36 Provinces), raising as major concerns international debt and inter-faith issues (18 July-9 August).
1998 42nd Meeting, Conference of Christian World Communions (CWCs), in Windsor (UK) (20-22 October).
1998 Baptist Youth Congress (sponsored by BWA), in Houston, TX (USA).
1998 8th International Convention, Baha'i Faith, held in Haifa (Israel) (April).
1998 18th Pentecostal World Conference (PWC), held in Seoul (Korea), with 100,000 attenders from 60 nations (22-25 September).
1998 5th Meeting for Dialogue between Churches of the Radical Reformation (Mennonite, Anabaptist) and Churches of the Classic Reformation (Lutheran, Reformed) (15-17 February).
1998 3rd Congress of the Union of Baptists in Latin America (UBLA), held in Guatemala, with 1,800 persons from 25 countries (25 March).
1998 International Congress of Ecclesial Movements, held in Rome with 350 participants from 50 different active movements, on theme 'Church Movements: Communion and Mission on the Threshold of the Third Millennium' (27-29 May).
1998 World Congress on Intercession, Spiritual Warfare and Evangelism (sponsored by International Spiritual Warfare Network), held in Guatemala City (27-31 October).
1998 3rd Himalayan Conference of Evangelism (HIM-COE 98), held in Darjeeling, Sikkim, with 1,200 participants from 13 major districts, on theme 'Himalayan People, Missionary People' (20-24 April).
1998 2nd Balkan Evangelical Conference, held in Sofia, Bulgaria (11-13 September).
1998 Nordic Pentecostal Missions Conference (sponsored by Finnish Free Foreign Missions), held in Finland to mobilize for reaching unreached peoples (26-29 March).
1998 Hispanic American Saturation Church Planting Congress, held in Colombia with 1,600 church leaders (16-19 November).
1998 Mission '99 Youth Congress, organized by TEMA (The European Missionary Association), held in Zuidlaren, Holland, with 7,000 young Europeans on theme 'You are a Chosen Generation (1 Peter 2:9)' (28 December-2 January 1999).
1998 4th CCR Anglophone Africa Consultative Meeting, held in Harare (Zimbabwe), followed by open Catholic Charismatic Conference (4-9 August).
1998 2nd Philippines National Catholic Charismatic Congress on the Holy Spirit, held in Manila with 300,000 attenders including 40 archbishops and bishops, 195 priests, 30 brothers and seminarians, 247 religious sisters and 3,883 lay leaders, on theme 'Holy Spirit, Renew the Face of the Earth!' (22-25 January).
1998 17th Latin American Catholic Charismatic Conference (ECCLA XVII), organized by CONCCLAT, held in Monterrey, Mexico (10-14 October), followed by Leaders' Conference, also International Priests' Retreat (12-16 October).
1998 Haiti: 6th National Conference of Catholic Charismatic Renewal (begun 1973), held in Port-au-Prince on theme 'Stir into flame the spiritual gift that God placed in you (2 Timothy 1:6)'; 50,000 attenders including 100 priests, 10 Haitian bishops, 4,000 Protestants (17-19 April).
1998 22nd National Conference of RnS (Rinnovamento nello Spirito, CCR), held in Rimini, Italy with 40,000 attenders under the theme 'Guided by the Holy Spirit Towards the Jubilee of the Year 2000'
1998 USA: 1st National Conference on Fasting and Prayer Sacred Assembly '98, one of largest prayer meetings ever, gathers 1.8 million to Houston, TX for prayer in English and Spanish (12-14 November 1998, also 11-13 November 1999, and 9-11 November 2000).
1998 8th International Conference of the Catholic

Fraternity of Charismatic Covenant Communities, held in Rome (31 May-3 June).
1998 Mexico: 13th National Youth Gathering in the Holy Spirit (ICCRS), held in Aguascalientes with over 14,000 youth (24-26 July).
1998 9th International Leaders' Conference, ICCRS, held in Fiuggi, Italy on theme 'Let the Fire Fall, Again!', with over 2,000 key world leaders (26-31 October).
1998 Mission '99 sponsored by European Missionary Association, held at Zuidlaren, Netherlands on theme 'Who Cares?' (28 December-2 January 1999).
1998 Holy Shroud of Turin again exhibited in Turin Cathedral, with 2 million viewers; carbon dating at AD 1260 becoming discounted by some experts.
1998 Special Assembly for Asia, Synod of Bishops, held in Vatican Synod Hall with 184 bishops and superiors general with 100 experts, on theme 'Jesus Christ the Saviour and His mission of love and service in Asia'. (19 April-14 May).

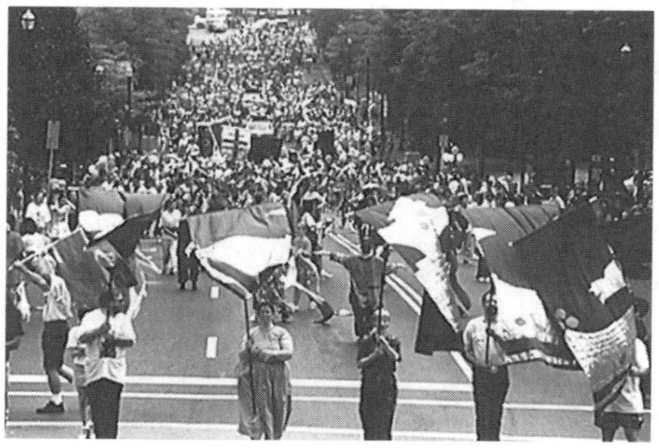

**AD 1998.** Since 1987, 100 million Christians in 500 cities worldwide have joined March for Jesus; *above*, 40,000 in Nashville, 1994.

1998 March for Jesus 98 sees over 10 million believers in 150 countries: Brazil 3 million in 1,000 cities, USA 700,000 in 625 cities, Russia 10,000 in Moscow.
1998 27th Annual AWCF World Congress (Apostolic World Christian Fellowship), held in Nashville, TN (12-15 May).
1998 10th Korean Urbana Mission Conference (IFES; biennial), held in Seoul (Korea) with 5,900 students (August).
1998 2 Anglican Charismatic Conferences, sponsored by SOMA and ARM, held in Canterbury to overlap 13th Lambeth Conference of Bishops: (1) Open Conference, with 754 attenders from 50 countries, on theme 'The Church for the Healing of the Nation', in 20 seminars and (2) Leaders' Retreat, with 485 from 51 countries (96 bishops, 40 bishops' wives, 170 clergy, 179 lay leaders).
1998 1st Next Generation Alliance Evangelists Conference (organized by Luis Palau Evangelistic Association), held in Portland, OR, with 70 evangelists from USA (May).
1998 World Future Society convenes special conference entitled 'Y2K—Scenarios and Strategies' dealing with the computer problem (as a date '00' being regarded as 1900 not 2000); in Washington, DC (16-17 December).
1998 Moribund USA Protestant plan COCU (Consultation on Church Union) holds first meeting since 1988, with 10 large denominations including UMC, PCUSA, UCC, AMEC, AMEZC, ICCC, Disciples of Christ.
1998 Saudi Arabia: pilgrims to 1998 Hajj to Mecca (29 March for a week) number 1,718,186 (585,842 being non-Saudi residents in the country), of whom 496,298 (44%) females, and 982,654 arrive by air, 117,162 by land, 32,528 by sea; pilgrims from USA 6,698 (in 1997, 5,968; in 1996, 5,339).
1998 3rd International Meeting for Priests (after 1st in Fatima, Portugal, and 2nd in Yamoussoukro, Ivory Coast), held in Mexico (7-12 July).
1998 OCIC-UNDA World Congress (International Catholic Association for Radio and Television), held in Montreal (Canada), on theme 'Creativity in the Media Sphere: a Spiritual Opportunity' (August).
1998 47th Congress of Euro-Asian Federation of the Unions of Evangelical Christians-Baptists (begun 1868), held in Minsk (Belarus) on theme 'You are a Letter of Christ (2 Corinthians 3:3)' (12-14 May); largest Protestant body in former USSR.
1998 Central African Congress of CCR, held in Libreville (Gabon) with 2,500 participants, for teaching, sharing, evangelization (27 July-2 August).
1998 France: 2nd Ecumenical Charismatic Meeting (after 1st in 1982), held in Charlety Stadium, Paris with 12,000 participants, organized by Fraternité Pentecôte and the French Ecumenical Charismatic Consultation (Catholics, Orthodox, Protestants, ecumenical leaders).
1998 Special Assembly for Oceania, Synod of Bishops, held in Vatican on theme 'Jesus Christ and the Peoples of Oceania: Walking His Way, Telling His Truth, and Living His Life' (22 November-12 December).
1998 10th Korea Urbana Student Mission, in Seoul, held every 2 years (patterned on Urbana USA) with 5,900 students attending (7 August).
1999 Estimated date for Prayalog, Hindu end of the world, at end of present Kali Yuga of decay, degeneration and guilt (Kali Age or Dark Ages, for last 5,000 years since Flood over whole Earth); final act of Lord Brahma's wrath; whole world disintegrates in chaos in natural disasters (according to 'Bhagwat' in Mahabharata), new life arises after Brahma completes 100,000 years of meditation.
1999 10th Ordinary Assembly, Synod of Bishops, held in Vatican.
1999 NASA launches detailed plan to expand efforts for radio search for extraterrestrial intelligence (SETI) 10 billionfold.
1999 43rd Meeting, Conference of Christian World Communions (CWCs), in Jerusalem. (2-5 December).
1999 3rd Christian Francophone Conference (COEF 5 International), held after series of continental conferences.
1999 On one long-anticipated scenario, war in Balkans escalates and involves more and more nations until World War III erupts: Western world and organized Christianity versus Asian powers and militant Islam; nuclear holocaust and chemical/biological warfare drag on for 22 years until 2021. (Nostradamus).
1999 VATs (voice-activated speech-recognition typewriters and word-processors) introduced, begin to displace 3 million typists and secretaries worldwide; sales in USA alone reach $3.5 billion a year by 2000.
1999 New Black Plague (immune system epidemic) begins (attacking immune systems) caused by pollution of air/water/food/environment, killing animals/insects/trees/planets/humans.
1999 Horrifying forms of warfare unleashed: nerve and other poison gas, biochemical weapons, immense swarms of killer bees, acid rain.
1999 Anti-eye low-energy laser weapons (LEL) deployed in armed services of most nations; future battlefields' most terrible weapon will have power to cause mass blindness, with aircraft pilots highest priority targets.
1999 World Convocation of Christianity proposed on initiative of Vatican; also, detailed plans announced for the Holy Year of the Great Jubilee of the Incarnation, AD 2000.
1999 Most large enterprises are becoming managed largely by artificial intelligence.
1999 Muslim end of world, as prophesied by traditional Islam: coming of Antichrist into godless world, Kaaba vanishes from Mecca, all copies of Quran suddenly become blank paper, all Quran's words disappear from human memory, final Mahdi appears, then Prophet Isa (Jesus) ushers in Islam as sole global religion, followed by Last Judgment.
1999 Global panic spreads as end of millennium approaches, widely believed to be 31 December 1999 (wrongly, since 20th century ends on 31 December 2000).
1999 Discovery in Vatican archive of lost document *Report on the Four Parts of the World* written about 1630 by Francesco Ingoli (1578-1649, first secretary of Sacred Congregation Propaganda Fide), a detailed description of missionary activity in Africa, America, Asia, and Europe, with prospects for future of world evangelization.
1999 International Conference 'Human Rights and Our Responsibilities towards Future Generations: an Inter-religious Perspective' (sponsored by UNESCO's Future Generations Project) and University of Malta), held in Valletta, Malta (6-8 May).
1999 European Monetary Union (11 nations) introduces new currency, *euro*, which results in major technical problems for foreign currency institutions, costing $400 billion to fix (1 January).
1999 Praying through the Window IV, involving over 50 million praying evangelicals all interceding for unreached peoples in 10/40 Window; coordinated by World Prayer Center, Colorado Springs (October).
1999 9th General Assembly, World Future Society (WFS), held in Washington, DC with 1,500 futurists attending, on theme 'Frontiers of the 21st Century' (29 July-1 August).
1999 54th Annual General Conference, Studiorum Novi Testamenti Societas (SNTS), held in Pretoria, South Africa, with postconference in Hammanskraal with African theologians and biblical scholars on 'African Hermeneutics and Theology' (1-10 August).
1999 World Congress on Deliverance: Equipping the Church for Revival (AD 2000 Movement), held in World Prayer Center, Colorado Springs; 14 speakers on aspects of deliverance ministries (exorcism, powers, curses, the occult, healings) (29-31 July).
1999 New Apostolic Reformation Summits (AD 2000 Movement), held in Colorado Springs and Nashville, TN, strategizing for foreign missions, worship, apostleship, intercession (1-2 March, 8-10 April, 24-26 June).
1999 7th General Assembly, Middle East Council of Churches (MECC), held in Lebanon, on theme 'Jesus Christ is the same yesterday and today and forever (Hebrews 13:8)' (26-29 April).
1999 Pacific Islands Chinese Mission Conferences: 1st Conference in Guam, with 60 Chinese pastors and mission leaders, focusing on Micronesia, (June); 2000, 2nd Conference, in Nadi (Fiji), focusing on Melanesia (6-9 June); 2001, 3rd Conference, in Tonga, focusing on Polynesia.
1999 6th Latin American Missionary Congress (COMLA VI, newly renamed American Congress CAM I because USA and Canada included), held in Parana (Argentina) with 3,030 participants on the Americas' missionary responsibility; one goal being 'to supply the world with Latin American missionaries'; theme 'America with Christ go out of your country!' (29 September-3 October).
1999 Latin American Congress of Catholic Arts (CONLARTE, sponsored by Catholic Charismatic Renewal), held in city of Cachoeira Paulista (Brazil), aiming to evangelize through dance and theater (14-17 January).
1999 Pan-African Congress of the Catholic Charismatic Renewal, held in Yaoundé (Cameroon) in May, Bangui (CAR) in December, culminating in the Jubilee of the Year 2000 in Kinshasa (August 2000).
1999 Internet Evangelism Conference (sponsored by Billy Graham Center, Illinois), held in northwest Chicago (18-20 April).
1999 1st International Consultation on Discipleship, held in Eastbourne, UK, with 500 invited denominational leaders from 100 countries, on theme of need for costly discipleship (21-24 September).
1999 Plenary Meeting, International Christian Maritime Association (ICMA), held in Durban (South Africa) (September).
1999 Special Synod of Bishops for Europe, held in Vatican for Europe's 720 Catholic dioceses/jurisdictions, on theme 'Jesus Christ living in his Church, source of hope for Europe' (1-23 October).
1999 New World Missions Congress for the Third Millennium (sponsored by Third World Missions Association/TWMA and Nippon Revival Association), held in Kyoto (Japan), with 2,000 delegates from 1,500 mission agencies worldwide (25-31 October).
1999 11th Meeting of Anglican Consultative Council (ACC-II), held in Dundee (Scotland) with representatives of the 38 Anglican Provinces, on theme 'The Communion We Share' (14-25 September).
1999 Conference of European Churches, with Ecumenical Forum of European Christian Women,hold consultation in Driebergen, Netherlands on outrage of 500,000 women worldwide being tricked and trafficked into forced marriages, labor, or prostitution in rich European Union countries (27 November–1 December).
1999 World Council of Churches launches plan named Decade to Overcome Violence 2001–2010.
1999 3rd Assembly, Parliament of the World's Religions (PWR, every 5 years now), held in Cape Town with 6,500 participants (1-8 December); announces 72-hour prayer meeting (31 December 1999–2 January, 2000; also, plans discussed for Millennium World Peace Summit/Summit of Spiritual and Religious Leaders (28-31 August 2000) organized by United Nations and PWR for 1,000 of world's religious and spiritual leaders, to be held at UN New York immediately before the UN Millennium Heads of State Summit.
1999 IBM Research, world's biggest network of computer research centers, announces $100 million research initiative to build, by AD 2005, Blue Gene ultracomputer with over a million 1-gigaflop processors in parallel, capable of one quadrillion (one million billion, or $10^{15}$) operations/calculations per second (one petaflop); initially to solve effects of protein-folding on genes, disease, and healthcare (6 December).

# COSMIC ERA III

## *The futurology of world evangelization*

### AN ESCHATO-SCIENTIFIC SCENARIO

The rest of the Chronology, here termed Cosmic Era III, deals with the future and in particular with the future of the Universe, of the Earth, of humanity, of religion, and of Christianity. In the tradition of Cosmic Eras I and II, it consists of a sequence of distinct miniscenarios (events or situations) arranged in a chronological order suggested or proposed by the background authors from whose writings the events have been condensed.

Cosmic Era III divides its presentation of possible, probable, and/or preferable future events into 2 distinct sequences. First comes (a) *a religio-scientific composite scenario of alternative futures*, derived from secular, religious, ecclesiastical, and other non-biblical sources, beginning with the last year of the 20th century, AD 2000, and extending into the far distant future described by physicists, mathematicians, astronomers, cosmologists, and even science-fiction novelists. Second comes (b) **the Christian eschatological schema**, based on the biblical materials and combining the interpretations, beliefs, and expectations of the whole range of exegetes and theologians, and indeed of the vast majority of Christians of all confessions. This schema, here named 'The Eschatology of World Evangelization', cannot be dated—it could occur today, tomorrow, next year, next century, next millennium—no one on Earth can know or even guess. But in order at least to portray it, it is placed here in a tinted, undated 5-page box located between the years AD 2049 and 2050.

### A RELIGIO-SCIENTIFIC COMPOSITE SCENARIO

#### *Notes on researching the future*

1. To assist us comprehend the study of the future, it is helpful to recognize 10 basic periods of the future, as follows. Of these, everybody is interested in periods (1) and (2); most futurists study periods (3) and (4); futurists involved in medicine and the sciences often make forecasts in periods (4) and (5); ecologists study periods (3) to (6); and astronomers and cosmologists specialize in periods (7) to (10).

(1) The immediate future (up to 1 year from now),
(2) The near-term future (1-5 years from now),
(3) The middle-range future (5-30 years from now),
(4) The long-range future (30-100 years from now, i.e. up to AD 2100),
(5) The distant future (100-1,000 years from now, i.e. AD 2100-3000),
(6) The far distant future (over 1,000 years hence, i.e. after AD 3000).
(7) The megafuture (after AD 1 million, up to end of Solar System),
(8) The gigafuture (after AD 1 billion, up to death of stars),
(9) The terafuture (after AD 1 trillion, up to supermassive black hole).
(10) The eschatofuture or exafuture (after AD 1 quintillion or $10^{18}$ years, up to end at $10^{100}$ years).

2. The following single continuous chronology is not intended to in any sense imply prediction, prophecy or predestination, nor should it be construed as presenting only one single coherent and consistent scenario. It combines numerous overlapping scenarios and miniscenarios and single scientifically-predicted or forecasted events with the entire range of possible and probable events envisaged by technological-social optimism, limits-to-growth secular pessimism, and extrabiblical Protestant and Catholic prophecy. In consequence, particular items or scenarios will often be inconsistent or even appear to be contradictory. The sequence should therefore be regarded as simply what it is: a set of possible or probable or preferable alternative futures, not necessarily connected or consistent.

3. A large number of Christian events, particularly international conferences, have already been arranged and announced for the period 2001-2010. They are here included together with places and themes and other details as planned and anticipated before the millennial year.

4. The years shown at the left margin are simply those forecasted or suggested by specialists in the particular items enumerated. They should be regarded not as exact predictions but as approximate milestones, probabilistic forecasts, or only conditional forecasts, claiming accuracy perhaps to 20% of the time distance from the year 2000 (thus the year '2100' below would mean somewhere between 2080-2120).

5. A large proportion of these items are secular events or situations. They are included here because all have ethical, theological and missiological significance, hence are given so that the reader can himself consider and assess their implications for global mission and world evangelization.

6. None of the individual items below should be taken as necessarily the personal opinions or position of the authors, who are here simply bringing together significant items from the vast extant literature on futurology, forecasting and alternative scenarios—possible, probable or preferable.

7. A more detailed discussion of the methodology used here to portray possible futures is given a few pages on, at the year 2050. It includes at that point a brief chronology of the biblical end-time whose dates however can not be proposed or even suggested.

### STATUS OF THE COSMOS IN AD 2000

2000 *Galactic civilizations*. Scientists estimate our Galaxy with its 400 billion stars has (1) some 300 billion planets suitable for life, (2) 100 billion inhabited worlds on which life forms have actually arisen, (3) 600 million planets that are Earthlike, bear life and are suitable for habitation by man, (4) between 1,000 and 1 billion developing planetary communicative civilizations with intelligent lifeforms, (5) between 100 and 1 million technical civilizations (those capable of interstellar radio communication) now existing out of 1 billion ever, increasing at rate of up to one new one every decade, with nearest one around 100 light-years from Earth, and (6) between 10 and 100,000 civilizations substantially or vastly in advance of Earth's. (C. Sagan, *Cosmos*, 1980).

2000 *Extragalactic civilizations*. Whole Universe with its 100 billion galaxies contains between 10 trillion ($10^{13}$) and 10,000 trillion ($10^{16}$) of these more advanced civilizations, with unimaginable technologies, together with between 100 trillion ($10^{14}$) and $10^{20}$ developing civilizations; however, none of all these extraterrestrial civilizations is likely to have produced anything resembling Homo Sapiens; all almost certainly have totally different lifeforms.

2000 *New worlds*. New suns (stars) are forming or being created across the Universe at a present rate of 10,000 suns every second, new planetary systems at 10 a second, new worlds with life on at 100 a day, and new technical civilizations at one a day.

2000 *Cosmic violence*. Our Galaxy experiences from 20-100 novas (binary hydrogen-fusion stars which explode) every year and one supernova (a single silicon-fusion star which explodes) every 30 years; whole Universe experiences vast, chaotic cosmic violence with 2 trillion novas a year, 2 billion supernovas a year (which then collapse into pulsars, spinning neutron stars, or black holes) also 10 million quasars (massive exploding galaxies, each destroying millions of stars and planets).

2000 *Ends of worlds*. This cosmic violence destroys related or nearby planetary civilizations at rate between 10,000 and 10 billion a year (27 a day to 300 every second), and vastly advanced civilizations at between 3 a day and 2 every minute.

2000 *Self-destroyed worlds*. Advanced technical civilizations across Universe last on average less than 10,000 years; before that time, at least 1% destroy themselves in wars or nuclear explosions, at rate of between 1 a year and 12 an hour.

### STATUS OF THE GLOBE IN AD 2000

2000 *Global Snapshot 1*. The following entries constitute a snapshot, at one specific point in time, of the world in all its complexity (Global Snapshot 2 follows in AD 2025).

2000 *Global categories*. World comprises 7 continents or continental areas, 21 regions, 238 countries with 3,030 major civil divisions; 4,050 rapidly growing metropolises (mother cities) of over 100,000 population each, housing 2.3 billion people, of which 456 are megacities (over 1 million population) housing 1 billion souls; world consists of 12,600 distinct ethnolinguistic peoples speaking 13,500 languages.

2000 *Megacrises*. Earth and its peoples and civilizations are progressively engulfed by massive crises in energy, pollution (water, air, soil), overpopulation, in a rushing vortex of convulsive social and ecological change causing dislocations globally and engendering widespread future shock.

2000 *Ecosystem*. Earth's capacity to support people is being irreversibly reduced by overpopulation and overconsumption.

2000 *Species*. Of world's present 8 million species (mostly invertebrates, with 500,000 plant species), 9,000 a year are being destroyed by man; rising by AD 2000 to 50,000 a year, with a million more at risk; also millions of new species of life are now being created artificially by man through insertion of genes from one species into another.

2000 *Environment*. Desertification spreads as world's great forest areas are destroyed (Sahara advances by 40 km a year); 25 square miles of arable land are engulfed by deserts every day; in last 100 years, 50% of virgin equatorial rainforest of Africa destroyed by man; in Amazon river basin, 1 million trees a day felled by man (1980), 110,000 square miles of forest disappear a year; present global rate 100 hectares per minute (2.5% of remaining forests per year).

2000 *Climate*. Greenhouse effect: since 1960, unregulated burning of fossil fuels increases carbon dioxide in atmosphere, heating it by 1°F more every 8 years; by AD 2045, reaches 7°F hotter at which point polar regions begin to thaw, ice caps melt, ocean levels rise 200 feet and flood much of Europe, UK, US, gulf States, eastern China, et alia.

2000 *Demographics*. World population (mid-2000), increasing at 1.18% per year; birth rate 2.05% per year, death rate 0.87% per year, life expectancy at birth 67 years.

2000 *Tourism*. International tourists per year rise from 25 million arrivals (1950) to 93 million (1963) to 141 million (1968) to 285 million (1980) to 450 million (AD 2000); total domestic as well as international movements per year, 4,500 million.

2000 *Networking*. Widespread phenomenon of innovating networks of shared attraction in all fields: health, space, human potential, environment, consciousness expansion, etc.

2000 *Megapoverty*. 2.8 billion people (46% of world) live in poverty, of whom 1.1 billion live in absolute poverty; 1.3 billion without adequate shelter, 2.2 billion without adequate water supply, 3 billion with unsafe water and bad sanitation, 991 million adults illiterate, 410 million with no access to schools, 1.5 billion with no access to medical care, 500 million on edge of starvation (22 million starvation-related deaths a year), 1.5 billion hungry or malnourished.

2000 *Handicapped*. World contains 540 million disabled persons (80% in developing countries, 60% being children, mostly among absolutely poor in Africa, Asia, Latin America): 19 million lepers, 33 million totally blind persons, 60 million psychotics (with severe mental disorders), 100 million severely handicapped children, 240 million partially handicapped children, 500 million deaf (372 million being partially deaf), 1 billion psychoneurotics.

2000 *Abortion*. 75% of world's population live in countries where abortion is legal, though regarded by most Christians as murder; 25% of all pregnancies worldwide end in abortion, resulting in 76 million abortions a year of which 38% are illegal.

2000 *Urbanization*. Greatest migration in history under way, in Third World, by 400 million underprivileged country-dwellers streaming into urban centres; urban dwellers rise to 47.6% of world, increasing by 1.3 million a week.

2000 *Skyscrapers*. Largest under development: 2,000-ft Braced Towers, New York; 2,500-ft 210-storey World Trade Center, Chicago; and 6,864-ft (1.3 miles) 500-storey Houston Tower, Houston, Texas.

2000 *Government*. Military coups and armed forces' takeovers of governments escalate to over 10% of world's countries.

2000 *Multinationals* or TNCs (transnational corporations) with affiliates outside their own countries number over 11,500, increasing annually, of which 250 are Communist transnationals; total short-term liquid assets (1971) $268 billion; a major political challenge to the world's 200 sovereign nation-states.

2000 *Transnational associations*. Global 'T-Net' grows from 1,300 transnational bodies in 1963 (political, cultural, ethnic, religious groupings, trade unions, non-governmental associations with millions of members) to 2,600 by 1975 and to 4,700 by 1987.

2000 *Inter-governmental organizations* (IGOs). Supranationals, largest of which is EEC (Common Market), coordinate global transport, communications, meteorology, atomic energy, free trade, oil, patents, etc; number grows from 139 in 1960 to 500 in AD 2000.

2000 *International non-governmental organizations*. Total NGOs across world number over 4,000 (2,000 in consultative status with United Nations Economic and Social Council, some 15% being Christian agencies).

2000 *Mega-industries*. 300 multinational corporations produce goods and services totaling US$300 billion a year (largest being General Motors USA with $25 billion annual sales); destabilizing effect on smaller and poorer nations.

2000 *Megafinance.* World largely controlled by money and power of the international banking community and gigantic oil companies with their allied banks through multinationals, controlling and even creating depressions, recessions, prosperity, inflation, money supply, interest rates, taxation, profits, losses, loans, localized conflicts and even full-scale wars; seeking the enormous profits to be made from a new world economic order and world socialistic government dominated by international finance.

2000 *International electronic fund transfers* (EFT) total US$7.3 trillion per year ($20 billion a day).

2000 *Debt.* Third World owes First World more than $1.6 trillion; corporate debt exceeds $1.7 trillion; possibility of global crash imminent.

2000 *Bureaucratization.* Political chaos spreads worldwide as corrupt bureaucracies strangle political leadership, orderly government, democratic procedures, and economic progress; popular outcry for tough, take-control, messianic global leader figures.

2000 *Human rights.* Increasing vulnerability of human rights; widespread government use of torture, increasing from 98 countries in 1980 to 150 countries, especially in South America (Colombia, Peru, Paraguay, Chile), Africa and Asia (Syria, Pakistan, Iran, etc). (Amnesty International).

2000 *Refugees.* World total of refugees of all kinds in asylum countries fluctuates around 25 million from 1965 to AD 2000.

2000 *Pain.* 20% of human race (1.2 billion persons) experience persistent or recurrent chronic pain (cancer, arthritis, migraine, shingles, sciatica, gout, etc).

2000 *Computers.* Total computers in world 496 million, some 323 million owned and operated by Christians and churches (98% in Western churches, 2% in Third- World churches mostly in Latin America); large number of Christian networks, all using Internet.

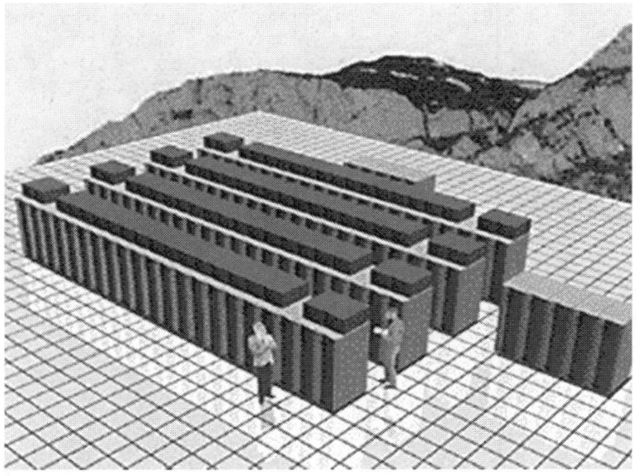

**AD 2000.** ASCI Red TFLOPS, world's first teraflop ultracomputer, at Sandia National Laboratory, New Mexico; operational since 1996.

2000 *Supercomputers* (4th-generation very large-scale integrated VLSIs, performing 2 billion operations per second) now operating at 180 sites in Western world; average cost $12 million each.

2000 *Ultracomputers.* World's first teraflop ultracomputer, ASCI Red TFLOPS, operates as a massively parallel, message-passing MIMD supercomputer, organized in 4 partitions (Compute, Service, System, I/O), with a system footprint of 1,000 square feet; peak performance 1.8 trillion computations per second.

2000 *Databases.* Commercially available databases accessible online grow from 20 in 1965 to 320 in 1979 and to 900 by AD 2000 (on a wide spectrum of subjects).

2000 *Information processing* now a $200-billion per year industry ($88 billion in USA); in USA and Europe, 86% of workforce involved in information gathering/processing/disseminating.

2000 *Electronic mail.* 300,000 systems (distinct company-wide organizations) in place in USA offices, rising by 1990 to 1.7 million systems (used by 1 million organizations).

2000 *Electronics.* As a Third-Wave industry, annual sales rise from $100 billion in 1977 to $400 billion by 1987; world's 4th-largest industry after steel, cars, and chemicals.

2000 *Communications.* 650 million telephones in world, 95% being direct-dial from London (72% dialable from USA).

2000 *Electronic bulletin boards* number 10,000, covering every interest.

2000 *Broadcasting.* Total radios in world 2,080 billion.

2000 *Space industries.* Manufacture, in space factories, of a thousand alloys and countless products that cannot be made in presence of Earth's gravity.

2000 *Informatics* (transborder data flow, TDF: computerized management techniques employed to transmit and use information without reference to national borders) assumes massive proportions, accounts for 90% of total worldwide information flow (other 10% being international news services); causes major Third-World discontent.

2000 *Counterfeiting.* Some 9% of all international trade ($36 billion in 1984) involves counterfeit products.

2000 *Megacrime.* International crime now costs $3.7 trillion a year: megafraud and computer crime $44 billion; illegal hard drug industry and traffic $200 billion, representing 38% of all organized crime; includes 25 million cocaine users in USA ($25 billion), 60 million marijuana users.

2000 *Secret police.* Scores of national police forces around world (KGB, DINA, SAVAK, BOSS, SIS, as well as in less recent history OGPU, NKVD, Gestapo) use surveillance, terror, imprisonment and torture to destroy human rights and to persecute alleged enemies of state.

2000 *Absolutism.* Number of citizens killed by totalitarian or extreme authoritarian governments reaches 130 million since 1900 (1918-53, USSR kills 40 million citizens, China under Mao 45 million, Cambodia 1975-79 2 million, et alia), far greater than 36 million combatants killed in wars since 1900; absolutist governments now mankind's deadliest scourge.

2000 *Warfare.* Persistent wars continue: since dawn of first literate civilization in BC 3500, historians have recorded a total of 14,500 wars (defined as armed conflicts each with over 50,000 combatants) with only 250 years of complete worldwide peace in the millennia since; during these wars 1,240 million people have been killed (2.9% of all humans born in this period).

2000 *Armed forces.* Total military in uniform: 23 million (18 million full-time soldiers); total combat aircraft 60,000; lethal poison-gas stockpiles include USA's 42,000 tons and USSR's 200,000 tons; in China, Peoples' Militia numbers 200 million part-time (75 million being women).

2000 *Strategic warfare.* USA's strategic plan designates 40,000 targets worldwide (60 within Moscow alone).

2000 *Strategic defense plans* take account of nuclear weapons delivery by ballistic missiles, cruise missiles, stealth technologies, bombers, small planes, terrorist groups; all defenses coordinated by huge battle management computers capable of tracking 20,000 strategic warheads and 1 million decoys likely to be used in a nuclear exchange.

2000 *Arms.* Worldwide annual military expenditure (arms race) rises from $2 billion in 1969 to $650 billion in 1982, to $940 billion in 1985, to $1 trillion in AD 2000, with $20 trillion from 1960-2000.

2000 *Technologists.* 40 million engineers and a million scientists work on Earth, of whom 40% are engaged in military/defense research and development.

2000 *Biochemical weapons.* 25 nations possess chemical or biological weaponry.

2000 *Nuclear weaponry.* Twelve countries achieve nuclear bomb capability; global arsenals now total 65,000 nuclear warheads or weapons (25,000 strategic, 35,000 tactical; USA 26,000, USSR 34,000) equivalent to 25 billion tons of TNT (2 million times size of Hiroshima bomb); scientists calculate world could not survive nuclear war if more than 1,000 warheads detonated.

2000 *International arms trade* in major weapons sold abroad now $48 billion per year, through 6 major exporters: USSR 36.5%, USA 33.6%, France 9.7%, Italy 4.3%, UK 3.6%, West Germany 3.0%.

2000 *Global terrorism.* International terrorism proliferates around world: blackmail, bombings, kidnappings, assassinations, hijackings.

2000 *Local terrorism.* Left-wing and right-wing terrorist gangs, political toughs, storm-trooper thugs, and paramilitary private armies proliferate across world's cities.

2000 *Religion.* Global status: 85% of world are religionists, 15% atheists (anti- religion) or agnostics (no religion).

2000 *Religious pluralism* widespread and accepted as the norm in most countries, cities and towns.

2000 *Quasi-religions.* Rapid increase in secular movements which are partly or virtually religions, whether anti-religious (atheism, communism, Leninism, Stalinism, etc) or non-religious (agnosticism, fascism, humanism, nationalism, etc).

2000 *Messiahs.* 75% of human race expects advent of a messiah figure: either Lord Maitreya as Boddhisattva (by Buddhists, numbering 6.2%), Kalki or Kalkin (the coming 10th Avatar/Incarnation of Vishnu, after Krishna the 8th and Buddha the 9th) (by Hindus, 13.5%), Jesus Son of Mary as Judge (by Muslims, 17.1%), Jesus Son of God as Judge (by Christians, 33.0%), Aquarian messiah (by New Age cultists, 0.6%), tribal messiahs (by 1.9%), New-Religionist messiahs (2.2%), Jewish Messiah (0.4%), et alia.

2000 *False messiahs* or would-be Christs (several with millions of followers) become a hundred times as numerous as in any previous era.

## GLOBAL OVERVIEW OF CHRISTIANITY, AD 2000

2000 *Respect for Christ:* person of Christ now widely known and respected throughout world, by all world religions, even among atheists and agnostics; also his teachings and his gospel (but not his church) are understood and valued, though not accepted or implemented, almost universally.

2000 *Christians* number 33.0% of world, receive annual income of $15.2 trillion (53% of entire world's annual income), spend 97% of it on themselves; donate 1% to secular charities and 2% ($270 billion) to operate global organized Christianity.

2000 *Massive global growth of electronic Christianity*: the electronic church, electronic evangelism, electronic worship, electronic religious education, electronic administration, electronic research, electronic communication.

2000 *Pentecostals/Charismatics.* 26% of organized Christianity are now Charismatics (12% of RCs, 34% of all Protestants, 5% of Anglicans); of world's 420,000 foreign missionaries, 25% are charismatics (20% of RCs, 40% of Protestants, 60% of Third-World missionaries).

2000 *Christian groupings.* Evangelicals worldwide number 211 million, neo-pentecostals (charismatics) in mainline denominations 173 million, premillennialists 90 million.

2000 *Ministries.* Christian experimental ministries multiply to cover whole range of human activity and human need: ministries to structures, discipling/ equipping models of pastoral leadership, whole-Body ministries.

2000 *Women.* Major increases in pastoral and other church leadership by women, also in seminary enrolment and ordained ministries of most major denominations.

2000 *Youth workers.* Western world's foreign missionary agencies send abroad, to 220 countries, 400,000 short-term young persons a year for evangelism.

2000 *Ecumenical conferences.* Total held under WCC auspices since 1948, at all levels, across world: 810 distinct consultations.

2000 *Conferences on evangelization.* Since 1945, some 7,000 conferences on mission and evangelism (at international, continental, regional or national level) have been held, via 5 groupings: 2,000 by Roman Catholic agencies; 2,100 by Ecumenical Movement agencies; 3,000 by Protestant and Anglican mission agencies; 1,500 by Evangelical mission agencies; and 1,000 by Charismatic Renewal agencies.

2000 *Unevangelized world.* 26.9% of world, or 1.6 billion, are unaware of Christianity, Christ or the gospel; in metropolises, 13%; unreached peoples (no disciples, no churches, no witness, no scriptures, no broadcasting) fall from 1,300 ethnolinguistic peoples in 1970 to 520 by 1988; no Christian broadcasting exists in 30 major languages with from 5 to 85 million native speakers each.

2000 *Pilgrims.* Some 7% of all Christians (150 million), of all traditions, are on the move as pilgrims every year, visiting national and international shrines; also 150 million Hindu, Buddhist, Muslim and other non-Christian pilgrims.

2000 *Christian lifestyles.* 52% of all Christians live in affluence, 21% are comparatively well off, 14% live in moderate poverty or near-poverty, and 13% (195 million) live in absolute poverty.

2000 *Churches of the poor* continue to spread gospel in almost every corner of Earth.

2000 *New construction* of religious buildings in USA peaks at $1.2 billion in 1965, falls to $0.9 billion in 1970, rises to $1.6 billion in 1980, and to $2.5 billion in 1987.

2000 *Megachurches.* Rise of huge individual local churches mostly in megacities: all over 5,000 members each, some with over 100,000; with multiple ministries of all kinds.

2000 *Christian activism.* Rapid spread of activism among Christians, especially in regard to pro-life issues, abortion, poverty, injustice, pornography, nuclear weaponry, war, euthanasia, child abuse, human rights, environment, et alia.

2000 *Christian unity.* Global Christian interest in church union plans declines as number of involved denominations and Christians in process of uniting decline drastically by comparison with mushrooming of 500 new denominations coming into existence each year; global ecumenical movement rejects model of 'reconciled diversity', in favor of 'conciliar fellowship', i.e. united local churches forming a universal fellowship excluding confessionalism.

2000 *Internal disarray.* Polarization between conservative/fundamentalist and liberal/radical constituencies grows rapidly worldwide in largest denominations, especially Roman Catholic, United Methodist, Presbyterian, Anglican, Lutheran and Southern Baptist.

2000 *Megaparachurch agencies.* Rise of ultralarge Christian transnationals--service agencies outside the control of churches or denominations, with global operations and huge though precarious annual budgets.

2000 *Scripture translation.* Total Common Bibles (interconfessional RC-Protestant collaboration) in preparation: 300 current active projects in 300 languages.

2000 *Christian literature.* New commercial book titles per year in all languages 26,100; new titles including devotional 73,600; Christian periodicals 27,700.

2000 *Literature on evangelization.* On narrower definition, titles strictly on 'evangelize', 'evangelism' or 'evangelization' total 100 new books and articles every year; on broader definition, titles on evangelization and synonyms total 3,500 a year.

2000 *Theological education by extension.* TEE organizations worldwide number over 300, with over 500 programs and 150,000 extension students in 120 countries.

2000 *Christian research.* Vast, loose network of 950 Christian or church-related research centers across world, very few controlled by denominations.

2000 *Paying for research.* Church-member Christians pay

out of their pockets 7,000 times as much for secular research (including on the arms race) as they pay for specifically Christian research to advance the kingdom of God.

2000 *Christian outreach.* Global foreign missions of Christian world operate on $12 billion a year; rest of organized Christianity's annual income, $254 billion (95%), goes on home church and its ministries.

2000 *Evangelistic mass campaigns.* Several hundred organized campaigns, usually multidenominational, are held in cities across the world each year.

2000 *Geostrategy.* Of 1,500 plans since AD 33 for completing world evangelization, 1,100 have fizzled out; of 400 plans extant now, 200 are in trouble; little or no cooperation between plans, nor any geostrategic framework for realistic planning.

2000 *Eschatology.* Popular books on premillennialist position (held by 41% of Evangelicals) sell 30 million copies in USA and a million copies abroad, 1970-85, especially H. Lindsay's 9-title series beginning with *The late great planet Earth* (19 million copies sold); these all however dismiss global mission and world evangelization after only miniscule passing mention (less than 1% of text).

2000 *Christian prophecy.* Millions of predictions, prophecies and proposed scenarios have been made throughout history; Catholic prophecy alone, not officially acknowledged by Rome, has produced over the centuries several thousand collected prophecies about End of World and the Antichrist, some by laypersons, some by clergy, some by monks and nuns, some by bishops, and some by popes.

2000 *Ecclesiastical gangsterism* proliferates in Third World: 5% of all churches' top leadership posts now occupied by corrupt accountants, embezzlers, swindlers, pirates, blackmailers, extortioners, liars, adulterers, thieves, thugs, vandals, even murderers; church and mission properties and funds regularly seized or looted (though still under 1% of the whole); vast increases in litigation and in illegal dealings.

2000 *Post-Christianity.* New Age Movement expands rapidly across world to embrace 1,100 million people (22% of world), based on self-realization, divinity of man, denial of Christ's bodily Incarnation, Hindu/Buddhist occultism, made up as follows: 16.4 million Christians as members in 176 countries in 1,500 marginal Christian denominations and churches; 25 million members of non-Christian religions, pseudo-churches and New Age cults; 60 million worldwide who dabble in the occult arts (witchcraft, black magic, orgies) of whom 15 million are devotees, with a further 80 million sympathetic and interested onlookers; 672 million Hindus in 84 countries, 12.0 million shamanists, 18.1 million Tantric Buddhists, 4.0 million Afro-American low spiritists, 3.1 million high spiritists in 20 countries, plus 200 million or so secularists committed to New Age philosophies.

## Epoch X:  AD 2000-AD 2050

### FINAL CLOSURE IN WORLD EVANGELIZATION

2000 **Global status:** 65.5 generations after Christ, world is 33.0% Christians (55% of them being Non-Whites, 45% Whites), 73.1% evangelized; with printed scriptures available in 2,600 languages; total martyrs since AD 33, 69,420,000 (0.8% of all Christians ever; recent rate 160,000 per year).

2000 World's 10 largest cities: Toyko/Yokohama 28,025,000, Mexico City 18,131,000, Bombay 18,042,000, Sao Paulo 17,711,000, New York/NENJ 16,626,000, Shanghai 14,173,000, Lagos 13,488,000, Los Angeles 13,129,000, Calcutta, 12,900,000, Buenos Aires 12,431,000.

2000 Jubilee Pilgrimage to Rome and Vatican (every 25 years) numbers 25 million pilgrims.

2000 World-level conference convened by Evangelicals with a representative from every people group on Earth, in last-minute attempt to complete evangelization of *panta ta ethne* by AD 2000.

2000 ICCOWE holds Consultation in Penang, Malaysia (27-31 March).

2000 4th Pan-European Charismatic Congress, sponsored by ECC and ICCOWE, held in Prague (23-27 August).

2000 World Hindu Conference 2000 convened in Port-of-Spain, Trinidad, with 1,000 Hindus attending representing total of 811 million Hindus worldwide (August).

2000 15th Assembly, World Convention of Churches of Christ (WCCC, with 5 main streams in 125 countries), in Brisbane (Australia), sponsored by Church of Christ (Disciples) (2-6 August).

2000 18th Baptist World Congress (BWA), held in Melbourne (Australia), with 15,000 attenders at close of 1997-2000 'plan for every Baptist to win one person to Christ by 2000' (January).

2000 Major Ecumenical Millennium Event, held in Jerusalem to mark the new Third Millennium, sponsored by all major confessions (and Conference of CWCs) and by Orthodox and Latin patriarchs of Jerusalem.

2000 Reunion of churches: faced with the world ridiculing the scandal of Christianity's fragmentation into 34,000 separate denominations, and under heavy governmental pressures, the world's largest churches (with 95% of all Christians) agree to begin acceptance of ministries and a common shared name, The Church of Jesus Christ.

2000 4th Japan Congress on Evangelism, held in Okinawa.

2000 Huge numbers of Asian and African and Latinamerican youth converts reject or ignore historic and Western Christianity; on world level, Christians henceforth align themselves not on confessional or denominational lines but on racial lines in 10 vast ethnolinguistic megaclusters.

2000 Emergence of hundreds of new shortlived millennial religions or belief systems at local, national and global levels; ultra-fast-growing religious cults and revivals, millions joining and leaving in rapid succession.

2000 All sizable nations and many private groups have nuclear weapons or can easily purchase them.

2000 Celebration 2000, a massive global event on the part of all Great Commission Christians, in myriads of locations; planned in detail since 1988; fizzles out.

2000 Celebrate Jesus 2000, organized by NARSC, held in St Louis, Missouri; celebrating Christ's achievements in 2 millennia; 8,000 registrants and 13,000 attenders, on theme 'Reconciliation, Repentance, Revival, Release, Renewal' (22-25 June).

2000 Proven exploitable reserves in barrels or barrels-equivalent: oil 1.5 trillion (enough to last 70 years), natural gas 500 billion, and coal to last 125 years.

2000 Ecological warfare perfected, including deliberate induction of earthquakes by triggering vibrations from a distance.

2000 Human transplant surgery multiplies; vast organ banks set up for freezing and storing of human organs, limbs, and undiseased youthful cadavers.

2000 Professional consultation on any subject available to all in any language at low cost by telephone, provided by computer expert systems.

2000 Palestinian Arabs now 5.3 million, 36% in Palestine (West Bank), 64% in exile in 25 countries.

2000 AIDS kills 20 million since 1970; deadly mutation HIV-7 devastates body's immune system 25 years after contact. (Wagar 1989:90).

2000 Japan: automatic-interpretation telephone systems introduced.

2000 NASA launches and deploys a satellite, MAP (Microwave Anisotropy Probe) to measure microwave background at high resolution; 2007, European counterpart Planck is launched; validity of Einstein's cosmological constant determined.

2000 3rd World Congress, World Assemblies of God Fellowship, in Indianapolis (USA), with 'New Millennium of Pentecosts' celebration (8-10 August).

2000 World Mission Congress (organized by Congregation for the Evangelization of Peoples), held in Rome with global participation, on theme 'Jesus Source of Life for All' (18-22 October).

2000 44th Meeting, Conference of CWCs, held in South Africa (24-26 October).

2000 'Celebrate Messiah 2000' (final meeting organized by AD 2000 Movement), in Jerusalem; cancelled.

2000 Missionary Exhibition for Holy Year 2000, held in Rome by Congregation for the Evangelization of Peoples; several previous Exhibitions in 1925, 1950 (open 10 June 2000 for 6 months).

2000 Korean World Mission Conference (KWMC 2000, sponsored by Korean World Mission Council for Christ), held in Wheaton, IL with 4,000 delegates from North America's 3,500 Korean-American churches and beyond; on 'completing world evangelization' (24-28 July).

2000 3rd World Conference of Itinerant Evangelists: 'Amsterdam 2000' (sponsored by BGEA) convened in Amsterdam by evangelist Billy Graham, with 10,000 invited preaching evangelists from 185 countries (29 July-6 August).

2000 Millennium World Peace Summit (UN-sponsored), in New York with 1,100 religious leaders, to resolve current religious conflicts worldwide, minorities, human rights abuses, the search for peace, formation of a continuing ongoing advisory committee (28-31 August).

2000 Techno-apocalypse threatened by Y2K computer bug ('Time Bomb 2000', due to failure of computers to recognize the 2-digit date '00'); fizzles out.

2000 EXPO 2000 World Exhibition in city of Hannover (Germany), attracting 40 million visitors from around world.

2000 Great Gathering of the Catholic Charismatic Family (RnS/NSC,ICCRS) held in Rimini, Italy (28 April-1 May); also Rome Jubilee 2000 Pilgrimage (ICCRS; 1-5 May).

2000 UBS World Assembly 2000 (United Bible Societies), held in Midrand, South Africa, on theme 'Word of God—Light for the World' (8-15 October).

2000 Final united organized March for Jesus, on 'Jesus Day' (10 June) with 20 million Christians across the world marching in cities.

2000 10th IAMS Conference (International Association of Mission Studies), held in Megawatt Park, South Africa, on theme 'Reflecting Christ Crucified and Living in a Broken World' (21-28 January).

2000 'All the World Sing Praise/1 January 2000' (ATWSP), greatest singing/praising event ever, a Millennium birthday tribute to Jesus beginning in New Zealand, then circling globe to finish 24 hours later.

2000 Urbana Convention (sponsored by Inter-Varsity with 530 USA campuses), held annually since 1948 (with 1,294 attenders) again held, at University of Illinois with 18,730 delegates (of whom 8,392 pledged Christian careers overseas) (26-31 December).

### 21st CENTURY BEGINS: CRISIS OR HOPE

2001 Third Millennium of Christian era begins (on 1 January 2001) which is also the beginning of 21st century AD.

2001 Over 500,000 Muslim preachers attend 3-day world's largest Islamic gathering, along Turag river outside industrial town of Tongi, Bangladesh; held there annually since 1962 (6-8 January).

2001 World Council of Churches launches Decade to Overcome Violence (DOV) (5 February).

2001 19th Pentecostal World Conference (PWC) and Centenary Celebration of Pentecostalism, held in Los Angeles (USA) (29 May-2 June).

2001 4th General Assembly, Latin American Council of Churches (CLAI).

2001 Three-quarters of world's nations involved in wars; fate of Earth lies in balance for 2 centuries more.

2001 Several communications satellites vital to global economy and nuclear balance of power are planned to be seized, disabled or taken over by techno-terrorists until demands met.

2001 Automatic language translation for telephone users, enabling speakers worldwide to converse each in his own language, under development.

2001 Japan becomes most informationized society on Earth, based on massive mainframe megacomputers storing vast data/information/knowledge banks; Japan now world's leading nation in design, manufacture and export of communications technology.

2001 Chemists create staggering compounds for every area of human experience, including the ultimate glue (adhesives that replace all existing fasteners).

2001 Most human genes now mapped (100,000 genes to build a human being), due to gene-splicing technology; many of medicine's problems and mysteries solved.

2001 Ocean level rises gradually by 5 feet until 2120 then falls, stabilizing from 2200-2400.

2001 Towing of asteroids Earthwards for mining planned, using mass driver (cost for 3-km-thick asteroid: $200 billion); over 60 asteroids are known to cross Earth's orbit; but whole scheme delayed.

2001 Holovision (life-size 3-dimensional pictures through use of laser holography) replaces television in homes.

2001 NASA and ESA (European Space Agency) put space platforms in position as satellites each with one million voice circuits.

2001 18th World Methodist Conference (WMC), held in Brighton (UK) with 4,000 delegates, on theme 'Jesus: God's Way of Salvation' (26-31 July).

2002 Synthetic blood in wide use.

2002 Memory metal Nitinol (and similar alloys) remembers its previous shape before crashes, etc; on heating, snaps back to its original shape, exerting enormous force in the process.

2002 First wristwatch computer perfected, accepting and imparting spoken instructions in English or any other language.

2002 Hospital (computerized health-care facility) in space being discussed by NASA (USA).

2002 One vast megacomputer established under UN auspices, with centralized global data facility giving wide public access to library, business and home terminals.

2002 Emergence of 7th-generation computers, powered not by electricity but by light beams.

2002 Startling influence of Christian world confessionalism continues to spread, at expense of world interdenominationalism, ecumenism and conciliarism; decline of WCC and its 200 associated continental and national councils of churches, under charges of having stood for ecumenical imperialism.

2002 Conquest of disease: every kind of cancer curable in early stages and treatable throughout; by 2015, all infectious and heritable diseases in humans, plants, and animals entirely eradicated.

2002 Civilian aerospace vehicles (CAVs) come into service, traveling at Mach 12 and carrying travelers half-way around the world in 2 hours.

2002 Worldwide emergence of natural economic regional states cutting across existing national political boundaries: Baden-Wurttemberg, Alsace-Lorraine, Catalonia, Wales, Vancouver-Seattle, Hong Kong-Guangdong, Fuzhou-Taiwan, and many more within China, Japan, Pacific Basin, et alia.

2002 National Computer Mercantile Network established, with superconducting supercomputers monitoring and recording every commercial and mercantile transaction in USA, including personal tax files, credit records.

2002 Proliferation of local organic church unions begins around world, as hostile governments order or force all churches in their countries, of totally different confessions, to unite under one single name in order to exercise total control over them.

2002 First commercial device producing clean safe power by low-temperature nuclear reactions goes on market; end of Fossil-Fuel Age.

2003 Substitutive medicine (replacement of defective parts by implants or transplants) replaces drug treatment; kidney dialysis patients wear device internally; by 2025, people being kept alive by spare parts number 1% of population in Western world.

2003 First prototype SPS (solar-power satellite) successfully beams energy from space to Earth, relaying solar power via low-density microwaves to become DC electrical current; 2021, over 20 SPS in geosynchronous Earth orbit each producing 10 gigawatts (10 billion watts) microbeamed to Earth to join existing electric-power grids; 2028, SPS supply 90% of Earth's energy requirements.

2003 Majority of countries enforce strict population control, including contraceptive injections and forced abortions.
2003 Accurate long-range weather forecasts now available over telephone, custom-made to any individual's or organization's detailed requirements.
2003 90% of all world's first-class mail now transmitted electronically (electronic mail).
2003 Corporate commercial warfare: giant multinational conglomerates engage in worldwide organized espionage, intimidation, threats, fraud, violence and terrorism to discourage competition.
2003 Full-immersion video rooms in homes for families to surround themselves with tropical rain forest, a Mars landscape, a movie epic, et alia.
2003 The 8 major obstacles to Christian world mission become megamaterialism, mega-affluence, mega-embezzlement, megapoverty, megapollution, megacrime, megaterrorism, megapersecution.

***Postindustrial societies and transindustrial economies***

2003 PLO splinter group, Sons of the Jihad, threatens to set off a squirt bomb in London, polluting 60% of city for next 70 years.
2003 Global killer pandemics arise, sweeping across (a) Third World with 'diseases of poverty' (malaria, bilharzia, filariasis, et alia) as parasites achieve full resistance to present drugs; (b) rest of world with revived deadly ancient diseases (smallpox, bubonic plague, pneumonic plague, et alia) as world loses its herd immunity and abandons vector control and vaccination; and (c) AIDS and related pandemics; hundreds of millions die.
2003 Biotechnologists succeed in mapping the complete neural signature of the entire human brain.
2003 Timolol and other drugs greatly reduce danger of heart attacks.
2003 One billion telephones in world, nearly all direct dial; everyone in world is offered a UN-designed 17-digit personal number, making him instantly accessible wherever he travels.
2003 Routine use of microcomputer implants in human brain proposed to control epilepsy, psychoses and other diseases.
2003 A newscaster using very powerful personal computer gets access to, and finally control over, all data banks in world. (A. Budrys' scenario *Michaelmas*, 1977).
2003 In democracies, citizens govern by televoting regularly every Sunday at noon.
2003 Worldwide disintegration of ecclesiastical coherence and centralized control.

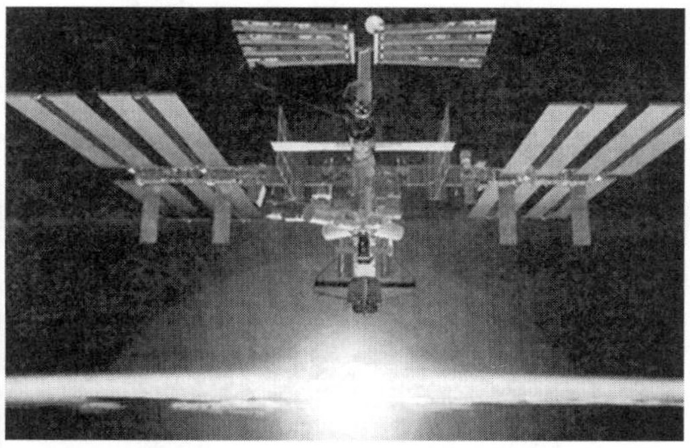

**AD 2003.** International Space Station with Milky Way galaxy in distance.

2003 NASA (USA) places Space Station in orbit, permanently-manned research laboratory, observatory and factory in space, involving 12 countries.
2003 Inexpensive wrist televisions with hundreds of channels available.
2003 14th Assembly, Mennonite World Conference (NWC), held in Africa.
2004 Computer robot designed to understand all 2,000 major languages and all 500 major lingua francas.
2004 First commercial computer to be completely conceived, designed, and manufactured by other computers and robots.
2004 Nuclear crime, blackmail and terrorism become rampant on all continents, especially in megacities and supercities.
2004 As result of microelectronics revolution, 50% of all jobs in industrial world have been eliminated over last 25 years; robots run 50% of world's industrial mass production.
2004 Research on control of aging well on way to perfection.
2004 Brazil, Mexico, Philippines and other Third-World countries default on total of $400 billion of international indebtedness; dozens of Western corporations, banks and cities go bankrupt.
2004 Hydrogen now the most popular small-scale energy source, powering commercial vehicles et alia.
2004 Seminaries, missionary training colleges, TEE (Theological Education by Extension) et alia revolutionized by chemical transfer of learning: memory pills, knowledge pills, new languages learned by injection.
2004 Public deliberately-staged TV trials and martyrdoms of Christian workers and leaders by fanatical Muslim and Communist regimes.
2004 Massive pentecostal-charismatic latter-rain revival sweeps across whole of Asia due to power evangelism with signs and wonders, with 150 million converts in Korea, Japan, China, Viet Nam, Thailand, Malaysia, Indonesia, Burma, Cambodia, India, Sri Lanka and Pakistan.
2004 Universe now found by astronomers to be not open (expanding forever) but closed, i.e. to have sufficient mass and energy for its receding galaxies to collapse back when expansion limit reached.
2004 World's greatest denominations continue to self-destruct over insoluble internal controversies: RCC, CofE, EKD, UMC, SBC, et alia.
2004 All cancers can now in principle be instantly arrested, cured and eliminated through reprogramming of DNA in individual body cells.
2004 Electronic mentors emerge, offering user personalized help in navigating the information age, sparking user's creativity with questions, taking dictation, placing and receiving phone calls, translating, and often using artificial intelligence.
2004 Mass production of implantable miniaturized artificial kidneys.
2004 HALO (High Altitude Large Optics) military satellite ready to place 10 million no-blink infrared detectors in space to protect USA from sneak missile launchings.
2004 Two-way wrist or pocket telephones/TVs/pagers/maintenance-free wrist computers/translatorfones in widespread use across globe.
2004 Ultrafast optical (fibre-optic) computers (for speedier informational transmission than by wires) produced by Bell Laboratories, IBM et alia.
2004 13th World Assembly, United Bible Societies (UBS), held in England on 200th anniversary of Bible Society movement.
2004 16th World Assembly, World Convention of Churches of Christ (WCCC), held in Brighton, England (27 July-1 August).
2004 First publicly admitted human clone, though claim doubted by many; scientists note clones age quicker than humans.
2005 Unified field theory finally constructed by physicists, a mathematical model tying together the 5 basic forces holding the Universe's particles together: gravity, electromagnetism, weak nuclear force, strong nuclear force, hypercharge.
2005 Eco-collapse scenario: initial worldwide eco-catastrophe due to unabated population growth, resource depletion, pollution of the biosphere, destruction of the ecosphere and the sociosphere, crop failures, starvation, megafamines, et alia. (Club of Rome).
2005 Russians develop psionics (science of electronics dealing with psychic phenomena) and place psionic weapon in orbit around Earth; Western world reacts belatedly by opening parapsychology laboratories.
2005 Polio as a children's disease is eliminated throughout world (goal of Rotarians since 1985).
2005 Centennial celebrations of Baptist World Alliance (BWA) held at 19th Baptist World Congress.
2005 First commercially viable biochip interface, linking a human by wire to multilingual interface computer.
2005 Total strategic nuclear warheads rise from 14,000 in 1982 (USA 9,000, USSR 5,000) to 35,000 by 1991, then fall to 5,000 by 2005.
2005 Self-replicating machines, computers, and factories begin to be produced in Japan, reproducing exact copies of themselves (initially for a limited range of products).
2005 Tourism continues as world's biggest industry, with 700 million people travelling abroad for pleasure each year.
2005 Telepathy in use for some types of communication, criminology, diplomacy, military intelligence, espionage.
2005 Parapsychology comes into use as a military weapon used by terrorists, private armies, vigilantes, and military regimes.
2005 Biotechnological disaster through a microbe spill: creation and accidental release of virulent microbes wipes out entire populations.
2005 Medical advances: antiviral drugs and vaccines wipe out communicable diseases; genetic manipulation removes congenital defects; lung and brain-cell transplants become routine; nerve tissue regenerated to rehabilitate paraplegics and quadriplegics.
2005 Beamlike gravitational radiation detected from super-heavy objects in outer space.
2005 Biomap: genomic inventory (mapping by molecular biologists of human genome or genetic complex) enables prediction of future health and pre-emptive treatment; but misuses increase (discrimination, invasion of privacy) until in 2010 uniform global policy on access is adopted by 145 countries; human biomap, with 3 billion separate genetic functions, not completed until 2086.
2005 Large numbers of substitute religions arise, mostly related to New Age movement; a vast amorphous hodgepodge of spiritualism, reincarnation, meditation, yoga, faith healing, macrobiotic diets, out-of-body experiences, altered-consciousness states, mystical environmentalism—all supported by empires of magazines, records, books, bulletin boards, broadcasts, telecasts, mass merchandizing.
2005 International Thermonuclear Experimental Reactor (ITER), producing nuclear power by fusion, completed by international team at San Diego, USA, and commissioned after cost of $7.5 billion; c2035, global chain of fusion reactor power stations at work.
2005 United Nations revokes license of sovereignty hitherto assumed by all sovereign nations.
2005 Citizens begin electing commercial firms instead of politicians to run their cities.
2005 Low intensity conflicts (LICs) proliferate, being USA responses to Third-World violence.
2005 Team of 150 terrorists uses man-transportable electromagnetic pulse generators (EMPGs) to attack transformers serving New York, Washington, Dallas, Atlanta, Boston, Chicago, and San Francisco; succeeds in erasing computer databases in those cities causing loss of social security records, tax records, bank records, pension plans, financial transactions, library holdings; all erased in a moment.
2005 International organization 'Honesty International' (modeled on Amnesty International) monitors corruption in government and corporate institutions around world, investigating bribery, embezzlement, with goal of deterring such activities.
2005 Sudden global power failure and total breakdown of sociosphere as domino effect destroys global infrastructures.
2005 Direct communication with computers by speech achieved by humans; talkwriters (transcribing speech) replace human transcribers.
2005 Historic abolition of all long-distance telephone charges (on December 31) transforms humanity into one huge gossiping family (A.C. Clarke 1987:17).
2005 Third-World nations led by Mexico repudiate $1,000 billion debts to Western banks; West and USSR retaliate, Latin American economy collapses, starvation sweeps Africa and Asia; huge Third-World terrorist operation smashes Western electronic economy, stock market crashes, world community disintegrates in chaos. (W. Clark's 1984 scenario *Cataclysm: the North-South conflict of 1987*).
2005 6th-generation computers with artificial intelligence emerge, equaling human brain in any intellectual activity.
2005 New weather patterns produce global crop failures and lead to megafamines, with hordes of starving people marching across continents in search of food.
2005 Personal computers incorporate TV and telephone; most people use handheld microcomputers.
2005 1st General Council of 3 ecumenical Communions/Agencies holding together each's previously separate confessional assemblies: WARC, LWF, WCC.
2006 Global collapse of organized Christian confessional monoliths begins.
2006 Global energy crisis finally solved as SPS (Solar Power Satellite) comes online; by 2021 becomes world's major energy source.
2006 Blatant state disinformation tactics cause havoc with organized Christianity: religious espionage, thefts of strategic plans, computerized embezzlement of funds, false accusations, forged documents, blackmail, heretical literature, pseudo-Christian broadcasting, terrorism falsely ascribed to Christian bodies.
2006 Accepted safeguards for religious liberty begin to collapse worldwide; as persecution spreads, bulk of local churches cut all ties with centralized denominational control, break all conciliar links, and retreat into nonconciliarism and ecclesiastical isolationism.
2006 Bionic eyes: artificial eyesight invented for blind people (the nonsighted); alternatively, whole-eye transplants become possible.
2006 Internationalists (people working for UN agencies) become major influence in world at all levels.
2006 Alien virus brought back by interplanetary spaceprobe wipes out 10% of population of Earth.
2006 Earth invaded from outer space by Overlords in giant spaceships, who then assist humanity to continue its evolution into a Galaxy-wide and ever-expanding Overmind; but in the end humans reactivate volcanic energies of Earth's core and destroy planet. (A.C. Clarke's scenario, *Childhood's end*, 1953).
2006 Conflict between science and religion finally disappears; physicists and biochemists become more concerned about questions of spirit, soul and creation than many theologians.
2006 Neurotransmitters activate human brains and change mental performance; brain radios communicate with electricity in brain, enabling people to dial into any emotional, mental or sensual experience.
2006 Declining Euroamerican denominations in Western world spark off itinerant tourist churches, groupings of believers ceaselessly travelling and witnessing around the Earth; Latin Americans independently form itinerant pilgrim churches which multiply phenomenally across world.
2006 Artificial intelligence (AI) affects 60%-90% of jobs in large organizations, augmenting, displacing, downgrading, eliminating workers.
2006 Diagnosis of almost any illness possible in a few hours by examining patient's Human Protein Index (human body contains 50,000 different kinds of protein).
2006 Anticipated medical advances: 2006, medical smart cards issued to all, animal testing of drugs replaced

by computer modeling; 2007, buying and selling of live organs legalized and closely regulated; 2009, spread of cancer tightly controlled by new drug; 2010, overall incidence of cancer decreased by 35%, memory improved with drug; 2011, aging slowed by new vitamins; 2013, use of animal organs for transplants; 2017, drug addiction conquered; 2019, polyvalent vaccine prevents 80% of colds; 2020, incidence of all cancer decreased by 80%, more than 90% of coronary disease eliminated; 2025, average life expectancy reaches 100 years; 2030, maximum human life-span increased to 150 years.

2006 Definitive alleviation of mental illness attained.

2006 Anti-Christian bodies hire (1) gangs of thugs, and (2) organized terrorist groups, specifically to harass and disrupt Western foreign mission operations and to kill their missionaries.

2006 People assisters (computer-assisted hydraulic mover systems with powered arms) worn by infirm or handicapped people to give them increased mobility; also, for healthy persons, personal maneuvering units (in space), Moon bugs, Mars rovers, submersibles, solarsail kites; also lighter-than-air skyships.

2006 People amplifiers (PAs) in use: portable computerized devices which assist average person perform as a pseudoexpert in several different spheres at once (e.g. law/accountancy/mathematics/astronomy/theology/missiology/homiletics).

2006 Experience-amplifiers in use, for magnifying human experiences: emotion-amplifiers, sensation-amplifiers, awareness-amplifiers, creativity-amplifiers.

2006 Intelligence-amplifiers (resulting in enhanced intelligence) create artificial personalities for secretaries, assistants, technicians et alii.

2006 All overt evangelistic activity prohibited or suppressed in over 50 countries.

2006 A new futuristic international city, Multifunction Polis, begins to be built in Australia.

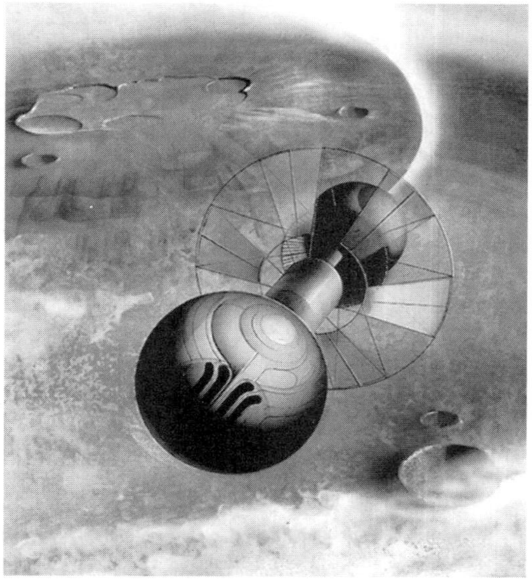

**AD 2006.** Manned starship orbits Mars above Olympus Mons in Amazonia Planitia region.

2006 Manned expedition to Mars launched by NASA (20 years after first landing of unmanned robot probe Viking).

2006 Distance learning widely used at all levels including doctoral research.

2006 Hyperinflation leads to general breakdown of world monetary system.

2007 Development of vast single computer which runs world, world economy and world government and monitors and controls all other computers. (I. Asimov, *The life and times of Multivac*, 1975).

2007 All Persian Gulf states run out of oil; virtual exhaustion of petroleum reserves; Saudi Arabia, Gulf states, Iran, Libya et alia lose accumulated oil wealth, revert to pauper status.

2007 Establishment of first nonterrestrial permanent resource base, either on Moon or Mars or in space.

2007 Cures found for every known 20th-century illness.

2007 21st-century epidemic Plague Wars, with appalling variety of new lethal diseases, begin with 15 million killed by influenza virus in southern Africa, leading to violent overthrow of governments; 2015, deliberately-engineered plague in Los Angeles, USA, kills 1 million; 2024, VD virus kills 5 million in Poland; 7 million in outbreak in Brussels; 2049, 38 million killed in China by lightning hepatitis; finally checked by 2060. (*The Third Millennium*, 1985).

2007 Computer work stations in offices equipped with expert systems function as dictionaries, directories, telephones; office typists and secretaries replaced by managers.

2007 Mind-reading computers invented, with direct telepathic reading of thoughts in the brain; telepathic machines pick up human thoughts, place them on screen in front of the thinker.

2007 Passive entertainment, passive listening to radio, passive TV watching, passive observing all disappear as reality becomes widely synthesized to give people active participation in sports, arts, wars, thrills et alia via sensavision head fittings.

2007 Organized hostage terrorism turns against foreign missionaries: scores rounded up as hostages, ransoms demanded, many murdered.

2007 OPEC cartel of oil-producing countries, which has rapidly accumulated unprecedented vast wealth, suddenly collapses and goes bankrupt.

2007 Synclavier invented: minicomputerized synthesizer capable of duplicating sounds of 25 musical instruments individually and as an orchestra; 2008, 'Music Minus One' company produces recordings leaving out one instrument for any amateur to join in.

2007 Wars fought with mercenary replicants (cloned humanoids with silicon intelligence), intelligent weapons, robot tanks, smart missiles, RPVs (remotely piloted vehicles), et alia.

2007 Earth unexpectedly enters dense belt of cosmic dust; temperatures fall catastrophically, new ice age begins.

2007 World's greatest natural explosion, of submerged volcano Krakatoa off Java, far larger than first cataclysm in 1883.

2007 Maglev (magnetic levitation) track reduces travel time from Los Angeles to Las Vegas (282 miles) to one hour, in trains flying on invisible magnetic cushion two-thirds inch off ground.

2007 Project Space Voyage, a low-Earth-orbit popular tour organized by Society Expeditions: 4 days' briefing, 12-hour trip, 2 days' debriefing.

2007 First of several global pandemics caused by new unstoppable viruses, killing millions through 'stealth' maladies attacking suddenly, silently, without warning, no cure, 100% fatalities; called prion diseases from eating meat (Mad Cow disease, etc; causing hole in human brain).

2007 Majority of books and publications are published online.

2007 Computerized info systems commonly used for medical care; genetic therapy routine.

2007 NASA's Next Generation Space Telescope, successor to the Hubble, is launched.

2008 Terrorist outrages against strategic Christian gatherings in church headquarters: Vatican devastated during conclave of all 200 cardinals, Ecumenical Center (Geneva) destroyed with heads of 300 major denominations, Canterbury Cathedral razed with 700 bishops at 14th Lambeth Conference, scores of cathedrals bombed during Easter services; end of mass public leaders' conferences.

2008 Lethal new space weapons introduced, including gamma-ray lasers (grasers) able to blow up planets and stars; arms race between Superpowers escalates again.

2008 Fanatical religious terrorism turns against Christian missionary bodies: selective or same-time assassinations of whole mission societies, or of all top mission executives.

2008 Russia attempts for political reasons to alter the past using scientific information carried by tachyons (particles that move backwards in time).

2008 Global church research project to determine which major events or situations in past history of evangelization should be changed by messages or messengers sent from today, as soon as science invents method of tachyonic time travel and alteration of the past; preference for rectifying the great missed opportunities of Christian history (as with China in 1266, 1644, 1843).

2008 Third-generation artificial experience developed through mammoth artificial-intelligence computer systems creating 3-dimensional holograms of any historical or future reality or event in the Universe.

2008 Final Return of Mahdi (Mirza Ghulam Ahmad), regarded as Christ/Vishnu/ Mohammed in Ahmadiyya belief expected, on centenary of his death; huge crowds of Ahmadis wait expectantly across world.

2008 Titanic nuclear accident as nuke (power plant) melts down in populous area: tens of thousands of casualties from radiation and mass panic; public outcry to shutdown all nukes.

2008 Scientists at International Astronomical Union announce Sun will go nova and explode in AD 3620; by 2553, 4 km-long seedships packed with data, life (species, DNA), technology and a million hibernating humans each, depart for Alpha Centauri A and 50 other planetary systems with oxygen; 3450, quantum drive invented making perpetual travel without fuel possible; 40 seedship voyages fail but 10 succeed including Mormon 'Ark of the Covenant' and other religious ones; 3617, starship Magellan leaves doomed Earth, 4135 arrives to begin life on planet Sagan Two. (A.C. Clarke, *The songs of* distant Earth, *1985).*

2008 Founding of Global Trade Consortium (GTC) in Zurich by megacorporate businessmen in developed countries; by 2015 all 12 megacorps enlist.

2008 European vigilantes' group called Speedwatch systematically assassinates dangerous, drunk or speeding car drivers.

2008 Cancer largely eliminated by immunization.

2008 A radical communications invention makes it possible to see, touch and speak with anyone in the world.

2008 First true space colony (High Frontier or O'Neill-type) built and inhabited in orbit between Earth and Moon; first children born off-Earth; 50,000 people now live and work in space.

2008 Global oil war erupts as Arabs cut off oil to USA: Russia's oil reserves also rapidly running out.

2008 Nuclear reactor disaster in Western capital city; millions killed, huge area contaminated; headquarters of major church and mission organizations there permanently abandoned.

2008 First submotel (submarine hotel) opens, with parking for tourist minisubmarines.

2008 80% of population in wealthy countries have access to information superhighway.

2008 Helvetian War (Secrecy War), last armed conflict on Earth, erupts to force Switzerland to reveal secret bank holdings; citizens of America and Pan-Europe attack Swiss-based laundered monies of drug merchants, tax cheats, and corrupt dictators shielded by banking `gnomes of Zurich' in their bank vault strongholds beneath the Glarus Alps; international banking secrecy finally destroyed.

## THE MIDDLE-RANGE FUTURE (5-30 years from now)

2009 Planetran world transportation network transports millions daily in electromagnetically-propelled cars travelling at 14,000 mph through evacuated tubes in underground tunnels.

2009 China invades Russia; nuclear exchange, then ground warfare drags on for 12 years.

2009 Development of direct brain-computer interfaces as means of extending human mental capacity; human brains linked to supercomputers; also direct communication between computers and human central nervous system.

2009 Terrorist outrages against world religions: Kaaba in Mecca razed with 1.8 million Muslim worshippers killed (700,000 inside); Kumbh Mela (Hindu 12-yearly festival at confluence of Ganges and Jumna) annihilated with 16 million worshippers present.

2009 Ecumenical Sharing of Resources (WCC program transmitting $65 million in 1983, $400 million in AD 2000) collapses catastrophically as banks disintegrate.

2009 Organized global moves against all Christian foreign missions: expulsions, prohibitions, seizure of properties, trials, assassinations, executions, massacres, eradication.

2009 Orient Express, or TAV (transatmospheric vehicle, a hypersonic space vehicle) takes off from and lands on conventional runways, deploys SDI payloads in space.

2009 Majority of global organized Christianity becomes underground or catacomb church as state surveillance, interference, persecution and suppression spread.

2009 Gigantic electromagnetic railguns, mounted on mountainsides, accelerate cargo-carrying missiles to hypersonic speeds out into space.

2009 Space-com wrist-radios enable user to speak with anyone in world; by 2010, 50 million users across globe.

2009 Cataract system, a network of orbiting nuclear mines, launched by USA to blind all enemy satellites before a nuclear preemptive first strike.

2009 Total global charismatic worship of Christ introduced, in which at a fixed time each Sunday one billion living believers across world are holographically present visibly at same location; the ultimate in inspiration and evangelistic converting power.

2009 Second Western Asia-Southern Asia war, spreading from Iran-Iraq war begun in 1980: both sides use nuclear weapons, destroying major cities.

2009 Terrorists in Africa seize and dominate world's supply of gold, diamonds and strategic metals.

2009 USA goes bankrupt as federal budget deficit increases from $4 trillion in 1992 to $8 trillion by AD 2009.

2009 Worst natural disaster of century as massive earthquake devastates most of Iran.

2009 United Religions Organization (URO) brought into being to parallel United Nations, to provide visions and moral power for world faiths; based in Jerusalem.

2009 NASA Shuttle passenger liner begins 74-passenger trips, ferrying 10,000 people into space annually.

2009 Control of human obesity attained.

2009 Race and class wars erupt across Southern Africa, Middle East, northern India, together with mass urban terrorism in urbanized Northern half of planet.

2009 An Asian city is devastated by accidental explosion of an atomic bomb in its armory; after uproar at UN, all nuclear weapons are destroyed.

## WORLD WAR III: NUCLEAR HOLOCAUST SCENARIO

2010 World's 10 largest cities: Toyko/Yokohama 28,840,000, Bombay 23,653,000, Lagos 20,956,000, Sao Paulo 19,659,000, Mexico City 18,682,000, New York,/NENJ 17,232,000, Karachi 16,669,000, Dhaka 16,663,000, Shanghai 16,578,000, Calcutta 15,640,000

2010 Universal Christian Church Council (WCC-RCC-Orthodoxy-Pentecostals) convened to resolve main outstanding issues dividing confessions and churches, including a role for primacy of bishop of Rome; leading to a common confession of faith, sanctioning total communion, and celebrating Eucharist together.

2010 Divine intervention scenario: Christ appears and

intervenes at last minute to save mankind from certain imminent self-destruction by nuclear holocaust; role as Savior now universally understood and acknowledged; evil held firmly in check as Millennium begins.

2010 On one widely-held premillennialist scenario, final Battle of Armageddon takes place in Israel, culminating in victory of Jesus the Messiah, overthrow of evil, and inauguration of the Millennium.

2010 After 38 years' preparation since 1961 1st Pan-Orthodox Conference (on island of Rhodes), Great & Holy Council of the Orthodox Church convenes in Greece as first fully-recognized ecumenical council of the entire church since 7th Ecumenical Council (Council of Nicaea II, last one recognized by Eastern Orthodox) in AD 787; statement promulgated on Orthodoxy's mission to the world; mission icon distributed.

2010 Astrophysicists test propulsion drive for speed-of-light starship; pilot ship said to be being readied to set out for Proxima Centauri star system.

2010 Definitive cures for cancer found in principle; universal cancer vaccine comes into wide use.

2010 All known human infectious diseases successfully eradicated in principle.

2010 Post-nuclear human mutants multiply and spread, with telepathic powers; several bizarre civilizations develop: telepathic societies, high-technology societies, barbarisms, dictatorships.

2010 Death of oceans scenario: terminal process leading to death of world's seas and oceans due to massive and irreversible pollution by industrial poisons, chemicals and sewage, leading to global disease, epidemics, famine, warfare and extinction.

2010 Computer-generated holocaust: all-out nuclear war erupts as superpowers' huge computer networks overreact.

2010 Technological collapse scenario: beginnings of collapse of global technology due to overload, exhaustion of minerals, warfare, terrorism; technological civilization disintegrates into barbarism.

2010 Rise of final Antichrist III (also known as Eighth & Final Antichrist), either (a) a polylingual ruthless Jewish despot from Israel's tribe of Dan posing as Messiah, (b) a blue-turbaned tyrant from Arabia espousing militaristic Islam and wielding the oil weapon, or (c) a professedly-Christian European dictator dominating 10-nation confederacy; each wielding nuclear weapons, global terror, and mass destruction. (Nostradamus).

2010 Last Pope of Rome elected, Peter II (Peter the Roman, 266th Pope, Pope of the Apocalypse; on St Malachy's reckoning, 112th since 1143); when he flees Rome, rival antipopes emerge over a Church of Darkness, as the Great Tribulation begins.

2010 Private transport severely restricted, even abolished by law in many vast areas.

2010 All information in a large library is storable on machine the size of a postage stamp and instantaneously retrievable.

2010 Psychiatry and medicine can now call on vast arrays of drugs.

2010 Antichrist III annihilates city of New York by missiles, reveals self's true identity in Horror of Horrors (Abomination of Desolation). (Nostradamus).

2010 Anti-aging drugs available on prescription to arrest and reverse aging in humans.

2010 Governments drug reservoirs and all water supplies with contraceptives to control population explosion.

2010 Intelligent machines tackle all mental activities somewhat better than humans can.

2010 World government arises as vastly complex polynucleated or decentralized matrix organization or network rather than all power being centrally concentrated.

2010 Mind-control and behavior-control chemicals widely used (via water and food supplies) by authoritarian governments to suppress dissension and unrest.

2010 Rise of totalitarianism produces mass religious revivals; bogus robot evangelists seduce ignorant with promises of immediate salvation.

2010 Vast growth of magical and pseudoscientific cults; governments use androids (chemically constructed beings) to deceive and manipulate religious followers.

2010 Formation of Arab Islamic Republic in Cairo, uniting several Arab states.

2010 Increasing influence of Christianity on secular worlds of science, politics, society, ideas; scientists in particular openly become more religious.

2010 Roman Catholic pope, a Black African, transfers Vatican to Jerusalem; church ends opposition to contraception, compulsory clerical celibacy, and ordination of women to priesthood, and seeks full rapprochement with separated Christians.

2010 Genetic manipulation allows humans to create evolutionary change: creating pilots with faster reaction times, workers happy with monotonous work, cloned soldiers to fight wars.

2010 Historic discovery: brain code deciphered, showing how human brain (most efficient and compact information storage system ever) works; direction communication with human minds achieved.

2010 Nuclear holocaust recovery scenario: due to warhead detonation patterns in global nuclear war, initial deaths 10% of world (including 50% of USA) but 90% of world survives (including 50% of USA) and 90% of world's surface remains unaffected; secondary deaths from fallout, wind-borne radiation followed by radiation sickness, contaminated food and water, breakdown of civilization, and decreased fertility, all kill another 10% of world; animal and plant life only marginally affected; world recovers fully within 20 years (USA 40 years).

2010 Nuclear holocaust median scenario: nuclear war between USA and other powers leaves initially 50% of both populations dead and all major urban cities destroyed; full-scale thermonuclear attack immediately kills 88% of USA and 50% of rest of world; a new Dark Ages era begins.

2010 Extinction scenario: nuclear war results in 6 billion deaths (6,000 megadeaths), end of civilization, destruction of the North, destruction of all global infrastructures, destruction of knowledge and know-how, mankind reduced to handful of demoralized tribal savages; eventually, final extinction of all human and animal life.

### *A new Golden Age of peace and prosperity*

2010 Widespread genetic engineering (gene splicing) to fix deformed arms or legs; all childhood diseases eliminated, also skin, breast and cervical cancer; by 2020, 90% of all forms of cancer eliminated, regeneration of fingers and toes accomplished, also plastic surgery without scalpel; by 2050, regeneration of human internal organs.

2010 Uniform global policy on access to biomaps adopted by 145 countries urged on by GTC.

2010 Whole world now looks to or follows 3 new global futures: (a) globalized liberal democratic technoliberal capitalism, with breakthroughs in technology (fusion power, artificial intelligence, et alia); (b) democratic socialism and world government, the workers' republic; (c) 2085 or 2130, self-sufficient advanced technologies scaled to local needs by neo-romantic counterculturalist values.

2010 World major wars (excluding regional and local wars): 3,500 were fought between BC 3600 and AD 2010, with 1.7 billion battle deaths.

2010 Since 1945, over 100 civil and international wars have caused deaths of over 300 million.

2010 A new kind of society emerges: post-capitalist but non-socialist, with knowledge as primary resource.

2010 World's 3 leading economic powers (USA, European Community, Japan) are joined by rapidly growing economic giant, China.

2010 Telephones in use that instantly translate foreign languages.

2010 Churches forced underground in many countries, into clandestine or illegal existence.

2010 Relaunching of world's largest particle accelerator, the Superconducting Supercollider (SSC), 54-mile circular tunnel under Waxahachie, Texas, USA, abandoned in 1993 as too expensive; aims include verifying Standard Model (4 particles, acted on by 4 forces), and identifying supersymmetric particles (dark matter, 99% of Universe).

2010 Energy use from alternative sources reaches 10%; 2016, energy efficiency improves by 50%.

2010 Expert systems (artificial intelligence) in wide use, with quick and accurate language translators routine.

2010 20% of all Americans now derive all their spiritual input through the Internet.

2010 First quantum generators tapping space energy are developed as portable and household units from a few kilowatts upwards, producing electricity indefinitely; central power stations close down, grid systems dismantled.

2010 Electronic monitoring virtually removes professional criminals from society.

2011 Revolution and civil war in South Africa lead to autocratic Black majority rule over White remnants and a shattered nation.

2011 Major shortages of vital metals (mercury, cadmium, copper, tin, silver) result in political blackmail and miniwars.

2011 Most forms of mental retardation now curable.

2011 Collapse of organized secularism, agnosticism (non-religion), atheism (anti-religion), and rise of spiritual movements with vast rash of sects and cults of all kinds.

2011 All texts published in English routinely put on electronic deposit; 2030, this becomes sole form of publication for scientific papers and other reference items, reproducible by printer only at point of consumption.

2011 All radio, telephone and televisual communication becomes integrated in single worldwide information-transfer network; satellite-relayed entertainment, English-language teletext library services, even for poorest nations; 2150, full integration universal.

2011 Great Cycle of the ancient Mayas of Meso-America due to be completed, ushering in end of whole Cosmos.

2011 Normal human lifespan extends to 150 years for 50% of Western world, but increased longevity only viable for future Homo species voyaging beyond Solar System.

2011 First of only 3 hostile nuclear incidents since 1945; 2011, Israelis destroy Libyan city, killing 78,000; 2020, Zaire accident detonates missile killing 7,000 with fallout throughout equatorial Africa; and 2079, city of Buenos Aires destroyed by Brazilian air force; thereafter, all nuclear weapons seized by superpowers, worldwide nuclear peace enforced. (*The Third Millennium*, 1985)

2011 Automated highways with central computer control of all vehicles moving at same speed at much greater densities than previously; all vehicles now have electronic collision-avoidance hardware.

## SPACE COLONIZATION SCENARIO

### *Human migration into space begins: origin of astroculture*

2011 Religious pilgrims become a major force in world, over 400 million religious zealots (50% being Christians) constantly on move from shrine to shrine and country to country, ignoring secular and state restrictions; Christian pilgrims form a vast unorganized network of continuously itinerant pilgrim churches.

2011 USA: Strategic Defense Initiative shield fully operational; similar shield over Europe and Russia by 2021.

2011 Time shown by scientists to be flowing at different rates in different parts of the Universe, including tachyons (particles that move faster than light) for which time moves backwards.

2012 Iran starts global conflict in Muslim world centered on Middle East by invading Macedonia and North Africa; Arab invasion of Europe, France, Italy. (Nostradamus).

2012 Orbital colonies commenced: one-mile-diameter Stanford torus space stations with living space for 10,000 people permanently resident (no return to Earth possible), each weighing 500,000 tons (materials from the Moon) and costing $30 billion and 10 years to build; several hundred artificial colonies around Earth by 2050, some 10,000 within Solar System by 2100, many millions throughout Galaxy by 2500, billions across Universe by AD 4000; but on other scenarios, endless delays and obstacles cause entire program to be abandoned until resurgence of interest in AD 2250.

2012 Space wars: incidents, conflicts and full-scale warfare in space erupt and proliferate.

2012 Long-predicted great earthquake in northern California strikes, with incredible force.

2012 International terrorist gang seize nuclear weapons, devastate a major capital city of over 5 million population.

2012 Solar Army (antinuclear movement) grows as quasi-religious movement with massive rallies, protests, lobbying.

2012 Revolution in Brazil kills millions, places workers in full control of world's second-largest economy.

2012 First commercial fusion plant opens in Tokyo.

2012 International Data Storage Center founded.

2012 Invention of programmable sound silencer to eliminate noise far better than brick or stone.

2012 Aerospace planes enter commercial service.

2013 Scientists perfect art of cloning (reproduction of infinite number of genetically identical people from cells of a single person, whose human body consists of $10^{28}$ atoms); first human is cloned.

2013 Futurists and others can file their prognostications (including 'random prophecy') with new World Predictions Registry, receiving annual scores or success ratings (worldwide average 5%, with 16%='brilliant foresight'); makes annual Prognostication Awards; 2040, new category of 'random prophecy' established based on huge databases.

2013 Church of the Absolutely Poor (260 million Christians in South Asia) finally revolts against all other churches; blackmail, hostages taken, forced reparations, arson, seizure of properties and money, thefts, violence, mass arming of members with weapons, sackings of mission stations and churches, massacres of missionaries and affluent Christians, huge armies on rampage across continent; ditto on all other impoverished continents.

2013 Beginning of protracted development of nuclear fusion power; 2039, fuser technology born in Spacelab IV orbiting laboratory; 2054, prototype fusion cell; 2070, first fusion reactors feeding power into national grids; 2090, true fusion-energy economy becomes widespread, world electrical grid set up, global use of fossil fuels abandoned.

2013 Beginning of freefly (flying for individuals) by means of jetpacks or rocket belts.

2014 Controlled thermonuclear power extracted from hydrogen isotopes; huge fusion power plants come online across world.

2014 On optimistic scenario, 1 million people now live permanently in space colonies.

2014 Manned exploration of Solar System expands to first human landing on planet Mars; no evidence of life found.

2014 Self-replicating factory placed on Moon, produces first exact copy in one year, and 1,000 replicas by 2025 thus creating major lunar manufacturing center.

2014 Construction of Hilton Orbiter Hotel begins in nearby space.

2015 Weather control on Earth achieved.

2015 Gradual military ascendancy of the North (Western world in new alliance with Russia) versus Islam and the South. (Nostradamus).

2015 Art of bodily healing becomes centered in self-regulation and self-regeneration, training our brains to produce exactly the right chemicals needed to heal the body of every disease including aging, and to develop optimal health and well-being.

2015 Pollution spreads: Caribbean Sea reduced to an ecological sewer.
2015 Catastrophic breakdown of world trade system.
2015 Small termite-like robots with nanomachine components lay fibre-optic cables connecting every house and office on Earth, linking everyone together into a vast planetary network for sharing information and doing advanced processing.
2015 Pax Nipponica begins: Japan has uncontested global dominance in every leading-edge industry, GNP twice that of USA, per capita GNP 4 times USA; Japan has now become world's financial center, a zaibatsu monolith of huge financial cliques of interlocking banks and companies dating back to 1890s, the directing apex of the new world economy, owning 45% of US manufacturing assets, holding 50% of US bank assets, with vast media holdings.
2015 USA stock market crashes, annihilating US economic stability; US economy destroyed, no longer a superpower.
2015 Artificial wombs widely available for women unable to bear children naturally.
2015 Conversion of Jewish race to faith in Christ takes place, during pontificate of last pope before Peter the Roman (St Malachy's Prophecy of the Popes); these Israelites then become End-time evangelists across the world.
2015 Context-recognition chips (anti-advertising modules) marketed: Adnix which mutes TV set when commercials begin, and Preachnix which switches channels when doctrinaire religious programs appear (at preselected keywords like 'Advent', 'Rapture', etc).
2015 Fuel cell electric cars widely available.
2015 By-product of quantum generator is complete control of matter at atomic level; lead and copper now cost twice as much as gold.

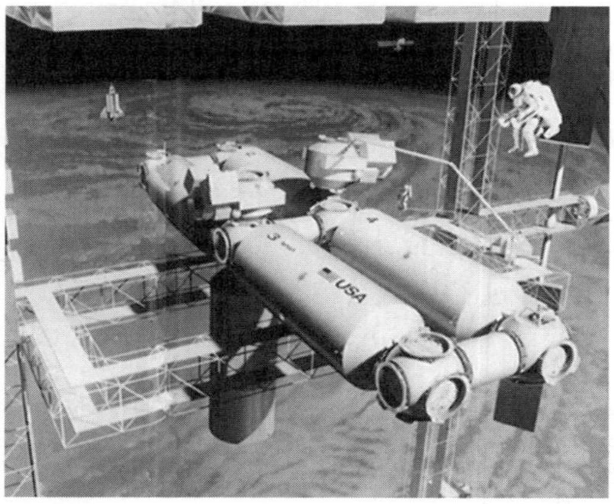

**AD 2016.** Complex multi-function Space Station launches interstellar spaceprobes.

2016 NASA launches 'Ambassador I', first robot interstellar data-gathering spaceprobe, on 20-year mission to Alpha Centauri star system; 2030, results in evidence of life there.
2016 Colonies of Earth move out from Moon to be set up on Mars, Venus and other planets of Solar System, including moons of Jupiter (Europa, Titan).
2016 After 2,000 years of predominance over 99% of all Catholics, Roman Latin rite breaks up and declines to 10% of all Catholics as hundreds of ethnolinguistic cultures defy Curia to form their own ecclesioliturgical rites.
2016 Arab People's Republic of the Holy War seizes power in Riyadh, Saudi Arabia; also, Islamic Republic of Palestine proclaimed in Amman.
2016 Worldwide financial collapse scenario: world's greatest economic depression begins, lasts until 2030; Third-World debt wipes out hundreds of major Western banks and institutions.
2016 Greenhouse gas emissions decline by 50% over 1996 level.
2016 Mobile robots that learn and make decisions become available.
2016 All existing currencies abolished; new unit of exchange becomes the megawatt hour.
2017 Nighttime eliminated from Earth through solar satellites.
2017 Tooth decay, dental cavities and pyorrhea eliminated for 95% of all persons accepting pre-decay treatment including vaccines.
2017 Biological computers developed as 8th generation of computer technology, with biochips and genetic codes assembling fully operational computers inside a cell each; computers increasingly participate in their own evolution.
2017 Medical science perfects implanting of silicon chips with over $10^{12}$ memory (greater than human brain), surgically linked to the brain, giving mankind a totally new order of development.
2017 Commercial applications of nanotechnology become numerous.
2018 Affiliated Christians (church members) rise to 2.5 billion worldwide, heavily infiltrated and monitored in many countries by police operatives, spies, informers, world government agents, computers, bugs and robots.
2018 Massive series of earthquakes over 50 years including in Greece, Turkey, Japan, China, Ecuador et alia.
2018 Reemergence in Atlantic Ocean of part of lost continent of Atlantis.
2019 Global megafamine sweeps Earth due to deliberate mismanagement and embezzlement; 2 billion die.
2019 Completion of Project Daedalus (British Interplanetary Society): unmanned spaceship accelerates to 13% of speed of light, in 50 years reaches Barnard's star (with view to possible space colonization) and sends back information.
2019 Petroleum metropolis of Cubatao, Brazil (population 500,000) disappears under massive landslides: 75,000 killed.
2019 City of Rome devastated by nuclear bomb; flight and murder of Peter the Roman, end of Roman papacy; Paris and cities across Europe also devastated. (St Malachy; Nostradamus).
2019 On pessimistic scenario, 90% of all governments in world have now become totalitarian, exercising total control over their own citizens.
2019 Urban greenhouses widespread for production of fruits and vegetables; artificial foods common, most seafood via aquaculture.
2019 In Western world, 80% of all employees telecommute, working at least part-time from remote locations.
2019 Major meteor impact on North Polar ice cap; resulting tsunamis cause heavy damage along coasts of Greenland and Canada; long-discussed Project Spaceguard to identify and deflect dangerous comets or asteroids finally activated.
2020 World's 10 largest cities: Tokyo-Yokohama 28,887,000, Bombay 28,499,000, Lagos 27,884,000, Karachi 22,135,000, Dhaka 21,951,000, Sao Paulo 20,703,000, Mexico City 19,967,000, Shanghai 19,377,000, Calcutta 19,143,000, Delhi 18,435,000.
2020 Robots and self-reproducing (self-replicating) machines go out in space to mine Moon and asteroids.
2020 Self-replicating uncrewed spaceprobes (von Neumann probes) embark on consecutive self-multiplying space exploration, taking 300 million years to explore entire Galaxy (2% of its lifetime).
2020 Regeneration medical techniques, by electrical stimulation of regenerative growth (e.g. new kidneys, amputated limbs), now replace substitutive medicine (replacement of defective parts by implants or transplants).
2020 Widely-developed urban systems of (a) covered cities on unused land masses, (b) subterranean cities especially in desert regions, (c) underwater cities in tropical and arctic regions, and (d) floating cities in mid-ocean.
2020 Major climate-control accident: attempts in upper levels of atmosphere to bring rain to desert areas get out of control; within 4 years a new catastrophic Ice Age has begun, obliterating 15 nations including Canada, UK, Scandinavia, Switzerland, New Zealand, with 2 billion deaths from starvation, panic and inability to flee.
2020 Worldwide fragmentation of global Christianity over last hundred years results in 50,000 distinct and separate denominations and paradenominations, as centralization and coordination become less possible.
2020 Widespread thought control and control of people's minds by drugs, subliminal techniques, psychological methods, and psychosurgery.
2020 Average lifespan in West increases to 97 years from 90 years in AD 2000, and to 200 years for large numbers of people.
2020 Final destruction of world's great forests by human encroachment.
2020 Nations possessing nuclear weapons total 50, including Libya, Cuba, Saudi Arabia, Nigeria, Indonesia, Zaire and Angola, all with long-range ballistic missiles.
2020 Overthrow and death of Antichrist III; end of militaristic Islam; conversion of Islam to Christianity. (Nostradamus).
2020 Alien civilization sends out probes to millions of planets, locates life on Earth, laser-transmits biological clones of its members ($10^{17}$ bits of information per individual), beaming them across space to Earth.
2020 Media revolution ushers in new era in total evangelization: instant communication, total knowledge, total teaching on any subject at any time; universal, continuous, non-stop, round-the-clock preaching and witnessing; global witness in all languages; full evangelization achieved in nearly all situations whether local, national, regional, continental or global.
2020 United Nations lunar base founded.
2020 Artificial singularity first constructed in laboratory, a micro black hole (a microscopic, titanically heavy fold of twisted space); new science of cavitronics allows quantum creations of space-warped sinkholes. (D. Brin, *Earth*, 1990).
2020 The long-predicted Great Earthquake, centered on San Andreas Fault, California, followed by unprecedented natural disasters including a Universal Famine leading to mass cannibalism. (Nostradamus).
2020 Vast populations of landless, stateless, disinherited populations and impoverished refugees take to permanent living on world's oceans, forming a new worldwide Sea State.
2020 Decay of marriage and family as stable and dependable way of life now reaches worldwide dire crisis threatening prospects of entire human race.
2020 Vegetarianism adopted worldwide, with more vegetarians than meat-eaters in Western world.
2020 Introduction of global government by direct democracy (phone votes, global referendum), with global agendas; also citizens elect commercial firms instead of politicians to run their districts, cities, education, health care, law and order, foreign affairs.
2020 Population density becomes intense: rise in Rwanda from 820 people per square mile in 1991, to 2,280 per square mile in 2020; and Bangladesh, 1991—2,250/square mile; AD 2020—4,060/square mile.
2020 Expert system allow users to have the knowledge of renowned heart surgeons, scientists, even cooks, available to anyone, anywhere in the world, anytime.
2020 Nanomachines complete tracking down and reading genome of every species now living, making a record of its genome, and delivering it to a central repository.
2020 Telecities merge as information societies become electronically united including JA-CAN-US, a specific telecity consisting of Japan, Canada, USA.
2020 Bundles of nanorobots weighing practically nothing are sent out across the Universe as explorer robots, reproducing themselves and their ships and building radio transmitters to report home for new instructions; the ultimate in interstellar emissaries.
2020 Collapse of most major currencies, with runaway global inflation.
2020 Nuclear power (fission) produces 50% of world's electricity, routinely using hydrogen; by 2026, fusion nuclear power used commercially.
2020 Artificial Intelligence (AI) reaches human level, creating a second intelligent species on planet Earth, evolving far more rapidly than biology permit.
2021 Voluntary surrender of sovereignty by all 300 previously independent nations to an enlarged United Nations organization, leading to a de facto world government.
2021 First manned interstellar expedition, intending only to explore nearest star systems.
2021 Electronic transfer of funds (ETF) largely replaces cash, but cash still valued for the privacy its use gives.
2021 Emerging worldwide data net reduces need for face-to-face communication in international business.
2021 Cold apocalypse scenario: pitch-dark bone-chilling nuclear winter brought on by limited nuclear war using 5,000 megatons (20% of current arsenals) in which 1.2-billion-ton cloud of dust (black snow) and smoke envelops northern hemisphere first, then southern; world freezes or starves to death except for bands of hunter-gatherers in south.
2021 As envisaged in C. Sagan's novel *Contact* (1985), Earth receives first extraterrestrial contact: a complex coded radio message is received from star Vega, being instructions to build an interstellar starship; 2023, dodecahedron Machine completed and activated, travels instantaneously to center of Galaxy and back via vast disused network of space wormholes in star systems with small double black holes (built by galactic civilization defunct 5 billion years ago).
2021 First humans land on Mars.
2022 Authoritarian/totalitarian/dictatorial world state arises after global nuclear war and famine kill over 600 million people (600 megadeaths); wields total world domination. (J.B.S. Haldane, H. Kahn, M. Bundy).
2022 Crime wiped out due to mind-reading police, telepaths, parapsychologists, psychiatrists, forensic scientists, and universal computerized surveillance.
2023 Demographic megacatastrophe scenario: massive 30-year population crash begins due to (a) mankind becoming sterile after nuclear testing or warfare, or (b) worldwide famine and drought catastrophe; 7 billion die from 2020 to 2050, leaving 3 billion alive.
2023 A free democratic United States of the World is established; all war finally outlawed; wars and threats of war disappear for first time in human history.
2023 Mass state expropriations globally of church institutions, properties, privileges, premises, plant, possessions, programs, and funds.
2023 Satellite colony ('Moontown') built on Moon.
2023 Dinosaur facsimiles cloned from computer-generated DNA; mini raptors start replacing guard dogs.
2024 After nuclear holocaust, Christians regroup as Luddite church savagely opposed to technology and machines. (E. Coopers's scenario, *The cloud walker*, 1973).
2024 Worldwide Authority set up after 65 million killed by nuclear war and famine; population control enforced by withholding food supplies. (McGeorge Bundy's 1974 scenario 'After the Deluge, the Covenant').
2024 Asian New Religions, and secular quasi-religions, with world government support sweep across entire world destroying infrastructure of global organized Christianity.
2024 Personal rapid transit installed in most metro areas.
2024 Hypersonic aircraft at 5 times speed of sound used for most transocean flights.
2024 Infra-red signals detected coming from centre of Milky Way galaxy, product of a technologically advanced civilization.

## STATUS OF THE GLOBE IN AD 2025

2025 *Global Snapshot 2.* The following 63 entries constitute a second snapshot, at one specific point in time, of the world in all its complexity (for Global Snapshot 1, see AD 2000).

2025 *Postindustrial age* begins, a fourth stage in human history beyond agriculturalism, industrialism, and the service economy.

2025 *Postindustrialism.* 25% of mankind live in societies with postindustrial (transindustrial) economies, where producing necessities of life becomes trivially easy technologically, and in which therefore knowledge and information replace capital as society's most important resource.

2025 *Demographics.* World population 7.8 billion (23.5% under 15, median age 32, life expectancy 73 years); 20-year period begins of probable population megadisasters due to famine, drought, crop failures, mismanagement, corruption, warfare (Neo-Malthusianism).

2025 *Urbanization.* Supercities (urban agglomerations with over 4 million inhabitants) total 114 (86 in developing countries); megacities (with over 1 million) 895; urban dwellers number 59% of world, increasing by 2 million a week; urban slums expand far faster than cities, producing 'a planet of slums'.

2025 *World's 10 largest cities:* Bombay 30,378,000, Lagos 30,372,000, Tokyo-Yokohama 28,887,000, Karachi 24,847,000, Dhaka 23,820,000, Calcutta 21,171,000, Mexico City 21,078,000, Sao Paulo 20,793,000, Shanghai 20,787,000, Delhi 19,838,000.

2025 *Industrialization.* World industrial robot population 35 million: Japan 11,000,000 (and a million new ones a year), USA 7,500,000, Russia 5,600,000, Germany 4,600,000, France 1,620,000, Italy 1,600,000, UK 820,000, Sweden 650,000, Brazil 550,000, others in 100 other countries.

2025 *Industry.* Only 4 automobile firms remain in world as all smaller ones consolidate into global giants, with production centered in Korea, Italy and Latin America.

2025 *Robots* of human complexity produced, with IQ of over 100. (A.C. Clarke).

2025 *Behavior.* Control of behavior by computerized monitoring of brain waves with automatic intervention to prevent misdeeds.

2025 *Work.* USA: 35% of all paid work is now done from people's homes.

2025 *Transportation.* Linear-motor trains become standard means of intercity transportation up to 1,000 km; ultra-highspeed, magnetic-levitation.

2025 *Society.* Mankind now more unified than at any time in the past; more standardized (English as lingua franca), more affluent, longer lived, more mobile, less religious, better educated; tourism by now world's largest industry, with 470 million foreign tourists a year.

2025 *Students.* USA colleges host 1 million foreign students from abroad.

2025 *Cashless society* in place, using a single world monetary unit for trade and exchange.

2025 *Unitary culture.* Creation of one single planetary culture and civilization finally achieved on Earth; planetization of human race well under way.

2025 *Regions.* Large number of small regional entities replace sovereign nation-states, and form themselves into United Regions, a single global body replacing United Nations, leading to a thoroughgoing world government by 2050; end of superpower conflicts and vast military expenditures.

2025 *Geopolitics.* Farthest extent of global penetration of Marxism, covering 90% of world including Australia and Canada; massive decline in influence suddenly begins; world Communism disintegrates by 2030.

2025 *Nations.* Nation states proliferate to over 500 in number.

2025 *Centralized world government* arises, based heavily on artificial intelligence.

2025 *Politics.* Instant polling of viewers' opinions and election choices over viewer-interactive cable TV.

2025 *Evolution of synocracy* government by synergy, by multiple mutual attraction not coercion.

2025 *Psychology.* Future shock becomes worldwide: breakdown of civilization because society's subsystems no longer function and people can no longer cope with accelerating change (pace of life too fast).

2025 *Ecosystem.* Human pressure on natural systems of Earth (consumption of raw materials) multiplies 70-fold in last hundred years.

2025 *Agriculture.* 30% of world's arable land destroyed by human encroachment in last 20 years; 20% of world's population are subsistence farmers, 20% more are poor farmers responsible for spread of desertification.

2025 *Mariculture.* Ocean farming begins to produce more food than agriculture, including 900 million metric tons of meat annually.

2025 *Biosphere.* 10% of world's 10 million animal and plant species destroyed in last 20 years due to deforestation, desertification and destruction of habitats; by AD 2030, possibly as high as 40%; since Earth's biosphere is a single complex system similar to a living organism (the Gaia theory), this extinction has vast adverse effects on human prosperity.

2025 *Evolution.* Two new human species of genus Homo with own distinct cultures begin to evolve and become recognized: (a) Homo Solaris, humans who function predominantly off-Earth in space, dependent on technology and alien life-support environments; and (b) Homo Posthumanus, arising from coalescence of humans and ultra-intelligent machines.

2025 *A new genus.* Next stage or giant leap in evolution begins to be manifested: the New Man in Christ (with resurrection body similar to Christ's), which will coexist on Earth with genus Homo during the Millennium.

2025 *Language.* New universal language evolves due to automated communication.

2025 *Medicine.* Drugless medical treatment attacks all illnesses electromagnetically, making body cells produce antibodies, new tissue, et alia.

2025 *Lethal new influenza virus* appears in India, decimates continents before burning out after 6 months.

2025 *Novel treatments.* Human hibernation developed for extensive periods (months to years).

2025 *Disease.* Global pandemics sweep across continents wiping out millions every few days; rapid destruction of Earth's ozone layer by aerosols (freon gas) results in increase in ultraviolet radiation, causes widespread cancer.

2025 *Pollution.* Urban pollution becomes deadly: Mexico City is world's most polluted city, with 6 million cars; Tokyo next; also Cubatao (Brazil), world's most polluted petrochemical center; and Cairo has world's worst noise pollution.

2025 *Communications.* Vast expansion of telephone systems: e.g. in Brazil, from 500,000 phones in 1967, to 7.6 million (1982) and to 125 million (AD 2000); total worldwide 2.2 billion, 98% being direct-dial.

2025 *Communications satellites* (a) enable instant global surveys of agriculture, minerals, hydrology, et alia, and (b) enable people to live anywhere they please, work anywhere including in electronic cottage industries, doing 90% of their business electronically at speed of light.

2025 *Communicators.* Anyone can own a personal computer-communicator, as powerful as any supercomputer of the past, containing all information in all libraries on Earth.

2025 *Global network.* Rapidly-growing global telecommunications network in its entirety now equals human brain in complexity.

2025 *Computerization.* World's 2.2 billion computers, from micros to mainframes, become connected to each other in a single global network.

2025 *Broadcasting.* Radios number 3.5 billion worldwide.

2025 *Television.* Subliminal TV in widespread use by countries for mass mind control.

2025 *Cable TV (CATV)* reaches 150 million households in USA (up from 14 million in 1982).

2025 *Data broadcasting* widespread, becomes norm for many professions.

2025 *Publishing.* Computer printout terminals in every neighborhood in Western world will publish and bind on demand any book requested before customer's eyes while he waits.

2025 *Litigation.* Disputes escalate over rights to information (copyrights, patents, industrial espionage, personal rights).

2025 *Energy.* Widespread use of renewable energy sources (invariant energy systems), i.e. solar energy (99.98% of all the energy Earth receives), geothermal energy, tidal energy; also, wireless transmission of energy comes into operation.

2025 *Commercial energy consumption* increases from 0.5 billion tonnes oil equivalent (1900) to 1.667 billion (1950) to 5.6 billion (1974; 1.4 tons per capita) to 15.5 billion (AD 2000; 2.5 tons per capita).

2025 *Warfare.* Inner solar system becomes vast arena for nuclear confrontation with locating of dark or hidden satellites, and nuclear missiles on Moon.

2025 *Nuclear power.* 100 large power plants worldwide become due for retirement after full working life, but their dismantling and disposal pose major problems.

2025 *Weaponry.* Countries owning nuclear power facilities proliferate, though over 100 exhausted or terminated nuclear plants exist, remaining lethally radioactive for thousands of years into future; total plutonium produced as by-product of global nuclear power reaches equivalent of one million atomic bombs; illegal nuclear weapons result, with disastrous consequences.

2025 *Nuclear powers.* Countries possessing clearcut nuclear weapons and means of delivery rise to 35, including Argentina, Egypt, India, Iraq, Israel, Kuwait, North Korea, Pakistan, Libya, Saudi Arabia, Turkey, Zaire.

2025 *China* now one of the world's 3 military and nuclear superpowers (with Russia and USA); latter 2 each have laser arsenals.

2025 *Biological warfare.* First use of deadly bacillus botulinus to destroy entire populations in a few hours.

2025 *Ethics.* Human selfishness and greed lead world inexorably towards eventual catastrophe or self-destruction.

2025 *Age of manufactured experience* begins: experiences of any kind (religious enlightenment, perception, insight, mystic contemplation, planetary consciousness, moods, orgasm, wellbeing, etc) available on order using chemical, physical and psychological stimulants (LSD, marijuana, peyote, mescaline, hallucinogenic drugs, etc).

## RELIGION AND CHRISTIANITY IN AD 2025

2025 **Global status of Christianity:** 65.6 generations after Christ, world is 33.4% Christians, 76.4% evangelized, with scriptures available in 10,000 languages.

2025 *Non-Christians.* 83% of world's 5.2 billion non-Christians now reside in 140 nations, many newly opened to traditional crosscultural foreign missionary endeavor and also to internal home mission or evangelism by nationals.

2025 *Agnosticism.* Abandoning of religion worldwide results in 160 million antireligious or atheists (2.0% of world) and 875 million non-religious or agnostics (11.2%).

2025 *Primal religion.* Despite attempts of missionary religions to convert them, adherents of traditional tribal religions (animism, shamanism, polytheism, pantheism, folk religion, fetishism, et alia) number 277 millions, over 2 times the same number in year 1900.

2025 *Mass movements.* Nativistic, messianic, cargo-cult and other mass religious movements of popular syncretism mushroom across Third World.

2025 *Respect for Christ.* Person of Christ now universally known and respected throughout world, by all world religions, even more so than in AD 2000; his teachings and his gospel (but not his church) are still understood and valued, though still not accepted or implemented universally.

2025 *Churchmanship.* Churches tend increasingly to combine 3 traditions or streams: (a) Catholic (liturgical or sacramental), (b) Protestant (Bible-based), (c) pentecostal (Spirit-filled, charismatic).

2025 *Final demise of denominational Christianity* and its complete abandonment by vast mass of rank-and-file lay Christians (99.8% of world Christianity), replaced by local combined approaches by all Christians together to local problems of the times, a diaspora church of small minority groupings, a future world utopian community. (J.C. Hoekendijk, Harvey Cox, et alii).

2025 *Christians.* At world level, Christians are now 65% Third-Worlders, 31% pentecostal-charismatics (5% in pentecostal denominations, 16% charismatics, 2.5% in Chinese house churches, and 11.4% inactive or unaffiliated).

2025 *Pentecostal-charismatics.* Organized Christianity's 31% charismatics constitute 20% of all RCs, 50% of all Protestants, 10% of Anglicans; of world's 600,000 foreign missionaries, 70% are charismatics (45% of RCs, 65% of Protestants, 90% of Third-World missionaries).

2025 *Evangelization.* Entire world finally reached with Christian gospel for first time in history, in the sense that everyone everywhere has heard or hears the gospel in depth with understanding and has access to Scripture, churches, missions, Christians, Christian broadcasting (with 4,000 Christian radio and TV stations worldwide), movies, literature and other means of grace.

2025 *Global church-planting goal* completed: at least one fellowship or church or congregation or nucleus of disciples has been planted as an ongoing indigenous witness in each of the world's 11,500 ethnolinguistic peoples and 4,000 metropolises of over 100,000 population.

2025 *Foreign missionaries* engaged in crosscultural ministries worldwide number 600,000, including citizens of 300 countries.

2025 *Spirituality.* Widespread revival of monasticism both eremitic (hermits) and cenobitic (communities), among young people of all churches across world, especially in Third-world countries.

2025 *Lifestyles.* Many segments of global church adopt radical and revolutionary personal, congregational and denominational lifestyles.

2025 *Growth.* Christianity and other world religions survive and flourish, also mysticism, magic, divination, cults, occult, astrology, numerology.

2025 *Mormonism.* Church of Jesus Christ of Latter-day Saints, as USA's fastest-growing religion, reaches 30 million members worldwide, with 50,000 missionaries, global television programs from Salt Lake City, et alia.

2025 *Theology of mission.* 100 years after J.R. Mott, Christian theology of religions, mission and evangelization (Protestant, Orthodox and Catholic) is still centered on Christ as sole Savior but has shifted radically towards a new universalism and recognition of value of world religions as ordinary or common ways of salvation, albeit incomplete without God's grace in Christ and his extraordinary or special way of salvation; world religions and Christianity are therefore widely regarded by many RCs and liberal Protestants (but denied by conservative evangelicals) as parallel paths to salvation, with final convergence reserved for the Eschaton.

## UNIVERSAL PEACE SCENARIO

2026 Common world language (evolved English) understood by 90% of Earth's people; also constructed languages (Esperanto, Glossa, Suma).
2026 9th generation of computers shift away from digital processing to analog processing whereby light waves are used to compute.
2026 Space industrialization: heavy industry and power generation relocated off Earth's surface so that waste heat and pollution can be harmlessly dissipated into space.
2026 2nd Vienna Conference reconstitutes United Nations as the Confederated States of Earth (CSE).
2026 Particles discovered capable of travelling faster than light: tachyons.
2026 Birth of first children altered by GTC gene surgery.
2026 Twelve children born to GTC executives, having been designed as 'perfect' by gene surgery, then live brilliant, charismatic, aggressive lives.
2026 Startling rise worldwide in crime rate, with most cities terrorized by gangs of alienated unteachable youths, international criminal empires (including 'Red Thumb' from Japan) based on electronic surveillance, psychochemical manipulation, invasion of computer networks.
2027 Christian broadcasting (overt and clandestine) utilizes vast range of 3,000 major languages, programs of every type; reputation for truth results in 90% of world as regular audience; but dangerously exposed to disinformation tactics and terrorism.
2027 Neurological research leads to direct inputs bypassing skin, eyes, ears, other organs; result is metal Braincap fitting over human skull, of which 20th century's Walkman was primitive precursor; wearer enters a whole universe of experience, real or imaginary, even merging in real time with other minds.
2027 In industry, composite materials replace metals, smart materials routinely used, self-assembling materials become widespread.
2028 New religious awareness results in interfaith convergence and union of all major world religions, despite core Christian opposition; emergence of totally new religions, cults, and messiahs using electronic communications techniques to gain power.
2028 All-purpose programmable microbiotic virucides developed, defeating all viruses including HIV by 2078.
2029 First signal received from extrasolar civilization, transmitted by neutrino stream; never decoded. (*A short history of the future, W.W. Wagar 1989:300*).

## THE LONG-RANGE FUTURE (30-100 years ahead)

c2030 Church of the future plays dynamic part in the evolution of mankind, bringing the world to final perfection in Point Omega. (Teilhard de Chardin).
c2030 Point Omega reached in noogenesis, emergence of a completely new evolutionary level (Fifth Level of Evolution: supermind): human minds of new species Homo Noeticus (Intellectual Man) become progressively integrated into some form of planetary consciousness or global social superorganism or supermind, a single living system or interthinking group or mind-linking process (Teilhard's noosphere, comprised of all consciousness minds; or, planetary Gaiafield; or, high-synergy society; or, New Age movement); expressed as synergy, syntony (superconscious learning), suprasex (empathy, mutual love for whole creation and minimal conflict between all, merging not of bodies for procreation but of minds).
2030 Age of universal peace begins: long period of global peace, the Millennium. (Nostradamus).
2030 After World War III nuclear holocaust, Christianity spreads again around world in global revival led by 'an ancient, Black and primitive Church'; ascendancy of Non-White indigenous Christianity.
2030 Capitalism now seen to have virtually destroyed itself as a viable ideology.
2030 Large-scale terraforming of other planets begins (transforming them to be habitable by humans).
2030 Western world relies on sun, wind and water for 60% of all power and heating needs.
2030 Continuing decline in rainfall by 55% over Africa; Sahara Desert, world's largest, advances 300 km farther south.
2030 In capitalist societies, most goods and services are now distributed and supplied free of charge; also, children attain virtually true equality with adults.
2030 Multinational companies of 20th century evolve into huge global corporations, each using a single global marketing strategy; top 50 are bigger and richer than many nations.
2030 Conversion of China to Christianity through multitude of Chinese house-church evangelists and witnesses, resulting in 1.5 billion zealous, neocharismatic, postdenominationalist Christians, who then launch their own global mission without reference to Western or Eastern churches and missions, or to historic Christianity, or to the 3,000 previously-proposed world evangelization plans.
2030 Consumption of red meat vanishes as flesh-eating is abandoned, replaced by vegetarianism, freeing millions of tons of grain formerly eaten by cattle.
2030 Coastal West Africa including Nigeria finally drowned as drenching rains engulf abandoned cities.
2030 Entire human genome now fully catalogued, with suite of all attributes at humans' disposal (such as wonderfully dexterous human hands); but no possibility yet of profiting from any other animal species' hard-won lessons, which remain each locked within one single species.
2030 World Data Net with 8 billion subscribers (80% of world) by 2040, grouped in rival cliques and alliances, all trying to sway the world's agenda; Net is accessed by plaques or wall-sized active-events screens; Net clipping service, ferret programs dispatched by one's autosec (automatic secretary), standard World Net tech-level press releases.
2030 90% of all archives and printed materials ever are now available in microcompact forms and can be transmitted anywhere by World Bibliotel system/network, which serves over 20 million institutional and individual subscribers in all countries.
2030 Global sources of energy: 71% fossil fuels (oil, gas, coal), 7% hydro-electric power, 6% solar power, rest 13% (especially nuclear power by means of fusion generators).
2030 Zimbabwe now a waterless desert, but Nigeria becomes land of rain-drenched abandoned cities; 2032, new nation Sea State, organized by millions permanently afloat across world, grows rapidly in size and influence.
2030 World Salvation Project organized to save wildlife and endangered species in South Africa and elsewhere; scientists recreate vast arks (arcologies), being entire ecosystems under multitiered vaulting domes, with all species of animals in natural habitats.
2030 21st-century Age of Faith established as result of science rediscovering the Creator through computer calculations showing improbable nature of random natural selection as sole explanation for ever-increasing intricacies found in biology, chemistry, physics, et alia; bolstered by discovery of multiple universes, found by astronomers at the macrocosmic level and by physicists at the microcosmic level.
2030 Technology fills world with intelligent machines, multi-sensual media, artificial creatures, big high-definition screens with large menu of interactive options.
2030 Nations in space are set up, living on very large orbiting space colonies, 20 miles long, 4 miles in diameter, 10 million population each; eventually 30% of human population lives in space by 2200.
2030 Colony world (Beltworld, later renamed Atlantis) built at virtually no cost in Asteroid Belt between Mars and Jupiter, built by AI (artificial intelligence) computers and their microbots, powered by direct solar radiation; 7,250 inhabitants; thousands more similar self-replicating worlds now immediately feasible; 2091, 44,000 pioneers live in 12 distant space colonies forming League of Space Cooperatives.
2030 UN finally revokes 400-year sovereignty of all nation-states, declaring its right to intervene in serious cases of national misgovernment, corruption, violation of civil rights, genocide, civil war.
2031 Advanced extraterrestrials, who have discarded biology in favor of electronics, become one gigantic collective intelligence, with immense computer as its only body; machine uses lasers to transmit instructions for its own replication on Earth.
2032 Telemedicine and computer diagnosis: computer replaces physician as primary agent of health care.
2032 Biological research extends possible normal human life-span to 800 years; by transcending nature, disease and death, man becomes potentially an immortal species.
2032 Standard Energy Corporation goes bankrupt due to hysterical overinvestment in fusion power.
2033 Mars colony finally established by GTC; 2035, abandoned by GTC for economic reasons; 2036, lunar colony abandoned also.
2034 Manipulation of genetic material (pantropy): genetic packages of fertilized human eggs begin to be altered before birth to fit alien environments, e.g. zero-gravity or high-gravity conditions, or deep water, or speed-of-light travel.
2035 Holography comes into universal use (projecting image of a 3-dimensional object in space); laser holography expands, replacing and duplicating museums and exhibitions; specialized museums now display holograms of priceless art treasures while originals remain securely stored; also 4-dimensional dynamic holograms for science and research.
2035 Invention of time-machine capable of viewing any event in history, in complete 3-dimensional color with stereophonic sound.
2035 Computers and robots become more intelligent than humans, make all major decisions.
2035 First major space city opened, on Moon; HQ of United Nations moves there.
2035 First Declaration of Independence by Spacekind from Earthkind: space colonies in orbit between Earth and Moon set up own government.
2035 Writers, researchers, preachers, anyone can now send word to his autosecretary to send out a ferret program to fetch in milliseconds any facts, information, or the whole truth about anything.
2035 Clean energy supplied to southwestern France through local Arcachon Tidal Power Barrage, generating pollution-free power from Moon's orbit.
2035 Giant gravity freighters haul huge loads from Earth up to Moon atop pillars of warped space-time.

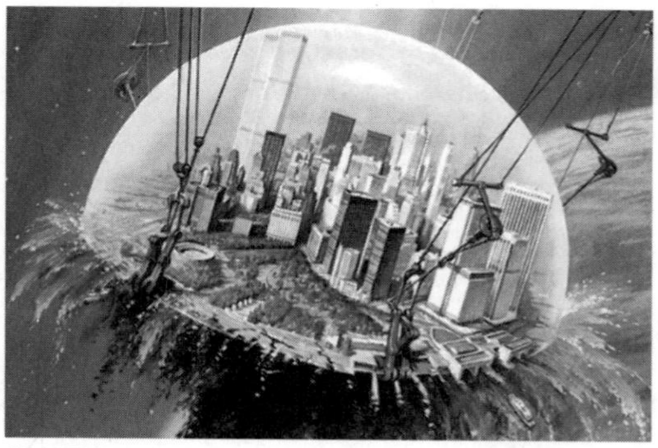

**AD 2035.** In macro-engineering scenario, alien civilization hijacks New York.

2035 Huge alien spaceship kidnaps and extricates dozens of whole cities from variety of planets, including Manhattan, USA, prior to destroying all life on those planets then terraforming them. (J.E. Stith, *Manhattan transfer, 1993*).
2036 In barbaric aftermath of 30-year world war, altruistic scientists help launch world's first interstellar space flight. (H.G. Wells' scenario and film, *The shape of things to come*, 1934-5).
2037 Manned mission to Mars finally completed.
2038 Over 250 million people live on High Orbital Mini Earths (HOMEs), 100 million having been born there; majority leaving Earth are female; majority can never return to Earth; violent competitive theocracies emerge, also varieties of crime.
2038 North America approaches 10-fold population increase (over 1980) to 2 billion persons in massive high-rise blocks.
2038 Worldwide equalization of economic opportunity arrives; age of universal abundance for all begins; money no longer matters.
2038 Scientific recognition of spiritual dimension in world; power of prayer explained in terms of Heisenberg's Uncertainty Principle.
2038 End of world, one of several dates predicted by Nostradamus (his earlier date: 1943).
2038 Church of the Purification founded in USA, a popular anti-modernist religious sect with 100,000 self-styled Crusaders in bands advocating nonviolent resistance and primitive Christianity; results in thousands of martyrs every year as it attempts to set up a Republic of Christ; 2058, pitched battles across North America.
2038 Of the Natural Tranquility Reserves (terrestrial silence zones) around Earth set up and promoted by United Nations, only 79 are left, declining by 2 or 3 each year.
2038 North American Church of Gaia (environmentalists worshiping Earth Mother, Gaia) now intervenes in favor of International Fish & Fowl Association (IFFA, duck-hunters) against animal rights group No-Flesh.
2038 Preservation Alliance of North Africa announce their creation and spread of a virus that will destroy entire world's population of goats who, as voracious eaters, are turning vast regions into barren desert.
2038 New government representing Gaia decrees no more mining of minerals or fuels, now to be obtained only from other planets; all criminals, polluters, conspirators, liars suddenly ripped to shreds by deadly gravity forces without warning or mercy. (*Earth*, 1990).
2038 Rival scientists construct first 2 micro black holes—artificial singularities (microscopic, titanically heavy folds of twisted space)—despite risk of them falling to Earth's center and orbiting there gradually devouring planet's interior (but losing matter by vacuum emission). (*Earth*, 1990).
2039 Microscopic black hole accidentally falls into Earth's core, capable of destroying planet in 2 years, extinguishing human race; some scientists argue for letting that happen and letting the million-year evolutionary clock rewind to start all over again. (*Earth*, 1990).
2039 Earth's colonies on other planets rebel; brief battle between their forces and Earth's, then their independence is recognized.
2040 Decline of great religions and quasi-religions, including Marxism.
2040 Worst anti-Christian persecution in history, involving terrorism, huge mob riots, fanaticism, racism, all instigated and coordinated by hostile world government.
2040 World's largest cities: Tokyo-Yokohama 47 million, Mexico City 38 million, São Paulo 35 million, Bombay 30 million, Teheran 28 million, Calcutta 28 million, Delhi 27 million, Dacca 25 million, Jakarta 23 million, Karachi 22 million.

## TERMINAL ECO-CATASTROPHE SCENARIOS

2040 In climax of hostility, world government turns definitively against churches, orders all followers of Christ worldwide without exception to identify themselves publicly and then to proceed within next 6 months to one central location (an island) where they will then be exterminated by nuclear device, in ultimate act of deliberate and voluntary martyrdom;

Christians refusing to do so being officially pronounced to have denied Christ and then rewarded with massive material benefits.

2040 Humanity discovers and taps into a galactic radio network, a cosmic encyclopedia in which cultures and histories of all civilizations are preserved and broadcast eternally; Earth becomes junior member of association of cultures thousands or even millions of years older.

2040 Magnetic floaters in operation: high-speed underground transport systems travelling in vacuum at 2,000 km per hour through Earth propelled by magnetic fields.

2040 Accelerating change, increasing since beginning of Industrial Revolution in AD 1775, now becomes critical (as measured by statistical indicator growth of mass of knowledge, doubling every 10 years in 1980 and every 2 years by 2040).

2040 Limits-to-growth end scenario: final collapse of world civilization (as predicted by Club of Rome in 1972) due to population increase and poverty in sociosphere, pollution and industrialization in ecosphere; supplies of many minerals and food items exhausted; freak weather conditions; collapse of world transport systems; famine among urban populations; runaway greenhouse effect on Earth, leaks of radioactive waste, pesticide-immune insects, corrosive rain, et alia.

2040 Universal information system on Earth: single global telephone and videophone system; instant access by all to contents of any book, magazine, document, program or fact ever published.

2040 Moon (Luna) acquires colony of several hundred thousand human contract workers (not permanent colonists, due to its low gravity) mining aluminum, iron, silicon.

2040 Earth's resources of numerous important essential minerals and metals finally exhausted.

2040 New macro geo-ideas passed regularly to Worldwide Long Range Solutions Special Interest Discussion Group, with 112 million members: dealing with such ideas as total global reforestation, orbital solar power, optional cryosuspension for a hundred or more years freezing Earth's surplus billions of people who at present have no prospects of quality life in 21st century.

2040 Recent new nations: Han China, Republic of Patagonia, Yakutsk SSR; also Sea State (largely young people, living in gargantuan ramshackle floating cities worldwide, slowly traversing the oceans, with own navy enforcing looting and destruction of mainland ports).

2040 Gaia worship (reverence for Earth Mother) becomes a church militant, mainly run by feminist environmentalists and ecoactivists.

2040 Another artificial singularity (microscopic mini black hole used as power plant) is accidentally released in a riot in Peruvian Amazon, falls into Earth's core devouring interior within 2 years; scientists frantically attempt to avert total disaster. (*Earth*, 1990).

2040 World Data Net in place and in universal use, accessible through personal plaques anywhere, with wall screens showing real-time views from random locations across Earth.

2040 Artificial intelligence (AI) thinking machines; molecular science and nanotechnologies create higher-speed microscopic brainlike computers and robots.

2040 Quantity of greenhouse gases (carbon dioxide, ozone, methane, nitrous oxide, chlorofluorocarbons) rises phenomenally since 1800 (275 parts $CO_2$ per million), 1960 (310), 2000 (365), 2040 (555).

2040 Mind-reading computers pick up multiple users' data, thoughts, ideas, and expertise, and then analyze them on computer screen—the ultimate in data entry.

2040 Universal replicator perfected based on nanotechnology: any object however complex can be created given the necessary raw material information matrix; agriculture and industry are phased out.

2041 Ubiquitous computing technologies place computers in walls, furniture, clothing, eyeglass lenses; world filled with small single-purpose semi-intelligent creatures.

2042 Spaceship launched to explore a neighboring star system.

2043 200 million persons have starved to death since AD 2000 (75% Africans, chiefly rural women and young children).

2044 Rebellion by Israelis in Autonomous District of Jordan Valley leads to World War III, with collapse of USA, UK, European Community, et alia; death toll in war and its aftermath reaches 5.8 billion.

2045 Global Bible distribution reaches optimal maximum level of 10 billion scriptures per year (whole Bibles, NTs, portions, selections), in languages understood by whole world's population; but highly susceptible both to antichristian terrorism and also to world government edicts.

2045 Self-contained, recycling, mobile homes perfected.

2046 Breeding of intelligent animals (apes, cetaceans, et alia) for low-grade labor.

2048 Drug offenders either executed, or neutralized by chemicals, or given brain implant, a micro-miniaturized nuclear-powered 'peacemaker' causing disabling pain when wearer becomes angry or hostile.

2048 North American Church of Gaia (NorA ChuGa) now intervenes on all ecological matters.

2049 World overpopulation crisis results in cryosuspension perfected at university of Beijing, offering option of being suspended 300 years into the 24th century; problem of logistics of safely freezing 5 billion people.

## THE ESCHATOLOGY OF WORLD EVANGELIZATION

The following short 5-page tinted box offers an excursus describing an undateable future sequence that all Christians look ahead to—the Christian eschatological schema, also known as the biblical end-time, or the period often called the Latter Days, the Last Days, or the End of the World.

***The eschato-scientific scenario continues***

This chronology has divided its presentation of possible, probable, and preferable future events into 2 distinct sections: (a) a religio-scientific composite scenario of alternative futures, derived from secular, religious, ecclesiastical and other non-biblical sources (which began here under the year 2000, the final year of the Second Millennium, and the year 2001, the start of the Third Millennium, and which will continue on to the last page of this chronology; and (b) the elements of the Christian eschatological schema as contained in the biblical materials (given below in this short 5-page tinted box).

## THE CHRISTIAN ESCHATOLOGICAL SCHEMA Notes.

1. In keeping with Christian tradition, no exact dates can be given for events in this short 5-page sequence here in section (b) of Cosmic Era III. No detailed apocalyptic timetable is possible. However, this eschatological scenario, which is a composite made up of numerous convergent and divergent alternative miniscenarios, may be imagined as slotting in anywhere in the dated sequence from 2000 onwards in section (a) entitled 'A Religio-Scientific Composite Scenario of Alternative Futures'.
2. This eschatological sequence contains (1) biblical material (followed by abbreviated scriptural references), plus (2) additional theological and other interpretative material that reasonably can be or has been attached to the biblical data by way of explanation and elaboration. Related scriptural references are given so that the reader may study them himself or herself to see if particular scenarios best represent likely or probable or accurate exegesis. These scenarios embody the varying eschatological interpretations proffered by scholars throughout Christian history: chiliasm (millennialism), amillennialism, nonmillennialism, postmillennialism, historic (posttribulational) premillennialism, dispensational (pretribulational) premillennialism, realized millennialism, inaugurated imminency, other varieties of tribulationism, and so on.
3. The End-time portrayed below can be interpreted as being either (a) allegorical, or spiritual, or symbolic, or (b) literal, or (c) a mixture of all of these. It can be seen as either (1) a series of apocalyptic vignettes or spiritual lessons in no particular order in time, or (2) a series of events in approximately chronological order. To the extent that this whole sequence is, or was, or is intended to be, a literal chronological sequence, the whole of this biblical End-time scenario, from its start (after Signs of the Times) to the onset of the Millennium, to the final New Creation, is usually regarded as occupying only a short 5-year, 7-year or 10-year period. Throughout Christian history, as described in the preceding pages of Cosmic Era II, Christian thinkers and ecclesiastics have imagined it as about to happen in their own immediate or near-term or middle-range future from one to 20 years ahead.
4. For purposes of understanding, interpretation and speculation, therefore, we can imagine this climactic period being placed at various concrete future points in our chronological scenario of the future, e.g. at AD 2000, or 2010, or 2050, or 2300, or 10,000, or 100,000, or 1 million, etc. We thus proffer below 2 alternative scenarios, combined for convenience into a single sequence. (1) Our Total Discontinuity scenario (nuclear holocausts or natural cataclysmic ends of the world) then envisages Christ returning in the aftermath of world annihilation and creating an entirely new world de novo. (2) More plausible is our Partial Discontinuity scenario which envisages Christ returning at one particular future date (unknown to us at present, of course), intervening in time to avert possible or even inevitable or imminent global disaster, and then taking control over the world in all its future aspects as shown below, thereby inaugurating a period we can recognize as the biblical Millennium, and controlling and guiding in person all the world's developments and potentialities as detailed below in 'A Religio-Scientific Composite Scenario of Alternative Futures' (continued), especially in the realms of science, technology, space, society, politics, government, human evolution, et alia.

**Epoch Omega**

## THE BIBLICAL END-TIME: A COMPOSITE SCENARIO

***The Signs of the Times***

Signs and portents arise in profusion, all being evangelistic, hortatory, warnings to rebellious mankind; Bible contains at least 22 major signs signalling the End-time, including international (wars), cultural (interest in occult), natural (famines, drought), mysterious (UFOs, etc), satanic (devil worship), et alia. (Mt 16:3, Mt 24:4).

Great Commission of Christ in the sense of universal preaching of the gospel to all nations (world evangelization, discipling of the peoples) now recognized as its central obligation by the church militant on Earth, with disciples and witnesses being sought in every race and people and language and nation. (Mt 24:14, 28:19-20).

Increasing global population mobility, global strife, disintegrating social order, vast increases in knowledge in all subjects. (Dan 12:4).

Jerusalem the Holy City trampled by Gentiles (Times of the Gentiles, under hostile Gentile powers from BC 586 and AD 135 up to state of Israel (1948) and future Advent). (Lk 21:24).

Wars and rumours of wars (cold wars), famines, earthquakes, epidemics, terrible sufferings, celestial portents. (Mt 24:6-7, Lk 21:9-11).

Beginning of the 2 great End-time revivals: (1) of good, (2) of evil. (Joel 2:28-29).

Revivals and rapid church growth with mass acceptance of gospel in some parts of the world, with mass rejection of gospel in others: millions converted in last great global spiritual revival; worldwide signs and wonders accompany proclamation of the gospel in every land.

Spread of false gospels increases, with rise of false prophets, false christs, false messiahs, and antichrists. (Mt 24:5,11,14, 1 Tim 4:1, 2 Pet 2:1, 1 John 1:18).

End-time apostasy within Christendom (represented by the 7 churches of the Apocalypse, Rev 1-3); abandonment of biblical Christianity by millions of nominal church members; polarization of global Christianity into the affluent middle-class Western-world church of the Rich ('the Laodicean Church'), the Church of the Poor (Africa, Latin America), and the Church of the Absolutely Poor (South and Central Asia) ('the Smyrna/Philadelphia Church'). (Mt 24:10-12, 2 Thess 2:3, Rev 2:9, 3:17).

Failure of the church to evangelize the world, part remaining still unevangelized until the Tribulation. (Mt 10:23b).

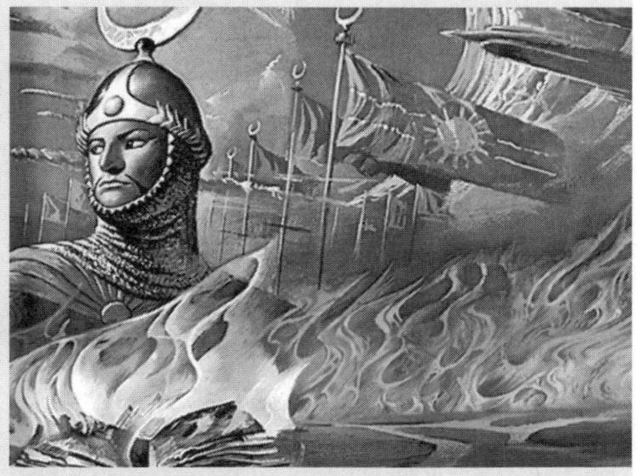

**The Ultimate Antichrist** arises as ruthless dictator annihilating peoples and metropolises.

Rise of a charismatic leader within 10-nation confederacy (European Economic Community, or a Mediterranean Confederacy, as revived Roman Empire), who seizes power and sets up a ruthless, totalitarian world government; who further is (a) a political genius with vast organizational and leadership abilities who creates a world socialist order, and (b) a psychic genius who creates a new universal world religion (based on occult Hinduism), mastery of secret cosmic forces, tremendous hypnotic powers; frightening display of psychic force, attempt to convert the whole world forcibly to occultism; later, ruler is revealed to be the final Antichrist, the Ultimate Antichrist, the Universal Monarch. (2 Thess 2:3-4).

## THE PRETRIBULATION RAPTURE SCENARIO

First or Secret Coming of Christ on the clouds of heaven (the private or invisible Coming 'for' his Saints) in his imperishable immortal resurrection body, imminent, sudden, unexpected, without prior signs or warnings, 'as a thief in the night'; announced with trumpet to the church but not publicly to the world. (1 Thess 4:16, 1 Cor 15:52).

First stage of calling out of the Elect (the Body of Christ): Translation of the Saints; imminent, sudden, secret Rapture of the Church, or part of it (only those prepared, worthy and expectant; or only the Confessing Church of prophets, apostles, martyrs, confessors and witnesses; or, 'God's preferential option for the poor', i.e. only the downtrodden, the persecuted, the deprived, the oppressed, the marginalized, the Church of the Poor, or the Church of the Absolutely Poor as the most faithful or most deserving Remnant), with the dead in Christ preceding them (the Church of the Martyrs, in the Out-Resurrection); Age of Grace with offer of salvation still open however until end of Great Tribulation. (1 Thess 4:16-17).

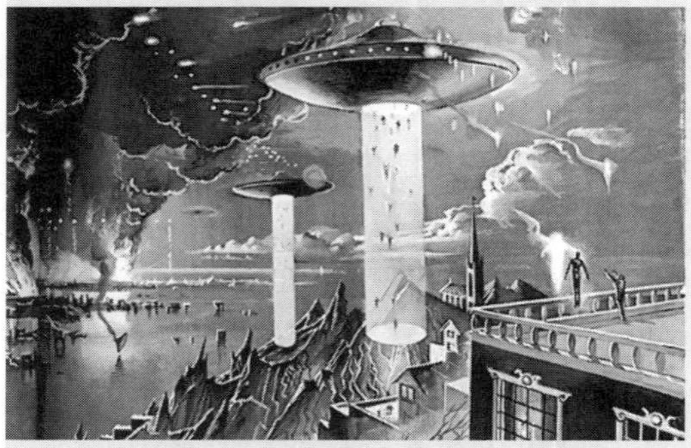

**Rapture** scenario as millions of believers are siphoned up out of imminent Tribulation.

The Rapture, with sudden disappearance of millions of Christians, is interpreted by hostile antichristian New Age Movement leaders as a mighty evolutionary quantum leap to a higher consciousness, the Cosmic Mind ejecting laggards of the species as a body rejects unwanted cells. (2 Peter 3:4).

On other scenarios, no secret coming or rapture takes place, but entire church moves forward as the suffering Body of Christ as it passes into and through the Great Tribulation.

## INAUGURATION OF NEW AGE ORDER AND RELIGION

Global inauguration of this-worldly New Age (the New Genesis), a pseudo-New Age biblically termed 'The Great Delusion', or 'The Lie', or the 'wicked deception', a 'false gospel', being widespread irresistible religious disinformation and deception as a 'Sign of the Times'; long period of unprecedented peace, prosperity and plenty, sharing and global euphoria on Earth, as satanic counterfeit and parody of promised Millennium; Western wealth redistributed among poorest countries; miracles, signs and wonders performed; millions of New-Agers agree to cooperate with newly-emerged World Ruler (the Antichrist) in building New Age Paradise on Earth. (Mt 24:24, 2 Thess 2:9-12).

Antichrist proclaims lasting and permanent peace settlement in Middle East including alliance with Israel; rebuilds great cities including Tyre as political capital. (Ezek 28).

Rebuilding of Temple in Jerusalem permitted and resumption of its sacrifices begun. (Dan 9:27).

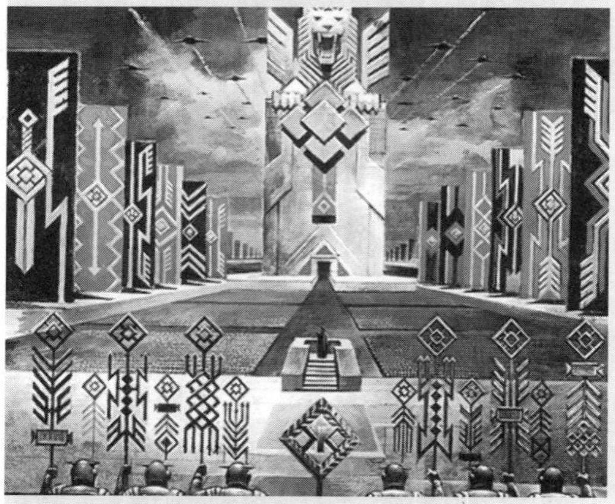

**Antichrist's New Age world order** begins with public refutation of Jesus and faith.

New Age world order inaugurated: Antichrist regulates international and local commerce and finance by ordering every person to have indelibly impregnated into his body an identifying number accessible to scanning devices, thus controlling all buying and selling; computer-controlled cashless society; total control of all personal and corporate wealth; ruler embraces number 666 to show rejection of Bible as myth. (Rev 13:2b,4b,7b,14-18).

New Age world religion inaugurated: blend of Western science and ancient Eastern wisdom or Hinduism/Buddhism/Lamaism/Tantrism, i.e. of elements of Hindu or Eastern philosophy, astrology, astral projection (out-of-body experiences), ancient pagan occultism, spiritism, medium religion, metaphysics, apostate modern or secular religion, denial of Incarnation of Christ, rejection of Bible as ultimate authority, mind power, self- realization (realizing one is God), deification of man, ESP, psychokinesis, psychology, parapsychology, telepathy, clairvoyance, precognition, hypnosis and hypnotherapy, autosuggestion, yoga, biofeedback ('electronic yoga'), witchcraft, shamanism, voodoo, satanism, chakras, reincarnation, vegetarianism, zen, demon possession, necromancy, overwhelming sense of universal consciousness.

Concrete embodiments of New Age religion, or Aquarian Age religion, include: Unity School of Christianity, Religious Science, Mind Science, Christian Science, Divine Science, Great White Brotherhood, Church Universal and Triumphant, White Eagle Brotherhood, Theosophical Society, Rosicrucians (AMORC), Human Potential Movement, TM, et alia; with elements of religious deception, delusion of divinity or godhead, higher or altered states of consciousness, exploitation of consciousness (inner space), based on belief in the oneness of all life and in themselves as part of the Universal Self or Consciousness, the Self's infinite potential, expecting an Aquarian messiah/saviour (Lord Maitreya, etc).

Mass media, computers, communications technology, Internet, artificial intelligence, mind control, hypnosis, drugs etc, all utilized by Antichrist to propagate pseudo-evangelization worldwide within days, i.e. establishment of the New Age world religion (based on man's divinity, self-realization, self-sufficiency, denial of Christ's bodily Incarnation).

Period of peace, plenty, prosperity under New Age world order begins to disintegrate as realities of human evil surface.

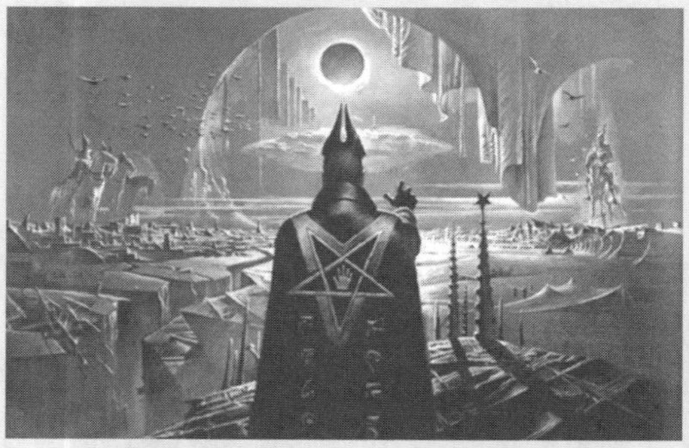

**Antichrist's iron grip** on world tightens: edicts, disasters, destruction, genocides begin, over territory prepared by the Four Horsemen of the Apocalypse (seen here in background).

## THE TRIBULATION BEGINS

Global peace and prosperity shattered in first half of a 7-year period of unprecedented terror, turmoil and bloodshed (the 'Great Disaster', the 'Great Chastisement' to Catholics, the 1st half of Daniel's 70th Week). (Dan 9:24, Mt 24:9, 2 Tim 3:1).

Northern power (Russia) launches all-out invasion of Middle East to obliterate Israel, but armies suddenly and inexplicably destroyed in northern Palestine; burial of corpses takes 7 months. (Ezek 38-39).

Antichrist renounces defense pact with Israel, breaks covenant with Jews, causes Temple sacrifices to cease, enters Temple and in Holy of Holies announces he is God (Abomination of Desolation, the Final Blasphemy), demands worship by whole world, sets up his own image as Prince of Peace in every city. (Mt 24:15, Ascension of Isaiah 4:11).

### *The 7 Seals are opened*

Vision of scroll or book of human destiny (God's purpose in judgment), sealed with 7 seals. (Rev 5, being Revelation's 1st of 7 groups of 7 visions each).

The 7 Seals opened by all-powerful and all-seeing Lamb: (1) conquest, (2) war, (3) famine, (4) death, (5) martyrdom, (6) anarchy, (7) judgment. (Rev 6:1-17, 8:1-2).

The Four Horsemen of the Apocalypse (opening of the first 4 Seals), white, red, black, pale: (1) war/conquest/deception/false religions/cults/ pseudo-messiah/antichrist, (2) slaughter, (3) famine, (4) death (or (1) missionary preaching of the gospel, (2) civil war/bloodshed, (3) famine/hunger/disease/poverty, (4) terror/pestilence/death/ destruction); 25% of world slaughtered. (Mt 24:7, Rev 6:1-8).

1st Persecution: storm of religious persecution sweeps across globe resulting in martyrdoms of vast numbers of Christians, especially in Western world's Church of the Rich (the Laodicean church), but including multitudes of new converts (after 5th Seal opened); persecuted Christians about to be martyred are told to be patient until foreordained total of all martyrs is completed. (Mt 24:9, Rev 6:9-11).

Collapse of governments—world, regional, local—into unprecedented global anarchy (after opening of 6th Seal); universal mass hysteria, total terror. (Rev 6:12-17).

False gospel of religious disinformation and deception now accepted worldwide: false christs and false prophets deceive vast mass of mankind by stupendous signs and wonders. (Mt 24:24).

Sealing begins of overcoming Christians and future martyrs on Earth; all 144,000 prospective martyrs are now permanently sealed for spiritual protection as the New Israel as Great Tribulation approaches. (Rev 7:1-8).

## THE 7 TRUMPETS SOUND

7th Seal opened: 7 Trumpet Woes herald plagues and curses: (1) natural calamities, (2) ships and seas destroyed, (3) rivers and water supplies ruined, (4) celestial bodies disorganized, (5) locusts from the Abyss (the bottomless pit), (6) Eastern army of 200 million kill a third of mankind; the 2nd Persecution. (Rev 8:1-9.21, being Revelation's 2nd group of 7 visions).

Sufferings of the church multiplied as it prophesies and witnesses to the world. (Rev 10:9-11).

Times of the Gentiles (period for God's punishment of Israel and their repentance and conversion) conclude with vicious persecution of Israel for three and a half years (literal or figurative) until end of Tribulation. (Lk 21:24, Rev 11:1-2).

The Two Witnesses (Olive Trees, Lampstands: Moses and Elijah, Law and Prophecy; Joshua and Zerubbabel the anointed religious and civil leaders; the witness-bearing two-sevenths of the universal church about to be martyred), after 42 months or three and a half years (literal or figurative) of preaching the gospel and opposing New Age philosophy, complete their task of world evangelization through bearing witness to claims of Christ, are slain by Antichrist symbolizing near-obliteration of the church, in 3rd Persecution; but then are raised from dead, symbolizing final global revival of faith in Christ with millions converted. (Zech 4:11-14, Rev 11:3-14).

Penultimate direct supernatural work of the Holy Spirit in proclamation, evangelization and conversions throughout world as Church Age draws to its close.

Midtribulation Rapture of the Saints: removal of confessing church before Great Tribulation escalates into total horror. (1 Thess 4:17).

## THE GREAT TRIBULATION ERUPTS

Second half of the Tribulation (2nd half of Daniel's 70th Week) eclipses terrors of first half now past. (Dan 9:24, Mt 24:21-28, Rev 11-18).

7th Trumpet sounds, announcing imminent end of present satanic world age and imminent commencement of Reign of Christ on Earth, with God's impending assumption of all power, preceded by second and more terrible half of the Great Tribulation. (Rev 11:15-19).

The Restrainer (=Holy Spirit; or Church before final rapture; or orderly process of government; or missionary preaching of the gospel) is removed from Earth, allowing evil full sway. (2 Thess 2:6-7).

### *The 7 Signs appear: a dragon and 2 beasts*

The 7 significant Signs of Revelation: woman clothed with Sun, Satan, war, 1st beast, 2nd beast, Lamb, harvest. (Rev12:1-14:20).

War in heaven (a legal battle between opposing counsel over the claims of Christ to be Lord and Messiah) between archangel Michael and the great blood-red 7-headed Dragon (the Devil or Satan, world deceiver, prince of the present world-system), who with his angels is then thrown down to Earth with great wrath; three and a half years (literal or figurative) of violent persecution of Israel and the Remnant and reign of terror against remaining Christians. (Rev12:1-17, being Revelation's 3rd group of 7 visions).

Emergence of Trinity of Evil (Satan, Antichrist, Pseudo-Christ): (1) rise of the Dragon (Satan) as final authority of evil; (2) rise from the sea ('the seething cauldron of unregenerate humanity') of 7-headed hydra, the beast Leviathan with blasphemous Name claiming Deity, the Antichrist as world political ruler over a global government (representing all such rulers and antichrists in history from 1st-century Roman emperor worshipped as divine, to Nero Redivivus, to final ruler of one last terrible empire, head of 10-nation confederacy of Europe or Mediterranean as revived Holy Roman Empire, one of whose 7 heads is killed but then resurrected); and (3) rise from the earth of the beast Behemoth, the False Prophet, religious incarnation of the final Antichrist, the Pseudo-Christ (the False Christ), the False Lamb (parodying Christ's death and resurrection), the Man of Sin, the Lawless One, the Little Horn, the Son of Perdition, the Pseudo-Messiah (symbolizing a long sequence from 1st-century imperial priesthood in charge of rites of emperor-worship whose cipher is 666); vicious religious persecution (the 4th Persecution) under universal world religion, psychotic hatred of Israel, totalitarian economic enslavement; Antichrist demands all take the mark of the Beast or die; millions slaughtered. (Rev 13:1-10, Mt 24:15-21, Mk 13:14-19, 2 Thess 2:3-12, Rev 13:11-18, 16:13, 19:20).

New Age world religion, which initially has been a universal religious movement emphasizing peace and prosperity, degenerates under control of Antichrist as supreme head; obligatory entry, on pain of death, by means of ancient Luciferic initiations; cult of worship of Antichrist enforced on all. (Rev 13:4,8,13-14).

## The Four Horsemen of the Apocalypse

This graphic subject has attracted more attention than any other for illustrators of the Book of Revelation: artists, engravers. Based on the biblical narrative of Revelation 6:1-8, the Horsemen are apocalyptic figures in the biblical end-times: the White horse representing Conquest (or, for Calvin, the missionary preaching of the gospel), the Red horse representing War and bloodshed, the Black horse representing Famine, and the Pale horse representing Death. All convey different aspects of the horror and terror they portray. The two at top right portray an additional theme—the total chaos that results from the Horsemen's arrival.

AD 1767. 'The Vision of the White Horse' (German Romantic painter P.J. de Loutherbourg).

AD 1150. 'The First Horseman' portrayed in 12th-century painting, reproduced in 1975 Portugal postage stamp.

AD 1555. Total destruction completed by 'The Four Horsemen' (Nostradamus, *Centuries*), as the Antichrist comes to the fore.

AD 1498. 'The 4 Horsemen', from Albrecht Durer's masterpiece on The Apocalypse.

AD 1840. 'The Riders of the Apocalypse' (German painter Peter von Cornelius).

AD 1940. 'The Four Horsemen of the Apocalypse' (woodcut by New Zealander J.B. Wright)

AD 1950.. 'The Four Horsemen of the Apocalypse' (wood engraving by B. Hughes-Stratton).

Image of the Resurrected Beast made and animated; huge size, utters oracles, universally believed. (Rev 13:14-15).

As full foreordained number of Gentile Christians is reached, mass conversion of Jews begins: a Remnant of 144,000 is converted out of Israel, together with vast numbers of new Gentile converts; all 144,000 prospective martyrs being sealed for spiritual protection against forces of evil. (Rom 11:25-27, Rev 7:1-17, 14:1-5).

The 144,000 converted Israelites become end-time evangelists who reach world's last unreached people groups and so complete task of world evangelization. (Rev 7:4-8).

Great Commission of Christ fulfilled in the sense that universal preaching of the gospel to all nations (world evangelization, discipling of the peoples) has been finally accomplished by the church militant on Earth, with disciples and witnesses found in every race and people and language and nation. (Mt 24:14, 28:19-20).

Vast worldwide satanic activity, under Antichrist as the Great Dictator (political tyrant with worldwide power); terrifying worldwide destruction.

Three-and-a-half-year (literal or figurative) reign of terror: (a) the 5th or Great Persecution, one last worldwide persecution, worst in history; ruthless total persecution of Israel and Jews, as ultimate scapegoat for ills of Earth, as Antichrist turns to 'the final solution'—total genocide; (b) the Great Falling Away (the Great Apostasy): millions of Christians from former Church of the Rich abandon their faith. (Mt 24:10, Lk 18:8, 2 Thess 2:3, Rev 13:7a).

## LAST DAYS OF THE AGE OF GRACE

Last supernatural proclamation from heaven of Everlasting Gospel of love in all its fullness to every nation, and kindred, and tongue, and people, either to convert or to seal doom of mankind; last appeal and announcement of final chance for repentance and salvation, imminent end of Age of Grace with following judgment upon wicked in climax of Great Tribulation. (Rev 14:6-7, being Revelation's 4th group of 7 visions; Lk 16:31).

Reaping of the harvest of Earth's peoples, and treading of 'the great winepress of the wrath of God', with total bloodshed throughout Israel. (Joel 3:13, Mk 4:29, Rev 14:14-20).

**Seven Angels with 7 Plagues** (Apocalypse of *Beatus of Liebana*, AD 1109).

### The 7 Last Plagues erupt

The 7 Last Plagues (the 7 Bowls of the wrath of God; terrible judgments, not chastisement but final and punitive): (1) foul bodily sores, (2) death of all seas, (3) pollution of all water supplies, (4) heat and fire, (5) darkness, (6) drought and plague of demons, (7) hail, thunder, lightning, mega-earthquakes. (Rev 15:1-16:21, being Revelation's 5th group of 7 visions; Mt 24:7).

### The fall of Babylon

Destruction of Great Babylon, city of Antichrist, the Great Harlot (Rome, the goddess Rome, et alia) seated on her paramour the 7-headed Dragon: (a) Religious Babylon (the apostate religious system); (b) Secular Babylon (civilized, urbanized man organized apart from God, man in organized but godless community); and (c) its destroyer, and usurper of its religious primacy, Political Babylon (the Antichrist's confederated 10-nation empire, the ruthless secular world of luxurious commerce, or the one-world politico-commercial system). (Rev 17:1-18:24, being Revelation's 6th group of 7 visions).

## THE DAY OF THE LORD

End to 20 centuries of delay over Parousia, a delay due to God's patience and forbearance 'not wanting anyone to perish but everyone to come to repentance'. (2 Peter 3:9).

The Day, the Day of Christ, the Great and Terrible Day of the Lord, the Last Day, the Day of Wrath (Rev 6:17, 19:11-21, being Revelation's 7th group of 7 visions; Mal 4:5).

Massing of 4 great confederations of Gentile nations: North (Russia and allies, Ezek 38-39) and South (Egypt and Arabs, Dan 11) mass to finally destroy Israel and God's people; opposed by West (10-nation confederation of Europe, Dan 2), with kings of the East (China and allies, Rev 16:12) also involved (USA having been destroyed after Rapture of church, on current premillennialist interpretation). (Mt 24:7, Rev 16:12-16, 19:17-19).

Battle or war of Armageddon (at Megiddo, scene of many decisive battles in history); the ultimate world war, greatest in history, with hundreds of millions of combatants, the entire armed might of the world, deployed for several hundred miles around Megiddo; last cataclysmic struggle between good and evil on the Day of the Lord, the Great Day of God's Wrath; slaughter of armies of Antichrist. (Rev. 16:16, 19:17-19).

### Total discontinuity scenario: complete destruction of old world

Celestial cataclysms, woes and terrors: Sun, Moon and stars disappear, 'great noise', 'fervent heat', 'earth burned up': a great celestial conflagration. (Mt 24:29, 2 Peter 3, Rev 6:12-14).

Jerusalem the scene of unparalleled warfare, with house-to-house fighting in streets; Mount of Olives suddenly splits with east-west chasm as Christ returns. (Zech 14:2,4).

The Last Trump: final consummation of all things in Christ, ending of all human history (Mt 24:31a, 1 Cor 15:52).

**Christ's Second Coming** (Beatus AD 1109).

## THE SECOND COMING OF CHRIST

Second Advent of Christ (Second Coming, Parousia, Arrival, Appearing, Return, Disclosure, Revelation, Revealing, Unveiling): premillennial, sudden, unexpected, public, visible Return of Jesus Christ as lightning with power and glory ('with ' his saints, 'revealed from Heaven with his mighty angels in flaming fire'), to Mount of Olives to establish the Millennial Kingdom, as king and great High Priest. (Mt 24:27, 2 Thess 1:7, Rev 19:11-16).

Final close of Age of Grace; universal mourning, and completion of number of the Elect (Body of Christ) who have come through the Great Tribulation and their gathering in from 4 quarters of Earth after Last Trump (Posttribulation Rapture of the Saints). (Mt 24:31b).

Judgment of All Nations on Earth: i.e. of living Gentile believers ('sheep'), of Israel's Gentile persecutors ('goats'), and of Israel itself and the Jews ('brethren'); the great eschatological reversal of fortunes. (Mt 25:31-46, Rom 14:10, 2 Cor 5:10).

The Last Day reveals final outcome of God's age-long cosmic dispute/ controversy/lawsuit against nations

of the world and their gods or idols to establish the claims of Jesus Christ. (OT, Jn 1-12, Jn 13:17, et alia).

Overthrow of Beast and False Prophet, cast into Lake of Fire with their followers (Rev 19:20).

Satan bound and thrown into Abyss (the bottomless pit); consummation and close of Age of Grace; 'End of the World' (end of entire satanic world- system). (Rev 20:1-3).

First Resurrection from the Dead (the resurrection of the just, the martyrs, the dead in Christ), who will live and reign with Christ 1,000 years (literal or figurative). (Rev 20:4-6).

## THE MILLENNIAL AGE: THE MESSIANIC KINGDOM

### Partial discontinuity scenario: Christ takes over existing world.

The Millennium is inaugurated, either (a) spiritual (allegorical, symbolic, nonmillennialist, amillennialist) i.e. the Church Age from AD 33 to Second Advent, with new birth as First Resurrection; or (b) literal transitional period of either 1,000 years, or 400 years, or 40 years, or a complete period of some sort, or one generation; or (c) Sabbath Day lasting a literal 1,000 years, after preceding 6 Days (6,000 years) of recorded secular history and Heilsgeschichte (salvation history); or (d) both spiritual and literal overlapping where Church Age overlaps with eternal Kingdom of God. (Rev 20:3-7).

The Messiah restores throne of David and sets up Millennial Kingdom at Jerusalem, over a restored Israel and subdued Gentile nations; Jews as a nation accept Jesus as their Messiah; earthly Jewish kingdom with restoration of Israel as God's people, rebuilt and restored Temple, daily sacrifices, annual feasts; but curse on humanity only partially lifted, people still born in sin, even allowing a small satanic following eventually to emerge.

Pacification, conquest and restoration of divine authority over entire world- system and all its peoples; gradual but final conquest of death, disease and sin; evil present but held firmly in check since Satan has been bound; all surviving persons and Christians on Earth at time of Parousia enter Millennium retaining their natural (mortal) bodies to repopulate the world, but Christians formerly raptured retain their heavenly bodies; eschatological union of Christ with Israel and Gentiles in his body, the church.

Universal spread and acceptance of the Kingdom of God (as envisaged by Irenaeus in AD 180); gradual conversion of vast numbers to Christ.

Conversion of the entire world (remaining humankind of all other religions, including 'anonymous Christianity'), under direct leadership of the Messiah, to open Christian faith; 'at the name of Jesus every knee would bow, every tongue confess that Jesus is Lord'; end of institutionalized Christian religion and worship. (Phil 2:10-11, Rom 14:11).

The Messianic Banquet (Marriage Supper of the Lamb, the Great Feast), attended by nations from North, South, East and West (Mt 26:26,29, Lk 13:29, 14:15-24, 22:16-18, Mt 24:31, Rev 19:7-9).

**King of Kings:** Jesus inaugurates the Millennial Age on Earth (Charles E. Butler).

Reign of Christ on Earth, presiding over annihilation of time itself, with resurrected apostles and martyrs from every race and people and culture and language as co-rulers, as a new species of Homo Sapiens i.e. immortal humans in the New Age (Mt 19:28, GNB), 'sitting on thrones ruling over the 12 Tribes of Israel'; the Golden Age of the Church, Reign of the Church in Society, the Eternal Sabbath rest of Creation, an earthly kingdom of peace, righteousness, justice and plenty, in which however flesh and blood (human nature in its weakness) cannot inherit the Kingdom of God. (Lk 22:30, Rev 20:4,6, 1 Cor 15:50, Heb 4:9).

### The Last Judgment: the Eschaton

Recapitulation of entire period since Jesus' Cross and Resurrection: Satan loosed from prison (the Abyss) to foment one last rebellion with vast host 'as the sand of the sea' led by the great persecutors Gog and Magog (Rome and Babylon); Satan finally overthrown and destroyed by fire. (Rev 20:7-9).
Postmillennial coming of Christ: final destruction of Satan with Beast and False Prophet in Lake of Fire (Rev 20:10).
Second or General Resurrection of the Dead, for judgment of the wicked, idolators, worshippers of the Beast, Christian apostates (Rev 20:12-13).

**AD 1536.** Michelangelo completes 'The Last Judgment' in Vatican's Sistine Chapel.

Last Judgment (Last Assize, Day of Judgment, Final Judgment, Great White Throne) invoking Lamb's Book of Life, based on people's response to persecuted church's witness and on loyalty to Christ under persecution. (Rev 20:11-15, Rom 14:10).
Death and Hades with their followers are cast into Lake of Fire; 'This is the Second Death' (Rev 20:14).
End of space-time continuum; specifically, end of 7 evils: death, mourning (sorrow), weeping (tears), pain, curse, night, and the sea (the unregenerate world of evil). (Rev 20:15; 21, 22).

## CONSUMMATION OF THE NEW CREATION

### God creates New Heavens and New Earth

Final fulfillment and completion of God's promise 'Behold, I create new heavens and a new earth' (Isaiah 65:17, RSV).

**AD 1000.** 'Das neue Jerusalem'—the New Jerusalem.

Beginning of the genuine New Age, the eternal state, the everlasting Kingdom of God, the Paradise of God, the New Eden, the New Jerusalem (1,500 miles cubed, an eternal Holy of Holies), 12 gates never closed (free access to God), River of Life and Tree of Life (knowledge of how creation works, with fruit conferring immortality), a place of light, glory, splendor, truth, universality, salvation, security, worship, work, service, responsibility, abundance, health, joy, enjoyment, the vision of Christ as Alpha and Omega; 12 zodiacal signs of the Old Age permanently reversed (Rev 21:19-20); a renovated Universe, a renewed Galaxy, a transformed Earth, built on Earth's different peoples (races), Israel and the church, and 'the unsearchable riches of Christ'. (Eph 2:7, Rev 2:7; 21-22).

**AD 1942.** The New Jerusalem as many envisage it— a huge futuristic science city conquering space and atom (Canto & Faliu).

---

## A Religio-Scientific Scenario (Continued)

2050 **Global status of Christianity:** 67.2 generations after Christ, world is 34.3% Christians, 79.7% evangelized; with scriptures available in all 13,000 languages.
2050 50% of all Christians are charismatics (pentecostals, neopentecostals, neocharismatics, apostolics, neo-apostolics, et alii), as are 70% of all church workers and 90% of all foreign missionaries.
2050 World's 10 largest cities: Lagos 46,566,000, Karachi 44,284,000, Bombay 41,803,000, Dhaka 35,841,000, Calcutta 35,027,000, Kinshasa 34,624,000, Addis Ababa 31,876,000, Shanghai 29,534,000, Tokyo 28,887,000, Delhi 28,627,000.
2050 Climate change disasters: unstoppable greenhouse effect, coastal flooding imperils 100 millions, Amazon rain forest now desert, 30 millions more starve as crops fail, malaria threatens large areas of world including all Europe.
2050 Christianity now dominated worldwide by Third-World indigenous pentecostal-charismatic bodies, spreading like wildfire through unorganized self-replicating media churches.
2050 Gantz organic homes produced by genetically-engineered bacteria manufacturing organic glues binding soil together; lifestyles transformed in crumbling Third-World cities.
2050 World Political Party issues Declaration of Human Sovereignty; by 2056, 35 countries have been mundialized (won or seized for Party by any means); CSE disbands, end of GTC; 2062, proclamation of the Commonwealth (capital Melbourne, later changed to Chungking, with 1,000 departments governing electronically), with World Militia (a million men and women, nuclear weapons) authorized to quell any resistance; 6 years of counterrevolutionary wars; 2070, all nations ratify Declaration.
2050 Molecular Revolution, resulting in Neomaterialism, a new worldview with massive impetus for sociopolitical change, arising from suite of 3 disciplines termed 'molecular sciences': molecular biology, molecular psychology, molecular technology (inventing microscopic robots).
2050 After 200 years of attempts, world at last adopts a single constructed international auxiliary language, a variant of Glossa, Suma or English. (A.C. Clarke).

2050 World's private cars and aircraft travel (latter at 350 mph) entirely under control of central traffic computers.
2050 Control of gravity on Earth achieved. (A.C. Clarke).
2050 Risk of total destruction of human race through nuclear war recedes as vast numbers emigrate to distant space colonies.
2050 'Freedom IV', first interstellar starship carrying humans intending to seek planets to colonize, departs for Alpha Centauri star system 4.3 light-years from Earth. (L.S. Wolfe & R.L. Wysack's scenario).
2050 Experimentation with human DNA reaches peak, leaving behind freak individuals, freak groups, freak colonies, freak races.
2050 World adult literacy rises from 15% in 1800, to 55% in 1960, to 70% by 2000, to 90% by 2050.
2050 Computer-controlled commercial factory farms become universal.
2050 Mankind's basic character fails to improve despite scientific advances; life still disrupted by greed, lust, dishonesty, corruption, and desire for power.

**AD 2050.** Space arks: spacefaring cities on a generation starship (T. Whitz).

2050 Multigeneration starships (taking several generations, e.g. 200 years, to reach destinations) built, with nuclear fusion reactors, travelling at 10% of speed of light.
2050 Relativistic spaceflight makes entire Universe accessible to those on the journey: starships that accelerate continuously at 1g reach 95% of speed of light within one year, reaching center of Galaxy in apparent 21 years (for an elapsed time of 30,000 years), circumnavigating entire Universe in 56 years ship time.
2050 Rise of eccentric religious cult, Neo-Manichees, an orbital religion with no meeting places except television screens; their 'statistical theology' disproves, and destroys faith in, a personal God.
2050 To solve massively accelerating overpopulation crisis, half the world (5 billions) otherwise condemned to die by starvation or epidemics finally agree to UN offer of cryosuspension and are frozen for 300 years until 24th century, with UN guaranteeing eventual wealth for all.
2050 Technical knowledge increases to 100,000 times that available in 1990.
2050 Nanotechnology nightmare scenario: accidentally-created omnivorous bacteria-size robot spreads like blowing pollen, replicates swiftly, reduces entire world biosphere to dust in matter of days.
2050 Millions decide to use cryonic suspension to emigrate into the future in search of adventure; vast hibernaculars are established in Antarctic and in regions of perpetual night at lunar poles.
2055 Cybernetic Wave (A. Toffler's Fourth Wave) arrives, based on artificial intelligence, brain-computer linkups, biochips, instant creativity.
2055 Cyborg minds widespread, through implanting electronic accessory brains in human brains, including biocomps (bionic-implant computer terminals) which monitor, calculate and advise the host brain.
2055 Religions become closely influenced by, even based on, chemistry once chemical basis of all life is understood.
2055 Human normal lifespan extends to 250 years for 75% of human race.
2055 Urban dwellers number 80% of world's population, 80% of them being in Third World.
2055 Plagues due to viruses from space ravage Earth killing billions. (M. Crichton, *The Andromeda strain*, 1969).
2060 Reunion of all major separated branches of

Christianity achieved: Catholic, Protestant, Anglican, Orthodox, organically united in 'the Coming Great Church'.
2060 Medical means discovered to achieve earthly immortality, even circumventing accidental death; open to 95% of Western world's population; also ability of individuals to change sex at will.
2060 Population increase deliberately reduced to near zero by proception, the procedure whereby every child born is deliberately chosen, wanted, and adored; birth defects a nightmare of the past.
2060 Synthetape replaces film: sophisticated software available for synthesizing visual images; human actors no longer necessary; by AD 2120, 3-D holographic epics made using 3-dimensional synthetape.
2060 Bus, subway and other transportation services in most of world's large cities are now provided free of charge.
2060 World energy demand reaches 4.4 times 1986 level, with electricity increasing 7.0 times.
2060 Zoo hypothesis: extraterrestrial ethics prevent other creatures from interfering with unusual developing species like Homo Sapiens.
2061 Return of Halley's Comet; first landing on nucleus by humans; sensational discovery of both dormant and active life leads to discovery that life is omnipresent throughout space.
2062 Spaceships or probes can now exceed 80% of speed of light.
2065 World population, on mediodemographic scenario, levels off at around 12 billion, well below Earth's absolute capacity. (*Interfutures OECD Project,* 1979).
2065 Small handheld pocket computers serve as audio translators into 300 different languages for instantaneous spoken translation, also for instantaneous transcribing and translated printout.
2070 Combining of ectogenesis with eugenics so that only superior humans can propagate.
2070 Educated classes in Europe and Eurasia become 70% nonreligious or antireligious.
2070 The Lost Billion: a 1,000 million subsistence farmers, displaced from their land, become religious cultists and urban guerrillas dedicated to mass assassination before being gradually destroyed.
2073 Planetary Restoration Authority created by People's Congress to oversee the Great Housecleaning restoring the biosphere.
2075 Human beings control spaceships via skull sockets linked to ships' computers.
2075 Man reaches travel at near-light speeds; participants' apparent longevity increases markedly.
2075 Islamic guerrillas on suicide missions across Middle East are disarmed by swift action of World Militia.
2080 Spread of Christianity throughout Chinese and Arab races generates vast missionary zeal to point where both launch independent schemes for total world evangelization and conversion.
2080 Transporting and storing of energy done through liquid hydrogen as preferred medium.
2080 Human race uses 15 times as much energy annually as it did in 1980.
2080 Stable world government in place: either a UN empire, or an American empire, or joint Chinese/American, based on English and/or Chinese; or the Millennial kingdom.
2080 Criminal procedures of all nations standardized everywhere.
2080 Uniform world monetary system established and enforced.
2080 All persons everywhere required to furnish total personal data annually for police work, social research, eugenic reform, et alia.
2080 Eugenic infanticide widespread (killing of handicapped children at birth).
2080 English becomes sole international language of science, technology, scholarship, culture, diplomacy, and Christianity.
2080 Runaway greenhouse effect as ocean levels rise (by 8 inches since 2000), flooding of world's coastal areas imperils 200 millions.
2082 Moon is now settled by humans, with 50,000 Lunarians (5,000 born on Moon, who have never visited Earth); at height of tourist season, total population rises to 110,000.
2082 Escalating arms race halted and finally terminated by (1) new generation of ultra-sophisticated computers in spy satellites, and (2) economic decline among superpowers, who finally hound international arms merchants into extinction.

## EXTRATERRESTRIAL INTELLIGENCE SCENARIOS

2085 First verifiable alien contact with extraterrestrial intelligence among our Galaxy's (Milky Way's) 400 billion stars, where between 100 and 1,000,000 other advanced technical civilizations (capable of interstellar radio communication) probably exist, as well as up to 1 billion lesser communicative civilizations (none resembling humanity); nearest is possibly only 100 light-years distant.
2085 Existence discovered of vast star empires, great civilizations, and alien cultures unimaginably far advanced.
2085 Planetary war scenario: alien beings from planet Mars, emotionless Martian killers, invade Earth; Darwinian struggle for survival of human race until Martians finally killed off by microbes. (H.G. Wells' scenario, *The War of the Worlds,* 1898).

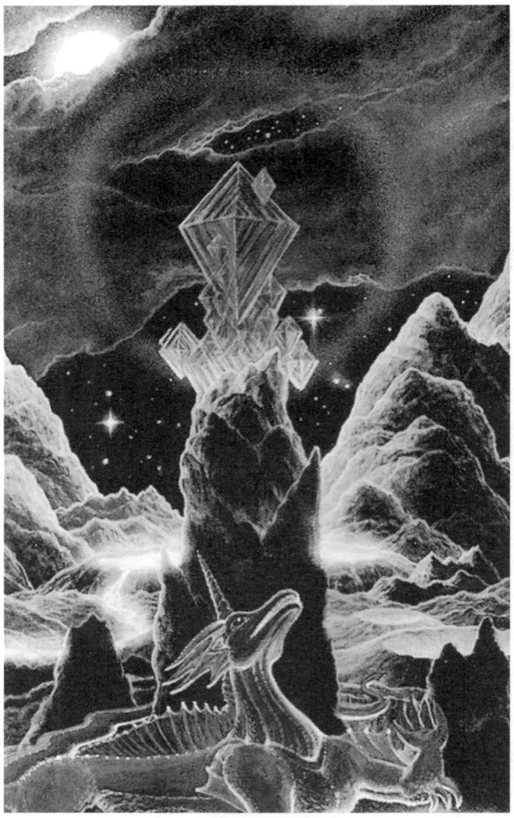

**AD 2085.** Many bizarre alien religions discovered on other planets (P. Nicholls 1982).

2085 Alien religion (religion of extraterrestrials, very popular theme of science fiction) found to take many bizarre forms: worship of sentient crystals, worship of intelligent polished black monoliths, etc.
2085 Holy Bible available translated into all 13,000 human languages, in numerous forms: print, comics, audio, signed, Braille, video, drama, pictodrama, psychodrama, holographic, telephonic, and computerized forms; with instant holographic commentary by galaxy of scholars, Bible teachers and preachers from throughout history.
2085 Biggest earthquake ever recorded devastates Japan, breaks Honshu in two, blasts Shikoku apart, killing 15 million; most Japanese emigrate worldwide to form a global technological diaspora.
2090 Church of the Martyrs: on one scenario, ruthless 80-year persecution by world government reaches climax, decimates global Christianity, reduces churches to a tiny minority, then liquidates all churches, which thus follow their Master to final execution and martyrdom.
2090 Mass global transportation systems, with zero energy loss, in operation: (a) through Earth in vacuum tubes; superspeed floater vehicles travelling at 7 miles a second, 39 minutes from one side of Earth to the other; and (b) into space, either using balloon-borne floater guideways, or space elevators riding up on superstrength cable.
2090 Military expenditures, 10% of world income in 1980, fall to 2% by 2090, eventually to 1% by 2200 and to 0.1% by 2500.
2090 Military arsenals include ultra-sophisticated weaponry: antimatter beams, laser rays, bullets near speed of light.
2090 Vast volumes of galactic space regularly monitored by remote sensing instead of by direct patrolling.
2090 First manned starship sent to nearby stars within 40 light-years known to have planets; interstellar manned flight within 1% of speed of light achieved, using ion drive, carbon-dioxide laser, composite optics, immensely potent energy source—reaction of matter with antimatter. (A.C. Clarke, G.K. O'Neill).
2090 Self-reproducing replicator factories, replicating exact copies of original machines/electronics/cybernetics; by 2380, up to any complexity reproducible within 10 years.
2090 New-style religions and mystical nature cults arise opposing biotechnology.
2090 Satellite solar power collection system ('Sun Ring') begins operation, by 2100 supplies 65% all energy needs on Earth.
2090 Most high-demand sects, cults, and religions have been rejected in favor of no-demand faiths; most are pantheist, neopagan, nature-love, and New Age groups and have long since merged in the World Soul Movement.
2090 Large-scale burning of fossil fuels is resumed to replace carbon dioxide mined from the air.
2092 Hinduism and Buddhism become sizeable and respectable religions in the Western world.
2095 Superpowers, faced by omniscient presence of alien beings of vastly superior technology, agree to abandon war and destroy all armaments.
2095 Genetic Initiative, to redesign the human race including program of raising intelligence by gene surgery, also cerebral enhancement, legislated by People's Congress; by 2147, 10 million children transformed by pre-natal surgery, creating a new human type, Homo Sapiens Altior.
2095 Workers: 3% are in agriculture, 6% factory and mine supervision, 15% technical consulting, 5% managerial consulting, 11% health and medicine, 21% public services, 7% personal services, 5% arts and letters, 8% research, 19% education. (Wagar 1989:182).
2095 Futures studies now known as prognostics; prognosticians chart and weigh alternative futures.
2095 Few people in world can read or bother to read; school children have become ignorant of Bible; theology has become a dying art.
2095 Development of true space drive, propulsion system reacting against structure of spacetime, permitting velocities close to that of light.
2100 Climate changes: land temperatures 6° C higher than in 2000, coastal flooding imperils 300 millions.

## THE DISTANT FUTURE (beyond 21st century AD)

2101 **Global status of Christianity:** 68.9 generations after Christ, world is 35.4% Christians (75% of them being Non-Whites), 81.6% evangelized; with printed and interactive scriptures available in all 13,000 languages.
2101 World census reveals 60% of adults live alone most of the time, 45% live with sex partner without contract and lasting 3 years on average, 20% opt for legalized alternatives (5-year marriage, group marriage); 2150, extinction of marriage as an institution.
2101 Women are in power everywhere including in all churches and denominations.
2101 90% of world's population reside in urban centers.

### *A new Dark Age begins*

2101 World population reaches a peak of 8,250 million, then starts to decline. (C. McEvedy & R. Jones scenario).
2101 World becomes either high-technology, ample-energy utopia, or a low-technology, overcrowded, energy-poor dystopia.
2101 First space arks begin to be made from hollowed-out asteroids.
2101 Some 10,000 orbiting space colonies exist around Earth; 100 million to 2 billion permanent population, including more USA citizens than remain in USA; after 5 generations their cultures draw apart even to mutual linguistic unintelligibility.
2101 Vast dispersion of human race into colonies across Galaxy makes humankind invulnerable to any single future disaster.
2101 Decline of industrial espionage, software sabotage, and computer crime, due to proficiency and omnipresence of police forces.
2101 A new Age of Barbarism arises, with world ground underfoot by war, religious fanaticism, neo-Islamic domination, terror, and Antichrist, for 2 centuries before final advent of the Golden Millennium in AD 2300. (Nostradamus).
2101 Cities of over 100 million inhabitants built, completely 3-dimensional and soundproofed, with varieties of transport on many levels; eventually cities each with over 1 billion residents, each with hundreds of thousands of museums, theaters, aquatic centers, recreation centers, universities, libraries, research institutes.
2101 Global dictatorship established under guise of a religious cult, the Prophets; a theocracy enforced by watchful 'Angels of the Lord'. (R. Heinlein, *Revolt in 2100,* 1940).
2102 Manufacture of androids: artificially-produced human creatures made out of organic materials.
2102 Immense macro-engineering projects arise: space elevators (skyhook), with 100-ton cars climbing cable at 3,700 miles per hour for 22,300 miles to satellite; 150-foot plastic pipe diverts Rhone river under Mediterranean to irrigate North African desert; shipment of Antarctic icebergs to Sahara desert.
2102 World's population rises to 10,185 million (Africa 2.5 billion, Latin America 1.3 billion, South Asia 3 billion, East Asia 1.8 billion, Northern America 400 million, Europe (stabilized since 2050) at 500 million. (UN projections 1984).
2102 'Blade runners' (replicant-killers) widely employed to kill or 'retire' renegade Nexus-6 replicants (4-year-life androids). (Movie 'Blade Runner', 1982).
2109 Sabbatical Law takes effect worldwide, guaranteeing all workers 12 months of educational leave every 7 years; soon adult citizens devote 85% of work time to education.
2110 Whole world now follows essentially a planned economy, due to proliferating UN agencies.
2110 Global sea-farming: seaweed becomes one of world's major food crops; 2130, Pacific coast of South America hosts long chain of kelp farms; vast regions of oceans sown with enriched plankton harvested by huge factory ships; 2180, whole ocean industry under UN control.
2110 Transition to zero population growth worldwide finally completed; all medical care, schooling, electrical

power, transportation free of charge, but no private vehicles allowed; no welfare since all adults earn 75% standard personal income whether they work or not.

2111 Resettlement of Mars colony, destroyed in chemical accident 4 years later, repopulated; by 2140, 20,000 inhabitants (mostly scientists and engineers); several hundred other space habitats with total population 5 million.

2112 'Albert Einstein', first faster-than-light starship, departs on exploratory mission to 10 star systems. (L.S. Wolfe & R.L. Wysack's scenario).

2120 Spacetorium, an orbiting clinic, established in space where 900 ultra-wealthy geriatrics with heart and degenerative problems can retire.

2120 Rising ocean levels finally destroy Shanghai, one of world's greatest trading cities.

2120 Fission-to-fusion drive in service for space travel.

2129 Small fleet of interstellar drones leaves Sun Ring to explore Alpha Centauri and other star systems at 7.5% speed of light (report expected back in 2258).

2130 Starship drives include (a) nuclear ion-drive, (b) propulsion by pressure of light, (c) pulsed fusion-bomb explosions at 250 per second, (d) Bussard ramscoop starship (designed in 1960), (e) antimatter/photon drive; at acceleration of 1 Earth gravity, ship reaches center of our Galaxy in 20 years (ship time) and any point in Universe within one lifetime; use of hyperspace and time warps developed.

2140 Federation of Galactic Civilizations proposed but comes to nothing.

2150 Widespread development of extrasensory perception (ESP), telepathy, telekinesis, teleportation (instant communication and transport), clairvoyance, precognition, remote viewing.

2150 Minute computer (size of a pinhead) stores for instant retrieval every word in every book entire human race has ever published.

2150 Universal use of synthetic foods.

2150 Free mass passenger transport provided universally: not only within large cities, but also globally and extraterrestrially.

2150 First manned long-distance starship leaves Earth for stars beyond 40 light-years distant, seeking any planets of theirs; millions of humans subsequently are transported across interstellar space.

2153 Successful tests of matter-antimatter blender; 2163, installed in spacecraft propulsion system.

2160 Definitive, permanent and universal cures finally achieved for cancer, aging, and all other human ailments; with bionic aid, man becomes virtually immortal either in same body or in succession of bodies; final end, after previous 2 billion years of evolution of life, of programmed death and also sexual reproduction to replace deaths.

2162 Formation of the Interstellar Expeditionary Service.

2166 Departure of pioneer interstellar expeditionary ship, with crew of 200 aboard; 2178, return from Alpha Centauri, reporting exploration of planet Elysium.

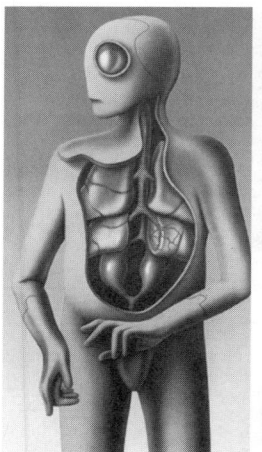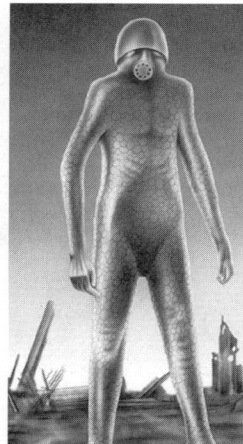

**AD 2170.** New human species engineered for (*left*) life unclothed in space, or (*right*) total warfare (B. Stableford).

2170 Several varieties of humans exist: those with prosthetic limbs or bodies, robots run by disembodied human brains, extraterrestrial humans, clones, cyborgs, androids, wholly artificial humanoids, replicants, mutants, et alii.

2170 Non-urgent flight including freight shifts to ubiquitous airships affordable by even poorest countries; widespread use in agriculture, reclaiming deserts et alia.

## AGE OF RECOVERY, AD 2175-2400

2175 Population of Earth 15 billion, gross world product US$300 trillion, per capita income $20,000 (at 1980 values).

2180 Human beings are everywhere numerous, rich, and in control of forces of nature; by contrast in AD 1780 human beings were relatively few, poor, and at mercy of forces of nature.

2180 UN's Land Use Committee attempts to turn entire world into a planned Garden of Eden, but thwarted by national jealousies.

2188 Use of hibertubes for forward time travel.

2189 Mind-net technique attempted with human volunteer; 2193 first successful human mind transfer.

2190 North American Church of Gaia (NorA ChuGa) continues to dictate ethics and intervene on all ecological matters.

2190 Explosive growth of cryonics corporations begins; 2210, over 10,000 persons 'frozen down'; 2214, lotteries offering treatment a huge success; 2230, 30,000 a year frozen down; 2244, massive electrical power failure in USA kills most off; cryonics industry finally collapses.

2200 Post-holocaust life on Earth now stabilized with, on minidemographic scenario, 2 billion population, homogeneous, largely self-supporting, no energy shortage, limited technology.

2200 On mediodemographic scenario, world population now 25 billion (or even as high as 75 billion in mile-high high-rise blocks, orbiting colonies and undersea city habitats), according to technological-social optimism scenario; world now in quaternary postindustrial phase, with all primary and secondary activities fully automated; many people in tertiary activities (research, industrial planning, operating the single world government, medicine, education).

2200 On maxidemographic scenario, population expands to 1,000 billion, crammed into 100,000 cities of 10 million people each, with thousand-storey tower blocks each housing a million people. (J. Blish & N.L. Knight, *A torrent of faces*, 1967).

2200 30% of humanity now lives in orbiting space colonies.

2200 Third interstellar expeditionary ship, returning from Sirius and Procyon, reports major archeological discoveries on planet circling companion star of Procyon.

2210 Computers designed and built with sense of identity, of self, of consciousness, self-designing, self-programming, self-maintaining, and self-replicating.

2210 Disembodied human brains function at center of machines, computers, vehicles, factories, spaceships.

2217 Space explorers from Earth encounter first spaceship of an alien species.

2220 First ectogenetic baby born from artificial womb; by 2300, 20,000 ectogenetic births in USA alone; 2302, Crusade for Moral Rearmament launched against ectogenesis.

2223 UN's Council of Justice set up; 2236, publishes its first Code of Rights.

2245 Deadly Sealed Laboratory in Antarctica, producing lethal micro-organisms in genetic research, relocated out in space.

2248 First successful experiments in large-scale human total rejuvenation.

2250 Americanized world state founded (First Men, on O. Stapledon's 1930 scenario); lasts until 6250, becoming rigidly stratified and regimented; power failure, breakdown of law and order, succeeded by Dark Age of semi-barbarism for 10,000 years; new civilization arises, destroyed by nuclear chain reaction.

2250 High Frontier (space colonization) makes comeback after 300 years' procrastination; 2285, O'Neill-I opened as first residential microworld, for 15,000 people; future of industry gets under way in space with specialist industrial microworlds; 2350, first lunar mass-driver (electromagnetic cannon on Moon accelerating buckets to escape velocity).

2250 Rapid growth of new mysticism and new monasticism.

2250 Instant travel anywhere, and astral travel anywhere, become both now commonplace.

2271 UN passes resolution enforcing universal sterilization to control population explosion; Ireland and Italy refuse, so are flooded with fanatical immigrants.

2275 Von Neumann machines (VNMs) or self-reproducing robot probes are dispatched beyond Solar System, mapping Universe and producing growing cloud of VNMs throughout space.

2282 SAP (solid artificial photosynthesis) results in colossal food-yields from restricted areas of land.

2285 Mauritania offers sanctuary to rival Roman papacy (conservative, anti-sterilization), which then builds headquarters at Kiffa, 300 miles inland in Sahara desert.

2289 Earth humans' first contact with an alien race, the Vegans; 2310, first interstellar war.

2291 Earth and 2 alien civilizations form Galactic Association of Intelligent Life.

2293 World divided into 3 distinct communities: Eternals, who rule; Brutals, poverty-stricken peons who worship a giant stone god, Zardoz; and Exterminators, barbarians trained by Eternals to restrict Brutals by killings and slavery. (J. Boorman's film 'Zardoz', 1974).

2300 Easily reachable coal reserves of world now all used up.

2300 Advent of Golden Millennium, on Nostradamus' predictions.

2300 Human fax invented: entire contents of a human brain are downloaded by computer and broadcast to a robot in a remote star system.

2305 Earth under complete control of a debased religion using science and psychology to keep man in subjection; rebellion comes via underground satanic cult with witches and warlocks. (F. Leiber, *Gather, Darkness*, 1943).

2310 First successful human analogues (artificial humans, sentient humanoids); 2325, wave of luddite or mechanophobic paranoia sweeps world as people

smash robots, computers, androids.

2310 Personal contact easier to avoid then ever before in history; people program electronic analogues of themselves to handle routine contacts.

2316 US Maglev Subway links east coast to west, with cars running in elevated transparent tubes floating on web of electromagnetism.

2350 A file on every known person in Galaxy exists in every starship's data bank.

2350 Universal immunization available; sophisticated cancer treatments available to half world's population; rejuvenation available only to the rich.

2350 Underwater acqua-cities, time travel, global police.

2355 World 95% urbanized and industrialized with all industries organized as monopolies.

2360 Humans now live dispersed in microworlds across Solar System.

2364 Totalitarian coup by admiral Hrunta who proclaims self emperor of all colonies; 3089, assassinated after 725 years of arbitrary personal rule. (J. Blish, *Cities in flight*, 1962).

2367 Tetroli disaster: first deaths of a microworld's entire complement: 615 perish in bacterial outbreak.

2380 Automation results in self-replicating devices of great complexity capable of self-reproduction, reproducing any apparatus no matter how complex, without human intervention, in under 10 years.

## AGE OF TRANSFORMATION, AD 2400-2650

2390 Humans have now discovered and colonized 8 planets within 78 light-years of Earth; outward migration continues across Galaxy's 100,000 light-year diameter.

2390 World population nearly homogenized into a single race (neo-Mongoloid) with a single culture and language (25th-century English); entire world urbanized, industrialized, homogenized, wired as a single global village.

2400 Aggregate households (6 adults and 3 children) replace nuclear family and become widespread, and by 2500 become the norm; by 2650, old-style 'family life' and biological parenthood abandoned worldwide except in space microworlds.

2400 Medical advances include repair of brain damage, regeneration of severed limbs, and regular body-scanning of entire populations in Western world (but only 1 in 10,000 in Third World).

2419 Date of Armageddon battle as postulated in original Buck Rogers stories and scenarios. (P.F. Nowlan, *Armageddon 2419 A.D.*, published 1928-29).

2425 As predicted since origin of Buddhism, a great war erupts with Buddhist forces based on Shambala defeating Muslims; Buddhism flourishes once more until decline and sudden and cataclysmic extinction in AD 4621.

2433 Ceres, largest asteroid of the Belt (760 km radius), cracked (blown apart) by engineers to provide $10^{18}$ tons of valuable mass (metals, ores); mass and energy now everywhere the key to space.

2460 Personality analogue transfer (PAT): people in distant space communicate with Earth via updated personality analogue constructs of themselves on Earth, who can converse with Earthdwellers with no time lag.

2465 Jupiter Bridge shuttle: fleets of robot shuttle-scoops transfer mass from Jupiter to moon Ganymede and its microworlds, making them refuelling bases for transJovian travellers.

2482 All world's nations merge into 12 large superstates (including North American Nation), governed by social scientists, under World Federal Union (world government) with world capital in Honolulu, using new language Voca scientifically designed to be easily teachable and learnable.

2485 Humans now diversified into 5 distinct species: (1) Homo Sapiens, or sapients, the 'ordinary humans' or 'normals'; (2) by 2485, merpeople as first radically modified humans, with gills, flippers etc; (3) by 2505, space-adapted humans (fabers, or ETs) with spaceships manned entirely by ETs in regular service by 2528, and nearly 3,000 ETs in Solar System by 2600; (4) by 2581, life-extended humans (emortals, or ZTs) interbreed successfully and thus become a new species; (5) by 2700, starpeople (emortal fabers) with further species being developed.

2490 With one trillion people living spread out across the Solar System, humans begin starship explorations into Galaxy beyond; meanwhile robots transform planet Mercury into giant solar-power station, beaming microwave energy throughout Solar System; Moon has become a mining and construction center.

2500 800-year decline of scientific profession, from overinflated novelty alone able to save the world, to more modest role in society: from AD 1740 to 1965, 90% of all scientists who ever lived were alive; by AD 2200, 45%; AD 2500, 18%; thereafter, further decline.

2500 Roofing-in of whole Earth as in effect a single several-mile-high tower block, housing around 400 billion people, fed either by artificial production or from extraterrestrial sources.

2510 Instantaneous teleportation now normal: all transport obsolete since people travel instantly by mind alone. (A. Bester's novel *The stars my destination*, 1956).

2512 Massive experimental manned ramjet starliner 'T.E. Lawrence' (6,000 feet long, with hydrogen funnel propulsion) travels around Sun and returns with more fuel than it began with.

2520 Daedalus-class robot starprobes, weighing 50,000 tons at departure, routinely make one-way exploratory trips to nearer stars.

2530 World rulers use genetic engineering to perpetuate society stratified by intelligence and physique; scheduled sexual orgies substitute for both marriage and religion. (Aldous Huxley's scenario, *Brave New World*, 1931).

2530 Whole ecosystems of genetically-engineered species assembled (Hanging Gardens of New Babylon, giant insect islands); genetic scientists recreate living monster dinosaurs by cloning from fossilized bones of extinct species, and place them in tropical neosaurian game parks; also herds of woolly mammoths for commercial meat industry.

2550 Laser lightsails in use: 60 starships without main engines, each with 1000-km sail driven at half lightspeed across space by light from 10 laser stations in close orbit around Sun.

2565 Interstellar ramjet 'Columbus', an entire microworld powered by cold-fusion torch using galactic hydrogen clouds for fuel, becomes first manned vehicle to orbit a star, averaging 20% of lightspeed; time of trip, 30 years; numerous microworlds established around Sirius and other stars; interstellar trade begins and flourishes.

2630 Gigantic spaceships or space arks begin to leave Earth on mission of 'zygotic evangelism': supermicroworlds each peopled by thousands of space-adapted humans, each cruising forever on its funneldrive at near-lightspeed, carrying (1) millions of frozen zygotes (life-building information in DNA coils), and (2) rest of entire human knowledge in its computer banks; also (3) Christian teams with full biblical and other materials.

## CREATION OF THE NEW WORLD, AD 2650-3000

2639 Antarctica becomes first genuinely international territory; 2650, Amundsen City built there as UN headquarters; whole continent and its resources rapidly developed.

2650 Life-extension technology available to every living person, through rejuvenation (NAR, nucleic acid renewal) or engineered longevity (Zaman transformation, ZT); all political power passes to rejuvenates, i.e. the old inherit the world; by 2700, over 99% of UN Council Chamber seats are occupied by NAR rejuvenates, and by 2950 by emortals (ZTs).

2650 UN decides all human embryos everywhere have right to engineered longevity free of charge.

2650 Direct brain linkups, body-part warehouses.

2700 Very little now proves to be impossible; almost everything is now practicable: e.g. faster-than-light travel, instantaneous matter transmission (teleportation), time travel, personality and memory transfer between humans, widespread telepathic communication.

2750 Dominant religion still Christianity, but dominant philosophy is now neo-Stoicism, fragmented into rival schisms and cults.

2750 Multi-planet communication established and now commonplace.

2800 Totality of human knowledge readily and instantly available to all human beings; life far more complex than in 20th century; life spans up to 900 years; no language barriers.

2800 World population restabilizes, at 2.5 billion, with global average life expectancy at birth of 180 years.

2800 Some 500 self-sufficient human communities live out in Solar System; by 2900, some 2,000, with 200 independent microworlds (population 100,000 starpeople) en route to other stars, and a dozen already arrived.

2850 Growth of science encompasses all paraconcepts as realities; space folding enables contact with any part of Universe.

2900 More human beings live in space than on Earth.

2967 Robot probe from Earth intercepted by alien sentients 75 light-years from Earth.

## THE FAR DISTANT FUTURE (beyond 30th century AD)

3000 Human species radiates out into many sub-species and subcultures alien to each other; telepathy and shared consciousness replace individuality; distinction between humans and other species blurs, with many different genetically engineered life forms derived from human and non-human stock; humans spread into diverse environments including cyberspace and sub-universes inside computer simulations.

3001 Interstellar distances finally recognized as too great to sustain any meaningful galactic communications or communities; no viable galactic empires or federations therefore possible; on alternative scenarios, however, humans discover flight at 30,000 times speed of light, quantum drives, and then instantaneous travel throughout Universe via black and white holes.

3001 Construction of a Dyson sphere (built from disassembly of gas giant planet Jupiter) enclosing everything within Earth's solar orbit (186 million miles diameter with Sun at center), in order to (1) gather up all the Sun's energy, and (2) provide living space for a million Earths with 400 trillion humans; creates vast civilization unique in history; but massive engineering know-how required also carries enormous potential for blackmail, evil, warfare and chaos.

3001 Extraterrestrial end scenario: human race wipes itself out by inept handling of alien (extraterrestrial) technology.

3001 Sudden, final disappearance of black alien megamonoliths dominating Jupiter, Earth, Moon, and the Solar System for past 4 million years. (A. C. Clarke's *3001: the final odyssey*, last of his series entitled *2001, 2010, 2060).*

3450 Geodynamics of superspace discovered; scientists find out inconceivably dense yet bubbling, foamlike structure of superspace: every empty space or vacuum contains massive infernos of energies and seething violence; harnessing these enormous subatomic quantum fluctuations leads to invention of ultimate propellant, the quantum drive; mankind now free to roam the Universe for ever. (A.C. Clarke 1986).

3500 Cosmic collision scenario: large astral body crashes into Earth catastrophically; previously, 500 meteorites crash annually, one asteroid collides every 1,000 years, and one comet (out of 100 billion circling the Sun) strikes Earth every 100,000 years.

**AD 3781.** After nuclear holocaust, monks leave Earth for Alpha Centauri.

3781 Monks of Order of Leibowitz, who have preserved knowledge through Dark Ages after 20th-century World War III nuclear holocaust, eventually see civilization rebuilt by AD 3100 to point where, again, a new industrial-scientific age culminates by AD 3781 in imminent nuclear World War IV; just before outbreak, discredited Order launches an ecclesiastical starship through which Church of New Rome transfers authority of St Peter from Earth to Alpha Centauri. (W.M. Miller's novel, *A canticle for Leibowitz*, 1960).

3797 End of world in cosmic explosion (as envisioned by Nostradamus as finale of his prophecies).

3936 End of world as predicted by Spanish Dominican monk Vincent Ferrer (c1350-1419).

4000 Human race is still Homo Sapiens Sapiens but has become alien by 1980 standards: communication and mutual understanding with humans of 1980 probably would be very difficult; no race problem since only one race (Mongoloid, tan); lifespans average several thousand years, with large numbers taking immortality drug or injection to become immortal at any particular age they wish.

## GOD BEGINS HIS NEW CREATION

4000 Eco-catastrophe as Earth's magnetic field (which lost 15% of its strength from AD 1670-2000) finally deteriorates to point of failure to ward off incoming radiation.

4100 Ice Age scenario: after interglacial (mild period) of 15,000 years, Earth enters new ice age, with famine reducing population from 10 billion to 1 billion, and freezing the rest to death by AD 12,000.

4104 Cosmos ends in stupendous collision of matter and antimatter, after which new Universe is created. (J. Blish's tetralogy *Cities in flight*, 1955-62).

4500 Cosmic rays scenario: Earth's magnetic field declines gradually to zero leaving humans unprotected for 500 years from cosmic radiation; a giant solar flare from Sun, or a star within 30 light-years which then explodes as a supernova, destroys Earth by radiation.

4600 Intelligent machines control world after outstripping now extinct creators. (O. Johannesson, *The great computer*, 1966).

4621 Sudden decline and cataclysmic total extinction of worldwide Buddhism as prophesied by the Buddha himself, after 5,100 years as a great world religion.

5000 Instantaneous communicators (superluminal faster-than-light connectors) across Universe include Dirac transmitter, sending messages that can be picked up by any Dirac receiver past, present, or future. (James Blish's scenario, *The Quicunx of Time*, 1973).

5000 Material from planets is used to construct immense spherical floor around Sun enclosing entire Solar System, with area of 160 quintillion ($1.6 \times 10^{20}$) square miles, capable of supporting human population of up to one septillion ($10^{24}$) persons.

5000 Supercivilizations are installed on rigid shells around black holes, extracting energy from hole by space-rubbish shuttle.

**AD 5000.** A spaceship approaches a black hole as a power source (A. McKie).

5000 Black holes prove to be time machines, wormholes or gravity tunnels providing a kind of instantaneous interstellar and intergalactic subway, emerging in remote parts of space-time through white holes (quasars); or even star gates out of this Cosmos and into totally different cosmoses.

6000 Intergalactic space-travel and time-travel underway using space and time machine: men construct a spinning or rotating black hole just outside Solar System, which instantaneously transports men and matter across millions of light-years, or across millions of years in time, spewing them out through white holes. (A. Berry's scenario, *The Iron Sun*, 1979).

6250 World supplies of energy finally fail; long Dark Ages of savagery begin, with scores of major disasters. (W.O. Stapledon's epic chronicle of future history, *Last and First Men*, 1930).

8000 Asteroidal collision scenario: large asteroid Ceres collides with Earth with 12,000 billion megatons impact energy, sterilizes Earth and shifts its orbit significantly.

9500 Planet Jupiter (a star that failed) supports human colonies in great balloon cities permanently floating in upper atmosphere.

10,000 Human race begins to evolve from Homo Sapiens Sapiens into a more advanced species Homo Noeticus Noeticus (Pan-Intellectual Man); evolution of humanity into a Galaxy-wide and continuously-growing cosmic Overmind.

10,150 Commission of Ecumenical Translators attempts to unite peoples of Universe, results in galactic Holy War. (F. Herbert, *Dune*, 1965).

12,000 Post-catastrophe scenario: 10,000 years after nuclear holocaust, sparsely-populated pastoral utopian matriarchy exists on Earth, marked by communal living, personal longevity, eugenics and superintelligent domestic animals. (W.H. Hudson's scenario, *A Crystal Age*, 1887).

20,000 Rise of pantropy, i.e. spread of human race throughout Galaxy, invading countless different environments by adapting mankind genetically to suit new conditions (life under sea, in flight, or on Mars, etc).

30,000 Supercivilizations move out to colonize whole galaxies at rate of 10 million years a galaxy; intergalactic travellers learn to utilize space warps and time warps (irregularities in space-time continuum) to traverse immense distances involved.

31,920 End of time as envisaged in G.B. Shaw's futurist drama *Back to Methuselah*, expounding creative evolution from Garden of Eden to end of world.

50,000 Exploding Sun scenario: a hostile alien civilization deliberately triggers solar cataclysm, Sun explodes as nova, flaring up in millionfold increase of brightness and heat to burn all Earthly life and vaporize the planet.

100,000 New Homo species, interstellar man (Homo Superior), evolves and outnumbers Homo Sapiens populations of Earth and its immediate colonies.

200,000 Mining of heaviest elements in Sun, by large magnetohydrodynamic machines built from Mercurian ores, provides Earth with unlimited energy for 300 million years, at the same time extending natural life of Sun from 8 billion years to 20 trillion years.

802,701 Human race degenerates by devolution into racial decadence with 2 separate races, the childish Eloi and the troglodyte cannibalistic Morlocks; humanity finally proves to be just another of Nature's unlucky failures; time travellers visiting them then move on to visit far future's last days of humanity and Earth. (H.G. Wells' scenario, *The Time Machine,* 1895).

## THE MEGAFUTURE (after AD 1 million)

1 million   Mankind evolves to Homo Galacticus: great unemotional intelligences, large-headed beings retaining no bodily parts except hands, 'floating in vats of amber nutritive fluid', doing little but think; a global brotherhood of enlightened supermen living in strongholds deep inside Earth whose surface is thickly mantled with ice at absolute zero temperature. (H.G. Wells' scenario, 'The Man of the Year Million', 1893).

2 million   Point Omega finally reached and consummated (as envisaged by Teilhard de Chardin), with Christ as Cosmocrat and perfector of human evolution, eventually (by AD 4 billion) with one decillion ($10^{33}$) believers.

2 million   Humanity completes its colonizing spread across the Galaxy (Milky Way), settling it in 2 million years.

3 million   Man's body height evolves to some 8 feet tall; tongue, palate and larynx increase in size to handle rapid complex speech.

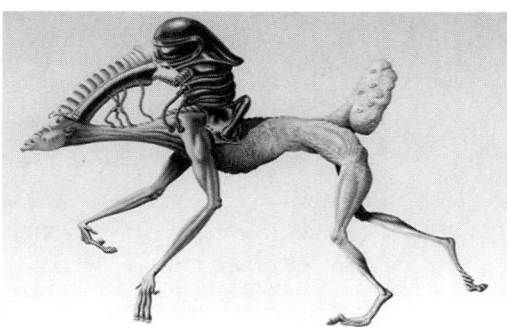

**AD 10 million.** Genetically-engineered Homo controls Homo workhorse by telepathy (D. Dixon 1990).

10 million   Superintelligent Second Men evolve, plagued by cloud-intelligences from Mars, then gradually stagnate. (W.O. Stapledon 1930).

15 million   Next scheduled mass collisions of Earth with comets/asteroids (every 26 million years, last being in BC 11 million), resulting in mass extinction of majority of remaining species including genus Homo.

40 million   Third Men evolve, midgets with massive ears, music as their religion, biogenetic control; then Fourth Men (Great Brains many feet across), who then design Fifth Men (huge intellectuals who migrate temporarily to Venus); AD 100 million, Sixth Men evolve, a barbarous throwback, also on Venus; AD 300 million, Seventh Men evolve: pygmy flying men uninterested in science or material progress. (W.O. Stapledon 1930).

100 million   Sun cools past point where it is visible from Earth, whose surface is too cold to support life; last human beings live 100 miles below surface in Pyramid (8-mile-high metal scientific marvel), with monsters outside in volcanic fireholes. (W.H. Hodgson's scenario *The night land*, 1912).

400 million   Eighth Men evolve, physically larger; science and progress resumed; they escape collision between Sun and gas cloud by migrating to planet Neptune; Ninth Men evolve as dwarfs, developed to survive on Pluto, but become degenerate and collapse. (W.O. Stapledon 1930).

500 million   Human race evolves into wealthy, powerful, coordinated universal society reaching across Galaxy and also across Universe; humans finally discover ultimate secrets of the Cosmos.

500 million   Emergence of Sixth Level of Evolution: galactic mind, i.e. galactic consciousness, with transition to a galactic superorganism; inter-Gaian interaction and communication reach sufficient complexity and synergy for all 10 billion Gaias (planets with life) in our Galaxy to integrate into a single system, a galactic society of communicating civilizations.

## THE GIGAFUTURE (after AD 1 billion)

1 billion   Sun begins to expand and turns Earth into tropical nightmare, with fantastic array of carnivorous and poisonous jungle plants and insects seizing telepathic control and destroying remaining civilization of devolved greenskinned descendants of Homo Sapiens. (B.W. Aldiss' scenario *Hothouse/The long afternoon of Earth*, 1962).

2 billion   Supernova end scenario: final extinction of human race by supernova, with Last Men (18th race after Homo Sapiens as First Men) as final form of civilized humanity, living on Neptune in virtual Paradise, one trillion strong; telepaths, virtually immortal, group mind. (W.O. Stapledon 1930).

3 billion   Disintegrating Moon scenario: Earth gradually pulls Moon closer, triggering earthquakes, volcanos, tidal waves engulfing continents; when Moon reaches 5,000 miles out, it disintegrates totally into planetary ring bombarding Earth with huge chunks.

4 billion   Final shape of man scenario—Homo Universalis, a non-material being with enormous powers, a sphere of force able to travel instantaneously across Galaxy or Universe at will.

5 billion   Emergence of Seventh or Final Level of Evolution: cosmic mind, i.e. universal consciousness, with all 100 billion galaxies or galactic superorganisms in Universe evolving into one single universal superorganism or being, the perfect Cosmos.

5.6 billion   Advent of next, fifth Buddha, Maitreya (Buddhist scholars vary over correct date, down to AD 560 million or even AD 4621), to be followed later, sequentially, by 995 other Buddhas with decline and then final demise of the Dharma.

6 billion   Sun evolves into luminous red giant with radius reaching planet Mercury; Earth's oceans and atmosphere have long since disappeared in intense heat; most stars very old, Galaxy (and most other galaxies) becoming a graveyard of stars at endpoint of stellar evolution; human race, if not yet extinct, embarks on its last journey.

7 billion   Sudden ice death of Earth scenario: huge alien star appears, loops around Sun, draws Earth off into icy depths of space.

8 billion   Solar end scenario: Sun, gradually expanding over last 13 billion years, engulfs Earth and all its related colonies, then collapses as a degenerate white dwarf and then finally a dead black dwarf.

15 billion   Universe's disorganization or entropy ('anti-information', e.g. decay, rusting, growing old, accumulated rubbish, deaths of stars, black dwarfs, neutron stars, dead hulks, multiple collisions, intergalactic chaos, supermassive black holes) rapidly increases with every energy transfer (2nd Law of Thermodynamics).

### Black holes engulf entire Cosmos

25 billion   Black hole at center of Galaxy (Milky Way) which has been devouring matter and stars for 40 billion years, emitting ever more intense radiation (and reaching a billion miles wide by AD 2000), finally consumes whole of Galaxy; most other galaxies similarly eaten up until all matter has been sucked into a number of gigantic black holes.

50 billion   Period of star formation ends, majority of stars begin to go out, whole Universe gradually becomes a graveyard of stars.

100 billion   After 100 billion ($10^{11}$) years, life and intelligence continue after end of Homo Sapiens (since essential feature of consciousness is not cells or DNA, but structural complexity) in forms of sentient computers, sentient clouds and other vastly complex structures.

## THE TERAFUTURE (after AD 1 trillion)

1 trillion   All stars in Milky Way galaxy become dark remnants; all galaxies now dead and invisible.

$10^{14}$ years   After 100 trillion ($10^{14}$) years, last remaining stars run out of nuclear fuel, contract and collapse under their own weight; all lose their planets through close encounters with other stars.

$10^{17}$ years   Dead stars break up, evaporate and are swallowed by massive black holes (one at center of every galaxy), which then all finally coalesce into one immense supermassive black hole coextensive with the still-expanding Universe.

$10^{18}$ years   Alternative end-time scenarios, after $10^{18}$ years: (1) Universe is open (with insufficient mass to halt expansion of galaxies, which thus continues for ever); or (2) Universe is flat (exactly flat, with just enough mass to halt expansion but not to reverse it), or (3) Universe is closed (with sufficient mass, especially nonluminous mass (cold dark matter) in haloes around galaxies, to halt expansion and reverse it).

## THE ESCHATOFUTURE—1: UNIVERSE IS OPEN

$10^{18}$ years   *The Expansion Heat Death Scenario:* in the eschatofuture or exafuture (after $10^{18}$ years), Universe gradually runs down in energy and temperature, in endless open expansion.

$10^{30}$ years   Some 40% of all matter in Universe with its $10^{80}$ elementary particles (protons, neutrons, electrons) has now totally decayed.

$10^{32}$ years   Life-span of all protons and neutrons ends as they disintegrate and all long-lived matter decays; nothing left in Universe except electrons, positrons, photons, neutrinos and black holes.

$10^{50}$ years   Universe continues expanding for ever; as its heat death approaches, humanity builds its own computer-god which duly creates another universe. (I. Asimov's scenario 'The Last Question', 1956).

$10^{95}$ years   Despite dying Universe, many advanced long-lived civilizations manage to maintain themselves by constructing rigid shells around rotating supermassive black holes and living off their energy until they decay and evaporate after $10^{100}$ (also termed 1 googol) years.

$10^{100}$ year   Final evolutionary heat death of Universe as entropy (disorder or chaos) reaches maximum: disappearance by quantum evaporation of all supermassive black-hole relics of collapsed galaxies, and elimination of all solid matter; lastly, remaining diffuse gas of low-energy particles vanishes, leaving nothing except cold, thin, expanding sea of radiation.

## THE ESCHATOFUTURE—2: UNIVERSE IS FLAT

$10^{18}$ years   *The Motionless Heat Death Scenario:* expansion of Universe slows, gradually comes to a permanent halt, declines toward ultimate heat death as entropy (disorder, chaos) approaches maximum.

$10^{20}$ years   Humans, huddled in space colonies across icy Universe, create new life forms based on plasma (remnants of interstellar gas), resulting in structured, constantly evolving plasmoid society and plasmoid creatures each living $10^{15}$ years in Universe's freezing night, using energy from black holes.

$10^{31}$ years   Final civilization: before plasmoid society disintegrates as protons decay, it creates enormously sluggish creatures of new kind of atom, positronium (orbiting electron and positron), forming its own vastly more diffuse plasma, powered by electron-positron antimatter clashes.

$10^{99}$ years   Space temperature only $10^{-60}$ degrees above absolute zero in stationary and motionless Universe.

$10^{100}$ years   Photons (light from earlier epochs) as only remaining entities in motion continue to expand, carrying the entire record of the Universe, galaxies, humanity and all creation, across limitless reaches of empty space.

## THE ESCHATOFUTURE—3: UNIVERSE IS CLOSED

$10^{25}$ years   *The Big Crunch or Big Squeeze Scenario:* at its maximum expansion, Universe is made up of dead stars, supermassive black-hole remnants of collapsed galaxies, and low-energy particles; gravity of Universe, especially nonluminous matter (over 99% of all matter), halts expansion and reverses it; dead stars begin to burn up and explode.

$10^{25}$ years   After expansion of Universe is halted and recession of galactic systems reversed, Universe begins to collapse rapidly and catastrophically.

$10^{32}$ years   A million years before the Big Crunch, photons dissociate interstellar hydrogen atoms into electrons and protons; one year before, stars break up; supermassive black holes swallow up matter and radiation; 3 minutes before, black holes coalesce, Universe becomes a single monster supermassive black hole.

$10^{32}$ years   The Big Crunch: in final collapse of Universe, at first galaxies then stars and lastly atoms, particles and quarks are crushed into each other in one overwhelming cataclysmic inferno, with collapsing Cosmos approaching a singularity of infinite density and temperature and reverting to primal chaos of original cosmic explosion and fireball, the primordial monobloc.

## GOD CREATES SUCCESSIVE UNIVERSES

After final collapse of our contracting Universe, a new and mightier Big Bang occurs and a totally new, more immense universe commences its vastly faster expansion; and ditto, in due course, for an endless sequence of progressively vaster universes. (Landsberg-Park model of universe bigger with each succeeding bounce).

## THE ESCHATOFUTURE—4: UNIVERSE IS EXPLODING

$10^{100}$ years   *The Eternally Accelerating Expansion Scenario:* vacuum energy, the antigravity energy existing everywhere in empty space, continues for ever to override gravity of all matter whether luminous or dark, creates titanically accelerating explosion of entire Universe, continuing outwards eternally for ever.

## GOD CREATES INFINITE PARALLEL UNIVERSES

Numerous cycles or bounces: our present Universe, which is only one in the current total of $10^{89}$ existing parallel universes, is no more than 100 bounces from cycle which lasted just long enough to create a single generation of stars.

Our Universe and its successors turn out to be only one bubble immersed in a froth of a billion trillion parallel sequences of infinitely evolving cyclic universes in superspace, each eternally expanding at the speed of light; awesome might, majesty, dominion, power, and glory of God the Almighty as Creator finally fully unveiled.

Part 3

# GEOCOMMISSION

Christ's Great Commission
from AD 33 to AD 2001

*The old command of Christ echoes down the long aisles of the ages, Evangelize!*
—A.T. Pierson, missiologist, *The New Acts of the Apostles*, 1898

*By evangelism is meant obedience to the Great Commission.*
—K. S. Latourette, historian, International Missionary Council, 1950

*The Great Commission is truly the most genuine utterance of the Risen Jesus.*
—Karl Barth (1886-1968), Swiss Protestant theologian, 1961

*All disciples stand under the Great Commission of the One Lord.*
—Report of 3rd Assembly, World Council of Churches, New Delhi 1961

Part 3 describes the origin of the church and its mission as a result of Christ's direct commission to his followers with its twofold commands 'Go into all the world!', and 'Evangelize!'. These complementary mandates are sufficiently concrete to have spawned a vast field of measurements across the centuries, as well as artistic representations. This Part begins a 7-fold analysis that is continued and completed throughout this volume.

# Christ's Great Commission from AD 33 to AD 2001

## TWO MASSIVE PHENOMENA

The Christian world mission is grounded on and springs out of 2 related key concepts or phenomena each based on vast quantities of biblical and current evidence in over 2,600 languages across the world. These 2 phenomena are clearly closely related, but equally clearly each is separate and distinct. These are (1) Christ's Great Commission, and (2) the Greek verb *euangelizo* and its English transliteration 'evangelize'. Wherever the Lordship of Christ is confessed, the Great Commission is rapidly becoming recognized as the most important task of the Christian church. And wherever Christians take seriously their obligation to obey God's commandments, the verb *euangelizo*/'evangelize' can be seen at its best as the imperative 'Evangelize!', namely as a universal command incumbent on every church and on every Christian. With its widespread usage within the Christian scriptures and throughout the Christian world, the original Greek verb *euangelizo* and its English transliteration 'evangelize' must be the richest Christian imperative. Because it epitomizes human responsibility for implementing God's plan for saving the peoples of the world, it remains arguably both the richest and the most important word in the entire Christian vocabulary.

This analysis begins by examining separately each of the 2 phenomena, leading on to how they relate to each other and in fact become a megaphenomenon. This analysis then creates a neologism for it and is terming it "GeoCommission".

## 1. THE GREAT COMMISSION

The first phenomenon to be examined here is centered on the scriptural accounts of Christ's last command on Earth before his Ascension. There is a vast amount to describe and to analyze.

### THE COMMISSION & ITS 7 MANDATES

At the end of his 3-year ministry in Palestine, Christ was betrayed and crucified, followed 3 days later by his resurrection from the dead. Then followed a 40-day period in which he appeared at different times to different followers, sometimes to groups and sometimes one at a time. During that period he commissioned his followers to carry on his work on earth. Six of those occasions are recorded in the New Testament in very specific form and with varying elements and instructions. These accounts are found in: Matthew 28:18-20, Mark 16:15-18, Luke 24:45-49, John 20:21-23, John 21:5-22, Acts 1:4-8. After the final instructions Jesus ascended into heaven. Ten days later on the Feast of Pentecost, the Holy Spirit descended on the disciples and the church was born.

### A variety of descriptive names

The accounts of the life and ministry of Jesus in the Four Gospels contain a large number of personal commissions, charges or commands of varying kinds from Jesus to individual disciples and to groups, instructing them to go out, announce, preach and heal. Early in his ministry in Palestine, he called the Twelve Apostles (Matthew 10:1-42), and later he commissioned the Seventy (Luke 10:1-12). All of these occasions, however, occurred before the Crucifixion and Resurrection of Christ. A special place of prominence is therefore to be accorded to the various commissions Christ then gave during the 40-day period between his Resurrection and Ascension. We read that during this period 'he had given commandment through the Holy Spirit to the apostles whom he had chosen' (Acts 1:2 RSV). Collectively, these have been regarded from the earliest years as a single, final or climactic mandate, imperative or commission.

The total list of all names or titles given to this commission throughout the history of Christianity is shown in Table 3–1, in English arranged alphabetically. The users or promulgators of these terms cover the entire spectrum of organized Christian communions. Thus, to give only 3 examples, the Syrian Orthodox communion speak of 'The Last Commission', the Methodist evangelist and statesman John R. Mott (1900) 'The Great Commission', and pope John Paul II (in his 'Redemptoris Missio', 1991) 'The Universal Commission'.

Of all these, that in widest use in our times as a title is 'The Great Commission'. In this study, the following definition is proposed and used:

> The Great Commission is defined as the sum total of all the imperatives, commands and mandates that the Risen Christ addressed to his followers, disciples and apostles together (corporately, collectively and individually) on all the varied occasions, recorded and unrecorded, during the 40-day period from his Resurrection to his Ascension; these commands and mandates being interpreted in the context of the totality of Christ's teaching before and after this period as recorded in the New Testament writings.

Six times during those 40 days between the Resurrection of Jesus Christ from the dead and his Ascension, as recorded in the New Testament, we read

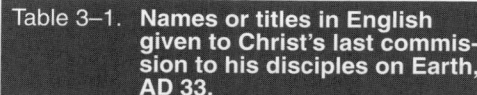

| Table 3–1. | Names or titles in English given to Christ's last commission to his disciples on Earth, AD 33. |
|---|---|

The Apostolic Commission
The Charter for Evangelization
Christ's Apostolic Mandate
Christ's Commission
Christ's Final Command
Christ's Mandate
The Christian Imperative
The Church's Commission
The Church's Mandate
The Commissioning of the Disciple Fellowship
The Divine Command
The Divine Commission
The Final Command
The Final Commission
The Great Command
The Great Commission
The Great Evangelistic Command
The Imperative
The Imperative Commission
The Last Charge
The Last Command
The Last Commission
The Missionary Command
The Missionary Commission
The Missionary Imperative
The Missionary Mandate
The New Commission
The Original Commission
The Royal Commission
The Solemn Command
The Solemn Mandate
The Universal Commission

that Jesus gave a comprehensive charge to his disciples concerning their future mission to the peoples of the world. These occasions, whether regarded as formalized into a single occasion or regarded as a series of parallel teachings at different times over the 40-day period, are the ones which are known to the Christian church as the Great Commission. The church's mandate to evangelize, and its obligation to work for the evangelization of the world, rest on that commission and draw their legitimation and authority from it. Ten days after the Ascension, on the Day of Pentecost the Holy Spirit descended to inaugurate the church and to give it the power necessary to implement its commission of evangelization.

### BIBLICAL ORIGINS

#### Old Testament foreshadowings

As a record of Heilsgeschichte (salvation history), the Old Testament contains several passages which foreshadow Christ's commission to evangelize the world. At the beginning of the first major division of the Jewish scripture, the Law, is recorded God's mandate to the first persons who peopled his world: 'Be fruitful and multiply, and fill the earth and subdue it; and have dominion over . . . every living thing that moves upon the earth' (Genesis 1:28). A similar mandate, 'Be fruitful and multiply', was repeated after the Flood to Noah and his relatives (Genesis 9:1-7). Later, Abram in Haran was given a commission that would benefit the entire world: 'Go from your country . . . to the land that I will show you. And I will make of you a great nation . . . and in you all the families of the earth will be blessed' (Genesis 12:1-3).

In the second major division of the Jewish scriptures, the Prophets, the most explicit statement of God's commission to the old Israel is found in the book of the prophet Isaiah: 'I will give you as a light to the nations, that my salvation may reach to the end of the earth' (Isaiah 49:6).

In the third and last division of the Jewish scriptures, the Psalms (or Writings), God's commission to his people becomes even more explicit. Many expositors of Scripture have found in the Psalms of David

**Title page, first Bible in English (Coverdale/Tyndale), AD 1535.** On this title page is shown (left) Moses receiving the Ten Commandments, centerpiece of the Old Testament, and (right) the Risen Christ giving his Great Commission 'Go into all the World', centerpiece of the New Testament.

## Table 3–2.  Christ's Great Commission analyzed under 7 Mandates.

This table analyzes the words used in the 6 New Testament narratives of Christ's Great Commission given to his followers in AD 33 (Matthew 28:16-20, Mark 16:14-18, Luke 24:36-49, John 20:19-23, John 21:1-22, Acts 1:3-14).

The Commission is first divided into 7 Mandates, and then described below in 8 columns.

Meanings of the 8 columns are as follows:

1. **Mandate imperative.** Lines 1-7 give the Big Seven—the 7 Mandates of the Great Commission—in English Bible usage.
2. **Greek keyword.** The related Greek verbs or derivatives central to the Great Commission narratives are given in lines 1-7.
3. **Usages.** Each Greek word is followed in this column by a figure which is the number of usages of the word, and its immediate cognates (adjectives or nouns), in the Greek New Testament.
4. **Characteristic.** The phrases here describe the differentia of the various Mandates.

5. **Other keywords.** These are keywords (related key nouns) from the Greek or Latin ('L') New Testaments which support or illustrate each Mandate.
6. **Usages.** The first figure gives the number of Greek or Latin New Testament usages of the exact noun opposite it in column 5; the second figure gives the total usages of the word together with its immediate cognates (adjectives, nouns, or verbs).
7. **Key synonyms.** The column lists a small alphabetized selection of examples of the previous column's total of synonyms, given in imperative mood as constituent commands under each Mandate. The 80 specific macrocommands in the Great Commission narratives are set out in Table 23-14.
8. **Facets.** The final column gives the total of all English verbs which are distinct aspects or facets (or synonyms or near-synonyms or part-synonyms) of each of the 7 Mandates.

| MANDATE IMPERATIVE English | KEYWORD NT Greek | Usages | DOMINANT CHARACTERISTIC | OTHER KEYWORDS (related nouns) Greek, Latin (L) | Usages | SYNONYMS Key English synonyms | FACETS English |
|---|---|---|---|---|---|---|---|
| 1 | 2 | 3 | 4 | 5 | 6 | 7 | 8 |
| CONSTITUENT MANDATES: | | | | | | | |
| 1. **Receive!** | labete verb: lambano | 263 | Spirit-dominated | parakletos dynamis pneumatikos exousia | 5/34 120/331 28/413 103/107 | Accompany, Be filled, Breathe, Be present, Follow, Participate, Pneumatize, Pray, Receive power, Stay, Wait | 33 |
| 2. **Go!** | poreuthentes verb: poreuomai | 154 | Person-implemented | apostole missio (L) | 4/255 900 | Act, Contact, Develop, Encounter, Engage, Extend, Go, Help, Impact, Influence, Itinerate, Liberate, Love, Make aware, Occupy, Permeate, Prepare, Reach, Seek, Send, Show Target, Touch, Transmit, Visit | 101 |
| 3. **Witness!** | martyres verb: martyreo | 173 | Unorganized, private | martyria praesencia (L) justitia (L) pax (L) dialogismos | 57/173 120 220 200 14/43 | Be martyred, Be present, Bring, Carry, Confess, Dialogue, Expose, Gossip, Inform, Propagate, Radiate, Report, Say, Share, Shine, Sow, Spread, Talk, Tell, Testify, Witness | 132 |
| 4. **Proclaim!** | keryxate verb: kerysso | 72 | Ordered, public | kerygma apologia therapeia | 8/72 8/18 3/47 | Advertise, Announce, Declare, Demonstrate, Do miracles, Exorcise, Explain, Expound, Give a message, Give opportunity, Heal, Herald, Make listen, Preach, Present, Proclaim, Prove, Publish, Read, Reason, Refute, Saturate, Translate | 85 |
| 5. **Disciple!** | matheteusate verb: matheteuo | 266 | Convert-oriented | paraklesis therismos mathetes | 29/34 13/36 261/266 | Appeal, Catch, Compel, Confront, Conquer, Convert, Convince, Denounce, Disciple, Exhort, Forgive, Give, Harvest, Impart, Implore, Invite, Offer, Persuade, Press, Reap, Retain, Urge, Warn, Win | 128 |
| 6. **Baptize!** | baptizontes verb: baptizo | 111 | Church-oriented | baptismos koinonia ekklesia leitourgeia eucharistia katechumenos | 23/111 19/59 115 6/15 15/54 8 | Affiliate, Baptize, Bless, Build, Catechize, Confirm, Enroll, Feed, Grow, Incorporate, Initiate, Minister, Multiply, Plant, Praise, Sacramentalize, Serve, Tend, Worship | 70 |
| 7. **Train!** | didaskontes verb: didasko | 212 | Ministry-oriented | didache diakonia oikodome | 30/212 34/101 18/59 | Broadcast, Celebrate, Cultivate, Edify, Educate, Follow-up, Instruct, Mobilize, Nurture, Program, Teach, Train | 43 |

a textbook for missionary study circles (see G.T. Manley, *The Gospel in the Psalms: being a study of the commission to evangelize the world as foreshadowed in the Psalms*, 1908).

Taken together, these Old Testament foreshadowings may be seen as a statement of the commissions given to old humanity (Genesis 1:28) and the old Israel (Isaiah 49:6), preparing the way for the Great Commission after Christ's Resurrection as the task given to the new humanity, the new Israel renewed in Christ.

### The 110 commands of the Risen Christ

In the New Testament, 6 distinct accounts are given of the 40-day period between Jesus' Resurrection from the dead and his Ascension into heaven. These are found at the ends of each of the Four Gospels with 2 distinct accounts in the Fourth Gospel, and at the beginning of The Acts of the Apostles. If we examine the narratives of the Forty Days we find that they record some 110 different commands or imperatives, 80 given personally on large-scale occasions in the 6 main narratives by the Risen Christ. The other 30 were more private, personal, individual, local or temporary commands made to individuals or small groups. The bulk of them, however, were the 80 or so which were public, universal and timeless commands made to the Apostles and the church in its entirety.

Of the less public occasions, 9 occur in Matthew's account, 4 in Mark, 4 in Luke, 18 in John, with none in Acts. Eleven commands were mediated through angels to the women at the Empty Tomb, and consist of the imperatives Fear not, Come, See, Go, Tell, Remember. The other private imperatives were given directly by Christ, 2 to the two Marys, 3 to Mary Magdalene alone, 6 to the Apostle Thomas, 5 to the Apostle Peter, and the like. These consist of the imperatives Fear not, Go Tell, See, Handle, Do not hold me, Say, Put, Look, Do not doubt, Believe, Cast the net, Bring, Come, Dine, Feed, Tend, Follow.

The 80 more universal commands are of the greatest interest. They are listed here in Part 23, Table 23-14. We have already defined these commands as constituting, in sum, 'The Great Commission'. Ten occur in Matthew's account, 20 in Mark, 16 in Luke, 24 in John and 10 in Acts. We will shortly demonstrate that the 215 commands can be subdivided into 7 major groups or mandates.

### THE NEW TESTAMENT NARRATIVES

#### Six accounts of the Commission

The promulgation of the Great Commission is unambiguously described 6 times in the New Testament. It clearly took place more than once, on different occasions, in different places, with different audiences, and with differing emphases. The 6 instances occur

as more or less clearcut utterances, reported once at the end of each of the Synoptic Gospels, twice at the end of the Johannine Gospel, and once at the beginning of the Acts of the Apostles. Five of these accounts describe verbal commissionings, and the sixth describes a commissioning under dramatic form as an acted parable. All 6 accounts are located in time after Christ's Resurrection and before his Ascension when the Resurrection appearances of Jesus terminated. Their approximate chronological order is as follows:

1. *John 20:19-23.* This commission was given to 'the disciples' (the Eleven plus others) in Jerusalem in the Upper room on the evening of Easter Day itself (John 20:19). Text of the commission: 'As the Father has sent me, even so I send you. Receive the Holy Spirit. If you forgive the sins of any, they are forgiven; if you retain the sins of any, they are retained'. This mandate says nothing about preaching to the nations, and instead it is very similar to the pre-Crucifixion mandate in Matthew 18:18.

2. *Mark 16:14-18.* This commissioning was given to the Eleven either (a) on the same occasion as John 20:19-23 on the evening of Easter Day (Mark 16:14), or (b) shortly after, or (c) 8 days later (John 20:26), or (d) as forecast (Mark 16:7), in Galilee. Text of the commission: 'Go into all the world and preach the gospel to the whole creation. He who believes and is baptized will be saved; but he who does not believe will be condemned. And these signs will accompany those who believe: in my name they will cast out demons; they will speak in new tongues; they will pick up serpents, and if they drink any deadly thing, it will not hurt them; they will lay their hands on the sick; and they will recover'.

3. *Luke 24:36-49.* This charge was given either (a) to the Eleven with a few others on the same occasion as John 20:19-23 on the evening of Easter Day (Luke 24:3, 33), or (b) 40 days later to the Apostles (Acts1:2) at Bethany on the Mount of Olives immediately prior to the Ascension (Luke 24:50-51). Text of the commission: 'Repentance and forgiveness of sins shall be preached in (my) name to all the nations, beginning from Jerusalem. You are witnesses of these things. And behold, I send you the promise of my Father upon you; but stay in the city, until you are clothed with power from on high'(47-49).

4. *Matthew 28:16-20.* This is the most authoritative and most often quoted of the commissionings. It was given to the Eleven with some 500 other disciples (as described in 1 Corinthians 15:6) on a mountain in Galilee as forecast (Matthew 28:7), a week or two after Easter Day. The account seems to parallel or supersede the giving of the Ten Commandments on Mount Sinai to Moses, and includes Old Testament prophetic language (Daniel 7). Text of the commission: 'Go therefore and make disciples of all nations, baptizing them in the name of the Father and of the Son and of the Holy Spirit, teaching them to observe all that I have commanded you; and lo, I am with you always, to the close of the age'.

5. *John 21:1-22.* The lengthiest of the commissionings, this was given to 'the disciples' (most probably, 7 of the Twelve Apostles) beside Lake Galilee well on in the 40-day period, when the Apostles had been puzzled at the long delay because nothing seemed to be happening; were becoming idle; had grown restless at the apparent absence of Jesus and were returning to a day's fishing as something to get on with. Whereas the other 5 accounts of the Commission are directly verbal, this occasion was a drama or acted parable. 'The catch of fish is the dramatic equivalent of the command given in the Matthean account of the Galilean appearance: Go therefore and make disciples of all nations'. 'Peter's words "I am going fishing" have a double meaning and refer to the apostolic mission of "catching men"'. In this drama, 'the commission of John 20:21 is being carried out'. This allegorical interpretation is evident from the use of the verb 'catch' in 21:6; elsewhere in John's Gospel (6:44, 12:32) it is used (as *elkein*) of men's being drawn to Christ, either by the Father or by Christ himself. The fishing expedition is thus the apostolic mission, and the fish are its converts. Text of the commission (GNB): 'Throw your net out on the right side of the boat, and you will catch some', 'Bring some of the fish you have just caught', 'Come and eat', 'Take care of my sheep', 'Follow Me'.

6. *Acts 1:3-14.* This was the final structured occasion, given to the Apostles (Acts 1:2) on the Mount of Olives (Luke 24:50) immediately prior to the Ascension (Acts 1:9-11).Verse 2 also contains a summary of

**CHRIST'S GREAT COMMISSION**
14 commands across 20 centuries

BOLD CAPITALS = The Seven Mandates
Medium type = Some lesser imperatives

*Notes.*
1. 'Ite!' (Latin, Go!): Miniature, Abdinghoven Gospel, AD 1060.
2. 'Offer salvation and charismata to all', on postage stamp, United Arab Emirates, 1970.
3. 'Departure of the Apostles' (Munich, German School): the Twelve preach and baptize in distant lands.
4. 'Make all nations My disciples': 'Christ Blessing', Great Tapestry, Coventry Cathedral, England.
5. 'Jesus appears, teaching the Apostles' (By Duccio, c1300 in Siena, Italy).
6. 'Witness to My Resurrection in every situation and encounter' (Joseph Aubert).
7. 'Christ in Majesty' (Llandaff Cathedral, Wales) proclaims His Gospel through His disciples.
8. Miraculous catch of 153 Fishes (C. Witz, AD 1444, on 1973 stamp).
9. Seal of Urban University, Vatican City, training evangelizers.
10. The Twelve receive the Holy Ghost (El Greco, c1600 in Toledo, Spain).
11. 'Praedicate!' (Latin, Preach!), on Italy commemorative postage stamp, 1922.
12. 'Wait till the Holy Spirit is given you!'; missionaries lie prostrate at ordination by pope in St Peter's Basilica, 1991.
13. The Twelve are told to go everywhere, preaching as they go (Bavarian State Library, Munich).
14. Since 1622 origin, this block has been used on title pages of publications of Congregation for Evangelization of Peoples.

**GO!**

**Offer!**

**BAPTIZE!**

**DISCIPLE!**

**Teach!**

**WITNESS!**

**PROCLAIM!**

**Preach!**

**Multiply!**

**TRAIN!**

**RECEIVE!**

**Wait!**

**Itinerate!**

**Tell!**

# Christ's Great Commission

the commission: 'He had given commandment through the Holy Spirit to the apostles'. Text of the commission: 'You shall receive power when the Spirit has come upon you; and you shall be my witnesses in Jerusalem and in all Judea and Samaria and to the end of the earth'.

Of these 6 accounts, those in Mark, Luke and Acts could also be interpreted as general summaries of Jesus' teachings and instructions to his disciples throughout the whole 40-day period. No doubt there were several other occasions during Jesus' post-Resurrection appearances on which he gave specific commissions or charges either to individuals (as with Peter in John 21:15-19) or to groups. Taken together, therefore, these 6 recorded occasions may be regarded as representative of often-given and repeated instructions during the 40 days to individuals and groups of varying sizes up to 500 believers.

Taken together, also, these accounts constitute a single commission to evangelize the peoples of the world. Samuel Zwemer, apostle to Islam (1867-1952), elaborated on this in his study '*Into all the world': The Great Commission, vindication and an interpretation* (1943): 'We note that Christ's command to evangelize the world is given and recorded no less than five times in the Gospels'. He then outlined the particular emphasis of each account: Matthew emphasizes Christ's authority, Mark the commission's universality in scope and result, Luke its message of repentance and forgiveness of sins, John the spiritual qualifications and demands it makes, and Acts its order of procedure—first Jerusalem (always the hardest place to begin), then Judea, Samaria, and finally the end of the earth.

### THE COMMISSION ANALYZED

Before briefly reviewing the history of Christian thought about, and interpretation of, the apostolic commission, we should analyze in detail the various elements of which it is composed. In the first place, this will assist us to comprehend the full range and scope of its components, and later it will enable us to quantify those components.

#### Elements in the Commission
Christ's commission as originally given consisted of a number of distinct and specific commands and elements. A glance at the Matthaean version gives us straightaway 4 of its keywords: Go, Disciple, Baptize, Teach. These commands, as well as the rest composing the Commission in its widest definition, are not placed in exact juxtaposition, nor is any relative importance stated or intended, since each forms an essential part of the one commission. Some exegeses have seen significance in the fact that, in the Greek text of Matthew 28:19-20, only one of these verbs is in the imperative: *Matheteusate*, i.e. 'Disciple' or 'Make disciples'. The other 3 verbs are said to be only participles: *Poreuthentes, baptizontes, didaskontes*, i.e. 'Going, baptizing, and teaching'; so that what Christ actually said was 'Going, baptizing, and teaching, make disciples!' This has then been taken to mean that 'Disciple' has some sort of priority among other components of the commission. Since we do not know the exact form of the original of Jesus' exact words which these Greek words translate, it is unwise to build too much on this distinction. Moreover, virtually all modern English versions of the New Testament ignore the distinction and render it invisible in English. They replace it either with 2 imperatives 'Go and make disciples' and 2 participles 'baptizing and teaching', as do the Authorized (King James) Version and the Revised Standard Version, or by 4 consecutive imperatives 'Go, make disciples, baptize, teach', as do the Good News Bible, the Jerusalem Bible, the New English Bible, the Revised English Bible, the Contemporary English Version, and others. In ignoring the distinction in this way, modern translators are stating that it is not part of the essential or original meaning. In our exposition, therefore, we will regard all the component verbs as imperatives and will assume that all are interdependent and equally essential to the full interpretation of the commission.

Altogether, the various accounts yield the 80 imperatives or commands listed in Table 23-14.

A number of writers have attempted to categorize or classify these commands under a handful of heads. In their 1975 study *What's gone wrong with the harvest? a communication strategy for the church and world evan-*

*gelization,* J. Engel and W. Norton proposed a 3-fold analysis as follows:

> The Great Commission contains three related but distinctly different communication mandates: (1) *to proclaim* the message; (2) *to persuade* the unbeliever; and (3) *to cultivate* the believer.

From the perspective of the present study, this is too simple and disconnected or disjointed a schema. Mandates (1) and (2) clearly cover much of the commission's meaning; but Mandate (3) seems to belong more in the realm of pastoralia or Christian nurture rather than in the initial confrontation of the pagan world by the gospel. Instead, we will now show that the commission in its various versions contains what may more naturally be seen as 7 distinct mandates: Receive! Go! Witness! Proclaim! Disciple! Baptize! Train! and that these 7 are all closely and integrally comprehended within the meaning of the word Evangelize. We can abbreviate each mandate into our 7 single key words in the imperative tense, as follows.

#### 1. Receive!
The first mandate concerns the necessary power to carry out the rest of the commission. Christian disciples must first receive the power of the Holy Spirit. The Johannine account, as mentioned above, contains the words 'Receive the Holy Spirit' (John 20:22). The Lukan narrative contains a similar statement: 'I send the promise of my Father upon you; but stay in the city until you are clothed with power from on high' (Luke 24:49), and in Acts carries on to elaborate: 'Do not depart from Jerusalem', 'Wait for the promise of the Father', 'Be baptized with the Holy Spirit', 'You shall receive power when the Holy Spirit has come upon you' (Acts 1:8). Without this power it is useless to undertake the subsequent mandates. At the start of their obedience to the commission, disciples are directed to 'Stay', 'Wait', 'Receive', and 'Be clothed'.

#### 2. Go!
The second mandate involves movement, mission, outreach, travel, presence elsewhere. The active form 'Go', which occurs in the Matthean and Markan accounts (Matthew 28:18, Mark 16:15), is paralleled by the Johannine 'I send you', i.e. the passive form 'Be sent' from which the word mission (or, *sending* in Dutch, Afrikaans; *Sendung* in German) is derived.'

#### 3. Witness!
The third mandate deals with the first aspect of communicating the gospel, namely witnessing. This usually refers to unstructured, spontaneous naming the Name of Christ in situations as they arise and as Christians find themselves in the events of everyday life. The imperative 'Witness' used as a verb is also rendered 'Bear witness' or 'Be witnesses'. In the 2 Lukan accounts, the disciples are already witnesses of the Resurrection of Christ (Luke 24:48) and are shortly to be witnesses to Christ spreading the knowledge of Him throughout the world.

#### 4. Proclaim!
The fourth mandate comes to the heart of the commission, which is to proclaim Christ to the world in a variety of ways. These include proclamation by words, by deeds, by the quality of disciples' lives, by signs, by healings, and by other acts of power. The emphasis here is on the plural rather than the singular, on corporate groups rather than on individuals: proclamation is a collective act or a collective of acts by the Christian community to corporate entities—to groups of people, to populations, to peoples, to nations, to the world. In the New Testament accounts, this involves 2 areas amongst others. (a) *Preach.* To preach is to announce the gospel or good news (Matthew 28:18, Mark 16:15) of forgiveness of sins (John 20:23, Luke 24:47) through Jesus Christ. It will involve, in some circumstances, speaking in new languages (Mark 16:17). (b) *Heal.* In Jesus' charges or commissions to his disciples before the Crucifixion, healing, cleansing of lepers, giving sight to the blind, raising the dead, and exorcism featured prominently in his definition of the Good News of the Kingdom of God (Luke 4:18-19). Peter's description of Jesus' ministry expands this: 'Jesus went everywhere, doing good and healing all who were under the power of the Devil' (Acts 10:38, GNB). After the Resurrection, it is therefore not surprising to find that the Markan account of the Great Commission indicates

that Spirit-filled proclamation will be accompanied by signs demonstrating the mighty acts of God, in particular exorcism, laying on of hands on the sick and other varieties of healing (Mark 16:17-18). The imperative 'Heal the sick' that occurred in Jesus' pre-Crucifixion commissions (Matthew 10:8, Luke 9:2, 10:9) is now spelled out in more detail: Give signs, Cast out demons, Lay hands on the sick, Pick up serpents, Heal.

#### 5. Disciple!
The fifth mandate takes the fourth mandate to the commission's next phase, namely, applying the publicly proclaimed message of the gospel to the particular needs and circumstances of receptive individuals, of receptive persons, of reception communities and peoples, of those interested, of those prepared to listen, of those who will treat it as seriously as a word from God deserves. This mandate introduces the important element of feedback or response on the part of those hearing the message. Individuals and receptive groups are now to have the gospel communicated to them and they are to be confronted with its demands on their lives. The commands in the biblical accounts are 'Forgive' and 'Retain' (John 20:23), 'Make disciples' (Matthew 28:19), and 'Make believers' (Mark 16:16). The third of these, 'Make disciples of all nations', is in Greek *Matheteusate panta ta ethne*. We here prefer to use the word 'Disciple' as a verb, and so to translate the phrase as 'Disciple the nations'.

#### 6. Baptize!
This sixth part of the Great Commission is often taken as a mandate for church planting, church extension and church growth, that is for the calling out of individuals, families, groups and peoples, out of the world and into the church. The church's attempt to obey 'Baptize' (Persuade people to accept baptism and become church members) will certainly produce some baptized church members; but it will also produce what we may call anti-baptized persons or anti-church-members—people who have been subject to the same persuasion but who have rejected the message or have otherwise decided not to accept baptism, or church membership.

#### 7. Train!
The commission concludes with a seventh mandate concerned with ensuring the continuity of the whole process represented by the commission and its mandates Receive, Go, Witness, Proclaim, Disciple, Baptize. This mandate is 'Teach', which occurs in specific form in the Matthean account only. Over the last 300 years, large numbers of Bible students in the English-speaking world have been conscious of this imperative because their major Bible translation, the Authorized or King James Version, has opened Matthew's account with the words: 'Go ye therefore, and teach all nations...' This usage had been perpetuated since Jerome's Latin Vulgate of the 6th century, which for this phrase had translated 'Euntes ergo docete omnes gentes', translating the Greek word *matheteusate* by the Latin word *docete*. Modern translations now render this Greek verb more accurately as the verb 'disciple' (ASV, margin) or 'make disciples' (RSV, NEB, et alia). Matthew 28:19 does however contain a further occurrence of this imperative, this time correctly rendered by the modern word 'teach': teaching them to observe all that I have commanded you' (28:20, RSV).

'Teach' or 'Train' refers to training with respect to the 6 previous mandates; in a word, to training for evangelism. 'Teach' therefore means 'Train people to receive the Spirit, to go, to witness, to proclaim the gospel, to disciple, to baptize'; or, 'Train believers to obey this Great Commission through which they themselves became disciples'. It means: 'Ensure the continuity of the witnessing process. Follow up new believers, and follow them through to full discipleship. Train Christians in obedience to this Great Commission. Train people for evangelism. Train people to train others also, for evangelism'. There is a parallel here with that first biblical commission. 'Be fruitful and multiply' (Genesis 1:28). Natural reproduction soon multiplies a population, and in the same way the process of training others for evangelism rapidly multiplies. Everybody is involved; not just the apostles, nor other key figures or special orders of ministry, but the entire active Christian community.

All of these 7 mandates composing the Great Commission—Receive, Go, Witness, Proclaim, Disciple, Baptize, Train—can be summed up in a single imperative which does not occur in the accounts of the Commission and which we have so far not employed: Evangelize, or in expanded form: 'Go and evangelize the world'. Over the last century during which the English word 'evangelize' has been returning to widespread use, this has been the usual interpretation as understood by the major Christian confessions. At the 1897 Lambeth Conference of the Anglican Communion, the first resolution on foreign missions spoke of 'Our Lord's great commission to evangelize all nations'. A year later, the Presbyterian missiologist A.T. Pierson wrote, in *The New Acts of the Apostles* (1898), 'The old command of Christ echoes down the long aisles of the ages, Evangelize!' (page 46). And in 1900 his seminal study *The evangelization of the world in this generation*, ecumenical statesman John R. Mott analyzed 'the Great Commission of Christ' on pages 23-24 and wrote 'The expression, the evangelization of the world in this generation, simply translates Christ's last command into terms of obligation concerning our own lifetime'. Within the early ecumenical movement, S. M. Zwemer summed up the widespread consensus in writing of 'Christ's command to evangelize the world'; and John R. Mott continued to write 'God has commissioned his true followers to evangelize the world'. Within the modern ecumenical movement, the prolific historian of missions, K. S. Latourette stated in a 1950 meeting of the International Missionary Council:

> By evangelism is meant obedience to the Great Commission. This includes not only preaching but also making disciples and teaching the observance of the whole range of commands of Christ. The Commission is as broad as the human race.

Among Evangelicals across the world there is the same understanding, as expressed in such books as R.Q. Leavell's *Evangelism: Christ's imperative commission* (1951).

For further examples the reader should consult the brief bibliography at the end of this Part.

### CATEGORIZING THE COMMISSION

To understand the Commission at this point. It is here first divided into two Mini-commissions 'Evangelize!' and 'Disciple!', then into seven distinct Mandates. This whole schema is set out in Global Diagram 6 in Part 1 of this volume and abbreviated here which is set out above as Table 3–2. It will be seen that column 7 near the end of this table speaks of and covers some 420 dimensions or aspects of the 7 Mandates. In other words, the Great Commission is such a complex and monumental command that its basic elements require of total of 420 synonyms in order to do them justice. And this is not all, for here we are only talking about the original commands in the language of New Testament Greek, and their translations and usages in contemporary English. Since the Christian church is a vast worldwide enterprise with Christians speaking and utilizing over 10,000 different languages, into 6,700 of which Christian Scripture has already been translated, it can be said that the Great Commission embraces at least 200 distinct synonyms or dimensions in each of those languages. The Great Commission therefore expresses itself in over a million commands or imperatives directed to Christ's followers across the face of the Earth.

## 2. THE VERB 'EVANGELIZE'

The second of the 2 empirical phenomena being examined here is the Greek verb *euangelizo* and its English transliteration 'evangelize'. Again, there is a vast amount of material to analyze.

### THE RICHEST CHRISTIAN WORD: *euangelizo/EVANGELIZE!*

#### Original of the word 'evangelize'
Any study of the central activities of the Christian church is faced with overwhelming masses of material. Instead of attempting to study everything, we are more likely to learn something new by narrowing the field to a single subject. So in this investigation we will narrow this examination of biblical mandates and words to the one singe word 'Evangelize!' and its cognates.

In its original language, Greek, the verb we are interested in is *euangelizo* (1st person singular), with its variant *euangelizomai* (1st person singular present indicative middle) and its infinitive form *euangelizein* (present infinitive) and *euangelizesthai* (present infinitive middle). Its most common cognate in those days was the noun *euangelion* (good news). All were derived from the 2 Greek words *eu* (good) and *angellein* (to bear a message, bring news of, announce, proclaim, report, command).

The verb transliterated directly into English as 'evangelize'. For the moment, let us assume that this is the best, or most useful, translation in contemporary English. We therefore now need to survey the usages of, firstly, the Greek verb, and then, secondly, the English verb, with some attention to Latin and contemporary European, and other major languages also. In doing so we will examine its contexts, meanings and implications in the Greek New Testament and will draw some conclusions about the correct or optimum usage of the English word today.

#### Usages before Christ
The earliest known usages of *euangelizesthai* were secular occurrences in classical Greek times. Greek dramatist Aristophanes (BC 450-388) used the term from BC 420 on, as did orator and statesman Demosthenes in the 4th century BC. The word then, as later, meant 'to carry good news'. There are also other secular usages in the papyri. It is used of a slave coming with news of a general's victory, or news of an approaching wedding, or deliverance from demonic powers, or some other reason for celebration. In later Roman times, also, *euangelion* was used in BC 9 to describe the advent of Octavian as the Roman emperor Augustus, whose birthday in BC 63 was described as 'the beginning for good tidings for the world'. A further aspect is that in pre-Christian days, *euangelion* had a 3-fold meaning: (1) good news, (2) the reward for good tidings given to the messenger, and (3) a sacrifice made in thanksgiving for the receipt of good news.

The earliest religious uses of the words occur in the Septuagint, the Greek translation of the Hebrew Old Testament made in the 3rd century BC. *Euangelion* occurs only 3 times, in the Second Book of Samuel. *Euangelizesthai* occurs 22 times: 3 times in the Psalms and 10 times in the historical books of the Writings, and 9 times in the Prophets. The simple meaning of the verb on each occasion is 'to carry or bring good news', or 'to act as the bringer of good news', such as telling a man that his wife has borne a son, 'making him very glad' (Jeremiah 20:15, RSV).

The news thus conveyed was not always or necessarily good news. It could be bad news from God—news of a defeat or a judgment. But it was always a public announcement of something wrought by God.

The word is used for the first time in its typically biblical meaning in Psalm 40:9 (Septuagint Psalm 39:10), translated as 'I have told the glad news of deliverance in the great congregation', in Psalm 92:2 'Tell of his salvation', and in Isaiah 52:7 'publish salvation and Isaiah 60:6 'proclaim the praise of the Lord'. This Jewish usage was continued into New Testament times by Philo (BC 20-AD 50), the historian Josephus (AD 37-100), and others.

A related word, *euangelos*, meaning sacral messenger or bearer of good tidings, was also in use by New Testament times, but only in secular Greek with no biblical usage.

#### Aramaic words
The language used by Jesus and the Apostles was Aramaic, a Semitic tongue with similarities to Hebrew. Only a handful of the actual Aramaic words used by Jesus have come down to us, embedded in our Four Gospels written in Koine Greek, the lingua franca of the day. These include 'Talitha cumi' (Mark 5:41, 'Little girl, arise'), 'Ephphatha' (Mark 7:34, 'Be opened') and 'Eloi, Eloi lama sabachthani' (Mark 15:34, from Psalm 22:1, 'My God, my God, why hast thou forsaken me?'), No Aramaic versions of the accounts of the Great Commission have come down to us or have been proposed, but it is reasonably certain that the Aramaic words later translated into Greek as *euangelion* (noun) and *euangelizo* (verb) were *sabarta* (noun; 'good news') and *sabar* (verb; 'tell good news') from the root *sbr*. The Hebrew equivalent was the similar *basar* from *bsr*, which in the Old Testament means 'proclaim good news' (as in 1 Kings 1:42 and Jeremiah 20:15). Another Aramaic word known to have been in Jesus' vocabulary was *akrez* ('proclaim').

#### Greek word frequencies
The words *euangelion* and *euangelizesthai* are used a total of 132 times in the Greek New Testament. By comparison with other key words in its 27 books, this is a significant amount. One must be careful not to allow statistical frequencies to mean too much. However, frequencies are important when establishing the significance of a concept for biblical theology, and in this case they establish these 2 concepts as of direct importance to the story of Christ.

Another type of frequency is usage by Christians outside the canon of Scripture. Such quotation frequencies must be very high indeed for our 2 words; they and their subsequent transliterations into scores of languages have been on Christians' lips and in their writings constantly ever since. The anthropologist Dillon-Malone recorded a typical instance of this in the 20th century, when, writing about a major African indigenous church in Zimbabwe-Rhodesia and their use of the final occurrence of both words in the New Testament, he stated: 'Revelation 14:6-7 is a text very dear to [the founder] Johane Masowe and his Vapostori [Apostles].' We need now to examine what those words and their other cognates and synonyms actually meant in those days of the Early Church.

#### Gospel: a 6-fold kerygma
The noun *euangelion* occurs 76 times in the Greek New Testament, in 17 of its 27 books: Matthew, Mark, Acts, Romans, 1 and 2 Corinthians, Galatians, Ephesians, Philippians, Colossians, 1 and 2 Thessalonians, 1 and 2 Timothy, Philemon, 1 Peter, and Revelation. It does not appear in Luke, John, Titus, Hebrews, James, 2 Peter, John's Epistles or Jude. It is always translated in the Authorized or King James Version (AV, KJV) of the Holy Bible, and in the Revised Standard Version (RSV) as 'the gospel'. In the New English Bible it is translated 'the good news' (as in Acts 14:7) and in that other major English translation, the Good News Bible, it is capitalized as 'Good News'.

What in fact was and is the good news? The classic discussion of this is C. H. Dodd's *The Apostolic preaching and its developments* (1936). *The translator's New Testament* summarizes Dodd's conclusions as follows. The *kerygma* (apostolic preaching) was: 'The age of fulfillment has dawned; this has taken place through the life, death, and resurrection of Jesus; Jesus, as Messiah, has been exalted to God's right hand; the Holy Spirit in the Church is the evidence of Christ's power and presence; Christ will return and bring in the New Age; therefore repent, receive forgiveness and the Holy Spirit and the promise of salvation.'

#### Occurrences of *euangelizo*
We come now to the usage of our major word, *euangelizo* or *euangelizesthai*, which for the moment we are transliterating as the English word 'evangelize'. It occurs 56 times in the Greek New Testament, in 12 of its 27 books: Matthew, Luke, Acts, Romans, 1 and 2 Corinthians, Galatians, Ephesians, 1 Thessalonians, Hebrews, 1 Peter, Revelation. It is found once in Matthew's Gospel, 10 times in Luke's Gospel, 16 times in Acts, 22 times in Pauline Epistles, 5 times in 2 other Epistles, and twice in Revelation.

It is therefore predominantly a word developed by Luke and Paul to explain the mission and message of Jesus. For Paul, this Greek term 'embraces the whole work of Jesus'; for Luke, it 'has almost become a technical term for proclamation'. In essence, its meaning in the New Testament writings in simply 'to offer or communicate good news, with whatever result'. As *The translator's New Testament* puts it, 'The fundamental idea is the telling of news to people who have not heard it before (evangelization).'

#### Who 'evangelizes'?
Examination of the subjects of the 56 occurrences of the verb *euangelizo* shows that the persons who 'evangelize' fall into 9 categories. In chronological order of appearance on the New Testament scene, with, in parentheses, the total occurrences of each, they are as follows.

1. Jesus (9 occurrences; 7 in the Gospels, also Ephesians 2:17, 1 Peter 4:6).
2. The archangel Gabriel (twice; Luke 1:19 and 2:10).

3. John the Baptist (once; Luke 3:18).
4. The Twelve (once; Luke 9:6).
5. The post-Pentecost church collectively, the believers (6 occurrences; 4 in Acts, twice in Romans 10:15).
6. Individual believers in the church (20 occurrences; Philip 3 times in Acts 8, Paul 15, Timothy 1, and 1 other).
7. Missionary pairs or teams of Apostles in the church (11 occurrences; Peter and John, Paul and Barnabas, Paul and his party, et alii).
8. God (4 occurrences; Acts 10:36, Hebrews 4:2, 4:6, Revelation 10:7).
9. An angel (twice; Galatians 1:8, Revelation 14:6).

Of these 56 occurrences, 17 (or 30%) refer to, or may be presumed to refer to, pre-Resurrection occasions or periods (before the Resurrection of Christ); whilst 39 (or 70%) refer to post-Pentecost occasions or peri-

ods. Of the 56, therefore, 17 (30%) have as subject God, Jesus, or God's immediate supernatural messengers, the angels; whilst 39 (70%) have as subjects the Church of sinful men, human believers. Stating this latter sentence in another way, 39 occurrences (70%) refer to ecclesiastical activity, i.e. human activity on the part of believers in Christ; whilst 17 occurrences (30%) refer to divine activity, i.e. divine initiatives on the part of God or Jesus (including 9 occurrences (16%) referring to the human activities of Jesus the Son of Man) that are or were nothing to do with direct ecclesiastical or believers' initiatives or activity.

We conclude that before the Resurrection of Christ, 'to evangelize' was largely (though not exclusively) used of divine evangelistic or evangelizing activity, while after Pentecost, it becomes largely (though not exclusively) used of human, ecclesiastical evangelistic activity, with this latter usage forming the bulk (70%) of all 56 occurrences in the New Testament.

### The Holy Spirit and 'evangelizing'

In 9 of the 56 occurrences of *euangelizo*, the verb is used in the context of activity on the part of the Holy Spirit. When Jesus began his ministry, he quoted the prophecy of Isaiah 61:1-2: 'The Spirit of the Lord is upon me, because he has chosen me to bring good news (*euangelizein*) to the poor.' In Acts 8:39-40, we read: 'The Spirit of the Lord took Philip away... and he preached the Good News in every town.' And in 1 Peter 1:12, 'The prophets spoke about those things which you have now heard from the messengers who announced the Good News (*euangelizein*) by the power of the Holy Spirit sent from heaven.'

We can say therefore that, in the New Testament, *euangelizein* is only possible when the Holy Spirit is present, at work, in action, and in control.

### *euangelizo in 2 Gospels*

Our eventual purpose in studying this biblical usage

---

**Graphic 3–1.    Greek origins of Christianity's richest word: 210 kaleidoscopic New Testament Greek verbs that are synonyms of the Christian keyword *euangelizo* (evangelize).**

This graphic below portrays schematically the relationship to *euangelizo* of 210 New Testament Greek synonyms and near-synonyms. The central word is portrayed by the heavy, central circle. English meanings of all Greek words are given in Table 3–3 on the next page.

Nine separate but overlapping categories or concentric zones of proximity can be distinguished. For full explanation and more detailed presentation, see Global Diagram 7 in Part 1 "GeoStatus".

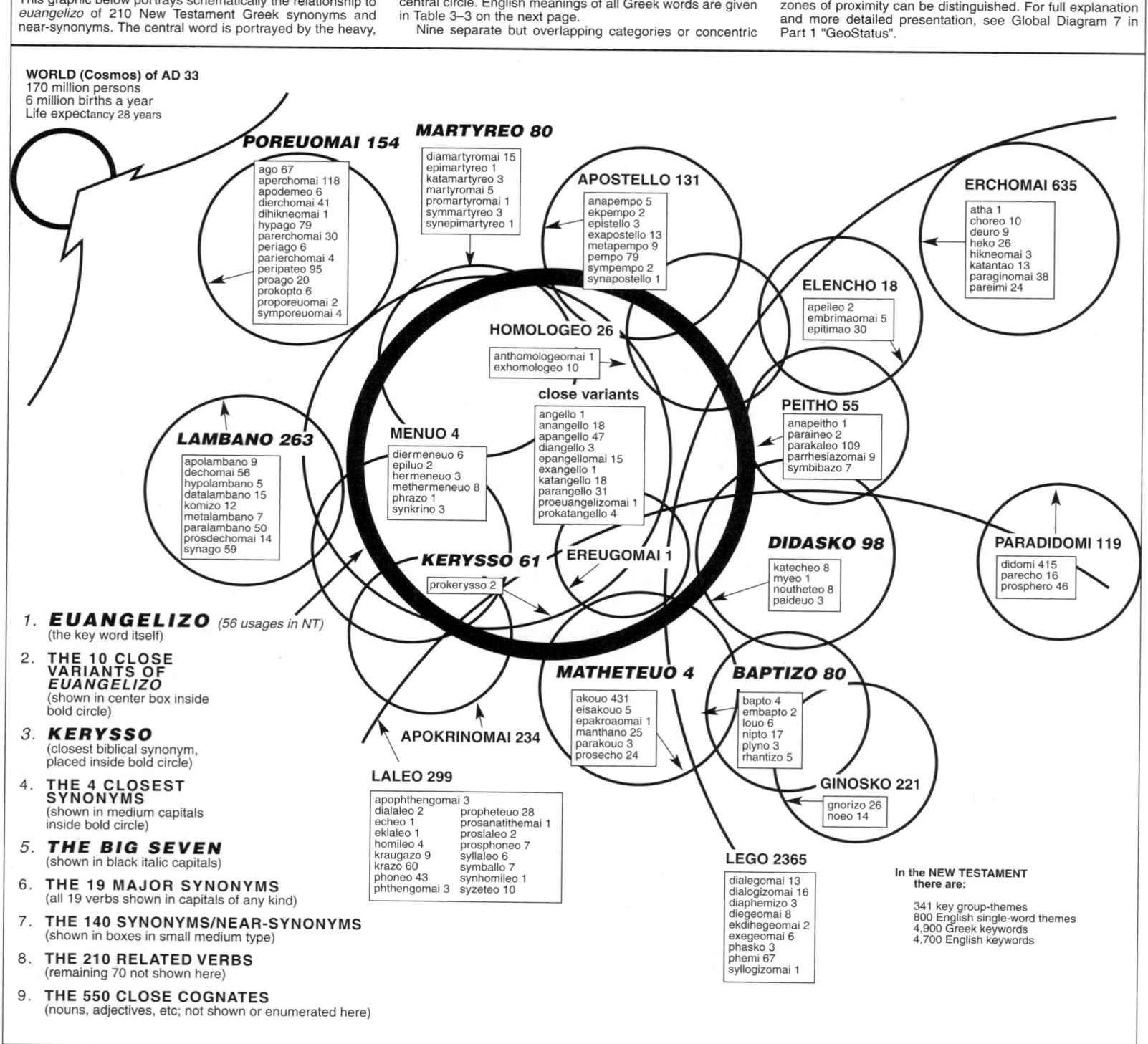

WORLD (Cosmos) of AD 33
170 million persons
6 million births a year
Life expectancy 28 years

**POREUOMAI 154**

ago 67
aperchomai 118
apodemeo 6
dierchomai 41
dihikneomai 1
hypago 79
parerchomai 30
periago 6
parierchomai 4
peripateo 95
proago 20
prokopto 6
proporeuomai 2
symporeuomai 4

**MARTYREO 80**

diamartyromai 15
epimartyreo 1
katamartyreo 3
martyromai 5
promartyromai 1
symmartyreo 3
synepimartyreo 1

**APOSTELLO 131**

anapempo 5
ekpempo 2
epistello 3
exapostello 13
metapempo 9
pempo 79
sympempo 2
synapostello 1

**ERCHOMAI 635**

atha 1
choreo 10
deuro 9
heko 26
hikneomai 3
katantao 13
paraginomai 38
pareimi 24

**ELENCHO 18**

apeileo 2
embrimaomai 5
epitimao 30

**HOMOLOGEO 26**

anthomologeomai 1
exhomologeo 10

**close variants**

angello 1
anangello 18
apangello 47
diangello 3
epangellomai 15
exangello 1
katangello 18
parangello 31
proeuangelizomai 1
prokatangello 4

**PEITHO 55**

anapeitho 1
paraineo 2
parakaleo 109
parrhesiazomai 9
symbibazo 7

**LAMBANO 263**

apolambano 9
dechomai 56
hypolambano 5
datalambano 15
komizo 12
metalambano 7
paralambano 50
prosdechomai 14
synago 59

**MENUO 4**

diermeneuo 6
epiluo 2
hermeneuo 3
methermeneuo 8
phrazo 1
synkrino 3

**DIDASKO 98**

katecheo 8
myeo 1
noutheteo 8
paideuo 3

**PARADIDOMI 119**

didomi 415
parecho 16
prosphero 46

**KERYSSO 61**

prokerysso 2

**EREUGOMAI 1**

1. **EUANGELIZO** (56 usages in NT)
(the key word itself)

2. **THE 10 CLOSE VARIANTS OF EUANGELIZO**
(shown in center box inside bold circle)

3. **KERYSSO**
(closest biblical synonym, placed inside bold circle)

4. **THE 4 CLOSEST SYNONYMS**
(shown in medium capitals inside bold circle)

5. **THE BIG SEVEN**
(shown in black italic capitals)

6. **THE 19 MAJOR SYNONYMS**
(all 19 verbs shown in capitals of any kind)

7. **THE 140 SYNONYMS/NEAR-SYNONYMS**
(shown in boxes in small medium type)

8. **THE 210 RELATED VERBS**
(remaining 70 not shown here)

9. **THE 550 CLOSE COGNATES**
(nouns, adjectives, etc; not shown or enumerated here)

**APOKRINOMAI 234**

**MATHETEUO 4**

akouo 431
eisakouo 5
epakroaomai 1
manthano 25
parakouo 3
prosecho 24

**BAPTIZO 80**

bapto 4
embapto 2
louo 6
nipto 17
plyno 3
rhantizo 5

**LALEO 299**

apophthengomai 3
dialaleo 2
echeo 1
eklaleo 1
homileo 4
kraugazo 9
krazo 60
phoneo 43
phthengomai 3

propheteuo 28
prosanatithemai 1
proslaleo 2
prosphoneo 7
syllaleo 6
symballo 7
synhomileo 1
syzeteo 10

**GINOSKO 221**

gnorizo 26
noeo 14

**LEGO 2365**

dialegomai 13
dialogizomai 16
diaphemizo 3
diegeomai 8
ekdihegeomai 2
exegeomai 6
phasko 3
phemi 67
syllogizomai 1

In the NEW TESTAMENT
there are:

341 key group-themes
800 English single-word themes
4,900 Greek keywords
4,700 English keywords

## Table 3–3. Glossary of 160 New Testament Greek words related to *euangelizo.*

This word list translates into English every Greek and Latin verb or noun shown on Global Diagrams 6 and 7. These number 160 biblical words. All occur in the original Greek New Testament with 5 words from the Latin New Testament. All are synonyms of the verb *euangelizo.* Their closeness to *euangelizo* is explained in Global Diagram 6. They are given here transliterated from Greek letters into roman letters. They are shown listed in alphabetical order; each followed by its meanings in English.

Almost all of these words are verbs with a sprinkling of nouns. Each word is followed by its English translation. Sometimes the translation is a single word. More usually, it is a range of several words. Each range is the full list of all English meanings in the priorities shown in *A Greek-English lexikon of the New Testament and other Early Christian literature* (W. F. Arndt & F. W. Gingrich, 2nd edition, University of Chicago, 1958). Transliterated spellings follow M. Darton, ed, *Modern concordance to the New Testament,* 1976.

**ago.** Lead, bring, take along, guide.
**akouo.** Hear, listen to.
**anangello.** Report, disclose, announce, proclaim, teach.
**anapeltho.** Persuade.
**anapempo**. Send.
**angello.** Announce.
**anthomologeomal.** Praise, thank publicly.
**apangello.** Report, announce, tell, proclaim.
**apelleo.** Threaten, warm.
**aperchomal**. Go away, depart, go, go out and spread, follow.
**apodemeo.** Go on a journey, be away, be absent.
**apokrinomal.** Answer, reply, speak up.
**apolambano.** Receive, recover, get back, take a person aside, welcome.
**apologia.** Defense.
**apophthengomal.** Speak out, declare boldly, declare loudly.
**apostello.** Send out, send away.
**apostole.** Apostleship, office of apostle.
**atha.** Come.
**baptisma.** Baptism.
**baptismos.** Dipping, washing, baptism.
**baptizo.** Dip, immerse, wash, baptize.
**baptizontes.** Baptizing.
**bapto.** Dip.
**choreo.** Go, go out, go away, go forward, make progress, grasp, accept, comprehend, understand.
**dechomal.** Take, receive, welcome, grasp, tolerate, approve, accept.
**deuro.** Come, follow.
**diakonia.** Service, office, aid, support, distribution.
**dialaleo.** Discuss.
**dialegomal.** Discuss, conduct a discussion, converse, speak, preach.
**dialogismos.** Thought, opinion, reasoning, design, dispute, argument.
**dialogizomal.** Consider, ponder, reason, discuss, argue.
**diamartyromal.** Charge, warn, adjure, testify, bear witness.
**diangello.** Proclaim far and wide, give notice, announce.
**diaphemizo.** Spread the news about, spread widely, disseminate.
**didache.** Teaching, instruction.
**didasko.** Teach, instruct.
**didaskontes.** Teach! teaching.
**didomi.** Give, grant, bestow, impart, speak plainly, give a sign, give out, hand over, hold out, entrust, yield, pay, make an effort.
**diegeomal.** Tell, relate, describe, recount.
**dierchomal.** Go through, pierce, come, go, review.
**diermeneuo.** Translate, complain, interpret.
**dihikneomal.** Pierce, penetrate.
**dynamis.** Power, might, strength, force, ability, capability, miracle, wonder, meaning.
**echeo.** Sound, ring out, roar, thunder.
**elsakouo.** Listen to, obey, hear.
**ekdihegeomai.** Tell in detail.
**ekklesia.** Assembly, congregation, church.
**eklaleo.** Tell.
**ekpempo.** Send out, send away.
**elencho.** Bring to light, expose, set forth, convict, convince, reprove, correct, punish, discipline.
**embapto.** Dip.
**embrimaomal.** Scold, censure.
**epakroaomal.** Listen.
**epangellomai.** Announce, proclaim, promise, offer, profess.
**epiluo.** Explain, interpret, set free, release, decide, settle.
**epimartyreo.** Bear witness.
**epistello.** Inform, instruct by letter, write.
**epitimao.** Rebuke, reprove, censure, speak seriously, warn, punish.
**erchomal.** Come, appear, appear in public, deal with, go.
**ereugomal.** Utter, proclaim.
**euangellon.** Good news, gospel.
**euangelizo** (euangelizomai, euangelizesthai). Evangelize: bring or announce good news, proclaim, preach.
**eucharistia.** Thankfulness, gratitude, thanksgiving, eucharist, Lord's Supper.
**evangelizatio** (Latin). Evangelization.
**exangello.** Proclaim, report.
**exapostello.** Send out, send away.
**exegeomal.** Explain, interpret, tell, report, describe, bring news.
**exhomologeo.** Promise, consent, confess, admit, acknowledge, praise.
**exousia.** Ability, capability, might, power, authority, warrant, government.
**ginosko.** Know, come to know, learn, ascertain, find out, understand, comprehend, perceive, notice, realize, acknowledge, recognize.
**gnorizo.** Make known, reveal, know.
**heko.** Be present, have come.
**hermeueuo.** Explain, interpret, translate.
**hikneomai** (aphikneomai, ephikneomai). Reach, come to.
**homileo.** Speak, converse, address, talk with.
**homologeo.** Promise, assure, agree, admit, confess, declare, acknowledge, praise.
**hypago.** Go, go away, leave, go home, return.
**hypolambano.** Take up, receive as guest, support, assume, think, believe, suppose, be of the opinion.
**justitla** (Latin). Justice.
**katalambano.** Seize, win, attain, make one's own, catch, detect, grasp, find, understand.
**katamartyreo.** Bear witness against, testify against.
**katantao.** Come, arrive, attain.
**katangello.** Solemnly proclaim, direct one's proclamation to.
**katecheo.** Make oneself understood, report, inform, teach, instruct.
**katechumenos.** Instructed in.
**keruxate.** Preach! (imperative of kerysso).
**kerygma.** Proclamation, announcement, preaching.
**kerysso.** Announce, make known, herald, proclaim aloud, mention publicly, praise publicly, spread widely, preach, preach against.
**koinonia.** Association, communion, fellowship, close relationship, generosity, participation.
**komizo.** Bring, carry off, get, receive, get back, recover.
**kraugazo.** Cry, cry loudly, scream, utter a loud sound.
**krazo.** Cry out, scream, shriek, call, call out, cry.
**labete.** Receive! (imperative of lambano).
**laleo.** Speak, express oneself, sound, assert, proclaim.
**lambano.** Take, take hold, grasp, find opportunity, take away, remove, receive, accept, take up, choose, select, apprehend, comprehend, get, obtain.
**lego.** Utter, say, tell, speak, express, mean, answer, order, command, enjoin, direct, recommend, assure, assert, maintain, declare, proclaim, report, call, name.
**leitourgela.** Service, priestly service.
**louo.** Wash, bathe.
**manthano.** Learn, come to know, find out, understand.
**martyreo.** Bear witness, testify, declare, confirm, witness unto death, be a martyr.
**martyres** (plural of martys). Witnesses.
**martyria.** Testimony, attestation, martyrdom.
**martyromal.** Testify, bear witness, affirm, insist, implore.
**martys.** Witness, martyr.
**mathetes.** Disciple, learner, pupil, apprentice, adherent.
**matheteuo.** Be instructed, become a pupil/disciple, make disciples, teach, train, instruct.
**matheteusate.** Make disciples!
**menuo.** Make known, reveal, report, give information.
**metalambano.** Share, receive, receive one's share.
**metapempo.** Summon.
**methermeneuo.** Translate.
**missio** (Latin). Sending, mission.
**myeo.** Initiate, learn.
**nipto.** Wash.
**noco.** Perceive, apprehend, understand, gain insight into, observe, comprehend, consider, take note of, think over, imagine.
**noutheteo.** Admonish, warn, instruct.
**oikodome.** Building, construction, edification, upbuilding.
**oikoumene.** Inhabited earth, world, humankind.
**paideuo.** Teach, discipline.
**paradidomi.** Hand over, give, deliver, entrust, turn over, give over, commend, commit, hand down, pass on, transmit, relate, teach, allow, permit.
**paraginomai.** Come, arrive, be present, appear, stand by, come to the aid of.
**paraineo.** Advise, recommend, urge.
**parakaleo.** Summon, invite, call upon, appeal, urge, exhort, encourage, request, implore, entreat, comfort, cheer up, console, conciliate.
**paraklesis.** Encouragement, exhortation, appeal, request, comfort, consolation.
**parakletos.** Mediator, intercessor, helper, paraclete.
**parakouo.** Overhear, ignore, refuse to listen.
**paralambano.** Take, take along. take over, receive, accept.
**parangello.** Give orders, command, instruct, direct, forbid.
**parecho.** Offer, present, grant, show, give up, cause, bring about, get.
**pareimi.** Be present.
**parerchomai.** Go by, go through, pass, pass by, pass away, disappear, neglect, come.
**parrhesiazomai.** Speak freely/open/fearlessly, deal openly.
**pax** (Latin). Peace.
**peitho.** Convince, persuade, appeal, conciliate, pacify, assure, obey, follow.
**pempo.** Send, write.
**perlago.** Lead around, go around, take along, accompany, travel.
**perierchomal.** Go around, circumambulate.
**peripateo.** Go about, walk, walk around.
**phasko.** Say, assert, claim.
**phemi.** Say, affirm, mean.
**phoneo.** Call, cry out, speak loudly, emphasize, summon, invite.
**phrazo.** Explain, interpret.
**phthengomai.** Speak, utter, proclaim, call out loudly.
**plyno.** Wash, free from.
**pneumatikos.** Spiritual, Spirit-related, filled with the Spirit, pneumatic.
**poreuomai.** Go, proceed, travel.
**poreuthentes.** Go! going.
**praesencia** (Latin). Presence.
**proago.** Lead, bring out, lead forward, go before, precede, lead the way, walk ahead.
**proeuangelizomai.** Proclaim good news in advance.
**prokatangello.** Announce beforehand, foretell.
**prokerysso.** Proclaim publicly, proclaim beforehand.
**prokopto.** Go forward, progress, make progress, advance, prosper.
**promartyromai.** Predict, bear witness beforehand.
**propheteuo.** Prophesy, proclaim revelation, reveal, foretell.
**proporeuomai.** Go before.
**prosanatithemai.** Contribute, add, consult.
**prosdechomai.** Take up, receive, welcome, deal with, wait, expect.
**prosecho.** Follow, give heed to, turn one's mind to, pay attention to, be alert, notice, care for, be concerned about, devote oneself to.
**proslaleo.** Address, speak with.
**prosphero.** Bring, offer, present, meet, deal with.
**prosphoneo.** Call out, address.
**rhantizo.** Sprinkle, cleanse, wash, purify.
**semela kai terata.** Signs and wonders.
**syllaleo.** Talk, converse, discuss.
**syllogizomai.** Reason, discuss, debate.
**symballo.** Converse, confer, consider, ponder, draw conclusions about, compare, meet, engage, help, assist.
**symbibazo.** Bring together, unite, conclude, infer, demonstrate, prove, instruct, teach, advise.
**symmartyreo.** Testify with, bear witness with, confirm, testify in support.
**sympempo.** Send with.
**symporeuomai.** Go along with, come together.
**synago.** Gather, bring, call together, reconcile, lead, advance, move.
**synapostello.** Send with, send at the same time.
**synepimartyreo.** Testify at the same time.
**synhomileo.** Talk, converse with, live with.
**synkrino.** Bring together, combine, compare, explain, interpret.
**syzeteo.** Discuss, dispute, debate, argue, reflect, meditate.
**therapeia.** Healing, treatment.
**therismos.** Harvest, crop.

of the Greek word is to obtain help in determining what the English word 'evangelize' and its cognates mean today, how they should correctly be used, and how they can then be quantified in order to assist the Christian world to assess its progress in obedience to its Lord.

The first 11 usages of the word in the New Testament occur in Matthew's and Luke's Gospels. There they refer to the earthly activity and ministry of Jesus the Son of God in proclaiming his own good news that 'The Kingdom of God has arrived'. These usages are unique to the pre-Resurrection ministry of Jesus and do not refer directly to the activity of Christians after that ministry. After Jesus' Resurrection, the new gospel proclaimed by the Apostles and disciples became 'God has raised Christ from the dead', and *euangelizesthai*—to evangelize—then became a major work of the newborn Church.

An important point which by the 20th century AD was to assume significant proportions concerns how all-inclusive the verb *euangelizo* was during the ministry of Jesus. Certainly its main meaning was 'proclaim the good news'. But already we find hints that its full meaning was intended to be very much more wide-ranging and all-inclusive. Thus in 1933 G. Friedrich had written of the ministry of Jesus, 'His manifestation, not merely His preaching but His whole work, is described in terms of *euangelizesthai.*'

### *euangelizo in the Acts of the Apostles*

The major and most typical usages of our word as an activity of the church, to help us in our inquiry, are the 16 occurrences in The Acts of the Apostles. We may note the following points.

*Subject.* In these 16 usages the verb is in the active voice. The subjects—the persons doing the evangelizing—are Philip, Peter, Paul, Barnabas, or the Church. Evangelizing is always done by active Christian believers.

*Object.* In half of the 16 cases in Acts, the verb is intransitive; it has no object. We are simply told 'And there they evangelized' (14:7), with no reference to the particular individuals, groups, or populations listening or otherwise involved. From this we deduce that evangelizing is an activity of the Church alone; one can describe evangelizing as simply what the Church does with no necessary explicit reference to any audience.

In the other 8 cases in Acts, the verb is transitive; it has an object. Thus 'Peter and John evangelized many villages of the Samaritans' (Acts 8:25); Philip evangelized the Ethiopian eunuch (8:35); he evangelized all the towns (8:40); likewise the other 5 cases.

In all these instances, the objects are non-believers. In general, therefore, in correct usage the objects of evangelizing are always non-Christians. Moreover, they are also usually non-believers who have not so far heard the good news; they are not unbelievers or disbelievers, terms which we reserve here for non-believers who have heard the good news but have not, or not yet, accepted it.

*Response.* In 9 of the 16 cases in Acts, no response on the part of the immediate hearers is reported on those occasions. No converts are mentioned. This seems to indicate, again, that evangelizing consists of preaching the gospel irrespective of any response or results. In the other 7 cases, a response is mentioned and described. Sometimes the success of the occasion is complete: as with Philip, the eunuch believed and was baptized. More usually, there is a modest response; there are a number of immediate converts (14:21), though these are usually a minority of the hearers or of the local population. At other times, there is a mixed response, as with Paul on Mars Hill: some mocked; some kept an open mind; others believed (17:32,34).

A brief examination of these 16 cases, using the English texts from the Good News Bible (and the Revised Standard Version where additionally helpful), will be a valuable guide as to the full meaning of *euangelizo* and its wider connotations and implications. We will give in quotation marks the exact English translations of the Greek verb.

In the first 3 cases, the verb is intransitive, with no object. In Acts 5:24, the Apostles continued to 'preach the Good News'. In 8:4, the believers went everywhere 'preaching the message'. In 8:12, we are further told what this news consists of: Philip 'preached good news' about the Kingdom of God and the name of Jesus Christ (RSV). In several of the cases that follow, the verb has an object and so a literal translation would be '*A* evangelized *B*'; but the English usage of 'preach' hides the full force of this. For instance, in 8:25 Peter and John 'preached the Good News in' many villages of Samaria (GNB) or 'preached the gospel to' many villages of the Samaritans (RSV). The English conjunctions 'in' and 'to' here are not found in the Greek, which we can translate literally as 'Peter and John evangelized many villages.' In 8:35, Philip expounded the Scriptures to the Ethiopian eunuch and 'told him the Good News' about Jesus. For Philip to evangelize this court official took only a number of minutes. In 8:40, Philip 'preached the Good News' in every town from Ashdod to Caesarea, which is most of the Mediterranean coastline of Palestine. Again, the English hides the fact that this string of towns is the direct object of our verb. In a comparatively short time, Philip evangelized every town over this strategic distance of 60 miles.

The point we are deducing from these usages is that, according to New Testament usage, it is correct and legitimate to speak of one or two individuals evangelizing a sizeable area or population, even in cases where no converts result or are reported. To evangelize either an individual or a substantial population is not necessarily a gradual, indefinite, lengthy, protracted, or interminable process; it is usually or normally a short definite accomplishment, completed over a relatively short, definite period of time.

In 10:36, our Greek verb first appears in an apostolic sermon. Peter describes how up till then God had dealt only with his people Israel, 'proclaiming the Good News' to them of peace through Jesus Christ. In 11:20 comes a further development. Believers from Cyprus and Cyrene 'proclaimed the message' for the first time to Gentiles also (Greek-speaking Jews and Gentiles). It is now clear that the people or populations whom believers evangelize are always non-Christians.

In 13:32, Paul tells his audience in Pisidian Antioch that he is 'here to bring the Good News to you'. The reason he is there is to evangelize them. On that occasion the response was mixed and his audience became polarized into believers and persecutors. In 14:7, the Apostles 'preached the Good News'; they evangelized, with nothing said about response or whether converts were made. In 14:15, Barnabas and Paul told their hearers that they were 'here to announce the Good News', to turn them away from worthless things to the living God. To evangelize appears to mean therefore both to preach and to polarize, to proclaim and to turn some of the people to God.

In 14:21, Paul and Barnabas 'preached the Good News' in Derbe and won many disciples (GNB; RSV, made many disciples; NEB, gained many converts). This is the only New Testament occasion outside the 3 instances in Matthew's Gospel where the Greek word *matheteuein* is used; it is a clear reminder of the Great Commission's mandate in Matthew 28:19. For our purpose at this point, we should note that Acts 14:21 indicates that to evangelize and to make disciples are not exact synonyms. They cover distinct and well-defined areas of activity. To make disciples is only one of the several component commands in the Great Commission to evangelize, as we will see in Part 23. One other point to note from 14:21 is that the response, although numerous, was clearly not universal. To evangelize therefore does not imply that all one's hearers must or will become disciples.

A further element is introduced in 15:35, in which Paul and Barnabas taught and 'preached' the word of the Lord. The use of the 2 verbs together implies that teaching is closely related to, or even part of, evangelizing. This demonstrates the seventh mandate of the Great Commission, 'Train'.

The remaining 3 usages in Acts cover the same ground. In 16:10 (one of the so-called 'We' passages), Paul and his companions including Luke prepare to leave for Macedonia to 'preach the Good News' to the people there. This illustrates the local application of the universal commission. Evangelizing cannot be done in vacuo or in general but must always be directed to specific individuals and peoples where they are, i.e. in their present geographical, political, social, linguistic, cultural, and religious situations.

In 16:17, a demon-possessed girl shouts out that Paul and his party 'announce' (GNB; RSV, proclaim) how to be saved. And lastly, in 17:18, Paul on Mars Hill was 'preaching' about Jesus and the Resurrection, leading once more to the polarization of his audience into believers, enquirers, nonbelievers, and mockers.

In sum, then, we may say that Acts portrays how the early Church proceeded to implement the Great Commission to evangelize, this consisting of a number of different mandates that will soon elaborate on.

### *euangelizo in the Epistles and Apocalypse*

The 28 remaining usages parallel those we have already discussed. Further points of interest, as translated in the Good News Bible, include: 'tell the Good News' (1 Corinthians 1:17), 'preaching the faith' (Galatians 1:23), 'taking the Good News' (Ephesians 3:8), 'bringing us welcome news' (1 Thessalonians 3:6, the only one of these references not related directly to preaching the gospel), 'heard the Good News' (Hebrews 4:2,6), 'announced the Good News' (1 Peter 1:12), 'the Good News that was proclaimed' (1 Peter 1:25), 'the Good News was preached also to the dead' (1 Peter 4:6)

A particularly noteworthy point comes in Hebrews 4:6. The reference is the the People of Israel in the wilderness when the opportunity to enter the Promised Land finally arrived. Those 'who received the good news (participle, *euangelisthentes*)', we are told, nevertheless 'failed to enter because of disobedience'. In other words, people can be evangelized but reject the message.

Once again, there are hints that *euangelizo* has both a clear, simple meaning ('proclaim the good news') and also a far wider, all-inclusive meaning. Thus Friedrich (1933) writes that for Paul *euangelizomai* is a missionary term, and that 'He can use *euangelizesthai* to describe his whole activity as an apostle.'

### *Summary: the usage of **euangelizo***

One can summarize the usage of the term *euangelizo* in the New Testament and the wider implications of this usage as follows. To evangelize after the Resurrection of Christ is almost always used in the active voice, as an activity of Christians. To evangelize is what the evangelizer does towards a target population or area. When the evangelizer has concluded, he or she is usually said to have evangelized that population or area. Christian believers evangelized, with or without mention of who was on the receiving end. Where this is mentioned, Christians always evangelized non-Christians, either individuals, or groups, audiences in synagogues or stadiums, whole populations, villages, towns, cities, whole areas, whole regions, or even Roman provinces as large as Asia Minor. Evangelizing is outreach beyond the existing Christian community; the extent of this outreach shows the extent of evangelizing.

### *The composition of the audience*

This New Testament usage enables us to define and categorize those who heard the gospel. Christians evangelized, either on a single definite occasion, or on several contiguous occasions, either in the open air or in enclosed buildings, either in public or in private. On almost all occasions, their hearers would be a group of people mixed with regard to receptivity to the gospel, both beforehand and afterwards At the start of any particular occasion of evangelizing.

I. Some of the audience were, or may well have been, already Christian believers.

II. The rest were, at that moment, not believers; they were non-Christians. Of these,

(A) Some already had, or may well have, heard the gospel before but had not accepted it then (here, we term such persons unbelievers).

(B) The rest had never heard it before (here, we term such persons non-believers).

These non-Christians then heard the gospel on this new occasion; as a result,

(i) Some responded, believed and became Christians as a result of this occasion.

(ii) the rest did not believe on this occasion.

(a) Some became seekers or enquirers who said 'We want to hear you speak about this again' (Acts 17:32, GNB).

(b) Others temporized or temporarily procrastinated, as is implied in a different translation of the above verse, saying 'We will hear you on this subject some other time' (Acts 17:32, NEB).

(c) Yet others perhaps either did not hear what was said, or did not understand the language adequately, or did not grasp the message at all, or did not listen.

(d) The rest rejected the message with varying degrees of finality.

### *Absences of **euangelizo***

We touch now on a problem that has puzzled Christians often: why *euangelizo* is absent where we would expect to find it. The usages of *euangelizo* in the New Testament are definitive for its meaning; but also significant and instructive are its absences at places where we would expect it to be present. Our word is not found at all in 15 of the 27 New Testament books. It is not used in several major books associated with leading Apostles: Mark, John, James, 2 Peter, 1 John, 2 John, 3 John, and Jude. Neither is it found in the accounts of the Great Commission nor in any of the records of the 40-day post-Resurrection period. These absences are similar to the absence of the more basic word *euangelion* (gospel), which does not occur in 10 New Testament books including the Fourth gospel, and which only occurs once (in Mark 16:15) in the accounts of the 40 days. Considering the centrality of this concept, this is surprising and needs investigation.

The problem is a very similar one to the question as to why John's Gospel omits all reference to a number of events in the ministry of Jesus which are recorded in the other 3 Gospels, the Synoptics, as being of major significance. These events, ignored by

John, are the Virgin Birth of Jesus, Baptism of Jesus by John, Temptation, exorcisms, Transfiguration, words explaining bread and wine at Last Supper, Agony in Gethsemane, et alia.

John's own answer is given in the last verse of his Gospel. 'There are many other things that Jesus did. If they were all written down one by one, I suppose that the whole world could not hold the books that would be written' (GNB). To have an impact, one must select. Writing many years later than the other 3 Evangelists, and for readers with different problems and interests, John's principles of selection were understandably very different.

A similar reason can explain the absence of *euangelizo* and *euangelion* also. The Apostle John preferred the verb *martyrein*, to testify or bear witness. Of the 80 occurrences of this verb in the New Testament, 33 are in John's Gospel and 15 in the Johannine Epistles and Revelation. He also used the noun *martyria* (witness) 14 times in his Gospel and 14 times elsewhere.

The reason for this state of affairs is that although our 2 words *euangelizo* and *euangelion* are major ones in the presentation of the story of Christ, they are not indispensable. There is a whole range of synonyms or part-synonyms for *euangelizo* which could be used, and which other writers preferred to use, knowing their own audiences' needs and with their own particular purposes in writing. We shall examine this range now.

### Scores of synonyms arise

In the New Testament, in addition to the word *euangelizo*, the writers employed a whole range of other Greek words of extraordinarily rich variety, to describe and cover the activity that we are terming 'to evangelize'. There were over 40 synonyms and part-synonyms, most of which had something to do with preaching, bringing, telling, proclaiming, announcing, declaring, speaking, or spreading good news.

The closest synonym to *euangelizo* was *kerysso* ('proclaim' or 'preach'), and the latter itself had 33 synonyms. Several of these were very close synonyms. Some had meanings only partially overlapping that of *euangelizo*. Most were more general words, with far wider use in secular life than in the church. Examples are *dialegein* (*dialegesthai*) meaning 'lecture' or 'argue with', as of Paul in Acts 17:2; and *lalein*, the common word for 'to speak' used 270 times in the New Testament, whose use in Acts 14:25 is translated 'There they preached the message' (GNB). Some of these were in use for the activities of evil men, and even of devils shouting and crying aloud during exorcism, as with *krazein* in Mark 5:7, 'He screamed in a loud voice, "Jesus, Son of the Most High God!"' (GNB).

To illustrate this point, one can arrange those synonyms closest to *euangelizo* in Table 3–3 in alphabetical order in Greek, with their English meanings. The frequencies of the major synonyms are shown in Graphic 3-1. In addition, Table 3–4 lists the current English meanings of the major Greek synonyms.

Each of these words has its own circle of synonyms and meanings. Thus *lalein* (to speak) can also mean a whole range obviously relevant to 'evangelize': speak, talk, say, tell, whisper, chat, proclaim, assert, express oneself, report, communicate, discourse.

The Greek verb that occurs most frequently is *legein*. This can best be translated in English as 'tell'.

Of all of these 42 words, the one with more common ground with the other 41 than any other is *euangelizesthai*. We here maintain that this verb is the best, most expressive, and most comprehensive, when it comes to describing the whole area of activity that we are investigating. Graphic 3-1 shows areas of meaning of several of these terms drawn in proportion to their importance in the New Testament record as measured by total numbers of occurrences.

The heavy circle in Graphic 3-1 represents the range of meaning of *euangelizesthai* and its 56 occurrences. It overlaps in meaning with 2 widely-used words, *legein* (1,210 usages) and *lalein* (270), and also with less-used words shown as smaller circles. Its closest synonym is *keryssein* (61). Even so, this is not an exact synonym, as can be seen from Luke 8:1 where Jesus went through cities and villages *kerusson kai euangelizomenos*, preaching and evangelizing. A noted Bible dictionary attempts to explain these nuances: 'The specific mode of communication implied in *euangelizesthai* is best brought to light by the two synonyms *keryssein* and *katangellein*, and by the interchangeable use of *kerygma* (proclamation) and

"gospel".'

What emerges from this survey of Greek usages is the extraordinary richness of the word *euangelizo*, which requires some 40 other words to display its full meaning. In New Testament usage, it touches on the whole range of activity involved in the spreading of the good news about Jesus Christ. In later Christian usage it would even become equivalent to the whole range itself.

What also emerges clearly is the vast number of times these words are used in the Greek New Testament—2,468 times in all. Evidently, the ideas behind these words were constantly in the minds of Jesus, the Apostles, the Early Church and the Four Evangelists.

A further point which emerges is that, in addition to the 41 fairly close synonyms, there are scores of other Greek verbs which although less close in meaning nevertheless overlap considerably with *euangelizesthai*. One well-known case is *apostello, -ein*. Its active voice means to send, send out, or despatch a message or messenger; its passive voice means to depart, go, be sent, or sent out. The 2 verbs are obviously related closely in meaning and usage.

After listing most of the 41 close synonyms, Kittel's *Theological dictionary of the New Testament* (1935 and 1964) commented:

> The New Testament is more dynamic and varied in its modes of expression than we are today . . . Our almost exclusive use of 'preach' for all of [these synonyms] is a sign, not merely of poverty of vocabulary, but of the loss of something which was a living reality in primitive Christianity.

This is a widespread view; but the present analysis demonstrates that the semantic situation is even richer and more complex in today's English (and also in German and in several other European languages) than it ever was in New Testament Greek. So also, as follows logically, is the living reality of today's empirical global Christianity.

### English meanings of synonyms for euangelizo

We will now construct a parallel list of all relevant words in current English (i.e. relevant to or with bearing on 'to evangelize') used by standard New Testament lexicons to translate these 42 Greek synonyms and part-synonyms. These lexicons usually give 2, 3, 4, or more English meanings for each Greek word, and (as our diagram shows) there is much overlapping, with several English meanings each shared by a number of Greek terms. A typical word, *kerussein*, for example is given 11 English meanings by Liddell & Scott's *Lexicon* (1889 Abridgement).

In Table 3–4 are arranged alphabetically the English terms for all 42 Greek words as given in Liddell & Scott. Note that the order of words is alphabetical and so bears no relation to that in Table 3–3. We should also note that this list is strictly limited to words occurring in this particular *Lexicon*. If we include all other parallel words used in 20th-century contemporary English, the total, as we will later show, mounts from 153 to around 700.

Seen in isolation out of context, some of these words may not appear to be much related to the activity of evangelizing. What we are doing at present, however, is simply to report actual Greek New Testament usage and its meanings. As with Table 3–3, we can arrange these meanings as a diagram of intersecting circles (see Graphic 3-1). Once again, the word with the most common ground with all others is the English transliteration of *euangelizein*, to evangelize.

One striking point that the diagram brings out is that certain synonyms are closer to 'evangelize' than all the rest. In the same way that the Gospels portray Jesus as frequently surrounded by an especially close group of 3 disciples—Peter, James and John—so the word 'evangelize' down the centuries in English usage has come to be surrounded most closely (as measured by frequency of usage by English speakers) by an especially close group of 10 synonyms which we will later be terming The Big Ten—the words preach, bring, tell, proclaim, declare, announce, evangelize, give, spread, make hear.

What this whole discussion illustrates is the extraordinary complexity of this whole concept. The English word 'evangelize', like *euangelizo*, lies at the center of a large range of overlapping synonyms, near-synonyms, and part-synonyms. All of these contribute part of their own meanings of the complete or

full meaning of 'evangelize', although 'evangelize' in its turn is only a part of each's own complete meaning. Inasmuch as no other word is an exact synonym, 'evangelize' is therefore an indispensable verbal component, in English, of any treatment of the subject. Like its Greek counterpart, 'evangelize' touches on and is to some degree equivalent to the whole range of activity involved in the spreading of the good news about Jesus Christ.

## 3. GEOCOMMISSION

The last few pages have examined the 2 biblical phenomena, the Great Commission, and the verb 'evangelize'. This Part 3 demonstrates that they are actually parallel and complementary, and that taken

| Table 3–4. | 153 current English meanings of 42 New Testament Greek verbs related to *euangelizo*. |
|---|---|

Source: H.G. Liddell & R. Scott, *A Greek-English lexicon* (1843, 1968, and 1889 Abridgement). This listing includes only meanings which are in some sense connected with or parallel to 'evangelize'.

| | |
|---|---|
| acknowledge | indicate |
| acquaint | induce |
| admit | inform |
| admonish | instruct |
| advertise | interpret |
| advise | invite |
| affirm | invoke |
| agree with | lead way to |
| announce | make known |
| argue with | make proclamation |
| asseverate | mean |
| attest | mobilize |
| be a witness | narrate |
| bear a message | noise abroad |
| bear witness to | notify |
| beg earnestly | obey |
| bellow | offer |
| beseech | order |
| beseech | pass on |
| bestow | pass word on |
| bless | persuade |
| bring convincing proof | point out |
| bring news of | praise |
| calculate | preach |
| call | prescribe |
| call to witness | prevail upon |
| carry tidings of | proclaim |
| carry back tidings of | profess |
| cause to be proclaimed | promise |
| censure | prophesy |
| certify | protest |
| charge | prove |
| chat | put in mind |
| chatter | read |
| command | reason |
| commend | rebuke |
| concede | recite |
| confess | recommend |
| confirm | recount |
| converse with | refute |
| corroborate | relate |
| count | relate in full |
| criticize | report |
| cry aloud | reveal |
| deal with | roar |
| declare | say |
| deliver | send as a message |
| demand | set out in detail |
| denounce | shout |
| depose to | show |
| describe | show by argument |
| detail | show a person up |
| dictate | show way to |
| disclose a secret | speak |
| discourse | speak out boldly |
| discuss | speak plainly |
| entreat | spread |
| evangelize | spread abroad |
| excite | summon |
| exhort | support |
| explain | talk |
| expound | teach |
| extol | teach aright |
| give | tell |
| give evidence of | tell at length |
| give good report of | tell over |
| give notice by messenger | testify |
| give orders | thank |
| give the word | train |
| grant | translate |
| hand down | transmit |
| hand over to | urge |
| have dealings with | utter |
| hear | visit |
| herald | warn |
| impart | win over |
| imply | witness |

together they form a vast new megaphenomenon that is being termed here "GeoCommission". The evidence for this can now be analyzed.

## 'EVANGELIZE' & THE GREAT COMMISSION

We return first to the problem noted earlier: the absence of the words *euangelizo* and 'evangelize' from, respectively, the Greek and English biblical accounts of the Great Commission. The verb had been employed 11 times before the Resurrection in Matthew's and Luke's Gospels, and was later employed 16 times in The Acts of the Apostles. Why then should it be absent from the entire records of the post-Resurrection 40-day period during which the Risen Christ promulgated his last commission? To answer this question, we must first make an analysis of the Commission itself.

### The centrality of Christ's Commission
In the 1960s, several missiologists were saying that the traditional emphasis upon the Great Commission of Christ as the main motivation for mission was misplaced. Instead, they said, the Day of Pentecost itself with the experience of the Holy Spirit should be regarded as the main motivation for mission. This was the thesis of Reformed missiologist Harry Boer.

By 1987 the pendulum appears to have swung back, and the Great Commission is once again widely seen as the major factor in mission and its motivation. Literature concerning this is multiplying in many languages of scholarship, although it is seldom treated with the depth of investigation and understanding that it requires. Some 30 alternative names for the Commission exist in English, with more in other languages, with 'Commission' often replaced by such words as Mandate, Command, Charge, Order, or Imperative, and 'Great' replaced by adjectives such as Last, Major, Final, Universal, Solemn, or Missionary.

### Locations in Scripture
The Great Commission is the term we use for the variety of directives the Risen Lord gave to his followers concerning their future mission. It was given probably on a number of occasions to different individuals or audiences and with different emphases during the 40-day period from the Resurrection to the Ascension. We have, in the New Testament, records of 6 such occasions. In imperative or verbal form, it is recorded at 5 points in the first 5 books of the New Testament: Matthew 28:18-20, Mark 16:15-18, Luke 24:45-49, John 20:21-23, and Acts 1:4-8. The sixth account of the Great Commission may be seen in the form of an acted parable in John 21.

Altogether, the 6 accounts document for us something like 50 distinct imperatives or verbs from the Risen Christ to his disciples. For the purposes of this investigation, we can divide them into 7 groups or mandates.

### Components of the Commission: The Big Seven
The 50 or so imperatives from Jesus to his disciples can be grouped together into 7 overarching mandates in imperative form (with the actual Greek words used) as follows:

These 7 New Testament Greek words, and the 7 English verbs they translate to, are so important to our subject that we are justified in giving them a popularized title: The Big Seven. This will help us to recognize their identity and their cohesiveness as a group. The Big Seven are by no means identical with, or synonymous with, that other grouping The Big Ten. But they are clearly closely related in concept and purpose. They will be examined in detail in a later study.

### Explaining the absence of euangelizo
We can now return to the problem raised earlier. The answer to this puzzle is twofold. The first answer is that the concept of *euangelizo* is in fact present in the form of its cognate noun *euangelion* (good news or gospel, used in Mark 16:15). The second answer can be seen in our argument that the verb *euangelizo* must be interpreted in the context of its 41 related Greek words and 152 related English words. Of all of these latter, a large number do occur in the post-Resurrection records.

This latter point also explains a further surprising fact. *Euangelizo* does not occur in the Bible in the imperative form. In other words, 'Evangelize!' as a command is not, strictly speaking, a biblical term. However, many of its synonyms—in Greek and in English—do occur as biblical imperatives (Preach! Bring! Tell! Proclaim! Announce! Declare! Disciple! et alia).

### Synonyms in the Commission
The 7 imperatives listed above may therefore be regarded as aspects of the single imperative Evangelize! or as dimensions of it or as synonyms of it. At the same time, however, they are clearly distinct from each other. Thus Witness!, which is the Apostle John's key word to the exclusion of *euangelizo* and *euangelizo*, is not the same as Proclaim! Each has its own important distinctives of meaning.

Taken together, the overall interpretation of the presence of all these synonyms of *euangelizo* in these 6 biblical accounts is that the initial thrust of the Great Commission can be summarized, in English, as: 'Go and evangelize the world.' To evangelize in New Testament usage, therefore, is essential to obeying and implementing Christ's Great Commission. To a large degree, also, to evangelize means to fulfill that same Commission.

---

**Table 3–5. GeoCommission as the product of 2 phenomena—2 strands of biblical emphasis and evidence in 2,600 languages.**

GeoCommission is defined here as the empirical megaphenomenon formed by the combining of 2 biblical empirical phenomena: (1) **the Great Commission**, evidenced by 200,000 Bible verses in 2,600 languages; and (2) **Evangelize!** evidenced by 105,000 usages of the biblical word in 2,600 languages. These 2 strands appear at first sight to be independent of each other but are found on analysis of all their synonyms and translations to be closely connected. In fact they are part of the same overall megaphenomenon articulating, describing, measuring, and analyzing human responsibility for global mission and world evangelization. This is the empirical reality here termed: **GeoCommission**.

| Aspect | First phenomenon | Second phenomenon | Synthesis |
|---|---|---|---|
| phenomenon | **1. The Great Commission** | **2. Evangelize!** *euangelizo* | **3. GeoCommission** |
| main title | the above name in 2,600 languages | its major translation in 2,600 languages | the above neologism |
| alternative names | 30 in English, 6,000 in other languages | 10,000 translations | a vast multilingual megaphenomenon |
| practitioners | Great Commission Christians | evangelizers, evangelists, evangelicals | geocommissioners |
| illustration | Global Diagram 6 | Global Diagrams 7, 33 | Global Diagrams 7, 33 |
| exegesis | Part 3 | Part 1 | Part 3 |
| source | Global Diagram 6 | Global Diagrams 7, 33 | Global Diagram 6 |
| languages | Each phenomenon has (a) 7 language spheres:<br>a. Old Testament Hebrew, Aramaic, Greek<br>b. New Testament Greek (Koine)<br>c. Contemporary English<br>d. 2,600 more print-scripture languages<br>e. 4,100 languages with only near-scriptures<br>f. 4,700 audio scripture languages (because using lingua francas)<br>g. 6,800 no-scripture languages | | |
| meanings | Each phenomenon has (b) 17 concentric circles of usage/meaning: | | |
| summary | Short sentence: 'The Great Commission is ...' | 'To evangelize is ... ' | 'GeoCommission is ... ' |
| scripture | 6 formal narrative NT accounts (61 verses) | 50 LXX usages & 54 NT usages | Some 200 Bible verses |
| | 8,000 accounts in 2,600 languages | 20,000 LXX & 85,000 NT usages | 200,000 Bible verses in 2,600 languages |
| | Briefer OT and NT references | | |
| dichotomy | 2 marching orders: Proclaim!, Baptize! | 2 meanings: Preach!, Convert! | The 2 Minicommissions: Evangelize! Disciple! |
| mandates | 7 Mandates, based on 7 Greek verbs | 7 related spheres of meaning | The Big Seven |
| roles | 7 human roles/responsibilities | 7 clusters of meanings of 'evangelize' | 7-P Evangelism, 7-P Evangelization |
| words | 7 descriptive overviews | 7 aspects of 'evangelize' | 7 types of Evangelizing Words |
| leading keywords | command, obey | 10 close variants (Greek), 10 most frequently used in English versions | The Big Ten (with 2 million usages in 1,100 languages) |
| macrotranslations | multiple translations in 1,000 languages | 28 English NT translations of 'evangelize' | The 51 Macrotranslations |
| macrocommands | 110 macrocommands | 100 English verbs as commands | The 110 Macrocommands |
| | the assumption of being obedient | | The 100,000 Imperatives |
| biblical synonyms | | *kerysso*, 4 closest, 19 major (Greek) | The 10 Million Commandments |
| nonbiblical synonyms | | | 140-420 synonyms per language |
| | | | The 900,000 biblical synonyms |
| ministries | 45 varieties of obeying the Commission | 45 ways to evangelize | The 45 Outreach Ministries/Evangelism |
| macrodefinitions | 30 major definitions | 250 definitions of 'evangelize' | The 250 Macrodefinitions |
| group-themes | | 344 key group-themes | The 344 Key Group-Themes |
| dimensions | 420 dimensions | The 420 dimensions of 'evangelize' | The 420 Dimensions |
| near-synonyms | | 140 Greek near-synonyms | |
| related verbs | | 210 related Greek verbs | |
| facets | | 620 English facets | The 620 Facets |
| single-word themes | | 800 English single-word themes | The 800 Single-Word Themes |
| cognates | | 2,400 English cognates of 'evangelize' | 550 Greek/2,400 English cognates |
| total keywords | | 4,700 English NT keywords | The 1 million cognates |
| | | 4,900 Greek NT keywords | The 3 million wider cognates/keywords |

*Thousands more synonymous imperatives*
This discussion so far has concerned only the New Testament Greek language and the contemporary English language. Table 3–5 takes into account the total of 10,000 other languages used by Christians. The central verb *euangelizo*/'evangelize' can be seen to have something of the order of 10 million commands or commandments, all being distinct and different synonyms in this multiplicity of languages.

## GEOCOMMISSION EMERGES

It can now be seen that the 2 related key phenomena that we observe in empirical global Christianity today are in fact very closely related. They appear to be two sides of the same coin. The proof of this is the

---

**Table 3–6. GeoCommission—a merger of 2 empirical biblical phenomena, (1) Christ's Great Commission, and (2) the richest biblical word *Evangelize!*—analyzed into 2 Minicommissions and 7 Mandates, resulting in and expounding 7-P evangelization calling for 7-P evangelism.**

This is an abbreviated version of the standalone Global Diagram 6 in Part 1 "GeoStatus". The table below analyzes the words used in the 6 New Testament narratives of Christ's Great Commission given to his followers in AD 33 (Matthew 28:16-20, Mark 16:14-18, Luke 24:36-49, John 20:19-23, John 21:1-22, Acts 1:3-14). At the same time it merges and combines (1) the whole phenomenon of the scriptural Great Commission narratives with (2) the quite distinct yet parallel phenomenon of the richest biblical word *euangelizo* (evangelize). The resulting merger is here termed—GeoCommission.

To understand GeoCommission here, it is first divided into 2 Minicommissions 'Evangelize!' and 'Disciple!', and then into 7 Mandates described in 14 columns.

Meanings of the 14 columns, including 3 giving statistics of usages (word frequency), are as follows. For meanings of all Greek words, see Table 3–3.
*Column 1. Mandate imperative.* Lines 1-7 give the Big Seven—the 7 Mandates of the Great Commission—in English Bible usage. These are given here as imperatives: *Receive* (the Holy Spirit)! *Go* (into all the world)! *Witness! Proclaim* (the gospel)! *Disciple* (the nations)! *Baptize! Train!* Note that what we are calling the overall imperative *Evangelize!* (Greek, *euangelizo*) does not occur in the Great Commission accounts although its cognate noun *euangelion*

(the Good News) does (in Mark 16:15). In that sense it is a distinct but parallel stream of apostolic commission.
*Column 2. Greek keyword.* The related Greek verbs or derivatives central to the Great Commission narratives are given in lines 1-7.
*Column 3. Usages.* Each Greek word is followed in this column by a figure which is the number of usages of the word, and its immediate cognates (adjectives or nouns) in the Greek New Testament.
*Column 4. Characteristic.* The phrases here describe the differentia of the various Mandates.
*Column 5. Human role.* The church's human response to GeoCommission is described under a spectrum of 7 generic types of evangelism, using a set of terms in 7-P format.
*Column 6. Sub-types.* The lists here (suggestive, not exhaustive or watertight or exclusive) give sub-types or varieties of evangelism or ministry for the stylized types in column 5.
*Column 7. Evangelizing words.* These 7 types of words corresponding to the 7 modes of evangelism in column 5.
*Column 8. Ministries.* The total number of distinct evangelistic outreach ministries classified here under each Mandate totals 45 (shown listed in Global Diagram 32).
*Column 9. Overview.* This defines the 7 Mandates using a

second set in 7-P format to describe the spectrum of 7 generic types of evangelization, as broadly defined.
*Column 10. Other keywords.* These are keywords (related key nouns) from the Greek or Latin ('L') New Testaments which support or illustrate each Mandate.
*Column 11. Usages.* The first figure gives the number of Greek or Latin New Testament usages of the exact noun opposite it in column 10; the second figure gives the total usages of the word together with its immediate cognates (adjectives, nouns, or verbs).
*Column 12. Dimensions.* The total number of dimensions of 'evangelize' related to each Mandate, namely major English synonyms which each contribute something unique to the full-orbed meaning of 'evangelize'; listed in Table 23-17 and divided here under each of the 7 Mandates.
*Column 13. Key dimensions.* The column lists a small alphabetized selection of examples of the previous column's total of dimensions of 'evangelize', given in imperative mood as constituent commands under the Mandate.
*Column 14. Facets.* The final column gives the total of all English verbs which are distinct aspects or facets (or synonyms or near-synonyms or part-synonyms) of 'evangelize' (again, listed in Table 23-17), arranged under each of the 7 Mandates.

| MANDATE IMPERATIVE English 1 | NT Greek 2 | Usages 3 | DOMINANT CHARACTERISTIC 4 | HUMAN ROLE 5 | SUB-TYPES OF EVANGELISM 6 | RESULTING WORDS 7 | OUTREACH MINISTRIES 8 | OVERVIEW 9 | OTHER KEYWORDS (related nouns) Greek, Latin (L) 10 | Usages 11 | Total 12 | Key dimensions 13 | FACETS English 14 |
|---|---|---|---|---|---|---|---|---|---|---|---|---|---|
| **OVERALL IMPERATIVE:** | | | | | | | | | | | | | |
| **Evangelize!** | *euangelizo* | 133 | Authoritative | **7-P Evangelism** | Pluriform evangelism Evangelistic work | Evangelizing words | 45 | **7-P Evangelization** | euangelion semeia kai terata evangelizatio (L) | 76/133 77/84 41 | 420 | Evangelize with signs following | 700 |
| **MINICOMMISSION I: EVANGELIZE!** CONSTITUENT MANDATES: | | | | | | | | | | | | | |
| 1. **Receive!** | *labete* verb: *lambano* | 263 | Spirit-dominated | **Prayer evangelism** | Baptism in the Spirit Spirit evangelism Pneumatization Renewal in the Spirit Intercession Power evangelism | HIDDEN WORDS | 2 | **Pneumatic evangelization** | parakletos dynamis pneumatikos exousia | 5/34 120/331 28/413 103/107 | 10 | Accompany, Be filled, Breathe, Cooperate, Follow, Participate, Pneumatize, Pray, Receive power, Stay, Wait | 33 |
| 2. **Go!** | *poreuthentes* verb: *poreuomai* | 154 | Person-implemented | **Pre-evangelism** | Apostolate Mission Extension Outreach Primary evangelism Visitation evangelism Visual evangelism Audiovisual evangelism | VISUAL WORDS | 11 | **Preparatory evangelization** | apostole missio (L) | 4/255 900 | 45 | Act, Contact, Develop, Encounter, Engage, Extend, Go, Help, Impact, Influence, Itinerate, Liberate, Love, Make aware, Occupy, Permeate, Prepare, Reach, Seek, Send, Show, Target, Touch, Transmit, Visit | 101 |
| 3. **Witness!** | *martyres* verb: *martyreo* | 173 | Unorganized, private | **Personal evangelism** | Person-to-person witness Personal work Individual evangelism Conversational evangelism Dialogue evangelism Gossiping the gospel Seed-sowing Prophetic evangelism | PERSONAL WORDS | 2 | **Presence evangelization** | martyria praesencia (L) justitia (L) pax (L) dialogismos | 57/173 120 220 200 14/43 | 60 | Be martyred, Be present, Bring, Carry, Confess, Dialogue, Expose, Gossip, Inform, Propagate, Radiate, Report, Say, Share, Shine, Sow, Spread, Talk, Tell, Testify, Witness | 132 |
| 4. **Proclaim!** | *keryxate* verb: *kerysso* | 72 | Ordered, public | **Preaching evangelism** | Public evangelism Mass evangelism Demonstration evangelism Deliverance evangelism Incarnational evangelism Power healing Saturation evangelism | PROCLAIMED WORDS | 6 | **Proclamation evangelization** | kerygma apologia therapeia | 8/72 8/18 3/47 | 48 | Advertise, Announce, Declare, Demonstrate, Do miracles, Exorcise, Explain, Expound, Give a message, Give opportunity, Heal, Herald, Make listen, Preach, Present, Proclaim, Prove, Publish, Read, Reason, Refute, Saturate, Translate | 85 |
| **MINICOMMISSION II: DISCIPLE!** | | | | | | | | | | | | | |
| 5. **Disciple!** | *matheteusate* verb: *matheteuo* | 266 | Convert-oriented | **Persuasion evangelism** | Paracletic evangelism Harvest evangelism Discipling evangelism Verdict evangelism Decision evangelism Lordship evangelism | WRITTEN WORDS | 9 | **Pressure evangelization** | paraklesis therismos mathetes | 29/34 13/36 261/266 | 63 | Appeal, Catch, Compel, Confront, Conquer, Convert, Convince, Denounce, Disciple, Exhort, Forgive, Give, Harvest, Impart, Implore, Invite, Offer, Persuade, Press, Reap, Retain, Urge, Warn, Win | 128 |
| 6. **Baptize!** | *baptizontes* verb: *baptizo* | 111 | Church-oriented | **Pastoral evangelism** | Baptism Baptizing evangelism Evangelism that results in churches Church planting Incorporation Shepherding Celebration evangelism | PRINTED WORDS | 9 | **Planting evangelization** | baptismos koinonia ekklesia leitourgeia eucharistia katechumenos | 23/111 19/59 115 6/15 15/54 8 | 35 | Affiliate, Baptize, Bless, Build, Catechize, Confirm, Enroll, Feed, Grow, Incorporate, Initiate, Minister, Multiply, Plant, Praise, Sacramentalize, Serve, Tend, Worship | 70 |
| 7. **Train!** | *didaskontes* verb: *didasko* | 212 | Ministry-oriented | **Programmed evangelism** | Teaching evangelism Electronic evangelism Broadcasting Radio/TV evangelism | ELECTRONIC WORDS | 6 | **Pedagogical evangelization** | didache diakonia oikodome | 30/212 34/101 18/59 | 21 | Broadcast, Celebrate, Cultivate, Edify, Educate, Follow-up, Instruct, Mobilize, Nurture, Program, Teach, Train | 43 |

discovery that they both share scores of biblical synonyms, numbering 200 or so in Greek and 400 or so in English and approaching at least a million in all the languages of the world. This is communication of the highest order. What it means is that if a certain range of synonyms for Christ's Commission as God's commands to the church has little appeal to certain populations, there are always scores of alternatives through which God's message can get access.

### Measuring the connection

In contemporary, scientific usage today, a 'dimension' is a characteristic which by definition can be measured. It can be enumerated, quantified, added up, computed and so on. Since it is now clear that the Great Commission is closely related to *euangelizo* and 'evangelize', the vast number of synonyms generated—any of which as a potential dimension can be measured—opens up vast vistas for social scientific investigation and discovery.

### EXTENDING THE CONNECTION OF COMMISSION & EVANGELIZE

Later Parts of this survey volume will attempt to measure these 2 phenomena in great detail and in addition will measure their connection to each other. The main variables derived are (1) evangelization, denoted by the variable E (the percentage of any population that has become evangelized, i.e. has become aware of Christianity, Christ and the gospel), and (2) Great Commission Christians (Christian believers who take seriously Christ's Great Commission and are in some way involved in implementing it). These computations are set out here in Part 22 "Evangelism", Part 23 "Evangelization", Part 24 "Microevangelistics", Part 25 "Macroevangelistics", and Part 21 "GeoPersonnel".

### GEOCOMMISSION IN CHURCH HISTORY

After the New Testament era, some 20 centuries of church history have flowed over the concepts. It is instructive to ask how the church has dealt with the Great Commission, or whether it has understood *euangelizo* sufficiently to have truly evangelized the world. The many and varied plans to do just this that Christians have produced over the centuries are worth investigating at this point. An overall summary then produces Global Diagrams 13 ('Global plans') and 9 ('Disobedience'). The Great Commission also produces a new megatypology, the first of 4 georenewal typologies with which to understand the empirical global Christian world.

### A variety of commissions, AD 30-33

Immediately after his temptation in the wilderness, Jesus began itinerating and witnessing to his Father's plan. His was first a ministry of announcement: Repent, for God's kingdom is at hand. His was a ministry of compassion and of evangelization. He also trained leaders for his future church. Healing, teaching, preaching, and making disciples comprised his immediate plan. Eventually, this culminated in his future global plan when he announced his Great Commission.

In his classic work, *The Master Plan of Evangelism* (1963), Robert Coleman expounds the evangelistic methods of Jesus. According to God's plan of global conquest, Jesus trained the twelve "to go with the gospel to the whole world."

During his three-year ministry, Jesus gave his disciples a variety of calls and commissions. First, he chose the twelve and gave them power and authority. He commissioned them to go initially to the Israelites (Matthew 10:1-6). Later, he commissioned the seventy to evangelize the seventy Gentile nations (compare Genesis 10 and Luke 10:1).

During the 40 days following his crucifixion and resurrection, Jesus delivered his Great Commission as the spiritual counterpart to Genesis 1:28. He specified two parts, evangelizing and discipling. 'Go forth to every part of the world (Greek, *cosmos*) and proclaim the Good News to the whole creation' (Mark 16:15, NEB). 'Go to all peoples everywhere and make them my disciples' (Matthew 28:19, GNB).

Probably Jesus gave various forms of his Great Commission to different groups at different times. Global Diagram 2 showed how he emphasized 7 distinct mandates: Receive! Go! Witness! Proclaim! Disciple! Baptize! Train! Today, the church employs a wide variety of terms and phrases for the different varieties of the ministry of evangelizing to which these lead.

In this way, then, Jesus launched the process of world evangelization. We pick up the story from there to find the answer to the all-important question: How did his followers respond? Did they obey his commission?

### The rise of global plans

How has the church responded to GeoCommission over the centuries? On the one hand, individuals have tried to obey it without considering what others might be doing. That's about as effective as an army issuing rifles to foot soldiers and asking them to fire at will. On the other hand, however, Christian churches and agencies have sought to obey GeoCommission without regard for what other churches and agencies are doing. That is equally chaotic and ineffective. The result has been the outpouring of an immense torrent of unrelated, uncoordinated plans for world evangelization. Our study shows that there must be a better way, which will be described later on, in Part 27 "GeoStrategies".

### BIBLIOGRAPHY

*An enquiry into the obligation of Christians to use means for the conversion of the heathen*. W. Carey. Leicester, UK: Ann Ireland, 1792. 87p.
'An exegetical study of Matthew 28:16–20,' K. Barth, in *The theology of the Christian mission*, p.55–71. G. Anderson (ed). New York: McGraw-Hill, 1961.
*Anglican cycle of prayer: praying together for persons and places around the world—1996*. London: Church House Publishing; Cincinnati, OH: Forward Movement Publications, 1995. 160p. (Annual publication of the Anglican Communion designed to focus attention on the world of Anglican missions worldwide).
*Churches that obey: taking the Great Commission seriously*. R. Forster & J. Richard (eds). Carlisle, UK: AD 2000 and M Publishers, 1995. 207p.
*DAWN 2000: 7 million churches to go: the personal story of the DAWN strategy for world evangelism*. J. Montgomery. Pasadena, CA: William Carey Library, 1989. 239p.
*Guardians of the Great Commission: the story of women in modern missions*. R. A. Tucker. Grand Rapids, MI: Academie Books, 1988. 278p.
*In search of the Great Commission: What did Jesus really say?* W. L. Banks. Chicago: Moody, 1991. 168p.
*New Life 2000: a revolutionary plan to help fulfill the Great Commission by AD 2000*. San Bernardino CA: Campus Crusade for Christ/Here's Life World, 1987.
*The earliest Christian mission to 'all nations': in the light of Matthew's gospel*. J. LeGrand. Atlanta: Scholar's Press, 1995. 301p.
*The evangelization of the world in this generation*. J. R. Mott. New York: Student Volunteer Movement for Foreign Missions, 1900. 253p.
*The Great Commission*. T. O. Jenkins. Darlington, SC: Evangelical Press, 1997. 174p.
*The Great Commission: biblical models for evangelism*. M. Arias. Nashville, TN: Abingdon Press, 1992. 142p.
*The Great Commission handbook*. Evanston, IL: Center for Information on Christian Student Opportunities, annual.
*The Great Commission lifestyle: conforming your life to Kingdom priorities*. R. E. Coleman. Grand Rapids, MI: Fleming H. Revell, 1992. 126p.
'The missionary mandate in the twentieth century,' J. T. Boberg, in *The gospel and frontier peoples*, p.17–31. R. P. Beaver (ed). Pasadena, CA: William Carey Library, 1973.

# Part 4

# MARTYROLOGY

## The demographics of Christian martyrdom, AD 33–AD 2001

*People will do to you exactly what they did to me.*
—Jesus to his disciples (John 15:21, Contemporary English Version)

*We share in the terrible sufferings of Christ.*
—Apostle Paul (2 Corinthians 1:5, Contemporary English Version)

*I saw under the altar the souls of those who had been slain for the word of God and for the witness they had borne... And I heard the number of the sealed: 144,000.*
—Revelation 6:9, 7:4, RSV; Sealing of the Martyrs

*Martyrdom is a charism of the Spirit.*
—C. H. Pinnock, *Flame of love: a theology of the Holy Spirit*, 1996

Demographics is both a science and an art. Part 4 applies this knowledge to a startling phenomenon: the killings of 70 million Christians across the centuries and in every country. The data are sufficiently dense, detailed, and incontrovertible that this Part arrives at firm totals and trends. Even ongoing rates of martyrdom are calculated, which bishops, evangelists, foreign missionaries, clergy, church leaders, as well as laypersons should be prepared to face.

# The demographics of Christian martyrdom, AD 33-AD 2001

## AN OVERVIEW OF MARTYRDOM

This section of the survey presents the evidence for the startling conclusion that, over the 20 centuries of the Christian faith, some 70 million Christians have been murdered for that faith and hence are called martyrs. And this number continues to grow in the new Millennium as over 400 new martyrs are being killed every day. The whole situation is summarized on a single sheet in Global Diagram 16 (in Part 1). Part of that diagram is shown here in Graphic 4-1 to the right.

### Christian vs. non-Christian martyrs

All religions have their own lists of martyrs. In their cases the term means 'members of our religion who have been killed for it'. A survey of human history reveals a large number of such martyrdom situations where hundreds, thousands, or on numerous occasions, millions of individuals have been killed because of their religion. Examples from the 20th century include the Jewish holocaust in Germany, the Muslim-Hindu wars since India's Partition in 1947, current Hindu-Sikh fighting in northern India, and the torture and murder of Confucianists under Communist Chinese rule. Throughout history, ethnic religionists have also suffered 'martyrdom' under the invasion of foreign peoples.

Martyrdom is even desired under certain circumstances. The role of Japanese *kamikazes* in World War II served this purpose, and certain fundamentalist Muslims deliberately fought to their deaths in the Iran/Iraq Persian Gulf War in the early 1980s.

A brief summary table of all such martyrdoms is given below in Table 4–1. The rest of this survey will then focus on Christian martyrdom.

| Table 4–1. | Martyrdom in world religions since each's origin. | |
|---|---|---|
| Islam | Muslim martyrs | 80 million |
| Christianity | Christian martyrs | 70 million |
| Hinduism | Hindu martyrs | 20 million |
| Buddhism | Buddhist martyrs | 10 million |
| Judaism | Jewish martyrs | 9 million |
| Ethnoreligions | Ethnic martyrs | 6 million |
| Sikhism | Sikh martyrs | 2 million |
| Baha'i | Baha'i martyrs | 1 million |
| Other religions | Other religious martyrs | 5 million |
| All religions | Total religious martyrs | 203 million |

### Origin of the word 'martyr'

The English word 'martyr' is derived from the Greek *martys*, which carries the meaning 'witness' in English. In New Testament usage, it meant 'a witness to the resurrection of Christ'. This witness resulted so frequently in death that by the end of the first century *martys* had come to mean a Christian who witnessed to Christ *by his or her death*. This enlarged meaning has become the accepted norm throughout church history.

### Definition of terms

For the purposes of this volume's primarily quantitative analysis of martyrdom, Christian martyrs are defined as 'believers in Christ who have lost their lives prematurely, in situations of witness, as a result of human hostility.' This definition has 5 essential and indeed indispensable elements which can be stated as follows:

1. *'Believers in Christ'*. These individuals include the entire Christian community including professing Christians, crypto-Christians, affiliated Christians, and unaffiliated Christians. In AD 2000, some 2.0 billion individuals match this description, and since the time of Christ over 8.3 billion have believed in Christ.

2. *'Lost their lives'*. Our definition is restricted to Christians actually put to death, for whatever reason.

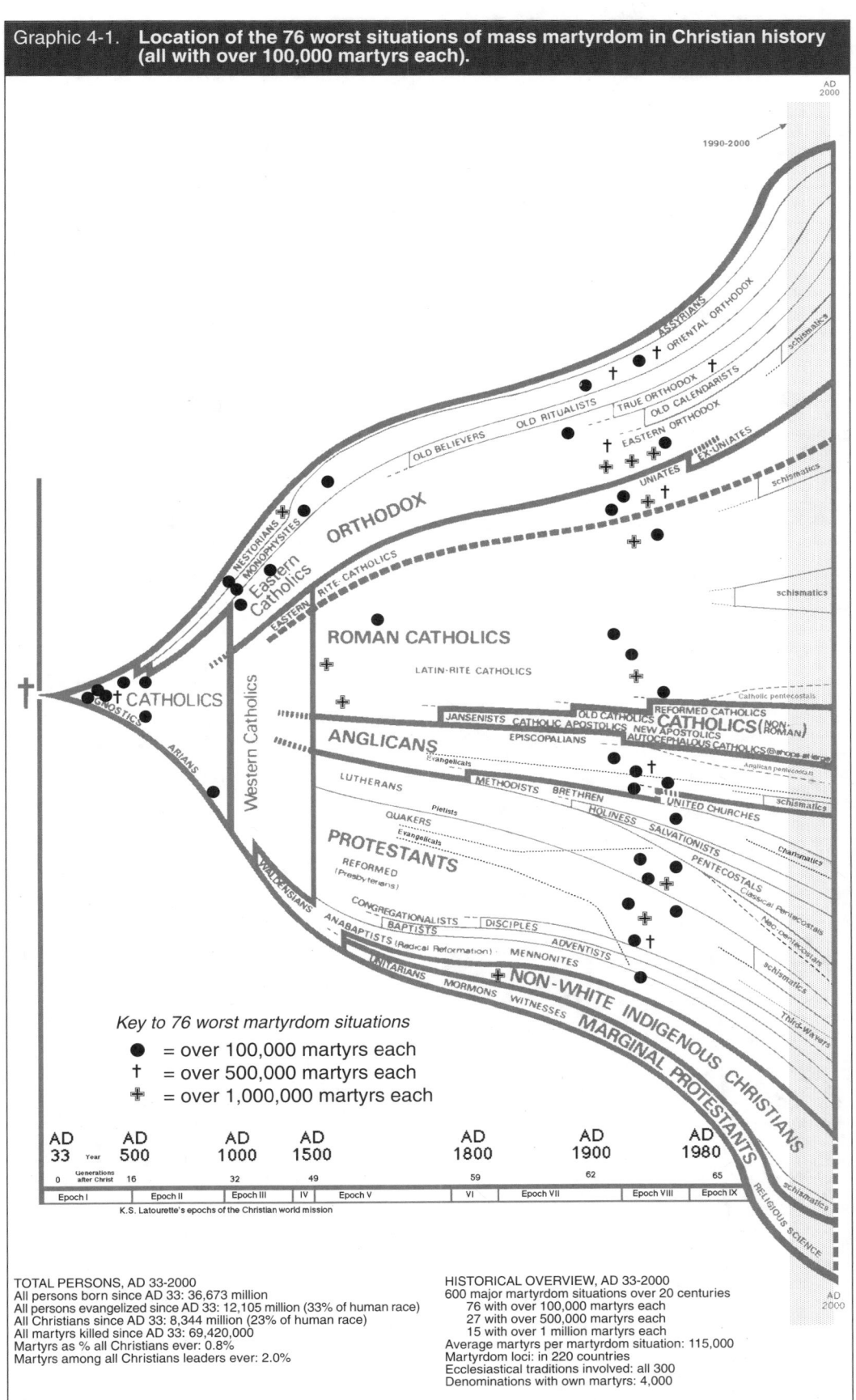

**Graphic 4-1.** Location of the 76 worst situations of mass martyrdom in Christian history (all with over 100,000 martyrs each).

Key to 76 worst martyrdom situations

● = over 100,000 martyrs each

† = over 500,000 martyrs each

✠ = over 1,000,000 martyrs each

K.S. Latourette's epochs of the Christian world mission

TOTAL PERSONS, AD 33-2000
All persons born since AD 33: 36,673 million
All persons evangelized since AD 33: 12,105 million (33% of human race)
All Christians since AD 33: 8,344 million (23% of human race)
All martyrs killed since AD 33: 69,420,000
Martyrs as % all Christians ever: 0.8%
Martyrs among all Christians leaders ever: 2.0%

HISTORICAL OVERVIEW, AD 33-2000
600 major martyrdom situations over 20 centuries
76 with over 100,000 martyrs each
27 with over 500,000 martyrs each
15 with over 1 million martyrs each
Average martyrs per martyrdom situation: 115,000
Martyrdom loci: in 220 countries
Ecclesiastical traditions involved: all 300
Denominations with own martyrs: 4,000

CHRIST POPULARIZED

CHRIST HISTORICIZED

CHRIST THREE-DIMENSIONALIZED

CHRIST REGNANT

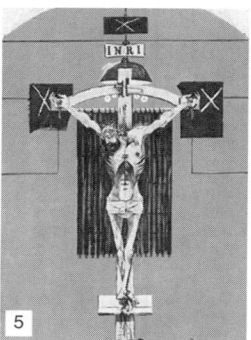

CHRIST SACRIFICED

CHRIST ACCURSED

CHRIST MOCKED

CHRIST EXHIBITED

CHRIST ROMANTICIZED

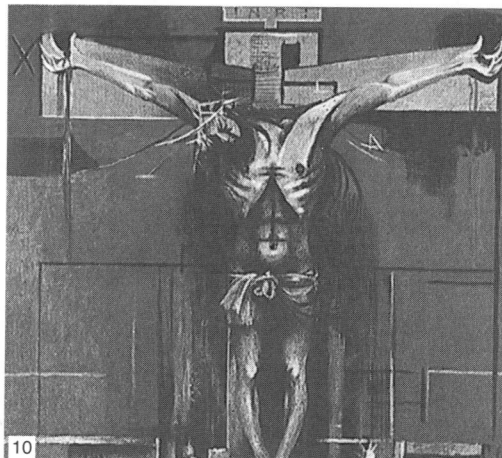

CHRIST DESTROYED

CHRIST REVILED

CHRIST UPLIFTED

CHRIST FOR SALE

CHRIST AUCTIONED

CHRIST AUTHENTICATED

CHRIST MULTIPLIED

# Jesus the Faithful and True *Martys*

(*Martys* is the Greek word for witness or martyr: see Revelation 3:14)
(see captions on facing page, bottom left)

## Table 4–2. Martyrdoms of The Twelve Apostles and of 12 other New Testament apostles.

The New Testament records the selection and subsequent ministries of the Twelve Apostles. Strong traditions exist that all were subsequently martyred for Christ, though the NT only records this for James son of Zebedee (Acts 12:2). The table below records what is known of the most likely fate of (a) each of the Twelve; (b) the 7 others named apostolos in the NT whose fate is partly known; and (c) the 5 others named apostolos in the NT about whose subsequent fate nothing whatever is known.

| Ref. 1 | Name in Mark's Gospel 2 | Other names 3 | Martyred 4 | How died 5 | Place 6 | Country 7 |
|---|---|---|---|---|---|---|
| **a.** | **The Twelve Apostles** | | | | | |
| 1 | Simon Peter | Cephas (Rock) | AD 64 | Crucified | Rome | Italy |
| 2 | James son of Zebedee | Boanerges (Son of Thunder) | 44 | Beheaded | Jerusalem | Palestine |
| 3 | John Boanerges | The Beloved Disciple | 96 | Boiled in oil | Ephesus | Turkey |
| 4 | Andrew | Andrea | 69 | Crucified | Patras | Greece |
| 5 | Philip | – | 60 | Hanged | Hierapolis | Turkey |
| 6 | Bartholomew | Nathanael, son of Ptolemy | 68 | Crucified | Albana | Armenia |
| 7 | Matthew | Levi | 70 | Stabbed | Nubia | Ethiopia |
| 8 | Thomas | Didymus (Twin) | 82 | Speared | Mylapore | India |
| 9 | James the Less | The Younger; son of Alphaeus | 54 | Stoned | Jerusalem | Palestine |
| 10 | Judas Thaddeus | Lebbaeus; son of James; Addai | 66 | Clubbed | Ardaze | Turkey |
| 11 | Simon Zelotes | The Zealot; the Canaanean | 61 | Crucified | Suanir | Iran |
| 12 | Judas Iscariot | Man of Kerioth; Assassin | 33 | (Suicide) | Jerusalem | Palestine |
| **b.** | **Other NT apostles** | | | | | |
| | Matthias | Mattaniah | 64 | Burned | Axum | Ethiopia |
| | Paul | Saul of Tarsus | 64 | Beheaded | Rome | Italy |
| | Barnabas | Joseph; Son of Consolation | 61 | Stoned | Salamis | Cyprus |
| | Mark the Evangelist | John Mark | 68 | Trampled | Alexandria | Egypt |
| | James the Just | The Brother of the Lord | 62 | Stoned | Jerusalem | Palestine |
| | Luke the Evangelist | The Good Physician | 91 | Hanged | Rome | Italy |
| | Timothy | Bishop of Ephesus | 90 | Beheaded | Ephesus | Turkey |
| **c.** | **Others of unknown fate** | | | | | |
| | These 5 are: Andronicus, Apollos, Epaphroditus, Junia, Silas (Silvanus). | | | | | |

*3. 'Prematurely'.* This word is important. Martyrdom is a disruption—sudden, abrupt, unexpected, unwanted.

*4. 'In situations of witness'.* This phrase incorporates the original heart of the etymology. However, "witness" in this definition does not mean only public testimony or proclamation concerning the Risen Christ. It refers to the entire lifestyle and way of life of the Christian believer, whether or not he or she is actively proclaiming at the time of being killed. In this sense all Great Commission Christians, committed to Christ's mission as by definition they are, are 'witnesses' to the Lordship of the Risen Christ daily and continuously, whether consciously or unknowingly.

*5. 'As a result of human hostility'.* This last element is the crucial one. It excludes deaths through accidents, crashes, earthquakes and other 'acts of God', illnesses, or other causes of death however tragic.

An important point to note is what this definition omits. The most important item omitted is a criterion considered essential by churches in their martyrologies—'heroic sanctity', by which is meant saintly life and fearless stance. Those are certainly essential for a martyrology if it is to have compelling educational and inspirational value for church members under persecution and in particular for new converts. Heroic sanctity is however not essential to our definition because many Christians have been killed shortly after their conversion and before they had any chance to develop Christian character, holiness, or courage.

### THE CHRISTIAN UNDERSTANDING OF MARTYRS

#### The fate of the Twelve Apostles

The New Testament records how the Risen Christ gave his disciples the Great Commission, and describes a few early cases of their obedience. But nothing is said about their ultimate fate as global missionaries. The murder of only one of the Twelve is recorded, that of James in AD 44 (Acts 12:2). But historical traditions, some strong, some weak, record that they all died as martyrs. Table 4–2 sets out this situation.

Since recording these martyrdoms was relatively unimportant in the early church, this should alert us to the proper significance to be attached to martyrdom. God evidently calls a number of his disciples to experience death as martyrs, but no additional salvation or pre-eminence in the Kingdom of God necessarily results. Their obedience however advanced the spread of the gospel across the world.

#### Martyrdom not exclusively an early Christian phenomenon

When most Christians hear the word 'martyr' they tend to think of the Roman persecution of early Christians. The *Ecclesia Martyrum* or Church of the Martyrs is often thought to refer only to the earliest period of church history, the 10 imperial Roman persecutions. This is not the case. Martyrdom instead is considered to be the 'common fate which the Church shares with its Lord'. Our survey of individual martyrs and of martyrdom situations reveals a startling fact: martyrdom is a consistent feature of church history and occurs in every Christian tradition and confession. This is evident in Tables 4-3 and 4-4, and is documented in detail later in Table 4–10. The rate of martyrdom across the world throughout the ages has been a remarkably constant 0.8%. One out of every 120 Christians in the past has been martyred, or in the future is likely to so be.

#### Martyrdom in Bible and church

The Christian view of martyr developed in the context of actual martyrdoms in the first and second centuries after Christ. Martyrdom came about because of persecution and resulted in a death that was in itself a witness for Christ. In the early church the idea developed that it was not enough to be called a Christian, one had to show some proof. That proof was normally some kind of verbal acknowledgement of identification with Christ, starting with the confession 'Jesus is Lord.' Baumeister writes: 'Dying because one is a Christian is the action par excellence in which the disciple who is called to this confirms his or her faith by following the example of Jesus' suffering and through action is able once again to become a word with power to speak to others'. Eventually confessors were distinguished from martyrs.

The first Christian document to have martyrdom as its exclusive subject was the letter written by the Christians of Smyrna describing the martyrdom of their bishop Polycarp. One key concept in this letter, important to our understanding of martyrdom, is the fact that Polycarp's death validated his discipleship—he followed his master unto death.

Justin Martyr took the subject of martyrdom further, portraying the martyr as the holder of truth, willing to die because of its value.

### Table 4–3. Global overview of Christian martyrdom, AD 2000.

**TOTAL PERSONS, AD 33-2000**
All persons born since AD 33: 36,673 million
All persons evangelized since AD 33: 12,105 million (33% of human race)
All Christians since AD 33: 8,344 million (23% of human race)
All martyrs killed since AD 33: 69,420,000
Martyrs as % all Christians ever: 0.8%
Martyrs among all Christian leaders ever: 2.0%

**HISTORICAL OVERVIEW, AD 33-2000**
600 major martyrdom situations over 20 centuries
  76 with over 100,000 martyrs each
  27 with over 500,000 martyrs each
  15 with over 1 million martyrs each
Average martyrs per martyrdom situation: 115,000
Martyrdom loci: in 220 countries
Ecclesiastical traditions involved: all 300
Denominations with own martyrs: 4,000

**CONFESSION OF VICTIMS, AD 33-2000**
(total martyrs of each tradition)
Orthodox .......................... 42,798,000
  Russian Orthodox .............. 21,626,400
  East Syrians (Nestorians) ......... 12,379,000
  Ukrainian Orthodox ............ 3,500,000
  Gregorians (Armenian Apostolic) .... 1,215,100
Roman Catholic .................... 12,210,000
  Catholics (before AD 1000) ........ 855,000
Independents ..................... 3,512,000
Protestants ...................... 3,172,000
Anglicans ........................ 1,046,000
Marginal Christians ................ 6,700
other and background martyrs ........ 6,675,700
                Total all martyrs 69,420,000

**PERSECUTORS AND THEIR VICTIMS, AD 33-2000**

| Persecutors responsible | Martyrs |
|---|---|
| State ruling power | 55,871,000 |
| Atheists (overlap with above) | 31,689,000 |
| Muslims | 9,121,000 |
| Ethnoreligionists (animists) | 7,469,000 |
| Roman Catholics | 5,171,000 |
| Quasi-religionists | 2,712,000 |
| Buddhists (Mahayana) | 1,651,000 |
| Hindus | 676,000 |
| Zoroastrians (Parsis) | 384,000 |
| Eastern Orthodox | 222,000 |
| Other non-Christians | 115,000 |
| Other Christians | 146,000 |
| SUBTOTALS: | |
| Non-Christian persecutors | 63,882,000 |
| Christian persecutors | 5,538,000 |
| Total all martyrs | 69,420,000 |

**SITUATION BY AD 2000 (P.A.= PER YEAR)**
Martyrs in 20th century (1900-2000): ... 45,400,000
Martyrs since 1950: ................ 13,300,000
Average annual martyrs since 1950: ... 278,000 p.a.
Recent annual martyrs: ............. 171,000 p.a.
Current annual martyrs: ............ 160,000 p.a.
Countries heavily involved in AD 2000: . 50

**CONFESSION OF VICTIMS, AD 2000**
(average annual martyrdom rates)
Roman Catholics .................... 93,000
Protestants ...................... 30,000
Orthodox ........................ 14,000
Non-White indigenous Christians ....... 10,000
Anglicans and Old Catholics .......... 8,000
Marginal Protestants ............... 5,000
          Total martyrs p.a 160,000

**LIKELIHOOD (L%) OF BEING MARTYRED**
(at current rates)

| Full-time workers | L% | Per year |
|---|---|---|
| Bishops | 5.0 | 15 |
| Evangelists | 4.0 | 133 |
| Catechists | 3.5 | 175 |
| Foreign missionaries | 3.0 | 131 |
| Clergy | 2.0 | 303 |
| All Christian workers | 2.0 | 1,700 |
| Monks, brothers | 1.9 | 63 |
| Sisters, nuns | 1.8 | 300 |
| *Other Christians:* | | |
| Great Commission Christians | 1.6 | 80,000 |
| Christians (all kinds) | 1.0 | 160,000 |

---

**Jesus the Faithful and True *Martys***
(captions for photo collage opposite)

1. **Christ popularized.** Public yearly enactment of Jesus carrying his Cross to Calvary (Mexico, and throughout Latin America).
2. **Christ historicized.** 3-dimensional tableau of Crucifixion, Einsiedeln Abbey (Switzerland).
3. **Christ three-dimensionalized.** Argentina's Roman Catholic bishops use life-size crucified Christ.
4. **Christ regnant.** 'Christ Triumphant' reigning from the Cross (Dogura, Papua).
5. **Christ sacrificed.** 'Crucifixion', Church of St Aidan, East Acton, UK (G. Sutherland).
6. **Christ accursed.** Christ bearing sins of the world (John Biggs).
7. **Christ mocked.** 'Christ Crowned with Thorns' (Hieronymus Bosch, c1510).
8. **Christ exhibited.** 'Christ Exhibited' (young woman artist Helina Kom).
9. **Christ romanticized.** Altarpiece by Raphael, Italian master.
10. **Christ destroyed.** A horrific crucifixion (Graham Sutherland), Church of St. Matthew, Northampton, UK.
11. **Christ reviled.** 'Crucifixion' (Herbert Seidel), in earlier East German atheist setting.
12. **Christ uplifted.** 'Christ of Saint John of the Cross' (Salvador Dali, 1951).
13. **Christ for sale.** Sought after by buyers: 'Crucifixion' by Duccio di Buonisegna, c1300.
14. **Christ auctioned.** Christies of London auction that Duccio (shown hung on right) for highest price ever in 1976, £1,000,000.
15. **Christ authenticated.** Holy Shroud of Turin (Christ's burial cloth) exhibited in Turin Cathedral, 1978.
16. **Christ multiplied.** Hill of Crosses in Lithuania, expanded daily throughout 46-year occupation by atheist USSR.

## Table 4–4. 112 methods used to kill 70 million martyrs, AD 33–2000.

This table lists the whole variety of means and methods used to kill Christian martyrs over the last 20 centuries. It then estimates the totals so killed by each means, using the following estimates of cases:

| | |
|---|---|
| 10 | Over 10 million |
| 9 | From 4-10 million |
| 8 | From 2-4 million |
| 7 | From 1-2 million |
| 6 | 500,000 to 1 million |
| 5 | 100,000 to 500,000 |
| 4 | 10,000 to 100,000 |
| 3 | 1,000 to 10,000 |
| 2 | 100 to 1,000 |
| 1 | Under 100 |

| Method | Magnitude | Method | Magnitude |
|---|---|---|---|
| assassinated | 3 | injected | 5 |
| annihilated | 7 | killed by contract | 3 |
| attacked during sleep | 5 | killed by mob | 8 |
| bayoneted | 7 | killed extrajudicially | 5 |
| beaten to death | 7 | killed during genocide | 9 |
| beheaded | 4 | killed with sword | 9 |
| bled to death | 6 | knifed | 7 |
| boiled in oil | 2 | lashed to death | 4 |
| blown up | 6 | left to die | 6 |
| brainwashed to death | 5 | liquidated | 7 |
| broken on wheel | 2 | lowered into sewage | 9 |
| buried alive | 5 | lynched | 4 |
| burned at stake | 4 | machine-gunned | 6 |
| buried in sand | 4 | massacred | 8 |
| butchered | 9 | murdered | 5 |
| cannibalized | 3 | mutilated to death | 4 |
| chemically killed | 8 | poisoned | 4 |
| clubbed to death | 6 | pushed under traffic | 3 |
| crucified | 4 | pushed under train | 3 |
| crushed to death | 3 | put to death | 5 |
| cut to pieces | 7 | quartered | 3 |
| decapitated | 4 | racked to death | 4 |
| deprived of medication | 7 | roasted alive | 4 |
| died after beating | 8 | run over by tank | 2 |
| died after prison release | 7 | run over by vehicle | 4 |
| died in custody | 6 | savaged by dogs | 3 |
| died in interrogation | 4 | savaged by wild animals | 5 |
| died in prison | 10 | sawed in two | 3 |
| died in slavery | 6 | shedding blood | 6 |
| died of injuries | 9 | shot | 10 |
| died on release | 4 | shot by sniper | 6 |
| died under torture | 6 | slashed to death | 7 |
| disemboweled | 3 | slaughtered | 7 |
| dismembered | 5 | speared to death | 4 |
| driven mad | 6 | stabbed to death | 5 |
| driven to suicide | 3 | starved to death | 10 |
| drowned | 7 | stoned | 3 |
| drugged to death | 4 | strangled | 4 |
| eaten alive | 3 | suffocated | 4 |
| eaten by piranhas | 3 | targeted in war | 5 |
| electrocuted | 4 | terrorized to death | 5 |
| electronically killed | 2 | throat slit | 9 |
| executed | 4 | thrown from aircraft | 4 |
| exposed to elements | 6 | thrown off building | 5 |
| frightened to death | 4 | thrown over cliff | 7 |
| frozen to death | 8 | thrown overboard | 4 |
| garroted | 4 | thrown to crocodiles | 3 |
| gassed | 7 | thrown to lions | 4 |
| gibbeted | 4 | thrown to sharks | 4 |
| guillotined | 4 | tied behind vehicle | 4 |
| hacked to death | 8 | torched | 5 |
| hanged | 6 | torn apart by horses | 3 |
| hanged upside down | 3 | tortured to death | 5 |
| hunted to death | 4 | trampled to death | 5 |
| immolated | 4 | wiped out | 6 |
| immured | 2 | | |
| impaled | 4 | Total | 70 million |

## Table 4–5. Persecutors and martyrs: 60 religious traditions and their related Christian martyrs, AD 33–2000.

| Religionists | As persecutors | | As victims | |
|---|---|---|---|---|
| 1 | Code 2 | Martyrs 3 | Code 4 | Martyrs 5 |
| *Non-Christian persecutors* | | | | |
| **Atheists** | a | 31,689,000 | – | |
| **Buddhists** | B | 1,651,000 | – | |
| **Confucianists** | G | 3,000 | – | |
| **Ethnoreligionists (pagans)** | T | 7,469,000 | – | |
| **Hindus** | H | 676,000 | – | |
| **Jews** | J | 60,100 | – | |
| **Manicheans (Gnostics)** | g | 10,000 | – | |
| **Muslims** | M | 9,121,000 | – | |
| **Quasireligionists** | Y | 2,712,000 | – | |
| **Shintoists** | S | 17,000 | – | |
| **Spiritists** | U | 25,000 | – | |
| **state ruling power** | x | 55,871,000 | – | |
| **Zoroastrians (Parsis)** | Z | 384,000 | – | |
| **other and background killers** | | 6,675,700 | – | |
| | | | | |
| *Christian persecutors and/or victims* | | | | |
| African Independent pentecostals | – | 0 | I-3pA | 6,700 |
| Anabaptists | – | 0 | P-Ana | 34,000 |
| **Anglicans** | A | 53,400 | A- | 1,046,000 |
| Apostolic era (AD 30-75) | – | 0 | I-Aps | 15,400 |
| **Arians** | n | 14,500 | – | 1,000 |
| **Armenian Apostolic (Gregorian)** | – | 0 | O-Arm | 1,215,000 |
| Baptists | – | 0 | P-Bap | 704,000 |
| Belorussian Orthodox | – | 0 | O-Bye | 670,000 |
| Bulgarian Orthodox | – | 0 | O-Bul | 112,000 |
| **Byzantines** (before 1000) | O | 222,000 | O-Byz | 1,527,000 |
| Cathari/Albigensians | – | 0 | I-Alg | 20,000 |
| **Catholics** (before AD 1000) | R | 57,000 | R-Lat | 855,000 |
| Celts | – | 0 | A-Cel | 53,500 |
| Chaldean Catholics | – | 0 | R-Cha | 450 |
| Chinese house churches | – | 0 | I-3hC | 700,000 |
| **Congregationalists** | – | 0 | P-Con | 2,200 |
| **Coptic Orthodox** | – | 0 | O-Cop | 1,068,000 |
| Czech Orthodox | – | 0 | O-Cze | 15,000 |
| Disciples | – | 0 | P-Dis | 4,000 |
| **Donatists** | – | 0 | I-Don | 24,000 |
| **East Syrians (Nestorians)** | – | 0 | O-Nes | 12,379,000 |
| **Eastern Orthodox** (after 1000) | – | 0 | O- | 42,773,000 |
| Ethiopian Orthodox | – | 0 | O-Eth | 651,000 |
| Georgian Orthodox | – | 0 | O-Geo | 210,000 |
| Independent Charismatics | – | 0 | I-3 | 1,889,000 |
| Independent Churches | I | 5,000 | I- | 3,512,000 |
| Jehovah's Witnesses | – | 0 | m-Jeh | 6,700 |
| Latter-day Saints (Mormons) | m | 10 | m-LdS | 30 |
| Lollards | – | 0 | I-Lol | 100 |
| **Lutherans** | – | 0 | P-Lut | 987,000 |
| Maronites | – | 0 | R-Mar | 152,700 |
| Marranos, Moriscos, Messianic, Jewish-Christian | – | 0 | I-Jew | 21,500 |
| **Melkites** | – | 0 | R-Mel | 30 |
| Messianic Jewish | – | 0 | I-3mJ | 1,000,000 |
| Montanists | – | 0 | I-Mon | 2,000 |
| Moravians | – | 0 | P-Mor | 6,000 |
| Old Believers | – | 0 | I-OBe | 3,200 |
| Paulicians | – | 0 | I-Pau | 100,000 |
| Pentecostals | – | 0 | P-Pen | 1,021,000 |
| **Presbyterians/Reformed** | – | 0 | P-Ref | 210,000 |
| **Protestants** | P | 16,200 | P- | 3,172,000 |
| Quakers | – | 0 | I-Qua | 500 |
| Quasi-Christians | – | 0 | I-qCh | 1,000,000 |
| **Roman Catholics** (after 1000) | R | 5,171,000 | R- | 11,355,000 |
| **Russian Orthodox** | – | 0 | O-Rus | 21,626,000 |
| Romanian Orthodox | – | 0 | O-Rum | 16,000 |
| Serbian Orthodox | – | 0 | O-Ser | 350,000 |
| **Ukrainian Orthodox** | – | 0 | O-Ukr | 3,500,000 |
| Waldensians | – | 0 | I-Wal | 6,100 |
| West Syrians (Jacobites) | – | 0 | O-Syr | 351,000 |
| other and background martyrs | – | – | – | 6,675,700 |

## Why are there martyrs?

According to Latin American radical theologian Leonardo Boff they exist for two reasons: (1) Christians prefer to sacrifice their lives rather than to be unfaithful to their convictions and, (2) those that reject proclamation persecute, torture and kill. This general presence of evil in the world, combined with Christian devotion is at the root of martyrdom.

When we examine a list of martyrs down the ages, as comprehensive as is known today, some startling findings emerge. Table 4–3 provides a global summary and overview. Table 4–5 analyses the grand total of 70 million martyrs separated out by which non-Christian authorities are responsible, and also by the Christian traditions or confessions of the victims. Surprisingly, Christians themselves have been the persecutors responsible for martyring 5,539,000 other Christians.

Another startling fact is the viciousness of killers hostile to Christians, Christianity, and Christian witness. Table 4–4 has already presented a horrifying listing of 112 ways in which killers have murdered Christians over the centuries.

## The martyrdom of Jesus

Jesus was the Christian martyr par excellence. It was he who provided the example for all Christian martyrs since. It is important to understand the varying reasons for his martyrdom. From the point of view of the Pharisees he was being punished for blasphemy and contempt for the law. The Romans saw him as a subversive. His followers later understood his death as a necessary price for the salvation of the world. Thus, the reasons Christians give to explain martyrdom, even in the case of Jesus, are very complex.

## The global presence of martyrs

Our survey reveals that martyrs have died in the 138 largest countries of the world. In many, the establishment of the church was the result of mass martyrdom. This was true in the early Roman empire, in Armenia, in Egypt, and in Palestine, and then subsequently in India, China, France, Japan, Britain, Viet Nam, Korea, the Americas, and Russia and the Ukraine.

## The many different kinds of martyrs

Karl Rahner expounds Thomas Aquinas' dictum that 'Someone is a martyr through a death that is clearly related to Christ if he is defending society against the attacks of its enemies who are trying to damage the Christian faith and if in this defense he suffers death'.

Edna McDonagh writes: 'Christian martyrs do not die solely even primarily for the sake of the Church community but for the kingdom which may be seeking expression and demanding recognition within the bounds of the historical Church, in causes not explicitly religious'.

Following in the footsteps of Jesus, Christians have been martyred for all kinds of reasons. Though the history of martyrdom illustrates the vast variety of reasons why Christians are martyred, Boff makes it clear that 'All those who have died, and those yet to die, for these causes, regardless of their ideological allegiance, are truly martyrs through the spilling of their blood because they perform virtuous actions in the spirit of Christ'.

## Analyzing martyrdom situations

The first way in which we can begin to understand the phenomenon of multiple or mass martyrdom is to analyze their features and their overall significance. This can be done by describing each individual situation by means of coded variables; this is done in

## Table 4–6.  Analysis of martyrs by 11 types of Christians.

In this table a variety of Christians together with a number of well-known martyrs are classified by type. To illustrate this typology, first come 11 categories then these categories with precise definitions. Then these categories are given again below together with a small selection of some of the best-known martyrs or martyr situations (names and dates) who fit in and illustrate each category.

```
 0 = non-witnessing Christians (nominals, etc)
Non-martyr witnesses (confessors)
 1 = Christians witnessing, but not suffering or persecuted
 2 = witnesses suffering, persecuted, or tortured but not killed
 3 = witnesses wanting or seeking martyrdom but not succeeding
Martyrs (Involuntary or inadvertent)
 4 = died during or after imprisonment or torture for being a Christian
 5 = killed for outwardly non-religious reasons
 6 = killed for being part of a Christian body being persecuted
 7 = killed because known individually or collectively as a Christian
Martyrs (voluntary or deliberate)
 8 = killed after deliberately provoking hostility or seeking martyrdom
 9 = killed after making a formal public witness in a hostile situation
 10 = publicly ordered to apostatize, refuses, confesses Christ, killed
```

 0 = *non-witnessing Christians.* (This refers to latent, unaffiliated, nominal, non-practicing, non-suffering Christians).
**Non-martyr witnesses (confessors)**
 1 = *Christians witnessing but not suffering or persecuted.* (By far the largest grouping, 83% of all active Great Commission Christians today, of whom 20% are harassed by state or society but not severely persecuted).
 2 = *witnesses persecuted but not killed.* (The underground church, which in 1988 numbered 16% of all Christians, including those tortured or imprisoned). A. Solzhenitsyn, R. Wurmbrandt, G. Vins.
 3 = *witnesses seeking martyrdom but not succeeding.* Pachomius, Anskar.
**Martyrs (involuntary or inadvertent)**
 4 = *died during or after imprisonment.* AD 254 Origen, 1920 abp Justin of Omsk, 1929 abp Peter of Voronezh, 1938 metropolitan Anatole of Odessa.
 5 = *killed for outwardly nonreligious reasons.* 1966 fr C. Torres, 1968 M. L. King Jr, 1977 abp J. Luwum.
 6 = *killed for being part of a persecuted body.* 1915, 600,000 Armenian Apostolics.
 7 = *killed because known as a Christian.* 1945 D. Bonhoeffer, M. Skobtsova, 1980 abp O. Romero.
**Martyrs (voluntary or deliberate)**
 8 = *killed after deliberately seeking martyrdom.* 628 Anastasius the Persian, 1531 Thomas Bilney, c1700 brother Markel & Old Believer monks, 1795 Greek neomartyrs.
 9 = *killed after formal public witness.* 1941 fr M. Kolbe.
 10 = *killed after being offered reprieve but refusing.* 33 Jesus, 36 Stephen, 64 Paul, 156 Polycarp, 1555 abp T. Cranmer.

Table 4–6. This provides a scale of varieties of martyrs, coded 0-10, is designed primarily to help classify individual martyrs. The scale provides a means of classifying and comparing the various types or degrees of martyrdom. It is descriptive, not evaluative. It describes circumstances, hence one cannot say that individuals killed in category 9 or 10 were better or more faithful witnesses than persons in category 1, or 4, etc. Neither does our definition of 'martyr' necessarily imply holiness of life or character, nor the 'heroic sanctity' that many Christian confessions require before persons can be formally recognized as saints. Category 1 gives in fact the original meaning of the New Testament Greek word *martys* (see Acts 1.8), but categories 0-3 are not properly called martyrs in today's English usage.

Another scale by which a country's experience of martyrdom can be measured is shown in Table 4–7; this can also measure a city's experience, or an ethnic people's experience.

Two more scales, this time describing each actual martyrdom situation, are given in Table 4–8. The whole range of situations is given values for these latter 2 variables in our major overall data compilation, Table 4–10, columns 9 and 10.

### Background murders and martyrs
At this point before examining our major datatable on martyrdom, it is important to note that we observers actually see only the tip of the iceberg, while a vast number of other martyrdoms take place every day, every week, every year, without anyone else hearing about them. Part of this phenomenon is termed here background martyrdom. It is defined and described in Table 4–9, and will then be utilized throughout Table 4–10.

### The impact of martyrdom on evangelization
Is there a correlation between martyrdom and evangelization? In some countries we find that martyrdom was followed by church growth. A contemporary example is the church in China. In 1949 there were only one million Christians. Forty years of anti-religious Communist rule produced some 1.2 million martyrs (see Table 4–10). The result: explosive church growth to today's 90 million believers.

### The future of martyrdom
We might be tempted to believe that mankind will gradually grow out of its violent nature and that, perhaps one hundred years in the future, will no longer be killing others, for whatever reason. However, this is not likely to be the case. The future almost certainly holds more martyrdom situations and the names of individual martyrs are likely to continue mounting

year after year at the same shocking rate of 160,000 a year or even higher.

### THE DEMOGRAPHICS OF MARTYRDOM

Our major compilation of data on Christian martyrs in all countries over the 20 centuries of Christian history is contained in the World Evangelization Database. This can be directly accessed via the CD related to this survey, the *World Christian database*. In print, most of these data are contained here in several large tables: (a) Table 4–10 describing 600 major martyrdom situations in 150 countries, AD 33-2000; (b) Table 4–11 'Alphabetical listing of 2,500 known Christian martyrs, AD 33-2000'; (c) Table 4–12 'Chronological listing of 2,500 known Christian martyrs, AD 33-2000'; and (d) Table 4–13 'Geographical listing of 2,500 known Christian martyrs, AD 33-2000'.

The most significant and informative of these tables in this Part 4 is Table 4–10, which will now be analyzed.

### The 500 major martyrdom situations in history
Table 4–10 describes the whole extent of Christian martyrdom and its martyrs—believers who have lost their lives prematurely because of their faith in Christ, in situations of witness, as a result of human hostility. The table lists a selection of the major or best-known martyr situations in the narrative of Christianity, arranged by the 10 major epochs in Christian history (in capital letters), with overall totals and analyses given at the end of each epoch. Names of a representative selection of 400 individual martyrs or groups are given throughout the table in bold type. Note these abbreviations: bp = bishop, abp = archbishop, msgr = monsignor, fr = father/priest, br = brother/monk, sr = sister/nun.

Definitions, sources, and meanings of the 11 columns and of the rows are appended in the following paragraphs. These explanations, qualifications and caveats must be carefully studied before the reader rushes into conclusions about the validity of the concept of martyrdom as presented here.

Briefly, note that column 5 = primary persecuting body, column 6 = Christian tradition of those martyred, column 7 = total martyrs as a result of that situation, 7a (on CD only) = total related Christians then, 8 = martyrdom ratio 7:7a as a percentage, 9 = magnitude of martyrs (code given in Index 1, Table 4–8), 10 = intensity of martyrdom (code given in Index 2, Table 4–8), 11 = total all Christians worldwide alive at that time, 11a = line number, for quick reference (on CD only).

For many dates, there are often many other well-

known martyrs too numerous to list in the table. Such additional names, numbering 2,500 individual martyrs, are given in Tables 4-11, 4-12, and 4-13.

It must be remembered again that although this table deals only with specifically Christian martyrdom, similar tables could be drawn up for martyrs in Judaism, Hinduism, Buddhism, Islam, and the other great religions. All share in this greatest of deprivations of human rights.

### ANALYSIS OF ALL MARTYR SITUATIONS, AD 33-2000

Each of the 11 Epochs has its martyrdom situations totaled and analyzed in the last 5 lines of each Epoch. Totals of all martyrs since AD 33 are then visible on that 5th line.

### Background martyrdom
This very significant aspect is enumerated for each Epoch in its last line but two. As mentioned briefly above, the term 'background martyrs' refers to the continuous stream of Christians killed as isolated victims or for individual reasons, usually without any particular ecclesiastical situation, often clouded by other kinds of violence (wars, killings, murders, etc). In such cases their ecclesiastical affiliation is either unknown or irrelevant. The term 'background killers' refers to those responsible for these killings. For fuller definition, see Table 4–9; for numbers, see Table 4–10.

### Some possible future scenarios
The rest of Table 4–10 after AD 2000 speculates on possible futures. It draws on material in Part 2 "CosmoChronology". It is based (purely for purposes of illustrating our method) on one of the possible suggested scenarios, namely with the 10-year End-time arbitrarily placed just after AD 2050, with a world population then of 8 billion and a church of 3 billion. Note that each of the lines anticipates not only the church having numerous martyrs but also, especially in the End-time, the church losing vast numbers through defections, apostasies, and non-martyr deaths.

### ESTABLISHING THE BOUNDARIES OF MARTYRDOM

### Detailed final definitions
In the light of the detailed data in Table 4–10, a recapitulation of the whole concept of martyrdom is in order at this point.

This analysis sees the term 'martyr' primarily as a religious one and in particular as a Christian one. We are looking at the phenomenon from the Christian point of view, as the Christian experiences it. The primary thing is—a Christian has lost his or her life due to human hostility. Who caused it, or in what hostile circumstances, or for what motivation, are all secondary.

The analysis therefore defines a 'martyr' as follows.
(i) *Brief definition.* A martyr is a Christian who loses his or her life prematurely due to hostility because of his or her faith in Christ.
(ii) *Expanded definition.* A martyr is a Christian who loses his or her life prematurely in circumstances related either directly or indirectly to witness to Christ, and as a result of human hostility or violence directed at him or her (but not simply as a result of natural causes, disease, famine, accident, warfare, or so-called

## Table 4–7.  Incidence of martyrdom in a country, city, or ethnolinguistic people.

```
 0 = no martyrs past or present
 1 = alien martyrs only (of an outside culture)
 2 = past martyrs of this people (over 3 generations ago)
 3 = one known recent protomartyr of this culture
 4 = several known recent martyrs of this culture
 5 = numerous martyrs but sporadic, local and under 0.1%
     of Christians
 6 = moderate martyrdom (0.1%-0.9% of all Christians at
     the time)
 7 = high martyrdom (1-9%)
 8 = severe martyrdom (10-49%)
 9 = intense martyrdom (50% or over)
 10 = total martyrdom (100%; virtually every Christian wiped
     out)
```

**Martyrs of the First Millennium**
1. Apostle Simon the Zealot, AD 61.
2. Apostle Jude (Thaddaeus), AD 66.
3. Apostle Thomas, in India, AD 82.
4. John on Patmos sees the 144,000 martyrs (Revelation 7,14).
5. India postage stamp on Thomas' 19th death centenary.
6. 'Diana or Christ?' (by A. Long): sacrifice to gods or die.
7. The 10,000 martyrs (AD 287, also AD 337), by Albrecht Dürer.
8. 'The Last Prayer' (Gerome): by martyrs on crosses in Colosseum, Rome.
9. Apostle John is boiled in oil as Emperor (left) watches, AD 95 (A. Durer, 1496).

# Martyrs of the First Millennium

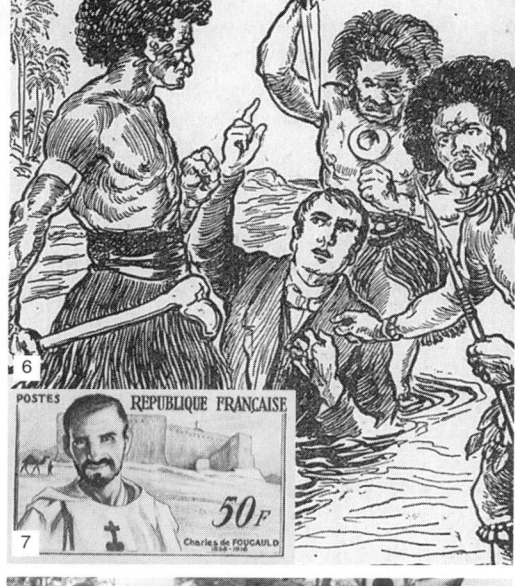

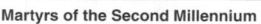

**Martyrs of the Second Millennium**
1. Murder in Canterbury Cathedral of archbishop Thomas Becket, 1170.
2. 20 OFM missionaries are crucified in Nagasaki, Japan, 1597.
3. Killing of bishop J.C. Patteson, Solomon Islands 1871.
4. Baptist missionary cardiologist C.H. Yi and wife K.W. Yi murdered in Khabarovsk, Russia, 1995.
5. Bible translator William Tyndale burned at stake in Belgium, 1536.
6. Murder of John Williams, New Hebrides, 1839.
7. Charles de Foucauld, killed in Tamanrassset, Algeria, 1916.

8. Bible translator Romulo Saune, (center) executed in Peru by Maoists, 1992.
9. Annual reenactment, martyrdom of prophet Simon Kimbangu by Belgian colonial authorities, 1951.
10. Assyrian Catholicos Mar Shimun XIX, killed by Turks, 1917.
11. Jesuit pioneers Rudolf Acquaviva, companions killed in India, 1583.
12. Catholic priest thrown into icy river by atheist mob, Croatia, 1970.
13. Oscar Romero, archbishop in El Salvador, murdered in San Salvador cathedral, 1980.

# Martyrs of the Second Millennium

## Table 4–8. Two persecution/martyrdom indexes, each of 10 levels of demographic martyrdom as experienced by the local Christian community in each of the 500 major historical martyrdom situations.

### Index 1. Magnitude of each martyrdom situation.

| Size | Martyrs per situation | Situations | Total Martyrs |
|---|---|---|---|
| 10 | Over 10 million martyrs | 1 | 15,000,000 |
| 9 | From 4 million to 10 million | 3 | 13,000,000 |
| 8 | From 2 million to 4 million | 2 | 4,900,000 |
| 7 | From 1 million to 2 million | 9 | 9,300,000 |
| 6 | From 500,000 to 1 million | 12 | 7,070,000 |
| 5 | From 100,000 to 500,000 | 48 | 9,330,000 |
| 4 | From 10,000 to 100,000 | 133 | 3,513,000 |
| 3 | From 1,000 to 10,000 | 178 | 589,900 |
| 2 | From 100 to 1,000 | 119 | 40,393 |
| 1 | Under 100 | 79 | 2,237 |
|  | Background and other martyrs | — | 6,675,700 |
|  | **TOTAL** | **584** | **69,420,000** |

### Index 2. Intensity of each martyrdom situation.

| Intensity | Martyrs as % local | Persecution | Situations | Total Martyrs |
|---|---|---|---|---|
|  | BELOW AVERAGE |  |  |  |
| 0 | Under 0.1% | Sporadic | 156 | 599,221 |
| 1 | From 0.1 to under 0.2% | Light | 45 | 543,690 |
| 2 | From 0.2 to under 0.5% | Moderate | 51 | 608,264 |
| 3 | From 0.5 to under 1% | Average | 35 | 1,482,670 |
|  | ABOVE AVERAGE |  |  |  |
| 4 | From 1 to under 2% | Heavy | 48 | 1,438,295 |
| 5 | From 2 to under 5% | Severe | 59 | 4,066,547 |
| 6 | From 5 to under 10% | Appalling | 51 | 10,603,711 |
| 7 | From 10 to under 20% | Catastrophic | 48 | 23,647,202 |
|  | GENOCIDAL |  |  |  |
| 8 | From 20 to under 50% | Horrifying | 57 | 13,451,163 |
| 9 | From 50 to under 90% | Terrifying | 33 | 6,304,367 |
| 10 | From 90 to under 100% | Annihilating | 1 | 400 |
|  | Background and other martyrs |  | — | 6,675,700 |
|  | **TOTAL** |  | **584** | **69,420,000** |

'acts of God' such as earthquakes, floods, etc; also excluding suicide, self-immolation, and the like).

(iii). *Standard short definition.* Our standardized summary definition should now be given again, as follows: *A martyr is a believer in Christ, who loses his or her life prematurely, in a situation of witness, as a result of human hostility.*

The key words to remember and insist on, when examining instances of possible martyrdom, are therefore these 5 words, which can be posed as questions:
—believer
—loses
—prematurely
—witness
—hostility

If any of these 5 key words do not apply to particular individuals or situations, then they should not be called martyrs in this precise sense.

(iv) *An even more detailed definition.* Our most complex definition sees a martyr as a Christian whose loyalty and witness to Christ (as a witness to the fact of Christ's resurrection, and also as a legal witness to, and advocate for, the claims of Christ in God's cosmic lawsuit against the world) lead directly or indirectly to a confrontation or clash with hostile opponents (either non-Christians, or Christians of another persuasion) as a result of him or her either (1) being a Christian, or (2) being part of a Christian body or community, or (3) being a Christian worker, or (4) averring the truth of Christianity, or (5) holding to some Christian tenet or principle or practice, or (6) holding to different Christian tenets to his or her opponents, or (7) speaking for Christ, or (8) refusing to deny Christ or his or her Christian convictions; which then results in violence and in him or her voluntarily or involuntarily losing his or her life prematurely (shedding his or her blood, being put to death, executed, assassinated, killed, stoned, clubbed to death, beheaded, guillotined, garroted, strangled, stabbed, eaten alive, gassed, injected, electrocuted, suffocated, boiled in oil, roasted alive, drowned, torched, burned massacred, crucified, lynched, hanged, shot, murdered, pushed under oncoming traffic, immured, buried alive, crushed to death, poisoned, drugged to death, starved, deprived of medication, chemically or electronically killed, killed extrajudicially, died under torture, died after beatings, died in custody, died in prison, died soon after release from prison, or allowed or left to die). Any of these may take place with or without prior demand or opportunity to recant. (See alphabetical listing in Table 4–4).

Note that (6) above means that most Christians killed as alleged 'heretics' down the ages should correctly be included in enumerations of martyrs. Item (3) above also includes Christian workers killed in the line of duty, or on active duty, or who lose their lives because they happen to be in the path of violence (this includes workers killed by robbers, soldiers, police, etc). Note also that our definition of demographic martyrdom includes and covers those children and infants who lose their lives along with adult martyrs.

### Sources

Data for many of the situations listed in Table 4–10 come from detailed entries in Part 2 "CosmoChronology", which should be consulted for additional details on any particular year and its context.

### Percentages

To give the reader an idea of the numerical significance of statistics of any particular martyrs or period he or she is interested, in, we produce in this table various differently-defined sets of percentages: (a) for a particular occasion, number of martyrs divided by total Christians of that time and place and/or denomination; (b) martyrs divided by nation's Christian population; (c) martyrs over a long period divided by total Christians alive at some median time during this period, as percent; and (d) martyrs per year divided by total Christian deaths (from all causes) per year, as percent. Readers will find some of these clearer or more helpful than others.

### DESCRIPTION OF COLUMNS IN TABLE 4–10

The meaning of columns and rows in the major table here, Table 4–10, are as follows:

1. *Year.* Date of first martyrdoms in a collective martyrdom situation, or of first or beginning of a prolonged series extending over either a few or many subsequent years. Note: 'c' = approximately.

2. *Main locus.* Place, country, or main area where situation of persecution or martyrdoms occurred. The name here is always either a country (using terminology of the time), or a continent or region, or occasionally one of the historical patriarchal metropolises (Jerusalem, Alexandria, Rome, Byzantium/Constantinople).

3. *Description of major martyrdom situation.* Details of group of martyrs concerned, or persecution, or context, or circumstances, i.e. the situation in its main particulars.

4. *Related individual martyrs.* Listed here in the table in bold type are a small selection of those persons whose names are known and whom the churches officially, or popularly, regard as 'martyrs' properly so-called. This includes many known exceptional individuals who died voluntarily or publicly for their faith or for refusing to deny Christ. Many of these persons thus named died as bishops. They are placed at the nearest appropriate date, in most cases on lines describing situations of which their martyrdoms formed part. Their dates are given if different from the line's date. Names of additional known or well-known martyrs are then given below in the 3 full listings of all individuals in Tables 4-11, 4-12, and 4-13.

Abbreviations in this column: bp = bishop (not used here for the original Apostles, but only after AD 100), abp = archbishop, msgr = monsignor (bishop), fr = father (a priest, noted and used here only from 1693 onwards), br = brother/monk, sr = sister/nun. Note: bps, abps, frs are the plural forms including all following names to next title or colon. Other similar titles are left unabbreviated: pope, patriarch, abba, mar, rabban. The symbol & (ampersand) here and throughout denotes persons martyred together. The phrase 'et alii' (and others) denotes several or numerous additional similar martyrs at the same time and place.

### SUMMARY OF TRADITIONS INVOLVED

The next 2 variables in Table 4–10 report quite different characteristics: firstly, persecutors; and secondly, the martyrs they persecute. These are set out in summary form in Table 4–5.

After these 2, there follow 4 variables reporting on the size and intensity of martyrdom in each situation.

5. *Persecutors.* Primary persecuting body, either secular or religious, or both (if 2 letters are given); i.e. the main persecutors of the martyrs described (in columns 3 and 4. There codes represent either (a) in the first half of the column, the state or ruling regime (shown by 'x', or a dot '.' meaning no state involvement); and (b) in the second half of the column, any religious body responsible or involved in killing the martyrs, which can be either non-Christian religious bodies, or Christian bodies themselves, or a dot '.' meaning no religious body is involved. In this column 5 there are always 2 code characters, side by side. As just noted, the code 'x' stands for the state

## Table 4–9. Multiple varieties of background martyrdom.

| Variety | Description |
|---|---|
| **Accidental martyrdom** | (Violence got out of control) |
| **Anonymous martyrdom** | (Nobody identifies the victims) |
| **Bounty martyrdom** | (Reward is offered and deliberate hunt ensues) |
| **Contract martyrdom** | (A price is put on a Christian's head) |
| **Criminal martyrdom** | (A killing breaks the law) |
| **Domestic martyrdom** | (Occurring during a family dispute) |
| **Family-related martyrdom** | (Such as new convert poisoned by relatives) |
| **Indirect martyrdom** | (Death comes as indirect product of hostility) |
| **Individual martyrdom** | (Killed without church involvement) |
| **Invisible martyrdom** | (Killers operate cautiously and out of sight) |
| **Isolated martyrdom** | (No apparent cause or connection) |
| **Laundered martyrdom** | (A killing has been covered up) |
| **Marginal martyrdom** | (At the edges of our definition) |
| **Mistaken martyrdom** | (Wrong target is killed) |
| **Money-related martyrdom** | (To cover embezzlement or theft) |
| **Petty martyrdom** | (Due to petty crime) |
| **Political martyrdom** | (Regime claims political justification) |
| **Quasi-martyrdom** | (Credentials as Christians appear uncertain) |
| **Revenge martyrdom** | (Settling of old scores) |
| **Subsequent martyrdom** | (Victim survives immediate attack but dies shortly after) |
| **Trivial martyrdom** | (Such as a killing during a robbery) |
| **Unconscious martyrdom** | (Nobody realizes what has happened except the victim) |
| **Unheralded martyrdom** | (Killers remain silent) |
| **Unintended martyrdom** | (Killing originally not planned) |
| **Unknown martyrdom** | (No reports ever surface) |
| **Unorganized martyrdom** | (No planning evident) |

secular, or other ruling power, civil or military (i.e. state involvement, excluding any temporary or invading power); this category is widely used here in combination with another code; thus, 'xa' means that the persecutors are the civil power (x) who are also expressly atheists (a)). The range is shown in Table 4–5.

6. *Tradition of martyrs.* Christian tradition, confession, or communion primarily involved as victims. The listing in Table 4–5 shows the various Christian bodies, traditions, and confessions involved, and also the various non-Christian bodies involved. The codes used are identical to codes for the 6 megablocs and 300 traditions as shown in Part 16 "GeoCodebook".

7. *Martyrs* (numerical total). Estimated number of Christian martyrs resulting from situation described in columns 1-3 of Table 4–10, defining 'martyrs' as all persons in categories 4-10 on our scale 'Analysis of martyrs by 11 types' in Table 4–6. Note that in any situation of mass deaths or killing of Christians, we do not automatically or necessarily define the entire total who have been killed as martyrs, but only that fraction whose deaths resulted from some form of Christian witness, individual or collective. Thus under '1095, Crusades', our table does not equate 'crusaders' with 'martyrs', but simply states that during the Crusades a number of zealous and overzealous Christians were in fact martyred as defined under 'Definitions' above. Likewise '1980, Latin America' does not count as martyrs all Christians who became victims of political killings, but only those whose situations involved Christian witness. Typical illustrations of the latter include the vast number of cases of an entire congregation singing hymns as soldiers lock their church's doors and proceed to burn it to the ground with no survivors.

The database here includes a further variable, 7a, available in the related CD but not in this print book.

7a. *Christians.* Local Christian population in that year and region, i.e. size of the related local Christian population to which columns 1-7 refer. Sometimes this means the total Christians in the country, of all denominations; sometimes it refers to a denominational or local grouping only. (Note: The only 3 exceptions are: AD 378 and 1648, where the figures of 120 million and 3,371 million refer to all Christians who ever lived up to that date; and AD 1697, where the figure refers to all Christians who have ever lived in Japan up to that date. They are shown in italics to indicate that they should not be included again in other totals or sub-totals).

8. *MR%.* In order to be able to assess and compare situations and their severity, we can speak of percentages. There are 5 or 6 different types we could use. Here, MR = martyrdom ratio for this incident or period, i.e. the number of those martyred as a percentage of the immediate Christian community (= columns 7 divided by 7a, times 100%)

9. *Magnitude.* The scale used here to measure magnitude of a martyrdom situation is as shown in Table 4–8, Index 1.

10. *Intensity.* The scale used here to measure intensity of a martyrdom situation is as shown in Table 4–8, Index 2.

11. *Global Christians.* This end column gives the total number of Christians of all types across the world alive at that time (expressed in millions).

11a. *Line.* In the related CD, this column gives an identification number to each line in the table, for quick reference.

### ARRIVING AT GLOBAL TOTALS

**World totals at the end of each Epoch**
At the end of each Epoch in Table 4–10, there are 5 standardized lines referring to the world situation with world totals at that time. These are as follows:

1. *Total of martyrs listed above that line, during that Epoch.*

2. *All other martyrdom situations, known or unknown, during that Epoch.*

3. *Background martyrdom during that Epoch (individual, domestic, family, isolated; see Table 4–9).*

4. *Global total of all martyrs during that Epoch (sum of 1, 2, 3).*

5. *Global cumulative total of all martyrs since AD 33.*

Additional notes on these 5 lines are as follows.

1. *Total of martyrs above.* Column 7 here simply totals all the martyrs enumerated in this column above for that Epoch.

2. *All other martyrdom situations, known or unknown.* This second line is self-explanatory, bearing in mind that all the most widely-known names of martyrs involved in the previous lines of situations just documented are merely the tip of the iceberg. We estimate the overall numerical size

of the iceberg, however, by adding this line to cover all unknown or undocumented situations.

3. *Background martyrdom.* The term is used here to cover a whole range of very small or isolated or individual situations, which can be termed non-ecclesiastical. They cover cases where a Christian is killed as a result of human hostility but where the circumstances are nothing directly or immediately to do with organized Christianity. These are set out in Table 4–9. Our general finding is that at every Epoch background martyrdoms of these kinds take place continually. Since they are largely isolated individual cases, usually there is no ecclesiastical situation nor ecclesiastical significance—they are just victims of background violence provoked further by Christian witness.

4. *Global total of all martyrs during Epoch.* Column 7 for this row gives total martyrs during the epoch, based on (a) total of all the specifically-named and detailed martyrdom situations described above (which themselves represent only a selection of the major situations) plus (b) the line immediately above, just described, which assesses the background martyrdom situation.

5. *Global cumulative total of all martyrs since AD 33.* Column 7 for this fifth row gives the total of all martyrs since the Crucifixion in AD 33, up to the year shown.

### NAMES OF INDIVIDUAL MARTYRS

The last 3 tables in this Part 4, Tables 4-11, 4-12, and 4-13, now give names of some 2,500 individual martyrs known to or recognized by one or more of the various Christian confessions and churches, or uncovered during the book's independent research over 35 years. They are here grouped firstly alphabetically, secondly chronologically, and thirdly by country. Many of those are individual or isolated martyrs whose deaths occurred outside major persecutions or similar martyrdom situations reported in Table 4–10. They are however summarized there at the end of each Epoch under the rubrics 'All other martyrdom situations, known or unknown' and 'Background martyrdom'.

**Summary**
This analysis has shown Christian martyrdom to be a phenomenon of enormous size and significance. Its statistics can be summarized in a single short table, and this has been done in Table 4–3 above.

### BIBLIOGRAPHY

'A bibliography of martyrology of Warmia, Masuria, and Powisla in the years 1939–1945,' M. Tarnowska, *Komunikaty, Mazursko-Warminskie* (Poland), 104 (1969), 229–266. (Bibliography of Polish martyrdom during World War II).
*A century of missionary martyrs.* S. F. Harris. London: James Nisbet, 1897. 159p.
*A martyr bishop: the life of St. Oliver Plunkett.* J. McKee. Houston, TX: Lumen Christi Press, 1975. 181p.
*A modern martyr: Theophane Venard.* J. A. Walsh. New York: Maryknoll, 1958. (Life and death of Paris Foreign Mission Society martyr in Vietnam).
*A noble death: suicide and martyrdom among Christians and Jews in antiquity.* A. J. Droge & J. D. Tabor. San Francisco: Harper San Francisco, 1992.
*A pilgrimage to the shrines of the North American martyrs.* G. F. Walter. N.p.: The Author, 1985.
*A question of conscience: the murder of the Jesuit priests in El Salvador.* L. Brown & I. Ziv. : First Run Features, 1990. (48 min. videocassette focusing on the November 16, 1989 murder of six Jesuit priests in El Salvador by uniformed soldiers. In English and Spanish with English subtitles).
*A Russian martyr.* I. V. Moiseyev. : Christ Nations.
*A tribute to the new martyrs of Russia.* London: Greek Orthodox Christian Brotherhood of St Athanasios, 1977.
*Account of the martyrs at Smyrna and Lyons in the second century.* Edinburgh: A. Murray, 1776.
'Actes des martyrs d'Aurelien en Gaule,' J. van der Straeten, *Analecta bollandiana,* LXXX (1962), 117.
*Acts of the Christian martyrs: introductions, texts and translations.* H. Musurillo. Oxford, UK: Clarendon Press, 1972.
*Ad martyras.* Origen.
*Adding Cross to crown: the political significance of Christ's Pas-*

*sion.* M. A. Noll. Washington, DC: Center for Public Justice; Grand Rapids, MI: Baker Book House, 1996. 95p.
*African Holocaust: the story of the Uganda martyrs.* J. F. Faupel. N.p.: P. J. Kennedy & Sons, 1962.
*African triumph: life of Charles Lwanga.* C. Dollen. Boston: St. Paul Editions, 1967.
*All for Christ: some twentieth century martyrs.* D. Dewar. Oxford, UK: Oxford University Press, 1980.
*American martyrs: from 1542.* A. J. Nevins. Huntington, IN: Our Sunday Visitor, 1987. 180p
*An early Christian Syrian martyrology: the names of our lords the confessors and victors and the days on which they gained their crowns.* W. Wright. (Eastern Orthodox).
*An hour with John and Betty Stam: martyred missionaries to China.* T. W. Engstrom. Grand Rapids, MI: Zondervan, 1942. (The Uganda martyrs).
*An universal history of Christian martyrdom.* J. Foxe. London: Sherwood, Jones & Co., 1824.
*Anuarite, vierge et martyre zaïroise.* P. X. Fernando da Riese. Kinshasa: Editions Saint Paul Afrique, 1978.
*Archbishop Romero: memories and reflections.* J. Sobrino. Maryknoll, NY: Orbis Books, 1990. 223p.
'Balthasar Hubmaier: martyr without honor,' W. R. Estep, *Baptist History and Heritage,* 13, 2 (1978), 5–10. (Swiss Anabaptist leader burned at the stake in 1528).
*Black martyrs.* J. P. Thoonen. New York: Sheed & Ward, 1941. (The Uganda martyrs).
'Blood in the Valdes Peninsula: the martyrdom of Father Bartolome Pogio,' R. A. Entraigas, *Bol. de la Acad. Nac. de la Hist.* (Argentina), 35, 303-326 (1965).
'Bloody Mary's victims: the iconography of John Foxe's *Book of Martyrs,*' O. T. Hargrave, *Historical Magazine of the Protestant Episcopal Church,* 51, 1 (1982), 7–21.
*Book of martyrs: an account of holy men who died for the Christian religion.* S. Hazard. London: J. Marshall, 1795.

*By their blood: Christian martyrs of the 20th century.* J. Hefley & M. Hefley. 2nd ed. Grand Rapids, MI: Baker Book House, 1996. (All continents and countries).
*Called to die: the story of American linguist Chet Bitterman, slain by terrorists.* S. Estes. Grand Rapids, MI: Zondervan, 1986. 214p.
*Called to suffer.* H. Schlossberg. N.p.: Multnomah, 1990.
*Candles in the dark: six modern martyrs.* M. Craig. London: Hodder & Stoughton, 1984. (Bonhoeffer, King, Kolbe, Luwum, Romero, Skobtsova).
*China! Christian martyrs of the 20th century.* J. Hefley & M. Hefley. Milford, MI: Mott Media, 1978.
*China's bloody century: genocide and mass murder since 1900.* R. J. Rummel. New Brunswick: Transaction Publishers, 1991. 348p.
*China's book of martyrs: a record of heroic martyrdoms and marvelous deliverances of Chinese Christians during the summer of 1900.* L. Miner. Cincinnati, OH: Jennings and Pye, [1903]. 512p
*Christian martyrs of Muslim Spain.* K. B. Wolf. Cambridge, UK: Cambridge University Press, 1988.
*Companions of Jesus: the Jesuit martyrs of El Salvador.* J. Sobrino et al. Maryknoll, NY: Orbis Books, 1990. 208p.
*Coptic martyrdoms, etc., in the dialect of Upper Egypt.* E. A. Budge (ed). 1914; reprint, New York: AMS Press, 1977. 609p.
*Coptic Martyrs.* O. de Lacy. London: Church Historical Society, 1937.
*Cry of the church: witness and martyrdom in the church of Latin America today.* J. Marins. Quezon City: Claretian Publications, 1983.
*Das altenglische Martyrologium.* G. Kotzor. Munich: Verlag der Bayerischen Akademie der Wissenschaft, 1981.
'Das Martyrium als Kampf mit dem Teufel,' F. J. Dögler, *Antike*

*und Christentum*, iii (1933), 177–188.
'Das vierte Makkabaerbuch, Ignatius von Antiochien und die ältesten Märtyrerberichte,' O. Perler, *Riv. di archeologia cristiana*, XXV (1949), 47–72.
*De morrtibus persecutorum (Ed. and French trans. J. Moreau, Sources chretiennes, 39).* Lactantius. Paris, 1954. 2 vols.(A fundamental work for the study of the Great Persecution.).
*De morte peregrini (Text and English trans. A.M. Harmon, Loeb Library, Lucian, v.).* Lucian of Samosata.
'Der M ärtyrertitel,' F. Kattenbusch, *Zeitschrift für Neutestamentum Wissenschaft*, IV (1903), 111–127.
'Die christlichen Martyrien,' J. Geffcken, *Hermes*, XLV (1910), 481–505.
'Die Idee des Märtyrers in Judentum und Urchristentum,' E. Lohmeyer, *Zeitschrift für Systematische Theologie*, V (1927), 222–249.
*Die Idee des Martyriums in der alten Kirche.* H. von Campenhausen. Göttingen, 1936.
*Die Kirche der Martyr.* A. Ehrhard. Munich, 1932.
'Die Martyrologien. Ihre Geschichte und ihr Wert,' H. Achelis, *Abhandlungen der Kön. Gesellschaft zu Göttingen*, (1900).
'Die Zahl der Martyrer bis 313,' L. Hertling, *Gregorianum*, XXV (1944), 103–129.
'Die Zahl der scillitanischen Märtyrer,' H. Karpp, *Vigiliae Christianae*, XV (1961), 165–172.
*Discourses of martyrdom in English literature, 1563–1694.* J. R. Knott. Cambridge, UK: Cambridge University Press, 1993. 294p.
'Documentation and bibliography on the Blessed Martyrs of the Rio de la Plata,' H. Storni, *Archivum Hist. Society Iesu* (Italy), 45, 90 (1976), 318–348. (Documents missionary martyrs in Argentina, Uruguay, and Paraguay in the 16th and 17th centuries).
*Dove at the windows: last letters of four Quaker martyrs.* G. Selleck (ed). Lincoln, MA: Penmaen, 1973.
*Drame d'une minorité religieuse: le martyre de l'église protestante en Colombie: avant le Concile, un interdit à lever.* E. Chastand. [Anduze, France]: The Author, [1961]. 37p.
'Dying for one's friends: the martyrological shape of Christian love,' P. J. Wojda, in *The annual of the society of Christian ethics*, p.121-42. J. Kelsay & S. B. Twiss (eds). Chicago: The Society of Christian Ethics, 1997.
*El martir de la castidad: vida y martirio del Siervo de Dios, Fernando Saperas Aluja, misionero hijo del Immaculado Corazon de Maria.* A. M. Arranz. Tarrega, Spain: F. Camps Calmet, 1976.
*El Padre Antonio Gonzalez, martir.* F. Villerreal. Leon, Spain: Institucion "Fray Bernardino de Sahagun, 1981.
*Essays on modern martyrs.* London: Paynes & Faulder, 1780.
*Eusebius, Bishop of Caesarea, The ecclesiastical history and martyrs of Palestine.* H. J. Lawlor & J. E. L. Oulton. London, 1928. 2 vols.
*Even unto death.* M. Ford. Elgin, IL: David C. Cook, 1978. 93p
*Exhortatio ad martyrum (English trans. J.E.L. Oulton & H. Chadwick, Alexandrian Christianity, vol II, Library of Christian Classics).* Origen. Ed., Koetschau. London: SCM Press.
*Faithful witnesses: records of early Christian martyrs.* E. R. Hardy (ed). London: Lutterworth Press, [1960]. 80p
*Fire against fire: Christian ministry face–to–face with persecution.* M. E. Gómez. Minneapolis, MN: Augsburg Press, 1990. 94p.
*Fire and sword in Shansi: the story of martyrdom of foreigners and Chinese Christians.* E. H. Edwards. New York: Revell, 1901.
*First victims of Communism: white book of the religious persecution in Ukraine.* Rome: Analecta O.S.B.M., 1953. 114p.
*Fools, martyrs, traitors: the story of martyrdom in the Western world.* L. B. Smith. New York: Alfred A. Knopf, 1997.
*For all the saints: changing perceptions of martyrdom and sainthood in the Lutheran Reformation.* R. Kolb. Macon, GA: Mercer University Press, 1987. 198p.
*Forty martyrs of England and Wales.* J. Walsh. London: Catholic Truth Society, 1972.
*Four martyrdoms from the Pierpont Morgan Coptic Codices.* E. A. E. Reymond & J. W. B. Barns (eds). Oxford, UK: Clarendon Press, 1973. 290p
*Foxe's Christian martyrs of the world.* J. Fox. Westwood, NJ: Barbour Books, 1989. 200p
*Franciscan martyrs of Damascus (1860): beatified on October 10th, 1926 by His Holiness Pope Pius XI.* Dublin: Franciscan Convent, [1927]. 39p
'From death we are reborn: martyrdom and resistance in El Salvador.' A. L. Peterson. Ph.D. dissertation, University of Chicago Divinity School, 1991. 343p.
*Genese et evolution de theologie du martyre dans l'Eglise ancienne.* T. Baumeister. Frankfurt am Main: Peter Lang, 1991. (Also in German).
*Heroes and martyrs of faith.* A. S. Peake. New York: Hodder & Stoughton, 1900. 222p
*Heroes and martyrs of the modern missionary enterprise.* L. E. Smith. Hartford, CT: P. Brockett & Co., 1854.
*Heroes of the cross: an American martyrology.* M. A. Habig. Paterson, NJ: St Anthony Guild Press, 1945.
'Hieronymian Martyrology,' *A.A.S.S.*, I (November 11, 1894).
*Histoire des persecutions pendant les deux premiers siecles.* P. Allard. 3rd ed. Paris, 1903.
*Historia de las persecuciones.* A. Torres de Castilla. Barcelona: Petronio, 1978.
*I martiri di Roma.* A. Amore. Rome: Antonianum, 1975.
*In the homes of martyrs.* J. A. Walsh. New York: Catholic Foreign Mission Society of America, [1922]. 160p
*In the lion's den: a primer on mounting Christian persecution around the world and how American Christians can respond.* Anderson, IN: Bristol House, 1996. 60p.
*In the lion's den: a shocking account of persecution and martyrdom of Christians today and how we should respond.* N. Shea. Nashville, TN: Broadman & Holman, 1997. 126p.
*In the prisons of Mao.* D. T. Yee-MIng. : Hong Kong, 1991. (By Catholic archbishop of Canton on his 22 years in Chinese prisons).
*Jean Pierre Neel: martyr et bienheureux.* J. Vuaillet. N.p.: Editions Gerbert, 1981.
*Jesuit saints and martyrs: short biographies of the saints, blessed, venerables, and servants of God of the Society of Jesus.* J. N. Tylenda. Chicago: Loyola University Press, 1984. 503p. (Accounts of 323 Jesuits).
'Jesus and Martyrdom,' J. Downing, *Journal of Theological Studies*, N.s. XIV, 2 (1963), 279–93.
*Judith: martyred missionary of Russia.* N. I. Saloff-Astakhoff. Grand Rapids, MI: Zondervan, 1941.
*Kikuyu martyrs.* E. H. M. Wiseman. London: Highway Press, 1958.
'La liste des martyrs de Lyon de l'an 177,' H. Quentin, *Analecta bollandiana*, XXXIX (1921).
*La persecution du christianisme dans l'empire romain.* J. Moreau. Paris, 1956.
*Land of crosses: the struggle for religious freedom in Lithuania, 1939–1978.* M. Bourdeaux. Devon, UK: Augustine Publishing Company, 1979. 359p.
*Last days of the earlier martyrs.* A. R. Bonar. Edinburgh: William Oliphant & Co., 1870. 144p.
*Le Bienheureux Francois–Isidore Gagelin: missionaire en Cochinchine, martyr, 1799–1833.* C. Barbier. Colmar, Germany: Editions d'Alsace, 1976.
*Le Chanione de Gouvets et les martyrs de l'Avranchin.* J. C. Toussaint. Avranches, France: Editions l'Avranchin, 1977.
'Le martyre de la legion Thebaine: Essai sur al formation d'une legende,' D. Van Berchem, 1956.
*Le martyrologe.* J. Baudot. , 1911.
'Le sens eccleial du martyre,' M. Pellegrino, *Reveu des sciences religieuses*, 35 (1961), 152–175.
'Le temoignage des martyrologies,' H. Delehaye, *Analecta bollandiana*, XXVI (1907), 78.
'Le veritable date du martyre de Saint Polycarpe,' H. Gregoire & P. Orgels, *Analecta bollandiana*, LXIX (1951), 1–38.
*Les actes des martyrs de l'Eglise Copte.* E. C. Amélineau. Paris: E. Leroux, 1890.
*Les Actes des martyrs de l'Egypte.* H. Hyvernat. New York, 1977.
'Les actes des martyrs de Pergame,' H. Delehaye, *Analecta bollandiana*, LVIII (1940), 142–176.
'Les actes du martyr Apollonius,' E. Griffe, *Bulletin de litterature ecclesiastique*, 53 (1952), 65–76.
*Les martyrologies hsitoriques du moyen age: Etude sur la formation du martyrologe romain.* H. Quentin. Paris, 1908.
'Les martyrs d'Ammaedara,' S. Gsell, *Bulletin archeologique du comité des travaux historiques*, (1934), 69–82.
*Les Martyrs d'Angers.* A. Merlaud. Paris: Editiions S.O.S., 1984.
*Les martyrs de l'Ouganda.* M. Takulaba. Issy-les-Moulineaux, France: Editions Saint-Paul, 1978.
'Les Martyrs d'Egypte,' H. Delahaye, *Analecta bollandiana*, (1922), 5–154.
*Les origines du culte des martyrs.* H. Delehaye. New York: AMS Press, 1980.
*Les passions des martyrs et les genres literaires.* H. Delahaye. Brussels, 1921.
*Les Saints Martyrs canadiens.* G. Laflèche. Laval, Québec: Singulier, 1988–89. 2 vols.
*Letters to the martyrs.* H. W. Homan. New York: David McKay, 1951.
*Lives of 103 martyr saints of Korea.* C. T. Kim. Seoul, Korea: Catholic Publishing House, 1984. 182p
*Livre des martyrs chrétiens.* B. Chenu et al. Paris: Éditions du Centurion, 1988.
*Loca sanctorum Africae: le culte des martyrs en Afrique du IVe au VIIe siècle.* Y. Duval. Rome: Ecole Francaise de Rome, 1982.
'Love in contemporary Christian ethics,' S. J. Pope, *Journal of religious ethics*, 23, 1 (Spring 1995). (Identifies martyrdom as a form of Christian love).
*Lutheran martyr.* N. S. Tjernagel. N.p.: Northwestern Publishing House, 1982.
*Magnificent witnesses: 40 English and Welsh martyrs.* M. P. Harney. Boston: St Paul Editions, 1970.
*Martires de Guatemala.* [Guatemala, 1988]. 231p.
*Martiri giudizio e dono per la Chiesa.* P. Siniscalco. Torino, Italy: Marietta, 1981.
*Martyrdom of the Serbs: persecutions of the Serbian Orthodox Church and massacre of the Serbian people.* N.p.: The Diocese, 1943.
'Martyr et confesseur,' H. Delehaye, *Analecta bollandiana*, XXXIX (1921).
*Martyr in Tibet: the heroic life and death of Father Maurice Tornay.* R. Loup. New York: David McKay, 1956.
*Martyr invictus.* T. Baumeister. Münster, 1972.
*Martyrdom and persecution in the Early Church: a study of conflict from the Maccabees to Donatus.* W. H. C. Frend. Oxford, UK: Blackwell, 1965.
*Martyrdom and Rome.* G. W. Bowersock. Cambridge, UK: Cambridge University Press, 1994.
*Martyrdom and the politics of religion: progressive Catholicism in El Salvador's civil war.* A. L. Peterson. Albany, NY: State University of New York Press, 1997. 235p.
*Martyrdom in El Salvador: the murders at the Central American University, San Salvador, 16 November 1989.* Trans., D. Livingston. *Church in the world*, 27. Sydney: Australian Catholic Relief, [1990]. 8p. (Funeral sermons by Jesuits on martyrdom in El Salvador).
'Martyrdom of the churches under the Soviet regime,' E. Pähn, in *Estonia Christiania: eximio domino Johanni Köpp*, p.286–301. U. S. P. Eesti (ed). Holmiae: Estonian Theological Society in Exile, 1965.
*Martyrdom of women in the Early Christian church.* A. F. Ide. Garland, TX: Tangelwuld, 1985. 106p.
*Martyrdom today.* J. -. Metz & E. Schillebeeckx (eds). Edinburgh: T. & T. Clark, 1983. 101p
*Martyred missionaries of the China Inland Mission.* M. Broomhall. London: Morgan & Scott, 1901. 354p
*Märtyrer der evangelischen Christenheit, 1933–1945.* W. Oehme. Berlin: Evangelische Verlagsanstalt, 1979.
*Märtyrer und Gottesknecht.* E. Lohse. Göttingen, 1955.
'Märtyrertheologie und Täuferbewegung,' E. Stauffer, *Zeitschrift für Kirchengeschichte*, III, Folge 3 (1933), 545–609.
*Martyria/mission: the witness of the Orthodox churches today.* I. Bria. N.p.: World Council of Churches, 1980.
'Martyrien in jüdischer und frühchristlicher Zeit,' H. W. Surkau,
*Martyrien und Martyrologien ältester Zeit.* E. Egli. *Altchristliche Studien.* Zurich, 1887.
*Martyrium recherches sur le culte des reliques et l'art chretien antique.* A. Grabar. London: Variorium Reprints, 1972.
*Martyrologium: an Old English martyrology.* G. Herzfeld. : Kraus Reprints, 1900.
*Martyrologium hieronymianum.* L. Duchesne & J. B. de Rossi (eds). Brussels, 1894. (Acta Sanctorum).
*Martyrology of Carthage//Syrian martyrology.* H. Lietzmann (Ed). Bonn, 1911. (Kleine Texte 2).
*Martyrology of St. Aengus.* S. Aengus. (Eastern Orthodox).
*Martyrology pronouncing dictionary.* A. I. Russo-Alesi. New York: Edward O'Toole, 1939; reprint, Detroit, MI: Gale Research, 1973. 191p.
'Martyrs and Martyrdom,' T. W. Manson, *Bulletin of John Rylands Library*, 39 (1957), 463–484.
*Martyrs and martyrdom in the Coptic church.* Los Angeles: Saint Shenouda the Archimandrite Coptic Society, [1984]. 229p.
*Martyrs and martyrologies.* D. Wood (ed). Oxford, UK: Blackwell, 1993.
*Martyrs and miracles: the inspiring lives of saints and martyrs.* C. Trickey–Bapty. Baltimore, MD: Halo Press, 1996. 220p.
*Martyrs and saints of the first twelve centuries: studies from the lives of the black letter saints of the English calendar.* E. R. Charles. London: SPCK, 1887. 476p
*Martyrs and witnesses.* F. Hendrickson. Detroit, MI: Protestant Missionary Publishers, 1917. 318p
*Martyrs: contemporary writers on modern lives of faith.* S. Bergman (ed). San Francisco: HarperSanFrancisco, 1996. 320p.
*Martyrs from St. Stephen to John Tung.* D. Attwater. London: Sheed & Ward, 1957.
*Martyrs grecs IIe–VIIes.* F. Halkin. London: Variorum Reprints, 1974.
*Martyrs in China.* J. Monsterleet. Chicago: Henry Regnery, 1956.
*Martyrs in flames: or the history of Popery, displaying the horrid persecutions and cruelties exercised upon Protestants by the Papists, for many hundred years past.* R. Burton. London: A. Betterworth, 1729.
*Martyrs mirror excerpts.* J. Isaac. Moundridge, KS: Gospel Publishers, 1988.
*Martyrs of our time.* W. Purcell. London: Mowbray, 1983. 161p. (15 individuals or groups).
*Martyrs of Palestine.* Eusebius. , Ca. 300.
*Martyrs of the Reformation: a history of martyrdoms, confessions, and sufferings from the dawn of the Reformation until the former part of the nineteenth century.* W. H. Rule. London: J. Mason, 1848–51. 666p
*Mashonaland martyr: Barnard Mizeki and the pioneer church.* J. C. Farrant. London: Oxford University Press, 1966. (A catechist of the Anglican church, killed 1896.).
*Massacre in Shansi.* N. Brandt. Syracuse, NY: Dædalus Books.
*Mazzucconi of Woddlark: biography of Blessed John Mazzucconi, priest and martyr of the P.I.M.E. missionaries.* N. Maestrini. Hong Kong: Catholic Truth Society, 1983.
*Mission und Martyrium: Studienzu Karl Hartenstein und zur Lausanner Bewegung.* C. Sauer. *Edition AFEM*, Bd. 5. Bonn: Verlag für Kultur und Wissenschaft, 1994. 140p.
*Missionari che sanno morire: P. Lazzaro da Sarcedo, P. Piergiovanni da Trieste, martiri cappuccini nell'Angola.* P. X. Fernando da Riese. Venezia: Curia Provinciale dei FF.MM. Cappuccini, 1961.
*Missionaries, martyrs, and modernizers: autobiography and reform thought in American Protestant missions.* P. W. Harris. , 1986.
*Missionaries, monks, and martyrs: making disciples of all nations.* L. A. Veronis. Minneapolis, MN: Light and Life Publishing, 1994. (Study of Orthodox missions with reference to martyrs).
*Missionary martyrs.* W. Moister. London: T. Wollmer, 1885. 242p
*Missions and martyrs in Madagascar.* N.p.: American Tract Society, 1864.
*Morts, martyrs, reliques en Afrique chretienne aux premiers siecles.* V. Saxer. Paris: Beauchesne, 1980.
*Murdered in Central America: the stories of 11 U.S. missionaries.* D. W. Brett & E. T. Brett. Maryknoll, NY: Orbis Books, 1988.
'Mysterious fall kills a minister,' M. Howe, *New York Times*, 140 (December 20, 1990), A20. (Concerns the death of Noah Lewis).
*New Martyrologium.* Nicodemos the Hagiorite. Venice, 1799. (Greek Orthodox New Martyrs; lists 87 neomartyrs since 1492).
*New martyrs of the Turkish yoke.* Seattle, WA: St. Nectarios Press, 1985. 409p.
*Nine martyr monks: the lives of the English Benedictine martyrs beatified in 1929.* D. B. Camm. London: Burns, Oates & Washbourne, 1931.
*No strangers to violence, no strangers to love: twentieth century Christian heroes.* B. Hanley. Notre Dame, IN: Ave Maria Press, 1983.
*No time for tombstones: life and death in the Vietnamese jungle.* J. Hefley & M. Hefley. Wheaton, IL: Tyndale House, 1974.
'Note sugli acta martyrum scillitanorum,' F. Corsaro, *Nuovo Didascaleion*, (1956), 5–51.
*Notes sur le livre des marturs de Jean Crespin.* A. Piaget. Neuchatel: Secretariat de l'Universite, 1930.
*Padre Ivan Betancur: mártir de la iglesia Latinoamericana.* B. Meza. Tegucigalpa: Editora Cultural, 1982.
*Perpetua's passion: the death and memory of a young Roman woman.* J. E. Salisbury. New York: Routledge, 1997. 228p.
*Persecution and destruction of the Ukrainian Church by the*

*Russian Bolsheviks.* G. Luznycky. New York: Ukrainian Congress Committee, 1960. 64p.
*Persecution in the early church: a chapter in the history of renunciation.* H. B. Workman. 4th ed. London: The Epworth Press, 1923. 402p.
*Pocket dictionary of saints.* J. J. Delaney. Abridged ed. Garden City, NY: Image, 1983. (1,500 entries).
*Pourpe des martyrs.* Remy. Paris: Librarie Artheme Fayard, 1953.
*Praxis del martirio: ayer y hoy.* Bogotá: Cepla Editores, 1977.
*Pre–Decian acts of martyrs and commentarii.* G. Bisbee. Philadelphia: Fortress Press, 1988.
*Promised land: death and life in El Salvador.* S. Wright. Maryknoll, NY: Orbis Books, 1994. 269p.
'Prophet ünd Martyrer,' O. Michel, *Beitrage zur Förderung christliche Theollogie*, XXXVII, tlft 2 (1932).
*Recuerdos de antaño los martires españoles de la Reforma del siglo XVI y la Inquisicion.* E. Martinez. Tarrasa, Barcelona: Clie, 1977.
*Resumen de la vida del glorioso martir San Pedro Pasgual de Valencia.* F. Colombo. Valencia: Librerias "Paris-Valencia", 1979.
'Ritualistic acts and compulsive behavior: the pattern of Tudor martyrdom,' S. Byman, *American historical review*, 83 (1978), 625–43.
'Roman Catholic 'martyrs' in the South Pacific, 1841–1855,' H. Laracy, *Journal of religious history* (Australia), 9 (1976), 189–202.
'Roman Catholic "martyrs" in the South Pacific, 1841–55,' H. Loracy, *Journal of Religious History* (Australia), 9, 2 (1976), 189–202. (Documents seven Marists killed by natives of Pacific Islands, 1841-55).
*Russia's catacomb saints: lives of the new martyrs.* I. M. Andreev. Platina, CA: Saint Herman of Alaska Press, 1982.
*Slovak bishops: martyrs of Christ.* T. J. Zubek. Toronto: Canadian Slovak League, 1963. 16p.
*Sobibor, martyrdom and revolt: documents and testimonies.* M. Novitch (ed). New York: Schocken Books, 1980. 176p
*Spirit and martyrdom: a study of the work of the Holy Spirit in contexts of persecution and martyrdom in the New Testament and early Christian literature.* W. C. Weinrich. Washington, DC: University Press of America.
*Stories of missionaries and martyrs.* J. Crowlesmith. : Goodship House, 1929.
*Strong in the faith: the witness of the Uganda martyrs.* L. Pirovet. Mukono, Uganda: Church of Uganda Literature Centre, 1969.
*Suffering, martyrdom, and rewards in heaven.* J. Ton. Lanham, MD: University Press of America, 1997. 516p. (Originally the author's doctoral dissertation at Evangelical Faculty of Theology, Heverlee, Belgium).
*Suffering and martyrdom in the New Testament.* W. Horbury & B. McNeil (eds). Cambridge, UK: Cambridge University Press, 1981.
*Ten lectures on the martyrs.* P. Allard. London: Kegan Paul, Trench, Trübner & Co., 1907.
*The acts of the Christian martyrs.* H. Musurillo. *Oxford early Christian texts.* Oxford, UK: Clarendon Press, 1972.
*The age of martyrs: Christianity from Diocletian to Constantine.* G. Ricciotti. Trans., A. Bull. Milwaukee, WI: Bruce Publishing Co., 1959.
*The biographical and martyrological dictionary containing the lives, sufferings, and deaths of the most eminent martyrs.* Newcastle upon Tyne: M. Angus, 1790.
*The blood of the martyrs.* N. Mitchison. London: Constable & Co., 1939.
*The book of Christian martyrs.* B. Chenu et al. New York: Crossroad, 1990.
*The book of martyrs, or, compleat history of martyrdom: from the crucifixion of our Blessed Saviour to the present times.* London: J. Cooke, 1764–[1975]. 5 vols.
*The book of martyrs: or, the history of paganism and popery.* London: J. Fuller, 1765.
*The book of martyrs, with an account of the acts and monuments of church and state, from the time of our blessed saviour, to the year 1701.* London: D. Browne, 1702.
*The case of martyrdom considered.* J. Williams. London: H. Walwyn, 1702.
*The China martyrs of 1900: a complete roll of the Christian heroes martyred in China in 1900, with narratives of survivors.* R. C. Forsyth (ed). New York: Revell, [1904]. 528p.
*The Christian holocaust.* A. Ugolnik. N.p.: Chautauqua Institution, 1991.
*The conflict between paganism and Christianity in the fourth century.* A. Momligliano (Ed). N.p.: Oxford University Press, 1963. (Important essays on martyrdom).
'The "Croatian Christian martyrs",' *East Europe*, 23 (August 1974), 12–15.
'The date of the "martyrs of Nagran",' F. d. Blois, *Arabian archaeology and epigraphy*, 1 (December 1990), 110–28.
*The drama of the martyrs: from the death of Jesus Christ up to the recent times.* J. Luiken. Lancaster, PA: Mennonite Historical Association, 1975.
*The early persecutions of the Christians.* L. H. Canfield. (Contains a full bibliography of the earlier works on the persecutions.).
*The eighty–five martyrs.* R. Connelly. Great Wakering, UK: McCrimmons, 1987. 108p.
'The evolution of the martyrology in medieval Armenian literature,' K. S. Ter-Davtian, *Istoriko-Filologicheskii Zhurnal*, 2 (1982), 22–33.
*The first martyrs of North America.* J. A. O'Brien. Notre Dame, IN: University of Notre Dame Press, 1953.
*The fulfilled promise: a documentary account of religious persecution in Albania.* G. Sinishta. Santa Clara, CA: Sinishta, 1976.
*The good spirit of the martyrs revived.* E. Hookes. London: J. Marshall, 1718.
*The hero of Auschwitz.* Franciscan Friars of Marytown (eds). : Prow Books-Franciscan, 1979.
*The historic martyrs of the primitive church.* A. J. Mason. London: Longman, Green & Co., 1905. 434p
*The history of Christian martyrdom.* F. W. Blagdon. Philadelphia: D. W. Farrand, 1814.
*The history of the martyrs epitomised.* T. Mall. Boston: Rogers and Fowis, 1747.
*The lives and sufferings of the English martyrs.* G. Burnet. London: H. Owen, 1755.
*The lives of the fathers, martyrs and other principle saints.* A. Butler. N.p.: Virtue & Co., 1876.
*The lives of the holy women martyrs.* Buena Vista, CO: Holy Apostles Convent, 1991. 587p. (A hagiography of the Greek Orthodox Church).
*The lives, tryals and sufferings of the holy apostles, primitive fathers, and martyrs.* J. Wheatley. Bristol: Samual Farley and Co., 1751.
*The Manchester martyrs: the story of a Fenian tragedy.* P. B. Rose. London: Lawrence & Wishart, 1970.
*The Marian martyrs and the Reformation in Bristol.* K. Powell. Bristol, UK: Historical Association, 1972.
*The martyr church and its book.* J. A. Patten & E. Shillito. London: British and Foreign Bible Society, 1935. 47p
*The martyrology of the Sacred Order of Friars Preachers.* W. R. Bonniwell (trans). Westminster, MD: Newman Press, 1955.
*The martyrs: a study in social control.* D. W. Riddle. Chicago: University of Chicago, 1931.
*The martyrs, heroes, and bards of the Scottish Covenant.* G. Gilfillan. N.p.: Robert Carter & Bros, 1854.
*The martyrs' isle, or Madagascar: the country, the people, and the missions.* A. Sharman. London: London Missionary Society, 1909. 174p
*The martyrs of Estonia: the suffering, ordeal, and annihilation of the churches under the Russian occupation.* A. Vööbus. *Papers of the Estonian Theological Society in Exile*, vol. 34. Stockholm: Estonian Theological Society in Exile, 1984. 158p.
*The martyrs of Mannar.* A. J. B. Antoninus. Colombo, Sri Lanka, 1944. (Recounts a massacre in 1544.).
*The martyrs of Najrân: new documents.* I. Shahîd. *Subsidia Hagiographica*, no. 49. Brussels: Société des Bollandistes, 1971. 306p.
*The martyrs of Northumberland and Durham.* W. Fee. London: Catholic Truth Society, 1979.
*The martyrs of Papua New Guinea: 333 missionary lives lost during World War II.* T. Aerts (ed). Port Moresby: University of Papua New Guinea Press, 1994. 276p.
*The martyrs of the Coliseum; or, historical records of the great amphitheater of ancient Rome.* A. J. O'Reilly. Baltimore, MD: Kelly, Piet, & Co., 1872. 396p
'The "neomartyrs" as evidence for methods and motives leading to conversion and martyrdom in the Ottoman Empire,' D. J. Constantelos, *Greek Orthodox Theological Review*, 23, 3-4 (1978), 216–234.
*The new book of martyrs or complete Christian martyrology.* H. Southwell. London: J. Cooke, 1765.
*The New Martyrs of Russia.* M. Polsky. Montreal: Russian Orthodox Church Outside of Russia, 1972. (names and descriptions of 230 martyrs during period 1917-1944).
*The New Testament concept of witness.* A. A. Trites. *Society for New Testament Studies.* Cambridge, UK: Cambridge University Press, 1977.
'The oldest manuscript of Justin's martyrdom,' F. C. Burkitt, *Journal of theological studies*, XI (1910), 61–66.
*The one hundred and five martyrs of Tyburn.* T. Convent. New York: P. J. Kennedy & Sons, 1917.
*The Oxford martyrs.* D. M. Loades. New York: Stein & Day, 1970.
*The Penguin dictionary of saints.* D. Attwater. 2nd ed. London: Penguin, 1983. (Over 750 saints).
*The priest who had to die: the tragedy of Father Jerzy Popieluszko.* R. Boyes & J. Moody. London: Victor Gollancz, 1986. 204p.
'The rhetoric of Christian martyrdom: an exploration of the homiletic uses of ultimate terms.' M. J. Hostetler. Ph.D. dissertation, Northwestern University, Evanston, IL, 1993. 246p
*The Roman catacombs and their martyrs.* L. Hertling & E. Kirschbaum. Milwaukee: Bruce, 1956.
*The Roman martyrology.* Westminster, MD: Newman Bookshop, 1947.
*The saints and martyrs of Ireland: feast days' calendar.* H. P. Montague. Gerrards Cross, UK: Colin Smythe, 1987. 138p
*The saints of Egypt.* D. L. O'Leary. London: SPCK, 1937. 293p
*The saints of Egypt: an alphabetical compendium of martyrs, patriarchs and sainted ascetes in the Coptic calendar.* D. L. E. O'Leary. Amsterdam: Philo Press, 1974.
*The seventeen Irish martyrs.* Dublin: Veritas, 1992.
*The shame and the sacrifice: the life and martyrdom of Dietrich Bonhoeffer.* E. H. Robertson. New York: Macmillan, 1996. 288p. (Bonhoeffer was martyred by hanging in a Nazi prison camp only weeks before it was liberated by the Allied forces in 1945. His writings, including those written in prison, have become classics of Christian literature).
*The Southwark martyrs.* M. Clifton. London: Catholic Truth Society, 1980.
*The spirit of the martyrs revived.* E. Hookes. London: J. Sowle, 1719.
*The story of the Uganda martyrs.* J. Barlow. Kampala: Uganda Bookshop, c1980. 63p
*The Sussex martyrs.* M. T. Elvins. London: Catholic Truth Society, 1983.
'The theme of martyrdom in the book of Revelation.' M. G. Reddish. Ph.D. dissertation, Southern Baptist Theological Seminary, Louisville, KY, 1982.
*The true heroes: or, the noble army of martyrs.* London: J. Marshall, 1796.
*The Uganda martyrs.* D. Kauulu. Kampala: Longmans of Uganda, 1969.
'The value of persecution to the Christian Church through the ages.' J. W. Allison. Thesis, Pasadena College, Pasadena, CA, 1949.
*The voice of the blood: five Christian martyrs of our time.* W. J. O'Malley. Maryknoll, NY: Orbis Books, 1980.
*The Welsh Elizabethan Catholic martyrs.* D. A. Thomas. Cardiff: University of Wales Press, 1971.
*The Word remains: a life of Oscar Romero.* J. R. Brockman. Maryknoll, NY: Orbis Books, 1982.
*Their blood cries out: the untold story of persecution against Christians in the modern world.* P. Marshall with L. Gilbert. Dallas: Word Publishing, 1997. 359p. (Analyzes the circumstances of the persecution of Christian minorities in particular places around the world).
*Through gates of splendor: the martyrdom of 5 missionaries in the Ecuador jungle.* E. Elliot. Wheaton, IL: Tyndale House, 1981. 273p. (Among the Auca Indians).
'Torture and eucharist in Pinochet's Chile.' W. Cavanaugh. Ph.D. dissertation, Duke University, Durham, NC, 1996.
*Torture and torments of the Christian martyrs.* A. Gallonio. Los Angeles: Feral House, 1989.
*Tortured for Christ.* R. Wurmbrand. Bartlesville, OK: Living Sacrifice Books Co., 1967. 139p
*Tratado da vida e martirio dos cinco martires de Marrocos.* A. Gomes (ed). N.p.: Impr. da Universidade, 1928.
*Triumph in death: the story of the Malagasy martyrs.* F. G. Smith. Welwyn, UK: Evangelical Press, 1987. 128p.
*Tudor book of saints and martyrs.* H. C. White. Madison, WI: University of Wisconsin Press, 1963. 387p
*Twentieth century martyrdom.* A. Chandler. London: Cassell, 1998. 256p.
*Uganda holocaust.* D. Wooding & R. Barnett. London: Pickering & Inglis, 1980.
'Une nouvelle passion des martyrs de Pergame,' F. Halkin, in *Mullus*, p.150–154. Münster: 1964.
*Victories of the martyrs.* St. Alphonsus de Liguori. Ed., E. Grimm. 1776; reprint, Brooklyn: Redemptorist Fathers, 1954. 552p.
*Witnesses of hope: the persecution of Christians in Latin America: a tract on martyrdom in the theology of liberation.* M. Lange & R. Iblacker (eds). Maryknoll, NY: Orbis Books, 1981.
*Witnessing and martyrdom: in the Second Vatican Council, in the New Testament, and in the Early and the Modern Church.* J. Aixala. [Bombay]: St Paul Publications, [1970]. 324p.
*Women of grace: a biographical dictionary of British women saints, martyrs and reformers.* K. Parbury. Stocksfield: Oriel, 1985. 207p
*Won by blood: the story of Erromanga, the martyr isle.* A. K. Langridge. N.p.: Covenanter Press, 1978.
'Zeuge der Warheit,' E. Peterson, in *Theologische Traktate.* Munich: Kösel Verlag, 1950.
*Zeuge und Märtyrer.* N. Brox. Munich, 1961.

**Table 4–10. The demographics of Christian martyrdom, AD 33–AD 2000: 70 million martyrs in 600 major martyrdom situations in 150 countries.**

| Year 1 | Main locus 2 | Description of major martyrdom situation 3 / Related individual martyrs (these are the names shown in boldface type) 4 | Pers 5 | Trad 6 | Martyrs 7 | MR% 8 | Mag 9 | Int 10 | Global Christians 11 millions |
|---|---|---|---|---|---|---|---|---|---|
| | | **EPOCH I: CHRISTIANITY WINS THE ROMAN EMPIRE, AD 33-500** | | | | | | | |
| AD 33 | Jerusalem | Crucifixion of **Jesus** the First Martyr, the 'Faithful and True *martys*' (Revelation 3:14). | xJ | I-Aps | 1 | 0.0 | 1 | 0 | 0.0 |
| 36 | Jerusalem | Jewish persecution of Early Church; **Stephen**, protomartyr; 44 **James son of Zebedee** beheaded. | xJ | I-Aps | 100 | 0.3 | 2 | 2 | 0.0 |
| 54 | World | Journeyings of the **Twelve Apostles**, all eventually martyred; 54 **James the Less**, 60 **Philip**, 61 **Simon Zelotes**, 70 **Matthew**, 82 **Thomas** (in India). | x. | I-Aps | 320 | 0.8 | 2 | 3 | 0.0 |
| 64 | Roman Empire | 1st Imperial Persecution, provoked by Nero; 64, apostles **Peter, Paul** executed, bp **Evodius** of Antioch, 68 **Mark** (in Alexandria), 69 **Andrew**. | x. | I-Aps | 5,000 | 1.7 | 3 | 4 | 0.1 |
| 66 | Armenia | Apostles **Judas Thaddaeus** in 66 and **Bartholomew** in 68 martyred with 1,000 believers; 76 patriarch **Zakaria**; c97 patriarch **Atirnerseh**. | x. | O-Arm | 1,000 | 0.8 | 3 | 3 | 0.1 |
| 70 | Judaea | 1st Jewish Rebellion, with 600,000 massacred; destruction of Jewish Christianity. | x. | I-Aps | 10,000 | 6.7 | 4 | 6 | 0.1 |
| 79 | Rome | Colosseum built for games (50,000 spectators); many martyrs thrown to lions and other beasts. | x. | R-Cat | 1,000 | 20.0 | 3 | 8 | 0.2 |
| 91 | Roman Empire | 2nd Imperial Persecution (Domitian); **Flavius Clemens**, **Antipas**, consul **Manius Acilius Glabrio**; 95 apostle **John**, 97 **Timothy**, **Clement** bp of Rome. | x. | R-Cat | 2,000 | 0.3 | 3 | 2 | 0.4 |
| 110 | Asia Minor | 3rd Imperial Persecution (Trajan); 108 bp **Symeon**, 115 **Ignatius** bp of Antioch, thrown to wild beasts; **Rufus** & **Zozimus**. | x. | O-Ort | 1,500 | 0.5 | 3 | 3 | 1.0 |
| 110 | Armenia | Persian tyrant Artaxerxes tries to eradicate Armenian Christianity: **Oski**, **Soukias**, & companions; c125 **Acacius** and 10,000 militiamen crucified on Ararat. | x. | O-Arm | 14,000 | 9.3 | 4 | 6 | 1.0 |
| 115 | Cyprus | Jewish population revolts, destroys Salamis, massacres 240,000 persons in Cyprus and Libya; suppressed by Hadrian, all Jews expelled. | .J | O-Gre | 10,000 | 10.0 | 4 | 7 | 1.0 |
| c117 | Asia Minor | Minor persecution (Hadrian); 2 bishops of Rome: **Sixtus I**, 130 **Telesphorus**. | x. | R-Cat | 300 | 0.1 | 2 | 0 | 1.1 |
| 132 | Jerusalem | 2nd Jewish Rebellion: messiah Bar-Kochba persecutes Christians, as do Romans. | xJ | O-Gre | 30,000 | 15.0 | 4 | 7 | 1.4 |
| 150 | Asia Minor | Minor persecution (Antoninus Pius); 156 bp **Polycarp**, **Felicitus Alexander**. | x. | R-Cat | 300 | 0.1 | 2 | 0 | 1.9 |
| 165 | Roman Empire | 4th Imperial Persecution (Marcus Aurelius): **Justin Martyr** & 5 others, **Felicity**, 178 **Marcellus**. | x. | R-Cat | 4,000 | 0.1 | 3 | 1 | 2.5 |
| 177 | France | Violent persecution in Lyons and Vienne; bp **Pothinus**, **Blandina**, **Ponticus**; 49 official martyrs. | x. | R-Cat | 300 | 1.0 | 2 | 4 | 3.1 |
| 180 | Carthage | African martyrs, in Numidia: 12 **Scillitans**, 4 **Madaurans** (**Lucitas**, **Miggin**, **Namphano**, **Sanam**). | x. | R-Cat | 100 | 0.0 | 2 | 0 | 3.3 |
| 190 | Phrygia | Protracted persecution of Montanist zealots, also of Armenian Apostolic Christians including in 193 patriarch **Ghevondius**. | x. | I-Mon | 2,000 | 2.0 | 3 | 5 | 3.9 |
| c200 | Egypt | Vicious persecution with thousands of Copts martyred: 202 **Potamiaena, Basilides**. | x. | O-Cop | 10,000 | 1.7 | 4 | 4 | 4.7 |
| 202 | North Africa | 5th Imperial Persecution (Septimius Severus); **Perpetua, Felicitas, Saturus; Leonidas**, father of Origen, in Alexandria; **Irenaeus** bp of Lyons. | x. | R-Cat | 30,000 | 3.0 | 4 | 5 | 4.8 |
| 235 | Italy | 6th Imperial Persecution (Maximinus Thrax); clergy singled out; antipope **Hippolytus, Demetrius**; pope **Pontian** in mines of Sardinia. | x. | R-Cat | 3,000 | 0.6 | 3 | 3 | 6.9 |
| 240 | Armenia | Armenian Christians almost blotted out in Shapur I's persecution. | xg | O-Arm | 10,000 | 5.6 | 4 | 6 | 7.2 |
| 245 | Alexandria | Violent local persecution with thousands of Copts killed, including aged deaconess **Appolonia**. | x. | O-Cop | 2,000 | 2.0 | 3 | 5 | 7.7 |
| 249 | Roman Empire | 7th Imperial Persecution (Decius); 250 pope **Fabian**, patriarch **Babylas**; 253 pope **Cornelius**, 255 pope **Stephen I**; mob riots in Alexandria. | x. | R-Cat | 120,000 | 1.0 | 5 | 4 | 8.0 |
| 257 | Roman Empire | 8th Imperial Persecution (Valerian); 258 bp **Cyprian**, pope **Sixtus II**, rival pope **Novatian**; bp **Denys** beheaded; many clergy (**Montanus, Lucius**) executed. | x. | R-Cat | 150,000 | 1.2 | 5 | 4 | 8.7 |
| 275 | Europe | 9th Imperial Persecution (Aurelian); martyrs in Phrygia, Italy; 278 **Marina**. | x. | R-Cat | 5,000 | 0.0 | 3 | 0 | 10.6 |
| 276 | Persia | First Persian Persecution, under shah Varahran II: 275 heresiarch Mani crucified, 286 Christian queen **Candida** executed. | xZ | O-Nes | 4,000 | 0.0 | 3 | 0 | 10.8 |
| 284 | Egypt | AD 284-311: Coptic 'Era of the Martyrs': in first phase, 50,000 martyrs by AD 300, then in second phase (see on AD 305 below), vast increase. | x. | O-Cop | 50,000 | 5.6 | 4 | 6 | 11.8 |
| 287 | Gaul | Martyrs of Agaunum: **Theban Legion** (Copts) all executed by emperor Maximian Herculius: **Maurice, Urs, Victor, Exuperius, Candidus**. | x. | O-Cop | 5,000 | 83.3 | 3 | 9 | 12.1 |
| 287 | Armenia | Major persecution under pagan king Tiridates III; abbess **Gayane**, **Hripsime**, 37 virgins, **Theodore Salahouni**. | x. | O-Arm | 20,000 | 8.0 | 4 | 6 | 12.1 |
| 303 | Roman Empire | 10th Imperial Persecution (Diocletian); 3,500 formal or official executions of bishops, clergy, leaders: bp **Anthimus of Nicomedia**. | x. | R-Cat | 300,000 | 1.6 | 5 | 4 | 14.3 |
| 304 | Carthage | *Acts of the Abitinian Martyrs* as proto-Donatist account provokes later Donatist church's schism; **Maxima, Donatilla, Secunda** killed. | xR | I-Don | 3,000 | 5.0 | 3 | 6 | 14.4 |
| 305 | Egypt | Over 700,000 Coptic Christians killed (50% of all martyrs ever): **Menas** governor of Mareotis beheaded; 311 patriarch **Peter I Ieromartyros** (Seal of Martyrs). | x. | O-Cop | 400,000 | 26.7 | 5 | 8 | 14.4 |
| 316 | Armenia | Licinius' persecution: bp **Blaize**, 320 **The Forty Martyrs of Sebastia**; 4 patriarchs: 333 **Aristakes I**, 347 **Houssik I** & **Daniel**, 373 catholicos **Nerses I**. | x. | O-Arm | 2,000 | 0.7 | 3 | 3 | 15.4 |
| 317 | North Africa | Constantine initiates 4-year state persecution of Donatists; whole congregation in Carthage's Basilica Maiorum slaughtered. | xR | I-Don | 10,000 | 20.0 | 4 | 8 | 15.5 |
| 327 | Persia | Sassanid persecutions kill 3 catholicoses: 341 **Simeon Barsabae** with 100 clergy, 342 **Shahdost**, 346 **Barbashmin**; also prefect **Pusak** & 100 clergy. | x. | O-Nes | 20,000 | 1.7 | 4 | 4 | 16.4 |
| 337 | Persia | Great Persian Persecution under Shapur II, lasts 40 years, most ferocious ever; 16,000 names of martyrs recorded in one town alone (Ledan). | x. | O-Nes | 100,000 | 10.0 | 5 | 7 | 17.4 |
| 338 | Egypt | After patriarch Athanasius' return, Arians massacre Copts and clergy in Alexandria. | .n | O-Cop | 500 | 0.0 | 2 | 0 | 17.5 |
| 346 | North Africa | Vicious persecution of Donatist church (Berbers, with 270 bishops); 347 bps **Marculus, Donatus of Bagai**; whole shipload of Donatists drowned. | xR | I-Don | 8,000 | 0.7 | 3 | 3 | 18.4 |
| 370 | Numidia | Circumcellions, armed Berber farmers, court martyrdom as Donatists; civil unrest: 398, bp **Optatus** of Thamugodi executed; civil unrest, new wave in 404-5. | xR | I-Don | 3,000 | 10.0 | 3 | 7 | 21.2 |
| 372 | Egypt | After patriarch Peter II succeeds Athanasius, violent Arian persecution of Copts aided by emperor Valens. | xn | O-Cop | 4,000 | 0.2 | 3 | 1 | 21.5 |
| 378 | World | Jerome's estimate of all martyrs since AD 33 (over 50% being Copts); AD 426, similar estimate by Augustine of Hippo. | - | - | ***1,900,000*** | 1.2 | 7 | 4 | 22.2 |
| 390 | Rome | Unrest up to 410 Visigoth sack of Rome; 391 **Telemachus**, 410 **Marcella**, c420 tribune **M. Flavius**. | xT | R-Cat | 10,000 | 5.0 | 4 | 6 | 23.9 |
| 420 | Persia | 3rd Persian Persecution, under Bahram V; 422 **Hormisdas**; **Chouchanik**, **Suenas**, **Benjamin**, **James**, **Peroz**. | xZ | O-Nes | 90,000 | 6.9 | 4 | 6 | 27.4 |
| 434 | Western Empire | Attila the Hun destroys Western empire; bp **Auraeus**, **Ursula** & virgins, **Gereon**, 451 **Livarius**. | .T | R-Cat | 200,000 | 1.0 | 5 | 4 | 29.0 |
| 439 | North Africa | Persecution of Catholics and Donatists under Arian Vandal kings Gaeseric and Huneric. | xn | R-Cat | 10,000 | 0.2 | 4 | 2 | 29.6 |
| c440 | Ireland | Patrick evangelizes Ireland; soldiers execute numerous converts; **Gwinear**. | x. | A-Cel | 500 | 2.5 | 2 | 5 | 29.7 |
| 442 | England | Over next 30 years, invading Anglo-Saxons wipe out Celts and the original British/Celtic church in England. | .T | A-Cel | 20,000 | 10.0 | 4 | 7 | 30.0 |
| 448 | Iraq | 4th Persian Persecution: Yazdegerd II massacres 153,000 East Syrian Christians with 10 bishops at Kirkuk: bp **John, Sirin, Tamasgerd**, bp **Dindui**. | xZ | O-Nes | 153,000 | 12.8 | 5 | 7 | 30.7 |
| c450 | Ethiopia | Persecution kills **Kharitas** and 10,000 companions. | x. | O-Eth | 11,000 | 11.0 | 4 | 7 | 30.9 |
| 451 | Egypt | After Council of Chalcedon, emperor Marcianus closes Coptic churches, murders bp **Macarl** of Edko. | x. | O-Cop | 500 | 0.0 | 2 | 0 | 31.1 |
| 451 | Armenia | Yazdegerd II enforces Zoroastrianism, killing **Vardan Mamikonian** & 1,035 Christian troops, **Atom** and his legion; 454 patriarch **Hovsep I**. | xZ | O-Arm | 25,000 | 6.3 | 4 | 6 | 31.1 |
| 459 | Egypt | Melkite patriarch **Proterius** killed by Coptic mob. | .O | R-Mel | 30 | 0.3 | 1 | 2 | 32.1 |
| c470 | Persia | 5th Persian Persecution: Sassanid king Firuz I massacres Monophysite priests, 484 crucifies catholicos **Babowi**; 493 bp **Barsumas**. | xZ | O-Nes | 2,000 | 2.0 | 3 | 5 | 33.5 |
| 476 | Rome | Sack of Rome by Barbarians under Odoacer; Goths ravage West, decapitate **Volusianus** bp of Tours. | xT | R-Cat | 1,000 | 0.3 | 3 | 2 | 34.3 |
| *500* | *World* | *Total of martyrs listed above during Epoch I.* | - | - | *1,864,451* | *4.9* | *3* | *4* | *37.8* |
| 500 | World | All other martyrdom situations, known or unknown, during Epoch I | - | - | 149,000 | 0.4 | 3 | 4 | 37.8 |
| 500 | World | Background martyrdom during Epoch I (individual, domestic, family, isolated) | - | - | 88,300 | 0.2 | 0 | 0 | 37.8 |
| **500** | **World** | **Global total of all martyrs during Epoch I** | **-** | **-** | **2,101,751** | **5.6** | **3** | **4** | **37.8** |
| **500** | **World** | **Global cumulative total of all martyrs since AD 33** | **-** | **-** | **2,101,751** | **0.8** | **3** | **4** | **37.8** |
| | | **EPOCH II: THE GREAT RECESSION (THE DARK AGES), AD 500-950** | | | | | | | |
| 500 | Europe | Scattered martyrs: 526 pope **John I**, 555 **Helier**, 570 bp **Cadoc**, 607 bp **Desiderius**, 617 **Donnan** & 52 companions, et alii. | x. | R-Cat | 1,000 | 0.0 | 3 | 0 | 37.8 |
| 518 | Syria | Violent 46-year persecution of Monophysites; many bishops and clergy killed. | x. | O-Syr | 30,000 | 2.0 | 4 | 5 | 38.3 |
| 523 | Yemen | 30,000 Arab Christians massacred by Jewish king Masruq (dhu-Nawas) in Najran and Himyar; **Aretas**; 427 monks and nuns burned alive. | xJ | O-Nes | 20,000 | 50.0 | 4 | 9 | 38.4 |
| 533 | Persia | 6th Persian Persecution, under Khosrow I: 533 patriarch of the East **Mar Aba**, 575 bp **Ahudemmeh**, 615 **George the Monk** crucified. | xZ | O-Nes | 5,000 | 0.4 | 3 | 2 | 38.6 |
| c550 | Armenia | Ongoing sporadic persecutions: **Grigor-Rajik, Adeodatus (Astouadzatour-Mapod)**; c650 **David of Douine**; c850 princes **Isaac** and **Joseph**. | xZ | O-Arm | 2,000 | 0.5 | 3 | 3 | 39.1 |
| 580 | Egypt | Byzantine emperors Tiberius, Maurice, Phocas ruthlessly persecute Copts, 606 Phocas seizes all churches. | xO | O-Cop | 5,000 | 0.2 | 3 | 1 | 39.9 |
| 615 | Palestine | Persians invade, drive Romans to Mediterranean, capture Jerusalem, massacre 90,000 Christian men, burn churches; patriarch **Zacharias**. | xZ | O-Syr | 90,000 | 50.0 | 4 | 9 | 40.4 |
| 616 | Wales | Ethelfrith king of Northumbria enforces Roman church rule on Celtic Church, massacres 12,000 Celtic monks at Bangor-is-Coed. | xR | A-Cel | 13,000 | 3.0 | 4 | 5 | 40.4 |
| 619 | Egypt | Persian king Khosrow II invades, massacres 10,000 Copts, destroys 30 monasteries. | xZ | O-Cop | 10,000 | 0.3 | 4 | 2 | 40.4 |
| 628 | Persia | 7th Persian Persecution, under Khosrow (Chosroes) II; **Anastasius the Persian** & 68 others. | xZ | O-Nes | 3,000 | 0.2 | 3 | 2 | 40.5 |
| 631 | Egypt | Melkites persecute Copts for 10 years, killing hermits, ascetics, patriarch's brother **Menas**. | .R | O-Cop | 20,000 | 0.6 | 4 | 3 | 40.5 |
| 637 | Palestine | Arabs capture Jerusalem, 80,000 Byzantines killed at Pilla. | xM | O-Byz | 5,000 | 5.0 | 3 | 6 | 40.5 |
| 689 | Germany | Martyrdom of Irish bishop **Kilian** & 11 companions; 695 the **Two Hewalds (The Dark**, and **The Fair)**. | .T | A-Cel | 30 | 0.1 | 1 | 1 | 40.6 |

Continued below

*Table 4–10 continued*

| Year | Main locus | Description of major martyrdom situation | Related individual martyrs (these are the names shown in boldface type) | Pers | Trad | Martyrs | MR% | Mag | Int | Global Christians |
|---|---|---|---|---|---|---|---|---|---|---|
| 1 | 2 | 3 | 4 | 5 | 6 | 7 | 8 | 9 | 10 | 11 |
| | | | | | | | | | | *millions* |
| 694 | Lebanon | Greeks sack Monastery of St Maro and kill 500 Maronite monks. | | .O | R-Mar | 700 | 0.2 | 2 | 2 | 40.6 |
| 698 | China | 1st Imperial Persecution of Nestorians under dowager Wu Hou; mobs sack church and monastery in capital Loyang. | | x. | O-Nes | 1,000 | 0.5 | 3 | 3 | 40.6 |
| 700 | North Africa | Destruction of Christianity by Arabs, with all priests killed or enslaved, although numbers of Berbers remain Christians for next 150 years. | | xM | O-Cop | 50,000 | 2.5 | 4 | 5 | 40.6 |
| 707 | Morocco | Arab Muslim conqueror Moussa massacres large number of Berber Christians in Tangiers | | xM | O-Cop | 30,000 | 5.0 | 4 | 6 | 40.6 |
| 712 | China | 2nd Imperial Persecution of Nestorians: in western capital Changan, hostile crowds violate first Christian church in China. | | x. | O-Nes | 2,000 | 1.0 | 3 | 4 | 40.6 |
| 717 | Middle East | Pious and zealous caliph Omar II destroys all new churches, instigates first general persecution of Christians; mass conversions to Islam, also mass martyrdoms. | | xM | O-Cop | 60,000 | 0.6 | 4 | 3 | 40.6 |
| 725 | Byzantium | Iconoclastic Controversy until 843: emperors Leo III and Constantine V destroy 15,000 icons, torture and kill monk artists; 764, abbot **Stephen the Younger**. | | xO | O-Byz | 15,000 | 0.0 | 4 | 0 | 40.6 |
| 754 | Europe | Numerous missionary martyrs including bps **Boniface, Eoban**, & 52 others in Frisia. | | .T | R-Lat | 4,000 | 0.0 | 3 | 0 | 40.7 |
| 754 | Belgium | Sporadic persecution results in numerous deaths: **Rombout** of Malines. | | x. | R-Lat | 1,000 | 0.1 | 3 | 1 | 40.7 |
| 807 | Europe | Viking raids slaughter thousands including 68 monks on Iona, 6,000 Christians in Spain, Italy. | | .T | A-Cel | 20,000 | 0.2 | 4 | 2 | 40.9 |
| 815 | Byzantium | Second violent iconoclastic persecution: thousands of monks process with icons, bloody massacres follow until end in 843. | | xO | O-Byz | 5,000 | 0.0 | 3 | 0 | 40.9 |
| 827 | Sicily | Christianity harassed by Arabs over next 230 years. | | xM | R-Lat | 2,000 | 1.0 | 3 | 4 | 40.9 |
| 832 | Egypt | Caliph Mamun massacres Copts after uprising; 837, all churches demolished. | | xM | O-Cop | 20,000 | 1.0 | 4 | 4 | 40.9 |
| 835 | China | 3rd Imperial Persecution; 845, 40,000 hermitages and temples and 4,600 monasteries with 265,500 monks and nuns destroyed or closed. | | x. | O-Nes | 40,000 | 13.3 | 4 | 7 | 40.9 |
| 842 | Cilicia | Savage persecution of Paulicians by Byzantine empire, with major revolt crushed in 874; 100,000 martyrs; 873, leader **Chrysocheir** murdered. | | xO | I-Pau | 100,000 | 33.3 | 5 | 8 | 40.9 |
| 847 | Iraq | Major 14-year persecution of Christians and Muslim sects under 10th caliph Mutawakkil; churches destroyed. | | xM | O-Nes | 30,000 | 1.0 | 4 | 4 | 40.9 |
| 850 | Arabia | Nestorianism eradicated after 200 years of persecution and attrition by Muslim caliphs. | | xM | O-Nes | 20,000 | 20.0 | 4 | 8 | 40.9 |
| 850 | Spain | Under Moorish rule, **Martyrs of Cordoba**: **Flora, Mary**, 853 **Columba, Pomposa, Eulogius**, et alii. | | xM | R-Lat | 50 | 0.0 | 1 | 0 | 40.9 |
| 870 | Malta | Saracens capture islands, enforce Islam; many Christian deaths. | | .M | R-Lat | 5,000 | 0.3 | 3 | 2 | 40.8 |
| 878 | China | Port city of Kan-fu (Canton) falls to rebels who then slaughter 120,000 Muslims, Jews, Christians, and Zoroastrians. | | x. | O-Nes | 35,000 | 0.3 | 4 | 2 | 40.8 |
| 916 | Bohemia | Christianization of Czechoslovakia; murders of **Ludmilla** (916) and 929 prince-duke **Wenceslas**. | | .T | O-Sla | 30 | 0.0 | 1 | 0 | 41.3 |
| 923 | Syria | Uprisings of Muslim mobs against Christians kill hundreds near Jerusalem, Hims, Damascus. | | .M | O-Syr | 900 | 0.8 | 2 | 3 | 41.5 |
| *950* | *World* | *Total of martyrs listed above during Epoch II* | | – | – | *645,710* | *1.5* | *3* | *3* | *42.4* |
| 950 | World | All other martyrdom situations, known or unknown, during Epoch II | | – | – | 51,700 | 0.1 | 3 | 3 | 42.4 |
| 950 | World | Background martyrdom during Epoch II (individual, domestic, family, isolated) | | – | – | 95,400 | 0.2 | 0 | 0 | 42.4 |
| **950** | **World** | **Global total of all martyrs during Epoch II** | | – | – | **792,810** | **1.9** | **3** | **3** | **42.4** |
| **950** | **World** | **Global cumulative total of all martyrs since AD 33** | | – | – | **2,894,561** | **0.3** | **3** | **4** | **42.4** |
| | **EPOCH III: RESURGENCE AND ADVANCE, AD 950-1350** | | | | | | | | | |
| 950 | Mongolia | Final disappearance of Christianity across Mongol heartlands. | | x. | O-Nes | 10,000 | 10.0 | 4 | 7 | 42.4 |
| c970 | China | Many Christians killed in rebellion in Canton; final imperial persecution results in extinction of all churches and Christians. | | xB | O-Nes | 3,000 | 6.0 | 3 | 6 | 43.3 |
| 990 | Europe | Numerous bishops martyred: 997 **Adalbert**, 1012 **Alphege**, 1038 **Eskil**, 1066 **Gottschalk**, 1116 **Magnus**, et alii. | | .T | R-Lat | 4,000 | 0.0 | 3 | 0 | 44.2 |
| 996 | Middle East | Severe persecution from Egypt to Persia under caliph al-Hakim; **Ghabrial**. | | xM | O-Cop | 50,000 | 1.0 | 4 | 4 | 44.5 |
| 1009 | Lithuania | **Bruno** (Boniface) bp of Querfurt evangelizes across Russia, but with 18 other missionaries is murdered by heathens. | | .T | R-Lat | 30 | 30.0 | 1 | 8 | 45.3 |
| 1012 | Austria | Scattered killings of Christian leaders: 1012 **Coloman**, 1145 abbot **C. Bosinlother**. | | x. | R-Lat | 100 | 0.0 | 2 | 0 | 45.5 |
| 1030 | Norway | **Olaf II Haraldsson** killed after 15 years violently converting Norway to Christianity. | | .T | R-Lat | 2,000 | 1.0 | 3 | 4 | 46.7 |
| 1064 | Armenia | Capital city Ani with its 1,001 churches destroyed by Seljuk Turks, population massacred. | | .M | O-Arm | 100,000 | 50.0 | 5 | 9 | 49.2 |
| 1095 | Palestine | Crusades to recapture Holy Land; numerous zealous martyrs. | | .M | R-Lat | 3,000 | 0.6 | 3 | 3 | 51.6 |
| 1096 | Cappadocia | Jacobites massacred by Turks in Malatya with bp **John (Said bar Sabhuni)**. | | .M | O-Syr | 200 | 0.0 | 2 | 0 | 51.7 |
| 1166 | Europe | 30 alleged heretics executed by King Henry II in England, also many heretics on Continent. | | xA | A-Ang | 2,000 | 0.0 | 3 | 0 | 60.7 |
| 1173 | Nubia | Invading army from Kurdish sultan Saladin of Egypt kills or enslaves 700,000 Nubian Christians. | | xM | O-Nub | 130,000 | 6.5 | 5 | 6 | 61.7 |
| 1187 | Palestine | Massacre in Galilee of 20,000 crusaders and lay Christians under Saladin; kills many Copts also, destroys cities. | | xM | R-Lat | 15,000 | 30.0 | 4 | 8 | 63.7 |
| 1202 | Byzantium | Constantinople sacked by Latins (French Catholic knights), Greek population massacred. | | .R | O-Byz | 30,000 | 15.0 | 4 | 7 | 66.0 |
| 1208 | France | 36-year papal Crusade against Albigensians (Cathar church); legate **Peter of Castelnau** et alii killed in Toulouse. | | .R | I-Alg | 20,000 | 22.2 | 4 | 8 | 67.0 |
| 1211 | France | Over 80 Waldensians burnt at stake as heretics in Strasbourg; intermittent persecutions. | | .R | I-Wal | 100 | 1.0 | 2 | 4 | 67.5 |
| 1212 | Near East | Children's Crusades end in disaster; many zealous child martyrs. | | .M | R-Lat | 1,000 | 2.0 | 3 | 5 | 67.7 |
| 1214 | Uzbekistan | Genghiz Khan massacres 6 million Christians destroying Christian strongholds of Bokhara, Samarkand, Tashkent. | | .T | O-Nes | 4,000,000 | 40.0 | 9 | 8 | 68.0 |
| 1214 | Afghanistan | Major Christian diocesan stronghold of Herat sacked by Genghiz Khan; 1.6 million killed in area. | | .T | O-Nes | 1,000,000 | 30.0 | 7 | 8 | 68.0 |
| 1220 | Morocco | First Franciscan martyrs: **Berard, Otho, Peter, Accursio, Aiuto**; 1227 **Daniel of Belvedere**; total Franciscan martyrs 158 by AD 1400. | | .M | R-Lat | 12 | 12.0 | 1 | 7 | 69.0 |
| 1220 | Persia, Iraq | Genghiz Khan pits Mongol military machine against Muslim states for first time, massacres 25% of population including Christians. | | xT | O-Nes | 150,000 | 25.0 | 5 | 8 | 69.0 |
| 1221 | Turkestan | Mongols destroy strongly Christian cities including Seljuk capital Merv and Khwarizm: 860,000 executed. | | xT | O-Nes | 600,000 | 30.0 | 6 | 8 | 69.2 |
| 1231 | Cyprus | Papal legate cardinal Pelagius tortures and burns 13 Cypriot monks. | | .R | O-Gre | 20 | 0.0 | 1 | 0 | 70.9 |
| 1231 | Europe | Inquisition established by Gregory IX; executes heretics for 300 years. | | .R | R-Lat | 10,000 | 0.0 | 4 | 0 | 70.9 |
| 1237 | Russia | Mongol armies under Ogodei destroy Moscow, Suzdal, Vladimir, Kiev (Greek Orthodox headquarters), 1241 Cracow. | | xT | O-Sla | 300,000 | 15.0 | 5 | 7 | 71.9 |
| 1241 | Hungary | Mongols destroy Hungarian army, ravage Hungary, destroying also the newly-established Diocese for Cumans. | | xT | R-Lat | 13,000 | 86.7 | 4 | 9 | 72.6 |
| 1258 | Syria | Many Christians in khan Hulegu's court executed by Mamelukes, including Mongol general **Kitbuqa**. | | xM | O-Nes | 1,000 | 0.1 | 3 | 1 | 75.7 |
| 1258 | Iraq | Baghdad captured by Hulaku Khan; end of Abbasid dynasty as caliph and 800,000 are massacred; Aleppo and Antioch likewise destroyed. | | xT | O-Nes | 1,100,000 | 50.0 | 7 | 9 | 75.7 |
| 1291 | Palestine | Turks finally succeed in destroying Carmelite monastery on Mount Carmel, murdering all monks. | | xM | R-Lat | 200 | 66.7 | 2 | 9 | 82.1 |
| 1295 | Persia | Kurds massacre Nestorians, especially in city of Maragha. | | .M | O-Nes | 3,000 | 0.6 | 3 | 3 | 82.9 |
| 1301 | Egypt, Syria | Mamelukes destroy all churches; Copts and Jacobites suffer a century of systematic persecution. | | xM | O-Cop | 80,000 | 2.7 | 4 | 5 | 84.0 |
| 1302 | South India | Roman Catholic missionary friars murdered by Muslim rulers. | | xM | R-Lat | 30 | 0.0 | 1 | 0 | 84.0 |
| 1310 | Iraq | Kurds and Arabs destroy Christian city of Arbela, massacre entire population. | | xM | O-Nes | 150,000 | 20.0 | 5 | 8 | 84.4 |
| 1317 | Turkey | Mongols enslave or kill 12,000 Nestorians at Amid; bp **Mar Gregorios** beaten to death. | | xT | O-Nes | 9,000 | 6.0 | 3 | 6 | 84.8 |
| 1321 | France | Final pogrom against Cathars: Cathar priest Guilhem Belibasta burned; last group buried alive. | | .R | R-Lat | 2,000 | 2.0 | 3 | 5 | 85.0 |
| 1321 | India | New missionary bishops to China decapitated by Muslims: **Thomas of Tolentino** & 3 other Dominicans at Tana, Bombay. | | xM | R-Lat | 100 | 10.0 | 2 | 7 | 85.0 |
| 1321 | Egypt | Mob fury: mass executions of Christians, monasteries destroyed, monks killed. | | .M | O-Cop | 30,000 | 3.8 | 4 | 5 | 85.0 |
| 1330 | India | Muslims conquer southwards to Vindhya mountains; 200,000 Christians slaughtered. | | .M | O-Nes | 180,000 | 36.0 | 5 | 8 | 85.4 |
| 1339 | China | Ruthless massacre of Christians in Mongol capital Almalik: bp **Richard**, 6 Franciscan missionary priests, vast number of laypersons. | | xM | R-Lat | 100,000 | 10.0 | 5 | 7 | 85.9 |
| *1350* | *World* | *Total of martyrs listed above during Epoch III* | | – | – | *8,098,792* | *9.4* | *4* | *5* | *86.5* |
| 1350 | World | All other martyrdom situations, known or unknown, during Epoch III | | – | – | 648,000 | 0.8 | 4 | 5 | 86.5 |
| 1350 | World | Background martyrdom during Epoch III (individual, domestic, family, isolated) | | – | – | 173,000 | 0.2 | 0 | 0 | 86.5 |
| **1350** | **World** | **Global total of all martyrs during Epoch III** | | – | – | **8,919,792** | **10.3** | **4** | **5** | **86.5** |
| **1350** | **World** | **Global cumulative total of all martyrs since AD 33** | | – | – | **11,814,353** | **0.6** | **3** | **4** | **86.5** |
| | **EPOCH IV: THE SECOND RECESSION: CONFUSION AND CORRUPTION, AD 1350-1500** | | | | | | | | | |
| 1358 | Asia | Tamerlane destroys 15-million-strong Catholic Apostolic Church of the East (Nestorians) across Asia. | | xM | O-Nes | 4,000,000 | 26.7 | 9 | 8 | 80.8 |
| c1375 | Georgia | In 20-year holy war, Tamerlane destroys 700 Georgian towns and all churches in the capital, Tiflis. | | xM | O-Geo | 150,000 | 20.0 | 5 | 8 | 70.0 |
| 1393 | Europe | Dissidents executed; **John of Nepomuk**, 1415 **John Hus**, 1416 **Jerome of Prague**. | | xR | R-Lat | 5,000 | 0.0 | 3 | 0 | 60.2 |

*Continued overleaf*

Table 4–10 continued

| Year 1 | Main locus 2 | Description of major martyrdom situation 3 / Related individual martyrs (these are the names shown in boldface type) 4 | Pers 5 | Trad 6 | Martyrs 7 | MR% 8 | Mag 9 | Int 10 | Global Christians 11 (millions) |
|---|---|---|---|---|---|---|---|---|---|
| 1394 | Mesopotamia | Tamerlane destroys West Syrian (Jacobite) churches and monasteries from Asia Minor to Persia. | xM | O-Syr | 200,000 | 10.0 | 5 | 7 | 59.7 |
| 1399 | England | Lollards executed: 1401 **W. Sawtrey**, 1410 **J. Badby**, 1413 Lord **Cobham**, 1418 Sir **John Oldcastle**. | xA | I-Lol | 100 | 0.1 | 2 | 1 | 57.2 |
| 1400 | Egypt | Vast number of Coptic martyrs during Mameluke age; **Saleeb**, **Ileya**, priest **Sidrak** & 5 monks, **Arsenius**; 1400, **Abu'l Farag** & 4 priests. | xM | O-Cop | 225,000 | 45.0 | 5 | 8 | 56.7 |
| 1400 | Europe | Inquisition begins systematic burning of accused witches, reaching a total of 30,000 by 1550. | xR | P-Chr | 10,000 | 0.1 | 4 | 1 | 56.7 |
| 1401 | Caucasus | Tamerlane sacks Sevauss, 4,000 Christians buried alive. | xM | O-Nes | 4,000 | 40.0 | 3 | 8 | 56.9 |
| 1401 | Iraq | Tamerlane massacres whole population of Baghdad, piles up skulls of Christians, liquidates church. | xM | O-Nes | 500,000 | 70.0 | 6 | 9 | 56.9 |
| 1453 | Greece | Start of neomartyr period, with Ottomans formally condemning and executing 172 Greek martyrs over period 1453-1867. | xM | O-Gre | 700 | 0.0 | 2 | 0 | 66.2 |
| 1478 | Spain | Spanish Inquisition: 120,000 Jews, intellectuals, and alleged crypto-Jews ruined during 1481-1498; 2,000 burned at stake. | xR | I-Jew | 1,000 | 2.0 | 3 | 5 | 71.2 |
| 1490 | Nubia | Extinction of Christianity after 3 centuries of apostasies, decline, many martyrdoms. | xM | O-Nub | 12,000 | 20.0 | 4 | 8 | 73.7 |
| 1492 | Spain | 12,000 Marranos and Moriscos executed as heretics by the Inquisition, insisting that they are crypto-Jews and crypto-Muslims. | xR | I-Jew | 10,000 | 33.3 | 4 | 8 | 74.1 |
| *1500* | *World* | *Total of martyrs listed above during Epoch IV.* | – | – | *5,117,800* | *6.7* | *4* | *5* | *75.9* |
| 1500 | World | All other martyrdom situations, known or unknown, during Epoch IV | – | – | 409,000 | 0.5 | 4 | 5 | 75.9 |
| 1500 | World | Background martyrdom during Epoch IV (individual, domestic, family, isolated) | – | – | 56,900 | 0.1 | 0 | 0 | 75.9 |
| **1500** | **World** | **Global total of all martyrs during Epoch IV** | – | – | **5,583,700** | **7.4** | **4** | **5** | **75.9** |
| **1500** | **World** | **Global cumulative total of all martyrs since AD 33** | – | – | **17,398,053** | **0.7** | **4** | **4** | **75.9** |
| | **EPOCH V: REFORM AND EXPANSION, AD 1500-1750** | | | | | | | | |
| 1500 | Latin America | First missionaries killed in the Americas: 1513 in Trinidad, 1518 in Brazil, 1523 by Caribs in Guadeloupe. | .T | R-Lat | 200 | 4.0 | 2 | 5 | 75.9 |
| 1500 | Europe | European Witch Craze accelerates; from 1400-1700, over 500,000 suspects (mostly innocent churchgoers) are executed. | xR | P-Lut | 100,000 | 0.2 | 5 | 2 | 75.9 |
| 1505 | Brazil | Start of evangelization in 1500 results in first 2 missionary protomartyrs of New World, with others, killed in 1505 by Indians near Porto Seguro. | .T | R-Lat | 50 | 0.0 | 1 | 0 | 76.9 |
| 1506 | Portugal | Massacre of New Christians (Marranos and Moriscos) in Lisbon. | .R | I-Jew | 10,000 | 7.7 | 4 | 6 | 77.1 |
| 1516 | Antilles | Carib cannibals kill fr **F. Salcedo**, **D. Botello**, and an unnamed friar. | .T | R-Lat | 50 | 25.0 | 1 | 8 | 79.3 |
| 1518 | Ceylon | Ceylon under Portuguese rule; several Franciscans martyred in Colombo. | .B | R-Lat | 20 | 1.0 | 1 | 4 | 79.7 |
| 1520 | Sweden | 'Stockholm Blood Bath': Christian II king of Denmark murders 80 Swedish leaders, ravages Sweden. | .R | P-Lut | 1,000 | 0.3 | 3 | 2 | 80.1 |
| c1520 | Scotland | Over next 250 years, 4,500 Christians are burned alive for alleged witchcraft. | .P | P-Ref | 4,000 | 0.0 | 3 | 0 | 80.1 |
| 1524 | Austria | Spread of Protestant Reformation results in persecution: 1524 first martyr **Caspar Tauber** tried, executed; 1528 Swiss Anabaptist leader **Balthasar Hubmaier**. | xR | P-Ana | 4,000 | 0.4 | 3 | 2 | 81.0 |
| 1525 | Low Countries | 30,000 Dutch Anabaptists executed; 1527 **F. Manz**, **M. Sattler**, 1536 **J. Hutter**, **John of Leiden**. | xR | P-Ana | 30,000 | 20.0 | 4 | 8 | 81.2 |
| 1526 | California | First Spanish missions and first martyrs; 1541 **J. de Padilla** OFM killed in Texas. | x. | R-Lat | 15 | 3.0 | 1 | 5 | 81.5 |
| 1526 | Hungary | Turkish sultan Suleiman I slaughters 200,000, enslaves 100,000 Protestants. | xM | P-Ref | 50,000 | 4.2 | 4 | 5 | 81.5 |
| 1527 | Ethiopia | Ahmed Gran destroys Amharic Orthodoxy in 15 years' savage pillaging. | xM | O-Eth | 100,000 | 20.0 | 5 | 8 | 81.7 |
| 1528 | England | Henry VIII executes 800; 1533 **J. Frith**, 1535 cardinal **J. Fisher**, **Thomas More**, 1536 **William Tyndale** captured in Belgium and burned at stake. | xA | A-Ang | 300 | 0.0 | 2 | 0 | 81.9 |
| 1535 | Ireland | Many clergy, religious and laity martyred under penal laws (1535-1714); chaplain **Maurice Kenraghty**; 107 Franciscan martyrs by 1707. | xA | A-Ang | 200 | 0.0 | 2 | 0 | 83.5 |
| 1536 | Mexico | Nearly 6 million Amerindians have been baptized since 1519; vast multitudes deliberately killed or slaughtered. | xR | R-Lat | 1,000,000 | 16.7 | 7 | 7 | 83.7 |
| 1536 | Paraguay | Mercedarian missionary **J. de Almasia** killed with companions by Agaces Indians. | .T | R-Lat | 40 | 0.0 | 1 | 0 | 83.7 |
| 1537 | Indonesia | On Halmahera, fierce Muslim rebellion leaves only 20,000 surviving Christians. | .M | R-Lat | 15,000 | 42.9 | 4 | 8 | 83.9 |
| c1540 | Egypt | Worst repression ever under Islam: monk **Yoannis al-Kalioobi** lashed to death by Turks. | xM | O-Cop | 3,000 | 0.8 | 3 | 3 | 84.6 |
| 1541 | Ecuador | Bishop **V. Valverde** OP killed in Guayaquil. | .T | R-Lat | 30 | 0.0 | 1 | 0 | 84.8 |
| 1544 | Ceylon | Ceylonese usurper king of Jaffna kills 600 out of 1,000 newly-baptized Manar islanders of Careas fisher caste. | xB | R-Lat | 600 | 46.2 | 2 | 8 | 85.5 |
| 1545 | France | French kings massacre Waldensians in Vaudois. | xR | I-Wal | 3,000 | 15.0 | 3 | 7 | 85.8 |
| 1547 | France | Many Protestants executed under Henri II, burned at stake for heresy; 1559 **Anne Du Bourg**, in Orleans. | xR | P-Ref | 10,000 | 5.0 | 4 | 6 | 86.2 |
| 1549 | Florida | From 1549-97, many missionaries evangelizing Florida (OFM, OP, SJ) are slaughtered; 1566 **P. Mart!nez** SJ. | .T | R-Lat | 100 | 1.0 | 2 | 4 | 86.7 |
| 1549 | India | Hindus, provoked by Portuguese, massacre fr **A. Criminali** SJ and other Christians in Malabar; 30 killed. | .H | R-Lat | 300 | 0.2 | 2 | 1 | 86.7 |
| 1550 | Nicaragua | Indian supporter bp **A. de Valdivieso** stabbed to death in Leon. | .T | R-Lat | 100 | 0.2 | 2 | 2 | 86.9 |
| c1550 | Uruguay | Catholic missionaries in Rio de la Plata area are resisted, several are killed over next 2 centuries. | .T | R-Lat | 50 | 0.0 | 1 | 0 | 86.9 |
| 1553 | England | Marian persecution burns 286 at stake: abp **T. Cranmer**, bps **N. Ridley**, **H. Latimer**, **J. Hooper**. | xA | A-Ang | 300 | 0.0 | 2 | 0 | 87.7 |
| 1554 | Turkey | Chaldean Catholic catholicos of India, **Yuhanna Sulaqa**, assassinated by Kurds at Diyarbakir. | .M | R-Cha | 400 | 8.0 | 2 | 6 | 88.0 |
| 1558 | Spain | Protestants virtually wiped out by Inquisition burning them at the stake. | xR | P-Ref | 300 | 0.0 | 2 | 0 | 89.0 |
| c1560 | Mexico | Bishop de Las Casas charges that conquistadors have killed 15 million Amerindians (many being baptized Christians). | xR | R-Lat | 2,200,000 | 66.7 | 8 | 9 | 89.5 |
| 1561 | Zimbabwe | Baptism of king of Monomotapa with 300 subjects; **G. da Silveira** SJ strangled soon after. | xT | R-Lat | 5 | 1.0 | 1 | 4 | 89.8 |
| 1562 | France | 1,200 Huguenots (French Protestants) killed in Massacre of Vassy, Toulouse; many others elsewhere. | xR | P-Ref | 3,000 | 1.5 | 3 | 4 | 90.0 |
| 1565 | Florida | French colony of Huguenots on St John's river savagely executed by Spaniards. | .R | P-Ref | 200 | 40.0 | 2 | 8 | 90.8 |
| 1567 | Low Countries | Spanish Council of Blood (1567-1574) executes heretics and Calvinists: **Lamoral of Egmont**. | xR | P-Ref | 5,000 | 0.2 | 3 | 1 | 91.3 |
| 1567 | Russia | Massacre in Moscow under tsar Ivan IV the Terrible; metropolitan of Moscow **Philip** strangled. | x. | O-Rus | 200 | 0.0 | 2 | 0 | 91.3 |
| 1569 | Siam | Muslim agitators and Burmese conquerors kill first missionaries **Jerome de la Croix**, **Sebastian Cantu**, and 2 colleagues. | xB | R-Lat | 4 | 0.3 | 1 | 2 | 91.8 |
| 1569 | Peru | Spanish Inquisition in Lima tortures 120,000 alleged heretics, burns 189 dissenters at stake. | xR | R-Lat | 500 | 0.1 | 2 | 1 | 91.8 |
| 1570 | Canary Islands | Huguenot corsairs murder at sea fr **I. de Azevedo** & 51 other Jesuit missionaries. | .P | R-Lat | 52 | 86.7 | 1 | 9 | 92.1 |
| 1570 | Cyprus | Turks invade, exterminate Copts including bishop and priests, annex Cyprus to Ottoman empire. | .M | O-Cop | 5,000 | 50.0 | 3 | 9 | 92.1 |
| 1571 | England | Elizabethan persecution of Catholics; 123 out of 438 priests executed; 1571 primate **J. Hamilton**. | xA | A-Ang | 400 | 0.0 | 2 | 0 | 92.4 |
| 1571 | America | 8 Jesuit priests killed in Virginia: **L. de Quiros**, **G. de Solis**, **J. B. Mendez**. | .T | R-Lat | 20 | 0.3 | 1 | 2 | 92.4 |
| 1572 | France | St Bartholomew's Day massacre of 72,000 to destroy Huguenot leaders under admiral **Gaspard de Coligny**. | xR | P-Ref | 70,000 | 28.0 | 4 | 8 | 92.6 |
| 1572 | Gold Coast | Augustinians inaugurate first mission, but are slaughtered. | .T | R-Lat | 10 | 2.0 | 1 | 5 | 92.6 |
| 1575 | Finland | At Valamo, Swedes murder 40 Russian monks, monastery destroyed. | .P | O-Rus | 100 | 0.1 | 2 | 0 | 93.5 |
| 1576 | Cambodia | Evangelization undertaken by Dominicans; **Silvestre de Azevedo** OP killed. | xB | R-Lat | 2 | 1.0 | 1 | 4 | 93.7 |
| 1581 | America | 14 Franciscan missionaries murdered in New Mexico (1581, 1631), Georgia (1597), Arizona (1632): **J. de Santa Maria**, **F. Lopez**. | .T | R-Lat | 30 | 0.0 | 1 | 0 | 95.1 |
| 1587 | Madagascar | First of numerous Roman Catholic missionaries killed, followed by many others up to AD 1800. | .T | R-Lat | 200 | 4.0 | 2 | 5 | 96.7 |
| 1597 | India | Several Nestorian metropolitans from Persia intercepted by Portuguese: mar **Simon**, mar **Joseph**, die in prison. | xR | O-Nes | 30 | 0.0 | 1 | 0 | 99.6 |
| 1597 | Japan | 20 Japanese Catholics (15 OFM) and 6 foreigners crucified in Nagasaki: **Paul Miki** SJ, **Leo Karasumaru**, **Francis of Miako**. | xB | R-Lat | 120 | 0.0 | 2 | 0 | 99.6 |
| 1600 | Nicaragua | Under Spanish rule, numerous Catholic martyrs over 70 years. | xR | R-Lat | 50 | 0.5 | 1 | 3 | 100.4 |
| 1603 | Philippines | Spanish rulers become fearful of rapid growth of Chinese converts, massacre 3,000 of them in Manila. | x. | R-Lat | 3,000 | 30.0 | 3 | 8 | 101.1 |
| 1612 | Chile | Araucanian Indians kill 3 Jesuit missionaries: frs **H. de Vecchi**, **M. de Aranda**, br **J. de Montalban**. | .T | R-Lat | 20 | 0.0 | 1 | 0 | 103.3 |
| 1612 | Honduras | Several Spanish Franciscan martyrs. | xT | R-Lat | 20 | 0.2 | 1 | 2 | 103.3 |
| 1614 | Japan | Ieyasu's Edict prohibiting Christianity; 205 martyrs (33 Jesuits): 1623 br **Simon Yempo**, 1627 fr **T. Tsuji**. | xB | R-Lat | 40,000 | 13.3 | 4 | 7 | 103.8 |
| 1616 | Mexico | Tepehuane Indians in Durango kill 8 Mexican and other Jesuits; frs **H. de Tovar**, **H. de Santarn**. | .T | R-Lat | 50 | 0.0 | 1 | 0 | 104.3 |
| 1617 | China | First general decree of persecution and banishment; missionaries imprisoned, banished; a few killings. | x. | R-Lat | 2,000 | 0.7 | 3 | 3 | 104.5 |
| 1618 | Europe | Thirty Years' War: numerous martyrs, 1631 priest **Liborius Wagner** of Schweinfurt. | x. | R-Lat | 15,000 | 0.1 | 4 | 0 | 104.7 |
| 1619 | Hungary | Martyrs of Kosice, beaten to death by Calvinists: frs **M. Crisinus**, **S. Pongracz** SJ, **M. Grodecz** SJ. | .P | R-Lat | 5 | 0.0 | 1 | 0 | 105.0 |
| 1620 | Italy | Massacre of Waldensians (11 July) at Tirano, Lombardy, near Swiss border. | .R | I-Wal | 1,000 | 50.0 | 3 | 9 | 105.2 |
| 1623 | Belorussia | Catholic priests and bishops killed by Orthodox mobs; **Josaphat Kuncevicz**, RC abp of Polotsk, killed outside Vitebsk cathedral. | .O | R-Lat | 200 | 0.0 | 2 | 0 | 106.0 |

Continued below

*Table 4–10 continued*

| Year 1 | Main locus 2 | *Description of major martyrdom situation* 3 / *Related individual martyrs (these are the names shown in boldface type)* 4 | Pers 5 | Trad 6 | Martyrs 7 | MR% 8 | Mag 9 | Int 10 | Global Christians 11 |
|---|---|---|---|---|---|---|---|---|---|
| | | | | | | | | | *millions* |
| 1624 | Tibet | First missionary fr A. de Andrade poisoned, survives; 1630, all 400 Tibetan Christians wiped out. | xT | R-Lat | 400 | 100.0 | 2 | 10 | 106.2 |
| 1628 | Paraguay | Reduction founder **Roque Gonzalez de Santa Cruz** SJ and 25 Jesuits killed by Guarani shamans. | xT | R-Lat | 250 | 0.3 | 2 | 2 | 107.2 |
| 1630 | Japan | Structure of Catholicism destroyed, 13% martyred, 1,900 Japanese Catholics crucified; 1632 fr **R.B. Gutierrez**, 1633 **fr J. K. G. Tomonaga** OP, **M. Kurobioye**. | xB | R-Lat | 100,000 | 20.0 | 5 | 8 | 107.7 |
| 1631 | Kenya | On Kenya coast, apostate sultan Chingulia kills 283 **Martyrs of Mombasa** in Fort Jesus, Mombasa. | xM | R-Lat | 283 | 31.4 | 2 | 8 | 108.0 |
| 1632 | Ethiopia | Emperor Susenyos kills 7 Jesuit priests: 1635 **G. Paes, J. Pereira**, 1638 bp **Apollinaris de Almeida**, 1640 **B. Bruni, L. Cardeira**; 1652 Lutheran **Peter Heyling**. | xO | R-Lat | 50 | 0.5 | 1 | 3 | 108.2 |
| 1637 | Japan | 35,000 Japanese Catholics executed at Shimabara on Kyushu; end of overt Christianity in Japan; **W. Courtet OP**. | xB | R-Lat | 35,000 | 70.0 | 4 | 9 | 109.5 |
| 1638 | Turkey | Ottoman sultan Murad IV murders 2 ecumenical patriarchs: **Cyril I, Cyril II**, for initiating reconciliation with Anglicanism, Protestantism, and Roman Catholicism. | xM | O-Gre | 300 | 0.0 | 2 | 0 | 109.7 |
| c1640 | India | Fierce persecutions of Christians and Hindus under Mughal emperors Shah Jahan and Aurangzeb (1659). | xM | R-Lat | 5,000 | 33.3 | 3 | 8 | 110.2 |
| 1641 | Ulster | 7,000 Scots Protestants including ministers and bishops massacred by Irish Catholics; 1649 Irish earl and parliamentarian **C. Plunkett**. | .R | P-Ref | 7,000 | 7.0 | 3 | 6 | 110.5 |
| 1642 | Canada | Numerous Jesuit missionaries killed by Iroquois and Huron Indians: 1646 **I. Jogues**, 1649 **G. Lalemant** & **J. de Brebeuf**. | .T | R-Lat | 100 | 0.1 | 2 | 1 | 110.8 |
| 1642 | England | Civil War (Puritan Revolution): many Anglican clergy, lay leaders, dissenters executed for treason: 1645 **William Laud** abp of Canterbury, 1648 king **Charles I**. | xA | A-Ang | 400 | 0.0 | 2 | 0 | 110.8 |
| 1644 | China | Manchus kill 10,000 Chinese Christians and behead Dominican protomartyr **F. de Capillas**. | xB | R-Lat | 10,000 | 6.7 | 4 | 6 | 111.3 |
| 1645 | Indochina | 1st Annam Persecution; A. de Rhodes expelled, 40 Christians put to death: Annamese catechists **André, Ignace, Vincent**. | xB | R-Lat | 40 | 0.0 | 1 | 0 | 111.5 |
| 1648 | Madagascar | First Lazarist mission at Fort-Dauphin; 4 Roman Catholic martyrs. | xT | R-Lat | 10 | 1.0 | 1 | 4 | 112.3 |
| 1648 | Lithuania | Cossacks and Tartars massacre Polish Catholics and Jews: 1648 fr **Adrian Chalinsky**; 1657 fr **Andrew Bobola** SJ. | .O | R-Lat | 3,000 | 0.1 | 3 | 1 | 112.3 |
| 1648 | World | Spanish Jesuit Ildefonso de Flores calculates all Christian martyrs to date at 11 million. | - | - | ***11,000,000*** | 0.3 | 10 | 2 | 112.3 |
| 1649 | Mexico | Inquisition ferrets out and executes Marranos (christianized Jews), including **Tomas Trevino de Sobremonte**. | xR | I-Jew | 500 | 16.7 | 2 | 7 | 112.6 |
| 1649 | Japan | Mass martyrdoms of underground Catholics still occur intermittently, when discovered: 1649, 1658, 1667. | x. | R-Lat | 1,000 | 5.0 | 3 | 6 | 112.6 |
| 1650 | Slovakia | Over next 50 years, several hundred Protestants executed in Presov and around. | xR | P-Lut | 800 | 10.0 | 2 | 7 | 112.8 |
| 1653 | India | Malabar church breaks with Rome; Nestorian metropolitan **Ahatalla** burned at stake in Goa by Portuguese. | .R | O-Nes | 500 | 0.6 | 2 | 3 | 113.8 |
| 1655 | Italy | Of Piedmont's 15,000 Waldensians, 2,000 massacred, part of 300-year persecution under Catholic House of Savoy. | .R | I-Wal | 2,000 | 2.0 | 3 | 5 | 114.5 |
| 1657 | England | Fifth Monarchy Men, extreme Puritan sect, launch 2 armed uprisings against Oliver Cromwell; 1661 leader **T. Venner** and others executed. | x. | A-Low | 300 | 1.0 | 2 | 4 | 115.1 |
| 1658 | Ceylon | Dutch conquer island; violent persecution of Roman Catholics ensues, especially 1689 Jaffna, 1706 Negumbo, 1720 Manar, 1729 Colombo. | xP | R-Lat | 300 | 0.1 | 2 | 1 | 115.4 |
| 1660 | Scotland | Scottish Covenanters brutally persecuted for 25 years; 1661 **James Guthrie** & **A. Campbell, Margaret Wilson**, 1680 **D. Cargill**, 1688 **J. Renwick**. | xA | P-Ref | 3,000 | 1.0 | 3 | 4 | 116.1 |
| 1661 | Formosa | Chinese pirate Koxinga kills 6,000 aborigine Reformed converts, crucifies Dutch missionaries: **A. Hambroek** and family publicly beheaded. | .T | P-Ref | 6,000 | 35.3 | 3 | 8 | 116.4 |
| 1662 | England | Under Charles II, 15,000 Quakers imprisoned, 500 deaths in prison; **Mary Dyre**. | xA | I-Qua | 500 | 0.8 | 2 | 3 | 116.8 |
| 1665 | Indochina | 2nd Annam Persecution; 45 Vietnamese martyrs officially recognized, but many others too. | x. | R-Lat | 600 | 0.2 | 2 | 2 | 117.8 |
| 1671 | Hungary | Ottoman Turk rulers launch violent attacks on Protestants. | xM | P-Ref | 1,000 | 2.0 | 3 | 5 | 119.8 |
| 1672 | Guam | Opposition from Chamorro sorcerers: 1672 **J. de San Vitores** SJ killed near Agaña, Guam. | .T | R-Lat | 10 | 0.1 | 1 | 1 | 120.1 |
| 1672 | India | In Sindh, persecution of Augustinian and Carmelite missions by Mughal emperor. | xM | R-Lat | 4 | 1.0 | 1 | 4 | 120.1 |
| 1672 | America | From 1542-1997, 117 Franciscan missionaries martyred, in New Mexico, Arizona, Illinois, Texas: **P. Avila y Ayala**. | .T | R-Lat | 350 | 1.5 | 2 | 4 | 120.1 |
| 1673 | Ireland | Roman Catholics persecuted; 1681 primate of Ireland **O. Plunket** becomes last martyr of Tyburn. | xA | R-Lat | 50 | 0.0 | 1 | 0 | 120.5 |
| 1676 | Russia | Czarist troops slaughter 190 Old Believer monks and other defenders of Solovki monastery in White Sea. | x. | I-OBe | 190 | 10.0 | 2 | 7 | 121.5 |
| 1680 | America | 22 Franciscan missionaries. | .T | R-Lat | 40 | 0.0 | 1 | 0 | 122.9 |
| 1682 | Russia | Old Believer archpriest **Avvakum Petrovich** burned at stake, monks massacred; thousands more executed; **Boyarina Morozova** dies in prison. | xI | I-OBe | 3,000 | 0.3 | 3 | 2 | 123.6 |
| 1685 | France | Edict of Nantes revoked, Huguenots flee or are killed; **Louis de Marolles, I. Le Fevre**. | xR | P-Ref | 5,000 | 1.3 | 3 | 4 | 124.7 |
| 1686 | Italy | With Edict of Nantes, 8,000 of the 16,000 Waldensians in Italy are massacred and the rest expelled | xR | P-Ref | 8,000 | 50.0 | 3 | 9 | 125.0 |
| 1687 | Hungary | Blood Trial of Eperies, persecution till 1781; large numbers of Protestants executed. | xM | P-Ref | 5,000 | 5.0 | 3 | 6 | 125.4 |
| 1691 | Bolivia | Jesuits work among Chiquito Indians; **Jose de Arce** killed. | .T | R-Lat | 2 | 0.0 | 1 | 0 | 126.8 |
| 1693 | India | Madras: persecution under Hindu Marava rajah Ranganagadeven; **J. de Brito** SJ beheaded outside Uraiyur. | xH | R-Lat | 100 | 0.1 | 2 | 0 | 127.5 |
| 1693 | Burma | King of Pegu drowns Paris missionaries; first Roman Catholic church built; frs **Genoud** and **Joret** martyred at capital city Ava. | xB | R-Lat | 4 | 1.0 | 1 | 4 | 127.5 |
| 1697 | Japan | Last great martyrdom in Japan, 35 victims in Mino; total all Japanese martyrs from 1614-1697 exceeds 200,000. | xB | R-Lat | 60,000 | 22.2 | 4 | 8 | 129.0 |
| 1698 | Indochina | 8 ongoing severe persecutions in 1698 (200 churches destroyed under king Min-Wong), 1712, 1721, 1723, 1737, 1745, 1750, 1773. | xB | R-Lat | 2,000 | 0.6 | 3 | 3 | 129.4 |
| 1699 | Trinidad | Carib Indians of San Francisco de los Avessales murder Capuchin friars; many Indians then hanged by Spaniards. | xR | R-Lat | 100 | 2.0 | 2 | 5 | 129.7 |
| 1702 | France | Camisards (Calvinist glossolalists) rebel, 12,000 executed in Languedoc alone. | xR | I-Ref | 15,000 | 15.0 | 4 | 7 | 131.0 |
| 1704 | China | Persecution throughout empire; many RC missionaries and converts killed. | xB | R-Lat | 10,000 | 3.3 | 4 | 5 | 131.9 |
| 1704 | America | Strong Capuchin missions in Florida destroyed by English governor, missionaries executed: 300 Christian Apalachee Indians killed, 1,000 enslaved. | x. | R-Lat | 400 | 30.8 | 2 | 8 | 131.9 |
| 1706 | Congo | Suppression of Antonian rising; Black prophetess **Donna Beatrice** burned at stake. | xR | I-CCa | 2,000 | 0.2 | 3 | 2 | 132.8 |
| 1714 | Romania | Executions by Ottoman Turks; Orthodox prince **Constantine Brankoveanu**, many youthful Neomartyrs. | xM | O-Rum | 1,000 | 0.0 | 3 | 0 | 136.6 |
| 1719 | Indochina | 11th Annam Persecution, 700 churches destroyed; 9 Vietnamese martyrs officially recognized. | xB | R-Lat | 5,000 | 1.4 | 3 | 4 | 139.0 |
| 1729 | Siam | Local persecutions of Roman Catholics. | .B | R-Lat | 200 | 10.0 | 2 | 7 | 143.9 |
| 1731 | Micronesia | Jesuit missionary **Juan Antonio Cantova** SJ killed at Mogmog in Caroline Islands. | .T | R-Lat | 10 | 0.3 | 1 | 2 | 144.9 |
| 1736 | Persia | Violent persecution under Nader Shah; Catholic work destroyed. | xM | R-Lat | 5,000 | 50.0 | 3 | 9 | 147.4 |
| 1737 | Tibet | Infuriated Buddhist monks persecute Jesuits and Capuchins, 1742 destroy first Tibetan church, and kill most of the 40 Tibetan believers. | .B | R-Lat | 35 | 70.0 | 1 | 9 | 147.9 |
| 1746 | China | Widespread, severe, intermittent 38-year persecutions: 1749 bp **P. Sanz** beheaded, 5 OP and 2 SJ missionaries strangled; also 1781, 1784. | xB | R-Lat | 20,000 | 8.0 | 4 | 6 | 152.6 |
| 1749 | America | Delawares, or Lenni-Lenape tribes (Amerindian Christians) massacred at Gnadenhuetten settlement; remnants flee to Ontario, Canada. | x. | I-Ang | 600 | 0.0 | 2 | 0 | 154.2 |
| *1750* | *World* | *Total of martyrs listed above during Epoch V* | – | – | *4,000,701* | *2.6* | *2* | *4* | *154.7* |
| 1750 | World | All other martyrdom situations, known or unknown, during Epoch V. | – | – | 320,000 | 0.2 | 2 | 4 | 154.7 |
| 1750 | World | Background martyrdom during Epoch V (individual, domestic, family, isolated). | – | – | 193,000 | 0.1 | 0 | 0 | 154.7 |
| **1750** | **World** | **Global total of all martyrs during Epoch V** | – | – | **4,513,701** | **2.9** | **2** | **4** | **154.7** |
| **1750** | **World** | **Global cumulative total of all martyrs since AD 33** | – | – | **21,911,754** | **0.6** | **3** | **4** | **154.7** |
| | **EPOCH VI: REPUDIATION AND REVIVAL, AD 1750-1815** | | | | | | | | |
| 1754 | Ottoman Empire | Steady stream of Orthodox killed (**The New Martyrs**); 1754 neomartyr **Nicholas**, 1771 **Damascenus**, 1794 **Polydorus the Cypriot**, 1795 **Theodore**. | xM | O-Gre | 30,000 | 0.3 | 4 | 2 | 158.2 |
| 1754 | Timor | Dutch colonists decimate Dominican work across island; 2,000 Catholics killed. | xP | R-Lat | 2,000 | 10.0 | 3 | 7 | 158.2 |
| 1754 | Greece | Numerous zealous Orthodox youths become neomartyrs: **Nicholas of Chios**, 1813 **Angelis**, 1838 **Georgios** tortured to death. | xM | O-Gre | 400 | 0.0 | 2 | 0 | 158.2 |
| c1760 | Russia | Alexander I's violent persecution of Dukhobors and other sectarians; 1771 in Plague Riot, mob murders abp **Ambrose of Krutitsy**. | xO | I-Rus | 1,000 | 0.0 | 3 | 0 | 163.7 |
| 1761 | Surinam | Three Amerindian converts of the Moravian Brethren are killed by fugitive slaves. | .T | P-Mor | 10 | 0.0 | 1 | 0 | 164.6 |
| 1764 | Siam | Roman Catholics annihilated by Burmese invaders. | xB | R-Lat | 2,000 | 50.0 | 3 | 9 | 167.4 |
| 1773 | Indochina | 12th Annam Persecution, in several waves: 1798 Vietnamese priests **E. Trieu, J. Dat** killed. | xB | R-Lat | 30 | 0.0 | 1 | 0 | 176.1 |
| 1780 | India | Under dewan Nagam Pillai, cruel persecution of Malabar Nestorians. | xH | O-Nes | 5,000 | 5.0 | 3 | 6 | 183.2 |
| c1780 | Egypt | Many Coptic government officials executed by Mamelukes, Turks: vizier **Rizk Agha**, 1822 scribe **Mu'allim Ghali** (an RC convert). | xM | O-Cop | 2,000 | 1.0 | 3 | 4 | 183.2 |
| 1780 | Argentina | Colonization of Patagonia from 1780 on is accompanied by martyrdoms: 1825 fr **B. Pogio**. | .T | R-Lat | 10 | 0.0 | 1 | 0 | 183.2 |
| 1782 | USA | Gnadenhutten Massacre: US militia slaughters entire Moravian village of 96 Delaware Indians, women, children; 1781 fr **F.T. Garces**; 1847 **M. & N. Whitman**. | x. | I-Con | 90 | 4.5 | 1 | 5 | 185.2 |
| 1784 | India | Tippu, Muslim sultan of Mysore, destroys 27 ancient churches, forcibly circumcises 50,000 Christians; 1798 kills 10,000. | xM | O-Nes | 10,000 | 5.0 | 4 | 6 | 187.3 |
| 1785 | Korea | Chin-san Incident as Confucianists attack Christians: first 10 converts executed; 1791 **Paul Yun**; then persecutions 1795, 1801, 1815, 1827, 1839, 1846, 1866. | xG | R-Lat | 500 | 50.0 | 2 | 9 | 188.4 |
| 1788 | Australia | Numerous tribal cultures destroyed as newly-arrived White settlers slaughter Aborigines as subhuman: though baptized, many are killed. | xA | I-Ang | 1,000 | 10.0 | 3 | 7 | 191.6 |
| 1789 | France | Many clergy executed during Terror; 1792 abp **J.M. Du Lau**, 1794 bp **L.A. Expilly**, fr **C. Carnus**, Carmelite Martyrs of Compiègne (also Laval, Orange). | xa | R-Lat | 5,000 | 0.0 | 3 | 0 | 192.7 |

*Continued overleaf*

*Table 4–10 continued*

| Year 1 | Main locus 2 | Description of major martyrdom situation 3 | Related individual martyrs (these are the names shown in boldface type) 4 | Pers 5 | Trad 6 | Martyrs 7 | MR% 8 | Mag 9 | Int 10 | Global Christians 11 |
|---|---|---|---|---|---|---|---|---|---|---|
| | | | | | | | | | | millions |
| 1791 | Haiti | Revolution by Black slaves begins; Spaniards slaughtered at mass; after 1800, a century of revolutions, assassinations, killings. | | x. | R-Lat | 3,000 | 0.7 | 3 | 3 | 194.9 |
| 1795 | Korea | 1st Great Persecution: 400 Korean Christians publicly executed: 1801 Chinese priest **James Cho Wen-Mo, S. C. Hwang**; many more in 1815, 1827. | | xG | R-Lat | 2,500 | 25.0 | 3 | 8 | 199.3 |
| 1799 | Tonga | First 3 missionaries of London Missionary Society are massacred. | | .T | P-Con | 3 | 3.0 | 1 | 5 | 203.8 |
| 1800 | USA | First major slave rebellion with Black Christian army of 10,000; leader **Gabriel Prosser** executed with 34 zealous followers. | | x. | I-Bap | 300 | 0.0 | 2 | 0 | 205.0 |
| 1801 | Egypt | Turks kill continuous stream of Copts; government official **Muallim Malati**. | | xM | O-Cop | 3,000 | 1.9 | 3 | 4 | 206.5 |
| 1809 | India | Dewan Velu Tampi massacres 3,000 Nestorian Christians and 9 clergy in Travancore and Cochin. | | xH | O-Nes | 3,000 | 10.0 | 3 | 7 | 219.3 |
| 1811 | China | Decree of Kia-tsing against Catholic preaching; **J.C. Tapeng, A. Chao, F. Clet**; 1816 fr **G. Lantrua**. | | xB | R-Lat | 2,000 | 0.9 | 3 | 3 | 222.6 |
| *1815* | *World* | *Total of martyrs listed above during Epoch VI.* | | – | – | *72,843* | *0.0* | *3* | *4* | *229.4* |
| 1815 | World | All other martyrdom situations, known or unknown, during Epoch VI | | – | – | 5,800 | 0.0 | 3 | 4 | 229.4 |
| 1815 | World | Background martyrdom during Epoch VI (individual, domestic, family, isolated) | | – | – | 74,600 | 0.0 | 0 | 0 | 229.4 |
| **1815** | **World** | **Global total of all martyrs during Epoch VI** | | – | – | **153,243** | **0.1** | **3** | **4** | **229.4** |
| **1815** | **World** | **Global cumulative total of all martyrs since AD 33** | | – | – | **22,064,997** | **0.6** | **3** | **4** | **229.4** |
| | **EPOCH VII: THE GREAT CENTURY, AD 1815-1914** | | | | | | | | | |
| 1817 | Venezuela | Murder of 30 Capuchin missionary priests and 4 brothers. | | .T | R-Lat | 34 | 0.0 | 1 | 0 | 234.0 |
| 1817 | Syria | Violent persecution of Catholics in Aleppo and Damascus. | | .M | R-Lat | 1,000 | 5.0 | 3 | 6 | 234.0 |
| 1817 | USA | Black African Methodist freed slave **Denmark Vesey** leads USA's largest slave insurrection, with army of 9,000; hanged, with 36 other Christian leaders. | | x. | I-Bap | 350 | 0.0 | 2 | 0 | 234.0 |
| 1821 | Cyprus | Turks hang Orthodox ethnarch abp **Kyprianos**, all 3 bishops, abbots, and 486 priests, and lay persons as alleged guerrilla reprisals. | | xM | O-Gre | 3,000 | 2.5 | 3 | 5 | 243.4 |
| 1821 | Indochina | 13th Annam Persecution, in a series of virulent waves: 1833 **F.-I. Gagelin**, 1837 fr **J.C. Cornay**, 1838 bp **I. Delgado**, 1857 bp **Diaz** beheaded. | | xB | R-Lat | 10,000 | 2.6 | 4 | 5 | 243.4 |
| 1821 | Greece | Ottoman Turk officials hang, lynch, or execute Greek Orthodox bishops and priests across Greece, also in Crete. | | xM | O-Gre | 5,000 | 0.3 | 3 | 2 | 243.4 |
| 1822 | Turkey | Greek Orthodox and Catholics massacred in Istanbul; ecumenical patriarch **Gregory V** and bishops hanged after Easter Day liturgy. | | xM | O-Gre | 23,000 | 1.1 | 4 | 4 | 245.8 |
| 1827 | China | Intermittent but violent persecutions: churches in Peking demolished, priests hunted down and executed including bp of Chengtu. | | xB | R-Lat | 400 | 0.0 | 2 | 0 | 258.2 |
| 1828 | Turkey | 20,000 Catholic Armenians expelled from Istanbul, many executed. | | xM | O-Arm | 1,000 | 5.0 | 3 | 6 | 260.8 |
| 1830 | Lithuania | Tsarist deportations of Roman Catholics (5,000 priests and nuns) to Siberia, and similarly in 1863. | | xO | R-Lat | 10,000 | 1.0 | 4 | 4 | 265.9 |
| 1831 | Iran, Iraq | Nestorians massacred by Kurds; also 1843, 1846. | | .M | O-Nes | 15,000 | 18.8 | 4 | 7 | 268.6 |
| 1831 | USA | Major violent Black slave insurrection, led by **Nat Turner**, a Black Baptist charismatic prophet; hanged, with a hundred followers; many others massacred. | | x. | I-Bap | 800 | 0.0 | 2 | 0 | 268.6 |
| 1834 | Sumatra | ABCFM missionaries **Henry Lyman** & **Samuel Munson**, inter alios, killed by Batak tribesmen. | | .T | P-Con | 100 | 20.0 | 2 | 8 | 276.6 |
| 1834 | Madagascar | Queen Ranavalona I's cruel 25-year persecution: 1834, converted idol-keeper **Rainitsiandavaka** & 200 followers killed. | | xT | I-Con | 1,800 | 45.0 | 3 | 8 | 276.6 |
| 1838 | Australia | Continuous White atrocities and police brutality kill 20% of all Aborigenes (20,000; many baptized) by 1948, especially in 1838, 1908, 1926, 1944, 1963. | | xA | I-Ang | 5,000 | 40.0 | 3 | 8 | 287.8 |
| 1839 | Oceania | Missionary martyrs: 1839 **J. Williams** (New Hebrides), 1841 fr **P.M. Chanel** (on Futuna) & 7 other Marists, 1871 bp **J.C. Patteson** (Solomons), J. Atkin. | | .T | A-Ang | 400 | 4.0 | 2 | 5 | 290.6 |
| 1839 | Korea | 2nd Great Persecution: **Martyrs of Korea** (81 RCs, 1839-46); bp **L. Imbert**, frs **P. Maubant, J.H. Chastan; J.Ri**; 1846, 3rd Great Persecution: fr **A. Kim**. | | xB | R-Lat | 2,000 | 20.0 | 3 | 8 | 290.6 |
| 1840 | Philippines | Revolutionaries: **A. De la Cruz**, 1872 frs **Gomez, Zamora, Burgos** garroted, 1896 **Jose Rizal**. | | xR | I-Cat | 2,000 | 0.1 | 3 | 0 | 293.5 |
| 1842 | Russia | Savage tsarist persecution of Catholics over protracted period; 1861 abp **J. Sokolskij** immured in Kiev. | | xO | R-Lat | 10,000 | 0.2 | 4 | 2 | 299.3 |
| 1843 | Turkey | Turkish officials use Kurdish leader Bedr Khan to massacre 20,000 Nestorians enslaving 50,000 others in Kurdistan mountains. | | xM | O-Nes | 20,000 | 80.0 | 4 | 9 | 302.3 |
| 1844 | USA | Mormon founders **Joseph** and **Hyrum Smith** lynched by mobs. | | .P | m-LdS | 20 | 0.4 | 1 | 2 | 305.3 |
| 1845 | Lebanon | Druzes kill 12,000 Maronites in 15 years up to 'Massacres of the Sixties'; 100,000 homeless. | | .M | R-Mar | 12,000 | 4.8 | 4 | 5 | 308.3 |
| 1846 | Solomons | Marist mission abandoned after 10 years; bishop **Epalle** killed. | | .T | R-Lat | 1 | 2.0 | 1 | 5 | 311.3 |
| 1847 | New Caledonia | Catholic mission abandoned in massacre; frère **Marmoiton**. | | .T | R-Lat | 10 | 20.0 | 1 | 8 | 314.4 |
| 1847 | Indochina | 14th Annam Persecution; 115 priests killed; **Martyrs of Tonkin**; several bishops executed; more persecutions 1851, 1856, 1884. | | xB | R-Lat | 18,000 | 4.0 | 4 | 5 | 314.4 |
| 1849 | Colombia | State persecution: Jesuits and 3 bishops deported, several killings. | | x. | R-Lat | 100 | 0.0 | 2 | 0 | 320.7 |
| 1849 | Thailand | All foreign missionaries expelled during local persecution which leaves little Christian presence left. | | xB | R-Lat | 40 | 0.0 | 1 | 0 | 320.7 |
| 1851 | Argentina | Tierra del Fuego: Patagonian Missionary Society party of 15 starved to death; **Allen Gardiner**; 1859, Aborigenes kill further party of 8. | | .T | A-Ang | 25 | 2.5 | 1 | 5 | 327.4 |
| 1855 | Ethiopia | Emperor Theodore II persecutes Roman Catholics; **fr Gabra Mikael**, 1860 bp **Justin de Jacobis**. | | xO | R-Lat | 2,000 | 20.0 | 3 | 8 | 342.0 |
| 1856 | USA | **James J. Strang**, founder in 1844 of CJCLdS (Strangites), is shot by 2 followers, sect then extinguished by fishermen near Great Lakes. | | .m | m-LdS | 10 | 0.2 | 1 | 2 | 345.7 |
| 1859 | Syria | **Martyrs of Damascus** (4 Spanish Catholic priests): **N. Ascanio, J.J. Fernandez, N.M. de Albera, P. Soler**. | | .M | R-Lat | 4 | 0.1 | 1 | 0 | 357.2 |
| 1860 | Egypt | Continuous Ottoman pressure on Copts; 1861 patriarch **Cyril IV** poisoned by khedive of Egypt. | | xM | O-Cop | 300 | 0.1 | 2 | 1 | 361.1 |
| 1860 | Lebanon, Syria | Full-fledged civil war: 11,000 Maronites (many wealthy) massacred by Druzes, 4,000 other Christians killed: fr **E. Billottet** SJ & 4 companions. | | .M | R-Mar | 15,000 | 8.0 | 4 | 6 | 361.1 |
| 1861 | Indochina | 16th Annam Persecution amidst massive church growth; formal executions of bps **H. Hermosilla** OP, **V.B. Ochoa**. | | xB | R-Lat | 3,000 | 0.8 | 3 | 3 | 365.1 |
| 1862 | China | Annihilation of 35 million Taiping quasi-Christians (Great Heavenly Kingdom) under Hung Hsiu-chuan based on Nanking. | | xB | I-qCh | 1,000,000 | 2.9 | 7 | 5 | 369.1 |
| 1865 | Paraguay | Over 60% of population killed in war with Brazil. | | x. | R-Lat | 1,000 | 0.1 | 3 | 1 | 381.3 |
| 1865 | Japan | Waves of persecution of Kakure Kirishitan (Hidden Christians) as they are discovered by entering Catholic missionaries; persecutions end 1873. | | xB | I-3mQ | 2,000 | 6.7 | 3 | 6 | 381.3 |
| 1866 | Korea | Final Great Persecution: bps **S.-F. Berneaux** & **M. A. N. Daveluy** beheaded, 7 priests, many catechists, 10,000 other believers killed; **R.J. Thomas, Peter Cho**. | | xB | R-Lat | 10,000 | 40.0 | 4 | 8 | 385.5 |
| 1868 | Mali | Two caravans of White Fathers missionaries massacred 1876-81, one by Tuareg nomads. | | .T | R-Lat | 30 | 50.0 | 1 | 9 | 394.0 |
| 1869 | Thailand | Northern prince Kawilorot of Chiangmai murders 2 key converts: ex-Buddhist abbot **Nan Chai**, and **Noi Sunya**. | | xB | P-Ref | 10 | 0.0 | 1 | 0 | 398.3 |
| 1870 | China | Tientsin Bloodbath: 2 French RC priests, 10 Sisters of Charity, and Chinese believers massacred. | | xB | R-Lat | 50 | 0.0 | 1 | 0 | 402.6 |
| 1871 | France | Paris: Commune executes **G. Darboy** archbishop of Paris, 60 priests and religious; 20,000 killed. | | xa | R-Lat | 300 | 0.1 | 2 | 1 | 407.0 |
| 1872 | Bulgaria | Bloody suppression of Bulgars, massacres by Turks till 1912. | | xM | O-Bul | 110,000 | 3.1 | 5 | 5 | 411.5 |
| 1875 | Papua | Missionary losses due to cannibalism become common in early years of mission work; on New Ireland, 4 Fijian missionaries killed and cannibalized. | | .T | P-Con | 60 | 0.0 | 1 | 0 | 425.2 |
| 1877 | Turkey | Uprising by Armenians, also by Syrian Christians. | | xM | O-Arm | 5,000 | 0.4 | 3 | 2 | 434.5 |
| 1878 | Italy | Old Catholic leader **David** shot as heretic after founding Chiesa Universale Giuris-Davidica. | | .R | I-OCa | 10 | 0.0 | 1 | 0 | 439.3 |
| 1880 | Britain | 1880-1885: peak of violent persecution of Salvationists: 660 brutally attacked, thrown into prison, where 20 die. | | .A | P-Sal | 50 | 0.1 | 1 | 1 | 448.9 |
| 1881 | Urundi | Massacre of White Fathers: frs **Augier, D'Hoop, Deniaud**. | | .T | R-Lat | 3 | 3.0 | 1 | 5 | 453.9 |
| 1883 | Madagascar | French wars 1883-96, waves of terror; many churches destroyed; 1896 fr **J. Berthieu** SJ clubbed by pagans. | | x. | R-Lat | 5,000 | 0.8 | 3 | 3 | 463.8 |
| 1883 | Kenya | Arabs plunder Fulodoya settlement for runaway slaves, behead teacher and protomartyr **David Koi**. | | .M | A-Ang | 200 | 2.0 | 2 | 5 | 463.8 |
| 1885 | Singapore | During big Chinese surge into Catholic Church 1885-1900, Triad secret societies kill 300 Chinese converts. | | .a | R-Lat | 300 | 10.0 | 2 | 7 | 474.1 |
| 1885 | Uganda | **Uganda Martyrs** (250 Anglicans and RCs; **Charles Lwanga**); bishop **J. Hannington**; 1897 **G.L. Pilkington**. | | x. | A-Ang | 1,000 | 10.0 | 3 | 7 | 474.1 |
| 1886 | Ethiopia | 30 Falasha Jewish families, converts to Anglican CMJ, martyred by Mahdists from Sudan. | | .M | A-Ang | 300 | 50.0 | 2 | 9 | 479.2 |
| 1886 | USA | In Alaska, sporadic killings of missionaries and Indian workers continue: abp **C. J. Seghers**. | | .T | R-Lat | 50 | 0.0 | 1 | 0 | 479.2 |
| 1887 | Togo | Catholic mission founded by fr **J. Moran**, who is then poisoned. | | .T | R-Lat | 1 | 5.0 | 1 | 6 | 484.5 |
| 1887 | Micronesia | On Ponape (Carolines), governor and party killed; 1890, Ponape Massacre of 1,500 Spaniards. | | .T | R-Lat | 1,500 | 3.0 | 3 | 5 | 484.5 |
| 1890 | Bhutan | Nepali and Lepcha converts from India (Ch of Scotland Mission) enter Bhutan as missionaries, but most die there, several being poisoned. | | xB | P-Ref | 40 | 40.0 | 1 | 8 | 500.6 |
| 1894 | Turkey | 300,000 Armenian Christians (10,000 Protestants) massacred: archimandrite **John Papizian**, 176 priests, 25 Protestant pastors. | | xM | O-Arm | 280,000 | 17.5 | 5 | 7 | 522.8 |
| 1896 | Mashonaland | Uprising against British; Africans killed are later canonized by African Independent Churches (AICs); Anglican catechist **Bernard Mizeki** killed. | | xA | I-3aA | 50 | 0.5 | 1 | 3 | 534.4 |
| 1896 | Turkey | Fr **Salvatore Lilli** OFM and 11 Catholics assassinated near Marash. | | .M | R-Lat | 20 | 0.0 | 1 | 0 | 534.4 |
| 1900 | North China | Boxer Revolt; 5 RC bishops, 31 priests, 188 Protestant missionaries killed, also 48,000 Chinese converts (3,500 Orthodox); **Wang Ten Ren, C. & E. Price**. | | xB | A-Ang | 49,000 | 2.9 | 4 | 5 | 558.1 |
| 1901 | Papua | Ordained LMS missionaries **J. Chalmers** and **O. Tomkins** murdered and cannibalized near Goaribari Island. | | .T | P-Con | 5 | 0.0 | 1 | 0 | 564.1 |
| 1904 | New Britain | At Baining, massacre of 2 RC priests, 3 brothers, 5 nuns. | | .T | R-Lat | 10 | 5.0 | 1 | 6 | 582.5 |
| 1904 | SW Africa | German troops kill 80,000 Hereros and Namas (10% Christians) from 1904-1908. | | xP | P-Lut | 6,000 | 30.0 | 3 | 8 | 582.5 |

*Continued below*

*Table 4–10 continued*

| Year 1 | Main locus 2 | Description of major martyrdom situation 3 / Related individual martyrs (these are the names shown in boldface type) 4 | Pers 5 | Trad 6 | Martyrs 7 | MR% 8 | Mag 9 | Int 10 | Global Christians 11 (millions) |
|---|---|---|---|---|---|---|---|---|---|
| 1905 | Manchuria | 2,000 Presbyterians killed by Japanese Shintoists; evangelists **Kim, Ni, An**. | xS | P-Ref | 2,000 | 10.0 | 3 | 7 | 588.7 |
| 1905 | Cilicia | Massacre of Armenian Christians by Turks in south. | xM | O-Arm | 20,000 | 1.2 | 4 | 4 | 588.7 |
| 1905 | Hong Kong | Violence and persecution: **Eleanor Chestnut** killed. | .B | P-Eva | 50 | 0.0 | 1 | 0 | 588.7 |
| 1905 | Burkina Faso | In Upper Volta, first Catholic baptisms result in severe persecution including deaths. | .T | R-Lat | 100 | 0.0 | 2 | 0 | 588.7 |
| 1905 | Azerbaijan | Baku massacres: 1905, governor goads local Tatars in 4-day slaughter of Armenian Christians; 1918, 20,000 Armenians massacred. | xM | O-Arm | 21,000 | 5.0 | 4 | 6 | 588.7 |
| 1906 | USA | Numerous Black pentecostal pioneers are murdered among 3,437 Negroes lynched by White racists, 1882-1922 (100 a year up to 1963). | .P | I-3pB | 2,300 | 7.7 | 3 | 6 | 595.0 |
| 1909 | Turkey | In Adana, largest city of Cilicia, further massacre of Armenians, including Armenian Evangelical Union at their annual conference. | xM | O-Arm | 45,000 | 2.7 | 4 | 5 | 614.4 |
| 1910 | Mexico | National Revolution kills 1,000,000 Christians (30,000 from 1927-29), mainly Catholics but with many Protestants; 1927 fr **M. Pro Juarez**. | x. | R-Lat | 70,000 | 0.5 | 4 | 3 | 620.9 |
| 1910 | Egypt | Last stages of Ottoman pressure on Copts; young deacon **Sidhom Bishai** killed. | xM | O-Cop | 600 | 0.0 | 2 | 0 | 620.9 |
| 1910 | Korea | 35-year Japanese occupation enforces Shintoism, kills thousands. | xS | R-Lat | 15,000 | 7.5 | 4 | 6 | 620.9 |
| *1914* | *World* | *Total of martyrs listed above during Epoch VII* | – | – | *1,809,433* | *0.3* | *3* | *4* | *648.0* |
| 1914 | World | All other martyrdom situations, known or unknown, during Epoch VII. | – | – | 145,000 | 0.0 | 3 | 4 | 648.0 |
| 1914 | World | Background martyrdom during Epoch VII (individual, domestic, family, isolated). | – | – | 321,000 | 0.1 | 0 | 0 | 648.0 |
| **1914** | **World** | **Global total of all martyrs during Epoch VII** | – | – | **2,275,433** | **0.4** | **3** | **4** | **648.0** |
| **1914** | **World** | **Global cumulative total of all martyrs since AD 33** | – | – | **24,340,430** | **0.5** | **3** | **4** | **648.0** |
| | **EPOCH VIII: VIGOUR AMIDST STORM, AD 1914-1950** | | | | | | | | |
| 1914 | Persia | Nestorians convert to Russian Orthodoxy under security guarantees but are betrayed, then annihilated by Turks at Urmia in Persia. | .M | O-Nes | 50,000 | 50.0 | 4 | 9 | 648.0 |
| 1914 | Europe | Out of 8.4 million killed in World War I, many individual martyrs for the faith. | x. | R-Lat | 100,000 | 0.0 | 5 | 0 | 648.0 |
| 1915 | Turkey | Final massacre of 600,000 Armenian Christians in Anatolia ; 600,000 more deported from Turkey, many dying by roadside or in Syrian desert. | xM | O-Arm | 600,000 | 34.3 | 6 | 8 | 653.0 |
| 1916 | Lebanon | Ottomans murder 100,000 Maronites (22% of Maronite population). | xM | R-Mar | 100,000 | 22.2 | 5 | 8 | 658.1 |
| 1917 | Iran, Turkey | Nestorians massacred by Turks and Kurds; catholicos mar **Benjamin Shimun XIX** assassinated. | xM | O-Nes | 20,000 | 40.0 | 4 | 8 | 663.2 |
| 1917 | USSR | Bolsheviks attack Russian Orthodox Church: 1917-26, 78 Orthodox bishops, 12,000 priests killed (8,100 in 1922); 1917-80, total clergy killed 200,000. | xa | O-Rus | 1,000,000 | 0.9 | 7 | 3 | 663.2 |
| 1918 | Iran | Killings of Chaldean Catholic archbishop **Audo**, apostolic delegate **Sontag**. | xM | R-Cha | 50 | 0.0 | 1 | 0 | 668.4 |
| 1918 | Turkey | Turks massacre 80% of all Syrian Orthodox: monks of Tur Abdin chained and buried alive. | xM | O-Syr | 30,000 | 75.0 | 4 | 9 | 668.4 |
| 1918 | Georgia | Orthodox Church crushed by Bolsheviks, 1920-40; 1918 catholicos **Kirion**, 1923 abp **Nasaire**. | xa | O-Geo | 60,000 | 12.0 | 4 | 7 | 668.4 |
| 1919 | Korea | Japanese rulers commence massive persecution; many Christians and missionaries killed; at Suwon, church filled with women and children burned down. | xB | R-Lat | 10,000 | 3.3 | 4 | 5 | 673.5 |
| 1920 | Turkey | Armenian Christians massacred by Turks at Marash and Hadjin. | .M | O-Arm | 30,000 | 5.0 | 4 | 6 | 678.8 |
| 1921 | Congo | 40-year Belgian persecution of EJCSK and other African Independent Churches (AICs); 1951 founder prophet **Simon Kimbangu** dies after 30 years in prison. | x. | I-3pA | 1,000 | 0.1 | 3 | 1 | 684.0 |
| 1921 | USSR | 1921-1950, 15 million Christians die in prison camps (=**New Martyrs**), including 30,000 clergy and 250 bishops, also pastors, evangelists, catechists. | xa | O-Rus | 15,000,000 | 13.6 | 10 | 7 | 684.0 |
| 1921 | USA | Tulsa Race Riot: White mobs torch 35-block Black business district, burn churches, burn or lynch 250 Blacks. | .P | I-3aB | 200 | 0.0 | 2 | 0 | 684.0 |
| 1922 | Kazakhstan | In Semipalatinsk, 12 Orthodox clergy tortured and shot, 84 more in Astrakhan, and hundreds elsewhere. | xa | O-Rus | 2,000 | 0.0 | 3 | 0 | 689.4 |
| 1923 | Turkey | In Greco-Turkish war, Greek and Armenian population of Smyrna (Izmir) massacred, city torched; metropolitan **Chrysostomos** of Smyrna (Neomartyr). | .M | O-Gre | 3,000 | 0.2 | 3 | 2 | 694.7 |
| 1925 | USSR | Soviets attempt to liquidate entire Roman Catholic Church, which falls from 9.2% in 1900 to 1.5% by 1950; 1935 exarch **L. Fedorov**, 1936 mother **C. Abrikosov**. | xa | R-Lat | 1,200,000 | 8.6 | 7 | 6 | 705.5 |
| 1927 | Ukraine | 34 Ukrainian Orthodox bishops, 2,000 priests, 20,000 lay officers, all martyred, many being crucified on iconostases; bp **N. Bretzkiy**. | xa | O-Ukr | 500,000 | 2.0 | 6 | 5 | 716.5 |
| 1927 | China | Civil wars, bandits, guerrillas; 1932 **W.E. Simpson**; 1934 **Y.C. Liu, J. & B. Stam**; 1940 fr **F.V. Lebbe**. | xB | P-Eva | 200,000 | 6.7 | 5 | 6 | 716.5 |
| 1927 | Belorussia | Autocephalous Church exterminated, 1927-1938; 3 bishops murdered: **Filaret** of Bobruisk, **Mikhail** of Slutsk, **Ioann** of Mozyr; 1943 RC exarch **Nemantsevich**. | xa | O-Bye | 120,000 | 2.0 | 5 | 5 | 716.5 |
| 1927 | Russia | Under Bolshevik dictator Stalin, a million German-origin Lutherans across Russia are liquidated, churches destroyed. | xa | P-Lut | 600,000 | 60.0 | 6 | 9 | 716.5 |
| 1928 | Ukraine | 95% of all Orthodox parishes destroyed, 16 UAOC bishops killed including 3 metropolitans: 1936 **I. Pavlivsky**, 1937 **M. Boretsky**, 1938 **V. Lypkivsky**. | xa | O-Ukr | 300,000 | 3.0 | 5 | 5 | 722.1 |
| 1930 | Kenya | In female circumcision controversy, African Independent Pentecostal Church is persecuted for 27 years; 30,000 Kikuyu killed; many Kikuyu Christian martyrs. | .T | I-3pA | 5,000 | 0.5 | 3 | 3 | 733.3 |
| 1930 | Russia | Soviets expand elimination of Russian Orthodox Church and its leadership: 1930-50, 100 more bishops killed or die in prison. | xa | O-Rus | 100 | 10.0 | 2 | 7 | 733.3 |
| 1931 | Spain | Separation of church from state; many priests and religious killed; 1936 historian **Z. Garcia Villada** SJ. | x. | R-Lat | 8,000 | 0.0 | 3 | 0 | 739.0 |
| 1932 | El Salvador | La Massacre: national army slaughters 31,000 Indians and peasants in 12 days. | x. | R-Lat | 5,000 | 0.3 | 3 | 2 | 744.8 |
| 1932 | Ukraine | 1929-37, The Terror-Famine: 14.5 million Orthodox peasants killed or starved to death on orders of Stalin. | xa | O-Ukr | 2,700,000 | 10.2 | 8 | 7 | 744.8 |
| 1933 | Germany | Nazis persecute Confessing Church, RC Church; fr **B. Lichtenberg**, 1944 fr **M.J. Metzger**, professor **J. Schmidlin**,1945 Lutheran theologian **D. Bonhoeffer**. | xY | P-Lut | 125,000 | 0.2 | 5 | 2 | 750.6 |
| 1933 | Iraq | Assyrians (Nestorians) murdered by Iraqi troops. | x. | O-Nes | 800 | 80.0 | 2 | 9 | 750.6 |
| 1933 | USA | Random assassinations: 1933 Armenian abp **Leontius Tourian** killed at Christmas Eve mass, New York City. | .O | O-Arm | 100 | 0.0 | 2 | 0 | 750.6 |
| 1934 | Mongolia | Stalinist purges liquidate 70,000 lamas, 30,000 intellectuals, and most crypto-Christians. | xa | I-3hZ | 1,000 | 71.4 | 3 | 9 | 756.4 |
| 1934 | Italy | Fascist persecution of Pentecostals kills many, especially in Assemblee di Dio in Italia. | x. | P-Pen | 2,000 | 0.0 | 3 | 0 | 756.4 |
| 1934 | Kazakhstan | Large numbers of Russian Orthodox clergy liquidated in prison camps: abp **Ambrose Poliansky** of Podolsk. | xa | O-Rus | 4,000 | 8.0 | 3 | 6 | 756.4 |
| 1934 | Latvia | Executions of clergy throughout Latvia: **John Pommer** abp of Riga. | xa | R-Lat | 500 | 0.0 | 2 | 0 | 756.4 |
| 1935 | USSR | Vicious persecution of underground churches ('catacomb church'); 1943 **I.E. Voronaev** shot. | xa | P-Pen | 1,000,000 | 5.0 | 7 | 6 | 762.3 |
| 1935 | Japan | Severe persecution, killings of members of Japan Holiness Church (Toyo Senkyokai, M=OMS). | x. | P-Hol | 1,000 | 0.1 | 3 | 0 | 762.3 |
| 1936 | Spain | Civil War: 13 bishops, 4,254 priests, 2,489 monks, 283 nuns, and 100,000 lay Catholics executed or assassinated: Jesuits **L. Isla, J. Valenti, T. Sitjar**. | x. | R-Lat | 107,000 | 0.5 | 5 | 2 | 768.2 |
| 1936 | Germany | Hitler orders city of Berlin 'cleaned up' by rounding up and massacring thousands of Sinti and Romani Gypsies. | x. | R-Lat | 50,000 | 29.9 | 4 | 8 | 768.2 |
| 1937 | Ethiopia | Italian conquest: Orthodox bishops **Petros, Mikael** murdered (pushed out of aircraft), scores of priests and monks massacred, churches razed. | xR | O-Eth | 500,000 | 10.0 | 6 | 7 | 774.1 |
| 1937 | Europe | Holocaust: Nazis kill 5 million religious Jews and 1 million Jewish Christians; 1942 **Edith Stein**, 1944 **Max Jacob**. | xY | I-3mJ | 1,000,000 | 71.4 | 7 | 9 | 774.1 |
| 1937 | Hispaniola | Troops and police of Dominican Republic massacre 5,000 Haitian migrant laborers. | x. | R-Lat | 1,500 | 0.0 | 3 | 0 | 774.1 |
| 1937 | Russia | Final attempt to liquidate Orthodox Church: 1937, 85,300 clergy shot; 1938, 21,500 clergy shot; 1939, 900 shot; 1939-45, 100 more each year. | xa | O-Rus | 120,000 | 25.0 | 5 | 8 | 774.1 |
| 1938 | Armenia | Systematic persecution of Armenian Orthodox and Armenian Catholics by Soviet secret police; catholicos **Khoren I** killed. | xa | O-Arm | 30,000 | 2.0 | 4 | 5 | 780.1 |
| 1938 | Sinkiang | Yarkand work (begun 1892) of Swedish Missionary Society destroyed by fanatical Muslims and Bolsheviks, Uighur church of 300 communicants obliterated. | xa | P-Lut | 1,000 | 33.3 | 3 | 8 | 780.1 |
| 1938 | Europe | Nazis exterminate 500,000 Gypsies across Europe in the Porajmos (Gypsy Holocaust), mostly Christians; 1938 **Joseph Horvath**. | xY | R-Lat | 350,000 | 89.7 | 5 | 9 | 780.1 |
| 1938 | Austria | Under Nazi occupation, outspoken preachers and lay Christians targeted en masse, with many killed. | xa | R-Lat | 4,000 | 0.0 | 3 | 0 | 780.1 |
| 1939 | Poland | Nazis execute 6 RC bishops, 2,030 priests, 173 brothers, 243 nuns; 1941 fr **M. Kolbe** OFM and others entombed alive in Auschwitz death camp. | xY | R-Lat | 1,000,000 | 3.9 | 7 | 5 | 786.2 |
| 1939 | World | Out of 55 million killed in World War II, many martyrs; 1942 fr **T. Brandsma** in Dachau death camp. | x. | R-Lat | 200,000 | 0.0 | 5 | 0 | 786.2 |
| 1940 | Greece | German, Italian, Bulgarian troops murder 350 Greek Orthodox priests. | xY | O-Gre | 21,000 | 0.3 | 4 | 2 | 792.3 |
| 1940 | Baltic states | 200,000 deported; 10,000 bps, clergy, nuns shot or killed in prison by Soviets; many Baptist, Lutheran martyrs (41 being pastors). | xa | P-Lut | 150,000 | 3.0 | 5 | 5 | 792.3 |
| 1940 | Germany | Jehovah's Witnesses savagely persecuted by Nazis; 10,000 incarcerated, 2,000 killed by 1945. | xa | m-Jeh | 2,000 | 0.0 | 3 | 0 | 792.3 |
| 1941 | Yugoslavia | In Croatia, 350,000 Serbian Orthodox massacred by Croats; 3 bishops, 220 priests martyred. | .R | O-Ser | 350,000 | 17.5 | 5 | 7 | 798.5 |
| 1941 | Lithuania | Nazis kill 200,000; 1944 Soviets kill 300,000; 1941 fr **V. Litaunieks**, 1953 abp **M. Reinys**, 1959 bp **P. Ramanauskas**. | xY | R-Lat | 100,000 | 5.0 | 5 | 6 | 798.5 |
| 1941 | Belorussia | A million Christians, clergy, bishops, killed (1) by Stalin 'eliminating all Belorussian enemies of the state', (2) by occupying Nazis, then (3) by returning Soviets. | xa | O-Bye | 550,000 | 8.0 | 6 | 6 | 798.5 |
| 1942 | Yugoslavia | Nazis and civil war kill vast numbers of clergy and laity; 1945 bishop **J. Simrak**, 270 Catholic priests. | xY | R-Lat | 100,000 | 1.0 | 5 | 4 | 804.7 |
| 1942 | Czechoslovakia | Nazis shoot Orthodox bishop **Pavlik Gorazd**, several of his clergy, many laity. | xY | O-Cze | 15,000 | 0.1 | 4 | 1 | 804.7 |
| 1942 | Papua | In Battle of Coral Sea, 118 RC priests and brothers, 78 nuns, killed by Japanese troops, totalling 333 Protestant & RC missionaries by 1945. | x. | R-Lat | 400 | 0.1 | 2 | 0 | 804.7 |
| 1942 | Taiwan | Many Aboriginal Christians killed by Japanese army of occupation. | x. | P-Ref | 10,000 | 3.7 | 4 | 5 | 804.7 |
| 1942 | Solomon Is | American missionaries murdered by Japanese troops: **A. C. Duhamel** SM, **J. G. Hennessey**. | x. | R-Lat | 300 | 0.0 | 2 | 0 | 804.7 |
| 1942 | Gilbert Islands | Japanese invasion results in persecutions: **A. Sadd** killed. | x. | I-Con | 200 | 0.0 | 2 | 0 | 804.7 |
| 1942 | Philippines | Bataan Death March: 70,000 USA prisoners in cruelest forced march in history; 10,000 killed by Japanese. | x. | P-Bap | 6,000 | 0.0 | 3 | 0 | 804.7 |

*Continued overleaf*

*Table 4–10 continued*

| Year 1 | Main locus 2 | Description of major martyrdom situation 3 / Related individual martyrs (these are the names shown in boldface type) 4 | Pers 5 | Trad 6 | Martyrs 7 | MR% 8 | Mag 9 | Int 10 | Global Christians 11 (millions) |
|---|---|---|---|---|---|---|---|---|---|
| 1943 | Bolivia | Ayore Indians massacre NTM missionaries: **D. Bacon, B. Dye, C. Dye, G. Hosback, E. Hunter**. | .T | P-Bap | 500 | 0.0 | 2 | 0 | 810.9 |
| 1943 | Philippines | Massacres by Japanese troops; **F. Meyer, F.H. Rose**, 10 other USA missionaries, many Filipinos. | x. | R-Lat | 3,000 | 0.0 | 3 | 0 | 810.9 |
| 1944 | Albania | Communist regime executes bishops: 1948 RC bps **Volai, Gigni, Gijni**, 1952 abp **N. Prennushi**; organized Christianity liquidated. | xa | R-Lat | 5,000 | 1.3 | 3 | 4 | 817.2 |
| 1944 | Mexico | In 34 years of Catholic persecution of Evangelicals and Indians since 1910, 400 pastors murdered. | .R | P-Eva | 10,000 | 0.1 | 4 | 0 | 817.2 |
| 1944 | Colombia | 1944-58, La Violencia civil war kills 300,000 Christians; 126 recognized Protestant martyrs; **Juan Coy**. | xR | P-Eva | 120,000 | 1.0 | 5 | 4 | 817.2 |
| 1945 | Ukraine | Soviets attempt to destroy 3.5 million-strong Ukrainian Catholic Uniates; 1946 bp **Kocylowskyj**, 1947 bp **T. Romza** poisoned, 1959 bp **A. Kherie**, many priests. | xa | R-Ukr | 70,000 | 2.0 | 4 | 5 | 823.5 |
| 1945 | Guam | Japanese occupiers kill first local Catholic priest, **Jesus Duenas**, et alii. | x. | R-Lat | 200 | 0.4 | 2 | 2 | 823.5 |
| 1945 | Burma | Baptist pastors and missionaries tortured by Japanese troops; pastor **Akya Nai, H. Devine**. | x. | P-Bap | 1,000 | 0.2 | 3 | 1 | 823.5 |
| 1945 | Mexico | Sporadic Protestant murders: in Veracruz, Catholic mob destroys Pentecostal church property, kills 9 Pentecostals. | .R | P-Pen | 100 | 0.0 | 2 | 0 | 823.5 |
| 1945 | Cyprus | EOKA guerrillas attempt to end British rule; 1948, lengthy campaign of terrorism until 1960 Independence; many killings. | x. | O-Gre | 500 | 0.1 | 2 | 1 | 823.5 |
| 1947 | India | Partition results in 1.1 million Muslim, Hindu, and Sikh deaths; 10,000 Christians killed or starve to death. | .H | P-Eva | 2,000 | 0.0 | 3 | 0 | 836.4 |
| 1947 | Madagascar | Insurrection against French rule: 11,000 executed, then 80,000 killed including many pastors and missionaries. | x. | P-Con | 2,000 | 0.1 | 3 | 0 | 836.4 |
| 1947 | Taiwan | 28,000 Taiwanese civilians, especially in Presbyterian Church in Taiwan, massacred in Taipei by Nationalist troops (28 February). | x. | P-Ref | 7,000 | 2.3 | 3 | 5 | 836.4 |
| 1947 | India | India government begins 53-year genocide to subdue 2 million Nagas (80% Baptists); 300,000 killed by 1999. | xH | P-Bap | 10,000 | 5.0 | 4 | 6 | 836.4 |
| 1948 | China | 50 Chinese Baptist leaders martyred, some buried alive; also 5 missionaries in North China. | xa | P-Bap | 70 | 0.1 | 1 | 0 | 842.9 |
| 1948 | Romania | Uniate churches destroyed: many priests killed; bps **Aftemie, Frentiu, Suciu**, 1970 bp **J. Hossu**; 500 priests (Oriental and Latin) die in prison. | xO | R-Byz | 50,000 | 3.1 | 4 | 5 | 842.9 |
| 1948 | Russia | MGB (ex NKVD) begins to destroy True Orthodox Church (3 million underground Russians). | xa | O-Rus | 500,000 | 16.7 | 6 | 7 | 842.9 |
| 1948 | Hungary | 40-year persecution under Communists begins: hundreds of bishops, priests, laity die in prison: Lutheran bishop **L. Ordacz**. | xa | P-Lut | 2,500 | 0.0 | 3 | 0 | 842.9 |
| 1949 | Tibet | Chinese Communists massacre 1.2 million Tibetans including all Christians discovered. | xa | I-rad | 500 | 0.0 | 2 | 0 | 849.4 |
| *1950* | *World* | *Total of martyrs listed above during Epoch VIII.* | – | – | *29,231,520* | *3.4* | *4* | *4* | *856.0* |
| 1950 | World | All other martyrdom situations, known or unknown, during Epoch VIII | – | – | 2,339,000 | 0.3 | 4 | 4 | 856.0 |
| 1950 | World | Background martyrdom during Epoch VIII (individual, domestic, family, isolated) | – | – | 154,000 | 0.0 | 0 | 0 | 856.0 |
| **1950** | **World** | **Global total of all martyrs during Epoch VIII** | **–** | **–** | **31,724,520** | **3.7** | **4** | **4** | **856.0** |
| **1950** | **World** | **Global cumulative total of all martyrs since AD 33** | **–** | **–** | **56,064,950** | **0.9** | **3** | **4** | **856.0** |
| | **EPOCH IX: SURGE IN THE THIRD WORLD, AD 1950-2000** | | | | | | | | |
| 1950 | China | Liquidation of churches, 1950-80; 1950-54, 800 Chinese RC priests killed; fr **Wang Ling-Tso**, fr **Tsiang Beda** SJ dies in prison. | xa | R-Lat | 500,000 | 9.3 | 6 | 6 | 856.0 |
| 1950 | North Korea | Mass slaughter of Christians: troops massacre 150 RC priests, and (1950-60) 500 pastors: **Tong-Sin, Sung Du**, bps **P.T. Brennan, P.J. Byrne**. | x. | R-Lat | 800,000 | 40.0 | 6 | 8 | 856.0 |
| 1950 | Viet Nam | From 1950, continuous Communist pressure; pastors **Nguyen, Phan Long, Thien Thi**. | xa | P-Eva | 20,000 | 1.0 | 4 | 3 | 856.0 |
| 1950 | Eastern Europe | 'Churches of Silence' liquidated in 8 countries, 1950-80, with 17 bishops; 1960 **Pavol Gojdic**, bp of Presov (Greek Catholic) dies in prison. | xa | R-Lat | 900,000 | 9.0 | 6 | 6 | 856.0 |
| 1950 | India | From 1950-1999, over 10,000 Christians, evangelists, workers killed each year due to mobs, infuriated relatives, RSS/VHP, etc.; 1995, nun sr **Rani Maria**. | .H | I-Bap | 400,000 | 5.6 | 5 | 6 | 856.0 |
| 1950 | USSR | From 1950-80, 5 million Christians die in prison camps; 1974 pastor **I.M. Ostapenko** hanged; **N. Rozanov**. | xa | O-Rus | 5,000,000 | 6.4 | 9 | 6 | 856.0 |
| 1950 | Nigeria | Over next 50 years, widespread anti-Christian riots sporadic in cities across north, led by Muslim mobs; pastors, lay leaders killed, churches targeted, burned. | .M | I-3cA | 1,000 | 0.0 | 3 | 0 | 856.0 |
| 1950 | South Africa | Start of 40 years' brutal repression of Blacks by Afrikaner security forces; thousands in AICs murdered; 1977 **Steve Biko**. | x. | I-3zA | 10,000 | 0.1 | 4 | 1 | 856.0 |
| 1951 | Russia | All 7,000 Jehovah's Witnesses forcibly scattered across Far North in Siberian labor camps. | xa | m-Jeh | 2,000 | 28.6 | 3 | 8 | 871.9 |
| 1952 | Kenya | Mau Mau rebellion: 1,500 officially recognized martyrs in Kikuyu churches: **G. & R. Gacigi, Mary Wancegi, W. Muriuki, J. Mungai**, 1953 **E. Gikonyo, A. Kaguru**. | .T | A-Ang | 1,800 | 0.5 | 3 | 2 | 888.1 |
| 1952 | West Irian | CMA, TEAM, RBMU missionaries killed, also converts; first Dani martyr **Selanuok**. | .T | P-Eva | 500 | 0.2 | 2 | 1 | 888.1 |
| 1952 | China | Chinese independent churches viciously persecuted: 1952, Little Flock's **Watchman Nee** arrested, 1972 dies in prison; 1955, regime destroys Jesus Family. | xa | I-3cC | 74,000 | 61.7 | 4 | 9 | 888.1 |
| 1952 | Bulgaria | Violent persecutions 1952-64 in Sofia, Plovdiv; 1952 bp **Basilikov**, exarch **Kirtoff**, 1956 metropolitan **Boris** of Nevrokop; in Nicopoli, Latin-rite bishop executed. | xa | O-Bul | 2,000 | 0.0 | 3 | 0 | 888.1 |
| 1953 | Viet Nam | In North Viet Nam, Communists execute 15,000 Catholic landlords and any rich peasants. | x. | R-Lat | 8,000 | 0.0 | 3 | 0 | 904.5 |
| 1954 | Algeria | 8-year civil war: French army kills a million Algerian Muslims, loses 17,500 troops; 3,000 French Catholic settlers murdered. | .M | R-Lat | 2,500 | 0.2 | 3 | 2 | 921.3 |
| 1956 | Ecuador | Aucas kill MAF/GMU/CMML missionaries: **J. Elliot, P. Fleming, E. McCully, N. Saint, R. Youdarian**. | .T | P-Eva | 5 | 0.0 | 1 | 0 | 955.8 |
| 1957 | Haiti | 29-year Voodoo terror under Duvaliers kills 50,000; 1961 fr **Yvon Emmanuel Moreau**. | xU | R-Lat | 25,000 | 0.7 | 4 | 3 | 973.6 |
| 1958 | Nepal | Numerous early converts murdered: Tamang ex-Buddhist lama **David Dapcha Lama** poisoned; 1970 Brahmin convert **Krishna Lamichami** beaten to death. | xB | I-3cZ | 50 | 0.0 | 1 | 0 | 991.6 |
| 1958 | Indonesia | For 7 years, Darul Islam (DITI) fundamentalist guerrilla fanatics murder 500 Makassarese Christians. | .M | R-Lat | 500 | 0.0 | 2 | 0 | 991.6 |
| 1959 | China | Great Leap Forward (1959-62) kills 25 million peasants, workers, pastors, priests; 1960 **H.H. Lin**. | xa | I-3hC | 300,000 | 10.0 | 5 | 7 | 1,010.0 |
| 1959 | Cuba | Castro's Communist revolution expels 590 RC priests, 970 brothers, 2,400 nuns, executes many who die shouting 'Long live Christ the King!' | xa | R-Lat | 15,000 | 0.3 | 4 | 2 | 1,010.0 |
| 1960 | Congo-Zaire | Mutinies, rebellions dislocate missions; 200 RC priests/nuns, 300 Protestant workers, killed: **E. Hodgson, P. Carlson, P. Rhine**, sr **M. C. Anuarite**. | .T | P-Eva | 15,000 | 0.1 | 4 | 1 | 1,028.8 |
| 1960 | Latin America | Christian radicals killed by troops; 1966 frs **Camilo Torres, H. Gallejo**, 1977 **A. Navarro**. | x. | R-Lat | 300,000 | 0.1 | 5 | 1 | 1,028.8 |
| 1960 | India | For next 40 years, every year 100 to 300 Christian Dalits (Untouchables, Outcastes) are murdered in inter-caste violence. | .H | R-Lat | 7,000 | 0.1 | 3 | 1 | 1,028.8 |
| 1961 | Congo | In and around Brazzaville, many killings of Europeans and missionaries: pastor **R. de Vos**. | x. | P-Eva | 400 | 0.0 | 2 | 0 | 1,047.8 |
| 1961 | Germany | Communist GDR erects 75-mile concrete Berlin Wall to prevent emigration; 5,000 escape, but 150 Christians trying to cross are killed by police. | xa | P-Lut | 100 | 0.0 | 2 | 0 | 1,047.8 |
| 1961 | Angola | Revolution and civil war: Portuguese troops and militias massacre Protestants, pastors, teachers: deacon **P. Rodrigues**. | x. | P-Eva | 5,000 | 2.0 | 3 | 5 | 1,047.8 |
| 1962 | Albania | Atheist state kills 10 more bishops, 100 priests: 1972 fr **S. Kurti**, 1979 bp **E. Coba**; and over 7,000 lay believers killed, 1962-1986. | xa | O-Alb | 7,200 | 3.8 | 3 | 5 | 1,067.3 |
| 1962 | Burma | 40-year civil war: army conducts many massacres of Hill Tribes (Karens, Kachins, et alii); churches burned, pastors tortured to death. | x. | P-Bap | 10,000 | 1.0 | 4 | 4 | 1,067.3 |
| 1962 | West Irian | Genocide: 150,000 West Papuans killed by Muslim troops, 1962-82; by 1995 total killed reaches 200,000. | x. | P-Eva | 70,000 | 7.9 | 4 | 6 | 1,067.3 |
| 1962 | Rwanda | Genocide: 150,000 Tutsis slaughtered by Hutus at Independence; pastor **Yona Kanamuzeyi**. | xR | A-Ang | 10,000 | 0.8 | 4 | 3 | 1,067.3 |
| 1962 | Russia | Leaders of unregistered Reform Baptists systematically liquidated by KGB: 1964 **N. Khmara**, 1972 **Melnikov** poisoned, 1975 **I. V. Biblenko**. | xa | I-3cW | 8,000 | 6.0 | 3 | 6 | 1,067.3 |
| 1962 | Eritrea | 30-year civil war led by Christian-dominated EPLF destroys churches, schools, missions, and kills scores of clergy, laity. | xa | O-Eth | 10,000 | 0.6 | 4 | 3 | 1,067.3 |
| 1963 | Guinea-Bissau | Portuguese kill Protestants (WEC): evangelists **Victor Vaz Martins, Formoso Mendes, Pedro da Silva**. | xR | P-Eva | 100 | 4.2 | 2 | 5 | 1,087.1 |
| 1963 | Sudan | Civil war: Arabs kill 64 missionaries and (1962-72) 600,000 Black Christians; pastor **G. Adwok**. | xM | A-Ang | 200,000 | 23.5 | 5 | 8 | 1,087.1 |
| 1964 | Brazil | 10,000 killings over 20 years by guerrillas, military, death squads; many priests murdered. | x. | R-Lat | 2,000 | 0.0 | 3 | 0 | 1,107.3 |
| 1964 | USA | In long and violent segregation struggle, civil rights workers murdered: **James Cheney** (Black Baptist) & colleagues; 1968 **Martin Luther King Jr** assassinated. | .Y | I-Bap | 20 | 0.0 | 1 | 0 | 1,107.3 |
| 1965 | Indonesia | Communists attempt to obliterate Christian leadership; crushed by army with 500,000 deaths. | .a | P-Ref | 8,000 | 0.1 | 3 | 0 | 1,127.8 |
| 1965 | Zambia | Lumpa Church (indigenous) crushed by military; 700 killed in holy village. | x. | I-3pA | 700 | 0.5 | 2 | 2 | 1,127.8 |
| 1965 | Lithuania | Soviets modify continuous persecution of RC bishops, target minor officials, harass by bureaucracy: 1975 **M. Tamonis**. | xa | R-Lat | 5,000 | 0.0 | 3 | 0 | 1,127.8 |
| 1965 | Cambodia | Mnong Christians fiercely persecuted, many killed with clergy (also 90% of Buddhist priests). | xB | R-Lat | 6,000 | 0.0 | 3 | 0 | 1,127.8 |
| 1966 | Nigeria | 30,000 Ibo Christians in Northern Nigeria massacred by Muslim mobs. | .M | A-Eva | 30,000 | 0.1 | 4 | 1 | 1,148.7 |
| 1966 | China | Great Proletarian Cultural Revolution: churches razed, 2,500,000 believers imprisoned; after 20 years jail and torture, in 1989 bp **Li Xinsheng** dies. | xa | I-3hC | 400,000 | 13.3 | 5 | 7 | 1,148.7 |
| 1967 | Nigeria | A million killed in 1967-70 Biafra civil war, including massacre of 150,000 Ibos by Muslims, also 10,000 Ogoni Christians slaughtered. | xM | R-Lat | 200,000 | 0.8 | 5 | 3 | 1,170.0 |
| c1968 | Somalia | Islamic hostility towards Christianity results in killings: **Musa Sheikow**, 1989 bp **P. S. Colombo** OFM, 1991 fr **P. Turati** OFM. | .M | I-3mM | 40 | 0.0 | 1 | 0 | 1,191.7 |
| 1968 | West Irian | Cannibalistic tribe, the Yali, kill and eat 2 NTM missionaries who destroyed village fetishes, **S. Dale** & **P. Masters**; 1976, tribe converts to Christianity. | .T | P-Eva | 10 | 0.0 | 1 | 0 | 1,191.7 |
| 1969 | Equat Guinea | 10-year reign of terror under dictator Macias; 80,000 deaths; crucifixions; 1975 **Raphael Nze** bp of Bata executed after torture; 50,000 Bubis murdered in 1978. | xR | R-Lat | 35,000 | 14.0 | 4 | 7 | 1,213.9 |
| 1969 | Malawi | Vicious state persecution of Jehovah's Witnesses. | x. | m-Jeh | 2,000 | 5.6 | 3 | 6 | 1,213.9 |
| 1969 | Czechoslovakia | State kills Roman Catholic leaders: 1974 cardinal **S. Trochta**, 1979 fr **M. Gono**, 1981 fr **P. Coufal**, 1982 fr **J. Barta**. | xa | R-Lat | 7,000 | 0.1 | 3 | 0 | 1,213.9 |
| 1970 | Cambodia | Massacres of 40,000 Vietnamese Catholics and 10,000 Protestants, 1970-77. | xB | R-Lat | 50,000 | 76.9 | 4 | 9 | 1,236.4 |
| 1970 | Paraguay | Genocide attempted by military against Ache Indians; 900 killed in repeated massacres, forced labor, resettlements. | .R | R-Lat | 100 | 33.3 | 2 | 8 | 1,236.4 |
| 1970 | USSR | Unregistered Protestants targeted by KGB for mass killings; 1980 **V.A. Shelkov, S. Bakholdin**, 1982 **N.P. Khrapov**. | xa | I-3cW | 60,000 | 6.7 | 4 | 6 | 1,236.4 |

*Continued below*

*Table 4–10 continued*

| Year 1 | Main locus 2 | Description of major martyrdom situation 3 / Related individual martyrs (these are the names shown in boldface type) 4 | Pers 5 | Trad 6 | Martyrs 7 | MR% 8 | Mag 9 | Int 10 | Global Christians 11 |
|---|---|---|---|---|---|---|---|---|---|
| | | | | | | | | | millions |
| 1970 | Cameroon | Jehovah's Witnesses banned by government, with continuous sporadic persecution since. | x. | m-Jeh | 600 | 0.0 | 2 | 0 | 1,236.4 |
| 1970 | Gabon | Banning and sporadic persecution of Jehovah's Witnesses, deliberately low-key and unreported. | x. | m-Jeh | 100 | 0.0 | 2 | 0 | 1,236.4 |
| 1971 | Uganda | 300,000 Christians killed in 7-year Amin terror; 1973 **J. Serwanika**, 1977 abp **Janani Luwum**, many Anglican and Catholic clergy. | xM | A-Ang | 200,000 | 2.8 | 5 | 5 | 1,259.9 |
| 1971 | Bangladesh | In civil war, 1,250,000 Bengalis executed. 5,700 leading Christians targeted and murdered with their children by Pakistani army, 1,500 Christian women raped. | xM | R-Lat | 13,000 | 5.2 | 4 | 6 | 1,259.9 |
| 1972 | Burundi | Genocide: 150,000 Hutus, especially intellectuals, massacred by Tutsis; 100 Anglican evangelists and 15 clergy murdered; **Abel Binyoni**. | xR | A-Ang | 15,000 | 0.7 | 4 | 3 | 1,284.0 |
| 1972 | Mozambique | Protestant persecution: Presbyterian leaders **Z. Manganhela, J. Sidumo** die in Machava prison. | xa | P-Ref | 200 | 0.0 | 2 | 0 | 1,284.0 |
| 1972 | Benin | Marxist military seize power, begin targeting clergy with death sentences; arrests, sporadic persecution and murders. | xa | R-Lat | 500 | 0.1 | 2 | 1 | 1,284.0 |
| 1972 | Ulster | Bloody Sunday: British army kills 17 Roman Catholic demonstrators; widespread violence by Protestant paramilitary forces. | x. | R-Lat | 2,000 | 0.2 | 3 | 2 | 1,284.0 |
| 1973 | Chad | Regime orders 2-year pagan initiation rites; many martyrs, including numerous pastors buried alive. | xT | P-Eva | 400 | 0.0 | 2 | 0 | 1,308.4 |
| 1973 | Chile | 2,500 Chileans executed by Pinochet military regime, including leftist Christian leaders. | x. | R-Lat | 2,100 | 0.0 | 3 | 0 | 1,308.4 |
| 1974 | Laos | Communists imprison and murder many of 20,000 tribal Miao (Hmong) and Khmu Protestants. | xa | P-Eva | 2,000 | 10.0 | 3 | 7 | 1,333.4 |
| 1974 | North Cyprus | Civil war escalates as Turkish army invades; 1983, Turks proclaim separate state; 2,000 Greek Orthodox murdered. | .M | O-Gre | 2,000 | 1.0 | 3 | 4 | 1,333.4 |
| 1974 | Bolivia | Government troops kill 200 devout RC peasants in Cochabamba valley. | x. | R-Lat | 100 | 1.0 | 2 | 4 | 1,333.4 |
| 1975 | Viet Nam | 10-year Communist persecution begins: churches closed, pastors executed; 1984, 65,000 butchered. | xa | P-Eva | 50,000 | 1.5 | 4 | 4 | 1,358.8 |
| 1975 | Ukraine | Uniate priests murdered: **M. Lutsky**, 1979 **Z.A. Kalienuk**, 1980 **A. Gurgula** and wife, 1984 **A. Potochnyak**. | xa | R-Byz | 500 | 0.0 | 2 | 0 | 1,358.8 |
| 1975 | Lebanon | 200,000 killed in 20-year civil war; thousands of Maronites, Orthodox, Evangelicals kidnapped and killed; 1987 fr **A. Masse** SJ. | .M | R-Mar | 25,000 | 1.4 | 4 | 4 | 1,358.8 |
| 1975 | Honduras | Christian radicals, Indians, murdered: 1975 frs **M.C. Cypher** OFM, **I. Betancur**, 1983 fr **J.G. Carney** SJ. | x. | R-Lat | 8,000 | 0.3 | 3 | 2 | 1,358.8 |
| 1975 | Cambodia | Khmer Rouge slaughter 2 million, execute 80% of all city dwellers including known Christians by 1979: bps **P. Tep Im, J.C. Salas, fr B.C. Chunsar.** | xa | P-Eva | 42,000 | 88.8 | 4 | 9 | 1,358.8 |
| 1975 | Timor | 200,000 Timorese (70% being RCs) killed in civil war over next 25 years; 1991, military kill 270 Catholic youths at a funeral in Santa Cruz massacre. | xM | R-Lat | 90,000 | 37.2 | 4 | 8 | 1,358.8 |
| 1975 | Paraguay | Army burns houses, seizes peasant cooperative funds, kills scores of peasants. | x. | R-Lat | 160 | 0.0 | 2 | 0 | 1,358.8 |
| 1975 | Bougainville | 23-year civil war attempting secession from Papua New Guinea, led by Catholic and Protestant bishops and clergy; many killed, starved, deprived of medicines. | x. | P-Eva | 3,000 | 4.0 | 3 | 5 | 1,358.8 |
| 1975 | Ireland | Irish Republican Army and other paramilitary groups target Christian activists; assassinations, bombings. | .R | P-Eva | 1,200 | 0.2 | 3 | 2 | 1,358.8 |
| 1976 | Argentina | 30,000 persons disappear 1976-79, killed by military junta (2,000 thrown alive out of Navy aircraft); many priests, bishops, activists, idealistic youth. | xR | R-Lat | 12,000 | 0.1 | 4 | 0 | 1,381.4 |
| 1976 | Zimbabwe | Civil war kills 50 missionaries: bp **A. Schmitt**, 6 nuns, 1978 **P.& S. Evans** & 12 Elim workers; 1987, 16 missionaries. | x. | P-Pen | 3,000 | 0.1 | 3 | 0 | 1,381.4 |
| 1976 | Guatemala | Army genocide against Mayans: 11 priests killed, 1982-3 15,000 killings; fr **H. Lopez**; 1980-82,100,000 Quiche Indians murdered, 1 million displaced. | x. | R-Lat | 20,000 | 0.3 | 4 | 2 | 1,381.4 |
| 1977 | Ethiopia | From 1977-80, 90,000 killed in Red Terror; 1980 patriarch **Theofilas**, abp **Samwel**, many priests; Protestant leader **S. B. Aleku**, 1979 **G. Tumsa**. | xa | O-Eth | 30,000 | 0.2 | 4 | 1 | 1,404.4 |
| 1977 | El Salvador | From 1977-89, 70,000 killings, massacres, crucifixions: 1980 abp **O. Romero**, 1981 4 USA nuns, 1988 4 Lutheran workers, 1989 6 Jesuit priests. | xR | R-Lat | 15,000 | 0.4 | 4 | 2 | 1,404.4 |
| 1977 | CAR | Brutal tyrant E. A. Bokasso seizes power as emperor, massacres thousands in churches and schools. | xa | P-Dis | 3,000 | 0.1 | 3 | 1 | 1,404.4 |
| 1977 | Mongolia | Many young Catholic Charismatics from India travel to witness and live as missionaries in Mongolia; a number are murdered. | xa | R-Lat | 50 | 20.0 | 1 | 8 | 1,404.4 |
| 1977 | Zaire | Mobutu regime executes, murders, assassinates, or massacres tribal or political opponents including church leaders. | x. | R-Lat | 4,000 | 0.1 | 3 | 1 | 1,404.4 |
| 1978 | Guyana | At Jonestown settlement, congregation of 900 are murdered by pastor J. Jones in suicide pact. | .P | P-Dis | 950 | 67.9 | 2 | 9 | 1,427.8 |
| 1978 | Angola | South African military bomb and kill 582 Namibian Christians at Kassinga refugee camp. | xP | P-Lut | 300 | 0.0 | 2 | 0 | 1,427.8 |
| 1979 | Iran | 100,000 Iranis executed under ayatollah Khomeini-Shias, Sunnis, Baha'is, Armenians; Anglican priest **Sayyad**. | xM | O-Arm | 8,000 | 2.5 | 3 | 5 | 1,451.5 |
| 1979 | Nicaragua | 50,000 die in Sandinista revolution, 20,000 later, many pastors; 1983, Pentecostal pastor **Noel Vargas** murdered by Contras; Miskito Christians massacred. | xa | P-Mor | 5,000 | 0.2 | 3 | 1 | 1,451.5 |
| 1979 | Malawi | Thousands including dissident churchmen tortured and murdered during Banda dictatorship, 1964-1993; 1979, **J. Sangaya**. | x. | P-Ref | 5,000 | 0.3 | 3 | 2 | 1,451.5 |
| 1980 | Lithuania | RC priests murdered: 1980 **L. Sapoka, V. Jaugelis**, 1981 **L. Mazeika, B. Laurinavicius**. | xa | R-Lat | 5,000 | 0.2 | 3 | 2 | 1,475.7 |
| 1980 | Bolivia | Assassinations and killings; 1980 fr **L. Espinal** SJ, editor exposing cocaine trade, assassinated. | .Y | R-Lat | 300 | 0.0 | 2 | 0 | 1,475.7 |
| 1980 | Iraq | Military regime murders 20,000 Christians over next 15 years: Assyrians, Chaldeans, Arabs. | xa | O-Nes | 20,000 | 4.0 | 4 | 5 | 1,475.7 |
| 1980 | Afghanistan | As Christian believers, a number of USSR Red Army soldiers refuse to kill Afghanis, so are executed. | xa | I-3pW | 400 | 0.0 | 2 | 0 | 1,475.7 |
| 1980 | India | In Nagaland, Indian Army continues 50-year genocide against 2 million Nagas; many Baptist churches destroyed | xH | P-Bap | 240,000 | 15.0 | 5 | 7 | 1,475.7 |
| 1980 | Peru | Maoist Shining Path guerrillas kill 30,000 peasant Christians before 1993 collapse; 1983 sr **Joan Sawyer**, many Pentecostals and Presbyterians murdered. | .a | P-Pen | 12,000 | 0.1 | 4 | 0 | 1,475.7 |
| 1981 | Romania | Police murder many Baptist and RC leaders: 1981 **S. Teodosiu**, bp **K. Kernweisz, I. Clipa**. | xa | P-Bap | 2,000 | 0.1 | 3 | 1 | 1,500.8 |
| 1981 | Egypt | Muslim Brotherhood killings; Coptic bp **Samuel (Makary El-Souriany)**, fr **Ghabrail Abd Mutagalli**. | .M | O-Cop | 1,000 | 0.0 | 3 | 0 | 1,500.8 |
| 1982 | Nicaragua | Sandinista military regime escalates 'reeducation' massacres of Miskito Indian Christians, pastors shot; 1982 **E. Smith, Lester Athers**. | xa | P-Mor | 1,000 | 3.3 | 3 | 5 | 1,526.2 |
| 1982 | Nigeria | Over next 14 years in Kaduna State, 18 major Muslim/Christian violent conflicts; over 600 Christians killed, 193 churches torched. | .M | A-Ang | 600 | 0.1 | 2 | 1 | 1,526.2 |
| 1983 | Guatemala | Mass killings of pentecostals by army, many pastors murdered; Full Gospel pastor **Nicolas Toma** shot. | x. | I-3pL | 11,000 | 0.2 | 4 | 2 | 1,552.2 |
| 1983 | Ecuador | Escalating violence against Quichua Protestants; churches burned, murders; 1987 Quichua pastor **Antonia Zuma** killed. | .R | P-Eva | 3,000 | 1.2 | 3 | 4 | 1,552.2 |
| 1983 | Ghana | African indigenous churches' prophets from Ashanti Spiritual Churches murdered by military regime; 1995, RC nuns **P. Maclese, C. Murphy** hacked to death. | x. | I-3sA | 200 | 0.0 | 2 | 0 | 1,552.2 |
| 1983 | Sri Lanka | Civil war kills 8,000 (450 RCs, 60 Protestants): fr **M.B. Manielpillai**, pastor **G. Jeyarajasingham**. | xB | R-Lat | 200 | 0.0 | 2 | 0 | 1,552.2 |
| 1983 | Sudan | Scores of Dinka and Shilluk pastors killed by Sudanese army, countless churches torched by Arab troops. | xM | A-Ang | 5,000 | 0.2 | 3 | 2 | 1,552.2 |
| 1984 | Poland | Continuous Communist harassment; priest **J. Popieluszko** (RC), 1985 fr **P. Poplawski** (Orthodox), et alii. | xa | R-Lat | 5,000 | 0.0 | 3 | 0 | 1,578.5 |
| 1984 | Uganda | Armed thugs murder **Godfrey Bazira** principal of Namugongo Martyrs Memorial Seminary, and 90 others. | .a | A-Ang | 95 | 0.0 | 1 | 0 | 1,578.5 |
| 1985 | Philippines | Clergy, laity murdered: frs **T. Favali, A. Romero, N. Valerio, R. Romano; M. Beling** (Episcopal). | .M | R-Lat | 40,000 | 0.1 | 4 | 0 | 1,605.3 |
| 1985 | Angola | Guerrilla violence kills workers: frs **J.E. Wasnak, J. Moretto, L. Sikufinde**, sr **L. Kautudja**. | x. | R-Lat | 10,000 | 0.1 | 4 | 1 | 1,605.3 |
| 1985 | India | 3,000 North Indian Christians murdered in mob riots instigated by politico-religious organizations (RSS/VHP, etc); 1995, in Bhopal, **John Kerkatta** killed by mob. | .H | P-Bap | 3,000 | 0.1 | 3 | 1 | 1,605.3 |
| c1985 | Kenya | Angarako bandits from Uganda destroy RC mission, kill 85 Turkana and priest. | .T | R-Lat | 50 | 0.0 | 1 | 0 | 1,605.3 |
| 1985 | Guatemala | Worst right-wing death-squad violence on continent: Indian catechist **Manuel de Jesus Tzalam Coj**, professor **C.H. Cabrera Rivera**. | xR | R-Lat | 10,000 | 0.1 | 4 | 1 | 1,605.3 |
| 1986 | Mozambique | 500,000 noncombatants (28,000 RCs, 7,000 Anglicans and Protestants) systematically slaughtered by Renamo rebels. | .a | R-Lat | 35,000 | 1.0 | 4 | 4 | 1,632.8 |
| 1986 | Africa | Marked continent-wide increase in killings of pastors, priests, missionaries, and laypersons. | x. | P-Eva | 20,000 | 0.0 | 4 | 0 | 1,632.8 |
| 1986 | Mexico | Outspoken newspaper staff begin to be targeted by drug cartels: publishers **J. Brennes, Ernesto Flores**, reporter **Norma Moreno**. | .a | R-Lat | 100 | 0.0 | 2 | 0 | 1,632.8 |
| 1987 | Ecuador | Auca arrows in jungle kill bp **A. Labaca Ugarte** OFMCap, sr **Ines Arango**; other killings also. | .T | R-Lat | 100 | 0.0 | 2 | 0 | 1,660.7 |
| 1987 | Sudan | 1,000 Christian Dinkas burned to death by Rizeigat Muslims in Diein. | .M | A-Ang | 1,000 | 0.5 | 3 | 2 | 1,660.7 |
| 1987 | Pakistan | Christians targeted: 1987 **Wahid**, 1994 **Manzoor Masih**; 1995, 12-year old **Iqbal Masih** near Lahore; 1995 **Javed Masih** in Hyderabad. | .M | P-Ref | 200 | 0.0 | 2 | 0 | 1,660.7 |
| 1987 | Azerbaijan | Religious warfare in Nagorno-Karabakh targets both Shia Muslims and Armenian Christian leaders; 10,000 killed over next 9 years; 1988 Sumgait Massacre. | xM | O-Arm | 1,000 | 0.2 | 3 | 2 | 1,660.7 |
| 1988 | Brazil | 14 Ticuna Indians massacred by traders; 30,000 gold prospectors attack other Amerindian tribes; 1995, hundreds of landless peasants killed by police. | .Y | I-3cL | 800 | 0.6 | 2 | 3 | 1,689.2 |
| 1988 | Colombia | Civil war versus cocaine drug lords with 500,000 employees; many judges assassinated; 1989 bp **Jesus E. Jaramillo** of Arauca. | .a | R-Lat | 1,000 | 0.0 | 3 | 0 | 1,689.2 |
| 1988 | Algeria | 1988 riots, 1992 army ousts victorious Islamic Fundamentalists who then murder 10,000 Christians; 1996, 7 Trappist monks beheaded, bp **P. Claverie**. | .M | R-Lat | 9,000 | 13.0 | 3 | 7 | 1,689.2 |
| 1988 | Myanmar | Mass uprising in Yangon crushed by military, 10,000 killed; thousands of Christians perish in vast slave camps. | x. | P-Bap | 30,000 | 1.0 | 4 | 4 | 1,689.2 |
| 1988 | Burundi | Genocide: Tutsi-dominated government kills 75,000 civilian Hutus in repeated massacres. | x. | R-Lat | 25,000 | 1.0 | 4 | 4 | 1,689.2 |
| 1989 | China | Army massacre of 3,000 mainly in Tiananmen Square, Beijing, kills 600 Christian student activists. | xa | I-3cC | 600 | 0.1 | 2 | 1 | 1,718.1 |
| 1989 | Romania | Secret police under dictator N. Ceausescu massacre 20,000 Christians, murder many activists. | xa | O-Rum | 15,000 | 0.1 | 4 | 1 | 1,718.1 |
| 1989 | World | Persecution during decade 1980-90 mushrooms, revealing Christ's people as the permanently Suffering Church, regularly enduring martyrdom. | xa | R-Lat | 190,000 | 12.7 | 5 | 7 | 1,718.1 |
| 1989 | Afghanistan | Underground Afghani Christians persecuted: blind leader **Zia Mohammed Nodrat** tortured to death; the Six Mullahs of Kabul confess Christ but are murdered. | xM | I-3mM | 30 | 0.0 | 1 | 0 | 1,718.1 |
| 1989 | Peru | 50 Assemblies of God worshippers machine-gunned while praying; 800 Christian leaders in Quechua High Andes murdered. | .a | P-Pen | 3,000 | 0.0 | 3 | 0 | 1,718.1 |
| 1990 | Iran | Radical Muslims kill prominent Iranian Pentecostal clergy: 1990 **H. Soodmand**, 1994 bp **Haik Hovsepian-Mehr, Mehdi Dibaj**; many laity executed. | xM | P-Pen | 720 | 0.0 | 2 | 0 | 1,747.5 |
| 1990 | Philippines | Islamic guerrillas in Jolo, Mindanao, kill many evangelizing Christians: 1995, **J. Solan**; 1996, pastor **Severino Bagtasos III** killed during worship. | .M | I-3cF | 10,000 | 0.1 | 4 | 1 | 1,747.5 |
| 1990 | Laos | 25-year Communist persecution of Christians intensifies, especially vicious in north with widespread continuous killings. | x. | R-Lat | 10,000 | 10.0 | 4 | 7 | 1,747.5 |
| 1990 | Mexico | Escalating violence against Oaxacan Protestants, often led by Catholic priests and local chiefs. | .R | P-Eva | 500 | 0.0 | 2 | 0 | 1,747.5 |

*Continued overleaf*

Table 4-10 concluded

| Year | Main locus | Description of major martyrdom situation / Related individual martyrs (these are the names shown in boldface type) | Pers | Trad | Martyrs | MR% | Mag | Int | Global Christians (millions) |
|---|---|---|---|---|---|---|---|---|---|
| 1 | 2 | 3 / 4 | 5 | 6 | 7 | 8 | 9 | 10 | 11 |
| 1991 | Bosnia | In vicious 4-year civil war, 200,000 including many clergy are killed by Muslim, Catholic Croat, and Orthodox Serb militias; Bosnian fr **N. Bagaric.** | .O | R-Lat | 20,000 | 0.1 | 4 | 1 | 1,772.7 |
| 1991 | Colombia | World's most violent country (38,000 killed p.a.), missionaries murdered by guerrillas, drug lords: 1995 **T. Van Dyke, S. Welsh;** many Pentecostal pastors. | .a | P-Eva | 5,000 | 1.0 | 3 | 4 | 1,772.7 |
| 1991 | Peru | Violent guerrilla warfare: **L. Gutierrez, M. Sarmiento, C. Casaverde, C. Vargas, N. Tattersall, J. Chuquin;** 1992 Bible translator **R. Saune.** | .a | P-Eva | 3,000 | 0.0 | 3 | 0 | 1,772.7 |
| 1991 | Haiti | Over 2,000 shot to death supporting RC priest elected president, J.-B. Aristide; 500 more die under torture; pastor **Sylvio Claude.** | .a | R-Lat | 1,500 | 0.0 | 3 | 0 | 1,772.7 |
| c1992 | Liberia | Civil war engulfs country, churches destroyed, Christians slaughtered; missionaries **Tom & June Jackson** (WEC); pastors **J. Fallah, D. Saah** disemboweled. | x. | P-Eva | 15,000 | 2.2 | 4 | 5 | 1,798.3 |
| 1992 | Angola | As civil war continues, numerous killings: sr **M. Pimentel,** sr **M. Culembee Munto,** fr **A. de Fonseca Guerra,** sr **Lourdes Aguiar.** | xa | R-Lat | 9,000 | 0.1 | 3 | 1 | 1,798.3 |
| 1992 | USA | Sporadic but continuous killings: news editor **Manuel de Dios** shot in New York bar for exposing cocaine cartels. | .a | P-Eva | 200 | 0.0 | 2 | 0 | 1,798.3 |
| 1993 | Burundi | 5th wave of violence since 1961: 200,000 Hutus killed by Tutsi army; clergy targeted; 1993 Bible Society's **G. Bimazubute,** 1996 abp **J. Ruhuna.** | xA | R-Lat | 40,000 | 1.0 | 4 | 4 | 1,824.3 |
| 1993 | Sudan | 500,000 Southern Black Christians driven into deserts and starve to death through deliberate diverting of famine relief food by Islamic state bureaucrats. | xA | R-Lat | 460,000 | 11.9 | 5 | 7 | 1,824.3 |
| 1994 | Rwanda | Genocide: ruling Hutu massacre 700,000 Tutsis (RCs, Anglicans, Revivalists); **I. Havugimana, T. Gatwa,** fr **J. Rutumbu,** 3 bishops, 101 priests, 64 nuns. | xR | R-Lat | 520,000 | 11.7 | 6 | 7 | 1,850.7 |
| 1994 | Egypt | Countrywide violence by militant Muslims burning Coptic churches, shops, businesses, villages, schools; 1,000 Copts killed; monk **Nur al-Qums Binyamin.** | .M | O-Cop | 1,000 | 0.0 | 0 | 0 | 1,850.7 |
| 1994 | Mexico | Catholic activists murdered in Zapatista guerrilla uprising; mainly women and children. | x. | R-Lat | 300 | 0.0 | 2 | 0 | 1,850.7 |
| 1995 | Palestine | Random killings of church workers: brother **B. Grassi** beaten to death. | .M | R-LEr | 200 | 0.0 | 0 | 0 | 1,877.4 |
| 1995 | Sudan | Sudanese air force drops napalm on 3 strongly-Christian cities in Nuba Mountains, killing thousands; Arab troops murder 50,000 more. | xM | A-Eva | 12,000 | 7.0 | 4 | 6 | 1,877.4 |
| 1996 | Uganda | Kidnappings, murders, massacres of schoolchildren continue, mainly by Lord's Resistance Army (LRA) rebels north of Gulu. | .I | A-Eva | 2,000 | 1.0 | 3 | 4 | 1,901.2 |
| 1996 | Zaire | Mutinies, rebellions, military rampages, refugees, mass lootings, sweep the country; thousands of laypersons, clergy, workers murdered, massacred. | x. | p-uni | 5,000 | 0.1 | 3 | 1 | 1,901.2 |
| 1997 | Indonesia | Large organized mob violence increases annually; 50 churches a year attacked, burned (200 in East Java). | .M | P-Ref | 500 | 0.0 | 2 | 0 | 1,925.4 |
| 1997 | Pakistan | Mobs of 30,000 Muslim rioters go on rampage, burning down churches, Christian homes, shops, businesses; lootings, murders, instant executions. | .M | P-uni | 1,000 | 0.1 | 3 | 1 | 1,925.4 |
| 1998 | Afghanistan | Taliban military regime (Sunnis) slaughters thousands of Hazaras (Shias) in Mazar-e-Sharif, including 500 Christians. | xM | I-3nZ | 500 | 20.0 | 3 | 8 | 1,949.8 |
| 1999 | India | Violent RSS/VHP activity supported by anti-Christian Hindu government kills nuns, priests, pastors, missionaries. | xH | R-Lat | 6,000 | 50.0 | 9 | 9 | 1,974.5 |
| 1999 | Timor | Timor UN-run plebiscite overwhelmingly votes for Independence: before and after, militias target Catholics, kill 7,000 clergy and laity. | x. | R-Lat | 4,000 | 2.0 | 3 | 0 | 1,974.5 |
| 2000 | *World* | *Total of martyrs listed above during Epoch IX.* | — | — | 11,904,280 | 0.6 | 3 | 3 | 1,999.6 |
| 2000 | *World* | All other martyrdom situations, known or unknown, during Epoch IX. | — | — | 952,000 | 0.1 | 3 | 3 | 1,999.6 |
| 2000 | *World* | Background martyrdom during Epoch IX (individual, domestic, family, isolated). | — | — | 500,000 | 0.0 | 0 | 3 | 1,999.6 |
| **2000** | **World** | **Global total of all martyrs during Epoch IX.** | — | — | **13,356,280** | **0.7** | **3** | **3** | 1,999.6 |
| **2000** | **World** | **Global cumulative total of all martyrs since AD 33.** | — | — | **69,421,230** | **0.8** | **3** | **4** | 1,999.6 |

**EPOCH X: FUTURE SCENARIOS OF MISSION AND MARTYRDOM, AD 2000-2050** (for details of numerous published scenarios, see Part 2 "CosmoChronology")

| Year | Main locus | Description | Pers | Trad | Martyrs | MR% | Mag | Int | Global Christians |
|---|---|---|---|---|---|---|---|---|---|
| — | World | Church in many Muslim countries forced underground into clandestine activity. | .a | I-3cZ | — | 1.0 | 4 | 4 | 1,999.6 |
| — | World | End of 2nd Millennium leads into breakdown of law and order, mass panic, chaos, killings, martyrdoms. | xQ | R-Lat | — | 1.0 | 9 | 4 | |
| — | World | Organized mass terrorism destroys cathedrals, Vatican, and other major Christian centers. | .a | R-Lat | — | 1.0 | 8 | 4 | |
| — | World | Suppression of all mission; global church forced into catacomb existence. | .a | I-Eva | — | 2.0 | 8 | 5 | |
| 2013 | World | Church of the Absolutely Poor goes on global rampage, killing millions. | .a | I-3cZ | — | 4.0 | 9 | 8 | 2,299.7 |
| 2025 | World | Final demise of organized denominational Christianity; mass apostasies. | .a | I-3cW | — | 1.0 | 8 | 4 | 2,616.7 |
| 2038 | World | Church of the Purification attempts to set up a Republic of Christ; pitched battles, thousands of martyrs each year. | x. | I-3pZ | — | 20.0 | 4 | 8 | 2,834.5 |
| 2040 | World | Worst anti-Christian persecution in history, instigated by world government ordering voluntary martyrdom of all followers of Christ. | xa | I-3pW | — | 5.0 | 10 | 6 | 2,869.6 |
| 2050 | World | Background martyrdom during Epoch X (individual, domestic, family, isolated). | — | — | large | 0.0 | 0 | 0 | |
| **2050** | **World** | **Global total of all martyrs during Epoch X.** | — | — | very large | **1.7** | **8** | **5** | 3,051.6 |

**EPOCH OMEGA: THE BIBLICAL END-TIME** (various biblical scenarios with some literal features)

| Year | Main locus | Description | Pers | Trad | Martyrs | MR% | Mag | Int | Global Christians |
|---|---|---|---|---|---|---|---|---|---|
| | World | 1st Persecution: 4 Horsemen of the Apocalypse, 25% of world killed (Revelation 6:8). | — | — | — | 25.0 | 10 | 8 | |
| | World | 2nd Persecution: 7th Seal, 6th Trumpet, 33% killed (Revelation 9:18). | — | — | — | 33.0 | 10 | 8 | |
| | World | 3rd Persecution: The 2 Witnesses: church all but obliterated (Revelation 11:4-8). | — | — | — | 90.0 | 10 | 10 | |
| | World | The Great Tribulation: Trinity of Evil, 4th Persecution (Revelation 12:11-17). | — | — | — | 10.0 | 10 | 7 | |
| | World | The Great (5th and Final) Persecution, with mass apostasies (Revelation 13:5-10). | — | — | — | 95.0 | 8 | 10 | |
| | World | Background martyrdom during Epoch Omega (individual, domestic, family, isolated). | — | — | formidable | 0.0 | 0 | 0 | |
| | **World** | **Global total of all martyrs during Epoch Omega.** | — | — | many millions | **2.0** | **10** | **9** | 3,051.6 |

## Table 4–11. Alphabetical listing of 2,550 known Christian martyrs, AD 30-2000.

***Definition.*** A Christian martyr is defined in this analysis as a person with 5 essential features. A martyr is (1) a believer in Christ who (2) loses his or her life (3) prematurely (4) in a situation of witness (5) as a result of human hostility.

***Dates and names.*** The first column for each entry gives the year of the martyr's death, A.D. The second column gives name and, occasionally, ecclesiastical occupation or rank.

***Country codes.*** The last of the 3 columns of information gives the country (using today's name) where the individual died. The 4-letter codes shown are this survey's standard short code for everything concerning the country in question. Any countries not included here may very well have martyrdom situations described in Table 4–10 but names of individuals involved may remain unknown.

***Description of this table.*** In the main, this is a listing of individuals, but with 3 exceptions to firm up the identities of some individuals. Firstly, spouses and other relatives may be added in a phrase ('and brothers', 'and 2 sons', etc). Secondly, widely-known pairs may be listed together, including named husbands and wives, but the second person is always given an additional separate entry under this second name. And thirdly, in well known group cases a group name may be briefly added ('Atom & his legion'). However, absence of such additions here does not imply absence of such extras. In fact, most persons in this listing of individuals lost their lives with one or more relatives, with companions, or in much larger incidents or events.

Note that in recent years in the interests of brevity and conciseness names have been reduced to surnames followed by initials, although full Christian names have occasionally been added to assist identification. Likewise, a person's occupation may be given, especially if ecclesiastical.

***Abbreviations.*** abp = archbishop, bp = bishop, br = brother or monk (only from AD 1330 onward), Canter = Canterbury, ecu = ecumenical, fr = father (priest, only given here after AD 1516), Jerus = Jerusalem, met = metro = metropolitan, msgr = monsignor, patr = patriarch, sr = sister (nun; only given here since 1950). Initials after the first name/surname = Roman Catholic order or congregation (e.g. SJ = Jesuit).

| | | |
|---|---|---|
| 254 | Aaron & Julius | brit |
| 552 | Aba, mar, patriarch catholicos | iraq |
| 1999 | Abadiano, Ted | phil |
| c300 | Abadion, bp of Antinoopolis | egyp |
| c291 | Abadir | egyp |
| c250 | Abadyus | egyp |
| 2000 | Abakumate, sr M | cent |
| c309 | Abamun of Tarnut | egyp |
| c309 | Abamun of Tukh | egyp |
| 1004 | Abbo | fran |
| 410 | Abda, mar | iraq |
| 375 | Abdas, metropolitan | iraq |
| 341 | Abdechalas & Ananias | iraq |
| 1996 | Abdel-Sayeda, H. L. | egyp |
| 309 | Abdon | ital |
| 1758 | Aberin, fr J. S. | usa |
| 786 | Abo | geor |
| 523 | Abraham | yeme |
| 1998 | Abrao | ango |
| 1936 | Abrikosov, mother C. | russ |
| 249 | Abu Sayfayn | egyp |
| 1400 | Abu'l Farag | egyp |
| 523 | Abu-Afr, governor | yeme |
| c125 | Acacius | arme |
| 1220 | Accursio | moro |
| 251 | Achatius, bp | turk |
| c100 | Achilleus | ital |
| 1583 | Acquaviva, fr R. | indi |
| 997 | Adalbert, bp of Prague | russ |
| 1222 | Adam, bp of Caithness | brit |
| c550 | Adeodatus (Astouadz-Mapod) | arme |
| 1632 | Adolphus, king Gustavus | germ |
| 304 | Adrian & Natalia | turk |
| 875 | Adrian of May, bp | brit |
| 1998 | Adrienne, sr | conz |
| 825 | Adulfus & John | spai |
| 1963 | Adwok, pastor G. | suda |
| c287 | Aesculapius | egyp |
| c305 | Aesi | egyp |
| 1932 | Afanassy, bp of Stavobelsk | russ |
| 1970 | Afonin, I.A. | russ |
| 303 | Afra | germ |
| 1948 | Aftemie, bp | roma |
| 304 | Agape | gree |
| 1932 | Agapit, abp of Ekaterinoslav | ukra |
| 259 | Agapitus of Praeneste | ital |
| c255 | Agapius, bp | tuni |
| 249 | Agatha | ital |
| c1640 | Agathangelo of Vendome, fr | fran |
| c300 | Agathon and brothers | egyp |
| c170 | Agathonice | turk |
| 1227 | Agnello | moro |
| c350 | Agnes | ital |
| 1794 | Agricola Viala | fran |
| 1992 | Aguiar, sr L. | ango |
| 1653 | Ahatalla, metropolitan | indi |
| 575 | Ahudemmeh, bp of Tagrit | iraq |
| 1779 | Aitolos, K. | alba |
| 1220 | Aiuto | moro |
| 2000 | Akullu, G. | ugan |
| 2000 | Akweyo, sr D. | ugan |
| 1945 | Akya Nai, pastor | myan |
| 1992 | Al-Hari, A. | phil |
| 1387 | al-Jadid, Jirjis | egyp |
| 959 | al-Muzahim, Jirjis | egyp |
| 1998 | Alam, pastor Noor | paki |
| 209 | Alban of Verulamium | brit |
| 577 | Aldate, bp of Gloucester | brit |
| 1282 | Aldobrand of Florence | iran |
| 1995 | Alean, pastor M. | colo |
| 1997 | Alege, prof A. | conz |
| 1985 | Aleku, B. | ethi |
| c117 | Alexander | ital |
| 397 | Alexander | ital |
| c260 | Alexander | pale |
| 284 | Alexander & Asterius | turk |
| 1720 | Alexander the Deacon | russ |
| 1932 | Alexander, abp | russ |
| 249 | Alexander, bp of Cappadocia | egyp |
| 840 | Alexander, bp of Fiesole | ital |
| 251 | Alexander, bp of Jerusalem | egyp |
| 1938 | Alexey, bp of Petrograd | russ |
| c800 | Alkelda, princess | brit |
| c360 | Alladyus, bp | egyp |
| 1871 | Allard, fr | fran |
| 1985 | Allende, S. N. | chil |
| 1861 | Almato OP, fr P. | viet |
| 1628 | Alonso Rodriguez SJ | para |
| 1633 | Alonso, fr L. | japa |
| 1999 | Aloysius, sr M. | sier |
| 1012 | Alphege, abp of Canterbury | brit |
| 1973 | Alsina, fr J. | chil |
| 1704 | Alverez, fr R. | mexi |
| 1996 | Alzate Varela, pastor P. | colo |
| 1993 | Alzokim, N.F. | egyp |
| 1995 | Amador, pastor Manuel | colo |
| 1794 | Ambroise, fr R. | fran |
| 1771 | Ambrose, abp of Krutitsy | russ |
| 1934 | Ambrose, bp of Podolsk | russ |
| 1918 | Ambrose, bp of Seroapulsk | russ |
| 1918 | Ambrose, fr | russ |
| 1927 | Amfiteatrov, P. | belo |
| 1992 | Amlak, fr A. | ethi |
| c320 | Ammonius, bp of Latopolis | egyp |
| c285 | Amsah of Qift | egyp |
| 2000 | Amzati, C.G. | conz |
| 1905 | An, evangelist | chin |
| 448 | Anahid | iraq |
| 341 | Ananias | iraq |
| 303 | Anastasia | croa |
| 628 | Anastasius the Persian | turk |
| 610 | Anastasius, patriarch | geor |
| 1938 | Anatole, metrop of Odessa | russ |
| c300 | Anatolius, general | egyp |
| 1997 | Anchanickal SJ, fr T. | indi |
| 1998 | Andeni, fr L. | keny |
| 1900 | Andlauer SJ, fr M. | chin |
| 1666 | Andrade, vicar apostolic | ethi |
| 1794 | Andre, fr J. | fran |
| 69 | Andrew, Apostle | gree |
| c355 | Andrew, monk | egyp |
| 1918 | Andronick, abp of Perm | russ |
| 304 | Andronicus | ital |
| 1645 | André, catechist | viet |
| 1998 | Anetta, sr | yeme |
| 1976 | Angelelli, bp Enrique | arge |
| 1813 | Angelis | gree |
| 1323 | Angelus of Spoleto | ital |
| c168 | Anicetus, pope | ital |
| 1704 | Anixa, A. | usa |
| 346 | Anna | iraq |
| 66 | Anna of Ormisdat | arme |
| 1979 | Annanias, fr O. | ugan |
| c660 | Annemond, bp of Lyons | fran |
| 1634 | Ansalone, fr G. | japa |
| 295 | Anthimus, bp of Nicomedia | turk |
| 1282 | Anthony of Armenia | iran |
| 91 | Antipas | turk |
| 1347 | Antoniy | lith |
| 1460 | Antony of Rivoli (Tunis) | tuni |
| 1932 | Antony, bp of Archangel | russ |
| 1964 | Anuarite, sr M.C. | conz |
| c290 | Anub | egyp |
| c295 | Apaiule | egyp |
| c300 | Apoli | egyp |
| c285 | Apollo | egyp |
| c290 | Apollonius | egyp |
| c185 | Apollonius, senator | ital |
| 1945 | Apor, bp Vilmos | hung |
| 245 | Appolonia, deaconess | egyp |
| 413 | Apringius, proconsul | tuni |
| 180 | Aquilinus | tuni |
| 1833 | Aquino, Anastasio | elsa |
| 1987 | Arango, sr Ines | ecua |
| 1583 | Aranha, F. | indi |
| 1550 | Arason, bp J. & 2 sons | denm |
| 1936 | Arbona, fr B. | spai |
| 1921 | Archangelsky, pastor T. | russ |
| 1934 | Arconada, fr J. B. | spai |
| 1985 | Arensen, J. | suda |
| 523 | Aretas | yeme |
| 1995 | Argelio, pastor J. | colo |
| 931 | Argentea | spai |
| 1977 | Argew, T. | ethi |
| c310 | Arianus, governor | egyp |
| 333 | Aristakes I, patriarch | arme |
| 1155 | Arnold of Brescia | fran |
| 1704 | Arraiyo, fr J. P. | usa |
| 1977 | Arreola, sr Silvia Maribel | elsa |
| 1628 | Arrowsmith, fr E. | brit |
| c298 | Arsenius | egyp |
| 1400 | Arsenius | egyp |
| 1935 | Arseny, abp of Serpuhov | russ |
| 1936 | Arseny, metrop of Novgorod | russ |
| 1936 | Artigues, fr R. | spai |
| 1830 | Asad es Shidiak | leba |
| 1859 | Ascanio OFM, fr N. | syri |
| c290 | Ascla | egyp |
| 2000 | Asienzo, sr P. | ugan |
| 284 | Asterius | turk |
| c296 | Athanasius | egyp |
| 258 | Athanasius, bp | egyp |
| c1982 | Athers, Lester | nica |
| c288 | Athom | egyp |
| c97 | Atirnerseh, patriarch | arme |
| 451 | Atom & his legion | arme |
| c120 | Atrasis, daughter of Hadrian | ital |
| 1936 | Audi, fr F. | spai |
| 1918 | Audo, abp | iraq |
| 1881 | Augier, fr | buru |
| 259 | Augurius | tuni |
| 1988 | Augusto, fr Giraldo Cesar | colo |
| 1736 | Aulneau, fr J. P. | usa |
| 434 | Auraeus, bp | fran |
| 850 | Aurea | spai |
| 91 | Aurelia Petronilla | ital |
| 852 | Aurelius | spai |
| 1977 | Avdeyev, M.V. | russ |
| 1672 | Avila y Ayala, fr P. | usa |
| 1682 | Avvakum Petrovich, archpriest | russ |
| 1989 | Ayap, pastor A. | phil |
| 1991 | Aziza, Adel | egyp |
| 467 | Azquir | saud |
| 112 | Babai | turk |
| 484 | Babowi, catholicos | iraq |
| 284 | Babylas, bp | egyp |
| 251 | Babylas, patriarch of Antioch | turk |
| 1992 | Bacabis, G. | phil |
| 315 | Bacchus | syri |
| 1943 | Bacon, D. | boli |
| 1410 | Badby, J. | brit |
| 1997 | Badiali, rev D. | peru |
| 1975 | Badre OSB, prior J. | camb |
| 1886 | Badzekuketta, A. | ugan |
| 1991 | Bagaric, fr N. | bosn |
| 1996 | Bagtasos III, pastor S. | phil |
| 1992 | Bakheit, dr S. | egyp |
| 1980 | Bakholdin, S. | russ |
| 285 | Balana, priest | egyp |
| 1959 | Balint, S. | hung |
| 1792 | Balmain SJ, fr F. | fran |
| 1966 | Bamba, Emmanuel | conz |
| 1886 | Banabakintu, Luke | ugan |
| c300 | Bandilaus, monk | egyp |
| 1987 | Bangirimana, Ernest | buru |
| c285 | Banina | egyp |
| 1279 | Bar Kaliq, bp of Tus | iran |
| 346 | Barbashmin, catholicos | iraq |
| 1963 | Barbosa, evangelist Dinis | gunb |
| 1981 | Barendsen, Eeva | afgh |
| 1981 | Barendsen, Erik | afgh |
| 2000 | Bargiggia, fr A. | buru |
| 1601 | Barkworth, fr M. | brit |
| 304 | Barlaam of Antioch | turk |
| 1641 | Barlow, fr. A. | brit |
| 61 | Barnabas, Apostle | cypr |
| 1540 | Barnes, Robert | brit |
| 1781 | Barreneche, fr J. A. | usa |
| 1593 | Barrow, Henry | brit |
| 112 | Barsamya | turk |
| c297 | Barsanuphius (Warshanufy) | egyp |
| c850 | Barsanuphius, monk | egyp |
| 493 | Barsumas, bp | iraq |
| 1982 | Barta, fr J. | czec |
| 68 | Bartholomew, Apostle | arme |
| 1936 | Bartholomew, bp | russ |
| 1534 | Barton, Elizabeth | brit |
| 1918 | Basil, abp of Chernigov | ukra |
| 298 | Basil, bp | egyp |
| c297 | Basilidas, general | egyp |
| 207 | Basilides | egyp |
| 1978 | Bassera, fr Ernesto | elsa |
| 1993 | Bassiliouss, P. | egyp |
| 1872 | Bassost, fr F. | usa |
| 1936 | Baste, fr N. | spai |
| 1997 | Batista, sr T. | braz |
| 250 | Batra | egyp |
| 1984 | Bazira, pastor G. | ugan |
| 1546 | Beaton, abp D. | brit |
| 1706 | Beatrice, Donna | conz |
| 1950 | Beda SJ, fr Tsiang | chin |
| 1997 | Bedoya, fr A. | colo |
| 1988 | Beebwa, sr M.T. | ugan |
| 1998 | Beheydt, pastor G. S. | ital |
| c355 | Behnam | egyp |
| 1321 | Belibasta, Guilhem | fran |
| 1985 | Beling, fr M. | phil |
| 2000 | Bello, fr C.O. | nige |
| 1997 | Beltran, A. | saud |
| 1684 | Beltran, fr M. | mexi |
| 1003 | Benedict of Benevento | pola |
| c150 | Benignus | fran |
| 1998 | Benimana, sr F. | rwan |
| 1686 | Benitez, fr E. | mexi |
| 1989 | Benitez, fr M.A. | colo |
| c291 | Benjamin | egyp |
| 422 | Benjamin | iraq |
| 1917 | Benjamin Simon, catholicos | iran |
| 1918 | Benjamin, fr | russ |
| 1922 | Benjamin, metrop of Petrograd | russ |
| 1220 | Berard | moro |
| 685 | Bercharius, abbot | fran |
| 1970 | Bergemann, F. | russ |
| 327 | Berikjesu | iraq |
| 1680 | Bernal, fr J. | usa |
| 1999 | Bernall, Cassie | usa |
| 2000 | Bernardo, fr J. | alba |
| 1866 | Berneux, bp S.-F. | souk |
| 1583 | Berno, P. | indi |
| 1612 | Bertelete, fr E. | hond |
| 884 | Bertharius, abbot | ital |
| 1638 | Berthelot, fr P. | indo |
| 1896 | Berthieu SJ, fr J. | mada |
| 1198 | Berthold, abbot | esto |
| c297 | Besamon | egyp |
| 1975 | Betancur, fr I. | hond |
| 1991 | Bethea, Lynda | keny |
| 1916 | Bettex, Paul | chin |
| 1999 | Bhatti, Sabir John | paki |
| 1977 | Biayenda, cardinal abp E. | cong |
| c360 | Bibiana | ital |
| 1975 | Biblenko, I.V. | russ |
| 1977 | Biko, Steve | soua |
| 1860 | Billottet SJ, fr E. | leba |
| 1531 | Bilney, Thomas | brit |
| 1993 | Bimazubute, G. | buru |
| 1972 | Binyoni, Abel | buru |
| 1945 | Birch, J. | chin |
| 1990 | Biscaro, fr Egidio | ugan |
| c1820 | Bishay, Sidhom | egyp |
| 1971 | Biswas, U. | bang |
| 1981 | Bitterman III, C.A. | colo |
| 316 | Blaize, bp | arme |
| 177 | Blandina | fran |
| 1597 | Blasquez, fr Pedro B. | japa |
| 1900 | Blind Chang Shen | chin |
| 1968 | Blood, H. | viet |
| 1657 | Bobola SJ, fr Andrew | belo |
| 1936 | Boguna, fr L. | spai |
| 1989 | Boisvert, fr A. | japa |
| 1860 | Bonacina, br F. | leba |
| 1388 | Bonaventure Peraga, cardinal | ital |
| 1945 | Bonhoeffer, Dietrich | germ |
| 754 | Boniface (Winfrith), bp | neth |
| 1792 | Bonnaud SJ, fr J. J. | fran |
| 1937 | Boretsky, M., metropolitan | ukra |
| 1936 | Bori, fr P. | spai |
| 1015 | Boris & Gleb | russ |
| 1956 | Boris, metrop of Nevrokop | bulg |
| 1946 | Borisevicius, V., bp of Telsiai | lith |
| 1989 | Bortolotti, fr F. | moza |
| 1145 | Bosinlother, abbot Conrad | ausz |
| 1997 | Bosmans, Sr M. | rwan |
| 1952 | Bossilkoff CP, bp E. | bulg |
| 1516 | Botello OP, Diego | trin |
| 1120 | Botvid | swed |
| 1998 | Boumans SVD, fr G. | para |
| 1838 | Bovie, fr P. D. | viet |
| 1555 | Bradford, John | brit |
| 1858 | Braeuninger, M. | usa |
| 1942 | Brandsma, fr Tiko | germ |
| 1714 | Brankoveanu, prince Constant | roma |
| 1950 | Brennan, bp P. T. | nork |
| 1986 | Brennes, J. | mexi |
| 1927 | Bretzkiy, bp N. | ukra |
| 1581 | Briant, fr A. | brit |
| 1560 | Brooks, J., bp of Gloucester | brit |
| c1970 | Brown, bp D. | libe |
| 1859 | Brown, John | usa |
| 1972 | Brown, pastor | bang |
| 1640 | Bruni SJ, fr B. | ethi |
| 1009 | Bruno, bp of Querfurt | lith |
| 1600 | Bruno, br G. | ital |
| 1997 | Buchwolder, sr C. | buru |
| 1923 | Budkiewicz, C., vicar | russ |
| c1250 | Bulus al-Habis | egyp |
| 1996 | Bumendwa, fr J. C. | conz |
| 1872 | Burgos, fr Jose | phil |
| 1942 | Bushiri, Mulumozi | conz |
| 1886 | Buzabaliawo, James | ugan |
| 1998 | Bwabulakombe, sr S. | conz |
| 1996 | Bwambale, pastor P. | conz |
| 1950 | Byrne, bp P. J. | nork |
| 1974 | Cabo, fr M. | usa |
| 1985 | Cabrera Rivera, prof C.H. | guat |
| 570 | Cadoc, bp | ital |
| c560 | Cadog | fran |
| c165 | Caecelia | ital |
| 1938 | Cairns, fr R. | chin |
| 1941 | Cairns, fr R. J. | chin |
| 1985 | Calderon, Z.S. | peru |
| 1541 | Calero, br J. | mexi |
| c286 | Callinicus | egyp |
| c300 | Callinicus | turk |
| c222 | Callistus I, pope | ital |
| 1976 | Calvan, pastor R. | phil |
| 1996 | Camacho, H. | phil |
| 1989 | Campanella, fr C. | moza |
| 1661 | Campbell, A. | brit |
| 1581 | Campion, fr E. | brit |
| 287 | Candidus | swit |
| 1086 | Canute IV, king | denm |
| 1131 | Canute Lavard | denm |
| 1991 | Capasilan, A. | phil |

*continued overleaf*

*Table 4–11 continued*

| | | |
|---|---|---|
| 1871 | Captier, fr E. | fran |
| 1936 | Carbonell, fr C. | spai |
| 1640 | Cardeira SJ, fr L. | ethi |
| 1661 | Cargill, D. | brit |
| 1900 | Carleson, N. | chin |
| 1950 | Carlo, bp A. | chin |
| 1964 | Carlson, P. | conz |
| 1999 | Carmeline, sr | sier |
| 1983 | Carney SJ, fr J.G. | hond |
| 1794 | Carnus, fr C. | fran |
| c170 | Carpus, bp | turk |
| 1734 | Carranco, fr L. | mexi |
| 1998 | Carreno, fr M. O. | mexi |
| 1936 | Carrio, fr A. | spai |
| 1996 | Carro, C. Quiroz | colo |
| 1624 | Carvalho, fr J. | japa |
| 1992 | Carzedda, fr S. | phil |
| 1597 | Casas Martinez, Felipe | japa |
| 1991 | Casaverde, C. | peru |
| 1925 | Cassels, bp W. C. | chin |
| 298 | Cassian | moro |
| 1638 | Cassian of Nantes, fr | ethi |
| 1986 | Castilblanco, N.A. | nica |
| c300 | Castorius | ital |
| 1605 | Catesby, Robert | brit |
| 307 | Catherine of Alexandria | egyp |
| 1871 | Caubert, fr J. | fran |
| 1626 | Caun, V. | japa |
| 1915 | Cavell, Edith | belg |
| c337 | Caxo, prince | iraq |
| 1985 | Ceballos, M. G. | chil |
| 178 | Cecilia | ital |
| 1992 | Celiz, Romeo | phil |
| 1649 | Chabenel, N. | cana |
| 1980 | Chacon, Juan | elsa |
| 1901 | Chalmers, pastor J. | papu |
| c299 | Chamoul | egyp |
| c286 | Chanazhum | egyp |
| 1988 | Chandra, fr F. | sril |
| 1841 | Chanel, fr P. M. | vanu |
| 1950 | Chang MM, sr Agneta | nork |
| 1996 | Chanthom, Toun | camb |
| 1900 | Chao Hsi Mao | chin |
| 1811 | Chao, A. | chin |
| 1985 | Chappell, R. | papu |
| 1648 | Charles I, king | brit |
| 1974 | Charlier, fr E. | conz |
| 1839 | Chastan, fr J. H. | souk |
| 1887 | Checa y Barba, abp J. I. | ecua |
| 1689 | Chefdeville, fr A. | usa |
| 1964 | Cheney, J. | usa |
| 1918 | Chernikh, S. | russ |
| 1996 | Cherukarokunnel, L. J. | indi |
| 1905 | Chestnut, Eleanor | hong |
| 1998 | Chicangana, fr A. J. | colo |
| 1915 | Chilembwe, John | mala |
| 304 | Chione | gree |
| 2000 | Chittinapilly, fr S.J. | indi |
| 1983 | Chiwanga | mala |
| 1866 | Cho, Peter | souk |
| 1998 | Chocho, Alber | pana |
| 1944 | Choo Kee Chul, pastor | nork |
| 422 | Chouchanik | iraq |
| 1996 | Christian, pastor Ishak | indo |
| 249 | Christopher | turk |
| 250 | Christophorus | egyp |
| 303 | Chrysogonus | ital |
| 1923 | Chrysostomos, met of Smyrna | turk |
| 1662 | Chu Tsu-hsuan, emperor | myan |
| 1801 | Chu, fr James | souk |
| 1801 | Chung, Augustine | souk |
| 1993 | Chunjee, bp P.S. | chin |
| 1976 | Chunsar OSB, fr B. C. | camb |
| 1991 | Chuquin, J. | peru |
| 1991 | Cisneros, fr Moises | guat |
| 180 | Cittinus | tuni |
| 283 | Cladius, Stratelates | egyp |
| 1980 | Clarke, sr M. | elsa |
| 1991 | Claude, pastor Sylvio | hait |
| c300 | Claudius | ital |
| 1996 | Claverie P., bp of Oran | alge |
| 99 | Clement, bp of Rome | ukra |
| 1871 | Clerc, fr A. | fran |
| 1811 | Clet, F. | chin |
| 1820 | Clet, fr F. R. | chin |
| c90 | Cletus, bp of Rome | ital |
| 1981 | Clipa, I. | roma |
| 1586 | Clitherow, Margaret | brit |
| 1979 | Coba, bp E. | alba |
| 1413 | Cobham, Lord | brit |
| 1678 | Coleman, Edward | brit |
| 1572 | Coligny, admiral Gaspard de | fran |
| 1997 | Collazo, S. | mexi |
| 1963 | Collins, Addie Mae | usa |
| 1012 | Coloman | ausz |
| 1989 | Colombo OFM, bp P.S. | soma |
| 1998 | Colorado, Adan | colo |
| 853 | Columba of Cordoba | spai |
| c299 | Comas | egyp |
| 1998 | Commissari, fr L. | braz |
| 1996 | Concesse, Sr | buru |
| 1998 | Conedera, bp J. G. | guat |
| c260 | Conon | turk |
| 1288 | Conrad of Saxony | geor |
| 1975 | Constable, pastor Eric | indo |
| 576 | Constantine, abbot | brit |
| 1622 | Constanzo, fr C. | japa |
| 1731 | Contova SJ, fr Juan Antonio | micr |
| c340 | Copres | egyp |
| 1644 | Corby, fr Ralph | brit |
| 1837 | Cornay, fr J. C. | viet |
| 1594 | Cornelius, fr J. | brit |
| 253 | Cornelius, pope | ital |
| 1989 | Corniall, sr Maurice | nica |
| 1996 | Coronel, J. D. | colo |
| 1936 | Corral, fr O. | spai |
| 1696 | Corvera, fr F. | usa |
| c300 | Cosmas & Damian | turk |
| 1564 | Cossin, fr B. | mexi |
| 1582 | Cottam, fr T. | brit |
| 1981 | Coufal, fr P. | czec |
| 1637 | Courtet OP, fr W. | japa |
| 1990 | Courtney, sr M. | nica |
| 1929 | Coveyou, fr W. | chin |
| 1944 | Coy, Juan | colo |
| 1921 | Coyle, J. E. | usa |
| 1553 | Cranmer, abp Thomas | brit |
| 2000 | Crasta, fr V. | indi |
| c302 | Crescentia | ital |
| 110 | Crescentius | turk |
| 1704 | Criado, fr D. | usa |
| 1549 | Criminali SJ, fr A. | indi |
| 1619 | Crisinus, fr M. | hung |
| c285 | Crispin | fran |
| 304 | Crispina of Tagora | alge |
| c285 | Crispinian | fran |
| 1991 | Cristovao, fr M.J. | moza |
| 1992 | Culembee Munto, sr M. | ango |
| 1998 | Curic, fr V. | rwan |
| 1684 | Custodio, fr F. | mexi |
| 1985 | Cuthbert, R. W. M. | jama |
| 1975 | Cypher OFM, fr M.C. | hond |
| 258 | Cyprian, bp of Carthage | tuni |
| c291 | Cyriacus | egyp |
| c260 | Cyril | turk |
| 1638 | Cyril I Lukaris, ecu patriarch | turk |
| 1638 | Cyril II Kontaris, ecu patriarch | turk |
| 1860 | Cyril IV, patriarch | egyp |
| c260 | Cyril, bp of Gortyna | gree |
| 1936 | Cyril, metropolitan of Kazan | russ |
| 303 | Cyrus & John | egyp |
| 1998 | Czuba, fr J. | cong |
| 1736 | d'Artiquette, P. | usa |
| 1736 | d'Esgly, F. M. | usa |
| 1997 | d'Herouville, Sr C. | chad |
| 1881 | D'Hoop, fr F. | buru |
| 1963 | da Costa, Joaquin | gunb |
| 1963 | da Silva, pastor Pedro | gunb |
| 1997 | da Silva, rev J. J. C. | braz |
| 1561 | da Silveira SJ, fr G. | zimb |
| c337 | Dado, governor | iraq |
| c360 | Dafrosa & Demetria | ital |
| 679 | Dagobert II, king | fran |
| c286 | Dalasina | egyp |
| 1968 | Dale, pastor Stan | indo |
| 1985 | Dalle Pezze, sr T.P. | moza |
| 1979 | Dalmajo, fr S. | ugan |
| 1771 | Damascenus | russ |
| 1935 | Damaskin, bp of Gluhov | ukra |
| c299 | Damian | egyp |
| c300 | Damian | turk |
| 1973 | Damian, abp of Tirane | alba |
| 345 | Daniel | iraq |
| 1227 | Daniel of Belvedere | span |
| 1648 | Daniel SJ, A. | cana |
| 347 | Daniel, patriarch | arme |
| 1965 | Daniels, J. | usa |
| 1958 | Dapcha, Lama David | nepa |
| 1871 | Darboy, G., abp of Paris | fran |
| 1936 | Darder, E. | spai |
| c286 | Dasyah | egyp |
| 1798 | Dat, fr J. | viet |
| 304 | Dativus | tuni |
| 1866 | Daveluy, bp M. A. N. | souk |
| c292 | David | egyp |
| c650 | David of Douine | arme |
| 1878 | David, fr | ital |
| 1567 | de Acevedo, fr P. | mexi |
| 1859 | de Albera OFM, fr. N. M. | syri |
| 1860 | de Albera, fr M. M. | syri |
| 1974 | de Alencar, F.T. | peru |
| 1536 | de Almasia, J. | para |
| 1638 | de Almeida, bp Apollinaris | ethi |
| 1606 | de Altamirano, fr M. | mexi |
| 1634 | de Andrade, fr A. | chin |
| 1623 | De Angelis, fr J. | japa |
| 1637 | de Aozaraza, fr M. | japa |
| 1612 | de Aranda SJ, fr M. | chil |
| 1696 | de Arbizu, fr J. | usa |
| 1691 | de Arce, Jose | boli |
| 1632 | de Arvide, fr M. | usa |
| 1597 | de Auñon, fr M. | usa |
| 1585 | de Ayala, fr A. | mexi |
| 1576 | de Azevedo OP, fr Silvestre | camb |
| 1570 | de Azevedo SJ, fr I. | spai |
| 1597 | de Badajoz, fr A. | usa |
| 1623 | de Baena, br J. | hond |
| 1549 | de Barbastro, fr L. C. | usa |
| 1871 | de Bengy, fr A. | fran |
| 1773 | de Bernave, fr J.C.G. | mexi |
| 1988 | de Boisseson, fr J. | mada |
| 1649 | de Brebeuf SJ, fr J. | cana |
| 1693 | de Britto SJ, fr J. | indi |
| 1567 | de Burgos, fr P. | mexi |
| 1644 | de Capillas OP, fr F. | chin |
| 1696 | de Carbonel, fr A. | usa |
| 1397 | de Cetina, J. | spai |
| 1996 | de Chergé OCSO, dom C. | alge |
| 1597 | de Corpa, fr P. | usa |
| 1736 | de Coulonge, L. d'A. | usa |
| 1541 | de Cuellar, fr A. | mexi |
| 1992 | de Dios, Manuel | usa |
| 1397 | de Duenas, P. | spai |
| 1680 | de Espeleta, fr J. | usa |
| 1680 | de Figuero, fr J. | usa |
| 1992 | de Fonseca Guerra, fr A. | ango |
| 1916 | de Foucauld, Charles | alge |
| 1972 | de Freitas, pastor F. | ango |
| 1597 | de Goto, fr J. S. | japa |
| 1567 | de Herrera, br J. | mexi |
| 1860 | de Jacobis, bp Justin | ethi |
| 1696 | de Jesus Maria Casañas, fr F. | usa |
| 1997 | de Jesus, bp B. | phil |
| 1680 | de Jesus, fr J. | usa |
| 1840 | de la Cruz, Apolinario | phil |
| c1976 | de la Cruz, fr C. | guat |
| 1553 | de la Cruz, fr D. | usa |
| 1542 | de la Cruz, fr J. | usa |
| 1996 | de la Fuente, br F. | conz |
| 1680 | de la Pedroso, fr J. | usa |
| 1586 | de la Puebla, fr A. | mexi |
| 1680 | de la Ribourde, fr G. | usa |
| 1928 | de la Vega, fr J. | mexi |
| 1730 | de Labrid, bp N. | vene |
| 1834 | de Leon, fr A. D. | usa |
| 1680 | de Lorenzana, fr F. | usa |
| 1685 | de Marolles, Louis | fran |
| 1680 | de Mdorales, fr L. | usa |
| 1553 | de Mena, fr J. | usa |
| 1704 | de Mendoza, fr M. | usa |
| 1792 | De Millou SJ, fr J. C. | fran |
| 1314 | de Molay, J., grand master | fran |
| 1612 | de Montalban SJ, br J. | chil |
| 1621 | de Montchretien, A. | fran |
| 1612 | de Monteagudo, fr J. | hond |
| 1718 | de Montesdoca, br L. | usa |
| 1680 | de Montesdoca, fr J. | usa |
| 1680 | de Mora, fr A. | usa |
| 1726 | de Oca, fr L. M. | usa |
| 1631 | de Ortega, fr P. | usa |
| 1704 | de Osorio, fr T. | usa |
| 1648 | de Oviedo, fr A. | pana |
| 1542 | de Padilla OFM, fr J. | usa |
| 1704 | de Parga, fr J. | usa |
| 1549 | de Pekalosa, fr D. | usa |
| 1680 | de Pro, fr A. S. | usa |
| 1571 | de Quiros, fr L. | usa |
| 1709 | de Rebullida, fr P. | cost |
| 1989 | de Rocha, fr A. | moza |
| 1597 | de Rodriguez, fr B. | usa |
| 1998 | de Rojas, M. R. | colo |
| 1314 | de Rosatis, A. of Milan | arme |
| 1516 | de Salcedo OP, fr F | trin |
| 1642 | de San Antonio, fr J. | pana |
| 1672 | de San Vitores SJ, fr J. | guam |
| 1680 | de Santa Maria, fr A. | usa |
| 1581 | de Santa Maria, fr J. | usa |
| 1616 | de Santarn, fr H. | mexi |
| 1731 | de Saraoz, fr D. | usa |
| 1571 | de Segura, fr J. B. | usa |
| 1950 | de Smedt, bp L. J. | chin |
| 1571 | de Solis, fr G. | usa |
| 1736 | de St Agne, L. G. | usa |
| 1706 | de St Cosme, fr J. F. B. | usa |
| 1326 | de Stapledon, Walter, bp | brit |
| 1680 | de Talban, fr J. | usa |
| 1564 | de Tapia, fr J. | mexi |
| 1758 | de Terreros, fr A. G. | usa |
| 1736 | de Tonty, P. A. | usa |
| 1626 | de Torres, fr B. | japa |
| 1680 | de Torres, fr T. | usa |
| 1616 | de Tovar, fr H. | mexi |
| 1680 | de Trujillo, fr J. | usa |
| 1542 | de Ubeda, fr L. D. | usa |
| 1792 | de Vafons, count | fran |
| 1550 | de Valdivieso, bp A. | nica |
| 1612 | de Vecchi SJ, fr H. | chil |
| 1680 | de Velasco, fr F. | usa |
| 1936 | de Velasco, fr I. | spai |
| 1680 | de Vera, fr D. | usa |
| 1582 | de Villalobos, fr L. | mexi |
| 1736 | de Vincennes, F. M. B. | usa |
| 1961 | de Vos, pastor R. | cong |
| 1709 | de Zamora, fr J.A. | cost |
| 1963 | Debior, P. | suda |
| c359 | Decius | egyp |
| 1871 | Deguerry, fr | fran |
| 1976 | Deinega, N.Y. | russ |
| 1586 | del Rio, fr J. | mexi |
| 1680 | del Val, fr J. | usa |
| 1792 | Delfaut SJ, fr W. A. | fran |
| 1838 | Delgado, bp I. | viet |
| 1624 | Delgado, fr D. | mexi |
| 1706 | Delhalle, fr C. | usa |
| 1945 | Delp, fr A. | germ |
| c360 | Demetria | ital |
| 1802 | Demetrios of Chios | gree |
| 235 | Demetrius | ital |
| 1321 | Demetrius, br | indi |
| 308 | Demetrius, megalomartyr | gree |
| 1529 | Denck, H. | neth |
| 1998 | Deng, A. Y. | suda |
| 1881 | Deniaud, fr | buru |
| 1900 | Denn, fr P. | chin |
| 259 | Denys, bp of Paris | fran |
| 411 | Desiderius, bp of Langres | fran |
| 607 | Desiderius, bp of Vienne | fran |
| 1998 | Desrumeaux, sr A. | conz |
| 834 | Deusdedit, abbot of M Cassino | ital |
| 1945 | Devine, H. | myan |
| 2000 | di Bari, fr R. | ugan |
| 1988 | Dias OFM, fr C. | paki |
| 2000 | Dias, J. da Rocha | ango |
| 1834 | Diaz OFM, fr | usa |
| 1781 | Diaz, fr J. M. | usa |
| 1994 | Diaz, Veronica J. | mexi |
| 1994 | Dibaj, pastor Mehdi | iran |
| 1838 | Diem, V. | viet |
| c1993 | Difen, bp Liu | chin |
| 1918 | Dimitri, pastor | russ |
| 1936 | Dimitry, abp of Gdovsk | russ |
| 305 | Dimyanah & her 40 Virgins | egyp |
| 448 | Dindui, metropolitan | iraq |
| c300 | Diomed | turk |
| 484 | Dionysia | tuni |
| 1261 | Dionysius, antipatriarch | iraq |
| 1976 | Dios Murias, fr C. | arge |
| c287 | Dioscorus | egyp |
| 1922 | Dobrolubov, pastor | russ |
| 1996 | Dochier OCSO, br L. | alge |
| 1227 | Domno | moro |
| 1997 | Donado, elder W. | colo |
| 180 | Donata | tuni |
| 304 | Donatilla | tuni |
| 347 | Donatus, bp of Bagai | tuni |
| 617 | Donnan & 52 companions | brit |
| 1938 | Donovan MM, fr G. | chin |
| 1980 | Donovan, sr J. | elsa |
| 1567 | Donzel, fr F. | mexi |
| 313 | Dorothy | turk |
| 1918 | Dovganav, P. | russ |
| 1970 | Druck, V. | russ |
| 1559 | Du Bourg, Anne | fran |
| 1792 | Du Lau, abp J. M. | fran |
| 1729 | du Poisson, fr P. | usa |
| 1736 | du Tisne, L. C. | usa |
| 1652 | du Tremblay, fr J. L. | ethi |
| 1871 | Ducoudray, fr L. | fran |
| 1944 | Duenas, fr Jesus | guam |
| 1942 | Duhamel, fr A. C. | solo |
| 1978 | Dunaway, Jr., A.G. | zimb |
| 2000 | Duque, fr H. | colo |
| 1954 | Durkovici, bp A. | roma |
| 1985 | Durksen, Y. | russ |
| 1964 | Dwatuka, fr B. | suda |
| 1943 | Dye, B. | boli |
| 1943 | Dye, C. | boli |
| c650 | Dympna of Ireland | belg |
| 1662 | Dyre, Mary | usa |
| c850 | Ebba, abbess | brit |
| 869 | Edmund the Martyr, king | brit |
| 979 | Edward the Martyr, king | brit |
| 1918 | Efrem, bp of Selenginsk | russ |
| 303 | Efrem, bp of Tomis | roma |
| 1989 | Ejeru, pastor Joseph | ugan |
| 1989 | Elba Ramos, Celina | elsa |
| 1989 | Elba Ramos, Julia & Celina | elsa |
| 523 | Elesbaan | yeme |
| 259 | Eleutherius | fran |
| 523 | Elias | yeme |
| 209 | Elias & companions | pale |
| c307 | Elias the eunuch | egyp |
| 523 | Elija | yeme |
| 1918 | Elizabeth, grand duchess | russ |
| 1989 | Ellacuria SJ, fr I. | elsa |
| 1956 | Elliot, J. | ecua |
| c300 | Elmo, bp of Formiae | ital |
| 2000 | Emmanuel, bp G. | indi |
| c660 | Emmeram, bp of Poitiers | fran |
| 754 | Eoban, bp | neth |
| 1846 | Epalle SM, bp | solo |
| 1682 | Epifanii, monk | russ |
| c286 | Epima | egyp |
| c292 | Epimachus | egyp |
| 303 | Epimachus of Pelusium | egyp |
| c800 | Erc, bp of Slane | irel |
| 1150 | Eric of Sweden | swed |
| 1075 | Erlembald | ital |
| 1121 | Erminold, abbot of Prufening | germ |
| 1148 | Ernest, abbot of Zwiefalten | saud |
| 1977 | Eschtruth, G.J.R. | conz |
| c1080 | Eskil, bp | swed |
| 1980 | Espinal SJ, fr L. | boli |
| 1985 | Espino, pastor E. F. | elsa |
| 1997 | Estafanos, K. | egyp |
| 1934 | Esteban, fr T. | chin |
| 1988 | Estorba, fr M. | phil |
| 794 | Ethelbert, king | brit |
| c291 | Eudoxia | egyp |
| c350 | Eudoxius & companions | pale |
| 304 | Eulalia of Merida | spai |
| 259 | Eulogius | tuni |
| 859 | Eulogius of Cordoba | spai |
| 1954 | Eunak, K. | souk |
| c355 | Eunapius, monk | egyp |
| c291 | Euphemia | egyp |
| 303 | Euphemia | turk |
| 379 | Eusebius, bp of Samosata | turk |
| 379 | Eustace of Mtskheta | geor |
| c111 | Eustathius, Roman general | ital |
| 419 | Eustochium | pale |
| 834 | Euthymius, metrop of Sardes | turk |
| c260 | Eutropius, bp of Saintes | fran |
| 1679 | Evans, fr D | brit |
| 1978 | Evans, P. & S. | zimb |
| 1978 | Evans, S. | zimb |
| 1347 | Evastafiy | lith |
| c117 | Eventius & Theodulus | ital |
| 64 | Evodius, bp of Antioch | turk |
| 1794 | Expilly, bp L. A. | fran |

*Continued opposite*

*Table 4–11 continued*

| | | |
|---|---|---|
| 287 | Exuperantius | swit |
| 287 | Exuperius | swit |
| 250 | Fabian, pope | ital |
| 252 | Fabius, bp of Antioch | turk |
| c250 | Faith (Foy) | fran |
| 1992 | Fallah, pastor J. | libe |
| 852 | Fandila of Cordoba | spai |
| 1932 | Farabundo, Marti | elsa |
| 1996 | Farris, Dr. Ron | como |
| 1757 | Faulhaber, fr A. | pola |
| 1985 | Favali, fr T. | phil |
| 1996 | Favre-Miville OCOS, br P. | alge |
| 303 | Febronia | iraq |
| c288 | Febronia, nun | egyp |
| 1935 | Fedorov, exarch L. | russ |
| c297 | Felician | ital |
| 1704 | Feliciano, A. C. | usa |
| 259 | Felicissimus & Agapitus | ital |
| 202 | Felicitas | tuni |
| 156 | Felicitus Alexander | turk |
| 165 | Felicity | turk |
| 287 | Felix | swit |
| 180 | Felix | tuni |
| 303 | Felix of Thibiuca | tuni |
| 1679 | Fenwick, fr J. | brit |
| 1859 | Fernandez, fr J. J. | syri |
| 1990 | Fernandez, fr T. | colo |
| 1996 | Fernando, SJ, R. M. | camb |
| 1553 | Ferrer, fr J. | usa |
| 1936 | Ferreres, fr J. B. | spai |
| 1622 | Fidelis of Sigmaringen | swit |
| 1981 | Fietje, K. | thai |
| 1986 | Figaroa, N.M. | mexi |
| 1903 | Figueroa, Juana | arge |
| c1927 | Filaret, bp of Bobruisk | byel |
| 1601 | Filcock, fr. R. | brit |
| c1995 | Finnemann, bp W. | phil |
| 1979 | Fiorantie, fr A. | ugan |
| 1992 | Fiorini, fr Alfredo | moza |
| c290 | Firmin, bp of Amiens | fran |
| 1535 | Fisher, cardinal John | brit |
| 1978 | Fisher, M. | zimb |
| 259 | Flavian | tuni |
| 449 | Flavian, patriarch | turk |
| 95 | Flavius Clemens | ital |
| 1956 | Fleming, P. | ecua |
| 1631 | Fleming, fr P. | czec |
| 1996 | Fleury OCSO, br M. | alge |
| 851 | Flora of Cordoba | spai |
| 1986 | Flores, Ernesto | mexi |
| 655 | Foillan, abbot | fran |
| 1952 | Ford, bp F.X. | chin |
| 1980 | Ford, sr I. | elsa |
| 1702 | Foucault, fr N. | usa |
| 1948 | Fowler, E. | colo |
| 1638 | Franceschi SJ, fr H. | ethi |
| 1339 | Francis of Alessandria | chin |
| 1314 | Francis of Borgo San Sepolcro | iran |
| 1314 | Francis of Fermo | arme |
| 1597 | Francis of Miako | japa |
| 1583 | Francisco, fr A. | indi |
| 1579 | Franz, David | hung |
| 866 | Fremund | brit |
| 1948 | Frentiu, bp | roma |
| 1922 | Friazinov, pastor | russ |
| 1533 | Frith, J. | brit |
| 1921 | Frolov, pastor J. | russ |
| 259 | Fructuosus, bp of Tarragona | spai |
| 1549 | Fuentes, br | usa |
| 1622 | Fugiscima, fr D. | japa |
| 1995 | Fumagalli, Graziella | soma |
| 1855 | Gabra Mikael, fr | ethi |
| 1996 | Gabriel, I. A. | egyp |
| 1952 | Gacigi, G. | keny |
| 1952 | Gacigi, R. | keny |
| 1983 | Gadama | mala |
| 1997 | Gadzhiyev, G. | russ |
| 1997 | Gadzhiyev, Tatiana | russ |
| 1997 | Gafney SJ, fr T. | nepa |
| 1833 | Gagelin, F.-I. | viet |
| 1990 | Gagnaux, dr R. | moza |
| 1996 | Gakobwa, Sr I. | buru |
| 1996 | Gakondo, sr J. A. | conz |
| 2000 | Gallardo, fr R. | phil |
| 1745 | Gallizia, bp | myan |
| 760 | Gangolf | fran |
| 1752 | Ganzabal, fr J. F. | usa |
| 1998 | Gaona, br M. A. Q. | colo |
| 1692 | Garangouas, M. | usa |
| 1781 | Garces OFM, fr F. T. | usa |
| 1936 | Garcia Villada SJ, fr Z. | spai |
| 1982 | Garcia, Anastasio | guat |
| 1996 | Garcia, br S. M. | conz |
| 1851 | Gardiner, Allen | arge |
| 1544 | Gardiner, J. | brit |
| 1608 | Garnet, fr T. | brit |
| 1649 | Garnier, fr C. | cana |
| 1998 | Gasigwa, sr E. | rwan |
| 1730 | Gaston, fr | usa |
| 1996 | Gatuku, fr C. | conz |
| 1996 | Gatunga, sr J. | conz |
| 1994 | Gatwa, T. | rwan |
| 1679 | Gavan, fr J. | brit |
| 290 | Gayane, abbess | arme |
| 2000 | Gaytan, rev J. | mexi |
| 1936 | Gelabert, P. | spai |
| 180 | Generosa | tuni |
| 250 | Genesius of Arles | fran |
| 303 | Genesius the Actor | turk |
| 1591 | Genings, fr E. | brit |
| 1693 | Genoud, fr | myan |
| 1340 | Gentle of Matelica | iran |
| 1514 | George Novi of Sophia | bulg |
| 1807 | George of Chios | gree |
| 850 | George of Cordoba | spai |
| 1652 | George of Ghiel, fr | conz |
| 615 | George the Monk | iran |
| 1595 | George, fr A. | ethi |
| 1972 | George, Margaret | iraq |
| 303 | George, megalomartyr | pale |
| 1838 | Georgios | gree |
| 1046 | Gerard, bp of Csanad | hung |
| 1962 | Gerber, D. | viet |
| 304 | Gereon | germ |
| 1998 | Germaine, sr | conz |
| 156 | Germanicus | turk |
| 675 | Germanus, abbot | fran |
| 729 | Germanus, ecu patriarch | turk |
| 799 | Gerold, duke of Bavaria | germ |
| 1540 | Gerrard, Thomas | brit |
| 750 | Gerulf | belg |
| 165 | Gervase & Protase | ital |
| 1608 | Gervase, fr. G. | brit |
| 1997 | Geyer-Iwand, V. | germ |
| 1981 | Ghabrail, fr Abd Mutagalli | egyp |
| 996 | Ghabrial | egyp |
| 193 | Ghevondius, patriarch | arme |
| 1954 | Ghika, fr V. | roma |
| 1983 | Gideon, dr | myan |
| 1948 | Gigni, bp | alba |
| 1948 | Gijni, bp | alba |
| 1953 | Gikonyo, E. | keny |
| 1585 | Gil, fr F. | mexi |
| 1339 | Gilotti, William | chin |
| 1988 | Giraldo, fr C. Augusto | colo |
| 1996 | Girgis, M. B. | egyp |
| 1989 | Giuliatti OFMCap, fr A. | ango |
| 91 | Glabrio, Manius Acilius, consul | ital |
| 1015 | Gleb | russ |
| 1952 | Gnidovec, dean | serb |
| 1794 | Gobel, J. B. J., bp of Paris | fran |
| c337 | Gobidlaha, princess | iraq |
| 1070 | Godelive | fran |
| 1965 | Goehring, H. | bang |
| c1150 | Goharin & companions | arme |
| 1960 | Gojdic, bp Pavol | slok |
| 1991 | Goldsworthy, K. | phil |
| 1970 | Golev, S.T. | russ |
| 1995 | Gomez Ramos, pastor A. | mexi |
| 1872 | Gomez, fr Mariano | phil |
| 1571 | Gomez, fr G. | usa |
| 1989 | Gomez, Maria Cristina | elsa |
| 1707 | Gomidas, fr K. | turk |
| 1692 | Gonannhatenha, F. | usa |
| 1985 | Goncalves Kamtedza SJ, fr J. | moza |
| 1992 | Goncalves, sr M.L. Granado | moza |
| 1979 | Gono, fr M. | czec |
| 1886 | Gonza, Gonzaga | ugan |
| 1637 | Gonzales, fr A. | japa |
| 1996 | Gonzales, J. L. | colo |
| 1628 | Gonzalez SJ, fr Roque | para |
| 1936 | Gonzalez, fr E. | spai |
| 1995 | Goobe, A. | soma |
| 1964 | Goodman | usa |
| 1979 | Goodman, Dave | turk |
| 1942 | Gorazd, bp Pavlik | czec |
| c292 | Gordian | egyp |
| c350 | Gordius | pale |
| 1885 | Gordon, general C. G. | suda |
| 1902 | Goretti, Maria | ital |
| 1066 | Gottschalk | germ |
| 1642 | Goupil SJ, R. | cana |
| c1976 | Gran, fr J.M. | guat |
| 1989 | Gran, Lovello | phil |
| 1989 | Gran, pastor Vizminda | phil |
| 1977 | Grande, fr R. | elsa |
| 2000 | Grange, fr R. | ivor |
| 1995 | Grassi, br B. | pale |
| 1708 | Gravier, fr J. | usa |
| 1942 | Gray, R. F. | phil |
| 1593 | Greenwood, John | brit |
| 1317 | Gregorios, Mar, bp | turk |
| 1822 | Gregory V, ecu patriarch | turk |
| c550 | Grigor-Rajik | arme |
| 337 | Grigoris, exarch | arme |
| 1936 | Grimaltos, R. | spai |
| 1619 | Grodecz SJ, fr M. | hung |
| 1944 | Gross, N. | germ |
| 1962 | Grove, M. | soma |
| 1679 | Grove, J. | brit |
| 1778 | Guillen, fr F. | mexi |
| 1900 | Guillon, bp L. | chin |
| 1992 | Guirguis, A.S. | egyp |
| 1992 | Guirguis, M.Q. | egyp |
| 1980 | Gurgula, fr A. | ukra |
| 315 | Gurias & companions | iraq |
| 1661 | Guthrie, James | brit |
| 1616 | Gutierrez, fr P. | mexi |
| 1632 | Gutierrez, fr R. B. | japa |
| 1991 | Gutierrez, L. | peru |
| c440 | Gwinear | irel |
| 1584 | Gwyn, R. | brit |
| 1886 | Gyavira | ugan |
| 1996 | Haaji, professor | soma |
| 1997 | Habakurama, rev I. | rwan |
| 309 | Habib the Deacon | turk |
| 523 | Habsa | yeme |
| 1613 | Hachikan, Joaquin | japa |
| 1387 | Hadid of Giza | egyp |
| 1919 | Hahn, G. H. & 32 pastors | germ |
| 731 | Hainmar, bp of Auxerre | fran |
| 1988 | Hairapetian, V. | azer |
| 1996 | Hakizimana, fr S. | buru |
| 1948 | Halan, Y. | ukra |
| 1043 | Hallvard Vebjornssen | norw |
| c450 | Hamai of Kahyor | egyp |
| 1662 | Hambroek, A. | taiw |
| 1992 | Hamill, J. | phil |
| 1528 | Hamilton, Patrick | brit |
| 1571 | Hamilton, primate J. | brit |
| 1985 | Hammes, W. | usa |
| 345 | Hanania | iraq |
| 1996 | Hanas, dr Michel Ayad | egyp |
| 1885 | Hannington, bp James | ugan |
| 1996 | Hansda, S. | indi |
| 1996 | Hapalla, J. | phil |
| 1992 | Hapalla, pastor Gregorio | phil |
| 1679 | Harcourt, fr W. | brit |
| 1991 | Hass, sr Claire | baha |
| 1997 | Hatagekimang, rev A. | conz |
| 1998 | Haviaropoulos, V. | turk |
| 1994 | Havugimana, evangelist I | rwan |
| 853 | Haymo, bp of Halberstadt | germ |
| 870 | Hedda of Peterborough, abbot | brit |
| 1908 | Heinrich, fr L. | usa |
| c286 | Helias, bp | egyp |
| 555 | Helier | chan |
| 1942 | Hennessey, J. G. | solo |
| 1624 | Henriquez, br J. | mexi |
| 1156 | Henry, bp of Uppsala | swed |
| 1996 | Her, Ah | laos |
| c300 | Heraclides | egyp |
| c291 | Herai | egyp |
| 1919 | Herman, bp of Kamychen | russ |
| 585 | Hermenegild of Spain | spai |
| 304 | Hermes | turk |
| 1918 | Hermogen, abp of Tobolsk | russ |
| 1861 | Hermosilla OP, bp H. | viet |
| 1995 | Hernandez Perez, pastor G. | mexi |
| 1997 | Hernandez, M. | mexi |
| 1974 | Hernandez, M. Gomez | mexi |
| 1974 | Hernandez, pastor | nica |
| 1704 | Hevia, fr D. | mexi |
| 695 | Hewald the Dark | germ |
| 695 | Hewald the Fair | germ |
| 1652 | Heyling, Peter | ethi |
| 1994 | Heyns, moderator Johan | soua |
| c1970 | Heywood, J. | viet |
| 1811 | Hidalgo y Costilla, fr M. | mexi |
| 1999 | Hindu, sr | sier |
| 297 | Hipparchus | turk |
| 235 | Hippolytus, antipope | ital |
| c1970 | Hmara of Kulunda | ukra |
| 1975 | Hoang, pastor Van Dat | viet |
| 1960 | Hodgson, E. | conz |
| 1942 | Hoeben, H. | neth |
| 1929 | Holbein, fr G. | chin |
| 1983 | Holdenried, F.X. | guat |
| 1642 | Holland, fr T. | brit |
| 1861 | Holmes, J. L. | chin |
| 1998 | Hood, Carl | colo |
| 1553 | Hooper, bp John | brit |
| 1567 | Hoorn, count | neth |
| 1973 | Hopewell, Gladys | taiw |
| 422 | Hormisdas | iraq |
| 408 | Hormizd of Sylvanus, rabban | iraq |
| 420 | Hormizdas | iraq |
| 1943 | Hosback, G. | boli |
| 1970 | Hossu, bp J. | roma |
| 1535 | Houghton, John, prior | brit |
| 347 | Houssik I, patriarch | arme |
| 454 | Hovsep I, patriarch | arme |
| 1994 | Hovsepian-Mehr, bp H. | iran |
| 1998 | Hoyo, br J. | indi |
| 290 | Hripsime | arme |
| 1217 | Hroznata | czec |
| 1528 | Hubmaier, B. | ausz |
| 1998 | Hubscher, fr M. | mada |
| 1998 | Hudon, fr B. | hait |
| 1998 | Hughes, B. | brit |
| 1227 | Hugolino | moro |
| 1601 | Hunt, Fr T. | brit |
| 1943 | Hunter, E. | boli |
| 1992 | Husband, sr G. | came |
| 1996 | Huseen, professor H. M. | soma |
| 1527 | Hut, H. | ausz |
| 1643 | Hutchinson, Anne | usa |
| 1536 | Hutter, J. | neth |
| 1606 | Hwang Ming-sha SJ, br | chin |
| 1801 | Hwang, S. C. | souk |
| 305 | Hypatius of Gangra | egyp |
| 1633 | Ibanez, fr D. | japa |
| c1925 | Ierofey, bp of Veliki-Ustinsk | russ |
| 1645 | Ignace, catechist | viet |
| 1814 | Ignanos | gree |
| 115 | Ignatius, bp of Antioch | ital |
| 1400 | Ileya | egyp |
| 1995 | Iloputaife, bp H. A. | nige |
| 1839 | Imbert, bp Laurence | souk |
| c700 | Indract | brit |
| 854 | Indrechtach, abbot of Iona | brit |
| 1954 | Indus, Artur | russ |
| 2000 | Inocencio, fr B. | phil |
| c240 | Intercisus, James | iraq |
| 1347 | Ioann | lith |
| c1930 | Ioann, bp of Mozyr | byel |
| 1689 | Iosif, hermit, & monks | russ |
| 1992 | Iqbal, Tahir | paki |
| 1679 | Ireland, fr W. | brit |
| 1544 | Ireland, J. | brit |
| 202 | Irenaeus, bp of Lyons | fran |
| 284 | Irene | turk |
| c359 | Irene | egyp |
| 304 | Irene | gree |
| 1996 | Irenee, sr | buru |
| 1918 | Irinarkh, fr | russ |
| 303 | Irineu, bp of Sirmium | croa |
| 1973 | Isa, Peter | ethi |
| 347 | Isaac | tuni |
| c299 | Isaac of Tiphre | egyp |
| 851 | Isaac, monk | spai |
| c850 | Isaac, prince | arme |
| 1996 | Ishak Christian, pastor | indo |
| 1995 | Isho, E.K. | iraq |
| 1997 | Isidi, rev N. | nige |
| c1480 | Isidor & followers | esto |
| c305 | Isidore of Takinash | egyp |
| c299 | Isidorus | egyp |
| c300 | Isidorus, monk | egyp |
| 1993 | Iskandar, E.N. | egyp |
| 1936 | Isla, fr L. | spai |
| 1900 | Isore, fr R. | chin |
| 1918 | Israel, monk | russ |
| 1918 | Issidor, bp of Mikhailov | russ |
| 1714 | Ivanov, Thomas | russ |
| 1977 | Ivanova, R. | russ |
| 1632 | Ixida SJ, fr A. | japa |
| 1993 | Izmery, A. | hait |
| 1940 | Jackson, F. C. | indo |
| 1992 | Jackson, J. | libe |
| 1992 | Jackson, T. & J. | libe |
| 337 | Jacob, bp | iraq |
| 1944 | Jacob, Max | fran |
| c300 | Jacob, The Soldier | egyp |
| 1943 | Jaegerstaetter, F. | germ |
| 1945 | Jaffray, R. A. | indo |
| 346 | James | iraq |
| 44 | James Boanerges, Apostle | pale |
| 259 | James of Cirta | tuni |
| 1321 | James of Padua | indi |
| 422 | James of Persia | iraq |
| 62 | James the Just, bp of Jerus | pale |
| 54 | James the Less, Apostle | pale |
| 1362 | James, abp of Zaitun | chin |
| 730 | James, bp of Catania | ital |
| 1997 | James, Jessica | usa |
| 2000 | Jami, fr Y. | indo |
| 1997 | Janda, R. | saud |
| 180 | Januaria | tuni |
| 305 | Januarius, bp of Benevento | ital |
| 1989 | Jaramillo, bp Jesus E. | colo |
| 1983 | Jarlan, A. | chil |
| 1980 | Jaugelis, fr V. | lith |
| 1991 | Jeanne SAM, fr A. | ivor |
| 1947 | Jensen, fr B. | chin |
| c258 | Jerasimus | egyp |
| 1569 | Jerome de la Croix | thai |
| 1416 | Jerome of Prague | czec |
| 1540 | Jerome, William | brit |
| 856 | Jeron | neth |
| 33 | Jesus | pale |
| 1985 | Jeyarajasingham, pastor G. | sril |
| 1936 | Jimenez Malla, Ceferino | spai |
| 1919 | Joachim, abp of Nizhni-Novgo | russ |
| 1431 | Joan of Arc | fran |
| 1822 | Joana Angelica, abbess | braz |
| 1646 | Jogues SJ, fr I. | cana |
| 303 | John | egyp |
| 1096 | John (Said bar Sabhuni), bp | turk |
| 1016 | John Baptist Vladimir, prince | alba |
| 407 | John Chrysostom, patriarch | turk |
| 1415 | John Hus | germ |
| 526 | John I, pope | ital |
| 825 | John of Cordoba | spai |
| 1339 | John of India, br | chin |
| 1536 | John of Leiden | germ |
| 1393 | John of Nepomuk | czec |
| 1209 | John of Phanidjoit | egyp |
| 1631 | John of Prado | moro |
| 1478 | John of Sahagun | spai |
| 1346 | John the Blind | luxe |
| c860 | John VII Grammaticus, patr | turk |
| 928 | John X, pope | ital |
| 95 | John, Apostle | turk |
| 337 | John, bp | iraq |
| 448 | John, bp of Karka | iraq |
| 1066 | John, bp of Mecklenburg | germ |
| 1960 | John, evangelist Esther | paki |
| c357 | John, The Soldier | egyp |
| 327 | Jonah | iraq |
| 1693 | Joret, fr | myan |
| 1996 | Jorge, br J. R. | conz |
| 1597 | Joseph, mar, metropolitan | indi |
| 1938 | Joseph, metro of Petrograd | russ |
| c850 | Joseph, prince | arme |
| 1628 | Juan del Castillo SJ | para |
| 1560 | Juan, br | mexi |
| 66 | Jude (Thaddaeus), Apostle | arme |
| 1992 | Juliet | phil |
| c291 | Julitta | egyp |
| 254 | Julius | brit |
| c302 | Julius of Durostorum | bulg |
| c120 | Junia | ital |
| 1996 | Jurcevic, sr D | bosn |
| 165 | Justin Martyr & 5 companions | ital |
| 1920 | Justin, abp of Omsk | russ |
| c286 | Justus, son of Numerianus | egyp |
| 1938 | Juvenal, abp of Riazan | russ |
| 1796 | Juvenal, hieromonk | usa |
| 1997 | Kabera, rev E. | conz |

*Continued overleaf*

*Table 4-11 continued*

| | | |
|---|---|---|
| 1383 | Kador, John | arme |
| 1998 | Kagabo, fr B. | rwan |
| 1886 | Kaggwa, Andrew | ugan |
| 1953 | Kaguru, A. | keny |
| 1973 | Kagwa, M. | ugan |
| 1996 | Kahegezo, fr B. K. | conz |
| 1527 | Kaiser | germ |
| 2000 | Kaiser, fr A. | keny |
| 1996 | Kajibwami, br F. | conz |
| 1886 | Kalemba, Matthias | ugan |
| 1979 | Kalienuk, fr Z.A. | ukra |
| 1962 | Kanamuzeyi, pastor Yona | rwan |
| 1996 | Kanyamanza, fr P. | conz |
| 1597 | Karasumaru, Leo | japa |
| 1992 | Kariuki, pastor H. | keny |
| 2000 | Karketta, fr R. | indi |
| 1994 | Karuhije, dean A. | rwan |
| 1996 | Kasati, fr J. | conz |
| 1998 | Kathihe, sr L. | ango |
| c1995 | Katoolig, C. | soma |
| c289 | Kau of Bismay | egyp |
| 1985 | Kautudja, sr L. | ango |
| 1980 | Kazel, sr D. | elsa |
| 1678 | Kemble, John | brit |
| 821 | Kenelm, prince | brit |
| 1535 | Kenraghty, chaplain Maurice | irel |
| 1902 | Kensit, John | brit |
| 1995 | Kerkatta, John | indi |
| 1981 | Kernweisz, bp K. | roma |
| 1624 | Ketevan, queen | iran |
| 1992 | Khalil, H.F. | egyp |
| c450 | Kharitas | ethi |
| 1959 | Kherie, bp A. | ukra |
| 1964 | Khmara, N. | russ |
| 1938 | Khoren I, catholicos | arme |
| 1982 | Khrapov, N.P. | russ |
| 1983 | Ki-Yoon, pastor I. | souk |
| 1886 | Kibuka, Ambrose | ugan |
| 1973 | Kiggundu, fr C. | ugan |
| 686 | Kilian, bp, & 11 companions | germ |
| 1846 | Kim Tai Kun, fr Andrew | souk |
| 1839 | Kim, Agatha | souk |
| 1943 | Kim, evangelist | chin |
| 1905 | Kim, evangelist | chin |
| c1990 | Kim, pastor | nork |
| 1951 | Kimbangu, prophet Simon | conz |
| 1622 | Kimura SJ, fr S. | japa |
| 1619 | Kimura, fr L. | japa |
| 1900 | King, A. | chin |
| 1968 | King, Jr, pastor Martin Luther | usa |
| 1886 | Kiriggwajjo, Anatole | ugan |
| 1918 | Kirion III, catholicos-patriarch | geor |
| 1886 | Kiriwawanvu, Mukasa | ugan |
| 1952 | Kirtoff, apostolic exarch | bulg |
| 1597 | Kisai, fr J. | japa |
| 1949 | Kisi, abp K. | alba |
| 1258 | Kitbuga, general | syri |
| 1886 | Kiwanuka, Achilles | ugan |
| 1972 | Kiwanuka, justice Benedicto | ugan |
| 1997 | Kiyumukiza, rev A. N. | conz |
| 1886 | Kizito | ugan |
| 1990 | Klein, Valve | esto |
| 1985 | Kluiters, fr N. | leba |
| 1960 | Knauf, E. | conz |
| 1988 | Knoerl, br K. | zimb |
| 1838 | Koa, P. | viet |
| 1917 | Kochurov, fr I. | russ |
| 1944 | Kocylowskyj, bp | ukra |
| 1944 | Koenzgen, G. | germ |
| 1633 | Kohioye, fr M. | japa |
| 1883 | Koi, David | keny |
| 1941 | Kolbe OFM, fr Maximilian | pola |
| 1860 | Kolland OFM, fr E. | syri |
| 1992 | Kolmer, sr J. | libe |
| 1992 | Kolmer, sr S. | libe |
| 1740 | Koman, pastor D. | slov |
| 1992 | Kon, Paul | suda |
| 1993 | Korfeh, pastor T. | libe |
| 1948 | Kostelnyk, fr H. | ukra |
| 1980 | Kotyk, fr Y. | ukra |
| c1942 | Kowalski, J., primate | pola |
| 1979 | Krasnova, T.K. | russ |
| 1962 | Kruegler MM, fr W.C. | boli |
| 1964 | Kucherenko | russ |
| 1999 | Kulakov, pastor A. | russ |
| 1919 | Kulbusch, bp Platon of Revel | esto |
| 1623 | Kuncevicz, abp Josaphat | belo |
| 1066 | Kuno, bp of Trier | germ |
| 1918 | Kuntsevich, L. | russ |
| 1633 | Kurobioye, M. | japa |
| 1972 | Kurti, fr Shtjefen | alba |
| 2000 | Kuzhikandom, fr G. | indi |
| 1627 | Kwon, Vincent | japa |
| 1821 | Kyprianos, abp | cypr |
| 1987 | Labaca Ugarte OFMCap, bp A. | ecua |
| 1645 | Labado, fr F. | mexi |
| 180 | Laetantius | tuni |
| 1944 | Lagerstadr, Farnz | germ |
| 1974 | Lain, fr Domingo | colo |
| 1646 | Lalande SJ, fr John de | cana |
| 1649 | Lalemant SJ, fr G. | cana |
| 705 | Lambert, bp of Maastricht | belg |
| 1970 | Lamichami, Krishna | nepa |
| 1567 | Lamoral of Egmont | neth |
| 1963 | Landim | gunb |
| 1792 | Lanfant, fr A. & 8 companions | fran |
| 1816 | Lantrua, fr G. | chin |
| 1544 | Larke, J. | brit |
| 1990 | Lasar, fr Hegumen | russ |
| 1996 | Lasker, evangelist Hussain | indi |
| 1553 | Latimer, bp Hugh | brit |
| 1645 | Laud, William, abp of Canter | brit |
| 1981 | Laurinavicius, fr B. | lith |
| c1985 | Lavina, J. | phil |
| 1919 | Lavrenty, bp of Balakhna | russ |
| 1991 | Lawi, Ezra | suda |
| 259 | Lawrence | ital |
| 1616 | Lawrence | japa |
| 1339 | Lawrence of Alessandria | chin |
| 1535 | Lawrence, Robert, prior | brit |
| 1802 | Lazarus the Bulgar | turk |
| 1637 | Lazzaro di Kyoto | japa |
| 1689 | Le Clercq, fr M. | usa |
| 1971 | Le Febre, M. | boli |
| 1685 | Le Fevre, I. | fran |
| 1405 | Le Scrope, abp R. | brit |
| 1683 | Le Vacher, bp J. | alge |
| 1992 | Leal, sr Torres N. | colo |
| 1940 | Lebbe, fr F. V. | chin |
| 1996 | Lebreton, OCSO, fr C. | alge |
| 1995 | Leclerc, sr D. | alge |
| 1866 | Lee, John | souk |
| 1942 | Lee, pastor Kipoong | souk |
| 1792 | Lefranc, fr F. | fran |
| 1588 | Leigh, fr R. | brit |
| c1940 | Leisner, fr K. | germ |
| 1996 | Lemarchand OCSO, fr Bruno | alge |
| 1227 | Leo | moro |
| 859 | Leocritia | spai |
| 679 | Leodegar, bp of Autun | fran |
| 1654 | Leonard of Chartres, fr | cana |
| 1992 | Leone, sr M. | came |
| 202 | Leonides | egyp |
| c360 | Leontius of Tripoli | syri |
| c260 | Leontius the Ascetic | turc |
| 1918 | Leonty, bp of Enotaev | russ |
| 1632 | Letrado, fr F. | usa |
| 1944 | Letterhaus, B. | germ |
| 1616 | Lewis | japa |
| 1678 | Lewis, David | brit |
| 1679 | Lewis, fr D | brit |
| 1990 | Lewis, pastor N. | usa |
| 1799 | Lewis, pastor T. | frep |
| 1900 | Li, fr J. | chin |
| 1941 | Lichtenberg, fr B. | germ |
| c580 | Licinianus, bp of Carthage | turk |
| 1945 | Liddell, Eric | chin |
| 1964 | Lifenya, director Pierre | conz |
| 1994 | Liibaan, Ibrahim | soma |
| 1998 | Lilia, sr | yeme |
| 1896 | Lilli OFM, fr Salvatore | turk |
| 1994 | Limar, br | taji |
| 1960 | Lin, H.H. | chin |
| 1571 | Linares, fr P. | usa |
| c76 | Linus, bp of Rome | ital |
| 1941 | Litaunieks, fr V. | lith |
| 1995 | Littlejohn, sr J. | alge |
| 1938 | Liu, H. | chin |
| 1934 | Liu, Y. C. | chin |
| 1968 | Liuzzo, Viola | usa |
| 451 | Livarius | fran |
| 1936 | Llatje, fr J. | spai |
| 1678 | Lloyd, John | brit |
| 1937 | Lo Pa Hong | chin |
| 1992 | Locatelli, A. | rwan |
| 1998 | Loften, pastor A. | usa |
| 1918 | Longin, pastor | russ |
| 1976 | Longueville, fr G. | arge |
| 1996 | Loperena Soto OP, fr W. | puer |
| 1989 | Lopez Lopez SJ, fr J. | elsa |
| 1989 | Lopez SJ, fr A. | elsa |
| 1623 | Lopez, fr B. | hond |
| 1582 | Lopez, fr F. | usa |
| 1976 | Lopez, fr H. | guat |
| 1560 | Lorenzo, fr F. | mexi |
| 1793 | Louis XVI | fran |
| 1998 | Louis, fr J-P. | hait |
| 1651 | Love, pastor Christopher | brit |
| 1837 | Lovejoy, Elijah P. | usa |
| 1847 | Lowrie, Walter M. | chin |
| 1996 | Luc, Father | alge |
| 1612 | Lucas of Tokyo | japa |
| 1564 | Lucas, br | mexi |
| 312 | Lucian of Antioch | turk |
| 1996 | Lucio, br M. A. I. | conz |
| 1996 | Lucio, sr M. A. I. | conz |
| 180 | Lucitas | tuni |
| c171 | Lucius | ital |
| 259 | Lucius | tuni |
| 303 | Lucy | ital |
| c1985 | Ludena, T. | peru |
| 1886 | Ludigo, Adolphus Mukasa | ugan |
| 916 | Ludmilla | czec |
| 96 | Luke the Evangelist | gree |
| 1802 | Luke the New | gree |
| 1992 | Lukkappa, sadhu | indi |
| 1315 | Lull, Ramon | alge |
| 1978 | Lunkebein, fr R. | braz |
| 1976 | Lunkenbein, fr R. | braz |
| 1936 | Luque, fr E. | spai |
| 1975 | Lutsky, fr M. | ukra |
| 1977 | Luwum, abp Janani | ugan |
| 1886 | Lwanga, Charles | ugan |
| 1834 | Lyman, H. | indo |
| 1978 | Lynn, R. & J. & Pamela | zimb |
| 1978 | Lynn, J. | zimb |
| 1978 | Lynn, Pamela | zimb |
| 1938 | Lypkivsky, V., metropolitan | ukra |
| 1860 | Mabeiche, br A. H. | leba |
| 1617 | Macaido, fr J. B. | japa |
| 451 | Macari of Edko, bp | egyp |
| c305 | Macarius | egyp |
| 455 | Macarius of Tkow, bp | egyp |
| 1906 | Macdonald, dr R. J. | chin |
| 511 | Macedonius II, patriarch | turk |
| 1990 | Mack, Myrna | guat |
| 1995 | Maclese, sr P. | ghan |
| 1634 | Maddalena of Nagasaki | japa |
| 275 | Magnus, bp of Fabrateria | ital |
| 1116 | Magnus, earl of Orkney | brit |
| 1997 | Magomedov, H & T. | russ |
| 1990 | Magorrian, H.L. | soua |
| c1995 | Mahamed, S. | soma |
| 1953 | Maina, E. | keny |
| 1989 | Maire, fr G.F. | braz |
| 484 | Majoricus | tuni |
| 1996 | Makaboge, moderator E. | soua |
| 1918 | Makarov, M. | russ |
| 1944 | Makary, abp | russ |
| 1919 | Makary, bp of Viazma | russ |
| c295 | Makrawi, bp of Nikiou | egyp |
| 1860 | Maksoud, br H. | leba |
| 1992 | Mal-Allah, S.A.K. | saud |
| 1761 | Malagrida, fr G. | port |
| 1989 | Malalay, fr D. | phil |
| 1811 | Malati, Muallim | egyp |
| c260 | Malchus | pale |
| 1680 | Maldonado, fr L. | usa |
| 1998 | Malenga, E. | conz |
| 1998 | Malesh, pastor J. | suda |
| 1936 | Malla, C. J. | spai |
| 1985 | Maluendo, J. M. P. | chil |
| 274 | Mamas | turk |
| 1990 | Mamma, pr | suda |
| 1998 | Mandro, J-F. K. | conz |
| 1972 | Manganhela, Z. | moza |
| 1900 | Mangin, fr L. I. | chin |
| 1992 | Maniafo, S.J. | keny |
| 1985 | Manielpillai, fr M.B. | sril |
| 1993 | Manping, Lai | chin |
| 1989 | Mansalve, bp Jesus E.J. | colo |
| 1527 | Manz, F. | neth |
| 1982 | Manzinger, fr | belo |
| 202 | Marcella | egyp |
| 410 | Marcella | ital |
| 1997 | Marcellina, sr A. T. S. | paki |
| 413 | Marcellinus Flavius, tribune | tuni |
| 178 | Marcellus | ital |
| 298 | Marcellus the Centurion | moro |
| 309 | Marcellus, pope | ital |
| 1835 | Marchand, fr J. | viet |
| 347 | Marculus, bp of S. Numidia | tuni |
| 305 | Marcus | egyp |
| 1176 | Marguerite of Roeskilde | denm |
| 1995 | Maria, sr Rani | indi |
| 66 | Mariam of Houssik | arme |
| 259 | Marian | tuni |
| 259 | Marianus | tuni |
| 1601 | Marin, fr Esteban | phil |
| 278 | Marina | turk |
| 1634 | Marina di Omura | japa |
| 262 | Marinus | pale |
| 68 | Mark the Evangelist | egyp |
| 1801 | Mark the New | gree |
| c364 | Mark, bp of Arethusa | ital |
| c1700 | Markel, br | russ |
| 1847 | Marmoiton, br | newc |
| 1998 | Marrero, mgr A. G. | vene |
| 1993 | Marsouk, H. | egyp |
| 1339 | Martel, Peter | chin |
| 346 | Martha | iraq |
| 66 | Martha of Makovtir | arme |
| c650 | Martin I, pope | ukra |
| 1989 | Martin-Baro SJ, fr I. | elsa |
| 1566 | Martinez SJ, fr P. | usa |
| 1928 | Martinez, br H. | mexi |
| 1936 | Martinez, fr B. | spai |
| 1934 | Martinez, fr E. | spai |
| c1956 | Martinuzzi, abp of Estergom | hung |
| 397 | Martyrius | ital |
| 346 | Mary | iraq |
| 851 | Mary of Cordoba | spai |
| 1860 | Masi, Francis | syri |
| 1860 | Masi, Muti | syri |
| 1860 | Masi, Raphael | syri |
| 1995 | Masih, Iqbal | paki |
| 1995 | Masih, Javed | paki |
| 1994 | Masih, Manzoor | paki |
| 2000 | Masih, Mushtaq | indi |
| 1999 | Massoud, Magdi F. | egyp |
| 1987 | Massé SJ, fr André | leba |
| 1968 | Masters, P. | indo |
| 1996 | Mataboge, rev E. | soua |
| 1983 | Matenje | mala |
| 1996 | Mathias, mrs. C. | usa |
| 1996 | Mathias, pastor C. & wife | usa |
| 249 | Matra | egyp |
| c70 | Matthew (Levi), Apostle | iraq |
| 1400 | Matthew of Escandel | chin |
| 64 | Matthias, Apostle | turk |
| 1534 | Matthys, Jan | germ |
| 1997 | Matti, Haval | iraq |
| 1991 | Matti, Lazar | iraq |
| 1962 | Matulionis, bp of Kaisiadorys | lith |
| 1839 | Maubant, fr P. | souk |
| 287 | Maurice | swit |
| 1886 | Mawaggali, Noe | ugan |
| 304 | Maxima | tuni |
| 347 | Maximian | tuni |
| 295 | Maximilian | alge |
| 178 | Maximus | ital |
| 662 | Maximus the Confessor, abbot | geor |
| 1950 | Maxville, Selma M. | myan |
| 1577 | Mayne, C. | brit |
| 1936 | Mayorga, fr M. | spai |
| 1981 | Mazeika, fr L. | lith |
| 1940 | Mazeika, L. | lith |
| 1855 | Mazzuconi, fr G. | papu |
| 1992 | Mbatha, S'Khumbuzo | soua |
| 1996 | McAleese, sr P. | ghan |
| c1965 | McBeth, fr | bang |
| 1978 | McCann, P. & S. & Joy | zimb |
| 1978 | McCann, Joy | zimb |
| 1978 | McCann, S. | zimb |
| 1991 | McCormack, sr Irene | peru |
| 1956 | McCully, E. | ecua |
| 1992 | McGuire, sr K. | libe |
| 1650 | McMahon, bp E. | irel |
| 1964 | McMillan, H. | conz |
| 1963 | McNair, Denise | usa |
| 861 | Meinrad of Einsiedeln, hermit | swit |
| 1972 | Melnikov | russ |
| 1689 | Membre, fr Z. | usa |
| 1661 | Menard, fr R. | usa |
| 631 | Menas | egyp |
| c717 | Menas of Al-Ashmunayn | egyp |
| 296 | Menas the Miracle Maker | egyp |
| 305 | Menas, governor | egyp |
| 1962 | Mendes, evangelist Formoso | gunb |
| 1553 | Mendez, fr H. | usa |
| 1571 | Mendez, fr J. B. | usa |
| 1961 | Mendez, Juana F. | arge |
| 1990 | Menn, fr Alexander | russ |
| 1120 | Merbot | ausz |
| c356 | Mercurius | egyp |
| 254 | Mercurius | brit |
| 1990 | Meri, dean Harald | esto |
| 311 | Methodius, bp of Olympus | turk |
| 1921 | Methody, bp of Petropavlovsk | russ |
| 1944 | Metzger, fr M. J. | germ |
| 1943 | Meyer, F. & 11 missionaries | phil |
| c1180 | Michael of Damietta | syri |
| 1998 | Michaela, sr | yeme |
| 1994 | Michaelian, pastor Tateos | iran |
| 1601 | Middleton, fr R. | brit |
| 1989 | Mien, fr Alexander | russ |
| 180 | Miggin | tuni |
| 1578 | Miguel de Medina | spai |
| 1997 | Mihingo, rev N. | conz |
| 1937 | Mikael, bp | ethi |
| 1400 | Mikhail Abu Mokaitef | egyp |
| c1930 | Mikhail, bp of Slutsk | byel |
| 1597 | Miki SJ, fr Paul | japa |
| 1993 | Mikic OFM, fr L. | bosn |
| 1993 | Milicevic OFM, fr N. | bosn |
| c305 | Milius | egyp |
| 1999 | Miller, Carla | usa |
| 1981 | Miller, fr J. | guat |
| 1999 | Miller, Jr., Shon | usa |
| 1918 | Miniatov, lawyer | russ |
| 1631 | Miranda, fr P. | usa |
| 1869 | Mirza Ibrahim | iran |
| 1962 | Mitchell, A. | viet |
| 1918 | Mitrophan, abp of Astrakhan | russ |
| 1996 | Miville OCSO, br P. F. | alge |
| 1896 | Mizeki, Bernard, catechist | zimb |
| 1918 | Modest, fr | russ |
| c302 | Modestus | ital |
| 1991 | Mohammed, br | nige |
| 1974 | Moiseyevich, pastor I. | russ |
| 1918 | Mokovsky, pastor G. & wife | russ |
| 1450 | Moleyns, A., bp of Chichester | brit |
| 1314 | Monold of Ancona | arme |
| 1989 | Monsalve, bp Jesus E. J. | colo |
| 259 | Montanus | tuni |
| 1647 | Montero, fr F. | mexi |
| 1989 | Montes SJ, fr S. | elsa |
| 1887 | Moran, fr J. | togo |
| 1535 | More, Thomas | brit |
| 1961 | Moreau, fr Yvon Emmanuel | hait |
| 1985 | Moreira SJ, fr S. | moza |
| 1815 | Morelos y Pavon, fr J. M. | mexi |
| 1696 | Moreno, fr A. | usa |
| 1781 | Moreno, fr J. M. | usa |
| 1986 | Moreno, Norma | mexi |
| 1934 | Moreno, Ramonita | arge |
| 1985 | Moretto, fr J. | ango |
| c1682 | Morozova, Boyarina | russ |
| 1645 | Morse, fr H. | brit |
| c197 | Moses | ital |
| 523 | Moses of Yemen | yeme |
| 1921 | Moslovsky, pastor J. | russ |
| 1996 | Mounabandi, sr C | conz |
| 1400 | Moussa, monk | egyp |
| 1996 | Mpengekeze, fr Y. | buru |
| 1822 | Muallim Ghali | egyp |
| 1801 | Muallim Malati | egyp |
| 1992 | Mueller, sr S. | libe |
| 1886 | Mugagga | ugan |
| c310 | Mui | egyp |
| 1998 | Mukagakwaya, sr X. | rwan |
| 1997 | Mukamihogo, sr F. | conz |
| 1998 | Mukamuhire, sr B. | rwan |
| 1998 | Mukanoheli, sr V. | rwan |
| 1885 | Mukasa, Joseph | ugan |
| 1996 | Mukeshimana, sr A. | rwan |
| 1973 | Mukhana, J. | ugan |
| 1952 | Mungai, J. | keny |
| 1944 | Munk, pastor Kaj | denm |
| 1834 | Munson, Samuel | indo |

*Continued opposite*

*Table 4–11 continued*

| | | |
|---|---|---|
| 1998 | Muntoni, fr G. | ital |
| 1997 | Munyakazy, rev E. | conz |
| 1996 | Munyankuyu, fr A. | conz |
| 1525 | Munzer, T. | germ |
| 1996 | Munzihirwa, abp C. | conz |
| 1996 | Munzombo, pasotr D. | conz |
| 1983 | Muothe, I.T. | soua |
| 1952 | Muriuki, W. | keny |
| 1684 | Muros, fr | mexi |
| 1798 | Murphy, fr J. | irel |
| 1996 | Murphy, sr C. | ghan |
| 1976 | Musaka, fr | ugan |
| 1994 | Musheng, Zheng | chin |
| 1992 | Muttra, sr B.A. | libe |
| 1997 | Muyoboke, rev F. | conz |
| 1887 | Muzeyi, Jean-Marie | ugan |
| c300 | Nabraha | egyp |
| 1922 | Nadezhdin, pastor | russ |
| 1628 | Nagascima SJ, br M. | japa |
| c304 | Naharuh | egyp |
| 1998 | Nakavoua, G. A. | cong |
| 180 | Namphano | tuni |
| 285 | Naou | egyp |
| 1680 | Naranjo, B. | usa |
| 180 | Nartzalus | tuni |
| 852 | Natalia | spai |
| 304 | Natalia of Nicomedia | turk |
| 1977 | Navarro, fr A. | elsa |
| 1921 | Nazary, metrop of Kutaisi | geor |
| 1996 | Ndacikiriwe, sr C. | buru |
| 1996 | Ndihokubwayo, sr L. | buru |
| c550 | Nectan | brit |
| 1997 | Nedumattahil, fr J. | indi |
| 1972 | Nee, Watchman | chin |
| 1862 | Neel, J. P. | chin |
| 1578 | Nelson, fr J. | brit |
| 1943 | Nemantsevich, exarch A. | byel |
| c100 | Nereus | ital |
| 1756 | Nerini, fr | myan |
| 373 | Nerses I, catholicos | arme |
| 250 | Nestor, bp of Perga | turk |
| 451 | Nestorius, patriarch | jord |
| 1679 | Nevill, fr F. | brit |
| 1996 | Ngabo SJ, abp C. M. M. | conz |
| 1886 | Ngondwe, Pontian | ugan |
| 1975 | Nguyen, Huy Mai | viet |
| 1975 | Nguyen, Van Hoa | viet |
| 1950 | Nguyen, pastor | viet |
| 1996 | Ngwije, fr A. K. | rwan |
| 1905 | Ni, evangelist | chin |
| 969 | Nicephorus, emperor | gree |
| c370 | Nicetas | roma |
| 1227 | Nicholas | moro |
| 1555 | Nicholas Novi of Sophia | bulg |
| 1754 | Nicholas of Chios | gree |
| 1990 | Nicholson, sr A.C. | ango |
| c300 | Nicostratus | ital |
| 1998 | Nielsen, B. M. | buru |
| 1994 | Nieto, F. A. E. | peru |
| c294 | Nikander | bulg |
| c1938 | Nikandr, metrop of Odessa | russ |
| 1919 | Nikodim, bp of Belgorod | russ |
| 1961 | Nikolai, metrop of Krutitsy | russ |
| 1938 | Nikon (Lebedev), bp | russ |
| 1938 | Nikon, bp of Belgorod | russ |
| 1996 | Nikwigize, bp P. | rwan |
| 304 | Nilus, bp | leba |
| 1996 | Nirere, fr B. | conz |
| 1634 | Nishi, fr T.H.R. | japa |
| 1918 | Nizza, L. | russ |
| 1989 | Nodrat, Zia Mohammed | afgh |
| 1868 | Noi Sunya | thai |
| 1869 | Non Chai, abbot | thai |
| 1622 | Novarra, fr P. P. | japa |
| 258 | Novatian, antipope | ital |
| 1994 | Nsengiyumva, abp V. | rwan |
| 1994 | Nsengiyumva, bp T. | rwan |
| 1996 | Nsengiyunva, fr E. | conz |
| 1994 | Nur al-Qums Binyamin | egyp |
| 1970 | Nyabadza, fr B. | zimb |
| 1997 | Nyirabakungu, sr C. | conz |
| 1997 | Nyirarukundu, sr M. | conz |
| 1926 | Nyirenda, Tomo | mala |
| 1975 | Nze, bp Abuy Raphael | equa |
| 2000 | Nzikobanyanka, rev P. | buru |
| 1651 | O'Brien, bp T. A. | irel |
| 1580 | O'Cullenan, G., abbot | irel |
| 1612 | O'Devany, C., bp | irel |
| 1575 | O'Donnell SJ, E. | irel |
| 1578 | O'Hely, P., bp | irel |
| 1584 | O'Hurley, D., abp | irel |
| 1995 | O'Neill, fr E. | soua |
| 1993 | Ocampo, cardinal Juan J.J.P. | mexi |
| 1861 | Ochoa, bp V. B. | viet |
| 1934 | Odongo, Alfayo | keny |
| 2000 | Ogbu, fr J.M.O. | nige |
| 1615 | Ogilvie SJ, J. | brit |
| 66 | Ogouhie, princess | arme |
| 1988 | Oido, fr C.O. | ugan |
| 1988 | Okagric, br A. | ugan |
| 1030 | Olav II Haraldsson, king | norw |
| 1418 | Oldcastle, Sir John | brit |
| 1619 | Oldenbarnevelt, J. van | neth |
| 1871 | Olivaint, fr P. | fran |
| 1968 | Olsen, Betty | viet |
| c301 | Olympius | egyp |
| 1795 | Oprea, Miclaus, monk | roma |
| 397 | Optatus, bp of Thamugadi | alge |
| 1948 | Ordacz, bp L. | hung |
| 254 | Origen | leba |
| 1922 | Orlov, pastor | russ |
| 1918 | Ornatsky, fr F. | russ |
| 1683 | Ortiz de Zarate, fr P. | arge |
| 1979 | Ortiz, fr Octavia | elsa |
| 110 | Oski | arme |
| 1974 | Ostapenko, pastor I.M. | russ |
| 642 | Oswald, king of Northumbria | brit |
| 651 | Oswin, king | brit |
| c65 | Osyth, queen | brit |
| 1622 | Ota, fr A. | japa |
| 1220 | Otho | moro |
| 1900 | Otu, Samuel | ghan |
| 1997 | Ozdemir, Ali | turk |
| 1954 | Pacha, bp | roma |
| 1583 | Pacheco, fr A. | indi |
| 1626 | Pacheco, fr F. | japa |
| 1993 | Packianathan, fr V.S. | indi |
| 1635 | Paes SJ, fr G. | ethi |
| c301 | Paese | egyp |
| 1988 | Paisai, G. | nepa |
| 1979 | Palacios, fr Rafael | elsa |
| 431 | Palladius | irel |
| 310 | Pamphilus | pale |
| 209 | Pamphilus | pale |
| 1383 | Panacea | ital |
| 304 | Pancras | ital |
| 1997 | Pande, evangelist M. | indi |
| c904 | Pandonia | brit |
| c290 | Panesneu, deacon | egyp |
| c313 | Pantaleon, physician | egyp |
| 130 | Papius | pale |
| c1898 | Papizian, archimandrite J. | turk |
| c170 | Papylus | turk |
| 1985 | Paredes, A.A. | ango |
| c260 | Paregorius | turc |
| 1987 | Park, Jong Ch'ol | souk |
| c98 | Parmenas the deacon | ital |
| 1339 | Pascal of Victoria | chin |
| c298 | Patape, bp of Coptos | egyp |
| 1972 | Pate, Mavis | pale |
| c260 | Patroclus | fran |
| 426 | Patroclus of Arles, primate | fran |
| 1871 | Patteson, bp J. C. | solo |
| c290 | Paul of Egypt | egyp |
| 309 | Paul of Jamnia | pale |
| 64 | Paul, Apostle | ital |
| 351 | Paul, patriarch | turk |
| 1936 | Pavlivsky, I., metropolitan | ukra |
| 1936 | Payan, fr A. | spai |
| c300 | Pelagia | turk |
| 1999 | Peleman, fr A. | soua |
| 304 | Peleus, bp | leba |
| 1997 | Pena, fr S. C. | colo |
| 2000 | Pepe, fr R. | conz |
| 1840 | Perboyre, fr J. G. | chin |
| 1840 | Perboyre, fr Jean G. | chin |
| 1928 | Perez, fr P. | mexi |
| 1627 | Perez, fr R. | cost |
| 1997 | Perez, M. | mexi |
| 850 | Perfectus of Cordoba | spai |
| 420 | Peroz | iraq |
| 202 | Perpetua | tuni |
| 1995 | Petcu, A. | mold |
| 1220 | Peter | moro |
| 311 | Peter I Ieromartyros, patriarch | egyp |
| 1133 | Peter of Bruys | fran |
| 1208 | Peter of Castelnau, legate | fran |
| 1365 | Peter of Ruffia | ital |
| 1321 | Peter of Siena | indi |
| 1252 | Peter of Verona (Peter Martyr) | ital |
| 1929 | Peter, abp of Voronezh | russ |
| 1936 | Peter, metropolitan of Krutitsy | russ |
| 448 | Pethiun, evangelist | iraq |
| 1937 | Petros, bp | ethi |
| 1936 | Peypoch, fr E. | spai |
| 1992 | Pfister, J. | ivor |
| 1950 | Phan Long, pastor | viet |
| 345 | Pherbutha | iraq |
| 1922 | Philaret, bp of Kostroma | russ |
| 304 | Phileas, bp of Thmuis | egyp |
| c290 | Philemon | egyp |
| 304 | Philip bp of Heraclea | turk |
| 1934 | Philip, abp | russ |
| 60 | Philip, Apostle | turk |
| 1567 | Philip, metropolitan of Moscow | russ |
| 297 | Philotheus of Antioch | turk |
| 518 | Philoxenus, bp of Mabbogh | iraq |
| 1985 | Philpot, J. | mexi |
| 1555 | Philpot, J., archdeacon | brit |
| c292 | Phiobammon of Preht | egyp |
| c120 | Phocas, bp of Bontos | ital |
| 315 | Phrebonia | iraq |
| 1978 | Picken, C. | zimb |
| 1679 | Pickering, T. | brit |
| 1569 | Pietersz, Pieter | neth |
| 1900 | Pigott, J. | chin |
| 1900 | Pigott, T. W. & J. | chin |
| 1897 | Pilkington, G. L. | ugan |
| 1752 | Pillai, D. | indi |
| 1919 | Pimen, bp of Verny | russ |
| 1992 | Pimentel, sr M. | ango |
| 1997 | Pinard WF, fr Guy | rwan |
| 1794 | Pinot, fr N. | fran |
| 1860 | Pinzano OFM, Francis | syri |
| 1680 | Pio, fr J. B. | usa |
| 250 | Pionius | turk |
| c288 | Piroou | egyp |
| c260 | Piscus | pale |
| c302 | Pisura, bp of Masil | egyp |
| 1938 | Pitirim, abp | russ |
| 1900 | Pitkin, H. T. | chin |
| 1991 | Plumey OMI, abp I. | came |
| 1681 | Plunket, primate O. | brit |
| 1649 | Plunkett, earl C. | brit |
| 1697 | Plunkett, fr C. | usa |
| 1825 | Pogio, fr Bartolome | arge |
| 1934 | Poliansky, abp Ambrose | kaza |
| 304 | Pollio | hung |
| 1918 | Polotnikov, abp of Petrograd | russ |
| 156 | Polycarp, bp of Smyrna | turk |
| 1794 | Polydorus the Cypriot | gree |
| c250 | Polyeuctus | arme |
| 1934 | Pommer, John, abp of Riga | latv |
| 853 | Pomposa | spai |
| 1704 | Ponce de Leon, fr A. | usa |
| 1619 | Pongracz SJ, fr S. | hung |
| 235 | Pontian, pope | ital |
| 177 | Ponticus | fran |
| c260 | Pontius | fran |
| 1984 | Popieluszko, fr J. | pola |
| 1985 | Poplawski, fr P. | pola |
| 1992 | Poppa, sr R. | rwan |
| 1310 | Porete, Marguerite | fran |
| c306 | Porphry | egyp |
| 309 | Porphyrius | pale |
| 1633 | Porras, fr F. | usa |
| 1993 | Posadas, cardinal J.J. | mexi |
| 1918 | Pospelov, abp G. | russ |
| 207 | Potamiana | egyp |
| 305 | Potamon of Heracla | egyp |
| 177 | Pothinus, bp | fran |
| 1984 | Potochnyak, fr A. | ukra |
| 1971 | Potter, Nancy | domr |
| 1971 | Potter, Paul E. & Nancy | domr |
| 1619 | Poulain, fr G. | cana |
| 1646 | Powel, fr. P. | brit |
| 1991 | Prada Pires, fr J.M. | braz |
| 586 | Praetextatus, bp of Rouen | fran |
| 1952 | Prennushi, abp N. | alba |
| 1995 | Prevost, sr O. | alge |
| 1900 | Price, Charles & Eva | chin |
| 1900 | Price, Eva | chin |
| 1644 | Price, fr Robert | brit |
| c297 | Primus | ital |
| 386 | Priscillian, bp | spai |
| c260 | Privatus | fran |
| 1990 | Priya SMA, sr | indi |
| 1927 | Pro Juarez, fr M. | mexi |
| 304 | Probus | brit |
| 303 | Procopius | pale |
| c305 | Procopius, governor | egyp |
| 1800 | Prosser, Gabriel | usa |
| 165 | Protase | ital |
| 459 | Proterius, patriarch | egyp |
| c306 | Psote of Psoi | egyp |
| c171 | Ptolemaus | ital |
| c171 | Publius, bp of Athens | ital |
| 202 | Pudens | ital |
| 1623 | Puerta, fr C.M. | hond |
| 1993 | Puglisi, pastor G. | ital |
| 339 | Pusak, prefect, & 100 clergy | iraq |
| 341 | Pusicius | iraq |
| 1682 | Pustosviat, Nikita | russ |
| 1998 | Puttaniyil, br L. | indi |
| 286 | Qndyr, queen | iraq |
| c258 | Quadratus, bp | tuni |
| 259 | Quartillosia | tuni |
| 1981 | Quilini, H. N. | egyp |
| 1998 | Quinn, Jason | brit |
| 1998 | Quinn, Mark | brit |
| 1998 | Quinn, Richard | brit |
| 1812 | Quintana, fr A. | usa |
| 1490 | Rabata, A. | ital |
| 1918 | Radion, fr | russ |
| 1981 | Raflan, B. | egyp |
| c870 | Ragener | brit |
| 1834 | Rainitsiandavaka | mada |
| c490 | Rajden | geor |
| 1998 | Rajiv, John | indi |
| 1724 | Rale SJ, fr S. | cana |
| 1996 | Ramanauskas, fr V. | lith |
| 1959 | Ramanauskas, P., bp of Telsiai | lith |
| 1988 | Ramaralahy, br I. | mada |
| 2000 | Ramirez, fr A.G. | colo |
| 1989 | Ramon Moreno SJ, fr J. | elsa |
| 1997 | Ramos SJ, fr W. G. | mexi |
| 1993 | Ramos, bp Robert J. | elsa |
| 1572 | Ramus, Peter | fran |
| 1995 | Rangell, Hugo | colo |
| 1837 | Rasalama | mada |
| 1945 | Rauschenbach MM, fr O. A. | chin |
| 1595 | Rawlins, A. | brit |
| c300 | Rebecca of Sunbat | egyp |
| 1652 | Redemptus of the Cross, br | indo |
| 1942 | Redlich, V. | papu |
| 1571 | Redondo, fr C. | usa |
| 287 | Regula | swit |
| 1974 | Reimer, G. | pana |
| 1989 | Reinkemeyer, sr A. | keny |
| 1953 | Reinys, M., abp of Vilnius | lith |
| 1680 | Rendon, fr M. | usa |
| 259 | Renus | tuni |
| 1661 | Renwick, J. | brit |
| c308 | Repsima & 78 companions | arme |
| 1989 | Restrepo, fr S. | colo |
| 202 | Revocatus | tuni |
| 1847 | Rey SJ, fr A. | mexi |
| 1964 | Rhine, Phyllis | conz |
| 1839 | Ri, J. | souk |
| 1918 | Riabuhin, pastor J. | russ |
| 1775 | Ricci SJ, general L. | ital |
| 1992 | Ricci, fr F. | ethi |
| 1339 | Richard, bp of Almalik | chin |
| 1553 | Ridley, bp Nicholas | brit |
| 1996 | Ringeard OCSO, fr C. | alge |
| 1626 | Rinscei, P. | japa |
| 1997 | Rio, pastor W. | phil |
| 1989 | Rivera, Rufino | phil |
| 1896 | Rizal, Jose | phil |
| c1780 | Rizk Agha, vizier | egyp |
| 1611 | Roberts, fr. J. | brit |
| 1963 | Robertson, Carole | usa |
| 1992 | Robinson, W. | leba |
| c1350 | Roch, healer | fran |
| 2000 | Rochester, fr H. | jama |
| 1987 | Rodrigo OMI, fr Miguel | sril |
| 1638 | Rodrigues SJ, fr F. | ethi |
| 1961 | Rodrigues, deacon Pedro | ango |
| 1582 | Rodriguez, fr A. | usa |
| 1970 | Rodriguez, fr Nicolas | elsa |
| 1642 | Roe, Alban | brit |
| 1985 | Rojas, C.M. | peru |
| 1999 | Rojas, fr H. F. | colo |
| 1985 | Romano, fr R. | phil |
| c1650 | Romanul, Ioan Valahul | roma |
| 884 | Rombout of Malines | belg |
| 1980 | Romero, abp Oscar | elsa |
| 1985 | Romero, fr A. | phil |
| 1645 | Romero, fr P. | para |
| 1947 | Romza, bp T. | ukra |
| 1989 | Rosales, sr Teresa | nica |
| 1985 | Rossiter, fr J. | usa |
| 1985 | Roth, F. | usa |
| 1849 | Roth, pastor S. L. | roma |
| 1981 | Rother, fr S. | guat |
| 1936 | Rovira, fr J. | spai |
| 1984 | Roxas, S. | phil |
| 1984 | Roy, fr | mada |
| 1974 | Rozanov, N. | russ |
| 1642 | Rubino, fr | japa |
| 1080 | Rudolf of Swabia | ital |
| 1989 | Ruelo, pastor Z. | phil |
| 1339 | Ruff, Raymond | chin |
| 258 | Rufina | ital |
| 115 | Rufus | gree |
| 1996 | Ruhuna, J., abp of Gitega | buru |
| 1995 | Ruibal, pastor Julio C. | colo |
| 1860 | Ruiz OFM, fr Emmanuel | syri |
| 1637 | Ruiz, L. | japa |
| 1997 | Ruiz, pastor N. H. | mexi |
| 259 | Rusticus | fran |
| 1997 | Ruterahagusha, pastor T. | rwan |
| 1997 | Ruterahagusha, T. | rwan |
| 1994 | Rutumbu, fr J. | rwan |
| 1994 | Ruzindana, bp J. | rwan |
| 1998 | Rwangeyo, sr D. | rwan |
| 1922 | Rybalkin, monk Fyodor | russ |
| 1992 | Saah, pastor D. | libe |
| 372 | Sabas the Goth | roma |
| 1996 | Sabuni, pastor M. | conz |
| 1626 | Sadamatzu, G. | japa |
| 1942 | Sadd, A. | kiri |
| 1998 | Saenz, J. D. | colo |
| 1992 | Sahihembo, Alfredo | ango |
| 1956 | Saint, Nate | ecua |
| 290 | Salahouni, Theodore | arme |
| 1976 | Salas, bp J. C. | camb |
| 1400 | Saleeb | egyp |
| 1593 | Sales, fr J. | fran |
| 1936 | Sales, V. | spai |
| c290 | Salfana | egyp |
| c800 | Salib | egyp |
| 1683 | Salinas, fr | arge |
| 1989 | Saltori, fr O. | moza |
| 1999 | Saluhaku, fr A. | ango |
| 1227 | Samuel | moro |
| 1981 | Samuel, bp Makary El-Souria | egyp |
| 66 | Samuel, satrap | arme |
| 1980 | Samwel, abp | ethi |
| 180 | Sanam | tuni |
| 1936 | Sanchez, fr J. | spai |
| 1696 | Sanchez, fr L. | usa |
| 851 | Sanctius of Cordoba | spai |
| 1622 | Sandaju, fr P. O. | japa |
| 66 | Sandoukhte, princess | arme |
| 1979 | Sangaya, J. | mala |
| 1963 | Sangueso, P. P. | arge |
| 1936 | Santaella, fr M. | spai |
| 1979 | Santi, fr G. | ugan |
| 1758 | Santiesteban, fr J. | usa |
| 1749 | Sanz, bp P. | chin |
| 1980 | Sapoka, fr L. | lith |
| 1995 | Saquic Vasquez, pastor M. | guat |
| c355 | Sarah | egyp |
| c197 | Sarah | ital |
| c290 | Sarah & children | egyp |
| 1795 | Sarai, Visarion, monk | roma |
| c287 | Sarapamon of Scetis, bp | egyp |
| 1921 | Sarichov, pastor S. | russ |
| 1620 | Sarkander, Jan | czec |
| 1991 | Sarmiento, M. | peru |
| 1995 | Saro-Wiwa, K. | nige |
| 1998 | Satchilombo, Francisco | ango |
| 1527 | Sattler, M. | germ |
| 1967 | Saturnino, fr | suda |
| 202 | Saturninus | tuni |
| 259 | Saturninus | fran |
| 202 | Saturus | tuni |
| 1593 | Saultemouche, fr W. | fran |
| 1992 | Saune, R. | peru |

*Continued overleaf*

*Table 4–11 concluded*

| | | |
|---|---|---|
| 1498 | Savonarola, G. | ital |
| 1401 | Sawtrey, W. | brit |
| 1983 | Sawyer, sr Joan | peru |
| 1979 | Sayyad, fr | iran |
| 1666 | Schall SJ, fr A. von Bell | chin |
| 1954 | Scheffler, bp | roma |
| 1996 | Schiavo, fr G. | tanz |
| 1534 | Schiemer, L., bp | germ |
| 1637 | Schiwozuka, fr V. | japa |
| 1944 | Schmidlin, professor J. | germ |
| 1976 | Schmitt, bp A. | zimb |
| 1988 | Schmitz, CP, fr Carl | phil |
| 1939 | Schneider, pasotr | germ |
| 1964 | Scholten, W.H. | conz |
| 1998 | Schreck, sr M. | soua |
| 1612 | Scott, fr. M. | brit |
| 1999 | Scott, Rachel | usa |
| 1996 | Sebalija, sr L. | conz |
| 1569 | Sebastian Cantu | thai |
| 288 | Sebastian of Milan | ital |
| 1886 | Sebuggwawo, Denis | ugan |
| 180 | Secunda | tuni |
| 258 | Secunda | ital |
| 304 | Secunda | tuni |
| 1978 | Sedletsky, V. | russ |
| 1886 | Seghers, abp C. J. | usa |
| 1952 | Selanuok | papu |
| 1977 | Selassie, emperor Haile | ethi |
| 309 | Seleucus | pale |
| 1995 | Sellekaerts IHM, sr C. | conz |
| 1997 | Selorio, pastor E. | phil |
| 123 | Semsoun, bp of Edessa | iraq |
| 1996 | Semutwe, sr M. A. | conz |
| 1736 | Senat SJ, fr A. | usa |
| 1953 | Seng, Joseph | chin |
| 309 | Sennen | ital |
| 1986 | Senter, L. & R. | libe |
| 1986 | Senter, R. | libe |
| 2000 | Sequeira, sr C. | paki |
| 1938 | Seraphim, bp | russ |
| 1932 | Seraphim, metro of Petrograd | russ |
| c365 | Serapion, bp of Thmuis | egyp |
| 1994 | Serech, P. | guat |
| 1929 | Serge, bp of Efremov | russ |
| 523 | Sergios | yeme |
| 315 | Sergius & Bacchus | syri |
| 1580 | Serrato, fr J. | mexi |
| 1886 | Serunkuma, Bruno | ugan |
| 484 | Servus | tuni |
| 1973 | Serwanika, J. | ugan |
| 524 | Severinus Boethius, consul | ital |
| 304 | Severus | turk |
| 1929 | Seybold, fr C. | chin |
| 1993 | Shafiq, S. | egyp |
| 1991 | Shaga, Nana | ethi |
| 342 | Shahdost, catholicos | iraq |
| 309 | Shamona | turk |
| 112 | Sharbil | turk |
| c1995 | Sheekhdoon, M. | soma |
| c1968 | Sheikow, Musa | soma |
| 1922 | Shein, S. | russ |
| 1980 | Shelkov, V. A. | russ |
| 1588 | Shelley, F. | brit |
| c299 | Shenufe | egyp |
| c299 | Shenute | egyp |
| 1830 | Shidiak, Asaad | leba |
| 1975 | Shimun, catholicos-patriarch | iraq |
| c650 | Shinudah, anba | egyp |
| 1979 | Shorrosh, A. | pale |
| 1984 | Shude SJ, fr F.Z. | chin |
| c473 | Shushanik, queen | geor |
| 1998 | Siahae, J. | indo |
| 1857 | Sibour, abp of Paris | fran |
| 1910 | Sidhom Bishai, deacon | egyp |
| 1714 | Sidotti, abbot G. B. | japa |
| 1400 | Sidrak, priest, & 5 monks | egyp |
| 1972 | Sidumo, J. | moza |
| 1997 | Sifer, M. H. | iraq |
| 1991 | Sigridsson, S. | phil |
| 1985 | Sikufinde, fr L. | ango |
| 1749 | Silva, fr F. X. | usa |
| 304 | Silvanus | syri |
| 537 | Silverius, pope | ital |
| 1998 | Simatupang, T. M. | indo |
| c800 | Simeon | egyp |
| 341 | Simeon Barsabae, catholicos | iraq |
| 1975 | Simescu, br | roma |
| 2000 | Simionato, sr G. | buru |
| 64 | Simon Peter, Apostle | ital |
| 61 | Simon Zelotes, Apostle | iraq |
| 1921 | Simon, bp of Ufa | russ |
| 1936 | Simon, fr A. | spai |
| 1597 | Simon, mar, metropolitan | indi |
| c300 | Simplicius | ital |
| c300 | Simpronian | ital |
| 1932 | Simpson, W. E. | chin |
| 1945 | Simrak, bp J. | croa |
| 1995 | Sinankwa, fr M. | buru |
| 448 | Sirin | iraq |
| 397 | Sisinnius | ital |
| 1936 | Sitjar, fr T. | spai |
| 1908 | Sivila, Visitación | arge |
| c117 | Sixtus I, bp of Rome | ital |
| 258 | Sixtus II, pope | ital |
| 1979 | Siyah, pastor Aristou | iran |
| 1918 | Skipetrov, fr A. | russ |
| 1940 | Skobtsova, mother M. | pola |
| 1982 | Smith, E. | nica |
| 1844 | Smith, Hyrum | usa |
| 1844 | Smith, Joseph | usa |
| 1908 | Sofiisky, exarch abp N. | geor |
| 1795 | Sofronie of Cioara, monk | roma |
| 1996 | Sokan, Khoun | camb |
| 1922 | Sokolov, pastor | russ |
| 1861 | Sokolskij, abp J. | russ |
| 1995 | Solan, Joel | phil |
| 1859 | Soler, fr P. | syri |
| 1950 | Son Yang Won, pastor | nork |
| 1918 | Sontag, apostolic delegate | iraq |
| 1990 | Soodmand, pastor H. | iran |
| c140 | Sophia | egyp |
| c286 | Sophronius | egyp |
| 1985 | Sorgon OCD, fr S. | mada |
| 1996 | Soto OP, fr W. L. | puer |
| 1729 | Souel, fr J. | usa |
| 110 | Soukias & companions | arme |
| 1595 | Southwell, fr R. | brit |
| 1654 | Southworth, fr J. | brit |
| 1991 | Speers, J. | phil |
| 180 | Speratus | tuni |
| 1988 | Spil MHM, fr C. | ugan |
| 1622 | Spinola SJ, fr C. | japa |
| 1941 | Sri-Phong, catechist P. | thai |
| 1998 | Sritharan, pastor Vasu | sril |
| 1999 | Staines, Graham | indi |
| 1999 | Staines, Philip | indi |
| 1999 | Staines, Timothy | indi |
| 1934 | Stam, Betty | chin |
| 1934 | Stam, John & Betty | chin |
| 1079 | Stanislas, bp of Cracow | pola |
| 1990 | Stanton, fr N. | soua |
| 1918 | Stavrovsky, fr A. | russ |
| 1997 | Stegar, Kayce | usa |
| 1942 | Stein, Edith | pola |
| 1942 | Stein, Rosa | pola |
| 1293 | Stepanos IV, patriarch | arme |
| 257 | Stephen I, pope | ital |
| 1334 | Stephen of Gross-Wardein | roma |
| 1288 | Stephen of Hungary | geor |
| 1242 | Stephen of Narbonne | fran |
| 347 | Stephen of Ulnia | arme |
| 36 | Stephen the Deacon | pale |
| 764 | Stephen the Younger, abbot | turk |
| 284 | Stephen, archdeacon | egyp |
| 1961 | Stepinac, cardinal abp A. | croa |
| 1988 | Stockton, Ann | phil |
| 1539 | Stone, J. | brit |
| 1856 | Strang, James J. | usa |
| 1991 | Strzalkowski, fr Z. | peru |
| 1990 | Stumpf, H. | keny |
| c810 | Subaljesu, monk | iraq |
| 1948 | Suciu, bp | roma |
| 422 | Suenas | iraq |
| 1900 | Sun Hwe Teh | chin |
| 1929 | Sundar Singh, sadhu | chin |
| 1950 | Sung Du, fr | nork |
| 451 | Suzanne | arme |
| 1981 | Svanda, fr P. | czec |
| 1999 | Sweva, sr | sier |
| 1990 | Sylvia SMA, sr | indi |
| 108 | Symeon, bp of Jerusalem | pale |
| c190 | Symphorian | fran |
| 1600 | Tadaoki, Gracia | japa |
| 1680 | Talbot, P., abp of Dublin | irel |
| 1734 | Tamaral, fr N. | mexi |
| 448 | Tamasgerd | iraq |
| 1975 | Tamonis, M. | lith |
| 870 | Tancred | brit |
| 1811 | Tapeng, J. C. | chin |
| 1942 | Tapiedi, Lucian | papu |
| 304 | Tarachus | brit |
| c300 | Taragus & companions | turk |
| 339 | Tarbo, deaconess | iraq |
| 1936 | Tarrats, J. | spai |
| c280 | Tarsicius | ital |
| 1988 | Tarzwell, John | paki |
| c228 | Tatiana, deaconess | ital |
| 1991 | Tattersall, N. | peru |
| 1524 | Tauber, Casper | ausz |
| c301 | Tecula | egyp |
| 1690 | Tegananokoa, S. | usa |
| 1971 | Tejerina, Silvita A. | arge |
| 1922 | Telegin, A. | russ |
| 391 | Telemachus | ital |
| 138 | Telesphorus, bp of Rome | ital |
| 1936 | Tena, fr R. | spai |
| 1981 | Teodosiu, S. | roma |
| 1975 | Tep Im, bp Paolo | camb |
| 1982 | Terelya, B.M. | ukra |
| 66 | Terentius | arme |
| 1990 | Tete, president Martin | indi |
| 284 | Thalelaeus | turk |
| c125 | Thalelaeus | turk |
| c50 | Thecla | turk |
| 220 | Theodorus of Peshotep | egyp |
| c306 | Theodorus, bp of Pentapolis | egyp |
| c725 | Theodosia | turk |
| 1918 | Theodot | russ |
| 258 | Theodotus | egyp |
| c117 | Theodulus | ital |
| 309 | Theodulus | pale |
| 1980 | Theofilas, patriarch | ethi |
| 1918 | Theophan, bp of Solikamsk | russ |
| 1993 | Theophiles, K.Y. | egyp |
| 1635 | Theophilus of Zakynthos | gree |
| c111 | Theopista | ital |
| 1950 | Thien Thi, pastor | viet |
| 1616 | Thomas | japa |
| 82 | Thomas (Didymus), Apostle | indi |
| 1170 | Thomas Becket, abp of Canter | brit |
| 1321 | Thomas of Tolentino | indi |
| 1997 | Thomas SJ, fr A. T. | indi |
| c900 | Thomas, bp of Damascus | syri |
| 1866 | Thomas, R. J. | souk |
| c306 | Tibarcius | egyp |
| 178 | Tiburtius | ital |
| 1919 | Tikhon, abp of Voronezh | russ |
| 1925 | Tikhon, patriarch | russ |
| c291 | Til, soldier | egyp |
| 1997 | Timmons, br L. | keny |
| c309 | Timothy of Memphis | egyp |
| 97 | Timothy, bp | turk |
| 1680 | Tinoco, fr M. | usa |
| 2000 | Tirelli, sr F. | zamb |
| 1989 | Tjibaou, Jean-Marie | newc |
| 1982 | Toj, Juan Garcia | guat |
| c295 | Tolemaeus | egyp |
| 1983 | Toma, pastor Nicolas | guat |
| 1991 | Tomaszek OFM, fr M. | peru |
| 1901 | Tomkins, pastor O. | papu |
| 1999 | Tomlin, John | usa |
| 1633 | Tomonaga OP, fr J. K. G. | japa |
| 1950 | Tong-Sin, fr | nork |
| 1984 | Torboli, fr S. | moza |
| 1949 | Tornay, fr M. | chin |
| c65 | Torquatus | spai |
| 1966 | Torres, fr Camilo | colo |
| 1977 | Torres, L.A. | elsa |
| 870 | Torthred | brit |
| 1933 | Tourian, abp Leontius | usa |
| 1803 | Toussaint-Louverture, F.D. | fran |
| 870 | Tova | brit |
| 1626 | Tozo, M. | japa |
| 1471 | Tresham, T. | brit |
| 1649 | Trevino de Sobremonte, T. | mexi |
| 1798 | Trieu, fr E. | viet |
| 1974 | Trochta, cardinal S. | czec |
| 1981 | Troyer, J.D. | guat |
| 643 | Trudpert | germ |
| 1981 | Tsachev, N.V. | bulg |
| 1997 | Tshisambu, fr F. | conz |
| 1992 | Tsotetsi, Saul | soua |
| 1627 | Tsuji, fr T. | japa |
| 1964 | Tucker, J. | conz |
| 1979 | Tumsa, Gudinsa | ethi |
| 1616 | Tunstall, fr. T. | brit |
| 1991 | Turati OFM, fr P. | soma |
| 1959 | Turcsanyi, msgr E. | hung |
| 1679 | Turner, fr A. | brit |
| 1831 | Turner, Nat | usa |
| 1886 | Tuzinde, Mbaga | ugan |
| 1997 | Twagirayezu, rev U. | conz |
| 1536 | Tyndale, William | belg |
| c310 | Tyrannio, bp of Tyre | turk |
| 1985 | Tzalam Coj, Manuel de Jesus | guat |
| 1852 | U, fr Moses Nya | myan |
| 345 | Uarda (Rose) | iraq |
| 1592 | Udall, J. | brit |
| c1200 | Uguzo (Lucio di Val Cavargna) | ital |
| 1984 | Ulcue Chocue, fr A. | colo |
| 1028 | Ulfrid | swed |
| 1999 | Umbarger, Deena M. | soma |
| 1940 | Urban SJ, fr J. | pola |
| 230 | Urban, pope | ital |
| c295 | Uri, priest of Shatanut | egyp |
| 287 | Urs | swit |
| 538 | Ursicinus, bp of Ravenna | ital |
| 451 | Ursula & virgins | germ |
| 287 | Ursus of Solothurn | swit |
| c345 | Usaghniyus | egyp |
| 341 | Usthazanes | iraq |
| 1997 | Uwizeyimana, rev J. | conz |
| 2000 | Uzcudum, fr I. | rwan |
| c750 | Vahan of Goghtn | syri |
| 309 | Valens | pale |
| 1936 | Valenti, fr T. | spai |
| 269 | Valentine | ital |
| 178 | Valerian | ital |
| c306 | Valerianus | egyp |
| 1985 | Valerio, fr N. | phil |
| 1541 | Valverde OP, bp V. | peru |
| 1995 | Van Dyke, T. | colo |
| 1989 | Van Kleef CM, fr N. | pana |
| 1619 | Vanini, L. | ital |
| 451 | Vardan Mamikonian | arme |
| 1991 | Vargas, C. | peru |
| 1983 | Vargas, pastor N. | nica |
| 1919 | Varsonoufy, bp of Kirillov | russ |
| c1968 | Vasilyevna, M. | russ |
| 1950 | Vasquez, Carmen | arge |
| 1995 | Vasquez, pastor M.S. | guat |
| 1989 | Vassallo, sr Emanuela | liby |
| 1963 | Vaz Martins, evangelist Victor | gunb |
| 1861 | Venard, fr J. T. | viet |
| 1661 | Venner, Thomas | brit |
| 1597 | Verascola, fr F. | usa |
| 1918 | Veraskin, abp A. | russ |
| 1936 | Verges, fr J. | spai |
| 1817 | Vesey, Denmark | usa |
| 180 | Vestia | tuni |
| 177 | Vettius Epagathus | fran |
| 180 | Veturius | tuni |
| 1974 | Viaene, fr L. | conz |
| c305 | Victor | ital |
| c359 | Victor | egyp |
| 303 | Victor Maurus | ital |
| c301 | Victor of Asyut | egyp |
| 287 | Victor of Marseilles | swit |
| c287 | Victor of Solothurn | swit |
| c310 | Victor of Stratelates | ital |
| 484 | Victorian | tuni |
| 258 | Victorinus | fran |
| 304 | Victorinus, bp of Pettau | slov |
| 1634 | Vieira, fr S. | japa |
| 1625 | Viel, fr N. | cana |
| 689 | Vigilius, bp of Auxerre | fran |
| 1616 | Vincent | japa |
| 304 | Vincent of Saragossa | spai |
| 1645 | Vincent, catechist | viet |
| 1994 | Vincent, pastor Jean-Marie | hait |
| 1922 | Vishniakov, pastor | russ |
| 1962 | Vitti, A. | viet |
| c302 | Vitus | ital |
| 1918 | Vladimir, metropolitan of Kiev | ukra |
| 1948 | Volai, bp | alba |
| 1865 | Volkner, Carl S. | newz |
| 1860 | Volta OFM, fr. C. | syri |
| 476 | Volusianus, bp of Tours | fran |
| c1935 | von Moltke, Helmut | germ |
| c1976 | Voordeckers, fr W. | guat |
| 1943 | Voronaev, I. E. | russ |
| 1918 | Vostorgov, fr J. | russ |
| 931 | Vulfura | spai |
| 1631 | Wagner, fr Liborius | germ |
| 1987 | Wahid | paki |
| c289 | Wakhus | egyp |
| 1679 | Wall, fr John | brit |
| 1951 | Wallace, W.L. | chin |
| c1975 | Wallenburg, Raoul | pola |
| 1595 | Walpole, H. | brit |
| 1801 | Wan-Suk, Columba | souk |
| 1952 | Wancegi, Mary | keny |
| 1950 | Wang Ling-Tso, fr | chin |
| 1900 | Wang Ten Ren | chin |
| 1588 | Ward, Margaret | brit |
| 1979 | Wasikye, John, bp of Mbale | ugan |
| 1985 | Wasnak, fr J.E. | ango |
| 1535 | Webster, Augustine, prior | brit |
| 1989 | Webster, David | soua |
| 1920 | Weinberg, Judith | russ |
| 1716 | Weiss, prefect L. | ethi |
| 1995 | Welsh, S. | colo |
| 929 | Wenceslas, prince-duke | czec |
| 1795 | Wenmo, fr J. Z. | souk |
| 726 | Werenfrid | neth |
| 1963 | Wesley, Cynthia | usa |
| 1880 | Westrup, J. O. | mexi |
| 1679 | Whitbread, fr T. | brit |
| 1428 | White, William | brit |
| 1539 | Whiting, R., abbot of Glastonb | brit |
| 1847 | Whitman, M. & N. | usa |
| 1847 | Whitman, N. | usa |
| c1990 | Wi-Foo | myan |
| 926 | Wiborada (Guiborat), recluse | swit |
| c1000 | Wigstan | brit |
| c1600 | Willems, D. | neth |
| 1242 | William of Arnaud | fran |
| 1362 | William of Campania | ital |
| 1334 | William of England | iran |
| 1144 | William of Norwich | brit |
| 1201 | William of Rochester | brit |
| 1154 | William, abp of York | brit |
| 1839 | Williams, John | vanu |
| 1972 | Williams, N. | phil |
| 1986 | Wilson, evangelist John E.H. | ugan |
| 1660 | Wilson, Margaret | brit |
| 1968 | Wilting, Ruth | viet |
| 1998 | Wimana, sr C. | rwan |
| 1528 | Winkler, pastor G. | germ |
| 1546 | Wishart, G. | brit |
| 1988 | Wojcickowski, sr S. | paki |
| 1573 | Woodhouse, fr T. | brit |
| 1976 | Woods MM, fr W. | guat |
| 1651 | Wright, Peter | brit |
| 1989 | Xinsheng, bp Li | chin |
| 1996 | Xiuju, Zhang | chin |
| c1990 | Xueyan, bp Fan | chin |
| 1972 | Yagozinsky, S. | russ |
| 1989 | Yeiwene Yeiwene | newc |
| c1930 | Yemelyanov, fr P. | russ |
| 1623 | Yempo, br Simon | japa |
| 1995 | Yi, C.H. | russ |
| 1995 | Yi, K. W. | russ |
| 1997 | Yirirwahandi, rev P. | rwan |
| c1540 | Yoannis al-Kalioobi, monk | egyp |
| 1991 | You WF, fr Alexander | ugan |
| 1956 | Youdarian, R. | ecua |
| 1860 | Younes, br E. | leba |
| 1866 | Yu, fr P. Chong-ryul | nork |
| 1554 | Yuhanna Sulaqa, catholicos | turk |
| 1600 | Yukinaga, general Konishi | japa |
| 1791 | Yun, Paul | souk |
| 1996 | Yusefi, pastor Mohammad B. | iran |
| 76 | Zakaria, bp | arme |
| 1971 | Zakharov | russ |
| 1872 | Zamora, fr Jacinto | phil |
| 1922 | Zaozersky, pastor | russ |
| 66 | Zarmandoukhte | arme |
| 1571 | Zeballos, fr S. | usa |
| 1975 | Zecianu, br | roma |
| 303 | Zeno of Rome | ital |
| 304 | Zenobius | turk |
| 1972 | Zhiming, pastor Wang | chin |
| 1645 | Zigarran, fr T. | mexi |
| 1795 | Zlata of Magden | bulg |
| 1626 | Zola, fr J. B. | japa |
| 115 | Zozimus | gree |
| 1996 | Zubiri, sr Carmen | rwan |
| 1993 | Zuma, Isaac | soua |
| 1987 | Zuma, pastor Antonio | ecua |
| 1993 | Zuma, Thandi | soua |
| 1622 | Zumarraga OP, fr | japa |

**Table 4–12. Chronological listing of 2,550 known Christian martyrs, AD 30-2000.**

| | | |
|---|---|---|
| 33 | Jesus | pale |
| 36 | Stephen the Deacon | pale |
| 44 | James Boanerges, Apostle | pale |
| c50 | Thecla | turk |
| 54 | James the Less, Apostle | pale |
| 60 | Philip, Apostle | turk |
| 61 | Barnabas, Apostle | cypr |
| 61 | Simon Zelotes, Apostle | iraq |
| 62 | James the Just, bp of Jerus | pale |
| 64 | Evodius, bp of Antioch | turk |
| 64 | Matthias, Apostle | turk |
| 64 | Paul, Apostle | ital |
| 64 | Simon Peter, Apostle | ital |
| c65 | Osyth, queen | brit |
| c65 | Torquatus | spai |
| 66 | Anna of Ormisdat | arme |
| 66 | Jude (Thaddaeus), Apostle | arme |
| 66 | Mariam of Houssik | arme |
| 66 | Martha of Makovtir | arme |
| 66 | Ogouhie, princess | arme |
| 66 | Samuel, satrap | arme |
| 66 | Sandoukhte, princess | arme |
| 66 | Terentius | arme |
| 66 | Zarmandoukhte | arme |
| 68 | Bartholomew, Apostle | arme |
| 68 | Mark the Evangelist | egyp |
| 69 | Andrew, Apostle | gree |
| c70 | Matthew (Levi), Apostle | iraq |
| c76 | Linus, bp of Rome | ital |
| 76 | Zakaria, bp | arme |
| 82 | Thomas (Didymus), Apostle | indi |
| c90 | Cletus, bp of Rome | ital |
| 91 | Antipas | turk |
| 91 | Aurelia Petronilla | ital |
| 91 | Glabrio, Manius Acilius, consul | ital |
| 95 | Flavius Clemens | ital |
| 95 | John, Apostle | turk |
| 96 | Luke the Evangelist | gree |
| c97 | Atirnerseh, patriarch | arme |
| 97 | Timothy, bp | turk |
| c98 | Parmenas the deacon | ital |
| 99 | Clement, bp of Rome | ukra |
| c100 | Achilleus | ital |
| c100 | Nereus | ital |
| 108 | Symeon, bp of Jerusalem | pale |
| 110 | Crescentius | turk |
| 110 | Oski | arme |
| 110 | Soukias & companions | arme |
| c111 | Eustathius, Roman general | ital |
| c111 | Theopista | ital |
| 112 | Babai | turk |
| 112 | Barsamya | turk |
| 112 | Sharbil | turk |
| 115 | Ignatius, bp of Antioch | ital |
| 115 | Rufus | gree |
| 115 | Zozimus | gree |
| c117 | Alexander | ital |
| c117 | Eventius & Theodulus | ital |
| c117 | Sixtus I, bp of Rome | ital |
| c117 | Theodulus | ital |
| c120 | Atrasis, daughter of Hadrian | ital |
| c120 | Junia | ital |
| c120 | Phocas, bp of Bontos | ital |
| 123 | Semsoun, bp of Edessa | iraq |
| c125 | Acacius | arme |
| c125 | Thalelaeus | turk |
| 130 | Papius | pale |
| 138 | Telesphorus, bp of Rome | ital |
| c140 | Sophia | egyp |
| c150 | Benignus | fran |
| 156 | Felicitus Alexander | turk |
| 156 | Germanicus | turk |
| 156 | Polycarp, bp of Smyrna | turk |
| c165 | Caecelia | ital |
| 165 | Felicity | turk |
| 165 | Gervase & Protase | ital |
| 165 | Justin Martyr & 5 companions | ital |
| 165 | Protase | ital |
| c168 | Anicetus, pope | ital |
| c170 | Agathonice | turk |
| c170 | Carpus, bp | turk |
| c170 | Papylus | turk |
| c171 | Lucius | ital |
| c171 | Ptolemaus | ital |
| c171 | Publius, bp of Athens | ital |
| 177 | Blandina | fran |
| 177 | Ponticus | fran |
| 177 | Pothinus, bp | fran |
| 177 | Vettius Epagathus | fran |
| 178 | Cecilia | ital |
| 178 | Marcellus | ital |
| 178 | Maximus | ital |
| 178 | Tiburtius | ital |
| 178 | Valerian | ital |
| 180 | Aquilinus | tuni |
| 180 | Cittinus | tuni |
| 180 | Donata | tuni |
| 180 | Felix | tuni |
| 180 | Generosa | tuni |
| 180 | Januaria | tuni |
| 180 | Laetantius | tuni |
| 180 | Lucitas | tuni |
| 180 | Miggin | tuni |
| 180 | Namphano | tuni |
| 180 | Nartzalus | tuni |
| 180 | Sanam | tuni |
| 180 | Secunda | tuni |
| 180 | Speratus | tuni |
| 180 | Vestia | tuni |
| 180 | Veturius | tuni |
| c185 | Apollonius, senator | ital |
| c190 | Symphorian | fran |
| 193 | Ghevondius, patriarch | arme |
| c197 | Moses | ital |
| c197 | Sarah | ital |
| 202 | Felicitas | tuni |
| 202 | Irenaeus, bp of Lyons | fran |
| 202 | Leonides | egyp |
| 202 | Marcella | egyp |
| 202 | Perpetua | tuni |
| 202 | Pudens | ital |
| 202 | Revocatus | tuni |
| 202 | Saturninus | tuni |
| 202 | Saturus | tuni |
| 207 | Basilides | egyp |
| 207 | Potamiana | egyp |
| 209 | Alban of Verulamium | brit |
| 209 | Elias & companions | pale |
| 209 | Pamphilus | pale |
| 220 | Theodorus of Peshotep | egyp |
| c222 | Callistus I, pope | ital |
| c228 | Tatiana, deaconess | ital |
| 230 | Urban, pope | ital |
| 235 | Demetrius | ital |
| 235 | Hippolytus, antipope | ital |
| 235 | Pontian, pope | ital |
| c240 | Intercisus, James | iraq |
| 245 | Appolonia, deaconess | egyp |
| 249 | Abu Sayfayn | egyp |
| 249 | Agatha | ital |
| 249 | Alexander, bp of Cappadocia | egyp |
| 249 | Christopher | turk |
| 249 | Matra | egyp |
| c250 | Abadyus | egyp |
| 250 | Batra | egyp |
| 250 | Christophorus | egyp |
| 250 | Fabian, pope | ital |
| c250 | Faith (Foy) | fran |
| 250 | Genesius of Arles | fran |
| 250 | Nestor, bp of Perga | turk |
| 250 | Pionius | turk |
| c250 | Polyeuctus | arme |
| 251 | Achatius, bp | turk |
| 251 | Alexander, bp of Jerusalem | egyp |
| 251 | Babylas, patriarch of Antioch | turk |
| 252 | Fabius, bp of Antioch | turk |
| 253 | Cornelius, pope | ital |
| 254 | Aaron & Julius | brit |
| 254 | Julius | brit |
| 254 | Mercurius | brit |
| 254 | Origen | leba |
| c255 | Agapius, bp | tuni |
| 257 | Stephen I, pope | ital |
| 258 | Athanasius, bp | egyp |
| 258 | Cyprian, bp of Carthage | tuni |
| c258 | Jerasimus | egyp |
| 258 | Novatian, antipope | ital |
| c258 | Quadratus, bp | tuni |
| 258 | Rufina | ital |
| 258 | Secunda | ital |
| 258 | Sixtus II, pope | ital |
| 258 | Theodotus | egyp |
| 258 | Victorinus | fran |
| 259 | Agapitus of Praeneste | ital |
| 259 | Augurius | tuni |
| 259 | Denys, bp of Paris | fran |
| 259 | Eleutherius | fran |
| 259 | Eulogius | tuni |
| 259 | Felicissimus & Agapitus | ital |
| 259 | Flavian | tuni |
| 259 | Fructuosus, bp of Tarragona | spai |
| 259 | James of Cirta | tuni |
| 259 | Lawrence | ital |
| 259 | Lucius | tuni |
| 259 | Marian | tuni |
| 259 | Marianus | tuni |
| 259 | Montanus | tuni |
| 259 | Quartillosia | tuni |
| 259 | Renus | tuni |
| 259 | Rusticus | fran |
| 259 | Saturninus | fran |
| c260 | Alexander | pale |
| c260 | Conon | turk |
| c260 | Cyril | turk |
| c260 | Cyril, bp of Gortyna | gree |
| c260 | Eutropius, bp of Saintes | fran |
| c260 | Leontius the Ascetic | turc |
| c260 | Malchus | pale |
| c260 | Paregorius | turc |
| c260 | Patroclus | fran |
| c260 | Piscus | pale |
| c260 | Pontius | fran |
| c260 | Privatus | fran |
| 262 | Marinus | pale |
| 269 | Valentine | ital |
| 274 | Mamas | turk |
| 275 | Magnus, bp of Fabrateria | ital |
| 278 | Marina | turk |
| c280 | Tarsicius | ital |
| 283 | Cladius, Stratelates | egyp |
| 284 | Alexander & Asterius | turk |
| 284 | Asterius | turk |
| 284 | Babylas, bp | egyp |
| 284 | Irene | turk |
| 284 | Stephen, archdeacon | egyp |
| 284 | Thalelaeus | turk |
| c285 | Amsah of Qift | egyp |
| c285 | Apollo | egyp |
| 285 | Balana, priest | egyp |
| c285 | Banina | egyp |
| c285 | Crispin | fran |
| c285 | Crispinian | fran |
| 285 | Naou | egyp |
| c286 | Callinicus | egyp |
| c286 | Chanazhum | egyp |
| c286 | Dalasina | egyp |
| c286 | Dasyah | egyp |
| c286 | Epima | egyp |
| c286 | Helias, bp | egyp |
| c286 | Justus, son of Numerianus | egyp |
| 286 | Qndyr, queen | iraq |
| c286 | Sophronius | egyp |
| c287 | Aesculapius | egyp |
| 287 | Candidus | swit |
| c287 | Dioscorus | egyp |
| 287 | Exuperantius | swit |
| 287 | Exuperius | swit |
| 287 | Felix | swit |
| 287 | Maurice | swit |
| 287 | Regula | swit |
| c287 | Sarapamon of Scetis, bp | egyp |
| 287 | Urs | swit |
| 287 | Ursus of Solothurn | swit |
| 287 | Victor of Marseilles | swit |
| c287 | Victor of Solothurn | swit |
| c288 | Athom | egyp |
| c288 | Febronia, nun | egyp |
| c288 | Piroou | egyp |
| 288 | Sebastian of Milan | ital |
| c289 | Kau of Bismay | egyp |
| c289 | Wakhus | egyp |
| c290 | Anub | egyp |
| c290 | Apollonius | egyp |
| c290 | Ascla | egyp |
| c290 | Firmin, bp of Amiens | fran |
| 290 | Gayane, abbess | arme |
| 290 | Hripsime | arme |
| c290 | Panesneu, deacon | egyp |
| c290 | Paul of Egypt | egyp |
| c290 | Philemon | egyp |
| 290 | Salahouni, Theodore | arme |
| c290 | Salfana | egyp |
| c290 | Sarah & children | egyp |
| c291 | Abadir | egyp |
| c291 | Benjamin | egyp |
| c291 | Cyriacus | egyp |
| c291 | Eudoxia | egyp |
| c291 | Euphemia | egyp |
| c291 | Herai | egyp |
| c291 | Julitta | egyp |
| c291 | Til, soldier | egyp |
| c292 | David | egyp |
| c292 | Epimachus | egyp |
| c292 | Gordian | egyp |
| c292 | Phiobammon of Preht | egyp |
| c294 | Nikander | bulg |
| 295 | Anthimus, bp of Nicomedia | turk |
| c295 | Apaiule | egyp |
| c295 | Makrawi, bp of Nikiou | egyp |
| 295 | Maximilian | alge |
| c295 | Tolemaeus | egyp |
| c295 | Uri, priest of Shatanut | egyp |
| c296 | Athanasius | egyp |
| 296 | Menas the Miracle Maker | egyp |
| c297 | Barsanuphius (Warshanufy) | egyp |
| c297 | Basilidas, general | egyp |
| c297 | Besamon | egyp |
| c297 | Felician | ital |
| 297 | Hipparchus | turk |
| 297 | Philotheus of Antioch | turk |
| c297 | Primus | ital |
| c298 | Arsenius | egyp |
| 298 | Basil, bp | egyp |
| 298 | Cassian | moro |
| 298 | Marcellus the Centurion | moro |
| c298 | Patape, bp of Coptos | egyp |
| c299 | Chamoul | egyp |
| c299 | Comas | egyp |
| c299 | Damian | egyp |
| c299 | Isaac of Tiphre | egyp |
| c299 | Isidorus | egyp |
| c299 | Shenufe | egyp |
| c299 | Shenute | egyp |
| c300 | Abadion, bp of Antinoopolis | egyp |
| c300 | Agathon and brothers | egyp |
| c300 | Anatolius, general | egyp |
| c300 | Apoli | egyp |
| c300 | Bandilaus, monk | egyp |
| c300 | Callinicus | turk |
| c300 | Castorius | ital |
| c300 | Claudius | ital |
| c300 | Cosmas & Damian | turk |
| c300 | Damian | turk |
| c300 | Diomed | turk |
| c300 | Elmo, bp of Formiae | ital |
| c300 | Heraclides | egyp |
| c300 | Isidorus, monk | egyp |
| c300 | Jacob, The Soldier | egyp |
| c300 | Nabraha | egyp |
| c300 | Nicostratus | ital |
| c300 | Pelagia | turk |
| c300 | Rebecca of Sunbat | egyp |
| c300 | Simplicius | ital |
| c300 | Simpronian | ital |
| c300 | Taragus & companions | turk |
| c301 | Olympius | egyp |
| c301 | Paese | egyp |
| c301 | Tecula | egyp |
| c301 | Victor of Asyut | egyp |
| c302 | Crescentia | ital |
| c302 | Julius of Durostorum | bulg |
| c302 | Modestus | ital |
| c302 | Pisura, bp of Masil | egyp |
| c302 | Vitus | ital |
| 303 | Afra | germ |
| 303 | Anastasia | croa |
| 303 | Chrysogonus | ital |
| 303 | Cyrus & John | egyp |
| 303 | Efrem, bp of Tomis | roma |
| 303 | Epimachus of Pelusium | egyp |
| 303 | Euphemia | turk |
| 303 | Febronia | iraq |
| 303 | Felix of Thibiuca | tuni |
| 303 | Genesius the Actor | turk |
| 303 | George, megalomartyr | pale |
| 303 | Irineu, bp of Sirmium | croa |
| 303 | John | egyp |
| 303 | Lucy | ital |
| 303 | Procopius | pale |
| 303 | Victor Maurus | ital |
| 303 | Zeno of Rome | ital |
| 304 | Adrian & Natalia | turk |
| 304 | Agape | gree |
| 304 | Andronicus | ital |
| 304 | Barlaam of Antioch | turk |
| 304 | Chione | gree |
| 304 | Crispina of Tagora | alge |
| 304 | Dativus | tuni |
| 304 | Donatilla | tuni |
| 304 | Eulalia of Merida | spai |
| 304 | Gereon | germ |
| 304 | Hermes | turk |
| 304 | Irene | gree |
| 304 | Maxima | tuni |
| c304 | Naharuh | egyp |
| 304 | Natalia of Nicomedia | turk |
| 304 | Nilus, bp | leba |
| 304 | Pancras | ital |
| 304 | Peleus, bp | leba |
| 304 | Phileas, bp of Thmuis | egyp |
| 304 | Philip bp of Heraclea | turk |
| 304 | Pollio | hung |
| 304 | Probus | brit |
| 304 | Secunda | tuni |
| 304 | Severus | turk |
| 304 | Silvanus | syri |
| 304 | Tarachus | brit |
| 304 | Victorinus, bp of Pettau | slov |
| 304 | Vincent of Saragossa | spai |
| 304 | Zenobius | turk |
| c305 | Aesi | egyp |
| 305 | Dimyanah & her 40 Virgins | egyp |
| 305 | Hypatius of Gangra | egyp |
| c305 | Isidore of Takinash | egyp |
| 305 | Januarius, bp of Benevento | ital |
| c305 | Macarius | egyp |
| 305 | Marcus | egyp |
| 305 | Menas, governor | egyp |
| c305 | Milius | egyp |
| 305 | Potamon of Heracla | egyp |
| c305 | Procopius, governor | egyp |
| c305 | Victor | ital |
| c306 | Porphry | egyp |
| c306 | Psote of Psoi | egyp |
| c306 | Theodorus, bp of Pentapolis | egyp |
| c306 | Tibarcius | egyp |
| c306 | Valerianus | egyp |
| 307 | Catherine of Alexandria | egyp |
| c307 | Elias the eunuch | egyp |
| 308 | Demetrius, megalomartyr | gree |
| c308 | Repsima & 78 companions | arme |
| c309 | Abamun of Tarnut | egyp |
| c309 | Abamun of Tukh | egyp |
| 309 | Abdon | ital |
| 309 | Habib the Deacon | turk |
| 309 | Marcellus, pope | ital |
| 309 | Paul of Jamnia | pale |
| 309 | Porphyrius | pale |
| 309 | Seleucus | pale |
| 309 | Sennen | ital |
| 309 | Shamona | turk |
| 309 | Theodulus | pale |
| c309 | Timothy of Memphis | egyp |
| 309 | Valens | pale |
| c310 | Arianus, governor | egyp |
| c310 | Mui | egyp |
| 310 | Pamphilus | pale |
| c310 | Tyrannio, bp of Tyre | turk |
| c310 | Victor of Stratelates | ital |
| 311 | Methodius, bp of Olympus | turk |
| 311 | Peter I Ieromartyros, patriarch | egyp |
| 312 | Lucian of Antioch | turk |
| 313 | Dorothy | turk |
| c313 | Pantaleon, physician | egyp |

*Continued overleaf*

*Table 4–12 continued*

| | | |
|---|---|---|
| 315 | Bacchus | syri |
| 315 | Gurias & companions | iraq |
| 315 | Phrebonia | iraq |
| 315 | Sergius & Bacchus | syri |
| 316 | Blaize, bp | arme |
| c320 | Ammonius, bp of Latopolis | egyp |
| 327 | Berikjesu | iraq |
| 327 | Jonah | iraq |
| 333 | Aristakes I, patriarch | arme |
| c337 | Caxo, prince | iraq |
| c337 | Dado, governor | iraq |
| c337 | Gobidlaha, princess | iraq |
| 337 | Grigoris, exarch | arme |
| 337 | Jacob, bp | iraq |
| 337 | John, bp | iraq |
| 339 | Pusak, prefect, & 100 clergy | iraq |
| 339 | Tarbo, deaconess | iraq |
| c340 | Copres | egyp |
| 341 | Abdechalas & Ananias | iraq |
| 341 | Ananias | iraq |
| 341 | Pusicius | iraq |
| 341 | Simeon Barsabae, catholicos | iraq |
| 341 | Usthazanes | iraq |
| 342 | Shahdost, catholicos | iraq |
| 345 | Daniel | iraq |
| 345 | Hanania | iraq |
| 345 | Pherbutha | iraq |
| 345 | Uarda (Rose) | iraq |
| c345 | Usaghniyus | egyp |
| 346 | Anna | iraq |
| 346 | Barbashmin, catholicos | iraq |
| 346 | James | iraq |
| 346 | Martha | iraq |
| 346 | Mary | iraq |
| 347 | Daniel, patriarch | arme |
| 347 | Donatus, bp of Bagai | tuni |
| 347 | Houssik I, patriarch | arme |
| 347 | Isaac | tuni |
| 347 | Marculus, bp of S. Numidia | tuni |
| 347 | Maximian | tuni |
| 347 | Stephen of Ulnia | arme |
| c350 | Agnes | ital |
| c350 | Eudoxius & companions | pale |
| c350 | Gordius | pale |
| 351 | Paul, patriarch | turk |
| c355 | Andrew, monk | egyp |
| c355 | Behnam | egyp |
| c355 | Eunapius, monk | egyp |
| c355 | Sarah | egyp |
| c356 | Mercurius | egyp |
| c357 | John, The Soldier | egyp |
| c359 | Decius | egyp |
| c359 | Irene | egyp |
| c359 | Victor | egyp |
| c360 | Alladyus, bp | egyp |
| c360 | Bibiana | ital |
| c360 | Dafrosa & Demetria | ital |
| c360 | Demetria | ital |
| c360 | Leontius of Tripoli | syri |
| c364 | Mark, bp of Arethusa | ital |
| c365 | Serapion, bp of Thmuis | egyp |
| c370 | Nicetas | roma |
| 372 | Sabas the Goth | roma |
| 373 | Nerses I, catholicos | arme |
| 375 | Abdas, metropolitan | iraq |
| 379 | Eusebius, bp of Samosata | turk |
| 379 | Eustace of Mtskheta | geor |
| 386 | Priscillian, bp | spai |
| 391 | Telemachus | ital |
| 397 | Alexander | ital |
| 397 | Martyrius | ital |
| 397 | Optatus, bp of Thamugadi | alge |
| 397 | Sisinnius | ital |
| 407 | John Chrysostom, patriarch | turk |
| 408 | Hormizd of Sylvanus, rabban | iraq |
| 410 | Abda, mar | iraq |
| 410 | Marcella | ital |
| 411 | Desiderius, bp of Langres | fran |
| 413 | Apringius, proconsul | tuni |
| 413 | Marcellinus Flavius, tribune | tuni |
| 419 | Eustochium | pale |
| 420 | Hormizdas | iraq |
| 420 | Peroz | iraq |
| 422 | Benjamin | iraq |
| 422 | Chouchanik | iraq |
| 422 | Hormisdas | iraq |
| 422 | James of Persia | iraq |
| 422 | Suenas | iraq |
| 426 | Patroclus of Arles, primate | fran |
| 431 | Palladius | irel |
| 434 | Auraeus, bp | fran |
| c440 | Gwinear | irel |
| 448 | Anahid | iraq |
| 448 | Dindui, metropolitan | iraq |
| 448 | John, bp of Karka | iraq |
| 448 | Pethiun, evangelist | iraq |
| 448 | Sirin | iraq |
| 448 | Tamasgerd | iraq |
| 449 | Flavian, patriarch | turk |
| c450 | Hamai of Kahyor | egyp |
| c450 | Kharitas | ethi |
| 451 | Atom & his legion | arme |
| 451 | Livarius | fran |
| 451 | Macari of Edko, bp | egyp |
| 451 | Nestorius, patriarch | jord |
| 451 | Suzanne | arme |
| 451 | Ursula & virgins | germ |
| 451 | Vardan Mamikonian | arme |
| 454 | Hovsep I, patriarch | arme |
| 455 | Macarius of Tkow, bp | egyp |
| 459 | Proterius, patriarch | egyp |
| 467 | Azquir | saud |
| c473 | Shushanik, queen | geor |
| 476 | Volusianus, bp of Tours | fran |
| 484 | Babowi, catholicos | iraq |
| 484 | Dionysia | tuni |
| 484 | Majoricus | tuni |
| 484 | Servus | tuni |
| 484 | Victorian | tuni |
| c490 | Rajden | geor |
| 493 | Barsumas, bp | iraq |
| 511 | Macedonius II, patriarch | turk |
| 518 | Philoxenus, bp of Mabbogh | iraq |
| 523 | Abraham | yeme |
| 523 | Abu-Afr, governor | yeme |
| 523 | Aretas | yeme |
| 523 | Elesbaan | yeme |
| 523 | Elias | yeme |
| 523 | Elija | yeme |
| 523 | Habsa | yeme |
| 523 | Moses of Yemen | yeme |
| 523 | Sergios | yeme |
| 524 | Severinus Boethius, consul | ital |
| 526 | John I, pope | ital |
| 537 | Silverius, pope | ital |
| 538 | Ursicinus, bp of Ravenna | ital |
| c550 | Adeodatus (Astouadz-Mapod) | arme |
| c550 | Grigor-Rajik | arme |
| c550 | Nectan | brit |
| 552 | Aba, mar, patriarch catholicos | iraq |
| 555 | Helier | chan |
| c560 | Cadoc | fran |
| 570 | Cadoc, bp | ital |
| 575 | Ahudemmeh, bp of Tagrit | iraq |
| 576 | Constantine, abbot | brit |
| 577 | Aldate, bp of Gloucester | brit |
| c580 | Licinianus, bp of Carthage | turk |
| 585 | Hermenegild of Spain | spai |
| 586 | Praetextatus, bp of Rouen | fran |
| 607 | Desiderius, bp of Vienne | fran |
| 610 | Anastasius, patriarch | geor |
| 615 | George the Monk | iran |
| 617 | Donnan & 52 companions | brit |
| 628 | Anastasius the Persian | turk |
| 631 | Menas | egyp |
| 642 | Oswald, king of Northumbria | brit |
| 643 | Trudpert | germ |
| c650 | David of Douine | arme |
| c650 | Dympna of Ireland | belg |
| c650 | Martin I, pope | ukra |
| c650 | Shinudah, anba | egyp |
| 651 | Oswin, king | brit |
| 655 | Foillan, abbot | fran |
| c660 | Annemond, bp of Lyons | fran |
| c660 | Emmeram, bp of Poitiers | fran |
| 662 | Maximus the Confessor, abbot | geor |
| 675 | Germanus, abbot | fran |
| 679 | Dagobert II, king | fran |
| 679 | Leodegar, bp of Autun | fran |
| 685 | Bercharius, abbot | fran |
| 686 | Kilian, bp, & 11 companions | germ |
| 689 | Vigilius, bp of Auxerre | fran |
| 695 | Hewald the Dark | germ |
| 695 | Hewald the Fair | germ |
| c700 | Indract | brit |
| 705 | Lambert, bp of Maastricht | belg |
| c717 | Menas of Al-Ashmunayn | egyp |
| c725 | Theodosia | turk |
| 726 | Werenfrid | neth |
| 729 | Germanus, ecu patriarch | turk |
| 730 | James, bp of Catania | ital |
| 731 | Hainmar, bp of Auxerre | fran |
| 750 | Gerulf | belg |
| c750 | Vahan of Goghtn | syri |
| 754 | Boniface (Winfrith), bp | neth |
| 754 | Eoban, bp | neth |
| 760 | Gangolf | fran |
| 764 | Stephen the Younger, abbot | turk |
| 786 | Abo | geor |
| 794 | Ethelbert, king | brit |
| 799 | Gerold, duke of Bavaria | germ |
| c800 | Alkelda, princess | brit |
| c800 | Erc, bp of Slane | irel |
| c800 | Salib | egyp |
| c800 | Simeon | egyp |
| c810 | Subaljesu, monk | iraq |
| 821 | Kenelm, prince | brit |
| 825 | Adulfus & John | spai |
| 825 | John of Cordoba | spai |
| 834 | Deusdedit, abbot of M Cassino | ital |
| 834 | Euthymius, metrop of Sardes | turk |
| 840 | Alexander, bp of Fiesole | ital |
| 850 | Aurea | spai |
| c850 | Barsanuphius, monk | egyp |
| c850 | Ebba, abbess | brit |
| 850 | George of Cordoba | spai |
| c850 | Isaac, prince | arme |
| c850 | Joseph, prince | arme |
| 850 | Perfectus of Cordoba | spai |
| 851 | Flora of Cordoba | spai |
| 851 | Isaac, monk | spai |
| 851 | Mary of Cordoba | spai |
| 851 | Sanctius of Cordoba | spai |
| 852 | Aurelius | spai |
| 852 | Fandila of Cordoba | spai |
| 852 | Natalia | spai |
| 853 | Columba of Cordoba | spai |
| 853 | Haymo, bp of Halberstadt | germ |
| 853 | Pomposa | spai |
| 854 | Indrechtach, abbot of Iona | brit |
| 856 | Jeron | neth |
| 859 | Eulogius of Cordoba | spai |
| 859 | Leocritia | spai |
| c860 | John VII Grammaticus, patr | turk |
| 861 | Meinrad of Einsiedeln, hermit | swit |
| 866 | Fremund | brit |
| 869 | Edmund the Martyr, king | brit |
| 870 | Hedda of Peterborough, abbot | brit |
| c870 | Ragener | brit |
| 870 | Tancred | brit |
| 870 | Torthred | brit |
| 870 | Tova | brit |
| 875 | Adrian of May, bp | brit |
| 884 | Bertharius, abbot | ital |
| 884 | Rombout of Malines | belg |
| c900 | Thomas, bp of Damascus | syri |
| c904 | Pandonia | brit |
| 916 | Ludmilla | czec |
| 926 | Wiborada (Guiborat), recluse | swit |
| 928 | John X, pope | ital |
| 929 | Wenceslas, prince-duke | czec |
| 931 | Argentea | spai |
| 931 | Vulfura | spai |
| 959 | al-Muzahim, Jirjis | egyp |
| 969 | Nicephorus, emperor | gree |
| 979 | Edward the Martyr, king | brit |
| 996 | Ghabrial | egyp |
| 997 | Adalbert, bp of Prague | russ |
| c1000 | Wigstan | brit |
| 1003 | Benedict of Benevento | pola |
| 1004 | Abbo | fran |
| 1009 | Bruno, bp of Querfurt | lith |
| 1012 | Alphege, abp of Canterbury | brit |
| 1012 | Coloman | ausz |
| 1015 | Boris & Gleb | russ |
| 1015 | Gleb | russ |
| 1016 | John Baptist Vladimir, prince | alba |
| 1028 | Ulfrid | swed |
| 1030 | Olav II Haraldsson, king | norw |
| 1043 | Hallvard Vebjornssen | norw |
| 1046 | Gerard, bp of Csanad | hung |
| 1066 | Gottschalk | germ |
| 1066 | John, bp of Mecklenburg | germ |
| 1066 | Kuno, bp of Trier | germ |
| 1070 | Godelive | fran |
| 1075 | Erlembald | ital |
| 1079 | Stanislas, bp of Cracow | pola |
| c1080 | Eskil, bp | swed |
| 1080 | Rudolf of Swabia | ital |
| 1086 | Canute IV, king | denm |
| 1096 | John (Said bar Sabhuni), bp | turk |
| 1116 | Magnus, earl of Orkney | brit |
| 1120 | Botvid | swed |
| 1120 | Merbot | ausz |
| 1121 | Erminold, abbot of Prufening | germ |
| 1131 | Canute Lavard | denm |
| 1133 | Peter of Bruys | fran |
| 1144 | William of Norwich | brit |
| 1145 | Bosinlother, abbot Conrad | ausz |
| 1148 | Ernest, abbot of Zwiefalten | saud |
| 1150 | Eric of Sweden | swed |
| c1150 | Goharin & companions | arme |
| 1154 | William, abp of York | brit |
| 1155 | Arnold of Brescia | fran |
| 1156 | Henry, bp of Uppsala | swed |
| 1170 | Thomas Becket, abp of Canter | brit |
| 1176 | Marguerite of Roeskilde | denm |
| c1180 | Michael of Damietta | syri |
| 1198 | Berthold, abbot | esto |
| c1200 | Uguzo (Lucio di Val Cavargna) | ital |
| 1201 | William of Rochester | brit |
| 1208 | Peter of Castelnau, legate | fran |
| 1209 | John of Phanidjoit | egyp |
| 1217 | Hroznata | czec |
| 1220 | Accursio | moro |
| 1220 | Aiuto | moro |
| 1220 | Berard | moro |
| 1220 | Otho | moro |
| 1220 | Peter | moro |
| 1222 | Adam, bp of Caithness | brit |
| 1227 | Agnello | moro |
| 1227 | Daniel of Belvedere | span |
| 1227 | Domno | moro |
| 1227 | Hugolino | moro |
| 1227 | Leo | moro |
| 1227 | Nicholas | moro |
| 1227 | Samuel | moro |
| 1242 | Stephen of Narbonne | fran |
| 1242 | William of Arnaud | fran |
| c1250 | Bulus al-Habis | egyp |
| 1252 | Peter of Verona (Peter Martyr) | ital |
| 1258 | Kitbuga, general | syri |
| 1261 | Dionysius, antipatriarch | iraq |
| 1279 | Bar Kaliq, bp of Tus | iran |
| 1282 | Aldobrand of Florence | iran |
| 1282 | Anthony of Armenia | iran |
| 1288 | Conrad of Saxony | geor |
| 1288 | Stephen of Hungary | geor |
| 1293 | Stepanos IV, patriarch | arme |
| 1310 | Porete, Marguerite | fran |
| 1314 | de Molay, J., grand master | fran |
| 1314 | de Rosatis, A. of Milan | arme |
| 1314 | Francis of Borgo San Sepolcro | iran |
| 1314 | Francis of Fermo | arme |
| 1314 | Monold of Ancona | arme |
| 1315 | Lull, Ramon | alge |
| 1317 | Gregorios, Mar, bp | turk |
| 1321 | Belibasta, Guilhem | fran |
| 1321 | Demetrius, br | indi |
| 1321 | James of Padua | indi |
| 1321 | Peter of Siena | indi |
| 1321 | Thomas of Tolentino | indi |
| 1323 | Angelus of Spoleto | ital |
| 1326 | de Stapledon, Walter, bp | brit |
| 1334 | Stephen of Gross-Wardein | roma |
| 1334 | William of England | iran |
| 1339 | Francis of Alessandria | chin |
| 1339 | Gilotti, William | chin |
| 1339 | John of India, br | chin |
| 1339 | Lawrence of Alessandria | chin |
| 1339 | Martel, Peter | chin |
| 1339 | Pascal of Victoria | chin |
| 1339 | Richard, bp of Almalik | chin |
| 1339 | Ruff, Raymond | chin |
| 1340 | Gentle of Matelica | iran |
| 1346 | John the Blind | luxe |
| 1347 | Antoniy | lith |
| 1347 | Evastafiy | lith |
| 1347 | Ioann | lith |
| c1350 | Roch, healer | fran |
| 1362 | James, abp of Zaitun | chin |
| 1362 | William of Campania | ital |
| 1365 | Peter of Ruffia | ital |
| 1383 | Kador, John | arme |
| 1383 | Panacea | ital |
| 1387 | al-Jadid, Jirjis | egyp |
| 1387 | Hadid of Giza | egyp |
| 1388 | Bonaventure Peraga, cardinal | ital |
| 1393 | John of Nepomuk | czec |
| 1397 | de Cetina, J. | spai |
| 1397 | de Duenas, P. | spai |
| 1400 | Abu'l Farag | egyp |
| 1400 | Arsenius | egyp |
| 1400 | Ileya | egyp |
| 1400 | Matthew of Escandel | chin |
| 1400 | Mikhail Abu Mokaitef | egyp |
| 1400 | Moussa, monk | egyp |
| 1400 | Saleeb | egyp |
| 1400 | Sidrak, priest, & 5 monks | egyp |
| 1401 | Sawtrey, W. | brit |
| 1405 | Le Scrope, abp R. | brit |
| 1410 | Badby, J. | brit |
| 1413 | Cobham, Lord | brit |
| 1415 | John Hus | germ |
| 1416 | Jerome of Prague | czec |
| 1418 | Oldcastle, Sir John | brit |
| 1428 | White, William | brit |
| 1431 | Joan of Arc | fran |
| 1450 | Moleyns, A., bp of Chichester | brit |
| 1460 | Antony of Rivoli (Tunis) | tuni |
| 1471 | Tresham, T. | brit |
| 1478 | John of Sahagun | spai |
| c1480 | Isidor & followers | esto |
| 1490 | Rabata, A. | ital |
| 1498 | Savonarola, G. | ital |
| 1514 | George Novi of Sophia | bulg |
| 1516 | Botello OP, Diego | trin |
| 1516 | de Salcedo OP, fr F | trin |
| 1524 | Tauber, Casper | ausz |
| 1525 | Munzer, T. | germ |
| 1527 | Hut, H. | ausz |
| 1527 | Kaiser | germ |
| 1527 | Manz, F. | neth |
| 1527 | Sattler, M. | germ |
| 1528 | Hamilton, Patrick | brit |
| 1528 | Hubmaier, B. | ausz |
| 1528 | Winkler, pastor G. | germ |
| 1529 | Denck, H. | neth |
| 1531 | Bilney, Thomas | brit |
| 1533 | Frith, J. | brit |
| 1534 | Barton, Elizabeth | brit |
| 1534 | Matthys, Jan | germ |
| 1534 | Schiemer, L., bp | germ |
| 1535 | Fisher, cardinal John | brit |
| 1535 | Houghton, John, prior | brit |
| 1535 | Kenraghty, chaplain Maurice | irel |
| 1535 | Lawrence, Robert, prior | brit |
| 1535 | More, Thomas | brit |
| 1535 | Webster, Augustine, prior | brit |
| 1536 | de Almasia, J. | para |
| 1536 | Hutter, J. | neth |
| 1536 | John of Leiden | germ |
| 1536 | Tyndale, William | belg |
| 1539 | Stone, J. | brit |
| 1539 | Whiting, R., abbot of Glastonb | brit |
| 1540 | Barnes, Robert | brit |
| 1540 | Gerrard, Thomas | brit |
| 1540 | Jerome, William | brit |
| c1540 | Yoannis al-Kalioobi, monk | egyp |
| 1541 | Calero, br J. | mexi |
| 1541 | de Cuellar, fr A. | mexi |
| 1541 | Valverde OP, bp V. | peru |
| 1542 | de la Cruz, fr J. | usa |
| 1542 | de Padilla OFM, fr J. | usa |
| 1542 | de Ubeda, fr L. D. | usa |
| 1544 | Gardiner, J. | brit |
| 1544 | Ireland, J. | brit |
| 1544 | Larke, J. | brit |
| 1546 | Beaton, abp D. | brit |
| 1546 | Wishart, G. | brit |
| 1549 | Criminali SJ, fr A. | indi |
| 1549 | de Barbastro, fr L. C. | usa |
| 1549 | de Pekalosa, fr D. | usa |
| 1549 | Fuentes, br | usa |
| 1550 | Arason, bp J. & 2 sons | denm |
| 1550 | de Valdivieso, bp A. | nica |

*Continued opposite*

*Table 4–12 continued*

| | | |
|---|---|---|
| 1553 | Cranmer, abp Thomas | brit |
| 1553 | de la Cruz, fr D. | usa |
| 1553 | de Mena, fr J. | usa |
| 1553 | Ferrer, fr J. | usa |
| 1553 | Hooper, bp John | brit |
| 1553 | Latimer, bp Hugh | brit |
| 1553 | Mendez, fr H. | usa |
| 1553 | Ridley, bp Nicholas | brit |
| 1554 | Yuhanna Sulaqa, catholicos | turk |
| 1555 | Bradford, John | brit |
| 1555 | Nicholas Novi of Sophia | bulg |
| 1555 | Philpot, J., archdeacon | brit |
| 1559 | Du Bourg, Anne | fran |
| 1560 | Brooks, J., bp of Gloucester | brit |
| 1560 | Juan, br | mexi |
| 1560 | Lorenzo, fr F. | mexi |
| 1561 | da Silveira SJ, fr G. | zimb |
| 1564 | Cossin, fr B. | mexi |
| 1564 | de Tapia, fr J. | mexi |
| 1564 | Lucas, br | mexi |
| 1566 | Martinez SJ, fr P. | usa |
| 1567 | de Acevedo, fr P. | mexi |
| 1567 | de Burgos, fr P. | mexi |
| 1567 | de Herrera, br J. | mexi |
| 1567 | Donzel, fr F. | mexi |
| 1567 | Hoorn, count | neth |
| 1567 | Lamoral of Egmont | neth |
| 1567 | Philip, metropolitan of Moscow | russ |
| 1569 | Jerome de la Croix | thai |
| 1569 | Pietersz, Pieter | neth |
| 1569 | Sebastian Cantu | thai |
| 1570 | de Azevedo SJ, fr I. | spai |
| 1571 | de Quiros, fr L. | usa |
| 1571 | de Segura, fr J. B. | usa |
| 1571 | de Solis, fr G. | usa |
| 1571 | Gomez, fr G. | usa |
| 1571 | Hamilton, primate J. | brit |
| 1571 | Linares, fr P. | usa |
| 1571 | Mendez, fr J. B. | usa |
| 1571 | Redondo, fr C. | usa |
| 1571 | Zeballos, fr S. | usa |
| 1572 | Coligny, admiral Gaspard de | fran |
| 1572 | Ramus, Peter | fran |
| 1573 | Woodhouse, fr T. | brit |
| 1575 | O'Donnell SJ, E. | irel |
| 1576 | de Azevedo OP, fr Silvestre | camb |
| 1577 | Mayne, C. | brit |
| 1578 | Miguel de Medina | spai |
| 1578 | Nelson, fr J. | brit |
| 1578 | O'Hely, P., bp | irel |
| 1579 | Franz, David | hung |
| 1580 | O'Cullenan, G., abbot | irel |
| 1580 | Serrato, fr J. | mexi |
| 1581 | Briant, fr A. | brit |
| 1581 | Campion, fr E. | brit |
| 1581 | de Santa Maria, fr J. | usa |
| 1582 | Cottam, fr T. | brit |
| 1582 | de Villalobos, fr L. | mexi |
| 1582 | Lopez, fr F. | usa |
| 1582 | Rodriguez, fr A. | usa |
| 1583 | Acquaviva, fr R. | indi |
| 1583 | Aranha, F. | indi |
| 1583 | Berno, P. | indi |
| 1583 | Francisco, fr A. | indi |
| 1583 | Pacheco, fr A. | indi |
| 1584 | Gwyn, R. | brit |
| 1584 | O'Hurley, D., abp | irel |
| 1585 | de Ayala, fr A. | mexi |
| 1585 | Gil, fr F. | mexi |
| 1586 | Clitherow, Margaret | brit |
| 1586 | de la Puebla, fr A. | mexi |
| 1586 | del Rio, fr J. | mexi |
| 1588 | Leigh, fr R. | brit |
| 1588 | Shelley, F. | brit |
| 1588 | Ward, Margaret | brit |
| 1591 | Genings, fr E. | brit |
| 1592 | Udall, J. | brit |
| 1593 | Barrow, Henry | brit |
| 1593 | Greenwood, John | brit |
| 1593 | Sales, fr J. | fran |
| 1593 | Saultemouche, fr W. | fran |
| 1594 | Cornelius, fr J. | brit |
| 1595 | George, fr A. | ethi |
| 1595 | Rawlins, A. | brit |
| 1595 | Southwell, fr R. | brit |
| 1595 | Walpole, H. | brit |
| 1597 | Blasquez, fr Pedro B. | japa |
| 1597 | Casas Martinez, Felipe | japa |
| 1597 | de Auñon, fr M. | usa |
| 1597 | de Badajoz, fr A. | usa |
| 1597 | de Corpa, fr P. | usa |
| 1597 | de Goto, fr J. S. | japa |
| 1597 | de Rodriguez, fr B. | usa |
| 1597 | Francis of Miako | japa |
| 1597 | Joseph, mar, metropolitan | indi |
| 1597 | Karasumaru, Leo | japa |
| 1597 | Kisai, fr J. | japa |
| 1597 | Miki SJ, fr Paul | japa |
| 1597 | Simon, mar, metropolitan | indi |
| 1597 | Verascola, fr F. | usa |
| 1600 | Bruno, br G. | ital |
| 1600 | Tadaoki, Gracia | japa |
| c1600 | Willems, D. | neth |
| 1600 | Yukinaga, general Konishi | japa |
| 1601 | Barkworth, fr M. | brit |
| 1601 | Filcock, fr. R. | brit |
| 1601 | Hunt, Fr T. | brit |
| 1601 | Marin, fr Esteban | phil |
| 1601 | Middleton, fr R. | brit |
| 1605 | Catesby, Robert | brit |
| 1606 | de Altamirano, fr M. | mexi |
| 1606 | Hwang Ming-sha SJ, br | chin |
| 1608 | Garnet, fr T. | brit |
| 1608 | Gervase, fr. G. | brit |
| 1611 | Roberts, fr. J. | brit |
| 1612 | Bertelete, fr E. | hond |
| 1612 | de Aranda SJ, fr M. | chil |
| 1612 | de Montalban SJ, br J. | chil |
| 1612 | de Monteagudo, fr J. | hond |
| 1612 | de Vecchi SJ, fr H. | chil |
| 1612 | Lucas of Tokyo | japa |
| 1612 | O'Devany, C., bp | irel |
| 1612 | Scott, fr. M. | brit |
| 1613 | Hachikan, Joaquin | japa |
| 1615 | Ogilvie SJ, J. | brit |
| 1616 | de Santarn, fr H. | mexi |
| 1616 | de Tovar, fr H. | mexi |
| 1616 | Gutierrez, fr P. | mexi |
| 1616 | Lawrence | japa |
| 1616 | Lewis | japa |
| 1616 | Thomas | japa |
| 1616 | Tunstall, fr. T. | brit |
| 1616 | Vincent | japa |
| 1617 | Macaido, fr J. B. | japa |
| 1619 | Crisinus, fr M. | hung |
| 1619 | Grodecz SJ, fr M. | hung |
| 1619 | Kimura, fr L. | japa |
| 1619 | Oldenbarnevelt, J. van | neth |
| 1619 | Pongracz SJ, fr S. | hung |
| 1619 | Poulain, fr G. | cana |
| 1619 | Vanini, L. | ital |
| 1620 | Sarkander, Jan | czec |
| 1621 | de Montchretien, A. | fran |
| 1622 | Constanzo, fr C. | japa |
| 1622 | Fidelis of Sigmaringen | swit |
| 1622 | Fugiscima, fr D. | japa |
| 1622 | Kimura SJ, fr S. | japa |
| 1622 | Novarra, fr P. P. | japa |
| 1622 | Ota, fr A. | japa |
| 1622 | Sandaju, fr P. O. | japa |
| 1622 | Spinola SJ, fr C. | japa |
| 1622 | Zumarraga OP, fr | japa |
| 1623 | De Angelis, fr J. | japa |
| 1623 | de Baena, br J. | hond |
| 1623 | Kuncevicz, abp Josaphat | belo |
| 1623 | Lopez, fr B. | hond |
| 1623 | Puerta, fr C.M. | hond |
| 1623 | Yempo, br Simon | japa |
| 1624 | Carvalho, fr J. | japa |
| 1624 | Delgado, fr D. | mexi |
| 1624 | Henriquez, br J. | mexi |
| 1624 | Ketevan, queen | iran |
| 1625 | Viel, fr N. | cana |
| 1626 | Caun, V. | japa |
| 1626 | de Torres, fr B. | japa |
| 1626 | Pacheco, fr F. | japa |
| 1626 | Rinscei, P. | japa |
| 1626 | Sadamatzu, G. | japa |
| 1626 | Tozo, M. | japa |
| 1626 | Zola, fr J. B. | japa |
| 1627 | Kwon, Vincent | japa |
| 1627 | Perez, fr R. | cost |
| 1627 | Tsuji, fr T. | japa |
| 1628 | Alonso Rodriguez SJ | para |
| 1628 | Arrowsmith, fr E. | brit |
| 1628 | Gonzalez SJ, fr Roque | para |
| 1628 | Juan del Castillo SJ | para |
| 1628 | Nagascima SJ, br M. | japa |
| 1631 | de Ortega, fr P. | usa |
| 1631 | Fleming, fr P. | czec |
| 1631 | John of Prado | moro |
| 1631 | Miranda, fr P. | usa |
| 1631 | Wagner, fr Liborius | germ |
| 1632 | Adolphus, king Gustavus | germ |
| 1632 | de Arvide, fr M. | usa |
| 1632 | Gutierrez, fr R. B. | japa |
| 1632 | Ixida SJ, fr A. | japa |
| 1632 | Letrado, fr F. | usa |
| 1633 | Alonso, fr L. | japa |
| 1633 | Ibanez, fr D. | japa |
| 1633 | Kohioye, fr M. | japa |
| 1633 | Kurobioye, M. | japa |
| 1633 | Porras, fr F. | usa |
| 1633 | Tomonaga OP, fr J. K. G. | japa |
| 1634 | Ansalone, fr G. | japa |
| 1634 | de Andrade, fr A. | chin |
| 1634 | Maddalena of Nagasaki | japa |
| 1634 | Marina di Omura | japa |
| 1634 | Nishi, fr T.H.R. | japa |
| 1634 | Vieira, fr S. | japa |
| 1635 | Paes SJ, fr G. | ethi |
| 1635 | Theophilus of Zakynthos | gree |
| 1637 | Courtet OP, fr W. | japa |
| 1637 | de Aozaraza, fr M. | japa |
| 1637 | Gonzales, fr A. | japa |
| 1637 | Lazzaro di Kyoto | japa |
| 1637 | Ruiz, L. | japa |
| 1637 | Schiwozuka, fr V. | japa |
| 1638 | Berthelot, fr P. | indo |
| 1638 | Cassian of Nantes, fr | ethi |
| 1638 | Cyril I Lukaris, ecu patriarch | turk |
| 1638 | Cyril II Kontaris, ecu patriarch | turk |
| 1638 | de Almeida, bp Apollinaris | ethi |
| 1638 | Franceschi SJ, fr H. | ethi |
| 1638 | Rodrigues SJ, fr F. | ethi |
| c1640 | Agathangelo of Vendome, fr | fran |
| 1640 | Bruni SJ, fr B. | ethi |
| 1640 | Cardeira SJ, fr L. | ethi |
| 1641 | Barlow, fr. A. | brit |
| 1642 | de San Antonio, fr J. | pana |
| 1642 | Goupil SJ, R. | cana |
| 1642 | Holland, fr T. | brit |
| 1642 | Roe, Alban | brit |
| 1642 | Rubino, fr | japa |
| 1643 | Hutchinson, Anne | usa |
| 1644 | Corby, fr Ralph | brit |
| 1644 | de Capillas OP, fr F. | chin |
| 1644 | Price, fr Robert | brit |
| 1645 | André, catechist | viet |
| 1645 | Ignace, catechist | viet |
| 1645 | Labado, fr F. | mexi |
| 1645 | Laud, William, abp of Canter | brit |
| 1645 | Morse, fr H. | brit |
| 1645 | Romero, fr P. | para |
| 1645 | Vincent, catechist | viet |
| 1645 | Zigarran, fr T. | mexi |
| 1646 | Jogues SJ, fr I. | cana |
| 1646 | Lalande SJ, fr John de | cana |
| 1646 | Powel, fr. P. | brit |
| 1647 | Montero, fr F. | mexi |
| 1648 | Charles I, king | brit |
| 1648 | Daniel SJ, A. | cana |
| 1648 | de Oviedo, fr A. | pana |
| 1649 | Chabenel, N. | cana |
| 1649 | de Brebeuf SJ, fr J. | cana |
| 1649 | Garnier, fr C. | cana |
| 1649 | Lalemant SJ, fr G. | cana |
| 1649 | Plunkett, earl C. | brit |
| 1649 | Trevino de Sobremonte, T. | mexi |
| 1650 | McMahon, bp E. | irel |
| c1650 | Romanul, Ioan Valahul | roma |
| 1651 | Love, pastor Christopher | brit |
| 1651 | O'Brien, bp T. A. | irel |
| 1651 | Wright, Peter | brit |
| 1652 | du Tremblay, fr J. L. | ethi |
| 1652 | George of Ghiel, fr | conz |
| 1652 | Heyling, Peter | ethi |
| 1652 | Redemptus of the Cross, br | indo |
| 1653 | Ahatalla, metropolitan | indi |
| 1654 | Leonard of Chartres, fr | cana |
| 1654 | Southworth, fr J. | brit |
| 1657 | Bobola SJ, fr Andrew | belo |
| 1660 | Wilson, Margaret | brit |
| 1661 | Campbell, A. | brit |
| 1661 | Cargill, D. | brit |
| 1661 | Guthrie, James | brit |
| 1661 | Menard, fr R. | usa |
| 1661 | Renwick, J. | brit |
| 1661 | Venner, Thomas | brit |
| 1662 | Chu Tsu-hsuan, emperor | myan |
| 1662 | Dyre, Mary | usa |
| 1662 | Hambroek, A. | taiw |
| 1666 | Andrade, vicar apostolic | ethi |
| 1666 | Schall SJ, fr A. von Bell | chin |
| 1672 | Avila y Ayala, fr P. | usa |
| 1672 | de San Vitores SJ, fr J. | guam |
| 1678 | Coleman, Edward | brit |
| 1678 | Kemble, John | brit |
| 1678 | Lewis, David | brit |
| 1678 | Lloyd, John | brit |
| 1679 | Evans, fr D | brit |
| 1679 | Fenwick, fr J. | brit |
| 1679 | Gavan, fr J. | brit |
| 1679 | Grove, J. | brit |
| 1679 | Harcourt, fr W. | brit |
| 1679 | Ireland, fr W. | brit |
| 1679 | Lewis, fr D | brit |
| 1679 | Nevill, fr F. | brit |
| 1679 | Pickering, T. | brit |
| 1679 | Turner, fr A. | brit |
| 1679 | Wall, fr John | brit |
| 1679 | Whitbread, fr T. | brit |
| 1680 | Bernal, fr J. | usa |
| 1680 | de Espeleta, fr J. | usa |
| 1680 | de Figuero, fr J. | usa |
| 1680 | de Jesus, fr J. | usa |
| 1680 | de la Pedroso, fr J. | usa |
| 1680 | de la Ribourde, fr G. | usa |
| 1680 | de Lorenzana, fr F. | usa |
| 1680 | de Mdorales, fr L. | usa |
| 1680 | de Montesdoca, fr J. | usa |
| 1680 | de Mora, fr A. | usa |
| 1680 | de Pro, fr A. S. | usa |
| 1680 | de Santa Maria, fr A. | usa |
| 1680 | de Talban, fr J. | usa |
| 1680 | de Torres, fr T. | usa |
| 1680 | de Trujillo, fr J. | usa |
| 1680 | de Velasco, fr F. | usa |
| 1680 | de Vera, fr D. | usa |
| 1680 | del Val, fr J. | usa |
| 1680 | Maldonado, fr L. | usa |
| 1680 | Naranjo, B. | usa |
| 1680 | Pio, fr J. B. | usa |
| 1680 | Rendon, fr M. | usa |
| 1680 | Talbot, P., abp of Dublin | irel |
| 1680 | Tinoco, fr M. | usa |
| 1681 | Plunket, primate O. | brit |
| 1682 | Avvakum Petrovich, archpriest | russ |
| 1682 | Epifanii, monk | russ |
| c1682 | Morozova, Boyarina | russ |
| 1682 | Pustosviat, Nikita | russ |
| 1683 | Le Vacher, bp J. | alge |
| 1683 | Ortiz de Zarate, fr P. | arge |
| 1683 | Salinas, fr J. | arge |
| 1684 | Beltran, fr M. | mexi |
| 1684 | Custodio, fr F. | mexi |
| 1684 | Muros, fr | mexi |
| 1685 | de Marolles, Louis | fran |
| 1685 | Le Fevre, I. | fran |
| 1686 | Benitez, fr E. | mexi |
| 1689 | Chefdeville, fr A. | usa |
| 1689 | Iosif, hermit, & monks | russ |
| 1689 | Le Clercq, fr M. | usa |
| 1689 | Membre, fr Z. | usa |
| 1690 | Tegananokoa, S. | usa |
| 1691 | de Arce, Jose | boli |
| 1692 | Garangouas, M. | usa |
| 1692 | Gonannhatenha, F. | usa |
| 1693 | de Britto SJ, fr J. | indi |
| 1693 | Genoud, fr | myan |
| 1693 | Joret, fr | myan |
| 1696 | Corvera, fr F. | usa |
| 1696 | de Arbizu, fr J. | usa |
| 1696 | de Carbonel, fr A. | usa |
| 1696 | de Jesus Maria Casañas, fr F. | usa |
| 1696 | Moreno, fr A. | usa |
| 1696 | Sanchez, fr L. | usa |
| 1697 | Plunkett, fr C. | usa |
| c1700 | Markel, br | russ |
| 1702 | Foucault, fr N. | usa |
| 1704 | Alverez, fr R. | mexi |
| 1704 | Anixa, A. | usa |
| 1704 | Arraiyo, fr J. P. | usa |
| 1704 | Criado, fr D. | usa |
| 1704 | de Mendoza, fr M. | usa |
| 1704 | de Osorio, fr T. | usa |
| 1704 | de Parga, fr J. | usa |
| 1704 | Feliciano, A. C. | usa |
| 1704 | Hevia, fr D. | mexi |
| 1704 | Ponce de Leon, fr A. | usa |
| 1706 | Beatrice, Donna | conz |
| 1706 | de St Cosme, fr J. F. B. | usa |
| 1706 | Delhalle, fr C. | usa |
| 1707 | Gomidas, fr K. | turk |
| 1708 | Gravier, fr J. | usa |
| 1709 | de Rebullida, fr P. | cost |
| 1709 | de Zamora, fr J.A. | cost |
| 1714 | Brankoveanu, prince Constant | roma |
| 1714 | Ivanov, Thomas | russ |
| 1714 | Sidotti, abbot G. B. | japa |
| 1716 | Weiss, prefect L. | ethi |
| 1718 | de Montesdoca, br L. | usa |
| 1720 | Alexander the Deacon | russ |
| 1724 | Rale SJ, fr S. | cana |
| 1726 | de Oca, fr L. M. | usa |
| 1729 | du Poisson, fr P. | usa |
| 1729 | Souel, fr J. | usa |
| 1730 | de Labrid, bp N. | vene |
| 1730 | Gaston, fr | usa |
| 1731 | Contova SJ, fr Juan Antonio | micr |
| 1731 | de Saraoz, fr D. | usa |
| 1734 | Carranco, fr L. | mexi |
| 1734 | Tamaral, fr N. | mexi |
| 1736 | Aulneau, fr J. P. | usa |
| 1736 | d'Artiquette, P. | usa |
| 1736 | d'Esgly, F. M. | usa |
| 1736 | de Coulonge, L. d'A. | usa |
| 1736 | de St Agne, L. G. | usa |
| 1736 | de Tonty, P. A. | usa |
| 1736 | de Vincennes, F. M. B. | usa |
| 1736 | du Tisne, L. C. | usa |
| 1736 | Senat SJ, fr A. | usa |
| 1740 | Koman, pastor D. | slov |
| 1745 | Gallizia, bp | myan |
| 1749 | Sanz, bp P. | chin |
| 1749 | Silva, fr F. X. | usa |
| 1752 | Ganzabal, fr J. F. | usa |
| 1752 | Pillai, D. | indi |
| 1754 | Nicholas of Chios | gree |
| 1756 | Nerini, fr | myan |
| 1757 | Faulhaber, fr A. | pola |
| 1758 | Aberin, fr J. S. | usa |
| 1758 | de Terreros, fr A. G. | usa |
| 1758 | Santiesteban, fr J. | usa |
| 1761 | Malagrida, fr G. | port |
| 1771 | Ambrose, abp of Krutitsy | russ |
| 1771 | Damascenus | russ |
| 1773 | de Bernave, fr J.C.G. | mexi |
| 1775 | Ricci SJ, general L. | ital |
| 1778 | Guillen, fr F. | mexi |
| 1779 | Aitolos, K. | alba |
| c1780 | Rizk Agha, vizier | egyp |
| 1781 | Barreneche, fr J. A. | usa |
| 1781 | Diaz, fr J. M. | usa |
| 1781 | Garces OFM, fr F. T. | usa |
| 1781 | Moreno, fr J. M. | usa |
| 1791 | Souk, Paul | souk |
| 1792 | Balmain SJ, fr F. | fran |
| 1792 | Bonnaud SJ, fr J. J. | fran |
| 1792 | De Millou SJ, fr J. C. | fran |
| 1792 | de Vafons, count | fran |
| 1792 | Delfaut SJ, fr W. A. | fran |
| 1792 | Du Lau, abp J. M. | fran |
| 1792 | Lanfant, fr A. & 8 companions | fran |
| 1792 | Lefranc, fr F. | fran |
| 1793 | Louis XVI | fran |
| 1794 | Agricola Viala | fran |
| 1794 | Ambroise, fr R. | fran |
| 1794 | Andre, fr J. | fran |
| 1794 | Carnus, fr C. | fran |
| 1794 | Expilly, bp L. A. | fran |
| 1794 | Gobel, J. B. J., bp of Paris | fran |
| 1794 | Pinot, fr N. | fran |
| 1794 | Polydorus the Cypriot | gree |
| 1795 | Oprea, Miclaus, monk | roma |
| 1795 | Sarai, Visarion, monk | roma |

*Continued overleaf*

*Table 4–12 continued*

| | | |
|---|---|---|
| 1795 | Sofronie of Cioara, monk | roma |
| 1795 | Wenmo, fr J. Z. | souk |
| 1795 | Zlata of Magden | bulg |
| 1796 | Juvenal, hieromonk | usa |
| 1798 | Dat, fr J. | viet |
| 1798 | Murphy, fr J. | irel |
| 1798 | Trieu, fr E. | viet |
| 1799 | Lewis, pastor T. | frep |
| 1800 | Prosser, Gabriel | usa |
| 1801 | Chu, fr James | souk |
| 1801 | Chung, Augustine | souk |
| 1801 | Hwang, S. C. | souk |
| 1801 | Mark the New | gree |
| 1801 | Muallim Malati | egyp |
| 1801 | Wan-Suk, Columba | souk |
| 1802 | Demetrios of Chios | gree |
| 1802 | Lazarus the Bulgar | turk |
| 1802 | Luke the New | gree |
| 1803 | Toussaint-Louverture, F.D. | fran |
| 1807 | George of Chios | gree |
| 1811 | Chao, A. | chin |
| 1811 | Clet, F. | chin |
| 1811 | Hidalgo y Costilla, fr M. | mexi |
| 1811 | Malati, Muallim | egyp |
| 1811 | Tapeng, J. C. | chin |
| 1812 | Quintana, fr A. | usa |
| 1813 | Angelis | gree |
| 1814 | Ignanos | gree |
| 1815 | Morelos y Pavon, fr J. M. | mexi |
| 1816 | Lantrua, fr G. | chin |
| 1817 | Vesey, Denmark | usa |
| c1820 | Bishay, Sidhom | egyp |
| 1820 | Clet, fr F. R. | chin |
| 1821 | Kyprianos, abp | cypr |
| 1822 | Gregory V, ecu patriarch | turk |
| 1822 | Joana Angelica, abbess | braz |
| 1822 | Muallim Ghali | egyp |
| 1825 | Pogio, fr Bartolome | arge |
| 1830 | Asad es Shidiak | leba |
| 1830 | Shidiak, Asaad | leba |
| 1831 | Turner, Nat | usa |
| 1833 | Aquino, Anastasio | elsa |
| 1833 | Gagelin, F.-I. | viet |
| 1834 | de Leon, fr A. D. | usa |
| 1834 | Diaz OFM, fr | usa |
| 1834 | Lyman, H. | indo |
| 1834 | Munson, Samuel | indo |
| 1834 | Rainitsiandavaka | mada |
| 1835 | Marchand, fr J. | viet |
| 1837 | Cornay, fr J. C. | viet |
| 1837 | Lovejoy, Elijah P. | usa |
| 1837 | Rasalama | mada |
| 1838 | Bovie, fr P. D. | viet |
| 1838 | Delgado, bp I. | viet |
| 1838 | Diem, V. | viet |
| 1838 | Georgios | gree |
| 1838 | Koa, P. | viet |
| 1839 | Chastan, fr J. H. | souk |
| 1839 | Imbert, bp Laurence | souk |
| 1839 | Kim, Agatha | souk |
| 1839 | Maubant, fr P. | souk |
| 1839 | Ri, J. | souk |
| 1839 | Williams, John | vanu |
| 1840 | de la Cruz, Apolinario | phil |
| 1840 | Perboyre, fr J. G. | chin |
| 1840 | Perboyre, fr Jean G. | chin |
| 1841 | Chanel, fr P. M. | vanu |
| 1844 | Smith, Hyrum | usa |
| 1844 | Smith, Joseph | usa |
| 1846 | Epalle SM, bp | solo |
| 1846 | Kim Tai Kun, fr Andrew | souk |
| 1847 | Lowrie, Walter M. | chin |
| 1847 | Marmoiton, br | newc |
| 1847 | Rey SJ, fr A. | mexi |
| 1847 | Whitman, M. & N. | usa |
| 1847 | Whitman, N. | usa |
| 1849 | Roth, pastor S. L. | roma |
| 1851 | Gardiner, Allen | arge |
| 1852 | U, fr Moses Nya | myan |
| 1855 | Gabra Mikael, fr | ethi |
| 1855 | Mazzuconi, fr G. | papu |
| 1856 | Strang, James J. | usa |
| 1857 | Sibour, abp of Paris | fran |
| 1858 | Braeuninger, M. | usa |
| 1859 | Ascanio OFM, fr N. | syri |
| 1859 | Brown, John | usa |
| 1859 | de Albera OFM, fr. N. M. | syri |
| 1859 | Fernandez, fr J. J. | syri |
| 1859 | Soler, fr P. | syri |
| 1860 | Billottet SJ, fr E. | leba |
| 1860 | Bonacina, br F. | leba |
| 1860 | Cyril IV, patriarch | egyp |
| 1860 | de Albera, fr M. M. | syri |
| 1860 | de Jacobis, bp Justin | ethi |
| 1860 | Kolland OFM, fr E. | syri |
| 1860 | Mabeiche, br A. H. | leba |
| 1860 | Maksoud, br H. | leba |
| 1860 | Masi, Francis | syri |
| 1860 | Masi, Muti | syri |
| 1860 | Masi, Raphael | syri |
| 1860 | Pinzano OFM, Francis | syri |
| 1860 | Ruiz OFM, fr Emmanuel | syri |
| 1860 | Volta OFM, fr. C. | syri |
| 1860 | Younes, br E. | leba |
| 1861 | Almato OP, fr P. | viet |
| 1861 | Hermosilla OP, bp H. | viet |
| 1861 | Holmes, J. L. | chin |
| 1861 | Ochoa, bp V. B. | viet |
| 1861 | Sokolskij, abp J. | russ |
| 1861 | Venard, fr J. T. | viet |
| 1862 | Neel, J. P. | chin |
| 1865 | Volkner, Carl S. | newz |
| 1866 | Berneux, bp S.-F. | souk |
| 1866 | Cho, Peter | souk |
| 1866 | Daveluy, bp M. A. N. | souk |
| 1866 | Lee, John | souk |
| 1866 | Thomas, R. J. | souk |
| 1866 | Yu, fr P. Chong-ryul | nork |
| 1868 | Noi Sunya | thai |
| 1869 | Mirza Ibrahim | iran |
| 1869 | Non Chai, abbot | thai |
| 1871 | Allard, fr | fran |
| 1871 | Captier, fr E. | fran |
| 1871 | Caubert, fr J. | fran |
| 1871 | Clerc, fr A. | fran |
| 1871 | Darboy, G., abp of Paris | fran |
| 1871 | de Bengy, fr A. | fran |
| 1871 | Deguerry, fr | fran |
| 1871 | Ducoudray, fr L. | fran |
| 1871 | Olivaint, fr P. | fran |
| 1871 | Patteson, bp J. C. | solo |
| 1872 | Bassost, fr F. | usa |
| 1872 | Burgos, fr Jose | phil |
| 1872 | Gomez, fr Mariano | phil |
| 1872 | Zamora, fr Jacinto | phil |
| 1878 | David, fr | ital |
| 1880 | Westrup, J. O. | mexi |
| 1881 | Augier, fr | buru |
| 1881 | D'Hoop, fr F. | buru |
| 1881 | Deniaud, fr | buru |
| 1883 | Koi, David | keny |
| 1885 | Gordon, general C. G. | suda |
| 1885 | Hannington, bp James | ugan |
| 1885 | Mukasa, Joseph | ugan |
| 1886 | Badzekuketta, A. | ugan |
| 1886 | Banabakintu, Luke | ugan |
| 1886 | Buzabaliawo, James | ugan |
| 1886 | Gonza, Gonzaga | ugan |
| 1886 | Gyavira | ugan |
| 1886 | Kaggwa, Andrew | ugan |
| 1886 | Kalemba, Matthias | ugan |
| 1886 | Kibuka, Ambrose | ugan |
| 1886 | Kiriggwajjo, Anatole | ugan |
| 1886 | Kiriwawanvu, Mukasa | ugan |
| 1886 | Kiwanuka, Achilles | ugan |
| 1886 | Kizito | ugan |
| 1886 | Ludigo, Adolphus Mukasa | ugan |
| 1886 | Lwanga, Charles | ugan |
| 1886 | Mawaggali, Noe | ugan |
| 1886 | Mugagga | ugan |
| 1886 | Ngondwe, Pontian | ugan |
| 1886 | Sebuggwawo, Denis | ugan |
| 1886 | Seghers, abp C. J. | usa |
| 1886 | Serunkuma, Bruno | ugan |
| 1886 | Tuzinde, Mbaga | ugan |
| 1887 | Checa y Barba, abp J. I. | ecua |
| 1887 | Moran, fr J. | togo |
| 1887 | Muzeyi, Jean-Marie | ugan |
| 1896 | Berthieu SJ, fr J. | mada |
| 1896 | Lilli OFM, fr Salvatore | turk |
| 1896 | Mizeki, Bernard, catechist | zimb |
| 1896 | Rizal, Jose | phil |
| 1897 | Pilkington, G. L. | ugan |
| c1898 | Papizian, archimandrite J. | turk |
| 1900 | Andlauer SJ, fr M. | chin |
| 1900 | Blind Chang Shen | chin |
| 1900 | Carleson, N. | chin |
| 1900 | Chao Hsi Mao | chin |
| 1900 | Denn, fr P. | chin |
| 1900 | Guillon, bp L. | chin |
| 1900 | Isore, fr R. | chin |
| 1900 | King, A. | chin |
| 1900 | Li, fr J. | chin |
| 1900 | Mangin, fr L. I. | chin |
| 1900 | Otu, Samuel | ghan |
| 1900 | Pigott, J. | chin |
| 1900 | Pigott, T. W. & J. | chin |
| 1900 | Pitkin, H. T. | chin |
| 1900 | Price, Charles & Eva | chin |
| 1900 | Price, Eva | chin |
| 1900 | Sun Hwe Teh | chin |
| 1900 | Wang Ten Ren | chin |
| 1901 | Chalmers, pastor J. | papu |
| 1901 | Tomkins, pastor O. | papu |
| 1902 | Goretti, Maria | ital |
| 1902 | Kensit, John | brit |
| 1903 | Figueroa, Juana | arge |
| 1905 | An, evangelist | chin |
| 1905 | Chestnut, Eleanor | hong |
| 1905 | Kim, evangelist | chin |
| 1905 | Ni, evangelist | chin |
| 1906 | Macdonald, dr R. J. | chin |
| 1908 | Heinrich, fr L. | usa |
| 1908 | Sivila, Visitación | arge |
| 1908 | Sofiisky, exarch abp N. | geor |
| 1910 | Sidhom Bishai, deacon | egyp |
| 1915 | Cavell, Edith | belg |
| 1915 | Chilembwe, John | mala |
| 1916 | Bettex, Paul | chin |
| 1916 | de Foucauld, Charles | alge |
| 1917 | Benjamin Simon, catholicos | iran |
| 1917 | Kochurov, fr I. | russ |
| 1918 | Ambrose, bp of Seroapulsk | russ |
| 1918 | Ambrose, fr | russ |
| 1918 | Andronick, abp of Perm | russ |
| 1918 | Audo, abp | iraq |
| 1918 | Basil, abp of Chernigov | ukra |
| 1918 | Benjamin, fr | russ |
| 1918 | Chernikh, S. | russ |
| 1918 | Dimitri, pastor | russ |
| 1918 | Dovganav, P. | russ |
| 1918 | Efrem, bp of Selenginsk | russ |
| 1918 | Elizabeth, grand duchess | russ |
| 1918 | Hermogen, abp of Tobolsk | russ |
| 1918 | Irinarkh, fr | russ |
| 1918 | Israel, monk | russ |
| 1918 | Issidor, bp of Mikhailov | russ |
| 1918 | Kirion III, catholicos-patriarch | geor |
| 1918 | Kuntsevich, L. | russ |
| 1918 | Leonty, bp of Enotaev | russ |
| 1918 | Longin, pastor | russ |
| 1918 | Makarov, M. | russ |
| 1918 | Miniatov, lawyer | russ |
| 1918 | Mitrophan, abp of Astrakhan | russ |
| 1918 | Modest, fr | russ |
| 1918 | Mokovsky, pastor G. & wife | russ |
| 1918 | Nizza, L. | russ |
| 1918 | Ornatsky, fr F. | russ |
| 1918 | Polotnikov, abp of Petrograd | russ |
| 1918 | Pospelov, abp G. | russ |
| 1918 | Radion, fr | russ |
| 1918 | Riabuhin, pastor J. | russ |
| 1918 | Skipetrov, fr A. | russ |
| 1918 | Sontag, apostolic delegate | iraq |
| 1918 | Stavrovsky, fr A. | russ |
| 1918 | Theodot | russ |
| 1918 | Theophan, bp of Solikamsk | russ |
| 1918 | Veraskin, abp A. | russ |
| 1918 | Vladimir, metropolitan of Kiev | ukra |
| 1918 | Vostorgov, fr J. | russ |
| 1919 | Hahn, G. H. & 32 pastors | germ |
| 1919 | Herman, bp of Kamychen | russ |
| 1919 | Joachim, abp of Nizhni-Novgo | russ |
| 1919 | Kulbusch, bp Platon of Revel | esto |
| 1919 | Lavrenty, bp of Balakhna | russ |
| 1919 | Makary, bp of Viazma | russ |
| 1919 | Nikodim, bp of Belgorod | russ |
| 1919 | Pimen, bp of Verny | russ |
| 1919 | Tikhon, abp of Voronezh | russ |
| 1919 | Varsonoufy, bp of Kirillov | russ |
| 1920 | Justin, abp of Omsk | russ |
| 1920 | Weinberg, Judith | russ |
| 1921 | Archangelsky, pastor T. | russ |
| 1921 | Coyle, J. E. | usa |
| 1921 | Frolov, pastor J. | russ |
| 1921 | Methody, bp of Petropavlovsk | russ |
| 1921 | Moslovsky, pastor J. | russ |
| 1921 | Nazary, metrop of Kutaisi | geor |
| 1921 | Sarichov, pastor S. | russ |
| 1921 | Simon, bp of Ufa | russ |
| 1922 | Benjamin, metrop of Petrograd | russ |
| 1922 | Dobrolubov, pastor | russ |
| 1922 | Friazinov, pastor | russ |
| 1922 | Nadezhdin, pastor | russ |
| 1922 | Orlov, pastor | russ |
| 1922 | Philaret, bp of Kostroma | russ |
| 1922 | Rybalkin, monk Fyodor | russ |
| 1922 | Shein, S. | russ |
| 1922 | Sokolov, pastor | russ |
| 1922 | Telegin, A. | russ |
| 1922 | Vishniakov, pastor | russ |
| 1922 | Zaozersky, pastor | russ |
| 1923 | Budkiewicz, C., vicar | russ |
| 1923 | Chrysostomos, met of Smyrna | turk |
| 1925 | Cassels, bp W. C. | chin |
| c1925 | Ierofey, bp of Veliki-Ustinsk | russ |
| 1925 | Tikhon, patriarch | russ |
| 1926 | Nyirenda, Tomo | mala |
| 1927 | Amfiteatrov, P. | belo |
| 1927 | Bretzkiy, bp N. | ukra |
| c1927 | Filaret, bp of Bobruisk | byel |
| 1927 | Pro Juarez, fr M. | mexi |
| 1928 | de la Vega, fr J. | mexi |
| 1928 | Martinez, br H. | mexi |
| 1928 | Perez, fr P. | mexi |
| 1929 | Coveyou, fr W. | chin |
| 1929 | Holbein, fr G. | chin |
| 1929 | Peter, abp of Voronezh | russ |
| 1929 | Serge, bp of Efremov | russ |
| 1929 | Seybold, fr C. | chin |
| 1929 | Sundar Singh, sadhu | chin |
| c1930 | Ioann, bp of Mozyr | byel |
| c1930 | Mikhail, bp of Slutsk | byel |
| c1930 | Yemelyanov, fr P. | russ |
| 1932 | Afanassy, bp of Stavobelsk | russ |
| 1932 | Agapit, abp of Ekaterinoslav | ukra |
| 1932 | Alexander, abp | russ |
| 1932 | Antony, bp of Archangel | russ |
| 1932 | Farabundo, Marti | elsa |
| 1932 | Seraphim, metro of Petrograd | russ |
| 1932 | Simpson, W. E. | chin |
| 1933 | Tourian, abp Leontius | usa |
| 1934 | Ambrose, bp of Podolsk | russ |
| 1934 | Arconada, fr J. B. | spai |
| 1934 | Esteban, fr T. | chin |
| 1934 | Liu, Y. C. | chin |
| 1934 | Martinez, fr E. | spai |
| 1934 | Moreno, Ramonita | arge |
| 1934 | Odongo, Alfayo | keny |
| 1934 | Philip, abp | russ |
| 1934 | Poliansky, abp Ambrose | kaza |
| 1934 | Pommer, John, abp of Riga | latv |
| 1934 | Stam, Betty | chin |
| 1934 | Stam, John & Betty | chin |
| 1935 | Arseny, abp of Serpuhov | russ |
| 1935 | Damaskin, bp of Gluhov | ukra |
| 1935 | Fedorov, exarch L. | russ |
| c1935 | von Moltke, Helmut | germ |
| 1936 | Abrikosov, mother C. | russ |
| 1936 | Arbona, fr B. | spai |
| 1936 | Arseny, metrop of Novgorod | russ |
| 1936 | Artigues, fr R. | spai |
| 1936 | Audi, fr F. | spai |
| 1936 | Bartholomew, bp | russ |
| 1936 | Baste, fr N. | spai |
| 1936 | Boguna, fr L. | spai |
| 1936 | Bori, fr P. | spai |
| 1936 | Carbonell, fr C. | spai |
| 1936 | Carrio, fr A. | spai |
| 1936 | Corral, fr O. | spai |
| 1936 | Cyril, metropolitan of Kazan | russ |
| 1936 | Darder, E. | spai |
| 1936 | de Velasco, fr I. | spai |
| 1936 | Dimitry, abp of Gdovsk | russ |
| 1936 | Ferreres, fr J. B. | spai |
| 1936 | Garcia Villada SJ, fr Z. | spai |
| 1936 | Gelabert, P. | spai |
| 1936 | Gonzalez, fr E. | spai |
| 1936 | Grimaltos, R. | spai |
| 1936 | Isla, fr L. | spai |
| 1936 | Jimenez Malla, Ceferino | spai |
| 1936 | Llatje, fr J. | spai |
| 1936 | Luque, fr E. | spai |
| 1936 | Malla, C. J. | spai |
| 1936 | Martinez, fr B. | spai |
| 1936 | Mayorga, fr M. | spai |
| 1936 | Pavlivsky, I., metropolitan | ukra |
| 1936 | Payan, fr A. | spai |
| 1936 | Peter, metropolitan of Krutitsy | russ |
| 1936 | Peypoch, fr E. | spai |
| 1936 | Rovira, fr J. | spai |
| 1936 | Sales, V. | spai |
| 1936 | Sanchez, fr J. | spai |
| 1936 | Santaella, fr M. | spai |
| 1939 | Schneider, pasotr | germ |
| 1936 | Simon, fr A. | spai |
| 1936 | Sitjar, fr T. | spai |
| 1936 | Tarrats, J. | spai |
| 1936 | Tena, fr R. | spai |
| 1936 | Valenti, fr T. | spai |
| 1936 | Verges, fr J. | spai |
| 1937 | Boretsky, M., metropolitan | ukra |
| 1937 | Lo Pa Hong | chin |
| 1937 | Mikael, bp | ethi |
| 1937 | Petros, bp | ethi |
| 1938 | Alexey, bp of Petrograd | russ |
| 1938 | Anatole, metrop of Odessa | russ |
| 1938 | Cairns, fr R. | chin |
| 1938 | Donovan MM, fr G. | chin |
| 1938 | Joseph, metro of Petrograd | russ |
| 1938 | Juvenal, abp of Riazan | russ |
| 1938 | Khoren I, catholicos | arme |
| 1938 | Liu, H. | chin |
| 1938 | Lypkivsky, V., metropolitan | ukra |
| c1938 | Nikandr, metrop of Odessa | russ |
| 1938 | Nikon (Lebedev), bp | russ |
| 1938 | Nikon, bp of Belgorod | russ |
| 1938 | Pitirim, abp | russ |
| 1938 | Seraphim, bp | russ |
| 1940 | Jackson, F. C. | indo |
| 1940 | Lebbe, fr F. V. | chin |
| c1940 | Leisner, fr K. | germ |
| 1940 | Mazeika, L. | lith |
| 1940 | Skobtsova, mother M. | pola |
| 1940 | Urban SJ, fr J. | pola |
| 1941 | Cairns, fr R. J. | chin |
| 1941 | Kolbe OFM, fr Maximilian | pola |
| 1941 | Lichtenberg, fr B. | germ |
| 1941 | Litaunieks, fr V. | lith |
| 1941 | Sri-Phong, catechist P. | thai |
| 1942 | Brandsma, fr Tiko | germ |
| 1942 | Bushiri, Mulumozi | conz |
| 1942 | Duhamel, fr A. C. | solo |
| 1942 | Gorazd, bp Pavlik | czec |
| 1942 | Gray, R. F. | phil |
| 1942 | Hennessey, J. G. | solo |
| 1942 | Hoeben, H. | neth |
| c1942 | Kowalski, J., primate | pola |
| 1942 | Lee, pastor Kipoong | souk |
| 1942 | Redlich, V. | papu |
| 1942 | Sadd, A. | kiri |
| 1942 | Stein, Edith | pola |
| 1942 | Stein, Rosa | pola |
| 1942 | Tapiedi, Lucian | papu |
| 1943 | Bacon, D. | boli |
| 1943 | Dye, B. | boli |
| 1943 | Dye, C. | boli |
| 1943 | Hosback, G. | boli |
| 1943 | Hunter, E. | boli |
| 1943 | Jaegerstaetter, F. | germ |
| 1943 | Kim, evangelist | chin |
| 1943 | Meyer, F. & 11 missionaries | phil |
| 1943 | Nemantsevich, exarch A. | byel |
| 1943 | Voronaev, I. E. | russ |
| 1944 | Choo Kee Chul, pastor | nork |
| 1944 | Coy, Juan | colo |
| 1944 | Duenas, fr Jesus | guam |
| 1944 | Gross, N. | germ |
| 1944 | Jacob, Max | fran |
| 1944 | Kocylowskyj, bp | ukra |
| 1944 | Koenzgen, G. | germ |
| 1944 | Lagerstadr, Farnz | germ |
| 1944 | Letterhaus, B. | germ |
| 1944 | Makary, abp | russ |
| 1944 | Metzger, fr M. J. | germ |
| 1944 | Munk, pastor Kaj | denm |

*Continued opposite*

*Table 4–12 continued*

| | | |
|---|---|---|
| 1944 | Schmidlin, professor J. | germ |
| 1945 | Akya Nai, pastor | myan |
| 1945 | Apor, bp Vilmos | hung |
| 1945 | Birch, J. | chin |
| 1945 | Bonhoeffer, Dietrich | germ |
| 1945 | Delp, fr A. | germ |
| 1945 | Devine, H. | myan |
| 1945 | Jaffray, R. A. | indo |
| 1945 | Liddell, Eric | chin |
| 1945 | Rauschenbach MM, fr O. A. | chin |
| 1945 | Simrak, bp J. | croa |
| 1946 | Borisevicius, V., bp of Telsiai | lith |
| 1947 | Jensen, fr B. | chin |
| 1947 | Romza, bp T. | ukra |
| 1948 | Aftemie, bp | roma |
| 1948 | Fowler, E. | colo |
| 1948 | Frentiu, bp | roma |
| 1948 | Gigni, bp | alba |
| 1948 | Gijni, bp | alba |
| 1948 | Halan, Y. | ukra |
| 1948 | Kostelnyk, fr H. | ukra |
| 1948 | Ordacz, bp L. | hung |
| 1948 | Suciu, bp | roma |
| 1948 | Volai, bp | alba |
| 1949 | Kisi, abp K. | alba |
| 1949 | Tornay, fr M. | chin |
| 1950 | Beda SJ, fr Tsiang | chin |
| 1950 | Brennan, bp P. T. | nork |
| 1950 | Byrne, bp P. J. | nork |
| 1950 | Carlo, bp A. | chin |
| 1950 | Chang MM, sr Agneta | nork |
| 1950 | de Smedt, bp L. J. | chin |
| 1950 | Maxville, Selma M. | myan |
| 1950 | Nguyen, pastor | viet |
| 1950 | Phan Long, pastor | viet |
| 1950 | Son Yang Won, pastor | nork |
| 1950 | Sung Du, fr | nork |
| 1950 | Thien Thi, pastor | viet |
| 1950 | Tong-Sin, fr | nork |
| 1950 | Vasquez, Carmen | arge |
| 1950 | Wang Ling-Tso, fr | chin |
| 1951 | Kimbangu, prophet Simon | conz |
| 1951 | Wallace, W.L. | chin |
| 1952 | Bossilkoff CP, bp E. | bulg |
| 1952 | Ford, bp F.X. | chin |
| 1952 | Gacigi, G. | keny |
| 1952 | Gacigi, R. | keny |
| 1952 | Gnidovec, dean | serb |
| 1952 | Kirtoff, apostolic exarch | bulg |
| 1952 | Mungai, J. | keny |
| 1952 | Muriuki, W. | keny |
| 1952 | Prennushi, abp N. | alba |
| 1952 | Selanuok | papu |
| 1952 | Wancegi, Mary | keny |
| 1953 | Gikonyo, E. | keny |
| 1953 | Kaguru, A. | keny |
| 1953 | Maina, E. | keny |
| 1953 | Reinys, M., abp of Vilnius | lith |
| 1953 | Seng, Joseph | chin |
| 1954 | Durkovici, bp A. | roma |
| 1954 | Eunak, K. | souk |
| 1954 | Ghika, fr V. | roma |
| 1954 | Indus, Artur | russ |
| 1954 | Pacha, bp | roma |
| 1954 | Scheffler, bp | roma |
| 1956 | Boris, metrop of Nevrokop | bulg |
| 1956 | Elliot, J. | ecua |
| 1956 | Fleming, P. | ecua |
| c1956 | Martinuzzi, abp of Estergom | hung |
| 1956 | McCully, E. | ecua |
| 1956 | Saint, Nate | ecua |
| 1956 | Youdarian, R. | ecua |
| 1958 | Dapcha, Lama David | nepa |
| 1959 | Balint, S. | hung |
| 1959 | Kherie, bp A. | ukra |
| 1959 | Ramanauskas, P., bp of Telsiai | lith |
| 1959 | Turcsanyi, msgr E. | hung |
| 1960 | Gojdic, bp Pavol | slok |
| 1960 | Hodgson, E. | conz |
| 1960 | John, evangelist Esther | paki |
| 1960 | Knauf, E. | conz |
| 1960 | Lin, H.H. | chin |
| 1961 | de Vos, pastor R. | cong |
| 1961 | Mendez, Juana F. | arge |
| 1961 | Moreau, fr Yvon Emmanuel | hait |
| 1961 | Nikolai, metrop of Krutitsy | russ |
| 1961 | Rodrigues, deacon Pedro | ango |
| 1961 | Stepinac, cardinal abp A. | croa |
| 1962 | Gerber, D. | viet |
| 1962 | Grove, M. | soma |
| 1962 | Kanamuzeyi, pastor Yona | rwan |
| 1962 | Kruegler MM, fr W.C. | boli |
| 1962 | Matulionis, bp of Kaisiadorys | lith |
| 1962 | Mendes, evangelist Formoso | gunb |
| 1962 | Mitchell, A. | viet |
| 1962 | Vitti, A. | viet |
| 1963 | Adwok, pastor G. | suda |
| 1963 | Barbosa, evangelist Dinis | gunb |
| 1963 | Collins, Addie Mae | usa |
| 1963 | da Costa, Joaquin | gunb |
| 1963 | da Silva, pastor Pedro | gunb |
| 1963 | Debior, P. | suda |
| 1963 | Landim | gunb |
| 1963 | McNair, Denise | usa |
| 1963 | Robertson, Carole | usa |
| 1963 | Sangueso, P. P. | arge |
| 1963 | Vaz Martins, evangelist Victor | gunb |
| 1963 | Wesley, Cynthia | usa |
| 1964 | Anuarite, sr M.C. | conz |
| 1964 | Carlson, P. | conz |
| 1964 | Cheney, J. | usa |
| 1964 | Dwatuka, fr B. | suda |
| 1964 | Goodman | usa |
| 1964 | Khmara, N. | russ |
| 1964 | Kucherenko | russ |
| 1964 | Lifenya, director Pierre | conz |
| 1964 | McMillan, H. | conz |
| 1964 | Rhine, Phyllis | conz |
| 1964 | Scholten, W.H. | conz |
| 1964 | Tucker, J. | conz |
| 1965 | Daniels, J. | usa |
| 1965 | Goehring, H. | bang |
| c1965 | McBeth, fr | bang |
| 1966 | Bamba, Emmanuel | conz |
| 1966 | Torres, fr Camilo | colo |
| 1967 | Saturnino, fr | suda |
| 1968 | Blood, H. | viet |
| 1968 | Dale, pastor Stan | indo |
| 1968 | King, Jr, pastor Martin Luther | usa |
| 1968 | Liuzzo, Viola | usa |
| 1968 | Masters, P. | indo |
| 1968 | Olsen, Betty | viet |
| c1968 | Sheikow, Musa | soma |
| c1968 | Vasilyevna, M. | russ |
| 1968 | Wilting, Ruth | viet |
| 1970 | Afonin, I.A. | russ |
| 1970 | Bergemann, F. | russ |
| c1970 | Brown, bp D. | libe |
| 1970 | Druck, V. | russ |
| 1970 | Golev, S.T. | russ |
| c1970 | Heywood, J. | viet |
| c1970 | Hmara of Kulunda | ukra |
| 1970 | Hossu, bp J. | roma |
| 1970 | Lamichami, Krishna | nepa |
| 1970 | Nyabadza, fr B. | zimb |
| 1970 | Rodriguez, fr Nicolas | elsa |
| 1971 | Biswas, U. | bang |
| 1971 | Le Febre, M. | boli |
| 1971 | Potter, Nancy | domr |
| 1971 | Potter, Paul E. & Nancy | domr |
| 1971 | Tejerina, Silvita A. | arge |
| 1971 | Zakharov | russ |
| 1972 | Binyoni, Abel | buru |
| 1972 | Brown, pastor | bang |
| 1972 | de Freitas, pastor F. | ango |
| 1972 | George, Margaret | iraq |
| 1972 | Kiwanuka, justice Benedicto | ugan |
| 1972 | Kurti, fr Shtjefen | alba |
| 1972 | Manganhela, Z. | moza |
| 1972 | Melnikov | russ |
| 1972 | Nee, Watchman | chin |
| 1972 | Pate, Mavis | pale |
| 1972 | Sidumo, J. | moza |
| 1972 | Williams, N. | phil |
| 1972 | Yagozinsky, S. | russ |
| 1972 | Zhiming, pastor Wang | chin |
| 1973 | Alsina, fr J. | chil |
| 1973 | Damian, abp of Tirane | alba |
| 1973 | Hopewell, Gladys | taiw |
| 1973 | Isa, Peter | ethi |
| 1973 | Kagwa, M. | ugan |
| 1973 | Kiggundu, fr C. | ugan |
| 1973 | Mukhana, J. | ugan |
| 1973 | Serwanika, J. | ugan |
| 1974 | Cabo, fr M. | usa |
| 1974 | Charlier, fr E. | conz |
| 1974 | de Alencar, F.T. | peru |
| 1974 | Hernandez, M. Gomez | mexi |
| 1974 | Hernandez, pastor | nica |
| 1974 | Lain, fr Domingo | colo |
| 1974 | Moiseyevich, pastor I. | russ |
| 1974 | Ostapenko, pastor I.M. | russ |
| 1974 | Reimer, G. | pana |
| 1974 | Rozanov, N. | russ |
| 1974 | Trochta, cardinal S. | czec |
| 1974 | Viaene, fr L. | conz |
| 1975 | Badre OSB, prior J. | camb |
| 1975 | Betancur, fr I. | hond |
| 1975 | Biblenko, I.V. | russ |
| 1975 | Constable, pastor Eric | indo |
| 1975 | Cypher OFM, fr M.C. | hond |
| 1975 | Hoang, pastor Van Dat | viet |
| 1975 | Lutsky, fr M. | ukra |
| 1975 | Nguyen, Huy Mai | viet |
| 1975 | Nguyen, Van Hoa | viet |
| 1975 | Nze, bp Abuy Raphael | equa |
| 1976 | Salas, bp J. C. | camb |
| 1975 | Shimun, catholicos-patriarch | iraq |
| 1975 | Simescu, br | roma |
| 1975 | Tamonis, M. | lith |
| 1975 | Tep Im, bp Paolo | camb |
| c1975 | Wallenburg, Raoul | pola |
| 1975 | Zecianu, br | roma |
| 1976 | Angelelli, bp Enrique | arge |
| 1976 | Calvan, pastor R. | phil |
| 1976 | Chunsar OSB, fr B. C. | camb |
| c1976 | de la Cruz, fr C. | guat |
| 1976 | Deinega, N.Y. | russ |
| 1976 | Dios Murias, fr C. | arge |
| c1976 | Gran, fr J.M. | guat |
| 1976 | Longueville, fr G. | arge |
| 1976 | Lopez, fr H. | guat |
| 1976 | Lunkenbein, fr R. | braz |
| 1976 | Musaka, fr | ugan |
| 1976 | Schmitt, bp A. | zimb |
| c1976 | Voordeckers, fr W. | guat |
| 1976 | Woods MM, fr W. | guat |
| 1977 | Argew, T. | ethi |
| 1977 | Arreola, sr Silvia Maribel | elsa |
| 1977 | Avdeyev, M.V. | russ |
| 1977 | Biayenda, cardinal abp E. | cong |
| 1977 | Biko, Steve | soua |
| 1977 | Eschtruth, G.J.R. | conz |
| 1977 | Grande, fr R. | elsa |
| 1977 | Ivanova, R. | russ |
| 1977 | Luwum, abp Janani | ugan |
| 1977 | Navarro, fr A. | elsa |
| 1977 | Selassie, emperor Haile | ethi |
| 1977 | Torres, L.A. | elsa |
| 1978 | Bassera, fr Ernesto | elsa |
| 1978 | Dunaway, Jr., A.G. | zimb |
| 1978 | Evans, P. & S. | zimb |
| 1978 | Evans, S. | zimb |
| 1978 | Fisher, M. | zimb |
| 1978 | Lunkebein, fr R. | braz |
| 1978 | Lynn, R. & J. & Pamela | zimb |
| 1978 | Lynn, J. | zimb |
| 1978 | Lynn, Pamela | zimb |
| 1978 | McCann, P. & S. & Joy | zimb |
| 1978 | McCann, Joy | zimb |
| 1978 | McCann, S. | zimb |
| 1978 | Picken, C. | zimb |
| 1978 | Sedletsky, V. | russ |
| 1979 | Annanias, fr O. | ugan |
| 1979 | Coba, bp E. | alba |
| 1979 | Dalmajo, fr S. | ugan |
| 1979 | Fiorantie, fr A. | ugan |
| 1979 | Gono, fr M. | czec |
| 1979 | Goodman, Dave | turk |
| 1979 | Kalienuk, fr Z.A. | ukra |
| 1979 | Krasnova, T.K. | russ |
| 1979 | Ortiz, fr Octavia | elsa |
| 1979 | Palacios, fr Rafael | elsa |
| 1979 | Sangaya, J. | mala |
| 1979 | Santi, fr G. | ugan |
| 1979 | Sayyad, fr | iran |
| 1979 | Shorrosh, A. | pale |
| 1979 | Siyah, pastor Aristou | iran |
| 1979 | Tumsa, Gudinsa | ethi |
| 1979 | Wasikye, John, bp of Mbale | ugan |
| 1980 | Bakholdin, S. | russ |
| 1980 | Chacon, Juan | elsa |
| 1980 | Clarke, sr M. | elsa |
| 1980 | Donovan, sr J. | elsa |
| 1980 | Espinal SJ, fr L. | boli |
| 1980 | Ford, sr I. | elsa |
| 1980 | Gurgula, fr A. | ukra |
| 1980 | Jaugelis, fr V. | lith |
| 1980 | Kazel, sr D. | elsa |
| 1980 | Kotyk, fr Y. | ukra |
| 1980 | Romero, abp Oscar | elsa |
| 1980 | Samwel, abp | ethi |
| 1980 | Sapoka, fr L. | lith |
| 1980 | Shelkov, V. A. | russ |
| 1980 | Theofilas, patriarch | ethi |
| 1981 | Barendsen, Eeva | afgh |
| 1981 | Barendsen, Erik | afgh |
| 1981 | Bitterman III, C.A. | colo |
| 1981 | Clipa, I. | roma |
| 1981 | Coufal, fr P. | czec |
| 1981 | Fietje, K. | thai |
| 1981 | Ghabrail, fr Abd Mutagalli | egyp |
| 1981 | Kernweisz, bp K. | roma |
| 1981 | Laurinavicius, fr B. | lith |
| 1981 | Mazeika, fr L. | lith |
| 1981 | Miller, fr J. | guat |
| 1981 | Quilini, H. N. | egyp |
| 1981 | Raflan, B. | egyp |
| 1981 | Rother, fr S. | guat |
| 1981 | Samuel, bp Makary El-Souria | egyp |
| 1981 | Svanda, fr P. | czec |
| 1981 | Teodosiu, S. | roma |
| 1981 | Troyer, J.D. | guat |
| 1981 | Tsachev, N.V. | bulg |
| c1982 | Athers, Lester | nica |
| 1982 | Barta, fr J. | czec |
| 1982 | Garcia, Anastasio | guat |
| 1982 | Khrapov, N.P. | russ |
| 1982 | Manzinger, fr | belo |
| 1982 | Smith, E. | nica |
| 1982 | Terelya, B.M. | ukra |
| 1982 | Toj, Juan Garcia | guat |
| 1983 | Carney SJ, fr J.G. | hond |
| 1983 | Chiwanga | mala |
| 1983 | Gadama | mala |
| 1983 | Gideon, dr | myan |
| 1983 | Holdenried, F.X. | guat |
| 1983 | Jarlan, A. | chil |
| 1983 | Ki-Yoon, pastor I. | souk |
| 1983 | Matenje | mala |
| 1983 | Muothe, I.T. | soua |
| 1983 | Sawyer, sr Joan | peru |
| 1983 | Toma, pastor Nicolas | guat |
| 1983 | Vargas, pastor N. | nica |
| 1984 | Bazira, pastor G. | ugan |
| 1984 | Popieluszko, fr J. | pola |
| 1984 | Potochnyak, fr A. | ukra |
| 1984 | Roxas, S. | phil |
| 1984 | Roy, fr | mada |
| 1984 | Shude SJ, fr F.Z. | chin |
| 1984 | Torboli, fr S. | moza |
| 1984 | Ulcue Chocue, fr A. | colo |
| 1985 | Aleku, B. | ethi |
| 1985 | Allende, S. N. | chil |
| 1985 | Arensen, J. | suda |
| 1985 | Beling, fr M. | phil |
| 1985 | Cabrera Rivera, prof C.H. | guat |
| 1985 | Calderon, Z.S. | peru |
| 1985 | Ceballos, M. G. | chil |
| 1985 | Chappell, R. | papu |
| 1985 | Cuthbert, R. W. M. | jama |
| 1985 | Dalle Pezze, sr T.P. | moza |
| 1985 | Durksen, Y. | russ |
| 1985 | Espino, pastor E. F. | elsa |
| 1985 | Favali, fr T. | phil |
| 1985 | Goncalves Kamtedza SJ, fr J. | moza |
| 1985 | Hammes, W. | usa |
| 1985 | Jeyarajasingham, pastor G. | sril |
| 1985 | Kautudja, sr L. | ango |
| 1985 | Kluiters, fr N. | leba |
| c1985 | Lavina, J. | phil |
| c1985 | Ludena, T. | peru |
| 1985 | Maluendo, J. M. P. | chil |
| 1985 | Manielpillai, fr M.B. | sril |
| 1985 | Moreira SJ, fr S. | moza |
| 1985 | Moretto, fr J. | ango |
| 1985 | Paredes, A.A. | ango |
| 1985 | Philpot, J. | mexi |
| 1985 | Poplawski, fr P. | pola |
| 1985 | Rojas, C.M. | peru |
| 1985 | Romano, fr R. | phil |
| 1985 | Romero, fr A. | phil |
| 1985 | Rossiter, fr J. | usa |
| 1985 | Roth, F. | usa |
| 1985 | Sikufinde, fr L. | ango |
| 1985 | Sorgon OCD, fr S. | mada |
| 1985 | Tzalam Coj, Manuel de Jesus | guat |
| 1985 | Valerio, fr N. | phil |
| 1985 | Wasnak, fr J.E. | ango |
| 1986 | Brennes, J. | mexi |
| 1986 | Castilblanco, N.A. | nica |
| 1986 | Figaroa, N.M. | mexi |
| 1986 | Flores, Ernesto | mexi |
| 1986 | Moreno, Norma | mexi |
| 1986 | Senter, L. & R. | libe |
| 1986 | Senter, R. | libe |
| 1986 | Wilson, evangelist John E.H. | ugan |
| 1987 | Arango, sr Ines | ecua |
| 1987 | Bangirimana, Ernest | buru |
| 1987 | Labaca Ugarte OFMCap, bp A. | ecua |
| 1987 | Massé SJ, fr André | leba |
| 1987 | Park, Jong Ch'ol | souk |
| 1987 | Rodrigo OMI, fr Miguel | sril |
| 1987 | Wahid | paki |
| 1987 | Zuma, pastor Antonio | ecua |
| 1988 | Augusto, fr Giraldo Cesar | colo |
| 1988 | Beebwa, sr M.T. | ugan |
| 1988 | Chandra, fr F. | sril |
| 1988 | de Boisseson, fr J. | mada |
| 1988 | Dias OFM, fr C. | paki |
| 1988 | Estorba, fr M. | phil |
| 1988 | Giraldo, fr C. Augusto | colo |
| 1988 | Hairapetian, V. | azer |
| 1988 | Knoerl, br K. | zimb |
| 1988 | Oido, fr C.O. | ugan |
| 1988 | Okagric, br A. | ugan |
| 1988 | Paisai, G. | nepa |
| 1988 | Ramaralahy, br I. | mada |
| 1988 | Schmitz, CP, fr Carl | phil |
| 1988 | Spil MHM, fr C. | ugan |
| 1988 | Stockton, Ann | phil |
| 1988 | Tarzwell, John | paki |
| 1988 | Wojcickowski, sr S. | paki |
| 1989 | Ayap, pastor A. | phil |
| 1989 | Benitez, fr M.A. | colo |
| 1989 | Boisvert, fr A. | japa |
| 1989 | Bortolotti, fr F. | moza |
| 1989 | Campanella, fr C. | moza |
| 1989 | Colombo OFM, bp P.S. | soma |
| 1989 | Corniall, sr Maurice | nica |
| 1989 | de Rocha, fr A. | moza |
| 1989 | Ejeru, pastor Joseph | ugan |
| 1989 | Elba Ramos, Celina | elsa |
| 1989 | Elba Ramos, Julia & Celina | elsa |
| 1989 | Ellacuria SJ, fr I. | elsa |
| 1989 | Giuliatti OFMCap, fr A. | ango |
| 1989 | Gomez, Maria Cristina | elsa |
| 1989 | Gran, Lovello | phil |
| 1989 | Gran, pastor Vizminda | phil |
| 1989 | Jaramillo, bp Jesus E. | colo |
| 1989 | Lopez Lopez SJ, fr J. | elsa |
| 1989 | Lopez SJ, fr A. | elsa |
| 1989 | Maire, fr G.F. | braz |
| 1989 | Malalay, fr D. | phil |
| 1989 | Mansalve, bp Jesus E.J. | colo |
| 1989 | Martin-Baro SJ, fr I. | elsa |
| 1989 | Mien, fr Alexander | russ |
| 1989 | Monsalve, bp Jesus E. J. | colo |
| 1989 | Montes SJ, fr S. | elsa |
| 1989 | Nodrat, Zia Mohammed | afgh |
| 1989 | Ramon Moreno SJ, fr J. | elsa |
| 1989 | Reinkemeyer, sr A. | keny |
| 1989 | Restrepo, fr S. | colo |
| 1989 | Rivera, Rufino | phil |
| 1989 | Rosales, sr Teresa | nica |
| 1989 | Ruelo, pastor Z. | phil |
| 1989 | Saltori, fr O. | moza |
| 1989 | Tjibaou, Jean-Marie | newc |
| 1989 | Van Kleef CM, fr N. | pana |
| 1989 | Vassallo, sr Emanuela | liby |
| 1989 | Webster, David | soua |
| 1989 | Xinsheng, bp Li | chin |
| 1989 | Yeiwene Yeiwene | newc |
| 1990 | Biscaro, fr Egidio | ugan |
| 1990 | Courtney, sr M. | nica |
| 1990 | Fernandez, fr T. | colo |

*Continued overleaf*

*Table 4-12 concluded*

| | | |
|---|---|---|
| 1990 | Gagnaux, dr R. | moza |
| c1990 | Kim, pastor | nork |
| 1990 | Klein, Valve | esto |
| 1990 | Lasar, fr Hegumen | russ |
| 1990 | Lewis, pastor N. | usa |
| 1990 | Mack, Myrna | guat |
| 1990 | Magorrian, H.L. | soua |
| 1990 | Mamma, pr | suda |
| 1990 | Menn, fr Alexander | russ |
| 1990 | Meri, dean Harald | esto |
| 1990 | Nicholson, sr A.C. | ango |
| 1990 | Priya SMA, sr | indi |
| 1990 | Soodmand, pastor H. | iran |
| 1990 | Stanton, fr N. | soua |
| 1990 | Stumpf, H. | keny |
| 1990 | Sylvia SMA, sr | indi |
| 1990 | Tete, president Martin | indi |
| c1990 | Wi-Foo | myan |
| c1990 | Xueyan, bp Fan | chin |
| 1991 | Aziza, Adel | egyp |
| 1991 | Bagaric, fr N. | bosn |
| 1991 | Bethea, Lynda | keny |
| 1991 | Capasilan, A. | phil |
| 1991 | Casaverde, C. | peru |
| 1991 | Chuquin, J. | peru |
| 1991 | Cisneros, fr Moises | guat |
| 1991 | Claude, pastor Sylvio | hait |
| 1991 | Cristovao, fr M.J. | moza |
| 1991 | Goldsworthy, K. | phil |
| 1991 | Gutierrez, L. | peru |
| 1991 | Hass, sr Claire | baha |
| 1991 | Lawi, Ezra | suda |
| 1991 | McCormack, sr Irene | peru |
| 1991 | Mohammed, br | nige |
| 1991 | Plumey OMI, abp I. | came |
| 1991 | Prada Pires, fr J.M. | braz |
| 1991 | Sarmiento, M. | peru |
| 1991 | Shaga, Nana | ethi |
| 1991 | Sigridsson, S. | phil |
| 1991 | Speers, J. | phil |
| 1991 | Strzalkowski, fr Z. | peru |
| 1991 | Tattersall, N. | peru |
| 1991 | Tomaszek OFM, fr M. | peru |
| 1991 | Turati OFM, fr P. | soma |
| 1991 | Vargas, C. | peru |
| 1991 | You WF, fr Alexander | ugan |
| 1992 | Aguiar, sr L. | ango |
| 1992 | Al-Hari, A. | phil |
| 1992 | Amlak, fr A. | ethi |
| 1992 | Bacabis, G. | phil |
| 1992 | Bakheit, dr S. | egyp |
| 1992 | Carzedda, fr S. | phil |
| 1992 | Celiz, Romeo | phil |
| 1992 | Culembee Munto, sr M. | ango |
| 1992 | de Dios, Manuel | usa |
| 1992 | de Fonseca Guerra, fr A. | ango |
| 1992 | Fallah, pastor J. | libe |
| 1992 | Fiorini, fr Alfredo | moza |
| 1992 | Goncalves, sr M.L. Granado | moza |
| 1992 | Guirguis, A.S. | egyp |
| 1992 | Guirguis, M.Q. | egyp |
| 1992 | Hamill, J. | phil |
| 1992 | Hapalla, pastor Gregorio | phil |
| 1992 | Husband, sr G. | came |
| 1992 | Iqbal, Tahir | paki |
| 1992 | Jackson, J. | libe |
| 1992 | Jackson, T. & J. | libe |
| 1992 | Juliet | phil |
| 1992 | Kariuki, pastor H. | keny |
| 1992 | Khalil, H.F. | egyp |
| 1992 | Kolmer, sr J. | libe |
| 1992 | Kolmer, sr S. | libe |
| 1992 | Kon, Paul | suda |
| 1992 | Leal, sr Torres N. | colo |
| 1992 | Leone, sr M. | came |
| 1992 | Locatelli, A. | rwan |
| 1992 | Lukkappa, sadhu | indi |
| 1992 | Mal-Allah, S.A.K. | saud |
| 1992 | Maniafo, S.J. | keny |
| 1992 | Mbatha, S'Khumbuzo | soua |
| 1992 | McGuire, sr K. | libe |
| 1992 | Mueller, sr S. | libe |
| 1992 | Muttra, sr B.A. | libe |
| 1992 | Pfister, J. | ivor |
| 1992 | Pimentel, sr M. | ango |
| 1992 | Poppa, sr R. | rwan |
| 1992 | Ricci, fr F. | ethi |
| 1992 | Robinson, W. | leba |
| 1992 | Saah, pastor D. | libe |
| 1992 | Sahihembo, Alfredo | ango |
| 1992 | Saune, R. | peru |
| 1992 | Tsotetsi, Saul | soua |
| 1993 | Alzokim, N.F. | egyp |
| 1993 | Bassiliouss, P. | egyp |
| 1993 | Bimazubute, G. | buru |
| 1993 | Chunjee, bp P.S. | chin |
| c1993 | Difen, bp Liu | chin |
| 1993 | Iskandar, E.N. | egyp |
| 1993 | Izmery, A. | hait |
| 1991 | Jeanne SAM, fr A. | ivor |
| 1993 | Korfeh, pastor T. | libe |
| 1993 | Manping, Lai | chin |
| 1993 | Marsouk, H. | egyp |
| 1993 | Mikic OFM, fr L. | bosn |
| 1993 | Milicevic OFM, fr N. | bosn |
| 1993 | Ocampo, cardinal Juan J.J.P. | mexi |
| 1993 | Packianathan, fr V.S. | indi |
| 1993 | Posadas, cardinal J.J. | mexi |
| 1993 | Puglisi, pastor G. | ital |
| 1993 | Ramos, bp Robert J. | elsa |
| 1993 | Shafiq, S. | egyp |
| 1993 | Theophiles, K.Y. | egyp |
| 1993 | Zuma, Isaac | soua |
| 1993 | Zuma, Thandi | soua |
| 1994 | Diaz, Veronica J. | mexi |
| 1994 | Dibaj, pastor Mehdi | iran |
| 1994 | Gatwa, T. | rwan |
| 1994 | Havugimana, evangelist I | rwan |
| 1994 | Heyns, moderator Johan | soua |
| 1994 | Hovsepian-Mehr, bp H. | iran |
| 1994 | Karuhije, dean A. | rwan |
| 1994 | Liibaan, Ibrahim | soma |
| 1994 | Limar, br | taji |
| 1994 | Masih, Manzoor | paki |
| 1994 | Michaelian, pastor Tateos | iran |
| 1994 | Musheng, Zheng | chin |
| 1994 | Nieto, F. A. E. | peru |
| 1994 | Nsengiyumva, abp V. | rwan |
| 1994 | Nsengiyumva, bp T. | rwan |
| 1994 | Nur al-Qums Binyamin | egyp |
| 1994 | Rutumbu, fr J. | rwan |
| 1994 | Ruzindana, bp J. | rwan |
| 1994 | Serech, P. | guat |
| 1995 | Van Dyke, T. | colo |
| 1994 | Vincent, pastor Jean-Marie | hait |
| 1995 | Welsh, S. | colo |
| 1995 | Alean, pastor M. | colo |
| 1995 | Argelio, pastor J. | colo |
| c1995 | Finnemann, bp W. | phil |
| 1995 | Fumagalli, Graziella | soma |
| 1995 | Gomez Ramos, pastor A. | mexi |
| 1995 | Goobe, A. | soma |
| 1995 | Grassi, br B. | pale |
| 1995 | Hernandez Perez, pastor G. | mexi |
| 1995 | Iloputaife, bp H. A. | nige |
| 1995 | Isho, E.K. | iraq |
| c1995 | Katoolig, C. | soma |
| 1995 | Kerkatta, John | indi |
| 1995 | Leclerc, sr D. | alge |
| 1995 | Littlejohn, sr J. | alge |
| 1995 | Maclese, sr P. | ghan |
| c1995 | Mahamed, S. | soma |
| 1995 | Maria, sr Rani | indi |
| 1995 | Masih, Iqbal | paki |
| 1995 | Masih, Javed | paki |
| 1996 | Murphy, sr C. | ghan |
| 1995 | O'Neill, fr E. | soua |
| 1995 | Petcu, A. | mold |
| 1995 | Prevost, sr O. | alge |
| 1995 | Rangell, Hugo | colo |
| 1995 | Ruibal, pastor Julio C. | colo |
| 1995 | Saquic Vasquez, pastor M. | guat |
| 1995 | Saro-Wiwa, K. | nige |
| 1995 | Sellekaerts IHM, sr C. | conz |
| c1995 | Sheekhdoon, M. | soma |
| 1995 | Sinankwa, fr M. | buru |
| 1995 | Solan, Joel | phil |
| 1995 | Vasquez, pastor M.S. | guat |
| 1995 | Yi, C.H. | russ |
| 1995 | Yi, K. W. | russ |
| 1996 | Abdel-Sayeda, H. L. | egyp |
| 1996 | Alzate Varela, pastor P. | colo |
| 1995 | Amador, pastor Manuel | colo |
| 1996 | Bagtasos III, pastor S. | phil |
| 1996 | Bumendwa, fr J. C. | conz |
| 1996 | Bwambale, pastor P. | conz |
| 1996 | Camacho, H. | phil |
| 1996 | Carro, C. Quiroz | colo |
| 1996 | Chanthom, Toun | camb |
| 1996 | Cherukarokunnel, L. J. | indi |
| 1996 | Christian, pastor Ishak | indo |
| 1996 | Claverie P., bp of Oran | alge |
| 1996 | Concesse, Sr | buru |
| 1996 | Coronel, J. D. | colo |
| 1996 | de Chergé OCSO, dom C. | alge |
| 1996 | de la Fuente, br F. | conz |
| 1996 | Dochier OCSO, br L. | alge |
| 1996 | Farris, Dr. Ron | como |
| 1996 | Favre-Miville OCOS, br P. | alge |
| 1996 | Fernando, SJ, R. M. | camb |
| 1996 | Fleury OCSO, br M. | alge |
| 1996 | Gabriel, I. A. | egyp |
| 1996 | Gakobwa, Sr I. | buru |
| 1996 | Gakondo, sr J. A. | conz |
| 1996 | Garcia, br S. M. | conz |
| 1996 | Gatuku, fr C. | conz |
| 1996 | Gatunga, sr J. | conz |
| 1996 | Girgis, M. B. | egyp |
| 1996 | Gonzales, J. L. | colo |
| 1996 | Haaji, professor | soma |
| 1996 | Hakizimana, fr S. | buru |
| 1996 | Hanas, dr Michel Ayad | egyp |
| 1996 | Hansda, S. | indi |
| 1996 | Hapalla, J. | phil |
| 1996 | Her, Ah | laos |
| 1996 | Huseen, professor H. M. | soma |
| 1996 | Irenee, sr | buru |
| 1996 | Ishak Christian, pastor | indo |
| 1996 | Jorge, br J. R. | conz |
| 1996 | Jurcevic, sr D | bosn |
| 1996 | Kahegezo, fr B. K. | conz |
| 1996 | Kajibwami, br F. | conz |
| 1996 | Kanyamanza, fr P. | conz |
| 1996 | Kasati, fr J. | conz |
| 1996 | Lasker, evangelist Hussain | indi |
| 1996 | Lebreton, OCSO, fr C. | alge |
| 1996 | Lemarchand OCSO, fr Bruno | alge |
| 1996 | Loperena Soto OP, fr W. | puer |
| 1996 | Luc, Father | alge |
| 1996 | Lucio, br M. A. I. | conz |
| 1996 | Lucio, sr M. A. I. | conz |
| 1996 | Makaboge, moderator E. | soua |
| 1996 | Mataboge, rev E. | soua |
| 1996 | Mathias, mrs. C. | usa |
| 1996 | Mathias, pastor C. & wife | usa |
| 1996 | McAleese, sr P. | ghan |
| 1996 | Miville OCSO, br P. F. | alge |
| 1996 | Mounabandi, sr C | conz |
| 1996 | Mpengekeze, fr Y. | buru |
| 1996 | Mukeshimana, sr A. | rwan |
| 1996 | Munyankuyu, fr A. | conz |
| 1996 | Munzihirwa, abp C. | conz |
| 1996 | Munzombo, pasotr D. | conz |
| 1996 | Ndacikiriwe, sr C. | buru |
| 1996 | Ndihokubwayo, sr L. | buru |
| 1996 | Ngabo SJ, abp C. M. M. | conz |
| 1996 | Ngwije, fr A. K. | rwan |
| 1996 | Nikwigize, bp P. | rwan |
| 1996 | Nirere, fr B. | conz |
| 1996 | Nsengiyunva, fr E. | conz |
| 1996 | Ramanauskas, fr V. | lith |
| 1996 | Ringeard OCSO, fr C. | alge |
| 1996 | Ruhuna, J., abp of Gitega | buru |
| 1996 | Sabuni, pastor M. | conz |
| 1996 | Schiavo, fr G. | tanz |
| 1996 | Sebalija, sr L. | conz |
| 1996 | Semutwe, sr M. A. | conz |
| 1996 | Sokan, Khoun | camb |
| 1996 | Soto OP, fr W. L. | puer |
| 1996 | Xiuju, Zhang | chin |
| 1996 | Yusefi, pastor Mohammad B. | iran |
| 1996 | Zubiri, sr Carmen | rwan |
| 1997 | Alege, prof A. | conz |
| 1997 | Anchanickal SJ, fr T. | indi |
| 1997 | Badiali, rev D. | peru |
| 1997 | Batista, sr T. | braz |
| 1997 | Bedoya, fr A. | colo |
| 1997 | Beltran, A. | saud |
| 1997 | Bosmans, Sr M. | rwan |
| 1997 | Buchwolder, sr C. | buru |
| 1997 | Collazo, S. | mexi |
| 1997 | d'Herouville, Sr C. | chad |
| 1997 | da Silva, rev J. J. C. | braz |
| 1997 | de Jesus, bp B. | phil |
| 1997 | Donado, elder W. | colo |
| 1997 | Estafanos, K. | egyp |
| 1997 | Gadzhiyev, G. | russ |
| 1997 | Gadzhiyev, Tatiana | russ |
| 1997 | Gafney SJ, fr T. | nepa |
| 1997 | Geyer-Iwand, V. | germ |
| 1997 | Habakurama, rev I. | rwan |
| 1997 | Hatagekimang, rev A. | conz |
| 1997 | Hernandez, M. | mexi |
| 1997 | Isidi, rev N. | nige |
| 1997 | James, Jessica | usa |
| 1997 | Janda, R. | saud |
| 1997 | Kabera, rev E. | conz |
| 1997 | Kiyumukiza, rev A. N. | conz |
| 1997 | Magomedov, H & T. | russ |
| 1997 | Marcellina, sr A. T. S. | paki |
| 1997 | Matti, Haval | iraq |
| 1991 | Matti, Lazar | iraq |
| 1997 | Mihingo, rev N. | conz |
| 1997 | Mukamihogo, sr F. | conz |
| 1997 | Munyakazy, rev E. | conz |
| 1997 | Muyoboke, rev F. | conz |
| 1997 | Nedumattahil, fr J. | indi |
| 1997 | Nyirabakungu, sr C. | conz |
| 1997 | Nyirarukundu, sr M. | conz |
| 1997 | Ozdemir, Ali | turk |
| 1997 | Pande, evangelist M. | indi |
| 1997 | Pena, fr S. C. | colo |
| 1997 | Perez, M. | mexi |
| 1997 | Pinard WF, fr Guy | rwan |
| 1997 | Ramos SJ, fr W. G. | mexi |
| 1997 | Rio, pastor W. | phil |
| 1997 | Ruiz, pastor N. H. | mexi |
| 1997 | Ruterahagusha, pastor T. | rwan |
| 1997 | Ruterahagusha, T. | rwan |
| 1997 | Selorio, pastor E. | phil |
| 1997 | Sifer, M. H. | iraq |
| 1997 | Stegar, Kayce | usa |
| 1997 | Thomas SJ, fr A. T. | indi |
| 1997 | Timmons, br L. | keny |
| 1997 | Tshisambu, fr F. | conz |
| 1997 | Twagirayezu, rev U. | conz |
| 1997 | Uwizeyimana, rev J. | conz |
| 1997 | Yirirwahandi, rev P. | rwan |
| 1998 | Abrao | ango |
| 1998 | Adrienne, sr | conz |
| 1998 | Alam, pastor Noor | paki |
| 1998 | Andeni, fr L. | keny |
| 1998 | Anetta, sr | yeme |
| 1998 | Beheydt, pastor G. S. | ital |
| 1998 | Benimana, sr F. | rwan |
| 1998 | Boumans SVD, fr G. | para |
| 1998 | Bwabulakombe, sr S. | conz |
| 1998 | Carreno, fr M. O. | mexi |
| 1998 | Chicangana, fr A. J. | colo |
| 1998 | Chocho, Alber | pana |
| 1998 | Colorado, Adan | colo |
| 1998 | Commissari, fr L. | braz |
| 1998 | Conedera, bp J. G. | guat |
| 1998 | Curic, fr V. | rwan |
| 1998 | Czuba, fr J. | cong |
| 1998 | de Rojas, M. R. | colo |
| 1998 | Deng, A. Y. | suda |
| 1998 | Desrumeaux, sr A. | conz |
| 1998 | Gaona, br M. A. Q. | colo |
| 1998 | Gasigwa, sr E. | rwan |
| 1998 | Germaine, sr | conz |
| 1998 | Haviaropoulos, V. | turk |
| 1998 | Hood, Carl | colo |
| 1998 | Hoyo, br J. | indi |
| 1998 | Hubscher, fr M. | mada |
| 1998 | Hudon, fr B. | hait |
| 1998 | Hughes, B. | brit |
| 1998 | Kagabo, fr B. | rwan |
| 1998 | Kathihe, sr L. | ango |
| 1998 | Lilia, sr | yeme |
| 1998 | Loften, pastor A. | usa |
| 1998 | Louis, fr J-P. | hait |
| 1998 | Malenga, E. | conz |
| 1998 | Malesh, pastor J. | suda |
| 1998 | Mandro, J-F. K. | conz |
| 1998 | Marrero, mgr A. G. | vene |
| 1998 | Michaela, sr | yeme |
| 1998 | Mukagakwaya, sr X. | rwan |
| 1998 | Mukamuhire, sr B. | rwan |
| 1998 | Mukanoheli, sr V. | rwan |
| 1998 | Muntoni, fr G. | ital |
| 1998 | Nakavoua, G. A. | cong |
| 1998 | Nielsen, B. M. | buru |
| 1998 | Puttaniyil, br L. | indi |
| 1998 | Quinn, Jason | brit |
| 1998 | Quinn, Mark | brit |
| 1998 | Quinn, Richard | brit |
| 1998 | Rajiv, John | indi |
| 1998 | Rwangeyo, sr D. | rwan |
| 1998 | Saenz, J. D. | colo |
| 1998 | Satchilombo, Francisco | ango |
| 1998 | Schreck, sr M. | soua |
| 1998 | Siahae, J. | indo |
| 1998 | Simatupang, T. M. | indo |
| 1998 | Sritharan, pastor Vasu | sril |
| 1998 | Wimana, sr C. | rwan |
| 1999 | Abadiano, Ted | phil |
| 1999 | Aloysius, sr M. | sier |
| 1999 | Bernall, Cassie | usa |
| 1999 | Bhatti, Sabir John | paki |
| 1999 | Carmeline, sr | sier |
| 1999 | Hindu, sr | sier |
| 1999 | Kulakov, pastor A. | russ |
| 1999 | Massoud, Magdi F. | egyp |
| 1999 | Miller, Carla | usa |
| 1999 | Miller, Jr., Shon | usa |
| 1999 | Peleman, fr A. | soua |
| 1999 | Rojas, fr H. F. | colo |
| 1999 | Saluhaku, fr A. | ango |
| 1999 | Scott, Rachel | usa |
| 1999 | Staines, Graham | indi |
| 1999 | Staines, Philip | indi |
| 1999 | Staines, Timothy | indi |
| 1999 | Sweva, sr | sier |
| 1999 | Tomlin, John | usa |
| 1999 | Umbarger, Deena M. | soma |
| 2000 | Abakumate, sr M | cent |
| 2000 | Akullu, G. | ugan |
| 2000 | Akweyo, sr D. | ugan |
| 2000 | Amzati, C.G. | conz |
| 2000 | Asienzo, sr P. | ugan |
| 2000 | Bargiggia, fr A. | buru |
| 2000 | Bello, fr C.O. | nige |
| 2000 | Bernardo, fr J. | alba |
| 2000 | Chittinapilly, fr S.J. | indi |
| 2000 | Crasta, fr V. | indi |
| 2000 | di Bari, fr R. | ugan |
| 2000 | Dias, J. da Rocha | ango |
| 2000 | Duque, fr H. | colo |
| 2000 | Emmanuel, bp G. | indi |
| 2000 | Gallardo, fr R. | phil |
| 2000 | Gaytan, rev J. | mexi |
| 2000 | Grange, fr R. | ivor |
| 2000 | Inocencio, fr B. | phil |
| 2000 | Jami, fr Y. | indo |
| 2000 | Kaiser, fr A. | keny |
| 2000 | Karketta, fr R. | indi |
| 2000 | Kuzhikandom, fr G. | indi |
| 2000 | Masih, Mushtaq | indi |
| 2000 | Nzikobanyanka, rev P. | buru |
| 2000 | Ogbu, fr J.M.O. | nige |
| 2000 | Pepe, fr R. | conz |
| 2000 | Ramirez, fr A.G. | colo |
| 2000 | Rochester, fr H. | jama |
| 2000 | Sequeira, sr C. | paki |
| 2000 | Simionato, sr G. | buru |
| 2000 | Tirelli, sr F. | zamb |
| 2000 | Uzcudum, fr I. | rwan |

## Table 4–13. Geographical listing of 2,550 known Christian martyrs, AD 33-2000.

| | | |
|---|---|---|
| 1981 | Barendsen, Eeva | afgh |
| 1981 | Barendsen, Erik | afgh |
| 1989 | Nodrat, Zia Mohammed | afgh |
| 1779 | Aitolos, K. | alba |
| 2000 | Bernardo, fr J. | alba |
| 1979 | Coba, bp E. | alba |
| 1973 | Damian, abp of Tirane | alba |
| 1948 | Gigni, bp | alba |
| 1948 | Gijni, bp | alba |
| 1016 | John Baptist Vladimir, prince | alba |
| 1949 | Kisi, abp K. | alba |
| 1972 | Kurti, fr Shtjefen | alba |
| 1952 | Prennushi, abp N. | alba |
| 1948 | Volai, bp | alba |
| 1996 | Claverie P., bp of Oran | alge |
| 304 | Crispina of Tagora | alge |
| 1996 | de Chergé OCSO, dom C. | alge |
| 1916 | de Foucauld, Charles | alge |
| 1996 | Dochier OCSO, br L. | alge |
| 1996 | Favre-Miville OCOS, br P. | alge |
| 1996 | Fleury OCSO, br M. | alge |
| 1683 | Le Vacher, bp J. | alge |
| 1996 | Lebreton, OCSO, fr C. | alge |
| 1995 | Leclerc, sr D. | alge |
| 1996 | Lemarchand OCSO, fr Bruno | alge |
| 1995 | Littlejohn, sr J. | alge |
| 1996 | Luc, Father | alge |
| 1315 | Lull, Ramon | alge |
| 295 | Maximilian | alge |
| 1996 | Miville OCSO, br P. F. | alge |
| 397 | Optatus, bp of Thamugadi | alge |
| 1995 | Prevost, sr O. | alge |
| 1996 | Ringeard OCSO, fr C. | alge |
| 1998 | Abrao | ango |
| 1992 | Aguiar, sr L. | ango |
| 1992 | Culembee Munto, sr M. | ango |
| 1992 | de Fonseca Guerra, fr A. | ango |
| 1972 | de Freitas, pastor F. | ango |
| 2000 | Dias, J. da Rocha | ango |
| 1989 | Giuliatti OFMCap, fr A. | ango |
| 1998 | Kathihe, sr L. | ango |
| 1985 | Kautudja, sr L. | ango |
| 1985 | Moretto, fr J. | ango |
| 1990 | Nicholson, sr A.C. | ango |
| 1985 | Paredes, A.A. | ango |
| 1992 | Pimentel, sr M. | ango |
| 1961 | Rodrigues, deacon Pedro | ango |
| 1992 | Sahihembo, Alfredo | ango |
| 1999 | Saluhaku, fr A. | ango |
| 1998 | Satchilombo, Francisco | ango |
| 1985 | Sikufinde, fr L. | ango |
| 1985 | Wasnak, fr J.E. | ango |
| 1976 | Angelelli, bp Enrique | arge |
| 1976 | Dios Murias, fr C. | arge |
| 1903 | Figueroa, Juana | arge |
| 1851 | Gardiner, Allen | arge |
| 1976 | Longueville, fr G. | arge |
| 1961 | Mendez, Juana F. | arge |
| 1934 | Moreno, Ramonita | arge |
| 1683 | Ortiz de Zarate, fr P. | arge |
| 1825 | Pogio, fr Bartolome | arge |
| 1683 | Salinas, fr | arge |
| 1963 | Sangueso, P. P. | arge |
| 1908 | Sivila, Visitación | arge |
| 1971 | Tejerina, Silvita A. | arge |
| 1950 | Vasquez, Carmen | arge |
| c125 | Acacius | arme |
| c550 | Adeodatus (Astouadz-Mapod) | arme |
| 66 | Anna of Ormisdat | arme |
| 333 | Aristakes I, patriarch | arme |
| c97 | Atirnerseh, patriarch | arme |
| 451 | Atom & his legion | arme |
| 68 | Bartholomew, Apostle | arme |
| 316 | Blaize, bp | arme |
| 347 | Daniel, patriarch | arme |
| c650 | David of Douine | arme |
| 1314 | de Rosatis, A. of Milan | arme |
| 1314 | Francis of Fermo | arme |
| 290 | Gayane, abbess | arme |
| 193 | Ghevondius, patriarch | arme |
| c1150 | Goharin & companions | arme |
| c550 | Grigor-Rajik | arme |
| 337 | Grigoris, exarch | arme |
| 347 | Houssik I, patriarch | arme |
| 454 | Hovsep I, patriarch | arme |
| 290 | Hripsime | arme |
| c850 | Isaac, prince | arme |
| c850 | Joseph, prince | arme |
| 66 | Jude (Thaddaeus), Apostle | arme |
| 1383 | Kador, John | arme |
| 1938 | Khoren I, catholicos | arme |
| 66 | Mariam of Houssik | arme |
| 66 | Martha of Makovtir | arme |
| 1314 | Monold of Ancona | arme |
| 373 | Nerses I, catholicos | arme |
| 66 | Ogouhie, princess | arme |
| 110 | Oski | arme |
| c250 | Polyeuctus | arme |
| c308 | Repsima & 78 companions | arme |
| 290 | Salahouni, Theodore | arme |
| 66 | Samuel, satrap | arme |
| 66 | Sandoukhte, princess | arme |
| 110 | Soukias & companions | arme |
| 1293 | Stepanos IV, patriarch | arme |
| 347 | Stephen of Ulnia | arme |
| 451 | Suzanne | arme |
| 66 | Terentius | arme |
| 451 | Vardan Mamikonian | arme |
| 76 | Zakaria, bp | arme |
| 66 | Zarmandoukhte | arme |
| 1145 | Bosinlother, abbot Conrad | ausz |
| 1012 | Coloman | ausz |
| 1528 | Hubmaier, B. | ausz |
| 1527 | Hut, H. | ausz |
| 1120 | Merbot | ausz |
| 1524 | Tauber, Casper | ausz |
| 1988 | Hairapetian, V. | azer |
| 1991 | Hass, sr Claire | baha |
| 1971 | Biswas, U. | bang |
| 1972 | Brown, pastor | bang |
| 1965 | Goehring, H. | bang |
| c1965 | McBeth, fr | bang |
| 1915 | Cavell, Edith | belg |
| c650 | Dympna of Ireland | belg |
| 750 | Gerulf | belg |
| 705 | Lambert, bp of Maastricht | belg |
| 884 | Rombout of Malines | belg |
| 1536 | Tyndale, William | belg |
| 1927 | Amfiteatrov, P. | belo |
| 1657 | Bobola SJ, fr Andrew | belo |
| 1623 | Kuncevicz, abp Josaphat | belo |
| 1982 | Manzinger, fr | belo |
| 1943 | Bacon, D. | boli |
| 1691 | de Arce, Jose | boli |
| 1943 | Dye, B. | boli |
| 1943 | Dye, C. | boli |
| 1980 | Espinal SJ, fr L. | boli |
| 1943 | Hosback, G. | boli |
| 1943 | Hunter, E. | boli |
| 1962 | Kruegler MM, fr W.C. | boli |
| 1971 | Le Febre, M. | boli |
| 1991 | Bagaric, fr N. | bosn |
| 1996 | Jurcevic, sr D | bosn |
| 1993 | Mikic OFM, fr L. | bosn |
| 1993 | Milicevic OFM, fr N. | bosn |
| 1997 | Batista, sr T. | braz |
| 1998 | Commissari, fr L. | braz |
| 1997 | da Silva, rev J. J. C. | braz |
| 1822 | Joana Angelica, abbess | braz |
| 1978 | Lunkebein, fr R. | braz |
| 1976 | Lunkenbein, fr R. | braz |
| 1989 | Maire, fr G.F. | braz |
| 1991 | Prada Pires, fr J.M. | braz |
| 254 | Aaron & Julius | brit |
| 1222 | Adam, bp of Caithness | brit |
| 875 | Adrian of May, bp | brit |
| 209 | Alban of Verulamium | brit |
| 577 | Aldate, bp of Gloucester | brit |
| c800 | Alkelda, princess | brit |
| 1012 | Alphege, abp of Canterbury | brit |
| 1628 | Arrowsmith, fr E. | brit |
| 1410 | Badby, J. | brit |
| 1601 | Barkworth, fr M. | brit |
| 1641 | Barlow, fr. A. | brit |
| 1540 | Barnes, Robert | brit |
| 1593 | Barrow, Henry | brit |
| 1534 | Barton, Elizabeth | brit |
| 1546 | Beaton, abp D. | brit |
| 1531 | Bilney, Thomas | brit |
| 1555 | Bradford, John | brit |
| 1581 | Briant, fr A. | brit |
| 1560 | Brooks, J., bp of Gloucester | brit |
| 1661 | Campbell, A. | brit |
| 1581 | Campion, fr E. | brit |
| 1661 | Cargill, D. | brit |
| 1605 | Catesby, Robert | brit |
| 1648 | Charles I, king | brit |
| 1586 | Clitherow, Margaret | brit |
| 1413 | Cobham, Lord | brit |
| 1678 | Coleman, Edward | brit |
| 576 | Constantine, abbot | brit |
| 1644 | Corby, fr Ralph | brit |
| 1594 | Cornelius, fr J. | brit |
| 1582 | Cottam, fr T. | brit |
| 1553 | Cranmer, abp Thomas | brit |
| 1326 | de Stapledon, Walter, bp | brit |
| 617 | Donnan & 52 companions | brit |
| c850 | Ebba, abbess | brit |
| 869 | Edmund the Martyr, king | brit |
| 979 | Edward the Martyr, king | brit |
| 794 | Ethelbert, king | brit |
| 1679 | Evans, fr D | brit |
| 1679 | Fenwick, fr J. | brit |
| 1601 | Filcock, fr. R. | brit |
| 1535 | Fisher, cardinal John | brit |
| 866 | Fremund | brit |
| 1533 | Frith, J. | brit |
| 1544 | Gardiner, J. | brit |
| 1608 | Garnet, fr T. | brit |
| 1679 | Gavan, fr J. | brit |
| 1591 | Genings, fr E. | brit |
| 1540 | Gerrard, Thomas | brit |
| 1608 | Gervase, fr. G. | brit |
| 1593 | Greenwood, John | brit |
| 1679 | Grove, J. | brit |
| 1661 | Guthrie, James | brit |
| 1584 | Gwyn, R. | brit |
| 1528 | Hamilton, Patrick | brit |
| 1571 | Hamilton, primate J. | brit |
| 1679 | Harcourt, fr W. | brit |
| 870 | Hedda of Peterborough, abbot | brit |
| 1642 | Holland, fr T. | brit |
| 1553 | Hooper, bp John | brit |
| 1535 | Houghton, John, prior | brit |
| 1998 | Hughes, B. | brit |
| 1601 | Hunt, Fr T. | brit |
| c700 | Indract | brit |
| 854 | Indrechtach, abbot of Iona | brit |
| 1679 | Ireland, fr W. | brit |
| 1544 | Ireland, J. | brit |
| 1540 | Jerome, William | brit |
| 254 | Julius | brit |
| 1678 | Kemble, John | brit |
| 821 | Kenelm, prince | brit |
| 1902 | Kensit, John | brit |
| 1544 | Larke, J. | brit |
| 1553 | Latimer, bp Hugh | brit |
| 1645 | Laud, William, abp of Canter | brit |
| 1535 | Lawrence, Robert, prior | brit |
| 1405 | Le Scrope, abp R. | brit |
| 1588 | Leigh, fr R. | brit |
| 1678 | Lewis, David | brit |
| 1679 | Lewis, fr D | brit |
| 1678 | Lloyd, John | brit |
| 1651 | Love, pastor Christopher | brit |
| 1116 | Magnus, earl of Orkney | brit |
| 1577 | Mayne, C. | brit |
| 254 | Mercurius | brit |
| 1601 | Middleton, fr R. | brit |
| 1450 | Moleyns, A., bp of Chichester | brit |
| 1535 | More, Thomas | brit |
| 1645 | Morse, fr H. | brit |
| c550 | Nectan | brit |
| 1578 | Nelson, fr J. | brit |
| 1679 | Nevill, fr F. | brit |
| 1615 | Ogilvie SJ, J. | brit |
| 1418 | Oldcastle, Sir John | brit |
| 642 | Oswald, king of Northumbria | brit |
| 651 | Oswin, king | brit |
| c65 | Osyth, queen | brit |
| c904 | Pandonia | brit |
| 1555 | Philpot, J., archdeacon | brit |
| 1679 | Pickering, T. | brit |
| 1681 | Plunket, primate O. | brit |
| 1649 | Plunkett, earl C. | brit |
| 1646 | Powel, fr. P. | brit |
| 1644 | Price, fr Robert | brit |
| 304 | Probus | brit |
| 1998 | Quinn, Jason | brit |
| 1998 | Quinn, Mark | brit |
| 1998 | Quinn, Richard | brit |
| c870 | Ragener | brit |
| 1595 | Rawlins, A. | brit |
| 1661 | Renwick, J. | brit |
| 1553 | Ridley, bp Nicholas | brit |
| 1611 | Roberts, fr. J. | brit |
| 1642 | Roe, Alban | brit |
| 1401 | Sawtrey, W. | brit |
| 1612 | Scott, fr. M. | brit |
| 1588 | Shelley, F. | brit |
| 1595 | Southwell, fr R. | brit |
| 1654 | Southworth, fr J. | brit |
| 1539 | Stone, J. | brit |
| 870 | Tancred | brit |
| 304 | Tarachus | brit |
| 1170 | Thomas Becket, abp of Canter | brit |
| 870 | Torthred | brit |
| 870 | Tova | brit |
| 1471 | Tresham, T. | brit |
| 1616 | Tunstall, fr. T. | brit |
| 1679 | Turner, fr A. | brit |
| 1592 | Udall, J. | brit |
| 1661 | Venner, Thomas | brit |
| 1679 | Wall, fr John | brit |
| 1595 | Walpole, H. | brit |
| 1588 | Ward, Margaret | brit |
| 1535 | Webster, Augustine, prior | brit |
| 1679 | Whitbread, fr T. | brit |
| 1428 | White, William | brit |
| 1539 | Whiting, R., abbot of Glastonb | brit |
| c1000 | Wigstan | brit |
| 1144 | William of Norwich | brit |
| 1201 | William of Rochester | brit |
| 1154 | William, abp of York | brit |
| 1660 | Wilson, Margaret | brit |
| 1546 | Wishart, G. | brit |
| 1573 | Woodhouse, fr T. | brit |
| 1651 | Wright, Peter | brit |
| 1956 | Boris, metrop of Nevrokop | bulg |
| 1952 | Bossilkoff CP, bp E. | bulg |
| 1514 | George Novi of Sophia | bulg |
| c302 | Julius of Durostorum | bulg |
| 1952 | Kirtoff, apostolic exarch | bulg |
| 1555 | Nicholas Novi of Sophia | bulg |
| c294 | Nikander | bulg |
| 1981 | Tsachev, N.V. | bulg |
| 1795 | Zlata of Magden | bulg |
| 1881 | Augier, fr | buru |
| 1987 | Bangirimana, Ernest | buru |
| 2000 | Bargiggia, fr A. | buru |
| 1993 | Bimazubute, G. | buru |
| 1972 | Binyoni, Abel | buru |
| 1997 | Buchwolder, sr C. | buru |
| 1996 | Concesse, Sr | buru |
| 1881 | D'Hoop, fr F. | buru |
| 1881 | Deniaud, fr | buru |
| 1996 | Gakobwa, Sr I. | buru |
| 1996 | Hakizimana, fr S. | buru |
| 1996 | Irenee, sr | buru |
| 1996 | Mpengekeze, fr Y. | buru |
| 1996 | Ndacikiriwe, sr C. | buru |
| 1996 | Ndihokubwayo, sr L. | buru |
| 1998 | Nielsen, B. M. | buru |
| 2000 | Nzikobanyanka, rev P. | buru |
| 1996 | Ruhuna, J., abp of Gitega | buru |
| 2000 | Simionato, sr G. | buru |
| 1995 | Sinankwa, fr M. | buru |
| c1927 | Filaret, bp of Bobruisk | byel |
| c1930 | Ioann, bp of Mozyr | byel |
| c1930 | Mikhail, bp of Slutsk | byel |
| 1943 | Nemantsevich, exarch A. | byel |
| 1975 | Badre OSB, prior J. | camb |
| 1996 | Chanthom, Toun | camb |
| 1976 | Chunsar OSB, fr B. C. | camb |
| 1576 | de Azevedo OP, fr Silvestre | camb |
| 1996 | Fernando, SJ, R. M. | camb |
| 1976 | Salas, bp J. C. | camb |
| 1996 | Sokan, Khoun | camb |
| 1975 | Tep Im, bp Paolo | camb |
| 1992 | Husband, sr G. | came |
| 1992 | Leone, sr M. | came |
| 1991 | Plumey OMI, abp I. | came |
| 1649 | Chabenel, N. | cana |
| 1648 | Daniel SJ, A. | cana |
| 1649 | de Brebeuf SJ, fr J. | cana |
| 1649 | Garnier, fr C. | cana |
| 1642 | Goupil SJ, R. | cana |
| 1646 | Jogues SJ, fr I. | cana |
| 1646 | Lalande SJ, fr John de | cana |
| 1649 | Lalemant SJ, fr G. | cana |
| 1654 | Leonard of Chartres, fr | cana |
| 1619 | Poulain, fr G. | cana |
| 1724 | Rale SJ, fr S. | cana |
| 1625 | Viel, fr N. | cana |
| 2000 | Abakumate, sr M | cent |
| 1997 | d'Herouville, Sr C. | chad |
| 555 | Helier | chan |
| 1985 | Allende, S. N. | chil |
| 1973 | Alsina, fr J. | chil |
| 1985 | Ceballos, M. G. | chil |
| 1612 | de Aranda SJ, fr M. | chil |
| 1612 | de Montalban SJ, br J. | chil |
| 1612 | de Vecchi SJ, fr H. | chil |
| 1983 | Jarlan, A. | chil |
| 1985 | Maluendo, J. M. P. | chil |
| 1905 | An, evangelist | chin |
| 1900 | Andlauer SJ, fr M. | chin |
| 1950 | Beda SJ, fr Tsiang | chin |
| 1916 | Bettex, Paul | chin |
| 1945 | Birch, J. | chin |
| 1900 | Blind Chang Shen | chin |
| 1938 | Cairns, fr R. | chin |
| 1941 | Cairns, fr R. J. | chin |
| 1900 | Carleson, N. | chin |
| 1950 | Carlo, bp A. | chin |
| 1925 | Cassels, bp W. C. | chin |
| 1900 | Chao Hsi Mao | chin |
| 1811 | Chao, A. | chin |
| 1993 | Chunjee, bp P.S. | chin |
| 1811 | Clet, F. | chin |
| 1820 | Clet, fr F. R. | chin |
| 1929 | Coveyou, fr W. | chin |
| 1634 | de Andrade, fr A. | chin |
| 1644 | de Capillas OP, fr F. | chin |
| 1950 | de Smedt, bp L. J. | chin |
| 1900 | Denn, fr P. | chin |
| c1993 | Difen, bp Liu | chin |
| 1938 | Donovan MM, fr G. | chin |
| 1934 | Esteban, fr T. | chin |
| 1952 | Ford, bp F.X. | chin |
| 1339 | Francis of Alessandria | chin |
| 1339 | Gilotti, William | chin |
| 1900 | Guillon, bp L. | chin |
| 1929 | Holbein, fr G. | chin |
| 1861 | Holmes, J. L. | chin |
| 1606 | Hwang Ming-sha SJ, br | chin |
| 1900 | Isore, fr R. | chin |
| 1362 | James, abp of Zaitun | chin |
| 1947 | Jensen, fr B. | chin |
| 1339 | John of India, br | chin |
| 1943 | Kim, evangelist | chin |
| 1905 | Kim, evangelist | chin |
| 1900 | King, A. | chin |
| 1816 | Lantrua, fr G. | chin |
| 1339 | Lawrence of Alessandria | chin |
| 1940 | Lebbe, fr F. V. | chin |
| 1900 | Li, fr J. | chin |
| 1945 | Liddell, Eric | chin |
| 1960 | Lin, H.H. | chin |
| 1938 | Liu, H. | chin |
| 1934 | Liu, Y. C. | chin |
| 1937 | Lo Pa Hong | chin |
| 1847 | Lowrie, Walter M. | chin |
| 1906 | Macdonald, dr R. J. | chin |
| 1900 | Mangin, fr L. I. | chin |
| 1993 | Manping, Lai | chin |
| 1339 | Martel, Peter | chin |
| 1400 | Matthew of Escandel | chin |
| 1994 | Musheng, Zheng | chin |
| 1972 | Nee, Watchman | chin |
| 1862 | Neel, J. P. | chin |
| 1905 | Ni, evangelist | chin |
| 1339 | Pascal of Victoria | chin |
| 1840 | Perboyre, fr J. G. | chin |

*Continued overleaf*

*Table 4–13 continued*

| | | |
|---|---|---|
| 1840 | Perboyre, fr Jean G. | chin |
| 1900 | Pigott, J. | chin |
| 1900 | Pigott, T. W. & J. | chin |
| 1900 | Pitkin, H. T. | chin |
| 1900 | Price, Charles & Eva | chin |
| 1900 | Price, Eva | chin |
| 1945 | Rauschenbach MM, fr O. A. | chin |
| 1339 | Richard, bp of Almalik | chin |
| 1339 | Ruff, Raymond | chin |
| 1749 | Sanz, bp P. | chin |
| 1666 | Schall SJ, fr A. von Bell | chin |
| 1953 | Seng, Joseph | chin |
| 1929 | Seybold, fr C. | chin |
| 1984 | Shude SJ, fr F.Z. | chin |
| 1932 | Simpson, W. E. | chin |
| 1934 | Stam, Betty | chin |
| 1934 | Stam, John & Betty | chin |
| 1900 | Sun Hwe Teh | chin |
| 1929 | Sundar Singh, sadhu | chin |
| 1811 | Tapeng, J. C. | chin |
| 1949 | Tornay, fr M. | chin |
| 1951 | Wallace, W.L. | chin |
| 1950 | Wang Ling-Tso, fr | chin |
| 1900 | Wang Ten Ren | chin |
| 1989 | Xinsheng, bp Li | chin |
| 1996 | Xiuju, Zhang | chin |
| c1990 | Xueyan, bp Fan | chin |
| 1972 | Zhiming, pastor Wang | chin |
| 1995 | Alean, pastor M. | colo |
| 1996 | Alzate Varela, pastor P. | colo |
| 1995 | Amador, pastor Manuel | colo |
| 1995 | Argelio, pastor J. | colo |
| 1988 | Augusto, fr Giraldo Cesar | colo |
| 1997 | Bedoya, fr A. | colo |
| 1989 | Benitez, fr M.A. | colo |
| 1981 | Bitterman III, C.A. | colo |
| 1996 | Carro, C. Quiroz | colo |
| 1998 | Chicangana, fr A. J. | colo |
| 1998 | Colorado, Adan | colo |
| 1996 | Coronel, J. D. | colo |
| 1944 | Coy, Juan | colo |
| 1998 | de Rojas, M. R. | colo |
| 1997 | Donado, elder W. | colo |
| 2000 | Duque, fr H. | colo |
| 1990 | Fernandez, fr T. | colo |
| 1948 | Fowler, E. | colo |
| 1998 | Gaona, br M. A. Q. | colo |
| 1988 | Giraldo, fr C. Augusto | colo |
| 1996 | Gonzales, J. L. | colo |
| 1998 | Hood, Carl | colo |
| 1989 | Jaramillo, bp Jesus E. | colo |
| 1974 | Lain, fr Domingo | colo |
| 1992 | Leal, sr Torres N. | colo |
| 1989 | Mansalve, bp Jesus E.J. | colo |
| 1989 | Monsalve, bp Jesus E. J. | colo |
| 1997 | Pena, fr S. C. | colo |
| 2000 | Ramirez, fr A.G. | colo |
| 1995 | Rangell, Hugo | colo |
| 1989 | Restrepo, fr S. | colo |
| 1999 | Rojas, fr H. F. | colo |
| 1995 | Ruibal, pastor Julio C. | colo |
| 1998 | Saenz, J. D. | colo |
| 1966 | Torres, fr Camilo | colo |
| 1984 | Ulcue Chocue, fr A. | colo |
| 1995 | Van Dyke, T. | colo |
| 1995 | Welsh, S. | colo |
| 1996 | Farris, Dr. Ron | como |
| 1977 | Biayenda, cardinal abp E. | cong |
| 1998 | Czuba, fr J. | cong |
| 1961 | de Vos, pastor R. | cong |
| 1998 | Nakavoua, G. A. | cong |
| 1998 | Adrienne, sr | conz |
| 1997 | Alege, prof A. | conz |
| 2000 | Amzati, C.G. | conz |
| 1964 | Anuarite, sr M.C. | conz |
| 1966 | Bamba, Emmanuel | conz |
| 1706 | Beatrice, Donna | conz |
| 1996 | Bumendwa, fr J. C. | conz |
| 1942 | Bushiri, Mulumozi | conz |
| 1998 | Bwabulakombe, sr S. | conz |
| 1996 | Bwambale, pastor P. | conz |
| 1964 | Carlson, P. | conz |
| 1974 | Charlier, fr E. | conz |
| 1996 | de la Fuente, br F. | conz |
| 1998 | Desrumeaux, sr A. | conz |
| 1977 | Eschtruth, G.J.R. | conz |
| 1996 | Gakondo, sr J. A. | conz |
| 1996 | Garcia, br S. M. | conz |
| 1996 | Gatuku, fr C. | conz |
| 1996 | Gatunga, sr J. | conz |
| 1652 | George of Ghiel, fr | conz |
| 1998 | Germaine, sr | conz |
| 1997 | Hatagekimang, rev A. | conz |
| 1960 | Hodgson, E. | conz |
| 1996 | Jorge, br J. R. | conz |
| 1997 | Kabera, rev E. | conz |
| 1996 | Kahegezo, fr B. K. | conz |
| 1996 | Kajibwami, br F. | conz |
| 1996 | Kanyamanza, fr P. | conz |
| 1996 | Kasati, fr J. | conz |
| 1951 | Kimbangu, prophet Simon | conz |
| 1997 | Kiyumukiza, rev A. N. | conz |
| 1960 | Knauf, E. | conz |
| 1964 | Lifenya, director Pierre | conz |
| 1996 | Lucio, br M. A. I. | conz |
| 1996 | Lucio, sr M. A. I. | conz |
| 1998 | Malenga, E. | conz |
| 1998 | Mandro, J-F. K. | conz |
| 1964 | McMillan, H. | conz |
| 1997 | Mihingo, rev N. | conz |
| 1996 | Mounabandi, sr C | conz |
| 1996 | Mukamihogo, sr F. | conz |
| 1997 | Munyakazy, rev E. | conz |
| 1996 | Munyankuyu, fr A. | conz |
| 1996 | Munzihirwa, abp C. | conz |
| 1996 | Munzombo, pasotr D. | conz |
| 1997 | Muyoboke, rev F. | conz |
| 1996 | Ngabo SJ, abp C. M. M. | conz |
| 1996 | Nirere, fr B. | conz |
| 1996 | Nsengiyunva, fr E. | conz |
| 1997 | Nyirabakungu, sr C. | conz |
| 1997 | Nyirarukundu, sr M. | conz |
| 2000 | Pepe, fr R. | conz |
| 1964 | Rhine, Phyllis | conz |
| 1996 | Sabuni, pastor M. | conz |
| 1964 | Scholten, W.H. | conz |
| 1996 | Sebalija, sr L. | conz |
| 1995 | Sellekaerts IHM, sr C. | conz |
| 1996 | Semutwe, sr M. A. | conz |
| 1997 | Tshisambu, fr F. | conz |
| 1964 | Tucker, J. | conz |
| 1997 | Twagirayezu, rev U. | conz |
| 1997 | Uwizeyimana, rev J. | conz |
| 1974 | Viaene, fr L. | conz |
| 1709 | de Rebullida, fr P. | cost |
| 1709 | de Zamora, fr J.A. | cost |
| 1627 | Perez, fr R. | cost |
| 303 | Anastasia | croa |
| 303 | Irineu, bp of Sirmium | croa |
| 1945 | Simrak, bp J. | croa |
| 1961 | Stepinac, cardinal abp A. | croa |
| 61 | Barnabas, Apostle | cypr |
| 1821 | Kyprianos, abp | cypr |
| 1982 | Barta, fr J. | czec |
| 1981 | Coufal, fr P. | czec |
| 1631 | Fleming, fr P. | czec |
| 1979 | Gono, fr M. | czec |
| 1942 | Gorazd, bp Pavlik | czec |
| 1217 | Hroznata | czec |
| 1416 | Jerome of Prague | czec |
| 1393 | John of Nepomuk | czec |
| 916 | Ludmilla | czec |
| 1620 | Sarkander, Jan | czec |
| 1981 | Svanda, fr P. | czec |
| 1974 | Trochta, cardinal S. | czec |
| 929 | Wenceslas, prince-duke | czec |
| 1550 | Arason, bp J. & 2 sons | denm |
| 1086 | Canute IV, king | denm |
| 1131 | Canute Lavard | denm |
| 1176 | Marguerite of Roeskilde | denm |
| 1944 | Munk, pastor Kaj | denm |
| 1971 | Potter, Nancy | domr |
| 1971 | Potter, Paul E. & Nancy | domr |
| 1987 | Arango, sr Ines | ecua |
| 1887 | Checa y Barba, abp J. I. | ecua |
| 1956 | Elliot, J. | ecua |
| 1956 | Fleming, P. | ecua |
| 1987 | Labaca Ugarte OFMCap, bp A. | ecua |
| 1956 | McCully, E. | ecua |
| 1956 | Saint, Nate | ecua |
| 1956 | Youdarian, R. | ecua |
| 1987 | Zuma, pastor Antonio | ecua |
| c300 | Abadion, bp of Antinoopolis | egyp |
| c291 | Abadir | egyp |
| c250 | Abadyus | egyp |
| c309 | Abamun of Tarnut | egyp |
| c309 | Abamun of Tukh | egyp |
| 1996 | Abdel-Sayeda, H. L. | egyp |
| 249 | Abu Sayfayn | egyp |
| 1400 | Abu'l Farag | egyp |
| c287 | Aesculapius | egyp |
| c305 | Aesi | egyp |
| c300 | Agathon and brothers | egyp |
| 1387 | al-Jadid, Jirjis | egyp |
| 959 | al-Muzahim, Jirjis | egyp |
| 249 | Alexander, bp of Cappadocia | egyp |
| 251 | Alexander, bp of Jerusalem | egyp |
| c360 | Alladyus, bp | egyp |
| 1993 | Alzokim, N.F. | egyp |
| c320 | Ammonius, bp of Latopolis | egyp |
| c285 | Amsah of Qift | egyp |
| c300 | Anatolius, general | egyp |
| c355 | Andrew, monk | egyp |
| c290 | Anub | egyp |
| c295 | Apaiule | egyp |
| c300 | Apoli | egyp |
| c285 | Apollo | egyp |
| c290 | Apollonius | egyp |
| 245 | Appolonia, deaconess | egyp |
| c310 | Arianus, governor | egyp |
| c298 | Arsenius | egyp |
| 1400 | Arsenius | egyp |
| c290 | Ascla | egyp |
| c296 | Athanasius | egyp |
| 258 | Athanasius, bp | egyp |
| c288 | Athom | egyp |
| 1991 | Aziza, Adel | egyp |
| 284 | Babylas, bp | egyp |
| 1992 | Bakheit, dr S. | egyp |
| 285 | Balana, priest | egyp |
| c300 | Bandilaus, monk | egyp |
| c285 | Banina | egyp |
| c297 | Barsanuphius (Warshanufy) | egyp |
| c850 | Barsanuphius, monk | egyp |
| 298 | Basil, bp | egyp |
| c297 | Basilidas, general | egyp |
| 207 | Basilides | egyp |
| 1993 | Bassiliouss, P. | egyp |
| 250 | Batra | egyp |
| c355 | Behnam | egyp |
| c291 | Benjamin | egyp |
| c297 | Besamon | egyp |
| c1820 | Bishay, Sidhom | egyp |
| c1250 | Bulus al-Habis | egyp |
| c286 | Callinicus | egyp |
| 307 | Catherine of Alexandria | egyp |
| c299 | Chamoul | egyp |
| c286 | Chanazhum | egyp |
| 250 | Christophorus | egyp |
| 283 | Cladius, Stratelates | egyp |
| c299 | Comas | egyp |
| c340 | Copres | egyp |
| c291 | Cyriacus | egyp |
| 1860 | Cyril IV, patriarch | egyp |
| 303 | Cyrus & John | egyp |
| c286 | Dalasina | egyp |
| c299 | Damian | egyp |
| c286 | Dasyah | egyp |
| c292 | David | egyp |
| c359 | Decius | egyp |
| 305 | Dimyanah & her 40 Virgins | egyp |
| c287 | Dioscorus | egyp |
| c307 | Elias the eunuch | egyp |
| c286 | Epima | egyp |
| c292 | Epimachus | egyp |
| 303 | Epimachus of Pelusium | egyp |
| 1997 | Estafanos, K. | egyp |
| c291 | Eudoxia | egyp |
| c355 | Eunapius, monk | egyp |
| c291 | Euphemia | egyp |
| c288 | Febronia, nun | egyp |
| 1996 | Gabriel, I. A. | egyp |
| 1981 | Ghabrail, fr Abd Mutagalli | egyp |
| 996 | Ghabrial | egyp |
| 1996 | Girgis, M. B. | egyp |
| c292 | Gordian | egyp |
| 1992 | Guirguis, A.S. | egyp |
| 1992 | Guirguis, M.Q. | egyp |
| 1387 | Hadid of Giza | egyp |
| c450 | Hamai of Kahyor | egyp |
| 1996 | Hanas, dr Michel Ayad | egyp |
| c286 | Helias, bp | egyp |
| c300 | Heraclides | egyp |
| c291 | Herai | egyp |
| 305 | Hypatius of Gangra | egyp |
| 1400 | Ileya | egyp |
| c359 | Irene | egyp |
| c299 | Isaac of Tiphre | egyp |
| c305 | Isidore of Takinash | egyp |
| c299 | Isidorus | egyp |
| c300 | Isidorus, monk | egyp |
| 1993 | Iskandar, E.N. | egyp |
| c300 | Jacob, The Soldier | egyp |
| c258 | Jerasimus | egyp |
| 303 | John | egyp |
| 1209 | John of Phanidjoit | egyp |
| c357 | John, The Soldier | egyp |
| c291 | Julitta | egyp |
| c286 | Justus, son of Numerianus | egyp |
| c289 | Kau of Bismay | egyp |
| 1992 | Khalil, H.F. | egyp |
| 202 | Leonides | egyp |
| 451 | Macari of Edko, bp | egyp |
| c305 | Macarius | egyp |
| 455 | Macarius of Tkow, bp | egyp |
| c295 | Makrawi, bp of Nikiou | egyp |
| 1811 | Malati, Muallim | egyp |
| 202 | Marcella | egyp |
| 305 | Marcus | egyp |
| 68 | Mark the Evangelist | egyp |
| 1993 | Marsouk, H. | egyp |
| 1999 | Massoud, Magdi F. | egyp |
| 249 | Matra | egyp |
| 631 | Menas | egyp |
| c717 | Menas of Al-Ashmunayn | egyp |
| 296 | Menas the Miracle Maker | egyp |
| 305 | Menas, governor | egyp |
| c356 | Mercurius | egyp |
| 1400 | Mikhail Abu Mokaitef | egyp |
| c305 | Milius | egyp |
| 1400 | Moussa, monk | egyp |
| 1822 | Muallim Ghali | egyp |
| 1801 | Muallim Malati | egyp |
| c310 | Mui | egyp |
| c300 | Nabraha | egyp |
| c304 | Naharuh | egyp |
| 285 | Naou | egyp |
| 1994 | Nur al-Qums Binyamin | egyp |
| c301 | Olympius | egyp |
| c301 | Paese | egyp |
| c290 | Panesneu, deacon | egyp |
| c313 | Pantaleon, physician | egyp |
| c298 | Patape, bp of Coptos | egyp |
| c290 | Paul of Egypt | egyp |
| 311 | Peter I Ieromartyros, patriarch | egyp |
| 304 | Phileas, bp of Thmuis | egyp |
| c290 | Philemon | egyp |
| c292 | Phiobammon of Preht | egyp |
| c288 | Piroou | egyp |
| c302 | Pisura, bp of Masil | egyp |
| c306 | Porphry | egyp |
| 207 | Potamiana | egyp |
| 305 | Potamon of Heracla | egyp |
| c305 | Procopius, governor | egyp |
| 459 | Proterius, patriarch | egyp |
| c306 | Psote of Psoi | egyp |
| 1981 | Quilini, H. N. | egyp |
| 1981 | Raflan, B. | egyp |
| c300 | Rebecca of Sunbat | egyp |
| c1780 | Rizk Agha, vizier | egyp |
| 1400 | Saleeb | egyp |
| c290 | Salfana | egyp |
| c800 | Salib | egyp |
| 1981 | Samuel, bp Makary El-Souria | egyp |
| c355 | Sarah | egyp |
| c290 | Sarah & children | egyp |
| c287 | Sarapamon of Scetis, bp | egyp |
| c365 | Serapion, bp of Thmuis | egyp |
| 1993 | Shafiq, S. | egyp |
| c299 | Shenufe | egyp |
| c299 | Shenute | egyp |
| c650 | Shinudah, anba | egyp |
| 1910 | Sidhom Bishai, deacon | egyp |
| 1400 | Sidrak, priest, & 5 monks | egyp |
| c800 | Simeon | egyp |
| c140 | Sophia | egyp |
| c286 | Sophronius | egyp |
| 284 | Stephen, archdeacon | egyp |
| c301 | Tecula | egyp |
| 220 | Theodorus of Peshotep | egyp |
| c306 | Theodorus, bp of Pentapolis | egyp |
| 258 | Theodotus | egyp |
| 1993 | Theophiles, K.Y. | egyp |
| c306 | Tibarcius | egyp |
| c291 | Til, soldier | egyp |
| c309 | Timothy of Memphis | egyp |
| c295 | Tolemaeus | egyp |
| c295 | Uri, priest of Shatanut | egyp |
| c345 | Usaghniyus | egyp |
| c306 | Valerianus | egyp |
| c359 | Victor | egyp |
| c301 | Victor of Asyut | egyp |
| c289 | Wakhus | egyp |
| c1540 | Yoannis al-Kalioobi, monk | egyp |
| 1833 | Aquino, Anastasio | elsa |
| 1977 | Arreola, sr Silvia Maribel | elsa |
| 1978 | Bassera, fr Ernesto | elsa |
| 1980 | Chacon, Juan | elsa |
| 1980 | Clarke, sr M. | elsa |
| 1980 | Donovan, sr J. | elsa |
| 1989 | Elba Ramos, Celina | elsa |
| 1989 | Elba Ramos, Julia & Celina | elsa |
| 1989 | Ellacuria SJ, fr I. | elsa |
| 1985 | Espino, pastor E. F. | elsa |
| 1932 | Farabundo, Marti | elsa |
| 1980 | Ford, sr I. | elsa |
| 1989 | Gomez, Maria Cristina | elsa |
| 1977 | Grande, fr R. | elsa |
| 1980 | Kazel, sr D. | elsa |
| 1989 | Lopez Lopez SJ, fr J. | elsa |
| 1989 | Lopez SJ, fr A. | elsa |
| 1989 | Martin-Baro SJ, fr I. | elsa |
| 1989 | Montes SJ, fr S. | elsa |
| 1977 | Navarro, fr A. | elsa |
| 1979 | Ortiz, fr Octavia | elsa |
| 1979 | Palacios, fr Rafael | elsa |
| 1989 | Ramon Moreno SJ, fr J. | elsa |
| 1993 | Ramos, bp Robert J. | elsa |
| 1970 | Rodriguez, fr Nicolas | elsa |
| 1980 | Romero, abp Oscar | elsa |
| 1977 | Torres, L.A. | elsa |
| 1975 | Nze, bp Abuy Raphael | equa |
| 1198 | Berthold, abbot | esto |
| c1480 | Isidor & followers | esto |
| 1990 | Klein, Valve | esto |
| 1919 | Kulbusch, bp Platon of Revel | esto |
| 1990 | Meri, dean Harald | esto |
| 1985 | Aleku, B. | ethi |
| 1992 | Amlak, fr A. | ethi |
| 1666 | Andrade, vicar apostolic | ethi |
| 1977 | Argew, T. | ethi |
| 1640 | Bruni SJ, fr B. | ethi |
| 1640 | Cardeira SJ, fr L. | ethi |
| 1638 | Cassian of Nantes, fr | ethi |
| 1638 | de Almeida, bp Apollinaris | ethi |
| 1860 | de Jacobis, bp Justin | ethi |
| 1652 | du Tremblay, fr J. L. | ethi |
| 1638 | Franceschi SJ, fr H. | ethi |
| 1855 | Gabra Mikael, fr | ethi |
| 1595 | George, fr A. | ethi |
| 1652 | Heyling, Peter | ethi |
| 1973 | Isa, Peter | ethi |
| c450 | Kharitas | ethi |
| 1937 | Mikael, bp | ethi |
| 1635 | Paes SJ, fr G. | ethi |
| 1937 | Petros, bp | ethi |
| 1992 | Ricci, fr F. | ethi |
| 1638 | Rodrigues SJ, fr F. | ethi |
| 1980 | Samwel, abp | ethi |
| 1977 | Selassie, emperor Haile | ethi |
| 1991 | Shaga, Nana | ethi |
| 1980 | Theofilas, patriarch | ethi |
| 1979 | Tumsa, Gudinsa | ethi |
| 1716 | Weiss, prefect L. | ethi |
| 1004 | Abbo | fran |
| c1640 | Agathangelo of Vendome, fr | fran |
| 1794 | Agricola Viala | fran |
| 1871 | Allard, fr | fran |
| 1794 | Ambroise, fr R. | fran |
| 1794 | Andre, fr J. | fran |
| c660 | Annemond, bp of Lyons | fran |
| 1155 | Arnold of Brescia | fran |
| 434 | Auraeus, bp | fran |
| 1792 | Balmain SJ, fr F. | fran |
| 1321 | Belibasta, Guilhem | fran |
| c150 | Benignus | fran |

*Continued opposite*

*Table 4–13 continued*

| | | |
|---|---|---|
| 685 | Bercharius, abbot | fran |
| 177 | Blandina | fran |
| 1792 | Bonnaud SJ, fr J. J. | fran |
| c560 | Cadog | fran |
| 1871 | Captier, fr E. | fran |
| 1794 | Carnus, fr C. | fran |
| 1871 | Caubert, fr J. | fran |
| 1871 | Clerc, fr A. | fran |
| 1572 | Coligny, admiral Gaspard de | fran |
| c285 | Crispin | fran |
| c285 | Crispinian | fran |
| 679 | Dagobert II, king | fran |
| 1871 | Darboy, G., abp of Paris | fran |
| 1871 | de Bengy, fr A. | fran |
| 1685 | de Marolles, Louis | fran |
| 1792 | De Millou SJ, fr J. C. | fran |
| 1314 | de Molay, J., grand master | fran |
| 1621 | de Montchretien, A. | fran |
| 1792 | de Vafons, count | fran |
| 1871 | Deguerry, fr | fran |
| 1792 | Delfaut SJ, fr W. A. | fran |
| 259 | Denys, bp of Paris | fran |
| 411 | Desiderius, bp of Langres | fran |
| 607 | Desiderius, bp of Vienne | fran |
| 1559 | Du Bourg, Anne | fran |
| 1792 | Du Lau, abp J. M. | fran |
| 1871 | Ducoudray, fr L. | fran |
| 259 | Eleutherius | fran |
| c660 | Emmeram, bp of Poitiers | fran |
| c260 | Eutropius, bp of Saintes | fran |
| 1794 | Expilly, bp L. A. | fran |
| c250 | Faith (Foy) | fran |
| c290 | Firmin, bp of Amiens | fran |
| 655 | Foillan, abbot | fran |
| 760 | Gangolf | fran |
| 250 | Genesius of Arles | fran |
| 675 | Germanus, abbot | fran |
| 1794 | Gobel, J. B. J., bp of Paris | fran |
| 1070 | Godelive | fran |
| 731 | Hainmar, bp of Auxerre | fran |
| 202 | Irenaeus, bp of Lyons | fran |
| 1944 | Jacob, Max | fran |
| 1431 | Joan of Arc | fran |
| 1792 | Lanfant, fr A. & 8 companions | fran |
| 1685 | Le Fevre, I. | fran |
| 1792 | Lefranc, fr F. | fran |
| 679 | Leodegar, bp of Autun | fran |
| 451 | Livarius | fran |
| 1793 | Louis XVI | fran |
| 1871 | Olivaint, fr P. | fran |
| c260 | Patroclus | fran |
| 426 | Patroclus of Arles, primate | fran |
| 1133 | Peter of Bruys | fran |
| 1208 | Peter of Castelnau, legate | fran |
| 1794 | Pinot, fr N. | fran |
| 177 | Ponticus | fran |
| c260 | Pontius | fran |
| 1310 | Porete, Marguerite | fran |
| 177 | Pothinus, bp | fran |
| 586 | Praetextatus, bp of Rouen | fran |
| c260 | Privatus | fran |
| 1572 | Ramus, Peter | fran |
| c1350 | Roch, healer | fran |
| 259 | Rusticus | fran |
| 1593 | Sales, fr J. | fran |
| 259 | Saturninus | fran |
| 1593 | Saultemouche, fr W. | fran |
| 1857 | Sibour, abp of Paris | fran |
| 1242 | Stephen of Narbonne | fran |
| c190 | Symphorian | fran |
| 1803 | Toussaint-Louverture, F.D. | fran |
| 177 | Vettius Epagathus | fran |
| 258 | Victorinus | fran |
| 689 | Vigilius, bp of Auxerre | fran |
| 476 | Volusianus, bp of Tours | fran |
| 1242 | William of Arnaud | fran |
| 1799 | Lewis, pastor T. | frep |
| 786 | Abo | geor |
| 610 | Anastasius, patriarch | geor |
| 1288 | Conrad of Saxony | geor |
| 379 | Eustace of Mtskheta | geor |
| 1918 | Kirion III, catholicos-patriarch | geor |
| 662 | Maximus the Confessor, abbot | geor |
| 1921 | Nazary, metrop of Kutaisi | geor |
| c490 | Rajden | geor |
| c473 | Shushanik, queen | geor |
| 1908 | Sofiisky, exarch abp N. | geor |
| 1288 | Stephen of Hungary | geor |
| 1632 | Adolphus, king Gustavus | germ |
| 303 | Afra | germ |
| 1945 | Bonhoeffer, Dietrich | germ |
| 1942 | Brandsma, fr Tiko | germ |
| 1945 | Delp, fr A. | germ |
| 1121 | Erminold, abbot of Prufening | germ |
| 304 | Gereon | germ |
| 799 | Gerold, duke of Bavaria | germ |
| 1997 | Geyer-Iwand, V. | germ |
| 1066 | Gottschalk | germ |
| 1944 | Gross, N. | germ |
| 1919 | Hahn, G. H. & 32 pastors | germ |
| 853 | Haymo, bp of Halberstadt | germ |
| 695 | Hewald the Dark | germ |
| 695 | Hewald the Fair | germ |
| 1943 | Jaegerstaetter, F. | germ |
| 1415 | John Hus | germ |
| 1536 | John of Leiden | germ |
| 1066 | John, bp of Mecklenburg | germ |
| 1527 | Kaiser | germ |
| 686 | Kilian, bp, & 11 companions | germ |
| 1944 | Koenzgen, G. | germ |
| 1066 | Kuno, bp of Trier | germ |
| 1944 | Lagerstadr, Farnz | germ |
| c1940 | Leisner, fr K. | germ |
| 1944 | Letterhaus, B. | germ |
| 1941 | Lichtenberg, fr B. | germ |
| 1534 | Matthys, Jan | germ |
| 1944 | Metzger, fr M. J. | germ |
| 1525 | Munzer, T. | germ |
| 1527 | Sattler, M. | germ |
| 1534 | Schiemer, L., bp | germ |
| 1944 | Schmidlin, professor J. | germ |
| 1939 | Schneider, pasotr | germ |
| 643 | Trudpert | germ |
| 451 | Ursula & virgins | germ |
| c1935 | von Moltke, Helmut | germ |
| 1631 | Wagner, fr Liborius | germ |
| 1528 | Winkler, pastor G. | germ |
| 1995 | Maclese, sr P. | ghan |
| 1996 | McAleese, sr P. | ghan |
| 1996 | Murphy, sr C. | ghan |
| 1900 | Otu, Samuel | ghan |
| 304 | Agape | gree |
| 69 | Andrew, Apostle | gree |
| 1813 | Angelis | gree |
| 304 | Chione | gree |
| c260 | Cyril, bp of Gortyna | gree |
| 1802 | Demetrios of Chios | gree |
| 308 | Demetrius, megalomartyr | gree |
| 1807 | George of Chios | gree |
| 1838 | Georgios | gree |
| 1814 | Ignanos | gree |
| 304 | Irene | gree |
| 96 | Luke the Evangelist | gree |
| 1802 | Luke the New | gree |
| 1801 | Mark the New | gree |
| 969 | Nicephorus, emperor | gree |
| 1754 | Nicholas of Chios | gree |
| 1794 | Polydorus the Cypriot | gree |
| 115 | Rufus | gree |
| 1635 | Theophilus of Zakynthos | gree |
| 115 | Zozimus | gree |
| 1672 | de San Vitores SJ, fr J. | guam |
| 1944 | Duenas, fr Jesus | guam |
| 1985 | Cabrera Rivera, prof C.H. | guat |
| 1991 | Cisneros, fr Moises | guat |
| 1998 | Conedera, bp J. G. | guat |
| c1976 | de la Cruz, fr C. | guat |
| 1982 | Garcia, Anastasio | guat |
| c1976 | Gran, fr J.M. | guat |
| 1983 | Holdenried, F.X. | guat |
| 1976 | Lopez, fr H. | guat |
| 1990 | Mack, Myrna | guat |
| 1981 | Miller, fr J. | guat |
| 1981 | Rother, fr S. | guat |
| 1995 | Saquic Vasquez, pastor M. | guat |
| 1994 | Serech, P. | guat |
| 1982 | Toj, Juan Garcia | guat |
| 1983 | Toma, pastor Nicolas | guat |
| 1981 | Troyer, J.D. | guat |
| 1985 | Tzalam Coj, Manuel de Jesus | guat |
| 1995 | Vasquez, pastor M.S. | guat |
| c1976 | Voordeckers, fr W. | guat |
| 1976 | Woods MM, fr W. | guat |
| 1963 | Barbosa, evangelist Dinis | gunb |
| 1963 | da Costa, Joaquin | gunb |
| 1963 | da Silva, pastor Pedro | gunb |
| 1963 | Landim | gunb |
| 1962 | Mendes, evangelist Formoso | gunb |
| 1963 | Vaz Martins, evangelist Victor | gunb |
| 1991 | Claude, pastor Sylvio | hait |
| 1998 | Hudon, fr B. | hait |
| 1993 | Izmery, A. | hait |
| 1998 | Louis, fr J-P. | hait |
| 1961 | Moreau, fr Yvon Emmanuel | hait |
| 1994 | Vincent, pastor Jean-Marie | hait |
| 1612 | Bertelete, fr E. | hond |
| 1975 | Betancur, fr I. | hond |
| 1983 | Carney SJ, fr J.G. | hond |
| 1975 | Cypher OFM, fr M.C. | hond |
| 1623 | de Baena, br J. | hond |
| 1612 | de Monteagudo, fr J. | hond |
| 1623 | Lopez, fr B. | hond |
| 1623 | Puerta, fr C.M. | hond |
| 1905 | Chestnut, Eleanor | hong |
| 1945 | Apor, bp Vilmos | hung |
| 1959 | Balint, S. | hung |
| 1619 | Crisinus, fr M. | hung |
| 1579 | Franz, David | hung |
| 1046 | Gerard, bp of Csanad | hung |
| 1619 | Grodecz SJ, fr M. | hung |
| c1956 | Martinuzzi, abp of Estergom | hung |
| 1948 | Ordacz, bp L. | hung |
| 304 | Pollio | hung |
| 1619 | Pongracz SJ, fr S. | hung |
| 1959 | Turcsanyi, msgr E. | hung |
| 1583 | Acquaviva, fr R. | indi |
| 1653 | Ahatalla, metropolitan | indi |
| 1997 | Anchanickal SJ, fr T. | indi |
| 1583 | Aranha, F. | indi |
| 1583 | Berno, P. | indi |
| 1996 | Cherukarokunnel, L. J. | indi |
| 2000 | Chittinapilly, fr S.J. | indi |
| 2000 | Crasta, fr V. | indi |
| 1549 | Criminali SJ, fr A. | indi |
| 1693 | de Britto SJ, fr J. | indi |
| 1321 | Demetrius, br | indi |
| 2000 | Emmanuel, bp G. | indi |
| 1583 | Francisco, fr A. | indi |
| 1996 | Hansda, S. | indi |
| 1998 | Hoyo, br J. | indi |
| 1321 | James of Padua | indi |
| 1597 | Joseph, mar, metropolitan | indi |
| 2000 | Karketta, fr R. | indi |
| 1995 | Kerkatta, John | indi |
| 2000 | Kuzhikandom, fr G. | indi |
| 1996 | Lasker, evangelist Hussain | indi |
| 1992 | Lukkappa, sadhu | indi |
| 1995 | Maria, sr Rani | indi |
| 2000 | Masih, Mushtaq | indi |
| 1997 | Nedumattahil, fr J. | indi |
| 1583 | Pacheco, fr A. | indi |
| 1993 | Packianathan, fr V.S. | indi |
| 1997 | Pande, evangelist M. | indi |
| 1321 | Peter of Siena | indi |
| 1752 | Pillai, D. | indi |
| 1990 | Priya SMA, sr | indi |
| 1998 | Puttaniyil, br L. | indi |
| 1998 | Rajiv, John | indi |
| 1597 | Simon, mar, metropolitan | indi |
| 1999 | Staines, Graham | indi |
| 1999 | Staines, Philip | indi |
| 1999 | Staines, Timothy | indi |
| 1990 | Sylvia SMA, sr | indi |
| 1990 | Tete, president Martin | indi |
| 82 | Thomas (Didymus), Apostle | indi |
| 1321 | Thomas of Tolentino | indi |
| 1997 | Thomas SJ, fr A. T. | indi |
| 1638 | Berthelot, fr P. | indo |
| 1996 | Christian, pastor Ishak | indo |
| 1975 | Constable, pastor Eric | indo |
| 1968 | Dale, pastor Stan | indo |
| 1996 | Ishak Christian, pastor | indo |
| 1940 | Jackson, F. C. | indo |
| 1945 | Jaffray, R. A. | indo |
| 2000 | Jami, fr Y. | indo |
| 1834 | Lyman, H. | indo |
| 1968 | Masters, P. | indo |
| 1834 | Munson, Samuel | indo |
| 1652 | Redemptus of the Cross, br | indo |
| 1998 | Siahae, J. | indo |
| 1998 | Simatupang, T. M. | indo |
| 1282 | Aldobrand of Florence | iran |
| 1282 | Anthony of Armenia | iran |
| 1279 | Bar Kaliq, bp of Tus | iran |
| 1917 | Benjamin Simon, catholicos | iran |
| 1994 | Dibaj, pastor Mehdi | iran |
| 1314 | Francis of Borgo San Sepolcro | iran |
| 1340 | Gentle of Matelica | iran |
| 615 | George the Monk | iran |
| 1994 | Hovsepian-Mehr, bp H. | iran |
| 1624 | Ketevan, queen | iran |
| 1994 | Michaelian, pastor Tateos | iran |
| 1869 | Mirza Ibrahim | iran |
| 1979 | Sayyad, fr | iran |
| 1979 | Siyah, pastor Aristou | iran |
| 1990 | Soodmand, pastor H. | iran |
| 1334 | William of England | iran |
| 1996 | Yusefi, pastor Mohammad B. | iran |
| 552 | Aba, mar, patriarch catholicos | iraq |
| 410 | Abda, mar | iraq |
| 375 | Abdas, metropolitan | iraq |
| 341 | Abdechalas & Ananias | iraq |
| 575 | Ahudemmeh, bp of Tagrit | iraq |
| 448 | Anahid | iraq |
| 341 | Ananias | iraq |
| 346 | Anna | iraq |
| 1918 | Audo, abp | iraq |
| 484 | Babowi, catholicos | iraq |
| 346 | Barbashmin, catholicos | iraq |
| 493 | Barsumas, bp | iraq |
| 422 | Benjamin | iraq |
| 327 | Berikjesu | iraq |
| c337 | Caxo, prince | iraq |
| 422 | Chouchanik | iraq |
| c337 | Dado, governor | iraq |
| 345 | Daniel | iraq |
| 448 | Dindui, metropolitan | iraq |
| 1261 | Dionysius, antipatriarch | iraq |
| 303 | Febronia | iraq |
| 1972 | George, Margaret | iraq |
| c337 | Gobidlaha, princess | iraq |
| 315 | Gurias & companions | iraq |
| 345 | Hanania | iraq |
| 422 | Hormisdas | iraq |
| 408 | Hormizd of Sylvanus, rabban | iraq |
| 420 | Hormizdas | iraq |
| c240 | Intercisus, James | iraq |
| 1995 | Isho, E.K. | iraq |
| 337 | Jacob, bp | iraq |
| 346 | James | iraq |
| 422 | James of Persia | iraq |
| 337 | John, bp | iraq |
| 448 | John, bp of Karka | iraq |
| 327 | Jonah | iraq |
| 346 | Martha | iraq |
| 346 | Mary | iraq |
| c70 | Matthew (Levi), Apostle | iraq |
| 1997 | Matti, Haval | iraq |
| 1991 | Matti, Lazar | iraq |
| 420 | Peroz | iraq |
| 448 | Pethiun, evangelist | iraq |
| 345 | Pherbutha | iraq |
| 518 | Philoxenus, bp of Mabbogh | iraq |
| 315 | Phrebonia | iraq |
| 339 | Pusak, prefect, & 100 clergy | iraq |
| 341 | Pusicius | iraq |
| 286 | Qndyr, queen | iraq |
| 123 | Semsoun, bp of Edessa | iraq |
| 342 | Shahdost, catholicos | iraq |
| 1975 | Shimun, catholicos-patriarch | iraq |
| 1997 | Sifer, M. H. | iraq |
| 341 | Simeon Barsabae, catholicos | iraq |
| 61 | Simon Zelotes, Apostle | iraq |
| 448 | Sirin | iraq |
| 1918 | Sontag, apostolic delegate | iraq |
| c810 | Subaljesu, monk | iraq |
| 422 | Suenas | iraq |
| 448 | Tamasgerd | iraq |
| 339 | Tarbo, deaconess | iraq |
| 345 | Uarda (Rose) | iraq |
| 341 | Usthazanes | iraq |
| c800 | Erc, bp of Slane | irel |
| c440 | Gwinear | irel |
| 1535 | Kenraghty, chaplain Maurice | irel |
| 1650 | McMahon, bp E. | irel |
| 1798 | Murphy, fr J. | irel |
| 1651 | O'Brien, bp T. A. | irel |
| 1580 | O'Cullenan, G., abbot | irel |
| 1612 | O'Devany, C., bp | irel |
| 1575 | O'Donnell SJ, E. | irel |
| 1578 | O'Hely, P., bp | irel |
| 1584 | O'Hurley, D., abp | irel |
| 431 | Palladius | irel |
| 1680 | Talbot, P., abp of Dublin | irel |
| 309 | Abdon | ital |
| c100 | Achilleus | ital |
| 259 | Agapitus of Praeneste | ital |
| 249 | Agatha | ital |
| c350 | Agnes | ital |
| c117 | Alexander | ital |
| 397 | Alexander | ital |
| 840 | Alexander, bp of Fiesole | ital |
| 304 | Andronicus | ital |
| 1323 | Angelus of Spoleto | ital |
| c168 | Anicetus, pope | ital |
| c185 | Apollonius, senator | ital |
| c120 | Atrasis, daughter of Hadrian | ital |
| 91 | Aurelia Petronilla | ital |
| 1998 | Beheydt, pastor G. S. | ital |
| 884 | Bertharius, abbot | ital |
| c360 | Bibiana | ital |
| 1388 | Bonaventure Peraga, cardinal | ital |
| 1600 | Bruno, br G. | ital |
| 570 | Cadoc, bp | ital |
| c165 | Caecelia | ital |
| c222 | Callistus I, pope | ital |
| c300 | Castorius | ital |
| 178 | Cecilia | ital |
| 303 | Chrysogonus | ital |
| c300 | Claudius | ital |
| c90 | Cletus, bp of Rome | ital |
| 253 | Cornelius, pope | ital |
| c302 | Crescentia | ital |
| c360 | Dafrosa & Demetria | ital |
| 1878 | David, fr | ital |
| c360 | Demetria | ital |
| 235 | Demetrius | ital |
| 834 | Deusdedit, abbot of M Cassino | ital |
| c300 | Elmo, bp of Formiae | ital |
| 1075 | Erlembald | ital |
| c111 | Eustathius, Roman general | ital |
| c117 | Eventius & Theodulus | ital |
| 250 | Fabian, pope | ital |
| c297 | Felician | ital |
| 259 | Felicissimus & Agapitus | ital |
| 95 | Flavius Clemens | ital |
| 165 | Gervase & Protase | ital |
| 91 | Glabrio, Manius Acilius, consul | ital |
| 1902 | Goretti, Maria | ital |
| 235 | Hippolytus, antipope | ital |
| 115 | Ignatius, bp of Antioch | ital |
| 730 | James, bp of Catania | ital |
| 305 | Januarius, bp of Benevento | ital |
| 526 | John I, pope | ital |
| 928 | John X, pope | ital |
| c120 | Junia | ital |
| 165 | Justin Martyr & 5 companions | ital |
| 259 | Lawrence | ital |
| c76 | Linus, bp of Rome | ital |
| c171 | Lucius | ital |
| 303 | Lucy | ital |
| 275 | Magnus, bp of Fabrateria | ital |
| 410 | Marcella | ital |
| 178 | Marcellus | ital |
| 309 | Marcellus, pope | ital |
| c364 | Mark, bp of Arethusa | ital |
| 397 | Martyrius | ital |
| 178 | Maximus | ital |
| c302 | Modestus | ital |
| c197 | Moses | ital |
| 1998 | Muntoni, fr G. | ital |
| c100 | Nereus | ital |
| c300 | Nicostratus | ital |
| 258 | Novatian, antipope | ital |
| 1383 | Panacea | ital |
| 304 | Pancras | ital |
| c98 | Parmenas the deacon | ital |
| 64 | Paul, Apostle | ital |
| 1365 | Peter of Ruffia | ital |
| 1252 | Peter of Verona (Peter Martyr) | ital |
| c120 | Phocas, bp of Bontos | ital |
| 235 | Pontian, pope | ital |
| c297 | Primus | ital |
| 165 | Protase | ital |
| c171 | Ptolemaus | ital |
| c171 | Publius, bp of Athens | ital |

*Continued overleaf*

*Table 4–13 continued*

| | | |
|---|---|---|
| 202 | Pudens | ital |
| 1993 | Puglisi, pastor G. | ital |
| 1490 | Rabata, A. | ital |
| 1775 | Ricci SJ, general L. | ital |
| 1080 | Rudolf of Swabia | ital |
| 258 | Rufina | ital |
| c197 | Sarah | ital |
| 1498 | Savonarola, G. | ital |
| 288 | Sebastian of Milan | ital |
| 258 | Secunda | ital |
| 309 | Sennen | ital |
| 524 | Severinus Boethius, consul | ital |
| 537 | Silverius, pope | ital |
| 64 | Simon Peter, Apostle | ital |
| c300 | Simplicius | ital |
| c300 | Simpronian | ital |
| 397 | Sisinnius | ital |
| c117 | Sixtus I, bp of Rome | ital |
| 258 | Sixtus II, pope | ital |
| 257 | Stephen I, pope | ital |
| c280 | Tarsicius | ital |
| c228 | Tatiana, deaconess | ital |
| 391 | Telemachus | ital |
| 138 | Telesphorus, bp of Rome | ital |
| c117 | Theodulus | ital |
| c111 | Theopista | ital |
| 178 | Tibúrtius | ital |
| c1200 | Uguzo (Lucio di Val Cavargna) | ital |
| 230 | Urban, pope | ital |
| 538 | Ursicinus, bp of Ravenna | ital |
| 269 | Valentine | ital |
| 178 | Valerian | ital |
| 1619 | Vanini, L. | ital |
| c305 | Victor | ital |
| 303 | Victor Maurus | ital |
| c310 | Victor of Stratelates | ital |
| c302 | Vitus | ital |
| 1362 | William of Campania | ital |
| 303 | Zeno of Rome | ital |
| 2000 | Grange, fr R. | ivor |
| 1991 | Jeanne SAM, fr A. | ivor |
| 1992 | Pfister, J. | ivor |
| 1985 | Cuthbert, R. W. M. | jama |
| 2000 | Rochester, fr H. | jama |
| 1633 | Alonso, fr L. | japa |
| 1634 | Ansalone, fr G. | japa |
| 1597 | Blasquez, fr Pedro B. | japa |
| 1989 | Boisvert, fr A. | japa |
| 1624 | Carvalho, fr J. | japa |
| 1597 | Casas Martinez, Felipe | japa |
| 1626 | Caun, V. | japa |
| 1622 | Constanzo, fr C. | japa |
| 1637 | Courtet OP, fr W. | japa |
| 1623 | De Angelis, fr J. | japa |
| 1637 | de Aozaraza, fr M. | japa |
| 1597 | de Goto, fr J. S. | japa |
| 1626 | de Torres, fr B. | japa |
| 1597 | Francis of Miako | japa |
| 1622 | Fugiscima, fr D. | japa |
| 1637 | Gonzales, fr A. | japa |
| 1632 | Gutierrez, fr R. B. | japa |
| 1613 | Hachikan, Joaquin | japa |
| 1633 | Ibanez, fr D. | japa |
| 1632 | Ixida SJ, fr A. | japa |
| 1597 | Karasumaru, Leo | japa |
| 1622 | Kimura SJ, fr S. | japa |
| 1619 | Kimura, fr L. | japa |
| 1597 | Kisai, fr J. | japa |
| 1633 | Kohioye, fr M. | japa |
| 1633 | Kurobioye, M. | japa |
| 1627 | Kwon, Vincent | japa |
| 1616 | Lawrence | japa |
| 1637 | Lazzaro di Kyoto | japa |
| 1616 | Lewis | japa |
| 1612 | Lucas of Tokyo | japa |
| 1617 | Macaido, fr J. B. | japa |
| 1634 | Maddalena of Nagasaki | japa |
| 1634 | Marina di Omura | japa |
| 1597 | Miki SJ, fr Paul | japa |
| 1628 | Nagascima SJ, br M. | japa |
| 1634 | Nishi, fr T.H.R. | japa |
| 1622 | Novarra, fr P. P. | japa |
| 1622 | Ota, fr A. | japa |
| 1626 | Pacheco, fr F. | japa |
| 1626 | Rinscei, P. | japa |
| 1642 | Rubino, fr | japa |
| 1637 | Ruiz, L. | japa |
| 1626 | Sadamatzu, G. | japa |
| 1622 | Sandaju, fr P. O. | japa |
| 1637 | Schiwozuka, fr V. | japa |
| 1714 | Sidotti, abbot G. B. | japa |
| 1622 | Spinola SJ, fr C. | japa |
| 1600 | Tadaoki, Gracia | japa |
| 1616 | Thomas | japa |
| 1633 | Tomonaga OP, fr J. K. G. | japa |
| 1626 | Tozo, M. | japa |
| 1627 | Tsuji, fr T. | japa |
| 1634 | Vieira, fr S. | japa |
| 1616 | Vincent | japa |
| 1623 | Yempo, br Simon | japa |
| 1600 | Yukinaga, general Konishi | japa |
| 1626 | Zola, fr J. B. | japa |
| 1622 | Zumarraga OP, fr | japa |
| 451 | Nestorius, patriarch | jord |
| 1934 | Poliansky, abp Ambrose | kaza |
| 1998 | Andeni, fr L. | keny |
| 1991 | Bethea, Lynda | keny |
| 1952 | Gacigi, G. | keny |
| 1952 | Gacigi, R. | keny |
| 1953 | Gikonyo, E. | keny |
| 1953 | Kaguru, A. | keny |
| 2000 | Kaiser, fr A. | keny |
| 1992 | Kariuki, pastor H. | keny |
| 1883 | Koi, David | keny |
| 1953 | Maina, E. | keny |
| 1992 | Maniafo, S.J. | keny |
| 1952 | Mungai, J. | keny |
| 1952 | Muriuki, W. | keny |
| 1934 | Odongo, Alfayo | keny |
| 1989 | Reinkemeyer, sr A. | keny |
| 1990 | Stumpf, H. | keny |
| 1997 | Timmons, br L. | keny |
| 1952 | Wancegi, Mary | keny |
| 1942 | Sadd, A. | kiri |
| 1996 | Her, Ah | laos |
| 1934 | Pommer, John, abp of Riga | latv |
| 1830 | Asad es Shidiak | leba |
| 1860 | Billottet SJ, fr E. | leba |
| 1860 | Bonacina, br F. | leba |
| 1985 | Kluiters, fr N. | leba |
| 1860 | Mabeiche, br A. H. | leba |
| 1860 | Maksoud, br H. | leba |
| 1987 | Massé SJ, fr André | leba |
| 304 | Nilus, bp | leba |
| 254 | Origen | leba |
| 304 | Peleus, bp | leba |
| 1992 | Robinson, W. | leba |
| 1830 | Shidiak, Asaad | leba |
| 1860 | Younes, br E. | leba |
| c1970 | Brown, bp D. | libe |
| 1992 | Fallah, pastor J. | libe |
| 1992 | Jackson, J. | libe |
| 1992 | Jackson, T. & J. | libe |
| 1992 | Kolmer, sr J. | libe |
| 1992 | Kolmer, sr S. | libe |
| 1993 | Korfeh, pastor T. | libe |
| 1992 | McGuire, sr K. | libe |
| 1992 | Mueller, sr S. | libe |
| 1992 | Muttra, sr B.A. | libe |
| 1992 | Saah, pastor D. | libe |
| 1986 | Senter, L. & R. | libe |
| 1986 | Senter, R. | libe |
| 1989 | Vassallo, sr Emanuela | liby |
| 1347 | Antoniy | lith |
| 1946 | Borisevicius, V., bp of Telsiai | lith |
| 1009 | Bruno, bp of Querfurt | lith |
| 1347 | Evastafiy | lith |
| 1347 | Ioann | lith |
| 1980 | Jaugelis, fr V. | lith |
| 1981 | Laurinavicius, fr B. | lith |
| 1941 | Litaunieks, fr V. | lith |
| 1962 | Matulionis, bp of Kaisiadorys | lith |
| 1981 | Mazeika, fr L. | lith |
| 1940 | Mazeika, L. | lith |
| 1996 | Ramanauskas, fr V. | lith |
| 1959 | Ramanauskas, P., bp of Telsiai | lith |
| 1953 | Reinys, M., abp of Vilnius | lith |
| 1980 | Sapoka, fr L. | lith |
| 1975 | Tamonis, M. | lith |
| 1346 | John the Blind | luxe |
| 1896 | Berthieu SJ, fr J. | mada |
| 1988 | de Boisseson, fr J. | mada |
| 1998 | Hubscher, fr M. | mada |
| 1834 | Rainitsiandavaka | mada |
| 1988 | Ramaralahy, br I. | mada |
| 1837 | Rasalama | mada |
| 1984 | Roy, fr | mada |
| 1985 | Sorgon OCD, fr S. | mada |
| 1915 | Chilembwe, John | mala |
| 1983 | Chiwanga | mala |
| 1983 | Gadama | mala |
| 1983 | Matenje | mala |
| 1926 | Nyirenda, Tomo | mala |
| 1979 | Sangaya, J. | mala |
| 1704 | Alverez, fr R. | mexi |
| 1684 | Beltran, fr M. | mexi |
| 1686 | Benitez, fr E. | mexi |
| 1986 | Brennes, J. | mexi |
| 1541 | Calero, br J. | mexi |
| 1734 | Carranco, fr L. | mexi |
| 1998 | Carreno, fr M. O. | mexi |
| 1997 | Collazo, S. | mexi |
| 1564 | Cossin, fr B. | mexi |
| 1684 | Custodio, fr F. | mexi |
| 1567 | de Acevedo, fr P. | mexi |
| 1606 | de Altamirano, fr M. | mexi |
| 1585 | de Ayala, fr A. | mexi |
| 1773 | de Bernave, fr J.C.G. | mexi |
| 1567 | de Burgos, fr P. | mexi |
| 1541 | de Cuellar, fr A. | mexi |
| 1567 | de Herrera, br J. | mexi |
| 1586 | de la Puebla, fr A. | mexi |
| 1928 | de la Vega, fr J. | mexi |
| 1616 | de Santarn, fr H. | mexi |
| 1564 | de Tapia, fr J. | mexi |
| 1616 | de Tovar, fr H. | mexi |
| 1582 | de Villalobos, fr L. | mexi |
| 1586 | del Rio, fr J. | mexi |
| 1624 | Delgado, fr D. | mexi |
| 1994 | Diaz, Veronica J. | mexi |
| 1567 | Donzel, fr F. | mexi |
| 1986 | Figaroa, N.M. | mexi |
| 1986 | Flores, Ernesto | mexi |
| 2000 | Gaytan, rev J. | mexi |
| 1585 | Gil, fr F. | mexi |
| 1995 | Gomez Ramos, pastor A. | mexi |
| 1778 | Guillen, fr F. | mexi |
| 1616 | Gutierrez, fr P. | mexi |
| 1624 | Henriquez, br J. | mexi |
| 1995 | Hernandez Perez, pastor G. | mexi |
| 1997 | Hernandez, M. | mexi |
| 1974 | Hernandez, M. Gomez | mexi |
| 1704 | Hevia, fr D. | mexi |
| 1811 | Hidalgo y Costilla, fr M. | mexi |
| 1560 | Juan, br | mexi |
| 1645 | Labado, fr F. | mexi |
| 1560 | Lorenzo, fr F. | mexi |
| 1564 | Lucas, br | mexi |
| 1928 | Martinez, br H. | mexi |
| 1647 | Montero, fr F. | mexi |
| 1815 | Morelos y Pavon, fr J. M. | mexi |
| 1986 | Moreno, Norma | mexi |
| 1684 | Muros, fr | mexi |
| 1993 | Ocampo, cardinal Juan J.J.P. | mexi |
| 1928 | Perez, fr P. | mexi |
| 1997 | Perez, M. | mexi |
| 1985 | Philpot, J. | mexi |
| 1993 | Posadas, cardinal J.J. | mexi |
| 1927 | Pro Juarez, fr M. | mexi |
| 1997 | Ramos SJ, fr W. G. | mexi |
| 1847 | Rey SJ, fr A. | mexi |
| 1997 | Ruiz, pastor N. H. | mexi |
| 1580 | Serrato, fr J. | mexi |
| 1734 | Tamaral, fr N. | mexi |
| 1649 | Trevino de Sobremonte, T. | mexi |
| 1880 | Westrup, J. O. | mexi |
| 1645 | Zigarran, fr T. | mexi |
| 1731 | Contova SJ, fr Juan Antonio | micr |
| 1995 | Petcu, A. | mold |
| 1220 | Accursio | moro |
| 1227 | Agnello | moro |
| 1220 | Aiuto | moro |
| 1220 | Berard | moro |
| 298 | Cassian | moro |
| 1227 | Domno | moro |
| 1227 | Hugolino | moro |
| 1631 | John of Prado | moro |
| 1227 | Leo | moro |
| 298 | Marcellus the Centurion | moro |
| 1227 | Nicholas | moro |
| 1220 | Otho | moro |
| 1220 | Peter | moro |
| 1227 | Samuel | moro |
| 1989 | Bortolotti, fr F. | moza |
| 1989 | Campanella, fr C. | moza |
| 1991 | Cristovao, fr M.J. | moza |
| 1985 | Dalle Pezze, sr T.P. | moza |
| 1989 | de Rocha, fr A. | moza |
| 1992 | Fiorini, fr Alfredo | moza |
| 1990 | Gagnaux, dr R. | moza |
| 1985 | Goncalves Kamtedza SJ, fr J. | moza |
| 1992 | Goncalves, sr M.L. Granado | moza |
| 1972 | Manganhela, Z. | moza |
| 1985 | Moreira SJ, fr S. | moza |
| 1989 | Saltori, fr O. | moza |
| 1972 | Sidumo, J. | moza |
| 1984 | Torboli, fr S. | moza |
| 1945 | Akya Nai, pastor | myan |
| 1662 | Chu Tsu-hsuan, emperor | myan |
| 1945 | Devine, H. | myan |
| 1745 | Gallizia, bp | myan |
| 1693 | Genoud, fr | myan |
| 1983 | Gideon, dr | myan |
| 1693 | Joret, fr | myan |
| 1950 | Maxville, Selma M. | myan |
| 1756 | Nerini, fr | myan |
| 1852 | U, fr Moses Nya | myan |
| c1990 | Wi-Foo | myan |
| 1958 | Dapcha, Lama David | nepa |
| 1997 | Gafney SJ, fr T. | nepa |
| 1970 | Lamichami, Krishna | nepa |
| 1988 | Paisai, G. | nepa |
| 754 | Boniface (Winfrith), bp | neth |
| 1529 | Denck, H. | neth |
| 754 | Eoban, bp | neth |
| 1942 | Hoeben, H. | neth |
| 1567 | Hoorn, count | neth |
| 1536 | Hutter, J. | neth |
| 856 | Jeron | neth |
| 1567 | Lamoral of Egmont | neth |
| 1527 | Manz, F. | neth |
| 1619 | Oldenbarnevelt, J. van | neth |
| 1569 | Pietersz, Pieter | neth |
| 726 | Werenfrid | neth |
| c1600 | Willems, D. | neth |
| 1847 | Marmoiton, br | newc |
| 1989 | Tjibaou, Jean-Marie | newc |
| 1989 | Yeiwene Yeiwene | newc |
| 1865 | Volkner, Carl S. | newz |
| c1982 | Athers, Lester | nica |
| 1986 | Castilblanco, N.A. | nica |
| 1989 | Corniall, sr Maurice | nica |
| 1990 | Courtney, sr M. | nica |
| 1550 | de Valdivieso, bp A. | nica |
| 1974 | Hernandez, pastor | nica |
| 1989 | Rosales, sr Teresa | nica |
| 1982 | Smith, E. | nica |
| 1983 | Vargas, pastor N. | nica |
| 2000 | Bello, fr C.O. | nige |
| 1995 | Iloputaife, bp H. A. | nige |
| 1997 | Isidi, rev N. | nige |
| 1991 | Mohammed, br | nige |
| 2000 | Ogbu, fr J.M.O. | nige |
| 1995 | Saro-Wiwa, K. | nige |
| 1950 | Brennan, bp P. T. | nork |
| 1950 | Byrne, bp P. J. | nork |
| 1950 | Chang MM, sr Agneta | nork |
| 1944 | Choo Kee Chul, pastor | nork |
| c1990 | Kim, pastor | nork |
| 1950 | Son Yang Won, pastor | nork |
| 1950 | Sung Du, fr | nork |
| 1950 | Tong-Sin, fr | nork |
| 1866 | Yu, fr P. Chong-ryul | nork |
| 1043 | Hallvard Vebjornssen | norw |
| 1030 | Olav II Haraldsson, king | norw |
| 1998 | Alam, pastor Noor | paki |
| 1999 | Bhatti, Sabir John | paki |
| 1988 | Dias OFM, fr C. | paki |
| 1992 | Iqbal, Tahir | paki |
| 1960 | John, evangelist Esther | paki |
| 1997 | Marcellina, sr A. T. S. | paki |
| 1995 | Masih, Iqbal | paki |
| 1995 | Masih, Javed | paki |
| 1994 | Masih, Manzoor | paki |
| 2000 | Sequeira, sr C. | paki |
| 1988 | Tarzwell, John | paki |
| 1987 | Wahid | paki |
| 1988 | Wojcickowski, sr S. | paki |
| c260 | Alexander | pale |
| 209 | Elias & companions | pale |
| c350 | Eudoxius & companions | pale |
| 419 | Eustochium | pale |
| 303 | George, megalomartyr | pale |
| c350 | Gordius | pale |
| 1995 | Grassi, br B. | pale |
| 44 | James Boanerges, Apostle | pale |
| 62 | James the Just, bp of Jerus | pale |
| 54 | James the Less, Apostle | pale |
| 33 | Jesus | pale |
| c260 | Malchus | pale |
| 262 | Marinus | pale |
| 310 | Pamphilus | pale |
| 209 | Pamphilus | pale |
| 130 | Papius | pale |
| 1972 | Pate, Mavis | pale |
| 309 | Paul of Jamnia | pale |
| c260 | Piscus | pale |
| 309 | Porphyrius | pale |
| 303 | Procopius | pale |
| 309 | Seleucus | pale |
| 1979 | Shorrosh, A. | pale |
| 36 | Stephen the Deacon | pale |
| 108 | Symeon, bp of Jerusalem | pale |
| 309 | Theodulus | pale |
| 309 | Valens | pale |
| 1998 | Chocho, Alber | pana |
| 1648 | de Oviedo, fr A. | pana |
| 1642 | de San Antonio, fr J. | pana |
| 1974 | Reimer, G. | pana |
| 1989 | Van Kleef CM, fr N. | pana |
| 1901 | Chalmers, pastor J. | papu |
| 1985 | Chappell, R. | papu |
| 1855 | Mazzuconi, fr G. | papu |
| 1942 | Redlich, V. | papu |
| 1952 | Selanuok | papu |
| 1942 | Tapiedi, Lucian | papu |
| 1901 | Tomkins, pastor O. | papu |
| 1628 | Alonso Rodriguez SJ | para |
| 1998 | Boumans SVD, fr G. | para |
| 1536 | de Almasia, J. | para |
| 1628 | Gonzalez SJ, fr Roque | para |
| 1628 | Juan del Castillo SJ | para |
| 1645 | Romero, fr P. | para |
| 1997 | Badiali, rev D. | peru |
| 1985 | Calderon, Z.S. | peru |
| 1991 | Casaverde, C. | peru |
| 1991 | Chuquin, J. | peru |
| 1974 | de Alencar, F.T. | peru |
| 1991 | Gutierrez, L. | peru |
| c1985 | Ludena, T. | peru |
| 1991 | McCormack, sr Irene | peru |
| 1994 | Nieto, F. A. E. | peru |
| 1985 | Rojas, C.M. | peru |
| 1991 | Sarmiento, M. | peru |
| 1992 | Saune, R. | peru |
| 1983 | Sawyer, sr Joan | peru |
| 1991 | Strzalkowski, fr Z. | peru |
| 1991 | Tattersall, N. | peru |
| 1991 | Tomaszek OFM, fr M. | peru |
| 1541 | Valverde OP, bp V. | peru |
| 1991 | Vargas, C. | peru |
| 1999 | Abadiano, Ted | phil |
| 1992 | Al-Hari, A. | phil |
| 1989 | Ayap, pastor A. | phil |
| 1992 | Bacabis, G. | phil |
| 1996 | Bagtasos III, pastor S. | phil |
| 1985 | Beling, fr M. | phil |
| 1872 | Burgos, fr Jose | phil |
| 1976 | Calvan, pastor R. | phil |
| 1996 | Camacho, H. | phil |
| 1991 | Capasilan, A. | phil |
| 1992 | Carzedda, fr S. | phil |
| 1992 | Celiz, Romeo | phil |
| 1997 | de Jesus, bp B. | phil |
| 1840 | de la Cruz, Apolinario | phil |
| 1988 | Estorba, fr M. | phil |
| 1985 | Favali, fr T. | phil |
| c1995 | Finnemann, bp W. | phil |
| 2000 | Gallardo, fr R. | phil |
| 1991 | Goldsworthy, K. | phil |
| 1872 | Gomez, fr Mariano | phil |
| 1989 | Gran, Lovello | phil |
| 1989 | Gran, pastor Vizminda | phil |
| 1942 | Gray, R. F. | phil |
| 1992 | Hamill, J. | phil |
| 1996 | Hapalla, J. | phil |

*Continued opposite*

*Table 4–13 continued*

| | | |
|---|---|---|
| 1992 | Hapalla, pastor Gregorio | phil |
| 2000 | Inocencio, fr B. | phil |
| 1992 | Juliet | phil |
| c1985 | Lavina, J. | phil |
| 1989 | Malalay, fr D. | phil |
| 1601 | Marin, fr Esteban | phil |
| 1943 | Meyer, F. & 11 missionaries | phil |
| 1997 | Rio, pastor W. | phil |
| 1989 | Rivera, Rufino | phil |
| 1896 | Rizal, Jose | phil |
| 1985 | Romano, fr R. | phil |
| 1985 | Romero, fr A. | phil |
| 1984 | Roxas, S. | phil |
| 1989 | Ruelo, pastor Z. | phil |
| 1988 | Schmitz, CP, fr Carl | phil |
| 1997 | Selorio, pastor E. | phil |
| 1991 | Sigridsson, S. | phil |
| 1995 | Solan, Joel | phil |
| 1991 | Speers, J. | phil |
| 1988 | Stockton, Ann | phil |
| 1985 | Valerio, fr N. | phil |
| 1972 | Williams, N. | phil |
| 1872 | Zamora, fr Jacinto | phil |
| 1003 | Benedict of Benevento | pola |
| 1757 | Faulhaber, fr A. | pola |
| 1941 | Kolbe OFM, fr Maximilian | pola |
| c1942 | Kowalski, J., primate | pola |
| 1984 | Popieluszko, fr J. | pola |
| 1985 | Poplawski, fr P. | pola |
| 1940 | Skobtsova, mother M. | pola |
| 1079 | Stanislas, bp of Cracow | pola |
| 1942 | Stein, Edith | pola |
| 1942 | Stein, Rosa | pola |
| 1940 | Urban SJ, fr J. | pola |
| c1975 | Wallenburg, Raoul | pola |
| 1761 | Malagrida, fr G. | port |
| 1996 | Loperena Soto OP, fr W. | puer |
| 1996 | Soto OP, fr W. L. | puer |
| 1948 | Aftemie, bp | roma |
| 1714 | Brankoveanu, prince Constant | roma |
| 1981 | Clipa, I. | roma |
| 1954 | Durkovici, bp A. | roma |
| 303 | Efrem, bp of Tomis | roma |
| 1948 | Frentiu, bp | roma |
| 1954 | Ghika, fr V. | roma |
| 1970 | Hossu, bp J. | roma |
| 1981 | Kernweisz, bp K. | roma |
| c370 | Nicetas | roma |
| 1795 | Oprea, Miclaus, monk | roma |
| 1954 | Pacha, bp | roma |
| c1650 | Romanul, Ioan Valahul | roma |
| 1849 | Roth, pastor S. L. | roma |
| 372 | Sabas the Goth | roma |
| 1795 | Sarai, Visarion, monk | roma |
| 1954 | Scheffler, bp | roma |
| 1975 | Simescu, br | roma |
| 1795 | Sofronie of Cioara, monk | roma |
| 1334 | Stephen of Gross-Wardein | roma |
| 1948 | Suciu, bp | roma |
| 1981 | Teodosiu, S. | roma |
| 1975 | Zecianu, br | roma |
| 1936 | Abrikosov, mother C. | russ |
| 997 | Adalbert, bp of Prague | russ |
| 1932 | Afanassy, bp of Stavobelsk | russ |
| 1970 | Afonin, I.A. | russ |
| 1720 | Alexander the Deacon | russ |
| 1932 | Alexander, abp | russ |
| 1938 | Alexey, bp of Petrograd | russ |
| 1771 | Ambrose, abp of Krutitsy | russ |
| 1934 | Ambrose, bp of Podolsk | russ |
| 1918 | Ambrose, bp of Seroapulsk | russ |
| 1918 | Ambrose, fr | russ |
| 1938 | Anatole, metrop of Odessa | russ |
| 1918 | Andronick, abp of Perm | russ |
| 1932 | Antony, bp of Archangel | russ |
| 1921 | Archangelsky, pastor T. | russ |
| 1935 | Arseny, abp of Serpuhov | russ |
| 1936 | Arseny, metrop of Novgorod | russ |
| 1977 | Avdeyev, M.V. | russ |
| 1682 | Avvakum Petrovich, archpriest | russ |
| 1980 | Bakholdin, S. | russ |
| 1936 | Bartholomew, bp | russ |
| 1918 | Benjamin, fr | russ |
| 1922 | Benjamin, metrop of Petrograd | russ |
| 1970 | Bergemann, F. | russ |
| 1975 | Biblenko, I.V. | russ |
| 1015 | Boris & Gleb | russ |
| 1923 | Budkiewicz, C., vicar | russ |
| 1918 | Chernikh, S. | russ |
| 1936 | Cyril, metropolitan of Kazan | russ |
| 1771 | Damascenus | russ |
| 1976 | Deinega, N.Y. | russ |
| 1918 | Dimitri, pastor | russ |
| 1936 | Dimitry, abp of Gdovsk | russ |
| 1922 | Dobrolubov, pastor | russ |
| 1918 | Dovganav, P. | russ |
| 1970 | Druck, V. | russ |
| 1985 | Durksen, Y. | russ |
| 1918 | Efrem, bp of Selenginsk | russ |
| 1918 | Elizabeth, grand duchess | russ |
| 1682 | Epifanii, monk | russ |
| 1935 | Fedorov, exarch L. | russ |
| 1922 | Friazinov, pastor | russ |
| 1921 | Frolov, pastor J. | russ |
| 1997 | Gadzhiyev, G. | russ |
| 1997 | Gadzhiyev, Tatiana | russ |
| 1015 | Gleb | russ |
| 1970 | Golev, S.T. | russ |
| 1919 | Herman, bp of Kamychen | russ |
| 1918 | Hermogen, abp of Tobolsk | russ |
| c1925 | Ierofey, bp of Veliki-Ustinsk | russ |
| 1954 | Indus, Artur | russ |
| 1689 | Iosif, hermit, & monks | russ |
| 1918 | Irinarkh, fr | russ |
| 1918 | Israel, monk | russ |
| 1918 | Issidor, bp of Mikhailov | russ |
| 1714 | Ivanov, Thomas | russ |
| 1977 | Ivanova, R. | russ |
| 1919 | Joachim, abp of Nizhni-Novgo | russ |
| 1938 | Joseph, metro of Petrograd | russ |
| 1920 | Justin, abp of Omsk | russ |
| 1938 | Juvenal, abp of Riazan | russ |
| 1964 | Khmara, N. | russ |
| 1982 | Khrapov, N.P. | russ |
| 1917 | Kochurov, fr I. | russ |
| 1979 | Krasnova, T.K. | russ |
| 1964 | Kucherenko | russ |
| 1999 | Kulakov, pastor A. | russ |
| 1918 | Kuntsevich, L. | russ |
| 1990 | Lasar, fr Hegumen | russ |
| 1919 | Lavrenty, bp of Balakhna | russ |
| 1918 | Leonty, bp of Enotaev | russ |
| 1918 | Longin, pastor | russ |
| 1997 | Magomedov, H & T. | russ |
| 1918 | Makarov, M. | russ |
| 1944 | Makary, abp | russ |
| 1919 | Makary, bp of Viazma | russ |
| c1700 | Markel, br | russ |
| 1972 | Melnikov | russ |
| 1990 | Menn, fr Alexander | russ |
| 1921 | Methody, bp of Petropavlovsk | russ |
| 1989 | Mien, fr Alexander | russ |
| 1918 | Miniatov, lawyer | russ |
| 1918 | Mitrophan, abp of Astrakhan | russ |
| 1918 | Modest, fr | russ |
| 1974 | Moiseyevich, pastor I. | russ |
| 1918 | Mokovsky, pastor G. & wife | russ |
| c1682 | Morozova, Boyarina | russ |
| 1921 | Moslovsky, pastor J. | russ |
| 1922 | Nadezhdin, pastor | russ |
| c1938 | Nikandr, metrop of Odessa | russ |
| 1919 | Nikodim, bp of Belgorod | russ |
| 1961 | Nikolai, metrop of Krutitsy | russ |
| 1938 | Nikon (Lebedev), bp | russ |
| 1938 | Nikon, bp of Belgorod | russ |
| 1918 | Nizza, L. | russ |
| 1922 | Orlov, pastor | russ |
| 1918 | Ornatsky, fr F. | russ |
| 1974 | Ostapenko, pastor I.M. | russ |
| 1929 | Peter, abp of Voronezh | russ |
| 1936 | Peter, metropolitan of Krutitsy | russ |
| 1922 | Philaret, bp of Kostroma | russ |
| 1934 | Philip, abp | russ |
| 1567 | Philip, metropolitan of Moscow | russ |
| 1919 | Pimen, bp of Verny | russ |
| 1938 | Pitirim, abp | russ |
| 1918 | Polotnikov, abp of Petrograd | russ |
| 1918 | Pospelov, abp G. | russ |
| 1682 | Pustosviat, Nikita | russ |
| 1918 | Radion, fr | russ |
| 1918 | Riabuhin, pastor J. | russ |
| 1974 | Rozanov, N. | russ |
| 1922 | Rybalkin, monk Fyodor | russ |
| 1921 | Sarichov, pastor S. | russ |
| 1978 | Sedletsky, V. | russ |
| 1938 | Seraphim, bp | russ |
| 1932 | Seraphim, metro of Petrograd | russ |
| 1929 | Serge, bp of Efremov | russ |
| 1922 | Shein, S. | russ |
| 1980 | Shelkov, V. A. | russ |
| 1921 | Simon, bp of Ufa | russ |
| 1918 | Skipetrov, fr A. | russ |
| 1922 | Sokolov, pastor | russ |
| 1861 | Sokolskij, abp J. | russ |
| 1918 | Stavrovsky, fr A. | russ |
| 1922 | Telegin, A. | russ |
| 1918 | Theodot | russ |
| 1918 | Theophan, bp of Solikamsk | russ |
| 1919 | Tikhon, abp of Voronezh | russ |
| 1925 | Tikhon, patriarch | russ |
| 1919 | Varsonoufy, bp of Kirillov | russ |
| c1968 | Vasilyevna, M. | russ |
| 1918 | Veraskin, abp A. | russ |
| 1922 | Vishniakov, pastor | russ |
| 1943 | Voronaev, I. E. | russ |
| 1918 | Vostorgov, fr J. | russ |
| 1920 | Weinberg, Judith | russ |
| 1972 | Yagozinsky, S. | russ |
| c1930 | Yemelyanov, fr P. | russ |
| 1995 | Yi, C.H. | russ |
| 1995 | Yi, K. W. | russ |
| 1971 | Zakharov | russ |
| 1922 | Zaozersky, pastor | russ |
| 1998 | Benimana, sr F. | rwan |
| 1997 | Bosmans, Sr M. | rwan |
| 1998 | Curic, fr V. | rwan |
| 1998 | Gasigwa, sr E. | rwan |
| 1994 | Gatwa, T. | rwan |
| 1997 | Habakurama, rev I. | rwan |
| 1994 | Havugimana, evangelist I | rwan |
| 1998 | Kagabo, fr B. | rwan |
| 1962 | Kanamuzeyi, pastor Yona | rwan |
| 1994 | Karuhije, dean A. | rwan |
| 1992 | Locatelli, A. | rwan |
| 1998 | Mukagakwaya, sr X. | rwan |
| 1998 | Mukamuhire, sr B. | rwan |
| 1998 | Mukanoheli, sr V. | rwan |
| 1996 | Mukeshimana, sr A. | rwan |
| 1996 | Ngwije, fr A. K. | rwan |
| 1996 | Nikwigize, bp P. | rwan |
| 1994 | Nsengiyumva, abp V. | rwan |
| 1994 | Nsengiyumva, bp T. | rwan |
| 1997 | Pinard WF, fr Guy | rwan |
| 1992 | Poppa, sr R. | rwan |
| 1997 | Ruterahagusha, pastor T. | rwan |
| 1997 | Ruterahagusha, T. | rwan |
| 1994 | Rutumbu, fr J. | rwan |
| 1994 | Ruzindana, bp J. | rwan |
| 1998 | Rwangeyo, sr D. | rwan |
| 2000 | Uzcudum, fr I. | rwan |
| 1998 | Wimana, sr C. | rwan |
| 1997 | Yirirwahandi, rev P. | rwan |
| 1996 | Zubiri, sr Carmen | rwan |
| 467 | Azquir | saud |
| 1997 | Beltran, A. | saud |
| 1148 | Ernest, abbot of Zwiefalten | saud |
| 1997 | Janda, R. | saud |
| 1992 | Mal-Allah, S.A.K. | saud |
| 1952 | Gnidovec, dean | serb |
| 1999 | Aloysius, sr M. | sier |
| 1999 | Carmeline, sr | sier |
| 1999 | Hindu, sr | sier |
| 1999 | Sweva, sr | sier |
| 1960 | Gojdic, bp Pavol | slok |
| 1740 | Koman, pastor D. | slov |
| 304 | Victorinus, bp of Pettau | slov |
| 1942 | Duhamel, fr A. C. | solo |
| 1846 | Epalle SM, bp | solo |
| 1942 | Hennessey, J. G. | solo |
| 1871 | Patteson, bp J. C. | solo |
| 1989 | Colombo OFM, bp P.S. | soma |
| 1995 | Fumagalli, Graziella | soma |
| 1995 | Goobe, A. | soma |
| 1962 | Grove, M. | soma |
| 1996 | Haaji, professor | soma |
| 1996 | Huseen, professor H. M. | soma |
| c1995 | Katoolig, C. | soma |
| 1994 | Liibaan, Ibrahim | soma |
| c1995 | Mahamed, S. | soma |
| c1995 | Sheekhdoon, M. | soma |
| c1968 | Sheikow, Musa | soma |
| 1991 | Turati OFM, fr P. | soma |
| 1999 | Umbarger, Deena M. | soma |
| 1977 | Biko, Steve | soua |
| 1994 | Heyns, moderator Johan | soua |
| 1990 | Magorrian, H.L. | soua |
| 1996 | Makaboge, moderator E. | soua |
| 1996 | Mataboge, rev E. | soua |
| 1992 | Mbatha, S'Khumbuzo | soua |
| 1983 | Muothe, I.T. | soua |
| 1995 | O'Neill, fr E. | soua |
| 1999 | Peleman, fr A. | soua |
| 1998 | Schreck, sr M. | soua |
| 1990 | Stanton, fr N. | soua |
| 1992 | Tsotetsi, Saul | soua |
| 1989 | Webster, David | soua |
| 1993 | Zuma, Isaac | soua |
| 1993 | Zuma, Thandi | soua |
| 1866 | Berneux, bp S.-F. | souk |
| 1839 | Chastan, fr J. H. | souk |
| 1866 | Cho, Peter | souk |
| 1801 | Chu, fr James | souk |
| 1801 | Chung, Augustine | souk |
| 1866 | Daveluy, bp M. A. N. | souk |
| 1954 | Eunak, K. | souk |
| 1801 | Hwang, S. C. | souk |
| 1839 | Imbert, bp Laurence | souk |
| 1983 | Ki-Yoon, pastor I. | souk |
| 1846 | Kim Tai Kun, fr Andrew | souk |
| 1839 | Kim, Agatha | souk |
| 1866 | Lee, John | souk |
| 1942 | Lee, pastor Kipoong | souk |
| 1839 | Maubant, fr P. | souk |
| 1987 | Park, Jong Ch'ol | souk |
| 1839 | Ri, J. | souk |
| 1866 | Thomas, R. J. | souk |
| 1801 | Wan-Suk, Columba | souk |
| 1795 | Wenmo, fr J. Z. | souk |
| 1791 | Yun, Paul | souk |
| 825 | Adulfus & John | spai |
| 1936 | Arbona, fr B. | spai |
| 1934 | Arconada, fr J. B. | spai |
| 931 | Argentea | spai |
| 1936 | Artigues, fr R. | spai |
| 1936 | Audi, fr F. | spai |
| 850 | Aurea | spai |
| 852 | Aurelius | spai |
| 1936 | Baste, fr N. | spai |
| 1936 | Boguna, fr L. | spai |
| 1936 | Bori, fr P. | spai |
| 1936 | Carbonell, fr C. | spai |
| 1936 | Carrio, fr A. | spai |
| 853 | Columba of Cordoba | spai |
| 1936 | Corral, fr O. | spai |
| 1936 | Darder, E. | spai |
| 1570 | de Azevedo SJ, fr I. | spai |
| 1397 | de Cetina, J. | spai |
| 1397 | de Duenas, P. | spai |
| 1936 | de Velasco, fr I. | spai |
| 304 | Eulalia of Merida | spai |
| 859 | Eulogius of Cordoba | spai |
| 852 | Fandila of Cordoba | spai |
| 1936 | Ferreres, fr J. B. | spai |
| 851 | Flora of Cordoba | spai |
| 259 | Fructuosus, bp of Tarragona | spai |
| 1936 | Garcia Villada SJ, fr Z. | spai |
| 1936 | Gelabert, P. | spai |
| 850 | George of Cordoba | spai |
| 1936 | Gonzalez, fr E. | spai |
| 1936 | Grimaltos, R. | spai |
| 585 | Hermenegild of Spain | spai |
| 851 | Isaac, monk | spai |
| 1936 | Isla, fr L. | spai |
| 1936 | Jimenez Malla, Ceferino | spai |
| 825 | John of Cordoba | spai |
| 1478 | John of Sahagun | spai |
| 859 | Leocritia | spai |
| 1936 | Llatje, fr J. | spai |
| 1936 | Luque, fr E. | spai |
| 1936 | Malla, C. J. | spai |
| 1936 | Martinez, fr B. | spai |
| 1934 | Martinez, fr E. | spai |
| 851 | Mary of Cordoba | spai |
| 1936 | Mayorga, fr M. | spai |
| 1578 | Miguel de Medina | spai |
| 852 | Natalia | spai |
| 1936 | Payan, fr A. | spai |
| 850 | Perfectus of Cordoba | spai |
| 1936 | Peypoch, fr E. | spai |
| 853 | Pomposa | spai |
| 386 | Priscillian, bp | spai |
| 1936 | Rovira, fr J. | spai |
| 1936 | Sales, V. | spai |
| 1936 | Sanchez, fr J. | spai |
| 851 | Sanctius of Cordoba | spai |
| 1936 | Santaella, fr M. | spai |
| 1936 | Simon, fr A. | spai |
| 1936 | Sitjar, fr T. | spai |
| 1936 | Tarrats, J. | spai |
| 1936 | Tena, fr R. | spai |
| c65 | Torquatus | spai |
| 1936 | Valenti, fr T. | spai |
| 1936 | Verges, fr J. | spai |
| 304 | Vincent of Saragossa | spai |
| 931 | Vulfura | spai |
| 1227 | Daniel of Belvedere | span |
| 1988 | Chandra, fr F. | sril |
| 1985 | Jeyarajasingham, pastor G. | sril |
| 1985 | Manielpillai, fr M.B. | sril |
| 1987 | Rodrigo OMI, fr Miguel | sril |
| 1998 | Sritharan, pastor Vasu | sril |
| 1963 | Adwok, pastor G. | suda |
| 1985 | Arensen, J. | suda |
| 1963 | Debior, P. | suda |
| 1998 | Deng, A. Y. | suda |
| 1964 | Dwatuka, fr B. | suda |
| 1885 | Gordon, general C. G. | suda |
| 1992 | Kon, Paul | suda |
| 1991 | Lawi, Ezra | suda |
| 1998 | Malesh, pastor J. | suda |
| 1990 | Mamma, pr | suda |
| 1967 | Saturnino, fr | suda |
| 1120 | Botvid | swed |
| 1150 | Eric of Sweden | swed |
| c1080 | Eskil, bp | swed |
| 1156 | Henry, bp of Uppsala | swed |
| 1028 | Ulfrid | swed |
| 287 | Candidus | swit |
| 287 | Exuperantius | swit |
| 287 | Exuperius | swit |
| 287 | Felix | swit |
| 1622 | Fidelis of Sigmaringen | swit |
| 287 | Maurice | swit |
| 861 | Meinrad of Einsiedeln, hermit | swit |
| 287 | Regula | swit |
| 287 | Urs | swit |
| 287 | Ursus of Solothurn | swit |
| 287 | Victor of Marseilles | swit |
| c287 | Victor of Solothurn | swit |
| 926 | Wiborada (Guiborat), recluse | swit |
| 1859 | Ascanio OFM, fr N. | syri |
| 315 | Bacchus | syri |
| 1859 | de Albera OFM, fr. N. M. | syri |
| 1860 | de Albera, fr M. M. | syri |
| 1859 | Fernandez, fr J. J. | syri |
| 1258 | Kitbuga, general | syri |
| 1860 | Kolland OFM, fr E. | syri |
| c360 | Leontius of Tripoli | syri |
| 1860 | Masi, Francis | syri |
| 1860 | Masi, Muti | syri |
| 1860 | Masi, Raphael | syri |
| c1180 | Michael of Damietta | syri |
| 1860 | Pinzano OFM, Francis | syri |
| 1860 | Ruiz OFM, fr Emmanuel | syri |
| 315 | Sergius & Bacchus | syri |
| 304 | Silvanus | syri |
| 1859 | Soler, fr P. | syri |
| c900 | Thomas, bp of Damascus | syri |
| c750 | Vahan of Goghtn | syri |
| 1860 | Volta OFM, fr. C. | syri |
| 1662 | Hambroek, A. | taiw |
| 1973 | Hopewell, Gladys | taiw |
| 1994 | Limar, br | taji |
| 1996 | Schiavo, fr G. | tanz |
| 1981 | Fietje, K. | thai |
| 1569 | Jerome de la Croix | thai |
| 1868 | Noi Sunya | thai |
| 1869 | Non Chai, abbot | thai |
| 1569 | Sebastian Cantu | thai |
| 1941 | Sri-Phong, catechist P. | thai |
| 1887 | Moran, fr J. | togo |
| 1516 | Botello OP, Diego | trin |
| 1516 | de Salcedo OP, fr F | trin |
| c255 | Agapius, bp | tuni |
| 1460 | Antony of Rivoli (Tunis) | tuni |
| 413 | Apringius, proconsul | tuni |

*Continued overleaf*

*Table 4–13 concluded*

| | | |
|---|---|---|
| 180 | Aquilinus | tuni |
| 259 | Augurius | tuni |
| 180 | Cittinus | tuni |
| 258 | Cyprian, bp of Carthage | tuni |
| 304 | Dativus | tuni |
| 484 | Dionysia | tuni |
| 180 | Donata | tuni |
| 304 | Donatilla | tuni |
| 347 | Donatus, bp of Bagai | tuni |
| 259 | Eulogius | tuni |
| 202 | Felicitas | tuni |
| 180 | Felix | tuni |
| 303 | Felix of Thibiuca | tuni |
| 259 | Flavian | tuni |
| 180 | Generosa | tuni |
| 347 | Isaac | tuni |
| 259 | James of Cirta | tuni |
| 180 | Januaria | tuni |
| 180 | Laetantius | tuni |
| 180 | Lucitas | tuni |
| 259 | Lucius | tuni |
| 484 | Majoricus | tuni |
| 413 | Marcellinus Flavius, tribune | tuni |
| 347 | Marculus, bp of S. Numidia | tuni |
| 259 | Marian | tuni |
| 259 | Marianus | tuni |
| 304 | Maxima | tuni |
| 347 | Maximian | tuni |
| 180 | Miggin | tuni |
| 259 | Montanus | tuni |
| 180 | Namphano | tuni |
| 180 | Nartzalus | tuni |
| 202 | Perpetua | tuni |
| c258 | Quadratus, bp | tuni |
| 259 | Quartillosia | tuni |
| 259 | Renus | tuni |
| 202 | Revocatus | tuni |
| 180 | Sanam | tuni |
| 202 | Saturninus | tuni |
| 202 | Saturus | tuni |
| 180 | Secunda | tuni |
| 304 | Secunda | tuni |
| 484 | Servus | tuni |
| 180 | Speratus | tuni |
| 180 | Vestia | tuni |
| 180 | Veturius | tuni |
| 484 | Victorian | tuni |
| c260 | Leontius the Ascetic | turc |
| c260 | Paregorius | turc |
| 251 | Achatius, bp | turk |
| 304 | Adrian & Natalia | turk |
| c170 | Agathonice | turk |
| 284 | Alexander & Asterius | turk |
| 628 | Anastasius the Persian | turk |
| 295 | Anthimus, bp of Nicomedia | turk |
| 91 | Antipas | turk |
| 284 | Asterius | turk |
| 112 | Babai | turk |
| 251 | Babylas, patriarch of Antioch | turk |
| 304 | Barlaam of Antioch | turk |
| 112 | Barsamya | turk |
| c300 | Callinicus | turk |
| c170 | Carpus, bp | turk |
| 249 | Christopher | turk |
| 1923 | Chrysostomos, met of Smyrna | turk |
| c260 | Conon | turk |
| c300 | Cosmas & Damian | turk |
| 110 | Crescentius | turk |
| c260 | Cyril | turk |
| 1638 | Cyril I Lukaris, ecu patriarch | turk |
| 1638 | Cyril II Kontaris, ecu patriarch | turk |
| c300 | Damian | turk |
| c300 | Diomed | turk |
| 313 | Dorothy | turk |
| 303 | Euphemia | turk |
| 379 | Eusebius, bp of Samosata | turk |
| 834 | Euthymius, metrop of Sardes | turk |
| 64 | Evodius, bp of Antioch | turk |
| 252 | Fabius, bp of Antioch | turk |
| 156 | Felicitus Alexander | turk |
| 165 | Felicity | turk |
| 449 | Flavian, patriarch | turk |
| 303 | Genesius the Actor | turk |
| 156 | Germanicus | turk |
| 729 | Germanus, ecu patriarch | turk |
| 1707 | Gomidas, fr K. | turk |
| 1979 | Goodman, Dave | turk |
| 1317 | Gregorios, Mar, bp | turk |
| 1822 | Gregory V, ecu patriarch | turk |
| 309 | Habib the Deacon | turk |
| 1998 | Haviaropoulos, V. | turk |
| 304 | Hermes | turk |
| 297 | Hipparchus | turk |
| 284 | Irene | turk |
| 1096 | John (Said bar Sabhuni), bp | turk |
| 407 | John Chrysostom, patriarch | turk |
| c860 | John VII Grammaticus, patr | turk |
| 95 | John, Apostle | turk |
| 1802 | Lazarus the Bulgar | turk |
| c580 | Licinianus, bp of Carthage | turk |
| 1896 | Lilli OFM, fr Salvatore | turk |
| 312 | Lucian of Antioch | turk |
| 511 | Macedonius II, patriarch | turk |
| 274 | Mamas | turk |
| 278 | Marina | turk |
| 64 | Matthias, Apostle | turk |
| 311 | Methodius, bp of Olympus | turk |
| 304 | Natalia of Nicomedia | turk |
| 250 | Nestor, bp of Perga | turk |
| 1997 | Ozdemir, Ali | turk |
| c1898 | Papizian, archimandrite J. | turk |
| c170 | Papylus | turk |
| 351 | Paul, patriarch | turk |
| c300 | Pelagia | turk |
| 304 | Philip bp of Heraclea | turk |
| 60 | Philip, Apostle | turk |
| 297 | Philotheus of Antioch | turk |
| 250 | Pionius | turk |
| 156 | Polycarp, bp of Smyrna | turk |
| 304 | Severus | turk |
| 309 | Shamona | turk |
| 112 | Sharbil | turk |
| 764 | Stephen the Younger, abbot | turk |
| c300 | Taragus & companions | turk |
| 284 | Thalelaeus | turk |
| c125 | Thalelaeus | turk |
| c50 | Thecla | turk |
| c725 | Theodosia | turk |
| 97 | Timothy, bp | turk |
| c310 | Tyrannio, bp of Tyre | turk |
| 1554 | Yuhanna Sulaqa, catholicos | turk |
| 304 | Zenobius | turk |
| 2000 | Akullu, G. | ugan |
| 2000 | Akweyo, sr D. | ugan |
| 1979 | Annanias, fr O. | ugan |
| 2000 | Asienzo, sr P. | ugan |
| 1886 | Badzekuketta, A. | ugan |
| 1886 | Banabakintu, Luke | ugan |
| 1984 | Bazira, pastor G. | ugan |
| 1988 | Beebwa, sr M.T. | ugan |
| 1990 | Biscaro, fr Egidio | ugan |
| 1886 | Buzabaliawo, James | ugan |
| 1979 | Dalmajo, fr S. | ugan |
| 2000 | di Bari, fr R. | ugan |
| 1989 | Ejeru, pastor Joseph | ugan |
| 1979 | Fiorantie, fr A. | ugan |
| 1886 | Gonza, Gonzaga | ugan |
| 1886 | Gyavira | ugan |
| 1885 | Hannington, bp James | ugan |
| 1886 | Kaggwa, Andrew | ugan |
| 1973 | Kagwa, M. | ugan |
| 1886 | Kalemba, Matthias | ugan |
| 1886 | Kibuka, Ambrose | ugan |
| 1973 | Kiggundu, fr C. | ugan |
| 1886 | Kiriggwajjo, Anatole | ugan |
| 1886 | Kiriwawanvu, Mukasa | ugan |
| 1886 | Kiwanuka, Achilles | ugan |
| 1972 | Kiwanuka, justice Benedicto | ugan |
| 1886 | Kizito | ugan |
| 1886 | Ludigo, Adolphus Mukasa | ugan |
| 1977 | Luwum, abp Janani | ugan |
| 1886 | Lwanga, Charles | ugan |
| 1886 | Mawaggali, Noe | ugan |
| 1886 | Mugagga | ugan |
| 1885 | Mukasa, Joseph | ugan |
| 1973 | Mukhana, J. | ugan |
| 1976 | Musaka, fr | ugan |
| 1887 | Muzeyi, Jean-Marie | ugan |
| 1886 | Ngondwe, Pontian | ugan |
| 1988 | Oido, fr C.O. | ugan |
| 1988 | Okagric, br A. | ugan |
| 1897 | Pilkington, G. L. | ugan |
| 1979 | Santi, fr G. | ugan |
| 1886 | Sebuggwawo, Denis | ugan |
| 1886 | Serunkuma, Bruno | ugan |
| 1973 | Serwanika, J. | ugan |
| 1988 | Spil MHM, fr C. | ugan |
| 1886 | Tuzinde, Mbaga | ugan |
| 1979 | Wasikye, John, bp of Mbale | ugan |
| 1986 | Wilson, evangelist John E.H. | ugan |
| 1991 | You WF, fr Alexander | ugan |
| 1932 | Agapit, abp of Ekaterinoslav | ukra |
| 1918 | Basil, abp of Chernigov | ukra |
| 1937 | Boretsky, M., metropolitan | ukra |
| 1927 | Bretzkiy, bp N. | ukra |
| 99 | Clement, bp of Rome | ukra |
| 1935 | Damaskin, bp of Gluhov | ukra |
| 1980 | Gurgula, fr A. | ukra |
| 1948 | Halan, Y. | ukra |
| c1970 | Hmara of Kulunda | ukra |
| 1979 | Kalienuk, fr Z.A. | ukra |
| 1959 | Kherie, bp A. | ukra |
| 1944 | Kocylowskyj, bp | ukra |
| 1948 | Kostelnyk, fr H. | ukra |
| 1980 | Kotyk, fr Y. | ukra |
| 1975 | Lutsky, fr M. | ukra |
| 1938 | Lypkivsky, V., metropolitan | ukra |
| c650 | Martin I, pope | ukra |
| 1936 | Pavlivsky, I., metropolitan | ukra |
| 1984 | Potochnyak, fr A. | ukra |
| 1947 | Romza, bp T. | ukra |
| 1982 | Terelya, B.M. | ukra |
| 1918 | Vladimir, metropolitan of Kiev | ukra |
| 1758 | Aberin, fr J. S. | usa |
| 1704 | Anixa, A. | usa |
| 1704 | Arraiyo, fr J. P. | usa |
| 1736 | Aulneau, fr J. P. | usa |
| 1672 | Avila y Ayala, fr P. | usa |
| 1781 | Barreneche, fr J. A. | usa |
| 1872 | Bassost, fr F. | usa |
| 1680 | Bernal, fr J. | usa |
| 1999 | Bernall, Cassie | usa |
| 1858 | Braeuninger, M. | usa |
| 1859 | Brown, John | usa |
| 1974 | Cabo, fr M. | usa |
| 1689 | Chefdeville, fr A. | usa |
| 1964 | Cheney, J. | usa |
| 1963 | Collins, Addie Mae | usa |
| 1696 | Corvera, fr F. | usa |
| 1921 | Coyle, J. E. | usa |
| 1704 | Criado, fr D. | usa |
| 1736 | d'Artiquette, P. | usa |
| 1736 | d'Esgly, F. M. | usa |
| 1965 | Daniels, J. | usa |
| 1696 | de Arbizu, fr J. | usa |
| 1632 | de Arvide, fr M. | usa |
| 1597 | de Auñon, fr M. | usa |
| 1597 | de Badajoz, fr A. | usa |
| 1549 | de Barbastro, fr L. C. | usa |
| 1696 | de Carbonel, fr A. | usa |
| 1597 | de Corpa, fr P. | usa |
| 1736 | de Coulonge, L. d'A. | usa |
| 1992 | de Dios, Manuel | usa |
| 1680 | de Espeleta, fr J. | usa |
| 1680 | de Figuero, fr J. | usa |
| 1696 | de Jesus Maria Casañas, fr F. | usa |
| 1680 | de Jesus, fr J. | usa |
| 1553 | de la Cruz, fr D. | usa |
| 1542 | de la Cruz, fr J. | usa |
| 1680 | de la Pedroso, fr J. | usa |
| 1680 | de la Ribourde, fr G. | usa |
| 1834 | de Leon, fr A. D. | usa |
| 1680 | de Lorenzana, fr F. | usa |
| 1680 | de Mdorales, fr L. | usa |
| 1553 | de Mena, fr J. | usa |
| 1704 | de Mendoza, fr M. | usa |
| 1718 | de Montesdoca, br L. | usa |
| 1680 | de Montesdoca, fr J. | usa |
| 1680 | de Mora, fr A. | usa |
| 1726 | de Oca, fr L. M. | usa |
| 1631 | de Ortega, fr P. | usa |
| 1704 | de Osorio, fr T. | usa |
| 1542 | de Padilla OFM, fr J. | usa |
| 1704 | de Parga, fr J. | usa |
| 1549 | de Pekalosa, fr D. | usa |
| 1680 | de Pro, fr A. S. | usa |
| 1571 | de Quiros, fr L. | usa |
| 1597 | de Rodriguez, fr B. | usa |
| 1680 | de Santa Maria, fr A. | usa |
| 1581 | de Santa Maria, fr J. | usa |
| 1731 | de Saraoz, fr D. | usa |
| 1571 | de Segura, fr J. B. | usa |
| 1571 | de Solis, fr G. | usa |
| 1736 | de St Agne, L. G. | usa |
| 1706 | de St Cosme, fr J. F. B. | usa |
| 1680 | de Talban, fr J. | usa |
| 1758 | de Terreros, fr A. G. | usa |
| 1736 | de Tonty, P. A. | usa |
| 1680 | de Torres, fr T. | usa |
| 1680 | de Trujillo, fr J. | usa |
| 1542 | de Ubeda, fr L. D. | usa |
| 1680 | de Velasco, fr F. | usa |
| 1680 | de Vera, fr D. | usa |
| 1736 | de Vincennes, F. M. B. | usa |
| 1680 | del Val, fr J. | usa |
| 1706 | Delhalle, fr C. | usa |
| 1834 | Diaz OFM, fr | usa |
| 1781 | Diaz, fr J. M. | usa |
| 1729 | du Poisson, fr P. | usa |
| 1736 | du Tisne, L. C. | usa |
| 1662 | Dyre, Mary | usa |
| 1704 | Feliciano, A. C. | usa |
| 1553 | Ferrer, fr J. | usa |
| 1702 | Foucault, fr N. | usa |
| 1549 | Fuentes, br | usa |
| 1752 | Ganzabal, fr J. F. | usa |
| 1692 | Garangouas, M. | usa |
| 1781 | Garces OFM, fr F. T. | usa |
| 1730 | Gaston, fr | usa |
| 1571 | Gomez, fr G. | usa |
| 1692 | Gonannhatenha, F. | usa |
| 1964 | Goodman | usa |
| 1708 | Gravier, fr J. | usa |
| 1985 | Hammes, W. | usa |
| 1908 | Heinrich, fr L. | usa |
| 1643 | Hutchinson, Anne | usa |
| 1997 | James, Jessica | usa |
| 1796 | Juvenal, hieromonk | usa |
| 1968 | King, Jr, pastor Martin Luther | usa |
| 1689 | Le Clercq, fr M. | usa |
| 1632 | Letrado, fr F. | usa |
| 1990 | Lewis, pastor N. | usa |
| 1571 | Linares, fr P. | usa |
| 1968 | Liuzzo, Viola | usa |
| 1998 | Loften, pastor A. | usa |
| 1582 | Lopez, fr F. | usa |
| 1837 | Lovejoy, Elijah P. | usa |
| 1680 | Maldonado, fr L. | usa |
| 1566 | Martinez SJ, fr P. | usa |
| 1996 | Mathias, mrs. C. | usa |
| 1996 | Mathias, pastor C. & wife | usa |
| 1963 | McNair, Denise | usa |
| 1689 | Membre, fr Z. | usa |
| 1661 | Menard, fr R. | usa |
| 1553 | Mendez, fr H. | usa |
| 1571 | Mendez, fr J. B. | usa |
| 1999 | Miller, Carla | usa |
| 1999 | Miller, Jr., Shon | usa |
| 1631 | Miranda, fr P. | usa |
| 1696 | Moreno, fr A. | usa |
| 1781 | Moreno, fr J. M. | usa |
| 1680 | Naranjo, B. | usa |
| 1680 | Pio, fr J. B. | usa |
| 1697 | Plunkett, fr C. | usa |
| 1704 | Ponce de Leon, fr A. | usa |
| 1633 | Porras, fr F. | usa |
| 1800 | Prosser, Gabriel | usa |
| 1812 | Quintana, fr A. | usa |
| 1571 | Redondo, fr C. | usa |
| 1680 | Rendon, fr M. | usa |
| 1963 | Robertson, Carole | usa |
| 1582 | Rodriguez, fr A. | usa |
| 1985 | Rossiter, fr J. | usa |
| 1985 | Roth, F. | usa |
| 1696 | Sanchez, fr L. | usa |
| 1758 | Santiesteban, fr J. | usa |
| 1999 | Scott, Rachel | usa |
| 1886 | Seghers, abp C. J. | usa |
| 1736 | Senat SJ, fr A. | usa |
| 1749 | Silva, fr F. X. | usa |
| 1844 | Smith, Hyrum | usa |
| 1844 | Smith, Joseph | usa |
| 1729 | Souel, fr J. | usa |
| 1997 | Stegar, Kayce | usa |
| 1856 | Strang, James J. | usa |
| 1690 | Teganankoa, S. | usa |
| 1680 | Tinoco, fr M. | usa |
| 1999 | Tomlin, John | usa |
| 1933 | Tourian, abp Leontius | usa |
| 1831 | Turner, Nat | usa |
| 1597 | Verascola, fr F. | usa |
| 1817 | Vesey, Denmark | usa |
| 1963 | Wesley, Cynthia | usa |
| 1847 | Whitman, M. & N. | usa |
| 1847 | Whitman, N. | usa |
| 1571 | Zeballos, fr S. | usa |
| 1841 | Chanel, fr P. M. | vanu |
| 1839 | Williams, John | vanu |
| 1730 | de Labrid, bp N. | vene |
| 1998 | Marrero, mgr A. G. | vene |
| 1861 | Almato OP, fr P. | viet |
| 1645 | André, catechist | viet |
| 1968 | Blood, H. | viet |
| 1838 | Bovie, fr P. D. | viet |
| 1837 | Cornay, fr J. C. | viet |
| 1798 | Dat, fr J. | viet |
| 1838 | Delgado, bp I. | viet |
| 1838 | Diem, V. | viet |
| 1833 | Gagelin, F.-I. | viet |
| 1962 | Gerber, D. | viet |
| 1861 | Hermosilla OP, bp H. | viet |
| c1970 | Heywood, J. | viet |
| 1975 | Hoang, pastor Van Dat | viet |
| 1645 | Ignace, catechist | viet |
| 1838 | Koa, P. | viet |
| 1835 | Marchand, fr J. | viet |
| 1962 | Mitchell, A. | viet |
| 1975 | Nguyen, Huy Mai | viet |
| 1975 | Nguyen, Van Hoa | viet |
| 1950 | Nguyen, pastor | viet |
| 1861 | Ochoa, bp V. B. | viet |
| 1968 | Olsen, Betty | viet |
| 1950 | Phan Long, pastor | viet |
| 1950 | Thien Thi, pastor | viet |
| 1798 | Trieu, fr E. | viet |
| 1861 | Venard, fr J. T. | viet |
| 1645 | Vincent, catechist | viet |
| 1962 | Vitti, A. | viet |
| 1968 | Wilting, Ruth | viet |
| 523 | Abraham | yeme |
| 523 | Abu-Afr, governor | yeme |
| 1998 | Anetta, sr | yeme |
| 523 | Aretas | yeme |
| 523 | Elesbaan | yeme |
| 523 | Elias | yeme |
| 523 | Elija | yeme |
| 523 | Habsa | yeme |
| 1998 | Lilia, sr | yeme |
| 1998 | Michaela, sr | yeme |
| 523 | Moses of Yemen | yeme |
| 523 | Sergios | yeme |
| 2000 | Tirelli, sr F. | zamb |
| 1561 | da Silveira SJ, fr G. | zimb |
| 1978 | Dunaway, Jr., A.G. | zimb |
| 1978 | Evans, P. & S. | zimb |
| 1978 | Evans, S. | zimb |
| 1978 | Fisher, M. | zimb |
| 1988 | Knoerl, br K. | zimb |
| 1978 | Lynn, R. & J. & Pamela | zimb |
| 1978 | Lynn, J. | zimb |
| 1978 | Lynn, Pamela | zimb |
| 1978 | McCann, P. & S. & Joy | zimb |
| 1978 | McCann, Joy | zimb |
| 1978 | McCann, S. | zimb |
| 1896 | Mizeki, Bernard, catechist | zimb |
| 1970 | Nyabadza, fr B. | zimb |
| 1978 | Picken, C. | zimb |
| 1976 | Schmitt, bp A. | zimb |

# Part 5

# GEORENEWAL

Four megatypologies analyzing empirical global Christianity

*God our Savior saved us through the washing of rebirth and renewal by the Holy Spirit,*
*whom He poured out on us generously through Jesus Christ our Savior.*
—Titus 3:5-6, New International Version

Part 5 describes 4 vast interlocking megatypologies under which empirical global Christianity and its followers are being described, enumerated, and analyzed today. Measurements are taken, and orders of magnitude and trends produced, at various stages in this process. In this Part, graphics, tables, maps, and photographs are combined to illustrate these phenomena.

# Four megatypologies analyzing empirical global Christianity

## Four varieties of renewal

Global Christianity can be described as a worldwide movement of renewal—renewal of human beings, renewal of Christians, renewal of the Earth, renewal of God's creation. Several useful typologies can be devised to describe these renewals. With regard to global Christianity, its adherents have been measured in detail over the 20 centuries of its history. To understand this complexity and to see the big picture at a glance, 4 megatypologies have been constructed over the last hundred years and are in use today. Each describes the whole phenomenon of global Christianity and sets out its structure under a handful of widely-used categories and subcategories.

The 4 are shown in Graphic 5–1 below as 4 spheres each representing the whole world. These 4 are then each briefly described, and in Graphic 5–2 are brought together into one single multi-megatypology which shows the characteristics and composition of each together with their many areas of overlap. The first 2 megatypologies are described in detail elsewhere: the first in Part 3 "GeoCommission" and Part 21 "GeoPersonnel", the second in Part 14 "Missiometrics" and in Country Tables 2 of *WCE* Part 4 "Countries".

The third megatypology is definitively described here in this Part 5. It then proceeds to review the much more detailed evidence, documentation, and description for the fourth and latest megatypology.

### BRIEF DESCRIPTIONS OF 4 MEGATYPOLOGIES

### I. The Great Commission GeoRenewal

The first megatypology describes global Christianity in terms of its origin as a mighty renewal of faith in God following Christ's death and resurrection. It enumerates the empirical obedience or disobedience of Christians to Christ's explicit commands known as the Great Commission. This commission with its 7 mandates has already been expounded in Part 3. It divides the Christian world into two: 648 million Christians who today are aware of the Commission and are in some manner, however humble, involving themselves in Christ's mission on Earth; and the 1,350 million Christians who are not.

### Table 5–1. A scale of confessional dogmatism.

This table sets out a graduated scale from 1 to 10 describing any church, denomination, network, or confession by each's degree of dogmatic assertion of its own uniqueness and significance on the world scene. The scale is further divided into 4 basic ecclesiastical stances, A, B, C, and D.

A. MONOCONFESSIONALISM: 'Our confession alone is the Body of Christ.'
1. 'Our confession is the one and only true church in the world', a claim widely and continuously publicized.
2. Belief 1 not widely publicized but amply attested by their major documents.
3. Belief 1 proclaimed verbally, though undocumented.
4. Belief 1 widely but only privately stated.
5. Belief 1 widely assumed; in practice, no need of or contact with other confessions.

B. CONCILIARISM: 'Our confession is a part of the Body of Christ.'
6. 'Our confession is one of the many confessions, but ours is the truest and best exemplar.'
7. 'Our confession is just one of the many, intrinsically no better and no worse than the rest.'
8. 'Our confession is just one of the many, but is among the worst of them.'

C. NONCONCILIARISM: 'Organized Christianity is not the Body of Christ.'
9. 'All historic confessions are misguided, unnecessary, and even wrong.'

D. POSTDENOMINATIONALISM: 'We are wholly independent of historic Christianity.'
10. 'All historic denominations are unnecessary, even wrong, to be replaced by loose networks of independent congregations like our own.'

### II. Six Ecclesiastical Megablocs in Renewal

The second megatypology describes the world in terms of how the initial mighty renewal has worked itself out historically resulting in the traditional ecclesiastico-cultural megablocs that have arisen over the last 20 centuries. An exposition is given in Part 14. In chronological order, these are the Orthodox, Roman Catholic, Anglican, Protestant, Independent, and marginal Christian churches. Total adherents of each are shown in *WCE* in all Country Tables 1. Each of these 6 empirical megablocs is then subdivided into a large number of ecclesiastical families or traditions. These are shown here in *WCE* in all Country Tables 2, and globally or by continent here in *WCT* Part 10.

A brief explanation should be noted in passing. First, this is here termed a megatypology of georenewal because virtually every megabloc, tradition, and ecclesiastical family of faith and experience, and still so regards itself. Second, virtually every megabloc, tradition, ecclesiastical family, and nowadays every denomination of any size, has within it an organized denominational expression of the 20th-century Charismatic Renewal in the Holy Spirit. This latter renewal is therefore part of

both Megatypology 2 and also of Megatypology 4, where it will be more fully documented and analyzed.

To illustrate this, Part 5 includes 2 specimen surveys of 4 pages each, printed on lightly screened paper, describing (1) a specimen megabloc minisurvey (of the Anglican Communion) and (2) another specimen megabloc minisurvey (of the Catholic Charismatic Renewal). The reader can apply this 4-page method to any entity or concept he or she wishes to publicize because much of the necessary documentation may well be found within this volume.

### III. The Evangelical GeoRenewal

The third megatypology describes global Christianity in terms of the great renewal of faith and obedience that arose from AD 1739 onwards, usually termed the Evangelical Revival. Two distinct usages have emerged and are reflected in our enumeration. In the first instance there are (1) core Evangelicals (written with a capital 'E') as the heart of the movement, consisting of a large number of specifically Evangelical national and international organizations, those denominations formally aligned with them, and all Christians anywhere in any churches who identify themselves individually as Evangelicals. These

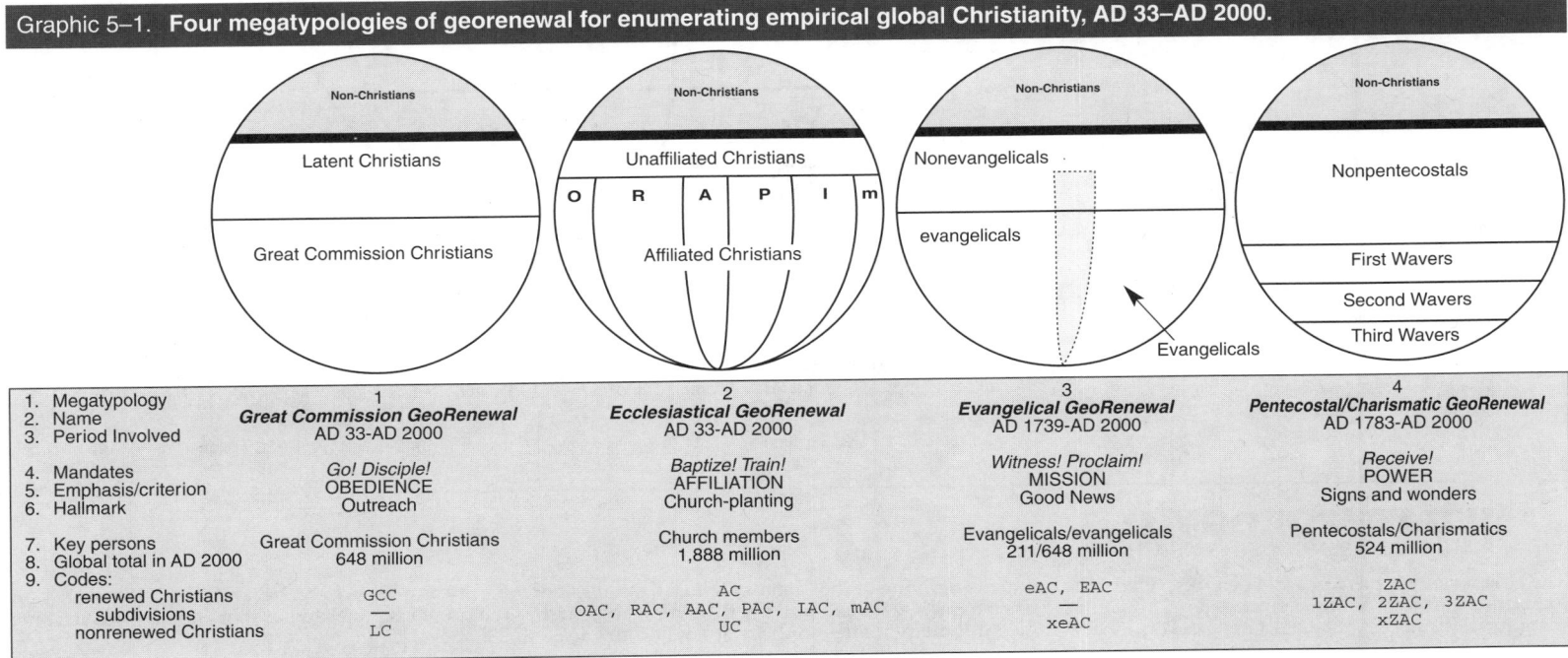

Graphic 5–1. Four megatypologies of georenewal for enumerating empirical global Christianity, AD 33–AD 2000.

| | 1 | 2 | 3 | 4 |
|---|---|---|---|---|
| 1. Megatypology | | | | |
| 2. Name | *Great Commission GeoRenewal* | *Ecclesiastical GeoRenewal* | *Evangelical GeoRenewal* | *Pentecostal/Charismatic GeoRenewal* |
| 3. Period Involved | AD 33-AD 2000 | AD 33-AD 2000 | AD 1739-AD 2000 | AD 1783-AD 2000 |
| 4. Mandates | *Go! Disciple!* | *Baptize! Train!* | *Witness! Proclaim!* | *Receive!* |
| 5. Emphasis/criterion | OBEDIENCE | AFFILIATION | MISSION | POWER |
| 6. Hallmark | Outreach | Church-planting | Good News | Signs and wonders |
| 7. Key persons | Great Commission Christians | Church members | Evangelicals/evangelicals | Pentecostals/Charismatics |
| 8. Global total in AD 2000 | 648 million | 1,888 million | 211/648 million | 524 million |
| 9. Codes: | | | | |
| renewed Christians | GCC | AC | eAC, EAC | ZAC |
| subdivisions | — | OAC, RAC, AAC, PAC, IAC, mAC | — | 1ZAC, 2ZAC, 3ZAC |
| nonrenewed Christians | LC | UC | xeAC | xZAC |

persons were, at the origin, largely Anglicans and now number 30 million; 144 million are Protestants; a smaller number, 27 million, are Independents; about 8 million are Roman Catholics; and a handful are Orthodox or Marginal Christians. As shown by the gray slice in Graphics 1 and 2, the organized Evangelical movement is still largely Anglican and Protestant. This whole phenomenon is depicted in Graphic 5–3. Secondly there are (2) the much wider constituency (usually written with lowercase 'e') defining as evangelicals all Christians who center their lives on 7 fundamental words and concepts: Jesus, evangel (gospel), Bible, witness, evangelism, mission, Advent. In practice this category is the same as those centered on obeying Christ's Great Commission; it is also the definition used here for 'practicing Christians' as opposed to Christians who are, regrettably, not practic-ing the full Christian faith as defined by Christ himself.

### IV. The Pentecostal/Charismatic GeoRenewal

The largest and best-known renewal today is often described by the single word Pentecostal, but is more accurately depicted by the title the Pentecostal/Charismatic Renewal in the Holy Spirit. In this survey we also term it, even more accurately, the Pentecostal/Charismatic/Neocharismatic Renewal. This refers to its 3 massive historical surges—First Wave, Second Wave, and Third Wave. The whole phenomenon is depicted in the 2 facing Tables 5-8 and 5-9.

### ONE SINGLE MULTI-MEGATYPOLOGY

These 4 megatypologies for enumerating global Christianity can now be combined into one single typology that shows how Christianity is being enumerated in these 4 ways, how its various component categories combine to form each megatypology, and how the 4 megatypologies relate to each other. This is shown in Graphic 5–2 below. It contains its own brief analysis and commentary. After this graphic, the 4 megatypologies are expounded separately, one by one, beginning with the short treatment of Megatypology 1 at the bottom of this page.

---

**Graphic 5–2.  A single multi-megatypology of empirical global Christianity, showing relationships, overlaps, and distinctives of the 4 major megatypologies of georenewal in Christianity, AD 30–AD 2000.**

This graphic divides empirical global Christianity into 7 major slices, 6 horizontal and 1 vertical (tinted light grey). It combines the 4 megatypologies and presents the same 7 global slices from 2 different standpoints. The first, shown by the vertical ar-rows to the right of the globe and by the 9 lines above the globe, shows how 9 well-known and widely-used aggregate categories are represented here, and how they overlap. The second, shown to the left of the globe, identifies by name, code, sta-tistics and arrows the precise meaning of each of the slices 0 through 7. Several of these slices, whose statistics are all known is detail, then form each of the 4 megatypologies 1 to 4.

#### HOW MAJOR AGGREGATE CATEGORIES OVERLAP (see arrows at below right)

| Aggregate categories | Groups of slices | Codes and their components | Total persons |
|---|---|---|---|
| Non-Christians | 0 | = X | 4,055 million |
| Christians | 1-6 | = C = UC + AC | 2,000 million |
| Affiliated Christians | 2-6 | = AC = OAC + RAC + AAC + PAC + IAC + mAC + 2AC | 1,888 million |
| Great Commission Christians | 3-6 | = GCC = pAC = eAC | 648 million |
| Pentecostals/Charismatics | 4-6 | = ZAC = 1ZAC + 2ZAC + 3ZAC | 524 million |
| Charismatics | 5 | = 2ZAC | 176 million |
| Neocharismatics (Third-Wavers) | 6 | = 3ZAC | 295 million |
| Nonpentecostals | 1-3 | = xZAC | 1,475 million |
| Evangelicals | 7 | = EAC | 211 million |
| evangelicals | 3-6 | = eAC | 648 million |
| Nonevangelicals | 1-2 | = xeAC | 1,352 million |
| Latent Christians | 1-2 | = LC | 1,352 million |

#### MEANING OF EACH SLICE, 0 TO 7

| Slice | Code | Meaning | Total persons |
|---|---|---|---|
| | | *Segments of the globe* | |
| 0 | X | Non-Christians | 4,055 million |
| 1 | UC | Unaffiliated Christians | 111 million |
| 2 | xpAC | Nonpractising members | 1,240 million |
| 3 | GCC - ZAC | Nonpentecostal GCCs | 124 million |
| 4 | 1ZAC | Pentecostals | 66 million |
| 5 | 2ZAC | Charismatics | 176 million |
| 6 | 3ZAC | Neocharismatics | 295 million |
| 7 | EAC | Evangelicals (grey) | 211 million |

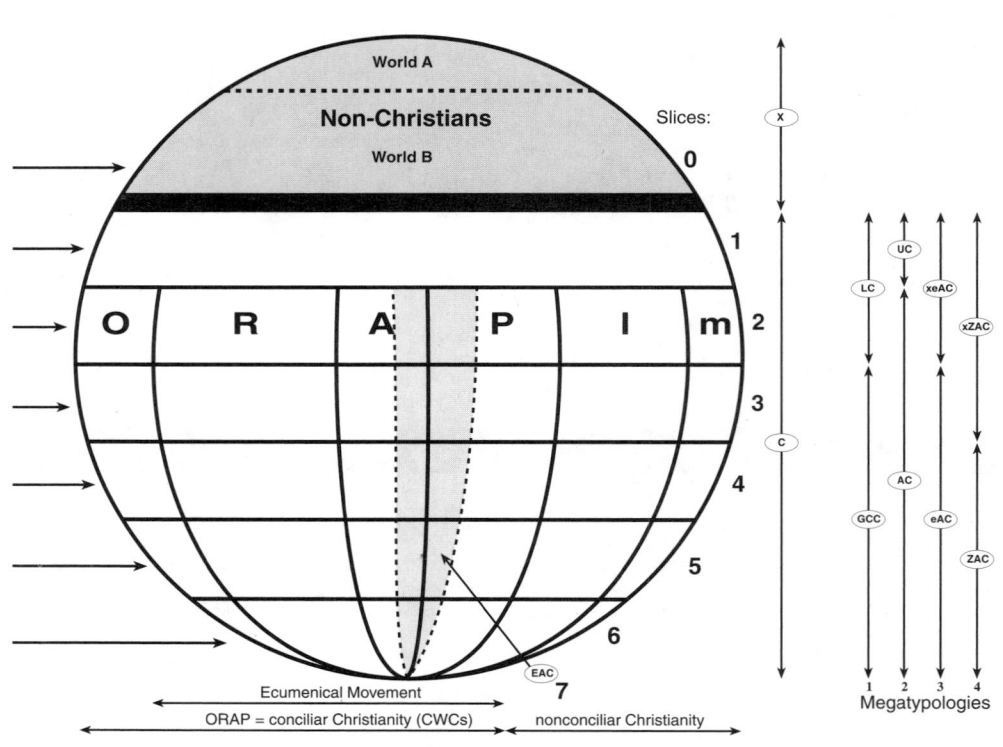

#### MEANING OF 6 VERTICAL MEGABLOCS (stretching from their code letters on the globe to the bottom)

| Megabloc: | Orthodox | Roman Catholics | Anglicans | Protestants | Independents | Marginal Christians |
|---|---|---|---|---|---|---|
| Code: | O– | R– | A– | P– | I– | m– |
| Traditions: | 40 | 20 | 25 | 100 | 200 | 30 |
| Total affiliated: | 215 million | 1,057 million | 80 million | 342 million | 386 million | 26 million |

---

# MEGATYPOLOGY 1:
## *GREAT COMMISSION GEORENEWAL*

The first typology has already been described and expounded in Part 3 "GeoCommission". Its enumeration is further set out in Part 21 "GeoPersonnel", with its deriving of the category 'Great Commission Christians'. A visual portrayal of how this first megatypology relates to the other 3, and to Chris-tianity as a whole, can be seen from Graphic 5-1 on the previous page, and in more detail from Graphic 5-2 above.

# MEGATYPOLOGY 2:
## *ECCLESIASTICAL GEORENEWAL*

Every ecclesiastical tradition or family regards itself as having originated in a definitive renewal of the Christian faith. This is true for all 6 major ecclesiastico-cultural megablocs, for the 300 or so traditions or families, and for most of the 33,000 denominations themselves. All of these concepts and the data supporting them are described in *WCT* Part 14 "Missiometrics" and *WCE* Part 4 "Countries". An overview is as follows.

### *6 major ecclesiastico-cultural megablocs*

Over the last 20 centuries, Christians have evolved into 6 major streams or megablocs. These are listed here as: Orthodox, Roman Catholics, Anglicans, Protestants, Independents, marginal Christians. Each has always regarded itself as the true church, the truest expression of Christianity, a georenewal restoring the original and genuine faith of Christ to the world.

### *300 Christian families or traditions*

Each ecclesiastical megabloc in turn can be divided into a multiplicity of families (Baptist, Methodist, Assyrian, Old Catholic, etc.). Each family or tradition regards itself as having originated in a renewal of New Testament Christianity, and often as a georenewal of worldwide proportions.

### *Christian World Communions (CWCs)*

This term, coined in 1970, describes the 250 distinct Christian traditions or families which have organized themselves into worldwide georenewals. Up to 1970 the accepted term was World Confessional Families (WCFs), or confessions, but this was unsatisfactory for the largest traditions which were not centered on specific historical confessions such as Augsburg or Westminster.

This relatively new development has now spread a long way past the 20 megacommunions that meet annually for the Conference of Christian World Communions (CCWC). These CWCs represent 90% of the entire Christian world, but there has been a huge mushrooming everywhere. This results in, by AD 2000, a total of 250 communions across the world. These are set out and described in Table 5–2.

### *Defining the Independency megabloc*

The least well-known or least recognized of the 6 megablocs is termed Independency in this book. Its relation to the other 5 megablocs is illustrated in Graphics 5-1 and 5-2. A full treatment of the subject, with enumeration of both its component memberships and its characteristics is given in Part 6 "Independency."

Defining the precise boundary between the Independency megabloc and the 4 ORAP megablocs, Protestantism in particular, is therefore done in Table 6-2. A quick overview of its component parts can be seen in Global Diagram 17 (or Table 6-3).

'Independency', in short, is defined here as that corporate and organized approach to Christian discipleship that either by design or due to circumstance regards itself collectively as being autonomous and independent of the whole range of historic Christianity—historic creeds, historic dogmas, historic churches, historic denominations, historic denominationalism (and in fact denominationalism in all its forms), historic conciliarism, historic confessions and confessionalism, historic scholarship, historic institutions—in brief, independent of any or all historic obligation to or control by mainline Christianity as it has evolved after the New Testament era over the last 20 centuries.

### *The 2 specimen minisurveys*

As described on the first page of this Part, after the photographic collage illustrating the 6 megablocs, there are the two specimen 4-page minisurveys: first the Anglican megabloc, and second the Catholic Charismatic Renewal. The latter is usually regarded as a part of the Second Wave of Megatypology 4, the Pentecostal/Charismatic/Neocharismatic Renewal in the Holy Spirit, and is so treated there at the end of this Part 5. But it is also an example of georenewal on a massive scale in the largest communion in Megatypology 2. Its survey is therefore placed here.

**Table 5–2. 250 Christian World Communions (CWCs) or World Confessional Families (WCFs) in 9 categories, ranked by attitudes to other communions in AD 2000.**

| *Mega-bloc* | *Code* | *Name of communion in English* | *Members, HQ, &c* |
|---|---|---|---|
| | | **1. Participants in Conference of Christian World Communions (CCWC), 1957-2000** | |
| R | R | Roman Catholic Church | 1,057 million in 235 countries. |
| R | b | Congregation for Bishops | Represents 901 million Catholics. |
| R | o | Congregation for the Oriental Churches | 3,700,000 Eastern-rite Catholics. |
| R | p | Congregation for the Evangelization of Peoples | 180 million in mission areas. |
| R | r | Catholic Charismatic Renewal (CCR) | 120 million in 233 countries. |
| - | - | World Council of Churches (WCC) | 460 million. HQ Geneva. |
| P | - | World Evangelical Fellowship (WEF) | 150 million. HQ Singapore. |
| - | - | United Bible Societies (UBS) | Begun 1946. HQ Reading, UK. |
| O | M | Orthodox Patriarchate of Moscow | 130 million. HQ Moscow. |
| P | L | Lutheran World Federation (LWF) | 80 million. HQ Geneva. |
| A | A | Anglican Consultative Council (ACC) | 80 million in 160 countries. |
| P | B | Baptist World Alliance (BWA) | 68 million. HQ Maclean, VA. |
| O | C | Ecumenical Patriarchate of Constantinople | 50 million. Eastern Orthodox. |
| P | P | World Alliance of Reformed Churches (WARC) | 60 million. HQ Geneva. |
| P | W | World Methodist Council (WMC) | 70 million in 108 countries. |
| P | Z | Pentecostal World Conference (PWC) | 68 million. HQ Zurich. |
| P | V | General Conference of Seventh-day Adventists (SDA) | 25 million, HQ Washington, DC. |
| P | T | World Convention of Churches of Christ (WCCC) | 10 million. Disciples. |
| I | J | International Old Catholic Bishops Conference (IOCBC) | 9 million. HQ Utrecht. |
| P | S | Salvation Army (SA), also in CHA | 2.3 million. HQ London. |
| P | s | Reformed Ecumenical Council (REC) | 5 million. HQ Grand Rapids, MI. |
| P | G | Mennonite World Conference (MWC) | 2 million. |
| P | Q | Friends World Committee for Consultation (FWCC) | 400,000 members. |
| P | D | Disciples Ecumenical Committee for Consultation (DECC) | 1.5 million. |
| P | i | Church of the Brethren | 210,000 adherents. HQ Illinois. |
| P | g | International Moravian Ch in Unity of Brethren (18 Provinces) | 582,000. HQ Bethlehem, PA. |
| | | **2. WCC-related bodies not participating in CCWC because never invited** | |
| - | K | International Charismatic Consultation on World Evangelization (ICCOWE) | 50 million. HQ Sussex, UK. |
| I | I | Organization of African Instituted Churches (OAIC) (WCC 1998) | 40 million. HQ Nairobi, Kenya. |
| O | - | Oriental Orthodox Churches Conference (= codes E,H,N,D,q) | 41.6 million. HQ Addis Ababa. |
| O | N | Coptic Orthodox Patriarchate of Alexandria (WCC 1948) | 9,800,000. HQ Cairo Egypt. |
| O | H | Ethiopian Orthodox Patriarchate of Addis Ababa (WCC 1948) | 20 million. HQ Addis Ababa. |
| O | E | Armenian Apostolic Catholicossate of Echmiadzin (WCC 1962) | 6 million, HQ Erevan, Armenia. |
| - | U | Consultation on Uniting and United Churches (CUUC) | 65 million. Every 4 years. |
| O | D | Syrian Orthodox Patriarchate of Antioch (WCC 1960) | 3.6 million. HQ Damascus. |
| O | q | Malankara Orthodox Syrian Catholicossate of the East (WCC 1948) | 2.2 million. Origin in AD 70. |
| O | Y | Ancient Assyrian Patriarchate of the East (WCC 1948) | 500,000. HQ Baghdad. |
| P | W | Waldensian Church (WCC 1948) | 42,000. United with Methodists. |
| I | v | Mar Thoma Syrian Church of Malabar (WCC 1948) | 875,000. 5 Dioceses. |
| I | e | Brazil for Christ Ev Pentecostal Church (OBPC) (WCC 1969) | 2 million. HQ São Paulo. |
| I | F | Philippine Independent Church (IFI/PIC) (WCC 1958) | 2.8 million. Ex RCC. |
| I | H | Czechoslovak Hussite Church (CCH/CHC) (WCC 1963) | 185,000. Split ex RCC. |
| | | **3. African/Amerindian/Asian/Black/Latino/Oceanic Independent minicommunions** | |
| I | c | Church of God in Christ (CoGiC) | 10 million. HQ Memphis, TN. |
| I | d | Deeper Life Bible Church (DLBC) | 9 million. HQ Lagos. |
| I | d | International Communion of Charismatic Churches (ICCC) | 6 million. HQ Nigeria. |
| I | f | Jesus is Lord Fellowship (JILF) | 2 million. In 25 countries. |
| I | B | Igreja Catolica Apostolica Brasileira (ICAB) | 3 million. 12 Dioceses. |
| I | C | Congregação Crista do Brasit (CCB) | 3.1 million. HQ São Paulo. |
| I | n | India Pentecostal Church of God (IPCG) | 900,000. In 10 countries. |
| I | s | Iglesia Metodista Pentecostal de Chile (IMPC) | 720,000. 20 schisms. |
| I | M | Iglesia ni Cristo (Manalista) | 1,750,000. TV stations. |
| I | j | African Apostolic Church of Johane Maranke (AACJM) | 1,400,000. Across central Africa. |
| I | x | 40 separate major Independent Neocharismatic minicommunions each with many members worldwide who maintain a separate communion: NMBCA, IFDA, CGMI, AIPCA, IPDA | 50 million in separate bodies. |
| | | **4. White-led Neocharismatic communions uninterested in CCWC** | |
| I | F | Chaplaincy of Full Gospel Churches (CFGC) | 7 million. Works in US armed forces. |
| I | w | Willow Creek Association of Churches (WCAC) | 500,000. HQ Barrington, IL. |
| I | j | Union of Messianic Jewish Congregations (UMJC) | 15,000, mainly in USA. |
| I | c | International Fellowship of Charismatic Churches (IFCC) | 2 million in Brazil, USA, et al. |
| I | k | Manna Church International | HQ Lisbon (Portugal). |
| I | f | Coalition of Spirit-filled Churches (CSC) | 500,000: rival to CFGC. |
| I | X | 30 other separate meganetworks uninterested in historic confessions: International Revival Network, ICF, UICC, EFICC, SACOC | 25 million in separate bodies. |
| | | **5. Conservative communions hostile to ecumenism, WCC, CCWC** | |
| P | z | World Assemblies of God Fellowship (WAGF), also in PWC | 43 million. HQ Seoul, Korea. |
| I | n | New Apostolic Church (NAC/NAK) | 11 million. HQ Zurich. |
| I | O | Apostolic World Christian Fellowship (AWCF) | Originally Black Oneness. |
| I | t | True Jesus Church (TJC) | 1,400,000. HQ Taipei, Taiwan. |
| I | u | Universal Church of the Kingdom of God (UCKG/IURD) | 5 million. In 50 countries. |
| P | e | International Lutheran Council (ILC) | 3 million. Conservative doctrine. |
| P | r | Alliance World Fellowship (AWF) | 2 million. HQ Colorado Springs. |
| I | k | International Federation of Free Evangelical Churches (IFFEC) | 580,000. HQ Stockholm, Sweden |
| I | o | Old Ritualist Churches (Old Believers, Old Calendarists) | 2 million. Most in Russia. |
| P | h | Christian Holiness Association (CHA) | 5 million. 22 denominations. |
| I | t | Assembly Hall Churches (Local Churches, Little Flock) | 2 million. Chinese. |
| I | b | Baptist Bible Fellowship International (BBFI) | 2.5 million. HQ Springfield, MO. |
| I | G | Gypsy Pentecostal Churches | 200,000. In 40 countries. |
| I | y | 25 other separate networks hostile to historic confessions: World Council of Biblical Churches, IARPC, ICRC | 9 million in separate bodies. |
| | | **6. Monodenominational Anglican minicommunions** | |
| I | a | International Communion of the Charismatic Episcopal church (ICCEC) | 100,000 in 60 countries. |
| I | a | 20 separate schismatic confessions or bodies ex Anglicanism/Episcopalianism, not in communion with Canterbury, including: Anglican Orthodox Communion (AOC), Communion of the Evangelical Episcopal Church (CEEC), Reformed Episcopal Church, Traditional Anglican Communion (International Anglican Fellowship) | 7.6 million in separate bodies. |
| | | **7. European/North American monodenominational Protestant minicommunions** | |
| P | x | 50 separate major denominations each linked with its worldwide daughter churches to form a separate communion: SIM, WEC, AIM, TEAM, CBI, CIPE, CAM, LAM, OMF, OMS, OD, OM, AEF, AWM, CMML, WCG, ARPC, EPC, EHC, GAGB, SDBWF, IGM, MEM, NLM, OCI, PCA, SSEM,BCU,WMPL,YFCI, BGC, ABA | 18 million in separate bodies. |
| | | **8. Worldwide communions with heterodox christologies** | |
| m | w | Jehovah's Christian Witnesses (Jehovah's Witnesses, Watch Tower, IBRA) | 13,000,000, 232 countries. |
| m | m | Church of Jesus Christ of Latter-day Saints (CJCLdS) | 8.6 million in 116 countries |
| m | h | Unification Church (Holy Spirit Association for Unification of World Christianity) | 1 million. HQ Seoul, Korea. |
| m | u | International Council of Unitarians and Universalists (ICUU) | 400,000. HQ Boston, MA. |
| m | v | Church of Christ, Scientist | 2.5 million, 63 countries. |
| m | m | 20 other separate heterodox communions: International New Thought Alliance (INTA), International Association for Liberal Christianity & Religious Freedom (IARF), International Alliance of Churches of the Truth (Divine Science, 1913), International General Assembly of Spiritualists (IGAS, 1936) | 2 million in separate bodies. |
| . | | **9. Unattached denominations with no CWC, no minicommunion, no claim to be one** | 100 million in 110 countries. |

## THE 6 MAJOR ECCLESIASTICO–CULTURAL MEGABLOCS

**White-initiated Christianity (White indigenous churches).** All of the world's 6 major ecclesiastico-cultural megablocs are predominantly European (White) in origin, history, culture, membership and leadership, as is indicated by the cities (given first in capitals) where their world spiritual headquarters are.

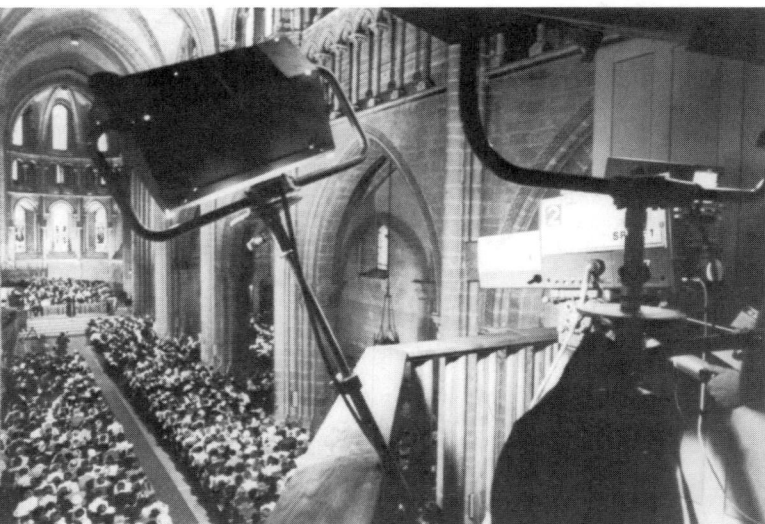

*Left.* **ROME. Roman Catholicism.** Second Vatican Council, 1962-65, attended by 2,540 bishops meets in St Peter's Basilica (Vatican City), presided over by His Holiness Pope Paul VI (inset), an Italian.
*Above.* **GENEVA. Protestantism.** 25th-anniversary celebrations in 1973 of World Council of Churches (whose constituents are 40% Protestants) in St Pierre Cathedral, Geneva (Switzerland), where Protestant reformer John Calvin (a Frenchman) labored and preached.

*Above.* **CONSTANTINOPLE. Orthodoxy.** Eastern Orthodox liturgy concelebrated by Metropolitans at First Pan-Orthodox Preconciliar Conference in Chambésy, November 1976. All are Caucasians or Whites, mostly Greeks or Slavs. From left to right: Dorothei of Prague. Archbishop of Cyprus; Stefan of Dalmatia (Yugoslavia); Germanos of Petra (Crete); Archbishop of Great Britain; Meliton of Chalcedon, Patriarch of Antioch, Philaret of Kiev, Patriarch of Romania, Alexandros of Peristenon (Greece), Nikodim of Sliven (Bulgaria), Paavah of Finland.

*Above.* **CANTERBURY. Anglicanism.** 11th Lambeth Conference in 1978 attended by 420 bishops meets in St Augustine's Cathedral, Canterbury (England), presided over by His Grace the Archbishop of Canterbury, an Englishman (center top, in St Augustine's Chair). *Insert.* Archbishop of Canterbury George Carey from 1990 (an Englishman), who convened the 13th Conference in 1998.

*Above.* **BOSTON. Marginal Christianity.** Christian Science Center, Boston (USA), world HQ of Church of Christ, Scientist, founded by Mary Baker Eddy, a USA White.

*Above.* **DORTMUND TO ZURICH. Independency.** Apostelversammlung (Council of Apostles) of 11 million-member New Apostolic Church meets at former world HQ in Dortmund (Germany), with 48 living Apostles presided over by Chief Apostle (a German) with quasi-papal powers regarded as sole successor of Apostle Peter and visible representative or incarnation of Christ on earth.

# THE ANGLICAN WORLD IN FIGURES (TAWIF-2000)

*A standardized 4-page comprehensive minisurvey of the life and activity of an entire megabloc*

The world we live in is changing fast. In the 10 years from the 12th Lambeth Conference to the 13th in 1998, 1.4 billion new persons entered the world (births) and 520 millions left it (deaths). This is a huge turnover. To help us grapple with our relation to these enormous numbers, this brief survey ('TAWIF-2000' for short) describes Anglicanism's global influence via a wide range of statistics. In doing this, we recall the dictum of prior Roger Schutz of Taizé: 'Les chiffres sont les signes de Dieu'/'Statistics are signs from God', empowering us to understand the world's dilemmas and how our ministry fits in.

## Vital statistics

Our survey begins with the current total of 102 million Anglicans affiliated and unaffiliated. Each year this grows by 2.4 million births and decreases by 906,000 deaths. Some 2 million new Anglicans are baptized each year. So the Anglican Communion is expanding at the rate of 1.5 million Anglicans each year. We illustrate this here with 2 tables each listing all the components of the Communion. Table 5–3 divides church members up by the 46 member Churches they belong to, and Table 5–4 divides them up by the 167 countries where they live.

## A brief history of 46 member Churches

Table 5–3 lists the component Churches of the Communion. From AD 400 for the next 11 centuries up to the Protestant Reformation in Europe, there were only 4 Anglican Churches—England, Wales, Scotland and Ireland. From 1550 to 1600 Anglicanism expanded to several British colonies. Before the year 1610, all Churches were British in origin, membership, and leadership. All services and documents were in the English language which today is the world's major global language with 1.3 billion speakers. But then from 1612-1640, it expanded to the Indian sub-continent and to the Caribbean, resulting in three of today's great churches: the CPWI, CSI, and CNI. In the 18th century 5 more churches were planted. The 19th century, termed by mission historian Latourette as the Great Century, saw 27 new Anglican Churches planted. The 20th century has seen mainly consolidation but far less new planting—only 3 new Churches have been planted since 1900.

## Latent Anglicans

Table 5–3 also shows that, in addition to the Anglican Communion, there are two other categories of Anglicans. Firstly, latent Anglicans (sometimes called dormant Anglicans) are those 21.7 million persons who profess to be Anglicans in censuses or public-opinion polls but who are

**1963.** 200 bishops enthrone Michael Ramsey as 100th Archbishop of Canterbury, leader of the Anglican Communion.

not affiliated to Anglican Churches. (In 1978 they numbered 13 million). Are these persons really Anglicans? Since 1948 the United Nations' Universal Declaration of Human Rights has insisted that every person has the right to say what his or her religion is. If a man says he is a Muslim, no one has the right to say to him 'No, you are not'. If a mother says she and her whole family are Anglicans, they are Anglicans. If we treat latent Anglicans as fellow Christians and extend to them friendship, evangelism, and pastoral care, then large numbers of them could well become active Anglicans.

## Anglicans outside the Communion

The second category are Anglicans in Churches not in communion with the See of Canterbury. Our survey for the 1978 Lambeth Conference enumerated 200,000 Anglicans involved in schismatic movements out of the Communion since the year 1844 (see Bibliography below, TAWIF-1978, pages 14-15). This has grown much larger by today to 40 denominations with 7.6 million members regarding themselves also as genuine Anglicans. Most are expanding rapidly. One such is the International Communion of the Charismatic Episcopal Church, ICCEC. Founded in 1992, it now has a worldwide episcopate claiming apostolic succession. It has just opened 43 new churches in Estonia, Eastern Europe. Another, the Communion of the Evangelical Episcopal Church claims over 3,000 parishes and is expanding rapidly in the Philippines and other long-time Anglican spheres. As with latent Anglicans, these Independent Anglicans should not be treated as outcastes but as fellow pilgrims and brethren in Christ in our global mission and ministry.

## The Anglican Communion expands

Global Map 5-1 below illustrates the growth of the Communion across the 20th century. In fact, it has expanded surprisingly uniformly over the last 300 years. In 1600 it had 4.5 million members, in 1800 7.2 million, in 1850 13.3 million. By 1900 it had 30 million, by 1970 47 million, by 1980 55 million, up to 80 million by AD 2000.

## Fifteen new Dioceses a year

Another way of showing this expansion is to enumerate dioceses, these being the basic structures of the Communion's members. These numbered 47 in the year 1600, 60 in 1800, 106 in 1850, 223 in 1900, 345 in 1968, 396 in 1978, 520 in 1988, up to 620 by AD 2000. In 1972 their annual increase was 6 new dioceses a year. At the time of the 1978 Lambeth Conference, 8 new dioceses were being begun each year. In AD 2000 it is 15 new dioceses a year.

## Parishes and congregations

These too have multiplied phenomenally. The Communion's parishes numbered 30,840 in 1977, and its total of congregations or worship centers numbered 63,500 in 1970 and 64,853 in 1977. By the year 2000 these are expected to have risen by 50%, resulting in today's count of 90,763 congregations.

## Evangelicals

Anglican Evangelicals organized and unorganized have increased from 15 million in 1970 to 30 million by AD 2000. Coordination is provided by activities of the Evangelical Fellowship of the Anglican Communion (EFAC).

## Renewed in the Spirit

The Charismatic Renewal in the Holy Spirit began within Anglicanism in a parish in Sunderland, England, in 1907. In the deadly worldwide influenza epidemic of 1918, charismatic prayer groups sprang up in Anglican parishes from Nigeria to Kenya to India to China. From 1960 large-scale revival began across Britain. Worldwide, Anglican Charismatics numbered over 810,000 in 1978, mushrooming to 17 million by AD 2000.

## Bishops

In 1900 there were 233 Anglican diocesan bishops worldwide. With suffragans and assistant bishops, across the 20th century the total has risen to 491 in 1968, 551 in 1978, 600 in 1988, and 880 in AD 2000. Some 68% are diocesan bishops and

THE LAMBETH BISHOPS PAY TRIBUTE TO THE BIBLE SOCIETY.

**1948.** 329 Bishops at LC 8 (8th Lambeth Conference, convened by 99th Archbishop of Canterbury Geoffrey Fisher, here standing at table) vote to wholeheartedly support the newly-founded United Bible Societies in their goal to distribute the Bible worldwide.

## Table 5–3.   AD 2000: 102 million Anglicans worldwide in 46 national or plurinational churches organized as the Anglican Communion, together with 21 million latent Anglicans (unaffiliated) and 7 million Independent Anglicans outside the Communion.

This table lists, in chronological order of their origin, the 46 churches constituting the Anglican Communion. Columns and rows have the following meanings.

**A. Member Churches of the Anglican Communion.**
1. *Begun.* This first column refers to the year of arrival of the first missionaries or other resident Christians, or planting of the first church or mission. (Note: c = circa, approximately).
2. *Present name in English.* Names shown are the official or formal full names used. Note that several bodies have more than one official or popular name in English, all have a name in their countries' national language, and all have additional names in all languages they work among.
3. *Status.* The third column describes each Church's stage of development, with these codes:
   M   Multiple-province autonomous Church

| | |
|---|---|
| S | Single-province autonomous Church |
| R | Nonfunctioning Church but now renewed by Diocese of Hong Kong and Macao |
| U | United Church with former Anglicans and others |
| d | Under Church of England & Convocation of American Churches in Europe |
| a | Church under See of Canterbury |
| h | Church under Metropolitan Council |
| c | Extra-provincial to See of Canterbury |
| e | Extra-provincial to ECUSA |

4. *Dioceses.* The fourth column gives the number of Dioceses in 1998, increasing by 15 each year.
5. *Members in AD 2000.* The last column gives baptized church members at the turn of the century (as projected from 1998).
6. *WCC.* Number of delegates from this Church appointed to attend the 8th Assembly of the World Council of Churches (its

50th anniversary) in Harare, Zimbabwe in December 1998.

**B. Latent Anglicans.** Persons calling themselves Anglicans, and thus professing in censuses or polls, but who are not affiliated church members. Sometimes called 'the nominal fringe' around the church, or 'dormant Anglicans'.

**C. Independent Anglicans outside the Communion.** This refers to the 40 or so new schismatic denominations that have broken from the Communion though still claiming to be Anglican.

**D. Total all Anglicans on broader definition.** All of the above millions are Anglicans, however imperfect, and should be regarded as such with a view to both reconciliation, fellowship, pastoral care, mutual love, aid, mission, and evangelization.

### A. Member Churches of the Anglican Communion, in order of origin

| Begun 1 | Present name in English 2 | Status 3 | Dioceses 4 | Members AD 2000 5 | WCC 6 |
|---|---|---|---|---|---|
| c100 | Church of England | M | 44 | 24,500,000 | 20 |
| c300 | Church in Wales | S | 6 | 1,300,000 | 2 |
| c350 | Church of Ireland | M | 12 | 410,000 | 2 |
| 397 | Scottish Episcopal Church | S | 7 | 53,100 | 2 |
| 1552 | Anglican Church in Europe | d | 1 | 125,430 | – |
| 1578 | Anglican Church of Canada (ACC) | M | 31 | 738,000 | 5 |
| 1578 | Episcopal Church in the USA (ECUSA) | M | 109 | 2,400,000 | 5 |
| 1609 | Anglican Church of Bermuda | c | 1 | 25,250 | – |
| 1612 | Church of North India (CNI) | U | 24 | 1,300,000 | 3 |
| 1623 | Church in the Province of the West Indies (CPWI) | S | 8 | 532,120 | 5 |
| 1640 | Church of South India (CSI) | U | 21 | 2,955,000 | 4 |
| 1656 | Lusitanian Catholic Apostolic Evangelical Ch (ILCAE) | a | 1 | 5,250 | – |
| 1740 | Church of the Province of the Central America Region | S | 5 | 35,800 | 1 |
| 1741 | Episcopal Church of Cuba (IEC) | h | 1 | 3,000 | – |
| 1752 | Church of the Province of West Africa (CPWA) | S | 12 | 268,360 | 2 |
| 1788 | Anglican Church of Australia (ACA) | M | 23 | 4,100,000 | 7 |
| 1796 | Church of Ceylon/Sri Lanka | S | 2 | 53,900 | 2 |
| 1805 | Church of Bangladesh | U | 2 | 13,600 | – |
| 1805 | Church of the Province of South East Asia (CPSEA) | S | 4 | 212,440 | – |
| 1806 | Church of the Province of Southern Africa (CPSA) | S | 23 | 2,800,000 | 5 |
| 1810 | Church of the Province in the Indian Ocean (CPIO) | S | 5 | 290,400 | 2 |
| 1810 | Episcopal Anglican Church of Brazil | S | 7 | 105,000 | 2 |
| 1811 | Episcopal Ch in Jerusalem & Middle East (ECJME) | S | 4 | 48,800 | 2 |
| 1814 | Anglican Ch in Aotearoa, New Zealand & Polynesia | S | 9 | 809,670 | 3 |
| 1824 | Anglican Ch of the Southern Cone of America (IACSA) | S | 7 | 51,850 | 1 |
| 1825 | Church of the Province of Myanmar (CPM) | S | 6 | 56,700 | 2 |
| 1832 | Anglican Church in Venezuela | e | 1 | 600 | – |
| 1842 | Anglican Church of Nigeria (ACN) | M | 61 | 17,900,000 | 6 |

| Begun 1 | Present name in English 2 | Status 3 | Dioceses 4 | Members AD 2000 5 | WCC 6 |
|---|---|---|---|---|---|
| 1843 | Holy Catholic Church in China (HKSKH Province) | R | 3 | 29,900 | – |
| 1844 | Anglican Church of Kenya (CPK/ACK) | S | 26 | 2,700,000 | 3 |
| 1846 | Holy Catholic Church in Japan (NSKK) | S | 11 | 62,000 | 2 |
| 1848 | Church of the Province of Melanesia (CM, CPM) | S | 8 | 186,800 | 2 |
| 1850 | Church of Pakistan (CP) | U | 8 | 1,160,000 | 2 |
| 1850 | Spanish Reformed Episcopal Church (IERE) | a | 1 | 28,870 | – |
| 1857 | Church of the Province of Mexico | S | 8 | 163,900 | – |
| 1861 | Church of the Province of Central Africa (CPCA) | S | 12 | 820,500 | 3 |
| 1864 | Church in the Province of Tanzania (CPT) | S | 16 | 2,300,000 | 3 |
| 1872 | Episcopal Church of Puerto Rico | e | 1 | 13,140 | 1 |
| 1875 | Church of Uganda | S | 28 | 7,400,000 | 6 |
| 1889 | Anglican Church of Korea | S | 3 | 100,780 | 2 |
| 1891 | Anglican Church of Papua New Guinea | S | 5 | 270,000 | 2 |
| 1895 | Province of the Anglican Ch of Congo-Zaire (EAC-Z) | S | 6 | 370,000 | – |
| 1898 | Philippine Episcopal Church (PEC) | S | 5 | 118,360 | 2 |
| 1899 | Province of the Episcopal Church of the Sudan | S | 24 | 2,106,000 | 3 |
| 1920 | Episcopal Church of the Province of Rwanda | S | 9 | 819,050 | 2 |
| 1934 | Protestant Episcopal Church of the Province of Burundi | S | 5 | 440,000 | 2 |

| | Dioceses | Members | WCC |
|---|---|---|---|
| **Anglican Communion (affiliated baptized)** | 593 | 80,186,970 | 113 |
| **B. Latent Anglicans (professing but unaffiliated, in 144 countries)** | | 21,764,000 | – |
| **C. Independent Anglicans outside the Communion** | | 7,600,000 | |
| **D. Total of all Anglicans on broader definition** | | 109,546,970 | 113 |

32% are suffragan, coadjutor, or assistant bishops. In a major development, there are now 11 women who are Anglican bishops, 4 being diocesans. Last, not included in the above totals are the 300 bishops who have retired, many of whom however still vote or are otherwise active in church life.

### Clergy
In 1968 Anglican clergy of all kinds numbered 39,800. In 1978 there were 43,740 including 122 women priests. This latter category has expanded rapidly to, by 1992, 1,400 women priests (1,000 in ECUSA alone), and to 7,000 by AD 2000.

Religious personnel—brothers, monks, and nuns—number 3,500. Men and women layworkers exceed 14,300. And ordinands—3,063 in 1967—now number 4,500.

In addition, lay readers perform an essential ministry role. In 1978 they numbered 43,796 men and 3,007 women. By 2000 their number approaches 70,000.

### Communications
Possibly the biggest new development worldwide since LC 12 (12th Lambeth Conference) is the emergence of e-mail, the Internet, web sites, and now Internet 2. Some 10 million Anglicans use these means of communication every day.

### The Communion in 167 Countries
Table 5–4 opposite lists all countries in the world which have an organized component of the Anglican Communion—at least a parish or congregation with regular Sunday services. It then shows the number of baptized Anglicans affiliated to the Communion in each country. In order to show the expansion or decline of each country's Anglican presence, the table provides

2 totals—for AD 1900 and for AD 2000.

### The center of gravity moves south
The demographic center of Anglicanism in the world has moved a long way from London since its origin. This can be shown by the following totals of Anglicans in the Churches in Britain, and their percentage of the entire Communion. In 1600, Britain's 4.4 million Anglicans formed 95% of the entire Communion; in 1800, 6.8 million were 94%; in 1850, 12.5 million were 93%; in 1900, 24 million were 80%; in 1968, 29 million were 63%; in 1978, 29.4 million were 54%; in 1988, 27 million were 48%; and by AD 2000, the Anglican Churches in Britain, declining considerably to 25 millions, make up only 35% of the entire Communion (see Global Map overleaf).

The largest move south has been to Africa. At 4.5% per year exponential growth Anglicans there have mushroomed 85-fold in 100 years.

**1968.** Convener of LC 10, Archbishop Ramsey dialogues about Jesus with Chief Rabbi over British Broadcasting Corporation.

### Persecution and martyrdom
On a quite different note, some 10 million Anglicans are suffering persecution in many countries as severe as Christians of any other Communion. The current rate of new Anglican martyrs—defined as believers in Christ who lose their lives, prematurely, in a situation of witness, due to human hostility—numbers some 8,000 per year (on average 22 each day). Since the 1988 Lambeth Conference at least 50,000 Anglicans—clergy, laity, children—have been martyred in this way.

Fittingly, the largest regular Anglican mass gathering, of 15,000, meets every 18 June at Marondera, Zimbabwe to celebrate a martyr—Anglican catechist Bernard Mizeki, killed in 1896.

### Money
In 1978, the personal income of all Anglicans added up to (in USA dollars) $150 billion a year. By AD 2000, this sum is likely to have reached $480 billion. The income and expenditure of the 46 member Churches has risen accordingly, from $4.5 billion a year in 1978 to $9.6 billion a year by AD 2000.

### Anglicans in world mission
From the start of the series of Lambeth Conferences in 1867, the Bishops have inspired and challenged the entire Christian world as it undertakes its world mission. In 1897 the 4th Lambeth Conference passed 14 resolutions on foreign missions, the first of which stated: 'We recommend prompt and continuous efforts be made to arouse the church to the fulfillment of our Lord's great commission to evangelize all nations.'

Episcopal challenges of this sort always galvanize the church. In that same year 1897, the House of Laymen, Province of Canterbury re-

## Table 5–4. Expansion of the organized Anglican Communion across 167 countries in the 20th century, AD 1900 – 2000.

The table divides up the total membership of the organized Anglican Communion into its 167 constituent countries (listed in the first columns below). It also provides a perspective on its expansion across the 20th century. In AD 1900, the Communion had organized churches and congregations in 112 countries, with 30,570,765 members (second columns below). By AD 2000 these totals increased to 167 countries, with 80,186,970 members (third columns below).

| Country | Organized Anglicans AD 1900 | Organized Anglicans AD 2000 |
|---|---|---|
| Afghanistan | 0 | 100 |
| Algeria | 100 | 200 |
| American Samoa | 0 | 190 |
| Angola | 0 | 3,400 |
| Anguilla | 1,970 | 2,700 |
| Antarctica | 0 | 300 |
| Antigua & Barbuda | 16,450 | 24,000 |
| Argentina | 1,000 | 19,000 |
| Aruba | 0 | 750 |
| Australia | 1,357,200 | 4,040,000 |
| Austria | 0 | 3,200 |
| Bahamas | 24,400 | 27,000 |
| Bahrain | 100 | 3,700 |
| Bangladesh | 5,000 | 13,600 |
| Barbados | 146,600 | 74,300 |
| Belgium | 1,000 | 10,500 |
| Belize | 8,000 | 9,500 |
| Bermuda | 13,000 | 25,250 |
| Bolivia | 0 | 1,150 |
| Botswana | 0 | 10,500 |
| Brazil | 300 | 105,000 |
| Britain | 24,537,000 | 25,970,223 |
| British Indian Ocean Territory | 50 | 200 |
| British Virgin Islands | 440 | 3,500 |
| Brunei | 40 | 5,000 |
| Burundi | 0 | 440,000 |
| Cambodia | 0 | 40 |
| Cameroon | 0 | 700 |
| Canada | 559,000 | 738,000 |
| Cayman Islands | 0 | 550 |
| Channel Islands | 58,930 | 64,300 |
| Chile | 1,000 | 12,500 |
| China | 30,000 | 29,900 |
| Christmas Island | 10 | 90 |
| Cocos (Keeling) Islands | 48 | 93 |
| Colombia | 0 | 4,000 |
| Congo-Zaire | 0 | 370,000 |
| Cook Islands | 0 | 100 |
| Costa Rica | 200 | 1,600 |
| Cuba | 1,000 | 3,000 |
| Cyprus | 200 | 3,300 |
| Czech Republic | 0 | 1,200 |
| Denmark | 200 | 4,500 |
| Dominica | 280 | 1,340 |
| Dominican Republic | 100 | 4,400 |
| Ecuador | 0 | 1,800 |
| Egypt | 12,000 | 2,600 |
| El Salvador | 0 | 400 |
| Ethiopia | 0 | 800 |
| Falkland Islands | 1,460 | 860 |
| Fiji | 200 | 8,000 |
| Finland | 0 | 160 |
| France | 500 | 13,100 |
| French Guiana | 0 | 100 |
| Gambia | 1,000 | 3,000 |
| Germany | 1,000 | 28,000 |
| Ghana | 2,000 | 210,000 |
| Gibraltar | 1,000 | 2,020 |
| Greece | 200 | 3,700 |
| Grenada | 22,200 | 14,300 |
| Guam | 0 | 1,000 |
| Guatemala | 100 | 2,000 |
| Guinea | 0 | 1,400 |
| Guinea-Bissau | 0 | 280 |
| Guyana | 62,700 | 68,000 |
| Haiti | 1,000 | 120,000 |
| Honduras | 0 | 6,000 |
| India | 550,000 | 4,255,000 |
| Indonesia | 0 | 3,400 |
| Iran | 300 | 1,200 |
| Iraq | 50 | 200 |
| Ireland | 264,000 | 140,000 |
| Isle of Man | 25,080 | 34,800 |
| Israel | 500 | 900 |
| Italy | 100 | 11,500 |
| Jamaica | 281,000 | 107,000 |
| Japan | 10,997 | 62,000 |
| Jordan | 400 | 7,200 |
| Kenya | 2,000 | 2,700,000 |
| Kiribati | 0 | 50 |
| Kuwait | 0 | 200 |
| Laos | 0 | 200 |
| Lebanon | 100 | 200 |
| Lesotho | 2,500 | 108,000 |
| Liberia | 2,200 | 27,500 |
| Libya | 0 | 150 |
| Luxembourg | 0 | 600 |
| Macedonia | 0 | 200 |
| Madagascar | 3,000 | 280,000 |
| Malawi | 3,100 | 200,000 |
| Malaysia | 10,000 | 180,000 |
| Malta | 10,000 | 1,100 |
| Mauritius | 4,100 | 4,800 |
| Mexico | 5,000 | 22,600 |
| Monaco | 100 | 320 |
| Montserrat | 6,100 | 3,000 |
| Morocco | 50 | 450 |
| Mozambique | 200 | 100,000 |
| Myanmar | 30,000 | 56,700 |
| Namibia | 0 | 110,000 |
| Nauru | 0 | 350 |
| Netherlands | 0 | 8,700 |
| Netherlands Antilles | 0 | 2,800 |
| New Caledonia | 0 | 200 |
| New Zealand | 320,000 | 800,000 |
| Nicaragua | 0 | 8,300 |
| Nigeria | 35,000 | 17,900,000 |
| Niue Island | 0 | 40 |
| Norfolk Island | 720 | 655 |
| Norway | 0 | 2,000 |
| Oman | 0 | 3,500 |
| Pakistan | 20,000 | 1,160,000 |
| Palestine | 1,000 | 3,200 |
| Panama | 6,000 | 23,500 |
| Papua New Guinea | 200 | 270,000 |
| Paraguay | 100 | 16,000 |
| Peru | 100 | 1,900 |
| Philippines | 0 | 118,362 |
| Portugal | 500 | 5,250 |
| Puerto Rico | 500 | 13,000 |
| Qatar | 20 | 8,300 |
| Romania | 0 | 450 |
| Russia | 1,500 | 3,300 |
| Rwanda | 0 | 819,050 |
| Saint Helena | 2,970 | 4,570 |
| Saint Kitts & Nevis | 12,000 | 10,000 |
| Saint Lucia | 5,970 | 4,700 |
| Saint Vincent & the Grenadines | 35,500 | 19,300 |
| Samoa | 0 | 550 |
| Saudi Arabia | 0 | 2,000 |
| Senegal | 0 | 180 |
| Seychelles | 1,500 | 5,400 |
| Sierre Leone | 20,000 | 26,000 |
| Singapore | 1,000 | 32,000 |
| Solomon Islands | 12,000 | 156,000 |
| Somalia | 0 | 30 |
| Somaliland | 0 | 300 |
| South Africa | 206,500 | 2,430,000 |
| South Korea | 100 | 100,780 |
| Spain | 1,000 | 28,870 |
| Sri Lanka | 41,000 | 53,900 |
| Sudan | 30 | 2,106,000 |
| Suriname | 100 | 780 |
| Swaziland | 80 | 16,600 |
| Sweden | 100 | 2,850 |
| Switzerland | 500 | 13,000 |
| Syria | 0 | 3,600 |
| Taiwan | 0 | 1,487 |
| Tanzania | 5,000 | 2,300,000 |
| Thailand | 100 | 400 |
| Tonga | 0 | 640 |
| Trinidad & Tobago | 73,100 | 162,000 |
| Tunisia | 50 | 80 |
| Turkey | 6,000 | 2,100 |
| Turks & Caicos Islands | 2,750 | 830 |
| Uganda | 60,000 | 7,400,000 |
| United Arab Emirates | 20 | 8,700 |
| United States of America | 1,600,000 | 2,400,000 |
| Uruguay | 0 | 1,300 |
| Vanuatu | 1,800 | 30,500 |
| Venezuela | 100 | 600 |
| Viet Nam | 0 | 3,200 |
| Virgin Islands of the US | 8,600 | 14,200 |
| Yemen | 2,000 | 200 |
| Yugoslavia | 0 | 400 |
| Zambia | 0 | 310,000 |
| Zimbabwe | 6,000 | 300,000 |
| **Anglicans in the Communion** | **30,570,765** | **80,186,970** |

solved: 'In view of the Great Commission to evangelize the world, and its long and serious neglect, the whole Church needs rousing on this question.' We still need this arousing today!

### Anglican foreign mission today

The Anglican world has a long and wide history of missions. The marks of this mission are evident around the world and in many forms. What are the current figures? The Anglican world now sends out and supports some 5,000 full-time foreign missionaries. This is up somewhat from the 1978 total of 3,634 clergy and laypersons serving abroad. Although numbers sent out from Britain and North America have since been falling drastically, numbers sent out from the newer Churches of Africa and Asia—especially Nigeria, Kenya, Southern Africa, and Singapore—are increasing rapidly. Nevertheless the overall level—48 foreign missionaries for every million Anglicans—is well below the global Christian average of 100 per million church members. And that level is recognized as the minimum level if any denomination is to be regarded as taking Christ's Great Commission seriously by obeying it and implementing it at the global level.

Anglican foreign missions attract less interest and support nowadays compared to 1897. Yet fully 25% of today's world is still totally unaware of the Gospel of Christ—there are 1.6 billion persons who have never heard of Anglicanism, nor of the Lambeth Conference, nor of the Bible, nor even of the name of Jesus himself. Some 8,000 ethnolinguistic peoples across the world are without any church of their own. And 200 mega-nationalities lack any Anglican expression of the Christian faith.

These facts indicate our present neglect of the Great Commission's imperative target 'the ends of the earth' (Acts 1:8). Difficult, yes; remote and hostile, often; but commanded and therefore expected of us, absolutely.

### Reaching the 1.6 billion unevangelized

One new initiative is currently being undertaken by the newest of the 25 Anglican foreign mission agencies, Anglican Frontier Missions. AFM, with the active support of 70 Anglican bishops, is halfway through its program of recruiting missionaries from any Church in the Anglican Communion in order to evangelize, specifically and exclusively, the top 25 least evangelized megapeoples on the face of the globe. These inhabit what we are calling World A, the unevangelized world, clearly a priority (even *the* priority) in any world mission that takes Christ's Commission seriously.

All of this survey's statistics, large or small, can help us see our vocations clearer so that for us, at least, 'Statistics are signs from God.'

## BIBLIOGRAPHY

*Anglicanism: a global communion.* A Wingate, ed. New York: Church Publishing Inc, 1998. 384p. (Over 60 contributors).

*Being Anglican in the Third Millennium.* Official Report of the 10th Meeting of the Anglican Consultative Council. J. Rosenthal & N. Currie, eds. New York: Morehouse Publishing, 1998. 320p.

*Church of England yearbook, 1998.* London: Church House Publishing, 1997. (Names, addresses, telephones, fax numbers, for all Churches of the Anglican Communion).

*Church on fire: the story of Anglican Evangelicals.* R. Steer.

**1973.** A master at befriending non-Christian leaders, Archbishop Ramsey welcomes the Dalai Lama to Lambeth for a discussion about Jesus.

(Near right). 101st Archbishop Donald Coggan, who in **1978** convened 420 bishops, shown here (Centre) worshiping in Canterbury Cathedral at the 11th Lambeth Conference. (Far right) 102nd Archbishop Robert Runcie, who in **1988** convened 500 bishops to the 12th Lambeth Conference.

*Episcopal Church Annual, 1998.* New York: Morehouse Publishing, 1998.

*Lambeth Conference 1978: Preparatory information: Statistics, documentation, addresses, maps.* London: CIO Publishing, 1978. (Contains survey 'The Anglican World in Figures' (TAWIF-1978), by D.B. Barrett, pages 1-37, with 15 statistical tables each describing the whole Communion and its component Churches).

*Membership, manpower and money in the Anglican Communion: a survey of 27 Churches and 360 Dioceses.* D.B. Barrett. London: ACC, 1973.

*Resolutions of the 12 Lambeth Conferences, 1867-1988.* R. Coleman, ed. Toronto: Anglican Book Centre, 1988.

*The Anglican cycle of prayer: 1998.* Cincinnati: Forward Movement Publications, 1997. 129p.

*The challenge of change: the Anglican Communion in the post-modern era.* M. Harris. New York: Church Publishing Inc, 1998.

*The essential guide to the Anglican Communion.* J. Rosenthal. London: Morehouse Publishing, 1998. 176p.

*The transformation of Anglicanism: from state church to global communion.* W.L. Sachs. Cambridge University Press, 1993. 386p.

## Global Map 5–1. **Growth of the Anglican Communion on the 7 Continents, AD 1900 – AD 2000.**

The map shows the growth in numbers of baptized Anglicans with organized church services within the 46 member Churches of the Anglican Communion, for the two years AD 1900 (light type) and AD 2000 (bold type). Our globe's 7 continents, their 238 countries and their boundaries are as defined in AD 2000 by the United Nations. Totals are derived from Table 5–4 above and have each been rounded below to the nearest 10.

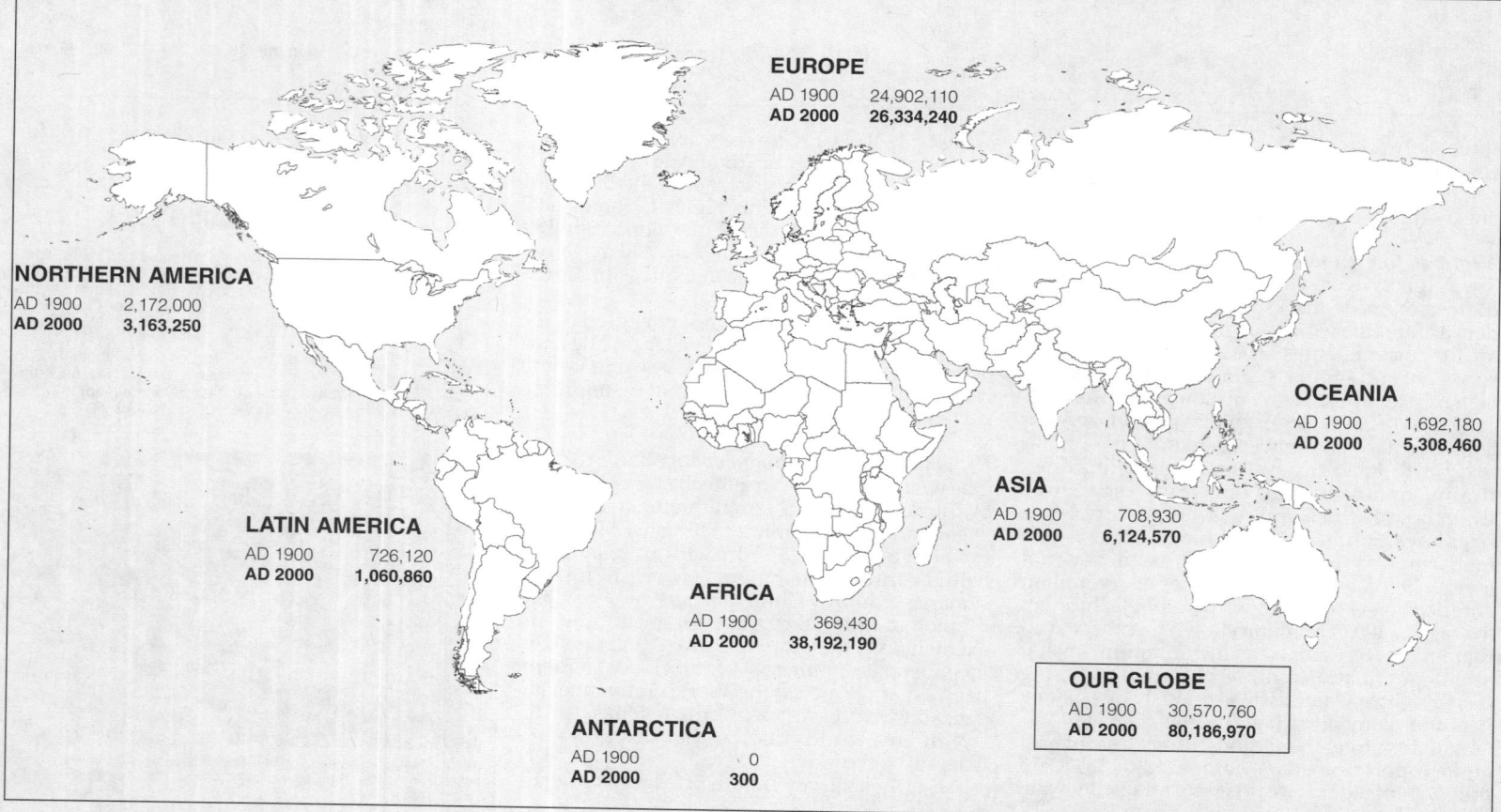

**EUROPE**
AD 1900  24,902,110
**AD 2000  26,334,240**

**NORTHERN AMERICA**
AD 1900  2,172,000
**AD 2000  3,163,250**

**OCEANIA**
AD 1900  1,692,180
**AD 2000  5,308,460**

**LATIN AMERICA**
AD 1900  726,120
**AD 2000  1,060,860**

**ASIA**
AD 1900  708,930
**AD 2000  6,124,570**

**AFRICA**
AD 1900  369,430
**AD 2000  38,192,190**

**OUR GLOBE**
AD 1900  30,570,760
**AD 2000  80,186,970**

**ANTARCTICA**
AD 1900  0
**AD 2000  300**

# THE CATHOLIC CHARISMATIC RENEWAL, 1959-2025

*A 4-page overview of the world's largest current renewal movement*

## ORIGINS OF RENEWAL

(*Left*). In 1959 John XXIII flung open the windows for the Holy Spirit to renew the entire church.
(*Right*). Catholic bishops led by cardinal L.-J. Suenens (architect of Renewal, center), in a charismatic celebration of the Lord's Supper.

### A brief history

One day in 1959 pope John XXIII startled Vatican bureaucrats by flinging open his office windows and calling for the Holy Spirit to send in a new wind of Pentecost to result in *aggiornamento* (updating or renewal) for the church. Among the 3,000 bishops present at the resulting Vatican Council II were several who would later be termed Charismatics. One leading advocate then was cardinal Leo-Joseph Suenens of Belgium. Suddenly in 1967 at Duquesne University, USA and in Bogota, Colombia the first charismatic prayer meetings erupted. The subsequent enormous mushrooming of what became known as the Catholic Charismatic Renewal (CCR) can be followed through Table 5–5 (which uses the same definitions as in Table 5–6).

It began in many different ways. In Italy, in 1971 the first prayer group was begun in English at the Gregorian University in Rome by a small group including Carlo Martini, now cardinal archbishop of Milan. As the Renewal spread like wildfire, in 1976 Suenens set up in Brussels an ICO which in 1981 became the International Catholic Charismatic Renewal Office (ICCRO) in Rome. In 1985 this relocated to the Vatican, and in 1993 became ICCRS (S=Services).

### MEASURING RENEWAL

### A detailed survey, 1995-2000

This present overview is the result of a 4-year survey. The ICCRS sent to its co-ordinator or correspondent in every country of the world a short one-page questionnaire containing 7 basic questions. Replies were faxed back and forth, additional information, facts, and figures were amassed. Extensive use was made of e-mail and the Internet. Results for all countries are shown here in Table 5–6.

### A sketch of each country

The table has 19 variables divided into 6 groups of columns. First is given the short *name* of each of the world's 238 countries. Second, the status of the Catholic Church in the year 2000 is sketched with 3 statistics: the numbers of *parishes*, *priests* at work, and *baptized Catholics*.

### A sketch of each country's Renewal

The third group describes the current status of the CCR in AD 2000. Column 5 gives the *year* Renewal began. Column 6 shows its current *magnitude* in each country, using the scale set out in Table 5–7. Column 7 describes the *organizational stage* now reached: - = none, c = at least a correspondent, h = head contact (relationship with a local leader), n = a service committee serving several countries, N = a National Service Committee (NSC) for a single country. One country, Britain, has 3 NSCs; the USA has two (one Hispanic). Next, column 8 shows organized *weekly prayer groups*. And column 9 gives *priests involved* in the CCR.

## SIX TYPES OF PARTICIPANTS

### A six-fold statistical typology of participants

Columns 10 to 15 then provide an enumeration of Charismatics themselves. With a mushrooming movement such as this it is essential to understand the exact definition of each and every statistic that is generated, published, or quoted. As the Pentecostal/Charismatic Renewal's best-documented membership data, Catholic statistics each refer to one of the following 6 types or categories, each of which includes the previous category. The first category is the basic grassroots head count, which is of weekly-attending adults who regularly attend their charismatic prayer group, which can vary in size from 2 persons to 1,000. The following 5 categories are then derived from it; the first 4 categories refer to adults only (over 15 years old); the last 2 categories are demographic totals including children and infants. These last two are just as important because the whole Renewal is not a movement of isolated adults but is largely a family movement in which the presence of children cannot be ignored.

**A. Active involved adults**. The first 3 categories now to be described refer to adults related to the mainline CCRs served by ICCRS.

*(1) Weekly-attender adult Charismatics* (column 10) These are defined as those adults actually attending (involved in/enrolled in/participating in) the Renewal's officially recognized prayer meetings regularly every week. These have been called the 'shock troops' of the movement. By 1995 this had increased to 11 million weekly adults, by 2000 to 13 million.

*(2) Monthly-attender adult Charismatics* (column 11). These are defined as adults attending the Renewal's prayer meetings once a month or more, enumerated at 7 million worldwide in 1985, 14 million in 1995, and 19 million in 2000 (including those in category (1) above).

*(3) Yearly-attender adult Charismatics* (column 12). This total covers all adults who attend less regularly, often only for a large annual congress or rally (including those in category (2) above).

*(4) Self-identifying involved adult Charismatics* (column 13). A somewhat larger number of adults identify themselves in public-opinion polls either as Catholic Charismatics or as otherwise involved in the Renewal (including those in category (3) above). Also included at this point are the large number of Catholics in charismatic renewal movements not related to ICCRS; in Italy, these amount to 30% more prayer groups and 20% more Charismatics than those under the ICCRS umbrella. (Example: Comunità Gesú Risorto, begun 1987, now with 160 communities and 12,000 regular adults).

**B. Active involved families.** To all these statistics of adults must now be added their children and infants, to get demographic figures or family figures which can be directly and legitimately compared with secular population figures, and also with standard Catholic statistics of baptized Catholics, both of which always include children and infants. Two more categories result, as follows.

*(5) Charismatic family members* (column 14). This is defined as active or involved adults plus their children and infants enumerated in this table at 30 million in 1980 and 71 million by AD 2000. This category also includes those enumerated under categories (1), (2), (3), and (4) above.

**C. Active and inactive Charismatic community**

*(6) Active Charismatic and Postcharismatic community* (column 15). This last category is defined as consisting of 2 distinct figures: (i) the active family of category (5) above, plus (ii) a large fringe of Catholic Postcharismatics (formerly active Charismatics who have become irregular, or less active, or inactive, or elsewhere active). Together these two constitute the total Catholic Charismatic demographic community amounting to 40 million in 1980, increasing to 63 million by 1985, to 104 million by 1995, and to 119 million by AD 2000.

### Table 5–5. Numerical growth of the Catholic Charismatic Renewal, 1967-2000.

| Year | Prayer groups | PARTICIPANTS: Weekly | Monthly | Yearly | Involved | Familial | Community | %Cath | Rate % p.a. | Countries |
|------|------|------|------|------|------|------|------|------|------|------|
| 1967 | 2 | First Charismatic prayer groups formed in USA and Colombia | | | | | | 0.0 | 500.0 | 2 |
| 1970 | 2,185 | 238,500 | 500,000 | 1,000,000 | 1,600,000 | 2,000,000 | 2,000,000 | 0.3 | 100.0 | 25 |
| 1973 | 3,000 | 900,000 | 2,000,000 | 3,500,000 | 5,000,000 | 7,000,000 | 8,000,000 | 1.1 | 58.7 | 71 |
| 1975 | 4,000 | 1,995,730 | 3,000,000 | 6,000,000 | 9,000,000 | 15,000,000 | 15,000,000 | 2.7 | 36.9 | 93 |
| 1980 | 12,000 | 3,000,000 | 4,771,390 | 7,700,000 | 16,000,000 | 30,000,000 | 40,000,000 | 5.0 | 21.6 | 110 |
| 1985 | 60,000 | 4,200,000 | 7,547,050 | 12,000,000 | 22,000,000 | 40,100,000 | 63,500,000 | 7.3 | 9.7 | 140 |
| 1990 | 90,000 | 7,000,000 | 10,100,000 | 17,000,000 | 30,000,000 | 45,000,000 | 85,000,000 | 9.2 | 6.0 | 180 |
| 1995 | 143,000 | 11,000,000 | 14,000,000 | 20,000,000 | 34,000,000 | 60,000,000 | 104,900,000 | 10.4 | 4.3 | 210 |
| 2000 | 160,000 | 13,400,000 | 19,300,000 | 28,700,000 | 44,300,000 | 71,300,000 | 119,900,000 | 11.3 | 2.7 | 233 |

### Reaching the whole world

The Renewal spread with incredible speed: by 1969, prayer groups had begun in 13 countries, by 1970 in 25, by 1975 in 93, and by AD 2000 in 233 countries. Table 5–7 shows its current status and size.

Since 1970, the Catholic Charismatic Renewal has held 5,000 large conferences (up to 200,000 attenders each). *Above*. At 1975 Dublin Conference, cardinal Suenens leads in charismatic worship. Three years later at the 1978 International conference in Dublin, Suenens concelebrated on television with 17 bishops and 1,500 priests in presence of 20,000.

**Table 5–6. The status, influence, and future prospects of the Catholic Charismatic Renewal, AD 1967–2025.**

| Country | Status of Catholic Church, AD 2000 | | | STATUS OF CATHOLIC CHARISMATIC RENEWAL, AD 2000 | | | | | Renewal participants: | | | | | | Influence of CCR (as % of cols 2,3,4) | | | CCR's Future |
|---|---|---|---|---|---|---|---|---|---|---|---|---|---|---|---|---|---|---|
| Name | Parishes | Priests | Catholics | Begun | Mag | Org | Prayer groups | Priests | Weekly | Monthly | Yearly | Involved | Familial | Community | Prayer groups | Priests | Cath | Community AD 2025 |
| 1 | 2 | 3 | 4 | 5 | 6 | 7 | 8 | 9 | 10 | 11 | 12 | 13 | 14 | 15 | 16 | 17 | 18 | 19 |
| Afghanistan | 1 | 0 | 1,497 | | 2 | - | 1 | 0 | 5 | 8 | 13 | 21 | 35 | 60 | 100 | 0 | 4 | 104 |
| Albania | 127 | 95 | 521,390 | 1993 | 5 | h | 10 | 1 | 1,000 | 1,598 | 2,554 | 4,082 | 6,524 | 10,428 | 7 | 1 | 2 | 38,650 |
| Algeria | 38 | 103 | 20,277 | | 2 | N | 2 | 0 | 100 | 170 | 289 | 491 | 835 | 1,419 | 5 | 0 | 7 | 3,181 |
| American Samoa | 10 | 10 | 9,470 | | 5 | - | 5 | 0 | 50 | 86 | 148 | 255 | 439 | 758 | 50 | 0 | 8 | 3,159 |
| Andorra | 7 | 18 | 69,535 | | 5 | - | 4 | 0 | 60 | 98 | 160 | 261 | 426 | 695 | 57 | 0 | 1 | 3,142 |
| Angola | 259 | 442 | 8,000,000 | | 6 | - | 200 | 50 | 20,000 | 38,946 | 75,839 | 147,681 | 287,578 | 560,000 | 77 | 11 | 7 | 2,936,919 |
| Antarctica | 0 | 3 | 1,400 | 1970 | 2 | - | 2 | 0 | 10 | 0 | 0 | 0 | 0 | 100 | | 0 | 7 | 0 |
| Antigua | 2 | 5 | 7,800 | | 2 | n | 2 | 0 | 30 | 50 | 84 | 140 | 234 | 390 | 100 | 0 | 5 | 819 |
| Argentina | 2,503 | 5,845 | 33,750,000 | 1972 | 7 | n | 3,000 | 500 | 100,000 | 216,212 | 467,477 | 1,010,743 | 2,185,351 | 4,725,000 | 119 | 9 | 14 | 7,988,750 |
| Armenia | 18 | 17 | 160,000 | | 5 | - | 10 | 0 | 200 | 348 | 606 | 1,055 | 1,837 | 3,200 | 55 | 0 | 2 | 6,854 |
| Aruba | 10 | 8 | 84,341 | | 5 | n | 20 | 0 | 400 | 641 | 1,027 | 1,645 | 2,635 | 4,217 | 200 | 0 | 5 | 29,822 |
| Australia | 1,418 | 3,462 | 5,400,000 | 1969 | 3 | N | 600 | 160 | 3,000 | 7,056 | 16,597 | 39,039 | 91,826 | 216,000 | 42 | 5 | 4 | 383,348 |
| Austria | 3,037 | 4,817 | 6,200,000 | 1971 | 6 | N | 420 | 120 | 5,500 | 11,781 | 25,235 | 54,053 | 115,781 | 248,000 | 13 | 2 | 4 | 342,536 |
| Azerbaijan | 1 | 0 | 7,500 | | 5 | - | 3 | 0 | 10 | 17 | 29 | 50 | 86 | 150 | 300 | 0 | 2 | 208 |
| Bahamas | 29 | 30 | 48,000 | | 5 | - | 4 | 0 | 50 | 104 | 216 | 448 | 929 | 1,919 | 13 | 0 | 4 | 3,350 |
| Bahrain | 1 | 3 | 25,000 | | 5 | h | 10 | 0 | 100 | 166 | 275 | 456 | 756 | 1,250 | 1000 | 0 | 5 | 3,315 |
| Bangladesh | 75 | 246 | 235,000 | 1972 | 5 | N | 19 | 20 | 500 | 1,006 | 2,023 | 4,069 | 8,183 | 16,450 | 25 | 8 | 7 | 39,101 |
| Barbados | 6 | 11 | 11,000 | c1973 | 2 | n | 2 | 0 | 40 | 65 | 105 | 170 | 275 | 440 | 33 | 0 | 4 | 797 |
| Belgium | 3,953 | 8,984 | 8,222,396 | 1970 | 6 | N | 350 | 110 | 6,500 | 13,451 | 27,835 | 57,601 | 119,199 | 246,672 | 8 | 1 | 3 | 315,738 |
| Belize | 13 | 37 | 136,939 | 1969 | 5 | N | 24 | 3 | 960 | 1,694 | 2,990 | 5,277 | 9,313 | 16,433 | 184 | 8 | 12 | 44,713 |
| Belorussia | 357 | 242 | 1,350,000 | | 5 | h | 20 | 0 | 1,000 | 1,683 | 2,832 | 4,766 | 8,021 | 13,500 | 5 | 0 | 1 | 20,657 |
| Benin | 151 | 341 | 1,266,195 | 1976 | 5 | N | 140 | 30 | 25,000 | 32,201 | 41,476 | 53,423 | 68,811 | 88,634 | 92 | 9 | 7 | 497,368 |
| Bermuda | 6 | 7 | 10,384 | | 2 | - | 2 | 0 | 30 | 48 | 77 | 123 | 196 | 311 | 33 | 0 | 3 | 488 |
| Bhutan | 1 | 0 | 600 | | 2 | - | 1 | 0 | 5 | 7 | 10 | 14 | 19 | 24 | 100 | 0 | 4 | 76 |
| Bolivia | 534 | 1,038 | 7,350,000 | 1969 | 6 | n | 600 | 35 | 12,000 | 28,343 | 66,943 | 158,111 | 373,439 | 881,999 | 112 | 3 | 12 | 2,420,740 |
| Bosnia-Herzegovina | 278 | 554 | 681,135 | c1980 | 5 | c | 30 | 0 | 3,000 | 4,664 | 7,251 | 11,273 | 17,526 | 27,245 | 10 | 0 | 4 | 21,296 |
| Botswana | 25 | 44 | 60,000 | 1985 | 2 | N | 2 | 3 | 35 | 71 | 144 | 292 | 592 | 1,200 | 8 | 7 | 2 | 3,525 |
| Bougainville | 2 | 39 | 148,401 | | 5 | - | 15 | 0 | 400 | 648 | 1,049 | 1,699 | 2,751 | 4,452 | 750 | 0 | 3 | 11,513 |
| Brazil | 8,096 | 15,568 | 153,300,000 | 1971 | 9 | n | 61,000 | 500 | 9,000,000 | 11,721,602 | 15,266,217 | 19,882,725 | 25,895,266 | 33,726,000 | 753 | 3 | 22 | 56,969,818 |
| Britain | 2,300 | 6,865 | 5,620,000 | 1969 | 4 | Nn | 250 | 180 | 15,500 | 28,871 | 53,776 | 100,164 | 186,567 | 347,493 | 10 | 3 | 6 | 455,494 |
| British Virgin Islands | 2 | 2 | 700 | | 2 | - | 1 | 0 | 10 | 13 | 17 | 22 | 28 | 35 | 50 | 0 | 5 | 80 |
| Brunei | 3 | 2 | 5,600 | | 2 | h | 1 | 0 | 20 | 32 | 52 | 84 | 136 | 224 | 33 | 0 | 4 | 484 |
| Bulgaria | 51 | 39 | 90,000 | | 5 | h | 3 | 0 | 100 | 155 | 241 | 374 | 580 | 900 | 5 | 0 | 1 | 1,000 |
| Burkina Faso | 108 | 491 | 1,129,078 | 1977 | 6 | N | 100 | 34 | 15,000 | 23,295 | 36,176 | 56,180 | 87,246 | 135,489 | 92 | 7 | 12 | 776,303 |
| Burundi | 123 | 296 | 3,827,541 | 1980 | 5 | h | 14 | 4 | 1,050 | 2,476 | 5,839 | 13,769 | 32,468 | 76,551 | 11 | 1 | 2 | 275,922 |
| Cambodia | 5 | 22 | 22,000 | | 5 | | 3 | 0 | 100 | 154 | 238 | 368 | 569 | 880 | 60 | 0 | 4 | 3,857 |
| Cameroon | 647 | 1,090 | 3,989,401 | 1975 | 6 | N̄ | 320 | 50 | 3,000 | 6,271 | 13,107 | 27,396 | 57,262 | 119,682 | 49 | 5 | 3 | 523,469 |
| Canada | 5,160 | 10,518 | 13,017,945 | 1968 | 7 | N | 862 | 175 | 20,730 | 45,374 | 99,315 | 217,381 | 475,804 | 1,041,436 | 16 | 2 | 8 | 1,681,355 |
| Cape Verde | 31 | 45 | 417,000 | 1992 | 5 | - | 10 | 0 | 300 | 670 | 1,497 | 3,344 | 7,469 | 16,680 | 32 | 0 | 4 | 52,492 |
| Cayman Islands | 1 | 2 | 200 | | 2 | - | 1 | 0 | 5 | 7 | 9 | 12 | 16 | 20 | 100 | 0 | 10 | 64 |
| Central African Republic | 108 | 277 | 664,639 | 1991 | 5 | N | 10 | 0 | 1,000 | 2,214 | 4,901 | 10,850 | 24,020 | 53,171 | 9 | 0 | 8 | 199,232 |
| Chad | 97 | 192 | 502,158 | | 5 | h | 12 | 0 | 1,100 | 2,056 | 3,843 | 7,184 | 13,429 | 25,108 | 12 | 0 | 5 | 127,300 |
| Channel Islands | 0 | 0 | 22,300 | | 5 | - | 4 | 0 | 50 | 77 | 119 | 184 | 285 | 446 | | 0 | 2 | 742 |
| Chile | 887 | 2,307 | 11,800,000 | 1972 | 7 | n | 705 | 15 | 21,000 | 50,278 | 120,375 | 288,200 | 690,005 | 1,652,000 | 79 | 1 | 14 | 2,780,379 |
| China | 17,500 | 4,000 | 7,500,000 | 1978 | 6 | Nh | 700 | 0 | 50,000 | 81,770 | 133,726 | 218,695 | 357,653 | 584,901 | 4 | 0 | 8 | 1,857,208 |
| Colombia | 3,023 | 6,912 | 40,670,000 | 1967 | 9 | n | 21,000 | 200 | 1,050,000 | 1,691,367 | 2,724,498 | 4,388,692 | 7,069,418 | 11,387,600 | 694 | 3 | 28 | 24,370,212 |
| Comoros | 2 | 2 | 5,751 | | 2 | - | 1 | 0 | 10 | 16 | 26 | 42 | 68 | 115 | 50 | 0 | 2 | 497 |
| Congo-Brazzaville | 11 | 277 | 1,451,178 | | 6 | N | 80 | 0 | 8,000 | 13,659 | 23,322 | 39,821 | 67,992 | 116,094 | 727 | 0 | 8 | 543,019 |
| Congo-Zaire | 1,208 | 3,695 | 26,300,000 | 1971 | 6 | N | 3,000 | 50 | 270,000 | 334,585 | 414,619 | 513,797 | 636,699 | 789,001 | 248 | 1 | 3 | 3,513,802 |
| Cook Islands | 15 | 8 | 3,650 | | 2 | - | 2 | 0 | 20 | 32 | 52 | 84 | 136 | 219 | 13 | 0 | 6 | 390 |
| Costa Rica | 241 | 700 | 3,660,000 | 1971 | 6 | n | 350 | 10 | 8,700 | 15,999 | 29,422 | 54,108 | 99,506 | 183,000 | 145 | 1 | 5 | 457,894 |
| Croatia | 1,498 | 2,221 | 3,960,000 | 1975 | 6 | hc | 30 | 0 | 4,000 | 7,882 | 15,531 | 30,602 | 60,298 | 118,800 | 2 | 0 | 3 | 142,647 |
| Cuba | 253 | 288 | 4,367,909 | 1977 | 6 | n | 120 | 20 | 3,600 | 8,989 | 22,445 | 56,044 | 139,940 | 349,433 | 47 | 7 | 8 | 515,810 |
| Cyprus | 13 | 17 | 9,800 | 1994 | 2 | h | 2 | 2 | 90 | 121 | 162 | 217 | 291 | 392 | 15 | 12 | 4 | 828 |
| Czech Republic | 3,121 | 1,852 | 4,135,936 | 1980 | 6 | h | 150 | 100 | 6,000 | 10,997 | 20,155 | 36,940 | 67,703 | 124,078 | 4 | 5 | 3 | 216,562 |
| Denmark | 50 | 98 | 33,200 | | 5 | N | 5 | 0 | 50 | 84 | 141 | 237 | 398 | 664 | 10 | 0 | 2 | 803 |
| Djibouti | 5 | 6 | 8,854 | | 2 | - | 2 | 0 | 20 | 31 | 48 | 74 | 115 | 178 | 40 | 0 | 2 | 500 |
| Dominica | 17 | 33 | 56,300 | | 5 | n | 5 | 0 | 100 | 162 | 263 | 427 | 693 | 1,126 | 29 | 0 | 2 | 1,590 |
| Dominican Republic | 329 | 643 | 7,522,305 | | 6 | N | 1,000 | 150 | 50,000 | 85,990 | 147,885 | 254,332 | 437,398 | 752,231 | 303 | 23 | 10 | 1,442,726 |
| Ecuador | 1,182 | 1,792 | 11,900,000 | 1970 | 7 | n | 604 | 30 | 23,000 | 50,640 | 111,496 | 245,484 | 540,489 | 1,190,000 | 51 | 2 | 10 | 2,808,510 |
| Egypt | 224 | 405 | 225,000 | | 5 | h | 10 | 0 | 500 | 841 | 1,415 | 2,381 | 4,007 | 6,750 | 4 | 0 | 3 | 18,167 |
| El Salvador | 298 | 558 | 5,723,000 | 1977 | 6 | n | 600 | 50 | 10,000 | 20,919 | 43,761 | 91,544 | 191,502 | 400,610 | 201 | 9 | 7 | 858,918 |
| Equatorial Guinea | 52 | 94 | 391,000 | | 5 | - | 10 | 0 | 500 | 867 | 1,503 | 2,605 | 4,515 | 7,820 | 19 | 0 | 2 | 30,415 |
| Eritrea | 91 | 319 | 130,000 | 1976 | 5 | h | 40 | 0 | 1,000 | 1,597 | 2,551 | 4,075 | 6,509 | 10,400 | 43 | 0 | 8 | 49,162 |
| Estonia | 7 | 12 | 5,875 | | 2 | - | 1 | 0 | 10 | 18 | 32 | 57 | 101 | 176 | 14 | 0 | 3 | 340 |
| Ethiopia | 186 | 393 | 450,000 | | 5 | c | 10 | 0 | 500 | 1,024 | 2,097 | 4,294 | 8,793 | 18,001 | 5 | 0 | 4 | 127,122 |
| Faeroe Islands | 1 | 0 | 130 | 1976 | 2 | h | 1 | 0 | 5 | 6 | 7 | 8 | 10 | 13 | 100 | 0 | 10 | 20 |
| Fiji | 34 | 108 | 85,000 | | 5 | N | 5 | 0 | 1,300 | 1,893 | 2,756 | 4,012 | 5,841 | 8,500 | 14 | 0 | 10 | 17,028 |
| Finland | 7 | 21 | 6,400 | | 2 | h | 1 | 0 | 15 | 25 | 42 | 70 | 117 | 192 | 14 | 0 | 3 | 268 |
| France | 30,709 | 27,781 | 48,600,000 | 1972 | 6 | N | 2,500 | 157 | 25,907 | 53,489 | 110,437 | 228,016 | 470,777 | 972,000 | 8 | 1 | 2 | 1,636,673 |
| French Guiana | 24 | 35 | 145,000 | | 5 | - | 10 | 0 | 300 | 542 | 980 | 1,772 | 3,204 | 5,800 | 41 | 0 | 4 | 33,846 |
| French Polynesia | 85 | 35 | 100,000 | | 5 | - | 10 | 0 | 400 | 663 | 1,099 | 1,821 | 3,018 | 5,000 | 11 | 0 | 5 | 11,000 |
| Gabon | 67 | 102 | 745,000 | | 5 | N | 30 | 0 | 1,000 | 1,716 | 2,946 | 5,057 | 8,680 | 14,901 | 44 | 0 | 2 | 48,782 |
| Gambia | 51 | 21 | 31,238 | | 2 | - | 2 | 0 | 50 | 83 | 138 | 229 | 380 | 625 | 3 | 0 | 2 | 2,181 |
| Georgia | 25 | 10 | 55,000 | | 5 | - | 5 | 0 | 100 | 162 | 262 | 423 | 683 | 1,100 | 20 | 0 | 2 | 2,100 |
| Germany | 12,491 | 20,490 | 28,700,000 | 1972 | 3 | N | 800 | 123 | 12,000 | 29,877 | 74,386 | 185,201 | 461,100 | 1,148,000 | 6 | 1 | 4 | 1,383,584 |
| Ghana | 255 | 851 | 1,925,000 | 1970 | 6 | N | 800 | 100 | 50,000 | 81,562 | 133,047 | 217,031 | 354,028 | 577,500 | 313 | 12 | 30 | 1,928,571 |
| Gibraltar | 5 | 14 | 21,200 | 1975 | 5 | N | 11 | 4 | 400 | 613 | 940 | 1,441 | 2,210 | 3,392 | 220 | 29 | 16 | 2,998 |
| Greece | 65 | 94 | 62,000 | | 5 | h | 5 | 0 | 100 | 165 | 273 | 452 | 748 | 1,240 | 7 | 0 | 2 | 1,573 |
| Greenland | 1 | 1 | 110 | | 2 | - | 1 | 0 | 1 | 1 | 1 | 1 | 1 | 2 | 100 | 0 | 2 | 10 |
| Grenada | 20 | 23 | 52,700 | 1971 | 3 | n | 10 | 0 | 200 | 335 | 561 | 940 | 1,574 | 2,635 | 50 | 0 | 5 | 3,746 |
| Guadeloupe | 45 | 59 | 433,000 | | 5 | c | 20 | 0 | 1,000 | 1,769 | 3,129 | 5,535 | 9,791 | 17,320 | 44 | 0 | 4 | 32,278 |
| Guam | 23 | 44 | 139,400 | | 5 | h | 4 | 0 | 200 | 367 | 674 | 1,238 | 2,274 | 4,182 | 17 | 0 | 3 | 8,969 |
| Guatemala | 410 | 901 | 9,600,000 | 1972 | 6 | n | 1,500 | 100 | 75,000 | 122,279 | 199,362 | 325,037 | 529,936 | 864,000 | 365 | 11 | 9 | 2,845,301 |
| Guinea | 51 | 80 | 117,000 | | 5 | - | 5 | 0 | 200 | 355 | 630 | 1,117 | 1,981 | 3,510 | 9 | 0 | 3 | 18,028 |
| Guinea-Bissau | 30 | 62 | 141,000 | 1992 | 2 | - | 2 | 0 | 100 | 195 | 380 | 741 | 1,445 | 2,820 | 6 | 0 | 2 | 9,655 |
| Guyana | 30 | 56 | 86,500 | 1969 | 4 | n | 10 | 7 | 700 | 1,045 | 1,560 | 2,329 | 3,477 | 5,190 | 33 | 13 | 6 | 6,719 |
| Haiti | 244 | 583 | 6,520,000 | 1972 | 6 | N | 150 | 50 | 18,200 | 38,614 | 81,925 | 173,815 | 368,773 | 782,400 | 61 | 9 | 12 | 1,771,123 |
| Honduras | 152 | 333 | 5,590,000 | 1971 | 6 | n | 1,057 | 7 | 12,983 | 26,979 | 56,064 | 116,504 | 242,101 | 503,100 | 695 | 2 | 9 | 1,498,604 |
| Hungary | 2,280 | 2,562 | 6,330,000 | 1976 | 6 | N | 300 | 65 | 23,000 | 38,856 | 65,643 | 110,896 | 187,346 | 316,500 | 13 | 3 | 5 | 306,811 |
| Iceland | 4 | 10 | 2,900 | | 2 | h | 1 | 0 | 10 | 16 | 26 | 42 | 69 | 116 | 25 | 0 | 4 | 208 |
| India | 7,613 | 17,042 | 15,500,000 | 1972 | 7 | N | 10,400 | 200 | 150,000 | 274,881 | 503,731 | 923,109 | 1,691,637 | 3,100,000 | 136 | 1 | 20 | 6,914,405 |
| Indonesia | 1,030 | 2,555 | 5,752,358 | 1975 | 6 | N | 397 | 75 | 20,000 | 36,460 | 66,466 | 121,166 | 220,884 | 402,665 | 38 | 3 | 7 | 912,962 |
| Iran | 19 | 13 | 16,400 | | 2 | - | 1 | 0 | 30 | 48 | 77 | 124 | 200 | 328 | 5 | 0 | 2 | 850 |
| Iraq | 88 | 131 | 268,000 | | 5 | - | 8 | 0 | 500 | 871 | 1,518 | 2,646 | 4,612 | 8,040 | 9 | 0 | 3 | 16,981 |
| Ireland | 1,244 | 5,525 | 3,159,896 | 1969 | 6 | N | 501 | 200 | 15,000 | 29,514 | 58,072 | 114,264 | 224,828 | 442,385 | 40 | 4 | 14 | 679,380 |
| Isle of Man | 0 | 0 | 6,800 | | 2 | - | 1 | 0 | 20 | 32 | 51 | 81 | 129 | 204 | | 0 | 3 | 360 |
| Israel | 85 | 402 | 140,000 | | 5 | h | 70 | 0 | 1,000 | 1,695 | 2,873 | 4,870 | 8,256 | 14,001 | 82 | 0 | 10 | 34,285 |
| Italy | 25,772 | 56,087 | 55,680,000 | 1971 | 7 | N | 1,500 | 850 | 50,000 | 115,863 | 268,486 | 622,154 | 1,441,697 | 3,340,800 | 5 | 2 | 6 | 3,278,581 |
| Ivory Coast | 235 | 684 | 2,182,882 | c1978 | 6 | h | 80 | 0 | 5,000 | 9,608 | 18,462 | 35,475 | 68,166 | 130,973 | 34 | 0 | 6 | 444,444 |
| Jamaica | 79 | 91 | 110,000 | | 4 | c | 10 | 0 | 500 | 928 | 1,722 | 3,195 | 5,929 | 11,000 | 12 | 0 | 10 | 15,532 |
| Japan | 869 | 1,828 | 460,000 | c1970 | 5 | N | 500 | 40 | 5,000 | 8,083 | 13,067 | 21,124 | 34,148 | 55,200 | 57 | 2 | 12 | 70,227 |
| Jordan | 71 | 86 | 48,000 | | 5 | h | 10 | 0 | 300 | 522 | 909 | 1,583 | 2,756 | 4,800 | 14 | 0 | 10 | 18,238 |
| Kazakhstan | 30 | 67 | 510,000 | | 5 | - | 20 | 0 | 600 | 1,057 | 1,863 | 3,283 | 5,786 | 10,200 | 66 | 0 | 2 | 21,951 |
| Kenya | 562 | 1,710 | 7,000,000 | 1975 | 6 | N | 60 | 31 | 3,000 | 7,432 | 18,413 | 45,618 | 113,017 | 280,000 | 10 | 2 | 4 | 642,092 |
| Kirghizia | 3 | 4 | 1,600 | | 2 | - | 1 | 0 | 5 | 7 | 10 | 14 | 20 | 32 | 33 | 0 | 2 | 98 |
| Kiribati | 22 | 21 | 44,100 | 1982 | 5 | N | 5 | 3 | 600 | 855 | 1,219 | 1,737 | 2,476 | 3,528 | 22 | 14 | 8 | 8,762 |
| Kuwait | 4 | 11 | 175,185 | 1981 | 5 | N | 9 | 5 | 2,500 | 3,072 | 3,775 | 4,639 | 5,701 | 7,007 | 225 | 45 | 4 | 21,029 |
| Laos | 29 | 19 | 32,000 | | 2 | - | 2 | 0 | 50 | 72 | 104 | 151 | 219 | 320 | 6 | 0 | 1 | 1,042 |
| Latvia | 206 | 111 | 490,000 | | 5 | h | 40 | 0 | 1,000 | 1,712 | 2,931 | 5,017 | 8,588 | 14,700 | 19 | 0 | 3 | 16,500 |
| Lebanon | 1,046 | 1,349 | 1,395,000 | 1969 | 5 | N | 15 | 15 | 1,000 | 2,110 | 4,453 | 9,397 | 19,830 | 41,850 | 1 | 1 | 3 | 81,961 |
| Lesotho | 79 | 139 | 806,529 | | 5 | - | 10 | 0 | 1,000 | 1,744 | 3,041 | 5,303 | 9,248 | 16,131 | 12 | 0 | 2 | 50,921 |
| Liberia | 50 | 55 | 150,000 | 1970 | 5 | N | 30 | 0 | 3,000 | 3,854 | 4,951 | 6,361 | 8,172 | 10,499 | 60 | 0 | 7 | 58,894 |
| Libya | 2 | 16 | 45,000 | | 5 | - | 10 | 0 | 100 | 168 | 283 | 476 | 801 | 1,350 | 500 | 0 | 3 | 4,083 |
| Liechtenstein | 11 | 25 | 24,381 | | 2 | - | 2 | 0 | 40 | 66 | 109 | 180 | 297 | 488 | 18 | 0 | 2 | 1,068 |
| Lithuania | 685 | 776 | 3,105,000 | 1986 | 5 | N | 40 | 0 | 1,500 | 2,750 | 5,041 | 9,241 | 16,940 | 31,050 | 5 | 0 | 1 | 38,011 |
| Luxembourg | 275 | 295 | 407,000 | 1973 | 5 | N | 20 | 10 | 400 | 839 | 1,761 | 3,696 | 7,756 | 16,280 | 7 | 3 | 4 | 21,717 |
| Macedonia | 30 | 61 | 70,600 | | 5 | - | 10 | 0 | 100 | 170 | 289 | 491 | 834 | 1,412 | 33 | 0 | 2 | 2,597 |
| Madagascar | 289 | 900 | 3,662,363 | 1973 | 6 | N | 500 | 5 | 50,000 | 61,993 | 76,862 | 95,298 | 118,156 | 146,495 | 173 | 1 | 4 | 695,727 |

Continued opposite

Table 5–6–concluded

| Country | Status of Catholic Church, AD 2000 | | | STATUS OF CATHOLIC CHARISMATIC RENEWAL, AD 2000 | | | | | Renewal participants: | | | | | | Influence of CCR, (as % of cols 2,3,4) | | | CCR's Future Community AD 2025 |
|---|---|---|---|---|---|---|---|---|---|---|---|---|---|---|---|---|---|---|
| Name | Parishes | Priests | Catholics | Begun | Mag | Org | Prayer groups | Priests | Weekly | Monthly | Yearly | Involved | Familial | Community | Prayer groups | Priests | Cath | |
| 1 | 2 | 3 | 4 | 5 | 6 | 7 | 8 | 9 | 10 | 11 | 12 | 13 | 14 | 15 | 16 | 17 | 18 | 19 |
| Malawi | 143 | 396 | 2,697,860 | | 5 | N | 60 | 0 | 6,000 | 10,096 | 16,988 | 28,585 | 48,099 | 80,936 | 41 | 0 | 3 | 299,690 |
| Malaysia | 143 | 212 | 721,889 | | 5 | N | 25 | 0 | 2,000 | 3,411 | 5,818 | 9,924 | 16,927 | 28,875 | 17 | 0 | 4 | 76,688 |
| Maldives | 1 | 0 | 80 | | 2 | - | 1 | 0 | 2 | 2 | 2 | 2 | 2 | 4 | 100 | 0 | 5 | 7 |
| Mali | 42 | 160 | 125,565 | 1982 | 5 | h | 11 | 3 | 1,230 | 1,539 | 1,925 | 2,408 | 3,012 | 3,767 | 26 | 2 | 3 | 18,904 |
| Malta | 80 | 977 | 367,501 | 1975 | 5 | N | 125 | 30 | 9,500 | 14,956 | 23,546 | 37,069 | 58,359 | 91,875 | 156 | 3 | 25 | 116,595 |
| Marshall Islands | 4 | 6 | 5,250 | | 2 | - | 1 | 0 | 10 | 17 | 30 | 52 | 90 | 158 | 25 | 0 | 3 | 680 |
| Martinique | 47 | 64 | 366,000 | | 5 | h | 10 | 0 | 500 | 855 | 1,462 | 2,501 | 4,278 | 7,320 | 21 | 0 | 2 | 12,246 |
| Mauritania | 6 | 7 | 4,216 | | 2 | - | 2 | 0 | 20 | 27 | 36 | 48 | 64 | 85 | 33 | 0 | 2 | 152 |
| Mauritius | 49 | 87 | 310,000 | 1975 | 6 | N | 70 | 0 | 9,000 | 16,493 | 30,224 | 55,387 | 101,499 | 186,000 | 142 | 0 | 60 | 274,986 |
| Mayotte | 0 | 0 | 1,256 | | 2 | - | 1 | 0 | 5 | 8 | 13 | 21 | 33 | 50 | | 0 | 4 | 300 |
| Mexico | 5,364 | 12,990 | 92,770,000 | 1971 | 8 | n | 6,000 | 200 | 400,000 | 750,118 | 1,406,692 | 2,637,962 | 4,946,956 | 9,277,000 | 111 | 2 | 10 | 17,645,977 |
| Micronesia | 23 | 22 | 74,578 | | 5 | - | 4 | 0 | 100 | 172 | 295 | 506 | 869 | 1,492 | 17 | 0 | 2 | 5,106 |
| Moldavia | 9 | 11 | 73,000 | | 5 | - | 7 | 0 | 100 | 171 | 292 | 499 | 853 | 1,460 | 77 | 0 | 2 | 2,653 |
| Monaco | 6 | 25 | 30,000 | | 5 | - | 6 | 0 | 80 | 130 | 211 | 342 | 555 | 900 | 100 | 0 | 3 | 1,519 |
| Mongolia | 1 | 3 | 350 | | 2 | - | 1 | 0 | 2 | 3 | 4 | 6 | 8 | 11 | 100 | 0 | 3 | 36 |
| Montserrat | 1 | 2 | 1,400 | | 2 | - | 1 | 0 | 10 | 12 | 15 | 18 | 22 | 28 | 100 | 0 | 2 | 30 |
| Morocco | 49 | 68 | 22,076 | | 5 | N | 10 | 0 | 70 | 110 | 172 | 270 | 423 | 662 | 20 | 0 | 3 | 960 |
| Mozambique | 285 | 397 | 3,110,000 | | 6 | h | 100 | 10 | 9,000 | 15,218 | 25,732 | 43,510 | 73,571 | 124,400 | 35 | 3 | 4 | 330,322 |
| Myanmar | 255 | 463 | 590,000 | | 5 | h | 10 | 0 | 1,000 | 1,638 | 2,683 | 4,395 | 7,200 | 11,800 | 3 | 0 | 2 | 37,578 |
| Namibia | 66 | 68 | 306,211 | | 5 | N | 15 | 0 | 1,000 | 1,558 | 2,428 | 3,783 | 5,895 | 9,186 | 22 | 0 | 3 | 21,717 |
| Nauru | 1 | 1 | 2,920 | | 2 | - | 1 | 0 | 10 | 14 | 20 | 28 | 40 | 58 | 100 | 0 | 2 | 174 |
| Nepal | 21 | 39 | 7,000 | 1975 | 2 | h | 2 | 0 | 10 | 17 | 29 | 49 | 83 | 139 | 9 | 0 | 2 | 767 |
| Netherlands | 1,696 | 4,387 | 5,450,000 | c1970 | 3 | N | 180 | 40 | 2,500 | 5,319 | 11,317 | 24,078 | 51,229 | 109,000 | 10 | 1 | 2 | 130,000 |
| Netherlands Antilles | 35 | 42 | 150,862 | | 3 | h | 3 | 0 | 200 | 344 | 592 | 1,019 | 1,753 | 3,017 | 8 | 0 | 2 | 5,023 |
| New Caledonia | 28 | 45 | 116,019 | | 2 | h | 2 | 0 | 200 | 327 | 534 | 872 | 1,424 | 2,320 | 7 | 0 | 2 | 5,084 |
| New Zealand | 285 | 643 | 495,000 | 1969 | 3 | N | 140 | 30 | 1,500 | 2,628 | 4,604 | 8,066 | 14,130 | 24,750 | 49 | 5 | 5 | 38,415 |
| Nicaragua | 214 | 400 | 4,320,000 | 1972 | 4 | n | 300 | 40 | 10,000 | 18,488 | 34,181 | 63,194 | 116,833 | 216,000 | 140 | 10 | 5 | 673,177 |
| Niger | 21 | 40 | 19,670 | c1975 | 5 | N | 4 | 0 | 40 | 63 | 99 | 156 | 246 | 393 | 19 | 0 | 2 | 1,488 |
| Nigeria | 1,454 | 3,096 | 13,400,000 | 1972 | 7 | c | 4,000 | 500 | 250,000 | 413,160 | 682,805 | 1,128,432 | 1,864,893 | 3,082,000 | 275 | 16 | 23 | 9,851,424 |
| North Korea | 1 | 0 | 55,000 | | 5 | - | 3 | 0 | 50 | 81 | 131 | 212 | 342 | 550 | 300 | 0 | 1 | 7,333 |
| Northern Cyprus | 0 | 0 | 0 | | 1 | - | 0 | 0 | 0 | 0 | 0 | 0 | 0 | 0 | | 0 | | 0 |
| Northern Mariana Islands | 10 | 35 | 69,300 | | 5 | - | 4 | 0 | 200 | 389 | 756 | 1,469 | 2,855 | 5,544 | 40 | 0 | 8 | 60,386 |
| Norway | 33 | 59 | 45,000 | | 5 | h | 3 | 0 | 50 | 89 | 159 | 283 | 504 | 900 | 9 | 0 | 2 | 1,393 |
| Oman | 4 | 7 | 53,000 | | 5 | N | 6 | 0 | 300 | 522 | 908 | 1,579 | 2,746 | 4,770 | 150 | 0 | 9 | 33,307 |
| Pakistan | 94 | 293 | 1,165,000 | 1972 | 5 | N | 50 | 4 | 2,000 | 4,199 | 8,815 | 18,506 | 38,850 | 81,550 | 53 | 1 | 7 | 304,075 |
| Palau | 2 | 5 | 8,600 | | 5 | - | 4 | 0 | 50 | 77 | 118 | 181 | 278 | 430 | 200 | 0 | 5 | 1,464 |
| Palestine | 0 | 0 | 28,000 | | 5 | - | 4 | 0 | 200 | 332 | 551 | 915 | 1,519 | 2,520 | | 0 | 9 | 8,074 |
| Panama | 175 | 400 | 2,210,000 | 1973 | 6 | n | 100 | 30 | 1,500 | 3,987 | 10,596 | 28,161 | 74,844 | 198,900 | 57 | 8 | 9 | 375,851 |
| Papua New Guinea | 339 | 500 | 1,380,000 | c1970 | 5 | N | 40 | 0 | 3,000 | 5,617 | 10,516 | 19,688 | 36,859 | 69,000 | 11 | 0 | 5 | 223,701 |
| Paraguay | 293 | 667 | 4,950,000 | | 5 | n | 50 | 0 | 4,000 | 7,599 | 14,437 | 27,428 | 52,109 | 99,000 | 17 | 0 | 2 | 377,272 |
| Peru | 1,382 | 2,514 | 24,550,000 | c1970 | 7 | n | 650 | 19 | 19,500 | 51,291 | 134,910 | 354,852 | 933,363 | 2,455,000 | 47 | 1 | 10 | 5,110,875 |
| Philippines | 2,615 | 6,942 | 62,570,000 | 1972 | 9 | N | 500 | 500 | 800,000 | 1,357,687 | 2,304,143 | 3,910,382 | 6,636,344 | 11,262,600 | 19 | 7 | 18 | 23,782,390 |
| Poland | 9,575 | 26,103 | 35,743,059 | c1972 | 7 | N | 711 | 300 | 26,850 | 62,171 | 143,957 | 333,331 | 771,826 | 1,787,153 | 7 | 1 | 5 | 2,255,583 |
| Portugal | 4,358 | 4,380 | 8,970,000 | 1974 | 6 | N | 280 | 120 | 12,000 | 22,353 | 41,637 | 77,558 | 144,468 | 269,100 | 6 | 3 | 3 | 271,495 |
| Puerto Rico | 324 | 791 | 2,900,000 | 1969 | 6 | n | 850 | 75 | 18,000 | 35,298 | 69,220 | 135,741 | 266,189 | 522,000 | 262 | 9 | 18 | 741,951 |
| Qatar | 1 | 1 | 37,578 | | 5 | h | 10 | 0 | 100 | 172 | 296 | 509 | 875 | 1,503 | 1000 | 0 | 4 | 4,170 |
| Reunion | 76 | 106 | 611,000 | | 5 | h | 20 | 0 | 2,000 | 3,450 | 5,951 | 10,266 | 17,709 | 30,550 | 26 | 0 | 5 | 62,727 |
| Romania | 1,735 | 1,565 | 3,237,000 | | 5 | h | 40 | 0 | 2,060 | 3,574 | 6,200 | 10,756 | 18,660 | 32,370 | 2 | 0 | 1 | 39,888 |
| Russia | 274 | 211 | 1,500,000 | | 5 | h | 100 | 5 | 2,000 | 3,728 | 6,949 | 12,953 | 24,144 | 45,000 | 36 | 2 | 3 | 69,011 |
| Rwanda | 129 | 442 | 3,948,000 | c1973 | 6 | N | 600 | 40 | 60,000 | 83,640 | 116,594 | 162,532 | 226,570 | 315,840 | 465 | 9 | 8 | 975,666 |
| Sahara | 2 | 3 | 140 | | 1 | - | 0 | 0 | 0 | 0 | 0 | 0 | 0 | 4 | 0 | 0 | 3 | 4 |
| Saint Helena | 1 | 2 | 40 | | 2 | - | 1 | 0 | 2 | 2 | 2 | 2 | 2 | 4 | 100 | 0 | 10 | 11 |
| Saint Kitts & Nevis | 4 | 4 | 4,850 | | 2 | - | 1 | 0 | 10 | 17 | 29 | 50 | 85 | 146 | 25 | 0 | 3 | 141 |
| Saint Lucia | 23 | 36 | 116,000 | c1973 | 4 | n | 20 | 0 | 200 | 327 | 534 | 872 | 1,424 | 2,320 | 86 | 0 | 2 | 4,904 |
| Saint Pierre & Miquelon | 3 | 2 | 6,465 | | 2 | - | 1 | 0 | 10 | 17 | 28 | 47 | 78 | 129 | 33 | 0 | 2 | 248 |
| Saint Vincent | 6 | 9 | 10,000 | c1973 | 2 | - | 1 | 0 | 20 | 32 | 51 | 81 | 128 | 200 | 16 | 0 | 2 | 293 |
| Samoa | 26 | 42 | 39,500 | | 5 | - | 10 | 0 | 100 | 164 | 269 | 441 | 723 | 1,185 | 38 | 0 | 3 | 2,877 |
| San Marino | 12 | 27 | 23,509 | | 2 | - | 2 | 0 | 40 | 65 | 106 | 174 | 285 | 470 | 16 | 0 | 2 | 871 |
| Sao Tome & Principe | 12 | 8 | 110,553 | | 5 | - | 15 | 0 | 200 | 351 | 615 | 1,078 | 1,890 | 3,316 | 125 | 0 | 3 | 8,075 |
| Saudi Arabia | 4 | 6 | 625,875 | | 5 | - | 150 | 5 | 1,500 | 2,634 | 4,625 | 8,121 | 14,259 | 25,035 | 3750 | 83 | 4 | 154,506 |
| Senegal | 89 | 332 | 441,031 | 1974 | 5 | N | 44 | 25 | 1,000 | 1,775 | 3,151 | 5,594 | 9,932 | 17,641 | 49 | 8 | 4 | 76,754 |
| Seychelles | 17 | 14 | 70,000 | | 5 | - | 20 | 0 | 200 | 320 | 512 | 820 | 1,312 | 2,101 | 117 | 0 | 3 | 4,355 |
| Sierra Leone | 37 | 121 | 169,140 | c1973 | 3 | h | 4 | 0 | 100 | 202 | 409 | 827 | 1,672 | 3,383 | 10 | 0 | 2 | 20,172 |
| Singapore | 30 | 123 | 143,000 | 1975 | 5 | N | 24 | 20 | 1,500 | 1,960 | 2,562 | 3,348 | 4,376 | 5,720 | 80 | 16 | 4 | 14,958 |
| Slovakia | 1,410 | 2,092 | 3,660,186 | | 6 | h | 500 | 20 | 10,000 | 17,105 | 29,257 | 50,043 | 85,596 | 146,407 | 35 | 1 | 4 | 180,487 |
| Slovenia | 799 | 1,117 | 1,659,006 | 1975 | 5 | h | 25 | 0 | 3,000 | 4,851 | 7,845 | 12,687 | 20,517 | 33,180 | 3 | 0 | 2 | 39,760 |
| Solomon Islands | 27 | 54 | 48,000 | | 5 | - | 3 | 0 | 100 | 170 | 290 | 494 | 842 | 1,440 | 11 | 0 | 3 | 5,443 |
| Somalia | 1 | 4 | 200 | | 2 | - | 1 | 0 | 30 | 22 | 16 | 12 | 9 | 6 | 100 | 0 | 3 | 16 |
| Somaliland | 1 | 0 | 31 | | 1 | - | 0 | 0 | 0 | 0 | 0 | 0 | 0 | 1 | 0 | 0 | 3 | 6 |
| South Africa | 744 | 1,169 | 3,350,000 | 1971 | 6 | N | 185 | 14 | 2,600 | 5,720 | 12,584 | 27,685 | 60,908 | 134,000 | 24 | 1 | 4 | 211,698 |
| South Korea | 985 | 2,232 | 3,700,000 | 1970 | 6 | h | 200 | 100 | 10,000 | 22,328 | 49,855 | 111,318 | 248,556 | 555,000 | 20 | 4 | 15 | 898,100 |
| Spain | 22,061 | 28,722 | 38,080,000 | c1970 | 6 | N | 360 | 30 | 25,000 | 49,511 | 98,053 | 194,186 | 384,570 | 761,600 | 1 | 0 | 2 | 895,483 |
| Spanish North Africa | 1 | 0 | 102,874 | | 5 | - | 5 | 0 | 200 | 319 | 508 | 810 | 1,291 | 2,057 | 500 | 0 | 2 | 3,510 |
| Sri Lanka | 374 | 850 | 1,260,000 | 1971 | 5 | N | 325 | 50 | 15,000 | 16,640 | 18,459 | 20,477 | 22,716 | 25,200 | 86 | 6 | 2 | 46,968 |
| Sudan | 103 | 273 | 3,148,593 | | 5 | N | 30 | 0 | 3,000 | 5,515 | 10,138 | 18,636 | 34,258 | 62,972 | 29 | 0 | 2 | 313,559 |
| Suriname | 30 | 22 | 93,000 | | 5 | N | 4 | 0 | 100 | 179 | 321 | 576 | 1,034 | 1,860 | 13 | 0 | 2 | 3,675 |
| Swaziland | 15 | 33 | 54,000 | | 5 | h | 4 | 0 | 100 | 161 | 259 | 417 | 671 | 1,080 | 26 | 0 | 2 | 3,375 |
| Sweden | 41 | 127 | 175,000 | 1972 | 5 | N | 15 | 8 | 200 | 355 | 629 | 1,115 | 1,976 | 3,500 | 36 | 6 | 2 | 6,260 |
| Switzerland | 1,671 | 3,433 | 3,260,000 | 1972 | 5 | N | 332 | 44 | 5,500 | 9,019 | 14,789 | 24,250 | 39,764 | 65,200 | 19 | 1 | 2 | 78,263 |
| Syria | 198 | 198 | 325,000 | | 5 | h | 20 | 0 | 500 | 835 | 1,395 | 2,330 | 3,892 | 6,501 | 10 | 0 | 2 | 20,236 |
| Taiwan | 447 | 700 | 300,000 | 1969 | 4 | N | 20 | 100 | 600 | 1,031 | 1,772 | 3,046 | 5,235 | 9,000 | 4 | 14 | 3 | 12,254 |
| Tajikistan | 1 | 2 | 4,412 | | 2 | - | 1 | 0 | 10 | 15 | 23 | 36 | 56 | 88 | 100 | 0 | 2 | 170 |
| Tanzania | 780 | 2,007 | 8,283,000 | 1981 | 6 | N | 83 | 26 | 3,170 | 6,993 | 15,427 | 34,034 | 75,084 | 165,660 | 10 | 1 | 2 | 811,697 |
| Thailand | 312 | 599 | 255,000 | c1973 | 5 | N | 20 | 0 | 1,000 | 1,664 | 2,769 | 4,607 | 7,665 | 12,750 | 6 | 0 | 5 | 20,267 |
| Timor | 31 | 100 | 796,000 | | 5 | - | 30 | 0 | 2,000 | 3,284 | 5,393 | 8,856 | 14,543 | 23,881 | 96 | 0 | 3 | 66,483 |
| Togo | 121 | 324 | 1,122,995 | 1976 | 6 | N | 150 | 106 | 15,000 | 22,436 | 33,559 | 50,196 | 75,080 | 112,300 | 123 | 33 | 10 | 630,466 |
| Tonga | 13 | 24 | 13,900 | | 2 | - | 1 | 0 | 20 | 34 | 58 | 98 | 166 | 278 | 7 | 0 | 2 | 346 |
| Trinidad & Tobago | 62 | 116 | 397,865 | 1971 | 3 | n | 20 | 0 | 1,000 | 1,642 | 2,696 | 4,427 | 7,269 | 11,936 | 32 | 0 | 3 | 15,799 |
| Tunisia | 13 | 36 | 19,000 | | 2 | h | 1 | 1 | 10 | 22 | 49 | 110 | 247 | 570 | 7 | 3 | 3 | 760 |
| Turkey | 51 | 65 | 30,500 | | 5 | h | 3 | 0 | 50 | 82 | 135 | 223 | 368 | 610 | 5 | 0 | 2 | 1,145 |
| Turkmenistan | 1 | 1 | 2,100 | | 2 | - | 1 | 0 | 10 | 13 | 17 | 23 | 31 | 42 | 100 | 0 | 2 | 115 |
| Turks & Caicos Islands | 2 | 1 | 750 | | 2 | - | 1 | 0 | 10 | 12 | 14 | 16 | 19 | 22 | 50 | 0 | 3 | 107 |
| Tuvalu | 1 | 1 | 95 | | 2 | - | 1 | 0 | 2 | 2 | 2 | 2 | 2 | 3 | 100 | 0 | 3 | 9 |
| Uganda | 374 | 1,358 | 9,130,000 | 1973 | 7 | N | 400 | 158 | 40,000 | 77,549 | 150,347 | 291,483 | 565,108 | 1,095,600 | 106 | 12 | 12 | 5,663,592 |
| Ukraine | 3,108 | 2,035 | 5,578,901 | | 6 | h | 200 | 50 | 8,000 | 15,567 | 30,291 | 58,941 | 114,689 | 223,156 | 6 | 2 | 4 | 258,117 |
| United Arab Emirates | 5 | 15 | 124,345 | | 5 | h | 3 | 0 | 100 | 206 | 425 | 876 | 1,807 | 3,730 | 60 | 0 | 3 | 9,722 |
| USA | 19,634 | 50,693 | 58,000,000 | 1967 | 3 | Nn | 4,800 | 2,000 | 200,000 | 425,332 | 904,536 | 1,923,640 | 4,090,926 | 8,700,000 | 24 | 4 | 15 | 13,515,288 |
| Uruguay | 229 | 520 | 2,608,000 | | 6 | n | 50 | 0 | 2,000 | 5,066 | 12,833 | 32,509 | 82,353 | 208,640 | 21 | 0 | 8 | 383,421 |
| Uzbekistan | 1 | 4 | 40,000 | | 5 | - | 3 | 0 | 40 | 63 | 100 | 158 | 250 | 400 | 300 | 0 | 1 | 466 |
| Vanuatu | 16 | 29 | 29,400 | | 5 | - | 4 | 0 | 40 | 68 | 116 | 199 | 341 | 588 | 25 | 0 | 2 | 2,043 |
| Venezuela | 1,116 | 2,406 | 22,400,000 | c1969 | 7 | n | 3,000 | 20 | 60,000 | 132,372 | 292,039 | 644,297 | 1,421,448 | 3,136,000 | 268 | 1 | 14 | 7,181,427 |
| Viet Nam | 2,154 | 2,239 | 5,320,822 | 1975 | 6 | h | 30 | 5 | 750 | 2,020 | 5,442 | 14,660 | 39,493 | 106,417 | 1 | 0 | 2 | 317,543 |
| Virgin Islands of the US | 8 | 14 | 29,000 | c1974 | 3 | n | 5 | 0 | 100 | 154 | 237 | 365 | 563 | 870 | 62 | 0 | 3 | 844 |
| Wallis & Futuna Islands | 5 | 12 | 13,936 | | 2 | - | 2 | 0 | 20 | 34 | 58 | 98 | 166 | 278 | 40 | 0 | 2 | 714 |
| Yemen | 4 | 4 | 6,000 | | 2 | - | 1 | 0 | 10 | 18 | 32 | 57 | 102 | 180 | 25 | 0 | 3 | 1,078 |
| Yugoslavia | 238 | 199 | 1,074,800 | 1975 | 5 | - | 20 | 2 | 1,000 | 1,847 | 3,411 | 6,300 | 11,636 | 21,497 | 8 | 1 | 2 | 40,000 |
| Zambia | 238 | 576 | 3,070,000 | 1973 | 5 | N | 160 | 20 | 11,000 | 16,825 | 25,735 | 39,364 | 60,211 | 92,100 | 67 | 3 | 3 | 325,172 |
| Zimbabwe | 142 | 420 | 1,120,000 | 1974 | 5 | N | 16 | 10 | 700 | 1,518 | 3,292 | 7,140 | 15,486 | 33,600 | 11 | 2 | 3 | 74,418 |
| 11 minicountries | 5 | 5 | 3,508 | | 4 | | 29 | 61 | 555 | 441 | 359 | 305 | 271 | 263 | 580 | | 7 | 361 |
| Africa | 10,048 | 24,679 | 120,392,235 | 1970 | | | 11,506 | 1,271 | 876,272 | 1,314,828 | 2,027,458 | 3,214,062 | 5,237,717 | 8,771,431 | 114 | 5 | 7 | 33,567,862 |
| Antarctica | 10 | 3 | 1,400 | 1970 | | | 2 | 0 | 10 | 20 | 30 | 40 | 50 | 100 | 20 | 0 | 7 | 200 |
| Asia | 36,264 | 42,922 | 110,481,491 | 1969 | | | 13,631 | 1,141 | 1,070,849 | 1,833,526 | 3,152,626 | 5,442,173 | 9,432,542 | 16,421,950 | 37 | 3 | 15 | 35,826,620 |
| Europe | 135,678 | 215,119 | 286,506,016 | 1969 | | | 9,936 | 2,629 | 280,647 | 566,538 | 1,163,286 | 2,426,620 | 5,136,644 | 11,020,755 | 7 | 1 | 4 | 13,317,506 |
| Latin America | 27,747 | 58,861 | 460,804,001 | 1967 | | | 102,873 | 2,061 | 10,905,935 | 15,093,368 | 21,331,403 | 31,001,335 | 46,711,912 | 73,604,186 | 370 | 4 | 16 | 139,435,238 |
| Northern America | 24,804 | 61,221 | 71,034,904 | 1967 | | | 5,666 | 2,175 | 220,771 | 470,772 | 1,003,957 | 2,141,192 | 4,567,005 | 9,741,878 | 22 | 4 | 14 | 15,197,392 |
| Oceania | 2,391 | 5,148 | 8,227,767 | 1969 | | | 868 | 193 | 11,340 | 21,334 | 41,284 | 82,107 | 167,579 | 350,209 | 36 | 4 | 4 | 790,683 |
| **World A (see line below)** | **1,223** | **2,513** | **6,798,452** | **1972** | | | **402** | **38** | **11,998** | **21,154** | **37,947** | **69,063** | **127,267** | **237,159** | **32** | **2** | **3** | **1,016,259** |
| **World B** | **42,500** | **50,445** | **100,135,588** | **1969** | | | **19,756** | **1,638** | **723,900** | **1,199,366** | **2,020,745** | **3,458,746** | **6,012,153** | **10,617,071** | **46** | **3** | **11** | **29,768,166** |
| **World C** | **193,209** | **354,995** | **950,513,774** | **1967** | | | **124,324** | **7,794** | **12,629,926** | **18,079,846** | **26,661,322** | **40,779,680** | **65,113,979** | **109,056,279** | **64** | **2** | **11** | **207,350,876** |
| **GLOBAL TOTAL** | **236,932** | **407,953** | **1,057,447,814** | **1967** | | | **144,482** | **9,470** | **13,365,824** | **19,300,366** | **28,720,014** | **44,307,489** | **71,253,399** | **119,910,509** | **60** | **2** | **11** | **238,135,301** |

Note on Worlds A, B, C: World A = unevangelized countries, World B = evangelized non-Christian countries, World C = Christian countries

### 140 million Catholic Charismatics

In addition to these 119 million Charismatics alive today, one must remember those who have died. Today's death rate among Charismatics is 1.2 million a year (3,300 every day), amounting to 20 million since the Renewal began. Since 1967, therefore, the total of all Catholics who have become Charismatics (which means persons baptized in the Holy Spirit) is around 140 million Charismatics.

## SOME OVERALL OBSERVATIONS

### CCR's status in 238 countries

All these columns of data portray numerous aspects of the Renewal. The short summary listing in Table 5–7 divides all the countries of the world by 9 codes or categories of the AD 2000 size of each country's Charismatic community.

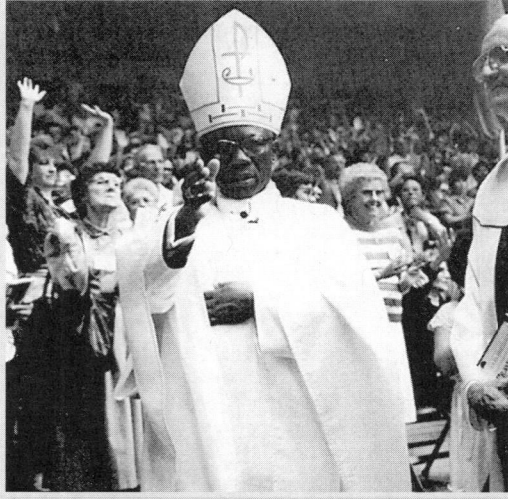

Cardinal Francis Arinze, a Nigerian, speaks at 1988 National CCR Conference, USA. Worldwide, 450 bishops are Charismatics.

At the 1990 International Priests Retreat, Mother Teresa greets 9,000 priests and addresses them on Renewal in Jesus.

| Table 5–7. | Magnitude of the Catholic Charismatic Renewal in 238 countries, AD 2000. | |
|---|---|---|
| Code | Country's CCR status in AD 2000 | Countries |
| 9. | Over 10 million Charismatics each and growing | 3 |
| 8. | Over 5 million Charismatics each and growing | 4 |
| 7. | Over 1 million Charismatics each and growing | 15 |
| 6. | Over 100,000 Charismatics each and growing | 61 |
| 5. | Under 100,000 but expanding fast | 101 |
| 4. | Numbers static since 1975 | 7 |
| 3. | Numbers in marked decline, 1975-2000 | 12 |
| 2. | Few Charismatics, under 3 prayer groups | 54 |
| 1. | No Charismatics | 3 |
| | Duplicates (status 6 includes 9, 8, 7) | -22 |
| | Total countries in world | 238 |

### Indicators of CCR's influence

Columns 16 to 18 of Table 5–6 now give 3 different numerical indicators of the extent to which the Renewal has penetrated the whole Catholic Church, expressed as a percentage. Column 16 shows *prayer groups* as percent of all parishes (from column 2). Column 17 gives *priests* in Renewal as a percentage of all priests (column 9 divided by column 3, x 100). Column 18 shows *Charismatics* (column 15) divided by all Catholics, x 100. Column 18 thus shows that the CCR is predominantly a lay movement, its percentages growing steadily from a world total of 1% of all Catholics in 1973 to 11.3% by AD 2000. In country after country this is consistently larger than the involvement of priests, which rose rapidly in the early years but which has remained for some years at 2% worldwide.

A final column, 19, projects current trends a generation into the *future* and estimates the likely size the Renewal may reach by AD 2025: 240 million live Charismatics, or, with the 70 million who will have died from 1967-2025, a total of 310 million baptized in the Spirit.

### Has the CCR peaked?

It is often heard in European and North American circles that the Renewal has passed its peak and is in decline. The data show that this has been the case in some 12 Western countries: Australia, Germany, Netherlands, New Zealand, USA, and 6 smaller Caribbean countries. The clearest example is the USA where participation rose rapidly to 1,613 prayer groups by 1973 (with 5% of all priests attending), to 6,500 by 1985, then to its 1987 level of a million Catholics attending 10,500 prayer groups in 12 major languages; but which has since dropped to 200,000 in 4,800 prayer groups. This decline contrasts with the explosive spreading of Renewal across Latin America, Western Africa, Southern Africa, India, the Philippines and a large number of other Third World countries.

### The 'revolving door' syndrome

After 1973 it began to be noticed that large numbers of active Charismatics ceased to be attenders after 3 or 4 years. Also called the 'alumni' of the Renewal, or Postcharismatics, most still regard themselves as Charismatics and are often found to be active in other less visible areas of the church's mission.

### The ecumenical context

It should be noted that the CCR has from its origins had close relations, fellowship, and cooperation with mainline Pentecostal denominations within Protestantism, also with Anglican and Orthodox Charismatics, also with the 220 million Independent Neocharismatics with their huge megachurches in Argentina, Brazil, Colombia, India, Indonesia, Mexico, Nigeria, Philippines, South Africa, et alia.

### A summary picture of CCR expansion

This whole history is set out in brief in Global Map 5-2 below. These figures give the number of Catholic Charismatics on each continent for the 3 years 1970, 1980, and AD 2000.

## BIBLIOGRAPHY

The best overall source of information on the Renewal is the bimonthly *ICCRS Newsletter* (published from the Vatican), now in its 26th annual volume. The most professional study is by an anthropologist, T. J. Csordas, *Language, charisma, and creativity: the ritual life of a religious movement* (University of California Press, 1997). The most readable account of the CCR's part in the entire context of the 20th-century Pentecostal/Charismatic Renewal in the Holy Spirit is by theologian Harvey Cox, *Fire from Heaven: the rise of Pentecostal spirituality and the re-shaping of religion in the 21st century* (Addison-Wesley, 1995).

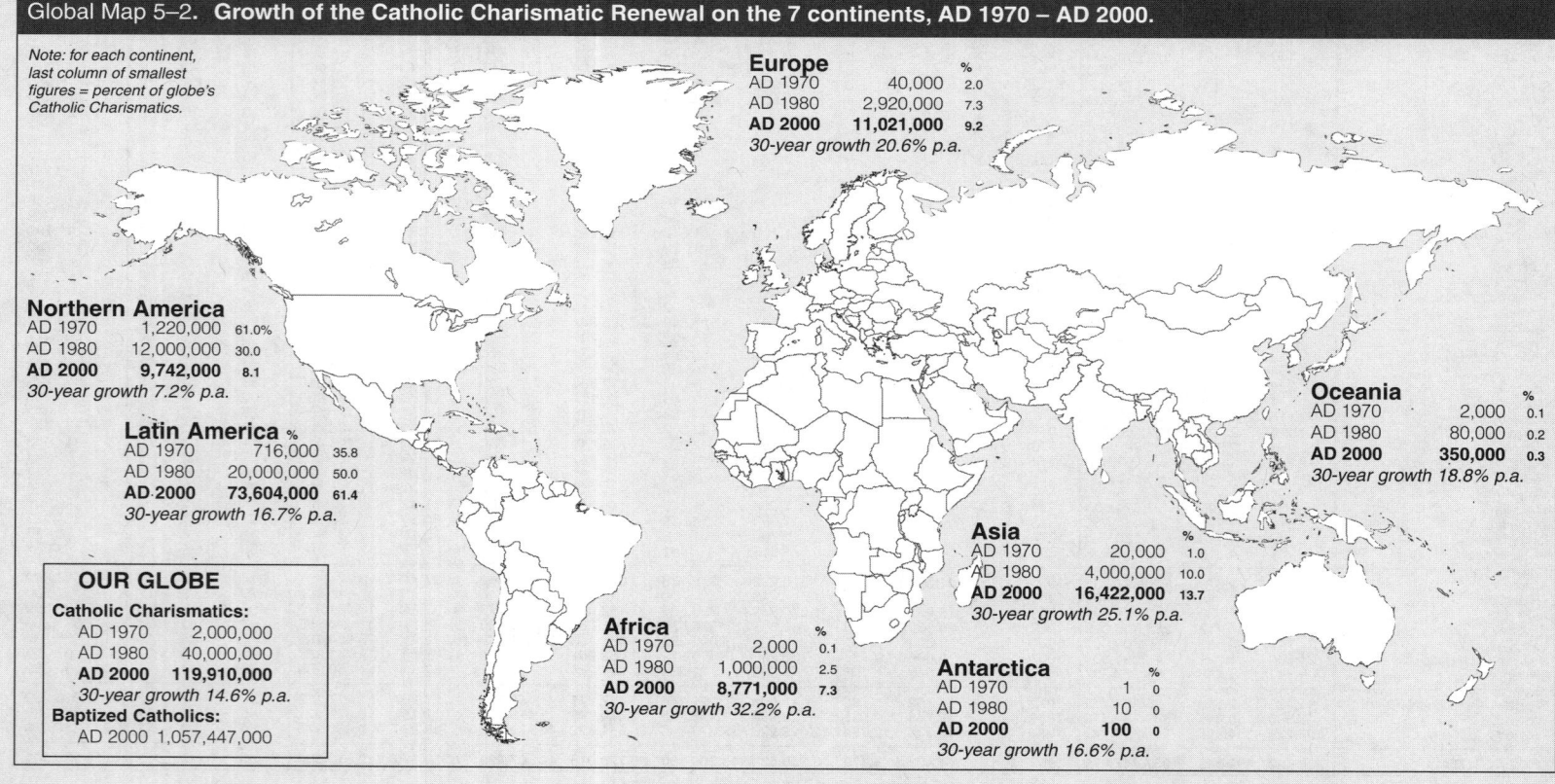

**Global Map 5–2.** Growth of the Catholic Charismatic Renewal on the 7 continents, AD 1970 – AD 2000.

Note: for each continent, last column of smallest figures = percent of globe's Catholic Charismatics.

**Europe**
| | | % |
|---|---|---|
| AD 1970 | 40,000 | 2.0 |
| AD 1980 | 2,920,000 | 7.3 |
| **AD 2000** | **11,021,000** | 9.2 |

*30-year growth 20.6% p.a.*

**Northern America**
| | | |
|---|---|---|
| AD 1970 | 1,220,000 | 61.0% |
| AD 1980 | 12,000,000 | 30.0 |
| **AD 2000** | **9,742,000** | 8.1 |

*30-year growth 7.2% p.a.*

**Latin America** %
| | | |
|---|---|---|
| AD 1970 | 716,000 | 35.8 |
| AD 1980 | 20,000,000 | 50.0 |
| **AD 2000** | **73,604,000** | 61.4 |

*30-year growth 16.7% p.a.*

**Oceania**
| | | % |
|---|---|---|
| AD 1970 | 2,000 | 0.1 |
| AD 1980 | 80,000 | 0.2 |
| **AD 2000** | **350,000** | 0.3 |

*30-year growth 18.8% p.a.*

**Asia**
| | | |
|---|---|---|
| AD 1970 | 20,000 | 1.0 |
| AD 1980 | 4,000,000 | 10.0 |
| **AD 2000** | **16,422,000** | 13.7 |

*30-year growth 25.1% p.a.*

**Africa**
| | | % |
|---|---|---|
| AD 1970 | 2,000 | 0.1 |
| AD 1980 | 1,000,000 | 2.5 |
| **AD 2000** | **8,771,000** | 7.3 |

*30-year growth 32.2% p.a.*

**Antarctica**
| | | % |
|---|---|---|
| AD 1970 | 1 | 0 |
| AD 1980 | 10 | 0 |
| **AD 2000** | **100** | 0 |

*30-year growth 16.6% p.a.*

**OUR GLOBE**

**Catholic Charismatics:**
| | |
|---|---|
| AD 1970 | 2,000,000 |
| AD 1980 | 40,000,000 |
| **AD 2000** | **119,910,000** |

*30-year growth 14.6% p.a.*

**Baptized Catholics:**
| | |
|---|---|
| AD 2000 | 1,057,447,000 |

# MEGATYPOLOGY 3:
*EVANGELICAL GEORENEWAL*

This megatypology defines and enumerates 2 distinct, different, but overlapping usages. These are distinguished in regular usage, both professional and popular, by spelling the first letter 'E' with either a capital letter or a lowercase letter. In brief, these describe 2 categories defined by (1) self-identification, or (2) personal practice of Christ's evangel, evangelism, and mission. These 2 usages can be expanded as follows.

(1) *Evangelicals* (with capital 'E') is a core historical term covering all persons who self-identify themselves by this term, either as members of specifically Evangelical denominations that are members of international or national Evangelical councils or alliances, or as individuals professing this self-identification though members of non-Evangelical denominations;

(2) *evangelicals* (with lowercase 'e') by contrast is a wider, more empirical term covering all Christians of evangelical conviction, however humble or unknown, of any and all cultures, whose lives center on Jesus, his evangel, evangelism, evangelizing, and evangelization, namely all who are attempting to practice obedience to Christ's command to follow him in the evangelical mandate to engage in mission, usu-ally expressed as awareness of and obedience to the Great Commission.

These 2 usages can now be further expanded in detail.

### 1. Definition of 'Evangelicals' and 'Evangelicalism'
In the first instance these terms in English are historical ones derived from 17th-century Puritanism and 18th-century Pietism, the 18th-century Evangelical Revival in Britain and America under John Wesley and George Whitefield, the 19th-century Great Awakenings in North America, which have produced all subsequent similar movements and organizations across the world with any claim to be historically de-

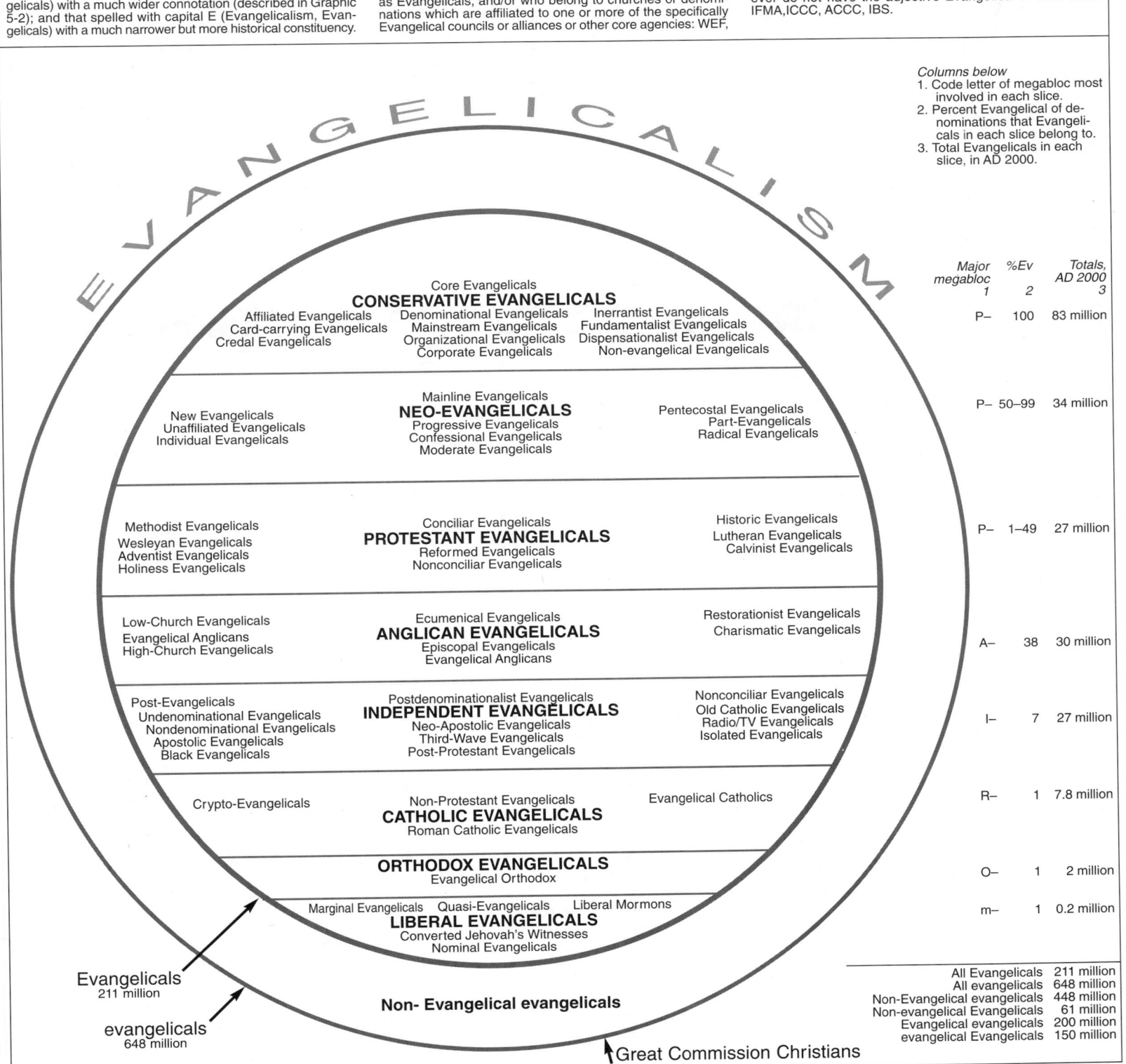

Graphic 5–3. Composition, definitions, and enumeration of evangelicalism, evangelicals, 69 varieties of Evangelicalism, and self-identified Evangelicals, AD 2000.

rived from them. Key initial dates were: 1725 Great Awakening in New England; 1739 conversion of John Wesley at Oxford; 1846 founding of the Evangelical Alliance in London, later the World's Evangelical Alliance; 1857 Evangelical Awakening in USA (under C.G. Finney); 1859 Second Evangelical Awakening in Britain; et alia. The crystalization of the earliest Evangelicals is well described by the title of Susan O'Brien's 1986 article 'A transatlantic community of Saints: the Great Awakening and the first Evangelical network, 1735-1755'. By AD 2000 organized specifically-Evangelical councils had expanded to 160 national, regional, continental, or global councils or alliances of churches or missions, all incorporating as key word the English adjective 'Evangelical'. Most of these are recorded in *WCE* Part 4 "Countries" at the end of each country's Country Table 2. Their member denominations are recorded in each table's column 4 'Councils'.

### Measuring Evangelicals and Evangelicalism

Vast numbers of Christians identify themselves by more than the one simple term 'Christians'. There are megabloc labels (Catholic, Protestant, Orthodox, Independent), confessional labels (Baptist, Lutheran, Methodist, Presbyterian), denominational labels (Southern Baptist, United Methodist), theological labels (Fundamentalist, Conservative, Moderate, Liberal), churchmanship labels (High Church, Low Church), experiential labels (Evangelical, Charismatic), and so on. The term 'Evangelicals' here applies not only to all Christians who belong to specifically Evangelical denominations as described above, but also to all Christians in non-Evangelical denominations who self-identify with the term by applying it regularly to themselves, used either in first place ('We are Evangelicals') or in a first batch of such adjectives ('I am a Charismatic Anglican Conservative Evangelical').

An added complication is that there are at least 68 types or subcategories of Evangelicals. These are set out here in Graphic 5–3. In this instance the circle represents, not the whole world, but the world of all Evangelicals. At the top are the core historic Evangelical organizations and their members. The 7 subsequent layers below then show successively less Evangelical layers scattered across the 6 megablocs forming the entirety of the Christian world.

Quantifying Evangelicals therefore combines 2 components. First, there are what we might call (1) corporate Evangelicals, namely all church members of all denominations which are members of or affiliated to the recognized Evangelical councils or alliances at world, continental, regional, or national level: specifically, WEF, EAE, EAGB, NAE, EMA, EFMA, etc. Most of these councils each have in their name the word 'Evangelical' (or Evangélique, Evangelico, etc), although a small handful of clearly Evangelical bodies do not (e.g. IFMA, ICCC, ACCC, IBS, etc). All these denominations can be identified in the *World Christian database* for Country Tables 2 by the figure 100% entered in the column for percentage Evangelical. Second, to this total are added (2) self-styled Evangelical individuals in non-Evangelical denominations that are unconnected with the recognized Evangelical bodies. Numbers are determined by multiplying the total affiliated adherents of every denomination, as listed in the database for Country Tables 2, by its percentage of Evangelicals also listed there.

We turn now to the second usage or variety, namely evangelicalism.

### 2. Definition of 'evangelicals' and 'evangelicalism'

a. *Etymology*. The renewal movement now known as evangelicalism was long seen as identical with Evangelicalism as defined above. With its lowercase 'e' its usage became widespread after World War II to denote a somewhat broader category of 'persons of evangelical conviction' many of whom did not dif-

ferentiate or distance themselves from their Anglican, Catholic, Protestant, or Orthodox identity by calling themselves by the label Evangelicals.

The term evangelicalism derives its actual name initially from its special emphasis on the 2 key biblical concepts gospel (*evangelion* in the Greek NT, in English usually gospel, evangel, or Good News) and evangelism (*evangelismos*, the spreading of the gospel, from the Greek OT and NT verb *euangelizo*). The shortest core meaning of the noun 'evangelicals' is therefore those Christians who constantly place at the center of their lives evangel and evangelism—the good news about Jesus and the urgency of spreading it.

Often, however, evangelicalism has been defined in terms of holding a large number of additional doctrines. Thus for many involved participants, evangelicals are Christians holding several or all of the following beliefs, often called the 5, 7, 9, 15, 20 or more 'Fundamentals' of the faith: the deity of Christ, his Virgin birth, his sinlessness, his miracles, his atonement on the Cross, his resurrection, the Holy Trinity, the Holy Spirit as Sanctifier, the total depravity of humankind, personal conversion, full plenary inspiration of the Bible (and for many, its infallibility or inerrancy), holiness of life, religious liberty, ministry and priesthood of all believers, world mission, world evangelization, the Second Coming, the rapture, the Great Tribulation, the Millennium, the final resurrection, the Last Judgment, and the New Jerusalem.

Most of the above beliefs, however, are held by the great majority of all Christians whether Anglican, Catholic, Protestant, Orthodox, or Independent, hence they cannot be said adequately to differentiate evangelicals from other Christians. The best differentia are contained in a number of other refinements of definitions in wide use. Extending the first definition given in (a) above, the list below describes 5 progressively more detailed definitions of the differentia of evangelicalism as widely understood today.

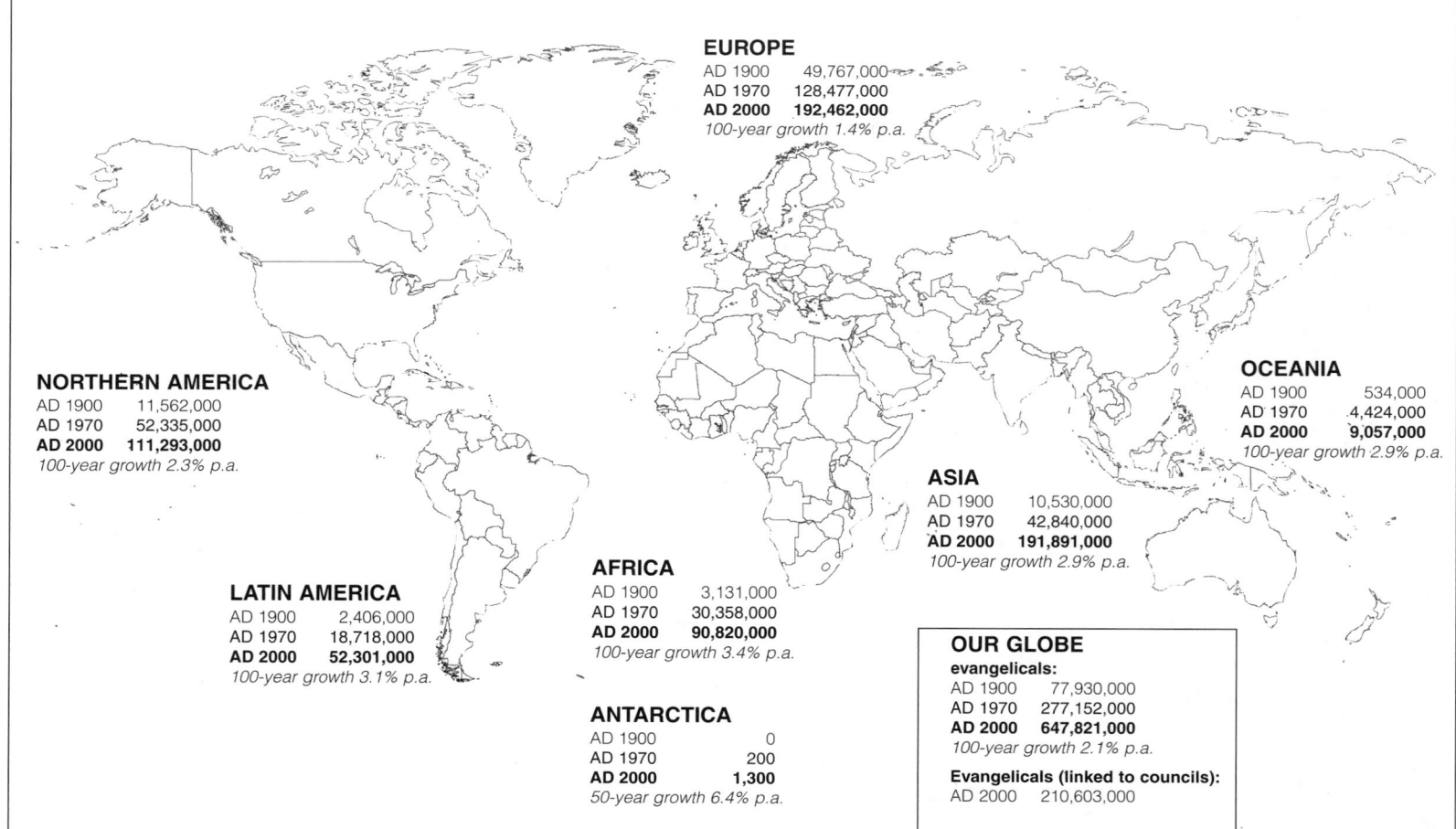

### Global Map 5–3. Growth of evangelicals on the world's 7 continents, AD 1900–AD 2000.

The map shows the growth in numbers of evangelicals (defined as all persons of evangelical conviction who are active in spreading the gospel) for the 3 years AD 1900 (light type), AD 1970 (medium type), and AD 2000 (bold type). Under each set of figures is given the exponential growth rate p.a. (per annum, per year) over the 100-year period shown. Our globe's 7 continents, their 238 countries and their boundaries are as recognized in AD 2000 by the United Nations. Under the global totals of evangelicals is a line 'Evangelicals (linked to councils)' which enumerates (a) all members of denominations affiliated to specifically Evangelical alliances, fellowships, and councils, to which is added (b) all persons in non-Evangelical denominations who identify themselves individually as Evangelicals. Note also: evangelicals = Great Commission Christians.

**EUROPE**
| | |
|---|---|
| AD 1900 | 49,767,000 |
| AD 1970 | 128,477,000 |
| **AD 2000** | **192,462,000** |

*100-year growth 1.4% p.a.*

**NORTHERN AMERICA**
| | |
|---|---|
| AD 1900 | 11,562,000 |
| AD 1970 | 52,335,000 |
| **AD 2000** | **111,293,000** |

*100-year growth 2.3% p.a.*

**OCEANIA**
| | |
|---|---|
| AD 1900 | 534,000 |
| AD 1970 | 4,424,000 |
| **AD 2000** | **9,057,000** |

*100-year growth 2.9% p.a.*

**ASIA**
| | |
|---|---|
| AD 1900 | 10,530,000 |
| AD 1970 | 42,840,000 |
| **AD 2000** | **191,891,000** |

*100-year growth 2.9% p.a.*

**LATIN AMERICA**
| | |
|---|---|
| AD 1900 | 2,406,000 |
| AD 1970 | 18,718,000 |
| **AD 2000** | **52,301,000** |

*100-year growth 3.1% p.a.*

**AFRICA**
| | |
|---|---|
| AD 1900 | 3,131,000 |
| AD 1970 | 30,358,000 |
| **AD 2000** | **90,820,000** |

*100-year growth 3.4% p.a.*

**ANTARCTICA**
| | |
|---|---|
| AD 1900 | 0 |
| AD 1970 | 200 |
| **AD 2000** | **1,300** |

*50-year growth 6.4% p.a.*

**OUR GLOBE**
**evangelicals:**
| | |
|---|---|
| AD 1900 | 77,930,000 |
| AD 1970 | 277,152,000 |
| **AD 2000** | **647,821,000** |

*100-year growth 2.1% p.a.*

**Evangelicals (linked to councils):**
| | |
|---|---|
| AD 2000 | 210,603,000 |

b. *Obedience to Christ*. Basically, evangelicals are defined as believers in Christ who are attempting to obey Jesus Christ as Lord, and in particular are in some measure obeying his final command to his disciples to propagate the evangel as embodied in the Great Commission; evangelicals can thus be alternatively labeled 'Great Commission Christians'. An example from America illustrates this. The large mainline body called the Evangelical Lutheran Church of America (ELCA) does not belong to WEF, NAE, or any other specifically Evangelical councils, although 18% of its members individually call themselves Evangelicals. For many of the latter this is not a satisfactory situation, so a large proportion of them have organized an overtly Evangelical body within the ELCA called Great Commission Network. Similar bodies within other large mainline Protestant bodies in the USA are: Presbyterians United for Biblical Concern (PCUSA et alia), and Confessing Movement within the UCC and United Methodist Church.

c. *Christ's mission*. A parallel briefest definition is: evangelicals are those believers in Jesus Christ who involve themselves in his mission to spread the evangel throughout the world.

d. *Seven key words*. The central meaning of evangelicalism can be expanded into a 7-fold definition centering on these 7 key words: Jesus, gospel, Bible, witness, evangelism, mission, Advent.

e. *A single-sentence definition*. These 7 key words can be expanded into a single sentence thus: evangelicals are believers centered on the person of **Jesus** as Lord and obedient to his Great Commission, committed to the evangel (the **gospel**), as set forth in the **Bible**, by means of their day-to-day personal **witness** to Christ, their organized **evangelism**, and their involvement in his **mission** to the world, looking and working toward his second and final **Advent.**

f. *A detailed definition*. These 7 key components of evangelicalism can be still further expounded as follows.

1. *Jesus.* The person of Christ the divine Son of God within the Holy Trinity is at the center of all evangelical faith and life. Jesus is acknowledged by evangelicals as Savior, Sanctifier, Baptizer in the Holy Spirit, Healer, and Returning King. These 5 titles can be expanded as he is portrayed in the 6 accounts of his Great Commission, as the following 5-fold listing shows: *Savior* ('Anyone who believes in me and is baptized will be saved', Mark 16:16, CEV; 'his sacred and everlasting message of how people can be saved forever', Mark 16:10 CEV); *Sanctifier* ('By using my name they will force out demons', Mark 16:17, CEV; 'Sanctify them by the truth', John 17:17, NIV); *Baptizer in the Holy Spirit* ('In a few days you will be baptized with the Holy Spirit', Acts 1:5 CEV); *Healer* ('By using my name... heal sick people', Mark 16:18, CEV); *Returning King* 'This same Jesus who was taken from you into heaven will return in the same way', Acts 1:11, NLV).

2. *Gospel*. Central to evangelical enterprise is proclaiming the evangel or **gospel**, as in Mark 16:15 'Go and preach the good news to everyone in the world'.

3. *Bible*. This gospel's implications are as set forth and expounded in the **Bible**, the Word of God, the inspired Holy Scriptures now available (in all 66 Books) in 400 major world languages and in part (at least one Book) in 2,500 languages.

4. *Witness*. A central emphasis is having a personal relationship with Christ as one's Savior and Lord and then giving personal **witness** to Jesus' resurrection and to his person as daily life gives opportunity ('You will be my witnesses', Acts 1:8, RSV; or 'You will tell everyone about me', CEV).

5. *Evangelism*. Banding with others in the church to evangelize results in corporate or collective or organized **evangelism** at home and abroad, so that the benefits of evangelization come to every unreached nation, people, and individual on earth.

6. *Mission*. All this entails becoming personally and actively involved in Christ's **mission** to the world, at home or abroad, which is usually interpreted as meaning awareness of and obedience to Christ's Great Commission ('Go to the people of all nations and make them my disciples. Baptize them', Matthew 28:19, CEV; 'I am sending you, just as the Father has sent me', John 20:21, CEV).

7. *Advent*. All definitions of evangelicalism require the keeping in sight of the final climax, the **Advent** of Jesus the ever-present Lord, the Coming Judge, the Returning King ('I will be with you always, even until the end of the world', Matthew 28:20, CEV; 'This same Jesus, who has been taken from you into heaven, will come back in the same way you have seen him go into heaven' (Acts 1:11, NIV).

### Pre-eminence of the Great Commission
The reader will have noted throughout the above analysis that the definition of 'evangelicals' is inextricably bound up with Christ's Great Commission. All the biblical references cited come from one or other New Testament account of the instituting of that Commission. This is the reasoning behind the treatment here of the 2 categories, evangelicals and Great Commission Christians, being defined as exact equivalents or synonyms.

### Measuring evangelicals and evangelicalism
Now that the definitions have been established, it is comparatively easy to measure the phenomenon itself. As with any large social phenomenon, there are several different approaches which hinge on measuring different variables, but which produce similar end results. The exact method followed here is described in detail in Part 21 "GeoPersonnel", at which point 'evangelicals' are more exactly linked by data to the alternate name 'Great Commission Christians'. The latter term is more self-explanatory and, with no previous history of use or abuse, may well be more helpful to readers, though this survey throughout quotes both usages in each's relevant context.

**NEW CHARISMATIC MOVEMENTS.** Charismatics worldwide have adopted the orant/orante position for prayer (standing upright with raised arms), standard attitude of prayer adopted by early Christians (see Early Christian art, 2nd-6th centuries, especially in Roman catacombs). *Left.* **Protestant Charismatics** (within non-Pentecostal Protestant denominations) numbered 35 million worldwide by 2000. From very numerous denominations, they often worship with Catholics and Black neo-pentecostals (as here). *Row below.* **Roman Catholic Charismatics** numbered 120 million worldwide by 2000, including *(below)* some 10,500 priests, *(center)* 150,000 nuns, *(center left)* 8,000 monks, and 450 bishops and cardinals. Although expanding phenomenally in numbers, the Renewal's major problem is the enormous turnover in active members. *Bottom.* **Anglican Charismatics,** of whom 3,000 are shown here at 1973 2nd Festival of Praise in Worcester Cathedral (Church of England), numbered 17.5 million worldwide by 2000, **Orthodox Charismatics** numbered 3.2 million worldwide in 2000: *bottom left.* 2nd Annual Orthodox Charismatic Conference, Ann Arbor (USA) July 1974, *insert,* Russian Orthodox charismatic expounds Jesus on the icon.

# CHARISMATICS
## (Second-Wavers)

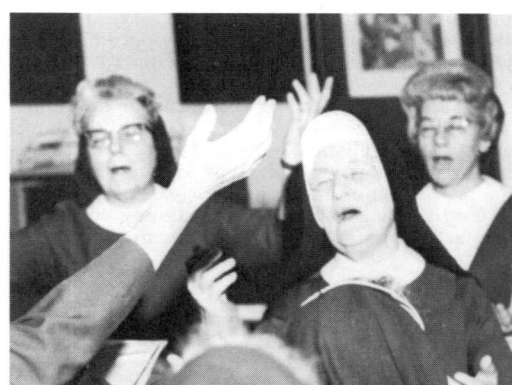

# MEGATYPOLOGY 4:

## PENTECOSTAL/CHARISMATIC GEORENEWAL

This 4th and final typology of empirical global Christianity has expanded with extreme rapidity throughout the 20th century. It will therefore be described here in considerable detail, utilizing 2 large tables and a mass of explanatory footnotes. First however an overall description will be given.

### THREE WAVES OF RENEWAL

The 2 tables that follow trace the expansion of this Renewal across 10 decades and two centuries, and also across 7 continents and the entire world. Historically, the Renewal can be seen to have arrived in 3 massive surges or waves whose origins are traced in Table 5–8 to the years 1886, 1907, and 1656 respectively. The first wave is known today as Pentecostalism or the Pentecostal Renewal (line 4), the second wave as the Charismatic movement or the Charismatic Renewal (line 12), followed by a third wave of nonpentecostal, noncharismatic but neocharismatic renewal (line 21). (References are to numbered lines in the tables plus their related numbered footnotes). The Pentecostals, Charismatics, and Neocharismatics who make up this Renewal today number 27.7% of organized global Christianity. They are here classified under 59 different categories (7 relating to Pentecostals, 8 to Charismatics, 44 to Neocharismatics).

The whole Renewal is excitingly new and photogenic. All 3 waves are extensively illustrated by photographs in WCT and WCE. The Pentecostal Renewal can be viewed via the Photographic Index in Part 32, Table 32-4 (see under Pentecostals). The Charismatic Renewal is illustrated in the page of photographs opposite to this page. And 40 component networks of the Neocharismatic Renewal are illustrated on the 2 facing pages of photographs in Part 6 "Independency".

Even with these 3 waves and 59 categories, an underlying unity pervades the movement. This survey views the Renewal in the Holy Spirit as one single cohesive movement into which a vast proliferation of all kinds of individuals and communities and cultures and languages have been drawn in a whole range of different circumstances. This explains the massive babel of diversity evident today.

These members are found in 740 Pentecostal denominations, 6,530 nonpentecostal mainline denominations with large organized internal Charismatic movements, and 18,810 independent Neocharismatic denominations and networks. Charismatics are now found across the entire spectrum of Christianity. They are found within all 150 traditional nonpentecostal ecclesiastical confessions, families, and traditions. Pentecostals/Charismatics (the shorthand generic term preferred here for the whole 3-Wave phenomenon) are found in 9,000 ethnolinguistic cultures, speaking 8,000 languages covering 95% of the world's total population.

The sheer magnitude and diversity of the numbers involved beggar the imagination. Table 5–8 and its footnotes document an AD 2000 total of 524 million affiliated church members (line 66). Of these, 66 million are Pentecostals, 176 million are Charismatics, and 295 million are Third-Wavers. Some 29% of all members worldwide are White, 71% Non-White. Members are more urban than rural, more female than male, more children (under 18) than adults, more Third-World (66%) than Western world (32%), more living in poverty (87%) than affluence (13%), more family-related than individualist.

These totals of believers today are not however the whole story. They do not include believers who died yesterday, or last month, or last year, or earlier in the 20th century. A complete tally of all Renewal believers throughout the century must therefore include the 176 million who are no longer alive. The total of all Renewal believers since AD 1900 can thus now be seen to amount to 796 millions (see lines 81 and 82 in Tables 5-8 and 5-9, and their footnotes).

### PERSECUTION AND DIVERSITY

Members are more harassed, persecuted, suffering, martyred than perhaps any other Christian tradition in recent history. They have been protected to some extent by the fact that their multiple cultures and vast diversity have made it virtually impossible for dictators, tyrants, archenemies, and totalitarian regimes to track them down and find them in order to liquidate them. Their incredible variety and diversity can be seen from the fact that to do justice to this diversity we have had to create a whole variety of neologisms and new statistical categories. Those described in the tables include: prepentecostals, quasi-pentecostals, indigenous pentecostals, ethnic pentecostals, isolated radio pentecostals, postpentecostals, non-Christian believers in Christ, postdenominationalists, neoapostolics, oneness apostolics, indigenous charismatics, grassroots neocharismatics, postcharismatics, crypto-charismatics, radio/TV charismatics, independent charismatics. Of these 16 categories only the last two have been universally recognized up to now as genuine pentecostals/charismatics. In this survey we are taking the position that all of these categories need to be recognized and enumerated as part of the Renewal.

### THE TIDE SURGES IN

All three waves are still continuing to surge in. Massive expansion and growth continue at a current rate of 9 million new members a year or over 25,000 a day. One-third of this is purely demographic (births minus deaths in the pentecostal/charismatic community); two-thirds are converts and other new members. In the early days of all three waves, annual rates of growth were enormous; now they have declined gradually to 2.7% per year for Pentecostals, 2.4% for Charismatics, 3.0% per year for Neocharismatics, and 3.2% per year for the Renewal as a whole (line 82). These overall figures hide a number of situations of saturation, some spheres of decline, and many situations of explosive, uncontrollable growth.

Charismatics greatly outnumber Pentecostals in numbers and in annual converts worldwide. They do, however, have a growing dilemma in that Charismatics in the nonpentecostal mainline Protestant and Catholic churches experience an average intense involvement of only two or three years—after this period as active weekly attenders at prayer meetings, they become irregular or nonattending, justifying our term postcharismatics (line 15). This 'revolving-door syndrome' results in an enormous annual turnover, a serious problem that has not yet begun to be adequately recognized or investigated.

### PERMEATION OF GLOBAL CHRISTIANITY

Table 5–8's lines 67-75 show the geographical spread of the Renewal today. Large numbers exist on every continent and in 236 countries. This table suggests the reason why Europe has always had the lowest response to Pentecostalism of any continent (less than 1%). Europeans rejected the First Wave because they were not prepared to leave the great state churches to become Pentecostals; since 1970, however, they have responded enormously as Charismatics within those churches. With 21 million Charismatics and 13 million Neocharismatics, Europe now has the highest ratio (6.6) of Charismatics to Pentecostals of all continents across the world.

At the other end of the spectrum from rejection to acceptance is Asia, whose Christians have become massively pentecostalized (line 70). This is due mainly to the phenomenal spread of the Renewal in Korea, India, the Philippines, Indonesia, and in mainland China.

All state churches and national denominations, with their myriads of agencies and institutions, are now rapidly becoming permeated with Charismatics. In addition, roughly 14% of Charismatics in these mainline churches have seceded or become independent each year since 1970. Altogether, White-led Independent charismatic churches across the world number over 100,000 loosely organized into 3,700 or so major denominations or networks (line 49).

The enormous force of the Renewal can be observed in many ways. One is that a majority of the fifty or so megachurches—the world's largest single congregations, each with over 50,000 members—are Pentecostal/Charismatic/Neocharismatic.

Another indication of its dynamic is the disproportionately high pentecostal/charismatic penetration of the media (see footnote to line 92). Charismatics in particular have seized the global initiative in radio, television, movies, audio, video, publishing, literature, magazines, citywide evangelistic campaigns (800 each year), and so on. Virtually all varieties of ministries engaged in by institutionalized Christianity worldwide have now been penetrated by stalwarts of the Renewal.

Finance, stewardship, and giving also have risen well above the global Christian average (lines 89-90). Personal annual income of church members in the Renewal has grown from $157 billion in 1970 to $1,550 billion by AD 2000 (line 89). Of this, $30 billion is donated to Christian causes (line 90). This means that the rank-and-file of the Renewal do not need to be further exhorted regarding stewardship. Its lay members are doing all they should, and more. There is, however, an almost universal failure by leaders of the Renewal to garner and organize these vast sums coherently for mission and ministry at the world level. In consequence, giving to global foreign missions per member per week is stuck at the paltry figure of 15 US cents.

A further illustration of the permeation of global Christianity lies in the huge numbers of ordained pastors, priests, ministers, bishops, and other church leaders involved (lines 93-95). Over one-third of the world's full-time Christian workers (38%) are Pentecostals/Charismatics/Neocharismatics.

### PENETRATION OF THE WORLD

Throughout the history of the Renewal, leaders have summoned members to the task of world evangelization. A favorite theme has been the saying of Jesus: 'The fields are white unto harvest.' The unharvested or unreached harvest field today consists of 1.6 billion unevangelized persons, who have never heard of Jesus Christ (line 101), in 3,000 unevangelized population segments (cities, peoples, countries). It includes 2,000 unreached ethnolinguistic peoples, 175 unreached megapeoples (of over 1 million population each), 140 unevangelized megacities, 300 unevangelized Islamic metropolises. The harvest force, or harvesters committed to harvesting, consists of 5.5 million full-time Christian workers: of these, 2.1 million are Pentecostals/Charismatics/Neocharismatics (38%; line no. 93).

Another indicator concerns global plans to evangelize the world (line 102). Of the world's 1,500 such plans since AD 30, some 12% have been definitively Pentecostal/Charismatic. Probably 20% altogether—300 plans—have had significant Charismatic participation. In the last twenty years, this percentage has risen markedly. Of the world's 24 current megaplans launched since 1960, 16, or 67%, are Pentecostal/Charismatic. So are 9 (64%) of the 14 current gigaplans (global plans to evangelize the world each spending over US $1 billion) launched since 1960.

New bodies are continually emerging. Over 100 new Charismatic mission agencies have recently been formed in the Western world, and over 300 more in the Third World. Many are taking on the challenge of unevangelized population segments in restricted-access countries by appointing nonresidential missionaries.

With Pentecostals/Charismatics/Neocharismatics now active in 80% of the world's 3,300 large metropolises, all in process of actively implementing networking and cooperation with Great Commission Christians of all confessions, a new era in world mission would clearly appear to have got under way.

## Table 5–8. The global expansion of the Pentecostal/Charismatic/Neocharismatic Renewal in the Holy Spirit, AD 1900–2025.

| Ref 1 | Category 2 | Begun 3 | Totals in AD 2000: Countries 4 | Denoms 5 | PARTICIPANTS in: 1900 6 | 1970 7 | 1995 8 | 2000 9 | 2025 10 |
|---|---|---|---|---|---|---|---|---|---|
| 1. | **PERIPHERAL QUASI-PENTECOSTALS** | | | | | | | | |
| 2. | Prepentecostals | 1739 | 100 | 2,600 | 2,500,000 | 3,824,000 | 5,000,000 | 7,300,000 | 18,800,000 |
| 3. | Postpentecostals | 1950 | 80 | 509 | 0 | 1,000,000 | 6,000,000 | 10,500,000 | 33,000,000 |
| 4. | **FIRST WAVE: PENTECOSTAL RENEWAL** | | | | | | | | |
| 5. | **Pentecostals** | 1886 | 225 | 740 | 20,000 | 15,382,330 | 57,424,520 | 65,832,970 | 97,876,000 |
| 6. | Denominational Pentecostals | 1910 | 225 | 740 | 20,000 | 15,382,330 | 57,424,520 | 65,832,970 | 97,876,000 |
| 7. | Classical Pentecostals | 1906 | 220 | 660 | 20,000 | 14,443,480 | 54,961,090 | 63,064,620 | 93,583,000 |
| 8. | Holiness Pentecostals | 1886 | 170 | 240 | 15,000 | 2,322,430 | 5,650,230 | 6,315,790 | 9,644,000 |
| 9. | Baptistic Pentecostals | 1906 | 210 | 390 | 5,000 | 11,415,390 | 47,713,650 | 54,973,310 | 81,272,000 |
| 10. | Apostolic Pentecostals | 1904 | 29 | 30 | 0 | 705,660 | 1,597,210 | 1,775,520 | 2,667,000 |
| 11. | Oneness Pentecostals | 1914 | 74 | 80 | 0 | 938,850 | 2,463,430 | 2,768,350 | 4,293,000 |
| 12. | **SECOND WAVE: CHARISMATIC RENEWAL** | | | | | | | | |
| 13. | **Charismatics** | 1907 | 235 | 6,530 | 12,000 | 3,349,400 | 156,041,320 | 175,856,690 | 274,934,000 |
| 14. | Mainline active Charismatics | 1960 | 225 | 6,500 | 12,000 | 3,349,400 | 100,841,320 | 114,029,250 | 179,969,000 |
| 15. | Mainline Postcharismatics | 1973 | 150 | 3,540 | 0 | 0 | 55,200,000 | 61,827,440 | 94,965,000 |
| 16. | Anglican Charismatics | 1907 | 163 | 165 | 1,000 | 509,900 | 15,980,520 | 17,562,110 | 25,470,000 |
| 17. | Catholic Charismatics | 1967 | 234 | 236 | 10,000 | 2,000,000 | 104,900,000 | 119,912,200 | 194,973,000 |
| 18. | Protestant Charismatics | 1959 | 231 | 5,780 | 1,000 | 824,100 | 32,208,900 | 35,200,000 | 50,156,000 |
| 19. | Orthodox Charismatics | 1970 | 87 | 219 | 0 | 15,200 | 2,941,900 | 3,167,380 | 4,295,000 |
| 20. | Marginal Charismatics | 1980 | 15 | 130 | 0 | 200 | 10,000 | 15,000 | 40,000 |
| 21. | **THIRD WAVE: NEOCHARISMATIC RENEWAL** | | | | | | | | |
| 22. | **Neocharismatics** (Independents, Postdenominationalists) | 1549 | 225 | 18,810 | 949,400 | 53,490,560 | 254,726,840 | 295,405,240 | 460,798,000 |
| 23. | (a) In 2 kinds of wholly Third Wave networks | 1656 | 220 | 17,125 | 949,300 | 36,854,370 | 217,689,150 | 253,936,540 | 401,173,000 |
| 24. | Non-White indigenous Neocharismatics | 1783 | 210 | 13,425 | 919,300 | 29,379,360 | 174,221,530 | 203,870,400 | 327,515,000 |
| 25. | African indigenous pentecostals/charismatics | 1864 | 60 | 9,300 | 890,000 | 12,569,300 | 56,520,100 | 65,910,530 | 99,263,000 |
| 26. | Afro-Caribbean pentecostals/charismatics | 1783 | 38 | 420 | 10,000 | 217,610 | 649,670 | 736,080 | 1,168,000 |
| 27. | Arab/Assyrian/Semitic neocharismatics | 1909 | 40 | 130 | 0 | 140,760 | 1,076,730 | 1,263,930 | 2,200,000 |
| 28. | Black American independent charismatics | 1955 | 4 | 10 | 0 | 62,500 | 1,236,800 | 1,471,660 | 2,646,000 |
| 29. | Black American indigenous pentecostals | 1889 | 20 | 90 | 15,000 | 2,820,540 | 6,832,460 | 7,634,850 | 11,647,000 |
| 30. | Black American Oneness Apostolics | 1886 | 10 | 150 | 0 | 559,120 | 2,560,600 | 2,960,900 | 4,962,000 |
| 31. | Brazilian/Portuguese grassroots neocharismatics | 1910 | 20 | 460 | 0 | 2,512,200 | 19,604,340 | 23,022,770 | 39,115,000 |
| 32. | Colored/Mixed-race indigenous charismatics | 1931 | 4 | 70 | 0 | 71,000 | 207,500 | 234,800 | 371,000 |
| 33. | Ethnic (Monoethnic) pentecostal churches | 1890 | 20 | 20 | 0 | 162,930 | 1,307,220 | 1,536,080 | 2,680,000 |
| 34. | Filipino indigenous pentecostals/charismatics | 1913 | 25 | 380 | 0 | 1,818,020 | 5,950,340 | 6,776,800 | 10,909,000 |
| 35. | Han Chinese indigenous pentecostals/charismatics | 1905 | 58 | 180 | 2,000 | 310,240 | 41,509,370 | 49,749,200 | 82,948,000 |
| 36. | Indian indigenous pentecostals/charismatics | 1911 | 25 | 580 | 1,000 | 1,421,310 | 14,081,380 | 16,613,400 | 29,274,000 |
| 37. | Indonesian indigenous pentecostals | 1920 | 5 | 170 | 0 | 2,649,780 | 6,076,000 | 6,761,240 | 10,187,000 |
| 38. | Japanese indigenous pentecostals | 1930 | 15 | 50 | 0 | 298,650 | 1,016,140 | 1,159,640 | 1,877,000 |
| 39. | Korean indigenous pentecostals/charismatics | 1910 | 30 | 170 | 500 | 100,700 | 2,799,030 | 3,338,700 | 6,037,000 |
| 40. | Latino-Hispanic grassroots believers | 1909 | 24 | 990 | 0 | 2,988,090 | 10,427,650 | 11,915.560 | 17,355,000 |
| 41. | Messianic Hindu believers in Christ | 1875 | 2 | 5 | 500 | 109,500 | 154,300 | 163,200 | 208,000 |
| 42. | Messianic Jewish believers in Christ | 1894 | 14 | 20 | 100 | 13,000 | 136,000 | 160,600 | 284,000 |
| 43. | Messianic Muslim believers in Christ | 1981 | 2 | 3 | 0 | 0 | 105,000 | 126,000 | 231,000 |
| 44. | Pacific/Oceanic indigenous charismatics | 1917 | 20 | 70 | 0 | 25,730 | 183,100 | 214,570 | 372,000 |
| 45. | Red Indian/Amerindian neopentecostals | 1870 | 3 | 4 | 0 | 361,000 | 506,300 | 535,360 | 681,000 |
| 46. | Vietnamese indigenous neocharismatics | 1952 | 2 | 3 | 0 | 12,600 | 195,000 | 231,480 | 414,000 |
| 47. | other Asian indigenous neocharismatics | 1948 | 40 | 130 | 100 | 153,780 | 986,500 | 1,153,050 | 1,986,000 |
| 48. | other Messianic non-Christian believers in Christ | 1950 | 15 | 20 | 100 | 1,000 | 100,000 | 200,000 | 700,000 |
| 49. | White-led Independent Postdenominationalists | 1805 | 210 | 3,700 | 30,000 | 7,475,010 | 43,467,620 | 50,066,140 | 73,658,000 |
| 50. | European/American White-led Neo-Apostolics | 1805 | 200 | 3,510 | 10,000 | 5,760,760 | 35,174,210 | 40,456,900 | 60,470,000 |
| 51. | European White-led New Apostolics | 1832 | 180 | 190 | 20,000 | 1,714,250 | 8,293,410 | 9,609,240 | 13,188,000 |
| 52. | (b) as % of 7 kinds of non-Third-Wave denominations | 1549 | 200 | 925 | 100 | 16,636,190 | 37,037,690 | 41,468,700 | 59,625,000 |
| 53. | Independent Anglican neocharismatics | 1925 | 80 | 130 | 0 | 10,000 | 1,595,000 | 1,716,000 | 2,321,000 |
| 54. | Independent Protestant neocharismatics | 1920 | 180 | 800 | 0 | 11,832,690 | 18,642,360 | 20,489,290 | 25,724,000 |
| 55. | Independent Catholic neocharismatics | 1724 | 30 | 70 | 0 | 700,000 | 1,187,260 | 1,314,800 | 1,953,000 |
| 56. | Independent Orthodox neocharismatics | 1666 | 20 | 90 | 0 | 1,000 | 538,310 | 584,200 | 814,000 |
| 57. | Nonhistorical Independent neocharismatics | 1549 | 62 | 300 | 0 | 1,000,000 | 3,200,000 | 3,500,000 | 5,000,000 |
| 58. | Isolated radio/TV neocharismatics | 1930 | 30 | 30 | 0 | 30,000 | 159,100 | 188,100 | 333,000 |
| 59. | Hidden non-Christian believers in Christ | 1800 | 70 | 290 | 100 | 3,062,500 | 11,715,660 | 13,676,310 | 23,480,000 |
| 60. | Hidden Hindu neocharismatics | 1800 | 4 | 10 | 0 | 3,000,000 | 8,637,500 | 9,715,000 | 15,103,000 |
| 61. | Hidden Muslim neocharismatics | 1930 | 15 | 15 | 0 | 2,000 | 348,560 | 417,790 | 764,000 |
| 62. | Hidden Buddhist neocharismatics | 1950 | 15 | 15 | 0 | 10,000 | 1,829,600 | 2,193,520 | 4,013,000 |
| 63. | Hidden Jewish neocharismatics | 1896 | 15 | 50 | 100 | 50,000 | 200,000 | 250,000 | 500,000 |
| 64. | Hidden other-religionist neocharismatics | 1980 | 50 | 200 | 0 | 500 | 700,000 | 1,100,000 | 3,100,000 |
| 65. | doubly-counted First/Second/Third Wavers (see footnote 65) | | | | | | | | |
| 66. | **Global affiliated Pentecostals/Charismatics/Neocharismatics** | | 236 | 21,080 | 981,400 | 72,223,000 | 477,378,000 | 523,778,000 | 811,551,600 |
| 67. | **RENEWAL MEMBERS ON 7 CONTINENTS** | | | | | | | | |
| 68. | Renewal members in Africa | 1830 | 60 | 9,990 | 901,000 | 17,049,020 | 110,409,270 | 126,010,200 | 227,819,720 |
| 69. | Renewal members in Antarctica | 1980 | 1 | 2 | 0 | 0 | 300 | 400 | 600 |
| 70. | Renewal members in Asia | 1870 | 50 | 2,690 | 4,300 | 10,144,120 | 122,691,990 | 134,889,530 | 217,550,600 |
| 71. | Renewal members in Europe | 1805 | 48 | 1,870 | 20,000 | 8,018,180 | 36,097,050 | 37,568,700 | 47,179,500 |
| 72. | Renewal members in Latin America | 1783 | 46 | 2,680 | 10,000 | 12,621,450 | 130,147,480 | 141,432,880 | 202,277,880 |
| 73. | Renewal members in Northern America | 1889 | 5 | 3,520 | 46,100 | 24,151,910 | 73,997,060 | 79,600,160 | 110,204,580 |
| 74. | Renewal members in Oceania | 1917 | 28 | 330 | 0 | 238,240 | 3,928,850 | 4,265,520 | 6,519,300 |
| 75. | Renewal members as % global church members | – | 238 | – | 0.2 | 6.4 | 26.9 | 27.7 | 32.5 |
| 76. | **PERIPHERAL CONSTITUENTS** | | | | | | | | |
| 77. | Quasi-Pentecostals (Prepentecostals, Postpentecostals) | 1739 | 110 | 2,700 | 2,500,000 | 4,824,000 | 11,000,000 | 17,800,000 | 51,800,000 |
| 78. | Unaffiliated believers professing Renewal | 1950 | 230 | 2,000 | 210,000 | 5,300,000 | 52,000,000 | 78,327,510 | 120,000,000 |
| 79. | **WIDER GLOBAL TOTALS OF RENEWAL** | | | | | | | | |
| 80. | Total all Renewal believers alive at mid-year | | 236 | 25,780 | 3,691,400 | 82,346,270 | 529,597,680 | 619,905,500 | 961,000,000 |
| 81. | Renewal believers dying since AD 1900 | | 236 | 11,565 | – | 34,657,900 | 146,743,000 | 175,728,800 | 270,000,000 |
| 82. | Total all Renewal believers ever, since AD 1900 | | 236 | 29,500 | 3,691,400 | 117,004,170 | 676,340,680 | 795,623,700 | 1,231,000,000 |
| 83. | **CHURCHES, FINANCE, AGENCIES, WORKERS** | | | | | | | | |
| 84. | Pentecostal churches, congregations (1st Wave) | | 225 | 740 | 10 | 94,200 | 360,000 | 480,000 | 1,080,000 |
| 85. | Mainline Charismatic prayer groups (2nd Wave) | | 235 | 4,450 | 0 | 35,000 | 370,000 | 550,000 | 1,450,000 |
| 86. | Catholic Charismatic weekly prayer groups | | 234 | 239 | 0 | 2,185 | 143,000 | 160,000 | 245,000 |
| 87. | Anglican & Protestant Charismatic groups | | 231 | 3,700 | 0 | 32,815 | 200,000 | 250,000 | 500,000 |
| 88. | Independent congregations, house churches (3rd Wave) | | – | – | 15,000 | 138,970 | 450,000 | 591,000 | 1,296,000 |
| 89. | Personal income of all Renewal members, $ p.a. | | – | – | 250 million | 157 billion | 1,280 billion | 1,550 billion | 2,400 billion |
| 90. | Renewal members' giving to all Christian causes, $ p.a. | | – | – | 7 million | 3 billion | 25 billion | 30 billion | 46 billion |
| 91. | Renewal service agencies | | – | – | 20 | 600 | 3,400 | 4,000 | 7,000 |
| 92. | Renewal institutions | | – | – | 100 | 1,300 | 13,000 | 14,000 | 19,000 |
| 93. | All pentecostal/charismatic full-time workers | | – | – | 2,010 | 240,790 | 1,200,000 | 2,100,000 | 4,300,000 |
| 94. | Nationals: pastors, clergy, evangelists, et alii | | – | – | 2,000 | 237,000 | 1,060,000 | 1,933,000 | 3,900,000 |
| 95. | Aliens: foreign missionaries | | – | – | 100 | 3,790 | 140,000 | 167,000 | 400,000 |
| 96. | **THE CONTEXT OF WORLD EVANGELIZATION** | | | | | | | | |
| 97. | Global population | | 238 | – | 1,619,626,000 | 3,696,148,000 | 5,666,360,000 | 6,055,049,000 | 7,823,703,000 |
| 98. | Christians (all varieties) | | 238 | 33,800 | 558,132,000 | 1,236,374,000 | 1,877,426,000 | 1,999,564,000 | 2,616,670,000 |
| 99. | Affiliated church members (baptized) | | 238 | 33,800 | 521,576,500 | 1,130,106,000 | 1,796,918,000 | 1,888,439,000 | 2,490,958,000 |
| 100. | Non-Christians | | 238 | – | 1,061,494,000 | 2,459,774,000 | 3,788,934,000 | 4,055,485,000 | 5,207,033,000 |
| 101. | Unevangelized persons | | 230 | – | 879,672,000 | 1,641,245,000 | 1,678,205,000 | 1,629,375,000 | 1,845,406,000 |
| 102. | World evangelization global plans since AD 30 | | 160 | – | 250 | 510 | 1,145 | 1,500 | 3,000 |

**Table 5–9. Codes and characteristics of each of the 95 generic categories and ministries of Pentecostals/Charismatics/Neocharismatics.**

| *Ref Column* 1 | *Category* 2 | *Country Table codes* *Table 1* 3 | *Table 2* 4 | *Definitions, characteristics, examples of major significant bodies* 5 | *Main country* 6 |
|---|---|---|---|---|---|
| 1. | **PERIPHERAL QUASI-PENTECOSTALS:** | ...... | ...... | Tables 5-6 and 5-7 divide all members into the 66 ecclesiastico-cultural categories below | |
| 2. | Prepentecostals | 0QZAC | ...... | Charismatic groups not officially in Renewal: numerous Salvationists, Holiness, Wesleyans | brit |
| 3. | Postpentecostals | 1QZAC | ...... | Former Denominational Pentecostals who have left to join nonpentecostal churches | usa |
| 4. | **FIRST WAVE: PENTECOSTAL RENEWAL** | ...... | ...... | Oldest part of Renewal, claiming name, history, experiences, and theology of Pentecostalism | usa |
| 5. | Pentecostals | 1ZAC | P-Pe | Churches of White origin (now 70% Non-White) requiring initial evidence of tongues-speaking | braz |
| 6. | Denominational Pentecostals | P1ZAC | P-Pe | Members in the older, larger, more traditional Pentecostal denominations | cana |
| 7. | Classical Pentecostals | CP1ZAC | P-Pe2/3 | Self-designation of older White denominations, usually excluding Black Pentecostals | usa |
| 8. | Holiness Pentecostals | ...... | P-Pe3 | Those holding 3-fold Wesleyan experience of conversion, sanctification, infilling: IPHC | chil |
| 9. | Baptistic Pentecostals | ...... | P-Pe2 | Emphasizing 2-fold Pentecostal experience of conversion, Spirit-baptism: AoG, COG, ICFG | arge |
| 10. | Apostolic Pentecostals | ...... | P-PeA | Denominations emphasizing Pentecostal church government by living apostles: ACG | ghan |
| 11. | Oneness Pentecostals | OP1ZAC | P-Pe1 | Denominations emphasizing baptism in name of 'Jesus Only'; anti-trinitarian: UPCI | colo |
| 12. | **SECOND WAVE: CHARISMATIC RENEWAL** | ...... | *Formula* | Members of nonpentecostal mainline churches who experience Pentecostal phenomena | ital |
| 13. | Charismatics | 2ZAC | ...... | All who have experienced Spirit-baptism but remain within nonpentecostal mainline churches | mexi |
| 14. | Mainline active charismatics | V2ZAC | ...... | All in nonpentecostal churches regularly attending Renewal activities | phil |
| 15. | Mainline postcharismatics | x2ZAC | ...... | Charismatics who no longer attend Renewal activities but still regard selves as Charismatics | fran |
| 16. | Anglican Charismatics | A2ZAC | %ΣA- . | Total Anglicans in Renewal, past and present, including children and infants | brit |
| 17. | Catholic Charismatics | R2ZAC | %ΣR- | Total baptized RCs in CCR, past and present, including children and infants | braz |
| 18. | Protestant Charismatics | P2ZAC | %ΣP- . | Total Protestants in Renewal, past and present, including children and infants | aust |
| 19. | Orthodox Charismatics | O2ZAC | %ΣO- | Total Orthodox in Renewal, past and present, including children and infants | arme |
| 20. | Marginal Charismatics | m2ZAC | %Σm- . | Total marginal Christians in Renewal, past and present, including children and infants | usa |
| 21. | **THIRD WAVE: NEOCHARISMATIC RENEWAL** | ...... | ...... | Spirit-led Independents rejecting White Pentecostal/Charismatic denominationalism | chin |
| 22. | Neocharismatics (Independents, Postdenominationalists) | 3ZAC .. | I-3+I- | All baptised in the Holy Spirit in new churches independent of historic Christianity | |
| 23. | (a) *In 2 kinds of wholly Third-Wave networks* | ...... | I-3 | (1) *Non-White and (2) White-led Neocharismatics in wholly Third-Wave networks/churches* | |
| 24. | Non-White indigenous Neocharismatics | N3ZAC | *End code* | Spirit-baptized Non-Whites in 26 varieties of indigenous, independent, apostolic churches | |
| 25. | African indigenous pentecostals/charismatics | ...... | A..... | Most AICs are Zionist, Apostolic, Spiritual: ZCC, CCC, AICN, DLBC, AACJM, EJCSK | zimb |
| 26. | Afro-Caribbean pentecostals/charismatics | ...... | U..... | West Indies churches of African origin: Spiritual Baptists/Shouters, Revival Zion, NESBC | trin |
| 27. | Arab/Assyrian/Semitic neocharismatics | ...... | S..... | Arabic/Aramaean/Assyrian/Berber/Semitic charismatic churches: Tree of Life Chs, GPC | iraq |
| 28. | Black American independent charismatics | ...... | D..... | African American independent charismatic bodies: Full Gospel Baptist Chs Fellowship | usa |
| 29. | Black American indigenous pentecostals | ...... | B..... | Black Pentecostalism: Church of God in Christ, UHCA, Full Gospel Catholic Ch | usa |
| 30. | Black American Oneness Apostolics | ...... | O..... | PAOW, AWCF, Bible Way Churches of Our Lord Jesus Christ WW, COLJCAF | usa |
| 31. | Brazilian/Portuguese grassroots neocharismatics | ...... | Y..... | OBPC (Brazil for Christ Ev Ch), IURD/UCKG, CCB, IPF, IPDA | braz |
| 32. | Colored/Mixed-race indigenous charismatics | ...... | N..... | Colored, Métis, mixed-race charismatics: Members in Christ Ch, Christen Gemeente | nami |
| 33. | Ethnic (Monoethnic) pentecostal churches | ...... | E..... | Yi Churches, Miao Churches, Nagaland Christian Revival Churches, Gypsy Ev Movement | chin |
| 34. | Filipino indigenous pentecostals/charismatics | ...... | F..... | Jesus is Lord Fellowship, CDCC, March of Faith, Ecclesiae Dei | phil |
| 35. | Han Chinese indigenous pentecostals/charismatics | ...... | C..... | True Jesus Church, NBM/BAM, AHC(Little Flock), Han Chinese house churches | chin |
| 36. | Indian indigenous pentecostals/charismatics | ...... | I..... | Indian Pentecostal Church of God, Believers' Chs of India, Christ Groups, IPA, MFGCM | indi |
| 37. | Indonesian indigenous pentecostals | ...... | G..... | Indonesia Pentecostal Church (GPI), GBI, GBIS, GPPS, GBT, GUP | indo |
| 38. | Japanese indigenous pentecostals | ...... | Q..... | Spirit of Jesus Church, Primitive Gospel Ch, Holy Ecclesia of Jesus, JJCC | japa |
| 39. | Korean indigenous pentecostals/charismatics | ...... | K..... | Yoido FGC, Grace & Truth Ch, FGIGM, Korea Full Gospel Chs of America | souk |
| 40. | Latino-Hispanic grassroots believers | ...... | L..... | Autochthonous grassroots (GR) churches, IMPC, IPP, IOAP, IEMP, IEPC | mexi |
| 41. | Messianic Hindu believers in Christ | ...... | H..... | Messianic temples, organized Hindu-Christian chs: Hindu Ch of the Lord Jesus, SRM | indi |
| 42. | Messianic Jewish believers in Christ | ...... | J..... | Messianic Jewish synagogues, Fellowship of Messianic Congregations, UMJC, IAMCS, JFJ | isra |
| 43. | Messianic Muslim believers in Christ | ...... | M..... | Messianic Muslim mosques: Jesus Mosques, Jamaat | bang |
| 44. | Pacific/Oceanic indigenous charismatics | ...... | P..... | Pacific indigenous churches: Christian Fellowship Ch, AGCFI, Samoan FGC | solo |
| 45. | Red Indian/Amerindian neopentecostals | ...... | R..... | Amerindian neopentecostals: UIEI, Halleluja Church | mexi |
| 46. | Vietnamese indigenous neocharismatics | ...... | V..... | Vietnamese churches: Good News house church movement | viet |
| 47. | Other Asian indigenous neocharismatics | ...... | Z..... | Other Asian churches: Hope of God Churches of Thailand, Latter Rain Ch of Malaysia | thai |
| 48. | Other Messianic non-Christian believers in Christ | ...... | T..... | Organized believers staying in Buddhism, Baha'i, Sikhism, &c | myan |
| 49. | White-led independent postdenominationalists | W3ZAC | ...... | Spirit-baptized Whites in non-Pentecostal/Charismatic apostolic networks | brit |
| 50. | European/American White-led Neo-Apostolics | ...... | W..... | AIGA, AVC, CEEC, COTRI, FCFI, IAOGI, ICCC, ICCEC, ICFCM, RBC-RMAI, UEC, VFM, &c | usa |
| 51. | European White-led New Apostolics | ...... | X..... | Neuapostolische Kirche (NAK), begun as Universal Catholic Ch, and 30 schismatic bodies | germ |
| 52. | (b) *as % of 6 kinds of non-Renewal denominations* | ...... | *Formula* | *Neocharismatics in non-pentecostal/charismatic (even anti-Renewal) denominations* | brit |
| 53. | Independent Anglican neocharismatics | A3ZAC | Σ%I-Ang | Neocharismatics within non-pentecostal/charismatic Independent Anglican bodies | brit |
| 54. | Independent Protestant neocharismatics | P3ZAC | Σ%I-Bap | Neocharismatics within non-pentecostal/charismatic Independent Protestant bodies | nige |
| 55. | Independent Catholic neocharismatics | R3ZAC | Σ%I-OCa | Neocharismatics within non-pentecostal/charismatic Independent Catholic bodies | neth |
| 56. | Independent Orthodox neocharismatics | O3ZAC | Σ%I-OBe | Neocharismatics within non-pentecostal/charismatic Independent Orthodox bodies | russ |
| 57. | Nonhistorical independent neocharismatics | I3ZAC | Σ%I-ind | Neocharismatics in other nonpentecostal Independent chs: PIC/IFI, NBCA | phil |
| 58. | Isolated radio/TV neocharismatics | r3ZAC | Σ%I-rad | Neocharismatics among non-pentecostal/charismatic Independent radio believers | chin |
| 59. | Hidden non-Christian believers in Christ | ...... | ...... | Hindu, Muslim, Buddhist, Jewish, Sikh, Baha'i, New Religionist converts who stay hidden | indi |
| 60. | Hidden Hindu neocharismatics | ...... | %I-Hin | Hindu believers in Christ (NBBCs) who have pentecostal/charismatic gifts | nepa |
| 61. | Hidden Muslim neocharismatics | ...... | %I-Mus | Muslim believers in Christ (NBBCs) who have pentecostal/charismatic gifts | turk |
| 62. | Hidden Buddhist neocharismatics | ...... | %I-Bud | Buddhist believers in Christ (NBBCs) who have pentecostal/charismatic gifts | myan |
| 63. | Hidden Jewish neocharismatics | ...... | %I-Jew | Jewish believers in Christ who have pentecostal/charismatic gifts | isra |
| 64. | Hidden other-religionist neocharismatics | ...... | %I-rel | Other religionist hidden believers in Christ who have pentecostal/charismatic gifts | japa |
| 65. | doubly-counted First/Second/Third Wavers | 4ZAC | ...... | Neocharismatics who join Pentecostal bodies; Charismatics who become Neocharismatics | souk |
| 66. | **Global Pentecostals/Charismatics/Neocharismatics** | ZAC | ...... | Total all church members in the Pentecostal/Charismatic/Neocharismatic Renewal | |
| 67. | **RENEWAL MEMBERS ON 7 CONTINENTS** | ..... | ..... | Renewal (which is 28% of globe) is: 12% Pentecostals, 33% Charismatics, 55% Neocharismatics. | |
| 68. | Renewal members in Africa | ...... | ...... | 12% Pentecostals, 25% Charismatics, 63% Neocharismatics. | |
| 69. | Renewal members in Antarctica | ...... | ...... | 1% Pentecostals, 95% Charismatics, 4% Neocharismatics. | |
| 70. | Renewal members in Asia | ...... | ...... | 5% Pentecostals, 16% Charismatics, 79% Neocharismatics. | |
| 71. | Renewal members in Europe | ...... | ...... | 8% Pentecostals, 56% Charismatics, 36% Neocharismatics. | |
| 72. | Renewal members in Latin America | ...... | ...... | 23% Pentecostals, 52% Charismatics, 24% Neocharismatics. | |
| 73. | Renewal members in Northern America | ...... | ...... | 7% Pentecostals, 28% Charismatics, 65% Neocharismatics. | |
| 74. | Renewal members in Oceania | ...... | ...... | 14% Pentecostals, 63% Charismatics, 24% Neocharismatics. | |
| 75. | Renewal members as % global church members | ...... | ...... | Rising rapidly at first to 6% by 1970 and to 28% by AD 2000. | |
| 76. | **PERIPHERAL CONSTITUENTS** | | | | |
| 77. | Quasi-Pentecostals (Prepentecostals, Postpentecostals) | QZAC . | ...... | Defined above for lines 2 and 3, not counted here as Renewal members but as Renewal believers. | |
| 78. | Unaffiliated believers professing Renewal | UZC .. | ...... | Individual believers experiencing Holy Spirit gifts but remaining unrelated to Renewal bodies. | |
| 79. | **WIDER GLOBAL TOTALS OF RENEWAL** | | | | |
| 80. | Total all Renewal believers alive at mid-year | ZC ... | ...... | Total of lines 66, 77, and 78. | |
| 81. | Renewal believers dying since AD 1900 | ...... | ...... | Former members of Renewal who have died by the year indicated. | |
| 82. | Total all Renewal believers ever, since AD 1900 | ...... | ...... | Total of lines 80 and 81. | |
| 83. | **CHURCHES, FINANCE, AGENCIES, WORKERS** | | | | |
| 84. | Pentecostal churches, congregations (1st Wave) | ...... | ...... | Mainly Assemblies of God buildings and properties. | |
| 85. | Mainline Charismatic prayer groups (2nd Wave) | ...... | ...... | These groups' regular weekly attenders are known as the 'shock troops' of the Renewal. | |
| 86. | Catholic Charismatic weekly prayer groups | ...... | ...... | Massive growth since origin in 1967, to 2,185 groups (1970), 12,000 (1980), 90,000 (1990), 160,000 (2000). | |
| 87. | Anglican & Protestant Charismatic groups | ...... | ...... | Large-scale lay and clerical leadership from 1960 onwards. | |
| 88. | Independent congregations, house churches (3rd Wave) | ...... | ...... | A huge number of smaller house groups, over half a billion. | |
| 89. | Personal income of all Renewal members, $ p.a. | ...... | ...... | Enormous wealth but no organized finance or central bank accounts. | |
| 90. | Renewal members' giving to all Christian causes, $ p.a. | ...... | ...... | Low at 2% of personal income given to Christian causes but higher than global Christian rates. | |
| 91. | Renewal service agencies | ...... | ...... | A huge and variegated number of agencies (listed here in footnote). | |
| 92. | Renewal institutions | ...... | ...... | Vast variety (listed here in footnote). | |
| 93. | All pentecostal/charismatic full-time workers | ...... | ...... | Full-time church workers of all kinds: total of next 2 lines, 94 and 95. | |
| 94. | Nationals: pastors, clergy, evangelists, et alii | ...... | ...... | Mostly well-documented by the major denominations and networks. | |
| 95. | Aliens: foreign missionaries | ...... | ...... | Large and rapidly growing numbers serving abroad for shorter or longer terms. | |
| 96. | **THE CONTEXT OF WORLD EVANGELIZATION** | | | | |
| 97. | Global population | ...... | ...... | Populations are shown at mid-year (30 June) for the years 1970, 1995, 2000, 2025. | |
| 98. | Christians (all varieties) | ...... | ...... | Professing plus crypto-Christians; affiliated plus unaffiliated; Great Commission plus latent Christians. | |
| 99. | Affiliated church members (baptized) | ...... | ...... | Baptized or other members of all the churches. | |
| 100. | Non-Christians | ...... | ...... | Now over 4 billion and growing rapidly. | |
| 101. | Unevangelized persons | ...... | ...... | All persons unaware of Christianity, Christ, and/or the gospel. | |
| 102. | World evangelization global plans since AD 30 | ...... | ...... | Distinct plans and proposals for completing world evangelization. | |

## METHODOLOGICAL NOTES ON TABLES 5-8, 5-9
This pair of Tables 5-8 and 5-9 presents a descriptive survey of the phenomenon usually known as the Pentecostal/Charismatic Renewal, or, by participants, as the Renewal in the Holy Spirit. It takes in the somewhat expanded boundaries of the movement that most leaders now understand it as inhabiting. At the same time, the Renewal recognizes the existence and reality of large numbers of other branches or segments of global Christianity, to which it is related in varying degrees of closeness. This means that these tables do not claim to be describing a tradition of Christianity distinct and separate from all other traditions but a contemporary movement that overlaps with the rest of the Christian world to a large degree (6% in 1970, rising to 28% by AD 2000). By 1985, in fact, the Renewal had penetrated, and had secured committed representation in, every one of the Christian world's 156 distinct ecclesiastical confessions, traditions, and families. By AD 2000 this had risen to all 300 traditions. The tables enumerate the progress of all branches of the Renewal across the century, with projections from AD 2000 to AD 2025 based on current long-term trends.

### DEFINITIONS AND ADDITIONAL DATA
(referring to numbered lines). Each line in Tables 5-8 and 5-9 above refers to the global (total, worldwide) situation, in which pentecostals/charismatics are found in 99% of the world's total of 238 countries (in which 99% of the world's population is found). A number of subjects are shown on the left broken down into divisions and subdivisions or components listed below them, indented. All indented titles in the tables therefore form part of, and are included in, unindented or less-indented categories above them. Lines are listed in approximate chronological order of their emergence (shown by dates in Table 5-8's column 3) and similarly with divisions, subdivisions, and components. Definitions of major categories are as given and explained throughout this volume, which contains details of all the denominations involved; additional data and explanations are given below. Basic data and bibliographies on the Pentecostal/Charismatic Renewal may be found in each country's article in WCE Part 4; also in C. E. Jones, A guide to the study of Pentecostalism (1983, 2 vols, 9,883 entries), also Jones, Black Holiness: A guide to the study of Black participation in Wesleyan Perfectionism and glossolalic Pentecostal movements (1987), and with W. J. Hollenweger, ed., Pentecostal research in Europe: problems, promises and people (1986), culminating in Hollenweger's 1997 magnum opus, Pentecostalism: origins and developments worldwide.

### COLUMNS 1-10 in Table 5-8
1. Reference number of line (same as in Table 5–9).
2. Usual current terminology for all major components and categories of the Renewal.
3. Year when first manifestations began.
4. Number of countries where category is in evidence in AD 2000.
5. Number of distinct denominations (including networks, paradenominations, quasi-denominations) involved in 2000.
6-10. Number of participants (total community or affiliated) at 1900, 1970, 1995, 2000, with projections to AD 2025 based on current trends.

### COLUMNS 1-6 in Table 5–9
1. Reference number of line (same as in Table 5–8).
2. Usual current terminology for all major components and categories of the Renewal (identical to listing in Table 5–8).
3. Code as utilized in Country Tables 1 (CD version).
4. Code as utilized in Country Tables 2, column 3 'Type'.
5. Definitions, characteristics, examples of major significant bodies within each category.
6. Major country where each category is involved (4-letter country code).

### OTHER COLUMNS in electronic World Christian database
a. Rate of change (% per year) in AD 2000.
b. Annual growth rate (% per year) in AD 2000 due to purely demographic factors (births minus deaths).
c. Annual converts (% per year) in AD 2000.

d. Church members in Renewal by 7 continental areas and 21 major regions of the world as standardized by the United Nations, in AD 2000.
e. Church members in Renewal by the 7 continental areas and 21 major regions of the world given as percent of total church members on each line.

### THE RENEWAL AS A SINGLE MOVEMENT
The tables above view the 20th century Renewal in the Holy Spirit as one single cohesive movement into which a vast proliferation of all kinds of individuals and communities have been drawn in a whole range of different circumstances over a period of 450 years. Whether termed pentecostals, charismatics, or third-wavers, they share a single basic experience. Their contribution to Christianity is a new awareness of spiritual gifts as a ministry to the life of the church. The case for this thesis could be made by listing historical, missiological, theological, sociological, and other data. It could also be made by drawing attention to the fact that in the 1900, 1904, 1906 revivals, news of these traveled throughout the globe (by rail, by ship, by telegraph) in a few days and weeks; while today, news of such happenings—conversions, blessings, healings, movements—travels worldwide within a few seconds by telephone, radio, television, electronic mail, Internet, World Wide Web, etc. Such rapid communication across time, space, and all varieties of the Renewal reinforces its underlying unity.

The case for the statistical presentation of the Renewal as a single interconnected movement can, however, best be made by considering how the movement starts off and spreads in any area, from the days of the earliest pentecostals to those of current charismatics and third-wavers.

The start of the movement anywhere has always been an unexpected or unpredictable happening rather than any result of human planning or organization. First, individuals (at random across the existing churches), then groups, then large numbers in organized movements become filled with the Spirit and embark on the common charismatic experience. All of them, originally, can collectively and correctly be termed charismatics. All these charismatics find themselves living initially within existing mainline nonpentecostal churches and denominations. There, over the last 200 years they have been termed or labeled as charismatics, revivalists, enthusiasts, spirituals, or pentecostals; and often have been dismissed as cranks, fanatics, sectarians, heretics, schismatics, or worse. However, all of them initially attempt to stay within, and work within, those churches. But before long evictions begin, and ejections, withdrawals, and secessions occur in varying degrees. First, various individuals, then groups, then whole movements are forced into schism or opt for it and so begin separate ecclesiastical structures and new denominations.

From its beginnings in this way, the Renewal has subsequently expanded in three massive surges or waves. We can further divide these waves into a typology of 9 states, explained and described in the table at the foot of this page.

These 9 stages and categories are approximate and descriptive, not watertight or exclusive. For instance, as a result of the global influenza pandemic of 1918, large numbers of Blacks in Anglican churches in Africa (Nigeria, Kenya, Uganda, South Africa) became charismatics and formed charismatic prayer groups within Anglican parishes. The majority, however, were soon evicted (and so are enumerated here in Tables 5-8 and 5-9 under line nos. 24, 25, 28, 29, 30, etc becoming what we now refer to as Black pentecostals); only a minority (10%) remained within Anglicanism as charismatics in what later became known as the Anglican Charismatic Renewal.

Having described the Renewal as a single movement, we shall next describe its component elements.

### THREE WAVES OF 20TH CENTURY RENEWAL.
The tables classify the various movements and types under the following 3 consecutive waves of the Renewal in the Holy Spirit, defining its 3 key terms as follows.

**1. Pentecostals.** These are defined as Christians who are

members of the major explicitly Pentecostal denominations in Pentecostalism or the Pentecostal Movement or the Pentecostal Renewal whose major characteristic is a rediscovery of, and a new experience of, the supernatural with a powerful and energizing ministry of the Holy Spirit in the realm of the miraculous that most other Christians have considered to be highly unusual. This is interpreted as a rediscovery of the spiritual gifts of New Testament times, and their restoration to ordinary Christian life and ministry. Pentecostalism is usually held to have begun in the USA in 1901 (although the present survey shows the year of origin as 1886). For a brief period it was a charismatic revival expecting to remain an interdenominational movement within the existing churches without beginning a new denomination; but from 1909 onward its members were increasingly ejected from all mainline bodies and so forced to begin new organized denominations. (See explanatory note no. 4, below, 'FIRST WAVE: PENTECOSTAL RENEWAL', for distinction between use of capital versus lower case 'p' in 'Pentecostal,' etc.)

Pentecostal denominations hold the distinctive teaching that all Christians should seek a postconversion religious experience called baptism in the Holy Spirit, and that a Spirit-baptized believer may receive one or more of the supernatural gifts known in the early church: instantaneous sanctification, the ability to prophesy, to practice divine healing through prayer, to speak in tongues (glossolalia), or to interpret tongues; singing in tongues, singing in the Spirit, dancing in the Spirit, praying with upraised hands; dreams, visions, discernment of spirits, words of wisdom, words of knowledge; emphasis on miracles, power encounters, exorcisms (casting out demons), resuscitations, deliverances, signs and wonders. From 1906 onward, the hallmark of explicitly Pentecostal denominations, by comparison with Holiness/Perfectionist denominations, has been the single addition of speaking with other tongues as the 'initial evidence' of one's having received the baptism of the Holy Ghost (or Holy Spirit), whether or not one subsequently experiences regularly the gift of tongues. Most Pentecostal denominations teach that tongues-speaking is mandatory for all members, but in practice today only from 5% to 35% of all members have practiced this gift either initially or as an ongoing experience. Pentecostal denominations proclaim a 'full' or 'fourfold' or 'fivefold' gospel of Christ as Savior, Sanctifier, Baptizer with the Holy Spirit, Healer, and Returning King. Collectively, all these denominations are sometimes referred to as the 'First Wave' of this whole 20th-century movement of Holy-Spirit-centered renewal. In the USA, Pentecostals usually name the entire body of these denominations founded before 1940 by the blanket term 'Classical Pentecostals' to distinguish them from the subsequent 'Neopentecostals' or 'Charismatics' in the nonpentecostal denominations.

**2. Charismatics.** These are defined as Christians affiliated to non-Pentecostal denominations (Anglican, Protestant, Catholic, Orthodox), who receive the experiences above in what then became termed the Charismatic Movement whose roots go back to 1907 and 1918 but whose rapid expansion has been mainly since 1950 (later called the Charismatic Renewal), usually describing themselves as having been renewed in the Spirit and experiencing the Spirit's supernatural and miraculous and energizing power, who remain within, and form organized renewal groups within, their older mainline nonpentecostal denominations (instead of leaving to join Pentecostal denominations). They demonstrate any or all of the charismata pneumatika (Greek New Testament: gifts of the Spirit) including signs and wonders (but with glossolalia regarded as optional). The whole Movement is sometimes termed the 'Second Wave' of the 20th-century Renewal. Concerning the key word, note that 'In the technical Pauline sense charismata (AV, gifts) denote extraordinary powers, distinguishing certain Christians and enabling them to serve the church of Christ, the reception of which is due to the power of divine grace operating in their souls by the Holy Spirit' (Thayer's Greek-English Lexicon of the New Testament, 1886, 1977: 667).

**3. Neocharismatics (or, Third-Wavers).** Since 1945 thousands of schismatic or other independent charismatic churches have come out of the Charismatic Movement; these independents have throughout the 20th century from 1900 to the present day numbered more than the first 2 waves combined. They consist of evangelicals and other Christians who, unrelated or no longer related to the Pentecostal or Charismatic Renewals, have become filled with the Spirit, or empowered or energized by the Spirit and experiencing the Spirit's supernatural and miraculous ministry (though usually without recognizing a baptism in the Spirit separate from conversion), who exercise gifts of the Spirit (with much less emphasis on tongues, as optional or even absent or unnecessary), and emphasize signs and wonders, supernatural miracles and power encounters, who leave their mainline nonpentecostal denominations but also do not identify themselves as either pentecostals or charismatics. In a number of countries they exhibit pentecostal and charismatic phenomena but combine this with rejection of pentecostal terminology. These believers are increasingly being identified by their leadership as Independent, Postdenominationalist, Restorationist, Radical, Neo-Apostolic, or the 'Third Wave' of the whole 20th-century Renewal, the terms 'Third Wave' and 'third-wavers' having been coined by a participant, C. Peter Wagner, in 1983. (See his articles 'A Third Wave?' in Pastoral renewal 8, no. 1 July-August 1983: 1-5, and 'The Third Wave' in Christian life, September 1984, p. 90, and his 1988 book The Third Wave of the Holy Spirit: encountering the power of signs and wonders today.) Because they constitute a major new revitalizing force, in this table we also term the movement the Neocharismatic Renewal.

**Layout of lines below.** The explanatory notes below have numbers referring to the numbered lines in Tables 5-8 and 5-

---

### A TYPOLOGY OF THE EVOLUTION OF CHARISMATICS WITHIN CHURCHES

Notes on the nine columns below:
1 = stage in evolution of new charismatic developments
2 = first year of start of new stage
3 = main or majority race involved in stage, either Whites or Non-Whites
4 = fate of charismatics in their existing parent churches
5 = percent of charismatics evicted from parent churches
6 = percent of charismatics who voluntarily secede from parent churches
7 = percent of charismatics lost to parent churches (= columns 5 + 6)
8 = percent remaining in parent churches (= 100 - column 7)
9 = new organizations or developments resulting

| Stage 1 | Start 2 | Race 3 | History of charismatics 4 | Fate, % 5 | 6 | 7 | 8 | Resulting organizations 9 |
|---|---|---|---|---|---|---|---|---|
| FIRST WAVE: Rejection, eviction, secession, new denominations/communions | | | | | | | | = PENTECOSTAL RENEWAL |
| 1. | 1741 | Non-White | Immediate eviction | 100 | 0 | 100 | 0 | Black/Non-White denominations |
| 2. | 1900 | Whites | Eventual secession | 90 | 6 | 96 | 4 | White denominations |
| SECOND WAVE: Friction, toleration, renewed parishes, mainline groups | | | | | | | | = CHARISMATIC RENEWAL |
| 3. | 1783 | Non-Whites | Majority eviction | 80 | 10 | 90 | 10 | Isolated mainline prayer groups |
| 4. | 1907 | Whites | Minority eviction | 40 | 30 | 70 | 30 | Isolated healing ministries |
| 5. | 1940 | Whites | Partial eviction | 10 | 15 | 25 | 75 | Large-scale mainline networks |
| 6. | 1960 | Whites | Few evictions | 4 | 10 | 14 | 86 | Denominational charismatic agencies |
| THIRD WAVE: Power evangelism, new structures, networks, megachurches | | | | | | | | = NEOCHARISMATIC RENEWAL |
| 7. | 1980 | Whites | Occasional evictions | 2 | 8 | 10 | 90 | Postdenominationalist structures |
| 8. | 1990 | Non-Whites | Rare evictions | 1 | 1 | 2 | 98 | New denominations and communions |
| 9. | 2000 | Non-Whites | No evictions | 0 | 0 | 0 | 100 | New global mission |

9. They are set out with each line's title in column 2 being given below in boldface type.

**1. PERIPHERAL QUASI-PENTECOSTALS**
(Line nos. 1, 2, 3, 77, with key years of origin or watersheds added).
**2. Prepentecostals**
Scattered individual quasi-pentecostals have long been observed in mainline nonpentecostal denominations ('quasi' means apparent, seemingly, largely, to a great extent, to some extent). There have always been sizeable numbers of such individuals who have experienced or demonstrated pentecostal phenomena in their own lives or ministries although they do not call themselves as, nor are regarded by others as Pentecostals. For many it is a stage in a process that ends in them essentially becoming members of Pentecostal bodies; for most however they do not reach that stage.

Those in the last 200 years, and which may reasonably be regarded as antecedents of the 20th-century Renewal, fall into four main categories: (1) Several thousands of individual monks, priests, brothers, sisters, in Catholic, Orthodox, Anglican, and other monastic and religious orders, who have been allowed unhindered to exercise personal gifts of the Spirit including glossolalia, faith healing, et alia. Many of these were indirectly responsible for the Encyclical Letter 'On the Holy Spirit' issued in 1897 by Pope Leo XIII, directing attention to the sevenfold gifts of the Spirit (Isaiah 11) and promoting a universal novena (9-day cycle of prayer) to the Holy Spirit before Pentecost Sunday each year, which influenced millions of Roman Catholics. (2) Numerous Mormons (Latter-day Saints) including founder Joseph Smith and organizer Brigham Young have practiced glossolalia (though not included here in the statistics of prepentecostals). (3) Charismatic groupings in new movements of the 19th century, which have now become denominations that define themselves as part of the Renewal; thus Salvation Army headquarters (London) states: 'The history of the Salvation Army (beginning in 1865) is only intelligible as a work of the Holy Spirit. For this reason, the Salvation Army could itself be called a charismatic movement and its early meetings resembled charismatic meetings of today' (A. Bittlinger, ed, *The Church is Charismatic*, 1981:42). (4) Sanctified/perfectionist Anglicans and Protestants in holiness movements within the churches. Especially in the years 1855-1900, which saw the rise in the USA of the doctrine of baptism in the Holy Spirit, the term 'prepentecostals' describes individuals with a perfectionist or 'second-blessing' experience plus related pentecostal phenomena but belonging as members to antipentecostal, nonpentecostal, or prepentecostal denominations, particularly Holiness/Perfectionist bodies, popular American revivalism, and other denominations opposed to pentecostal phenomena (especially glossolalia), which claim instead that conversion and sanctification (often termed 'infilling with the Spirit') are the only two necessary and complete experiences promised to believers. On the eve of the year 1900, this category included (a) in the USA alone, several thousand scattered glossolalists, 100,000 'come-outers' (adults in Holiness split-offs and higher-life movements), and over 1,000,000 White (with some Black) 'loyalists' with the sanctification/infilling experience, belonging to Holiness, Wesleyan, and Methodist denominations; and (b) similar numbers abroad in Holiness/Wesleyan/Methodist denominations and movements and missions in Europe, South Africa, India, Chile, et alia. (For detailed treatment of the relation between the Holiness and Pentecostal movements, see H. V. Synan, *The Holiness-Pentecostal Movement in the United States*, 1971.) Historically, the prototype prepentecostal has been regarded as the Anglican revivalist priest John Wesley (1703-1791). For this reason, the first two words of Synan's study were deliberately chosen as 'John Wesley' (Synan 1971:13—'John Wesley, the indomitable founder of Methodism, was also the spiritual and intellectual father of the modern holiness and pentecostal movements which have issued from Methodism within the last century'). The best-known prepentecostal preacher before 1900 was the evangelist Dwight L. Moody, whose preaching from 1875 onward sometimes resulted in glossolalia (Synan 1971:99; the term 'pre-pentecostal' appears to have originated in this passage). Before 1900 there were many such cases: thus, tongues were a significant feature, according to some scholars, of the Camp Creek holiness revival in North Carolina in 1896; other scholars produce contrary evidence.

For the years 1970-2000 on line no. 2, the statistics refer mainly to similar 'sanctified Methodists' and other phenomenological pentecostals and quasipentecostals in these nonpentecostal denominations at present (especially in Church of the Nazarene, Wesleyan Church, Free Methodist Church, Salvation Army), most of which differ from pentecostalism only in the absence of tongues-speaking or in the absence of a doctrine that tongues-speaking is the essential evidence of baptism in the Holy Spirit. Most of these prepentecostals are unrelated to, and are uninvolved with, either Pentecostalism, or the Charismatic Movement, or the Third Wave of the 1980s; they do not identify themselves by the terms 'pentecostals,' 'charismatics,' or 'third-wavers.' However, a new complication is that a number of these denominations' largest congregations in the Third World have independently become Third-Wave; these are not enumerated on line no. 2 but later in the tables.
**3. Postpentecostals**
Former members of Pentecostal denominations who have left to join nonpentecostal denominations (due to marriage, family moves, job transfers, upward mobility, new interests in liturgy and theology, et alia), but who have not renounced their pentecostal experience, and who still identify themselves as pentecostal. Example: active postpentecostals formerly members of the International Pentecostal Holiness Church are nowadays estimated at 450,000 in the USA which is three times IPHC's present membership of 150,000.

**Notes on lines 4-64.**
Total Christian community affiliated to (on the rolls of) denominations, churches, or groups, including baptized members, their children and infants, catechumens, inquirers, attenders, but excluding interested non-Christian attenders, casual attenders, visitors, et alia. Many Pentecostal denominations enumerate their children and infants, and a number are paedobapitst (infant-baptizing). Most, however, ignore their children's statistics, which has led to serious undernumeration of the spread of the Renewal. Whenever statistics of church members are compared to total population figures (which almost always include children and infants), such membership figures must also include its children and infants. Like must always be compared with like.

**4. FIRST WAVE: PENTECOSTAL RENEWAL**
Pentecostals are defined here as all associated with explicitly Pentecostal denominations that identify themselves in explicitly Pentecostal terms (see definition of 'Pentecostals' near the beginning of these footnotes), or with other denominations that as a whole are phenomenologically pentecostal in teaching and practice. Current practice in the USA is to analyze the phenomenon as basically an American one, and as one distinct from Neopentecostalism (the Charismatic Movement), and so to label the whole of denominational Pentecostalism worldwide by the parallel or synonymous term 'Classical Pentecostalism'. In the present table, however, we are concerned more to see the entire phenomenon as a global one requiring a different set of descriptive terms. We therefore divide the movement into two major streams as shown by two different spellings: (1) the term 'Pentecostal' with a capital P denotes what we are terming Classical Pentecostalism (which is mainly White-originated), whereas (2) the term 'pentecostal' with a lowercase 'p' refers to the huge phenomenon of Black/Non-White/Third-World indigenous pentecostalism unrelated to Western Classical Pentecostalism (see notes below on line nos. 6-12). To avoid excessive repetition of the comprehensive adjective 'Pentecostal/pentecostal' the adjective 'pentecostal' is often used below to denote the whole. Historically, the First Wave developed out of Black slavery in the USA, the Evangelical (Wesleyan) Revival from 1738 in Britain, and the Holiness (Perfectionist) movement in Britain, the USA, and its world wide missions in the 19th century. Although many Pentecostal/pentecostal denominations had antecedents going back to the 18th century, the year 1901 is usually quoted as the year of origin of Pentecostalism because that is when the movement took off on a massive universal scale with widespread tongues and other pentecostal phenomena. Other scholars cite 1906 (Azusa Street), for the same reasons.
**5. Pentecostals**
(This line's statistics are computed as the sum of line nos. 7 + 11). These totals of all associated with explicitly Pentecostal denominations as elaborated above are derived from *WCE* Country Tables 2.
**6. Denominational Pentecostals**
In 740 major recognized, clear-cut, wholly Pentecostal denominations of Pentecostal theology or practice or stance, committed as denominations to Pentecostal distinctives; these include many minor or very small denominations in 225 different countries. (This line is the same as no. 5).
**7. Classical Pentecostals**
As explained above, in this global classification we define this as a blanket term for those in 660 traditional Western-related denominations which identify themselves as explicitly Pentecostal; almost all of White origin in USA, but now worldwide with adherents in all races, found in 220 countries (sum of line nos. 8-10). USA Pentecostal spokespersons use a somewhat wider definition which identifies 'Classical Pentecostals' (a term that dates from 1970) with all denominational Pentecostals in contrast to Neopentecostals (Charismatics); they therefore include under this term the major early Black pentecostal denominations in the USA, notably the Church of God in Christ with its 6 million members today (which, however, we here classify under line no. 29). In essence, our procedure is saying that the whole phenomenon of denominational Pentecostalism/pentecostalism is best understood when classified into the two subdivisions, (a) Black-originated pentecostalism and (b) White-originated Pentecostalism. As the better-organized and better-articulated form, category (b) then better merits the appellation 'classical' Pentecostalism.

There has been a certain amount of blurred boundaries and movement between Pentecostalism and the Charismatic Movement. Thus in 1948 the Latter Rain Revival (New Order of the Latter Rain) erupted among classical Pentecostals in Saskatchewan, Canada, and spread rapidly to Europe, USA, and across the world. It emphasized laying on of hands with prophecy, and government by an order of living apostles; it began Global Missions Broadcast (over radio); but from 1965, it merged into the Charismatic Movement.
**8. Holiness Pentecostals**
Also known as Wesleyan Pentecostals, or Methodistic Pentecostals, this was the universal Pentecostal position until the 1910 Northern USA change (see note 18, below), and still remains the major Southern USA position. It is found today in 240 denominations worldwide, teaching a 3-crisis experience (conversion, sanctification, baptism in the Spirit). First claimed glossolalia manifestations: 1897 Fire-Baptized Holiness Church, 1896 Church of God (Cleveland), 1906 Pentecostal Holiness Church. Total countries involved: 170.
**9. Baptistic Pentecostals**
Mainline Classical Pentecostals teaching 'finished work' or 2-crisis experience (conversion, baptism in the Spirit); in 390 denominations in 210 countries. Scores of Pentecostal denominations trace their origin to the 1906-9 Azusa Street Revival in Los Angeles, USA, under Bishop W. J. Seymour et alii, at which thousands first spoke in tongues; but the 'finished work' teaching (combining conversion with sanctification or 'second blessing') of W. H. Durham in 1910 shifted many Northern USA Pentecostals out of the Wesleyan 3-crisis teaching into the 2-crisis position now known as Baptistic Pentecostalism. The first new denomination to hold this position was the Assemblies of God, founded in 1914, which with its foreign mission work now in 118 countries is by far the largest Pentecostal worldwide denomination. Its meticulously kept annual statistics for each country form Pentecostalism's most solid body of statistical data and hence the main documentation for the Renewal's phenomenal growth.
**10. Apostolic Pentecostals**
The 1904 Welsh Revival under Evan Roberts, which is often regarded by European writers as the origin of the worldwide Pentecostal movement, prepared the way for British Pentecostalism, especially Apostolic-type teaching resulting in 1908 in the Apostolic Faith Church (Bournemouth), from which a schism in 1916 formed the Apostolic Church (HQ in Wales). Apostolics are now found worldwide in 30 denominations, stressing complex hierarchy of living apostles, prophets, and other charismatic officials. Total countries involved: 29.
**11. Oneness Pentecostals**
In 80 denominations in 74 countries; termed by outsiders Unitarian Pentecostals or Jesus-Only Pentecostals, but calling themselves Oneness-Pentecostals or Jesus Name Pentecostals; baptism in name of Jesus only; widely accepted ecclesiastically as Evangelicals but theologically as modal monarchians; since 1920 they have included 25% of all Pentecostals in the USA. The major denomination is the United Pentecostal Church, a 1945 union of the Pentecostal Assemblies of Jesus Christ (1913) and the Pentecostal Church (1916). In contrast to this emphasis within denominational Pentecostalism, the Charismatic Movement has remained explicitly Trinitarian throughout.

Many Third-Wave denominations (True Jesus Church, etc) also hold Oneness theologies, but are listed not here but under line nos. 25-48 as they occur.

**12. SECOND WAVE: CHARISMATIC RENEWAL**
Charismatics (or, until recently, Neopentecostals) are usually defined as those baptized or renewed in the Spirit within the mainline nonpentecostal denominations, from its first mass stirrings in 1918 in Africa on to the large-scale rise from 1950 of the Charismatic Movement (initially also termed Neopentecostalism to distinguish it from Classical Pentecostalism) who remain within their mainline nonpentecostal denominations. The Movement was later called the Charismatic Renewal. The exact definition used here is given above near the beginning of these footnotes. Note that many individuals and groups in the mainline churches had already received baptism in the Spirit without publicity for many years before the usually quoted beginning dates of 1900, 1907, 1924, 1950, 1959, 1962, 1967, etc. Note also that column 5 'Denominations' for the Charismatic Renewal means totals of nonpentecostal noncharismatic bodies with organized Renewal agencies within them: total is 6,530 denominations in 235 countries.
**13. Charismatics**
(This line's statistics of members are computed as the sum of line nos. 14-15, or 16-20). These totals of all associated explicitly with the Charismatic Renewal in the mainline nonpentecostal denominations are derived from detailed surveys summarized in *WCE* Country Tables 1 and 2 and given in full in *World Christian database*.
**14. Mainline active Charismatics**
Active members regularly (weekly, monthly, annually, including members' children) involved in prayer groups within the Charismatic Renewal in the older mainline denominations. During the period 1906-1950, many thousands of mainline clergy and hundreds of thousands of laity received the pentecostal experience and spoke in tongues, but many were ejected and later joined the Pentecostal denominations. By 2000 the Renewal had penetrated every one of the Christian world's 300 distinct ecclesiastical confessions, traditions, and families, with Charismatics within every tradition, and in the 6,530 denominations.
**15. Mainline Postcharismatics**
Self-identified charismatics within mainline nonpentecostal denominations who are no longer regularly active in the Charismatic Renewal but have moved into other spheres of witness and service in their churches. There are 3 major categories here. (1) **Protestant Postcharismatics** are Charismatics formerly active in Renewal, now inactive but in wider ministries; these inactive persons are much fewer than inactive Catholics because of the more developed teaching, pastoral care, and ministry opportunities offered by the 20 or so organized denominational renewal fellowships in the USA and their counterparts in Europe. An indication of the rapid turnover in membership is the fact that 25% of the 12,000 attenders at the Lutheran ILCOHS annual charismatic conferences in Minneapolis (USA) are first-timers, which implies an average 4-year turnover. (2) **Catholic Postcharismatics** are Charismatics formerly active in the Catholic Charismatic Renewal (for average turnover period of 2 to 3 years of active involvement in officially recognized Catholic Charismatic prayer groups), now in wider ministries; inaccurately called 'graduates' or 'alumni' of Renewal; in the USA, these consist of 4.6 million inactive in addition to active Catholic charismatic community including children. Added to active persons this means that in 1985 Catholic Charismatics worldwide numbered 63.5 million (7.3% of the entire Roman Catholic Church), rising to 11.3% by AD 2000). A number of Catholic theologians hold that Spirit baptism is as irreversible as water baptism. Lastly, (3) **Anglican Postcharismatics** likewise are Charismatics formerly active in the Anglican Charismatic Renewal, often as far back as 1953, but who are now not actively involved though usually involved in foreign mission or other ministries.
**16. Anglican Charismatics**
Anglican pentecostals, begun 1907 with clergyman A. A. Boddy (Sunderland, England); then from 1918, due to the

global influenza pandemic, numerous prayer and healing groups in the Anglican churches of Nigeria and Kenya, inter alia; then from 1925 the Spirit Movement (Aladura), which was then expelled and seceded as today's African indigenous churches (with total membership of 50 million, here enumerated in line no. 25); subsequently numerous isolated clergy and groups in several countries up to US Episcopalian Agnes Sanford's healing ministry from 1953, priests R. Winkler in 1956 and D. Bennett in 1959, Blessed Trinity Society (1961), and Church of England clergyman M. C. Harper in 1962 (who then founded Fountain Trust in 1964); in 18 countries by 1978, expanding to 95 countries by 1987 (with 850,000 active adherents in UK served by Anglican Renewal Ministries (ARM); 520,000 (18% of all Episcopalians) in USA served by Episcopal Renewal Ministries; with branches of ARM in other countries also); with by AD 2000 rapid increase to 17.5 million in 165 denominations in 163 countries. Much of this expansion is due to a unique structured international Charismatic ministry body, SOMA (Sharing of Ministries Abroad), begun 1979, which now covers 27 of the 37 Anglican Provinces worldwide and partially covers more, working by 1987 in 70 countries.

### 17. Catholic Charismatics
Known at first as Catholic pentecostals or neopentecostals, then as the Catholic Charismatic Renewal, begun with early stirrings in Third-World countries (Africa, Latin America), then definitively in 1967 in USA; in 1985, 60,000 prayer groups in 140 countries worldwide (in USA 10,500 English, Vietnamese, Korean, Filipino, Haitian, Hispanic, and several other language groups), rising to 143,000 by 1995. Since 1978 there have been National Service Committees in over 120 countries uniting Catholic Charismatics. Streams of different emphasis in the USA and several other countries: (a) that centered on Word of God Community (Servant Ministries, University Christian Outreach, *New Covenant* magazine, in Ann Arbor, Mich., with overseas communities and work in Belgium, Honduras, Hong Kong, India, Indonesia, Lebanon, Nicaragua, Northern Ireland, Philippines, South Africa, Sri Lanka) with cohesive, authoritarian leadership, which originated ICCRO in Brussels, Belgium; and (b) that centered on People of Praise Community (South Bend, Ind.), ICCRO after its relocation in Vatican City in 1987, and a wide international network of covenant communities, with a less authoritarian structure and leadership style. *Priests.* Since 1974 some 4% of USA priests have been active in the Renewal, including 2% now Postcharismatics. Priests worldwide (now 9,470) are less involved than bishops (now 450); foreign missionaries are more involved than home clergy.

A full interpretation of the methodology of this survey of the Catholic Charismatic Renewal is given above in the 4-page minisurvey and analysis itself.

### 18. Protestant Charismatics
Origins: 1909 Lutheran prayer groups in state churches (Germany), 1918 charismatics in African countries secede to form AICs (African indigenous churches), 1931 Reformed groups related to 1946 Union de Prière (south of France), 1932 charismatic revival in Methodist Church (Southern Rhodesia) leading to massive AACJM schism, 1945 Darmstadt Sisters of Mary (Germany), 1950 Dutch Reformed Church (Netherlands); 1950 origins of Protestant neopentecostals in USA; 1958 large-scale neopentecostal movements in Brazil's Protestant churches (Renovação); in 38 countries by 1978, in 130 by 1987, and in 5,780 denominations in 231 countries by 2000. Some representative figures: East Germany, 500,000 participants (7% of all members) in state Lutheran church.

### 19. Orthodox Charismatics
Contemporary successors of scores of charismatic movements within Russian Orthodox Church dating from Spiritual Christians (AD 1650); also charismatics in Greek Orthodox Church in Greece, and Eastern and Oriental Orthodox churches in USA (1967, Fr. A. Emmert, who by 1987 had become a Melkite Catholic convert), Canada, Australia, Lebanon, Uganda, Kenya, Tanzania, Egypt, and some 30 other countries. Agency: Service Committee for Orthodox Spiritual Renewal (SCOSR). A recent significant development is the rapid spread of the Brotherhood of Lovers of the Church, a charismatic renewal within the Armenian Apostolic church in the USSR. Despite these stirrings, Orthodox authorities have general harassed charismatics relentlessly, this hostility being due to the Orthodox assertion that they never lost the Spirit or the charismata.

### 20. Marginal Charismatics
There has always been a small nucleus of practicing Charismatics within the various heterodox organizations in the marginal Christian megabloc.

### 21. THIRD WAVE: NEOCHARISMATIC RENEWAL
These terms describe a new wave of the 20th-century Renewal in the Holy Spirit gathering momentum in the 1980s and 1990s with no direct affiliation with either Pentecostalism or the Charismatic Renewal. Note that large numbers of phenomenological charismatics (in Korea, East Germany, Poland, et alia) do not identify themselves as either pentecostal or charismatic, and instead exhibit a marked rejection of pentecostal terminology.

### 22. Neocharismatics (Third-Wavers, Independents, Post-denominationalists, Neo-Apostolics)
Persons in mainline nonpentecostal denominations, recently filled with or empowered with the Spirit but usually nonglossolalic, who do not identify themselves with the terms 'pentecostal' or 'charismatic.' Because they demonstrate the charismata and the phenomena of pentecostalism, they are also being termed (by outside observers) 'quasicharismatics'. Totals in AD 2000: 295,405,240 members in 18,810 denominations or networks, in 225 countries. Neocharismatics can be divided into 2 categories: (a) those in networks entirely (100%) Neocharismatics (see line no. 23); and (b) Neocharismatic individuals in nonpentecostal/charismatic denominations (see line no. 52).

### 23. (a) In 2 kinds of wholly Third-Wave networks
These 100% Neocharismatic bodies have 253,936,500 members in 17,125 denominations/networks in 220 countries.

### 24. Non-White indigenous Neocharismatics
Apparent/seemingly/largely pentecostal or semipentecostal members of this 250-year-old movement of churches indigenous to Christians in Non-White races across the world, and begun without reference to Western Christianity; estimated in 1970 as 60% (rising by 1985 to 75%) of all members of the over 1,000 Non-White/Third-World indigenous denominations, which, though not all explicitly pentecostal, nevertheless have the main phenomenological hallmarks of pentecostalism (charismatic spirituality, oral liturgy, narrative witness/theology, dreams and visions, emphasis on filling with the Holy Spirit, healing by prayer, atmospheric communication [simultaneous audible prayer], emotive fellowship, et alia). These denominations are found in AD 2000 in 210 different countries on all continents, in 13,425 denominations, numbering 203,870,000 persons. The case for enumerating adherents of these movements as pentecostals has been fully made by W. J. Hollenweger in his writings, most recently in 'After twenty years' research on Pentecostalism,' *International review of mission* (April 1986), and *Pentecostalism* (1997). Note that the term 'indigenous' as used here refers to the auto-origination of these movements, begun among Non-White races without Western or White missionary support.

This whole category can be divided into various subcategories. **Indigenous holiness-pentecostals** are found in some 60 denominations, teaching 3-crisis experience (conversion, sanctification, baptism in the Spirit); in 35 different countries. **Indigenous baptistic-pentecostals** exist in 70 denominations, teaching 2-crisis experience (conversion, baptism in the Spirit); in 45 different countries. **Indigenous oneness-pentecostals** are widespread in 60 denominations practicing baptism in name of Jesus only; the major such body with missions worldwide is the True Jesus Church (begun in China, 1917). The first such new denomination, a schism from the (mainly White) Assemblies of God (USA), was the Pentecostal Assemblies of the World (1916). These bodies are found in 38 countries today. **Indigenous pentecostal-apostolics** have over 60 denominations in 18 countries; stress on complex hierarchy of living apostles, prophets, and other charismatic officials. **Indigenous radical-pentecostals** are found in over 100 deliverance-pentecostal denominations in at least 40 countries and expanding rapidly. Most of the mushrooming new youth churches, hotel churches, theater churches, cinema churches, store churches, and open-air churches are in this category. This category is also known as perfectionist-pentecostals, free pentecostals, deliverance-pentecostals, revivalist-pentecostals, teaching 4-crisis experience including deliverance/ecstatic-confession/ascension/perfectionism/prophecy; in over 40 denominations, in over 30 countries and rapidly expanding.

### 25. African indigenous pentecostals/charismatics
In 60 countries and 9,300 denominations with 66 million members, 92 national councils of AICs, and the continent-wide Organization of African Instituted (formerly Independent) Churches, based in Nairobi, Kenya. Origins: 1864.

An important historical note must be added here. In the year 1900 the mainline mission bodies in Africa (Catholic, Anglican, Protestant) regarded these believers as, at best, 'nominal' Christians or 'unaffiliated' Christians, and this is how they appear in *WCE*'s Country Tables 1 (for Nigeria, South Africa, et alia). Today they are classified, as here, as Independent Neocharismatics.

### 26. Afro-Caribbean pentecostals/charismatics
Begun in 1783 in Jamaica (Native Baptists, Revival Zionists, Shouters, Shakers, et alia), in 1860 in Trinidad and Tobago (West Indies Spiritual Baptist Churches, National Evangelical Spiritual Baptist Church, National Spiritual Baptist Council of Churches), now in 420 denominations in 38 countries across the world.

### 27. Arab/Assyrian/Semitic neocharismatics
There are only some 130 denominations in 40 countries. Membership stands at 1.3 million.

### 28. Black American independent charismatics
Only recently begun, with one large body: Full Gospel Baptist Churches Fellowship (New Orleans, USA); 10 denominations, 1.5 million members.

### 29. Black American indigenous pentecostals
Black Christians in explicitly pentecostal denominations in 20 countries, indigenous to Non-White races in that they were begun without outside Western or White missionary assistance or support. The largest is the Church of God in Christ (begun 1895). Most Pentecostal spokespersons in the USA define this variety as an integral part of Classical Pentecostalism, although in this table we give this term a more restricted definition (see line no 7). Our reasoning is that, seen in the total global perspective, this variety is far more accurately located as the archetype of global Non-White pentecostalism. Furthermore, many Black pentecostals regard the terms 'Pentecostal' and 'Charismatic' as largely White in origin, and have traditionally preferred the term 'sanctified.' Denominations: 90, with 7.6 million members.

### 30. Black American Oneness Apostolics
Some 150 denominations in 10 countries with 3 million membership. Most belong to the Apostolic World Christian Fellowship (150 denominations).

### 31. Brazilian/Portuguese grassroots neocharismatics
There were numerous early movements in Portuguese Africa (Angola): 2 prophet movements, Nkimba and Kimpasi, had broken from Jesuit missions by 1656; later, prophetess Fumaria; Donna Beatrice's attempt to found an independent Catholic church, for which king Pedro IV had her burned alive in 1706; 1872, Kiyoka; 1904 Epikilipikili; et alia. By AD 2000 independent pentecostal bodies in Portuguese-speaking countries on 5 continents numbered 460 denominations with 23 million members in 20 countries; including IURD, OBPC, CCB, IPDA, MC (Portugal).

### 32. Colored/Mixed-race indigenous charismatics
In 4 countries of Southern Africa, 70 denominations for Coloreds: Christen Gemeente, et alia.

### 33. Ethnic (Monoethnic) pentecostal churches
In 20 denominations with 1.5 million members in 20 countries.

### 34. Filipino indigenous pentecostals/charismatics
6.8 million members in 380 denominations in 25 countries; the earliest began in 1913.

### 35. Han Chinese indigenous pentecostals/ charismatics
A strong tradition beginning in 1905, widespread by 1955, expanding rapidly throughout mainland China by 1982; by 1985, almost 25% of all Protestants were tongues-speakers; estimates of the proportion of all Chinese Christians who are phenomenologically pentecostals/charismatics range from 50% to 85%, in large numbers and networks of de-facto independent pentecostal or charismatic churches. Total: 50 million members in 180 denominations in 58 countries.

### 36. Indian indigenous pentecostals/charismatics
With 16.6 million members in 580 denominations in 25 countries including Europe and the USA.

### 37. Indonesian indigenous pentecostals
Over 6.8 million members in 170 major denominations in 5 countries.

### 38. Japanese indigenous pentecostals
There are 50 denominations with 1.2 million adherents, in 15 countries.

### 39. Korean indigenous pentecostals/charismatics
Begun 1910, there are now 170 denominations with 3.3 million members in 30 countries worldwide.

### 40. Latino-Hispanic grassroots believers
There are 11.9 million believers in 990 denominations or networks in 24 countries. 'Grassroots' churches is the name given in preference to Western terminology.

### 41. Messianic Hindu believers in Christ
Since 1921, 5 denominations or networks have arisen, now with 163,000 members.

### 42. Messianic Jewish believers in Christ
Some 2% of all Jews (350,000) are believers in Jesus Christ (Yeshua the Mashiach/Messiah), also known as Jewish Christians, Christian Jews, Hebrew Christians, or Messianic Jews (the latter being those who emphasize Jewish roots and rituals). Of the 150,000 Messianic Jews, 75% (110,000) identify themselves as charismatic, particularly in the 53 churches of the Union of Messianic Jewish Congregations (USA); other charismatics are found in Britain (London Messianic Fellowship), France (Paris), Italy, USSR (aided by Finnish Lutheran Jewish missions broadcasts), Argentina, Israel (3,000, including Beth Emmanuel, Tel Aviv). A smaller number of other Jewish charismatics are found in Pentecostal denominations (Assemblies of God with 37 centers in USA, International Church of the Foursquare Gospel, et alia), or in Anglican/Catholic/Protestant charismatic groupings, so are classified here under line nos. 16, 17, 18.

### 43. Messianic Muslim believers in Christ
The 126,000 believers in Jesus mosques are in 2 countries, but many more are incipient movements elsewhere.

### 44. Pacific/Oceanic indigenous charismatics
214,600 members in 70 denominations in 20 countries.

### 45. Red Indian/AmerIndian neopentecostals
Over 530,000 members in 3 countries in 4 bodies, but not much growth or spreading elsewhere.

### 46. Vietnamese indigenous neocharismatics
There are at least 230,000 believers in the Good News house church movement; much opposition and persecution.

### 47. Other Asian indigenous neocharismatics
1.2 million believers in 130 denominations in 40 countries (Thailand, Malaysia, et alia).

### 48. Other Messianic non-Christian believers in Christ
Some 200,000 believers in 20 denominations in 15 countries not covered by the above categories; most are hidden believers.

### 49. White-led Independent Postdenominationalists
Independent charismatic and neocharismatic churches that either have separated from the Charismatic Renewal in parent mainline denominations (thus 50% of all Presbyterian charismatics in USA are known to have left to join these new churches), or have recently been founded independently (though from out of the same milieux), all being either independent congregations or in loose networks, and all being mainly or predominantly of White membership (Europeans, North Americans) or under overall White leadership or initiative. Total: 50 million members in 3,700 denominations in 210 countries.

### 50. European/American White-led Neo-Apostolics
These number 41 millions in 3,510 denominations or networks in 200 countries. Examples: house church movements in England (Restor-ation, and 5 other major groupings), Scotland, Norway, Sweden (many, including Rhema Fellowship), Denmark, Hungary, Poland, France (several communities), Switzerland, Spain (Witnessing), Netherlands (many), New Zealand, South Africa (many, including International Fellowship of Charismatic Churches, with 300 churches, Hatfield Christian Centre [162 churches], etc), former Soviet Union/USSR (in Central Russia, Northern Russia, Ukraine, Baltic, Georgia, et alia), and USA (60,000 recently formed churches in several major groupings or networks, with some overlap: International Fellowship of Faith Ministries [2,000 churches], International Convention of Faith Churches and Ministries [495 churches; in Tulsa], Faith Christian Fellowship International [1,000 ordained ministers], Melodyland Christian Center, People of Destiny, International Communion of Charismatic Churches [former classical Pentecostals, very large, fastest growing network in 1988], Network of Christian Ministries [Latter Rain emphasis], Fellowship of Christian Assemblies [101 churches], Marantha Christian Churches [57 churches], Fellowship of Covenant Ministers & Churches [250 churches], Association of Vineyard Churches [200 churches, founder John Wimber; note that he and the churches have regarded themselves as Third-Wavers rather than Charismatics, though most observers hold the

reverse is truer], National Leadership Conference, Charismatic Bible Ministries [1,500 ministers], Word Churches [Word of Faith Movement], Calvary Ministries International [200 churches], Local Covenant Churches [Shepherding], Rhema Ministerial Association [525 churches], International Ministers Forum [500 churches], Full Gospel Chaplaincy [3 million independent charismatics], Christ for the Nations [600 churches], Abundant Life Community Churches [25 churches], et alia. This category also includes quasidenominational networks such as Full Gospel Fellowship of Churches and Ministers International (begun 1962; 425 churches). There are thus similar movements, related and unrelated, in 84% of all the countries of the world.

### 51. European White-led New Apostolics
Origins: 1832 schism (Irvingites) in London ex-Church of Scotland (Presbyterian) stressing Catholic features, hierarchy of living apostles, glossolalia, and that all the New Testament charismata have now been restored; Old Apostolics; 1863 formation of Universal Catholic Church (Germany), later renamed New Apostolic Church, emphasizing the gifts of the Holy Spirit including prophecy, tongues interpretation of tongues, miraculous healing, sacraments, hierarchy of 48 living Apostles (1970: 1,700,000 members worldwide; AD 2000, 9,600,000). Total countries involved: 48 in 1980, increasing by AD 2000 to 180.

### 52. (b) as % of 7 kinds of non-Third-Wave denominations
This category summarizes Neocharismatic individuals who are members of Independent denominations or networks that are nonpentecostal/noncharismatic or even antipentecostal/ant100charismatic. As shown in the *World Christian database*, each such body is assigned a percent figure estimating the size of its Neocharismatic members. Total in AD 2000: 41,468,700 in 925 denominations in 200 countries.

### 53. Independent Anglican neocharismatics
1.7 million in 130 denominations claiming to be true Anglicans; in 80 countries since 1925.

### 54. Independent Protestant neocharismatics
Some 20.5 millions are in 800 denominations of Protestant origin, background, or ethos, in 180 countries since 1920.

### 55. Independent Catholic neocharismatics
Mainly within Old Catholic Churches in Netherlands, USA, and 10 other countries. At its origin in the Netherlands in the 1723 Schism of Utrecht, the Jansenist Church (later Old Catholic Church) specifically embraced 'signs and wonders' (miracles, healings, supernatural signs, spiritual gifts).

### 56. Independent Orthodox neocharismatics
Some 580,000 since the 1666 origin in Russia of Old Believers; 90 denominations in 20 countries.

### 57. Nonhistorical Independent neocharismatics
3.5 million Black neopentecostals within Black Baptist and Methodist and other denominations in the Independent megabloc in around 60 countries.

### 58. Isolated radio/TV neocharismatics
Those in isolated regions with no denominations or churches, whose on-going Christian life derives only from foreign radio broadcasts: 188,000 in 30 countries.

### 59. Hidden non-Christian believers in Christ
Often termed NBBCs (non-baptized believers in Christ), these number over 13 million since 1800, in 290 networks.

### 60. Hidden Hindu neocharismatics
With 9.7 million NBBCs mainly in India and 3 other countries.

### 61. Hidden Muslim neocharismatics
About 418,000 believers in 15 countries.

### 62. Hidden Buddhist neocharismatics
2.2 million believers in 15 countries.

### 63. Hidden Jewish neocharismatics
Members are thought to number 250,000 in 50 groupings in 15 countries.

### 64. Hidden other-religionist neocharismatics
Some 1.1 million believers in 200 networks in 50 countries.

### 65. doubly-counted First/Second/Third Wavers
This category numbering several million persons is difficult to assess because of differences in definition and enumeration procedures. An estimate may be obtained as the totals of line nos. 4-64 minus line no. 66. The category enumerates the growing number of believers and congregations who are enumerated as either Pentecostals (within the First Wave) or Charismatics (within the Second Wave), but who also are in addition regarded or regard themselves as Neocharismatics within the Third Wave. Many Methodist, Baptist, Assemblies of God, and other congregations are in this position and thus are counted twice in our enumeration. The grand total on line no. 65 is therefore shown as a negative quantity to arrive at accurate overall totals. Examples include many African, Asian, and Latin American believers; this category includes many large, widely known or outstanding Third-World churches and congregations belonging to nonpentecostal denominations founded by nonpentecostal or even antipentecostal mission boards from Europe and North America. Among the most prominent of such congregations are 4 from Korea: Sung Rak Baptist Church, Seoul (at 25,000 members the largest Southern Baptist-related congregation in the world until its secession in September 1987); Central Evangelical Holiness Church, Seoul (at 6,000 members the largest Holiness congregation in the world); and the world's two largest Methodist congregations, in Inchon and Seoul (25,000 members each). All of these congregations exhibit charismatic and pentecostal phenomena.

### 66. Global Pentecostals/Charismatics/Neocharismatics (affiliated).
Sum of lines nos. 5, 13, 22 minus line 65 (the Three Waves of Renewal).

## 67. RENEWAL MEMBERS ON 7 CONTINENTS
Ranked by size: 1. Latin America, 2. Asia, 3. Africa, 4. Northern America, 5. Europe, 6. Oceania, 7. Antarctica.

### 68. Renewal members in Africa
Total 126,000,000: 12% Pentecostals, 25% Charismatics, 63% Neocharismatics.

### 69. Renewal members in Antarctica
Total 400: 50% Catholics, 30% Protestants.

### 70. Renewal members in Asia
Total 134,890,000: 5% Pentecostals, 16% Charismatics, 79% Neocharismatics.

### 71. Renewal members in Europe
Total 37,569,000: 8% Pentecostals, 56% Charismatics, 36% Neocharismatics.

### 72. Renewal members in Latin America
Total 141,433,000: 23% Pentecostals, 52% Charismatics, 24% Neocharismatics.

### 73. Renewal members in Northern America
Total 79,600,000: 7% Pentecostals, 28% Charismatics, 65% Neocharismatics.

### 74. Renewal members in Oceania
Total 4,266,000: 14% Pentecostals, 63% Charismatics, 24% Neocharismatics.

### 75. Renewal members as % global church members
Computed as line no. 66 divided by line no. 99, times 100.

## 76. PERIPHERAL CONSTITUENTS
Not counted as Renewal members, but clearly related to it or close to it are 2 more categories.

### 77. Quasi-Pentecostals
This first category consists of Prepentecostals (of whom John Wesley is the archetype), and Postpentecostals (former members of Pentecostal denominations who have left to join such nonpentecostal mainline bodies as Anglicanism, Catholicism, Lutheranism, etc).

### 78. Unaffiliated believers professing Renewal
This use of the term 'believers' refers to persons with pentecostal gifts or experience who are professing pentecostals/charismatics but who do not, or do not yet, belong to pentecostal or charismatic or third-wave organized churches or groups or communities or denominations. Large numbers become pentecostals/charismatics in personal experience several weeks, months, or even years before they find a church or group and get enrolled and therefore enumerated. They can be estimated, as here, by careful comparison of polls of those professing with those affiliated (enrolled).

## 79. WIDER GLOBAL TOTALS OF RENEWAL
Living persons associated with Renewal consisting of (a) column 66, (b) column 78, and column 77.

### 80. Total all Renewal believers alive at mid-year
It is important to remember that virtually all Pentecostal or Charismatic or Neocharismatic statistics collected, published, or quoted by members or observers are of living believers only and do not include believers who have just died or just been martyred. To balance this bias, line number 81 has been added here.

### 81. Renewal believers dying since AD 1900
These figure give a much truer picture of the size of Renewal if one is speaking about the whole of the 20th century. The formula used is: Dead believers = death rate (averaging 1% per year/100x$(P_2-P_1)/^{(P_2/P_1)}\frac{1}{t_2-t_1}$-1 where $P_1$ = total live believers initially at year $t_1$, and $P_2$ = total live believers at end at year $t_2$.

### 82. Total all Renewal believers ever, since AD 1900
Calculated as columns 80 plus 81. By mid AD 2000 this total had passed 795 millions.

## 83. CHURCHES, FINANCE, AGENCIES, WORKERS
All distinct organized local congregations, worship centers, parishes, fellowships or groupings of all kinds, which are explicitly identified with or attached to the Renewal. *Megachurches*. A majority of the 150 or so largest megachurches (the world's largest single congregations, each with over 50,000 members) are pentecostal/charismatic. The largest Protestant church is Full Gospel Central

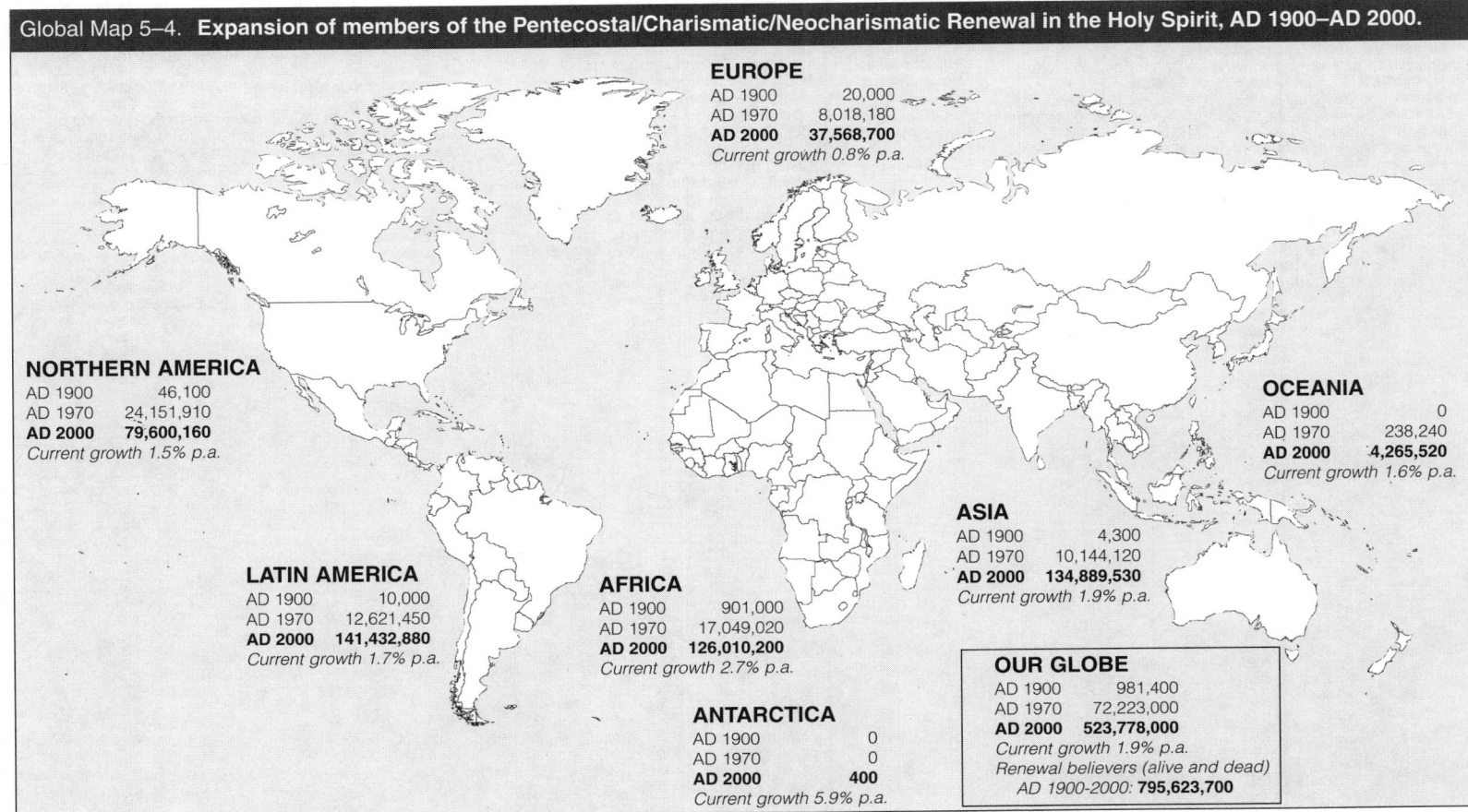

**Global Map 5–4.   Expansion of members of the Pentecostal/Charismatic/Neocharismatic Renewal in the Holy Spirit, AD 1900–AD 2000.**

**EUROPE**
AD 1900          20,000
AD 1970       8,018,180
**AD 2000    37,568,700**
*Current growth 0.8% p.a.*

**NORTHERN AMERICA**
AD 1900          46,100
AD 1970      24,151,910
**AD 2000    79,600,160**
*Current growth 1.5% p.a.*

**OCEANIA**
AD 1900               0
AD 1970         238,240
**AD 2000     4,265,520**
*Current growth 1.6% p.a.*

**ASIA**
AD 1900           4,300
AD 1970      10,144,120
**AD 2000   134,889,530**
*Current growth 1.9% p.a.*

**LATIN AMERICA**
AD 1900          10,000
AD 1970      12,621,450
**AD 2000   141,432,880**
*Current growth 1.7% p.a.*

**AFRICA**
AD 1900         901,000
AD 1970      17,049,020
**AD 2000   126,010,200**
*Current growth 2.7% p.a.*

**ANTARCTICA**
AD 1900               0
AD 1970               0
**AD 2000             400**
*Current growth 5.9% p.a.*

**OUR GLOBE**
AD 1900         981,400
AD 1970      72,223,000
**AD 2000   523,778,000**
*Current growth 1.9% p.a.*
*Renewal believers (alive and dead)*
*AD 1900-2000:* **795,623,700**

Church, Seoul, Korea, with 600,000 members by 1988, and 800,000 by 1998.

### 84. Pentecostal churches, congregations (1st Wave)
Largest grouping, Assemblies of God (U.S.A. and overseas): churches excluding outstations (1985) 77,976, (1986) 92,355 (15.6% per year increase). All denominations: 480,000 congregations.

### 85. Mainline Charismatic prayer groups (2nd Wave)
Growth of weekly groups: (1960) 10,000, rising to (AD 2000) 550,000.

### 86. Catholic Charismatic weekly prayer groups
Growth of weekly groups: (1970) 2,185; (1980) 12,000; (1990) 90,000; (2000) 160,000.

### 87. Anglican & Protestant Charismatic groups
Some 250,000 regular prayer groups were meeting by AD 2000.

### 88. Independent congregations, house churches (3rd Wave)
Around 591,000 by AD 2000.

### 89. Personal income of all Renewal members, $ p.a.
Defined as in article 'Silver and gold have I none,' in *International bulletin of missionary research* (October 1983), p. 150. By 2000, personal income of all Renewal members reached US$1,550 billion per year.

### 90. Renewal members' giving to all Christian causes, $ p.a.
By AD 2000 this amounted to at least $30 billion per year.

### 91. Renewal service agencies
National, countrywide, regional or international bodies, parachurch organizations and agencies which assist or serve the churches but are not themselves denominations or church-planting mission bodies. Among the most significant categories are (a) Pentecostal agencies (missions, evangelism, publishing, etc.), (b) denominational charismatic agencies: Anglican Renewal Ministries (U.K.), Episcopal Renewal Ministries (USA), International Catholic Charismatic Renewal Services (Vatican City), National Service Committees for the Catholic Charismatic Renewal (in over 120 countries), and 100 more such bodies, (c) global mission agencies: SOMA, Advance, AIMS, and other missionary bodies serving the Charismatic Renewal, and (d) Third-World mission agencies: over 500 locally organized and supported charismatic sending bodies. One of the fastest-growing varieties of renewal agency is TV production organizations, numbering over 500 by 1987 and 1,000 by AD 2000. Grand total by AD 2000: 4,000 agencies.

### 92. Renewal institutions
Major pentecostal/charismatic church-operated or -related institutions of all kinds, i.e., fixed centers with premises, plant, and permanent staff, excluding church buildings, worship centers, church headquarters or offices; including high schools, colleges, universities, medical centers, hospitals, clinics presses, bookshops, libraries, radio/TV stations and studios, conference centers, study centers, research centers, seminaries, religious communities (monasteries, abbeys, convents, houses), etc. Many of these have been originated by Pentecostal bodies, a growing number by mainline Charismatics, and a vast mushrooming of new institutions have been begun by Third-Wave networks and churches. But in countries where new initiatives have been prohibited or repressed (e.g., before 1989 East Germany, Poland), thousands of traditionally Christian institutions have been infiltrated and virtually taken over by charismatics. *Charismatic covenant communities.* Since 1958 (Community of Jesus, Cape Cod, Mass., now with 900 members) and 1965 (Episcopal Church of the Redeemer, Houston, Tex.), residential communities committed to intentional corporate charismatic life, service and mission, mainly ecumenical or interdenominational, with married couples and families as well as celibates, have arisen in 50 countries across the world. Size varies from under 20 persons each to 4,000 (Emmanuel Community, Paris, France, begun 1972). Total communities in 1987: some 2,000 with over quarter of a million members; rising to treble that number by 1998. A very detailed survey is given by P. Hocken, 'The Significance of Charismatic Communities,' in P. Elbert, ed., *Charismatic Renewal in the Churches* (1990). Grand total by AD 2000: 14,000.

### 93. All pentecostal/charismatic full-time workers
Full-time church workers, pastors, clergy, ministers, evangelists, missionaries, executives, administrators, bishops, moderators, church leaders, et alia. This line is the sum of the next two, nos. 94 and 95. Grand total by AD 2000: 2,100,000.

### 94. Nationals: pastors, clergy, evangelists, et alii
Some representative statistics: (1) *Pentecostal Renewal.* Assemblies of God (USA and overseas) credentialed ministers 11,788 (1985), 121,425 (1986), annual increase 8% per year. (2) *Charismatic Renewal.* Percentage of charismatics among clergy (some representative figures): (East Germany) Bund der Evangelische Kirchen in der DDR (state Lutheran church): 500 pastors (10% of all clergy) are charismatics. (U.K.) Church of England: 25% of all 17,000 clergy. (USA)

Episcopal Church in the U.S.A.: 21% of 14,111 clergy are involved, and 64% receive ERM periodicals. Lutheran Church Missouri Synod: 400 out of 6,000 clergy are charismatic; several clergy have been unfrocked since 1970. Many ecumenical and evangelical parachurch agencies have 20-60% charismatics on staff. In the 2,000 or so Pentecostal agencies, virtually all staff are Pentecostal. Grand total by AD 2000: 1,933,000.

### 95. Aliens: foreign missionaries
These include Pentecostals, and the following varieties of Charismatics and Neocharismatics (renewed in the Spirit): (1985) 25% of all Anglican foreign missionaries, 20% of all RCs, 40% of all Protestants (60% of WEC, 42% of ABCIM, etc.); by AD 2000, these figures are likely to have increased at least to 50% of Anglicans, 25% of RCs, 50% of Protestants, and 90% of Third-World missionaries. Grand total by AD 2000: 167,000.

## 96. THE CONTEXT OF WORLD EVANGELIZATION
This last section is added to illustrate what has always been the focus and goal of the Renewal as a whole.

### 97. Global population
In mid-2000: 6,055,049,000.

### 98. Christians (all varieties)
In mid-2000: 1,999,564,000.

### 99. Affiliated church members (baptized)
Persons (adults and children) on the rolls of the churches and so of organized Christianity; in mid-2000, 1,888,439,000.

### 100. Non-Christians
In mid-2000: 4,055,485,000.

### 101. Unevangelized persons
Total persons in the world who have never heard the name of Jesus Christ and remain unaware of Christianity, Christ, and the gospel. Total in mid-2000: 1,629,375,000.

### 102. World evangelization global plans since AD 30
Grand total of all distinct plans and proposals for accomplishing world evangelization made by Christians since AD 30. Most of these are each described in Part 27 "GeoStrategies", with their historical context in Part 2 "CosmoChronology". All 770 global plans by 1987 rising to 1,500 by AD 2000 are listed, enumerated, described, analyzed, and interpreted in Part 27 also.

---

## BIBLIOGRAPHY

*A guide to the study of the Pentecostal movement.* C. E. Jones. ATLA Bibliographic Series, 6. Metuchen, NJ and London: American Theological Library Association and Scarecrow Press, 1983. 1,245p in 2 vols. (An important bibliography of the Pentecostal movement).

'A survey of the 20th century Pentecostal/Charismatic Renewal in the Holy Spirit, with its goal of world evangelization,' D. B. Barrett, *International bulletin of missionary research*, 12, 3 (July 1988).

*As by a new Pentecost: the dramatic beginnings of the Catholic Charismatic renewal.* P. G. Mansfield. Steubenville, OH: Franciscan University Press, 1992.

*Carisma e institución en la renovación carismática.* T. I. J. Urresti. Barcelona: Editorial Roma, 1979.

*Charismatic challenge: four key questions.* J. Napier. Nashville, TN: Providence House Publishers, 1995.

*Charismatic Christianity as a global culture.* K. Poewe (ed). *Studies in comparative religion.* Columbia, SC: University of South Carolina Press, 1994. 316p.

*Charismatic experiences in history.* C. M. Robeck Jr (ed). Peabody, MA: Hendrickson Publishing, 1985. 186p.

*Dictionary of pentecostal and charismatic movements.* S. M. Burgess & G. B. McGee (eds). Grand Rapids, MI: Zondervan, 1988. 927p.

*Faces of renewal: studies in honor of Stanley M. Horton.* P. Elbert (ed). Peabody, MA: Hendrickson Publishers, 1988.

*Fire from heaven: the rise of Pentecostal spirituality and the reshaping of religion in the twenty-first century.* H. Cox.

Reading, MA: Addison–Wesley, 1995. 339p.

*Haven of the masses: a study of the Pentecostal movement in Chile.* C. L. d'Epinay. London: Lutterworth Press, 1969.

*Historia de la Asamblea Apostólica de La Fe en Cristo Jesus.* E. Cantú & J. A. Ortega (eds). Mentone, CA: Sal's Printing Service, 1966.

*Historia del Concilio Latino Americano de Iglesias Cristianas.* M. Guillen. Brownsville, TX, 1982.

'Origins, development and perspectives of La Luz del Mundo,' P. F. Loret de Mola, *Religion,* 25 (1995), 147–62.

*Pentecost, mission and ecumenism: essays on intercultural theology.* J. A. B. Jongeneel et al. (eds). *Studies in the intercultural history of Christianity,* 75. Frankfurt am Main: Peter Lang, 1992. 386p.

'Pentecostal churches and Nicaraguan politics,' R. Nauta, *Exchange,* (April 1994), 25–43.

*Pentecostalism: origins and development worldwide.* W. J. Hollenweger. Peabody, MA: Hendrickson, 1997. 500p.

*Perspectives on the new pentecostalism.* R. P. Spittler (ed). Grand Rapids, MI: Baker Book House, 1976. 268p.

*Pioneros de Pentecostés.* R. Dominguez. Barcelona: Editorial CLIE, 1990. 3 vols.

*Presence, power, praise: documents on the Charismatic renewal.* K. McDonnell. Collegeville, MN: The Liturgical Press, 1980. 3 vols.

'Readings in the church growth dynamics of the missionary expansion of the Pentecostal movement.' L. G. McClung. MTM thesis, Fuller Theological Seminary, Pasadena, CA, 1984.

*Restoring the kingdom: the radical Christianity of the house church movement.* A. Walker. London: Hodder &

Stoughton, 1988.

*Spontaneous combustion: grass–roots Christianity, Latin American style.* M. Berg & P. Pretiz. Pasadena, CA: William Carey Library, 1996. 296p.

*The Catholic Charismatics: the anatomy of a modern religious movement.* R. J. Bord & J. E. Faulkner. University Park, PA: Pennsylvania State University Press, 1983.

*The charismatic movement: a guide to the study of neo–pentecostalism with emphasis on Anglo–American sources.* C. E. Jones. ATLA Bibliographic Series, 30. Metuchen, NJ and London: American Theological Library Association and Scarecrow Press, 1995. 1,266p in 2 vols.

*The flaming tongue: the impact of 20th century revivals.* J. E. Orr. Chicago: Moody Press, 1973. 255p.

*The Holiness Pentecostal movement in the United States.* H. V. Synan. Rev. ed. Grand Rapids, MI: Eerdmans, 1997.

*The life and theology of Watchman Nee, including a study of the Little Flock Movement.* N. H. Cliff. Leiden: Pharos, 1994. 300p.

*The rise of the charismatic movement in the mainline churches.* A. O. Atiemo. Accra, Ghana: Asempa Publishers, Christian Council of Ghana, 1993. 84p.

*The serpent and the dove: the history of the Apostolic Church of the Faith in Christ Jesus in Mexico, 1914–1968.* M. Gaxiola–Gaxiola. South Pasadena, CA: WIlliam Carey Library, 1969.

*The third wave of the Holy Spirit: encountering the power of signs and wonders today.* C. P. Wagner. Ann Arbor, MI: Servant Publications, Vine Books, 1988. 133p.

*Tongues of fire: the explosion of Protestantism in Latin America.* D. Martin. Oxford, UK: Basil Blackwell, 1990.

Part 6

# INDEPENDENCY

The shift to postdenominationalism
in church lifestyles worldwide

*Tradition is the living faith of the dead, traditionalism is the dead faith of the living.*
—Jaroslav Pelikan, Jefferson Lectures, 1983

*Denominations as we know them may well be breaking up… Denominationalism is a relatively recent phenomenon and may have outlived its usefulness.*
—Russell E. Richey, *Reimagining denominationalism*, 1994

Part 6 provides a history and analysis of a major trend involving over 385 million Christians who have discarded historic denominationalism and even any dependence on historic Christianity. Documentation, enumeration, instrumentation, photographs, statistics, and other measurements, though not easy to obtain, are all adequate to certify this century-long shift in worldwide church lifestyles.

This Independency megabloc may be interpreted as demonstrating the translatability of the Christian gospel into the pluralistic and multifaceted cultures and populations of the world. Moreover, in many cases this is now succeeding spectacularly via Independency precisely where the 5 older Christian megablocs have singularly failed to establish even a beachhead.

# The shift to postdenominationalism in church lifestyles worldwide

## A massive new realignment

Postdenominationalism is the latest in a long line of major historical realignments within global Christianity. These realignments are here briefly listed in chronological order in Table 6–1.

Contemporary postdenominationalism is a movement sweeping throughout the churches worldwide. It is a vast, scattered movement of many distinct and separate protests, revolts, schisms, secessions, rebellions, independencies, reformations, renewals.

With the passage of time all these newer movements tend to become established denominations themselves. They become recognized as part of the establishment of mainline Christianity. With the passage of time, their enthusiasm and zeal cool and they become themselves in need of renewal and reformation. Before long they in turn are confronted with independency movements against them from within their own ranks.

## Five paramount characteristics

From Table 6–1 and its listing of independency movements down the ages, some recurring hallmarks can be noted. First, many church members in the parent body experience dissatisfaction or disagreement on matters concerning 3 areas—authority, lifestyle, and gifts of the Spirit. New desires emerge: a desire for independence from restrictive or overbearing centralized authority; a desire to abandon an ineffective lifestyle; and a desire to receive more of God's empowering for the Christian life than has hitherto been disclosed to them.

The result is the emergence of 5 dominant characteristics—independency, postdenominationalism, radicalism, restorationism, and neo-apostolic experience. The individual Christians who battle through this struggle can be given the 5-fold descriptive terms: *Independents, Postdenominationalists, Radicals, Restorationists,* and *Neo-Apostolics.* In this analysis these labels are treated as different facets or aspects of the same phenomenon, and therefore complementary and virtually synonymous.

## Defining Postdenominationalism

So then, the following definition emerges, arising from the numbered columns in Table 6–1, and also with the help of Table 6–2 which defines the boundary between mainline Christianity (the 4 megablocs, coded ORAP) and the Independency megabloc (coded I).

Postdenominationalism results from longstanding dissatisfaction and differences between one of the segments of organized, established mainline Christianity (column 1) which before long results in a crisis point (column 2) at which the new postdenominationalist movement (column 3) comes into being. It consists of congregations or churches or networks/associations/paradenominations of significant size (column 4), historical race (column 5), ethnolinguistic category (column 6) and ecclesiastical category at origin (column 7), which either eventually pass into oblivion or in most cases result in ongoing entities today with categories as shown in column 8. At origin these unilaterally adopt a markedly different church lifestyle from their parent bodies, rejecting the authority of existing parent denominations and many established aspects of denominationalist faith and life, and putting in their place new authority, new structures, new names, new beliefs, new solutions, and new forms of church life. Up to the present, several still exist and have not or not yet moved out of this radical category by either (a) being accepted by mainstream Christianity as a legitimate part of that establishment (this being indicated by A- and P- in column 8), or (b) evolving into a marginal Chris-

tian body with heterodox christology or other deviations, or (c) evolving into a non-Christian religion, or (d) collapsing, dying, or otherwise going out of existence (shown by hyphen in column 8). Of these variables, a major explanatory variable is the movement's main racial or ethnolinguistic character of its population (column 5).

## Two major Postdenominationalist streams

Examination of Table 6–1 shows that many of the movements of the past have now become mainline denominations themselves (e.g. Lutheranism, Methodism, Pentecostalism), and still other once-powerful movements have collapsed and faded from the scene (Montanism, Donatism). Those which are still alive and well today, having rejected established mainline denominationalism over the years, are here defined as the phenomenon of Postdenominationalism.

Closer examination of these Christians, who they are, and what they stand for, leads to examination of their present ecclesiastical codes (column 6 of Table 6–3). By means of these codes they can be delineated, described, and enumerated. Two main types of independency emerge, as follows.

1. *Non-White indigenous Christians,* from the period AD 1500-2000. 'Non-White' here refers to peoples not of European or White American origin. Their races are shown in Table 6–1, columns 5 and 6. It may be noted that the table demonstrates that this postdenominationalist initiative began first among Africans, Asians, Latin Americans, and Oceanic peoples, and has erupted many times over the last 2, 3, or even 4 centuries ago.

2. *White-led Independents/Postdenominationalists/Neocharismatics,* mainly of much more recent origin

## Table 6–1. Mainline Christianity and its succession of independency movements, AD 33-2000.

| Mainline Christianity | Begun | Independents | Members | Historical Race | Ethnic code | Ecclesiastical Origin | Today |
|---|---|---|---|---|---|---|---|
| 1 | 2 | 3 | 4 | 5 | 6 | 7 | 8 |
| European Catholicism | AD 61 | Celtic churches | 2,000,000 | Celts | CEW18 | I-Cel | A-Eva |
| West Asian Catholicism | 156 | Montanists | 100,000 | Phrygians | CEW17 | I-Mon | I-3pW |
| Latin Catholicism | 320 | Donatists | 3,000,000 | Berbers | CMT32 | I-Don | I-Lat |
| Byzantine Orthodoxy | 400 | Monophysites | 20,100,000 | Copts | CMT30 | O-Cop | O-Cop |
| Italian Catholicism | 318 | Arians | 2,000,000 | Germans | CEW19m | I-Ari | R-Lat |
| Roman Catholicism | 900 | Cathari | 500,000 | French | CEW21b | I-Pau | I-Pau |
| Balkan Orthodoxy | 1070 | Bogomils | 200,000 | Bulgarians | CEW22b | I-Pau | I-Pau |
| Italian Catholicism | 1200 | Waldensians | 50,000 | Italians | CEW21e | I-Wal | P-Wal |
| Anglicanism | 1350 | Lollards | 20,000 | English | CEW19i | I-Ang | A-Eva |
| German Catholicism | 1517 | Lutherans | 80,000,000 | Germans | CEW19m | I-Lut | P-Lut |
| French Catholicism | 1536 | Calvinists | 50,000,000 | French | CEW21b | I-Ref | P-Ref |
| Japanese Catholicism | 1549 | Hidden Christians | 30,000 | Japanese | MSY45a | I-Lat | I-CCa |
| Russian Orthodoxy | 1666 | Old Believers | 3,000,000 | Russians | CEW22j | I-OBe | I-OBe |
| Anglicanism | 1609 | Baptists | 50,000,000 | English | CEW19i | I-Bap | P-Bap |
| Anglicanism | 1558 | Puritans | 100,000 | English | CEW19i | I-Ang | A-Eva |
| Anglicanism | 1739 | Methodists | 40,000,000 | English | CEW19i | I-Met | P-Met |
| Colonial missions | 1815 | African Independents | 55,000,000 | Africans | NAB57 | I-Ang | I-3pA |
| Methodism | 1865 | Salvationists | 4,000,000 | English | CEW19i | I-Sal | P-Sal |
| White Protestantism | 1900 | Classical Pentecostals | 45,000,000 | Americans | CEW19s | I-Pen | P-Pen |
| Denominationalist Pentecostalism | 1959 | Latin Charismatics | 120,000,000 | Brazilians | CLT26 | I-3cL | I-3cL |
| Chinese denominationalism | 1950 | House churches | 80,000,000 | Chinese | MSY42a | I-3pC | I-3nC |
| Latin American Catholicism | 1909 | Grassroots (GR) churches | 28,000,000 | Mestizos | CLN29 | I-3gL | I-3gL |
| Mainline Charismatic renewal | 1970 | Independent Charismatics | 150,000,000 | Europeans | CEW21 | I-3cW | I-3cW |
| White denominationalism | 1975 | Postdenominationalists | 380,000,000 | Americans | CEW19s | I-3nW | I-3cW |
| Independency megabloc | 1980 | Neocharismatics | 230,000,000 | Non-Whites | MSY44 | I-3nI | I-3nG |

## Table 6–2. Defining the boundary between the Independency megabloc and the 4 ORAP megablocs (Orthodoxy, Roman Catholicism, Anglicanism, Protestantism).

This scale of 10 questions attempts to define the difference or distance or boundary between Christianity's 4 traditional or historical major ecclesiastico-cultural megablocs (Orthodoxy, Roman Catholicism, Anglicanism, Protestantism, these being abbreviated here as ORAP) and the newest megabloc here termed Independency. Many Independent denominations are characterized by 'Yes' answers to all 10 questions; most are not as clearcut, having 9, 8, 7, or 6 'Yes' answers; and a small number may have only 5, 4, 3, 2, or 1 'Yes' answers but still be indisputably in the Independent category.

The general rule observed here is therefore to define the

boundary by the following 2 statements. Any denomination or network with over 5 'Yes' answers to the 10 questions is here defined as 'Independent' and as part of the Independency megabloc (coded I- ). Any denomination with over 5 'No' answers to the 10 questions is almost certainly part of one of the 4 historic megablocs (coded O-, R-, A-, or P-).

The 10 dichotomies are the opening lines of a far more detailed set of 280 dichotomies showing the contrast between denominationalism (ORAP) and postdenominationalism (Independency). set out here in Table 6–9 in this Part 6.

| | ORAP megablocs | Independency megabloc (I) |
|---|---|---|
| Name of denomination or network: _____ | | |
| NAME 'INDEPENDENT' | | |
| 1. Does this body, leaders and members, self-identify as 'Independent'? | No | Yes |
| 2. Does its name include 'Independent' or a synonym ('Free', 'Autonomous')? | No | Yes |
| 3. Does its name avoid using any ORAP family name? ('Anglican', 'Baptist', &c) | No | Yes |
| 4. Does literature about this body describe it as 'Independent'? | No | Yes |
| ORIGIN | | |
| 5. Was it begun after 1940 or less than 60 years (2 generations) ago? | No | Yes |
| 6. Did it originate by schism, secession, or founding, since 1940? | No | Yes |
| WIDER CHRISTIANITY | | |
| 7. Is it uninterested in historic ORAP Christianity? | No | Yes |
| 8. Is it uninterested in the entirety of contemporary ORAP global Christianity? | No | Yes |
| 9. Does it avoid conciliarism (membership in any Christian council or alliance)? | No | Yes |
| RENEWAL | | |
| 10. Is this body based on the pentecostal/charismatic experience? | No | Yes |
| Probable identity of denomination: = ORAP if over 5 'No's | | = I if over 5 'Yes' |

## AFRICA    84 million

**Malagasy Church of Spiritual Revival:** word 'Repent!' is inscribed over founder in rear (Madagascar).

**Organization of African Instituted Churches** (OAIC): 1978 founding Conference, Cairo (Egypt).

**Legion of Mary Church:** founder (1962) Gaudencia Aoko (Kenya); largest Africa schism ex Rome.

**Deeper Life Bible Church, Lagos:** congregations in 45 countries (mainly Nigeria).

**Zion Christian Church** (ZCC): 2 million at Easter Pasaka/Passover/Communion (South Africa).

**Kimbanguist Church** (EJCSK): inside vast cathedral, Kinshasa (Congo-Zaire).

**New Jerusalem Church:** opening worship service, Chingola (Zambia).

**African Apostolic Church of Johane Maranke:** AACJM apostle and prophet (Zimbabwe).

**Celestial Church of Christ:** sign to one of its 2,000 churches (Benin, Nigeria, Europe, USA).

**Full Gospel Believers Church,** begun 1965 (Ethiopia).

**National Association of Aladura Churches** (NAAC), linking 150 denominations (Nigeria).

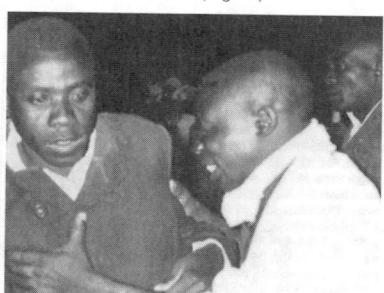

**Zion Apostolic Church** (ZAC): prophet detects unconfessed sinner at communion (Zimbabwe).

**Lumpa (Visible Salvation) Church:** founder Alice Lenshina (Zambia).

## ASIA    155 million

**House church, Phnom Penh:** communion meal (Cambodia).

**True Jesus Church:** one of 4,000 churches; striking Taiwanese architecture (Taiwan).

**True Jesus Church** (China) moves into disused Scottish church in Edinburgh.

**Subba Rao Movement:** high-caste Hindu non-baptized believers in Christ, known as 'NBBCs' (India).

**Church of Christ (Manalista):** Executive Minister E.G. Manalo greets followers (Philippines).

**Good News Mission**, city of Bishkek: pastor Vladimir baptizes prison inmate, 1995 (Kirghizia).

**Philippine Independent Church:** postage stamp celebrating Aglipay's 1902 schism ex Rome.

**Hope of God International:** 900 churches, converted Buddhists (Thailand).

**Banner of the Race Church:** Catholic-style priests, officials, rites, claims (Philippines).

**Assembly Hall Churches (Little Flock):** 2 seminarians studying in TSPM seminary, Nanjing (China).

## CARIBBEAN 1.1 million
(listed also as part of Latin America)

**Revival Zion**, begun 1783; 1861-2 Great Christian Revival (Jamaica).

**National Spiritual Baptist Council of Churches**, 'dancing, trumping and laboring' (Trinidad).

**Shiloh United Church of Christ Apostolic,** a Oneness or Jesus Only church (Jamaica).

## EUROPE 26 million

**Old Ritualist Church** (Old Believers), Moscow, with members across Europe to Siberia (Russia).

**Traditionalist Catholic Church:** schismatic Archbishop M.Lefebvre consecrates 4 bishops (France).

**Good Samaritan Mission**, Kiev: baptism of 130 new converts (Ukraine).

**Czechoslovak Hussite Church:** founded 1920 when 20% of all Czech Roman Catholics seceded.

**New Apostolic Church** (NAK) 9.6 million, begun 1863: Council of Apostles meets in Germany.

**Old Catholics:** 25th International Congress, 1990 (world HQ: Utrecht, Netherlands).

**Bishops-at-large:** one of 900 episcopi vagantes, Mar Georgius I, Patriarch of the West (Britain).

**Manna Christian Church**, Lisbon; founder J. Tadeu; huge cell-based churches, tents (Portugal).

## LATIN AMERICA 40 million

**Pentecostal Church of Chile** (IEP): 6,000 begin dancing in the Spirit, at annual conference.

**Pentecostal Church Brazil for Christ** (1.5 million): leader de Mello preaches to 30,000-seat church.

**Prince of Peace Church:** 161 pastors from across Central America at pastors' conference (Honduras).

**Union of Independent Evangelical Churches**, Otomi Indian pentecostals (Mexico).

## NORTHERN AMERICA 80 million

**International Revival Fellowship** (Toronto Blessing); pastor J. Arnott in center (Canada).

**Church of God in Christ:** Bishop B.R. Stewart celebrates a rock star's marriage, New York (USA).

**Willow Creek Association of Churches:** pastor Hybels addresses 15,000 at HQ church, Chicago.

**Native American Church** of North America: Navajo peyote session (USA).

## OCEANIA 1.5 million

**Ratana Church** leader, a Maori parliamentarian, addresses NCCNZ (New Zealand).

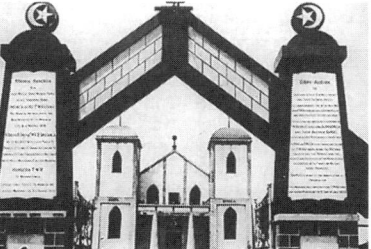

**Ratana Church,** begun 1918 in Maori holy city Ratanapa; 141 apostles now (New Zealand).

during the period 1940-2000. 'White-led' here is simply an objective descriptive term. It is noteworthy that these European and White American initiatives followed their Non-White counterparts by several centuries and many decades.

In this book's analysis, these 2 types or streams form one single ecclesiastico-cultural megabloc here termed 'Independency', parallel to but distinct from the other 5 megablocs—Orthodoxy, Roman Catholicism, Anglicanism, Protestantism, and marginal Christianity. The adjective 'Independent' here must again be precisely understood. It does not refer only to local autonomy or freedom from centralized authority or meddling—it refers to a thorough-going attitude of being independent of or from historic Christianity (the other 5 megablocs).

Actual examples of these postdenominationalist bodies can now be given to show the global range of this spectrum of independent movements. Some 40 are illustrated here in the 2-page photographic collage. Then Table 6–3 lists the 9 major varieties under which these Independent bodies are classified here. Table 6–4 takes the classification a stage further by listing the 313 largest bodies numerically (over 100,000 followers each) and describes their salient features. Table 6–4 then examines the range of pentecostal/charismatic bodies involved by applying a detailed code to each in the table's end column 7. Each code is listed and named in Part 16 "GeoCodebook" under Country Tables 2, and is expounded here in Table 6–5.

Using these codes Table 6–5 summarizes the varieties of Neocharismatics in each of Independency's many categories. Table 6–6 then lists the various components of that part of Independency which can be clearly seen as a part of the Pentecostal/Charismatic Renewal in the Holy Spirit. Table 6–7 gives exact definitions of the various neologisms involved.

This whole subject is then summed up in the single-page Table 6–8, presenting a statistical overview of the entire phenomenon of Postdenominationalism by contrasting its numbers with those of Denominationalism. Its dichotomies result in 91 pairs of figures which illustrate the statistical evolution from AD 1970 to AD 2000 with its current short-term and long-term trends.

Next, Table 6–9 goes into vastly greater detail by describing the 2 underlying phenomena—denominationalism and postdenominationalism—under a series of 280 dichotomies or dichotomous situations or aspects.

Lastly, Table 6–10 shows the negative side of Independency—the chaotic world of failed Independent movements which started with the best of intentions but then foundered from lack of interest or support.

### INDEPENDENTS— POSTDENOMINATIONALISTS—RADICALS— RESTORATIONISTS—NEO-APOSTOLICS

All bodies in this major ecclesiastico-cultural megabloc are identified by the letter "I" in each's code shown in WCE Part 4's Country Tables 2, column 3.

The shortest definitions of these 5 terms can be seen in these 5 adjectives or nouns each describing this whole megabloc, and used in this survey as complementary or coterminous synonyms:

• **Independents**—independent of historic, organized, institutionalized, denominationalist Christianity;

• **Postdenominationalists**—replacing mainline denominationalism by completely new forms;

• **Radicals**—returning to the basic biblical roots, beliefs, practices, and lifestyles;

• **Restorationists**—heralding and working for the full restoration of New Testament church ministries, offices, order, and polity;

• **Neo-Apostolics**—emphasizing the office of today's Apostles with Apostolic initiatives and roles springing from the power and charisms of the Holy Spirit.

This major ecclesiastico-cultural megabloc is best briefly summarized by the single noun *Independents*; and it consists of 9 distinct varieties as listed here in

Table 6–3 and is further explained in the Pentecostal/Charismatic context in Part 5 "GeoRenewal", in the facing Tables 5-8 and 5-9. The codes applicable to all these movements are shown in Country Tables 2, column 3, and are listed here in order in Part 16 "GeoCodebook".

### The 5 overall synonyms more fully described
Fuller definitions of the 5 new overall descriptive synonymous terms are as follows.

• **Independents**—these are Christian groupings that develop a church lifestyle that is, or is claimed to be, completely independent of historic, organized Christianity as represented in the 5 other major ecclesiastico-cultural megablocs which have been White-initiated, -dominated, and -led since the origins of Christianity and especially since the Middle Ages—Orthodox, Roman Catholics, Anglicans, Protestants, and marginal Christians.

• **Postdenominationalists**—these are Christian groupings that have abandoned using the names of the 4 major ecclesiastico-cultural megablocs (Orthodox, Catholic, Anglican, Protestant) as well as the names of the 100 historic Christian confessions or families (Lutheran, Reformed, etc) and hence reject the nomenclature and terminology of, and have rejected many organizational and lifestyle forms of, traditional mainline denominationalism and its 5,000 historic denominations;

• **Radicals**—Radical Christians are Christian groupings dissatisfied with status quo religion who therefore deliberately go back beyond their parent bodies to the original biblical roots and sources and who construct on them their basic fundamental beliefs, practices, and lifestyles.

• **Restorationists**—movements and groupings with the avowed aim of working for the full restoration of New Testament church ministry, ministries, offices, order, and polity have arisen often throughout church history. Two major examples are (a) the Restoration movement under Alexander Campbell from 1832 onward, which became the Church of Christ, Christian Church, and/or Disciples of Christ, and has resulted in today's massive denominations termed Churches of Christ; and (2) the Restoration movement in Britain from 1960 onward, in a pentecostal renewal which produced the independent charismatic house-church movement, the New Churches, also termed the Restoration-1 and Restoration-2 plethora of apostolic networks.

• **Neo-Apostolics**—these are Christian groupings that emphasize the Apostolic role of beginning Christian outreach in new spheres in fresh new ways supported by the power, gifts, charismata, and charisms of the Holy Spirit, with the caveat that some 15% do not accept the appellations pentecostals nor charismatics nor all their related theologies and practices.

The great majority of all Neo-Apostolics—the other 85%—are also widely termed the Third Wave of the Pentecostal/Charismatic Renewal in the Holy Spirit. These are renewed churches and Christians akin to mainline Pentecostals/Charismatics but who have rejected the denominationalism of the First Wave (Classical Pentecostal denominations) and also of the Second Wave (the Charismatic Renewal within the nonpentecostal mainline denominations). In thus rejecting historic denominationalism, and thence also

affiliation with historic Christianity, whilst embracing the full range of gifts of the Holy Spirit, these Christians explain and justify their use of their description as Independents, as Postdenominationalists, and also as Neo-Apostolics. This is highlighted by the virtually complete absence of historic denominational/confessional labels or adjectives like Anglican, Baptist, Catholic, Congregationalist, Ecumenical, Episcopalian, Evangelical, Fundamentalist, Holiness, Lutheran, Mennonite, Methodist, Moravian, Orthodox, Pentecost-al, Presbyterian, Quaker, Reformed, Salvationist, Unitarian, Wesleyan, etc. By the 1990s the Third Wave has thus within its own sphere completely swept aside, ignored, and replaced the entire historic nomenclature of 20th-century denominationalism.

To clearly distinguish the Third Wave from the First and Second Waves, this principle of classification is followed in this survey: First-Wave denominations and members are termed Pentecostals, always with a capital P; and Second-Wave participants are termed Charismatics, always with a capital C. By contrast, all Third-Wave movements, networks, denominations, and members are formally termed Neocharismatics. Note two usages introduced here. 'Neocharismatic' with capital N implies a formal proper noun or adjective and refers to its use as a name. In addition, however, these terms can be used not as formal proper nouns or names but simply as descriptive adjectives where this seems appropriate. Thus specific Third-Wave movements or participants may also occasionally be descriptively termed pentecostal, charismatic, or neocharismatic, but always with lowercase p, c, or n, except for proper nouns or adjectives which may sometimes occur in their official names.

### DEFINITIONS OF 9 VARIETIES OF INDEPENDENTS

The first interpretation of this megabloc, this whole category of Independents/Postdenominationalists/Radicals/Restorationists/Neo-Apostolics, divides them into 9 distinct branches, separated by chronological, geographical, cultural, linguistic, racial, and ecclesiastical differences. Though racially distinct, they are not racist and most have at least a few members of other races. The 9 branches are:

(1) **Non-White indigenous Christians**. In colonial Africa from 1864, large numbers of African Christians seceded from the Western-related mission churches and denominations and opted for complete spiritual and ecclesiastical independence. Similar Non-White movements had begun even earlier on all other non-Western continents including Asia, Latin America, and Northern America. Nearly all are independent charismatics or independent pentecostals. Note that until the 1980s most of these indigenous bodies tended to claim a Western denominational label (Baptist, Lutheran, Methodist, Pentecostal, etc), but by the 1990s the newest movements did not want even these labels.

(2) **Independent Orthodox**. A similar phenomenon of renewal and schism began among Russian Orthodox in 1617 in Sweden and in Poland in 1634 with the emergence of the Old Believers (Old Ritualists). Over the next few centuries, other major schisms began: Old Calendarists (Paleohemerologites, 1924), True Orthodox (1900), Mar Thoma Syrian Church of Malabar (1843), and a vast range of more radical bodies:

Table 6–3. **Nine categories of Independent Christians (ecclesiastically independent denominations or networks) composing the Independent megabloc in the global Christian megatypology, AD 1549-AD 2000.**

| Name of type 1 | Year begun 2 | Denoms 3 | Status in AD 2000 | | Example of codes 6 |
|---|---|---|---|---|---|
| | | | Churches 4 | Affiliated 5 | |
| 1. Non-White indigenous Christians | 1783 | 13,830 | 709,000 | 180,082,000 | I-3aA, I-3cC |
| 2. Independent Orthodox | 1617 | 160 | 21,000 | 13,873,000 | I-OBe, I-Byz |
| 3. Independent Catholics | 1549 | 490 | 35,000 | 18,275,000 | I-OCa, I-Epi |
| 4. Independent Anglicans | 1833 | 150 | 9,000 | 1,812,000 | I-ReA, I-Eva |
| 5. Independent Protestants | 1680 | 2,080 | 359,000 | 88,533,000 | I-Bap, I-Uni |
| 6. Nonhistorical Independents | 1769 | 1,650 | 20,000 | 4,450,000 | I-Jeh, I-mar |
| 7. Isolated radio/TV believers | 1931 | 70 | 233,000 | 16,493,000 | I-rad, I-3rA |
| 8. White-led Postdenominationalists | 1656 | 3,640 | 301,000 | 47,863,000 | I-3aW, I-3aX |
| 9. Hidden non-Christian believers in Christ | 1800 | 30 | 45,000 | 14,364,000 | I-Hin, I-Mus |
| **TOTAL Independents** | | 22,100 | 1,732,000 | 385,745,000 | I- |

Spiritual Christians (Molokans) (1765), Whippers (1650), Castrated Ones (1765), Spirit-Wrestlers (1650), et alia. Most still regard themselves as embodying the authentic Orthodox tradition. A few (10%) have sizable charismatic minorities.

(3) **Independent Catholics.** Another parallel phenomenon can be seen in schisms from the Roman Catholic world, the largest being the Old Catholics (1723 onwards), Reformed Catholics, and a host of 19th- and 20th-century movements: Philippine Independent Church (1902), Czechoslovak Hussite Church (1920), Igreja Catolica Apostolica Brasileira (1945), Iglesia Ortodoxa Catolica Apostolica Mexicana (1926), Polish National Catholic Church (1897), etc. Several have over a million members each. Also, quite a number have sizable charismatic minorities, especially the Old Catholic churches since their origin in 1723 in the Jansenist Church which practiced and still today values the range of charismatic manifestations.

(4) **Independent Anglicans.** These are schisms which retain the label and claims of Anglicanism, but are not in communion with the see of Canterbury and so not part of the global Anglican Communion. These include: Reformed Episcopal Church (1873), Evangelical Church of England (1922), and the multinational Anglican Orthodox Communion (1963). Most have sizable charismatic minorities, and several such as the International Communion of the Charismatic Episcopal Church (1992) are entirely Neocharismatic.

(5) **Independent Protestants.** These are the whole range of schisms and renewals out of Protestantism which regard themselves as still Protestants (Baptists, Methodists, Lutherans, Presbyterians/Reformed, Pentecostals, etc) but which reject Protestant denominationalism or other organic links with historic Protestant bodies. Around 10% are pentecostal or charismatic; 30% have sizable charismatic minorities; by contrast, most (60%) reject all pentecostal, charismatic, and postdenominational labels and theologies.

(6) **Nonhistorical Independents.** These are Independent bodies with no clear or obvious confessional linkages, past or present, and which have no interest whatever in the above 4 megablocs—Orthodox, Catholic, Anglican, or Protestant—and which are not themselves pentecostal/charismatic. A large proportion in fact disown pentecostal or charismatic beliefs and practices, although at the same time sizeable percentages of their constituent members, churches, networks, or even denominations may be pentecostal/charismatic/neocharismatic (this is shown in the relevant tables here).

(7) **Isolated radio/TV believers**. This category enumerates all of any race or religion who are, or have recently become, believers in Christ as a result of Christian radio or satellite TV programs, who now regard themselves as Christians, but who have no nearby church or denomination to join although they may be able to start their own house church. Sizable numbers, and even large majorities, are charismatics.

(8) **White-led Postdenominationalists**. Seen in Portugal as early as 1656, and in many countries from 1805 onwards, by the 1960s, the same phenomenon of Independency began on a large scale as White-initiated, White-instituted, or White-led movements among European and White American peoples in their own home countries. Here the main emphasis was postdenominationalist in that it rejected all denominational labels and ties and also a number of dysfunctional aspects of historic White denominationalism—big government, large headquarters buildings, expensive budgets, liberal staffs, centralization, institutionalism, radical sociopolitical agendas. In addition to being post-Baptist, post-Lutheran, post-Mennonite, post-Methodist, post-Presbyterian, and post-Reformed, large parts of this phenomenon can also be termed post-Evangelical and post-Fundamentalist since Evangelicalism and Fundamentalism have been closely related to Protestant denominationalism for many decades.

(9) **Hidden non-Christian believers in Christ**. In addition to the organized messianic movements just described, there are also, in countries with large non-Christian religions hostile to Christianity, vast numbers of individual non-Christian religionists who

Table 6–4. **Independents: the 313 largest independency movements (Non-White/White-led) of 100,000 members each, and the 60 over one million each, in AD 1995.**

| *Begun* 1 | *Movement* 2 | *Main country* 3 | *Churches* 4 | *Adults* 5 | *Affiliated* 6 | *Eccles* 7 |
|---|---|---|---|---|---|---|
| c1950 | Han charismatic house churches | China | 198,000 | 11,200,000 | 29,740,000 | I-3cC |
| 1807 | Han Chinese Three-Self Churches | China | 27,000 | 4,000,000 | 10,500,000 | I-Uni |
| 1950 | Han unregistered house churches | China | 62,000 | 3,800,000 | 9,910,000 | I-Non |
| 1773 | National Baptist Convention, USA | USA | 44,444 | 8,200,000 | 9,410,000 | I-Bap |
| 1952 | Isolated radio churches | India | 100,000 | 6,000,000 | 9,000,000 | I-3rI |
| c1800 | Low-caste Hindu believers in Christ | India | 10,000 | 5,000,000 | 7,500,000 | I-Hin |
| 1921 | EdeJC sur la Terre par le Prophète SK | Congo-Zaire | 12,000 | 4,000,000 | 7,500,000 | I-3nA |
| 1914 | Zion Christian Church | South Africa | 4,800 | 2,500,000 | 7,100,000 | I-3zA |
| 1895 | Church of God in Christ | USA | 15,300 | 4,281,000 | 5,499,875 | I-3pB |
| 1957 | Chinese Catholic Church (Patriotic) | China | 15,500 | 3,384,000 | 4,600,000 | I-Lat |
| 1880 | National Baptist Conv of America | USA | 19,744 | 3,500,000 | 4,270,000 | I-Bap |
| c1980 | New Birth Movement | China | 10,000 | 2,943,000 | 4,000,000 | I-3cC |
| 1977 | Igreja Universal do Reino de Deus | Brazil | 10,000 | 2,000,000 | 4,000,000 | I-3pY |
| 1991 | Ukrainian Orthodox Ch: P Kiev | Ukraine | 1,332 | 1,800,000 | 3,800,000 | I-Ukr |
| 1978 | Fullness/Praise Network of Churches | USA | 6,000 | 1,800,000 | 3,300,000 | I-3cW |
| 1787 | African Methodist Episcopal Church | USA | 10,789 | 2,050,000 | 3,300,000 | I-Met |
| 1910 | Congregação Cristã do Brasil | Brazil | 15,294 | 1,560,000 | 3,120,000 | I-3pY |
| 1952 | Celestial Church of Christ | Nigeria | 1,140 | 1,708,000 | 3,085,000 | I-3aA |
| 1961 | Progressive National Baptist Conv | USA | 1,800 | 2,500,000 | 3,000,000 | I-Bap |
| 1988 | National Missionary Baptist Conv of A | USA | 1,000 | 2,500,000 | 3,000,000 | I-Bap |
| 1939 | Isolated radio churches | Russia | 50,000 | 2,000,000 | 3,000,000 | I-3rW |
| 1945 | Igreja Católica Apostólica Brasileira | Brazil | 300 | 1,500,000 | 3,000,000 | I-CCa |
| 1890 | Philippine Independent Church | Philippines | 5,751 | 2,000,000 | 2,800,000 | I-ReC |
| | Igreja Pentecostal Deus e Amor | Brazil | 3,200 | 1,600,000 | 2,670,000 | I-3pY |
| c1800 | High-caste Hindu believers in Christ | India | 3,000 | 1,800,000 | 2,500,000 | I-Hin |
| 1933 | Isolated radio churches | China | 40,000 | 1,200,000 | 2,500,000 | I-3rC |
| c1970 | Igreja Pedra Fundamental | Brazil | 2,000 | 1,000,000 | 2,400,000 | I-3pY |
| 1951 | Pr C in K (Reunited Anti-Ecumenical) | South Korea | 4,561 | 772,000 | 2,158,597 | I-Ref |
| 1952 | Redeemed Christian Church of God | Nigeria | 2,220 | 635,618 | 2,100,000 | I-3aA |
| 1981 | Philippine Independent Catholic Church | Philippines | 3,000 | 1,000,000 | 2,000,000 | I-ReC |
| 1978 | Jesus is Lord Fellowship | Philippines | 3,000 | 1,200,000 | 2,000,000 | I-3fF |
| c1995 | People's Organization churches | China | 4,200 | 1,200,000 | 2,000,000 | I-3cC |
| 1939 | Isolated radio churches | Ukraine | 30,000 | 1,200,000 | 2,000,000 | I-3rW |
| 1955 | Igreja Ev Pente 'O Brasil para Cristo' | Brazil | 5,000 | 1,000,000 | 2,000,000 | I-3pY |
| 1913 | Church of Christ (Manalista) | Philippines | 8,400 | 1,050,000 | 1,750,000 | I-3nF |
| c1870 | Chs of Christ (Non-Instrumental) | USA | 13,097 | 1,280,000 | 1,681,013 | I-Dis |
| 1950 | Baptist Bible Fellowship International | USA | 3,500 | 900,000 | 1,500,000 | I-Bap |
| 1943 | African Assemb of God (Back to God) | South Africa | 700 | 900,000 | 1,500,000 | I-3pA |
| 1969 | New Apostolic Church | India | 3,400 | 530,000 | 1,448,209 | I-3aX |
| c1970 | Eglise Neo-Apostolique | Congo-Zaire | 700 | 500,000 | 1,421,425 | I-3aX |
| 1930 | Church of the Lord (Aladura) | Nigeria | 2,888 | 462,000 | 1,400,000 | I-3pA |
| 1865 | National Primitive Baptist Convention | USA | 1,530 | 1,000,000 | 1,300,000 | I-Bap |
| 1917 | Christ Apostolic Church | Nigeria | 4,952 | 520,000 | 1,300,000 | I-3aA |
| 1920 | Pentecostal Church of Indonesia | Indonesia | 1,540 | 770,000 | 1,280,000 | I-3oG |
| 1906 | Pentecostal Assemblies of the World | USA | 1,600 | 950,000 | 1,270,000 | I-3aO |
| c1935 | Christian Churches & Chs of Christ | USA | 5,238 | 966,976 | 1,213,188 | I-Dis |
| 1913 | Russian Unified Fellowship of CEF | Russia | 1,300 | 600,000 | 1,200,000 | I-3pW |
| 1968 | Church of God Mission International | Nigeria | 3,200 | 880,000 | 1,200,000 | I-3aA |
| 1925 | African Indep Pentecostal Ch of Africa | Kenya | 408 | 400,000 | 1,200,000 | I-Ref |
| 1922 | Assembly Hall Churches | China | 4,000 | 800,000 | 1,200,000 | I-3nC |
| 1953 | Gospel Faith Mission | Nigeria | 6,000 | 642,000 | 1,185,000 | I-3aA |
| 1796 | African Methodist Episcopal Zion Ch | USA | 3,000 | 942,857 | 1,142,016 | I-Met |
| 1993 | Full Gospel Baptist Church Fellowship | USA | 5,000 | 500,000 | 1,100,000 | I-3fD |
| 1979 | Catholic Church in China (Underground) | China | 2,000 | 400,000 | 1,100,000 | I-Lat |
| 1990 | Ukrainian Orthodox Ch: P Kiev | Russia | 200 | 500,500 | 1,100,000 | I-Ukr |
| 1956 | Brotherhood of the Cross and Star | Nigeria | 3,200 | 600,000 | 1,074,000 | I-3nA |
| 1923 | Zion Christian Church | Zimbabwe | 1,400 | 480,000 | 1,044,000 | I-3zA |
| 1973 | New Apostolic Church | Kenya | 3,000 | 403,000 | 1,011,531 | I-3aX |
| 1925 | Eternal Sacred Order of Cherubim & S | Nigeria | 3,500 | 350,000 | 1,000,000 | I-3aA |
| 1917 | True Jesus Church | China | 3,500 | 400,000 | 1,000,000 | I-3oC |
| | Nigerian Christian Fellowship | Nigeria | 5,375 | 430,000 | 956,000 | I-3pA |
| 1898 | Presbyterian Church of Africa | South Africa | 9,600 | 426,000 | 927,000 | I-Ref |
| 1932 | African Apost Ch of Johane Maranke | Zimbabwe | 500 | 420,000 | 910,000 | I-3aA |
| 1976 | Eglise Catholique Traditionalle | France | 500 | 400,000 | 900,000 | I-CCa |
| 1905 | American Baptist Association | USA | 1,849 | 270,000 | 900,000 | I-Bap |
| 1958 | Yoido Full Gospel Churches | South Korea | 100 | 700,000 | 900,000 | I-3kK |
| 1924 | Indian Pentecostal Church of God | India | 9,950 | 581,000 | 900,000 | I-3pI |
| 1843 | Mar Thoma Syrian Church of Malabar | India | 1,000 | 550,000 | 875,000 | I-ReO |
| 1870 | Christian Methodist Episcopal Church | USA | 3,000 | 438,000 | 800,000 | I-Met |
| | Gen As of Pres Ch in K (BoSu) I | South Korea | 1,292 | 589,000 | 769,343 | I-Ref |
| 1922 | Zion Apostolic Churches | Zimbabwe | 1,300 | 430,000 | 760,000 | I-3zA |
| 1962 | International Pentecost Church | South Africa | 165 | 300,000 | 750,000 | I-3pA |
| c1915 | New Apostolic Church | Zambia | 435 | 376,000 | 728,063 | I-3aX |
| 1909 | Iglesia Metodista Pentecostal de Chile | Chile | 3,250 | 520,000 | 720,000 | I-3pL |
| 1666 | Old Ritualist Ch Belokrinitsa Concord | Russia | 1,600 | 400,000 | 710,000 | I-OBe |
| 1911 | Assemblies of God Fellowship Int | USA | 700 | 550,000 | 700,000 | I-3pW |
| 1910 | Nazarite Baptist Church | South Africa | 300 | 300,000 | 700,000 | I-3pA |
| c1980 | International Fell of Charismatic Chs | South Africa | 600 | 400,000 | 700,000 | I-3cW |
| c1970 | Hidden Buddhist believers in Christ | China | 10,000 | 350,000 | 693,000 | I-Bud |
| 1993 | Metropolitan Church of Bessarabia | Moldavia | 40 | 400,000 | 630,000 | I-Mol |
| 1973 | Deeper Life Bible Church of Nigeria | Nigeria | 5,733 | 348,980 | 612,641 | I-3pA |
| 1951 | Bible Way Chs of Our Lord JC WW | USA | 1,000 | 412,000 | 600,600 | I-3oO |
| c1990 | Russian Orthodox Ch in Exile | Ukraine | 200 | 400,000 | 600,000 | I-Rus |
| 1965 | Zimbabwe Assemblies of God Africa | Zimbabwe | 1,709 | 300,000 | 600,000 | I-3pA |
| c1940 | St John's Apostolic Faith Mission | South Africa | 300 | 300,000 | 600,000 | I-3pA |
| 1970 | Bethel Full Gospel Church | Indonesia | 1,200 | 360,000 | 600,000 | I-3fG |
| | Unaffiliated fundamentalist chapels | Britain | 2,800 | 300,000 | 600,000 | I-Fun |
| 1933 | Iglesia Evangélica Pentecostal de Chile | Chile | 1,680 | 400,000 | 571,000 | I-3pL |
| 1918 | Ukrainian Autocephalous Orthodox Ch | Ukraine | 1,200 | 360,000 | 554,000 | I-Ukr |
| c1985 | Word of Faith Ministries | Nigeria | 300 | 277,000 | 500,000 | I-3wA |
| 1964 | International Evangelical Churches | USA | 70 | 360,000 | 500,000 | I-3cB |
| 1975 | Willow Creek Association of Chs | USA | 2,700 | 200,000 | 500,000 | I-Eva |
| 1954 | American Evangelistic Association | USA | 2,000 | 200,000 | 500,000 | I-3pW |
| 1960 | Rhema Bible Churches | USA | 1,500 | 272,456 | 500,000 | I-3wW |
| 1992 | Orthodox Church of Bulgaria | Bulgaria | 200 | 200,000 | 500,000 | I-Bul |
| 1948 | Cherubim & Seraphim Ch of Zion of N | Nigeria | 1,087 | 250,000 | 500,000 | I-3aA |
| 1923 | Unión de Iglesias Ev Independientes | Mexico | 1,000 | 300,000 | 500,000 | I-3pR |
| 1952 | Isolated radio churches | Japan | 8,000 | 300,000 | 500,000 | I-3rQ |
| 1952 | Isolated radio churches | Indonesia | 15,000 | 300,000 | 500,000 | I-3rG |
| 1963 | Indonesia Protestant Christian Church | Indonesia | 797 | 192,000 | 497,054 | I-Lut |
| 1968 | New Life Fellowship | India | 2,050 | 240,000 | 480,000 | I-3pI |
| c1900 | Ukrainian Orthodox P Kiev | Kazakhstan | 50 | 300,000 | 450,000 | I-Ukr |

*Continued overleaf*

Table 6–4 continued

| Begun 1 | Movement 2 | Main country 3 | Churches 4 | Adults 5 | Affiliated 6 | Eccles 7 |
|---|---|---|---|---|---|---|
| c1980 | New Apostolic Church | Ghana | 700 | 200,000 | 434,666 | I-3aX |
| 1937 | Spirit of Jesus Church | Japan | 470 | 353,000 | 420,000 | I-3oQ |
| 1863 | Neuapostolische Kirche | Germany | 3,050 | 350,000 | 401,179 | I-3aX |
| 1962 | International Gospel Assemblies | USA | 500 | 300,000 | 400,000 | I-3pW |
| 1985 | Iglesia Ondas de Amor & Paz | Argentina | 110 | 275,000 | 400,000 | I-3gL |
| 1965 | Calvary Chapels International | USA | 750 | 275,000 | 400,000 | I-3cW |
| 1945 | Korea Assembly of God | South Korea | 530 | 220,000 | 400,000 | I-3pK |
| 1940 | Iglesia La Luz del Mundo (Aaronistas) | Mexico | 400 | 258,000 | 400,000 | I-3oL |
| 1946 | Iglesia Pentecostal de Chile | Chile | 300 | 150,000 | 400,000 | I-3pL |
| 1962 | Maria Legio of Africa | Kenya | 962 | 130,000 | 385,000 | I-3sA |
| c1890 | Lisu Church | China | 1,800 | 160,000 | 380,000 | I-eth |
| 1913 | Eglise Harriste | Ivory Coast | 290 | 158,100 | 376,000 | I-Met |
| c1985 | New Apostolic Church | Tanzania | 1,200 | 210,000 | 375,432 | I-3aX |
| 1955 | Crusaders of the Divine Ch of Christ | Philippines | 1,692 | 225,000 | 375,000 | I-ind |
| 1961 | Jesus Korean Holiness Church | South Korea | 819 | 184,443 | 362,346 | I-Hol |
| c1910 | Korean Churches | China | 2,000 | 150,000 | 360,000 | I-3hK |
| 1967 | Convenção Batista Nacional | Brazil | 900 | 200,000 | 360,000 | I-3cY |
| 1930 | Mariavite Old Catholic Church | USA | 200 | 220,000 | 358,176 | I-OCa |
| 1897 | Polish National Catholic Ch of America | USA | 260 | 210,000 | 350,000 | I-OCa |
| 1666 | Old Ritualist Ch Belokrinitsa Concord | Ukraine | 1,200 | 260,000 | 350,000 | I-OBe |
| 1957 | Church of Christ in Africa | Kenya | 879 | 150,000 | 350,000 | I-Ang |
| 1927 | Indonesian Christian Church (HKI) | Indonesia | 590 | 230,800 | 342,300 | I-Lut |
| 1946 | Presbyterian Church in Korea (Kosin) | South Korea | 1,361 | 258,500 | 336,620 | I-Ref |
| 1932 | General Assoc of Regular Baptist Chs | USA | 1,582 | 216,408 | 333,000 | I-Bap |
|  | Pentecostal Union | Ukraine | 900 | 100,000 | 333,000 | I-3pW |
| c1958 | Igreja Adventista da Promessa | Brazil | 2,727 | 150,000 | 333,000 | I-3pY |
|  | Association of Christian Foundations | Indonesia | 824 | 140,000 | 326,000 | I-3nG |
| 1962 | Full Gospel Fell of Chs & Ministries | USA | 650 | 195,000 | 320,000 | I-3fW |
| c1970 | Hidden Buddhist believers in Christ | Japan | 2,000 | 200,000 | 320,000 | I-Bud |
| c1900 | Miao (Meo) Churches | China | 1,400 | 120,000 | 320,000 | I-3pE |
| 1927 | Igreja Kimbanguista | Angola | 425 | 106,000 | 320,000 | I-3aA |
| c1980 | Faith Gospel Ministry | Ghana | 2,000 | 150,000 | 300,000 | I-3pA |
| 1950 | Calvary Temple | USA | 3,000 | 200,000 | 300,000 | I-3oW |
| c1970 | House Church movement | North Korea | 20,000 | 170,000 | 300,000 | I-3hK |
| 1953 | Eglise Apost Africaine de J Maranke | Congo-Zaire | 1,100 | 160,000 | 300,000 | I-3aA |
| 1870 | Native American Ch of North America | USA | 450 | 110,000 | 300,000 | I-mar |
| 1970 | Christian Growth Ministries | USA | 3,000 | 150,000 | 300,000 | I-3cW |
| 1952 | Isolated radio churches | Thailand | 5,000 | 200,000 | 300,000 | I-3rZ |
| c1710 | Old Ritualist Church (Priestless) | Russia | 50 | 100,000 | 300,000 | I-OBe |
| c1960 | Full Gospel Believers Church | Ethiopia | 1,200 | 150,000 | 300,000 | I-3fA |
| c1979 | Local Church (Shouters/Yellers) | China | 2,000 | 120,000 | 300,000 | I-3nC |
| 1947 | Conservative Bapt Assoc of America | USA | 1,121 | 204,496 | 292,000 | I-Bap |
| 1903 | New Apostolic Church | South Africa | 1,500 | 150,000 | 291,528 | I-3aX |
| 1914 | Nomiya Luo Church | Kenya | 600 | 90,000 | 290,000 | I-Ang |
| 1950 | Baptist Missionary Assoc of America | USA | 1,374 | 228,287 | 289,969 | I-Bap |
| c1970 | Hidden Buddhist believers in Christ | Viet Nam | 1,400 | 130,000 | 288,000 | I-Bud |
| c1968 | Manna Full Gospel Chs & Ministries | India | 5,000 | 140,000 | 275,000 | I-3fI |
| c1910 | Cooneyites (Tramp-Preachers) | USA | 200 | 130,000 | 270,000 | I-Fun |
| c1890 | Yi Churches | China | 1,000 | 110,000 | 270,000 | I-3pE |
| 1962 | Assoc of Intern Gospel Assemblies | USA | 458 | 210,000 | 260,000 | I-3fW |
| 1952 | Nagaland Christian Revival Churches | India | 855 | 185,000 | 260,000 | I-3pE |
| c1980 | New Apostolic Church | Nigeria | 600 | 110,000 | 256,046 | I-3aX |
| 1976 | Christ Chosen Ch of God of N | Nigeria | 70 | 180,000 | 250,000 | I-3pA |
| c1950 | Hidden nonreligious believers in Christ | China | 5,000 | 200,000 | 250,000 | I-Non |
| 1956 | Liberty Baptist Churches | USA | 510 | 200,000 | 250,000 | I-Fun |
| 1910 | Church of Christ | South Africa | 1,500 | 100,000 | 250,000 | I-3pA |
| c1860 | Old Ritualist Ancient Orth Christians | Russia | 20 | 180,000 | 250,000 | I-OBe |
| 1959 | International Evangelism Crusaders | USA | 50 | 175,000 | 240,000 | I-3fW |
| c1970 | Christ Groups | India | 9,364 | 80,000 | 233,000 | I-3hI |
| c1940 | New Apostolic Church | Pakistan | 1,000 | 150,000 | 231,656 | I-3aX |
| c1960 | Omega Full Gospel Assembly | India | 50 | 180,000 | 230,000 | I-3fI |
| 1960 | Network of Kingdom Churches | USA | 900 | 200,000 | 230,000 | I-3pW |
| 1951 | EdeJC sur la Terre par le St-Esprit | Congo-Zaire | 140 | 70,000 | 230,000 | I-3pA |
| 1969 | Iglesia Pentecostal Unida de Colombia | Colombia | 1,006 | 80,500 | 230,000 | I-3oL |
|  | New Apostolic Church | Uganda | 200 | 110,000 | 228,595 | I-3aX |
| c1960 | Anglican Church of India | India | 114 | 150,000 | 225,000 | I-Ang |
| 1970 | Presbyterian Church in America | USA | 1,161 | 183,090 | 221,392 | I-Ref |
| 1941 | Assemblies (Jehova Shammah) | India | 1,350 | 140,000 | 216,000 | I-CBr |
| 1890 | Igreja Evangélica Luterana do Brasil | Brazil | 1,426 | 128,000 | 216,000 | I-Lut |
| 1924 | Authentic Old Calendar Orthodox Ch | Greece | 180 | 106,000 | 212,000 | I-OCd |
| c1990 | Holy Spirit Ministries International | Nigeria | 100 | 116,000 | 210,000 | I-3wA |
| c1980 | Hidden Hindu believers in Christ | Nepal | 800 | 120,000 | 210,000 | I-Hin |
| 1927 | True Orthodox Church | Russia | 2,000 | 100,000 | 210,000 | I-Tru |
| 1968 | Episcopal Church of Africa | Kenya | 440 | 102,000 | 206,000 | I-3cA |
| c1980 | Reformed Christian Church | South Africa | 1,300 | 112,000 | 204,000 | I-3oA |
| c1970 | Intern Fellowship of Faith Ministries | USA | 2,000 | 150,000 | 200,000 | I-3wW |
| c1980 | Korean Full Gospel Chs of America | USA | 600 | 100,000 | 200,000 | I-3fK |
| 1948 | Worldwide/Last Churches | USA | 250 | 150,000 | 200,000 | I-3jW |
| 1977 | Faith Christian Fellowship Intern | USA | 272 | 89,500 | 200,000 | I-3cW |
| c1940 | Assembly Hall Churches | Philippines | 700 | 60,000 | 200,000 | I-3nC |
| c1960 | Believers' Churches in India | India | 3,000 | 120,000 | 200,000 | I-3nI |
| c1970 | Hidden Hindu believers in Christ | Bangladesh | 4,000 | 120,000 | 200,000 | I-Hin |
| 1923 | Eglise Kitawala | Congo-Zaire | 1,000 | 120,000 | 200,000 | I-Jeh |
| 1973 | Eglise du Christ Unie de l'Angola | Congo-Zaire | 200 | 100,000 | 200,000 | I-Uni |
| 1971 | Eglise Apostolique Unie en Afrique | Congo-Zaire | 500 | 90,000 | 200,000 | I-3aA |
| c1915 | Assemblies of God (Spanish) | USA | 500 | 90,000 | 200,000 | I-3pL |
|  | Iglesia Evangélica Filadelfia | Spain | 363 | 168,000 | 200,000 | I-3pE |
| c1991 | Full Gospel Church | South Korea | 20 | 90,000 | 200,000 | I-3kK |
|  | Bantu Bethlehem Ch of Zion in SA | South Africa | 250 | 100,000 | 200,000 | I-3zA |
| 1927 | Holy Order of Cherubim & Seraphim | Nigeria | 400 | 120,000 | 200,000 | I-3aA |
| 1947 | Churches of Christ | Nigeria | 1,050 | 99,800 | 200,000 | I-Dis |
| 1942 | African Israel Church Nineveh | Kenya | 500 | 108,000 | 200,000 | I-3pA |
| c1950 | Isolated radio churches | Iraq | 4,000 | 120,000 | 200,000 | I-3rS |
| 1959 | Surabaya Pentecostal Church | Indonesia | 500 | 70,000 | 200,000 | I-3pG |
|  | Pentecostal Church (Sihombing) | Indonesia | 400 | 60,000 | 200,000 | I-3pG |
| 1954 | Divine Healer's Church | Ghana | 170 | 120,700 | 200,000 | I-3pA |
| 1966 | God's All Times Association | Ethiopia | 240 | 60,000 | 200,000 | I-3cA |
|  | Gen As of Pres Chs (Hap-tong Bo-Su) II | South Korea | 807 | 88,900 | 197,511 | I-Ref |
| c1970 | Hidden Buddhist believers in Christ | Thailand | 1,500 | 140,000 | 195,100 | I-Bud |
| c1970 | Hidden Buddhist believers in Christ | Myanmar | 900 | 80,000 | 192,300 | I-Bud |
| c1975 | Indian Pentecostal Ch of America | USA | 300 | 80,000 | 190,000 | I-3pI |
| 1978 | Int Convention of Faith Chs & Minis | USA | 1,000 | 172,864 | 190,000 | I-3wW |
| 1965 | Visión del Futuro | Argentina | 339 | 95,000 | 190,000 | I-3gL |
| 1957 | Bethel Tabernacle Church | Indonesia | 500 | 75,000 | 188,000 | I-3pG |
|  | Gen As of Pres Chs (Haptong Bo-Su) III | South Korea | 213 | 74,200 | 185,431 | I-Ref |
| 1920 | Hussite Church of the Czech Republic | Czech Republic | 432 | 130,000 | 185,000 | I-ReC |

Continued opposite

claim to have had a vision or dream or theophany of Jesus Christ and who now follow him, openly witnessing within their non-Christian family, caste, society, and religion, but without joining the organized Christian churches. A large majority are charismatics. This type of response appears to be generated only within Hindu, Muslim, or Buddhist countries when adherents exceed 15 million for any or each religion.

## A CHARISMATIC—NONCHARISMATIC TYPOLOGY

A second interpretation of this whole category Independency recognizes that the vast bulk of all these movements center on new experiences of the gifts and charismata of God the Holy Spirit. At the same time, many of these movements dislike or disown the labels 'pentecostal' and 'charismatic', especially Latin American bodies who reject fellowship with the Catholic Charismatic Renewal. In Latin America, bodies are usually termed GR (grassroots) churches instead. The classificatory solution proposed here is to term those bodies that emphasize gifts of the Spirit collectively as Neocharismatics. This leads to a further typology, a simple dichotomy, recognized in our coding system as follows:

(a) **Independent pentecostals/charismatics/neo-charismatics.** All movements openly emphasizing the gifts and charisms of the Holy Spirit, whether predominantly Black or White, have their members here termed pentecostals or charismatics, and more properly independent pentecostals or independent charismatics. They make up 85% of all Independents and in our typology are called Third-Wavers or, synonymously, Neocharismatics. They are coded here each with 3 separate characters after the leading I, giving the reader data on 3 additional different characteristics.

The reader should note that this survey's usage of these terms, especially 'charismatic', is phenomenological, that is, based on visible/observable/measurable phenomena. Thus a network or denomination may dislike the term charismatic, or even strongly deny it or oppose it, but will be classified here as charismatic if it exhibits the range of recognized beliefs and practices that relate to the term charismatic in the wider Christian world.

(b) **Nonpentecostals/noncharismatics.** A number of other movements, some huge some small, some old some new, some dynamic some moribund, emphasize gifts of the Spirit but reject the descriptive terms pentecostal or charismatic and their related beliefs and practices and instead claim some sort of link with the older nonpentecostal denominational terminology, often including a historic denominational term in their titles ('Baptist', 'Methodist', etc.) For this reason they are coded in WCE Part 4's Country Tables 2, column 3b 'Type' with one of the 3-character nonpentecostal denominationalist codes applying to the older mainline denominations, especially Protestant ones. Individually these movements and their members are seen here as only loosely or broadly related to the Third Wave but in contact with it in varying degrees of closeness. They are clearly independent, postdenominationalist, and have many renewal features, hence they have much in common with the core or nucleus of the Third Wave. An additional consideration is that even when the church is officially not pentecostal or charismatic, many of its members *are* (and so in all cases are given a 'percent charismatic or neocharismatic' figure in the appropriate column), while the rest are not.

Most of these nonpentecostal noncharismatic bodies are either predominantly Non-White/Black, or predominantly White. This distinction is made in the 3-letter codes as follows:

(1) White-led bodies have their 3-letter codes always beginning with a capital letter, thus: Bap, Met, Lut, Ang, etc. This is because in most cases there is some clear link with the denominational stream. Orthodox, Catholic, Anglican, and Protestant independents can all be precisely identified by their 3-letter codes, as in fully set out in Part 16 "GeoCodebook".

(2) Non-White indigenous bodies by contrast have their 3-letter codes beginning with a capital letter only if there is a clear or strong link to that tradition; otherwise the code starts with the numeral 3 to indicate

the new entity—Neocharismatic. In many cases there is no clear link, historical or otherwise, with the denominational stream; the users merely like the tradition being claimed, or claim to represent the tradition more faithfully than the originators.

Further, isolated or hidden non-Christian believers in Christ who are neither pentecostal nor charismatic nor neocharismatic may also be recognized by (a) their codes, thus: Hindus = I-Hin, Muslims = I-Mus, Buddhists = I-Bud, and Jews = I-Jew, together with (b) the % neocharismatic which enables division of the total into neocharismatic and non-neocharismatic individuals.

### *THE THIRD WAVE AND ITS 29 VARIETIES (NEOCHARISMATICS)*

***A new variety of Radical Christians***

This analysis describes the 20th-century Renewal in the Holy Spirit as consisting of a First Wave (Classical Pentecostals, originally mainly in the Americas), a Second Wave (Charismatics in the nonpentecostal mainline Catholic and Protestant churches in the Western world, mainly in Europe), and a Third Wave (Independents rejecting, or uninterested in, both previous waves). As often happens in successive waves of a movement, this Third Wave demonstrates a new and disturbingly different kind of Christian renewal. Its members can accurately be called: Radical Christians with some pente-costal/charismatic parallels. In varying degrees they demonstrate some or even many (but not all) of the recognized pentecostal and charismatic gifts—enthusiasm, joy, glossolalia, words of knowledge, prophecies, power encounters, power evangelism, power healing, exotic manifestations.

But Third-Wavers are also characterized by a far more radical Christian lifestyle than has been evident recently in the Western churches. They live in a context of ministry described in the reply of Jesus when John's disciples questioned his credentials: 'Go and tell John what you hear and see: the blind receive their sight and the lame walk, lepers are cleansed and the deaf hear, and the dead are raised up, and the poor have good news preached to them' (Matthew 11:4-5, RSV). These Radical Christians experience healings, liberations, releases from prison, miracles, physical as well as spiritual restoration of sight and hearing, exorcisms, conversions. But the biggest difference is the fact that most members and church workers live this apostolic or neo-apostolic life with a far lower standard of living than their Western counterparts. The average Third-Wave evangelist in India supports his ministry and his family with wages averaging the national per capita income (US$290, or $25 a month). First-Wave and Second-Wave workers in Europe or the USA likewise receive wages averaging the national per capita income, but this is 80 times larger than in India (US$24,000, or $2,000 a month in the USA, France, Germany). Third-Wavers thus live a life without security in a material context only 1% of that in the West. But they also demonstrate other gifts—endurance and victory under recurring hostility, harassment, persecution, suffering, beatings, violent assault, martyrdom, massacre, and even genocide.

The listing of codes in Table 6–4 demonstrates the range and diversity of bodies making up this category of Radical Christians in the Third Wave. Collectively, this further justifies terming them here 'Neocharismatics'.

***Messianic non-Christian believers in Christ***

One very significant newly-recognized element in the Third Wave must be briefly described at this point. This concerns a number of movements within non-Christian religions which have come to accept and follow Jesus Christ as Lord and Messiah but which accept it as their Spirit-led witness to remain within their religion instead of joining the Christian churches or seeking baptism. India and most other large non-Christian countries provide detailed examples, as follows.

Since the year 1800, many organized movements have arisen in all countries with large non-Christian religions hostile to Christianity (listed in Part 21 "GeoPersonnel", as those over 5 million in size). These organize themselves around Jesus Christ as their Lord, Messiah, Savior, and Liberator, but remain within their original religion without calling themselves Christians or joining the Christian churches. A brief listing from India is: Hindu Church of the Lord

*Table 6–4 concluded*

| Begun 1 | Movement 2 | Main country 3 | Churches 4 | Adults 5 | Affiliated 6 | Eccles 7 |
|---|---|---|---|---|---|---|
| 1958 | International Ministerial Fellowship | USA | 110 | 58,690 | 182,500 | I-3cW |
| 1976 | Association of Ev Lutheran Chs | USA | 320 | 120,000 | 180,000 | I-Lut |
| 1945 | Iglesia Evangélica del Principe de Paz | Guatemala | 900 | 72,000 | 180,000 | I-3pL |
| 1914 | Iglesia Apostólica de la Fe en CJ | Mexico | 1,520 | 138,000 | 176,000 | I-3oL |
| 1967 | Friends Missionary Prayer Band | India | 1,950 | 90,500 | 175,500 | I-Non |
| c1965 | Misión Cristiana Elim | El Salvador | 71 | 72,000 | 175,000 | I-3kL |
| | Iglesia Pentecoste Naciente | Chile | 1,500 | 120,000 | 171,000 | I-3pL |
| 1950 | Iglesia Evangélica Metodista Pentecostal | Chile | 1,500 | 120,000 | 171,000 | I-3pL |
| 1918 | Independent Assemblies of God Intern | USA | 800 | 100,000 | 170,000 | I-3pW |
| 1991 | Igreja Universal do Reino do Deus | Portugal | 320 | 90,000 | 170,000 | I-3pY |
| 1945 | African Brotherhood Church | Kenya | 765 | 76,500 | 170,000 | I-Non |
| 1942 | Iglesia Ev Cristiana Calvario | Guatemala | 462 | 60,000 | 167,000 | I-3pL |
| 1978 | Association of Vineyard Churches | USA | 505 | 115,000 | 165,000 | I-3cW |
| 1962 | Church of the Living God | Philippines | 350 | 80,000 | 160,000 | I-3pF |
| c1930 | Iglesias Evangélicas Independientes | Mexico | 727 | 80,000 | 160,000 | I-3pL |
| | Igreja da Restauração | Brazil | 280 | 70,000 | 156,000 | I-3cY |
| 1979 | International Churches of Christ | USA | 124 | 110,000 | 152,600 | I-3cW |
| 1968 | Universal Fellowship of MCCs | USA | 300 | 119,000 | 152,296 | I-Gay |
| 1979 | Tribal Gospel Mission | India | 149 | 83,000 | 152,000 | I-3cI |
| 1907 | World Missionary Association | South Africa | 300 | 97,000 | 151,400 | I-Eva |
| c1965 | Intern Conf of Charismatic Chs | USA | 3,000 | 100,000 | 150,000 | I-3cW |
| 1961 | Council of Churches of Ev Chr-Baptists | Ukraine | 1,200 | 70,000 | 150,000 | I-Bap |
| 1896 | Zulu Congregational Church | South Africa | 274 | 80,000 | 150,000 | I-Con |
| 1975 | Peoples Churches (Kwasizabantu) | South Africa | 140 | 80,000 | 150,000 | I-3cA |
| 1939 | Isolated radio churches | Poland | 3,000 | 100,000 | 150,000 | I-rad |
| 1948 | God, Mysterious Mother | Philippines | 200 | 70,000 | 150,000 | I-mar |
| 1920 | Igl de Dios en la República Mexicana | Mexico | 625 | 75,000 | 150,000 | I-3pL |
| 1942 | Subba Rao Movement | India | 500 | 50,000 | 150,000 | I-3mH |
| c1930 | Iglesia Nueva Apostólica | Argentina | 135 | 103,000 | 145,008 | I-3aX |
| 1978 | Association of Faith Chs & Ministries | USA | 800 | 126,868 | 145,000 | I-3wW |
| c1980 | New Apostolic Church | Philippines | 200 | 90,000 | 140,267 | I-3aX |
| c1960 | Victory Fellowship of Ministries | USA | 400 | 95,300 | 140,000 | I-3vW |
| 1950 | International Ministers Forum | USA | 400 | 99,750 | 140,000 | I-3fW |
| 1922 | Eglise Déimatiste | Ivory Coast | 840 | 84,000 | 140,000 | I-mar |
| | Chiese Pentecostali Autonome | Italy | 350 | 70,000 | 140,000 | I-3pW |
| c1930 | Lahu Churches | China | 1,000 | 60,000 | 140,000 | I-eth |
| 1955 | Congregational Christian Churches | USA | 399 | 79,255 | 139,999 | I-Con |
| c1970 | Hidden Hindu believers in Christ | Indonesia | 700 | 60,000 | 135,000 | I-Hin |
| 1958 | Pentecostal Protestant Church | South Africa | 500 | 88,000 | 135,000 | I-3pW |
| 1952 | Assemblies of the Lord Jesus Christ | USA | 500 | 40,000 | 130,000 | I-3oW |
| 1935 | Pentecostal Missionary Church | Indonesia | 266 | 58,500 | 130,000 | I-3pG |
| | Indonesia Pentecostal Church | Indonesia | 247 | 49,400 | 130,000 | I-3pG |
| 1922 | Indep Fundamental Chs of America | USA | 698 | 82,400 | 127,000 | I-Fun |
| c1830 | Primitive Baptists | USA | 2,647 | 90,000 | 125,000 | I-Bap |
| 1927 | Pentecostal Mission | India | 1,071 | 75,000 | 125,000 | I-3pI |
| 1922 | Army of the Cross of Christ Church | Ghana | 1,094 | 69,000 | 125,000 | I-3sA |
| c1890 | Eglise des Banzie (Bwiti) | Gabon | 1,200 | 77,000 | 125,000 | I-mar |
| c1945 | Iglesia del Principe de Paz | El Salvador | 556 | 50,000 | 125,000 | I-3pL |
| 1956 | Iglesia Panamericana de Colombia | Colombia | 250 | 82,000 | 125,000 | I-3aL |
| 1924 | Churches of Christ, Philippine Mission | Philippines | 281 | 85,000 | 121,000 | I-Dis |
| 1950 | Churches on the Rock International | USA | 115 | 40,500 | 120,000 | I-3cW |
| 1934 | Christian Evangelistic Assemblies | USA | 82 | 92,158 | 120,000 | I-3fW |
| 1927 | Church of Jesus Christ | USA | 500 | 100,000 | 120,000 | I-3pW |
| 1980 | New Frontiers International | Britain | 710 | 58,000 | 120,000 | I-3tW |
| 1965 | Eglise Unie du Saint-Esprit | Congo-Zaire | 140 | 50,000 | 120,000 | I-3pA |
| 1935 | Eglise Libre Méthodiste au Rwanda | Rwanda | 38 | 64,000 | 120,000 | I-Hol |
| 1975 | Charismatic youth movements | Nigeria | 500 | 60,000 | 120,000 | I-3cA |
| 1958 | Eglises radiophoniques isolées | Morocco | 1,000 | 60,000 | 120,000 | I-3rS |
| 1966 | CMS Anglican Church of India | India | 310 | 90,000 | 120,000 | I-Ang |
| 1918 | Ukrainian Greek-Orthodox Ch of C | Canada | 258 | 85,200 | 120,000 | I-Ukr |
| 1919 | African Faith Tabernacle Church | Ghana | 860 | 92,900 | 116,000 | I-3oA |
| 1909 | Evangelical Methodist Church in the P | Philippines | 295 | 44,964 | 112,000 | I-Met |
| 1955 | Igreja Evangélica Pentecostal Unida | Brazil | 252 | 37,000 | 112,000 | I-3pY |
| c1980 | Thai Ezra Churches | Thailand | 15,000 | 75,000 | 110,000 | I-3nZ |
| c1670 | Old Ritualist Church | Latvia | 56 | 50,000 | 110,000 | I-OBe |
| 1901 | United Free Will Baptist Church | USA | 750 | 90,000 | 110,000 | I-3pB |
| 1920 | Christian Spiritist Union of the P | Philippines | 180 | 60,000 | 110,000 | I-Spi |
| 1906 | Associate Reformed Presbyterian Ch | Pakistan | 176 | 63,000 | 110,000 | I-Ref |
| c1920 | African Methodist Episcopal Church | Nigeria | 450 | 45,000 | 110,000 | I-Met |
| c1925 | Fellowship of Ev Baptist Churches in C | Canada | 492 | 60,566 | 110,000 | I-Bap |
| c1920 | Cooneyites (Go Preachers) | Australia | 500 | 60,000 | 110,000 | I-Fun |
| c1986 | Korean Baptist Convention | South Korea | 151 | 82,000 | 107,500 | I-Bap |
| 1870 | Church of England in South Africa | South Africa | 160 | 68,000 | 107,046 | I-ReA |
| 1884 | Eglise Baptiste Camerounaise | Cameroon | 142 | 55,936 | 106,000 | I-Bap |
| 1896 | Iglesia Unión Misionera Ev en el E | Ecuador | 474 | 61,165 | 105,141 | I-Hol |
| 1955 | Eglise Réformée Evangélique de M | Madagascar | 500 | 87,500 | 105,000 | I-Con |
| 1950 | IEvMP Reunida en el Nombre de Jesús | Chile | 200 | 65,000 | 105,000 | I-3gL |
| 1930 | Association of Christian Churches | South Korea | 309 | 56,800 | 103,265 | I-Non |
| 1943 | Church of God (Huntsville) | USA | 2,027 | 75,000 | 103,000 | I-3pW |
| 1963 | Full Gospel International General Mtg | South Korea | 54 | 78,000 | 101,233 | I-3fK |
| 1996 | Charismatic Church of Uganda | Uganda | 210 | 40,600 | 101,000 | I-3cW |
| 1990 | Integrity Leadership Ministries | USA | 60 | 60,000 | 100,000 | I-3cW |
| c1922 | Independent Assemblies of God Int | India | 250 | 70,000 | 100,000 | I-3pI |
| 1960 | Deliverance Evangelistic Church | USA | 32 | 83,000 | 100,000 | I-3vB |
| | Trinity Church Network | USA | 15 | 70,000 | 100,000 | I-3cW |
| 1945 | United Ch of Jesus Christ (Apostolic) | USA | 80 | 50,000 | 100,000 | I-3aO |
| 1970 | Apos Ministers Conf of Philadelphia | USA | 300 | 80,000 | 100,000 | I-3aO |
| | Evangelistic Messengers Association | USA | 400 | 70,000 | 100,000 | I-3cW |
| c1970 | Immanuel Bible College | India | 1,700 | 50,000 | 100,000 | I-3nI |
| c1980 | Missão Ev Pentecostal de Angola | Angola | 600 | 75,460 | 100,000 | I-3pA |
| 1922 | Congregational Bible Churches | USA | 450 | 80,000 | 100,000 | I-3pW |
| c1960 | Independent charismatic churches | Russia | 500 | 50,000 | 100,000 | I-3cW |
| 1981 | Jamaat (Messianic Muslims) | Bangladesh | 1,000 | 60,000 | 100,000 | I-3mM |
| 1910 | Churches of Christ (Non-Instrumental) | Zambia | 909 | 40,000 | 100,000 | I-Dis |
| 1952 | Isolated radio churches | Viet Nam | 2,000 | 60,000 | 100,000 | I-3rV |
| c1960 | Isolated radio churches | Sudan | 1,600 | 50,000 | 100,000 | I-3rA |
| c1990 | Full Gospel Church of God | South Africa | 336 | 90,000 | 100,000 | I-3fW |
| 1947 | African Gospel Church | South Africa | 90 | 40,000 | 100,000 | I-3fA |
| 1944 | True Orthodox Christians | Russia | 5,000 | 60,000 | 100,000 | I-Tru |
| 1921 | Christians of Evangelical Faith | Russia | 500 | 40,000 | 100,000 | I-3pW |
| 1957 | Church of God (Ecclesiae Dei) | Philippines | 150 | 70,000 | 100,000 | I-3pF |
| c1950 | Isolated radio churches | Lebanon | 1,000 | 60,000 | 100,000 | I-3rS |
| | Iglesia Após de los Apóstoles y Profetas | El Salvador | 300 | 45,000 | 100,000 | I-3pL |
| 1920 | Eglises Baptistes de la RCA | Central African Rep | 118 | 40,000 | 100,000 | I-Fun |
| 1967 | Eglise Presb Camerounaise Orthodoxe | Cameroon | 700 | 78,600 | 100,000 | I-Ref |

## Table 6–5. Third-Wave Independents: 4-character codes for 26 generic types and 26 varieties of Neocharismatics (Third-Wavers).

In every Country Table 2, in *WCE* Part 4, column 3 gives a 4-character code which identifies each denomination's type, tradition, and family. The table below sets out those codes for the megabloc termed Independents. Example: I-3pA signifies Independents who are *Third-Wavers*, *pentecostals*, and *African*.

**1. First character: Megabloc code.** The first letter, a capital I, is the global code in all tables referring to the Independent/Postdenominationalist megabloc. It is followed by a hyphen and then by 3 further characters describing tradition or family. These further 3 characters are as shown below.

**2. Second character: Third Wave.** The numeral 3 identifies all those independent charismatic/pentecostal entities which indisputably form the nucleus or core or the heart of the

Third Wave. The reader can thus rapidly glance over any Country Table 2 and see immediately which bodies constitute or belong to this Third Wave.

**3. Third character: Generic type.** This lowercase letter identifies each entity by whichever of 26 generic adjectives forms its *primary* description or generic differentium, even though in many cases several adjectives might well legitimately be applied to a single entity. These are as shown below left, arranged in alphabetic order. Note that these are not global codes (as set out in Table 16–2); these are values that apply only to this specific third-character variable shown in Country Tables 2, column 3.

**4. Fourth character: Specific identity.** The last letter in

the 4-character code, always a capital, identifies each entity's main or major *geographico-cultural* or *ethnic* or *racial differentium*—its persona/primary identity/ecclesiology. Some 26 such major current descriptors can be identified, shown below at the right, subdivided into the 2 main varieties of Independents (Non-White, and White). Codes describe both *individuals*, and their *churches* or other groupings. Most of these codes can appear combined with and following any of the third-character codes listed at left.

Again, the list at below right is not listing all global codes but only giving values of this specific fourth-character variable shown in Country Tables 2, column 3.

*Third character: Generic type*

a = apostolic
b = baptistic pentecostal (4-square)
c = charismatic
d = doubly-affiliated (mainliners, also 3rd-Wave)
e = earthkeeping pentecostal
f = full gospel (5-fold) pentecostal
g = grassroots (GR/autochthonous)
h = house church
i = holiness pentecostal
j = healing, exorcisms
k = cell-based full gospel
l = latter rain pentecostal
m = messianic
n = neocharismatic
o = oneness pentecostal
p = pentecostal
q = neopentecostal
r = radio/TV
s = spiritual (Spiritual Christian)
t = restorationist (Kingdom, New Churches)
u = undenominational (single-church)
v = victory, deliverance, perfectionist
w = word of faith (faith/word)
x = mixed
y = high church pentecostal (liturgical)
z = zionist

*Fourth character: Specific identity*

(1) **Non-White indigenous Neocharismatics**, described under each's most prominent *geographico-ethnoculturo-racial* description (either of individuals or of their churches) as shown by one of the following capital letters:

A = African indigenous pentecostals/charismatics (Zionist, Apostolic, Spiritual churches; e.g. ZCC, EJCSK)
B = Black American indigenous pentecostals (e.g. Church of God in Christ, Full Gospel Catholic Ch)
C = Han Chinese indigenous pentecostal/charismatic churches (e.g. True Jesus Church, NBM/BAM)
D = Black American independent charismatics (e.g. FGBCF)
E = Ethnic (monoethnic) pentecostal churches (e.g. Yi Churches, Miao Churches)
F = Filipino indigenous pentecostals/charismatics (e.g. Jesus is Lord Fellowship)
G = Indonesian indigenous pentecostal churches (e.g. GPI, GBI, GBIS, GPPS)
H = Messianic Hindu temples or organized Hindu-Christian churches (e.g. Subba Rao Movement)
I = Indian indigenous pentecostals/charismatics (e.g. Believers' Chs of India, Christ Groups)
J = Messianic Jewish synagogues (organized, e.g. FMC, UMJC, IAMCS)
K = Korean indigenous pentecostal/charismatic churches (e.g. KFGCA)
L = Latin American/Hispanic autochthonous grassroots (GR) churches (e.g. IMPC, IPP)
M = Messianic Muslim mosques (Jesus Mosques; some organizing)
N = Colored/Creole/Pijin/Mixed-race indigenous charismatics or pentecostals
O = Black American Oneness Apostolics (e.g. COLJCAF)
P = Pacific/Oceanic/Australasian indigenous pentecostals/charismatics
Q = Japanese indigenous pentecostal/charismatic churches (e.g. Spirit of Jesus Church, OGM)
R = Red Indian (Amerindian) indigenous neopentecostal or charismatic churches (e.g. UIEI, IEUT)
S = Arab/Assyrian/Semitic indigenous charismatic churches
T = other Messianic non-Christian believers in Christ
U = Afro-Caribbean indigenous pentecostals/charismatics (e.g. Spiritual Baptists/Shouters)
V = Vietnamese indigenous churches (e.g. Good News house church movement)
Y = Brazilian/Portuguese grassroots (GR) churches (e.g. OBPC, IURD)
Z = other Asian indigenous neocharismatics (e.g. Hope of God Churches of Thailand)

(2) **White-led Postdenominationalists**/Neo-Apostolics/pentecostals/charismatics/neocharismatics, deriving from European/American initiative or ancestry:

W = European/American/White-led Neo-Apostolics (pentecostals, charismatics, or neocharismatics)
X = European White-led New Apostolics (the Neuapostolische Kirche, and its many schisms)

---

### Table 6–6. Neocharismatic components of Renewal, AD 2000.

Neocharismatics of all kinds number 295,405,000, which is 77% of all Independents and 56% of all Renewal members. For sizes of all components below, see Table 5-8.

**NEOCHARISMATIC RENEWAL**
Neocharismatics (Independents, Postdenominationalists)
(a) In 2 kinds of wholly Third Wave networks
  Non-White indigenous Neocharismatics
    African indigenous pentecostals/charismatics
    Afro-Caribbean pentecostals/charismatics
    Arab/Assyrian/Semitic neocharismatics
    Black American independent charismatics
    Black American indigenous pentecostals
    Black American Oneness Apostolics
    Brazilian/Portuguese grassroots neocharismatics
    Colored/Mixed-race indigenous charismatics
    Ethnic (Monoethnic) pentecostal churches
    Filipino indigenous pentecostals/charismatics
    Han Chinese indigenous pentecostals/charismatics
    Indian indigenous pentecostals/charismatics
    Indonesian indigenous pentecostals
    Japanese indigenous pentecostals
    Korean indigenous pentecostals/charismatics
    Latino-Hispanic grassroots believers
    Messianic Hindu believers in Christ
    Messianic Jewish believers in Christ
    Messianic Muslim believers in Christ
    Pacific/Oceanic indigenous charismatics
    Red Indian/Amerindian neopentecostals
    Vietnamese indigenous neocharismatics
    other Asian indigenous neocharismatics
    other Messianic non-Christian believers in Christ
  White-led independent postdenominationalists
    European/American White-led Neo-Apostolics
    European White-led New Apostolics
(b) as % of 7 kinds of non-Third-Wave denominations
  Independent Anglican neocharismatics
  Independent Protestant neocharismatics
  Independent Catholic neocharismatics
  Independent Orthodox neocharismatics
  Nonhistorical Independent neocharismatics
  Isolated radio/TV neocharismatics
  Hidden non-Christian believers in Christ
    Hidden Hindu neocharismatics
    Hidden Muslim neocharismatics
    Hidden Buddhist neocharismatics
    Hidden Jewish neocharismatics
    Hidden other religionist neocharismatics

Jesus (1858), National Church of Bengal (1868), Church of the New Dispensation (1880), Calcutta Christo Samaj (1887), National Church in India (1893), Fellowship of the Followers of Jesus (1933), Subba Rao Movement (1942). Although not all professedly pentecostal or charismatic, a majority of their members exhibit the related phenomena and so these movements as a whole can be regarded as unanticipated but legitimate components of the Third Wave of 20th-century renewal.

### Definitions of the Third Wave

All these considerations enable us in this survey to define the Third Wave precisely as consisting of 2 elements, as follows:

(i) All independent/postdenominationalist pentecostal/charismatic bodies of any race, which are now identified by a 4-character code (in column 3 'Type') beginning with the code I-3, as for example 'I-3pG' (an indigenous pentecostal church in Indonesia); and

(ii) All independent charismatic or neocharismatic *individuals* in any nonpentecostal/noncharismatic postdenominationalist bodies, identified in this survey as a percentage of each such body.

In defining the Third Wave of the Pentecostal/Charismatic Renewal in this way, and in labeling its adherents by our neologisms Neocharismatics and Radical Christians, we are demonstrating the autonomy of these 295 million believers in Christ, which disturbs Western and Eastern Christianity at present. In other words, in the same way that the mainline denominations were disturbed in 1900 by the irruption of Pentecostalism, and in the same way that First-Wavers (Classical Pentecostals) were disturbed in 1968 by the Second Wave when it erupted, so First-Wavers and Second-Wavers alike are disturbed today by the Third Wave and resist recognizing it as the next phase in God's global renewal of Christianity. This has been a regularly-occurring sequence of reactions throughout Christian history.

### 26 generic types and 26 varieties of Third-Wave bodies

The 4-character code describing each of these bodies is not a coherent single term but is made up of 4 separate characters, each with its own meaning. This code as shown in Table 6–4 analyzes the ecclesiastical identity of each Third-Wave network/association/denomination/paradenomination/entity which is given a line to itself in Country Tables 2. There is the single first-character code defining the megabloc (I), a second-character code ('3'), a third-character code with 26 generic types, and a fourth-character code with 26 specific varieties. Altogether this yields a grand total of 676 possible types of Third-Wave entity, although in practice many combinations have no examples existing.

Here is a typical example: a grouping of churches coded 'I-3pK' is thus identified as being *Independents, Third-Wave*, of *pentecostal* emphasis, among *Koreans*. All the characters in existence are coded as shown in Table 6–4. And Table 6–5 gives the global overview of Neocharismatics related to all these codes, in the order shown in the whole Renewal's listing in Table 5-8 which also gives each line's statistics.

### DOUBLE AFFILIATION

### Final considerations: doubly-affiliated bodies

Note that a small percentage of all Third-Wave churches or denominations or networks begin independently but later become also nominally affiliated with First-Wave Pentecostal denominations, mainly with the Assemblies of God. Where this is so, this fact is stated in Country Tables 2's column 10. Because all these are thus counted and reported twice, a negative figure for these doubly-affiliated persons is added at the end of the listing of denominations in Country Tables 2, thereby rectifying the enumeration.

Secondly, note that groupings identified and coded above as 'I-3d' are mainline-denominationalist First-Wavers (such as with the Assemblies of God), or mainline-nonpentecostal-denominationalists (such as Anglicans, Roman Catholics, Methodists, etc), who

## Table 6–7.  Definitions of key terms in the denominationalist/postdenominationalist analysis.

**apostle.** A charismatic preacher or minister who experiences a call to leadership under the Holy Spirit and who becomes convinced through the witness of colleagues that he (or occasionally she) is called to the biblical office of apostle, this being similar to the New Testament offices of pioneer evangelist and bishop providing cover or accountability for a large body of pastors.

**apostolic network.** A grouping of churches, ministers, and ministries centering on one particular apostle.

**borderline.** In Tables 6-8 and 6-9 this refers to an individual or organization which is on the edges of both denominationalism and postdenominationalism as defined here.

**charismata.** The classic gifts of the Holy Spirit.

**Charismatic.** The Charismatic Renewal within mainline denominations only (Catholic, Anglican, Protestant, et al), and its members, making up the Second Wave of Renewal.

**charismatic.** Applied to any individual or church evidencing the charismata but not in a First- or Second-Wave situation.

**Classical Pentecostal.** Denominations, churches, and members making up the First Wave of Renewal (Pentecostalism), originally mainly with White or European members.

**denomination.** A grouping or network of linked churches or congregations within a single nation.

**denominationalism.** Stance or ideology surrounding denominations as authorities over congregations and members.

**denominationalist.** One who accepts or promotes the primary role of a denomination as to regulate congregations and members.

**First Wave.** Classical Pentecostal mainline denominations, congregations, and members.

**First-Wavers.** Denominational Pentecostals (Classical Pentecostals), members of mainline USA churches and their worldwide constituencies.

**historic denomination.** A mainline denomination.

**independency.** The ecclesiastical position rejecting control of churches by centralized denominationalist headquarters.

**Independents.** Christians or churches having nothing to do with historical, organized, denominationalist Christianity; also

termed Postdenominationalists, or Neo-Apostolics.

**Independent.** In this context, refers to churches and paradenominations rejecting historic, traditional, mainline Christianity.

**Independent single congregation.** An autonomous local church with no outside affiliations or structural relationships.

**mainline denomination.** A historic, traditional Christian denomination of any confession.

**mainstream.** The main, central part of a denomination, or a confession, or of Christianity as a whole, where the currents of movement are strongest.

**megabloc.** One of 6 major ecclesiastico-cultural subdivisions of affiliated Christians and their churches.

**minidenomination.** A very small denomination of minimal significance consisting of from 2 to 10 congregations only.

**Neo-Apostolics,** describing the movement as a whole. Alternative term for independents or Postdenominationalists.

**Neocharismatic.** An adherent of the Third Wave of the Pentecostal/Charismatic Renewal in the Holy Spirit.

**neocharismatic.** A religious person or movement similar to a charismatic but unconnected with mainline pentecostal or nonpentecostal congregations.

**network.** An electronic linking of 3 or more computers.

**noncharismatic.** A person or congregation disclaiming or rejecting the appellation charismatic.

**nonpentecostal.** A person or congregation disclaiming or rejecting the appellation pentecostal.

**nonpentecostal/noncharismatic.** A person or congregation disclaiming or rejecting both the appellations pentecostal and charismatic. As everywhere, many persons may hold these disclaimers yet nevertheless be enumerated as members of First-Wave or Second-Wave congregations or denominations.

**paradenomination.** Almost a denomination; a de facto denomination in process of formation, or a denomination whose members deny it is one.

**Pentecostal.** Classical Pentecostal denomination, congregation, or individual, professing initial evidence (tongues).

**pentecostal.** Applied to any individual or church holding to ini-

tial evidence (tongues) but in a Third-Wave situation rather than in a First-Wave or Second-Wave situation.

**Pentecostal/Charismatic.** Referring to the First and Second Waves of the 20th-century Renewal in the Holy Spirit.

**pentecostal/charismatic.** Applied to any individual or church evidencing charismata or tongues but outside, or not within, a First- or Second-Wave situation.

**personal charismatic, personal pentecostal.** Persons of these convictions but found in bodies or denominations not describing themselves in this way.

**postdenominationalism.** Stance or ideology rejecting denominationalism, especially denominations as regulatory bodies over congregations and members.

**postdenominationalist.** One who accepts or promotes rejection of historic mainline denominationalist Christianity.

**Postdenominationalists.** Also termed Independents, or Neo-Apostolics; that segment of global Christianity unrelated to denominationalism or historic Christianity.

**Renewal.** Shorthand term for the entire Pentecostal/Charismatic/Neocharismatic Renewal in the Holy Spirit.

**Second Wave.** The Charismatic Renewal within mainline denominations only, enumerated as denominational services, prayer groups, and individual members.

**Second-Wavers.** Charismatics in the Renewal within mainline nonpentecostal churches.

**Third Wave.** Third stage in the 20th-Century Pentecostal/Charismatic Renewal in the Holy Spirit known primarily as Neocharismatics; also making up the greater part of the major ecclesiastico-cultural megabloc termed Independents, or Postdenominationalists, or Neo-Apostolics

**Third-Wavers.** Believers baptized in the Holy Spirit but who do not affiliate with First-Wavers or Second-Wavers but join Independent churches.

**traditional denomination.** A mainline denomination, in one or other of the 4 megablocs O, R, A, or P.

(For further definitions, see Part 30 "Glossary").

---

then later also adopt the additional identity of Third-Wavers. Generically they are often referred to by mainline missiologists as 'Apostolic congregations'. They are doubly counted in our enumeration because they identify themselves and/or their congregations as belonging to postdenominationalist networks (and are therefore listed as such within a line each in Country Tables 2) but they also retain their mainline de-

nominational affiliation (often hidden, or not mentioned, or otherwise played down) and so are also counted by their mainline denominations. A negative figure rectifying the enumeration is therefore included in Country Tables 2's line 'Doubly-affiliated' (global code 2AC). If both of a body's affiliations are pentecostal, charismatic, or neocharismatic, their component of double affiliation is here labeled 'Doubly-

counted 1st-/2nd-/3rd-Wavers' (global code 4ZAC).

These 2 sources of double affiliation for Third-Wavers are combined in this single line 'Doubly-affiliated'.

---

## BIBLIOGRAPHY - a small selection

*A guide to the study of the Pentecostal movement.* C. E. Jones. ATLA Bibliographic Series, 6. Metuchen, NJ and London: American Theological Library Association and Scarecrow Press, 1983. 1,245p in 2 vols. (Though dated, remains an important bibliography of the Pentecostal movement).

*African independent church.* H. W. Turner. London: Oxford University Press, 1967. 2 vols. (On the Church of the Lord [Aladura]).

*American denominational organization: a sociological view.* R. P. Scherer. Pasadena, CA: William Carey Library, 1980. 386p.

*Charismatic Christianity as a global culture.* K. Poewe (ed). Studies in comparative religion. Columbia, SC: University of South Carolina Press, 1994. 316p.

*Deeper life: the extraordinary growth of the Deeper Life Bible Church.* A. Isaacson. London: Hodder & Stoughton, 1990. 254p. (Chronicles the origins and development of an African Independent Church in Nigeria from a Bible study group in 1973 to over one thousand congregations today).

*From rags to riches: an analysis of the Faith movement and its relation to the classical Pentecostal movement.* J. H. Horn. Pretoria: UNISA, 1989. 147p.

*Habits of the heart: individualism and commitment in American life.* R. N. Bellah et al. Berkeley, CA: University of California Press, 1985. (An influential study of the loss of the 'second language' of piety in American culture).

*Modern Christian revivals.* E. L. Blumhofer & R. Balmer (eds). Bloomington, IN: Indiana University Press, 1993.

*Nova religio: the journal of alternative and emergent religions.* 1997.

*Perspectives on the new pentecostalism.* R. P. Spittler (ed). Grand Rapids, MI: Baker Book House, 1976. 268p. (Provides a variety of pentecostal and non-pentecostal perspectives on the movement).

*Reimagining denominationalism: interpretive essays.* R. B. Mullin & R. E. Richey (eds). Religion in America series. New York and Oxford, UK: Oxford University Press, 1994. 336p.

*Religion in sociological perspective: essays in the empirical study of religion.* C. Y. Glock. The Wadsworth series in sociology. Belmont, CA: Wadsworth, 1973. 325p.

*Religion in the modern world: from cathedral to cults.* S. Bruce. Oxford and New York: Oxford University Press, 1996. 267p.

*Restoring the kingdom: the radical Christianity of the house church movement.* A. Walker. London: Hodder & Stoughton, 1988.

*Rise up and walk! Conciliarism and the African indigenous churches, 1815–1987.* D. B. Barrett. Nairobi: Oxford University Press, 1988.

*Spontaneous combustion: grass–roots Christianity, Latin American style.* M. Berg & P. Pretiz. Pasadena, CA: William Carey Library, 1996. 296p.

*The charismatic movement: a guide to the study of neo–pentecostalism with emphasis on Anglo–American sources.* C. E. Jones. ATLA Bibliographic Series, 30. Metuchen, NJ and London: American Theological Library Association and Scarecrow Press, 1995. 1,266p in 2 vols. (A major bibliography of the charismatic movement).

*The empty church: the suicide of liberal Christianity.* T. C. Reeves. New York: The Free Press, 1996. 286p.

*The freedom of the Spirit: African indigenous churches in Kenya.* F. K. Githieya. Atlanta: Scholars Press, 1997. 304p.

*The good society.* R. N. Bellah et al. New York: Knopf, 1991.

*The life and theology of Watchman Nee, including a study of the Little Flock Movement.* N. H. Cliff. Leiden: Pharos, 1994. 300p.

*The rise of independent churches in Ghana.* Accra: Asempa Publishers, 1990. 92p.

*The social dimensions of sectarianism: sects and new religious movements in contemporary society.* B. R. Wilson. Oxford, UK and New York: Clarendon, 1992. 311p.

*The spirit–seekers: new religious movements in southern Ghana.* R. W. Wyllie. American Academy of Religion. Studies in religion, no. 21. Missoula, MT: Scholars Press, 1980.

*The third wave of the Holy Spirit: encountering the power of signs and wonders today.* C. P. Wagner. Ann Arbor, MI: Servant Publications, Vine Books, 1988. 133p.

*Unity of the churches: an actual possibility.* H. Fires & K. Rahner. New York: Paulist Press; Philadelphia: Fortress Press, 1985. 153p.

*Zulu Zion and some Swazi Zionists.* B. Sundkler. Oxford studies in African affairs. Oxford, UK: Oxford University Press, 1976. 337p.

**Table 6–8. Global Christianity dichotomized into denominationalism versus postdenominationalism (Independency), AD 1970-2000.**

*In the year 1970 (light figures)*
*In the year AD 2000 (**black** figures)*

# GLOBAL CHRISTIANITY

*had*
18,630  **33,820** denominations/paradenominations
*with*
1,449,600  **3,447,900** congregations/churches
*composed of*
1,130 million  **1,888 million** affiliated Christians
*dichotomized into*
*the 2 global categories below*

## 1. DENOMINATIONALISM (in megablocs O,R,A,P,m)

|  |  | % | % |
|---|---|---|---|
| *which had* | | | |
| 7,610 **11,680** traditional denominations .......... | | 41 | **35** |
| *of which* | | | |
| 7,080 **7,160** were clearcut denominationalist ..................... | | 93 | **60** |
| 380 **2,920** were less markedly denominationalist .............. | | 5 | **25** |
| 150 **1,750** were borderline denominationalist/postdenominationalist | | 2 | **15** |

|  | % | % |
|---|---|---|
| *all of which had* | | |
| 1,040,200 **1,715,700** congregations/churches ......... | 72 | **50** |
| *of which* | | |
| 1,029,800 **1,201,000** were clearcut denominationalist ................ | 99 | **70** |
| 10,400 **514,700** were borderline denominationalist ................ | 1 | **30** |
| 988,200 **1,458,400** were affiliated to mainline denominations ........ | 95 | **85** |
| 52,000 **257,400** were in minor minidenominations .................. | 5 | **15** |
| 82,100 **303,400** were Pentecostal/Charismatic .................... | 8 | **18** |
| 958,000 **1,412,400** were nonpentecostal/noncharismatic .......... | 92 | **82** |

|  | % | % |
|---|---|---|
| *all of which had* | | |
| 1,075 million **1,720 million** Christians (in O,R,A,P,m) ....... | 92 | **82** |
| *of whom* | | |
| 645 million **516 million** were personal denominationalists .............. | 60 | **30** |
| 430 million **1,204 million** were just Christians who happened to be there . | 40 | **70** |
| 1,043 million **1,376 million** were in mainline denominations .............. | 97 | **80** |
| 32 million **344 million** were in minor minidenominations .............. | 3 | **20** |
| 1,056 million **1,478 million** were nonpentecostal/noncharismatic Christians | 98 | **87** |
| 19 million **242 million** were Pentecostals/Charismatics ............... | 2 | **13** |
| *of this line above (which = the First & Second Waves)* | | |
| 15 million **66 million** were Pentecostals (First-Wavers) .............. | 1 | **4** |
| 3 million **176 million** were Charismatics (Second-Wavers) .......... | 0 | **10** |
| *and of that same line above* | | |
| 1 million **19 million** also adopted Third-Wave identity ............... | 0 | **1** |
| 18 million **222 million** did not relate to Third-Wave activities .......... | 2 | **12** |

## 2. POSTDENOMINATIONALISM (in megabloc I)

|  | % | % |
|---|---|---|
| *which had* | | |
| 11,000 **22,100** paradenominations/networks ........ | 59 | **65** |
| *of which* | | |
| 2000 **1,350** were clearcut apostolic networks ................... | 2 | **2** |
| 7,600 **5,500** were looser groupings of churches ............... | 69 | **25** |
| 3,300 **16,300** were postdenominationalist new denominations ...... | 29 | **74** |

|  | % | % |
|---|---|---|
| *all of which had* | | |
| 409,400 **1,732,200** congregations/churches ......... | 28 | **50** |
| *of which* | | |
| 327,500 **1,773,000** were clearcut postdenominationalist ............. | 80 | **99** |
| 81,900 **18,000** were borderline postdenominationalist ............ | 20 | **1** |
| 163,700 **1,433,000** were affiliated to independent networks ......... | 40 | **80** |
| 245,600 **358,000** were independent single congregations ........... | 60 | **20** |
| 195,400 **1,367,600** were clearly pentecostal/charismatic ........... | 48 | **79** |
| 214,000 **364,500** were nonpentecostal/noncharismatic ........... | 52 | **21** |

|  | % | % |
|---|---|---|
| *all of which had* | | |
| 95 million **386 million** Christians (Independents, I) ...... | 8 | **18** |
| *of whom* | | |
| 38 million **270 million** were personal postdenominationalists .......... | 40 | **70** |
| 57 million **116 million** were just Christians who happened to be there .. | 60 | **30** |
| 29 million **289 million** were in independent networks ................ | 30 | **75** |
| 67 million **96 million** were in independent single congregations ........ | 70 | **25** |
| 42 million **90 million** were nonpentecostals/noncharismatics .......... | 44 | **26** |
| 53 million **295 million** were independent pentecostals/charismatics/ neocharismatics ............................. | | **56** **74** |
| *of this line above (which = the Third Wave, termed Neocharismatics)* | | |
| 18 million **94 million** were personal pentecostals (Third-Wavers) ...... | 19 | **23** |
| 35 million **201 million** were personal charismatics (Third-Wavers) ..... | 37 | **50** |
| *and of that same line above* | | |
| 1 million **32 million** subsequently affiliated also to the First Wave ... | 1 | **8** |
| 52 million **263 million** did not relate to First or Second Waves ........ | 55 | **66** |

**Notes.** The rise and growth of global Independency is shown in the globes below covering the years 1900, 1970, 2000, and 2025. Vertical slices represent the 6 megablocs (Orthodox, Roman Catholic, Anglican, Protestant, Independent, marginal Christian). The light grey balloon from 1970 to 2025 represents the size and ecclesiastical location of the whole Pentecostal/Charismatic/Neocharismatic Renewal in the Holy Spirit.

This table analyzes the 6 totals for global Christianity shown at top center. It does it for the year 1970, shown throughout by all numbers in light type. It does the same for the year AD 2000, shown throughout by all numbers in **black** type. This results in 91 pairs of figures showing AD 1970-2000 trends.

Next, the table dichotomizes the whole of Christianity into the *de-nominationalist* world (Christians organized into the 5 historic megablocs Orthodox, Roman Catholic, Anglican, Protestant, marginal Christian; shown in the lefthand half of the table), and the *postdenominationalist* world (the more recent Independent megabloc that rejects historic denominationalism; shown in the righthand half of the table). This results in 88 direct numerical denominationalist/postdenominationalist comparisons.

Large-size numbers are meant primarily to be compared horizontally (% meaning percent of each's global total at top).

Small-size numbers are meant primarily to be compared vertically (% meaning percent of nearest large-size number above each).

The table then gives 176 numbers which, when read horizontally an-alyze Christianity into 88 dichotomous pairs or parallels between the 1970 situation and the AD 2000 situation. These numbers can also be read vertically as 72 vertical comparisons arranged in 8 vertical trichotomies followed by 64 vertical dichotomies.

The bottom 5 lines enumerate the 3 Waves of the Pentecostal/Charismatic/Neocharismatic Renewal by means of 40 different numbers. The first of these 5 lines gives 8 figures enumerating the whole Renewal (First and Second Waves on the left, Third Wave on the right. The following 2 pairs of 2 lines each analyze the Renewal in 16 horizontal dichotomies and 16 vertical dichotomies.

The rise of Renewal since 1900 (= the gray oblong at bottom of globe)

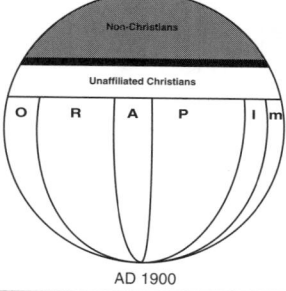

AD 1900

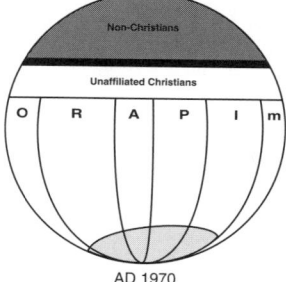

AD 1970

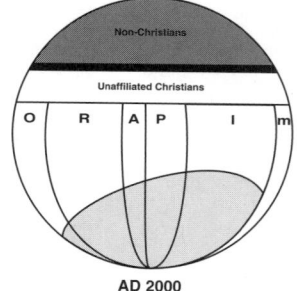

AD 2000

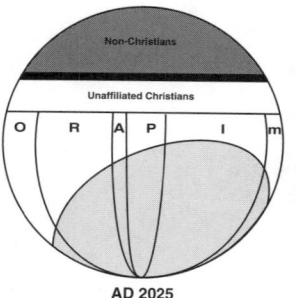

AD 2025

## Table 6–9. Two worldwide church lifestyles: the shift from denominationalism to postdenominationalism, analyzed under 280 dichotomies.

The table describes the characteristics of two divergent church lifestyles which have come into prominence in the 1980s and 1990s. This description is made up of 280 distinct dichotomies, here divided into 2 columns under 'Denominationalism' and 'Postdenominationalism'. The opposing features are given on the same line below, with a common reference number on the left.

The best interpretation of this new phenomenon is in terms not of conflict, but of choice: the 2 church lifestyles, now worldwide in extent, are not so much conflicting rivals as alternate lifestyles that have crystallized out for historical reasons.

This is a listing of 280 differing dichotomies which are applicable selectively to specific cases. Although no single Independency situation is characterized by all 280, most are characterized by a majority of them.

| | DENOMINATIONALISM | POSTDENOMINATIONALISM |
|---|---|---|
| | **OLDER IDENTITY** | **NEWER IDENTITY** |
| 1. | Orthodox, Roman Catholic, Anglican, or Protestant identity | Recognized and claimed by members as 'Independent' |
| 2. | Name excludes 'Independent' or similar claim | Name includes 'Independent', 'Free', or synonym |
| 3. | Name includes an ORAP family name | Name excludes any ORAP family name |
| 4. | Vast literature (250,000 book titles) identifies ORAP traditions | Sizeable literature (15,000 titles) identifies 'Independency' |
| 5. | Begun before 1940 (60 years, 2 generations ago) | Begun after 1940 (60 years, 2 generations ago) |
| 6. | Originating by schism or secession long ago | Originating by schism or secession since 1940 |
| 7. | Grounded on history of ORAP Christianity | Uninterested in historic ORAP Christianity |
| 8. | Supportive of current ORAP global Christianity | Uninterested in contemporary ORAP global Christianity |
| 9. | Commitment to conciliar memberships | Rejecting conciliarism (membership in councils or alliances) |
| 10. | Opposed to pentecostal/charismatic experience | Based on pentecostal/charismatic experience |
| | **HISTORIC CHRISTIANITY** | **NON-HISTORIC CHRISTIANITY** |
| 11. | Continuity with historic Christianity | No continuity with historic Christianity |
| 12. | Importance of historic Christianity | Insignificance of historic Christianity |
| 13. | Rooted in historic Christianity | Independence from historic Christianity |
| 14. | Member of one of the 90 historic confessions | Unaligned with any of the 90 historic confessions |
| 15. | Part of historic Christianity | Unrelated to the entirety of historic Christianity |
| 16. | Built on centuries of European church tradition and habit | Abandonment of European church history, tradition, habit |
| 17. | Respect for and imitation of old-church European institutions | Rejection of European atmospherics, ritual, language, institutions |
| 18. | Denominations as centerpiece | Replacement of mainline denominations by paradenominations |
| 19. | Denominational history: pride, publicity, literature | No interest in denominational history |
| 20. | Dependence on organized Christianity | Independence from organized Christianity |
| 21. | Institutional religion | Rejection of institutional religion |
| 22. | Widespread national, international, and global structures | Rejection of any wider structures or structuring |
| 23. | Churches started mostly well before 1965 | Churches begun mainly long after 1965 |
| 24. | Embodiment of traditional Christianity | Unrelated to traditional Christianity |
| 25. | Denominational distinctives | No denominational distinctives |
| 26. | Denominational traditions | No denominational traditions |
| 27. | Ongoing reliance on traditional Christianity | No organized relations with traditional Christianity |
| 28. | Denominationalism: institutionalized divisionings | Historical divisionings ignored and abandoned |
| 29. | Denominational labels seen as guarantors of legitimacy | Denominational labels seen as anathema to the unchurched |
| 30. | Labels: Catholic, Protestant, Evangelical, &c | Post-Catholic, post-Protestant, post-Evangelical, &c |
| 31. | Ecumenism as main hope of Christianity | Independence from organized ecumenism |
| 32. | Integral part of contemporary mainline Christianity | Unrelated to contemporary mainline Christianity |
| 33. | Mainline Christianity as the true church today | No interest in today's mainline or mainstream Christianity |
| 34. | Confessionalism as major 20th-century phenomenon | Rejection of historic and contemporary confessionalism |
| 35. | Denominationalism: eclipse, ambiguity, rebirth, renewal | Denominationalism definitively abandoned |
| 36. | Church Universal displaced by Church Denominational | Return to ideal of one sole universal Body of Christ |
| | **TRADITIONAL CHURCHES** | **NEW-PARADIGM CHURCHES** |
| 37. | Centrality of the Word preached and the Sacraments administered | Centrality of the Holy Spirit (uMoya, Espiritu, Roho) |
| 38. | Pride in the label denominationalist | Pride in the label postdenominationalist |
| 39. | Acceptance of denominational pluralism | Rejection of denominational pluralism |
| 40. | Recognition of other denominations' validity | Rejection of rightness of multiple denominations |
| 41. | Churches relevant to past contexts, irrelevant to present | Churches answer current need for community, civic structure |
| 42. | Offering insiders a time-honored place in Christian history | Offering outsiders a new place to belong, a place to feel at home |
| 43. | Churches of the Confessional Paradigm | Churches of the New Apostolic Paradigm |
| 44. | Roots in Protestant Reformation or in Vatican II | Part of an emerging New Apostolic Reformation |
| 45. | Continuity with First Church (Rome), Second Church (Geneva) | Renewal as the Third Church, the Next Church |
| 46. | Churches: historic architectural masterpieces, but irrelevant relics | Full-service churches, shopping-mall churches, pastoral churches |
| 47. | Unclear value of historic churches for today's populations | New deeper roles as seeker-sensitive churches, teaching churches |
| 48. | Church names identify denomination or tradition | Church names never employ denominational labels |
| 49. | Preference for ecclesiastical church names ("St Mary's") | Churches reject ecclesiastical names, prefer geographical ones |
| 50. | Church names avoid biblical/spiritual themes | Many churches use hitherto unused biblical/spiritual names |
| 51. | Recognizable/identifiable local church names | Unrecognizable/unidentifiable local church names |
| 52. | Open acknowledgement of denominational affiliation | Hiding of any denominational affiliation or linkage |
| 53. | Publicizing of previous denominational backgrounds | Hiding of any previous denominational backgrounds or past |
| 54. | Claim to offer the Whole Gospel to the Whole World | Claim to offer the Full Gospel in all respects |
| 55. | White-led initiatives, control, and leadership predominate | Non-White initiatives and leadership predominate |
| 56. | Elitist-religion aspects | Popular religion, but held in check |
| 57. | White denominationalism excludes Blacks from leadership | Blacks embrace postdenominationalism in creative leadership |
| 58. | Most denominations are more than 50 years old | Most paradenominations are under 10 years old |
| 59. | Many members were born before 1945 | Members were almost all born after 1945 |
| 60. | Average age of members: 40 years old | Average age of members: 25 years old |
| 61. | Average age of today's congregations: 50 years | Average age of today's congregations: 5 years |
| 62. | Denominationalism as the current Christian mainstream | Postdenominationalism flourishes outside the mainstream |
| | **MEGADENOMINATIONS (= over 1 million members each)** | **MEGACHURCHES (= over 2,000 members each)** |
| 63. | Spectacular rise of 100 megadenominations | Spectacular emergence of 5,000 megachurches |
| 64. | A multiplicity of 12,000 denominations | 22,000 denominations/paradenominations/networks/associations |
| 65. | 1,715,700 denominationalist congregations/churches | 1,791,000 postdenominationalist congregations/churches |
| 66. | 1,700 million Christians in these 12,000 denominations | 380 million Christians in these 22,000 networks/denominations |
| 67. | Worldwide, every week 300 older churches close | Worldwide, every week 400 new independent churches begin |
| 68. | Of 15,000 older churches closing each year, 90% are White | Of 20,000 new churches opening each year, 90% are Non-White/Black |
| 69. | Widespread decline of older big-city churches | Meteoric growth of newest big-city churches |
| 70. | Leaders downplay recruiting, decry triumphalist church growth | Leaders intentional about recruiting, hence rapid numerical growth |
| 71. | Average Christians per denomination: 147,000 | Average Christians per paradenomination: 17,400 |
| 72. | Average size of a congregation: 1,003 members | Average size of a congregation: 223 members |
| 73. | Average size of a denomination: 147 churches | Average size of a paradenomination: 78 churches |

*Continued overleaf*

*Table 6–9 continued*

| LIMITED CHOICES | MASSIVE OPTIONS |
|---|---|
| 74. Context of collapsing families, schools, social institutions | Wholesale reorganizing of religious life as newest form of community |
| 75. Little or no attention paid to marketing, recruiting, fundraising | Bold market-driven but culturally-sensitive approaches |
| 76. Traditional churches offer preaching, sacraments, little else | Megachurches as churches of options: a panoply of choices under one roof |
| 77. Relatively few services or activities offered: 1 to 4 hours a day | Continuous 24-hour round-the clock activities, services, meetings |
| 78. Weekday groups cater primarily to members' needs | Support groups cater to outsiders: illness, divorce, grief support ministries |
| 79. Limited unpaid volunteerism: Sunday-school teachers, ushers | Huge volunteer pools (70% of all members), unpaid for their services |
| 80. Basic unit of church life: Sunday morning service/eucharist/mass | Basic unit of church life: small 10-person cells in homes on weeknights |
| 81. Limited choices restrict growth to the already interested | Massive choices plus cell-groups ensure ongoing permanent growth |

| CHURCH LOYALISTS | NEOCHARISMATICS |
|---|---|
| 82. Uncomfortable with unusual charismata | Tongues, prophecy, knowledge, healing, deliverance |
| 83. Denial that such gifts can be from God | Affirmation of gifts of the Holy Spirit |
| 84. New Testament charismata: only for the Apostolic Age | All New Testament gifts can be experienced today |
| 85. A church life based on the 2 or 7 Sacraments | A church life of experiencing signs and wonders |
| 86. Liturgical evangelism | Unstructured evangelism |
| 87. Low-profile healings | High-profile healings |
| 88. Carefully-regulated exorcisms | Unregulated exorcisms |
| 89. Exorcism by licensed professionals only | Demonic deliverance in the name of Jesus |
| 90. Little emphasis on spirits or demons | Continuous concern with spirits and demons |
| 91. Avoidance of encounters with evil | Power encounters, confrontations with evil |

| LAY MEMBERSHIP | LAY LEADERSHIP |
|---|---|
| 92. Dependence on denominational leadership | Independence from denominational leadership |
| 93. Acceptance of outside control | Rejection of outside control |
| 94. Undemocratic rule by seminary-trained priesthood | Democratizing the priesthood of all believers |
| 95. Leadership by outsiders | Indigenous local leadership |
| 96. Leadership by clergy | Lay leadership empowered to initiate |
| 97. Clergy initiate and control any small groups and cells | Laity control cells in cell-based churches |
| 98. Decisions by committee | Decisions by anointed individuals |
| 99. Dependence on entrenched office-holders | Dependence on charismatic prima donnas |
| 100. Total dependence on hierarchy | Total dependence on gifted leaders |

| BISHOPS AND CLERGY | APOSTLES AND PROPHETS |
|---|---|
| 101. Episcopal leadership, by bishops | Apostolic leadership, by apostles |
| 102. Apostles were appointed only for NT era | Apostles are being appointed by God today |
| 103. Later Apostles: only a few heroic country-openers | Apostles now: restricted to a few outstanding claimants |
| 104. Apostolic succession | Apostolic success |
| 105. Leadership by ordained clergy formally appointed | Leadership by prophets as well as apostles |
| 106. No prophetic utterances noticeable | Prophets, prophecies, prophetic churches prominent |
| 107. A professional, trained, paid clergy and workers | No professional clergy or workers |
| 108. Standard clerical dress and robes | No dress or robe standards |
| 109. Clerical collars, insignia, titles, styles | No clerical collars, insignia, titles, styles |
| 110. Formal dress, attention to proper clothing | Casual informal dress for leaders as well as laity |
| 111. Basic building block: the denomination | Basic building block: pastor with congregation |
| 112. Pastor controlled by boards, committees | Pastor as chief decision-maker |
| 113. Vision controlled by committees | Pastor as chief visionary |
| 114. Little new varieties of ministerial roles | New roles (Minister of Prayer, or of Spiritual Formation) |
| 115. Dominance of bishops, executives, political personalities | Ministers as teachers, facilitators, TV "talk-show host" image |
| 116. Ministers mainly function in community context | Individuals exercise authority |
| 117. Leadership shared by clergy and laity | Autocratic leadership by apostolic claimants |
| 118. Leadership through office | Leadership through charisma, with strongly charismatic leadership |
| 119. Clergy get automatic, permanent authority and trust | Leaders must continually re-earn authority and trust |
| 120. Clear and stiff criteria for ordination | Minimal or unclear local criteria for ordination |

| CENTRALIZING | DECENTRALIZING |
|---|---|
| 121. 600,000 denomination-related institutions | 10,000 postdenominationalist institutions |
| 122. Centralist view of life | Decentralized mind-set |
| 123. Hierarchical ecclesiastical structures | Flat ecclesiastical structures |
| 124. Hierarchically-controlled churches | New churches are organizationally flat |
| 125. Centralization of many aspects of church life | Decentralization of almost all aspects of church life |
| 126. Bureaucratization grows steadily since 1800 | Nonbureaucratic administrative procedures |
| 127. Centrally-controlled by elites | People-controlled local churches |
| 128. Massive centrally-controlled computers | Massive networks of small PCs in parallel under local control |
| 129. Interdenominational contacts/cooperation | Apostolic networks |
| 130. Personal camaraderie among bishops, leaders | Fellowship mainly with other network leaders |
| 131. Pursuit of organic church unity, now losing steam | Defense of luxuriant neofragmentation |
| 132. Conciliarism: memberships in 6,000 councils of churches | Nonconciliarism: unrelated to any Christian councils anywhere |
| 133. Most councils now formalized with constitutions, rules | Networks/associations function as loose conciliarism |
| 134. Interdenominational cooperation | Strategic alliances |
| 135. Conference of Christian World Communions (CWCs) | Loose meganetworks of hundreds of apostolic networks |

| REGULATING | EMPOWERING |
|---|---|
| 136. Overall reliance on denominational polities | Independence from denominational polities |
| 137. Impressive denominational headquarters buildings | Network headquarters: none, or small part-time offices |
| 138. Large headquarters staffs, small local church staffs | Few or no headquarters staffs, large local church staffs |
| 139. Centralized sociopolitical agendas | No centralized agendas |
| 140. Agreed statements on issues | No agreed statements on issues |
| 141. Lecturing the laity | Trusting the laity |
| 142. Preachers urge liberal views and positions on laity | Leaders accept members' intense views (abortion, homosexuality) |
| 143. Controlling the laity | Empowering the laity |
| 144. Clergy in control | Lay persons in control |
| 145. Dependence of local church on central offices | Complete autonomy of local church |
| 146. Cautious approach to the digital revolution | Immediate embrace of the digital revolution |
| 147. Difficulty of controlling digital approach | Empowering nature of digital approach |
| 148. Proliferation of record-keeping since 1920 | Scarcity of record-keeping |
| 149. Mass multiplication of paper and paperwork | Paperwork replaced by computer, e-mail, fax, web, internet, phone |
| 150. Churches required to report annual statistics, budgets to HQ | No requirements for annual reporting |

| APOLOGETICS | EVANGELIZATION |
|---|---|
| 151. Emphasis on the ecclesiastical apostolate | Emphasis on the missionary apostolate |
| 152. Under 10% of members are active evangelizers | Over 60% of members are active evangelizers |
| 153. Low-key self-identifying personal insignia (e.g. small lapel cross) | T-shirts proclaiming acronym FDFX (Fully Devoted Followers of Christ) |

*Continued opposite*

*Table 6—9 continued*

| | |
|---|---|
| 154. 30% of members are Great Commission Christians | 80% of members are Great Commission Christians |
| 155. Cautious inviting of outsiders to come to church | Direct outreach to outsiders at home, work, or play |
| 156. Discreet use of mailings to inform members of future events | Enormous 100,000-piece mail drops inviting outsiders in |
| 157. Evangelism under its 45 main varieties | Power evangelism confronting the spiritual powers |
| 158. Organized foreign mission agencies | Unstructured foreign missions |
| 159. Mission as consolidating the church in Worlds C and B | Mission as reaching unreached peoples in World A |
| 160. Foreign missions as partnership, interchurch aid | Foreign mission as pioneer, experimental, frontier missions |
| 161. Preaching as verbal, thoughtful, quiet, reasoned | Emphasis on preaching as shouting the message |
| 162. Sermons often 30-minute monologues | 'Sermons' replaced by 'messages', with testimonies, video clips |
| 163. Teaching God's preferential option for the poor | Teaching and preaching a prosperity gospel |
| 164. Reliance on historic symbols of Christianity | Resymbolizing of the entire Christian message |

### MINISTRY PROGRAMS / POWER MINISTRIES

| | |
|---|---|
| 165. Approval for ethical members, censure for the rest | Direct ministry to millions with a major failure in their lives |
| 166. Institutionalized ministries | Free ministries |
| 167. Programmed ministries | Widespread use of power ministries |
| 168. Empowering of oneself for ministry | Empowering of all and any others for ministry |
| 169. Neglect of music for recruiting | Enormous recruiting power of music |
| 170. Drama, passion plays, religious theatre | Mime, skits, street-acting as witness |
| 171. Reliance on centralized denominational programs | Independence from centralized denominational programs |
| 172. Lecturing/sermonizing | Storying (narrating Bible stories) |
| 173. Little emphasis on healing | Body-mind relationship in ministry of healing |
| 174. New experimental ministries | Prophetic ministries |
| 175. Attempts to update traditional ministries | Apostolic networking in contemporary forms |
| 176. Local pastors' fellowships | Apostolic teams arise |
| 177. Emphasis on well-run large church services | Extensive small-group ministry |
| 178. Encouraging of house meetings for interested members | Networks of small groups compulsory for all church members |
| 179. Little interest in cell-based church concept | Multiplication of cell-based churches |
| 180. Decline of church youth groups | Millions of youths in Bible study groups |
| 181. Home study groups on weeknights | Apostolic team ministries for specific roles |
| 182. Christian standards in business, politics, academia | Spirit-filled lifestyle affecting personal Christian standards |
| 183. Centrality of reason, rules, regulations, tradition | Centrality of relationships |
| 184. No ecclesiastical discipline enforced | Strict discipline expected and enforced |
| 185. Excommunication rarely mentioned | Excommunication as a real option for disciplining offenders |
| 186. Tradition-oriented planning for congregations | Market-driven planning for congregations |
| 187. Stagnant expansion | Constantly-growing planting churches |
| 188. Introverted non-growing congregations | Apostolic congregations continuously growing |
| 189. Limited or no use of television | Widespread use of television |
| 190. Reliance on printed denominational literature | Independence from denominational literature |
| 191. Book publishing: theology, administration, computers | Vast numbers of bestseller paperbacks on spirituality |

### HOME PRIORITIZING / GLOBALIZING ENDEAVOR

| | |
|---|---|
| 192. Retrenchment from former foreign mission programs | New foreign mission programs unrelated to mainline ones |
| 193. 97% of all Christians' incomes now spent only on Christians | Disavowing of past financial obligations to mainline churches abroad |
| 194. Only 3% of Christians' income now spent on non-Christian world | Attempts to spend 10% of income on non-Christian world |
| 195. Former foreign mission resources rerouted to home mission | Creation of new independent linked congregations worldwide |

### TRADITIONAL MUSIC / CONTEMPORARY MUSIC

| | |
|---|---|
| 196. Use of ecclesiastical music familiar to members | Use of every variety of contemporary, secular music |
| 197. In worship, time-honored church music, hymns, language, words | In worship, music and lyrics that are contemporary, accessible, authentic |
| 198. Dislike of popular musical idiom, pop culture, rock | Gospel-music tradition related to Black culture |
| 199. Worship geared to some one great historical musical tradition | Seamless multimedia worship created for today |
| 200. Pipe organs, harmoniums, pianos | Culturally authentic church music, worship bands, orchestras |
| 201. A selection of acceptable musical instruments | Employment of entire spectrum of musical instruments |
| 202. Single-instrument accompaniment | Complex, multi-instrument music |
| 203. Preference for organ, piano, occasionally stringed instruments | 12-piece orchestras: saxophones, synthesizers, guitars, trumpets, drums |
| 204. Restrained musical presentations | Immensely loud volumes of deafening music |
| 205. Formal, stylized, routine choir/music practices | Perfectionist rehearsings of music to professional standards |

### TRADITIONAL HYMNODY / NEW SINGING

| | |
|---|---|
| 206. Hymnals consist mainly of hymns composed AD 70–1950 | Few or no public worship songs were composed before 1990 |
| 207. Expensive hymnals, requiring heads-bowed page-flipping | Overhead projectors showing Scripture and song lyrics |
| 208. Hymns sung standing for up to 5 minutes only at a time | Sustained celebration in song, often for 45 minutes standing |
| 209. Once-only singing of hymn lines | Protracted repetition of new song lines |
| 210. Repeating hymn verses extremely rare | Repetitive singing of lyrics and verses is the norm |

### LITURGICAL WORSHIP / INTERCESSORY WORSHIP

| | |
|---|---|
| 211. Institutional resistance to innovations in worship | Relentless search for culturally authentic new worship forms |
| 212. Fixed worship styles and patterns, unchanging from week to week | Creativity in developing new forms of worship from one week to the next |
| 213. Prayer by clergy and leaders | Full participation in prayer by entire congregation |
| 214. Liturgical prayer | Concert prayer |
| 215. Set or fixed prayers read aloud by officiant | Simultaneous audible prayer by whole congregation |
| 216. Medieval worship | Contemporary worship |
| 217. Stained-glass windows as nonverbal storytelling devices | Overhead projectors instead of hymnals and prayer books |
| 218. Under 5% of church members are home-based intercessors | Over 50% of members are home-based intercessors |
| 219. Theological debate | Spiritual warfare |
| 220. Dull weekly Sunday worship services | Appealing and exciting Sunday worship experience |
| 221. Dislike of emotionalism in worship | Joy, weeping, forgiveness, celebration, ecstasy, shouting |
| 222. Discouragement of body movements, interjections, reactions | Spontaneous movements, interjections accepted and acceptable |
| 223. Opposition to hand-raising, swaying, in worship | Bodily participation in worship: swaying, hand-raising |
| 224. Emphasis on silence, meditation, awe before God | Emphasis on loudness, noise, shouts, excitement |
| 225. No applause, clapping, or cheering in worship | Applause, clapping, and cheering in worship |
| 226. Body subordination | Body language and expression |
| 227. Traditional worship styles | New worship and praise styles |
| 228. Ushers with collection plates pressure worshippers to contribute | No collections, no collection plates, no ushers noting gifts |
| 229. Planning for worship | Spontaneity in worship |
| 230. Written liturgy | Oral liturgy |
| 231. Word-centered | Narrative style in preaching and witness |
| 232. Clergy-led liturgical activities | Total congregational participation in liturgy |
| 233. No dreams or visions in worship | Use of dreams and visions in worship |
| 234. Traditionally-sanctified forms of worship | Highly specialized new forms of worship |

*Continued overleaf*

*Table 6–9 concluded*

| CHILDREN IGNORED | CHILDREN PROMINENT |
|---|---|
| 235. Children have little or no role in denominational life | Birth of own children brings in lapsed or unchurched couples |
| 236. Most older churches have no daily child-oriented programs | 7-days-a-week continuous kid-oriented activities |
| 237. Often no provision at all for infants or older children in church | Full child care, children's education, teen activities |
| 238. Children's church-sponsored games, teams, matches rare | Sports options for all children and adults: basketball, baseball clinics |

| AFFLUENT PROPERTY | MINIMAL PROPERTY |
|---|---|
| 239. Denominationalists own 59% of the world | Postdenominationalists own 1% of the world |
| 240. Property centrally owned | Property locally owned |
| 241. Architecturally-striking church buildings | Churches meet in warehouses, shops, malls, cinemas, schools |
| 242. Architecture: Gothic, Baroque, spires, crosses, statues, pews | Architecture: secular, contemporary, functional, warehouse, supermarket |
| 243. Church edifices seen as pious, demanding, threatening | Huge auditoriums, atriums, food courts, boutiques, parking, clean restrooms |
| 244. Church sanctuaries and worship buildings unused on weekdays | Multi-use church facilities all open to any community activities |
| 245. Old-style churches help members feel comfortable | New-style churches appeal to seekers and the unchurched |
| 246. Reluctance to employ hi-tech media | Emphasis on new hi-tech media |
| 247. No administrative use of Internet or World Wide Web | Continuous administrative use of Internet and World Wide Web |
| 248. Little hi-tech ministry visible | Visible hi-tech ministries |
| 249. Church offices: computers to staff <0.5 (1:2) | Church offices: computers to staff >0.5 (2:1) |
| 250. Clerical control of digital equipment and data | Lay control of digital networks and databases |
| 251. Handfuls of experts controlling digital agendas | Thousands of lay youths implementing digital agendas |
| 252. Little use of new or untried resources | Constant and widespread use of hundreds of new resources |

| CENTRALLY-MANAGED FINANCES | LOCALLY-MANAGED FINANCES |
|---|---|
| 253. Denominationalists earn $10,800 billion p.a. | Postdenominationalists earn $200 billion p.a. |
| 254. Financial dues/quotas to denominational HQs | No central financial obligation |
| 255. Centralized budget | Little or no centralized budget |
| 256. Denominations: churches must pay annual quotas | Rejection of compulsory centralized annual quota payments |
| 257. Publicly-announced fixed quotas payable to HQ | No fixed quotas |
| 258. Centralized salaries or scales for workers | No centralized salaries or scales |
| 259. Centrally-salaried clergy | Ministries locally salaried |
| 260. Pension funds properly managed | No pension funds |
| 261. Suspicion of marketing as unspiritual | Marketing expertise welcomed |
| 262. Accountability to center | No accountability to center |
| 263. Little accountability both ways (clergy/laity) | Mutual accountability (leaders/members) |

| SEMINARY TRAINING | MENTORED APPRENTICESHIP |
|---|---|
| 264. Seminary training required for clergy and lay leaders | Mentoring during ministry now replacing seminary |
| 265. Denominations train clergy mainly in own seminaries | Megachurches train their own pastoral staffs on the job |
| 266. Training for running a church is learned when seminarians | 40 megachurches train 9,000 pastors via Teaching Church Network |
| 267. Denominational educational curricula | No standard educational curricula |
| 268. Professional educational programs | Locally created educational programs |
| 269. Scientific worldview with Christian commentary | Demonology and related spiritual warfare worldview |
| 270. Classroom lectures | Courses by e-mail and Internet |
| 271. Supervision of students | Mentoring of students |
| 272. Denominational liberalism | Independence from denominational liberalism |
| 273. Denominational theologies | No dependence on denominational theologies |
| 274. Liberation theology | Theologies of gifts, intercession, spiritual mapping, spiritual warfare |

| POSSIBLE FUTURES | PROBABLE FUTURES |
|---|---|
| 275. Continued decline of large-scale denominationalism | Continued expansion of postdenominationalist networks |
| 276. Degeneration into hyperdenominationalism | Mass moves of Christians from denominationalism to networks |
| 277. Breakup of major megadenominations | Global meganetworks and matrices evolve |
| 278. Demise of historic confessionalism | Emergence of postdenominational confessionalism |
| 279. Lifestyle of many small denominations survives | Postdenominationalist networks multiply as alternate lifestyle |
| 280. Decline or demise of historic ecumenism | Emergence and global mushrooming of postdenominationalist ecumenism |

## Table 6–10. Autocephalous episcopal churches with disputed or unrecognized apostolic succession, AD 1650–2000, here categorized as Independent but also Noncharismatic.

This table describes a less successful component of Independency—a major attempt to achieve Independency or Post-denominationalism by claiming to start, de novo, Christ's one, true, original and only church. Using the entire spectrum of ecclesiastical terms, jargon, and claims, these bodies have launched themselves onto the global Christian world. Upon coming into existence, many of them each immediately write to the leading figures of mainstream Christianity—popes, patriarchs, archbishops, moderators—announcing this new creation and urging these leaders all to abandon their current titles and pretensions and implement at one stroke Christ's plea 'Ut Unum Omnes Sint' by joining the new entity.

At the same time, regrettably, all these bodies claim to be spiritual renewals sent by the Holy Spirit but do not evidence the traditional elements of renewals and revivals—signs and wonders, miracles, healings, charismata, enthusiasm, zeal, crowds, conversions, supernatural manifestations, et alia. None align themselves with the 20th century's Pentecostal/Charismatic/Neocharismatic Renewal in the Holy Spirit, and many are strongly anticharismatic.

From the standpoint of this present analysis, therefore, this table documents the chaotic side of Independency, of fragmentation run riot without the saving grace of charismatic manifestations. However, as a major religious phenomenon those bodies need to be objectively documented and described, and this will now be attempted.

Most episcopal churches in the world (churches governed by a bishop or a hierarchy of bishops) have some form of recognized procedure for the selection, appointment, and consecration of new bishops. This procedure can usually only take place with the consent and co-operation of one or more existing bishops. As a result, as a church's history extends over a long period of time, the succession of the episcopate becomes important. A number of large episcopal churches (e.g. United Methodist Church, USA) have maintained a succession over 200 years but are not concerned to claim that the succession goes back in unbroken line to the time of the first Apostles. Very many other major episcopal churches, however—Roman Catholic, Orthodox, Old Catholic, Anglican, Scandinavian Lutheran—do make this claim and contend that a bishop cannot have regular or valid orders unless he has been consecrated in this apostolic succession. The table below excludes all these recognized episcopal churches (such as all Old Catholics in communion with Utrecht): it also excludes the many schisms from these episcopal churches which either possess undisputed succession or make no attempt or claim to possess such succession.

In addition to those larger churches whose claim is recognized by large segments of historic Christianity, there are across the world at least 450 autocephalous episcopal churches which claim to have bishops in this historic succession of the episcopate, but whose claim is disputed or contested or not recognized by any of those major historic episcopal churches. Or, the validity of their succession is at present especially opposed or contested by one or more of those churches. Over half of these, some 250 churches in 120 countries, are large or sizeable secessions from Roman Catholicism, or Orthodoxy, or Anglicanism. The other half (170) are minuscule (with only 100 or under members) autocephalous Catholic churches under bishops-at-large (episcopi vagantes) with irregular or unrecognized orders, almost all confined to the Western world, and with few or sometimes even no lay followers. A fairly complete listing of 760 such bishops-at-large is given in E. Plazinski, *Mit Krummstab und Mitra* (1970, p. 239-255), which also gives a detailed list of 15 of the major disputed lines of apostolic succession (notably, Ferrette, Vilatte, Mathew). Over 700 bishops are also listed, and described with historical narrative, in P.F. Anson, *Bishops at large: some autocephalous churches of the past hundred years and their founders* (London, 1964). Biographical details of nearly 470 of them are given in H.R.T. Brandreth, *'Are they bishops? a handbook of certain episcopal sects and their founders'* (London, 1972; typescript). The most thorough documentation to date is *Independent bishops: an international directory* (eds G.L. Ward, B. Persson, A. Bain, Apogee Books 1990, 524 pages).

The table below lists the majority of both these 2 types of bodies, sizeable and minuscule, and includes a variety of sizeable non-Catholic churches which nevertheless lay claim to apostolic succession in some form and have gone to considerable pains to have their bishops consecrated by bishops of other churches they regard as in that succession: many of these bodies are in Third-World countries. It also includes the fair number of minuscule bodies which once existed but are now defunct. Note that the table excludes the large number of episcopal churches in the Third World (especially African indigenous churches) which, though governed by bishops, do not lay claim to any historic apostolic succession. The table also lists only autonomous churches and denominations and excludes episcopal orders, jurisdictions, abbeys, colleges and other related types of ecclesiastical organizations.

One object of this listing is to enable the reader, who has heard of or from a specific episcopal body which is not listed in *WCE* Part 4's Country Table 2 for its country (e.g. 'British Orthodox Catholic Church'), to locate and identify it and to assess its numerical significance if any. Each line below describes one distinct body, whether still existing or long defunct; alternative names for each body are all given on the same line. Each line also describes one distinct body together with all its organically-related international branches in other countries, if any. The meaning of the 4 columns is as follows:

**Name.** Each official name is given here in the major European language it uses (of the 6 employed in this book: English, French, German, Italian, Portuguese, Spanish. Note D=Diocese, AD=Archdiocese, M=Metropolitan See, P=Patriarchate.

**Size.** Churches with numerically large or sizeable or significant following are also given a line each in their country's statistical Country Table 2 in *WCE* Part 4, where fuller details including each's conciliar relationships will be found. Those with only small, or very small, or minuscule following are enumerated in Country Tables 2 only on lines at the end ('Other Catholic churches') and in corresponding footnotes.

**Begun.** Year of foundation or origin.

**Type.** 1st letter: ecclesiastical megabloc, all being classified here as I = Independent.
2nd-4th letters: ecclesiastical tradition (see "GeoCodebook", Part 16). Note that the recurring code Epi = minuscule unrecognized church under bishops-at-large (with 100 or fewer members).

**Notes.** Descriptive notes on each body, including some of the following: initials if commonly used, offical name (if in italics), translation of name, alternative names, former names, title of chief bishop, line of apostolic succession adopted or claimed (about 20 distinct lines are involved), headquarters, country or countries in which present, total affiliated members if significant, and whether or not still in existence or recently defunct.

| *Name* | *Begun* | *Type* | *Names, notes, comments, adherents, clergy, and other data* |
|---|---|---|---|
| African Orthodox Church | 1919 | I-ARo | *AOC,* Schism ex PECUSA; Vilatte succession, West Indian Blacks, HA New York (USA). In Bahamas, Cuba, SAfrica. |
| African Orthodox Ch of New York & Massachusetts | 1938 | I-ARo | Black. Large schism ex AOC. Vilatte succession. HQ New York 27 (USA). |
| Afro-American Catholic Church | 1938 | I-Epi | Black. Schism ex AOC by suspended bishop. Vilatte succession. HQ USA. |
| Alexandrian Orthodox Church in America | 1963 | I-Rus | Former Russian and Ukrainian Orthodox now linked with American Orthodox Catholic Ch. High % Blacks. |
| All Nations Reformed Orthodox Catholic Church | | I-Epi | Body set up in USA, applied to join WCC; rejected. |
| Altrömisch-Katholische Kirche von Deutschland | 1949 | I-Epi | *ORCC* in Germany. Split ex Catholicate of the West (UK), in Vilatte succession. HQ Cologne (Germany). |
| American Catholic Church | 1927 | I-ARo | Black. Ex African Orthodox Ch, claiming Syrian Orthodox (Jacobite) succession. HQ New York (USA). |
| American Catholic Church (Syro-Antiochian) | 1915 | I-CCa | *Assyrian Jacobite Apost Ch.* Split ex ACC (Vilatte), in Jacobite succession. HA Miami (USA). 1,800 members. |
| American Catholic Church (Western Orthodox) | 1914 | I-CCa | *Holy Cath Ch in America.* Ex RCC, begun by Vilatte as primate (Jacobite succession). Virtually defunct. |
| American Episcopal Church (ACC) | 1943 | I-Epi | Split ex American Catholic Ch by bishop. Vilatte succession, plus 7 other lines claimed. Short-lived. |
| American Holy Orthodox Catholic Apostolic Eastern Ch | 1932 | I-ARo | Ex African Orthodox Ch by bishop. Vilatte succession. HQ New York 35 (USA). Decline to 3,000 members. |
| American National Catholic Church | | I-Epi | *Diocese of New Jersey.* HQ New Jersey (USA). |
| American Old Catholic Church | 1927 | I-CCa | Split ex NAORCC by bishop in Mathew succession. Formerly 1,000 members, in Louisiana; defunct 1945. |
| American Orthodox Catholic Church | 1961 | I-ReO | New York Branch, Denver Branch. Rival White (Russian) and Black groups. Continuous mergers, fresh schisms. |
| American Orthodox Catholic Church (AD N&S America) | 1964 | I-ReO | Ex Ukrainian Orth Ch of USA. 8 bishops. Dioceses in USA, US Virgin Is, Argentina, France, Nigeria, Zaire. |
| American Orthodox Missionary Church | | I-CCa | *Eastern Orthodox Catholic Ch in America,* under Russian Orth Ch Outside of Russia. Ex Holy Orth Ch in America. |
| Ancient Apostolic Catholic Church | 1951 | I-Epi | Schism by a bishop ex Ancient Catholic Church (Chelsea, UK) and Catholicate of the West. Defunct. |
| Ancient British Church | 1874 | I-ARo | *ABC.* First British Patriarch (ex CofE) consecrated by Ferrette, in Caerleon, Wales (UK). |
| Ancient British Church (Agnostic) | 1937 | I-Lib | 1937 Jesuene Ch, or Free Orth Cath Ch. 1957 new name. Agnostic=rejecting Christendom. Vilatte succession. |
| Ancient Catholic Church | 1946 | I-ARo | Until 1950, *New Pentecostal Ch of Christ.* Spiritual healing, animals' services. Cathedral in Chelsea (UK). |
| Ancient Universal Orthodox Catholic Church | 1943 | I-Lib | Theosophical and occult religious branch of Ekklesia Agiae Sophiae (Order of Holy Wisdom). UK. |
| Anglican Orthodox Church of North America | 1963 | I-ReA | Schism ex PECUSA in North Carolina (USA). Promotes Anglican Orthodox Communion in 10 nations. 4,360 in USA. |
| Anglican Orthodox Church: D Pakistan | 1967 | I-ReA | *Episcopal Ch of Pakistan.* Schism ex Anglican Ch, Sialkot. M=AOC(USA). Bishop, 14,300 members, 19 priests. |
| Antiochian Orthodox Archdiocese of Toledo | 1940 | I-Ara | Arabs in USA. In communion with Greek P Antioch, but not accepted as canonical. 30,000 members. |
| Apostolic Catholic Church | | I-Epi | Split by bishop ex Ancient Catholic Ch. Ferrette succession. HQ London NW6 (UK). Defunct 1952. |
| Apostolic Church of St. Peter | 1935 | I-Epi | Dutch primate. Amalgamation of esoteric sects. HQ Kensington (UK). |
| Apostolic Episcopal Church | 1925 | I-ARo | *Holy Eastern Cath & Apost Orth Ch.* Ex PECUSA. Chaldean rite. HQ Long Island, NY. 3,000, in 5 European nations. |
| Apostolic Polish Catholic Church of Canada | | I-Epi | Ex North American Old Roman Catholic Church. Attempt to create body from Polish Old Catholics. |
| Aumónerie Générale Indép Mixte Orient-Occident | | I-Epi | *Abbaye Missionnaire de Behéme, Exarchat de Diaspora.* 1968 applied to join WCC, rejected. HQ Gagny (France). |
| Authentic Old Calendar Greek Orthodox Church | 1924 | I-Gre | *Paleohemerologites.* Schism ex Ch of Greece (Greece, USA, Canada). 200,000 adherents, 250 priests. |
| Autonomous African Universal Church | 1935 | I-CCa | Founded in Hornsey (UK) by a Ghanaian. Vilatte succession. HQ in Ghana. |
| Autonomous British Eastern Church | 1935 | I-Epi | *Orthodox-Cath Prov of Our Lady of England in Devon & Cornwall.* Several lines of succession. Defunct 1940. |
| British Orthodox Catholic Church | 1935 | I-Epi | Small group. 1944, united with ABC and OCOC to form Western Orthodox Catholic Ch (Catholicate of the West). |
| Brotherhood of the Blessed Sacrament | 1959 | I-Lib | *Broederschap van het Heilig Sacrament.* Schism ex Liberal Catholic Ch. in Netherlands. |
| Byelorussian Autocephalic Orthodox Church | | I-Bye | Refugees from White Russian church begun AD 1291, HQ Brooklyn (USA). USA 20,000; UK 1,500; Australia 1,000 |
| Byzantine American Church | 1942 | I-CCa | Schism ex RCC by Melkite priest from Lebanon. Syrians. HQ San Francisco (USA). |
| Canadian Catholic Church | 1946 | I-Epi | Melkite, Vilatte and 3 other successions. Canada, New Zealand, Ceylon. |
| Catholic Apostolic Church (Catholicate of the West) | 1944 | I-ARo | *Western Orth Cath Ch.* Patriarch ex CAC(Irvingite); 23 lines of succession. 1947, applied to WCC; rejected. |
| Catholic Christian Church | 1933 | I-Epi | Begun in England by bishop in Vilatte succession. HQ Bournemouth (UK). Defunct c1945. |
| Catholic Church of America | 1930 | I-Epi | Lithuanians. Split ex Lithuanian National Catholic Ch. Defunct c1935. |
| Catholic Tridentine Church | 1976 | I-CCa | De facto schism ex Ch of Rome, supporting archbishop Lefebvre (Latin mass,&c). Also USA, NZ Europe, LAmerica. |
| Chiesa Cattolica Nazionale | | I-CCa | First attempt in Italy to set up a national church, ex RCC. Short-lived. |

*Continued overleaf*

*Table 6–10 continued*

| *Name* | *Begun* | *Type* | *Names, notes, comments, adherents, clergy, and other data* |
|---|---|---|---|
| Chiesa Cattolica Nazionale d'Italia | 1882 | I-CCa | Schism ex RCC by canon of Vatican Basilica. Support from Old Catholics across Europe. Defunct 1903. |
| Chiesa Cattolica Riformata d'Italia | 1881 | I-ReC | Schism ex RCC by 12 priests and 6 churches. Support from Swiss Old Catholics. HQ Milan (Italy). 500 members. |
| Chiesa Episcopale Nazionale Italiana | 1900 | I-Epi | Old Catholic bishop of Piacenza consecrated by Vilatte (Jacobite succession). Soon defunct. |
| Christ Catholic Ch of America & Europe: D Boston | 1965 | I-OCa | Old Catholic teachings. Aims at total comprehensiveness. HQ New Jersey (USA). 1,000 members, 5 priests. |
| Christ Orthodox Cath Exarchate of Americas & Europe | 1959 | I-CCa | Byelorussian origins. 1959 merger Old Catholic and Orthodox. 5,513 members, 21 priests. |
| Christian Community (Anthroposophical Society) | 1922 | I-Gno | *Natural Catholicism.* Theosophical, ESP. Black Templars succession. 7 sacraments. In 8 nations. |
| Church Catholic, The (The Sanctuary) | 1919 | I-Epi | Mathew succession. HQ Knightsbridge (UK). Theosophical. Defunct 1940. |
| Church of the East | | I-Nes | Assyrian schism ex Ancient Ch of the East(P Baghdad)(Iraq). 3 Dioceses, 5,000 members, 11 priests. |
| Church of the Virgin Mary & Mar Gaura | | I-Nes | Assyrian (Nestorian) schism ex P Baghdad in dispute over authority. In Iraq. 2 priests, 200 members. |
| CMS Anglican Church of India | 1966 | I-Ang | *D Travancore & Cochin.* Pulaya outcaste schism ex Ch of South India (D Madhya Kerala). 24 priests; 107,000 |
| Communion Evangelica Catholica Eucharistica | 1930 | I-Epi | *Cath Ev Ch of Germany.* Founded by ex-RC Lutheran mystic Friedrich Heiler. Syro-Jacobite (Vilatte) succession. |
| Coptic Orthodox Church Apostolicf | 1942 | I-Epi | *Ch of the Living God.* Begun by US Black, links with Father Divine Peace Mission. HQ Manhattan (USA). |
| Croatian Old Catholic Church | 1923 | I-OCa | Ex RCC in Croatia (Yugoslavia). 1938 repudiated by Union of Utrecht. 5,000 members, 4 priests. |
| Czechoslovak Hussite Church | 1920 | I-ReC | *Los von Rom.* Schism of 20% ex RCC (Czechoslovakia). c1935 apostolic succession (Mathew) adopted. 650,000 members. |
| Eastern Apostolic Episcopal Church | 1946 | I-Epi | Begun by Missionary Bishop for Holland & Indonesia. Chaldean succession and rite. HQ Amersfoort (Holland). |
| Eastern Orthodox Catholic Church in America | 1927 | I-Epi | Schism ex American Orthodox Ch. Russian Orthodox and Viatte successions. HQ New York (USA). Defunct 1959. |
| Eglise Apostolique de Madagascar | 1968 | I-Ang | *Apostolic Ch of Madagascar.* Schism ex Eglise Episcopale (Anglican Ch). M=AOC(USA). Bishop, 15,000 adherents. |
| Eglise Catholique Apostolique de France | 1951 | I-CCa | Schism ex Old Cath Mariavite Ch (Poland). HQ Nantes (France). 400 adherents. |
| Eglise Catholique Apostolique et Gallicane Autoéphale | 1950 | I-Epi | Split ex Eglise Universalle Gnostique en France. Partiarch. HQ Bordeaux (France); Lyons, Cannes; Belgium. |
| Eglise Catholique Apostolique Gallicane | 1935 | I-CCa | *Cath Apost Gallican Ch.* Ex RCC. 1975, large Synod in Bordeaux. 40,000 members. Applied to WCC, rejected. |
| Eglise Catholique Apostolique Orthodoxe de France | | I-Epi | Split ex Eglise Gallicane. Linked with Eglise Catholique Ancienne. HQ Angers (France). |
| Eglise Cath Apost Primitive d'Antioche Orthodoxe | 1956 | I-CCa | Egl Cath Ancienne, Syro-Byzantine. HQ Paris. 2,000 members in 19 nations: Canada, Germany, Holland, Africa, &c. |
| Eglise Catholique de France | 1951 | I-CCa | Schism ex Polish Mariavite Ch. |
| Eglise Catholique du Rite Dominicain | 1947 | I-CCa | Schism ex RCC (Belgium). Metropolitan. HQ Schaerbeik-Brussels. |
| Eglise Catholique Orthodoxe do France | 1924 | I-Lib | *Eglise Cath Ev.* Ex Liberal CC. HQ St-Denys, Paris. 1937, joined P Moscow, later ROCOR, later P Bucharest. |
| Eglise Catholique Francaise (Eglise Gallicane) | 1883 | I-CCa | 1907, restored in Paris (France) by Vilatte. Attempt to revive Gnosticism. Occultism, faith-healing, magic. |
| Eglise Catholique Française (Mgr Chatel) | 1831 | I-Lib | Founded by Gallican RC's in France & (1837) Belgium. Suppressed by 1870. |
| Eglise Catholique Gallicane Autocéphale | 1959 | I-Lib | *Eglise Vieille Cath Libérale,* D Normandie. Succession Apost Oecuménique. Applied to WCC, rejected. 2,000. |
| Eglise Christique Primitive | 1938 | I-ReC | Founded by Catholic faith-healer. Sin, repentance not preached. In France, Germany, Switzerland. |
| Eglise Constitutionnelle de France | 1790 | I-CCa | Ordered to adhere to civil constitution by France. 130 RC dioceses suppressed, until 1801. |
| Eglise du Christ-Roi Renovée | 1951 | I-CCa | *Holy Cath Apost & Roman Renewed Ch.* Ex RCC(D Nancy). Papal claimant Clement XV. France 4,000, Canada 2,000. |
| Eglise Gnostique Apostolique | 1953 | I-Lib | *Apost Gnostic Ch.* Closed group protecting Gospel from world. France, Belgium, Brazil, Italy. 5,000 members. |
| Eglise Gnostique de France | 1914 | I-Lib | Orders through Eglise Gallicane. Vilatte succession. |
| Eglise Johannite des Chrétiens Primitifs | 1803 | I-Lib | Revived Templars; Masonic dogmas. Secret society. Many bishops (ex RC's). Suppressed by 1870. |
| Eglise Orthodoxe Apostolique Haitienne | 1861 | I-Hig | Schism ex RCC in Haiti. Black. 1913, Missionary District of PECUSA. 38,452 members, 26 priests. |
| Eglise Orthodoxe Gallicane Autocéphale | | I-Epi | Split in Belgium, related to Eglise Catholique Apostolique et Gallicane (France). Vilatte succession. |
| Eglise Primitive Catholique et Apostolique | 1937 | I-CCa | *Eglise Catholique Primitive.* HQ Paris. Bishop a former Liberal Catholic Priest; in Vilatte succession. |
| Eglise Rosicrucienne Apostolique | | I-Lib | *Apostolic Rosicrucian Ch.* Bishop in Brussels (Belgium). Gnostic teachings. Applied to join WCC, rejected. |
| Eglise Universell Gnostique en France | 1890 | I-Lib | France, Switzerland. Magic, occultism. Missions in Portugal,Italy, Belgium, Brazil, NAfrica. Suppressed 1944. |
| Eglise Vieille Catholique Romaine en France | 1960 | I-CCa | *Old Roman Catholic Ch in France.* Rapid expansion claimed since 1960. 7 priests, 1 seminary. |
| Eglise Vintrassienne | 1839 | I-Spi | *Oeuvre de la Miséricorde.* Founder Vitras (Bayeux, France). Miracles, occultism, spiritism. |
| Eglise Catholiques Apostoliques Orthodoxes d'Occident | | I-Epi | *Cath Apost Orth Churches of the West.* HQ Alouette-Pessac (Gironde) (France). 1947, applied to WCC, rejected. |
| English Episcopal Church | 1947 | I-ReA | *Ch of England (Ev).* Ex Ev Ch of England. HQ Acton, London (UK). Use 1662 Book of Common Prayer. West Indians. |
| English Orthodox Church | 1950 | I-Epi | Split ex Cathokicate of the West. 1952, merged in Free Catholic Church. |
| English (Old Roman Catholic) Rite | 1948 | I-Epi | Schism ex ORCC (Pro-Uniate Rite) by 2 deposed priests. Mathew succession. London. Elaborate rituals. |
| Episcopal Orthodox Church (Greek Communion) | | I-Lib | Founded in Trinidad; 1921, Cuba; 1939, New York (USA). West Indian Blacks. HQ Barbados. |
| Essene Church in the Hashemite Kingdom of Jordan | | I-Epi | Small group in Jordan claiming Essene or Gnostic doctrines. Under a primate in an oriental succession. |
| Evangelical Catholic Church | 1903 | I-Nes | *Ev Catholic Communion, Church Universal.* Nestorian/Chaldean succession from South India. HQ Oxford. Defunct. |
| Evangelical Catholic Church of New York | 1927 | I-Epi | Split by deposed bishop ex NAORCC. Mathew succession. Defunct 1945. |
| Evangelical Church of England | 1922 | I-ReA | Anglicans opposing Anglo-Catholicism. Archbishop, in Ferrette succession. 10 churches in Lancashire (UK). |
| Free Anglo-Catholic Church | 1948 | I-Epi | *Order of Llanthony Brothers.* 3 bishops, in Mathew succession. Extinct 1957. |
| Free Catholic Church | 1930 | I-ARo | Ex Church of England. Anglo-Catholic. Bishop, in Ferrette succession. HQ Forest Gate, London E7 (UK). |
| Free Catholic Church in Germany | | I-Epi | *Ch of the Servants of Christ. Catholic Episcopal Ch.* Ex Ancient Catholic Ch (UK). Women consecrated as bishops. |
| Free Church of England | 1844 | I-ReA | Linked with Reformed Episcopal Ch (USA). Ex Ch of England. 2 Dioceses. Declining. 3,194 members, 5 bishops. |
| Free Holy Catholic Church of England (D Mercia) | 1952 | I-Epi | *Free Protestant Catholic Communion.* |
| Free Protestant Episcopal Church | 1897 | I-ARo | *FPEC. Ecumenical Church Foundation.* Ex REC(USA). Armenian succession. UK 3,000; USA, Canada, W Africa, WIndies. |
| Gnostic Catholic Church | 1960 | I-Epi | *Old Cath Orth Western Primitive Rite Synod of the One Holy Cath & Apostolic Ch.* Mathew succession. USA. |
| Hochkirche in Österreich | 1958 | I-Epi | Ephemeral body under bishop in Vilatte succession. In Austria. |
| Holy Apostolic Catholic Church | 1963 | I-Epi | *Autocephalous Chaldean Rite.* Nestorian succession through Catholicate of the West (UK). HQ Bremerton (USA). |
| Holy Catholic Church of the Apostles in D Louisiana | 1929 | I-Epi | Split by deposed bishop ex NAORCC. Archbishop in Mathew succession. Defunct 1942. |
| Holy Orthodox Church in America | 1925 | I-CCa | Begun by P Moscow as American Orthodox Ch. 1961. Western Rite Vicariate in Antiochian OC AD NY (USA). |
| Holy Orth Ch in America (Eastern Catholic & Apostolic) | 1926 | I-lib | Begun as Anglican Universal Ch. Ex RCC. Vilatte succession. Rosicrucianism. 5 bishops. HQ NY (USA). |
| Hungarian Orthodox Greek Catholic Church | 1933 | I-Hun | Begun by P Belgrade (Serbian Orth Ch) in Hungary. 1934, Syrian (Jacobite) succession. In Hungary and USA. |
| Iglesia Católica Americana Ortodoxa | | I-CCa | Schism in Argentina by RC priests, bishop. M=AOCC(USA). Maintains an Apostolic Exarchate in Rome. 30,000. |
| Iglesia Católica Apostólica Venezolana | 1946 | I-CCa | *Cath Apostolic Ch.* Schism ex Rome by 33 priests. ICAB (Brazil) succession. Under Free Cath Ch in Germany. |
| Iglesia Católica Romana Antigua | 1935 | I-CCa | *Ecclesia Veteris Romanae Catholicae.* ORCC. Ex RCC, Mexico. Mathew succession. 1965, applied to WCC, rejected. |
| Iglesia Española Reformada Episcopal | 1880 | I-Ang | *Spanish Reformed Episcopal Ch.* Split ex Spanish Ev Ch. 1894 Anglican succession. In Union of Utrecht. 1,000. |
| Iglesia Ortodoxa Católica Mexicana | 1926 | I-CCa | *National Ch.* State-aided schism ex RCC, Mexico. 10 bishops, Mathew succession. Decline since 1940. 60,000. |
| Igreja Brasileira | 1961 | I-CCa | Schism ex Ch of Rome. 1963, 6 bishops; applied to join WCC, also to rejoin RCC; rejected. 2,000 members. |
| Igreja Católica Apostólica Brasileira | 1945 | I-CCa | *ICAB.* Schism ex RCC in Brazil by former RC bishop of Botucatú. Clerical celibacy abolished. 2 million. |
| Igreja Católica Livre no Brasil | 1936 | I-CCa | *Free Catholic Ch in Brazil.* Schism ex RCC. 1945, Durate (Roman Catholic) succession adopted. 3,000 adherents. |
| Igreja Lusitana Católica Apostólica Evangélica | 1871 | I-ReC | *Lusitanian Ch.* Schism ex RCC (Portugal) by 11 priests. 1958, Anglican succession. 4,500 members. |
| Independent Catholic Church | 1922 | I-Epi | Short-lived body begun by patriarch-archbishop, in Mathew succession. HQ East Molesey (UK) |
| Independent Catholic Church of Ceylon, Goa & India | 1866 | I-CCa | Schism of 5,000 Latin-rite Catholics ex RCC opposing Propaganda. Jacobite (Antioch) succession. Defunct 1950. |
| Independent Church of Filipino Christians | 1946 | I-Lib | Schism ex Philippine Independent Ch by deposed primate Fonacier. Unitarian. HQ Baangas (Philippines). 1,700. |
| Independent Episcopal Church of the US & Canada | | I-ARo | Schism ex Protestant Episcopal Ch (USA), by bishop in Mathew succession in ORCC (USA). |
| Independent Syrian Church of Malabar | 1771 | I-ReO | *Malabar Swathanthra Suriani Sabha. D Thozhiyur.* Schism ex Orthodox Syrian Ch. 3,780 members, 8 priests. |
| Indian National Church | 1955 | I-ARo | Ex CIPBC (Anglican). Archbishop and several bishops, in Vilatte succession. HQ Delhi (India). 1,000 members. |
| Indian Orthodox Church: Patriarchate of India | 1956 | I-CCa | Ex RCC. Ferrette succession. Linked with Catholicate of the West, FPEC. |
| Katholische Kirche in Deutschland | 1845 | I-CCa | Short-lived schism ex Roman Catholic Church (Germany). |
| Liberal Catholic Church | 1915 | I-Lib | *LCC.* Schism ex ORCC. Mathew succession. Theosophical, Masonic. HQ London (UK). In 18 nations. |
| Liberal Catholic Church, Order of St Germain | 1969 | I-Lib | Split ex LCC. In USA (Texas, Colorado, Oklahoma, California). 3,000 members, 22 priests. |
| Liberal Catholic Church (California) | 1947 | I-Lib | Schism ex original LCC opposing Theosophy. HQ USA. 4,000 members, 5 bishops, 62 priests. |
| Liberal Christian Episcopal Church | | I-Epi | *Apostolic Eastern Succession of Antioch.* Archbishop. HQ USA. 1954, applied to join WCC; rejected. |
| Lutheran Episcopal Church of England | | I-Epi | Schism ex English Episcopal Ch, by former minister of Reformed Presbyterian Ch in Ireland. Defunct 1956. |
| Mar Thoma Syrian Church of Malabar | 1843 | I-ReO | Schism ex Orthodox Syrian Ch (India). Jacobite (Antioch) succession, disputed. 5 Dioceses. 350,000 members. |
| Mariavite Church of Ancient Catholic Rite | 1936 | I-CCa | *Catholic Mariavite Ch.* Schism ex Old Catholic Mariavite Ch of Poland. HQ Felicijanow (Poland). 4,000 members. |
| National Catholic Apostolic Church of the Philippines | 1930 | I-CCa | *Iglesia Catolica Apostolica Nacional.* Schism ex RCC. HQ Cabanatuan Cith (Philippines). 35,000 members. |
| Nazarene Episcopal Ecclesia | 1873 | I-Epi | British-Israelite. Ex Reformed Episcopal CH (USA). Ferrette succession. HQ Sydenham (UK). |
| New Catholic and Free Church | | I-Epi | Schism ex Catholic Apostolic Ch (Catholicate of the West). Spiritism, theosophy. HQ London N10 (UK). |
| North American Old Roman Catholic Church | 1912 | I-CCa | *NAORCC.* ORCC in USA. Ex RCC. Mathew succession. Italians, Poles, Lithuanians. HQ Chicago. 60,098 members. |
| North American (Old Roman) Catholic Church | 1958 | I-CCa | *North American Catholic Ch.* Schism ex original NAORCC. Mathew succession. HQ Brooklyn (USA). 1,290 members. |
| Old Catholic Archdiocese for Americas & Europe | 1940 | I-Epi | Schism ex OCCA, in Mathew succession. HQ Bronx 58 (USA). |

*Continued opposite*

Table 6–10 concluded

| Name | Begun | Type | Names, notes, comments, adherents, clergy, and other data |
|---|---|---|---|
| Old Catholic Ch in America (Catholic Ch of North A) | 1917 | I-CCa | *OCCA. Orth Old Cath Ch in America.* Mathew succession. HQ NY USA. 6,000; 1962, received into ROC (P Moscow). |
| Old Catholic Church in Bosnia & Herzegovina | 1965 | I-OCa | Founded separate from other 4 old Catholic churches in Yugoslavia. Not under Utrecht. 1,000 members. |
| Old Catholic Church in Ireland | 1916 | I-Epi | Schism ex RCC and ORCC. Mathew succession, Regionary Bishop. Defunct 1960. |
| Old Catholic Church in Portugal | 1918 | I-Epi | Attempt to start Old Catholic movement, by bishop in Mathew succession. Short-lived. |
| Old Catholic Church of Hungary | 1945 | I-CCa | Small group ex RCC in Hungary. Close links with Mariavite Church (Poland), who provided succession. |
| Old Catholic Church of Poland | 1946 | I-CCa | Schism ex RCC. Joined by Mariavite remnants. Mathew succession. Links with NAORCC (USA). |
| Old Catholic Church (Vilatte) | 1892 | I-CCa | Begun by Vilatte, Jacobite (Antioch) succession. 1903, UK, 1915, dissolved into American Catholic Ch. |
| Old Catholic Evangelical Church of God | 1924 | I-ARo | Anglo-Saxon rite. Mathew succession. 5 bishops, 33 priests. HQ Greenwich (UK). Defunct. |
| Old Catholic Mariavite Church of Poland | 1906 | I-CCA | Excommunicated by Pius X. 1906: 500,000 declining to 24,000 (1970). Women bishops. In 9 nations. |
| Old Catholic Orthodox Church | 1925 | I-ARo | Schism by laity after infallibility claim by primate of Old RCC (Pro-Uniate Rite). Mathew succession. In UK. |
| Old Catholic Orthodox Church (Apostolic Serive Ch) | 1925 | I-Epi | Formerly Independent Catholic Ch. Mathew succession. Nationalist; spiritual healing. HQ Strand, London (UK). |
| Old Holy Catholic Church (Church of the One Life)f | 1955 | I-ARo | *OHCC.* Schism ex Old Catholic Evangelical Ch of God. Mathew succession. In UK. |
| Old Ritualist Ancient Orthodox Christians | | I-OBe | *AD Moscow. Old Believers. Beglopopytsy (Ch of Fugitive Priests),* Ex Popovtsy. 200,000 in USSR. |
| Old Ritualist Church of Belokrinitsa Concord | 1666 | I-OBe | *AD Moscow. Raskolniki (Schismatics).* ex ROC (P Moscow). Popoytsy (Priestists). 5 dioceses. 1 mission in USSR. |
| Old Roman Catholic Apostolic Church | | I-CCa | Italians, ex Church of Rome, in New York state (USA). Bishop, ex RCC, in Vilatte succession. 2,500 members. |
| Old Roman Catholic Church | 1908 | I-CCa | *Ancient Cath Ch of England, English CC. Old CC in GB. Western Uniate CC.* 1915, ORCC. Bishop AH Mathew, ex RC. |
| Old Roman Catholic Church in North America | 1958 | I-CCa | Schism ex NAORCC. Mathew succession. Two rival groups using same name. |
| Old Roman Catholic Church (D Niagara Falls) | 1952 | I-Epi | Ex NAORCC. HQ Niagara Falls, NY (USA). |
| Old Roman Catholic Church (English Rite) | 1950 | I-CCa | Schism ex ORCC. Mathew succession. 12 churches in UK; 1963, large USA branch of 65,000 added (HQ Chicago). |
| Old Roman Catholic Church (Orthodox Orders) | | I-CCa | Split ex ORCC in Canada. Rules by a cardinal. HA Havelock, Ontario (Canada). 1967, applied to WCC, rejected. |
| Old Roman Catholic Church (Pro-Uniate Rite) | 1915 | I-ARo | *Western Catholic Uniate Rite.* Canonical ORC Ch. Mathew succession. 2 bishops, 6 priests until 1915 LCC schism. |
| Orthodox Catholic Church in England | 1929 | I-Epi | UK branch of Vilatte's American Catholic CH (USA), with Metropolitan for the British Empire. Defunct 1938. |
| Orthodox Catholic Patriarchate of America | | I-Epi | Linked with American Holy Orthodox Catholic Apostolic Eastern Ch. HQs New York, Springfield (Mass) (USA). |
| Orthodox Church of Sardinia | 1961 | I-Epi | Mariavite links, claiming Russian Orthodox succession. |
| Orthodox Ecclesia | | I-Epi | Short-lived attempt to found church based on Llanthony abbey, Wales. Mathew succession. Defunct. |
| Orthodox Old Catholic Church | 1964 | I-Epi | *OOCC,* Second Movement. Primate-Bishop. HQ Philadelphia (USA). 1965, applied to join WCC; rejected. |
| Orthodox-Keltic Church of British Commonwealth of N | 1935 | I-Epi | *N=Nations.* British Orthodox Cath Ch. British-Israelite. Vilatte succession. HQ London N7 (UK). Defunct 1942. |
| Petite Eglise (Vendéene) | 1801 | I-CCa | *Little Ch.* Schism of 38 bishops ex Rome, rejecting 1801 concordat with France. Declining; no clergy left. 5,000 members. |
| Philippine Church (Adarnista) | 1901 | I-mar | *Iglesia Filipina (Adarnistas).* Followers of bishop Adarna. Rizalist (marginal Catholic) type. 15,000. |
| Philippine Independent Church | 1890 | I-ReC | *Iglesia Filipina Independiente.* Ex RCC (Philippines). 1948, Anglican succession adopted. 3,500,000 adherents. |
| Polish Catholic Church | | I-CCa | Handful of Polish followers. Ex RCC before PNCC fully organized, in USA> |
| Pre-Nicene Gnostic Catholic Church | 1952 | I-Lib | Founded by ex-priests of Liberal Catholic Ch (Australia). Theosophical, esoteric, mystical. UK, Australia, NZ. |
| Primitive Church of Antioch | 1951 | I-Epi | Set up by Primate, ex Catholicate of Austria; Vilatte succession. HQ Cologne (Germany). |
| Protestant Orthodox Western Church | 1943 | I-Epi | Bishop for NAORCC Mathew succession. USA. |
| Reformed Catholic Church (Utrecht Confession) | | I-ARo | Schism ex OC Ev Ch of God. Mathew succession. 2,217 members in USA; also in UK, France, Germany. |
| Reformed Episcopal Church | 1873 | I-ReA | *REC.* Ex PECUSA opposing ritualism. 1927, communion with Free Ch of England (UK). Enquiry re joining WCC. |
| Russian Orthodox Church Outside of Russia | 1920 | I-Rus | *ROCOR.* Exiles from USSR. Ultra-conservative. 1950, world HQ moved to New York (USA). 13 Dioceses in world. |
| Russian Orthodox Living Church | 1922 | I-Rus | State-aided schism of 30% all parishes ex (USSR). 1929: controlled 35% all ROC churches. Defunct 1943. |
| St Thomas Evangelical Church of India | 1961 | I-Reo | *Pathiopadesa Samita.* Schism ex Mar Thoma Syrian Ch. HQ Tiruvella (India). 25,000 members, 29 priests. |
| Sainte Eglise Apostolique | 1955 | I-Lib | Uniate Armenian succession. Militantly Gallican. Healing, occult. HQ Coloms (Seine) (France). 1,5000 members. |
| Sainte Eglise Apostolique Orth Celtique en Brétagne | 1956 | I-CCa | 10 bishops, 300 Celtic-rite families. Breton nationalism (Brittany). Druidic rites, midnight sea baptism. |
| Sainte Eglise Apostolique Orth Gallicane Autocéphale | 1955 | I-CCa | PR=Puerto Rico. Ex RCC, aided by Polish NCC(USA), 1,000 members. HQ Bayamon. 1968 applied to WCC, rejected. |
| South African Episcopal Church | 1950 | I-Epi | Ex Ch of England. Bishop, in Ferrette succession. 1662 Anglican Book of Common Prayer used. |
| True Orthodox Christian Wanderers | 1956 | I-Tru | *IPKh, Stranniki.* Underground schism ex Russian Orthodox Ch (P Moscow), across USSR. Highly-organized. |
| True Orthodox Church | 1927 | I-Tru | *IPTS. Istinno-Pravoslavnaya Tserkov.* Remnants of underground church (ex Russian OC) across USSR smashed by KGB. |
| Turkish Orthodox Church: P Istanbul | 1922 | I-ReO | State-aided schism in Turkey ex Ecumenical Patriarchate. Adherents: 300 in Turkey, 14,800 in USA. |
| Ukrainian Autocephalic Orthodox Church | 1947 | I-Ukr | Ukrainian refugees in UK. Linked to UOC of the USA. 30,000 members in UK, also several other nations. |
| Ukrainian Greek-Orthodox Church of Canada | 1918 | I-Ukr | Former Uniates; schism ex RCC in Canada. 3 Dioceses. 95 clergy. |
| Ukrainian Orthodox Church of the USA | 1919 | I-Ukr | From USSR. Disputed succession through hand of dead saint. 9 Dioceses in 5 nations (USA, 87,475 members). |
| Ukrainian Orthodox Church (Democratic) | 1947 | I-Ukr | *UOC (Sobornopravna).* Ex UOCUSA. Bishop in Chicago (USA), also for Europe in Geneva (Switzerland). 2,000. |
| United Armenian Catholic Church in the British Isles | 1890 | I-Epi | Ireland, UK. Primate, in Ferrette succession. Linked with Catholicate of the West. Defunct c1920. |
| United Episcopal Ch (Christian Cath/Church Universal) | 1959 | I-Epi | Split ex Liberal Catholic Ch. Theosophical. HQ Los Angeles (USA). |
| United Old Catholic Church | 1964 | I-OCa | Attempt in USA to unite all Catholic factions. 1 monastery, 3,000 members, 28 priests. |
| United Orthodox Catholicate | 1953 | I-Epi | Organization replacing temporarily-dissolved Catholicate of the West, in UK. |
| Universal Apostolic Church of Life | 1955 | I-Epi | *Sedes Universalis Apostolica. Universal Life Foundation.* HQ North Burnaby, BC (Canada). |
| Universal Christian Communion | 1931 | I-Epi | *Universal Episcopal Communion.* Attempt to unite all Old Catholic bodies in USA. HQ Chicago 21 (USA). |
| Vrai Eglise Catholique | 1964 | I-3cW | *True Catholic Ch.* In Lorraine (France) and Belgium, begun by excommunicated RC priests. 1,000 members. |
| Other sizeable episcopal churches | | | At least 20 more bodies, mainly in Europe and USA. Adherents at least 10,000. |
| Other minuscule episcopal churches | | | At least 85 more bodies, mainly in Europe and USA (see list below). Adherents around 3,000. |
| | | | |
| Total sizeable episcopal churches | | | About 250 churches in 120 countries, with total adherents about 10,280,000, (1975) increasing to 25,000,000 (1995). |
| Total minuscule episcopal churches | | | About 170 churches or bodies in 40 countries, with total adherents around 5,000 (1975) increasing to 10,000 (1995). |
| Total all disputed episcopal churches | | | About 420 distinct churches or denominations in 130 countries, with around 10,285,000 (1975) increasing to 25,010,000 (1995). |

OTHER MINUSCULE EPISCOPAL CHURCHES. There were in 1970 a large number of other bodies under bishops-at-large, many ephemeral or short-lived. These include such titles as: Byzantine Primitive Catholic Ch, Latin American Ecumenical Patriarchate, Orthodox Catholic Diocese of the Holy Spirit, Orthodoxe Ökumenische Cleryker, Slavonic Orthodox Ch. Totals in the 7 major nations concerned, with a selection of names, are as follows.

*France.* About 10 more bodies, in addition to those listed, including: Eglise Catholique Apostalique Indépendente, Eglise Orthodoxe Française. *Germany.* About 5 more, including Evangelisch-Ökumenische Vereinigung des Augsburger Bekenntnis. *Italy.* About 10 more, including: Chiesa Cattolica Apostolica Ortodossa, Chiesa Cattolica Liberale, Chiesa Cattolica Ortodossa in Italia, Chiesa Ortodossa (D Patrasso), Chiesa Vetero-Cattolica, Pia

Unione delle Chiese Cristiane. *Philippines.* At least 10 more small Aglipayan and Rizalist schisms. *Switzerland.* About 10 more. *UK.* At least 15 more, including: English Old Catholic Ch, Free Catholic Communion of the Old Catholic Ch. *USA.* At least 15 more, including: American Rite Byzantine Catholic Ch, Catholic Ch of the North American Rite, North American Orthodox Catholic Ch, Russian American Orthodox Catholic Ch.

# Part 7

# GEOTRENDS

Trends and megatrends throughout
the world, AD 30–AD 2200

*Day by day the Lord added new converts to their number.*
—Acts of the Apostles 2:47, Revised English Bible

*I dare affirm a man shall more profit, in one week, by figures and charts, well and per-
fectly made, than he shall by the only reading or hearing the rules of that science by
the space of half a year at the least.*
—Sir Thomas Elyot, lexicographer, 1531 (on geometry, and cosmography)

*When you can measure what you are speaking about and express it in numbers, you
know something about it; but when you cannot express it in numbers, your
knowledge is of a meager and unsatisfactory kind.*
—Lord Kelvin (William Thomson), 1891

The bibliography at the end of this Part lists 70 items with titles combining the word 'trend' or 'trends' with the subject of religion—either Christianity, Hinduism, Islam, Buddhism, Judaism, or even 'world religions'. These draw attention to the changing face not only of Christianity but also of all other religions too.

This Part 7 therefore starts by defining 13 distinct variables or meanings of the English word 'trend'. This leads into an overall global survey of 26 Christian variables, measured for each of our world's 28 geopolitical areas (the globe, 7 continents, 20 regions as defined by United Nations' demographers), and then further measured for each end of century over the period AD 30-AD 2200. This produces a grid of 16,016 numerical trends. Results are given on 28 semilogarithmic graphs with each's statistical box on its facing page.

# Trends and megatrends throughout the world, AD 30-AD 2200

The English word 'trend' is explained and utilized in a vast literature. At last count in AD 2001, the world's 50,000 largest libraries had on their shelves 72,344 distinct and different book titles in English classified by the US Library of Congress under the keyword 'trend' (or 'trends'). Some 46,114 of these books also had this keyword in their titles. Narrowing the search by adding a second keyword 'religion' produced a listing of 372 books. And lastly, main subject 'religion' and use of 'trends' in titles produced 86 books, the most significant of which are appended at the end of this Part 7. This bibliography, if shown in chronological sequence would make the titles themselves a trend listing of major books on religious trends.

A similar investigation of books in other languages reveals a parallel plethora of titles on this subject. Major titles exist in German, French, Spanish, Portuguese, Italian, Russian, Chinese, Arabic, Japanese, Hindi, and at least a thousand other languages of scholarship.

Part 7 utilizes this vast range of scholarship concerning the concept 'trends' to set out a comprehensive overview of the whole range of Christian membership trends across 20 centuries and across the 7 continents. The attempt is made to show how today's trends are related to, and have evolved from, the trends of the past; and how they suggest what the trends of the future are likely to be.

## REVIEWING CONTEMPORARY DEFINITIONS

It must first be noted that the word 'trend' is a complex one with a number of meanings in today's dictionaries, in the literature, and in current technical reports describing specific trends. Synonyms of this word are many, and include: general direction, tendency, drift, tenor, inclination, disposition, predisposition, movement, motion, rate. In our survey here, these meanings are categorized under 13 heads labeled from Trend A to Trend M.

Usages of this word can be divided into 2 generic kinds: non-numeric (without numbers or statistics), and numeric (with both).

## MAJOR CATEGORIES OF TRENDS
## 1. NON-NUMERIC DEFINITIONS

First comes the widest or most comprehensive usage.

*Trend A*. **General direction.** This is the main definition found in dictionaries. A trend is the **general direction** of any descriptive entity—a coast, a river, a road, a population, a period of time, or any other **line of development**. It is the general direction or **prevailing tendency** or course, indefinite without goals, as of events; subject to change caused by external forces. For many users, trend is used primarily in reference to something that follows an **irregular** or winding course, and denotes the general direction maintained in spite of these irregularities. Thus the river Jordan forming the boundary between Israel and the kingdom of Jordan meanders a good deal throughout its length but in its general direction it follows a clear southwards trend.

*Trend B*. **Status description.** Trend, however, is often used in a general or vague sense for a general discussion or description of the **current status** of any major subject or concern or problem.

*Trend C*. **Time period with title.** For many users, an indispensible component of any trend is the time factor. This may be indicated by 2 or more points in time (e.g. 'AD 1000 and 1100', or '11th century') each with a short 2-6 word title such as 'End of the Dark Ages'.

*Trend D*. **Descriptive sentences.** A trend can likewise be indicated if 2 or more longer **descriptive sentences**, each with attached time period, are listed one under the other.

## 2. NUMERIC DEFINITIONS

The main value of trend studies comes when measurements, quantification, numbers, statistics, mathematics, and computing are invoked.

*Trend E*. **Measurement.** The combination of a series of numbers with each's own date or time attached immediately reveals hitherto hidden relationships. Visual inspection often enables the trend to be seen in past, present, and future. Thus 'A trend is a definite, **predictable** direction or **sequence of events**' (G. Celente, *Trend tracking*, 1990:3). To find or identify such trends, the enquirer must look at relevant events and watch for a direction or a significant measurable sequence to emerge.

*Trend F*. **Quantification.** A trend based on employing quantification in space and time may illuminate an otherwise hidden situation.

It should be noted that there exist a number of complex and sophisticated scientific applications based on quantified data. One such is trend surface analysis, a technique in multidimensional mathematical modeling which has applications in engineering, sociology, and economics especially in demonstrating how a microcosm operates. Applications to data from the churches' annual megacensus await only an initiative by interested Christians.

*Trend G*. **Statistics at 2 points in time.** The introduction of statistics as the art of precise counting and analysis now provides trends of considerable sophistication. Two definitions from Webster's *Third new international dictionary of the English language* illustrate this:
(a) 'Trend: the general **movement** over a sufficiently long **period of time** of some statistical progressive **change**' (e.g. 'population trend')
(b) 'Trend: a straight line or other **statistical curve** showing the tendency of some function to grow or decline over a period of time' (e.g. 'trends through mass mailings').

*Trend H*. **Graphic measures.** Values of the 2 or more points in time may be plotted on regular graph paper (equal spacing on both axes) or semi-logarithmic graph paper (vertical scale being logarithmic with 1, 10, 100, 1000, etc being equidistant). On the latter a fixed exponential rate of change results in an exact straight line.

*Trend I*. **Linear rates.** A trend between 2 points in time may be approximately estimated by joining them graphically in a straight line. This is a rapid first step that can be done through mental arithmetic.

*Trend J*. **Exponential growth rates.** This is the well-known principle of compound interest. For any specific time period between 2 known points, a single precise trend figure—rate of increase or decrease as % per year, being the same at every point in the period—may be computed by using any handheld scientific calculator, or spreadsheet subroutine.

*Trend K*. **Yearly increase.** A valuable trend figure is the annual increase (absolute number) at one of the 2 points in time. This is obtained by multiplying the exponential growth rate (divided by 100) by the actual number of persons at the later date.

*Trend L*. **Daily increase.** Dividing the yearly increase shown in K above by 365 gives the increase per day (per diem, p.d.). This has the potential of being the most valuable of the various long-term trend figures by virtue of the degree of microscopic examination that it imparts concerning the whole process.

*Trend M*. **Other related variables.** When the main variable (members, adherents) has been analyzed and its trend numbers worked out, it is now useful to do the same for other quantified variables related in interest though their numbers may be derived independently.

Summing up, the concept 'trend' can be defined and used in at least 13 different ways, termed above as Trends A to M. In this analysis, we give emphasis primarily to the more precise definitions enabling exact quantification, measurement, enumeration, computation, analysis, and on to interpretation. These are Trends E to M above. Thus the preferred overall definition is as follows:

A trend is the average **general direction** of movement taken by a specific secular or religious **variable**, or indicator of any property or activity or **line of development**, in **numeric** form to show **precise magnitude**, between any **2 points**, at 2 different times and/or places or stages (1 minute, 1 hour, 1 day, 1 week, 1 month, 1 quarter, 1 year, 1 decade, 1 century, 1 millennium, 1 million years, or any other period of time) or as a **sequence of events**, expressed, **measured**, and **quantified** to produce **statistics of change** either (a) as a single linear or **exponential growth rate** of change (G% per year/annum, p.a.); or (b) as the increment between those 2 points in absolute numbers (e.g. 200,000 per year); or (c) as the exponential growth rate multiplied by the year's absolute value to arrive at the rate of increase—the nett absolute **number of new adherents** per year—at that one point in time; or (d) as the average **daily increase** at that precise year; or (e) **graphical illustration** (often on semi-logarithmic paper) of this precise trend in the context of any or all other related trends.

## APPLICATION TO CHRISTIAN TRENDS

Trends can be measured not only for the present but also for the past. In fact, past Christian history can be greatly illuminated by measuring annual trends every 50 years or so, to cover the entire period AD 30 to AD 2000 and even projected into the future to AD 2200.

Many of the global diagrams in Part 1 show the world as a 3-dimensional sphere on which variables are shown which can be extended to show geographical location, chronological status, and trends either annual or centennial or even millennial. For many data it can be seen as a single sphere representing the globe, with multidimensional representation on the series of global diagrams. Hence the reader can extend any diagram chronologically, or geographically, or politically, or ethnically, or linguistically, or religiously, or ecclesiastically, or topically, as he or she wishes.

These 13 distinct varieties of trends can now be applied to the narrative of Christian expansion. First, a few classics in the literature dealing with secular trends will be mentioned. Then follows a review of literature on religious trends. After this comes a description of the 2 main tables in this Part 7. First, Table 7–1 sets out the numerical growth of Christianity from its origins in Palestine in AD 30 to successive years throughout the 1st century AD to its contemporary worldwide spread to 238 countries today, and then on 2 centuries into the future. The much longer Table 7–2 then extends this coverage to 26 variables at 23 different dates in time, for the whole world followed by 27 other geopolitical areas.

## Table 7–1. Numerical trends in the worldwide expansion of Christianity, AD 30–AD 2200, with special reference to the 1st century AD.

The table charts the numerical progress of global Christianity century by century, with detailed attention to the 1st century AD. For precise dates of events, major stages, and statistical origins, consult Part 2 "CosmoChronology".

*Columns*

1. *Year.* Statistics in columns 5 to 11 refer precisely to each year shown in column 1 (with fraction of year, up to AD 58). Events and evidence in columns 2 and 4 illustrate progress or decline at the year shown during the 1st century AD, but after AD 100 exact dates of events described in column 2 may be ascertained from "CosmoChronology".
2. *Event.* A major activity or trend regarding growth or decline around or after the year indicated.
3. *Scripture.* Up to the end of The Acts of the Apostles in AD 61, the verses shown represent major developments in the narrative of the immediate expansion of Christianity. Each such verse presents evidence, initially of rapid growth, which is then fitted into the mathematical grid in columns 5 to 11 and also as in Table 7–2. *Note*: Sentences or phrases in quotation marks show the exact wording in the CEV (Contemporary English Version); or, occasionally, in KJV (King James Version), RSV (Revised Standard Version), NEB (New English Bible), GNB (Good News Bible), or NRSV (New Revised Standard Version).
4. *Evidence.* In the Acts, precise statistics of the total size of the Christian community are rare, but the 50 sequential sentences shown can be fitted into the numerical grid from AD 400–2000 without difficulty.
5. *Evangelized.* Total evangelized persons, meaning all persons adequately aware of Christianity, Christ, and the gospel.
6. *Outreach per Christian.* Evangelized non-Christians (World B) divided by Christians, or (E/AC)-1, or (E-AC)/AC.
7. *Followers.* Total living Christian community, including children. (Widely used in CEV instead of 'disciples').
8. *Increase per year* (as at the date in column 1). Average figure, computed as column 10 divided by 100, multiplied by column 7.
9. *Increase per day.* Average figure, computed as column 8 divided by 365.
10. *Rate, % per year.* This is the exponential growth rate of column 7 at the one point of the exact year shown in column 1, which rate remains unaltered throughout the previous period covered back to the previous line here, which is the period of 1, 2, 5, 10, 100, or other number of years that the table shows ending in the year indicated. Note also that for the years to AD 57, each year with multiple lines requires growth to be calculated for 6, 4, 3 or 2 month periods only, although it is then reported here as an annual rate at that particular point in time.
11. *Martyrs.* Defined here by 5 criteria: *Believers in Christ* who *lose their lives, prematurely*, in situations of *witness*, as a result of *human hostility*. Statistics shown here are of total martyrs ever, cumulatively (not annual rates), at the year shown. Sources: consult "CosmoChronology" and Part 4 "Martyrology", especially Table 4-10.

| *Year* 1 | *Event* 2 | *Scripture* 3 | *Evidence of expansion, growth, or decline (quotes = exact words from Scripture verse in column 3)* 4 | *Evangelized* 5 | *E/AC-1* 6 | *Followers* 7 | *Increase per year* 8 | *Increase per day* 9 | *Rate % pa* 10 | *Martyrs ever* 11 |
|---|---|---|---|---|---|---|---|---|---|---|
| AD 30 | Start of Jesus' ministry | Mark 1:16 | First disciples chosen as Twelve Apostles; Kingdom of God told in parables | 1,000 | 4 | 200 | 2000 | 5 | – | – |
| 31 | Signs and wonders | John 2:11 | Localized miracles, signs, healings as followers multiply | 200,000 | 199 | 1,000 | 4,000 | 11 | – | – |
| 32 | Vast audiences | Luke 10:14 | Mass feedings (5,000 and 4,000); mass healings, mass teachings | 800,000 | 199 | 4,000 | 12,000 | 33 | – | – |
| 33.3 | Crucifixion | Matthew 26:56 | Disciples scattered, deserting Jesus, who is then crucified | 1,600,000 | 15,999 | 100 | 0 | 0 | 0 | 5 |
| 33.3 | The Forty Days | 1 Corinthians 15:6 | The Risen Lord meets individuals, then The Twelve, then 500 at once | 1,700,000 | 2,124 | 800 | 800 | 2 | – | 5 |
| 33.4 | Ascension | Matthew 28:19 | Christ's Great Commission: 'Go! Witness! Proclaim! Disciple! Baptize! Train!' | 1,800,000 | 1,199 | 1,500 | 1,500 | 4 | – | 5 |
| 33.5 | Pentecost | Acts 2:41 | 3,000 new converts from wider Jewish Diaspora baptized, then return home | 2,000,000 | 249 | 8,000 | 8,000 | 22 | 100.0 | 5 |
| 33.6 | Daily increases | Acts 2:47 | 'Day by day the Lord added to their number those whom He was saving' (NEB) | 2,010,000 | 235 | 8,500 | 7,085 | 19 | 83.4 | 5 |
| 33.8 | Peter arrested | Acts 4:4 | Despite arrests, adult men believers number 'about 5,000 followers of the Lord' | 2,020,000 | 223 | 9,000 | 2,977 | 8 | 33.1 | 8 |
| 34 | Mass movement | Acts 4:32 | Large-scale people movement into the church now under way | 2,030,000 | 213 | 9,500 | 2,949 | 8 | 31.0 | 8 |
| 34.2 | Signs and wonders | Acts 5:14 | 'Many men and women started having faith in the Lord' ('multitudes', KJV) | 2,040,000 | 203 | 10,000 | 2,924 | 8 | 29.2 | 10 |
| 34.4 | Mass healings | Acts 5:16 | Many town-dwellers healed; followers including women and children over 10,000 | 2,050,000 | 194 | 10,500 | 2,901 | 8 | 27.6 | 15 |
| 34.7 | Daily evangelism | Acts 5:42 | Evangelism—witnessing 'every day… in one home after another' | 2,060,000 | 185 | 11,100 | 2,259 | 6 | 20.3 | 20 |
| 35 | Greek/Aramaic split | Acts 6:1 | 'A lot of people were now becoming followers of the Lord' | 2,080,000 | 177 | 11,700 | 2,244 | 6 | 19.2 | 30 |
| 35.3 | Priests converted | Acts 6:7 | 'The number of the disciples multiplied greatly… a great many priests' (RSV) | 2,090,000 | 168 | 12,400 | 2,650 | 7 | 21.4 | 50 |
| 35.7 | Violent persecution | Acts 8:1 | Persecuted believers scattered from Jerusalem throughout Judea and Samaria | 2,110,000 | 156 | 13,400 | 2,867 | 8 | 21.4 | 200 |
| 36.1 | Mission to Samaritans | Acts 8:4 | Philip, Peter, John 'went everywhere preaching the word' (KJV) | 2,130,000 | 147 | 14,400 | 2,839 | 8 | 19.7 | 200 |
| 36.5 | Relative peace | Acts 9:31 | 'Through the help of the Holy Spirit (the church)… grew in numbers' (GNB) | 2,160,000 | 139 | 15,400 | 2,814 | 8 | 18.3 | 200 |
| 37 | Ceaseless itineration | Acts 9:32 | Constant itinerant evangelism: 'While Peter was travelling from place to place…' | 2,180,000 | 130 | 16,600 | 2,688 | 7 | 16.2 | 210 |
| 37.6 | Coast evangelized | Acts 9:35 | 'Many people in the towns of Lydda and Sharon… became followers of the Lord' | 2,220,000 | 122 | 18,000 | 2,601 | 7 | 14.4 | 210 |
| 38 | City-wide conversions | Acts 9:42 | 'Everyone in Joppa heard… many of them put their faith in the Lord' | 2,240,000 | 117 | 19,000 | 2,750 | 8 | 14.5 | 210 |
| 39.1 | First Gentiles converted | Acts 10:48 | Large influx of Italian believers from Cohors II Italica | 2,300,000 | 104 | 22,000 | 3,136 | 9 | 14.3 | 220 |
| 40.3 | Mission to Gentile world | Acts 11:1 | 'The apostles and the followers heard that Gentiles had accepted God's message' | 2,370,000 | 92 | 25,500 | 3,338 | 9 | 13.1 | 220 |
| 42.2 | Conversions in Antioch | Acts 11:21 | 'A great number that believed turned to the Lord' (RSV) | 2,490,000 | 76 | 32,200 | 4,207 | 12 | 13.1 | 230 |
| 43.2 | Ongoing conversions | Acts 11:24 | 'Many more people turned to the Lord' ('A large company was added', RSV) | 2,550,000 | 70 | 36,000 | 4,248 | 12 | 11.8 | 240 |
| 44.2 | Evangelization spreads | Acts 12:24 | 'God's message kept spreading' ('grew and multiplied', RSV) | 2,620,000 | 65 | 40,000 | 4,444 | 12 | 11.1 | 250 |
| 45.1 | Paul's 1st missionary journey | Acts 13:43 | 'Many Jews and devout converts to Judaism followed Paul and Barnabas' (RSV) | 2,680,000 | 60 | 44,000 | 4,915 | 13 | 11.2 | 250 |
| 46.1 | Paul's global mandate | Acts 13:47 | 'Take the saving power of God to people everywhere on Earth' | 2,740,000 | 55 | 49,000 | 5,568 | 15 | 11.4 | 260 |
| 47.1 | Saturating regions | Acts 13:49 | 'The message about the Lord spread all over that region' | 2,810,000 | 51 | 54,000 | 5,510 | 15 | 10.2 | 260 |
| 48 | Acceptance and rejection | Acts 14:1 | 'Many Jews and Gentiles put their faith in the Lord' | 2,880,000 | 48 | 59,000 | 6,100 | 17 | 10.3 | 270 |
| 50 | Paul's 2nd missionary journey | Acts 16:5 | 'The churches were strengthened in the faith and increased in numbers daily' | 3,030,000 | 42 | 71,000 | 6,886 | 19 | 9.7 | 280 |
| 51.2 | Corinthians hear Paul | Acts 18:8 | 'Many of the Corinthians hearing Paul believed and were baptized' (RSV) | 3,120,000 | 39 | 78,000 | 6,358 | 17 | 8.2 | 290 |
| 51.8 | City-wide faith at Corinth | Acts 18:10 | 'The Lord said… "Many people in this city belong to Me" ' | 3,160,000 | 38 | 82,000 | 7,128 | 20 | 8.7 | 290 |
| 52.4 | India reached | – | First missionaries (Thomas and party) reach India | 3,210,000 | 36 | 86,000 | 7,105 | 19 | 8.3 | 300 |
| 53.1 | Paul's 3rd missionary journey | Acts 19:9 | Normal evangelism—proclamation 'every day for two years' | 3,270,000 | 35 | 91,000 | 7,651 | 21 | 8.4 | 340 |
| 55.5 | Asia Minor evangelized | Acts 19:10 | 'Every Jew and Gentile in Asia had heard the Lord's message' | 3,470,000 | 31 | 110,000 | 9,044 | 25 | 8.2 | 350 |
| 56.5 | Paul's ministry in Ephesus | Acts 19:20 | 'The Lord's message spread and became even more powerful' | 3,560,000 | 29 | 118,000 | 8,582 | 24 | 7.3 | 400 |
| 57.4 | James' report to Paul | Acts 21:20 | 'See how many tens of thousands of our people have become followers' | 3,640,000 | 28 | 125,000 | 8,266 | 23 | 6.6 | 450 |
| 58 | Balkans reached | Romans 15:19 | From Jerusalem to Illyricum Paul had 'fully preached the gospel' | 3,700,000 | 27 | 130,000 | 8,782 | 24 | 6.8 | 500 |
| 62 | Paul evangelizes in Rome | Acts 28:23 | 'Many came to [Paul] in great numbers' (RSV) | 4,090,000 | 23 | 170,000 | 11,792 | 32 | 6.9 | 1000 |
| 64 | Nero's persecution | | 1st Roman Imperial Persecution: 5,000 executed | 4,300,000 | 22 | 190,000 | 10,866 | 30 | 5.7 | 5,500 |
| 70 | Sack of Jerusalem | | Titus obliterates Jerusalem, crucifies 10,000, kills 600,000 | 5,000,000 | 18 | 270,000 | 16,285 | 45 | 6.0 | 17,000 |
| 80 | Ephesus main center of mission | | Under Apostle John ongoing struggle against influence of Diana queen of heaven | 6,420,000 | 14 | 440,000 | 22,021 | 60 | 5.0 | 18,000 |
| 90 | Domitian's persecution | | 2nd Roman Imperial Persecution, over emperor-worship as 'Our Lord and God' | 8,250,000 | 12 | 640,000 | 24,435 | 67 | 3.8 | 20,000 |
| 100 | Massive spread of churches | | Christians predominantly urban, spreading rapidly along trade routes | 10,600,000 | 12 | 800,000 | 18,052 | 49 | 2.3 | 53,000 |
| 200 | Severus' persecution | | 5th Roman Imperial Persecution: for months, 100 a day martyred in Thebes | 17,760,000 | 2.81 | 4,660,000 | 82,844 | 227 | 1.8 | 177,000 |
| 300 | Diocletian's persecution | | 10th and final Roman Imperial Persecution | 32,820,000 | 1.34 | 14,010,000 | 155,068 | 425 | 1.1 | 627,000 |
| 350 | Shapur II's persecutions | | Great Persian Persecutions: 100,000 believers martyred | 42,000,000 | 1.00 | 21,000,000 | 170,685 | 468 | 0.8 | 1,200,000 |
| 400 | Continued expansion across Asia | | Christians now 25% of population in Persian Empire and 80% of Roman Empire | 45,920,000 | 0.81 | 25,320,000 | 94,911 | 260 | 0.4 | 1,538,000 |
| 500 | The Dark Ages begin | | Disappearance of urban life; collapse of Christian enthusiasm and mission | 59,400,000 | 0.57 | 37,800,000 | 151,774 | 416 | 0.4 | 2,102,000 |
| 600 | Rise of militant Islam | | Muslim conquest complete in 20 years; 1000s of churches destroyed | 64,450,000 | 0.60 | 40,400,000 | 26,883 | 74 | 0.1 | 2,197,000 |
| 700 | China reached | | Nestorians reach Hsian, churches spread; but by 845 all obliterated. | 60,050,000 | 0.48 | 40,570,000 | 1,704 | 5 | 0.0 | 2,423,000 |
| 800 | Church in Africa destroyed | | Saracens destroy Christianity and its 1,200 bishoprics across North Africa | 57,530,000 | 0.41 | 40,870,000 | 3,011 | 8 | 0.0 | 2,568,000 |
| 900 | Christian losses proliferate | | 50% of former Christendom now under Islamic rule | 57,270,000 | 0.40 | 40,830,000 | -400 | -1 | 0.0 | 2,877,000 |
| 1000 | All Europe now evangelized | | Prussians and Magyars, last remaining pagans in Europe, become christianized | 56,170,000 | 0.26 | 44,670,000 | 40,170 | 110 | 0.1 | 3,064,000 |
| 1100 | End of the Dark Ages | | Renewal of Europe's intellectual life reinvigorates Christianity | 63,810,000 | 0.23 | 51,960,000 | 78,608 | 215 | 0.2 | 3,375,000 |
| 1200 | Genghiz Khan's massacres | | Mongol emperors massacre 7 million Christians across Asia | 81,310,000 | 0.24 | 65,710,000 | 154,453 | 423 | 0.2 | 3,727,000 |
| 1300 | Kublai Khan requests baptism | | Empire of 80 million asks for missions; ignored; greatest missed opportunity ever | 102,260,000 | 0.22 | 83,910,000 | 205,406 | 563 | 0.2 | 11,161,000 |
| 1400 | Massive losses by plague | | Christians killed: 5 million by Tamerlane, 25 million by Black Death | 66,660,000 | 0.18 | 56,730,000 | -221,631 | -607 | -0.4 | 16,560,000 |
| 1500 | Losses to Islam continue | | Fall of Constantinople to Ottoman Turkish Empire | 86,750,000 | 0.14 | 75,890,000 | 221,148 | 606 | 0.3 | 17,398,000 |
| 1600 | Expansion by Spain and Portugal | | Huge colonial empires baptize millions of Amerindians, Asians, Africans | 114,660,000 | 0.14 | 100,440,000 | 281,904 | 772 | 0.3 | 21,221,000 |
| 1700 | Awakenings and revivals | | Evangelical Revival begins under Wesleys; many mission agencies are begun | 148,300,000 | 0.14 | 130,110,000 | 337,186 | 924 | 0.3 | 21,750,000 |
| 1800 | Great Century of missions begins | | New mission fields around the world are opened | 229,305,000 | 0.12 | 204,980,000 | 933,821 | 2558 | 0.5 | 22,038,000 |
| 1900 | Vast range of new ministries | | Pentecostal/Charismatic/Neocharismatic Renewal erupts across world | 739,954,000 | 0.33 | 558,132,000 | 5,618,808 | 15394 | 1.0 | 24,092,000 |
| 2000 | Great Commission closure | | 1,500 global plans fail to evangelize world's 1.6 billion unevangelized | 4,425,674,000 | 1.21 | 1,999,564,000 | 25,679,715 | 70355 | 1.3 | 69,420,000 |
| 2100 | Century of mission through Asians | | Asia's churches (China,India) dominate global mission expansion | 8,250,113,000 | 1.30 | 3,583,017,000 | 20,959,947 | 57425 | 0.6 | 90,000,000 |
| 2200 | Century of servant mission | | End of global population explosion; churches clearer on servant role | 8,792,809,000 | 1.29 | 3,843,539,000 | 2,698,664 | 7394 | 0.1 | 110,000,000 |

## NON-NUMERIC USAGES

Over 50,000 books use the first 3 definitions of 'trends', A, B, and C, which avoid numbers and statistics and their analysis.

*Trend A.* **General direction**. Historians writing on the fortunes of the Christian faith over its 20 centuries of existence have generally followed the main non-numeric dictionary definitions in their use of the concept 'trend'. Numbers and statistics, though often copiously incorporated, are seldom added up or analyzed to produce clear trend rates. Secular studies are seldom numeric. Two standard works are: *Megatrends: 10 new directions transforming our lives* (1982); and *Megatrends for women* (1993). And two such works dealing with religion are: *Future trends: religion, politics, psychology* (1983); and *Religion and modern social trends* (1938).

*Trend B.* **Status description**. Large numbers of Christian, Muslim, and other religion studies, though often clearly scholarly, use the word 'trends' to mean little or no more than 'current issues' or 'current status'. In such works there is no numeric treatment, no reference to any clearly stated period of time, nor any sequence of related events. If therefore one does not speak of any line of development, or sequence of events, then one can only be speaking of trends in the vaguest of senses. The earliest of such books include: *Trends of thought and Christian truth* (1915); also *A critical evaluation of the modernist trends in Hinduism* (1925). From after that era were *Religious trends in modern China* (1953); *Modern trends in world religions* (1934); *Modern trends in Siamese culture: religion* (1942); *Trends in theology, 1870-1970* (1970); *Major trends in Jewish mysticism* (1953); *Contemporary trends in Christology* (1958); *Present trends among the Disciples* (1930).

Recent books in this category include: *New trends and developments in African religions* (1998); *Muslim religious trends in Kashmir in modern times* (1997); *Religious trends in Israel* (1983); *Religious trends in Singapore, with special reference to Christianity* (1982); *New trends in black theology* (1972); *Trends in American eschatology* (1976); *New evangelism: a review of trends, developments, and events during 1990* (1991).

Perhaps the best example of vague usage of 'trends' in literature on Christian mission is an otherwise excellent and influential series from the years 1976-1981 entitled *Mission trends, Nos. 1-5*. These 5 books marshalled ground-breaking articles contributed by 124 Christian leaders and scholars. Subtitles were: *No. 1 Crucial issues in mission today; No. 2 Evangelization; No. 3 Third World theologies; No. 4 Liberation theologies in North America and Europe; and No. 5 Faith meets faith*. The subject of numerical data was raised only by the editor, and only once, in his opening *No. 1* (1974: 138-139). There he drew attention to the drastically falling numbers of foreign missionaries being sent out from the USA. Subsequently, none of the 124 contributors took up his lead, and in fact numbers and statistics were ignored in virtually the entire series.

*Trend C.* **Time period with title**. Many writers on Christian subjects assist the reader by following a chronological sequence and by dividing up their material by time periods to each of which they give a series of short titles. Among the best-known historical works on global Christianity employing this aid are K.S. Latourette's 7-volume series *A history of the expansion of Christianity* (1937-45), and also his *A history of Christianity* (1953), and *Christianity throughout the ages* (1965). In these he divided the 20 centuries of Christian history into 10 clearly-dated and aptly-titled epochs. This schema, slightly modified and extended, is followed in the present *World Christian trends*, Part 2 "CosmoChronology". And this defining of a clearly-dated period plus a short 3- or 4-word descriptive title is also followed here in Table 7–1, columns 1 and 2.

*Trend D.* **Descriptive sentences**. We can now move toward the construction of tables to illustrate more clearly-defined meanings of 'trend'. This is done in Table 7–1, column 4, by compiling a series of short, dated sentences on the subject in question (in this case the worldwide expansion of Christianity). Here the 1st century AD is described by means of a sequence of 40 short sentences of 10 to15 words each (in column 4) covering the New Testament period from AD 30 to AD 62 by means of precise Scriptural references (in column 3), with each's related year (in column 1).

Although these columns 1-4 indicate that massive trends are taking place, they remain non-numeric trends since those columns have no numeric data to permit mathematical analysis. Numeric usages will now be examined.

## NUMERIC USAGES

*Trend E.* **Measurement**. There is a vast range of numeric studies—at least 20,000 distinct books by the year 2000. The most comprehensive in scope is: *Global trends: the world almanac of development and peace* (1994), with scores of tables, maps, with a time axis, and graphics. This presents a vast amount of data on 7 major subjects: world development, world order, world society (including human rights), world peace, world economy, world ecology, and world culture (including religion).

A second landmark on this subject, published in 1990, was The United Nations' book *Global outlook 2000: an economic, social, and environmental perspective*. This study grew out of work prepared for the UN General Assembly on macroeconomic variables of the world economy. It employed the Global Econometric Model (GEM) of the UN Secretariat. Chapter headings included 'Long-term trends, 1960-1990', 'Historical trends', 'Future trends in energy consumption and production', 'Demographic and labour force trends and issues', 'Trends in the growth and function of urban areas', 'Projection of enrollment trends' (in schools), 'Trends in life expectancy and mortality', and 'Trends in social welfare policy'.

In 340 pages the book provided a wealth of statistics, statistical trends, and their interpretations on the whole spectrum of secular issues within the UN's orbit. Nothing on religion was dealt with, as has been UN policy from its foundation.

Other books are valuable for setting forth usable methodologies for tracking and measuring trends. These include *Trend tracking: the system to profit from today's trends* (1990); *Tracking tomorrow's trends: what we think about our lives and our future* (1986); *The first measured century: an illustrated guide to trends in America, 1900-2000* (2000).

Other works involving religious measurement include: *Trends in the geography of belief systems* (1987); *Trends in the geography of pilgrimages* (1987). A fuller list is given in the bibliography at the end of this Part 7.

There is a no single procedure for arriving at numerical trend figures. It all depends on what types of statistical data are available. In Table 7–1, our starting points are (1) numbers and indicators of rapid growth in its sequence of sentences (column 4), (2) a handful of data on followers during AD 30-62 (column 7), (3) a vast mass of census and other statistical data from the modern period (AD 1900-AD 2000), (4) a number of reasonably reliable totals of Christians at intermediate points (AD 350, 1000, 1500, 1800), and (5) a proven precise mathematical framework or grid that data must be situated in. This grid here is based on exponential growth over all longer or shorter periods of time.

In this case, column 7 was constructed first, guided by columns 4, 10, 11; column 10 was deduced from column 7; column 8 from column 7; and column 9 (numeric increase per day) by dividing column 8 by 365.

*Trend F.* **Quantification**. If a decision has been reached to undertake measurement of any trend, a researcher can find ways to quantify categories which in many cases will never have been measured before. The starting point is to employ a very precise definition and then to create imaginative ways to relate it to quantities. One example comes from the continent-wide spread of the African Independent Churches. Few censuses or headcounts of followers have been possible. However, many churches publish unique hymnals for their members' use. Researchers therefore quantified members by counting the number of hymnals printed, sold, circulated or in regular use. From this has emerged today's Africa-wide enumeration of 65 million AIC members.

A surprisingly vast amount of hard statistical data exists on a large number of religious variables. Table 7–2 shows 26 of the main variables necessary to portray the expansion of Christianity from AD 30 to AD 2200 and does this for each of the globe's 28 basic geopolitical areas. This produces a grand total of 16,016 numerical trend figures. This mass of data can be fitted comfortably into 7 pages as Table 7–2 shows.

*Trend G.* **Statistics at 2 points in time**. Table 7–1, column 7 and Table 7–2, row 'Christians' consist of precise totals for the number of followers at 60 different years. If the column is inspected visually the reader can easily—without any further mathematics—get an impression of how its growth is faring.

The Gallup Organization has a 70-year record of creating and publishing statistics on religion in the USA and more recently in Europe and other continents. Among its recent books are: *Surveying the religious landscape: trends in U.S. beliefs* (1999), and *Emerging trends in religion in America* (1973, updated irregularly); also *Seven trends facing the church in 1988 and beyond* (1988). Since their entire literature is meticulously defined, dated, and explained, the production of precise trend statistics on any of the subjects they cover becomes relatively easy.

*Trend H.* **Graphic measures**. Graph 7-1 illustrates in diagrammatic form on semi-logarithmic paper the church growth data in Tables 7-1 and 7-2. Lines represent world population, number of live Christians, number of all Christians ever, number of the evangelized, number of unorganized charismatics, numbers of new Christian martyrs each year, and number of martyred Christians ever. All start from zero with very high rates of increase per year. For instance, 100% p.a. is equivalent to getting a first convert on 1 January in Year 1, followed by a second in January one year later and two more converts after one more year.

*Trend I.* **Linear rates**. In Table 7–1 this method is used to derive intermediate points in column 5 (evangelized persons) where data support is weak. The variable describes the extent of Christian influence and the spread across the world of awareness of Christianity, Christ, and the gospel.

The method is easy and quick to work out by mental arithmetic. In Tables 7-1 and 7-2, the linear growth of followers from the year 1900 to 2000 is $(1,999,600,000 - 558,100,000)/100 = 14,415,000$ every year including in AD 2000. The method is not used in our table because we use the more accurate exponential growth rate, which as column 8 indicates, gives in AD 2000 a total growth of 25,679,700. This is almost double the linear figure.

*Trend J.* **Exponential growth rates**. Table 7–1, column 10 and Table 7–2 'Christian growth rate, % p.a.' give the exponential rate of increase for each of the periods shown separated by 2 points in time.

*Trend K.* **Yearly increase**. This variable is more easily visualized than the rate in Trend J. It consists of the number of new followers each year at the end of a time period during which the exponential growth rate has been as shown in column 10 of Table 7–1. Multiplying this rate (divided by 100) by the number of followers in column 7 on that line gives the increase per year as shown in column 8. Likewise with Table 7–2: the line is 'Christian nett increase p.a., millions'.

At this point clear thinking on the meaning of 'increase' is needed. 'Christian nett increase p.a.', elaborated, means 'Gains (births + converts) minus losses (deaths + defectors)'. The word 'nett' is added to avoid a reader thinking 'increase' here means only 'births' or 'converts' without 'deaths' or 'defectors'..

*Trend L.* **Daily increase**. In Table 7–1, the increase per year in column 8 is divided by 365 to produce the daily rate in column 9, which is the increase per day in the number of followers at that point in time. This leads to a major analytical finding, discussed below.

*Trend M.* **Martyrs**. Shown in Table 7–1 as the final column 10, this variable is not directly related to, or derived from columns 5-9. It is however indirectly related and it is included because it is readily measurable and quantifiable (see data in Table 4-10, columns 1 to 11). At the same time, it is valuable evidence of the magnitude of the number of Christians year by year.

An important benefit of this column and its magnitude is that it corrects a major scholarly misunderstanding. Some Western historians of the rise of Christianity have ignored the number of martyrs reported here as exaggerated. The reason lies in their own omission of Egyptian martyrs of the Coptic Orthodox tradition. The 8-volume authority, *The Coptic encyclopedia* edited by Aziz S. Atiya (Macmillan, 1991) has 3 separate articles on Coptic martyrs, martyrdom, and martyrology. These categorically state and document the fact that the first 3 centuries of savage persecutions and killings culminated in the Coptic Age of Persecution with its Anno Martyrii calendar in AD 284. The accepted total of all martyrs in Egypt by the end of the 10 Roman Imperial Persecutions in AD 320 is stated as one million Coptic Christian men and women from all walks of life, including many clergy, bishops, patriarchs, and scholars. The *Coptic encyclopedia* goes on to list and enumerate this further, with listings and biographies of some 320 of these Coptic martyrs. Similar totals and details are given in Part 4 "Martyrology" in Tables 4-10 to 4-13.

### EXPOSITION OF TABLE 7–1

#### Sparse but totally adequate data
From several points of view the total data at our disposal is very thin. It seems inadequate. Likewise to try to compress this vast 20-century story into a single table with 39 Scripture verses and 67 historical lines seems too ambitious. But the Four Gospels themselves set the precedent. They reduce, select, summarize.

#### The need for an overall grid
This table therefore supplies a compact one-page overview of the whole 20 centuries of Christian history, beginning with a detailed covering of the New Testament era and the 1st century AD. Its figures of the numbers of Christians are based upon 4 widely-agreed considerations: (a) a clear starting-point in AD 33 when on the Day of Pentecost 3,000 Jews from this worldwide diaspora were converted and baptized in 'the birthday of the church'; (b) the detailed statistical coverage of 20th-century Christianity from 1900's 558 million church members to AD 2000's 1,999 million, described here in Part 1 et alia; (c) a large number of numerically authenticated intermediate points such as the ballpark figure of 21 million or thereabouts after Constantine's reign by AD 350, or the Christian megadeaths in Europe's Black Death from 1347 to 1353 killing 75 millions of Christians and non-Christians, and millions more under Tamerlane's massacres; and (d) the need for an overall mathematical rationale or grid to link convincingly each and all of these numbers as an organic series across the 20 centuries.

#### Parallels to cosmology and creation
There are striking parallels between the creation and expansion of the universe and creation and expansion of the Christian church. We can observe 4 stages. (1) In cosmology as understood by most scientists and many Christians (see Part 2 "CosmoChronology"), first came the zero of cosmic time, the Big Bang. Then, (2) this was followed after $10^{-35}$ seconds by a massive inflation involving unimaginably high temperatures during which the primordial fireball exploded outwards. (3) Next, the rates of temperature rapidly fell. Finally, (4) these early stages were succeeded by 15 billion years in which expansion slowed, life emerged, and eventually conditions reached the situation of today's expanding universe.

These 4 event-stages are strikingly similar to the rise and expansion of Christianity. (1) The creation of the church began with the Day of Pentecost in Jerusalem with its sudden, massive, descent of the Holy Spirit with conversion and baptism of 3,000 Jews from across the worldwide Jewish diaspora. (2) The whole phenomenon was described by observers in terms of the Holy Spirit as fire, with tongues of fire visible on all the converts. Then (3) over the next 2 generations there took place rapid decline of rates of expansion and growth to seemingly very small rates of increase each day. And (4) subsequently there has been the passage of vast centuries of time with, numerically, very little apparently happening. One could conclude that God seems to be in no particular need to hurry.

#### A massive expanding people movement
The evidence makes it clear that a truly momentous creative movement took place in the generation after Pentecost, from AD 33 to the close of Paul's ministry in AD 64. The main historical document is The Acts of the Apostles. In Table 7–1, column 4 sets out 39 short sentences describing the expansion from 39 Scripture verses mostly from The Acts. These abound in movement, drama, travel, action, expansion. The column records 22 large-scale superlatives describing the excitement of this early period. Here in chronological order are the 22 Scripture phrases extracted verbatim from various English Bible versions:

"many men and women, multitudes, in one house after another, a lot of people, multiplied greatly, a great many priests, went everywhere preaching, grew in numbers, everyone in Joppa, large influx, a great number, a large company, grew and multiplied, people everywhere on Earth, all over that region, increased in numbers, 'Many people in this city belong to Me', every day for 2 years, every Gentile in Asia, tens of thousands of our people, fully preached, in great numbers..."

Some analysts of this period have taken the easy route of dismissing all the above descriptive phrases as improbable fiction dreamed up by early Christians. In that case someone must explain how this fiction has grown to today's 2 billion church members. It makes far more sense to accept the veracity of the above description of massive happenings as recorded by eye-witnesses.

#### A daily minimum of conversions
Here we meet an extraordinary paradox. Despite the massive flurry of activity and results just listed above, it appears from our mathematical grid that only a handful of new converts were being made each day. In fact, Table 7–1 column 9 indicates that average daily converts remained as no more than single-digit (under 10) for the first 84 months or 7 years of church expansion, and remained as no more than double-digit (under 100) to the end of the 1st century reaching 49 per day by AD 100. Thereafter, daily converts remained no more than triple-digit (under 1,000) throughout the Dark Ages, Middle Ages, and Reformation period right up to the year 1700. This seemingly interminable slow growth has worried countless Christians since the 7 Apostles by Lake Tiberias lost patience hanging around for the next appearance of the Risen Christ and decided instead with Peter to get on with their profession as fishermen (John 21:3). But this slow development of God's plans occurs throughout God's creation: the 15 billion years before the human race appears, the 12 centuries after Moses before the Incarnation, Jesus's 30 years of silence growing up in Nazareth, the 40 days of the Risen Lord's unexpectedly unpredictable appearances. So it should not be surprising to find the growth of the Christian faith following the same pattern.

#### The Holy Spirit's timetable is slow but sure
The reaction of some readers to Table 7–1's columns 8 and 9 is often ambivalent. Comment is twofold. To many readers, (1) the numbers in column 8 seem surprisingly high, surely too high for the sparse historical evidence in each year; but also (2) to the same readers the numbers in column 9 seem surprisingly low, surely too low for the evidence. In fact, of course, the 2 columns express identical data.

A theological exegesis can be constructed at this point. The Acts of the Apostles is a historico-theological narrative describing the extraordinary rise of the Christian movement. The sequence of sentences in column 4 gives only a few clues as to the processes going on. It does however provide a major clue not brought out until column 9.

Dominant throughout this narrative, yet often hidden from immediate view, is the person and work of the Holy Spirit. He is seen speaking, empowering, guiding, directing, commanding, initiating, forbidding. He is also seen selecting a small number of key events and key persons for particular roles at particular moments. First comes the enormous manifestation of God's power and purpose on the Day of Pentecost. Thousands of Jews from across the Jewish diaspora, throughout the Roman empire and beyond, had gathered there for the Jewish festival of wheat harvest called Pentecost. Suddenly the Holy Spirit 'took control of everyone' as he fell on the Lord's followers with tongues of fire, who began speaking in new and unknown languages. Three thousand hearers were converted and baptized. Soon after, they all left for their home countries, where we can visualize them immediately evangelizing wives, family, colleagues, and friends. Over the next 10 years these converts must have converted and baptized thousands more.

The Holy Spirit nevertheless remains mainly out of sight in the background, despite being mentioned 65 times throughout the Acts of the Apostles. God's whole operation is almost leisurely or timeless. In Old Testament times it was 2,000 years after Abraham and 1,000 years after David and Solomon before the Messiah finally came. Throughout that time the Holy Spirit called or empowered a handful of prophets on a handful of occasions. It was the same with the Forty Days of the Risen Christ's appearances—on the first Sunday after the Resurrection, then the next Sunday, much later the breakfast on Lake Tiberias.

It is the same with the early growth of the church—a massive, explosive start at Pentecost, then a handful of disciples selected and called out. One can imagine the process: the Holy Spirit deciding 'Today We will convert seven people: Saul of Tarsus, those 2 soldiers with him, that family in Jerusalem, that slave in Rome'.

To return to Table 7–1, column 9: these figures show the church growing by an average of only 6, 7, 8, or 9 converts a day from Pentecost to AD 40 seven years later, then increasing very gradually after, only reaching 45 a day by the time Jerusalem was destroyed in AD 70, and 49 a day by the end of the 1st century.

Yet the remarkable fact becomes evident that this minuscule daily increase produced the massive church of 0.8 million followers by AD 100 and 21 million by AD 350. It is the main trend variable explaining the numerical capture of the Roman empire by Christianity.

#### The Holy Spirit remains in full control
It seems a clear deduction that the expansion of the Christian faith has proceeded from the start under the invisible, background control of the Holy Spirit. It is not surprising therefore that in the end this slow day-by-day process turns out to be the sure way for tens to become 100s, 100s to become 1000s, 1000s to become millions, up to today's church of 2 billion believers.

#### Daily increments provide the mechanism
The immense power of minute changes implemented unfailingly day by day has parallels throughout life and nature. In the case of church growth, it is clear from Table 7–1 that it solves the immense problem mentioned earlier—of how Christians grew from 3,000 to 2 billion in 20 centuries.

There is no need therefore for the hypothetical sudden mass movement into the church in the late 3rd century, postulated by Harnack and other historians as essential to explain the massive numbers by Constantine's reign. Neither is it necessary to postulate a single fixed growth rate from Pentecost to Constantine. Sociologist R. Stark showed in his study *The rise of Christianity* (1996) that a fixed annual growth rate of 3.4% would take Christians from his starting point of 1,000 Christians by AD 40 to 30 million by AD 350. But that assumption produces only 7,000 Christians by AD 100, with an unlikely annual increase then of only 214 converts giving a daily figure of 0.7. The whole movement had become immensely more influential by that time.

What actually happens with these huge religious movements is what is portrayed in Graph 7-1. In the earliest days, annual and daily rates of increase are enormous. A situation where the first convert is followed by a second a year later, then 2 more after a further year, is an annual growth rate of 100%. Then as the days, months, and years pass, these high rates gradually decrease to zero as the number of believers meet natural barriers or high natural ceilings ending when the entire population has become 100% followers.

#### The slow progress of evangelization
Table 7–1 column 5 estimates the number of persons who have heard the gospel, proclaimed publicly or in private, whether they have responded by becoming believers or not. Running one's eye down this column to perceive trends reveals a surprising finding: the number of evangelized persons does not increase as dramatically as does the number of Christians in column 7. In fact the evangelized grow only very slowly and stay more or less unchanged between 2

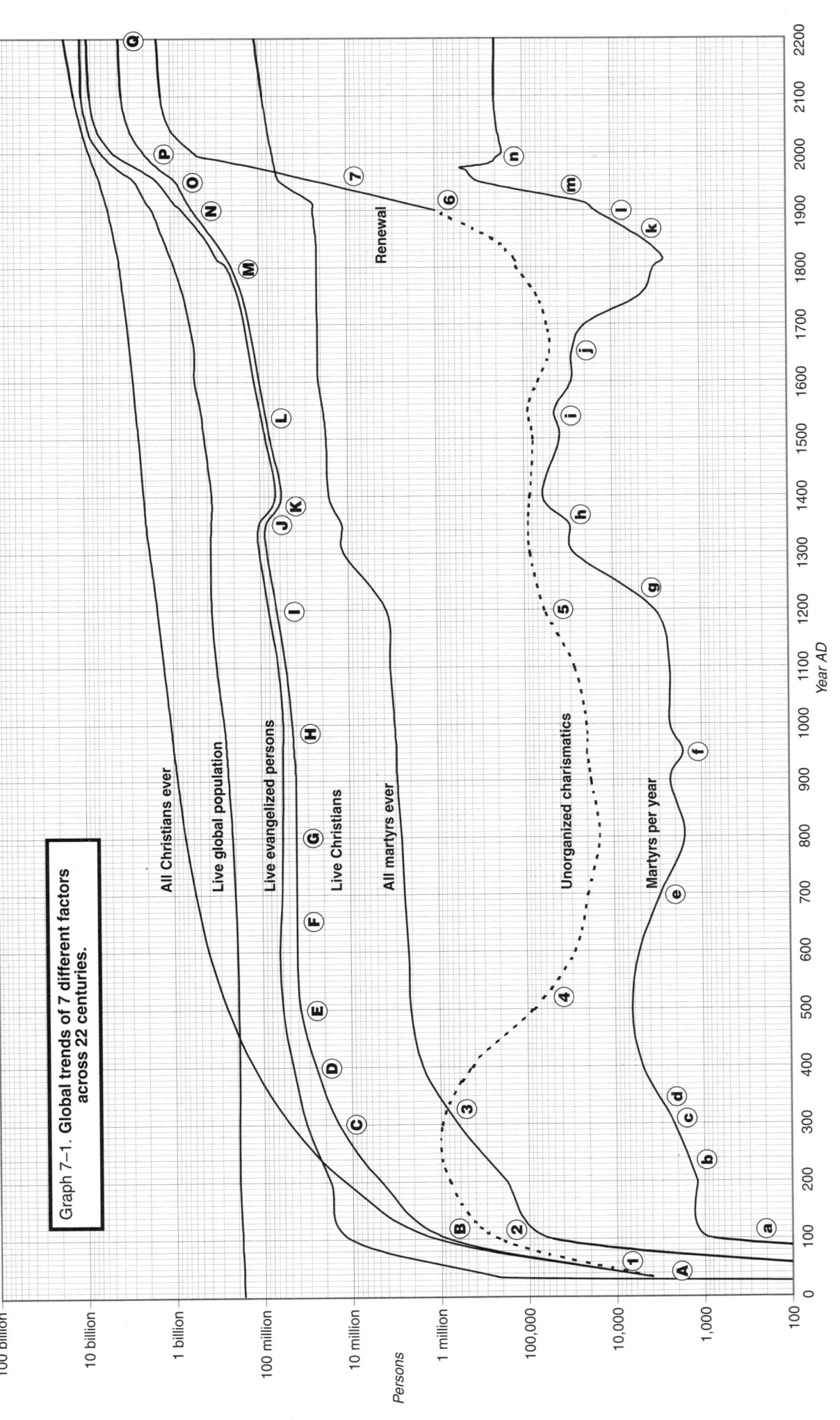

Graph 7–1. Global trends of 7 different factors across 22 centuries.

**CHRISTIANS**

A = AD 30   Jesus begins ministry in Palestine
B =    100   Church grows in North Africa, Western Asia, and Southern Europe
C =    313   Edict of Milan ends persecution of Christians
D =    400   Roman Empire over 50% Christian
E =    500   Germanic tribes convert to Christianity; Celtic missions begin
F =    650   Church of the East reaches China; Islam spreads to North Africa
G =    800   Vikings invade Europe and are eventually converted to Christianity
H =    988   Mass conversion of the Rus under Vladimir
I =   1200   Friars spread message across Europe
J =   1350   Black Death kills 75 million in Europe and Asia
K =   1380   Tamerlane wipes out Church of the East

L =   1540   Roman Catholic missions to Africa, America, and Asia
M =   1800   Protestant missions begin
N =   1900   Tribal religionists convert to Christianity in large numbers
O =   1950   Independent churches in Africa and Asia grow rapidly
P =   2000   World is 33% Christian, 73% evangelized; worldwide growth begins to rapidly taper off as population explosion ends.
Q =   2200   World is 36% Christian, 83% evangelized

**MARTYRDOM**

a = AD 64   First five Roman Imperial Persecutions
b =    235   Second five Roman Imperial Persecutions intensify culminating with Diocletian's

c =    305   Over 700,000 Coptic Christians killed
d =    337   Persian persecutions of Nestorians begin; continue until 628
e =    698   Chinese persecutions of Nestorians begin; continue until 845
f =    950   Muslim persecution of Christians in the Middle East and North Africa intensifies
g =   1214   Genghiz Khan begins massacre of Christians in Central Asia
h =   1358   Tamerlane begins destroying Church of the East across Asia
i =   1536   Millions of Amerindians baptized and later slaughtered
j =   1649   Over 200,000 Japanese Christians martyred
k =   1862   Chinese annihilate Taiping quasi-Christians
l =   1894   Armenian Christians in Turkey massacred

m = 1921   Soviet Communists begin largest massacre of Christians ever
n = 1995   Christians of southern Sudan starved to death by Muslim government

**PENTECOSTAL/CHARISMATIC RENEWAL**

1 = AD 33   Holy Spirit poured out on Day of Pentecost
2 =    100   Early believers practice gifts of the Spirit
3 =    320   Interest in spiritual gifts declines as Christianity takes on official status in Roman Empire
4 =    520   Celtic missions movement mildly charismatic
5 =   1200   Many Franciscan and Dominican friars practice spiritual gifts
6 =   1900   Pentecostal movement begins in USA
7 =   1950   Independent churches around the world practice gifts of the Spirit

and 5 million from the day of Pentecost in AD 33 up to the destruction of Jerusalem under Titus in AD 70. An explanation might be as follows.

During Jesus' ministry he evangelized virtually the whole of Palestine's population of 800,000. Everybody had heard of him and his message of the kingdom of God. Then at Pentecost, 3,000 Jewish pilgrims were converted and baptized, after which they returned home to evangelize wives, families, friends, and co-religionists in the worldwide diaspora. By this time the total evangelized persons can be estimated at 2 million. But the early church up to AD 70 remained, at 270,000, small enough for it not to influence the wider population of the Roman empire until later—10,600,000 by AD 100.

### Christian personal outreach declines
Examination of Table 7–1's column 6 reveals another major trend: the number of non-Christians becoming evangelized per Christian fell markedly from the Day of Pentecost onwards. In fact it continued to fall throughout 18 centuries reaching its lowest point of 0.12 per Christian in the year 1800. The whole of Christian history is often portrayed by church historians as the history of the obedience of Christians fulfilling Christ's Great Commission. Instead, this trend portrays it as 18 centuries of the disobedience of Christians failing to obey Christ's central command to the church.

### Decline of Christianity: the Dark and Middle Ages
The first half of Table 7–1 has set forth the Apostolic age as described by eyewitnesses at the time up to AD 62. The rest of the table now deals with the historical evolution of the faith over the decades AD 70 to AD 100 and then at the end of every subsequent century. The trends that follow, particularly outreach per Christian, are widely noted by scholars and other observers. Outreach fell drastically, to less than 1.0 from Constantine's reign right through to AD 2000. The Christian growth rate also fell drastically from 6.9% p.a. in AD 62, to 1.1% p.a. in AD 300, then fell below this level—usually drastically below—throughout history right up to AD 2000 and beyond.

These long-term trends can be seen visually in Graph 7-1. The church's predicament is most evident when one compares the 2 layers above the line 'live Christians'. The first layer above consists of World B—the number of evangelized non-Christians, which remains minute right up to the 20th century. This is a portrayal of Christian lukewarmness, even of disobedience. The next layer above is World A, the number of unevangelized persons unaware of Christianity, Christ, or the gospel. This is a portrayal of the challenge to Christians, the unfinished task. This overall trend indicates that from AD 350 to 1900 Christians largely ignored the challenge presented by World A. Theologically, the mass of Christians ignored mission and evangelism.

### Persecution and martyrdom
It is often thought that, after the end of the 10 great Roman Imperial Persecutions in AD 312, Christianity became the established religion and the quality of Christian living went into decline. But in point of fact persecution and martyrdom did not end in AD 312 but have continued up to the present at the same global level of 0.8% of all Christians, though continually moving to different continents and countries. The tyrants have become more diverse—Genghiz Khan, Tamerlane, Stalin, Hitler, Mao Zedong. Instead, in Graph 7-1 a trend can be observed linking martyrdom with the rise and fall of charismatics over the centuries and eventually, in the 20th century with the Pentecostal/Charismatic/Neocharismatic Renewal in the Holy Spirit.

### COVERAGE BY TABLES 7-1 AND 7-2

#### A large variety of variables and trends
These 2 tables emerge from a single common database and have wide coverage. Together they span 22 centuries with 76 specific year dates (54 in Table 7–1, 22 in Table 7–2). While the first table covers only the

whole globe, the second presents 27 more subtables covering the world's 28 geopolitical areas. As defined by the United Nations, these are the 20 regions of the world, the 7 continents (termed 'major areas'), and the whole globe itself. Between them the tables represent a database containing a vast number of trends as understood here; 195 are non-numeric trends and the rest numeric. Table 7–1 contains 540 trend numbers unique to it; Table 7–2 has 16,016. Together they include all the 13 varieties of trends described earlier, 4 non-numeric (Trends A-D) and 9 numeric (Trends E-M). They also present 31 different variables: 11 in Table 7–1 (6 being shared), and 26 in Table 7–2.

### Exposition of Table 7–2's 26 variables
Each of the 28 subtables sets out 26 data subjects. The 10 in italics below are trends proper, per annum. The 26 can be described under the following 6 headings.

| Subject | Trend variables |
|---|---|
| 1. Total population: | number, *rate, increase* |
| 2. Evangelized population: | number, percent, ratio |
| 3. Christians (World C): | number, the 6 megablocs |
| 4. Christians: | number, *rate, increase, gains, losses* |
| 5. World B (evangelized non-Christians): | number, percent, *rate, increase* |
| 6. World A (unevangelized): | number, percent, *rate, increase* |

### 6,160 spot trends
Table 7–2 contains 728 lines across the page, each describing one variable. The 10 items above in italics describe the value of the trend at each specific point or spot in the horizontal scale of years, hence are termed here 'spot trends'.

### 9,856 status points
The majority of numbers in Table 7–2 are not themselves trends, but are status points describing a certain value for its exact time and place. For any variable, any 2 of them at 2 different points in time constitute a trend that can be enumerated.

### Visualizing trends
Starting from status points, a vast number of trends can be observed by eye by moving horizontally for any or each of the 728 lines of numbers across the page in Table 7–2. To assist the reader to navigate through this ocean of data, every subtable is identically laid out, with 2 lines (Christians, and Christians %) printed in bold type. Also, all data for the years AD 1000 and AD 2000 on each page are placed in vertical screened columns. The value of this whole grid is that the whole layout is standardized for ease of navigation.

It is straightforward for a reader to read rapidly across one of these lines in Table 7–2 (or a column in Table 7–1) in order to derive impressionistic opinions of how things are trending from one year's column to the next. This can be done without resorting to numbers: as with the first variety Trend A one looks for the general direction. If one wishes to progress to numbers, they are right there waiting for analysis.

### Four varieties of trends proper
The user of Tables 7-1 or 7-2 can at any point select one of 4 different kinds of time periods (t) to measure a trend. These 4 are:

(a) a *spot trend*, already defined as a rate or increase per annum at a specific point;

(b) a *short-term trend* can be defined as one whose starting year and ending year are 25 years or less apart (t≤25);

(c) a *medium-term trend* arises for 2 points between 25 and 100 years apart; (100>t>25);

(d) a *long-term trend* arises from 2 points 100 years or more apart (t≥100).

### Effect of varying time periods
Some examples illustrate how choosing different periods gives differing results. At what rate are Christians growing in numbers from Pentecost in AD 33 with 8,000 adherents to AD 2000 with 2,000 million, using the exponential model of growth (compound interest)? Use of a scientific calculator or spreadsheet

program yields the answer: 0.63% per annum throughout the 1,967 years, a long-term result. Divide the time period into 2 and one gets: across the First Millennium (AD 33-AD 1000): 0.90% p.a.; across the Second Millennium (AD 1000-AD 2000): 0.38% p.a. Another example is shown in 6 contrasting lines:

*Spot trend at AD 2000 using differing periods*

| Period | Annual growth, % p.a. |
|---|---|
| AD 33-2000 | 0.63 |
| 1000-2000 | 0.38 |
| 1900-2000 | 1.28 |
| 1970-2000 | 1.62 |
| 1990-2000 | 1.36 |
| 1995-2000 | 1.27 |

Each of these has yielded a valuable figure but the method and context requires explanation.

### Sensitivity to the starting number
There is not too much drastic divergence in the effect of high or low starting numbers. This table below shows the spot trend % p.a. in the year 2000 for the whole 1,967 years, when one assumes 4 different starting points:

*Spot trend at AD 2000 using differing starting number*

| Christians in AD 33 | Annual growth, 2000 |
|---|---|
| 10 | 0.98% p.a. |
| 100 | 0.86 |
| 3,000 | 0.68 |
| 8,000 | 0.63 |

Table 7–1 uses the bottom line in its assumptions.

### Aggregating areas in Table 7–2
Each UN region is made up of its countries; each continent is made up of its regions; the globe is made up of its 7 continents. Simple addition of any of the 17 variables of absolute numbers (identified by having m=millions, added) will give correct results allowing for minor differences due to rounding to 2 places of decimals. Rates and percentages in regions can also be aggregated accurately, but not by addition; likewise from continents to global totals.

### Visualizing the 20 centuries
These data have been brought into visual form as Graph 7-1 using a semi-logarithmic scale with linear horizontal axis representing the 20 centuries and logarithmic vertical axis representing number of persons involved. Thirty-eight letters or numbers have been added to explain a series of the more outstanding causes of variations in the lines.

### Commentary on the 20 geographical areas
In order to assist the reader through the mass of data reported in Table 7–2, both in graphic and table form, a series of letters has been added to each graph. In general, these letters pinpoint the following phenomena: (1) the presence of civilizations previously uncontacted by Christians; (2) the arrival of Christianity in the area or region; (3) significant events in either the growth or decline of Christianity; (4) the status of Christianity and evangelization in AD 2000; and (5) future prospects for Christianity.

For further documentation of the events depicted in short-hand on each graph see the relevant dates in Part 2 "CosmoChronology."

### A PANORAMA OF 16,016 TRENDS

Table 7–2 thus presents the major statistical and graphical data necessary for any assessment of numerical trends at any time or location in the 20 centuries of Christian history. The very different shapes of the lines on the 28 smaller graphs depict the startlingly different fortunes and calamities that Christians have experienced from one part of the world to another.

**Table 7–2.** A panorama of 16,016 numerical trends of 26 varieties, measuring the advances and reverses of Christianity at 22 points in time from AD 33 to AD 2200, for each of the world's 28 component geographical areas (globe, 7 continents, 20 regions), with each preceded by a historical graph showing the growth of its population, its evangelized persons, and its Christians.

This 8-page table and its 8 pages of graphs form a panoramic grid of 28 geographic or geopolitical blocs or subtables separated by horizontal rules and each identical in length and format. The global data across 22 centuries are also illustrated in the semilogarithmic Graph 7-1. In this, each rectangle in the grid is divided up horizontally and vertically into 10 smaller rectangles. The reader thus can place on the grid any other horizontal line of data across this table, in order to visualize any other variables or trends.

26 TREND VARIETIES
Each subtable starts in its first column with an identical listing of 26 trends with identical names and definitions, as set out here on the right. All the resulting numbers across the grid are given to 2 places of decimals, and all are either (a) absolute numbers in millions (shown by 'm' after any trend's name), or (b) percentages (shown by '%'), or (c) on one line 'Outreach per Christian', the number shown. Ten of the trends represent annual change (shown by 'p.a.', per annum). The first 3 trends measure total population; the remaining 23 measure religious numbers. This standard listing of trends for each of the 28 subtables is defined as shown at right.

22 POINTS IN TIME
The line of years along the top of each subtable specifies significant dates in the expansion of Christianity. A dark screen locates all data for AD 1000 and AD 2000. Each year with its major statistics may be seen, summarized and contexualized, in Part 2 "CosmoChronology". See Table 7–1 for a detailed analysis of the 1st century AD, followed by end-of-century statistics for the subsequent 21 centuries.

28 GEOPOLITICAL AREAS
The names, definitions, and order of these areas follow exactly United Nations' usage, being one globe, 7 continents (UN-termed 'major areas', with Antarctica added), and their 20 component regions made up of 238 countries. These are set out in Table A below. These 28 geopolitical areas are assumed to have identical geographic boundaries—those existing in AD 2000—throughout this grid of 20 centuries.

| | |
|---|---|
| **Area** . . . . . . . . . . . . . . . . . . | Name, followed by number of countries in AD 2000 |
| Population (m=millions) . . . . . . . | From *Atlas of world population history* |
| Growth rate, % p.a. . . . . . . . . . | Exponential rate since previous column's year |
| Increase p.a., m . . . . . . . . . . | Line above, over 100, times population |
| Evangelized persons, m . . . . . . | All aware of Christianity, Christ, and the gospel |
| Evangelized persons, % . . . . . . | Line above, over population, times 100 |
| Outreach per Christian . . . . . . | World B divided by Christians (E-AC ÷ AC) |
| **Christians,** m . . . . . . . . . . . . . | Total affiliated (church members) plus unaffiliated. |
| Orthodox, m . . . . . . . . . . . . | Affiliated (church members) |
| Roman Catholics, m . . . . . . . | Affiliated (church members) |
| Anglicans, m . . . . . . . . . . . | Affiliated (church members) |
| Protestants, m . . . . . . . . . . | Affiliated (church members) |
| Independents, m . . . . . . . . . | Affiliated (church members) |
| Marginal Christians, m . . . . . . | Affiliated (church members) |
| **Christians, %** . . . . . . . . . . . . . | Christians as percent of population of area |
| Christian growth rate, % p.a. . . . | Exponential rate since previous column's year |
| Christian nett increase p.a., m . . | Gains minus losses: line above, x 0.01 Christians. |
| Gains: births + converts, m . . . | Annual births to Christians plus conversions |
| Losses: deaths + defectors, m . | Annual deaths plus annual defections |
| World B, m . . . . . . . . . . . . . . . | Total evangelized non-Christians |
| World B, % . . . . . . . . . . . . . . | World B persons as % of area's population |
| World B growth rate, % p.a. . . . | Exponential rate since previous column's year |
| World B increase p.a., m . . . . . . | Line above, over 100, times World B |
| World A, m . . . . . . . . . . . . . . . | Total unevangelized, unaware of Christianity or Christ. |
| World A, % . . . . . . . . . . . . . . | World A persons as % of area's population |
| World A growth rate, % p.a. . . . . | Exponential rate since previous column's year |
| World A increase p.a., m . . . . . . | Line above, over 100, times World A |

28 HISTORICAL GRAPHS
Each statistical subtable is preceded, on its opposite facing page, by a historical overview graph with highlights briefly elucidated.

**Table A. The world's 238 countries classified by 7 continents (UN major areas, in bold capitals) and 20 regions (in bold upper/lowercase), AD 2000.**

The following is the full listing utilized by the United Nations, with the addition of 12 countries not recognized or included by the UN: Antarctica, Bougainville, British Indian Ocean Territory, Christmas Island, Cocos Islands, Mayotte, Norfolk Island, Northern Cyprus, Somaliland, Spanish North Africa, Svalbard & Jan Mayen Islands, Taiwan.

**AFRICA** (60 countries.)

| **Eastern Africa** (21) | | **Middle Africa** (9) | **Northern Africa** (8) | **Southern Africa** (5) | **Western Africa** (17) | |
|---|---|---|---|---|---|---|
| British Indian Ocean Territory | Mozambique | Angola | Algeria | Botswana | Benin | Mali |
| Burundi | Reunion | Cameroon | Egypt | Lesotho | Burkina Faso | Mauritania |
| Comoros | Rwanda | Central African Republic | Libya | Namibia | Cape Verde | Niger |
| Djibouti | Seychelles | Chad | Morocco | South Africa | Gambia | Nigeria |
| Eritrea | Somalia | Congo (Brazzaville) | Sahara | Swaziland | Ghana | Saint Helena |
| Ethiopia | Somaliland | Congo–Zaire | Spanish North Africa | | Guinea | Senegal |
| Kenya | Tanzania | Equatorial Guinea | Sudan | | Guinea–Bissau | Sierra Leone |
| Madagascar | Uganda | Gabon | Tunisia | | Ivory Coast | Togo |
| Malawi | Zambia | Sao Tome & Principe | | | Liberia | |
| Mauritius | Zimbabwe | | | | | |
| Mayotte | | | | | | |

**ANTARCTICA** (territories claimed by 39 nations)

**ASIA** (50 countries)

| **Eastern Asia** (6) | **South–central Asia** (14) | | **South–eastern Asia** (11) | | **Western Asia** (19) | |
|---|---|---|---|---|---|---|
| China | Afghanistan | Sri Lanka | Brunei | Timor | Armenia | Northern Cyprus |
| Japan | Bangladesh | Tajikistan | Cambodia | Viet Nam | Azerbaijan | Oman |
| Mongolia | Bhutan | Turkmenistan | Indonesia | | Bahrain | Palestine |
| North Korea | India | Uzbekistan | Laos | | Cyprus | Qatar |
| South Korea | Iran | | Malaysia | | Georgia | Saudi Arabia |
| Taiwan | Kazakhstan | | Myanmar | | Iraq | Syria |
| | Kirghizstan | | Philippines | | Israel | Turkey |
| | Maldives | | Singapore | | Jordan | United Arab Emirates |
| | Nepal | | Thailand | | Kuwait | Yemen |
| | Pakistan | | | | Lebanon | |

**EUROPE** (48 countries)

| **Eastern Europe** (10) | **Northern Europe** (14) | | **Southern Europe** (15) | | **Western Europe** (9) |
|---|---|---|---|---|---|
| Belorussia | Britain | Ireland | Albania | Macedonia | Austria |
| Bulgaria | Channel Islands | Isle of Man | Andorra | Malta | Belgium |
| Czech Republic | Denmark | Latvia | Bosnia–Herzegovina | Portugal | France |
| Hungary | Estonia | Lithuania | Croatia | San Marino | Germany |
| Poland | Faeroe Islands | Norway | Gibraltar | Slovenia | Liechtenstein |
| Moldavia | Finland | Svalbard & Jan Mayen Is | Greece | Spain | Luxembourg |
| Romania | Iceland | Sweden | Holy See | Yugoslavia | Monaco |
| Russia | | | Italy | | Netherlands |
| Slovakia | | | | | Switzerland |
| Ukraine | | | | | |

**LATIN AMERICA AND THE CARIBBEAN** (46 countries)

| **Caribbean** (24) | | | **Central America** (8) | **South America** (14) | |
|---|---|---|---|---|---|
| Anguilla | Dominican Republic | Saint Kitts & Nevis | Belize | Argentina | French Guiana |
| Antigua & Barbuda | Grenada | Saint Lucia | Costa Rica | Bolivia | Guyana |
| Aruba | Guadeloupe | Saint Vincent & Grenadines | El Salvador | Brazil | Paraguay |
| Bahamas | Haiti | Trinidad & Tobago | Guatemala | Chile | Peru |
| Barbados | Jamaica | Turks & Caicos Islands | Honduras | Colombia | Suriname |
| British Virgin Islands | Martinique | Virgin Islands of the US | Mexico | Ecuador | Uruguay |
| Cayman Islands | Montserrat | | Nicaragua | Falkland Islands | Venezuela |
| Cuba | Netherlands Antilles | | Panama | | |
| Dominica | Puerto Rico | | | | |

**NORTHERN AMERICA** (5 countries)

| | |
|---|---|
| Bermuda | Saint Pierre & Miquelon |
| Canada | United States of America |
| Greenland | |

**OCEANIA** (28 countries)

| **Australia/New Zealand** (5) | **Melanesia** (6) | **Micronesia** (7) | **Polynesia** (10) | |
|---|---|---|---|---|
| Australia | Bougainville | Guam | American Samoa | Tonga |
| Christmas Island | Fiji | Kiribati | Cook Islands | Tuvalu |
| Cocos Islands | New Caledonia | Marshall Islands | French Polynesia | Wallis & Futuna Islands |
| New Zealand | Papua New Guinea | Micronesia | Niue | |
| Norfolk Island | Solomon Islands | Nauru | Pitcairn Islands | |
| | Vanuatu | Northern Mariana Islands | Samoa | |
| | | Palau | Tokelau | |

The **2 axes** below are: horizontally, years AD by 20-year gaps; vertically, persons (logarithmic scale).
The **3 lines** on each graph are, from top to bottom: live **population**, live **evangelized persons**, live **Christians**.
**Statistics** and trends for 22 years are given, for each geopolitical area, in its facing table opposite.

## GLOBE

**A** = AD 30   Jesus preaches good news in Palestine
**B** =   300   Church grows rapidly in Roman Empire
**C** =   500   Goths, Visigoths accept Christian message
**D** =   700   Islam spreads across formerly Christian lands
**E** = 1200   Friars spread message across Europe
**F** = 1350   Black Death kills 75 million in Europe and Asia
**G** = 1400   Tamerlane wipes out Church of the East
**H** = 1500   Roman Catholic missions to Africa, America, and Asia
**I** = 1800   Protestant missions begin
**J** = 1950   Tribal religionists convert to Christianity in large numbers
**K** = 2000   World is 33% Christian, 73% evangelized
**L** = 2050   World population explosion now virtually halted

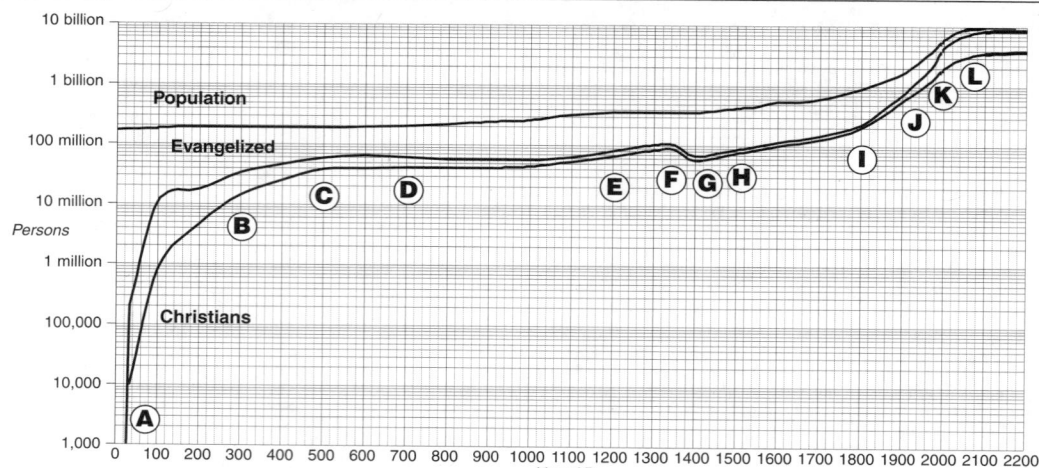

## AFRICA

**A** = AD 33   Gospel introduced to Egypt; Alexandria and Carthage become strong centers of Christianity
**B** =   500   Latinized peoples nearly all Christians; Berbers begin to join churches
**C** =   700   Mass conversions to Islam steadily erode Christian population
**D** = 1450   Roman Catholic missions initiated in sub-Saharan Africa
**E** = 1870   Bible is translated into main languages.
**F** = 1900   African Independent churches grow rapidly
**G** = 2000   Continent is 46% Christian, 78% evangelized

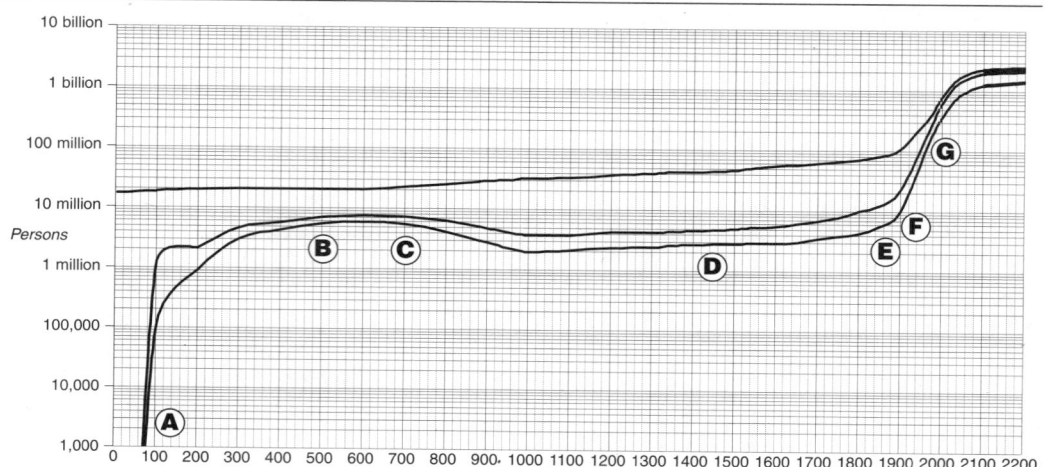

## Eastern Africa

**A** = AD 39   Gospel introduced to Ethiopia by pilgrims returning from Jerusalem
**B** =   332   Frumentius in Ethiopia: Orthodox church rises to 16% of the population, remains there for 1,500 years
**C** = 1449   Roman Catholic missionaries arrive in Tanzania
**D** = 1868   Bible is translated into main languages
**E** = 1940   Radio broadcasting begins
**F** = 2000   Region is 60% Christian; 86% evangelized

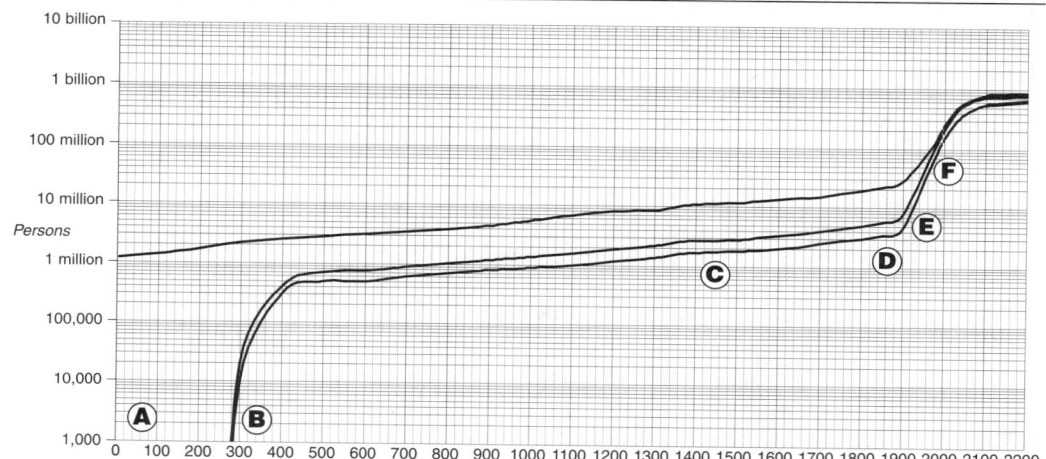

## Middle Africa

**A** = c800   Bantu states uncontacted by African Christians from the north for 1,500 years
**B** = 1482   Roman Catholic missionaries arrive in Congo-Zaire
**C** = 1900   Few converts. Region is 1% Christian
**D** = 1950   Roman Catholics, Anglicans, Protestants, and Independents mushroom 1000-fold in all 9 countries
**E** = 2000   Region is 82% Christian; 92% evangelized

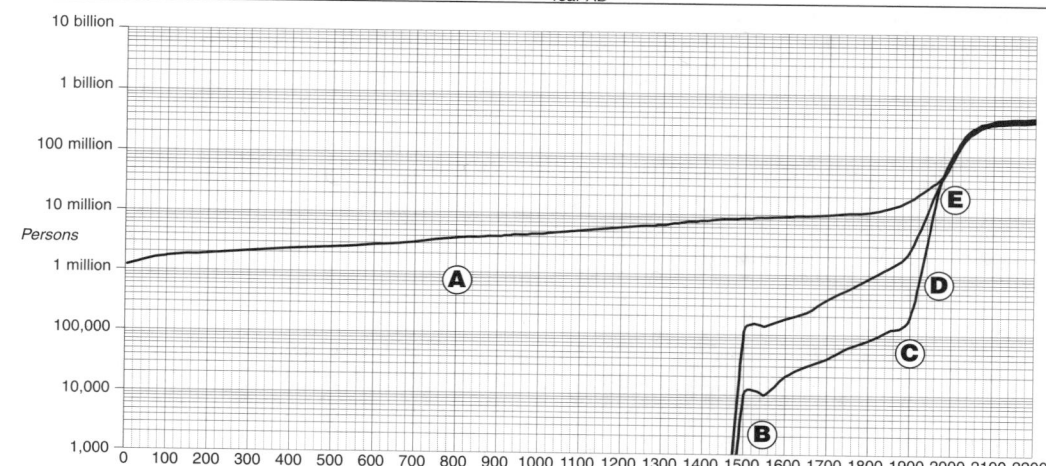

| Area / Year, AD | 33 | 100 | 300 | 500 | 800 | 1000 | 1200 | 1350 | 1500 | 1650 | 1750 | 1800 | 1850 | 1900 | 1970 | 1990 | 1995 | 2000 | 2025 | 2050 | 2100 | 2200 |
|---|---|---|---|---|---|---|---|---|---|---|---|---|---|---|---|---|---|---|---|---|---|---|
| 1 | 2 | 3 | 4 | 5 | 6 | 7 | 8 | 9 | 10 | 11 | 12 | 13 | 14 | 15 | 16 | 17 | 18 | 19 | 20 | 21 | 22 | 23 |
| **GLOBE** (238 countries in 2000) | | | | | | | | | | | | | | | | | | | | | | |
| Population, m(=millions) | 170.66 | 179.51 | 191.93 | 190.32 | 217.92 | 263.65 | 357.44 | 361.04 | 422.95 | 546.66 | 719.19 | 903.65 | 1,202.87 | 1,619.63 | 3,696.15 | 5,266.44 | 5,666.36 | 6,055.05 | 7,823.70 | 8,909.10 | 10,109.28 | 10,561.48 |
| Growth rate, % p.a. | 0.08 | 0.08 | 0.03 | 0.00 | 0.05 | 0.10 | 0.15 | 0.01 | 0.11 | 0.17 | 0.27 | 0.46 | 0.57 | 0.60 | 1.19 | 1.79 | 1.47 | 1.34 | 1.03 | 0.52 | 0.25 | 0.04 |
| Increase p.a., m | 0.13 | 0.14 | 0.06 | -0.01 | 0.10 | 0.25 | 0.54 | 0.02 | 0.45 | 0.94 | 1.98 | 4.14 | 6.90 | 9.67 | 43.82 | 94.06 | 83.56 | 80.88 | 80.61 | 46.42 | 25.58 | 4.62 |
| Evangelized persons, m | 0.21 | 10.60 | 32.82 | 59.40 | 57.53 | 56.17 | 81.31 | 103.17 | 86.75 | 129.76 | 174.96 | 229.31 | 401.24 | 739.95 | 2,054.90 | 3,600.97 | 3,988.16 | 4,425.67 | 5,978.30 | 7,103.04 | 8,250.11 | 8,792.81 |
| Evangelized persons % | 0.12 | 5.90 | 17.10 | 31.21 | 26.40 | 21.30 | 22.75 | 28.58 | 20.51 | 23.74 | 24.33 | 25.38 | 33.36 | 45.69 | 55.60 | 68.38 | 70.38 | 73.09 | 76.41 | 79.73 | 81.61 | 83.25 |
| Outreach per Christian | 20.00 | 12.25 | 1.34 | 0.57 | 0.41 | 0.26 | 0.24 | 0.19 | 0.14 | 0.15 | 0.13 | 0.12 | 0.24 | 0.33 | 0.66 | 1.06 | 1.12 | 1.21 | 1.28 | 1.33 | 1.30 | 1.29 |
| **Christians, m** | **0.01** | **0.80** | **14.01** | **37.80** | **40.87** | **44.67** | **65.71** | **86.47** | **75.89** | **112.84** | **154.69** | **204.98** | **323.86** | **558.13** | **1,236.37** | **1,747.46** | **1,877.43** | **1,999.56** | **2,616.67** | **3,051.56** | **3,583.02** | **3,843.54** |
| Orthodox, m | 0.00 | 0.61 | 8.90 | 24.48 | 24.44 | 23.99 | 29.07 | 35.06 | 25.87 | 33.18 | 45.01 | 55.22 | 75.46 | 115.84 | 139.66 | 203.77 | 209.62 | 215.13 | 252.72 | 266.81 | 278.12 | 292.97 |
| Roman Catholics, m | 0.01 | 0.17 | 4.91 | 12.72 | 15.93 | 18.88 | 33.24 | 47.26 | 44.83 | 60.10 | 82.39 | 106.43 | 163.20 | 266.55 | 665.95 | 929.70 | 994.15 | 1,057.33 | 1,361.97 | 1,564.60 | 1,695.10 | 1,849.70 |
| Anglicans, m | 0.00 | 0.01 | 0.20 | 0.60 | 0.50 | 1.80 | 3.40 | 4.15 | 5.18 | 4.84 | 6.20 | 11.91 | 21.85 | 30.57 | 47.50 | 68.20 | 74.52 | 79.65 | 113.75 | 145.98 | 167.81 | 194.59 |
| Protestants, m | 0.00 | 0.00 | 0.00 | 0.00 | 0.00 | 0.00 | 0.00 | 0.00 | 0.01 | 14.69 | 21.02 | 30.98 | 60.86 | 103.02 | 210.76 | 296.35 | 319.68 | 342.00 | 468.63 | 574.42 | 643.38 | 725.79 |
| Independents, m | 0.00 | 0.00 | 0.00 | 0.00 | 0.00 | 0.00 | 0.00 | 0.00 | 0.00 | 0.03 | 0.06 | 0.40 | 2.14 | 7.93 | 95.60 | 301.54 | 346.54 | 385.75 | 581.64 | 752.84 | 861.56 | 989.95 |
| Marginal Christians, m | 0.00 | 0.00 | 0.00 | 0.00 | 0.00 | 0.00 | 0.00 | 0.00 | 0.00 | 0.00 | 0.01 | 0.04 | 0.35 | 0.93 | 11.10 | 21.83 | 23.85 | 26.06 | 45.55 | 62.20 | 73.25 | 86.72 |
| **Christians %** | **0.01** | **0.45** | **7.30** | **19.86** | **18.75** | **16.94** | **18.38** | **23.95** | **17.94** | **20.64** | **21.51** | **22.68** | **26.92** | **34.46** | **33.45** | **33.18** | **33.13** | **33.02** | **33.45** | **34.25** | **35.44** | **36.39** |
| Christian growth rate, % p.a. | 0.00 | 6.76 | 1.44 | 0.50 | 0.03 | 0.04 | 0.19 | 0.18 | -0.09 | 0.26 | 0.32 | 0.56 | 0.92 | 1.09 | 1.14 | 1.74 | 1.45 | 1.27 | 1.08 | 0.62 | 0.32 | 0.07 |
| Christian nett increase p.a., m | 0.00 | 0.04 | 0.21 | 0.21 | 0.03 | 0.04 | 0.15 | 0.17 | 0.01 | 0.50 | 0.54 | 1.25 | 3.29 | 6.60 | 20.52 | 37.32 | 27.72 | 25.90 | 30.98 | 20.65 | 12.20 | 2.79 |
| Gains: births+converts,m | 0.00 | 0.08 | 0.79 | 1.78 | 1.74 | 1.92 | 2.94 | 3.85 | 2.96 | 3.96 | 4.87 | 6.42 | 9.71 | 16.13 | 41.23 | 63.47 | 55.27 | 55.11 | 66.05 | 63.85 | 66.76 | 68.39 |
| Losses: deaths+defectors,m | 0.00 | 0.03 | 0.58 | 1.58 | 1.71 | 1.88 | 2.79 | 3.68 | 2.95 | 3.46 | 4.34 | 5.17 | 6.42 | 9.53 | 20.70 | 26.15 | 27.55 | 29.20 | 35.07 | 43.20 | 54.56 | 65.60 |
| World B, m | 0.20 | 9.80 | 18.81 | 21.60 | 16.66 | 11.50 | 15.60 | 16.70 | 10.86 | 16.92 | 20.27 | 24.33 | 77.38 | 181.82 | 818.53 | 1,853.51 | 2,110.73 | 2,426.11 | 3,361.63 | 4,051.48 | 4,667.10 | 4,949.27 |
| World B % | 0.12 | 5.46 | 9.80 | 11.35 | 7.65 | 4.36 | 4.36 | 4.63 | 2.57 | 3.10 | 2.82 | 2.69 | 6.43 | 11.23 | 22.15 | 35.19 | 37.25 | 40.07 | 42.97 | 45.48 | 46.17 | 46.86 |
| World B growth rate, % p.a. | 27.91 | 5.98 | 0.33 | 0.07 | -0.09 | -0.19 | 0.15 | 0.05 | -0.29 | 0.30 | 0.18 | 0.37 | 2.34 | 1.72 | 2.17 | 4.17 | 2.63 | 2.82 | 1.31 | 0.75 | 0.28 | 0.06 |
| World B increase p.a., m | 0.03 | 0.33 | 0.03 | 0.01 | -0.01 | -0.01 | 0.01 | 0.00 | -0.01 | 0.01 | 0.01 | 0.01 | 0.15 | 0.19 | 0.48 | 1.47 | 0.98 | 1.13 | 0.56 | 0.34 | 0.13 | 0.03 |
| World A, m | 170.45 | 168.91 | 159.11 | 130.92 | 160.39 | 207.48 | 276.13 | 257.87 | 336.20 | 416.90 | 544.23 | 674.35 | 801.63 | 879.67 | 1,641.25 | 1,665.47 | 1,678.20 | 1,629.37 | 1,845.41 | 1,806.05 | 1,859.17 | 1,768.67 |
| World A % | 99.88 | 94.10 | 82.90 | 68.79 | 73.60 | 78.70 | 77.25 | 71.42 | 79.49 | 76.26 | 75.67 | 74.62 | 66.64 | 54.31 | 44.40 | 31.62 | 29.62 | 26.91 | 23.59 | 20.27 | 18.39 | 16.75 |
| World A growth rate, % p.a. | 0.08 | -0.01 | -0.03 | -0.10 | 0.07 | 0.13 | 0.14 | -0.05 | 0.18 | 0.14 | 0.27 | 0.43 | 0.35 | 0.19 | 0.89 | 0.07 | 0.15 | -0.59 | 0.50 | -0.09 | 0.06 | -0.05 |
| World A increase p.a., m | 0.13 | -0.02 | -0.05 | -0.13 | 0.11 | 0.27 | 0.39 | -0.12 | 0.60 | 0.60 | 1.45 | 2.90 | 2.78 | 1.64 | 14.69 | 1.22 | 2.56 | -9.59 | 9.21 | -1.56 | 1.08 | -0.88 |
| **AFRICA** (60 countries in 2000) | | | | | | | | | | | | | | | | | | | | | | |
| Population, m(=millions) | 17.16 | 18.01 | 20.48 | 20.02 | 25.07 | 32.30 | 36.62 | 42.25 | 46.55 | 57.71 | 66.34 | 70.00 | 81.62 | 107.81 | 357.04 | 614.77 | 696.96 | 784.45 | 1,298.31 | 1,766.08 | 2,243.42 | 2,431.29 |
| Growth rate, % p.a. | 0.07 | 0.07 | 0.06 | -0.01 | 0.08 | 0.13 | 0.06 | 0.10 | 0.06 | 0.14 | 0.14 | 0.11 | 0.31 | 0.56 | 1.73 | 2.75 | 2.54 | 2.39 | 2.04 | 1.24 | 0.48 | 0.08 |
| Increase p.a., m | 0.01 | 0.01 | 0.01 | 0.00 | 0.02 | 0.04 | 0.02 | 0.04 | 0.03 | 0.08 | 0.09 | 0.08 | 0.25 | 0.60 | 6.16 | 16.93 | 17.71 | 18.77 | 26.43 | 21.87 | 10.76 | 1.96 |
| Evangelized persons, m | 0.00 | 1.09 | 4.52 | 7.10 | 6.33 | 3.66 | 4.20 | 4.50 | 4.84 | 6.00 | 7.81 | 9.88 | 12.52 | 22.22 | 217.07 | 455.19 | 528.12 | 607.65 | 1,056.90 | 1,489.13 | 1,949.92 | 2,150.79 |
| Evangelized persons % | 0.00 | 6.05 | 22.07 | 35.46 | 25.25 | 11.33 | 11.47 | 10.65 | 10.40 | 10.40 | 11.77 | 14.11 | 15.34 | 20.61 | 60.80 | 74.04 | 75.77 | 77.46 | 81.41 | 84.32 | 86.92 | 88.46 |
| Outreach per Christian | — | 11.11 | 0.50 | 0.29 | 0.52 | 0.87 | 0.83 | 0.73 | 0.70 | 0.97 | 1.01 | 1.28 | 1.19 | 1.24 | 0.51 | 0.65 | 0.66 | 0.69 | 0.67 | 0.65 | 0.57 | 0.51 |
| **Christians, m** | **0.00** | **0.09** | **3.01** | **5.50** | **4.16** | **1.96** | **2.30** | **2.60** | **2.84** | **3.04** | **3.89** | **4.33** | **5.72** | **9.94** | **143.82** | **276.50** | **317.63** | **360.23** | **633.80** | **903.21** | **1,243.50** | **1,420.50** |
| Orthodox, m | 0.00 | 0.09 | 2.01 | 4.00 | 2.96 | 1.91 | 2.28 | 2.58 | 2.79 | 2.85 | 3.48 | 3.65 | 3.92 | 4.60 | 18.40 | 28.00 | 31.69 | 35.30 | 59.78 | 83.71 | 99.36 | 118.14 |
| Roman Catholics, m | 0.00 | 0.00 | 1.00 | 1.50 | 1.20 | 0.05 | 0.02 | 0.02 | 0.05 | 0.19 | 0.39 | 0.58 | 1.04 | 1.91 | 45.07 | 90.66 | 105.62 | 120.39 | 228.29 | 341.89 | 418.88 | 513.57 |
| Anglicans, m | 0.00 | 0.00 | 0.00 | 0.00 | 0.00 | 0.00 | 0.00 | 0.00 | 0.00 | 0.00 | 0.00 | 0.01 | 0.16 | 0.37 | 7.73 | 31.82 | 37.59 | 42.54 | 76.12 | 109.28 | 131.41 | 158.39 |
| Protestants, m | 0.00 | 0.00 | 0.00 | 0.00 | 0.00 | 0.00 | 0.00 | 0.00 | 0.00 | 0.00 | 0.02 | 0.09 | 0.59 | 1.84 | 27.29 | 67.03 | 78.22 | 89.00 | 157.30 | 227.15 | 273.42 | 329.44 |
| Independents, m | 0.00 | 0.00 | 0.00 | 0.00 | 0.00 | 0.00 | 0.00 | 0.00 | 0.00 | 0.00 | 0.00 | 0.00 | 0.01 | 0.04 | 17.94 | 62.60 | 73.78 | 83.84 | 139.81 | 209.11 | 256.80 | 316.15 |
| Marginal Christians, m | 0.00 | 0.00 | 0.00 | 0.00 | 0.00 | 0.00 | 0.00 | 0.00 | 0.00 | 0.00 | 0.00 | 0.00 | 0.00 | 0.00 | 1.00 | 1.81 | 2.10 | 2.43 | 5.55 | 9.10 | 11.69 | 15.07 |
| **Christians %** | **0.00** | **0.50** | **14.70** | **27.47** | **16.59** | **6.07** | **6.28** | **6.15** | **6.10** | **5.27** | **5.86** | **6.19** | **7.01** | **9.22** | **40.28** | **44.98** | **45.57** | **45.92** | **48.82** | **51.14** | **55.43** | **58.43** |
| Christian growth rate, % p.a. | 0.00 | 3.33 | 1.77 | 0.30 | -0.09 | -0.38 | 0.08 | 0.08 | 0.06 | 0.05 | 0.25 | 0.21 | 0.56 | 1.11 | 3.89 | 3.32 | 2.81 | 2.55 | 2.29 | 1.43 | 0.64 | 0.13 |
| Christian nett increase p.a., m | 0.00 | 0.00 | 0.05 | 0.02 | 0.00 | -0.01 | 0.00 | 0.00 | 0.00 | 0.00 | 0.01 | 0.01 | 0.04 | 0.13 | 6.94 | 9.24 | 8.96 | 9.20 | 14.73 | 12.96 | 8.02 | 1.90 |
| Gains: births+converts,m | 0.00 | 0.01 | 0.18 | 0.25 | 0.17 | 0.08 | 0.10 | 0.11 | 0.11 | 0.11 | 0.13 | 0.15 | 0.22 | 0.40 | 10.03 | 14.12 | 14.50 | 15.48 | 21.16 | 21.32 | 18.54 | 13.02 |
| Losses: deaths+defectors,m | 0.00 | 0.00 | 0.12 | 0.23 | 0.17 | 0.08 | 0.09 | 0.11 | 0.11 | 0.11 | 0.12 | 0.14 | 0.18 | 0.27 | 3.09 | 4.88 | 5.55 | 6.28 | 6.43 | 8.36 | 10.52 | 11.12 |
| World B, m | 0.00 | 1.00 | 1.51 | 1.60 | 2.17 | 1.70 | 1.90 | 1.90 | 2.00 | 2.96 | 3.92 | 5.55 | 6.80 | 12.28 | 73.25 | 178.70 | 210.50 | 247.42 | 423.09 | 585.93 | 706.42 | 730.29 |
| World B % | 0.00 | 5.55 | 7.37 | 7.99 | 8.66 | 5.26 | 5.19 | 4.50 | 4.30 | 5.13 | 5.91 | 7.93 | 8.33 | 11.39 | 20.52 | 29.07 | 30.20 | 31.54 | 32.59 | 33.18 | 31.49 | 30.04 |
| World B growth rate, % p.a. | 0.00 | 6.01 | 0.21 | 0.03 | 0.10 | -0.12 | 0.06 | 0.00 | 0.03 | 0.26 | 0.28 | 0.70 | 0.41 | 1.19 | 2.58 | 4.56 | 3.33 | 3.28 | 2.17 | 1.31 | 0.37 | 0.03 |
| World B increase p.a., m | 0.00 | 0.33 | 0.02 | 0.00 | 0.01 | -0.01 | 0.00 | 0.00 | 0.00 | 0.01 | 0.02 | 0.06 | 0.03 | 0.14 | 0.53 | 1.33 | 1.01 | 1.04 | 0.71 | 0.43 | 0.12 | 0.01 |
| World A, m | 17.16 | 16.92 | 15.96 | 12.92 | 18.74 | 28.64 | 32.42 | 37.75 | 41.71 | 51.71 | 58.53 | 60.12 | 69.10 | 85.59 | 139.97 | 159.57 | 168.84 | 176.79 | 241.42 | 276.95 | 293.50 | 280.50 |
| World A % | 100.00 | 93.95 | 77.93 | 64.54 | 74.75 | 88.67 | 88.53 | 89.35 | 89.60 | 89.60 | 88.23 | 85.89 | 84.66 | 79.39 | 39.20 | 25.96 | 24.23 | 22.54 | 18.59 | 15.68 | 13.08 | 11.54 |
| World A growth rate, % p.a. | 0.07 | -0.02 | -0.03 | -0.11 | 0.12 | 0.21 | 0.06 | 0.10 | 0.07 | 0.14 | 0.12 | 0.05 | 0.28 | 0.43 | 0.71 | 0.66 | 1.14 | 0.93 | 1.25 | 0.55 | 0.12 | -0.05 |
| World A increase p.a., m | 0.01 | 0.00 | 0.00 | -0.01 | 0.02 | 0.06 | 0.02 | 0.04 | 0.03 | 0.07 | 0.07 | 0.03 | 0.19 | 0.37 | 0.99 | 1.05 | 1.92 | 1.64 | 3.03 | 1.53 | 0.34 | -0.13 |
| **Eastern Africa** (21 countries in 2000) | | | | | | | | | | | | | | | | | | | | | | |
| Population, m(=millions) | 1.20 | 1.40 | 2.20 | 2.80 | 3.90 | 5.40 | 8.10 | 9.70 | 11.50 | 14.10 | 16.80 | 18.75 | 21.55 | 28.04 | 108.45 | 191.72 | 217.15 | 246.97 | 426.18 | 595.56 | 767.08 | 834.72 |
| Growth rate, % p.a. | 0.23 | 0.23 | 0.23 | 0.12 | 0.11 | 0.16 | 0.20 | 0.12 | 0.11 | 0.14 | 0.18 | 0.22 | 0.28 | 0.53 | 1.95 | 2.89 | 2.52 | 2.61 | 2.21 | 1.35 | 0.51 | 0.08 |
| Increase p.a., m | 0.00 | 0.00 | 0.00 | 0.00 | 0.00 | 0.01 | 0.02 | 0.01 | 0.01 | 0.02 | 0.03 | 0.04 | 0.06 | 0.15 | 2.12 | 5.54 | 5.48 | 6.44 | 9.40 | 8.03 | 3.89 | 0.71 |
| Evangelized persons, m | 0.00 | 0.00 | 0.02 | 0.70 | 1.05 | 1.40 | 1.90 | 2.50 | 2.80 | 3.60 | 4.40 | 4.90 | 5.70 | 7.77 | 81.69 | 160.53 | 184.74 | 213.21 | 380.12 | 542.05 | 715.08 | 789.72 |
| Evangelized persons % | 0.00 | 0.00 | 0.91 | 25.00 | 26.92 | 25.93 | 23.46 | 25.77 | 24.35 | 25.53 | 26.19 | 26.13 | 26.45 | 27.71 | 75.32 | 83.73 | 85.08 | 86.33 | 89.19 | 91.02 | 93.22 | 94.61 |
| Outreach per Christian | — | — | 1.00 | 0.40 | 0.50 | 0.56 | 0.58 | 0.56 | 0.56 | 0.64 | 0.57 | 0.63 | 0.63 | 0.72 | 0.47 | 0.38 | 0.40 | 0.41 | 0.40 | 0.39 | 0.30 | 0.23 |
| **Christians, m** | **0.00** | **0.00** | **0.01** | **0.50** | **0.70** | **0.90** | **1.20** | **1.60** | **1.80** | **2.20** | **2.80** | **3.00** | **3.50** | **4.52** | **55.45** | **116.36** | **132.27** | **151.12** | **271.31** | **389.13** | **550.00** | **640.00** |
| Orthodox, m | 0.00 | 0.00 | 0.01 | 0.50 | 0.70 | 0.90 | 1.20 | 1.60 | 1.80 | 2.19 | 2.75 | 2.90 | 3.02 | 2.80 | 12.19 | 19.66 | 22.56 | 25.54 | 47.15 | 68.86 | 83.25 | 100.66 |
| Roman Catholics, m | 0.00 | 0.00 | 0.00 | 0.00 | 0.00 | 0.00 | 0.00 | 0.00 | 0.00 | 0.01 | 0.05 | 0.10 | 0.30 | 0.78 | 18.47 | 36.73 | 41.92 | 47.43 | 85.90 | 123.93 | 148.90 | 178.93 |
| Anglicans, m | 0.00 | 0.00 | 0.00 | 0.00 | 0.00 | 0.00 | 0.00 | 0.00 | 0.00 | 0.00 | 0.00 | 0.00 | 0.03 | 0.08 | 2.89 | 12.38 | 14.73 | 16.54 | 32.57 | 51.41 | 64.63 | 81.27 |
| Protestants, m | 0.00 | 0.00 | 0.00 | 0.00 | 0.00 | 0.00 | 0.00 | 0.00 | 0.00 | 0.00 | 0.00 | 0.00 | 0.15 | 0.51 | 7.78 | 26.41 | 31.26 | 35.72 | 66.25 | 96.82 | 117.10 | 141.64 |
| Independents, m | 0.00 | 0.00 | 0.00 | 0.00 | 0.00 | 0.00 | 0.00 | 0.00 | 0.00 | 0.00 | 0.00 | 0.00 | 0.00 | 0.00 | 3.39 | 14.29 | 17.03 | 19.17 | 34.62 | 53.50 | 66.53 | 82.77 |
| Marginal Christians, m | 0.00 | 0.00 | 0.00 | 0.00 | 0.00 | 0.00 | 0.00 | 0.00 | 0.00 | 0.00 | 0.00 | 0.00 | 0.00 | 0.00 | 0.60 | 0.68 | 0.70 | 0.75 | 1.11 | 1.62 | 1.95 | 2.36 |
| **Christians %** | **0.00** | **0.00** | **0.45** | **17.86** | **17.95** | **16.67** | **14.81** | **16.49** | **15.65** | **15.60** | **16.67** | **16.00** | **16.24** | **16.10** | **51.13** | **60.69** | **60.91** | **61.19** | **63.66** | **65.34** | **71.70** | **76.67** |
| Christian growth rate, % p.a. | 0.00 | 0.00 | 2.33 | 1.98 | 0.11 | 0.13 | 0.14 | 0.19 | 0.08 | 0.13 | 0.24 | 0.14 | 0.31 | 0.51 | 3.65 | 3.78 | 2.60 | 2.70 | 2.37 | 1.45 | 0.69 | 0.15 |
| Christian nett increase p.a., m | 0.00 | 0.00 | 0.00 | 0.01 | 0.00 | 0.00 | 0.00 | 0.00 | 0.00 | 0.00 | 0.01 | 0.00 | 0.01 | 0.02 | 2.02 | 4.39 | 3.43 | 4.08 | 6.43 | 5.65 | 3.82 | 0.97 |
| Gains: births+converts,m | 0.00 | 0.00 | 0.00 | 0.03 | 0.03 | 0.04 | 0.05 | 0.07 | 0.07 | 0.08 | 0.10 | 0.10 | 0.12 | 0.16 | 3.25 | 6.72 | 6.02 | 6.98 | 9.27 | 9.32 | 8.49 | 5.88 |
| Losses: deaths+defectors,m | 0.00 | 0.00 | 0.00 | 0.02 | 0.03 | 0.04 | 0.05 | 0.07 | 0.07 | 0.08 | 0.09 | 0.10 | 0.11 | 0.14 | 1.22 | 2.33 | 2.58 | 2.90 | 2.85 | 3.67 | 4.67 | 4.91 |
| World B, m | 0.00 | 0.00 | 0.01 | 0.20 | 0.35 | 0.50 | 0.70 | 0.90 | 1.00 | 1.40 | 1.60 | 1.90 | 2.20 | 3.26 | 26.24 | 44.17 | 52.47 | 62.10 | 108.81 | 152.93 | 165.08 | 149.72 |
| World B % | 0.00 | 0.00 | 0.45 | 7.14 | 8.97 | 9.26 | 8.64 | 9.28 | 8.70 | 9.93 | 9.52 | 10.13 | 10.21 | 11.61 | 24.20 | 23.04 | 24.16 | 25.14 | 25.53 | 25.68 | 21.52 | 17.94 |
| World B growth rate, % p.a. | 0.00 | 0.00 | 1.98 | 1.51 | 0.19 | 0.18 | 0.17 | 0.17 | 0.07 | 0.22 | 0.13 | 0.34 | 0.29 | 0.79 | 3.03 | 2.64 | 3.50 | 3.43 | 2.27 | 1.37 | 0.15 | -0.10 |
| World B increase p.a., m | 0.00 | 0.00 | 0.01 | 0.11 | 0.02 | 0.02 | 0.01 | 0.02 | 0.01 | 0.02 | 0.01 | 0.03 | 0.03 | 0.09 | 0.73 | 0.61 | 0.85 | 0.86 | 0.58 | 0.35 | 0.03 | -0.02 |
| World A, m | 1.20 | 1.40 | 2.18 | 2.10 | 2.85 | 4.00 | 6.20 | 7.20 | 8.70 | 10.50 | 12.40 | 13.85 | 15.85 | 20.27 | 26.76 | 31.18 | 32.40 | 33.75 | 46.06 | 53.51 | 52.00 | 45.00 |
| World A % | 100.00 | 100.00 | 99.09 | 75.00 | 73.08 | 74.07 | 76.54 | 74.23 | 75.65 | 74.47 | 73.81 | 73.87 | 73.55 | 72.29 | 24.68 | 16.27 | 14.92 | 13.67 | 10.81 | 8.98 | 6.78 | 5.39 |
| World A growth rate, % p.a. | 0.23 | 0.23 | 0.22 | -0.02 | 0.10 | 0.17 | 0.22 | 0.10 | 0.13 | 0.13 | 0.17 | 0.22 | 0.27 | 0.49 | 0.40 | 0.77 | 0.77 | 0.82 | 1.25 | 0.60 | -0.06 | -0.14 |
| World A increase p.a., m | 0.00 | 0.00 | 0.00 | 0.00 | 0.00 | 0.01 | 0.01 | 0.01 | 0.01 | 0.01 | 0.02 | 0.03 | 0.04 | 0.10 | 0.11 | 0.24 | 0.25 | 0.28 | 0.58 | 0.32 | -0.03 | -0.07 |
| **Middle Africa** (9 countries in 2000) | | | | | | | | | | | | | | | | | | | | | | |
| Population, m(=millions) | 1.35 | 1.70 | 2.10 | 2.55 | 3.75 | 4.50 | 5.80 | 7.15 | 8.75 | 9.60 | 10.55 | 11.20 | 13.30 | 18.08 | 40.10 | 70.38 | 83.74 | 95.65 | 184.67 | 274.63 | 372.06 | 411.77 |
| Growth rate, % p.a. | 0.34 | 0.34 | 0.11 | 0.10 | 0.13 | 0.09 | 0.13 | 0.14 | 0.13 | 0.06 | 0.09 | 0.12 | 0.34 | 0.62 | 1.14 | 2.85 | 3.54 | 2.70 | 2.67 | 1.60 | 0.61 | 0.10 |
| Increase p.a., m | 0.00 | 0.01 | 0.00 | 0.00 | 0.00 | 0.00 | 0.01 | 0.01 | 0.01 | 0.01 | 0.01 | 0.01 | 0.05 | 0.11 | 0.46 | 2.01 | 2.96 | 2.58 | 4.92 | 4.39 | 2.27 | 0.42 |
| Evangelized persons, m | 0.00 | 0.00 | 0.00 | 0.00 | 0.00 | 0.00 | 0.00 | 0.00 | 0.11 | 0.23 | 0.56 | 0.88 | 1.32 | 2.56 | 33.07 | 63.69 | 76.25 | 87.62 | 172.55 | 259.76 | 357.06 | 397.77 |
| Evangelized persons % | 0.00 | 0.00 | 0.00 | 0.00 | 0.00 | 0.00 | 0.00 | 0.00 | 1.26 | 2.40 | 5.31 | 7.86 | 9.92 | 14.17 | 82.45 | 90.49 | 91.05 | 91.60 | 93.44 | 94.59 | 95.97 | 96.60 |
| Outreach per Christian | — | — | — | — | — | — | — | — | 10.00 | 6.67 | 8.33 | 10.00 | 10.00 | 12.25 | 0.09 | 0.12 | 0.12 | 0.12 | 0.10 | 0.10 | 0.07 | 0.06 |
| **Christians, m** | **0.00** | **0.00** | **0.00** | **0.00** | **0.00** | **0.00** | **0.00** | **0.00** | **0.01** | **0.03** | **0.06** | **0.08** | **0.12** | **0.19** | **30.29** | **56.65** | **68.13** | **78.08** | **156.49** | **237.10** | **335.00** | **375.00** |
| Orthodox, m | 0.00 | 0.00 | 0.00 | 0.00 | 0.00 | 0.00 | 0.00 | 0.00 | 0.00 | 0.00 | 0.00 | 0.00 | 0.00 | 0.00 | 0.01 | 0.01 | 0.01 | 0.01 | 0.01 | 0.02 | 0.02 | 0.02 |
| Roman Catholics, m | 0.00 | 0.00 | 0.00 | 0.00 | 0.00 | 0.00 | 0.00 | 0.00 | 0.01 | 0.03 | 0.06 | 0.08 | 0.11 | 0.12 | 15.63 | 30.24 | 36.55 | 42.15 | 86.49 | 135.75 | 170.16 | 213.35 |
| Anglicans, m | 0.00 | 0.00 | 0.00 | 0.00 | 0.00 | 0.00 | 0.00 | 0.00 | 0.00 | 0.00 | 0.00 | 0.00 | 0.00 | 0.00 | 0.10 | 0.31 | 0.38 | 0.44 | 0.97 | 1.61 | 2.08 | 2.68 |
| Protestants, m | 0.00 | 0.00 | 0.00 | 0.00 | 0.00 | 0.00 | 0.00 | 0.00 | 0.00 | 0.00 | 0.00 | 0.00 | 0.01 | 0.06 | 6.49 | 12.77 | 15.35 | 17.59 | 33.35 | 48.55 | 58.60 | 70.74 |
| Independents, m | 0.00 | 0.00 | 0.00 | 0.00 | 0.00 | 0.00 | 0.00 | 0.00 | 0.00 | 0.00 | 0.00 | 0.00 | 0.00 | 0.00 | 4.77 | 10.45 | 12.72 | 14.67 | 32.87 | 54.54 | 70.30 | 90.64 |
| Marginal Christians, m | 0.00 | 0.00 | 0.00 | 0.00 | 0.00 | 0.00 | 0.00 | 0.00 | 0.00 | 0.00 | 0.00 | 0.00 | 0.00 | 0.00 | 0.06 | 0.37 | 0.46 | 0.57 | 1.74 | 2.71 | 3.38 | 4.22 |
| **Christians %** | **0.00** | **0.00** | **0.00** | **0.00** | **0.00** | **0.00** | **0.00** | **0.00** | **0.11** | **0.31** | **0.57** | **0.71** | **0.90** | **1.07** | **75.53** | **80.49** | **81.36** | **81.62** | **84.74** | **86.33** | **90.04** | **91.07** |
| Christian growth rate, % p.a. | 0.00 | 0.00 | 0.00 | 0.00 | 0.00 | 0.00 | 0.00 | 0.00 | 3.93 | 0.74 | 0.70 | 0.58 | 0.81 | 0.96 | 7.49 | 3.18 | 3.76 | 2.76 | 2.82 | 1.68 | 0.69 | 0.11 |
| Christian nett increase p.a., m | 0.00 | 0.00 | 0.00 | 0.00 | 0.00 | 0.00 | 0.00 | 0.00 | 0.00 | 0.00 | 0.00 | 0.00 | 0.00 | 0.00 | 2.27 | 1.80 | 2.56 | 2.16 | 4.41 | 3.97 | 2.32 | 0.42 |
| Gains: births+converts,m | 0.00 | 0.00 | 0.00 | 0.00 | 0.00 | 0.00 | 0.00 | 0.00 | 0.00 | 0.00 | 0.00 | 0.00 | 0.00 | 0.01 | 2.96 | 2.80 | 3.74 | 3.40 | 5.82 | 5.85 | 4.68 | 2.77 |
| Losses: deaths+defectors,m | 0.00 | 0.00 | 0.00 | 0.00 | 0.00 | 0.00 | 0.00 | 0.00 | 0.00 | 0.00 | 0.00 | 0.00 | 0.00 | 0.01 | 0.69 | 0.99 | 1.18 | 1.24 | 1.41 | 1.88 | 2.35 | 2.35 |
| World B, m | 0.00 | 0.00 | 0.00 | 0.00 | 0.00 | 0.00 | 0.00 | 0.00 | 0.10 | 0.20 | 0.50 | 0.80 | 1.20 | 2.37 | 2.77 | 7.04 | 8.11 | 9.54 | 16.07 | 22.66 | 22.06 | 22.77 |
| World B % | 0.00 | 0.00 | 0.00 | 0.00 | 0.00 | 0.00 | 0.00 | 0.00 | 1.14 | 2.08 | 4.74 | 7.14 | 9.02 | 13.10 | 6.92 | 10.00 | 9.69 | 9.98 | 8.70 | 8.25 | 5.93 | 5.53 |
| World B growth rate, % p.a. | 0.00 | 0.00 | 0.00 | 0.00 | 0.00 | 0.00 | 0.00 | 0.00 | 9.35 | 0.46 | 0.92 | 0.94 | 0.81 | 1.37 | 0.23 | 4.77 | 2.88 | 3.30 | 2.11 | 1.39 | -0.05 | 0.03 |
| World B increase p.a., m | 0.00 | 0.00 | 0.00 | 0.00 | 0.00 | 0.00 | 0.00 | 0.00 | 0.11 | 0.01 | 0.04 | 0.07 | 0.07 | 0.18 | 0.02 | 0.48 | 0.28 | 0.33 | 0.18 | 0.11 | 0.00 | 0.00 |
| World A, m | 1.35 | 1.70 | 2.10 | 2.55 | 3.75 | 4.50 | 5.80 | 7.15 | 8.64 | 9.37 | 9.99 | 10.32 | 11.98 | 15.52 | 7.04 | 6.69 | 7.49 | 8.04 | 12.12 | 14.87 | 15.00 | 14.00 |
| World A % | 100.00 | 100.00 | 100.00 | 100.00 | 100.00 | 100.00 | 100.00 | 100.00 | 98.74 | 97.60 | 94.69 | 92.14 | 90.08 | 85.83 | 17.55 | 9.51 | 8.95 | 8.40 | 6.56 | 5.41 | 4.03 | 3.40 |
| World A growth rate, % p.a. | 0.34 | 0.34 | 0.11 | 0.10 | 0.13 | 0.09 | 0.13 | 0.14 | 0.13 | 0.05 | 0.06 | 0.07 | 0.30 | 0.52 | -1.12 | -0.25 | 2.29 | 1.41 | 1.66 | 0.82 | 0.02 | -0.07 |
| World A increase p.a., m | 0.00 | 0.01 | 0.00 | 0.00 | 0.00 | 0.00 | 0.01 | 0.01 | 0.01 | 0.01 | 0.01 | 0.01 | 0.04 | 0.08 | -0.08 | -0.02 | 0.17 | 0.11 | 0.20 | 0.12 | 0.00 | -0.01 |

The **2 axes** below are: horizontally, years AD by 20-year gaps; vertically, persons (logarithmic scale).
The **3 lines** on each graph are, from top to bottom: live **population**, live **evangelized persons**, live **Christians**.
**Statistics** and trends for 22 years are given, for each geopolitical area, in its facing table opposite.

## Northern Africa

**A** = AD 33  Gospel introduced to Egypt; Alexandria and Carthage become strong centers of Christianity
**B** =   500  Latinized peoples nearly all Christians; Berbers begin to join churches; Region over 50% Christian
**C** =   700  Mass conversions to Islam steadily erode Christian population
**D** =  1000  Small church in Egypt and Sudan survives under Islam for several centuries
**E** =  1850  Roman Catholic missions enjoy mild success in French and Italian colonies
**F** =  2000  Region is 9% Christian; 60% evangelized

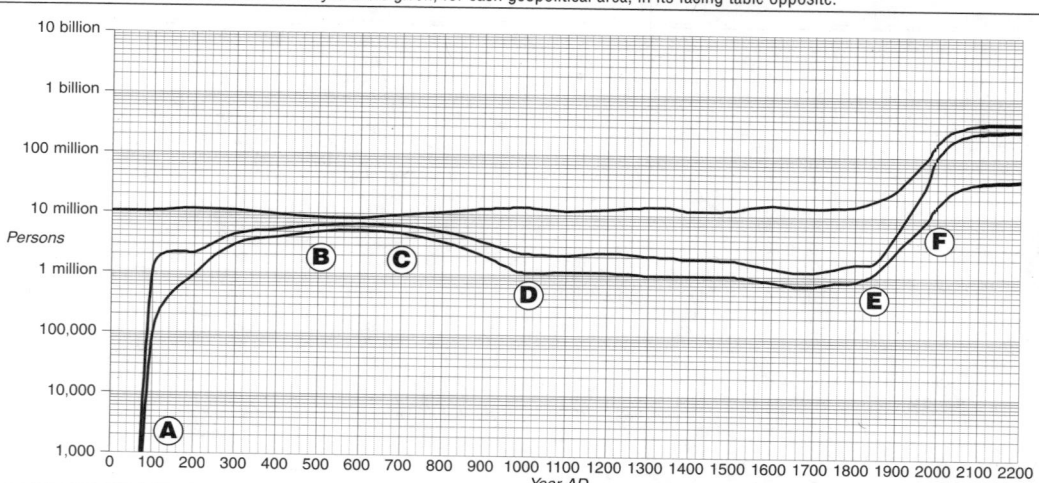

## Southern Africa

**A** = 1300  Great Zimbabwe kingdom uncontacted by Christians
**B** = 1500  Roman Catholics begin work in South Africa
**C** = 1700  Christian growth among colonists and some Africans
**D** = 1900  Major African tribes converted; Independent churches emerge
**E** = 2000  Region is 83% Christian; 98% evangelized

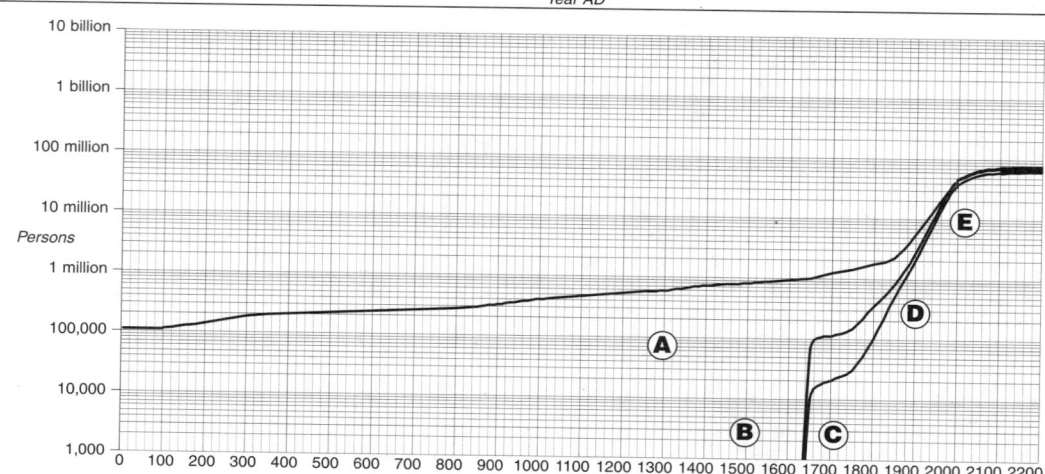

## Western Africa

**A** = c700  Small Christian community of Tuaregs and other Berbers, forced south by Muslim conquest, appears in Niger, later disappears
**B** = 1445  Roman Catholics begin work in Senegal
**C** = 1950  All Christian traditions enjoy success, especially along the coast
**D** = 2000  Region is 34% Christian; 71% evangelized

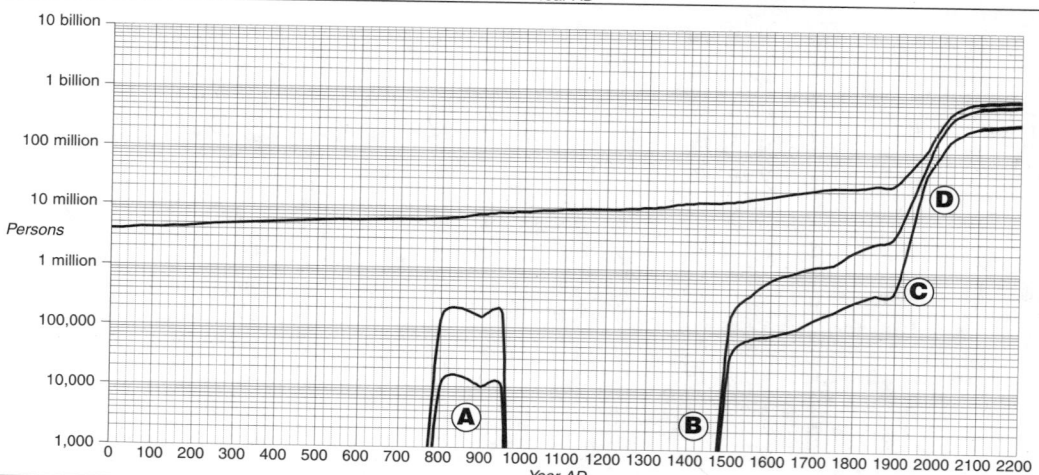

## ANTARCTICA

**A** = 1700  Continent not yet discovered by humans
**B** = 1900  First explorers spend extensive periods of time on continent
**C** = 1961  Antarctic Treaty signed; territories later claimed by 39 nations
**D** = 2000  Population (scientists, engineers, technicians) is 75% Christian; 95% evangelized

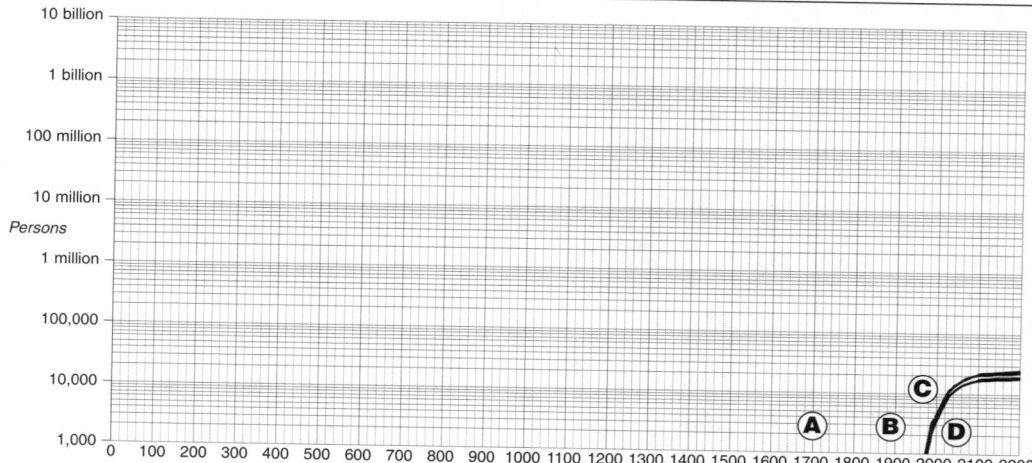

| Area / Year, AD | 33 | 100 | 300 | 500 | 800 | 1000 | 1200 | 1350 | 1500 | 1650 | 1750 | 1800 | 1850 | 1900 | 1970 | 1990 | 1995 | 2000 | 2025 | 2050 | 2100 | 2200 |
|---|---|---|---|---|---|---|---|---|---|---|---|---|---|---|---|---|---|---|---|---|---|---|
| 1 | 2 | 3 | 4 | 5 | 6 | 7 | 8 | 9 | 10 | 11 | 12 | 13 | 14 | 15 | 16 | 17 | 18 | 19 | 20 | 21 | 22 | 23 |
| **Northern Africa** (8 countries in 2000) | | | | | | | | | | | | | | | | | | | | | | |
| Population, m(=millions) | 10.65 | 10.70 | 11.10 | 8.80 | 10.80 | 13.50 | 12.40 | 13.70 | 12.25 | 14.20 | 14.30 | 14.75 | 18.60 | 28.21 | 85.39 | 142.04 | 157.08 | 173.27 | 249.12 | 303.76 | 356.85 | 376.55 |
| Growth rate, % p.a. | 0.01 | 0.01 | 0.02 | -0.12 | 0.07 | 0.11 | -0.04 | 0.07 | -0.07 | 0.10 | 0.01 | 0.06 | 0.46 | 0.84 | 1.59 | 2.58 | 2.03 | 1.98 | 1.46 | 0.80 | 0.32 | 0.05 |
| Increase p.a., m | 0.00 | 0.00 | 0.00 | -0.01 | 0.01 | 0.02 | -0.01 | 0.01 | -0.01 | 0.01 | 0.00 | 0.01 | 0.09 | 0.24 | 1.36 | 3.66 | 3.19 | 3.43 | 3.64 | 2.42 | 1.15 | 0.20 |
| Evangelized persons, m | 0.00 | 1.09 | 4.50 | 6.40 | 5.15 | 2.26 | 2.30 | 2.00 | 1.80 | 1.20 | 1.40 | 1.65 | 1.80 | 5.24 | 29.67 | 79.05 | 91.15 | 104.00 | 161.39 | 207.92 | 256.85 | 276.55 |
| Evangelized persons % | 0.00 | 10.19 | 40.54 | 72.73 | 47.69 | 16.74 | 18.55 | 14.60 | 14.69 | 8.45 | 9.79 | 11.19 | 9.68 | 18.58 | 34.74 | 55.65 | 58.03 | 60.03 | 64.78 | 68.45 | 71.98 | 73.44 |
| Outreach per Christian | — | 11.11 | 0.50 | 0.28 | 0.49 | 1.13 | 1.09 | 1.00 | 0.80 | 0.71 | 0.75 | 0.94 | 0.50 | 0.94 | 2.71 | 5.00 | 5.23 | 5.56 | 5.98 | 5.93 | 5.94 | 5.75 |
| **Christians, m** | **0.00** | **0.09** | **3.00** | **5.00** | **3.45** | **1.06** | **1.10** | **1.00** | **1.00** | **0.70** | **0.80** | **0.85** | **1.20** | **2.70** | **8.00** | **13.18** | **14.63** | **15.86** | **23.13** | **29.99** | **37.00** | **41.00** |
| Orthodox, m | 0.00 | 0.09 | 2.00 | 3.50 | 2.25 | 1.01 | 1.08 | 0.98 | 0.99 | 0.66 | 0.73 | 0.75 | 0.90 | 1.80 | 6.16 | 8.20 | 8.95 | 9.58 | 12.38 | 14.48 | 15.67 | 16.94 |
| Roman Catholics, m | 0.00 | 0.00 | 1.00 | 1.50 | 1.20 | 0.05 | 0.02 | 0.02 | 0.01 | 0.04 | 0.07 | 0.10 | 0.30 | 0.82 | 1.18 | 2.89 | 3.20 | 3.58 | 6.12 | 8.52 | 10.05 | 11.87 |
| Anglicans, m | 0.00 | 0.00 | 0.00 | 0.00 | 0.00 | 0.00 | 0.00 | 0.00 | 0.00 | 0.00 | 0.00 | 0.00 | 0.00 | 0.01 | 0.30 | 1.80 | 2.10 | 2.32 | 3.60 | 4.60 | 5.21 | 5.89 |
| Protestants, m | 0.00 | 0.00 | 0.00 | 0.00 | 0.00 | 0.00 | 0.00 | 0.00 | 0.00 | 0.00 | 0.00 | 0.00 | 0.00 | 0.05 | 0.22 | 0.99 | 1.15 | 1.36 | 2.28 | 3.29 | 3.96 | 4.77 |
| Independents, m | 0.00 | 0.00 | 0.00 | 0.00 | 0.00 | 0.00 | 0.00 | 0.00 | 0.00 | 0.00 | 0.00 | 0.00 | 0.00 | 0.00 | 0.13 | 0.46 | 0.56 | 0.63 | 1.35 | 2.29 | 2.98 | 3.89 |
| Marginal Christians, m | 0.00 | 0.00 | 0.00 | 0.00 | 0.00 | 0.00 | 0.00 | 0.00 | 0.00 | 0.00 | 0.00 | 0.00 | 0.00 | 0.00 | 0.00 | 0.00 | 0.00 | 0.00 | 0.01 | 0.02 | 0.03 | 0.05 |
| **Christians %** | **0.00** | **0.84** | **27.03** | **56.82** | **31.94** | **7.85** | **8.87** | **7.30** | **8.16** | **4.93** | **5.59** | **5.76** | **6.45** | **9.57** | **9.37** | **9.28** | **9.31** | **9.16** | **9.28** | **9.87** | **10.37** | **10.89** |
| Christian growth rate, % p.a. | 0.00 | 3.33 | 1.77 | 0.26 | -0.12 | -0.59 | 0.02 | -0.06 | 0.00 | -0.24 | 0.13 | 0.12 | 0.69 | 1.64 | 1.56 | 2.53 | 2.11 | 1.63 | 1.52 | 1.04 | 0.42 | 0.10 |
| Christian nett increase p.a., m | 0.00 | 0.00 | 0.05 | 0.01 | 0.00 | -0.01 | 0.00 | 0.00 | 0.00 | 0.00 | 0.00 | 0.00 | 0.01 | 0.04 | 0.13 | 0.33 | 0.31 | 0.26 | 0.35 | 0.31 | 0.16 | 0.04 |
| Gains: births+converts,m | 0.00 | 0.01 | 0.18 | 0.22 | 0.14 | 0.04 | 0.05 | 0.04 | 0.04 | 0.02 | 0.03 | 0.03 | 0.05 | 0.12 | 0.27 | 0.47 | 0.45 | 0.40 | 0.54 | 0.62 | 0.62 | 0.69 |
| Losses: deaths+defectors,m | 0.00 | 0.00 | 0.12 | 0.21 | 0.14 | 0.04 | 0.05 | 0.04 | 0.04 | 0.02 | 0.03 | 0.03 | 0.04 | 0.07 | 0.15 | 0.14 | 0.14 | 0.14 | 0.19 | 0.30 | 0.47 | 0.65 |
| World B, m | 0.00 | 1.00 | 1.50 | 1.40 | 1.70 | 1.20 | 1.20 | 1.00 | 0.80 | 0.50 | 0.60 | 0.80 | 0.60 | 2.54 | 21.67 | 65.87 | 76.52 | 88.14 | 138.26 | 177.93 | 219.85 | 235.55 |
| World B % | 0.00 | 9.35 | 13.51 | 15.91 | 15.74 | 8.89 | 9.68 | 7.30 | 6.53 | 3.52 | 4.20 | 5.42 | 3.23 | 9.01 | 25.38 | 46.37 | 48.71 | 50.87 | 55.50 | 58.58 | 61.61 | 62.55 |
| World B growth rate, % p.a. | 0.00 | 6.01 | 0.20 | -0.03 | 0.06 | -0.17 | 0.00 | -0.12 | -0.15 | -0.31 | 0.18 | 0.58 | -0.57 | 2.93 | 3.11 | 5.72 | 3.04 | 2.87 | 1.82 | 1.01 | 0.42 | 0.07 |
| World B increase p.a., m | 0.00 | 0.56 | 0.03 | -0.01 | 0.01 | -0.02 | 0.00 | -0.01 | -0.01 | -0.01 | 0.01 | 0.03 | -0.02 | 0.26 | 0.79 | 2.65 | 1.48 | 1.46 | 1.01 | 0.59 | 0.26 | 0.04 |
| World A, m | 10.65 | 9.61 | 6.60 | 2.40 | 5.65 | 11.24 | 10.10 | 11.70 | 10.45 | 13.00 | 12.90 | 13.10 | 16.80 | 22.97 | 55.72 | 62.99 | 65.93 | 69.26 | 87.73 | 95.84 | 100.00 | 100.00 |
| World A % | 100.00 | 89.81 | 59.46 | 27.27 | 52.31 | 83.26 | 81.45 | 85.40 | 85.31 | 91.55 | 90.21 | 88.81 | 90.32 | 81.42 | 65.26 | 44.35 | 41.97 | 39.97 | 35.22 | 31.55 | 28.02 | 26.56 |
| World A growth rate, % p.a. | 0.01 | -0.15 | -0.19 | -0.50 | 0.29 | 0.34 | -0.05 | 0.10 | -0.08 | 0.15 | -0.01 | 0.03 | 0.50 | 0.63 | 1.27 | 0.62 | 0.92 | 0.99 | 0.95 | 0.35 | 0.08 | 0.00 |
| World A increase p.a., m | 0.00 | -0.01 | -0.01 | -0.01 | 0.02 | 0.04 | -0.01 | 0.01 | -0.01 | 0.02 | 0.00 | 0.00 | 0.08 | 0.14 | 0.71 | 0.39 | 0.60 | 0.69 | 0.83 | 0.34 | 0.08 | 0.00 |
| **Southern Africa** (5 countries in 2000) | | | | | | | | | | | | | | | | | | | | | | |
| Population, m(=millions) | 0.11 | 0.11 | 0.18 | 0.22 | 0.27 | 0.40 | 0.52 | 0.65 | 0.80 | 1.01 | 1.44 | 1.75 | 2.27 | 5.55 | 25.00 | 39.11 | 43.29 | 46.89 | 55.89 | 65.54 | 72.13 | 74.48 |
| Growth rate, % p.a. | 0.00 | 0.00 | 0.25 | 0.10 | 0.07 | 0.20 | 0.13 | 0.15 | 0.14 | 0.16 | 0.36 | 0.39 | 0.52 | 1.80 | 2.17 | 2.26 | 2.05 | 1.61 | 0.70 | 0.64 | 0.19 | 0.03 |
| Increase p.a., m | 0.00 | 0.00 | 0.00 | 0.00 | 0.00 | 0.00 | 0.00 | 0.00 | 0.00 | 0.00 | 0.01 | 0.01 | 0.01 | 0.10 | 0.54 | 0.89 | 0.89 | 0.75 | 0.39 | 0.42 | 0.14 | 0.02 |
| Evangelized persons, m | 0.00 | 0.00 | 0.00 | 0.00 | 0.00 | 0.00 | 0.00 | 0.00 | 0.00 | 0.07 | 0.15 | 0.35 | 0.80 | 2.69 | 23.71 | 38.18 | 42.29 | 45.97 | 54.59 | 64.03 | 70.63 | 72.98 |
| Evangelized persons % | 0.00 | 0.00 | 0.00 | 0.00 | 0.00 | 0.00 | 0.00 | 0.00 | 0.00 | 6.93 | 10.42 | 20.00 | 35.24 | 48.43 | 94.86 | 97.61 | 97.71 | 98.04 | 97.68 | 97.70 | 97.92 | 97.99 |
| Outreach per Christian | — | — | — | — | — | — | — | — | — | 6.00 | 4.00 | 2.50 | 0.60 | 0.31 | 0.23 | 0.20 | 0.18 | 0.18 | 0.17 | 0.16 | 0.15 | 0.13 |
| **Christians, m** | **0.00** | **0.00** | **0.00** | **0.00** | **0.00** | **0.00** | **0.00** | **0.00** | **0.00** | **0.01** | **0.03** | **0.10** | **0.50** | **2.06** | **19.26** | **31.94** | **35.71** | **38.96** | **46.78** | **55.09** | **61.50** | **64.50** |
| Orthodox, m | 0.00 | 0.00 | 0.00 | 0.00 | 0.00 | 0.00 | 0.00 | 0.00 | 0.00 | 0.00 | 0.00 | 0.00 | 0.00 | 0.00 | 0.03 | 0.11 | 0.13 | 0.15 | 0.20 | 0.30 | 0.37 | 0.45 |
| Roman Catholics, m | 0.00 | 0.00 | 0.00 | 0.00 | 0.00 | 0.00 | 0.00 | 0.00 | 0.00 | 0.01 | 0.01 | 0.02 | 0.04 | 0.06 | 2.17 | 3.68 | 4.16 | 4.58 | 6.41 | 8.37 | 9.57 | 10.94 |
| Anglicans, m | 0.00 | 0.00 | 0.00 | 0.00 | 0.00 | 0.00 | 0.00 | 0.00 | 0.00 | 0.00 | 0.00 | 0.00 | 0.10 | 0.21 | 1.35 | 2.31 | 2.60 | 2.84 | 3.59 | 4.29 | 4.68 | 5.11 |
| Protestants, m | 0.00 | 0.00 | 0.00 | 0.00 | 0.00 | 0.00 | 0.00 | 0.00 | 0.00 | 0.00 | 0.02 | 0.08 | 0.36 | 1.07 | 7.26 | 11.52 | 12.75 | 13.84 | 16.60 | 19.98 | 21.92 | 24.06 |
| Independents, m | 0.00 | 0.00 | 0.00 | 0.00 | 0.00 | 0.00 | 0.00 | 0.00 | 0.00 | 0.00 | 0.00 | 0.00 | 0.00 | 0.02 | 4.86 | 15.96 | 18.16 | 19.90 | 25.49 | 30.99 | 34.17 | 37.69 |
| Marginal Christians, m | 0.00 | 0.00 | 0.00 | 0.00 | 0.00 | 0.00 | 0.00 | 0.00 | 0.00 | 0.00 | 0.00 | 0.00 | 0.00 | 0.00 | 0.09 | 0.16 | 0.19 | 0.21 | 0.44 | 0.68 | 0.84 | 1.05 |
| **Christians %** | **0.00** | **0.00** | **0.00** | **0.00** | **0.00** | **0.00** | **0.00** | **0.00** | **0.00** | **0.99** | **2.08** | **5.71** | **22.03** | **37.07** | **77.03** | **81.65** | **82.51** | **83.10** | **83.70** | **84.06** | **85.26** | **86.60** |
| Christian growth rate, % p.a. | 0.00 | 0.00 | 0.00 | 0.00 | 0.00 | 0.00 | 0.00 | 0.00 | 0.00 | 3.12 | 1.10 | 2.44 | 3.27 | 2.87 | 3.25 | 2.56 | 2.26 | 1.76 | 0.73 | 0.66 | 0.22 | 0.05 |
| Christian nett increase p.a., m | 0.00 | 0.00 | 0.00 | 0.00 | 0.00 | 0.00 | 0.00 | 0.00 | 0.00 | 0.00 | 0.00 | 0.00 | 0.02 | 0.06 | 0.63 | 0.82 | 0.81 | 0.68 | 0.34 | 0.36 | 0.14 | 0.03 |
| Gains: births+converts,m | 0.00 | 0.00 | 0.00 | 0.00 | 0.00 | 0.00 | 0.00 | 0.00 | 0.00 | 0.00 | 0.00 | 0.01 | 0.03 | 0.11 | 0.93 | 1.20 | 1.32 | 1.46 | 0.97 | 1.11 | 0.98 | 0.92 |
| Losses: deaths+defectors,m | 0.00 | 0.00 | 0.00 | 0.00 | 0.00 | 0.00 | 0.00 | 0.00 | 0.00 | 0.00 | 0.00 | 0.00 | 0.01 | 0.05 | 0.30 | 0.38 | 0.51 | 0.78 | 0.63 | 0.75 | 0.84 | 0.89 |
| World B, m | 0.00 | 0.00 | 0.00 | 0.00 | 0.00 | 0.00 | 0.00 | 0.00 | 0.00 | 0.06 | 0.12 | 0.25 | 0.30 | 0.63 | 4.46 | 6.24 | 6.58 | 7.00 | 7.81 | 8.94 | 9.13 | 8.48 |
| World B % | 0.00 | 0.00 | 0.00 | 0.00 | 0.00 | 0.00 | 0.00 | 0.00 | 0.00 | 5.94 | 8.33 | 14.29 | 13.22 | 11.36 | 17.82 | 15.96 | 15.20 | 14.94 | 13.98 | 13.64 | 12.66 | 11.38 |
| World B growth rate, % p.a. | 0.00 | 0.00 | 0.00 | 0.00 | 0.00 | 0.00 | 0.00 | 0.00 | 0.00 | 1.12 | 0.70 | 1.48 | 0.37 | 1.50 | 2.83 | 1.70 | 1.05 | 1.25 | 0.44 | 0.54 | 0.04 | -0.07 |
| World B increase p.a., m | 0.00 | 0.00 | 0.00 | 0.00 | 0.00 | 0.00 | 0.00 | 0.00 | 0.00 | 0.07 | 0.06 | 0.21 | 0.05 | 0.17 | 0.51 | 0.27 | 0.16 | 0.19 | 0.06 | 0.07 | 0.01 | -0.01 |
| World A, m | 0.11 | 0.11 | 0.18 | 0.22 | 0.27 | 0.40 | 0.52 | 0.65 | 0.80 | 0.94 | 1.29 | 1.40 | 1.47 | 2.86 | 1.29 | 0.93 | 0.99 | 0.92 | 1.30 | 1.51 | 1.50 | 1.50 |
| World A % | 100.00 | 100.00 | 100.00 | 100.00 | 100.00 | 100.00 | 100.00 | 100.00 | 100.00 | 93.07 | 89.58 | 80.00 | 64.76 | 51.57 | 5.14 | 2.39 | 2.29 | 1.96 | 2.32 | 2.30 | 2.08 | 2.01 |
| World A growth rate, % p.a. | 0.00 | 0.00 | 0.25 | 0.10 | 0.07 | 0.20 | 0.13 | 0.15 | 0.14 | 0.11 | 0.32 | 0.16 | 0.10 | 1.34 | -1.14 | -1.59 | 1.24 | -1.53 | 1.38 | 0.61 | -0.01 | 0.00 |
| World A increase p.a., m | 0.00 | 0.00 | 0.00 | 0.00 | 0.00 | 0.00 | 0.00 | 0.00 | 0.00 | 0.00 | 0.00 | 0.00 | 0.00 | 0.04 | -0.01 | -0.01 | 0.01 | -0.01 | 0.02 | 0.01 | 0.00 | 0.00 |
| **Western Africa** (17 countries in 2000) | | | | | | | | | | | | | | | | | | | | | | |
| Population, m(=millions) | 3.85 | 4.10 | 4.90 | 5.65 | 6.35 | 8.50 | 9.80 | 11.05 | 13.25 | 18.80 | 23.25 | 23.55 | 25.90 | 27.93 | 98.10 | 171.52 | 195.71 | 221.67 | 382.45 | 526.59 | 675.30 | 733.78 |
| Growth rate, % p.a. | 0.09 | 0.09 | 0.09 | 0.07 | 0.04 | 0.15 | 0.07 | 0.08 | 0.12 | 0.23 | 0.21 | 0.03 | 0.19 | 0.15 | 1.81 | 2.83 | 2.67 | 2.52 | 2.21 | 1.29 | 0.50 | 0.08 |
| Increase p.a., m | 0.00 | 0.00 | 0.00 | 0.00 | 0.00 | 0.01 | 0.01 | 0.01 | 0.02 | 0.04 | 0.05 | 0.01 | 0.05 | 0.04 | 1.78 | 4.86 | 5.23 | 5.59 | 8.44 | 6.78 | 3.37 | 0.61 |
| Evangelized persons, m | 0.00 | 0.00 | 0.00 | 0.00 | 0.13 | 0.00 | 0.00 | 0.00 | 0.13 | 0.90 | 1.30 | 2.10 | 2.90 | 3.96 | 48.93 | 113.75 | 133.69 | 156.85 | 288.24 | 415.36 | 550.30 | 613.78 |
| Evangelized persons % | 0.00 | 0.00 | 0.00 | 0.00 | 2.05 | 0.00 | 0.00 | 0.00 | 0.98 | 4.79 | 5.59 | 8.92 | 11.20 | 14.18 | 49.88 | 66.32 | 68.31 | 70.76 | 75.37 | 78.88 | 81.49 | 83.65 |
| Outreach per Christian | — | — | — | — | — | — | — | — | 3.33 | 8.00 | 5.50 | 6.00 | 6.25 | 7.38 | 0.59 | 0.95 | 1.00 | 1.06 | 1.12 | 1.16 | 1.12 | 1.05 |
| **Christians, m** | **0.00** | **0.00** | **0.00** | **0.00** | **0.01** | **0.00** | **0.00** | **0.00** | **0.03** | **0.10** | **0.20** | **0.30** | **0.40** | **0.47** | **30.82** | **58.37** | **66.87** | **76.21** | **136.10** | **191.90** | **260.00** | **300.00** |
| Orthodox, m | 0.00 | 0.00 | 0.00 | 0.00 | 0.01 | 0.00 | 0.00 | 0.00 | 0.00 | 0.00 | 0.00 | 0.00 | 0.00 | 0.00 | 0.01 | 0.02 | 0.02 | 0.03 | 0.04 | 0.05 | 0.06 | 0.07 |
| Roman Catholics, m | 0.00 | 0.00 | 0.00 | 0.00 | 0.00 | 0.00 | 0.00 | 0.00 | 0.03 | 0.10 | 0.20 | 0.28 | 0.29 | 0.13 | 7.62 | 17.12 | 19.79 | 22.64 | 43.38 | 65.33 | 80.20 | 98.48 |
| Anglicans, m | 0.00 | 0.00 | 0.00 | 0.00 | 0.00 | 0.00 | 0.00 | 0.00 | 0.00 | 0.00 | 0.00 | 0.01 | 0.03 | 0.06 | 3.09 | 15.01 | 17.77 | 20.39 | 35.38 | 47.36 | 54.81 | 63.44 |
| Protestants, m | 0.00 | 0.00 | 0.00 | 0.00 | 0.00 | 0.00 | 0.00 | 0.00 | 0.00 | 0.00 | 0.00 | 0.01 | 0.07 | 0.15 | 5.55 | 15.35 | 17.71 | 20.48 | 38.83 | 58.51 | 71.84 | 88.24 |
| Independents, m | 0.00 | 0.00 | 0.00 | 0.00 | 0.00 | 0.00 | 0.00 | 0.00 | 0.00 | 0.00 | 0.00 | 0.00 | 0.01 | 0.02 | 4.79 | 21.44 | 25.31 | 29.46 | 45.49 | 67.80 | 82.81 | 101.16 |
| Marginal Christians, m | 0.00 | 0.00 | 0.00 | 0.00 | 0.00 | 0.00 | 0.00 | 0.00 | 0.00 | 0.00 | 0.00 | 0.00 | 0.00 | 0.00 | 0.26 | 0.60 | 0.75 | 0.90 | 2.25 | 4.08 | 5.49 | 7.39 |
| **Christians %** | **0.00** | **0.00** | **0.00** | **0.00** | **0.16** | **0.00** | **0.00** | **0.00** | **0.23** | **0.53** | **0.86** | **1.27** | **1.54** | **1.69** | **31.42** | **34.03** | **34.17** | **34.38** | **35.59** | **36.44** | **38.50** | **40.88** |
| Christian growth rate, % p.a. | 0.00 | 0.00 | 0.00 | 0.00 | 0.77 | -8.80 | 0.00 | 0.00 | 2.29 | 0.81 | 0.70 | 0.81 | 0.58 | 0.33 | 6.15 | 3.24 | 2.76 | 2.65 | 2.35 | 1.38 | 0.61 | 0.14 |
| Christian nett increase p.a., m | 0.00 | 0.00 | 0.00 | 0.00 | 0.00 | 0.00 | 0.00 | 0.00 | 0.00 | 0.00 | 0.00 | 0.00 | 0.00 | 0.00 | 1.90 | 1.89 | 1.84 | 2.02 | 3.19 | 2.66 | 1.58 | 0.43 |
| Gains: births+converts,m | 0.00 | 0.00 | 0.00 | 0.00 | 0.00 | 0.00 | 0.00 | 0.00 | 0.00 | 0.00 | 0.01 | 0.01 | 0.02 | 0.02 | 2.62 | 2.94 | 2.98 | 3.24 | 4.56 | 4.42 | 3.77 | 2.75 |
| Losses: deaths+defectors,m | 0.00 | 0.00 | 0.00 | 0.00 | 0.00 | 0.00 | 0.00 | 0.00 | 0.00 | 0.00 | 0.01 | 0.01 | 0.01 | 0.01 | 0.73 | 1.05 | 1.13 | 1.22 | 1.36 | 1.76 | 2.19 | 2.32 |
| World B, m | 0.00 | 0.00 | 0.00 | 0.00 | 0.12 | 0.00 | 0.00 | 0.00 | 0.10 | 0.80 | 1.10 | 1.80 | 2.50 | 3.49 | 18.11 | 55.37 | 66.81 | 80.64 | 152.14 | 223.46 | 290.30 | 313.78 |
| World B % | 0.00 | 0.00 | 0.00 | 0.00 | 1.89 | 0.00 | 0.00 | 0.00 | 0.75 | 4.26 | 4.73 | 7.64 | 9.65 | 12.49 | 18.46 | 32.28 | 34.14 | 36.38 | 39.78 | 42.44 | 42.99 | 42.76 |
| World B growth rate, % p.a. | 0.00 | 0.00 | 0.00 | 0.00 | 1.06 | -100.00 | 0.00 | 0.00 | 2.64 | 1.40 | 0.32 | 0.99 | 0.66 | 0.67 | 2.38 | 5.75 | 3.83 | 3.83 | 2.57 | 1.55 | 0.52 | 0.08 |
| World B increase p.a., m | 0.00 | 0.00 | 0.00 | 0.00 | 0.02 | 0.00 | 0.00 | 0.00 | 0.02 | 0.06 | 0.02 | 0.08 | 0.06 | 0.08 | 0.44 | 1.86 | 1.31 | 1.39 | 1.02 | 0.66 | 0.23 | 0.03 |
| World A, m | 3.85 | 4.10 | 4.90 | 5.65 | 6.22 | 8.50 | 9.80 | 11.05 | 13.12 | 17.90 | 21.95 | 21.45 | 23.00 | 23.97 | 49.17 | 57.77 | 62.02 | 64.82 | 94.21 | 111.23 | 125.00 | 120.00 |
| World A % | 100.00 | 100.00 | 100.00 | 100.00 | 97.95 | 100.00 | 100.00 | 100.00 | 99.02 | 95.21 | 94.41 | 91.08 | 88.80 | 85.82 | 50.12 | 33.68 | 31.69 | 29.24 | 24.63 | 21.12 | 18.51 | 16.35 |
| World A growth rate, % p.a. | 0.09 | 0.09 | 0.09 | 0.07 | 0.03 | 0.16 | 0.07 | 0.08 | 0.11 | 0.21 | 0.20 | -0.05 | 0.14 | 0.08 | 1.03 | 0.81 | 1.43 | 0.89 | 1.51 | 0.67 | 0.23 | -0.04 |
| World A increase p.a., m | 0.00 | 0.00 | 0.00 | 0.00 | 0.00 | 0.01 | 0.01 | 0.01 | 0.02 | 0.04 | 0.04 | -0.01 | 0.03 | 0.02 | 0.51 | 0.47 | 0.89 | 0.58 | 1.42 | 0.74 | 0.29 | -0.05 |
| **ANTARCTICA** (territories claimed by 39 nations) | | | | | | | | | | | | | | | | | | | | | | |
| Population, m(=millions) | 0.00 | 0.00 | 0.00 | 0.00 | 0.00 | 0.00 | 0.00 | 0.00 | 0.00 | 0.00 | 0.00 | 0.00 | 0.00 | 0.00 | 0.00 | 0.00 | 0.00 | 0.00 | 0.01 | 0.02 | 0.02 | 0.02 |
| Growth rate, % p.a. | 0.00 | 0.00 | 0.00 | 0.00 | 0.00 | 0.00 | 0.00 | 0.00 | 0.00 | 0.00 | 0.00 | 0.00 | 0.00 | 0.00 | 9.89 | 9.89 | 3.40 | 2.90 | 3.25 | 1.64 | 0.70 | 0.12 |
| Increase p.a., m | 0.00 | 0.00 | 0.00 | 0.00 | 0.00 | 0.00 | 0.00 | 0.00 | 0.00 | 0.00 | 0.00 | 0.00 | 0.00 | 0.00 | 0.00 | 0.00 | 0.00 | 0.00 | 0.00 | 0.00 | 0.00 | 0.00 |
| Evangelized persons, m | 0.00 | 0.00 | 0.00 | 0.00 | 0.00 | 0.00 | 0.00 | 0.00 | 0.00 | 0.00 | 0.00 | 0.00 | 0.00 | 0.00 | 0.00 | 0.00 | 0.00 | 0.00 | 0.01 | 0.01 | 0.02 | 0.02 |
| Evangelized persons % | 0.00 | 0.00 | 0.00 | 0.00 | 0.00 | 0.00 | 0.00 | 0.00 | 0.00 | 0.00 | 0.00 | 0.00 | 0.00 | 0.00 | 90.00 | 93.94 | 94.36 | 94.60 | 96.50 | 97.33 | 97.64 | 97.90 |
| Outreach per Christian | — | — | — | — | — | — | — | — | — | — | — | — | — | — | 0.22 | 0.35 | 0.27 | 0.25 | 0.21 | 0.19 | 0.22 | 0.23 |
| **Christians, m** | **0.00** | **0.00** | **0.00** | **0.00** | **0.00** | **0.00** | **0.00** | **0.00** | **0.00** | **0.00** | **0.00** | **0.00** | **0.00** | **0.00** | **0.00** | **0.00** | **0.00** | **0.00** | **0.01** | **0.01** | **0.02** | **0.02** |
| Orthodox, m | 0.00 | 0.00 | 0.00 | 0.00 | 0.00 | 0.00 | 0.00 | 0.00 | 0.00 | 0.00 | 0.00 | 0.00 | 0.00 | 0.00 | 0.00 | 0.00 | 0.00 | 0.00 | 0.00 | 0.00 | 0.00 | 0.00 |
| Roman Catholics, m | 0.00 | 0.00 | 0.00 | 0.00 | 0.00 | 0.00 | 0.00 | 0.00 | 0.00 | 0.00 | 0.00 | 0.00 | 0.00 | 0.00 | 0.00 | 0.00 | 0.00 | 0.00 | 0.00 | 0.00 | 0.01 | 0.01 |
| Anglicans, m | 0.00 | 0.00 | 0.00 | 0.00 | 0.00 | 0.00 | 0.00 | 0.00 | 0.00 | 0.00 | 0.00 | 0.00 | 0.00 | 0.00 | 0.00 | 0.00 | 0.00 | 0.00 | 0.00 | 0.00 | 0.00 | 0.00 |
| Protestants, m | 0.00 | 0.00 | 0.00 | 0.00 | 0.00 | 0.00 | 0.00 | 0.00 | 0.00 | 0.00 | 0.00 | 0.00 | 0.00 | 0.00 | 0.00 | 0.00 | 0.00 | 0.00 | 0.00 | 0.00 | 0.01 | 0.01 |
| Independents, m | 0.00 | 0.00 | 0.00 | 0.00 | 0.00 | 0.00 | 0.00 | 0.00 | 0.00 | 0.00 | 0.00 | 0.00 | 0.00 | 0.00 | 0.00 | 0.00 | 0.00 | 0.00 | 0.00 | 0.00 | 0.00 | 0.00 |
| Marginal Christians, m | 0.00 | 0.00 | 0.00 | 0.00 | 0.00 | 0.00 | 0.00 | 0.00 | 0.00 | 0.00 | 0.00 | 0.00 | 0.00 | 0.00 | 0.00 | 0.00 | 0.00 | 0.00 | 0.00 | 0.00 | 0.00 | 0.00 |
| **Christians %** | **0.00** | **0.00** | **0.00** | **0.00** | **0.00** | **0.00** | **0.00** | **0.00** | **0.00** | **0.00** | **0.00** | **0.00** | **0.00** | **0.00** | **74.00** | **69.70** | **74.36** | **75.56** | **80.00** | **82.00** | **80.11** | **79.73** |
| Christian growth rate, % p.a. | 0.00 | 0.00 | 0.00 | 0.00 | 0.00 | 0.00 | 0.00 | 0.00 | 0.00 | 0.00 | 0.00 | 0.00 | 0.00 | 0.00 | 9.57 | 9.57 | 4.75 | 3.23 | 3.48 | 1.74 | 0.65 | 0.11 |
| Christian nett increase p.a., m | 0.00 | 0.00 | 0.00 | 0.00 | 0.00 | 0.00 | 0.00 | 0.00 | 0.00 | 0.00 | 0.00 | 0.00 | 0.00 | 0.00 | 0.00 | 0.00 | 0.00 | 0.00 | 0.00 | 0.00 | 0.00 | 0.00 |
| Gains: births+converts,m | 0.00 | 0.00 | 0.00 | 0.00 | 0.00 | 0.00 | 0.00 | 0.00 | 0.00 | 0.00 | 0.00 | 0.00 | 0.00 | 0.00 | 0.00 | 0.00 | 0.00 | 0.00 | 0.00 | 0.00 | 0.00 | 0.00 |
| Losses: deaths+defectors,m | 0.00 | 0.00 | 0.00 | 0.00 | 0.00 | 0.00 | 0.00 | 0.00 | 0.00 | 0.00 | 0.00 | 0.00 | 0.00 | 0.00 | 0.00 | 0.00 | 0.00 | 0.00 | 0.00 | 0.00 | 0.00 | 0.00 |
| World B, m | 0.00 | 0.00 | 0.00 | 0.00 | 0.00 | 0.00 | 0.00 | 0.00 | 0.00 | 0.00 | 0.00 | 0.00 | 0.00 | 0.00 | 0.00 | 0.00 | 0.00 | 0.00 | 0.00 | 0.00 | 0.00 | 0.00 |
| World B % | 0.00 | 0.00 | 0.00 | 0.00 | 0.00 | 0.00 | 0.00 | 0.00 | 0.00 | 0.00 | 0.00 | 0.00 | 0.00 | 0.00 | 16.00 | 24.24 | 20.00 | 19.04 | 16.50 | 15.33 | 17.54 | 18.17 |
| World B growth rate, % p.a. | 0.00 | 0.00 | 0.00 | 0.00 | 0.00 | 0.00 | 0.00 | 0.00 | 0.00 | 0.00 | 0.00 | 0.00 | 0.00 | 0.00 | 12.20 | 12.20 | -0.51 | 1.90 | 2.66 | 1.34 | 0.97 | 0.15 |
| World B increase p.a., m | 0.00 | 0.00 | 0.00 | 0.00 | 0.00 | 0.00 | 0.00 | 0.00 | 0.00 | 0.00 | 0.00 | 0.00 | 0.00 | 0.00 | 1.95 | 2.96 | -0.10 | 0.36 | 0.44 | 0.21 | 0.17 | 0.03 |
| World A, m | 0.00 | 0.00 | 0.00 | 0.00 | 0.00 | 0.00 | 0.00 | 0.00 | 0.00 | 0.00 | 0.00 | 0.00 | 0.00 | 0.00 | 0.00 | 0.00 | 0.00 | 0.00 | 0.00 | 0.00 | 0.00 | 0.00 |
| World A % | 0.00 | 0.00 | 0.00 | 0.00 | 0.00 | 0.00 | 0.00 | 0.00 | 0.00 | 0.00 | 0.00 | 0.00 | 0.00 | 0.00 | 10.00 | 6.06 | 5.64 | 5.40 | 3.50 | 2.67 | 2.36 | 2.10 |
| World A growth rate, % p.a. | 0.00 | 0.00 | 0.00 | 0.00 | 0.00 | 0.00 | 0.00 | 0.00 | 0.00 | 0.00 | 0.00 | 0.00 | 0.00 | 0.00 | 7.18 | 7.18 | 1.92 | 2.01 | 1.47 | 0.54 | 0.45 | 0.00 |
| World A increase p.a., m | 0.00 | 0.00 | 0.00 | 0.00 | 0.00 | 0.00 | 0.00 | 0.00 | 0.00 | 0.00 | 0.00 | 0.00 | 0.00 | 0.00 | 0.00 | 0.00 | 0.00 | 0.00 | 0.00 | 0.00 | 0.00 | 0.00 |

The **2 axes** below are: horizontally, years AD by 20-year gaps; vertically, persons (logarithmic scale).
The **3 lines** on each graph are, from top to bottom: live **population**, live **evangelized persons**, live **Christians**.
**Statistics** and trends for 22 years are given, for each geopolitical area, in its facing table opposite.

## ASIA

**A** = AD 30  Jesus begins ministry in Palestine
**B** =  150  Orthodox churches grow in Western Asia
**C** =  650  Church of the East expands all across Asia
**D** = 1200  Mongols favor growth of Christianity
**E** = 1350  Black Death, then Tamerlane, kills millions
**F** = 1540  Jesuits enter India, Malaysia, Japan, China
**G** = 1800  Protestants begin work in India, China
**H** = 1980  Massive growth of house church movement in China
**I** = 2000  Continent is 8.5% Christian; 61% evangelized

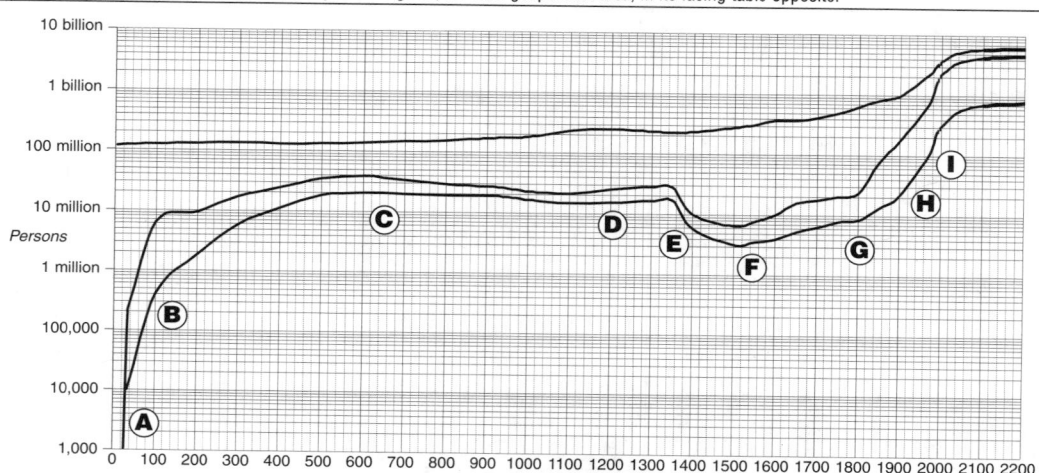

## Eastern Asia

**A** =  635  Church of the East arrives in China
**B** =  845  Major decline under Taoist emperor Wu Tsung
**C** = 1000  Keraits converted; later Mongols favor Church of the East
**D** = 1360  Tamerlane deliberately targets Church of the East, killing millions
**E** = 1540  Society of Jesus enters Japan and China
**F** = 1840  Protestants enter Japan, Korea, and China
**G** = 1950  All foreign missionaries expelled from China
**H** = 1980  Chinese house churches mushroom
**I** = 2000  Region is 7.7% Christian; 66% evangelized

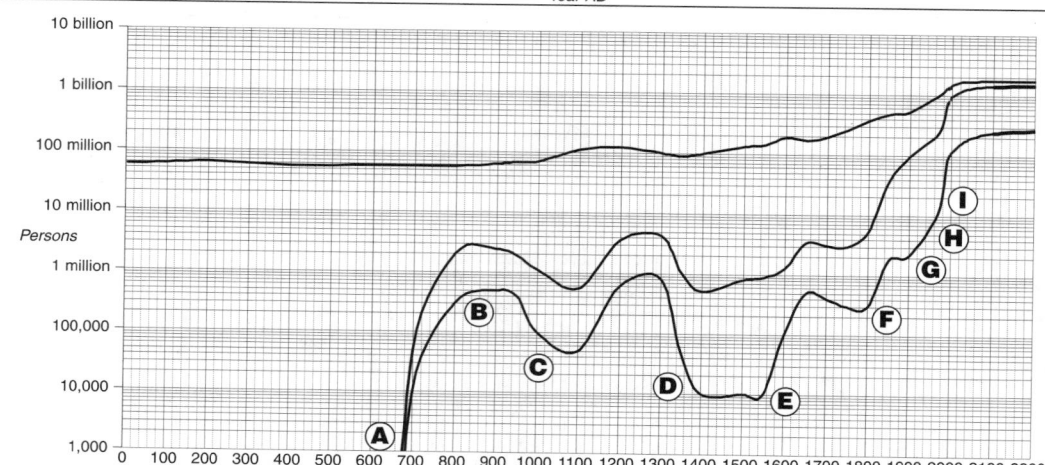

## South-central Asia

**A** = AD 52  Thomas arrives in south India
**B** =  600  Church of the East strong in the north
**C** = 1380  Church of the East extinguished by Tamerlane
**D** = 1800  Roman Catholics grow to 2 million by 1700 and then decline amongst numerous controversies
**E** = 1900  Roman Catholics, Anglicans, Protestants, and Independents are successful, especially among tribal groups
**F** = 1970  Millions of hidden believers in Christ emerge among Hindus and Muslims
**G** = 2000  Region is 5% Christian; 56% evangelized

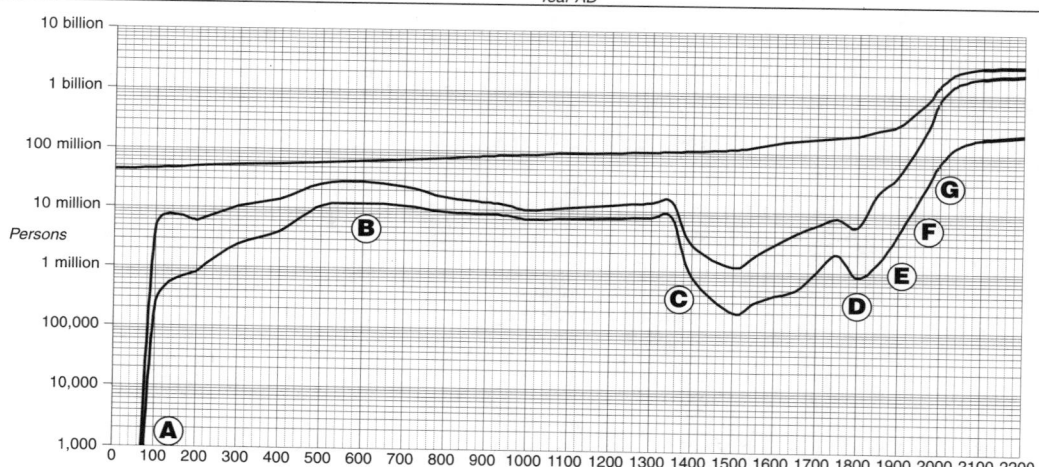

## South-eastern Asia

**A** =  600  Empires and civilizations uncontacted by Christians
**B** =  650  Small community of Roman Catholics survives in enclave in Sumatra
**C** = 1550  Jesuits arrive and church grows, especially in the Philippines
**D** = 1900  Protestants and Independents grow, especially among tribal groups
**E** = 2000  Region is 21% Christian; 67% evangelized

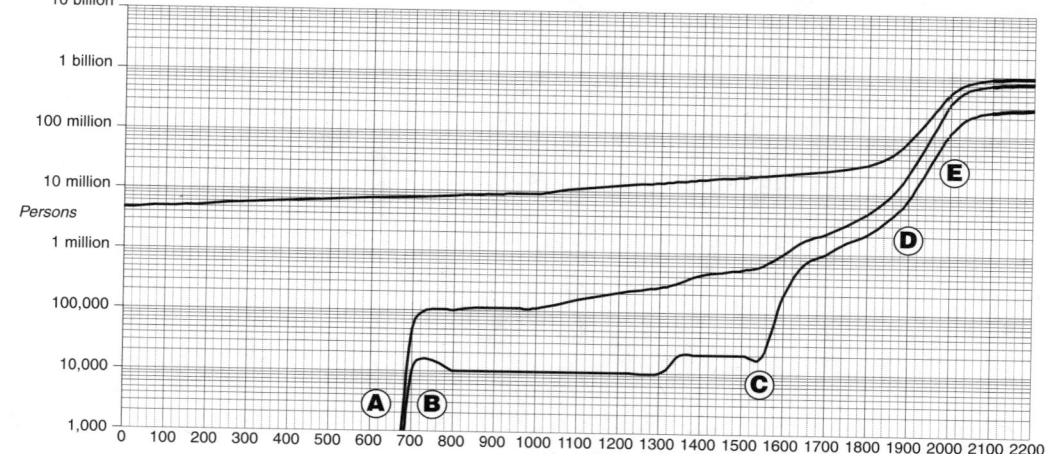

| *Area* *Year, AD* | 33 | 100 | 300 | 500 | 800 | 1000 | 1200 | 1350 | 1500 | 1650 | 1750 | 1800 | 1850 | 1900 | 1970 | 1990 | 1995 | 2000 | 2025 | 2050 | 2100 | 2200 |
|---|---|---|---|---|---|---|---|---|---|---|---|---|---|---|---|---|---|---|---|---|---|---|
| *1* | *2* | *3* | *4* | *5* | *6* | *7* | *8* | *9* | *10* | *11* | *12* | *13* | *14* | *15* | *16* | *17* | *18* | *19* | *20* | *21* | *22* | *23* |
| **ASIA** (50 countries in 2000) | | | | | | | | | | | | | | | | | | | | | | |
| Population, m(=millions) | 116.00 | 122.10 | 131.20 | 134.00 | 155.00 | 185.00 | 250.00 | 225.00 | 280.00 | 370.00 | 495.00 | 625.00 | 795.00 | 956.20 | 2,147.02 | 3,180.59 | 3,436.28 | 3,682.55 | 4,723.14 | 5,268.45 | 5,875.32 | 6,096.71 |
| Growth rate, % p.a. | 0.08 | 0.08 | 0.04 | 0.01 | 0.05 | 0.09 | 0.15 | -0.07 | 0.15 | 0.19 | 0.29 | 0.47 | 0.48 | 0.37 | 1.16 | 1.98 | 1.56 | 1.39 | 1.00 | 0.44 | 0.22 | 0.04 |
| Increase p.a., m | 0.09 | 0.09 | 0.05 | 0.01 | 0.08 | 0.16 | 0.38 | -0.16 | 0.41 | 0.69 | 1.44 | 2.92 | 3.83 | 3.54 | 24.95 | 63.11 | 53.55 | 51.33 | 47.25 | 23.08 | 12.83 | 2.26 |
| Evangelized persons, m | 0.21 | 6.40 | 16.90 | 34.50 | 29.00 | 22.71 | 24.81 | 27.87 | 6.53 | 15.70 | 20.60 | 23.35 | 75.90 | 174.90 | 691.85 | 1,707.75 | 1,957.75 | 2,258.73 | 3,150.66 | 3,771.83 | 4,345.32 | 4,646.71 |
| Evangelized persons % | 0.18 | 5.24 | 12.88 | 25.75 | 18.71 | 12.28 | 9.92 | 12.39 | 2.33 | 4.24 | 4.16 | 3.74 | 9.55 | 18.29 | 32.22 | 53.69 | 56.97 | 61.34 | 66.71 | 71.59 | 73.96 | 76.22 |
| Outreach per Christian | 20.00 | 15.00 | 1.86 | 0.86 | 0.54 | 0.37 | 0.64 | 0.63 | 1.02 | 2.02 | 1.61 | 1.80 | 4.79 | 6.99 | 5.78 | 5.87 | 5.94 | 6.22 | 5.78 | 5.45 | 5.20 | 4.91 |
| **Christians, m** | **0.01** | **0.40** | **5.90** | **18.50** | **18.81** | **16.61** | **15.11** | **17.07** | **3.23** | **5.20** | **7.90** | **8.35** | **13.10** | **21.90** | **101.39** | **248.73** | **281.91** | **312.85** | **464.80** | **584.72** | **701.00** | **786.00** |
| Orthodox, m | 0.00 | 0.39 | 5.89 | 18.48 | 18.78 | 16.58 | 15.09 | 17.03 | 3.17 | 3.64 | 4.10 | 5.08 | 6.02 | 6.86 | 8.97 | 13.93 | 14.35 | 14.11 | 17.35 | 19.08 | 20.03 | 21.03 |
| Roman Catholics, m | 0.01 | 0.01 | 0.01 | 0.02 | 0.03 | 0.03 | 0.02 | 0.04 | 0.06 | 1.32 | 3.43 | 2.78 | 6.03 | 11.16 | 50.96 | 90.59 | 100.63 | 110.48 | 159.58 | 193.93 | 213.84 | 235.84 |
| Anglicans, m | 0.00 | 0.00 | 0.00 | 0.00 | 0.00 | 0.00 | 0.00 | 0.00 | 0.00 | 0.01 | 0.01 | 0.02 | 0.27 | 0.71 | 0.36 | 0.60 | 0.68 | 0.73 | 0.95 | 1.14 | 1.25 | 1.37 |
| Protestants, m | 0.00 | 0.00 | 0.00 | 0.00 | 0.00 | 0.00 | 0.00 | 0.00 | 0.00 | 0.21 | 0.35 | 0.45 | 0.73 | 1.92 | 21.75 | 41.64 | 45.96 | 49.97 | 73.27 | 92.84 | 104.74 | 118.33 |
| Independents, m | 0.00 | 0.00 | 0.00 | 0.00 | 0.00 | 0.00 | 0.00 | 0.00 | 0.00 | 0.02 | 0.01 | 0.02 | 0.05 | 1.91 | 21.58 | 113.23 | 135.41 | 154.73 | 247.28 | 318.58 | 361.95 | 411.49 |
| Marginal Christians, m | 0.00 | 0.00 | 0.00 | 0.00 | 0.00 | 0.00 | 0.00 | 0.00 | 0.00 | 0.00 | 0.00 | 0.00 | 0.00 | 0.00 | 0.76 | 2.11 | 2.29 | 2.49 | 3.60 | 4.96 | 5.91 | 7.13 |
| **Christians %** | **0.01** | **0.33** | **4.50** | **13.81** | **12.14** | **8.98** | **6.04** | **7.59** | **1.15** | **1.41** | **1.60** | **1.34** | **1.65** | **2.29** | **4.72** | **7.82** | **8.20** | **8.50** | **9.84** | **11.10** | **11.93** | **12.89** |
| Christian growth rate, % p.a. | 0.00 | 5.66 | 1.35 | 0.57 | 0.01 | -0.06 | -0.05 | 0.08 | -1.10 | 0.32 | 0.42 | 0.11 | 0.90 | 1.03 | 2.21 | 4.59 | 2.54 | 2.10 | 1.60 | 0.92 | 0.36 | 0.11 |
| Christian nett increase p.a., m | 0.00 | 0.03 | 0.08 | 0.11 | 0.01 | -0.01 | 0.00 | 0.02 | -0.03 | 0.04 | 0.05 | 0.02 | 0.15 | 0.26 | 2.53 | 14.16 | 7.17 | 6.59 | 7.43 | 5.40 | 2.55 | 0.90 |
| Gains: births+converts,m | 0.00 | 0.04 | 0.32 | 0.87 | 0.78 | 0.67 | 0.62 | 0.72 | 0.09 | 0.20 | 0.30 | 0.29 | 0.50 | 0.82 | 4.29 | 16.97 | 10.18 | 9.83 | 12.52 | 13.29 | 14.41 | 17.82 |
| Losses: deaths+defectors,m | 0.00 | 0.02 | 0.24 | 0.76 | 0.77 | 0.68 | 0.62 | 0.70 | 0.12 | 0.17 | 0.25 | 0.27 | 0.35 | 0.56 | 1.76 | 2.81 | 3.01 | 3.25 | 5.09 | 7.89 | 11.85 | 16.91 |
| World B, m | 0.20 | 6.00 | 11.00 | 16.00 | 10.19 | 6.10 | 9.70 | 10.80 | 3.30 | 10.50 | 12.70 | 15.00 | 62.80 | 153.00 | 590.45 | 1,459.03 | 1,675.85 | 1,945.88 | 2,685.86 | 3,187.12 | 3,644.32 | 3,860.71 |
| World B % | 0.17 | 4.91 | 8.38 | 11.94 | 6.57 | 3.30 | 3.88 | 4.80 | 1.18 | 2.84 | 2.57 | 2.40 | 7.90 | 16.00 | 27.50 | 45.87 | 48.77 | 52.84 | 56.87 | 60.49 | 62.03 | 63.32 |
| World B growth rate, % p.a. | 0.00 | 5.21 | 0.30 | 0.19 | -0.15 | -0.26 | 0.23 | 0.07 | -0.79 | 0.77 | 0.19 | 0.33 | 2.91 | 1.80 | 1.95 | 4.63 | 2.81 | 3.03 | 1.30 | 0.69 | 0.27 | 0.06 |
| World B increase p.a., m | 0.00 | 0.26 | 0.03 | 0.02 | -0.01 | -0.01 | 0.01 | 0.00 | -0.01 | 0.02 | 0.00 | 0.01 | 0.23 | 0.29 | 0.54 | 2.12 | 1.37 | 1.60 | 0.74 | 0.42 | 0.17 | 0.04 |
| World A, m | 115.79 | 115.70 | 114.30 | 99.50 | 126.00 | 162.29 | 225.19 | 197.13 | 273.47 | 354.30 | 474.40 | 601.65 | 719.10 | 781.29 | 1,455.18 | 1,472.84 | 1,478.53 | 1,423.82 | 1,572.48 | 1,496.62 | 1,530.00 | 1,450.00 |
| World A % | 99.82 | 94.76 | 87.12 | 74.25 | 81.29 | 87.72 | 90.08 | 87.61 | 97.67 | 95.76 | 95.84 | 96.26 | 90.45 | 81.71 | 67.78 | 46.31 | 43.03 | 38.66 | 33.29 | 28.41 | 26.04 | 23.78 |
| World A growth rate, % p.a. | 0.08 | 0.00 | -0.01 | -0.07 | 0.08 | 0.13 | 0.16 | -0.09 | 0.22 | 0.17 | 0.29 | 0.48 | 0.36 | 0.17 | 0.89 | 0.06 | 0.08 | -0.75 | 0.40 | -0.20 | 0.04 | -0.05 |
| World A increase p.a., m | 0.09 | 0.00 | -0.01 | -0.07 | 0.10 | 0.21 | 0.37 | -0.17 | 0.60 | 0.61 | 1.39 | 2.87 | 2.57 | 1.30 | 12.99 | 0.89 | 1.14 | -10.70 | 6.26 | -2.96 | 0.68 | -0.78 |
| **Eastern Asia** (6 countries in 2000) | | | | | | | | | | | | | | | | | | | | | | |
| Population, m(=millions) | 56.39 | 59.29 | 59.67 | 54.35 | 57.67 | 71.35 | 125.20 | 91.15 | 131.95 | 168.00 | 261.60 | 368.90 | 480.60 | 532.55 | 986.64 | 1,350.47 | 1,422.28 | 1,485.22 | 1,695.44 | 1,676.25 | 1,735.26 | 1,755.39 |
| Growth rate, % p.a. | 0.07 | 0.07 | 0.00 | -0.05 | 0.02 | 0.11 | 0.28 | -0.21 | 0.25 | 0.16 | 0.44 | 0.69 | 0.53 | 0.21 | 0.88 | 1.58 | 1.04 | 0.87 | 0.53 | -0.05 | 0.07 | 0.01 |
| Increase p.a., m | 0.04 | 0.04 | 0.00 | -0.03 | 0.01 | 0.08 | 0.35 | -0.19 | 0.33 | 0.27 | 1.16 | 2.54 | 2.55 | 1.09 | 8.73 | 21.36 | 14.82 | 12.92 | 9.00 | -0.76 | 1.20 | 0.20 |
| Evangelized persons, m | 0.00 | 0.00 | 0.00 | 0.00 | 2.00 | 1.10 | 3.60 | 1.05 | 0.81 | 3.50 | 3.00 | 5.30 | 36.80 | 96.26 | 241.98 | 746.77 | 838.90 | 978.03 | 1,214.75 | 1,319.01 | 1,415.26 | 1,475.39 |
| Evangelized persons % | 0.00 | 0.00 | 0.00 | 0.00 | 3.47 | 1.54 | 2.88 | 1.15 | 0.61 | 2.08 | 1.15 | 1.44 | 7.66 | 18.08 | 24.53 | 55.30 | 58.98 | 65.85 | 71.65 | 78.69 | 81.56 | 84.05 |
| Outreach per Christian | — | — | — | — | 5.67 | 10.00 | 5.00 | 20.00 | 80.00 | 6.00 | 9.00 | 16.67 | 19.44 | 43.44 | 19.88 | 7.48 | 7.16 | 7.53 | 6.31 | 5.52 | 4.90 | 4.46 |
| **Christians, m** | **0.00** | **0.00** | **0.00** | **0.00** | **0.30** | **0.10** | **0.60** | **0.05** | **0.01** | **0.50** | **0.30** | **0.30** | **1.80** | **2.17** | **11.59** | **88.07** | **102.87** | **114.66** | **166.08** | **202.33** | **240.00** | **270.00** |
| Orthodox, m | 0.00 | 0.00 | 0.00 | 0.00 | 0.30 | 0.10 | 0.60 | 0.04 | 0.00 | 0.00 | 0.01 | 0.01 | 0.03 | 0.06 | 0.04 | 0.07 | 0.07 | 0.09 | 0.13 | 0.20 | 0.24 | 0.30 |
| Roman Catholics, m | 0.00 | 0.00 | 0.00 | 0.00 | 0.00 | 0.00 | 0.00 | 0.01 | 0.01 | 0.48 | 0.28 | 0.28 | 1.74 | 1.19 | 1.89 | 10.26 | 11.16 | 12.02 | 19.90 | 23.87 | 26.15 | 28.64 |
| Anglicans, m | 0.00 | 0.00 | 0.00 | 0.00 | 0.00 | 0.00 | 0.00 | 0.00 | 0.00 | 0.00 | 0.00 | 0.00 | 0.00 | 0.04 | 0.11 | 0.17 | 0.19 | 0.19 | 0.24 | 0.26 | 0.27 | 0.28 |
| Protestants, m | 0.00 | 0.00 | 0.00 | 0.00 | 0.00 | 0.00 | 0.00 | 0.00 | 0.00 | 0.00 | 0.00 | 0.00 | 0.02 | 0.45 | 3.25 | 9.41 | 9.96 | 10.51 | 13.37 | 14.74 | 15.48 | 16.26 |
| Independents, m | 0.00 | 0.00 | 0.00 | 0.00 | 0.00 | 0.00 | 0.00 | 0.00 | 0.00 | 0.02 | 0.01 | 0.01 | 0.01 | 0.01 | 3.54 | 67.21 | 80.59 | 90.90 | 132.89 | 164.79 | 183.52 | 204.40 |
| Marginal Christians, m | 0.00 | 0.00 | 0.00 | 0.00 | 0.00 | 0.00 | 0.00 | 0.00 | 0.00 | 0.00 | 0.00 | 0.00 | 0.00 | 0.00 | 0.54 | 1.48 | 1.55 | 1.63 | 2.06 | 2.31 | 2.45 | 2.60 |
| **Christians %** | **0.00** | **0.00** | **0.00** | **0.00** | **0.52** | **0.14** | **0.48** | **0.05** | **0.01** | **0.30** | **0.11** | **0.08** | **0.37** | **0.41** | **1.17** | **6.52** | **7.23** | **7.72** | **9.80** | **12.07** | **13.83** | **15.38** |
| Christian growth rate, % p.a. | 0.00 | 0.00 | 0.00 | 0.00 | 1.92 | -0.55 | 0.90 | -1.64 | -1.07 | 2.64 | -0.51 | 0.00 | 3.65 | 0.37 | 2.43 | 10.67 | 3.15 | 2.19 | 1.49 | 0.79 | 0.34 | 0.12 |
| Christian nett increase p.a., m | 0.00 | 0.00 | 0.00 | 0.00 | 0.01 | 0.00 | 0.01 | 0.00 | 0.00 | 0.01 | 0.00 | 0.00 | 0.07 | 0.01 | 0.28 | 9.40 | 3.25 | 2.52 | 2.48 | 1.60 | 0.82 | 0.32 |
| Gains: births+converts,m | 0.00 | 0.00 | 0.00 | 0.00 | 0.02 | 0.00 | 0.03 | 0.00 | 0.00 | 0.03 | 0.01 | 0.01 | 0.11 | 0.06 | 0.39 | 10.29 | 4.27 | 3.67 | 4.55 | 4.85 | 5.86 | 7.83 |
| Losses: deaths+defectors,m | 0.00 | 0.00 | 0.00 | 0.00 | 0.01 | 0.00 | 0.02 | 0.00 | 0.00 | 0.02 | 0.01 | 0.01 | 0.05 | 0.05 | 0.11 | 0.89 | 1.03 | 1.16 | 2.07 | 3.25 | 5.04 | 7.52 |
| World B, m | 0.00 | 0.00 | 0.00 | 0.00 | 1.70 | 1.00 | 3.00 | 1.00 | 0.80 | 3.00 | 2.70 | 5.00 | 35.00 | 94.10 | 230.39 | 658.70 | 736.04 | 863.37 | 1,048.67 | 1,116.68 | 1,175.26 | 1,205.39 |
| World B % | 0.00 | 0.00 | 0.00 | 0.00 | 2.95 | 1.40 | 2.40 | 1.10 | 0.61 | 1.79 | 1.03 | 1.36 | 7.28 | 17.67 | 23.35 | 48.78 | 51.75 | 58.13 | 61.85 | 66.62 | 67.73 | 68.67 |
| World B growth rate, % p.a. | 0.00 | 0.00 | 0.00 | 0.00 | 2.27 | -0.26 | 0.55 | -0.73 | -0.15 | 0.89 | -0.11 | 1.24 | 3.97 | 2.00 | 1.29 | 5.39 | 2.24 | 3.24 | 0.78 | 0.25 | 0.10 | 0.03 |
| World B increase p.a., m | 0.00 | 0.00 | 0.00 | 0.00 | 0.07 | 0.00 | 0.01 | -0.01 | 0.00 | 0.02 | 0.00 | 0.02 | 0.29 | 0.35 | 0.30 | 2.63 | 1.16 | 1.89 | 0.48 | 0.17 | 0.07 | 0.02 |
| World A, m | 56.39 | 59.29 | 59.67 | 54.35 | 55.67 | 70.25 | 121.60 | 90.10 | 131.14 | 164.50 | 258.60 | 363.60 | 443.80 | 436.28 | 744.66 | 603.69 | 583.38 | 507.19 | 480.70 | 357.23 | 320.00 | 280.00 |
| World A % | 100.00 | 100.00 | 100.00 | 100.00 | 96.53 | 98.46 | 97.12 | 98.85 | 99.39 | 97.92 | 98.85 | 98.56 | 92.34 | 81.92 | 75.47 | 44.70 | 41.02 | 34.15 | 28.35 | 21.31 | 18.44 | 15.95 |
| World A growth rate, % p.a. | 0.07 | 0.07 | 0.00 | -0.05 | 0.01 | 0.12 | 0.27 | -0.20 | 0.25 | 0.15 | 0.45 | 0.68 | 0.40 | -0.03 | 0.77 | -1.04 | -0.68 | -2.76 | -0.21 | -1.18 | -0.22 | -0.13 |
| World A increase p.a., m | 0.04 | 0.04 | 0.00 | -0.03 | 0.00 | 0.08 | 0.33 | -0.18 | 0.33 | 0.25 | 1.17 | 2.49 | 1.77 | -0.15 | 5.71 | -6.30 | -3.98 | -14.00 | -1.03 | -4.22 | -0.70 | -0.37 |
| **South-central Asia** (14 countries in 2000) | | | | | | | | | | | | | | | | | | | | | | |
| Population, m(=millions) | 42.50 | 44.70 | 52.10 | 59.10 | 72.70 | 88.25 | 96.40 | 102.60 | 114.50 | 161.70 | 188.00 | 205.00 | 249.25 | 313.33 | 787.54 | 1,238.82 | 1,365.19 | 1,490.78 | 2,049.85 | 2,430.00 | 2,795.41 | 2,929.17 |
| Growth rate, % p.a. | 0.08 | 0.08 | 0.08 | 0.06 | 0.07 | 0.10 | 0.04 | 0.04 | 0.07 | 0.23 | 0.15 | 0.17 | 0.39 | 0.46 | 1.33 | 2.29 | 1.96 | 1.78 | 1.28 | 0.68 | 0.28 | 0.05 |
| Increase p.a., m | 0.03 | 0.03 | 0.04 | 0.04 | 0.05 | 0.09 | 0.04 | 0.04 | 0.08 | 0.37 | 0.28 | 0.36 | 0.98 | 1.44 | 10.44 | 28.38 | 26.78 | 26.47 | 26.28 | 16.59 | 7.84 | 1.37 |
| Evangelized persons, m | 0.00 | 4.20 | 10.40 | 24.90 | 15.60 | 10.00 | 12.50 | 15.00 | 1.20 | 4.50 | 8.00 | 5.85 | 21.50 | 44.31 | 273.97 | 621.40 | 727.39 | 832.91 | 1,259.49 | 1,601.28 | 1,915.41 | 2,069.17 |
| Evangelized persons % | 0.00 | 9.40 | 19.96 | 42.13 | 21.46 | 11.33 | 12.97 | 14.62 | 1.05 | 2.78 | 4.26 | 2.85 | 8.63 | 14.14 | 34.79 | 50.16 | 53.28 | 55.87 | 61.44 | 65.90 | 68.52 | 70.64 |
| Outreach per Christian | — | 20.00 | 3.33 | 1.28 | 0.73 | 0.43 | 0.67 | 0.88 | 5.00 | 8.00 | 3.00 | 5.88 | 13.33 | 8.63 | 8.13 | 9.55 | 10.07 | 10.30 | 9.92 | 9.79 | 9.35 | 8.85 |
| **Christians, m** | **0.00** | **0.20** | **2.40** | **10.90** | **9.00** | **7.00** | **7.50** | **8.00** | **0.20** | **0.50** | **2.00** | **0.85** | **1.50** | **4.60** | **30.01** | **58.88** | **65.69** | **73.68** | **115.37** | **148.36** | **185.00** | **210.00** |
| Orthodox, m | 0.00 | 0.20 | 2.40 | 10.90 | 9.00 | 7.00 | 7.50 | 8.00 | 0.20 | 0.20 | 0.20 | 0.28 | 0.31 | 0.81 | 4.91 | 6.14 | 5.88 | 5.43 | 6.53 | 7.40 | 7.87 | 8.38 |
| Roman Catholics, m | 0.00 | 0.00 | 0.00 | 0.00 | 0.00 | 0.00 | 0.00 | 0.00 | 0.00 | 0.10 | 1.50 | 0.20 | 0.40 | 2.31 | 9.90 | 15.76 | 17.30 | 18.74 | 25.32 | 30.35 | 33.22 | 36.38 |
| Anglicans, m | 0.00 | 0.00 | 0.00 | 0.00 | 0.00 | 0.00 | 0.00 | 0.00 | 0.00 | 0.00 | 0.00 | 0.01 | 0.25 | 0.62 | 0.05 | 0.05 | 0.05 | 0.06 | 0.07 | 0.07 | 0.08 | 0.08 |
| Protestants, m | 0.00 | 0.00 | 0.00 | 0.00 | 0.00 | 0.00 | 0.00 | 0.00 | 0.00 | 0.20 | 0.30 | 0.35 | 0.50 | 0.78 | 9.21 | 15.34 | 17.31 | 19.04 | 27.17 | 33.72 | 37.57 | 41.86 |
| Independents, m | 0.00 | 0.00 | 0.00 | 0.00 | 0.00 | 0.00 | 0.00 | 0.00 | 0.00 | 0.00 | 0.00 | 0.01 | 0.04 | 0.09 | 7.44 | 25.10 | 31.11 | 37.43 | 71.31 | 94.16 | 108.23 | 124.41 |
| Marginal Christians, m | 0.00 | 0.00 | 0.00 | 0.00 | 0.00 | 0.00 | 0.00 | 0.00 | 0.00 | 0.00 | 0.00 | 0.00 | 0.00 | 0.00 | 0.02 | 0.05 | 0.06 | 0.07 | 0.12 | 0.21 | 0.27 | 0.36 |
| **Christians %** | **0.00** | **0.45** | **4.61** | **18.44** | **12.38** | **7.93** | **7.78** | **7.80** | **0.17** | **0.31** | **1.06** | **0.41** | **0.60** | **1.47** | **3.81** | **4.75** | **4.81** | **4.94** | **5.63** | **6.11** | **6.62** | **7.17** |
| Christian growth rate, % p.a. | 0.00 | 8.23 | 1.25 | 0.76 | -0.06 | -0.13 | 0.03 | 0.04 | -2.43 | 0.61 | 1.40 | -1.70 | 1.14 | 2.27 | 2.71 | 3.43 | 2.21 | 2.32 | 1.81 | 1.01 | 0.44 | 0.13 |
| Christian nett increase p.a., m | 0.00 | 0.02 | 0.03 | 0.08 | -0.01 | -0.01 | 0.00 | 0.00 | 0.00 | 0.00 | 0.03 | -0.01 | 0.02 | 0.10 | 0.81 | 2.02 | 1.45 | 1.71 | 2.09 | 1.50 | 0.82 | 0.27 |
| Gains: births+converts,m | 0.00 | 0.02 | 0.13 | 0.53 | 0.36 | 0.28 | 0.31 | 0.33 | 0.00 | 0.02 | 0.09 | 0.01 | 0.06 | 0.23 | 1.34 | 2.66 | 2.13 | 2.44 | 3.25 | 3.37 | 3.76 | 4.55 |
| Losses: deaths+defectors,m | 0.00 | 0.01 | 0.10 | 0.45 | 0.37 | 0.29 | 0.31 | 0.33 | 0.01 | 0.02 | 0.06 | 0.03 | 0.04 | 0.12 | 0.53 | 0.65 | 0.68 | 0.73 | 1.17 | 1.86 | 2.94 | 4.28 |
| World B, m | 0.00 | 4.00 | 8.00 | 14.00 | 6.60 | 3.00 | 5.00 | 7.00 | 1.00 | 4.00 | 6.00 | 5.00 | 20.00 | 39.71 | 243.96 | 562.52 | 661.70 | 759.24 | 1,144.13 | 1,452.92 | 1,730.41 | 1,859.17 |
| World B % | 0.00 | 8.95 | 15.36 | 23.69 | 9.08 | 3.40 | 5.19 | 6.82 | 0.87 | 2.47 | 3.19 | 2.44 | 8.02 | 12.67 | 30.98 | 45.41 | 48.47 | 50.93 | 55.82 | 59.79 | 61.90 | 63.47 |
| World B growth rate, % p.a. | 0.00 | 5.66 | 0.35 | 0.28 | -0.25 | -0.39 | 0.26 | 0.22 | -1.29 | 0.93 | 0.41 | -0.36 | 2.81 | 1.38 | 2.63 | 4.27 | 3.30 | 2.79 | 1.65 | 0.96 | 0.35 | 0.07 |
| World B increase p.a., m | 0.00 | 0.51 | 0.05 | 0.07 | -0.02 | -0.01 | 0.01 | 0.02 | -0.01 | 0.02 | 0.01 | -0.01 | 0.23 | 0.18 | 0.81 | 1.94 | 1.60 | 1.42 | 0.92 | 0.57 | 0.22 | 0.05 |
| World A, m | 42.50 | 40.50 | 41.70 | 34.20 | 57.10 | 78.25 | 83.90 | 87.60 | 113.30 | 157.20 | 180.00 | 199.15 | 227.75 | 269.02 | 513.56 | 617.42 | 637.80 | 657.86 | 790.36 | 828.73 | 880.00 | 860.00 |
| World A % | 100.00 | 90.60 | 80.04 | 57.87 | 78.54 | 88.67 | 87.03 | 85.38 | 98.95 | 97.22 | 95.74 | 97.15 | 91.37 | 85.86 | 65.21 | 49.84 | 46.72 | 44.13 | 38.56 | 34.10 | 31.48 | 29.36 |
| World A growth rate, % p.a. | 0.08 | -0.07 | 0.01 | -0.10 | 0.17 | 0.16 | 0.03 | 0.03 | 0.17 | 0.22 | 0.14 | 0.20 | 0.27 | 0.33 | 0.93 | 0.93 | 0.65 | 0.62 | 0.74 | 0.19 | 0.12 | -0.02 |
| World A increase p.a., m | 0.03 | -0.03 | 0.01 | -0.03 | 0.10 | 0.12 | 0.03 | 0.03 | 0.19 | 0.34 | 0.24 | 0.40 | 0.61 | 0.90 | 4.77 | 5.71 | 4.15 | 4.09 | 5.82 | 1.57 | 1.06 | -0.20 |
| **South-eastern Asia** (11 countries in 2000) | | | | | | | | | | | | | | | | | | | | | | |
| Population, m(=millions) | 4.51 | 4.91 | 5.83 | 6.75 | 8.08 | 9.10 | 13.00 | 15.30 | 18.50 | 22.30 | 27.00 | 31.50 | 42.00 | 80.63 | 286.71 | 440.97 | 480.46 | 518.54 | 683.53 | 785.58 | 884.89 | 920.74 |
| Growth rate, % p.a. | 0.13 | 0.13 | 0.09 | 0.07 | 0.06 | 0.06 | 0.18 | 0.11 | 0.13 | 0.12 | 0.19 | 0.31 | 0.58 | 1.31 | 1.83 | 2.18 | 1.73 | 1.54 | 1.11 | 0.56 | 0.24 | 0.04 |
| Increase p.a., m | 0.01 | 0.01 | 0.01 | 0.00 | 0.00 | 0.01 | 0.02 | 0.02 | 0.02 | 0.03 | 0.05 | 0.10 | 0.24 | 1.06 | 5.24 | 9.59 | 8.31 | 7.97 | 7.59 | 4.39 | 2.11 | 0.37 |
| Evangelized persons, m | 0.00 | 0.00 | 0.00 | 0.00 | 0.10 | 0.11 | 0.21 | 0.32 | 0.52 | 1.70 | 3.10 | 4.70 | 8.80 | 22.82 | 148.94 | 269.18 | 306.40 | 346.85 | 500.92 | 609.50 | 704.89 | 750.74 |
| Evangelized persons % | 0.00 | 0.00 | 0.00 | 0.00 | 1.24 | 1.21 | 1.62 | 2.09 | 2.81 | 7.62 | 11.48 | 14.92 | 20.95 | 28.30 | 51.95 | 61.04 | 63.77 | 66.89 | 73.28 | 77.59 | 79.66 | 81.54 |
| Outreach per Christian | — | — | — | — | 9.00 | 10.00 | 20.00 | 15.00 | 25.00 | 1.43 | 0.94 | 1.14 | 1.32 | 1.72 | 1.77 | 1.98 | 2.04 | 2.12 | 2.05 | 1.89 | 1.82 | 1.68 |
| **Christians, m** | **0.00** | **0.00** | **0.00** | **0.00** | **0.01** | **0.01** | **0.01** | **0.02** | **0.02** | **0.70** | **1.60** | **2.20** | **3.80** | **8.39** | **53.70** | **90.24** | **100.69** | **111.03** | **164.44** | **210.84** | **250.00** | **280.00** |
| Orthodox, m | 0.00 | 0.00 | 0.00 | 0.00 | 0.00 | 0.00 | 0.00 | 0.00 | 0.00 | 0.00 | 0.00 | 0.00 | 0.00 | 0.00 | 0.00 | 0.00 | 0.00 | 0.00 | 0.01 | 0.01 | 0.01 | 0.01 |
| Roman Catholics, m | 0.00 | 0.00 | 0.00 | 0.00 | 0.01 | 0.01 | 0.01 | 0.02 | 0.02 | 0.69 | 1.55 | 2.10 | 3.59 | 7.15 | 37.46 | 61.87 | 69.02 | 76.21 | 108.86 | 132.29 | 145.85 | 160.81 |
| Anglicans, m | 0.00 | 0.00 | 0.00 | 0.00 | 0.00 | 0.00 | 0.00 | 0.00 | 0.00 | 0.00 | 0.00 | 0.00 | 0.01 | 0.04 | 0.18 | 0.34 | 0.39 | 0.43 | 0.57 | 0.72 | 0.81 | 0.90 |
| Protestants, m | 0.00 | 0.00 | 0.00 | 0.00 | 0.00 | 0.00 | 0.00 | 0.00 | 0.00 | 0.01 | 0.05 | 0.10 | 0.20 | 0.62 | 9.17 | 16.71 | 18.48 | 20.19 | 32.36 | 43.83 | 51.03 | 59.41 |
| Independents, m | 0.00 | 0.00 | 0.00 | 0.00 | 0.00 | 0.00 | 0.00 | 0.00 | 0.00 | 0.00 | 0.00 | 0.00 | 0.00 | 1.80 | 10.51 | 20.05 | 22.69 | 25.16 | 40.50 | 55.52 | 65.03 | 76.17 |
| Marginal Christians, m | 0.00 | 0.00 | 0.00 | 0.00 | 0.00 | 0.00 | 0.00 | 0.00 | 0.00 | 0.00 | 0.00 | 0.00 | 0.00 | 0.00 | 0.19 | 0.57 | 0.67 | 0.77 | 1.38 | 2.33 | 3.04 | 3.96 |
| **Christians %** | **0.00** | **0.00** | **0.00** | **0.00** | **0.12** | **0.11** | **0.08** | **0.13** | **0.11** | **3.14** | **5.93** | **6.98** | **9.05** | **10.40** | **18.73** | **20.46** | **20.96** | **21.41** | **24.06** | **26.84** | **28.25** | **30.41** |
| Christian growth rate, % p.a. | 0.00 | 0.00 | 0.00 | 0.00 | 0.77 | 0.00 | 0.00 | 0.46 | 0.00 | 2.40 | 0.83 | 0.64 | 1.10 | 1.60 | 2.69 | 2.63 | 2.21 | 1.98 | 1.58 | 1.00 | 0.34 | 0.11 |
| Christian nett increase p.a., m | 0.00 | 0.00 | 0.00 | 0.00 | 0.00 | 0.00 | 0.00 | 0.00 | 0.00 | 0.02 | 0.01 | 0.01 | 0.04 | 0.13 | 1.44 | 2.37 | 2.23 | 2.19 | 2.60 | 2.11 | 0.85 | 0.32 |
| Gains: births+converts,m | 0.00 | 0.00 | 0.00 | 0.00 | 0.00 | 0.00 | 0.00 | 0.00 | 0.00 | 0.04 | 0.06 | 0.08 | 0.14 | 0.36 | 2.47 | 3.53 | 3.42 | 3.43 | 4.30 | 4.64 | 4.41 | 5.05 |
| Losses: deaths+defectors,m | 0.00 | 0.00 | 0.00 | 0.00 | 0.00 | 0.00 | 0.00 | 0.00 | 0.00 | 0.02 | 0.05 | 0.07 | 0.10 | 0.22 | 1.03 | 1.16 | 1.19 | 1.24 | 1.69 | 2.54 | 3.55 | 4.73 |
| World B, m | 0.00 | 0.00 | 0.00 | 0.00 | 0.09 | 0.10 | 0.20 | 0.30 | 0.50 | 1.00 | 1.50 | 2.50 | 5.00 | 14.44 | 95.25 | 178.94 | 205.71 | 235.82 | 336.47 | 398.66 | 454.89 | 470.74 |
| World B % | 0.00 | 0.00 | 0.00 | 0.00 | 1.11 | 1.10 | 1.54 | 1.96 | 2.70 | 4.48 | 5.56 | 7.94 | 11.90 | 17.90 | 33.22 | 40.58 | 42.82 | 45.48 | 49.23 | 50.75 | 51.41 | 51.13 |
| World B growth rate, % p.a. | 0.00 | 0.00 | 0.00 | 0.00 | 1.14 | 0.05 | 0.35 | 0.27 | 0.34 | 0.46 | 0.41 | 1.03 | 1.40 | 2.14 | 2.73 | 3.20 | 2.83 | 2.77 | 1.43 | 0.68 | 0.26 | 0.03 |
| World B increase p.a., m | 0.00 | 0.00 | 0.00 | 0.00 | 0.01 | 0.00 | 0.01 | 0.01 | 0.01 | 0.02 | 0.02 | 0.08 | 0.17 | 0.38 | 0.91 | 1.30 | 1.21 | 1.26 | 0.70 | 0.35 | 0.14 | 0.02 |
| World A, m | 4.51 | 4.91 | 5.83 | 6.75 | 7.98 | 8.99 | 12.79 | 14.98 | 17.98 | 20.60 | 23.90 | 26.80 | 33.20 | 57.81 | 137.76 | 171.78 | 174.06 | 171.69 | 182.61 | 176.08 | 180.00 | 170.00 |
| World A % | 100.00 | 100.00 | 100.00 | 100.00 | 98.76 | 98.79 | 98.38 | 97.91 | 97.19 | 92.38 | 88.52 | 85.08 | 79.05 | 71.70 | 48.05 | 38.96 | 36.23 | 33.11 | 26.72 | 22.41 | 20.34 | 18.46 |
| World A growth rate, % p.a. | 0.13 | 0.13 | 0.09 | 0.07 | 0.06 | 0.06 | 0.18 | 0.11 | 0.12 | 0.09 | 0.15 | 0.23 | 0.43 | 1.12 | 1.25 | 1.11 | 0.26 | -0.27 | 0.25 | -0.15 | 0.04 | -0.06 |
| World A increase p.a., m | 0.01 | 0.01 | 0.01 | 0.00 | 0.00 | 0.01 | 0.02 | 0.02 | 0.02 | 0.02 | 0.04 | 0.06 | 0.14 | 0.64 | 1.72 | 1.91 | 0.46 | -0.47 | 0.45 | -0.26 | 0.08 | -0.10 |

The **2 axes** below are: horizontally, years AD by 20-year gaps; vertically, persons (logarithmic scale).
The **3 lines** on each graph are, from top to bottom: live **population**, live **evangelized persons**, live **Christians**.
**Statistics** and trends for 22 years are given, for each geopolitical area, in its facing table opposite.

## Western Asia

**A** = AD 30  Jesus begins ministry in Palestine
**B** =  150  Orthodox church grows in Turkey, Syria, and Iraq
**C** =  500  Church of the East strong in Syria and Iraq
**D** = 1300  Roman Catholic missions begin successful work in Iraq
**E** = 1350  Black Death kills hundreds of thousands
**F** = 2000  Region is 7% Christian; 54% evangelized

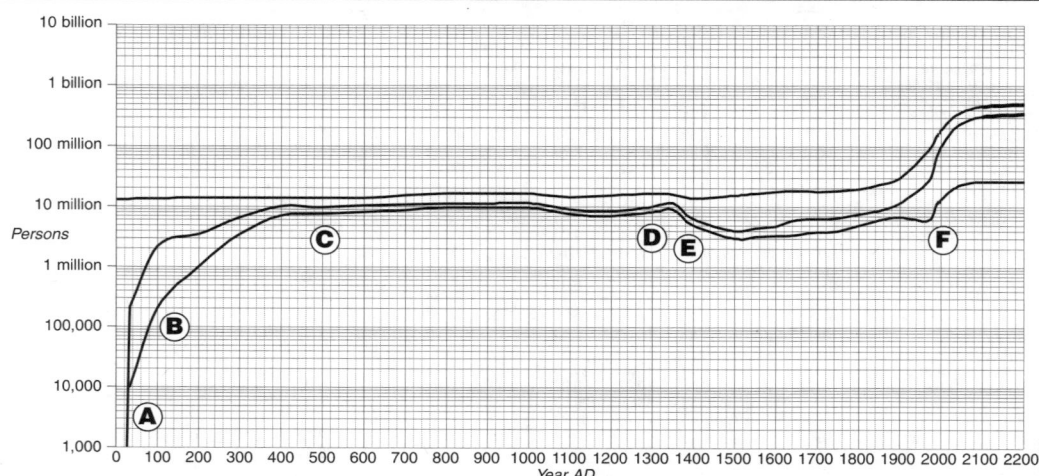

## EUROPE

**A** = AD 35  Gospel spreads to all regions in Europe by the end of the first one hundred years of Christianity
**B** =  380  Roman Empire officially Christian
**C** =  410  Barbarians destroy Roman Empire but are converted to Christianity in the process
**D** =  500  After conversion of Ireland, Celtic mission movement evangelizes northern Europe
**E** =  700  Islam spreads to Western Europe
**F** =  988  Mass conversion of the Rus under Prince Vladimir
**G** = 1200  Friars bring renewal to Europe
**H** = 1350  Black Death kills millions
**I** = 1800  French Revolution begins slow decline of church authority and membership
**J** = 1990  Collapse of Communism in Eastern Europe; churches grow
**K** = 1350  Continent is 77% Christian; 97% evangelized

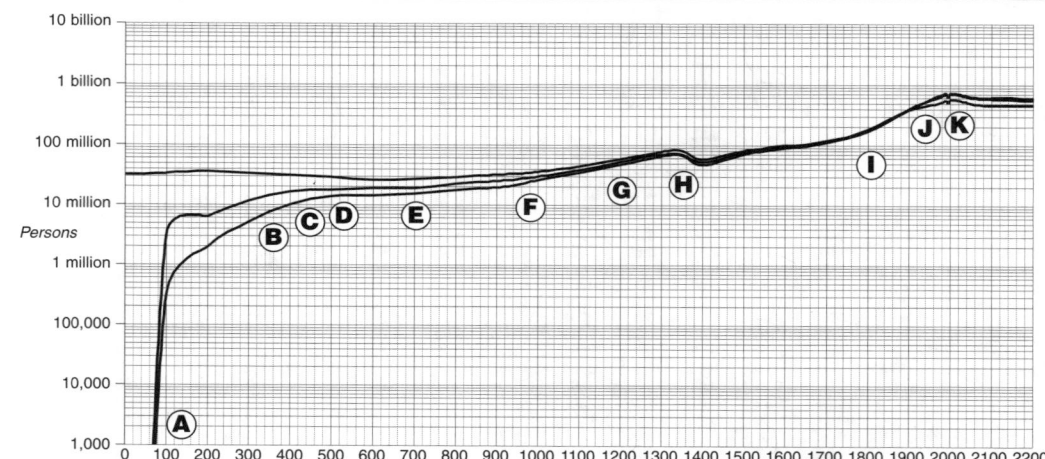

## Eastern Europe

**A** = AD 35  Gospel introduced to Romania and Russia by Apostle Andrew
**B** =  850  Cyril and Methodius work among the Slavs
**C** =  988  Mass conversion of the Rus under Prince Vladimir
**D** = 1350  Black Death kills hundreds of thousands
**E** = 1917  70 years of Soviet Communist domination followed by 1989 collapse
**F** = 2000  Region is 72% Christian; 96% evangelized

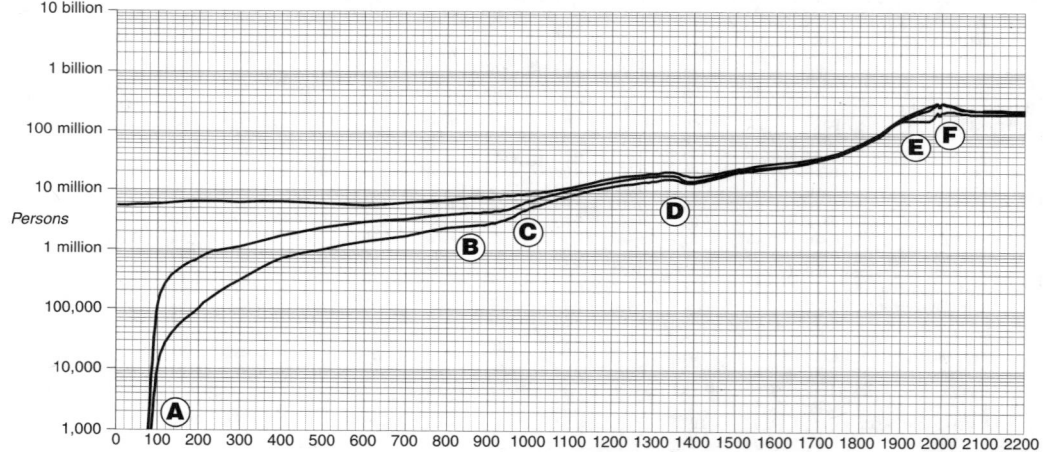

## Northern Europe

**A** = AD 61  First church erected at Glastonbury in Britain
**B** =  400  Conversion of Ireland and subsequent Celtic missions movement
**C** =  800  Viking invasions followed by their conversion
**D** = 1350  Black Death kills millions
**E** = 1950  Secularization begins to erode church membership
**F** = 2000  Region is 83% Christian; 98% evangelized

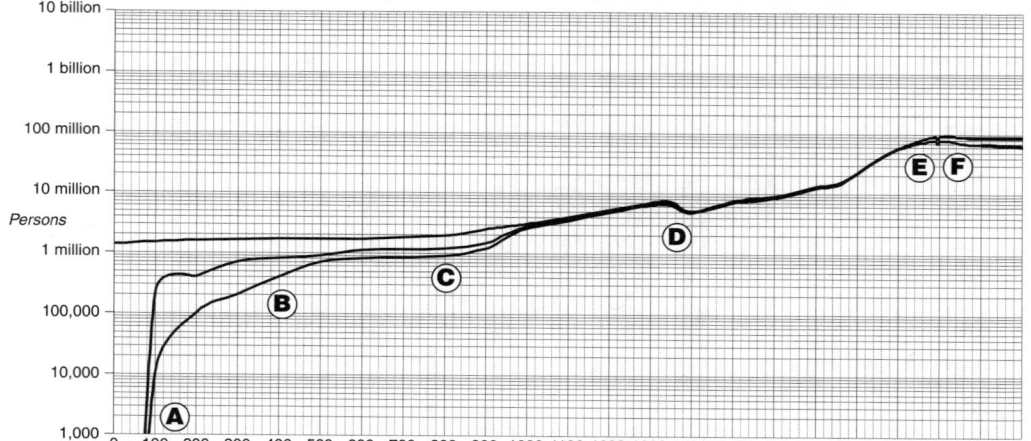

| Area Year, AD | 33 | 100 | 300 | 500 | 800 | 1000 | 1200 | 1350 | 1500 | 1650 | 1750 | 1800 | 1850 | 1900 | 1970 | 1990 | 1995 | 2000 | 2025 | 2050 | 2100 | 2200 |
|---|---|---|---|---|---|---|---|---|---|---|---|---|---|---|---|---|---|---|---|---|---|---|
| *1* | *2* | *3* | *4* | *5* | *6* | *7* | *8* | *9* | *10* | *11* | *12* | *13* | *14* | *15* | *16* | *17* | *18* | *19* | *20* | *21* | *22* | *23* |
| **Western Asia** (19 countries in 2000) | | | | | | | | | | | | | | | | | | | | | | |
| Population, m(=millions) | 12.60 | 13.20 | 13.60 | 13.80 | 16.55 | 16.30 | 15.40 | 15.95 | 15.05 | 18.00 | 18.40 | 19.60 | 23.15 | 29.69 | 86.13 | 150.34 | 168.35 | 188.02 | 294.32 | 376.62 | 459.76 | 491.41 |
| Growth rate, % p.a. | 0.07 | 0.07 | 0.01 | 0.01 | 0.06 | -0.01 | -0.03 | 0.02 | -0.04 | 0.12 | 0.02 | 0.13 | 0.33 | 0.50 | 1.53 | 2.82 | 2.29 | 2.23 | 1.81 | 0.99 | 0.40 | 0.07 |
| Increase p.a., m | 0.01 | 0.01 | 0.00 | 0.00 | 0.01 | 0.00 | 0.00 | 0.00 | -0.01 | 0.02 | 0.00 | 0.02 | 0.08 | 0.15 | 1.32 | 4.25 | 3.85 | 4.20 | 5.32 | 3.73 | 1.84 | 0.33 |
| Evangelized persons, m | 0.21 | 2.20 | 6.50 | 9.60 | 11.30 | 11.50 | 8.50 | 11.50 | 4.00 | 6.00 | 6.50 | 7.50 | 8.80 | 11.51 | 26.95 | 70.40 | 85.06 | 100.93 | 175.50 | 242.04 | 309.76 | 351.41 |
| Evangelized persons % | 1.67 | 16.67 | 47.79 | 69.57 | 68.28 | 70.55 | 55.19 | 72.10 | 26.58 | 33.33 | 35.33 | 38.27 | 38.01 | 38.76 | 31.28 | 46.82 | 50.53 | 53.68 | 59.63 | 64.27 | 67.37 | 71.51 |
| Outreach per Christian | 20.00 | 10.00 | 0.86 | 0.26 | 0.19 | 0.21 | 0.21 | 0.28 | 0.33 | 0.71 | 0.63 | 0.50 | 0.47 | 0.71 | 3.42 | 5.10 | 5.72 | 6.49 | 8.28 | 9.44 | 10.91 | 12.52 |
| **Christians, m** | **0.01** | **0.20** | **3.50** | **7.60** | **9.50** | **9.50** | **7.00** | **9.00** | **3.00** | **3.50** | **4.00** | **5.00** | **6.00** | **6.74** | **6.10** | **11.54** | **12.67** | **13.48** | **18.91** | **23.18** | **26.00** | **26.00** |
| Orthodox, m | 0.00 | 0.19 | 3.49 | 7.58 | 9.48 | 9.48 | 6.99 | 8.99 | 2.97 | 3.44 | 3.89 | 4.79 | 5.68 | 6.00 | 4.02 | 7.72 | 8.39 | 8.60 | 10.69 | 11.48 | 11.90 | 12.34 |
| Roman Catholics, m | 0.01 | 0.01 | 0.01 | 0.02 | 0.02 | 0.02 | 0.01 | 0.01 | 0.03 | 0.05 | 0.10 | 0.20 | 0.30 | 0.51 | 1.72 | 2.70 | 3.16 | 3.51 | 5.49 | 7.42 | 8.62 | 10.02 |
| Anglicans, m | 0.00 | 0.00 | 0.00 | 0.00 | 0.00 | 0.00 | 0.00 | 0.00 | 0.00 | 0.01 | 0.01 | 0.01 | 0.01 | 0.01 | 0.03 | 0.04 | 0.05 | 0.05 | 0.06 | 0.08 | 0.09 | 0.10 |
| Protestants, m | 0.00 | 0.00 | 0.00 | 0.00 | 0.00 | 0.00 | 0.00 | 0.00 | 0.00 | 0.00 | 0.00 | 0.00 | 0.01 | 0.07 | 0.12 | 0.19 | 0.21 | 0.23 | 0.38 | 0.55 | 0.67 | 0.81 |
| Independents, m | 0.00 | 0.00 | 0.00 | 0.00 | 0.00 | 0.00 | 0.00 | 0.00 | 0.00 | 0.00 | 0.00 | 0.00 | 0.00 | 0.00 | 0.10 | 0.87 | 1.03 | 1.24 | 2.59 | 4.11 | 5.17 | 6.51 |
| Marginal Christians, m | 0.00 | 0.00 | 0.00 | 0.00 | 0.00 | 0.00 | 0.00 | 0.00 | 0.00 | 0.00 | 0.00 | 0.00 | 0.00 | 0.00 | 0.01 | 0.02 | 0.02 | 0.02 | 0.05 | 0.11 | 0.15 | 0.21 |
| **Christians %** | **0.08** | **1.52** | **25.74** | **55.07** | **57.40** | **58.28** | **45.45** | **56.43** | **19.93** | **19.44** | **21.74** | **25.51** | **25.92** | **22.71** | **7.08** | **7.68** | **7.52** | **7.17** | **6.43** | **6.15** | **5.66** | **5.29** |
| Christian growth rate, % p.a. | 0.00 | 4.57 | 1.44 | 0.39 | 0.07 | 0.00 | -0.15 | 0.17 | -0.73 | 0.10 | 0.13 | 0.45 | 0.37 | 0.23 | -0.14 | 3.24 | 1.88 | 1.25 | 1.36 | 0.82 | 0.23 | 0.00 |
| Christian nett increase p.a., m | 0.00 | 0.01 | 0.05 | 0.03 | 0.01 | 0.00 | -0.01 | 0.02 | -0.02 | 0.00 | 0.01 | 0.02 | 0.02 | 0.02 | -0.01 | 0.37 | 0.24 | 0.17 | 0.26 | 0.19 | 0.06 | 0.00 |
| Gains: births+converts,m | 0.00 | 0.02 | 0.19 | 0.34 | 0.40 | 0.39 | 0.28 | 0.38 | 0.09 | 0.12 | 0.13 | 0.18 | 0.18 | 0.18 | 0.08 | 0.49 | 0.36 | 0.29 | 0.42 | 0.43 | 0.38 | 0.39 |
| Losses: deaths+defectors,m | 0.00 | 0.01 | 0.14 | 0.31 | 0.39 | 0.39 | 0.29 | 0.37 | 0.11 | 0.11 | 0.13 | 0.16 | 0.16 | 0.16 | 0.09 | 0.12 | 0.12 | 0.12 | 0.16 | 0.24 | 0.32 | 0.39 |
| World B, m | 0.20 | 2.00 | 3.00 | 2.00 | 1.80 | 2.00 | 1.50 | 2.50 | 1.00 | 2.50 | 2.50 | 2.50 | 2.80 | 4.77 | 20.85 | 58.86 | 72.39 | 87.45 | 156.59 | 218.86 | 283.76 | 325.41 |
| World B % | 1.59 | 15.15 | 22.06 | 14.49 | 10.88 | 12.27 | 9.74 | 15.67 | 6.64 | 13.89 | 13.59 | 12.76 | 12.10 | 16.05 | 24.21 | 39.15 | 43.00 | 46.51 | 53.20 | 58.11 | 61.72 | 66.22 |
| World B growth rate, % p.a. | 0.00 | 3.50 | 0.20 | -0.20 | -0.04 | 0.05 | -0.14 | 0.34 | -0.61 | 0.61 | 0.00 | 0.00 | 0.23 | 1.07 | 2.13 | 5.33 | 4.23 | 3.85 | 2.36 | 1.35 | 0.52 | 0.14 |
| World B increase p.a., m | 0.00 | 0.53 | 0.04 | -0.03 | 0.00 | 0.01 | -0.01 | 0.05 | -0.04 | 0.09 | 0.00 | 0.00 | 0.03 | 0.17 | 0.52 | 2.09 | 1.82 | 1.79 | 1.25 | 0.78 | 0.32 | 0.09 |
| World A, m | 12.39 | 11.00 | 7.10 | 4.20 | 5.25 | 4.80 | 6.90 | 4.45 | 11.05 | 12.00 | 11.90 | 12.10 | 14.35 | 18.18 | 59.19 | 79.95 | 83.29 | 87.08 | 118.82 | 134.58 | 150.00 | 140.00 |
| World A % | 98.33 | 83.33 | 52.21 | 30.43 | 31.72 | 29.45 | 44.81 | 27.90 | 73.42 | 66.67 | 64.67 | 61.73 | 61.99 | 61.24 | 68.72 | 53.18 | 49.47 | 46.32 | 40.37 | 35.73 | 32.63 | 28.49 |
| World A growth rate, % p.a. | 0.07 | -0.18 | -0.22 | -0.26 | 0.07 | -0.04 | 0.18 | -0.29 | 0.61 | 0.05 | -0.01 | 0.03 | 0.34 | 0.47 | 1.70 | 1.51 | 0.82 | 0.90 | 1.25 | 0.50 | 0.22 | -0.07 |
| World A increase p.a., m | 0.01 | -0.02 | -0.02 | -0.01 | 0.00 | 0.00 | 0.01 | -0.01 | 0.07 | 0.01 | 0.00 | 0.00 | 0.05 | 0.09 | 1.01 | 1.21 | 0.69 | 0.78 | 1.49 | 0.67 | 0.33 | -0.10 |
| **EUROPE** (48 countries in 2000) | | | | | | | | | | | | | | | | | | | | | | |
| Population, m(=millions) | 31.90 | 33.50 | 33.65 | 28.70 | 28.85 | 35.85 | 58.12 | 79.44 | 80.40 | 104.75 | 139.55 | 182.15 | 265.00 | 402.61 | 656.44 | 722.21 | 727.91 | 728.89 | 702.34 | 627.69 | 600.17 | 591.34 |
| Growth rate, % p.a. | 0.07 | 0.07 | 0.00 | -0.08 | 0.00 | 0.11 | 0.24 | 0.21 | 0.01 | 0.18 | 0.29 | 0.53 | 0.75 | 0.84 | 0.70 | 0.48 | 0.16 | 0.03 | -0.15 | -0.45 | -0.09 | -0.01 |
| Increase p.a., m | 0.02 | 0.02 | 0.00 | -0.02 | 0.00 | 0.04 | 0.14 | 0.17 | 0.01 | 0.18 | 0.40 | 0.97 | 1.99 | 3.38 | 4.60 | 3.46 | 1.15 | 0.20 | -1.04 | -2.81 | -0.54 | -0.09 |
| Evangelized persons, m | 0.00 | 3.11 | 11.40 | 17.80 | 22.20 | 29.80 | 52.30 | 70.80 | 74.40 | 99.90 | 132.90 | 173.90 | 255.30 | 392.85 | 616.72 | 695.76 | 704.09 | 707.41 | 682.88 | 609.98 | 582.47 | 573.74 |
| Evangelized persons % | 0.00 | 9.28 | 33.88 | 62.02 | 76.95 | 83.12 | 89.99 | 89.12 | 92.54 | 95.37 | 95.23 | 95.47 | 96.34 | 97.58 | 93.95 | 96.34 | 96.73 | 97.05 | 97.23 | 97.18 | 97.05 | 97.02 |
| Outreach per Christian | — | 9.03 | 1.24 | 0.29 | 0.24 | 0.14 | 0.08 | 0.06 | 0.07 | 0.02 | 0.01 | 0.01 | 0.02 | 0.03 | 0.25 | 0.26 | 0.26 | 0.26 | 0.23 | 0.24 | 0.25 | 0.27 |
| **Christians, m** | **0.00** | **0.31** | **5.10** | **13.80** | **17.90** | **26.10** | **48.30** | **66.80** | **69.70** | **98.00** | **131.20** | **171.70** | **249.80** | **380.64** | **492.69** | **550.42** | **557.49** | **559.64** | **554.59** | **492.73** | **465.00** | **451.00** |
| Orthodox, m | 0.00 | 0.13 | 1.00 | 2.00 | 2.70 | 5.50 | 11.70 | 15.45 | 19.91 | 26.69 | 37.43 | 46.48 | 65.37 | 103.95 | 107.13 | 155.12 | 156.45 | 158.11 | 165.80 | 152.71 | 146.58 | 140.72 |
| Roman Catholics, m | 0.00 | 0.16 | 3.90 | 11.20 | 14.70 | 18.80 | 33.20 | 47.20 | 44.60 | 52.09 | 68.38 | 88.54 | 126.06 | 180.72 | 256.16 | 281.45 | 284.43 | 285.98 | 276.27 | 243.55 | 228.99 | 215.49 |
| Anglicans, m | 0.00 | 0.01 | 0.20 | 0.60 | 0.50 | 1.80 | 3.40 | 4.15 | 5.18 | 4.80 | 6.04 | 11.38 | 19.58 | 24.90 | 29.47 | 26.30 | 26.59 | 26.64 | 26.41 | 24.65 | 23.81 | 23.01 |
| Protestants, m | 0.00 | 0.00 | 0.00 | 0.00 | 0.00 | 0.00 | 0.00 | 0.00 | 0.01 | 14.41 | 19.32 | 25.25 | 38.70 | 59.49 | 82.13 | 76.38 | 76.87 | 77.53 | 77.09 | 70.23 | 67.14 | 64.27 |
| Independents, m | 0.00 | 0.00 | 0.00 | 0.00 | 0.00 | 0.00 | 0.00 | 0.00 | 0.00 | 0.01 | 0.02 | 0.03 | 0.04 | 0.08 | 9.89 | 23.28 | 25.09 | 25.72 | 29.30 | 30.21 | 30.74 | 31.32 |
| Marginal Christians, m | 0.00 | 0.00 | 0.00 | 0.00 | 0.00 | 0.00 | 0.00 | 0.00 | 0.00 | 0.00 | 0.01 | 0.02 | 0.05 | 0.10 | 1.81 | 3.17 | 3.36 | 3.56 | 4.86 | 6.09 | 6.83 | 7.67 |
| **Christians %** | **0.00** | **0.93** | **15.16** | **48.08** | **62.05** | **72.80** | **83.10** | **84.09** | **86.69** | **93.56** | **94.02** | **94.26** | **94.26** | **94.54** | **75.06** | **76.21** | **76.59** | **76.78** | **78.96** | **78.50** | **77.48** | **76.27** |
| Christian growth rate, % p.a. | 0.00 | 8.94 | 1.41 | 0.50 | 0.09 | 0.19 | 0.31 | 0.22 | 0.03 | 0.23 | 0.29 | 0.54 | 0.75 | 0.85 | 0.37 | 0.56 | 0.26 | 0.08 | -0.04 | -0.47 | -0.12 | -0.03 |
| Christian nett increase p.a., m | 0.00 | 0.01 | 0.07 | 0.07 | 0.03 | 0.05 | 0.15 | 0.15 | 0.02 | 0.22 | 0.39 | 0.94 | 1.90 | 3.27 | 1.93 | 3.43 | 1.43 | 0.43 | -0.17 | -2.31 | -0.54 | -0.14 |
| Gains: births+converts,m | 0.00 | 0.03 | 0.29 | 0.66 | 0.79 | 1.18 | 2.23 | 3.02 | 2.74 | 3.20 | 4.02 | 5.23 | 6.71 | 9.58 | 10.40 | 13.48 | 11.60 | 10.77 | 10.91 | 8.70 | 11.13 | 12.65 |
| Losses: deaths+defectors,m | 0.00 | 0.01 | 0.21 | 0.59 | 0.77 | 1.12 | 2.08 | 2.87 | 2.72 | 2.98 | 3.64 | 4.29 | 4.81 | 6.32 | 8.47 | 10.05 | 10.17 | 10.34 | 11.09 | 11.01 | 11.67 | 12.79 |
| World B, m | 0.00 | 2.80 | 6.30 | 4.00 | 4.30 | 3.70 | 4.00 | 4.00 | 4.70 | 1.90 | 1.70 | 2.20 | 5.50 | 12.21 | 124.02 | 145.34 | 146.60 | 147.77 | 128.29 | 117.26 | 117.47 | 122.74 |
| World B % | 0.00 | 8.36 | 18.72 | 13.94 | 14.90 | 10.32 | 6.88 | 5.04 | 5.85 | 1.81 | 1.22 | 1.21 | 2.08 | 3.03 | 18.89 | 20.12 | 20.14 | 20.27 | 18.27 | 18.68 | 19.57 | 20.76 |
| World B growth rate, % p.a. | 0.00 | 8.77 | 0.41 | -0.23 | 0.02 | -0.08 | 0.04 | 0.00 | 0.11 | -0.60 | -0.11 | 0.52 | 1.85 | 1.61 | 3.37 | 0.80 | 0.17 | 0.16 | -0.56 | -0.36 | 0.00 | 0.04 |
| World B increase p.a., m | 0.00 | 0.73 | 0.08 | -0.03 | 0.00 | -0.01 | 0.00 | 0.00 | 0.01 | -0.01 | 0.00 | 0.01 | 0.04 | 0.05 | 0.64 | 0.16 | 0.03 | 0.03 | -0.10 | -0.07 | 0.00 | 0.01 |
| World A, m | 31.90 | 30.39 | 22.25 | 10.90 | 6.65 | 6.05 | 5.82 | 8.64 | 6.00 | 4.85 | 6.65 | 8.25 | 9.70 | 9.76 | 39.72 | 26.44 | 23.82 | 21.47 | 19.45 | 17.71 | 17.70 | 17.60 |
| World A % | 100.00 | 90.72 | 66.12 | 37.98 | 23.05 | 16.88 | 10.01 | 10.88 | 7.46 | 4.63 | 4.77 | 4.53 | 3.66 | 2.42 | 6.05 | 3.66 | 3.27 | 2.95 | 2.77 | 2.82 | 2.95 | 2.98 |
| World A growth rate, % p.a. | 0.07 | -0.07 | -0.16 | -0.36 | -0.16 | -0.05 | -0.02 | 0.26 | -0.24 | -0.14 | 0.32 | 0.43 | 0.32 | 0.01 | 2.03 | -2.01 | -2.07 | -2.05 | -0.39 | -0.38 | 0.00 | -0.01 |
| World A increase p.a., m | 0.02 | -0.02 | -0.03 | -0.04 | -0.01 | 0.00 | 0.00 | 0.02 | -0.01 | -0.01 | 0.02 | 0.04 | 0.03 | 0.00 | 0.80 | -0.53 | -0.49 | -0.44 | -0.08 | -0.07 | 0.00 | 0.00 |
| **Eastern Europe** (10 countries in 2000) | | | | | | | | | | | | | | | | | | | | | | |
| Population, m(=millions) | 5.22 | 5.66 | 6.19 | 5.83 | 6.86 | 8.54 | 15.76 | 19.99 | 22.77 | 30.57 | 44.70 | 62.05 | 97.10 | 169.36 | 276.28 | 310.78 | 310.04 | 306.99 | 287.51 | 251.89 | 238.07 | 233.64 |
| Growth rate, % p.a. | 0.12 | 0.12 | 0.04 | -0.03 | 0.05 | 0.11 | 0.31 | 0.16 | 0.09 | 0.20 | 0.38 | 0.66 | 0.90 | 1.12 | 0.70 | 0.59 | -0.05 | -0.20 | -0.26 | -0.53 | -0.11 | -0.02 |
| Increase p.a., m | 0.01 | 0.01 | 0.00 | 0.00 | 0.00 | 0.01 | 0.05 | 0.03 | 0.02 | 0.06 | 0.17 | 0.41 | 0.87 | 1.89 | 1.94 | 1.83 | -0.15 | -0.61 | -0.75 | -1.33 | -0.27 | -0.04 |
| Evangelized persons, m | 0.00 | 0.11 | 1.10 | 2.30 | 3.80 | 6.50 | 14.00 | 17.60 | 20.80 | 28.00 | 40.60 | 56.80 | 89.80 | 161.23 | 246.31 | 294.76 | 296.26 | 295.19 | 279.57 | 245.93 | 233.07 | 229.64 |
| Evangelized persons % | 0.00 | 1.94 | 17.77 | 39.45 | 55.39 | 76.11 | 88.83 | 88.04 | 91.35 | 91.59 | 90.83 | 91.54 | 92.48 | 95.20 | 89.15 | 94.85 | 95.55 | 96.16 | 97.24 | 97.63 | 97.90 | 98.29 |
| Outreach per Christian | — | 10.00 | 2.67 | 1.30 | 0.65 | 0.30 | 0.22 | 0.14 | 0.05 | 0.04 | 0.03 | 0.01 | 0.03 | 0.06 | 0.56 | 0.36 | 0.35 | 0.34 | 0.22 | 0.16 | 0.14 | 0.12 |
| **Christians, m** | **0.00** | **0.01** | **0.30** | **1.00** | **2.30** | **5.00** | **11.50** | **15.50** | **19.80** | **27.00** | **39.60** | **56.00** | **87.30** | **151.94** | **158.20** | **216.54** | **219.56** | **220.27** | **229.85** | **212.11** | **205.00** | **205.00** |
| Orthodox, m | 0.00 | 0.00 | 0.00 | 0.50 | 1.40 | 4.00 | 9.80 | 13.30 | 17.79 | 23.79 | 33.78 | 41.78 | 59.67 | 96.54 | 89.34 | 134.03 | 134.98 | 136.37 | 143.62 | 131.65 | 126.05 | 120.68 |
| Roman Catholics, m | 0.00 | 0.00 | 0.30 | 0.50 | 0.90 | 1.00 | 1.70 | 2.20 | 2.00 | 3.00 | 5.00 | 13.00 | 25.00 | 41.11 | 49.63 | 60.31 | 61.17 | 61.70 | 62.93 | 58.33 | 56.16 | 54.07 |
| Anglicans, m | 0.00 | 0.00 | 0.00 | 0.00 | 0.00 | 0.00 | 0.00 | 0.00 | 0.00 | 0.00 | 0.00 | 0.00 | 0.00 | 0.00 | 0.00 | 0.00 | 0.00 | 0.00 | 0.01 | 0.01 | 0.02 | 0.03 |
| Protestants, m | 0.00 | 0.00 | 0.00 | 0.00 | 0.00 | 0.00 | 0.00 | 0.00 | 0.01 | 0.20 | 0.80 | 1.20 | 2.60 | 4.52 | 7.27 | 8.94 | 9.09 | 9.33 | 10.24 | 10.41 | 10.49 | 10.57 |
| Independents, m | 0.00 | 0.00 | 0.00 | 0.00 | 0.00 | 0.00 | 0.00 | 0.00 | 0.00 | 0.01 | 0.01 | 0.01 | 0.00 | 0.00 | 7.07 | 16.92 | 18.34 | 18.74 | 20.61 | 20.40 | 20.30 | 20.19 |
| Marginal Christians, m | 0.00 | 0.00 | 0.00 | 0.00 | 0.00 | 0.00 | 0.00 | 0.00 | 0.00 | 0.00 | 0.01 | 0.01 | 0.03 | 0.06 | 0.19 | 0.67 | 0.75 | 0.82 | 1.14 | 1.48 | 1.69 | 1.93 |
| **Christians %** | **0.00** | **0.18** | **4.85** | **17.15** | **33.53** | **58.55** | **72.97** | **77.54** | **86.96** | **88.32** | **88.59** | **90.25** | **89.91** | **89.71** | **57.26** | **69.68** | **70.82** | **71.75** | **79.95** | **84.21** | **86.11** | **87.74** |
| Christian growth rate, % p.a. | 0.00 | 0.00 | 1.72 | 0.60 | 0.28 | 0.39 | 0.42 | 0.20 | 0.16 | 0.21 | 0.38 | 0.70 | 0.89 | 1.11 | 0.06 | 1.58 | 0.28 | 0.06 | 0.17 | -0.32 | -0.07 | 0.00 |
| Christian nett increase p.a., m | 0.00 | 0.00 | 0.01 | 0.01 | 0.01 | 0.02 | 0.05 | 0.03 | 0.03 | 0.06 | 0.15 | 0.39 | 0.78 | 1.69 | 0.09 | 3.43 | 0.61 | 0.14 | 0.39 | -0.68 | -0.14 | 0.00 |
| Gains: births+converts,m | 0.00 | 0.00 | 0.02 | 0.05 | 0.11 | 0.23 | 0.54 | 0.70 | 0.80 | 0.97 | 1.34 | 1.79 | 2.18 | 4.10 | 2.68 | 7.69 | 4.99 | 4.59 | 5.12 | 4.13 | 5.01 | 5.73 |
| Losses: deaths+defectors,m | 0.00 | 0.00 | 0.01 | 0.04 | 0.10 | 0.22 | 0.49 | 0.67 | 0.77 | 0.92 | 1.19 | 1.40 | 1.40 | 2.40 | 2.59 | 4.26 | 4.38 | 4.45 | 4.73 | 4.81 | 5.15 | 5.73 |
| World B, m | 0.00 | 0.10 | 0.80 | 1.30 | 1.50 | 1.50 | 2.50 | 2.10 | 1.00 | 1.00 | 1.00 | 0.80 | 2.50 | 9.29 | 88.10 | 78.22 | 76.70 | 74.92 | 49.72 | 33.81 | 28.07 | 24.64 |
| World B % | 0.00 | 1.77 | 12.92 | 22.30 | 21.87 | 17.56 | 15.86 | 10.51 | 4.39 | 3.27 | 2.24 | 1.29 | 2.57 | 5.48 | 31.89 | 25.17 | 24.74 | 24.40 | 17.29 | 13.42 | 11.79 | 10.54 |
| World B growth rate, % p.a. | 0.00 | 0.00 | 1.05 | 0.24 | 0.05 | 0.00 | 0.26 | -0.12 | -0.49 | 0.00 | 0.00 | -0.45 | 2.31 | 2.66 | 3.27 | -0.59 | -0.39 | -0.47 | -1.63 | -1.53 | -0.37 | -0.13 |
| World B increase p.a., m | 0.00 | 0.00 | 0.14 | 0.05 | 0.01 | 0.00 | 0.04 | -0.01 | -0.02 | 0.00 | 0.00 | -0.01 | 0.06 | 0.15 | 1.04 | -0.15 | -0.10 | -0.11 | -0.28 | -0.21 | -0.04 | -0.01 |
| World A, m | 5.22 | 5.55 | 5.09 | 3.53 | 3.06 | 2.04 | 1.76 | 2.39 | 1.97 | 2.57 | 4.10 | 5.25 | 7.30 | 8.13 | 29.97 | 16.02 | 13.78 | 11.80 | 7.93 | 5.97 | 5.00 | 4.00 |
| World A % | 100.00 | 98.06 | 82.23 | 60.55 | 44.61 | 23.89 | 11.17 | 11.96 | 8.65 | 8.41 | 9.17 | 8.46 | 7.52 | 4.80 | 10.85 | 5.15 | 4.45 | 3.84 | 2.76 | 2.37 | 2.10 | 1.71 |
| World A growth rate, % p.a. | 0.12 | 0.09 | -0.04 | -0.18 | -0.05 | -0.20 | -0.07 | 0.20 | -0.13 | 0.18 | 0.47 | 0.50 | 0.66 | 0.22 | 1.88 | -3.08 | -2.97 | -3.06 | -1.58 | -1.13 | -0.35 | -0.22 |
| World A increase p.a., m | 0.01 | 0.01 | 0.00 | -0.01 | 0.00 | 0.00 | 0.00 | 0.00 | 0.00 | 0.00 | 0.02 | 0.03 | 0.05 | 0.02 | 0.56 | -0.49 | -0.41 | -0.36 | -0.12 | -0.07 | -0.02 | -0.01 |
| **Northern Europe** (14 countries in 2000) | | | | | | | | | | | | | | | | | | | | | | |
| Population, m(=millions) | 1.38 | 1.49 | 1.66 | 1.72 | 1.94 | 3.16 | 5.36 | 7.15 | 7.48 | 10.68 | 14.75 | 22.70 | 38.40 | 57.98 | 87.35 | 92.50 | 93.68 | 94.38 | 95.88 | 90.66 | 89.45 | 89.05 |
| Growth rate, % p.a. | 0.11 | 0.11 | 0.05 | 0.02 | 0.04 | 0.24 | 0.26 | 0.19 | 0.03 | 0.24 | 0.32 | 0.87 | 1.06 | 0.83 | 0.59 | 0.29 | 0.26 | 0.15 | 0.06 | -0.22 | -0.03 | 0.00 |
| Increase p.a., m | 0.00 | 0.00 | 0.00 | 0.00 | 0.00 | 0.01 | 0.01 | 0.01 | 0.00 | 0.03 | 0.05 | 0.20 | 0.41 | 0.48 | 0.51 | 0.27 | 0.24 | 0.14 | 0.06 | -0.20 | -0.02 | 0.00 |
| Evangelized persons, m | 0.00 | 0.21 | 0.70 | 0.90 | 1.20 | 2.80 | 5.10 | 6.80 | 7.30 | 10.40 | 14.40 | 22.30 | 38.00 | 57.93 | 86.58 | 91.06 | 92.24 | 92.93 | 94.03 | 88.53 | 87.05 | 86.35 |
| Evangelized persons % | 0.00 | 14.09 | 42.17 | 52.33 | 61.86 | 88.61 | 95.15 | 95.10 | 97.59 | 97.38 | 97.63 | 98.24 | 98.96 | 99.91 | 99.13 | 98.45 | 98.46 | 98.46 | 98.07 | 97.66 | 97.32 | 96.97 |
| Outreach per Christian | — | 20.00 | 2.50 | 0.29 | 0.33 | 0.08 | 0.06 | 0.08 | 0.06 | 0.04 | 0.03 | 0.03 | 0.03 | 0.02 | 0.14 | 0.18 | 0.18 | 0.19 | 0.20 | 0.26 | 0.30 | 0.35 |
| **Christians, m** | **0.00** | **0.01** | **0.20** | **0.70** | **0.90** | **2.60** | **4.80** | **6.30** | **6.90** | **10.00** | **14.00** | **21.70** | **37.00** | **56.89** | **75.76** | **77.10** | **77.88** | **78.31** | **78.10** | **70.54** | **67.00** | **64.00** |
| Orthodox, m | 0.00 | 0.00 | 0.00 | 0.00 | 0.00 | 0.00 | 0.20 | 0.15 | 0.12 | 0.20 | 0.25 | 0.30 | 0.40 | 0.57 | 1.30 | 1.45 | 1.43 | 1.45 | 1.61 | 1.72 | 1.78 | 1.84 |
| Roman Catholics, m | 0.00 | 0.00 | 0.00 | 0.10 | 0.40 | 0.80 | 1.20 | 2.00 | 1.60 | 2.00 | 3.20 | 4.00 | 5.00 | 7.57 | 10.76 | 12.46 | 12.58 | 12.67 | 13.17 | 12.94 | 12.82 | 12.71 |
| Anglicans, m | 0.00 | 0.01 | 0.20 | 0.60 | 0.50 | 1.80 | 3.40 | 4.15 | 5.18 | 4.80 | 6.04 | 11.38 | 19.58 | 24.88 | 29.36 | 26.19 | 26.48 | 26.52 | 26.29 | 24.52 | 23.68 | 22.88 |
| Protestants, m | 0.00 | 0.00 | 0.00 | 0.00 | 0.00 | 0.00 | 0.00 | 0.00 | 0.00 | 3.00 | 4.50 | 6.00 | 12.00 | 22.91 | 30.74 | 27.73 | 27.90 | 28.13 | 27.90 | 25.75 | 24.73 | 23.76 |
| Independents, m | 0.00 | 0.00 | 0.00 | 0.00 | 0.00 | 0.00 | 0.00 | 0.00 | 0.00 | 0.00 | 0.01 | 0.01 | 0.01 | 0.01 | 0.98 | 2.44 | 2.57 | 2.67 | 3.73 | 4.42 | 4.81 | 5.24 |
| Marginal Christians, m | 0.00 | 0.00 | 0.00 | 0.00 | 0.00 | 0.00 | 0.00 | 0.00 | 0.00 | 0.00 | 0.00 | 0.01 | 0.01 | 0.01 | 0.58 | 0.68 | 0.70 | 0.73 | 1.04 | 1.34 | 1.53 | 1.74 |
| **Christians %** | **0.00** | **0.67** | **12.05** | **40.70** | **46.39** | **82.28** | **89.55** | **88.11** | **92.25** | **93.63** | **94.92** | **95.59** | **96.35** | **98.13** | **86.73** | **83.36** | **83.13** | **82.97** | **81.46** | **77.81** | **74.90** | **71.87** |
| Christian growth rate, % p.a. | 0.00 | 3.50 | 1.51 | 0.63 | 0.08 | 0.53 | 0.31 | 0.18 | 0.06 | 0.25 | 0.34 | 0.88 | 1.07 | 0.86 | 0.41 | 0.09 | 0.20 | 0.11 | -0.01 | -0.41 | -0.10 | -0.05 |
| Christian nett increase p.a., m | 0.00 | 0.00 | 0.00 | 0.00 | 0.00 | 0.01 | 0.01 | 0.01 | 0.00 | 0.02 | 0.05 | 0.19 | 0.40 | 0.49 | 0.31 | 0.07 | 0.16 | 0.09 | -0.01 | -0.29 | -0.07 | -0.03 |
| Gains: births+converts,m | 0.00 | 0.00 | 0.01 | 0.03 | 0.04 | 0.13 | 0.22 | 0.28 | 0.27 | 0.31 | 0.40 | 0.73 | 1.17 | 1.47 | 1.68 | 1.48 | 1.55 | 1.48 | 1.47 | 1.17 | 1.44 | 1.55 |
| Losses: deaths+defectors,m | 0.00 | 0.00 | 0.01 | 0.03 | 0.04 | 0.11 | 0.21 | 0.27 | 0.27 | 0.29 | 0.35 | 0.54 | 0.78 | 0.97 | 1.37 | 1.41 | 1.39 | 1.39 | 1.48 | 1.46 | 1.51 | 1.58 |
| World B, m | 0.00 | 0.20 | 0.50 | 0.20 | 0.30 | 0.20 | 0.30 | 0.50 | 0.40 | 0.40 | 0.40 | 0.60 | 1.00 | 1.04 | 10.83 | 13.96 | 14.36 | 14.62 | 15.93 | 17.99 | 20.05 | 22.35 |
| World B % | 0.00 | 13.42 | 30.12 | 11.63 | 15.46 | 6.33 | 5.60 | 6.99 | 5.35 | 3.75 | 2.71 | 2.64 | 2.60 | 1.79 | 12.40 | 15.10 | 15.33 | 15.49 | 16.61 | 19.84 | 22.42 | 25.10 |
| World B growth rate, % p.a. | 0.00 | 5.66 | 0.46 | -0.46 | 0.14 | -0.20 | 0.20 | 0.34 | -0.15 | 0.00 | 0.00 | 0.81 | 1.03 | 0.07 | 3.41 | 1.28 | 0.56 | 0.36 | 0.34 | 0.49 | 0.22 | 0.11 |
| World B increase p.a., m | 0.00 | 0.76 | 0.14 | -0.05 | 0.02 | -0.01 | 0.01 | 0.02 | -0.01 | 0.00 | 0.00 | 0.02 | 0.03 | 0.00 | 0.42 | 0.19 | 0.09 | 0.06 | 0.06 | 0.10 | 0.05 | 0.03 |
| World A, m | 1.38 | 1.28 | 0.96 | 0.82 | 0.74 | 0.36 | 0.26 | 0.35 | 0.18 | 0.28 | 0.35 | 0.40 | 0.40 | 0.05 | 0.76 | 1.43 | 1.44 | 1.45 | 1.85 | 2.13 | 2.40 | 2.70 |
| World A % | 100.00 | 85.91 | 57.83 | 47.67 | 38.14 | 11.39 | 4.85 | 4.90 | 2.41 | 2.62 | 2.37 | 1.76 | 1.04 | 0.09 | 0.87 | 1.55 | 1.54 | 1.54 | 1.93 | 2.34 | 2.68 | 3.03 |
| World A growth rate, % p.a. | 0.11 | -0.11 | -0.14 | -0.08 | -0.03 | -0.36 | -0.16 | 0.20 | -0.44 | 0.29 | 0.22 | 0.27 | 0.00 | -4.10 | 3.99 | 3.20 | 0.12 | 0.14 | 0.98 | 0.56 | 0.24 | 0.12 |
| World A increase p.a., m | 0.00 | 0.00 | 0.00 | 0.00 | 0.00 | 0.00 | 0.00 | 0.00 | 0.00 | 0.00 | 0.00 | 0.00 | 0.00 | 0.00 | 0.03 | 0.05 | 0.00 | 0.00 | 0.02 | 0.01 | 0.01 | 0.00 |

The **2 axes** below are: horizontally, years AD by 20-year gaps; vertically, persons (logarithmic scale).
The **3 lines** on each graph are, from top to bottom: live **population**, live **evangelized persons**, live **Christians**.
**Statistics** and trends for 22 years are given, for each geopolitical area, in its facing table opposite.

## Southern Europe

**A** = AD 40   Gospel spreads to Greece, Italy, and Yugoslavia
**B** =   313   Edict of Milan ends persecution of Christians
**C** =   700   Islam spreads to Spain
**D** = 1350   Black Death kills millions
**E** = 1950   Secularization begins to erode church membership
**F** = 2000   Region is 84% Christian; 98% evangelized

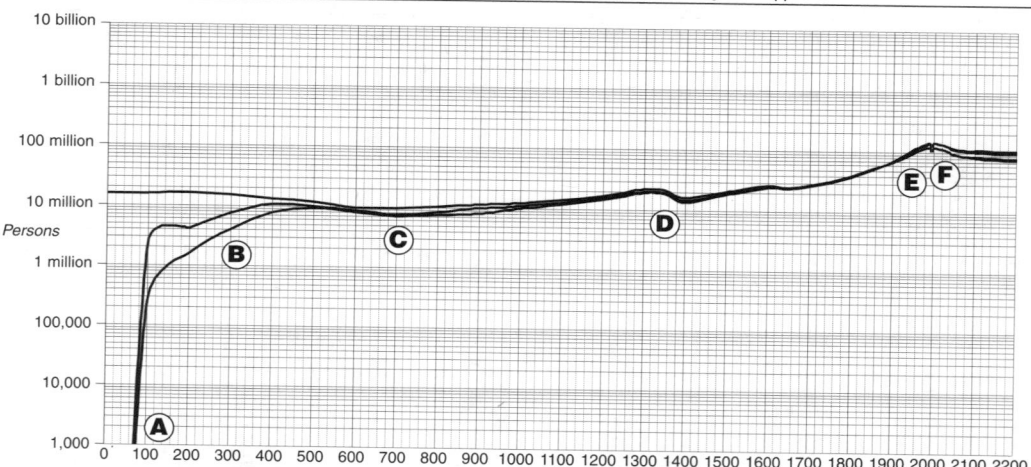

## Western Europe

**A** = AD 80   Gospel enters Gaul along Mediterranean Sea
**B** =   500   Barbarians invade the Roman Empire and are converted over time
**C** =   600   Celtic monks evangelize in the Low Countries, Gaul, and Germany
**D** = 1350   Black Death kills millions
**E** = 1800   French Revolution begins slow decline of church authority and membership
**F** = 2000   Region is 76% Christian; 97% evangelized

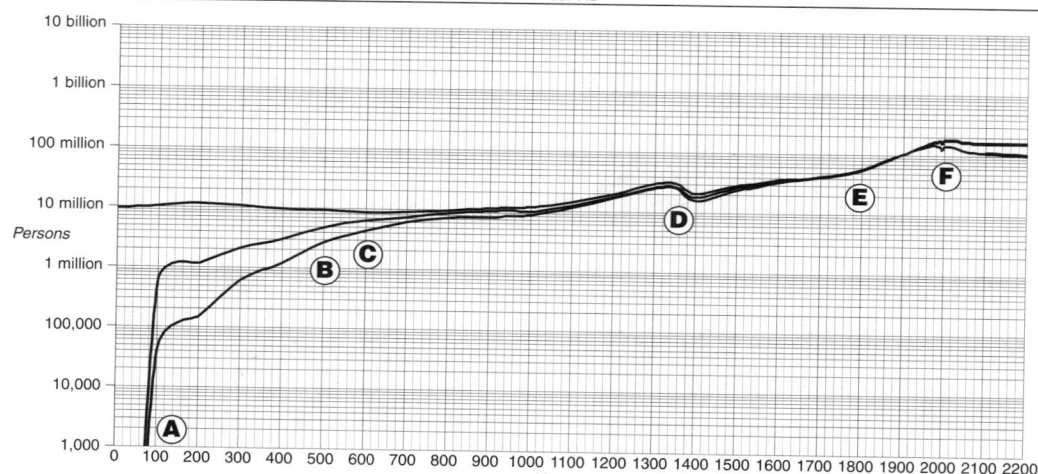

## LATIN AMERICA AND THE CARIBBEAN

**A** = 1000   Aztec, Inca, Maya, and other major civilizations uncontacted by Christians
**B** = 1500   Europeans arrive along with first missionaries
**C** = 1520   Native populations begin to succomb to European diseases; millions perish
**D** = 1530   Mass conversions of Amerindians begin in Mexico
**E** = 1580   Jesuit work in South America strong
**F** = 1900   Protestant and Indepedent churches begin to grow
**G** = 2000   Continent is 93% Christian; 99.6% evangelized

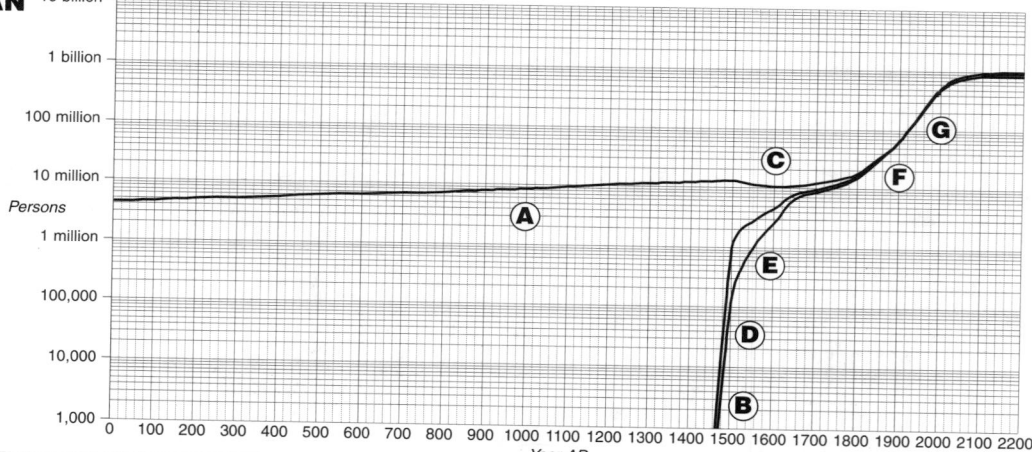

## Caribbean

**A** = 1200   Region uncontacted by Christians for 1,500 years
**B** = 1493   Franciscans and Dominicans begin work in Haiti and Dominican Republic
**C** = 1600   Slaves from Africa brought to work in sugar plantations
**D** = 1700   Successful Roman Catholic missions to most islands
**E** = 1900   Protestant missions begun; especially in Haiti
**F** = 1950   Secularization begins to impact churches
**G** = 2000   Region is 79%; 99 evangelized

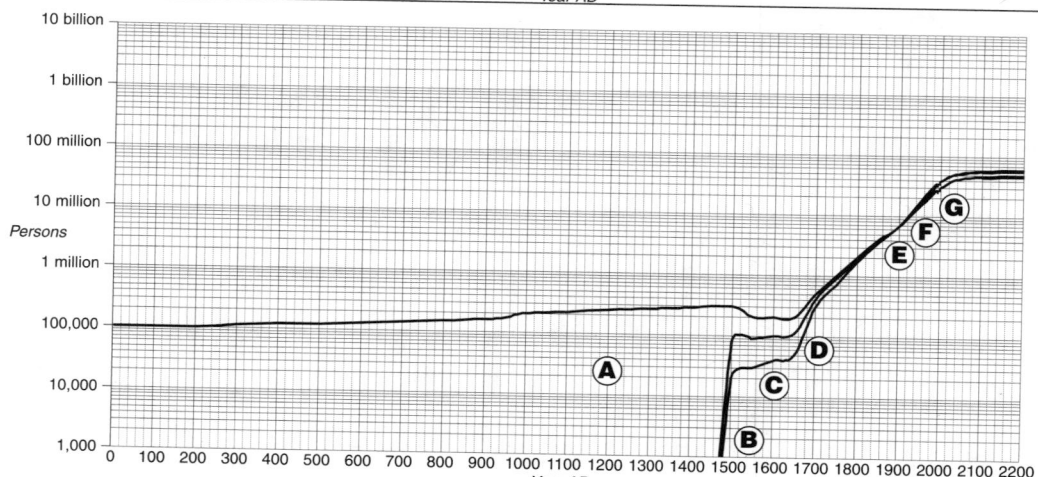

| *Area* *Year, AD* | 33 | 100 | 300 | 500 | 800 | 1000 | 1200 | 1350 | 1500 | 1650 | 1750 | 1800 | 1850 | 1900 | 1970 | 1990 | 1995 | 2000 | 2025 | 2050 | 2100 | 2200 |
|---|---|---|---|---|---|---|---|---|---|---|---|---|---|---|---|---|---|---|---|---|---|---|
| *1* | *2* | *3* | *4* | *5* | *6* | *7* | *8* | *9* | *10* | *11* | *12* | *13* | *14* | *15* | *16* | *17* | *18* | *19* | *20* | *21* | *22* | *23* |
| **Southern Europe** (15 countries in 2000) | | | | | | | | | | | | | | | | | | | | | | |
| Population, m(=millions) | 15.80 | 16.05 | 15.10 | 11.80 | 10.50 | 12.45 | 17.25 | 21.45 | 21.20 | 24.75 | 32.60 | 40.40 | 52.50 | 70.68 | 127.61 | 142.97 | 143.35 | 144.17 | 135.03 | 114.53 | 106.08 | 103.40 |
| Growth rate, % p.a. | 0.02 | 0.02 | -0.03 | -0.12 | -0.04 | 0.09 | 0.16 | 0.15 | -0.01 | 0.10 | 0.28 | 0.43 | 0.53 | 0.60 | 0.85 | 0.57 | 0.05 | 0.11 | -0.26 | -0.66 | -0.15 | -0.03 |
| Increase p.a., m | 0.00 | 0.00 | 0.00 | -0.01 | 0.00 | 0.01 | 0.03 | 0.03 | 0.00 | 0.03 | 0.09 | 0.17 | 0.28 | 0.42 | 1.08 | 0.82 | 0.08 | 0.17 | -0.35 | -0.75 | -0.16 | -0.03 |
| Evangelized persons, m | 0.00 | 2.25 | 7.50 | 9.90 | 8.50 | 11.00 | 15.60 | 19.60 | 19.60 | 24.20 | 31.80 | 39.40 | 51.50 | 69.31 | 123.06 | 138.97 | 139.90 | 140.92 | 131.78 | 111.77 | 103.28 | 100.50 |
| Evangelized persons % | 0.00 | 14.02 | 49.67 | 83.90 | 80.95 | 88.35 | 90.43 | 91.38 | 92.45 | 97.78 | 97.55 | 97.52 | 98.10 | 98.07 | 96.44 | 97.20 | 97.59 | 97.75 | 97.59 | 97.59 | 97.36 | 97.20 |
| Outreach per Christian | — | 8.00 | 0.88 | 0.05 | 0.13 | 0.10 | 0.04 | 0.03 | 0.03 | 0.01 | 0.01 | 0.01 | 0.02 | 0.01 | 0.10 | 0.15 | 0.16 | 0.17 | 0.19 | 0.22 | 0.24 | 0.29 |
| **Christians, m** | **0.00** | **0.25** | **4.00** | **9.40** | **7.50** | **10.00** | **15.00** | **19.00** | **19.00** | **24.00** | **31.60** | **39.00** | **50.50** | **68.54** | **112.24** | **120.48** | **121.00** | **120.92** | **110.78** | **91.96** | **83.00** | **78.00** |
| Orthodox, m | 0.00 | 0.13 | 1.00 | 1.50 | 1.30 | 1.50 | 1.70 | 2.00 | 2.00 | 2.70 | 3.40 | 4.40 | 5.30 | 6.69 | 15.43 | 18.18 | 18.54 | 18.70 | 18.73 | 17.40 | 16.78 | 16.17 |
| Roman Catholics, m | 0.00 | 0.12 | 3.00 | 7.90 | 6.20 | 8.50 | 13.30 | 17.00 | 17.00 | 21.29 | 28.18 | 34.55 | 45.10 | 61.23 | 99.40 | 110.20 | 110.64 | 110.71 | 100.57 | 82.04 | 74.11 | 66.95 |
| Anglicans, m | 0.00 | 0.00 | 0.00 | 0.00 | 0.00 | 0.00 | 0.00 | 0.00 | 0.00 | 0.00 | 0.00 | 0.00 | 0.00 | 0.01 | 0.03 | 0.03 | 0.03 | 0.03 | 0.04 | 0.04 | 0.04 | 0.04 |
| Protestants, m | 0.00 | 0.00 | 0.00 | 0.00 | 0.00 | 0.00 | 0.00 | 0.00 | 0.00 | 0.01 | 0.02 | 0.05 | 0.10 | 0.25 | 0.76 | 0.85 | 0.89 | 0.91 | 1.09 | 1.29 | 1.41 | 1.53 |
| Independents, m | 0.00 | 0.00 | 0.00 | 0.00 | 0.00 | 0.00 | 0.00 | 0.00 | 0.00 | 0.00 | 0.00 | 0.00 | 0.00 | 0.00 | 0.37 | 1.36 | 1.48 | 1.49 | 1.81 | 2.13 | 2.31 | 2.51 |
| Marginal Christians, m | 0.00 | 0.00 | 0.00 | 0.00 | 0.00 | 0.00 | 0.00 | 0.00 | 0.00 | 0.00 | 0.00 | 0.00 | 0.00 | 0.00 | 0.21 | 0.70 | 0.74 | 0.79 | 1.20 | 1.57 | 1.79 | 2.04 |
| **Christians %** | **0.00** | **1.56** | **26.49** | **79.66** | **71.43** | **80.32** | **86.96** | **88.58** | **89.62** | **96.97** | **96.93** | **96.53** | **96.19** | **96.98** | **87.96** | **84.27** | **84.41** | **83.87** | **82.04** | **80.29** | **78.24** | **75.43** |
| Christian growth rate, % p.a. | 0.00 | 4.92 | 1.40 | 0.43 | -0.08 | 0.14 | 0.20 | 0.16 | 0.00 | 0.16 | 0.28 | 0.42 | 0.52 | 0.61 | 0.71 | 0.35 | 0.09 | -0.01 | -0.35 | -0.74 | -0.20 | -0.06 |
| Christian nett increase p.a., m | 0.00 | 0.01 | 0.06 | 0.04 | -0.01 | 0.01 | 0.03 | 0.03 | 0.00 | 0.04 | 0.09 | 0.16 | 0.26 | 0.42 | 0.79 | 0.43 | 0.10 | -0.02 | -0.39 | -0.68 | -0.17 | -0.05 |
| Gains: births+converts,m | 0.00 | 0.02 | 0.22 | 0.44 | 0.32 | 0.44 | 0.68 | 0.85 | 0.74 | 0.73 | 1.04 | 1.14 | 1.32 | 1.56 | 2.61 | 2.45 | 2.14 | 2.08 | 1.85 | 1.49 | 2.14 | 2.55 |
| Losses: deaths+defectors,m | 0.00 | 0.01 | 0.17 | 0.40 | 0.32 | 0.43 | 0.65 | 0.82 | 0.74 | 0.70 | 0.95 | 0.98 | 1.06 | 1.14 | 1.82 | 2.03 | 2.03 | 2.09 | 2.24 | 2.17 | 2.31 | 2.59 |
| World B, m | 0.00 | 2.00 | 3.50 | 0.50 | 1.00 | 1.00 | 0.60 | 0.60 | 0.60 | 0.20 | 0.20 | 0.40 | 1.00 | 0.77 | 10.82 | 18.50 | 18.90 | 20.01 | 21.00 | 19.81 | 20.28 | 22.50 |
| World B % | 0.00 | 12.46 | 23.18 | 4.24 | 9.52 | 8.03 | 3.48 | 2.80 | 2.83 | 0.81 | 0.61 | 0.99 | 1.90 | 1.09 | 8.48 | 12.94 | 13.19 | 13.88 | 15.55 | 17.30 | 19.12 | 21.76 |
| World B growth rate, % p.a. | 0.00 | 7.12 | 0.28 | -0.97 | 0.23 | 0.00 | -0.26 | 0.00 | 0.00 | -0.73 | 0.00 | 1.40 | 1.85 | -0.52 | 3.85 | 2.71 | 0.44 | 1.14 | 0.19 | -0.23 | 0.05 | 0.10 |
| World B increase p.a., m | 0.00 | 0.89 | 0.06 | -0.04 | 0.02 | 0.00 | -0.01 | 0.00 | 0.00 | -0.01 | 0.00 | 0.01 | 0.04 | -0.01 | 0.33 | 0.35 | 0.06 | 0.16 | 0.03 | -0.04 | 0.01 | 0.02 |
| World A, m | 15.80 | 13.80 | 7.60 | 1.90 | 2.00 | 1.45 | 1.65 | 1.85 | 1.60 | 0.55 | 0.80 | 1.00 | 1.00 | 1.36 | 4.54 | 4.00 | 3.45 | 3.25 | 3.26 | 2.76 | 2.80 | 2.90 |
| World A % | 100.00 | 85.98 | 50.33 | 16.10 | 19.05 | 11.65 | 9.57 | 8.62 | 7.55 | 2.22 | 2.45 | 2.48 | 1.90 | 1.93 | 3.56 | 2.80 | 2.41 | 2.25 | 2.41 | 2.41 | 2.64 | 2.80 |
| World A growth rate, % p.a. | 0.02 | -0.20 | -0.30 | -0.69 | 0.02 | -0.16 | 0.06 | 0.08 | -0.10 | -0.71 | 0.38 | 0.45 | 0.00 | 0.62 | 1.74 | -0.64 | -2.90 | -1.19 | 0.01 | -0.67 | 0.03 | 0.04 |
| World A increase p.a., m | 0.00 | -0.03 | -0.02 | -0.01 | 0.00 | 0.00 | 0.00 | 0.00 | 0.00 | 0.00 | 0.00 | 0.00 | 0.00 | 0.01 | 0.08 | -0.03 | -0.10 | -0.04 | 0.00 | -0.02 | 0.00 | 0.00 |
| **Western Europe** (9 countries in 2000) | | | | | | | | | | | | | | | | | | | | | | |
| Population, m(=millions) | 9.50 | 10.30 | 10.70 | 9.35 | 9.55 | 11.70 | 19.75 | 30.85 | 28.95 | 38.75 | 47.50 | 57.00 | 77.00 | 104.59 | 165.21 | 175.96 | 180.84 | 183.34 | 183.92 | 170.61 | 166.57 | 165.24 |
| Growth rate, % p.a. | 0.12 | 0.12 | 0.02 | -0.07 | 0.01 | 0.10 | 0.26 | 0.30 | -0.04 | 0.19 | 0.20 | 0.37 | 0.60 | 0.61 | 0.66 | 0.32 | 0.55 | 0.27 | 0.01 | -0.30 | -0.05 | -0.01 |
| Increase p.a., m | 0.01 | 0.01 | 0.00 | -0.01 | 0.00 | 0.01 | 0.05 | 0.09 | -0.01 | 0.08 | 0.10 | 0.21 | 0.46 | 0.64 | 1.08 | 0.56 | 0.99 | 0.50 | 0.02 | -0.51 | -0.08 | -0.01 |
| Evangelized persons, m | 0.00 | 0.54 | 2.10 | 4.70 | 8.70 | 9.50 | 17.60 | 26.80 | 26.70 | 37.30 | 46.10 | 55.40 | 76.00 | 104.38 | 160.76 | 170.97 | 175.69 | 178.37 | 177.51 | 163.75 | 159.07 | 157.24 |
| Evangelized persons % | 0.00 | 5.24 | 19.63 | 50.27 | 91.10 | 81.20 | 89.11 | 86.87 | 92.23 | 96.26 | 97.05 | 97.19 | 98.70 | 99.80 | 97.31 | 97.16 | 97.15 | 97.29 | 96.51 | 95.98 | 95.50 | 95.16 |
| Outreach per Christian | — | 12.50 | 2.50 | 0.74 | 0.21 | 0.12 | 0.04 | 0.03 | 0.11 | 0.01 | 0.00 | 0.01 | 0.01 | 0.01 | 0.10 | 0.25 | 0.26 | 0.27 | 0.31 | 0.39 | 0.45 | 0.51 |
| **Christians, m** | **0.00** | **0.04** | **0.60** | **2.70** | **7.20** | **8.50** | **17.00** | **26.00** | **24.00** | **37.00** | **46.00** | **55.00** | **75.00** | **103.27** | **146.50** | **136.30** | **139.05** | **140.14** | **135.86** | **118.11** | **110.00** | **104.00** |
| Orthodox, m | 0.00 | 0.00 | 0.00 | 0.00 | 0.00 | 0.00 | 0.00 | 0.00 | 0.00 | 0.00 | 0.00 | 0.00 | 0.00 | 0.15 | 1.06 | 1.46 | 1.50 | 1.58 | 1.84 | 1.93 | 1.98 | 2.02 |
| Roman Catholics, m | 0.00 | 0.04 | 0.60 | 2.70 | 7.20 | 8.50 | 17.00 | 26.00 | 24.00 | 25.80 | 32.00 | 36.99 | 50.96 | 70.80 | 96.37 | 98.48 | 100.04 | 100.89 | 99.60 | 90.24 | 85.90 | 81.77 |
| Anglicans, m | 0.00 | 0.00 | 0.00 | 0.00 | 0.00 | 0.00 | 0.00 | 0.00 | 0.00 | 0.00 | 0.00 | 0.00 | 0.00 | 0.00 | 0.07 | 0.07 | 0.08 | 0.08 | 0.08 | 0.08 | 0.07 | 0.07 |
| Protestants, m | 0.00 | 0.00 | 0.00 | 0.00 | 0.00 | 0.00 | 0.00 | 0.00 | 0.00 | 11.20 | 14.00 | 18.00 | 24.00 | 31.80 | 43.37 | 38.86 | 38.99 | 39.16 | 37.86 | 32.79 | 30.52 | 28.40 |
| Independents, m | 0.00 | 0.00 | 0.00 | 0.00 | 0.00 | 0.00 | 0.00 | 0.00 | 0.00 | 0.00 | 0.00 | 0.01 | 0.03 | 0.08 | 1.47 | 2.55 | 2.70 | 2.82 | 3.15 | 3.26 | 3.32 | 3.37 |
| Marginal Christians, m | 0.00 | 0.00 | 0.00 | 0.00 | 0.00 | 0.00 | 0.00 | 0.00 | 0.00 | 0.00 | 0.00 | 0.00 | 0.01 | 0.03 | 0.83 | 1.12 | 1.17 | 1.22 | 1.49 | 1.70 | 1.82 | 1.95 |
| **Christians %** | **0.00** | **0.39** | **5.61** | **28.88** | **75.39** | **72.65** | **86.08** | **84.28** | **82.90** | **95.48** | **96.84** | **96.49** | **97.40** | **98.73** | **88.67** | **77.46** | **76.89** | **76.44** | **73.87** | **69.23** | **66.04** | **62.94** |
| Christian growth rate, % p.a. | 0.00 | 5.66 | 1.36 | 0.75 | 0.33 | 0.08 | 0.35 | 0.28 | -0.05 | 0.29 | 0.22 | 0.36 | 0.62 | 0.64 | 0.50 | -0.36 | 0.40 | 0.16 | -0.12 | -0.56 | -0.14 | -0.06 |
| Christian nett increase p.a., m | 0.00 | 0.00 | 0.01 | 0.02 | 0.02 | 0.01 | 0.06 | 0.07 | -0.01 | 0.11 | 0.10 | 0.20 | 0.47 | 0.66 | 0.73 | -0.49 | 0.56 | 0.22 | -0.17 | -0.66 | -0.16 | -0.06 |
| Gains: births+converts,m | 0.00 | 0.00 | 0.03 | 0.14 | 0.33 | 0.37 | 0.79 | 1.19 | 0.92 | 1.18 | 1.25 | 1.57 | 2.04 | 2.46 | 3.42 | 1.86 | 2.92 | 2.63 | 2.47 | 1.91 | 2.54 | 2.83 |
| Losses: deaths+defectors,m | 0.00 | 0.00 | 0.03 | 0.12 | 0.31 | 0.37 | 0.73 | 1.12 | 0.94 | 1.07 | 1.15 | 1.38 | 1.58 | 1.80 | 2.69 | 2.36 | 2.36 | 2.41 | 2.64 | 2.57 | 2.69 | 2.89 |
| World B, m | 0.00 | 0.50 | 1.50 | 2.00 | 1.50 | 1.00 | 0.60 | 0.80 | 2.70 | 0.30 | 0.10 | 0.40 | 1.00 | 1.11 | 14.27 | 34.67 | 36.64 | 38.23 | 41.65 | 45.64 | 49.07 | 53.24 |
| World B % | 0.00 | 4.85 | 14.02 | 21.39 | 15.71 | 8.55 | 3.04 | 2.59 | 9.33 | 0.77 | 0.21 | 0.70 | 1.30 | 1.06 | 8.63 | 19.70 | 20.26 | 20.85 | 22.65 | 26.75 | 29.46 | 32.22 |
| World B growth rate, % p.a. | 0.00 | 7.12 | 0.55 | 0.14 | -0.10 | -0.20 | -0.26 | 0.19 | 0.81 | -1.45 | -1.09 | 2.81 | 1.85 | 0.21 | 3.71 | 4.54 | 1.11 | 0.85 | 0.34 | 0.37 | 0.14 | 0.08 |
| World B increase p.a., m | 0.00 | 0.35 | 0.08 | 0.03 | -0.02 | -0.02 | -0.01 | 0.00 | 0.08 | -0.01 | 0.00 | 0.02 | 0.02 | 0.00 | 0.32 | 0.89 | 0.22 | 0.18 | 0.08 | 0.10 | 0.04 | 0.03 |
| World A, m | 9.50 | 9.76 | 8.60 | 4.65 | 0.85 | 2.20 | 2.15 | 4.05 | 2.25 | 1.45 | 1.40 | 1.60 | 1.00 | 0.21 | 4.45 | 5.00 | 5.15 | 4.98 | 6.41 | 6.86 | 7.50 | 8.00 |
| World A % | 100.00 | 94.76 | 80.37 | 49.73 | 8.90 | 18.80 | 10.89 | 13.13 | 7.77 | 3.74 | 2.95 | 2.81 | 1.30 | 0.20 | 2.69 | 2.84 | 2.85 | 2.71 | 3.49 | 4.02 | 4.50 | 4.84 |
| World A growth rate, % p.a. | 0.12 | 0.04 | -0.06 | -0.31 | -0.56 | 0.48 | -0.01 | 0.42 | -0.39 | -0.29 | -0.04 | 0.27 | -0.94 | -3.07 | 4.45 | 0.59 | 0.61 | -0.69 | 1.02 | 0.27 | 0.18 | 0.06 |
| World A increase p.a., m | 0.01 | 0.00 | -0.01 | -0.01 | 0.00 | 0.01 | 0.00 | 0.02 | -0.01 | 0.00 | 0.00 | 0.00 | -0.01 | -0.01 | 0.20 | 0.03 | 0.03 | -0.03 | 0.07 | 0.02 | 0.01 | 0.01 |
| **LATIN AMERICA AND THE CARIBBEAN** (46 countries in 2000) | | | | | | | | | | | | | | | | | | | | | | |
| Population, m(=millions) | 4.30 | 4.50 | 5.10 | 6.00 | 7.10 | 8.50 | 10.28 | 11.65 | 13.00 | 10.90 | 13.70 | 17.50 | 32.50 | 65.14 | 284.80 | 440.47 | 479.95 | 519.14 | 696.65 | 808.89 | 918.91 | 958.87 |
| Growth rate, % p.a. | 0.07 | 0.07 | 0.06 | 0.08 | 0.06 | 0.09 | 0.10 | 0.08 | 0.07 | -0.12 | 0.23 | 0.49 | 1.25 | 1.40 | 2.13 | 2.20 | 1.73 | 1.58 | 1.18 | 0.60 | 0.26 | 0.04 |
| Increase p.a., m | 0.00 | 0.00 | 0.00 | 0.00 | 0.00 | 0.01 | 0.01 | 0.01 | 0.01 | -0.01 | 0.03 | 0.09 | 0.40 | 0.91 | 6.07 | 9.71 | 8.31 | 8.21 | 8.24 | 4.85 | 2.35 | 0.41 |
| Evangelized persons, m | 0.00 | 0.00 | 0.00 | 0.00 | 0.00 | 0.00 | 0.00 | 0.00 | 0.98 | 7.76 | 11.70 | 15.85 | 30.50 | 63.38 | 279.89 | 438.45 | 477.95 | 517.19 | 694.10 | 805.98 | 915.49 | 955.17 |
| Evangelized persons % | 0.00 | 0.00 | 0.00 | 0.00 | 0.00 | 0.00 | 0.00 | 0.00 | 7.54 | 71.19 | 85.40 | 90.57 | 93.85 | 97.29 | 98.28 | 99.54 | 99.58 | 99.63 | 99.63 | 99.64 | 99.63 | 99.61 |
| Outreach per Christian | — | — | — | — | — | — | — | — | 7.17 | 0.19 | 0.14 | 0.06 | 0.04 | 0.02 | 0.04 | 0.07 | 0.07 | 0.08 | 0.08 | 0.10 | 0.11 | 0.14 |
| **Christians, m** | **0.00** | **0.00** | **0.00** | **0.00** | **0.00** | **0.00** | **0.00** | **0.00** | **0.12** | **6.50** | **10.30** | **14.90** | **29.30** | **62.00** | **269.20** | **409.35** | **445.27** | **481.10** | **641.12** | **734.44** | **823.50** | **841.00** |
| Orthodox, m | 0.00 | 0.00 | 0.00 | 0.00 | 0.00 | 0.00 | 0.00 | 0.00 | 0.00 | 0.00 | 0.00 | 0.00 | 0.00 | 0.01 | 0.36 | 0.48 | 0.49 | 0.56 | 0.76 | 0.91 | 1.00 | 1.09 |
| Roman Catholics, m | 0.00 | 0.00 | 0.00 | 0.00 | 0.00 | 0.00 | 0.00 | 0.00 | 0.12 | 6.49 | 10.18 | 14.46 | 28.38 | 58.69 | 251.79 | 391.77 | 426.73 | 461.22 | 606.06 | 688.83 | 734.44 | 783.12 |
| Anglicans, m | 0.00 | 0.00 | 0.00 | 0.00 | 0.00 | 0.00 | 0.00 | 0.00 | 0.00 | 0.01 | 0.08 | 0.22 | 0.44 | 0.73 | 0.77 | 0.99 | 1.05 | 1.09 | 1.35 | 1.62 | 1.78 | 1.95 |
| Protestants, m | 0.00 | 0.00 | 0.00 | 0.00 | 0.00 | 0.00 | 0.00 | 0.00 | 0.00 | 0.00 | 0.04 | 0.17 | 0.45 | 0.93 | 12.51 | 39.84 | 44.06 | 48.13 | 76.19 | 96.44 | 108.65 | 122.52 |
| Independents, m | 0.00 | 0.00 | 0.00 | 0.00 | 0.00 | 0.00 | 0.00 | 0.00 | 0.00 | 0.00 | 0.00 | 0.05 | 0.03 | 0.03 | 9.24 | 32.90 | 36.36 | 39.71 | 60.02 | 75.17 | 84.26 | 94.55 |
| Marginal Christians, m | 0.00 | 0.00 | 0.00 | 0.00 | 0.00 | 0.00 | 0.00 | 0.00 | 0.00 | 0.00 | 0.00 | 0.00 | 0.00 | 0.00 | 0.85 | 5.01 | 5.74 | 6.60 | 13.21 | 19.94 | 24.52 | 30.16 |
| **Christians %** | **0.00** | **0.00** | **0.00** | **0.00** | **0.00** | **0.00** | **0.00** | **0.00** | **0.92** | **59.63** | **75.18** | **85.14** | **90.15** | **95.18** | **94.52** | **92.93** | **92.77** | **92.67** | **92.03** | **90.80** | **89.62** | **87.71** |
| Christian growth rate, % p.a. | 0.00 | 0.00 | 0.00 | 0.00 | 0.00 | 0.00 | 0.00 | 0.00 | 1.61 | 2.70 | 0.46 | 0.74 | 1.36 | 1.51 | 2.12 | 2.12 | 1.70 | 1.56 | 1.16 | 0.55 | 0.23 | 0.02 |
| Christian nett increase p.a., m | 0.00 | 0.00 | 0.00 | 0.00 | 0.00 | 0.00 | 0.00 | 0.00 | 0.01 | 0.23 | 0.06 | 0.11 | 0.40 | 0.94 | 5.76 | 8.69 | 7.56 | 7.51 | 7.41 | 4.01 | 1.89 | 0.18 |
| Gains: births+converts,m | 0.00 | 0.00 | 0.00 | 0.00 | 0.00 | 0.00 | 0.00 | 0.00 | 0.02 | 0.44 | 0.34 | 0.48 | 1.00 | 2.04 | 9.50 | 13.08 | 12.22 | 12.50 | 14.58 | 13.80 | 15.21 | 16.92 |
| Losses: deaths+defectors,m | 0.00 | 0.00 | 0.00 | 0.00 | 0.00 | 0.00 | 0.00 | 0.00 | 0.00 | 0.21 | 0.29 | 0.36 | 0.60 | 1.10 | 3.73 | 4.39 | 4.66 | 4.99 | 7.17 | 9.80 | 13.32 | 16.74 |
| World B, m | 0.00 | 0.00 | 0.00 | 0.00 | 0.00 | 0.00 | 0.00 | 0.00 | 0.86 | 1.26 | 1.40 | 0.95 | 1.20 | 1.38 | 10.69 | 29.10 | 32.68 | 36.09 | 52.99 | 71.55 | 91.99 | 114.17 |
| World B % | 0.00 | 0.00 | 0.00 | 0.00 | 0.00 | 0.00 | 0.00 | 0.00 | 6.62 | 11.56 | 10.22 | 5.43 | 3.69 | 2.11 | 3.75 | 6.61 | 6.81 | 6.95 | 7.61 | 8.84 | 10.01 | 11.91 |
| World B growth rate, % p.a. | 0.00 | 0.00 | 0.00 | 0.00 | 0.00 | 0.00 | 0.00 | 0.00 | 1.26 | 0.25 | 0.11 | -0.77 | 0.47 | 0.27 | 2.97 | 5.14 | 2.34 | 2.01 | 1.55 | 1.21 | 0.50 | 0.22 |
| World B increase p.a., m | 0.00 | 0.00 | 0.00 | 0.00 | 0.00 | 0.00 | 0.00 | 0.00 | 0.08 | 0.03 | 0.01 | -0.04 | 0.02 | 0.01 | 0.11 | 0.34 | 0.16 | 0.14 | 0.12 | 0.11 | 0.05 | 0.03 |
| World A, m | 4.30 | 4.50 | 5.10 | 6.00 | 7.10 | 8.50 | 10.28 | 11.65 | 12.02 | 3.14 | 2.00 | 1.65 | 2.00 | 1.76 | 4.91 | 2.02 | 2.00 | 1.94 | 2.54 | 2.91 | 3.42 | 3.70 |
| World A % | 100.00 | 100.00 | 100.00 | 100.00 | 100.00 | 100.00 | 100.00 | 100.00 | 92.46 | 28.81 | 14.60 | 9.43 | 6.15 | 2.71 | 1.72 | 0.46 | 0.42 | 0.37 | 0.37 | 0.36 | 0.37 | 0.39 |
| World A growth rate, % p.a. | 0.07 | 0.07 | 0.06 | 0.08 | 0.06 | 0.09 | 0.10 | 0.08 | 0.02 | -0.89 | -0.45 | -0.38 | 0.39 | -0.25 | 1.47 | -4.34 | -0.20 | -0.57 | 1.08 | 0.54 | 0.32 | 0.08 |
| World A increase p.a., m | 0.00 | 0.00 | 0.00 | 0.00 | 0.00 | 0.01 | 0.01 | 0.01 | 0.00 | -0.03 | -0.01 | -0.01 | 0.01 | 0.00 | 0.07 | -0.09 | 0.00 | -0.01 | 0.03 | 0.02 | 0.01 | 0.00 |
| **Caribbean** (24 countries in 2000) | | | | | | | | | | | | | | | | | | | | | | |
| Population, m(=millions) | 0.10 | 0.10 | 0.11 | 0.12 | 0.15 | 0.20 | 0.24 | 0.27 | 0.30 | 0.20 | 1.00 | 2.00 | 4.00 | 6.87 | 24.86 | 33.96 | 36.14 | 38.14 | 47.29 | 52.03 | 56.86 | 58.58 |
| Growth rate, % p.a. | 0.00 | 0.00 | 0.05 | 0.04 | 0.07 | 0.14 | 0.09 | 0.08 | 0.07 | -0.27 | 1.62 | 1.40 | 1.40 | 1.09 | 1.85 | 1.57 | 1.25 | 1.08 | 0.86 | 0.38 | 0.18 | 0.03 |
| Increase p.a., m | 0.00 | 0.00 | 0.00 | 0.00 | 0.00 | 0.00 | 0.00 | 0.00 | 0.00 | 0.00 | 0.02 | 0.03 | 0.06 | 0.07 | 0.46 | 0.53 | 0.45 | 0.41 | 0.41 | 0.20 | 0.10 | 0.02 |
| Evangelized persons, m | 0.00 | 0.00 | 0.00 | 0.00 | 0.00 | 0.00 | 0.00 | 0.00 | 0.08 | 0.11 | 0.90 | 1.85 | 3.80 | 6.84 | 21.65 | 33.54 | 35.82 | 37.87 | 47.01 | 51.77 | 56.64 | 58.38 |
| Evangelized persons % | 0.00 | 0.00 | 0.00 | 0.00 | 0.00 | 0.00 | 0.00 | 0.00 | 26.67 | 55.00 | 90.00 | 92.50 | 95.00 | 99.51 | 87.08 | 98.75 | 99.13 | 99.31 | 99.42 | 99.51 | 99.61 | 99.66 |
| Outreach per Christian | — | — | — | — | — | — | — | — | 3.00 | 1.20 | 0.29 | 0.09 | 0.06 | 0.02 | 0.11 | 0.26 | 0.26 | 0.26 | 0.23 | 0.22 | 0.22 | 0.22 |
| **Christians, m** | **0.00** | **0.00** | **0.00** | **0.00** | **0.00** | **0.00** | **0.00** | **0.00** | **0.02** | **0.05** | **0.70** | **1.70** | **3.60** | **6.72** | **19.58** | **26.55** | **28.38** | **30.05** | **38.19** | **42.37** | **46.50** | **48.00** |
| Orthodox, m | 0.00 | 0.00 | 0.00 | 0.00 | 0.00 | 0.00 | 0.00 | 0.00 | 0.00 | 0.00 | 0.00 | 0.00 | 0.00 | 0.00 | 0.01 | 0.01 | 0.01 | 0.02 | 0.02 | 0.03 | 0.03 | 0.03 |
| Roman Catholics, m | 0.00 | 0.00 | 0.00 | 0.00 | 0.00 | 0.00 | 0.00 | 0.00 | 0.02 | 0.04 | 0.59 | 1.35 | 2.94 | 5.06 | 15.55 | 20.52 | 21.88 | 23.19 | 29.11 | 31.55 | 32.85 | 34.20 |
| Anglicans, m | 0.00 | 0.00 | 0.00 | 0.00 | 0.00 | 0.00 | 0.00 | 0.00 | 0.00 | 0.01 | 0.08 | 0.20 | 0.40 | 0.64 | 0.55 | 0.57 | 0.59 | 0.59 | 0.70 | 0.84 | 0.92 | 1.01 |
| Protestants, m | 0.00 | 0.00 | 0.00 | 0.00 | 0.00 | 0.00 | 0.00 | 0.00 | 0.00 | 0.00 | 0.03 | 0.10 | 0.23 | 0.47 | 1.76 | 3.28 | 3.56 | 3.86 | 5.47 | 7.02 | 7.96 | 9.02 |
| Independents, m | 0.00 | 0.00 | 0.00 | 0.00 | 0.00 | 0.00 | 0.00 | 0.00 | 0.00 | 0.00 | 0.00 | 0.05 | 0.03 | 0.02 | 0.54 | 1.10 | 1.16 | 1.31 | 2.16 | 2.98 | 3.50 | 4.12 |
| Marginal Christians, m | 0.00 | 0.00 | 0.00 | 0.00 | 0.00 | 0.00 | 0.00 | 0.00 | 0.00 | 0.00 | 0.00 | 0.00 | 0.00 | 0.00 | 0.07 | 0.34 | 0.38 | 0.43 | 0.84 | 1.40 | 1.81 | 2.34 |
| **Christians %** | **0.00** | **0.00** | **0.00** | **0.00** | **0.00** | **0.00** | **0.00** | **0.00** | **6.67** | **25.00** | **70.00** | **85.00** | **90.00** | **97.72** | **78.77** | **78.18** | **78.54** | **78.79** | **80.77** | **81.43** | **81.77** | **81.95** |
| Christian growth rate, % p.a. | 0.00 | 0.00 | 0.00 | 0.00 | 0.00 | 0.00 | 0.00 | 0.00 | 7.18 | 0.61 | 2.67 | 1.79 | 1.51 | 1.25 | 1.54 | 1.53 | 1.34 | 1.15 | 0.96 | 0.42 | 0.19 | 0.03 |
| Christian nett increase p.a., m | 0.00 | 0.00 | 0.00 | 0.00 | 0.00 | 0.00 | 0.00 | 0.00 | 0.00 | 0.00 | 0.02 | 0.03 | 0.05 | 0.08 | 0.30 | 0.41 | 0.38 | 0.35 | 0.37 | 0.18 | 0.09 | 0.02 |
| Gains: births+converts,m | 0.00 | 0.00 | 0.00 | 0.00 | 0.00 | 0.00 | 0.00 | 0.00 | 0.00 | 0.00 | 0.04 | 0.08 | 0.13 | 0.20 | 0.57 | 0.72 | 0.71 | 0.70 | 0.83 | 0.79 | 0.90 | 1.04 |
| Losses: deaths+defectors,m | 0.00 | 0.00 | 0.00 | 0.00 | 0.00 | 0.00 | 0.00 | 0.00 | 0.00 | 0.00 | 0.02 | 0.05 | 0.08 | 0.12 | 0.26 | 0.32 | 0.33 | 0.35 | 0.47 | 0.61 | 0.81 | 1.02 |
| World B, m | 0.00 | 0.00 | 0.00 | 0.00 | 0.00 | 0.00 | 0.00 | 0.00 | 0.06 | 0.06 | 0.20 | 0.15 | 0.20 | 0.12 | 2.07 | 6.99 | 7.44 | 7.83 | 8.82 | 9.41 | 10.14 | 10.38 |
| World B % | 0.00 | 0.00 | 0.00 | 0.00 | 0.00 | 0.00 | 0.00 | 0.00 | 20.00 | 30.00 | 20.00 | 7.50 | 5.00 | 1.79 | 8.31 | 20.57 | 20.59 | 20.52 | 18.65 | 18.08 | 17.84 | 17.71 |
| World B growth rate, % p.a. | 0.00 | 0.00 | 0.00 | 0.00 | 0.00 | 0.00 | 0.00 | 0.00 | 11.61 | 0.00 | 1.21 | -0.57 | 0.58 | -0.97 | 4.11 | 6.28 | 1.27 | 1.01 | 0.48 | 0.26 | 0.15 | 0.02 |
| World B increase p.a., m | 0.00 | 0.00 | 0.00 | 0.00 | 0.00 | 0.00 | 0.00 | 0.00 | 2.32 | 0.00 | 0.24 | -0.04 | 0.03 | -0.02 | 0.34 | 1.29 | 0.26 | 0.21 | 0.09 | 0.05 | 0.03 | 0.00 |
| World A, m | 0.10 | 0.10 | 0.11 | 0.12 | 0.15 | 0.20 | 0.24 | 0.27 | 0.22 | 0.09 | 0.10 | 0.15 | 0.20 | 0.03 | 3.21 | 0.42 | 0.31 | 0.26 | 0.27 | 0.25 | 0.22 | 0.20 |
| World A % | 100.00 | 100.00 | 100.00 | 100.00 | 100.00 | 100.00 | 100.00 | 100.00 | 73.33 | 45.00 | 10.00 | 7.50 | 5.00 | 0.49 | 12.92 | 1.25 | 0.87 | 0.69 | 0.58 | 0.49 | 0.39 | 0.34 |
| World A growth rate, % p.a. | 0.00 | 0.00 | 0.05 | 0.04 | 0.07 | 0.14 | 0.09 | 0.08 | -0.14 | -0.59 | 0.11 | 0.81 | 0.58 | -3.49 | 6.72 | -9.63 | -5.79 | -3.43 | 0.15 | -0.32 | -0.28 | -0.10 |
| World A increase p.a., m | 0.00 | 0.00 | 0.00 | 0.00 | 0.00 | 0.00 | 0.00 | 0.00 | 0.00 | 0.00 | 0.00 | 0.00 | 0.00 | 0.00 | 0.22 | -0.04 | -0.02 | -0.01 | 0.00 | 0.00 | 0.00 | 0.00 |

The **2 axes** below are: horizontally, years AD by 20-year gaps; vertically, persons (logarithmic scale).
The **3 lines** on each graph are, from top to bottom: live **population**, live **evangelized persons**, live **Christians**.
**Statistics** and trends for 22 years are given, for each geopolitical area, in its facing table opposite.

## Central America

**A** = 1000   Mayan and Aztec civilizations uncontacted by Christians for 1,500 years
**B** = 1500   Spanish settlers arrive in Mexico followed by missionaries
**C** = 1518   Native populations succumb to European disease
**D** = 1523   Cortes orders mass conversion of Amerindians
**E** = 1900   Protestant and Independent churches grow
**F** = 2000   Region is 96% Christian; 99.8% evangelized

## South America

**A** = 1000   Indigenous tribes and civilizations not contacted by Christians
**B** = 1549   Portuguese settlers and Jesuits arrive in Brazil
**C** = 1560   Native populations killed by disease and European conquest
**D** = 1580   Jesuit reducciones rescue large numbers of indigenous converts in Bolivia, Paraguay, Argentina, and Brazil
**E** = 1900   Protestants and Independents grow in Brazil and other countries
**F** = 2000   Region is 93% Christian; 99.6% evangelized

## NORTHERN AMERICA

**A** = 1400   Amerindians uncontacted by Christians
**B** = 1607   British Anglicans land in Virginia; Protestant Pilgrims later land in New England
**C** = 1700   European immigrants rapidly outnumber native Americans
**D** = 1776   Disestablishment of churches and independence from Britain
**E** = 1950   Secularization and massive immigration of non-Christians erode Christian percentage
**F** = 2000   Region is 84% Christian; 98% evangelized

## OCEANIA

**A** = 1600   Indigenous populations uncontacted by Christians
**B** = 1660   Roman Catholic missionaries arrive in the islands
**C** = 1780   British Anglicans establish presence in Australia
**D** = 1835   Protestants arrive in the islands
**E** = 1850   Native populations succomb to European diseases
**F** = 1880   Mass movements into the churches begin
**G** = 2000   Continent is 83% Christian; 98% evangelized

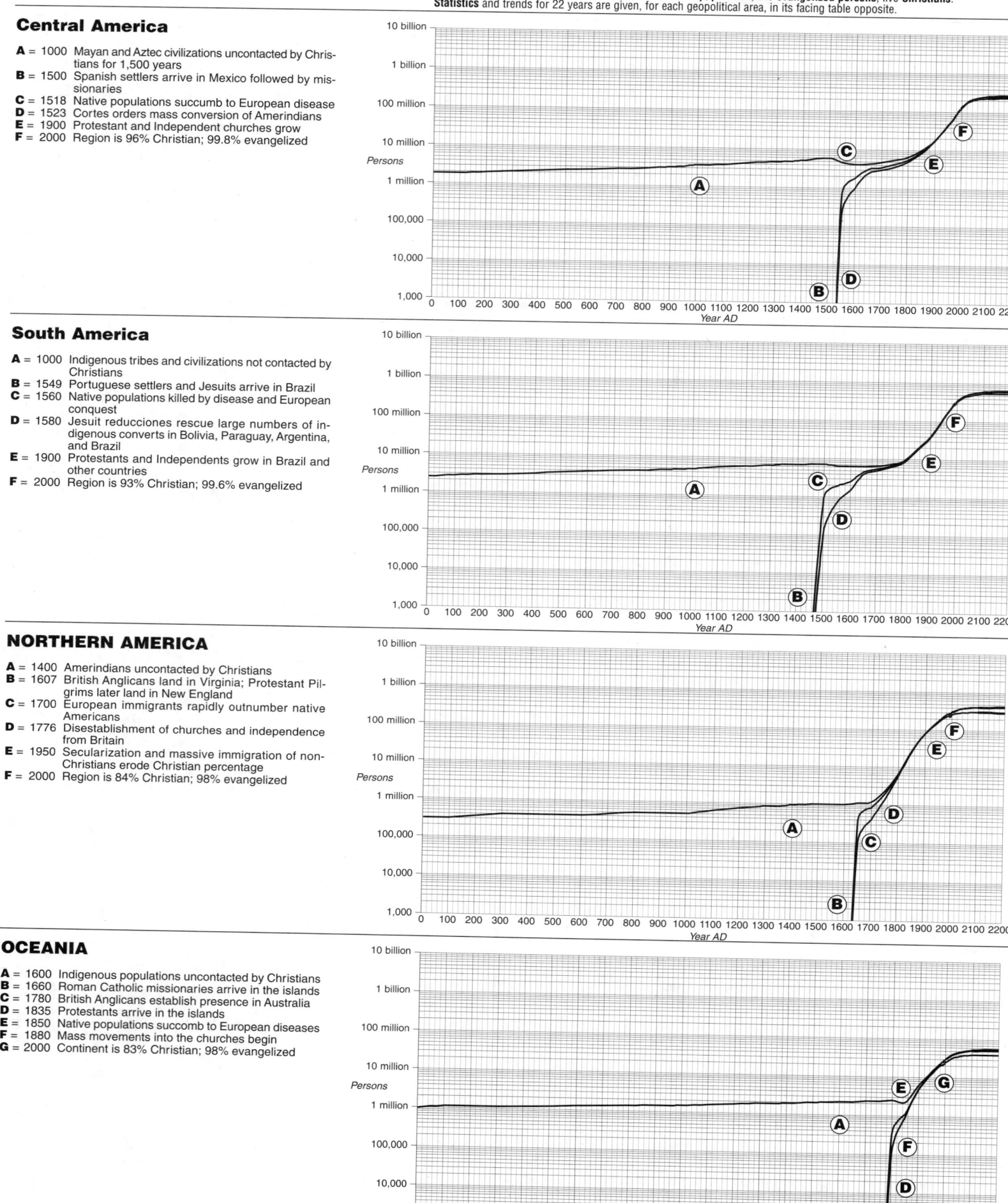

| Area / Year, AD<br>1 | 33<br>2 | 100<br>3 | 300<br>4 | 500<br>5 | 800<br>6 | 1000<br>7 | 1200<br>8 | 1350<br>9 | 1500<br>10 | 1650<br>11 | 1750<br>12 | 1800<br>13 | 1850<br>14 | 1900<br>15 | 1970<br>16 | 1990<br>17 | 1995<br>18 | 2000<br>19 | 2025<br>20 | 2050<br>21 | 2100<br>22 | 2200<br>23 |
|---|---|---|---|---|---|---|---|---|---|---|---|---|---|---|---|---|---|---|---|---|---|---|
| **Central America** (8 countries in 2000) | | | | | | | | | | | | | | | | | | | | | | |
| Population, m(=millions) | 1.80 | 1.82 | 2.10 | 2.44 | 2.80 | 3.60 | 4.24 | 4.68 | 5.80 | 4.30 | 5.55 | 6.50 | 10.00 | 17.95 | 67.51 | 111.42 | 123.27 | 135.22 | 188.50 | 222.50 | 256.66 | 269.18 |
| Growth rate, % p.a. | 0.02 | 0.02 | 0.07 | 0.08 | 0.05 | 0.13 | 0.08 | 0.07 | 0.14 | -0.20 | 0.26 | 0.32 | 0.87 | 1.18 | 1.91 | 2.54 | 2.04 | 1.87 | 1.34 | 0.67 | 0.29 | 0.05 |
| Increase p.a., m | 0.00 | 0.00 | 0.00 | 0.00 | 0.00 | 0.00 | 0.00 | 0.00 | 0.01 | -0.01 | 0.01 | 0.02 | 0.09 | 0.21 | 1.29 | 2.83 | 2.52 | 2.53 | 2.52 | 1.48 | 0.73 | 0.13 |
| Evangelized persons, m | 0.00 | 0.00 | 0.00 | 0.00 | 0.00 | 0.00 | 0.00 | 0.00 | 0.00 | 3.10 | 4.20 | 5.50 | 9.10 | 17.90 | 67.37 | 111.21 | 123.04 | 134.99 | 188.14 | 222.03 | 255.86 | 268.18 |
| Evangelized persons % | 0.00 | 0.00 | 0.00 | 0.00 | 0.00 | 0.00 | 0.00 | 0.00 | 0.00 | 72.09 | 75.68 | 84.62 | 91.00 | 99.73 | 99.79 | 99.80 | 99.82 | 99.83 | 99.81 | 99.79 | 99.69 | 99.63 |
| Outreach per Christian | — | — | — | — | — | — | — | — | — | 0.29 | 0.17 | 0.10 | 0.07 | 0.01 | 0.02 | 0.03 | 0.04 | 0.04 | 0.05 | 0.06 | 0.08 | 0.10 |
| **Christians, m** | **0.00** | **0.00** | **0.00** | **0.00** | **0.00** | **0.00** | **0.00** | **0.00** | **0.00** | **2.40** | **3.60** | **5.00** | **8.50** | **17.77** | **66.26** | **107.52** | **118.81** | **130.21** | **179.74** | **209.65** | **237.00** | **243.00** |
| Orthodox, m | 0.00 | 0.00 | 0.00 | 0.00 | 0.00 | 0.00 | 0.00 | 0.00 | 0.00 | 0.00 | 0.00 | 0.00 | 0.00 | 0.00 | 0.06 | 0.09 | 0.10 | 0.11 | 0.14 | 0.17 | 0.18 | 0.19 |
| Roman Catholics, m | 0.00 | 0.00 | 0.00 | 0.00 | 0.00 | 0.00 | 0.00 | 0.00 | 0.00 | 2.40 | 3.60 | 4.99 | 8.47 | 16.43 | 61.96 | 102.40 | 113.16 | 124.01 | 169.85 | 195.70 | 210.08 | 225.51 |
| Anglicans, m | 0.00 | 0.00 | 0.00 | 0.00 | 0.00 | 0.00 | 0.00 | 0.00 | 0.00 | 0.00 | 0.00 | 0.01 | 0.01 | 0.02 | 0.05 | 0.20 | 0.21 | 0.24 | 0.32 | 0.37 | 0.40 | 0.43 |
| Protestants, m | 0.00 | 0.00 | 0.00 | 0.00 | 0.00 | 0.00 | 0.00 | 0.00 | 0.00 | 0.00 | 0.00 | 0.00 | 0.02 | 0.09 | 1.44 | 5.36 | 6.18 | 6.98 | 12.75 | 18.18 | 21.71 | 25.93 |
| Independents, m | 0.00 | 0.00 | 0.00 | 0.00 | 0.00 | 0.00 | 0.00 | 0.00 | 0.00 | 0.00 | 0.00 | 0.00 | 0.00 | 0.00 | 1.42 | 4.00 | 4.56 | 5.16 | 9.65 | 13.70 | 16.32 | 19.44 |
| Marginal Christians, m | 0.00 | 0.00 | 0.00 | 0.00 | 0.00 | 0.00 | 0.00 | 0.00 | 0.00 | 0.00 | 0.00 | 0.00 | 0.00 | 0.00 | 0.28 | 1.94 | 2.20 | 2.46 | 4.91 | 7.38 | 9.05 | 11.10 |
| **Christians %** | **0.00** | **0.00** | **0.00** | **0.00** | **0.00** | **0.00** | **0.00** | **0.00** | **0.00** | **55.81** | **64.86** | **76.92** | **85.00** | **98.98** | **98.15** | **96.49** | **96.38** | **96.30** | **95.35** | **94.22** | **92.34** | **90.27** |
| Christian growth rate, % p.a. | 0.00 | 0.00 | 0.00 | 0.00 | 0.00 | 0.00 | 0.00 | 0.00 | 0.00 | 5.33 | 0.41 | 0.66 | 1.07 | 1.49 | 1.90 | 2.45 | 2.02 | 1.85 | 1.30 | 0.62 | 0.25 | 0.03 |
| Christian nett increase p.a., m | 0.00 | 0.00 | 0.00 | 0.00 | 0.00 | 0.00 | 0.00 | 0.00 | 0.00 | 0.13 | 0.01 | 0.03 | 0.09 | 0.26 | 1.26 | 2.63 | 2.40 | 2.41 | 2.33 | 1.29 | 0.58 | 0.06 |
| Gains: births+converts,m | 0.00 | 0.00 | 0.00 | 0.00 | 0.00 | 0.00 | 0.00 | 0.00 | 0.00 | 0.20 | 0.12 | 0.17 | 0.28 | 0.62 | 2.19 | 3.66 | 3.50 | 3.61 | 4.15 | 3.91 | 4.32 | 4.99 |
| Losses: deaths+defectors,m | 0.00 | 0.00 | 0.00 | 0.00 | 0.00 | 0.00 | 0.00 | 0.00 | 0.00 | 0.08 | 0.11 | 0.14 | 0.19 | 0.35 | 0.93 | 1.03 | 1.11 | 1.20 | 1.82 | 2.62 | 3.73 | 4.93 |
| World B, m | 0.00 | 0.00 | 0.00 | 0.00 | 0.00 | 0.00 | 0.00 | 0.00 | 0.00 | 0.70 | 0.60 | 0.50 | 0.60 | 0.13 | 1.11 | 3.69 | 4.23 | 4.78 | 8.40 | 12.38 | 18.86 | 25.18 |
| World B % | 0.00 | 0.00 | 0.00 | 0.00 | 0.00 | 0.00 | 0.00 | 0.00 | 0.00 | 16.28 | 10.81 | 7.69 | 6.00 | 0.74 | 1.64 | 3.31 | 3.43 | 3.53 | 4.46 | 5.57 | 7.35 | 9.35 |
| World B growth rate, % p.a. | 0.00 | 0.00 | 0.00 | 0.00 | 0.00 | 0.00 | 0.00 | 0.00 | 0.00 | 3.70 | -0.15 | -0.36 | 0.37 | -2.97 | 3.07 | 6.20 | 2.79 | 2.45 | 2.28 | 1.57 | 0.84 | 0.29 |
| World B increase p.a., m | 0.00 | 0.00 | 0.00 | 0.00 | 0.00 | 0.00 | 0.00 | 0.00 | 0.00 | 0.60 | -0.02 | -0.03 | 0.02 | -0.02 | 0.05 | 0.21 | 0.10 | 0.09 | 0.10 | 0.09 | 0.06 | 0.03 |
| World A, m | 1.80 | 1.82 | 2.10 | 2.44 | 2.80 | 3.60 | 4.24 | 4.68 | 5.80 | 1.20 | 1.35 | 1.00 | 0.90 | 0.05 | 0.14 | 0.22 | 0.23 | 0.23 | 0.36 | 0.47 | 0.80 | 1.00 |
| World A % | 100.00 | 100.00 | 100.00 | 100.00 | 100.00 | 100.00 | 100.00 | 100.00 | 100.00 | 27.91 | 24.32 | 15.38 | 9.00 | 0.27 | 0.21 | 0.20 | 0.18 | 0.17 | 0.19 | 0.21 | 0.31 | 0.37 |
| World A growth rate, % p.a. | 0.02 | 0.02 | 0.07 | 0.08 | 0.05 | 0.13 | 0.08 | 0.07 | 0.14 | -1.04 | 0.12 | -0.60 | -0.21 | -5.64 | 1.53 | 2.17 | 0.78 | 0.42 | 1.77 | 1.04 | 1.08 | 0.22 |
| World A increase p.a., m | 0.00 | 0.00 | 0.00 | 0.00 | 0.00 | 0.00 | 0.00 | 0.00 | 0.01 | -0.01 | 0.00 | -0.01 | 0.00 | 0.00 | 0.00 | 0.00 | 0.00 | 0.00 | 0.01 | 0.00 | 0.01 | 0.00 |
| **South America** (14 countries in 2000) | | | | | | | | | | | | | | | | | | | | | | |
| Population, m(=millions) | 2.40 | 2.58 | 2.89 | 3.44 | 4.15 | 4.70 | 5.80 | 6.70 | 6.90 | 6.40 | 7.15 | 9.00 | 18.50 | 40.31 | 192.43 | 295.08 | 320.55 | 345.78 | 460.86 | 534.37 | 605.39 | 631.12 |
| Growth rate, % p.a. | 0.11 | 0.11 | 0.06 | 0.09 | 0.06 | 0.06 | 0.11 | 0.10 | 0.02 | -0.05 | 0.11 | 0.46 | 1.45 | 1.57 | 2.26 | 2.16 | 1.67 | 1.53 | 1.16 | 0.59 | 0.25 | 0.04 |
| Increase p.a., m | 0.00 | 0.00 | 0.00 | 0.00 | 0.00 | 0.00 | 0.01 | 0.01 | 0.00 | 0.00 | 0.01 | 0.04 | 0.27 | 0.63 | 4.34 | 6.38 | 5.35 | 5.28 | 5.33 | 3.17 | 1.51 | 0.26 |
| Evangelized persons, m | 0.00 | 0.00 | 0.00 | 0.00 | 0.00 | 0.00 | 0.00 | 0.00 | 0.90 | 4.55 | 6.60 | 8.50 | 17.60 | 38.64 | 190.87 | 293.70 | 319.09 | 344.33 | 458.95 | 532.18 | 602.99 | 628.62 |
| Evangelized persons % | 0.00 | 0.00 | 0.00 | 0.00 | 0.00 | 0.00 | 0.00 | 0.00 | 13.04 | 71.09 | 92.31 | 94.44 | 95.14 | 95.84 | 99.19 | 99.53 | 99.54 | 99.58 | 99.59 | 99.59 | 99.60 | 99.60 |
| Outreach per Christian | — | — | — | — | — | — | — | — | 8.00 | 0.12 | 0.10 | 0.04 | 0.02 | 0.03 | 0.04 | 0.07 | 0.07 | 0.07 | 0.08 | 0.10 | 0.12 | 0.14 |
| **Christians, m** | **0.00** | **0.00** | **0.00** | **0.00** | **0.00** | **0.00** | **0.00** | **0.00** | **0.10** | **4.05** | **6.00** | **8.20** | **17.20** | **37.52** | **183.36** | **275.27** | **298.08** | **320.84** | **423.18** | **482.42** | **540.00** | **550.00** |
| Orthodox, m | 0.00 | 0.00 | 0.00 | 0.00 | 0.00 | 0.00 | 0.00 | 0.00 | 0.00 | 0.00 | 0.00 | 0.00 | 0.00 | 0.01 | 0.29 | 0.37 | 0.38 | 0.43 | 0.59 | 0.72 | 0.79 | 0.87 |
| Roman Catholics, m | 0.00 | 0.00 | 0.00 | 0.00 | 0.00 | 0.00 | 0.00 | 0.00 | 0.10 | 4.05 | 5.99 | 8.12 | 16.97 | 37.20 | 174.28 | 268.86 | 291.69 | 314.02 | 407.10 | 461.58 | 491.52 | 523.41 |
| Anglicans, m | 0.00 | 0.00 | 0.00 | 0.00 | 0.00 | 0.00 | 0.00 | 0.00 | 0.00 | 0.00 | 0.00 | 0.01 | 0.03 | 0.07 | 0.17 | 0.23 | 0.24 | 0.26 | 0.33 | 0.41 | 0.46 | 0.51 |
| Protestants, m | 0.00 | 0.00 | 0.00 | 0.00 | 0.00 | 0.00 | 0.00 | 0.00 | 0.00 | 0.00 | 0.01 | 0.07 | 0.20 | 0.37 | 9.31 | 31.20 | 34.32 | 37.28 | 57.97 | 71.24 | 78.98 | 87.57 |
| Independents, m | 0.00 | 0.00 | 0.00 | 0.00 | 0.00 | 0.00 | 0.00 | 0.00 | 0.00 | 0.00 | 0.00 | 0.00 | 0.00 | 0.00 | 7.28 | 27.80 | 30.63 | 33.24 | 48.21 | 58.50 | 64.44 | 70.99 |
| Marginal Christians, m | 0.00 | 0.00 | 0.00 | 0.00 | 0.00 | 0.00 | 0.00 | 0.00 | 0.00 | 0.00 | 0.00 | 0.00 | 0.00 | 0.00 | 0.49 | 2.73 | 3.16 | 3.70 | 7.47 | 11.17 | 13.66 | 16.72 |
| **Christians %** | **0.00** | **0.00** | **0.00** | **0.00** | **0.00** | **0.00** | **0.00** | **0.00** | **1.45** | **63.28** | **83.92** | **91.11** | **92.97** | **93.06** | **95.29** | **93.29** | **92.99** | **92.79** | **91.82** | **90.28** | **89.20** | **87.15** |
| Christian growth rate, % p.a. | 0.00 | 0.00 | 0.00 | 0.00 | 0.00 | 0.00 | 0.00 | 0.00 | 12.20 | 2.50 | 0.39 | 0.63 | 1.49 | 1.57 | 2.29 | 2.05 | 1.60 | 1.48 | 1.11 | 0.53 | 0.23 | 0.02 |
| Christian nett increase p.a., m | 0.00 | 0.00 | 0.00 | 0.00 | 0.00 | 0.00 | 0.00 | 0.00 | 0.01 | 0.10 | 0.02 | 0.05 | 0.26 | 0.59 | 4.20 | 5.65 | 4.78 | 4.76 | 4.71 | 2.53 | 1.22 | 0.10 |
| Gains: births+converts,m | 0.00 | 0.00 | 0.00 | 0.00 | 0.00 | 0.00 | 0.00 | 0.00 | 0.02 | 0.23 | 0.19 | 0.23 | 0.59 | 1.22 | 6.74 | 8.70 | 8.01 | 8.19 | 9.60 | 9.10 | 9.99 | 10.89 |
| Losses: deaths+defectors,m | 0.00 | 0.00 | 0.00 | 0.00 | 0.00 | 0.00 | 0.00 | 0.00 | 0.00 | 0.13 | 0.16 | 0.18 | 0.34 | 0.63 | 2.54 | 3.05 | 3.22 | 3.43 | 4.88 | 6.57 | 8.77 | 10.79 |
| World B, m | 0.00 | 0.00 | 0.00 | 0.00 | 0.00 | 0.00 | 0.00 | 0.00 | 0.80 | 0.50 | 0.60 | 0.30 | 0.40 | 1.12 | 7.52 | 18.43 | 21.00 | 23.49 | 35.77 | 49.76 | 62.99 | 78.62 |
| World B % | 0.00 | 0.00 | 0.00 | 0.00 | 0.00 | 0.00 | 0.00 | 0.00 | 11.59 | 7.81 | 8.39 | 3.33 | 2.16 | 2.78 | 3.91 | 6.25 | 6.55 | 6.79 | 7.76 | 9.31 | 10.40 | 12.46 |
| World B growth rate, % p.a. | 0.00 | 0.00 | 0.00 | 0.00 | 0.00 | 0.00 | 0.00 | 0.00 | 20.25 | -0.31 | 0.18 | -1.38 | 0.58 | 2.08 | 2.76 | 4.59 | 2.65 | 2.26 | 1.70 | 1.33 | 0.47 | 0.22 |
| World B increase p.a., m | 0.00 | 0.00 | 0.00 | 0.00 | 0.00 | 0.00 | 0.00 | 0.00 | 2.35 | -0.02 | 0.02 | -0.05 | 0.01 | 0.06 | 0.11 | 0.29 | 0.17 | 0.15 | 0.13 | 0.12 | 0.05 | 0.03 |
| World A, m | 2.40 | 2.58 | 2.89 | 3.44 | 4.15 | 4.70 | 5.80 | 6.70 | 6.00 | 1.85 | 0.55 | 0.50 | 0.90 | 1.68 | 1.55 | 1.38 | 1.46 | 1.45 | 1.91 | 2.19 | 2.40 | 2.50 |
| World A % | 100.00 | 100.00 | 100.00 | 100.00 | 100.00 | 100.00 | 100.00 | 100.00 | 86.96 | 28.91 | 7.69 | 5.56 | 4.86 | 4.16 | 0.81 | 0.47 | 0.46 | 0.42 | 0.41 | 0.41 | 0.40 | 0.40 |
| World A growth rate, % p.a. | 0.11 | 0.11 | 0.06 | 0.09 | 0.06 | 0.06 | 0.11 | 0.10 | -0.07 | -0.78 | -1.21 | -0.19 | 1.18 | 1.26 | -0.11 | -0.60 | 1.15 | -0.15 | 1.11 | 0.55 | 0.18 | 0.04 |
| World A increase p.a., m | 0.00 | 0.00 | 0.00 | 0.00 | 0.00 | 0.00 | 0.01 | 0.01 | 0.00 | -0.01 | -0.01 | 0.00 | 0.01 | 0.02 | 0.00 | -0.01 | 0.02 | 0.00 | 0.02 | 0.01 | 0.00 | 0.00 |
| **NORTHERN AMERICA** (5 countries in 2000) | | | | | | | | | | | | | | | | | | | | | | |
| Population, m(=millions) | 0.30 | 0.30 | 0.40 | 0.40 | 0.50 | 0.50 | 0.72 | 0.85 | 1.00 | 1.10 | 2.30 | 6.50 | 26.50 | 81.63 | 231.54 | 281.99 | 296.76 | 309.63 | 363.61 | 391.78 | 419.08 | 428.59 |
| Growth rate, % p.a. | 0.00 | 0.00 | 0.14 | 0.00 | 0.07 | 0.00 | 0.18 | 0.11 | 0.11 | 0.06 | 0.74 | 2.10 | 2.85 | 2.28 | 1.50 | 0.99 | 1.03 | 0.85 | 0.64 | 0.30 | 0.13 | 0.02 |
| Increase p.a., m | 0.00 | 0.00 | 0.00 | 0.00 | 0.00 | 0.00 | 0.00 | 0.00 | 0.00 | 0.00 | 0.02 | 0.14 | 0.76 | 1.86 | 3.47 | 2.79 | 3.05 | 2.64 | 2.34 | 1.17 | 0.56 | 0.10 |
| Evangelized persons, m | 0.00 | 0.00 | 0.00 | 0.00 | 0.00 | 0.00 | 0.00 | 0.00 | 0.00 | 0.40 | 1.95 | 6.00 | 25.90 | 81.47 | 230.41 | 277.88 | 292.29 | 304.86 | 354.99 | 381.09 | 406.08 | 413.59 |
| Evangelized persons % | 0.00 | 0.00 | 0.00 | 0.00 | 0.00 | 0.00 | 0.00 | 0.00 | 0.00 | 36.36 | 84.78 | 92.31 | 97.74 | 99.81 | 99.51 | 98.54 | 98.49 | 98.46 | 97.63 | 97.27 | 96.90 | 96.50 |
| Outreach per Christian | — | — | — | — | — | — | — | — | — | 3.00 | 0.39 | 0.07 | 0.04 | 0.03 | 0.09 | 0.16 | 0.16 | 0.17 | 0.22 | 0.27 | 0.31 | 0.36 |
| **Christians, m** | **0.00** | **0.00** | **0.00** | **0.00** | **0.00** | **0.00** | **0.00** | **0.00** | **0.00** | **0.10** | **1.40** | **5.60** | **25.00** | **78.81** | **211.42** | **240.46** | **251.48** | **260.62** | **290.35** | **300.68** | **310.00** | **305.00** |
| Orthodox, m | 0.00 | 0.00 | 0.00 | 0.00 | 0.00 | 0.00 | 0.00 | 0.00 | 0.00 | 0.00 | 0.00 | 0.01 | 0.15 | 0.42 | 4.54 | 5.66 | 6.02 | 6.34 | 7.96 | 9.23 | 9.94 | 10.70 |
| Roman Catholics, m | 0.00 | 0.00 | 0.00 | 0.00 | 0.00 | 0.00 | 0.00 | 0.00 | 0.00 | 0.01 | 0.01 | 0.05 | 1.50 | 13.01 | 57.41 | 68.24 | 69.14 | 71.03 | 80.52 | 82.82 | 84.00 | 85.19 |
| Anglicans, m | 0.00 | 0.00 | 0.00 | 0.00 | 0.00 | 0.00 | 0.00 | 0.00 | 0.00 | 0.02 | 0.07 | 0.20 | 1.00 | 2.17 | 4.40 | 3.35 | 3.32 | 3.24 | 2.92 | 2.77 | 2.70 | 2.63 |
| Protestants, m | 0.00 | 0.00 | 0.00 | 0.00 | 0.00 | 0.00 | 0.00 | 0.00 | 0.00 | 0.07 | 1.29 | 5.02 | 20.05 | 37.30 | 62.81 | 65.14 | 67.73 | 69.98 | 74.77 | 75.87 | 76.43 | 76.99 |
| Independents, m | 0.00 | 0.00 | 0.00 | 0.00 | 0.00 | 0.00 | 0.00 | 0.00 | 0.00 | 0.00 | 0.03 | 0.30 | 2.00 | 5.86 | 36.32 | 68.31 | 74.53 | 80.24 | 102.71 | 116.41 | 123.94 | 131.95 |
| Marginal Christians, m | 0.00 | 0.00 | 0.00 | 0.00 | 0.00 | 0.00 | 0.00 | 0.00 | 0.00 | 0.00 | 0.00 | 0.02 | 0.30 | 0.82 | 6.47 | 9.36 | 9.94 | 10.53 | 17.50 | 21.01 | 23.03 | 25.24 |
| **Christians %** | **0.00** | **0.00** | **0.00** | **0.00** | **0.00** | **0.00** | **0.00** | **0.00** | **0.00** | **9.09** | **60.87** | **86.15** | **94.34** | **96.55** | **91.31** | **85.27** | **84.74** | **84.17** | **79.85** | **76.75** | **73.97** | **71.16** |
| Christian growth rate, % p.a. | 0.00 | 0.00 | 0.00 | 0.00 | 0.00 | 0.00 | 0.00 | 0.00 | 0.00 | 1.55 | 2.67 | 2.81 | 3.04 | 2.32 | 1.42 | 0.65 | 0.90 | 0.72 | 0.43 | 0.14 | 0.06 | -0.02 |
| Christian nett increase p.a., m | 0.00 | 0.00 | 0.00 | 0.00 | 0.00 | 0.00 | 0.00 | 0.00 | 0.00 | 0.00 | 0.04 | 0.16 | 0.76 | 1.83 | 3.00 | 1.55 | 2.26 | 1.87 | 1.26 | 0.42 | 0.19 | -0.05 |
| Gains: births+converts,m | 0.00 | 0.00 | 0.00 | 0.00 | 0.00 | 0.00 | 0.00 | 0.00 | 0.00 | 0.00 | 0.07 | 0.27 | 1.22 | 3.05 | 6.39 | 5.29 | 6.12 | 5.90 | 6.13 | 6.05 | 6.73 | 7.24 |
| Losses: deaths+defectors,m | 0.00 | 0.00 | 0.00 | 0.00 | 0.00 | 0.00 | 0.00 | 0.00 | 0.00 | 0.00 | 0.04 | 0.11 | 0.46 | 1.22 | 3.39 | 3.74 | 3.86 | 4.03 | 4.87 | 5.63 | 6.54 | 7.29 |
| World B, m | 0.00 | 0.00 | 0.00 | 0.00 | 0.00 | 0.00 | 0.00 | 0.00 | 0.00 | 0.30 | 0.55 | 0.40 | 0.90 | 2.66 | 18.99 | 37.42 | 40.81 | 44.23 | 64.64 | 80.41 | 96.08 | 108.59 |
| World B % | 0.00 | 0.00 | 0.00 | 0.00 | 0.00 | 0.00 | 0.00 | 0.00 | 0.00 | 27.27 | 23.91 | 6.15 | 3.40 | 3.26 | 8.20 | 13.27 | 13.75 | 14.29 | 17.78 | 20.52 | 22.93 | 25.34 |
| World B growth rate, % p.a. | 0.00 | 0.00 | 0.00 | 0.00 | 0.00 | 0.00 | 0.00 | 0.00 | 0.00 | 1.82 | 0.61 | -0.63 | 1.64 | 2.19 | 2.85 | 3.45 | 1.75 | 1.63 | 1.53 | 0.88 | 0.36 | 0.12 |
| World B increase p.a., m | 0.00 | 0.00 | 0.00 | 0.00 | 0.00 | 0.00 | 0.00 | 0.00 | 0.00 | 0.50 | 0.15 | -0.04 | 0.06 | 0.07 | 0.23 | 0.46 | 0.24 | 0.23 | 0.27 | 0.18 | 0.08 | 0.03 |
| World A, m | 0.30 | 0.30 | 0.40 | 0.40 | 0.50 | 0.50 | 0.72 | 0.85 | 1.00 | 0.70 | 0.35 | 0.50 | 0.60 | 0.16 | 1.13 | 4.11 | 4.47 | 4.77 | 8.63 | 10.69 | 13.00 | 15.00 |
| World A % | 100.00 | 100.00 | 100.00 | 100.00 | 100.00 | 100.00 | 100.00 | 100.00 | 100.00 | 63.64 | 15.22 | 7.69 | 2.26 | 0.19 | 0.49 | 1.46 | 1.51 | 1.54 | 2.37 | 2.73 | 3.10 | 3.50 |
| World A growth rate, % p.a. | 0.00 | 0.00 | 0.14 | 0.00 | 0.07 | 0.00 | 0.18 | 0.11 | 0.11 | -0.24 | -0.69 | 0.72 | 0.37 | -2.65 | 2.87 | 6.66 | 1.72 | 1.31 | 2.39 | 0.86 | 0.39 | 0.14 |
| World A increase p.a., m | 0.00 | 0.00 | 0.00 | 0.00 | 0.00 | 0.00 | 0.00 | 0.00 | 0.00 | 0.00 | 0.00 | 0.00 | 0.00 | 0.00 | 0.03 | 0.27 | 0.08 | 0.06 | 0.21 | 0.09 | 0.05 | 0.02 |
| **OCEANIA** (28 countries in 2000) | | | | | | | | | | | | | | | | | | | | | | |
| Population, m(=millions) | 1.00 | 1.10 | 1.10 | 1.20 | 1.40 | 1.50 | 1.70 | 1.85 | 2.00 | 2.20 | 2.30 | 2.50 | 2.25 | 6.25 | 19.31 | 26.41 | 28.49 | 30.39 | 39.65 | 46.18 | 52.37 | 54.65 |
| Growth rate, % p.a. | 0.14 | 0.14 | 0.00 | 0.04 | 0.05 | 0.03 | 0.06 | 0.06 | 0.05 | 0.06 | 0.04 | 0.17 | -0.21 | 2.06 | 1.63 | 1.58 | 1.52 | 1.30 | 1.07 | 0.61 | 0.25 | 0.04 |
| Increase p.a., m | 0.00 | 0.00 | 0.00 | 0.00 | 0.00 | 0.00 | 0.00 | 0.00 | 0.00 | 0.00 | 0.00 | 0.00 | 0.00 | 0.13 | 0.31 | 0.42 | 0.43 | 0.40 | 0.42 | 0.28 | 0.13 | 0.02 |
| Evangelized persons, m | 0.00 | 0.00 | 0.00 | 0.00 | 0.00 | 0.00 | 0.00 | 0.00 | 0.00 | 0.00 | 0.00 | 0.33 | 1.12 | 5.13 | 18.98 | 25.93 | 27.94 | 29.83 | 38.77 | 45.01 | 50.82 | 52.78 |
| Evangelized persons % | 0.00 | 0.00 | 0.00 | 0.00 | 0.00 | 0.00 | 0.00 | 0.00 | 0.00 | 0.00 | 0.00 | 13.00 | 49.78 | 82.13 | 98.27 | 98.17 | 98.09 | 98.15 | 97.78 | 97.47 | 97.04 | 96.57 |
| Outreach per Christian | — | — | — | — | — | — | — | — | — | — | — | 2.25 | 0.19 | 0.06 | 0.06 | 0.18 | 0.18 | 0.19 | 0.21 | 0.26 | 0.27 | 0.32 |
| **Christians, m** | **0.00** | **0.00** | **0.00** | **0.00** | **0.00** | **0.00** | **0.00** | **0.00** | **0.00** | **0.00** | **0.00** | **0.10** | **0.94** | **4.84** | **17.85** | **22.01** | **23.64** | **25.11** | **32.01** | **35.79** | **40.00** | **40.02** |
| Orthodox, m | 0.00 | 0.00 | 0.00 | 0.00 | 0.00 | 0.00 | 0.00 | 0.00 | 0.00 | 0.00 | 0.00 | 0.00 | 0.00 | 0.00 | 0.27 | 0.59 | 0.63 | 0.71 | 1.06 | 1.16 | 1.22 | 1.28 |
| Roman Catholics, m | 0.00 | 0.00 | 0.00 | 0.00 | 0.00 | 0.00 | 0.00 | 0.00 | 0.00 | 0.00 | 0.00 | 0.02 | 0.19 | 1.05 | 4.55 | 6.99 | 7.59 | 8.23 | 11.24 | 13.57 | 14.94 | 16.48 |
| Anglicans, m | 0.00 | 0.00 | 0.00 | 0.00 | 0.00 | 0.00 | 0.00 | 0.00 | 0.00 | 0.00 | 0.00 | 0.08 | 0.40 | 1.69 | 4.78 | 5.13 | 5.29 | 5.41 | 6.00 | 6.52 | 6.85 | 7.25 |
| Protestants, m | 0.00 | 0.00 | 0.00 | 0.00 | 0.00 | 0.00 | 0.00 | 0.00 | 0.00 | 0.00 | 0.00 | 0.00 | 0.34 | 1.55 | 4.27 | 6.32 | 6.84 | 7.39 | 10.02 | 11.88 | 12.99 | 14.23 |
| Independents, m | 0.00 | 0.00 | 0.00 | 0.00 | 0.00 | 0.00 | 0.00 | 0.00 | 0.00 | 0.00 | 0.00 | 0.00 | 0.01 | 0.02 | 0.62 | 1.21 | 1.38 | 1.50 | 2.52 | 3.35 | 3.88 | 4.48 |
| Marginal Christians, m | 0.00 | 0.00 | 0.00 | 0.00 | 0.00 | 0.00 | 0.00 | 0.00 | 0.00 | 0.00 | 0.00 | 0.00 | 0.00 | 0.00 | 0.21 | 0.37 | 0.42 | 0.46 | 0.83 | 1.10 | 1.27 | 1.46 |
| **Christians %** | **0.00** | **0.00** | **0.00** | **0.00** | **0.00** | **0.00** | **0.00** | **0.00** | **0.00** | **0.00** | **0.00** | **4.00** | **41.78** | **77.45** | **92.42** | **83.33** | **82.99** | **82.62** | **80.74** | **77.50** | **76.38** | **73.23** |
| Christian growth rate, % p.a. | 0.00 | 0.00 | 0.00 | 0.00 | 0.00 | 0.00 | 0.00 | 0.00 | 0.00 | 0.00 | 0.00 | 4.71 | 4.58 | 3.33 | 1.88 | 1.05 | 1.44 | 1.21 | 0.98 | 0.45 | 0.22 | 0.00 |
| Christian nett increase p.a., m | 0.00 | 0.00 | 0.00 | 0.00 | 0.00 | 0.00 | 0.00 | 0.00 | 0.00 | 0.00 | 0.00 | 0.00 | 0.04 | 0.17 | 0.36 | 0.24 | 0.34 | 0.31 | 0.33 | 0.17 | 0.09 | 0.00 |
| Gains: births+converts,m | 0.00 | 0.00 | 0.00 | 0.00 | 0.00 | 0.00 | 0.00 | 0.00 | 0.00 | 0.00 | 0.00 | 0.01 | 0.05 | 0.23 | 0.62 | 0.52 | 0.64 | 0.62 | 0.75 | 0.69 | 0.75 | 0.74 |
| Losses: deaths+defectors,m | 0.00 | 0.00 | 0.00 | 0.00 | 0.00 | 0.00 | 0.00 | 0.00 | 0.00 | 0.00 | 0.00 | 0.00 | 0.02 | 0.06 | 0.26 | 0.27 | 0.30 | 0.32 | 0.42 | 0.52 | 0.66 | 0.74 |
| World B, m | 0.00 | 0.00 | 0.00 | 0.00 | 0.00 | 0.00 | 0.00 | 0.00 | 0.00 | 0.00 | 0.00 | 0.23 | 0.18 | 0.29 | 1.13 | 3.92 | 4.30 | 4.72 | 6.76 | 9.22 | 10.82 | 12.76 |
| World B % | 0.00 | 0.00 | 0.00 | 0.00 | 0.00 | 0.00 | 0.00 | 0.00 | 0.00 | 0.00 | 0.00 | 9.00 | 8.00 | 4.68 | 5.85 | 14.83 | 15.10 | 15.53 | 17.04 | 19.97 | 20.66 | 23.34 |
| World B growth rate, % p.a. | 0.00 | 0.00 | 0.00 | 0.00 | 0.00 | 0.00 | 0.00 | 0.00 | 0.00 | 0.00 | 0.00 | 4.96 | -0.45 | 0.98 | 1.95 | 6.41 | 1.89 | 1.87 | 1.44 | 1.25 | 0.32 | 0.16 |
| World B increase p.a., m | 0.00 | 0.00 | 0.00 | 0.00 | 0.00 | 0.00 | 0.00 | 0.00 | 0.00 | 0.00 | 0.00 | 0.45 | -0.04 | 0.05 | 0.11 | 0.95 | 0.29 | 0.29 | 0.25 | 0.25 | 0.07 | 0.04 |
| World A, m | 1.00 | 1.10 | 1.10 | 1.20 | 1.40 | 1.50 | 1.70 | 1.85 | 2.00 | 2.20 | 2.30 | 2.18 | 1.13 | 1.12 | 0.33 | 0.48 | 0.54 | 0.56 | 0.88 | 1.17 | 1.55 | 1.87 |
| World A % | 100.00 | 100.00 | 100.00 | 100.00 | 100.00 | 100.00 | 100.00 | 100.00 | 100.00 | 100.00 | 100.00 | 87.00 | 50.22 | 17.87 | 1.73 | 1.83 | 1.91 | 1.85 | 2.22 | 2.53 | 2.96 | 3.43 |
| World A growth rate, % p.a. | 0.14 | 0.14 | 0.00 | 0.04 | 0.05 | 0.03 | 0.06 | 0.06 | 0.05 | 0.06 | 0.04 | -0.11 | -1.30 | -0.02 | -1.71 | 1.86 | 2.37 | 0.70 | 1.80 | 1.14 | 0.57 | 0.19 |
| World A increase p.a., m | 0.00 | 0.00 | 0.00 | 0.00 | 0.00 | 0.00 | 0.00 | 0.00 | 0.00 | 0.00 | 0.00 | 0.00 | -0.01 | 0.00 | -0.01 | 0.01 | 0.01 | 0.00 | 0.02 | 0.01 | 0.01 | 0.00 |

The **2 axes** below are: horizontally, years AD by 20-year gaps; vertically, persons (logarithmic scale).
The **3 lines** on each graph are, from top to bottom: live **population**, live **evangelized persons**, live **Christians**.
**Statistics** and trends for 22 years are given, for each geopolitical area, in its facing table opposite.

## Australia/New Zealand

**A** = 1600  Aboriginals uncontacted by Christians
**B** = 1788  British Anglican convicts land at Botany Bay
**C** = 1850  European immigrants rapidly outnumber aborigi-
nals
**D** = 1950  Secularization and non-Christian immigrants erode
Christian majority
**E** = 2000  Region is 80% Christian; 98% evangelized

## Melanesia

**A** = 1600  Islanders uncontacted by Christians
**B** = 1835  Methodist missionaries arrive in Fiji
**C** = 1850  European disease and conquest kills many is-
landers
**D** = 1920  Massive church growth begins in Papua New
Guinea
**E** = 2000  Region is 90% Christian; 97% evangelized

## Micronesia

**A** = 1600  Islanders uncontacted by Christians
**B** = 1668  Roman Catholic missionaries arrive in Guam
**C** = 1700  Islanders begin to succomb to European diseases
**D** = 1852  American Board missionaries land in Micronesia
**E** = 1880  Mass movements into the churches begin in Mi-
cronesia and Northern Mariana Islands
**F** = 2000  Region is 93% Christian; 99% evangelized

## Polynesia

**A** = 1600  Islanders uncontacted by Christians
**B** = 1659  Roman Catholic missionaries arrive in French Poly-
nesia
**C** = 1700  Islanders succumb to European diseases
**D** = 1830  Massive church growth in American Samoa, French
Polynesia, and Tonga
**E** = 2000  Region is 93% Christian; 99.5% evangelized

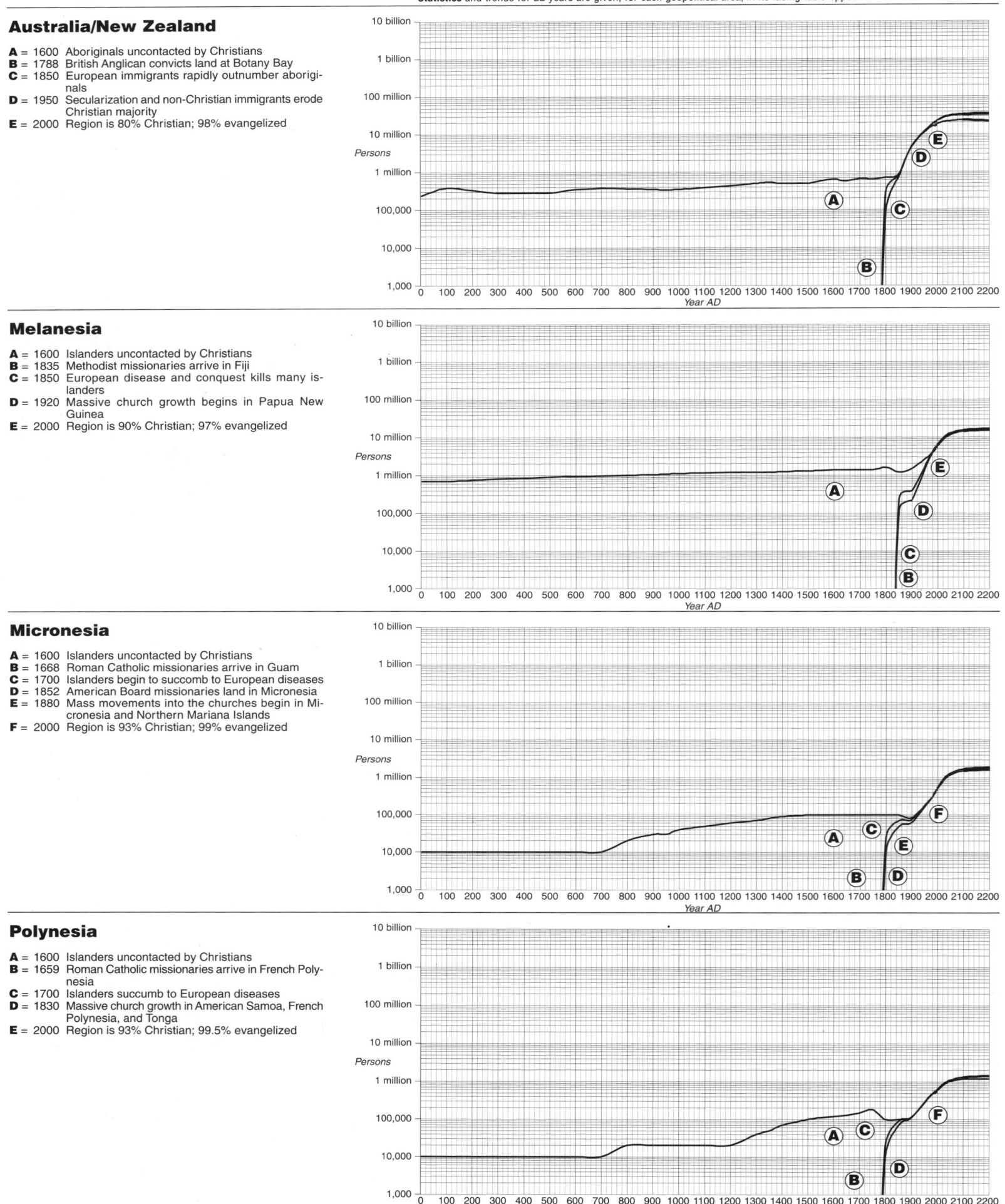

| *Area* *Year, AD* | 33 | 100 | 300 | 500 | 800 | 1000 | 1200 | 1350 | 1500 | 1650 | 1750 | 1800 | 1850 | 1900 | 1970 | 1990 | 1995 | 2000 | 2025 | 2050 | 2100 | 2200 |
|---|---|---|---|---|---|---|---|---|---|---|---|---|---|---|---|---|---|---|---|---|---|---|
| *1* | *2* | *3* | *4* | *5* | *6* | *7* | *8* | *9* | *10* | *11* | *12* | *13* | *14* | *15* | *16* | *17* | *18* | *19* | *20* | *21* | *22* | *23* |
| **Australia/New Zealand** (5 countries in 2000) | | | | | | | | | | | | | | | | | | | | | | |
| Population, m(=millions) | 0.28 | 0.38 | 0.28 | 0.28 | 0.36 | 0.34 | 0.42 | 0.52 | 0.50 | 0.57 | 0.62 | 0.70 | 0.85 | 4.59 | 15.35 | 20.25 | 21.62 | 22.75 | 27.79 | 31.01 | 33.89 | 34.90 |
| Growth rate, % p.a. | 0.46 | 0.46 | -0.15 | 0.00 | 0.08 | -0.03 | 0.11 | 0.14 | -0.03 | 0.09 | 0.08 | 0.24 | 0.39 | 3.43 | 1.74 | 1.39 | 1.32 | 1.02 | 0.80 | 0.44 | 0.18 | 0.03 |
| Increase p.a., m | 0.00 | 0.00 | 0.00 | 0.00 | 0.00 | 0.00 | 0.00 | 0.00 | 0.00 | 0.00 | 0.00 | 0.00 | 0.00 | 0.16 | 0.27 | 0.28 | 0.28 | 0.23 | 0.22 | 0.14 | 0.06 | 0.01 |
| Evangelized persons, m | 0.00 | 0.00 | 0.00 | 0.00 | 0.00 | 0.00 | 0.00 | 0.00 | 0.00 | 0.00 | 0.00 | 0.28 | 0.72 | 4.56 | 15.28 | 19.98 | 21.30 | 22.40 | 27.18 | 30.15 | 32.69 | 33.40 |
| Evangelized persons % | 0.00 | 0.00 | 0.00 | 0.00 | 0.00 | 0.00 | 0.00 | 0.00 | 0.00 | 0.00 | 0.00 | 40.00 | 84.71 | 99.29 | 99.49 | 98.68 | 98.51 | 98.48 | 97.79 | 97.24 | 96.46 | 95.70 |
| Outreach per Christian | — | — | — | — | — | — | — | — | — | — | — | 2.50 | 0.03 | 0.03 | 0.07 | 0.21 | 0.22 | 0.23 | 0.28 | 0.38 | 0.42 | 0.52 |
| **Christians, m** | **0.00** | **0.00** | **0.00** | **0.00** | **0.00** | **0.00** | **0.00** | **0.00** | **0.00** | **0.00** | **0.00** | **0.08** | **0.70** | **4.44** | **14.33** | **16.46** | **17.45** | **18.20** | **21.17** | **21.85** | **23.00** | **22.00** |
| Orthodox, m | 0.00 | 0.00 | 0.00 | 0.00 | 0.00 | 0.00 | 0.00 | 0.00 | 0.00 | 0.00 | 0.00 | 0.00 | 0.00 | 0.00 | 0.27 | 0.59 | 0.63 | 0.71 | 1.06 | 1.16 | 1.22 | 1.27 |
| Roman Catholics, m | 0.00 | 0.00 | 0.00 | 0.00 | 0.00 | 0.00 | 0.00 | 0.00 | 0.00 | 0.00 | 0.00 | 0.00 | 0.10 | 0.95 | 3.46 | 5.16 | 5.52 | 5.90 | 7.35 | 8.40 | 8.98 | 9.60 |
| Anglicans, m | 0.00 | 0.00 | 0.00 | 0.00 | 0.00 | 0.00 | 0.00 | 0.00 | 0.00 | 0.00 | 0.00 | 0.08 | 0.40 | 1.68 | 4.65 | 4.75 | 4.84 | 4.89 | 5.05 | 5.15 | 5.20 | 5.25 |
| Protestants, m | 0.00 | 0.00 | 0.00 | 0.00 | 0.00 | 0.00 | 0.00 | 0.00 | 0.00 | 0.00 | 0.00 | 0.00 | 0.20 | 1.33 | 2.76 | 3.32 | 3.46 | 3.56 | 4.05 | 4.25 | 4.35 | 4.46 |
| Independents, m | 0.00 | 0.00 | 0.00 | 0.00 | 0.00 | 0.00 | 0.00 | 0.00 | 0.00 | 0.00 | 0.00 | 0.00 | 0.00 | 0.00 | 0.54 | 0.85 | 0.97 | 1.03 | 1.66 | 2.15 | 2.45 | 2.79 |
| Marginal Christians, m | 0.00 | 0.00 | 0.00 | 0.00 | 0.00 | 0.00 | 0.00 | 0.00 | 0.00 | 0.00 | 0.00 | 0.00 | 0.00 | 0.00 | 0.15 | 0.27 | 0.31 | 0.34 | 0.62 | 0.80 | 0.91 | 1.03 |
| **Christians %** | **0.00** | **0.00** | **0.00** | **0.00** | **0.00** | **0.00** | **0.00** | **0.00** | **0.00** | **0.00** | **0.00** | **11.43** | **82.35** | **96.84** | **93.33** | **81.31** | **80.70** | **80.01** | **76.16** | **70.45** | **67.88** | **63.03** |
| Christian growth rate, % p.a. | 0.00 | 0.00 | 0.00 | 0.00 | 0.00 | 0.00 | 0.00 | 0.00 | 0.00 | 0.00 | 0.00 | 4.25 | 4.43 | 3.77 | 1.69 | 0.70 | 1.16 | 0.85 | 0.61 | 0.13 | 0.10 | -0.04 |
| Christian nett increase p.a., m | 0.00 | 0.00 | 0.00 | 0.00 | 0.00 | 0.00 | 0.00 | 0.00 | 0.00 | 0.00 | 0.00 | 0.00 | 0.03 | 0.17 | 0.24 | 0.11 | 0.20 | 0.15 | 0.13 | 0.03 | 0.02 | -0.01 |
| Gains: births+converts,m | 0.00 | 0.00 | 0.00 | 0.00 | 0.00 | 0.00 | 0.00 | 0.00 | 0.00 | 0.00 | 0.00 | 0.00 | 0.04 | 0.22 | 0.44 | 0.31 | 0.42 | 0.39 | 0.43 | 0.38 | 0.44 | 0.45 |
| Losses: deaths+defectors,m | 0.00 | 0.00 | 0.00 | 0.00 | 0.00 | 0.00 | 0.00 | 0.00 | 0.00 | 0.00 | 0.00 | 0.00 | 0.01 | 0.05 | 0.19 | 0.20 | 0.22 | 0.23 | 0.30 | 0.35 | 0.42 | 0.46 |
| World B, m | 0.00 | 0.00 | 0.00 | 0.00 | 0.00 | 0.00 | 0.00 | 0.00 | 0.00 | 0.00 | 0.00 | 0.20 | 0.02 | 0.11 | 0.95 | 3.52 | 3.85 | 4.20 | 6.01 | 8.31 | 9.69 | 11.40 |
| World B % | 0.00 | 0.00 | 0.00 | 0.00 | 0.00 | 0.00 | 0.00 | 0.00 | 0.00 | 0.00 | 0.00 | 28.57 | 2.35 | 2.45 | 6.16 | 17.37 | 17.81 | 18.48 | 21.63 | 26.79 | 28.58 | 32.67 |
| World B growth rate, % p.a. | 0.00 | 0.00 | 0.00 | 0.00 | 0.00 | 0.00 | 0.00 | 0.00 | 0.00 | 0.00 | 0.00 | 4.71 | -4.50 | 3.51 | 3.09 | 6.79 | 1.83 | 1.77 | 1.44 | 1.30 | 0.31 | 0.16 |
| World B increase p.a., m | 0.00 | 0.00 | 0.00 | 0.00 | 0.00 | 0.00 | 0.00 | 0.00 | 0.00 | 0.00 | 0.00 | 1.35 | -0.11 | 0.09 | 0.19 | 1.18 | 0.33 | 0.33 | 0.31 | 0.35 | 0.09 | 0.05 |
| World A, m | 0.28 | 0.38 | 0.28 | 0.28 | 0.36 | 0.34 | 0.42 | 0.52 | 0.50 | 0.57 | 0.62 | 0.42 | 0.13 | 0.03 | 0.08 | 0.27 | 0.32 | 0.35 | 0.61 | 0.86 | 1.20 | 1.50 |
| World A % | 100.00 | 100.00 | 100.00 | 100.00 | 100.00 | 100.00 | 100.00 | 100.00 | 100.00 | 100.00 | 100.00 | 60.00 | 15.29 | 0.71 | 0.51 | 1.32 | 1.49 | 1.52 | 2.21 | 2.76 | 3.54 | 4.30 |
| World A growth rate, % p.a. | 0.46 | 0.46 | -0.15 | 0.00 | 0.08 | -0.03 | 0.11 | 0.14 | -0.03 | 0.09 | 0.08 | -0.78 | -2.32 | -2.72 | 1.24 | 6.36 | 3.83 | 1.44 | 2.33 | 1.34 | 0.68 | 0.22 |
| World A increase p.a., m | 0.00 | 0.00 | 0.00 | 0.00 | 0.00 | 0.00 | 0.00 | 0.00 | 0.00 | 0.00 | 0.00 | 0.00 | 0.00 | 0.00 | 0.00 | 0.02 | 0.01 | 0.00 | 0.01 | 0.01 | 0.01 | 0.00 |
| **Melanesia** (6 countries in 2000) | | | | | | | | | | | | | | | | | | | | | | |
| Population, m(=millions) | 0.70 | 0.70 | 0.80 | 0.90 | 1.00 | 1.10 | 1.20 | 1.20 | 1.30 | 1.40 | 1.40 | 1.60 | 1.20 | 1.46 | 3.30 | 5.20 | 5.81 | 6.47 | 9.99 | 12.71 | 15.43 | 16.47 |
| Growth rate, % p.a. | 0.00 | 0.00 | 0.07 | 0.06 | 0.04 | 0.05 | 0.04 | 0.00 | 0.05 | 0.05 | 0.00 | 0.27 | -0.57 | 0.40 | 1.17 | 2.31 | 2.23 | 2.18 | 1.75 | 0.97 | 0.39 | 0.06 |
| Increase p.a., m | 0.00 | 0.00 | 0.00 | 0.00 | 0.00 | 0.00 | 0.00 | 0.00 | 0.00 | 0.00 | 0.00 | 0.00 | -0.01 | 0.01 | 0.04 | 0.12 | 0.13 | 0.14 | 0.17 | 0.12 | 0.06 | 0.01 |
| Evangelized persons, m | 0.00 | 0.00 | 0.00 | 0.00 | 0.00 | 0.00 | 0.00 | 0.00 | 0.00 | 0.00 | 0.00 | 0.00 | 0.24 | 0.39 | 3.05 | 4.99 | 5.59 | 6.26 | 9.73 | 12.42 | 15.10 | 16.12 |
| Evangelized persons % | 0.00 | 0.00 | 0.00 | 0.00 | 0.00 | 0.00 | 0.00 | 0.00 | 0.00 | 0.00 | 0.00 | 0.00 | 20.00 | 26.41 | 92.34 | 95.94 | 96.29 | 96.75 | 97.46 | 97.68 | 97.86 | 97.87 |
| Outreach per Christian | — | — | — | — | — | — | — | — | — | — | — | — | 1.00 | 0.76 | 0.06 | 0.07 | 0.07 | 0.08 | 0.07 | 0.06 | 0.06 | 0.06 |
| **Christians, m** | **0.00** | **0.00** | **0.00** | **0.00** | **0.00** | **0.00** | **0.00** | **0.00** | **0.00** | **0.00** | **0.00** | **0.00** | **0.12** | **0.22** | **2.88** | **4.65** | **5.21** | **5.82** | **9.13** | **11.72** | **14.30** | **15.20** |
| Orthodox, m | 0.00 | 0.00 | 0.00 | 0.00 | 0.00 | 0.00 | 0.00 | 0.00 | 0.00 | 0.00 | 0.00 | 0.00 | 0.00 | 0.00 | 0.00 | 0.00 | 0.00 | 0.00 | 0.00 | 0.00 | 0.00 | 0.00 |
| Roman Catholics, m | 0.00 | 0.00 | 0.00 | 0.00 | 0.00 | 0.00 | 0.00 | 0.00 | 0.00 | 0.00 | 0.00 | 0.00 | 0.03 | 0.06 | 0.86 | 1.43 | 1.61 | 1.81 | 3.02 | 4.02 | 4.63 | 5.34 |
| Anglicans, m | 0.00 | 0.00 | 0.00 | 0.00 | 0.00 | 0.00 | 0.00 | 0.00 | 0.00 | 0.00 | 0.00 | 0.00 | 0.00 | 0.01 | 0.13 | 0.38 | 0.45 | 0.52 | 0.94 | 1.37 | 1.65 | 1.99 |
| Protestants, m | 0.00 | 0.00 | 0.00 | 0.00 | 0.00 | 0.00 | 0.00 | 0.00 | 0.00 | 0.00 | 0.00 | 0.00 | 0.09 | 0.11 | 1.21 | 2.56 | 2.90 | 3.30 | 5.16 | 6.61 | 7.49 | 8.48 |
| Independents, m | 0.00 | 0.00 | 0.00 | 0.00 | 0.00 | 0.00 | 0.00 | 0.00 | 0.00 | 0.00 | 0.00 | 0.00 | 0.00 | 0.00 | 0.06 | 0.32 | 0.37 | 0.42 | 0.75 | 1.06 | 1.25 | 1.48 |
| Marginal Christians, m | 0.00 | 0.00 | 0.00 | 0.00 | 0.00 | 0.00 | 0.00 | 0.00 | 0.00 | 0.00 | 0.00 | 0.00 | 0.00 | 0.00 | 0.01 | 0.03 | 0.04 | 0.04 | 0.08 | 0.13 | 0.16 | 0.20 |
| **Christians %** | **0.00** | **0.00** | **0.00** | **0.00** | **0.00** | **0.00** | **0.00** | **0.00** | **0.00** | **0.00** | **0.00** | **0.00** | **10.00** | **15.01** | **87.23** | **89.28** | **89.63** | **89.93** | **91.47** | **92.20** | **92.65** | **92.32** |
| Christian growth rate, % p.a. | 0.00 | 0.00 | 0.00 | 0.00 | 0.00 | 0.00 | 0.00 | 0.00 | 0.00 | 0.00 | 0.00 | 0.00 | 2.52 | 1.22 | 3.74 | 2.42 | 2.31 | 2.25 | 1.82 | 1.00 | 0.40 | 0.06 |
| Christian nett increase p.a., m | 0.00 | 0.00 | 0.00 | 0.00 | 0.00 | 0.00 | 0.00 | 0.00 | 0.00 | 0.00 | 0.00 | 0.00 | 0.00 | 0.00 | 0.11 | 0.11 | 0.12 | 0.13 | 0.17 | 0.12 | 0.06 | 0.01 |
| Gains: births+converts,m | 0.00 | 0.00 | 0.00 | 0.00 | 0.00 | 0.00 | 0.00 | 0.00 | 0.00 | 0.00 | 0.00 | 0.00 | 0.01 | 0.01 | 0.16 | 0.18 | 0.19 | 0.21 | 0.27 | 0.26 | 0.25 | 0.24 |
| Losses: deaths+defectors,m | 0.00 | 0.00 | 0.00 | 0.00 | 0.00 | 0.00 | 0.00 | 0.00 | 0.00 | 0.00 | 0.00 | 0.00 | 0.00 | 0.01 | 0.06 | 0.07 | 0.07 | 0.07 | 0.10 | 0.15 | 0.20 | 0.23 |
| World B, m | 0.00 | 0.00 | 0.00 | 0.00 | 0.00 | 0.00 | 0.00 | 0.00 | 0.00 | 0.00 | 0.00 | 0.00 | 0.12 | 0.17 | 0.17 | 0.35 | 0.39 | 0.44 | 0.60 | 0.70 | 0.80 | 0.92 |
| World B % | 0.00 | 0.00 | 0.00 | 0.00 | 0.00 | 0.00 | 0.00 | 0.00 | 0.00 | 0.00 | 0.00 | 0.00 | 10.00 | 11.39 | 5.11 | 6.66 | 6.66 | 6.82 | 5.99 | 5.48 | 5.21 | 5.56 |
| World B growth rate, % p.a. | 0.00 | 0.00 | 0.00 | 0.00 | 0.00 | 0.00 | 0.00 | 0.00 | 0.00 | 0.00 | 0.00 | 0.00 | 1.81 | 0.66 | 0.02 | 3.67 | 2.22 | 2.67 | 1.23 | 0.61 | 0.29 | 0.13 |
| World B increase p.a., m | 0.00 | 0.00 | 0.00 | 0.00 | 0.00 | 0.00 | 0.00 | 0.00 | 0.00 | 0.00 | 0.00 | 0.00 | 0.18 | 0.07 | 0.00 | 0.24 | 0.15 | 0.18 | 0.07 | 0.03 | 0.01 | 0.01 |
| World A, m | 0.70 | 0.70 | 0.80 | 0.90 | 1.00 | 1.10 | 1.20 | 1.20 | 1.30 | 1.40 | 1.40 | 1.60 | 0.96 | 1.08 | 0.25 | 0.21 | 0.22 | 0.21 | 0.25 | 0.30 | 0.33 | 0.35 |
| World A % | 100.00 | 100.00 | 100.00 | 100.00 | 100.00 | 100.00 | 100.00 | 100.00 | 100.00 | 100.00 | 100.00 | 100.00 | 80.00 | 73.59 | 7.66 | 4.06 | 3.71 | 3.25 | 2.54 | 2.32 | 2.14 | 2.13 |
| World A growth rate, % p.a. | 0.00 | 0.00 | 0.07 | 0.06 | 0.04 | 0.05 | 0.04 | 0.00 | 0.05 | 0.05 | 0.00 | 0.27 | -1.02 | 0.23 | -2.05 | -0.89 | 0.41 | -0.46 | 0.74 | 0.61 | 0.22 | 0.06 |
| World A increase p.a., m | 0.00 | 0.00 | 0.00 | 0.00 | 0.00 | 0.00 | 0.00 | 0.00 | 0.00 | 0.00 | 0.00 | 0.00 | -0.01 | 0.00 | -0.01 | 0.00 | 0.00 | 0.00 | 0.00 | 0.00 | 0.00 | 0.00 |
| **Micronesia** (7 countries in 2000) | | | | | | | | | | | | | | | | | | | | | | |
| Population, m(=millions) | 0.01 | 0.01 | 0.01 | 0.01 | 0.02 | 0.04 | 0.06 | 0.08 | 0.10 | 0.10 | 0.10 | 0.10 | 0.10 | 0.08 | 0.25 | 0.42 | 0.48 | 0.54 | 0.96 | 1.33 | 1.72 | 1.87 |
| Growth rate, % p.a. | 0.00 | 0.00 | 0.00 | 0.00 | 0.23 | 0.35 | 0.20 | 0.19 | 0.15 | 0.00 | 0.00 | 0.00 | 0.00 | -0.38 | 1.59 | 2.60 | 2.73 | 2.62 | 2.30 | 1.31 | 0.52 | 0.09 |
| Increase p.a., m | 0.00 | 0.00 | 0.00 | 0.00 | 0.00 | 0.00 | 0.00 | 0.00 | 0.00 | 0.00 | 0.00 | 0.00 | 0.00 | 0.00 | 0.00 | 0.01 | 0.01 | 0.01 | 0.02 | 0.02 | 0.01 | 0.00 |
| Evangelized persons, m | 0.00 | 0.00 | 0.00 | 0.00 | 0.00 | 0.00 | 0.00 | 0.00 | 0.00 | 0.00 | 0.00 | 0.03 | 0.07 | 0.08 | 0.25 | 0.41 | 0.47 | 0.54 | 0.95 | 1.32 | 1.70 | 1.86 |
| Evangelized persons % | 0.00 | 0.00 | 0.00 | 0.00 | 0.00 | 0.00 | 0.00 | 0.00 | 0.00 | 0.00 | 0.00 | 25.00 | 70.00 | 91.05 | 99.35 | 99.32 | 99.31 | 99.35 | 99.25 | 99.24 | 99.18 | 99.15 |
| Outreach per Christian | — | — | — | — | — | — | — | — | — | — | — | 1.50 | 0.40 | 0.21 | 0.04 | 0.06 | 0.06 | 0.07 | 0.08 | 0.10 | 0.12 | 0.15 |
| **Christians, m** | **0.00** | **0.00** | **0.00** | **0.00** | **0.00** | **0.00** | **0.00** | **0.00** | **0.00** | **0.00** | **0.00** | **0.01** | **0.05** | **0.06** | **0.24** | **0.39** | **0.45** | **0.51** | **0.88** | **1.20** | **1.52** | **1.62** |
| Orthodox, m | 0.00 | 0.00 | 0.00 | 0.00 | 0.00 | 0.00 | 0.00 | 0.00 | 0.00 | 0.00 | 0.00 | 0.00 | 0.00 | 0.00 | 0.00 | 0.00 | 0.00 | 0.00 | 0.00 | 0.00 | 0.00 | 0.00 |
| Roman Catholics, m | 0.00 | 0.00 | 0.00 | 0.00 | 0.00 | 0.00 | 0.00 | 0.00 | 0.00 | 0.00 | 0.00 | 0.01 | 0.05 | 0.03 | 0.13 | 0.26 | 0.30 | 0.34 | 0.61 | 0.85 | 0.99 | 1.16 |
| Anglicans, m | 0.00 | 0.00 | 0.00 | 0.00 | 0.00 | 0.00 | 0.00 | 0.00 | 0.00 | 0.00 | 0.00 | 0.00 | 0.00 | 0.00 | 0.00 | 0.00 | 0.00 | 0.00 | 0.00 | 0.00 | 0.00 | 0.00 |
| Protestants, m | 0.00 | 0.00 | 0.00 | 0.00 | 0.00 | 0.00 | 0.00 | 0.00 | 0.00 | 0.00 | 0.00 | 0.00 | 0.00 | 0.04 | 0.08 | 0.15 | 0.17 | 0.19 | 0.31 | 0.41 | 0.47 | 0.55 |
| Independents, m | 0.00 | 0.00 | 0.00 | 0.00 | 0.00 | 0.00 | 0.00 | 0.00 | 0.00 | 0.00 | 0.00 | 0.00 | 0.00 | 0.00 | 0.01 | 0.02 | 0.02 | 0.03 | 0.06 | 0.09 | 0.12 | 0.15 |
| Marginal Christians, m | 0.00 | 0.00 | 0.00 | 0.00 | 0.00 | 0.00 | 0.00 | 0.00 | 0.00 | 0.00 | 0.00 | 0.00 | 0.00 | 0.00 | 0.00 | 0.01 | 0.01 | 0.01 | 0.04 | 0.06 | 0.07 | 0.09 |
| **Christians %** | **0.00** | **0.00** | **0.00** | **0.00** | **0.00** | **0.00** | **0.00** | **0.00** | **0.00** | **0.00** | **0.00** | **10.00** | **50.00** | **75.53** | **95.63** | **93.73** | **93.35** | **93.13** | **91.60** | **90.23** | **88.50** | **86.57** |
| Christian growth rate, % p.a. | 0.00 | 0.00 | 0.00 | 0.00 | 0.00 | 0.00 | 0.00 | 0.00 | 0.00 | 0.00 | 0.00 | 4.71 | 3.27 | 0.45 | 1.93 | 2.50 | 2.64 | 2.57 | 2.24 | 1.25 | 0.48 | 0.06 |
| Christian nett increase p.a., m | 0.00 | 0.00 | 0.00 | 0.00 | 0.00 | 0.00 | 0.00 | 0.00 | 0.00 | 0.00 | 0.00 | 0.00 | 0.00 | 0.00 | 0.00 | 0.01 | 0.01 | 0.01 | 0.02 | 0.01 | 0.01 | 0.00 |
| Gains: births+converts,m | 0.00 | 0.00 | 0.00 | 0.00 | 0.00 | 0.00 | 0.00 | 0.00 | 0.00 | 0.00 | 0.00 | 0.00 | 0.00 | 0.00 | 0.01 | 0.01 | 0.02 | 0.02 | 0.03 | 0.03 | 0.03 | 0.03 |
| Losses: deaths+defectors,m | 0.00 | 0.00 | 0.00 | 0.00 | 0.00 | 0.00 | 0.00 | 0.00 | 0.00 | 0.00 | 0.00 | 0.00 | 0.00 | 0.00 | 0.00 | 0.00 | 0.00 | 0.01 | 0.01 | 0.01 | 0.02 | 0.03 |
| World B, m | 0.00 | 0.00 | 0.00 | 0.00 | 0.00 | 0.00 | 0.00 | 0.00 | 0.00 | 0.00 | 0.00 | 0.02 | 0.02 | 0.01 | 0.01 | 0.02 | 0.03 | 0.03 | 0.07 | 0.12 | 0.18 | 0.24 |
| World B % | 0.00 | 0.00 | 0.00 | 0.00 | 0.00 | 0.00 | 0.00 | 0.00 | 0.00 | 0.00 | 0.00 | 15.00 | 20.00 | 15.52 | 3.72 | 5.59 | 5.96 | 6.22 | 7.65 | 9.01 | 10.68 | 12.58 |
| World B growth rate, % p.a. | 0.00 | 0.00 | 0.00 | 0.00 | 0.00 | 0.00 | 0.00 | 0.00 | 0.00 | 0.00 | 0.00 | 4.11 | 0.58 | -0.88 | -0.46 | 4.72 | 4.05 | 3.51 | 3.15 | 1.97 | 0.86 | 0.25 |
| World B increase p.a., m | 0.00 | 0.00 | 0.00 | 0.00 | 0.00 | 0.00 | 0.00 | 0.00 | 0.00 | 0.00 | 0.00 | 0.62 | 0.12 | -0.14 | -0.02 | 0.26 | 0.24 | 0.22 | 0.24 | 0.18 | 0.09 | 0.03 |
| World A, m | 0.01 | 0.01 | 0.01 | 0.01 | 0.02 | 0.04 | 0.06 | 0.08 | 0.10 | 0.10 | 0.10 | 0.08 | 0.03 | 0.01 | 0.00 | 0.00 | 0.00 | 0.00 | 0.01 | 0.01 | 0.01 | 0.02 |
| World A % | 100.00 | 100.00 | 100.00 | 100.00 | 100.00 | 100.00 | 100.00 | 100.00 | 100.00 | 100.00 | 100.00 | 75.00 | 30.00 | 8.95 | 0.65 | 0.68 | 0.69 | 0.65 | 0.75 | 0.76 | 0.82 | 0.85 |
| World A growth rate, % p.a. | 0.00 | 0.00 | 0.00 | 0.00 | 0.23 | 0.35 | 0.20 | 0.19 | 0.15 | 0.00 | 0.00 | -0.57 | -1.82 | -2.76 | -2.15 | 2.83 | 3.09 | 1.26 | 2.90 | 1.39 | 0.65 | 0.13 |
| World A increase p.a., m | 0.00 | 0.00 | 0.00 | 0.00 | 0.00 | 0.00 | 0.00 | 0.00 | 0.00 | 0.00 | 0.00 | 0.00 | 0.00 | 0.00 | 0.00 | 0.00 | 0.00 | 0.00 | 0.00 | 0.00 | 0.00 | 0.00 |
| **Polynesia** (10 countries in 2000) | | | | | | | | | | | | | | | | | | | | | | |
| Population, m(=millions) | 0.01 | 0.01 | 0.01 | 0.01 | 0.02 | 0.02 | 0.02 | 0.05 | 0.10 | 0.13 | 0.18 | 0.10 | 0.10 | 0.11 | 0.41 | 0.54 | 0.58 | 0.63 | 0.91 | 1.13 | 1.33 | 1.41 |
| Growth rate, % p.a. | 0.00 | 0.00 | 0.00 | 0.00 | 0.23 | 0.00 | 0.00 | 0.61 | 0.46 | 0.18 | 0.33 | -1.17 | 0.00 | 0.25 | 1.84 | 1.46 | 1.45 | 1.57 | 1.47 | 0.87 | 0.33 | 0.06 |
| Increase p.a., m | 0.00 | 0.00 | 0.00 | 0.00 | 0.00 | 0.00 | 0.00 | 0.00 | 0.00 | 0.00 | 0.00 | 0.00 | 0.00 | 0.00 | 0.01 | 0.01 | 0.01 | 0.01 | 0.01 | 0.01 | 0.00 | 0.00 |
| Evangelized persons, m | 0.00 | 0.00 | 0.00 | 0.00 | 0.00 | 0.00 | 0.00 | 0.00 | 0.00 | 0.00 | 0.00 | 0.02 | 0.09 | 0.11 | 0.40 | 0.54 | 0.58 | 0.63 | 0.90 | 1.12 | 1.33 | 1.40 |
| Evangelized persons % | 0.00 | 0.00 | 0.00 | 0.00 | 0.00 | 0.00 | 0.00 | 0.00 | 0.00 | 0.00 | 0.00 | 20.00 | 90.00 | 99.93 | 99.41 | 99.40 | 99.41 | 99.42 | 99.43 | 99.46 | 99.48 | 99.50 |
| Outreach per Christian | — | — | — | — | — | — | — | — | — | — | — | 1.00 | 0.29 | 0.01 | 0.02 | 0.06 | 0.07 | 0.07 | 0.09 | 0.10 | 0.12 | 0.17 |
| **Christians, m** | **0.00** | **0.00** | **0.00** | **0.00** | **0.00** | **0.00** | **0.00** | **0.00** | **0.00** | **0.00** | **0.00** | **0.01** | **0.07** | **0.11** | **0.40** | **0.51** | **0.54** | **0.58** | **0.83** | **1.02** | **1.18** | **1.20** |
| Orthodox, m | 0.00 | 0.00 | 0.00 | 0.00 | 0.00 | 0.00 | 0.00 | 0.00 | 0.00 | 0.00 | 0.00 | 0.00 | 0.00 | 0.00 | 0.00 | 0.00 | 0.00 | 0.00 | 0.00 | 0.00 | 0.00 | 0.00 |
| Roman Catholics, m | 0.00 | 0.00 | 0.00 | 0.00 | 0.00 | 0.00 | 0.00 | 0.00 | 0.00 | 0.00 | 0.00 | 0.01 | 0.01 | 0.01 | 0.10 | 0.15 | 0.17 | 0.18 | 0.25 | 0.30 | 0.33 | 0.37 |
| Anglicans, m | 0.00 | 0.00 | 0.00 | 0.00 | 0.00 | 0.00 | 0.00 | 0.00 | 0.00 | 0.00 | 0.00 | 0.00 | 0.00 | 0.00 | 0.00 | 0.00 | 0.00 | 0.00 | 0.00 | 0.00 | 0.00 | 0.00 |
| Protestants, m | 0.00 | 0.00 | 0.00 | 0.00 | 0.00 | 0.00 | 0.00 | 0.00 | 0.00 | 0.00 | 0.00 | 0.00 | 0.05 | 0.08 | 0.21 | 0.30 | 0.32 | 0.34 | 0.50 | 0.61 | 0.67 | 0.74 |
| Independents, m | 0.00 | 0.00 | 0.00 | 0.00 | 0.00 | 0.00 | 0.00 | 0.00 | 0.00 | 0.00 | 0.00 | 0.00 | 0.01 | 0.02 | 0.02 | 0.03 | 0.03 | 0.03 | 0.04 | 0.06 | 0.06 | 0.07 |
| Marginal Christians, m | 0.00 | 0.00 | 0.00 | 0.00 | 0.00 | 0.00 | 0.00 | 0.00 | 0.00 | 0.00 | 0.00 | 0.00 | 0.00 | 0.00 | 0.05 | 0.06 | 0.06 | 0.07 | 0.09 | 0.11 | 0.13 | 0.14 |
| **Christians %** | **0.00** | **0.00** | **0.00** | **0.00** | **0.00** | **0.00** | **0.00** | **0.00** | **0.00** | **0.00** | **0.00** | **10.00** | **70.00** | **99.38** | **97.82** | **93.69** | **93.09** | **92.66** | **91.47** | **90.49** | **88.45** | **85.08** |
| Christian growth rate, % p.a. | 0.00 | 0.00 | 0.00 | 0.00 | 0.00 | 0.00 | 0.00 | 0.00 | 0.00 | 0.00 | 0.00 | 4.71 | 3.97 | 0.96 | 1.82 | 1.24 | 1.32 | 1.48 | 1.42 | 0.83 | 0.29 | 0.02 |
| Christian nett increase p.a., m | 0.00 | 0.00 | 0.00 | 0.00 | 0.00 | 0.00 | 0.00 | 0.00 | 0.00 | 0.00 | 0.00 | 0.00 | 0.00 | 0.00 | 0.01 | 0.01 | 0.01 | 0.01 | 0.01 | 0.01 | 0.00 | 0.00 |
| Gains: births+converts,m | 0.00 | 0.00 | 0.00 | 0.00 | 0.00 | 0.00 | 0.00 | 0.00 | 0.00 | 0.00 | 0.00 | 0.00 | 0.00 | 0.00 | 0.01 | 0.01 | 0.01 | 0.01 | 0.02 | 0.02 | 0.02 | 0.02 |
| Losses: deaths+defectors,m | 0.00 | 0.00 | 0.00 | 0.00 | 0.00 | 0.00 | 0.00 | 0.00 | 0.00 | 0.00 | 0.00 | 0.00 | 0.00 | 0.00 | 0.01 | 0.01 | 0.01 | 0.01 | 0.01 | 0.01 | 0.02 | 0.02 |
| World B, m | 0.00 | 0.00 | 0.00 | 0.00 | 0.00 | 0.00 | 0.00 | 0.00 | 0.00 | 0.00 | 0.00 | 0.01 | 0.02 | 0.00 | 0.01 | 0.03 | 0.04 | 0.04 | 0.07 | 0.10 | 0.15 | 0.20 |
| World B % | 0.00 | 0.00 | 0.00 | 0.00 | 0.00 | 0.00 | 0.00 | 0.00 | 0.00 | 0.00 | 0.00 | 10.00 | 20.00 | 0.55 | 1.60 | 5.71 | 6.32 | 6.76 | 7.95 | 8.97 | 11.03 | 14.43 |
| World B growth rate, % p.a. | 0.00 | 0.00 | 0.00 | 0.00 | 0.00 | 0.00 | 0.00 | 0.00 | 0.00 | 0.00 | 0.00 | 3.27 | 1.40 | -6.71 | 3.41 | 8.13 | 3.53 | 2.95 | 2.13 | 1.36 | 0.75 | 0.33 |
| World B increase p.a., m | 0.00 | 0.00 | 0.00 | 0.00 | 0.00 | 0.00 | 0.00 | 0.00 | 0.00 | 0.00 | 0.00 | 0.33 | 0.28 | -0.04 | 0.05 | 0.46 | 0.22 | 0.20 | 0.17 | 0.12 | 0.08 | 0.05 |
| World A, m | 0.01 | 0.01 | 0.01 | 0.01 | 0.02 | 0.02 | 0.02 | 0.05 | 0.10 | 0.13 | 0.18 | 0.08 | 0.01 | 0.00 | 0.00 | 0.00 | 0.00 | 0.00 | 0.01 | 0.01 | 0.01 | 0.01 |
| World A % | 100.00 | 100.00 | 100.00 | 100.00 | 100.00 | 100.00 | 100.00 | 100.00 | 100.00 | 100.00 | 100.00 | 80.00 | 10.00 | 0.07 | 0.59 | 0.60 | 0.59 | 0.58 | 0.57 | 0.54 | 0.52 | 0.50 |
| World A growth rate, % p.a. | 0.00 | 0.00 | 0.00 | 0.00 | 0.23 | 0.00 | 0.00 | 0.61 | 0.46 | 0.18 | 0.33 | -1.61 | -4.07 | -9.21 | 4.97 | 1.61 | 1.08 | 1.31 | 1.41 | 0.64 | 0.27 | 0.00 |
| World A increase p.a., m | 0.00 | 0.00 | 0.00 | 0.00 | 0.00 | 0.00 | 0.00 | 0.00 | 0.00 | 0.00 | 0.00 | 0.00 | 0.00 | 0.00 | 0.00 | 0.00 | 0.00 | 0.00 | 0.00 | 0.00 | 0.00 | 0.00 |

# BIBLIOGRAPHY

*A critical evaluation of the modernist trends in Hinduism.* Eno, Engla. 1925.

*A place for baptism: new trends in baptismal architecture since the Second Vatican Council.* van Parys, Johan M. J. 1998.

*An exploration of the contemporary trends in the psychology of religious experience.* Oates, Wayne Edward. 1973.

*Build my church: trends and possibilities for Australian churches.* Kaldor, Peter. Adelaide: Openbook/NCLS, 1999.

*Church-state separation: recent trends and developments.* Sinensky, Jeffrey P. New York, N.Y.: Anti-Defamation League of B'nai B'rith, 1984.

*Contemporary trends in Christology. 1. The Christ of our Christian faith.* Pittenger, W. Norman. 1958.

*Current conditions and trends in relations between religion and mental health.* Anderson, George Christian. New York: Academy of Religion and Mental Health, 1960.

*Current trends of religious liberty in Southeastern Africa.* Dos Santos, Joao E. B. 1976.

*Dangerous trends: an analysis of the social repercussions of the new religions and the anti-religious movement.* Verity, Leslie. Bondi: Better Family Relations Association, 1977.

*Decade of volatility: ten powerful trends facing the church.* Anderson, Leith. Eden Prairie, MN: Leith Anderson, 1991.

*Emerging trends in religion in America.* Gallup, George. Chautaqua, NY: Chautaqua Institute, 1990.

*Emerging trends Main Series: Current periodical series.* Princeton, N.J.: Princeton Religion Research Center, 1979-99.

*Future trends: religion, politics, psychology.* Gillett, Grover & Grace Gage. Dallas, TX: World View Publishers, 1983.

*Global outlook 2000: an economic, social, and environmental perspective.* United Nations. New York and Geneva: UN Publications, 1990. (Long-term trends).

*Global trends: the world almanac of development and peace.* I. Hauchler & P.M. Kennedy, eds. New York: Continuum, 1994.

*Hsien tai Chung kuo ti tsung chiao ch'ü shih.* Chan, Wing-tsit & Shih-te Liao. T'aipei: Wen shu ch'u pan she, 1987.

*Issues and trends in contemporary African American religion.* Rigmaiden, Paul Quinlan. 1996.

*Kung yüan 2000 tsung chiao ta ch'ü shih.* Yang, Mu-ku.T'aipei: Hsiso yüan shu fang ch'u pan she, 1990.

*Major trends in Jewish mysticism [Based on the Hilda Stroo[c]k lectures delivered at the Jewish Institute of Religion, New York]* Scholem, Gershom Gerhard. London: Thames and Hudson 1953.

*Megatrends for women.* Aburdene, Patricia & John Naisbitt. New York: Fawcett Columbine, 1993.

*Modern Japan and Shinto nationalism: a study of present-day trends in Japanese religions.* Holtom, Daniel Clarence. Chicago: University of Chicago Press, 1943.

*Modern trends in Islam.* Gibb, Hamilton Alexander Rosskeen. Chicago: University of Chicago Press, 1947.

*Modern trends in Siamese culture: religion.* Landon, Kenneth Perry. 1942.

*Modern trends in the religion of the American Negro.* Eubanks, John Bunyan, University Microfilms, 1959.

*Modern trends in world religions.* Haydon, A. Eustace, ed. Chicago: University of Chicago Press, 1934.

*Modern trends in world religions: Paul Carus Memorial Symposium.* Kitagawa, Joseph Mitsuo. La Salle, IL: Open Court Pub. Co., 1959.

*Modernist versus post-modernist trends in ethnography: the case of the Yaqui.* Carsten, Cynthia G. 1993.

*Muslim religious trends in Kashmir in modern times.* Wani, Mushtaq Ahmad. Patna: Khuda Bakhsh Oriental Public Library, 1997.

*Muslim tradition in psychotherapy and modern trends.* Rizvi, Syed Azhar Ali. Lahore, Pakistan: Institute of Islamic Culture, 1989.

*New evangelism: a review of trends, developments, and events during 1990.*1991.

*New trends and developments in African religions.* Clarke, Peter B. Westport, CT.: Greenwood Press, 1998.

*New trends in black theology.* Jones, William Ronald. Creative Sights,1972.

*On the way to the future: a Christian view of eschatology in the light of current trends in religion, philosophy, and science.* Schwarz, Hans. Minneapolis: Augsburg Publishing House, 1979.

*Pastoral investigation of social trends: working paper. Major Religious Superiors of England and Wales by the Liverpool Institute of Socio-Religious Studies.* Liverpool. Published on behalf of the Conferences of 1976, 1978.

*Present trends among the Disciples.* West, George D. Nashville, 1930.

*Problems and trends in religion.* Hudson, Tom. 1974.

*Protestant church trends of New York City, 1900-1936: causes, correlates, consequences.* Dodson, Dan William. New York: Dodson, 1940.

*Punjab crisis: context and trends.* Pramod Kumar. Chandigarh: Centre for Research in Rural and Industrial, 1984.

*Reflections on pilgrimages in Ethiopia.* Pankhurst, Alula.1994.

*Regressive trends in Turkey since 1923: translation with explanatory notes of Neset Çagatay's Türkiye de gerici eylemler (1923' den buyana).* Çagatay, Neset & Maribel Aydiner Donat. 1978.

*Religion and modern social trends.* Bruton, Marie Josephine. 1938.

*Religion and politics emerging trends.* Clark, Dick Clarence. Pittsburgh, 1981.

*Religious change in America.* Greeley, Andrew M. Cambridge, MA: Harvard University Press, 1989.

*Religious trends in English poetry.* Fairchild, Hoxie Neale. New York: Columbia University Press, 1957.

*Religious trends in Israel.* Hardan, David. Jerusalem: Center for Programming, 1983.

*Religious trends in modern China.* Chan, Wing-tsit. New York: Columbia University Press, 1983.

*Religious trends in Singapore: with special reference to Christianity.* Sng, Bobby E. K. & Poh Seng You. Singapore: Graduates' Christian Fellowship, 1982.

*Seven trends facing the church in 1988 and beyond.* Barna, George. 1988.

*Sharing Jesus in the two thirds world: the papers of the First Conference of Evangelical Mission Theologians from the Two Thirds World.* Samuel, Vinay & Chris Sugden. Grand Rapids, MI: Eerdmans, 1984.

*Some trends in precolonial religious thought in Kenya and Tanzania.* Ehret, Christopher. 1974.

*Surveying the religious landscape: trends in U.S. beliefs.* Gallup, George & D. Michael Lindsay. Harrisburg, PA: Morehouse, 1999.

*Tendencias religiosas de la China moderna.* Chan, Wing-tsit. Madrid: Espasa-Calpe, 1955.

*The creation of several paintings with consideration given to the need for a more meaningful integration between art and contemporary trends in religion.* Buckley, Frank Joseph. 1965.

*The future: trends and developments through the 21st century.* R. D. Rotstein. New York: Carol, 1990.

*The state, religious fundamentalism and women: trends in South Asia.* Chhachhi, Amrita. The Hague, 1988.

*The United Church of Christ in Japan: an analysis of the background of and trends toward unity in religion and state resulting in the creation of the United Protestant Church in Japan.* Best, Earl Van. 1948.

*The United States and its churches: some facts and trends.* Whitman, Lauris B. New York: National Council of the Churches of Christ, 1963.

*Trend tracking: the system to profit from today's trends.* G. Celente. New York: Wiley. 1990.

*Trends in American eschatology: an application of Skinnerian concepts in an analysis of changes in religion and culture.* Armstrong, James Robert. Chestnut Hill, MA, 1976.

*Trends in American religion and the Protestant world.* Marty, Martin. E. Meckler, 1991.

*Trends in American religion, 1964-1986: implications for the future.* Nauta, André. 1991.

*Trends in Far East broadcasting.* Bowman, James & David Adams. Morristown, NJ: National Religious Broadcasters, 1982.

*Trends in Protestant giving: a study of church finance in the United States.* C. Fahs. New York: Institute of Social and Religious Research, 1929.

*Trends in religious thought that affect social outlook.* Tillich, Paul. New York: Harper, 1944.

*Trends in the geography of belief systems: festschrift to Angelika Sievers.* Singh, R. L. & Rana P. Varanasi: National Geographical Society of India, 1987.

*Trends in the geography of pilgrimages: homage to David E. Sopher.* Singh, R. L. & Rana P. Varanasi: National Geographical Society of India, 1987.

*Trends in theology, 1870-1970.* Griffin, V. G. Dublin: APCK, 1970.

*Trends of modern religion.* Ames, Edward Scribner & William Bower, 1930.

*Trends of thought and Christian truth.* Haas, John A. W. Boston: R. G. Badger, 1915.

*Twentieth-century British social trends.* Halsey, A. H. & Josephine Webb. New York: St. Martin's Press, 2000.

*Universalism and syncretism trends.* Climenhaga, Arthur. Springfield, MO: Assemblies of God Audiovisual Services, 1967.

*Waking up tomorrow: top ten major trends shaping the twenty-first century.* Valerie, Julie. 1999.

*We beheld His glory: the primitive Christian message and present-day religious trends.* Arsen, Nikolai Sergeevich. London: Society for Promoting Christian Knowledge, 1937.

*Xian dai Zhongguo di zong jiao qu shi.* Chan, Wing-tsit. Taipei: Wen shu chu ban she, 1987.

Part 8

# WHO'S WHO

Leaders in the Christian and non-Christian worlds, AD 30–AD 2001

*God watches over good people and places them in positions of power and honor forever.*
—Job 36:7, Contemporary English Version

*This is a true saying: If a man is eager to be a church leader,*
*he desires an excellent work.*
—1 Timothy 3:1, Good News Bible

Leaders of the Christian world through its 2,000 years are often listed and described in terms of their achievements, authority, power, prestige, and influence. Part 8 records these elements over the past but then goes on to list current leaders in terms of accountability for the current status of global Christianity both good and bad. Leaders who navigated the church through the 1990s (the Decade of Evangelism) have had control over massive resources of personnel, finance, and global expertise. They are accountable to the rest of the church who would have questions to ask about certain major failures to reach widely-proclaimed AD 2000 goals. A final brief section lists some of their non-Christian counterparts.

# Leaders in the Christian and non-Christian worlds, AD 30-AD 2001

## THREE APPROACHES TO THE WHO'S WHO

One important element in understanding both the historical and present status of the world's religions is its leaders. Unfortunately, this involves millions of individuals, each making some important contribution to the religious history of the world. To provide some guide to the reader we have chosen three representative approaches. First, we examine the history of Christianity and present a highly selective list of its great evangelizers under the title 'Who's Who in world evangelization, AD 30–AD 2000.' Second, we present a selection of the Christian world's current and recent leadership in the last 3 decades, under the title 'Who's Who in the Christian World, AD 1970–AD 2000.' Finally, a brief overview of leadership in the non-Christian world is added under the title 'Who's Who in the non-Christian world, AD 1900–AD 2000.' For each of these a rationale and explanation of methodology is given below.

### Who's Who in world evangelization, AD 30–AD 2000

Millions of Christians since the time of Christ have contributed to the evangelization of the world. This includes over 2 billion Great Commission Christians, 214 million pastoral workers, 33 million near-cultural home missionaries, 3.6 million cross-cultural home missionaries, and over 6 million foreign missionaries. How does one choose the great evangelizers from this enormous pool of candidates? To begin with we looked for the following: (1) foreign missionaries who have made a major contribution to the spreading of the gospel into new cultural basins or nation states; thus, Patrick is included for his role in the conversion of Ireland; (2) evangelists and pastors who are widely known; (3) theologians whose writings have encouraged missionary or evangelistic expansion; (4) martyrs whose deaths have resulted in a marked increase in the preaching of the gospel; (5) church leaders who have provided oversight and leadership to the expansion of Christianity; and (6) any others whose evangelistic or missionary effort has resulted in significant evangelization. A small number appear both in this list and in the 'Who's Who in the Christian World' because they made recent but significant contributions to world evangelization.

Many Christians who are not listed here can be found in other parts of this survey. Significant evangelizers appear in (1) Part 2 "CosmoChronology"; (2) Part 4 "Martyrology"; and (3) the texts accompanying each country in *WCE* Part 4 "Countries".

### Who's Who in the Christian World, AD 1970–AD 2000

This listing gives approximately 1,000 names of church and council executives and other persons prominent in the contemporary Christian world in or around the period 1970–2000. All 490 names from the *World Christian encyclopedia*, first edition, are included, shown in medium typeface, contrasting them with the newer names from the 1990–2000 period in bold type. One should note that many leaders from the earlier period are still in positions of leadership in the later period.

The object of the Who's Who should be clearly stated. It is not to inform the reader about who the bishop or general secretary of this of that organization is, since such appointments change too rapidly for a survey of this nature. (See any directory for clues on how to find current leadership). Our object is the reverse: to inform the reader who knows a leading executive's name and wants to know what church or council or organization he or she directed or headed during the period 1970–1980 or 1980–2000. Another purpose is to enable the reader to get a general idea of the global spread of Christian leaders and decision-makers during these periods, and also an idea of the titles, ages, nationalities and denominational affiliations of the executives involved.

In the world's 33,800 distinct Christian denominations today, there are over 21,000 bishops, over 20,000 moderators and church presidents, over one million priests, pastors, ministers and clergy, some 420,000 foreign missionaries and personnel, over 5 million men and women church workers and personnel of all kinds, to say nothing of the 648 million lay persons who are practicing, activist Christians. It is therefore an impossible task to draw up any concise yet balanced selection of all names of importance. So that our selection will not be too arbitrary, we need to employ and to set out certain guiding principles.

The present listing of 800 persons therefore brings together the names of most of the individuals in the

following 8 categories: (1) executive heads of all national, regional, continental, international, and confessional councils or alliances of churches, Christian councils, fellowships of churches, and episcopal conferences; (2) executive heads of the 64 major Protestant, Orthodox, Anglican, and other denominations with over one million affiliated members each in the period 1970–2000; (3) heads of all 63 Roman Catholic local (nation-wide) churches with over one million Catholics each in the period 1970–2000 (most of whom are also presidents of Catholic national episcopal conferences); (4) heads of a representative range of major postdenominational networks and quasi-denominations; (5) executive heads of a representative range of major international Christian service agencies or organizations; (6) executive heads of a representative range of major international missionary organizations; (7) a selection of leaders among the most prominent Christian martyrs in the period 1970–2000 (who were alive at some time during that period), and (8) a selection of other prominent figures who are of note on the international Christian scene. On principle, for almost all organizations only one office-holder is listed, usually the main executive, and usually the one in office in or around 1970–1980 for the earlier period, and 1980–2000 for the later period. If he or she has subsequently died, however, the year of death is added, and his or her successor is usually included in the listing also.

Information on each person is arranged in a standard order. The churches and organizations listed here are mentioned only by name; further information on them may be found either in *WCE* Part 4's Country Table 2 for the given country or in *WCE* Part 14 "Directory".

### Who's Who in the Non-Christian World, AD 1900–AD 2000

Our third approach to describing leadership in religion is to present a small selection of leaders from the non-Christian world. This includes (1) leaders of organized structures within the world's great religions; (2) recognized persons whose followers are not in an organized structure; and (3) leaders in the nonreligious and atheist worlds.

# Who's Who in world evangelization, AD 30–AD 2000

**Abelard, Peter** (1079-1142). Catholic. Theologian. France.
**Aberhart, William** (1878-1943). Baptist. Radio broadcaster. Canada.
**Adalbert of Prague** (956-997). Catholic. Missionary. Hungary.
**Addams, Jane** (1860-1935). Presbyterian. Founder of Hull House. USA.
**Adelaide** (931-999). Catholic. Empress. Germany.
**Adrian I** (c730-795). Roman Catholic. Pope. Italy.
**Agbebi, Mojola** (1860-1917). Independent. Church leader. Nigeria.
**Aggrey, James Emman** (1875-1927). Methodist Episcopal. Apologist. Ghana.
**Aglipay, Gregorio** (1860-1940). RC/Indigenous. Priest. Philippines.
**Agricola, Mikael** (1510-1557). Lutheran. Reformer. Finland.
**Aidan** (c600-651). Celtic. Bishop. England.
**Aitken, R.** (1800-1878). Anglo-Catholic. Clergy. UK.
**Aitolos, Kosmas** (1714-1779). Orthodox. Athonite monk. Albania.
**Akinyele, Isaac Babalola** (1882-1964). Independent. Church leader. Nigeria.
**Alain of Lille** (1125-1202). Roman Catholic. Apologist. France.

Theologian ALBERTUS     Missionary ANDREWS

**Albertus, Magnus** (1193-1280). Roman Catholic. Theologian. Germany.
**Albright, William F.** (1891-1971). Methodist. Biblical archeologist. USA.
**Alcuin of York** (732-804). Catholic. Advisor to Charlemagne. France.
**Alexander, C.M.** (1867-1920). Protestant. Evangelistic gospel singer. USA.
**Alexander, Daniel W.** (c1890-c1950). African Orthodox. Primate. Africa.
**Alfred the Great** (849-899). Anglican. King. Britain.
**Allen, Richard** (1760-1831). African Methodist. Founder. USA.
**Allen, Roland** (1868-1947). Anglican, S.P.G.. Missionary strategist. China.
**Alopen** (c590-c655). Nestorian. Missionary. Thailand.
**Ambrose of Milan** (339-397). Catholic. Bishop. Italy.
**Anderson, Rufus** (1796-1880). Congregational. Missions secretary/author. USA.
**Andrei Rublev** (1360-1430). Orthodox. Iconographer. Russia.
**Andrew** (c5-c70). Jew. Apostle. Russia.
**Andrews, C. F.** (1871-1940). Anglican. Missionary. India.
**Angus, Joseph** (1816-1902). Baptist. Missionary. England.
**Anselm of Cantebury** (1033-1109). Anglican. Founder of scholasticism. England.
**Anselm of Laon** (c1040-1117). Catholic. Theologian. France.
**Anskar** (801-865). Catholic. Missionary. Denmark.
**Anthony of Egypt** (c251-356). Orthodox. Eremetical monk. Egypt.
**Antony of Padua** (1195-1231). Franciscan. Teacher/evangelist. Italy.
**Apollonia of Alexandria** (c200-c249). Orthodox. Martyr. Egypt.
**Aquaviva, Claudio** (1543-1615). Jesuit. Missionary director. Italy.
**Aquinas, Thomas** (1225-1274). Catholic. Theologian/apologist. Italy.
**Aristo of Pella** (c100-c160). Orthodox. Apologist to the Jews. Jordan.
**Arius** (256-336). Heretic. Presbyter of Alexandria. Egypt.
**Arminius, Jacobus** (1560-1609). Dutch Reformed. Theologian. Netherlands.
**Arndt, John** (1555-1621). Pietist. Evangelist. Germany.
**Arnot, Frederick Stanley** (1858-1914). Plymouth Brethren. Missionary. Zaire.
**Arthington, Robert** (1823-1900). Quaker. Philanthropist. UK.
**Asbury, Francis** (1745-1816). Methodist. Missionary. USA.
**Atallah, Ignatius Mar** (c1600-1653). Syrian Orthodox. Bishop. India.
**Athanasius** (c293-373). Coptic Orthodox. Bishop. Egypt.
**Athanasius the Athonite** (c920-1003). Orthodox. Founder of monasteries. Greece.

**Athenagoras** (c100-c170). Catholic. Apologist. Greece.
**Athenagoras I** (1886-1972). Orthodox. Ecumenical patriarch. Turkey.
**Augustine** (c530-604). Catholic. Missionary. England.
**Augustine of Hippo** (354-430). Catholic. Bishop. Tunisia.
**Aylward, Gladys** (1902-1970). Primitive Methodist. Missionary. China.
**Azariah, V.S.** (1874-1945). Anglican. Bishop. India.
**Babalola, Joseph** (1904-1959). Independent. Founder/prophet. Nigeria.
**Bach, Johann Sebastian** (1685-1750). Lutheran. Composer. Germany.
**Backus, Isaac** (1724-1806). Baptist. Evangelist. USA.
**Bacon, Francis** (1561-1626). Anglican. Philosopher of science. UK.
**Bacon, Roger** (1214-1292). Franciscan. Philosopher. France.
**Baedekev, Freidrich W.** (1823-1906). Anglican. Evangelist. Russia.
**Barclay, Robert** (1648-1690). Quaker. Apologist. Scotland.
**Baring-Gould, Sabina** (1834-1924). Anglican. Hymn writer. England.
**Barnabas** (c70-c90). Jew. Apostle. Palestine.
**Barnardo, Thomas John** (1845-1905). Anglican. Social reformer. England.
**Barratt, T.B.** (1862-1940). Methodist. Prophet. Norway.
**Barth, Karl** (1886-1968). Protestant. Theologian. Switzerland.
**Basil The Great** (c329-379). Catholic. Church father. Palestine.
**Bavinck, Johan H.** (1895-1964). Dutch Reformed. Missiologist. Indonesia.
**Becker, Carl K.** (1884-1990). Protestant. Missionary. Congo.
**Becket, Thomas** (1118-1170). Anglican. Archbishop of Canterbury. England.
**Bede** (c672-735). Anglican. Historian. England.
**Beecher, Lyman** (1775-1865). Presbyterian. Revivalist. USA.
**Bell, L. Nelson** (1894-1973). Presbyterian. Missionary. China.
**Benedict of Nursia** (c480-547). Catholic. Monk. Italy.
**Benedict XV** (1854-1922). Roman Catholic. Pope/ promoter of foreign missions. Rome.
**Bernadette (Soubirous)** (1844-1879). Roman Catholic. Mystic. France.
**Bernard of Clairvaux** (1090-1153). Catholic. Monk. Gaul.
**Bernini, G. L.** (1598-1680). Roman Catholic. Sculptor. Italy.
**Bhengu, Nicholas** (1909-1986). Assembies of God. Evangelist. South Africa.
**Bingham, Hiram** (1789-1869). United Church of Christ. Missionary. USA.
**Bingham, Rowland V.** (1872-1942). Salvation Army. Founder of SIM. Nigeria.
**Blackstone, W.E.** (1841-1935). Methodist. Theologian. USA.
**Blake, William** (1757-1827). Dissenter. Mystic. England.
**Blanche of Castile** (1188-1252). Roman Catholic. Mother of Louis IX. France.
**Boehme, Jacob** (1575-1624). Lutheran. Mystic. Germany.
**Boisemenu, Alain de** (1870-1953). Roman Catholic. Missionary. Papua New Guinea.
**Bolanos, Luis** (1549-1629). Franciscan. Missionary. Argentina.
**Bonaventure** (1221-1274). Franciscan. Theologian. France.
**Bonhoeffer, Dietrich** (1906-1945). Lutheran. Pastor/martyr. Germany.

Bishop ATHANASIUS     Missionary BONIFACE

**Boniface** (680-754). Catholic. Missionary. Germany.
**Boos, Martin** (1762-1825). Roman Catholic. Revivalist. Bavaria.
**Booth, Catherine M.** (1829-1890). Methodist. Co-founder of Salvation Army. UK.
**Booth, William** (1829-1912). Methodist. Co-founder of Salvation Army. UK.
**Boris** (c830-907). Orthodox. Khan. Bulgaria.
**Bosch, David** (1929-1992). Reformed. Missiologist. South Africa.
**Bosco, John** (1815-1888). Roman Catholic. Founder of Salesian Order. Italy.
**Botticelli, Sandro** (1445-1510). Roman Catholic. Renaissance painter. Italy.

**Bowen, George** (1816-1888). Methodist. Missionary. India.
**Boyle, Robert** (1627-1691). Anglican. Scientist/apologist. UK.
**Brahms, Johannes** (1833-1897). Lutheran. Pianist and composer. Germany.
**Braide, Garrick** (1880-1918). Independent. Prophet. Nigeria.
**Brainerd, David** (1718-1747). Presbyterian. Missionary. USA.
**Bray, Thomas** (1656-1730). Anglican. Founder of SPG/SPCK. England.
**Brenz, Johannes** (1499-1570). Protestant. Itinerant preacher. Germany.
**Bridget of Sweden** (c1303-1373). Roman Catholic. Mystic/papal advisor. Rome.
**Brigid of Kildare** (c460-c525). Celtic. Founder of monastery. Ireland.
**Bunyan, John** (1628-1688). Nonconformist. Lay preacher. England.
**Burchard** (c960-1025). Catholic. Bishop/canonist. Germany.
**Cable, Mildred** (1877-1952). Anglican. Missionary. China.
**Cabrini, F. X.** (1850-1917). Roman Catholic. Founder of missionary sisters. USA.
**Caedmon** (c620-678). Anglican. Poet. England.
**Cakobau** (1817-1883). Wesleyan. Chief. Fiji.
**Calvert, James** (1813-1892). Wesleyan. Missionary. Fiji.
**Calvin, John** (1509-1564). Protestant. Reformer. Switzerland.
**Campbell, Alexander** (1788-1866). Disciples of Christ. Founder. USA.
**Candidius, Georgius** (c1610-c1670). Dutch Reformed. Pioneer missionary. Formosa.
**Capito, Wolfgang** (1478-1541). Lutheran. Itinerate preacher. Germany.

Reformer CALVIN     Missionary CAREY

**Carey, William** (1761-1834). Baptist. Missionary. India.
**Carlile, Wilson** (1847-1942). Anglican. Founder, Church Army. UK.
**Carmichael, Amy** (1867-1951). Presbyterian. Missionary. India.
**Carroll, John** (1735-1815). Roman Catholic. Archbishop. USA.
**Carver, W.O.** (1868-1954). Southern Baptist. Missiologist. USA.
**Catherine of Siena** (1347-1380). Dominican. Mystic. Italy.
**Catholicos John** (c1050-c1120). Orthodox. Catholicos. Georgia.
**Caughey, James** (c1800-c1860). Protestant. Preacher. USA.
**Challoner, Richard** (1691-1781). Roman Catholic. Bible translator. England.
**Chalmers, James** (1841-1901). Congregational. Missionary. Papua New Guinea.
**Chambers, Oswald** (1874-1917). Baptist. Devotional writer/missionary. UK.
**Chapman, J. Wilbur** (1859-1918). Presbyterian. Evangelist. USA.
**Charlemagne** (742-814). Catholic. Emperor. Germany.
**Chatterton, Percy** (1898-1984). Congregational. Missionary statesman. Papua New Guinea.
**Chesterton, G. K.** (1874-1936). Anglican. Prolific author. UK.
**Chotuncevski, Josef** (c1700-c1760). Orthodox. Missionary. Kamchatka.
**Chu, James** (c1750-1801). Chinese Catholic. Priest. Korea.
**Church, Joe** (1899-1989). Anglican. Missionary. Rwanda.
**Clare of Assisi** (1194-1253). Catholic. Founder of Poor Clares. Italy.
**Clark, Francis E.** (1851-1927). Congregational. Founder of Christian Endeavor. USA.
**Claver, Peter** (1580-1654). Jesuit. Missionary. Colombia.
**Clement bishop of Rome** (c40-c100). Catholic. Bishop. Rome.
**Clement of Alexandria** (c150-215). Orthodox. Theologian. Egypt.
**Clough, John E.** (1836-1910). Baptist. Missionary to the Telugus. India.
**Clovis** (466-511). Catholic. King. France.
**Coke, Thomas** (1747-1814). Methodist. Bishop. USA.
**Columba** (521-597). Celtic. Monk. Scotland.
**Columbanus** (c543-615). Celtic. Monk. Gaul.
**Comboni, Daniele** (1831-1881). Roman Catholic. Missionary. Sudan.

Constantine (285-337). Catholic. Emperor. Rome.
Cosmas Indicopleustes (c500-c570). Nestorian. Geographer. Egypt.
Crawford, Daniel (1870-1926). Plymouth Brethren. Missionary. Zaire.
Crosby, Fanny J. (1820-1915). Protestant. Blind hymn writer. USA.

Bishop CROWTHER

Martyr DE FOUCAULD

Crowther, Samuel (c1809-1891). Anglican. Bishop. Nigeria.
Crummell, Alexander (1819-1898). Episcopal. Afro-American missionary. Liberia.
Cyprian (200-258). Catholic. Bishop. Carthage.
Cyril (826-869). Orthodox. Missionary. Bohemia.
Cyril bishop of Jerusalem (310-386). Orthodox. Bishop. Palestine.
Cyril I Lukaris (c1580-1638). Orthodox. Ecumenical patriarch. Turkey.
Cyril VI (1902-1971). Coptic Orthodox. Pope. Egypt.
Damascus I (304-384). Catholic. Pope/promoted the Vulgate. Rome.
Damien, Father (1840-1889). Roman Catholic. Missionary to lepers. USA.
Dante, Alighieri (1265-1321). Roman Catholic. Poet. Italy.
David of Basra (c260-c330). Orthodox. Missionary. India.
Day, Dorothy (1897-1980). Roman Catholic. Social reformer. USA.
de Acosta, Jose (1539-1600). Jesuit. Missionary. Peru.
de Andrade, Antoine (c1590-1634). Jesuit. Missionary. Tibet.
de Foucauld, Charles (1858-1916). Roman Catholic. Missionary martyr. Algeria.
de la Trinite, sr M.A. (1920-1996). Roman Catholic. Little Sisters superior general. France.
de Labadie, J. (1610-1674). Pietist. Evangelist. Germany.
de Nobili, Robert (1577-1656). Jesuit. Missionary. India.
de Rhodes, Alexander (1591-1660). Jesuit. Pioneer missionary. Viet Nam.
de Viler, Felix (c1600-c1660). Roman Catholic. Missionary. Congo.
Del Bufalo, Caspar (1786-1837). Roman Catholic. Missions founder. Italy.
Delitzsch, F. (1813-1890). Lutheran. Missions founder. Israel.
des Places, C.F.P. (1679-1709). Spiritans (RC). Missions founder. Italy.
Devananden, P. D. (1901-1962). Protestant. Theologian. India.
Didymus the Blind (313-398). Catholic. Theologian. Egypt.
Dionysius the Great (c200-264). Orthodox. Bishop/author. Egypt.

Theologian DODD

Preacher DOMINIC

Dodd, C.H. (1884-1973). Congregational. Scholar. USA.
Dominic (1170-1221). Dominican. Founder. France.
Domitilla Flavia (c10-c65). Catholic. Matron of Imperial family. Rome.
Donne, John (1572-1631). Anglican. Poet and preacher. UK.
Dositheos (1641-1707). Orthodox. Patriarch. Israel.
Dostoyevsky, Fyodor (1821-1881). Orthodox. Novelist. Russia.
Drummond, Henry (1851-1897). Anglican. Scientist/Bible teacher. UK.
Du Plessis, J. (1905-1987). Pentecostal. Historian. South Africa.
Duff, Alexander (1806-1878). Anglican. Missionary. India.
Duns Scotos, John (1266-1308). Franciscan. Apologist. France.
Dunstan (924-988). Anglican. Illuminator of manuscripts. England.
Durer, Albrecht (1471-1528). Roman Catholic. Wood carver. Germany.
Dwight, Timothy (1752-1817). Congregational. University president. USA.
Eddy, Sherwood (1871-1963). YMCA. Promoter of social gospel/evangelist. India.

Edersheim, Alfred (1825-1889). Anglican. Bible scholar/missionary. UK.
Edwards, Jonathan (1703-1758). Congregational. Revivalist. USA.

Missionary EGEDE

Apologist ERASMUS

Egede, Hans (1686-1758). Protestant. Missionary. Greenland.
Eliot, John (1604-1690). Puritan. Missionary. North America.
Eliot, T. S. (1888-1965). Anglican. Poet. UK.
Elliot, Jim (1927-1956). Brethren. Missionary martyr. Ecuador.
Elmo (Peter Gonzales) (1190-1246). Dominican. Preacher/patron saint of sailors. Spain.
Ephraem Syrus (c306-373). Catholic. Ascetic. Syria.
Erasmus, D. (1469-1536). Roman Catholic. Apologist. Italy.
Eusebius of Caesarea (c265-339). Catholic. Historian. Caesarea.
Evans, Christmas (1766-1838). Anglican. Revivalist. Wales.
Excell, E.O. (1851-1921). Methodist. Song writer/evangelist. USA.
Farquhar, John Nicol (1861-1929). London Missionary Society. Missionary author. India.
Ferrer, Vincent (c1350-1419). Dominican. Wandering preacher. Europe.
Finney, Charles G. (1792-1875). Presbyterian. Revivalist. USA.
Flavian (320-404). Orthodox. Bishop of Antioch. Syria.
Forman, Charles W. (1821-1894). Presbyterian. Missionary. Pakistan.
Fox, George (1624-1691). Quakers. Founder. UK.

Revivalist FINNEY

Mystic FRANCIS

Francis of Assisi (1182-1226). Franciscan. Founder. Italy.
Francis of Sales (1567-1622). Roman Catholic. Bishop/apologist. Switzerland.
Francke, August Hermann (1663-1727). Lutheran Pietist. Training school founder. Germany.
Franson, Fredrik (1852-1908). Evangelical Free. Mission founder. USA.
Fraser, James O. (1886-1938). CIM. Missionary. China.
Freeman, Thomas Birch (1806-1890). Wesleyan. Afro-American missionary. Ghana.
Frelinghuysen, T.J. (1691-1748). Dutch Reformed. Evangelist. USA.
Friedrich, G. (c1880-c1940). Protestant. Bible scholar. Germany.
Frumentius (c320-c380). Orthodox. Missionary. Ethiopia.
Fry, Elizabeth (1780-1845). Quaker. Prison ministry. UK.
Fuller, Andrew (1754-1815). Baptist. Minister. England.
Fuller, C.E. (1887-1968). Independent. Radio evangelist. USA.
Gaebelien, Arno Clemens (1861-1945). Methodist Episcopal. Missionary to Jews. USA.
Gairdner, W. H. Temple (1873-1928). Anglican. Missionary. Egypt.
Gardiner, Allen (1794-1851). Anglican. Missionary. Argentina.
Gaussen, F. (1790-1863). Evangelical. Revivalist. Switzerland.
Geddie, John (1815-1872). Presbyterian. Mission founder. Canada.
Gerbillon, Jean Francois (1654-1707). Jesuit. Missionary. China.
Germanus (c496-576). Catholic. Bishop/champion of the poor. France.
Gilmour, James (1843-1891). Congregational. Missionary. Mongolia.
Glegg, Alexander Lindsay (1882-1975). Anglican. Lay evangelist. UK.
Glukharev, Macarius (1792-1847). Orthodox. Apostle. Russia.
Goforth, Jonathan (1859-1936). Presbyterian. Missionary. China.
Goodell, William (1792-1867). Congregational. Missionary to Armenians. Turkey.

Gordon, Adoniram Judson (1836-1895). Baptist. Missions advocate. USA.
Gordon, S. D. (1859-1936). Protestant. Devotional writer. USA.
Goszner, Johannes (1773-1858). Roman Catholic. Revivalist. Bavaria.
Gowry (c1500-c1560). Russian Orthodox. Missionary. Russia.
Grebel, Conrad (1490-1526). Anabaptist. Reformer. Switzerland.
Green, Bryan (1901-c1992). Anglican. Evangelist. UK.
Gregory of Tours (538-594). Catholic. Bishop. Gaul.
Gregory Thaumaturgos (c213-270). Catholic. Bishop. Pontus.
Gregory the Great (540-604). Catholic. Pope. Rome.
Gregory the Illuminator (240-332). Orthodox. Missionary. Armenia.
Gregory VII Hildebrand (1020-1085). Roman Catholic. Pope. Rome.
Gregory XV (1554-1623). Roman Catholic. Pope. Vatican.
Grenfell, George (1849-1906). Baptist. Missionary. Congo.
Grenfell, Wilfred T. (1865-1940). Anglican. Medical missionary. Labrador.
Grenz, T. (c1780-c1835). Lutheran. Evangelist. Lithuania.
Groote, Gerard (1340-1383). Roman Catholic. Founder of Devotio Moderna. Netherlands.
Groves, Anthony N. (1795-1853). Plymouth Brethren. Missionary. Iraq.
Grubb, Kenneth G. (1900-1980). Anglican. Researcher. UK.
Grubb, Wilfred B. (1865-1930). Anglican. Missionary. South America.
Grunewald, Stonemason (c1800-c1860). Lutheran. Evangelist. Germany.
Guinness, H.G. (1835-1910). Anglican. Missions founder. UK.

Printer GUTENBERG

Composer HANDEL

Gutenberg, Johan (c1395-1468). Catholic. Printer. Germany.
Gutzlaff, Karl (1803-1851). Lutheran. Missionary. China.
Haldane, Robert (1764-1842). Evangelical. Revivalist. Switzerland.
Hall, Gordon (1784-1826). Congregational. Missionary. India.
Hallesby, Ole K. (1879-1961). Evangelical. Theologian/writer. Norway.
Ham, Mordecai (1877-1961). Baptist. Evangelist. USA.
Hamlin, Cyrus (1811-1900). Congregational. Missionary. Turkey.
Handel, G.F. (1685-1759). Lutheran. Composer. Germany.
Harald I (c910-c985). Lutheran. First Christian king. Denmark.
Harris, Howell (1714-1773). Anglican. Itinerant evangelist. Wales.
Harris, William Wade (c1850-1929). Independent. Prophet. Liberia.
Havergal, Frances R. (1836-1879). Anglican. Hymn writer. England.
Haydn, Franz Joseph (1732-1809). Roman Catholic. Composer. Austria.
Hegesippus (c120-190). Catholic. Apologist. Palestine.
Helms, Edgar J. (1863-1942). Methodist. Founder of Goodwill Industries. USA.
Henry of Uppsala (c1100-1155). Catholic. King. Finland.
Hepburn, James Curtis (1815-1911). Presbyterian. Missionary. Japan.
Herman of Alaska (1757-1837). Orthodox. Missionary. USA.
Hermann von Reichenau (1013-1054). Catholic. Musician/Gregorian Chant. Switzerland.
Hermas (c100-150). Catholic. Author. Rome.
Hervas, J. (c1900-c1960). Roman Catholic. Cursillo founder. Spain.
Heyling, Peter (1607-1652). Lutheran. Missionary. Eqypt.
Hicks, Tommy (1909-1973). Pentecostal. Evangelist. Argentina.
Higginbottom, Sam (1874-1958). Presbyterian. Missionary. India.
Hilarion of Gaza (291-371). Orthodox. Monk. Palestine.
Hilda of Whitby (614-671). Celtic. Abbotess. England.
Hildegarde (1098-1179). Catholic. Abbess of Rupertsberg. Germany.
Hill, David (1840-1896). Methodist. Missionary. China.
Hoekendijk, J.C. (1912-1975). Dutch Reformed. Missiologist. Indonesia.
Hofmann, Melchior (1495-1543). Anabaptist. Pastor. Germany.
Honda, Koji (c1920-c1980). Presbyterian. Evangelist. Japan.
Honorius III (c1160-1227). Catholic. Pope. Italy.
Hoste, D.E. (1861-1946). China Inland Mission. Mission executive. China.
Hsi, Pastor (1830-1896). Independent. Preacher/evangelist. China.
Hsiu-chuan, Hung (1814-1864). Quasi-Christian. Sect founder. China.
Huc, Evarisle Regis (1813-1860). Roman Catholic. Missionary. Tibet.

**Hughes, Hugh Price** (1847-1902). Methodist. Social reformer. UK.

**Hunain ibn Ishaq** (808-873). Nestorian. Scholar. Iraq.

**Hunt, John** (1812-1848). Wesleyan. Missionary. Fiji.

**Hunter, George** (c1870-1946). Anglican. Missionary to Turkestan. China.

**Huss, Jan** (1373-1415). Roman Catholic. Preacher. Bohemia.

**Hyde, John** (1865-1912). Presbyterian. Missionary/prayer. India.

**Ignatius of Antioch** (c50-c110). Catholic. Bishop. Antioch.

**Il'minskii, Nikolai** (1822-1891). Orthodox. Missionary educator. Russia.

**Innocent III** (1160-1216). Roman Catholic. Pope. Italy.

**Irenaeus bishop of Lyons** (c135-203). Catholic. Bishop. Lyons.

**Irving, Edward** (1792-1834). Catholic Apostolic Church. Founder. Scotland.

**Isaac of Ninevah** (c640-700). Nestorian. Bishop/theologian. Iraq.

**Isidore of Seville** (560-636). Catholic. Theologian. Spain.

**Jacob Baradaeus** (c510-578). Syrian. Founder of Jacobites. Egypt.

**Jaeschke, Heinrich August** (1817-1883). Moravian. Missionary/linguist. Tibet.

**Jaffray, Robert A.** (1873-1945). Alliance. Missionary. Indo China.

**James** (c1-c65). Jew. Apostle. Palestine.

**James the Just** (c5-c70). Jew. Apostle. Palestine.

**James the Less** (c5-c65). Jew. Apostle. Palestine.

**Javouhey, Anne-Marie** (1779-1850). Roman Catholic. Missionary/advocate. France.

**Jeffreys, G.** (1889-1962). Pentecostal. Healer. UK.

**Jerome** (c347-419). Catholic. Bible translator. Rome.

**Jesus of Nazareth** (Bc4-29). Jew. Founder. Palestine.

**Joachim of Fiore** (c1130-1202). Cistercian. Mystic. Italy.

**Joan of Arc** (1412-1431). Roman Catholic. Martyr. France.

**John Cassian** (360-435). Catholic. Monk. Gaul.

**John Chrysostom** (c347-407). Catholic. Theologian. Constantinople.

**John of Damascus** (c675-749). Greek Orthodox. Theologian. Syria.

**John of Kronstadt** (1829-1908). Russian Orthodox. Priest/evangelist. Russia.

**John of Montecorvino** (1246-1328). Franciscan. Missionary. China.

**John of the Cross** (1542-1591). Roman Catholic. Reformer/mystic. Spain.

**John the Baptist** (cBC15-c28). Jew. Prophet. Palestine.

**John the Divine** (c5-c95). Jew. Apostle. Palestine.

**John XXIII** (1881-1963). Roman Catholic. Pope. Vatican.

**John, Griffith** (1831-1912). Congregational. Missionary. China.

**Jones, E. Stanley** (1884-1973). Methodist. Missionary. India.

**Jones, Samuel Porter** (1847-1906). Methodist Episcopal. Evangelist. USA.

**Judson, Adoniram** (1788-1850). ABCFM. Missionary. Burma.

**Justin Martyr** (c100-165). Catholic. Theologian/martyr. Rome.

**Justinian I** (482-565). Orthodox. Emperor. Constantinople.

**Kagawa, Toyohiko** (1888-1960). Presbyterian. Evangelist. Japan.

**Kamwana, Elliott** (c1870-1956). Independent. Pastor. Central Africa.

**Kasatkin, Ivan** (1836-1912). Russian Orthodox. Missionary. Japan.

**Kazacev of Tobolsk, Eugene** (c1780-c1840). Russian Orthodox. Metropolitan. Siberia.

**Keith-Falconer, Ion** (1856-1887). Free Church. Missionary. Yemen.

**Kentigern** (c530-603). Anglican. Missionary. UK.

**Keysser, Christian** (1877-1961). Lutheran. Missionary. Papua New Guinea.

**Kilian** (c640-689). Celtic. Missionary. Germany.

**Kimbangu, Simon** (1889-1951). Independent. Founder. Congo.

Abbess HILDEGARDE          Missionary KIVEBULAYA

**Kivebulaya, Apolo** (1864-1933). Anglican. African missionary. Zaire.

**Kivengere** (1919-1988). Anglican. Bishop. Uganda.

**Knox, John** (1514-1572). Protestant. Reformer. Scotland.

**Ko Tha Byu** (1778-1840). Baptist. Karen evangelist. Burma.

**Kraemer, Hendrik** (1888-1965). Dutch Reformed. Missiologist. Netherlands.

**Krapf, J.L.** (1810-1881). Anglican. Missionary. Kenya.

**Krishna Pillai** (1827-1900). Church of South India. Tamil author/evangelist. India.

**Kuhn, Isobel** (1901-1957). Presbyterian. Missionary. China.

**Kuyper, A.** (1837-1920). Dutch Reformed. Theologian. Netherlands.

**La Salle, Jean Raptse de** (1651-1719). Roman Catholic. Founder of lay schools. France.

**Lactantius** (c240-320). Catholic. Apologist/historian. North Africa.

**Laestadius, L.L.** (1800-1861). Lutheran. Pastor. Finland.

**Langton, Stephen** (c1160-1228). Anglican. Archbishop of Canterbury. England.

**Las Casas, Bartolomo'de** (1474-1566). Dominican. Missionary/advocate. Spain.

**Latourette, K.S.** (1884-1968). Baptist. Historian. USA.

**Laubach, Frank C.** (1884-1970). Congregational. Literacy evangelist. Asia.

**Lavigerie, cardinal Charles** (1825-1892). White Fathers. Founder. Algeria.

**Lebbaeus** (c5-c70). Jew. Apostle. Palestine.

**Lebbe, Vincent** (1877-1940). Roman Catholic. Missionary. China.

**Leo XIII** (1810-1903). Roman Catholic. Pope. Vatican.

**Leonardo da Vinci** (1452-1519). Roman Catholic. Inventor/artist. Italy.

**Leszczynski, Filofei** (1650-1722). Orthodox. Missionary to Siberia. Russia.

**Lewis, C.S.** (1898-1963). Anglican. Apologist. UK.

**Libermann, Francois Marie Paul** (1802-1852). Roman Catholic. Mission founder. France.

**Liddell, Eric** (1902-1945). Anglican. Athlete/missionary. China.

**Liguori, Alphonsius** (1696-1787). Roman Catholic. Founder of Redemptorists. Italy.

**Lindl, Ignatius** (1774-1834). Roman Catholic. Revivalist. Bavaria.

**Lioba** (c710-780). Catholic. Founder of monasteries. Germany.

**Livingstone, David** (1813-1873). Anglican. Missionary explorer. Africa.

**Lo, Gregory** (1611-1691). Roman Catholic. Priest. China.

**Locke, John** (1632-1704). Anglican. Philosopher. UK.

**Longinus** (c530-c600). Orthodox. Missionary. Nubia.

**Longley, C.T.** (1794-1868). Anglican. Archbishop of Cantebury. UK.

**Louise de Marillac** (1589-1660). Roman Catholic. Founder of Daughters of Charity. France.

**Loyola, Ignatius** (1491-1556). Jesuit. Founder. Palestine.

**Ludmila of Bohemia** (c860-921). Orthodox. Queen/martyr. Bohemia.

**Luke** (c10-c95). Gentile Christian. Physician/author. Palestine.

**Lull, Ramon** (1232-1316). Franciscan. Missionary. Tunisia.

Reformer KNOX          Reformer LUTHER

**Luther, Martin** (1483-1546). Lutheran. Reformer. Germany.

**MacDonald, George** (1824-1905). Anglican. Writer and poet. Scotland.

**Mackay, Alexander** (1849-1890). Anglican. Missionary. Uganda.

**MacKay, George L.** (1844-1901). Presbyterian. Missionary. Taiwan.

**Macrina of Cappadocia** (327-379). Orthodox. Nun. Turkey.

**Maftaa, Dallington** (c1840-c1900). Anglican. Evangelist. Uganda.

**Maranke, Johane** (1912-1963). Independent. Founder. Rhodesia.

**Margaret of Scotland** (1045-1093). Anglican. Queen. Scotland.

**Maritain, Jacques** (1882-1973). Roman Catholic. Philosopher. France.

**Mark the Evangelist** (c10-c68). Jew. Apostle. Palestine.

**Marsden, Samuel** (1764-1838). Anglican. Chaplain. New Zealand.

Prophet MARANKE          Missionary MARSHMAN

**Marshman, Joshua** (1768-1837). Baptist. Missionary. India.

**Martin of Tours** (335-397). Catholic. Bishop. Gaul.

**Martyn, Henry** (1781-1812). Anglican. Missionary. Persia.

**Mashtotz (Mesrob)** (c360-440). Orthodox. Bible translator. Armenia.

**Mason, A.J.** (1851-1928). Anglo-Catholic. Clergy. UK.

**Massaja, Guglielmo (Lorenzo)** (1809-1889). Roman Catholic. Missionary. Ethiopia.

**Mather, Cottor** (1663-1728). Congregational. Founder of Yale University. USA.

**Matthew** (c5-c75). Jew. Apostle. Palestine.

**Matthew, Paris** (c1195-1259). Anglican. Historian. UK.

**Matthias** (c5-c70). Jew. Apostle. Palestine.

**Mauriac, Francois** (1885-1970). Roman Catholic. Novelist. France.

**Maximus the Confessor** (580-662). Orthodox. Theologian. North Africa.

Missiologist MCGAVRAN          Mobilizer MONTGOMERY

**McGavran, D.A.** (1897-1990). Disciples of Christ. Missionary statesman. India.

**McGready, James** (c1760-1817). Presbyterian. Frontier revivalist. USA.

**McPherson, Aimee Semple** (1890-1944). Foursquare. Founder. USA.

**Mede, Joseph** (1586-1638). Anglican. Premillennialist scholar. England.

**Melito** (c100-c160). Catholic. Bishop of Sardis/first known pilgrim. Turkey.

**Merton, Thomas** (1915-1968). Roman Catholic. Trappist monk / author. USA.

**Methodius** (c788-885). Orthodox. Missionary. Bohemia.

**Meyer, F. B.** (1847-1929). Baptist. Preacher. UK.

**Michelangelo Buonarroti** (1475-1554). Roman Catholic. Artist. Rome.

**Mills, B. Fay** (1857-1916). Presbyterian. Social gospel promoter. USA.

**Mills, Samuel J.** (1783-1818). Congregational. Founder of ABCFM. USA.

**Milton, John** (1608-1674). Anglican. Writer/poet. UK.

**Moffat, Robert** (1795-1883). Anglican. Missionary. South Africa.

**Moffett, Samuel A.** (1864-1939). Presbyterian. Missionary. Korea.

**Mohan Rai, Ram** (1772-1833). Quasi-Protestant. Reformer. India.

**Monod, F.** (1794-1863). Protestant. Revivalist. France.

**Montgomery, Helen Barrett** (1861-1934). Baptist. Missions advocate. USA.

Evangelist MOODY          Theologian ORIGEN

**Moody, D.L.** (1837-1899). Congregational. Evangelist. USA.

**Moon, Charlotte (Lottie)** (1840-1912). Baptist. Missionary. China.

**Morrison, Robert** (1782-1834). Protestant. Missionary. China.

**Mott, John R.** (1865-1955). Methodist. Missionary statesman. USA.

**Muller, George** (1805-1898). Plymouth Brethren. Orphanage founder. UK.

**Murray, Andrew** (1828-1917). Dutch Reformed. Prayer. South Africa.

**Myklebust, O.G.** (1905-1998). Lutheran. Missiologist. Norway.

**Nagenda, William** (1912-1973). Anglican. Revivalist. Uganda.

**Neander, J.** (1650-1680). Pietist. Evangelist. Germany.

**Neander, Johann A. W.** (1789-1850). Lutheran. Historian. Germany.

**Nee, Watchman** (1903-1972). Independent. Founder. China.

**Nektarios Kephalas** (1846-1920). Greek Orthodox. Bishop of Pentapolis. Greece.

**Neri, Philip** (1515-1595). Roman Catholic. Founder of Congregation of the Oratory. Italy.

**Nestorius** (c380-c451). Orthodox. Founder of missionary movement. Turkey.

**Nevius, John** (1829-1893). Presbyterian. Missionary. China.

**Newell, Samuel** (1784-1821). Congregational. Missionary. India.

**Newman, J. H.** (1801-1890). Roman Catholic. Cardinal/author. England.

**Newton, John** (1725-1807). Anglican. Preacher/hymn writer. UK.
**Nicholas of Cusa** (1401-1464). Catholic. Scholar/author. Germany.
**Nicolai (Kasatkin), Ivan** (1836-1912). Russian Orthodox. Missionary. Japan.
**Nielsen Hauge, Hans** (1771-1824). Lutheran. Revivalist. Norway.
**Nightingale, Florence** (1820-1910). Anglican. Nurse. England.
**Niles, D.T.** (1908-1970). Methodist. Pastor/theologian. Sri Lanka.
**Ninian** (c360-c432). Catholic. Bishop. Scotland.
**Nino** (c300-c360). Orthodox. Woman slave/missionary. Georgia.
**Nommensen, Ludwig I.** (1834-1918). Dutch Reformed. Missionary to Bataks. Indonesia.
**Norbert of Xanten** (c1080-1134). Roman Catholic. Founder of Premonstratensian order. Italy.
**Novatian** (c200-258). Catholic. Theologian. Rome.
**O'Morgain, Malachy** (c1094-1148). Catholic. Monk. Ireland.
**Occom, Samson** (1723-1792). Presbyterian. American Indian preacher. USA.
**Odilo** (962-1049). Catholic. Fifth abbot of Cluny. Germany.
**Odo** (879-942). Catholic. Cluny monastic reform. Germany.
**Olaf Haraldson** (995-1030). Lutheran. Christian king. Norway.
**Oldham, J.H.** (1874-1969). United Free Church. Missions activist. Scotland.
**Origen** (c185-254). Orthodox. Theologian. Alexandria.
**Orosius, Paulus** (c370-c430). Catholic. Historian/apologist. North Africa.
**Otto of Bamberg** (1062-1139). Catholic. Missionary. Poland.
**Pachomius** (c290-346). Orthodox. Cenobitic monk. Egypt.
**Padwick, Constance** (1886-1968). Anglican. Missionary. Eqypt.
**Pantaenus** (c120-190). Orthodox. Missionary. India.
**Parham, Charles F.** (1873-1929). Methodist. Pentecostal founder. USA.
**Parker, Joel** (1799-1873). Presbyterian. Pastor/missions advocate. USA.
**Parker, Peter** (1804-1888). Congregational. Medical missionary. China.
**Pascal, Blaise** (1623-1662). Roman Catholic. Scientist/apologist. France.
**Paton, John G.** (1824-1907). Presbyterian. Missionary. New Hebrides.
**Paton, William** (1886-1943). Presbyterian. Missions advocate. UK.
**Patrick** (389-461). Catholic. Missionary. Ireland.
**Patteson, John C.** (1827-1871). Anglican. Missionary. Melanesia.
**Paul VI** (1897-1978). Roman Catholic. Pope. Vatican.
**Paul, J.A.A.B.** (1853-1931). Lutheran. Pastor. Germany.
**Paulinus of York** (c584-644). Catholic. Missionary. England.
**Penzotti, F.G.** (1851-1925). Evangelical. Bible colporteur. Peru.
**Perpetua** (c150-203). Catholic. Martyr. Italy.
**Peter I Ieromartyros** (c260-311). Orthodox. Bishop. Egypt.
**Philip the Evangelist** (c10-c70). Jew. Apostle. Palestine.
**Phillips, J. B.** (1906-1982). Anglican. Bible paraphraser. UK.
**Photius** (821-891). Orthodox. Patriarch. Constantinople.
**Pierson, A.T.** (1837-1911). Presbyterian. Missions advocate. USA.
**Pius XI** (1857-1939). Roman Catholic. Pope. Vatican.
**Pius XII** (1876-1958). Roman Catholic. Pope. Vatican.
**Pollard, Samuel** (1864-1915). Methodist. Missionary to Miao. China.
**Polycarp bishop of Smyrna** (69-156). Catholic. Bishop/martyr. Smyrna.
**Pratt, Josiah** (1768-1844). Anglican. Missionary. England.
**Priscilla** (c10-c80). Jew. Evangelist/teacher. Palestine.
**Prudentius Clemens, Aurelius** (348-c405). Catholic. Latin poet. Spain.
**Pulcheria of Constantinople** (399-453). Orthodox. Empress. Turkey.
**Raikes, Robert** (1735-1811). Anglican. Sunday school advocate. England.
**Ramabai, Pandita** (1858-1922). Independent. Evangelist. India.
**Ramsey, A.M.** (1904-1988). Anglican. Archbishop of Canterbury. UK.
**Rattenbury, J.E.** (c1910-c1970). Methodist. Evangelist. UK.
**Rauschenbusch, Walter** (1861-1948). Baptist. Social gospel. USA.
**Rehberger** (1716-1769). Pietist. Preacher. Bavaria.
**Reichelt, Karl Ludwig** (1877-1952). Lutheran. Missionary. China.
**Rembrandt Harmensz van Rijn** (1606-1669). Dutch Reformed. Artist. Netherlands.
**Rhenius, Karl** (1790-1838). Lutheran. Missionary to Shenan caste. India.
**Ricci, Matteo** (1552-1610). Jesuit. Missionary. China.
**Richard, Timothy** (1845-1919). Baptist. Missionary. China.
**Richter, Julius** (1862-1940). Lutheran. Professor of missiology. Germany.
**Roberts, Evan** (1878-1951). Calvinist Methodist. Revivalist. Wales.
**Rodeheaver, Homer A.** (1880-1955). Methodist. Publisher of gospel music. USA.
**Romero, Oscar** (1917-1980). Roman Catholic. Archbishop, martyr. El Salvador.
**Rowland, Daniel** (c1713-1790). Anglican. Revivalist. Wales.
**Russell, Charles T.** (1852-1916). Jehovah Witnesses. Founder. USA.
**Sabaryeshu III** (c1050-c1110). Nestorian. Bishop. China.
**Sailer, Johann** (1751-1832). Roman Catholic. Revivalist. Bavaria.
**Salazar, Domingo de** (1512-1594). Dominican. Missionary. Phillipines.

**Sallman, Warner** (1892-1968). Protestant. Artist. USA.
**Samuel the Confessor** (c590-c660). Coptic. Monk. Egypt.
**Sanchez, Alonso** (1547-1593). Jesuit. Missionary. China.

Missionary RICCI          Songwriter SANKEY

**Sankey, Ira D.** (1840-1908). Methodist. Songwriter/evangelist. USA.
**Saravia, Hadrian** (1531-1613). Anglican. Advocate of Great Commission. England.
**Saul of Tarsus** (c10-c70). Jew. Apostle. Asia Minor.
**Savonarola, Girolamo** (1452-1498). Dominican. Preacher. Italy.
**Sayers, Dorothy L.** (1893-1957). Anglican. Writer. UK.
**Schaeffer, Francis A.** (1912-1984). Presbyterian. Apologist. Switzerland.
**Schaff, P.** (1819-1893). Presbyterian. Historian. Germany.
**Schall Von Bell, J.A.** (1591-1666). Jesuit. Missionary. China.
**Schmidlin, Joseph** (1876-1944). Roman Catholic. Missiologist. Germany.
**Schmidt, W.** (1868-1954). RC Divine Word. Anthropologist. Germany.
**Schwartz, Christian F.** (1726-1798). Lutheran. Missionary. India.

Apostle PAUL (right)       Missionary SCHWEITZER

**Schweitzer, Albert** (1875-1965). German Evangelical. Missionary doctor. Africa.
**Schwenkfeld, Kaspar von Ossig** (1489-1561). Anabaptist. Evangelist. Germany.
**Scudder, Ida S.** (1870-1959). Reformed. Medical missionary. India.
**Seraphim of Sarov** (1759-1833). Orthodox. Mystic. Russia.
**Sergius of Radonezh** (1314-1392). Orthodox. Monastery founder. Russia.
**Serra, Junipero** (1713-1784). Franciscan. Founder of missions. USA.
**Seton, Elizabeth Ann** (1774-1821). Roman Catholic. Founder of Sisters of Charity. USA.
**Severus of Antioch** (c465-538). Coptic Orthodox. Monk. Eqypt.
**Seymour, W.J.** (1870-1922). Black Holiness. Preacher. USA.
**Shaftesbury, Earl of (A. A. Cooper)** (1801-1885). Anglican. Social reformer. UK.
**Shahbaz, Imam-U Din** (1844-1924). Anglican. Bible translator/poet. Pakistan.
**Shakarian, D.** (1913-1993). Pentecostal. Full Gospel Businessmen. USA.
**Shangjie, Song** (1901-1944). Independent. Preacher. China.
**Sheen, Fulton J.** (1895-1979). Roman Catholic. Broadcaster. USA.
**Simeon, Charles** (1759-1836). Anglican. Vicar. England.
**Simon Peter** (cBC5-c64). Jew. Apostle. Palestine.
**Simon Zelotes** (c5-c80). Jew. Apostle. Palestine.
**Simons, Menno** (1496-1561). Dutch Anabaptist. Founder of Mennonites. Netherlands.
**Simpson, A. B.** (1844-1919). Christian and Missionary Alliance. Founder. USA.

Evangelist SINGH          Evangelist SMITH

**Singh, Bakht** (1903-c1998). Independent. Evangelist. India.
**Singh, Sadhu Sundar** (1889-c1929). Independent. Evangelist. India.
**Slepcov, G.** (c1760-c1820). Roman Catholic. Missionary. Siberia.
**Slessor, Mary** (1848-1915). United Presbyterian. Missionary. Calabar (Nigeria).
**Smith, Gipsy** (1860-1947). Salvation Army. Evangelist. UK.
**Smith, Oswald J.** (1889-1986). Presbyterian. Missions advocate. Canada.
**Sojourner Truth** (c1797-1883). Independent. Black slave. USA.
**Speer, Robert E.** (1867-1947). Presbyterian. Missionary statesman. USA.
**Spener, Philip Jakob** (1635-1705). Pietist. Evangelist. Germany.
**Speratus, Paul** (1484-1551). Lutheran. Itinerate preacher. Germany.

Preacher SPURGEON          Missionary TAYLOR

**Spurgeon, C.H.** (1834-1892). Baptist. Expositor. UK.
**Stearns, Shumbal** (1706-1771). Baptist. Evangelist. USA.
**Stephen** (cBC5-c36). Jew. Apostle. Palestine.
**Stephen of Perm** (1335-1384). Orthodox. Missionary. Russia.
**Stern, Henry Aaron** (1820-1885). Orthodox. Missionary to Jews. Ethiopia.
**Stewart, James** (1831-1905). Presbyterian. Missionary statesman. East Africa.
**Strachen, Kenneth** (1910-1965). Protestant. Mission founder. Costa Rica.
**Streit, Robert** (1875-1930). RC Propaganda. Editor. Rome.
**Studd, C.T.** (1862-1931). Anglican. Missionary. Central Africa.
**Suenens, L.-J.** (1904-1995). Roman Catholic. Cardinal. Belgium.
**Sumitada, Omura** (c1520-c1600). Roman Catholic. Evangelist. Japan.
**Sunday, Billy** (1862-1935). Presbyterian. Mass evangelist. USA.
**Sung, John** (1901-1944). Independent. Evangelist. China.
**Swain, Clara A.** (1834-1910). Methodist Episcopal. Medical missionary. India.
**Sylvester II** (c945-1003). Roman Catholic. Pope. Rome.
**Tatian** (110-172). Catholic. Apologist. Syrian.
**Taylor, J. Hudson** (1832-1905). China Inland Mission. Missions founder. China.
**Taylor, M.** (c1910-c1980). Nazarene. Theologian. USA.
**Teilhard de Chardin, Pierre** (1881-1955). Jesuit. Priest & paleontologist. France.
**Temple, William** (1881-1944). Anglican. Archbishop of Canterbury. Britain.
**Tennent, William** (1673-1746). Presbyterian. Missionary trainer. USA.
**Teresa of Avila** (1515-1582). Roman Catholic. Nun/mystic. Spain.
**Teresa of Lisieux** (1873-1897). Carmelite. Patroness of foreign missions. France.
**Teresa, Mother** (1910-1997). Roman Catholic. Advocate for the poor. India.
**Tertullian** (c155-222). Catholic. Theologian. Carthage.
**Thaddeus & Bartholomew** (c5-c75). Jew. Apostle. Palestine.
**Theodosius I** (347-395). Catholic. Emperor. Rome.
**Thoburn, J.M.** (1836-1922). Methodist. Missionary. India.

Apostle THOMAS          Patriarch TIKHON

**Thomas** (cBC5-c53). Jew. Apostle. India.
**Thomas a Jesu** (1564-1627). Discalced Carmelite. Monk. Spain.
**Thomas a Kempis** (c1380-1471). Mystic. Writer. Germany.
**Thomson, D.P.** (1896-1974). Anglican. Evangelist. Scotland.
**Thornton, Henry** (1760-1815). Anglican. Philanthropist. England.
**Tikhon, Patriarch** (1866-1925). Russian Orthodox. Patriarch. USSR.

**Tilak, Narayan Vaman** (1862-1919). Presbyterian. Minister/hymn writer. India.
**Timothy** (728-823). Nestorian. Patriarch. Iraq.
**Torrey, R.A.** (1856-1928). Congregationalist. Evangelist. USA.

Evangelist TORREY        Translator TOWNSEND

**Townsend, W. Cameron** (1896-1982). WBT/SIL. Bible translator. Latin America.
**Trifo** (c1410-c1460). Roman Catholic. Missionary. Scandinavia.
**Trotter, Isabella L.** (1853-1928). Anglican. Founder of Algiers Mission Board. Algeria.
**Tyndale, William** (1494-1536). Anglican. Bible translator. Germany.
**Uchimura, Kanzo** (1861-1930). Independent. Founder of "No Church" movement. Japan.
**Uemura, Masahisa** (1858-1925). Protestant. Evangelist. Japan.
**Ulfilas** (311-381). Arian. Missionary. Goths.
**Underwood, Horace G.** (1859-1916). Presbyterian. Missionary. Korea.
**Untereyck, T.** (1635-1693). Pietist. Evangelist. Germany.
**van Prinsterer, G.** (1801-1876). Dutch Reformed. Preacher. Netherlands.
**Vanderkemp, Johannes T.** (1747-1811). Dutch Reformed. Missionary. South Africa.
**Varonaev, I.E.** (1892-1943). Pentecostal. Church planter. USSR.
**Veniaminov, I.** (1797-1879). Orthodox. Missionary. Russia.
**Venn, Henry** (1796-1873). Anglican. Missions executive. England.
**Vincent de Paul** (1580-1660). Roman Catholic. Founder of Lazarists. France.

**Vladimir** (956-1015). Orthodox. Czar. Russia.
**Voetius, G.** (1588-1676). Pietist. Evangelist. Germany.
**von Canstein, Karl** (1667-1719). Lutheran. Bible Society. Germany.
**von Harnack, Adolf** (1851-1930). Lutheran. Theologian. Germany.
**von Hochenau, E.C.H.** (1670-1721). Pietist/Lutheran. Evangelist. Germany.
**von Lodenstein, J.** (1620-1677). Pietist. Evangelist. Germany.
**von Regensburg, Berthold** (c1210-1272). Franciscan. Evangelist. Germany.
**von Weltz, Justinian** (1621-1668). Pietist. Missionary advocate. Germany.
**von Zinzendorf, N.L.** (1700-1760). Moravian. Missions advocate. Moravia.
**Waldo, Peter** (c1140-1218). Waldenses. Mendicant preacher. Gaul.
**Warneck, Gustav** (1834-1910). Lutheran. Missiologist. Germany.
**Watts, Isaac** (1674-1748). Anglican. Hymn writer. England.
**Webb, Mary** (1779-1861). Women's society. Founder. USA.
**Wesley, Charles** (1707-1788). Anglican. Hymn writer. UK.
**Wesley, John** (1703-1791). Anglican. Evangelist. UK.
**White, Ellen G.** (1827-1915). Seventh Day Adventist. Founder. USA.
**Whitefield, George** (1714-1770). Anglican. Evangelist. UK.
**Wigglesworth, Smith** (1859-1947). Pentecostal. Healing evangelist. USA.

Abolitionist WILBERFORCE        Missionary WILLIBRORD

**Wilberforce, William** (1759-1833). Anglican. Abolitionist. England.
**Wilder, Robert P.** (1863-1938). Presbyterian. Missions advocate. USA.
**Wilfrid** (634-709). Roman Catholic. Bishop. England.
**Wilkinson, G.H.** (1833-1907). Anglo-Catholic. Clergy. UK.
**William of Tripoli** (c1225-c1280). Dominican. Missionary. Palestine.
**Williams, Sir George** (1821-1905). Anglican. Founder of YMCA. UK.
**Williams, William** (1717-1791). Anglican. Revivalist. Wales.
**Willibrord** (658-739). Celtic. Missionary. Netherlands.
**Wilson, John** (1804-1875). Scottish Presbyterian. Missionary. India.
**Woodbury, W.E.** (c1890-c1950). Baptist. Printed Page evangelist. USA.
**Wycliffe, John** (c1330-1384). Anglican. Bible translator. England.

Missionary XAVIER        Reformer ZWINGLI

**Xavier, Francis** (1506-1552). Jesuit. Missionary. India/Japan.
**Xavier, Jerome** (1549-1617). Jesuit. Missionary. India.
**Yabalaha III** (c1245-1317). Nestorian. Bishop. Mongolia.
**Young, Brigham** (1801-1877). Mormon. Church leader. USA.
**Yun (Baron) Tchi-ho** (1865-1945). Methodist. Diplomat. Korea.
**Ziegenbalg, Bartholomew** (1682-1719). Lutheran. Mssionary. India.
**Zwemer, Samuel** (1867-1952). Presbyterian. Missionary. Arabia.
**Zwingli, Huldreich** (1484-1531). Protestant. Reformer. Switzerland.

# Who's who in the Christian world,
# AD 1970–AD 2000

Note: medium type = leaders in 1970-80, **bold** type = leaders in 1980-2000

Abainza, Bishop Estanilao Q., General Secretary, United Church of Christ in the Philippines (UCCP). Born 1923. Nationality: Philippines. United.

**Abastoflor Montero**, Edmundo Luis Flavio, Archbishop of La Paz, Conferencia Episcopal de Bolivia, President. Born 1943. Nationality: Bolivia. Roman Catholic.

Mother ABIODUN          Primate ADEJOBI

Abiodun, Most Rev. Mother Captain Christiana Emmanuel, Living Founder & Supreme Head, Sacred Order of Cherubim & Seraphim Society. Born 1908. Died c1980. Nationality: Nigeria. African Independent.

Abiola, Most Elder Apostle Adekunle Ayodele, General Superintendent & Supreme Head, Sacred Cherubim & Seraphim Society of Nigeria, Chairman-General, Nigerian Association of Aladura Churches (NAAC). Born 1899. Died c1980. Nationality: Nigeria. African Independent.

**Abraham**, Daniel, President, Federation of Evangelical Churches of India. Born c1950. Nationality: India. Protestant.

Adam, Right Rev. François Nestor, Bishop of Zion, President, Conférence des Evêques Suisses. Born 1903. Nationality: Switzerland. Roman Catholic.

Adejobi, Most Rev. Dr. Emmanuel Owoade Adeleke Sunday, Archbishop and Primate, Church of the Lord (Aladura), Chairman, Organization of African Independent Churches (OAIC). Born 1922. Died 1992. Nationality: Nigeria. African Independent.

Secretary ADEYEMO          Secretary ADOLF

Adeyemo, Rev. Dr. Tokunboh, General Secretary, Association of Evangelicals of Africa (AEA). Born 1944. Nationality: Nigeria. Evangelical (ECWA).

**Adhikary**, Rev. Subodh, General Secretary, National Council of Churches of Bangladesh. Nationality: Bangladesh. Protestant.

Adimou, Most Rev. Christopher, Archbishop of Cotonou, President, Conférence Episcopale du Benin. Born 1916. Nationality: Benin. Roman Catholic.

**Adolf**, Felipe, General Secretary, Council of Latin American Churches. Nationality: Brazil. Protestant.

**Agré**, Bernard, Archbishop of Abidjan. Born 1926. Nationality: Ivory Coast. Roman Catholic.

Aier, Rev. K. Imotemjen, General Secretary, Council of Baptist Churches in North East India. Nationality: India. Baptist.

Aires da Cruz, Most Rev. José, Archbishop & Second Primate (elected 1961), Igreja Católica Apostólica Brasileira (ICAB). Nationality: Brazil. Independent Catholic.

**Ajuoga**, Matthew, Founder, Church of Christ in Africa, Chairman, Organization of African Instituted Churches. Born 1925. Nationality: Kenya. Independent Anglican.

**Alexy II**, Patriarch of Moscow and All Russia. Born 1929. Nationality: Russia. Russian Orthodox.

Allin, Right Rev. John Maury, Presiding Bishop, Episcopal Church in the USA (ECUSA). Born 1921. Nationality: USA. Episcopalian (Anglican).

Allison, Rev. Canon R. G., General Secretary, United Christian Council in Israel (UCCI). Nationality: UK. Anglican.

Chairman AJUOGA          Patriarch ALEXY II

Alton, Bishop Ralph T., Secretary, Council of Bishops, United Methodist Church (USA). Nationality: USA. Methodist.

Alves, J. V., President, Christian Council of St Vincent. Nationality: St Vincent. Protestant.

**Alves**, João, Bishop of Coimbra, Conferencia Episcopal Portuguesa da Metropole, Presidente. Born 1925. Nationality: Portugal. Roman Catholic.

**Amos**, Barbara, Bishop, Faith Deliverance Christian Center (FDCC), Norfolk, VA. Born 1957. Nationality: USA. Independent pentecostal.

Andersen, Miss Birte, Administrative Secretary, Danish Missionary Council. Nationality: Denmark. Lutheran.

**Andoh**, Right Rev. Dominic Kodwo, Bishop of Accra, President, Ghana Bishops Conference. Born 1929. Nationality: Ghana. Roman Catholic.

Brother ANDREW          Pastor ANNACONDIA

**Andrew**, Brother, Founder and President Emeritus, Open Doors. Born 1928. Nationality: Netherlands. Reformed.

Andrews, Rev. James E., Stated Clerk, Presbyterian Church in the US. Nationality: USA. Presbyterian.

**Anguilé**, Most Rev. André F., Archbishop of Libreville, Président, Conférence Episcopale du Gabon. Born 1922. Nationality: Gabon. Roman Catholic.

**Annacondia**, Pastor Carlos, Pastor, Church of the Salvation message. Born 1944. Nationality: Argentina. Independent.

Ansa, Rev. Charles A., General Secretary, Christian Council of Ghana. Born 1922. Nationality: Ghana. Presbyterian.

Aponte Martinez, His Eminence Cardinal Luis, Archbishop of San Juan of Puerto Rico, Conferencia Episcopal Puertorique-a, Presidente. Born 1922. Nationality: Puerto Rico. Roman Catholic.

**Aram I**, Catholicos of Cilicia, Armenian Apostolic Church. Born 1940. Nationality: Armenia. Armenian Apostolic.

Arden, Most Rev. Donald Seymour, Archbishop of Central Africa, Secretary, Conference of Anglican Provinces in Africa (CAPA). Born 1916. Nationality: UK. Anglican.

Catholicos ARAM I          Cardinal ARINZE

**Arinze**, Cardinal Francis, President, Pontifical Council for Inter-Religious Dialogue. Born 1932. Nationality: Nigeria.

Roman Catholic.

Arlow, Rev. William J., Secretary, Irish Council of Churches. Nationality: Ireland. Protestant.

**Armstrong**, Herbert W., Founder, Worldwide Church of God. Born 1892. Died 1986. Nationality: USA. Marginal Christian.

**Arnold**, Canon John, President, Conference of European Churches. Nationality: Britain. Anglican.

Arrieta Villalobos, Right Rev. Roman, Bishop of Tilarán, Presidente, Conferencia Episcopal de Costa Rica (CECOR). Born 1924. Nationality: Costa Rica. Roman Catholic.

**Arrieta Villalobos**, Román, Archbishop of San José de Costa Rica, Conferencia Episcopal de Costa Rica (CECOR), President. Born 1924. Nationality: Costa Rica. Roman Catholic.

Arrupe, Rev. Fr. Pedro, SJ, General of Society of Jesus, Presidente, Unione dei Superiori Generali. Born 1907. Died 1991. Nationality: Spain (Basque). Roman Catholic.

Aru, Pastor Simeon, Chairman, Vanuatu Christian Council. Nationality: Vanuatu. Protestant.

**Athyal**, Saphir, Director of Missions and Evangelism, World Vision, Founder, Asia Theological Association. Born 1931. Nationality: India. Protestant.

President ARNOLD          Theologian AUGUST

**August**, Lydia. Nationality: South Africa. Independent.

**Avila del Aguila**, S.E.R. Mons. Jorge Mario, Bishop of Jalapa, Episcopal Conference of Guatemala, President. Born 1924. Nationality: Guatemala. Roman Catholic.

**Baba**, Panya, President, Evangelical Churches of West Africa, Director, Evangelical Missionary Society. Born 1932. Nationality: Nigeria. Evangelical.

Baccino, Right Rev. Luis, Bishop of San José de Mayo, Presidente, Conferencia Episcopal Uruguaya. Born 1905. Nationality: Uruguay. Roman Catholic.

**Backis**, Audrys Juozas, Archbishop of Vilnius, Episcopal Conference of Lithuania, President. Born 1937. Nationality: Latvia. Roman Catholic.

**Bada**, Pastor A.A., Head, Celestial Church of Christ (CCC). Born c1920. Nationality: Nigeria. Independent.

Baggio, His Eminence Cardinal Sabastiano, Prefect, Sacred Congregation for Bishops, Roman Curia (Vatican City). Born 1913. Nationality: Italy. Roman Catholic.

Bailey, Rev. C. Evans, Executive Secretary, Jamaica Council of Churches. Nationality: Jamaica. Protestant.

**Bakker**, Dr. Ineke, General Secretary, Council of Churches in the Netherlands. Nationality: Netherlands. Reformed.

Baksa, Pastor Arpad, Secretary, Ecumenical Council of Churches in Yugoslavia. Nationality: Yugoslavia. Orthodox.

**Baltasar Marcelino**, António, Bishop of Aveiro. Born 1930. Nationality: Portugal. Roman Catholic.

**Bam**, Ms. Brigalia Hlophe, General Secretary, South African Council of Churches (SACC). Protestant.

Bamrungtrakul, Right Rev. Robert Ratna, Bishop of Ratchaburi, President, Bishops' Conference of Thailand. Born 1916. Nationality: Thailand. Roman Catholic.

Barnes, D. J., Honorary Secretary, Fiji Council of Churches. Protestant.

**Barnes**, Brian James, OFM, Bishop of Aitape. Born 1933. Nationality: Australia. Roman Catholic.

Barrera y Rayes, Right Rev. Benjamin, MI, Bishop of Santa Ana, Presidente, Conferencia Episcopal del El Salvador. Born 1902. Nationality: El Salvador. Roman Catholic.

Bartha, Right Rev. Bishop (Fotiszteletü Püspök) Dr Tibor, Clerical President of General Synod (A Zsinat Lelkészi Elnöke)(since 1957), Reformed Church of Hungary. Born 1912. Nationality: Hungary. Reformed.

**Bartholomaios**, His All-Holiness, Archbishop of Constantinople, New Rome & Ecumenical Patriarch. Born 1940. Nationality: Turkey. Greek Orthodox.

Baselius Augen I, His Holiness Moran Mar, Catholicos of the East & Metropolitan of Malankara (since 1962). Born 1884. Nationality: India. Syrian Orthodox.

Batanian, see Ignatius Peter XVI.

**Batantu**, Barthélémy, Archbishop of Brazzaville. Born 1925. Nationality: Congo. Roman Catholic.

Beach, Dr. Bert Beverly, Secretary, Conference of Secretaries of Christian World Communion. Born 1928. Nationality: USA. Seventh-day Adventist.

**Begu**, Eugen, General Secretary, Albanian Evangelical Alliance. Born c1960. Nationality: Albania. Evangelical.

Bekish, J., see Ireney.

Bello, Rev. I. B., Secretary, Evangelical Churches of West Africa (ECWA). Nationality: Nigeria. Evangelical.

Beltritti, His Beatitude Giacoma, Latin Patriarch of Jerusalem, Conférence des Evêques Latins dans les Régions Arabes (CELRA), Président. Born 1910. Nationality: Italy. Roman Catholic.

Benech, Carlos Enrique, Executive Secretary, Federación de Iglesias Evangélicas del Uruguay (FIEU). Nationality: Uruguay. Protestant.

Benediktos I (Vassilios Papadopoulos), His Holiness (or His Beatitude), Patriarch of the Holy City of Jerusalem & All Palestine. Born 1892. Nationality: Israel/Greece. Greek Orthodox.

Bengsch, His Eminence Cardinal Alfred, Archbishop of Berlin, President, Berliner Ordinarienkonferenz (HQ German Democratic Republic). Born 1921. Nationality: German Democratic Republic. Roman Catholic.

Benítez Avalos, Right Rev. Felipe Santiago, Bishop of Villarríca, Presidente, Conferencia Episcopal Paraguaya. Born 1926. Nationality: Paraguay. Roman Catholic.

Benítez Fonturvel, Most Rev. Críspulo, Archbishop of Barquisimeto, Presidente, Conferencia Episcopal de Venezuela. Born 1905. Nationality: Venezuela. Roman Catholic.

Beras Rojas, Most Rev. Octavio Antonio, Archbishop of Santo Domingo, Presidente, Conferencia del Episcopado Dominicano. Born 1906. Nationality: Dominican Republic. Roman Catholic.

**Bertuzzi**, Rev. Federico, Executive Secretary, COMIBAM, Founder & Director, Misiones Mundiales. Born 1948. Nationality: Argentina. Evangelical.

Patriarch BARTHOLOMAIOS    Moderator BEST

**Best**, Marian, Moderator, United Church of Canada. Nationality: Canada. Protestant.

**Bhengu**, Nicholas, Founder, Assemblies of God/Back to God Movement. Born 1909. Died 1986. Nationality: South Africa. Independent.

Biayenda, His Eminence Cardinal Emile, Archbishop of Brazzaville, President, Conference Episcopale du Congo (Brazzaville). Born 1927. Murdered 1977. Nationality: Congo. Roman Catholic.

**Bidawid**, S.B. Raphaël I., Patriarch of Babylon of the Chaldeans, Riunione Interrituale Dei Vescovi Dell'Iraq, Head of the Chaldean "Della Chiesa" Synod. Nationality: Iraq. Roman Catholic.

**Biffi**, Cardinal Giacomo, Archbishop of Bologna. Born 1928. Nationality: Italy. Roman Catholic.

**Bille**, S.E.R. Mons. Louis Marie, Archbishop of Aix, Conference Episcopale Francaise, President. Born 1938. Nationality: France. Roman Catholic.

**Bitsoane**, Evaristus Thatho, Bishop of Qacha's Nek, Lesotho Catholics Bishops Conference, President. Born 1938. Nationality: Lesotho. Roman Catholic.

Bjerno, Aage, President, Evangelical Alliance of Denmark. Nationality: Denmark. Protestant.

Blanch, Most Rev. & Right Hon. Stuart Yarworth, Archbishop of York & Primate of England & Metropolitan. Born 1918. Nationality: UK. Anglican.

Evangelist BHENGU    Director BODNAR

**Bodnar**, Mikhael, Director, Interconfessional Bible Society of Moldava. Nationality: Moldavia. Protestant.

Bokeleale, Rev. Dr. Itofo Bokambanza, Président, Eglise du Christ au Zaïare (ECZ). Born 1919. Nationality: Zaire. Disciples.

**Bonnke**, Reinhard, Evangelist, Nationality: Germany. Pentecostal.

---

**Boonstra**, Juan S., Radio speaker and writer, Christian Reformed Church. Born 1926. Nationality: Argentina. Reformed.

**Bordeaux**, Michael A., Founder and Director, Keston College. Born 1934. Nationality: England. Anglican.

**Borgomeo**, Rev. Pasquale P., Director, Vatican Radio. Nationality: Italy. Roman Catholic.

**Bosch**, Dr. David J., Professor of Missiology, University of South Africa. Born 1929. Died 1992. Nationality: South Africa. Reformed.

Boseto, Rev. Leslie, Moderator, United Church in Papua New Guinea & the Solomon Islands. Born 1933. Nationality: Papua New Guinea. United.

**Bovone**, Ser. Mons. Alberto, Pro Prefect, Sacred Congregation for the Causes of Saints, Roman Curia (Vatican City). Born 1922. Nationality: Italy. Roman Catholic.

**Boyle**, Leonard Anthony, Bishop of Dunedin, New Zealand Episcopal Conference, President. Born 1930. Nationality: New Zealand. Roman Catholic.

**Brady**, Most Rev. Seán B., Archbishop of Armagh, Episcopal Conference of Ireland, President. Born 1939. Nationality: Ireland. Roman Catholic.

Evangelist BONNKE    Founder BRIGHT

Bright, Dr. William R., Founder and President, Campus Crusade for Christ International (CCCI). Born 1921. Nationality: USA. Presbyterian.

Brosnanhan, Most Rev. Thomas J, CSSp, Archbishop of Freetown and Bo, President, Inter-territorial Episcopal Conference of Gambia, Liberia and Sierra Leone. Born 1905. Nationality: Sierra Leone. Roman Catholic.

Brown, General, Eleventh General of the Salvation Army. Born 1913. Nationality: Canada. Salvationist.

**Brunner**, Norbert, Bishop of Sion, Sitten. Born 1942. Nationality: Switzerland. Roman Catholic.

**Bryce**, Bishop Jabez, President, Fiji Council of Churches. Anglican.

**Bududira**, Bernard, Bishop of Bururi, Conférence des Evêques Catholiques du Burundi (CECAB), President. Born 1934. Nationality: Burundi. Roman Catholic.

Burnett, Most Rev. Bill Bendyshe, Archbishop of Cape Town & Metropolitan of South Africa, Church of the Province of the Province of South Africa (CPSA). Born 1917. Nationality: South Africa. Anglican.

**Burrows**, Eva Evelyn, General, Salvation Army. Born 1929. Retired. Nationality: Australia.

**Bush**, Luis, International Director, AD 2000 and Beyond Movement, Inc. Born 1946. Nationality: Argentina. Protestant.

**Butelezi**, Peter Fanyana John, O.M.I., Archbishop of Bloemfontein. Born 1930. Nationality: South Africa. Roman Catholic.

Buttler, Pastor P. G., Secretary, Deutscher Evangelischer Missions-Rat. Nationality: FR Germany. Protestant.

Bychkov, Rev. Alexei M., General Secretary, Union of Evangelical Christians-Baptists of USSR (AUCECB). Born 1928. Nationality: USSR. Baptist.

**Cabrera Ovalle**, Julio Edgar, Bishop of Santa Cruz del Quiché. Born 1939. Nationality: Guatemala. Roman Catholic.

**Calvet**, Michael-Marie-Bernard, Archbishop of Nouméa, Conferentia Episcopalis fPacifici (C.E.PAC.), President. Born 1944. Nationality: France. Roman Catholic.

Campbell, Rev. Robert C., General Secretary, American Baptist Churches in the USA. Nationality: USA. Baptist.

Campi, Rev. Dr. Emidio, General Secretary, World Student Christian Federation (WSCF). Born 1943. Nationality: Italy. Waldensian.

Papal Preacher CANTALAMESSA    Director CAPPELLO

**Cantalamessa OFM Cap.**, Raniero, Papal Preacher. Nationality: Italy. Roman Catholic.

**Cappello**, Mario, International Director, International

---

Catholic Programme of Evangelization. Nationality: Malta. Roman Catholic.

**Cardoso Sobrinho, O.C.**, José, Archbishop of Olinda & Recife. Born 1933. Nationality: Brazil. Roman Catholic.

**Carey**, Dr. George L., Archbishop of Canterbury. Born 1935. Nationality: Britain. Anglican.

Secretary CARINO    Cardinal CASSIDY

**Carino**, Feliciano, General Secretary, Christian Conference of Asia. Born 1940. Protestant.

Carr, Rev. Canon Burgess, General Secretary, All Africa Conference of Churches (AACC) (until 1979). Born 1935. Nationality: Liberia. Episcopalian.

Carter, Most Rev. Samuel Emmanuel, SJ, Archbishop of Kingston in Jamaica, President, Antilles Episcopal Conference (AEC). Born 1919. Nationality: Jamaica. Roman Catholic.

**Casaroli**, Cardinal Agostino, Former Secretary of State (1979-1990), Holy See. Born 1914. Died 1998. Nationality: Italy, Holy See. Roman Catholic.

**Cassidy**, Michael, Founder, African Enterprise. Born 1936. Nationality: South Africa. Anglican.

**Cassidy**, Cardinal Edward Idris, President, Pontifical Council for Promoting Christian Unity. Born 1924. Nationality: Australia. Roman Catholic.

**Castrillón**, S.E.R. Mons. Hoyos Dario, Pro Prefect, Sacred Congregation for the Clergy, Roman Curia (Vatican City). Born 1929. Nationality: Colombia. Roman Catholic.

**Castro**, Dr. Emilio, General Secretary, World Council of Churches, Director, WCC Commission on World Mission and Evangelism. Born 1927. Nationality: Uruguay. Evangelical Methodist.

Castrén, Miss Inga-Brita, General Secretary, Ecumenical Council of Finland. Born 1919. Nationality: Finland. Lutheran.

**Cedeño Delgado**, José Dimas, Archbishop of Panama, Conferencia Episcopal de Panama (CEP), President. Born 1933. Nationality: Panama. Roman Catholic.

Evangelist CERULLO    Pastor CHAREONWONGSAK

**Cerullo**, Morris, President, World Evangelism. Nationality: USA. Assemblies of God.

**Chareonwongsak**, Dr. Kriengsak, Founder, Hope of Bangkok Church. Nationality: Thailand. Independent.

Cheikho, see Paul II.

**Cheong Jin-Suk**, Nicholas, Bishop of Ch'ongju, Catholic Conference of Korea, President. Born 1931. Nationality: South Korea. Roman Catholic.

Chiona, Most Rev. James, Archbishop of Blantyre. Born 1924. Nationality: Malawi. Roman Catholic.

**Chirivella Varela**, Tulio Manuel, Archbishop of Barquisimeto, Conferencia Episcopal de Venezuela, Presidente. Born 1932. Nationality: Venezuela. Roman Catholic.

**Cho**, Dr. David Yonggi, Pastor, Full Gospel Central Church.

Pastor CHO    Archbishop CHRYSOSTOMOS

Born 1936. Nationality: South Korea. Full Gospel pentecostal.
**Christodoulos of Dimitriada**, Archbishop of Athens and All Greece, Greek Orthodox Church. Born 1939. Nationality: Greece. Greek Orthodox.
**Chrysostomos**, Archbishop of Cyprus. Born 1940. Nationality: Cyprus. Greek Orthodox.
**Chuabsamai**, John Bosco Manat, Bishop of Ratchaburi. Born 1935. Nationality: Thailand. Roman Catholic.
**Chung Hoan Ting**, S.E.R. Mons. Peter, Archbishop of Kuching, Catholic Bishops Conference of Malaysia, Singapore and Brunei, President. Born 1928. Nationality: Malaysia. Roman Catholic.
**Clancy**, Cardinal Edward Bede, Archbishop of Sydney, Australian Catholic Bishops' Conference, President. Born 1923. Nationality: Australia. Roman Catholic.
**Clarke**, Edgerton Roland, Archbishop of Kingston in Jamaica. Born 1929. Nationality: Jamaica. Roman Catholic.
Class, Bishop Helmut, Landesbischof, Evangelische Landeskirche in Württemberg, Vorsitzender, Rat der Evangelischen Kirche in Deutschland (Chairman, EKD Council of Bishops). Nationality: FR Germany. Protestant.
**Clements**, Rev. Dr Keith W., General Secretary, Conference of European Churches. Born 1943. Nationality: Britain. Baptist.
Coggan, Most Rev. & Right Hon. Frederick Donald, Archbishop of Canterbury and Primate of All England (retired 1980). Born 1909. Nationality: Britain. Anglican.
Coggins, Dr. Wade T., Executive Director, Evangelical Foreign Missions Association (EFMA). Nationality: USA. Protestant.
**Colson**, Charles W., Chairman of the Board, Prison Fellowship (founded by him in 1976). Nationality: USA. Protestant.
Comba, Rev. Pastor Aldo, Secretary, Federazione delle Chiese Evangeliche in Italia (FCEI). Born 1924. Nationality: Italy. Protestant.
**Compaoré**, Jean-Marie Untaani, Archbishop of Ouagadougou. Born 1933. Nationality: Burkina Faso. Roman Catholic.
**Constant**, Right Rev. Emmanuel, Bishop of Les Gonaïves, Président, Conférence Episcopale de Haiti. Born 1928. Nationality: Haiti. Roman Catholic.
Conway, His Eminence Cardinal William, Archbishop of Armagh, Episcopal Conference of Ireland, President. Born 1913. Died 1977. Nationality: Ireland. Roman Catholic.
Cooray, His Eminence Cardinal Thomas B., OMI, Archbishop of Colombo, President, Bishops' Conference of Sri Lanka. Born 1901. Nationality: Sri Lanka. Roman Catholic.
Cordeiro, His Eminence Cardinal Joseph, Archbishop of Karachi, President, Pakistan Episcopal Conference. Born 1918. Died Pakistan. Nationality: Pakistan. Roman Catholic.
**Couture**, Maurice, Archbishop of Quebec. Born 1926. Nationality: Canada. Roman Catholic.
**Crimmins**, Ms. Judith, National Administrator, Conference of Churches in Aotearoa New Zealand. Protestant.
Cruz, Rev. Orestes Gonzales, Executive Secretary, Consejo de Iglesias Evangélicas de Cuba. Nationality: Cuba. Protestant.
**Cruz**, Oscar V., Archbishop of Lingayen-Dagupan, Catholic Bishops' Conference of the Philippines, President. Born 1934. Nationality: Philippines. Roman Catholic.
Cunha, Rev. Ireneu da Silva, General Secretary, Conselho Português de Igrejas Cristãs. Nationality: Portugal. Protestant.
Câmara, see Pessoa Câmara.
D'Almeida Trindade, Right Rev. Manuel, Bishop of Aveiro, Presidente, Conferência Episcopal Portuguesa da Metrópole. Born 1918. Nationality: Portugal. Roman Catholic.
Dalmais, Most Rev. Paul, SJ, Archbishop of N'Djamena, Président, Association des Conférences Episcopales du Congo, de la République Centrafricaine, et du Tchad (ACECCT). Born 1917. Nationality: Chad. Roman Catholic.
Damaris, Rev. Stephanus, Secretary General, Indonesia Evangelical Fellowship. Nationality: Indonesia. Protestant.
Damien, Most Rev., Archbishop of Tirana. Died 1973. Nationality: Albania. Greek Orthodox.
**Dankó**, László, Archbishop of Kalocsa-Kecskemét. Born 1939. Nationality: Hungary. Roman Catholic.

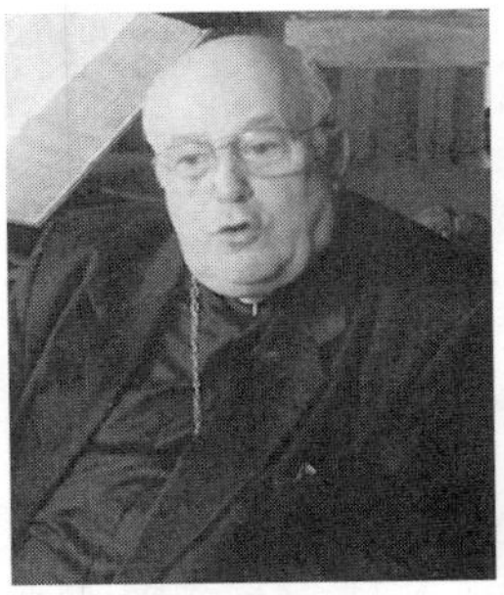
Cardinal DANNEELS

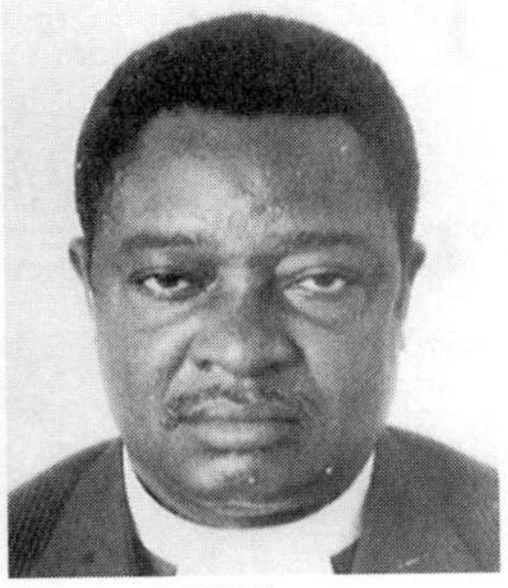
Secretary DARTEY

**Danneels**, Cardinal Godfried, Archbishop of Brussels, Conference Episcopale de Belgique, President. Born 1933. Nationality: Belgium. Roman Catholic.
**Darmaatmadja**, Cardinal Julius Riyadi, Archbishop of Jakarta, Konperensi Waligereja Indonesia (KWI), President. Born 1934. Nationality: Indonesia. Roman Catholic.
Darmojuwono, His Eminence Cardinal Justinus, Archbishop of Semarang, President, General Conference of Ordinaries of Indonesia (MAWI). Born 1914. Nationality: Indonesia. Roman Catholic.
**Dartey**, David A., General Secretary, Christian Council of Ghana. Nationality: Ghana. Protestant.
David V (Gregory Sidamonidze), His Beatitude, Archbishop of Mtzkheta, Metropolitan of Tiflis and Catholicos-Patriarch of All Georgia. Born 1896. Died 1977. Nationality: USSR. Georgian Orthodox.
Davies, J. E. (Ted), Honorary Secretary, New Zealand Evangelical Alliance. Nationality: New Zealand. Protestant.
Davies, Rev. Meiron Lloyd, General Secretary, Council of Churches for Wales. Nationality: UK. Protestant.
Davies, Mrs. P. W., Secretary, Isle of Man Council of Churches. Nationality: UK. Protestant.
Daws, Rev. C. K., President General, Methodist Church of Australia. Nationality: Australia. Methodist.
de Mello Silva, Pastor Manoel, President, Evangelical Pentecostal Church 'Brazil for Christ' (OBPC). Born 1929. Nationality: Brazil. Indigenous pentecostal.
de Run, Rev. Lloyd B., Chairman, National Evangelical Fellowship of Malaysia. Nationality: Malaysia. Evangelical.
**de Souza**, Isidore, Archbishop of Cotonou. Born 1934. Nationality: Benin. Roman Catholic.
Demetrios I (Dimitrios Papadopoulos), His All-Holiness, Archbishop of Constantinople, New Rome & Ecumenical Patriarch (elected 1971). Born 1914. Nationality: Turkey. Greek Orthodox.
Deng, Right Rev. Pio Yukwan, Bishop of Malakal, President, Sudan Episcopal Conference. Nationality: Sudan. Roman Catholic.
Denisenko, see Filaret.
Denny, Dr. Robert S., General Secretary, Baptist World Alliance (BWA). Nationality: USA. Baptist.

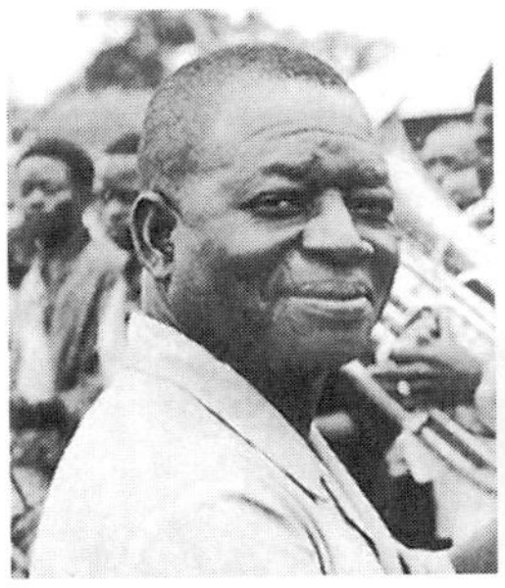
Prophet DIANGIENDA

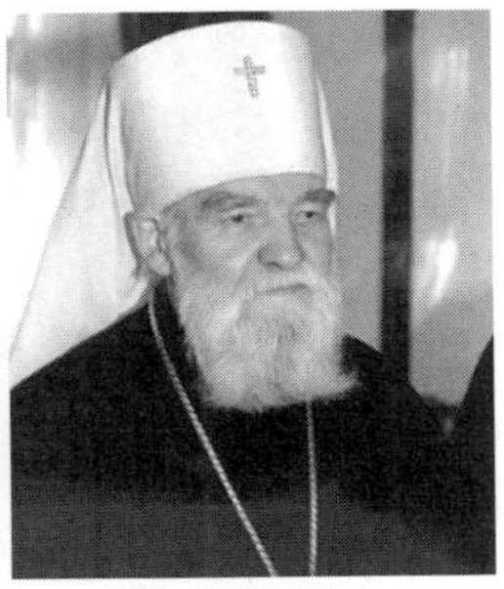
Metropolitan DOROTEY

Diangienda, His Eminence Joseph Ku Ntima, Chef Spirituel, Eglise de Jésus-Christ sur la Terre par le Prophète Simon Kimbangu (EJCSK). Born 1918. Died 1995. Nationality: Zaire. African Independent.
Dinkha IV, His Holiness Mar (Dinkha Khananyia), High Catholicos Patriarch of the East, Ancient Assyrian Church of the East, elected 1977. Born 1936. Nationality: Iran. Assyrian Orthodox.
**do Nascimento**, Cardinal Alexandre, Archbishop of Luanda, Conferencia Episcopal de Angola e São Tomé (CEAST), President. Born 1925. Nationality: Angola. Roman Catholic.
Dombrava, Rev. Mother Florina Jana, Mother Superior, Pasarea Monastery, Romanian Orthodox Church. Born 1930. Nationality: Romania. Orthodox.
Domínguez y Rodriguez, Right Rev. José Maximino Eusebio, Bishop of Matanzas, Presidente, Conferencia Episcopal de Cuba. Born 1915. Nationality: Cuba. Roman Catholic.
**Dorotey (Filipp)**, His Beatitude, Metropolitan of Prague & All Czechoslovakia. Born 1913. Nationality: Czechoslovakia. Greek Orthodox.
Dositey (Stoykovsky), His Beatitude, Archbishop of Ochrid & Macedonia, Metropolitan of the Macedonian Orthodox Church. Born 1906. Nationality: Macedonia. Orthodox.
Dosseh Anyron, Most Rev. Robert, Archbishop of Lomé, Président, Conférence Plénière des Ordinaires de l'Afrique Occidentale, Président, Conférence Episcopale du Togo. Born 1925. Nationality: Togo. Roman Catholic.
**Douglass**, Dr. Jane Dempsey, President, World Alliance of Reformed Churches. Nationality: USA. Presbyterian.

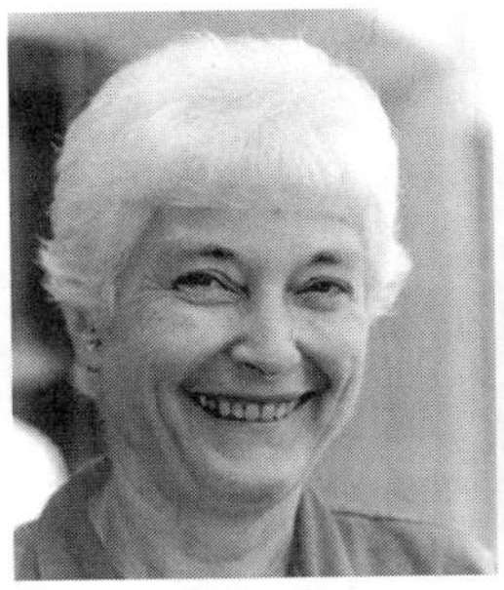
President DOUGLASS

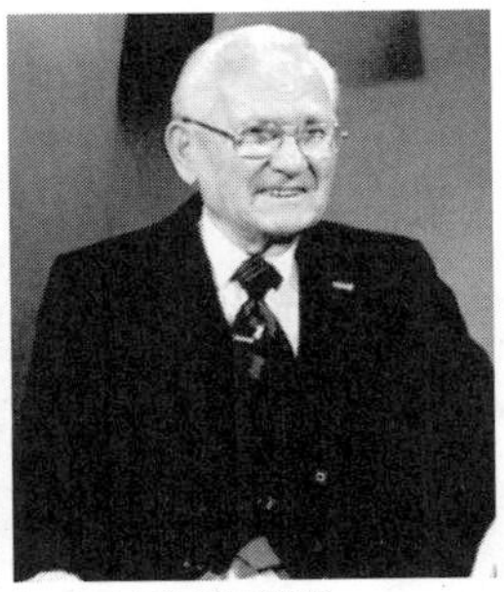
Apologist DU PLESSIS

Du Plessis, Rev. David Johannes, Ecumenical Pentecostal apologist. Born 1905. Nationality: USA. Assemblies of God.
Dube, Rev. Joseph James, Secretary, Christian Apostolic Church in Zion, Secretary, League of Independent Churches of Swaziland. Born 1915. Nationality: Swaziland. African Independent.

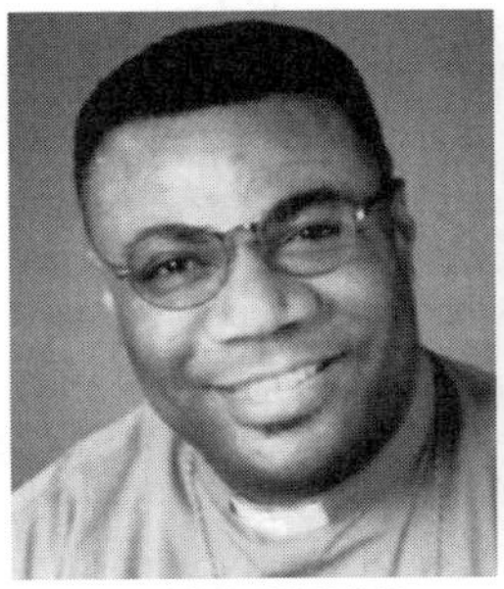
Pastor DUNCAN-WILLIAMS

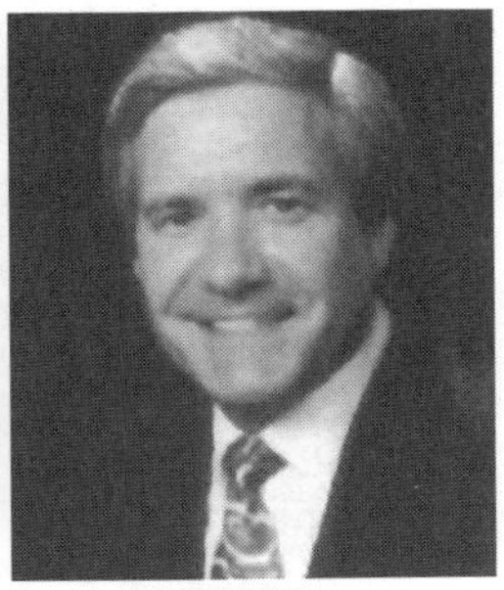
President EASTMAN

**Duncan-Williams**, Nicholas, Charismatic pastor, ACTION. Nationality: Ghana. Independent.
Dutta, Dilip Kumar, Executive Secretary, National Council of Churches of Bangladesh. Born 1942. Nationality: Bangladesh. Baptist.
Dutton, Rev. Denis C., General Secretary, Council of Churches of Malaysia. Protestant.
Duval, His Eminence Cardinal Léon-Etienne, Archbishop of Algiers, Président, Conférence Episcopale d'Afrique du Nord. Born 1903. Nationality: Algeria. Roman Catholic.
Döpfner, His Eminence Cardinal Julius, Archbishop of Munich and Friesing, President, Deutsche Bischofskonferenz, and Bayerische Bischofskonferenz. Born 1913. Nationality: FR Germany. Roman Catholic.
**Eastman**, Dick, President, Every Home for Christ. Nationality: USA. Evangelical.
Echeverria Ruiz, Most Rev. Bernardino, OFM, Archbishop of Guayaquil, Presidente, Conferencia Episcopal Ecuatoriana. Born 1912. Nationality: Ecuador. Roman Catholic.
Ekandem, His Eminence Cardinal Dominic, Bishop of Ikot Ekpene, President, National Episcopal Conference of Nigeria. Born 1917. Nationality: Nigeria. Roman Catholic.
Elias IV (Mo'awad), His Holiness (or His Beatitude), Patriarch of Antioch and All the East. Born 1914. Died 1979. Nationality: Syria. Greek Orthodox.
Elisha (Yeghishe II (Derderian), His Beatitude, Armenian Patriarch of Jerusalem. Born 1910. Armenian Apostolic.
Ellison, Rev. Father R., Secretary, Gambia Christian Council. Anglican.
**Endo**, Shusako, World-renowned Japanese novelist. Born 1923. Died 1996. Nationality: Japan. Catholic.
Engel, Rev. Frank Graham, General Secretary, Australian Council of Churches (ACC). Nationality: Australia. Presbyterian.

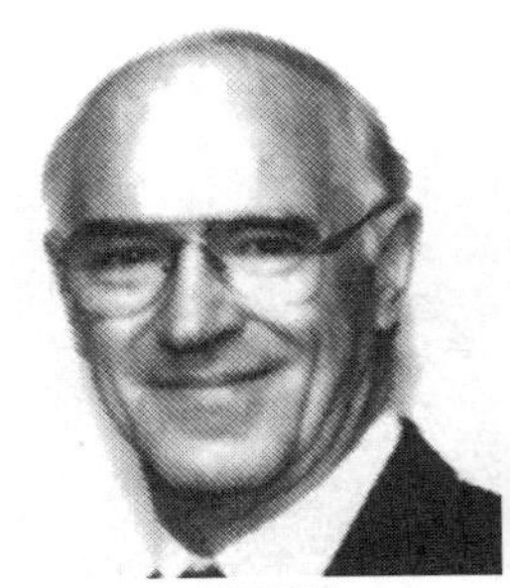
Chairperson ENGLISH

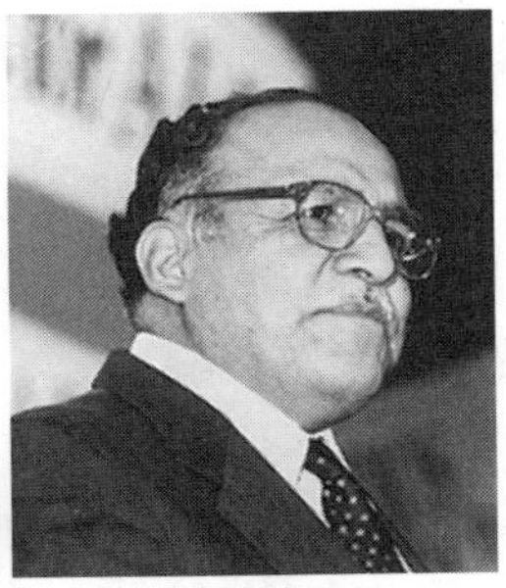
President ESCOBAR

**English**, Donald, Vice-Chairperson, World Methodist Council. Born 1940. Nationality: Britain. Methodist.
Enrique y Tarancón, His Eminence Cardinal Vicente, Archbishop of Madrid, Presidente, Conferencia Episcopal Española. Born 1907. Nationality: Spain. Roman Catholic.
**Escobar**, Samuel, President, United Bible Societies, Born 1934. Nationality: Peru. Baptist.
Etchegaray, Cardinal Roger, Archbishop of Marseilles, President, Consilium Conferentiarum Episcopalium Europae (CCEE). President, Pontifical Council for Justice and Peace. Born 1922. Nationality: France. Roman Catholic.

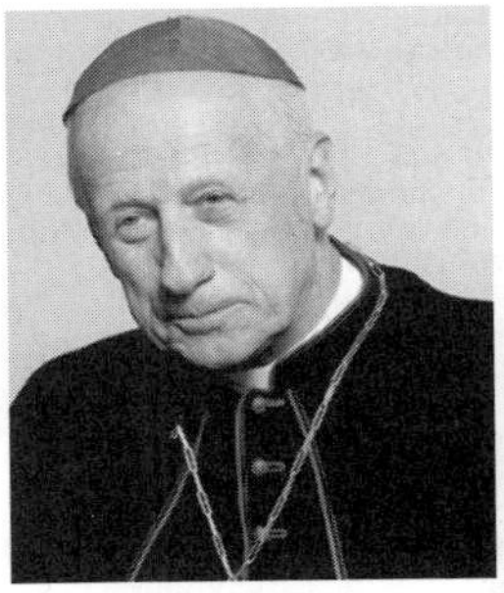
Cardinal ETCHEGARAY

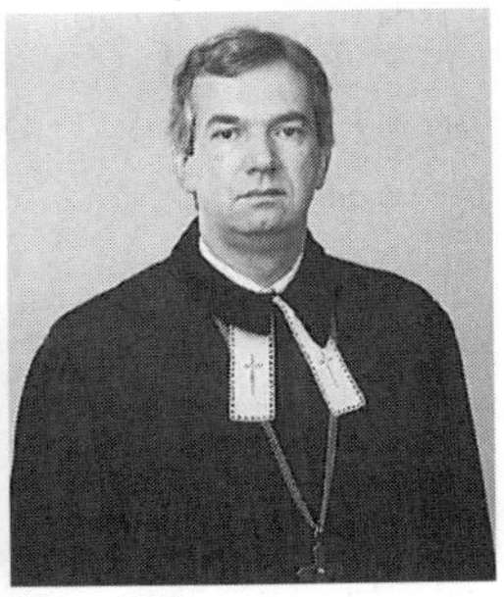
Bishop FILO

**Etokudoh**, Camillus Archibong, Bishop of Ikot Ekpene. Born 1949. Nationality: Nigeria. Roman Catholic.

**Etsou-Nzabi-Bamungwabi**, Cardinal Frédéric, Archbishop of Kinshasa. Born 1930. Nationality: Zaire. Roman Catholic.

Faichney, Right Rev. N., Moderator-General, Presbyterian Church of Australia. Nationality: Australia. Presbyterian.

**Felix**, Kelvin Edward, Archbishop of Castries, Antilles Episcopal Conference (AEC), President. Born 1933. Nationality: Jamaica. Roman Catholic.

Feller, A. E., Secretary General, Fédération des Eglises Protestantes de la Suisse (FEPS). Nationality: Switzerland. Reformed.

Fen, Li Shih, President, China Evangelical Fellowship, Taiwan. Nationality: Taiwan. Protestant.

**Fernando**, Nicholas Marcus, Archbishop of Colombo. Born 1932. Nationality: Sri Lanka. Roman Catholic.

**Fernando**, Joseph Vianney, Bishop of Kandy, Bishops' Conference of Sri Lanka, President. Born 1942. Nationality: Sri Lanka. Roman Catholic.

Ferraz, Rev. José Coelho, Executive Secretary, Confederaçâo Evangélica do Brasil. Died 1998. Nationality: Brazil.

Fick, Rev. Ulrich, General Secretary, United Bible Societies (UBS). Born 1922. Nationality: FR Germany. Lutheran.

Filaret (Michael Antonovic Denisenko), Exarch of the Ukraine, Archbishop of Kiev and Galicia, Russian Orthodox Church. Born 1929. Nationality: Ukraine. Orthodox.

Filaret (Voznessenskiy), His Eminence, Metropolitan of East America and New York, Primate, Russian Orthodox Church Outside of Russia. Born 1902. Nationality: USA. Russian Orthodox.

**Filo**, Bishop Julius, President, Ecumenical Council of Churches in the Slovak Republic. Born 1940. Nationality: Slovakia. Lutheran.

Fiolet, Dr. H. A. H., Secretary, Council of Churches in the Netherlands. Nationality: Netherlands. Reformed.

**Fischer**, Mr. Jean, General Secretary, Conference of European Churches (CEC). Born 1934. Nationality: Switzerland. Swiss Reformed.

Fitzgerald, Most Rev. Joseph P., OMI, Archbishop of Bloemfontein, President (1975), Southern Africa Catholic Bishops' Conference. Born 1914. Nationality: South Africa. Roman Catholic.

Forck, Rev. Dr. Gottfried, General Superintendent, Federation of Evangelical Churches in the GDR. Born 1923. Nationality: German Democratic Republic. Lutheran.

**Ford**, Louis Henry, Bishop, Church of God in Christ. Born 1916. Nationality: USA. Church of God in Christ. Independent.

Fortier, Most Rev. Jean-Marie, Archbishop of Sherbrooke, President, Canadian Catholic Conference (CCC). Born 1920. Nationality: Canada. Roman Catholic.

Director FOX            Prefect GANTIN

**Fox**, N. Eddie, World Director, Methodist Evangelism. Born 1945. Methodist.

**Fragasso, A.S.C.**, Sr. Giuseppina, President, Unione Internazionale delle Superiore Generali (UISG). Nationality: Italy. Roman Catholic.

Franklin, Fredrik, Secretary General, World Alliance of YMCAs. Protestant.

**Franz**, Frederick, President, Watchtower Bible and Tract Society (1977-1992). Born 1894. Died 1992. Nationality: USA. Jehovah's Witnesses.

Fraser, Rev. Wilfred, Secretary, Guyana Council of Churches. Nationality: Guyana. Protestant.

Freeman, His Eminence Cardinal James Darcy, Archbishop of Sydney, President, Australian Episcopal Conference. Born 1907. Nationality: Australia. Roman Catholic.

Frizen, Edwin L., Jr., Executive Director, Interdenominational Foreign Mission Association (IFMA). Nationality: USA. Evangelical.

**Fóscolos**, S.E.R. Mons. Nikolaos, Archbishop of Athens, President. Born 1936. Nationality: Greece. Roman Catholic.

Ga, Right Rev. Macario V., Obispo Maximo, Iglesia Filipina Independiente (Philippine Independent Church). Nationality: Philippines. Independent Catholic.

Gaillard, Yves, Secretary, Swiss Evangelical Fellowship. Nationality: Switzerland. Evangelical.

**Galimberti di Vietri**, Pablo Jaime, Bishop of San José de Mayo. Born 1941. Nationality: Uruguay. Roman Catholic.

Galvin, Right Rev. Anthony Dénis, MHM, Vicar Apostolic of Miri, President, Catholic Bishops' Conference of Malaysia-Singapore. Born 1919. Nationality: Roman Catholic.

**Ganda**, Joseph Henry, Archbishop of Freetown and Bo. Born 1932. Nationality: Sierra Leone. Roman Catholic.

Ganguli, Most Rev. Theotonius A., CSC, Archbishop of Dacca, President, Catholic Bishops' Conference of Bangladesh. Born 1920. Nationality: Bangladesh. Roman

Catholic.

**Gantin**, Cardinal Bernardin, Prefect, Sacred Congregation for Bishops, Roman Curia (Vatican City). Born 1922. Nationality: Benin. Roman Catholic.

Garrone, His Eminence Cardinal Gabriel-Marie, Prefect, Sacred Congregation for Catholic Education, Roman Curia (Vatican City). Born 1901. Nationality: Holy See. Roman Catholic.

Gatu, Rev. John G., Chairman, All Africa Conference of Churches (AACC). Born 1925. Nationality: Kenya. Presbyterian.

**Gaumond**, André, Archbishop of Sherbrooke. Born 1936. Nationality: Canada. Roman Catholic.

Gaxiola, Rev. Manuel J., Bishop, Apostolic Church of the Faith in Christ Jesus. Nationality: Mexico. Independent Oneness.

**Gayot**, François, S.M.M. Archbishop of Cap-Haïtien, Conference Episcopale de Haiti, President. Born 1927. Nationality: Haiti. Roman Catholic.

Gegeyo, Rev. Kingsley, Executive Secretary, Melanesian Council of Churches. Nationality: Papau New Guinea. Protestant.

Genheimer, Rev. Don, Chairman, Association of Evangelicals of South Africa. Nationality: South Africa. Evangelical.

Gerardi, Conedera, Right Rev. Juan, Bishop of Santa Cruz del Quiché, Presidente, Conferencia Episcopal de Guatemala. Born 1922. Nationality: Guatemala. Roman Catholic.

German (Djorich), His Holiness, Archbishop of Pec, Metropolitan of Belgrade & Karlovitz, Patriarch of Serbia. Born 1899. Nationality: Yugoslavia. Serbian Orthodox.

**Ghattas**, S.B. Stéphanos II, CM, Coptic Patriarch of Alexandria, Synod della Chiesa Copta Catholic, Head, Assembly della Gerarchia Cattolica D'Egitto, President. Born 1920. Nationality: Egypt. Roman Catholic.

Secretary GIBBENS            Secretary GILL

**Gibbens**, Altaa, Executive Secretary, Mongolian Bible Society. Nationality: Mongolia. Independent.

Gill, Rev. William, Chairman, Evangelical Fellowship of Pakistan. Nationality: Pakistan. Evangelical.

**Gill**, Rev. David, General Secretary, National Council of Churches in Australia. Nationality: Australia. Protestant.

Gilson-Rome, Mme C., Secretary, Fédération des Eglises Protestantes de Belgique. Nationality: Belgium. Protestant.

**Giraldo Jaramillo**, S.E.R. Mons Alberto, Archbishop of Popayán, Conferencia Episcopal de Colombia, President. Born 1934. Nationality: Colombia. Roman Catholic.

Gjerding, Uffe, General Secretary, Ecumenical Council of Denmark. Nationality: Denmark. Lutheran.

**Glazemaker**, A.J., Archbishop of Utrecht, Old Catholic Church. Born 1935. Nationality: Netherlands. Old Catholic.

**Glemp**, Cardinal Józef, Archbishop of Warsaw, Polish Episcopal Conference, President. Born 1929. Nationality: Poland. Roman Catholic.

Goncalves, Most Rev. Raul Nicolau, Archbishop of Goa & Damao, Patriarch of the East Indies. Born 1927. Nationality: India. Roman Catholic.

Archbishop GLAZEMAKER            Cardinal GONG

**Gong**, Cardinal Pin-Mei Ignatius, Archbishop of Shanghai. Born 1901. Nationality: China. Roman Catholic.

**Gonsalves**, Raul Nicolau, Archbishop of Goa & Damao, Patriarch of E. Indies. Born 1927. Nationality: India. Roman Catholic.

Gonzi, Most Rev. Michael, Archbishop of Malta, Maltese Episcopal Conference, President. Born 1885. Nationality: Malta. Roman Catholic.

Gottschald, Rev. K., President, Evangelical Federation of Brazil. Nationality: Brazil. Evangelical.

**Governo**, Bernardo Felipe, Bishop of Quelimone. Born 1939. Nationality: Mozambique. Roman Catholic.

**Gowans**, John, General (from 1999), Salvation Army. Born 1935. Nationality: Britain. Salvationist.

Evangelist GRAHAM            Founder GUTI

Graham, Rev. Dr. William Frankin (Billy), World evangelist. Born 1918. Nationality: USA. Southern Baptist.

Gray, His Eminence Cardinal Gordon J., Archbishop of St Andrews and Edinburgh, President, Bishops' Conference of Scotland. Born 1910. Nationality: UK. Roman Catholic.

Greet, Rev. Kenneth Gerald, Secretary of the Conference (since 1971), Methodist Church of Great Britain. Nationality: UK. Methodist.

Gregory, Archbishop-Abbot, Church of Sinai, St Catherine's Monastery, Mount Sinai (Egypt). Greek Orthodox.

**Griswold, III**, Right Rev. Frank T., Presiding Bishop, Episcopal Church in the USA (ECUSA). Born 1937. Nationality: USA. Episcopalian (Anglican).

Gruhn, Dr. Klaus, Executive Secretary, Deutscher Evangelischer Missionsrat. Nationality: FR Germany. Protestant.

Guelly, Joseph, General Secretary, Sudan Council of Churches. Born 1938. Died 1978. Nationality: Sudan. Anglican.

**Guti**, Ezekiel, Founder, Forward in Faith. Nationality: Zimbabwe. Independent.

**Gyi**, Saw Mar Gay, General Secretary, Myanmar Baptist Convention. Nationality: Myanmar. Baptist.

Haddad, Fuad, General Secretary, United Christian Council of Israel (UCCI). Nationality: Israel. Protestant.

Hadley, Herbert M., Secretary, Friends World Committee for Consultation (FWCC). Nationality: USA. Quaker.

Hakim, see Maximos V..

Secretary HALDER            President HANSEN

**Halder**, James, Executive Secretary, Bangladesh Bible Society. Nationality: Bangladesh. Protestant.

Hale, Rev. Joe, General Secretary, World Methodist Council (WMC). Nationality: USA. Methodist.

Hallencreutz, Dr. Carl-Fredrik, Assistant General Secretary, Svenska Missionsradet. Born 1934. Nationality: Sweden. Lutheran (Church of Sweden).

**Hamao**, Stephen Fumio, Bishop of Yokohama, Catholic Bishops Conference of Japan, President. Born 1930. Nationality: Japan. Roman Catholic.

**Hamm**, Richard L., General Minister & President, Christian Church (Disciples of Christ).

Hand, Most Rev. Geoffrey David, Archbishop of Papua New Guinea, South Pacific Anglican Council (SPAC), Chairman. Born 1918. Nationality: Papua New Guinea. Anglican.

**Hansen**, Jane, President, Women's Aglow Ministries. Nationality: USA. Protestant.

**Harper**, Michael, International Director, International Charismatic Consultation for World Evangelization. Nationality: Britain. Orthodox.

**Hayek (Haik)**, Ignace Antony II, Syrian Catholic Patriarch of Antioch of the Syrians, Syrian Patriarchal Synod, Syrian Patriarchal Synod. Born 1910. Roman Catholic.

**Held**, Hans-Joachim, Moderator, World Council of Churches. Nationality: Germany. Lutheran.

Moderator HELD            President HINCKLEY

Hermaniuk, Most Rev. Maxim, CSSR, Archbishop of Winnipeg, President, Conference of the Ukrainian Catholic Hierarchy. Born 1911. Nationality: Canada. Roman Catholic.

Hian, Chua Wee, General Secretary, International Fellowship of Evangelical Students (IFES). Evangelical.

**Hinckley**, Gordon, President, Church of Jesus Christ of Latter-day Saints. Nationality: USA. Mormon.

Hmyin, Rev. U Ba, General Secretary, Burma Baptist Convention. Nationality: Myanmar. Baptist.

**Hocken**, Peter, Charismatic Historian. Nationality: Britain. Roman Catholic.

Honey, Dr. T. E. Floyd, General Secretary, Canadian Council of Churches (until 1976). Nationality: Canada. United.

**Houston**, Reverend Tom, LCWE Minister at Large, Lausanne Committee for World Evangelization (LCWE). Nationality: Britain. Baptist.

Howe, Right Rev. John William Alexander, Secretary General, Anglican Consultative Council (ACC), Secretary, Lambeth Conference. Born 1920. Nationality: UK. Anglican.

Hoyois, Pastor M. Wilfred, Président, Departement Missionnaire Protestant de Belgique. Nationality: Belgium. Protestant.

Hughes, Dr. Ray H., General Overseer, Church of God (Cleveland), Chairperson, Pentecostal Fellowship of North America (PFNA). Nationality: USA. Pentecostal.

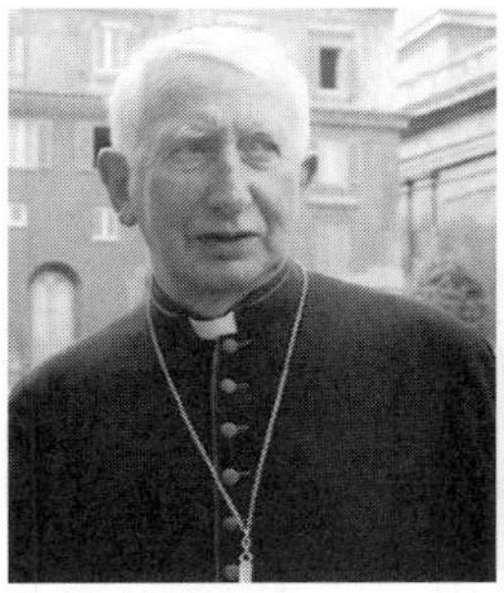
Cardinal HUME

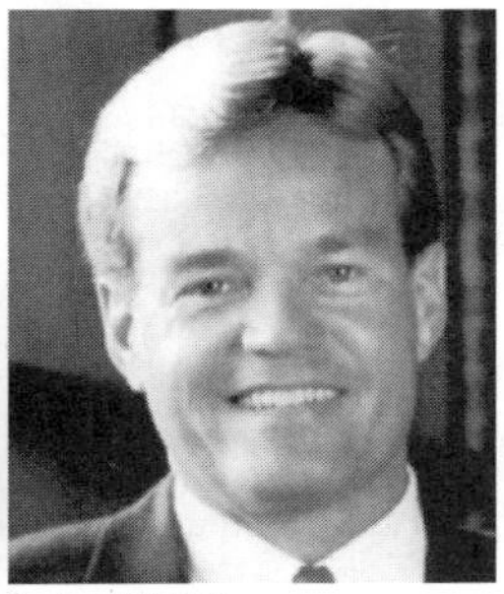
Pastor HYBELS

**Hume**, Cardinal George Basil, Archbishop of Westminster, Bishops' Conference of England & Wales, President. Born 1923. Died 1999. Nationality: UK. Roman Catholic.

**Hummes**, Cláudio, O.F.M., Archbishop of Fortaleza. Born 1934. Nationality: Brazil. Roman Catholic.

Humphries, Rev. M., Secretary-Treasurer, New Hebrides Christian Council. Protestant.

**Hybels**, Pastor Bill, Pastor, Willow Creek Community Church. Nationality: USA. Independent.

Iakovos (James Coucouzis), His Eminence Archbishop, Exarch of the Ecumenical Patriarch and Primate of the Greek Orthodox Church in North and South America, Chairperson, Standing Conference of Canonical Orthodox Bishops in the Americas (SCOBA). Born 1911. Nationality: USA. Greek Orthodox.

Ibrahim, Rev. Simon A., General Secretary, Evangelical Churches of West Africa (ECWA). Born 1942. Nationality: Nigeria. Evangelical.

**Idahosa**, Benson, Founder and Archbishop, Church of God Mission International. Born 1939. Died 1998. Nationality: Nigeria. Independent.

Idowu, His Pre-Eminence Rev. Prof Emmanuel Bolaji, Archbishop & Patriarch, Patriarchat Conference, Methodist Church Nigeria. Born 1913. Nationality: Nigeria. Methodist.

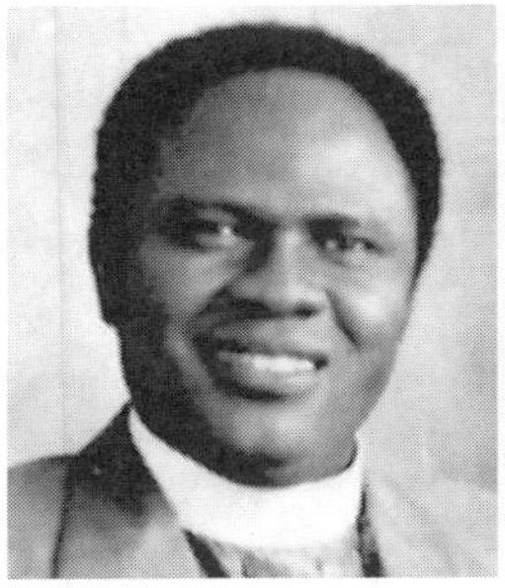
Founder IDAHOSA

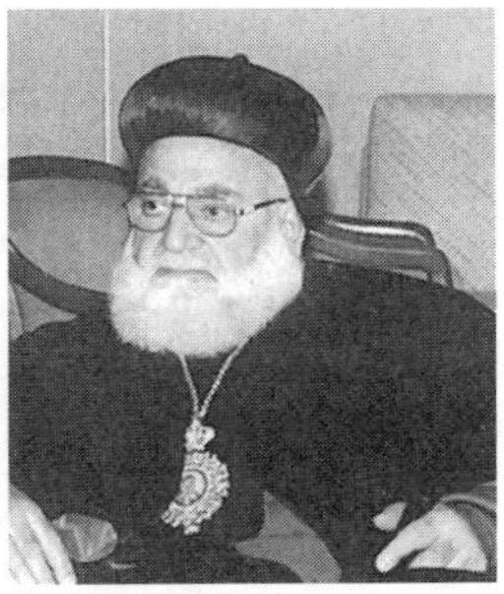
Patriarch IGNATIUS

**Ignatius**, Zakka I, Patriarch of Antioch, Syrian Orthodox Church. Born 1930. Nationality: Syria. Syrian Orthodox.

Ignatius IV (Habeeb Hazim), His Holiness (or, His Beatitude), Patriarch of Antioch and All the East. Born 1920. Nationality: Syria. Greek Orthodox.

Ignatius Peter XVI (Batanian), His Beatitude, Patriarch of Cilicia of the Armenians, Head, Armenian Patriarchal Synod. Born 1899. Nationality: Lebanon. Roman Catholic.

Ignatius Yacub III (Severios Jacob Tuma), His Holiness Moran Mar, Patriarch of Antioch & All the East (since 1957), Supreme Head of the Orthodox Syrian Church. Born 1912. Died 1980. Nationality: Syria. Syrian Orthodox.

Ijjas, Most Rev. Jozsef, Archbishop of Kalocsa, President, Magyar Puspoki Kar. Born 1901. Nationality: Hungary. Roman Catholic.

Ilya II (Shiolashvili), His Beatitude, Archbishop of Mcheta, Metropolitan of Tiflis, Catholicos-Patriarch of All Georgia, since 1977. Born 1933. Nationality: USSR. Georgian Orthodox.

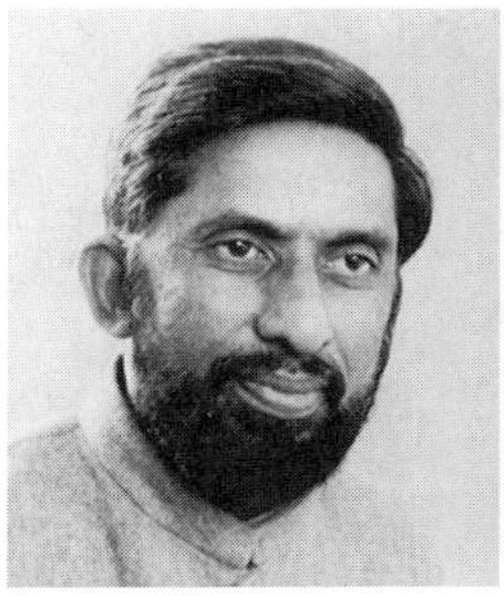
Secretary IPE

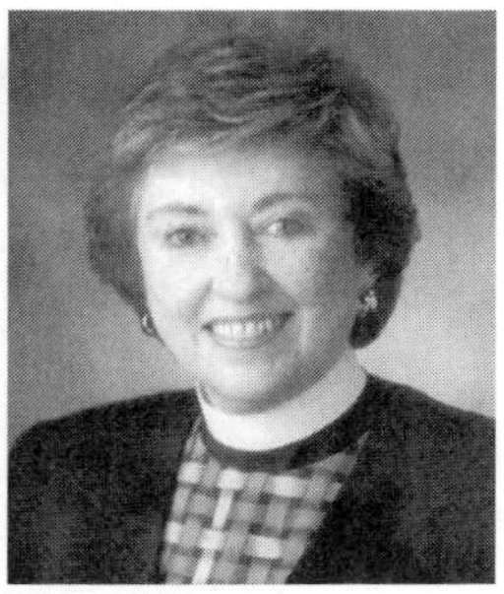
Bishop IRISH

**Ipe**, Joseph, General Secretary, National Council of Churches in India. Born 1940. Nationality: India. Protestant.

Ireney (John Bekish), His Beatitude, Archbishop of New York, Metropolitan of All America & Canada, Primate, Orthodox Church of America, until 1977. Born 1892. Nationality: USA. Russian Orthodox.

**Irish**, Carolyn Tanner, Bishop, Episcopal Church in the USA. Nationality: USA. Anglican.

Ishai (Jesse) Shimun XXIII, Mar, Patriarch-Catholicos of the Assyrians, Ancient Church of the East (resigned 1973). Died Assassinated 1975. Nationality: Iraq, then naturalized USA citizen. Assyrian Orthodox.

Isteero, Rev. Albert, General Secretary, Middle East Council of Churches (MECC). Born 1930. Nationality: Egypt. Coptic Evangelical.

Izvekov, see Pimen.

Jackson, Rev. Dr. Joseph H., President, National Baptist Convention. Nationality: USA. Baptist.

Jacob, Very Rev. W. Ungoed, President, Council of Churches for Wales (UK). Nationality: UK. Anglican.

**Jacobs**, Lorraine and Lindsay, General Secretary, World Convention of Churches of Christ. Disciples.

**Jagessar**, Rev. Michael N., President, Curacao Council of Churches. Protestant.

Jaime, Rev. Angel Luis, Coordinator, UNELAM (Movimiento Pro Unidad Evangélica Latinoamericana). Nationality: Puerto Rico. Protestant.

**Jakubìnyi**, György-Miklós, Archbishop of Alba Julia. Born 1946. Nationality: Romanian. Roman Catholic.

**Janda**, Canon Clement, General Secretary, All Africa Conference of Churches (AACC). Born 1941. Nationality: Sudan. Episcopal (Anglican).

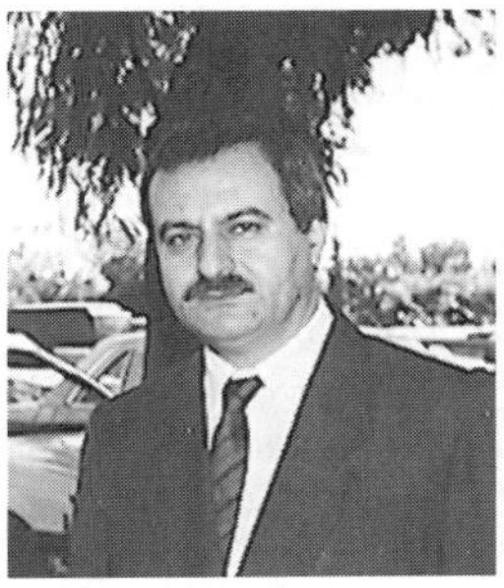
Secretary JARJOUR

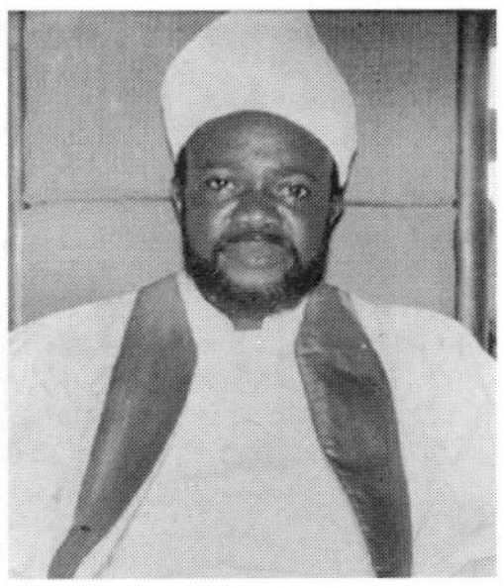
Bishop JEHU-APPIAH II

**Jarjour**, Rev. Dr. Riad, General Secretary, Middle East Council of Churches (MECC). Born c1940. Nationality: Syria. Presbyterian.

**Jean Pierre XVIII Kasparian**, His Beatitude, Patriarch of Cilicia of the Armenians, Sinodo Della Chiesa Armena Cattolica, Head. Born 1927. Nationality: Lebanon. Roman Catholic.

Jegasothy, J. S., General Secretary, National Christian Council of Sri Lanka. Nationality: Sri Lanka. Protestant.

**Jehu-Appiah II**, Bishop, Army of the Cross of Christ Church. Nationality: Ghana. Independent.

Jimenez-Perez, Mrs. Alda de, Secretary, Christian Council of Trinidad and Tobago. Nationality: Trinidad & Tobago. Protestant.

**Johannes**, His Eminence, Archbishop of Karelia & All Finland. Born 1923. Nationality: Finland. Greek Orthodox.

John Paul I (Albino Luciani), His Holiness the Pope (elected 1978), Bishop of Rome, Sovereign of Vatican City State. Born 1912. Died 1978. Nationality: Holy See, and Italy. Roman Catholic.

**John Paul II (Karol Wojtyla)**, His Holiness the Pope (elected 1978), Bishop of Rome, Vicar of Jesus Christ, Successor of the Prince of the Apostles, Supreme Pontifex of the Universal Church, Patriarch of the West, Primate of Italy, Sovereign of Vatican City State. Born 1920. Nationality: Holy See, and Poland. Roman Catholic.

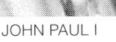

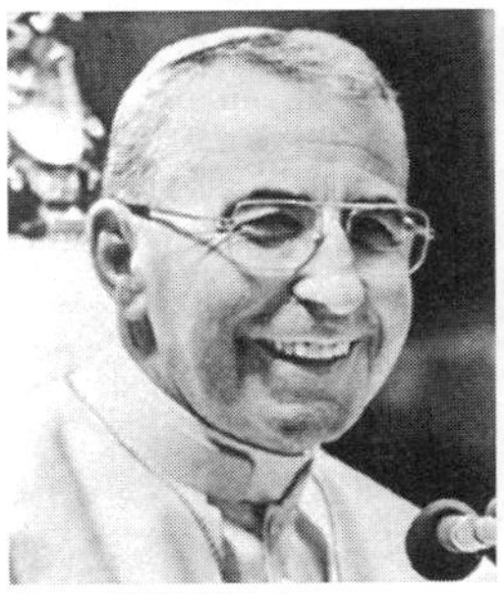
Pope JOHN PAUL I

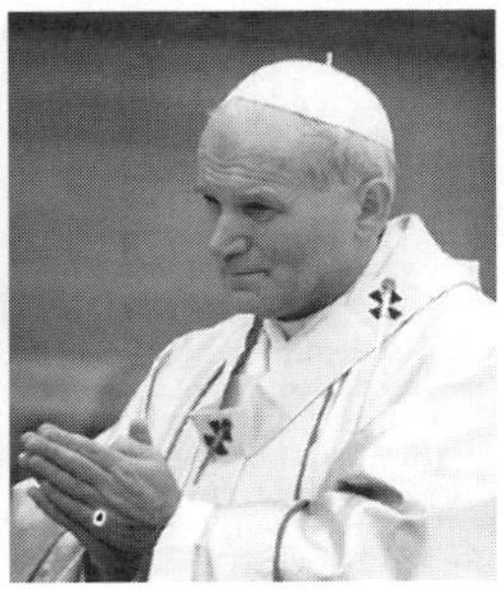
Pope JOHN PAUL II

Johnson, Rev. E. H., Moderator, Presbyterian Church in Canada. Nationality: Canada. Presbyterian.

Johnston, Most Rev. Allen Howard, Archbishop, Church of the Province of New Zealand (CPNZ). Born 1912. Nationality: New Zealand. Anglican.

**Jones**, Dr. E. Edward, President, National Baptist Convention of America. Nationality: USA. Baptist.

Juhanon Mar Thoma, Most Rev. Dr., Metropolitan of Mar Thoma Syrian Church of Malabar (since 1947). Died 1976. Nationality: India. Independent Orthodox.

Justin (Moisescu), His Holiness (or His Beatitude), Archbishop of Bucharest, Metropolitan of Ungrovalacia, Patriarch of Romania from 1977. Born 1910. Nationality: Romania. Romanian Orthodox.

Justinian (Ioan Marina), His Holiness (or His Beatitude), Archbishop of Bucharest, Metropolitan of Ungrovalacia, Patriarch of Romania. Born 1901. Died 1977. Nationality: Romania. Romanian Orthodox.

Kachaje, Rev. Gibiel Adam, General Secretary, Christian Council of Malawi. Born 1930. Nationality: Malawi. Anglican.

Kahihia, Right Rev. Benjamin, Bishop, African Independent Pentecostal Church of Africa. Nationality: Kenya. African Independent.

**Kalanda**, S.E.R. Mons. Paul L., Bishop of Fort Portal, Uganda Episcopal Conference, President. Born 1927. Nationality: Uganda. Roman Catholic.

Kaldy, Bishop Zoltan, Lutheran Church in Hungary. Born 1919. Nationality: Hungary. Lutheran.

Kale, Right Rev. Seth Irunsewe, Bishop of Lagos (since 1963), Anglican Church in Nigeria. Nationality: Nigeria. Anglican.

**Kalisz**, Raymond Philip, S.V.D. Bishop of Wewak, Bishops' Conference of Papua New Guinea & the Solomon Islands, President. Born 1927. Nationality: Papua New Guinea. Roman Catholic.

Kalustian (Shnork), His Beatitude, Armenian Patriarch of Constantinople. Born 1907. Nationality: Turkey. Armenian Apostolic.

Kamau, John C., General Secretary, National Christian Council of Kenya (NCCK). Born 1923. Nationality: Kenya. Presbyterian.

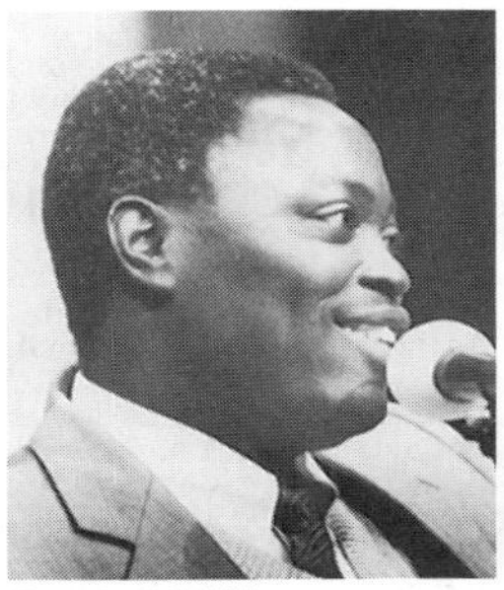
Founder KAMUYI

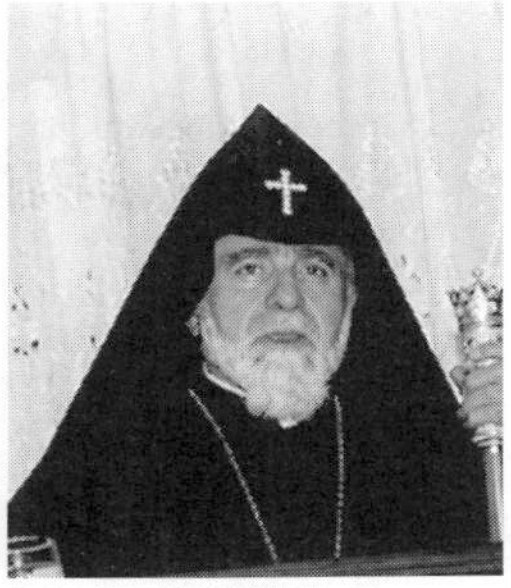
Catholicos KAREKIN I

**Kamuyi**, William, Founder, Deeper Life Bible Church. Nationality: Nigeria. Independent.

Kanyonza, Rev. Fr. Vincent, Executive Secretary, Uganda Joint Christian Council. Born 1930. Nationality: Uganda. Roman Catholic.

Kao, Rev. Dr. Chun-Ming, General Secretary, Presbyterian Church of Taiwan. Born 1929. Nationality: Taiwan. Presbyterian.

**Karekin I**, His Holiness, Supreme Patriarch and Catholicos of All Armenians, Archbishop of Ararat. Born 1932. Died 1999. Nationality: Armenia. Armenian Apostolic.

**Karlic**, Estanislao Esteban, Archbishop of Paraná, Conferencia Episcopal Argentina, President. Born 1926. Nationality: Argentina. Roman Catholic.

Kavanagh, Right Rev. John Patrick, Bishop of Dunedin, President, New Zealand Episcopal Conference. Born 1913. Nationality: New Zealand. Roman Catholic.

Kayuwa-Tshibumbu wa Kahinga, Patriarch, President, Church of Christ in Zaire, Community Christ the Light. Born 1931. Nationality: Zaire. African Independent.

Keijer, Magister Augustinus, General Secretary, International Federation of Free Evangelical Churches (IFFEC). Nationality: Sweden.

**Kendrick**, Graeham, Founder, March for Jesus. Born 1955. Nationality: Britain. Independent.

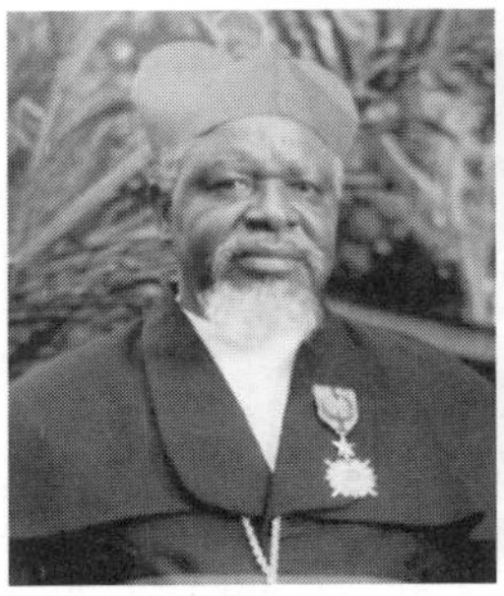
Patriarch KAYUWA

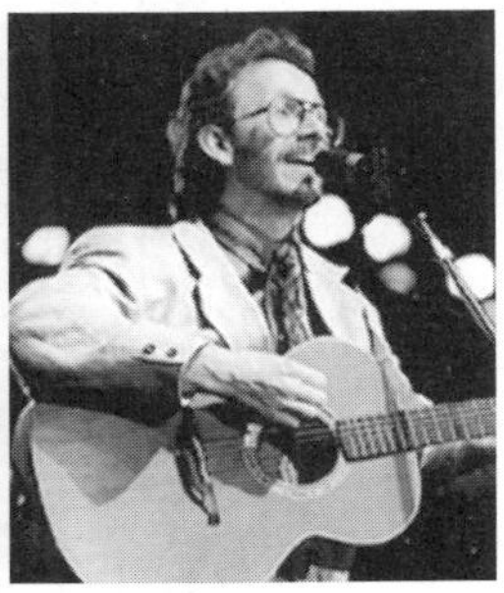
Musician KENDRICK

**Khamsé Vithavong**, Jean, O.M.I. Vicariati Apostolici of Vientianne, Bishop of Moglena. Born 1942. Nationality: Laos. Roman Catholic.
Khin, Rev. U Aungh, General Secretary, Burma Council of Churches. Nationality: Myanmar. Protestant.
Khoabane, Jubilee Tseliso, General Secretary, Christian Council of Lesotho. Nationality: Lesotho. Protestant.
Khoren I (Paroján), His Holiness, Catholicos of the Great House of Cilicia (Sis) (since 1963). Born Born 1914. Nationality: Cyprus and Lebanon. Armenian Apostolic.
Kibira, Right Rev. Dr. Josiah M., Bishop of North West Tanzania, Evangelical Lutheran Church in Tanzania (ELCT). Born 1925. Nationality: Tanzania. Lutheran.
Kim, Rev. Kwan Suk, General Secretary, National Council of Churches in Korea. Born 1918. Nationality: South Korea. Presbyterian.
Kim, His Eminence Cardinal Stephen Sou Hwan, Archbishop of Seoul, President, Catholic Conference of Korea, President, Federation of Asian Bishops' Conferences. Born 1922. Nationality: Korea. Roman Catholic.
Kimball, Spencer, 12th President of the Church (elected 1973), Church of Jesus Christ of Latter-day Saints. Born 1895. Nationality: USA. Mormon.
Kipe, Rev. H. Frank, Chairman, Evangelical Fellowship of Zambia. Nationality: Zambia. Evangelical.
**Kitbunchu**, Cardinal Michael Michai, Archbishop of Bangkok, Bishops' Conference of Thailand, President. Born 1929. Nationality: Thailand. Roman Catholic.

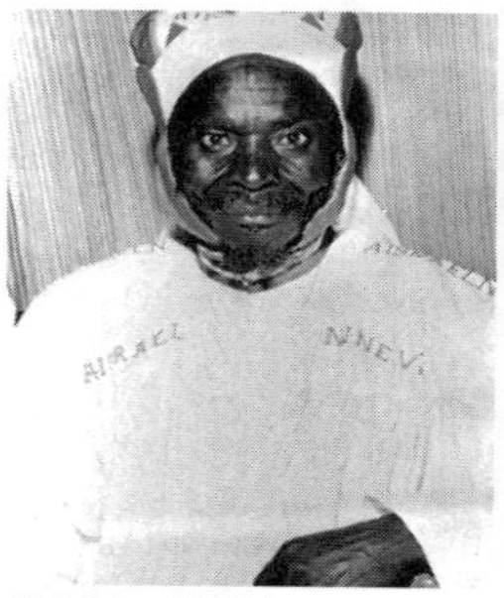
High Priest KIVULI

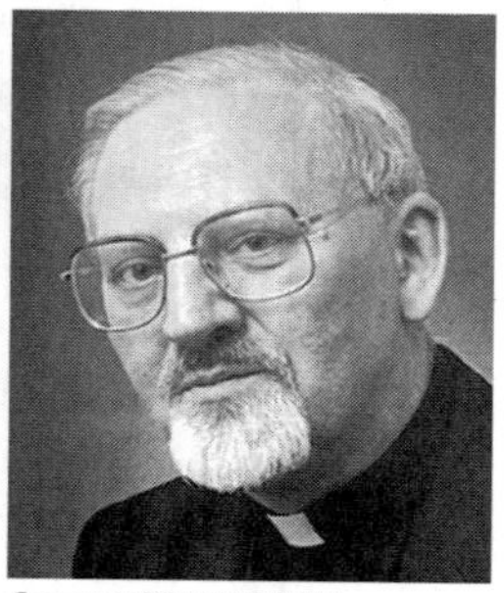
General KOLVENBACH

Kivuli, Baba M. P. D. Zakayo, High Priest, African Israel Church Nineveh (AICN), Chairman, Kenya Independent Churches Fellowship. Born 1896. Died 1974. Nationality: Kenya. African Independent.
Kjaer, Karlo, Secretary, Ecumenical Council of Denmark. Nationality: Denmark. Lutheran.
Knight, Rev. Howard, Executive Secretary, Australian Evangelical Alliance. Nationality: Australia. Evangelical.
Knight, Rev. S., President, Antigua Christian Council. Nationality: Antigua. Protestant.
Knorr, Brother Nathan H., President 1942-77, Watch Tower Bible & Tract Societies of Pennsylvania and New York, President, International Bible Students Association (Jehovah's Christian Witnesses). Born 1905. Died 1977. Nationality: USA. Jehovah's Witnesses.
Knox, His Eminence Cardinal James Robert, Prefect, Sacred Congregation for the Sacraments and Divine Worship, Roman Curia (Vatican City). Born 1914. Nationality: Australia. Roman Catholic.
Kok, Most Rev. Professor Marinus, Archbishop of Utecht & Metropolitan of the Church Province of the Netherlands, President, International Conference of Old Catholic Bishops. Born 1916. Nationality: Netherlands. Old Catholic.
Kolowa, Bishop Sabastian, Bishop of the North-Eastern Diocese and Presiding Bishop of the Evangelical Lutheran Church in Tanzania (ELCT). Born 1933. Nationality: Tanzania. Lutheran.
**Kolvenbach**, S.J., Peter-Hans, Superior General, Society of Jesus. Roman Catholic.
**Kon Avalchek**, Peter, President, Union of Evangelical Christians-Baptists of the Russian Federation. Nationality: Russia. Baptist.
Kotto, Pastor Jean, President, Fédération des Eglises et Missions Evangéliques du Cameroun (FEMEC). Born 1918. Nationality: Cameroon. Evangelical Church of Cameroon.
**Kpodzro**, Philippe Fanoko Kossi, Archbishop of Lomé, Conference Episcopale du Togo, President. Born 1930. Nationality: Togo. Roman Catholic.
Kraybil, Rev. Paul N., Executive Secretary, Mennonite World Conference. Nationality: USA. Mennonite.
Kreuzeder, Dr. Ernest, Chairman, Ecumenical Council of Churches in Austria. Nationality: Austria. Old Catholic.
Kristensen, Dr. Invar, Chairman, Curaçao Council of Churches. Nationality: Netherlands Antilles. Protestant.
Kryuchkov, Gennadi Konstantinovich, Chairman, Council of Churches of Evangelical Christians and Baptists, USSR. Born 1926. Nationality: USSR. Baptist.
Krüger, Oberkirchenrat D. Dr. H., Secretary, Arbeitsgemeinschaft Christlicher Kirchen in der BRD und Berlin. Born 1914. Nationality: FR Germany. Lutheran.
**Kuharic**, Cardinal Franjo, Archbishop of Zagreb, Hrvatska Biskupska Konferencija, President. Born 1919. Nationality: Croatia. Roman Catholic.
Kujok, Rev. Ezekiel, General Secretary, Sudan Council of Churches. Born 1938. Nationality: Sudan. Presbyterian.
Kunene, Rev. Z., President, Swaziland Conference of Churches. Nationality: Swaziland. Protestant.
Kuria, Most Rev. Manasses, Archbishop of Kenya and Bishop of Nairobi, Church of the Province of Kenya (CPK). Born 1927. Nationality: Kenya. Anglican.

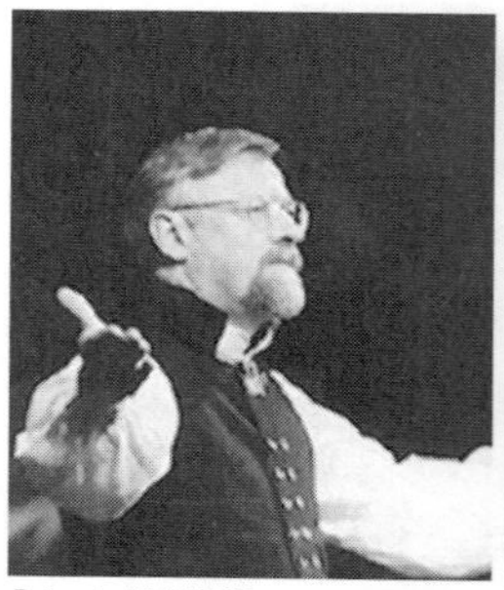
Primate KVARME

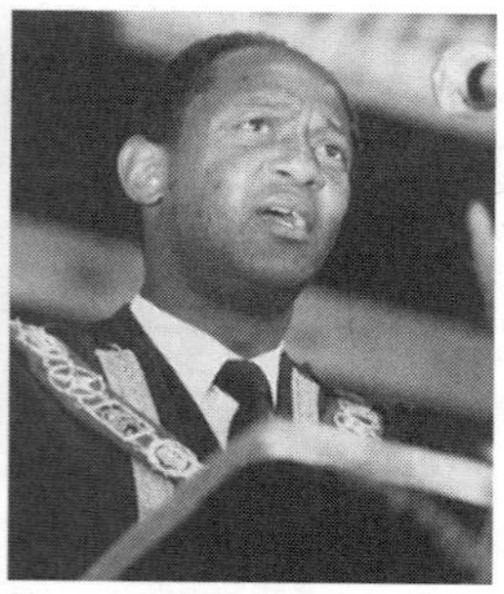
Bishop LEKGANYANE

**Kvarme**, Ole Christian, Primate, Church of Norway. Nationality: Norway. Lutheran.
König, His Eminence Cardinal Franz, Archbishop of Vienna, President, Österreichische Bischofskonferenz. Born 1905. Nationality: Austria. Roman Catholic.
**Küng**, Dr. Hans, Professor, Institute of Ecumenical Research, University of Tübingen. Born 1928. Nationality: Germany. Roman Catholic.
**Laghi**, Cardinal Pio, Prefect, Sacred Congregation for Catholic Education, Roman Curia (Vatican City). Born 1922. Nationality: Italy. Roman Catholic.
Lagos, Rev. Sepulveda, General Secretary, Unión de Misiones Pentecostales Libres de Chile. Nationality: Chile. Independent pentecostal.
Lanarès, Dr. Pierre, Secrétaire général, Association Internationale pour la Défense de la Liberté Religieuse.
Landreth, Gordon, General Secretary, Evangelical Alliance of Great Britain (EAGB). Nationality: UK. Anglican.
Landázuri Ricketts, His Eminence Cardinal Juan, OFM, Archbishop of Lima, Presidente, Conferencia Episcopal Peruana. Born 1913. Nationality: Peru. Roman Catholic.
**Larrea Holguin**, Juan Ignacio, Archbishop of Guayaquil. Born 1927. Nationality: Ecuador. Roman Catholic.
Latyshev, see Nikodim.
Laws, Rev. W. R, Secretary, Methodist Church of New Zealand. Nationality: New Zealand. Methodist.
Lee, Dr. Allan W., General Secretary, World Convention of Churches of Christ. Born 1924. Nationality: USA. Disciples.
**Lehman**, Karl, S.E.R. Mons., Bishop of Mainz, Deutsche Bischofkonferenz, President. Born 1936. Nationality: Germany. Roman Catholic.
**Lehmann**, Mons. Karl, S.E.R., Bishop of Mainz, Deutsche Bischofskonferenz, President. Born 1936. Nationality: Germany. Roman Catholic.
**Leite**, Pastor José, President, Conselho Portugues de Igrejas Cristas (COPIC). Protestant.
**Lekganyane**, Bishop Barnabas, Bishop, Zion Christian Church. Nationality: South Africa. Independent.
**Levada**, William Joseph, Archbishop of San Francisco. Born 1936. Nationality: USA. Roman Catholic.
**Lewis-Cooper**, Rev. Marjorie, General Secretary, Jamaica Council of Churches. Nationality: Jamaica. Protestant.
Lichtenberger, Ms. Ruth, General Director, Nurses Christian Fellowship International. Protestant.
**Lindsay**, Right Reverend Orland, Antigua Christian Council, President. Anglican.
Linscott, Sister Mary, Superior General, Sisters of Our Lady of Namur, Presidente, Unione Internazionale delle Superiore Generali (UISG). Roman Catholic.
Lissy, Pfarrer Rudolf, General Secretary, Österreichischer Missionsrat. Nationality: Austria. Catholic.
Livingston, Elder F. L., President, National Convention, National Primitive Baptist Convention. Nationality: USA. Baptist.

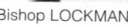

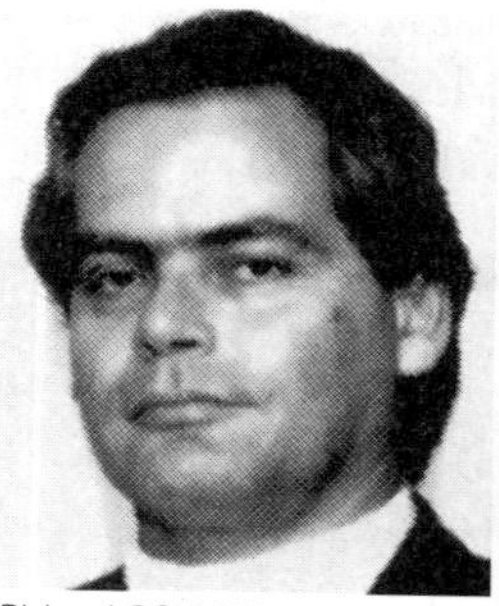
Bishop LOCKMAN

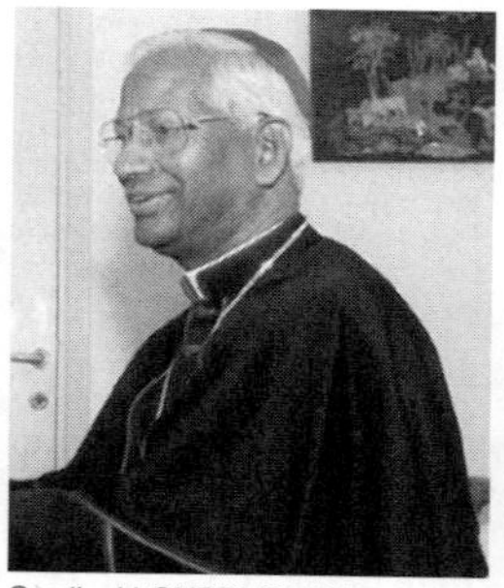
Cardinal LOURDUSAMY

**Lockman**, Paulo, Bishop, Methodist Church of Brazil. Born 1945. Nationality: Brazil. Methodist.
**Lodonu**, Francis Anani Kofi, Bishop of Ho, Ghana Bishops Conference, President. Born 1937. Nationality: Ghana. Roman Catholic.
Loosdregt, Right Rev. Etienne Auguste Germain, OMI, Vicar Apostolic of Vientiane, Président, Conférence Episcopale du Laos et de la République Khmère. Born 1908. Roman Catholic.
Lorscheider, Most Rev. Aloisio, OFM, Archbishop of Fortaleza, Presidente, Conferência Nacional dos Bispos do Brasil. Born 1924. Nationality: Brazil. Roman Catholic.
**Lotz**, Denton, General Secretary, Baptist World Alliance (BWA). Nationality: USA. American Baptist.
**Louden**, Harry, General Director, Nurses Christian Fellowship International. Protestant.
**Lourdusamy**, Cardinal D. Simon, Prefect, Congregation for the Oriental Churches. Born 1924. Nationality: India. Roman Catholic.
Luciani, A., see John Paul I.
Lunga, M., Secretary, Evangelical Alliance of the South Pacific Islands. Evangelical.
**Lustiger**, Cardinal Jean Marie, Archbishop of Paris, Consiglio della II Sezione, Secretary of State. Born 1926. Nationality: France. Roman Catholic.
Luwum, Most Rev. Janani, Archbishop of Uganda & Bishop of Kampala, Church of Uganda, Rwanda, Burundi & Boga-Zaire. Born 1925. Murdered 1977. Nationality: Uganda. Anglican.
**Lyons**, Dr. Henry J., President, National Baptist Convention. Imprisoned 1999. Nationality: USA. Baptist.
**López Rodríguez**, Cardinal Nicolás Jesús, Archbishop of Santo Domingo, Conferencia del Episcopado Dominicano, Presidente. Born 1936. Nationality: Dominican Republic. Roman Catholic.
Maasdorp, Pastor Albertus, Administrative Secretary, Evangelical Lutheran Church of South West Africa. Nationality: South Africa. Lutheran.

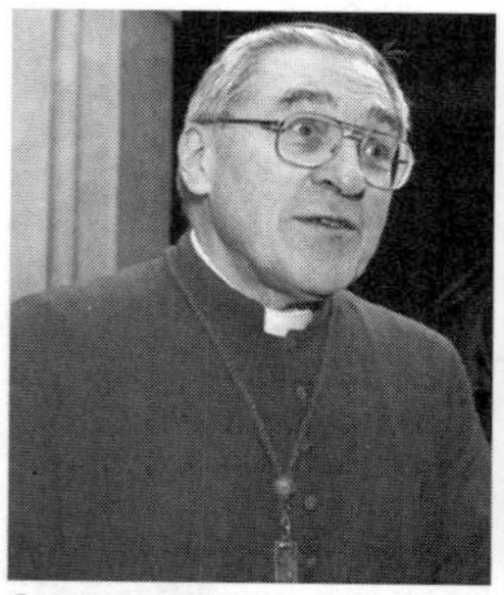
Cardinal LUSTIGER

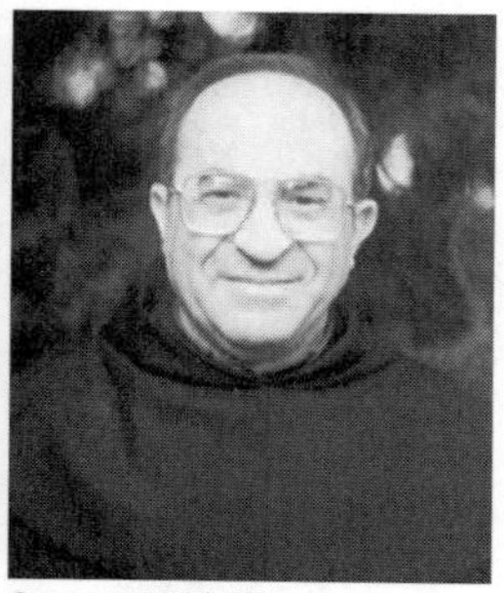
General MACCISE

**Maccise O.C.D.**, Camilo, General, Scalzi Carmelites.
**Macdonald**, Rev. Fergus, General Secretary, United Bible Societies. Born 1936. Nationality: Britain. Presbyterian.
**Macedo**, Edir, Bishop, Universal Church of the Kingdom of God (IURD). Born c1940. Nationality: Brazil. Independent.
Machunga, Rev. A. W., General Secretary, Fellowship of Churches of Christ in Nigeria (TEKAN). Nationality: Nigeria. Evangelical.
MacLeod, Rev. Angus Hamilton, General Secretary, National Council of Churches in New Zealand (NCCZ). Born 1926. Nationality: UK. Baptist.
Maillis, Alexander P., Secretary, Bahamas Christian Council. Nationality: Bahamas. Greek Orthodox.
Makarakiza, Most Rev. André, Archbishop of Gitega, Président, Conférence des Ordinaires du Rwanda et du Burundi (COREB). Born 1919. Nationality: Burundi. Roman Catholic.
Makarios III (Mihail Christodoulou Mouskos), His Beatitude, Archbishop of New Justiniana & All Cyprus. Born 1913. Died 1977. Nationality: Cyprus. Greek Orthodox.
Makokwe, Rev. J. W., General Secretary, Protestant Alliance of Burundi. Nationality: Burundi. Protestant.
Mall, William K., Executive Secretary, National Council of Churches in Pakistan. Born 1912. Nationality: Pakistan. United Presbyterian.
**Mallona Txertudi, C.P.**, S.E.R. Mons. Iñaki, Vesc. di Arecibo, Conferencia Episcopal Puertorique-a, President. Born 1932. Nationality: Puerto Rico. Roman Catholic.
Malula, His Eminence Cardinal Joseph, Archbishop of Kinshasa, Former Président, Conférence Plénière des Ordinaires du Zaïre. Born 1917. Nationality: Zaire. Roman Catholic.
Manalo, Brother Eraño G., Executive Minister, Eglesia ni Cristo (INC). Nationality: Philippines. Independent.
**Mandysova**, Mrs. Nadeje, General Secretary, Ecumenical Council of Churches in the CSR. Protestant.
**Manougian**, Torkom, His Beatitude, Armenian Patriarch of Jerusalem, Patriarch of the Apostolic Throne of St. James, Archbishop of Jerusalem. Armenian Apostolic.
Mans, Rev. Sedu Joseph, President, Evangelical Fellowship of Sierra Leone. Nationality: Sierra Leone. Evangelical.

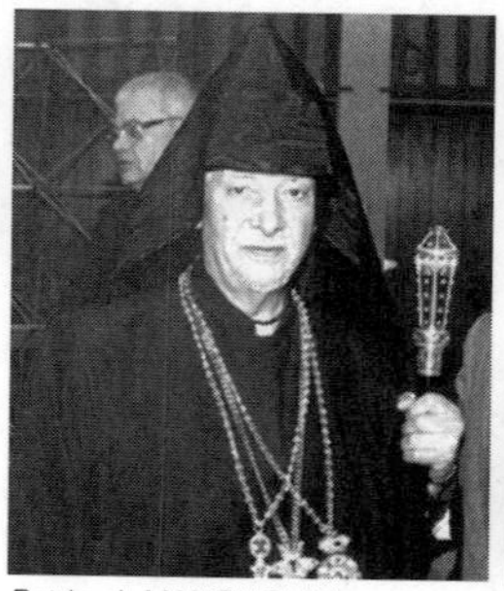
Patriarch MANOUGIAN

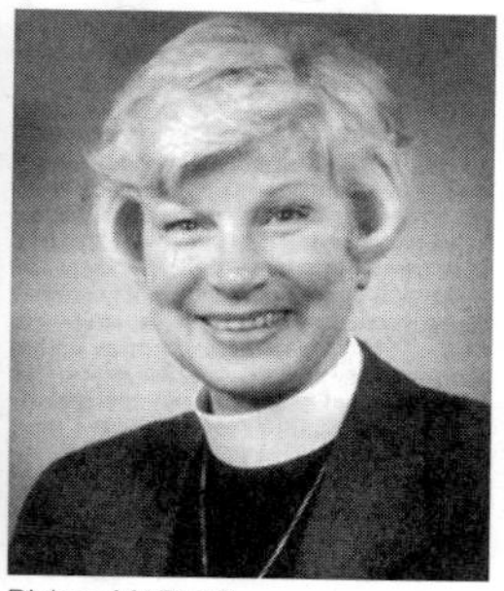
Bishop MAPLES

**Maples**, Katherine Elizabeth, Bishop, Episcopal Church in the USA. Nationality: USA. Anglican.
Maqina, Rev. E. V. M., National President, African Independent Churches Association (AICA). Nationality: South Africa. African Independent.
**Maradiaga**, S.E.R. Mons. Oscar Andres Rodriguez, Bishop of Tegucigalpa, Consejo Episcopal Latinoamericano (CELAM), President. Born 1942. Nationality: Honduras. Roman Catholic.

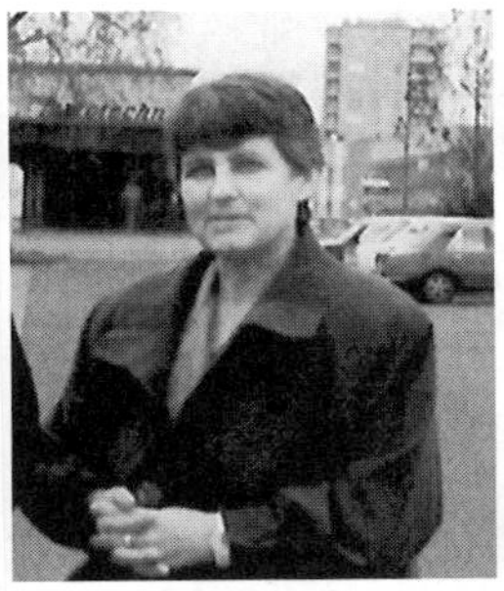
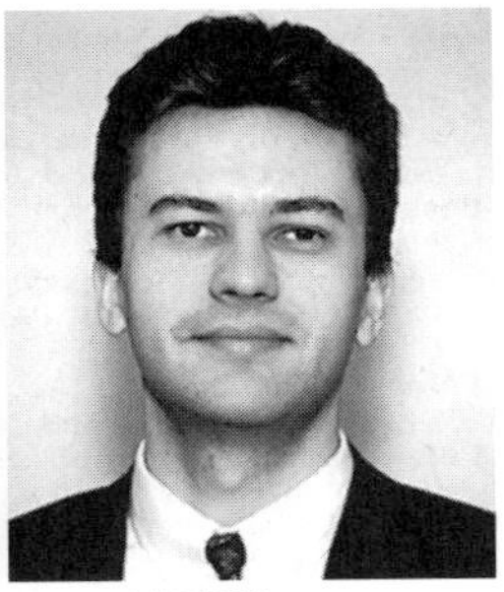

Secretary MARDYOVO  Director MARICAK

**Mardyovo**, Nadeje, Secretary General, Ecumenical Council of Churches in The Czech Republic. Nationality: Czech Republic. Protestant.
**Maricak**, Robert, Director, Network of Christian Ministries. Nationality: Croatia. Independent.
Marina, I., see Justinian.
Markos, His Grace Anba Antonious (Magdy Sobhy Mikhail), Bishop of African Affairs, Coptic Orthodox Church, Organizing Secretary, Organization of African Independent Churches (OAIC). Born 1936. Nationality: Egypt. Coptic Orthodox.
Marsh, Rev. Dr. Clinton M., Stated Clerk, United Presbyterian Church in the USA. Born 1916. Nationality: USA. Presbyterian.
Marshall, Rev. Dr. Robert James, President, Lutheran Church in America (LCA). Born 1918. Nationality: USA. Lutheran.
Martin, Most Rev. Pierre, former Archbishop of Nouméa, Président, Conférence des Evêques du Pacifique. Born 1910. Roman Catholic.
**Martinez**, Cardinal Somalo Eduardo, Prefect, Congregazione per GLI Instituti di Vita Consacrata e le Società di Vita Apostolica, Roman Curia (Vatican City). Born 1927. Nationality: Spain. Roman Catholic.

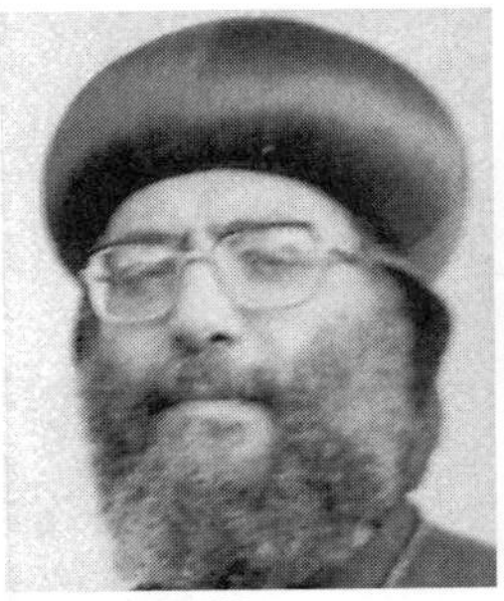
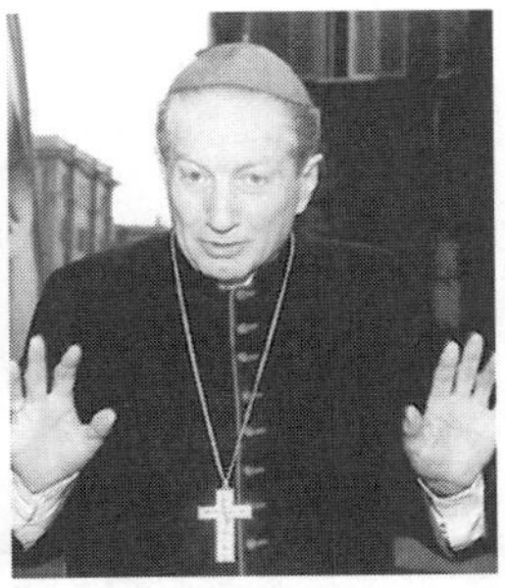

Bishop MARKOS  Cardinal MARTINI

**Martini**, Cardinal Carlo Maria, Archbishop of Milan. Born 1927. Nationality: Italy. Roman Catholic.
Marton, Right Rev. Aaron, Bishop of Alba Julia, President, Romanian Catholic Episcopal Conference. Born 1896. Nationality: Romania. Roman Catholic.
Marty, His Eminence Cardinal François, Archbishop of Paris, Conférence Episcopale Française, Président. Born 1904. Nationality: France. Roman Catholic.
**Marty**, Dr. Martin E., Professor, Divinity School, University of Chicago. Born 1928. Nationality: USA. Lutheran.
**Masih**, J.F., General Secretary, Council of Baptist Churches in North East India. Nationality: India. Baptist.
Matthews, Bishop Marjorie Swank, Area Bishop for Wisconsin, North Central Jurisdictional Conference, United Methodist Church, USA. Born 1916. Nationality: USA. Methodist.
Matulaitis-Labukas, Right Rev. Giuseppe, Apostolic Administrator of Kaunas and Vilkaviskis, President, Catholic Bishops Conference of Lithuania. Born 1894. Nationality: USSR. Roman Catholic.
Mau, Dr. Carl Henning, General Secretary, Lutheran World Federation (LWF). Born 1922. Nationality: USA. American Lutheran.
**Maunganidze**, Mrs. Mbuya, Founder and Leader, Pentecostal Apostolic Church of God. Born 1935. Nationality: Zimbabwe. Independent pentecostal.
Maurer, His Eminence Cardinal José Clemente, CSSR, Archbishop of Sucre, Presidente, Conferencia Episcopal de Bolivia. Born 1900. Nationality: Bolivia. Roman Catholic.
Maury, Pastor Jacques, Président, Eglise Réformée de France. Born 1920. Nationality: France. Reformed.
Maxim (Neidenov-Minkov), His Holiness, Patriarch of Bulgaria & Metropolitan of Sofia. Born 1914. Nationality: Bulgaria. Orthodox.
**Maximos V Hakim**, His Beatitude, Greek Catholic Patriarch of Antioch and All the East, Alexandria and Jerusalem, President, Assembly of Bishops of Syria, and Melkite Patriarchal Synod. Born 1908. Died 2001. Nationality: Syria. Roman Catholic.
Mazombwe, Right Rev. Médard Joseph, Bishop of Chipata, Zambia Episcopal Conference, President. Born 1931. Nationality: Zambia. Roman Catholic.
Mbiti, Rev. Professor John Samuel, Director, Ecumenical Institute, Bossey (Switzerland); University of Bern. Born 1931. Nationality: Kenya. Anglican.
McCann, His Eminence Cardinal Owen, Archbishop of Cape Town, Southern Africa Catholic Bishops' Conference, President (1974). Born 1907. Nationality: South Africa. Roman Catholic.
McCauley, Most Rev. Vincent, CSC, former Bishop of Fort Portal, Executive Secretary, Association of Member Episcopal Conferences in Eastern Africa (AMECEA). Born 1906. Nationality: USA. Roman Catholic.
McClure, Dr. Robert B., Moderator, United Church of Canada. Nationality: Canada. United.
**McCormack**, Mr. Michael, Executive Secretary, Guyana Council of Churches. Protestant.
**McDonnell**, O.S.B. Killian, Charismatic Theologian, St. John's University. Nationality: USA. Roman Catholic.
McIntire, Rev. Dr. Carl, President, International Council of Christian Churches (ICCC). Born 1906. Nationality: USA. Presbyterian.
McLean, Ralph, Editor, Christian Churches & Churches of Christ (no central organization), Directory of the Ministry. Nationality: USA. Churches of Christ.
**Medina Estévez**, S.E.R. Mons. Jorge Arturo, Pro Prefect, Sacred Congregation for the Sacraments and Divine Worship (Vatican City). Born 1926. Nationality: Chile. Roman Catholic.
Meeking, Rev. Basil, Executive Secretary, Secretariat for Christian Unity (Vatican). Born 1929. Nationality: New Zealand. Roman Catholic.
Melaku, see Tekle-Haimonot.
Melvin, Dr. Billy, Executive Director, National Association of Evangelicals (NEA). Nationality: USA. Evangelical.
Méouchi, His Eminence Cardinal Paul Pierre, Maronite Patriarch of Antioch, President, Assembly of Catholic Patriarchs and Bishops of Lebanon, and Maronite Patriarchal Synod. Born 1894. Roman Catholic.
Mercado, Rev. LaVerne Diwa, General Secretary, National Council of Churches in the Philippines (NCCP). Born 1921. Nationality: Philippines. United Methodist.
**Mercieca**, Most Rev. Joseph, Archbishop of Malta, Maltese Episcopal Conference, President. Born 1928. Nationality: Malta. Roman Catholic.
Mercier, Pastor Henri, Secretary, Conseil Suisse des Missions Evangéliques/Schweizerischer Evangelischer Missionsrat. Nationality: Switzerland. Evangelical.
Mickelson, Dr. Arnold R., General Secretary, American Lutheran Church (ALC). Born 1922. Nationality: USA. Lutheran.

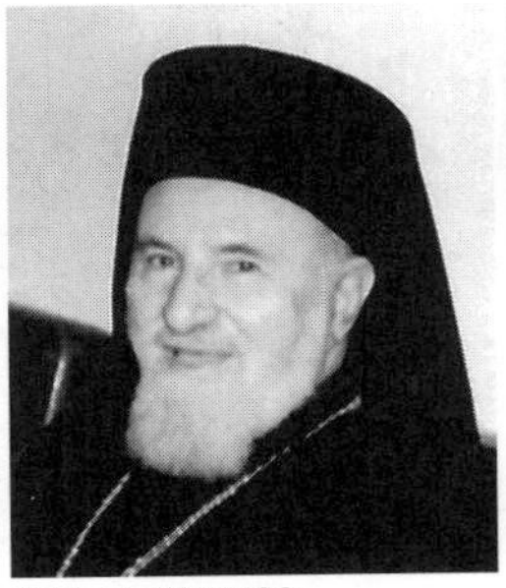
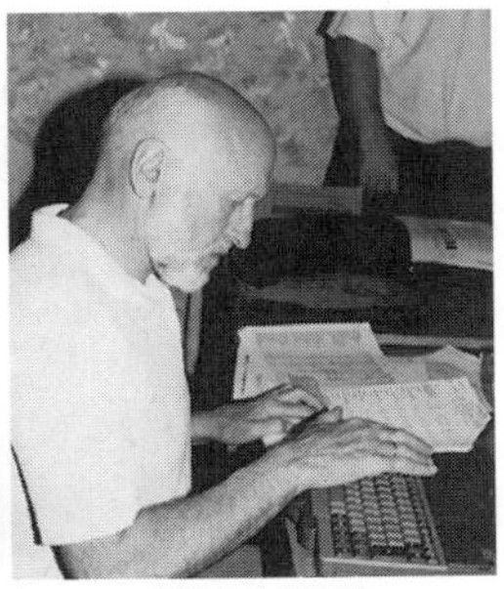

Patriarch MAXIMOS  Secretary MIKALAJUNAS

**Mikalajunas**, Mykolas, Executive Secretary, Latvian Bible society. Nationality: Latvia. Lutheran.
**Mills**, Rev. Robert H., International General Secretary, Canadian Council of Churches. Protestant.
**Mitin**, Sergei, Executive Secretary, Bible Society in Uzbekistan. Nationality: Uzbekistan. Independent.
**Mkhori**, S.E.R. Mons. Felix Eugenio, Archbishop of Chikwawa, Episcopal Conference of Malawi, President. Born 1931. Nationality: Malawi. Roman Catholic.

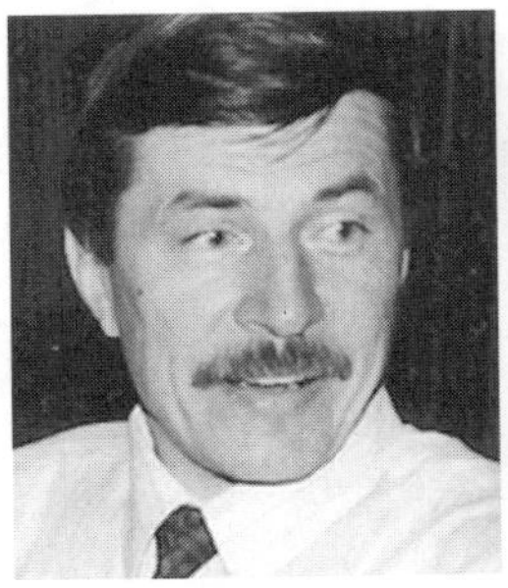
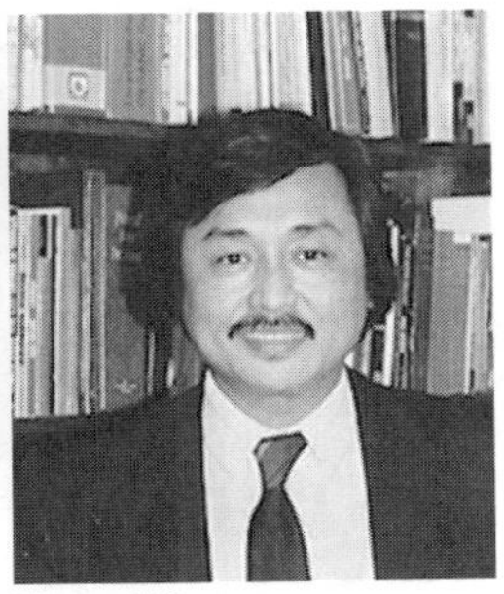

Secretary MITIN  Director MO

**Mo**, David Yone, Director, Myanmar Young Crusaders. Nationality: Myanmar. Independent.
Mo'awad, see Elias IV.
**Modiega**, David, Deputy General Secretary, Botswana Christian Council. Nationality: Botswana. Protestant.
**Mohlalisi**, O.M.I. Bernard, Archbishop of Maseru. Born 1933. Nationality: Lesotho. Roman Catholic.
**Mojwok Nyiker**, Vincent, Bishop of Malakal. Born 1933. Nationality: Sudan. Roman Catholic.
**Monsi-Agboka**, Lucien, Bishop of Abomey, Conference Episcopale du Benin, President. Born 1926. Nationality: Benin. Roman Catholic.
Montini, G. B., see Paul VI.
Moon, Rev. Sun Myung, Prophet & Founder (1954), Unification Church International (Holy Spirit Association for the Unification of World Christianity). Born 1920. Nationality: Korea. Independent.
Mooneyham, Dr. W. Stanley, President, World Vision (USA). Born 1926. Nationality: USA. Baptist.
Morapeli, Most Rev. Alfonso Liguori, OMI, Archbishop of Maseru. Born 1929. Nationality: Lesotho. Roman Catholic.
**Moreira Neves**, Lucas, Cardinal, Archbishop of São Salvador da Bahia, Conferencia Nacional do Bishops do Brasil, President. Born 1925. Nationality: Brazil. Roman Catholic.
**Morera Vega**, Héctor, Bishop of Tilaván. Born 1926. Nationality: Costa Rica. Roman Catholic.
Morton, Rev. Harry Osborne, General Secretary, British Council of Churches (BCC). Born 1925. Nationality: UK. Methodist.
Moshi, Right Rev. Dr. Stefano R., President, Evangelical Lutheran Church in Tanzania (ELCT). Born 1906. Died 1976. Nationality: Tanzania. Lutheran.
Moss, Rev. Dr. Robert V., President, United Church of Christ. Born 1922. Nationality: USA. United.
Mouskos, M. C., see Makarios III.
**Mpundu**, S.E.R. Mons. Telesphore George, Bishop of Mbala-Mpika, Zambia Episcopal Conference, President. Born 1947. Nationality: Zambia. Roman Catholic.
**Mqathazane**, Rev. Ishmael, General Secretary, Christian Council of Lesotho. Protestant.
Mugambe, Rev. Father Francis Xavier, Joint Secretary, Uganda Joint Christian Council. Nationality: Uganda. Roman Catholic.

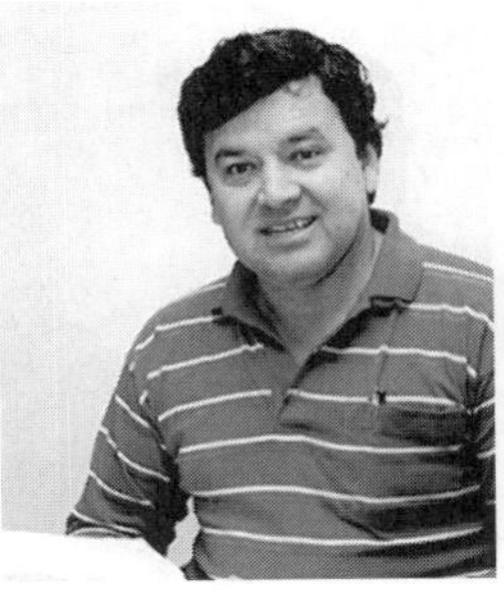
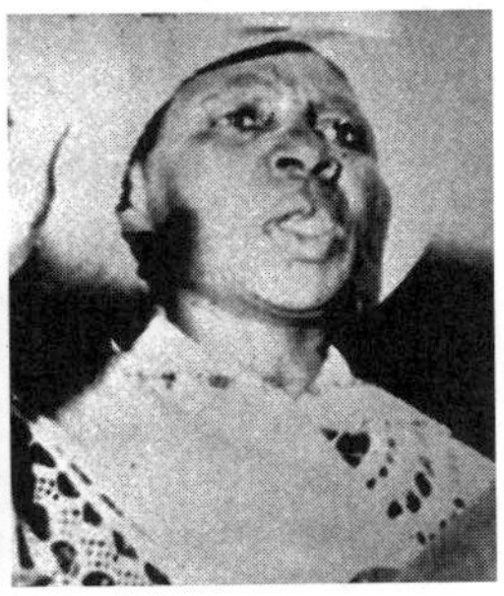

Director MUNOZ  Mother NKU

**Munoz**, Josue, Mission Director, Church of the Prince of Peace. Nationality: Guatemala. Independent.
Murrieta, Rev. Israel Ortiz, Executive Secretary, Federación Evangélica de México. Nationality: Mexico. Evangelical.
**Musa**, Victor, President, Evangelical Churches of West Africa. Evangelical.
Musu, Rev. Posenai, General Secretary, Pacific Conference of Churches (PCC). Died 1976. Protestant.
**Muszynski**, Archbishop Henryk, Archbishop of Gniezno. Born 1933. Nationality: Poland. Roman Catholic.
**Mvé Engone S.D.B.**, Basile, Bishop of Oyem, Conference Episcopale du Gabon, Preisdent. Born 1941. Nationality: Gabon. Roman Catholic.
Mwenda, Rev. Kingsley C., General Secretary, Christian Council of Zambia (CCZ). Born 1930. Nationality: Zambia. United Church of Zambia. Protestant.
**N'Dayen**, Most Rev. Joachim, Archbishop of Bangui, Président, Conférence Episcopale de la République Centrafricaine. Born 1934. Nationality: CAR. Roman Catholic.
Nababan, Rev. Dr. Soritua A. E., General Secretary, Council of Churches in Indonesia (DGI). Born 1933. Nationality: Indonesia. Lutheran (HKBP).
Nakajima, Rev. John Masaaki, General Secretary, National Christian Council of Japan (NCCJ). Born 1928. Nationality: Japan. United (UCCJ).
Nasir, Bishop Dr. Eric Samuel, Bishop in Delhi, Church of North India (CNI), Moderator. Nationality: India. United.
Ndandali, Right Rev. Justin, Bishop of Butare, Conseil Protestant du Rwanda, Secretary. Born 1942. Nationality: Rwanda. Anglican.
Ndebele, Rev. P. J. M., General Secretary, Christian Council of Botswana. Nationality: Botswana. Protestant.
**Ndlovu**, Louis Ncamiso, O.S.M., Bishop of Manzini, Southern Africa Catholic Bishops' Conference, President. Born 1945. Nationality: South Africa. Roman Catholic.
**Ndlovu O.S.M.**, S.E.R. Mons. Louis Ncamiso, Vesc. di Manzini, Southern Africa Catholic Bishops' Conference, President. Born 1945. Nationality: Swaziland. Roman Catholic.
Neehall, Rev. Dr. Roy Gilbert, General Secretary, Caribbean Conference of Churches (CCC). Born 1928. Nationality: Trinidad & Tobago. Presbyterian.
**Ngabu**, Faustin, Bishop of Goma, Conférence Episcopale du Zaire, President. Born 1935. Nationality: Zaire. Roman Catholic.
Ngomberume, Abel, High Priest, African Apostolic Church of Johane Maranke (AACJM). Born 1925. Nationality: Zimbabwe. African Independent.
Nguyên van Binh, Most Rev. Paul, Archbishop of Saigon, Président, Conférence Episcopale du Viêtnam. Born 1910. Nationality: Viet Nam. Roman Catholic.
Nicolas, Pastor Albert Jean, General Secretary, Fédération Protestante de France (FPF). Born 1918. Nationality: France. Reformed.
Nicole, Dr. Jules-Marcel, Secretary, French Evangelical Alliance. Nationality: France. Evangelical.
Nikodim (Boris Georgievic Rotov), Metropolitan of Leningrad & Ladoga, Chairman of Holy Synod, Russian Orthodox Church. Born 1929. Died 1978. Nationality: USSR. Russian Orthodox.
Nikodim (Latyshev), Archbishop of Moscow & All Russia (since 1971), Old Ritualist Church of the Belokrinitsa Concord (Old Believers). Nationality: USSR. Old Believer.
Nikolaos VI (Varelopoulo), His Beatitude, Pope & Patriarch of Alexandria, All Egypt & All Africa. Born 1915. Nationality: Greece. Greek Orthodox.

Nku, Mother Christina Mokutudu (Ma Nku), Founder, Head, & Life General President, St John's Apostolic Faith Mission of South Africa. Born 1894. Nationality: South Africa. African Independent.
**Nobou**, S.E.R. Mons. Auguste, Archbishop of Korhogo, Episcopal Conference de la Côte d'Ivoire, President. Born 1928. Nationality: Ivory Coast. Roman Catholic.
Noel, Rev. Claude, General Secretary, Concile des Eglises Evangéliques d'Haiti. Nationality: Haiti. Evangelical.
Norniella, Rev. Francisco, President, Presbyterian Reformed Church in Cuba. Born 1914. Nationality: Cuba. Presbyterian.
Novak, Patriarch Dr. Miroslav, President, Czechoslovak Hussite Church. Born 1907. Nationality: Czechoslovakia. Catholic Independent.
**Nsayi**, Bernard, Bishop of Nkayi, Conference Episcopale du Congo (Brazzaville), President. Born 1943. Nationality: Congo. Roman Catholic.
Nsubuga, His Eminence Cardinal Emmanuel, Archbishop of Kampala, President, Uganda Episcopal Conference. Born 1914. Nationality: Uganda. Roman Catholic.
Nunes Gabriel, Most Rev. Manuel, Archbishop of Luanda, Presidente, Conferência Episcopal de Angola e São Tomé (CEAST). Born 1912. Nationality: Angola. Roman Catholic.
Nunes Teixeira, Right Rev. Francisco, Bishop of Quelimane, Presidente, Conferência Episcopal de Moçambique. Born 1910. Nationality: Mozambique. Roman Catholic.
**Nuñez**, Right Rev. Daniel Enrique, Bishop of David. Born 1927. Nationality: Panama. Roman Catholic.
Nyangor, Rev. Albert Boaz Ogadason, General Secretary, African Israel Church Ninevah (AICN). Born 1923. Nationality: Kenya. African Independent.
**O'Brien**, Keith Michael Patrick, Archbishop of St. Andrews and Edinburgh. Born 1938. Nationality: UK. Roman Catholic.
**Obando Bravo** SDB, Miguel. Cardinal, Archbishop of Managua, Presidente, Conferencia Episcopal de Nicaragua. Born 1926. Nationality: Nicaragua. Roman Catholic.
**Obeso Rivera**, Sergio, Archbishop of Jalap, Conferencia del Episcopado Mexicano, President. Born 1931. Nationality: Mexico. Roman Catholic.
**Obiefuna**, Albert Kanene, Archbishop of Onitsha, Catholic Bishops' Conference of Nigeria, President. Born 1930. Nationality: Nigeria. Roman Catholic.
**Oh**, Sr. Emi Frances, General Secretary, Fiji Council of Churches. Protestant.
**Okoth**, Zacchaeus, Archbishop of Kisumu, Kenya Episcopal Conference (KEC), President. Born 1942. Nationality: Kenya. Roman Catholic.
Oliver, Mr. Ernest, Secretary, Evangelical Missionary Alliance of Great Britain. Nationality: UK. Evangelical.
Olufusoye, Most Rev. Timothy Omotayo, Archbishop of Nigeria, Church of Nigeria. Born 1918. Nationality: Nigerian. Anglican.
Ondeto, Holy Father (Baba Mtakatifu) Simeon, Maria Legio of Africa. Born 1910. Nationality: Kenya. African Independent.

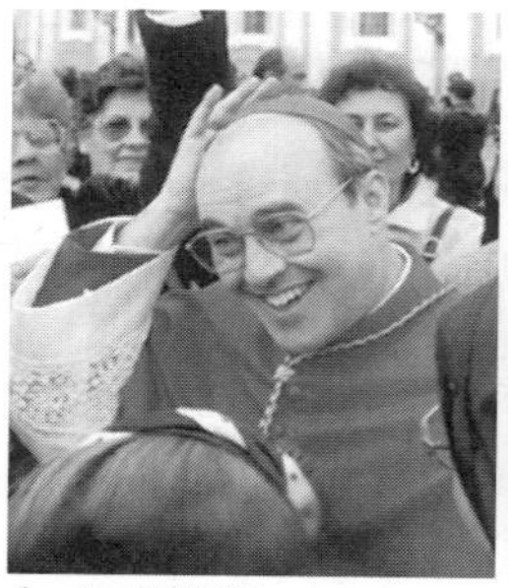
Cardinal ORTEGA

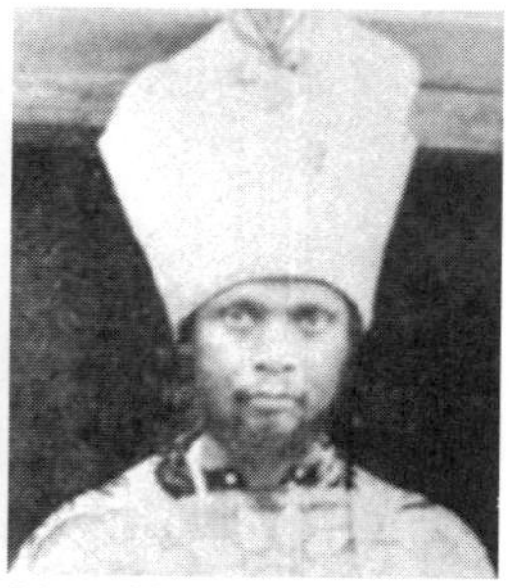
Primate OSHITELU

**Ortega y Alamino**, Cardinal Jaime Lucas, Archbishop of San Cristóbal de la Habana, Conferencia Episcopal de Cuba, Presidente. Born 1936. Nationality: Cuba. Roman Catholic.
Osborne, Charles, Président, Fraternité Evangélique du Sénégal. Nationality: Senegal. Evangelical.
Osei-Mensah, Rev. Gottfried, Executive Secretary, Lausanne Committee for World Evangelization (LCWE), Nairobi, Kenya. Born 1934. Nationality: Ghana. Baptist.
**Oshitelu**, J.O., Founder and Primate, Church of the Lord Aladura. Nationality: Nigeria. Independent.
**Otobu**, His Most Eminence G.I.M., Baba Aladura of the Eternal Sacred Order of the Cherubim & Seraphim. Born c1920. Nationality: Nigeria. Independent.
**Otsu**, Rev. Kenichi, General Secretary, National Christian Council in Japan. Nationality: Japan. Protestant.
Otunga, His Eminence Cardinal Maurice M., Archbishop of Nairobi. Born 1923. Nationality: Kenya. Roman Catholic.
**Oviedo Cavada**, Cardinal Carlos, Archbishop of Santiago de Chile, Conferencia Episcopal de Chile (CECH), President. Born 1927. Nationality: Chile. Roman Catholic.
**Owens**, Chandler David, Presiding Bishop, Church of God in Christ. Born c1935. Nationality: USA. Independent pentecostal.
Paavali Olmari, Most Rev., Archbishop of Karelia & All Finland. Born 1914. Nationality: Finland. Greek Orthodox.
Pabst, Oberkirchenrat Dr Walter, Geschäftsführer, Arbeitsgemeinschaft Christlicher Kirchen in der DDR. Born 1912. Nationality: German Democratic Republic. Lutheran.
**Páez**, Garcete, Oscar, Conferencia Episcopal Paraguaya, Presidente. Born 1937. Nationality: Paraguay. Roman Catholic.
**Page**, Reverend Dr. Rodney, Director, Church World Service and Witness Unit (former Div. of Overseas Ministries). Protestant.

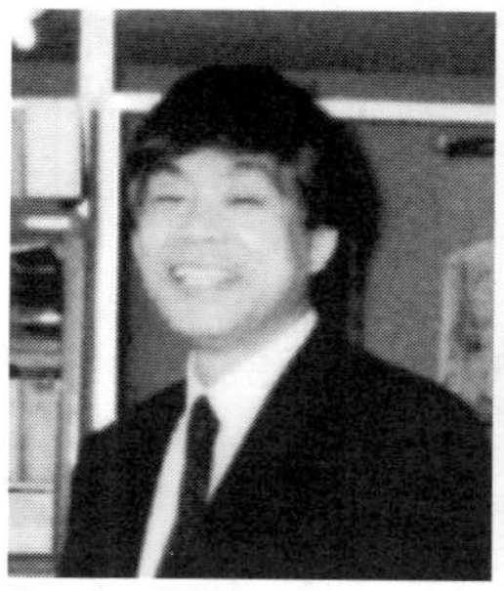
Secretary OTSU

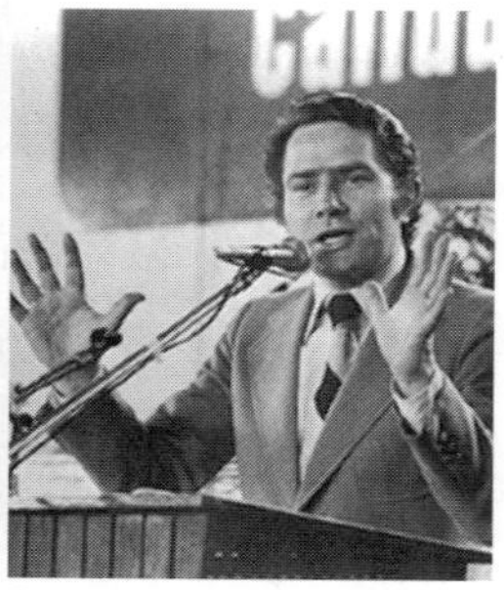
Evangelist PALAU

**Palau**, Rev. Dr. Luis, International evangelist. Born 1934. Nationality: Argentina & USA. Evangelical.
Palchian, see Vasken I.
Palmer, Ms. Elizabeth, General Secretary, World Young Women's Christian Association (YWCA). Protestant.
**Panafieu**, Bernard, Archbishop of Marseilles. Born 1931. Nationality: France. Roman Catholic.
Papadopoulos, D., see Demetrios I.
Papadopoulos, V., see Benediktos I.
Parecattil, His Eminence Cardinal Joseph, Archbishop of Ernakulam, President, Catholic Bishops' Conference of India (CBCI). Born 1912. Nationality: India. Roman Catholic.
Patterson, Bishop J. O., Sr., Presiding Bishop, Church of God in Christ. Nationality: USA. Black pentecostal.
Patterson, Rev. Thomas Carlisle, General Secretary, Conference of Missionary Societies in Great Britain and Ireland (CBMS). Born 1922. Nationality: UK. Presbyterian Church in Ireland.

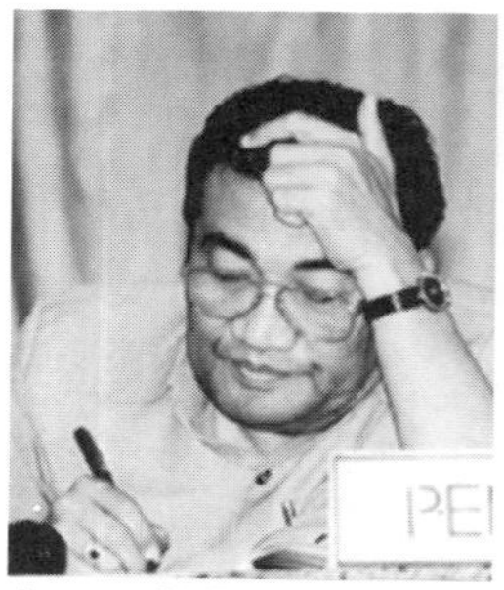
Secretary PATTIASINO

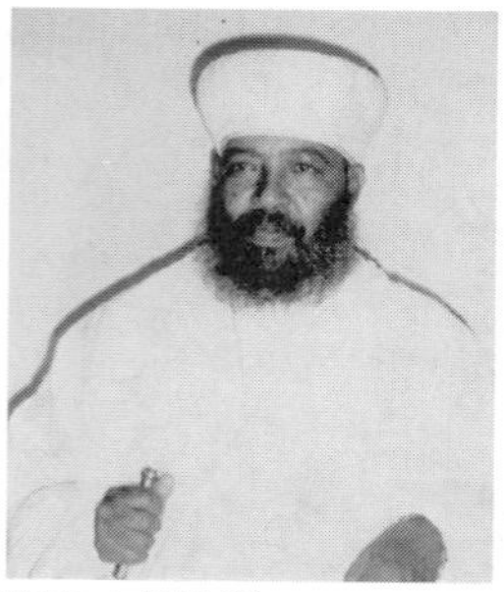
Patriarch PAULOS

**Pattiasino**, Joseph M., General Secretary, Communion of Churches in Indonesia. Nationality: Indonesia. Protestant.
**Paul**, Cyril, Right Reverend, Christian Council of Trinidad and Tobago, Chairman. Protestant.
Paul II, His Beatitude Mar Cheikho, Patriarch of Babylon of the Chaldeans (since 1958), Chaldean Catholic Church, Head of the Chaldean Patriarchal Synod. Born 1906. Nationality: Iraq. Roman Catholic.
Paul VI (Paolo VI) (Giovanni Battista Montini), His Holiness the Pope (elected 1963), Bishop of Rome, Sovereign of Vatican City State. Born 1897. Died 1978. Nationality: Holy See and Italy. Roman Catholic.
**Paulos**, His Holiness Abuna, Patriarch of the Ethiopian Orthodox Church. Born 1935. Nationality: Ethiopian. Oriental Orthodox.

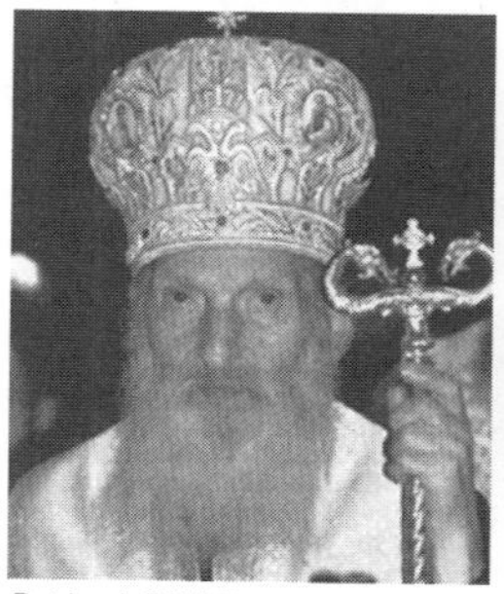
Patriarch PAVLE

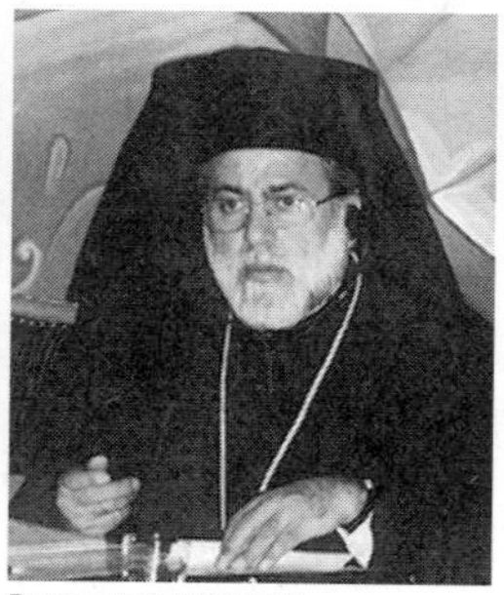
Patriarch PETROS VII

**Pavle**, Patriarch, Serbian Orthodox Church. Born 1915. Nationality: Yugoslavia. Orthodox.
Pawlik, Rev. Pastor Zdzislaw, General Secretary, Polish Ecumenical Council. Nationality: Poland. Protestant.
**Pengo**, Polycarp, Archbishop of Dar Es Salaam. Born 1944. Nationality: Tanzania. Roman Catholic.
**Pereira**, Simeon Anthony, Archbishop of Karachi. Born 1927. Nationality: Pakistan. Roman Catholic.
**Perera**, Rev. Dr. Rienzie, General Secretary, National Christian Council of Sri Lanka. Nationality: Sri Lanka. Protestant.
**Pérez**, Pedro, General Secretary, Alianza Evangelica Espanala. Nationality: Spain. Evangelical.
**Pérez Rodríguez**, Jesús, Archbishop of Sucre. Born 1936. Nationality: Bolivia. Roman Catholic.
Perret, Rev. Dr. Edmond Jean, General Secretary, World Alliance of Reformed Churches (WARC). Born 1925. Nationality: Switzerland. Reformed.
**Pesare**, Oreste, Director, ICCRS, Vatican City. Born 1960. Nationality: Italy. Roman Catholic.
Pessoa Câmara, Most Rev. Dom Helder, Archbishop of Olinda & Ricife. Born 1909. Nationality: Brazil. Roman Catholic.
**Peters**, Miss Hannah Acy, General Secretary, Gambia Christian Council. Protestant.
**Peterson**, Canon John, Secretary General, Anglican Consultative Council. Born c1940. Nationality: USA. Episcopalian.
**Petros VII**, His Divine Beatitude, Pope & Patriarch of Alexandria, All Egypt & All Africa. Born 1949. Nationality: Greece. Greek Orthodox.
**Pham Dinh Tung**, Cardinal Paul Joseph, Archbishop of Hà Nôi, Conference Episcopale du Vietnam, President. Born 1919. Nationality: Vietnam. Roman Catholic.
**Philipos I**, His Holiness Patriarch, Eritrean Orthodox Church. Nationality: Eritrea. Orthodox.
Philippe, His Eminence Cardinal Paul, OP, Prefect, Sacred Congregation for the Oriental Churches, Roman Curia (Vatican City). Born 1905. Nationality: France. Roman Catholic.
**Phipps**, William, Moderator, United Church of Canada. Born 1942. Nationality: Canada. United Church.
Pierson, Robert H., President, General Conference of Seventh-day Adventists, until 1978. Nationality: USA. Adventist.
Pignedoli, His Eminence Cardinal Sergio, President, Secretariat for Non-Christians, Roman Curia (Vatican City). Born 1910. Died 1980. Nationality: Italy. Roman Catholic.
**Pilla**, Anthony Michael, S.E.R. Mons., Bishop of Cleveland, National Conference of Catholic Bishops (NCCB), USA, President. Born 1932. Nationality: USA. Roman Catholic.
Pimen (Sergij Izvekov), His Holiness, Patriarch of Moscow & All Russia (elected 1971). Born 1910. Nationality: USSR. Russian Orthodox.
Pimiento Rodriguez, Right Rev. José de Jesús, Bishop of Garzón, Conferencia Episcopal de Colombia, Presidente. Born 1919. Nationality: Colombia. Roman Catholic.
Pironio, Right Rev. Eduardo, Bishop of Mar del Plata, Consejo Episcopal Latinoamericano (CELAM), Presidente. Born 1920. Nationality: Argentina. Roman Catholic.
Pitts, Rev. S. G., President, Methodist Church of South Africa. Nationality: South Africa. Methodist.

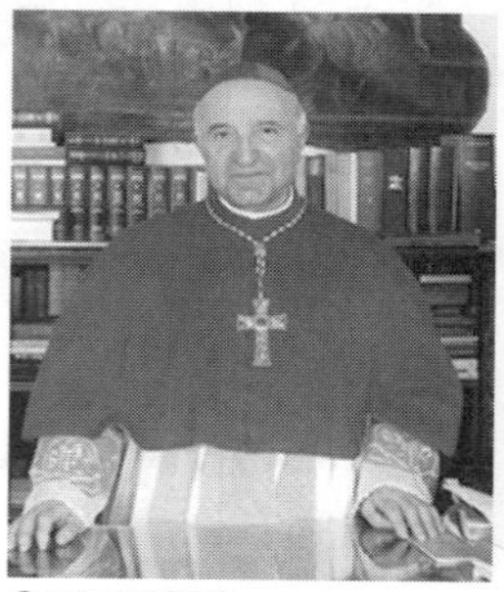
Cardinal POGGI

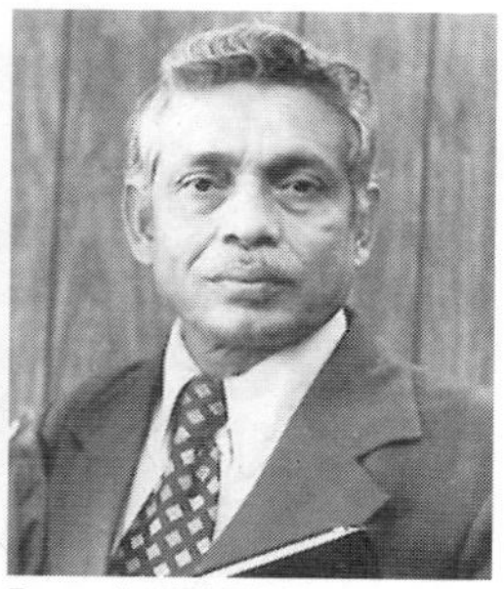
Evangelist PRADHAN

**Poggi**, Cardinal Luigi, Archivist & Librarian, College of Cardinals. Born 1917. Nationality: Italy. Roman Catholic.
Poma, His Eminence Cardinal Antonio, Archbishop of Bologna, Presidente, Conferenza Episcopale Italiana. Born 1910. Nationality: Italy. Roman Catholic.
Pong, Right Rev. James, Bishop of Taiwan, Chairman, Council of the Church in East Asia (CCEA). Born 1911. Nationality: Taiwan. Episcopalian (Anglican).
Pont, Pastor Maurice Paul, General Secretary, Department Evangélique Français d'Action Apostolique (DEFAP). Born 1919. Nationality: France. Reformed Church of France.
Potter, Rev. Dr. Philip Alford, General Secretary, World Council of Churches (WCC). Born 1921. Nationality: UK. Methodist.
**Powathill**, S.E.R. Mons. Joseph, Archbishop of Changanacherry, Catholic Bishops' Conference of India (CBCI), President. Born 1930. Nationality: India. Roman Catholic.
**Pradhan**, Prem, Pioneer Evangelist, Churches of Nepal. Nationality: Nepal. Independent.
Preus, Rev. Dr. David W., General President, American Lutheran Church (ALC). Born 1922. Nationality: USA. Lutheran.
Preus, Rev. Dr. Jacob Aall O., President, Lutheran Church—Missouri Synod. Born 1920. Nationality: USA. Lutheran.
**Prieto Vega**, Right Rev. Ignacio, Bishop of Wankie (Hwange), President, Rhodesia Catholic Bishops' Conference. Born 1923. Nationality: Spain. Roman Catholic.
Pröhle, Professor Dr Karoly, General Secretary, Ecumenical Council of Hungarian Churches. Born 1911. Nationality: Hungary. Lutheran.
**Proykov**, S.E.R. Mons Christo, Vesc. tit. di Briula, Bulgarian Catholic Bishops Conference, President. Born 1946. Nationality: Bulgaria. Roman Catholic.
Quinn, Most Rev. John Raphael, Archbishop of San Francisco, President, National Conference of Catholic Bishops (NCCB), USA. Born 1929. Nationality: USA. Roman Catholic.
**Radchuk**, Slavik, Evangelist. Nationality: Ukraine. Independent.

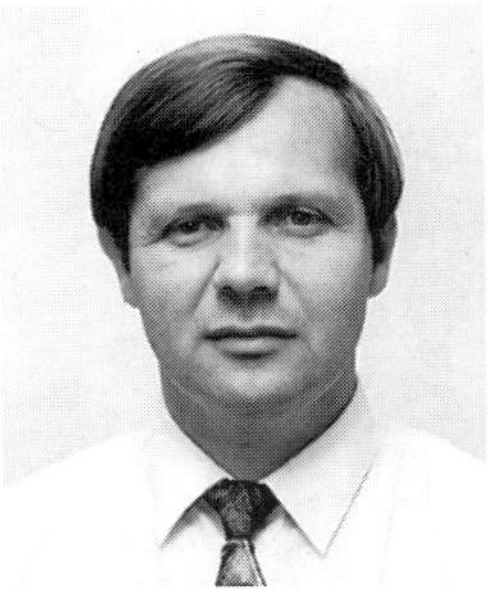

Evangelist RADCHUK

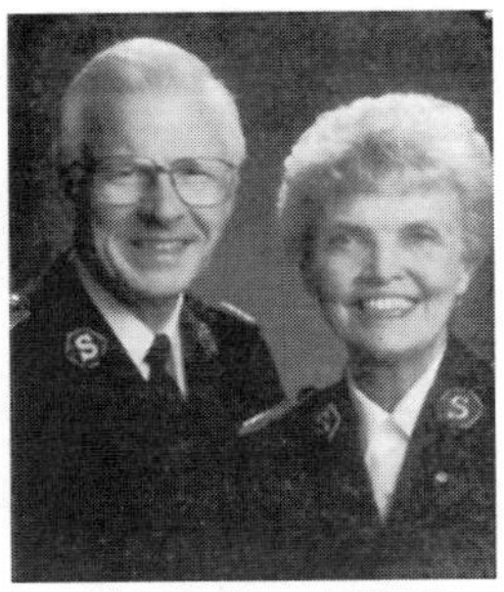

General & Mrs General RADER

**Rader**, Paul and Kay, General and Mrs General, Salvation Army. Born 1934. Nationality: USA. Salvationist.

Rafransoa, Rev. Dr. Maxime Victor, General Secretary, All Africa Conference of Churches (AACC). Born 1934. Nationality: Madagascar. Reformed.

Raimondi, His Eminence Cardinal Luigi, Prefect, Sacred Congregation for the Causes of Saints, Roman Curia (Vatican City). Born 1912. Nationality: Italy. Roman Catholic.

Rairi, Nga, General Secretary, Cook Islands Christian Church. Born 1932. Nationality: New Zealand. Congregationalist.

**Raiser**, Conrad, General Secretary, World Council of Churches. Nationality: Germany. Protestant.

**Rakic**, Rev. Radomir, General Secretary, Ecumenical Council of Churches in Yugoslavia. Protestant.

Rakotoarimanana, Pastor Victor, Secretary General, Communauté Evangélique d'Action Apostolique (CEVAA). Nationality: Madagascar. United (FJKM).

**Rakotonirina**, Charles Rémy, S.E. Bishop of Farafangana. Born 1928. Nationality: Madagascar. Roman Catholic.

Ramambasoa, Pastor Joseph Joelson, President, Eglise du Jésus-Christ à Madagascar. Born 1925. Nationality: Madagascar. United (FJKM).

**Ramousse**, Yves-Georges-René, M.E.P., Vesc. tit. of Pisita, Conference Episcopale du Laos et de la Republique Khmere, President. Born 1928. Nationality: Laos. Roman Catholic.

Ramsey, Most Rev. & Right Hon. Arthur Michael, Archbishop of Canterbury and Primate of All England (retired 1974). Born 1904. Nationality: UK. Anglican.

Randall, Dr. Claire, General Secretary, National Council of Churches of Christ in the USA(NCCCUSA). Born 1919. Nationality: USA. United Presbyterian.

**Rankin**, Jerry, President, International Mission Board (IMB), Southern Baptist Convention. Nationality: USA. Southern Baptist.

**Ratanabutra**, Rev. Charan, President, Evangelical Fellowship of Thailand, Chairman, Protestant Association of Thailand. Nationality: Thailand. Evangelical.

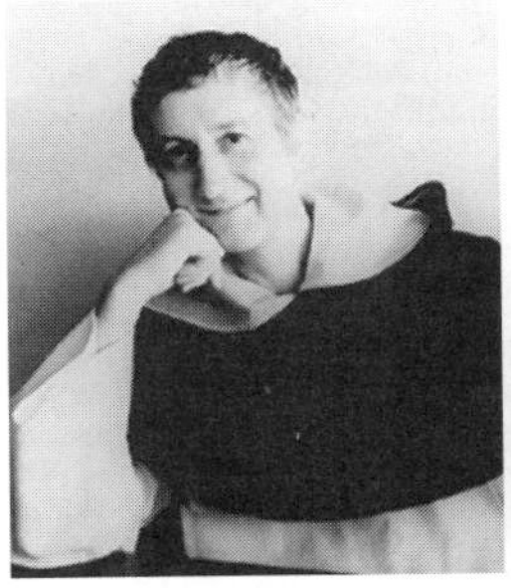

Maestro RATCLIFFE

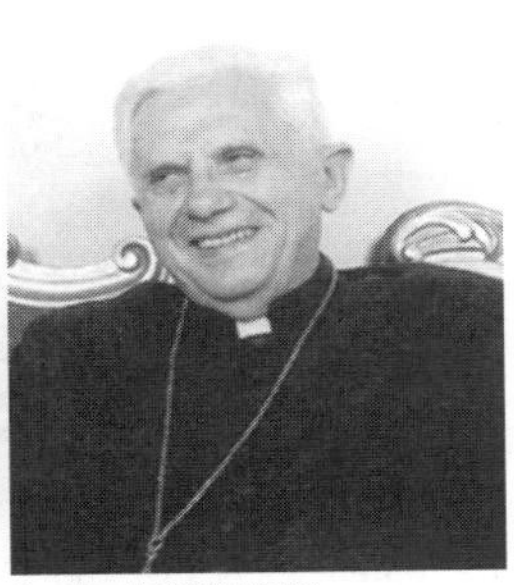

Cardinal RATZINGER

**Ratcliffe O.P.**, Timothy, Maestro of the Dominican Order. Nationality: Britain. Roman Catholic.

**Ratzinger**, Cardinal Joseph, Prefect, Sacred Congregation for the Doctrine of the Faith, Roman Curia (Vatican City). Born 1927. Nationality: Vatican City & Germany. Roman Catholic.

Ratéfy, Rev. Pastor Daniel, General Secretary, Christian Council of Madagascar (FFPM). Born 1913. Nationality: Madagascar. United (FJKM).

**Razafimahatratra**, His Eminence Cardinal Victor, Président, Conférence Episcopale de Madagascar. Born 1921. Nationality: Madagascar. Roman Catholic.

Reed, Dr. Roy M., President, American Baptist Association (ABA). Nationality: USA. Baptist.

Rees, John Charles, General Secretary (until 1977), South African Council of Churches (SACC). Born 1937. Nationality: South Africa. Methodist.

**Revelo Contreras**, Marco René, Bishop of Santa Ana, Episcopal Conference of El Salvador, President. Born 1923. Nationality: El Salvador. Roman Catholic.

Ribeiro, His Eminence Cardinal Antonio, Patriarch of Lisbon. Born 1928. Nationality: Portugal. Roman Catholic.

Ricciardi, Rev. Salvatore, Secretary, Federazione delle Chiese Evangeliche in Italia (FCEI). Nationality: Italy. Evangelical.

**Richardson**, Art, American Baptist Association (ABA), President. Nationality: USA. Baptist.

**Roberts**, Oral, Founder, Oral Roberts University. Nationality: USA. Methodist.

Robinson, Bishop Hubert N., President, Bishops Council, African Methodist Episcopal Church. Nationality: USA. Methodist.

**Robu**, Ioan, S.E.R. Mons., Archbishop of Bucharest, Romanian Catholic Episcopal Conference, President. Born 1944. Nationality: Romania. Roman Catholic.

Rocchietti, Marcos, Executive Secretary, Federación de Iglesias Evangélicas del Uruguay (FIEU). Nationality: Uruguay. Protestant.

Rodriguez, Rev. Antonio Rivera, Presidente, Concilio Evangélico de Puerto Rico. Nationality: Puerto Rico. Evangelical.

**Rodriguez Maradiaga**, Oscar Andrés, Archbishop of Tegucigalpa, Conferencia Episcopal de Honduras, President. Born 1942. Nationality: Honduras. Roman Catholic.

Rolston, Rev. M. A. Z., General Secretary, National Christian Council of India (NCCI). Nationality: India. Protestant.

**Romero Caberera**, Orlando, Bishop of Canelones, Conferencia Episcopal Uruguaya, Presidente. Born 1933. Nationality: Uruguay. Roman Catholic.

Rompas, Rev. Paul Hein, Moderator, Protestant Church in Indonesia. Born 1921. Nationality: Indonesia. Reformed.

**Rosa**, Moisés, Secretary, Concilio Evangelico de Puerto Rico. Evangelical.

Rosales, His Eminence Cardinal Julio, Archbishop of Cebu, President, Catholic Bishops' Conference of the Philippines. Born 1906. Nationality: Philippines. Roman Catholic.

Rossi, His Eminence Cardinal Agnelo, Prefect, Sacred Congregation for the Evangelization of Peoples (Propaganda Fide), Roman Curia (Vatican City). Born 1913. Nationality: Brazil. Roman Catholic.

Rotov, see Nikodim.

**Rouco Varela**, Antonio Mana, Archbishop of Madrid. Born 1936. Nationality: Spain. Roman Catholic.

Routh, Porter Wroe, Executive Secretary-Treasurer, Southern Baptist Convention. Nationality: USA. Southern Baptist.

Rowell, Right Rev. Kevin William, OFM, Bishop of Aitape, President, Bishops' Conference of Papua New Guinea & the Solomon Islands. Born 1927. Nationality: Australia. Roman Catholic.

Roy, His Eminence Cardinal Maurice, Archbishop of Quebec, President, Consilium de Laicis (HQ VAtican City). Born 1905. Nationality: Canada. Roman Catholic.

**Rozario**, Michael, Archbishop of Dhaka, Catholic Bishops' Conference of Bangladesh, President. Born 1926. Nationality: Bangladesh. Roman Catholic.

Rugambwa, His Eminence Cardinal Laurean, Archbishop of Dar es Salaam, Former President, Tanzania Episcopal Conference. Born 1912. Nationality: Tanzania. Roman Catholic.

**Ruini**, Cardinal Camillo, President, Conferenza Episcopale Italiana. Born 1931. Nationality: Italy. Roman Catholic.

Ruivivar, Faustino, Jr., Chairman, Philippine Council of Evangelical Churches. Nationality: Philippines. Evangelical.

**Ruiz Nava**, José Mario, Archbishop of Portoviejo, Conferencia Episcopal Ecuatoriana, Presidente. Born 1930. Nationality: Ecuador. Roman Catholic.

Runcie, Most Rev. & Right Hon. Robert, Archbishop of Canterbury and Primate of All England. Born 1921. Nationality: UK. Anglican.

**Runn**, Harunn, General Secretary, New Sudan Council of Churches. Born c1960. Nationality: Sudan. Protestant.

Russell, Rev. Dr. David Syme, General Secretary, Baptist Union of Great Britain and Ireland. Born 1916. Nationality: UK. Baptist.

**Sabbah**, S.B. (His Beatitude) Michel, Latin Patriarch of Jerusalem, Conference des Eveques Latins dans les Regions Arabes (CELRA), President. Born 1933. Nationality: Israel. Roman Catholic.

Salajka, Professor Dr. Milan, Secretary, Ecumenical Council of Churches in the CSR. Nationality: Czechoslovakia. Protestant.

Salazar López, His Eminence Cardinal José, Archbishop of Guadalajara, Presidente, Conferencia del Episcopado Mexicano. Born 1910. Nationality: Mexico. Roman Catholic.

**Salina**, Henri, Vesc. tit. of Monte di Mauritania, Conference des Eveques Suisses, President. Born 1926. Nationality: Switzerland. Roman Catholic.

**Samba**, Justin Tetemu, Bishop of Musoma, Tanzania Episcopal Conference, President. Born 1950. Nationality: Tanzania. Roman Catholic.

Sams, Dr. James C., President, National Baptist Convention of America. Nationality: USA. Baptist.

Samuel, His Grace Anba, Bishop for Public, Ecumenical and Social Services, Coptic Orthodox Church, Chairman, Ecumenical Advisory Council for Church Services in Egypt. Born 1920. Nationality: Egypt. Coptic Orthodox.

Samuel, Most Rev. Ananda Rao, Bishop in Krishna-Godavari, Church of South India, Moderator. Nationality: India. United.

Samuel, Right Rev. John Victor, Moderator, Church of Pakistan. Born 1930. Nationality: Pakistan. United.

**Samuels**, Elder T.W., President, National Convention, Natl. Primitive Baptist Convention. Nationality: USA. Baptist.

**Sandoval Iñiguez**, Cardinal Juan, Archbishop of Guadalajara. Born 1933. Nationality: Mexico. Roman Catholic.

**Sangaré**, Most Rev. Luc Auguste, Archbishop of Bamako, Président, Conférence Episcopale du Mali. Born 1925. Nationality: Mali. Roman Catholic.

**Sanon**, Anselme Titianma, Bishop of Bobo-Dioulasso, Conferences Episcopale de l'Afrique de l'Ouest Francophone (Africa Occidentale), President. Born 1937. Nationality: Burkina Faso. Roman Catholic.

Santos Hernández, Most Rev. Hector Enrique, SDB, Archbishop of Tegucigalpa, Presidente, Conferencia Episcopal de Honduras. Born 1917. Nationality: Honduras. Roman Catholic.

**Sarah**, Robert, Archbishop of Conakry, Conference Episcopale de la Guinie, President. Born 1945. Nationality: Guinea. Roman Catholic.

Sarli, Rev. Feliciano A., Presidente, Federación Argentina de Iglesias Evangélicas (FAIE). Nationality: Argentina. Evangelical.

**Sarr**, Théodore-Adrien, Bishop of Kaolack, Senegal, Mauritania, Capo Verde E Guinea Bissau, President. Born 1936. Nationality: Senegal. Roman Catholic.

Schmale, Pastor K. H., Secretary, Federation of Evangelical Lutheran Churches in South Africa (FELCSA). Nationality: South Africa. Lutheran.

Schmidt, Chief Apostle Walter, Stammapostel (elected 1960), New Apostolic Church (Neuapostolische Kirche). Born 1891. Nationality: FR Germany. New Apostolic.

Schneider, Peter, General Secretary, Germany Evangelical Alliance. Nationality: FR Germany. Evangelical.

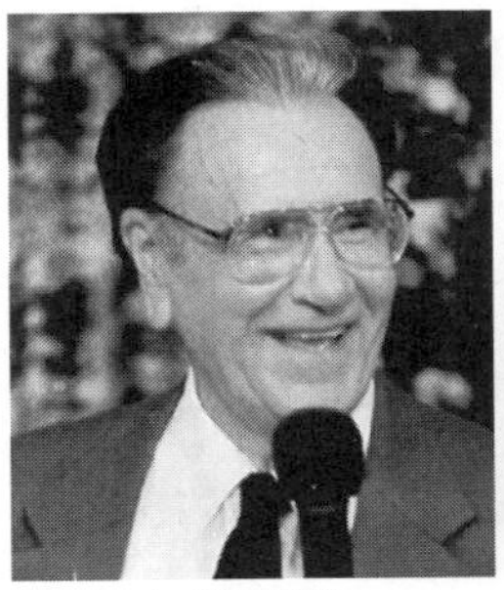

Broadcaster ROBERTS

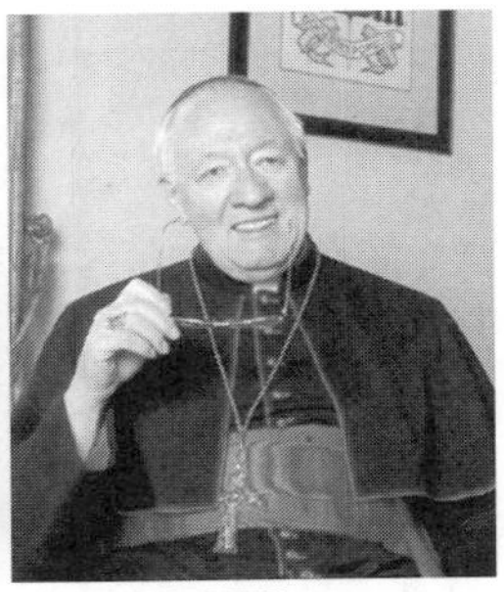

Cardinal SCHOTTE

**Schotte CICM**, Cardinal Jan Peiter, Secretary General, Synod of Bishops. Born 1928. Nationality: Belgium. Roman Catholic.

Schrotenboer, Rev. Dr. Paul Gerard, General Secretary, Christian Reformed Church USA. Born 1922. Nationality: USA. Reformed.

**Schönborn**, Christoph, Archbishop of Vienna. Born 1945. Nationality: Austria. Roman Catholic.

Scott, Most Rev. Archbishop Edward Walter, Primate, Anglican Church of Canada (Eglise Episcopale du Canada). Born 1919. Nationality: Canada. Anglican.

Scott, Most Rev. Moses Nathaniel Christopher Omobiala, Archbishop of West Africa & Bishop of Sierra Leone, Church of the Province of West Africa (CPWA). Born 1911. Nationality: Sierra Leone. Anglican.

Seidenspinner, Dr. Charles, President, Evangelical Fellowship of Canada. Nationality: Canada. Evangelical.

**Sekey**, Benedict Dotu, Bishop of Gbarnga, Inter-territorial Catholic Bishops' Conference of the Gambia, Liberia, and Sierra Leone (ITCABIC), President. Born 1940. Nationality: Liberia. Roman Catholic.

Seper, His Eminence Cardinal Franjo, Prefect, Sacred Congregation for the Doctrine of the Faith, Roman Curia, Vatican City. Born 1905. Nationality: Yugoslavia. Roman Catholic.

Seraphim (Tikas), His Beatitude, Archbishop of Athens & Primate of All Greece. Born 1913. Died 1998. Nationality: Greece. Greek Orthodox.

**Seregély**, István, President, Magyar Püspöki Kar Konferenciája. Born 1931. Nationality: Hungary. Roman Catholic.

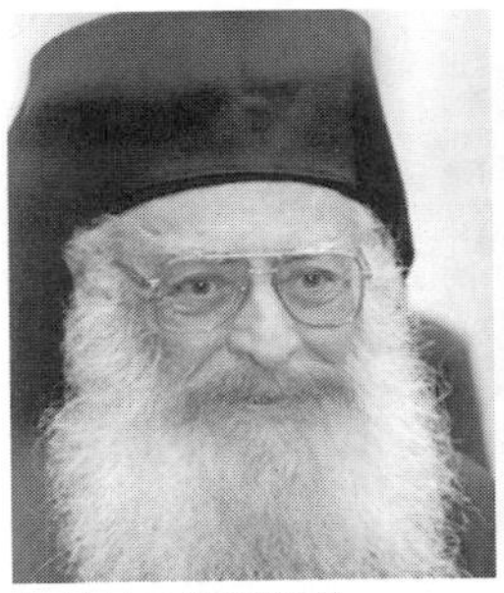

Archbishop SERAPHIM

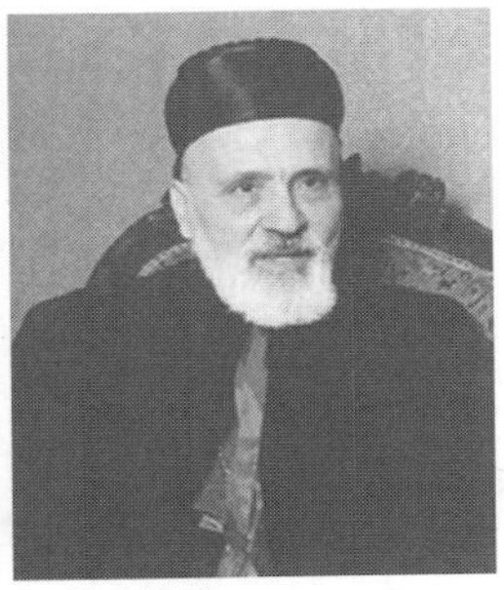

Cardinal SFEIR

**Sfeir**, Cardinal Nasrallah Pierre, Maronite Patriarch of Antioch, Sinodo Della Chiesa Maronita, President, Assembly of Catholic Patriarchs and Bishops of Lebanon, President. Born 1920. Nationality: Syria. Maronite Catholic.

**Shan Kuo-hsi**, S.E.R. Mons. Paul, Bishop of Kaohsiung, Regional Conference of China, President. Born 1923. Nationality: China. Roman Catholic.

**Shastri**, Rev. Dr. Hermen, General Secretary, Council of Churches of Malaysia. Protestant.

Shauri, Stanford Abraham, General Secretary, Christian Council of Tanzania (CCT). Born 1929. Nationality: Tanzania. Anglican.

Shenk, Rev. Jacob, Chairman, Evangelical Fellowship of Zimbabwe-Rhodesia. Nationality: USA. Mennonite.

Shenouda III (Nazeer Gayed), His Holiness Anba, Pope and Patriarch of Alexandria, All Egypt & All Africa (elected 1971). Born 1923. Nationality: Egypt. Coptic Orthodox.

Shiolashvili, see Iliya.

Shnork, see Kalustian.

**Showell-Rogers**, Gordon John, General Secretary, European Evangelical Alliance (EEA). Born 1953. Nationality: Britain. Baptist.

Sianipar, Rev. Professor Frans Hanaehan, General Secretary, Batak Protestant Christian Church (HKBP). Born 1929. Nationality: Indonesia. Lutheran.

Sidamonidze, G., see David V..
Sidarouss, His Eminence Cardinal Stephanos I., CM, Coptic Patriarch of Alexandria, Head, Coptic Patriarchal Synod, President, Assembly of Bishops of Egypt. Born 1904. Nationality: Egypt. Roman Catholic.
Sigrist, Dr. Walter, Président, Fédération des Eglises Protestantes de la Suisse (FEPS). Nationality: Switzerland. Reformed.
Sikakane, Rev. Enos, Programme Director, Interdenominational African Ministers Association of Southern Africa (IDAMASA). Nationality: South Africa. Independent.
**Silota**, Francisco João, Bishop of Chimoio, Conferência Episcopal de Moçambique, President. Born 1941. Nationality: Mozambique. Roman Catholic.
Silva Henríquez, His Eminence Cardinal Raúl, SDB, Archbishop of Santiago de Chile, Presidente, Conferencia Episcopal de Chile (CECH). Born 1907. Died 1999. Nationality: Chile. Roman Catholic.

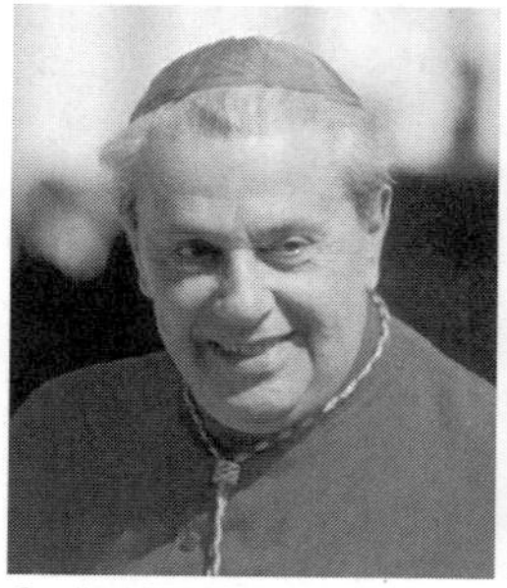
Cardinal SILVESTRINI

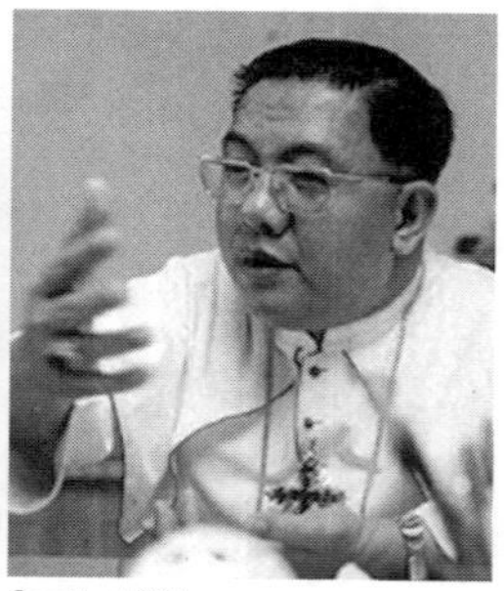
Cardinal SIN

**Silvestrini**, Cardinal Achille, Prefect, Sacred Congregation for the Oriental Churches, Roman Curia (Vatican City). Born 1923. Nationality: Italy. Roman Catholic.
Simojoki, Most Rev. Martii I., Archbishop of Turku (Abo) & Primate, Evangelical Lutheran Church of Finland. Born 1908. Nationality: Finland. Lutheran.
**Simonis**, Cardinal Adrianus Johannes, Archbishop of Utrecht, Netherlands Bishops' Conference, President. Born 1931. Nationality: Netherlands. Roman Catholic.
**Sin**, Cardinal Jaime L., Archbishop of Manila. Born 1928. Nationality: Philippines. Roman Catholic.
**Sindamuka**, Most Reverend Samuel, Archbishop of Burundi, Bishop of Matana. Nationality: Burundi. Anglican.
Sintim-Misa, Right Rev. Gottfried Kwadwo, Moderator, Presbyterian Church of Ghana. Born 1912. Nationality: Ghana. Presbyterian.
Sipilä, Miss Annikki, Secretary, Finnish Missionary Council. Nationality: Finland. Lutheran.
Skrypnyk, His Eminence Mstyslav, Metropolitan of the Ukrainian Autocephalous Orthodox Church in Exile & in the USA. Born 1898. Nationality: USA. Ukrainian Orthodox.
Slack, Rev. Dr Kenneth, Director, Christian Aid. Born 1917. Nationality: UK. United Reformed.
Smail, Rev. Thomas A., Director, Fountain Trust (Charismatic). Nationality: UK. Presbyterian (Church of Scotland).
Smith, Dr. Nelson Henry, President, Progressive National Baptist Convention. Born 1930. Nationality: USA. Baptist.
**Smith**, Dr. Bennett W., President, Progressive National Baptist Convention. Nationality: USA. Baptist.
**Sodano**, Cardinal Angelo, Secretary of State, Holy See. Born 1927. Nationality: Italy. Roman Catholic.
Solzhenitsyn, Alexandr, Writer. Born 1918. Nationality: USSR (deprived 1974). Russian Orthodox.
**Somé**, Jean-Baptiste, S.E.R. Mons, Bishop of Diébougou, Conference des Evêques de Burkina Faso et du Niger, President. Born 1930. Nationality: Burkina Faso. Roman Catholic.

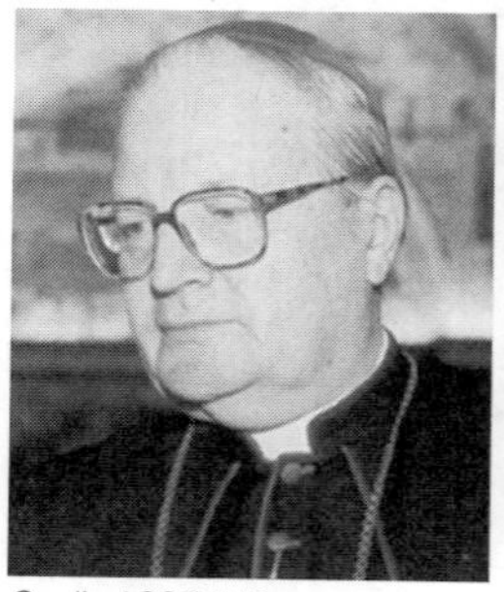
Cardinal SODANO

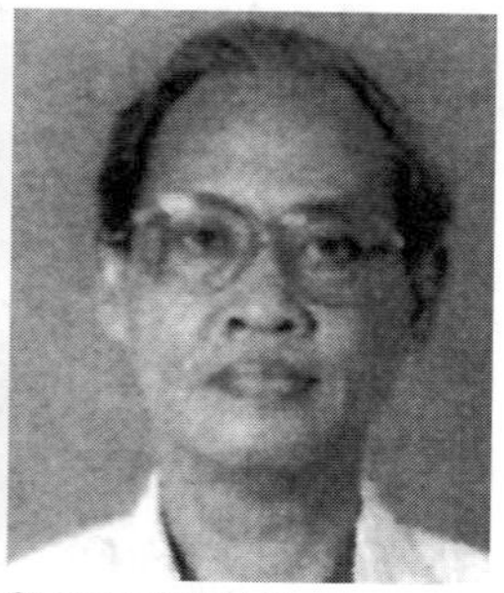
Chairman SOPATER

**Sopater**, Sularso, General Chairman, Communion of Churches in Indonesia. Born 1945. Nationality: Indonesia. Protestant.
Spae, Rev. Dr Joseph J., CICM, General Secretary, SODEPAX, Author. Born 1913. Nationality: Belgium. Roman Catholic.
**Spence**, Francis John, Archbishop of Kingston, Conference Eveques Catholiques du Canada (C.E.C.C.), President, Canadian Conference of Catholic Bishops (C.C.C.B.). Born 1926. Nationality: Canada. Roman Catholic.
Srisang, Dr. Koson, General Secretary, Church of Christ in Thailand. Born 1938. Nationality: Thailand. United.
**Stephen**, Reverend Enock Tombe, General Secretary, Sudan Council of Churches. Nationality: Sudan. Protestant.
**Sterzinsky**, Cardinal Georg Maximilian, Archbishop of Berlin. Born 1936. Nationality: Poland. Roman Catholic.
**Stevens**, Dr. R.D., General Secretary, Irish Council of Churches. Protestant.
Stewart, Rev. W., Chairman, Scottish Churches Council. Nationality: UK. Protestant.
**Stockwell**, Rev. Eugene, Chairman, National Council of Churches, Div. of Overseas Ministries (1972-1984). Died 1996. Nationality: USA. Protestant.
Stratiew, Msgr. Metodio Dimitrow, Exarch of Sofia, President, Bulgarian Catholic Bishops Conference. Born 1916. Nationality: Bulgaria. Roman Catholic.
Stöylen, Right Rev. Kaare, Bishop of Oslo, Chairman of Bishops' Conference, Church of Norway. Born 1909. Nationality: Norway. Lutheran.
Suenens, His Eminence Cardinal Leo Jozef, Archbishop of Malines-Brussels & Primate of Belgium, Président, Conférence Episcopale de Belgique. Born 1904. Nationality: Belgium. Roman Catholic.
Sundby, Most Rev. Olof Carl, Archbishop of Uppsala & Primate, Church of Sweden. Born 1917. Nationality: Sweden. Lutheran.
**Sunderaraj**, Francis, General Secretary, Evangelical Fellowship of Asia. Born c1950. Nationality: India. Evangelical.
Sundholm, Nils, Secretary, Swedish Ecumenical Council. Nationality: Sweden. Lutheran.

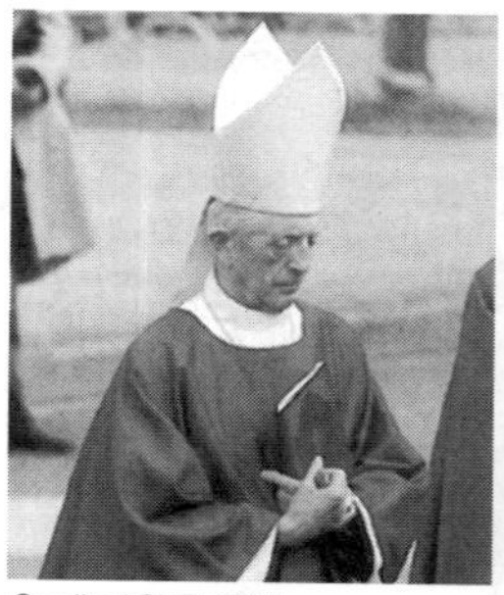
Cardinal SUENENS

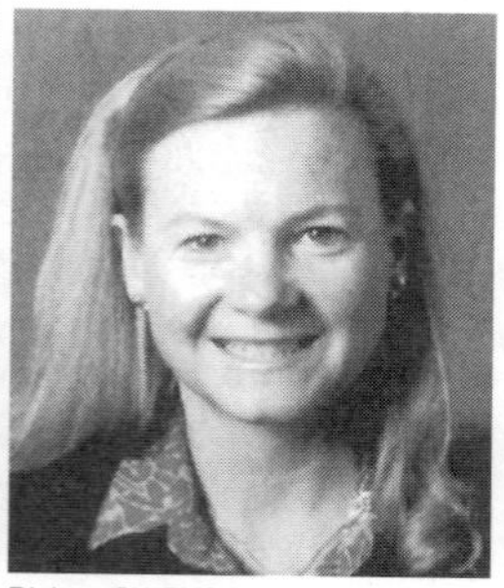
Bishop SWENSON

**Swenson**, Mary Ann, Bishop of Denver Area, United Methodist Church. Nationality: USA. Methodist.
Tabera, His Eminence Cardinal Araoz Arturo, CMF, Prefect, Sacred Congregation for Religious and Secular Institutes, Roman Curia (Vatican City). Born 1903. Nationality: Spain. Roman Catholic.
**Tadeu**, Jorge, Founder, Manna Church. Born 1960. Nationality: Portugal. Independent charismatic.
Taguchi, His Eminence Cardinal Paul Yoshigoro, Archbishop of Osaka, Japan Catholic Bishops' Conference, President. Born 1902. Died 1978. Nationality: Japan. Roman Catholic.
**Tamkevicius**, Sigitas, S.I., Archbishop of Kaunas. Born 1938. Nationality: Latvia. Roman Catholic.
Tan, Rev. Stephen, Honorary General Secretary, National Council of Churches of Singapore. Nationality: Singapore. Protestant.

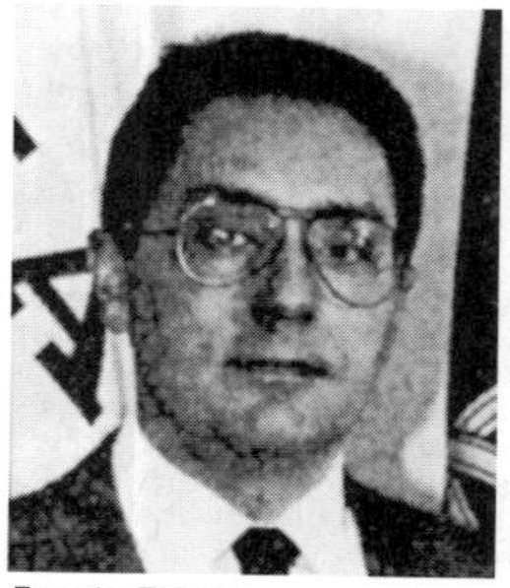
Founder TADEU

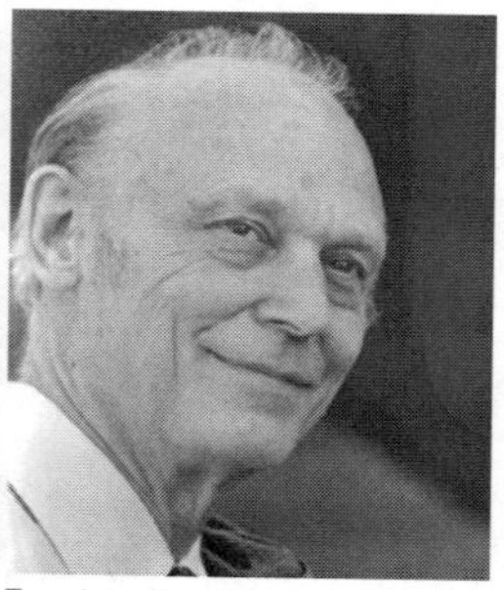
Translator TAYLOR

**Taylor**, Kenneth, Translator, Living Bible. Nationality: USA. Baptist.
**Tchidimbo**, Most Rev. Raymond-Marie, CSSp, Archbishop of Conakry, Président, Conférence Episcopale de la Guinée. Born 1920. Nationality: Guinea. Roman Catholic.
Teegarden, Dr. Kenneth L., General Minister & President, Christian Church (Disciples of Christ). Nationality: USA. Disicples.
**Teissier**, Henri, Archbishop of Algiers, Conference Episcopale d'Afrique du Nord, President. Born 1929. Nationality: Algeria. Roman Catholic.
Tekle-Haimanot, His Holiness Abuna (Abba Wolde-Mikael Melaku), Patriarch, Ethiopian Orthodox Church. Born 1918. Nationality: Ethiopia. Orthodox.
**Templeton**, John Marks, Founder, Templeton Prize for Progress in Religion. Born 1912. Nationality: USA. Presbyterian.
**Teodua**, Cardinal Paulos, Archbishop of Addis Ababa, Conferenza Episcopale di Etiopia, President. Born 1921. Nationality: Ethiopia. Roman Catholic.
**Teresa**, Mother (Agnes G. Bojaxhiu), Founder, Sisters of Charity. Born 1910. Died 1997. Nationality: Albania. Roman Catholic.
**Thapa**, Sundar, Secretary, Christian Fellowship of Nepal. Evangelical.

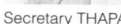

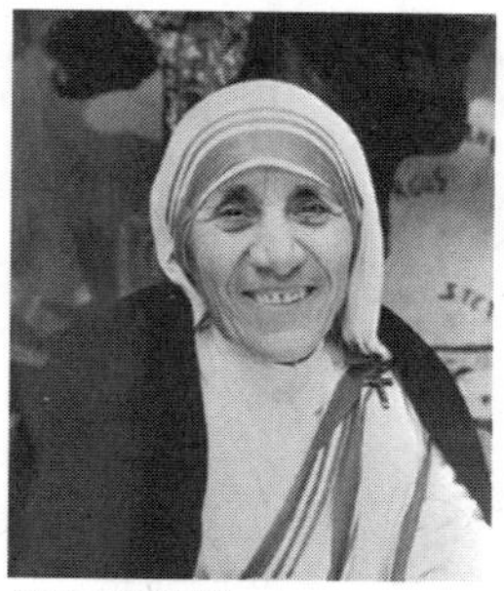
Mother TERESA

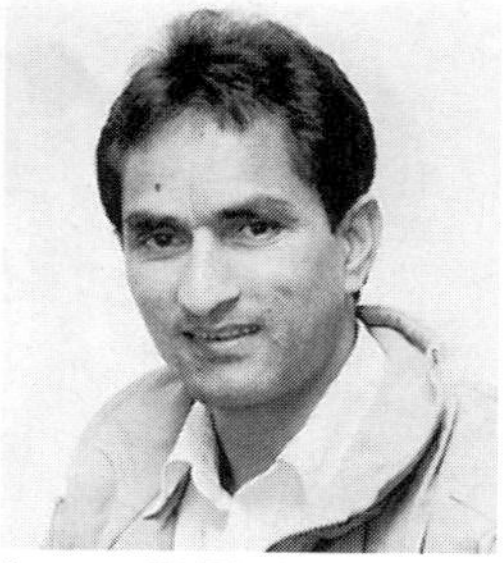
Secretary THAPA

Theodosius (Lazor), His Beatitude, Archbishop of New York, Metropolitan of All America and Canada, Primate, Orthodox Church in America, since 1977. Born 1933. Nationality: USA. Orthodox.
Theophilus I (Tewoflos), His Holiness Abuna (Anba, Abba), Patriarch of Ethiopia 1971-76. Deposed by military regime 1976. Nationality: Ethiopian. Ethiopian Orthodox.
Thevabalasingham, Sam, Secretary, Evangelical Alliance of Ceylon. Nationality: Sri Lanka. Evangelical.
**Thiandoum**, Cardinal Hyacinthe, Archbishop of Dakar, Président, Conférence Episcopale du Sénégal-Mauritanie. Born 1921. Nationality: Senegal. Roman Catholic.
Thohey Mahn Gaby, Gabriel, Archbishop of Yangon. Born 1927. Nationality: Burma. Roman Catholic.
Thompson, William P., Stated Clerk, United Presbyterian Church in the USA. Nationality: USA. Presbyterian.

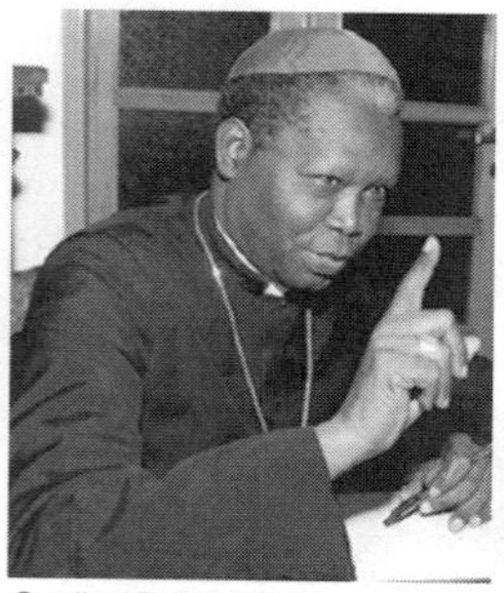
Cardinal THIANDOUM

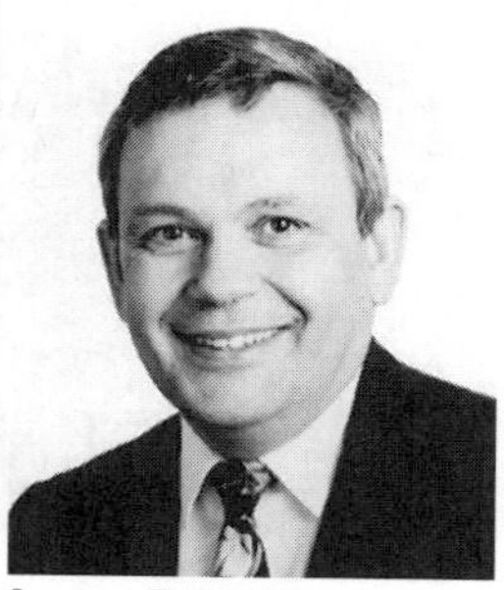
Secretary THORDSON

**Thordson**, Thord-Ove, General Secretary, Christian Council of Sweden. Nationality: Sweden. Lutheran.
Thorne, Rev. John Francis, General Secretary, United Congregational Church of Southern Africa. Born 1926. Nationality: South Africa. Congregationalist.
Ting, Bishop Kuang-Hsun (Ding Guangxun), President, China Christian Council (1980), Chairperson, Chinese Christian Three-Self Patriotic Movement. Born 1915. Nationality: PR China. Anglican, Postdenominationalist.
Tomasek, His Eminence Cardinal Frantisek, Archbishop of Prague. Born 1899. Nationality: Czechoslovakia. Roman Catholic.
**Tomko**, Cardinal Jozef, Prefect, Sacred Congregation for the Evangelization of Peoples (Propaganda Fide), Roman Curia (Vatican City). Born 1924. Nationality: Slovenia. Roman Catholic.
Torrance, Right Rev. Professor Thomas F., Moderator (1976-77), Church of Scotland. Nationality: UK. Presbyterian.
Tortolo, Most Rev. Adolfo Servando, Archbishop of Paraná, Presidente, Conferencia Episcopal Argentina. Born 1911. Nationality: Argentina. Roman Catholic.
Toth, Rev. Dr. Karoly, General Secretary, Christian Peace Conference (CPC). Born 1931. Nationality: Hungary. Reformed Church in Hungary.
**Trindade**, Armando, Archbishop of Lahore, Pakistan Episcopal Conference, President. Born 1927. Nationality: Pakistan. Roman Catholic.
Tuboku-Metzger, Rev. Dr. C. E., General Secretary, United Christian Council of Sierra Leone. Nationality: Sierra Leone. Protestant.
**Tucci**, Rev. Roberto P., President, Vatican Radio. Born 1921. Nationality: Italy. Roman Catholic.
Tung, Rev. William C., General Secretary, Hong Kong Christian Council (HKCC). Born 1936. Nationality: Hong Kong/UK. Methodist.
**Turaki**, Dr. Yusufu, General Secretary, Evangelical Churches of West Africa (ECWA). Evangelical.
Tutu, Right Rev. Desmond, former Bishop of Lesotho, General Secretary, South African Council of Churches (SACC). Born 1935. Nationality: South Africa. Anglican.
**U Shwe**, Matthias, Bishop of Taunggyi, Myanmar Catholic Bishops Conference, President. Born 1943. Nationality: Burma (Myanmar). Roman Catholic.
Vaivods, Right Rev. Giuliano, Apostolic Administrator of Riga & Leipaja, President, Catholic Bishops Conference of Latvia. Born 1895. Nationality: USSR. Roman Catholic.
van den Heuvel, Rev. Dr Albert Hendrik, General Secretary, Netherlands Reformed Church (NHK). Born 1932. Nationality: Netherlands. Reformed.
van der Merwe, Ds. (Rev.) Dr. Willem Jacobus, Moderator, Federal Council of dutch Reformed Churches. Born 1907. Nationality: South Africa. Reformed.
van der Veen, Rev. Rein Jan, General Secretary, Netherlands Missionary Council. Born 1921. Nationality: Netherlands. Reformed Churches in the Netherlands.
Van Meing, Rev. Doan, Chairman, Evangelical Fellowship of Viet Nam. Nationality: Viet Nam. Evangelical.

**Vandame**, Charles, S.I. Archbishop of N'Djamena, Episcopal Conference of Chad, President. Born 1928. Nationality: Chad. Roman Catholic.

**Vargas Alzamora**, Cardinal Augusto, Archbishop of Lima, Conferencia Episcopal Peruana, President. Born 1922. Nationality: Peru. Roman Catholic.

Varthalítis, Most Rev. António, Archbishop of Corfú, Zante and Cefalonia, President, Catholic Episcopal Conference of Greece. Born 1924. Nationality: Greece. Roman Catholic.

Vasken I (Palchian), His Holiness, Supreme Patriarch, Catholicos & Chief Bishop of All the Armenians (since 1955), Echmiadzin. Born 1908. Died 1978. Nationality: USSR. Armenian Apostolic.

Prefect TOMKO                    Metropolitan VASSILIY

**Vassiliy (Basil Doroshkevich)**, His Beatitude, Metropolitan of Warsaw & All Poland. Born 1914. Nationality: Poland. Eastern Orthodox.

Vazgen, See Vasken I.

**Vencer**, Jun, President, World Evangelical Fellowship (WEF). Nationality: Philippines. Evangelical.

**Verschuren**, Right Rev. Paul, SCI, Bishop of Helsinki, President, Scandinavian Episcopal Conference. Born 1925. Nationality: Finland. Roman Catholic.

**Vidal**, Cardinal Ricardo J., Archbishop of Cebu. Born 1931. Nationality: Philippines. Roman Catholic.

Villot, His Eminence Cardinal Jean, Secretary of State, Holy See, Prefect, Council for the Public Affairs of the Church, Roman Curia (Vatican City). Born 1905. Died 1980. Nationality: Holy See and France. Roman Catholic.

**Vivanco Valiente**, Mariano, Bishop of Matanzas. Born 1933. Nationality: Cuba. Roman Catholic.

**Vlk**, Cardinal Miloslav, Archbishop of Prague, Bishops Conference of Czech Republic, President, Consilium Conferentiarum Episcopalium Europae, President. Born 1932. Nationality: Czechoslavakia. Roman Catholic.

von Heyl, Rechtsanwalt Cornelius A., Präses, Präsidum der Synode, Evangelische Kirche in Deutschland (EKD). Nationality: FR Germany. Lutheran.

Vorster, Dominie (Rev.) Dr Jacobus Daniel, Moderator, Algemene Synode van die Nederduitse Gereformeerde Kerk, (Moederkerk), General Synod of the Dutch Reformed Church (Mother Church) of South Africa. Born 1910. Nationality: South Africa. Reformed.

**Wagner**, C. Peter, Professor of Church Growth, Fuller Theological Seminary. Nationality: USA. New Apostolic/Postdenominationalist.

**Walker**, Rev. Paul L., General Overseer, Church of God. Born 1924. Nationality: USA. Protestant.

Professor WAGNER              Director WALKER

**Walker**, Sir Alan, World Director, Methodist Evangelism. Born 1920. Nationality: Australia. Methodist.

**Wall**, Leonard James, Archbishop of Winnipeg. Born 1924. Nationality: Canada. Roman Catholic.

**Wamala**, Cardinal Emmanuel, Archbishop of Kampala. Born 1926. Nationality: Uganda. Roman Catholic.

**Ward**, Kay, Bishop, Moravian Church. Born 1942. Nationality: USA. Moravian.

Wasikye, Rev. Canon J., Joint Secretary, Uganda Joint Christian Council. Nationality: Uganda. Anglican.

Wati, Dr I. Ben, Executive Secretary, Evangelical Fellowship of India (EFI). Nationality: India. Evangelical.

Watyoka, Cornelius Dick, General Secretary, Christian Council of Rhodesia. Born 1934. Nationality: UK. Methodist.

**Weber**, Johann, Bishop of Graz-Seckau, Österreichische Bischofskonferenz, President. Born 1927. Nationality: Austria. Roman Catholic.

**Weiss**, Daniel E., General Secretary, American Baptist Churches in the USA. Nationality: USA. Baptist.

Westergard-Madsen, Right Rev. Willy, Bishop of Copenhagen & Primate, National Church of Denmark. Born 1907. Nationality: Denmark. Lutheran.

**Wetter**, Cardinal Friedrich, Archbishop of Munich i Friesing. Born 1928. Nationality: Germany. Roman Catholic.

Wickham, D. Pablo, Secretary, Alianza Evangélica Espanõla. Nationality: Spain. Evangelical.

Willebrands, His Eminence Cardinal Johannes Gerardus Maria, Archbishop of Utrecht & Primate of the Netherlands, President, Netherlands Bishops' Conference, President, Secretariat for Christian Unity (Vatican City). Born 1909. Nationality: Netherlands. Roman Catholic.

**Williams**, C. O., General Secretary, Christian Council of Nigeria. Nationality: Nigeria. Protestant.

Williams, Dr. Glen Garfield, General Secretary, Conference of European Churches (CEC). Protestant.

Williams, Most Rev. Gwilym Owen, Archbishop of Wales & Bishop of Bangor, Church of Wales. Born 1913. Nationality: UK. Anglican.

**Williams**, Mr. Carlton, Chairperson, St. Vincent and the Grenadines Christian Council. Protestant.

**Wimber**, John, International Director, Association of Vineyard Churches. Born 1934. Died 1997. Nationality: USA. Independent.

**Winning**, Cardinal Thomas Joseph, Archbishop of Glasgow, Bishops' Conference of Scotland, President. Born 1925. Nationality: UK. Roman Catholic.

Wiseman, General Clarence, Tenth General (1974), Salvation Army International. Born 1907, retired 1977. Nationality: Canada. Salvationist.

Wojtyla, see John Paul II.

Wong, Rev. Dr. Peter, General Secretary, Church of Christ in China (Hong Kong Council). Born 1913. Nationality: Hong Kong/UK. United.

**Wong**, Rev. Canon Dr. James, President, National Council of Churches of Singapore. Nationality: Singapore. Anglican.

Woods, Most Rev. Frank, Archbishop of Melbourne, Metropolitan of the Province of Victoria & Primate of Australia, Church of England in Australia. Born 1907, retired 1977. Nationality: Australia. Anglican.

**Wouking**, André, Bishop of Bafoussam, Episcopal Conference of Cameroon, President. Born 1930. Nationality: Cameroon. Roman Catholic.

Wright, Cardinal John Joseph, Prefect, Sacred Congregation for the Clergy, Roman Curia (Vatican City). Born 1909. Nationality: USA and Holy See. Roman Catholic.

Wyszysnki, Cardinal Stefan, Archbishop of Gniezno and Warsaw, President, Polish Episcopal Conference. Born 1901. Nationality: Poland. Roman Catholic.

Yago, Most Rev. Bernard, Archbishop of Abidjan, Président, Conférence Episcopale de la Côte d'Ivoire. Born 1916. Nationality: Ivory Coast. Roman Catholic.

**Yanes Alvarez**, Elías, Archbishop of Zaragoza, Conferencia Episcopal Española, Presidente. Born 1928. Nationality: Spain. Roman Catholic.

Yap, Kim-Hao, Bishop Dr., Methodist Church in Malaysia & Singapore, General Secretary, Christian Conference of Asia (CCA). Born 1929. Nationality: Malaysia. Methodist.

**Yasuda**, Most Rev. Paul Hisao, Archbishop of Osaka. Born 1921. Nationality: Japan. Roman Catholic.

Yemmeru, Most Rev. Asrate M., Archbishop-Metropolitan of Addis Ababa, Presidente, Conferenza Episcopale di Etiopia. Born 1904. Nationality: Ethiopian. Roman Catholic.

**Yongze**, Peter Xu, Leader, Born Again Movement (BAM) China. Born 1940. Nationality: China. Independent.

Yü Pin, His Eminence Cardinal Paul, Archbishop of Nanking, President, Regional Episcopal Conference of China (Taiwan). Born 1901. Nationality: China. Roman Catholic.

**Zemaitis**, Juozas, M.I.C., Bishop of Vilkaviskis. Born 1926. Nationality: Latvia. Roman Catholic.

Zimmerman, Rev. Dr. Thomas F., General Superintendent, Assemblies of God, Chairman, World Pentecostal Conference. Nationality: USA. Pentecostal.

**Zoa**, His Eminence Cardinal Jean, Archbishop of Yaoundé. Born 1924. Nationality: Cameroon. Roman Catholic.

Zoungrana, His Eminence Cardinal Paul, WF, Archbishop of Ouagadougou, Président, Conférence des Evêques de la Haute Volta et du Niger, Président, Symposium des Conférences Episcopales d'Afrique et de Madagascar (SCEAM). Born 1917. Nationality: Upper Volta. Roman Catholic.

**Zubeir Wako**, Gabriel, Archbishop of Khartoum, Sudan Catholic Bishops' Conference (SCBC), President. Born 1941. Nationality: Sudan. Roman Catholic.

Zurenuo, Right Rev. Zurewe K., Bishop, Evangelical Lutheran Church of Papua New Guinea. Nationality: Papua New Guinea. Lutheran.

# Who's Who in the Non-Christian world, AD 1900–AD 2000

**Aandamayi Ma (Nirmala Sundari Devi)**, (1896-1982), Hinduism, Responsive teacher and spiritual attainer who reached Hindu goal without studying the scriptures and without a guru. Traveled widely in India.

**Abd al-Baha**, (1844-1921), Baha'i, Son and Successor of Baha Allah a.k.a. Abdul-Baha Abbas. Led Bahais from 1892-1921. Systematized father's teachings. Travelled extensively in the west 1900-1920.

Imam AGA KHAN IV

Professor AL-HIBRI

**Aga Khan IV (Karim Al-Hussain Shah)**, (1937- ), Imam, Ismaili Muslim. Imamate of the Nizari Ismailite sect of Islam since 1957.

**Agnihotri, Satya Nand**, (1859-1928), Hinduism, Founder of Dev Samaj. Broke with Brahmo Samaj in 1887. Developed a religious atheism. Loyal following among Punjabi Hindus.

**Al Huang, Chungliang**, (1930- ), Taoism, Founder, Living Tao Foundation.

**al-Banna, Hasan**, (1906-1949), Islam, Founder of the Society of Muslim Brothers (1928). Assassinated by Egyptian secret police 12 February 1949.

**al-Hibri, Azizah**, (1950- ), Islam, Leading Muslim feminist. Founder Muslim American Bar Association. President of the Parliament of the World's Religions (1993-1995).

**al-Sadr, Al-Sayyid Musa**, (1928-1978), Islam, Leader of Shi'i Muslim Community in Lebanon, Chairman of Supreme Islamic Shi'i Council (SISC).

**al-Sadr, Muhammed Baqer**, (1935-1980), Islam, Important Iraqi cleric, author of *Falsafatuna* (" Our Philosophy") and *Iqtisaduna*, ("Our Economic System"). Executed April 1980

**Ambedkar, Bhimrao Ramji**, (1891-1956), Buddhism, Political leader, social reformer, and founder of a new Buddhist movement in independent India. Four million Indian Hindus became Buddhists in 1956.

**Anandamurti, Shrii Shrii**, (1923-1990), Hinduism, Founder of Ananda Marga in 1954, an international socio-spiritual organization teaching tantra yoga.

**Ariyaratne, Dr. A. T.**, (1930- ), Buddhism, Founder of Sarvodaya movement in 1960s in Sri Lanka.

**Avrobindo, Si**, (1872-1950), Hinduism, Indian nationalist & Hindu philosopher who developed a new system of Vedanta in which Bualiman is the sole reality.

**Avtar Singh**, (1899-1939), Sikhism, Second guru of the Sant Nirankaris. Many Hindu & Muslim followers.

**Baeck, Leo**, (1873-1956), Judaism, Influential rabbi & theologian who represented German Jewry during the holocaust. Wrote *The Essence of Judaism* (1905).

**Bandido Hamba Lama H. Ga'akan**, (1940- ), Buddhist, Leader of Mongolia's Buddhists. President, Asian Buddhist Conference for Peace.

Taoist AL-HUANG

Hopi leader BANYACYA

**Banyacya, Thomas**, (1930-1999), Native American religion, Interpreter and spokesman for Hopi traditional spiritual leaders.

**Bdud-joms rin-po-che**, (1904-1987), Tibetan Buddhism, Supreme head of the Rnying-ma-pa sect of Tibetan Buddhism.

**Bennett, John Godolphin**, (1897-1974), New Age, Thinker, writer, & teacher. Promoter of Subud. Founded International Academy for Continuous Education in 1970.

**Besant, Annie**, (1847-1933), Theosophy, English theosophist and social reformer. President of Theosophical Society (1907). Author of *Esoteric Christianity* (1902).

**Bhajan, Yogi**, (1929- ), Sikhism, Founder of 3HO (The Healthy, Happy, Holy Organization), educational branch of Sikh Dharma.

**Bhownagree, Muncherji Merwanji**, (1851-1933), Zorastrianism, Influential leader of the Zorastrian Association in India.

**Black Elk**, (1863-1950), Ethnic religion, Oglala Lakota Shaman, spokesman for traditional religions.

**Brahmachari, Dhirendra**, (1925-1994), Hinduism, Guru and teacher of yoga. Exercised much influence on Indira Gandhi, persuading her that yoga classes should be taught in all Indian schools.

**Buber, Martin**, (1878-1965), Judaism, Jewish philosopher and educator; *I and Thou* (1923).

**Buddhadasa**, (1906- ), Buddhism, Thai Buddhist intellectual and monk. Large number of publications aimed at reforming Buddhism.

**Castaneda, Carlos**, (1925-1998), Indian Sorcerer, Author of series of books (awarded Ph.D. by University of California for *Journey to Ixtlan*). Advocated use of pychotropical drugs.

**Cayce, Edgar**, (1877-1945), New Age, Founder of the Association for Research and Enlightenment (ARE) in 1931 with headquarters in Virginia Beach, Virginia, USA.

**Chidananda, Swami**, (1916- ), Hinduism, President of Divine Life Society. Personal representative of Swami Sivananda to Western society.

**Chinmoy, Sri Kumar Ghose**, (1931- ), New religions, Leader of Sri Chinmoy: The Peace Meditation at the United Nations. Author of 700 books and founder of 100 meditation centers.

**Creme, Benjamin**, (1922- ), New Age, Leader of Tava Centers. Claims to have been receiving messages from spiritual masters since 1959.

**Crowley, Aleister**, (1875-1947), Occultist, English occultist-widely read author. *The book of the law: Magick in theory and practice* (1929).

**Da Free John (Franklyn Albert Jones)**, (1939- ), New religion, Founder of the Free Daist Communion. Seven Stages to Enlightenment.

**Daiun Sogaku Harada**, (1870-1961), Zen Buddhism, Japanese Zen master. Received the seal of recognition from Dokutan Roshi and became abbot of Hosshinji.

Swami CHIDANANDA

Dalai LAMA

**Dalai Lama (Tenzin Gyatso)**, (1935- ), Tibetan Buddhism, Considered an incarnation of celestial bodhisattua. Exiled in India seeking independence for Tibet. Recipient of 1989 Nobel Peace Prize.

**Deguchi Nao**, (1837-1918), New religion, Founder of Omotokyo, a Japanese new religion emphasizing eschatology.

**Delahunt, Jacqueline Left Hand Bull**, (1943- ), Baha'i, Member of Continental Board of Counsellors for the Protection and Propagation of the Baha'i Faith in the Americas.

**Dev, Guru**, (1890-1953), Hinduism, Teacher of Yogi Maharishi Mahesh, founder of Transcendental Meditation.

**Dhalla, M. N.**, (1875-1956), Zorastrianism, Parsi reformer, priest and scholar. His main books in English are *Zorastrian Theology* (1914), *Zorastrian Civilization* (1920), and *On Perfecting World* (1930).

**Dharmapala, Anagarika**, (1864-1933), Buddhism, Founder of "Protestant Buddhism" in Sri LankaNemphasized a spiritual egalitarianism influenced by theosophists.

**Eisendrath, M.N.**, (1902-1973), Judaism, USA Reform rabbi, president of the Union of American Hebrew Congregations.

**Elijah Muhammad (Elijah Poole)**, (1897-1975), Muslim, Leader of the Nation of Islam. Preached Black nationalism combined with elements of Christianity and Islam.

**Erhard, Werner (John Paul Rosenberg)**, (1935- ), New Age, Founded Erhard Seminars Training (EST) in 1971. Later called The Forum.

**Fard, Wallace**, (1877-1940), Islam, Founded the Black Muslim Movement.

**Finkelstein, Louis**, (1895- ), Judaism, USA Conservative rabbi. President of Jewish Theological Seminary and the Rabbinical Assembly (1940-1951).

**Fortune, Dion (Violet Mary Firth)**, (1890-1946), Occultist, Wrote classic *The Mystical Qabalah* (1935). Initiated in 1919 into Golden Dawn, now reformed as Stella Matutina.

**Gandhi, Mohanadas Karamachand**, (1869-1948), Hinduism, Indian political and spiritual leader assassinated in 1948 by right-wing Hindus.

**Garvey, Marcus Mosiah**, (1887-1940), Rastafarianism, Proponent of black nationalism in Jamaica. Founded Universal Negro Improvement and Conservation Society and African Communities League (UNIA).

**Ginzberg, Louis**, (1873-1953), Judaism, USA Talmudic and rabbinical scholar. Author of *The legends of the Jews* published in seven volumes (1908-1938).

**Govinda, Lama Anagarika**, (1898-1985), Tibetan Buddhism, Interpreter of Tibetan Buddhism to the West and founder of Arya Maitreya Mandala. Lived in Sri Lanka and Tibet.

**Greenberg, Rabbi Irving**, (1930- ), Jewish, The National Jewish Center for Learning and Leadership (CLAL).

**Gruenbaum, Yitzhak**, (1879-1970), Judaism, Polish Jewish leader and Zionist. Editor of *Encyclopedia of the diaspora*.

**Hakuun Ryoko Yasutani**, (1885-1973), Zen Buddhism, Japanese Zen Buddhist master who received the seal of recognition from Daiun Sogaku Harada. Visited USA frequently.

**Hasan al-Banna**, (1904-1949), Muslim, Founder of Muslim BrotherhoodNinfluenced long-term direction of radical Islamic politics.

Hazrat Inayat KHAN

Theologian HESCHEL

**Hazrat Inayat Khan**, (1882-1927), Islam, From Baroda, India. Established in London in 1910 the Sufi Order in the West acting as bridge between East and West.

**Henderson, Dr. Robert C.**, (1940- ), Baha'i, Secretary-General of the National Spiritual Assembly of the Baha'is of the United States.

**Herzog, Isaac Ha-Levi**, (1888-1959), Judaism, Rabbinic scholar and second Ashkenazi Chief Rabbi of modern Israel. Author of *Main institutions of Jewish law*.

**Heschel, Abraham Joshua**, (1909-1972), Jewish, Theologian and philosopher. Author of *The Sabbath*.

**Heschel, Susannah**, (1960- ), Judaism, Leading Jewish feminist. Abba Hillel Silver Associate Professor of Judaic Studies at Case Western Reserve University.

**Hubbard, Lafayette Ronald**, (1911-1986), New Age, Founder of Scientology. Published *Dianetics: the modern science of mental health* (1950) combining Buddhist ideas and psychology.

**Ikeda Daisaku**, (1928- ), Buddhism, Third president of Soka Gakkai, a Nichiven Buddhist sect. Founded The Clean Government Party (1964).

**Iqbal, Sir Muhammad**, (1876-1938), Islam, Indian Muslim poet and philosopher. His poetry was one of the chief forces behind the creation of Pakistan.

**Irani, Dr. Kaikhosrov**, (1920- ), Zoroastrianism, Member, Board of Directors, World Zorastrian Organization. Professor Emeritus of Philosophy, City College, New York.

**Jabotinsky, Vladimir**, (1880-1940), Judaism, Zionist leader. Founder and head of the Revisionist movement in Zionism. Author of biblical novel *Samson the Nazirite*.

**Jayanti, Sister**, (1955- ), Hinduism, Director of London branch of Brahma Kumaris World Spiritual University. BKSWU's NGO representative to the United Nations.

**Kabilsingh, Dr. Chatsumarn**, (1940- ), Buddhism, Thailand, Professor of Religion and Philosophy at Thammasat University in Bangkok.

**Kahane, Meir**, (1932-1990), Judaism, Rabbi and Jewish activist. Founder of the Jewish Defense League (JDL) and Kach movement.

**Kahn Singh Nabha**, (1861-1938), Sikhism, Erudite Sikh

Scholar. Best known for 4-volume encyclopedia of Sikh literature (1930). Author of *Ham Hindu Nahin* ('We are not Hindus).

**Kanji Svami**, (1889-1980), Jainism, Jain reformer. Renounced his monastic background, founded a lay movement in Gujarat, India.

**Kaplan, Mordecai**, (1881-1983), Judaism, American rabbi and founder of Reconstructionist Movement. Founded Society for the Advancement of Judaism (1922). Author of *Judaism as a Civilization*.

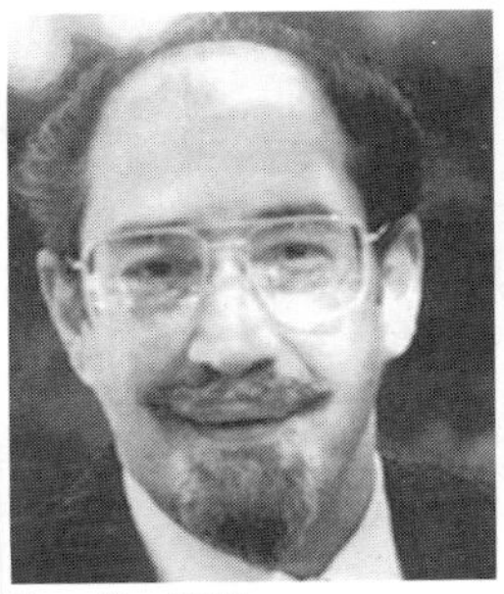

Zorastrian IRANI

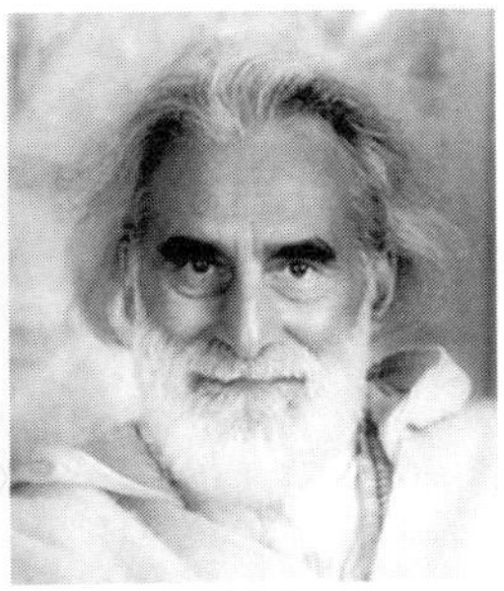

Vilayat Inayat KHAN

**Khan, Pir Vilayat Inayat**, (1917- ), Islam, Leader of Sufi Movement. Founder of Hope Project providing food, education, and health care for slum dwellers.

**Khumayni, Ayat Allah Ruh Allah (Imam Khomeini)**, (1902-1989), Islam, Twelver Shiite leader in Iran, figurehead of Islamic Revolution (1979). Opposed Pahlavi secularism. Developed vilayat-ifaqih ('Government of the Clergy').

**King, George**, (1919- ), New Age, Founder and president of the Aetherius Society, "An International Spiritual Brotherhood" (1955). Invented Spiritual Energy Radiators and Spiritual Energy Battery.

**Kitamura Sayo**, (1900-1967), New Religion, Founder of Japanese new religion Tensho Kotai Jingukyo. In 1945 proclaimed herself universal savior.

**Kook, Abraham Isaac**, (1865-1935), Judaism, Religious thinker. First Chief Rabbi of Palestine. Founded the rabbinical academy Merkaz ha-Rav.

**Kotani Kimi**, (1901-1971), Buddhism, Co-founder and leader of Reiyukai Kyodan ('The Society of Friends of the Spirits) a Japanese lay Buddhist organization.

**Krishnamurti, Jiddu**, (1895-1989), Hinduism, Advocated for life at the "unconditioned" human level. Author of *The First and Last Freedom* (1954).

**Kumar, Acharya Sushil**, (1926-1994), Jainaism, Founder, Mahavir Jain Mission, World Jain Congress.

**Lieberman, Saul**, (1898-1983), Judaism, Jewish Talmudic scholar. Born in Belorussia but settled in Jerusalem and taught at Jewish Theological Seminary.

**Magnes, Judah Leib**, (1877-1948), Judaism, U.S. Reform rabbi. First chancellor of the Hebrew University of Jerusalem.

**Maharaj, Sri Swami Sivananda**, (1887-1963), Hinduism, Established the Divine Life Society.

**Maharaji (Prem Pal Singh Rawat)**, (1957- ), New Age, Founder of Elan Vital, The Sucessor to the Divine Light Mission. Thousands of Western devotees.

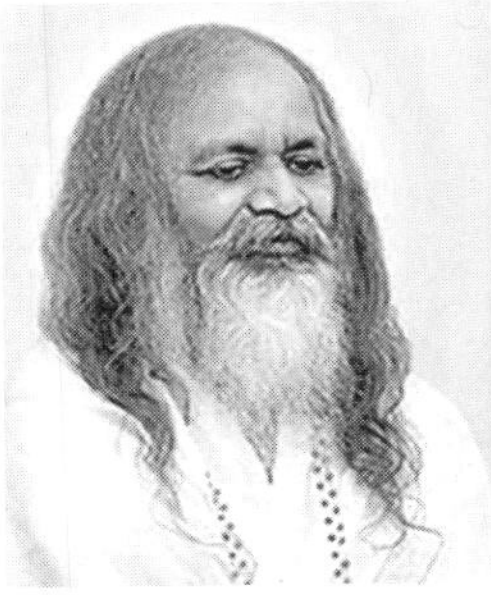

Maharishi MAHESH YOGI

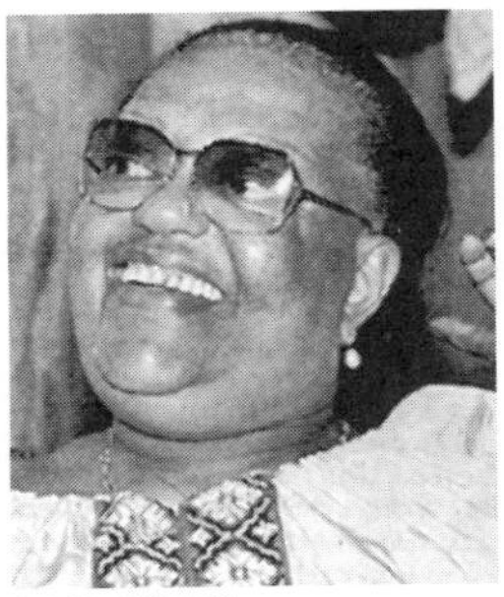

Spiritist MILLET

**Maharishi Mahesh Yogi (Mahesh Prasan Varma)**, (1911- ), New Age, Founder of Transcendatal Meditation (TM) movement. Founded Science of Creative Intelligence and Maharishi International University (1971).

**Makiguchi Tsunesaburo**, (1871-1944), Buddhism, Co-founder of Soka Gakkai. Author of Soka Kyoikugaku taikei (A System of Value-Creation Education) (1930-1934).

**Malcolm X (Malcolm Little)**, (1925-1965), Islam, First Plenipotentiary of The Nation of Islam. Left Nation of Islam in 1964 for Sunni Islam. Assassinated 1965.

**Mawdudi, Mawlana Sayyid Abul-ala**, (1903-1979), Islam, Founder of the Jama'at-i Islami in India (1941) and major religious political leader in Pakistan. Editor of *Tarjuman al-Quran* (1933-1979). Author of *Rasaili Diniyat* (Towards Understanding Isl

**Mawlana Ilyas**, (1885-1944), Islam, Founder of Islamic movement in India (1921), Tablighi Jamaat ('Party which propagates').

**Meher Baba (Merwan Shehiar Irani)**, (1894-1969), Hinduism, Indian guru who built up following of 'Baba lovers' among Muslims, Hindus, and Zorastraians. Claimed to be Avatar of the Age.

**Miki Tokuchika**, (1900- ), New religions, Son and successor of Miki Tokuharu. Re-established Hito-no-michi and Perfect Liberty Kyodan. Taught that everyday activities are forms of art.

**Miki Tokuharu**, (1871-1938), New religions, Founder of Hito-no-michi, a Japanese new religion. (The Way of Man). Practiced *ofurikae* where he, as founder, took on the sufferings of his followers.

**Millet, Mother Cleusa**, (1932-1999), Spiritism, Spritual leader, Candomble Temple, Alto do Gantois, Salvador, Brazil. Afro-Brazilian syncretistic Spiritism.

**Mohan Singh Vaid**, (1881-1936), Sikhism, A distinguished doctor who promoted social reform, education, and Punjabi language among the Sikhs. He advocated separating Sikhs from Hindus and wrote hundreds of books and tracts.

**Muktananda, Paramahansa (Baba)**, (1908-1982), Hinduism, Founder of the SYDA Foundation. Revered by his followers as a Perfected Being. Western converts include Franklyn Jones (Da Free John).

**Murray, Margaret**, (1863-1963), Occultism, Anthropologist who promoted witchcraft. *The God of the Witches* (1933).

**Nakagawa Soen**, (1908-1983), Zen Buddhism, Leading Zen master of the Rinzai school, dharma-successor of Yamamoto Gempo.

**Nanjio Bunyu**, (1849-1927), Buddhism, Japanese Buddhist scholar. President of Otani University (Jodo Shinshu). Studied under Max Muller.

**Nichidatsu, Fujii**, (1884-1985), Buddhism, Founder of Japanese Buddhist revival movement (Nipponzan Myohoji) in 1917. Also known as Movement of the Wonderous Law of the Lotus Sutra.

**Nishida Kitaro**, (1870-1945), Buddhism, Leading Japanese Buddhist philosopher and founder of the Kyoto school of philosophy.

**Niwano, Nikkyo**, (1906- ), Buddhism, Co-founder with Naganuma Myodo of Dai Nippon Rissho Koseikai (The Great Society to Establish Righteousness and Foster Fellowship). The Lotus Sutra is key to universal salvations.

**Okada Mokichi**, (1882-1955), New religion, Founder of Sekai Kyuseikyo ('The Church of World Messianity'). Faith-healer. Distributed 600,000 pieces of paper on which he had written Chinese character for 'light'.

**Onisaburo, Deguchi**, (1871-1948), New Religion, Co-founder of Omoto-kyo (Teaching of the Great Origin) in 1892, reorganized in 1905.

**Prabhupada (Abhay Charan De)**, (1896-1977), Hinduism, Founder of International Society for Krishna Consciousness (ISKCON). In 1965 moved to USA and attracted thousands of "Hare Krishna" followers.

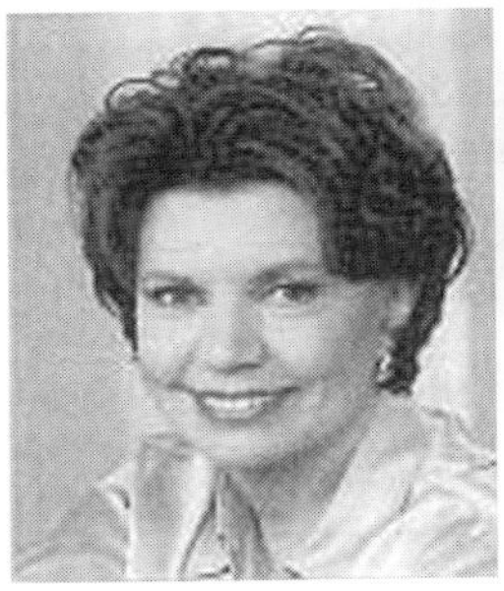

Guru Ma PROPHET

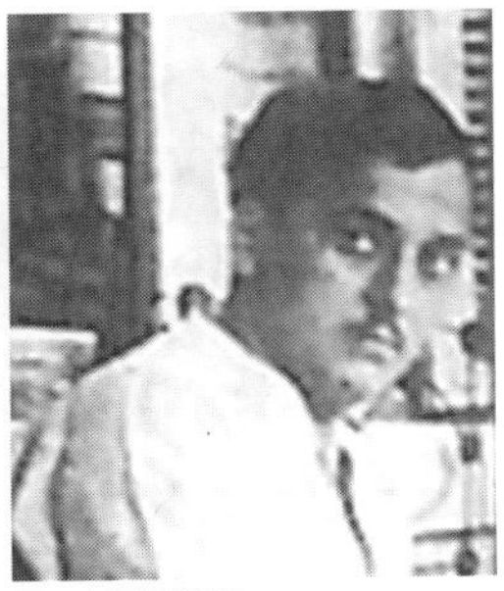

Shoghi EFFENDI

**Prophet, Elizabeth Clare**, (1940-1999), New religion, Leader of The Summit Lighthouse. Known to her students as Guru Ma. Church Universal & Triumphant sees itself as following both Jesus Christ and Gautama Buddha.

**Qutb, Sayyid**, (1906-1966), Islam, Intellectual spokesperson for the Egyptian Muslim Brotherhood. Advocated a purely Islamic state. Executed for conspiring to kill Egyptian president Abdel Nasser.

**Radhakrishnan, Sarvepalli**, (1888-1975), Hinduism, Philosopher and president of India (1962-67). Promoted Hinduism through a number of substantial works including *The Hindu View of Life*.

**Raj, Dada Lekh**, (1900- ), Hindu, Founder of the Brahma Kumaris World Spiritual University (1937).

**Rajneesh, Bhagwan Shree**, (1931-1990), Hinduism, Contemporary guru who advocated meditation techniques and free sex. Formed communities in Poona, India and Oregon, USA.

**Ramana Maharshi**, (1879-1950), Hinduism, Hindu spiritual leader in South India. Gave counsel to a number of prominent westerners like Jung, Somerset and Zimmer.

**Ramon Medina Silva**, (1925-1971), Shamanism, Huichol mara'akame (shaman priest) in Mexico. Musician, artist and communicator of peyoe pilgrimage.

**Rashid Rida**, (1870-1933), Islam, Syrian Muslim scholar. President of Syrian National Congress (1920). Chief disciple and interpreter of Islamic thinker Muhammad Abduh.

**Said Nursi**, (1873-1960), Islam, Turkish religious scholar. Author of *Risala-i-Nur* (The Treatise of Light) prominent in current Islamic revival.

**Satya Mitra Nandgiri (Swami Jagatguru Shankar Acharya)**, (1920- ), Hinduism, Spiritual head of Hindu religion worldwide, 1960-1974. Head of Dandi Sanyasis, Head of Central India Math (Bhanpur, Ujjain).

**Scholem, Gershom Gerhard**, (1897-1982), Judaism, Scholar of Jewish mysticism. Major works include *Major trends in Jewish mysticism, Jewish gnosticism*, and *Sabbatai Sevi*.

**Shahroky, Kay Khosrow**, (1880-1940), Zorastrianism, Parsi reformer. Maintained that Zoraster taught a simple monotheism, high morality, and virtually no observances.

**Shar-rdza Bkra-shis rgyal-mtshan**, (1859-1935), Tibetan Buddhism, Monk from Shar-rdza in east Tibet. Proponent of the Bon religion which predates Tibetan Buddhism. Worked for rapprochement between Bon and Buddhism.

**Sharawi, Sheikh Mohammed Mutwali**, (1911-1998), Islam, Egypt's leading Islamic authority. Served as Minister of Religious Endowments under President A. Sadat

**Shari'ati, Ali**, (1933-1977), Islam, Leading lay theorist of modern revolutionary Shi'ism. As professor and author, he influenced many young people to see Islam as a political force against Western influence.

**Shoghi Effendi (Rabbani)**, (1897-1957), Baha'i, Head of Baha'i from 1921-1957. Great grandson of Baha'Allah. Facilitated the global spread of the religion.

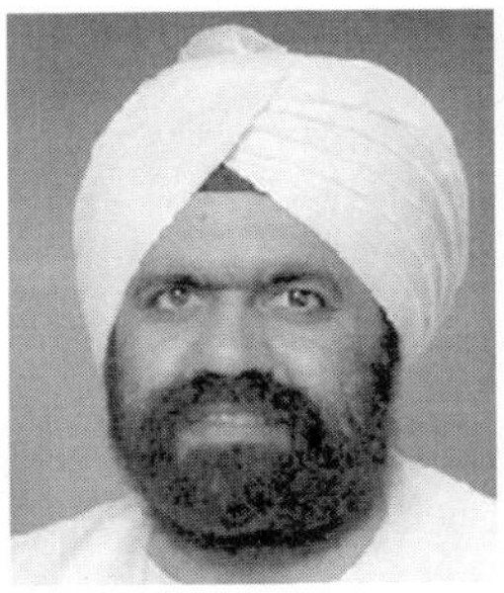

Rajinder SINGH

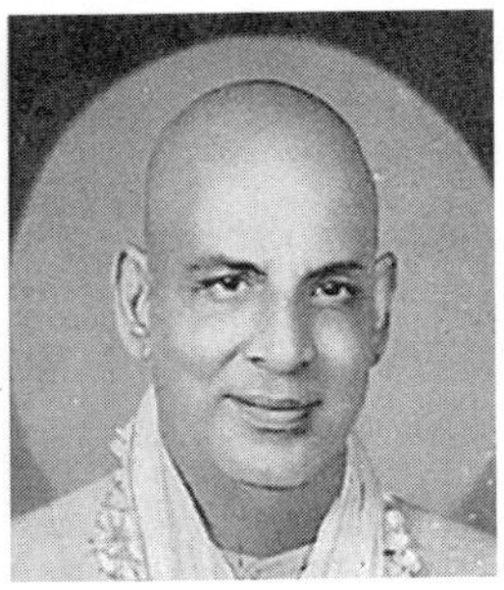

Swami SIVADANANDA

**Singh, Sant Rajinder**, (1940- ), Sikhism, President, World Fellowship of Religions; spiritual head, Science of Spirituality.

**Sivadananda, Swami**, (1887-1963), Hinduism, Holy man and founder of The Divine Life Mission, claiming to represent a synthesis of the fundamentals of all religions.

**Soe-tae San**, (1891-1943), Buddhism, Founder of Korean Buddhist movement, Won Buddhism. Founded the Association for the Study of Buddha-Dharma (1924).

**Soloveichik, Joseph Bev**, (1903-1993), Jewish, Jewish Orthodox thinker in the United States. Laid down guidelines for Jewish-Christian dialogue.

**Steiner, Rudolph**, (1861-1925), Anthroposophy, Founder of Anthroposophy (wisdom of humanity) a breakoff from Theosophy in 1913. Emphasizes the central place of humanity in spiritual science.

**Sumohadiwidjojo, Muhammad Subuh**, (1901-1987), Islam, Founder and spiritual guide of the spiritual brotherhood of Subud. Began in Indonesia, spread to Western world in 1957.

**Suzuki, Daisetz Teitaro**, (1870-1966), Zen Buddhism, Japanese Zen Buddhist laymen who by lectures and writings made "Zen" a household word in the Western world. Published nearly 30 works in English.

**T'ai-hsu**, (1889-1947), Buddhism, Reformer of Chinese Buddhism. Monk. Wrote *The Reorganization of the Buddhist Community* (1915). Founded Chinese Buddhist Society in 1929.

**Tagore, Robindvanath**, (1861-1941), Hinduism, Bengali poet. Secretary of Adi Brahmo Samaj (1884) but mainly influential through his writings. First Indian to win Nobel Prize for Literature.

**Taniguchi Masahuru**, (1893-1985), New-Religion, Founder of Seicho no ie (The Household of Growth) a Japanese new religion. Taught that sin and divine punishment are unreal; only reality is the mind. Wrote 300 books and thousands of articles.

**Tara Singh, Master**, (1885-1967), Sikhism, Sikh political and religious leader vigourously pushed for a Sikh majority state in independent India.

**Teja Singh Bhasaur**, (1866-1933), Sikhism, Sikh religious leader who founded a branch of the Singh Sabha in his village (1893) which he turned into a powerful vehicle to advance Sikhism. Excommunicated (1928).

**Toda Josei**, (1900-1958), Buddhism, Co-founder of Soka Gokkai. Restructured Soka Gakkai in 1952 after being released from prison.

**Trungpa, Chogyam**, (1939-1987), Buddhism, Recognized as 11th incarnation of Trungpa lamas. Popularized Tibetan Buddhism in the West. Organized the Vajradhatu Association of Buddhist Churches in North America.

**Twitchell, Paul**, (1908-1971), New Age, Founder of Eckankar in 1965. Former member of Church of Scientology.

**U Nu**, (1907- ), Buddhism, Burmese nationalist and prime minister of Burma (1948-58, 1960-62). Proponent of Buddhist Socialism.

**Vajirananavarorasa (Wachirayan Warorot)**, (1860-1921), Buddhism, Thai Buddhist reformer, son of King Mongkut. Patriarch of monastic community in Thailand (1910).

**Vinoba Bhave**, (1895-1982), Hinduism, Social and religious reformer. Co-worker with M. Gandhi. From 1951 began huge journeys on foot through the villages of India advocating the donation of land for redistribution.

**Vir Singh**, (1872-1957), Sikhism, Leading intellectual of the Singh Sabha movement. Founded Punjabi newspaper Khalsa Samachar (1899). Wrote hundreds of books and articles.

**Watts, Alan**, (1915-1973), New Religion, Comparative religionist, theologian, synthesist. Counter-culture guru in California, USA. Connected with Esalen Institute and Human Potential Movement.

**Wise, Stephen Samuel**, (1874-1949), Judaism, Reform rabbi, Jewish and Zionist leader, and civic activist. Co-founder of American Jewish Congress (1915).

**Yamamoto Gempo**, (1866-1961), Buddhism, Prominent Zen Buddhist specializing in the way of writing. Received the seal of recognition from Sohan.

**Yogananda, Paramhansa**, (1893-1953), Hinduism, Founder of the Self-Realization Fellowship (Boston, USA, 1920). Taught specific yoga techniques.

Part 9

# GLOBALISTICS

Quick-reference global statistical index on 4,200 subjects

*Beloved parish priests, pay attention, we beg you, to accurate and well-studied statistics.*
*They are a very important task in governing a parish.*
—John XXIII, Synod of the Diocese of Rome, 1960

*Facts are the fingers of God.*
—A. T. Pierson, *Missionary review of the world*, 1888

Speakers, writers, planners, leaders, and executives often need instant access to an exact statistic for a topic that has suddenly emerged in conversation. Part 9 is a quick-reference global statistical index for 4,200 subjects that relate to global Christianity and its world mission. The great majority of these statistics are here because churches, missions, and agencies have measured them, checked them, compiled them, and published them.

Most of these figures occur again in Part 1 in one or other of the series of Global Diagrams 1 to 74. There the reader may see any figure in its wider context.

# Quick-reference global statistical index on 4,200 subjects

The Bible as the Word of God includes surprisingly numerous figures, totals, numbers, censuses, and statistics—surprising, that is, when we realize that it is God's primary revelation to the human race. One lengthy book of the Bible is almost entirely on the subject and indeed is called by the actual name 'Numbers' (in the Greek Old Testament, 'Arithmoi', from which we get the word 'arithmetic'). At the very least, therefore, Christians need to appreciate the positive role of statistics.

As soon as the Scriptures were penned from BC 2000 onwards, exegetes began to expound its more elaborate statistics such as the dimensions of Noah's Ark. Jerome and other early Greek and Latin Fathers came out with elaborate allegorical analyses of the 153 fishes (John 21:11), the 276 persons saved in Paul's shipwreck (Acts 27:37), and the like. With the advent of computers from 1945 on, statistical analysis of the biblical texts has become a major new science with a vast amount of literature on the subject. Today the Hebrew Old Testament, the Greek Bible, the Latin Bible, and about 100 modern-language translations of the Bible are available on compact disc and can be analyzed using personal computers and a variety of sophisticated techniques including lexicostatistics, word frequencies, and similar means.

The value of statistics for the Christian has been best summed up by the Protestant theologian Roger Schutz of France: 'Statistics are signs from God.' They alert us to the magnitude of the human dilemma, the size of Christian resources, and a clearer vision of what we Christians should do. The value of statistics for the churches can be summarized in a nutshell as (a) understanding the past, (b) analyzing the present, and (c) planning for the future.

## A new menace in missions—innumeracy
Innumeracy is the inability to understand numbers, to see the importance of numbers, and to handle numbers in everyday life. Basically it's an inability to deal comfortably with the fundamental notions of numbers and chance—which is a malady that often strikes otherwise knowledgeable people. Innumerate people characteristically have a strong tendency to personalize—to be misled by their own experiences, or by the media's focus on individuals and drama.

## Casinos and world evangelization
We start with a quotation from a very important recent book dealing with innumeracy. 'There is a strong tendency to filter out the bad and the failed and to focus on the good and the successful. Casinos encourage this tendency by making sure that every quarter that is won in a slot machine causes lights to blink and makes its own little tinkle in the metal tray. Seeing all the lights and hearing all the tinkles, it is not hard to get the impression that everyone is winning. Losses or failures are silent' (*Innumeracy: mathematical illiteracy and its consequences*, John Allen Paulos, 1988). Similarly, mission agencies and churches are not anxious to report failures or even mundane results. Instead, the fantastic and positive are highlighted, giving the impression that things are much better than they actually are.

A parallel situation is that international news is usually worse than national news which is worse than state news which is worse than local news. At the international level there is such a huge pool of events that abnormal or catastrophic events are usually highlighted.

If unusual or catastrophic events are highlighted in mission, the overall picture is obscured and distorted. What overall progress is being made is seldom apparent from selective reporting of either spectacular success or spectacular failure.

## Mathematical illiterates are preventing missiological analysis
How do innumerates frustrate missionary outreach? Consider the global missions situation. Every year, the world's 33,800 denominations and 4,000 Great Commission mission agencies instruct some 10 million Christian leaders—pastors, clergy, bishops, catechists, evangelists, lay officers—to fill out and return detailed statistical questionnaires. This has become the world's biggest single new outreach. Enter innumerate bureaucrats. We've investigated what happens to the accumulated mountains of paper after they arrive at all these headquarters. The short answer is—nothing. Apart from publishing simple totals, little or no statistical analysis of any kind is done with these statistics. We encourage Christians to undertake such analysis and to tap this unique gold mine of annual data.

## Don't be a missiological innumerate!
A tendency to drastically underestimate the frequency of coincidences is typical of innumerates. Consequently they attribute great importance to correspondences of all sorts that they come across without being interested in clear statistical evidence.

Many correspondences simply don't stand up to logic. For example, to be absolutely certain that at least two people have the same birthday you would need to gather 367 people (366 days if you count February 29 and one more person in case everyone gathered matches one day of the year each). What if you only wanted to be 50% certain of this fact? It would seem logical that 183 or half of 366 would be the answer. But the answer is 23. In other words, if you randomly gather 23 people, half the time two will share a birthday. This is perhaps obvious only to the numerate who work with probabilities.

People also confuse correspondence with causation. For example, it has been found that where people drink more milk the cancer rate is much higher. One might deduce that drinking milk causes cancer, but this is not so. As it turns out wealthier people with health-threatening lifestyles also drink more milk. The side effects of affluence cause the cancer.

Innumeracy is often the result of two misconceptions. First, the impression that mathematics is cold and abstract. This tends to be true in pure mathematics but is not generally true when one thinks of the myriad of daily experiences built around numbers and math (counting change, reading sports statistics, cooking with precise amounts of ingredients, calculating how long it will take to get somewhere, etc).

Second is the feeling that numbers somehow depersonalize humans—diminishing their individuality. Quite to the contrary, if you think about it, identification numbers enhance individuality by their unique nature. There may be two John Smiths, or Mohammed Alis, or Wan Lees, but they all each have unique ID numbers.

Others are concerned that statistics will somehow predetermine our future. But normally, rather than constraining, they empower—as tools to be used for anyone who knows how and has some application that requires them.

## Being numerate is vital for mission strategy
How can we avoid the hazards of innumeracy? For one, those who use numbers every day in relation to mission strategy need to be much more careful in their use. Many of us need refresher courses in basic mathematics and probabilities. Others could benefit from advanced courses in statistics. The goal should be the proper handling of quantities necessary to describe world evangelization.

Second, the church at large has a responsibility to back up its mission with the most accurate assessment of progress being made. Scoffing at numbers one doesn't understand is not helpful or legitimate. Without some sort of enumeration we will continue to blindly set agendas and plans for world evangelization that cannot be evaluated. But if we are open to being monitored we will be able to see our way to the goals that God has led us to set. Then, some day, these will coordinate with Christians of other traditions so that no people remains beyond the reach of the Father's love.

As John Allen Paulos says, 'In an increasingly complex world full of senseless coincidence, what's required in many situations is not more facts—we're inundated already—but a better command of known facts, and for this a course in probability is invaluable... Probability, like logic, is not just for mathematicians anymore. It permeates our lives.'

## Our findings
The results of our analysis are presented within this Part 9 in the form of a list of statistics. To provide a rapid means of navigating through these stormy waters, what follows is a Quick-Reference Global Statistical Index to all topics, statistics, trends, megatrends, and global diagrams. This should help the busy reader, speaker, executive, or other Christian worker to locate any particular statistic he or she needs, and to do it within 10 seconds or so. Note the following 15 points.

1. The Index which follows is alphabetized A-Z in order to help the user find, within a few seconds (or, in its computer form, immediately), any global statistic related to any subject he can put a name to.

2. The first column gives the name of each category; the second column gives the related global statistic (or a dash meaning the category is not precise but is a non-measurable heading); the third column gives, for reference purposes, the sources of the data (these are in most cases the 74 Global Diagrams, with all their own sources, which are described and listed in Part 1 "GeoStatus"). For each entry, only one source diagram is listed, this being the major diagram where the subject is enumerated. Numerous subjects are however addressed on several diagrams. A hyphen '-' means the statistic is not immediately found on a Global Diagram but in a related statistical table.

3. All categories throughout refer to the situation in AD 2000, usually mid-2000, unless another date is specified (usually AD 2025).

4. Each category is included in the Index only once, though a number of items are entered under different wordings to assist the user to locate them rapidly.

5. All categories of this Index are global, referring to the entire world as a whole, unless clearly stated to be restricted geographically or otherwise (e.g. to 'Africa', 'Third World', etc).

6. The abbreviation 'p.a.' means 'per annum', or 'per year', or 'each year'. Sums of money are given in US$ (US dollars).

7. Exact definitions of categories are essential to a full understanding of each statistic. The reader can rely on the exact meaning of the English words and phrases used to be an accurate definition of each category. Additional explanations (e.g. for Worlds A, B, C, or for Millennial Scenarios I, II, III) are given below in paragraphs 10 and 13 respectively and in Part 30 "Glossary".

8. Numbers are given in differing degrees of precision. In this Index we use 'million', 'billion', 'trillion', in words or in figures. This varied use is designed to assist the reader with the form that is most illustra-

tive and most easy to quote. The degree of either precision or approximation is indicated by the form employed. Thus '2 million' claims less precision than '2.0 million'. In order of ascending accuracy or precision claimed, a given number may be entered as 1 billion, 1.0 billion, 1,001 million, 1,001,361,000, or 1,001,361,256. The first 2 are easy-to-quote figures. The first 3 are general-order-of-magnitude totals. The fourth one is a rounded total (rounded to the nearest thousand). The last one is (or claims to be) an exact count to the last digit. The reader wanting to quote should use the simplest form that suits his audience or his purpose.

9. The Index contains a number of words in italic type: these are Greek or Latin words important for the understanding of evangelization. The New Testament Greek word *euangelizo* has 140 Greek synonyms (shown in this Index, with their word counts or frequencies of usage in the New Testament) and 210 related Greek verbs. The word frequencies shown after each word are essential starting-points for exegesis. Similar word counts are also shown here after English verbs which translate *euangelizo* for English Bibles.

10. To portray today's status of world evangelization, the globe is divided here into 3 worlds each with distinct populations. World C is the Christian World (all who individually are Christians). World A is the Unevangelized World (persons who have not heard of Christianity, Christ, or the gospel and who remain unreached by the gospel). World B is the Evangelized Non-Christian World (all non-Christians who nevertheless have heard and understood the good news, without accepting it yet).

11. The term 'plans' occurs often in this Index. 'Global plans' are those which present a scheme for evangelizing the entire world. 'Nonglobal plans' are those restricted to part of the globe, such as Africa, or Europe. 'Megaplans' are global plans each expending over US$100 million in a decade; 'gigaplans' are those each expending over US$1 billion in a decade.

12. Many figures describe tomorrow's globe; these are shown in the Index with the phrase 'AD 2025'. These geopolitical and religious statistics are based on current trends and are the best AD 2025 projections or estimates made by specialists in the various fields. They show what the world is likely to look like in AD 2025. Differing scenarios would vary most of these figures by plus or minus 4%.

13. Numerous AD 2025 figures deal with tomorrow's global Christianity. The figures project the status of Christianity in AD 2025 with 3 main scenarios. Millennial Scenario I posits little or no church growth. Millennial Scenario II posits moderate growth at today's level, with some progress by AD 2025 but no completion of the task. Millennial Scenario III posits closure with world evangelization successfully completed and over half the world now Christians.

14. Sources for the data in this Index (shown after each statistic) are important for their credibility. As noted above, they are the 74 Global Diagrams, together with the fuller documentation available via the related electronic versions.

15. This whole process is not completed once and for all. It is an ongoing process in which the authors invite the user to cooperate. New data are being added every week; older information is being updated as soon as newer versions become available. The authors' responsibility is to coordinate the new with the old and to produce a single, agreed, internally-consistent, externally-credible, global picture.

## BIBLIOGRAPHY

*A handbook of numerical and statistical techniques: with examples mainly from the life sciences.* J. H. Pollard. Cambridge: Cambridge University Press, 1977. 349p.

*A statistics primer for managers: how to read a statistical report or a computer printout and get the right answers.* J. J. Clark and M. T. Clark. New York: The Free Press, 1983. 258p.

*An Eerdmans handbook: Christianity in today's world.* R. Keeley et al. (eds). Grand Rapids, MI: Eerdmans, 1985. 384p.

*Atlas of world population history.* C. McEvedy & R. Jones. Harmondsworth, UK and New York: Penguin Books, 1978. 368p.

*Church and denomination growth.* D. A. Roozen & C. K. Hadaway (eds). Nashville, TN: Abingdon Press, 1993.

*Datawars: the politics of modeling in federal policymaking.* K. L. Kraemer et al. New York: Columbia University Press, 1987. 342p.

*Envisioning information.* E. R. Tufte. Cheshire, CT: Graphics Press, 1990. 126p.

*Ethnostatistics: qualitative foundations for quantitative research.* R. P. Gephart Jr. *Qualitative research methods,* 12. Newbury Park, CA and London: Sage Publications, 1988. 72p.

*Global health statistics.* C. J. L. Murray and A. D. Lopez (eds). Boston, MA: Harvard University Press, 1996. 906p.

*Global trends: the world almanac of development and peace.* I. Hauchler & P. M. Kennedy (eds). New York: Continuum, 1994. 416p.

*Global warming unchecked: signs to watch for.* H. Bernard Jr. Bloomington, IN: Indiana University Press, 1993.

*How many people can the earth support?* J. E. Cohen. New York and London: Norton, 1995. 542p.

*Human rights and statistics: getting the record straight.* T. B. Jabine & R. P. Claude (eds). *Pennsylvania studies in human rights.* Philadelphia: University of Pennsylvania Press, 1992. 476p.

*Innumeracy: mathematical illiteracy and its consequences.* J. A. Paulos. New York: Hill and Wang, 1988. 135p.

*Looking forward: the next forty years.* J. M. Templeton (ed). New York: Giniger Books of HarperBusiness, 1993. 229p.

*Mapping it out: expository cartography for the humanities and social studies.* M. Monmonier. Chicago: University of Chicago Press, 1993. 316p.

*On the shoulders of giants: new approaches to numeracy.* L. A. Steen (ed). Washington, D.C.: National Academy Press, 1990. 232p.

*Physiology by the numbers: an encouragement to quantitative thinking.* R. F. Burton. Cambridge: Cambridge University Press, 1994. 185p.

*Quantitative methods for historians: a guide to research, data, and statistics.* K. H. Jarausch & K. A. Hardy. Chapel Hill, NC and London: University of North Carolina Press, 1991. 265p.

*Reading between the numbers: statistical thinking in everyday life.* J. Tal. New York: McGraw Hill, 2001. 285p.

*Say it with figures.* H. Zeisel. New York: Harper & Row, Publishers, 1968. 248p.

*Sharing social science data: advantages and challenges.* J. Sieber (ed). *Sage focus editions,* 128. Newbury Park, CA and London: Sage Publications, 1991. 176p.

*Social statistics.* H. M. Blalock Jr. 2nd ed. New York: McGraw-Hill, 1972.

*State of the world: a Worldwatch Institute report on progress toward a sustainable society.* L. R. Brown, C. Flavin & H. Kane. New York and London: W. W. Norton/Worldwatch Books, 2000. 247p. (An annual report of the Worldwatch Institute. Analytical essays on the environment and development).

*The 1996 index of economic freedom.* B. T. Johnson & T. P. Sheehy. Washington, DC: The Heritage Foundation, 1996. 394p.

*The 2000 Information Please environmental almanac.* A. Hammond (ed). Boston: Houghton Mifflin, 2000. 606p. (Compiled by the World Resources Institute).

*The 21st century.* G. T. Kurian and G. T. T. Molitor (eds). New York: Macmillan Publishing, 1999. 999p.

*The Cambridge survey of world migration.* R. Cohen (ed). New York and Cambridge, UK: Cambridge University Press, 1995. 592p.

*The Christian book of lists.* R. Peterson. Wheaton, IL: Tyndale, 1997. 256p.

*The data game: controversies in social science statistics.* M. H. Maier. Armonk, NY and London: M. E. Sharpe, 1991. 261p.

*The Economist book of vital world statistics: a portrait of everything significant in the world today.* M. Smith-Morris (ed). New York: Times Books, 1990. 254p.

'The future of world population,' W. Lutz, *Population Bulletin,* 49, 1 (June 1994), 1–47. (The entire issue of this journal is devoted to this article).

*The Gaia atlas of future worlds: challenge and opportunity in an age of change.* N. Myers. New York: Doubleday, 1991. 190p.

*The global burden of disease.* C. J. L. Murray and A. D. Lopez (eds). Boston, MA: Harvard University Press, 1996. 990p.

*The great human diasporas: the history of diversity and evolution.* L. L. Cavalli-Sforza & F. Cavalli-Sforza. Trans., S. Thorne. Reading, MA: Helix Books of Addison-Wesley, 1995. 311p.

'The homeless poor: what is the church doing for America's destitute?,' M. Hope & J. Young, *Christianity Today,* 29, 14 (October 14, 1985), 30–35.

*The state of humanity.* J. L. Simon (ed). Oxford, UK and Cambridge, MA: Blackwell Publishers and the Cato Institute, 1995. 704p.

*The true state of the planet.* R. Bailey (ed). New York and London: Free Press, 1995. 480p. (Presents opposing viewpoints to the environmental movement).

*The tyranny of numbers; mismeasurement and misrule.* N. Eberstadt. Washington, D.C.: AEI Press, 1995. 303p.

*The women's chronology: a year–by–year record, from prehistory to the present.* J. Trager. New York: Henry Holt, 1994. 799p.

*The world in figures.* London: The Economist Newspaper Limited, 1976. 294p.

*Understanding ethnographic texts.* P. Atkinson. *Qualitative research methods series,* no. 25. Newbury Park, CA and London: Sage Publications, 1992. 66p.

*Vital signs 2000: the trends that are shaping our future.* L. R. Brown, C. Flavin & H. Kane. New York: W. W. Norton/Worldwatch Books, 2000. 169p. (Tracks historic trends in food production, energy production and consumption, environmental activity, and six other areas as indicators of the state of the world).

*Why numbers count: quantitative literacy for tomorrow's America.* L. A. Steen (ed). New York: College Entrance Examination Board, 1997. 194p.

| Category | Statistic | Diag |
|---|---|---|
| 300 DIMENSIONS OF EVANGELIZATION | — | 33 |
| abandoned children and infants | 70 million | 18 |
| abortions a year | 76 million | 21 |
| abortions p.a., illegal (38%) | 29 million | 21 |
| absenteeism at work, cost of p.a. | $7 billion | 18 |
| absolutely poor Christians | 260 million | 24 |
| absolutely poor Christians, % of all Christians | 13% | 24 |
| absolutely poor Christians, AD 2025 | 262 million | 67 |
| absolutely poor Christians, AD 2025, % of all Christians | 10% | 67 |
| absolutely poor in AD 2025 (those in absolute poverty) | 1.41 billion | 66 |
| absolutely poor, % of world | 18% | 18 |
| absolutely poor, the | 1.09 billion | 18 |
| access to Scripture in mother tongue, % of world population | 96% | 28 |
| access to Scripture in understood language, % of world population | 98.7% | 28 |
| access to whole Bible in mother tongue, % of world | 86% | 28 |
| action points, world Christian global plan | 109 | 61 |
| active global plans | 845 | 61 |
| activism, countries with marked Christian | 150 | 53 |
| AD 2025 GLOBAL GOALS | — | 59 |
| AD 33 | — | 7 |
| adequate shelter, persons without | 1.3 billion | 18 |
| ADHERENTS OF NON-CHRISTIAN RELIGIONS | — | 23 |
| ADHERENTS OF NON-CHRISTIAN RELIGIONS IN AD 2025 | — | 66 |
| ADHERENTS OF RELIGIONS | — | 23 |
| ADHERENTS OF RELIGIONS IN AD 2025 | — | 66 |
| administrative units, political | 1 million | 22 |
| adolescents (teenagers, ages 13-19) | 789 million | 34 |
| adolescents (teenagers, ages 13-19) in AD 2025 | 814 million | 66 |
| adoptions p.a. | 3.5 million | 21 |
| adult nonliterates | 990 million | 34 |
| adults (ages 15 and over) | 4.25 billion | 34 |
| adults (ages 15 and over), % of world | 70.30% | 34 |
| adults (ages 15 and over), AD 2025 | 5.99 billion | 66 |
| adults (ages 15 and over), AD 2025, % of world | 76.50% | 66 |
| Adventists (including Independents) | 12.5 million | 44 |
| Adventists (including Independents) in AD 2025 | 22.4 million | 68 |
| Adventists, % of all Christians | 0.63% | — |
| Adventists, % of all Christians, in AD 2025 | 0.86% | — |
| Adventists, % of world | 0.21% | — |
| Adventists, % of world, in AD 2025 | 0.29% | — |
| Adventists, annual growth rate, % | 2.35% | — |
| Adventists, annual growth rate, %, in AD 2025 | 2.35% | — |
| Adventists, annual increase | 295,000 | — |
| Adventists, annual increase in AD 2025 | 527,000 | — |
| advertising, sums spent on all, p.a. | $150 billion | 20 |
| affiliated Christians (church members) | 1,888 million | 24 |
| affiliated Christians (church members), AD 2025 | 2,491 million | 68 |
| affiliated Christians, % of all Christians | 94.44% | 24 |
| affiliated Christians, % of world | 31.19% | 24 |
| affluent Christians, % of all Christians | 11% | 24 |
| affluent Christians, % of all Christians, AD 2025 | 10% | 67 |
| affluent, the (9% of world) | 545 million | 18 |
| Africa, church members | 335.1 million | 44 |
| Africa, church members in AD 2025 | 600.5 million | 68 |
| Africa, church members, annual growth rate | 2.62% | — |
| Africa, church members, annual growth rate in AD 2025 | 2.36% | — |
| Africa, church members, annual increase | 8.8 million | — |
| Africa, church members, annual increase, in AD 2025 | 14.2 million | — |
| Africa, church members, as % of region | 42.72% | — |
| Africa, church members, as % of region, in AD 2025 | 46.25% | — |
| Africa, church members, as % of world members | 17.75% | — |
| Africa, church members, as % of world members, in AD 2025 | 24.11% | — |
| Africa, population | 784.4 million | 47 |
| Africa, population in AD 2025 | 1,298 million | — |
| Africa, population, annual growth rate | 2.39% | — |
| Africa, population, annual growth rate in AD 2025 | 2.04% | — |
| Africa, population, annual increase | 18.8 million | — |
| Africa, population, annual increase, in AD 2025 | 26.4 million | — |
| Africa, population, as % of world | 12.96% | — |
| Africa, population, as % of world, in AD 2025 | 16.59% | — |
| Afro-American spiritists | 5.65 million | — |
| Afro-American spiritists in AD 2025 | 7.71 million | — |
| Afro-American spiritists, % of world | 0.09% | — |
| Afro-American spiritists, % of world, in AD 2025 | 0.10% | — |
| Afro-American spiritists, annual growth rate, % | 2.13% | — |
| Afro-American spiritists, annual growth rate, %, in AD 2025 | 1.25% | — |
| Afro-American spiritists, annual increase | 118,000 | — |
| Afro-American spiritists, annual increase in AD 2025 | 95,300 | — |
| Afro-Caribbean spiritists | 107,000 | — |
| Afro-Caribbean spiritists in AD 2025 | 184,000 | — |
| Afro-Caribbean spiritists, annual growth rate, % | 3.30% | — |
| Afro-Caribbean spiritists, annual growth rate, %, in AD 2025 | 2.17% | — |
| Afro-Caribbean spiritists, annual increase | 3,430 | — |
| Afro-Caribbean spiritists, annual increase in AD 2025 | 3,910 | — |
| age, median | 26.6 | 46 |
| age, median in AD 2150 | 42.7 | 46 |
| agencies, parachurch or service | 23,000 | 24 |
| ago, usages in NT | 67 | 7 |
| agricultural land as % of all land | 8.54% | 21 |
| agricultural land, sq km | 12.9 million | 21 |
| agricultural production growth p.a. | 2.80% | 21 |
| agricultural research, global, p.a. | $10.5 billion | 21 |
| AGRICULTURE | — | 21 |
| Ahmadis (Ahmadi Muslims) | 8.0 million | 23 |
| Ahmadis in AD 2025 | 14.7 million | 66 |
| Ahmadis, % of all Muslims | 0.67% | — |
| Ahmadis, % of all Muslims, in AD 2025 | 0.82% | — |
| Ahmadis, % of world | 0.13% | — |
| Ahmadis, % of world, in AD 2025 | 0.19% | — |
| Ahmadis, annual growth rate, % | 3.25% | 23 |
| Ahmadis, annual growth rate, %, in AD 2025 | 2.49% | — |
| Ahmadis, annual increase | 258,000 | — |
| Ahmadis, annual increase in AD 2025 | 366,000 | 66 |
| AIDS carriers | 41 million | 18 |
| AIDS carriers, AD 2025 (on Millennial Scenario I) | 223 million | 66 |
| AIDS carriers, AD 2025 (on Millennial Scenario III) | 139 million | 66 |
| AIDS carriers, growth rate % p.a. | 25% | 18 |

| Category | Statistic | Diag |
|---|---|---|
| AIDS cases | 5 million | 18 |
| AIDS cases, AD 2025 (on Millennial Scenario I) | 27.1 million | 66 |
| AIDS deaths p.a. | 2.5 million | 18 |
| AIDS deaths p.a., AD 2025 (on Millennial Scenario I) | 13.6 million | 66 |
| AIDS deaths: cumulative total by AD 2025 | 136 million | 66 |
| AIDS deaths: cumulative total since 1970 | 19.5 million | — |
| air cargo, ton-km | 46 billion | 20 |
| air distance flown, civil, km | 12 billion | 20 |
| air traffic, passenger-km | 1.6 trillion | 20 |
| aircraft carriers, nuclear | 30 | 19 |
| aircraft, combat | 60,000 | 19 |
| airports and airfields | 65,000 | 20 |
| akouo, usages in NT | 431 | 7 |
| Alawites (Alawite Shia Muslims) | 1.6 million | — |
| Alawites in AD 2025 | 2.7 million | — |
| Alawites, % of all Muslims | 0.14% | — |
| Alawites, % of all Muslims, in AD 2025 | 0.15% | — |
| Alawites, % of world | 0.03% | — |
| Alawites, % of world, in AD 2025 | 0.03% | — |
| Alawites, annual growth rate, % | 2.20% | — |
| Alawites, annual growth rate, %, in AD 2025 | 2.01% | — |
| Alawites, annual increase | 35,800 | — |
| Alawites, annual increase in AD 2025 | 53,800 | — |
| albino-gene carriers | 100 million | 18 |
| albinos (homozygous persons) | 524,000 | 18 |
| alcoholic drink, world expenditure on, p.a. | $408 trillion | 19 |
| alcoholics | 198 million | 18 |
| alcoholism, cost of, p.a. | $81 billion | 19 |
| Alzheimer's disease, sufferers worldwide | 23 million | — |
| Alzheimer's disease: economic cost in USA, p.a. | $100 billion | — |
| AMATEUR RADIO | — | 29 |
| amateur radio operators | 1.5 million | 29 |
| anangello, usages in NT | 18 | 7 |
| anapeitho, usages in NT | 1 | 7 |
| anapempo, usages in NT | 5 | 7 |
| anemia sufferers | 2.0 billion | 18 |
| anemic women (iron-deficient) | 700 million | 18 |
| angello, usages in NT | 1 | 7 |
| Anglican Charismatics | 17.6 million | 30 |
| Anglican congregations | 100,000 | 64 |
| Anglican Evangelicals | 30 million | 30 |
| Anglican foreign missionaries, % in World A, 1990 | 2.6% | 38 |
| Anglican foreign missionaries, 1990 | 4,170 | 38 |
| Anglican, number of traditions | 25 | 10 |
| Anglicans | 79.7 million | — |
| Anglicans in AD 2025 | 113.7 million | — |
| Anglicans, % of all Christians | 3.98% | — |
| Anglicans, % of all Christians, in AD 2025 | 4.35% | — |
| Anglicans, % of world | 1.32% | — |
| Anglicans, % of world, in AD 2025 | 1.45% | — |
| Anglicans, annual growth rate, % | 1.34% | — |
| Anglicans, annual growth rate, %, in AD 2025 | 1.44% | — |
| Anglicans, annual increase | 1.1 million | — |
| Anglicans, annual increase in AD 2025 | 1.6 million | — |
| Anglicans, professing | 110 million | 30 |
| Anglo-Saxon net, total speakers | 1.46 billion | 27 |
| Animists | 216.2 million | 23 |
| Animists in AD 2025 | 264.0 million | — |
| Animists, % of ethnoreligionists | 94.66% | — |
| Animists, % of ethnoreligionists, in AD 2025 | 95.22% | — |
| Animists, % of world | 3.57% | — |
| Animists, % of world, in AD 2025 | 3.37% | — |
| Animists, annual growth rate, % | 1.35% | 23 |
| Animists, annual growth rate, %, in AD 2025 | 0.80% | — |
| Animists, annual increase | 2.9 million | — |
| Animists, annual increase in AD 2025 | 2.1 million | — |
| announce, usages in GNB/NT | 25 | 33 |
| ANNUAL SCRIPTURE DISTRIBUTION | — | 28 |
| Antarctica, church members | 3,400 | 44 |
| Antarctica, church members in AD 2025 | 8,000 | 68 |
| anthomologeomai, usages in NT | 1 | 7 |
| apangello, usages in NT | 47 | 7 |
| apeileo, usages in NT | 2 | 7 |
| aperchomai, usages in NT | 118 | 7 |
| Apocrypha/Deuterocanonical Books (RSV), books in | 19 | — |
| Apocrypha/Deuterocanonical Books (RSV), words in | 155,875 | — |
| apodemeo, usages in NT | 6 | 7 |
| apokrinomai, usages in NT | 234 | 7 |
| apolambano, usages in NT | 9 | 7 |
| apologia, usages in NT | 18 | 6 |
| apophthengomai, usages in NT | 3 | 7 |
| apostello, usages in NT | 131 | 7 |
| apostle, apostolic, titles (books) on | 40,300 | — |
| apostle, apostolic, titles (books) on since 1970 | 11,700 | — |
| apostole, usages in NT | 255 | 6 |
| Arabic net, total speakers | 328 million | 27 |
| arable land as % global land area | 11% | 34 |
| arable land destroyed 1980-2000, % | 35% | 66 |
| armed conflict (internal or external), countries with significant | 60 | 19 |
| armed forces, troops in | 22.7 million | 19 |
| arms black market p.a. | $5.8 billion | 19 |
| arms trade p.a. | $48 billion | 19 |
| arms trade, international, in AD 2025 p.a. | $135 billion | 66 |
| art, major works of, sales p.a. | $58 billion | 19 |
| art, theft of major works of, p.a. | $29 billion | 19 |
| arthritics | 350 million | 18 |
| artificial implants (pacemakers, prostheses), persons with | 3.5 million | 18 |
| artificial kidneys, persons kept alive by | 350,000 | 18 |
| ARTIFICIAL LANGUAGES | — | 28 |
| Ashkenazis (Ashkenazi Jews) | 11.1 million | 23 |
| Ashkenazis in AD 2025 | 12.3 million | — |
| Ashkenazis, % of all Jews | 76.76% | — |
| Ashkenazis, % of all Jews, in AD 2025 | 76.75% | — |
| Ashkenazis, % of world | 0.18% | — |
| Ashkenazis, % of world, in AD 2025 | 0.16% | — |
| Ashkenazis, annual growth rate, % | 0.79% | 23 |
| Ashkenazis, annual growth rate, %, in AD 2025 | 0.43% | — |

| Category | Statistic | Diag |
|---|---|---|
| Ashkenazis, annual increase | 87,200 | — |
| Ashkenazis, annual increase in AD 2025 | 52,500 | — |
| Asia, church members | 307.3 million | 44 |
| Asia, church members in AD 2025 | 459.0 million | 68 |
| Asia, church members, annual growth rate | 2.12% | — |
| Asia, church members, annual growth rate in AD 2025 | 1.62% | — |
| Asia, church members, annual increase | 6.5 million | — |
| Asia, church members, annual increase, in AD 2025 | 7.4 million | — |
| Asia, church members, as % of region | 8.34% | — |
| Asia, church members, as % of region, in AD 2025 | 9.72% | — |
| Asia, church members, as % of world members | 16.27% | — |
| Asia, church members, as % of world members, in AD 2025 | 18.43% | — |
| Asia, population | 3,683 million | 47 |
| Asia, population in AD 2025 | 4,723 million | — |
| Asia, population, annual growth rate | 1.39% | — |
| Asia, population, annual growth rate in AD 2025 | 1.00% | — |
| Asia, population, annual increase | 51.3 million | — |
| Asia, population, annual increase, in AD 2025 | 47.3 million | — |
| Asia, population, as % of world | 60.82% | — |
| Asia, population, as % of world, in AD 2025 | 60.37% | — |
| Assemblies of God USA, missionaries, % in World A, 1990 | 2% | 39 |
| Assemblies of God USA, missionaries, 1990 | 1,565 | 39 |
| ASSOCIATIONS OF COUNTRIES | — | 23 |
| *atha*, usages in NT | 1 | 7 |
| atheistic countries (1989) | 30 | 23 |
| atheistic regimes, persons under (1989) | 1.5 billion | 18 |
| atheists (antireligious persons) | 150.1 million | 23 |
| atheists in AD 2025 | 159.5 million | 66 |
| atheists, % of world | 2.48% | — |
| atheists, % of world, in AD 2025 | 2.04% | — |
| atheists, annual growth rate, % | 0.24% | 23 |
| atheists, annual growth rate, %, in AD 2025 | 0.24% | — |
| atheists, annual increase | 357,000 | — |
| atheists, annual increase in AD 2025 | 390,000 | — |
| audio languages | 6,500 | 22 |
| audio scripture selections, languages with | 4,700 | 28 |
| AUDIO SCRIPTURES | — | 28 |
| audio scriptures in preparation, languages with | 300 | 28 |
| audio scriptures, languages with at least one complete Book on | 700 | 28 |
| audits, cost of annual Christian | $810 million | — |
| Australoid race | 69.9 million | 25 |
| Australoid race, % of world | 1% | 25 |
| autocracies/dictatorships, countries with | 40 | 23 |
| automobile thefts p.a. | 3.4 million | 19 |
| automobile thefts, cost of p.a. | $23 billion | 19 |
| babies born malnourished, p.a. | 15 million | 18 |
| babies p.a. born to young women (15-19) | 17 million | — |
| Baha'is | 7.1 million | 23 |
| Baha'is in AD 2025 | 12.1 million | 66 |
| Baha'is, % of world | 0.12% | — |
| Baha'is, % of world, in AD 2025 | 0.15% | — |
| Baha'is, annual growth rate, % | 2.52% | 23 |
| Baha'is, annual growth rate, %, in AD 2025 | 2.14% | — |
| Baha'is, annual increase | 179,000 | — |
| Baha'is, annual increase in AD 2025 | 258,000 | 66 |
| balance of trade p.a., world | $116 billion | 21 |
| ballistic-missile warheads, submarine-launched | 10,720 | 19 |
| baptism rate, % of all church members p.a. | 3.6 | — |
| baptism, books on | 16,600 | — |
| *baptismos*, usages in NT | 23 | 6 |
| baptisms p.a. | 44.5 million | 44 |
| baptisms p.a., AD 2025 | 53.5 million | 68 |
| baptisms, annual rate in AD 2025, % p.a. | 2.04% | 68 |
| baptisms, annual rate, % p.a. | 2.20% | 44 |
| Baptists (including Independents) | 81.8 million | 44 |
| Baptists (including Independents) in AD 2025 | 121.0 million | 68 |
| Baptists, % of all Christians | 4.09% | — |
| Baptists, % of all Christians, in AD 2025 | 4.63% | — |
| Baptists, % of world | 1.35% | — |
| Baptists, % of world, in AD 2025 | 1.55% | — |
| Baptists, annual growth rate, % | 1.58% | — |
| Baptists, annual growth rate, %, in AD 2025 | 1.58% | — |
| Baptists, annual increase | 1.3 million | — |
| Baptists, annual increase in AD 2025 | 1.9 million | — |
| Baptize!, facets of "evangelize" related to | 70 | 6 |
| baptize, usages in GNB/NT | 89 | 33 |
| *baptizo*, usages in NT | 80 | 7 |
| *baptizontes*, usages in NT | 111 | 6 |
| *bapto*, usages in NT | 4 | 7 |
| base ecclesial communities, AD 2025 | 1.35 million | 67 |
| basic (base) ecclesial communities (BECs) | 400,000 | 24 |
| basic ecclesial communities (BECs), persons related to | 4 million | 12 |
| BASIC RIGHTS | — | 18 |
| battered women | 250 million | 19 |
| bedridden or housebound radio/TV regular worshippers | 70 million | 29 |
| beggars | 93 million | 18 |
| Bengali cluster, native speakers | 217 million | 27 |
| Bengali cluster, total speakers | 278 million | 27 |
| bereaved each year | 233 million | 21 |
| betting and gambling, cost p.a. | $815 billion | 19 |
| BEYOND AD 2025 | — | 70 |
| BIBLE | — | 28 |
| Bible (complete), languages possessing | 392 | 28 |
| Bible, books on or about | 449,000 | — |
| Bible, books on since 1970 | 186,500 | — |
| Bibles and NTs a year | 149 million | 28 |
| Bibles and NTs a year, AD 2025 | 243 million | 67 |
| Bibles distributed p.a. | 53.7 million | 28 |
| Biblical renewal, Christians involved in | 200 million | 12 |
| bicycles | 932 million | 20 |
| bicycles per 1000 | 154 | 20 |
| Big Seven, usages in Greek NT | 1,251 | 7 |
| Bihari cluster, native speakers | 90 million | 27 |
| Bihari cluster, total speakers | 130 million | 27 |
| billionaires (each worth over US$1 billion) | 500 | 19 |
| birth rate, % p.a. | 2.07% | 18 |
| birth rate, % p.a., AD 2025 | 1.55% | 66 |

| Category | Statistic | Diag |
|---|---|---|
| births a day | 354,000 | 34 |
| births a year | 129.2 million | 18 |
| births a year in AD 33 | 6 million | 7 |
| births a year, AD 2025 | 122 million | 66 |
| births per childbearing woman | 2.64 | 21 |
| births per year, non-Christian | 87.7 million | 41 |
| births per year, World A | 40.2 million | 41 |
| births per year, World B | 47.5 million | 41 |
| births per year, World C | 36.6 million | 41 |
| bisexuals (men) | 175 million | 21 |
| bishops | 21,000 | 44 |
| bishops, AD 2025 | 30,000 | 68 |
| Black Christians as % of all Christians | 19% | 67 |
| black money (banked profits from criminal enterprise), p.a. | $300 billion | 19 |
| Black Muslims | 1.6 million | — |
| Black Muslims in AD 2025 | 2.9 million | — |
| Black Muslims, % of all Muslims | 0.14% | — |
| Black Muslims, % of all Muslims, in AD 2025 | 0.16% | — |
| Black Muslims, % of world | 0.03% | — |
| Black Muslims, % of world, in AD 2025 | 0.04% | — |
| Black Muslims, annual growth rate, % | 2.48% | — |
| Black Muslims, annual growth rate, %, in 2025 | 2.30% | — |
| Black Muslims, annual increase | 40,900 | — |
| Black Muslims, annual increase in AD 2025 | 66,800 | — |
| Black Pentecostals, church members | 13 million | — |
| blind (non-sighted), totally | 19.3 million | 18 |
| blind, legally | 49 million | 18 |
| blocs, ecclesiastico-cultural major | 6 | 44 |
| blocs, major religious and anti-religious | 33 | 23 |
| book new titles (Christian) including devotional p.a. | 73,600 | 28 |
| book new titles (Christian) p.a. | 26,100 | 28 |
| book new titles (Christian) p.a., AD 2025 | 29,130 | 67 |
| book new titles p.a. per million | 190 | 28 |
| book titles a year, new | 1.0 million | 28 |
| book titles a year, new, AD 2025 | 1.3 million | 66 |
| book titles cataloged by OCLC to 1998 | 41 million | — |
| book titles on all subjects, distinct | 45.0 million | 3 |
| book titles, Christian, new p.a. | 26,100 | 24 |
| booklet new titles (Christian) p.a., AD 2025 | 50,000 | 67 |
| books cataloged by OCLC, total copies to 1998 | 652 million | — |
| books in Apocrypha (RSV) | 19 | 28 |
| books in English Bible | 66 | 28 |
| books in English NT | 27 | 28 |
| books in English OT | 39 | 28 |
| books in largest public library (New York) | 11.5 million | — |
| books in world's largest library (US Congress) | 23.6 million | — |
| books on Christianity in a country | 380,300 | — |
| books printed a year, copies | 34.9 billion | 28 |
| books, Christian p.a., % circulating in World A countries | 0.1% | 37 |
| books, Christian, copies printed p.a. | 3.5 billion | 28 |
| books, total titles about Christianity | 5.03 million | — |
| books/articles on mission p.a. | 12,800 | 24 |
| bookshops | 700,000 | 28 |
| bookshops, Christian | 73,500 | 28 |
| branches (language sets) | 684 | 22 |
| bridge peoples (socio-peoples) | 2 million | 42 |
| bring, usages in GNB/NT | 250 | 33 |
| broadcast hours available per programming year | 8,760 | 29 |
| BROADCASTING | — | 29 |
| broadcasting (radio/TV), Christian, cost p.a. | $5.8 billion | 24 |
| broadcasting agencies, Christian national or international | 1,050 | 24 |
| broadcasting, % world's population with mother-tongue Christian | 87.5% | 29 |
| broadcasting, Baha'i, countries originating | 80 | 29 |
| broadcasting, Buddhist, countries originating | 85 | 29 |
| broadcasting, Christian, full-time personnel in | 120,000 | 24 |
| broadcasting, cost of Christian, p.a. | $5.8 billion | 37 |
| broadcasting, cost of Christian, p.a., benefiting World A countries | 0.1% | 37 |
| broadcasting, Hindu, countries originating | 78 | 29 |
| broadcasting, Muslim, countries originating | 168 | 29 |
| broadcasting, New-Religionist, countries originating | 25 | 29 |
| broadcasting, persons offered mother-tongue Christian | 5.3 billion | 29 |
| broadcasting, persons offered mother-tongue Christian, % world | 87.5% | 29 |
| broadcasting, persons offered mother-tongue foreign Christian | 4 billion | 29 |
| broadcasting, persons offered mother-tongue foreign Christian, % | 66% | 29 |
| broadcasting, persons with no mother-tongue (secular or Christian) | 570 million | 29 |
| broadcasting, persons with no mother-tongue Christian | 770 million | 29 |
| broadcasting, persons with no mother-tongue Christian, % world | 12.7% | 29 |
| broadcasting, persons with only internal mother-tongue Christian | 160 million | 29 |
| broadcasting, persons with only internal mother-tongue Christian, % | 2.6% | 29 |
| Brown Christians as % of all Christians | 13% | 67 |
| bubonic plague, cases of since 1980 | 400,000 | 21 |
| Buddhist religions, distinct | 270 | 1 |
| Buddhists | 360.0 million | 23 |
| Buddhists in AD 2025 | 418.3 million | 66 |
| Buddhists, % of world | 5.95% | — |
| Buddhists, % of world, in AD 2025 | 5.35% | — |
| Buddhists, annual growth rate, % | 1.04% | 23 |
| Buddhists, annual growth rate, %, in AD 2025 | 0.60% | — |
| Buddhists, annual increase | 3.8 million | — |
| Buddhists, annual increase in AD 2025 | 2.5 million | 66 |
| buffaloes and camels | 178 million | 21 |
| buildings, new Christian p.a. | $8 billion | 24 |
| bulletin boards, electronic (BSS), total since origin in 1983 | 150,000 | 20 |
| bulletin boards, electronic, active | 10,000 | 20 |
| bureaucrats | 186 million | 19 |
| businesses failing each year | 291,300 | 19 |
| cable TV: households reached, AD 2025 | 500 million | 66 |
| calls, appeals, or slogans (global plans) | 132 | 13 |
| calorie deficiency, children with (20% of all children) | 365 million | — |
| calorie supply per capita per day, minimal | 2,600 | 18 |
| campaigns, mass evangelistic, p.a. | 3,000 | 24 |
| Campus Crusade for Christ, missionaries, % in World A, 1990 | 2.5% | 39 |
| Campus Crusade for Christ, missionaries, 1990 | 6,698 | 39 |
| cancer deaths p.a. | 6.2 million | 18 |
| Cantonese cluster, native speakers | 66.4 million | 27 |
| Cantonese cluster, total speakers | 132 million | 27 |
| Capoid race | 1.2 million | 25 |

| *Category* | *Statistic* | *Diag* |
|---|---|---|
| church members, annual increase, in AD 2025 | 27.7 million | — |
| church members, as % of all Christians | 94.44% | — |
| church members, as % of all Christians, in AD 2025 | 95.20% | — |
| church members, as % of world | 31.19% | — |
| church members, as % of world, in AD 2025 | 31.84% | — |
| church members, global increase of p.a. | 19.5 million | 34 |
| CHURCH MEMBERSHIP BY CONTINENTS, AD 2000 | — | 44 |
| CHURCH MEMBERSHIP BY CONTINENTS, AD 2025 | — | 68 |
| Church of the Absolutely Poor | 245 million | 24 |
| Church of the Absolutely Poor, AD 2025 | 262 million | 67 |
| Church of the Affluent | 208 million | 24 |
| Church of the Affluent, AD 2025 | 262 million | 67 |
| Church of the Poor | 793 million | 24 |
| Church of the Poor, AD 2025 | 1.31 billion | 67 |
| Church of the Rich | 1.1 billion | 24 |
| Church of the Rich, AD 2025 | 1.31 billion | 67 |
| CHURCH PLANTING BY RADIO | — | 29 |
| church, books on | 915,200 | — |
| church, books on, since 1970 | 211,000 | — |
| church/agency income | $270 billion | 24 |
| church/agency income, AD 2025 | $500 billion | — |
| churches (worship centers) | 3.45 million | 24 |
| churches (worship centers) in AD 2025 | 5 million | 68 |
| churches closed or suppressed each year | 6,000 | 44 |
| churches closed or suppressed p.a., AD 2025 | 10,000 | 68 |
| churches in christianized areas newly arising p.a. due to radio/TV | 20,000 | 29 |
| Churches that are 0% Great Commission Christians | nil | 44 |
| Churches that are 0% Great Commission Christians, in AD 2025 | nil | 68 |
| Churches that are 100% Great Commission Christians | nil | 44 |
| Churches that are 100% Great Commission Christians in AD 2025 | nil | 68 |
| churches, new, planted or opened each year | 58,000 | 44 |
| churches, new, planted or opened p.a., AD 2025 | 100,000 | 68 |
| cigarettes smoked each year | 5.5 trillion | — |
| cigarettes smoked per capita p.a. | 950 | — |
| cigarettes smoked per smoker p.a. | 5,500 | — |
| cigarettes, world expenditure on, p.a. | $338 billion | 19 |
| cinema attendance p.a. | 17 billion | 20 |
| cinema seats | 85 million | 20 |
| cinemas | 290,000 | 20 |
| circulatory disease deaths p.a. | 15.3 million | 18 |
| CITIES | — | 21 |
| CITIES IN AD 2025 | — | 66 |
| cities, anti-Christian megacities (under 1% Christian) | 28 | 21 |
| cities, christianized metropolises (World C) | 2,380 | — |
| cities, evangelized non-Christian metropolises (World B) | 1,860 | — |
| cities, megacities over 1 million | 402 | 21 |
| cities, megacities over 1 million, evangelized but non-Christian | 185 | 21 |
| cities, megacities over 1 million, in AD 2025 | 602 | — |
| cities, megacities over 1 million, in AD 2050 | 806 | — |
| cities, megacities over 1 million, under 1% Christian | 28 | — |
| cities, megacities over 1 million, under 50% Christian | 216 | — |
| cities, megacities over 1 million, World A | 41 | 54 |
| cities, megacities over 1 million, World A, in AD 2025 | 82 | — |
| cities, megacities over 1 million, World B | 185 | 54 |
| cities, megacities over 1 million, World B, in AD 2025 | 294 | — |
| cities, megacities over 1 million, World C | 176 | 54 |
| cities, megacities over 1 million, World C, in AD 2025 | 226 | — |
| cities, metrodwellers (in cities over 50,000 plus capitals) | 2.03 billion | 21 |
| cities, metrodwellers, AD 2025 | 3.08 billion | 66 |
| cities, metropolises over 50,000 | 5,080 | 21 |
| cities, metropolises over 50,000, AD 2025 | 6,690 | 66 |
| cities, non-Christian | 226 | 21 |
| cities, nonmetro urbanites | 849 million | 21 |
| cities, nonmetro urbanites in AD 2025 | 1.54 billion | — |
| cities, over 10,000 | 50,000 | 21 |
| cities, over 100,000 | 4,050 | 54 |
| cities, over 100,000, in AD 2025 | 4,190 | 66 |
| cities, over 100,000, under 1% Christian | 472 | — |
| cities, over 100,000, under 50% Christian | 1,600 | — |
| cities, over 100,000, World A | 596 | — |
| cities, over 100,000, World B | 2,015 | 54 |
| cities, over 100,000, World C | 1,439 | 54 |
| cities, over 300,000 | 1,240 | — |
| cities, over 300,000, in AD 2025 | 1,830 | — |
| cities, over 300,000, under 1% Christian | 119 | — |
| cities, over 300,000, under 50% Christian | 667 | — |
| cities, over 300,000, World A | 167 | — |
| cities, over 300,000, World B | 562 | — |
| cities, over 300,000, World C | 512 | — |
| cities, over 500,000 | 756 | 21 |
| cities, supercities over 4 million | 60 | 21 |
| cities, supercities over 4 million, in AD 2025 | 118 | 66 |
| cities, supercities over 4 million, in AD 2050 | 174 | — |
| cities, supercities over 4 million, under 1% Christian | 2 | — |
| cities, supercities over 4 million, under 50% Christian | 36 | — |
| cities, supercities over 4 million, World A | 2 | 54 |
| cities, supercities over 4 million, World B | 34 | 54 |
| cities, supercities over 4 million, World C | 24 | 54 |
| cities, supergiants over 10 million | 20 | 21 |
| cities, supergiants over 10 million, in AD 2025 | 31 | 66 |
| cities, supergiants over 10 million, in AD 2050 | 49 | — |
| cities, supergiants over 10 million, under 1% Christian | 0 | — |
| cities, supergiants over 10 million, under 50% Christian | 13 | — |
| cities, supergiants over 10 million, World A | 0 | 54 |
| cities, supergiants over 10 million, World B | 13 | 54 |
| cities, supergiants over 10 million, World C | 7 | 54 |
| cities, unevangelized metropolises (World A) | 979 | — |
| cities, unevangelized metropolises over 50,000 (World A) | 1,397 | 54 |
| cities, urbanites, evangelized | 2.25 billion | 34 |
| cities, urbanites, evangelized, % | 78.20% | 34 |
| cities, urbanites, unevangelized | 629 million | 34 |
| cities, urbanites, unevangelized, % | 21.80% | 34 |
| citizen full-time Christian workers, % of all workers | 93% | 24 |
| citizens killed by own governments since 1900 | 151 million | 18 |
| citizens without full political and civil rights, % of world (1989) | 80% | 19 |
| city-dwellers, cities over 100,000 | 1.89 billion | 21 |
| city-dwellers, cities over 100,000, in AD 2025 | 3.01 billion | — |

| *Category* | *Statistic* | *Diag* |
|---|---|---|
| city-dwellers, cities over 100,000, under 1% Christian | 162 million | — |
| city-dwellers, cities over 100,000, under 50% Christian | 1.02 billion | — |
| city-dwellers, cities over 100,000, World A | 210 million | — |
| city-dwellers, cities over 100,000, World B | 866 million | — |
| city-dwellers, cities over 100,000, World C | 813 million | — |
| city-dwellers, cities over 300,000 | 1.56 billion | — |
| city-dwellers, cities over 300,000, in AD 2025 | 2.59 billion | — |
| city-dwellers, cities over 300,000, under 1% Christian | 105 million | — |
| city-dwellers, cities over 300,000, under 50% Christian | 864 million | — |
| city-dwellers, cities over 300,000, World A | 139 million | — |
| city-dwellers, cities over 300,000, World B | 767 million | — |
| city-dwellers, cities over 300,000, World C | 658 million | — |
| city-dwellers, megacities over 1 million | 1.13 billion | — |
| city-dwellers, megacities over 1 million, in AD 2025 | 1.95 billion | — |
| city-dwellers, megacities over 1 million, in AD 2050 | 2.95 billion | — |
| city-dwellers, megacities over 1 million, under 1% Christian | 59.5 million | — |
| city-dwellers, megacities over 1 million, under 50% Christian | 628 million | — |
| city-dwellers, megacities over 1 million, World A | 76.6 million | — |
| city-dwellers, megacities over 1 million, World B | 566 million | — |
| city-dwellers, megacities over 1 million, World C | 484 million | — |
| city-dwellers, supercities over 4 million | 514 million | — |
| city-dwellers, supercities over 4 million, in AD 2025 | 1.03 billion | — |
| city-dwellers, supercities over 4 million, in AD 2050 | 1.75 billion | — |
| city-dwellers, supercities over 4 million, under 1% Christian | 11.8 million | — |
| city-dwellers, supercities over 4 million, under 50% Christian | 311 million | — |
| city-dwellers, supercities over 4 million, World A | 11.5 million | — |
| city-dwellers, supercities over 4 million, World B | 300 million | — |
| city-dwellers, supercities over 4 million, World C | 202 million | — |
| city-dwellers, supergiants over 10 million | 276 million | — |
| city-dwellers, supergiants over 10 million, in AD 2025 | 526 million | — |
| city-dwellers, supergiants over 10 million, in AD 2050 | 968 million | — |
| city-dwellers, supergiants over 10 million, under 1% Christian | 0 | — |
| city-dwellers, supergiants over 10 million, under 50% Christian | 177 million | — |
| city-dwellers, supergiants over 10 million, World A | 0 | — |
| city-dwellers, supergiants over 10 million, World B | 177 million | — |
| city-dwellers, supergiants over 10 million, World C | 99.4 million | — |
| citywide evangelistic campaigns, % in World A countries | 0% | 37 |
| citywide evangelistic campaigns, cities involved in World B, p.a. | 300 | 24 |
| citywide evangelistic campaigns, cities involved in World C, p.a. | 1,300 | 24 |
| citywide evangelistic campaigns, cities involved p.a. | 1,600 | 24 |
| civilians employed by national ministries of defense | 116 million | 19 |
| civilizations | 20 | 22 |
| clandestine foreign evangelizers, in closed/restricted-access countries | 5,000 | 43 |
| clans (microcultures) | 250,000 | 22 |
| clergy (ordained clergy, ministers, pastors, priests) | 1.1 million | 44 |
| clergy/ministers, ordained women | 80,000 | 24 |
| closed countries (severely-restricted-access) | 43 | 43 |
| closed/closing/restricted-access countries in Worlds A,B,C | 86 | 43 |
| closed/closing/restricted-access countries, AD 2025 | 100 | 66 |
| closed/closing/restricted-access countries, new each year | 1 | 43 |
| closed/restricted-access countries in World B | 31 | 42 |
| closed/restricted-access countries in World B, Christians in | 290 million | 43 |
| closed/restricted-access countries in World C, Christians in | 560 million | 43 |
| closed/restricted-access countries now newly opening, p.a. | 2 | 43 |
| closed/restricted-access countries, persons in | 3.0 billion | 43 |
| closest biblical synonyms of "evangelize" | 10 | 33 |
| clothing, persons without adequate daily | 1.4 billion | 18 |
| cocaine traffic, cost p.a. | $47 billion | 19 |
| cognates of "evangelize" and synonyms | 2,400 | 33 |
| college graduates | 175 million | 21 |
| college students | 70 million | 21 |
| college students, AD 2025 | 94 million | 66 |
| college students, women | 31 million | 21 |
| Colloquial Arabic cluster, native speakers | 174.4 million | 27 |
| Colloquial Arabic cluster, total speakers | 212 million | 27 |
| colonies | 39 | 23 |
| color zones | 7 | 22 |
| colorblind persons in world (females) | 13 million | — |
| colorblind persons in world (males) | 250 million | — |
| colorblind persons, world total | 263 million | — |
| colors, major stylized racial skin | 7 | 22 |
| combat aircraft | 70,000 | 19 |
| combatants killed in wars since 1900 | 42 million | 19 |
| commentaries on Bible, languages with printed | 150 | 28 |
| commercial Bible distribution p.a. | 28 million | 28 |
| commercial NT distribution p.a. | 45 million | 28 |
| commercial scripture distribution p.a. | 470 million | 28 |
| commercial vehicles | 134 million | 20 |
| commercial vehicles per 1000 | 22 | 20 |
| Common Bibles in preparation | 300 | 28 |
| Common Language Bibles, languages with | 220 | 28 |
| COMMUNICATION | — | 20 |
| COMMUNICATIONS IN AD 2025 | — | 66 |
| Communist front organizations, affiliates of | 1,400 | 23 |
| Communist front organizations, international | 12 | 23 |
| Communist party members (1989) | 88.7 million | 23 |
| Communist party members in Communist states (1989) | 83 million | 23 |
| Communist world as % of world population (1989) | 33% | 23 |
| Communist world, countries in (1989) | 30 | 23 |
| Communist-ruled states (1989) | 16 | 23 |
| Communist/Leninist/Marxist parties (1989) | 122 | 23 |
| completely unreached peoples | 1,240 | 42 |
| computer crime, cost p.a. | $51 billion | 19 |
| computer languages | 180 | 28 |
| computer power, new Christian-purchase per day, MIPS | 14 million | 24 |
| computer power, trillion instructions per second, world total | 4 | 20 |
| computer professionals who are Great Commission Christians | 20 million | 64 |
| computer professionals, Christian | 100 million | 24 |
| computer sales p.a. | 100 million | 20 |
| computer sales p.a., value of | $300 billion | 20 |
| computer screens/terminals | 600 million | 20 |
| computer screens/terminals, Christian-owned | 350 million | 24 |
| computer users, Christian | 400 million | 24 |
| computer users, Christian, % in World A countries | 0.1% | 37 |
| computer users, Christian, in AD 2025 | 1.7 billion | 67 |
| computerized Great Commission networks | 5,000 | 44 |
| computerized Great Commission networks, AD 2025 | 10,000 | 68 |

| Category | Statistic | Diag |
|---|---|---|
| computerized Scripture languages | 1,500 | 28 |
| COMPUTERS AND NETWORKS | — | 20 |
| computers benefiting Christians, % of all | 90% | 34 |
| computers, AD 2025 | 2.2 billion | 66 |
| computers, Christian owned | 332 million | 37 |
| computers, Christian owned, % in World A countries | 0.05% | 37 |
| computers, Christian owned or operated | 332 million | 24 |
| computers, Christian-owned or operated, AD 2025 | 1.5 billion | 68 |
| computers, Christian-owned, % of all | 70% | 34 |
| computers, Christian-owned, value of | $1.5 trillion | 24 |
| computers, general-purpose | 509 million | 20 |
| computers, new Christian-owned per day | 250,000 | 24 |
| computers, new sales of, p.a. | 100 million | 20 |
| computers, World A's share of | 2.8% | 34 |
| computers, World B's share of | 23.4% | 34 |
| computers, World C's share of | 73.8% | 34 |
| CONCILIARISM IN AD 2025 | — | 68 |
| concordance to Bible, languages with at least one | 200 | 28 |
| Conf of Christian World Communions, member confessions in, AD 2025 | 70 | 68 |
| Conference of Christian World Communions, member confessions in | 23 | 44 |
| conferences on evangelization p.a. | 500 | 53 |
| CONFESSION OF MARTYRDOM VICTIMS, AD 2000 | — | 16 |
| CONFESSION OF MARTYRDOM VICTIMS, AD 33-AD 2000 | — | 16 |
| CONFESSIONAL CONCILIARISM | — | 44 |
| confessions, major Christian | 100 | 44 |
| Confucianists | 6.3 million | — |
| Confucianists, % of world | 0.10% | — |
| Confucianists, % of world, in AD 2025 | 0.09% | — |
| Confucianists, annual growth rate, % | 0.72% | — |
| Confucianists, annual growth rate, %, in AD 2025 | 0.32% | — |
| Confucianists, annual increase | 45,500 | — |
| Confucianists, annual increase in AD 2025 | 21,600 | — |
| Confucianists, in AD 2025 | 6.8 million | — |
| congregation/churches, pentecostal/charismatic | 1,367,600 | 17 |
| congregations, Anglican | 100,000 | 64 |
| congregations, Evangelical | 477,000 | 64 |
| congregations, Independent | 1.7 million | 64 |
| congregations, Marginal Christian | 116,000 | 64 |
| congregations, Orthodox | 99,000 | 64 |
| congregations, Pentecostal/Charismatic | 1.8 million | 64 |
| congregations, Protestant | 1.04 million | 64 |
| congregations, Roman Catholic | 358,000 | 64 |
| congregations/churches | 3,448,000 | 17 |
| congregations/churches, 1970 | 1,450,000 | 17 |
| congregations/churches, Pentecostal/Charismatic | 303,400 | 17 |
| congregations/churches, pentecostal/charismatic, 1970 | 195,400 | 17 |
| congregations/churches, Pentecostal/Charismatic, 1970 | 82,100 | 17 |
| congregations/churches, Postdenominationalist | 1,773,000 | 17 |
| congregations/churches, Postdenominationalist, 1970 | 327,500 | 17 |
| constructed international languages | 10 | 28 |
| consultations, medical, in Christian centers, p.a. | 55 million | 24 |
| continent-wide councils of churches | 30 | 44 |
| continental areas (macro regions) | 7 | 22 |
| continental Christian councils or councils of churches, AD 2025 | 30 | 68 |
| CONTINENTAL CONCILIARISM | — | 44 |
| continents | 7 | 22 |
| CONTINENTS AND REGIONS | — | 23 |
| contraceptives, % of child-bearing women using | 60% | 21 |
| converts from Christianity to other religions p.a. | 16.5 million | 41 |
| converts to Christianity from World A, p.a. | 1 million | 41 |
| converts to Christianity from World B, p.a. | 19.0 million | 41 |
| convicted murderers a year | 350,000 | 19 |
| convicted murderers a year per 100,000 | 5.8 | 19 |
| cooperatives, modern business, persons in | 700 million | — |
| copies of new Christian books printed p.a. | 116 million | 24 |
| corporate debt | $1.7 trillion | 19 |
| corruption, victims of | 1.2 billion | 18 |
| cost of annual church megacensus | $1.1 billion | 3 |
| cost per baptism | $330,000 | — |
| councils of churches, local | 20,000 | 44 |
| councils of churches, major | 6,500 | 44 |
| councils of churches, national or international | 1,500 | 44 |
| counties (districts) | 20,000 | 22 |
| countries | 238 | 42 |
| COUNTRIES | — | 23 |
| countries (with over 1,000 population) | 235 | 23 |
| countries (with under 1,000 population) | 3 | 23 |
| countries below population replacement level, 1955 | 3 | — |
| countries below population replacement level, 2025 | 102 | — |
| COUNTRIES IN AD 2025 | — | 66 |
| countries in AD 2025 | 238 | 66 |
| countries in world | 238 | 23 |
| countries in World A (with E%≤U>50%) | 38 | 34 |
| countries in World B (E>50%, C | 59 | 34 |
| countries in World C (C%≥60%, E%≥95%) | 141 | 34 |
| countries involved in human-rights violations | 150 | 19 |
| countries involved in significant armed conflict | 60 | 19 |
| countries members of United Nations | 185 | 23 |
| countries partially politically free (1989) | 87 | 23 |
| countries politically free (1989) | 79 | 23 |
| countries politically not free (1989) | 85 | 23 |
| countries sending foreign missionaries | 231 | 63 |
| countries uncontrolled by popular vote (1989) | 154 | 18 |
| countries where calorie supply too low | 50 | 18 |
| countries with Christians and churches in | 238 | 34 |
| countries with Communist/Leninist/Marxist parties (1989) | 122 | 23 |
| countries with heavy external debt, Third-World | 120 | 19 |
| countries with isolated radio churches | 80 | 29 |
| countries with new radio/TV converts regularly | 170 | 29 |
| countries with no TV service | 30 | 29 |
| countries with nuclear technology | 60 | 19 |
| countries with own-language radio service | 238 | 29 |
| countries with own-language TV service | 208 | 29 |
| countries with polio endemic | 116 | — |
| countries with polio eradicated | 155 | — |
| countries with population over 10 million | 77 | 3 |
| countries with severe safe water shortages | 80 | — |
| countries with TEE programs | 120 | 24 |
| countries without full political and civil rights (1989) | 180 | 19 |
| countries, % totalitarian by AD 2025 | 40% | 66 |
| countries, nonsovereign (dependencies) | 39 | 23 |
| countries, nonsovereign, % | 9.64 million | 23 |
| countries, nonsovereign, population in | 9.64 million | 23 |
| countries, sovereign (nations) | 195 | 23 |
| couriers, alien, in closed/restricted-access countries | 10,000 | 43 |
| covert evangelizers | 123.7 million | 30 |
| Creation, stages of | 7 | 69 |
| credit card fraud, cost of p.a. | $582 million | 19 |
| CRIME | — | 19 |
| crime in AD 2025, international organized, cost p.a. | $1 trillion | 66 |
| crime victims p.a. | 594 million | 18 |
| crime, organized, cost p.a. | $750 billion | 19 |
| crime, total cost p.a. of all varieties | $5.7 trillion | 19 |
| crimes p.a. per 1000 | 117 | 19 |
| crimes per year | 73.6 million | 19 |
| crimes, property, p.a. | 16.0 million | 19 |
| crimes, violent, p.a. | 3.40 million | 19 |
| criminals p.a. | 750 million | 19 |
| criminals, % of population | 12.4% | 19 |
| Crucifixion, books on | 5,000 | — |
| Crucifixion, books on, since 1970 | 2,500 | — |
| crypto-Christians (secret believers) | 123.7 million | 43 |
| crypto-Christians in AD 2025 | 190.5 million | — |
| crypto-Christians, % of all Christians | 6.19% | 43 |
| crypto-Christians, % of all Christians, in AD 2025 | 7.28% | — |
| crypto-Christians, % of world | 2.04% | — |
| crypto-Christians, % of world, in AD 2025 | 2.43% | — |
| crypto-Christians, annual growth rate, % | 2.18% | — |
| crypto-Christians, annual growth rate, %, in AD 2025 | 1.74% | — |
| crypto-Christians, annual increase | 2.7 million | — |
| crypto-Christians, annual increase in AD 2025 | 3.3 million | — |
| culture areas | 71 | 22 |
| culture clusters | 430 | 22 |
| culture complexes (microcultures) | 250,000 | 22 |
| culture provinces (culture areas) | 71 | 22 |
| culture units (cultures) | 6,629 | 22 |
| culture worlds | 17 | 25 |
| culture zones | 20 | 22 |
| cultures | 6,629 | 22 |
| Cursillistas (Catholic and Protestant) | 1 million | 12 |
| cyclones, deaths from 1960-2000 | 750,000 | 18 |
| cyclones, major, since 1960 | 300 | 18 |
| daily evangelizers, AD 2025 | 820 million | 68 |
| daily intercessors | 200 million | 44 |
| daily intercessors, AD 2025 | 300 million | 68 |
| daily newspapers | 6,170 | 20 |
| daily-evangelizing Christians (daily evangelizers) | 600 million | 44 |
| daily-evangelizing Christians, AD 2025 | 820 million | 68 |
| daily-praying intercessors for world mission | 200 million | 24 |
| databases, secular commercial | 10,000 | 24 |
| deaf (hearing-impaired), partially | 365 million | 18 |
| deaf, severely | 150 million | 18 |
| deaf, totally | 23 million | 18 |
| deaf-mutes (deaf and dumb) | 11.6 million | 18 |
| death rate, % p.a. | 0.87% | 18 |
| death rate, % p.a., AD 2025 | 0.84% | 66 |
| death squads, nations tolerating local or international | 35 | 19 |
| deaths a year | 54.3 million | 18 |
| deaths a year, AD 2025 | 65.7 million | 66 |
| deaths of Christians p.a., due to accidents | 508,000 | 12 |
| deaths of Christians p.a., due to AIDS | 1.50 million | 12 |
| deaths of Christians p.a., due to cancer | 2.11 million | 12 |
| deaths of Christians p.a., due to cardiovascular disease | 3.03 million | 12 |
| deaths of Christians p.a., due to childhood diseases (under 15s) | 4.63 million | 12 |
| deaths of Christians p.a., due to circulatory diseases | 4.02 million | 12 |
| deaths of Christians p.a., due to diarrhea (under 5s) | 1.50 million | 12 |
| deaths of Christians p.a., due to dirty water | 3.03 million | 12 |
| deaths of Christians p.a., due to earthquakes | 35,000 | 12 |
| deaths of Christians p.a., due to execution by governments | 20,000 | 12 |
| deaths of Christians p.a., due to floods | 3,000 | 12 |
| deaths of Christians p.a., due to homicide | 410,000 | 12 |
| deaths of Christians p.a., due to hunger (under 5s) | 5.04 million | 12 |
| deaths of Christians p.a., due to infant mortality (under 1 year) | 3.22 million | 12 |
| deaths of Christians p.a., due to injury and poisoning | 898,000 | 12 |
| deaths of Christians p.a., due to malaria | 1.50 million | 12 |
| deaths of Christians p.a., due to man-made disasters | 312,000 | 12 |
| deaths of Christians p.a., due to martyrdom for Christ | 160,000 | 12 |
| deaths of Christians p.a., due to maternal mortality | 156,000 | 12 |
| deaths of Christians p.a., due to motor vehicles | 97,600 | 12 |
| deaths of Christians p.a., due to murder | 273,000 | 12 |
| deaths of Christians p.a., due to natural causes | 9.76 million | 12 |
| deaths of Christians p.a., due to natural disasters | 58,600 | 12 |
| deaths of Christians p.a., due to parasitic diseases | 5.04 million | 12 |
| deaths of Christians p.a., due to perinatal diseases | 1.02 million | 12 |
| deaths of Christians p.a., due to pesticide poisoning | 293,000 | 12 |
| deaths of Christians p.a., due to pneumonia (under 15s) | 1.21 million | 12 |
| deaths of Christians p.a., due to pollution | 3.03 million | 12 |
| deaths of Christians p.a., due to starvation | 6.03 million | 12 |
| deaths of Christians p.a., due to suicide | 195,000 | 12 |
| deaths of Christians p.a., due to terrorism | 4,000 | 12 |
| deaths of Christians p.a., due to tobacco-related causes | 605,000 | 12 |
| deaths of Christians p.a., due to torture | 25,000 | 12 |
| deaths of Christians p.a., due to tuberculosis | 1.11 million | 12 |
| deaths of Christians p.a., due to venomous snakebite | 12,000 | 12 |
| deaths of Christians p.a., due to wars | 312,000 | 12 |
| deaths per year, non-Christian | 34.3 million | 41 |
| deaths per year, World A | 13.2 million | 41 |
| deaths per year, World B | 21.1 million | 41 |
| deaths per year, World C | 18.4 million | 41 |
| DEBT | — | 19 |
| debt servicing, Third-World, p.a. | $100 billion | 19 |
| debt, Third-World, repayable | $160 billion | 19 |
| debt, Third-World, total | $1.6 trillion | 19 |
| debt, unrepayable Third-World | $1.4 trillion | 19 |
| DECADE PLANS, 1990-2000 | — | 13 |

| Category | Statistic | Diag |
|---|---|---|
| Decades of Evangelism, confessional | 10 | 13 |
| Decades of Evangelism, denominational | 25 | 13 |
| Decades of Evangelism, interdenominational | 10 | 13 |
| Decades of Evangelism, nondenominational | 30 | 13 |
| *dechomai*, usages in NT | 56 | 7 |
| declare, usages in GNB/NT | 19 | 33 |
| defections (apostasies) among Christians p.a., AD 2025 | 15 million | 68 |
| definitions of "evangelize" | 250 | 33 |
| defunct plans for world evangelization | 527 | 13 |
| Denominational Charismatics (2nd Wave of Renewal) | 176 million | 44 |
| Denominational Charismatics (2nd Wave of Renewal), AD 2025 | 279 million | 68 |
| Denominational Pentecostalism, members of | 66 million | 12 |
| Denominational Pentecostalism, members of, in AD 2025 | 101 million | — |
| denominations (Christian), AD 2025 | 50,000 | 68 |
| denominations and paradenominations, 1970 | 18,630 | 17 |
| denominations and paradenominations, 2000 | 33,820 | 17 |
| denominations merged (organic union) since 1900 | 400 | 44 |
| denominations with own martyrs | 5,000 | 16 |
| denominations, Christian (distinct and separate) | 33,800 | 24 |
| denominations, clearcut denominationalist, 1970 | 7,080 | 17 |
| denominations, clearcut denominationalist, 2000 | 7,160 | 17 |
| denominations, traditional, 1970 | 7,610 | 17 |
| denominations, traditional, 2000 | 11,680 | 17 |
| density, people per sq km | 41 | 34 |
| density, people per sq km, AD 2025 | 53 | 66 |
| dentists | 570,000 | 21 |
| dependencies/colonies | 39 | 23 |
| dependent countries/territories, population of | 9.64 million | 23 |
| deportees a year | 14 million | 18 |
| desertification victims added each year | 1.16 million | 18 |
| desertification, % world's land in danger from | 33% | 19 |
| desertification, new p.a., sq km | 210,000 | 19 |
| desertification, people at risk | 1.0 billion | 18 |
| deserts, land engulfed a day through mismanagement by, sq km | 165 | 19 |
| *deuro*, usages in NT | 9 | 7 |
| developing countries, % of world's population increase occurring in | 93% | 18 |
| developing countries, persons in | 4.8 billion | — |
| DEVELOPMENT | — | 23 |
| diabetics adults | 145 million | 18 |
| diabetics, adults, 2025 | 300 million | — |
| *diakonia*, usages in NT | 101 | 6 |
| *dialaleo*, usages in NT | 2 | 7 |
| dialects | 30,000 | 22 |
| *dialegomai*, usages in NT | 13 | 7 |
| *dialogismos*, usages in NT | 43 | 6 |
| *dialogizomai*, usages in NT | 16 | 7 |
| *diamartyromai*, usages in NT | 15 | 7 |
| *diangello*, usages in NT | 3 | 7 |
| *diaphemizo*, usages in NT | 3 | 7 |
| diarrheal deaths of under 5s p.a. | 2.5 million | 18 |
| dictatorships, national | 7 | 23 |
| *didache*, usages in NT | 212 | 6 |
| *didasko*, usages in NT | 98 | 7 |
| *didaskontes*, usages in NT | 212 | 6 |
| *didomi*, usages in NT | 415 | 7 |
| *diegeomai*, usages in NT | 8 | 7 |
| *dierchomai*, usages in NT | 41 | 7 |
| *diermeneuo*, usages in NT | 6 | 7 |
| *dihikneomai*, usages in NT | 1 | 7 |
| dimensions of "evangelize" | 420 | 33 |
| direct-dial telephones (95% of total) | 679 million | 20 |
| dirty money, % of all financial transactions | 25% | 19 |
| dirty water, persons killed each day by | 25,000 | 18 |
| disabled children, AD 2025 | 500 million | 66 |
| disabled persons (handicapped) | 1.0 billion | 18 |
| disabled, AD 2025 | 1.5 billion | 66 |
| disaffiliated | -22.7 million | 30 |
| disarmament treaties, nations signing | 150 | 19 |
| DISASTERS AND DESERTIFICATION | — | 18 |
| Disciple!, facets of "evangelize" related to | 266 | 6 |
| disciple, usages in GNB/NT | 350 | 33 |
| disciple-opportunities (offers) each year | 938 billion | 32 |
| disciple-opportunities p.a., % in World A | 0.2% | 40 |
| disciple-opportunities p.a., % in World B | 17% | 40 |
| disciple-opportunities p.a., % in World C | 82.8% | 40 |
| disciple-opportunities per capita p.a. | 155 | 32 |
| disciple-opportunities per day | 2.6 billion | 40 |
| disciple-opportunities per day per person | 0.42 | 40 |
| disciple-opportunities per day, World A | 5 million | 40 |
| disciple-opportunities per day, World B | 436 million | 40 |
| disciple-opportunities per day, World C | 2.13 billion | 40 |
| disciplines | 50 | 69 |
| DISCIPLINES | — | 69 |
| disenfranchised (no vote)(1989) | 2.8 billion | 18 |
| districts (counties) | 20,000 | 22 |
| divorce rate per 1000 population p.a., 1993 | 0.4 | 48 |
| divorce rate per 1000 population p.a., 2025 | 1 | 48 |
| divorcees (divorced persons) | 86 million | 21 |
| divorces per year | 9.3 million | 21 |
| doctors (physicians) | 7.45 million | 21 |
| documents, reports, or books (global plans) | 200 | 13 |
| domestic letters per capita p.a. | 50 | 20 |
| domestic pets | 1.2 billion | 21 |
| domestic tourists a year | 4 billion | 21 |
| domestic tourists, AD 2025 | 6 billion | 66 |
| domestic tourists, Christian, p.a. | 3.3 billion | 24 |
| doubly-affiliated Christians | 194.8 million | 30 |
| doubly-counted First/Second/Third Wavers | 13.3 million | 30 |
| Downs-syndrome (mongoloid) births p.a. | 256,000 | 18 |
| dracunculiasis, persons with | 11.5 million | 18 |
| drive-in cinemas | 3,500 | 20 |
| drug addicts (illicit drug users) | 64 million | 18 |
| DRUG TRAFFIC | — | 19 |
| drug traffic (illegal), cost p.a. | $250 billion | 19 |
| drug traffickers (persons employed) | 46 million | 19 |
| drugs: illegal traffic p.a., in AD 2025 | $500 billion | 66 |
| Druzes (Druze Muslims) | 834,000 | — |

| Category | Statistic | Diag |
|---|---|---|
| Druzes in AD 2025 | 1.4 million | — |
| Druzes, % of all Muslims | 0.07% | — |
| Druzes, % of all Muslims, in AD 2025 | 0.08% | — |
| Druzes, % of world | 0.01% | — |
| Druzes, % of world, in AD 2025 | 0.02% | — |
| Druzes, annual growth rate, % | 2.31% | — |
| Druzes, annual growth rate, %, in AD 2025 | 2.10% | — |
| Druzes, annual increase | 19,300 | — |
| Druzes, annual increase in AD 2025 | 29,400 | — |
| dumb (deaf-mutes) | 11.6 million | 18 |
| dwarfs (little people) | 3.4 million | 18 |
| dwellings | 1.3 billion | 21 |
| dwellings, % self-built | 97% | 21 |
| dwellings, self-built | 1.3 billion | 21 |
| *dynamis*, usages in NT | 331 | 6 |
| Earth satellites in orbit, artificial | 4,000 | 20 |
| earthquake deaths, 1900-2000 | 2.1 million | 18 |
| earthquake victims (deaths) a year | 21,000 | 18 |
| earthquakes, major, 1900-2000 | 1,900 | 18 |
| East African Revival, Christians involved in | 3 million | 12 |
| East Asian colossus, Christians in | 115 million | 53 |
| East Bantu-Inner net, total speakers | 216 million | 27 |
| Eastern Orthodox church members | 172.7 million | 44 |
| Eastern Orthodox church members in AD 2025 | 199.9 million | 68 |
| Eastern Orthodox church members, % of all Christians | 8.98% | — |
| Eastern Orthodox church members, % of all Christians, in AD 2025 | 8.85% | — |
| Eastern Orthodox church members, % of world | 2.97% | — |
| Eastern Orthodox church members, % of world, in AD 2025 | 3.09% | — |
| Eastern Orthodox church members, annual growth rate, % | 1.24% | — |
| Eastern Orthodox church members, annual growth rate, %, in AD 2025 | 1.20% | — |
| Eastern Orthodox church members, annual increase | 2.2 million | — |
| Eastern Orthodox church members, annual increase in AD 2025 | 2.9 million | — |
| Eastern-rite Catholics | 17.9 million | 44 |
| Eastern-rite Catholics in AD 2025 | 27.4 million | 68 |
| Eastern-rite Catholics, % of all Christians | 0.89% | — |
| Eastern-rite Catholics, % of all Christians, in AD 2025 | 1.05% | — |
| Eastern-rite Catholics, % of world | 0.30% | — |
| Eastern-rite Catholics, % of world, in AD 2025 | 0.35% | — |
| Eastern-rite Catholics, annual growth rate, % | 1.72% | — |
| Eastern-rite Catholics, annual growth rate, %, in AD 2025 | 1.72% | — |
| Eastern-rite Catholics, annual increase | 308,000 | — |
| Eastern-rite Catholics, annual increase in AD 2025 | 471,000 | — |
| ecclesiastical crime p.a. | $16 billion | 19 |
| ecclesiastical traditions/families | 312 | 44 |
| ecclesiastical traditions/families, AD 2025 | 400 | 68 |
| ecclesiastico-cultural megablocs (historico-cultural blocs of Christianity) | 6 | 44 |
| *echeo*, usages in NT | 1 | 7 |
| economic aid for developing countries, world | $38.5 billion | 21 |
| economically active persons | 2.6 billion | 20 |
| economically active persons, AD 2025 | 4.0 billion | 66 |
| ecumenical centers | 400 | 24 |
| Ecumenical Movement, Christians related to | 460 million | 12 |
| EDUCATION | — | 21 |
| education costs p.a. | $1 trillion | 21 |
| education costs per capita, p.a. | $165 | 21 |
| education costs per child, p.a. | $1,000 | 21 |
| education costs, % of GWP | 3.5% | 21 |
| *eisakouo*, usages in NT | 5 | 7 |
| *ekdihegeomai*, usages in NT | 2 | 7 |
| *ekklesia*, usages in NT | 115 | 6 |
| *eklaleo*, usages in NT | 1 | 7 |
| *ekpempo*, usages in NT | 2 | 7 |
| elderly (ages 65 and over) | 419 million | 34 |
| elderly (ages 65 and over), % of world | 6.91% | 34 |
| elderly (ages 65 and over), AD 2025 | 817 million | 66 |
| elderly (ages 65 and over), AD 2025, % of world | 10.40% | 66 |
| elderly (ages 80 and over) | 69.5 million | 34 |
| elderly (ages 80 and over), AD 2025 | 149 million | — |
| electrical energy grid, cost of proposed global | $25 billion | 20 |
| electricity production, growth p.a. | 3.20% | 20 |
| electricity production, kWh | 11 trillion | 20 |
| electricity production, kWh per capita | 1,817 | 20 |
| electricity, persons without access to | 40% | 18 |
| electronic Christianity, listeners/viewers | 2.1 billion | 53 |
| electronic Christianity, listeners/viewers, % of world | 35% | 53 |
| electronic fund transfers a day | $20 billion | 23 |
| electronic mail systems (95% secular) | 5 million | 24 |
| electronic warfare, cost p.a. | $5.8 billion | 19 |
| electronic-mail messages p.a. | 20 billion | 20 |
| *elencho*, usages in NT | 18 | 7 |
| elephantiasis, persons with | 314 million | 18 |
| *embapto*, usages in NT | 2 | 7 |
| embezzlements (Christian funds stolen by top custodians), p.a. | $16 billion | — |
| *embrimaomai*, usages in NT | 5 | 7 |
| emigrants/immigrants per year | 29 million | 18 |
| *en cristo*, usages of term in Pauline Epistles (Greek NT) | 164 | 28 |
| encyclopedias | 800 | 28 |
| encyclopedias in English | 400 | 28 |
| encyclopedias, general | 150 | 28 |
| encyclopedias, subject | 650 | 28 |
| ENERGY | — | 20 |
| energy consumed by humans as % total available on earth p.a. | 40% | 20 |
| energy consumed by humans as % total available on earth p.a., AD 2025 | 70% | 66 |
| energy consumption per person, in kg of coal | 2,000 | 20 |
| energy, metric tons of oil equivalent | 8 billion | 20 |
| English Bible translations (distinct) published | 400 | 28 |
| English keywords in NT | 4,700 | 28 |
| English mother-tongue speakers | 234 million | 28 |
| English mother-tongue speakers, AD 2025 | 800 million | 66 |
| English NT keywords | 4,700 | 28 |
| English readers, AD 2025 | 940 million | 66 |
| English single-word themes in NT | 800 | 7 |
| English speakers | 1.32 billion | 28 |
| English speakers, AD 2025 | 2,800 million | 66 |
| English words (distinct) in GNB | 10,500 | 28 |
| English words (distinct) in KJV/AV | 7,200 | 28 |
| English words in NT (GNB), total | 181,253 | 28 |

| Category | Statistic | Diag |
|---|---|---|
| Great Commission Christians, annual growth rate, %, in AD 2025 | 1.27% | — |
| Great Commission Christians, annual increase | 9.3 million | — |
| Great Commission Christians, annual increase in AD 2025 | 11.3 million | — |
| Great Commission Christians, peoples with members who are | 10,850 | 44 |
| Great Commission church and agency leaders | 40,000 | 44 |
| Great Commission computer professionals | 20 million | 44 |
| Great Commission computer users | 130 million | 44 |
| Great Commission computerized networks | 5,000 | 24 |
| Great Commission expert systems by AD 2025 | 2,000 | 60 |
| Great Commission full-time workers | 5.52 million | 44 |
| Great Commission full-time workers, AD 2025 | 6 million | 68 |
| Great Commission giganetwork | 1 | 44 |
| Great Commission giganetwork, in AD 2025 | 5 | 68 |
| Great Commission global meganetworks | 9 | 24 |
| Great Commission global networks | 100 | 24 |
| Great Commission global networks, AD 2025 | 500 | 68 |
| GREAT COMMISSION IN TIME AND SPACE | — | 5 |
| Great Commission leaders | 40,000 | 44 |
| Great Commission leaders, AD 2025 | 60,000 | 68 |
| GREAT COMMISSION NETWORKS, AD 2000 | — | 44 |
| GREAT COMMISSION NETWORKS, AD 2025 | — | 68 |
| Great Commission plans announced by mid-AD 2000 | 1,510 | 13 |
| Great Commission research centers | 200 | 44 |
| Great Commission research centers, AD 2025 | 600 | 68 |
| Great Commission, Greek commands in | 210 | 5 |
| GREAT WORLD RELIGIONS | — | 23 |
| GREAT WORLD RELIGIONS IN AD 2025 | — | 66 |
| Greek commands in Great Commission | 210 | 7 |
| Greek NT keywords | 4,900 | 7 |
| Greek verbs of command in Great Commission | 210 | 5 |
| GREEK VERBS RELATED TO *EUANGELIZO* | — | 7 |
| Greek words in NT (distinct) | 5,600 | 7 |
| Greek words in OT (LXX), total | 623,684 | 28 |
| gross reproduction rate, per woman, 1993 | 1.61 | 48 |
| gross reproduction rate, per woman, 2025 | 1.09 | 48 |
| gross world product (GWP, global income) p.a. | $28.9 trillion | 21 |
| gross world product, increase p.a. | 4.00% | 19 |
| guerrilla evangelizers, in closed countries | 6,000 | 43 |
| Gujarati cluster, native speakers | 50.1 million | 27 |
| Gujarati cluster, total speakers | 80 million | 27 |
| guns (firearms), personal, owners of | 291 million | 19 |
| GWP (gross world product), % by richest 20% of people | 74.20% | 19 |
| gypsies, unassimilated | 6.6 million | 21 |
| ham radio operators | 1.5 million | 29 |
| Han-Yu net, total speakers | 1.86 billion | 27 |
| Hanafis (Hanafi Sunni Muslims) | 531.4 million | — |
| Hanafites in AD 2025 | 724.4 million | — |
| Hanafites, % of all Muslims | 44.72% | — |
| Hanafites, % of all Muslims, in AD 2025 | 40.58% | — |
| Hanafites, % of world | 8.78% | — |
| Hanafites, % of world, in AD 2025 | 9.26% | — |
| Hanafites, annual growth rate, % | 2.03% | — |
| Hanafites, annual growth rate, %, in AD 2025 | 1.25% | — |
| Hanafites, annual increase | 10.8 million | — |
| Hanafites, annual increase in AD 2025 | 9.0 million | — |
| Hanbalites (Hanbalite Sunni Muslims) | 2.3 million | — |
| Hanbalites in AD 2025 | 3.4 million | — |
| Hanbalites, % of all Muslims | 0.20% | — |
| Hanbalites, % of all Muslims, in AD 2025 | 0.19% | — |
| Hanbalites, % of world | 0.04% | — |
| Hanbalites, % of world, in AD 2025 | 0.04% | — |
| Hanbalites, annual growth rate, % | 2.20% | — |
| Hanbalites, annual growth rate, %, in AD 2025 | 1.50% | — |
| Hanbalites, annual increase | 51,200 | — |
| Hanbalites, annual increase in AD 2025 | 50,400 | — |
| handicapped children | 340 million | 18 |
| handicapped children, severely | 100 million | 18 |
| handicapped persons | 1.0 billion | 18 |
| harvest categories | 70 | 60 |
| harvested land as % of all arable | 77% | 21 |
| Hausa cluster, native speakers | 29.9 million | 27 |
| Hausa cluster, total speakers | 79 million | 27 |
| HEALTH | — | 21 |
| health costs p.a. | $1.45 trillion | 21 |
| health costs, % of GWP | 5% | 21 |
| hear, usages in GNB/NT | 360 | 33 |
| hearing-impaired | 365 million | 18 |
| heart transplants a year | 3,500 | 18 |
| Hebrew words in OT (Masoretic Text), total | 424,037 | 28 |
| *heko*, usages in NT | 26 | 7 |
| hemophiliacs (all males) | 303,000 | 18 |
| hepatitis B virus, persons infected by | 350 million | — |
| *hermeneuo*, usages in NT | 3 | 7 |
| heroin traffic, cost p.a. | $5.8 billion | 19 |
| hidden religions | 2,000 | 1 |
| High German cluster, native speakers | 71.1 million | 27 |
| High German cluster, total speakers | 167 million | 27 |
| High Spiritists | 3.75 million | — |
| High Spiritists in AD 2025 | 5.10 million | — |
| High Spiritists, % of Spiritists | 30.40% | — |
| High Spiritists, % of Spiritists, in AD 2025 | 31.46% | — |
| High Spiritists, % of world | 0.06% | — |
| High Spiritists, % of world, in AD 2025 | 0.07% | — |
| High Spiritists, annual growth rate, % | 2.53% | — |
| High Spiritists, annual growth rate, %, in AD 2025 | 1.24% | — |
| High Spiritists, annual increase | 92,700 | — |
| High Spiritists, annual increase in AD 2025 | 62,300 | — |
| highly-indebted countries | 25 | 19 |
| *hikneomai*, usages in NT | 3 | 7 |
| Hindi-Urdu cluster, native speakers | 264 million | 27 |
| Hindi-Urdu cluster, total speakers | 492 million | 27 |
| Hindu religions, distinct | 90 | 1 |
| Hindus | 811.3 million | 23 |
| Hindus in AD 2025 | 1,049 million | 66 |
| Hindus, % of world | 13.40% | — |
| Hindus, % of world, in AD 2025 | 13.41% | — |
| Hindus, annual growth rate, % | 1.54% | 23 |

| Category | Statistic | Diag |
|---|---|---|
| Hindus, annual growth rate, %, in AD 2025 | 1.03% | — |
| Hindus, annual increase | 12.5 million | — |
| Hindus, annual increase in AD 2025 | 10.8 million | 66 |
| HIV/AIDS, adult deaths p.a. | 1.8 million | — |
| HIV/AIDS, children under 15 infected p.a. | 590,000 | — |
| Holiness movement, adherents (including Independents) | 9.6 million | 12 |
| Holiness movement, adherents in AD 2025 | 14.7 million | — |
| Holiness movement, adherents, % of all Christians | 0.48% | — |
| Holiness movement, adherents, % of all Christians, in AD 2025 | 0.56% | — |
| Holiness movement, adherents, % of world | 0.16% | — |
| Holiness movement, adherents, % of world, in AD 2025 | 0.19% | — |
| Holiness movement, adherents, annual growth rate, % | 1.73% | — |
| Holiness movement, adherents, annual growth rate, %, in AD 2025 | 1.73% | — |
| Holiness movement, adherents, annual increase | 166,000 | — |
| Holiness movement, adherents, annual increase in AD 2025 | 255,000 | — |
| Holy Spirit, books on | 13,500 | — |
| Holy Spirit, books on, since 1970 | 7,700 | — |
| home apostolate, workers in | 5.1 million | 15 |
| home Christianity, cost p.a. | $163 billion | 24 |
| home mission boards, agencies, or societies | 5,800 | 24 |
| home missionaries (working in own nation) | 1,135,000 | 24 |
| home missionaries, % in World A countries | 0.2% | 37 |
| home missionaries, AD 2025 | 1.2 million | 67 |
| homeless, persons without adequate shelter | 1.3 billion | 18 |
| homeless/family-less children | 349 million | 18 |
| homes | 1.3 billion | 21 |
| *homileo*, usages in NT | 4 | 7 |
| homogeneous segments | 18 million | 22 |
| *homologeo*, usages in NT | 26 | 7 |
| homosexuals | 93 million | 21 |
| horses, mules, asses | 139 million | 21 |
| hospital beds | 18.8 million | 21 |
| hospitals | 248,000 | 21 |
| hospitals, Christian | 5,500 | 24 |
| hotel beds, registered | 16 million | 21 |
| hours available per programming year (broadcasting) | 8,760 | 29 |
| HOURS BROADCAST | — | 29 |
| hours broadcast p.a., radio | 40 million | 29 |
| hours broadcast p.a., TV | 30 million | 29 |
| House church movement, Christians involved in | 100 million | 12 |
| house churches/cells, isolated, arising each year due to radio/TV | 20,000 | 29 |
| household size in AD 2025, persons | 3.9 | 66 |
| household size, average persons | 4.22 | 21 |
| households (families, homes, dwellings) | 1.43 billion | 21 |
| HOUSEHOLDS AND FAMILIES | — | 21 |
| households reached by cable TV, AD 2025 | 500 million | 66 |
| households, AD 2025 | 1.79 billion | 66 |
| human energy consumption as % total available on Earth p.a. | 40% | 20 |
| HUMAN NEED | — | 18 |
| HUMAN NEED IN AD 2025 | — | 66 |
| human need, money needed to relieve poor in, p.a. | $700 billion | 18 |
| human rights performance (worldwide) | 55% | 18 |
| human rights violations, nations involved in | 150 | 19 |
| human rights, % violated | 45% | 18 |
| human rights, nations dishonoring UN-defined | 130 | 19 |
| HUMAN SCIENCES | — | 69 |
| hunger, annual deaths due to | 30 million | — |
| hunger-related deaths of under 5s p.a. | 18 million | 18 |
| hungry | 1.2 billion | 18 |
| *hypago*, usages in NT | 79 | 7 |
| *hypolambano*, usages in NT | 5 | 7 |
| IAEA, member countries in | 121 | 23 |
| IBRD, member countries in | 177 | 23 |
| ICAO, member countries in | 180 | 23 |
| IDA, member countries in | 177 | 23 |
| IDEOLOGY | — | 23 |
| IFAD, member countries in | 142 | 23 |
| IFC, member countries in | 161 | 23 |
| IGOs (intergovernmental organizations) | 500 | 23 |
| illegal drug traffic, cost p.a. | $250 billion | 19 |
| illegitimate births p.a. | 19 million | 21 |
| illegitimate births, % of all births | 15% | 21 |
| illiterate adults, increase p.a. | 10 million | 18 |
| illiterate/nonliterate adults | 991 million | 18 |
| illiterate/nonliterate, % of all adult | 23.30% | 18 |
| ILLNESS/DISEASE | — | 18 |
| ILO, member countries in | 168 | 23 |
| IMF, member countries in | 179 | 23 |
| IMO, member countries in | 149 | 23 |
| imperatives of the 7 Mandates, synonyms of in 10,000 languages | 600,000 | 5 |
| imprisoned each year | 120 million | 18 |
| income of Christians, personal, per capita p.a. | $8,050 | 24 |
| income of non-Christians, per capita p.a. | $3,380 | 24 |
| income p.a., churches | $108 billion | 24 |
| income p.a., parachurch/institutional | $162 billion | 24 |
| income per person p.a. | $4,770 | 34 |
| income per person, AD 2025 | $9,842 | 66 |
| income, family, p.a. | $20,200 | 34 |
| income, global average per capita p.a. | $4,770 | 34 |
| income, global p.a. | $28.9 trillion | 21 |
| income, per capita p.a., global average | $4,770 | 18 |
| incomes of Christians, personal p.a. | $8,050 | 24 |
| incomes of Christians, personal, in AD 2025 | $44.2 trillion | 67 |
| Independent Charismatics (3rd Wave of Renewal) | 295 million | 12 |
| Independent Charismatics (3rd Wave of Renewal), AD 2025 | 432 million | 68 |
| Independent Charismatics, growth rate, AD 2025 | 1.77% | — |
| Independent congregations | 1.7 million | 64 |
| Independent missionaries, % in World A, 1990 | 0% | 38 |
| Independent missionaries, 1990 | 280 | 38 |
| Independent, number of traditions | 200 | 10 |
| Independents in AD 2025 | 581.6 million | — |
| Independents, % of all Christians | 19.29% | — |
| Independents, % of all Christians, in AD 2025 | 22.23% | — |
| Independents, % of world | 6.37% | — |
| Independents, % of world, in AD 2025 | 7.43% | — |
| Independents, annual growth rate, % | 2.17% | — |
| Independents, annual growth rate, %, in AD 2025 | 1.66% | — |

| Category | Statistic | Diag |
|---|---|---|
| Independents, annual increase | 8.4 million | — |
| Independents, annual increase in AD 2025 | 9.6 million | — |
| Independents, church members | 385.7 million | — |
| Independents, professing | 250.0 million | 30 |
| Indic-Central net, total speakers | 1.63 billion | 27 |
| INDIVIDUALS IN AD 2025 | — | 66 |
| Indonesian cluster, native speakers | 55.5 million | 27 |
| Indonesian cluster, total speakers | 229 million | 27 |
| induced abortions, p.a., 1993 | 60 | 48 |
| induced abortions, p.a., 2025 | 130 | 48 |
| industrial growth (global) p.a. | 1.90% | 20 |
| INDUSTRIALIZATION | — | 20 |
| industry, % run by robots in AD 2025 | 50% | 66 |
| inequality of income, rich:poor, 1960 | 30 | — |
| inequality of income, rich:poor, 2000 | 85 | — |
| infant mortality (under 1) p.a., 1993 | 6.3% | 48 |
| infant mortality (under 1) p.a., % 2025 | 2.8% | 48 |
| infant mortality in AD 1950 | 163.75 | — |
| infant mortality in AD 2025 | 28.6 | — |
| infant mortality per 1000 live births | 51.6 | 18 |
| infectious diseases, deaths of unimmunized children from, p.a. | 5 million | 18 |
| infectious/parasitic diseases, deaths p.a. due to | 17.3 million | — |
| injury/poisoning deaths p.a. | 2.7 million | 18 |
| institutions, Christian or church-related, minor | 376,000 | 24 |
| institutions, Christian, major | 105,000 | 24 |
| institutions, Christian, major, AD 2025 | 168,000 | 68 |
| instrument panels | 201 | — |
| INSTRUMENTATION FOR MISSIONS | — | 31 |
| instruments monitoring global mission | 1,020 | 3 |
| instruments, missiological | 1,198 | — |
| INTERCESSION | — | 24 |
| intercessors, daily | 200 million | 44 |
| intercessors, daily, in AD 2025 | 300 million | 68 |
| intercessory networks, worldwide | 50 | 24 |
| intergovernmental organizations (IGOs) | 500 | 23 |
| interlibrary loans made (OCLC) | 79 million | — |
| international arms trade p.a. | $48 billion | 19 |
| international foreign exchange transactions, p.a. | $120 trillion | 23 |
| international languages | 70 | 22 |
| International Mission Board, SBC, missionaries, % in World A, 1990 | 3% | 39 |
| International Mission Board, SBC, missionaries, 1990 | 3,715 | 39 |
| international peace-keeping forces p.a. | $250 million | 19 |
| internationals (persons living abroad) | 100 million | 23 |
| Internet, number of Christian users | 198 million | — |
| Internet, number of users | 277 million | 20 |
| irrigation, % global water used in | 70% | 21 |
| Islamic schismatics (Schismatic Muslims) | 14.9 million | — |
| Islamic schismatics in AD 2025 | 27.7 million | 66 |
| Islamic schismatics, % of all Muslims | 1.26% | — |
| Islamic schismatics, % of all Muslims, in AD 2025 | 1.55% | — |
| Islamic schismatics, % of world | 0.25% | — |
| Islamic schismatics, % of world, in AD 2025 | 0.35% | — |
| Islamic schismatics, annual growth rate, % | 2.99% | — |
| Islamic schismatics, annual growth rate, %, in AD 2025 | 2.50% | — |
| Islamic schismatics, annual increase | 448,000 | — |
| Islamic schismatics, annual increase in AD 2025 | 692,000 | — |
| Islamic supergiants (cities over 10 million) | 3 | 21 |
| Ismailis (Ismaili Shia Muslims) | 23.8 million | 23 |
| Ismailis in AD 2025 | 41.0 million | 66 |
| Ismailis, % of all Muslims | 2.00% | — |
| Ismailis, % of all Muslims, in AD 2025 | 2.29% | — |
| Ismailis, % of world | 0.39% | — |
| Ismailis, % of world, in AD 2025 | 0.52% | — |
| Ismailis, annual growth rate, % | 2.70% | 23 |
| Ismailis, annual growth rate, %, in AD 2025 | 2.20% | — |
| Ismailis, annual increase | 642,000 | — |
| Ismailis, annual increase in AD 2025 | 901,000 | 66 |
| isolated house churches/cells, new p.a. | 20,000 | 29 |
| isolated radio believers | 25 million | 29 |
| isolated radio believers in AD 2025 | 80 million | — |
| isolated radio believers, annual increase | 1 million | 29 |
| isolated radio congregations | 300,000 | 29 |
| Italian cluster, native speakers | 36.5 million | 27 |
| Italian cluster, total speakers | 86 million | 27 |
| Ithna-Asharis (Ithna-Ashari Shiite Muslims) | 136.7 million | — |
| Ithna-Asharis in AD 2025 | 229.2 million | — |
| Ithna-Asharis, % of all Muslims | 11.50% | — |
| Ithna-Asharis, % of all Muslims, in AD 2025 | 12.84% | — |
| Ithna-Asharis, % of world | 2.26% | — |
| Ithna-Asharis, % of world, in AD 2025 | 2.93% | — |
| Ithna-Asharis, annual growth rate, % | 2.24% | — |
| Ithna-Asharis, annual growth rate, %, in AD 2025 | 2.09% | — |
| Ithna-Asharis, annual increase | 3.1 million | — |
| Ithna-Asharis, annual increase in AD 2025 | 4.8 million | — |
| itinerant charismatic evangelists | 50,000 | — |
| itinerant charismatic evangelists, AD 2025 (Millennial Scenario II) | 50,000 | 67 |
| itinerant charismatic evangelists, AD 2025 (Millennial Scenario III) | 300,000 | 67 |
| itinerant pilgrim churches, AD 2025 | 50,000 | 67 |
| itinerant tourist churches, AD 2025 | 75,000 | 67 |
| ITU, member countries in | 166 | 23 |
| Jain religions, distinct | 16 | 1 |
| Jains | 4.2 million | 23 |
| Jains in AD 2025 | 6.1 million | — |
| Jains, % of world | 0.07% | — |
| Jains, % of world, in AD 2025 | 0.08% | — |
| Jains, annual growth rate, % | 1.61% | 23 |
| Jains, annual growth rate, %, in AD 2025 | 1.50% | — |
| Jains, annual increase | 67,900 | — |
| Jains, annual increase in AD 2025 | 91,600 | — |
| Japanese cluster, native speakers | 129.0 million | 27 |
| Japanese cluster, total speakers | 134 million | 27 |
| Japanese-Central net, total speakers | 134 million | 27 |
| Javanese cluster, native speakers | 56.3 million | 27 |
| Javanese cluster, total speakers | 88 million | 27 |
| Javanese net, total speakers | 89 million | 27 |
| Jehovah's Witnesses, missionaries, % in World A, 1990 | 0.1% | 39 |
| Jehovah's Witnesses, missionaries, 1990 | 16,113 | 39 |
| Jesus, books about | 174,900 | — |
| Jesus, books about, since 1970 | 87,600 | — |
| Jesus, books with name in title | 71,700 | — |
| Jesus, distinct titles of, in 10,000 languages | 100,000 | 5 |
| Jesus, usages of name in NT (NIV) | 1,275 | 28 |
| Jewish religions, distinct | 63 | 1 |
| Jews | 14.4 million | 23 |
| Jews in AD 2025 | 16.1 million | 66 |
| Jews, % of world | 0.24% | — |
| Jews, % of world, in AD 2025 | 0.21% | — |
| Jews, annual growth rate, % | 0.81% | 23 |
| Jews, annual growth rate, %, in AD 2025 | 0.43% | — |
| Jews, annual increase | 118,000 | — |
| Jews, annual increase in AD 2025 | 68,400 | 66 |
| just coping Christians, % of all Christians | 10% | 24 |
| just coping, those (10% of world) | 606 million | 18 |
| just-coping Christians, AD 2025, % of all Christians | 15% | 67 |
| justitia (Latin), usages in NT | 220 | 6 |
| Karaites (Karaite Jews) | 24,100 | 23 |
| Karaites in AD 2025 | 26,800 | — |
| Karaites, % of all Jews | 0.17% | — |
| Karaites, % of all Jews, in AD 2025 | 0.17% | — |
| Karaites, annual growth rate, % | 0.85% | 23 |
| Karaites, annual growth rate, %, in AD 2025 | 0.43% | — |
| Karaites, annual increase | 210 | — |
| Karaites, annual increase in AD 2025 | 110 | — |
| katalambano, usages in NT | 15 | 7 |
| katamartyreo, usages in NT | 3 | 7 |
| katangello, usages in NT | 18 | 7 |
| katantao, usages in NT | 13 | 7 |
| katecheo, usages in NT | 8 | 7 |
| katechumenos, usages in NT | 8 | 6 |
| keruxate, usages in NT | 72 | 6 |
| kerygma, usages in NT | 8 | 6 |
| kerysso, usages in NT | 61 | 7 |
| Keswick Movement, persons involved in | 40,000 | 12 |
| key group-themes in NT (Greek, English) | 341 | 28 |
| Kharijites (Kharijite Muslims; Ibadis) | 1.6 million | — |
| Kharijites in AD 2025 | 2.6 million | — |
| Kharijites, % of all Muslims | 0.14% | — |
| Kharijites, % of all Muslims, in AD 2025 | 0.15% | — |
| Kharijites, % of world | 0.03% | — |
| Kharijites, % of world, in AD 2025 | 0.03% | — |
| Kharijites, annual growth rate, % | 2.09% | — |
| Kharijites, annual growth rate, %, in AD 2025 | 1.90% | — |
| Kharijites, annual increase | 34,300 | — |
| Kharijites, annual increase in AD 2025 | 49,800 | — |
| killed in wars each year, persons | 1 million | 19 |
| killed in wars since 1960 | 15 million | 19 |
| killed in wars since 1960, civilians | 84% | 19 |
| killed in wars since AD 1700 | 150 million | 19 |
| killed in wars since AD 1700, civilian | 55% | 19 |
| killings, states responsible for mass | 50 | 19 |
| KNOWLEDGE | — | 28 |
| knowledge expansion rate, words per year | 2.0 trillion | 28 |
| koinonia, usages in NT | 59 | 6 |
| komizo, usages in NT | 12 | 7 |
| Korean cluster, native speakers | 75.7 million | 27 |
| Korean cluster, total speakers | 78 million | 27 |
| kraugazo, usages in NT | 9 | 7 |
| krazo, usages in NT | 60 | 7 |
| Kulturkreis (minicultures) | 24,000 | 22 |
| labete, usages in NT | 263 | 6 |
| labor force growth, p.a. | 1.90% | 20 |
| LABOR FORCE IN AD 2025 | — | 66 |
| labor force in agriculture, % | 49% | 21 |
| labor force, % women | 37% | 20 |
| labor force, persons | 2.1 billion | 20 |
| labor migrants, resident | 30 million | 21 |
| labor migrants, seasonal | 120 million | 21 |
| laity | 1,883 million | 24 |
| laity, % of whole church | 99.8% | 24 |
| laleo, usages in NT | 299 | 7 |
| Lamaist Buddhists | 21.5 million | 23 |
| Lamaists in AD 2025 | 25.0 million | 66 |
| Lamaists, % of Buddhists | 5.97% | — |
| Lamaists, % of Buddhists, in AD 2025 | 5.97% | — |
| Lamaists, % of world | 0.35% | — |
| Lamaists, % of world, in AD 2025 | 0.32% | — |
| Lamaists, annual growth rate, % | 1.10% | 23 |
| Lamaists, annual growth rate, %, in AD 2025 | 0.60% | — |
| Lamaists, annual increase | 236,000 | — |
| Lamaists, annual increase in AD 2025 | 151,000 | 66 |
| lambano, usages in NT | 263 | 7 |
| land area, sq km | 148.9 million | 23 |
| land engulfed a day by deserts by mismanagement, sq. km. | 165 | 19 |
| land surface of Earth endangered | 33% | 19 |
| land surface under permanent crops | 11% | 21 |
| landmines, anti-personnel | 100 million | — |
| language chains | 1,400 | 26 |
| language clusters (outer-languages) | 4,962 | 26 |
| language glossozones (zones, microzones) | 100 | 26 |
| language handicaps, persons with | 300 million | 18 |
| language macrozones | 10 | 26 |
| language nets | 2,690 | 26 |
| language sets (groupings of chains and nets) | 684 | 26 |
| language(s), books about | 1.053 million | — |
| languages (inner-languages) | 13,510 | 26 |
| languages in AD 2025 | 13,000 | 66 |
| LANGUAGES IN AD 2025 | — | 66 |
| LANGUAGES IN WORLD | — | 28 |
| languages not reduced to writing | 5,000 | 28 |
| languages of annual church megacensus | 3,000 | 3 |
| languages understood per person | 13 | 27 |
| languages used in broadcasts by Christian radio/TV stations | 300 | 29 |
| languages used in Christian broadcasts over state/secular stations | 2,700 | 29 |
| languages with 'Jesus' Film (Gospel of Luke) available or near | 2,360 | 28 |

| Category | Statistic | Diag |
|---|---|---|
| languages with 'Jesus' Film in preparation | 609 | 28 |
| languages with a complete Portion (gospel) | 2,600 | 28 |
| languages with active RC/Protestant translation cooperation | 400 | 28 |
| languages with any Christian literature (apart from Scripture) | 1,000 | 28 |
| languages with any Scripture endeavor | 6,900 | 28 |
| languages with Christian radio broadcasts | 2,800 | 29 |
| languages with Christians with no own-language Christian broadcasting | 10,500 | 29 |
| languages with direct-access scriptures | 2,500 | 28 |
| languages with first-scripture translation under way | 550 | 28 |
| languages with gospel only (P..) | 520 | 26 |
| languages with gospel, near-NT only (Pn.) | 140 | 26 |
| languages with gospel, near-NT, near-Bible (Pnb) | 100 | 26 |
| languages with gospel, New Testament only (PN.) | 700 | 26 |
| languages with gospel, NT, near-Bible (PNb) | 110 | 26 |
| languages with gospel, NT, whole Bible (PNB) | 392 | 26 |
| languages with indirect-access scriptures only | 4,100 | 28 |
| languages with major name of God used in scriptures | 7,100 | 5 |
| languages with near-gospel only (p..) | 1,300 | 26 |
| languages with near-gospel, near-NT (pn.) | 2,100 | 26 |
| languages with near-gospel, near-NT, near-Bible (pnb) | 1,300 | 26 |
| languages with New Reader Portion | 600 | 28 |
| languages with New Reader Selections | 800 | 28 |
| languages with New Testament in mother-tongue | 800 | 28 |
| languages with New Testament only (no Bible) | 950 | 28 |
| languages with no Christian radio broadcasts | 10,700 | 29 |
| languages with no scriptures but with some Christian literature | 1,000 | 28 |
| languages with no scriptures or Christian literature | 3,000 | 28 |
| languages with no scriptures or Christian literature, but with Christians | 2,800 | 28 |
| languages with no scriptures published (...) | 6,800 | 26 |
| languages with non-roman script | 1,300 | 28 |
| languages with obsolete Scripture only (out of print / incomprehensible) | 700 | 28 |
| languages with older scriptures but with new translations under way | 265 | 28 |
| languages with over 1 million speakers | 380 | 26 |
| languages with partial scriptures (uncompleted) only | 5,600 | 28 |
| languages with Portion only (no Testaments) in mother-tongue | 1,800 | 28 |
| languages with roman script, Scripture | 6,500 | 28 |
| languages with Scripture revised versions under way | 300 | 28 |
| languages with Scripture translation projects under way | 1,200 | 28 |
| languages with selections | 5,100 | 28 |
| languages with under 1 million speakers | 13,100 | 26 |
| languages with whole Bible in mother-tongue | 392 | 28 |
| languages without Christian radio broadcasts | 10,700 | 29 |
| latent (inactive) Christians | 1,352 million | 30 |
| Latin America, church members | 475.7 million | 44 |
| Latin America, church members in AD 2025 | 635.3 million | 68 |
| Latin America, church members, annual growth rate | 1.57% | — |
| Latin America, church members, annual growth rate in AD 2025 | 1.16% | — |
| Latin America, church members, annual increase | 7.5 million | — |
| Latin America, church members, annual increase, in AD 2025 | 7.4 million | — |
| Latin America, church members, as % of region | 91.62% | — |
| Latin America, church members, as % of region, in AD 2025 | 91.19% | — |
| Latin America, church members, as % of world members | 25.19% | — |
| Latin America, church members, as % of world members, in AD 2025 | 25.50% | — |
| Latin America, population | 519.1 million | 47 |
| Latin America, population in AD 2025 | 696.6 million | — |
| Latin America, population, annual growth rate | 1.58% | — |
| Latin America, population, annual growth rate in AD 2025 | 1.18% | — |
| Latin America, population, annual increase | 8.2 million | — |
| Latin America, population, annual increase, in AD 2025 | 8.2 million | — |
| Latin America, population, as % of world | 8.57% | — |
| Latin America, population, as % of world, in AD 2025 | 8.90% | — |
| Latter-day Saints (Mormons), missionaries, % in World A, 1990 | 0.1% | 39 |
| Latter-day Saints (Mormons), missionaries, 1990 | 43,000 | 39 |
| lawyers (advocates, solicitors, attorneys) | 6.5 million | 20 |
| lay apostalate | 624.3 million | 15 |
| lay Christians residing abroad | 40 million | 24 |
| lay Christians residing abroad in closed countries | 50,000 | 24 |
| lay Christians residing abroad, AD 2025 | 75 million | 67 |
| lay renewals, Christians involved in | 1.2 billion | 12 |
| laypersons (lay Christians) | 1,883 million | 24 |
| laypersons, % in World A countries | 0.5% | 37 |
| laypersons, % of church members | 99.8% | 24 |
| least developed countries (LDCs) | 48 | 23 |
| least developed countries, persons in | 642 million | 23 |
| lego, usages in NT | 2,365 | 7 |
| leitourgeia, usages in NT | 15 | 6 |
| leprosy sufferers (lepers) | 19.2 million | 18 |
| lesbians, overt | 35 million | 21 |
| less developed countries | 130 | 23 |
| less developed regions, persons in | 4.2 billion | 23 |
| letters in KJV/AV English Bible | 3,566,480 | 28 |
| Liberation theology, Christians involved in | 25 million | 12 |
| LIBRARIES | — | 28 |
| libraries participating in OCLC | 27,000 | — |
| libraries, large Christian (over 35,000 volumes each) | 2,200 | 28 |
| libraries, largest Christian (over 120,000 volumes each) | 130 | — |
| libraries, major religious (Christian) | 12,000 | 24 |
| libraries, public | 12,100 | 28 |
| libraries, religious (Christian) | 16,000 | 28 |
| library borrowers or users | 200 million | 28 |
| library volumes (books) | 4.5 billion | 28 |
| library volumes, increase p.a. | 50 million | 28 |
| library, books in largest university (Harvard) | 13.4 million | — |
| library, books in, world's largest | 23.6 million | — |
| life expectancy at birth | 66.5 | 18 |
| life expectancy at birth, in AD 1950 | 45 | — |
| life expectancy at birth, in AD 2025 | 73 | 66 |
| life expectancy at birth, in AD 2050 | 76 | — |
| life expectancy at birth, World A | 61 | 41 |
| life expectancy at birth, World C | 73 | 41 |
| life expectancy in AD 33, years | 28 | 7 |
| LIFE SCIENCES | — | 69 |
| LIKELIHOOD (L%) OF BEING MARTYRED | — | 16 |
| limited-access (partially-restricted) countries | 25 | 43 |
| lingua francas > 1 million non-native speakers | 407 | 27 |
| lingua francas > 1 million speakers | 774 | 27 |
| lingua francas > 10 million speakers | 228 | 27 |

| Category | Statistic | Diag |
|---|---|---|
| lingua francas > 100 million speakers | 41 | 27 |
| lingua francas > 100,000 non-native speakers | 983 | 27 |
| lingua francas > 100,000 speakers | 2,178 | 27 |
| lingua francas > 50 million speakers | 85 | 27 |
| listeners/viewers (regular) to Christian radio/TV programs | 1,150 million | 29 |
| listeners/viewers (regular) to Christian radio/TV stations | 600 million | 29 |
| LISTENERS/VIEWERS OF CHRISTIAN PROGRAM | — | 29 |
| listeners/viewers to Christian radio/TV over state/secular stations | 1 billion | 29 |
| literacy rate (% of world's adults) | 76.70% | 34 |
| literacy rate, (% of Christian adults) | 90% | 24 |
| literary languages | 1,000 | 28 |
| literate Christians, (adults) | 1.29 billion | 24 |
| literates (adult) | 3.26 billion | 34 |
| literates (adult), AD 2025 | 5.09 billion | 66 |
| LITERATURE | — | 28 |
| LITERATURE AND MEDIA IN AD 2025 | — | 67 |
| LITERATURE ON "evangelize"- | — | 28 |
| literature on evangelization, new items p.a. | 13,000 | 53 |
| literature, published Christian p.a. | 12 billion | 37 |
| literature, published Christian p.a., % in World A countries | 0.1% | 37 |
| Liturgical renewal, Christians involved in | 15 million | 12 |
| live births per 1000 females | 43.15 | 21 |
| LIVESTOCK | — | 21 |
| livestock, investment in domestic | $450 billion | 21 |
| living together as unmarried couples, persons | 1.5 billion | 21 |
| living together, unmarried couples | 750 million | 21 |
| local churches (worship centers) | 3.45 million | 24 |
| local churches (worship centers), AD 2025 | 5 million | 68 |
| local councils of churches | 20,000 | 44 |
| local councils of churches, AD 2025 | 40,000 | 68 |
| LOCAL OR SUBNATIONAL CONCILIARISM | — | 44 |
| local races (culture areas) | 71 | 22 |
| LOCATION OF WORKERS IN AD 2025 | — | 67 |
| long-term future Scenarios | 4 | 70 |
| LORD (Yahweh), uses of in KJV/AV | 1,855 | 28 |
| Lord's Army, persons involved in | 300,000 | 12 |
| louo, usages in NT | 6 | 7 |
| low-birthweight babies born p.a. | 24 million | — |
| lung cancer, deaths p.a. due to | 1.1 million | — |
| Lutherans (including Independents) | 63.7 million | 44 |
| Lutherans (including Independents) in AD 2025 | 71.0 million | 68 |
| Lutherans, % of all Christians | 3.19% | — |
| Lutherans, % of all Christians, in AD 2025 | 2.71% | — |
| Lutherans, % of world | 1.05% | — |
| Lutherans, % of world, in AD 2025 | 0.91% | — |
| Lutherans, annual growth rate, % | 0.43% | — |
| Lutherans, annual growth rate, %, in AD 2025 | 0.43% | — |
| Lutherans, annual increase | 275,000 | — |
| Lutherans, annual increase in AD 2025 | 306,000 | — |
| macro regions (continents) | 7 | 22 |
| MACRO SEGMENTS | — | 42 |
| macro-evangelists | 1,000 | — |
| macropeoples | 432 | 22 |
| macrophyla | 5 | 22 |
| macroraces (major races) | 5 | 22 |
| macrozones | 10 | 22 |
| Madagascar Revival, persons involved in | 1 million | 12 |
| magazine titles | 600,000 | 28 |
| Mahayana Buddhists | 202.2 million | 23 |
| Mahayana in AD 2025 | 235.3 million | 66 |
| Mahayana, % of Buddhists | 56.18% | — |
| Mahayana, % of Buddhists, in AD 2025 | 56.24% | — |
| Mahayana, % of world | 3.34% | — |
| Mahayana, % of world, in AD 2025 | 3.01% | — |
| Mahayana, annual growth rate, % | 1.00% | 23 |
| Mahayana, annual growth rate, %, in AD 2025 | 0.61% | — |
| Mahayana, annual increase | 2.0 million | — |
| Mahayana, annual increase in AD 2025 | 1.4 million | 66 |
| mail, pieces delivered p.a. | 350 billion | 20 |
| mainframe computer sales p.a. | 2,000 | 20 |
| mainframe computers | 25,000 | 20 |
| major civil divisions (MCDs) | 3,030 | 22 |
| major culture areas (culture zones) | 20 | 22 |
| major peoples (macropeoples) | 432 | 22 |
| major population segments | 19,550 | 42 |
| major races | 5 | 22 |
| make known, usages in GNB/NT | 580 | 33 |
| malaria deaths p.a. | 2.7 million | 18 |
| malaria, new cases p.a. | 450 million | 18 |
| malaria, persons at risk | 3.2 billion | 18 |
| Malayu net, total speakers | 242 million | 27 |
| Malikites | 221.9 million | — |
| Malikites in AD 2025 | 346.6 million | — |
| Malikites, % of all Muslims | 18.67% | — |
| Malikites, % of all Muslims, in AD 2025 | 19.42% | — |
| Malikites, % of world | 3.66% | — |
| Malikites, % of world, in AD 2025 | 4.43% | — |
| Malikites, annual growth rate, % | 2.00% | — |
| Malikites, annual growth rate, %, in AD 2025 | 1.80% | — |
| Malikites, annual increase | 4.4 million | — |
| Malikites, annual increase in AD 2025 | 6.2 million | — |
| malnourished babies born p.a. | 15 million | 18 |
| malnutrition, % of childhood (under 5) deaths caused by | 50% | — |
| malnutrition, sufferers from chronic | 700 million | 18 |
| man-made disaster victims (deaths) p.a. | 1.5 million | 18 |
| Mandarin Chinese cluster, native speakers | 882.1 million | 27 |
| Mandarin Chinese cluster, total speakers | 1.32 billion | 27 |
| Mandates disobeyed | 4 | 9 |
| Mandates obeyed | 3 | 9 |
| Mandates of the Great Commission | 7 | 6 |
| Mandates, Greek synonyms related to the Seven | 140 | 6 |
| Mandates, synonyms of in 10,000 languages | 600,000 | 5 |
| manthano, usages in NT | 25 | 7 |
| Marathi cluster, native speakers | 106.5 million | 27 |
| Marathi cluster, total speakers | 164 million | 27 |
| MARGINAL CHRISTIAN BROADCASTING | — | 29 |
| Marginal Christian congregations | 116,000 | 64 |

| *Category* | *Statistic* | *Diag* |
|---|---|---|
| MINISTRY TO CLOSED COUNTRIES | — | 43 |
| minor religions | 500 | 1 |
| MINOR RELIGIONS AND QUASI-RELIGIONS | — | 23 |
| MINOR RELIGIONS AND QUASI-RELIGIONS IN AD 2025 | — | 66 |
| *missio* (Latin), usages in NT | 900 | 6 |
| missiologists, professional | 20,000 | 24 |
| mission agencies | 4,000 | 44 |
| mission agencies, AD 2025 | 6,000 | 68 |
| mission boards or societies, foreign | 4,000 | 24 |
| mission boards, agencies or societies, home | 5,800 | 24 |
| mission, % that is aid and relief | 1% | 64 |
| mission, % that is counterwitness | 5% | 64 |
| mission, % that is cross-cultural discipling | 1% | 64 |
| mission, % that is dialogue | 0.1% | 64 |
| mission, % that is discipling the evangelized | 8% | 64 |
| mission, % that is domestic mission | 3% | 64 |
| mission, % that is edification of Christians | 40% | 64 |
| mission, % that is evangelization of the unevangelized | 1% | 64 |
| mission, % that is frontier mission | 0.6% | 64 |
| mission, % that is monocultural ministry | 10% | 64 |
| mission, % that is nonresidential mission | 0.1% | 64 |
| mission, % that is partnership with other Christians | 91% | 64 |
| mission, % that is proselytization of other Christians | 20% | 64 |
| mission, % that is psuedo-frontier mission | 2% | 64 |
| mission, % that is re-evangelization of Christians | 1% | 64 |
| mission, % that is renewal of Christians | 10% | 64 |
| mission, % that is sociopolitical action | 5% | 64 |
| mission, % that is tentmaking | 1% | 64 |
| mission, % that is witness | 0.2% | 64 |
| missionaries (home or foreign) | 1.6 million | 64 |
| missionaries deployed to World A peoples | 18,000 | 62 |
| missionaries deployed to World B peoples | 68,000 | 62 |
| missionaries deployed to World C peoples | 335,000 | 62 |
| missionaries required for World A peoples on evangelized basis | 177,000 | 62 |
| missionaries required for World A peoples on population basis | 77,000 | 62 |
| missionaries required for World B peoples on evangelized basis | 242,000 | 62 |
| missionaries required for World B peoples on population basis | 211,000 | 62 |
| missionaries required for World C peoples on evangelized basis | 1,000 | 62 |
| missionaries required for World C peoples on population basis | 132,000 | 62 |
| missionaries, cross-cultural | 630,000 | 15 |
| missionaries, cross-cultural, home | 210,000 | 15 |
| missionaries, foreign | 419,500 | 24 |
| missionaries, Third-World citizens who are foreign | 5,360 | 24 |
| MISSIONARY CONCILIARISM | — | 44 |
| missionary sending, countries with adequate S | 27 | 36 |
| missionary sending, countries with adequate S (%) | 20% | 36 |
| missionary sending, countries with adequate SS | 26 | 45 |
| missionary sending, countries with adequate SS (%) | 19.4% | 45 |
| missionary sending, countries with barely adequate S | 12 | 36 |
| missionary sending, countries with barely adequate S (%) | 9% | 36 |
| missionary sending, countries with barely adequate SS | 16 | 45 |
| missionary sending, countries with barely adequate SS (%) | 11.9% | 45 |
| missionary sending, countries with exemplary S | 33 | 36 |
| missionary sending, countries with exemplary S (%) | 25% | 36 |
| missionary sending, countries with exemplary SS | 27 | 45 |
| missionary sending, countries with exemplary SS (%) | 20.1% | 45 |
| missionary sending, countries with inadequate S | 60 | 36 |
| missionary sending, countries with inadequate S (%) | 44% | 36 |
| missionary sending, countries with inadequate SS | 61 | 45 |
| missionary sending, countries with inadequate SS (%) | 45.5% | 45 |
| missionary sending, countries with negligible S | 2 | 36 |
| missionary sending, countries with negligible S (%) | 1.5% | 36 |
| missionary sending, countries with negligible SS | 4 | 45 |
| missionary sending, countries with negligible SS (%) | 3.0% | 45 |
| missionary-donating Christian countries | 26 | 45 |
| missionary-draining Christian countries | 44 | 45 |
| missionary-looting Christian countries | 52 | 45 |
| missions councils (national or international) | 60 | 44 |
| missions councils, AD 2025 | 100 | 68 |
| missions, books about | 111,500 | — |
| mobile cinemas | 35,000 | 20 |
| modems, microcomputers with | 100 million | 20 |
| moderators or other denominational heads | 20,000 | 44 |
| moderators or other denominational heads, AD 2025 | 25,000 | 68 |
| moles, in closed/restricted-access countries | 800 | 43 |
| monasteries, ashrams, convents, abbeys, priories | 8,000 | 24 |
| Monastic renewal, Christians involved in | 700,000 | 12 |
| money and quasi-money, annual increase | 20% | 19 |
| money in use, annual increase | 19% | 19 |
| money needed p.a. for adequate global food, water, health, education | $700 billion | 18 |
| money to buy food, persons without | 1.5 billion | 18 |
| money-laundering through banks (gray or black money), p.a. | $1.8 trillion | 19 |
| Mongoloid race | 2,266 million | 25 |
| Mongoloid race, % of world | 37% | 25 |
| monks including friars | 500,000 | 24 |
| MONODENOMINATIONALISM (SCENARIO 1) | — | 70 |
| MONOLITHS, CHRISTIAN ORGANIZATIONAL | — | 74 |
| Monoliths, Global Christian | 80 | 14 |
| more developed countries | 60 | 23 |
| more developed countries, persons in | 1.2 billion | 23 |
| mother tongues | 13,500 | 28 |
| mother-tongue broadcasting, persons with none (religious or secular) | 570 million | 29 |
| mother-tongue Christian broadcasting, persons exposed to | 5.3 billion | 29 |
| mother-tongue Christian broadcasting, persons exposed to foreign | 4.0 billion | 29 |
| mother-tongue Christian broadcasting, persons who get none | 770 million | 29 |
| mother-tongue Christian broadcasting, persons who get none, % world | 12.70% | 29 |
| mother-tongue Christian broadcasting, persons with as % world | 87.5% | 29 |
| mother-tongue Christian broadcasting, persons with foreign, % world | 66% | 29 |
| mother-tongue Christian broadcasting, persons with only internal | 160 million | 29 |
| MULTICHANNELING | — | 61 |
| multimillionaires | 75,000 | 19 |
| MULTINATIONALS | — | 23 |
| multiparty democratic states (1990) | 82 | 23 |
| murder squads, nations tolerating local or international | 35 | 19 |
| murderers convicted p.a. | 350,000 | 19 |
| murders: victims murdered a year | 975,000 | 18 |
| museum visitors a year | 1.3 billion | 20 |

| *Category* | *Statistic* | *Diag* |
|---|---|---|
| museums | 23,000 | 20 |
| Muslim religions, distinct | 270 | 1 |
| Muslims | 1,188 million | 23 |
| Muslims in AD 2025 | 1,785 million | 66 |
| Muslims, % of world | 19.62% | — |
| Muslims, % of world, in AD 2025 | 22.81% | — |
| Muslims, annual growth rate, % | 2.11% | 23 |
| Muslims, annual growth rate, %, in AD 2025 | 1.64% | — |
| Muslims, annual increase | 25.1 million | — |
| Muslims, annual increase in AD 2025 | 29.3 million | 66 |
| *myeo*, usages in NT | 1 | 7 |
| names of God, languages with distinct, in scriptures | 7,100 | 5 |
| narcotraffickers (persons employed in drug traffic) | 46 million | 19 |
| national (citizen) full-time Christian workers | 5.10 million | 24 |
| national (citizen) full-time Christian workers, % of all workers | 92.4% | 24 |
| national (citizen) full-time Christian workers, AD 2025 | 8 million | 68 |
| national Christian councils with Roman Catholic membership | 50 | 44 |
| NATIONAL CONCILIARISM | — | 44 |
| national evangelizers in closed/restricted-access countries, types of | 8 | 43 |
| nations (sovereign states) | 195 | 23 |
| nations (sovereign) without own TV service | 30 | 29 |
| nations belonging to United Nations | 185 | 23 |
| nations dishonoring UN-defined human rights | 130 | 19 |
| nations operating torture | 110 | 19 |
| nations responsible for extrajudicial killings | 80 | 19 |
| nations tolerating local or international murder squads | 35 | 19 |
| nations with human rights violations | 150 | 19 |
| nationwide Christian councils | 1,200 | 44 |
| nationwide Christian councils, AD 2025 | 2,000 | 68 |
| near-scriptures, languages with indirect-access only | 4,100 | 28 |
| near-synonyms of "evangelize" | 620 | 33 |
| needy Christians, % of all Christians | 29% | 24 |
| needy Christians, AD 2025, % of all Christians | 40% | 67 |
| needy, the (30% of world) | 1.8 billion | 18 |
| Negroid race | 648.1 million | 25 |
| Negroid race, % of world | 11% | 25 |
| Neo-Evangelicalism, persons involved in | 34 million | 12 |
| Neo-Evangelicals | 34 million | 11 |
| Neo-Hindus | 17.4 million | 23 |
| Neo-Hindus in AD 2025 | 23.2 million | 66 |
| Neo-Hindus, % of all Hindus | 2.14% | — |
| Neo-Hindus, % of all Hindus, in AD 2025 | 2.21% | — |
| Neo-Hindus, % of world | 0.29% | — |
| Neo-Hindus, % of world, in AD 2025 | 0.30% | — |
| Neo-Hindus, annual growth rate, % | 2.70% | 23 |
| Neo-Hindus, annual growth rate, %, in AD 2025 | 1.16% | — |
| Neo-Hindus, annual increase | 470,000 | — |
| Neo-Hindus, annual increase in AD 2025 | 269,000 | 66 |
| Neocharismatic types | 144 | — |
| neofundamentalists, non-Christian | 250 million | 19 |
| Neoreligionists (New-Religionist) religions, distinct | 160 | 1 |
| net reproduction rate, per woman, 1993 | 1.4 | 48 |
| net reproduction rate, per woman, AD 2025 | 1.03 | 48 |
| NETWORKS | — | 24 |
| networks (computer), Great Commission | 5,000 | 24 |
| New Age religionists | 500 million | 19 |
| New Age/millennialist/messianic cults or sects, AD 2025 | 750 million | 66 |
| New Age/occult/neo-Hindu cultists | 500 million | 23 |
| new bibliographical items a year on mission | 16,000 | 28 |
| new books and articles on evangelization p.a. | 12,000 | 28 |
| new Christians, increase p.a. | 55.6 million | 44 |
| new church member rate (baptism rate) | 2.23% | — |
| new families each year, 1993 | 33 | 48 |
| new families each year, AD 2025 | 50 | 48 |
| new homes/families a year | 38 million | 21 |
| new homes/families a year, AD 2025 | 50 million | 66 |
| new knowledge, pages p.a. | 20 billion | 28 |
| new knowledge, words p.a. | 6 trillion | 28 |
| NEW LIFE MOVEMENTS, AD 1700-AD 2000 | — | 12 |
| New Reader Portions distributed p.a. | 30 million | 28 |
| New Reader Portions, languages able to use | 1,956 | 28 |
| new religions in Western world | 4,000 | 53 |
| new religious buildings (Christian), cost p.a. | $8 billion | 24 |
| new souls on Earth each year | 129.2 million | 33 |
| NEW TESTAMENT | — | 28 |
| New Testament key group-themes | 341 | 7 |
| New Testament, languages possessing | 1,200 | 28 |
| New Testament, languages possessing (but not the whole Bible) | 800 | 28 |
| New Testaments distributed p.a. | 120.7 million | 28 |
| New-Religionists | 102.4 million | 23 |
| New-Religionists | 102.4 million | 23 |
| New-Religionists in AD 2025 | 114.7 million | 66 |
| New-Religionists, % of world | 1.69% | — |
| New-Religionists, % of world, in AD 2025 | 1.47% | — |
| New-Religionists, annual growth rate, % | 0.94% | 23 |
| New-Religionists, annual growth rate, %, in AD 2025 | 0.46% | — |
| New-Religionists, annual increase | 958,000 | — |
| New-Religionists, annual increase in AD 2025 | 524,000 | 66 |
| newly evangelized p.a. | 78.1 million | 41 |
| newly-closed countries in World A, p.a. | 1 | 43 |
| newly-closed/restricted-access countries each year | 2 | 43 |
| newly-evangelized every day | 166,000 | 34 |
| newly-evangelized every year | 60.5 million | 34 |
| news and information, % of radio and TV time | 17% | 29 |
| newspaper circulation | 509 million | 20 |
| newspaper circulation per 1000 | 84 | 20 |
| newspaper circulation, daily, AD 2025 | 1.2 billion | 66 |
| newspapers (daily, non-daily), AD 2025 | 10,000 | 66 |
| newspapers, daily | 6,170 | 20 |
| newsprint, lbs. consumed per person p.a. | 12 | 20 |
| newsprint, metric tons p.a. | 30 million | 20 |
| NGOs (nongovernmental organizations) | 4,000 | 23 |
| *nipto*, usages in NT | 17 | 7 |
| no past schooling, persons with | 850 million | 18 |
| no vote, populations with (1989) | 2.8 billion | 18 |
| NO-SCRIPTURE LANGUAGES | — | 28 |
| no-Scripture languages (with no scriptures or selections translated yet) | 6,850 | 28 |

| Category | Statistic | Diag |
|---|---|---|
| Protestants, professing | 310.0 million | 30 |
| provinces | 3,030 | 23 |
| PSEUDO-RELIGION | — | 19 |
| psychoneurotics | 1 billion | 18 |
| psychotics | 60 million | 18 |
| psychotics, AD 2025 | 80 million | 66 |
| public health expenditures per capita, p.a. | $239 | 21 |
| public libraries | 290,000 | 28 |
| publish, usages in KJV-AV/NT | 7 | 33 |
| Punjabi cluster, native speakers | 136.0 million | 27 |
| Punjabi cluster, total speakers | 212 million | 27 |
| pupils enrolled (first/primary level) | 95% | 24 |
| pupils in Christian primary and secondary schools | 400 million | 24 |
| quasipentecostals | 18 million | 12 |
| quasireligionist religions, distinct | 8 | 1 |
| quasireligionists | 1.1 million | — |
| quasireligionists, % of world | 0.02% | — |
| quasireligionists, % of world, in AD 2025 | 0.02% | — |
| quasireligionists, annual growth rate, % | 0.96% | — |
| quasireligionists, annual growth rate, %, in AD 2025 | 1.37% | — |
| quasireligionists, annual increase | 10,300 | — |
| quasireligionists, annual increase in AD 2025 | 20,600 | — |
| quasireligionists, in AD 2025 | 1.5 million | — |
| questionnaires in annual church megacensus | 10 million | 3 |
| questions in annual church megacensus | 2,056 | 3 |
| questions, basic, in research process | 8 | 69 |
| race, Australoid | 69.9 million | 25 |
| race, Australoid, % of world | 1% | 25 |
| race, Capoid | 1.2 million | 25 |
| race, Capoid, % of world | 0.02% | 25 |
| race, Caucasoid | 3,057 million | 25 |
| race, Caucasoid, % of world | 50% | 25 |
| RACE, COLOR, ETHNICITY | — | 22 |
| race, Mongoloid | 2,266 million | 25 |
| race, Mongoloid, % of world | 37% | 25 |
| race, Negroid | 648.1 million | 25 |
| race, Negroid, % of world | 11% | 25 |
| races | 5 | 22 |
| racist regimes, persons under | 80 million | 18 |
| radio or TV sets, persons without | 2.6 billion | 29 |
| radio or TV, persons without, % world | 43.50% | 18 |
| radio scripture selections, languages with | 4,000 | 28 |
| radio scriptures in preparation, languages with | 100 | 28 |
| radio scriptures, languages quoting Scripture texts/passages/selections | 2,600 | 28 |
| radio scriptures, languages with at least one complete Book broadcast | 1,400 | 28 |
| radio sets in use | 2.08 billion | 20 |
| radio sets per 1000 | 343 | 20 |
| radio sets, AD 2025 | 3.5 billion | 66 |
| radio sets, World A countries' share of | 4.35% | — |
| radio sets, World A individuals' share of | 14.00% | — |
| radio sets, World B countries' share of | 35.40% | — |
| radio sets, World B individuals' share of | 29.50% | — |
| radio sets, World C countries' share of | 60.30% | — |
| radio sets, World C individuals' share of | 56.50% | — |
| radio transmitters | 35,000 | 20 |
| radio/TV audience for all Christian programs, % of world | 30% | 29 |
| radio/TV audience for Christian programs, regular | 1.5 billion | 24 |
| radio/TV bedridden or housebound regular worshippers | 70 million | 29 |
| radio/TV believers (not joining any local church) | 30 million | 29 |
| radio/TV converts (new believers) p.a. | 3.5 million | 29 |
| radio/TV converts (new believers) p.a. isolated | 1 million | 29 |
| radio/TV global meganetworks, marginal/quasi-Christian | 3 | 29 |
| radio/TV global networks, marginal/quasi-Christian | 16 | 29 |
| radio/TV stations, Christian | 4,000 | 29 |
| radio: hours broadcast a week | 770,000 | 29 |
| radio: hours broadcast p.a. | 40 million | 29 |
| rail freight, ton-km p.a. | 8.4 trillion | 20 |
| rail passenger-km p.a. | 2.0 trillion | 20 |
| railway trackage, km | 1.63 million | 20 |
| rape, women victims a year | 2.5 million | 19 |
| rats | 30 billion | 21 |
| rats, % of world's food destroyed by, p.a. | 25% | 21 |
| rats, rural | 22.5 billion | 21 |
| rats, urban | 7.5 billion | 21 |
| rats, value of food and property destroyed by, p.a. | $400 billion | 21 |
| reached agglomerated christianized minipeoples | 14,000 | 42 |
| reached megapeoples (Worlds B & C) | 384 | 42 |
| reached micropeoples (in Worlds B and C) | 200,000 | 42 |
| reached minipeoples | 14,000 | 42 |
| reached minipeoples in 1974 | 11,000 | 42 |
| reached minipeoples in 1989 | 12,000 | 42 |
| reached peoples (with own churches) | 8,690 | 42 |
| reached socio-peoples (in Worlds B and C) | 1.7 million | 42 |
| Receive!, facets of "evangelize" related to | 33 | 6 |
| receive, usages in GNB/NT | 194 | 33 |
| Red (Amerindian) Christians as % of all Christians | 4% | 67 |
| Reform Hindus | 4.5 million | 23 |
| Reform Hindus in AD 2025 | 5.8 million | 66 |
| Reform Hindus, % of all Hindus | 0.55% | — |
| Reform Hindus, % of all Hindus, in AD 2025 | 0.55% | — |
| Reform Hindus, % of world | 0.07% | — |
| Reform Hindus, % of world, in AD 2025 | 0.07% | — |
| Reform Hindus, annual growth rate, % | 1.80% | 23 |
| Reform Hindus, annual growth rate, %, in AD 2025 | 1.07% | — |
| Reform Hindus, annual increase | 80,100 | — |
| Reform Hindus, annual increase in AD 2025 | 62,300 | 66 |
| Reformed, church members (incl. Independents) in AD 2025 | 74.4 million | 68 |
| Reformed, church members (including Independents) | 55.0 million | 44 |
| Reformed, church members, % of all Christians | 2.75% | — |
| Reformed, church members, % of all Christians, in AD 2025 | 2.84% | — |
| Reformed, church members, % of world | 0.91% | — |
| Reformed, church members, % of world, in AD 2025 | 0.95% | — |
| Reformed, church members, annual growth rate, % | 1.21% | — |
| Reformed, church members, annual growth rate, %, in AD 2025 | 1.21% | — |
| Reformed, church members, annual increase | 668,000 | — |
| Reformed, church members, annual increase in AD 2025 | 904,000 | — |
| refugees (external and internal) | 27.3 million | 66 |

| Category | Statistic | Diag |
|---|---|---|
| refugees, environmental | 11.6 million | 18 |
| refugees, permanently unsettled | 15 million | 18 |
| regimes using brutal violence against citizens | 70 | 19 |
| regional Christian councils or council of churches, AD 2025 | 60 | 68 |
| regional councils of churches | 70 | 44 |
| regions of world (UN) | 21 | 23 |
| registered national workers, in closed/restricted-access countries | 70,000 | 43 |
| regular audience for Christian program, all stations | 1.15 billion | 29 |
| regular audience for Christian program, over secular stations | 1 billion | 29 |
| regular audience for Christian radio/TV, over Christian stations | 600 million | 29 |
| regular radio/TV audience for Christian programs | 1.1 billion | 24 |
| regular radio/TV audience for Christian programs, AD 2025 | 2.5 billion | 67 |
| RELIGION IN AD 2025 | — | 66 |
| religionists (all religions) | 5.14 billion | 23 |
| religionists in AD 2025 | 6.81 billion | 66 |
| religionists, % of world | 84.80% | — |
| religionists, % of world, in AD 2025 | 87.00% | — |
| religionists, annual growth rate, % | 1.53% | 23 |
| religionists, annual growth rate, %, in AD 2025 | 1.12% | — |
| religionists, annual increase | 77.6 million | — |
| religionists, annual increase in AD 2025 | 75.6 million | — |
| religions in world, total | 8,400 | 53 |
| religions, distinct | 9,900 | 1 |
| religious (Christian) libraries | 16,000 | 28 |
| religious and anti-religious blocs | 33 | 23 |
| religious countries | 113 | 23 |
| religious countries, persons in | 1.96 billion | 18 |
| religious institutes (orders, societies for religious life based on prayer) | 2,400 | 24 |
| religious major subjects measured annually | 180 | 3 |
| religious pluralism: new religions spreading across Western world | 4,000 | 53 |
| RENEWAL | — | 12 |
| renewals, Christians involved in | 1.3 billion | 12 |
| reproduction rate for zero population increase | 2.1 | 47 |
| reproductive rate, babies per woman, 1955 | 5 | — |
| reproductive rate, babies per woman, 2025 | 2.3 | — |
| reproductive rate, babies per woman, AD 2000 | 2.64 | 21 |
| research and development (R&D), cost p.a. | $650 billion | 20 |
| research and development , cost p.a., in AD 2025 | $3 trillion | 66 |
| research and development, military, p.a. | $80 billion | 19 |
| research centers, church-related | 300 | 24 |
| research centers, Great Commission | 200 | 44 |
| research centers, Great Commission, in AD 2025 | 600 | 68 |
| research/scholarly books on Christian faith, new p.a. | 110,000 | 24 |
| researchers with access to supercomputers | 1 million | 20 |
| residential foreign missionaries in closed countries in Worlds A,B,C | 80,000 | 43 |
| RESOURCES | — | 24 |
| respiratory diseases, deaths p.a. due to | 2.9 million | — |
| restricted access countries in World A | 26 | 43 |
| restricted-access countries | 86 | 43 |
| restricted-access countries in World B | 31 | 43 |
| restricted-access countries in World C | 29 | 42 |
| restricted-access countries, AD 2025 | 100 | 66 |
| restricted-access countries, persons in | 3.0 billion | 19 |
| restricted-access countries, persons in, % of world | 50% | 19 |
| restricted-access countries, persons in, % of world, AD 2025 | 60% | 66 |
| restricted-access countries, persons in, AD 2025 | 4.7 billion | 66 |
| revisions (revised translations) of Scripture under way, languages with | 600 | 28 |
| *rhantizo*, usages in NT | 5 | 7 |
| Rheumatoid arthritis sufferers | 165 million | — |
| rich Christians (both affluent, and well off), AD 2025 | 1.3 billion | 67 |
| rich Christians, % of all Christians | 58% | 24 |
| rich Christians, AD 2025, % of all Christians | 50% | 67 |
| rich, the (54% of world) | 3.3 billion | 18 |
| riots, large-scale violent (over 1,000 persons each), p.a. | 250 | 19 |
| riots, violent, 1948-1977 | 10,893 | 19 |
| river blindness, persons at risk | 100 million | 18 |
| river blindness, persons with | 20 million | 18 |
| roads, km | 25 million | 20 |
| robbers/burglars per year | 360 million | 19 |
| robots, industrial | 25 million | 20 |
| robots, industrial, AD 2025 | 75 million | 66 |
| Roman Catholic congregations (churches) | 358,000 | 64 |
| Roman Catholic foreign missionaries in World A, 1990 | 5,830 | 38 |
| Roman Catholic foreign missionaries, 1990 | 200,430 | 38 |
| Roman Catholic membership, national Christian councils with | 50 | 44 |
| Roman Catholic missionaries, % in World A, 1990 | 2.9% | 38 |
| Roman Catholic, number of traditions/rites | 20 | 10 |
| Roman Catholics in AD 2025 | 1,362 million | — |
| Roman Catholics in ecumenical Bible translation: languages | 200 | 28 |
| Roman Catholics, % of all Christians | 52.88% | — |
| Roman Catholics, % of all Christians, in AD 2025 | 52.05% | — |
| Roman Catholics, % of world | 17.46% | — |
| Roman Catholics, % of world, in AD 2025 | 17.41% | — |
| Roman Catholics, annual growth rate, % | 1.24% | — |
| Roman Catholics, annual growth rate, %, in AD 2025 | 1.02% | — |
| Roman Catholics, annual increase | 13.1 million | — |
| Roman Catholics, annual increase in AD 2025 | 13.9 million | — |
| Roman Catholics, church members | 1,057 million | — |
| Roman Catholics, professing | 1,021 million | 30 |
| rural dwellers | 3.17 billion | 21 |
| rural dwellers, % of world | 52.40% | 21 |
| rural dwellers, % of world in AD 2025 | 40.9% | 66 |
| rural dwellers, AD 2025 | 3.20 billion | 66 |
| rural growth rate p.a. | 0.32% | 21 |
| rural poor migrating to cities each day | 100,000 | 21 |
| Russian cluster, native speakers | 200.9 million | 27 |
| Russian cluster, total speakers | 269 million | 27 |
| safe water supply, persons without adequate | 3.0 billion | 18 |
| safe water to drink, persons without | 2.2 billion | 18 |
| Saktists (Saktist Hindus) | 25.7 million | 23 |
| Saktists in AD 2025 | 33.1 million | 66 |
| Saktists, % of all Hindus | 3.17% | — |
| Saktists, % of all Hindus, in AD 2025 | 3.16% | — |
| Saktists, % of world | 0.42% | — |
| Saktists, % of world, in AD 2025 | 0.42% | — |
| Saktists, annual growth rate, % | 1.69% | 23 |
| Saktists, annual growth rate, %, in AD 2025 | 1.02% | — |

| Category | Statistic | Diag |
|---|---|---|
| Saktists, annual increase | 435,000 | — |
| Saktists, annual increase in AD 2025 | 338,000 | 66 |
| Samaritans | 500 | — |
| Samaritans in AD 2025 | 500 | — |
| sanitation, % rural developing world with inadequate | 88% | 18 |
| sanitation, persons living without | 3 billion | — |
| schistosomiasis, persons at risk | 700 million | 18 |
| schistosomiasis, persons with | 250 million | 18 |
| schizophrenics | 15 million | 18 |
| school age, children reaching, p.a. | 28 million | 18 |
| school pupils | 1 billion | 21 |
| school pupils, % of all eligible | 60% | 21 |
| school-age children | 1.4 billion | 18 |
| school-age population per teacher | 38 | 21 |
| school-agers not in schools | 670 million | 18 |
| schools, persons with access to (% of those eligible) | 33% | 18 |
| schools, persons with little or no access to | 940 million | 18 |
| schools, persons with no access to (24%) | 340 million | 18 |
| schoolteachers, Christian | 18 million | 24 |
| scientific articles a year | 2.5 million | 28 |
| scientific explanation, levels of | 4 | 69 |
| scientific journals | 390,000 | 28 |
| scientific journals, AD 2025 | 950,000 | 66 |
| scientific research, cost p.a. | $140 billion | 20 |
| scientists and engineers | 40 million | 20 |
| scientists and engineers in military work | 500,000 | 19 |
| scientists and engineers in R&D | 5 million | 20 |
| scientists, pure | 1.2 million | 20 |
| screens and terminals, Christian-owned | 350 million | 24 |
| screens/terminals, computer | 600 million | 20 |
| Scripture distribution p.a. | 4,600 million | 37 |
| Scripture distribution p.a., % in World A countries | 0.4% | 37 |
| Scripture languages | 6,700 | 28 |
| SCRIPTURE LANGUAGES | — | 28 |
| Scripture languages in audio versions | 800 | 28 |
| Scripture languages in print versions | 2,800 | 28 |
| Scripture languages in video versions | 700 | 28 |
| Scripture languages, % in World A countries | 3% | 37 |
| Scripture languages, complete (complete books translated) | 2,600 | 28 |
| Scripture languages, partial only (no complete books) | 6,900 | 28 |
| scriptures (all varieties) distributed p.a. | 4.6 billion | 28 |
| scriptures distributed each year, AD 2025 | 10 billion | — |
| SCRIPTURES IN PREPARATION | — | 28 |
| sea cargo, tons p.a. | 4 billion | 20 |
| sea levels, annual rise, inches | 0.6 | 19 |
| sea traffic: merchant ships | 67,300 | 20 |
| seamen (merchant seafarers) | 11 million | 21 |
| secondary schools, Christian | 50,000 | 24 |
| secondary/high schools | 700,000 | 21 |
| secret believers | 123.7 million | 43 |
| secret police forces, nations with | 100 | 19 |
| secular countries | 102 | 23 |
| secular countries, persons in | 2.40 billion | 18 |
| Sefardis (Sefardi Jews) | 952,000 | 23 |
| Sefardis in AD 2025 | 1.1 million | — |
| Sefardis, % of all Jews | 6.60% | — |
| Sefardis, % of all Jews, in AD 2025 | 6.60% | — |
| Sefardis, % of world | 0.02% | — |
| Sefardis, % of world, in AD 2025 | 0.01% | — |
| Sefardis, annual growth rate, % | 0.91% | 23 |
| Sefardis, annual growth rate, %, in AD 2025 | 0.43% | — |
| Sefardis, annual increase | 8,600 | — |
| Sefardis, annual increase in AD 2025 | 4,600 | — |
| SEGMENTIZATION | — | 22 |
| SEGMENTIZED GLOBE | — | 42 |
| segments | 18 million | 22 |
| selections (of Scripture) distributed p.a. | 4.1 billion | 28 |
| selections (Scripture texts), language producing leaflets of | 1,500 | 28 |
| selections of Scripture (print/audio/video/radio), languages using | 5,600 | 28 |
| semeia kai terata, usages in NT | 84 | 6 |
| seminarians | 1.1 million | 24 |
| seminaries and theological colleges | 4,800 | 24 |
| senior citizens (over 65 years) | 419 million | 21 |
| seniors (ages over 65) in AD 2025 | 817 million | — |
| serious global plans with some details | 229 | 13 |
| service agencies | 23,000 | 24 |
| SEVEN MANDATES OF CHRIST'S GREAT COMMISSION | — | 6 |
| severely deaf | 150 million | 18 |
| severely handicapped children | 100 million | 18 |
| severely malnourished | 700 million | 18 |
| sex ratio (males per 100 females), 1993 | 101.5 | 48 |
| sex ratio (males per 100 females), 2025 | 100.9 | 48 |
| sexually-exploited children, increase p.a. | 1 million | — |
| sexually-exploited children, world total | 40 million | — |
| Shafiites (Shafiite Sunni Muslims) | 239.9 million | — |
| Shafiites in AD 2025 | 393.5 million | — |
| Shafiites, % of all Muslims | 20.19% | — |
| Shafiites, % of all Muslims, in AD 2025 | 22.05% | — |
| Shafiites, % of world | 3.96% | — |
| Shafiites, % of world, in AD 2025 | 5.03% | — |
| Shafiites, annual growth rate, % | 2.20% | — |
| Shafiites, annual growth rate, %, in AD 2025 | 2.00% | — |
| Shafiites, annual increase | 5.3 million | — |
| Shafiites, annual increase in AD 2025 | 7.9 million | — |
| Shaivites (Shaivite Hindus) | 216.3 million | 23 |
| Shaivites in AD 2025 | 278.9 million | 66 |
| Shaivites, % of all Hindus | 26.65% | — |
| Shaivites, % of all Hindus, in AD 2025 | 26.58% | — |
| Shaivites, % of world | 3.57% | — |
| Shaivites, % of world, in AD 2025 | 3.56% | — |
| Shaivites, annual growth rate, % | 1.70% | 23 |
| Shaivites, annual growth rate, %, in AD 2025 | 1.02% | — |
| Shaivites, annual increase | 3.7 million | — |
| Shaivites, annual increase in AD 2025 | 2.9 million | 66 |
| Shanghainese cluster, native speakers | 94.9 million | 27 |
| Shanghainese cluster, total speakers | 153 million | 27 |
| shanty-dwellers or slum-dwellers | 700 million | 18 |

| Category | Statistic | Diag |
|---|---|---|
| sheep | 1.2 billion | 21 |
| shelter, persons without any kind of | 150 million | 18 |
| shelter, persons without decent or adequate | 1.3 billion | 18 |
| Shias (Shia Muslims) | 170.1 million | 23 |
| Shias in AD 2025 | 286.0 million | 66 |
| Shias, % of all Muslims | 14.32% | — |
| Shias, % of all Muslims, in AD 2025 | 16.02% | — |
| Shias, % of world | 2.81% | — |
| Shias, % of world, in AD 2025 | 3.66% | — |
| Shias, annual growth rate, % | 2.30% | 23 |
| Shias, annual growth rate, %, in AD 2025 | 2.10% | — |
| Shias, annual increase | 3.9 million | — |
| Shias, annual increase in AD 2025 | 6.0 million | 66 |
| Shintoist religions, distinct | 150 | 1 |
| Shintoists | 2.8 million | 23 |
| Shintoists in AD 2025 | 2.1 million | — |
| Shintoists, % of world | 0.05% | — |
| Shintoists, % of world, in AD 2025 | 0.03% | — |
| Shintoists, annual growth rate, % | -0.55% | 23 |
| Shintoists, annual growth rate, %, in AD 2025 | -1.05% | — |
| Shintoists, annual increase | -15,100 | — |
| Shintoists, annual increase in AD 2025 | -22,200 | — |
| ships (naval) with nuclear weapons | 950 | 19 |
| ships (naval), reactor-driven | 450 | 19 |
| shoplifting, cost of p.a. | $100 billion | 19 |
| short-term foreign missionaries | 400,000 | 44 |
| short-term foreign missionaries, AD 2025 | 700,000 | 67 |
| show, usages in GNB/NT | 325 | 33 |
| sick/ill children | 700 million | 18 |
| sick/ill persons | 2.2 billion | 18 |
| Sikh religions, distinct | 21 | 1 |
| Sikhs | 23.3 million | 23 |
| Sikhs in AD 2025 | 31.4 million | 66 |
| Sikhs, % of world | 0.38% | — |
| Sikhs, % of world, in AD 2025 | 0.40% | — |
| Sikhs, annual growth rate, % | 1.85% | 23 |
| Sikhs, annual growth rate, %, in AD 2025 | 1.20% | — |
| Sikhs, annual increase | 429,000 | — |
| Sikhs, annual increase in AD 2025 | 378,000 | 66 |
| singles (unmarrieds over 15) | 750 million | 21 |
| slaves (bought and sold, including bonded labor) | 35 million | 18 |
| Slavonic net, total speakers | 376 million | 27 |
| slumdwellers or shanty-dwellers | 700 million | 18 |
| slumdwellers, AD 2025 | 1.5 billion | 66 |
| slumdwellers, annual increase | 80 million | 18 |
| slums in AD 2025, as % of all metropolitan areas | 30% | 66 |
| slums, % of all metropolitan areas | 25% | 21 |
| smart cards in circulation, 1995 | 505 million | — |
| smart cards in circulation, AD 2000 | 3.1 billion | — |
| smokers killed by tobacco p.a. | 2.2 million | — |
| smokers killed by tobacco p.a. in 2025 | 4 million | — |
| smokers killed by tobacco per day | 6,000 | — |
| smugglers (closed-country alien evangelizers) | 2,000 | 43 |
| snake-bites, venomous, deaths p.a. due to | 50,000 | 18 |
| snakes, venomous, persons bitten by p. | 1.2 million | 18 |
| social people groups | 2 million | 22 |
| social surgery, genitally-mutilated women due to | 100 million | 19 |
| societies (cultures) | 6,629 | 22 |
| Society of Jesus (Jesuits), missionaries, % in World A, 1990 | 1.3% | 39 |
| Society of Jesus (Jesuits), missionaries, 1990 | 24,421 | 39 |
| Society of the Divine Word (SVD), missionaries, 1990 | 5,648 | 39 |
| Society of the Divine Word, missionaries, % in World A, 1990 | 1.7% | 39 |
| socio-peoples | 2 million | 22 |
| sociocultures | — | 22 |
| socioeconomic groups | 500,000 | 22 |
| sociolects | 100,000 | 22 |
| SOCIOPOLITICAL RIGHTS | — | 18 |
| sociopolitico-religious groups | 1 million | 22 |
| soil erosion, topsoil lost from cropland, tons p.a. | 27 billion | 19 |
| Southwest Turkic net, total speakers | 191 million | 27 |
| sovereign nations | 195 | 23 |
| space in AD 2025, persons living and working in | 1,000 | 66 |
| Spanish cluster, native speakers | 337 million | 27 |
| Spanish cluster, total speakers | 543 million | 27 |
| Spanish speakers | 543 million | 28 |
| Spanish speakers, AD 2025 | 800 million | 66 |
| speak, usages in GNB/NT | 310 | 33 |
| speakers of languages with gospel only | 129 million | 26 |
| speakers of languages with gospel, New Testament | 477 million | 26 |
| speakers of languages with gospel, NT, whole Bible | 5.22 billion | 26 |
| speakers of languages with no scriptures published | 254 million | 26 |
| special sermons, or encyclicals (global plans) | 68 | 13 |
| specialist groups | 5 million | 22 |
| species of life destroyed p.a. | 75,000 | 19 |
| species, % of 1990 total extinct by AD 2025 | 20% | 66 |
| species, world total of | 35 million | 66 |
| speech communities (idioms) | 15,000 | 28 |
| speech forms in AD 2025 | 13,000 | 66 |
| Spiritist Catholics, professing | 82.0 million | 30 |
| Spiritist religions, distinct | 36 | 1 |
| Spiritists (non-Christian) | 12.3 million | 23 |
| Spiritists in AD 2025 | 16.2 million | 66 |
| Spiritists, % of world | 0.20% | — |
| Spiritists, % of world, in AD 2025 | 0.21% | — |
| Spiritists, annual growth rate, % | 2.05% | 23 |
| Spiritists, annual growth rate, %, in AD 2025 | 1.10% | — |
| Spiritists, annual increase | 253,000 | — |
| Spiritists, annual increase in AD 2025 | 178,000 | 66 |
| SPIRITUAL SCIENCES | — | 69 |
| spread, usages in GNB/NT | 45 | 33 |
| standalone plans for evangelization | 1,500 | 61 |
| starvation, persons on verge of | 500 million | 18 |
| starvation-related Christian deaths p.a. | 6 million | 12 |
| starvation-related deaths p.a. | 22 million | 18 |
| starving persons (on edge of starvation), AD 2025 | 750 million | 66 |
| stateless (no nationality) | 10 million | 18 |
| statements (global plans) by organized bodies | 101 | 13 |

Part 10

# GEOSTATISTICS

Global tables on religionists, Christians, urbanites, and literates, AD 1900-AD 2025

*The message was told everywhere on earth. It was announced all over the world.*
—Paul in Romans 10:18 CEV quoting Psalm 19:4 LXX

*The good news is spreading all over the world with great success.*
—Colossians 1:6, CEV

Part 10 offers the reader several statistical views of the big picture—the whole world (Greek, *ge*) and the whole of global Christianity divided up by its continents, its regions, its cities, its literacy, its religions, its ecclesiastical varieties.

Inclusion of data from 1900 to AD 2000 enables the reader to perceive the whole variety of long-term trends, but also the immediate spot trends of year-by-year annual rates of change (see column 'Rate' or 'Trend' in Tables 1-2, 10-2, 10-6, 10-7, 10-8, 10-10, 10-11, 10-12).

# Global tables on religionists, Christians, urbanites, and literates, AD 1900-AD 2025

The Global Tables in Parts 1 and 10 form a series of 14 interconnected statistical tables. They are derived from the computerized World Christian Database, which covers all nations, languages, ethnolinguistic groups, religions, blocs, traditions, denominations, and Christian activities. This database will be available on the CD *World Christian database*.

Most figures in these tables are given to the nearest 1,000 or 100 or 10. Many, however, are given to the last digit. This latter should not be taken as implying any bogus claim to precision or exactitude. The reason they are given to the last digit is in order that all totals and sub-totals should add up exactly,

and be seen to add up exactly, without which their comprehensibility and credibility would be less satisfactory. When using or quoting all such individual figures, therefore, especially for publication elsewhere, the reader is advised to round them off to the nearest 100 or 1,000, 10,000 or 100,000, or even million, as may best serve his purpose.

These tables are built on precisely defined and exactly delimited definitions, which should be carefully examined when particular figures are wanted or are to be used or quoted elsewhere. In particular, our fundamental statistical distinction between 'global Christianity' (world total of all Christians of all categories)

and 'global church membership' (world total of Christians affiliated to churches) should be borne in mind throughout.

Also to be remembered throughout is that all figures, especially those of change or changing situations, report *net* (or 'nett') totals of the categories concerned, i.e. births minus deaths, gains minus losses, immigrants minus emigrants, conversions minus defections, and so on.

## Table 10–1. Organized Christianity: denominations and memberships on 6 continents in 6 ecclesiastical megablocs, AD 1900–AD 2025.

| Continent | Megabloc Code | Congs 1970 | Adults 1970 | Congs 1995 | Adults 1995 | 1900 | 1970 | Affiliated, 1900-2025 1990 | 1995 | 2000 | 2025 | Denoms Total 1970 | 1995 | Countries |
|---|---|---|---|---|---|---|---|---|---|---|---|---|---|---|
| 1 | 2  3 | 4 | 5 | 6 | 7 | 8 | 9 | 10 | 11 | 12 | 13 | 14 | 15 | 16 |
| **AFRICA** | | | | | | | | | | | | | | |
| | Total | 247,100 | 63,193,000 | 551,700 | 151,866,000 | 8,756,000 | 117,070,000 | 255,621,000 | 294,507,000 | 335,116,000 | 600,527,000 | 5,622 | 11,496 | 60 |
| A | Anglicans | 23,600 | 4,489,000 | 45,600 | 19,575,000 | 369,000 | 7,729,000 | 31,820,000 | 37,595,000 | 42,542,000 | 76,119,000 | 39 | 40 | 39 |
| I | Independents | 60,500 | 9,066,000 | 213,500 | 35,555,000 | 39,000 | 17,944,000 | 62,602,000 | 73,779,000 | 83,841,000 | 139,813,000 | 4,460 | 9,603 | 59 |
| m | Marginals | 5,300 | 380,000 | 12,600 | 749,000 | 1,000 | 1,004,000 | 1,811,000 | 2,098,000 | 2,427,000 | 5,547,000 | 113 | 183 | 53 |
| O | Orthodox | 15,100 | 10,745,000 | 16,000 | 16,134,000 | 4,600,000 | 18,395,000 | 27,996,000 | 31,686,000 | 35,304,000 | 59,783,000 | 59 | 82 | 31 |
| P | Protestants | 127,500 | 12,974,000 | 252,100 | 39,755,000 | 1,837,000 | 27,292,000 | 67,032,000 | 78,224,000 | 89,000,000 | 157,300,000 | 891 | 1,528 | 58 |
| R | Roman Catholics | 15,100 | 25,737,000 | 11,900 | 57,522,000 | 1,910,000 | 45,073,000 | 90,655,000 | 105,622,000 | 120,386,000 | 228,295,000 | 60 | 60 | 60 |
| – | doubly-affiliated | | -198,000 | | -16,377,000 | | | -367,000 | -26,295,000 | -32,499,000 | -38,384,000 | -66,330,000 | | |
| – | disaffiliated | | | | -1,047,000 | | | | | -1,998,000 | | | | |
| **ASIA** | | | | | | | | | | | | | | |
| | Total | 192,100 | 52,179,000 | 993,400 | 148,134,000 | 20,758,300 | 97,329,000 | 243,535,000 | 276,724,000 | 307,288,000 | 459,029,000 | 2,856 | 5,258 | 50 |
| A | Anglicans | 1,200 | 202,000 | 1,700 | 388,000 | 709,000 | 361,000 | 598,000 | 677,000 | 727,000 | 946,000 | 33 | 33 | 32 |
| I | Independents | 80,700 | 11,104,000 | 781,300 | 69,019,000 | 1,906,000 | 21,582,000 | 113,234,000 | 135,410,000 | 154,732,000 | 247,278,000 | 1,625 | 3,308 | 49 |
| m | Marginals | 3,700 | 323,000 | 10,600 | 1,412,000 | 300 | 759,000 | 2,115,000 | 2,292,000 | 2,486,000 | 3,604,000 | 87 | 120 | 41 |
| O | Orthodox | 3,500 | 5,406,000 | 6,500 | 8,041,000 | 6,864,000 | 8,967,000 | 13,926,000 | 14,351,000 | 14,113,000 | 17,351,000 | 131 | 191 | 36 |
| P | Protestants | 89,000 | 10,398,000 | 150,800 | 25,486,000 | 1,916,000 | 21,745,000 | 41,640,000 | 45,956,000 | 49,970,000 | 73,270,000 | 930 | 1,555 | 49 |
| R | Roman Catholics | 14,000 | 28,512,000 | 42,500 | 56,462,000 | 11,163,000 | 50,964,000 | 90,594,000 | 100,635,000 | 110,480,000 | 159,576,000 | 50 | 51 | 49 |
| – | doubly-affiliated | | -3,766,000 | | -12,674,000 | -1,800,000 | -7,049,000 | -18,572,000 | -22,597,000 | -25,220,000 | -42,996,000 | | |
| **EUROPE** | | | | | | | | | | | | | | |
| | Total | 432,900 | 326,555,000 | 538,900 | 370,444,000 | 368,210,000 | 468,479,000 | 528,848,000 | 534,778,000 | 536,832,000 | 532,861,000 | 2,693 | 5,083 | 48 |
| A | Anglicans | 22,200 | 14,386,000 | 20,700 | 13,226,000 | 24,902,000 | 29,468,000 | 26,302,000 | 26,592,000 | 26,637,000 | 26,410,000 | 29 | 30 | 26 |
| I | Independents | 88,300 | 6,010,000 | 150,000 | 13,994,000 | 82,000 | 9,894,000 | 23,281,000 | 25,089,000 | 25,724,000 | 29,302,000 | 861 | 1,962 | 42 |
| m | Marginals | 11,900 | 891,000 | 20,500 | 1,825,000 | 103,000 | 1,806,000 | 3,168,000 | 3,363,000 | 3,564,000 | 4,859,000 | 270 | 437 | 45 |
| O | Orthodox | 55,200 | 74,990,000 | 65,100 | 102,631,000 | 103,954,000 | 107,126,000 | 155,120,000 | 156,451,000 | 158,105,000 | 165,804,000 | 212 | 319 | 40 |
| P | Protestants | 112,800 | 54,906,000 | 123,600 | 52,554,000 | 59,487,000 | 82,132,000 | 76,377,000 | 76,867,000 | 77,529,000 | 77,089,000 | 1,271 | 2,285 | 46 |
| R | Roman Catholics | 142,500 | 187,635,000 | 159,000 | 213,516,000 | 180,722,000 | 256,162,000 | 281,450,000 | 284,434,000 | 285,978,000 | 276,272,000 | 50 | 50 | 47 |
| – | doubly-affiliated | | -5,851,000 | | -12,060,000 | -529,000 | -8,181,000 | -17,140,000 | -17,527,000 | -19,737,000 | -24,525,000 | | |
| – | disaffiliated | | -6,412,000 | | -15,242,000 | -511,000 | -9,928,000 | -19,710,000 | -20,491,000 | -20,968,000 | -22,350,000 | | |
| **LATIN AMERICA** | | | | | | | | | | | | | | |
| | Total | 128,200 | 149,654,000 | 419,000 | 246,880,000 | 60,026,000 | 263,595,000 | 404,399,000 | 440,039,000 | 475,660,000 | 635,271,000 | 2,814 | 5,324 | 46 |
| A | Anglicans | 1,800 | 376,000 | 2,100 | 590,000 | 726,000 | 768,000 | 989,000 | 1,045,000 | 1,090,000 | 1,353,000 | 44 | 44 | 44 |
| I | Independents | 32,500 | 4,807,000 | 115,100 | 19,086,000 | 29,000 | 9,242,000 | 32,902,000 | 36,357,000 | 39,706,000 | 60,022,000 | 1,174 | 2,719 | 44 |
| m | Marginals | 5,600 | 433,000 | 28,100 | 2,368,000 | 4,000 | 847,000 | 5,014,000 | 5,739,000 | 6,595,000 | 13,212,000 | 165 | 264 | 46 |
| O | Orthodox | 300 | 199,000 | 400 | 275,000 | 6,000 | 364,000 | 477,000 | 490,000 | 558,000 | 755,000 | 53 | 67 | 21 |
| P | Protestants | 65,500 | 7,066,000 | 189,500 | 25,763,000 | 933,000 | 12,505,000 | 39,842,000 | 44,056,000 | 48,132,000 | 76,191,000 | 1,332 | 2,184 | 46 |
| R | Roman Catholics | 22,500 | 143,689,000 | 83,800 | 241,369,000 | 58,689,000 | 251,791,000 | 391,772,000 | 426,725,000 | 461,220,000 | 606,059,000 | 46 | 46 | 46 |
| – | doubly-affiliated | | -6,454,000 | | -41,600,000 | -280,000 | -11,156,000 | -65,113,000 | -72,762,000 | -79,915,000 | -119,774,000 | | |
| – | disaffiliated | | -462,000 | | -971,000 | -81,000 | -766,000 | -1,484,000 | -1,611,000 | -1,726,000 | -2,547,000 | | |
| **NORTHERN AMERICA** | | | | | | | | | | | | | | |
| | Total | 407,200 | 115,477,000 | 601,800 | 141,017,000 | 59,570,000 | 168,932,000 | 194,457,000 | 203,742,000 | 212,166,000 | 235,111,000 | 1,577 | 4,986 | 5 |
| A | Anglicans | 10,800 | 2,824,000 | 9,100 | 2,243,000 | 2,172,000 | 4,395,000 | 3,354,000 | 3,318,000 | 3,244,000 | 2,923,000 | 3 | 3 | 3 |
| I | Independents | 144,300 | 24,455,000 | 320,300 | 52,044,000 | 5,857,000 | 36,320,000 | 68,306,000 | 74,525,000 | 80,237,000 | 102,710,000 | 749 | 3,687 | 4 |
| m | Marginals | 29,200 | 3,904,000 | 32,100 | 5,758,000 | 815,000 | 6,469,000 | 9,359,000 | 9,937,000 | 10,532,000 | 17,503,000 | 240 | 374 | 5 |
| O | Orthodox | 1,700 | 2,995,000 | 2,600 | 3,272,000 | 415,000 | 4,539,000 | 5,660,000 | 6,015,000 | 6,342,000 | 7,962,000 | 54 | 67 | 2 |
| P | Protestants | 197,100 | 44,012,000 | 209,800 | 48,994,000 | 37,300,000 | 62,812,000 | 65,135,000 | 67,732,000 | 69,978,000 | 74,765,000 | 526 | 850 | 5 |
| R | Roman Catholics | 24,100 | 39,346,000 | 27,900 | 47,363,000 | 13,011,000 | 57,413,000 | 68,236,000 | 69,140,000 | 71,035,000 | 80,520,000 | 5 | 5 | 5 |
| – | doubly-affiliated | | -2,059,000 | | -18,655,000 | | -3,016,000 | -25,593,000 | -26,925,000 | -29,202,000 | -51,272,000 | | |
| **OCEANIA** | | | | | | | | | | | | | | |
| | Total | 42,100 | 7,996,000 | 51,800 | 11,590,000 | 4,321,000 | 14,699,000 | 18,710,000 | 20,123,000 | 21,375,000 | 28,152,000 | 512 | 942 | 28 |
| A | Anglicans | 10,800 | 2,052,000 | 12,500 | 2,369,000 | 1,692,000 | 4,781,000 | 5,132,000 | 5,294,000 | 5,409,000 | 5,996,000 | 18 | 18 | 18 |
| I | Independents | 2,900 | 364,000 | 7,000 | 785,000 | 18,000 | 622,000 | 1,212,000 | 1,382,000 | 1,505,000 | 2,516,000 | 120 | 303 | 22 |
| m | Marginals | 1,400 | 131,000 | 2,200 | 250,000 | 4,000 | 215,000 | 365,000 | 422,000 | 457,000 | 829,000 | 71 | 110 | 25 |
| O | Orthodox | 200 | 188,000 | 300 | 407,000 | 4,000 | 271,000 | 586,000 | 631,000 | 706,000 | 1,060,000 | 24 | 38 | 3 |
| P | Protestants | 23,800 | 2,244,000 | 27,000 | 3,952,000 | 1,551,000 | 4,273,000 | 6,323,000 | 6,843,000 | 7,392,000 | 10,015,000 | 252 | 446 | 27 |
| R | Roman Catholics | 3,000 | 3,023,000 | 2,800 | 4,967,000 | 1,052,000 | 4,549,000 | 6,994,000 | 7,595,000 | 8,228,000 | 11,240,000 | 27 | 27 | 27 |
| – | doubly-affiliated | | -6,000 | | -1,140,000 | | -12,000 | -1,902,000 | -2,044,000 | -2,322,000 | -3,504,000 | | |
| **GLOBE** | | | | | | | | | | | | | | |
| | Total | 1,449,600 | 715,054,000 | 3,156,600 | 1,069,933,000 | 521,641,300 | 1,130,104,000 | 1,645,570,000 | 1,769,913,000 | 1,888,437,000 | 2,490,951,000 | 16,074 | 33,089 | 237 |
| A | Anglicans | 70,400 | 24,329,000 | 91,700 | 38,391,000 | 30,570,000 | 47,502,000 | 68,195,000 | 74,521,000 | 79,649,000 | 113,747,000 | 166 | 168 | 162 |
| I | Independents | 409,200 | 55,806,000 | 1,587,200 | 190,483,000 | 7,931,000 | 95,604,000 | 301,537,000 | 346,542,000 | 385,745,000 | 581,641,000 | 8,989 | 21,582 | 220 |
| m | Marginals | 57,100 | 6,062,000 | 106,100 | 12,362,000 | 927,300 | 11,100,000 | 21,832,000 | 23,851,000 | 26,061,000 | 45,554,000 | 946 | 1,488 | 215 |
| O | Orthodox | 76,000 | 94,523,000 | 90,900 | 130,760,000 | 115,843,000 | 139,662,000 | 203,765,000 | 209,624,000 | 215,128,000 | 252,715,000 | 533 | 764 | 133 |
| P | Protestants | 615,700 | 131,600,000 | 952,800 | 196,504,000 | 103,024,000 | 210,759,000 | 296,349,000 | 319,678,000 | 342,001,000 | 468,630,000 | 5,202 | 8,848 | 231 |
| R | Roman Catholics | 221,200 | 427,942,000 | 327,900 | 621,199,000 | 266,547,000 | 665,952,000 | 929,701,000 | 994,151,000 | 1,057,327,000 | 1,361,962,000 | 238 | 239 | 234 |
| – | doubly-affiliated | | -18,334,000 | | -102,506,000 | -2,609,000 | -29,781,000 | -154,615,000 | -174,354,000 | -194,780,000 | -308,401,000 | | |
| – | disaffiliated | | -6,874,000 | | -17,260,000 | -592,000 | -10,694,000 | -21,194,000 | -24,100,000 | -22,694,000 | -24,897,000 | | |

## Table 10–2. Status and trends in global mission as revealed by the annual Christian megacensus, AD 1800–AD 2025.

| Year: | 1800 | 1900 | 1970 | mid-2000 | trend. % p.a | mid-2002 | 2025 |
|---|---|---|---|---|---|---|---|
| **GLOBAL POPULATION** | | | | | | | |
| 1. Total population | 903,650,000 | 1,619,626,000 | 3,696,148,000 | 6,055,049,000 | 1.22 | 6,203,789,000 | 7,823,703,000 |
| 2. Urban dwellers (urbanites) | 36,146,000 | 232,695,000 | 1,353,370,000 | 2,881,079,000 | 1.90 | 2,991,572,000 | 4,611,677,000 |
| 3. Rural dwellers | 867,504,000 | 1,386,931,000 | 2,342,778,000 | 3,173,970,000 | 0.60 | 3,212,217,000 | 3,212,026,000 |
| 4. Adult population (over 15s) | 619,000,000 | 1,074,058,000 | 2,310,543,000 | 4,254,647,000 | 1.76 | 4,405,603,000 | 5,987,079,000 |
| 5. Literates | 123,800,000 | 296,258,000 | 1,475,194,000 | 3,261,345,000 | 1.76 | 3,377,265,000 | 5,046,637,000 |
| 6. Nonliterates | 495,200,000 | 777,800,000 | 835,349,000 | 993,302,000 | 1.75 | 1,028,338,000 | 940,442,000 |
| **WORLDWIDE EXPANSION OF CITIES** | | | | | | | |
| 7. Metropolises (over 100,000 population) | 40 | 300 | 2,400 | 4,050 | 1.84 | 4,200 | 6,500 |
| 8. Megacities (over 1 million population) | 1 | 20 | 161 | 402 | 2.21 | 420 | 650 |
| 9. Urban poor | 18 million | 100 million | 650 million | 1,400 million | 3.16 | 1,490 million | 3,000 million |
| 10. Urban slumdwellers | 3 million | 20 million | 260 million | 700 million | 2.82 | 740 million | 1,500 million |
| **GLOBAL POPULATION BY RELIGION** | | | | | | | |
| 11. Total all distinct religions | 700 | 1,000 | 6,000 | 9,900 | 1.70 | 10,200 | 15,000 |
| 12. Christians (total all kinds) (=World C) | 204,980,000 | 558,132,000 | 1,236,374,000 | 1,999,564,000 | 1.27 | 2,050,616,000 | 2,616,670,000 |
| 13. Muslims | 90,500,000 | 199,941,000 | 553,528,000 | 1,188,243,000 | 2.11 | 1,239,029,000 | 1,784,876,000 |
| 14. Nonreligious | 300,000 | 3,024,000 | 532,096,000 | 768,159,000 | 0.80 | 780,557,000 | 875,121,000 |
| 15. Hindus | 108,000,000 | 203,003,000 | 462,598,000 | 811,336,000 | 1.54 | 836,543,000 | 1,049,231,000 |
| 16. Buddhists | 69,400,000 | 127,077,000 | 233,424,000 | 359,982,000 | 1.04 | 367,538,000 | 418,345,000 |
| 17. Atheists | 10,000 | 226,000 | 165,400,000 | 150,090,000 | 0.24 | 150,804,000 | 159,544,000 |
| 18. New-Religionists | 0 | 5,910,000 | 77,762,000 | 102,356,000 | 0.94 | 104,280,000 | 114,720,000 |
| 19. Ethnoreligionists | 92,000,000 | 117,558,000 | 160,278,000 | 228,367,000 | 1.30 | 234,341,000 | 277,247,000 |
| 20. Sikhs | 1,800,000 | 2,962,000 | 10,618,000 | 23,258,000 | 1.84 | 24,124,000 | 31,378,000 |
| 21. Jews | 9,000,000 | 12,292,000 | 14,763,000 | 14,434,000 | 0.81 | 14,670,000 | 16,053,000 |
| 22. Non-Christians (=Worlds A and B) | 698,670,000 | 1,061,494,000 | 2,459,774,000 | 4,055,485,000 | 1.20 | 4,153,173,000 | 5,207,033,000 |
| **GLOBAL CHRISTIANITY** | | | | | | | |
| 23. Total Christians as % of world (=World C) | 22.7 | 34.5 | 33.5 | 33.0 | 0.05 | 33.1 | 33.4 |
| 24. Unaffiliated Christians | 9,300,000 | 36,489,000 | 106,268,000 | 111,125,000 | 0.65 | 112,575,000 | 125,712,000 |
| 25. Affiliated Christians (church members) | 195,680,000 | 521,643,000 | 1,130,106,000 | 1,888,439,000 | 1.30 | 1,938,041,000 | 2,490,958,000 |
| 26. Crypto-Christians | 900,000 | 3,571,000 | 59,195,000 | 123,727,000 | 2.18 | 129,173,000 | 190,490,000 |
| 27. Great Commission Christians | 21,000,000 | 77,931,000 | 277,152,000 | 647,821,000 | 1.44 | 666,640,000 | 887,579,000 |
| 28. Church attenders | 180,100,000 | 469,303,000 | 885,777,000 | 1,359,420,000 | 1.04 | 1,387,834,000 | 1,760,568,000 |
| 29. Evangelicals | 25,000,000 | 71,726,000 | 93,449,000 | 210,603,000 | 1.72 | 217,896,000 | 327,835,000 |
| 30. evangelicals | 21,000,000 | 77,931,000 | 277,152,000 | 647,821,000 | 1.44 | 666,640,000 | 887,579,000 |
| 31. Pentecostals/Charismatics/Neocharismatics | 0 | 981,000 | 72,223,000 | 523,767,000 | 1.87 | 543,578,000 | 811,552,000 |
| 32. Average Christian martyrs per year | 2,500 | 34,400 | 377,000 | 160,000 | 1.24 | 164,000 | 210,000 |
| **MEMBERSHIP BY 6 ECCLESIASTICAL MEGABLOCS** | | | | | | | |
| 33. Anglicans | 11,910,000 | 30,571,000 | 47,501,000 | 79,650,000 | 1.34 | 81,799,000 | 113,746,000 |
| 34. Independents | 400,000 | 7,931,000 | 95,605,000 | 385,745,000 | 2.17 | 402,641,000 | 581,642,000 |
| 35. Marginal Christians | 40,000 | 928,000 | 11,100,000 | 26,060,000 | 1.79 | 27,000,000 | 45,555,000 |
| 36. Orthodox | 55,220,000 | 115,844,000 | 139,662,000 | 215,129,000 | 0.52 | 217,371,000 | 252,716,000 |
| 37. Protestants | 30,980,000 | 103,024,000 | 210,759,000 | 342,002,000 | 1.36 | 351,362,000 | 468,633,000 |
| 38. Roman Catholics | 106,430,000 | 266,548,000 | 665,954,000 | 1,057,328,000 | 1.24 | 1,083,708,000 | 1,361,965,000 |
| **MEMBERSHIP BY 7 CONTINENTS, 21 UN REGIONS** | | | | | | | |
| 39. Africa (5 regions) | 4,330,000 | 8,756,000 | 117,069,000 | 335,116,000 | 2.62 | 352,886,000 | 600,526,000 |
| 40. Antarctica (1 region) | 0 | 0 | 370 | 3,400 | 2.90 | 3,600 | 8,000 |
| 41. Asia (4 regions) | 8,350,000 | 20,759,000 | 97,329,000 | 307,288,000 | 1.62 | 317,314,000 | 459,029,000 |
| 42. Europe (including Russia; 4 regions) | 171,700,000 | 368,210,000 | 468,480,000 | 536,832,000 | 0.08 | 537,656,000 | 532,861,000 |
| 43. Latin America (3 regions) | 14,900,000 | 60,027,000 | 263,597,000 | 475,659,000 | 1.57 | 490,701,000 | 635,271,000 |
| 44. Northern America (1 region) | 5,600,000 | 59,570,000 | 168,932,000 | 212,167,000 | 0.81 | 215,633,000 | 235,112,000 |
| 45. Oceania (4 regions) | 100,000 | 4,322,000 | 14,699,000 | 21,375,000 | 1.22 | 21,898,000 | 28,152,000 |
| **CHRISTIAN ORGANIZATIONS** | | | | | | | |
| 46. Denominations | 800 | 1,900 | 18,600 | 33,800 | 2.48 | 35,500 | 63,000 |
| 47. Congregations (worship centers) | 150,000 | 400,000 | 1,450,000 | 3,448,000 | 1.53 | 3,554,000 | 5,035,000 |
| 48. Service agencies | 600 | 1,500 | 14,100 | 23,000 | 2.15 | 24,000 | 40,000 |
| 49. Foreign-mission sending agencies | 200 | 600 | 2,200 | 4,000 | 1.24 | 4,100 | 6,000 |
| 50. Standalone global monoliths | 5 | 35 | 62 | 80 | 6.07 | 90 | 300 |
| **CHRISTIAN WORKERS** (clergy, laypersons) | | | | | | | |
| 51. Nationals (citizens; all denominations) | 400,000 | 1,050,000 | 2,350,000 | 5,104,000 | 0.97 | 5,204,000 | 6,500,000 |
| 52. Aliens (foreign missionaries) | 25,000 | 62,000 | 240,000 | 420,000 | 1.07 | 429,000 | 550,000 |
| **CHRISTIAN FINANCE** (in US$, per year) | | | | | | | |
| 53. Personal income of church members, $ | 40 billion | 270 billion | 4,100 billion | 15,198 billion | 2.28 | 15,900 billion | 26,000 billion |
| 54. Personal income of Pentecostals/Charismatics, $ | 0 | 250,000,000 | 157 billion | 3,508 billion | 4.08 | 3,800 billion | 9,500 billion |
| 55. Giving to Christian causes, $ | 1 billion | 8 billion | 70 billion | 270 billion | 5.41 | 300 billion | 870 billion |
| 56. Churches' income, $ | 950 million | 7 billion | 50 billion | 108 billion | 4.53 | 118 billion | 300 billion |
| 57. Parachurch and institutional income, $ | 50 million | 1 billion | 20 billion | 162 billion | 5.99 | 182 billion | 570 billion |
| 58. Cost-effectiveness (cost per baptism, $) | 7,500 | 17,500 | 128,000 | 330,000 | 2.80 | 349,000 | 650,000 |
| 59. Ecclesiastical crime, $ | 100,000 | 300,000 | 5,000,000 | 16 billion | 6.07 | 18 billion | 65 billion |
| 60. Income of global foreign missions, $ | 25,000,000 | 200,000,000 | 3.0 billion | 15 billion | 6.46 | 17 billion | 60 billion |
| 61. Computers in Christian use (numbers) | 0 | 0 | 1,000 | 332 million | 6.40 | 370 million | 1.5 billion |
| **CHRISTIAN LITERATURE** (titles) | | | | | | | |
| 62. Books about Christianity | 75,000 | 300,000 | 1.8 million | 4.5 million | 3.28 | 4.8 million | 11.8 million |
| 63. Books on Christian mission | 3,000 | 15,000 | 65,000 | 95,000 | 2.00 | 99,000 | 195,000 |
| 64. New commercial book titles per year | 500 | 2,200 | 17,100 | 25,000 | 3.92 | 27,000 | 70,000 |
| 65. Christian periodicals | 800 | 3,500 | 23,000 | 35,000 | 4.20 | 38,000 | 100,000 |
| 66. New books/articles on evangelization p.a. | 50 | 500 | 3,100 | 16,000 | 6.07 | 18,000 | 80,000 |
| **SCRIPTURE DISTRIBUTION** (all sources, per year/p.a.) | | | | | | | |
| 67. Bibles, p.a. | 500,000 | 5,452,600 | 25,000,000 | 53,700,000 | 4.96 | 59,156,000 | 180,000,000 |
| 68. New Testaments, p.a. | 800,000 | 7,300,000 | 45,000,000 | 120,700,000 | 2.96 | 127,940,000 | 250,000,000 |
| 69. Scriptures including gospels, selections, p.a. | 1,500,000 | 20 million | 281 million | 4,600 million | 1.08 | 4,700 million | 8,000 million |
| 70. Bible density (copies in place) | 20 million | 108 million | 443 million | 1,400 million | 2.12 | 1,460 million | 2,280 million |
| **CHRISTIAN BROADCASTING** | | | | | | | |
| 71. Christian radio/TV stations | 0 | 0 | 1,230 | 4,000 | 0.62 | 4,050 | 5,400 |
| 72. Total monthly listeners/viewers | 0 | 0 | 750,000,000 | 2,150,000,000 | 2.30 | 2,250,226,000 | 3,800,000,000 |
| 73. for Christian stations | 0 | 0 | 150,000,000 | 600,000,000 | 3.14 | 638,285,000 | 1,300,000,000 |
| 74. for secular stations | 0 | 0 | 650,000,000 | 1,810,000,000 | 1.76 | 1,874,291,000 | 2,800,000,000 |
| **CHRISTIAN URBAN MISSION** | | | | | | | |
| 75. Non-Christian megacities | 1 | 5 | 65 | 226 | 1.10 | 231 | 300 |
| 76. New non-Christian urban dwellers per day | 500 | 5,200 | 51,100 | 129,000 | 1.77 | 133,600 | 200,000 |
| 77. Urban Christians | 5,500,000 | 159,600,000 | 660,800,000 | 1,160,000,000 | 1.58 | 1,197,000,000 | 1,720,000,000 |
| **CHRISTIAN EVANGELISM** | | | | | | | |
| 78. Evangelism-hours per year | 600 million | 5 billion | 25 billion | 165 billion | 4.45 | 180 billion | 425 billion |
| 79. Offers per year (hearer-hours p.a.) | 900 million | 10 billion | 99 billion | 938 billion | 6.30 | 1,060 billion | 4,250 billion |
| 80. Disciple-opportunities per capita per year | 1 | 6 | 27 | 155 | 5.03 | 171 | 529 |
| **WORLD EVANGELIZATION** | | | | | | | |
| 81. Unevangelized population (=World A) | 674,350,000 | 879,672,000 | 1,641,245,000 | 1,629,375,000 | 0.50 | 1,645,685,000 | 1,845,406,000 |
| 82. Unevangelized as % of world | 74.6 | 54.3 | 44.4 | 26.9 | -0.71 | 26.5 | 23.6 |
| 83. World evangelization plans since AD 30 | 160 | 250 | 510 | 1,500 | 2.96 | 1,590 | 3,000 |

## Table 10–3. World population ranked by the world's 104 official state languages, AD 2000.

1. The table gives the totals in AD 2000, ranked by magnitude, of all populations of countries for whom the languages shown are their official state languages (including official national languages) throughout their country. Data for individual countries are given, coded, in column 14 of Global Table 12-1. The full codes are given in Part 16 "GeoCodebook".
2. Note that the table contains 1.9 billion duplications; several countries have 2, 3 or even 4 country-wide official languages, hence many populations have more than one official state language.

| Language Rank | Code | Name | Population |
|---|---|---|---|
| 1 | E | English | 2,047,163,000 |
| 2 | C | Chinese (Mandarin) | 1,288,524,000 |
| 3 | H | Hindi | 1,013,662,000 |
| 4 | S | Spanish | 448,924,000 |
| 5 | F | French | 309,305,000 |
| 6 | A | Arabic | 303,153,000 |
| 7 | P | Portuguese | 214,337,000 |
| 8 | X | Indonesian | 212,992,000 |
| 9 | R | Russian | 161,551,000 |
| 10 | U | Urdu | 156,483,000 |
| 11 | B | Bengali | 129,155,000 |
| 12 | J | Japanese | 126,714,000 |
| 13 | S | Swahili | 115,252,000 |
| 14 | G | German | 108,441,000 |
| 15 | V | Vietnamese | 79,832,000 |
| 16 | O | Filipino | 75,967,000 |
| 17 | K | Korean | 70,883,000 |
| 18 | N | Persian | 67,702,000 |
| 19 | T | Turkish | 66,776,000 |
| 20 | I | Italian | 64,710,000 |
| 21 | L | Amharic | 62,565,000 |
| 22 | Z | Thai | 61,399,000 |
| 23 | U | Ukrainian | 50,456,000 |
| 24 | W | Burmese | 45,611,000 |
| 25 | M | Afrikaans | 42,102,000 |
| 26 | Y | Polish | 38,765,000 |
| 27 | q | Quechua | 33,990,000 |
| 28 | y | Aymara | 33,990,000 |
| 29 | D | Dutch | 26,684,000 |
| 30 | m | Malay | 26,139,000 |
| 31 | Z | Uzbek | 24,318,000 |
| 32 | n | Nepali | 23,930,000 |
| 33 | P | Pushtu | 22,720,000 |
| 34 | D | Dari | 22,720,000 |
| 35 | t | Tamil | 22,394,000 |
| 36 | R | Romanian | 22,327,000 |
| 37 | u | Sinhalese | 18,827,000 |
| 38 | K | Kazakh | 16,223,000 |
| 39 | m | Malagasy | 15,942,000 |
| 40 | s | Swedish | 14,086,000 |
| 41 | g | Greek | 11,245,000 |
| 42 | k | Khmer | 11,168,000 |
| 43 | c | Chewa | 10,925,000 |
| 44 | Y | Serbian | 10,640,000 |
| 45 | c | Czech | 10,244,000 |
| 46 | B | Belorussian | 10,236,000 |
| 47 | v | Somali | 10,097,000 |
| 48 | h | Hungarian | 10,036,000 |
| 49 | b | Bulgarian | 8,225,000 |
| 50 | h | Haitian Creol | 8,222,000 |
| 51 | A | Azerbaijani | 7,734,000 |
| 52 | r | Rwandese | 7,733,000 |
| 53 | r | Romansch | 7,386,000 |
| 54 | y | Rundi | 6,695,000 |
| 55 | T | Tajik | 6,188,000 |
| 56 | g | Guarani | 5,496,000 |
| 57 | l | Lao | 5,433,000 |
| 58 | d | Danish | 5,392,000 |
| 59 | u | Slovak | 5,387,000 |
| 60 | f | Finnish | 5,176,000 |
| 61 | e | Hebrew | 5,122,000 |
| 62 | G | Georgian | 4,968,000 |
| 63 | t | Tok Pisin | 4,807,000 |
| 64 | k | Kirghiz | 4,699,000 |
| 65 | C | Croatian | 4,473,000 |
| 66 | j | Norwegian | 4,465,000 |
| 67 | V | Turkmen | 4,459,000 |
| 68 | Q | Moldavian | 4,380,000 |
| 69 | Q | Serbo-Croatia | 3,972,000 |
| 70 | I | Maori | 3,862,000 |
| 71 | q | Tigrinya | 3,850,000 |
| 72 | i | Irish | 3,730,000 |
| 73 | e | Lithuanian | 3,670,000 |
| 74 | x | Sango | 3,615,000 |
| 75 | a | Armenian | 3,520,000 |
| 76 | a | Albanian | 3,113,000 |
| 77 | b | Monokutuba | 2,943,000 |
| 78 | o | Mongolian | 2,662,000 |
| 79 | L | Latvian | 2,357,000 |
| 80 | w | Sotho | 2,153,000 |
| 81 | z | Dzongkha | 2,124,000 |
| 82 | M | Macedonian | 2,024,000 |
| 83 | W | Slovenian | 1,986,000 |
| 84 | X | Tswana | 1,622,000 |
| 85 | E | Estonian | 1,396,000 |
| 86 | x | Swazi | 1,008,000 |
| 87 | j | Comorian | 593,000 |
| 88 | O | Luxemburgish | 431,000 |
| 89 | o | Maltese | 389,000 |
| 90 | f | Divehi | 286,000 |
| 91 | i | Icelandic | 281,000 |
| 92 | w | Samoan | 248,000 |
| 93 | N | Tahitian | 235,000 |
| 94 | p | Bislama | 190,000 |
| 95 | v | Chamorro | 168,000 |
| 96 | z | Tongan | 99,000 |
| 97 | F | Catalan | 78,000 |
| 98 | s | Seselwa | 77,000 |
| 99 | d | Marshallese | 64,000 |
| 100 | H | Greenlandic | 56,000 |
| 101 | J | Faeroese | 43,000 |
| 102 | p | Palauan | 19,000 |
| 103 | n | Nauruan | 12,000 |
| 104 | l | Latin | 1,000 |

## Table 10–4. Christians ranked by the world's 104 official state languages, AD 2000.

1. The table gives the totals ranked by magnitude of total Christians in AD 2000 in countries for whom the languages shown are their official state languages (including official national languages) throughout their country.
2. Note that the table contains 585 million duplications, i.e. Christians who have more than one official state language.

| Language Rank | Code | Name | Christians |
|---|---|---|---|
| 1 | E | English | 655,400,000 |
| 2 | S | Spanish | 411,723,000 |
| 3 | P | Portuguese | 182,645,000 |
| 4 | F | French | 177,961,000 |
| 5 | R | Russian | 93,001,000 |
| 6 | C | Chinese (Mandarin) | 90,538,000 |
| 7 | S | Swahili | 85,352,000 |
| 8 | G | German | 81,087,000 |
| 9 | O | Filipino | 66,600,000 |
| 10 | H | Hindi | 62,257,000 |
| 11 | I | Italian | 53,391,000 |
| 12 | U | Ukrainian | 41,669,000 |
| 13 | Y | Polish | 37,498,000 |
| 14 | M | Afrikaans | 33,150,000 |
| 15 | q | Quechua | 32,488,000 |
| 16 | y | Aymara | 32,488,000 |
| 17 | L | Amharic | 31,161,000 |
| 18 | X | Indonesian | 27,180,000 |
| 19 | A | Arabic | 25,250,000 |
| 20 | R | Romanian | 19,627,000 |
| 21 | D | Dutch | 19,254,000 |
| 22 | K | Korean | 19,182,000 |
| 23 | g | Greek | 10,613,000 |
| 24 | s | Swedish | 10,580,000 |
| 25 | h | Hungarian | 8,750,000 |
| 26 | h | Haitian Creol | 7,639,000 |
| 27 | m | Malagasy | 7,629,000 |
| 28 | c | Chewa | 7,032,000 |
| 29 | Y | Serbian | 6,886,000 |
| 30 | b | Bulgarian | 6,658,000 |
| 31 | B | Belorussian | 6,584,000 |
| 32 | V | Vietnamese | 6,568,000 |
| 33 | r | Romansch | 6,446,000 |
| 34 | r | Rwandese | 6,337,000 |
| 35 | g | Guarani | 5,174,000 |
| 36 | y | Rundi | 5,153,000 |
| 37 | d | Danish | 4,830,000 |
| 38 | c | Czech | 4,819,000 |
| 39 | f | Finnish | 4,579,000 |
| 40 | u | Slovak | 4,324,000 |
| 41 | C | Croatian | 4,256,000 |
| 42 | j | Norwegian | 4,203,000 |
| 43 | t | Tok Pisin | 3,971,000 |
| 44 | U | Urdu | 3,812,000 |
| 45 | W | Burmese | 3,741,000 |
| 46 | J | Japanese | 3,437,000 |
| 47 | i | Irish | 3,355,000 |
| 48 | e | Lithuanian | 3,213,000 |
| 49 | G | Georgian | 3,009,000 |
| 50 | a | Armenian | 2,954,000 |
| 51 | Q | Moldavian | 2,799,000 |
| 52 | K | Kazakh | 2,592,000 |
| 53 | I | Maori | 2,562,000 |
| 54 | b | Monokutuba | 2,333,000 |
| 55 | m | Malay | 2,199,000 |
| 56 | t | Tamil | 2,158,000 |
| 57 | q | Tigrinya | 1,934,000 |
| 58 | u | Sinhalese | 1,755,000 |
| 59 | W | Slovenian | 1,737,000 |
| 60 | x | Sango | 1,609,000 |
| 61 | L | Latvian | 1,576,000 |
| 62 | w | Sotho | 1,445,000 |
| 63 | Q | Serbo-Croatia | 1,386,000 |
| 64 | Z | Thai | 1,345,000 |
| 65 | M | Macedonian | 1,287,000 |
| 66 | a | Albanian | 1,070,000 |
| 67 | B | Bengali | 932,000 |
| 68 | X | Tswana | 751,000 |
| 69 | x | Swazi | 681,000 |
| 70 | n | Nepali | 576,000 |
| 71 | E | Estonian | 530,000 |
| 72 | k | Kirghiz | 466,000 |
| 73 | O | Luxemburgish | 403,000 |
| 74 | Z | Uzbek | 394,000 |
| 75 | T | Turkish | 389,000 |
| 76 | o | Maltese | 371,000 |
| 77 | A | Azerbaijani | 358,000 |
| 78 | N | Persian | 314,000 |
| 79 | e | Hebrew | 294,000 |
| 80 | i | Icelandic | 265,000 |
| 81 | w | Samoan | 224,000 |
| 82 | N | Tahitian | 199,000 |
| 83 | p | Bislama | 170,000 |
| 84 | v | Chamorro | 157,000 |
| 85 | T | Tajik | 130,000 |
| 86 | k | Khmer | 118,000 |
| 87 | l | Lao | 113,000 |
| 88 | v | Somali | 107,000 |
| 89 | V | Turkmen | 99,000 |
| 90 | z | Tongan | 90,000 |
| 91 | s | Seselwa | 72,000 |
| 92 | F | Catalan | 70,000 |
| 93 | d | Marshallese | 60,000 |
| 94 | J | Faeroese | 40,000 |
| 95 | H | Greenlandic | 39,000 |
| 96 | o | Mongolian | 33,000 |
| 97 | p | Palauan | 18,000 |
| 98 | z | Dzongkha | 10,000 |
| 99 | n | Nauruan | 8,000 |
| 100 | j | Comorian | 7,000 |
| 101 | P | Pushtu | 7,000 |
| 102 | D | Dari | 7,000 |
| 103 | l | Latin | 1,000 |
| 104 | f | Divehi | 400 |

## Table 10–5. Official state languages ranked by number of mother-tongue speakers, AD 2000.

1. The table gives the totals of mother-tongue speakers, ranked by size, for the world's 104 official state languages in AD 2000.
2. This table contains no duplications.
3. The third column contains the language code (World Language Classification), from which proximity of languages may be noted.

| Language Rank | Code | Language ID | Name | Population |
|---|---|---|---|---|
| 1 | C | 79-AAAB | Chinese (Mandarin) | 882,103,000 |
| 2 | S | 51-AABB | Spanish | 336,909,000 |
| 3 | A | 12-AAC | Arabic | 247,771,000 |
| 4 | E | 52-ABAC | English | 231,598,000 |
| 5 | B | 59-AAFT | Bengali | 217,240,000 |
| 6 | P | 51-AABA | Portuguese | 184,264,000 |
| 7 | R | 53-AAAE-d | Russian | 145,587,000 |
| 8 | J | 45-CAAA | Japanese | 128,987,000 |
| 9 | K | 45-AAAA | Korean | 75,665,000 |
| 10 | t | 49-EBEA | Tamil | 72,690,000 |
| 11 | V | 46-EBAA | Vietnamese | 72,047,000 |
| 12 | G | 52-ABCE | German | 71,117,000 |
| 13 | U | 59-AAFO-d | Urdu | 66,314,000 |
| 14 | H | 59-AAFO-e | Hindi | 64,508,000 |
| 15 | T | 44-AABA-a | Turkish | 59,476,000 |
| 16 | F | 51-AABI | French | 48,629,000 |
| 17 | U | 53-AAAE-b | Ukrainian | 43,955,000 |
| 18 | Y | 53-AAAC | Polish | 42,280,000 |
| 19 | X | 31-PHAA-c | Indonesian | 41,103,000 |
| 20 | Z | 47-AAAB | Thai | 39,481,000 |
| 21 | I | 51-AABQ | Italian | 36,509,000 |
| 22 | N | 58-AACC | Persian | 34,566,000 |
| 23 | P | 58-ABDA | Pushtu | 32,313,000 |
| 24 | W | 77-AABA | Burmese | 30,542,000 |
| 25 | Z | 44-AABD-a | Uzbek | 22,854,000 |
| 26 | O | 31-CKAA | Filipino | 22,509,000 |
| 27 | n | 59-AAFD | Nepali | 22,100,000 |
| 28 | D | 52-ABCA | Dutch | 21,736,000 |
| 29 | A | 44-AABA-f | Azerbaijani | 20,658,000 |
| 30 | R | 51-AADC-a | Romanian | 20,308,000 |
| 31 | L | 12-ACBA | Amharic | 19,977,000 |
| 32 | l | 47-AAAC | Lao | 19,410,000 |
| 33 | h | 41-BAAA | Hungarian | 15,383,000 |
| 34 | g | 56-AAAA | Greek | 14,088,000 |
| 35 | u | 59-ABBA | Sinhalese | 13,931,000 |
| 36 | v | 14-GAGA | Somali | 13,690,000 |
| 37 | s | 52-AAAD-r | Swedish | 13,380,000 |
| 38 | Q | 53-AAAG-a | Serbo-Croatia | 12,513,000 |
| 39 | Y | 53-AAAG-a | Serbian | 12,513,000 |
| 40 | k | 46-FBAA | Khmer | 11,941,000 |
| 41 | K | 44-AABC-c | Kazakh | 11,812,000 |
| 42 | F | 51-AABE | Catalan | 11,731,000 |
| 43 | m | 31-PHAA-b | Malay | 11,644,000 |
| 44 | c | 53-AAAD-a | Czech | 11,220,000 |
| 45 | B | 53-AAAE-c | Belorussian | 10,175,000 |
| 46 | r | 99-AUSD-f | Rwandese | 9,711,000 |
| 47 | m | 31-LDAA | Malagasy | 9,549,000 |
| 48 | h | 51-AACC-b | Haitian Creol | 9,339,000 |
| 49 | j | 52-AAAC | Norwegian | 8,638,000 |
| 50 | b | 53-AAAH-b | Bulgarian | 8,302,000 |
| 51 | D | 58-AACC-f | Dari | 7,594,000 |
| 52 | y | 99-AUSD-c | Rundi | 7,545,000 |
| 53 | u | 53-AAAD-b | Slovak | 7,334,000 |
| 54 | d | 52-AAAD-c | Danish | 6,976,000 |
| 55 | a | 57-AAAA | Armenian | 6,966,000 |
| 56 | M | 52-ABCB | Afrikaans | 6,550,000 |
| 57 | f | 41-AAAA | Finnish | 6,024,000 |
| 58 | C | 53-AAAG-b | Croatian | 5,820,000 |
| 59 | c | 99-AUSX-a | Chewa | 5,813,000 |
| 60 | g | 82-AAIF | Guarani | 5,705,000 |
| 61 | q | 12-ACAC-a | Tigrinya | 5,466,000 |
| 62 | T | 58-AACC-j | Tajik | 5,434,000 |
| 63 | V | 44-AABA-e | Turkmen | 5,398,000 |
| 64 | e | 54-AAAA | Lithuanian | 4,043,000 |
| 65 | w | 99-AUTE-e | Sotho | 4,019,000 |
| 66 | X | 99-AUTE-g | Tswana | 3,689,000 |
| 67 | S | 99-AUSM | Swahili | 3,657,000 |
| 68 | b | 99-AURG-a | Monokutuba | 3,481,000 |
| 69 | k | 44-AABC-d | Kirghiz | 3,323,000 |
| 70 | G | 42-CABB | Georgian | 3,163,000 |
| 71 | y | 85-JABA | Aymara | 3,011,000 |
| 72 | Q | 51-AADC-ab | Moldavian | 2,687,000 |
| 73 | a | 55-AAAA | Albanian | 2,596,000 |
| 74 | W | 53-AAAF-a | Slovenian | 2,265,000 |
| 75 | o | 44-BAAB-c | Mongolian | 1,987,000 |
| 76 | x | 99-AUTF-e | Swazi | 1,873,000 |
| 77 | e | 12-AABA | Hebrew | 1,741,000 |
| 78 | M | 53-AAAH-a | Macedonian | 1,684,000 |
| 79 | L | 54-AABA | Latvian | 1,544,000 |
| 80 | E | 41-AAAC | Estonian | 1,090,000 |
| 81 | i | 50-AAAA-g | Irish | 1,036,000 |
| 82 | q | 85-FAAF | Quechua | 883,000 |
| 83 | o | 12-AACC-a | Maltese | 563,000 |
| 84 | z | 70-AAAB | Dzongkha | 531,000 |
| 85 | t | 52-ABAI-c | Tok Pisin | 502,000 |
| 86 | x | 93-ABBA-a | Sango | 469,000 |
| 87 | O | 52-ABCD-b | Luxemburgish | 413,000 |
| 88 | I | 39-CAQA | Maori | 401,000 |
| 89 | w | 39-CAOA | Samoan | 354,000 |
| 90 | i | 52-AAAB-a | Icelandic | 328,000 |
| 91 | f | 59-ABAA | Divehi | 291,000 |
| 92 | v | 31-UAAA | Chamorro | 150,000 |
| 93 | z | 39-CAPB | Tongan | 136,000 |
| 94 | r | 51-AABK | Romansch | 130,000 |
| 95 | N | 39-CAQH | Tahitian | 107,000 |
| 96 | j | 99-AUSM-v | Comorian | 94,000 |
| 97 | s | 51-AACC-k | Seselwa | 80,000 |
| 98 | H | 60-ABBC | Greenlandic | 64,000 |
| 99 | d | 38-CAAA | Marshallese | 57,000 |
| 100 | p | 52-ABAI-e | Bislama | 48,000 |
| 101 | J | 52-AAAB-b | Faeroese | 47,000 |
| 102 | p | 31-SAAA | Palauan | 23,000 |
| 103 | n | 38-EAAA-a | Nauruan | 5,500 |
| 104 | l | 51-AAAA | Latin | 30 |

## Table 10–6. Adherents of all religions on 6 continents, AD 1900–AD 2000.

1. This table is an expanded version of Table 1-2 in Part 1, adding, as a variable, continents as standardized by the United Nations. Corresponding world totals are given only in Table 1-2 and are not repeated below.
2. Indented rows are sub-divisions of the unindented names, and are included in the latter's totals.
3. The order in which all rows are listed is in descending order of total adherents in AD 2000. The same applies to indented listings.
4. For exact definitions of all categories, see (a) Part 16 "GeoCodebook" for brief definitions: (b) Part 30 "Glossary" for expanded definitions; and (c) Part 14 "Missiometrics" for their origination.
5. The table is derived from the 238 Country Tables 1 presented in *WCE* Part 4 for all countries.

| Continent | 1900 Adherents | % | mid-1970 Adherents | % | 1990 Adherents | % | Annual change, 1990-2000 Natural | Conversion | Total | Rate | mid–1995 Adherents | % | mid–2000 Adherents | % | mid–2025 Adherents | % | Countries |
|---|---|---|---|---|---|---|---|---|---|---|---|---|---|---|---|---|---|
| **AFRICA** | | | | | | | | | | | | | | | | | |
| **Christians** | 9,938,588 | 9.2 | 143,818,494 | 40.3 | 276,497,939 | 45.0 | 7,934,453 | 438,975 | 8,373,428 | 2.68 | 317,625,134 | 45.6 | 360,232,182 | 45.9 | 633,803,970 | 48.8 | 60 |
| crypto-Christians | 1,182,778 | 1.1 | 4,828,791 | 1.4 | 6,897,060 | 1.1 | 152,927 | 16,107 | 169,034 | 2.22 | 7,741,480 | 1.1 | 8,587,400 | 1.1 | 12,856,150 | 1.0 | 19 |
| **professing Christians** | 8,755,810 | 8.1 | 138,989,703 | 38.9 | 269,600,879 | 43.9 | 7,781,526 | 422,868 | 8,204,394 | 2.69 | 309,883,654 | 44.5 | 351,644,782 | 44.8 | 620,947,820 | 47.8 | 60 |
| unaffiliated Christians | 1,182,116 | 1.1 | 26,749,534 | 7.5 | 20,876,949 | 3.4 | 601,857 | -177,906 | 423,951 | 1.87 | 23,118,061 | 3.3 | 25,116,432 | 3.2 | 33,277,700 | 2.6 | 60 |
| **affiliated Christians** | 8,756,472 | 8.1 | 117,068,960 | 32.8 | 255,620,990 | 41.6 | 7,332,594 | 616,885 | 7,949,479 | 2.74 | 294,507,073 | 42.3 | 335,115,750 | 42.7 | 600,526,270 | 46.3 | 60 |
| Roman Catholics | 1,909,812 | 1.8 | 45,072,986 | 12.6 | 90,655,340 | 14.7 | 2,754,331 | 218,760 | 2,973,091 | 2.88 | 105,621,883 | 15.2 | 120,386,235 | 15.3 | 228,294,600 | 17.6 | 60 |
| Protestants | 1,836,980 | 1.7 | 27,291,581 | 7.6 | 67,031,580 | 10.9 | 1,897,041 | 299,794 | 2,196,835 | 2.88 | 78,224,292 | 11.2 | 88,999,928 | 11.3 | 157,299,850 | 12.1 | 58 |
| Independents | 39,200 | 0.0 | 17,944,214 | 5.0 | 62,601,520 | 10.2 | 1,681,764 | 442,148 | 2,123,912 | 2.96 | 73,779,292 | 10.6 | 83,840,642 | 10.7 | 139,812,970 | 10.8 | 59 |
| Anglicans | 369,430 | 0.3 | 7,728,519 | 2.2 | 31,819,805 | 5.2 | 885,332 | 186,878 | 1,072,210 | 2.95 | 37,594,899 | 5.4 | 42,541,902 | 5.4 | 76,118,630 | 5.9 | 39 |
| Orthodox | 4,600,250 | 4.3 | 18,395,020 | 5.2 | 27,996,330 | 4.6 | 774,636 | -43,852 | 730,784 | 2.35 | 31,685,766 | 4.6 | 35,304,168 | 4.5 | 59,783,200 | 4.6 | 31 |
| Marginal Christians | 800 | 0.0 | 1,004,113 | 0.3 | 1,811,015 | 0.3 | 51,883 | 9,671 | 61,554 | 2.97 | 2,097,874 | 0.3 | 2,426,550 | 0.3 | 5,547,290 | 0.4 | 53 |
| doubly-affiliated | 0 | 0.0 | -367,473 | -0.1 | -26,294,600 | -4.3 | -712,389 | -496,521 | -1,208,910 | 3.86 | -32,499,389 | -4.7 | -38,383,675 | -4.9 | -66,330,270 | -5.1 | 59 |
| *Trans-megabloc groupings* | | | | | | | | | | | | | | | | | |
| Evangelicals | 1,635,410 | 1.5 | 16,248,140 | 4.6 | 50,590,045 | 8.2 | 1,438,677 | 460,149 | 1,898,826 | 3.24 | 60,995,123 | 8.8 | 69,578,305 | 8.9 | 136,111,730 | 10.5 | 60 |
| Pentecostals/Charismatics | 901,000 | 0.8 | 17,049,020 | 4.8 | 93,703,065 | 15.2 | 2,589,538 | 642,277 | 3,231,815 | 3.01 | 110,454,194 | 15.9 | 126,021,202 | 16.1 | 227,819,720 | 17.6 | 60 |
| **Great Commission Christians** | 3,131,290 | 2.9 | 30,357,970 | 8.5 | 68,029,710 | 11.1 | 1,874,816 | 404,240 | 2,279,056 | 2.93 | 78,433,785 | 11.3 | 90,820,254 | 11.6 | 168,833,430 | 13.0 | 60 |
| Muslims | 34,485,292 | 32.0 | 143,095,965 | 40.1 | 251,066,766 | 40.8 | 6,500,296 | 130,471 | 6,630,767 | 2.37 | 282,641,990 | 40.6 | 317,374,423 | 40.5 | 519,347,830 | 40.0 | 58 |
| Ethnoreligionists | 62,685,865 | 58.2 | 67,429,897 | 18.9 | 79,519,748 | 12.9 | 2,345,361 | -616,792 | 1,728,569 | 1.99 | 87,804,160 | 12.6 | 96,805,405 | 12.3 | 126,051,000 | 9.7 | 49 |
| Nonreligious | 7,210 | 0.0 | 583,740 | 0.2 | 3,588,570 | 0.6 | 90,144 | 53,373 | 143,517 | 3.42 | 4,329,925 | 0.6 | 5,023,704 | 0.6 | 10,575,560 | 0.8 | 60 |
| Hindus | 279,120 | 0.3 | 994,450 | 0.3 | 1,939,600 | 0.3 | 39,529 | 1,650 | 41,179 | 1.94 | 2,162,771 | 0.3 | 2,351,390 | 0.3 | 3,426,660 | 0.3 | 32 |
| Baha'is | 225 | 0.0 | 698,094 | 0.2 | 1,383,320 | 0.2 | 38,634 | -3,679 | 34,955 | 2.28 | 1,546,330 | 0.2 | 1,732,816 | 0.2 | 3,396,180 | 0.3 | 58 |
| Atheists | 1,020 | 0.0 | 102,600 | 0.0 | 332,742 | 0.1 | 8,594 | 135 | 8,729 | 2.36 | 375,570 | 0.1 | 420,039 | 0.1 | 890,200 | 0.1 | 37 |
| Jews | 397,900 | 0.4 | 205,470 | 0.1 | 201,320 | 0.0 | 3,962 | -2,686 | 1,276 | 0.62 | 205,960 | 0.0 | 214,055 | 0.0 | 234,100 | 0.0 | 22 |
| Buddhists | 3,400 | 0.0 | 11,650 | 0.0 | 107,640 | 0.0 | 2,764 | -86 | 2,678 | 2.25 | 122,250 | 0.0 | 134,409 | 0.0 | 293,750 | 0.0 | 14 |
| Jains | 3,180 | 0.0 | 32,810 | 0.0 | 56,630 | 0.0 | 1,591 | -648 | 943 | 1.55 | 60,750 | 0.0 | 66,061 | 0.0 | 94,650 | 0.0 | 5 |
| Other religionists | 1,000 | 0.0 | 28,750 | 0.0 | 54,350 | 0.0 | 1,410 | -273 | 1,137 | 1.92 | 62,720 | 0.0 | 65,707 | 0.0 | 121,800 | 0.0 | 18 |
| Sikhs | 2,200 | 0.0 | 25,900 | 0.0 | 45,540 | 0.0 | 1,180 | -425 | 755 | 1.54 | 49,980 | 0.0 | 53,076 | 0.0 | 100,900 | 0.0 | 9 |
| Chinese folk-religionists | 1,900 | 0.0 | 7,300 | 0.0 | 28,285 | 0.0 | 573 | -166 | 407 | 1.35 | 30,910 | 0.0 | 32,351 | 0.0 | 57,490 | 0.0 | 9 |
| New-Religionists | 0 | 0.0 | 700 | 0.0 | 20,300 | 0.0 | 667 | 147 | 814 | 3.43 | 24,700 | 0.0 | 28,436 | 0.0 | 43,000 | 0.0 | 3 |
| Spiritists | 1,000 | 0.0 | 2,300 | 0.0 | 2,500 | 0.0 | 46 | -45 | 1 | 0.04 | 2,630 | 0.0 | 2,509 | 0.0 | 4,400 | 0.0 | 2 |
| Zoroastrians | 200 | 0.0 | 480 | 0.0 | 720 | 0.0 | 20 | -4 | 16 | 2.04 | 780 | 0.0 | 881 | 0.0 | 1,810 | 0.0 | 4 |
| Confucianists | 0 | 0.0 | 0 | 0.0 | 230 | 0.0 | 4 | -3 | 1 | 0.51 | 240 | 0.0 | 242 | 0.0 | 500 | 0.0 | 1 |
| doubly-professing | 0 | 0.0 | 0 | 0.0 | -76,300 | 0.0 | -1,690 | 56 | -1,634 | 1.96 | -84,400 | 0.0 | -92,652 | 0.0 | -135,000 | 0.0 | 4 |
| World A (unevangelized persons) | 85,586,225 | 79.4 | 139,973,054 | 39.2 | 159,574,355 | 26.0 | 4,306,250 | -2,584,202 | 1,722,048 | 1.03 | 168,839,893 | 24.2 | 176,794,822 | 22.5 | 241,415,415 | 18.6 | 60 |
| World B (evangelized non-Christians) | 12,283,287 | 11.4 | 73,247,052 | 20.5 | 178,773,906 | 29.1 | 4,726,835 | 2,145,487 | 6,872,062 | 3.31 | 210,581,773 | 30.2 | 247,510,682 | 31.6 | 423,224,415 | 32.6 | 60 |
| World C (Christians) | 9,938,588 | 9.2 | 143,818,494 | 40.3 | 276,497,939 | 45.0 | 7,934,453 | 438,975 | 8,373,428 | 2.68 | 317,625,134 | 45.6 | 360,232,182 | 45.9 | 633,803,970 | 48.8 | 60 |
| CONTINENT'S POPULATION | 107,808,100 | 100.0 | 357,038,600 | 100.0 | 614,846,200 | 100.0 | 16,967,538 | 0 | 16,967,538 | 2.47 | 697,046,800 | 100.0 | 784,537,686 | 100.0 | 1,298,443,800 | 100.0 | 60 |
| **ASIA** | | | | | | | | | | | | | | | | | |
| Muslims | 156,139,610 | 16.3 | 391,407,279 | 18.2 | 676,677,775 | 21.2 | 15,156,918 | 463,200 | 15,620,118 | 2.10 | 751,779,485 | 21.8 | 832,878,936 | 22.5 | 1,219,867,350 | 25.7 | 50 |
| Hindus | 202,546,700 | 21.2 | 460,498,800 | 21.4 | 680,830,450 | 21.3 | 13,134,205 | -705,258 | 12,428,947 | 1.69 | 745,833,820 | 21.6 | 805,119,915 | 21.8 | 1,040,588,600 | 21.9 | 30 |
| Nonreligious | 47,100 | 0.0 | 428,361,350 | 19.9 | 554,696,790 | 17.4 | 6,051,811 | -662,047 | 5,389,764 | 0.93 | 581,093,525 | 16.9 | 608,594,416 | 16.5 | 702,802,500 | 14.8 | 50 |
| Chinese folk-religionists | 379,914,740 | 39.7 | 231,589,753 | 10.8 | 346,421,374 | 10.9 | 3,786,798 | -88,160 | 3,698,638 | 1.02 | 367,875,620 | 10.7 | 383,407,747 | 10.4 | 447,120,300 | 9.4 | 23 |
| Buddhists | 126,619,501 | 13.2 | 232,239,001 | 10.8 | 318,863,450 | 10.0 | 3,494,084 | 84,715 | 3,578,799 | 1.07 | 336,973,085 | 9.8 | 354,651,462 | 9.6 | 408,835,280 | 8.6 | 37 |
| **Christians** | 21,897,519 | 2.3 | 101,394,552 | 4.7 | 248,728,290 | 7.8 | 4,046,396 | 2,365,720 | 6,412,116 | 2.32 | 281,908,145 | 8.2 | 312,849,430 | 8.5 | 464,800,100 | 9.8 | 50 |
| crypto-Christians | 2,388,299 | 0.3 | 18,185,055 | 0.9 | 93,838,820 | 2.9 | 1,255,122 | 754,905 | 2,010,027 | 1.96 | 102,163,531 | 3.0 | 113,939,089 | 3.1 | 176,334,100 | 3.7 | 45 |
| **professing Christians** | 19,509,220 | 2.0 | 83,209,197 | 3.9 | 154,885,130 | 4.9 | 2,791,188 | 1,610,678 | 4,401,866 | 2.53 | 179,739,214 | 5.2 | 198,903,786 | 5.4 | 288,451,700 | 6.1 | 49 |
| unaffiliated Christians | 1,138,810 | 0.1 | 4,065,302 | 0.2 | 5,194,370 | 0.2 | 67,929 | -31,253 | 36,676 | 0.68 | 5,183,841 | 0.2 | 5,561,122 | 0.2 | 5,771,540 | 0.1 | 50 |
| **affiliated Christians** | 20,758,709 | 2.2 | 97,329,250 | 4.5 | 243,533,920 | 7.6 | 3,978,465 | 2,396,976 | 6,375,441 | 2.35 | 276,724,304 | 8.0 | 307,288,308 | 8.3 | 459,028,560 | 9.7 | 50 |
| Independents | 1,906,100 | 0.2 | 21,581,887 | 1.0 | 113,234,010 | 3.6 | 1,619,315 | 2,530,488 | 4,149,803 | 3.17 | 135,410,109 | 3.9 | 154,732,021 | 4.2 | 247,278,100 | 5.2 | 49 |
| Roman Catholics | 11,162,799 | 1.2 | 50,964,406 | 2.4 | 90,593,690 | 2.8 | 1,943,413 | 45,221 | 1,988,634 | 2.00 | 100,634,847 | 2.9 | 110,480,013 | 3.0 | 159,576,400 | 3.4 | 49 |
| Protestants | 1,916,480 | 0.2 | 21,745,218 | 1.0 | 41,639,670 | 1.3 | 689,419 | 143,564 | 832,983 | 1.84 | 45,955,800 | 1.3 | 49,969,501 | 1.4 | 73,269,600 | 1.5 | 49 |
| Orthodox | 6,864,220 | 0.7 | 8,967,132 | 0.4 | 13,926,370 | 0.4 | 97,226 | -78,518 | 18,708 | 0.13 | 14,351,180 | 0.4 | 14,113,465 | 0.4 | 17,351,300 | 0.4 | 37 |
| Marginal Christians | 280 | 0.0 | 758,913 | 0.0 | 2,114,595 | 0.1 | 24,240 | 12,862 | 37,102 | 1.63 | 2,291,773 | 0.1 | 2,485,605 | 0.1 | 3,604,060 | 0.1 | 41 |
| Anglicans | 708,930 | 0.1 | 360,997 | 0.0 | 598,035 | 0.0 | 10,618 | 2,300 | 12,918 | 1.97 | 677,146 | 0.0 | 727,212 | 0.0 | 945,500 | 0.0 | 35 |
| doubly-affiliated | -1,800,100 | -0.2 | -7,049,303 | -0.3 | -18,572,450 | -0.6 | -405,766 | -258,939 | -664,705 | 3.11 | -22,596,551 | -0.7 | -25,219,509 | -0.7 | -42,996,400 | -0.9 | 50 |
| *Trans-megabloc groupings* | | | | | | | | | | | | | | | | | |
| Evangelicals | 1,332,180 | 0.1 | 9,605,330 | 0.5 | 25,526,820 | 0.8 | 385,199 | 212,516 | 597,715 | 2.13 | 28,654,777 | 0.8 | 31,503,970 | 0.9 | 49,075,500 | 1.0 | 50 |
| Pentecostals/Charismatics | 4,300 | 0.0 | 10,144,120 | 0.5 | 108,921,565 | 3.4 | 1,690,301 | 906,496 | 2,596,797 | 2.16 | 122,696,550 | 3.6 | 134,889,530 | 3.7 | 217,550,606 | 4.6 | 50 |
| **Great Commission Christians** | 10,529,965 | 1.1 | 42,840,670 | 2.0 | 157,136,380 | 4.9 | 2,201,952 | 1,273,447 | 3,475,399 | 2.02 | 173,140,495 | 5.0 | 191,890,345 | 5.2 | 292,839,260 | 6.2 | 50 |
| Ethnoreligionists | 50,564,090 | 5.3 | 90,872,440 | 4.2 | 117,696,230 | 3.7 | 1,723,368 | -663,140 | 1,060,228 | 0.87 | 123,190,410 | 3.6 | 128,298,498 | 3.5 | 147,975,620 | 3.1 | 35 |
| Atheists | 7,000 | 0.0 | 109,602,500 | 5.1 | 115,632,080 | 3.6 | 1,262,073 | -630,754 | 631,319 | 0.53 | 119,570,720 | 3.5 | 121,945,250 | 3.3 | 135,461,900 | 2.9 | 43 |
| New-Religionists | 5,910,000 | 0.6 | 77,448,720 | 3.6 | 91,097,790 | 2.9 | 1,017,149 | -62,994 | 954,155 | 1.00 | 96,191,135 | 2.8 | 100,639,356 | 2.7 | 112,430,400 | 2.4 | 21 |
| Sikhs | 2,959,900 | 0.3 | 10,378,800 | 0.5 | 18,645,520 | 0.6 | 357,406 | 20,107 | 377,513 | 1.86 | 20,465,290 | 0.6 | 22,420,618 | 0.6 | 30,206,460 | 0.6 | 17 |
| Confucianists | 640,050 | 0.1 | 4,758,050 | 0.2 | 5,823,610 | 0.2 | 55,441 | -11,452 | 43,989 | 0.73 | 6,042,160 | 0.2 | 6,263,506 | 0.2 | 6,771,100 | 0.1 | 7 |
| Jews | 411,200 | 0.0 | 2,418,950 | 0.1 | 3,298,630 | 0.1 | 115,036 | -1,975 | 113,061 | 2.99 | 3,924,295 | 0.1 | 4,429,230 | 0.1 | 5,811,500 | 0.1 | 29 |
| Jains | 1,320,100 | 0.1 | 2,585,000 | 0.1 | 3,806,840 | 0.1 | 72,900 | -39,088 | 33,812 | 0.85 | 3,827,370 | 0.1 | 4,144,959 | 0.1 | 6,014,000 | 0.1 | 4 |
| Baha'is | 5,900 | 0.0 | 1,411,530 | 0.1 | 2,811,995 | 0.1 | 55,963 | 10,355 | 66,318 | 2.14 | 3,034,140 | 0.1 | 3,475,167 | 0.1 | 5,483,000 | 0.1 | 46 |
| Shintoists | 6,720,000 | 0.7 | 4,173,000 | 0.2 | 3,025,790 | 0.1 | 7,966 | -40,662 | -32,696 | -1.14 | 2,778,340 | 0.1 | 2,698,820 | 0.1 | 2,042,950 | 0.0 | 6 |
| Taoists | 375,000 | 0.0 | 1,734,000 | 0.1 | 2,392,090 | 0.1 | 25,301 | -172 | 25,129 | 1.00 | 2,541,250 | 0.1 | 2,643,380 | 0.1 | 3,052,800 | 0.1 | 4 |
| Zoroastrians | 108,290 | 0.0 | 121,000 | 0.0 | 1,895,530 | 0.1 | 44,723 | 12,066 | 56,789 | 2.66 | 2,193,650 | 0.1 | 2,463,407 | 0.1 | 4,311,140 | 0.1 | 14 |
| Mandeans | 8,000 | 0.0 | 23,000 | 0.0 | 31,600 | 0.0 | 823 | -85 | 738 | 2.12 | 35,000 | 0.0 | 38,977 | 0.0 | 58,000 | 0.0 | 2 |
| Other religionists | 1,000 | 0.0 | 10,950 | 0.0 | 19,286 | 0.0 | 339 | 42 | 381 | 1.82 | 21,260 | 0.0 | 23,094 | 0.0 | 35,000 | 0.0 | 5 |
| Spiritists | 500 | 0.0 | 1,200 | 0.0 | 1,880 | 0.0 | 20 | -16 | 4 | 0.21 | 1,900 | 0.0 | 1,919 | 0.0 | 3,000 | 0.0 | 1 |
| doubly-professing | 0 | 0.0 | -4,000,000 | -0.2 | -11,803,000 | -0.4 | -213,094 | -50,402 | -263,496 | 2.04 | -12,998,600 | -0.4 | -14,437,985 | -0.4 | -20,530,000 | -0.4 | 20 |
| World A (unevangelized persons) | 781,294,400 | 81.7 | 1,455,175,150 | 67.7 | 1,472,841,080 | 46.1 | 23,976,662 | -28,878,336 | -4,901,674 | -0.34 | 1,478,527,050 | 42.9 | 1,423,824,293 | 38.5 | 1,572,484,800 | 33.2 | 50 |
| World B (evangelized non-Christians) | 153,004,281 | 16.0 | 594,460,173 | 27.6 | 1,470,827,630 | 46.1 | 22,172,722 | 26,512,539 | 48,685,184 | 2.91 | 1,688,845,405 | 49 | 1,960,314,364 | 53 | 2,706,386,100 | 57.1 | 50 |
| World C (Christians) | 21,897,519 | 2.3 | 101,394,552 | 4.7 | 248,728,290 | 7.8 | 4,046,396 | 2,365,720 | 6,412,116 | 2.32 | 281,908,145 | 8.2 | 312,849,430 | 8.5 | 464,800,100 | 9.8 | 50 |
| CONTINENT'S POPULATION | 956,196,200 | 100.0 | 2,151,029,875 | 100.0 | 3,192,397,000 | 100.0 | 50,195,626 | 0 | 50,195,626 | 1.48 | 3,449,280,600 | 100.0 | 3,696,988,087 | 100.0 | 4,743,671,000 | 100.0 | 50 |

*Continued opposite*

*Table 10–6 continued*

| Continent | 1900 Adherents | 1900 % | mid-1970 Adherents | mid-1970 % | 1990 Adherents | 1990 % | Annual change, 1990-2000 Natural | Conversion | Total | Rate | mid–1995 Adherents | mid–1995 % | mid–2000 Adherents | mid–2000 % | mid–2025 Adherents | mid–2025 % | Countries |
|---|---|---|---|---|---|---|---|---|---|---|---|---|---|---|---|---|---|
| **EUROPE** | | | | | | | | | | | | | | | | | |
| **Christians** | 380,642,840 | 94.5 | 492,694,892 | 75.1 | 550,418,843 | 76.2 | 606,981 | 315,389 | 922,370 | 0.17 | 557,493,375 | 76.6 | 559,642,545 | 76.8 | 554,586,470 | 79.0 | 48 |
| crypto-Christians | 0 | 0.0 | 35,683,780 | 5.4 | 965,000 | 0.1 | -4,138 | -69,362 | -73,500 | -13.36 | 250,000 | 0.0 | 230,000 | 0.0 | 200,000 | 0.0 | 20 |
| **professing Christians** | 380,642,840 | 94.5 | 457,011,112 | 69.6 | 549,453,843 | 76.1 | 611,118 | 384,752 | 995,870 | 0.18 | 557,243,375 | 76.6 | 559,412,545 | 76.8 | 554,386,470 | 78.9 | 48 |
| unaffiliated Christians | 12,433,130 | 3.1 | 24,215,164 | 3.7 | 21,570,990 | 3.0 | 49,825 | 74,175 | 124,000 | 0.56 | 22,715,007 | 3.1 | 22,810,974 | 3.1 | 21,725,420 | 3.1 | 48 |
| **affiliated Christians** | 368,209,710 | 91.5 | 468,479,728 | 71.4 | 528,847,853 | 73.2 | 557,158 | 241,216 | 798,374 | 0.15 | 534,778,368 | 73.5 | 536,831,571 | 73.7 | 532,861,050 | 75.9 | 48 |
| Roman Catholics | 180,722,280 | 44.9 | 256,162,441 | 39.1 | 281,449,879 | 39.0 | 512,817 | -60,025 | 452,792 | 0.16 | 284,434,435 | 39.1 | 285,977,773 | 39.2 | 276,272,080 | 39.3 | 47 |
| Orthodox | 103,954,150 | 25.8 | 107,125,809 | 16.3 | 155,120,280 | 21.5 | -190,755 | 489,243 | 298,488 | 0.19 | 156,451,050 | 21.5 | 158,105,154 | 21.7 | 165,804,370 | 23.6 | 40 |
| Protestants | 59,486,600 | 14.8 | 82,131,881 | 12.5 | 76,376,594 | 10.6 | 232,580 | -117,342 | 115,238 | 0.15 | 76,867,425 | 10.6 | 77,528,973 | 10.6 | 77,089,120 | 11.0 | 46 |
| Anglicans | 24,902,110 | 6.2 | 29,467,936 | 4.5 | 26,302,100 | 3.6 | 59,403 | -25,865 | 33,538 | 0.13 | 26,591,699 | 3.7 | 26,637,479 | 3.7 | 26,410,100 | 3.8 | 26 |
| Independents | 81,880 | 0.0 | 9,894,261 | 1.5 | 23,280,700 | 3.2 | -12,095 | 256,396 | 244,301 | 1.00 | 25,088,864 | 3.5 | 25,723,708 | 3.5 | 29,301,690 | 4.2 | 42 |
| Marginal Christians | 103,400 | 0.0 | 1,806,202 | 0.3 | 3,168,280 | 0.4 | 6,307 | 33,253 | 39,560 | 1.18 | 3,363,096 | 0.5 | 3,563,880 | 0.5 | 4,858,970 | 0.7 | 45 |
| doubly-affiliated | -529,310 | -0.1 | -8,180,697 | -1.3 | -17,140,346 | -2.4 | -6,682 | -252,993 | -259,675 | 1.42 | -17,527,431 | -2.4 | -19,737,096 | -2.7 | -24,525,280 | -3.5 | 48 |
| disaffiliated | -511,400 | -0.1 | -9,928,105 | -1.6 | -19,709,634 | -2.7 | -44,420 | -81,447 | -125,867 | 0.62 | -20,490,770 | -2.8 | -20,968,300 | -2.9 | -22,350,000 | -3.2 | 4 |
| *Trans-megabloc groupings* | | | | | | | | | | | | | | | | | |
| Evangelicals | 32,357,300 | 8.0 | 22,026,770 | 3.4 | 20,899,286 | 2.9 | 36,546 | 27,884 | 64,430 | 0.30 | 21,385,735 | 2.9 | 21,543,577 | 3.0 | 22,043,420 | 3.1 | 48 |
| Pentecostals/Charismatics | 20,000 | 0.0 | 8,018,180 | 1.2 | 33,455,365 | 4.6 | 35,970 | 375,364 | 411,334 | 1.17 | 36,097,106 | 5.0 | 37,568,700 | 5.2 | 47,179,505 | 6.7 | 48 |
| **Great Commission Christians** | 49,767,490 | 12.4 | 128,476,980 | 19.6 | 185,297,970 | 25.7 | 305,743 | 410,668 | 716,411 | 0.38 | 189,712,000 | 26.1 | 192,462,065 | 26.4 | 198,404,720 | 28.3 | 48 |
| Nonreligious | 1,543,180 | 0.4 | 85,949,228 | 13.1 | 109,190,130 | 15.1 | 48,724 | -283,602 | -234,878 | -0.22 | 108,755,640 | 14.9 | 106,841,391 | 14.7 | 86,237,350 | 12.3 | 47 |
| Muslims | 9,234,890 | 2.3 | 17,622,610 | 2.7 | 29,206,045 | 4.0 | 6,035 | 229,994 | 236,029 | 0.78 | 29,866,635 | 4.1 | 31,566,311 | 4.3 | 36,004,880 | 5.1 | 44 |
| Atheists | 205,300 | 0.1 | 53,915,110 | 8.2 | 25,883,952 | 3.6 | -1,250 | -294,909 | -296,159 | -1.21 | 24,030,535 | 3.3 | 22,922,349 | 3.1 | 16,767,600 | 2.4 | 41 |
| Jews | 9,926,800 | 2.5 | 4,283,800 | 0.7 | 2,654,830 | 0.4 | 1,654 | -14,430 | -12,776 | -0.49 | 2,564,160 | 0.4 | 2,527,051 | 0.4 | 2,107,420 | 0.3 | 43 |
| Buddhists | 401,000 | 0.1 | 551,700 | 0.1 | 1,347,265 | 0.2 | 2,336 | 17,644 | 19,980 | 1.39 | 1,477,595 | 0.2 | 1,547,050 | 0.2 | 2,236,220 | 0.3 | 21 |
| Hindus | 60 | 0.0 | 243,390 | 0.0 | 1,243,370 | 0.2 | 1,133 | 16,115 | 17,248 | 1.31 | 1,343,165 | 0.2 | 1,415,843 | 0.2 | 1,706,770 | 0.2 | 15 |
| Ethnoreligionists | 619,500 | 0.2 | 586,100 | 0.1 | 1,213,860 | 0.2 | -633 | 5,523 | 4,890 | 0.40 | 1,270,120 | 0.2 | 1,262,760 | 0.2 | 1,150,570 | 0.2 | 17 |
| Chinese folk-religionists | 0 | 0.0 | 60,000 | 0.0 | 228,650 | 0.0 | 662 | 2,004 | 2,666 | 1.11 | 243,450 | 0.0 | 255,310 | 0.0 | 350,600 | 0.1 | 11 |
| Sikhs | 0 | 0.0 | 200,000 | 0.0 | 228,200 | 0.0 | 508 | 574 | 1,082 | 0.46 | 233,560 | 0.0 | 239,021 | 0.0 | 281,300 | 0.0 | 3 |
| Other religionists | 23,770 | 0.0 | 209,650 | 0.0 | 222,180 | 0.0 | 765 | 583 | 1,348 | 0.59 | 231,310 | 0.0 | 235,660 | 0.0 | 294,600 | 0.0 | 17 |
| New-Religionists | 0 | 0.0 | 33,100 | 0.0 | 141,400 | 0.0 | 561 | 1,088 | 1,649 | 1.11 | 150,040 | 0.0 | 157,887 | 0.0 | 223,200 | 0.0 | 9 |
| Spiritists | 10,000 | 0.0 | 36,400 | 0.0 | 110,170 | 0.0 | 348 | 1,908 | 2,256 | 1.88 | 123,800 | 0.0 | 132,711 | 0.0 | 167,100 | 0.0 | 9 |
| Baha'is | 210 | 0.0 | 56,810 | 0.0 | 106,635 | 0.0 | 246 | 2,066 | 2,312 | 1.98 | 120,275 | 0.0 | 129,706 | 0.0 | 204,440 | 0.0 | 39 |
| Confucianists | 0 | 0.0 | 1,000 | 0.0 | 9,960 | 0.0 | 24 | 50 | 74 | 0.72 | 10,500 | 0.0 | 10,697 | 0.0 | 14,600 | 0.0 | 3 |
| Zoroastrians | 0 | 0.0 | 410 | 0.0 | 610 | 0.0 | 2 | 3 | 5 | 0.75 | 640 | 0.0 | 657 | 0.0 | 980 | 0.0 | 3 |
| World A (unevangelized persons) | 9,756,171 | 2.4 | 39,724,130 | 6.1 | 26,444,795 | 3.7 | -5,200 | -491,862 | -497,062 | -2.06 | 23,820,585 | 3.3 | 21,474,187 | 3.0 | 19,454,895 | 2.8 | 48 |
| World B (evangelized non-Christians) | 12,208,539 | 3.0 | 124,025,178 | 18.9 | 145,342,462 | 20.1 | 66,903 | 176,179 | 242,788 | 0.17 | 146,600,840 | 20.1 | 147,770,217 | 20.3 | 128,292,735 | 18.3 | 48 |
| World C (Christians) | 380,642,840 | 94.5 | 492,694,892 | 75.1 | 550,418,843 | 76.2 | 606,981 | 315,389 | 922,370 | 0.17 | 557,493,375 | 76.6 | 559,642,545 | 76.8 | 554,586,470 | 79.0 | 48 |
| CONTINENT'S POPULATION | 402,607,550 | 100.0 | 656,444,200 | 100.0 | 722,206,100 | 100.0 | 668,096 | 0 | 668,096 | 0.09 | 727,914,800 | 100.0 | 728,886,949 | 100.0 | 702,334,100 | 100.0 | 48 |
| **LATIN AMERICA** | | | | | | | | | | | | | | | | | |
| **Christians** | 62,002,925 | 95.2 | 269,200,550 | 94.5 | 409,345,790 | 92.9 | 7,426,256 | -250,598 | 7,175,658 | 1.63 | 445,272,855 | 92.8 | 481,102,373 | 92.7 | 641,115,950 | 92.0 | 46 |
| crypto-Christians | 0 | 0.0 | 497,700 | 0.2 | 900,000 | 0.2 | 4,852 | 2,148 | 7,000 | 0.75 | 940,000 | 0.2 | 970,000 | 0.2 | 1,100,000 | 0.2 | 1 |
| **professing Christians** | 62,002,925 | 95.2 | 268,702,850 | 94.4 | 408,445,790 | 92.7 | 7,421,404 | -252,746 | 7,168,658 | 1.63 | 444,332,855 | 92.6 | 480,132,373 | 92.5 | 640,015,950 | 91.9 | 46 |
| unaffiliated Christians | 1,976,165 | 3.0 | 5,603,853 | 2.0 | 4,946,049 | 1.1 | 86,666 | -36,923 | 49,743 | 0.96 | 5,232,160 | 1.1 | 5,443,473 | 1.1 | 5,845,230 | 0.8 | 46 |
| **affiliated Christians** | 60,026,760 | 92.2 | 263,596,697 | 92.6 | 404,399,741 | 91.8 | 7,339,592 | -213,676 | 7,125,916 | 1.64 | 440,040,695 | 91.7 | 475,658,900 | 91.6 | 635,270,720 | 91.2 | 46 |
| Roman Catholics | 58,689,470 | 90.1 | 251,791,319 | 88.4 | 391,772,330 | 88.9 | 7,116,888 | -172,120 | 6,944,768 | 1.65 | 426,725,018 | 88.9 | 461,220,001 | 88.8 | 606,059,020 | 87.0 | 46 |
| Protestants | 932,550 | 1.4 | 12,505,263 | 4.4 | 39,842,016 | 9.1 | 657,274 | 171,695 | 828,969 | 1.91 | 44,056,347 | 9.2 | 48,131,716 | 9.3 | 76,191,140 | 10.9 | 46 |
| Independents | 29,400 | 0.1 | 9,242,347 | 3.3 | 32,901,772 | 7.5 | 531,782 | 148,677 | 680,459 | 1.90 | 36,357,171 | 7.6 | 39,706,358 | 7.7 | 60,021,780 | 8.6 | 44 |
| Marginal Christians | 3,820 | 0.0 | 847,347 | 0.3 | 5,014,205 | 1.1 | 91,012 | 67,098 | 158,110 | 2.78 | 5,739,146 | 1.2 | 6,595,300 | 1.3 | 13,211,790 | 1.9 | 46 |
| Anglicans | 726,120 | 1.1 | 767,559 | 0.3 | 989,380 | 0.2 | 12,199 | -2,177 | 10,022 | 0.97 | 1,045,447 | 0.2 | 1,089,611 | 0.2 | 1,352,770 | 0.2 | 44 |
| Orthodox | 6,400 | 0.0 | 364,263 | 0.1 | 477,000 | 0.1 | 7,470 | 580 | 8,050 | 1.57 | 490,315 | 0.1 | 557,500 | 0.1 | 755,170 | 0.1 | 21 |
| disaffiliated | -81,000 | -0.1 | -765,843 | -0.3 | -1,483,500 | -0.3 | -23,366 | -904 | -24,270 | 1.53 | -1,610,984 | -0.3 | -1,726,200 | -0.3 | -2,547,450 | -0.4 | 6 |
| doubly-affiliated | -280,000 | -0.4 | -11,155,558 | -3.9 | -65,113,462 | -14.8 | -1,053,669 | -426,523 | -1,480,192 | 2.07 | -72,761,765 | -15.2 | -79,915,386 | -15.4 | -119,773,500 | -17.2 | 46 |
| *Trans-megabloc groupings* | | | | | | | | | | | | | | | | | |
| Evangelicals | 766,300 | 1.2 | 9,565,160 | 3.4 | 32,743,665 | 7.4 | 535,045 | 224,713 | 759,758 | 2.11 | 36,638,382 | 7.6 | 40,341,240 | 7.8 | 64,498,400 | 9.3 | 46 |
| Pentecostals/Charismatics | 10,000 | 0.0 | 12,621,450 | 4.4 | 118,629,420 | 26.9 | 1,994,890 | 285,456 | 2,280,346 | 1.77 | 130,166,167 | 27.1 | 141,432,880 | 27.2 | 202,277,880 | 29.0 | 46 |
| **Great Commission Christians** | 2,406,110 | 3.7 | 18,717,550 | 6.6 | 43,679,515 | 9.9 | 721,004 | 141,193 | 862,197 | 1.82 | 47,937,015 | 10.0 | 52,301,448 | 10.1 | 79,053,905 | 11.4 | 46 |
| Nonreligious | 372,340 | 0.6 | 5,842,940 | 2.1 | 12,657,905 | 2.9 | 175,515 | 151,524 | 327,039 | 2.32 | 14,489,910 | 3.0 | 15,928,252 | 3.1 | 25,799,710 | 3.7 | 46 |
| Spiritists | 257,040 | 0.4 | 4,557,880 | 1.6 | 9,902,865 | 2.3 | 135,393 | 78,217 | 213,610 | 1.97 | 10,863,185 | 2.3 | 12,038,942 | 2.3 | 15,836,080 | 2.3 | 38 |
| Atheists | 9,900 | 0.0 | 1,265,110 | 0.4 | 2,359,000 | 0.5 | 29,565 | 10,238 | 39,803 | 1.57 | 2,564,010 | 0.5 | 2,757,006 | 0.5 | 3,671,800 | 0.5 | 32 |
| Muslims | 57,710 | 0.1 | 488,630 | 0.2 | 1,373,320 | 0.3 | 20,296 | 9,572 | 29,868 | 1.99 | 1,546,300 | 0.3 | 1,672,011 | 0.3 | 2,638,130 | 0.4 | 40 |
| Ethnoreligionists | 2,244,540 | 3.5 | 1,150,610 | 0.4 | 1,094,475 | 0.3 | 21,914 | -2,518 | 19,396 | 1.64 | 1,181,245 | 0.3 | 1,288,429 | 0.3 | 1,304,850 | 0.2 | 21 |
| Jews | 23,110 | 0.0 | 794,580 | 0.3 | 1,060,995 | 0.2 | 16,123 | -7,974 | 8,149 | 0.74 | 1,094,265 | 0.2 | 1,142,465 | 0.2 | 1,227,360 | 0.2 | 33 |
| Baha'is | 0 | 0.0 | 299,350 | 0.1 | 657,845 | 0.2 | 14,700 | 6,795 | 21,495 | 2.87 | 763,205 | 0.2 | 872,757 | 0.2 | 1,577,280 | 0.2 | 46 |
| Hindus | 163,160 | 0.3 | 527,340 | 0.2 | 702,710 | 0.2 | 5,490 | 996 | 6,486 | 0.89 | 732,870 | 0.2 | 767,572 | 0.2 | 968,750 | 0.1 | 29 |
| Buddhists | 5,930 | 0.0 | 389,200 | 0.1 | 546,700 | 0.1 | 9,038 | 996 | 10,034 | 1.70 | 590,030 | 0.1 | 647,013 | 0.1 | 1,081,660 | 0.2 | 31 |
| New-Religionists | 0 | 0.0 | 167,910 | 0.1 | 518,835 | 0.1 | 7,907 | 2,406 | 10,313 | 1.83 | 578,025 | 0.1 | 621,961 | 0.1 | 982,860 | 0.1 | 16 |
| Chinese folk-religionists | 1,600 | 0.0 | 68,870 | 0.0 | 161,650 | 0.0 | 3,248 | -21 | 3,227 | 1.84 | 176,085 | 0.0 | 193,932 | 0.0 | 281,920 | 0.0 | 29 |
| Other religionists | 4,045 | 0.0 | 40,530 | 0.0 | 81,210 | 0.0 | 1,301 | 378 | 1,679 | 1.89 | 89,995 | 0.0 | 97,974 | 0.0 | 149,850 | 0.0 | 29 |
| Shintoists | 0 | 0.0 | 2,000 | 0.0 | 6,000 | 0.0 | 90 | -9 | 81 | 1.27 | 6,300 | 0.0 | 6,805 | 0.0 | 10,000 | 0.0 | 1 |
| Confucianists | 0 | 0.0 | 0 | 0.0 | 400 | 0.0 | 6 | -2 | 4 | 1.05 | 420 | 0.0 | 444 | 0.0 | 600 | 0.0 | 1 |
| World A (unevangelized persons) | 1,762,315 | 2.7 | 4,906,660 | 1.7 | 2,020,630 | 0.5 | 28,229 | -35,832 | -7,603 | -0.38 | 2,000,893 | 0.4 | 1,944,600 | 0.4 | 2,544,325 | 0.4 | 46 |
| World B (evangelized non-Christians) | 1,377,060 | 2.1 | 10,688,290 | 3.8 | 29,103,280 | 6.6 | 412,357 | 286,703 | 698,787 | 2.18 | 32,674,952 | 6.8 | 36,090,963 | 7 | 52,986,525 | 7.6 | 46 |
| World C (Christians) | 62,002,925 | 95.2 | 269,200,550 | 94.5 | 409,345,790 | 92.9 | 7,426,256 | -250,598 | 7,175,658 | 1.63 | 445,272,855 | 92.8 | 481,102,373 | 92.7 | 641,115,950 | 92.0 | 46 |
| CONTINENT'S POPULATION | 65,142,300 | 100.0 | 284,795,500 | 100.0 | 440,469,700 | 100.0 | 7,866,842 | 0 | 7,866,842 | 1.66 | 479,948,700 | 100.0 | 519,137,936 | 100.0 | 696,646,800 | 100.0 | 46 |

*Continued overleaf*

Table 10-6 concluded

| Continent | 1900 Adherents | 1900 % | mid-1970 Adherents | mid-1970 % | 1990 Adherents | 1990 % | Annual change, 1990-2000 Natural | Conversion | Total | Rate | mid-1995 Adherents | mid-1995 % | mid-2000 Adherents | mid-2000 % | mid-2025 Adherents | mid-2025 % | Countries |
|---|---|---|---|---|---|---|---|---|---|---|---|---|---|---|---|---|---|
| **NORTHERN AMERICA** | | | | | | | | | | | | | | | | | |
| Christians | 78,811,550 | 96.6 | 211,419,760 | 91.3 | 240,458,450 | 85.3 | 2,354,524 | -337,930 | 2,016,594 | 0.81 | 251,482,205 | 84.7 | 260,624,388 | 84.2 | 290,345,170 | 79.9 | 5 |
| professing Christians | 78,811,550 | 96.6 | 211,419,760 | 91.3 | 240,458,450 | 85.3 | 2,354,524 | -337,930 | 2,016,594 | 0.81 | 251,482,205 | 84.7 | 260,624,388 | 84.2 | 290,345,170 | 79.9 | 5 |
| unaffiliated Christians | 19,241,860 | 23.6 | 42,487,820 | 18.4 | 46,001,485 | 16.3 | 449,770 | -204,161 | 245,609 | 0.52 | 47,739,109 | 16.1 | 48,457,570 | 15.7 | 55,233,100 | 15.2 | 5 |
| affiliated Christians | 59,569,690 | 73.0 | 168,931,940 | 73.0 | 194,456,965 | 69.0 | 1,904,754 | -133,768 | 1,770,986 | 0.88 | 203,743,096 | 68.7 | 212,166,818 | 68.5 | 235,112,070 | 64.7 | 5 |
| Independents | 5,856,800 | 7.2 | 36,320,074 | 15.7 | 68,305,890 | 24.2 | 656,301 | 536,822 | 1,193,123 | 1.62 | 74,525,264 | 25.1 | 80,237,120 | 25.9 | 102,710,200 | 28.3 | 4 |
| Roman Catholics | 13,011,300 | 15.9 | 57,413,009 | 24.8 | 68,235,790 | 24.2 | 681,677 | -401,765 | 279,912 | 0.40 | 69,140,333 | 23.3 | 71,034,904 | 22.9 | 80,520,490 | 22.1 | 5 |
| Protestants | 37,299,590 | 45.7 | 62,811,885 | 27.1 | 65,135,355 | 23.1 | 634,364 | -150,054 | 484,310 | 0.72 | 67,732,067 | 22.8 | 69,978,450 | 22.6 | 74,765,120 | 20.6 | 5 |
| Marginal Christians | 815,000 | 1.0 | 6,469,233 | 2.8 | 9,359,145 | 3.3 | 90,494 | 26,785 | 117,279 | 1.19 | 9,937,278 | 3.4 | 10,531,930 | 3.4 | 17,503,380 | 4.8 | 5 |
| Orthodox | 415,000 | 0.5 | 4,538,550 | 2.0 | 5,660,000 | 2.0 | 55,375 | 12,825 | 68,200 | 1.14 | 6,015,253 | 2.0 | 6,342,000 | 2.1 | 7,962,000 | 2.2 | 2 |
| Anglicans | 2,172,000 | 2.7 | 4,395,191 | 1.9 | 3,353,700 | 1.2 | 34,282 | -45,232 | -10,950 | -0.33 | 3,318,042 | 1.1 | 3,244,200 | 1.1 | 2,922,700 | 0.8 | 3 |
| doubly-affiliated | 0 | 0.0 | -3,016,002 | -1.3 | -25,592,915 | -9.1 | -247,737 | -113,150 | -360,887 | 1.33 | -26,925,141 | -9.1 | -29,201,786 | -9.4 | -51,271,840 | -14.1 | 5 |
| *Trans-megabloc groupings* | | | | | | | | | | | | | | | | | |
| Evangelicals | 33,479,300 | 41.0 | 33,103,210 | 14.3 | 39,598,010 | 14.0 | 384,047 | -24,867 | 359,180 | 0.87 | 41,725,462 | 14.1 | 43,189,810 | 14.0 | 50,365,020 | 13.9 | 5 |
| Pentecostals/Charismatics | 46,100 | 0.1 | 24,151,910 | 10.4 | 67,231,220 | 23.8 | 651,772 | 585,122 | 1,236,894 | 1.70 | 73,997,060 | 24.9 | 79,600,160 | 25.7 | 110,204,580 | 30.3 | 5 |
| Great Commission Christians | 11,562,270 | 14.2 | 52,335,120 | 22.6 | 98,657,250 | 35.0 | 970,387 | 293,187 | 1,263,574 | 1.21 | 105,328,980 | 35.5 | 111,292,984 | 35.9 | 136,413,220 | 37.5 | 5 |
| Nonreligious | 1,010,000 | 1.9 | 10,699,100 | 4.6 | 24,142,465 | 8.6 | 237,460 | 195,549 | 433,009 | 1.66 | 26,281,665 | 8.9 | 28,472,554 | 9.2 | 44,855,650 | 12.3 | 5 |
| Muslims | 1,516,400 | 1.9 | 6,994,020 | 3.0 | 5,885,020 | 2.1 | 57,123 | -43,203 | 13,920 | 0.23 | 5,980,020 | 2.0 | 6,024,219 | 2.0 | 6,560,040 | 1.8 | 5 |
| Jews | 10,050 | 0.0 | 842,000 | 0.4 | 3,810,010 | 1.4 | 37,040 | 26,929 | 63,969 | 1.56 | 4,105,010 | 1.4 | 4,449,696 | 1.4 | 6,520,040 | 1.8 | 3 |
| Buddhists | 40,410 | 0.1 | 216,050 | 0.1 | 2,060,025 | 0.7 | 20,140 | 43,935 | 64,075 | 2.75 | 2,350,020 | 0.8 | 2,700,766 | 0.9 | 5,420,020 | 1.5 | 3 |
| Atheists | 2,000 | 0.0 | 300,000 | 0.1 | 1,190,000 | 0.4 | 12,431 | 36,601 | 49,032 | 3.51 | 1,435,010 | 0.5 | 1,680,320 | 0.5 | 2,250,000 | 0.6 | 2 |
| Hindus | 1,000 | 0.0 | 120,000 | 0.1 | 975,000 | 0.4 | 9,884 | 25,303 | 35,187 | 3.13 | 1,190,000 | 0.4 | 1,326,862 | 0.4 | 2,050,000 | 0.6 | 2 |
| Chinese folk-religionists | 75,120 | 0.1 | 120,000 | 0.1 | 756,000 | 0.3 | 8,938 | 851 | 9,789 | 1.23 | 807,000 | 0.3 | 853,886 | 0.3 | 945,000 | 0.3 | 2 |
| New-Religionists | 0 | 0.0 | 112,000 | 0.1 | 590,000 | 0.2 | 5,676 | 19,541 | 25,217 | 3.62 | 707,000 | 0.2 | 842,169 | 0.3 | 961,000 | 0.3 | 3 |
| Baha'is | 2,800 | 0.0 | 162,350 | 0.1 | 628,675 | 0.2 | 6,076 | 9,616 | 15,692 | 2.25 | 712,335 | 0.2 | 785,587 | 0.2 | 1,201,400 | 0.3 | 5 |
| Other religionists | 11,000 | 0.0 | 460,020 | 0.2 | 546,045 | 0.2 | 5,258 | -197 | 5,061 | 0.89 | 568,445 | 0.2 | 596,648 | 0.2 | 830,080 | 0.2 | 3 |
| Sikhs | 0 | 0.0 | 8,000 | 0.0 | 400,000 | 0.1 | 4,427 | 8,326 | 12,753 | 2.81 | 462,300 | 0.1 | 527,533 | 0.2 | 760,000 | 0.2 | 2 |
| Ethnoreligionists | 145,170 | 0.2 | 82,500 | 0.0 | 289,460 | 0.1 | 2,785 | 12,654 | 15,439 | 4.37 | 395,970 | 0.1 | 443,860 | 0.1 | 506,300 | 0.1 | 3 |
| Spiritists | 0 | 0.0 | 4,000 | 0.0 | 130,650 | 0.1 | 1,274 | 726 | 2,000 | 1.43 | 144,300 | 0.0 | 150,653 | 0.1 | 192,200 | 0.1 | 3 |
| Zoroastrians | 0 | | 0 | | 61,400 | 0.0 | 634 | 990 | 1,624 | 2.37 | 69,530 | 0.0 | 77,638 | 0.0 | 124,000 | 0.0 | 2 |
| Shintoists | 0 | | 0 | | 50,000 | 0.0 | 478 | 144 | 622 | 1.18 | 53,900 | 0.0 | 56,220 | 0.0 | 70,000 | 0.0 | 1 |
| Taoists | 0 | | 0 | | 10,000 | 0.0 | 96 | 17 | 113 | 1.08 | 10,600 | 0.0 | 11,134 | 0.0 | 13,500 | 0.0 | 1 |
| Jains | 0 | | 0 | | 5,000 | 0.0 | 48 | 148 | 196 | 3.36 | 6,000 | 0.0 | 6,959 | 0.0 | 7,000 | 0.0 | 1 |
| World A (unevangelized persons) | 156,300 | 0.2 | 1,131,727 | 0.5 | 4,106,052 | 1.5 | 40,639 | 26,108 | 66,747 | 1.52 | 4,472,272 | 1.5 | 4,773,514 | 1.5 | 8,625,455 | 2.4 | 5 |
| World B (evangelized non-Christians) | 2,657,650 | 3.3 | 18,988,313 | 8.2 | 37,423,698 | 13.3 | 369,365 | 311,704 | 680,951 | 1.69 | 40,806,823 | 13.8 | 44,233,190 | 14.3 | 64,640,775 | 17.8 | 5 |
| World C (Christians) | 78,811,550 | 96.6 | 211,419,760 | 91.3 | 240,458,450 | 85.3 | 2,354,524 | -337,930 | 2,016,594 | 0.81 | 251,482,205 | 84.7 | 260,624,388 | 84.2 | 290,345,170 | 79.9 | 5 |
| CONTINENT'S POPULATION | 81,625,500 | 100.0 | 231,539,800 | 100.0 | 281,988,200 | 100.0 | 2,764,292 | 0 | 2,764,292 | 0.94 | 296,761,300 | 100.0 | 309,631,092 | 100.0 | 363,611,400 | 100.0 | 5 |
| **OCEANIA** | | | | | | | | | | | | | | | | | |
| Christians | 4,838,150 | 77.5 | 17,845,126 | 92.4 | 22,010,352 | 83.3 | 340,036 | -30,117 | 309,919 | 1.33 | 23,641,309 | 83.0 | 25,109,520 | 82.6 | 32,010,392 | 80.7 | 28 |
| professing Christians | 4,838,150 | 77.5 | 17,845,126 | 92.4 | 22,010,352 | 83.3 | 340,036 | -30,117 | 309,919 | 1.33 | 23,641,309 | 83.0 | 25,109,520 | 82.6 | 32,010,392 | 80.7 | 28 |
| unaffiliated Christians | 516,431 | 8.3 | 3,146,438 | 16.3 | 3,299,410 | 12.5 | 49,095 | -5,535 | 43,560 | 1.25 | 3,519,505 | 12.4 | 3,734,974 | 12.3 | 3,858,795 | 9.7 | 27 |
| affiliated Christians | 4,321,719 | 69.2 | 14,698,688 | 76.1 | 18,710,942 | 70.8 | 290,939 | -24,579 | 266,360 | 1.34 | 20,121,804 | 70.6 | 21,374,546 | 70.3 | 28,151,597 | 71.0 | 27 |
| Independents | 1,052,096 | 16.8 | 4,549,395 | 23.6 | 6,993,955 | 26.5 | 108,615 | 14,766 | 123,381 | 1.64 | 7,594,923 | 26.7 | 8,227,767 | 27.1 | 11,239,665 | 28.4 | 27 |
| Roman Catholics | 1,551,415 | 24.8 | 4,273,450 | 22.1 | 6,323,401 | 23.9 | 113,356 | -6,488 | 106,868 | 1.43 | 6,842,666 | 24.0 | 7,392,067 | 24.3 | 10,015,097 | 25.3 | 28 |
| Protestants | 1,692,178 | 27.1 | 4,780,810 | 24.8 | 5,132,405 | 19.4 | 69,656 | -42,004 | 27,652 | 0.53 | 5,293,760 | 18.6 | 5,408,938 | 17.8 | 5,996,255 | 15.1 | 18 |
| Anglicans | 17,560 | 0.3 | 621,951 | 3.2 | 1,211,960 | 4.6 | 18,791 | 10,499 | 29,290 | 2.19 | 1,381,589 | 4.9 | 1,504,858 | 5.0 | 2,515,860 | 6.4 | 22 |
| Marginal Christians | 4,190 | 0.1 | 270,800 | 1.4 | 585,600 | 2.2 | 6,948 | 5,132 | 12,080 | 1.89 | 630,828 | 2.2 | 706,400 | 2.3 | 1,059,800 | 2.7 | 17 |
| Orthodox | 4,280 | 0.1 | 214,616 | 1.1 | 365,275 | 1.4 | 5,356 | 3,813 | 9,169 | 2.26 | 421,770 | 1.5 | 456,965 | 1.5 | 829,240 | 2.1 | 24 |
| doubly-affiliated | 0 | 0.0 | -12,334 | -0.1 | -1,901,654 | -7.2 | -31,782 | -10,298 | -42,080 | 2.02 | -2,043,732 | -7.2 | -2,322,449 | -7.6 | -3,504,320 | -8.8 | 28 |
| *Trans-megabloc groupings* | | | | | | | | | | | | | | | | | |
| Evangelicals | 2,155,730 | 34.5 | 2,900,548 | 15.0 | 3,914,329 | 14.8 | 60,088 | -6,911 | 53,177 | 1.28 | 4,020,269 | 14.1 | 4,446,081 | 14.6 | 5,740,665 | 14.5 | 28 |
| Pentecostals/Charismatics | 0 | | 238,240 | 1.2 | 3,545,837 | 13.4 | 54,432 | 17,539 | 71,971 | 1.87 | 3,928,858 | 13.8 | 4,265,522 | 14.0 | 6,519,303 | 16.4 | 28 |
| Great Commission Christians | 533,975 | 8.6 | 4,424,195 | 22.9 | 7,865,136 | 29.8 | 106,123 | 12,755 | 118,878 | 1.42 | 8,511,344 | 29.9 | 9,053,891 | 29.8 | 12,034,360 | 30.4 | 28 |
| Nonreligious | 43,800 | 0.7 | 659,109 | 3.4 | 2,841,189 | 10.8 | 35,293 | 10,362 | 45,655 | 1.50 | 3,066,174 | 10.8 | 3,297,727 | 10.9 | 4,848,625 | 12.2 | 27 |
| Atheists | 900 | 0.0 | 0 | 0.0 | 320,830 | 1.2 | 3,909 | 462 | 4,371 | 1.29 | 342,820 | 1.2 | 364,544 | 1.2 | 502,580 | 1.3 | 6 |
| Muslims | 13,400 | 0.2 | 215,000 | 1.1 | 307,780 | 1.2 | 3,868 | 818 | 4,686 | 1.43 | 328,855 | 1.2 | 354,643 | 1.2 | 489,760 | 1.2 | 5 |
| Hindus | 13,372 | 0.2 | 213,730 | 1.1 | 223,279 | 0.9 | 2,790 | 5,012 | 7,802 | 3.04 | 259,295 | 0.9 | 301,292 | 1.0 | 497,223 | 1.3 | 8 |
| Buddhists | 6,530 | 0.1 | 71,309 | 0.4 | 181,450 | 0.7 | 2,555 | 9,405 | 11,960 | 5.19 | 251,830 | 0.9 | 301,027 | 1.0 | 477,700 | 1.2 | 19 |
| Ethnoreligionists | 1,299,320 | 20.8 | 156,810 | 0.8 | 221,635 | 0.8 | 5,131 | -537 | 4,594 | 1.90 | 246,805 | 0.9 | 267,563 | 0.9 | 258,810 | 0.7 | 17 |
| Baha'is | 400 | 0.0 | 29,215 | 0.2 | 83,217 | 0.3 | 1,539 | 1,180 | 2,719 | 2.87 | 91,505 | 0.3 | 110,387 | 0.4 | 199,850 | 0.5 | 24 |
| Jews | 16,800 | 0.3 | 66,600 | 0.3 | 88,160 | 0.3 | 1,064 | -179 | 885 | 0.96 | 97,595 | 0.3 | 97,019 | 0.3 | 112,930 | 0.3 | 4 |
| New-Religionists | 0 | 0.0 | 0 | 0.0 | 28,030 | 0.1 | 440 | 3,407 | 3,847 | 9.02 | 48,735 | 0.2 | 66,488 | 0.2 | 79,750 | 0.2 | 9 |
| Chinese folk-religionists | 12,678 | 0.2 | 19,310 | 0.1 | 55,293 | 0.2 | 907 | -86 | 821 | 1.39 | 59,314 | 0.2 | 63,506 | 0.2 | 87,250 | 0.2 | 15 |
| Confucianists | 0 | | 150 | 0.0 | 21,340 | 0.1 | 264 | -27 | 237 | 1.06 | 22,400 | 0.1 | 23,708 | 0.1 | 31,150 | 0.1 | 3 |
| Sikhs | 200 | 0.0 | 5,000 | 0.0 | 12,820 | 0.1 | 156 | 379 | 535 | 3.55 | 15,350 | 0.1 | 18,164 | 0.1 | 29,200 | 0.1 | 3 |
| Other religionists | 300 | 0.0 | 11,200 | 0.1 | 8,900 | 0.0 | 116 | -62 | 54 | 0.59 | 8,820 | 0.0 | 9,436 | 0.0 | 11,100 | 0.0 | 4 |
| Spiritists | 500 | 0.0 | 1,000 | 0.0 | 6,600 | 0.0 | 82 | -42 | 40 | 0.59 | 6,740 | 0.0 | 7,001 | 0.0 | 9,000 | 0.0 | |
| Zoroastrians | 0 | 0.0 | 0 | 0.0 | 600 | 0.0 | 12 | 25 | 37 | 3.18 | 1,200 | 0.0 | 1,367 | 0.0 | 2,000 | 0.0 | 1 |
| World A (unevangelized persons) | 1,116,325 | 17.9 | 334,390 | 1.7 | 483,818 | 1.8 | 7,327 | 621 | 7,948 | 1.53 | 543,904 | 1.9 | 563,298 | 1.9 | 880,428 | 2.2 | 28 |
| World B (evangelized non-Christians) | 291,875 | 4.7 | 1,130,534 | 5.9 | 3,917,705 | 14.8 | 50,917 | 29,437 | 80,295 | 1.88 | 4,303,534 | 15.1 | 4,720,574 | 15.5 | 6,756,500 | 17 | 28 |
| World C (Christians) | 4,838,150 | 77.5 | 17,845,126 | 92.4 | 22,010,352 | 83.3 | 340,036 | -30,117 | 309,919 | 1.33 | 23,641,309 | 83.0 | 25,109,520 | 82.6 | 32,010,392 | 80.7 | 28 |
| CONTINENT'S POPULATION | 6,246,350 | 100.0 | 19,310,139 | 100.0 | 26,411,875 | 100.0 | 398,162 | 0 | 398,162 | 1.41 | 28,488,747 | 100.0 | 30,393,392 | 100.0 | 39,647,320 | 100.0 | 28 |

## Table 10–7. Global Christianity: Christians on 7 continents and in Worlds A, B, and C, AD 1900–AD 2025.

1. All figures in this table refer to Christians except (for purposes of comparison) the last line which refers to total world population.
2. Of the 2 adjacent columns of percentages, the first gives the preceding absolute number of Christians as a percentage of all Christians (global Christianity), and the second as a percentage of total world population. A third variety (Christians as a percentage of their continent's total population) is given in Table 10–8. Note that totals of percentages may not always add up exactly (e.g. to 100.0%), due to rounding.
3. Note that our Worlds A, B, and C trichotomy here refers to countries. See Part 30 "Glossary" for precise definitions.

| CONTINENT Code | Name | 1900 Adherents | % | % | mid-1970 Adherents | % | % | mid-1990 Adherents | % | % | Annual change 1990-2000 Natural | Conversions | Total | Rate | mid-1995 Adherents | % | % | mid-2000 Adherents | % | % | 2025 Adherents | % | % | Countries Count |
|---|---|---|---|---|---|---|---|---|---|---|---|---|---|---|---|---|---|---|---|---|---|---|---|---|
| | AFRICA | 9,938,588 | 1.8 | 0.6 | 143,818,494 | 11.6 | 3.9 | 276,497,939 | 15.8 | 5.3 | 7,934,453 | 438,975 | 8,373,428 | 2.68 | 317,625,134 | 16.9 | 5.6 | 360,232,182 | 18.0 | 5.9 | 633,803,970 | 24.2 | 8.1 | 60 |
| | ANTARCTICA | 0 | 0.0 | 0.0 | 370 | 0.0 | 0.0 | 0 | 0.0 | 0.0 | 153 | -43 | 110 | 3.99 | 2,900 | 0.0 | 0.0 | 3,400 | 0.0 | 0.0 | 8,000 | 0.0 | 0.0 | 1 |
| | ASIA | 21,897,519 | 3.9 | 1.4 | 101,394,552 | 8.2 | 2.7 | 248,728,290 | 14.2 | 4.7 | 4,046,396 | 2,365,720 | 6,412,116 | 2.32 | 281,908,145 | 15.0 | 5.0 | 312,849,430 | 15.6 | 5.2 | 464,800,100 | 17.8 | 5.9 | 50 |
| | EUROPE | 380,642,840 | 68.2 | 23.5 | 492,694,892 | 39.8 | 13.3 | 550,418,843 | 31.5 | 10.5 | 606,981 | 315,389 | 922,370 | 0.17 | 557,493,375 | 29.7 | 9.8 | 559,642,545 | 28.0 | 9.2 | 554,586,470 | 21.2 | 7.1 | 48 |
| | LATIN AMERICA | 62,002,925 | 11.1 | 3.8 | 269,200,550 | 21.8 | 7.3 | 409,345,790 | 23.4 | 7.8 | 7,426,256 | -250,598 | 7,175,658 | 1.63 | 445,272,855 | 23.7 | 7.9 | 481,102,373 | 24.1 | 7.9 | 641,115,950 | 24.5 | 8.2 | 46 |
| | NORTHERN AMERICA | 78,811,550 | 14.1 | 4.9 | 211,419,760 | 17.1 | 5.7 | 240,458,450 | 13.8 | 4.6 | 2,354,524 | -337,930 | 2,016,594 | 0.81 | 251,482,205 | 13.4 | 4.4 | 260,624,388 | 13.0 | 4.3 | 290,345,170 | 11.1 | 3.7 | 5 |
| | OCEANIA | 4,838,150 | 0.9 | 0.3 | 17,845,126 | 1.4 | 0.5 | 22,010,352 | 1.3 | 0.4 | 340,036 | -30,117 | 309,919 | 1.33 | 23,641,309 | 1.3 | 0.4 | 25,109,520 | 1.3 | 0.4 | 32,010,392 | 1.2 | 0.4 | 28 |
| | WORLDS (BY COUNTRY) | | | | | | | | | | | | | | | | | | | | | | | |
| | World A (38 countries) | 4,455,333 | 0.8 | 0.3 | 4,909,914 | 0.4 | 0.1 | 8,765,520 | 0.5 | 0.2 | 217,954 | -61,818 | 156,136 | 1.65 | 9,482,580 | 0.5 | 0.2 | 10,326,848 | 0.5 | 0.2 | 18,708,960 | 0.7 | 0.2 | 38 |
| | World B (59 countries) | 89,219,764 | 16.0 | 5.5 | 199,636,587 | 16.1 | 5.4 | 418,871,750 | 24.0 | 8.0 | 6,482,200 | 2,933,763 | 9,415,963 | 2.05 | 467,589,919 | 24.9 | 8.3 | 513,031,343 | 25.7 | 8.5 | 784,158,220 | 30.0 | 10.0 | 59 |
| | World C (141 countries) | 464,456,475 | 83.2 | 28.7 | 1,031,827,243 | 83.5 | 27.9 | 1,319,824,694 | 75.5 | 25.1 | 16,008,645 | -370,549 | 15,638,096 | 1.13 | 1,400,353,424 | 74.6 | 24.7 | 1,476,205,647 | 73.8 | 24.4 | 1,813,802,872 | 69.3 | 23.2 | 141 |
| | Global Christianity (238 countries) | 558,131,572 | 100.0 | 34.5 | 1,236,373,744 | 100.0 | 33.5 | 1,747,461,964 | 100.0 | 33.2 | 22,708,799 | 2,501,396 | 25,210,195 | 1.36 | 1,877,425,923 | 100.0 | 33.1 | 1,999,563,838 | 100.0 | 33.0 | 2,616,670,052 | 100.0 | 33.4 | 238 |
| | Global population (238 countries) | 1,619,625,741 | – | 100.0 | 3,696,148,148 | – | 100.0 | 5,266,441,768 | – | 100.0 | 22,708,799 | 2,501,396 | 25,210,195 | 1.36 | 5,666,360,221 | – | 100.0 | 6,055,049,115 | – | 100.0 | 7,823,703,142 | – | 100.0 | 238 |

## Table 10–8. Christians on 7 continents, 21 UN regions, and in Worlds A, B, and C, AD 1900–AD 2025.

This table is an expanded version of Table 10–7 above, setting out, as variables, major areas and regions as standardized by the United Nations, in the numerical order assigned to regions in *WCE* Part 4 "Countries" for all countries. The term 'Christians' = unaffiliated plus affiliated Christians of all 300 ecclesiastical traditions enumerated in Table 10–9).

| CONTINENT Code | Region | 1900 Adherents | % | mid-1970 Adherents | % | mid-1990 Adherents | % | Annual change 1990-2000 Natural | Conversions | Total | Rate | mid-1995 Adherents | % | mid-2000 Adherents | % | 2025 Adherents | % | Countries Count |
|---|---|---|---|---|---|---|---|---|---|---|---|---|---|---|---|---|---|---|
| | AFRICA | 9,938,588 | 1.8 | 143,818,494 | 11.6 | 276,497,939 | 15.8 | 7,934,453 | 438,975 | 8,373,428 | 2.68 | 317,625,134 | 16.9 | 360,232,182 | 18.0 | 633,803,970 | 24.2 | 60 |
| 1 | Eastern Africa | 4,515,970 | 0.8 | 55,447,650 | 4.5 | 116,359,799 | 6.7 | 3,246,676 | 229,063 | 3,475,739 | 2.65 | 132,271,469 | 7.0 | 151,117,180 | 7.6 | 271,312,920 | 10.4 | 21 |
| 2 | Middle Africa | 193,350 | 0.0 | 30,290,407 | 2.4 | 56,648,030 | 3.2 | 2,077,941 | 64,784 | 2,142,725 | 3.26 | 68,134,525 | 3.6 | 78,075,281 | 3.9 | 156,486,000 | 6.0 | 9 |
| 3 | Northern Africa | 2,700,645 | 0.5 | 7,997,855 | 0.6 | 13,179,700 | 0.8 | 286,438 | -17,908 | 268,530 | 1.87 | 14,631,220 | 0.8 | 15,864,986 | 0.8 | 23,128,000 | 0.9 | 8 |
| 4 | Southern Africa | 2,056,300 | 0.4 | 19,258,000 | 1.6 | 31,935,470 | 1.8 | 634,517 | 68,304 | 702,821 | 2.01 | 35,714,000 | 1.9 | 38,963,681 | 1.9 | 46,777,900 | 1.8 | 5 |
| 5 | Western Africa | 472,323 | 0.1 | 30,824,582 | 2.5 | 58,374,940 | 3.3 | 1,688,881 | 94,732 | 1,783,613 | 2.7 | 66,873,920 | 3.6 | 76,211,054 | 3.8 | 136,099,150 | 5.2 | 17 |
| | ANTARCTICA | 0 | 0.0 | 370 | 0.0 | 0 | 0.0 | 153 | -43 | 110 | 3.99 | 2,900 | 0.0 | 3,400 | 0.0 | 8,000 | 0.0 | 1 |
| | ASIA | 21,897,519 | 3.9 | 101,394,552 | 8.2 | 248,728,290 | 14.2 | 4,046,396 | 2,365,720 | 6,412,116 | 2.32 | 281,908,145 | 15.0 | 312,849,430 | 15.6 | 464,800,100 | 17.8 | 50 |
| 6 | Eastern Asia | 2,166,150 | 0.4 | 11,591,500 | 0.9 | 88,069,500 | 5.0 | 881,499 | 1,777,489 | 2,658,988 | 2.67 | 102,866,000 | 5.5 | 114,659,379 | 5.5 | 166,077,900 | 6.3 | 6 |
| 7 | South-central Asia | 8,386,150 | 1.5 | 53,697,226 | 4.3 | 90,243,050 | 5.2 | 1,966,605 | 112,485 | 2,079,090 | 2.09 | 100,687,445 | 5.4 | 111,033,948 | 5.6 | 164,443,100 | 6.3 | 11 |
| 8 | South-eastern Asia | 4,603,309 | 0.8 | 30,009,573 | 2.4 | 58,876,090 | 3.4 | 1,069,652 | 410,481 | 1,480,133 | 2.27 | 65,688,830 | 3.5 | 73,677,421 | 3.7 | 115,365,500 | 4.4 | 14 |
| 9 | Western Asia | 6,741,950 | 1.2 | 6,096,253 | 0.5 | 11,539,650 | 0.7 | 128,640 | 65,265 | 193,905 | 1.57 | 12,665,870 | 0.7 | 13,478,682 | 0.7 | 18,913,600 | 0.7 | 19 |
| | EUROPE | 380,642,840 | 68.2 | 492,694,892 | 39.8 | 550,418,843 | 31.5 | 606,981 | 315,389 | 922,370 | 0.17 | 557,493,375 | 29.7 | 559,642,545 | 28.0 | 554,586,470 | 21.2 | 48 |
| 10 | Eastern Europe | 151,940,840 | 27.2 | 158,204,825 | 12.8 | 216,541,650 | 12.4 | 636,946 | -263,650 | 373,296 | 0.17 | 219,563,100 | 11.7 | 220,274,611 | 11.0 | 229,853,700 | 8.8 | 10 |
| 11 | Northern Europe | 56,892,190 | 10.2 | 75,756,800 | 6.1 | 77,102,050 | 4.4 | 172,648 | -51,638 | 121,010 | 0.16 | 77,880,340 | 4.1 | 78,312,145 | 3.9 | 78,097,850 | 3.0 | 14 |
| 12 | Southern Europe | 68,542,170 | 12.3 | 112,237,930 | 9.1 | 120,476,663 | 6.9 | 121,515 | -77,491 | 44,024 | 0.04 | 120,995,155 | 6.4 | 120,916,908 | 6.0 | 110,776,980 | 4.2 | 15 |
| 13 | Western Europe | 103,267,640 | 18.5 | 146,495,337 | 11.8 | 136,298,480 | 7.8 | 576,468 | -192,428 | 384,040 | 0.28 | 139,054,780 | 7.4 | 140,138,881 | 7.0 | 135,857,940 | 5.2 | 9 |
| | LATIN AMERICA | 62,002,925 | 11.1 | 269,200,550 | 21.8 | 409,345,790 | 23.4 | 7,426,256 | -250,598 | 7,175,658 | 1.63 | 445,272,855 | 23.7 | 481,102,373 | 24.1 | 641,115,950 | 24.5 | 46 |
| 14 | Caribbean | 6,715,620 | 1.2 | 19,579,310 | 1.6 | 26,552,450 | 1.5 | 366,585 | -16,976 | 349,609 | 1.24 | 28,379,965 | 1.5 | 30,048,543 | 1.5 | 38,193,320 | 1.5 | 24 |
| 15 | Central America | 17,772,050 | 3.2 | 66,263,650 | 5.4 | 107,518,360 | 6.2 | 2,298,473 | -28,887 | 2,269,586 | 1.93 | 118,808,090 | 6.3 | 130,214,224 | 6.5 | 179,744,750 | 6.9 | 8 |
| 16 | South America | 37,515,255 | 6.7 | 183,357,590 | 14.8 | 275,274,980 | 15.8 | 4,761,198 | -204,735 | 4,556,463 | 1.54 | 298,084,800 | 15.9 | 320,839,606 | 16.0 | 423,177,880 | 16.2 | 14 |
| | NORTHERN AMERICA | 78,811,550 | 14.1 | 211,419,760 | 17.1 | 240,458,450 | 13.8 | 2,354,524 | -337,930 | 2,016,594 | 0.81 | 251,482,205 | 13.4 | 260,624,388 | 13.0 | 290,345,170 | 11.1 | 5 |
| 17 | Northern America | 78,811,550 | 14.1 | 211,419,760 | 17.1 | 240,458,450 | 13.8 | 2,354,524 | -337,930 | 2,016,594 | 0.81 | 251,482,205 | 13.4 | 260,624,388 | 13.0 | 290,345,170 | 11.1 | 5 |
| | OCEANIA | 4,838,150 | 0.9 | 17,845,126 | 1.4 | 22,010,352 | 1.3 | 340,036 | -30,117 | 309,919 | 1.33 | 23,641,309 | 1.3 | 25,109,520 | 1.3 | 32,010,392 | 1.2 | 28 |
| 18 | Australia-New Zealand | 4,443,320 | 0.8 | 14,331,461 | 1.2 | 16,464,640 | 0.9 | 203,538 | -30,061 | 173,477 | 1.01 | 17,445,035 | 0.9 | 18,199,401 | 0.9 | 21,166,580 | 0.8 | 5 |
| 19 | Melanesia | 219,520 | 0.0 | 2,877,390 | 0.2 | 4,645,810 | 0.3 | 116,484 | 903 | 117,387 | 2.28 | 5,207,510 | 0.3 | 5,819,667 | 0.3 | 9,133,400 | 0.3 | 6 |
| 20 | Micronesia | 62,560 | 0.0 | 238,690 | 0.0 | 391,058 | 0.0 | 11,743 | -265 | 11,478 | 2.61 | 445,515 | 0.0 | 505,842 | 0.0 | 879,320 | 0.0 | 7 |
| 21 | Polynesia | 112,750 | 0.0 | 397,585 | 0.0 | 508,844 | 0.0 | 8,271 | -694 | 7,577 | 1.4 | 543,249 | 0.0 | 584,610 | 0.0 | 831,092 | 0.0 | 10 |
| | WORLDS (BY COUNTRY) | | | | | | | | | | | | | | | | | |
| | World A (38 countries) | 4,455,333 | 0.8 | 4,909,914 | 0.4 | 8,765,520 | 0.5 | 217,954 | -61,818 | 156,136 | 1.65 | 9,482,580 | 0.5 | 10,326,848 | 0.5 | 18,708,960 | 0.7 | 38 |
| | World B (59 countries) | 89,219,764 | 16.0 | 199,636,587 | 16.1 | 418,871,750 | 24.0 | 6,482,200 | 2,933,763 | 9,415,963 | 2.05 | 467,589,919 | 24.9 | 513,031,343 | 25.7 | 784,158,220 | 30.0 | 59 |
| | World C (141 countries) | 464,456,475 | 83.2 | 1,031,827,243 | 83.5 | 1,319,824,694 | 75.5 | 16,008,645 | -370,549 | 15,638,096 | 1.13 | 1,400,353,424 | 74.6 | 1,476,205,647 | 73.8 | 1,813,802,872 | 69.3 | 141 |
| | GLOBAL CHRISTIANITY (238 countries) | 558,131,572 | 100.0 | 1,236,373,744 | 100.0 | 1,747,461,964 | 100.0 | 22,708,799 | 2,501,396 | 25,210,195 | 1.36 | 1,877,425,923 | 100.0 | 1,999,563,838 | 100.0 | 2,616,670,052 | 100.0 | 238 |

## Table 10–9. Organized Christianity: global membership ranked by 6 ecclesiastico-cultural megablocs and 300 major traditions, AD 1970–AD 2025.

a. This table is derived from the 238 Country Tables 2 in *WCE* Part 4 "Countries" for all countries.

b. All figures are given to the last digit in order that totals here, and in all other tables, shall add up exactly. When quoting any aggregate or global figures in these tables, therefore, they should be rounded, either to the nearest thousand, or ten thousand, or 0.1%, or 1% as may be appropriate to the reader's requirements.

c. *Meaning of columns.*

1. *Ecclesiastical bloc.* On these 6 lines are given the global statistical totals applicable to each bloc, and also, at the end of the table, for global church membership.

1-2. *Ecclesiastical tradition.* Under each of the 6 blocs are specified each's major constituent ecclesiastical traditions, listed in their codes' alphabetical order. First comes the 3-letter code as used in Tables 2, then the full name of each tradition. Totals include traditions which are part of a larger denomination which has been sub-divided in Tables 2 into different traditions.

3-4. *Congregations* (worship centers) and adult church members (all referring to the year 1995). These two columns are totals derived directly by addition from columns in Tables 2 for all countries..

5-6. *Affiliated church members* (total Christian community) in 1970 and 1995.

7-12. *Denominations.* A denomination is defined in this book as an organized aggregate of worship centers or congregations of similar ecclesiastical tradition within a specific country; i.e as an organized Christian church or tradition or religious group or community of believers, within a specific country, whose component congregations and members are called by the same denominational name in different areas, regarding themselves as one autonomous Christian church distinct from other denominations, churches and traditions. As defined here, world Christianity consists of 6 major ecclesiastico-cultural blocs, divided into 300 major ecclesiastical traditions, composed of over 33,000 distinct denominations in 238 countries, these denominations themselves being composed of over 3,400,000 worship centers, churches or congregations.

7-8. *Significant.* This word refers to those denominations which are significantly large, important or otherwise significant in a country's context for each to have its own single line in the country's Table 2.

9-12. *Total distinct denominations,* significant and less significant (or relatively insignificant), the latter being smaller bodies too small to each be enumerated with its own single line in Tables 2; for the years 1970, 1990, 1995, 2000, and 2025.

13. *Countries.* Number of countries (out of 238) where this tradition exists.

| Megabloc Tradition code 1 | name 2 | Congs 1995 3 | Adults 1995 4 | Affiliated 1970 5 | Affiliated 1995 6 | Denominations Sig 1970 7 | Sig 1995 8 | Total 1970 9 | 1995 10 | 2000 11 | 2025 12 | Countries Count 13 |
|---|---|---|---|---|---|---|---|---|---|---|---|---|
| **ORTHODOX** | | 90,900 | 130,759,000 | 139,662,000 | 209,624,000 | 431 | 466 | 519 | 764 | 781 | 887 | 133 |
| O-Alb | Albanian/Greek-speaking (Orthodox) | 600 | 221,000 | 198,000 | 537,000 | 6 | 6 | 6 | 6 | 6 | 6 | 4 |
| O-Ara | Arabic- or Arabic/Greek-speaking Orthodox | 1,100 | 722,000 | 777,000 | 1,380,000 | 31 | 31 | 31 | 31 | 31 | 31 | 29 |
| O-Arm | Armenian Orthodox (Gregorian) | 1,100 | 3,314,000 | 2,573,000 | 5,593,000 | 49 | 50 | 49 | 50 | 50 | 51 | 47 |
| O-Bul | Bulgarian Orthodox | 4,200 | 4,636,000 | 5,688,000 | 6,384,000 | 18 | 20 | 18 | 20 | 20 | 22 | 20 |
| O-Bye | Byelorussian/Belorussian (White Russian/White Ruthenian) | 900 | 3,177,000 | 4,528,000 | 4,854,000 | 7 | 7 | 7 | 7 | 7 | 7 | 6 |
| O-Cop | Coptic Orthodox | 2,500 | 5,403,000 | 6,180,000 | 9,234,000 | 20 | 24 | 20 | 24 | 25 | 28 | 24 |
| O-Cze | Czech/Slavonic-speaking Orthodox | 100 | 40,000 | 60,000 | 50,000 | 1 | 1 | 1 | 1 | 1 | 1 | 1 |
| O-Est | Estonian Orthodox | 100 | 130,000 | 277,000 | 209,000 | 5 | 5 | 5 | 5 | 5 | 5 | 5 |
| O-Eth | Ethiopic, Ethiopian Orthodox, GeOez-speaking | 13,100 | 10,647,000 | 11,932,000 | 21,902,000 | 13 | 15 | 13 | 15 | 15 | 17 | 15 |
| O-Fin | Finnish/Slavonic-speaking Orthodox | 40 | 44,000 | 58,000 | 65,000 | 2 | 2 | 2 | 2 | 2 | 2 | 2 |
| O-Geo | Georgian Orthodox | 600 | 1,156,000 | 1,268,000 | 2,589,000 | 9 | 9 | 9 | 9 | 9 | 9 | 9 |
| O-Gre | Greek Orthodox | 36,000 | 10,315,000 | 12,280,000 | 14,912,000 | 77 | 78 | 77 | 78 | 78 | 79 | 72 |
| O-Hun | Hungarian/Slavonic-speaking Orthodox | 40 | 30,000 | 40,000 | 50,000 | 1 | 1 | 1 | 1 | 1 | 1 | 1 |
| O-Lav | Latvian Orthodox | 100 | 200,000 | 200,000 | 250,000 | 1 | 1 | 1 | 1 | 1 | 1 | 1 |
| O-Mac | Macedonian Orthodox | 1,000 | 922,000 | 1,128,000 | 1,259,000 | 5 | 5 | 5 | 5 | 5 | 5 | 5 |
| O-Mol | Moldavian Orthodox | 200 | 902,000 | 1,151,000 | 1,303,000 | 2 | 3 | 2 | 3 | 3 | 4 | 3 |
| O-Nes | Assyrian or Nestoran (East Syrian, Messihaye (Christians) | 200 | 138,000 | 121,000 | 243,000 | 18 | 19 | 18 | 19 | 19 | 20 | 18 |
| O-Pol | Polish/Slavonic-speaking Orthodox | 400 | 642,000 | 547,000 | 1,021,000 | 2 | 2 | 2 | 2 | 2 | 2 | 2 |
| O-Rum | Romanian Orthodox | 8,300 | 13,135,000 | 16,108,000 | 19,271,000 | 21 | 23 | 21 | 23 | 23 | 25 | 23 |
| O-Rus | Russian Orthodox | 11,200 | 50,310,000 | 41,570,000 | 80,451,000 | 55 | 58 | 55 | 58 | 59 | 61 | 51 |
| O-Ser | Serbian Orthodox | 3,100 | 3,963,000 | 6,284,000 | 7,286,000 | 19 | 22 | 19 | 22 | 23 | 25 | 21 |
| O-Slo | Slovak Orthodox | 10 | 11,000 | 216,000 | 22,000 | 1 | 1 | 1 | 1 | 1 | 1 | 1 |
| O-SyM | Syro-Malabarese (Eastern Syrian), Syriac/Malayalam-speaking | 1,600 | 1,339,000 | 1,424,000 | 2,251,000 | 11 | 12 | 11 | 12 | 12 | 13 | 12 |
| O-Syr | Syrian, Syriac-speaking Orthodox or Syro-Antiochian | 700 | 449,000 | 208,000 | 1,018,000 | 17 | 24 | 17 | 24 | 25 | 31 | 24 |
| O-Ukr | Ukrainian Orthodox | 3,100 | 18,703,000 | 24,686,000 | 27,121,000 | 9 | 10 | 9 | 10 | 10 | 11 | 9 |
| **ROMAN CATHOLIC** | | 328,000 | 621,200,000 | 665,954,000 | 994,154,000 | 239 | 240 | 239 | 240 | 242 | 245 | 235 |
| R-Arm | Armenian (Eastern-rite Catholic) | 100 | 98,000 | 189,000 | 151,000 | – | – | – | – | – | – | 15 |
| R-Bul | Bulgarian (Byzantine rite) | 30 | 12,000 | 7,000 | 20,000 | – | – | – | – | – | – | 1 |
| R-Byz | Byzantine-rite (jurisdiction for more than one ethnic group) | 100 | 112,000 | 190,000 | 154,000 | – | – | – | – | – | – | 3 |
| R-Cha | Chaldean (Eastern Syrian rite) | 100 | 178,000 | 281,000 | 312,000 | – | – | – | – | – | – | 9 |
| R-Cop | Coptic (Alexandrian rite) | 200 | 111,000 | 107,000 | 190,000 | – | – | – | – | – | – | 1 |
| R-Eth | Ethiopic, Alexandrian rite | 200 | 83,000 | 87,000 | 141,000 | – | – | – | – | – | – | 2 |
| R-Gre | Greek (Byzantine rite) | 10 | 2,000 | 3,000 | 2,000 | – | – | – | – | – | – | 2 |
| R-Hun | Hungarian (Byzantine rite) | 200 | 211,000 | 269,000 | 281,000 | – | – | – | – | – | – | 1 |
| R-IAb | Italo-Albanian (Byzantine rite) | 100 | 52,000 | 68,000 | 62,000 | – | – | – | – | – | – | 1 |
| R-LEr | jurisdiction for both Latin-rite and Eastern-rite Catholics | 600 | 782,000 | 2,110,000 | 1,599,000 | 36 | 37 | 36 | 37 | 38 | 40 | 9 |
| R-Lat | Latin-rite Catholic | 315,300 | 609,777,000 | 653,710,000 | 975,673,000 | 203 | 203 | 203 | 203 | 204 | 205 | 229 |
| R-Mal | Malankara (Syro-Antiochian,Eastern Syrian), Syro-Malankarese | 900 | 183,000 | 202,000 | 311,000 | – | – | – | – | – | – | 1 |
| R-Mar | Maronite (Syro-Antiochian, Western Syrian) | 1,000 | 1,802,000 | 1,030,000 | 2,976,000 | – | – | – | – | – | – | 11 |
| R-Mel | Melkite (Byzantine, Greek Catholic; Arabic-speaking) | 500 | 633,000 | 353,000 | 1,116,000 | – | – | – | – | – | – | 12 |
| R-Ori | plural Oriental (jurisdiction for several Eastern rites) | 40 | 172,000 | 129,000 | 255,000 | – | – | – | – | – | – | 3 |
| R-Rum | Romanian Byzantine rite | 1,600 | 1,509,000 | 1,563,000 | 2,012,000 | – | – | – | – | – | – | 2 |
| R-Rus | Russian (Byzantine rite) | 2 | 7,000 | 3,000 | 10,000 | – | – | – | – | – | – | 1 |
| R-Rut | Ruthenian (Byzantine rite) | 400 | 249,000 | 130,000 | 391,000 | – | – | – | – | – | – | 2 |
| R-Slo | Slovak (Byzantine rite) | 300 | 170,000 | 10,000 | 239,000 | – | – | – | – | – | – | 2 |
| R-SyM | Syro-Malabarese (Eastern Syrian) | 2,600 | 1,797,000 | 2,017,000 | 3,055,000 | – | – | – | – | – | – | 1 |
| R-Syr | Syrian, Syriac-speaking (Syro-Antiochian, West Syrian) | 100 | 61,000 | 75,000 | 111,000 | – | – | – | – | – | – | 7 |
| R-Ukr | Ukrainian Byzantine rite | 3,700 | 3,201,000 | 3,422,000 | 5,093,000 | – | – | – | – | – | – | 10 |
| **ANGLICAN** | | 91,800 | 38,392,000 | 47,501,000 | 74,521,000 | 166 | 168 | 166 | 168 | 168 | 179 | 162 |
| A-ACa | Anglo-Catholic | 5,000 | 1,105,000 | 1,424,000 | 1,965,000 | 38 | 38 | 38 | 38 | 38 | 38 | 39 |
| A-Cen | Central or Broad Church Anglican | 5,500 | 5,094,000 | 10,204,000 | 9,292,000 | 31 | 31 | 31 | 31 | 31 | 32 | 32 |
| A-Ecu | Ecumenical (Anglican/Protestant/Orthodox joint parishes) | 700 | 80,000 | 0 | 120,000 | 0 | 1 | 0 | 1 | 1 | 1 | 1 |
| A-Eva | Anglican Evangelical, Evangelical Anglican | 18,500 | 7,841,000 | 5,355,000 | 15,345,000 | 11 | 11 | 11 | 11 | 11 | 14 | 12 |
| A-Hig | High Church Anglican (Prayer Book Catholic) | 12,800 | 3,452,000 | 5,805,000 | 7,604,000 | 31 | 31 | 31 | 31 | 31 | 33 | 30 |
| A-Low | Low Church Anglican (Conservative Evangelical) | 15,800 | 10,786,000 | 4,459,000 | 20,065,000 | 15 | 15 | 15 | 15 | 15 | 16 | 15 |
| A-plu | Anglican, of plural or mixed traditions | 33,500 | 10,034,000 | 20,254,000 | 20,129,000 | 40 | 41 | 40 | 41 | 41 | 45 | 41 |
| **PROTESTANT** | | 947,000 | 195,757,000 | 210,037,000 | 318,027,000 | 2,933 | 3,399 | 5,621 | 8,844 | 8,973 | 9,490 | 231 |
| P-Adv | Adventist | 34,000 | 5,966,000 | 4,189,000 | 11,011,000 | 195 | 214 | 195 | 214 | 218 | 233 | 199 |
| P-Bap | Baptist | 125,400 | 31,520,000 | 27,726,000 | 48,133,000 | 266 | 313 | 266 | 313 | 322 | 360 | 163 |
| P-CBr | Christian Brethren (Plymouth Brethren; Open only) | 16,700 | 1,341,000 | 1,535,000 | 2,798,000 | 120 | 124 | 120 | 124 | 125 | 128 | 113 |
| P-Con | Congregational, Congregationalist | 11,500 | 1,385,000 | 1,893,000 | 2,438,000 | 81 | 85 | 81 | 85 | 86 | 89 | 55 |
| P-Dis | Disciple, Restorationist, Restorationist Baptist, Christian | 6,700 | 1,053,000 | 2,455,000 | 1,919,000 | 13 | 17 | 13 | 17 | 18 | 21 | 18 |
| P-Dun | Dunker (Tunker), Dipper, German Baptist, Brethren | 2,100 | 322,000 | 465,000 | 603,000 | 10 | 10 | 10 | 10 | 10 | 10 | 7 |
| P-EBr | Exclusive Brethren (Plymouth Brethren, Closed, Strict) | 2,500 | 107,000 | 175,000 | 211,000 | 20 | 20 | 20 | 20 | 20 | 20 | 18 |
| P-Eva | Anglican Evangelical, Independent Evangelical | 20,100 | 2,842,000 | 1,824,000 | 5,482,000 | 112 | 135 | 112 | 138 | 143 | 164 | 89 |
| P-Fun | Fundamentalist | 2,600 | 122,000 | 67,000 | 211,000 | 13 | 16 | 13 | 16 | 17 | 19 | 14 |
| P-Hol | Holiness (Conservative Methodist, Wesleyan, Free Methodist) | 43,600 | 3,978,000 | 4,111,000 | 7,387,000 | 283 | 339 | 283 | 339 | 350 | 395 | 117 |
| P-LuR | Lutheran/Reformed united church or joint misssion | 10,800 | 11,626,000 | 18,525,000 | 15,041,000 | 23 | 24 | 23 | 24 | 24 | 25 | 22 |
| P-Lut | Lutheran | 81,900 | 39,853,000 | 54,717,000 | 60,696,000 | 231 | 249 | 231 | 249 | 253 | 267 | 122 |
| P-Men | Mennonite, Anabaptist (Left Wing or Radical Reformation) | 9,500 | 1,166,000 | 1,117,000 | 2,009,000 | 99 | 123 | 99 | 123 | 128 | 147 | 59 |
| P-Met | Methodist (mainline Methodist, United Methodist) | 89,500 | 13,860,000 | 21,933,000 | 22,902,000 | 113 | 121 | 113 | 121 | 123 | 129 | 108 |
| P-Mor | Moravian (Continental Pietist) | 1,200 | 302,000 | 478,000 | 582,000 | 27 | 29 | 27 | 29 | 29 | 31 | 27 |
| P-Non | Nondenominational (no church or anti-church groups) | 11,800 | 1,938,000 | 886,000 | 3,434,000 | 125 | 142 | 166 | 191 | 196 | 216 | 76 |
| P-Pe1 | Oneness-Pentecostal or Unitarian-Pentecostal: Jesus Only | 11,600 | 1,326,000 | 939,000 | 2,463,000 | 57 | 80 | 57 | 80 | 85 | 103 | 74 |
| P-Pe2 | Baptistic-Pentecostal or Keswick-Pentecostal | 232,000 | 30,284,000 | 12,006,000 | 49,420,000 | 311 | 380 | 311 | 382 | 396 | 453 | 174 |
| P-Pe3 | Holiness-Pentecostal: 3-crisis-experience | 28,800 | 3,219,000 | 2,322,000 | 5,650,000 | 167 | 233 | 167 | 233 | 246 | 299 | 118 |
| P-PeA | Apostolic, or Pentecostal Apostolic (living apostles) | 11,500 | 762,000 | 706,000 | 1,597,000 | 29 | 31 | 29 | 31 | 31 | 33 | 30 |
| P-Pen | Pentecostal (Protestant; Classical Pentecostal | 20 | 1,000 | 0 | 3,000 | 0 | 1 | 0 | 1 | 1 | 2 | 1 |
| P-Qua | Friends (Quaker) | 4,900 | 222,000 | 348,000 | 403,000 | 50 | 53 | 50 | 53 | 54 | 56 | 43 |
| P-Ref | Reformed, Presbyterian | 97,700 | 26,318,000 | 33,121,000 | 43,902,000 | 269 | 295 | 269 | 295 | 300 | 321 | 141 |
| P-Sal | Salvationist (Salvation Army) | 14,100 | 1,467,000 | 2,910,000 | 2,378,000 | 79 | 85 | 79 | 85 | 86 | 91 | 84 |
| P-Uni | United church (union of bodies of different traditions) | 50,300 | 12,348,000 | 13,608,000 | 22,266,000 | 49 | 53 | 49 | 53 | 54 | 57 | 45 |
| P-Wal | Waldensian | 200 | 31,000 | 37,000 | 41,000 | 2 | 2 | 2 | 2 | 2 | 2 | 2 |
| P-com | community church or union congregation | 50 | 12,000 | 19,000 | 20,000 | 19 | 19 | 20 | 23 | 24 | 26 | 18 |
| **INDEPENDENT** | | 1,593,100 | 191,227,000 | 96,327,000 | 348,196,000 | 2,835 | 4,043 | 11,024 | 21,586 | 22,148 | 49,431 | 220 |
| I-3aA | African Independent Apostolic | 30,800 | 6,497,000 | 2,035,000 | 13,504,000 | 76 | 89 | 76 | 89 | 92 | 102 | 24 |
| I-3aB | Black American Apostolic | 200 | 19,000 | 16,000 | 31,000 | 3 | 4 | 3 | 4 | 4 | 5 | 2 |
| I-3aF | Filipino Apostolic | 20 | 1,000 | 1,000 | 1,000 | 1 | 1 | 1 | 1 | 1 | 1 | 1 |
| I-3aI | Indian Apostolic | 200 | 28,000 | 7,000 | 50,000 | 3 | 3 | 3 | 3 | 3 | 3 | 2 |
| I-3aK | Korean Apostolic | 20 | 4,000 | 0 | 7,000 | 0 | 1 | 0 | 1 | 1 | 2 | 1 |
| I-3aL | Latin American Apostolic | 800 | 178,000 | 49,000 | 271,000 | 13 | 14 | 13 | 14 | 14 | 15 | 6 |

*Continued opposite*

*Table 10–9 continued*

| Megabloc Tradition code 1 | Name 2 | Congs 1995 3 | Adults 1995 4 | Affiliated 1970 5 | Affiliated 1995 6 | Denominations Sig 1970 7 | Denominations Sig 1995 8 | Denominations Total 1970 9 | Denominations 1995 10 | Denominations 2000 11 | Denominations 2025 12 | Countries Count 13 |
|---|---|---|---|---|---|---|---|---|---|---|---|---|
| I-3aO | Black American Oneness Apostolic | 3,400 | 1,368,000 | 418,000 | 1,873,000 | 20 | 26 | 20 | 26 | 27 | 32 | 3 |
| I-3aP | Pacific Apostolic | 20 | 4,000 | 0 | 5,000 | 0 | 1 | 0 | 1 | 1 | 2 | 1 |
| I-3aS | Arab Apostolic | 30 | 1,000 | 1,000 | 4,000 | 1 | 2 | 1 | 4 | 5 | 7 | 2 |
| I-3aU | Afro-Caribbean Apostolic | 100 | 11,000 | 1,000 | 16,000 | 2 | 2 | 2 | 2 | 2 | 2 | 2 |
| I-3aW | White-led Apostolic | 1,000 | 132,000 | 22,000 | 199,000 | 4 | 18 | 4 | 18 | 21 | 32 | 4 |
| I-3aX | New Apostolic, Catholic Apostolic (Irvingite), Old Apostolic | 23,700 | 3,976,000 | 1,714,000 | 8,293,000 | 76 | 176 | 77 | 186 | 208 | 295 | 149 |
| I-3cA | African Independent charismatic | 12,400 | 1,041,000 | 98,000 | 1,935,000 | 9 | 68 | 57 | 517 | 609 | 977 | 30 |
| I-3cB | Black American charismatic | 100 | 360,000 | 80,000 | 500,000 | 1 | 1 | 1 | 1 | 1 | 1 | 1 |
| I-3cC | Chinese charismatic | 212,400 | 15,361,000 | 18,000 | 35,778,000 | 5 | 10 | 17 | 62 | 71 | 107 | 3 |
| I-3cD | Black American Independent charismatic | 200 | 89,000 | 63,000 | 137,000 | 3 | 5 | 3 | 5 | 5 | 7 | 2 |
| I-3cE | Monoethnic charismatic | 100 | 2,000 | 30 | 4,000 | 1 | 2 | 1 | 2 | 2 | 3 | 1 |
| I-3cF | Filipino charismatic | 1,700 | 640,000 | 0 | 1,289,000 | 0 | 5 | 0 | 54 | 65 | 108 | 2 |
| I-3cI | Indian charismatic | 6,800 | 528,000 | 8,000 | 971,000 | 16 | 44 | 18 | 399 | 475 | 780 | 5 |
| I-3cK | Korean charismatic | 200 | 35,000 | 5,000 | 72,000 | 1 | 2 | 1 | 2 | 2 | 3 | 1 |
| I-3cL | Latin American charismatic | 3,900 | 129,000 | 4,000 | 269,000 | 3 | 13 | 3 | 77 | 92 | 151 | 8 |
| I-3cP | Pacific charismatic | 500 | 27,000 | 1,000 | 64,000 | 1 | 9 | 4 | 42 | 50 | 80 | 6 |
| I-3cQ | Japanese charismatic | 300 | 19,000 | 6,000 | 28,000 | 7 | 14 | 11 | 30 | 34 | 49 | 1 |
| I-3cS | Arab charismatic | 900 | 33,000 | 7,000 | 61,000 | 5 | 13 | 10 | 87 | 102 | 164 | 9 |
| I-3cU | Afro-Caribbean charismatic | 40 | 2,000 | 0 | 4,000 | 0 | 5 | 0 | 8 | 10 | 16 | 3 |
| I-3cW | White-led charismatic | 111,900 | 10,406,000 | 548,000 | 17,478,000 | 30 | 152 | 118 | 2,400 | 2,856 | 4,682 | 43 |
| I-3cY | Brazilian/Portuguese charismatic | 1,400 | 360,000 | 42,000 | 651,000 | 4 | 6 | 4 | 6 | 6 | 8 | 2 |
| I-3cZ | other Asian charismatic | 200 | 53,000 | 0 | 94,000 | 0 | 11 | 0 | 15 | 18 | 30 | 6 |
| I-3dW | White-led neocharismatic mainliners | 20 | 10,000 | 0 | 15,000 | 0 | 1 | 0 | 1 | 1 | 2 | 1 |
| I-3dZ | other Asian, doubly-affiliated mainliners | 30 | 5,000 | 0 | 10,000 | 0 | 3 | 0 | 3 | 4 | 6 | 2 |
| I-3fA | African Independent Full Gospel | 1,900 | 264,000 | 157,000 | 517,000 | 8 | 17 | 8 | 17 | 19 | 26 | 12 |
| I-3fB | Black American Full Gospel | 30 | 11,000 | 0 | 15,000 | 0 | 3 | 0 | 3 | 4 | 6 | 1 |
| I-3fC | Chinese Full Gospel | 100 | 7,000 | 0 | 15,000 | 0 | 1 | 0 | 1 | 1 | 2 | 1 |
| I-3fD | Black American charismatic Full Gospel | 5,000 | 500,000 | 0 | 1,100,000 | 0 | 1 | 0 | 1 | 1 | 2 | 1 |
| I-3fF | Filipino Full Gospel | 3,300 | 1,225,000 | 9,000 | 2,050,000 | 2 | 5 | 2 | 5 | 6 | 8 | 4 |
| I-3fG | Indonesian Full Gospel | 1,200 | 362,000 | 51,000 | 603,000 | 1 | 2 | 1 | 2 | 2 | 3 | 2 |
| I-3fI | Indian Full Gospel | 6,300 | 390,000 | 31,000 | 631,000 | 7 | 10 | 7 | 10 | 11 | 13 | 1 |
| I-3fK | Korean Full Gospel | 700 | 180,000 | 4,000 | 308,000 | 1 | 5 | 1 | 5 | 6 | 9 | 5 |
| I-3fL | Latin American Full Gospel | 500 | 43,000 | 10,000 | 92,000 | 1 | 2 | 1 | 2 | 2 | 3 | 2 |
| I-3fP | Pacific Full Gospel | 200 | 6,000 | 4,000 | 13,000 | 3 | 3 | 3 | 3 | 3 | 3 | 3 |
| I-3fW | White-led Full Gospel | 9,200 | 1,730,000 | 519,000 | 2,537,000 | 21 | 43 | 21 | 192 | 226 | 363 | 6 |
| I-3fY | Brazilian/Portuguese Full Gospel | 300 | 15,000 | 0 | 30,000 | 0 | 1 | 0 | 1 | 1 | 2 | 1 |
| I-3fZ | other Asian Full Gospel | 40 | 16,000 | 0 | 27,000 | 0 | 5 | 0 | 5 | 6 | 10 | 4 |
| I-3gL | Latin American grassroots | 5,900 | 1,342,000 | 182,000 | 2,245,000 | 35 | 68 | 57 | 244 | 281 | 431 | 15 |
| I-3gU | Afro-Caribbean grassroots | 40 | 3,000 | 2,000 | 5,000 | 1 | 1 | 4 | 10 | 11 | 16 | 1 |
| I-3gY | Brazilian grassroots | 3,000 | 1,600,000 | 0 | 3,000,000 | 0 | 1 | 0 | 250 | 300 | 500 | 1 |
| I-3hA | African house-church network | 200 | 5,000 | 0 | 12,000 | 0 | 2 | 0 | 2 | 2 | 4 | 2 |
| I-3hE | Monoethnic house-church network | 20 | 1,000 | 20 | 2,000 | 1 | 1 | 1 | 1 | 1 | 1 | 1 |
| I-3hG | Indonesian house-church network | 300 | 9,000 | 0 | 20,000 | 0 | 1 | 0 | 1 | 1 | 2 | 1 |
| I-3hI | Indian house-church network | 11,500 | 106,000 | 0 | 304,000 | 0 | 4 | 0 | 4 | 5 | 8 | 3 |
| I-3hK | Korean house-church network | 22,000 | 330,000 | 10,000 | 672,000 | 1 | 3 | 1 | 3 | 3 | 5 | 2 |
| I-3hL | Latin American house-church network | 300 | 28,000 | 0 | 50,000 | 0 | 4 | 0 | 4 | 5 | 8 | 3 |
| I-3hP | Pacific house-church network | 600 | 21,000 | 0 | 52,000 | 0 | 3 | 0 | 3 | 4 | 6 | 3 |
| I-3hS | Arab house-church network | 1,100 | 12,000 | 1,000 | 18,000 | 1 | 1 | 1 | 1 | 1 | 1 | 1 |
| I-3hV | Vietnamese house-church network | 300 | 38,000 | 0 | 95,000 | 0 | 1 | 0 | 1 | 1 | 2 | 1 |
| I-3hW | White-led house-church network | 300 | 5,000 | 60 | 12,000 | 1 | 5 | 1 | 5 | 6 | 9 | 5 |
| I-3hZ | other Asian house-church network | 30 | 1,000 | 10 | 2,000 | 1 | 2 | 1 | 2 | 2 | 3 | 2 |
| I-3jA | African healing network | 100 | 27,000 | 20,000 | 43,000 | 5 | 9 | 5 | 9 | 10 | 13 | 3 |
| I-3jW | White-led healing network | 300 | 154,000 | 303,000 | 207,000 | 2 | 3 | 2 | 3 | 3 | 4 | 2 |
| I-3kA | African cell-based network | 100 | 15,000 | 0 | 45,000 | 0 | 1 | 0 | 1 | 1 | 2 | 1 |
| I-3kB | Black American cell-based network | 10 | 18,000 | 200 | 24,000 | 1 | 1 | 1 | 1 | 1 | 1 | 1 |
| I-3kC | Chinese cell-based network | 20 | 12,000 | 0 | 23,000 | 0 | 1 | 0 | 1 | 1 | 2 | 1 |
| I-3kK | Korean cell-based network | 100 | 790,000 | 23,000 | 1,100,000 | 1 | 2 | 1 | 2 | 2 | 3 | 1 |
| I-3kL | Latin American cell-based network | 100 | 97,000 | 1,000 | 235,000 | 1 | 2 | 1 | 2 | 2 | 3 | 2 |
| I-3kW | White-led cell-based network | 50 | 42,000 | 0 | 78,000 | 0 | 2 | 0 | 2 | 2 | 4 | 2 |
| I-3kZ | other Asian cell-based network | 800 | 15,000 | 0 | 36,000 | 0 | 1 | 0 | 1 | 1 | 2 | 1 |
| I-3mA | Messianic African Independent | 10 | 1,000 | 2,000 | 2,000 | 1 | 1 | 1 | 1 | 1 | 1 | 1 |
| I-3mC | Messianic Chinese | 2 | 70 | 0 | 150 | 0 | 1 | 0 | 1 | 1 | 2 | 1 |
| I-3mH | Messianic Hindu temples | 500 | 53,000 | 110,000 | 154,000 | 4 | 4 | 4 | 4 | 4 | 4 | 1 |
| I-3mJ | Messianic Jewish | 1,800 | 81,000 | 13,000 | 136,000 | 3 | 15 | 3 | 15 | 17 | 27 | 9 |
| I-3mM | Messianic Muslim mosques | 1,200 | 64,000 | 0 | 105,000 | 0 | 2 | 0 | 2 | 2 | 4 | 2 |
| I-3nA | African Independent neocharismatic | 17,800 | 4,684,000 | 3,842,000 | 8,730,000 | 6 | 19 | 12 | 33 | 37 | 54 | 13 |
| I-3nB | Black American neocharismatic | 4 | 0 | 1,000 | 1,000 | 1 | 1 | 3 | 7 | 8 | 11 | 1 |
| I-3nC | Chinese neocharismatic | 8,600 | 1,126,000 | 152,000 | 1,973,000 | 11 | 60 | 11 | 60 | 70 | 109 | 57 |
| I-3nE | Monoethnic neocharismatic | 400 | 18,000 | 14,000 | 60,000 | 1 | 1 | 1 | 1 | 1 | 1 | 1 |
| I-3nF | Filipino neocharismatic | 9,500 | 1,158,000 | 1,551,000 | 2,013,000 | 3 | 4 | 113 | 253 | 281 | 393 | 2 |
| I-3nG | Indonesian neocharismatic | 800 | 140,000 | 70,000 | 326,000 | 1 | 1 | 1 | 1 | 1 | 1 | 1 |
| I-3nI | Indian neocharismatic | 10,600 | 353,000 | 20,000 | 631,000 | 2 | 13 | 2 | 20 | 24 | 38 | 2 |
| I-3nL | Latin American neocharismatic | 32 | 1,000 | 150 | 4,000 | 1 | 2 | 1 | 2 | 2 | 3 | 2 |
| I-3nN | Creole neocharismatic | 300 | 32,000 | 6,000 | 63,000 | 2 | 2 | 20 | 45 | 50 | 70 | 2 |
| I-3nP | Pacific neocharismatic | 100 | 6,000 | 4,000 | 10,000 | 1 | 2 | 1 | 2 | 2 | 3 | 2 |
| I-3nS | Arab neocharismatic | 10 | 5,000 | 0 | 10,000 | 0 | 1 | 0 | 1 | 1 | 2 | 1 |
| I-3nU | Afro-Caribbean neocharismatics | 30 | 1,000 | 200 | 2,000 | 1 | 2 | 2 | 11 | 13 | 20 | 2 |
| I-3nW | White-led neocharismatic | 100 | 5,000 | 5,000 | 7,000 | 1 | 3 | 1 | 3 | 3 | 5 | 3 |
| I-3nZ | other Asian neocharismatic | 15,400 | 108,000 | 11,000 | 165,000 | 2 | 6 | 23 | 58 | 65 | 93 | 5 |
| I-3oA | African Oneness pentecostal | 4,300 | 408,000 | 83,000 | 707,000 | 7 | 28 | 7 | 81 | 96 | 155 | 15 |
| I-3oC | Chinese Oneness pentecostal | 4,000 | 455,000 | 71,000 | 1,084,000 | 12 | 12 | 12 | 12 | 12 | 12 | 11 |
| I-3oF | Filipino Oneness pentecostal | 700 | 41,000 | 3,000 | 99,000 | 3 | 6 | 3 | 35 | 41 | 67 | 1 |
| I-3oG | Indonesian Oneness pentecostal | 1,500 | 770,000 | 1,000,000 | 1,280,000 | 1 | 1 | 1 | 1 | 1 | 1 | 1 |
| I-3oI | Indian Oneness pentecostal | 200 | 121,000 | 5,000 | 232,000 | 1 | 3 | 1 | 42 | 50 | 83 | 1 |
| I-3oL | Latin American Oneness pentecostal | 5,100 | 647,000 | 467,000 | 1,136,000 | 19 | 26 | 19 | 30 | 32 | 41 | 14 |
| I-3oO | Black American Oneness pentecostal | 1,400 | 447,000 | 141,000 | 687,000 | 5 | 5 | 78 | 124 | 133 | 170 | 2 |
| I-3oQ | Japanese Oneness pentecostal | 600 | 361,000 | 65,000 | 435,000 | 2 | 3 | 2 | 12 | 14 | 22 | 2 |
| I-3oU | Afro-Caribbean Oneness pentecostal | 700 | 61,000 | 19,000 | 112,000 | 9 | 26 | 9 | 73 | 86 | 137 | 7 |
| I-3oW | White-led Oneness pentecostal | 6,300 | 469,000 | 135,000 | 796,000 | 14 | 21 | 14 | 85 | 99 | 156 | 8 |
| I-3oY | Brazilian/Portuguese Oneness pentecostal | 100 | 7,000 | 1,000 | 13,000 | 1 | 3 | 1 | 3 | 3 | 5 | 1 |
| I-3oZ | other Asian Oneness pentecostal | 10 | 200 | 110 | 300 | 1 | 1 | 1 | 1 | 1 | 1 | 1 |
| I-3pA | African Independent pentecostal | 55,900 | 8,998,000 | 4,339,000 | 18,943,000 | 169 | 219 | 2,234 | 4,860 | 5,385 | 7,486 | 41 |
| I-3pB | Black American pentecostal | 19,100 | 4,713,000 | 2,699,000 | 6,162,000 | 35 | 38 | 35 | 71 | 78 | 107 | 18 |
| I-3pC | Chinese pentecostal | 300 | 65,000 | 54,000 | 118,000 | 11 | 12 | 23 | 41 | 45 | 59 | 4 |
| I-3pE | Monoethnic pentecostal | 4,800 | 688,000 | 148,000 | 1,242,000 | 19 | 20 | 19 | 20 | 20 | 21 | 15 |
| I-3pF | Filipino pentecostal | 1,800 | 258,000 | 254,000 | 474,000 | 13 | 22 | 13 | 22 | 24 | 31 | 5 |
| I-3pG | Indonesian pentecostal | 10,700 | 1,253,000 | 1,462,000 | 3,347,000 | 12 | 12 | 77 | 160 | 177 | 243 | 2 |
| I-3pI | Indian pentecostal | 17,000 | 1,311,000 | 696,000 | 2,243,000 | 23 | 34 | 46 | 87 | 95 | 128 | 12 |
| I-3pK | Korean pentecostal | 600 | 232,000 | 21,000 | 420,000 | 4 | 7 | 4 | 7 | 8 | 10 | 5 |
| I-3pL | Latin American pentecostal | 27,300 | 3,281,000 | 2,264,000 | 6,027,000 | 161 | 192 | 333 | 592 | 644 | 851 | 22 |
| I-3pN | Creole pentecostal | 400 | 68,000 | 65,000 | 145,000 | 3 | 3 | 14 | 28 | 31 | 42 | 3 |
| I-3pP | Pacific pentecostal | 200 | 17,000 | 15,000 | 35,000 | 14 | 18 | 14 | 18 | 19 | 22 | 11 |
| I-3pQ | Japanese pentecostal | 300 | 30,000 | 64,000 | 56,000 | 11 | 11 | 11 | 11 | 11 | 11 | 1 |
| I-3pR | Amerindian pentecostal | 1,000 | 303,000 | 361,000 | 506,000 | 3 | 3 | 3 | 3 | 3 | 3 | 3 |
| I-3pS | Arab pentecostal | 100 | 11,000 | 10,000 | 22,000 | 8 | 10 | 8 | 16 | 18 | 24 | 7 |
| I-3pU | Afro-Caribbean pentecostal | 2,700 | 212,000 | 154,000 | 464,000 | 41 | 50 | 141 | 309 | 343 | 477 | 19 |
| I-3pW | White-led pentecostal | 28,900 | 3,816,000 | 2,436,000 | 6,553,000 | 131 | 172 | 207 | 712 | 813 | 1,217 | 55 |
| I-3pY | Brazilian/Portuguese pentecostal | 44,300 | 8,047,000 | 2,468,000 | 15,896,000 | 17 | 23 | 72 | 196 | 221 | 320 | 6 |
| I-3pZ | other Asian pentecostal | 600 | 27,000 | 6,000 | 50,000 | 7 | 13 | 9 | 27 | 31 | 45 | 10 |
| I-3rA | African radio/TV believers | 4,300 | 78,000 | 7,000 | 150,000 | 9 | 11 | 9 | 11 | 11 | 13 | 11 |
| I-3rC | Chinese radio/TV believers | 40,400 | 1,212,000 | 15,000 | 2,519,000 | 3 | 3 | 3 | 3 | 3 | 3 | 2 |
| I-3rG | Indonesian radio/TV believers | 15,000 | 300,000 | 66,000 | 500,000 | 1 | 1 | 1 | 1 | 1 | 1 | 1 |
| I-3rI | Indian radio/TV believers | 100,500 | 6,012,000 | 654,000 | 9,020,000 | 4 | 4 | 4 | 4 | 4 | 4 | 4 |
| I-3rK | Korean radio/TV believers | 600 | 69,000 | 8,000 | 80,000 | 1 | 1 | 1 | 1 | 1 | 1 | 1 |
| I-3rL | Latin American radio/TV network | 2,400 | 50,000 | 13,000 | 79,000 | 7 | 7 | 7 | 7 | 7 | 7 | 7 |
| I-3rQ | Japanese radio/TV believers | 8,000 | 300,000 | 165,000 | 500,000 | 1 | 1 | 1 | 1 | 1 | 1 | 1 |
| I-3rS | Arab radio/TV network | 20,700 | 557,000 | 121,000 | 963,000 | 18 | 19 | 18 | 19 | 19 | 20 | 19 |
| I-3rV | Vietnamese radio/TV believers | 2,000 | 60,000 | 13,000 | 100,000 | 1 | 1 | 1 | 1 | 1 | 1 | 1 |
| I-3rW | European White radio/TV believers | 83,900 | 3,262,000 | 1,599,000 | 5,128,000 | 11 | 11 | 11 | 11 | 11 | 11 | 11 |
| I-3rY | Brazilian/Portuguese radio/TV believers | 300 | 10,000 | 2,000 | 15,000 | 1 | 1 | 1 | 1 | 1 | 1 | 1 |
| I-3rZ | other Asian radio/TV believers | 12,500 | 369,000 | 137,000 | 602,000 | 10 | 13 | 10 | 13 | 14 | 16 | 13 |
| I-3sA | African Independent Spiritual | 8,300 | 586,000 | 475,000 | 1,186,000 | 29 | 29 | 315 | 418 | 439 | 521 | 8 |
| I-3sU | Afro-Caribbean Spiritual | 100 | 6,000 | 6,000 | 11,000 | 5 | 5 | 5 | 5 | 5 | 5 | 4 |

*Continued overleaf*

*Table 10–9 concluded*

| Megabloc Tradition code 1 | Name 2 | Congs 1995 3 | Adults 1995 4 | Affiliated 1970 5 | Affiliated 1995 6 | Denominations Sig 1970 7 | Sig 1995 8 | Total 1970 9 | 1995 10 | 2000 11 | 2025 12 | Countries Count 13 |
|---|---|---|---|---|---|---|---|---|---|---|---|---|
| I-3sW | White-led signs and wonders | 40 | 2,000 | 0 | 6,000 | 0 | 3 | 0 | 3 | 4 | 6 | 3 |
| I-3tW | White-led restorationist | 1,600 | 132,000 | 0 | 280,000 | 0 | 10 | 0 | 10 | 12 | 20 | 1 |
| I-3vA | African Independent deliverance | 40 | 8,000 | 0 | 21,000 | 0 | 2 | 0 | 2 | 2 | 4 | 2 |
| I-3vB | Black American deliverance pentecostal | 30 | 83,000 | 25,000 | 100,000 | 1 | 1 | 1 | 1 | 1 | 1 | 1 |
| I-3vW | White-led deliverance pentecostal | 600 | 127,000 | 100,000 | 209,000 | 1 | 5 | 1 | 5 | 6 | 9 | 3 |
| I-3wA | African Word of Faith/Prosperity | 300 | 170,000 | 0 | 332,000 | 0 | 6 | 0 | 6 | 7 | 12 | 3 |
| I-3wF | Filipino Word of Faith/Prosperity | 40 | 15,000 | 0 | 25,000 | 0 | 1 | 0 | 1 | 1 | 2 | 1 |
| I-3wP | Pacific Word-of-Faith/Prosperity | 100 | 4,000 | 2,000 | 5,000 | 1 | 2 | 1 | 2 | 2 | 3 | 2 |
| I-3wW | White-led Word of Faith/Prosperity | 6,700 | 1,051,000 | 102,000 | 1,619,000 | 3 | 15 | 3 | 15 | 17 | 27 | 7 |
| I-3xA | African neocharismatic of mixed traditions | 4,200 | 950,000 | 850,000 | 1,500,000 | 1 | 1 | 3,000 | 3,000 | 3,333 | 4,667 | 1 |
| I-3xK | Korean pentecostal of mixed traditions | 3,000 | 50,000 | 30,000 | 140,000 | 1 | 1 | 67 | 150 | 167 | 233 | 1 |
| I-3xL | Latin American neocharismatic of mixed traditions | 30 | 15,000 | 0 | 19,000 | 0 | 1 | 0 | 1 | 1 | 2 | 1 |
| I-3xW | European charismatic of mixed traditions | 600 | 30,000 | 0 | 59,000 | 0 | 2 | 0 | 2 | 2 | 4 | 1 |
| I-3zA | Zionist African Independent | 12,200 | 4,067,000 | 999,000 | 10,140,000 | 41 | 49 | 93 | 147 | 158 | 201 | 6 |
| I-3zU | Afro-Caribbean Zionist | 400 | 21,000 | 35,000 | 37,000 | 1 | 1 | 1 | 1 | 1 | 1 | 1 |
| I-ACa | Independent Anglo-Catholic | 100 | 8,000 | 2,000 | 14,000 | 1 | 3 | 1 | 3 | 3 | 5 | 2 |
| I-ARo | Anglo-Roman (schism ex Anglicanism in Roman direction) | 500 | 43,000 | 83,000 | 80,000 | 18 | 18 | 18 | 18 | 18 | 18 | 13 |
| I-Adv | Independent Adventist | 1,100 | 71,000 | 91,000 | 141,000 | 22 | 25 | 22 | 25 | 26 | 28 | 19 |
| I-Ang | schism ex Anglicanism in Protestant direction | 4,500 | 721,000 | 875,000 | 1,460,000 | 40 | 40 | 44 | 59 | 62 | 74 | 14 |
| I-Apo | apocalyptic, eschatological | 100 | 2,000 | 2,000 | 4,000 | 2 | 3 | 2 | 3 | 3 | 4 | 2 |
| I-Bap | Independent Baptist | 97,900 | 21,314,000 | 17,048,000 | 27,547,000 | 184 | 238 | 192 | 258 | 271 | 324 | 95 |
| I-BrI | British-Israelite | 400 | 57,000 | 210,000 | 99,000 | 4 | 7 | 4 | 7 | 8 | 10 | 5 |
| I-Bud | Hidden Buddhist believers in Christ | 17,100 | 971,000 | 10,000 | 1,830,000 | 1 | 8 | 1 | 8 | 9 | 15 | 8 |
| I-Bul | Independent Bulgarian Orthodox | 200 | 200,000 | 0 | 500,000 | 0 | 1 | 0 | 1 | 1 | 2 | 1 |
| I-Byz | Independent Byzantine-rite | 30 | 3,000 | 0 | 6,000 | 0 | 1 | 0 | 1 | 1 | 2 | 1 |
| I-CBr | Christian Brethren (Plymouth Brethren; Open only) | 2,100 | 198,000 | 194,000 | 339,000 | 25 | 25 | 25 | 25 | 25 | 25 | 24 |
| I-CCa | Conservative Catholic (schism ex Rome) | 3,000 | 2,244,000 | 2,602,000 | 4,518,000 | 67 | 70 | 236 | 402 | 435 | 568 | 30 |
| I-Con | Independent Congregational, Congregationalist | 4,300 | 525,000 | 628,000 | 921,000 | 27 | 32 | 27 | 32 | 33 | 37 | 22 |
| I-Dis | Independent Disciple, Restorationist, Christian | 31,100 | 2,964,000 | 6,081,000 | 4,289,000 | 111 | 129 | 111 | 129 | 133 | 147 | 96 |
| I-Dun | Independent Dunker (Tunker, Dipper) | 600 | 80,000 | 70,000 | 115,000 | 3 | 3 | 3 | 3 | 3 | 3 | 1 |
| I-EBr | Independent Exclusive Brethren (Closed, Strict) | 400 | 21,000 | 30,000 | 42,000 | 5 | 7 | 5 | 7 | 7 | 9 | 5 |
| I-Epi | episcopi vagantes (bishops-at-large) (under 100 members) | 10 | 1,000 | 2,000 | 3,000 | 5 | 5 | 7 | 11 | 12 | 15 | 4 |
| I-Est | Independent Estonian Orthodox | 10 | 5,000 | 6,000 | 9,000 | 2 | 2 | 2 | 2 | 2 | 2 | 2 |
| I-Eva | Anglican Evangelical, Independent Evangelical | 6,800 | 684,000 | 461,000 | 1,357,000 | 67 | 88 | 67 | 88 | 92 | 109 | 48 |
| I-Fun | Independent Fundamentalist | 7,200 | 1,034,000 | 1,349,000 | 1,915,000 | 45 | 52 | 45 | 52 | 53 | 59 | 31 |
| I-Gay | Gay/Lesbian homosexual tradition | 300 | 121,000 | 30,000 | 154,000 | 1 | 2 | 1 | 2 | 2 | 3 | 2 |
| I-Gre | Independent Greek Orthodox | 20 | 11,000 | 13,000 | 16,000 | 2 | 2 | 2 | 2 | 2 | 2 | 1 |
| I-Hin | Hidden Hindu believers in Christ | 20,400 | 7,146,000 | 4,002,000 | 10,637,000 | 3 | 9 | 3 | 9 | 10 | 15 | 7 |
| I-Hol | Holiness (Conservative Methodist, non-Pentecostal) | 7,700 | 733,000 | 727,000 | 1,393,000 | 71 | 80 | 71 | 80 | 82 | 89 | 39 |
| I-Hun | Independent Hungarian Orthodox | 1 | 200 | 400 | 1,000 | 1 | 1 | 1 | 1 | 1 | 1 | 1 |
| I-Jeh | Independent Jehovahs Witnesses (Jehovahs Christian Witnesses | 1,200 | 198,000 | 111,000 | 323,000 | 8 | 8 | 8 | 8 | 8 | 8 | 7 |
| I-Jew | Messianic, Jewish-Christian | 200 | 20,000 | 50,000 | 30,000 | 1 | 1 | 1 | 1 | 1 | 1 | 1 |
| I-Lat | Latin-rite Catholic | 18,300 | 3,839,000 | 11,000 | 5,828,000 | 4 | 5 | 4 | 5 | 5 | 6 | 1 |
| I-Lib | Liberal Catholic (Theosophical, Masonic, Gnostic) | 300 | 55,000 | 87,000 | 106,000 | 27 | 27 | 27 | 27 | 27 | 27 | 18 |
| I-LuR | Independent Lutheran/Reformed united church | 10 | 1,000 | 2,000 | 2,000 | 1 | 1 | 1 | 1 | 1 | 1 | 1 |
| I-Lut | Independent Lutheran | 4,900 | 921,000 | 902,000 | 1,690,000 | 44 | 49 | 44 | 49 | 50 | 54 | 20 |
| I-Mac | Independent Macedonian Orthodox | 3 | 1,000 | 200 | 1,000 | 1 | 1 | 1 | 1 | 1 | 1 | 1 |
| I-Men | Independent Mennonite, Anabaptist | 800 | 70,000 | 71,000 | 130,000 | 6 | 10 | 6 | 10 | 11 | 14 | 7 |
| I-Met | Independent Methodist | 22,900 | 4,209,000 | 4,706,000 | 6,862,000 | 86 | 91 | 86 | 91 | 92 | 96 | 46 |
| I-Mol | Independent Moldavian Orthodox | 40 | 400,000 | 0 | 630,000 | 0 | 1 | 0 | 1 | 1 | 2 | 1 |
| I-Mor | Independent Moravian (Continental Pietist) | 1 | 100 | 200 | 200 | 1 | 1 | 1 | 1 | 1 | 1 | 1 |
| I-Mus | Hidden Muslim believers in Christ | 3,700 | 252,000 | 3,000 | 448,000 | 2 | 15 | 2 | 15 | 18 | 28 | 15 |
| I-Nes | Independent Assyrian or Nestorian (East Syrian) | 100 | 38,000 | 31,000 | 74,000 | 5 | 5 | 5 | 5 | 5 | 5 | 3 |
| I-NoC | No-Church movement | 100 | 2,000 | 3,000 | 3,000 | 2 | 2 | 2 | 2 | 2 | 2 | 2 |
| I-Non | Nondenominational (no church or anti-church group) | 15,200 | 1,188,000 | 1,091,000 | 2,109,000 | 179 | 206 | 188 | 228 | 236 | 268 | 71 |
| I-OBe | Old Believer, Old Ritualist | 3,300 | 1,135,000 | 2,631,000 | 1,957,000 | 23 | 24 | 23 | 25 | 25 | 27 | 19 |
| I-OCa | Old Catholic | 1,100 | 518,000 | 647,000 | 866,000 | 26 | 26 | 26 | 26 | 26 | 26 | 19 |
| I-OCd | Old Calendarist, Authentic Orthodox | 300 | 136,000 | 215,000 | 261,000 | 8 | 8 | 8 | 8 | 8 | 8 | 4 |
| I-Ort | schism from Orthodoxy, in Protestant direction | 300 | 58,000 | 50,000 | 95,000 | 6 | 6 | 11 | 25 | 28 | 39 | 6 |
| I-Ose | Orthodox sect/sectarian | 900 | 75,000 | 264,000 | 139,000 | 9 | 9 | 17 | 28 | 30 | 39 | 3 |
| I-Qua | Independent Friends (Quaker) | 200 | 22,000 | 40,000 | 37,000 | 2 | 2 | 2 | 2 | 2 | 2 | 2 |
| I-ReA | Reformed Anglican | 800 | 103,000 | 111,000 | 168,000 | 16 | 20 | 24 | 39 | 42 | 54 | 10 |
| I-ReC | Reformed Catholic, retaining Roman Catholic claims | 9,500 | 3,188,000 | 4,200,000 | 5,110,000 | 14 | 16 | 14 | 16 | 16 | 18 | 11 |
| I-ReO | Reformed Orthodox (uncanonical reform movement) | 1,800 | 641,000 | 420,000 | 1,023,000 | 22 | 23 | 22 | 23 | 23 | 24 | 15 |
| I-Ref | Independent Reformed, Presbyterian | 29,200 | 3,806,000 | 2,628,000 | 7,884,000 | 104 | 131 | 104 | 131 | 136 | 158 | 51 |
| I-Rum | Independent Romanian Orthodox | 100 | 73,000 | 67,000 | 110,000 | 3 | 3 | 3 | 3 | 3 | 3 | 3 |
| I-Rus | Independent Russian Orthodox | 700 | 610,000 | 219,000 | 921,000 | 27 | 31 | 27 | 31 | 32 | 35 | 30 |
| I-Sal | Independent Salvationist | 400 | 63,000 | 113,000 | 140,000 | 8 | 8 | 8 | 8 | 8 | 8 | 5 |
| I-Ser | Independent Serbian Orthodox | 50 | 20,000 | 17,000 | 34,000 | 4 | 5 | 4 | 5 | 5 | 6 | 5 |
| I-Spi | Spiritualist, Spiritist (thaumaturgical), occult | 200 | 61,000 | 107,000 | 114,000 | 3 | 3 | 3 | 3 | 3 | 3 | 1 |
| I-TrA | Traditional Anglican, Traditionalist | 100 | 7,000 | 0 | 10,000 | 0 | 1 | 0 | 1 | 1 | 2 | 1 |
| I-Tru | True Orthodox (devoutly conservative Russian Orthodox) | 8,100 | 185,000 | 259,000 | 358,000 | 6 | 6 | 6 | 6 | 6 | 6 | 4 |
| I-Ukr | Independent Ukrainian Orthodox | 3,400 | 3,238,000 | 661,000 | 6,324,000 | 20 | 23 | 20 | 23 | 24 | 26 | 18 |
| I-Uni | United church (union of bodies of different traditions) | 27,200 | 4,101,000 | 300,000 | 10,701,000 | 2 | 3 | 2 | 3 | 3 | 4 | 3 |
| I-com | community church or union congregation | 1 | 100 | 100 | 200 | 1 | 1 | 1 | 1 | 1 | 1 | 1 |
| I-eth | ethnic or monoethnic denomination | 6,700 | 451,000 | 52,000 | 1,092,000 | 15 | 15 | 161 | 214 | 225 | 267 | 2 |
| I-ind | independent evangelical (dispensationalist) | 1,700 | 228,000 | 304,000 | 380,000 | 2 | 3 | 2 | 3 | 3 | 4 | 2 |
| I-mar | marginal independent Christian (Black/Third-World indigenous | 4,500 | 599,000 | 2,017,000 | 1,211,000 | 54 | 76 | 59 | 90 | 96 | 121 | 48 |
| I-rad | isolated radio churches (unorganized) | 7,000 | 197,000 | 28,000 | 301,000 | 7 | 7 | 7 | 7 | 7 | 7 | 7 |
| I-sin | single congregation(s): one single autonomous congregation | 10,600 | 1,088,000 | 1,287,000 | 1,996,000 | 7 | 7 | 445 | 745 | 805 | 1,045 | 7 |
| **MARGINAL CHRISTIAN** | | 106,200 | 12,362,000 | 11,100,000 | 23,851,000 | 493 | 545 | 1,061 | 1,488 | 1,596 | 2,030 | 215 |
| m-Ade | Christadelphian | 1,200 | 43,000 | 97,000 | 71,000 | 21 | 21 | 21 | 21 | 21 | 21 | 20 |
| m-Apo | apocalyptic, eschatological | 1 | 1,000 | 10,000 | 1,000 | 1 | 1 | 1 | 1 | 1 | 1 | 1 |
| m-Div | Divine Science | 20 | 1,000 | 0 | 1,000 | 0 | 1 | 0 | 1 | 1 | 2 | 1 |
| m-Gno | Gnostic, esoteric, anthroposophical | 200 | 58,000 | 53,000 | 70,000 | 5 | 5 | 5 | 5 | 5 | 5 | 3 |
| m-HSA | Holy Spirit Assoc. for Unification of World Christianity | 900 | 713,000 | 454,000 | 926,000 | 5 | 8 | 5 | 8 | 9 | 11 | 8 |
| m-Jeh | Jehovah's Witnesses (Russellites) | 70,500 | 4,466,000 | 4,017,000 | 11,305,000 | 204 | 222 | 204 | 222 | 226 | 240 | 212 |
| m-LdS | Latter-day Saints (Mormons), including Mormon schismatics | 20,000 | 5,117,000 | 3,111,000 | 7,985,000 | 88 | 116 | 88 | 116 | 122 | 144 | 102 |
| m-Lib | Liberal Catholic (Theosophical, Masonic, Gnostic) | 200 | 22,000 | 2,000 | 31,000 | 1 | 1 | 1 | 1 | 1 | 1 | 1 |
| m-Ort | schism from Orthodoxy, in marginal direction | 500 | 50,000 | 71,000 | 85,000 | 2 | 2 | 2 | 2 | 2 | 2 | 2 |
| m-Pau | Paulician, Bogomil | 30 | 4,000 | 5,000 | 6,000 | 2 | 2 | 2 | 2 | 2 | 2 | 2 |
| m-Sci | metaphysical science, Divine Science, Religious Science | 3,600 | 488,000 | 1,220,000 | 1,097,000 | 59 | 59 | 59 | 59 | 59 | 59 | 55 |
| m-Spi | Spiritualist, Spiritist (thaumaturgical), psychic, occult | 1,100 | 83,000 | 357,000 | 145,000 | 20 | 20 | 20 | 20 | 20 | 20 | 10 |
| m-Swe | Swedenborgian (Church of the New Jerusalem; spiritualistic) | 300 | 19,000 | 44,000 | 31,000 | 18 | 18 | 18 | 18 | 18 | 18 | 15 |
| m-The | Theosophist, Theosophical, synthesist | 100 | 3,000 | 6,000 | 5,000 | 3 | 3 | 3 | 3 | 3 | 3 | 3 |
| m-Unt | Unitarian, Universalist, Free Christian, Liberal Christian | 1,700 | 249,000 | 469,000 | 378,000 | 29 | 29 | 29 | 29 | 29 | 29 | 26 |
| **DOUBLY AFFILIATED / DISAFFILIATED** | | | -119,766,000 | -40,475,000 | -198,453,000 | | | | | | | 93 |
| 2-Aff | Doubly-affiliated | | -102,506,000 | -29,781,000 | -174,354,000 | | | | | | | 93 |
| X-Aff | Disaffiliated | | -17,260,000 | -10,694,000 | -24,099,000 | | | | | | | 11 |
| **GLOBAL TOTALS** | | **3,157,000** | **1,069,931,000** | **1,130,106,000** | **1,769,920,000** | **7,097** | **8,861** | **18,630** | **33,090** | **33,909** | **62,262** | **238** |

## Table 10–10   Urban and rural Christians and populations on 6 continents, AD 1900–AD 2025.

1. The table gives statistics of urban and rural dwellers, using United Nations' definitions of urbanized populations.
2. All percentages in this table are %s of the relevant continent's total population, except the last 6 lines which give percentages of the world population;

4. 'Rate' gives the rate of increase as percent per year.
5. The last column 'Cites' gives the number of cities in AD 2000 with over 100,000 population, and also over 1 million populations.

3. and except for the column 'Rate' which gives annual increase. Annual change is here divided into (a natural increase (births minus deaths), (b) conversion increase (nett converts minus nett defections), and (c) transfer increase (nett immigration from rural areas to urban areas).

| | 1900 adherents | % | 1970 Adherents | % | 1990 Adherents | % | Annual Change, 1990-2000 — Natural | Conversions | Transfer | Total | Rate | 1995 Adherents | % | 2000 Adherents | % | 2025 Adherents | % | Cities 2000 over 100,000 | over 1 million |
|---|---|---|---|---|---|---|---|---|---|---|---|---|---|---|---|---|---|---|---|
| **AFRICA** | | | | | | | | | | | | | | | | | | | |
| Population | 107,808,260 | 100.0 | 357,040,697 | 100.0 | 614,768,549 | 100.0 | 16,967,278 | 0 | | 16,967,278 | 2.47 | 696,963,168 | 100.0 | 784,445,039 | 100.0 | 1,298,310,949 | 100.0 | 334 | 40 |
| Urban population | 4,312,330 | 4.0 | 82,342,277 | 23.0 | 196,814,475 | 32.0 | 5,431,972 | 0 | 4,411,169 | 9,843,141 | 4.14 | 242,718,319 | 34.8 | 295,249,605 | 37.6 | 666,825,948 | 51.3 | | |
| Rural population | 103,495,930 | 100.0 | 274,698,420 | 76.9 | 417,954,074 | 67.9 | 11,535,305 | 0 | -4,411,169 | 7,124,136 | 1.59 | 454,244,849 | 65.1 | 489,195,434 | 62.3 | 631,485,001 | 48.6 | | |
| Christian population | 9,938,588 | 9.2 | 143,818,494 | 40.2 | 276,497,939 | 44.9 | 7,934,453 | 438,975 | 0 | 8,373,428 | 2.68 | 317,625,134 | 45.5 | 360,232,182 | 45.9 | 633,803,970 | 48.8 | | |
| Urban Christians | 318,035 | 3.2 | 33,168,046 | 9.2 | 88,519,162 | 14.4 | 2,540,167 | 140,535 | 1,727,372 | 4,408,074 | 4.36 | 110,613,361 | 15.8 | 135,584,272 | 17.2 | 325,528,282 | 25.0 | | |
| Rural Christians | 9,620,553 | 6.0 | 110,650,448 | 30.9 | 187,978,777 | 30.5 | 5,394,285 | 298,440 | -1,727,372 | 3,965,353 | 1.80 | 207,011,773 | 29.7 | 224,647,910 | 28.6 | 308,275,688 | 23.7 | | |
| **ASIA** | | | | | | | | | | | | | | | | | | | |
| Population | 956,196,550 | 100.0 | 2,147,021,065 | 100.0 | 3,180,594,448 | 100.0 | 50,195,703 | 0 | | 50,195,703 | 1.48 | 3,436,281,411 | 100.0 | 3,682,550,093 | 100.0 | 4,723,140,220 | 100.0 | 1,373 | 195 |
| Urban population | 62,152,776 | 6.5 | 507,098,558 | 23.6 | 1,018,185,600 | 32.0 | 16,068,864 | 0 | 20,927,233 | 36,996,097 | 3.15 | 1,195,459,687 | 34.7 | 1,388,145,191 | 37.7 | 2,472,984,601 | 52.3 | | |
| Rural population | 894,043,774 | 100.0 | 1,639,922,507 | 76.3 | 2,162,408,848 | 67.9 | 34,126,838 | 0 | -20,927,233 | 13,199,605 | 0.59 | 2,240,821,724 | 65.2 | 2,294,404,902 | 62.3 | 2,250,155,619 | 47.6 | | |
| Christian population | 21,897,519 | 2.2 | 101,394,552 | 4.7 | 248,728,290 | 7.8 | 4,046,396 | 2,365,720 | 0 | 6,412,116 | 2.32 | 281,908,145 | 8.2 | 312,849,430 | 8.5 | 464,800,100 | 9.8 | | |
| Urban Christians | 109,488 | 0.5 | 23,948,079 | 1.1 | 79,623,972 | 2.5 | 1,295,349 | 757,324 | 169,461 | 2,222,134 | 4.01 | 98,073,988 | 2.8 | 117,929,267 | 3.2 | 243,364,253 | 5.1 | | |
| Rural Christians | 21,788,031 | 1.7 | 77,446,473 | 3.6 | 169,104,318 | 5.3 | 2,751,046 | 1,608,396 | -169,461 | 4,189,981 | 1.43 | 183,834,157 | 5.3 | 194,920,163 | 5.2 | 221,435,847 | 4.6 | | |
| **EUROPE** | | | | | | | | | | | | | | | | | | | |
| Population | 402,606,400 | 100.0 | 656,441,036 | 100.0 | 722,206,284 | 100.0 | 668,390 | 0 | | 668,390 | 0.09 | 727,912,397 | 100.0 | 728,886,951 | 100.0 | 702,335,374 | 100.0 | 735 | 66 |
| Urban population | 152,990,432 | 38.0 | 423,544,554 | 64.5 | 520,579,792 | 72.0 | 481,788 | 0 | 2,069,722 | 2,551,510 | 0.48 | 535,277,051 | 73.5 | 546,091,672 | 74.9 | 574,131,311 | 81.7 | | |
| Rural population | 249,615,968 | 100.0 | 232,896,482 | 35.4 | 201,626,492 | 27.9 | 186,601 | 0 | -2,069,722 | -1,883,121 | -0.98 | 192,635,346 | 26.4 | 182,795,279 | 25.0 | 128,204,063 | 18.2 | | |
| Christian population | 380,642,840 | 94.5 | 492,694,892 | 75.0 | 550,418,843 | 76.2 | 606,981 | 315,389 | 0 | 922,370 | 0.17 | 557,493,375 | 76.5 | 559,642,545 | 76.7 | 554,586,470 | 78.9 | | |
| Urban Christians | 134,747,565 | 35.4 | 317,893,347 | 48.4 | 396,752,193 | 54.9 | 437,523 | 227,338 | 1,501,022 | 2,165,883 | 0.55 | 409,957,862 | 56.3 | 419,291,541 | 57.5 | 453,352,442 | 64.5 | | |
| Rural Christians | 245,895,275 | 59.1 | 174,801,545 | 26.6 | 153,666,650 | 21.2 | 169,457 | 88,051 | -1,501,022 | -1,243,514 | -0.90 | 147,535,513 | 20.2 | 140,351,004 | 19.2 | 101,234,028 | 14.4 | | |
| **LATIN AMERICA** | | | | | | | | | | | | | | | | | | | |
| Population | 65,141,790 | 100.0 | 284,795,464 | 100.0 | 440,468,913 | 100.0 | 7,866,569 | 0 | | 7,866,569 | 1.66 | 479,949,705 | 100.0 | 519,138,048 | 100.0 | 696,648,086 | 100.0 | 420 | 52 |
| Urban population | 8,468,433 | 13.0 | 163,481,642 | 57.4 | 312,929,153 | 71.0 | 5,588,768 | 0 | 2,251,663 | 7,840,431 | 2.26 | 352,208,905 | 73.3 | 391,336,920 | 75.3 | 573,018,922 | 82.2 | | |
| Rural population | 56,673,357 | 100.0 | 121,313,822 | 42.6 | 127,539,760 | 28.9 | 2,277,800 | 0 | -2,251,663 | 26,137 | 0.02 | 127,740,800 | 26.6 | 127,801,128 | 24.6 | 123,629,164 | 17.7 | | |
| Christian population | 62,002,925 | 95.1 | 269,200,550 | 94.5 | 409,345,790 | 92.9 | 7,426,256 | -250,598 | 0 | 7,175,658 | 1.63 | 445,272,855 | 92.7 | 481,102,373 | 92.6 | 641,115,950 | 92.0 | | |
| Urban Christians | 7,068,333 | 11.4 | 154,529,666 | 54.2 | 290,817,871 | 66.0 | 5,275,950 | -178,036 | 2,159,344 | 7,257,258 | 2.23 | 326,761,457 | 68.0 | 362,664,847 | 69.8 | 527,341,678 | 75.7 | | |
| Rural Christians | 54,934,592 | 83.7 | 114,670,884 | 40.2 | 118,527,919 | 26.9 | 2,150,305 | -72,562 | -2,159,344 | -81,601 | -0.01 | 118,511,398 | 24.6 | 118,437,526 | 22.8 | 113,774,272 | 16.3 | | |
| **NORTHERN AMERICA** | | | | | | | | | | | | | | | | | | | |
| Population | 81,625,761 | 100.0 | 231,539,903 | 100.0 | 281,988,054 | 100.0 | 2,764,410 | 0 | | 2,764,410 | 0.94 | 296,761,566 | 100.0 | 309,631,093 | 100.0 | 363,611,501 | 100.0 | 292 | 43 |
| Urban population | 35,915,335 | 44.0 | 170,865,148 | 73.8 | 212,558,213 | 75.3 | 2,083,769 | 0 | 564,630 | 2,648,399 | 1.18 | 226,159,367 | 76.2 | 239,041,153 | 77.2 | 302,844,913 | 83.2 | | |
| Rural population | 45,710,426 | 100.0 | 60,674,755 | 26.2 | 69,429,841 | 24.6 | 680,640 | 0 | -564,630 | 116,010 | 0.17 | 70,602,199 | 23.7 | 70,589,940 | 22.8 | 60,766,588 | 16.7 | | |
| Christian population | 78,811,550 | 96.5 | 211,419,760 | 91.3 | 240,458,450 | 85.2 | 2,354,524 | -337,930 | 0 | 2,016,594 | 0.81 | 251,482,205 | 84.7 | 260,624,388 | 84.1 | 290,345,170 | 79.8 | | |
| Urban Christians | 32,549,170 | 41.3 | 156,017,464 | 67.3 | 181,253,843 | 64.2 | 1,774,803 | -254,726 | 558,445 | 2,078,522 | 1.05 | 191,652,366 | 64.5 | 201,207,035 | 64.9 | 241,822,818 | 66.5 | | |
| Rural Christians | 46,262,380 | 55.2 | 55,402,296 | 23.9 | 59,204,607 | 21.0 | 579,720 | -83,204 | -558,445 | -61,929 | 0.04 | 59,829,839 | 20.1 | 59,417,353 | 19.1 | 48,522,352 | 13.3 | | |
| **OCEANIA** | | | | | | | | | | | | | | | | | | | |
| Population | 6,246,980 | 100.0 | 19,309,483 | 100.0 | 26,412,220 | 100.0 | 398,221 | 0 | | 398,221 | 1.41 | 28,488,074 | 100.0 | 30,393,391 | 100.0 | 39,647,012 | 100.0 | 25 | 6 |
| Urban population | 2,623,732 | 42.0 | 13,678,312 | 70.8 | 18,642,839 | 70.5 | 281,080 | 0 | -13,044 | 268,036 | 1.35 | 20,020,674 | 70.2 | 21,322,165 | 70.1 | 29,058,578 | 73.2 | | |
| Rural population | 3,623,248 | 100.0 | 5,631,171 | 29.1 | 7,769,381 | 29.4 | 117,140 | 0 | 13,044 | 130,185 | 1.56 | 8,467,400 | 29.7 | 9,071,226 | 29.8 | 10,588,434 | 26.7 | | |
| Christian population | 4,838,150 | 77.4 | 17,845,126 | 92.4 | 22,010,352 | 83.3 | 340,036 | -30,117 | 0 | 309,919 | 1.33 | 23,641,309 | 82.9 | 25,109,520 | 82.6 | 32,010,392 | 80.7 | | |
| Urban Christians | 1,577,237 | 32.6 | 12,641,001 | 65.4 | 15,535,818 | 58.8 | 240,011 | -21,258 | -1,942 | 216,811 | 1.26 | 16,614,494 | 58.3 | 17,615,321 | 57.9 | 23,461,452 | 59.1 | | |
| Rural Christians | 3,260,913 | 44.8 | 5,204,125 | 26.9 | 6,474,534 | 24.5 | 100,024 | -8,859 | 1,942 | 93,107 | 1.47 | 7,026,815 | 24.6 | 7,494,199 | 24.6 | 8,548,940 | 21.5 | | |
| **GLOBE** | | | | | | | | | | | | | | | | | | | |
| Population | 1,619,625,741 | 100.0 | 3,696,147,648 | 100.0 | 5,266,438,468 | 100.0 | 78,860,571 | 0 | | 78,860,571 | 1.41 | 5,666,356,321 | 100.0 | 6,055,044,615 | 100.0 | 7,823,693,142 | 100.0 | 3,179 | 402 |
| Urban population | 266,463,037 | 16.5 | 1,361,010,491 | 36.8 | 2,279,710,072 | 43.3 | 29,936,241 | 0 | 30,211,373 | 60,147,614 | 2.37 | 2,571,844,003 | 45.4 | 2,881,186,706 | 47.6 | 4,618,864,273 | 59.0 | | |
| Rural population | 1,353,162,704 | 83.5 | 2,335,137,157 | 63.2 | 2,986,728,396 | 56.7 | 48,924,324 | 0 | -30,211,373 | 18,712,952 | 0.61 | 3,094,512,318 | 54.6 | 3,173,857,909 | 52.4 | 3,204,828,869 | 41.0 | | |
| Christian population | 558,131,572 | 34.5 | 1,236,373,374 | 33.5 | 1,747,459,664 | 33.2 | 22,708,646 | 2,501,439 | 0 | 25,210,085 | 1.36 | 1,877,423,023 | 33.1 | 1,999,560,438 | 33.0 | 2,616,662,052 | 33.4 | | |
| Urban Christians | 176,369,828 | 10.9 | 698,197,603 | 18.9 | 1,052,502,859 | 20.0 | 11,563,803 | 1,273,794 | 6,113,702 | 18,348,682 | 1.77 | 1,153,673,528 | 20.4 | 1,254,292,283 | 20.7 | 1,814,870,925 | 23.2 | | |
| Rural Christians | 381,761,744 | 23.6 | 538,175,771 | 14.6 | 694,956,805 | 13.2 | 11,144,837 | 1,227,645 | -6,113,702 | 6,861,397 | 0.70 | 723,749,495 | 12.8 | 745,268,155 | 12.3 | 801,791,127 | 10.2 | | |

## Table 10–11. Evangelized, unevangelized, and evangelizing populations on 6 continents, AD 1900–AD 2025.

1. *Derivation*, definitions, and methodology for enumerating evangelization are as explained in Part 23 "Evangelization" and Part 24 "Microevangelistics".
2. *Rows*. Each successive indentation below divides up the preceding category immediately above it. Thus, global population is divided below into 2 categories, Unevangelized and Evangelized; the latter is then divided into 2 categories, Evangelized non-Christians, and Christians; and so on.
3. *Columns*. The heading "%" in all cases throughout this table refers to the preceding absolute number as a percentage of its continent's population at that date, except for the last 7 lines which refer to global population.
4. *Natural*. This component of annual numerical change refers, for all 7 rows, to natural (biological plus transfer) growth.
5. *Conversion*. This component of annual numerical change refers to change of
allegiance or status from the category indicated.
6. *Total*. This column refers to the nett annual total of annual numerical change, equal to the sum of the 2 preceding columns.
7. *Rate*. Calculated as exponential growth rate from 1990-2000, p. a. Note that some percentages do not total to 100% because of rounding.

| CONTINENT | 1900 Adherents | 1900 % | mid-1970 Adherents | mid-1970 % | mid-1990 Adherents | mid-1990 % | Annual change, 1990-2000 Natural | Conversions | Total | Rate | mid-1995 Adherents | mid-1995 % | mid-2000 Adherents | mid-2000 % | 2025 Adherents | 2025 % |
|---|---|---|---|---|---|---|---|---|---|---|---|---|---|---|---|---|
| **AFRICA** | | | | | | | | | | | | | | | | |
| Total population | 107,808,260 | 100.0 | 357,040,697 | 100.0 | 614,768,549 | 100.0 | 16,967,538 | 0 | 16,967,538 | 2.47 | 696,963,168 | 100.0 | 784,445,039 | 100.0 | 1,298,310,949 | 100.0 |
| Unevangelized | 85,586,225 | 79.3 | 139,974,054 | 39.2 | 159,574,355 | 25.9 | 4,306,250 | -2,584,202 | 1,722,048 | 1.03 | 168,839,893 | 24.2 | 176,794,822 | 22.5 | 241,415,415 | 18.5 |
| Evangelized | 22,222,035 | 20.6 | 217,067,643 | 60.8 | 455,194,194 | 74.0 | 12,661,028 | 2,584,462 | 15,245,490 | 2.93 | 528,123,275 | 75.7 | 607,650,217 | 77.4 | 1,056,895,534 | 81.4 |
| Evangelized non-Christians | 12,283,447 | 11.3 | 73,249,149 | 20.5 | 178,696,255 | 29.0 | 4,726,575 | 2,145,487 | 6,872,062 | 3.31 | 210,498,141 | 30.2 | 247,418,035 | 31.5 | 423,091,564 | 32.5 |
| Christians | 9,938,588 | 9.2 | 143,818,494 | 40.2 | 276,497,939 | 44.9 | 7,934,453 | 438,975 | 8,373,428 | 2.68 | 317,625,134 | 45.5 | 360,232,182 | 45.9 | 633,803,970 | 48.8 |
| Non-evangelizing Christians | 6,807,298 | 6.3 | 113,460,524 | 31.7 | 208,468,229 | 33.9 | 6,059,637 | 34,735 | 6,094,372 | 2.60 | 239,191,349 | 34.3 | 269,411,928 | 34.3 | 464,970,540 | 35.8 |
| Evangelizing Christians | 3,131,290 | 2.9 | 30,357,970 | 8.5 | 68,029,710 | 11.0 | 1,874,816 | 404,240 | 2,279,056 | 2.93 | 78,433,785 | 11.2 | 90,820,254 | 11.5 | 168,833,430 | 13.0 |
| **ASIA** | | | | | | | | | | | | | | | | |
| Total population | 956,196,550 | 100.0 | 2,147,021,065 | 100.0 | 3,180,594,448 | 100.0 | 50,195,626 | 0 | 50,195,626 | 1.48 | 3,436,281,411 | 100.0 | 3,682,550,093 | 100.0 | 4,723,140,220 | 100.0 |
| Unevangelized | 781,294,400 | 81.7 | 1,455,175,150 | 67.7 | 1,472,841,080 | 46.3 | 23,976,662 | -28,878,336 | -4,901,674 | -0.34 | 1,478,527,050 | 43.0 | 1,423,824,293 | 38.6 | 1,572,484,800 | 33.2 |
| Evangelized | 174,902,150 | 18.2 | 691,845,915 | 32.2 | 1,707,753,368 | 53.6 | 26,219,041 | 28,878,259 | 55,097,300 | 2.84 | 1,957,754,361 | 56.9 | 2,258,725,800 | 61.3 | 3,150,655,420 | 66.7 |
| Evangelized non-Christians | 153,004,631 | 16.0 | 590,451,363 | 27.5 | 1,459,025,078 | 45.8 | 22,172,645 | 26,512,539 | 48,685,184 | 2.92 | 1,675,846,216 | 48.7 | 1,945,876,370 | 52.8 | 2,685,855,320 | 56.8 |
| Christians | 21,897,519 | 2.2 | 101,394,552 | 4.7 | 248,728,290 | 7.8 | 4,046,396 | 2,365,720 | 6,412,116 | 2.32 | 281,908,145 | 8.2 | 312,849,430 | 8.5 | 464,800,100 | 9.8 |
| Non-evangelizing Christians | 11,367,554 | 1.1 | 58,553,882 | 2.7 | 91,591,910 | 2.8 | 1,844,444 | 1,092,273 | 2,936,717 | 2.82 | 108,767,650 | 3.1 | 120,959,085 | 3.2 | 171,960,840 | 3.6 |
| Evangelizing Christians | 10,529,965 | 1.1 | 42,840,670 | 2.0 | 157,136,380 | 4.9 | 2,201,952 | 1,273,447 | 3,475,399 | 2.02 | 173,140,495 | 5.0 | 191,890,345 | 5.2 | 292,839,260 | 6.2 |
| **EUROPE** | | | | | | | | | | | | | | | | |
| Total population | 402,606,400 | 100.0 | 656,441,036 | 100.0 | 722,206,284 | 100.0 | 668,096 | 0 | 668,096 | 0.09 | 727,912,397 | 100.0 | 728,886,951 | 100.0 | 702,335,374 | 100.0 |
| Unevangelized | 9,756,171 | 2.4 | 39,724,130 | 6.0 | 26,444,795 | 3.6 | -5,200 | -491,862 | -497,062 | -2.06 | 23,820,585 | 3.2 | 21,474,187 | 2.9 | 19,454,895 | 2.7 |
| Evangelized | 392,850,229 | 97.5 | 616,716,906 | 93.9 | 695,761,489 | 96.3 | 673,590 | 491,568 | 1,165,158 | 0.17 | 704,091,812 | 96.7 | 707,412,764 | 97.0 | 682,880,479 | 97.2 |
| Evangelized non-Christians | 12,207,389 | 3.0 | 124,022,014 | 18.8 | 145,342,646 | 20.1 | 66,609 | 176,179 | 242,788 | 0.17 | 146,598,437 | 20.1 | 147,770,219 | 20.2 | 128,294,009 | 18.2 |
| Christians | 380,642,840 | 94.5 | 492,694,892 | 75.0 | 550,418,843 | 76.2 | 606,981 | 315,389 | 922,370 | 0.17 | 557,493,375 | 76.5 | 559,642,545 | 76.7 | 554,586,470 | 78.9 |
| Non-evangelizing Christians | 330,875,350 | 82.1 | 364,217,912 | 55.4 | 365,120,873 | 50.5 | 301,238 | -95,279 | 205,959 | 0.06 | 367,781,375 | 50.5 | 367,180,480 | 50.3 | 356,181,750 | 50.7 |
| Evangelizing Christians | 49,767,490 | 12.3 | 128,476,980 | 19.5 | 185,297,970 | 25.6 | 305,743 | 410,668 | 716,411 | 0.38 | 189,712,000 | 26.0 | 192,462,065 | 26.4 | 198,404,720 | 28.2 |
| **LATIN AMERICA** | | | | | | | | | | | | | | | | |
| Total population | 65,141,790 | 100.0 | 284,795,464 | 100.0 | 440,468,913 | 100.0 | 7,866,842 | 0 | 7,866,842 | 1.66 | 479,949,705 | 100.0 | 519,138,048 | 100.0 | 696,648,086 | 100.0 |
| Unevangelized | 1,762,315 | 2.7 | 4,906,660 | 1.7 | 2,020,630 | 0.4 | 28,229 | -35,832 | -7,603 | -0.38 | 2,000,893 | 0.4 | 1,944,600 | 0.3 | 2,544,325 | 0.3 |
| Evangelized | 63,379,475 | 97.2 | 279,888,804 | 98.2 | 438,448,283 | 99.5 | 7,838,340 | 36,105 | 7,874,445 | 1.67 | 477,948,812 | 99.5 | 517,193,448 | 99.6 | 694,103,761 | 99.6 |
| Evangelized non-Christians | 1,376,550 | 2.1 | 10,688,254 | 3.7 | 29,102,493 | 6.6 | 412,084 | 286,703 | 698,787 | 2.18 | 32,675,957 | 6.8 | 36,091,075 | 6.9 | 52,987,811 | 7.6 |
| Christians | 62,002,925 | 95.1 | 269,200,550 | 94.5 | 409,345,790 | 92.9 | 7,426,256 | -250,598 | 7,175,658 | 1.63 | 445,272,855 | 92.7 | 481,102,373 | 92.6 | 641,115,950 | 92.0 |
| Non-evangelizing Christians | 59,596,815 | 91.4 | 250,483,000 | 87.9 | 365,666,275 | 83.0 | 6,705,252 | -391,791 | 6,313,461 | 1.61 | 397,335,840 | 82.7 | 428,800,925 | 82.6 | 562,062,045 | 80.6 |
| Evangelizing Christians | 2,406,110 | 3.6 | 18,717,550 | 6.5 | 43,679,515 | 9.9 | 721,004 | 141,193 | 862,197 | 1.82 | 47,937,015 | 9.9 | 52,301,448 | 10.0 | 79,053,905 | 11.3 |
| **NORTHERN AMERICA** | | | | | | | | | | | | | | | | |
| Total population | 81,625,761 | 100.0 | 231,539,903 | 100.0 | 281,988,054 | 100.0 | 2,764,292 | 0 | 2,764,292 | 0.94 | 296,761,566 | 100.0 | 309,631,093 | 100.0 | 363,611,501 | 100.0 |
| Unevangelized | 156,300 | 0.1 | 1,131,727 | 0.4 | 4,106,052 | 1.4 | 40,639 | 26,108 | 66,747 | 1.52 | 4,472,272 | 1.5 | 4,773,514 | 1.5 | 8,625,455 | 2.3 |
| Evangelized | 81,469,461 | 99.8 | 230,408,176 | 99.5 | 277,882,002 | 98.5 | 2,723,771 | -26,226 | 2,697,545 | 0.93 | 292,289,294 | 98.4 | 304,857,579 | 98.4 | 354,986,046 | 97.6 |
| Evangelized non-Christians | 2,657,911 | 3.2 | 18,998,416 | 8.2 | 37,423,552 | 13.2 | 369,247 | 311,704 | 680,951 | 1.69 | 40,807,089 | 13.7 | 44,233,191 | 14.2 | 64,640,876 | 17.7 |
| Christians | 78,811,550 | 96.5 | 211,419,760 | 91.3 | 240,458,450 | 85.2 | 2,354,524 | -337,930 | 2,016,594 | 0.81 | 251,482,205 | 84.7 | 260,624,388 | 84.1 | 290,345,170 | 79.8 |
| Non-evangelizing Christians | 67,249,280 | 82.3 | 159,084,640 | 68.7 | 141,801,200 | 50.2 | 1,384,137 | -631,117 | 753,020 | 0.52 | 146,153,225 | 49.2 | 149,331,404 | 48.2 | 153,931,950 | 42.3 |
| Evangelizing Christians | 11,562,270 | 14.1 | 52,335,120 | 22.6 | 98,657,250 | 34.9 | 970,387 | 293,187 | 1,263,574 | 1.21 | 105,328,980 | 35.4 | 111,292,984 | 35.9 | 136,413,220 | 37.5 |
| **OCEANIA** | | | | | | | | | | | | | | | | |
| Total population | 6,246,980 | 100.0 | 19,309,483 | 100.0 | 26,412,220 | 100.0 | 398,162 | 0 | 398,162 | 1.41 | 28,488,074 | 100.0 | 30,393,391 | 100.0 | 39,647,012 | 100.0 |
| Unevangelized | 1,116,325 | 17.8 | 334,390 | 1.7 | 483,818 | 1.8 | 7,327 | 621 | 7,948 | 1.53 | 543,904 | 1.9 | 563,298 | 1.8 | 880,428 | 2.2 |
| Evangelized | 5,130,655 | 82.1 | 18,975,093 | 98.2 | 25,928,402 | 98.1 | 390,894 | -680 | 390,214 | 1.41 | 27,944,170 | 98.0 | 29,830,093 | 98.1 | 38,766,584 | 97.7 |
| Evangelized non-Christians | 292,505 | 4.6 | 1,129,967 | 5.8 | 3,918,050 | 14.8 | 50,858 | 29,437 | 80,295 | 1.88 | 4,302,861 | 15.1 | 4,720,573 | 15.5 | 6,756,192 | 17.0 |
| Christians | 4,838,150 | 77.4 | 17,845,126 | 92.4 | 22,010,352 | 83.3 | 340,036 | -30,117 | 309,919 | 1.33 | 23,641,309 | 82.9 | 25,109,520 | 82.6 | 32,010,392 | 80.7 |
| Non-evangelizing Christians | 4,304,175 | 68.9 | 13,420,931 | 69.5 | 14,145,216 | 53.5 | 233,913 | -42,872 | 191,041 | 1.27 | 15,129,965 | 53.1 | 16,055,629 | 52.8 | 19,976,032 | 50.3 |
| Evangelizing Christians | 533,975 | 8.5 | 4,424,195 | 22.9 | 7,865,136 | 29.7 | 106,123 | 12,755 | 118,878 | 1.42 | 8,511,344 | 29.8 | 9,053,891 | 29.7 | 12,034,360 | 30.3 |
| **GLOBE** | | | | | | | | | | | | | | | | |
| Total population | 1,619,625,741 | 100.0 | 3,696,147,648 | 100.0 | 5,266,438,468 | 100.0 | 78,860,556 | 0 | 78,860,556 | 1.41 | 5,666,356,321 | 100.0 | 6,055,044,615 | 100.0 | 7,823,693,142 | 100.0 |
| Unevangelized | 879,671,736 | 54.3 | 1,641,245,111 | 44.4 | 1,665,470,730 | 31.6 | 28,353,907 | -31,963,503 | -3,609,596 | -0.22 | 1,678,204,597 | 29.6 | 1,629,374,714 | 26.9 | 1,845,405,318 | 23.5 |
| Evangelized | 739,954,005 | 45.6 | 2,054,902,537 | 55.6 | 3,600,967,738 | 68.3 | 50,506,664 | 31,963,488 | 82,470,152 | 2.08 | 3,988,151,724 | 70.3 | 4,425,669,901 | 73.0 | 5,978,287,824 | 76.4 |
| Evangelized non-Christians | 181,822,433 | 11.2 | 818,529,163 | 22.1 | 1,853,508,074 | 35.1 | 27,798,018 | 29,462,049 | 57,260,067 | 2.73 | 2,110,728,701 | 37.2 | 2,426,109,463 | 40.0 | 3,361,625,772 | 42.9 |
| Christians | 558,131,572 | 34.4 | 1,236,373,374 | 33.4 | 1,747,459,664 | 33.1 | 22,708,646 | 2,501,439 | 25,210,085 | 1.36 | 1,877,423,023 | 33.1 | 1,999,560,438 | 33.0 | 2,616,662,052 | 33.4 |
| Non-evangelizing Christians | 480,200,472 | 29.6 | 959,220,889 | 25.9 | 1,186,793,703 | 22.5 | 16,528,621 | -34,051 | 16,494,570 | 1.31 | 1,274,359,404 | 22.4 | 1,351,739,451 | 22.3 | 1,729,083,157 | 22.1 |
| Evangelizing Christians | 77,931,100 | 4.8 | 277,152,485 | 7.5 | 560,665,961 | 10.6 | 6,180,025 | 2,535,490 | 8,715,515 | 1.46 | 603,063,619 | 10.6 | 647,820,987 | 10.7 | 887,578,895 | 11.3 |

## Table 10–12. Literate and nonliterate Christians and populations on 6 continents, AD 1900–AD 2025.

1. Literacy is measured as the number of literates in the adult population (over 15 years).
2. All percentages in this table are %s of the relevant continent's adult population, except the last 6 lines which give percentages of the world's adult population; and except also the column 'Rate' which gives annual increase as percentage per year.

| | 1900 | | mid–1970 | | mid–1990 | | Annual change, 1990–2000 | | 1995 | | 2000 | | 2025 | |
|---|---|---|---|---|---|---|---|---|---|---|---|---|---|---|
| | Adherents | % | Adherents | % | Adherents | % | Total | Rate | Adherents | % | Adherents | % | Adherents | % |
| **AFRICA** | | | | | | | | | | | | | | |
| Adult population | 61,935,000 | 100.0 | 197,282,000 | 100.0 | 342,113,000 | 100.0 | 10,916,000 | 2.8 | 393,238,000 | 100.0 | 451,270,000 | 100.0 | 849,733,000 | 100.0 |
| Literates | 2,292,000 | 3.7 | 55,831,000 | 28.3 | 153,327,000 | 44.8 | 10,119,000 | 5.2 | 197,705,000 | 50.3 | 254,516,000 | 56.4 | 594,813,000 | 70.0 |
| Nonliterates | 59,643,000 | 96.3 | 141,452,000 | 71.7 | 188,786,000 | 55.2 | 797,000 | 0.4 | 195,532,000 | 49.7 | 196,754,000 | 43.6 | 254,920,000 | 30.0 |
| Adult Christians | 5,710,000 | 9.2 | 79,467,000 | 40.3 | 153,869,000 | 45.0 | 5,336,000 | 3.0 | 179,209,000 | 45.6 | 207,232,000 | 45.9 | 414,819,000 | 48.8 |
| Literate Christians | 1,142,000 | 1.8 | 37,349,000 | 18.9 | 87,452,000 | 25.6 | 4,207,000 | 4.0 | 106,809,000 | 27.2 | 129,520,000 | 28.7 | 331,855,000 | 39.1 |
| Nonliterate Christians | 4,568,000 | 7.4 | 42,117,000 | 21.3 | 66,417,000 | 19.4 | 1,130,000 | 1.6 | 72,400,000 | 18.4 | 77,712,000 | 17.2 | 82,964,000 | 9.8 |
| **ASIA** | | | | | | | | | | | | | | |
| Adult population | 611,741,000 | 100.0 | 1,280,579,000 | 100.0 | 2,124,538,000 | 100.0 | 45,514,000 | 2.0 | 2,343,758,000 | 100.0 | 2,579,677,000 | 100.0 | 3,677,080,000 | 100.0 |
| Literates | 47,716,000 | 7.8 | 650,534,000 | 50.8 | 1,363,042,000 | 64.2 | 49,691,000 | 3.2 | 1,594,053,000 | 68.0 | 1,859,947,000 | 72.1 | 3,088,748,000 | 84.0 |
| Nonliterates | 564,025,000 | 92.2 | 630,045,000 | 49.2 | 761,496,000 | 35.8 | -4,177,000 | -0.6 | 749,705,000 | 32.0 | 719,730,000 | 27.9 | 588,333,000 | 16.0 |
| Adult Christians | 14,009,000 | 2.3 | 60,476,000 | 4.7 | 166,143,000 | 7.8 | 5,301,000 | 2.8 | 192,279,000 | 8.2 | 219,155,000 | 8.5 | 361,858,000 | 9.8 |
| Literate Christians | 10,507,000 | 1.7 | 47,474,000 | 3.7 | 132,078,000 | 6.2 | 4,325,000 | 2.9 | 153,339,000 | 6.5 | 175,324,000 | 6.8 | 318,435,000 | 8.7 |
| Nonliterate Christians | 3,502,000 | 0.6 | 13,002,000 | 1.0 | 34,065,000 | 1.6 | 977,000 | 2.6 | 38,940,000 | 1.7 | 43,831,000 | 1.7 | 43,423,000 | 1.2 |
| **EUROPE** | | | | | | | | | | | | | | |
| Adult population | 297,658,000 | 100.0 | 490,087,000 | 100.0 | 574,617,000 | 100.0 | 2,692,000 | 0.5 | 588,442,000 | 100.0 | 601,533,000 | 100.0 | 599,111,000 | 100.0 |
| Literates | 214,611,000 | 72.1 | 473,914,000 | 96.7 | 557,569,000 | 97.0 | 2,712,000 | 0.5 | 571,474,000 | 97.1 | 584,691,000 | 97.2 | 577,543,000 | 96.4 |
| Nonliterates | 83,047,000 | 27.9 | 16,173,000 | 3.3 | 17,049,000 | 3.0 | -21,000 | -0.1 | 16,968,000 | 2.9 | 16,843,000 | 2.8 | 21,568,000 | 3.6 |
| Adult Christians | 281,420,000 | 94.5 | 367,837,000 | 75.1 | 437,936,000 | 76.2 | 2,392,000 | 0.5 | 450,676,000 | 76.6 | 461,860,000 | 76.8 | 473,077,000 | 79.0 |
| Literate Christians | 203,467,000 | 68.4 | 363,791,000 | 74.2 | 428,435,000 | 74.6 | 2,096,000 | 0.5 | 439,701,000 | 74.7 | 449,390,000 | 74.7 | 456,519,000 | 76.2 |
| Nonliterate Christians | 77,953,000 | 26.2 | 4,046,000 | 0.8 | 9,501,000 | 1.7 | 297,000 | 2.8 | 10,975,000 | 1.9 | 12,470,000 | 2.1 | 16,558,000 | 2.8 |
| **LATIN AMERICA** | | | | | | | | | | | | | | |
| Adult population | 38,908,000 | 100.0 | 163,995,000 | 100.0 | 281,961,000 | 115.2 | 7,350,000 | 2.3 | 318,067,000 | 100.0 | 355,460,000 | 100.0 | 531,967,000 | 100.0 |
| Literates | 10,544,000 | 27.1 | 120,208,000 | 73.3 | 230,799,000 | 97.0 | 7,667,000 | 2.9 | 267,639,000 | 84.1 | 307,473,000 | 86.5 | 478,770,000 | 90.0 |
| Nonliterates | 28,364,000 | 72.9 | 43,787,000 | 26.7 | 51,162,000 | 18.1 | -317,000 | -0.6 | 50,428,000 | 15.9 | 47,987,000 | 13.5 | 53,197,000 | 10.0 |
| Adult Christians | 37,034,000 | 95.2 | 155,014,000 | 94.5 | 262,038,000 | 92.9 | 6,738,000 | 2.3 | 295,087,000 | 92.8 | 329,416,000 | 92.7 | 489,562,000 | 92.0 |
| Literate Christians | 10,147,000 | 26.1 | 116,416,000 | 71.0 | 216,066,000 | 76.6 | 6,855,000 | 2.8 | 249,068,000 | 78.3 | 284,616,000 | 80.1 | 440,606,000 | 82.8 |
| Nonliterate Christians | 26,886,000 | 69.1 | 38,599,000 | 23.5 | 45,972,000 | 16.3 | -117,000 | -0.3 | 46,019,000 | 14.5 | 44,801,000 | 12.6 | 48,956,000 | 9.2 |
| **NORTHERN AMERICA** | | | | | | | | | | | | | | |
| Adult population | 59,446,000 | 100.0 | 165,500,000 | 100.0 | 220,526,000 | 100.0 | 2,341,000 | 1.0 | 231,577,000 | 100.0 | 243,938,000 | 100.0 | 297,899,000 | 100.0 |
| Literates | 52,848,000 | 88.9 | 162,852,000 | 98.4 | 212,862,000 | 96.5 | 2,034,000 | 0.9 | 222,455,000 | 96.1 | 233,204,000 | 95.6 | 277,046,000 | 93.0 |
| Nonliterates | 6,599,000 | 11.1 | 2,648,000 | 1.6 | 7,665,000 | 3.5 | 307,000 | 3.4 | 9,122,000 | 3.9 | 10,733,000 | 4.4 | 20,853,000 | 7.0 |
| Adult Christians | 57,397,000 | 96.6 | 151,119,000 | 91.3 | 188,049,000 | 85.3 | 1,728,000 | 0.9 | 196,243,000 | 84.7 | 205,329,000 | 84.2 | 237,873,000 | 79.9 |
| Literate Christians | 52,001,000 | 87.5 | 149,457,000 | 90.3 | 181,820,000 | 82.4 | 1,447,000 | 0.8 | 188,673,000 | 81.5 | 196,294,000 | 80.5 | 221,222,000 | 74.3 |
| Nonliterate Christians | 5,395,000 | 9.1 | 1,662,000 | 1.0 | 6,229,000 | 2.8 | 281,000 | 3.8 | 7,571,000 | 3.3 | 9,034,000 | 3.7 | 16,651,000 | 5.6 |
| **OCEANIA** | | | | | | | | | | | | | | |
| Adult population | 4,370,000 | 100.0 | 13,099,000 | 100.0 | 19,498,000 | 100.0 | 327,000 | 1.6 | 21,133,000 | 100.0 | 22,766,000 | 100.0 | 31,282,000 | 100.0 |
| Literates | 2,194,000 | 50.2 | 11,855,000 | 90.5 | 18,162,000 | 93.1 | 335,000 | 1.7 | 19,828,000 | 93.8 | 21,513,000 | 94.5 | 29,718,000 | 95.0 |
| Nonliterates | 2,176,000 | 49.8 | 1,244,000 | 9.5 | 1,336,000 | 6.9 | -8,000 | -0.6 | 1,306,000 | 6.2 | 1,252,000 | 5.5 | 1,564,000 | 5.0 |
| Adult Christians | 3,384,000 | 77.4 | 12,106,000 | 92.4 | 16,249,000 | 83.3 | 256,000 | 1.5 | 17,538,000 | 83.0 | 18,808,000 | 82.6 | 25,256,000 | 80.7 |
| Literate Christians | 2,091,000 | 47.8 | 11,416,000 | 87.2 | 15,344,000 | 78.7 | 243,000 | 1.5 | 16,567,000 | 78.4 | 17,773,000 | 78.1 | 23,994,000 | 76.7 |
| Nonliterate Christians | 1,293,000 | 29.6 | 690,000 | 5.3 | 905,000 | 4.6 | 13,000 | 1.3 | 970,000 | 4.6 | 1,034,000 | 4.5 | 1,263,000 | 4.0 |
| **WORLD GLOBE** | | | | | | | | | | | | | | |
| Adult population | 1,074,058,000 | 100.0 | 2,310,543,000 | 100.0 | 3,563,254,000 | 100.0 | 69,139,000 | 1.8 | 3,896,215,000 | 100.0 | 4,254,644,000 | 100.0 | 5,987,071,000 | 100.0 |
| Literates | 330,204,000 | 30.7 | 1,475,194,000 | 63.8 | 2,535,761,000 | 71.2 | 72,558,000 | 2.5 | 2,873,155,000 | 73.7 | 3,261,345,000 | 76.7 | 5,046,637,000 | 84.3 |
| Nonliterates | 743,854,000 | 69.3 | 835,348,000 | 36.2 | 1,027,493,000 | 28.8 | -3,419,000 | -0.3 | 1,023,060,000 | 26.3 | 993,299,000 | 23.3 | 940,434,000 | 15.7 |
| Adult Christians | 398,953,000 | 37.1 | 826,019,000 | 35.7 | 1,224,283,000 | 34.4 | 21,752,000 | 1.6 | 1,331,032,000 | 34.2 | 1,441,800,000 | 33.9 | 2,002,446,000 | 33.4 |
| Literate Christians | 279,355,000 | 26.0 | 725,902,000 | 31.4 | 1,061,195,000 | 29.8 | 19,172,000 | 1.7 | 1,154,157,000 | 29.6 | 1,252,917,000 | 29.4 | 1,792,631,000 | 29.9 |
| Nonliterate Christians | 119,598,000 | 11.1 | 100,117,000 | 4.3 | 163,088,000 | 4.6 | 2,579,000 | 1.5 | 176,874,000 | 4.5 | 188,883,000 | 4.4 | 209,815,000 | 3.5 |

## Table 10–13. World population and Christians by state attitude to religion, AD 1900–AD 2000.

| | State religion or philosophy | year Code | 1900 adherents | % | Countries | mid-1970 adherents | % | Countries | mid-1990 adherents | % | Countries | mid-2000 adherents | % | Countries |
|---|---|---|---|---|---|---|---|---|---|---|---|---|---|---|
| 1. | GLOBAL POPULATION | | | | | | | | | | | | | |
| | Atheistic | A | 0 | 0.0 | 0 | 1,185,969,946 | 32.0 | 33 | 1,644,200,985 | 31.2 | 31 | 1,701,043,125 | 28.0 | 23 |
| | Secular | S | 436,251,210 | 26.9 | 76 | 1,315,150,405 | 35.5 | 91 | 2,005,292,272 | 38.0 | 99 | 2,396,865,408 | 39.5 | 102 |
| | Religious | R | 1,183,374,531 | 73.0 | 161 | 1,195,027,797 | 32.3 | 114 | 1,616,948,511 | 30.7 | 108 | 1,957,140,582 | 32.3 | 113 |
| | Adventist | RD | 150 | 0.0 | 1 | 90 | 0.0 | 1 | 66 | 0.0 | 1 | 47 | 0.0 | 1 |
| | Anglican | RA | 38,492,761 | 2.3 | 7 | 56,275,789 | 1.5 | 7 | 58,033,064 | 1.1 | 5 | 59,375,046 | 0.9 | 5 |
| | Buddhist | RB | 14,441,400 | 0.8 | 6 | 58,968,576 | 1.6 | 5 | 74,337,208 | 1.4 | 3 | 82,350,273 | 1.3 | 3 |
| | Confucian | RG | 487,198,000 | 30.0 | 4 | 0 | 0.0 | 0 | 0 | 0.0 | 0 | 0 | 0.0 | 0 |
| | Hindu | RH | 4,430,000 | 0.2 | 1 | 11,326,500 | 0.3 | 1 | 18,771,878 | 0.3 | 1 | 23,930,490 | 0.4 | 1 |
| | Islamic | RI | 73,295,000 | 4.5 | 29 | 328,355,521 | 8.8 | 27 | 545,962,121 | 10.3 | 29 | 713,757,507 | 11.7 | 32 |
| | Jewish | RJ | 0 | 0.0 | 0 | 13,622,581 | 0.3 | 1 | 3,767,295 | 0.0 | 1 | 5,121,683 | 0.0 | 1 |
| | Lutheran | RL | 9,911,700 | 0.6 | 7 | 17,138,293 | 0.4 | 7 | 18,297,354 | 0.3 | 7 | 19,048,036 | 0.3 | 7 |
| | Methodist | RM | 20,000 | 0.0 | 1 | 81,750 | 0.0 | 1 | 95,758 | 0.0 | 1 | 98,546 | 0.0 | 1 |
| | Orthodox | RO | 147,172,150 | 9.0 | 20 | 39,558,789 | 1.0 | 4 | 73,847,150 | 1.4 | 6 | 88,213,664 | 1.4 | 8 |
| | Reformed | RR | 38,920,000 | 2.4 | 2 | 0 | 0.0 | 0 | 0 | 0.0 | 0 | 0 | 0.0 | 0 |
| | Roman Catholic | RC | 124,193,040 | 7.6 | 36 | 217,498,277 | 5.8 | 30 | 269,992,302 | 5.1 | 25 | 314,246,814 | 5.1 | 26 |
| | Shinto | RS | 44,825,000 | 2.7 | 1 | 0 | 0.0 | 0 | 0 | 0.0 | 0 | 0 | 0.0 | 0 |
| | Tribal | RT | 6,650,000 | 0.4 | 7 | 0 | 0.0 | 0 | 0 | 0.0 | 0 | 0 | 0.0 | 0 |
| | Christian (unspecified) | RX | 3,055,800 | 0.1 | 3 | 6,135,671 | 0.1 | 3 | 7,874,790 | 0.1 | 4 | 8,700,234 | 0.1 | 4 |
| | Religious (unspecified) | R | 190,769,530 | 11.7 | 36 | 446,065,960 | 12.0 | 27 | 545,969,525 | 10.3 | 25 | 642,298,242 | 10.6 | 24 |
| | Global population | | 1,619,625,741 | 100.0 | 238 | 3,696,148,148 | 100.0 | 238 | 5,266,441,768 | 100.0 | 238 | 6,055,049,115 | 100.0 | 238 |
| 2. | GLOBAL CHRISTIANITY | | | | | | | | | | | | | |
| | Atheistic | A | 0 | 0.0 | 0 | 177,755,785 | 15.7 | 33 | 299,710,464 | 18.2 | 31 | 297,944,214 | 15.7 | 23 |
| | Secular | S | 85,629,144 | 16.4 | 76 | 369,943,251 | 32.7 | 91 | 621,382,270 | 37.7 | 99 | 750,435,138 | 39.7 | 102 |
| | Religious | R | 436,013,916 | 83.5 | 161 | 582,406,597 | 51.5 | 114 | 724,479,977 | 44.0 | 108 | 840,059,941 | 44.4 | 113 |
| | Adventist | RD | 150 | 0.0 | 1 | 90 | 0.0 | 1 | 62 | 0.0 | 1 | 42 | 0.0 | 1 |
| | Anglican | RA | 36,478,990 | 6.9 | 7 | 44,465,936 | 3.9 | 7 | 39,577,460 | 2.4 | 5 | 39,478,553 | 2.0 | 5 |
| | Buddhist | RB | 459,869 | 0.0 | 6 | 1,513,582 | 0.1 | 5 | 2,744,030 | 0.1 | 3 | 3,109,936 | 0.1 | 3 |
| | Confucian | RG | 1,573,750 | 0.3 | 4 | 0 | 0.0 | 0 | 0 | 0.0 | 0 | 0 | 0.0 | 0 |
| | Hindu | RH | 0 | 0.0 | 1 | 7,450 | 0.0 | 1 | 373,500 | 0.0 | 1 | 576,061 | 0.0 | 1 |
| | Islamic | RI | 7,069,255 | 1.3 | 29 | 16,781,474 | 1.4 | 27 | 21,794,885 | 1.3 | 29 | 28,074,207 | 1.4 | 32 |
| | Jewish | RJ | 0 | 0.0 | 0 | 4,020 | 0.0 | 1 | 211,600 | 0.0 | 1 | 294,078 | 0.0 | 1 |
| | Lutheran | RL | 9,817,250 | 1.8 | 7 | 14,859,001 | 1.3 | 7 | 14,889,620 | 0.9 | 7 | 15,298,676 | 0.8 | 7 |
| | Methodist | RM | 19,920 | 0.0 | 1 | 80,125 | 0.0 | 1 | 89,020 | 0.0 | 1 | 89,688 | 0.0 | 1 |
| | Orthodox | RO | 113,138,250 | 21.6 | 20 | 21,552,498 | 1.9 | 4 | 59,197,980 | 3.6 | 6 | 70,099,257 | 3.7 | 8 |
| | Reformed | RR | 549,150 | 0.1 | 2 | 0 | 0.0 | 0 | 0 | 0.0 | 0 | 0 | 0.0 | 0 |
| | Roman Catholic | RC | 105,890,940 | 20.3 | 36 | 194,025,666 | 17.1 | 30 | 248,597,790 | 15.1 | 25 | 284,127,278 | 15.0 | 26 |
| | Shinto | RS | 177,090 | 0.0 | 1 | 0 | 0.0 | 0 | 0 | 0.0 | 0 | 0 | 0.0 | 0 |
| | Tribal | RT | 7,164 | 0.0 | 7 | 0 | 0.0 | 0 | 0 | 0.0 | 0 | 0 | 0.0 | 0 |
| | Christian (unspecified) | RX | 2,738,000 | 0.5 | 3 | 4,852,473 | 0.4 | 3 | 5,399,570 | 0.3 | 4 | 5,850,694 | 0.3 | 4 |
| | Religious (unspecified) | R | 158,094,138 | 30.3 | 36 | 284,264,282 | 25.1 | 27 | 331,604,460 | 20.1 | 25 | 393,061,471 | 20.8 | 24 |
| | Global Christianity | | 521,643,060 | 100.0 | 238 | 1,130,105,633 | 100.0 | 238 | 1,645,572,711 | 100.0 | 238 | 1,888,439,293 | 100.0 | 238 |

Part 11

# LISTINGS

Global Top Ten lists on 145 major missiometric categories

*List the names of all the men twenty years or older.*
—Numbers 1:2-3, Good News Bible, and New Living Translation

*This is the list of the descendants of Adam...This is the list of
the ancestors of Jesus Christ.*
—Genesis 5:1, Matthew 1:1, Good News Bible

'Top Ten' listings have become very useful communication and information tools in many walks of life. Part 11 offers 145 such statistical lists for a whole range of missiometric subjects measured by churches and missions.

# Global Top Ten lists on 145 major missiometric categories

A book of lists is a unique and effective tool for organizing and presenting information. Used by both the researcher and the communicator, lists present data in a way that joins simplicity and directness with the potential for instructive discoveries and surprises. They can be lively and engaging, and at the same time stimulate serious study in basic research questions of interest to scholars. Lists provide perspective on a wide range of knowledge, and, in the present case, on the phenomena of global Christianity.

The 145 lists in this section are each global in scope. Each pertain to Christianity or religion. A few provide context by referring only to secular matters in their title (e.g. 'The ten largest cities in the world'), but the vast majority provide information of special

interest to readers of the present volume. Included lists do not touch upon all matters of interest to Christians, but are chosen with an emphasis on world evangelization and the global reach of Christianity. Thus this Part does not duplicate other Christian books of lists such as *The book of Bible lists*, for example. This is different also from works such as *The Christian almanac* which seek to present information of general interest without subjecting it to the particular discipline of list-making; in almanacs, some data is presented in list format, much is not.

In every case, the following lists are based on firm, quantifiable criteria. All of these lists are derived from data in the *World Christian database*, which are represented in various sections of this volume. In most

cases, the data refer to AD 2000 unless otherwise indicated.

The lists are organized in categories, noted in their headings. The number and name of each list is then presented. With many lists there are more than one column of information. From them the reader can deduce the objective, statistical criteria on which the list is based.

The lists draw very much from many other Parts of this volume and *WCE*, thus providing highlights (though not a summary; for that see Part 1 "GeoStatus") of the facts and findings presented. The rationale and methodology for the data and databases are found in the Part from which the 'Top Ten' list is derived.

## MARTYRS

**List 1. Largest martyrdom situations**

| | Situation | Martyrs |
|---|---|---|
| 1. | 1921-1950, Christians die in Soviet prison camps | 15,000,000 |
| 2. | 1950-80, Christians die in Soviet prison camps | 5,000,000 |
| 3. | 1214, Genghiz Khan massacres 6 million Christians | 4,000,000 |
| 4. | 1358, Tamerlane destroys 15-million-strong Nestorians | 4,000,000 |
| 5. | 1929-37, 14.5 million Orthodox killed by Stalin | 2,700,000 |
| 6. | 1560, Conquistadors kill 15 million Amerindians | 2,000,000 |
| 7. | 1925, Soviets attempt to liquidate Roman Catholics | 1,200,000 |
| 8. | 1258, Baghdad captured in massacre by Hulaku Khan | 1,100,000 |
| 9. | 1214, Diocese of Herat sacked by Genghiz Khan | 1,000,000 |
| 10. | 1939, Nazis execute thousands in death camps | 1,000,000 |

**List 2. Most severe martyrdom situations**

| | Situation | M% |
|---|---|---|
| 1. | 1630, all 400 Tibetan Christians wiped out. | 100.00% |
| 2. | 1938, Nazis exterminate 500,000 Gypsies | 89.74% |
| 3. | 1975, Khmer Rouge slaughter 2 million | 88.79% |
| 4. | 1570, Huguenot corsairs murder 52 Jesuits | 86.67% |
| 5. | 1241, Mongols ravage Hungary killing Christians | 86.67% |
| 6. | 287, Martyrs of Agaunum | 83.33% |
| 7. | 1933, Assyrians (Nestorians) murdered by Iraqi troops | 80.00% |
| 8. | 1843, Turks use Kurds to massacre 20,000 Nestorians | 80.00% |
| 9. | 1970, Massacre of 40,000 Vietnamese Catholics | 76.92% |
| 10. | 1918, Turks massacre 80% of all Syrian Orthodox | 75.00% |

**List 3. Persecutors of most martyrs**

| | Persecutor | Martyrs |
|---|---|---|
| 1. | State ruling power | 55,777,000 |
| 2. | Atheists | 31,699,000 |
| 3. | Shamanists | 14,937,000 |
| 4. | Roman Catholics | 10,016,000 |
| 5. | Muslims | 9,101,000 |
| 6. | Quasireligionists | 2,711,000 |
| 7. | Buddhists | 1,811,000 |
| 8. | Hindus | 676,000 |
| 9. | Zoroastrians (Parsis) | 384,000 |
| 10. | Byzantines | 222,000 |

**List 4. Countries with most martyrs (in the past)**

| | Country | Martyrs |
|---|---|---|
| 1. | USSR | 23,260,000 |
| 2. | Uzbekistan | 4,000,000 |
| 3. | Iraq | 1,954,000 |
| 4. | Russia | 1,544,000 |
| 5. | Turkey | 1,047,000 |
| 6. | Sudan | 668,000 |
| 7. | Turkestan | 600,000 |
| 8. | Yugoslavia | 450,000 |
| 9. | Uganda | 203,000 |
| 10. | Western Empire | 200,000 |

**List 5. Traditions with most martyrs**

| | Tradition | Martyrs |
|---|---|---|
| 1. | Russian Orthodox | 21,626,000 |
| 2. | Assyrian or Nestoran (East Syrian, Messihaye) | 12,379,000 |
| 3. | Latin-rite Catholic | 11,024,000 |
| 4. | Ukrainian Orthodox | 3,500,000 |
| 5. | Armenian Orthodox (Gregorian) | 1,215,000 |
| 6. | Coptic Orthodox | 1,068,000 |
| 7. | Pentecostal (Protestant; Classical Pentecostal) | 1,021,000 |
| 8. | Messianic Jewish | 1,000,000 |
| 9. | Quasi-Christians | 1,000,000 |
| 10. | Lutheran | 987,000 |

**List 6. Centuries with most martyrs**

| | Century | Martyrs |
|---|---|---|
| 1. | 1900s | 41,323,000 |
| 2. | 1600s | 11,484,000 |
| 3. | 1200s | 7,228,000 |
| 4. | 1300s | 4,906,000 |
| 5. | 1500s | 3,418,000 |
| 6. | 300s | 2,761,000 |
| 7. | 1800s | 1,577,000 |
| 8. | 1400s | 763,000 |
| 9. | 400s | 513,000 |
| 10. | 200s | 409,000 |

## COUNTRIES

**List 7. Most populous, AD 1900**

| | Country | Population |
|---|---|---|
| 1. | China | 472,000,000 |
| 2. | India | 229,900,000 |
| 3. | USA | 75,995,000 |
| 4. | Russia | 73,758,000 |
| 5. | Japan | 44,825,000 |
| 6. | Germany | 42,138,000 |
| 7. | France | 41,000,000 |
| 8. | Indonesia | 38,800,000 |
| 9. | Britain | 38,100,000 |
| 10. | Italy | 33,000,000 |

**List 8. Most populous, AD 2000**

| | Country | Population |
|---|---|---|
| 1. | China | 1,262,557,000 |
| 2. | India | 1,013,662,000 |
| 3. | USA | 278,357,000 |
| 4. | Indonesia | 212,107,000 |
| 5. | Brazil | 170,115,000 |
| 6. | Pakistan | 156,483,000 |
| 7. | Russia | 146,934,000 |
| 8. | Bangladesh | 129,155,000 |
| 9. | Japan | 126,714,000 |
| 10. | Nigeria | 111,506,000 |

**List 9. Most populous, AD 2025**

| | Country | Population |
|---|---|---|
| 1. | China | 1,462,931,000 |
| 2. | India | 1,330,449,000 |
| 3. | USA | 325,573,000 |
| 4. | Indonesia | 273,442,000 |
| 5. | Pakistan | 263,000,000 |
| 6. | Brazil | 217,930,000 |
| 7. | Nigeria | 183,041,000 |
| 8. | Bangladesh | 178,751,000 |
| 9. | Russia | 137,933,000 |
| 10. | Mexico | 130,196,000 |

**List 10. Most ethnic peoples**

| | Country | Number of peoples |
|---|---|---|
| 1. | Papua New Guinea | 862 |
| 2. | Indonesia | 744 |
| 3. | Nigeria | 491 |
| 4. | India | 439 |
| 5. | USA | 307 |
| 6. | Cameroon | 297 |
| 7. | Mexico | 278 |
| 8. | Congo-Zaire | 260 |
| 9. | China | 254 |
| 10. | Sudan | 245 |

**List 11. Lowest HDI**

| | Country | HDI |
|---|---|---|
| 1. | Sierra Leone | 17.6 |
| 2. | Rwanda | 18.7 |
| 3. | Niger | 20.6 |
| 4. | Burkina Faso | 22.1 |
| 5. | Somalia | 22.1 |
| 6. | Afghanistan | 22.9 |
| 7. | Mali | 22.9 |
| 8. | Sahara | 24.2 |
| 9. | Ethiopia | 24.4 |
| 10. | Burundi | 24.7 |

**List 12. Highest HDI**

| | Country | HDI |
|---|---|---|
| 1. | San Marino | 96.3 |
| 2. | Canada | 96.0 |
| 3. | Holy See | 95.0 |
| 4. | France | 94.6 |
| 5. | Norway | 94.3 |
| 6. | USA | 94.2 |
| 7. | Iceland | 94.2 |
| 8. | Netherlands | 94.0 |
| 9. | Monaco | 94.0 |
| 10. | Japan | 94.0 |

**List 13. Lowest GNP per capita**

| | Country | GNP p.c. |
|---|---|---|
| 1. | Mozambique | $ 80 |
| 2. | Ethiopia | $ 100 |
| 3. | Congo-Zaire | $ 120 |
| 4. | Tanzania | $ 120 |
| 5. | Somaliland | $ 155 |
| 6. | Burundi | $ 160 |
| 7. | Malawi | $ 170 |
| 8. | Chad | $ 180 |
| 9. | Rwanda | $ 180 |
| 10. | Sierra Leone | $ 180 |

**List 14. Highest GNP per capita**

| | Country | GNP p.c. |
|---|---|---|
| 1. | Luxembourg | $ 41,210 |
| 2. | Switzerland | $ 40,630 |
| 3. | Japan | $ 39,640 |
| 4. | Liechtenstein | $ 33,000 |
| 5. | Bermuda | $ 31,870 |
| 6. | Norway | $ 31,250 |
| 7. | Denmark | $ 29,890 |
| 8. | Germany | $ 27,510 |
| 9. | USA | $ 26,980 |
| 10. | Austria | $ 26,890 |

**List 15. Most urbanized (countries over 1 million each)**

| | Country | % urban |
|---|---|---|
| 1. | Singapore | 100.00% |
| 2. | Kuwait | 97.59% |
| 3. | Belgium | 97.35% |
| 4. | Palestine | 94.56% |
| 5. | Uruguay | 91.33% |
| 6. | Israel | 91.17% |
| 7. | Lebanon | 89.74% |
| 8. | Britain | 89.48% |
| 9. | Argentina | 89.35% |
| 10. | Netherlands | 89.35% |

**List 16. Least urbanized (countries over 1 million each)**

| | Country | % urban |
|---|---|---|
| 1. | Rwanda | 6.15% |
| 2. | Bhutan | 7.14% |
| 3. | Burundi | 8.96% |
| 4. | Nepal | 11.88% |
| 5. | Uganda | 14.16% |
| 6. | Malawi | 15.35% |
| 7. | Papua New Guinea | 17.41% |
| 8. | Ethiopia | 17.65% |
| 9. | Burkina Faso | 18.46% |
| 10. | Eritrea | 18.74% |

**List 17. Most cities over 50,000**

| | Country | Cities over 50,000 |
|---|---|---|
| 1. | India | 644 |
| 2. | China | 493 |
| 3. | USA | 346 |
| 4. | Russia | 318 |
| 5. | Japan | 223 |
| 6. | Brazil | 187 |
| 7. | Germany | 150 |
| 8. | Mexico | 134 |
| 9. | France | 121 |
| 10. | Italy | 117 |

**List 18. Most blind persons**

| | Country | Blind |
|---|---|---|
| 1. | India | 9,000,000 |
| 2. | China | 2,000,000 |
| 3. | Indonesia | 1,000,000 |
| 4. | Pakistan | 900,000 |
| 5. | USA | 482,850 |
| 6. | Nigeria | 420,000 |
| 7. | Russia | 350,000 |
| 8. | Japan | 256,455 |
| 9. | Saudi Arabia | 230,000 |
| 10. | Thailand | 210,000 |

# COUNTRIES (continued)

### List 19. Most deaf persons

| Country | Deaf |
|---|---|
| 1. China | 75,234,000 |
| 2. India | 60,406,200 |
| 3. USA | 16,669,300 |
| 4. Indonesia | 12,753,900 |
| 5. Brazil | 10,152,100 |
| 6. Pakistan | 9,360,400 |
| 7. Russia | 8,771,700 |
| 8. Nigeria | 7,727,100 |
| 9. Bangladesh | 7,698,600 |
| 10. Japan | 7,585,700 |

### List 20. Most lepers

| Country | Lepers |
|---|---|
| 1. India | 5,500,000 |
| 2. China | 3,500,000 |
| 3. Nigeria | 1,000,000 |
| 4. Myanmar | 880,000 |
| 5. Congo-Zaire | 800,000 |
| 6. Bangladesh | 700,000 |
| 7. Thailand | 500,000 |
| 8. Burkina Faso | 450,000 |
| 9. Ethiopia | 400,000 |
| 10. Brazil | 280,000 |

### List 21. Most Christian income

| Country | Total Christian income |
|---|---|
| 1. USA | $ 5,175,509 million |
| 2. Germany | $ 1,617,126 million |
| 3. France | $ 1,027,512 million |
| 4. Italy | $ 892,459 million |
| 5. Britain | $ 730,293 million |
| 6. Brazil | $ 565,931 million |
| 7. Spain | $ 503,460 million |
| 8. Canada | $ 392,208 million |
| 9. Mexico | $ 311,438 million |
| 10. Argentina | $ 272,906 million |

### List 22. Least Christian income

| Country | Total Christian income |
|---|---|
| 1. Sahara | $ 100,809 |
| 2. Cocos (Keeling) Is | $ 110,700 |
| 3. Maldives | $ 354,420 |
| 4. Christmas Island | $ 442,000 |
| 5. Pitcairn Islands | $ 504,000 |
| 6. Mayotte | $ 1,119,600 |
| 7. Somaliland | $ 1,299,055 |
| 8. Mauritania | $ 3,001,960 |
| 9. Comoros | $ 3,319,140 |
| 10. Norfolk Island | $ 3,380,000 |

### List 23. Most cost effective

| Country | Cost per baptism |
|---|---|
| 1. Mozambique | $ 1,366 |
| 2. Ethiopia | $ 2,127 |
| 3. Tanzania | $ 2,495 |
| 4. Congo-Zaire | $ 2,619 |
| 5. Sierra Leone | $ 3,623 |
| 6. Nepal | $ 3,715 |
| 7. Chad | $ 3,865 |
| 8. Burundi | $ 3,986 |
| 9. Somaliland | $ 4,245 |
| 10. Cambodia | $ 4,292 |

### List 24. Least cost effective

| Country | Cost per baptism |
|---|---|
| 1. Japan | $ 2,721,000 |
| 2. Switzerland | $ 2,656,000 |
| 3. Bermuda | $ 2,507,000 |
| 4. Denmark | $ 2,337,000 |
| 5. Belgium | $ 2,202,000 |
| 6. Norway | $ 2,190,000 |
| 7. Germany | $ 2,119,000 |
| 8. France | $ 2,030,000 |
| 9. Austria | $ 1,943,000 |
| 10. Italy | $ 1,902,000 |

# RELIGIONS

### List 25. Most Christians in 1900

| Country | Christians |
|---|---|
| 1. USA | 73,270,000 |
| 2. Russia | 61,545,000 |
| 3. Germany | 41,533,000 |
| 4. France | 40,731,000 |
| 5. Britain | 37,125,000 |
| 6. Italy | 32,903,000 |
| 7. Ukraine | 28,501,000 |
| 8. Poland | 21,990,000 |
| 9. Spain | 18,797,000 |
| 10. Brazil | 17,319,000 |

### List 26. Over 99% Christian in 1900

| Country | Christians |
|---|---|
| 1. Finland | 5,176,000 |
| 2. Slovenia | 1,986,000 |
| 3. Barbados | 270,000 |
| 4. Netherlands Antilles | 217,000 |
| 5. Samoa | 180,000 |
| 6. Aruba | 103,000 |
| 7. Tonga | 99,000 |
| 8. Virgin Is of the US | 93,000 |
| 9. Kiribati | 83,000 |
| 10. Dominica | 71,000 |

### List 27. Most Christians in 2000

| Country | Christians |
|---|---|
| 1. USA | 235,742,000 |
| 2. Brazil | 155,545,000 |
| 3. Mexico | 95,169,000 |
| 4. China | 89,056,000 |
| 5. Russia | 84,308,000 |
| 6. Philippines | 68,151,000 |
| 7. India | 62,341,000 |
| 8. Germany | 62,326,000 |
| 9. Nigeria | 51,123,000 |
| 10. Congo-Zaire | 49,256,000 |

### List 28. Highest % Christians in 2000

| Country | % Christian |
|---|---|
| 1. Holy See | 100.0% |
| 2. Malta | 98.3% |
| 3. Faeroe Islands | 98.1% |
| 4. Cook Islands | 97.7% |
| 5. Wallis & Futuna Is | 97.7% |
| 6. Paraguay | 97.7% |
| 7. Guatemala | 97.7% |
| 8. Ecuador | 97.5% |
| 9. El Salvador | 97.5% |
| 10. Poland | 97.4% |

### List 29. Most Christians in 2025

| Country | Christians |
|---|---|
| 1. USA | 261,349,000 |
| 2. Brazil | 195,848,000 |
| 3. China | 135,190,000 |
| 4. Mexico | 123,979,000 |
| 5. Congo-Zaire | 100,936,000 |
| 6. India | 98,200,000 |
| 7. Philippines | 96,611,000 |
| 8. Russia | 95,791,000 |
| 9. Nigeria | 86,000,000 |
| 10. Ethiopia | 68,488,000 |

### List 30. Highest % Christians in 2025

| Country | % Christian |
|---|---|
| 1. Holy See | 100.0% |
| 2. Poland | 97.9% |
| 3. Wallis & Futuna Is | 97.7% |
| 4. Malta | 97.5% |
| 5. Paraguay | 97.4% |
| 6. Angola | 97.3% |
| 7. Guatemala | 96.9% |
| 8. Ecuador | 96.8% |
| 9. Faeroe Islands | 96.7% |
| 10. Marshall Islands | 96.6% |

### List 31. Most Muslims in 2000

| Country | Muslims |
|---|---|
| 1. Pakistan | 150,365,000 |
| 2. India | 122,570,000 |
| 3. Indonesia | 116,105,000 |
| 4. Bangladesh | 110,849,000 |
| 5. Turkey | 64,714,000 |
| 6. Iran | 64,707,000 |
| 7. Egypt | 57,780,000 |
| 8. Nigeria | 49,000,000 |
| 9. Algeria | 30,442,000 |
| 10. Morocco | 27,736,000 |

### List 32. Highest % Muslims in 2000

| Country | % Muslim |
|---|---|
| 1. Somaliland | 99.5% |
| 2. Sahara | 99.4% |
| 3. Mauritania | 99.1% |
| 4. Maldives | 99.0% |
| 5. Tunisia | 98.9% |
| 6. Yemen | 98.9% |
| 7. Somalia | 98.3% |
| 8. Morocco | 98.2% |
| 9. Afghanistan | 98.1% |
| 10. Comoros | 98.0% |

### List 33. Most Hindus in 2000

| Country | Hindus |
|---|---|
| 1. India | 755,135,000 |
| 2. Nepal | 18,354,000 |
| 3. Bangladesh | 15,995,000 |
| 4. Indonesia | 7,259,000 |
| 5. Sri Lanka | 2,124,000 |
| 6. Pakistan | 1,868,000 |
| 7. Malaysia | 1,630,000 |
| 8. USA | 1,032,000 |
| 9. South Africa | 959,000 |
| 10. Myanmar | 893,000 |

### List 34. Highest % Hindu in 2000

| Country | % Hindu |
|---|---|
| 1. Nepal | 76.7% |
| 2. India | 74.5% |
| 3. Mauritius | 43.9% |
| 4. British Indian Ocean | 38.2% |
| 5. Fiji | 33.3% |
| 6. Guyana | 32.5% |
| 7. Trinidad & Tobago | 22.7% |
| 8. Bhutan | 20.5% |
| 9. Surinam | 17.8% |
| 10. Bangladesh | 12.3% |

### List 35. Most Buddhists in 2000

| Country | Buddhists |
|---|---|
| 1. China | 105,829,000 |
| 2. Japan | 69,931,000 |
| 3. Thailand | 52,383,000 |
| 4. Viet Nam | 39,534,000 |
| 5. Myanmar | 33,145,000 |
| 6. Sri Lanka | 12,879,000 |
| 7. Cambodia | 9,462,000 |
| 8. India | 7,249,000 |
| 9. South Korea | 7,174,000 |
| 10. Taiwan | 4,686,000 |

### List 36. Highest % Buddhist in 2000

| Country | % Buddhist |
|---|---|
| 1. Thailand | 85.3% |
| 2. Cambodia | 84.7% |
| 3. Bhutan | 73.9% |
| 4. Myanmar | 72.6% |
| 5. Sri Lanka | 68.4% |
| 6. Japan | 55.1% |
| 7. Viet Nam | 49.5% |
| 8. Laos | 48.7% |
| 9. Mongolia | 22.4% |
| 10. Taiwan | 20.9% |

### List 37. Most Chinese folk-religionists in 2000

| Country | Chinese folk-religionists |
|---|---|
| 1. China | 359,618,000 |
| 2. Taiwan | 11,356,000 |
| 3. Malaysia | 5,364,000 |
| 4. Indonesia | 3,039,000 |
| 5. Singapore | 1,521,000 |
| 6. Viet Nam | 798,000 |
| 7. Canada | 775,000 |
| 8. Thailand | 530,000 |
| 9. Cambodia | 524,000 |
| 10. Japan | 149,000 |

### List 38. Highest % Chinese folk-religionists in 2000

| Country | % Chinese folk-religionists |
|---|---|
| 1. Taiwan | 50.6% |
| 2. Singapore | 42.6% |
| 3. Christmas Island | 29.8% |
| 4. China | 28.4% |
| 5. Malaysia | 24.1% |
| 6. Nauru | 10.4% |
| 7. French Polynesia | 7.8% |
| 8. Cambodia | 4.6% |
| 9. French Guiana | 3.5% |
| 10. Brunei | 3.5% |

### List 39. Most ethnoreligionists in 2000

| Country | ethnoreligionists |
|---|---|
| 1. China | 54,152,000 |
| 2. India | 34,761,000 |
| 3. Nigeria | 10,964,000 |
| 4. Mozambique | 9,909,000 |
| 5. Madagascar | 7,648,000 |
| 6. South Korea | 7,325,000 |
| 7. Ethiopia | 7,312,000 |
| 8. Viet Nam | 6,793,000 |
| 9. Myanmar | 5,749,000 |
| 10. Ivory Coast | 5,555,000 |

### List 40. Highest % ethnoreligionists in 2000

| Country | % ethnoreligionists |
|---|---|
| 1. Benin | 51.5% |
| 2. Mozambique | 50.3% |
| 3. Madagascar | 47.9% |
| 4. Guinea-Bissau | 45.2% |
| 5. Liberia | 42.9% |
| 6. Laos | 41.7% |
| 7. Sierra Leone | 40.3% |
| 8. Botswana | 38.7% |
| 9. Togo | 37.7% |
| 10. Ivory Coast | 37.5% |

### List 41. Most Jews in 2000

| Country | Jews |
|---|---|
| 1. USA | 5,621,000 |
| 2. Israel | 3,951,000 |
| 3. Russia | 951,000 |
| 4. France | 591,000 |
| 5. Argentina | 490,000 |
| 6. Canada | 403,000 |
| 7. Brazil | 357,000 |
| 8. Britain | 302,000 |
| 9. Palestine | 273,000 |
| 10. Ukraine | 220,000 |

### List 42. Highest % Jewish in 2000

| Country | % Jewish |
|---|---|
| 1. Israel | 77.1% |
| 2. Palestine | 12.3% |
| 3. USA | 2.0% |
| 4. Gibraltar | 1.9% |
| 5. Cayman Islands | 1.7% |
| 6. Monaco | 1.7% |
| 7. Argentina | 1.3% |
| 8. Canada | 1.2% |
| 9. Uruguay | 1.2% |
| 10. Moldavia | 1.1% |

### List 43. Most nonreligious in 2000

| Country | nonreligious |
|---|---|
| 1. China | 532,568,000 |
| 2. Russia | 40,410,000 |
| 3. USA | 25,078,000 |
| 4. Germany | 14,131,000 |
| 5. North Korea | 13,361,000 |
| 6. Japan | 12,906,000 |
| 7. India | 12,849,000 |
| 8. Viet Nam | 10,809,000 |
| 9. France | 9,229,000 |
| 10. Italy | 7,535,000 |

### List 44. Highest % nonreligious in 2000

| Country | % nonreligious |
|---|---|
| 1. North Korea | 55.5% |
| 2. Svalbard & Jan Mayen | 47.7% |
| 3. China | 42.1% |
| 4. Czech Republic | 31.8% |
| 5. Mongolia | 30.6% |
| 6. Cuba | 29.8% |
| 7. Kazakhstan | 29.3% |
| 8. Russia | 27.5% |
| 9. Uruguay | 26.8% |
| 10. Latvia | 26.0% |

### List 45. Most atheists in 2000

| Country | atheists |
|---|---|
| 1. China | 102,238,000 |
| 2. Russia | 7,634,000 |
| 3. Viet Nam | 5,603,000 |
| 4. North Korea | 3,745,000 |
| 5. Japan | 3,642,000 |
| 6. France | 2,381,000 |
| 7. Ukraine | 2,012,000 |
| 8. Italy | 1,965,000 |
| 9. Germany | 1,793,000 |
| 10. Kazakhstan | 1,771,000 |

## RELIGIONS (continued)

### List 46. Highest % atheist in 2000

| | Country | % Atheist |
|---|---|---|
| 1. | North Korea | 15.5% |
| 2. | Sweden | 11.8% |
| 3. | Estonia | 10.9% |
| 4. | Kazakhstan | 10.9% |
| 5. | Mongolia | 9.0% |
| 6. | Albania | 9.0% |
| 7. | China | 8.1% |
| 8. | Cuba | 7.2% |
| 9. | Viet Nam | 7.0% |
| 10. | Kirghizia | 6.2% |

### List 47. Most Roman Catholics in 2000

| | Country | Roman Catholics |
|---|---|---|
| 1. | Brazil | 153,300,000 |
| 2. | Mexico | 92,770,000 |
| 3. | Philippines | 62,570,000 |
| 4. | USA | 58,000,000 |
| 5. | Italy | 55,680,000 |
| 6. | France | 48,600,000 |
| 7. | Colombia | 40,670,000 |
| 8. | Spain | 38,080,000 |
| 9. | Poland | 35,743,000 |
| 10. | Argentina | 33,750,000 |

### List 48. Highest % Roman Catholic in 2000

| | Country | % Roman Catholic |
|---|---|---|
| 1. | Saint Pierre & Miquelon | 98.4% |
| 2. | Holy See | 98.0% |
| 3. | Cape Verde | 97.4% |
| 4. | Italy | 97.1% |
| 5. | Colombia | 96.1% |
| 6. | Spain | 96.0% |
| 7. | Wallis & Futuna Is | 96.0% |
| 8. | Peru | 95.6% |
| 9. | Guadeloupe | 95.0% |
| 10. | Malta | 94.5% |

### List 49. Most Orthodox in 2000

| | Country | Orthodox |
|---|---|---|
| 1. | Russia | 75,950,000 |
| 2. | Ukraine | 27,400,000 |
| 3. | Ethiopia | 22,838,000 |
| 4. | Romania | 19,000,000 |
| 5. | Greece | 9,900,000 |
| 6. | Egypt | 9,317,000 |
| 7. | Yugoslavia | 6,046,000 |
| 8. | Bulgaria | 5,886,000 |
| 9. | USA | 5,762,000 |
| 10. | Belorussia | 4,986,000 |

### List 50. Highest % Orthodox in 2000

| | Country | % Orthodox |
|---|---|---|
| 1. | Greece | 93.0% |
| 2. | Cyprus | 87.4% |
| 3. | Romania | 85.1% |
| 4. | Armenia | 78.2% |
| 5. | Bulgaria | 71.5% |
| 6. | Macedonia | 59.3% |
| 7. | Georgia | 58.1% |
| 8. | Yugoslavia | 56.8% |
| 9. | Ukraine | 54.3% |
| 10. | Russia | 51.6% |

### List 51. Most Protestants in 2000

| | Country | Protestants |
|---|---|---|
| 1. | USA | 64,570,000 |
| 2. | Germany | 30,420,000 |
| 3. | Brazil | 30,200,000 |
| 4. | India | 16,826,000 |
| 5. | Nigeria | 14,050,000 |
| 6. | South Africa | 12,410,000 |
| 7. | Indonesia | 12,125,000 |
| 8. | Congo-Zaire | 10,485,000 |
| 9. | South Korea | 8,870,000 |
| 10. | Ethiopia | 8,510,000 |

### List 52. Highest % Protestant in 2000

| | Country | % Protestant |
|---|---|---|
| 1. | Marshall Islands | 105.0% |
| 2. | Tuvalu | 102.4% |
| 3. | Sweden | 94.5% |
| 4. | Norway | 94.1% |
| 5. | Faeroe Islands | 90.9% |
| 6. | Finland | 89.5% |
| 7. | Pitcairn Islands | 89.3% |
| 8. | Iceland | 89.1% |
| 9. | Denmark | 87.6% |
| 10. | Cook Islands | 72.7% |

### List 53. Most Independents in 2000

| | Country | Independents |
|---|---|---|
| 1. | China | 80,708,000 |
| 2. | USA | 78,550,000 |
| 3. | India | 34,200,000 |
| 4. | Brazil | 25,500,000 |
| 5. | Nigeria | 23,975,000 |
| 6. | South Africa | 18,500,000 |
| 7. | Philippines | 14,330,000 |
| 8. | Congo-Zaire | 12,050,000 |
| 9. | Ukraine | 8,500,000 |
| 10. | Indonesia | 8,436,000 |

### List 54. Highest % Independent in 2000

| | Country | % Independent |
|---|---|---|
| 1. | South Africa | 45.8% |
| 2. | Swaziland | 45.6% |
| 3. | Zimbabwe | 40.2% |
| 4. | Botswana | 30.7% |
| 5. | USA | 28.2% |
| 6. | Chile | 25.1% |
| 7. | Congo-Zaire | 23.3% |
| 8. | Kenya | 21.9% |
| 9. | Nigeria | 21.5% |
| 10. | Palau | 21.1% |

### List 55. Most Anglicans in 2000

| | Country | Anglicans |
|---|---|---|
| 1. | Britain | 26,278,000 |
| 2. | Nigeria | 20,070,000 |
| 3. | Uganda | 8,580,000 |
| 4. | Australia | 4,060,000 |
| 5. | Kenya | 3,000,000 |
| 6. | South Africa | 2,660,000 |
| 7. | Tanzania | 2,650,000 |
| 8. | USA | 2,400,000 |
| 9. | Sudan | 2,320,000 |
| 10. | New Zealand | 825,000 |

### List 56. Highest % Anglican in 2000

| | Country | % Anglican |
|---|---|---|
| 1. | Saint Helena | 70.1% |
| 2. | Britain | 44.6% |
| 3. | Channel Islands | 44.1% |
| 4. | Isle of Man | 42.4% |
| 5. | Uganda | 39.4% |
| 6. | Solomon Islands | 38.2% |
| 7. | Bermuda | 37.4% |
| 8. | Falkland Islands | 36.5% |
| 9. | Antigua | 33.4% |
| 10. | Anguilla | 31.8% |

### List 57. Most Marginal Christians in 2000

| | Country | Marginal |
|---|---|---|
| 1. | USA | 10,080,000 |
| 2. | Mexico | 1,950,000 |
| 3. | Brazil | 1,420,000 |
| 4. | South Korea | 850,000 |
| 5. | Japan | 720,000 |
| 6. | Philippines | 670,000 |
| 7. | Nigeria | 600,000 |
| 8. | Britain | 550,000 |
| 9. | Germany | 540,000 |
| 10. | Argentina | 500,000 |

### List 58. Countries with the greatest % Marginal in 2000

| | Country | % Marginal |
|---|---|---|
| 1. | Niue Island | 23.4% |
| 2. | Tonga | 14.5% |
| 3. | American Samoa | 11.7% |
| 4. | French Polynesia | 10.6% |
| 5. | Samoa | 9.4% |
| 6. | Cook Islands | 8.4% |
| 7. | Guadeloupe | 4.3% |
| 8. | Zambia | 4.1% |
| 9. | Marshall Islands | 3.8% |
| 10. | USA | 3.6% |

### List 59. Most Great Commission Christians in 2000

| | Country | Great Commission Christians |
|---|---|---|
| 1. | USA | 98,662,000 |
| 2. | China | 81,353,000 |
| 3. | India | 50,364,000 |
| 4. | Russia | 29,373,000 |
| 5. | Germany | 26,147,000 |
| 6. | France | 24,540,000 |
| 7. | Italy | 24,221,000 |
| 8. | Brazil | 24,207,000 |
| 9. | Britain | 21,121,000 |
| 10. | Spain | 17,132,000 |

### List 60. Highest % Great Commission Christian in 2000

| | Country | % Great Commission Christians |
|---|---|---|
| 1. | San Marino | 48.6% |
| 2. | Ireland | 48.4% |
| 3. | Samoa | 47.4% |
| 4. | Holy See | 46.1% |
| 5. | Belgium | 46.0% |
| 6. | American Samoa | 44.4% |
| 7. | Malta | 43.7% |
| 8. | Spain | 43.2% |
| 9. | Liechtenstein | 43.1% |
| 10. | Italy | 42.2% |

### List 61. Most Pentecostal/Charismatics in 2000

| | Country | Pentecostal/charismatic |
|---|---|---|
| 1. | Brazil | 79,950,000 |
| 2. | USA | 75,156,000 |
| 3. | China | 54,275,000 |
| 4. | Nigeria | 35,885,000 |
| 5. | India | 33,530,000 |
| 6. | South Africa | 21,200,000 |
| 7. | Philippines | 20,050,000 |
| 8. | Congo-Zaire | 17,750,000 |
| 9. | Mexico | 13,050,000 |
| 10. | Colombia | 12,585,000 |

### List 62. Highest % Pentecostal/Charismatic in 2000

| | Country | % Pentecostal/charismatic |
|---|---|---|
| 1. | South Africa | 52.5% |
| 2. | Swaziland | 52.0% |
| 3. | Marshall Islands | 47.0% |
| 4. | Brazil | 47.0% |
| 5. | Zimbabwe | 42.2% |
| 6. | Chile | 36.4% |
| 7. | Congo-Zaire | 34.3% |
| 8. | Montserrat | 33.3% |
| 9. | Botswana | 32.9% |
| 10. | Nigeria | 32.1% |

### List 63. Highest Christian rate in 2000

| | Country | Growth rate |
|---|---|---|
| 1. | Northern Mariana Is | 6.07% |
| 2. | Cambodia | 5.09% |
| 3. | Aruba | 4.91% |
| 4. | Oman | 4.70% |
| 5. | Nepal | 4.43% |
| 6. | Kuwait | 4.42% |
| 7. | French Guiana | 4.37% |
| 8. | Jordan | 4.21% |
| 9. | Comoros | 4.13% |
| 10. | Andorra | 4.08% |

### List 64. Highest Muslim rate 2000

| | Country | Growth rate |
|---|---|---|
| 1. | Andorra | 11.26% |
| 2. | Aruba | 7.33% |
| 3. | Namibia | 5.36% |
| 4. | Czech Republic | 4.98% |
| 5. | French Guiana | 4.64% |
| 6. | Yemen | 4.57% |
| 7. | Malta | 4.53% |
| 8. | Afghanistan | 4.43% |
| 9. | Anguilla | 4.37% |
| 10. | Cape Verde | 4.27% |

### List 65. Highest Hindu rate in 2000

| | Country | Growth rate |
|---|---|---|
| 1. | Sweden | 67.99% |
| 2. | Andorra | 15.94% |
| 3. | Tonga | 12.68% |
| 4. | Anguilla | 5.45% |
| 5. | Christmas Island | 5.14% |
| 6. | French Guiana | 5.12% |
| 7. | Austria | 5.08% |
| 8. | Oman | 4.90% |
| 9. | Yemen | 4.56% |
| 10. | Costa Rica | 4.22% |

### List 66. Highest Buddhist rate in 2000

| | Country | Growth rate |
|---|---|---|
| 1. | Falkland Islands | 17.46% |
| 2. | Austria | 13.20% |
| 3. | Tuvalu | 10.84% |
| 4. | American Samoa | 8.18% |
| 5. | Vanuatu | 6.46% |
| 6. | Northern Mariana Is | 6.23% |
| 7. | Bahrain | 6.05% |
| 8. | Paraguay | 5.95% |
| 9. | Australia | 5.62% |
| 10. | Guam | 5.59% |

### List 67. Highest Jewish rate in 2000

| | Country | Growth rate |
|---|---|---|
| 1. | Germany | 7.41% |
| 2. | Palestine | 4.67% |
| 3. | Andorra | 4.62% |
| 4. | Cayman Islands | 3.17% |
| 5. | Israel | 3.12% |
| 6. | Botswana | 3.03% |
| 7. | Aruba | 2.73% |
| 8. | French Guiana | 2.71% |
| 9. | Tanzania | 2.57% |
| 10. | Nicaragua | 2.19% |

### List 68. Highest ethnoreligionist rate in 2000

| | Country | Growth rate |
|---|---|---|
| 1. | Austria | 44.97% |
| 2. | Bahrain | 11.98% |
| 3. | Saudi Arabia | 8.75% |
| 4. | Northern Mariana Is | 5.55% |
| 5. | USA | 4.50% |
| 6. | Nicaragua | 3.75% |
| 7. | Cape Verde | 3.46% |
| 8. | French Guiana | 3.36% |
| 9. | Mozambique | 3.21% |
| 10. | Mexico | 3.18% |

### List 69. Highest nonreligious rate in 2000

| | Country | Growth rate |
|---|---|---|
| 1. | Saint Vincent | 9.09% |
| 2. | Bahrain | 8.63% |
| 3. | Northern Mariana Is | 8.14% |
| 4. | Niue Island | 7.70% |
| 5. | Cayman Islands | 7.55% |
| 6. | Palau | 7.46% |
| 7. | Paraguay | 7.19% |
| 8. | French Guiana | 6.87% |
| 9. | Malta | 6.74% |
| 10. | Guatemala | 6.71% |

### List 70. Highest atheist rate in 2000

| | Country | Growth rate |
|---|---|---|
| 1. | Nicaragua | 6.86% |
| 2. | Haiti | 6.09% |
| 3. | Isle of Man | 5.66% |
| 4. | Turks & Caicos Is | 5.45% |
| 5. | Mozambique | 5.43% |
| 6. | Guinea-Bissau | 5.24% |
| 7. | French Guiana | 5.17% |
| 8. | Suriname | 4.94% |
| 9. | Aruba | 4.85% |
| 10. | Jordan | 4.49% |

### List 71. Highest Roman Catholic rate in 2000

| | Country | Growth rate |
|---|---|---|
| 1. | Nepal | 6.88% |
| 2. | Northern Mariana Is | 6.11% |
| 3. | Kuwait | 5.77% |
| 4. | Aruba | 5.17% |
| 5. | Georgia | 4.93% |
| 6. | Ethiopia | 4.86% |
| 7. | Armenia | 4.81% |
| 8. | Russia | 4.67% |
| 9. | Turks & Caicos Is | 4.56% |
| 10. | Liberia | 4.35% |

### List 72. Highest Protestant rate in 2000

| | Country | Growth rate |
|---|---|---|
| 1. | Albania | 14.87% |
| 2. | Armenia | 10.31% |
| 3. | Nepal | 6.17% |
| 4. | Andorra | 5.76% |
| 5. | Oman | 5.62% |
| 6. | Djibouti | 4.81% |
| 7. | Northern Mariana Is | 4.72% |
| 8. | Benin | 4.51% |
| 9. | Malta | 4.40% |
| 10. | Mauritania | 4.14% |

## RELIGIONS (continued)

### List 73. Highest Anglican rate in 2000

| Country | Growth rate |
|---|---|
| 1. Cameroon | 97.44% |
| 2. Madagascar | 6.98% |
| 3. Ghana | 5.24% |
| 4. Cayman Islands | 4.56% |
| 5. Honduras | 4.14% |
| 6. Swaziland | 4.01% |
| 7. Angola | 4.01% |
| 8. Solomon Islands | 3.96% |
| 9. Mozambique | 3.90% |
| 10. Zambia | 3.90% |

### List 74. Highest Independent rate in 2000

| Country | Growth rate |
|---|---|
| 1. Guadeloupe | 30.20% |
| 2. Bulgaria | 23.73% |
| 3. Cyprus | 14.87% |
| 4. Djibouti | 9.60% |
| 5. Estonia | 8.69% |
| 6. Armenia | 7.97% |
| 7. Northern Mariana Is | 7.95% |
| 8. Liechtenstein | 7.18% |
| 9. Rwanda | 6.25% |
| 10. Iran | 6.16% |

### List 75. Highest Orthodox rate in 2000

| Country | Growth rate |
|---|---|
| 1. Nepal | 5.97% |
| 2. Madagascar | 5.82% |
| 3. Malawi | 5.20% |
| 4. Oman | 5.14% |
| 5. Uganda | 4.81% |
| 6. Jordan | 4.70% |
| 7. China | 4.62% |
| 8. Botswana | 4.14% |
| 9. Saudi Arabia | 3.71% |
| 10. Yemen | 3.51% |

### List 76. Highest Marginal Christian rate in 2000

| Country | Growth rate |
|---|---|
| 1. Mauritania | 25.89% |
| 2. Armenia | 14.87% |
| 3. Saint Pierre & Miquelon | 10.31% |
| 4. Belorussia | 10.31% |
| 5. Brunei | 9.60% |
| 6. Georgia | 9.60% |
| 7. Cambodia | 7.92% |
| 8. Norfolk Island | 7.18% |
| 9. Nepal | 7.18% |
| 10. Uganda | 7.18% |

### List 77. Highest Great Commission Christian rate in 2000

| Country | Growth rate |
|---|---|
| 1. Northern Mariana Is | 6.64% |
| 2. Cameroon | 6.07% |
| 3. Aruba | 5.88% |
| 4. Guinea | 5.02% |
| 5. Togo | 4.77% |
| 6. French Guiana | 4.77% |
| 7. Nepal | 4.69% |
| 8. Jordan | 4.64% |
| 9. Oman | 4.43% |
| 10. Cambodia | 4.43% |

### List 78. Highest Evangelical rate in 2000

| Country | Growth rate |
|---|---|
| 1. Northern Mariana Is | 7.48% |
| 2. Sahara | 7.18% |
| 3. Andorra | 7.18% |
| 4. Albania | 7.18% |
| 5. Somaliland | 6.25% |
| 6. Yemen | 4.81% |
| 7. Tuvalu | 4.81% |
| 8. Afghanistan | 4.81% |
| 9. Togo | 4.70% |
| 10. Jordan | 4.60% |

### List 79. Highest Renewal rate in 2000

| Country | Growth rate |
|---|---|
| 1. Albania | 9.60% |
| 2. Maldives | 7.18% |
| 3. Northern Mariana Is | 6.80% |
| 4. Andorra | 5.76% |
| 5. Jordan | 5.61% |
| 6. French Guiana | 5.31% |
| 7. Somalia | 5.24% |
| 8. Estonia | 5.24% |
| 9. Aruba | 5.22% |
| 10. Niger | 5.18% |

### List 80. Largest in World C, AD 1900

| Country | Population |
|---|---|
| 1. USA | 75,995,000 |
| 2. Russia | 73,758,000 |
| 3. Germany | 42,138,000 |
| 4. France | 41,000,000 |
| 5. Britain | 38,100,000 |
| 6. Italy | 33,000,000 |
| 7. Ukraine | 29,333,000 |
| 8. Poland | 24,200,000 |
| 9. Spain | 18,800,000 |
| 10. Brazil | 17,984,000 |

### List 81. Largest in World B, AD 1900

| Country | Population |
|---|---|
| 1. Ethiopia | 7,560,000 |
| 2. South Africa | 4,900,000 |
| 3. Madagascar | 2,580,000 |
| 4. Bosnia-Herzegovina | 1,139,000 |
| 5. Guyana | 285,000 |
| 6. Reunion | 173,000 |
| 7. Suriname | 76,000 |
| 8. Nauru | 2,000 |
| 9. British Indian Ocean | 1,000 |
| 10. — | — |

### List 82. Largest in World A, AD 1900

| Country | Population |
|---|---|
| 1. China | 472,000,000 |
| 2. India | 229,900,000 |
| 3. Japan | 44,825,000 |
| 4. Indonesia | 38,800,000 |
| 5. Bangladesh | 28,673,000 |
| 6. Pakistan | 25,455,000 |
| 7. Nigeria | 16,200,000 |
| 8. Iran | 9,700,000 |
| 9. Myanmar | 10,450,000 |
| 10. Viet Nam | 11,000,000 |

### List 83. Largest in World C, AD 2000

| Country | Population |
|---|---|
| 1. USA | 278,357,000 |
| 2. Brazil | 170,115,000 |
| 3. Mexico | 98,881,000 |
| 4. Philippines | 75,967,000 |
| 5. Germany | 82,220,000 |
| 6. Congo-Zaire | 51,654,000 |
| 7. Britain | 58,830,000 |
| 8. Italy | 57,298,000 |
| 9. Ukraine | 50,456,000 |
| 10. France | 59,080,000 |

### List 84. Largest in World B, AD 2000

| Country | Population |
|---|---|
| 1. China | 1,262,557,000 |
| 2. India | 1,013,662,000 |
| 3. Indonesia | 212,107,000 |
| 4. Russia | 146,934,000 |
| 5. Bangladesh | 129,155,000 |
| 6. Japan | 126,714,000 |
| 7. Nigeria | 111,506,000 |
| 8. Viet Nam | 79,832,000 |
| 9. Egypt | 68,470,000 |
| 10. Ethiopia | 62,565,000 |

### List 85. Largest in World A, AD 2000

| Country | Population |
|---|---|
| 1. Pakistan | 156,483,000 |
| 2. Iran | 67,702,000 |
| 3. Turkey | 66,591,000 |
| 4. Morocco | 28,221,000 |
| 5. Afghanistan | 22,720,000 |
| 6. Algeria | 31,471,000 |
| 7. Nepal | 23,930,000 |
| 8. Uzbekistan | 24,318,000 |
| 9. North Korea | 24,039,000 |
| 10. Iraq | 23,115,000 |

### List 86. Largest in World C, AD 2025

| Country | Population |
|---|---|
| 1. USA | 325,573,000 |
| 2. Brazil | 217,930,000 |
| 3. Mexico | 130,196,000 |
| 4. Congo-Zaire | 104,788,000 |
| 5. Philippines | 108,251,000 |
| 6. Russia | 137,933,000 |
| 7. Germany | 80,238,000 |
| 8. Colombia | 59,758,000 |
| 9. Britain | 59,961,000 |
| 10. Argentina | 47,150,000 |

### List 87. Largest in World B, AD 2025

| Country | Population |
|---|---|
| 1. China | 1,462,931,000 |
| 2. India | 1,330,449,000 |
| 3. Indonesia | 273,442,000 |
| 4. Pakistan | 263,000,000 |
| 5. Nigeria | 183,041,000 |
| 6. Bangladesh | 178,751,000 |
| 7. Japan | 121,150,000 |
| 8. Ethiopia | 115,382,000 |
| 9. Viet Nam | 108,037,000 |
| 10. Egypt | 95,615,000 |

### List 88. Largest in World A, AD 2025

| Country | Population |
|---|---|
| 1. Iran | 94,463,000 |
| 2. Afghanistan | 44,934,000 |
| 3. Morocco | 38,530,000 |
| 4. Niger | 21,495,000 |
| 5. Mali | 21,295,000 |
| 6. Somalia | 16,227,000 |
| 7. Senegal | 16,743,000 |
| 8. Guinea | 12,497,000 |
| 9. Azerbaijan | 9,403,000 |
| 10. Laos | 9,653,000 |

### List 89. Least-evangelized, AD 1900

| Country | unevangelized |
|---|---|
| 1. Bhutan | 306,000 |
| 2. Burkina Faso | 1,400,000 |
| 3. Chad | 1,700,000 |
| 4. Maldives | 72,000 |
| 5. Nepal | 4,430,000 |
| 6. Niger | 910,000 |
| 7. Somaliland | 164,000 |
| 8. Oman | 280,000 |
| 9. Burundi | 1,009,000 |
| 10. Central African Rep | 769,000 |

### List 90. Least-evangelized, AD 2000

| Country | unevangelized |
|---|---|
| 1. Maldives | 230,000 |
| 2. Bhutan | 1,683,000 |
| 3. Sahara | 221,000 |
| 4. Afghanistan | 16,000,000 |
| 5. Mauritania | 1,818,000 |
| 6. Turkmenistan | 2,919,000 |
| 7. Azerbaijan | 4,873,000 |
| 8. Iran | 42,507,000 |
| 9. Comoros | 371,000 |
| 10. Mayotte | 60,000 |

### List 91. Least-evangelized, AD 2025

| Country | unevangelized |
|---|---|
| 1. Maldives | 395,000 |
| 2. Bhutan | 2,950,000 |
| 3. Sahara | 320,000 |
| 4. Afghanistan | 29,207,000 |
| 5. Mauritania | 3,000,000 |
| 6. Turkmenistan | 3,800,000 |
| 7. Azerbaijan | 5,500,000 |
| 8. Iran | 52,500,000 |
| 9. Comoros | 550,000 |
| 10. Guinea | 6,800,000 |

## DENOMINATIONS

### List 92. Largest, AD 1970

| Denomination | Country | Members |
|---|---|---|
| 1. Igreja Católica no Brasil | Brazil | 85,119,000 |
| 2. Chiesa Cattolica in Italia | Italy | 51,353,000 |
| 3. Catholic Church in the USA | USA | 48,305,000 |
| 4. Iglesia Católica en México | Mexico | 47,029,000 |
| 5. Eglise Catholique de France | France | 44,579,000 |
| 6. Russian Orthodox Church | Russia | 36,080,000 |
| 7. Iglesia Católica en España | Spain | 33,596,000 |
| 8. Evangelische Kirche in Deutschland | Germany | 33,417,000 |
| 9. Catholic Church in the Philippines | Philippines | 30,860,000 |
| 10. Catholic Church in Poland | Poland | 28,783,000 |

### List 93. Largest, AD 1995

| Denomination | Country | Members |
|---|---|---|
| 1. Igreja Católica no Brasil | Brazil | 144,000,000 |
| 2. Iglesia Católica en México | Mexico | 85,500,000 |
| 3. Russian Orthodox Church | Russia | 73,998,000 |
| 4. Catholic Church in the USA | USA | 56,715,000 |
| 5. Catholic Church in the Philippines | Philippines | 56,554,000 |
| 6. Chiesa Cattolica in Italia | Italy | 55,750,000 |
| 7. Eglise Catholique de France | France | 48,064,000 |
| 8. Iglesia Católica en España | Spain | 38,057,000 |
| 9. Iglesia Católica en Colombia | Colombia | 37,064,000 |
| 10. Catholic Church in Poland | Poland | 35,475,000 |

### List 94. Fastest growing

| Denomination | Country | Rate |
|---|---|---|
| 1. Independent charismatic chs | Brazil | 81.59% |
| 2. New Apostolic Church | Bulgaria | 80.76% |
| 3. Igreja Pedra Fundamental | Brazil | 79.97% |
| 4. Eglise Neo-Apostolique | Congo-Zaire | 76.24% |
| 5. Ibero-Hispanic churches | USA | 67.53% |
| 6. Hidden Buddhist believers in Christ | Japan | 66.04% |
| 7. Independent pentecostal chs | USA | 65.61% |
| 8. House Church movement | North Korea | 65.61% |
| 9. Hidden Buddhist believers in Christ | Viet Nam | 65.34% |
| 10. Christ Groups | India | 63.94% |

### List 95. Largest Catholic, AD 1970

| Denomination | Country | Members |
|---|---|---|
| 1. Igreja Católica no Brasil | Brazil | 85,119,000 |
| 2. Chiesa Cattolica in Italia | Italy | 51,353,000 |
| 3. Catholic Church in the USA | USA | 48,305,000 |
| 4. Iglesia Católica en México | Mexico | 47,029,000 |
| 5. Eglise Catholique de France | France | 44,579,000 |
| 6. Iglesia Católica en España | Spain | 33,596,000 |
| 7. Catholic Church in the Philippines | Philippines | 30,860,000 |
| 8. Catholic Church in Poland | Poland | 28,783,000 |
| 9. Katholische Kirche Deutschlands | Germany | 27,957,000 |
| 10. Iglesia Católica en la Argentina | Argentina | 22,432,000 |

### List 96. Largest Catholic, AD 1995

| Denomination | Country | Members |
|---|---|---|
| 1. Igreja Católica no Brasil | Brazil | 144,000,000 |
| 2. Iglesia Católica en México | Mexico | 85,500,000 |
| 3. Catholic Church in the USA | USA | 56,715,000 |
| 4. Catholic Church in the Philippines | Philippines | 56,554,000 |
| 5. Chiesa Cattolica in Italia | Italy | 55,750,000 |
| 6. Eglise Catholique de France | France | 48,064,000 |
| 7. Iglesia Católica en España | Spain | 38,057,000 |
| 8. Iglesia Católica en Colombia | Colombia | 37,064,000 |
| 9. Catholic Church in Poland | Poland | 35,475,000 |
| 10. Iglesia Católica en la Argentina | Argentina | 31,800,000 |

### List 97. Fastest-growing Catholic

| Denomination | Country | Rate |
|---|---|---|
| 1. Catholic Church in Russia | Russia | 25.83% |
| 2. Catholic Church in Armenia | Armenia | 25.00% |
| 3. Catholic Church (VA Arabia) | Saudi Arabia | 23.61% |
| 4. Catholic Church (VA Arabia) | Oman | 19.89% |
| 5. Catholic Church in China (Clandestine) | China | 18.24% |
| 6. Catholic Church (VA Arabia) | Qatar | 16.94% |
| 7. Catholic Church (VA Arabia) | UAE | 16.53% |
| 8. Catholic Church (VA Arabia) | Yemen | 16.09% |
| 9. Catholic Church  AA Kazakhstan | Kazakhstan | 13.74% |
| 10. Catholic Church (D Patna) | Nepal | 11.98% |

# DENOMINATIONS (continued)

### List 98. Largest Anglican, AD 1970

| Denomination | Country | Members |
|---|---|---|
| 1. Church of England | Britain | 27,659,000 |
| 2. Anglican Church of Australia | Australia | 3,775,000 |
| 3. Episcopal Church in the USA | USA | 3,196,000 |
| 4. Anglican Church of Nigeria | Nigeria | 2,941,000 |
| 5. Church of Uganda | Uganda | 1,281,000 |
| 6. Ch of the Province of Southern Africa | South Africa | 1,236,000 |
| 7. Anglican Church of Canada | Canada | 1,177,000 |
| 8. Church in Wales | Britain | 1,000,000 |
| 9. Angl Ch in Aotearoa, NZ, & Polynesia | New Zealand | 877,000 |
| 10. Anglican Church of Kenya | Kenya | 583,000 |

### List 99. Largest Anglican, AD 1995

| Denomination | Country | Members |
|---|---|---|
| 1. Church of England | Britain | 24,493,000 |
| 2. Anglican Church of Nigeria | Nigeria | 17,500,000 |
| 3. Church of Uganda | Uganda | 7,400,000 |
| 4. Anglican Church of Australia | Australia | 4,040,000 |
| 5. Anglican Church of Kenya | Kenya | 2,700,000 |
| 6. Episcopal Church in the USA | USA | 2,445,000 |
| 7. Ch of the Province of Southern Africa | South Africa | 2,430,000 |
| 8. Church of the Province of Tanzania | Tanzania | 2,300,000 |
| 9. Province of the Epis Ch of the Sudan | Sudan | 2,100,000 |
| 10. Church in Wales | Britain | 1,300,000 |

### List 100. Fastest growing Anglican

| Denomination | Country | Rate |
|---|---|---|
| 1. Anglican Church of Cameroon | Cameroon | 29.96% |
| 2. Iglesia Episcopal Hondureña | Honduras | 13.33% |
| 3. Iglesia Episcopal Mexicana | Mexico | 12.37% |
| 4. Anglican Ch (D Cyprus & the Gulf) | Qatar | 10.24% |
| 5. Egl Protestante Episcopale du Burundi | Burundi | 9.58% |
| 6. Anglican Church D Swaziland | Swaziland | 9.22% |
| 7. Province of the Epis Ch of the Sudan | Sudan | 8.09% |
| 8. Anglican Ch (North & Central Europe) | Russia | 7.43% |
| 9. Church of the Province of Tanzania | Tanzania | 7.40% |
| 10. Anglican Church of Nigeria | Nigeria | 7.39% |

### List 101. Largest Protestant, AD 1970

| Denomination | Country | Members |
|---|---|---|
| 1. Evangelische Kirche in Deutschland | Germany | 33,417,000 |
| 2. United Methodist Church | USA | 14,353,000 |
| 3. Southern Baptist Convention | USA | 14,200,000 |
| 4. Church of Sweden | Sweden | 7,942,000 |
| 5. Evangelical Lutheran Ch in America | USA | 5,772,000 |
| 6. Presbyterian Church (USA) | USA | 4,767,000 |
| 7. National Church of Denmark | Denmark | 4,700,000 |
| 8. Eglise du Christ au Congo-Zaire | Congo-Zaire | 4,628,000 |
| 9. Evangelical Lutheran Ch of Finland | Finland | 4,361,000 |
| 10. United Protestant Ch in the N | Netherlands | 4,079,000 |

### List 102. Largest Protestant, AD 1995

| Denomination | Country | Members |
|---|---|---|
| 1. Evangelische Kirche in Deutschland | Germany | 29,205,000 |
| 2. Assembleias de Deus | Brazil | 22,000,000 |
| 3. Southern Baptist Convention | USA | 21,500,000 |
| 4. United Methodist Church | USA | 11,091,000 |
| 5. Eglise du Christ au Congo-Zaire | Congo-Zaire | 9,260,000 |
| 6. Church of Sweden | Sweden | 7,630,000 |
| 7. Evangelical Lutheran Ch in America | USA | 5,227,000 |
| 8. National Church of Denmark | Denmark | 4,540,000 |
| 9. Evangelical Lutheran Ch of Finland | Finland | 4,473,000 |
| 10. Word of Life Evangelical Church | Ethiopia | 4,000,000 |

### List 103. Fastest growing Protestant

| Denomination | Country | Rate |
|---|---|---|
| 1. Korean Baptist Convention | USA | 63.26% |
| 2. Eglises de Dieu du Congo | Congo-Brazzaville | 51.97% |
| 3. Igreja Cristiana do Timur | Timor | 51.91% |
| 4. Chiese Elim in Italia | Italy | 50.00% |
| 5. Congregazioni Cristiane Pentecostal | Italy | 48.61% |
| 6. Church of Norway | Sweden | 45.10% |
| 7. Ev Lutheran Church of Finland | Estonia | 43.94% |
| 8. Evangelical Church of Germany | Sweden | 43.94% |
| 9. Eglise Baptiste | Benin | 43.94% |
| 10. Igreja de Cristo do Angola | Angola | 43.03% |

### List 104. Largest Orthodox, AD 1970

| Denomination | Country | Members |
|---|---|---|
| 1. Russian Orthodox Church | Russia | 36,080,000 |
| 2. Ukrainian Orthodox Ch (P Moscow) | Ukraine | 24,480,000 |
| 3. Romanian Orthodox Ch, P Bucuresti | Romania | 16,000,000 |
| 4. Ethiopian Orthodox Church | Ethiopia | 11,066,000 |
| 5. Church of Greece | Greece | 7,720,000 |
| 6. Coptic Orthodox Church | Egypt | 5,950,000 |
| 7. Bulgarian Orthodox Church | Bulgaria | 5,500,000 |
| 8. Belorussian Orth Ch  D Minsk | Belorussia | 4,500,000 |
| 9. Serbian Orthodox Church | Yugoslavia | 4,047,000 |
| 10. Russian Orthodox Ch  D Almaty | Kazakhstan | 1,950,000 |

### List 105. Largest Orthodox, AD 1995

| Denomination | Country | Members |
|---|---|---|
| 1. Russian Orthodox Church | Russia | 73,998,000 |
| 2. Ukrainian Orthodox Ch  (P  Moscow) | Ukraine | 26,994,000 |
| 3. Ethiopian Orthodox Church | Ethiopia | 20,250,000 |
| 4. Romanian Orthodox Ch, P Bucuresti | Romania | 19,040,000 |
| 5. Church of Greece | Greece | 9,098,000 |
| 6. Coptic Orthodox Church | Egypt | 8,670,000 |
| 7. Bulgarian Orthodox Church | Bulgaria | 6,000,000 |
| 8. Serbian Orthodox Church | Yugoslavia | 5,359,000 |
| 9. Belorussian Orth Ch  D Minsk & B | Belorussia | 4,800,000 |
| 10. Armenian Apostolic Church | Armenia | 2,600,000 |

### List 106. Fastest growing Orthodox

| Denomination | Country | Rate |
|---|---|---|
| 1. Coptic Orthodox Ch (P Alexandria) | UAE | 48.90% |
| 2. Serbian Orthodox Church | Libya | 44.54% |
| 3. Coptic Orthodox Church | Yemen | 42.50% |
| 4. Aethiopische Orthodoxe Kirche | Germany | 40.59% |
| 5. Holy Ap Cath Assyrian Ch of the East | Australia | 37.75% |
| 6. Eglise Orthodoxe Russe | Madagascar | 37.37% |
| 7. Armenian Apostolic Church | Sweden | 36.17% |
| 8. Iglesia Ortodoxa Syriana | Argentina | 35.53% |
| 9. Bulgarian Orthodox Church | Libya | 34.65% |
| 10. Serbian Orthodox Church | Zambia | 33.98% |

### List 107. Largest Independent, AD 1970

| Denomination | Country | Members |
|---|---|---|
| 1. National Baptist Convention, USA | USA | 6,426,000 |
| 2. Chs of Christ (Non-Instrumental) | USA | 4,000,000 |
| 3. EdeJC sur la Terre par le Prophète SK | Congo-Zaire | 3,500,000 |
| 4. Philippine Independent Church | Philippines | 3,500,000 |
| 5. National Baptist Conv of America | USA | 3,300,000 |
| 6. Low-caste Hindu believers in Christ | India | 3,000,000 |
| 7. National Primitive Baptist Convention | USA | 2,007,000 |
| 8. Igreja Católica Apostólica Brasileira | Brazil | 2,000,000 |
| 9. Church of God in Christ | USA | 1,600,000 |
| 10. African Methodist Episcopal Church | USA | 1,529,000 |

### List 108. Largest Independent, AD 1995

| Denomination | Country | Members |
|---|---|---|
| 1. Han charismatic house churches | China | 29,740,000 |
| 2. Han Chinese Three-Self Churches | China | 10,500,000 |
| 3. National Baptist Convention, USA | USA | 9,410,000 |
| 4. Isolated radio churches | India | 9,000,000 |
| 5. Low-caste Hindu believers in Christ | India | 7,500,000 |
| 6. EdeJC sur la Terre par le Prophète SK | Congo-Zaire | 7,500,000 |
| 7. Zion Christian Church | South Africa | 7,100,000 |
| 8. Church of God in Christ | USA | 5,500,000 |
| 9. Independent charismatic chs | USA | 5,000,000 |
| 10. Chinese Catholic Church (Patriotic) | China | 4,600,000 |

### List 109. Fastest growing Independent

| Denomination | Country | Rate |
|---|---|---|
| 1. Independent charismatic chs | Brazil | 81.59% |
| 2. New Apostolic Church | Bulgaria | 80.76% |
| 3. Igreja Pedra Fundamental | Brazil | 79.97% |
| 4. Eglise Neo-Apostolique | Congo-Zaire | 76.24% |
| 5. Ibero-Hispanic churches | USA | 67.53% |
| 6. Hidden Buddhist believers in Christ | Japan | 66.04% |
| 7. Independent pentecostal chs | USA | 65.61% |
| 8. House Church movement | North Korea | 65.61% |
| 9. Hidden Buddhist believers in Christ | Viet Nam | 65.34% |
| 10. Christ Groups | India | 63.94% |

### List 110. Largest Marginal Christian, AD 1970

| Denomination | Country | Members |
|---|---|---|
| 1. Ch of Jesus Christ of Latter-day Saints | USA | 2,186,000 |
| 2. Jehovah's Witnesses | USA | 1,000,000 |
| 3. Church of Christ, Scientist | USA | 1,000,000 |
| 4. Jehovah's Witnesses | Zambia | 450,000 |
| 5. Holy Spirit Association for U of WC | South Korea | 305,000 |
| 6. Unitarian Universalist Association | USA | 265,000 |
| 7. Reorganized Ch of JC of LD Saints | USA | 203,000 |
| 8. Jehovah's Witnesses | Britain | 200,000 |
| 9. Jehovah's Witnesses | Canada | 175,000 |
| 10. Jehovah's Witnesses | Nigeria | 170,000 |

### List 111. Largest Marginal Christian, AD 1995

| Denomination | Country | Members |
|---|---|---|
| 1. Ch of Jesus Christ of Latter-day Saints | USA | 4,430,000 |
| 2. Jehovah's Witnesses | USA | 2,260,000 |
| 3. Testigos de Jehová | Mexico | 1,200,000 |
| 4. Church of Christ, Scientist | USA | 900,000 |
| 5. Testemunhas de Jeová | Brazil | 779,000 |
| 6. Iglesia de JC de los Santos de los UD | Mexico | 570,000 |
| 7. Holy Spirit Association for U of WC | South Korea | 550,000 |
| 8. Jehovah's Witnesses | Nigeria | 440,000 |
| 9. Testimoni di Geova | Italy | 377,000 |
| 10. Jehovah's Witnesses | Zambia | 370,000 |

### List 112. Fastest growing Marginal Christian

| Denomination | Country | Rate |
|---|---|---|
| 1. Témoins de Jeova | Cambodia | 58.49% |
| 2. Igreja de J C dos SUD | Portugal | 49.44% |
| 3. Ch of Jesus Christ of Latter-day Saints | Jamaica | 35.80% |
| 4. Iglesia de Jesu Cristo de los SUD | Andorra | 33.33% |
| 5. Iglesia Unificación | Panama | 28.22% |
| 6. Jehovah's Witnesses | Kirghizia | 27.68% |
| 7. Ch of Jesus C of Latter-day Saints | Estonia | 26.40% |
| 8. Jehovah's Witnesses | Moldavia | 21.05% |
| 9. Iglesia Unificación | Andorra | 20.00% |
| 10. Jehovah's Witnesses | Mongolia | 20.00% |

### List 113. Megablocs/traditions in most countries

| Tradition | Number of Countries |
|---|---|
| 1. Roman Catholic | 235 |
| 2. Protestant | 231 |
| 3. Independent | 230 |
| 4. Jehovah's Witnesses | 212 |
| 5. Adventist | 199 |
| 6. Baptist | 163 |
| 7. Anglican | 162 |
| 8. New Apostolic | 149 |
| 9. Reformed, Presbyterian | 141 |
| 10. Orthodox | 133 |

# PEOPLES

### List 114. Largest

| People | Country | Population |
|---|---|---|
| 1. Han Chinese (Mandarin) | China | 803,194,000 |
| 2. Japanese | Japan | 121,326,000 |
| 3. Russian | Russia | 117,800,000 |
| 4. USA White | USA | 115,353,000 |
| 5. Bengali | Bangladesh | 102,112,000 |
| 6. Han Chinese (Wu) | China | 94,770,000 |
| 7. Brazilian White (Branco) | Brazil | 88,062,000 |
| 8. Maratha (Maharathi) | India | 75,633,000 |
| 9. Bengali | India | 74,157,000 |
| 10. Telugu (Andhra, Tolangan) | India | 73,183,000 |

### List 115. Greatest number of Christians

| People | Country | Christians |
|---|---|---|
| 1. Brazilian White (Branco) | Brazil | 80,577,000 |
| 2. USA White | USA | 75,441,000 |
| 3. Russian | Russia | 74,450,000 |
| 4. Han Chinese (Mandarin) | China | 61,525,000 |
| 5. Mexican Mestizo | Mexico | 52,395,000 |
| 6. German (High German) | Germany | 40,458,000 |
| 7. Brazilian Mulato | Brazil | 35,180,000 |
| 8. Polish (Pole, Silesian) | Poland | 34,053,000 |
| 9. Ukrainian | Ukraine | 31,508,000 |
| 10. English (British) | Britain | 28,924,000 |

### List 116. Greatest number of Muslims

| People | Country | Muslims |
|---|---|---|
| 1. Bengali | Bangladesh | 101,948,000 |
| 2. Western Punjabi (Lahnda) | Pakistan | 63,931,000 |
| 3. Urdu (Islami, Undri) | India | 49,350,000 |
| 4. Egyptian Arab | Egypt | 47,534,000 |
| 5. Turk | Turkey | 42,076,000 |
| 6. Persian (Irani) | Iran | 21,220,000 |
| 7. Javanese (Orang Jawa) | Indonesia | 19,627,000 |
| 8. Hausa (Hausawa) | Nigeria | 19,184,000 |
| 9. Sindhi | Pakistan | 18,239,000 |
| 10. Algerian Arab | Algeria | 17,653,000 |

### List 117. Greatest number of Hindus

| People | Country | Hindus |
|---|---|---|
| 1. Bengali | India | 58,954,000 |
| 2. Hindi (High Hindi) | India | 58,457,000 |
| 3. Maratha (Maharathi) | India | 57,367,000 |
| 4. Telugu (Andhra, Tolangan) | India | 57,083,000 |
| 5. Hindi (Bazaar, Popular) | India | 53,330,000 |
| 6. Tamil (Madrasi, Tamalsan) | India | 48,691,000 |
| 7. Gujarati | India | 43,379,000 |
| 8. Awadhi (Baiswari, Bagheli) | India | 34,625,000 |
| 9. Kanarese (Canarese) | India | 33,210,000 |
| 10. Orisi (Utkali, Vadiya) | India | 32,032,000 |

### List 118. Greatest number of Buddhists

| People | Country | Buddhists |
|---|---|---|
| 1. Japanese | Japan | 66,377,000 |
| 2. Han Chinese (Mandarin) | China | 56,224,000 |
| 3. Vietnamese (Kinh) | Viet Nam | 37,187,000 |
| 4. Burmese (Myen, Bhama) | Myanmar | 24,731,000 |
| 5. Central Thai (Siamese) | Thailand | 20,509,000 |
| 6. Northeastern Tai (Isan) | Thailand | 15,938,000 |
| 7. Sinhalese (Singhalese) | Sri Lanka | 12,846,000 |
| 8. Han Chinese (Cantonese) | China | 11,372,000 |
| 9. Central Khmer (Cambodian) | Cambodia | 9,016,000 |
| 10. Han Chinese (Wu) | China | 6,729,000 |

### List 119. Greatest number of Jews

| People | Country | Jews |
|---|---|---|
| 1. Jewish | USA | 4,893,000 |
| 2. Israeli Jewish (Sabra) | Israel | 1,271,000 |
| 3. Jewish | Russia | 624,000 |
| 4. Jewish (Judeo-German) | USA | 540,000 |
| 5. Jewish | Argentina | 435,000 |
| 6. Jewish | France | 378,000 |
| 7. Russian Jew | Israel | 340,000 |
| 8. Anglo-Canadian Jew | Canada | 339,000 |
| 9. Jewish | Russia | 315,000 |
| 10. Jewish | Brazil | 306,000 |

### List 120. Greatest number of ethnoreligionists

| People | Country | ethnoreligionists |
|---|---|---|
| 1. Northern Zhuang (Chwang) | China | 10,237,000 |
| 2. South Korean | South Korea | 7,325,000 |
| 3. Tujia (Tuchia) | China | 6,327,000 |
| 4. Central Bhil | India | 4,449,000 |
| 5. Southern Zhuang | China | 4,009,000 |
| 6. Western Meo (Peh, Tak) | China | 3,492,000 |
| 7. North Korean | North Korea | 2,952,000 |
| 8. Eastern Bhil (Vil) | India | 2,676,000 |
| 9. Yao (Highland Yao, Man) | China | 2,360,000 |
| 10. Puyi (Bouyei, Pu-I) | China | 2,267,000 |

### List 121. Greatest number of atheists

| People | Country | atheists |
|---|---|---|
| 1. Han Chinese (Mandarin) | China | 96,383,000 |
| 2. Russian | Russia | 6,762,000 |
| 3. Han Chinese (Jinyu) | China | 5,682,000 |
| 4. Vietnamese (Kinh) | Viet Nam | 5,429,000 |
| 5. North Korean | North Korea | 3,714,000 |
| 6. Japanese | Japan | 3,640,000 |
| 7. French | France | 1,449,000 |
| 8. German (High German) | Germany | 1,428,000 |
| 9. Ukrainian | Ukraine | 1,067,000 |
| 10. Swedish (Swede) | Sweden | 1,042,000 |

### List 122. Greatest number of nonreligious

| People | Country | nonreligious |
|---|---|---|
| 1. Han Chinese (Mandarin) | China | 453,322,000 |
| 2. Russian | Russia | 35,340,000 |
| 3. Han Chinese (Jinyu) | China | 26,990,000 |
| 4. Han Chinese (Wu) | China | 18,954,000 |
| 5. USA White | USA | 13,450,000 |
| 6. North Korean | North Korea | 13,196,000 |
| 7. Japanese | Japan | 12,133,000 |
| 8. German (High German) | Germany | 11,333,000 |
| 9. Vietnamese (Kinh) | Viet Nam | 10,179,000 |
| 10. Han Chinese (Cantonese) | China | 9,439,000 |

## PEOPLES (continued)

### List 123. Greatest number of Baha'is

| People | Country | Baha'is |
|---|---|---|
| 1. Telugu (Andhra, Tolangan) | India | 585,000 |
| 2. Persian (Irani) | Iran | 463,000 |
| 3. Vietnamese (Kinh) | Viet Nam | 339,000 |
| 4. Hindi (Bazaar, Popular) | India | 279,000 |
| 5. Hindi (High Hindi) | India | 252,000 |
| 6. USA White | USA | 231,000 |
| 7. Central Aymara | Bolivia | 170,000 |
| 8. Indo-Pakistani | USA | 139,000 |
| 9. USA Black (Afro-American) | USA | 121,000 |
| 10. Levantine Arab | USA | 111,000 |

### List 124. Least-evangelized megapeoples

| People | Country | % evangelized |
|---|---|---|
| 1. Bakhtiari | Iran | 10.0% |
| 2. Dimili Kurd (Southern Zaza) | Turkey | 12.0% |
| 3. Banjarese (Banjar Malay) | Indonesia | 13.0% |
| 4. Bedouin | Egypt | 16.0% |
| 5. Lampungese (Lamponger) | Indonesia | 16.0% |
| 6. Luri (Lori, Feyli) | Iran | 16.0% |
| 7. Khandeshi | India | 17.2% |
| 8. Western Baluch | Pakistan | 18.0% |
| 9. Khamba (Khams Bhotia) | China | 19.0% |
| 10. Tajakant Bedouin | Algeria | 20.0% |

### List 125. Largest World A peoples

| People | Country | Population |
|---|---|---|
| 1. Western Punjabi (Lahnda) | Pakistan | 66,810,000 |
| 2. Han Chinese (Jinyu) | China | 47,351,000 |
| 3. Han Chinese (Hunanese) | China | 44,226,000 |
| 4. Awadhi (Baiswari, Bagheli) | India | 37,352,000 |
| 5. Bhojpuri Bihari (Deswali) | India | 36,071,000 |
| 6. Maitili (Maithili, Tharu) | India | 31,636,000 |
| 7. Han Chinese (Kan) | China | 25,272,000 |
| 8. Northern Uzbek | Uzbekistan | 19,024,000 |
| 9. Sindhi | Pakistan | 18,259,000 |
| 10. Braj Bhakha (Antarbedi) | India | 17,990,000 |

### List 126. Largest World B peoples

| People | Country | Population |
|---|---|---|
| 1. Han Chinese (Mandarin) | China | 803,194,000 |
| 2. Japanese | Japan | 121,326,000 |
| 3. Bengali | Bangladesh | 102,112,000 |
| 4. Han Chinese (Wu) | China | 94,770,000 |
| 5. Maratha (Maharathi) | India | 75,633,000 |
| 6. Bengali | India | 74,157,000 |
| 7. Telugu (Andhra, Tolangan) | India | 73,183,000 |
| 8. Vietnamese (Kinh) | Viet Nam | 67,859,000 |
| 9. Tamil (Madrasi, Tamalsan) | India | 64,663,000 |
| 10. Hindi (High Hindi) | India | 63,061,000 |

### List 127. Largest World C peoples

| People | Country | Population |
|---|---|---|
| 1. Russian | Russia | 117,800,000 |
| 2. USA White | USA | 115,353,000 |
| 3. Brazilian White (Branco) | Brazil | 88,062,000 |
| 4. German (High German) | Germany | 56,664,000 |
| 5. Mexican Mestizo | Mexico | 54,038,000 |
| 6. English (British) | Britain | 43,957,000 |
| 7. Brazilian Mulato | Brazil | 37,425,000 |
| 8. Ukrainian | Ukraine | 35,562,000 |
| 9. Polish (Pole, Silesian) | Poland | 34,873,000 |
| 10. Argentinian White | Argentina | 27,170,000 |

### List 128. Largest with no Scriptures

| People | Country | Population |
|---|---|---|
| 1. Han Chinese (Hunanese) | China | 44,226,000 |
| 2. Han Chinese (Kan) | China | 25,272,000 |
| 3. Tujia (Tuchia) | China | 6,353,000 |
| 4. Han Chinese (Peranakan) | Indonesia | 5,621,000 |
| 5. Luri (Lori, Feyli) | Iran | 4,870,000 |
| 6. Mazanderani (Tabri) | Iran | 3,445,000 |
| 7. Gilaki | Iran | 3,445,000 |
| 8. Jakarta Malay (Batavi) | Indonesia | 2,970,000 |
| 9. Puyi (Bouyei, Pu-I) | China | 2,834,000 |
| 10. Northern Tung (Dong, Kam) | China | 2,800,000 |

### List 129. Largest without own Bible

| People | Country | Population |
|---|---|---|
| 1. Telugu (Andhra, Tolangan) | India | 73,183,000 |
| 2. Western Punjabi (Lahnda) | Pakistan | 66,810,000 |
| 3. Hindi (Bazaar, Popular) | India | 55,726,000 |
| 4. Han Chinese (Jinyu) | China | 47,351,000 |
| 5. Han Chinese (Hunanese) | China | 44,226,000 |
| 6. Awadhi (Baiswari, Bagheli) | India | 37,352,000 |
| 7. Bhojpuri Bihari (Deswali) | India | 36,071,000 |
| 8. Maitili (Maithili, Tharu) | India | 31,636,000 |
| 9. Han Chinese (Kan) | China | 25,272,000 |
| 10. Northern Uzbek | Uzbekistan | 19,024,000 |

### List 130. Largest without own New Testament

| People | Country | Population |
|---|---|---|
| 1. Telugu (Andhra, Tolangan) | India | 73,183,000 |
| 2. Western Punjabi (Lahnda) | Pakistan | 66,810,000 |
| 3. Hindi (Bazaar, Popular) | India | 55,726,000 |
| 4. Han Chinese (Jinyu) | China | 47,351,000 |
| 5. Han Chinese (Hunanese) | China | 44,226,000 |
| 6. Awadhi (Baiswari, Bagheli) | India | 37,352,000 |
| 7. Bhojpuri Bihari (Deswali) | India | 36,071,000 |
| 8. Maitili (Maithili, Tharu) | India | 31,636,000 |
| 9. Han Chinese (Kan) | China | 25,272,000 |
| 10. Yemeni Arab | Yemen | 16,189,000 |

### List 131. Largest with no Gospel

| People | Country | Population |
|---|---|---|
| 1. Telugu (Andhra, Tolangan) | India | 73,183,000 |
| 2. Hindi (Bazaar, Popular) | India | 55,726,000 |
| 3. Han Chinese (Jinyu) | China | 47,351,000 |
| 4. Han Chinese (Hunanese) | China | 44,226,000 |
| 5. Han Chinese (Kan) | China | 25,272,000 |
| 6. Yemeni Arab | Yemen | 16,189,000 |
| 7. Saudi Arab | Saudi Arabia | 16,031,000 |
| 8. Bangri (Deswali, Hariani) | India | 14,900,000 |
| 9. Sinhalese (Singhalese) | Sri Lanka | 13,639,000 |
| 10. Iraqi Arab | Iraq | 13,311,000 |

### List 132. Largest with no access to any Scripture

| People | Country | Population |
|---|---|---|
| 1. Luri (Lori, Feyli) | Iran | 4,870,000 |
| 2. Northern Tung (Dong, Kam) | China | 2,800,000 |
| 3. Bai (Baizi, Whites) | China | 1,776,000 |
| 4. Northern Yi (I, Lolo) | China | 1,757,000 |
| 5. Khandeshi | India | 1,660,000 |
| 6. Dimili Kurd (Southern Zaza) | Turkey | 1,145,000 |
| 7. Bakhtiari | Iran | 1,137,000 |
| 8. Antaisaka | Madagascar | 943,000 |
| 9. Beja (Beni-Amer, Ababda) | Sudan | 905,000 |
| 10. Kuruba (Urali, Kurumvari) | India | 885,000 |

### List 133. Largest with no denominations

| People | Country | Population |
|---|---|---|
| 1. Han Chinese (Jinyu) | China | 47,351,000 |
| 2. Braj Bhakha (Antarbedi) | India | 17,990,000 |
| 3. Deccani | India | 12,726,000 |
| 4. Bundelkhandi (Bondili) | India | 12,515,000 |
| 5. Jat (Jati, Bangri) | India | 12,164,000 |
| 6. Pathan (Pukhtun, Afghani) | Afghanistan | 10,807,000 |
| 7. Hui (Dungan, Tunya, Huizui) | China | 9,581,000 |
| 8. Uighur (Kashgar) | China | 8,035,000 |
| 9. Sylhetti Bengali | Bangladesh | 6,052,000 |
| 10. Jewish | USA | 5,331,000 |

### List 134. Largest with no mission agencies

| People | Country | Population |
|---|---|---|
| 1. Han Chinese (Jinyu) | China | 47,351,000 |
| 2. Sylhetti Bengali | Bangladesh | 6,052,000 |
| 3. Luri (Lori, Feyli) | Iran | 4,870,000 |
| 4. Crimean Tatar | Turkey | 4,661,000 |
| 5. Iranian Kurd | Iran | 4,062,000 |
| 6. Eta | Japan | 2,534,000 |
| 7. White Moor (Bidan) | Morocco | 2,258,000 |
| 8. Hamyan Bedouin | Algeria | 2,197,000 |
| 9. Banjarese (Banjar Malay) | Indonesia | 2,085,000 |
| 10. Sahel Bedouin | Tunisia | 2,051,000 |

### List 135. Largest with no Christian broadcasting

| People | Country | Population |
|---|---|---|
| 1. Han Chinese (Hunanese) | China | 44,226,000 |
| 2. Awadhi (Baiswari, Bagheli) | India | 37,352,000 |
| 3. Bhojpuri Bihari (Deswali) | India | 36,071,000 |
| 4. Maitili (Maithili, Tharu) | India | 31,636,000 |
| 5. Han Chinese (Kan) | China | 25,272,000 |
| 6. Braj Bhakha (Antarbedi) | India | 17,990,000 |
| 7. Bangri (Deswali, Hariani) | India | 14,900,000 |
| 8. Deccani | India | 12,726,000 |
| 9. Magadhi Bihari (Maghori) | India | 11,941,000 |
| 10. Manchu (Man) | China | 10,938,000 |

### List 136. Megapeoples with least evangelistic offers

| People | Country | Offers per capita |
|---|---|---|
| 1. Shawiya (Chaouia) | Algeria | 0.00 |
| 2. Tajakant Bedouin | Algeria | 0.00 |
| 3. Hui (Dungan, Tunya, Huizui) | China | 0.00 |
| 4. Kazakh | China | 0.00 |
| 5. Uighur (Kashgar) | China | 0.00 |
| 6. Bedouin | Egypt | 0.00 |
| 7. Deccani | India | 0.00 |
| 8. Banjarese (Banjar Malay) | Indonesia | 0.00 |
| 9. Lampungese (Lamponger) | Indonesia | 0.00 |
| 10. Azerbaijani (Turk) | Iran | 0.00 |

### List 137. Most responsive megapeoples

| People | Country | Response |
|---|---|---|
| 1. Khandeshi | India | 1,112 |
| 2. Awadhi (Baiswari, Bagheli) | India | 1,074 |
| 3. Magadhi Bihari (Maghori) | India | 931 |
| 4. Bai (Baizi, Whites) | China | 913 |
| 5. Berar Marathi (Brahmani) | India | 895 |
| 6. Khamba (Khams Bhotia) | China | 895 |
| 7. Maitili (Maithili, Tharu) | India | 885 |
| 8. Hani (Uni, Ouni) | China | 861 |
| 9. Tho (Tai Tho) | China | 851 |
| 10. Kumaoni (Central Pahari) | India | 832 |

### List 138. Least responsive megapeoples

| People | Country | Response |
|---|---|---|
| 1. Swedish | Sweden | 2 |
| 2. Russian | Belorussia | 2 |
| 3. Lithuanian | Lithuania | 8 |
| 4. Polish | Poland | 9 |
| 5. Georgian | Georgia | 9 |
| 6. Serb | Yugoslavia | 13 |
| 7. French | France | 13 |
| 8. Irish | Ireland | 16 |
| 9. Czech | Czech Republic | 17 |
| 10. Italian | Italy | 19 |

### List 139. Megapeoples with highest Christian rate, 1900-2000

| People | Country | Growth Rate |
|---|---|---|
| 1. Southern Nyanja (Maravi) | Malawi | 5.54 |
| 2. Chewa (Western Nyanja) | Malawi | 5.54 |
| 3. Southern Uzbek | Afghanistan | 5.20 |
| 4. Pathan (Pukhtun, Afghani) | Afghanistan | 5.20 |
| 5. Hazara (Berberi) | Afghanistan | 5.20 |
| 6. Afghani Tajik (Tadzhik) | Afghanistan | 5.20 |
| 7. Teso (Iteso) | Uganda | 5.15 |
| 8. Soga (Kenyi) | Uganda | 5.15 |
| 9. Rwandese Hutu | Uganda | 5.15 |
| 10. Nkole (Nkore) | Uganda | 5.15 |

### List 140. Largest top priority targets

| People | Country | Population |
|---|---|---|
| 1. Atuentse | China | 579,000 |
| 2. Southern Pathan | Afghanistan | 227,000 |
| 3. Pashayi (Pashai) | Afghanistan | 159,000 |
| 4. Ngolok (Golog) | China | 107,000 |
| 5. Persian | Japan | 51,000 |
| 6. Jiddu | Somalia | 37,000 |
| 7. Tunni | Somalia | 36,000 |
| 8. Dabarre | Somalia | 32,000 |
| 9. Thami | Nepal | 28,000 |
| 10. Loba (Mustang) | Nepal | 28,000 |

## CITIES

### List 141. Largest, AD 2000

| City | Country | Population |
|---|---|---|
| 1. TOKYO-Yokohama | Japan | 28,025,000 |
| 2. Ciudad de Mexico (Mexico City) | Mexico | 18,131,000 |
| 3. Mumbai (Bombay) | India | 18,042,000 |
| 4. Sao Paulo | Brazil | 17,711,000 |
| 5. New York-N New Jersey-Long Island | USA | 16,626,000 |
| 6. Shanghai (Shang-hai) | China | 14,173,000 |
| 7. Lagos | Nigeria | 13,488,000 |
| 8. Los Angeles-Anaheim-Riverside, CA | USA | 13,129,000 |
| 9. Calcutta | India | 12,900,000 |
| 10. BUENOS AIRES | Argentina | 12,431,000 |

### List 142. Largest in World C, AD 2000

| City | Country | Population |
|---|---|---|
| 1. Ciudad de Mexico (Mexico City) | Mexico | 18,131,000 |
| 2. Sao Paulo | Brazil | 17,711,000 |
| 3. New York-N New Jersey-Long Island | USA | 16,626,000 |
| 4. Los Angeles-Anaheim-Riverside, CA | USA | 13,129,000 |
| 5. BUENOS AIRES | Argentina | 12,431,000 |
| 6. MANILA-Quezon (Metro Manila) | Philippines | 10,818,000 |
| 7. Rio de Janeiro (Rio) | Brazil | 10,556,000 |
| 8. PARIS | France | 9,638,000 |
| 9. MOSKVA (Moscow) | Russia | 9,299,000 |
| 10. LONDON (Greater London) | Britain | 7,640,000 |

### List 143. Largest in World B, AD 2000

| City | Country | Population |
|---|---|---|
| 1. TOKYO-Yokohama | Japan | 28,025,000 |
| 2. Mumbai (Bombay) | India | 18,042,000 |
| 3. Shanghai (Shang-hai) | China | 14,173,000 |
| 4. Lagos | Nigeria | 13,488,000 |
| 5. Calcutta | India | 12,900,000 |
| 6. SOUL (Seoul, Kyongsong) | South Korea | 12,215,000 |
| 7. BEIJING (Pei-Ching, Peking) | China | 12,033,000 |
| 8. Karachi | Pakistan | 11,774,000 |
| 9. Delhi | India | 11,680,000 |
| 10. DHAKA (Dacca) | Bangladesh | 10,979,000 |

### List 144. Largest in World A, AD 2000

| City | Country | Population |
|---|---|---|
| 1. TEHRAN (Teheran) | Iran | 7,380,000 |
| 2. Ahmadabad (Ahmedabad) | India | 4,154,000 |
| 3. Casablanca (Dar el Beida) | Morocco | 3,535,000 |
| 4. ANKARA (Ancyra, Angora) | Turkey | 3,190,000 |
| 5. KABOL (Kabul) | Afghanistan | 2,716,000 |
| 6. Lucknow | India | 2,565,000 |
| 7. Kanpur (Cawnpore) | India | 2,447,000 |
| 8. Mashhad (Meshed) | Iran | 2,378,000 |
| 9. Surat | India | 2,341,000 |
| 10. Jaipur (Jeypore) | India | 2,143,000 |

### List 145. Least-evangelized, AD 2000

| City | Country | Population |
|---|---|---|
| 1. Paro | Bhutan | 4,000 |
| 2. EL AAIUN (Laayoun) | Sahara | 216,000 |
| 3. THIMPHU (Thimbu) | Bhutan | 17,000 |
| 4. MALE | Maldives | 76,000 |
| 5. Bushehr (Bushire) | Iran | 213,000 |
| 6. Ilam | Iran | 131,000 |
| 7. Shirvan | Iran | 71,000 |
| 8. Shushtar | Iran | 96,000 |
| 9. Agha Jari | Iran | 112,000 |
| 10. Ahar | Iran | 91,000 |

Part 12

# COUNTRYTRENDS

Comprehensive summary table of 191 indicators for all 238 countries

*Missionary statistics, to be sure, are mere figures,*
*but they stand for immense and thrilling facts.*
—James S. Dennis, *Christian missions and social progress*, 1897

*Les chiffres sont les signes de Dieu—Statistics are signs from God.*
—Prior Roger Schutz of Taizé Community, 1960

Christian churches and missions worldwide activate every year several hundred scientific measuring devices (instruments). These can be called 'scientific' for 4 reasons: (1) they produce hitherto unknown data, information, and knowledge, (2) other observers can use the same instruments to repeat the investigations to exactly verify the measurements, (3) the resulting new data fit well into existing knowledge, and (4) they enable future projections to be calculated, in the shape here of 24 variables describing for every country the probable situation in AD 2025 and in AD 2050.

Part 12 contains the largest concentration of these instruments and measurements in this volume: 191 instruments arranged into 50 instrument panels resulting in 45,649 measurements shown on 12 sets of 2-facing-page sections, each section listing on average 14 variables for all countries and major geopolitical entities. Most of Table 12–1's columns report numbers; for the meaning of columns with symbols, consult the facing page or Part 16 "GeoCodebook".

## Table 12–1. Geopolitico-religious data and typologies via 191 instruments including 110 trend variables for all 238 countries and 7 continents, AD 1900-AD 2050.

### Notes

1. This table is the original source from which many tables elsewhere in *WCT* and *WCE* have been derived. It summarizes much of the material in *WCE* Part 4, "Countries," especially in the footnotes under Country Tables 1 and 2, concerning Christian resources, organizations, institutions, personnel, activities and attributes in the 20th century at various points from AD 1900-2000 and beyond to AD 2050.
2. The table is spread out over 24 pages making up 12 pairs of facing pages. Each pair lists all countries of the world with totals for continents and for the world. Each pair then gives the statistics, codes or values for between 12 and 26 variables (in 12 to 20 columns).
3. To locate specific data for a country, the reader should use a ruler or straight edge. From the listing below, or from Part 16 "GeoCodebook", obtain the column number of the data you require. Locate the country (whose physical position on the pair of pages is exactly the same for all 14 pairs), locate the column number, and read off the data.
4. *Rows.* These list the 227 countries of the world whose AD 2000 population is each over 4,500.
5. *Minicountries.* The 11 smallest countries with population each under 5,000 are combined here in the single line '11 minicountries' in the same position for all 14 pairs of tables. With each's AD 2000 population (in parentheses) they are: Antarctica (4,500), British Indian Ocean Territory (2,000), Christmas Island (3,424), Cocos (Keeling) Islands (726), Falkland Islands (2,255), Holy See (5,000), Niue Island (1,876), Norfolk Island (2,075), Pitcairn Islands (47), Svalbard & Jan Mayen Islands (3,676), Tokelau Islands (1,500).
6. *Columns.* These give the values of 191 variables whose meaning is given below, and in more detail set out in Part 16 "GeoCodebook" and at the end of Part 14 "Missiometrics". The numbers of the columns are given at the top of each column.
7. *Abbreviations.* The abbreviation 'p.m.' throughout means total per million population of the country; 'p.m.a.' means total per million of the country's affiliated church members; 'p.a.' means per annum, per year.
8. *Dating.* All data refer to the year AD 2000 at its midpoint, except (a) columns clearly identified at other dates (columns 6, 7, 58, 59, 60, 61, 62, 116, 152-156, 158, 167-191), and (b) the analysis in columns 120-146 which is based on a detailed study of empirical numbers in 1995.
9. *Totals.* At the end of the listings for countries, totals are given for each of the 7 continents (UN major areas); for Worlds A, B, C (as countries, not as peoples or as individuals); and lastly for the entire globe.

### BRIEF MEANINGS OF COLUMNS 1-191 IN TABLE 12–1: COLUMN NUMBERS, HEADINGS, AND SUBJECTS

| Column | Heading | Subject |
|---|---|---|
| **COUNTRY** | | |
| 1. | *code* | 4-letter country code |
| 2. | *short name* | as in *WCE* Part 4 |
| 3. | *UN* | UN major area and region |
| 4. | *prov* | major civil divisions (provinces, states) |
| **DEMOGRAPHICS** | | |
| 5. | *pop 2000* | population, mid-AD 2000 |
| 6. | *pop 2010* | population, mid-AD 2010 |
| 7. | *pop 2025* | population, mid-AD 2025 |
| 8. | *adults* | population age 15 and over |
| 9. | *apop* | adults as % population |
| 10. | *bpop* | birth rate, % per year |
| 11. | *dpop* | death rate, % per year |
| 12. | *npop* | natural increase, % per year |
| 13. | *life* | life expectancy, years |
| 14. | *hom* | household size (adults, children) |
| 15. | *spac* | floor area per person, sq. meters |
| 16. | *den* | density of population per sq. kilometer |
| 17. | *peop* | total ethnolinguistic peoples |
| 18. | *langs* | official and national state language(s) |
| **GEOPOLITICAL TYPOLOGIES** | | |
| 19. | *dev* | more/less/least-developed |
| 20. | *HDI* | human development index |
| 21. | *HFI* | human freedom index |
| 22. | *HSI* | human suffering index |
| 23. | *liter* | literacy as % population over 15 |
| 24. | *literates* | adult literates (over 15) |
| **SOCIETY** | | |
| ECONOMICS | | |
| 25. | *GNP* | gross national product p.a. per capita |
| 26. | *EFL* | economic freedom level |
| URBANIZATION | | |
| 27. | *rural* | ruralites, country-dwellers (millions) |
| 28. | *urban* | urbanites, town/city dwellers (millions) |
| 29. | *metro* | metropolitan urbanites (millions) |
| METROSCAN | | |
| 30. | *cit50* | cities over 50,000 persons |
| 31. | *cit100* | cities over 100,000 persons |
| 32. | *mega* | megacities over 1 million persons |
| HEALTH | | |
| 33. | *access* | people's access to health services, % |
| 34. | *water* | people's access to safe water, % |
| 35. | *mat-m* | maternal mortality, per 100,000 births |
| 36. | *inf-m* | infant mortality, per 1000 live births |
| 37. | *hosp* | hospitals |
| 38. | *beds* | beds, per 10,000 population |
| 39. | *doct* | doctors |
| 40. | *blind* | nonsighted persons |
| 41. | *deaf* | hearing-impaired persons |
| 42. | *lepers* | persons with leprosy |
| 43. | *murder* | murders per 100,000 per year |
| EDUCATION | | |
| 44. | *educ* | rate % school enrolments, female/male |
| 45. | *schools* | elementary, secondary, high |
| 46. | *univs* | degree-granting colleges, universities |
| COMMUNICATION | | |
| 47. | *news* | daily newspaper copies per 1000 persons |
| 48. | *radios* | radio sets per 1000 persons |
| 49. | *TVs* | TV sets per 1000 persons |
| 50. | *fones* | telephones per 1000 persons |
| 51. | *faxes* | fax machines per 1000 persons |
| 52. | *computers* | general-purpose computers in use |
| 53. | *Internet* | users of Internet, e-mail, www |
| **RELIGIOUS RELATIONS** | | |
| RELIGIONS | | |
| 54. | *religs* | total major religions in country |
| 55. | *indig* | ethnoreligions indigenous to this country |
| RELIGIOUS PERSECUTION | | |
| 56. | *liberty* | religious liberty or persecution |
| 57. | *CSI* | Christian Safety Index, 0-100 |
| 58. | *martyrs* | martyrs ever (less background martyrs) |
| 59. | *martyrs p.a.* | annual average, 1950-2000 |
| CHURCH/STATE RELATIONS: state religion or philosophy | | |
| 60. | *1900* | situation in 1900 |
| 61. | *1970* | situation in 1970 |
| 62. | *1990* | situation in 1990 |
| 63. | *2000* | situation in AD 2000 |
| BIBLIOGRAPHY | | |
| 64. | *items listed* | listed in *WCE* Part 4 after each country's text |
| **CHRISTIANITY** | | |
| CHURCH MEMBERS | | |
| 65. | *affiliated* | affiliated church members |
| 66. | *AC* | affiliated church members, % |
| **FOUR MEGATYPOLOGIES OF RENEWAL** | | |
| 1. THE GREAT COMMISSION | | |
| 67. | *GCCs* | Great Commission Christians |
| 68. | *GCC* | Great Commission Christians, % country |
| 2. ECCLESIASTICAL RENEWAL: 6 MEGABLOCS | | |
| 69. | *Megabloc O* | Orthodox, affiliated |
| 70. | *Megabloc R* | Roman Catholics, affiliated |
| 71. | *Megabloc A* | Anglicans, affiliated |
| 72. | *Megabloc P* | Protestants, affiliated |
| 73. | *Megabloc I* | Independents, affiliated |
| 74. | *Megabloc m* | Marginal Christians, affiliated |
| 3. EVANGELICAL RENEWAL | | |
| 75. | *Evangelicals* | Evangelicals (linked to Ev councils) |
| 76. | *evangelicals* | evangelicals (all varieties) |
| 4. PENTECOSTAL/CHARISMATIC RENEWAL | | |
| 77. | *1st-Wavers* | Pentecostals (Classical denominations) |
| 78. | *2nd-Wavers* | Charismatics (in non-Pentecostal churches) |
| 79. | *3rd-Wavers* | Neocharismatics (Independents) |
| **CHURCHES** | | |
| STRUCTURES | | |
| 80. | *denom* | denominations |
| 81. | *p.m.* | denominations per million |
| 82. | *worship* | worship centers (churches, congregations) |
| 83. | *p.m.* | worship centers per million |
| FINANCE, US$ | | |
| 84. | *personal* | personal income p.a. of all affiliated |
| 85. | *church* | churches' income per year |
| 86. | *parachurch* | parachurch income per year |
| 87. | *ecc crime* | ecclesiastical crime p.a. (embezzlements) |
| **MISSION** | | |
| STATUS OF MISSIONS | | |
| 88. | *stat* | current status of foreign missions, 1-7 |
| 89. | *misags* | foreign mission agencies present |
| 90. | *all orgs* | all service agencies |
| 91. | *p.m.* | all organizations per million |
| MISSION INSTITUTIONS | | |
| 92. | *major* | major institutions |
| 93. | *p.m.* | major institutions per million |
| 94. | *minor* | minor institutions |
| 95. | *p.m.* | minor institutions per million |
| RESPONSE/GROWTH | | |
| 96. | *CG%* | annual church growth 1900-2000, % p.a. |
| 97. | *g%* | new Christians per year, % |
| 98. | *bapt p.a.* | newly baptized persons per year |
| 99. | *resp R* | responsiveness to evangelism |
| 100. | *cost-eff, $* | cost-effectiveness: $ cost per baptism |
| WORLDS A, B, and C | | |
| 101. | *A-individuals* | World A individuals, 2000 |
| 102. | *B-individuals* | World B individuals, 2000 |
| 103. | *C-individuals* | World C individuals, 2000 |
| MINISTRIES | | |
| 104. | *peo-ags* | total agencies-in-peoples |
| **CHRISTIAN PERSONNEL** | | |
| ALL WORKERS | | |
| 105. | *workers* | full-time Christian workers in country |
| 106. | *w.p.m.* | Christian workers per million population |
| CITIZENS | | |
| 107. | *workers* | citizen Christian workers in country |
| 108. | *citw p.m.* | citizen Christian workers per million |
| **GLOBAL MISSION SHARING** | | |
| CITIZENS SENT ABROAD | | |
| 109. | *total* | citizen missionaries working abroad |
| 110. | *p.m.a.* | citizen missionaries abroad, p.m. affiliated |
| ALIENS RECEIVED FROM ABROAD | | |
| 111. | *total* | aliens at work as missionaries |
| 112. | *p.m.* | aliens at work as missionaries, p.m. |
| **CHRISTIAN LITERATURE** | | |
| LIBRARIES | | |
| 113. | *total* | Christian or religious libraries |
| 114. | *p.m.* | Christian or religious libraries, p.m. |
| BOOKS ON CHRISTIANITY IN EACH COUNTRY | | |
| 115. | *total* | all books describing this country's Christians |
| 116. | *1970-99* | such books published since 1970 |
| 117. | *p.a.* | books published per year in AD 2000 |
| PERIODICALS | | |
| 118. | *total* | Christian periodicals |
| 119. | *p.m.* | Christian periodicals, per million |
| **SCRIPTURES** | | |
| BIBLE DISTRIBUTION | | |
| 120. | *goal* | goal for all Bibles in place |
| 121. | *goal p.a.* | required Bibles distributed p.a. |
| 122. | *UBS p.a.* | UBS Bibles distributed p.a. |
| 123. | *other p.a.* | all other Bibles distributed p.a. |
| 124. | *total p.a.* | total all Bibles distributed p.a. |
| 125. | *T/G%* | ratio Bible total (col 124) to goal (col 121), % |
| NEW TESTAMENT DISTRIBUTION | | |
| 126. | *goal* | goal for all NTs in place |
| 127. | *goal p.a.* | required NTs distributed p.a. |
| 128. | *UBS p.a.* | UBS NTs distributed p.a. |
| 129. | *other p.a.* | all other NTs distributed p.a. |
| 130. | *duplicates* | NTs distributed via Bibles p.a. |
| 131. | *total p.a.* | total all NTs distributed p.a. |
| 132. | *T/G%* | ratio NT total (col 131) to goal (col 127), % |
| PORTIONS DISTRIBUTION (GOSPELS) | | |
| 133. | *goal* | goal for all gospels in place |
| 134. | *goal p.a.* | required gospels distributed p.a. |
| 135. | *UBS p.a.* | UBS portions (gospels) distributed p.a. |
| 136. | *other p.a.* | all other gospels distributed p.a. |
| 137. | *duplicates* | gospels distributed via Bibles & NTs p.a. |
| 138. | *total p.a.* | total all gospels distributed p.a. |
| 139. | *T/G %* | ratio gospel total (col 138) to goal (col 134),% |
| SELECTIONS DISTRIBUTION | | |
| 140. | *goal* | goal for all selections in place |
| 141. | *goal p.a.* | required selections distributed p.a. |
| 142. | *UBS p.a.* | UBS selections distributed p.a. |
| 143. | *other p.a.* | all other selections distributed p.a. |
| 144. | *duplicates* | selections distributed via gospels,N or B p.a. |
| 145. | *total p.a.* | total all selections distributed p.a. |
| 146. | *T/G %* | ratio selection total (col 145) to goal (col 141),% |
| **BROADCASTING** | | |
| RADIO/TV AUDIENCES | | |
| 147. | *cb aud* | regular audience for Christian programs, % |
| 148. | *cstat* | audience via Christian stations, % |
| 149. | *secstat* | audience via secular stations, % |
| **EVANGELISM** | | |
| OFFERS VIA 45 MINISTRIES | | |
| 150. | *q per day* | offers (disciple-opportunities) per day |
| 151. | *e p.a.p.c.* | offers per year per capita |
| **EVANGELIZATION** | | |
| WHEN BEGUN | | |
| 152. | *year begun* | year first Christians resident |
| STATUS OF EVANGELIZATION, E | | |
| 153. | *1900* | E (% population evangelized), 1900 |
| 154. | *1970* | E (% population evangelized), 1970 |
| 155. | *1990* | E (% population evangelized), 1990 |
| 156. | *1995* | E (% population evangelized), 1995 |
| 157. | *2000* | E (% population evangelized), 2000 |
| 158. | *2025* | E (% population evangelized), 2025 |
| SOURCE OF E IN AD 2000 | | |
| 159. | *internal* | evangelized by population's Christians |
| 160. | *external* | evangelized by Christians from outside |
| UNEVANGELIZED, AD 2000 | | |
| 161. | *U* | U, % population unevangelized |
| 162. | *total* | unevangelized persons |
| STRATEGIES | | |
| 163. | *World* | 3-fold trichotomy: A, B, C |
| 164. | *plans* | plans to evangelize globe (less 'other plans') |
| 165. | *target* | total top priority target peoples (T=1) |
| FUTURES (CHRISTIAN FUTURISTICS) | | |
| 166. | *growth index* | growth relative to demographics |
| 167. | *prospects* | outlook during 21st century (+2 to -2) |
| **COUNTRY TRENDS IN AD 2025** | | |
| DEMOGRAPHIC TRENDS | | |
| 168. | *pop 2025* | population in AD 2025 |
| 169. | *npop* | natural increase, % per year |
| 170. | *increase p.a.* | total increase per year |
| EVANGELIZATION TRENDS | | |
| 171. | *evangelized* | persons now evangelized |
| 172. | *E* | % of population evangelized |
| 173. | *outreach* | outreach per Christian = (E-C)/C |
| CHRISTIAN TRENDS | | |
| 174. | *Christians* | total all Christians |
| 175. | *C%* | Christians, % |
| 176. | *G%* | Christian growth rate, % p.a., AD 2000-2025 |
| 177. | *increase p.a.* | nett new Christians, p.a. (= 178 minus 179) |
| 178. | *gains p.a.* | Christian births + converts, p.a. |
| 179. | *losses p.a.* | Christian deaths + defectors, p.a. |
| **COUNTRY TRENDS IN AD 2050** | | |
| DEMOGRAPHIC TRENDS | | |
| 180. | *pop 2050* | population in AD 2050 |
| 181. | *npop* | natural increase, % per year |
| 182. | *increase p.a.* | total increase per year |
| EVANGELIZATION TRENDS | | |
| 183. | *evangelized* | persons now evangelized |
| 184. | *E* | % of population evangelized |
| 185. | *outreach* | outreach per Christian = (E-C)/C |
| CHRISTIAN TRENDS | | |
| 186. | *Christians* | total all Christians |
| 187. | *C%* | Christians, % |
| 188. | *G%* | Christian growth rate, % p.a., AD 2025-2050 |
| 189. | *increase p.a.* | nett new Christians, p.a. (= 190 minus 191) |
| 190. | *gains p.a.* | Christian births + converts, p.a. |
| 191. | *losses p.a.* | Christian deaths + defectors, p.a. |

| COUNTRY | | | | DEMOGRAPHICS | | | | | | | | | | | | | | GEOPOLITICAL TYPOLOGIES | | | | | |
|---|---|---|---|---|---|---|---|---|---|---|---|---|---|---|---|---|---|---|---|---|---|---|---|
| | | | | | | | | | | | | | | | | | | | SCALES, 0-100 | | | | |
| code | short name | UN | prov | pop 2000 | pop 2010 | pop 2025 | adults | apop | bpop | dpop | npop | life | hom | spac | den | peop | langs | dev | HDI | HFI | HSI | liter | literates |
| 1 | 2 | 3 | 4 | 5 | 6 | 7 | 8 | 9 | 10 | 11 | 12 | 13 | 14 | 15 | 16 | 17 | 18 | 19 | 20 | 21 | 22 | 23 | 24 |
| afgh | Afghanistan | C2 | 29 | 22,720,416 | 32,901,664 | 44,934,122 | 12,782,506 | 56.3 | 4.65 | 1.83 | 2.82 | 47 | 6.2 | 2 | 35 | 70 | PD | 3 | 23 | 5 | 11 | 32 | 4,029,000 |
| alba | Albania | E3 | 26 | 3,113,434 | 3,346,892 | 3,819,763 | 2,195,905 | 70.5 | 1.81 | 0.55 | 1.25 | 74 | 4.7 | 8 | 108 | 12 | a | 1 | 66 | 30 | 53 | 92 | 2,017,000 |
| alge | Algeria | A3 | 48 | 31,471,278 | 38,303,706 | 46,610,551 | 19,940,202 | 63.4 | 2.67 | 0.51 | 2.16 | 70 | 6.9 | 7 | 13 | 44 | A | 2 | 74 | 20 | 46 | 62 | 12,284,000 |
| amer | American Samoa | P4 | 3 | 68,089 | 94,712 | 142,680 | 42,093 | 61.8 | 2.73 | 0.46 | 2.27 | 73 | 7.0 | 15 | 342 | 10 | Ew | 2 | 67 | 80 | 75 | 96 | 40,400 |
| ando | Andorra | E3 | 7 | 77,985 | 108,765 | 154,335 | 63,402 | 81.3 | 1.19 | 0.95 | 0.23 | 79 | 3.0 | 40 | 167 | 11 | F | 1 | 89 | 90 | 80 | 100 | 63,400 |
| ango | Angola | A2 | 18 | 12,878,188 | 17,235,659 | 25,106,861 | 6,761,049 | 52.5 | 4.56 | 1.65 | 2.92 | 49 | 4.8 | 7 | 10 | 60 | P | 3 | 34 | 30 | 14 | 42 | 2,833,000 |
| angu | Anguilla | L1 | 1 | 8,309 | 9,361 | 10,984 | 6,326 | 76.1 | 1.53 | 0.58 | 0.95 | 78 | 4.0 | 18 | 91 | 5 | E | 2 | 85 | 70 | 80 | 90 | 5,700 |
| anti | Antigua | L1 | 7 | 67,560 | 70,919 | 75,080 | 51,433 | 76.1 | 1.53 | 0.58 | 0.95 | 78 | 3.5 | 25 | 153 | 6 | E | 2 | 89 | 70 | 80 | 90 | 46,200 |
| arge | Argentina | L3 | 24 | 37,027,297 | 41,467,500 | 47,150,313 | 26,763,330 | 72.3 | 1.91 | 0.78 | 1.13 | 74 | 3.2 | 20 | 13 | 64 | S | 2 | 88 | 63 | 61 | 96 | 25,746,000 |
| arme | Armenia | C4 | 11 | 3,519,569 | 3,697,258 | 3,946,381 | 2,656,923 | 75.5 | 1.40 | 0.79 | 0.61 | 71 | 4.7 | 15 | 118 | 25 | a | 2 | 65 | 40 | 55 | 99 | 2,623,000 |
| arub | Aruba | L1 | 1 | 102,747 | 154,785 | 250,376 | 77,112 | 75.1 | 1.53 | 0.61 | 0.92 | 76 | 3.6 | 35 | 532 | 7 | D | 2 | 90 | 80 | 90 | 95 | 73,200 |
| aust | Australia | P1 | 8 | 18,879,524 | 20,608,386 | 23,090,790 | 14,982,790 | 79.4 | 1.26 | 0.77 | 0.49 | 79 | 3.0 | 50 | 2 | 133 | E | 1 | 93 | 83 | 96 | 100 | 14,908,000 |
| ausz | Austria | E4 | 9 | 8,210,520 | 8,347,849 | 8,185,725 | 6,814,732 | 83.0 | 0.94 | 0.99 | -0.05 | 78 | 2.6 | 55 | 98 | 36 | G | 1 | 93 | 90 | 94 | 100 | 6,815,000 |
| azer | Azerbaijan | C4 | 4 | 7,734,015 | 8,411,360 | 9,402,570 | 5,520,540 | 71.4 | 1.57 | 0.67 | 0.90 | 71 | 4.8 | 12 | 89 | 35 | A | 2 | 64 | 25 | 25 | 97 | 5,375,000 |
| baha | Bahamas | L1 | 19 | 306,529 | 354,213 | 414,631 | 213,405 | 69.6 | 2.06 | 0.50 | 1.56 | 75 | 3.8 | 40 | 22 | 9 | E | 2 | 89 | 90 | 90 | 98 | 210,000 |
| bahr | Bahrain | C4 | 12 | 617,217 | 713,145 | 858,368 | 434,953 | 70.5 | 1.61 | 0.38 | 1.23 | 74 | 6.5 | 25 | 889 | 14 | A | 2 | 87 | 30 | 71 | 85 | 369,000 |
| bang | Bangladesh | C2 | 6 | 129,155,152 | 151,799,126 | 178,751,214 | 83,795,863 | 64.9 | 2.64 | 0.86 | 1.78 | 61 | 5.3 | 5 | 875 | 61 | B | 3 | 37 | 18 | 32 | 38 | 31,867,000 |
| barb | Barbados | L1 | 11 | 270,449 | 282,304 | 296,753 | 213,601 | 79.0 | 1.21 | 0.79 | 0.43 | 77 | 3.7 | 30 | 629 | 11 | E | 2 | 91 | 80 | 89 | 97 | 208,000 |
| belg | Belgium | E4 | 11 | 10,161,164 | 10,135,688 | 9,917,861 | 8,420,557 | 82.9 | 1.00 | 1.07 | -0.07 | 78 | 2.7 | 50 | 333 | 34 | DFG | 1 | 93 | 88 | 98 | 100 | 8,421,000 |
| beli | Belize | L2 | 6 | 240,709 | 294,499 | 370,035 | 144,955 | 60.2 | 2.73 | 0.39 | 2.34 | 76 | 4.9 | 18 | 10 | 19 | E | 2 | 81 | 70 | 75 | 70 | 102,000 |
| belo | Belorussia | E1 | 6 | 10,236,181 | 9,973,382 | 9,495,683 | 8,322,015 | 81.3 | 1.05 | 1.37 | -0.32 | 68 | 3.2 | 19 | 49 | 26 | BR | 1 | 81 | 55 | 50 | 98 | 8,122,000 |
| beni | Benin | A5 | 6 | 6,096,559 | 7,902,809 | 11,109,357 | 3,303,725 | 54.2 | 3.95 | 1.24 | 2.72 | 54 | 5.4 | 6 | 54 | 58 | F | 3 | 37 | 33 | 38 | 37 | 1,225,000 |
| berm | Bermuda | N1 | 10 | 64,590 | 69,443 | 75,613 | 44,968 | 69.6 | 2.06 | 0.50 | 1.56 | 75 | 2.6 | 45 | 1,196 | 7 | E | 1 | 92 | 90 | 95 | 97 | 43,600 |
| bhut | Bhutan | C2 | 17 | 2,123,970 | 2,753,954 | 3,903,897 | 1,219,796 | 57.4 | 3.50 | 0.85 | 2.64 | 63 | 5.4 | 5 | 45 | 27 | z | 3 | 34 | 10 | 27 | 42 | 516,000 |
| boli | Bolivia | L3 | 9 | 8,328,665 | 10,229,354 | 13,131,183 | 5,028,848 | 60.4 | 3.05 | 0.82 | 2.23 | 63 | 3.8 | 7 | 8 | 58 | Syq | 2 | 59 | 45 | 32 | 83 | 4,185,000 |
| bosn | Bosnia-Herzegovina | E3 | 8 | 3,971,813 | 4,329,808 | 4,323,818 | 3,223,921 | 81.2 | 1.11 | 0.81 | 0.30 | 74 | 3.6 | 12 | 78 | 20 | Q | 1 | 72 | 35 | 20 | 86 | 2,787,000 |
| bots | Botswana | A4 | 19 | 1,622,220 | 1,831,933 | 2,241,857 | 938,454 | 57.9 | 3.18 | 1.99 | 1.19 | 41 | 5.7 | 8 | 3 | 54 | EX | 2 | 67 | 65 | 43 | 70 | 657,000 |
| boug | Bougainville | P2 | 1 | 198,495 | 229,750 | 286,097 | 121,757 | 61.3 | 3.04 | 0.90 | 2.14 | 60 | 4.0 | 7 | 20 | 35 | tE | 2 | 48 | 30 | 30 | 80 | 97,600 |
| braz | Brazil | L3 | 27 | 170,115,463 | 190,875,224 | 217,929,781 | 121,037,152 | 71.2 | 1.92 | 0.72 | 1.20 | 68 | 4.2 | 10 | 20 | 224 | P | 2 | 78 | 45 | 50 | 83 | 100,763,000 |
| brit | Britain | E2 | 64 | 58,830,160 | 59,331,486 | 59,960,856 | 47,758,324 | 81.2 | 1.11 | 1.07 | 0.04 | 78 | 2.7 | 50 | 241 | 95 | E | 1 | 93 | 80 | 84 | 94 | 45,127,000 |
| briz | British Virgin Is | L1 | 1 | 21,366 | 27,248 | 36,663 | 14,734 | 69.0 | 2.00 | 0.56 | 1.43 | 76 | 4.0 | 45 | 140 | 8 | E | 2 | 88 | 90 | 90 | 93 | 13,700 |
| brun | Brunei | C3 | 4 | 328,080 | 384,439 | 458,972 | 222,110 | 67.7 | 1.88 | 0.32 | 1.56 | 76 | 5.8 | 15 | 57 | 27 | m | 2 | 88 | 40 | 55 | 88 | 195,000 |
| bulg | Bulgaria | E1 | 9 | 8,225,045 | 7,752,691 | 7,023,064 | 6,890,120 | 83.8 | 0.88 | 1.38 | -0.50 | 72 | 3.3 | 17 | 74 | 35 | b | 1 | 78 | 10 | 68 | 98 | 6,744,000 |
| burk | Burkina Faso | A5 | 30 | 11,936,823 | 15,751,319 | 23,321,336 | 6,287,125 | 52.7 | 4.43 | 1.69 | 2.74 | 46 | 6.2 | 6 | 44 | 80 | F | 3 | 22 | 15 | 27 | 19 | 1,216,000 |
| buru | Burundi | A1 | 15 | 6,695,001 | 8,496,970 | 11,568,648 | 3,591,199 | 53.6 | 3.97 | 1.82 | 2.14 | 44 | 4.6 | 7 | 241 | 14 | yF | 3 | 25 | 20 | 25 | 36 | 1,279,000 |
| camb | Cambodia | C3 | 20 | 11,167,719 | 13,250,035 | 16,526,449 | 6,603,472 | 59.1 | 2.97 | 1.20 | 1.77 | 54 | 5.6 | 4 | 61 | 37 | k | 3 | 35 | 10 | 16 | 66 | 4,369,000 |
| came | Cameroon | A2 | 10 | 15,084,969 | 19,239,891 | 26,484,402 | 8,524,516 | 56.5 | 3.78 | 1.26 | 2.52 | 54 | 5.2 | 9 | 32 | 297 | EF | 2 | 47 | 20 | 23 | 63 | 5,412,000 |
| cana | Canada | N1 | 12 | 31,146,639 | 33,928,551 | 37,896,497 | 25,247,466 | 81.1 | 1.10 | 0.75 | 0.35 | 79 | 2.7 | 50 | 3 | 152 | EF | 1 | 96 | 85 | 97 | 96 | 24,362,000 |
| cape | Cape Verde | A5 | 9 | 427,724 | 529,110 | 670,931 | 259,244 | 60.6 | 2.92 | 0.56 | 2.36 | 71 | 5.1 | 15 | 106 | 7 | P | 3 | 55 | 45 | 70 | 72 | 187,000 |
| caym | Cayman Islands | L1 | 1 | 38,371 | 53,015 | 77,938 | 26,461 | 69.0 | 2.00 | 0.56 | 1.43 | 76 | 4.0 | 40 | 148 | 6 | E | 2 | 89 | 85 | 90 | 93 | 24,600 |
| cent | Central African Rep | A2 | 17 | 3,615,266 | 4,333,276 | 5,703,795 | 2,078,416 | 57.5 | 3.63 | 1.84 | 1.80 | 45 | 4.7 | 6 | 6 | 95 | Fx | 3 | 36 | 30 | 27 | 60 | 1,252,000 |
| chad | Chad | A2 | 14 | 7,650,982 | 9,887,331 | 13,908,122 | 4,165,195 | 54.4 | 4.19 | 1.62 | 2.58 | 49 | 3.9 | 5 | 6 | 136 | FA | 3 | 29 | 12 | 18 | 48 | 2,010,000 |
| chan | Channel Islands | E2 | 1 | 152,898 | 162,284 | 173,400 | 124,123 | 81.2 | 1.11 | 1.07 | 0.04 | 78 | 2.0 | 45 | 788 | 6 | EF | 1 | 92 | 85 | 85 | 98 | 122,000 |
| chil | Chile | L3 | 13 | 15,211,294 | 17,010,268 | 19,547,916 | 10,883,681 | 71.6 | 1.82 | 0.57 | 1.24 | 76 | 4.1 | 14 | 20 | 25 | S | 2 | 89 | 20 | 63 | 95 | 10,361,000 |
| chin | China | C1 | 33 | 1,262,556,787 | 1,356,939,193 | 1,462,931,461 | 949,063,937 | 75.2 | 1.46 | 0.70 | 0.76 | 71 | 4.1 | 10 | 132 | 254 | C | 2 | 63 | 5 | 39 | 82 | 773,923,000 |
| colo | Colombia | L3 | 26 | 42,321,361 | 49,665,304 | 59,757,874 | 28,469,580 | 67.3 | 2.23 | 0.55 | 1.68 | 72 | 5.4 | 11 | 37 | 99 | S | 2 | 85 | 35 | 49 | 91 | 25,993,000 |
| como | Comoros | A1 | 3 | 592,749 | 766,305 | 989,515 | 343,261 | 57.9 | 3.48 | 0.84 | 2.64 | 61 | 5.6 | 9 | 318 | 11 | AFj | 3 | 41 | 15 | 37 | 57 | 197,000 |
| cong | Congo-Brazzaville | A2 | 15 | 2,943,464 | 3,858,198 | 5,689,140 | 1,579,463 | 53.7 | 4.13 | 1.42 | 2.70 | 50 | 4.7 | 12 | 9 | 79 | Fb | 2 | 50 | 20 | 36 | 75 | 1,184,000 |
| conz | Congo-Zaire | A2 | 11 | 51,654,496 | 69,389,334 | 104,787,601 | 26,684,713 | 51.7 | 4.29 | 1.29 | 3.00 | 53 | 6.0 | 11 | 22 | 260 | FES | 3 | 38 | 13 | 12 | 77 | 20,562,000 |
| cook | Cook Islands | P4 | 1 | 19,522 | 20,968 | 23,736 | 12,069 | 61.8 | 2.73 | 0.46 | 2.27 | 73 | 5.0 | 20 | 84 | 8 | E | 2 | 71 | 70 | 85 | 92 | 11,100 |
| cost | Costa Rica | L2 | 7 | 4,023,422 | 4,856,685 | 5,928,508 | 2,721,443 | 67.6 | 2.19 | 0.40 | 1.79 | 77 | 4.2 | 17 | 79 | 22 | S | 2 | 89 | 78 | 66 | 95 | 2,581,000 |
| croa | Croatia | E3 | 21 | 4,472,600 | 4,402,743 | 4,193,413 | 3,709,127 | 82.9 | 1.04 | 1.18 | -0.14 | 74 | 3.1 | 22 | 79 | 31 | C | 1 | 76 | 30 | 40 | 97 | 3,588,000 |
| cuba | Cuba | L1 | 15 | 11,200,684 | 11,516,190 | 11,798,235 | 8,823,899 | 78.8 | 1.17 | 0.72 | 0.44 | 76 | 3.7 | 18 | 101 | 15 | S | 2 | 72 | 13 | 62 | 96 | 8,449,000 |
| cypr | Cyprus | C4 | 5 | 600,506 | 647,453 | 687,811 | 460,948 | 76.8 | 1.36 | 0.76 | 0.61 | 78 | 3.5 | 30 | 102 | 10 | g | 2 | 91 | 40 | 50 | 95 | 439,000 |
| czec | Czech Republic | E1 | 8 | 10,244,177 | 10,066,401 | 9,512,292 | 8,547,741 | 83.4 | 0.89 | 1.08 | -0.19 | 75 | 2.7 | 25 | 130 | 26 | c | 1 | 88 | 15 | 75 | 100 | 8,548,000 |
| denm | Denmark | E2 | 16 | 5,293,239 | 5,327,432 | 5,238,499 | 4,341,515 | 82.0 | 1.13 | 1.17 | -0.04 | 76 | 2.2 | 51 | 123 | 29 | d | 1 | 93 | 95 | 99 | 100 | 4,342,000 |
| djib | Djibouti | A1 | 5 | 637,634 | 785,170 | 1,026,235 | 373,462 | 58.6 | 3.47 | 1.36 | 2.11 | 52 | 5.6 | 13 | 27 | 10 | AF | 3 | 32 | 15 | 18 | 46 | 173,000 |
| domi | Dominica | L1 | 10 | 70,714 | 71,045 | 73,442 | 53,835 | 76.1 | 1.53 | 0.58 | 0.95 | 78 | 4.3 | 15 | 94 | 10 | E | 2 | 87 | 45 | 40 | 90 | 48,400 |
| domr | Dominican Republic | L1 | 30 | 8,495,338 | 9,708,026 | 11,164,412 | 5,687,629 | 67.0 | 2.18 | 0.52 | 1.66 | 72 | 5.1 | 14 | 175 | 14 | S | 2 | 72 | 53 | 47 | 82 | 4,669,000 |
| ecua | Ecuador | L3 | 21 | 12,646,068 | 14,898,509 | 17,796,101 | 8,367,903 | 66.2 | 2.32 | 0.58 | 1.74 | 70 | 4.1 | 17 | 46 | 33 | S | 2 | 78 | 60 | 42 | 90 | 7,540,000 |
| egyp | Egypt | A3 | 27 | 68,469,695 | 80,063,292 | 95,615,454 | 44,272,505 | 64.7 | 2.35 | 0.61 | 1.74 | 68 | 4.9 | 12 | 69 | 38 | A | 2 | 61 | 28 | 41 | 51 | 22,745,000 |
| elsa | El Salvador | L2 | 14 | 6,276,023 | 7,440,647 | 9,062,331 | 4,041,759 | 64.4 | 2.53 | 0.59 | 1.94 | 70 | 4.9 | 11 | 298 | 15 | S | 2 | 59 | 50 | 36 | 74 | 3,003,000 |
| equa | Equatorial Guinea | A2 | 7 | 452,661 | 575,328 | 794,724 | 257,021 | 56.8 | 3.88 | 1.46 | 2.42 | 52 | 4.5 | 8 | 16 | 23 | SF | 3 | 46 | 40 | 40 | 79 | 202,000 |
| erit | Eritrea | A1 | 6 | 3,850,388 | 4,909,569 | 6,680,653 | 2,151,597 | 55.9 | 3.82 | 1.33 | 2.49 | 52 | 4.0 | 9 | 33 | 16 | qEA | 3 | 27 | 30 | 45 | 20 | 429,000 |
| esto | Estonia | E2 | 15 | 1,396,158 | 1,260,920 | 1,131,222 | 1,152,389 | 82.5 | 0.91 | 1.35 | -0.43 | 70 | 3.1 | 21 | 31 | 24 | E | 1 | 78 | 35 | 50 | 100 | 1,149,000 |
| ethi | Ethiopia | A1 | 10 | 62,564,875 | 79,943,539 | 115,382,091 | 33,691,185 | 53.9 | 4.31 | 1.88 | 2.43 | 44 | 4.5 | 11 | 55 | 145 | L | 3 | 24 | 5 | 15 | 35 | 11,939,000 |
| faer | Faeroe Islands | E2 | 1 | 42,749 | 39,703 | 36,604 | 35,063 | 82.0 | 1.13 | 1.17 | -0.04 | 76 | 3.0 | 30 | 31 | 5 | Jd | 1 | 92 | 80 | 90 | 99 | 34,700 |
| fiji | Fiji | P2 | 15 | 816,905 | 936,229 | 1,104,141 | 561,295 | 68.7 | 2.10 | 0.47 | 1.63 | 74 | 6.0 | 18 | 45 | 30 | E | 2 | 86 | 40 | 60 | 92 | 514,000 |
| finl | Finland | E2 | 12 | 5,175,743 | 5,235,338 | 5,253,863 | 4,239,451 | 81.9 | 1.08 | 0.99 | 0.09 | 78 | 2.3 | 45 | 15 | 31 | fs | 1 | 94 | 90 | 92 | 100 | 4,239,000 |
| fran | France | E4 | 96 | 59,079,709 | 60,596,993 | 61,661,804 | 48,031,803 | 81.3 | 1.19 | 0.95 | 0.23 | 79 | 2.6 | 50 | 109 | 97 | F | 1 | 95 | 88 | 93 | 99 | 47,454,000 |
| freg | French Guiana | L3 | 2 | 181,313 | 264,502 | 416,191 | 127,209 | 70.2 | 1.88 | 0.69 | 1.19 | 66 | 3.4 | 15 | 2 | 24 | F | 2 | 77 | 30 | 60 | 83 | 106,000 |
| frep | French Polynesia | P4 | 5 | 235,061 | 272,750 | 324,439 | 157,185 | 66.9 | 2.11 | 0.47 | 1.64 | 73 | 4.7 | 18 | 59 | 15 | FN | 2 | 87 | 70 | 65 | 95 | 149,000 |
| gabo | Gabon | A2 | 9 | 1,226,127 | 1,506,584 | 1,981,233 | 733,469 | 59.8 | 3.48 | 1.55 | 1.93 | 52 | 4.0 | 9 | 5 | 51 | F | 2 | 56 | 25 | 45 | 63 | 465,000 |
| gamb | Gambia | A5 | 7 | 1,305,363 | 1,651,481 | 2,150,833 | 778,910 | 59.7 | 3.74 | 1.58 | 2.16 | 49 | 8.3 | 7 | 122 | 32 | E | 3 | 28 | 20 | 36 | 39 | 301,000 |
| geor | Georgia | C4 | 13 | 4,967,561 | 5,010,697 | 5,178,116 | 3,868,737 | 77.9 | 1.38 | 0.97 | 0.41 | 74 | 4.1 | 18 | 71 | 35 | G | 2 | 64 | 40 | 45 | 100 | 3,851,000 |
| germ | Germany | E4 | 16 | 82,220,490 | 82,032,281 | 80,238,159 | 69,468,092 | 84.5 | 0.84 | 1.10 | -0.26 | 78 | 2.3 | 36 | 230 | 79 | G | 1 | 92 | 88 | 94 | 100 | 69,468,000 |
| ghan | Ghana | A5 | 10 | 20,212,495 | 26,366,959 | 36,876,215 | 11,488,782 | 56.8 | 3.55 | 0.85 | 2.70 | 62 | 4.9 | 5 | 85 | 108 | E | 2 | 47 | 28 | 19 | 65 | 7,427,000 |
| gibr | Gibraltar | E3 | 1 | 25,082 | 23,454 | 21,393 | 20,364 | 81.2 | 1.11 | 1.07 | 0.04 | 78 | 3.2 | 28 | 4,180 | 7 | E | 1 | 93 | 80 | 80 | 99 | 20,200 |
| gree | Greece | E3 | 13 | 10,644,744 | 10,554,397 | 9,862,572 | 9,052,290 | 85.0 | 0.88 | 1.03 | -0.15 | 79 | 3.3 | 26 | 81 | 31 | g | 1 | 92 | 78 | 81 | 95 | 8,628,000 |
| grel | Greenland | N1 | 6 | 56,156 | 57,200 | 59,634 | 46,059 | 82.0 | 1.13 | 1.17 | -0.04 | 76 | 1.8 | 15 | <1 | 5 | Hd | 1 | 86 | 75 | 75 | 100 | 46,100 |
| gren | Grenada | L1 | 9 | 93,717 | 97,453 | 104,647 | 70,269 | 75.0 | 1.37 | 0.60 | 0.77 | 75 | 3.7 | 16 | 272 | 10 | E | 2 | 84 | 60 | 70 | 85 | 59,700 |
| guad | Guadeloupe | L1 | 3 | 455,687 | 509,648 | 569,216 | 346,915 | 76.1 | 1.53 | 0.58 | 0.95 | 78 | 3.4 | 14 | 256 | 7 | F | 2 | 87 | 60 | 70 | 90 | 313,000 |
| guam | Guam | P3 | 1 | 167,556 | 193,836 | 227,634 | 112,430 | 67.1 | 2.07 | 0.47 | 1.60 | 76 | 4.0 | 20 | 113 | 13 | yE | 2 | 90 | 80 | 80 | 99 | 111,000 |
| guat | Guatemala | L2 | 22 | 11,385,295 | 14,631,050 | 19,816,134 | 6,420,168 | 56.4 | 3.42 | 0.68 | 2.74 | 66 | 5.4 | 15 | 105 | 65 | S | 2 | 57 | 50 | 31 | 56 | 3,570,000 |
| guin | Guinea | A5 | 33 | 7,430,346 | 9,427,100 | 12,496,941 | 4,160,994 | 56.0 | 4.04 | 1.60 | 2.44 | 49 | 4.7 | 10 | 30 | 44 | F | 3 | 27 | 15 | 14 | 36 | 1,497,000 |
| gunb | Guinea-Bissau | A5 | 9 | 1,213,111 | 1,480,638 | 1,946,020 | 696,690 | 57.4 | 4.03 | 1.95 | 2.07 | 45 | 4.1 | 9 | 34 | 32 | P | 3 | 29 | 20 | 18 | 55 | 384,000 |
| guya | Guyana | L3 | 10 | 861,334 | 922,942 | 1,044,669 | 604,312 | 70.2 | 1.88 | 0.69 | 1.19 | 66 | 5.1 | 13 | 4 | 24 | E | 2 | 65 | 55 | 39 | 98 | 592,000 |
| hait | Haiti | L1 | 9 | 8,222,025 | 9,669,191 | 11,988,232 | 4,874,839 | 59.3 | 3.06 | 1.17 | 1.88 | 55 | 4.4 | 10 | 297 | 9 | hF | 3 | 34 | 23 | 11 | 45 | 2,196,000 |
| hond | Honduras | L2 | 18 | 6,485,445 | 8,202,633 | 10,656,044 | 3,784,257 | 58.4 | 3.00 | 0.51 | 2.49 | 71 | 5.7 | 14 | 58 | 27 | S | 2 | 58 | 45 | 38 | 73 | 2,749,000 |
| hung | Hungary | E1 | 20 | 10,035,568 | 9,626,550 | 8,900,388 | 8,329,521 | 83.0 | 0.93 | 1.33 | -0.40 | 72 | 2.9 | 29 | 108 | 23 | h | 1 | 86 | 18 | 68 | 99 | 8,237,000 |
| icel | Iceland | E2 | 7 | 280,969 | 303,644 | 328,356 | 215,419 | 76.7 | 1.51 | 0.68 | 0.83 | 80 | 2.9 | 38 | 3 | 10 | i | 1 | 94 | 85 | 93 | 100 | 215,000 |
| indi | India | C2 | 32 | 1,013,661,777 | 1,152,163,518 | 1,330,448,707 | 676,011,039 | 66.7 | 2.26 | 0.84 | 1.42 | 64 | 5.6 | 12 | 320 | 439 | HE | 2 | 45 | 35 | 37 | 52 | 351,847,000 |
| indo | Indonesia | C3 | 26 | 212,107,385 | 238,011,716 | 273,442,120 | 147,181,314 | 69.4 | 2.01 | 0.70 | 1.31 | 67 | 4.5 | 14 | 111 | 744 | X | 2 | 67 | 13 | 36 | 84 | 123,321,000 |
| iran | Iran | C2 | 27 | 67,702,199 | 76,931,899 | 94,462,501 | 43,180,463 | 63.8 | 2.12 | 0.52 | 1.60 | 71 | 5.1 | 15 | 41 | 78 | N | 2 | 78 | 10 | 44 | 72 | 31,173,000 |
| iraq | Iraq | C4 | 18 | 23,114,884 | 30,338,663 | 41,013,588 | 13,559,191 | 58.7 | 3.38 | 0.54 | 2.84 | 69 | 8.9 | 13 | 53 | 36 | A | 2 | 53 | 0 | 35 | 58 | 7,874,000 |
| irel | Ireland | E2 | 4 | 3,730,239 | 4,016,447 | 4,403,843 | 2,938,309 | 78.8 | 1.45 | 0.81 | 0.64 | 77 | 3.9 | 48 | 53 | 21 | iE | 1 | 93 | 68 | 89 | 100 | 2,938,000 |
| isle | Isle of Man | E2 | 1 | 79,166 | 88,814 | 100,891 | 64,275 | 81.2 | 1.11 | 1.07 | 0.04 | 78 | 2.0 | 42 | 138 | 5 | E | 1 | 92 | 80 | 85 | 96 | 61,700 |
| isra | Israel | C4 | 6 | 5,121,683 | 6,017,886 | 6,926,755 | 3,701,440 | 72.3 | 1.82 | 0.62 | 1.20 | 78 | 3.7 | 28 | 251 | 53 | eA | 2 | 91 | 48 | 79 | 96 | 3,540,000 |
| ital | Italy | E3 | 20 | 57,297,886 | 55,781,181 | 51,269,528 | 49,132,937 | 85.8 | 0.85 | 1.09 | -0.24 | 79 | 2.8 | 50 | 190 | 60 | I | 1 | 92 | 73 | 88 | 97 | 47,698,000 |
| ivor | Ivory Coast | A5 | 50 | 14,785,832 | 18,200,343 | 23,345,116 | 8,364,345 | 56.6 | 3.60 | 1.53 | 2.07 | 48 | 5.4 | 10 | 46 | 103 | F | 2 | 37 | 35 | 26 | 40 | 3,356,000 |
| jama | Jamaica | L1 | 13 | 2,582,577 | 2,815,869 | 3,244,840 | 1,780,945 | 69.0 | 2.00 | 0.56 | 1.43 | 76 | 4.2 | 18 | 235 | 14 | E | 2 | 74 | 63 | 56 | 85 | 1,513,000 |
| japa | Japan | C1 | 47 | 126,714,220 | 127,315,474 | 121,150,001 | 107,947,844 | 85.2 | 1.01 | 0.90 | 0.12 | 80 | 3.0 | 38 | 335 | 34 | J | 1 | 94 | 80 | 93 | 100 | 107,948,000 |
| jord | Jordan | C4 | 12 | 6,669,341 | 8,797,930 | 12,062,895 | 3,871,552 | 58.1 | 3.30 | 0.41 | 2.89 | 72 | 6.0 | 25 | 75 | 20 | A | 2 | 73 | 20 | 59 | 87 | 3,354,000 |
| kaza | Kazakhstan | C2 | 16 | 16,222,563 | 16,492,359 | 17,698,360 | 11,751,625 | 72.4 | 1.72 | 0.83 | 0.89 | 69 | 4.0 | 18 | 6 | 49 | K | 2 | 71 | 40 | 35 | 98 | 11,465,000 |
| keny | Kenya | A1 | 8 | 30,080,372 | 35,204,705 | 41,755,990 | 17,136,788 | 57.0 | 3.20 | 1.41 | 1.79 | 48 | 6.2 | 10 | 52 | 124 | ES | 2 | 46 | 20 | 25 | 78 | 13,396,000 |
| kirg | Kirgizstan | C2 | 7 | 4,699,337 | 5,188,282 | 6,096,197 | 3,054,569 | 65.0 | 2.31 | 0.68 | 1.62 | 69 | 4.2 | 15 | 24 | 42 | k | 2 | 64 | 15 | 30 | 97 | 2,962,000 |
| kiri | Kiribati | P3 | 3 | 83,387 | 96,191 | 119,324 | 55,953 | 67.1 | 2.07 | 0.47 | 1.60 | 76 | 6.6 | 20 | 103 | 6 | E | 3 | 53 | 60 | 50 | 90 | 50,400 |
| kuwa | Kuwait | C4 | 5 | 1,971,634 | 2,419,713 | 2,974,454 | 1,306,996 | 66.3 | 2.02 | 0.24 | 1.78 | 77 | 7.4 | 25 | 111 | 27 | A | 2 | 84 | 20 | 72 | 79 | 1,029,000 |
| laos | Laos | C3 | 18 | 5,433,036 | 6,964,623 | 9,652,526 | 3,044,673 | 56.0 | 3.70 | 1.19 | 2.52 | 56 | 6.0 | 5 | 23 | 97 | l | 3 | 46 | 5 | 13 | 57 | 1,735,000 |
| latv | Latvia | E2 | 33 | 2,356,508 | 2,137,362 | 1,936,009 | 1,940,113 | 82.3 | 0.91 | 1.40 | -0.48 | 70 | 3.1 | 19 | 36 | 35 | L | 1 | 71 | 35 | 55 | 99 | 1,930,000 |
| leba | Lebanon | C4 | 5 | 3,281,787 | 3,722,943 | 4,399,649 | 2,208,643 | 67.3 | 1.98 | 0.61 | 1.37 | 71 | 5.3 | 18 | 321 | 19 | A | 2 | 79 | 30 | 39 | 92 | 2,042,000 |
| leso | Lesotho | A4 | 10 | 2,152,553 | 2,609,785 | 3,506,420 | 1,294,115 | 60.1 | 3.39 | 1.40 | 1.99 | 52 | 4.8 | 10 | 71 | 13 | wE | 3 | 46 | 40 | 30 | 72 | 926,000 |
| libe | Liberia | A5 | 12 | 3,154,001 | 4,443,705 | 6,617,526 | 1,824,590 | 57.9 | 4.77 | 1.19 | 3.58 | 55 | 5.0 | 8 | 32 | 47 | E | 3 | 31 | 18 | 24 | 38 | 697,000 |
| liby | Libya | A3 | 13 | 5,604,722 | 6,981,828 | 8,646,769 | 3,495,665 | 62.4 | 2.78 | 0.46 | 2.33 | 71 | 5.4 | 12 | 3 | 40 | A | 2 | 80 | 3 | 49 | 76 | 2,653,000 |
| liec | Liechtenstein | E4 | 2 | 32,843 | 36,668 | 41,252 | 27,112 | 82.6 | 1.01 | 0.89 | 0.12 | 79 | 3.0 | 45 | 205 | 6 | G | 1 | 93 | 80 | 85 | 100 | 27,100 |
| lith | Lithuania | E2 | 10 | 3,670,269 | 3,565,746 | 3,398,950 | 2,964,843 | 80.8 | 0.98 | 1.19 | -0.21 | 77 | 3.2 | 16 | 56 | 24 | e | 1 | 76 | 55 | 65 | 99 | 2,948,000 |
| luxe | Luxembourg | E4 | 3 | 430,615 | 456,615 | 463,356 | 352,932 | 82.0 | 1.15 | 0.94 | 0.21 | 77 | 2.8 | 40 | 167 | 15 | OG | 1 | 90 | 85 | 93 | 100 | 353,000 |
| mace | Macedonia | E3 | 30 | 2,023,580 | 2,142,050 | 2,257,977 | 1,559,371 | 77.1 | 1.56 | 0.81 | 0.75 | 74 | 4.4 | 32 | 79 | 24 | M | 1 | 75 | 50 | 65 | 89 | 1,388,000 |
| mada | Madagascar | A1 | 6 | 15,941,727 | 20,691,738 | 28,963,663 | 8,854,035 | 55.5 | 3.62 | 0.93 | 2.69 | 60 | 4.7 | 5 | 27 | 55 | mF | 3 | 35 | 40 | 25 | 80 | 7,105,000 |
| mala | Malawi | A1 | 24 | 10,925,238 | 13,912,265 | 19,958,349 | 5,773,988 | 52.9 | 4.51 | 2.14 | 2.37 | 40 | 4.3 | 7 | 92 | 31 | Ec | 3 | 32 | 35 | 21 | 57 | 3,276,000 |
| malb | Malaysia | C3 | 15 | 22,244,062 | 25,919,134 | 30,968,453 | 14,678,857 | 66.0 | 2.15 | 0.47 | 1.69 | 73 | 4.9 | 12 | 67 | 174 | m | 2 | 83 | 23 | 60 | 84 | 12,283,000 |

| COUNTRY | | | | DEMOGRAPHICS | | | | | | | | | | | | | | GEOPOLITICAL TYPOLOGIES | | | | | |
|---|---|---|---|---|---|---|---|---|---|---|---|---|---|---|---|---|---|---|---|---|---|---|---|
| | | | | | | | | | | | | | | | | | | | SCALES, 0–100 | | | | |
| code 1 | short name 2 | UN 3 | prov 4 | pop 2000 5 | pop 2010 6 | pop 2025 7 | adults 8 | apop 9 | bpop 10 | dpop 11 | npop 12 | life 13 | hom 14 | spac 15 | den 16 | peop 17 | langs 18 | dev 19 | HDI 20 | HFI 21 | HSI 22 | liter 23 | literates 24 |
| mald | Maldives | C2 | 19 | 286,223 | 373,116 | 501,456 | 163,405 | 57.1 | 3.33 | 0.63 | 2.70 | 67 | 7.1 | 10 | 960 | 9 | f | 3 | 61 | 10 | 30 | 93 | 152,000 |
| mali | Mali | A5 | 8 | 11,233,821 | 14,558,463 | 21,295,460 | 6,034,809 | 53.7 | 4.47 | 1.44 | 3.03 | 55 | 5.6 | 7 | 9 | 45 | F | 3 | 23 | 10 | 30 | 31 | 1,880,000 |
| malt | Malta | E3 | 6 | 388,544 | 412,587 | 429,847 | 309,825 | 79.7 | 1.32 | 0.78 | 0.54 | 78 | 3.6 | 17 | 1,230 | 11 | oE | 1 | 89 | 70 | 80 | 96 | 298,000 |
| mars | Marshall Islands | P3 | 24 | 64,220 | 86,434 | 127,147 | 43,092 | 67.1 | 2.07 | 0.47 | 1.60 | 76 | 8.7 | 15 | 355 | 3 | dE | 2 | 58 | 70 | 70 | 91 | 39,300 |
| mart | Martinique | L1 | 3 | 395,362 | 420,797 | 450,094 | 306,406 | 77.5 | 1.34 | 0.66 | 0.68 | 79 | 3.3 | 12 | 350 | 9 | F | 2 | 91 | 50 | 65 | 93 | 283,000 |
| maur | Mauritania | A5 | 13 | 2,669,547 | 3,455,905 | 4,766,399 | 1,511,231 | 56.6 | 3.86 | 1.20 | 2.66 | 56 | 5.0 | 4 | 3 | 26 | A | 3 | 36 | 5 | 23 | 38 | 572,000 |
| maus | Mauritius | A1 | 11 | 1,156,498 | 1,254,018 | 1,377,463 | 863,788 | 74.7 | 1.58 | 0.66 | 0.92 | 73 | 5.3 | 7 | 567 | 24 | E | 2 | 83 | 35 | 60 | 83 | 716,000 |
| mayo | Mayotte | A1 | 2 | 101,621 | 129,559 | 186,507 | 58,849 | 57.9 | 3.48 | 0.84 | 2.64 | 61 | 4.9 | 8 | 272 | 10 | AF | 2 | 49 | 20 | 35 | 91 | 53,600 |
| mexi | Mexico | L2 | 32 | 98,881,289 | 112,890,609 | 130,196,156 | 66,102,142 | 66.9 | 2.22 | 0.51 | 1.71 | 73 | 5.1 | 6 | 50 | 278 | S | 2 | 85 | 38 | 47 | 90 | 59,212,000 |
| micr | Micronesia | P3 | 4 | 118,689 | 144,265 | 189,609 | 79,640 | 67.1 | 2.07 | 0.47 | 1.60 | 76 | 7.0 | 12 | 169 | 22 | E | 2 | 56 | 65 | 65 | 77 | 61,000 |
| mold | Moldavia | E1 | 50 | 4,380,492 | 4,424,179 | 4,546,842 | 3,360,713 | 76.7 | 1.29 | 1.07 | 0.21 | 69 | 3.4 | 18 | 130 | 32 | QR | 1 | 61 | 40 | 60 | 96 | 3,240,000 |
| mona | Monaco | E4 | 1 | 33,597 | 36,867 | 40,692 | 27,314 | 81.3 | 1.19 | 0.95 | 0.23 | 79 | 2.2 | 35 | 16,799 | 15 | F | 1 | 94 | 85 | 95 | 99 | 27,000 |
| mong | Mongolia | C1 | 21 | 2,662,020 | 3,083,289 | 3,708,989 | 1,740,695 | 65.4 | 2.09 | 0.59 | 1.50 | 68 | 4.8 | 10 | 2 | 21 | o | 2 | 66 | 5 | 57 | 83 | 1,443,000 |
| mont | Montserrat | L1 | 1 | 10,629 | 10,502 | 10,658 | 8,091 | 76.1 | 1.53 | 0.58 | 0.95 | 78 | 4.0 | 18 | 104 | 8 | E | 2 | 84 | 65 | 70 | 82 | 6,600 |
| moro | Morocco | A3 | 43 | 28,220,843 | 32,682,965 | 38,529,890 | 19,034,959 | 67.5 | 2.28 | 0.61 | 1.67 | 69 | 5.8 | 10 | 62 | 32 | A | 2 | 57 | 18 | 41 | 44 | 8,340,000 |
| moza | Mozambique | A1 | 11 | 19,680,456 | 23,116,593 | 30,611,842 | 10,845,899 | 55.1 | 4.12 | 2.39 | 1.73 | 38 | 4.4 | 8 | 24 | 57 | P | 3 | 28 | 15 | 7 | 40 | 4,371,000 |
| myan | Myanmar | C3 | 14 | 45,611,177 | 50,902,661 | 58,120,485 | 32,885,659 | 72.1 | 1.99 | 0.86 | 1.13 | 63 | 5.2 | 7 | 67 | 133 | W | 3 | 48 | 7 | 19 | 83 | 27,353,000 |
| nami | Namibia | A4 | 13 | 1,725,868 | 1,915,827 | 2,337,592 | 1,008,425 | 58.4 | 3.42 | 2.20 | 1.22 | 41 | 4.8 | 3 | 2 | 33 | EM | 2 | 57 | 60 | 60 | 76 | 765,000 |
| naur | Nauru | P3 | 1 | 11,519 | 13,790 | 17,821 | 7,728 | 67.1 | 2.07 | 0.47 | 1.60 | 76 | 8.0 | 10 | 549 | 9 | nE | 2 | 86 | 65 | 65 | 99 | 7,700 |
| nepa | Nepal | C2 | 14 | 23,930,490 | 29,715,459 | 38,010,174 | 14,123,775 | 59.0 | 3.19 | 0.95 | 2.23 | 60 | 5.5 | 14 | 163 | 118 | n | 3 | 35 | 10 | 31 | 28 | 3,903,000 |
| neth | Netherlands | E4 | 12 | 15,785,699 | 15,972,738 | 15,781,965 | 12,926,909 | 81.9 | 1.03 | 0.90 | 0.13 | 78 | 2.4 | 48 | 380 | 46 | D | 1 | 94 | 93 | 98 | 100 | 12,927,000 |
| nets | Netherlands Antilles | L1 | 5 | 216,775 | 236,607 | 258,459 | 162,690 | 75.1 | 1.53 | 0.61 | 0.92 | 76 | 3.7 | 40 | 271 | 15 | D | 2 | 89 | 70 | 80 | 94 | 153,000 |
| newc | New Caledonia | P2 | 3 | 214,029 | 245,885 | 285,515 | 150,163 | 70.2 | 2.06 | 0.54 | 1.53 | 74 | 4.1 | 30 | 12 | 50 | F | 2 | 71 | 75 | 80 | 58 | 86,900 |
| newz | New Zealand | P1 | 16 | 3,861,905 | 4,207,078 | 4,694,964 | 2,986,411 | 77.3 | 1.42 | 0.79 | 0.63 | 78 | 2.9 | 45 | 14 | 48 | EI | 1 | 94 | 90 | 92 | 100 | 2,986,000 |
| nica | Nicaragua | L2 | 17 | 5,074,194 | 6,529,320 | 8,696,054 | 2,905,483 | 57.3 | 3.28 | 0.54 | 2.74 | 69 | 6.9 | 25 | 39 | 22 | S | 2 | 53 | 50 | 34 | 66 | 1,906,000 |
| niga | Niger | A5 | 7 | 10,730,102 | 14,485,881 | 21,495,434 | 5,559,266 | 51.8 | 4.56 | 1.51 | 3.05 | 51 | 6.4 | 10 | 8 | 37 | F | 3 | 21 | 20 | 30 | 14 | 760,000 |
| nige | Nigeria | A5 | 31 | 111,506,095 | 138,698,398 | 183,041,179 | 63,469,269 | 56.9 | 3.72 | 1.44 | 2.28 | 50 | 5.0 | 12 | 121 | 491 | E | 2 | 39 | 33 | 30 | 57 | 36,318,000 |
| nork | North Korea | C1 | 13 | 24,039,193 | 26,451,118 | 29,387,635 | 17,399,568 | 72.4 | 1.68 | 0.55 | 1.13 | 73 | 4.8 | 14 | 196 | 7 | K | 2 | 77 | 35 | 63 | 95 | 16,530,000 |
| norl | Northern Cyprus | C4 | 1 | 185,045 | 195,562 | 212,470 | 142,041 | 76.8 | 1.36 | 0.76 | 0.61 | 78 | 3.0 | 18 | 55 | 4 | T | 2 | 88 | 25 | 45 | 85 | 121,000 |
| norm | Northern Mariana Is | P3 | 1 | 78,356 | 131,073 | 245,191 | 52,577 | 67.1 | 2.07 | 0.47 | 1.60 | 76 | 4.6 | 15 | 164 | 10 | E | 2 | 84 | 70 | 55 | 96 | 50,600 |
| norw | Norway | E2 | 19 | 4,461,033 | 4,643,522 | 4,812,063 | 3,585,332 | 80.4 | 1.22 | 1.00 | 0.23 | 79 | 2.2 | 38 | 14 | 32 | j | 1 | 94 | 88 | 96 | 100 | 3,585,000 |
| oman | Oman | C4 | 8 | 2,541,739 | 3,517,471 | 5,351,885 | 1,420,578 | 55.9 | 3.58 | 0.39 | 3.19 | 72 | 3.7 | 24 | 8 | 26 | A | 2 | 72 | 20 | 50 | 59 | 844,000 |
| paki | Pakistan | C2 | 6 | 156,483,155 | 199,744,986 | 262,999,723 | 91,041,900 | 58.2 | 3.29 | 0.68 | 2.62 | 66 | 6.3 | 1 | 197 | 93 | UE | 2 | 45 | 13 | 33 | 38 | 34,238,000 |
| pala | Palau | P3 | 1 | 19,426 | 24,391 | 33,228 | 13,035 | 67.1 | 2.07 | 0.47 | 1.60 | 76 | 6.0 | 10 | 12 | 5 | pE | 2 | 67 | 75 | 60 | 97 | 12,700 |
| pale | Palestine | C4 | 2 | 2,215,393 | 2,845,762 | 4,132,562 | 1,070,699 | 48.3 | 4.38 | 0.38 | 3.99 | 73 | 6.0 | 12 | 355 | 21 | A | 2 | 79 | 25 | 30 | 72 | 772,000 |
| pana | Panama | L2 | 11 | 2,855,683 | 3,266,131 | 3,779,174 | 1,961,854 | 68.7 | 2.03 | 0.51 | 1.53 | 74 | 4.4 | 14 | 38 | 33 | S | 2 | 86 | 53 | 62 | 91 | 1,781,000 |
| papu | Papua New Guinea | P2 | 20 | 4,608,145 | 5,687,355 | 7,173,798 | 2,826,636 | 61.3 | 3.04 | 0.90 | 2.14 | 60 | 4.6 | 8 | 10 | 862 | tE | 2 | 53 | 75 | 34 | 72 | 2,039,000 |
| para | Paraguay | L3 | 18 | 5,496,453 | 6,980,320 | 9,355,207 | 3,323,705 | 60.5 | 2.96 | 0.51 | 2.46 | 71 | 4.7 | 10 | 14 | 45 | Sg | 2 | 71 | 25 | 37 | 92 | 3,060,000 |
| peru | Peru | L3 | 14 | 25,661,669 | 29,885,322 | 35,518,199 | 17,093,238 | 66.6 | 2.26 | 0.62 | 1.64 | 70 | 5.1 | 12 | 20 | 111 | Syq | 2 | 72 | 40 | 37 | 89 | 15,162,000 |
| phil | Philippines | C3 | 16 | 75,966,500 | 90,544,498 | 108,251,048 | 48,094,391 | 63.3 | 2.56 | 0.53 | 2.03 | 70 | 5.7 | 22 | 253 | 183 | OES | 2 | 67 | 25 | 50 | 95 | 45,523,000 |
| pola | Poland | E1 | 49 | 38,765,085 | 39,190,093 | 39,069,168 | 31,240,782 | 80.6 | 1.11 | 0.99 | 0.12 | 74 | 3.6 | 18 | 124 | 24 | Y | 1 | 83 | 25 | 67 | 99 | 30,846,000 |
| port | Portugal | E3 | 20 | 9,874,853 | 9,776,944 | 9,348,354 | 8,261,302 | 83.7 | 1.00 | 1.09 | -0.09 | 76 | 3.8 | 30 | 107 | 30 | P | 1 | 89 | 75 | 75 | 90 | 7,406,000 |
| puer | Puerto Rico | L1 | 7 | 3,868,602 | 4,158,727 | 4,477,962 | 2,928,145 | 75.7 | 1.66 | 0.81 | 0.85 | 75 | 3.6 | 40 | 425 | 12 | SE | 2 | 88 | 75 | 85 | 90 | 2,625,000 |
| qata | Qatar | C4 | 9 | 599,065 | 692,178 | 778,537 | 442,889 | 73.9 | 1.81 | 0.44 | 1.37 | 73 | 6.4 | 25 | 52 | 21 | A | 2 | 84 | 20 | 68 | 79 | 352,000 |
| reun | Reunion | A1 | 4 | 699,406 | 777,722 | 879,761 | 507,699 | 72.6 | 1.67 | 0.52 | 1.14 | 77 | 3.8 | 20 | 278 | 17 | F | 2 | 84 | 35 | 55 | 78 | 397,000 |
| roma | Romania | E1 | 41 | 22,326,502 | 21,524,798 | 19,945,452 | 18,363,548 | 82.3 | 0.92 | 1.18 | -0.26 | 71 | 3.1 | 22 | 94 | 29 | R | 1 | 75 | 3 | 56 | 97 | 17,761,000 |
| russ | Russia | E1 | 21 | 146,933,847 | 144,418,309 | 137,932,932 | 120,250,660 | 81.8 | 1.04 | 1.44 | -0.39 | 67 | 3.2 | 17 | 9 | 169 | R | 1 | 79 | 8 | 69 | 98 | 117,920,000 |
| rwan | Rwanda | A1 | 10 | 7,733,127 | 9,534,549 | 12,426,835 | 4,223,834 | 54.6 | 4.12 | 2.02 | 2.10 | 41 | 4.7 | 10 | 294 | 13 | FrE | 3 | 19 | 15 | 24 | 61 | 2,559,000 |
| saha | Sahara | A3 | 1 | 293,357 | 386,057 | 469,946 | 182,116 | 62.1 | 2.86 | 0.76 | 2.10 | 64 | 5.0 | 3 | 1 | 12 | A | 2 | 24 | 5 | 5 | 10 | 18,200 |
| saih | Saint Helena | A5 | 1 | 6,293 | 6,841 | 7,756 | 5,109 | 81.2 | 1.11 | 1.07 | 0.04 | 78 | 3.0 | 20 | 52 | 4 | E | 2 | 75 | 70 | 75 | 98 | 5,000 |
| saik | Saint Kitts & Nevis | L1 | 2 | 38,473 | 36,321 | 35,052 | 29,289 | 76.1 | 1.53 | 0.58 | 0.95 | 78 | 4.0 | 15 | 143 | 6 | E | 2 | 85 | 70 | 75 | 90 | 26,400 |
| sail | Saint Lucia | L1 | 10 | 154,366 | 175,541 | 208,093 | 117,519 | 76.1 | 1.53 | 0.58 | 0.95 | 78 | 4.0 | 18 | 250 | 7 | E | 2 | 84 | 75 | 80 | 80 | 94,000 |
| saip | Saint Pierre & Miquelon | N1 | 1 | 6,567 | 6,778 | 7,171 | 5,340 | 81.3 | 1.19 | 0.95 | 0.23 | 79 | 3.0 | 22 | 27 | 3 | F | 1 | 75 | 75 | 80 | 99 | 5,300 |
| saiv | Saint Vincent | L1 | 13 | 113,954 | 121,403 | 130,781 | 86,753 | 76.1 | 1.53 | 0.58 | 0.95 | 78 | 4.0 | 17 | 293 | 13 | E | 2 | 84 | 80 | 75 | 96 | 83,300 |
| samo | Samoa | P4 | 2 | 180,073 | 216,958 | 271,417 | 111,321 | 61.8 | 2.73 | 0.46 | 2.27 | 73 | 7.8 | 14 | 64 | 8 | wE | 3 | 68 | 70 | 60 | 100 | 111,000 |
| sanm | San Marino | E3 | 9 | 26,514 | 29,407 | 32,392 | 22,736 | 85.8 | 0.85 | 1.09 | -0.24 | 79 | 2.7 | 40 | 435 | 4 | I | 1 | 96 | 85 | 95 | 99 | 22,500 |
| saot | Sao Tome & Principe | A2 | 7 | 146,775 | 175,794 | 217,146 | 84,381 | 57.5 | 3.63 | 1.84 | 1.80 | 45 | 4.0 | 10 | 147 | 7 | P | 3 | 53 | 10 | 20 | 54 | 45,800 |
| saud | Saudi Arabia | C4 | 5 | 21,606,691 | 28,778,495 | 39,964,965 | 12,849,499 | 59.5 | 3.22 | 0.38 | 2.84 | 73 | 6.6 | 15 | 10 | 39 | A | 2 | 77 | 15 | 56 | 62 | 7,962,000 |
| sene | Senegal | A5 | 10 | 9,481,161 | 12,166,453 | 16,742,579 | 5,244,978 | 55.3 | 3.79 | 1.16 | 2.63 | 54 | 8.8 | 8 | 48 | 58 | F | 2 | 33 | 58 | 34 | 33 | 1,735,000 |
| seyc | Seychelles | A1 | 5 | 77,435 | 85,582 | 97,962 | 57,836 | 74.7 | 1.58 | 0.66 | 0.92 | 73 | 4.8 | 10 | 170 | 10 | sEF | 2 | 85 | 10 | 56 | 84 | 48,800 |
| sier | Sierra Leone | A5 | 4 | 4,854,383 | 6,017,780 | 8,085,454 | 2,716,513 | 56.0 | 4.39 | 2.23 | 2.17 | 41 | 4.7 | 6 | 68 | 31 | E | 3 | 18 | 35 | 16 | 32 | 857,000 |
| sing | Singapore | C3 | 1 | 3,566,614 | 3,885,328 | 4,167,756 | 2,778,749 | 77.9 | 1.28 | 0.53 | 0.75 | 78 | 3.9 | 25 | 5,564 | 47 | CmtE | 2 | 90 | 28 | 72 | 89 | 2,476,000 |
| slok | Slovakia | E1 | 4 | 5,387,191 | 5,456,375 | 5,392,691 | 4,326,992 | 80.3 | 1.11 | 0.96 | 0.15 | 74 | 3.0 | 22 | 110 | 19 | u | 1 | 87 | 25 | 60 | 100 | 4,327,000 |
| slov | Slovenia | E3 | 12 | 1,985,557 | 1,950,573 | 1,817,953 | 1,669,059 | 84.1 | 0.89 | 1.05 | -0.16 | 75 | 3.1 | 21 | 98 | 15 | W | 1 | 89 | 25 | 55 | 100 | 1,669,000 |
| solo | Solomon Islands | P2 | 8 | 443,643 | 587,925 | 816,561 | 253,542 | 57.2 | 3.30 | 0.37 | 2.93 | 73 | 5.6 | 18 | 16 | 76 | E | 3 | 56 | 30 | 51 | 54 | 137,000 |
| soma | Somalia | A1 | 13 | 7,264,500 | 10,579,797 | 16,227,263 | 3,780,446 | 52.0 | 4.99 | 1.67 | 3.32 | 49 | 4.9 | 4 | 15 | 29 | vA | 3 | 22 | 5 | 8 | 25 | 942,000 |
| somi | Somaliland | A1 | 3 | 2,832,677 | 3,550,995 | 4,984,017 | 1,474,125 | 52.0 | 4.99 | 1.67 | 3.32 | 49 | 5.0 | 3 | 20 | 11 | vA | 2 | 28 | 15 | 20 | 25 | 367,000 |
| soua | South Africa | A4 | 9 | 40,376,579 | 42,514,924 | 46,015,286 | 26,236,701 | 65.0 | 2.52 | 1.81 | 0.71 | 47 | 4.6 | 27 | 33 | 70 | ME | 2 | 72 | 8 | 39 | 82 | 21,461,000 |
| souk | South Korea | C1 | 15 | 46,843,989 | 49,975,564 | 52,532,789 | 36,777,216 | 78.5 | 1.41 | 0.66 | 0.76 | 74 | 3.8 | 25 | 472 | 9 | K | 2 | 71 | 13 | 66 | 98 | 36,046,000 |
| spai | Spain | E3 | 17 | 39,629,775 | 39,089,282 | 36,658,293 | 33,863,643 | 85.5 | 0.89 | 1.00 | -0.11 | 79 | 3.5 | 25 | 79 | 36 | S | 1 | 93 | 65 | 89 | 97 | 32,701,000 |
| span | Spanish North Africa | A3 | 2 | 130,000 | 133,911 | 140,000 | 87,685 | 67.5 | 2.28 | 0.61 | 1.67 | 69 | 3.0 | 20 | 3,939 | 5 | S | 2 | 91 | 70 | 70 | 92 | 80,700 |
| sril | Sri Lanka | C2 | 25 | 18,827,054 | 20,869,505 | 23,546,757 | 13,913,193 | 73.9 | 1.72 | 0.59 | 1.13 | 74 | 5.2 | 15 | 287 | 22 | ut | 2 | 71 | 28 | 42 | 90 | 12,559,000 |
| suda | Sudan | A3 | 9 | 29,489,719 | 36,256,579 | 46,264,179 | 17,864,872 | 60.6 | 3.17 | 1.07 | 2.10 | 57 | 5.3 | 5 | 12 | 245 | A | 3 | 33 | 5 | 11 | 46 | 8,250,000 |
| suri | Suriname | L3 | 10 | 417,130 | 452,074 | 524,642 | 290,030 | 69.5 | 1.89 | 0.60 | 1.29 | 71 | 3.9 | 7 | 3 | 28 | D | 2 | 79 | 15 | 45 | 93 | 270,000 |
| swaz | Swaziland | A4 | 4 | 1,007,895 | 1,310,450 | 1,784,790 | 574,601 | 57.0 | 3.51 | 0.79 | 2.73 | 63 | 5.7 | 12 | 58 | 12 | xE | 2 | 58 | 60 | 34 | 77 | 441,000 |
| swed | Sweden | E2 | 23 | 8,910,214 | 9,039,070 | 9,096,927 | 7,288,555 | 81.8 | 0.98 | 1.11 | -0.13 | 79 | 2.2 | 50 | 20 | 51 | s | 1 | 94 | 95 | 89 | 100 | 7,289,000 |
| swit | Switzerland | E4 | 26 | 7,385,708 | 7,602,762 | 7,586,992 | 6,097,641 | 82.6 | 1.01 | 0.89 | 0.12 | 79 | 2.2 | 50 | 179 | 39 | GFrI | 1 | 93 | 85 | 97 | 100 | 6,098,000 |
| syri | Syria | C4 | 14 | 16,124,618 | 20,464,138 | 26,291,810 | 9,547,386 | 59.2 | 2.92 | 0.45 | 2.47 | 70 | 6.2 | 30 | 87 | 28 | A | 2 | 76 | 13 | 36 | 71 | 6,769,000 |
| taiw | Taiwan | C1 | 23 | 22,401,000 | 24,033,000 | 25,730,000 | 16,838,832 | 75.2 | 1.46 | 0.70 | 0.76 | 71 | 3.8 | 25 | 619 | 30 | C | 2 | 90 | 55 | 75 | 94 | 15,829,000 |
| taji | Tajikistan | C2 | 6 | 6,188,201 | 7,133,677 | 8,856,904 | 3,692,500 | 59.7 | 2.87 | 0.63 | 2.24 | 69 | 6.1 | 20 | 43 | 41 | T | 2 | 58 | 5 | 10 | 98 | 3,607,000 |
| tanz | Tanzania | A1 | 25 | 33,517,014 | 42,235,298 | 57,918,322 | 18,290,235 | 54.6 | 3.90 | 1.50 | 2.40 | 48 | 5.1 | 17 | 36 | 163 | SE | 3 | 36 | 25 | 29 | 68 | 12,438,000 |
| thai | Thailand | C3 | 7 | 61,399,249 | 66,510,844 | 72,716,978 | 45,908,218 | 74.8 | 1.58 | 0.72 | 0.86 | 69 | 5.3 | 15 | 120 | 95 | Z | 2 | 83 | 35 | 46 | 94 | 43,059,000 |
| timo | Timor | C3 | 1 | 884,541 | 1,015,062 | 1,184,977 | 540,720 | 61.1 | 2.76 | 1.35 | 1.41 | 50 | 4.0 | 10 | 59 | 22 | X | 2 | 52 | 10 | 20 | 90 | 487,000 |
| togo | Togo | A5 | 5 | 4,629,218 | 5,953,281 | 8,482,467 | 2,506,722 | 54.2 | 3.95 | 1.43 | 2.51 | 50 | 5.6 | 8 | 82 | 53 | F | 3 | 37 | 20 | 29 | 52 | 1,300,000 |
| tong | Tonga | P4 | 5 | 98,546 | 101,251 | 105,126 | 60,921 | 61.8 | 2.73 | 0.46 | 2.27 | 73 | 6.1 | 13 | 131 | 10 | zE | 2 | 63 | 65 | 70 | 93 | 56,600 |
| trin | Trinidad & Tobago | L1 | 12 | 1,294,958 | 1,374,007 | 1,493,418 | 970,960 | 75.0 | 1.37 | 0.60 | 0.77 | 75 | 4.1 | 14 | 253 | 16 | E | 2 | 88 | 63 | 71 | 98 | 951,000 |
| tuni | Tunisia | A3 | 23 | 9,585,611 | 10,928,892 | 12,843,081 | 6,678,295 | 69.7 | 1.97 | 0.64 | 1.34 | 71 | 5.1 | 12 | 58 | 25 | A | 2 | 75 | 28 | 47 | 67 | 4,456,000 |
| turk | Turkey | C4 | 8 | 66,590,940 | 76,054,450 | 87,869,200 | 47,745,704 | 71.7 | 1.98 | 0.63 | 1.35 | 71 | 4.5 | 18 | 85 | 57 | T | 2 | 77 | 18 | 47 | 82 | 39,221,000 |
| turm | Turkmenistan | C2 | 6 | 4,459,293 | 5,218,906 | 6,286,522 | 2,779,923 | 62.3 | 2.53 | 0.65 | 1.88 | 67 | 5.6 | 10 | 9 | 38 | V | 2 | 72 | 5 | 10 | 98 | 2,716,000 |
| turs | Turks & Caicos Is | L1 | 1 | 16,760 | 23,068 | 33,769 | 12,759 | 76.1 | 1.53 | 0.58 | 0.95 | 78 | 3.0 | 15 | 34 | 5 | E | 2 | 67 | 65 | 70 | 93 | 11,900 |
| tuva | Tuvalu | P4 | 9 | 11,719 | 15,022 | 20,674 | 7,245 | 61.8 | 2.73 | 0.46 | 2.27 | 73 | 6.4 | 12 | 488 | 7 | E | 3 | 57 | 70 | 70 | 96 | 6,900 |
| ugan | Uganda | A1 | 38 | 21,778,450 | 29,830,737 | 44,435,310 | 10,876,158 | 49.9 | 4.92 | 1.72 | 3.20 | 45 | 4.8 | 10 | 90 | 63 | E | 3 | 33 | 30 | 15 | 62 | 6,732,000 |
| ukra | Ukraine | E1 | 25 | 50,455,980 | 48,723,593 | 45,687,963 | 41,489,952 | 82.2 | 0.97 | 1.38 | -0.41 | 70 | 3.2 | 21 | 84 | 66 | U | 1 | 69 | 35 | 55 | 98 | 40,817,000 |
| unia | United Arab Emirates | C4 | 7 | 2,441,436 | 2,851,247 | 3,283,949 | 1,757,590 | 72.0 | 1.79 | 0.33 | 1.46 | 76 | 6.8 | 18 | 29 | 39 | A | 2 | 87 | 15 | 66 | 79 | 1,393,000 |
| usa | USA | N1 | 51 | 278,357,141 | 297,998,958 | 325,572,586 | 218,593,863 | 78.5 | 1.30 | 0.86 | 0.44 | 77 | 2.6 | 50 | 29 | 307 | E | 1 | 94 | 83 | 95 | 95 | 208,751,000 |
| uuay | Uruguay | L3 | 19 | 3,337,058 | 3,565,821 | 3,906,674 | 2,509,801 | 75.2 | 1.69 | 0.93 | 0.75 | 75 | 3.3 | 22 | 19 | 32 | S | 2 | 88 | 20 | 63 | 97 | 2,442,000 |
| uzbe | Uzbekistan | C2 | 13 | 24,317,851 | 28,170,066 | 33,354,778 | 15,210,816 | 62.6 | 2.57 | 0.62 | 1.96 | 69 | 5.5 | 20 | 54 | 64 | Z | 2 | 66 | 10 | 45 | 97 | 14,791,000 |
| vanu | Vanuatu | P2 | 11 | 190,417 | 239,668 | 319,146 | 111,622 | 58.6 | 3.00 | 0.53 | 2.46 | 69 | 5.1 | 18 | 16 | 123 | FEp | 3 | 55 | 55 | 55 | 53 | 58,700 |
| vene | Venezuela | L3 | 23 | 24,169,722 | 28,715,855 | 34,775,110 | 15,942,349 | 66.0 | 2.28 | 0.47 | 1.82 | 73 | 5.3 | 15 | 27 | 70 | S | 2 | 86 | 73 | 49 | 91 | 14,516,000 |
| viet | Viet Nam | C3 | 7 | 79,831,650 | 90,764,274 | 108,037,101 | 53,319,559 | 66.8 | 1.95 | 0.63 | 1.33 | 69 | 4.8 | 12 | 241 | 100 | V | 2 | 56 | 13 | 24 | 94 | 50,023,000 |
| virg | Virgin Is of the US | L1 | 3 | 92,954 | 87,198 | 83,559 | 70,766 | 76.1 | 1.53 | 0.58 | 0.95 | 78 | 3.1 | 35 | 264 | 9 | E | 2 | 88 | 85 | 90 | 95 | 67,200 |
| wall | Wallis & Futuna Is | P4 | 1 | 14,517 | 15,529 | 17,500 | 8,974 | 61.8 | 2.73 | 0.46 | 2.27 | 73 | 5.0 | 20 | 60 | 4 | F | 2 | 80 | 70 | 70 | 95 | 8,500 |
| yeme | Yemen | C4 | 17 | 18,112,066 | 25,366,187 | 38,985,203 | 9,363,938 | 51.7 | 4.33 | 0.87 | 3.46 | 61 | 5.6 | 10 | 38 | 22 | A | 3 | 36 | 15 | 25 | 46 | 4,310,000 |
| yugo | Yugoslavia | E3 | 4 | 10,640,150 | 10,762,337 | 10,844,276 | 8,508,928 | 80.0 | 1.27 | 1.01 | 0.26 | 74 | 3.0 | 20 | 104 | 35 | Y | 1 | 63 | 20 | 56 | 93 | 7,945,000 |
| zamb | Zambia | A1 | 9 | 9,168,700 | 11,426,935 | 15,616,246 | 4,837,406 | 52.8 | 4.06 | 1.79 | 2.27 | 42 | 4.4 | 6 | 12 | 86 | E | 3 | 37 | 23 | 32 | 78 | 3,791,000 |
| zimb | Zimbabwe | A1 | 10 | 11,669,029 | 12,863,136 | 15,092,435 | 6,847,386 | 58.7 | 2.97 | 2.00 | 0.97 | 41 | 4.8 | 7 | 30 | 42 | E | 2 | 51 | 20 | 34 | 85 | 5,828,000 |
| | 11 minicountries | | 11 | 23,079 | 25,481 | 30,666 | 17,447 | 75.6 | 1.59 | 0.79 | 0.80 | 76 | 3.3 | 21 | <1 | 48 | – | – | 78 | 77 | 79 | 90 | 15,800 |
| | Africa | A | 793 | 784,445,039 | 973,315,192 | 1,298,310,949 | 451,269,790 | 57.5 | 3.59 | 1.36 | 2.22 | 54 | 5.2 | 10 | 26 | 3,823 | – | – | 42 | 22 | 27 | 56 | 252,800,000 |
| | Antarctica | B | 1 | 4,500 | 6,193 | 10,000 | 3,253 | 72.3 | 1.91 | 0.78 | 1.13 | 74 | 2.0 | 15 | <1 | 1 | – | – | 80 | 80 | 70 | 100 | 3,300 |
| | Asia | C | 666 | 3,682,550,093 | 4,135,949,307 | 4,723,140,220 | 2,579,677,434 | 70.1 | 1.99 | 0.74 | 1.25 | 69 | 4.9 | 12 | 116 | 3,696 | – | – | 58 | 20 | 40 | 72 | 1,860,609,000 |
| | Europe | E | 811 | 728,886,951 | 724,242,074 | 702,335,374 | 601,533,471 | 82.5 | 1.01 | 1.16 | -0.15 | 75 | 2.9 | 32 | 32 | 1,518 | – | – | 86 | 52 | 78 | 98 | 588,366,000 |
| | Latin America | L | 531 | 519,138,048 | 595,030,371 | 696,648,086 | 355,459,810 | 68.5 | 2.14 | 0.64 | 1.50 | 73 | 4.6 | 11 | 25 | 1,555 | – | – | 79 | 44 | 49 | 87 | 307,774,000 |
| | Northern America | N | 80 | 309,631,093 | 332,050,930 | 363,611,501 | 243,937,696 | 78.8 | 1.28 | 0.85 | 0.43 | 77 | 2.6 | 49 | 14 | 474 | – | – | 94 | 83 | 95 | 96 | 233,208,000 |
| | Oceania | P | 149 | 30,393,391 | 34,179,316 | 39,647,012 | 22,765,535 | 74.9 | 1.67 | 0.76 | 0.91 | 73 | 3.5 | 39 | 4 | 1,516 | – | – | 85 | 79 | 83 | 95 | 21,550,000 |
| | **World A** | | **517** | **605,303,996** | **744,275,621** | **953,171,604** | **373,218,956** | **61.7** | **2.95** | **0.77** | **2.18** | **62** | **5.8** | **9** | **33** | **1,448** | – | – | **55** | **14** | **36** | **58** | **216,596,000** |
| | **World B** | | **812** | **3,755,011,992** | **4,193,116,856** | **4,783,698,891** | **2,636,973,009** | **70.2** | **2.02** | **0.85** | **1.16** | **64** | **4.7** | **12** | **71** | **5,192** | – | – | **57** | **21** | **40** | **72** | **1,907,017,000** |
| | **World C** | | **1,702** | **1,694,733,127** | **1,857,380,906** | **2,086,832,647** | **1,244,455,024** | **73.4** | **1.82** | **0.94** | **0.87** | **71** | **3.8** | **27** | **21** | **5,943** | – | – | **80** | **55** | **65** | **92** | **1,140,698,000** |
| | **GLOBAL TOTAL** | | **3,031** | **6,055,049,115** | **6,794,773,383** | **7,823,703,142** | **4,254,646,989** | **70.3** | **2.05** | **0.87** | **1.18** | **68** | **4.5** | **16** | **40** | **12,583** | – | – | **63** | **30** | **47** | **77** | **3,264,311,000** |

| COUNTRY | | SOCIETY | | | | | | | | | | | | | | | | | | | | | |
|---|---|---|---|---|---|---|---|---|---|---|---|---|---|---|---|---|---|---|---|---|---|---|---|
| | | ECONOMIC | | URBANIZATION | | | METROSCAN | | | HEALTH | | | | | | | | | | | EDUCATION | | |
| code | short name | GNP | EFL | rural | urban | metro | cit50 | cit100 | mega | acces | water | mat-m | inf-m | hosp | beds | doct | blind | deaf | lepers | murd | educ | schools | univs |
| 1 | 2 | 25 | 26 | 27 | 28 | 29 | 30 | 31 | 32 | 33 | 34 | 35 | 36 | 37 | 38 | 39 | 40 | 41 | 42 | 43 | 44 | 45 | 46 |
| afgh | Afghanistan | 600 | 2 | 17.7 | 5.0 | 4.9 | 10 | 8 | 1 | 29 | 12 | 1,700 | 142 | 250 | 3 | 2,233 | 200,000 | 1,535,500 | 8,000 | 90.0 | 36 | 2,605 | 5 |
| alba | Albania | 670 | 31 | 1.9 | 1.2 | 0.7 | 6 | 1 | 0 | 45 | 50 | 65 | 26 | 895 | 57 | 4,467 | 2,000 | 209,600 | 500 | 50.0 | 79 | 2,290 | 8 |
| alge | Algeria | 1,600 | 35 | 12.8 | 18.7 | 11.3 | 44 | 26 | 2 | 98 | 78 | 160 | 36 | 284 | 22 | 25,304 | 25,000 | 1,895,900 | 44,000 | 1.0 | 84 | 17,372 | 40 |
| amer | American Samoa | 2,600 | 50 | 0.0 | 0.0 | 0.0 | 0 | 0 | 0 | 80 | 80 | 30 | 19 | 1 | 27 | 34 | 50 | 3,800 | 550 | 8.0 | 95 | 38 | 2 |
| ando | Andorra | 16,200 | 45 | 0.0 | 0.1 | 0.0 | 0 | 0 | 0 | 95 | 90 | 10 | 5 | 1 | 20 | 110 | 50 | 4,900 | 0 | 1.6 | 90 | 18 | 0 |
| ango | Angola | 410 | 13 | 8.5 | 4.4 | 3.9 | 6 | 6 | 1 | 30 | 32 | 1,500 | 112 | 58 | 12 | 662 | 12,000 | 766,800 | 50,000 | 3.4 | 45 | 6,308 | 1 |
| angu | Anguilla | 2,000 | 40 | 0.0 | 0.0 | 0.0 | 0 | 0 | 0 | 70 | 90 | 30 | 7 | 1 | 50 | 10 | 10 | 500 | 0 | 3.0 | 90 | 7 | 0 |
| anti | Antigua | 7,690 | 45 | 0.0 | 0.0 | 0.0 | 0 | 0 | 0 | 90 | 95 | 40 | 7 | 2 | 65 | 59 | 120 | 4,100 | 200 | 4.7 | 90 | 56 | 1 |
| arge | Argentina | 8,030 | 47 | 3.9 | 33.1 | 22.7 | 43 | 26 | 3 | 71 | 64 | 100 | 20 | 2,000 | 44 | 88,800 | 14,300 | 2,221,800 | 40,000 | 2.3 | 94 | 31,735 | 1,540 |
| arme | Armenia | 730 | 25 | 1.1 | 2.5 | 1.8 | 5 | 3 | 1 | 50 | 60 | 50 | 24 | 183 | 83 | 14,000 | 3,000 | 219,700 | 1,000 | 5.4 | 87 | 1,443 | 14 |
| arub | Aruba | 15,890 | 46 | 0.0 | 0.1 | 0.0 | 0 | 0 | 0 | 90 | 90 | 30 | 12 | 2 | 44 | 74 | 60 | 4,400 | 0 | 1.2 | 85 | 56 | 1 |
| aust | Australia | 18,720 | 58 | 2.9 | 16.0 | 13.8 | 25 | 15 | 5 | 90 | 95 | 9 | 5 | 1,071 | 50 | 38,800 | 18,820 | 1,129,900 | 1,800 | 1.8 | 96 | 9,865 | 95 |
| ausz | Austria | 26,890 | 59 | 2.9 | 5.3 | 3.8 | 12 | 6 | 1 | 95 | 100 | 10 | 5 | 324 | 92 | 26,121 | 11,000 | 497,500 | 300 | 2.5 | 106 | 6,311 | 44 |
| azer | Azerbaijan | 480 | 6 | 3.3 | 4.4 | 2.6 | 7 | 3 | 1 | 30 | 50 | 22 | 32 | 749 | 105 | 29,000 | 7,000 | 469,700 | 10,000 | 8.1 | 97 | 4,578 | 23 |
| baha | Bahamas | 11,940 | 60 | 0.0 | 0.3 | 0.2 | 1 | 1 | 0 | 95 | 97 | 100 | 13 | 5 | 40 | 357 | 110 | 18,100 | 60 | 17.6 | 98 | 227 | 1 |
| bahr | Bahrain | 7,840 | 66 | 0.0 | 0.6 | 0.4 | 1 | 1 | 0 | 80 | 100 | 60 | 14 | 12 | 23 | 542 | 62 | 37,100 | 100 | 1.8 | 106 | 118 | 4 |
| bang | Bangladesh | 240 | 27 | 101.8 | 27.4 | 19.8 | 35 | 24 | 3 | 45 | 83 | 850 | 67 | 891 | 3 | 21,749 | 200,000 | 7,698,600 | 700,000 | 1.9 | 46 | 62,433 | 1,046 |
| barb | Barbados | 6,560 | 40 | 0.1 | 0.1 | 0.1 | 1 | 1 | 0 | 90 | 100 | 43 | 10 | 10 | 75 | 312 | 250 | 15,900 | 180 | 6.8 | 90 | 139 | 1 |
| belg | Belgium | 24,710 | 58 | 0.3 | 9.9 | 4.7 | 17 | 13 | 1 | 92 | 89 | 10 | 6 | 363 | 76 | 37,792 | 4,780 | 615,400 | 200 | 3.1 | 102 | 6,707 | 21 |
| beli | Belize | 2,630 | 46 | 0.1 | 0.1 | 0.1 | 1 | 0 | 0 | 70 | 89 | 70 | 26 | 7 | 29 | 110 | 80 | 14,500 | 1,000 | 33.2 | 92 | 267 | 4 |
| belo | Belorussia | 2,070 | 29 | 2.6 | 7.6 | 5.3 | 22 | 12 | 1 | 65 | 80 | 37 | 21 | 868 | 122 | 45,000 | 9,000 | 617,100 | 300 | 2.9 | 95 | 5,047 | 38 |
| beni | Benin | 370 | 41 | 3.5 | 2.6 | 1.3 | 4 | 3 | 0 | 18 | 50 | 990 | 80 | 50 | 10 | 323 | 5,000 | 373,300 | 100,000 | 0.9 | 40 | 3,048 | 13 |
| berm | Bermuda | 31,870 | 50 | 0.0 | 0.1 | 0.0 | 0 | 0 | 0 | 95 | 85 | 30 | 13 | 2 | 42 | 91 | 25 | 3,900 | 0 | 5.1 | 75 | 36 | 1 |
| bhut | Bhutan | 420 | 2 | 2.0 | 0.2 | 0.0 | 0 | 0 | 0 | 65 | 58 | 1,600 | 53 | 27 | 12 | 141 | 10,000 | 121,900 | 9,000 | 6.0 | 30 | 187 | 2 |
| boli | Bolivia | 800 | 45 | 2.9 | 5.4 | 3.8 | 8 | 6 | 2 | 67 | 55 | 650 | 55 | 336 | 15 | 3,392 | 1,070 | 499,700 | 6,500 | 5.0 | 77 | 10,529 | 10 |
| bosn | Bosnia-Herzegovina | 300 | 10 | 2.3 | 1.7 | 1.2 | 6 | 6 | 0 | 40 | 50 | 50 | 14 | 200 | 46 | 6,929 | 4,000 | 260,300 | 500 | 2.5 | 70 | 2,443 | 44 |
| bots | Botswana | 3,020 | 44 | 0.4 | 1.2 | 0.3 | 2 | 1 | 0 | 89 | 70 | 250 | 58 | 30 | 25 | 240 | 1,880 | 97,100 | 6,000 | 12.7 | 92 | 1,025 | 1 |
| boug | Bougainville | 1,400 | 25 | 0.2 | 0.0 | 0.0 | 0 | 0 | 0 | 20 | 30 | 20 | 54 | 5 | 20 | 15 | 200 | 11,900 | 7,000 | 7.0 | 50 | 140 | 0 |
| braz | Brazil | 3,640 | 31 | 31.8 | 138.3 | 92.3 | 185 | 143 | 14 | 45 | 72 | 220 | 38 | 35,701 | 37 | 208,966 | 60,700 | 10,152,100 | 280,000 | 12.0 | 96 | 208,147 | 873 |
| brit | Britain | 18,700 | 61 | 6.2 | 52.6 | 36.8 | 111 | 65 | 5 | 95 | 100 | 9 | 6 | 2,423 | 54 | 87,000 | 116,414 | 3,500,200 | 500 | 2.5 | 104 | 28,169 | 820 |
| briz | British Virgin Is | 8,000 | 50 | 0.0 | 0.0 | 0.0 | 0 | 0 | 0 | 90 | 90 | 10 | 19 | 1 | 50 | 60 | 20 | 1,300 | 20 | 2.0 | 95 | 18 | 1 |
| brun | Brunei | 15,800 | 45 | 0.1 | 0.2 | 0.1 | 1 | 0 | 0 | 80 | 90 | 60 | 8 | 10 | 36 | 197 | 300 | 19,500 | 500 | 1.5 | 89 | 187 | 4 |
| bulg | Bulgaria | 1,330 | 30 | 2.5 | 5.8 | 3.9 | 26 | 10 | 1 | 75 | 99 | 27 | 14 | 287 | 106 | 28,457 | 3,312 | 498,300 | 400 | 5.9 | 81 | 3,881 | 88 |
| burk | Burkina Faso | 230 | 26 | 9.7 | 2.2 | 1.6 | 4 | 2 | 1 | 90 | 78 | 930 | 91 | 78 | 5 | 341 | 90,000 | 723,400 | 450,000 | 0.2 | 25 | 2,936 | 9 |
| buru | Burundi | 160 | 25 | 6.1 | 0.6 | 0.4 | 2 | 2 | 0 | 80 | 52 | 1,300 | 109 | 264 | 19 | 317 | 11,000 | 418,400 | 70,000 | 3.3 | 40 | 1,531 | 8 |
| camb | Cambodia | 270 | 5 | 8.5 | 2.6 | 1.1 | 6 | 3 | 0 | 53 | 13 | 900 | 92 | 188 | 16 | 600 | 40,000 | 672,400 | 47,000 | 70.0 | 75 | 5,044 | 9 |
| came | Cameroon | 650 | 28 | 7.7 | 7.4 | 4.1 | 10 | 8 | 2 | 70 | 41 | 550 | 66 | 629 | 27 | 945 | 15,630 | 907,700 | 200,000 | 0.1 | 58 | 6,763 | 5 |
| cana | Canada | 19,380 | 60 | 7.1 | 24.0 | 21.1 | 49 | 34 | 4 | 95 | 100 | 6 | 5 | 1,079 | 50 | 60,559 | 27,184 | 1,840,700 | 500 | 5.2 | 105 | 16,231 | 272 |
| cape | Cape Verde | 960 | 31 | 0.2 | 0.3 | 0.1 | 2 | 0 | 0 | 80 | 51 | 100 | 49 | 75 | 15 | 112 | 400 | 26,200 | 3,000 | 7.0 | 83 | 367 | 3 |
| caym | Cayman Islands | 5,000 | 60 | 0.0 | 0.0 | 0.0 | 0 | 0 | 0 | 95 | 90 | 10 | 19 | 5 | 65 | 50 | 10 | 2,200 | 0 | 1.0 | 95 | 20 | 1 |
| cent | Central African Rep | 340 | 22 | 2.1 | 1.5 | 1.0 | 4 | 2 | 0 | 45 | 18 | 700 | 92 | 133 | 15 | 170 | 27,000 | 218,400 | 200,000 | 1.6 | 43 | 976 | 1 |
| chad | Chad | 180 | 10 | 5.8 | 1.8 | 1.3 | 4 | 3 | 1 | 30 | 24 | 1,500 | 103 | 40 | 7 | 217 | 175,000 | 436,200 | 25,000 | 45.0 | 33 | 2,610 | 4 |
| chan | Channel Islands | 12,000 | 60 | 0.1 | 0.1 | 0.1 | 0 | 0 | 0 | 95 | 90 | 10 | 6 | 70 | 50 | 230 | 120 | 9,200 | 0 | 1.0 | 95 | 50 | 2 |
| chil | Chile | 4,160 | 51 | 2.3 | 12.9 | 10.3 | 28 | 17 | 1 | 97 | 85 | 65 | 11 | 217 | 32 | 15,015 | 2,910 | 912,700 | 1,000 | 11.0 | 89 | 8,626 | 201 |
| chin | China | 620 | 24 | 829.0 | 433.6 | 329.6 | 491 | 332 | 92 | 92 | 90 | 95 | 36 | 60,784 | 24 | 1,832,000 | 2,000,000 | 75,234,000 | 3,500,000 | 0.2 | 86 | 953,807 | 1,065 |
| colo | Colombia | 1,910 | 40 | 10.6 | 31.7 | 21.1 | 35 | 26 | 4 | 60 | 76 | 100 | 25 | 947 | 14 | 36,551 | 30,000 | 2,334,300 | 50,000 | 81.9 | 89 | 44,693 | 235 |
| como | Comoros | 470 | 25 | 0.4 | 0.2 | 0.0 | 0 | 0 | 0 | 55 | 48 | 950 | 67 | 20 | 25 | 57 | 500 | 36,700 | 3,000 | 10.0 | 49 | 275 | 2 |
| cong | Congo-Brazzaville | 680 | 24 | 1.1 | 1.8 | 1.8 | 4 | 2 | 1 | 83 | 60 | 890 | 85 | 500 | 33 | 613 | 4,000 | 178,900 | 66,000 | 5.0 | 40 | 1,623 | 124 |
| conz | Congo-Zaire | 120 | 16 | 36.0 | 15.6 | 12.3 | 30 | 24 | 1 | 26 | 27 | 870 | 76 | 400 | 21 | 2,469 | 73,000 | 3,105,000 | 800,000 | 1.5 | 49 | 12,987 | 0 |
| cook | Cook Islands | 2,000 | 60 | 0.0 | 0.0 | 0.0 | 0 | 0 | 0 | 90 | 90 | 30 | 19 | 18 | 100 | 25 | 20 | 1,200 | 700 | 3.0 | 90 | 35 | 0 |
| cost | Costa Rica | 2,610 | 44 | 1.9 | 2.1 | 1.1 | 2 | 1 | 1 | 80 | 92 | 55 | 10 | 33 | 21 | 4,027 | 2,000 | 227,900 | 3,000 | 5.3 | 82 | 3,729 | 6 |
| croa | Croatia | 3,250 | 26 | 1.9 | 2.6 | 2.0 | 7 | 7 | 1 | 75 | 96 | 35 | 9 | 98 | 61 | 9,280 | 3,700 | 269,100 | 500 | 7.4 | 84 | 2,413 | 54 |
| cuba | Cuba | 1,300 | 15 | 2.5 | 8.7 | 5.2 | 19 | 16 | 1 | 98 | 93 | 95 | 8 | 244 | 61 | 46,860 | 4,600 | 672,000 | 11,000 | 5.0 | 90 | 12,233 | 35 |
| cypr | Cyprus | 13,420 | 48 | 0.3 | 0.3 | 0.3 | 3 | 1 | 0 | 90 | 100 | 5 | 8 | 110 | 18 | 1,441 | 1,209 | 36,500 | 700 | 1.9 | 95 | 501 | 30 |
| czec | Czech Republic | 3,870 | 60 | 3.5 | 6.8 | 4.4 | 23 | 11 | 1 | 85 | 100 | 15 | 6 | 287 | 98 | 31,897 | 10,000 | 611,700 | 500 | 2.0 | 95 | 5,344 | 23 |
| denm | Denmark | 29,890 | 61 | 0.8 | 4.5 | 2.3 | 9 | 4 | 1 | 95 | 100 | 9 | 6 | 163 | 35 | 14,497 | 8,000 | 316,500 | 300 | 4.9 | 108 | 2,952 | 235 |
| djib | Djibouti | 850 | 5 | 0.1 | 0.5 | 0.4 | 1 | 1 | 0 | 40 | 90 | 570 | 97 | 8 | 27 | 97 | 300 | 41,200 | 9,000 | 4.4 | 26 | 82 | 1 |
| domi | Dominica | 2,990 | 28 | 0.0 | 0.1 | 0.0 | 0 | 0 | 0 | 70 | 77 | 50 | 7 | 53 | 25 | 38 | 60 | 4,300 | 400 | 4.2 | 70 | 77 | 2 |
| domr | Dominican Republic | 1,460 | 31 | 3.0 | 5.5 | 6.5 | 11 | 9 | 2 | 80 | 71 | 110 | 30 | 103 | 20 | 11,130 | 2,850 | 509,700 | 528 | 11.9 | 84 | 6,207 | 7 |
| ecua | Ecuador | 1,390 | 37 | 4.8 | 7.9 | 5.5 | 16 | 13 | 2 | 88 | 70 | 150 | 41 | 429 | 16 | 12,853 | 10,000 | 758,800 | 6,300 | 10.5 | 91 | 18,353 | 21 |
| egyp | Egypt | 790 | 31 | 37.0 | 31.5 | 24.2 | 60 | 29 | 2 | 99 | 64 | 170 | 40 | 6,418 | 20 | 101,500 | 75,000 | 4,087,100 | 115,000 | 1.6 | 87 | 19,150 | 12 |
| elsa | El Salvador | 1,610 | 51 | 3.3 | 2.9 | 1.8 | 4 | 3 | 1 | 40 | 55 | 300 | 26 | 78 | 17 | 4,525 | 3,961 | 379,200 | 600 | 25.0 | 68 | 3,806 | 6 |
| equa | Equatorial Guinea | 380 | 22 | 0.2 | 0.2 | 0.1 | 1 | 1 | 0 | 35 | 95 | 820 | 98 | 15 | 29 | 99 | 800 | 27,100 | 16,000 | 12.0 | 40 | 713 | 4 |
| erit | Eritrea | 570 | 20 | 3.1 | 0.7 | 0.5 | 2 | 1 | 0 | 30 | 25 | 1,400 | 81 | 7 | 9 | 68 | 3,200 | 228,500 | 25,000 | 20.0 | 33 | 581 | 1 |
| esto | Estonia | 2,860 | 53 | 0.4 | 1.0 | 0.8 | 5 | 2 | 0 | 85 | 90 | 41 | 14 | 115 | 84 | 4,680 | 1,200 | 85,100 | 200 | 24.3 | 96 | 825 | 22 |
| ethi | Ethiopia | 100 | 26 | 51.5 | 11.0 | 4.1 | 10 | 7 | 1 | 46 | 27 | 1,400 | 103 | 86 | 3 | 1,466 | 90,000 | 3,970,500 | 400,000 | 16.4 | 20 | 8,120 | 11 |
| faer | Faeroe Islands | 15,000 | 50 | 0.0 | 0.0 | 0.0 | 0 | 0 | 0 | 95 | 90 | 12 | 6 | 3 | 57 | 81 | 20 | 2,900 | 0 | 2.0 | 95 | 77 | 1 |
| fiji | Fiji | 2,440 | 38 | 0.5 | 0.3 | 0.2 | 1 | 1 | 0 | 75 | 100 | 90 | 17 | 25 | 22 | 426 | 4,000 | 50,900 | 8,000 | 11.5 | 97 | 693 | 5 |
| finl | Finland | 20,580 | 54 | 1.8 | 3.4 | 2.4 | 12 | 5 | 1 | 95 | 100 | 11 | 5 | 317 | 90 | 13,344 | 3,345 | 310,700 | 300 | 0.6 | 110 | 5,490 | 20 |
| fran | France | 24,990 | 54 | 14.4 | 44.6 | 30.2 | 108 | 59 | 3 | 90 | 100 | 15 | 5 | 3,834 | 120 | 155,896 | 43,000 | 3,543,600 | 400 | 4.7 | 106 | 52,981 | 1,062 |
| freg | French Guiana | 10,580 | 24 | 0.0 | 0.1 | 0.1 | 1 | 0 | 0 | 75 | 60 | 70 | 51 | 6 | 66 | 200 | 150 | 10,700 | 8,500 | 27.2 | 60 | 110 | 1 |
| frep | French Polynesia | 16,940 | 30 | 0.1 | 0.1 | 0.1 | 1 | 1 | 0 | 80 | 70 | 20 | 10 | 34 | 58 | 323 | 96 | 14,400 | 2,200 | 0.9 | 99 | 316 | 4 |
| gabo | Gabon | 3,490 | 39 | 0.5 | 0.7 | 0.7 | 4 | 2 | 0 | 90 | 67 | 500 | 81 | 27 | 51 | 448 | 1,300 | 74,100 | 40,000 | 1.4 | 40 | 1,024 | 1 |
| gamb | Gambia | 320 | 20 | 0.9 | 0.4 | 0.3 | 1 | 1 | 0 | 93 | 76 | 1,100 | 112 | 13 | 7 | 61 | 2,700 | 74,600 | 33,000 | 0.4 | 44 | 277 | 9 |
| geor | Georgia | 440 | 23 | 2.0 | 3.0 | 2.1 | 7 | 4 | 1 | 80 | 90 | 33 | 18 | 422 | 105 | 30,000 | 4,500 | 325,100 | 500 | 10.7 | 75 | 3,808 | 19 |
| germ | Germany | 27,510 | 58 | 10.2 | 72.0 | 52.3 | 137 | 74 | 12 | 95 | 100 | 22 | 4 | 2,381 | 80 | 259,981 | 15,000 | 4,961,300 | 1,000 | 4.6 | 100 | 18,867 | 314 |
| ghan | Ghana | 390 | 36 | 12.5 | 7.8 | 4.0 | 7 | 5 | 1 | 60 | 56 | 740 | 58 | 121 | 13 | 628 | 65,000 | 1,195,700 | 120,000 | 2.1 | 58 | 16,653 | 16 |
| gibr | Gibraltar | 6,600 | 40 | 0.0 | 0.0 | 0.0 | 0 | 0 | 0 | 90 | 90 | 12 | 6 | 2 | 86 | 29 | 140 | 1,700 | 20 | 3.7 | 95 | 22 | 1 |
| gree | Greece | 8,210 | 44 | 4.2 | 6.4 | 5.3 | 15 | 6 | 2 | 95 | 99 | 10 | 7 | 372 | 50 | 40,116 | 13,000 | 635,800 | 5,000 | 2.6 | 96 | 11,317 | 17 |
| grel | Greenland | 15,500 | 40 | 0.0 | 0.0 | 0.0 | 0 | 0 | 0 | 80 | 90 | 25 | 6 | 16 | 75 | 78 | 50 | 3,600 | 0 | 18.1 | 60 | 88 | 2 |
| gren | Grenada | 2,980 | 35 | 0.1 | 0.0 | 0.0 | 0 | 0 | 0 | 75 | 85 | 30 | 12 | 3 | 38 | 47 | 90 | 5,600 | 50 | 7.8 | 95 | 76 | 1 |
| guad | Guadeloupe | 9,200 | 40 | 0.0 | 0.5 | 0.2 | 2 | 1 | 0 | 70 | 80 | 20 | 7 | 30 | 80 | 590 | 90 | 27,400 | 2,500 | 13.2 | 90 | 418 | 1 |
| guam | Guam | 20,300 | 50 | 0.1 | 0.1 | 0.1 | 1 | 0 | 0 | 85 | 90 | 15 | 9 | 1 | 6 | 147 | 150 | 9,900 | 800 | 7.9 | 95 | 63 | 1 |
| guat | Guatemala | 1,340 | 43 | 6.8 | 4.6 | 2.9 | 3 | 2 | 1 | 34 | 64 | 200 | 41 | 160 | 16 | 7,601 | 6,000 | 733,300 | 1,200 | 27.4 | 57 | 12,670 | 5 |
| guin | Guinea | 550 | 33 | 5.0 | 2.4 | 2.4 | 5 | 4 | 1 | 80 | 62 | 1,600 | 114 | 38 | 6 | 773 | 45,000 | 471,700 | 250,000 | 0.5 | 30 | 2,849 | 10 |
| gunb | Guinea-Bissau | 250 | 20 | 0.9 | 0.3 | 0.2 | 1 | 1 | 0 | 40 | 53 | 910 | 122 | 16 | 13 | 274 | 5,000 | 70,800 | 35,000 | 0.5 | 38 | 648 | 4 |
| guya | Guyana | 590 | 32 | 0.5 | 0.3 | 0.2 | 1 | 1 | 0 | 50 | 61 | 500 | 51 | 30 | 33 | 138 | 1,300 | 52,400 | 4,400 | 4.5 | 82 | 524 | 1 |
| hait | Haiti | 250 | 16 | 5.4 | 2.9 | 1.9 | 2 | 1 | 1 | 50 | 28 | 1,000 | 61 | 87 | 8 | 564 | 9,000 | 469,000 | 1,500 | 18.0 | 40 | 6,741 | 2 |
| hond | Honduras | 600 | 37 | 3.4 | 3.0 | 1.9 | 5 | 2 | 1 | 64 | 65 | 220 | 31 | 86 | 12 | 3,803 | 1,000 | 389,100 | 1,300 | 9.4 | 77 | 8,838 | 10 |
| hung | Hungary | 4,120 | 42 | 3.3 | 6.7 | 4.0 | 20 | 8 | 1 | 70 | 94 | 30 | 9 | 148 | 98 | 36,643 | 10,000 | 588,700 | 1,000 | 4.3 | 91 | 5,094 | 91 |
| icel | Iceland | 24,950 | 55 | 0.0 | 0.3 | 0.2 | 1 | 1 | 0 | 95 | 100 | 10 | 5 | 26 | 111 | 726 | 434 | 16,900 | 0 | 0.9 | 102 | 80 | 5 |
| indi | India | 340 | 25 | 725.4 | 288.3 | 206.1 | 642 | 346 | 33 | 85 | 81 | 570 | 64 | 15,067 | 8 | 405,253 | 9,000,000 | 60,406,200 | 5,500,000 | 4.6 | 73 | 812,975 | 7,958 |
| indo | Indonesia | 980 | 43 | 126.8 | 85.3 | 39.3 | 94 | 65 | 6 | 80 | 62 | 650 | 39 | 971 | 6 | 25,135 | 1,000,000 | 12,753,900 | 200,000 | 0.8 | 80 | 180,604 | 1,000 |
| iran | Iran | 4,700 | 6 | 26.0 | 41.7 | 31.1 | 80 | 65 | 6 | 80 | 83 | 120 | 29 | 609 | 15 | 37,000 | 200,000 | 4,585,700 | 30,000 | 0.5 | 84 | 81,134 | 0 |
| iraq | Iraq | 2,000 | 2 | 5.4 | 17.8 | 12.3 | 16 | 16 | 3 | 93 | 44 | 310 | 39 | 177 | 18 | 9,366 | 75,000 | 1,386,500 | 7,000 | 7.1 | 69 | 11,045 | 20 |
| irel | Ireland | 14,710 | 56 | 1.5 | 2.2 | 1.3 | 3 | 2 | 0 | 95 | 100 | 10 | 6 | 63 | 34 | 6,036 | 7,000 | 214,500 | 0 | 1.2 | 108 | 4,103 | 26 |
| isle | Isle of Man | 10,800 | 58 | 0.0 | 0.1 | 0.0 | 0 | 0 | 0 | 95 | 100 | 10 | 6 | 3 | 50 | 86 | 60 | 4,700 | 0 | 0.7 | 95 | 40 | 1 |
| isra | Israel | 15,920 | 42 | 0.5 | 4.7 | 4.0 | 9 | 5 | 1 | 80 | 99 | 7 | 7 | 244 | 63 | 24,344 | 5,285 | 298,900 | 500 | 2.1 | 92 | 3,065 | 7 |
| ital | Italy | 19,020 | 46 | 18.9 | 38.4 | 26.3 | 107 | 52 | 4 | 40 | 100 | 12 | 6 | 1,926 | 68 | 296,385 | 110,000 | 3,431,700 | 1,000 | 4.7 | 87 | 38,459 | 50 |
| ivor | Ivory Coast | 660 | 35 | 7.9 | 6.9 | 4.7 | 7 | 6 | 1 | 30 | 72 | 810 | 79 | 100 | 8 | 2,020 | 50,000 | 908,600 | 250,000 | 2.5 | 49 | 7,249 | 1 |
| jama | Jamaica | 1,510 | 46 | 1.1 | 1.4 | 1.0 | 2 | 2 | 0 | 90 | 70 | 120 | 19 | 30 | 22 | 1,589 | 3,100 | 155,200 | 2,500 | 27.6 | 86 | 932 | 15 |
| japa | Japan | 39,640 | 59 | 26.8 | 100.0 | 83.5 | 216 | 108 | 6 | 95 | 95 | 18 | 4 | 9,963 | 136 | 219,704 | 256,455 | 7,585,700 | 15,000 | 1.0 | 101 | 48,002 | 1,207 |
| jord | Jordan | 1,510 | 44 | 1.7 | 4.9 | 2.3 | 4 | 3 | 1 | 97 | 89 | 150 | 21 | 53 | 11 | 6,395 | 9,000 | 379,800 | 600 | 2.0 | 92 | 3,277 | 55 |
| kaza | Kazakhstan | 1,330 | 20 | 6.2 | 10.0 | 7.5 | 34 | 21 | 1 | 80 | 70 | 80 | 30 | 1,805 | 134 | 66,000 | 15,000 | 1,015,700 | 2,000 | 12.0 | 89 | 11,956 | 61 |
| keny | Kenya | 280 | 39 | 20.1 | 10.0 | 3.9 | 7 | 7 | 1 | 77 | 53 | 650 | 63 | 877 | 14 | 3,794 | 65,000 | 1,820,400 | 120,000 | 6.4 | 72 | 18,506 | 14 |
| kirg | Kirgizstan | 700 | 15 | 2.8 | 1.9 | 1.4 | 7 | 2 | 0 | 70 | 75 | 110 | 35 | 396 | 99 | 14,674 | 4,000 | 272,600 | 1,000 | 10.4 | 95 | 3,359 | 12 |
| kiri | Kiribati | 920 | 30 | 0.1 | 0.0 | 0.0 | 0 | 0 | 0 | 90 | 99 | 300 | 9 | 4 | 40 | 10 | 100 | 5,200 | 1,000 | 5.1 | 90 | 107 | 0 |
| kuwa | Kuwait | 17,390 | 52 | 0.0 | 1.9 | 1.5 | 2 | 2 | 1 | 100 | 100 | 29 | 10 | 22 | 26 | 2,717 | 1,000 | 118,000 | 200 | 1.7 | 66 | 671 | 1 |
| laos | Laos | 350 | 5 | 4.2 | 1.3 | 0.8 | 4 | 1 | 0 | 67 | 39 | 650 | 82 | 1,074 | 25 | 1,173 | 10,000 | 341,600 | 20,000 | 15.0 | 67 | 9,250 | 9 |
| latv | Latvia | 2,270 | 39 | 0.6 | 1.8 | 1.3 | 4 | 3 | 0 | 90 | 90 | 40 | 15 | 170 | 121 | 7,714 | 2,000 | 143,800 | 200 | 14.6 | 85 | 978 | 14 |
| leba | Lebanon | 2,660 | 41 | 0.3 | 2.9 | 2.7 | 4 | 4 | 1 | 95 | 100 | 300 | 25 | 25 | 50 | 6,638 | 5,000 | 197,300 | 1,000 | 4.3 | 94 | 2,100 | 20 |
| leso | Lesotho | 770 | 27 | 1.6 | 0.6 | 0.2 | 1 | 1 | 0 | 80 | 52 | 610 | 87 | 22 | 15 | 136 | 3,000 | 137,600 | 40,000 | 33.9 | 73 | 1,397 | 1 |
| libe | Liberia | 770 | 20 | 1.6 | 1.5 | 1.4 | 1 | 1 | 1 | 39 | 30 | 560 | 75 | 92 | 13 | 89 | 15,000 | 195,400 | 39,000 | 20.0 | 45 | 2,076 | 3 |
| liby | Libya | 6,510 | 6 | 0.7 | 4.9 | 3.6 | 6 | 6 | 1 | 45 | 30 | 220 | 25 | 75 | 41 | 4,749 | 10,000 | 383,200 | 7,700 | 1.3 | 105 | 4,494 | 10 |
| liec | Liechtenstein | 33,000 | 55 | 0.0 | 0.0 | 0.0 | 0 | 0 | 0 | 95 | 95 | 9 | 5 | 1 | 35 | 32 | 30 | 2,000 | 50 | 5.0 | 100 | 23 | 0 |
| lith | Lithuania | 1,900 | 30 | 0.9 | 2.7 | 1.6 | 6 | 5 | 0 | 90 | 90 | 36 | 14 | 198 | 117 | 14,670 | 3,000 | 221,400 | 100 | 6.9 | 87 | 2,485 | 14 |
| luxe | Luxembourg | 41,210 | 61 | 0.0 | 0.4 | 0.2 | 2 | 1 | 0 | 95 | 95 | 8 | 6 | 34 | 115 | 848 | 204 | 25,800 | 50 | 13.2 | 81 | 100 | 1 |
| mace | Macedonia | 860 | 25 | 0.8 | 1.3 | 0.9 | 3 | 3 | 0 | 80 | 80 | 70 | 20 | 61 | 52 | 4,528 | 2,000 | 134,000 | 200 | 3.9 | 77 | 1,145 | 27 |
| mada | Madagascar | 230 | 33 | 11.2 | 4.7 | 2.9 | 7 | 7 | 1 | 65 | 29 | 490 | 73 | 250 | 9 | 1,392 | 40,000 | 1,043,700 | 120,000 | 0.6 | 43 | 14,766 | 5 |
| mala | Malawi | 170 | 32 | 9.2 | 1.7 | 0.9 | 2 | 2 | 0 | 80 | 45 | 560 | 126 | 395 | 16 | 186 | 18,400 | 659,000 | 70,000 | 3.1 | 88 | 3,225 | 4 |
| malb | Malaysia | 3,890 | 52 | 9.5 | 12.7 | 5.8 | 21 | 17 | 1 | 70 | 90 | 80 | 10 | 264 | 22 | 7,012 | 50,000 | 1,337,900 | 30,000 | 2.1 | 78 | 8,379 | 54 |

| COUNTRY | | SOCIETY | | | | | | | | | | | | | | | | | | | | | |
|---|---|---|---|---|---|---|---|---|---|---|---|---|---|---|---|---|---|---|---|---|---|---|---|
| | | ECONOMIC | | URBANIZATION | | | METROSCAN | | | HEALTH | | | | | | | | | | | EDUCATION | | |
| code | short name | GNP | EFL | rural | urban | metro | cit50 | cit100 | mega | acces | water | mat-m | inf-m | hosp | beds | doct | blind | deaf | lepers | murd | educ | schools | univs |
| 1 | 2 | 25 | 26 | 27 | 28 | 29 | 30 | 31 | 32 | 33 | 34 | 35 | 36 | 37 | 38 | 39 | 40 | 41 | 42 | 43 | 44 | 45 | 46 |
| mald | Maldives | 990 | 8 | 0.2 | 0.1 | 0.1 | 1 | 0 | 0 | 50 | 89 | 200 | 40 | 5 | 8 | 45 | 128 | 18,100 | 100 | 1.9 | 90 | 262 | 0 |
| mali | Mali | 250 | 38 | 7.9 | 3.4 | 1.7 | 7 | 4 | 1 | 30 | 37 | 1,200 | 109 | 15 | 4 | 435 | 110,000 | 753,600 | 270,000 | 6.0 | 21 | 1,821 | 7 |
| malt | Malta | 12,000 | 39 | 0.0 | 0.4 | 0.2 | 1 | 1 | 0 | 95 | 100 | 10 | 7 | 7 | 58 | 900 | 570 | 22,700 | 500 | 3.0 | 98 | 192 | 1 |
| mars | Marshall Islands | 1,890 | 40 | 0.0 | 0.0 | 0.0 | 0 | 0 | 0 | 70 | 31 | 100 | 9 | 2 | 14 | 20 | 50 | 3,900 | 50 | 7.0 | 75 | 115 | 0 |
| mart | Martinique | 10,000 | 35 | 0.0 | 0.4 | 0.1 | 1 | 1 | 0 | 75 | 80 | 20 | 7 | 20 | 103 | 625 | 100 | 23,900 | 4,000 | 5.8 | 90 | 361 | 1 |
| maur | Mauritania | 460 | 24 | 1.1 | 1.5 | 0.4 | 1 | 1 | 0 | 63 | 76 | 930 | 83 | 16 | 7 | 135 | 15,000 | 154,800 | 9,000 | 1.8 | 44 | 1,696 | 4 |
| maus | Mauritius | 3,380 | 15 | 0.7 | 0.5 | 0.5 | 1 | 1 | 0 | 100 | 98 | 120 | 13 | 23 | 28 | 941 | 250 | 70,600 | 400 | 3.2 | 80 | 421 | 2 |
| mayo | Mayotte | 600 | 20 | 0.1 | 0.0 | 0.0 | 0 | 0 | 0 | 50 | 60 | 600 | 67 | 2 | 11 | 9 | 80 | 6,100 | 200 | 11.0 | 40 | 95 | 1 |
| mexi | Mexico | 3,320 | 33 | 25.3 | 73.6 | 56.5 | 132 | 85 | 8 | 78 | 83 | 110 | 28 | 1,539 | 10 | 149,432 | 60,000 | 5,932,900 | 40,000 | 7.3 | 86 | 112,624 | 13,000 |
| micr | Micronesia | 2,010 | 35 | 0.1 | 0.0 | 0.0 | 0 | 0 | 0 | 70 | 100 | 700 | 9 | 4 | 31 | 50 | 200 | 8,500 | 600 | 6.0 | 90 | 193 | 1 |
| mold | Moldavia | 920 | 31 | 2.0 | 2.4 | 1.4 | 5 | 4 | 0 | 75 | 80 | 60 | 24 | 335 | 122 | 18,000 | 3,700 | 267,500 | 500 | 8.8 | 80 | 1,700 | 18 |
| mona | Monaco | 25,000 | 60 | 0.0 | 0.0 | 0.0 | 0 | 0 | 0 | 95 | 100 | 10 | 5 | 1 | 168 | 112 | 15 | 2,000 | 0 | 0.5 | 100 | 6 | 0 |
| mong | Mongolia | 310 | 30 | 1.0 | 1.7 | 0.8 | 2 | 1 | 0 | 95 | 54 | 65 | 44 | 475 | 105 | 5,911 | 4,000 | 164,200 | 200 | 19.0 | 68 | 708 | 9 |
| mont | Montserrat | 12,527 | 45 | 0.0 | 0.0 | 0.0 | 0 | 0 | 0 | 90 | 90 | 35 | 7 | 2 | 55 | 10 | 10 | 600 | 0 | 4.0 | 90 | 15 | 1 |
| moro | Morocco | 1,110 | 46 | 12.6 | 15.6 | 10.6 | 26 | 17 | 2 | 70 | 52 | 610 | 41 | 203 | 11 | 7,695 | 35,000 | 1,731,200 | 40,000 | 1.4 | 59 | 6,474 | 50 |
| moza | Mozambique | 80 | 19 | 11.8 | 7.9 | 4.4 | 10 | 6 | 1 | 39 | 32 | 1,500 | 115 | 238 | 9 | 388 | 28,000 | 1,173,800 | 20,000 | 4.2 | 35 | 4,035 | 2 |
| myan | Myanmar | 1,790 | 14 | 33.0 | 12.6 | 8.4 | 29 | 16 | 1 | 60 | 38 | 580 | 69 | 717 | 6 | 12,245 | 210,000 | 2,960,500 | 880,000 | 4.1 | 62 | 38,754 | 40 |
| nami | Namibia | 2,000 | 25 | 1.0 | 0.7 | 0.2 | 1 | 1 | 0 | 62 | 57 | 370 | 74 | 47 | 45 | 324 | 1,400 | 104,000 | 1,500 | 72.4 | 109 | 1,064 | 7 |
| naur | Nauru | 8,070 | 30 | 0.0 | 0.0 | 0.0 | 0 | 0 | 0 | 70 | 60 | 100 | 9 | 1 | 40 | 5 | 10 | 700 | 100 | 25.0 | 70 | 6 | 1 |
| nepa | Nepal | 200 | 30 | 21.1 | 2.8 | 0.8 | 3 | 2 | 0 | 35 | 44 | 1,500 | 70 | 114 | 3 | 1,497 | 60,000 | 1,460,800 | 120,000 | 2.5 | 74 | 26,835 | 3 |
| neth | Netherlands | 24,000 | 63 | 1.7 | 14.1 | 8.6 | 38 | 23 | 2 | 85 | 100 | 12 | 5 | 236 | 57 | 39,069 | 8,000 | 952,300 | 500 | 24.9 | 110 | 10,888 | 206 |
| nets | Netherlands Antilles | 10,400 | 35 | 0.1 | 0.2 | 0.2 | 1 | 1 | 0 | 85 | 90 | 15 | 12 | 11 | 73 | 291 | 500 | 12,100 | 30 | 7.0 | 95 | 142 | 1 |
| newc | New Caledonia | 8,000 | 40 | 0.1 | 0.1 | 0.1 | 1 | 1 | 0 | 70 | 90 | 40 | 9 | 8 | 62 | 370 | 30 | 11,700 | 3,500 | 5.0 | 101 | 342 | 6 |
| newz | New Zealand | 14,340 | 65 | 0.5 | 3.4 | 2.5 | 10 | 6 | 1 | 95 | 100 | 25 | 6 | 330 | 77 | 11,413 | 3,687 | 225,600 | 50 | 3.9 | 108 | 2,772 | 7 |
| nica | Nicaragua | 380 | 28 | 1.8 | 3.3 | 1.9 | 6 | 6 | 1 | 83 | 61 | 160 | 38 | 56 | 12 | 2,554 | 1,800 | 281,700 | 900 | 25.6 | 79 | 7,544 | 4 |
| niga | Niger | 220 | 26 | 8.5 | 2.2 | 1.1 | 5 | 3 | 0 | 32 | 53 | 1,200 | 105 | 15 | 5 | 142 | 50,000 | 648,300 | 75,000 | 0.2 | 18 | 2,768 | 3 |
| nige | Nigeria | 260 | 35 | 62.5 | 49.1 | 35.7 | 110 | 70 | 2 | 66 | 39 | 1,000 | 76 | 11,588 | 12 | 17,954 | 420,000 | 7,727,100 | 1,000,000 | 15.0 | 63 | 44,723 | 31 |
| nork | North Korea | 950 | 2 | 8.9 | 15.1 | 7.0 | 12 | 12 | 1 | 40 | 100 | 70 | 19 | 2,500 | 135 | 57,690 | 48,000 | 1,434,800 | 40,000 | 5.0 | 80 | 6,122 | 281 |
| norl | Northern Cyprus | 12,402 | 15 | 0.1 | 0.1 | 0.0 | 0 | 0 | 0 | 70 | 100 | 40 | 8 | 25 | 15 | 250 | 150 | 11,100 | 500 | 20.0 | 90 | 80 | 2 |
| norm | Northern Mariana Is | 10,500 | 40 | 0.0 | 0.0 | 0.0 | 0 | 0 | 0 | 75 | 70 | 20 | 9 | 1 | 19 | 23 | 40 | 3,200 | 100 | 3.8 | 90 | 27 | 1 |
| norw | Norway | 31,250 | 51 | 1.2 | 3.3 | 1.6 | 9 | 4 | 0 | 95 | 100 | 6 | 4 | 350 | 53 | 14,497 | 4,000 | 264,200 | 200 | 1.0 | 108 | 4,096 | 195 |
| oman | Oman | 4,820 | 43 | 0.4 | 2.1 | 0.1 | 1 | 0 | 0 | 96 | 63 | 190 | 21 | 180 | 23 | 2,095 | 23,000 | 163,000 | 250 | 0.8 | 75 | 568 | 5 |
| paki | Pakistan | 460 | 39 | 98.5 | 58.0 | 38.7 | 63 | 55 | 8 | 55 | 60 | 340 | 65 | 10,905 | 6 | 63,033 | 900,000 | 9,360,400 | 150,000 | 6.4 | 42 | 156,450 | 804 |
| pala | Palau | 5,000 | 40 | 0.0 | 0.0 | 0.0 | 0 | 0 | 0 | 75 | 90 | 20 | 9 | 1 | 45 | 10 | 10 | 1,100 | 0 | 5.0 | 90 | 32 | 1 |
| pale | Palestine | 14,584 | 25 | 0.1 | 2.1 | 0.9 | 5 | 5 | 0 | 70 | 85 | 200 | 20 | 100 | 50 | 9,000 | 2,000 | 124,200 | 500 | 20.0 | 85 | 500 | 1 |
| pana | Panama | 2,750 | 52 | 1.2 | 1.6 | 1.3 | 3 | 2 | 1 | 80 | 83 | 55 | 18 | 60 | 29 | 3,168 | 2,000 | 171,300 | 850 | 13.9 | 85 | 3,141 | 8 |
| papu | Papua New Guinea | 1,160 | 38 | 3.8 | 0.8 | 0.3 | 2 | 1 | 0 | 96 | 28 | 930 | 54 | 150 | 40 | 301 | 9,000 | 276,700 | 20,000 | 8.6 | 51 | 3,073 | 2 |
| para | Paraguay | 1,690 | 47 | 2.4 | 3.1 | 1.7 | 5 | 3 | 1 | 63 | 8 | 160 | 37 | 100 | 12 | 2,924 | 4,000 | 329,800 | 14,000 | 15.6 | 79 | 6,282 | 2 |
| peru | Peru | 2,310 | 40 | 7.0 | 18.7 | 12.1 | 24 | 15 | 1 | 75 | 60 | 280 | 37 | 427 | 17 | 23,771 | 23,000 | 1,539,700 | 12,000 | 9.3 | 101 | 63,551 | 655 |
| phil | Philippines | 1,050 | 42 | 31.4 | 44.5 | 21.9 | 51 | 44 | 3 | 76 | 85 | 280 | 29 | 1,723 | 11 | 78,445 | 80,000 | 4,502,200 | 67,000 | 30.1 | 99 | 42,228 | 809 |
| pola | Poland | 2,790 | 39 | 13.4 | 25.4 | 17.6 | 74 | 34 | 3 | 90 | 100 | 19 | 13 | 752 | 63 | 87,706 | 21,523 | 2,323,600 | 1,000 | 3.1 | 98 | 31,813 | 140 |
| port | Portugal | 9,740 | 48 | 6.1 | 3.8 | 3.4 | 5 | 2 | 2 | 95 | 100 | 15 | 8 | 335 | 42 | 24,499 | 8,225 | 587,300 | 4,000 | 4.2 | 92 | 14,140 | 250 |
| puer | Puerto Rico | 7,800 | 50 | 1.0 | 2.9 | 2.0 | 4 | 4 | 1 | 95 | 95 | 12 | 11 | 72 | 26 | 6,269 | 4,500 | 232,600 | 1,800 | 26.8 | 95 | 1,989 | 45 |
| qata | Qatar | 11,600 | 30 | 0.0 | 0.6 | 0.5 | 1 | 1 | 0 | 90 | 100 | 50 | 15 | 3 | 20 | 758 | 200 | 36,000 | 1,000 | 1.8 | 85 | 197 | 1 |
| reun | Reunion | 4,300 | 35 | 0.2 | 0.5 | 0.1 | 1 | 1 | 0 | 80 | 90 | 30 | 8 | 20 | 44 | 1,061 | 1,000 | 41,900 | 1,400 | 7.8 | 75 | 445 | 1 |
| roma | Romania | 1,480 | 26 | 9.3 | 13.0 | 8.9 | 48 | 24 | 1 | 60 | 100 | 130 | 19 | 300 | 95 | 42,808 | 15,918 | 1,350,300 | 4,500 | 3.3 | 83 | 16,769 | 63 |
| russ | Russia | 2,240 | 30 | 32.8 | 114.1 | 78.4 | 293 | 152 | 13 | 65 | 90 | 75 | 17 | 12,265 | 119 | 612,400 | 350,000 | 8,771,700 | 20,000 | 21.8 | 94 | 72,574 | 569 |
| rwan | Rwanda | 180 | 20 | 7.3 | 0.5 | 0.3 | 1 | 1 | 0 | 80 | 66 | 1,300 | 115 | 220 | 9 | 272 | 7,000 | 460,400 | 80,000 | 85.0 | 50 | 1,724 | 3 |
| saha | Sahara | 207 | 5 | 0.0 | 0.3 | 0.2 | 1 | 1 | 0 | 25 | 40 | 800 | 53 | 2 | 10 | 50 | 1,000 | 17,400 | 100 | 25.0 | 30 | 45 | 1 |
| saih | Saint Helena | 9,000 | 40 | 0.0 | 0.0 | 0.0 | 0 | 0 | 0 | 75 | 75 | 40 | 6 | 1 | 30 | 10 | 12 | 400 | 0 | 4.0 | 75 | 8 | 0 |
| saik | Saint Kitts & Nevis | 5,170 | 45 | 0.0 | 0.0 | 0.0 | 0 | 0 | 0 | 90 | 100 | 70 | 7 | 0 | 0 | 0 | 0 | 2,500 | 100 | 14.0 | 95 | 0 | 0 |
| sail | Saint Lucia | 3,370 | 48 | 0.1 | 0.1 | 0.1 | 1 | 0 | 0 | 95 | 100 | 50 | 7 | 4 | 37 | 64 | 200 | 9,100 | 100 | 17.0 | 90 | 84 | 0 |
| saip | Saint Pierre & Miquelon | 11,000 | 45 | 0.0 | 0.0 | 0.0 | 0 | 0 | 0 | 80 | 80 | 40 | 5 | 1 | 40 | 10 | 10 | 400 | 0 | 4.0 | 80 | 9 | 0 |
| saiv | Saint Vincent | 2,280 | 46 | 0.1 | 0.1 | 0.0 | 0 | 0 | 0 | 90 | 100 | 40 | 7 | 0 | 44 | 40 | 100 | 7,000 | 100 | 10.3 | 95 | 60 | 0 |
| samo | Samoa | 1,120 | 44 | 0.1 | 0.0 | 0.0 | 0 | 0 | 0 | 80 | 90 | 35 | 19 | 16 | 20 | 50 | 200 | 10,500 | 1,000 | 7.0 | 75 | 206 | 6 |
| sanm | San Marino | 24,700 | 60 | 0.0 | 0.0 | 0.0 | 0 | 0 | 0 | 95 | 100 | 10 | 6 | 5 | 66 | 60 | 100 | 1,600 | 0 | 4.1 | 100 | 17 | 0 |
| saot | Sao Tome & Principe | 350 | 20 | 0.1 | 0.1 | 0.0 | 0 | 0 | 0 | 30 | 70 | 1,200 | 92 | 5 | 10 | 61 | 200 | 8,800 | 200 | 4.0 | 50 | 64 | 2 |
| saud | Saudi Arabia | 7,040 | 42 | 3.1 | 18.5 | 9.9 | 17 | 16 | 2 | 97 | 93 | 130 | 18 | 229 | 21 | 25,543 | 230,000 | 1,299,700 | 2,000 | 0.9 | 66 | 17,338 | 72 |
| sene | Senegal | 600 | 32 | 5.0 | 4.5 | 3.0 | 6 | 6 | 1 | 40 | 50 | 1,200 | 58 | 20 | 10 | 520 | 22,000 | 569,700 | 100,000 | 1.4 | 38 | 2,832 | 18 |
| seyc | Seychelles | 6,620 | 20 | 0.0 | 0.0 | 0.0 | 0 | 0 | 0 | 70 | 97 | 200 | 13 | 7 | 56 | 72 | 150 | 4,600 | 100 | 2.7 | 90 | 45 | 1 |
| sier | Sierra Leone | 180 | 25 | 3.1 | 1.8 | 1.1 | 5 | 2 | 0 | 38 | 34 | 1,800 | 145 | 219 | 10 | 404 | 28,000 | 291,900 | 150,000 | 12.0 | 36 | 2,039 | 2 |
| sing | Singapore | 26,730 | 74 | 0.0 | 3.6 | 3.6 | 1 | 1 | 1 | 100 | 100 | 10 | 4 | 22 | 36 | 4,301 | 427 | 215,200 | 12,000 | 1.7 | 86 | 392 | 7 |
| slok | Slovakia | 2,950 | 41 | 2.1 | 3.3 | 1.4 | 11 | 2 | 0 | 65 | 90 | 17 | 10 | 111 | 91 | 15,767 | 4,500 | 322,300 | 700 | 2.4 | 0 | 3,386 | 14 |
| slov | Slovenia | 8,200 | 33 | 0.9 | 1.0 | 0.5 | 2 | 2 | 0 | 75 | 95 | 13 | 6 | 24 | 58 | 4,086 | 1,600 | 114,800 | 1,000 | 4.9 | 90 | 1,067 | 28 |
| solo | Solomon Islands | 910 | 30 | 0.4 | 0.1 | 0.0 | 0 | 0 | 0 | 60 | 90 | 70 | 19 | 8 | 53 | 52 | 370 | 26,600 | 4,000 | 10.0 | 64 | 544 | 1 |
| soma | Somalia | 500 | 6 | 5.3 | 2.0 | 1.5 | 3 | 1 | 1 | 27 | 25 | 1,600 | 112 | 90 | 7 | 450 | 10,000 | 521,800 | 14,000 | 1.5 | 10 | 1,125 | 1 |
| somi | Somaliland | 155 | 2 | 2.1 | 0.8 | 0.2 | 2 | 1 | 0 | 25 | 20 | 1,700 | 112 | 10 | 5 | 50 | 2,500 | 170,000 | 4,500 | 2.0 | 10 | 200 | 0 |
| soua | South Africa | 3,160 | 40 | 20.0 | 20.3 | 13.3 | 15 | 14 | 6 | 75 | 70 | 230 | 63 | 834 | 39 | 25,967 | 62,000 | 2,775,400 | 36,000 | 8.0 | 104 | 22,447 | 32 |
| souk | South Korea | 9,700 | 54 | 6.5 | 40.4 | 31.2 | 55 | 31 | 5 | 100 | 89 | 130 | 9 | 600 | 29 | 51,518 | 110,000 | 2,813,000 | 90,000 | 1.4 | 98 | 10,312 | 645 |
| spai | Spain | 13,580 | 46 | 8.9 | 30.8 | 19.3 | 69 | 44 | 3 | 90 | 99 | 7 | 6 | 813 | 42 | 159,291 | 30,000 | 2,388,100 | 4,000 | 2.6 | 110 | 42,315 | 1,415 |
| span | Spanish North Africa | 8,000 | 30 | 0.0 | 0.1 | 0.2 | 2 | 0 | 0 | 90 | 57 | 250 | 41 | 3 | 40 | 100 | 150 | 7,800 | 100 | 2.0 | 80 | 20 | 1 |
| sril | Sri Lanka | 700 | 47 | 14.4 | 4.4 | 2.9 | 7 | 3 | 1 | 93 | 46 | 140 | 15 | 422 | 28 | 3,345 | 65,000 | 1,129,200 | 13,000 | 8.2 | 87 | 18,654 | 8 |
| suda | Sudan | 800 | 18 | 18.8 | 10.7 | 4.8 | 12 | 12 | 1 | 70 | 50 | 660 | 64 | 200 | 8 | 2,400 | 110,000 | 1,789,400 | 150,000 | 4.2 | 39 | 10,661 | 24 |
| suri | Suriname | 880 | 22 | 0.2 | 0.2 | 0.3 | 1 | 1 | 0 | 40 | 72 | 100 | 25 | 40 | 47 | 329 | 1,300 | 27,100 | 3,700 | 7.6 | 70 | 454 | 1 |
| swaz | Swaziland | 1,170 | 42 | 0.6 | 0.4 | 0.1 | 1 | 0 | 0 | 45 | 43 | 560 | 55 | 24 | 0 | 83 | 1,000 | 59,000 | 10,000 | 88.1 | 95 | 705 | 1 |
| swed | Sweden | 23,750 | 49 | 1.5 | 7.4 | 4.7 | 21 | 11 | 1 | 95 | 100 | 7 | 5 | 700 | 52 | 22,200 | 15,716 | 533,900 | 200 | 4.5 | 100 | 5,426 | 100 |
| swit | Switzerland | 40,630 | 64 | 2.8 | 4.6 | 4.0 | 18 | 9 | 0 | 95 | 100 | 6 | 5 | 500 | 78 | 23,000 | 9,000 | 444,700 | 300 | 2.3 | 96 | 3,000 | 12 |
| syri | Syria | 1,120 | 16 | 7.3 | 8.8 | 7.1 | 15 | 10 | 2 | 90 | 85 | 180 | 28 | 213 | 12 | 11,808 | 12,000 | 967,600 | 6,500 | 1.4 | 77 | 10,219 | 47 |
| taiw | Taiwan | 12,400 | 61 | 5.4 | 17.0 | 10.7 | 28 | 23 | 2 | 75 | 80 | 50 | 36 | 810 | 48 | 27,288 | 18,510 | 1,344,100 | 55,000 | 8.2 | 90 | 3,654 | 125 |
| taji | Tajikistan | 340 | 20 | 4.2 | 2.0 | 1.1 | 4 | 3 | 0 | 60 | 50 | 130 | 51 | 449 | 88 | 13,084 | 6,000 | 383,900 | 1,500 | 2.5 | 83 | 3,350 | 22 |
| tanz | Tanzania | 120 | 31 | 24.2 | 9.3 | 5.0 | 13 | 10 | 2 | 80 | 49 | 770 | 74 | 170 | 11 | 1,065 | 40,000 | 2,021,200 | 200,000 | 6.4 | 44 | 10,892 | 4 |
| thai | Thailand | 2,740 | 54 | 48.1 | 13.2 | 9.0 | 18 | 7 | 1 | 90 | 81 | 200 | 24 | 1,097 | 17 | 13,398 | 210,000 | 3,629,700 | 500,000 | 7.7 | 67 | 37,409 | 84 |
| timo | Timor | 644 | 30 | 0.8 | 0.1 | 0.1 | 1 | 1 | 0 | 40 | 60 | 1,000 | 120 | 5 | 5 | 100 | 800 | 53,000 | 1,000 | 5.0 | 75 | 750 | 5 |
| togo | Togo | 310 | 22 | 3.1 | 1.5 | 0.8 | 2 | 1 | 0 | 61 | 63 | 640 | 76 | 30 | 16 | 319 | 9,000 | 280,600 | 80,000 | 7.0 | 64 | 2,594 | 1 |
| tong | Tonga | 1,630 | 35 | 0.1 | 0.0 | 0.0 | 0 | 0 | 0 | 80 | 100 | 60 | 19 | 4 | 31 | 46 | 80 | 6,000 | 200 | 3.0 | 90 | 163 | 1 |
| trin | Trinidad & Tobago | 3,770 | 50 | 0.3 | 1.0 | 0.5 | 2 | 1 | 0 | 100 | 82 | 90 | 12 | 31 | 33 | 1,051 | 1,300 | 80,400 | 3,000 | 11.7 | 87 | 576 | 1 |
| tuni | Tunisia | 1,820 | 47 | 3.3 | 6.3 | 3.3 | 11 | 6 | 1 | 90 | 99 | 170 | 25 | 138 | 20 | 4,670 | 25,000 | 590,200 | 10,000 | 2.1 | 86 | 4,998 | 0 |
| turk | Turkey | 2,780 | 40 | 16.4 | 50.2 | 32.4 | 102 | 48 | 5 | 75 | 92 | 180 | 38 | 857 | 24 | 50,639 | 38,178 | 3,943,900 | 50,000 | 3.6 | 80 | 50,701 | 424 |
| turm | Turkmenistan | 920 | 15 | 2.4 | 2.0 | 1.2 | 7 | 5 | 0 | 70 | 85 | 55 | 49 | 368 | 115 | 14,000 | 4,000 | 268,800 | 500 | 5.0 | 60 | 1,832 | 9 |
| turs | Turks & Caicos Is | 2,172 | 45 | 0.0 | 0.0 | 0.0 | 0 | 0 | 0 | 65 | 90 | 40 | 7 | 1 | 20 | 7 | 10 | 1,000 | 0 | 4.0 | 90 | 20 | 0 |
| tuva | Tuvalu | 800 | 30 | 0.0 | 0.0 | 0.0 | 0 | 0 | 0 | 70 | 100 | 200 | 19 | 8 | 36 | 8 | 10 | 600 | 50 | 3.0 | 85 | 11 | 0 |
| ugan | Uganda | 240 | 43 | 18.7 | 3.1 | 1.4 | 4 | 1 | 1 | 49 | 34 | 1,200 | 94 | 89 | 12 | 774 | 209,000 | 1,347,500 | 200,000 | 9.5 | 47 | 8,815 | 9 |
| ukra | Ukraine | 1,630 | 20 | 13.9 | 36.6 | 24.9 | 87 | 49 | 5 | 75 | 97 | 50 | 15 | 3,900 | 130 | 230,000 | 43,000 | 3,048,100 | 1,000 | 8.8 | 90 | 22,448 | 159 |
| unia | United Arab Emirates | 17,400 | 58 | 0.3 | 2.1 | 2.0 | 5 | 4 | 0 | 99 | 98 | 26 | 13 | 35 | 21 | 3,090 | 400 | 146,600 | 50 | 1.1 | 103 | 363 | 1 |
| usa | USA | 26,980 | 62 | 63.4 | 214.9 | 188.2 | 344 | 258 | 39 | 85 | 90 | 12 | 6 | 6,580 | 46 | 670,300 | 482,850 | 16,669,300 | 1,000 | 9.0 | 103 | 85,393 | 5,758 |
| uuay | Uruguay | 5,170 | 44 | 0.3 | 3.0 | 1.7 | 4 | 1 | 1 | 82 | 34 | 85 | 13 | 112 | 45 | 11,201 | 3,000 | 196,500 | 2,000 | 4.1 | 95 | 2,862 | 2 |
| uzbe | Uzbekistan | 970 | 25 | 14.0 | 10.3 | 6.5 | 24 | 17 | 1 | 75 | 90 | 55 | 39 | 1,388 | 85 | 79,000 | 22,000 | 1,501,100 | 1,000 | 5.5 | 87 | 9,347 | 52 |
| vanu | Vanuatu | 1,200 | 35 | 0.2 | 0.0 | 0.0 | 0 | 0 | 0 | 70 | 72 | 280 | 31 | 90 | 22 | 12 | 200 | 11,500 | 400 | 4.0 | 66 | 272 | 1 |
| vene | Venezuela | 3,020 | 30 | 3.1 | 21.1 | 14.0 | 40 | 29 | 4 | 60 | 79 | 120 | 18 | 610 | 26 | 32,616 | 18,000 | 1,450,200 | 40,000 | 22.1 | 85 | 17,421 | 99 |
| viet | Viet Nam | 240 | 6 | 64.1 | 15.8 | 12.7 | 43 | 29 | 3 | 90 | 38 | 160 | 31 | 12,500 | 27 | 28,500 | 200,000 | 4,832,900 | 240,000 | 6.0 | 55 | 19,841 | 104 |
| virg | Virgin Is of the US | 11,740 | 60 | 0.0 | 0.0 | 0.0 | 0 | 0 | 0 | 95 | 95 | 20 | 7 | 5 | 49 | 250 | 20 | 6,500 | 100 | 22.3 | 95 | 20 | 1 |
| wall | Wallis & Futuna Is | 4,654 | 40 | 0.0 | 0.0 | 0.0 | 0 | 0 | 0 | 90 | 90 | 70 | 19 | 1 | 45 | 20 | 10 | 900 | 20 | 2.0 | 85 | 20 | 0 |
| yeme | Yemen | 260 | 25 | 11.2 | 6.9 | 2.0 | 5 | 5 | 0 | 38 | 52 | 1,400 | 68 | 75 | 8 | 3,065 | 16,000 | 1,087,100 | 3,600 | 1.5 | 70 | 7,313 | 1 |
| yugo | Yugoslavia | 2,000 | 35 | 4.3 | 6.4 | 4.1 | 18 | 18 | 1 | 80 | 85 | 25 | 16 | 1,000 | 55 | 22,000 | 10,000 | 630,100 | 100 | 7.0 | 65 | 4,996 | 146 |
| zamb | Zambia | 400 | 41 | 5.1 | 4.1 | 3.8 | 10 | 9 | 1 | 75 | 43 | 940 | 74 | 965 | 29 | 713 | 38,000 | 548,000 | 50,000 | 9.8 | 62 | 3,995 | 2 |
| zimb | Zimbabwe | 540 | 26 | 7.5 | 4.1 | 2.9 | 4 | 4 | 1 | 85 | 74 | 570 | 67 | 1,378 | 15 | 1,551 | 15,000 | 745,400 | 60,000 | 5.0 | 66 | 6,193 | 28 |
| | 11 minicountries | 21,015 | 48 | 0.0 | 0.0 | 0.0 | 0 | 0 | 0 | 77 | 89 | 236 | 112 | 11 | 29 | 93 | 142 | 1,312 | 120 | 2.9 | 85 | 15 | 1 |
| | Africa | 657 | 30 | 489.2 | 295.2 | 190.6 | 493 | 334 | 40 | 63 | 48 | 819 | 75 | 27,694 | 15 | 218,175 | 2,170,862 | 49,194,200 | 6,269,200 | 7.9 | 57 | 302,576 | 556 |
| | Antarctica | 80,000 | 50 | 0.0 | 0.0 | 0.0 | 0 | 0 | 0 | 80 | 100 | 10 | 20 | 1 | 20 | 20 | 10 | 300 | 0 | 1.0 | 100 | 0 | 0 |
| | Asia | 2,396 | 28 | 2,294.4 | 1,388.1 | 972.4 | 2,199 | 1,373 | 195 | 82 | 80 | 338 | 46 | 130,113 | 22 | 3,316,962 | 15,357,604 | 220,900,900 | 12,319,800 | 4.0 | 77 | 2,674,707 | 16,186 |
| | Europe | 12,714 | 43 | 182.8 | 546.1 | 371.1 | 1,361 | 735 | 66 | 78 | 96 | 34 | 11 | 37,269 | 88 | 2,450,000 | 908,711 | 43,759,900 | 52,020 | 8.5 | 96 | 442,546 | 6,360 |
| | Latin America | 3,302 | 35 | 127.8 | 391.3 | 271.5 | 594 | 420 | 52 | 63 | 72 | 181 | 31 | 43,697 | 26 | 682,333 | 273,691 | 30,881,200 | 545,418 | 16.9 | 89 | 596,382 | 16,803 |
| | Northern America | 26,214 | 62 | 70.6 | 239.0 | 209.4 | 393 | 292 | 43 | 86 | 91 | 11 | 7 | 7,678 | 46 | 731,038 | 510,119 | 18,517,900 | 1,500 | 8.6 | 103 | 101,757 | 6,033 |
| | Oceania | 14,091 | 54 | 9.1 | 21.3 | 17.4 | 41 | 25 | 6 | 89 | 84 | 160 | 14 | 1,789 | 50 | 52,183 | 37,410 | 1,815,212 | 52,240 | 3.7 | 90 | 19,043 | 135 |
| | **World A** | **1,464** | **26** | **315.0** | **290.3** | **185.2** | **475** | **325** | **36** | **61** | **64** | **496** | **57** | **21,762** | **24** | **429,916** | **2,026,691** | **37,328,710** | **1,404,150** | **8.5** | **63** | **428,932** | **1,855** |
| | **World B** | **2,284** | **29** | **2,342.0** | **1,413.0** | **1,000.2** | **2,413** | **1,448** | **197** | **82** | **78** | **378** | **47** | **142,888** | **25** | **3,652,694** | **15,284,994** | **225,955,000** | **15,511,650** | **4.0** | **76** | **2,510,926** | **14,514** |
| | **World C** | **11,448** | **44** | **516.8** | **1,177.9** | **847.0** | **2,193** | **1,406** | **169** | **73** | **81** | **174** | **25** | **83,591** | **47** | **3,368,101** | **1,946,722** | **101,785,902** | **2,324,378** | **10.9** | **92** | **1,197,153** | **29,704** |
| | **GLOBAL TOTAL** | **4,767** | **33** | **3,173.9** | **2,881.2** | **2,032.3** | **5,081** | **3,179** | **402** | **78** | **77** | **333** | **42** | **248,241** | **31** | **7,450,711** | **19,258,407** | **365,069,612** | **19,240,178** | **6.4** | **79** | **4,137,011** | **46,073** |

| COUNTRY | | SOCIETY (continued) | | | | | | | RELIGIOUS RELATIONS | | | | | | | | | | | CHRISTIANITY | |
|---|---|---|---|---|---|---|---|---|---|---|---|---|---|---|---|---|---|---|---|---|---|
| | | COMMUNICATION per 1000 | | | | | | | RELIGIONS | | RELIGIOUS PERSECUTION | | | | CHURCH/STATE RELATIONS | | | | bibliography | church members | |
| code | short name | news | radios | TVs | fones | faxes | computers | internet | religs | indig | liberty | CSI | martyrs | mar-pa | 1900 | 1970 | 1990 | 2000 | items listed | affiliated | AC |
| 1 | 2 | 47 | 48 | 49 | 50 | 51 | 52 | 53 | 54 | 55 | 56 | 57 | 58 | 59 | 60 | 61 | 62 | 63 | 64 | 65 | 66 |
| afgh | Afghanistan | 11 | 73.7 | 10.0 | 1.4 | 0.1 | 25,592 | 1,000 | 10 | 3 | 9 | 9 | 1,000,430 | 12 | RI | RI | A | RI | 17 | 6,897 | 0.0 |
| alba | Albania | 54 | 157.0 | 89.0 | 12.0 | 0.3 | 122,252 | 20,000 | 6 | 0 | 7 | 39 | 12,200 | 99 | RI | A | S | S | 18 | 1,070,390 | 34.4 |
| alge | Algeria | 46 | 125.0 | 71.0 | 42.0 | 0.2 | 221,190 | 25,000 | 6 | 0 | 8 | 39 | 30,833 | 153 | RI | RI | RI | RI | 22 | 90,877 | 0.3 |
| amer | American Samoa | 51 | 330.0 | 130.0 | 136.0 | 15.0 | 3,134 | 5,000 | 5 | 0 | 5 | 67 | 0 | 0 | S | S | S | S | 5 | 55,240 | 81.1 |
| ando | Andorra | 63 | 6.0 | 360.0 | 438.0 | 20.0 | 20,248 | 4,000 | 6 | 0 | 3 | 80 | 0 | 0 | RC | RC | RC | RC | 6 | 70,205 | 90.0 |
| ango | Angola | 11 | 39.0 | 51.0 | 5.6 | 0.8 | 127,806 | 10,000 | 7 | 36 | 7 | 46 | 24,300 | 367 | RC | RC | A | A | 32 | 10,934,238 | 84.9 |
| angu | Anguilla | 1 | 700.0 | 500.0 | 350.0 | 25.0 | 8,304 | 500 | 6 | 0 | 4 | 74 | 0 | 0 | S | S | S | S | 2 | 7,186 | 86.5 |
| anti | Antigua | 94 | 778.0 | 419.0 | 311.0 | 7.5 | 6,791 | 3,000 | 6 | 0 | 5 | 68 | 0 | 1 | S | S | S | S | 9 | 53,713 | 79.5 |
| arge | Argentina | 138 | 637.0 | 347.0 | 160.0 | 1.6 | 2,329,017 | 300,000 | 14 | 15 | 7 | 56 | 12,035 | 527 | RC | RC | RC | RC | 46 | 33,985,872 | 91.8 |
| arme | Armenia | 23 | 250.0 | 241.0 | 155.0 | 0.3 | 128,163 | 30,000 | 6 | 0 | 3 | 73 | 204,000 | 9 | RO | A | RO | RO | 31 | 2,953,693 | 83.9 |
| arub | Aruba | 757 | 571.0 | 471.0 | 390.0 | 6.8 | 5,856 | 2,000 | 10 | 0 | 5 | 72 | 0 | 1 | S | S | S | S | 5 | 95,241 | 92.7 |
| aust | Australia | 255 | 1,152.0 | 641.0 | 510.0 | 32.0 | 10,600,000 | 800,000 | 16 | 61 | 3 | 81 | 6,000 | 46 | R | R | R | R | 61 | 12,587,959 | 66.7 |
| ausz | Austria | 465 | 584.0 | 497.0 | 466.0 | 61.0 | 2,871,633 | 100,000 | 14 | 0 | 2 | 87 | 8,100 | 23 | R | S | S | S | 25 | 6,909,670 | 84.2 |
| azer | Azerbaijan | 28 | 200.0 | 212.0 | 85.0 | 0.4 | 156,561 | 20,000 | 6 | 0 | 9 | 29 | 22,000 | 14 | RI | A | A | RI | 6 | 357,802 | 4.6 |
| baha | Bahamas | 126 | 282.0 | 233.0 | 277.0 | 2.0 | 75,487 | 25,000 | 6 | 0 | 4 | 73 | 0 | 3 | RA | RA | RA | RA | 17 | 266,851 | 87.1 |
| bahr | Bahrain | 128 | 542.0 | 442.0 | 242.0 | 13.0 | 43,256 | 25,000 | 9 | 0 | 7 | 50 | 0 | 0 | RI | RI | RI | RI | 7 | 62,698 | 10.2 |
| bang | Bangladesh | 6 | 67.0 | 7.0 | 2.4 | 0.0 | 384,930 | 80,000 | 10 | 17 | 4 | 56 | 13,000 | 175 | S | RI | RI | RI | 40 | 931,740 | 0.7 |
| barb | Barbados | 159 | 1,132.0 | 284.0 | 345.0 | 7.0 | 23,791 | 10,000 | 10 | 0 | 2 | 84 | 0 | 3 | RA | RA | R | R | 21 | 196,858 | 72.8 |
| belg | Belgium | 321 | 500.0 | 464.0 | 458.0 | 22.0 | 4,156,023 | 300,000 | 13 | 0 | 2 | 87 | 1,000 | 27 | R | R | R | R | 17 | 8,518,696 | 83.8 |
| beli | Belize | 100 | 140.0 | 167.0 | 134.0 | 3.3 | 12,079 | 5,000 | 9 | 1 | 4 | 67 | 0 | 2 | S | S | S | S | 20 | 197,139 | 81.9 |
| belo | Belorussia | 187 | 311.0 | 265.0 | 190.0 | 0.6 | 411,376 | 60,000 | 8 | 0 | 7 | 51 | 550,000 | 382 | RO | A | A | RO | 10 | 6,584,077 | 64.3 |
| beni | Benin | 2 | 73.0 | 73.0 | 5.2 | 0.2 | 93,323 | 5,000 | 7 | 38 | 6 | 50 | 500 | 13 | RT | S | A | A | 17 | 1,684,195 | 27.6 |
| berm | Bermuda | 254 | 1,311.0 | 460.0 | 900.0 | 40.0 | 13,061 | 12,000 | 7 | 0 | 3 | 82 | 0 | 0 | RA | RA | R | R | 3 | 55,675 | 86.2 |
| bhut | Bhutan | 6 | 28.0 | 3.0 | 6.3 | 0.4 | 2,032 | 500 | 7 | 4 | 9 | 29 | 40 | 0 | RB | RB | RB | RB | 16 | 9,649 | 0.5 |
| boli | Bolivia | 69 | 553.0 | 202.0 | 47.0 | 0.8 | 166,573 | 50,000 | 11 | 27 | 2 | 75 | 902 | 89 | RC | RC | RC | RC | 32 | 7,786,232 | 93.5 |
| bosn | Bosnia-Herzegovina | 131 | 263.0 | 111.0 | 69.0 | 0.7 | 151,842 | 40,000 | 5 | 0 | 8 | 37 | 53,333 | 269 | R | A | R | RI | 37 | 1,385,885 | 34.9 |
| bots | Botswana | 29 | 206.0 | 24.0 | 41.0 | 2.1 | 24,286 | 3,000 | 8 | 31 | 4 | 61 | 0 | 4 | RR | S | S | S | 34 | 751,073 | 46.3 |
| boug | Bougainville | 15 | 72.0 | 163.0 | 8.0 | 1.0 | 1,985 | 500 | 4 | 31 | 4 | 64 | 3,000 | 40 | S | S | S | S | 7 | 185,331 | 93.4 |
| braz | Brazil | 45 | 340.0 | 278.0 | 78.0 | 3.0 | 8,500,000 | 520,000 | 14 | 145 | 7 | 52 | 50 | 1,703 | RC | R | R | R | 57 | 155,475,609 | 91.4 |
| brit | Britain | 351 | 1,109.0 | 612.0 | 502.0 | 69.0 | 26,000,000 | 17,000,000 | 14 | 0 | 3 | 78 | 70,933 | 149 | RA | RA | RA | RA | 88 | 39,053,151 | 66.4 |
| briz | British Virgin Is | 250 | 625.0 | 234.0 | 370.0 | 35.0 | 6,365 | 4,000 | 6 | 0 | 5 | 70 | 0 | 0 | S | S | S | S | 9 | 14,892 | 69.7 |
| brun | Brunei | 71 | 417.0 | 609.0 | 240.0 | 7.0 | 26,063 | 5,000 | 10 | 7 | 6 | 51 | 0 | 0 | RI | RI | RI | RI | 10 | 24,592 | 7.5 |
| bulg | Bulgaria | 141 | 437.0 | 359.0 | 306.0 | 2.4 | 646,172 | 200,000 | 6 | 0 | 8 | 51 | 102,000 | 381 | R | A | A | A | 25 | 6,657,950 | 81.0 |
| burk | Burkina Faso | 1 | 48.0 | 4.0 | 2.9 | 0.5 | 24,114 | 10,000 | 6 | 52 | 5 | 52 | 100 | 7 | RT | S | S | S | 35 | 1,984,078 | 16.6 |
| buru | Burundi | 3 | 47.0 | 7.0 | 2.7 | 0.1 | 6,974 | 2,000 | 6 | 3 | 3 | 67 | 80,003 | 1,082 | RT | S | S | S | 23 | 5,152,841 | 77.0 |
| camb | Cambodia | 5 | 150.0 | 8.0 | 0.5 | 0.1 | 16,811 | 2,000 | 10 | 13 | 9 | 14 | 98,002 | 1,298 | RB | RB | A | A | 12 | 118,398 | 1.1 |
| came | Cameroon | 4 | 115.0 | 75.0 | 4.5 | 0.7 | 30,258 | 4,000 | 7 | 241 | 4 | 60 | 600 | 39 | S | S | S | S | 47 | 7,761,501 | 51.5 |
| cana | Canada | 189 | 803.0 | 647.0 | 590.0 | 32.7 | 16,000,000 | 11,600,000 | 15 | 0 | 3 | 80 | 100 | 76 | S | S | S | S | 56 | 20,237,778 | 65.0 |
| cape | Cape Verde | 40 | 135.0 | 3.0 | 55.0 | 2.6 | 1,093 | 500 | 6 | 0 | 7 | 57 | 0 | 2 | RC | RC | S | S | 15 | 406,880 | 95.1 |
| caym | Cayman Islands | 700 | 1,450.0 | 800.0 | 700.0 | 5.0 | 14,410 | 10,000 | 7 | 0 | 5 | 70 | 0 | 0 | S | S | S | S | 4 | 25,820 | 67.3 |
| cent | Central African Rep | 1 | 55.0 | 5.0 | 2.3 | 0.1 | 3,640 | 1,000 | 5 | 59 | 4 | 60 | 3,000 | 49 | RT | S | S | S | 14 | 1,608,999 | 44.5 |
| chad | Chad | 0 | 240.0 | 2.0 | 0.8 | 0.0 | 7,270 | 2,000 | 5 | 61 | 6 | 36 | 400 | 12 | RT | S | S | S | 8 | 1,438,014 | 18.8 |
| chan | Channel Islands | 300 | 900.0 | 500.0 | 700.0 | 30.0 | 38,223 | 15,000 | 8 | 0 | 3 | 78 | 0 | 0 | RA | RA | RA | RA | 2 | 100,781 | 65.9 |
| chil | Chile | 99 | 317.0 | 280.0 | 132.0 | 2.0 | 886,818 | 20,000 | 10 | 5 | 3 | 74 | 2,120 | 173 | RC | S | S | S | 40 | 13,358,340 | 87.8 |
| chin | China | 23 | 178.0 | 247.0 | 34.0 | 1.0 | 15,900,000 | 3,800,000 | 17 | 109 | 9 | 33 | 2,753,055 | 17,146 | RG | A | A | A | 148 | 88,955,347 | 7.1 |
| colo | Colombia | 64 | 150.0 | 188.0 | 100.0 | 3.0 | 1,968,576 | 350,000 | 12 | 64 | 7 | 38 | 126,100 | 518 | RC | RC | RC | RC | 44 | 40,935,888 | 96.7 |
| como | Comoros | 100 | 97.0 | 5.0 | 8.2 | 0.3 | 1,530 | 500 | 5 | 0 | 7 | 41 | 0 | 0 | S | S | S | S | 7 | 7,061 | 1.2 |
| cong | Congo-Brazzaville | 8 | 95.0 | 17.0 | 8.1 | 0.1 | 2,982 | 1,000 | 10 | 47 | 7 | 49 | 400 | 15 | S | A | A | A | 18 | 2,332,878 | 79.3 |
| conz | Congo-Zaire | 3 | 81.0 | 41.0 | 0.8 | 0.1 | 113,849 | 20,000 | 10 | 159 | 6 | 51 | 0 | 502 | RC | R | R | R | 52 | 47,151,525 | 91.3 |
| cook | Cook Islands | 100 | 200.0 | 700.0 | 200.0 | 20.0 | 1,005 | 500 | 3 | 0 | 3 | 81 | 0 | 0 | S | S | S | S | 7 | 18,492 | 94.7 |
| cost | Costa Rica | 102 | 224.0 | 220.0 | 167.0 | 0.7 | 303,816 | 25,000 | 10 | 3 | 2 | 82 | 0 | 42 | RC | RC | RC | RC | 24 | 3,870,161 | 96.2 |
| croa | Croatia | 575 | 230.0 | 230.0 | 269.0 | 14.5 | 313,947 | 50,000 | 5 | 0 | 5 | 61 | 33,333 | 13 | RC | A | RC | RC | 41 | 4,256,386 | 95.2 |
| cuba | Cuba | 120 | 326.0 | 200.0 | 32.0 | 0.1 | 448,020 | 10,000 | 11 | 0 | 8 | 46 | 15,000 | 252 | RC | A | A | A | 34 | 4,822,909 | 43.1 |
| cypr | Cyprus | 110 | 288.0 | 143.0 | 474.0 | 16.0 | 48,630 | 10,000 | 6 | 0 | 7 | 54 | 17,520 | 28 | R | R | R | R | 19 | 551,594 | 91.9 |
| czec | Czech Republic | 219 | 884.0 | 406.0 | 237.0 | 10.0 | 1,336,540 | 300,000 | 6 | 0 | 9 | 44 | 19,530 | 436 | R | A | A | RC | 31 | 4,819,136 | 47.0 |
| denm | Denmark | 308 | 988.0 | 536.0 | 612.0 | 57.0 | 2,691,014 | 1,200,000 | 9 | 0 | 2 | 88 | 0 | 15 | RL | RL | RL | RL | 24 | 4,751,110 | 89.8 |
| djib | Djibouti | 7 | 61.0 | 73.0 | 13.0 | 0.2 | 1,373 | 400 | 5 | 0 | 4 | 68 | 0 | 0 | S | S | S | S | 8 | 28,194 | 4.4 |
| domi | Dominica | 60 | 875.0 | 141.0 | 240.0 | 5.6 | 1,067 | 200 | 9 | 0 | 5 | 62 | 0 | 1 | S | S | S | S | 6 | 66,757 | 94.4 |
| domr | Dominican Republic | 35 | 154.0 | 87.0 | 76.0 | 0.5 | 84,953 | 5,000 | 11 | 0 | 2 | 76 | 1,500 | 87 | RC | RC | RC | RC | 34 | 8,026,705 | 94.5 |
| ecua | Ecuador | 72 | 277.0 | 148.0 | 65.0 | 2.6 | 885,225 | 50,000 | 10 | 15 | 3 | 71 | 3,135 | 173 | R | R | R | R | 22 | 12,307,787 | 97.3 |
| egyp | Egypt | 64 | 265.0 | 126.0 | 46.0 | 0.9 | 1,362,372 | 40,000 | 7 | 0 | 8 | 39 | 1,056,263 | 65 | RI | RI | RI | RI | 51 | 10,320,466 | 15.1 |
| elsa | El Salvador | 53 | 373.0 | 241.0 | 53.0 | 0.8 | 315,970 | 45,000 | 10 | 3 | 6 | 52 | 20,000 | 264 | RC | RC | RC | RC | 22 | 6,098,022 | 97.2 |
| equa | Equatorial Guinea | 2 | 488.0 | 92.0 | 6.3 | 0.4 | 6,777 | 1,000 | 7 | 3 | 6 | 54 | 35,000 | 465 | RC | A | S | S | 18 | 394,698 | 87.2 |
| erit | Eritrea | 5 | 80.0 | 6.0 | 4.8 | 0.3 | 95,224 | 4,000 | 7 | 2 | 4 | 60 | 10,000 | 140 | RO | RO | A | S | 9 | 1,934,358 | 50.2 |
| esto | Estonia | 242 | 400.0 | 411.0 | 277.0 | 14.3 | 56,706 | 3,000 | 6 | 0 | 5 | 54 | 50,000 | 3 | R | A | A | S | 21 | 529,875 | 38.0 |
| ethi | Ethiopia | 10 | 167.0 | 4.0 | 2.5 | 0.0 | 1,654,380 | 50,000 | 8 | 107 | 8 | 35 | 643,350 | 532 | RO | RO | A | S | 43 | 31,161,159 | 49.8 |
| faer | Faeroe Islands | 100 | 447.0 | 286.0 | 400.0 | 42.0 | 9,579 | 1,000 | 3 | 0 | 2 | 87 | 0 | 0 | RL | RL | RL | RL | 14 | 39,590 | 92.6 |
| fiji | Fiji | 45 | 574.0 | 89.0 | 83.0 | 5.9 | 67,812 | 10,000 | 9 | 2 | 4 | 65 | 0 | 1 | R | R | R | R | 40 | 459,745 | 56.3 |
| finl | Finland | 464 | 966.0 | 519.0 | 547.0 | 40.0 | 2,615,352 | 800,000 | 10 | 0 | 2 | 87 | 100 | 15 | RX | RX | RX | RX | 32 | 4,579,451 | 88.5 |
| fran | France | 237 | 862.0 | 579.0 | 558.0 | 45.0 | 21,800,000 | 12,600,000 | 14 | 5 | 4 | 75 | 174,617 | 128 | R | S | S | S | 47 | 41,116,959 | 69.6 |
| freg | French Guiana | 11 | 486.0 | 170.0 | 288.0 | 1.1 | 5,358 | 500 | 12 | 3 | 5 | 60 | 0 | 2 | S | S | S | S | 4 | 152,736 | 84.2 |
| frep | French Polynesia | 112 | 488.0 | 177.0 | 219.0 | 4.0 | 14,424 | 1,000 | 7 | 1 | 4 | 71 | 0 | 1 | S | S | S | S | 17 | 198,725 | 84.5 |
| gabo | Gabon | 16 | 119.0 | 76.0 | 24.0 | 0.4 | 24,709 | 2,000 | 8 | 25 | 4 | 68 | 100 | 5 | R | R | R | R | 27 | 1,085,756 | 88.6 |
| gamb | Gambia | 2 | 125.0 | 5.0 | 17.0 | 0.9 | 18,653 | 500 | 6 | 5 | 5 | 52 | 0 | 0 | S | S | S | S | 14 | 47,198 | 3.6 |
| geor | Georgia | 703 | 400.0 | 220.0 | 103.0 | 0.1 | 162,547 | 10,000 | 6 | 0 | 5 | 58 | 210,000 | 9 | RO | A | A | RO | 9 | 3,008,814 | 60.6 |
| germ | Germany | 317 | 1,875.0 | 550.0 | 494.0 | 32.0 | 30,600,000 | 22,900,000 | 14 | 0 | 5 | 70 | 799,547 | 192 | R | R | S | S | 41 | 58,783,222 | 71.5 |
| ghan | Ghana | 18 | 76.0 | 16.0 | 3.5 | 0.4 | 498,210 | 20,000 | 11 | 74 | 4 | 58 | 210 | 45 | R | R | R | R | 57 | 8,666,976 | 42.9 |
| gibr | Gibraltar | 214 | 573.0 | 275.0 | 696.0 | 10.7 | 2,816 | 1,000 | 6 | 0 | 2 | 84 | 0 | 0 | S | S | S | S | 10 | 21,368 | 85.2 |
| gree | Greece | 156 | 400.0 | 442.0 | 493.0 | 3.0 | 1,321,445 | 800,000 | 8 | 0 | 2 | 85 | 5,000 | 31 | RO | RO | RO | RO | 25 | 10,061,020 | 94.5 |
| grel | Greenland | 150 | 374.0 | 380.0 | 305.0 | 20.3 | 5,995 | 1,000 | 4 | 1 | 2 | 78 | 0 | 0 | RL | RL | RL | RL | 23 | 39,350 | 70.1 |
| gren | Grenada | 45 | 489.0 | 158.0 | 255.0 | 4.3 | 7,525 | 1,500 | 7 | 0 | 6 | 62 | 0 | 1 | R | R | A | A | 13 | 90,745 | 96.8 |
| guad | Guadeloupe | 83 | 208.0 | 262.0 | 378.0 | 8.1 | 31,936 | 3,000 | 8 | 0 | 7 | 56 | 67 | 5 | S | S | S | S | 10 | 432,948 | 95.0 |
| guam | Guam | 170 | 1,827.0 | 648.0 | 461.0 | 10.0 | 19,736 | 7,000 | 8 | 0 | 2 | 84 | 210 | 0 | R | R | R | R | 5 | 156,656 | 93.5 |
| guat | Guatemala | 23 | 52.0 | 122.0 | 27.0 | 1.6 | 733,299 | 250,000 | 11 | 1 | 3 | 65 | 41,000 | 662 | RC | RC | RC | RC | 50 | 10,684,153 | 93.8 |
| guin | Guinea | 2 | 35.0 | 9.7 | 1.6 | 0.1 | 23,584 | 1,000 | 6 | 12 | 8 | 33 | 100 | 2 | S | A | A | A | 7 | 231,322 | 3.1 |
| gunb | Guinea-Bissau | 6 | 36.0 | 10.0 | 8.8 | 0.5 | 4,719 | 500 | 6 | 13 | 7 | 40 | 0 | 1 | RC | RC | A | A | 20 | 155,645 | 12.8 |
| guya | Guyana | 63 | 454.0 | 42.0 | 63.0 | 0.3 | 15,734 | 2,000 | 11 | 8 | 6 | 51 | 950 | 17 | R | R | R | R | 16 | 374,036 | 43.4 |
| hait | Haiti | 7 | 41.0 | 5.0 | 8.4 | 2.0 | 117,250 | 5,000 | 9 | 0 | 8 | 38 | 29,500 | 435 | RC | RC | RC | RC | 37 | 7,639,424 | 92.9 |
| hond | Honduras | 44 | 354.0 | 80.0 | 29.0 | 1.2 | 194,563 | 25,000 | 11 | 5 | 6 | 55 | 8,020 | 173 | RC | RC | RC | RC | 16 | 6,057,600 | 93.4 |
| hung | Hungary | 228 | 590.0 | 444.0 | 185.0 | 4.4 | 1,504,063 | 200,000 | 7 | 0 | 8 | 51 | 71,505 | 466 | R | A | A | A | 39 | 8,749,732 | 87.2 |
| icel | Iceland | 515 | 733.0 | 447.0 | 556.0 | 17.8 | 84,571 | 150,000 | 9 | 1 | 2 | 88 | 0 | 1 | RL | RL | RL | RL | 17 | 265,259 | 94.4 |
| indi | India | 21 | 121.0 | 61.0 | 13.0 | 0.2 | 6,241,974 | 600,000 | 13 | 199 | 5 | 52 | 866,064 | 8,875 | S | S | S | S | 121 | 62,243,546 | 6.1 |
| indo | Indonesia | 20 | 132.0 | 147.0 | 17.0 | 0.8 | 3,294,753 | 150,000 | 11 | 505 | 3 | 63 | 94,610 | 1,138 | RR | R | R | R | 73 | 26,364,858 | 12.4 |
| iran | Iran | 20 | 213.0 | 134.0 | 85.0 | 0.8 | 3,057,144 | 300,000 | 12 | 0 | 7 | 44 | 227,270 | 117 | RI | RI | RI | RI | 40 | 313,990 | 0.5 |
| iraq | Iraq | 27 | 630.0 | 74.0 | 33.0 | 0.4 | 462,180 | 80,000 | 8 | 0 | 8 | 36 | 2,262,300 | 267 | RI | RI | RI | RI | 24 | 724,662 | 3.1 |
| irel | Ireland | 170 | 610.0 | 382.0 | 365.0 | 32.0 | 1,444,394 | 200,000 | 7 | 0 | 5 | 72 | 3,950 | 53 | RC | RC | R | R | 35 | 3,355,446 | 90.0 |
| isle | Isle of Man | 300 | 900.0 | 500.0 | 700.0 | 25.0 | 11,874 | 3,000 | 4 | 0 | 3 | 78 | 0 | 0 | RA | RA | RA | RA | 12 | 52,438 | 66.2 |
| isra | Israel | 281 | 481.0 | 303.0 | 418.0 | 25.5 | 1,598,856 | 1,000,000 | 7 | 0 | 6 | 56 | 65 | 1 | R | RJ | RJ | RJ | 38 | 294,078 | 5.7 |
| ital | Italy | 105 | 801.0 | 436.0 | 433.0 | 4.4 | 17,500,000 | 10,600,000 | 12 | 1 | 3 | 80 | 236,260 | 144 | RC | RC | RC | RC | 25 | 46,922,140 | 81.9 |
| ivor | Ivory Coast | 7 | 110.0 | 59.0 | 8.1 | 0.5 | 227,154 | 15,000 | 7 | 69 | 3 | 63 | 0 | 18 | S | S | S | S | 25 | 4,353,882 | 29.5 |
| jama | Jamaica | 66 | 747.0 | 306.0 | 116.0 | 0.8 | 129,334 | 30,000 | 11 | 0 | 3 | 65 | 0 | 23 | S | S | S | S | 36 | 1,121,713 | 43.4 |
| japa | Japan | 576 | 801.0 | 619.0 | 488.0 | 79.0 | 49,900,000 | 21,900,000 | 13 | 1 | 5 | 64 | 399,120 | 14 | RS | S | S | S | 72 | 3,436,881 | 2.7 |
| jord | Jordan | 48 | 234.0 | 175.0 | 73.0 | 8.0 | 379,811 | 20,000 | 5 | 0 | 4 | 62 | 10,064 | 1 | RI | RI | RI | RI | 8 | 273,522 | 4.1 |
| kaza | Kazakhstan | 400 | 150.0 | 275.0 | 118.0 | 0.4 | 507,835 | 25,000 | 8 | 1 | 8 | 36 | 6,000 | 8 | RO | A | S | S | 9 | 2,591,803 | 16.0 |
| keny | Kenya | 13 | 103.0 | 18.0 | 9.0 | 0.2 | 758,507 | 35,000 | 11 | 55 | 4 | 61 | 7,333 | 114 | S | S | S | S | 49 | 22,477,365 | 74.7 |
| kirg | Kirgizstan | 11 | 183.0 | 238.0 | 77.0 | 0.1 | 113,565 | 15,000 | 8 | 1 | 8 | 35 | 0 | 1 | RO | A | RI | RI | 7 | 465,665 | 9.9 |
| kiri | Kiribati | 100 | 79.0 | 25.0 | 26.0 | 2.3 | 8,619 | 2,000 | 4 | 0 | 4 | 68 | 200 | 0 | S | S | S | S | 10 | 77,331 | 92.7 |
| kuwa | Kuwait | 387 | 591.0 | 373.0 | 226.0 | 21.0 | 167,098 | 40,000 | 6 | 0 | 8 | 45 | 0 | 1 | RI | RI | RI | RI | 12 | 247,535 | 12.6 |
| laos | Laos | 3 | 121.0 | 7.0 | 4.1 | 0.2 | 56,927 | 3,000 | 11 | 64 | 8 | 30 | 12,000 | 159 | RB | RB | A | A | 27 | 112,563 | 2.1 |
| latv | Latvia | 228 | 547.0 | 482.0 | 280.0 | 0.5 | 95,870 | 12,000 | 7 | 0 | 6 | 55 | 50,500 | 5 | RO | A | S | S | 18 | 1,576,425 | 66.9 |
| leba | Lebanon | 135 | 601.0 | 291.0 | 89.0 | 1.9 | 115,104 | 10,000 | 6 | 0 | 4 | 62 | 170,264 | 336 | RI | R | R | R | 41 | 1,734,821 | 52.9 |
| leso | Lesotho | 7 | 569.0 | 7.0 | 9.0 | 0.5 | 91,766 | 3,000 | 7 | 1 | 6 | 46 | 0 | 7 | S | S | S | S | 22 | 1,445,329 | 67.1 |
| libe | Liberia | 14 | 275.0 | 25.0 | 2.1 | 0.3 | 65,125 | 2,500 | 5 | 28 | 4 | 54 | 15,000 | 203 | RX | RX | RX | RX | 24 | 932,060 | 29.6 |
| liby | Libya | 13 | 190.0 | 138.0 | 59.0 | 2.0 | 159,684 | 5,000 | 11 | 0 | 9 | 35 | 12,500 | 1 | RI | RI | RI | RI | 14 | 170,352 | 3.0 |
| liec | Liechtenstein | 581 | 384.0 | 371.0 | 638.0 | 30.0 | 5,000 | 8,000 | 5 | 0 | 2 | 84 | 0 | 0 | RC | RC | RC | RC | 5 | 27,051 | 82.4 |
| lith | Lithuania | 136 | 381.0 | 364.0 | 254.0 | 1.1 | 147,603 | 18,000 | 6 | 1 | 5 | 65 | 173,030 | 142 | RO | A | S | S | 22 | 3,213,397 | 87.6 |
| luxe | Luxembourg | 384 | 586.0 | 593.0 | 550.0 | 18.3 | 107,444 | 40,000 | 6 | 0 | 2 | 85 | 0 | 1 | RC | RC | RC | RC | 8 | 402,674 | 93.5 |
| mace | Macedonia | 21 | 179.0 | 179.0 | 179.0 | 1.3 | 100,504 | 15,000 | 5 | 0 | 5 | 64 | 0 | 4 | RO | A | RO | RO | 34 | 1,287,192 | 63.6 |
| mada | Madagascar | 4 | 173.0 | 24.0 | 2.4 | 0.3 | 260,922 | 20,000 | 10 | 34 | 3 | 65 | 9,010 | 30 | R | R | S | S | 36 | 7,629,263 | 47.9 |
| mala | Malawi | 2 | 112.0 | 70.0 | 3.6 | 0.1 | 54,920 | 3,000 | 9 | 6 | 4 | 60 | 7,000 | 124 | S | S | S | S | 31 | 7,032,260 | 64.4 |
| malb | Malaysia | 142 | 476.0 | 226.0 | 166.0 | 4.5 | 2,539,817 | 800,000 | 12 | 110 | 8 | 42 | 0 | 6 | RI | RI | RI | RI | 58 | 1,771,189 | 8.0 |

| COUNTRY | | SOCIETY (continued) | | | | | | | RELIGIOUS RELATIONS | | | | | | | | | | | | CHRISTIANITY | |
|---|---|---|---|---|---|---|---|---|---|---|---|---|---|---|---|---|---|---|---|---|---|
| | | COMMUNICATION per 1000 | | | | | | | RELIGIONS | | RELIGIOUS PERSECUTION | | | | CHURCH/STATE RELATIONS | | | | bibliography | church members | |
| code | short name | news | radios | TVs | fones | faxes | computers | internet | religs | indig | liberty | CSI | martyrs | mar-pa | 1900 | 1970 | 1990 | 2000 | items listed | affiliated | AC |
| 1 | 2 | 47 | 48 | 49 | 50 | 51 | 52 | 53 | 54 | 55 | 56 | 57 | 58 | 59 | 60 | 61 | 62 | 63 | 64 | 65 | 66 |
| mald | Maldives | 12 | 99.0 | 40.0 | 57.0 | 14.0 | 4,533 | 1,000 | 6 | 0 | 5 | 51 | 0 | 0 | RI | RI | RI | RI | 7 | 358 | 0.1 |
| mali | Mali | 4 | 176.0 | 12.0 | 1.7 | 0.1 | 50,237 | 5,000 | 6 | 17 | 4 | 55 | 30 | 1 | R | S | S | S | 18 | 224,365 | 2.0 |
| malt | Malta | 145 | 260.0 | 448.0 | 459.0 | 13.2 | 94,558 | 35,000 | 7 | 0 | 3 | 80 | 5,000 | 1 | RC | RC | RC | RC | 16 | 371,381 | 95.6 |
| mars | Marshall Islands | 20 | 500.0 | 20.0 | 44.2 | 3.8 | 13,039 | 6,000 | 4 | 1 | 5 | 67 | 0 | 0 | S | S | S | S | 7 | 60,103 | 93.6 |
| mart | Martinique | 84 | 187.0 | 137.0 | 381.0 | 9.0 | 47,878 | 5,000 | 11 | 0 | 5 | 66 | 0 | 4 | S | S | S | S | 10 | 373,372 | 94.4 |
| maur | Mauritania | 0 | 444.0 | 58.0 | 4.1 | 0.2 | 7,739 | 500 | 6 | 0 | 5 | 49 | 0 | 0 | RI | RI | RI | RI | 14 | 6,526 | 0.2 |
| maus | Mauritius | 68 | 353.0 | 187.0 | 131.0 | 18.0 | 58,833 | 7,000 | 11 | 0 | 2 | 75 | 0 | 1 | S | S | S | S | 26 | 369,432 | 31.9 |
| mayo | Mayotte | 15 | 427.0 | 1.0 | 48.0 | 1.0 | 203 | 100 | 4 | 0 | 5 | 50 | 0 | 0 | S | S | S | S | 6 | 1,866 | 1.8 |
| mexi | Mexico | 113 | 230.0 | 192.0 | 96.0 | 3.5 | 6,300,000 | 200,000 | 12 | 20 | 6 | 57 | 3,081,550 | 1,031 | S | S | S | S | 54 | 93,806,927 | 94.9 |
| micr | Micronesia | 25 | 667.0 | 21.0 | 74.0 | 4.3 | 9,879 | 1,500 | 7 | 6 | 5 | 66 | 1,510 | 0 | S | S | S | S | 17 | 108,662 | 91.6 |
| mold | Moldavia | 24 | 358.0 | 300.0 | 131.0 | 0.2 | 200,629 | 20,000 | 6 | 0 | 5 | 62 | 0 | 160 | RO | A | RO | RO | 3 | 2,798,558 | 63.9 |
| mona | Monaco | 263 | 987.0 | 670.0 | 876.0 | 61.0 | 10,080 | 10,000 | 5 | 0 | 2 | 88 | 0 | 0 | RC | RC | RC | RC | 12 | 31,101 | 92.6 |
| mong | Mongolia | 88 | 121.0 | 59.0 | 32.0 | 0.9 | 5,472 | 1,000 | 8 | 10 | 10 | 28 | 11,050 | 1 | RB | A | A | A | 25 | 33,393 | 1.3 |
| mont | Montserrat | 150 | 1,935.0 | 125.0 | 350.0 | 25.0 | 1,605 | 500 | 5 | 0 | 5 | 68 | 0 | 0 | S | S | S | S | 10 | 10,170 | 95.7 |
| moro | Morocco | 13 | 194.0 | 145.0 | 43.0 | 0.7 | 288,536 | 25,000 | 6 | 0 | 9 | 33 | 30,512 | 1 | RI | RI | RI | RI | 40 | 174,476 | 0.6 |
| moza | Mozambique | 5 | 36.0 | 3.0 | 3.4 | 0.8 | 156,503 | 10,000 | 8 | 24 | 8 | 34 | 35,200 | 494 | RC | RC | A | A | 30 | 6,460,533 | 32.8 |
| myan | Myanmar | 23 | 72.0 | 76.0 | 3.3 | 0.0 | 74,013 | 1,000 | 14 | 71 | 8 | 34 | 41,004 | 541 | R | S | S | S | 48 | 3,741,464 | 8.2 |
| nami | Namibia | 93 | 136.0 | 29.0 | 51.0 | 8.0 | 69,335 | 7,000 | 6 | 8 | 6 | 45 | 0 | 6 | R | R | R | R | 27 | 1,349,211 | 78.2 |
| naur | Nauru | 20 | 577.0 | 300.0 | 250.0 | 5.0 | 585 | 200 | 5 | 0 | 4 | 65 | 0 | 0 | R | R | R | R | 3 | 8,341 | 72.4 |
| nepa | Nepal | 8 | 29.0 | 3.0 | 3.6 | 0.0 | 97,389 | 1,000 | 11 | 67 | 8 | 36 | 50 | 2 | RH | RH | RH | RH | 70 | 576,061 | 2.4 |
| neth | Netherlands | 299 | 775.0 | 495.0 | 525.0 | 38.0 | 7,146,914 | 5,400,000 | 14 | 0 | 3 | 76 | 36,333 | 39 | S | S | S | S | 39 | 10,282,853 | 65.1 |
| nets | Netherlands Antilles | 260 | 1,009.0 | 325.0 | 374.0 | 25.0 | 30,128 | 5,000 | 11 | 0 | 2 | 83 | 50 | 2 | S | S | S | S | 14 | 184,912 | 85.3 |
| newc | New Caledonia | 123 | 495.0 | 380.0 | 236.0 | 20.6 | 38,946 | 5,000 | 9 | 1 | 4 | 73 | 10 | 1 | S | S | S | S | 16 | 161,679 | 75.5 |
| newz | New Zealand | 297 | 866.0 | 506.0 | 479.0 | 24.0 | 1,876,902 | 800,000 | 14 | 1 | 3 | 79 | 0 | 10 | S | S | S | S | 35 | 2,562,219 | 66.4 |
| nica | Nicaragua | 30 | 222.0 | 170.0 | 23.0 | 2.0 | 70,416 | 15,000 | 11 | 5 | 6 | 51 | 6,150 | 132 | R | R | A | A | 35 | 4,857,432 | 95.7 |
| niga | Niger | 1 | 48.0 | 23.0 | 1.5 | 0.1 | 32,415 | 7,000 | 5 | 3 | 4 | 56 | 0 | 0 | R | S | S | S | 19 | 58,270 | 0.5 |
| nige | Nigeria | 18 | 170.0 | 38.0 | 3.6 | 0.3 | 1,030,285 | 120,000 | 10 | 424 | 3 | 63 | 231,600 | 3,257 | S | S | S | S | 85 | 50,965,002 | 45.7 |
| nork | North Korea | 213 | 211.0 | 115.0 | 46.0 | 0.2 | 23,913 | 1,000 | 8 | 1 | 10 | 32 | 820,000 | 10,592 | RG | A | A | A | 19 | 500,213 | 2.1 |
| norl | Northern Cyprus | 90 | 220.0 | 100.0 | 350.0 | 8.0 | 9,252 | 2,000 | 3 | 0 | 9 | 31 | 0 | 0 | RO | RO | RI | RI | 5 | 16,106 | 8.7 |
| norm | Northern Mariana Is | 20 | 190.0 | 82.0 | 100.0 | 38.0 | 526 | 200 | 8 | 0 | 5 | 64 | 0 | 0 | S | S | S | S | 1 | 69,260 | 88.4 |
| norw | Norway | 498 | 767.0 | 561.0 | 558.0 | 39.0 | 2,271,390 | 1,000,000 | 12 | 1 | 2 | 88 | 2,000 | 13 | RL | RL | RL | RL | 34 | 4,201,262 | 94.2 |
| oman | Oman | 30 | 416.0 | 61.0 | 79.0 | 1.0 | 108,694 | 20,000 | 10 | 0 | 6 | 50 | 0 | 0 | RI | RI | RI | RI | 21 | 121,916 | 4.8 |
| paki | Pakistan | 22 | 76.0 | 22.0 | 16.0 | 1.2 | 780,037 | 200,000 | 12 | 14 | 4 | 56 | 1,200 | 28 | S | RI | RI | RI | 54 | 3,812,245 | 2.4 |
| pala | Palau | 15 | 536.0 | 89.0 | 90.0 | 3.0 | 363 | 100 | 6 | 1 | 5 | 65 | 0 | 0 | S | S | S | S | 5 | 18,371 | 94.6 |
| pale | Palestine | 200 | 300.0 | 150.0 | 300.0 | 10.0 | 434,679 | 20,000 | 6 | 0 | 6 | 43 | 168,564 | 3 | RI | S | S | S | 17 | 188,289 | 8.5 |
| pana | Panama | 62 | 200.0 | 229.0 | 116.0 | 2.0 | 85,670 | 20,000 | 13 | 8 | 7 | 53 | 0 | 27 | RC | RC | RC | RC | 10 | 2,457,064 | 86.0 |
| papu | Papua New Guinea | 15 | 72.0 | 163.0 | 10.0 | 0.3 | 46,125 | 5,000 | 9 | 634 | 3 | 68 | 475 | 13 | S | S | S | S | 57 | 3,785,528 | 82.2 |
| para | Paraguay | 42 | 144.0 | 144.0 | 34.0 | 0.5 | 192,376 | 15,000 | 8 | 15 | 2 | 74 | 1,550 | 61 | RC | RC | RC | RC | 19 | 5,173,602 | 94.1 |
| peru | Peru | 86 | 225.0 | 100.0 | 47.0 | 0.6 | 1,134,246 | 100,000 | 11 | 55 | 2 | 75 | 18,500 | 509 | RC | RC | RC | RC | 42 | 24,702,049 | 96.3 |
| phil | Philippines | 65 | 116.0 | 129.0 | 25.0 | 0.8 | 1,583,276 | 250,000 | 13 | 131 | 3 | 68 | 64,000 | 871 | R | R | R | R | 53 | 66,600,057 | 87.7 |
| pola | Poland | 141 | 421.0 | 408.0 | 148.0 | 1.4 | 3,686,795 | 1,000,000 | 9 | 0 | 8 | 52 | 1,592,500 | 2,073 | R | A | A | A | 57 | 37,498,059 | 96.7 |
| port | Portugal | 41 | 224.0 | 333.0 | 362.0 | 6.1 | 1,567,058 | 400,000 | 10 | 1 | 3 | 78 | 10,000 | 28 | RC | RC | RC | RC | 29 | 9,080,231 | 92.0 |
| puer | Puerto Rico | 184 | 666.0 | 311.0 | 321.0 | 140.0 | 697,935 | 250,000 | 11 | 0 | 3 | 76 | 0 | 40 | S | S | S | S | 40 | 3,722,291 | 96.2 |
| qata | Qatar | 138 | 311.0 | 451.0 | 212.0 | 33.0 | 35,970 | 15,000 | 7 | 0 | 8 | 44 | 0 | 0 | RI | RI | RI | RI | 7 | 59,635 | 10.0 |
| reun | Reunion | 83 | 265.0 | 205.0 | 329.0 | 5.7 | 20,966 | 4,000 | 11 | 0 | 5 | 63 | 0 | 2 | S | S | S | S | 14 | 607,104 | 86.8 |
| roma | Romania | 297 | 198.0 | 201.0 | 131.0 | 0.4 | 1,005,968 | 120,000 | 7 | 0 | 8 | 49 | 155,500 | 1,269 | RO | A | A | A | 39 | 19,627,363 | 87.9 |
| russ | Russia | 267 | 341.0 | 380.0 | 170.0 | 0.7 | 9,200,000 | 5,000,000 | 10 | 47 | 9 | 40 | 24,004,490 | 71,595 | RO | A | A | A | 83 | 83,618,357 | 56.9 |
| rwan | Rwanda | 0 | 78.0 | 2.0 | 2.5 | 0.1 | 61,391 | 5,000 | 6 | 3 | 4 | 46 | 510,000 | 7,040 | RT | R | R | R | 40 | 6,336,822 | 81.9 |
| saha | Sahara | 1 | 50.0 | 10.0 | 10.0 | 0.0 | 289 | 50 | 5 | 0 | 3 | 51 | 0 | 0 | R | S | S | S | 11 | 487 | 0.2 |
| saih | Saint Helena | 0 | 600.0 | 150.0 | 100.0 | 10.0 | 4,406 | 200 | 3 | 0 | 3 | 78 | 0 | 0 | RA | RA | RA | RA | 3 | 5,332 | 84.7 |
| saik | Saint Kitts & Nevis | 600 | 650.0 | 241.0 | 355.0 | 20.0 | 3,707 | 1,000 | 7 | 0 | 4 | 72 | 0 | 0 | S | S | S | S | 10 | 36,000 | 93.6 |
| sail | Saint Lucia | 700 | 699.0 | 172.0 | 211.0 | 10.0 | 10,628 | 3,000 | 7 | 0 | 2 | 82 | 0 | 2 | S | S | S | S | 12 | 144,339 | 93.5 |
| saip | Saint Pierre & Miquelon | 0 | 900.0 | 200.0 | 150.0 | 15.0 | 6,691 | 300 | 4 | 0 | 5 | 70 | 0 | 0 | S | S | S | S | 1 | 6,388 | 97.3 |
| saiv | Saint Vincent | 500 | 565.0 | 161.0 | 165.0 | 8.6 | 9,333 | 2,500 | 7 | 0 | 4 | 70 | 0 | 1 | S | S | S | S | 8 | 78,439 | 68.8 |
| samo | Samoa | 122 | 448.0 | 38.0 | 47.0 | 4.6 | 6,968 | 1,000 | 5 | 0 | 4 | 70 | 0 | 1 | RX | RX | RX | RX | 20 | 169,129 | 93.9 |
| sanm | San Marino | 82 | 522.0 | 367.0 | 571.0 | 192.0 | 8,025 | 4,000 | 5 | 0 | 3 | 82 | 0 | 0 | S | S | S | S | 2 | 23,779 | 89.7 |
| saot | Sao Tome & Principe | 20 | 237.0 | 154.0 | 19.0 | 2.0 | 2,197 | 500 | 5 | 1 | 3 | 67 | 0 | 1 | RC | RC | A | A | 9 | 132,103 | 90.0 |
| saud | Saudi Arabia | 54 | 213.0 | 257.0 | 96.0 | 5.8 | 1,470,808 | 35,000 | 11 | 0 | 9 | 36 | 20,000 | 2 | RI | RI | RI | RI | 26 | 786,985 | 3.6 |
| sene | Senegal | 6 | 93.0 | 37.0 | 9.8 | 0.1 | 75,961 | 10,000 | 7 | 24 | 4 | 57 | 0 | 2 | S | S | S | S | 38 | 467,291 | 4.9 |
| seyc | Seychelles | 40 | 667.0 | 184.0 | 187.0 | 9.1 | 1,546 | 500 | 8 | 0 | 4 | 70 | 0 | 0 | S | S | S | S | 9 | 71,795 | 92.7 |
| sier | Sierra Leone | 2 | 221.0 | 16.0 | 3.7 | 0.3 | 19,463 | 2,000 | 8 | 16 | 4 | 52 | 0 | 2 | S | S | S | S | 33 | 510,494 | 10.5 |
| sing | Singapore | 340 | 275.0 | 218.0 | 478.0 | 28.5 | 1,477,954 | 900,000 | 14 | 1 | 5 | 60 | 300 | 1 | S | S | S | S | 49 | 402,936 | 11.3 |
| slok | Slovakia | 256 | 118.0 | 216.0 | 208.0 | 11.3 | 602,696 | 300,000 | 6 | 0 | 5 | 65 | 8,300 | 245 | R | A | S | S | 33 | 4,324,186 | 80.3 |
| slov | Slovenia | 183 | 320.0 | 374.0 | 309.0 | 10.5 | 191,369 | 200,000 | 6 | 0 | 5 | 64 | 0 | 6 | RO | A | RO | RO | 36 | 1,736,806 | 87.5 |
| solo | Solomon Islands | 15 | 117.0 | 16.0 | 17.0 | 2.2 | 22,200 | 5,000 | 7 | 64 | 4 | 67 | 301 | 1 | S | S | S | S | 27 | 403,203 | 90.9 |
| soma | Somalia | 1 | 41.0 | 13.0 | 1.7 | 0.1 | 17,394 | 2,000 | 7 | 2 | 8 | 31 | 40 | 1 | RI | RI | RI | RI | 17 | 98,583 | 1.4 |
| somi | Somaliland | 0 | 20.0 | 5.0 | 1.0 | 0.0 | 2,833 | 200 | 6 | 0 | 9 | 29 | 0 | 0 | RI | RI | RI | RI | 8 | 8,381 | 0.3 |
| soua | South Africa | 33 | 273.0 | 101.0 | 95.0 | 2.2 | 2,118,564 | 1,200,000 | 14 | 27 | 6 | 54 | 10,000 | 258 | R | R | R | R | 91 | 31,800,789 | 78.8 |
| souk | South Korea | 405 | 928.0 | 321.0 | 415.0 | 13.0 | 10,600,000 | 3,200,000 | 11 | 1 | 6 | 57 | 20,000 | 59 | RG | S | S | S | 51 | 18,681,876 | 39.9 |
| spai | Spain | 104 | 304.0 | 490.0 | 385.0 | 7.5 | 8,100,000 | 4,400,000 | 7 | 0 | 2 | 87 | 141,402 | 114 | RC | RC | RC | RC | 51 | 37,073,672 | 93.6 |
| span | Spanish North Africa | 90 | 250.0 | 400.0 | 350.0 | 3.0 | 23,400 | 3,000 | 5 | 0 | 2 | 82 | 0 | 0 | RC | RC | RC | RC | 4 | 104,324 | 80.3 |
| sril | Sri Lanka | 25 | 182.0 | 66.0 | 11.0 | 0.8 | 150,564 | 20,000 | 13 | 1 | 6 | 48 | 1,120 | 8 | RB | RB | RB | RB | 45 | 1,755,120 | 9.3 |
| suda | Sudan | 23 | 193.0 | 76.0 | 2.7 | 0.3 | 59,646 | 5,000 | 8 | 107 | 8 | 33 | 810,000 | 8,994 | RI | RI | RI | RI | 49 | 4,874,391 | 16.5 |
| suri | Suriname | 103 | 609.0 | 186.0 | 123.0 | 2.2 | 6,784 | 1,000 | 13 | 9 | 2 | 72 | 10 | 2 | S | S | S | S | 24 | 172,334 | 41.3 |
| swaz | Swaziland | 14 | 550.0 | 96.0 | 21.0 | 2.0 | 39,345 | 6,000 | 7 | 1 | 4 | 46 | 0 | 3 | RT | R | R | R | 22 | 680,841 | 67.6 |
| swed | Sweden | 515 | 844.0 | 476.0 | 681.0 | 56.0 | 4,528,309 | 3,700,000 | 9 | 0 | 2 | 84 | 1,000 | 19 | RL | RL | RL | RL | 24 | 6,000,356 | 67.3 |
| swit | Switzerland | 415 | 791.0 | 370.0 | 613.0 | 40.0 | 3,288,599 | 1,300,000 | 9 | 0 | 2 | 88 | 0 | 20 | R | R | R | R | 33 | 6,445,548 | 87.3 |
| syri | Syria | 18 | 207.0 | 89.0 | 63.0 | 0.3 | 1,128,841 | 110,000 | 7 | 0 | 7 | 43 | 145,468 | 4 | RI | RI | S | S | 29 | 1,257,709 | 7.8 |
| taiw | Taiwan | 188 | 402.0 | 327.0 | 467.0 | 25.0 | 5,199,272 | 1,500,000 | 11 | 15 | 6 | 54 | 7,000 | 4 | RG | S | S | S | 46 | 1,179,743 | 5.3 |
| taji | Tajikistan | 13 | 100.0 | 258.0 | 45.0 | 0.3 | 127,966 | 2,000 | 9 | 0 | 9 | 27 | 0 | 0 | RO | A | RI | RI | 7 | 129,612 | 2.1 |
| tanz | Tanzania | 8 | 123.0 | 16.0 | 3.0 | 0.2 | 336,872 | 25,000 | 12 | 104 | 5 | 54 | 0 | 63 | S | S | S | S | 43 | 15,722,778 | 46.9 |
| thai | Thailand | 47 | 167.0 | 227.0 | 59.0 | 1.6 | 3,127,602 | 200,000 | 14 | 33 | 3 | 63 | 2,244 | 4 | RB | RB | RB | RB | 57 | 1,345,167 | 2.2 |
| timo | Timor | 15 | 100.0 | 100.0 | 15.0 | 0.4 | 4,421 | 1,000 | 9 | 14 | 3 | 67 | 96,000 | 1,247 | RC | RC | RC | RC | 27 | 815,391 | 92.2 |
| togo | Togo | 2 | 170.0 | 12.0 | 5.2 | 2.1 | 37,408 | 6,000 | 7 | 23 | 7 | 43 | 1 | 7 | S | S | S | S | 22 | 1,749,095 | 37.8 |
| tong | Tonga | 73 | 400.0 | 20.0 | 67.0 | 3.0 | 3,001 | 500 | 6 | 0 | 2 | 83 | 3 | 0 | RM | RM | RM | RM | 22 | 89,688 | 91.0 |
| trin | Trinidad & Tobago | 135 | 433.0 | 328.0 | 166.0 | 1.9 | 67,036 | 10,000 | 11 | 0 | 2 | 78 | 167 | 9 | R | R | R | R | 39 | 795,865 | 61.5 |
| tuni | Tunisia | 46 | 193.0 | 156.0 | 58.0 | 4.1 | 98,366 | 5,000 | 6 | 0 | 5 | 54 | 178,933 | 0 | RI | RI | RI | RI | 27 | 50,503 | 0.5 |
| turk | Turkey | 44 | 141.0 | 240.0 | 215.0 | 1.8 | 1,801,043 | 120,000 | 9 | 0 | 8 | 39 | 1,369,520 | 1 | RI | S | S | S | 37 | 373,155 | 0.6 |
| turm | Turkmenistan | 250 | 189.0 | 189.0 | 71.0 | 0.3 | 35,834 | 5,000 | 8 | 0 | 9 | 26 | 2,600,000 | 0 | RO | A | RI | RI | 14 | 98,883 | 2.2 |
| turs | Turks & Caicos Is | 80 | 190.0 | 150.0 | 127.0 | 12.5 | 414 | 200 | 5 | 0 | 5 | 66 | 0 | 0 | S | S | S | S | 2 | 13,262 | 79.1 |
| tuva | Tuvalu | 60 | 320.0 | 200.0 | 165.0 | 1.0 | 204 | 100 | 5 | 0 | 4 | 72 | 0 | 0 | S | S | S | S | 9 | 9,745 | 83.2 |
| ugan | Uganda | 2 | 507.0 | 26.0 | 2.3 | 0.2 | 224,587 | 15,000 | 10 | 33 | 7 | 45 | 203,095 | 2,748 | S | S | S | S | 51 | 18,944,173 | 87.0 |
| ukra | Ukraine | 118 | 346.0 | 233.0 | 161.0 | 0.1 | 2,301,278 | 500,000 | 8 | 1 | 5 | 62 | 3,970,500 | 2,232 | RO | A | RO | RO | 43 | 41,669,097 | 82.6 |
| unia | United Arab Emirates | 126 | 206.0 | 26.0 | 283.0 | 16.6 | 244,382 | 80,000 | 9 | 0 | 6 | 54 | 0 | 1 | RI | RI | RI | RI | 15 | 262,745 | 10.8 |
| usa | USA | 228 | 1,976.0 | 780.0 | 626.0 | 108.0 | 164,100,000 | 132,300,000 | 18 | 49 | 4 | 74 | 600 | 725 | S | S | S | S | 119 | 191,827,627 | 68.9 |
| uuay | Uruguay | 237 | 591.0 | 310.0 | 199.0 | 3.7 | 98,234 | 20,000 | 9 | 0 | 3 | 73 | 0 | 23 | R | S | S | S | 22 | 2,161,729 | 64.8 |
| uzbe | Uzbekistan | 264 | 250.0 | 176.0 | 76.0 | 0.2 | 875,640 | 15,000 | 10 | 0 | 8 | 38 | 2,000,000 | 1 | RO | A | RI | RI | 14 | 394,334 | 1.6 |
| vanu | Vanuatu | 70 | 327.0 | 12.0 | 250.0 | 4.0 | 2,876 | 500 | 7 | 54 | 3 | 74 | 0 | 1 | S | S | RX | RX | 22 | 170,054 | 89.3 |
| vene | Venezuela | 215 | 372.0 | 183.0 | 111.0 | 1.0 | 1,488,855 | 35,000 | 11 | 23 | 2 | 75 | 34 | 245 | RC | RC | RC | RC | 34 | 22,735,834 | 94.1 |
| viet | Viet Nam | 8 | 95.0 | 163.0 | 11.0 | 0.3 | 966,584 | 25,000 | 12 | 59 | 8 | 34 | 116,670 | 1,053 | S | S | A | A | 35 | 6,567,922 | 8.2 |
| virg | Virgin Is of the US | 267 | 1,029.0 | 315.0 | 597.0 | 50.0 | 54,227 | 20,000 | 6 | 0 | 4 | 73 | 0 | 1 | S | S | S | S | 16 | 86,159 | 92.7 |
| wall | Wallis & Futuna Is | 30 | 100.0 | 80.0 | 26.0 | 10.0 | 305 | 100 | 4 | 2 | 4 | 73 | 400 | 0 | S | S | S | S | 1 | 14,021 | 96.6 |
| yeme | Yemen | 17 | 48.0 | 243.0 | 12.0 | 0.2 | 452,952 | 5,000 | 10 | 0 | 8 | 35 | 20,000 | 0 | RI | RI | RI | RI | 24 | 30,656 | 0.2 |
| yugo | Yugoslavia | 90 | 256.0 | 170.0 | 192.0 | 1.6 | 1,050,206 | 150,000 | 8 | 1 | 6 | 56 | 0 | 22 | R | A | A | A | 38 | 6,885,557 | 64.7 |
| zamb | Zambia | 13 | 139.0 | 64.0 | 8.2 | 0.1 | 27,398 | 5,000 | 9 | 51 | 6 | 52 | 700 | 38 | S | S | S | S | 44 | 7,052,080 | 76.9 |
| zimb | Zimbabwe | 17 | 113.0 | 27.0 | 14.0 | 1.0 | 99,381 | 10,000 | 11 | 12 | 6 | 52 | 3,055 | 69 | R | R | A | A | 46 | 6,917,360 | 59.3 |
| | 11 minicountries | 0 | 1,054.0 | 206.0 | 183.0 | 43.0 | 19,692 | 4,235 | 10 | 0 | 4 | 73 | | 0 | - | - | - | - | 86 | 13,876 | 60.1 |
| | Africa | 18 | 163.0 | 51.0 | 17.0 | 1.0 | 10,933,293 | 1,773,450 | 17 | 2,041 | 6 | 49 | 3,949,169 | 26,985 | - | - | - | - | 1,627 | 335,115,750 | 42.7 |
| | Antarctica | 0 | 2,000.0 | 200.0 | 200.0 | 100.0 | 9,000 | 2,000 | 5 | 0 | 3 | 76 | 0 | 0 | - | - | - | - | 17 | 3,400 | 75.6 |
| | Asia | 55 | 184.0 | 169.0 | 55.0 | 4.0 | 116,150,740 | 35,656,500 | 19 | 1,452 | 7 | 45 | 15,869,994 | 44,038 | - | - | - | - | 1,647 | 307,288,308 | 8.3 |
| | Europe | 236 | 698.0 | 431.0 | 341.0 | 19.0 | 161,425,041 | 91,179,950 | 16 | 59 | 5 | 64 | 32,341,964 | 80,815 | - | - | - | - | 1,319 | 536,831,571 | 73.7 |
| | Latin America | 83 | 311.0 | 223.0 | 90.0 | 3.0 | 27,578,722 | 2,455,200 | 15 | 430 | 6 | 57 | 3,368,389 | 7,246 | - | - | - | - | 1,043 | 475,658,900 | 91.6 |
| | Northern America | 224 | 1,858.0 | 766.0 | 622.0 | 100.0 | 180,125,747 | 143,913,300 | 18 | 50 | 4 | 75 | 700 | 801 | - | - | - | - | 202 | 212,166,818 | 68.5 |
| | Oceania | 205 | 884.0 | 500.0 | 391.0 | 24.0 | 12,742,117 | 1,651,685 | 16 | 859 | 3 | 77 | 12,109 | 115 | - | - | - | - | 431 | 21,374,546 | 70.3 |
| | **World A** | **41** | **149.0** | **95.0** | **53.0** | **1.0** | **9,235,090** | **885,260** | **19** | **260** | **7** | **42** | **10,696,811** | **12,655** | - | - | - | - | **744** | **10,026,564** | **1.7** |
| | **World B** | **60** | **196.0** | **172.0** | **55.0** | **4.0** | **123,679,836** | **40,336,450** | **19** | **2,695** | **7** | **46** | **31,808,415** | **116,122** | - | - | - | - | **2,137** | **491,326,295** | **13.1** |
| | **World C** | **152** | **739.0** | **377.0** | **283.0** | **28.0** | **376,049,734** | **235,410,375** | **19** | **1,936** | **5** | **66** | **13,037,100** | **31,223** | - | - | - | - | **3,405** | **1,387,086,434** | **81.8** |
| | **GLOBAL TOTAL** | **84** | **343.0** | **222.0** | **118.0** | **10.0** | **508,964,660** | **276,632,085** | **19** | **4,891** | **6** | **51** | **55,542,325** | **160,000** | - | - | - | - | **6,286** | **1,888,439,293** | **31.2** |

| COUNTRY | | FOUR MEGATYPOLOGIES OF RENEWAL IN GLOBAL CHRISTIANITY, AD 30–AD 2000 | | | | | | | | | | | | |
|---|---|---|---|---|---|---|---|---|---|---|---|---|---|---|
| | | 1. The Great Commission | | 2. Ecclesiastical Renewal: 6 megablocs | | | | | | 3. Evangelical Renewal | | 4. Pentecostal/Charismatic Renewal | | |
| code | short name | GCCs | GCC | Megabloc O | Megabloc R | Megabloc A | Megabloc P | Megabloc I | Megabloc m | Evangelicals | evangelicals | 1st -Wavers | 2nd-Wavers | 3rd-Wavers |
| 1 | 2 | 67 | 68 | 69 | 70 | 71 | 72 | 73 | 74 | 75 | 76 | 77 | 78 | 79 |
| afgh | Afghanistan | 4,081 | 0.0 | 100 | 1,497 | 100 | 2,000 | 3,000 | 200 | 800 | 4,081 | 48 | 267 | 1,985 |
| alba | Albania | 614,345 | 19.7 | 500,000 | 521,390 | 0 | 20,000 | 17,000 | 12,000 | 6,000 | 614,345 | 2,868 | 40,946 | 56,186 |
| alge | Algeria | 65,098 | 0.2 | 1,800 | 20,277 | 200 | 3,400 | 65,000 | 200 | 5,700 | 65,098 | 0 | 1,543 | 53,457 |
| amer | American Samoa | 30,261 | 44.4 | 0 | 9,470 | 190 | 35,800 | 1,780 | 8,000 | 5,450 | 30,261 | 3,570 | 5,527 | 803 |
| ando | Andorra | 26,551 | 34.1 | 0 | 69,535 | 0 | 140 | 80 | 450 | 20 | 26,551 | 0 | 758 | 82 |
| ango | Angola | 1,545,888 | 12.0 | 0 | 8,000,000 | 4,000 | 1,930,238 | 880,000 | 120,000 | 1,227,000 | 1,545,888 | 414,526 | 783,776 | 846,698 |
| angu | Anguilla | 1,098 | 13.2 | 0 | 310 | 2,650 | 4,126 | 0 | 100 | 800 | 1,098 | 0 | 1,040 | 0 |
| anti | Antigua | 10,329 | 15.3 | 0 | 7,800 | 22,613 | 21,000 | 1,200 | 1,100 | 7,000 | 10,329 | 2,249 | 5,280 | 891 |
| arge | Argentina | 2,739,882 | 7.4 | 158,000 | 33,750,000 | 19,000 | 2,295,000 | 2,050,000 | 500,000 | 1,960,000 | 2,739,882 | 1,659,492 | 4,657,566 | 2,082,942 |
| arme | Armenia | 395,380 | 11.2 | 2,752,493 | 160,000 | 0 | 12,000 | 28,000 | 1,200 | 1,900 | 395,380 | 0 | 59,228 | 17,672 |
| arub | Aruba | 5,402 | 5.3 | 0 | 84,341 | 750 | 7,500 | 1,350 | 1,300 | 4,100 | 5,402 | 2,550 | 4,668 | 1,232 |
| aust | Australia | 6,485,759 | 34.4 | 700,000 | 5,400,000 | 4,060,000 | 2,630,000 | 840,000 | 220,000 | 2,598,851 | 6,485,759 | 146,247 | 1,776,680 | 532,073 |
| ausz | Austria | 1,722,957 | 21.0 | 155,000 | 6,200,000 | 3,100 | 413,570 | 73,000 | 65,000 | 46,000 | 1,722,957 | 17,316 | 269,594 | 11,590 |
| azer | Azerbaijan | 126,853 | 1.6 | 345,302 | 7,500 | 0 | 1,400 | 3,600 | 0 | 450 | 126,853 | 0 | 6,259 | 3,741 |
| baha | Bahamas | 40,536 | 13.2 | 380 | 48,000 | 27,300 | 167,171 | 19,000 | 5,000 | 90,600 | 40,536 | 28,127 | 10,937 | 9,936 |
| bahr | Bahrain | 21,414 | 3.5 | 2,500 | 25,000 | 3,000 | 5,100 | 27,058 | 40 | 3,700 | 21,414 | 0 | 2,372 | 26,028 |
| bang | Bangladesh | 639,011 | 0.5 | 160 | 235,000 | 0 | 160,490 | 536,000 | 90 | 72,000 | 639,011 | 17,556 | 28,804 | 433,639 |
| barb | Barbados | 49,919 | 18.5 | 300 | 11,000 | 77,300 | 85,158 | 17,500 | 5,600 | 80,400 | 49,919 | 31,428 | 10,732 | 6,740 |
| belg | Belgium | 4,675,333 | 46.0 | 48,500 | 8,222,396 | 10,800 | 125,000 | 40,000 | 72,000 | 27,700 | 4,675,333 | 13,310 | 267,136 | 22,054 |
| beli | Belize | 28,865 | 12.0 | 0 | 136,939 | 10,500 | 39,500 | 5,200 | 5,000 | 17,100 | 28,865 | 7,082 | 20,089 | 4,229 |
| belo | Belorussia | 2,162,574 | 21.1 | 4,986,077 | 1,350,000 | 0 | 130,000 | 110,000 | 8,000 | 30,800 | 2,162,574 | 63,842 | 22,035 | 9,123 |
| beni | Benin | 1,004,584 | 16.5 | 0 | 1,266,195 | 0 | 230,000 | 175,000 | 13,000 | 112,000 | 1,004,584 | 84,306 | 104,526 | 153,168 |
| berm | Bermuda | 11,327 | 17.5 | 0 | 10,384 | 24,200 | 19,500 | 7,000 | 1,650 | 7,700 | 11,327 | 2,421 | 8,335 | 2,644 |
| bhut | Bhutan | 8,666 | 0.4 | 0 | 600 | 0 | 3,200 | 5,849 | 0 | 1,100 | 8,666 | 231 | 304 | 4,965 |
| boli | Bolivia | 1,724,676 | 20.7 | 3,100 | 7,350,000 | 1,100 | 530,000 | 145,000 | 135,000 | 375,000 | 1,724,676 | 145,271 | 951,855 | 117,874 |
| bosn | Bosnia-Herzegovina | 368,217 | 9.3 | 700,000 | 681,135 | 0 | 2,700 | 750 | 1,300 | 400 | 368,217 | 479 | 31,631 | 290 |
| bots | Botswana | 384,089 | 23.7 | 120 | 60,000 | 10,500 | 178,000 | 498,253 | 4,200 | 51,800 | 384,089 | 29,479 | 26,639 | 478,882 |
| boug | Bougainville | 16,167 | 8.1 | 0 | 148,401 | 0 | 22,650 | 14,000 | 280 | 5,200 | 16,167 | 0 | 6,658 | 2,642 |
| braz | Brazil | 24,207,478 | 14.2 | 170,000 | 153,300,000 | 125,000 | 30,200,000 | 25,500,000 | 1,420,000 | 27,749,000 | 24,207,478 | 25,234,662 | 33,185,413 | 21,529,926 |
| brit | Britain | 21,120,856 | 35.9 | 370,000 | 5,620,000 | 26,278,000 | 5,050,000 | 2,140,000 | 550,000 | 11,560,000 | 21,120,856 | 277,128 | 4,089,776 | 1,453,096 |
| briz | British Virgin Is | 6,229 | 29.2 | 0 | 700 | 2,800 | 9,792 | 1,000 | 600 | 3,650 | 6,229 | 705 | 1,607 | 359 |
| brun | Brunei | 18,199 | 5.6 | 0 | 5,600 | 4,592 | 6,000 | 8,300 | 100 | 6,350 | 18,199 | 0 | 2,509 | 6,341 |
| bulg | Bulgaria | 493,299 | 6.0 | 5,886,450 | 90,000 | 0 | 95,000 | 580,000 | 6,500 | 120,000 | 493,299 | 55,894 | 3,778 | 80,328 |
| burk | Burkina Faso | 1,521,822 | 12.8 | 0 | 1,129,078 | 0 | 799,000 | 54,000 | 2,000 | 765,000 | 1,521,822 | 635,430 | 151,853 | 56,717 |
| buru | Burundi | 1,144,771 | 17.1 | 1,400 | 3,827,541 | 500,000 | 800,000 | 23,000 | 900 | 850,000 | 1,144,771 | 497,639 | 257,824 | 19,537 |
| camb | Cambodia | 103,375 | 0.9 | 0 | 22,000 | 40 | 21,500 | 74,708 | 150 | 20,000 | 103,375 | 1,187 | 2,716 | 52,097 |
| came | Cameroon | 3,388,574 | 22.5 | 1,200 | 3,989,401 | 900 | 3,120,000 | 590,000 | 60,000 | 620,000 | 3,388,574 | 99,499 | 554,497 | 326,004 |
| cana | Canada | 12,604,889 | 40.5 | 580,000 | 13,017,945 | 820,000 | 5,350,000 | 1,680,000 | 450,000 | 2,540,000 | 12,604,889 | 504,551 | 2,596,361 | 1,324,088 |
| cape | Cape Verde | 55,921 | 13.1 | 0 | 417,000 | 0 | 15,500 | 12,800 | 4,800 | 10,900 | 55,921 | 499 | 17,621 | 13,580 |
| caym | Cayman Islands | 7,430 | 19.4 | 0 | 200 | 500 | 20,690 | 4,050 | 380 | 5,600 | 7,430 | 601 | 3,683 | 2,216 |
| cent | Central African Rep | 811,638 | 22.5 | 0 | 664,639 | 0 | 520,800 | 418,000 | 5,560 | 630,000 | 811,638 | 103,705 | 123,870 | 257,425 |
| chad | Chad | 718,153 | 9.4 | 0 | 502,158 | 0 | 782,756 | 152,000 | 1,100 | 653,000 | 718,153 | 17,107 | 149,905 | 82,988 |
| chan | Channel Islands | 40,543 | 26.5 | 200 | 22,300 | 67,511 | 10,500 | 0 | 270 | 20,000 | 40,543 | 1,419 | 6,981 | 0 |
| chil | Chile | 2,222,359 | 14.6 | 23,750 | 11,800,000 | 12,000 | 382,000 | 3,820,000 | 420,000 | 250,000 | 2,222,359 | 90,791 | 1,635,173 | 3,811,036 |
| chin | China | 81,352,742 | 6.4 | 55,000 | 7,500,000 | 23,000 | 640,000 | 80,708,347 | 29,000 | 2,521,500 | 81,352,742 | 47,686 | 629,491 | 53,597,823 |
| colo | Colombia | 2,673,679 | 6.3 | 7,200 | 40,670,000 | 3,600 | 1,100,000 | 535,000 | 275,000 | 590,000 | 2,673,679 | 512,397 | 11,522,127 | 550,476 |
| como | Comoros | 3,558 | 0.6 | 0 | 5,751 | 0 | 900 | 400 | 10 | 220 | 3,558 | 0 | 198 | 362 |
| cong | Congo-Brazzaville | 567,743 | 19.3 | 400 | 1,451,178 | 0 | 500,000 | 370,000 | 11,300 | 195,000 | 567,743 | 53,479 | 195,925 | 339,595 |
| conz | Congo-Zaire | 3,898,238 | 7.6 | 8,100 | 26,300,000 | 440,000 | 10,485,000 | 12,050,000 | 360,000 | 4,440,000 | 3,898,238 | 78,344 | 2,780,182 | 14,891,474 |
| cook | Cook Islands | 2,521 | 12.9 | 0 | 3,650 | 100 | 14,200 | 60 | 1,650 | 1,530 | 2,521 | 1,278 | 1,816 | 6 |
| cost | Costa Rica | 514,542 | 12.8 | 0 | 3,660,000 | 1,600 | 330,000 | 108,000 | 75,000 | 280,000 | 514,542 | 223,063 | 199,841 | 71,095 |
| croa | Croatia | 233,171 | 5.2 | 250,000 | 3,960,000 | 0 | 26,000 | 11,386 | 9,000 | 6,700 | 233,171 | 2,909 | 119,765 | 5,146 |
| cuba | Cuba | 2,584,208 | 23.1 | 1,400 | 4,367,909 | 3,600 | 190,000 | 135,000 | 125,000 | 134,400 | 2,584,208 | 68,215 | 366,011 | 136,774 |
| cypr | Cyprus | 66,156 | 11.0 | 525,294 | 9,800 | 3,300 | 4,600 | 400 | 8,200 | 3,050 | 66,156 | 1,398 | 1,543 | 260 |
| czec | Czech Republic | 2,591,316 | 25.3 | 60,000 | 4,135,936 | 1,200 | 320,000 | 270,000 | 32,000 | 127,000 | 2,591,316 | 9,451 | 155,059 | 91,490 |
| denm | Denmark | 682,522 | 12.9 | 1,400 | 33,200 | 4,800 | 4,639,710 | 36,000 | 36,000 | 264,000 | 682,522 | 27,390 | 141,621 | 36,989 |
| djib | Djibouti | 11,995 | 1.9 | 18,900 | 8,854 | 0 | 240 | 200 | 0 | 70 | 11,995 | 0 | 984 | 16 |
| domi | Dominica | 5,057 | 7.2 | 0 | 56,300 | 1,320 | 11,200 | 2,100 | 750 | 4,700 | 5,057 | 1,202 | 2,355 | 1,443 |
| domr | Dominican Republic | 496,611 | 5.9 | 0 | 7,522,305 | 4,400 | 360,000 | 130,000 | 60,000 | 267,000 | 496,611 | 169,018 | 770,066 | 96,916 |
| ecua | Ecuador | 646,048 | 5.1 | 1,800 | 11,900,000 | 1,600 | 240,000 | 225,000 | 185,000 | 295,000 | 646,048 | 129,230 | 1,218,821 | 61,949 |
| egyp | Egypt | 8,196,488 | 12.0 | 9,317,066 | 225,000 | 2,500 | 550,000 | 225,000 | 900 | 408,000 | 8,196,488 | 165,338 | 422,795 | 164,868 |
| elsa | El Salvador | 510,916 | 8.1 | 0 | 5,723,000 | 400 | 530,000 | 710,000 | 110,000 | 423,000 | 510,916 | 385,343 | 400,452 | 694,205 |
| equa | Equatorial Guinea | 63,372 | 14.0 | 0 | 391,000 | 0 | 15,200 | 18,000 | 1,200 | 11,200 | 63,372 | 3,389 | 10,314 | 11,197 |
| erit | Eritrea | 286,321 | 7.4 | 1,774,558 | 130,000 | 0 | 22,000 | 7,800 | 0 | 13,700 | 286,321 | 0 | 34,452 | 3,348 |
| esto | Estonia | 292,255 | 20.9 | 230,000 | 5,875 | 0 | 240,000 | 46,000 | 8,000 | 72,000 | 292,255 | 6,488 | 18,862 | 34,650 |
| ethi | Ethiopia | 9,745,644 | 15.6 | 22,837,859 | 450,000 | 800 | 8,510,000 | 860,000 | 12,500 | 6,569,000 | 9,745,644 | 1,095,426 | 2,229,221 | 741,353 |
| faer | Faeroe Islands | 11,794 | 27.6 | 0 | 130 | 0 | 38,860 | 400 | 200 | 7,500 | 11,794 | 691 | 1,940 | 349 |
| fiji | Fiji | 105,120 | 12.9 | 0 | 85,000 | 8,300 | 375,000 | 86,000 | 15,000 | 106,200 | 105,120 | 65,206 | 35,740 | 84,054 |
| finl | Finland | 1,033,772 | 20.0 | 55,900 | 6,400 | 170 | 4,635,000 | 77,700 | 38,000 | 740,585 | 1,033,772 | 73,741 | 513,445 | 79,813 |
| fran | France | 24,539,680 | 41.5 | 660,000 | 48,600,000 | 13,200 | 910,000 | 1,325,000 | 330,000 | 236,000 | 24,539,680 | 161,535 | 1,114,446 | 191,019 |
| freg | French Guiana | 23,745 | 13.1 | 0 | 145,000 | 90 | 7,000 | 1,700 | 5,500 | 3,600 | 23,745 | 2,116 | 6,509 | 1,775 |
| frep | French Polynesia | 32,345 | 13.8 | 0 | 100,000 | 0 | 110,000 | 4,800 | 25,000 | 6,130 | 32,345 | 1,374 | 20,188 | 3,238 |
| gabo | Gabon | 102,629 | 8.4 | 0 | 745,000 | 0 | 233,000 | 180,000 | 7,500 | 57,500 | 102,629 | 12,144 | 41,662 | 35,694 |
| gamb | Gambia | 30,607 | 2.3 | 450 | 31,238 | 2,800 | 3,670 | 8,950 | 90 | 1,200 | 30,607 | 197 | 1,618 | 9,185 |
| geor | Georgia | 742,337 | 14.9 | 2,886,814 | 55,000 | 0 | 24,000 | 42,000 | 1,000 | 9,200 | 742,337 | 0 | 20,609 | 9,391 |
| germ | Germany | 26,146,513 | 31.8 | 680,000 | 28,700,000 | 27,000 | 30,420,000 | 728,000 | 540,000 | 1,323,000 | 26,146,513 | 145,957 | 1,904,070 | 549,974 |
| ghan | Ghana | 3,925,064 | 19.4 | 1,600 | 1,925,000 | 250,000 | 3,360,000 | 2,920,376 | 210,000 | 1,490,000 | 3,925,064 | 858,349 | 889,035 | 2,732,617 |
| gibr | Gibraltar | 2,285 | 9.1 | 0 | 21,200 | 1,900 | 380 | 0 | 240 | 340 | 2,285 | 0 | 3,900 | 0 |
| gree | Greece | 262,176 | 2.5 | 9,900,000 | 62,000 | 3,600 | 21,400 | 228,000 | 40,000 | 12,300 | 262,176 | 3,157 | 104,249 | 14,594 |
| grel | Greenland | 12,438 | 22.2 | 0 | 110 | 0 | 38,880 | 120 | 240 | 2,100 | 12,438 | 2,206 | 3,277 | 117 |
| gren | Grenada | 6,456 | 6.9 | 0 | 52,700 | 14,400 | 19,100 | 3,700 | 1,400 | 10,100 | 6,456 | 5,684 | 5,656 | 2,861 |
| guad | Guadeloupe | 65,752 | 14.4 | 0 | 433,000 | 0 | 22,500 | 1,120 | 19,700 | 13,650 | 65,752 | 4,294 | 18,236 | 281 |
| guam | Guam | 16,931 | 10.1 | 0 | 139,400 | 900 | 17,500 | 2,900 | 4,300 | 8,500 | 16,931 | 2,410 | 6,694 | 797 |
| guat | Guatemala | 974,549 | 8.6 | 0 | 9,600,000 | 1,800 | 1,450,000 | 1,030,000 | 160,000 | 1,180,000 | 974,549 | 698,717 | 921,741 | 869,542 |
| guin | Guinea | 169,775 | 2.3 | 0 | 117,000 | 1,400 | 69,182 | 43,000 | 740 | 54,100 | 169,775 | 8,646 | 11,841 | 41,913 |
| gunb | Guinea-Bissau | 97,900 | 8.1 | 0 | 141,000 | 280 | 9,500 | 31,000 | 70 | 9,400 | 97,900 | 347 | 4,928 | 29,025 |
| guya | Guyana | 104,650 | 12.2 | 8,800 | 86,500 | 77,000 | 168,636 | 27,000 | 6,100 | 105,000 | 104,650 | 76,242 | 28,351 | 21,407 |
| hait | Haiti | 535,309 | 6.5 | 0 | 6,520,000 | 105,000 | 1,440,000 | 430,000 | 50,000 | 1,170,000 | 535,309 | 327,903 | 973,804 | 194,293 |
| hond | Honduras | 414,293 | 6.4 | 7,200 | 5,590,000 | 6,000 | 425,000 | 180,000 | 70,000 | 310,000 | 414,293 | 199,438 | 531,984 | 128,578 |
| hung | Hungary | 1,066,779 | 10.6 | 90,000 | 6,330,000 | 0 | 2,560,000 | 165,000 | 40,000 | 455,000 | 1,066,779 | 11,202 | 514,103 | 164,694 |
| icel | Iceland | 30,470 | 10.8 | 0 | 2,900 | 0 | 250,459 | 11,000 | 900 | 6,500 | 30,470 | 878 | 18,109 | 4,013 |
| indi | India | 50,364,266 | 5.0 | 3,100,000 | 15,500,000 | 0 | 16,826,000 | 34,200,000 | 50,000 | 9,300,000 | 50,364,266 | 1,263,041 | 5,032,741 | 27,234,219 |
| indo | Indonesia | 14,599,219 | 6.9 | 100 | 5,752,358 | 3,400 | 12,125,000 | 8,436,000 | 48,000 | 4,030,000 | 14,599,219 | 1,395,797 | 971,415 | 7,082,789 |
| iran | Iran | 129,374 | 0.2 | 202,290 | 16,400 | 1,200 | 13,800 | 80,000 | 300 | 20,000 | 129,374 | 5,070 | 3,967 | 66,963 |
| iraq | Iraq | 196,953 | 0.9 | 139,485 | 268,000 | 200 | 1,400 | 315,547 | 30 | 69,000 | 196,953 | 340 | 9,050 | 255,610 |
| irel | Ireland | 1,805,772 | 48.4 | 1,550 | 3,159,896 | 134,000 | 31,500 | 19,000 | 9,500 | 124,000 | 1,805,772 | 3,056 | 466,998 | 19,946 |
| isle | Isle of Man | 25,633 | 32.4 | 0 | 6,800 | 33,588 | 11,200 | 210 | 640 | 17,700 | 25,633 | 181 | 5,625 | 194 |
| isra | Israel | 192,425 | 3.8 | 46,878 | 140,000 | 2,200 | 19,000 | 85,000 | 1,000 | 30,600 | 192,425 | 2,692 | 17,668 | 84,640 |
| ital | Italy | 24,220,748 | 42.3 | 91,000 | 55,680,000 | 10,600 | 446,000 | 415,000 | 420,000 | 340,000 | 24,220,748 | 320,346 | 3,407,064 | 452,590 |
| ivor | Ivory Coast | 2,035,544 | 13.8 | 20,000 | 2,182,882 | 0 | 760,000 | 1,373,000 | 18,000 | 665,000 | 2,035,544 | 216,484 | 191,221 | 807,294 |
| jama | Jamaica | 635,819 | 24.6 | 3,300 | 110,000 | 103,000 | 643,413 | 232,000 | 30,000 | 304,000 | 635,819 | 169,902 | 63,604 | 151,494 |
| japa | Japan | 3,116,536 | 2.5 | 26,000 | 460,000 | 60,000 | 570,881 | 1,600,000 | 720,000 | 455,140 | 3,116,536 | 55,740 | 152,234 | 1,552,026 |
| jord | Jordan | 228,157 | 3.4 | 131,330 | 48,000 | 7,200 | 9,822 | 77,000 | 170 | 29,800 | 228,157 | 2,653 | 8,467 | 76,879 |
| kaza | Kazakhstan | 1,443,467 | 8.9 | 1,401,803 | 510,000 | 0 | 25,000 | 650,000 | 5,000 | 10,000 | 1,443,467 | 0 | 43,986 | 38,014 |
| keny | Kenya | 3,693,709 | 12.3 | 740,000 | 7,000,000 | 3,000,000 | 6,375,000 | 6,607,000 | 30,000 | 6,750,000 | 3,693,709 | 2,077,689 | 1,730,553 | 4,541,758 |
| kirg | Kirgizstan | 225,162 | 4.8 | 363,065 | 1,600 | 0 | 30,000 | 70,500 | 500 | 3,000 | 225,162 | 4,008 | 6,042 | 7,750 |
| kiri | Kiribati | 10,228 | 12.3 | 0 | 44,100 | 50 | 37,000 | 1,300 | 1,700 | 5,950 | 10,228 | 4,246 | 7,005 | 1,449 |
| kuwa | Kuwait | 163,948 | 8.3 | 7,000 | 175,185 | 200 | 1,100 | 64,000 | 50 | 18,000 | 163,948 | 0 | 7,493 | 60,507 |
| laos | Laos | 100,576 | 1.9 | 0 | 32,000 | 200 | 34,400 | 45,613 | 350 | 40,000 | 100,576 | 0 | 3,178 | 46,822 |
| latv | Latvia | 471,566 | 20.0 | 555,000 | 490,000 | 0 | 560,000 | 115,000 | 2,500 | 168,000 | 471,566 | 9,698 | 73,574 | 6,728 |
| leba | Lebanon | 720,781 | 22.0 | 535,000 | 1,395,000 | 200 | 20,000 | 118,000 | 8,000 | 58,000 | 720,781 | 1,194 | 47,802 | 118,004 |
| leso | Lesotho | 510,738 | 23.7 | 0 | 806,529 | 102,000 | 279,000 | 254,000 | 3,800 | 76,000 | 510,738 | 25,102 | 68,896 | 248,003 |
| libe | Liberia | 542,686 | 17.2 | 0 | 150,000 | 34,500 | 430,000 | 538,500 | 8,000 | 335,000 | 542,686 | 152,946 | 48,602 | 318,452 |
| liby | Libya | 93,153 | 1.7 | 106,642 | 45,000 | 150 | 4,500 | 14,000 | 60 | 5,500 | 93,153 | 0 | 4,730 | 13,270 |
| liec | Liechtenstein | 14,173 | 43.2 | 0 | 24,381 | 0 | 2,520 | 40 | 110 | 125 | 14,173 | 0 | 763 | 37 |
| lith | Lithuania | 429,935 | 11.7 | 114,000 | 3,105,000 | 0 | 44,000 | 32,000 | 4,300 | 8,900 | 429,935 | 3,197 | 35,829 | 12,274 |
| luxe | Luxembourg | 75,421 | 17.5 | 1,100 | 407,000 | 600 | 7,500 | 2,200 | 3,000 | 1,100 | 75,421 | 223 | 17,652 | 1,925 |
| mace | Macedonia | 212,563 | 10.5 | 1,200,000 | 70,600 | 0 | 7,000 | 8,192 | 1,400 | 3,120 | 212,563 | 221 | 2,171 | 5,308 |
| mada | Madagascar | 2,487,601 | 15.6 | 4,400 | 3,662,363 | 320,000 | 4,090,000 | 510,000 | 27,500 | 950,000 | 2,487,601 | 15,252 | 467,847 | 251,901 |
| mala | Malawi | 2,457,034 | 22.5 | 4,400 | 2,697,860 | 230,000 | 2,140,000 | 1,830,000 | 130,000 | 940,000 | 2,457,034 | 130,999 | 346,922 | 1,462,079 |
| malb | Malaysia | 1,355,307 | 6.1 | 2,300 | 721,889 | 205,000 | 660,000 | 178,000 | 4,000 | 500,000 | 1,355,307 | 51,215 | 328,689 | 160,096 |

| COUNTRY | | FOUR MEGATYPOLOGIES OF RENEWAL IN GLOBAL CHRISTIANITY, AD 30–AD 2000 | | | | | | | | | | | | |
|---|---|---|---|---|---|---|---|---|---|---|---|---|---|---|
| | | 1. The Great Commission | | 2. Ecclesiastical Renewal: 6 megablocs | | | | | | 3. Evangelical Renewal | | 4. Pentecostal/Charismatic Renewal | | |
| code 1 | short name 2 | GCCs 67 | GCC 68 | Megabloc O 69 | Megabloc R 70 | Megabloc A 71 | Megabloc P 72 | Megabloc I 73 | Megabloc m 74 | Evangelicals 75 | evangelicals 76 | 1st -Wavers 77 | 2nd-Wavers 78 | 3rd-Wavers 79 |
| mald | Maldives | 300 | 0.1 | 0 | 80 | 0 | 258 | 20 | 0 | 60 | 300 | 0 | 29 | 21 |
| mali | Mali | 200,207 | 1.8 | 0 | 125,565 | 0 | 82,000 | 16,300 | 500 | 87,900 | 200,207 | 1,599 | 12,156 | 15,444 |
| malt | Malta | 170,064 | 43.8 | 130 | 367,501 | 1,100 | 1,000 | 750 | 900 | 550 | 170,064 | 523 | 95,811 | 666 |
| mars | Marshall Islands | 7,300 | 11.4 | 0 | 5,250 | 0 | 67,431 | 8,100 | 2,500 | 19,900 | 7,300 | 19,189 | 7,434 | 3,577 |
| mart | Martinique | 42,790 | 10.8 | 0 | 366,000 | 0 | 23,700 | 4,349 | 8,000 | 16,000 | 42,790 | 4,579 | 9,080 | 1,741 |
| maur | Mauritania | 3,914 | 0.2 | 0 | 4,216 | 0 | 600 | 1,700 | 10 | 600 | 3,914 | 0 | 154 | 1,946 |
| maus | Mauritius | 88,727 | 7.7 | 0 | 310,000 | 5,000 | 110,000 | 3,400 | 2,500 | 102,000 | 88,727 | 112,576 | 180,422 | 3,002 |
| mayo | Mayotte | 929 | 0.9 | 0 | 1,256 | 0 | 350 | 160 | 100 | 120 | 929 | 0 | 86 | 114 |
| mexi | Mexico | 5,123,454 | 5.2 | 100,000 | 92,770,000 | 187,800 | 3,280,000 | 2,900,000 | 1,950,000 | 1,740,000 | 5,123,454 | 861,284 | 9,497,650 | 2,691,066 |
| micr | Micronesia | 22,442 | 18.9 | 0 | 74,578 | 0 | 47,000 | 1,700 | 3,300 | 13,900 | 22,442 | 1,081 | 7,480 | 839 |
| mold | Moldavia | 836,487 | 19.1 | 1,950,558 | 73,000 | 0 | 78,000 | 670,000 | 27,000 | 20,000 | 836,487 | 16,451 | 31,334 | 1,214 |
| mona | Monaco | 8,786 | 26.2 | 90 | 30,000 | 330 | 681 | 0 | 0 | 65 | 8,786 | 0 | 1,060 | 0 |
| mong | Mongolia | 29,582 | 1.1 | 1,400 | 350 | 0 | 21,573 | 10,000 | 70 | 1,100 | 29,582 | 0 | 3,093 | 6,807 |
| mont | Montserrat | 1,946 | 18.3 | 0 | 1,400 | 3,100 | 5,500 | 1,050 | 130 | 2,650 | 1,946 | 1,654 | 777 | 1,109 |
| moro | Morocco | 109,745 | 0.4 | 740 | 22,076 | 450 | 4,100 | 147,000 | 110 | 43,200 | 109,745 | 89 | 775 | 149,136 |
| moza | Mozambique | 3,554,815 | 18.1 | 500 | 3,110,000 | 110,000 | 1,750,000 | 1,422,033 | 68,000 | 1,350,000 | 3,554,815 | 684,668 | 241,992 | 1,398,340 |
| myan | Myanmar | 2,257,465 | 5.0 | 0 | 590,000 | 58,000 | 2,511,664 | 575,000 | 6,800 | 1,120,000 | 2,257,465 | 298,025 | 249,765 | 412,210 |
| nami | Namibia | 295,226 | 17.1 | 0 | 306,211 | 31,000 | 820,000 | 187,000 | 5,000 | 160,000 | 295,226 | 23,749 | 87,174 | 119,077 |
| naur | Nauru | 2,187 | 19.0 | 0 | 2,920 | 320 | 5,840 | 380 | 40 | 310 | 2,187 | 0 | 708 | 392 |
| nepa | Nepal | 543,340 | 2.3 | 2,500 | 7,000 | 0 | 14,561 | 551,000 | 1,000 | 185,000 | 543,340 | 4,865 | 1,318 | 501,817 |
| neth | Netherlands | 6,515,668 | 41.3 | 7,400 | 5,450,000 | 8,600 | 4,238,853 | 490,000 | 88,000 | 614,000 | 6,515,668 | 52,390 | 537,922 | 449,688 |
| nets | Netherlands Antilles | 38,128 | 17.6 | 0 | 150,862 | 2,550 | 23,000 | 2,100 | 6,400 | 7,000 | 38,128 | 3,229 | 5,172 | 1,798 |
| newc | New Caledonia | 40,236 | 18.8 | 0 | 116,019 | 160 | 30,000 | 11,000 | 4,500 | 10,800 | 40,236 | 3,936 | 4,618 | 3,246 |
| newz | New Zealand | 1,541,611 | 39.9 | 6,000 | 495,000 | 825,000 | 931,219 | 190,000 | 115,000 | 660,000 | 1,541,611 | 37,262 | 419,689 | 133,049 |
| nica | Nicaragua | 307,306 | 6.1 | 0 | 4,320,000 | 8,300 | 590,000 | 155,000 | 51,000 | 446,000 | 307,306 | 378,967 | 238,016 | 103,017 |
| niga | Niger | 44,186 | 0.4 | 0 | 19,670 | 0 | 13,000 | 25,000 | 600 | 12,200 | 44,186 | 526 | 2,087 | 24,387 |
| nige | Nigeria | 11,252,805 | 10.1 | 3,100 | 13,400,000 | 20,070,000 | 14,050,000 | 23,975,000 | 600,000 | 22,300,000 | 11,252,805 | 3,034,330 | 9,793,479 | 23,057,191 |
| nork | North Korea | 468,670 | 2.0 | 0 | 55,000 | 0 | 10,000 | 432,413 | 2,800 | 20,000 | 468,670 | 0 | 715 | 449,285 |
| norl | Northern Cyprus | 4,479 | 2.4 | 13,870 | 0 | 0 | 0 | 2,236 | 0 | 220 | 4,479 | 0 | 0 | 2,180 |
| norm | Northern Mariana Is | 7,226 | 9.2 | 0 | 69,300 | 0 | 6,500 | 6,660 | 1,870 | 3,290 | 7,226 | 983 | 6,232 | 1,085 |
| norw | Norway | 1,074,638 | 24.1 | 1,600 | 45,000 | 2,000 | 4,200,000 | 136,000 | 24,000 | 485,000 | 1,074,638 | 70,742 | 1,031,297 | 146,961 |
| oman | Oman | 55,517 | 2.2 | 16,500 | 53,000 | 2,800 | 5,700 | 43,916 | 0 | 6,600 | 55,517 | 0 | 7,139 | 39,861 |
| paki | Pakistan | 3,520,938 | 2.3 | 0 | 1,165,000 | 0 | 1,796,000 | 850,000 | 1,245 | 626,000 | 3,520,938 | 77,920 | 292,012 | 520,068 |
| pala | Palau | 2,814 | 14.5 | 0 | 8,600 | 0 | 5,600 | 4,100 | 650 | 1,950 | 2,814 | 243 | 900 | 127 |
| pale | Palestine | 169,540 | 7.7 | 48,140 | 28,000 | 3,500 | 3,900 | 103,349 | 1,400 | 13,600 | 169,540 | 1,665 | 3,857 | 101,478 |
| pana | Panama | 445,061 | 15.6 | 1,400 | 2,210,000 | 23,500 | 340,000 | 73,000 | 42,000 | 263,000 | 445,061 | 225,235 | 207,163 | 57,602 |
| papu | Papua New Guinea | 523,096 | 11.4 | 400 | 1,380,000 | 308,000 | 2,610,000 | 270,000 | 15,400 | 810,000 | 523,096 | 238,143 | 310,060 | 202,797 |
| para | Paraguay | 429,463 | 7.8 | 2,000 | 4,950,000 | 17,600 | 200,000 | 70,800 | 26,000 | 159,000 | 429,463 | 76,990 | 107,312 | 57,698 |
| peru | Peru | 968,929 | 3.8 | 5,500 | 24,550,000 | 2,000 | 1,480,000 | 456,000 | 330,000 | 1,129,000 | 968,929 | 449,618 | 2,605,445 | 384,937 |
| phil | Philippines | 3,915,959 | 5.2 | 0 | 62,570,000 | 120,000 | 3,775,000 | 14,330,000 | 670,000 | 1,825,000 | 3,915,959 | 765,813 | 11,659,457 | 7,624,730 |
| pola | Poland | 2,958,523 | 7.6 | 1,030,000 | 35,743,059 | 0 | 195,000 | 330,000 | 200,000 | 140,000 | 2,958,523 | 42,155 | 1,823,326 | 149,519 |
| port | Portugal | 3,570,189 | 36.2 | 1,200 | 8,970,000 | 3,050 | 135,000 | 277,000 | 98,000 | 108,000 | 3,570,189 | 89,340 | 256,631 | 296,030 |
| puer | Puerto Rico | 544,610 | 14.1 | 1,300 | 2,900,000 | 12,400 | 505,000 | 249,000 | 95,000 | 348,000 | 544,610 | 239,572 | 544,717 | 240,711 |
| qata | Qatar | 30,261 | 5.1 | 1,300 | 36,100 | 8,000 | 4,000 | 10,235 | 0 | 4,300 | 30,261 | 0 | 4,019 | 10,381 |
| reun | Reunion | 56,272 | 8.1 | 0 | 611,000 | 0 | 31,500 | 700 | 6,000 | 26,900 | 56,272 | 23,624 | 30,727 | 649 |
| roma | Romania | 1,857,773 | 8.3 | 19,000,000 | 3,237,000 | 450 | 2,380,000 | 290,000 | 150,000 | 1,395,302 | 1,857,773 | 864,250 | 360,247 | 125,503 |
| russ | Russia | 29,373,498 | 20.0 | 75,950,000 | 1,500,000 | 3,300 | 1,630,000 | 7,800,000 | 200,000 | 560,000 | 29,373,498 | 140,319 | 1,001,265 | 5,333,416 |
| rwan | Rwanda | 960,617 | 12.4 | 2,000 | 3,942,000 | 600,000 | 1,619,822 | 165,000 | 8,000 | 1,505,000 | 960,617 | 636,449 | 502,657 | 97,893 |
| saha | Sahara | 284 | 0.1 | 0 | 140 | 0 | 0 | 347 | 0 | 40 | 284 | 0 | 0 | 370 |
| saih | Saint Helena | 1,167 | 18.5 | 0 | 40 | 4,412 | 520 | 160 | 200 | 155 | 1,167 | 0 | 765 | 165 |
| saik | Saint Kitts & Nevis | 2,098 | 5.5 | 0 | 4,850 | 9,700 | 22,270 | 1,500 | 510 | 7,100 | 2,098 | 2,591 | 3,570 | 989 |
| sail | Saint Lucia | 9,556 | 6.2 | 0 | 116,000 | 4,400 | 20,500 | 3,239 | 1,400 | 10,400 | 9,556 | 7,702 | 3,392 | 1,657 |
| saip | Saint Pierre & Miquelon | 2,251 | 34.3 | 0 | 6,465 | 0 | 70 | 0 | 40 | 10 | 2,251 | 0 | 160 | 0 |
| saiv | Saint Vincent | 24,080 | 21.1 | 70 | 10,000 | 19,715 | 33,854 | 13,300 | 1,500 | 15,050 | 24,080 | 8,551 | 4,485 | 10,964 |
| samo | Samoa | 85,350 | 47.4 | 0 | 39,500 | 450 | 128,000 | 2,000 | 17,000 | 26,830 | 85,350 | 18,962 | 7,849 | 1,489 |
| sanm | San Marino | 12,895 | 48.6 | 0 | 23,509 | 0 | 0 | 0 | 270 | 0 | 12,895 | 0 | 485 | 0 |
| saot | Sao Tome & Principe | 21,628 | 14.7 | 0 | 110,553 | 0 | 5,450 | 15,500 | 600 | 4,620 | 21,628 | 3,974 | 3,222 | 13,904 |
| saud | Saudi Arabia | 417,623 | 1.9 | 36,000 | 625,875 | 2,000 | 38,000 | 85,000 | 110 | 26,000 | 417,623 | 0 | 33,133 | 83,367 |
| sene | Senegal | 300,623 | 3.2 | 0 | 441,031 | 160 | 9,800 | 14,000 | 2,300 | 6,000 | 300,623 | 3,281 | 18,139 | 13,580 |
| seyc | Seychelles | 9,236 | 11.9 | 0 | 70,000 | 5,200 | 1,950 | 50 | 270 | 2,550 | 9,236 | 789 | 3,212 | 49 |
| sier | Sierra Leone | 389,099 | 8.0 | 610 | 169,140 | 25,000 | 171,000 | 165,000 | 2,700 | 86,000 | 389,099 | 25,234 | 23,666 | 151,100 |
| sing | Singapore | 292,499 | 8.2 | 1,400 | 143,000 | 34,000 | 126,536 | 94,000 | 4,000 | 118,000 | 292,499 | 31,469 | 51,856 | 62,675 |
| slok | Slovakia | 761,996 | 14.1 | 21,000 | 3,660,186 | 0 | 600,000 | 23,000 | 20,000 | 115,000 | 761,996 | 5,262 | 236,722 | 4,016 |
| slov | Slovenia | 264,345 | 13.3 | 12,000 | 1,659,006 | 0 | 32,000 | 31,000 | 2,800 | 13,800 | 264,345 | 973 | 36,117 | 32,409 |
| solo | Solomon Islands | 59,890 | 13.5 | 0 | 48,000 | 169,503 | 159,000 | 22,500 | 4,200 | 99,400 | 59,890 | 4,626 | 37,230 | 20,145 |
| soma | Somalia | 13,606 | 0.2 | 91,753 | 200 | 30 | 1,100 | 5,500 | 0 | 870 | 13,606 | 0 | 120 | 6,880 |
| somi | Somaliland | 3,120 | 0.1 | 4,400 | 31 | 320 | 330 | 3,300 | 0 | 550 | 3,120 | 0 | 59 | 3,621 |
| soua | South Africa | 7,717,095 | 19.1 | 150,000 | 3,350,000 | 2,660,000 | 12,410,000 | 18,500,000 | 190,000 | 4,522,000 | 7,717,095 | 1,772,371 | 2,331,365 | 17,096,264 |
| souk | South Korea | 13,329,255 | 28.5 | 5,000 | 3,700,000 | 110,000 | 8,870,000 | 7,700,000 | 850,000 | 9,142,000 | 13,329,255 | 2,393,749 | 2,020,598 | 3,165,652 |
| spai | Spain | 17,132,496 | 43.2 | 2,250 | 38,080,000 | 12,000 | 120,000 | 320,000 | 200,000 | 120,000 | 17,132,496 | 18,048 | 752,763 | 314,189 |
| span | Spanish North Africa | 11,344 | 8.7 | 0 | 102,874 | 0 | 650 | 800 | 0 | 300 | 11,344 | 66 | 2,167 | 767 |
| sril | Sri Lanka | 1,402,374 | 7.5 | 0 | 1,260,000 | 55,000 | 102,000 | 331,120 | 7,000 | 86,500 | 1,402,374 | 53,731 | 35,836 | 310,432 |
| suda | Sudan | 1,910,208 | 6.5 | 155,000 | 3,148,593 | 2,320,000 | 796,000 | 150,000 | 900 | 781,000 | 1,910,208 | 7,282 | 511,678 | 130,039 |
| suri | Suriname | 70,952 | 17.0 | 0 | 93,000 | 800 | 71,334 | 2,800 | 4,400 | 11,700 | 70,952 | 1,413 | 7,129 | 2,558 |
| swaz | Swaziland | 271,534 | 26.9 | 0 | 54,000 | 40,000 | 153,200 | 460,000 | 5,500 | 123,000 | 271,534 | 53,612 | 16,100 | 455,288 |
| swed | Sweden | 2,499,326 | 28.1 | 120,000 | 175,000 | 2,880 | 8,420,000 | 60,000 | 56,000 | 890,000 | 2,499,326 | 182,053 | 382,949 | 57,999 |
| swit | Switzerland | 2,541,157 | 34.4 | 26,000 | 3,260,000 | 13,300 | 3,040,000 | 160,000 | 122,000 | 298,500 | 2,541,157 | 40,562 | 313,236 | 118,702 |
| syri | Syria | 791,510 | 4.9 | 798,269 | 325,000 | 4,000 | 30,040 | 100,000 | 400 | 40,300 | 791,510 | 343 | 17,346 | 92,311 |
| taiw | Taiwan | 820,752 | 3.7 | 0 | 300,000 | 1,650 | 400,000 | 451,093 | 27,000 | 215,000 | 820,752 | 26,554 | 66,246 | 266,200 |
| taji | Tajikistan | 50,711 | 0.8 | 93,000 | 4,412 | 0 | 17,000 | 15,000 | 200 | 1,900 | 50,711 | 416 | 1,562 | 1,221 |
| tanz | Tanzania | 5,627,411 | 16.8 | 12,500 | 8,283,000 | 2,650,000 | 5,530,000 | 638,000 | 18,000 | 4,860,000 | 5,627,411 | 1,464,786 | 1,328,831 | 631,383 |
| thai | Thailand | 1,187,923 | 1.9 | 0 | 255,000 | 450 | 303,000 | 778,717 | 8,000 | 194,000 | 1,187,923 | 33,905 | 52,065 | 742,930 |
| timo | Timor | 39,435 | 4.5 | 0 | 796,000 | 0 | 47,000 | 0 | 0 | 4,800 | 39,435 | 3,783 | 42,417 | 0 |
| togo | Togo | 917,794 | 19.8 | 0 | 1,122,995 | 0 | 480,000 | 110,000 | 36,100 | 139,000 | 917,794 | 87,526 | 177,221 | 110,253 |
| tong | Tonga | 27,926 | 28.3 | 0 | 13,900 | 660 | 42,320 | 20,798 | 14,350 | 7,350 | 27,926 | 1,306 | 3,695 | 7,300 |
| trin | Trinidad & Tobago | 287,827 | 22.2 | 8,500 | 397,865 | 154,000 | 179,000 | 42,000 | 14,500 | 164,000 | 287,827 | 53,935 | 47,560 | 35,505 |
| tuni | Tunisia | 36,504 | 0.4 | 270 | 19,000 | 100 | 670 | 30,413 | 50 | 7,000 | 36,504 | 5 | 659 | 15,636 |
| turk | Turkey | 198,054 | 0.3 | 227,655 | 30,500 | 2,100 | 32,500 | 78,000 | 2,400 | 13,500 | 198,054 | 0 | 8,959 | 56,041 |
| turm | Turkmenistan | 48,002 | 1.1 | 74,583 | 2,100 | 0 | 2,800 | 19,000 | 400 | 900 | 48,002 | 0 | 739 | 10,011 |
| turs | Turks & Caicos Is | 3,513 | 21.0 | 0 | 750 | 2,000 | 8,112 | 2,000 | 400 | 3,000 | 3,513 | 1,141 | 1,234 | 1,924 |
| tuva | Tuvalu | 2,240 | 19.1 | 0 | 95 | 0 | 12,000 | 250 | 290 | 560 | 2,240 | 0 | 1,836 | 264 |
| ugan | Uganda | 3,019,984 | 13.9 | 32,000 | 9,130,000 | 8,580,000 | 596,000 | 815,000 | 6,000 | 3,890,000 | 3,019,984 | 371,193 | 3,879,073 | 759,734 |
| ukra | Ukraine | 6,110,588 | 12.1 | 27,400,000 | 5,578,901 | 0 | 1,340,000 | 8,500,000 | 135,000 | 1,016,000 | 6,110,588 | 399,462 | 589,113 | 3,046,426 |
| unia | United Arab Emirates | 137,255 | 5.6 | 70,000 | 124,345 | 8,600 | 12,800 | 47,000 | 0 | 13,500 | 137,255 | 0 | 8,696 | 45,304 |
| usa | USA | 98,662,079 | 35.4 | 5,762,000 | 58,000,000 | 2,400,000 | 64,570,000 | 78,550,000 | 10,080,000 | 40,640,000 | 98,662,079 | 4,946,390 | 19,473,158 | 50,736,451 |
| uuay | Uruguay | 891,482 | 26.7 | 26,500 | 2,608,000 | 1,200 | 110,000 | 52,500 | 95,000 | 64,800 | 891,482 | 38,878 | 215,453 | 49,669 |
| uzbe | Uzbekistan | 244,386 | 1.0 | 188,934 | 40,000 | 0 | 44,000 | 120,000 | 1,400 | 12,500 | 244,386 | 0 | 13,669 | 136,331 |
| vanu | Vanuatu | 28,820 | 15.1 | 0 | 29,400 | 34,500 | 102,254 | 16,500 | 1,400 | 53,300 | 28,820 | 27,708 | 15,111 | 4,381 |
| vene | Venezuela | 1,861,728 | 7.7 | 27,000 | 22,816,000 | 600 | 500,000 | 350,000 | 300,000 | 302,000 | 1,861,728 | 160,593 | 3,203,257 | 306,151 |
| viet | Viet Nam | 5,597,118 | 7.0 | 0 | 5,320,822 | 3,100 | 580,000 | 640,000 | 24,000 | 628,000 | 5,597,118 | 52,101 | 157,802 | 588,097 |
| virg | Virgin Is of the US | 11,931 | 12.8 | 0 | 29,000 | 13,800 | 40,000 | 12,800 | 1,500 | 18,500 | 11,931 | 7,149 | 7,290 | 7,911 |
| wall | Wallis & Futuna Is | 1,885 | 13.0 | 0 | 13,936 | 0 | 40 | 0 | 45 | 15 | 1,885 | 8 | 322 | 0 |
| yeme | Yemen | 23,012 | 0.1 | 12,000 | 6,000 | 180 | 4,476 | 8,000 | 0 | 1,600 | 23,012 | 0 | 1,388 | 7,112 |
| yugo | Yugoslavia | 1,398,890 | 13.2 | 6,046,000 | 546,557 | 400 | 99,000 | 185,000 | 8,600 | 42,400 | 1,398,890 | 11,064 | 78,057 | 160,879 |
| zamb | Zambia | 1,506,682 | 16.4 | 6,400 | 3,070,000 | 220,000 | 2,705,000 | 1,580,000 | 375,680 | 1,146,000 | 1,506,682 | 311,113 | 427,400 | 1,278,487 |
| zimb | Zimbabwe | 2,934,675 | 25.2 | 6,000 | 1,120,000 | 320,000 | 1,440,000 | 4,700,000 | 64,000 | 525,000 | 2,934,675 | 164,858 | 241,644 | 4,523,498 |
| | 11 minicountries | 5,300 | 23.0 | 779 | 4,598 | 2,128 | 5,343 | 730 | 520 | 1,685 | 5,300 | 0 | 1,105 | 44 |
| | Africa | 90,820,254 | 11.6 | 35,304,168 | 120,386,235 | 42,541,902 | 88,999,928 | 83,840,642 | 2,426,550 | 69,578,305 | 90,820,254 | 15,560,021 | 31,471,122 | 78,990,057 |
| | Antarctica | 1,000 | 22.2 | 30 | 1,400 | 300 | 970 | 700 | 0 | 500 | 1000 | 110 | 300 | 500 |
| | Asia | 191,890,345 | 5.2 | 14,113,465 | 110,480,013 | 727,212 | 49,969,501 | 154,732,021 | 2,485,605 | 31,503,970 | 191,890,345 | 6,594,195 | 22,120,550 | 106,174,533 |
| | Europe | 192,462,065 | 26.4 | 158,105,154 | 285,977,773 | 26,637,479 | 77,528,973 | 25,723,708 | 3,563,880 | 21,543,577 | 192,462,065 | 3,146,061 | 20,880,130 | 13,542,099 |
| | Latin America | 52,301,448 | 10.1 | 557,500 | 461,220,001 | 1,089,611 | 48,131,716 | 39,706,358 | 6,595,300 | 40,341,240 | 52,301,448 | 32,698,803 | 74,226,603 | 34,507,227 |
| | Northern America | 111,292,984 | 35.9 | 6,342,000 | 71,034,904 | 3,244,200 | 69,978,450 | 80,237,120 | 10,531,930 | 43,189,810 | 111,292,984 | 5,455,568 | 22,081,291 | 52,063,300 |
| | Oceania | 9,053,891 | 29.8 | 706,400 | 8,227,767 | 5,408,938 | 7,392,067 | 1,504,858 | 456,965 | 4,446,081 | 9,053,891 | 577,778 | 2,683,950 | 1,003,797 |
| | **World A** | **7,281,018** | **1.2** | **1,891,769** | **2,720,984** | **17,385** | **2,265,910** | **3,140,736** | **15,985** | **1,264,540** | **7,281,018** | **108,775** | **425,007** | **2,553,191** |
| | **World B** | **279,101,242** | **7.4** | **117,870,812** | **103,758,713** | **26,909,172** | **95,386,092** | **185,699,067** | **3,382,820** | **73,462,585** | **279,101,242** | **15,324,280** | **29,614,682** | **138,640,023** |
| | **World C** | **361,439,727** | **21.3** | **95,366,136** | **950,848,396** | **52,723,085** | **244,349,603** | **196,905,604** | **22,661,425** | **135,876,358** | **361,439,727** | **48,599,481** | **143,424,257** | **145,088,299** |
| | **GLOBAL TOTAL** | **647,821,987** | **10.7** | **215,128,717** | **1,057,328,093** | **79,649,642** | **342,001,605** | **385,745,407** | **26,060,230** | **210,603,483** | **647,821,987** | **64,032,536** | **173,463,946** | **286,281,513** |

| COUNTRY | | CHURCHES | | | | | | | | MISSION | | | | | | | |
|---|---|---|---|---|---|---|---|---|---|---|---|---|---|---|---|---|---|
| | | STRUCTURES | | | | FINANCE, US $ | | | | STATUS OF MISSIONS | | | | MISSION INSTITUTIONS | | | |
| code | short name | denom | p.m. | worship | p.m. | personal | church | parachurch | ecc crime | stat | misags | all orgs | p.m. | major | p.m. | minor | p.m. |
| 1 | 2 | 80 | 81 | 82 | 83 | 84 | 85 | 86 | 87 | 88 | 89 | 90 | 91 | 92 | 93 | 94 | 95 |
| afgh | Afghanistan | 9 | 0 | 49 | 2 | 4,138,200 | 29,381 | 44,278 | 4,552 | 1 | 29 | 12 | 1 | 0 | 0 | 0 | 0 |
| alba | Albania | 51 | 16 | 1,010 | 324 | 717,161,300 | 5,091,845 | 7,673,625 | 788,877 | 6 | 79 | 0 | 0 | 5 | 2 | 10 | 3 |
| alge | Algeria | 33 | 1 | 1,100 | 35 | 145,403,200 | 1,032,362 | 1,555,814 | 159,943 | 4 | 37 | 26 | 1 | 70 | 2 | 50 | 2 |
| amer | American Samoa | 25 | 367 | 130 | 1,909 | 143,624,000 | 1,019,730 | 1,536,776 | 157,986 | 7 | 18 | 5 | 73 | 10 | 147 | 15 | 220 |
| ando | Andorra | 11 | 141 | 20 | 256 | 1,137,321,000 | 8,074,979 | 12,169,334 | 1,251,053 | 5 | 1 | 2 | 26 | 1 | 13 | 5 | 64 |
| ango | Angola | 42 | 3 | 11,000 | 854 | 4,483,037,580 | 31,829,566 | 47,968,502 | 4,931,341 | 2 | 68 | 20 | 2 | 350 | 27 | 1,000 | 78 |
| angu | Anguilla | 17 | 2,046 | 25 | 3,009 | 14,372,000 | 102,041 | 153,780 | 15,809 | 7 | 3 | 2 | 241 | 0 | 0 | 0 | 0 |
| anti | Antigua | 25 | 370 | 140 | 2,072 | 413,052,970 | 2,932,676 | 4,419,666 | 454,358 | 2 | 25 | 9 | 133 | 6 | 89 | 25 | 370 |
| arge | Argentina | 193 | 5 | 24,000 | 648 | 272,906,552,160 | 1,937,636,520 | 2,920,100,108 | 300,197,207 | 6 | 207 | 140 | 4 | 1,500 | 41 | 7,000 | 189 |
| arme | Armenia | 27 | 8 | 300 | 85 | 2,156,195,890 | 15,308,990 | 23,071,296 | 2,371,815 | 2 | 10 | 0 | 0 | 10 | 3 | 20 | 6 |
| arub | Aruba | 25 | 243 | 90 | 876 | 1,513,379,490 | 10,744,994 | 16,193,160 | 1,664,717 | 6 | 3 | 0 | 0 | 2 | 20 | 5 | 49 |
| aust | Australia | 267 | 14 | 24,000 | 1,271 | 235,646,592,480 | 1,673,090,806 | 2,521,418,539 | 259,211,251 | 5 | 200 | 190 | 10 | 1,300 | 69 | 4,000 | 212 |
| ausz | Austria | 70 | 9 | 5,400 | 658 | 185,801,026,300 | 1,319,187,286 | 1,988,070,981 | 204,381,128 | 5 | 133 | 195 | 24 | 250 | 30 | 1,000 | 122 |
| azer | Azerbaijan | 19 | 2 | 100 | 13 | 171,744,960 | 1,219,389 | 1,837,671 | 188,919 | 3 | 4 | 0 | 0 | 0 | 0 | 10 | 1 |
| baha | Bahamas | 47 | 153 | 1,000 | 3,262 | 3,186,200,940 | 22,622,026 | 34,092,350 | 3,504,821 | 6 | 39 | 22 | 72 | 25 | 82 | 50 | 163 |
| bahr | Bahrain | 22 | 36 | 180 | 292 | 491,552,320 | 3,490,021 | 5,259,609 | 540,707 | 6 | 9 | 0 | 0 | 3 | 5 | 15 | 24 |
| bang | Bangladesh | 42 | 0 | 9,000 | 70 | 223,617,600 | 1,587,684 | 2,392,708 | 245,979 | 2 | 116 | 40 | 0 | 250 | 2 | 600 | 5 |
| barb | Barbados | 52 | 192 | 550 | 2,034 | 1,291,388,480 | 9,168,858 | 13,817,856 | 1,420,527 | 6 | 37 | 25 | 92 | 20 | 74 | 70 | 259 |
| belg | Belgium | 99 | 10 | 5,500 | 541 | 210,496,978,160 | 1,494,528,544 | 2,252,317,666 | 231,546,675 | 5 | 130 | 330 | 33 | 2,100 | 207 | 7,500 | 738 |
| beli | Belize | 43 | 179 | 600 | 2,493 | 518,475,570 | 3,681,176 | 5,547,688 | 570,323 | 6 | 61 | 13 | 54 | 40 | 166 | 100 | 415 |
| belo | Belorussia | 31 | 3 | 2,030 | 198 | 13,629,039,390 | 96,766,179 | 145,830,721 | 14,991,943 | 2 | 18 | 0 | 0 | 5 | 1 | 40 | 4 |
| beni | Benin | 46 | 8 | 2,400 | 394 | 623,152,150 | 4,424,380 | 6,667,728 | 685,467 | 2 | 51 | 35 | 6 | 75 | 12 | 350 | 57 |
| berm | Bermuda | 71 | 1,099 | 190 | 2,942 | 1,774,362,250 | 12,597,971 | 18,985,676 | 1,951,798 | 7 | 12 | 6 | 93 | 2 | 31 | 10 | 155 |
| bhut | Bhutan | 32 | 15 | 200 | 94 | 4,052,580 | 28,773 | 43,362 | 4,457 | 5 | 20 | 6 | 3 | 3 | 1 | 5 | 2 |
| boli | Bolivia | 131 | 16 | 7,000 | 840 | 6,228,985,600 | 44,225,797 | 66,650,145 | 6,851,884 | 7 | 190 | 90 | 11 | 500 | 60 | 2,700 | 324 |
| bosn | Bosnia-Herzegovina | 30 | 8 | 700 | 176 | 415,765,500 | 2,951,935 | 4,448,690 | 457,342 | 5 | 13 | 0 | 0 | 5 | 1 | 30 | 8 |
| bots | Botswana | 196 | 121 | 3,900 | 2,404 | 2,268,240,460 | 16,104,507 | 24,270,172 | 2,495,064 | 7 | 66 | 25 | 15 | 150 | 93 | 300 | 185 |
| boug | Bougainville | 11 | 55 | 430 | 2,166 | 259,463,400 | 1,842,190 | 2,776,258 | 285,409 | 6 | 0 | 0 | 0 | 10 | 50 | 10 | 50 |
| braz | Brazil | 1,581 | 9 | 220,000 | 1,293 | 565,931,216,760 | 4,018,111,638 | 6,055,464,019 | 622,524,338 | 7 | 453 | 250 | 2 | 4,500 | 27 | 15,000 | 88 |
| brit | Britain | 828 | 14 | 66,000 | 1,122 | 730,293,923,700 | 5,185,086,858 | 7,814,144,983 | 803,323,316 | 5 | 369 | 1,300 | 22 | 2,400 | 41 | 10,000 | 170 |
| briz | British Virgin Is | 19 | 889 | 45 | 2,106 | 119,136,000 | 845,865 | 1,274,755 | 131,049 | 7 | 6 | 3 | 140 | 1 | 47 | 5 | 234 |
| brun | Brunei | 20 | 61 | 140 | 427 | 388,553,600 | 2,758,730 | 4,157,523 | 427,408 | 6 | 3 | 0 | 0 | 3 | 9 | 10 | 30 |
| bulg | Bulgaria | 54 | 7 | 5,600 | 681 | 8,855,073,500 | 62,871,021 | 94,749,286 | 9,740,580 | 2 | 42 | 10 | 1 | 200 | 24 | 800 | 97 |
| burk | Burkina Faso | 40 | 3 | 4,000 | 335 | 456,337,940 | 3,239,999 | 4,882,815 | 501,971 | 2 | 54 | 30 | 3 | 100 | 8 | 600 | 50 |
| buru | Burundi | 34 | 5 | 5,100 | 762 | 824,454,560 | 5,853,627 | 8,821,663 | 906,900 | 2 | 37 | 40 | 6 | 220 | 33 | 800 | 119 |
| camb | Cambodia | 23 | 2 | 2,300 | 206 | 31,967,460 | 226,968 | 342,051 | 35,164 | 2 | 35 | 4 | 0 | 25 | 2 | 100 | 9 |
| came | Cameroon | 103 | 7 | 17,000 | 1,127 | 5,044,975,650 | 35,819,327 | 53,981,239 | 5,549,473 | 6 | 120 | 57 | 4 | 400 | 27 | 1,500 | 99 |
| cana | Canada | 469 | 15 | 35,000 | 1,124 | 392,208,137,640 | 2,784,677,777 | 4,196,627,072 | 431,428,951 | 5 | 178 | 350 | 11 | 900 | 29 | 3,000 | 96 |
| cape | Cape Verde | 12 | 28 | 130 | 304 | 390,604,800 | 2,773,294 | 4,179,471 | 429,665 | 7 | 16 | 8 | 19 | 7 | 16 | 40 | 94 |
| caym | Cayman Islands | 25 | 652 | 160 | 4,170 | 129,100,000 | 916,610 | 1,381,370 | 142,010 | 6 | 12 | 0 | 0 | 1 | 26 | 5 | 130 |
| cent | Central African Rep | 62 | 17 | 4,000 | 1,106 | 547,059,660 | 3,884,123 | 5,853,538 | 601,765 | 6 | 44 | 28 | 8 | 300 | 83 | 1,400 | 387 |
| chad | Chad | 51 | 7 | 3,800 | 497 | 258,842,520 | 1,837,781 | 2,769,614 | 284,726 | 2 | 53 | 26 | 3 | 70 | 9 | 300 | 39 |
| chan | Channel Islands | 22 | 144 | 120 | 785 | 1,209,372,000 | 8,586,541 | 12,940,280 | 1,330,309 | 5 | 1 | 12 | 79 | 4 | 26 | 20 | 131 |
| chil | Chile | 252 | 17 | 23,000 | 1,512 | 55,570,694,400 | 394,551,930 | 594,606,430 | 61,127,763 | 7 | 147 | 95 | 6 | 2,000 | 132 | 10,000 | 657 |
| chin | China | 546 | 0 | 520,000 | 412 | 55,152,315,140 | 391,581,437 | 590,129,771 | 60,667,546 | 3 | 122 | 0 | 0 | 50 | 0 | 1,000 | 1 |
| colo | Colombia | 175 | 4 | 9,000 | 213 | 78,187,546,080 | 555,131,577 | 836,606,743 | 86,006,300 | 6 | 188 | 140 | 3 | 2,500 | 59 | 9,000 | 213 |
| como | Comoros | 6 | 10 | 50 | 84 | 3,318,670 | 23,562 | 35,509 | 3,650 | 5 | 8 | 8 | 14 | 2 | 3 | 10 | 17 |
| cong | Congo-Brazzaville | 65 | 22 | 2,200 | 747 | 1,586,357,040 | 11,263,134 | 16,974,020 | 1,744,992 | 6 | 64 | 13 | 4 | 100 | 34 | 500 | 170 |
| conz | Congo-Zaire | 864 | 17 | 49,000 | 949 | 5,658,183,000 | 40,173,099 | 60,542,558 | 6,224,001 | 2 | 218 | 95 | 2 | 2,500 | 48 | 11,000 | 213 |
| cook | Cook Islands | 13 | 666 | 160 | 8,196 | 36,984,000 | 262,586 | 395,728 | 40,682 | 7 | 5 | 0 | 0 | 2 | 102 | 10 | 512 |
| cost | Costa Rica | 122 | 30 | 4,500 | 1,118 | 10,101,120,210 | 71,717,953 | 108,081,986 | 11,111,232 | 7 | 140 | 76 | 19 | 200 | 50 | 1,000 | 249 |
| croa | Croatia | 48 | 11 | 2,200 | 492 | 13,833,254,500 | 98,216,106 | 148,015,823 | 15,216,579 | 6 | 25 | 0 | 0 | 20 | 5 | 150 | 34 |
| cuba | Cuba | 69 | 6 | 3,900 | 348 | 6,269,781,700 | 44,515,450 | 67,086,664 | 6,896,759 | 1 | 53 | 20 | 2 | 25 | 2 | 120 | 11 |
| cypr | Cyprus | 30 | 50 | 750 | 1,249 | 7,402,391,480 | 52,556,979 | 79,205,588 | 8,142,630 | 6 | 49 | 10 | 17 | 30 | 50 | 150 | 250 |
| czec | Czech Republic | 56 | 5 | 6,100 | 595 | 18,650,056,320 | 132,415,399 | 199,555,602 | 20,515,061 | 6 | 69 | 20 | 2 | 50 | 5 | 280 | 27 |
| denm | Denmark | 88 | 17 | 3,010 | 569 | 142,010,677,900 | 1,008,275,813 | 1,519,514,253 | 156,211,745 | 7 | 34 | 90 | 17 | 150 | 28 | 500 | 94 |
| djib | Djibouti | 6 | 9 | 20 | 31 | 23,964,900 | 170,150 | 256,424 | 26,361 | 5 | 7 | 0 | 0 | 2 | 3 | 10 | 16 |
| domi | Dominica | 23 | 325 | 120 | 1,697 | 199,603,430 | 1,417,184 | 2,135,756 | 219,563 | 6 | 16 | 14 | 198 | 8 | 113 | 30 | 424 |
| domr | Dominican Republic | 81 | 10 | 6,000 | 706 | 11,718,989,300 | 83,204,824 | 125,393,185 | 12,890,888 | 2 | 102 | 40 | 5 | 250 | 29 | 700 | 82 |
| ecua | Ecuador | 122 | 10 | 6,200 | 490 | 17,107,823,930 | 121,465,549 | 183,053,716 | 18,818,606 | 2 | 167 | 58 | 5 | 500 | 40 | 2,000 | 158 |
| egyp | Egypt | 68 | 1 | 6,500 | 95 | 8,153,168,140 | 57,887,493 | 87,238,899 | 8,968,484 | 2 | 103 | 60 | 1 | 300 | 4 | 1,500 | 22 |
| elsa | El Salvador | 87 | 14 | 9,500 | 1,514 | 9,817,815,420 | 69,706,489 | 105,050,624 | 10,799,596 | 2 | 83 | 39 | 6 | 200 | 32 | 650 | 104 |
| equa | Equatorial Guinea | 16 | 35 | 620 | 1,370 | 149,985,240 | 1,064,895 | 1,604,842 | 164,983 | 7 | 28 | 4 | 9 | 90 | 199 | 400 | 884 |
| erit | Eritrea | 32 | 8 | 1,200 | 312 | 1,102,584,060 | 7,828,346 | 11,797,649 | 1,212,842 | 5 | 11 | 0 | 0 | 40 | 10 | 200 | 52 |
| esto | Estonia | 26 | 19 | 580 | 415 | 1,515,442,500 | 10,759,641 | 16,215,234 | 1,666,986 | 6 | 15 | 0 | 0 | 50 | 36 | 270 | 193 |
| ethi | Ethiopia | 52 | 1 | 30,000 | 480 | 3,116,115,900 | 22,124,422 | 33,342,440 | 3,427,727 | 2 | 107 | 69 | 1 | 3,500 | 56 | 8,500 | 136 |
| faer | Faeroe Islands | 8 | 187 | 90 | 2,105 | 593,850,000 | 4,216,335 | 6,354,195 | 653,235 | 5 | 4 | 4 | 94 | 0 | 0 | 5 | 117 |
| fiji | Fiji | 45 | 55 | 4,000 | 4,897 | 1,121,777,800 | 7,964,622 | 12,003,022 | 1,233,955 | 7 | 48 | 34 | 42 | 40 | 49 | 150 | 184 |
| finl | Finland | 56 | 11 | 1,740 | 336 | 94,245,101,580 | 669,140,221 | 1,008,422,586 | 103,669,611 | 5 | 27 | 55 | 11 | 150 | 29 | 750 | 145 |
| fran | France | 429 | 7 | 43,000 | 728 | 1,027,512,805,410 | 7,295,340,918 | 10,994,387,017 | 1,130,264,085 | 5 | 252 | 610 | 10 | 4,200 | 71 | 13,000 | 220 |
| freg | French Guiana | 15 | 83 | 100 | 552 | 1,615,946,880 | 11,473,222 | 17,290,631 | 1,777,541 | 7 | 16 | 12 | 66 | 10 | 55 | 50 | 276 |
| frep | French Polynesia | 15 | 64 | 320 | 1,361 | 3,366,401,500 | 23,901,450 | 36,020,496 | 3,703,041 | 7 | 7 | 12 | 51 | 30 | 128 | 180 | 766 |
| gabo | Gabon | 23 | 19 | 3,000 | 2,447 | 3,789,288,440 | 26,903,947 | 40,545,386 | 4,168,217 | 2 | 17 | 20 | 16 | 60 | 49 | 250 | 204 |
| gamb | Gambia | 37 | 28 | 200 | 153 | 15,103,360 | 107,233 | 161,605 | 16,613 | 6 | 29 | 17 | 13 | 15 | 12 | 80 | 61 |
| geor | Georgia | 31 | 6 | 990 | 199 | 1,323,878,160 | 9,399,534 | 14,165,496 | 1,456,265 | 2 | 7 | 0 | 0 | 50 | 10 | 300 | 60 |
| germ | Germany | 342 | 4 | 47,500 | 578 | 1,617,126,437,220 | 11,481,597,704 | 17,303,252,878 | 1,778,839,080 | 5 | 279 | 0 | 0 | 5,000 | 61 | 25,000 | 304 |
| ghan | Ghana | 598 | 30 | 40,500 | 2,004 | 3,380,120,640 | 23,998,856 | 36,167,290 | 3,718,132 | 6 | 183 | 65 | 3 | 500 | 25 | 3,000 | 148 |
| gibr | Gibraltar | 8 | 319 | 20 | 797 | 141,028,800 | 1,001,304 | 1,509,008 | 155,131 | 7 | 7 | 3 | 120 | 1 | 40 | 5 | 199 |
| gree | Greece | 64 | 6 | 34,800 | 3,269 | 82,600,974,200 | 586,466,916 | 883,830,423 | 90,861,071 | 2 | 69 | 60 | 6 | 700 | 66 | 1,800 | 169 |
| grel | Greenland | 13 | 231 | 130 | 2,315 | 609,925,000 | 4,330,467 | 6,526,197 | 670,917 | 6 | 11 | 3 | 53 | 2 | 36 | 10 | 178 |
| gren | Grenada | 41 | 437 | 220 | 2,347 | 270,420,100 | 1,919,982 | 2,893,495 | 297,462 | 7 | 21 | 21 | 224 | 15 | 160 | 50 | 534 |
| guad | Guadeloupe | 14 | 31 | 310 | 680 | 3,983,121,600 | 28,280,163 | 42,619,401 | 4,381,433 | 7 | 11 | 15 | 33 | 35 | 77 | 120 | 263 |
| guam | Guam | 47 | 281 | 150 | 895 | 3,180,116,800 | 22,578,829 | 34,027,249 | 3,498,128 | 7 | 30 | 15 | 90 | 30 | 179 | 50 | 298 |
| guat | Guatemala | 162 | 14 | 17,000 | 1,493 | 14,316,765,020 | 101,649,031 | 153,189,385 | 15,748,441 | 6 | 159 | 50 | 4 | 700 | 62 | 3,500 | 307 |
| guin | Guinea | 51 | 7 | 700 | 94 | 127,227,100 | 903,312 | 1,361,329 | 139,949 | 2 | 43 | 3 | 0 | 5 | 1 | 25 | 3 |
| gunb | Guinea-Bissau | 7 | 6 | 190 | 157 | 38,911,250 | 276,269 | 416,350 | 42,802 | 6 | 38 | 1 | 1 | 25 | 21 | 120 | 99 |
| guya | Guyana | 76 | 88 | 1,500 | 1,741 | 220,681,240 | 1,566,836 | 2,361,289 | 242,749 | 2 | 50 | 19 | 22 | 80 | 93 | 400 | 464 |
| hait | Haiti | 234 | 28 | 6,500 | 791 | 1,909,856,000 | 13,559,977 | 20,435,459 | 2,100,841 | 1 | 169 | 35 | 4 | 300 | 37 | 1,200 | 146 |
| hond | Honduras | 100 | 15 | 5,200 | 802 | 3,634,560,000 | 25,805,376 | 38,889,792 | 3,998,016 | 2 | 143 | 35 | 5 | 200 | 31 | 1,000 | 154 |
| hung | Hungary | 72 | 7 | 6,800 | 678 | 36,048,895,840 | 255,947,160 | 385,723,185 | 39,653,785 | 2 | 80 | 24 | 2 | 50 | 5 | 400 | 40 |
| icel | Iceland | 30 | 107 | 410 | 1,459 | 6,618,212,050 | 46,989,305 | 70,814,868 | 7,280,033 | 5 | 16 | 20 | 71 | 10 | 36 | 50 | 178 |
| indi | India | 1,327 | 1 | 280,000 | 276 | 21,162,805,640 | 150,255,920 | 226,442,020 | 23,279,086 | 4 | 720 | 320 | 0 | 7,500 | 7 | 35,000 | 35 |
| indo | Indonesia | 276 | 1 | 63,000 | 297 | 25,837,560,840 | 183,446,681 | 276,461,900 | 28,421,316 | 2 | 234 | 105 | 0 | 3,500 | 17 | 12,500 | 59 |
| iran | Iran | 36 | 1 | 990 | 15 | 1,475,753,000 | 10,477,846 | 15,790,557 | 1,623,328 | 3 | 26 | 24 | 0 | 40 | 1 | 200 | 3 |
| iraq | Iraq | 34 | 1 | 5,000 | 216 | 1,449,324,000 | 10,290,200 | 15,507,766 | 1,594,256 | 3 | 23 | 15 | 1 | 30 | 1 | 100 | 4 |
| irel | Ireland | 64 | 17 | 2,850 | 764 | 49,358,610,660 | 350,446,135 | 528,137,134 | 54,294,471 | 5 | 112 | 105 | 28 | 1,000 | 268 | 3,000 | 804 |
| isle | Isle of Man | 21 | 265 | 119 | 1,503 | 566,330,400 | 4,020,945 | 6,059,735 | 622,963 | 5 | 2 | 8 | 101 | 0 | 0 | 5 | 63 |
| isra | Israel | 109 | 21 | 1,700 | 332 | 4,681,721,760 | 33,240,224 | 50,094,422 | 5,149,893 | 7 | 146 | 60 | 12 | 200 | 39 | 1,500 | 293 |
| ital | Italy | 337 | 6 | 38,000 | 663 | 892,459,102,800 | 6,336,459,629 | 9,549,312,399 | 981,705,013 | 5 | 199 | 850 | 15 | 13,500 | 236 | 25,000 | 436 |
| ivor | Ivory Coast | 80 | 5 | 8,500 | 575 | 2,873,562,120 | 20,402,291 | 30,747,114 | 3,160,918 | 6 | 96 | 56 | 4 | 200 | 14 | 800 | 54 |
| jama | Jamaica | 173 | 67 | 5,000 | 1,936 | 1,693,786,630 | 12,025,885 | 18,123,516 | 1,863,165 | 6 | 127 | 29 | 11 | 150 | 58 | 600 | 232 |
| japa | Japan | 262 | 2 | 25,000 | 197 | 136,237,962,840 | 967,289,536 | 1,457,746,202 | 149,861,759 | 5 | 334 | 250 | 2 | 900 | 7 | 2,500 | 20 |
| jord | Jordan | 33 | 5 | 1,200 | 180 | 413,018,220 | 2,932,429 | 4,419,294 | 454,320 | 3 | 57 | 8 | 1 | 40 | 6 | 200 | 30 |
| kaza | Kazakhstan | 77 | 5 | 650 | 40 | 3,447,097,990 | 24,474,395 | 36,883,948 | 3,791,807 | 2 | 15 | 0 | 0 | 5 | 0 | 40 | 2 |
| keny | Kenya | 825 | 27 | 55,000 | 1,828 | 6,293,662,200 | 44,685,001 | 67,342,185 | 6,923,028 | 2 | 345 | 180 | 6 | 1,500 | 50 | 7,500 | 249 |
| kirg | Kirgizstan | 39 | 8 | 530 | 113 | 325,965,500 | 2,314,355 | 3,487,830 | 358,562 | 3 | 9 | 0 | 0 | 3 | 1 | 15 | 3 |
| kiri | Kiribati | 16 | 192 | 300 | 3,598 | 71,144,520 | 505,126 | 761,246 | 78,258 | 7 | 5 | 4 | 48 | 13 | 156 | 45 | 540 |
| kuwa | Kuwait | 18 | 9 | 2,300 | 1,167 | 4,304,633,650 | 30,562,898 | 46,059,580 | 4,735,097 | 6 | 5 | 2 | 1 | 5 | 3 | 20 | 10 |
| laos | Laos | 24 | 4 | 900 | 166 | 39,397,050 | 279,719 | 421,548 | 43,336 | 3 | 15 | 15 | 3 | 80 | 15 | 250 | 46 |
| latv | Latvia | 45 | 19 | 1,000 | 424 | 3,578,484,750 | 25,407,241 | 38,289,786 | 3,936,333 | 2 | 14 | 0 | 0 | 10 | 4 | 50 | 21 |
| leba | Lebanon | 69 | 21 | 3,100 | 945 | 4,614,623,860 | 32,763,829 | 49,376,475 | 5,076,086 | 7 | 81 | 140 | 43 | 250 | 76 | 500 | 152 |
| leso | Lesotho | 322 | 150 | 2,200 | 1,022 | 1,112,903,330 | 7,901,613 | 11,908,065 | 1,224,193 | 2 | 65 | 55 | 26 | 200 | 93 | 1,000 | 465 |
| libe | Liberia | 327 | 104 | 5,000 | 1,585 | 717,686,200 | 5,095,572 | 7,679,242 | 789,454 | 6 | 110 | 35 | 11 | 150 | 48 | 700 | 222 |
| liby | Libya | 35 | 6 | 370 | 66 | 1,108,991,520 | 7,873,839 | 11,866,209 | 1,219,890 | 2 | 13 | 0 | 0 | 0 | 0 | 10 | 2 |
| liec | Liechtenstein | 16 | 487 | 40 | 1,218 | 892,683,000 | 6,338,049 | 9,551,708 | 981,951 | 5 | 1 | 3 | 91 | 2 | 61 | 10 | 304 |
| lith | Lithuania | 28 | 8 | 910 | 248 | 6,105,454,300 | 43,348,725 | 65,328,361 | 6,715,999 | 6 | 9 | 0 | 0 | 15 | 4 | 40 | 11 |
| luxe | Luxembourg | 32 | 74 | 360 | 836 | 16,594,195,540 | 117,818,788 | 177,557,892 | 18,253,615 | 5 | 17 | 45 | 105 | 40 | 93 | 100 | 232 |
| mace | Macedonia | 38 | 19 | 1,000 | 494 | 1,106,985,120 | 7,859,594 | 11,844,740 | 1,217,683 | 2 | 4 | 0 | 0 | 10 | 5 | 50 | 25 |
| mada | Madagascar | 49 | 3 | 14,000 | 878 | 1,754,730,490 | 12,458,586 | 18,775,616 | 1,930,203 | 2 | 57 | 58 | 4 | 450 | 28 | 1,200 | 75 |
| mala | Malawi | 401 | 37 | 17,000 | 1,556 | 1,195,484,200 | 8,487,937 | 12,791,680 | 1,315,032 | 6 | 124 | 50 | 5 | 200 | 18 | 1,000 | 92 |
| malb | Malaysia | 70 | 3 | 6,000 | 270 | 6,889,925,210 | 48,918,468 | 73,722,199 | 7,578,917 | 5 | 98 | 41 | 2 | 250 | 11 | 750 | 34 |

| COUNTRY | | CHURCHES | | | | | | | | MISSION | | | | | | | |
|---|---|---|---|---|---|---|---|---|---|---|---|---|---|---|---|---|---|
| | | STRUCTURES | | | | FINANCE, US $ | | | | STATUS OF MISSIONS | | | | MISSION INSTITUTIONS | | | |
| code | short name | denom | p.m. | worship | p.m. | personal | church | parachurch | ecc crime | stat | misags | all orgs | p.m. | major | p.m. | minor | p.m. |
| 1 | 2 | 80 | 81 | 82 | 83 | 84 | 85 | 86 | 87 | 88 | 89 | 90 | 91 | 92 | 93 | 94 | 95 |
| mald | Maldives | 8 | 28 | 10 | 35 | 354,420 | 2,516 | 3,792 | 389 | 1 | 1 | 0 | 0 | 0 | 0 | 0 | 0 |
| mali | Mali | 39 | 3 | 1,400 | 125 | 56,091,250 | 398,247 | 600,176 | 61,700 | 6 | 48 | 17 | 2 | 70 | 6 | 300 | 27 |
| malt | Malta | 17 | 44 | 160 | 412 | 4,456,572,000 | 31,641,661 | 47,685,320 | 4,902,229 | 5 | 20 | 48 | 124 | 20 | 52 | 100 | 257 |
| mars | Marshall Islands | 17 | 265 | 400 | 6,229 | 113,594,670 | 806,522 | 1,215,462 | 124,954 | 7 | 11 | 0 | 0 | 0 | 0 | 10 | 156 |
| mart | Martinique | 47 | 119 | 290 | 734 | 3,733,720,000 | 26,509,412 | 39,950,804 | 4,107,092 | 7 | 11 | 25 | 63 | 10 | 25 | 50 | 126 |
| maur | Mauritania | 31 | 12 | 70 | 26 | 3,001,960 | 21,313 | 32,120 | 3,302 | 1 | 20 | 1 | 0 | 0 | 0 | 0 | 0 |
| maus | Mauritius | 25 | 22 | 380 | 329 | 1,248,680,160 | 8,865,629 | 13,360,877 | 1,373,548 | 7 | 14 | 41 | 36 | 30 | 26 | 100 | 86 |
| mayo | Mayotte | 5 | 49 | 10 | 98 | 1,119,600 | 7,949 | 11,979 | 1,231 | 1 | 0 | 0 | 0 | 0 | 0 | 5 | 49 |
| mexi | Mexico | 297 | 3 | 65,000 | 657 | 311,438,997,640 | 2,211,216,883 | 3,332,397,274 | 342,582,897 | 6 | 395 | 205 | 2 | 1,500 | 15 | 5,000 | 51 |
| micr | Micronesia | 14 | 118 | 270 | 2,275 | 218,410,620 | 1,550,715 | 2,336,993 | 240,251 | 7 | 20 | 0 | 0 | 10 | 84 | 50 | 421 |
| mold | Moldavia | 28 | 6 | 1,100 | 251 | 2,574,673,360 | 18,280,180 | 27,549,004 | 2,832,140 | 2 | 7 | 0 | 0 | 15 | 3 | 60 | 14 |
| mona | Monaco | 4 | 119 | 12 | 357 | 777,525,000 | 5,520,427 | 8,319,517 | 855,277 | 7 | 6 | 20 | 595 | 7 | 208 | 25 | 744 |
| mong | Mongolia | 27 | 10 | 350 | 131 | 10,351,830 | 73,497 | 110,764 | 11,387 | 7 | 23 | 0 | 0 | 2 | 1 | 15 | 6 |
| mont | Montserrat | 21 | 1,976 | 80 | 7,527 | 127,399,590 | 904,537 | 1,363,175 | 140,139 | 7 | 8 | 4 | 376 | 2 | 188 | 10 | 941 |
| moro | Morocco | 32 | 1 | 1,900 | 67 | 193,668,360 | 1,375,045 | 2,072,251 | 213,035 | 5 | 47 | 31 | 1 | 50 | 2 | 250 | 9 |
| moza | Mozambique | 308 | 16 | 15,000 | 762 | 516,842,640 | 3,669,582 | 5,530,216 | 568,526 | 2 | 120 | 20 | 1 | 350 | 18 | 1,000 | 51 |
| myan | Myanmar | 118 | 3 | 12,000 | 263 | 6,697,220,560 | 47,550,265 | 71,660,259 | 7,366,942 | 3 | 72 | 20 | 0 | 60 | 1 | 300 | 7 |
| nami | Namibia | 104 | 60 | 3,100 | 1,796 | 2,698,422,000 | 19,158,796 | 28,873,115 | 2,968,264 | 2 | 42 | 12 | 7 | 200 | 116 | 1,000 | 579 |
| naur | Nauru | 12 | 1,042 | 50 | 4,341 | 67,311,870 | 477,914 | 720,237 | 74,043 | 7 | 2 | 0 | 0 | 2 | 174 | 10 | 868 |
| nepa | Nepal | 57 | 2 | 4,700 | 196 | 115,212,200 | 818,006 | 1,232,770 | 126,733 | 4 | 115 | 50 | 2 | 35 | 2 | 200 | 8 |
| neth | Netherlands | 393 | 25 | 10,000 | 633 | 246,788,472,000 | 1,752,198,151 | 2,640,636,650 | 271,467,319 | 5 | 125 | 340 | 22 | 1,800 | 114 | 4,500 | 285 |
| nets | Netherlands Antilles | 48 | 221 | 210 | 969 | 1,923,084,800 | 13,653,902 | 20,577,007 | 2,115,393 | 7 | 26 | 20 | 92 | 70 | 323 | 250 | 1,153 |
| newc | New Caledonia | 12 | 56 | 260 | 1,215 | 1,293,432,000 | 9,183,367 | 13,839,722 | 1,422,775 | 7 | 16 | 12 | 56 | 40 | 187 | 150 | 701 |
| newz | New Zealand | 175 | 45 | 6,200 | 1,605 | 36,742,220,460 | 260,869,765 | 393,141,758 | 40,416,442 | 5 | 119 | 150 | 39 | 300 | 78 | 1,500 | 388 |
| nica | Nicaragua | 95 | 19 | 5,000 | 985 | 1,845,824,160 | 13,105,351 | 19,750,318 | 2,030,406 | 6 | 108 | 40 | 8 | 250 | 49 | 1,250 | 246 |
| niga | Niger | 65 | 6 | 1,400 | 130 | 12,819,400 | 91,017 | 137,167 | 14,101 | 5 | 38 | 12 | 1 | 20 | 2 | 100 | 9 |
| nige | Nigeria | 2,079 | 19 | 109,000 | 978 | 13,250,900,520 | 94,081,393 | 141,784,635 | 14,575,990 | 5 | 246 | 105 | 1 | 1,500 | 14 | 8,000 | 72 |
| nork | North Korea | 18 | 1 | 20,900 | 869 | 475,202,350 | 3,373,936 | 5,084,665 | 522,722 | 1 | 1 | 0 | 0 | 2 | 0 | 20 | 1 |
| norl | Northern Cyprus | 3 | 16 | 120 | 648 | 199,746,612 | 1,418,200 | 2,137,288 | 219,721 | 7 | 0 | 0 | 0 | 0 | 0 | 10 | 54 |
| norm | Northern Mariana Is | 23 | 294 | 70 | 893 | 727,230,000 | 5,163,333 | 7,781,361 | 799,953 | 6 | 14 | 0 | 0 | 5 | 64 | 25 | 319 |
| norw | Norway | 92 | 21 | 3,000 | 672 | 131,289,437,500 | 932,155,006 | 1,404,796,981 | 144,418,381 | 5 | 36 | 110 | 25 | 80 | 18 | 250 | 56 |
| oman | Oman | 37 | 15 | 300 | 118 | 587,635,120 | 4,172,209 | 6,287,695 | 646,398 | 2 | 7 | 2 | 1 | 2 | 1 | 10 | 4 |
| paki | Pakistan | 56 | 0 | 8,000 | 51 | 1,753,632,700 | 12,450,792 | 18,763,869 | 1,928,995 | 2 | 150 | 45 | 0 | 300 | 2 | 1,500 | 10 |
| pala | Palau | 11 | 566 | 60 | 3,089 | 91,855,000 | 652,170 | 982,848 | 101,040 | 7 | 1 | 0 | 0 | 0 | 0 | 10 | 515 |
| pale | Palestine | 71 | 32 | 2,300 | 1,038 | 2,746,006,776 | 19,496,648 | 29,382,272 | 3,020,607 | 5 | 10 | 40 | 18 | 150 | 68 | 400 | 181 |
| pana | Panama | 88 | 31 | 2,500 | 875 | 6,756,926,000 | 47,974,174 | 72,299,108 | 7,432,618 | 7 | 87 | 47 | 17 | 100 | 35 | 500 | 175 |
| papu | Papua New Guinea | 100 | 22 | 13,000 | 2,821 | 4,391,212,480 | 31,177,608 | 46,985,973 | 4,830,333 | 2 | 140 | 130 | 28 | 700 | 152 | 2,500 | 543 |
| para | Paraguay | 96 | 17 | 2,800 | 509 | 8,743,387,380 | 62,078,050 | 93,554,244 | 9,617,726 | 6 | 136 | 54 | 10 | 300 | 55 | 1,500 | 273 |
| peru | Peru | 134 | 5 | 15,000 | 585 | 57,061,733,190 | 405,138,305 | 610,560,545 | 62,767,906 | 2 | 237 | 130 | 5 | 600 | 23 | 2,500 | 97 |
| phil | Philippines | 598 | 8 | 65,000 | 856 | 69,930,059,850 | 496,503,424 | 748,251,640 | 76,923,065 | 2 | 2,766 | 190 | 3 | 2,000 | 26 | 10,000 | 132 |
| pola | Poland | 66 | 2 | 17,000 | 439 | 104,619,584,610 | 742,799,050 | 1,119,429,555 | 115,081,543 | 3 | 91 | 45 | 1 | 400 | 10 | 2,000 | 52 |
| port | Portugal | 91 | 9 | 9,200 | 932 | 88,441,449,940 | 627,934,294 | 946,323,514 | 97,285,594 | 5 | 140 | 130 | 13 | 380 | 39 | 2,100 | 213 |
| puer | Puerto Rico | 135 | 35 | 5,000 | 1,292 | 29,033,869,800 | 206,140,475 | 310,662,406 | 31,937,256 | 7 | 90 | 50 | 13 | 150 | 39 | 700 | 181 |
| qata | Qatar | 35 | 58 | 200 | 334 | 691,766,000 | 4,911,538 | 7,401,896 | 760,942 | 3 | 0 | 0 | 0 | 0 | 0 | 10 | 17 |
| reun | Reunion | 17 | 24 | 290 | 415 | 2,610,547,200 | 18,534,885 | 27,932,855 | 2,871,601 | 2 | 16 | 18 | 26 | 20 | 29 | 100 | 143 |
| roma | Romania | 55 | 2 | 38,000 | 1,702 | 29,048,497,240 | 206,244,330 | 310,818,920 | 31,953,346 | 2 | 82 | 20 | 1 | 300 | 13 | 1,500 | 67 |
| russ | Russia | 470 | 3 | 84,000 | 572 | 187,305,119,680 | 1,329,866,349 | 2,004,164,780 | 206,035,631 | 2 | 112 | 120 | 1 | 400 | 3 | 2,500 | 17 |
| rwan | Rwanda | 44 | 6 | 7,000 | 905 | 1,140,627,960 | 8,098,458 | 12,204,719 | 1,254,690 | 2 | 57 | 38 | 5 | 200 | 26 | 1,000 | 129 |
| saha | Sahara | 2 | 7 | 30 | 102 | 100,809 | 715 | 1,078 | 110 | 1 | 3 | 0 | 0 | 2 | 7 | 10 | 34 |
| saih | Saint Helena | 12 | 1,907 | 30 | 4,767 | 47,988,000 | 340,714 | 513,471 | 52,786 | 7 | 4 | 2 | 318 | 0 | 0 | 10 | 1,589 |
| saik | Saint Kitts & Nevis | 38 | 988 | 160 | 4,159 | 186,120,000 | 1,321,452 | 1,991,484 | 204,732 | 6 | 7 | 8 | 208 | 0 | 0 | 5 | 130 |
| sail | Saint Lucia | 36 | 233 | 180 | 1,166 | 486,422,430 | 3,453,599 | 5,204,720 | 535,064 | 2 | 13 | 13 | 84 | 7 | 45 | 20 | 130 |
| saip | Saint Pierre & Miquelon | 3 | 457 | 6 | 914 | 70,268,000 | 498,902 | 751,867 | 77,294 | 7 | 3 | 5 | 761 | 2 | 305 | 10 | 1,523 |
| saiv | Saint Vincent | 42 | 369 | 300 | 2,633 | 178,840,920 | 1,269,770 | 1,913,597 | 196,725 | 2 | 18 | 7 | 61 | 6 | 53 | 20 | 176 |
| samo | Samoa | 27 | 150 | 640 | 3,554 | 189,424,480 | 1,344,913 | 2,026,841 | 208,366 | 7 | 16 | 12 | 67 | 18 | 100 | 50 | 278 |
| sanm | San Marino | 2 | 75 | 14 | 528 | 587,341,300 | 4,170,123 | 6,284,551 | 646,075 | 7 | 1 | 0 | 0 | 1 | 38 | 5 | 189 |
| saot | Sao Tome & Principe | 9 | 61 | 140 | 954 | 46,236,050 | 328,275 | 494,725 | 50,859 | 7 | 7 | 5 | 34 | 2 | 14 | 10 | 68 |
| saud | Saudi Arabia | 42 | 2 | 4,000 | 185 | 5,540,374,400 | 39,336,658 | 59,282,006 | 6,094,411 | 2 | 12 | 0 | 0 | 0 | 0 | 5 | 0 |
| sene | Senegal | 37 | 4 | 450 | 47 | 280,374,600 | 1,990,659 | 3,000,008 | 308,412 | 5 | 71 | 35 | 4 | 150 | 16 | 750 | 79 |
| seyc | Seychelles | 12 | 155 | 50 | 646 | 475,282,900 | 3,374,508 | 5,085,527 | 522,811 | 7 | 7 | 14 | 181 | 20 | 258 | 100 | 1,291 |
| sier | Sierra Leone | 67 | 14 | 2,000 | 412 | 91,888,920 | 652,411 | 983,211 | 101,077 | 2 | 82 | 24 | 5 | 100 | 21 | 400 | 82 |
| sing | Singapore | 92 | 26 | 520 | 146 | 10,770,479,280 | 76,470,402 | 115,244,128 | 11,847,527 | 5 | 112 | 60 | 17 | 20 | 6 | 150 | 42 |
| slok | Slovakia | 49 | 9 | 3,100 | 575 | 12,756,348,700 | 90,570,075 | 136,492,931 | 14,031,983 | 2 | 20 | 0 | 0 | 20 | 4 | 100 | 19 |
| slov | Slovenia | 39 | 20 | 1,700 | 856 | 14,241,809,200 | 101,116,845 | 152,387,358 | 15,665,990 | 6 | 17 | 0 | 0 | 10 | 5 | 50 | 25 |
| solo | Solomon Islands | 37 | 83 | 2,500 | 5,635 | 366,914,730 | 2,605,094 | 3,925,987 | 403,606 | 7 | 30 | 9 | 20 | 70 | 158 | 300 | 676 |
| soma | Somalia | 11 | 2 | 250 | 34 | 49,291,500 | 349,969 | 527,419 | 54,220 | 3 | 22 | 5 | 1 | 10 | 1 | 30 | 4 |
| somi | Somaliland | 5 | 2 | 80 | 28 | 1,299,055 | 9,223 | 13,899 | 1,428 | 1 | 0 | 0 | 0 | 0 | 0 | 5 | 2 |
| soua | South Africa | 3,364 | 83 | 80,000 | 1,981 | 100,490,493,240 | 713,482,502 | 1,075,248,277 | 110,539,542 | 7 | 271 | 160 | 4 | 2,000 | 50 | 8,000 | 198 |
| souk | South Korea | 385 | 8 | 45,000 | 961 | 181,214,197,200 | 1,286,620,800 | 1,938,991,910 | 199,335,616 | 5 | 161 | 120 | 3 | 1,000 | 21 | 5,000 | 107 |
| spai | Spain | 315 | 8 | 30,000 | 757 | 503,460,465,760 | 3,574,569,306 | 5,387,026,983 | 553,806,512 | 5 | 303 | 300 | 8 | 4,100 | 104 | 9,500 | 240 |
| span | Spanish North Africa | 6 | 46 | 30 | 231 | 834,592,000 | 5,925,603 | 8,930,134 | 918,051 | 6 | 1 | 5 | 39 | 2 | 15 | 10 | 77 |
| sril | Sri Lanka | 61 | 3 | 3,900 | 207 | 1,228,584,000 | 8,722,946 | 13,145,848 | 1,351,442 | 5 | 93 | 45 | 2 | 150 | 8 | 600 | 32 |
| suda | Sudan | 37 | 1 | 4,400 | 149 | 3,899,512,800 | 27,686,540 | 41,724,786 | 4,289,464 | 2 | 68 | 27 | 1 | 60 | 2 | 250 | 8 |
| suri | Suriname | 33 | 79 | 250 | 599 | 151,653,920 | 1,076,742 | 1,622,696 | 166,819 | 7 | 38 | 24 | 58 | 50 | 120 | 200 | 479 |
| swaz | Swaziland | 103 | 102 | 2,400 | 2,381 | 796,583,970 | 5,655,746 | 8,523,448 | 876,242 | 7 | 53 | 18 | 18 | 100 | 99 | 500 | 496 |
| swed | Sweden | 156 | 18 | 9,500 | 1,066 | 142,508,455,000 | 1,011,810,030 | 1,524,840,468 | 156,759,300 | 5 | 52 | 90 | 10 | 75 | 8 | 250 | 28 |
| swit | Switzerland | 182 | 25 | 6,900 | 934 | 261,882,615,240 | 1,859,366,568 | 2,802,143,983 | 288,070,876 | 5 | 106 | 480 | 65 | 220 | 30 | 700 | 95 |
| syri | Syria | 29 | 2 | 3,800 | 236 | 1,408,634,080 | 10,001,301 | 15,072,384 | 1,549,497 | 4 | 20 | 29 | 2 | 40 | 3 | 200 | 12 |
| taiw | Taiwan | 153 | 7 | 4,200 | 187 | 14,628,813,200 | 103,864,573 | 156,528,301 | 16,091,694 | 5 | 229 | 90 | 4 | 300 | 13 | 1,200 | 54 |
| taji | Tajikistan | 26 | 4 | 100 | 16 | 44,068,080 | 312,883 | 471,528 | 48,474 | 2 | 3 | 0 | 0 | 0 | 0 | 10 | 2 |
| tanz | Tanzania | 81 | 2 | 24,000 | 716 | 1,886,733,360 | 13,395,806 | 20,188,046 | 2,075,406 | 2 | 183 | 75 | 2 | 500 | 15 | 2,500 | 75 |
| thai | Thailand | 58 | 1 | 30,000 | 489 | 3,685,757,580 | 26,168,878 | 39,437,606 | 4,054,333 | 2 | 176 | 90 | 2 | 300 | 5 | 1,500 | 24 |
| timo | Timor | 10 | 11 | 200 | 226 | 525,111,804 | 3,728,293 | 5,618,696 | 577,622 | 6 | 3 | 3 | 3 | 15 | 17 | 70 | 79 |
| togo | Togo | 45 | 10 | 3,200 | 691 | 542,219,450 | 3,849,758 | 5,801,748 | 596,441 | 6 | 49 | 32 | 7 | 100 | 22 | 400 | 86 |
| tong | Tonga | 26 | 264 | 600 | 6,089 | 146,191,440 | 1,037,959 | 1,564,248 | 160,810 | 7 | 15 | 6 | 61 | 25 | 254 | 120 | 1,218 |
| trin | Trinidad & Tobago | 97 | 75 | 1,400 | 1,081 | 3,000,411,050 | 21,302,918 | 32,104,398 | 3,300,452 | 7 | 51 | 30 | 23 | 80 | 62 | 300 | 232 |
| tuni | Tunisia | 20 | 2 | 360 | 38 | 91,915,460 | 652,599 | 983,495 | 101,107 | 3 | 19 | 18 | 2 | 25 | 3 | 100 | 10 |
| turk | Turkey | 56 | 1 | 1,370 | 21 | 1,037,370,900 | 7,365,333 | 11,099,868 | 1,141,107 | 3 | 48 | 17 | 0 | 50 | 1 | 200 | 3 |
| turm | Turkmenistan | 23 | 5 | 100 | 22 | 90,972,360 | 645,903 | 973,404 | 100,069 | 2 | 11 | 0 | 0 | 0 | 0 | 5 | 1 |
| turs | Turks & Caicos Is | 17 | 1,014 | 50 | 2,983 | 28,805,064 | 204,515 | 308,214 | 31,685 | 7 | 2 | 3 | 179 | 1 | 60 | 5 | 298 |
| tuva | Tuvalu | 9 | 768 | 30 | 2,560 | 7,796,000 | 55,351 | 83,417 | 8,575 | 7 | 2 | 0 | 0 | 2 | 171 | 10 | 853 |
| ugan | Uganda | 78 | 4 | 25,000 | 1,148 | 4,546,601,520 | 32,280,870 | 48,648,636 | 5,001,261 | 2 | 150 | 59 | 3 | 350 | 16 | 1,350 | 62 |
| ukra | Ukraine | 124 | 2 | 51,000 | 1,011 | 67,920,628,110 | 482,236,459 | 726,750,720 | 74,712,690 | 2 | 56 | 0 | 0 | 100 | 2 | 500 | 10 |
| unia | United Arab Emirates | 72 | 29 | 1,800 | 737 | 4,571,763,000 | 32,459,517 | 48,917,864 | 5,028,939 | 2 | 12 | 6 | 3 | 5 | 2 | 20 | 8 |
| usa | USA | 4,684 | 17 | 600,000 | 2,156 | 5,175,509,376,460 | 36,746,116,572 | 55,377,950,328 | 5,693,060,314 | 5 | 256 | 2,300 | 8 | 9,000 | 32 | 25,000 | 90 |
| uuay | Uruguay | 132 | 40 | 2,200 | 659 | 11,176,138,930 | 79,350,586 | 119,584,686 | 12,293,752 | 7 | 105 | 68 | 20 | 150 | 45 | 700 | 210 |
| uzbe | Uzbekistan | 80 | 3 | 1,000 | 41 | 382,503,980 | 2,715,778 | 4,092,792 | 420,754 | 2 | 9 | 0 | 0 | 3 | 0 | 10 | 0 |
| vanu | Vanuatu | 29 | 152 | 1,150 | 6,039 | 204,064,800 | 1,448,860 | 2,183,493 | 224,471 | 6 | 15 | 8 | 42 | 20 | 105 | 100 | 525 |
| vene | Venezuela | 110 | 5 | 9,500 | 393 | 68,662,218,680 | 487,501,752 | 734,685,739 | 75,528,440 | 2 | 124 | 78 | 3 | 450 | 19 | 1,500 | 62 |
| viet | Viet Nam | 68 | 1 | 11,000 | 138 | 1,576,301,280 | 11,191,739 | 16,866,423 | 1,733,931 | 4 | 51 | 62 | 1 | 800 | 10 | 2,000 | 25 |
| virg | Virgin Is of the US | 80 | 861 | 250 | 2,690 | 1,011,506,660 | 7,181,697 | 10,823,121 | 1,112,657 | 7 | 33 | 10 | 108 | 10 | 108 | 50 | 538 |
| wall | Wallis & Futuna Is | 4 | 276 | 8 | 551 | 65,253,734 | 463,301 | 698,214 | 71,779 | 7 | 3 | 6 | 413 | 2 | 138 | 10 | 689 |
| yeme | Yemen | 20 | 1 | 600 | 33 | 7,970,560 | 56,590 | 85,284 | 8,767 | 3 | 12 | 0 | 0 | 0 | 0 | 10 | 1 |
| yugo | Yugoslavia | 102 | 10 | 4,500 | 423 | 13,771,114,000 | 97,774,909 | 147,350,919 | 15,148,225 | 6 | 16 | 40 | 4 | 400 | 38 | 1,800 | 169 |
| zamb | Zambia | 209 | 23 | 13,000 | 1,418 | 2,820,832,000 | 20,027,907 | 30,182,902 | 3,102,915 | 2 | 141 | 78 | 9 | 250 | 27 | 950 | 104 |
| zimb | Zimbabwe | 348 | 30 | 20,000 | 1,714 | 3,735,374,400 | 26,521,158 | 39,968,506 | 4,108,911 | 6 | 159 | 58 | 5 | 500 | 43 | 2,000 | 171 |
| | 11 minicountries | 41 | 1,777 | 193 | 8,363 | 349,448,200 | 2,481,079 | 3,739,091 | 384,390 | 5 | 14 | 150 | 6,499 | 2 | 87 | 110 | 4,766 |
| | Africa | 11,680 | 15 | 603,662 | 770 | 199,617,997,404 | 1,417,287,750 | 2,135,912,544 | 219,579,767 | 6 | 4,150 | 1,994 | 3 | 18,192 | 23 | 73,375 | 94 |
| | Antarctica | 2 | 444 | 20 | 4,444 | 272,000,000 | 1,931,200 | 2,910,400 | 299,200 | 1 | 1 | 0 | 0 | 0 | 0 | 0 | 0 |
| | Asia | 5,378 | 1 | 1,145,849 | 311 | 588,150,287,072 | 4,175,867,011 | 6,293,208,046 | 646,965,289 | 3 | 6,264 | 1,921 | 1 | 18,461 | 5 | 79,230 | 22 |
| | Europe | 5,192 | 7 | 546,167 | 749 | 6,976,591,936,380 | 49,533,802,725 | 74,649,533,695 | 7,674,251,106 | 5 | 3,218 | 5,639 | 8 | 38,258 | 52 | 115,912 | 159 |
| | Latin America | 5,456 | 11 | 461,860 | 890 | 1,574,429,913,124 | 11,178,452,364 | 16,846,400,051 | 1,731,872,886 | 6 | 4,122 | 2,068 | 4 | 17,504 | 34 | 69,942 | 135 |
| | Northern America | 5,240 | 17 | 635,326 | 2,052 | 5,570,172,069,350 | 39,548,221,689 | 59,600,841,140 | 6,127,189,274 | 5 | 460 | 2,664 | 9 | 9,906 | 32 | 28,030 | 91 |
| | Oceania | 963 | 32 | 54,787 | 1,803 | 288,463,899,984 | 2,048,093,679 | 3,086,563,715 | 317,310,277 | 7 | 718 | 593 | 20 | 2,629 | 86 | 9,311 | 306 |
| | **World A** | **1,068** | **2** | **56,222** | **93** | **10,548,883,544** | **74,897,052** | **112,873,033** | **11,603,752** | **3** | **987** | **364** | **1** | **1,024** | **2** | **4,526** | **7** |
| | **World B** | **9,769** | **3** | **1,456,811** | **388** | **771,979,359,808** | **5,481,053,425** | **8,260,179,119** | **849,177,266** | **3** | **5,466** | **2,720** | **1** | **26,008** | **7** | **105,582** | **28** |
| | **World C** | **23,074** | **14** | **1,934,638** | **1,142** | **14,415,169,859,962** | **102,347,705,941** | **154,242,317,439** | **15,856,686,781** | **5** | **12,480** | **11,795** | **7** | **77,918** | **46** | **265,692** | **157** |
| | **GLOBAL TOTAL** | **33,911** | **6** | **3,447,671** | **569** | **15,197,698,103,314** | **107,903,656,418** | **162,615,369,591** | **16,717,467,799** | **5** | **18,933** | **14,879** | **2** | **104,950** | **17** | **375,800** | **62** |

| COUNTRY | | MISSION (continued) | | | | | | | | | CHRISTIAN PERSONNEL | | | |
|---|---|---|---|---|---|---|---|---|---|---|---|---|---|---|
| | | RESPONSE/GROWTH | | | | | WORLDS A,B, and C | | | ministries | ALL WORKERS | | CITIZENS | |
| code | short name | CG% | g % | bapt p.a. | resp R | cost-eff, $ | A -individuals | B-individuals | C-individuals | peo-ags | workers | w.p.m. | workers | citw p.m. |
| 1 | 2 | 96 | 97 | 98 | 99 | 100 | 101 | 102 | 103 | 104 | 105 | 106 | 107 | 108 |
| afgh | Afghanistan | 6.8 | 2.0 | 136 | 97 | 30,410 | 16,000,408 | 6,712,933 | 7,075 | 64 | 70 | 3.1 | 20 | 0.9 |
| alba | Albania | 1.6 | 3.8 | 40,396 | 118 | 17,753 | 454,107 | 1,558,097 | 1,101,230 | 23 | 1,800 | 578.1 | 1,000 | 321.2 |
| alge | Algeria | -1.8 | 2.0 | 1,824 | 118 | 79,681 | 15,876,006 | 15,504,320 | 90,952 | 53 | 620 | 19.7 | 120 | 3.8 |
| amer | American Samoa | 2.3 | 3.9 | 2,178 | 71 | 65,922 | 252 | 2,613 | 65,224 | 11 | 350 | 5,140.3 | 150 | 2,203.0 |
| ando | Andorra | 2.8 | 5.0 | 3,532 | 88 | 322,003 | 734 | 4,368 | 72,883 | 4 | 30 | 384.7 | 20 | 256.5 |
| ango | Angola | 7.0 | 5.4 | 593,401 | 106 | 7,554 | 91,226 | 671,654 | 12,115,308 | 98 | 27,000 | 2,096.6 | 25,000 | 1,941.3 |
| angu | Anguilla | 0.6 | 2.0 | 144 | 38 | 99,157 | 17 | 688 | 7,604 | 11 | 30 | 3,610.5 | 20 | 2,407.0 |
| anti | Antigua | 0.6 | 0.9 | 476 | 17 | 866,967 | 157 | 3,962 | 63,441 | 9 | 170 | 2,516.3 | 100 | 1,480.2 |
| arge | Argentina | 2.1 | 2.0 | 685,834 | 34 | 397,918 | 242,999 | 2,384,300 | 34,399,998 | 119 | 36,000 | 972.3 | 24,000 | 648.2 |
| arme | Armenia | 1.9 | 2.9 | 85,716 | 53 | 25,155 | 77,944 | 485,574 | 2,956,051 | 47 | 300 | 85.2 | 250 | 71.0 |
| arub | Aruba | 2.0 | 5.3 | 5,086 | 91 | 297,509 | 475 | 3,178 | 99,094 | 9 | 51 | 496.4 | 40 | 389.3 |
| aust | Australia | 1.4 | 1.7 | 213,365 | 34 | 1,104,424 | 307,968 | 3,598,791 | 14,972,765 | 206 | 59,400 | 3,146.3 | 55,000 | 2,913.2 |
| ausz | Austria | 0.2 | 1.4 | 95,629 | 25 | 1,942,919 | 115,508 | 724,934 | 7,370,078 | 42 | 25,500 | 3,105.8 | 24,000 | 2,923.1 |
| azer | Azerbaijan | 0.9 | 0.8 | 3,012 | 58 | 57,007 | 4,872,856 | 2,503,202 | 357,957 | 50 | 150 | 19.4 | 50 | 6.5 |
| baha | Bahamas | 1.7 | 2.2 | 5,873 | 39 | 542,480 | 859 | 22,465 | 283,205 | 20 | 720 | 2,348.9 | 420 | 1,370.2 |
| bahr | Bahrain | 5.9 | 3.4 | 2,110 | 149 | 232,917 | 264,134 | 288,608 | 64,475 | 16 | 110 | 178.2 | 60 | 97.2 |
| bang | Bangladesh | 3.3 | 3.4 | 31,231 | 157 | 7,159 | 55,267,877 | 72,953,499 | 933,776 | 103 | 3,400 | 26.3 | 2,400 | 18.6 |
| barb | Barbados | 0.2 | 1.3 | 2,496 | 25 | 517,350 | 2,159 | 6,415 | 261,875 | 10 | 550 | 2,033.7 | 350 | 1,294.1 |
| belg | Belgium | 0.3 | 1.1 | 95,579 | 20 | 2,202,317 | 219,444 | 972,518 | 8,969,202 | 54 | 57,600 | 5,668.6 | 55,000 | 5,412.8 |
| beli | Belize | 1.9 | 2.8 | 5,482 | 52 | 94,570 | 5,155 | 16,631 | 218,923 | 41 | 800 | 3,323.5 | 400 | 1,661.8 |
| belo | Belorussia | 0.0 | 2.1 | 136,751 | 42 | 99,662 | 86,904 | 2,958,209 | 7,191,068 | 58 | 1,700 | 166.1 | 1,200 | 117.2 |
| beni | Benin | 5.7 | 4.5 | 75,064 | 158 | 8,301 | 1,574,060 | 2,817,682 | 1,704,817 | 104 | 2,200 | 360.9 | 1,600 | 262.4 |
| berm | Bermuda | 1.1 | 1.3 | 707 | 22 | 2,507,474 | 121 | 4,239 | 60,230 | 8 | 250 | 3,870.6 | 150 | 2,322.3 |
| bhut | Bhutan | 7.1 | 2.3 | 217 | 284 | 18,641 | 1,683,112 | 431,209 | 9,649 | 17 | 250 | 117.7 | 50 | 23.5 |
| boli | Bolivia | 1.7 | 3.1 | 245,110 | 54 | 25,412 | 24,406 | 469,058 | 7,835,201 | 135 | 7,200 | 864.5 | 3,000 | 360.2 |
| bosn | Bosnia-Herzegovina | 0.7 | 1.0 | 13,858 | 29 | 30,000 | 1,045,717 | 1,535,294 | 1,390,802 | 57 | 1,050 | 264.4 | 500 | 125.9 |
| bots | Botswana | 4.1 | 5.2 | 39,311 | 136 | 57,699 | 83,331 | 566,698 | 972,191 | 78 | 1,400 | 863.0 | 1,000 | 616.4 |
| boug | Bougainville | 5.1 | 2.8 | 5,263 | 56 | 49,295 | 256 | 10,063 | 188,176 | 57 | 200 | 1,007.6 | 100 | 503.8 |
| braz | Brazil | 2.2 | 2.0 | 3,174,811 | 33 | 178,256 | 425,724 | 14,144,725 | 155,545,014 | 461 | 150,000 | 881.8 | 125,000 | 734.8 |
| brit | Britain | 0.1 | 1.0 | 402,247 | 20 | 1,815,533 | 1,116,976 | 9,132,524 | 48,580,660 | 244 | 215,000 | 3,654.6 | 200,000 | 3,399.6 |
| briz | British Virgin Is | 1.2 | 2.8 | 411 | 60 | 289,645 | 90 | 2,815 | 18,461 | 14 | 30 | 1,404.1 | 20 | 936.1 |
| brun | Brunei | 5.7 | 2.1 | 526 | 128 | 738,662 | 180,020 | 122,877 | 25,183 | 32 | 70 | 213.4 | 40 | 121.9 |
| bulg | Bulgaria | 0.8 | 1.3 | 84,223 | 24 | 105,138 | 454,079 | 1,106,963 | 6,664,003 | 39 | 3,200 | 389.1 | 3,000 | 364.7 |
| burk | Burkina Faso | 13.0 | 4.9 | 97,378 | 212 | 4,686 | 4,406,314 | 5,542,063 | 1,988,446 | 183 | 7,000 | 586.4 | 6,000 | 502.6 |
| buru | Burundi | 14.1 | 4.0 | 206,835 | 79 | 3,986 | 54,611 | 502,751 | 6,137,639 | 21 | 9,200 | 1,374.2 | 8,000 | 1,194.9 |
| camb | Cambodia | 1.2 | 6.3 | 7,447 | 353 | 4,292 | 5,685,563 | 5,363,556 | 118,600 | 48 | 600 | 53.7 | 300 | 26.9 |
| came | Cameroon | 7.2 | 4.7 | 361,608 | 134 | 13,951 | 3,027,138 | 3,884,172 | 8,173,659 | 402 | 18,500 | 1,226.4 | 15,000 | 994.4 |
| cana | Canada | 1.4 | 1.6 | 329,875 | 32 | 1,188,957 | 688,856 | 5,695,795 | 24,761,988 | 236 | 138,000 | 4,430.7 | 130,000 | 4,173.8 |
| cape | Cape Verde | 1.8 | 2.8 | 11,299 | 50 | 34,569 | 202 | 20,642 | 406,880 | 8 | 300 | 701.4 | 200 | 467.6 |
| caym | Cayman Islands | 1.8 | 4.1 | 1,054 | 86 | 122,488 | 749 | 7,856 | 29,766 | 11 | 120 | 3,127.4 | 100 | 2,606.1 |
| cent | Central African Rep | 10.5 | 4.5 | 72,018 | 134 | 7,596 | 578,728 | 586,294 | 2,450,244 | 105 | 6,000 | 1,659.6 | 5,000 | 1,383.0 |
| chad | Chad | 12.6 | 4.7 | 66,968 | 251 | 3,865 | 3,818,667 | 2,086,520 | 1,745,795 | 167 | 3,250 | 424.8 | 2,500 | 326.8 |
| chan | Channel Islands | 0.2 | 1.3 | 1,320 | 25 | 916,030 | 719 | 20,599 | 131,580 | 8 | 60 | 392.4 | 50 | 327.0 |
| chil | Chile | 1.6 | 2.1 | 278,387 | 36 | 199,616 | 61,134 | 1,586,996 | 13,563,164 | 39 | 23,000 | 1,512.0 | 15,000 | 986.1 |
| chin | China | 4.2 | 3.9 | 3,484,380 | 165 | 15,828 | 444,210,082 | 729,291,154 | 89,055,551 | 369 | 104,000 | 82.4 | 100,000 | 79.2 |
| colo | Colombia | 2.6 | 2.4 | 1,002,110 | 41 | 78,022 | 119,613 | 1,258,792 | 40,942,956 | 161 | 42,000 | 992.4 | 35,000 | 827.0 |
| como | Comoros | 4.4 | 5.0 | 353 | 361 | 9,379 | 371,333 | 214,224 | 7,192 | 12 | 60 | 101.2 | 20 | 33.7 |
| cong | Congo-Brazzaville | 5.8 | 4.5 | 106,006 | 95 | 14,964 | 28,634 | 232,228 | 2,682,602 | 108 | 7,800 | 2,649.9 | 7,000 | 2,378.2 |
| conz | Congo-Zaire | 6.1 | 4.6 | 2,160,011 | 86 | 2,619 | 461,513 | 1,937,082 | 49,255,901 | 566 | 80,000 | 1,548.8 | 65,000 | 1,258.4 |
| cook | Cook Islands | 0.8 | 1.1 | 198 | 18 | 186,219 | 10 | 424 | 19,088 | 13 | 130 | 6,659.2 | 60 | 3,073.5 |
| cost | Costa Rica | 2.5 | 3.2 | 124,154 | 54 | 81,359 | 4,553 | 133,901 | 3,884,968 | 39 | 5,000 | 1,242.7 | 3,600 | 894.8 |
| croa | Croatia | 0.5 | 1.2 | 52,098 | 20 | 265,522 | 33,972 | 179,825 | 4,258,803 | 76 | 2,700 | 603.7 | 1,200 | 268.3 |
| cuba | Cuba | 1.1 | 1.1 | 53,148 | 28 | 117,967 | 100,633 | 6,116,018 | 4,984,033 | 26 | 1,750 | 156.2 | 1,500 | 133.9 |
| cypr | Cyprus | 1.1 | 2.4 | 13,061 | 41 | 566,722 | 1,086 | 33,820 | 565,600 | 10 | 1,600 | 2,664.4 | 1,400 | 2,331.4 |
| czec | Czech Republic | -0.4 | 1.2 | 56,094 | 27 | 332,474 | 59,480 | 3,727,387 | 6,457,310 | 33 | 5,500 | 536.9 | 4,000 | 390.5 |
| denm | Denmark | 0.7 | 1.3 | 60,766 | 22 | 2,336,982 | 41,131 | 405,164 | 4,846,944 | 36 | 4,400 | 831.2 | 3,000 | 566.8 |
| djib | Djibouti | 5.8 | 2.5 | 699 | 142 | 34,274 | 345,336 | 263,782 | 28,516 | 15 | 123 | 192.9 | 50 | 78.4 |
| domi | Dominica | 0.9 | 0.4 | 298 | 8 | 668,903 | 62 | 3,600 | 67,052 | 17 | 230 | 3,252.5 | 150 | 2,121.2 |
| domr | Dominican Republic | 2.7 | 2.3 | 184,453 | 39 | 63,533 | 6,278 | 405,568 | 8,083,492 | 20 | 3,000 | 353.1 | 1,000 | 117.7 |
| ecua | Ecuador | 2.2 | 2.7 | 328,741 | 44 | 52,040 | 71,415 | 234,516 | 12,340,137 | 94 | 10,500 | 830.3 | 7,000 | 553.5 |
| egyp | Egypt | 1.7 | 2.3 | 238,712 | 81 | 34,154 | 15,303,820 | 42,820,086 | 10,345,789 | 47 | 6,500 | 94.9 | 5,000 | 73.0 |
| elsa | El Salvador | 1.8 | 2.7 | 163,061 | 46 | 60,209 | 6,319 | 147,733 | 6,121,971 | 27 | 3,400 | 541.7 | 2,000 | 318.7 |
| equa | Equatorial Guinea | 4.2 | 4.1 | 16,076 | 77 | 9,329 | 6,462 | 45,879 | 400,320 | 44 | 800 | 1,767.3 | 500 | 1,104.6 |
| erit | Eritrea | 3.5 | 4.3 | 82,384 | 113 | 13,383 | 1,017,551 | 889,321 | 1,943,516 | 42 | 1,000 | 259.7 | 800 | 207.8 |
| esto | Estonia | -0.2 | 1.6 | 8,562 | 42 | 176,980 | 26,919 | 482,686 | 886,553 | 59 | 650 | 465.6 | 500 | 358.1 |
| ethi | Ethiopia | 2.5 | 4.7 | 1,464,574 | 124 | 2,127 | 9,707,024 | 16,749,811 | 36,108,040 | 211 | 252,500 | 4,035.8 | 250,000 | 3,995.9 |
| faer | Faeroe Islands | 1.0 | 1.5 | 593 | 26 | 1,000,000 | 30 | 766 | 41,953 | 10 | 70 | 1,637.5 | 40 | 935.7 |
| fiji | Fiji | 1.6 | 1.7 | 8,031 | 41 | 139,668 | 91,621 | 261,649 | 463,635 | 77 | 2,600 | 3,182.7 | 2,000 | 2,448.3 |
| finl | Finland | 0.5 | 1.3 | 58,754 | 23 | 1,604,053 | 14,982 | 357,193 | 4,803,568 | 53 | 3,100 | 598.9 | 2,600 | 502.3 |
| fran | France | 0.0 | 1.2 | 506,149 | 24 | 2,030,056 | 2,188,393 | 15,105,381 | 41,785,935 | 173 | 216,000 | 3,656.1 | 200,000 | 3,385.3 |
| freg | French Guiana | 2.1 | 5.1 | 7,730 | 94 | 209,049 | 2,240 | 25,711 | 153,362 | 32 | 300 | 1,654.6 | 100 | 551.5 |
| frep | French Polynesia | 1.8 | 2.4 | 4,759 | 45 | 707,306 | 3,191 | 25,038 | 206,832 | 46 | 600 | 2,552.5 | 200 | 850.8 |
| gabo | Gabon | 4.2 | 4.2 | 46,112 | 83 | 82,175 | 23,478 | 91,756 | 1,110,893 | 77 | 2,400 | 1,957.4 | 2,000 | 1,631.2 |
| gamb | Gambia | 2.6 | 4.8 | 2,276 | 295 | 6,633 | 730,102 | 524,794 | 50,467 | 55 | 670 | 513.3 | 500 | 383.0 |
| geor | Georgia | 0.5 | 0.9 | 26,387 | 20 | 50,171 | 565,806 | 1,311,275 | 3,090,480 | 52 | 1,000 | 201.3 | 900 | 181.2 |
| germ | Germany | 0.4 | 1.3 | 763,006 | 24 | 2,119,414 | 1,942,922 | 17,951,407 | 62,326,161 | 133 | 310,000 | 3,770.3 | 300,000 | 3,648.7 |
| ghan | Ghana | 4.8 | 4.0 | 348,932 | 115 | 9,687 | 3,106,004 | 5,911,396 | 11,195,095 | 369 | 27,000 | 1,335.8 | 25,000 | 1,236.9 |
| gibr | Gibraltar | 0.1 | 1.5 | 320 | 27 | 440,000 | 1,359 | 2,105 | 21,618 | 13 | 60 | 2,392.2 | 20 | 797.4 |
| gree | Greece | 1.4 | 1.4 | 140,049 | 24 | 589,798 | 165,750 | 396,020 | 10,082,974 | 36 | 17,500 | 1,644.0 | 17,000 | 1,597.0 |
| grel | Greenland | 1.5 | 1.2 | 479 | 25 | 1,271,534 | 166 | 1,867 | 54,123 | 11 | 260 | 4,630.0 | 200 | 3,561.5 |
| gren | Grenada | 0.4 | 0.9 | 799 | 15 | 338,251 | 28 | 2,754 | 90,935 | 16 | 220 | 2,347.5 | 100 | 1,067.0 |
| guad | Guadeloupe | 0.9 | 2.1 | 9,078 | 36 | 438,721 | 434 | 20,980 | 434,273 | 17 | 2,400 | 5,266.8 | 2,000 | 4,389.0 |
| guam | Guam | 2.8 | 2.6 | 4,121 | 46 | 771,569 | 1,708 | 8,125 | 157,723 | 29 | 550 | 3,282.5 | 100 | 596.8 |
| guat | Guatemala | 1.9 | 3.3 | 353,324 | 58 | 40,520 | 7,929 | 253,700 | 11,123,666 | 225 | 7,500 | 658.7 | 4,000 | 351.3 |
| guin | Guinea | 5.0 | 5.1 | 11,765 | 335 | 10,814 | 4,337,014 | 2,798,103 | 295,229 | 76 | 450 | 60.6 | 350 | 47.1 |
| gunb | Guinea-Bissau | 3.5 | 4.3 | 6,742 | 233 | 5,771 | 628,702 | 424,479 | 159,930 | 59 | 230 | 189.6 | 40 | 33.0 |
| guya | Guyana | 1.0 | 1.3 | 4,754 | 35 | 46,420 | 161,535 | 260,619 | 439,180 | 42 | 1,200 | 1,393.2 | 900 | 1,044.9 |
| hait | Haiti | 1.8 | 2.8 | 215,737 | 48 | 8,852 | 5,934 | 341,421 | 7,874,670 | 21 | 4,600 | 559.5 | 3,100 | 377.0 |
| hond | Honduras | 2.5 | 3.3 | 202,808 | 58 | 17,921 | 6,422 | 187,257 | 6,291,766 | 74 | 3,300 | 508.8 | 2,500 | 385.5 |
| hung | Hungary | 0.4 | 1.1 | 98,172 | 20 | 367,201 | 65,545 | 1,206,351 | 8,763,672 | 36 | 8,200 | 817.1 | 7,000 | 697.5 |
| icel | Iceland | 1.2 | 1.5 | 4,016 | 27 | 1,647,952 | 154 | 7,726 | 273,089 | 12 | 340 | 1,210.1 | 300 | 1,067.7 |
| indi | India | 2.8 | 3.5 | 2,158,606 | 159 | 9,803 | 412,122,495 | 539,198,276 | 62,341,006 | 835 | 308,000 | 303.8 | 300,000 | 296.0 |
| indo | Indonesia | 4.0 | 2.4 | 633,811 | 102 | 40,765 | 78,805,877 | 105,497,392 | 27,804,116 | 730 | 56,000 | 264.0 | 50,000 | 235.7 |
| iran | Iran | 1.0 | 2.2 | 6,841 | 164 | 215,695 | 42,507,292 | 24,831,853 | 363,054 | 61 | 600 | 8.9 | 400 | 5.9 |
| iraq | Iraq | 1.6 | 2.1 | 15,399 | 117 | 94,117 | 11,916,962 | 10,457,144 | 740,778 | 70 | 1,580 | 68.4 | 1,500 | 64.9 |
| irel | Ireland | 0.1 | 1.3 | 44,526 | 23 | 1,108,515 | 10,277 | 96,195 | 3,623,767 | 55 | 25,500 | 6,836.0 | 25,000 | 6,702.0 |
| isle | Isle of Man | 0.4 | 1.8 | 954 | 36 | 593,406 | 292 | 8,494 | 70,380 | 9 | 124 | 1,566.3 | 120 | 1,515.8 |
| isra | Israel | 2.3 | 4.0 | 11,683 | 193 | 400,704 | 2,252,726 | 2,571,811 | 297,146 | 58 | 1,500 | 292.9 | 500 | 97.6 |
| ital | Italy | 0.4 | 1.0 | 469,221 | 19 | 1,902,000 | 436,987 | 9,850,473 | 47,010,426 | 72 | 282,000 | 4,921.6 | 270,000 | 4,712.2 |
| ivor | Ivory Coast | 9.3 | 4.2 | 183,733 | 146 | 15,639 | 4,029,608 | 6,054,370 | 4,701,854 | 235 | 9,720 | 657.4 | 8,000 | 541.1 |
| jama | Jamaica | 0.7 | 1.3 | 13,483 | 31 | 125,623 | 27,592 | 384,458 | 2,170,527 | 43 | 3,700 | 1,432.7 | 3,000 | 1,161.6 |
| japa | Japan | 3.0 | 1.5 | 50,075 | 60 | 2,720,658 | 41,890,821 | 80,263,826 | 4,559,573 | 58 | 23,500 | 185.5 | 16,000 | 126.3 |
| jord | Jordan | 3.0 | 4.6 | 12,669 | 232 | 32,599 | 3,051,282 | 3,344,170 | 273,889 | 32 | 1,000 | 149.9 | 800 | 120.0 |
| kaza | Kazakhstan | 3.2 | 2.0 | 51,836 | 78 | 66,500 | 5,799,212 | 7,713,371 | 2,709,980 | 85 | 500 | 30.8 | 300 | 18.5 |
| keny | Kenya | 8.8 | 4.1 | 931,911 | 84 | 6,753 | 1,742,085 | 4,478,448 | 23,859,839 | 330 | 41,000 | 1,363.0 | 35,000 | 1,163.5 |
| kirg | Kirgizstan | 3.4 | 3.0 | 13,970 | 159 | 23,333 | 2,473,100 | 1,737,992 | 488,245 | 68 | 200 | 42.6 | 150 | 31.9 |
| kiri | Kiribati | 1.3 | 1.8 | 1,408 | 32 | 50,521 | 60 | 4,639 | 78,688 | 11 | 550 | 6,595.8 | 500 | 5,996.1 |
| kuwa | Kuwait | 7.4 | 4.7 | 11,656 | 194 | 369,292 | 700,639 | 1,021,449 | 249,546 | 33 | 120 | 60.9 | 20 | 10.1 |
| laos | Laos | 2.7 | 3.3 | 3,697 | 190 | 10,654 | 2,849,470 | 2,470,957 | 112,609 | 82 | 620 | 114.1 | 540 | 99.4 |
| latv | Latvia | 0.3 | 0.7 | 10,987 | 14 | 325,681 | 22,603 | 756,035 | 1,577,870 | 78 | 1,200 | 509.2 | 800 | 339.5 |
| leba | Lebanon | 1.7 | 3.0 | 52,582 | 69 | 87,759 | 266,666 | 1,276,767 | 1,738,354 | 41 | 6,600 | 2,011.1 | 6,000 | 1,828.3 |
| leso | Lesotho | 4.0 | 3.2 | 46,655 | 65 | 23,853 | 8,139 | 184,442 | 1,959,972 | 40 | 4,250 | 1,974.4 | 3,600 | 1,672.4 |
| libe | Liberia | 3.6 | 4.5 | 42,194 | 164 | 17,009 | 867,108 | 1,048,172 | 1,238,721 | 152 | 2,900 | 919.5 | 2,400 | 760.9 |
| liby | Libya | 2.9 | 2.3 | 3,948 | 135 | 280,845 | 3,019,596 | 2,409,648 | 175,478 | 31 | 140 | 25.0 | 40 | 7.1 |
| liec | Liechtenstein | 1.1 | 2.0 | 541 | 37 | 1,650,000 | 538 | 1,775 | 30,530 | 11 | 50 | 1,522.4 | 30 | 913.4 |
| lith | Lithuania | 0.5 | 1.3 | 41,742 | 23 | 146,266 | 14,620 | 441,709 | 3,213,940 | 48 | 1,900 | 517.7 | 1,500 | 408.7 |
| luxe | Luxembourg | 0.6 | 2.2 | 8,742 | 38 | 1,898,203 | 3,931 | 22,270 | 404,414 | 32 | 2,040 | 4,737.4 | 2,000 | 4,644.5 |
| mace | Macedonia | 0.9 | 0.6 | 8,263 | 14 | 133,956 | 241,781 | 493,480 | 1,288,319 | 69 | 450 | 222.4 | 300 | 148.3 |
| mada | Madagascar | 2.2 | 4.4 | 332,864 | 120 | 5,271 | 2,712,337 | 5,339,031 | 7,890,359 | 85 | 16,000 | 1,003.7 | 14,000 | 878.2 |
| mala | Malawi | 6.7 | 3.9 | 277,282 | 88 | 4,311 | 431,511 | 2,105,620 | 8,388,107 | 82 | 7,500 | 686.5 | 6,000 | 549.2 |
| malb | Malaysia | 4.1 | 3.0 | 53,401 | 129 | 129,021 | 8,081,332 | 12,315,745 | 1,846,985 | 231 | 4,000 | 179.8 | 3,000 | 134.9 |

| COUNTRY | | MISSION (continued) | | | | | | | | | CHRISTIAN PERSONNEL | | | |
|---|---|---|---|---|---|---|---|---|---|---|---|---|---|---|
| | | RESPONSE/GROWTH | | | | | WORLDS A,B, and C | | | ministries | ALL WORKERS | | CITIZENS | |
| code | short name | CG% | g % | bapt p.a. | resp R | cost-eff, $ | A -individuals | B-individuals | C-individuals | peo-ags | workers | w.p.m. | workers | citw p.m. |
| 1 | 2 | 96 | 97 | 98 | 99 | 100 | 101 | 102 | 103 | 104 | 105 | 106 | 107 | 108 |
| mald | Maldives | 3.6 | 2.8 | 9 | 434 | 35,895 | 230,137 | 55,717 | 369 | 12 | 10 | 34.9 | 0 | 0.0 |
| mali | Mali | 6.0 | 4.4 | 9,869 | 275 | 5,683 | 6,340,283 | 4,668,098 | 225,440 | 108 | 1,000 | 89.0 | 400 | 35.6 |
| malt | Malta | 0.7 | 1.6 | 6,046 | 27 | 737,100 | 220 | 6,285 | 382,039 | 29 | 3,230 | 8,313.1 | 3,200 | 8,235.9 |
| mars | Marshall Islands | 2.5 | 4.2 | 2,506 | 74 | 45,312 | 42 | 2,136 | 62,042 | 6 | 130 | 2,024.3 | 50 | 778.6 |
| mart | Martinique | 0.6 | 1.6 | 5,791 | 26 | 644,745 | 507 | 11,559 | 383,296 | 16 | 1,200 | 3,035.2 | 1,000 | 2,529.3 |
| maur | Mauritania | 5.1 | 0.6 | 41 | 57 | 71,987 | 1,818,258 | 844,720 | 6,569 | 31 | 60 | 22.5 | 10 | 3.7 |
| maus | Mauritius | 1.1 | 1.7 | 6,446 | 52 | 193,696 | 290,720 | 488,624 | 377,154 | 42 | 700 | 605.3 | 400 | 345.9 |
| mayo | Mayotte | 4.2 | 4.6 | 85 | 304 | 13,040 | 60,252 | 39,147 | 2,222 | 8 | 40 | 393.6 | 10 | 98.4 |
| mexi | Mexico | 2.0 | 2.3 | 2,117,222 | 38 | 147,097 | 147,917 | 3,564,338 | 95,169,034 | 394 | 98,000 | 991.1 | 90,000 | 910.2 |
| micr | Micronesia | 1.6 | 2.5 | 2,761 | 48 | 79,102 | 441 | 7,720 | 110,528 | 34 | 580 | 4,886.7 | 100 | 842.5 |
| mold | Moldavia | 0.8 | 2.0 | 55,523 | 44 | 46,370 | 252,923 | 1,113,616 | 3,013,953 | 58 | 1,200 | 273.9 | 700 | 159.8 |
| mona | Monaco | 0.7 | 2.0 | 606 | 33 | 1,281,394 | 392 | 1,892 | 31,313 | 17 | 260 | 7,738.8 | 110 | 3,274.1 |
| mong | Mongolia | 4.2 | 3.2 | 1,056 | 202 | 9,797 | 1,522,030 | 1,106,075 | 33,915 | 25 | 500 | 187.8 | 100 | 37.6 |
| mont | Montserrat | -0.1 | 1.5 | 152 | 27 | 835,133 | 7 | 413 | 10,209 | 13 | 30 | 2,822.5 | 20 | 1,881.6 |
| moro | Morocco | 1.8 | 2.5 | 4,279 | 159 | 45,250 | 16,314,645 | 11,730,763 | 175,435 | 42 | 1,800 | 63.8 | 300 | 10.6 |
| moza | Mozambique | 6.4 | 5.9 | 378,135 | 191 | 1,366 | 4,521,300 | 7,606,979 | 7,552,177 | 140 | 11,200 | 569.1 | 8,000 | 406.5 |
| myan | Myanmar | 2.8 | 2.9 | 109,662 | 129 | 61,071 | 17,852,271 | 23,985,544 | 3,773,362 | 127 | 7,700 | 168.8 | 7,500 | 164.4 |
| nami | Namibia | 5.2 | 4.8 | 64,654 | 92 | 41,736 | 39,161 | 94,399 | 1,592,308 | 63 | 2,800 | 1,622.4 | 1,600 | 927.1 |
| naur | Nauru | 3.4 | 2.2 | 186 | 46 | 360,107 | 410 | 2,472 | 8,637 | 14 | 30 | 2,604.4 | 10 | 868.1 |
| nepa | Nepal | 11.6 | 5.4 | 31,009 | 319 | 3,715 | 12,866,777 | 10,487,030 | 576,683 | 65 | 1,500 | 62.7 | 600 | 25.1 |
| neth | Netherlands | 0.7 | 1.3 | 134,705 | 26 | 1,832,061 | 373,557 | 2,718,199 | 12,693,943 | 74 | 47,100 | 2,983.7 | 45,000 | 2,850.7 |
| nets | Netherlands Antilles | 1.8 | 1.9 | 3,570 | 35 | 538,581 | 1,547 | 10,498 | 204,730 | 35 | 750 | 3,459.8 | 150 | 692.0 |
| newc | New Caledonia | 1.5 | 2.8 | 4,472 | 56 | 289,226 | 2,965 | 24,869 | 186,195 | 108 | 600 | 2,803.4 | 300 | 1,401.7 |
| newz | New Zealand | 1.3 | 1.9 | 48,169 | 37 | 762,765 | 35,988 | 601,577 | 3,224,340 | 154 | 9,300 | 2,408.1 | 6,500 | 1,683.1 |
| nica | Nicaragua | 2.4 | 3.4 | 164,472 | 57 | 11,222 | 7,125 | 181,337 | 4,885,732 | 78 | 5,000 | 985.4 | 3,000 | 591.2 |
| niga | Niger | 9.1 | 4.9 | 2,850 | 318 | 4,497 | 6,208,244 | 4,463,281 | 58,577 | 97 | 530 | 49.4 | 80 | 7.5 |
| nige | Nigeria | 6.4 | 4.1 | 2,072,237 | 111 | 6,394 | 22,559,535 | 37,823,393 | 51,123,167 | 661 | 55,300 | 495.9 | 50,000 | 448.4 |
| nork | North Korea | 3.6 | 2.5 | 12,380 | 136 | 38,383 | 12,026,315 | 11,510,232 | 502,646 | 4 | 170 | 7.1 | 150 | 6.2 |
| norl | Northern Cyprus | 4.8 | 1.7 | 270 | 75 | 739,094 | 81,374 | 87,269 | 16,402 | 1 | 90 | 486.4 | 50 | 270.2 |
| norm | Northern Mariana Is | 3.4 | 6.5 | 4,523 | 122 | 160,771 | 836 | 7,889 | 69,631 | 3 | 160 | 2,042.0 | 40 | 510.5 |
| norw | Norway | 0.7 | 1.4 | 59,952 | 23 | 2,189,908 | 61,076 | 191,843 | 4,208,114 | 55 | 3,700 | 829.4 | 2,700 | 605.2 |
| oman | Oman | 8.7 | 5.3 | 6,425 | 302 | 91,461 | 1,347,866 | 1,069,746 | 124,127 | 10 | 90 | 35.4 | 50 | 19.7 |
| paki | Pakistan | 3.8 | 3.8 | 144,674 | 223 | 12,121 | 83,307,766 | 69,324,793 | 3,850,596 | 153 | 4,500 | 28.8 | 3,000 | 19.2 |
| pala | Palau | 2.2 | 2.9 | 525 | 52 | 174,764 | 11 | 822 | 18,593 | 6 | 40 | 2,059.1 | 20 | 1,029.5 |
| pale | Palestine | 1.8 | 3.3 | 6,238 | 127 | 440,205 | 650,425 | 1,375,327 | 189,641 | 32 | 1,600 | 722.2 | 400 | 180.6 |
| pana | Panama | 2.6 | 2.1 | 52,802 | 38 | 127,966 | 47,114 | 290,405 | 2,518,164 | 97 | 2,800 | 980.5 | 700 | 245.1 |
| papu | Papua New Guinea | 5.0 | 3.4 | 127,572 | 76 | 34,421 | 113,957 | 114,273 | 4,379,915 | 932 | 17,600 | 3,819.3 | 14,000 | 3,038.1 |
| para | Paraguay | 2.2 | 3.2 | 164,365 | 54 | 53,194 | 10,063 | 115,564 | 5,370,826 | 123 | 3,500 | 636.8 | 2,300 | 418.5 |
| peru | Peru | 2.0 | 2.3 | 574,569 | 39 | 99,312 | 68,433 | 644,093 | 24,949,143 | 321 | 15,800 | 615.7 | 9,000 | 350.7 |
| phil | Philippines | 2.4 | 2.8 | 1,840,825 | 51 | 37,988 | 4,222,787 | 3,592,289 | 68,151,424 | 532 | 59,500 | 783.2 | 50,000 | 658.2 |
| pola | Poland | 0.6 | 1.2 | 464,601 | 21 | 225,181 | 16,713 | 990,216 | 37,758,156 | 45 | 75,700 | 1,952.8 | 75,000 | 1,934.7 |
| port | Portugal | 0.5 | 1.0 | 94,162 | 16 | 939,247 | 35,999 | 717,800 | 9,121,054 | 66 | 14,750 | 1,493.7 | 14,000 | 1,417.7 |
| puer | Puerto Rico | 1.4 | 1.7 | 63,390 | 28 | 458,015 | 3,864 | 111,138 | 3,753,600 | 32 | 5,500 | 1,421.7 | 3,000 | 775.5 |
| qata | Qatar | 7.0 | 3.3 | 1,968 | 152 | 351,515 | 261,389 | 275,417 | 62,259 | 28 | 40 | 66.8 | 30 | 50.1 |
| reun | Reunion | 2.3 | 1.9 | 11,735 | 35 | 222,452 | 19,656 | 65,959 | 613,791 | 22 | 2,640 | 3,774.6 | 2,400 | 3,431.5 |
| roma | Romania | 0.7 | 1.0 | 202,358 | 18 | 143,549 | 162,918 | 2,524,231 | 19,639,353 | 43 | 30,000 | 1,343.7 | 29,000 | 1,298.9 |
| russ | Russia | 0.4 | 1.7 | 1,442,416 | 37 | 129,855 | 9,923,477 | 52,702,172 | 84,308,198 | 183 | 219,000 | 1,490.5 | 200,000 | 1,361.2 |
| rwan | Rwanda | 11.6 | 3.2 | 202,017 | 60 | 5,646 | 88,387 | 1,247,774 | 6,396,966 | 43 | 5,200 | 672.4 | 4,000 | 517.3 |
| saha | Sahara | 1.6 | 1.3 | 6 | 164 | 15,622 | 221,118 | 71,752 | 487 | 2 | 10 | 34.1 | 0 | 0.0 |
| saih | Saint Helena | 0.6 | 1.6 | 84 | 28 | 569,620 | 9 | 223 | 6,061 | 13 | 30 | 4,767.2 | 10 | 1,589.1 |
| saik | Saint Kitts & Nevis | -0.1 | 1.5 | 540 | 27 | 344,666 | 28 | 1,974 | 36,471 | 24 | 140 | 3,638.9 | 100 | 2,599.2 |
| sail | Saint Lucia | 1.1 | 2.0 | 2,824 | 35 | 172,202 | 1,573 | 4,413 | 148,380 | 20 | 300 | 1,943.4 | 150 | 971.7 |
| saip | Saint Pierre & Miquelon | 0.2 | 1.2 | 74 | 20 | 947,459 | 4 | 168 | 6,395 | 3 | 55 | 8,375.2 | 15 | 2,284.1 |
| saiv | Saint Vincent | 0.6 | 1.2 | 907 | 25 | 197,061 | 1,389 | 10,996 | 101,569 | 36 | 160 | 1,404.1 | 80 | 702.0 |
| samo | Samoa | 1.7 | 1.6 | 2,662 | 26 | 71,156 | 113 | 6,032 | 173,928 | 24 | 3,300 | 18,325.9 | 2,500 | 13,883.3 |
| sanm | San Marino | 1.1 | 2.3 | 542 | 37 | 1,083,333 | 31 | 2,049 | 24,434 | 6 | 40 | 1,508.6 | 20 | 754.3 |
| saot | Sao Tome & Principe | 5.0 | 3.7 | 4,935 | 67 | 9,368 | 142 | 6,074 | 140,559 | 11 | 120 | 817.6 | 20 | 136.3 |
| saud | Saudi Arabia | 11.9 | 3.8 | 29,763 | 185 | 186,144 | 9,735,310 | 11,073,316 | 798,065 | 38 | 130 | 6.0 | 30 | 1.4 |
| sene | Senegal | 3.5 | 4.0 | 18,869 | 235 | 14,858 | 5,118,446 | 3,840,197 | 522,518 | 123 | 2,000 | 210.9 | 800 | 84.4 |
| seyc | Seychelles | 1.4 | 1.7 | 1,195 | 29 | 397,597 | 348 | 2,091 | 74,996 | 9 | 220 | 2,841.1 | 70 | 904.0 |
| sier | Sierra Leone | 2.5 | 5.0 | 25,356 | 230 | 3,623 | 1,981,739 | 2,316,971 | 555,673 | 95 | 1,900 | 391.4 | 1,200 | 247.2 |
| sing | Singapore | 3.9 | 2.7 | 10,899 | 99 | 988,170 | 974,057 | 2,154,964 | 437,593 | 124 | 1,800 | 504.7 | 800 | 224.3 |
| slok | Slovakia | 0.1 | 1.1 | 46,830 | 23 | 272,391 | 25,349 | 751,390 | 4,610,452 | 0 | 2,800 | 519.8 | 1,800 | 334.1 |
| slov | Slovenia | 0.7 | 1.4 | 24,836 | 25 | 573,426 | 3,933 | 152,143 | 1,829,481 | 52 | 2,200 | 1,108.0 | 1,400 | 705.1 |
| solo | Solomon Islands | 3.5 | 3.9 | 15,575 | 78 | 23,556 | 471 | 18,548 | 424,624 | 112 | 1,700 | 3,831.9 | 1,200 | 2,704.9 |
| soma | Somalia | 5.2 | 0.9 | 927 | 57 | 53,134 | 4,080,364 | 3,082,255 | 101,881 | 19 | 80 | 11.0 | 30 | 4.1 |
| somi | Somaliland | 7.0 | 3.7 | 306 | 219 | 4,245 | 1,566,720 | 1,257,556 | 8,401 | 6 | 20 | 7.1 | 10 | 3.5 |
| soua | South Africa | 3.3 | 3.8 | 1,212,882 | 70 | 82,852 | 781,832 | 6,030,845 | 33,563,902 | 169 | 92,000 | 2,278.5 | 80,000 | 1,981.3 |
| souk | South Korea | 6.3 | 1.8 | 344,680 | 48 | 525,745 | 560,817 | 27,185,788 | 19,097,384 | 19 | 52,800 | 1,127.1 | 50,000 | 1,067.4 |
| spai | Spain | 0.7 | 1.0 | 381,117 | 17 | 1,321,011 | 125,103 | 2,397,563 | 37,107,109 | 81 | 172,500 | 4,352.8 | 170,000 | 4,289.7 |
| span | Spanish North Africa | 1.6 | 0.5 | 503 | 9 | 1,656,314 | 8,550 | 17,126 | 104,324 | 6 | 60 | 461.5 | 10 | 76.9 |
| sril | Sri Lanka | 1.6 | 1.7 | 30,205 | 73 | 40,674 | 6,670,591 | 10,392,860 | 1,763,603 | 57 | 4,200 | 223.1 | 2,500 | 132.8 |
| suda | Sudan | 8.0 | 3.4 | 165,095 | 163 | 23,619 | 13,620,937 | 10,947,827 | 4,920,955 | 177 | 3,700 | 125.5 | 3,000 | 101.7 |
| suri | Suriname | 1.7 | 0.9 | 1,478 | 25 | 102,564 | 67,699 | 139,228 | 210,203 | 66 | 700 | 1,678.1 | 300 | 719.2 |
| swaz | Swaziland | 7.2 | 4.2 | 28,915 | 86 | 27,548 | 6,491 | 126,096 | 875,308 | 34 | 2,800 | 2,778.1 | 2,000 | 1,984.3 |
| swed | Sweden | 0.2 | 1.4 | 83,164 | 27 | 1,713,564 | 140,311 | 2,718,098 | 6,051,805 | 112 | 9,000 | 1,010.1 | 8,000 | 897.8 |
| swit | Switzerland | 0.7 | 1.5 | 98,616 | 26 | 2,655,555 | 130,557 | 727,846 | 6,527,305 | 85 | 20,200 | 2,735.0 | 18,000 | 2,437.1 |
| syri | Syria | 1.5 | 2.4 | 30,574 | 103 | 46,071 | 6,092,966 | 8,768,933 | 1,262,719 | 54 | 800 | 49.6 | 700 | 43.4 |
| taiw | Taiwan | 5.3 | 1.6 | 18,486 | 62 | 791,321 | 6,977,716 | 14,012,974 | 1,410,310 | 73 | 7,000 | 312.5 | 4,000 | 178.6 |
| taji | Tajikistan | 3.3 | 2.5 | 3,240 | 152 | 13,600 | 3,457,770 | 2,599,837 | 130,594 | 61 | 70 | 11.3 | 30 | 4.8 |
| tanz | Tanzania | 5.5 | 4.8 | 756,108 | 139 | 2,495 | 6,227,819 | 10,406,634 | 16,882,561 | 376 | 27,500 | 820.5 | 23,000 | 686.2 |
| thai | Thailand | 3.7 | 2.1 | 28,907 | 103 | 127,501 | 26,509,177 | 33,528,284 | 1,361,788 | 265 | 4,000 | 65.1 | 2,000 | 32.6 |
| timo | Timor | 2.9 | 3.2 | 26,386 | 67 | 19,901 | 10,692 | 57,890 | 815,959 | 43 | 300 | 339.2 | 200 | 226.1 |
| togo | Togo | 6.5 | 4.8 | 83,326 | 148 | 6,507 | 1,118,285 | 1,539,323 | 1,971,610 | 154 | 1,800 | 388.8 | 1,200 | 259.2 |
| tong | Tonga | 1.5 | 0.5 | 478 | 9 | 305,243 | 91 | 6,867 | 91,588 | 22 | 1,000 | 10,147.5 | 600 | 6,088.5 |
| trin | Trinidad & Tobago | 1.4 | 1.0 | 8,125 | 23 | 369,245 | 109,423 | 348,544 | 836,991 | 48 | 1,200 | 926.7 | 700 | 540.6 |
| tuni | Tunisia | -0.9 | 1.7 | 840 | 92 | 109,309 | 4,897,282 | 4,636,763 | 51,566 | 27 | 240 | 25.0 | 40 | 4.2 |
| turk | Turkey | -2.1 | 1.2 | 4,533 | 66 | 228,806 | 34,243,536 | 31,958,647 | 388,757 | 78 | 900 | 13.5 | 400 | 6.0 |
| turm | Turkmenistan | 3.1 | 2.5 | 2,472 | 195 | 36,800 | 2,918,902 | 1,438,743 | 101,648 | 64 | 70 | 15.7 | 20 | 4.5 |
| turs | Turks & Caicos Is | 1.0 | 3.8 | 508 | 75 | 56,606 | 35 | 1,376 | 15,349 | 20 | 30 | 1,790.0 | 20 | 1,193.3 |
| tuva | Tuvalu | 1.4 | 3.1 | 300 | 58 | 25,940 | 20 | 1,238 | 10,461 | 18 | 40 | 3,413.3 | 30 | 2,559.9 |
| ugan | Uganda | 5.1 | 4.8 | 907,994 | 89 | 5,007 | 195,502 | 2,261,835 | 19,321,113 | 175 | 32,600 | 1,496.9 | 30,000 | 1,377.5 |
| ukra | Ukraine | 0.5 | 1.4 | 588,367 | 25 | 115,439 | 752,837 | 7,834,697 | 41,868,446 | 93 | 10,200 | 202.2 | 6,000 | 118.9 |
| unia | United Arab Emirates | 8.9 | 3.3 | 8,623 | 147 | 530,164 | 1,028,415 | 1,142,777 | 270,244 | 67 | 220 | 90.1 | 100 | 41.0 |
| usa | USA | 1.3 | 1.7 | 3,335,882 | 32 | 1,551,466 | 4,084,367 | 38,531,122 | 235,741,652 | 519 | 1,533,200 | 5,508.0 | 1,500,000 | 5,388.8 |
| uuay | Uruguay | 1.3 | 1.6 | 34,198 | 33 | 326,801 | 43,093 | 1,115,569 | 2,178,396 | 66 | 5,200 | 1,558.3 | 2,200 | 659.3 |
| uzbe | Uzbekistan | 3.1 | 2.0 | 7,886 | 113 | 48,500 | 12,558,682 | 11,358,026 | 401,143 | 81 | 250 | 10.3 | 50 | 2.1 |
| vanu | Vanuatu | 2.6 | 3.2 | 5,431 | 63 | 37,570 | 1,304 | 11,991 | 177,122 | 226 | 700 | 3,676.1 | 400 | 2,100.7 |
| vene | Venezuela | 2.3 | 2.6 | 599,771 | 44 | 114,480 | 149,477 | 1,110,150 | 22,910,095 | 126 | 14,000 | 579.2 | 7,000 | 289.6 |
| viet | Viet Nam | 2.0 | 3.0 | 197,431 | 123 | 7,984 | 26,516,153 | 46,729,168 | 6,586,329 | 107 | 17,200 | 215.5 | 16,000 | 200.4 |
| virg | Virgin Is of the US | 1.1 | 1.5 | 1,292 | 26 | 782,666 | 390 | 3,044 | 89,520 | 35 | 300 | 3,227.4 | 150 | 1,613.7 |
| wall | Wallis & Futuna Is | 2.3 | 1.1 | 149 | 21 | 437,406 | 5 | 323 | 14,189 | 5 | 80 | 5,510.8 | 50 | 3,444.2 |
| yeme | Yemen | 1.9 | 4.6 | 1,423 | 282 | 5,601 | 9,673,610 | 8,406,264 | 32,192 | 32 | 230 | 12.7 | 80 | 4.4 |
| yugo | Yugoslavia | 0.8 | 1.9 | 132,133 | 40 | 104,220 | 702,914 | 2,712,500 | 7,224,736 | 75 | 9,000 | 845.9 | 8,000 | 751.9 |
| zamb | Zambia | 8.5 | 4.4 | 313,465 | 90 | 8,998 | 113,566 | 1,503,728 | 7,551,406 | 207 | 7,200 | 785.3 | 4,000 | 436.3 |
| zimb | Zimbabwe | 6.3 | 3.9 | 271,298 | 87 | 13,768 | 207,516 | 3,591,134 | 7,870,379 | 153 | 8,700 | 745.6 | 6,000 | 514.2 |
| | 11 minicountries | 0.2 | 1.7 | 258 | 40 | 1,349,544 | 1,924 | 6,381 | 14,774 | 54 | 1,221 | 52,905.2 | 950 | 41,163.0 |
| | Africa | 3.7 | 4.1 | 14,373,418 | 117 | 13,888 | 176,794,822 | 247,418,035 | 360,232,182 | 6,872 | 798,793 | 1,018.3 | 708,330 | 903.0 |
| | Antarctica | 6.0 | 4.8 | 162 | 138 | 1,677,852 | 243 | 857 | 3,400 | 0 | 30 | 6,666.7 | 20 | 4,444.4 |
| | Asia | 2.7 | 3.1 | 9,630,494 | 135 | 61,071 | 1,423,824,293 | 1,945,876,370 | 312,849,430 | 5,344 | 681,440 | 185.0 | 623,470 | 169.3 |
| | Europe | 0.4 | 1.3 | 7,023,145 | 25 | 993,371 | 21,474,187 | 147,770,219 | 559,642,545 | 2,653 | 1,809,539 | 2,482.6 | 1,703,840 | 2,337.6 |
| | Latin America | 2.1 | 2.3 | 10,864,866 | 38 | 144,910 | 1,944,600 | 36,091,075 | 481,102,373 | 3,291 | 462,401 | 890.7 | 354,280 | 682.4 |
| | Northern America | 1.3 | 1.7 | 3,667,019 | 32 | 1,518,991 | 4,773,514 | 44,233,191 | 260,624,388 | 777 | 1,671,765 | 5,399.2 | 1,630,365 | 5,265.5 |
| | Oceania | 1.6 | 2.1 | 454,646 | 43 | 634,479 | 563,298 | 4,720,573 | 25,109,520 | 2,150 | 99,846 | 3,285.1 | 84,080 | 2,766.4 |
| | **World A** | **0.8** | **2.4** | **332,049** | **149** | **31,768** | **334,256,241** | **260,720,907** | **10,326,848** | **1,848** | **20,518** | **33.9** | **10,340** | **17.1** |
| | **World B** | **1.8** | **2.9** | **16,177,799** | **115** | **47,718** | **1,269,343,426** | **1,972,637,223** | **513,031,343** | **8,181** | **1,309,120** | **348.6** | **1,206,055** | **321.2** |
| | **World C** | **1.2** | **2.1** | **29,503,902** | **38** | **488,585** | **25,775,290** | **192,752,190** | **1,476,205,647** | **11,058** | **4,194,176** | **2,474.8** | **3,887,990** | **2,294.2** |
| | **GLOBAL TOTAL** | **1.3** | **2.3** | **46,013,752** | **68** | **330,286** | **1,629,374,957** | **2,426,110,320** | **1,999,563,838** | **21,087** | **5,523,814** | **912.3** | **5,104,385** | **843.0** |

| COUNTRY | | GLOBAL MISSION SHARING | | | | CHRISTIAN LITERATURE | | | | | | | SCRIPTURES | | | | | |
|---|---|---|---|---|---|---|---|---|---|---|---|---|---|---|---|---|---|---|
| | | citizens sent | | aliens received | | libraries | | book on country's Christians | | | periodicals | | Bible distribution | | | | | |
| code | short name | total | p.m.a. | total | p.m. | total | p.m. | total | 1970–99 | p.a. | total | p.m. | goal | goal p.a. | UBS p.a. | other p.a. | total p.a. | T/G% |
| 1 | 2 | 109 | 110 | 111 | 112 | 113 | 114 | 115 | 116 | 117 | 118 | 119 | 120 | 121 | 122 | 123 | 124 | 125 |
| afgh | Afghanistan | 0 | 0.0 | 50 | 2.2 | 0 | 0.0 | 20 | 8 | 0 | 0 | 0 | 399 | 19 | 40 | 10 | 50 | 250 |
| alba | Albania | 50 | 46.7 | 800 | 257.0 | 0 | 0.0 | 72 | 64 | 3 | 5 | 2 | 201,647 | 10,082 | 8,002 | 5,334 | 13,336 | 132 |
| alge | Algeria | 20 | 220.1 | 500 | 15.9 | 10 | 0.3 | 470 | 230 | 9 | 10 | 0 | 7,502 | 375 | 300 | 33 | 333 | 88 |
| amer | American Samoa | 60 | 1,086.2 | 200 | 2,937.3 | 0 | 0.0 | 10 | 0 | 0 | 8 | 117 | 6,373 | 318 | 1,400 | 73 | 1,473 | 462 |
| ando | Andorra | 40 | 569.8 | 10 | 128.2 | 1 | 12.8 | 9 | 9 | 0 | 1 | 13 | 19,326 | 966 | 1,300 | 144 | 1,444 | 149 |
| ango | Angola | 320 | 29.3 | 2,000 | 155.3 | 12 | 0.9 | 122 | 49 | 2 | 40 | 3 | 796,991 | 39,849 | 70,702 | 4,593 | 75,295 | 188 |
| angu | Anguilla | 5 | 695.8 | 10 | 1,203.5 | 1 | 120.4 | 4 | 0 | 0 | 4 | 481 | 1,498 | 74 | 200 | 10 | 210 | 280 |
| anti | Antigua | 2 | 37.2 | 70 | 1,036.1 | 0 | 0.0 | 10 | 2 | 0 | 7 | 104 | 13,576 | 678 | 700 | 77 | 777 | 114 |
| arge | Argentina | 1,800 | 53.0 | 12,000 | 324.1 | 90 | 2.4 | 1,001 | 591 | 24 | 200 | 5 | 9,606,646 | 480,332 | 145,797 | 198,876 | 344,673 | 71 |
| arme | Armenia | 100 | 33.9 | 50 | 14.2 | 0 | 0.0 | 501 | 260 | 10 | 10 | 3 | 584,002 | 29,200 | 7,819 | 44,307 | 52,126 | 178 |
| arub | Aruba | 4 | 42.0 | 11 | 107.1 | 0 | 0.0 | 6 | 4 | 0 | 1 | 10 | 20,015 | 1,000 | 1,000 | 666 | 1,666 | 166 |
| aust | Australia | 5,500 | 436.7 | 4,400 | 233.1 | 110 | 5.8 | 3,195 | 2,459 | 98 | 400 | 21 | 4,013,329 | 200,666 | 323,195 | 91,157 | 414,352 | 206 |
| ausz | Austria | 2,500 | 361.8 | 1,500 | 182.7 | 190 | 23.1 | 2,185 | 1,093 | 44 | 550 | 67 | 2,613,771 | 130,688 | 12,698 | 52,755 | 65,453 | 50 |
| azer | Azerbaijan | 15 | 41.9 | 100 | 12.9 | 0 | 0.0 | 18 | 15 | 1 | 1 | 0 | 74,505 | 3,725 | 18,542 | 187 | 18,729 | 502 |
| baha | Bahamas | 20 | 74.9 | 300 | 978.7 | 2 | 6.5 | 45 | 32 | 1 | 12 | 39 | 63,559 | 3,177 | 2,000 | 4,666 | 6,666 | 209 |
| bahr | Bahrain | 5 | 79.7 | 50 | 81.0 | 0 | 0.0 | 10 | 7 | 0 | 4 | 6 | 7,132 | 356 | 200 | 600 | 800 | 224 |
| bang | Bangladesh | 30 | 32.2 | 1,000 | 7.7 | 20 | 0.2 | 68 | 58 | 2 | 40 | 0 | 59,688 | 2,984 | 3,225 | 402 | 3,627 | 121 |
| barb | Barbados | 10 | 50.8 | 200 | 739.5 | 5 | 18.5 | 62 | 40 | 2 | 15 | 55 | 50,728 | 2,536 | 10,600 | 2,650 | 13,250 | 522 |
| belg | Belgium | 10,200 | 1,197.4 | 2,600 | 255.9 | 260 | 25.6 | 1,594 | 721 | 29 | 300 | 30 | 3,125,982 | 156,299 | 13,750 | 50,203 | 63,953 | 40 |
| beli | Belize | 10 | 50.7 | 400 | 1,661.8 | 0 | 0.0 | 27 | 23 | 1 | 10 | 42 | 25,140 | 1,257 | 2,000 | 500 | 2,500 | 198 |
| belo | Belorussia | 100 | 15.2 | 500 | 48.8 | 0 | 0.0 | 97 | 66 | 3 | 20 | 2 | 1,940,202 | 97,010 | 35,710 | 35,710 | 71,420 | 73 |
| beni | Benin | 50 | 29.7 | 600 | 98.4 | 13 | 2.1 | 60 | 38 | 2 | 25 | 4 | 99,188 | 4,959 | 29,349 | 1,544 | 30,893 | 622 |
| berm | Bermuda | 10 | 179.6 | 100 | 1,548.2 | 0 | 0.0 | 43 | 14 | 1 | 40 | 619 | 20,001 | 1,000 | 1,000 | 666 | 1,666 | 166 |
| bhut | Bhutan | 2 | 207.3 | 200 | 94.2 | 0 | 0.0 | 20 | 15 | 1 | 0 | 0 | 692 | 34 | 40 | 2 | 42 | 121 |
| boli | Bolivia | 2,800 | 359.6 | 4,200 | 504.3 | 62 | 7.4 | 392 | 242 | 10 | 100 | 12 | 1,520,924 | 76,046 | 81,550 | 20,771 | 102,321 | 134 |
| bosn | Bosnia-Herzegovina | 250 | 180.4 | 550 | 138.5 | 0 | 0.0 | 50 | 3 | 0 | 20 | 5 | 378,487 | 18,924 | 9,000 | 1,000 | 10,000 | 52 |
| bots | Botswana | 80 | 106.5 | 400 | 246.6 | 5 | 3.1 | 52 | 43 | 2 | 40 | 25 | 79,665 | 3,983 | 20,617 | 1,085 | 21,702 | 544 |
| boug | Bougainville | 10 | 54.0 | 100 | 503.8 | 0 | 0.0 | 5 | 3 | 0 | 10 | 50 | 34,383 | 1,719 | 3,000 | 92 | 3,092 | 179 |
| braz | Brazil | 20,000 | 128.6 | 25,000 | 147.0 | 450 | 2.6 | 3,280 | 2,351 | 94 | 500 | 3 | 28,993,076 | 1,449,653 | 1,838,680 | 4,751,570 | 6,590,250 | 454 |
| brit | Britain | 18,500 | 473.7 | 15,000 | 255.0 | 480 | 8.2 | 18,527 | 4,662 | 186 | 2,000 | 34 | 13,701,830 | 685,091 | 247,014 | 855,727 | 1,102,741 | 161 |
| briz | British Virgin Is | 4 | 268.6 | 10 | 468.0 | 0 | 0.0 | 12 | 5 | 0 | 2 | 94 | 3,070 | 153 | 400 | 600 | 1,000 | 651 |
| brun | Brunei | 2 | 81.3 | 30 | 91.4 | 0 | 0.0 | 12 | 2 | 0 | 4 | 12 | 3,509 | 175 | 300 | 75 | 375 | 213 |
| bulg | Bulgaria | 100 | 15.0 | 200 | 24.3 | 135 | 16.4 | 768 | 380 | 15 | 20 | 2 | 2,012,363 | 100,618 | 22,593 | 52,717 | 75,310 | 74 |
| burk | Burkina Faso | 40 | 20.2 | 1,000 | 83.8 | 14 | 1.2 | 41 | 25 | 1 | 10 | 1 | 52,537 | 2,626 | 15,133 | 796 | 15,929 | 606 |
| buru | Burundi | 150 | 29.1 | 1,200 | 179.2 | 17 | 2.5 | 55 | 28 | 1 | 20 | 3 | 362,725 | 18,136 | 8,927 | 5,951 | 14,878 | 82 |
| camb | Cambodia | 4 | 33.8 | 300 | 26.9 | 0 | 0.0 | 29 | 22 | 1 | 5 | 0 | 12,052 | 602 | 4,927 | 49 | 4,976 | 825 |
| came | Cameroon | 400 | 51.5 | 3,500 | 232.0 | 21 | 1.4 | 291 | 228 | 9 | 40 | 3 | 801,509 | 40,075 | 28,117 | 2,985 | 31,102 | 77 |
| cana | Canada | 16,500 | 815.3 | 8,000 | 256.8 | 250 | 8.0 | 5,856 | 2,578 | 103 | 800 | 26 | 6,940,684 | 347,034 | 87,294 | 300,679 | 387,973 | 111 |
| cape | Cape Verde | 80 | 196.6 | 100 | 233.8 | 3 | 7.0 | 28 | 15 | 1 | 5 | 12 | 50,827 | 2,541 | 3,000 | 157 | 3,157 | 124 |
| caym | Cayman Islands | 2 | 77.5 | 20 | 521.2 | 0 | 0.0 | 5 | 3 | 0 | 4 | 104 | 5,067 | 253 | 300 | 75 | 375 | 148 |
| cent | Central African Rep | 80 | 49.7 | 1,000 | 276.6 | 8 | 2.2 | 40 | 33 | 1 | 20 | 6 | 180,773 | 9,038 | 18,724 | 189 | 18,913 | 209 |
| chad | Chad | 30 | 20.9 | 750 | 98.0 | 8 | 1.0 | 24 | 23 | 1 | 15 | 2 | 154,448 | 7,722 | 11,698 | 118 | 11,816 | 153 |
| chan | Channel Islands | 15 | 148.8 | 10 | 65.4 | 5 | 32.7 | 30 | 9 | 0 | 10 | 65 | 48,809 | 2,440 | 4,000 | 6,000 | 10,000 | 409 |
| chil | Chile | 1,700 | 127.3 | 8,000 | 525.9 | 50 | 3.3 | 1,160 | 779 | 31 | 200 | 13 | 2,898,028 | 144,901 | 89,305 | 124,343 | 213,648 | 147 |
| chin | China | 5,000 | 56.2 | 4,000 | 3.2 | 10 | 0.0 | 4,645 | 1,956 | 78 | 50 | 0 | 15,601,316 | 780,065 | 3,400,000 | 600,000 | 4,000,000 | 512 |
| colo | Colombia | 3,500 | 85.5 | 7,000 | 165.4 | 120 | 2.8 | 910 | 460 | 18 | 150 | 4 | 6,315,030 | 315,751 | 419,202 | 553,424 | 972,626 | 308 |
| como | Comoros | 2 | 283.2 | 40 | 67.5 | 0 | 0.0 | 10 | 8 | 0 | 0 | 0 | 617 | 30 | 40 | 17 | 57 | 185 |
| cong | Congo-Brazzaville | 120 | 51.4 | 800 | 271.8 | 7 | 2.4 | 34 | 15 | 1 | 20 | 7 | 320,867 | 16,043 | 12,594 | 29,386 | 41,980 | 261 |
| conz | Congo-Zaire | 1,000 | 21.2 | 15,000 | 290.4 | 130 | 2.5 | 1,011 | 600 | 24 | 150 | 3 | 5,340,910 | 267,045 | 294,827 | 64,718 | 359,545 | 134 |
| cook | Cook Islands | 10 | 540.8 | 70 | 3,585.7 | 2 | 102.4 | 9 | 7 | 0 | 5 | 256 | 3,293 | 164 | 600 | 257 | 857 | 520 |
| cost | Costa Rica | 700 | 180.9 | 1,400 | 348.0 | 20 | 5.0 | 223 | 169 | 7 | 50 | 12 | 771,920 | 38,596 | 88,581 | 124,867 | 213,448 | 553 |
| croa | Croatia | 300 | 70.5 | 1,500 | 335.4 | 0 | 0.0 | 512 | 376 | 15 | 30 | 7 | 1,305,774 | 65,288 | 1,800 | 4,200 | 6,000 | 9 |
| cuba | Cuba | 20 | 4.1 | 250 | 22.3 | 11 | 1.0 | 441 | 254 | 10 | 20 | 2 | 1,224,535 | 61,226 | 106,765 | 11,862 | 118,627 | 193 |
| cypr | Cyprus | 50 | 90.6 | 200 | 333.1 | 16 | 26.6 | 212 | 144 | 6 | 10 | 17 | 141,301 | 7,065 | 1,725 | 3,733 | 5,458 | 77 |
| czec | Czech Republic | 250 | 51.9 | 1,500 | 146.4 | 14 | 1.4 | 708 | 291 | 12 | 30 | 3 | 1,756,067 | 87,803 | 24,211 | 6,052 | 30,263 | 34 |
| denm | Denmark | 600 | 126.3 | 1,400 | 264.5 | 30 | 5.7 | 1,773 | 681 | 27 | 250 | 47 | 2,143,367 | 107,168 | 29,537 | 19,691 | 49,228 | 45 |
| djib | Djibouti | 5 | 177.3 | 73 | 114.5 | 0 | 0.0 | 10 | 1 | 0 | 0 | 0 | 2,388 | 119 | 100 | 42 | 142 | 119 |
| domi | Dominica | 5 | 74.9 | 80 | 1,131.3 | 1 | 14.1 | 14 | 12 | 0 | 10 | 141 | 14,040 | 702 | 800 | 88 | 888 | 126 |
| domr | Dominican Republic | 130 | 16.2 | 2,000 | 235.4 | 12 | 1.4 | 253 | 191 | 8 | 25 | 3 | 1,192,644 | 59,632 | 68,464 | 31,629 | 100,093 | 167 |
| ecua | Ecuador | 400 | 32.5 | 3,500 | 276.8 | 45 | 3.6 | 1,021 | 348 | 14 | 100 | 8 | 2,453,197 | 122,659 | 95,396 | 131,197 | 226,593 | 184 |
| egyp | Egypt | 300 | 29.1 | 1,500 | 21.9 | 52 | 0.8 | 1,211 | 674 | 27 | 50 | 1 | 1,002,195 | 50,109 | 68,979 | 12,749 | 81,728 | 163 |
| elsa | El Salvador | 200 | 32.8 | 1,400 | 223.1 | 12 | 1.9 | 430 | 381 | 15 | 40 | 6 | 832,542 | 41,627 | 100,940 | 122,378 | 223,318 | 536 |
| equa | Equatorial Guinea | 50 | 126.7 | 300 | 662.7 | 6 | 13.3 | 20 | 13 | 1 | 15 | 33 | 60,677 | 3,033 | 4,000 | 444 | 4,444 | 146 |
| erit | Eritrea | 120 | 62.0 | 200 | 51.9 | 0 | 0.0 | 10 | 9 | 0 | 10 | 3 | 80,020 | 4,001 | 19,485 | 602 | 20,087 | 502 |
| esto | Estonia | 40 | 75.5 | 150 | 107.4 | 0 | 0.0 | 105 | 53 | 2 | 40 | 29 | 151,944 | 7,597 | 4,164 | 6,246 | 10,410 | 137 |
| ethi | Ethiopia | 250 | 8.0 | 2,500 | 40.0 | 60 | 1.0 | 553 | 316 | 13 | 40 | 1 | 2,161,999 | 108,099 | 215,421 | 26,353 | 241,774 | 223 |
| faer | Faeroe Islands | 50 | 1,262.9 | 30 | 701.8 | 0 | 0.0 | 20 | 10 | 0 | 7 | 164 | 13,686 | 684 | 600 | 200 | 800 | 116 |
| fiji | Fiji | 100 | 217.5 | 600 | 734.5 | 8 | 9.8 | 83 | 46 | 2 | 25 | 31 | 65,575 | 3,278 | 23,700 | 2,633 | 26,333 | 803 |
| finl | Finland | 1,400 | 305.7 | 500 | 96.6 | 60 | 11.6 | 662 | 394 | 16 | 150 | 29 | 1,968,946 | 98,447 | 44,151 | 3,476 | 47,627 | 48 |
| fran | France | 30,500 | 741.8 | 16,000 | 270.8 | 670 | 11.3 | 19,811 | 6,662 | 266 | 1,800 | 30 | 15,448,745 | 772,437 | 71,769 | 618,317 | 690,086 | 89 |
| freg | French Guiana | 20 | 130.9 | 200 | 1,103.1 | 0 | 0.0 | 10 | 5 | 0 | 4 | 22 | 30,341 | 1,517 | 2,000 | 105 | 2,105 | 138 |
| frep | French Polynesia | 30 | 151.0 | 400 | 1,701.7 | 2 | 8.5 | 33 | 16 | 1 | 20 | 85 | 36,884 | 1,844 | 2,100 | 134 | 2,234 | 121 |
| gabo | Gabon | 20 | 18.4 | 400 | 326.2 | 4 | 3.3 | 38 | 24 | 1 | 10 | 8 | 150,924 | 7,546 | 8,452 | 1,491 | 9,943 | 131 |
| gamb | Gambia | 4 | 84.7 | 170 | 130.2 | 0 | 0.0 | 18 | 11 | 0 | 4 | 3 | 1,916 | 95 | 100 | 5 | 105 | 109 |
| geor | Georgia | 60 | 19.9 | 100 | 20.1 | 0 | 0.0 | 11 | 8 | 0 | 10 | 2 | 753,102 | 37,655 | 2,730 | 4,095 | 6,825 | 18 |
| germ | Germany | 26,500 | 450.8 | 10,000 | 121.6 | 0 | 0.0 | 20,911 | 9,677 | 387 | 3,600 | 44 | 24,772,421 | 1,238,621 | 498,426 | 717,247 | 1,215,673 | 98 |
| ghan | Ghana | 550 | 63.5 | 2,000 | 98.9 | 35 | 1.7 | 373 | 288 | 12 | 150 | 7 | 985,972 | 49,298 | 219,339 | 81,125 | 300,464 | 609 |
| gibr | Gibraltar | 10 | 468.0 | 40 | 1,594.8 | 0 | 0.0 | 12 | 3 | 0 | 5 | 199 | 6,863 | 343 | 300 | 52 | 352 | 102 |
| gree | Greece | 400 | 39.8 | 500 | 47.0 | 500 | 47.0 | 3,186 | 1,115 | 45 | 110 | 10 | 2,863,481 | 143,174 | 8,233 | 12,349 | 20,582 | 14 |
| grel | Greenland | 2 | 50.8 | 60 | 1,068.5 | 1 | 17.8 | 103 | 20 | 1 | 2 | 36 | 21,608 | 1,080 | 400 | 400 | 800 | 74 |
| gren | Grenada | 10 | 110.2 | 120 | 1,280.5 | 0 | 0.0 | 20 | 16 | 1 | 15 | 160 | 20,524 | 1,026 | 900 | 385 | 1,285 | 125 |
| guad | Guadeloupe | 140 | 323.4 | 400 | 877.8 | 4 | 8.8 | 29 | 18 | 1 | 15 | 33 | 106,920 | 5,346 | 16,000 | 4,000 | 20,000 | 374 |
| guam | Guam | 25 | 159.6 | 450 | 2,685.7 | 2 | 11.9 | 12 | 10 | 0 | 18 | 107 | 35,126 | 1,756 | 2,000 | 222 | 2,222 | 126 |
| guat | Guatemala | 450 | 42.1 | 3,500 | 307.4 | 60 | 5.3 | 628 | 346 | 14 | 80 | 7 | 965,826 | 48,291 | 117,124 | 183,965 | 301,089 | 623 |
| guin | Guinea | 2 | 8.6 | 100 | 13.5 | 0 | 0.0 | 561 | 304 | 12 | 4 | 1 | 16,171 | 808 | 2,918 | 153 | 3,071 | 379 |
| gunb | Guinea-Bissau | 10 | 64.2 | 190 | 156.6 | 4 | 3.3 | 40 | 25 | 1 | 5 | 4 | 18,483 | 924 | 1,000 | 111 | 1,111 | 120 |
| guya | Guyana | 10 | 26.7 | 300 | 348.3 | 7 | 8.1 | 63 | 31 | 1 | 30 | 35 | 69,436 | 3,471 | 4,000 | 347 | 4,347 | 125 |
| hait | Haiti | 30 | 3.9 | 1,500 | 182.4 | 20 | 2.4 | 325 | 222 | 9 | 50 | 6 | 723,114 | 36,155 | 78,280 | 11,080 | 89,360 | 247 |
| hond | Honduras | 200 | 33.0 | 800 | 123.4 | 19 | 2.9 | 177 | 140 | 6 | 40 | 6 | 675,930 | 33,796 | 70,879 | 101,157 | 172,036 | 509 |
| hung | Hungary | 250 | 28.6 | 1,200 | 119.6 | 45 | 4.5 | 1,551 | 573 | 23 | 50 | 5 | 3,023,496 | 151,174 | 86,711 | 1,769 | 88,480 | 58 |
| icel | Iceland | 40 | 150.8 | 40 | 142.4 | 2 | 7.1 | 141 | 64 | 3 | 30 | 107 | 88,006 | 4,400 | 3,134 | 579 | 3,713 | 84 |
| indi | India | 7,000 | 112.4 | 8,000 | 7.9 | 580 | 0.6 | 5,141 | 2,003 | 80 | 1,200 | 1 | 5,054,462 | 252,723 | 762,776 | 362,262 | 1,125,038 | 445 |
| indo | Indonesia | 600 | 22.8 | 6,000 | 28.3 | 150 | 0.7 | 1,262 | 764 | 31 | 400 | 2 | 4,534,021 | 226,701 | 448,218 | 215,808 | 664,026 | 292 |
| iran | Iran | 20 | 63.7 | 200 | 3.0 | 5 | 0.1 | 212 | 90 | 4 | 30 | 0 | 38,768 | 1,938 | 500 | 190 | 690 | 35 |
| iraq | Iraq | 40 | 55.2 | 80 | 3.5 | 8 | 0.3 | 271 | 23 | 1 | 25 | 1 | 42,821 | 2,141 | 18,049 | 2,117 | 20,166 | 941 |
| irel | Ireland | 9,300 | 2,771.6 | 500 | 134.0 | 60 | 16.1 | 6,604 | 2,017 | 81 | 200 | 54 | 836,770 | 41,838 | 6,800 | 16,567 | 23,367 | 55 |
| isle | Isle of Man | 20 | 381.4 | 4 | 50.5 | 0 | 0.0 | 30 | 5 | 0 | 15 | 189 | 24,131 | 1,206 | 400 | 1,600 | 2,000 | 165 |
| isra | Israel | 50 | 170.0 | 1,000 | 195.2 | 32 | 6.2 | 4,100 | 793 | 32 | 150 | 29 | 65,678 | 3,283 | 3,997 | 1,088 | 5,085 | 154 |
| ital | Italy | 31,500 | 671.3 | 12,000 | 209.4 | 850 | 14.8 | 16,618 | 9,672 | 387 | 2,000 | 35 | 16,374,428 | 818,721 | 33,213 | 1,548,358 | 1,581,571 | 193 |
| ivor | Ivory Coast | 300 | 68.9 | 1,720 | 116.3 | 13 | 0.9 | 40 | 20 | 1 | 40 | 3 | 293,344 | 14,667 | 44,755 | 19,180 | 63,935 | 435 |
| jama | Jamaica | 45 | 40.1 | 700 | 271.0 | 15 | 5.8 | 276 | 140 | 6 | 80 | 31 | 219,107 | 10,955 | 71,961 | 2,998 | 74,959 | 684 |
| japa | Japan | 800 | 232.8 | 7,500 | 59.2 | 120 | 0.9 | 3,157 | 1,467 | 59 | 400 | 3 | 1,112,518 | 55,625 | 184,172 | 25,591 | 209,763 | 377 |
| jord | Jordan | 12 | 43.9 | 200 | 30.0 | 0 | 0.0 | 138 | 93 | 4 | 20 | 3 | 32,689 | 1,634 | 8,051 | 7,582 | 15,633 | 956 |
| kaza | Kazakhstan | 30 | 11.6 | 200 | 12.3 | 0 | 0.0 | 20 | 10 | 0 | 5 | 0 | 757,244 | 37,862 | 51,880 | 2,730 | 54,610 | 144 |
| keny | Kenya | 800 | 35.6 | 6,000 | 199.5 | 28 | 0.9 | 651 | 578 | 23 | 200 | 7 | 2,524,927 | 126,246 | 161,240 | 34,915 | 196,155 | 155 |
| kirg | Kirgizstan | 30 | 64.4 | 50 | 10.6 | 0 | 0.0 | 10 | 8 | 0 | 1 | 0 | 113,496 | 5,674 | 5,000 | 50 | 5,050 | 89 |
| kiri | Kiribati | 10 | 129.3 | 50 | 599.6 | 3 | 36.0 | 12 | 9 | 0 | 10 | 120 | 9,867 | 493 | 600 | 25 | 625 | 126 |
| kuwa | Kuwait | 10 | 40.4 | 100 | 50.7 | 0 | 0.0 | 20 | 4 | 0 | 5 | 3 | 22,180 | 1,109 | 800 | 200 | 1,000 | 90 |
| laos | Laos | 5 | 44.4 | 80 | 14.7 | 0 | 0.0 | 36 | 22 | 1 | 4 | 1 | 9,681 | 484 | 500 | 26 | 526 | 108 |
| latv | Latvia | 60 | 38.1 | 400 | 169.7 | 0 | 0.0 | 130 | 62 | 2 | 25 | 11 | 528,902 | 26,445 | 12,662 | 8,441 | 21,103 | 79 |
| leba | Lebanon | 200 | 115.3 | 600 | 182.8 | 55 | 16.8 | 560 | 321 | 13 | 60 | 18 | 279,000 | 13,950 | 10,330 | 15,495 | 25,825 | 185 |
| leso | Lesotho | 50 | 34.6 | 650 | 302.0 | 14 | 6.5 | 72 | 53 | 2 | 40 | 19 | 194,898 | 9,744 | 13,193 | 408 | 13,601 | 139 |
| libe | Liberia | 70 | 75.1 | 500 | 158.5 | 16 | 5.1 | 248 | 132 | 5 | 50 | 16 | 44,301 | 2,215 | 28,679 | 10,715 | 39,394 | 1,778 |
| liby | Libya | 5 | 29.4 | 100 | 17.8 | 0 | 0.0 | 11 | 8 | 0 | 2 | 0 | 23,129 | 1,156 | 100 | 900 | 1,000 | 86 |
| liec | Liechtenstein | 25 | 924.2 | 20 | 609.0 | 0 | 0.0 | 6 | 4 | 0 | 5 | 152 | 8,556 | 427 | 60 | 240 | 300 | 70 |
| lith | Lithuania | 220 | 68.5 | 400 | 109.0 | 0 | 0.0 | 355 | 210 | 8 | 25 | 7 | 991,076 | 49,553 | 1,065 | 1,065 | 2,130 | 4 |
| luxe | Luxembourg | 120 | 298.0 | 40 | 92.9 | 10 | 23.2 | 71 | 31 | 1 | 30 | 70 | 135,890 | 6,794 | 2,000 | 3,000 | 5,000 | 73 |
| mace | Macedonia | 50 | 38.8 | 150 | 74.1 | 0 | 0.0 | 218 | 147 | 6 | 10 | 5 | 273,672 | 13,683 | 1,763 | 440 | 2,203 | 16 |
| mada | Madagascar | 300 | 39.3 | 2,000 | 125.5 | 23 | 1.4 | 212 | 93 | 4 | 45 | 3 | 1,111,671 | 55,583 | 21,269 | 1,381 | 22,650 | 40 |
| mala | Malawi | 400 | 56.9 | 1,500 | 137.3 | 22 | 2.0 | 192 | 146 | 6 | 50 | 5 | 807,961 | 40,398 | 99,528 | 10,447 | 109,975 | 272 |
| malb | Malaysia | 90 | 50.8 | 1,000 | 45.0 | 10 | 0.4 | 218 | 143 | 6 | 50 | 2 | 268,305 | 13,415 | 28,618 | 1,506 | 30,124 | 224 |

| COUNTRY ° | | GLOBAL MISSION SHARING | | | | CHRISTIAN LITERATURE | | | | | | | SCRIPTURES | | | | | |
|---|---|---|---|---|---|---|---|---|---|---|---|---|---|---|---|---|---|---|
| | | citizens sent | | aliens received | | libraries | | book on country's Christians | | | periodicals | | Bible distribution | | | | | |
| code | short name | total | p.m.a. | total | p.m. | total | p.m. | total | 1970–99 | p.a. | total | p.m. | goal | goal p.a. | UBS p.a. | other p.a. | total p.a. | T/G% |
| 1 | 2 | 109 | 110 | 111 | 112 | 113 | 114 | 115 | 116 | 117 | 118 | 119 | 120 | 121 | 122 | 123 | 124 | 125 |
| mald | Maldives | 0 | 0.0 | 10 | 34.9 | 0 | 0.0 | 8 | 6 | 0 | 0 | 0 | 49 | 2 | 5 | 0 | 5 | 226 |
| mali | Mali | 10 | 44.6 | 600 | 53.4 | 6 | 0.5 | 20 | 12 | 0 | 10 | 1 | 10,789 | 539 | 4,068 | 353 | 4,421 | 819 |
| malt | Malta | 1,000 | 2,692.7 | 30 | 77.2 | 8 | 20.6 | 137 | 69 | 3 | 80 | 206 | 95,996 | 4,799 | 7,500 | 5,000 | 12,500 | 260 |
| mars | Marshall Islands | 10 | 166.4 | 80 | 1,245.7 | 0 | 0.0 | 15 | 3 | 0 | 5 | 78 | 5,283 | 264 | 300 | 12 | 312 | 118 |
| mart | Martinique | 80 | 214.3 | 200 | 505.9 | 2 | 5.1 | 18 | 10 | 0 | 5 | 13 | 100,747 | 5,037 | 10,000 | 2,500 | 12,500 | 248 |
| maur | Mauritania | 0 | 0.0 | 50 | 18.7 | 0 | 0.0 | 17 | 13 | 1 | 1 | 0 | 491 | 24 | 30 | 0 | 30 | 123 |
| maus | Mauritius | 40 | 108.3 | 300 | 259.4 | 2 | 1.7 | 58 | 48 | 2 | 5 | 4 | 55,050 | 2,752 | 8,769 | 2,634 | 11,403 | 414 |
| mayo | Mayotte | 0 | 0.0 | 30 | 295.2 | 0 | 0.0 | 7 | 5 | 0 | 0 | 0 | 292 | 14 | 10 | 5 | 15 | 105 |
| mexi | Mexico | 4,500 | 48.0 | 8,000 | 80.9 | 180 | 1.8 | 6,891 | 2,554 | 102 | 900 | 9 | 15,178,697 | 758,934 | 181,426 | 134,097 | 315,523 | 41 |
| micr | Micronesia | 50 | 460.1 | 480 | 4,044.2 | 0 | 0.0 | 43 | 15 | 1 | 20 | 169 | 10,762 | 538 | 3,711 | 412 | 4,123 | 766 |
| mold | Moldavia | 100 | 35.7 | 500 | 114.1 | 0 | 0.0 | 45 | 23 | 1 | 25 | 6 | 766,724 | 38,336 | 46,874 | 46,874 | 93,748 | 244 |
| mona | Monaco | 20 | 643.1 | 150 | 4,464.7 | 1 | 29.8 | 15 | 8 | 0 | 8 | 238 | 13,352 | 667 | 100 | 900 | 1,000 | 149 |
| mong | Mongolia | 5 | 149.7 | 400 | 150.3 | 0 | 0.0 | 29 | 8 | 0 | 1 | 0 | 5,080 | 254 | 1,261 | 12 | 1,273 | 501 |
| mont | Montserrat | 2 | 196.7 | 10 | 940.8 | 0 | 0.0 | 15 | 6 | 0 | 4 | 376 | 2,114 | 105 | 100 | 11 | 111 | 105 |
| moro | Morocco | 15 | 86.0 | 1,500 | 53.2 | 4 | 0.1 | 43 | 9 | 0 | 20 | 1 | 12,069 | 603 | 399 | 171 | 570 | 94 |
| moza | Mozambique | 150 | 23.2 | 3,200 | 162.6 | 13 | 0.7 | 164 | 99 | 4 | 40 | 2 | 514,540 | 25,727 | 22,266 | 1,196 | 23,462 | 91 |
| myan | Myanmar | 250 | 66.8 | 200 | 4.4 | 33 | 0.7 | 241 | 17 | 1 | 20 | 0 | 546,104 | 27,305 | 4,782 | 1,195 | 5,977 | 21 |
| nami | Namibia | 50 | 37.1 | 1,200 | 695.3 | 5 | 2.9 | 195 | 155 | 6 | 40 | 23 | 189,744 | 9,487 | 17,071 | 1,896 | 18,967 | 199 |
| naur | Nauru | 2 | 239.8 | 20 | 1,736.3 | 0 | 0.0 | 3 | 2 | 0 | 2 | 174 | 942 | 47 | 50 | 12 | 62 | 132 |
| nepa | Nepal | 100 | 173.6 | 900 | 37.6 | 2 | 0.1 | 45 | 30 | 1 | 15 | 1 | 24,462 | 1,223 | 9,344 | 491 | 9,835 | 804 |
| neth | Netherlands | 10,200 | 991.9 | 2,100 | 133.0 | 300 | 19.0 | 3,973 | 1,673 | 67 | 700 | 44 | 4,231,832 | 211,591 | 83,194 | 194,119 | 277,313 | 131 |
| nets | Netherlands Antilles | 20 | 108.2 | 600 | 2,767.8 | 4 | 18.5 | 17 | 9 | 0 | 20 | 92 | 44,635 | 2,231 | 3,302 | 5,078 | 8,380 | 375 |
| newc | New Caledonia | 30 | 185.6 | 300 | 1,401.7 | 4 | 18.7 | 30 | 18 | 1 | 10 | 47 | 20,818 | 1,040 | 1,000 | 250 | 1,250 | 120 |
| newz | New Zealand | 2,100 | 819.6 | 2,800 | 725.0 | 30 | 7.8 | 658 | 331 | 13 | 250 | 65 | 852,259 | 42,612 | 33,527 | 12,909 | 46,436 | 109 |
| nica | Nicaragua | 250 | 51.5 | 2,000 | 394.2 | 16 | 3.2 | 578 | 501 | 20 | 40 | 8 | 403,824 | 20,191 | 39,717 | 5,830 | 45,547 | 225 |
| niga | Niger | 10 | 171.6 | 450 | 41.9 | 0 | 0.0 | 32 | 20 | 1 | 5 | 0 | 1,049 | 52 | 100 | 1 | 101 | 192 |
| nige | Nigeria | 2,500 | 49.1 | 5,300 | 47.5 | 80 | 0.7 | 1,403 | 1,158 | 46 | 300 | 3 | 5,139,377 | 256,968 | 276,174 | 31,369 | 307,543 | 119 |
| nork | North Korea | 2 | 4.0 | 20 | 0.8 | 0 | 0.0 | 150 | 29 | 1 | 0 | 0 | 89,788 | 4,489 | 1,600 | 177 | 1,777 | 39 |
| norl | Northern Cyprus | 2 | 124.2 | 40 | 216.2 | 0 | 0.0 | 10 | 5 | 0 | 2 | 11 | 4,406 | 220 | 200 | 133 | 333 | 151 |
| norm | Northern Mariana Is | 5 | 72.2 | 120 | 1,531.5 | 0 | 0.0 | 2 | 2 | 0 | 5 | 64 | 10,911 | 545 | 600 | 66 | 666 | 122 |
| norw | Norway | 1,800 | 428.4 | 1,000 | 224.2 | 30 | 6.7 | 1,213 | 481 | 19 | 140 | 31 | 1,866,629 | 93,331 | 63,542 | 12,283 | 75,825 | 81 |
| oman | Oman | 2 | 16.4 | 40 | 15.7 | 0 | 0.0 | 24 | 13 | 1 | 5 | 2 | 11,295 | 564 | 200 | 22 | 222 | 39 |
| paki | Pakistan | 50 | 13.1 | 1,500 | 9.6 | 15 | 0.1 | 258 | 127 | 5 | 50 | 0 | 197,826 | 9,891 | 34,941 | 502,612 | 537,553 | 5,434 |
| pala | Palau | 10 | 544.3 | 20 | 1,029.5 | 0 | 0.0 | 22 | 16 | 1 | 2 | 103 | 2,663 | 133 | 100 | 66 | 166 | 125 |
| pale | Palestine | 250 | 1,327.7 | 1,200 | 541.7 | 30 | 13.5 | 2,700 | 1,023 | 41 | 40 | 18 | 20,131 | 1,006 | 2,000 | 1,636 | 3,636 | 361 |
| pana | Panama | 600 | 244.2 | 2,100 | 735.4 | 20 | 7.0 | 139 | 65 | 3 | 40 | 14 | 468,666 | 23,433 | 52,016 | 22,935 | 74,951 | 319 |
| papu | Papua New Guinea | 100 | 26.4 | 3,600 | 781.2 | 34 | 7.4 | 356 | 254 | 10 | 50 | 11 | 525,576 | 26,278 | 49,451 | 6,174 | 55,625 | 211 |
| para | Paraguay | 450 | 87.0 | 1,200 | 218.3 | 16 | 2.9 | 249 | 143 | 6 | 40 | 7 | 890,730 | 44,536 | 33,178 | 23,633 | 56,811 | 127 |
| peru | Peru | 800 | 32.4 | 6,800 | 265.0 | 65 | 2.5 | 1,039 | 594 | 24 | 100 | 4 | 3,946,150 | 197,307 | 168,828 | 127,882 | 296,710 | 150 |
| phil | Philippines | 2,000 | 30.0 | 9,500 | 125.1 | 195 | 2.6 | 1,692 | 992 | 40 | 300 | 4 | 9,960,360 | 498,018 | 456,758 | 1,204,180 | 1,660,938 | 333 |
| pola | Poland | 2,500 | 66.7 | 700 | 18.1 | 76 | 2.0 | 3,716 | 2,305 | 92 | 200 | 5 | 10,179,134 | 508,956 | 46,913 | 41,269 | 88,182 | 17 |
| port | Portugal | 5,000 | 550.6 | 750 | 76.0 | 35 | 3.5 | 1,151 | 563 | 23 | 300 | 30 | 2,073,046 | 103,652 | 51,391 | 75,814 | 127,205 | 122 |
| puer | Puerto Rico | 900 | 241.8 | 2,500 | 646.2 | 25 | 6.5 | 381 | 252 | 10 | 50 | 13 | 892,086 | 44,604 | 93,128 | 41,062 | 134,190 | 300 |
| qata | Qatar | 4 | 67.1 | 10 | 16.7 | 0 | 0.0 | 10 | 6 | 0 | 0 | 0 | 6,975 | 348 | 300 | 33 | 333 | 95 |
| reun | Reunion | 10 | 16.5 | 240 | 343.1 | 2 | 2.9 | 18 | 11 | 0 | 2 | 3 | 117,428 | 5,871 | 5,000 | 2,142 | 7,142 | 121 |
| roma | Romania | 200 | 10.2 | 1,000 | 44.8 | 200 | 9.0 | 1,622 | 388 | 16 | 70 | 3 | 6,169,502 | 308,475 | 48,724 | 146,172 | 194,896 | 63 |
| russ | Russia | 1,000 | 12.0 | 19,000 | 129.3 | 72 | 0.5 | 3,421 | 1,693 | 68 | 150 | 1 | 25,416,691 | 1,270,834 | 303,275 | 707,641 | 1,010,916 | 79 |
| rwan | Rwanda | 120 | 18.9 | 1,200 | 155.2 | 17 | 2.2 | 120 | 80 | 3 | 20 | 3 | 547,003 | 27,350 | 48,493 | 5,388 | 53,881 | 197 |
| saha | Sahara | 0 | 0.0 | 10 | 34.1 | 0 | 0.0 | 12 | 5 | 0 | 0 | 0 | 9 | 0 | 1 | 0 | 1 | 265 |
| saih | Saint Helena | 5 | 937.7 | 20 | 3,178.1 | 1 | 158.9 | 25 | 0 | 0 | 3 | 477 | 1,707 | 85 | 100 | 42 | 142 | 167 |
| saik | Saint Kitts & Nevis | 2 | 55.6 | 40 | 1,039.7 | 0 | 0.0 | 15 | 10 | 0 | 7 | 182 | 8,442 | 422 | 700 | 77 | 777 | 184 |
| sail | Saint Lucia | 4 | 27.7 | 150 | 971.7 | 0 | 0.0 | 13 | 5 | 0 | 8 | 52 | 26,952 | 1,347 | 1,000 | 428 | 1,428 | 106 |
| saip | Saint Pierre & Miquelon | 10 | 1,565.4 | 40 | 6,091.1 | 1 | 152.3 | 2 | 0 | 0 | 2 | 305 | 2,084 | 104 | 100 | 25 | 125 | 120 |
| saiv | Saint Vincent | 2 | 25.5 | 80 | 702.0 | 1 | 8.8 | 10 | 6 | 0 | 5 | 44 | 18,257 | 912 | 1,100 | 122 | 1,222 | 133 |
| samo | Samoa | 300 | 1,773.8 | 800 | 4,442.6 | 3 | 16.7 | 54 | 42 | 2 | 20 | 111 | 19,845 | 992 | 2,000 | 222 | 2,222 | 224 |
| sanm | San Marino | 6 | 252.3 | 20 | 754.3 | 0 | 0.0 | 13 | 10 | 0 | 3 | 113 | 8,177 | 408 | 300 | 200 | 500 | 122 |
| saot | Sao Tome & Principe | 20 | 151.4 | 100 | 681.3 | 0 | 0.0 | 11 | 5 | 0 | 2 | 14 | 16,268 | 813 | 500 | 214 | 714 | 87 |
| saud | Saudi Arabia | 10 | 12.7 | 100 | 4.6 | 0 | 0.0 | 28 | 14 | 1 | 0 | 0 | 62,002 | 3,100 | 3,000 | 750 | 3,750 | 121 |
| sene | Senegal | 90 | 192.6 | 1,200 | 126.6 | 8 | 0.8 | 44 | 29 | 1 | 20 | 2 | 15,133 | 756 | 1,000 | 176 | 1,176 | 155 |
| seyc | Seychelles | 15 | 208.9 | 150 | 1,937.1 | 2 | 25.8 | 12 | 8 | 0 | 4 | 52 | 11,995 | 599 | 700 | 77 | 777 | 129 |
| sier | Sierra Leone | 10 | 19.6 | 700 | 144.2 | 8 | 1.6 | 122 | 60 | 2 | 25 | 5 | 28,595 | 1,429 | 8,368 | 1,098 | 9,466 | 662 |
| sing | Singapore | 500 | 1,240.9 | 1,000 | 280.4 | 10 | 2.8 | 180 | 144 | 6 | 50 | 14 | 85,945 | 4,297 | 32,656 | 8,164 | 40,820 | 949 |
| slok | Slovakia | 70 | 16.2 | 1,000 | 185.6 | 0 | 0.0 | 227 | 139 | 6 | 20 | 4 | 1,424,158 | 71,207 | 7,436 | 826 | 8,262 | 11 |
| slov | Slovenia | 150 | 86.4 | 800 | 402.9 | 0 | 0.0 | 267 | 195 | 8 | 20 | 10 | 553,570 | 27,678 | 14,700 | 6,300 | 21,000 | 75 |
| solo | Solomon Islands | 45 | 111.6 | 500 | 1,127.0 | 5 | 11.3 | 103 | 60 | 2 | 10 | 23 | 33,104 | 1,655 | 2,000 | 222 | 2,222 | 134 |
| soma | Somalia | 4 | 40.6 | 50 | 6.9 | 0 | 0.0 | 20 | 12 | 0 | 0 | 0 | 5,443 | 272 | 600 | 66 | 666 | 244 |
| somi | Somaliland | 0 | 0.0 | 10 | 3.5 | 0 | 0.0 | 6 | 3 | 0 | 0 | 0 | 379 | 18 | 50 | 2 | 52 | 277 |
| soua | South Africa | 7,000 | 220.1 | 12,000 | 297.2 | 150 | 3.7 | 2,626 | 1,644 | 66 | 400 | 10 | 5,195,286 | 259,764 | 664,374 | 17,734 | 682,108 | 262 |
| souk | South Korea | 5,500 | 294.4 | 2,800 | 59.8 | 160 | 3.4 | 845 | 758 | 30 | 200 | 4 | 4,544,073 | 227,203 | 1,209,905 | 42,584 | 1,252,489 | 551 |
| spai | Spain | 30,500 | 822.7 | 2,500 | 63.1 | 300 | 7.6 | 7,716 | 4,578 | 183 | 1,500 | 38 | 10,162,121 | 508,106 | 31,938 | 1,964,187 | 1,996,125 | 392 |
| span | Spanish North Africa | 10 | 95.9 | 50 | 384.6 | 0 | 0.0 | 5 | 3 | 0 | 0 | 0 | 32,035 | 1,601 | 1,800 | 34,200 | 36,000 | 2,247 |
| sril | Sri Lanka | 200 | 114.0 | 1,700 | 90.3 | 25 | 1.3 | 249 | 129 | 5 | 100 | 5 | 288,151 | 14,407 | 29,463 | 3,716 | 33,179 | 230 |
| suda | Sudan | 100 | 20.5 | 700 | 23.7 | 5 | 0.2 | 230 | 150 | 6 | 20 | 1 | 387,100 | 19,355 | 25,681 | 524 | 26,205 | 135 |
| suri | Suriname | 25 | 145.1 | 400 | 958.9 | 2 | 4.8 | 25 | 13 | 1 | 10 | 24 | 40,596 | 2,029 | 16,268 | 677 | 16,945 | 834 |
| swaz | Swaziland | 100 | 146.9 | 800 | 793.7 | 3 | 3.0 | 53 | 41 | 2 | 40 | 40 | 78,008 | 3,900 | 10,270 | 427 | 10,697 | 274 |
| swed | Sweden | 2,000 | 333.3 | 1,000 | 112.2 | 40 | 4.5 | 2,025 | 713 | 29 | 450 | 51 | 2,705,595 | 135,279 | 65,796 | 1,069 | 66,865 | 49 |
| swit | Switzerland | 3,400 | 527.5 | 2,200 | 297.9 | 150 | 20.3 | 2,738 | 1,200 | 48 | 400 | 54 | 2,856,836 | 142,841 | 51,238 | 204,952 | 256,190 | 179 |
| syri | Syria | 150 | 119.3 | 100 | 6.2 | 0 | 0.0 | 340 | 163 | 7 | 40 | 2 | 130,371 | 6,518 | 5,294 | 2,268 | 7,562 | 116 |
| taiw | Taiwan | 400 | 339.1 | 3,000 | 133.9 | 60 | 2.7 | 404 | 283 | 11 | 20 | 1 | 277,162 | 13,858 | 92,049 | 18,454 | 110,503 | 797 |
| taji | Tajikistan | 5 | 38.6 | 40 | 6.5 | 0 | 0.0 | 8 | 5 | 0 | 1 | 0 | 22,196 | 1,109 | 4,000 | 40 | 4,040 | 364 |
| tanz | Tanzania | 300 | 19.1 | 4,500 | 134.3 | 60 | 1.8 | 341 | 253 | 10 | 100 | 3 | 1,830,026 | 91,501 | 212,278 | 12,117 | 224,395 | 245 |
| thai | Thailand | 30 | 22.3 | 2,000 | 32.6 | 15 | 0.2 | 283 | 202 | 8 | 30 | 0 | 226,129 | 11,306 | 25,977 | 18,051 | 44,028 | 389 |
| timo | Timor | 40 | 49.1 | 100 | 113.1 | 0 | 0.0 | 29 | 16 | 1 | 5 | 6 | 168,386 | 8,419 | 5,000 | 11,666 | 16,666 | 198 |
| togo | Togo | 80 | 45.7 | 600 | 129.6 | 5 | 1.1 | 41 | 24 | 1 | 20 | 4 | 137,059 | 6,852 | 22,873 | 2,541 | 25,414 | 370 |
| tong | Tonga | 50 | 557.5 | 400 | 4,059.0 | 2 | 20.3 | 121 | 87 | 3 | 15 | 152 | 13,541 | 677 | 700 | 175 | 875 | 129 |
| trin | Trinidad & Tobago | 150 | 188.5 | 500 | 386.1 | 10 | 7.7 | 49 | 43 | 2 | 30 | 23 | 187,956 | 9,397 | 9,000 | 2,250 | 11,250 | 119 |
| tuni | Tunisia | 4 | 79.2 | 200 | 20.9 | 2 | 0.2 | 65 | 46 | 2 | 1 | 0 | 6,432 | 321 | 200 | 85 | 285 | 88 |
| turk | Turkey | 30 | 80.4 | 500 | 7.5 | 7 | 0.1 | 1,338 | 702 | 28 | 15 | 0 | 66,119 | 3,305 | 14,029 | 769 | 14,798 | 447 |
| turm | Turkmenistan | 2 | 20.2 | 50 | 11.2 | 0 | 0.0 | 15 | 11 | 0 | 1 | 0 | 18,426 | 921 | 2,000 | 20 | 2,020 | 219 |
| turs | Turks & Caicos Is | 2 | 150.8 | 10 | 596.7 | 0 | 0.0 | 2 | 2 | 0 | 2 | 119 | 3,477 | 173 | 100 | 66 | 166 | 95 |
| tuva | Tuvalu | 2 | 205.2 | 10 | 853.3 | 0 | 0.0 | 10 | 6 | 0 | 2 | 171 | 1,279 | 63 | 100 | 42 | 142 | 223 |
| ugan | Uganda | 500 | 26.4 | 2,600 | 119.4 | 28 | 1.3 | 357 | 211 | 8 | 40 | 2 | 2,109,730 | 105,486 | 69,473 | 9,116 | 78,589 | 74 |
| ukra | Ukraine | 400 | 9.6 | 4,200 | 83.2 | 0 | 0.0 | 1,360 | 749 | 30 | 70 | 1 | 12,851,431 | 642,571 | 160,476 | 481,428 | 641,904 | 99 |
| unia | United Arab Emirates | 10 | 38.1 | 120 | 49.2 | 0 | 0.0 | 18 | 12 | 0 | 5 | 2 | 26,997 | 1,349 | 2,000 | 500 | 2,500 | 185 |
| usa | USA | 118,600 | 618.8 | 33,200 | 119.3 | 2,700 | 9.7 | 41,948 | 21,067 | 843 | 8,000 | 29 | 67,674,125 | 3,383,706 | 1,989,928 | 16,100,326 | 18,090,254 | 534 |
| uuay | Uruguay | 600 | 277.6 | 3,000 | 899.0 | 20 | 6.0 | 219 | 141 | 6 | 70 | 21 | 616,295 | 30,814 | 17,920 | 8,549 | 26,469 | 85 |
| uzbe | Uzbekistan | 5 | 12.7 | 200 | 8.2 | 0 | 0.0 | 15 | 10 | 0 | 5 | 0 | 88,595 | 4,429 | 40,562 | 409 | 40,971 | 924 |
| vanu | Vanuatu | 10 | 58.8 | 300 | 1,575.5 | 2 | 10.5 | 90 | 51 | 2 | 10 | 53 | 15,496 | 774 | 900 | 100 | 1,000 | 129 |
| vene | Venezuela | 900 | 39.6 | 7,000 | 289.6 | 44 | 1.8 | 498 | 264 | 11 | 70 | 3 | 3,532,494 | 176,624 | 91,241 | 121,441 | 212,682 | 120 |
| viet | Viet Nam | 800 | 121.8 | 1,200 | 15.0 | 65 | 0.8 | 110 | 50 | 2 | 50 | 1 | 1,154,978 | 57,748 | 20,000 | 10,075 | 30,075 | 52 |
| virg | Virgin Is of the US | 20 | 232.1 | 150 | 1,613.7 | 0 | 0.0 | 17 | 10 | 0 | 15 | 161 | 27,642 | 1,382 | 3,000 | 12,000 | 15,000 | 1,085 |
| wall | Wallis & Futuna Is | 2 | 142.6 | 30 | 2,066.5 | 0 | 0.0 | 8 | 5 | 0 | 2 | 138 | 2,579 | 128 | 200 | 133 | 333 | 258 |
| yeme | Yemen | 2 | 65.2 | 150 | 8.3 | 0 | 0.0 | 26 | 17 | 1 | 0 | 0 | 1,755 | 87 | 100 | 100 | 200 | 227 |
| yugo | Yugoslavia | 500 | 72.6 | 1,000 | 94.0 | 280 | 26.3 | 769 | 475 | 19 | 150 | 14 | 2,046,035 | 102,301 | 9,539 | 38,156 | 47,695 | 46 |
| zamb | Zambia | 250 | 35.5 | 3,200 | 349.0 | 33 | 3.6 | 198 | 153 | 6 | 70 | 8 | 1,094,611 | 54,730 | 65,694 | 6,576 | 72,270 | 132 |
| zimb | Zimbabwe | 400 | 57.8 | 2,700 | 231.4 | 25 | 2.1 | 310 | 237 | 9 | 60 | 5 | 1,131,167 | 56,558 | 105,155 | 39,090 | 144,245 | 255 |
| | 11 minicountries | 181 | 12,681.9 | 271 | 11,742.3 | 71 | 3076.4 | 31,718 | 0 | 0 | 153 | 6,629 | 4,550 | 227 | 244 | 1,049 | 1,293 | 568 |
| | Africa | 17,406 | 51.9 | 90,463 | 115.3 | 985 | 1.3 | 13,056 | 8,524 | 338 | 2,358 | 3 | 36,398,525 | 1,819,926 | 2,994,093 | 481,858 | 3,475,951 | 190 |
| | Antarctica | 0 | 0.0 | 10 | 2,222.2 | 1 | 222.2 | 15 | 0 | 0 | 0 | 0 | 1,450 | 72 | 0 | 0 | 0 | 0 |
| | Asia | 24,504 | 79.7 | 57,970 | 15.7 | 1,623 | 0.4 | 29,746 | 13,008 | 520 | 3,439 | 1 | 47,596,347 | 2,379,817 | 6,959,865 | 3,116,180 | 10,076,045 | 423 |
| | Europe | 192,351 | 358.3 | 105,699 | 145.0 | 4,866 | 6.7 | 158,802 | 54,316 | 2,173 | 15,774 | 22 | 180,180,811 | 9,009,040 | 2,178,112 | 7,957,672 | 10,135,784 | 112 |
| | Latin America | 41,544 | 87.3 | 108,121 | 208.3 | 1,412 | 2.7 | 21,015 | 11,433 | 458 | 3,180 | 6 | 85,206,783 | 4,260,339 | 4,135,898 | 6,892,994 | 11,028,892 | 258 |
| | Northern America | 135,122 | 637.3 | 41,400 | 133.7 | 2,952 | 9.5 | 47,952 | 23,679 | 948 | 8,844 | 29 | 74,658,503 | 3,732,925 | 2,078,722 | 16,402,097 | 18,480,819 | 495 |
| | Oceania | 8,502 | 397.6 | 15,766 | 518.7 | 213 | 7.0 | 4,920 | 3,442 | 136 | 902 | 30 | 5,720,961 | 286,048 | 451,308 | 115,404 | 566,712 | 198 |
| | **World A** | **507** | **50.6** | **10,178** | **16.8** | **72** | **0.1** | **3,935** | **1,904** | **73** | **245** | **0** | **943,843** | **47,192** | **166,959** | **509,493** | **676,452** | **1,433** |
| | **World B** | **29,898** | **60.9** | **103,065** | **27.4** | **1,974** | **0.5** | **35,832** | **16,964** | **680** | **4,456** | **1** | **80,963,360** | **4,048,168** | **8,324,398** | **2,335,117** | **10,659,515** | **263** |
| | **World C** | **389,024** | **280.5** | **306,186** | **180.7** | **10,006** | **5.9** | **235,739** | **95,534** | **3,820** | **29,796** | **18** | **347,856,179** | **17,392,808** | **10,306,641** | **32,121,596** | **42,428,237** | **243** |
| | **GLOBAL TOTAL** | **419,429** | **222.2** | **419,429** | **69.3** | **12,052** | **2.0** | **275,506** | **114,402** | **4,573** | **34,497** | **6** | **429,763,383** | **21,488,169** | **18,797,998** | **34,966,207** | **53,764,205** | **250** |

| COUNTRY | | SCRIPTURES (continued): NEW TESTAMENT DISTRIBUTION | | | | | | | PORTIONS DISTRIBUTION (Gospels) | | | | | | |
|---|---|---|---|---|---|---|---|---|---|---|---|---|---|---|---|
| code 1 | short name 2 | goal 126 | goal p.a. 127 | UBS p.a. 128 | other p.a. 129 | duplicates 130 | total p.a. 131 | T/G% 132 | goal 133 | goal p.a. 134 | UBS p.a. 135 | other p.a. 136 | duplicates 137 | total p.a. 138 | T/G% 139 |
| afgh | Afghanistan | 1,393 | 69 | 100 | 11 | 50 | 161 | 231.2 | 3,484,672 | 348,467 | 1,000 | 52 | 161 | 1,213 | 0.3 |
| alba | Albania | 668,444 | 33,422 | 25,002 | 6,250 | 13,336 | 44,589 | 133.4 | 2,056,753 | 205,675 | 413,180 | 413,180 | 44,589 | 870,949 | 423.5 |
| alge | Algeria | 32,800 | 1,640 | 700 | 36 | 333 | 1,070 | 65.3 | 10,933,335 | 1,093,333 | 3,500 | 388 | 1,070 | 4,959 | 0.5 |
| amer | American Samoa | 27,580 | 1,379 | 1,500 | 78 | 1,473 | 3,052 | 221.4 | 33,647 | 3,364 | 3,800 | 3,800 | 3,052 | 10,652 | 316.6 |
| ando | Andorra | 47,138 | 2,356 | 2,000 | 150 | 1,444 | 3,594 | 152.5 | 52,109 | 5,210 | 700 | 175 | 3,594 | 4,469 | 85.8 |
| ango | Angola | 2,008,419 | 100,420 | 9,097 | 1,193 | 75,295 | 85,585 | 85.2 | 2,402,128 | 240,212 | 25,655 | 4,527 | 85,585 | 115,768 | 48.2 |
| angu | Anguilla | 4,563 | 228 | 3,000 | 260 | 210 | 3,471 | 1,521.2 | 5,342 | 534 | 500 | 26 | 3,471 | 3,997 | 748.2 |
| anti | Antigua | 36,174 | 1,808 | 2,000 | 222 | 777 | 3,000 | 165.9 | 45,038 | 4,503 | 2,000 | 105 | 3,000 | 5,105 | 113.4 |
| arge | Argentina | 22,219,788 | 1,110,989 | 79,137 | 113,410 | 344,673 | 537,221 | 48.4 | 24,172,963 | 2,417,296 | 748,279 | 187,069 | 537,221 | 1,472,569 | 60.9 |
| arme | Armenia | 2,072,060 | 103,603 | 4,394 | 39,546 | 52,126 | 96,066 | 92.7 | 2,665,714 | 266,571 | 29,985 | 269,865 | 96,066 | 395,916 | 148.5 |
| arub | Aruba | 54,076 | 2,703 | 2,000 | 857 | 1,666 | 4,523 | 167.3 | 58,109 | 5,810 | 1,000 | 52 | 4,523 | 5,576 | 96.0 |
| aust | Australia | 9,554,935 | 477,746 | 173,835 | 305,049 | 414,352 | 893,236 | 187.0 | 14,165,953 | 1,416,595 | 437,470 | 187,487 | 893,236 | 1,518,194 | 107.2 |
| ausz | Austria | 5,640,517 | 282,025 | 5,975 | 28,966 | 65,453 | 100,395 | 35.6 | 6,640,590 | 664,059 | 6,492 | 1,623 | 100,395 | 108,510 | 16.3 |
| azer | Azerbaijan | 255,275 | 12,763 | 4,519 | 45 | 18,729 | 23,293 | 182.5 | 5,252,575 | 525,257 | 23,190 | 473 | 23,293 | 46,957 | 8.9 |
| baha | Bahamas | 168,151 | 8,407 | 3,000 | 7,000 | 6,666 | 16,666 | 198.2 | 191,691 | 19,169 | 2,000 | 500 | 16,666 | 19,166 | 100.0 |
| bahr | Bahrain | 32,672 | 1,633 | 1,400 | 2,975 | 800 | 5,175 | 316.8 | 334,763 | 33,476 | 1,000 | 52 | 5,175 | 6,227 | 18.6 |
| bang | Bangladesh | 205,246 | 10,262 | 3,881 | 12,494 | 3,627 | 20,003 | 194.9 | 29,320,947 | 2,932,094 | 484,740 | 261,013 | 20,003 | 765,757 | 26.1 |
| barb | Barbados | 148,241 | 7,412 | 5,000 | 2,142 | 13,250 | 20,392 | 275.1 | 203,321 | 20,332 | 5,000 | 555 | 20,392 | 25,948 | 127.6 |
| belg | Belgium | 6,994,354 | 349,717 | 17,104 | 62,821 | 63,953 | 143,878 | 41.1 | 8,276,363 | 827,636 | 6,775 | 15,808 | 143,878 | 166,462 | 20.1 |
| beli | Belize | 74,183 | 3,709 | 3,000 | 1,285 | 2,500 | 6,785 | 182.9 | 90,313 | 9,031 | 2,000 | 222 | 6,785 | 9,007 | 99.7 |
| belo | Belorussia | 5,047,631 | 252,381 | 3,745 | 1,248 | 71,420 | 76,413 | 30.3 | 8,270,737 | 827,073 | 54,005 | 29,079 | 76,413 | 159,497 | 19.3 |
| beni | Benin | 290,250 | 14,512 | 12,695 | 1,410 | 30,893 | 44,999 | 310.1 | 1,069,849 | 106,984 | 25,655 | 10,995 | 44,999 | 81,649 | 76.3 |
| berm | Bermuda | 36,204 | 1,810 | 2,000 | 857 | 1,666 | 4,523 | 249.9 | 41,826 | 4,182 | 5,000 | 5,000 | 4,523 | 14,523 | 347.2 |
| bhut | Bhutan | 2,148 | 107 | 120 | 11 | 42 | 173 | 161.9 | 447,656 | 44,765 | 600 | 12 | 173 | 786 | 1.8 |
| boli | Bolivia | 3,489,669 | 174,483 | 28,781 | 360,151 | 102,321 | 491,253 | 281.5 | 3,719,933 | 371,993 | 1,069,216 | 118,801 | 491,253 | 1,679,271 | 451.4 |
| bosn | Bosnia-Herzegovina | 1,105,985 | 55,299 | 10,000 | 2,500 | 10,000 | 22,500 | 40.7 | 2,370,307 | 237,030 | 10,000 | 10,000 | 22,500 | 42,500 | 17.9 |
| bots | Botswana | 262,694 | 13,134 | 4,392 | 488 | 21,702 | 26,582 | 202.4 | 595,273 | 59,527 | 30,339 | 7,584 | 26,582 | 64,505 | 108.4 |
| boug | Bougainville | 84,363 | 4,218 | 8,000 | 333 | 3,092 | 11,426 | 270.9 | 90,537 | 9,053 | 2,000 | 3,000 | 11,426 | 16,426 | 181.4 |
| braz | Brazil | 86,640,011 | 4,332,000 | 64,161 | 2,148,287 | 6,590,250 | 8,802,699 | 203.2 | 94,440,823 | 9,444,082 | 1,541,991 | 8,737,949 | 8,802,699 | 19,082,639 | 202.1 |
| brit | Britain | 30,032,493 | 1,501,624 | 55,000 | 165,000 | 1,102,741 | 1,322,741 | 88.1 | 44,731,149 | 4,473,114 | 729,598 | 6,566,382 | 1,322,741 | 8,618,721 | 192.7 |
| briz | British Virgin Is | 8,469 | 423 | 1,500 | 2,250 | 1,000 | 4,750 | 1,121.7 | 11,970 | 1,197 | 1,000 | 428 | 4,750 | 6,178 | 516.2 |
| brun | Brunei | 13,779 | 688 | 800 | 141 | 375 | 1,316 | 191.0 | 175,758 | 17,575 | 300 | 33 | 1,316 | 1,649 | 9.4 |
| bulg | Bulgaria | 5,562,996 | 278,149 | 100,000 | 150,000 | 75,310 | 325,310 | 117.0 | 6,970,300 | 697,030 | 28,640 | 28,640 | 325,310 | 382,590 | 54.9 |
| burk | Burkina Faso | 171,564 | 8,578 | 16,446 | 865 | 15,929 | 33,241 | 387.5 | 1,053,188 | 105,318 | 57,977 | 585 | 33,241 | 91,803 | 87.2 |
| buru | Burundi | 895,002 | 44,750 | 10,634 | 7,089 | 14,878 | 32,601 | 72.9 | 1,165,670 | 116,567 | 7,516 | 1,879 | 32,601 | 41,996 | 36.0 |
| camb | Cambodia | 39,907 | 1,995 | 1,498 | 15 | 4,976 | 6,489 | 325.2 | 4,385,473 | 438,547 | 13,295 | 134 | 6,489 | 19,919 | 4.5 |
| came | Cameroon | 2,355,250 | 117,762 | 7,982 | 376 | 31,102 | 39,460 | 33.5 | 4,722,780 | 472,278 | 83,258 | 2,574 | 39,460 | 125,293 | 26.5 |
| cana | Canada | 15,190,520 | 759,526 | 137,303 | 446,965 | 387,973 | 972,241 | 128.0 | 23,191,634 | 2,319,163 | 140,860 | 563,440 | 972,241 | 1,676,541 | 72.3 |
| cape | Cape Verde | 157,112 | 7,855 | 7,000 | 216 | 3,157 | 10,374 | 132.1 | 165,137 | 16,513 | 1,000 | 30 | 10,374 | 11,405 | 69.1 |
| caym | Cayman Islands | 13,977 | 698 | 900 | 385 | 375 | 1,660 | 237.6 | 20,522 | 2,052 | 2,000 | 222 | 1,660 | 3,882 | 189.2 |
| cent | Central African Rep | 488,456 | 24,422 | 6,508 | 723 | 18,913 | 26,144 | 107.0 | 1,134,099 | 113,409 | 10,004 | 526 | 26,144 | 36,674 | 32.3 |
| chad | Chad | 327,918 | 16,395 | 12,109 | 247 | 11,816 | 24,172 | 147.4 | 1,756,395 | 175,639 | 25,714 | 259 | 24,172 | 50,146 | 28.6 |
| chan | Channel Islands | 79,246 | 3,962 | 5,000 | 7,500 | 10,000 | 22,500 | 567.8 | 117,524 | 11,752 | 5,000 | 20,000 | 22,500 | 47,500 | 404.2 |
| chil | Chile | 8,501,511 | 425,075 | 23,602 | 57,226 | 213,648 | 294,477 | 69.3 | 9,679,508 | 967,950 | 412,772 | 766,576 | 294,477 | 1,473,825 | 152.3 |
| chin | China | 48,082,788 | 2,404,139 | 200,000 | 85,714 | 4,000,000 | 4,285,714 | 178.3 | 738,598,894 | 73,859,889 | 660,000 | 220,000 | 4,285,714 | 5,165,714 | 7.0 |
| colo | Colombia | 22,939,853 | 1,146,992 | 46,611 | 174,294 | 972,626 | 1,193,531 | 104.1 | 23,671,296 | 2,367,129 | 1,164,809 | 776,539 | 1,193,531 | 3,134,880 | 132.4 |
| como | Comoros | 2,003 | 100 | 100 | 42 | 57 | 200 | 199.6 | 171,245 | 17,124 | 2,000 | 105 | 200 | 2,305 | 13.5 |
| cong | Congo-Brazzaville | 809,234 | 40,461 | 4,480 | 10,453 | 41,980 | 56,913 | 140.7 | 1,029,167 | 102,916 | 19,988 | 13,325 | 56,913 | 90,226 | 87.7 |
| conz | Congo-Zaire | 16,554,686 | 827,734 | 54,264 | 11,911 | 359,545 | 425,720 | 51.4 | 18,138,147 | 1,813,814 | 200,360 | 35,357 | 425,720 | 661,438 | 36.5 |
| cook | Cook Islands | 10,180 | 509 | 1,000 | 428 | 857 | 2,285 | 449.0 | 10,749 | 1,074 | 1,000 | 111 | 2,285 | 3,396 | 316.0 |
| cost | Costa Rica | 2,192,932 | 109,646 | 13,643 | 23,531 | 213,448 | 250,622 | 228.6 | 2,278,845 | 227,884 | 69,413 | 46,275 | 250,622 | 366,310 | 160.7 |
| croa | Croatia | 3,356,924 | 167,846 | 128 | 298 | 6,000 | 6,426 | 3.8 | 3,603,010 | 360,301 | 51,362 | 27,656 | 6,426 | 85,445 | 23.7 |
| cuba | Cuba | 3,569,348 | 178,467 | 162,277 | 8,540 | 118,627 | 289,445 | 162.2 | 8,266,207 | 826,620 | 1,138,930 | 35,224 | 289,445 | 1,463,600 | 177.1 |
| cypr | Cyprus | 379,620 | 18,981 | 5,243 | 5,243 | 5,458 | 15,944 | 84.0 | 412,138 | 41,213 | 262 | 112 | 15,944 | 16,319 | 39.6 |
| czec | Czech Republic | 3,956,208 | 197,810 | 18,844 | 3,325 | 30,263 | 52,433 | 26.5 | 8,615,436 | 861,543 | 7,341 | 1,835 | 52,433 | 61,609 | 7.2 |
| denm | Denmark | 3,867,577 | 193,378 | 76,793 | 19,801 | 49,228 | 145,823 | 75.4 | 4,285,404 | 428,540 | 22,279 | 3,931 | 145,823 | 172,033 | 40.1 |
| djib | Djibouti | 7,834 | 391 | 300 | 128 | 142 | 571 | 145.9 | 162,542 | 16,254 | 2,000 | 105 | 571 | 2,676 | 16.5 |
| domi | Dominica | 45,963 | 2,298 | 2,500 | 131 | 888 | 3,520 | 153.2 | 48,592 | 4,859 | 3,000 | 61 | 3,520 | 6,581 | 135.4 |
| domr | Dominican Republic | 4,072,225 | 203,611 | 20,305 | 42,950 | 100,093 | 163,349 | 80.2 | 4,300,132 | 430,013 | 164,117 | 70,335 | 163,349 | 397,801 | 92.5 |
| ecua | Ecuador | 6,655,449 | 332,772 | 105,721 | 263,932 | 226,593 | 596,247 | 179.2 | 6,832,409 | 683,240 | 135,392 | 72,903 | 596,247 | 804,543 | 117.8 |
| egyp | Egypt | 3,175,296 | 158,764 | 74,754 | 2,872 | 81,728 | 159,354 | 100.4 | 20,699,453 | 2,069,945 | 353,670 | 10,938 | 159,354 | 523,963 | 25.3 |
| elsa | El Salvador | 2,627,170 | 131,358 | 18,368 | 17,437 | 223,318 | 259,123 | 197.3 | 2,705,076 | 270,507 | 247,659 | 61,914 | 259,123 | 568,697 | 210.2 |
| equa | Equatorial Guinea | 155,036 | 7,751 | 8,000 | 888 | 4,444 | 13,333 | 172.0 | 178,060 | 17,806 | 2,000 | 61 | 13,333 | 15,395 | 86.5 |
| erit | Eritrea | 178,860 | 8,943 | 19,377 | 395 | 20,087 | 39,860 | 445.7 | 356,154 | 35,615 | 8,921 | 90 | 39,860 | 48,871 | 137.2 |
| esto | Estonia | 388,785 | 19,439 | 2,738 | 6,388 | 10,410 | 19,536 | 100.5 | 1,222,597 | 122,259 | 4,571 | 4,571 | 19,536 | 28,678 | 23.5 |
| ethi | Ethiopia | 5,239,064 | 261,953 | 75,863 | 19,084 | 241,774 | 336,721 | 128.5 | 10,581,830 | 1,058,183 | 148,379 | 20,233 | 336,721 | 505,334 | 47.8 |
| faer | Faeroe Islands | 33,677 | 1,683 | 2,000 | 857 | 800 | 3,657 | 217.2 | 36,232 | 3,623 | 2,000 | 222 | 3,657 | 5,879 | 162.3 |
| fiji | Fiji | 270,341 | 13,517 | 10,000 | 1,764 | 26,333 | 38,098 | 281.9 | 483,184 | 48,318 | 10,000 | 1,111 | 38,098 | 49,209 | 101.8 |
| finl | Finland | 3,709,357 | 185,467 | 4,954 | 707 | 47,627 | 53,289 | 28.7 | 4,183,800 | 418,380 | 14,280 | 2,520 | 53,289 | 70,089 | 16.8 |
| fran | France | 32,655,557 | 1,632,777 | 83,055 | 399,822 | 690,086 | 1,172,964 | 71.8 | 46,604,192 | 4,660,419 | 150,009 | 1,350,081 | 1,172,964 | 2,673,054 | 57.4 |
| freg | French Guiana | 72,377 | 3,618 | 3,000 | 92 | 2,105 | 5,198 | 143.6 | 85,461 | 8,546 | 3,000 | 61 | 5,198 | 8,259 | 96.6 |
| frep | French Polynesia | 115,922 | 5,796 | 3,500 | 145 | 2,234 | 5,879 | 101.4 | 136,717 | 13,671 | 4,000 | 123 | 5,879 | 10,003 | 73.2 |
| gabo | Gabon | 361,132 | 18,056 | 3,874 | 968 | 9,943 | 14,786 | 81.9 | 407,277 | 40,727 | 13,382 | 1,486 | 14,786 | 29,654 | 72.8 |
| gamb | Gambia | 9,490 | 474 | 500 | 55 | 105 | 660 | 139.3 | 255,807 | 25,580 | 3,000 | 157 | 660 | 3,818 | 14.9 |
| geor | Georgia | 2,404,716 | 120,235 | 2,610 | 3,915 | 6,825 | 13,350 | 11.1 | 4,047,662 | 404,766 | 68,058 | 29,167 | 13,350 | 110,575 | 27.3 |
| germ | Germany | 48,139,504 | 2,406,975 | 92,323 | 112,839 | 1,215,673 | 1,420,835 | 59.0 | 66,925,488 | 6,692,548 | 320,883 | 1,283,532 | 1,420,835 | 3,025,250 | 45.2 |
| ghan | Ghana | 2,746,090 | 137,304 | 27,520 | 27,520 | 300,464 | 355,504 | 258.9 | 6,470,523 | 647,052 | 381,613 | 163,548 | 355,504 | 900,665 | 139.2 |
| gibr | Gibraltar | 17,831 | 891 | 1,000 | 250 | 352 | 1,602 | 179.8 | 20,884 | 2,088 | 1,000 | 111 | 1,602 | 2,714 | 130.0 |
| gree | Greece | 8,035,844 | 401,792 | 39,781 | 92,822 | 20,582 | 153,185 | 38.1 | 8,491,857 | 849,185 | 12,144 | 48,576 | 153,185 | 213,905 | 25.2 |
| grel | Greenland | 31,901 | 1,595 | 1,000 | 1,000 | 800 | 2,800 | 175.5 | 45,307 | 4,530 | 1,000 | 111 | 2,800 | 3,911 | 86.3 |
| gren | Grenada | 56,941 | 2,847 | 3,000 | 1,000 | 1,285 | 5,285 | 185.7 | 58,720 | 5,872 | 1,500 | 224 | 5,285 | 7,009 | 119.4 |
| guad | Guadeloupe | 276,755 | 13,837 | 9,500 | 2,375 | 20,000 | 31,875 | 230.3 | 291,015 | 29,101 | 5,000 | 1,250 | 31,875 | 38,125 | 131.0 |
| guam | Guam | 94,278 | 4,713 | 3,100 | 547 | 2,222 | 5,869 | 124.5 | 100,370 | 10,037 | 6,000 | 315 | 5,869 | 12,185 | 121.4 |
| guat | Guatemala | 2,941,001 | 147,050 | 30,630 | 28,615 | 301,089 | 360,335 | 245.0 | 3,127,726 | 312,772 | 179,876 | 44,969 | 360,335 | 585,180 | 187.1 |
| guin | Guinea | 42,563 | 2,128 | 2,577 | 286 | 3,071 | 5,934 | 278.9 | 1,437,959 | 143,795 | 7,922 | 416 | 5,934 | 14,273 | 9.9 |
| gunb | Guinea-Bissau | 43,521 | 2,176 | 95 | 23 | 1,111 | 1,229 | 56.5 | 342,417 | 34,241 | 10,000 | 526 | 1,229 | 11,756 | 34.3 |
| guya | Guyana | 248,455 | 12,422 | 90 | 15 | 4,347 | 4,453 | 35.9 | 571,161 | 57,116 | 12,000 | 1,333 | 4,453 | 17,787 | 31.1 |
| hait | Haiti | 1,886,432 | 94,321 | 4,195 | 6,137 | 89,360 | 99,693 | 105.7 | 2,017,143 | 201,714 | 74,460 | 31,911 | 99,693 | 206,064 | 102.2 |
| hond | Honduras | 2,248,112 | 112,405 | 27,527 | 58,226 | 172,036 | 257,790 | 229.3 | 2,398,242 | 239,824 | 124,939 | 31,234 | 257,790 | 413,964 | 172.6 |
| hung | Hungary | 7,277,555 | 363,877 | 3,904 | 976 | 88,480 | 93,360 | 25.7 | 8,394,919 | 839,491 | 5,830 | 647 | 93,360 | 99,838 | 11.9 |
| icel | Iceland | 195,676 | 9,783 | 7,249 | 8,076 | 3,713 | 19,038 | 194.6 | 205,780 | 20,578 | 42 | 42 | 19,038 | 19,122 | 92.9 |
| indi | India | 18,876,599 | 943,829 | 1,811,385 | 4,287,554 | 1,125,038 | 7,223,977 | 765.4 | 323,783,860 | 32,378,386 | 19,402,010 | 41,229,271 | 7,223,977 | 67,855,258 | 209.6 |
| indo | Indonesia | 14,157,709 | 707,885 | 1,072,504 | 357,501 | 664,026 | 2,094,032 | 295.8 | 114,823,272 | 11,482,327 | 467,280 | 116,820 | 2,094,032 | 2,678,132 | 23.3 |
| iran | Iran | 126,104 | 6,305 | 0 | 0 | 690 | 690 | 11.0 | 28,660,089 | 2,866,008 | 50,000 | 1,020 | 690 | 51,711 | 1.8 |
| iraq | Iraq | 223,562 | 11,178 | 52,012 | 525 | 20,166 | 72,703 | 650.4 | 6,836,763 | 683,676 | 200,512 | 2,025 | 72,703 | 275,241 | 40.3 |
| irel | Ireland | 2,570,584 | 128,529 | 1,750 | 8,920 | 23,367 | 34,038 | 26.5 | 2,842,938 | 284,293 | 14,000 | 6,000 | 34,038 | 54,038 | 19.0 |
| isle | Isle of Man | 39,184 | 1,959 | 2,000 | 8,000 | 2,000 | 12,000 | 612.5 | 57,734 | 5,773 | 2,000 | 6,000 | 12,000 | 20,000 | 346.4 |
| isra | Israel | 175,623 | 8,781 | 9,550 | 4,391 | 5,085 | 19,026 | 216.7 | 3,097,409 | 309,740 | 37,502 | 12,500 | 19,026 | 69,029 | 22.3 |
| ital | Italy | 39,315,003 | 1,965,750 | 17,360 | 705,973 | 1,581,571 | 2,304,904 | 117.3 | 47,741,351 | 4,774,135 | 2,139 | 2,139 | 2,304,904 | 2,309,182 | 48.4 |
| ivor | Ivory Coast | 896,103 | 44,805 | 17,916 | 746 | 63,935 | 82,598 | 184.3 | 3,068,848 | 306,884 | 65,824 | 2,035 | 82,598 | 150,458 | 49.0 |
| jama | Jamaica | 634,604 | 31,730 | 5,918 | 1,479 | 74,959 | 82,356 | 259.6 | 1,449,530 | 144,953 | 30,000 | 5,294 | 82,356 | 117,650 | 81.2 |
| japa | Japan | 2,843,263 | 142,163 | 377,038 | 397,167 | 209,763 | 983,968 | 692.1 | 106,889,597 | 10,688,959 | 29,272 | 19,514 | 983,968 | 1,032,755 | 9.7 |
| jord | Jordan | 113,856 | 5,692 | 52,824 | 2,780 | 15,633 | 71,237 | 1,251.4 | 2,882,438 | 288,243 | 65,150 | 2,714 | 71,237 | 139,101 | 48.3 |
| kaza | Kazakhstan | 2,194,193 | 109,709 | 10,924 | 574 | 54,610 | 66,109 | 60.3 | 11,658,836 | 1,165,883 | 139,651 | 4,319 | 66,109 | 210,079 | 18.0 |
| keny | Kenya | 8,918,397 | 445,919 | 32,516 | 7,380 | 196,155 | 236,052 | 52.9 | 12,109,162 | 1,210,916 | 60,152 | 8,988 | 236,052 | 305,192 | 25.2 |
| kirg | Kirgizstan | 309,845 | 15,492 | 600 | 18 | 5,050 | 5,669 | 36.6 | 2,882,287 | 288,228 | 10,000 | 309 | 5,669 | 15,978 | 5.5 |
| kiri | Kiribati | 43,699 | 2,184 | 500 | 20 | 625 | 1,145 | 52.4 | 46,897 | 4,689 | 2,000 | 40 | 1,145 | 3,186 | 67.9 |
| kuwa | Kuwait | 108,806 | 5,440 | 3,000 | 333 | 1,000 | 4,333 | 79.7 | 880,313 | 88,031 | 5,000 | 555 | 4,333 | 9,888 | 11.2 |
| laos | Laos | 32,551 | 1,627 | 1,500 | 264 | 526 | 2,291 | 140.8 | 1,514,033 | 151,403 | 1,000 | 52 | 2,291 | 3,343 | 2.2 |
| latv | Latvia | 1,349,880 | 67,494 | 911 | 227 | 21,103 | 22,242 | 33.0 | 2,078,017 | 207,801 | 8,640 | 1,524 | 22,242 | 32,406 | 15.6 |
| leba | Lebanon | 995,168 | 49,758 | 49,015 | 73,522 | 25,825 | 148,362 | 298.2 | 1,870,968 | 187,096 | 231,670 | 154,446 | 148,362 | 534,479 | 285.7 |
| leso | Lesotho | 562,429 | 28,121 | 188 | 9 | 13,601 | 13,798 | 49.1 | 825,766 | 82,576 | 12,270 | 511 | 13,798 | 26,580 | 32.2 |
| libe | Liberia | 128,141 | 6,407 | 13,447 | 14,982 | 39,394 | 67,823 | 1,058.6 | 463,104 | 46,310 | 9,595 | 3,198 | 67,823 | 80,616 | 174.1 |
| liby | Libya | 77,898 | 3,894 | 200 | 1,800 | 1,000 | 3,000 | 77.0 | 2,360,573 | 236,057 | 200 | 1,800 | 3,000 | 5,000 | 2.1 |
| liec | Liechtenstein | 21,190 | 1,059 | 300 | 1,200 | 300 | 1,800 | 169.9 | 25,417 | 2,541 | 2,000 | 1,333 | 1,800 | 5,133 | 202.0 |
| lith | Lithuania | 2,561,892 | 128,094 | 4,238 | 1,816 | 2,130 | 8,184 | 6.4 | 2,961,383 | 296,138 | 14,077 | 3,519 | 8,184 | 25,780 | 8.7 |
| luxe | Luxembourg | 311,851 | 15,592 | 2,000 | 3,000 | 5,000 | 10,000 | 64.1 | 333,495 | 33,349 | 10,000 | 15,000 | 10,000 | 35,000 | 104.9 |
| mace | Macedonia | 927,924 | 46,396 | 638 | 70 | 2,203 | 2,912 | 6.3 | 1,348,139 | 134,813 | 1,000 | 111 | 2,912 | 4,023 | 3.0 |
| mada | Madagascar | 2,901,885 | 145,094 | 7,246 | 778 | 22,650 | 30,675 | 21.1 | 6,122,120 | 612,212 | 190,938 | 10,049 | 30,675 | 231,662 | 37.8 |
| mala | Malawi | 1,836,133 | 91,806 | 18,813 | 28,574 | 109,975 | 157,363 | 171.4 | 2,882,469 | 288,246 | 60,074 | 20,024 | 157,363 | 237,462 | 82.4 |
| malb | Malaysia | 867,568 | 43,378 | 9,716 | 1,079 | 30,124 | 40,919 | 94.3 | 11,080,057 | 1,108,005 | 78,486 | 4,130 | 40,919 | 123,536 | 11.1 |

| COUNTRY | | SCRIPTURES (continued) | | | | | | | | | | | | | |
|---|---|---|---|---|---|---|---|---|---|---|---|---|---|---|---|
| | | NEW TESTAMENT DISTRIBUTION | | | | | | | PORTIONS DISTRIBUTION (Gospels) | | | | | | |
| code | short name | goal | goal p.a. | UBS p.a. | other p.a. | duplicates | total p.a. | T/G% | goal | goal p.a. | UBS p.a. | other p.a. | duplicates | total p.a. | T/G% |
| 1 | 2 | 126 | 127 | 128 | 129 | 130 | 131 | 132 | 133 | 134 | 135 | 136 | 137 | 138 | 139 |
| mald | Maldives | 198 | 9 | 10 | 0 | 5 | 16 | 161.8 | 132,519 | 13,251 | 0 | 0 | 16 | 16 | 0.1 |
| mali | Mali | 32,457 | 1,622 | 2,049 | 227 | 4,421 | 6,698 | 412.8 | 1,655,990 | 165,599 | 35,521 | 1,869 | 6,698 | 44,088 | 26.6 |
| malt | Malta | 275,571 | 13,778 | 4,000 | 2,666 | 12,500 | 19,166 | 139.1 | 287,083 | 28,708 | 1,500 | 1,000 | 19,166 | 21,666 | 75.5 |
| mars | Marshall Islands | 30,842 | 1,542 | 1,900 | 100 | 312 | 2,312 | 150.0 | 33,473 | 3,347 | 0 | 0 | 2,312 | 2,312 | 69.1 |
| mart | Martinique | 257,661 | 12,883 | 15,000 | 789 | 12,500 | 28,289 | 219.6 | 271,565 | 27,156 | 0 | 0 | 28,289 | 28,289 | 104.2 |
| maur | Mauritania | 1,391 | 69 | 200 | 2 | 30 | 232 | 333.8 | 497,100 | 49,710 | 0 | 0 | 232 | 232 | 0.5 |
| maus | Mauritius | 217,922 | 10,896 | 9,490 | 134 | 11,403 | 21,027 | 193.0 | 688,538 | 68,853 | 259,611 | 2,622 | 21,027 | 283,261 | 411.4 |
| mayo | Mayotte | 828 | 41 | 70 | 37 | 15 | 123 | 297.1 | 47,897 | 4,789 | 0 | 0 | 123 | 123 | 2.6 |
| mexi | Mexico | 51,749,491 | 2,587,474 | 142,932 | 396,434 | 315,523 | 854,889 | 33.0 | 54,593,830 | 5,459,383 | 501,959 | 2,007,836 | 854,889 | 3,364,684 | 61.6 |
| micr | Micronesia | 50,549 | 2,527 | 5,595 | 621 | 4,123 | 10,340 | 409.1 | 55,191 | 5,519 | 1,662 | 87 | 10,340 | 12,089 | 219.0 |
| mold | Moldavia | 1,999,984 | 99,999 | 10,721 | 2,680 | 93,748 | 107,149 | 107.2 | 3,236,220 | 323,622 | 19,572 | 2,174 | 107,149 | 128,895 | 39.8 |
| mona | Monaco | 23,882 | 1,194 | 1,000 | 250 | 1,000 | 2,250 | 188.4 | 25,605 | 2,560 | 0 | 0 | 2,250 | 2,250 | 87.9 |
| mong | Mongolia | 15,946 | 797 | 4,561 | 141 | 1,273 | 5,975 | 749.5 | 1,328,880 | 132,888 | 16,443 | 335 | 5,975 | 22,754 | 17.1 |
| mont | Montserrat | 6,438 | 321 | 400 | 21 | 111 | 532 | 165.3 | 6,718 | 671 | 0 | 0 | 532 | 532 | 79.2 |
| moro | Morocco | 47,217 | 2,360 | 201 | 50 | 570 | 821 | 34.8 | 7,615,695 | 761,569 | 98 | 10 | 821 | 930 | 0.1 |
| moza | Mozambique | 1,247,677 | 62,383 | 12,746 | 9,420 | 23,462 | 45,629 | 73.1 | 3,842,554 | 384,255 | 8,069 | 1,423 | 45,629 | 55,122 | 14.3 |
| myan | Myanmar | 2,047,456 | 102,372 | 4,283 | 225 | 5,977 | 10,485 | 10.2 | 25,689,540 | 2,568,954 | 60,980 | 2,540 | 10,485 | 74,006 | 2.9 |
| nami | Namibia | 532,163 | 26,608 | 739 | 30 | 18,967 | 19,737 | 74.2 | 683,575 | 68,357 | 14,245 | 440 | 19,737 | 34,423 | 50.4 |
| naur | Nauru | 5,061 | 253 | 200 | 22 | 62 | 284 | 112.5 | 6,974 | 697 | 0 | 0 | 284 | 284 | 40.8 |
| nepa | Nepal | 79,407 | 3,970 | 15,484 | 316 | 9,835 | 25,635 | 645.7 | 3,452,514 | 345,251 | 127,512 | 1,288 | 25,635 | 154,435 | 44.7 |
| neth | Netherlands | 8,317,074 | 415,853 | 4,951 | 7,364 | 277,313 | 289,629 | 69.6 | 12,659,170 | 1,265,917 | 87,382 | 37,449 | 289,629 | 414,460 | 32.7 |
| nets | Netherlands Antilles | 123,946 | 6,197 | 2,867 | 2,532 | 8,380 | 13,779 | 222.4 | 144,443 | 14,444 | 26,982 | 8,994 | 13,779 | 49,755 | 344.5 |
| newc | New Caledonia | 59,885 | 2,994 | 3,200 | 355 | 1,250 | 4,805 | 160.5 | 78,404 | 7,840 | 0 | 0 | 4,805 | 4,805 | 61.3 |
| newz | New Zealand | 1,911,252 | 95,562 | 14,774 | 30,824 | 46,436 | 92,035 | 96.3 | 2,839,055 | 283,905 | 73,171 | 109,756 | 92,035 | 274,962 | 96.9 |
| nica | Nicaragua | 1,595,486 | 79,774 | 10,591 | 10,054 | 45,547 | 66,192 | 83.0 | 1,664,912 | 166,491 | 60,962 | 26,126 | 66,192 | 153,280 | 92.1 |
| niga | Niger | 3,481 | 174 | 200 | 2 | 101 | 303 | 174.1 | 644,737 | 64,473 | 0 | 0 | 303 | 303 | 0.5 |
| nige | Nigeria | 14,626,669 | 731,333 | 11,312 | 11,868 | 307,543 | 330,723 | 45.2 | 32,160,662 | 3,216,066 | 222,676 | 2,004,084 | 330,723 | 2,557,483 | 79.5 |
| nork | North Korea | 311,947 | 15,597 | 2,000 | 857 | 1,777 | 4,634 | 29.7 | 15,291,520 | 1,529,152 | 0 | 0 | 4,634 | 4,634 | 0.3 |
| norl | Northern Cyprus | 10,147 | 507 | 500 | 55 | 333 | 888 | 175.2 | 117,442 | 11,744 | 0 | 0 | 888 | 888 | 7.6 |
| norm | Northern Mariana Is | 33,678 | 1,683 | 2,300 | 121 | 666 | 3,087 | 183.4 | 38,024 | 3,802 | 0 | 0 | 3,087 | 3,087 | 81.2 |
| norw | Norway | 3,300,462 | 165,023 | 45,241 | 3,352 | 75,825 | 124,419 | 75.4 | 3,492,553 | 349,255 | 15,450 | 3,862 | 124,419 | 143,732 | 41.2 |
| oman | Oman | 23,359 | 1,167 | 600 | 31 | 222 | 853 | 73.1 | 493,848 | 49,384 | 0 | 0 | 853 | 853 | 1.7 |
| paki | Pakistan | 725,102 | 36,255 | 20,129 | 3,141 | 537,553 | 560,824 | 1,546.9 | 29,962,913 | 2,996,291 | 606,562 | 31,924 | 560,824 | 1,199,310 | 40.0 |
| pala | Palau | 10,723 | 536 | 1,000 | 111 | 166 | 1,277 | 238.3 | 11,280 | 1,128 | 0 | 0 | 1,277 | 1,277 | 113.3 |
| pale | Palestine | 58,376 | 2,918 | 5,000 | 2,142 | 3,636 | 10,779 | 369.3 | 680,380 | 68,038 | 8,275 | 3,546 | 10,779 | 22,600 | 33.2 |
| pana | Panama | 1,416,686 | 70,834 | 15,848 | 26,300 | 74,951 | 117,099 | 165.3 | 1,641,202 | 164,120 | 112,572 | 28,143 | 117,099 | 257,814 | 157.1 |
| papu | Papua New Guinea | 1,482,986 | 74,149 | 60,706 | 3,737 | 55,625 | 120,069 | 161.9 | 1,823,195 | 182,319 | 1,056,637 | 1,056,637 | 120,069 | 2,233,343 | 1,225.0 |
| para | Paraguay | 2,531,535 | 126,576 | 21,314 | 28,023 | 56,811 | 106,149 | 83.9 | 2,689,117 | 268,911 | 205,198 | 87,942 | 106,149 | 399,289 | 148.5 |
| peru | Peru | 13,405,505 | 670,275 | 50,326 | 130,053 | 296,710 | 477,089 | 71.2 | 13,903,241 | 1,390,324 | 400,826 | 601,239 | 477,089 | 1,479,154 | 106.4 |
| phil | Philippines | 35,943,655 | 1,797,182 | 1,255,897 | 6,593,459 | 1,660,938 | 9,510,294 | 529.2 | 40,938,104 | 4,093,810 | 426,158 | 1,704,632 | 9,510,294 | 11,641,084 | 284.4 |
| pola | Poland | 29,532,112 | 1,476,605 | 10,226 | 15,794 | 88,182 | 114,202 | 7.7 | 30,711,431 | 3,071,143 | 43,237 | 129,711 | 114,202 | 287,150 | 9.3 |
| port | Portugal | 6,590,379 | 329,518 | 11,164 | 31,609 | 127,205 | 169,979 | 51.6 | 7,157,232 | 715,723 | 8,253 | 21,222 | 169,979 | 199,454 | 27.9 |
| puer | Puerto Rico | 2,430,792 | 121,539 | 21,886 | 85,398 | 134,190 | 241,474 | 198.7 | 2,522,353 | 252,235 | 213,698 | 142,465 | 241,474 | 597,637 | 236.9 |
| qata | Qatar | 33,003 | 1,650 | 1,000 | 111 | 333 | 1,444 | 87.5 | 321,670 | 32,167 | 0 | 0 | 1,444 | 1,444 | 4.5 |
| reun | Reunion | 323,918 | 16,195 | 5,000 | 2,142 | 7,142 | 14,285 | 88.2 | 371,764 | 37,176 | 0 | 0 | 14,285 | 14,285 | 38.4 |
| roma | Romania | 15,730,688 | 786,534 | 2,415 | 7,245 | 194,896 | 204,556 | 26.0 | 18,079,173 | 1,807,917 | 43,850 | 102,316 | 204,556 | 350,722 | 19.4 |
| russ | Russia | 66,563,265 | 3,328,163 | 51,626 | 120,460 | 1,010,916 | 1,183,003 | 35.5 | 118,778,132 | 11,877,813 | 574,058 | 5,166,522 | 1,183,003 | 6,923,583 | 58.3 |
| rwan | Rwanda | 1,404,233 | 70,211 | 22,080 | 1,162 | 53,881 | 77,123 | 109.8 | 1,737,698 | 173,769 | 156,384 | 4,836 | 77,123 | 238,343 | 137.2 |
| saha | Sahara | 29 | 1 | 2 | 0 | 1 | 3 | 256.6 | 15,380 | 1,538 | 0 | 0 | 3 | 3 | 0.2 |
| saih | Saint Helena | 4,158 | 207 | 300 | 100 | 142 | 542 | 261.1 | 4,801 | 480 | 0 | 0 | 542 | 542 | 113.1 |
| saik | Saint Kitts & Nevis | 25,707 | 1,285 | 3,000 | 658 | 777 | 4,436 | 345.1 | 27,406 | 2,740 | 0 | 0 | 4,436 | 4,436 | 161.9 |
| sail | Saint Lucia | 82,075 | 4,103 | 3,000 | 529 | 1,428 | 4,957 | 120.8 | 87,762 | 8,776 | 0 | 0 | 4,957 | 4,957 | 56.5 |
| saip | Saint Pierre & Miquelon | 5,084 | 254 | 300 | 75 | 125 | 500 | 196.7 | 5,212 | 521 | 0 | 0 | 500 | 500 | 95.9 |
| saiv | Saint Vincent | 55,598 | 2,779 | 4,500 | 500 | 1,222 | 6,222 | 223.8 | 80,356 | 8,035 | 0 | 0 | 6,222 | 6,222 | 77.4 |
| samo | Samoa | 95,691 | 4,784 | 6,000 | 666 | 2,222 | 8,888 | 185.8 | 101,551 | 10,155 | 0 | 0 | 8,888 | 8,888 | 87.5 |
| sanm | San Marino | 18,933 | 946 | 1,000 | 1,000 | 500 | 2,500 | 264.1 | 20,909 | 2,090 | 0 | 0 | 2,500 | 2,500 | 119.6 |
| saot | Sao Tome & Principe | 37,410 | 1,870 | 3,000 | 1,285 | 714 | 5,000 | 267.3 | 41,296 | 4,129 | 0 | 0 | 5,000 | 5,000 | 121.1 |
| saud | Saudi Arabia | 243,359 | 12,168 | 2,000 | 500 | 3,750 | 6,250 | 51.4 | 6,816,803 | 681,680 | 0 | 0 | 6,250 | 6,250 | 0.9 |
| sene | Senegal | 73,672 | 3,683 | 3,500 | 1,166 | 1,176 | 5,843 | 158.6 | 1,525,319 | 152,531 | 0 | 0 | 5,843 | 5,843 | 3.8 |
| seyc | Seychelles | 43,006 | 2,150 | 3,000 | 750 | 777 | 4,527 | 210.6 | 46,183 | 4,618 | 0 | 0 | 4,527 | 4,527 | 98.0 |
| sier | Sierra Leone | 75,209 | 3,760 | 3,111 | 10,015 | 9,466 | 22,592 | 600.8 | 735,907 | 73,590 | 14,820 | 6,351 | 22,592 | 43,764 | 59.5 |
| sing | Singapore | 261,144 | 13,057 | 4,353 | 12,784 | 40,820 | 57,957 | 443.9 | 2,356,896 | 235,689 | 61,414 | 61,414 | 57,957 | 180,785 | 76.7 |
| slok | Slovakia | 3,431,653 | 171,582 | 8,276 | 435 | 8,262 | 16,973 | 9.9 | 4,300,856 | 430,085 | 21,624 | 901 | 16,973 | 39,498 | 9.2 |
| slov | Slovenia | 1,442,526 | 72,126 | 3,908 | 1,302 | 21,000 | 26,210 | 36.3 | 1,659,411 | 165,941 | 9 | 1 | 26,210 | 26,221 | 15.8 |
| solo | Solomon Islands | 105,947 | 5,297 | 7,000 | 291 | 2,222 | 9,513 | 179.6 | 117,224 | 11,722 | 0 | 0 | 9,513 | 9,513 | 81.2 |
| soma | Somalia | 13,881 | 694 | 1,000 | 30 | 667 | 1,697 | 244.6 | 708,238 | 70,823 | 0 | 0 | 1,697 | 1,697 | 2.4 |
| somi | Somaliland | 987 | 49 | 60 | 1 | 52 | 113 | 230.6 | 329,153 | 32,915 | 0 | 0 | 113 | 113 | 0.3 |
| soua | South Africa | 15,529,127 | 776,456 | 99,690 | 32,876 | 682,108 | 814,675 | 104.9 | 19,916,798 | 1,991,679 | 267,718 | 29,746 | 814,675 | 1,112,139 | 55.8 |
| souk | South Korea | 13,556,698 | 677,834 | 1,502,864 | 1,214,792 | 1,252,489 | 3,970,146 | 585.7 | 34,583,413 | 3,458,341 | 1,543,703 | 435,403 | 3,970,146 | 5,949,252 | 172.0 |
| spai | Spain | 30,392,364 | 1,519,618 | 26,501 | 1,125,716 | 1,996,125 | 3,148,342 | 207.2 | 32,390,881 | 3,239,088 | 1,263,734 | 1,263,734 | 3,148,342 | 5,675,810 | 175.2 |
| span | Spanish North Africa | 64,823 | 3,241 | 3,000 | 27,000 | 36,000 | 66,000 | 2,036.3 | 79,733 | 7,973 | 0 | 0 | 66,000 | 66,000 | 827.8 |
| sril | Sri Lanka | 1,107,307 | 55,365 | 26,791 | 53,421 | 33,179 | 113,391 | 204.8 | 11,945,066 | 1,194,506 | 202,937 | 86,973 | 113,391 | 403,301 | 33.8 |
| suda | Sudan | 1,242,880 | 62,144 | 125,455 | 1,267 | 26,205 | 152,927 | 246.1 | 7,433,496 | 743,349 | 239,712 | 7,413 | 152,927 | 400,053 | 53.8 |
| suri | Suriname | 110,083 | 5,504 | 11,583 | 1,838 | 16,945 | 30,367 | 551.7 | 264,496 | 26,449 | 116,616 | 12,957 | 30,367 | 159,940 | 604.7 |
| swaz | Swaziland | 253,494 | 12,674 | 2,210 | 68 | 10,697 | 12,976 | 102.4 | 381,538 | 38,153 | 12,116 | 247 | 12,976 | 25,339 | 66.4 |
| swed | Sweden | 4,868,990 | 243,449 | 19,503 | 175,527 | 66,865 | 261,895 | 107.6 | 7,198,388 | 719,838 | 169,596 | 638,004 | 261,895 | 1,069,495 | 148.6 |
| swit | Switzerland | 5,188,930 | 259,446 | 13,162 | 13,162 | 256,190 | 282,514 | 108.9 | 5,897,181 | 589,718 | 117,101 | 468,404 | 282,514 | 868,019 | 147.2 |
| syri | Syria | 478,595 | 23,929 | 7,773 | 7,773 | 7,562 | 23,108 | 96.6 | 5,952,677 | 595,267 | 54,350 | 126,816 | 23,108 | 204,275 | 34.3 |
| taiw | Taiwan | 791,702 | 39,585 | 443,392 | 617,354 | 110,503 | 1,171,249 | 2,958.8 | 15,137,715 | 1,513,771 | 188,142 | 438,998 | 1,171,249 | 1,798,389 | 118.8 |
| taji | Tajikistan | 80,792 | 4,039 | 3,000 | 30 | 4,040 | 7,070 | 175.0 | 3,352,401 | 335,240 | 0 | 0 | 7,070 | 7,070 | 2.1 |
| tanz | Tanzania | 5,093,091 | 254,654 | 54,967 | 1,064 | 224,395 | 280,426 | 110.1 | 11,071,938 | 1,107,193 | 94,232 | 951 | 280,426 | 375,610 | 33.9 |
| thai | Thailand | 896,108 | 44,805 | 15,280 | 73,043 | 44,028 | 132,352 | 295.4 | 41,105,910 | 4,110,591 | 261,499 | 2,353,491 | 132,352 | 2,747,342 | 66.8 |
| timo | Timor | 411,739 | 20,586 | 2,000 | 3,714 | 16,666 | 22,380 | 108.7 | 447,786 | 44,778 | 0 | 0 | 22,380 | 22,380 | 50.0 |
| togo | Togo | 415,618 | 20,780 | 4,729 | 248 | 25,414 | 30,392 | 146.3 | 1,136,500 | 113,650 | 29,359 | 908 | 30,392 | 60,659 | 53.4 |
| tong | Tonga | 51,064 | 2,553 | 3,800 | 422 | 875 | 5,097 | 199.6 | 55,740 | 5,574 | 0 | 0 | 5,097 | 5,097 | 91.4 |
| trin | Trinidad & Tobago | 577,812 | 28,890 | 320 | 35 | 11,250 | 11,605 | 40.2 | 926,724 | 92,672 | 0 | 0 | 11,605 | 11,605 | 12.5 |
| tuni | Tunisia | 22,857 | 1,142 | 400 | 21 | 285 | 706 | 61.8 | 4,155,825 | 415,582 | 0 | 0 | 706 | 706 | 0.2 |
| turk | Turkey | 213,333 | 10,666 | 44,663 | 10,004 | 14,798 | 69,465 | 651.2 | 36,158,183 | 3,615,818 | 23,471 | 211,239 | 69,465 | 304,175 | 8.4 |
| turm | Turkmenistan | 64,326 | 3,216 | 2,000 | 20 | 2,020 | 4,040 | 125.6 | 2,483,665 | 248,366 | 0 | 0 | 4,040 | 4,040 | 1.6 |
| turs | Turks & Caicos Is | 7,943 | 397 | 400 | 266 | 166 | 833 | 209.8 | 9,917 | 991 | 0 | 0 | 833 | 833 | 84.0 |
| tuva | Tuvalu | 5,062 | 253 | 700 | 233 | 142 | 1,076 | 425.1 | 6,046 | 604 | 0 | 0 | 1,076 | 1,076 | 178.0 |
| ugan | Uganda | 5,057,278 | 252,863 | 20,197 | 8,780 | 78,589 | 107,566 | 42.5 | 5,843,861 | 584,386 | 67,696 | 22,565 | 107,566 | 197,827 | 33.9 |
| ukra | Ukraine | 33,816,743 | 1,690,837 | 31,897 | 74,426 | 641,904 | 748,227 | 44.3 | 41,615,485 | 4,161,548 | 188,796 | 283,194 | 748,227 | 1,220,217 | 29.3 |
| unia | United Arab Emirates | 132,163 | 6,608 | 2,000 | 352 | 2,500 | 4,852 | 73.4 | 1,259,902 | 125,990 | 0 | 0 | 4,852 | 4,852 | 3.9 |
| usa | USA | 138,175,676 | 6,908,783 | 1,696,117 | 32,226,223 | 18,090,254 | 52,012,594 | 752.8 | 200,254,603 | 20,025,460 | 2,188,717 | 70,768,516 | 52,012,594 | 124,969,827 | 624.1 |
| uuay | Uruguay | 1,529,603 | 76,480 | 5,267 | 11,400 | 26,469 | 43,137 | 56.4 | 2,355,047 | 235,504 | 86,680 | 202,253 | 43,137 | 332,070 | 141.0 |
| uzbe | Uzbekistan | 304,789 | 15,239 | 27,805 | 280 | 40,971 | 69,057 | 453.1 | 13,667,699 | 1,366,769 | 73,222 | 739 | 69,057 | 143,019 | 10.5 |
| vanu | Vanuatu | 46,329 | 2,316 | 3,000 | 296 | 1,000 | 4,296 | 185.5 | 52,355 | 5,235 | 0 | 0 | 4,296 | 4,296 | 82.1 |
| vene | Venezuela | 12,349,178 | 617,458 | 6,508 | 58,572 | 212,682 | 277,762 | 45.0 | 13,126,252 | 1,312,625 | 202,647 | 810,588 | 277,762 | 1,290,997 | 98.4 |
| viet | Viet Nam | 3,702,767 | 185,138 | 159,300 | 240,951 | 30,075 | 430,326 | 232.4 | 46,226,812 | 4,622,681 | 0 | 0 | 430,326 | 430,326 | 9.3 |
| virg | Virgin Is of the US | 65,236 | 3,261 | 7,000 | 28,000 | 15,000 | 50,000 | 1,532.9 | 70,153 | 7,015 | 0 | 0 | 50,000 | 50,000 | 712.7 |
| wall | Wallis & Futuna Is | 7,974 | 398 | 1,000 | 428 | 333 | 1,761 | 441.9 | 8,273 | 827 | 0 | 0 | 1,761 | 1,761 | 213.0 |
| yeme | Yemen | 5,083 | 254 | 300 | 33 | 200 | 533 | 209.8 | 2,990,001 | 299,000 | 0 | 0 | 533 | 533 | 0.2 |
| yugo | Yugoslavia | 4,908,643 | 245,432 | 9,037 | 21,086 | 47,695 | 77,818 | 31.7 | 7,884,104 | 788,410 | 185 | 226 | 77,818 | 78,229 | 9.9 |
| zamb | Zambia | 2,541,075 | 127,053 | 17,605 | 18,470 | 72,270 | 108,346 | 85.3 | 3,380,438 | 338,043 | 60,404 | 90,606 | 108,346 | 259,356 | 76.7 |
| zimb | Zimbabwe | 3,186,090 | 159,304 | 14,602 | 29,646 | 144,245 | 188,494 | 118.3 | 5,428,677 | 542,867 | 66,687 | 92,091 | 188,494 | 347,272 | 64.0 |
| | 11 minicountries | 9,402 | 470 | 621 | 642 | 1,293 | 2,556 | 543.8 | 15,113 | 1,511 | 471 | 728 | 2,556 | 3,755 | 248.5 |
| | Africa | 103,728,365 | 5,186,418 | 870,548 | 299,425 | 3,475,951 | 4,645,925 | 89.6 | 225,242,765 | 22,524,276 | 3,372,274 | 2,588,483 | 4,645,925 | 10,606,683 | 47.1 |
| | Antarctica | 2,096 | 104 | 0 | 0 | 0 | 0 | 0.0 | 2,818 | 281 | 100 | 100 | 0 | 200 | 70.9 |
| | Asia | 156,012,976 | 7,800,648 | 7,227,618 | 14,111,365 | 10,076,045 | 31,415,028 | 402.7 | 1,748,880,458 | 174,888,045 | 25,654,631 | 47,787,940 | 31,415,028 | 104,857,599 | 60.0 |
| | Europe | 430,315,211 | 21,515,760 | 840,470 | 3,404,343 | 10,135,784 | 14,380,597 | 66.8 | 584,861,414 | 58,486,141 | 4,454,434 | 17,962,989 | 14,380,597 | 36,798,021 | 62.9 |
| | Latin America | 260,148,612 | 13,007,430 | 992,208 | 4,103,718 | 11,028,892 | 16,124,818 | 124.0 | 285,128,350 | 28,512,835 | 9,070,093 | 14,920,598 | 16,124,818 | 40,115,510 | 140.7 |
| | Northern America | 153,439,387 | 7,671,969 | 1,836,720 | 32,675,120 | 18,480,819 | 52,992,659 | 690.7 | 223,538,585 | 22,353,858 | 2,335,577 | 71,337,067 | 52,992,659 | 126,665,304 | 566.6 |
| | Oceania | 14,101,655 | 705,082 | 313,041 | 346,727 | 566,712 | 1,226,480 | 173.9 | 20,300,756 | 2,030,075 | 1,597,891 | 1,363,062 | 1,226,480 | 4,187,434 | 206.3 |
| | **World A** | **3,241,833** | **162,091** | **193,865** | **19,827** | **676,452** | **890,145** | **549.2** | **195,813,022** | **19,581,302** | **1,211,398** | **255,113** | **890,145** | **2,356,657** | **12.0** |
| | **World B** | **234,756,609** | **11,737,830** | **6,606,618** | **7,736,859** | **10,659,515** | **25,002,993** | **213.0** | **1,802,090,967** | **180,209,096** | **28,626,930** | **53,535,419** | **25,002,993** | **107,165,342** | **59.5** |
| | **World C** | **879,749,863** | **43,987,493** | **5,280,122** | **47,184,013** | **42,428,237** | **94,892,372** | **215.7** | **1,090,051,160** | **109,005,116** | **16,646,672** | **102,169,708** | **94,892,372** | **213,708,753** | **196.0** |
| | **GLOBAL TOTAL** | **1,117,748,305** | **55,887,415** | **12,080,605** | **54,940,701** | **53,764,205** | **120,785,511** | **216.1** | **3,087,955,150** | **308,795,515** | **46,485,000** | **155,960,241** | **120,785,511** | **323,230,753** | **104.7** |

| COUNTRY | | SCRIPTURES (continued) | | | | | | | BROADCASTING | | | EVANGELISM | |
|---|---|---|---|---|---|---|---|---|---|---|---|---|---|
| | | SELECTIONS DISTRIBUTION | | | | | | | RADIO/TV AUDIENCES | | | offers via 45 ministries | |
| code | short name | goal | goal p.a. | UBS p.a. | other p.a. | duplicates | total p.a. | T/G% | cb aud | cstat | secstat | q per day | e p.a.p.c. |
| 1 | 2 | 140 | 141 | 142 | 143 | 144 | 145 | 146 | 147 | 148 | 149 | 150 | 151 |
| afgh | Afghanistan | 999,011 | 499,505 | 227,204 | 11,958 | 1,213 | 240,376 | 48.1 | 0.3 | 0.3 | 0.0 | 2,040 | <1 |
| alba | Albania | 620,455 | 310,227 | 31,134 | 31,134 | 870,949 | 933,217 | 300.8 | 20.0 | 10.0 | 15.0 | 939,481 | 110 |
| alge | Algeria | 2,500,854 | 1,250,427 | 314,712 | 34,968 | 4,959 | 354,639 | 28.4 | 5.0 | 5.0 | 0.0 | 45,093 | <1 |
| amer | American Samoa | 7,775 | 3,887 | 680 | 680 | 10,652 | 12,014 | 309.0 | 80.0 | 15.0 | 75.0 | 83,937 | 450 |
| ando | Andorra | 21,365 | 10,682 | 779 | 194 | 4,469 | 5,444 | 51.0 | 75.0 | 10.0 | 70.0 | 110,355 | 516 |
| ango | Angola | 953,225 | 476,612 | 21,253 | 3,750 | 115,768 | 140,771 | 29.5 | 9.0 | 3.0 | 7.0 | 15,268,570 | 432 |
| angu | Anguilla | 1,754 | 877 | 83 | 4 | 3,997 | 4,085 | 465.7 | 52.0 | 5.0 | 50.0 | 10,310 | 452 |
| anti | Antigua | 16,902 | 8,451 | 675 | 35 | 5,105 | 5,816 | 68.8 | 62.0 | 4.0 | 60.0 | 74,393 | 401 |
| arge | Argentina | 10,451,094 | 5,225,547 | 14,058,031 | 3,514,507 | 1,472,569 | 19,045,108 | 364.5 | 70.0 | 10.0 | 65.0 | 55,335,797 | 545 |
| arme | Armenia | 751,322 | 375,661 | 65,654 | 590,886 | 395,916 | 1,052,456 | 280.2 | 12.0 | 3.0 | 10.0 | 4,426,109 | 459 |
| arub | Aruba | 21,507 | 10,753 | 1,027 | 54 | 5,576 | 6,657 | 61.9 | 75.0 | 20.0 | 60.0 | 152,671 | 542 |
| aust | Australia | 5,950,081 | 2,975,040 | 1,235,596 | 529,541 | 1,518,194 | 3,283,331 | 110.4 | 62.0 | 15.0 | 50.0 | 17,396,559 | 336 |
| ausz | Austria | 3,077,196 | 1,538,598 | 38,746 | 9,686 | 108,510 | 156,942 | 10.2 | 77.0 | 3.0 | 75.0 | 10,294,026 | 457 |
| azer | Azerbaijan | 1,533,043 | 766,521 | 2,009 | 41 | 46,957 | 49,007 | 6.4 | 0.8 | 0.8 | 0.0 | 140,652 | 6 |
| baha | Bahamas | 72,457 | 36,228 | 3,065 | 766 | 19,166 | 22,998 | 63.5 | 77.0 | 2.5 | 75.0 | 412,498 | 491 |
| bahr | Bahrain | 73,083 | 36,541 | 6,172 | 324 | 6,227 | 12,724 | 34.8 | 15.5 | 15.5 | 0.0 | 38,910 | 23 |
| bang | Bangladesh | 8,526,902 | 4,263,451 | 608,673 | 327,747 | 765,757 | 1,702,177 | 39.9 | 0.8 | 0.8 | 0.0 | 533,701 | 1 |
| barb | Barbados | 69,576 | 34,788 | 2,704 | 300 | 25,948 | 28,953 | 83.2 | 72.0 | 3.0 | 70.0 | 267,176 | 360 |
| belg | Belgium | 3,698,949 | 1,849,474 | 2,094 | 4,886 | 166,462 | 173,442 | 9.4 | 68.0 | 4.0 | 65.0 | 13,226,127 | 475 |
| beli | Belize | 30,606 | 15,303 | 2,407 | 267 | 9,007 | 11,682 | 76.3 | 84.0 | 15.0 | 75.0 | 285,083 | 432 |
| belo | Belorussia | 3,179,096 | 1,589,548 | 6,687 | 3,600 | 159,497 | 169,785 | 10.7 | 19.0 | 10.0 | 10.0 | 8,829,247 | 314 |
| beni | Benin | 365,603 | 182,801 | 142,430 | 61,041 | 81,649 | 285,120 | 156.0 | 7.5 | 3.0 | 5.0 | 1,300,872 | 77 |
| berm | Bermuda | 23,106 | 11,553 | 645 | 645 | 14,523 | 15,815 | 136.9 | 78.0 | 5.0 | 75.0 | 86,413 | 488 |
| bhut | Bhutan | 144,348 | 72,174 | 21,239 | 433 | 786 | 22,459 | 31.1 | 3.0 | 3.0 | 0.0 | 2,003 | <1 |
| boli | Bolivia | 1,621,281 | 810,640 | 11,246,626 | 1,249,625 | 1,679,271 | 14,175,522 | 1,748.7 | 55.0 | 8.0 | 50.0 | 12,508,582 | 548 |
| bosn | Bosnia-Herzegovina | 811,160 | 405,580 | 39,718 | 39,718 | 42,500 | 121,936 | 30.1 | 10.0 | 7.0 | 5.0 | 1,311,740 | 120 |
| bots | Botswana | 180,525 | 90,262 | 8,440 | 2,110 | 64,505 | 75,055 | 83.2 | 20.0 | 8.0 | 15.0 | 793,734 | 178 |
| boug | Bougainville | 36,900 | 18,450 | 1,984 | 2,977 | 16,426 | 21,388 | 115.9 | 44.0 | 5.0 | 40.0 | 255,127 | 469 |
| braz | Brazil | 31,603,528 | 15,801,764 | 164,859,596 | 934,204,377 | 19,082,639 | 1,118,146,612 | 7,076.1 | 70.0 | 25.0 | 50.0 | 262,023,044 | 562 |
| brit | Britain | 20,407,849 | 10,203,924 | 174,712 | 1,572,408 | 8,618,721 | 10,365,841 | 101.6 | 65.0 | 15.0 | 55.0 | 56,338,076 | 349 |
| briz | British Virgin Is | 4,339 | 2,169 | 213 | 91 | 6,178 | 6,483 | 298.8 | 75.0 | 7.0 | 70.0 | 19,016 | 324 |
| brun | Brunei | 44,761 | 22,380 | 3,280 | 364 | 1,649 | 5,294 | 23.7 | 3.0 | 3.0 | 0.0 | 11,275 | 12 |
| bulg | Bulgaria | 2,521,442 | 1,260,721 | 82,250 | 82,250 | 382,590 | 547,090 | 43.4 | 6.0 | 3.0 | 3.0 | 9,476,260 | 420 |
| burk | Burkina Faso | 322,515 | 161,257 | 110,000 | 1,111 | 91,803 | 202,914 | 125.8 | 8.7 | 1.0 | 8.0 | 1,255,326 | 38 |
| buru | Burundi | 472,421 | 236,210 | 10,012 | 2,503 | 41,996 | 54,511 | 23.1 | 12.0 | 3.0 | 10.0 | 7,154,204 | 390 |
| camb | Cambodia | 1,324,404 | 662,202 | 65,426 | 660 | 19,919 | 86,006 | 13.0 | 6.5 | 5.5 | 1.0 | 58,157 | 1 |
| came | Cameroon | 1,607,196 | 803,598 | 53,175 | 1,644 | 125,293 | 180,113 | 22.4 | 22.0 | 3.0 | 20.0 | 7,396,710 | 179 |
| cana | Canada | 10,596,464 | 5,298,232 | 5,383,873 | 21,535,492 | 1,676,541 | 28,595,906 | 539.7 | 80.0 | 20.0 | 65.0 | 28,268,128 | 331 |
| cape | Cape Verde | 53,423 | 26,711 | 4,277 | 132 | 11,405 | 15,814 | 59.2 | 7.0 | 3.0 | 5.0 | 621,713 | 530 |
| caym | Cayman Islands | 7,440 | 3,720 | 383 | 42 | 3,882 | 4,309 | 115.8 | 28.0 | 25.0 | 5.0 | 33,349 | 317 |
| cent | Central African Rep | 419,721 | 209,860 | 12,784 | 672 | 36,674 | 50,131 | 23.9 | 25.0 | 8.0 | 20.0 | 1,474,165 | 148 |
| chad | Chad | 827,255 | 413,627 | 63,370 | 640 | 50,146 | 114,156 | 27.6 | 9.5 | 2.0 | 8.0 | 731,518 | 34 |
| chan | Channel Islands | 72,385 | 36,192 | 1,528 | 6,115 | 47,500 | 55,144 | 152.4 | 77.0 | 10.0 | 70.0 | 142,766 | 340 |
| chil | Chile | 3,299,588 | 1,649,794 | 4,718,174 | 8,762,323 | 1,473,825 | 14,954,322 | 906.4 | 60.0 | 6.0 | 55.0 | 20,915,153 | 501 |
| chin | China | 239,651,552 | 119,825,776 | 17,641,828 | 5,880,609 | 5,165,714 | 28,688,151 | 23.9 | 15.0 | 15.0 | 0.0 | 57,687,543 | 16 |
| colo | Colombia | 6,516,386 | 3,258,193 | 12,760,796 | 8,507,197 | 3,134,880 | 24,402,873 | 749.0 | 68.0 | 15.0 | 60.0 | 67,012,049 | 577 |
| como | Comoros | 52,805 | 26,402 | 5,927 | 311 | 2,305 | 8,544 | 32.4 | 2.0 | 2.0 | 0.0 | 2,656 | 1 |
| cong | Congo-Brazzaville | 408,072 | 204,036 | 45,743 | 30,495 | 90,226 | 166,465 | 81.6 | 7.0 | 3.0 | 5.0 | 3,061,436 | 379 |
| conz | Congo-Zaire | 5,851,770 | 2,925,885 | 602,800 | 106,376 | 661,438 | 1,370,614 | 46.8 | 21.0 | 8.0 | 15.0 | 68,605,469 | 484 |
| cook | Cook Islands | 3,477 | 1,738 | 195 | 21 | 3,396 | 3,613 | 207.8 | 45.0 | 10.0 | 40.0 | 28,903 | 540 |
| cost | Costa Rica | 802,161 | 401,080 | 1,265,112 | 843,408 | 366,310 | 2,474,830 | 617.0 | 63.0 | 10.0 | 55.0 | 6,354,804 | 576 |
| croa | Croatia | 1,401,496 | 700,748 | 44,726 | 24,083 | 85,445 | 154,254 | 22.0 | 18.0 | 4.0 | 15.0 | 7,094,544 | 579 |
| cuba | Cuba | 2,835,884 | 1,417,942 | 686,779 | 21,240 | 1,463,600 | 2,171,619 | 153.2 | 10.0 | 10.0 | 0.0 | 5,108,908 | 166 |
| cypr | Cyprus | 153,405 | 76,702 | 6,005 | 2,573 | 16,319 | 24,897 | 32.5 | 42.0 | 3.0 | 40.0 | 877,476 | 533 |
| czec | Czech Republic | 3,824,187 | 1,912,093 | 2,280 | 570 | 61,609 | 64,459 | 3.4 | 9.0 | 5.0 | 5.0 | 5,667,786 | 201 |
| denm | Denmark | 2,374,922 | 1,187,461 | 52,932 | 9,341 | 172,033 | 234,307 | 19.7 | 62.0 | 5.0 | 60.0 | 7,667,816 | 528 |
| djib | Djibouti | 49,556 | 24,778 | 6,376 | 335 | 2,676 | 9,388 | 37.9 | 2.5 | 0.5 | 2.0 | 13,471 | 7 |
| domi | Dominica | 14,843 | 7,421 | 707 | 14 | 6,581 | 7,303 | 98.4 | 45.0 | 6.0 | 40.0 | 101,404 | 523 |
| domr | Dominican Republic | 1,259,392 | 629,696 | 3,699,857 | 1,585,653 | 397,801 | 5,683,311 | 902.5 | 48.0 | 20.0 | 40.0 | 12,987,209 | 558 |
| ecua | Ecuador | 2,518,424 | 1,259,212 | 2,347,994 | 1,264,304 | 804,543 | 4,416,841 | 350.8 | 85.0 | 45.0 | 60.0 | 20,386,618 | 588 |
| egyp | Egypt | 6,533,217 | 3,266,608 | 1,025,480 | 31,715 | 523,963 | 1,581,158 | 48.4 | 11.0 | 4.0 | 8.0 | 8,055,124 | 42 |
| elsa | El Salvador | 857,230 | 428,615 | 2,606,856 | 651,714 | 568,697 | 3,827,267 | 892.9 | 43.0 | 5.0 | 40.0 | 9,797,692 | 569 |
| equa | Equatorial Guinea | 69,688 | 34,844 | 54,897 | 1,697 | 15,395 | 71,990 | 206.6 | 24.0 | 20.0 | 5.0 | 571,996 | 461 |
| erit | Eritrea | 159,339 | 79,669 | 22,382 | 226 | 48,871 | 71,479 | 89.7 | 22.0 | 16.0 | 10.0 | 2,001,093 | 189 |
| esto | Estonia | 477,812 | 238,906 | 13,961 | 13,961 | 28,678 | 56,601 | 23.7 | 30.0 | 15.0 | 20.0 | 561,191 | 146 |
| ethi | Ethiopia | 4,366,792 | 2,183,396 | 882,126 | 120,289 | 505,334 | 1,507,750 | 69.1 | 30.0 | 25.0 | 10.0 | 32,276,728 | 188 |
| faer | Faeroe Islands | 14,724 | 7,362 | 427 | 47 | 5,879 | 6,354 | 86.3 | 44.0 | 6.0 | 40.0 | 61,677 | 526 |
| fiji | Fiji | 117,203 | 58,601 | 8,169 | 907 | 49,209 | 58,285 | 99.5 | 43.0 | 5.0 | 40.0 | 539,097 | 240 |
| finl | Finland | 2,220,783 | 1,110,391 | 10,905 | 1,924 | 70,089 | 82,918 | 7.5 | 57.0 | 3.0 | 55.0 | 7,171,420 | 505 |
| fran | France | 22,047,588 | 11,023,794 | 38,032 | 342,288 | 2,673,054 | 3,053,374 | 27.7 | 64.0 | 5.0 | 60.0 | 58,324,406 | 360 |
| freg | French Guiana | 35,826 | 17,913 | 1,813 | 37 | 8,259 | 10,109 | 56.4 | 45.5 | 1.0 | 45.0 | 225,667 | 454 |
| frep | French Polynesia | 43,500 | 21,750 | 2,350 | 72 | 10,003 | 12,426 | 57.1 | 62.0 | 3.0 | 60.0 | 293,119 | 455 |
| gabo | Gabon | 170,209 | 85,104 | 31,000 | 3,444 | 29,654 | 64,099 | 75.3 | 26.5 | 2.0 | 25.0 | 1,523,859 | 453 |
| gamb | Gambia | 51,650 | 25,825 | 13,053 | 687 | 3,818 | 17,559 | 68.0 | 20.5 | 1.0 | 20.0 | 21,088 | 5 |
| geor | Georgia | 1,267,635 | 633,817 | 2,000 | 857 | 110,575 | 113,432 | 17.9 | 23.0 | 5.0 | 20.0 | 3,565,445 | 262 |
| germ | Germany | 34,439,624 | 17,219,812 | 721,556 | 2,886,224 | 3,025,250 | 6,633,030 | 38.5 | 58.0 | 10.0 | 50.0 | 86,029,245 | 381 |
| ghan | Ghana | 2,323,214 | 1,161,607 | 1,008,423 | 432,181 | 900,665 | 2,341,270 | 201.6 | 36.0 | 8.0 | 30.0 | 8,336,764 | 150 |
| gibr | Gibraltar | 8,038 | 4,019 | 250 | 27 | 2,714 | 2,992 | 74.5 | 33.0 | 4.0 | 30.0 | 32,986 | 480 |
| gree | Greece | 3,025,976 | 1,512,988 | 106,447 | 425,789 | 213,905 | 746,143 | 49.3 | 62.0 | 3.0 | 60.0 | 16,213,334 | 555 |
| grel | Greenland | 30,688 | 15,344 | 561 | 62 | 3,911 | 4,535 | 29.6 | 21.5 | 2.0 | 20.0 | 51,450 | 334 |
| gren | Grenada | 21,166 | 10,583 | 937 | 140 | 7,009 | 8,087 | 76.4 | 61.5 | 2.0 | 60.0 | 145,655 | 567 |
| guad | Guadeloupe | 112,429 | 56,214 | 4,556 | 1,139 | 38,125 | 43,821 | 78.0 | 41.5 | 2.0 | 40.0 | 698,605 | 559 |
| guam | Guam | 37,396 | 18,698 | 1,675 | 88 | 12,185 | 13,948 | 74.6 | 86.0 | 7.0 | 80.0 | 246,248 | 536 |
| guat | Guatemala | 1,027,147 | 513,573 | 3,800,725 | 950,181 | 585,180 | 5,336,086 | 1,039.0 | 60.0 | 20.0 | 50.0 | 16,831,815 | 539 |
| guin | Guinea | 546,337 | 273,168 | 2,000 | 105 | 14,273 | 16,379 | 6.0 | 0.7 | 0.2 | 0.5 | 96,415 | 4 |
| gunb | Guinea-Bissau | 145,423 | 72,711 | 12,131 | 638 | 11,756 | 24,525 | 33.7 | 6.0 | 2.0 | 5.0 | 79,426 | 23 |
| guya | Guyana | 159,624 | 79,812 | 8,613 | 957 | 17,787 | 27,357 | 34.3 | 36.5 | 2.0 | 35.0 | 375,046 | 158 |
| hait | Haiti | 773,219 | 386,609 | 940,409 | 403,032 | 206,064 | 1,549,506 | 400.8 | 21.0 | 4.0 | 18.0 | 12,359,824 | 548 |
| hond | Honduras | 721,069 | 360,534 | 1,029,310 | 257,327 | 413,964 | 1,700,601 | 471.7 | 40.0 | 6.0 | 36.0 | 9,596,450 | 540 |
| hung | Hungary | 3,487,710 | 1,743,855 | 832 | 92 | 99,838 | 100,762 | 5.8 | 64.0 | 5.0 | 60.0 | 13,735,329 | 499 |
| icel | Iceland | 92,551 | 46,275 | 36 | 36 | 19,122 | 19,194 | 41.5 | 72.0 | 3.0 | 70.0 | 409,772 | 532 |
| indi | India | 86,697,475 | 43,348,737 | 108,079,130 | 229,668,151 | 67,855,258 | 405,602,540 | 935.7 | 24.0 | 5.0 | 20.0 | 37,196,743 | 13 |
| indo | Indonesia | 36,772,276 | 18,386,138 | 3,122,859 | 780,714 | 2,678,132 | 6,581,705 | 35.8 | 23.0 | 6.0 | 18.0 | 17,094,974 | 29 |
| iran | Iran | 8,810,952 | 4,405,476 | 677,021 | 13,816 | 51,711 | 742,549 | 16.9 | 2.0 | 1.0 | 1.0 | 117,464 | <1 |
| iraq | Iraq | 1,309,539 | 654,769 | 348,157 | 3,516 | 275,241 | 626,914 | 95.7 | 4.0 | 4.0 | 0.0 | 361,244 | 5 |
| irel | Ireland | 925,426 | 462,713 | 37,302 | 15,986 | 54,038 | 107,327 | 23.2 | 82.0 | 3.0 | 80.0 | 5,419,381 | 530 |
| isle | Isle of Man | 35,555 | 17,777 | 791 | 2,374 | 20,000 | 23,166 | 130.3 | 78.0 | 4.0 | 75.0 | 73,733 | 340 |
| isra | Israel | 1,158,347 | 579,173 | 1,157 | 385 | 69,029 | 70,572 | 12.2 | 9.5 | 2.0 | 8.0 | 165,684 | 11 |
| ital | Italy | 19,883,944 | 9,941,972 | 5,126 | 5,126 | 2,309,182 | 2,319,434 | 23.3 | 67.0 | 3.0 | 65.0 | 69,060,006 | 439 |
| ivor | Ivory Coast | 1,004,605 | 502,302 | 200,500 | 6,201 | 150,458 | 357,159 | 71.1 | 22.0 | 16.0 | 8.0 | 3,433,471 | 84 |
| jama | Jamaica | 500,473 | 250,236 | 25,825 | 4,557 | 117,650 | 148,034 | 59.2 | 41.0 | 8.0 | 35.0 | 1,176,116 | 166 |
| japa | Japan | 41,824,000 | 20,912,000 | 4,403,130 | 2,935,420 | 1,032,755 | 8,371,305 | 40.0 | 37.0 | 10.0 | 30.0 | 2,304,429 | 6 |
| jord | Jordan | 827,573 | 413,786 | 72,506 | 3,021 | 139,101 | 214,628 | 51.9 | 9.5 | 7.0 | 3.0 | 149,097 | 8 |
| kaza | Kazakhstan | 4,023,618 | 2,011,809 | 162,225 | 5,017 | 210,079 | 377,322 | 18.8 | 6.5 | 2.0 | 5.0 | 1,812,189 | 40 |
| keny | Kenya | 3,428,279 | 1,714,139 | 136,902 | 20,456 | 305,192 | 462,551 | 27.0 | 45.0 | 8.0 | 40.0 | 30,405,132 | 368 |
| kirg | Kirgizstan | 1,055,783 | 527,891 | 46,993 | 1,453 | 15,978 | 64,425 | 12.2 | 3.0 | 3.0 | 0.0 | 240,423 | 18 |
| kiri | Kiribati | 10,589 | 5,294 | 833 | 17 | 3,186 | 4,037 | 76.3 | 66.0 | 2.0 | 65.0 | 120,466 | 527 |
| kuwa | Kuwait | 179,455 | 89,727 | 19,716 | 2,190 | 9,888 | 31,795 | 35.4 | 15.0 | 15.0 | 0.0 | 164,982 | 30 |
| laos | Laos | 450,283 | 225,141 | 54,330 | 2,859 | 3,343 | 60,533 | 26.9 | 3.0 | 3.0 | 0.0 | 53,546 | 3 |
| latv | Latvia | 814,196 | 407,098 | 3,545 | 625 | 32,406 | 36,577 | 9.0 | 33.0 | 4.0 | 30.0 | 2,137,002 | 331 |
| leba | Lebanon | 524,536 | 262,268 | 203,574 | 135,716 | 534,479 | 873,769 | 333.2 | 70.0 | 17.0 | 60.0 | 2,081,785 | 231 |
| leso | Lesotho | 286,152 | 143,076 | 3,000 | 125 | 26,580 | 29,705 | 20.8 | 13.0 | 4.0 | 10.0 | 1,977,210 | 335 |
| libe | Liberia | 160,105 | 80,052 | 5,700 | 1,900 | 80,616 | 88,216 | 110.2 | 35.0 | 10.0 | 30.0 | 706,315 | 81 |
| liby | Libya | 700,886 | 350,443 | 56,047 | 504,424 | 5,000 | 565,472 | 161.4 | 1.0 | 1.0 | 0.0 | 80,014 | 5 |
| liec | Liechtenstein | 10,263 | 5,131 | 328 | 218 | 5,133 | 5,680 | 110.7 | 63.0 | 4.0 | 60.0 | 40,282 | 447 |
| lith | Lithuania | 1,145,620 | 572,810 | 15,221 | 3,805 | 25,780 | 44,806 | 7.8 | 27.0 | 3.0 | 25.0 | 5,004,866 | 497 |
| luxe | Luxembourg | 145,321 | 72,660 | 4,306 | 6,459 | 35,000 | 45,765 | 63.0 | 74.0 | 5.0 | 70.0 | 632,883 | 536 |
| mace | Macedonia | 397,606 | 198,803 | 20,235 | 2,248 | 4,023 | 26,507 | 13.3 | 21.5 | 2.0 | 20.0 | 1,622,634 | 292 |
| mada | Madagascar | 2,345,298 | 1,172,649 | 506,259 | 26,645 | 231,662 | 764,566 | 65.2 | 38.0 | 10.0 | 30.0 | 7,619,345 | 174 |
| mala | Malawi | 1,268,385 | 634,192 | 515,000 | 171,666 | 237,462 | 924,128 | 145.7 | 19.0 | 5.0 | 15.0 | 8,591,312 | 287 |
| malb | Malaysia | 3,426,634 | 1,713,317 | 1,353,878 | 71,256 | 123,536 | 1,548,671 | 90.4 | 9.0 | 9.0 | 0.0 | 1,135,332 | 18 |

| COUNTRY | | SCRIPTURES (continued) | | | | | | | BROADCASTING | | | EVANGELISM | |
|---|---|---|---|---|---|---|---|---|---|---|---|---|---|
| | | SELECTIONS DISTRIBUTION | | | | | | | RADIO/TV AUDIENCES | | | offers via 45 ministries | |
| code | short name | goal | goal p.a. | UBS p.a. | other p.a. | duplicates | total p.a. | T/G% | cb aud | cstat | secstat | q per day | e p.a.p.c. |
| 1 | 2 | 140 | 141 | 142 | 143 | 144 | 145 | 146 | 147 | 148 | 149 | 150 | 151 |
| mald | Maldives | 32,693 | 16,346 | 2,862 | 58 | 16 | 2,936 | 18.0 | 2.0 | 2.0 | 0.0 | 70 | <1 |
| mali | Mali | 550,470 | 275,235 | 40,000 | 2,105 | 44,088 | 86,194 | 31.3 | 7.5 | 2.0 | 6.0 | 97,868 | 3 |
| malt | Malta | 100,006 | 50,003 | 3,885 | 2,590 | 21,666 | 28,142 | 56.3 | 73.0 | 7.0 | 70.0 | 611,887 | 574 |
| mars | Marshall Islands | 5,734 | 2,867 | 642 | 26 | 2,312 | 2,981 | 104.0 | 91.0 | 8.0 | 90.0 | 92,559 | 526 |
| mart | Martinique | 106,184 | 53,092 | 3,953 | 439 | 28,289 | 32,682 | 61.6 | 36.5 | 2.0 | 35.0 | 601,913 | 555 |
| maur | Mauritania | 175,622 | 87,811 | 26,695 | 269 | 232 | 27,197 | 31.0 | 3.0 | 3.0 | 0.0 | 2,086 | <1 |
| maus | Mauritius | 173,936 | 86,968 | 386,870 | 3,907 | 283,261 | 674,038 | 775.0 | 16.5 | 2.0 | 15.0 | 339,914 | 107 |
| mayo | Mayotte | 16,879 | 8,439 | 1,016 | 435 | 123 | 1,574 | 18.7 | 2.0 | 2.0 | 0.0 | 775 | 2 |
| mexi | Mexico | 16,012,973 | 8,006,486 | 3,011,786 | 12,047,144 | 3,364,684 | 18,423,614 | 230.1 | 84.0 | 5.0 | 80.0 | 151,910,938 | 560 |
| micr | Micronesia | 11,750 | 5,875 | 4,000 | 210 | 12,089 | 16,300 | 277.4 | 91.0 | 8.0 | 90.0 | 158,364 | 487 |
| mold | Moldavia | 1,240,653 | 620,326 | 43,804 | 4,867 | 128,895 | 177,568 | 28.6 | 19.0 | 10.0 | 10.0 | 3,489,522 | 290 |
| mona | Monaco | 14,315 | 7,157 | 335 | 59 | 2,250 | 2,645 | 37.0 | 83.0 | 6.0 | 80.0 | 50,365 | 547 |
| mong | Mongolia | 423,383 | 211,691 | 1,290 | 26 | 22,754 | 24,070 | 11.4 | 3.0 | 3.0 | 0.0 | 14,312 | 2 |
| mont | Montserrat | 2,206 | 1,103 | 106 | 1 | 532 | 639 | 58.0 | 64.0 | 6.0 | 60.0 | 15,272 | 524 |
| moro | Morocco | 1,946,702 | 973,351 | 6,072 | 674 | 930 | 7,676 | 0.8 | 10.0 | 10.0 | 0.0 | 73,925 | 1 |
| moza | Mozambique | 1,584,662 | 792,331 | 2,945 | 519 | 55,122 | 58,587 | 7.4 | 3.5 | 2.0 | 2.0 | 5,411,988 | 100 |
| myan | Myanmar | 6,852,006 | 3,426,003 | 616,690 | 25,695 | 74,006 | 716,392 | 20.9 | 3.0 | 3.0 | 0.0 | 2,332,055 | 18 |
| nami | Namibia | 243,730 | 121,865 | 17,258 | 533 | 34,423 | 52,215 | 42.8 | 33.0 | 4.0 | 30.0 | 1,919,388 | 405 |
| naur | Nauru | 1,299 | 649 | 115 | 6 | 284 | 405 | 62.5 | 57.0 | 3.0 | 55.0 | 11,409 | 361 |
| nepa | Nepal | 1,063,588 | 531,794 | 709,675 | 7,168 | 154,435 | 871,279 | 163.8 | 4.5 | 2.0 | 3.0 | 266,428 | 4 |
| neth | Netherlands | 6,441,145 | 3,220,572 | 7,615 | 3,263 | 414,460 | 425,339 | 13.2 | 52.0 | 4.0 | 50.0 | 14,171,828 | 327 |
| nets | Netherlands Antilles | 52,016 | 26,008 | 303,561 | 101,187 | 49,755 | 454,503 | 1,747.5 | 75.0 | 20.0 | 60.0 | 281,861 | 474 |
| newc | New Caledonia | 27,256 | 13,628 | 2,140 | 89 | 4,805 | 7,035 | 51.6 | 56.5 | 2.0 | 55.0 | 221,953 | 378 |
| newz | New Zealand | 1,265,983 | 632,991 | 2,413,210 | 3,619,815 | 274,962 | 6,307,987 | 996.5 | 66.0 | 12.0 | 60.0 | 3,543,036 | 334 |
| nica | Nicaragua | 421,396 | 210,698 | 746,845 | 320,076 | 153,280 | 1,220,202 | 579.1 | 45.0 | 6.0 | 40.0 | 7,920,529 | 569 |
| niga | Niger | 194,441 | 97,220 | 107,301 | 1,083 | 303 | 108,687 | 111.8 | 5.5 | 2.0 | 4.0 | 24,584 | <1 |
| nige | Nigeria | 11,300,302 | 5,650,151 | 1,002,604 | 9,023,436 | 2,557,483 | 12,583,523 | 222.7 | 45.0 | 20.0 | 30.0 | 51,347,240 | 168 |
| nork | North Korea | 4,401,400 | 2,200,700 | 240,391 | 103,025 | 4,634 | 348,051 | 15.8 | 4.0 | 4.0 | 0.0 | 249,956 | 3 |
| norl | Northern Cyprus | 51,000 | 25,500 | 1,850 | 97 | 888 | 2,836 | 11.1 | 11.5 | 2.0 | 10.0 | 9,759 | 19 |
| norm | Northern Mariana Is | 12,319 | 6,159 | 783 | 24 | 3,087 | 3,895 | 63.2 | 83.0 | 8.0 | 80.0 | 101,750 | 474 |
| norw | Norway | 1,975,269 | 987,634 | 30,876 | 7,719 | 143,732 | 182,327 | 18.5 | 75.0 | 7.0 | 70.0 | 7,113,157 | 582 |
| oman | Oman | 238,813 | 119,406 | 25,417 | 1,059 | 853 | 27,330 | 22.9 | 4.0 | 4.0 | 0.0 | 58,288 | 8 |
| paki | Pakistan | 8,174,661 | 4,087,330 | 9,320,863 | 490,571 | 1,199,310 | 11,010,745 | 269.4 | 1.0 | 1.0 | 0.0 | 1,782,987 | 4 |
| pala | Palau | 2,801 | 1,400 | 194 | 3 | 1,277 | 1,476 | 105.4 | 92.0 | 3.0 | 90.0 | 27,806 | 522 |
| pale | Palestine | 234,630 | 117,315 | 221 | 94 | 22,600 | 22,916 | 19.5 | 6.5 | 2.0 | 5.0 | 133,986 | 22 |
| pana | Panama | 542,941 | 271,470 | 1,929,404 | 482,351 | 257,814 | 2,669,569 | 983.4 | 69.0 | 5.0 | 65.0 | 3,770,119 | 481 |
| papu | Papua New Guinea | 646,147 | 323,073 | 156,150 | 156,150 | 2,233,343 | 2,545,643 | 787.9 | 44.0 | 5.0 | 40.0 | 4,626,672 | 366 |
| para | Paraguay | 946,176 | 473,088 | 1,530,794 | 656,054 | 399,289 | 2,586,138 | 546.7 | 36.0 | 8.0 | 30.0 | 8,359,506 | 555 |
| peru | Peru | 4,092,667 | 2,046,333 | 5,320,872 | 7,981,308 | 1,479,154 | 14,781,334 | 722.3 | 44.0 | 6.0 | 40.0 | 40,763,321 | 579 |
| phil | Philippines | 11,344,374 | 5,672,187 | 11,099,395 | 44,397,580 | 11,641,084 | 67,138,059 | 1,183.6 | 55.0 | 10.0 | 50.0 | 99,946,706 | 480 |
| pola | Poland | 10,585,622 | 5,292,811 | 844 | 2,532 | 287,150 | 290,526 | 5.5 | 76.0 | 12.0 | 70.0 | 60,660,610 | 571 |
| port | Portugal | 2,251,353 | 1,125,676 | 120,657 | 310,260 | 199,454 | 630,372 | 56.0 | 52.0 | 5.0 | 50.0 | 15,783,258 | 583 |
| puer | Puerto Rico | 925,688 | 462,844 | 2,312,687 | 1,541,791 | 597,637 | 4,452,116 | 961.9 | 84.0 | 7.0 | 80.0 | 6,316,728 | 596 |
| qata | Qatar | 67,984 | 33,992 | 5,990 | 315 | 1,444 | 7,750 | 22.8 | 3.0 | 3.0 | 0.0 | 35,423 | 21 |
| reun | Reunion | 134,774 | 67,387 | 6,994 | 1,748 | 14,285 | 23,028 | 34.2 | 38.0 | 4.0 | 35.0 | 919,398 | 479 |
| roma | Romania | 7,090,567 | 3,545,283 | 223,265 | 520,951 | 350,722 | 1,094,939 | 30.9 | 23.0 | 15.0 | 10.0 | 30,911,134 | 505 |
| russ | Russia | 45,354,553 | 22,677,276 | 26,579 | 239,211 | 6,923,583 | 7,189,373 | 31.7 | 30.0 | 20.0 | 15.0 | 108,009,832 | 268 |
| rwan | Rwanda | 676,900 | 338,450 | 29,885 | 924 | 238,343 | 269,153 | 79.5 | 12.0 | 3.0 | 10.0 | 9,299,920 | 439 |
| saha | Sahara | 4,955 | 2,477 | 2,933 | 325 | 3 | 3,263 | 131.7 | 0.5 | 0.5 | 0.0 | 120 | <1 |
| saih | Saint Helena | 1,971 | 985 | 62 | 15 | 542 | 621 | 63.1 | 55.0 | 6.0 | 50.0 | 8,235 | 477 |
| saik | Saint Kitts & Nevis | 9,000 | 4,500 | 384 | 42 | 4,436 | 4,863 | 108.1 | 57.5 | 3.0 | 55.0 | 54,324 | 515 |
| sail | Saint Lucia | 28,820 | 14,410 | 1,543 | 81 | 4,957 | 6,582 | 45.7 | 71.5 | 2.0 | 70.0 | 217,865 | 515 |
| saip | Saint Pierre & Miquelon | 2,136 | 1,068 | 65 | 7 | 500 | 572 | 53.6 | 67.0 | 3.0 | 65.0 | 10,232 | 568 |
| saiv | Saint Vincent | 26,387 | 13,193 | 1,139 | 59 | 6,222 | 7,421 | 56.3 | 61.5 | 2.0 | 60.0 | 101,830 | 326 |
| samo | Samoa | 21,060 | 10,530 | 1,800 | 94 | 8,888 | 10,784 | 102.4 | 73.0 | 5.0 | 70.0 | 280,111 | 567 |
| sanm | San Marino | 9,031 | 4,515 | 265 | 397 | 2,500 | 3,162 | 70.0 | 72.0 | 3.0 | 70.0 | 39,994 | 550 |
| saot | Sao Tome & Principe | 17,957 | 8,978 | 1,467 | 366 | 5,000 | 6,834 | 76.1 | 27.0 | 3.0 | 25.0 | 201,840 | 501 |
| saud | Saudi Arabia | 1,736,756 | 868,378 | 216,066 | 144,044 | 6,250 | 366,361 | 42.2 | 7.0 | 7.0 | 0.0 | 441,262 | 7 |
| sene | Senegal | 313,325 | 156,662 | 94,811 | 23,702 | 5,843 | 124,357 | 79.4 | 12.5 | 1.0 | 12.0 | 220,608 | 8 |
| seyc | Seychelles | 12,882 | 6,441 | 774 | 86 | 4,527 | 5,388 | 83.7 | 49.0 | 5.0 | 45.0 | 112,173 | 528 |
| sier | Sierra Leone | 279,799 | 139,899 | 11,187 | 4,794 | 43,764 | 59,745 | 42.7 | 13.0 | 4.0 | 10.0 | 302,876 | 22 |
| sing | Singapore | 775,680 | 387,840 | 1,015,654 | 1,015,654 | 180,785 | 2,212,093 | 570.4 | 22.0 | 12.0 | 15.0 | 299,905 | 30 |
| slok | Slovakia | 1,784,884 | 892,442 | 53,871 | 2,244 | 39,498 | 95,615 | 10.7 | 9.0 | 5.0 | 5.0 | 5,528,472 | 374 |
| slov | Slovenia | 636,800 | 318,400 | 16,729 | 2,952 | 26,221 | 45,902 | 14.4 | 21.5 | 2.0 | 20.0 | 2,736,859 | 503 |
| solo | Solomon Islands | 36,628 | 18,314 | 4,436 | 137 | 9,513 | 14,087 | 76.9 | 43.0 | 5.0 | 40.0 | 544,808 | 448 |
| soma | Somalia | 277,745 | 138,872 | 72,645 | 1,482 | 1,697 | 75,825 | 54.6 | 0.5 | 0.5 | 0.0 | 44,007 | 2 |
| somi | Somaliland | 126,500 | 63,250 | 28,326 | 286 | 113 | 28,726 | 45.4 | 0.5 | 0.5 | 0.0 | 3,756 | <1 |
| soua | South Africa | 6,663,186 | 3,331,593 | 3,986 | 442 | 1,112,139 | 1,116,568 | 33.5 | 55.0 | 8.0 | 50.0 | 47,484,938 | 429 |
| souk | South Korea | 11,592,024 | 5,796,012 | 30,099,374 | 8,489,567 | 5,949,252 | 44,538,193 | 768.4 | 44.0 | 15.0 | 35.0 | 19,604,761 | 152 |
| spai | Spain | 10,830,354 | 5,415,177 | 73,223 | 73,223 | 5,675,810 | 5,822,256 | 107.5 | 62.0 | 3.0 | 60.0 | 62,524,748 | 575 |
| span | Spanish North Africa | 39,403 | 19,701 | 1,300 | 3,033 | 66,000 | 70,333 | 357.0 | 42.0 | 3.0 | 40.0 | 159,167 | 446 |
| sril | Sri Lanka | 3,108,427 | 1,554,213 | 1,620,718 | 694,593 | 403,301 | 2,718,613 | 174.9 | 10.0 | 5.0 | 7.0 | 1,136,791 | 22 |
| suda | Sudan | 2,315,197 | 1,157,598 | 993,471 | 30,725 | 400,053 | 1,424,250 | 123.0 | 12.0 | 4.0 | 9.0 | 2,772,066 | 34 |
| suri | Suriname | 97,540 | 48,770 | 681,200 | 75,688 | 159,940 | 916,829 | 1,879.9 | 66.5 | 2.0 | 65.0 | 165,234 | 144 |
| swaz | Swaziland | 117,412 | 58,706 | 10,078 | 205 | 25,339 | 35,624 | 60.7 | 42.0 | 10.0 | 35.0 | 920,157 | 333 |
| swed | Sweden | 3,999,993 | 1,999,996 | 88,596 | 333,289 | 1,069,495 | 1,491,381 | 74.6 | 63.0 | 5.0 | 60.0 | 8,318,294 | 340 |
| swit | Switzerland | 3,246,774 | 1,623,387 | 85,794 | 343,176 | 868,019 | 1,296,989 | 79.9 | 68.0 | 5.0 | 65.0 | 10,296,118 | 508 |
| syri | Syria | 1,621,532 | 810,766 | 9,735 | 22,715 | 204,275 | 236,725 | 29.2 | 5.0 | 5.0 | 0.0 | 810,468 | 18 |
| taiw | Taiwan | 5,299,466 | 2,649,733 | 10,174,695 | 23,740,955 | 1,798,389 | 35,714,039 | 1,347.8 | 52.0 | 15.0 | 40.0 | 821,337 | 13 |
| taji | Tajikistan | 921,022 | 460,511 | 61,882 | 625 | 7,070 | 69,577 | 15.1 | 0.5 | 0.5 | 0.0 | 58,442 | 3 |
| tanz | Tanzania | 3,978,318 | 1,989,159 | 335,170 | 3,385 | 375,610 | 714,166 | 35.9 | 17.0 | 3.0 | 15.0 | 14,876,893 | 162 |
| thai | Thailand | 10,372,919 | 5,186,459 | 2,549,517 | 22,945,653 | 2,747,342 | 28,242,512 | 544.5 | 13.5 | 4.0 | 10.0 | 764,862 | 4 |
| timo | Timor | 183,128 | 91,564 | 8,845 | 20,639 | 22,380 | 51,865 | 56.6 | 23.0 | 4.0 | 20.0 | 1,075,256 | 443 |
| togo | Togo | 374,785 | 187,392 | 20,000 | 618 | 60,659 | 81,277 | 43.4 | 18.0 | 3.0 | 16.0 | 1,544,801 | 121 |
| tong | Tonga | 14,781 | 7,390 | 985 | 51 | 5,097 | 6,134 | 83.0 | 54.0 | 6.0 | 50.0 | 145,617 | 539 |
| trin | Trinidad & Tobago | 301,454 | 150,727 | 12,949 | 826 | 11,605 | 25,381 | 16.8 | 63.0 | 4.0 | 60.0 | 975,253 | 274 |
| tuni | Tunisia | 1,169,610 | 584,805 | 95,856 | 5,045 | 706 | 101,607 | 17.4 | 4.0 | 4.0 | 0.0 | 24,777 | <1 |
| turk | Turkey | 11,206,627 | 5,603,313 | 105,421 | 948,789 | 304,175 | 1,358,385 | 24.2 | 1.5 | 1.5 | 0.0 | 182,137 | 1 |
| turm | Turkmenistan | 711,440 | 355,720 | 44,592 | 450 | 4,040 | 49,083 | 13.8 | 0.5 | 0.5 | 0.0 | 34,777 | 2 |
| turs | Turks & Caicos Is | 4,342 | 2,171 | 167 | 111 | 833 | 1,112 | 51.2 | 70.0 | 15.0 | 60.0 | 18,690 | 407 |
| tuva | Tuvalu | 1,528 | 764 | 117 | 20 | 1,076 | 1,214 | 158.9 | 68.0 | 5.0 | 65.0 | 14,256 | 444 |
| ugan | Uganda | 2,437,867 | 1,218,933 | 102,278 | 34,092 | 197,827 | 334,198 | 27.4 | 40.0 | 15.0 | 30.0 | 27,895,295 | 467 |
| ukra | Ukraine | 15,815,200 | 7,907,600 | 504,559 | 756,839 | 1,220,217 | 2,481,616 | 31.4 | 40.0 | 20.0 | 25.0 | 64,170,409 | 464 |
| unia | United Arab Emirates | 257,368 | 128,684 | 24,414 | 2,712 | 4,852 | 31,980 | 24.9 | 3.0 | 3.0 | 0.0 | 161,352 | 24 |
| usa | USA | 98,078,443 | 49,039,221 | 57,801,656 | 1,868,920,210 | 124,969,827 | 2,051,691,694 | 4,183.8 | 82.0 | 60.0 | 75.0 | 280,931,560 | 368 |
| uuay | Uruguay | 948,877 | 474,438 | 1,261,271 | 2,942,965 | 332,070 | 4,536,307 | 956.1 | 57.0 | 3.0 | 55.0 | 2,858,670 | 312 |
| uzbe | Uzbekistan | 3,972,879 | 1,986,439 | 243,178 | 2,456 | 143,019 | 388,654 | 19.6 | 3.5 | 2.0 | 2.0 | 191,686 | 2 |
| vanu | Vanuatu | 17,512 | 8,756 | 1,904 | 100 | 4,296 | 6,301 | 72.0 | 23.0 | 4.0 | 20.0 | 232,583 | 445 |
| vene | Venezuela | 3,754,777 | 1,877,388 | 2,881,434 | 11,525,736 | 1,290,997 | 15,698,167 | 836.2 | 70.0 | 15.0 | 60.0 | 36,995,749 | 558 |
| viet | Viet Nam | 14,419,203 | 7,209,601 | 798,316 | 1,197,474 | 430,326 | 2,426,117 | 33.7 | 5.0 | 5.0 | 0.0 | 4,416,271 | 20 |
| virg | Virgin Is of the US | 29,725 | 14,862 | 929 | 2,788 | 50,000 | 53,718 | 361.4 | 79.0 | 5.0 | 75.0 | 137,088 | 538 |
| wall | Wallis & Futuna Is | 2,676 | 1,338 | 145 | 36 | 1,761 | 1,943 | 145.2 | 78.0 | 5.0 | 75.0 | 19,728 | 496 |
| yeme | Yemen | 1,032,744 | 516,372 | 181,120 | 9,532 | 533 | 191,186 | 37.0 | 1.0 | 1.0 | 0.0 | 14,292 | <1 |
| yugo | Yugoslavia | 3,286,276 | 1,643,138 | 106,401 | 130,046 | 78,229 | 314,677 | 19.2 | 44.0 | 6.0 | 40.0 | 9,020,080 | 309 |
| zamb | Zambia | 1,456,181 | 728,090 | 34,224 | 51,336 | 259,356 | 344,916 | 47.4 | 28.0 | 4.0 | 25.0 | 9,573,904 | 381 |
| zimb | Zimbabwe | 1,927,359 | 963,679 | 564,740 | 779,879 | 347,272 | 1,691,891 | 175.6 | 38.5 | 5.0 | 35.0 | 8,547,782 | 267 |
| | 11 minicountries | 7,126 | 3,563 | 231 | 310 | 3,755 | 4,297 | 120.6 | 44.0 | 11.7 | 39.3 | 17,204 | 272 |
| | Africa | 76,137,742 | 38,068,871 | 9,877,176 | 11,543,963 | 10,606,683 | 32,027,823 | 84.1 | 24.4 | 9.3 | 17.2 | 397,631,611 | 185 |
| | Antarctica | 1,950 | 975 | 45 | 45 | 200 | 290 | 29.7 | 60.0 | 20.0 | 50.0 | 3,216 | 260 |
| | Asia | 541,625,705 | 270,812,852 | 206,372,348 | 344,701,530 | 104,857,599 | 655,931,478 | 242.2 | 17.4 | 8.4 | 9.7 | 265,064,772 | 26 |
| | Europe | 245,848,304 | 122,924,152 | 2,844,243 | 8,224,861 | 36,798,021 | 47,867,126 | 38.9 | 49.9 | 10.9 | 42.0 | 791,068,562 | 396 |
| | Latin America | 93,659,253 | 46,829,626 | 244,074,329 | 999,901,956 | 40,115,510 | 1,284,091,796 | 2,742.1 | 66.8 | 15.1 | 56.0 | 776,662,515 | 546 |
| | Northern America | 108,730,840 | 54,365,420 | 63,186,802 | 1,890,456,418 | 126,665,304 | 2,080,308,524 | 3,826.5 | 81.8 | 56.0 | 74.0 | 309,347,783 | 364 |
| | Oceania | 8,276,287 | 4,138,143 | 3,838,207 | 4,311,324 | 4,187,434 | 12,336,966 | 298.1 | 59.1 | 12.1 | 49.9 | 28,990,880 | 348 |
| | **World A** | **56,675,257** | **28,337,628** | **13,268,270** | **2,175,763** | **2,356,657** | **17,800,691** | **62.8** | **2.9** | **2.2** | **0.8** | **4,670,919** | **2** |
| | **World B** | **577,425,774** | **288,712,887** | **191,690,499** | **309,051,866** | **107,165,342** | **607,907,708** | **210.6** | **20.1** | **10.0** | **11.2** | **435,715,991** | **42** |
| | **World C** | **440,179,052** | **220,089,526** | **325,234,383** | **2,947,912,469** | **213,708,753** | **3,486,855,605** | **1,584.3** | **61.4** | **19.2** | **53.7** | **2,128,382,429** | **458** |
| | **GLOBAL TOTAL** | **1,074,280,084** | **537,140,042** | **530,193,153** | **3,259,140,099** | **323,230,753** | **4,112,564,005** | **765.6** | **29.9** | **11.8** | **22.0** | **2,568,769,339** | **155** |

| COUNTRY | | EVANGELIZATION | | | | | | | | | | | | STRATEGIES | | FUTURES | |
|---|---|---|---|---|---|---|---|---|---|---|---|---|---|---|---|---|---|
| code 1 | short name 2 | when begun: year begun 152 | status of evangelization, E: 1900 153 | 1970 154 | 1990 155 | 1995 156 | 2000 157 | 2025 158 | source of E: internal 159 | external 160 | unevangelized: U 161 | total 162 | world 163 | plans 164 | target 165 | growth 166 | prospect 167 |
| afgh | Afghanistan | c300 | 3.0 | 14.0 | 25.0 | 27.0 | 29.6 | 35.0 | 2.5 | 27.1 | 70.4 | 16,000,408 | A | 0 | 47 | 1 | -2 |
| alba | Albania | c70 | 39.0 | 34.0 | 75.7 | 81.1 | 85.4 | 90.8 | 43.4 | 42.0 | 14.6 | 454,107 | B | 0 | 1 | 24 | 2 |
| alge | Algeria | c100 | 15.0 | 24.0 | 43.9 | 47.1 | 49.6 | 55.0 | 4.4 | 45.2 | 50.5 | 15,876,006 | A | 2 | 22 | 18 | -2 |
| amer | American Samoa | 1827 | 100.0 | 100.0 | 99.6 | 99.6 | 99.6 | 99.4 | 91.0 | 8.6 | 0.4 | 252 | C | 0 | 0 | 0 | 0 |
| ando | Andorra | c600 | 100.0 | 100.0 | 99.1 | 99.1 | 99.1 | 98.7 | 97.7 | 1.4 | 0.9 | 734 | C | 0 | 1 | -2 | 0 |
| ango | Angola | 1491 | 15.0 | 86.0 | 99.1 | 99.2 | 99.3 | 99.5 | 94.1 | 5.2 | 0.7 | 91,226 | C | 0 | 0 | 3 | 1 |
| angu | Anguilla | c1650 | 100.0 | 100.0 | 99.8 | 99.8 | 99.8 | 99.5 | 96.5 | 3.3 | 0.2 | 17 | C | 0 | 0 | -2 | 0 |
| anti | Antigua | 1634 | 100.0 | 99.9 | 99.8 | 99.8 | 99.8 | 99.7 | 89.5 | 10.3 | 0.2 | 157 | C | 0 | 0 | -1 | 0 |
| arge | Argentina | 1527 | 99.5 | 99.7 | 99.4 | 99.4 | 99.3 | 98.9 | 96.4 | 2.9 | 0.7 | 242,999 | C | 2 | 0 | -1 | 1 |
| arme | Armenia | c60 | 95.0 | 93.0 | 96.5 | 97.4 | 97.8 | 98.9 | 93.8 | 4.0 | 2.2 | 77,944 | C | 0 | 6 | 10 | 2 |
| arub | Aruba | 1499 | 100.0 | 99.9 | 99.6 | 99.6 | 99.5 | 99.4 | 98.6 | 0.9 | 0.5 | 475 | C | 0 | 2 | -1 | 0 |
| aust | Australia | 1788 | 99.2 | 99.5 | 98.6 | 98.4 | 98.4 | 97.7 | 76.5 | 21.9 | 1.6 | 307,968 | C | 6 | 0 | -5 | -1 |
| ausz | Austria | 174 | 99.8 | 99.9 | 98.7 | 98.6 | 98.6 | 97.8 | 93.9 | 4.7 | 1.4 | 115,508 | C | 0 | 1 | -3 | 0 |
| azer | Azerbaijan | c270 | 18.0 | 25.0 | 33.8 | 34.6 | 37.0 | 41.5 | 8.1 | 28.9 | 63.0 | 4,872,856 | A | 0 | 14 | -16 | 1 |
| baha | Bahamas | c1670 | 99.8 | 99.9 | 99.8 | 99.7 | 99.7 | 99.6 | 96.9 | 2.8 | 0.3 | 859 | C | 0 | 0 | -2 | 0 |
| bahr | Bahrain | c250 | 8.9 | 40.1 | 53.1 | 55.4 | 57.2 | 65.0 | 16.0 | 41.2 | 42.8 | 264,134 | B | 0 | 1 | 8 | 1 |
| bang | Bangladesh | 1536 | 15.0 | 43.0 | 53.0 | 55.1 | 57.2 | 62.0 | 5.8 | 51.4 | 42.8 | 55,267,877 | B | 0 | 3 | 17 | 2 |
| barb | Barbados | 1626 | 100.0 | 99.8 | 99.3 | 99.2 | 99.2 | 99.0 | 82.7 | 16.5 | 0.8 | 2,159 | C | 0 | 1 | -1 | 0 |
| belg | Belgium | c200 | 100.0 | 99.5 | 98.2 | 98.0 | 97.8 | 97.2 | 93.6 | 4.2 | 2.2 | 219,444 | C | 5 | 0 | -3 | -1 |
| beli | Belize | c1650 | 99.0 | 99.0 | 98.0 | 97.9 | 97.9 | 97.3 | 90.6 | 7.3 | 2.1 | 5,155 | C | 0 | 0 | -1 | 0 |
| belo | Belorussia | c960 | 99.9 | 97.8 | 98.5 | 99.1 | 99.2 | 99.2 | 74.2 | 25.0 | 0.9 | 86,904 | C | 0 | 4 | 22 | 1 |
| beni | Benin | 1680 | 12.9 | 52.2 | 67.1 | 71.0 | 74.2 | 79.8 | 36.1 | 38.1 | 25.8 | 1,574,060 | B | 0 | 1 | 24 | 1 |
| berm | Bermuda | 1609 | 100.0 | 100.0 | 99.8 | 99.8 | 99.8 | 99.7 | 95.9 | 3.9 | 0.2 | 121 | C | 0 | 1 | -2 | 0 |
| bhut | Bhutan | 1626 | 0.0 | 15.5 | 19.0 | 20.0 | 20.8 | 24.4 | 4.9 | 15.9 | 79.2 | 1,683,112 | A | 0 | 3 | -18 | -1 |
| boli | Bolivia | 1537 | 96.1 | 99.0 | 99.7 | 99.7 | 99.7 | 99.7 | 98.5 | 1.2 | 0.3 | 24,406 | C | 1 | 0 | -2 | 0 |
| bosn | Bosnia-Herzegovina | c90 | 64.9 | 65.0 | 70.8 | 71.6 | 73.7 | 74.6 | 40.7 | 33.0 | 26.3 | 1,045,717 | B | 0 | 0 | -27 | -1 |
| bots | Botswana | 1816 | 18.0 | 85.0 | 91.0 | 93.0 | 94.9 | 96.0 | 55.7 | 39.2 | 5.1 | 83,331 | B | 0 | 0 | 11 | 2 |
| boug | Bougainville | 1900 | 5.0 | 99.6 | 99.8 | 99.9 | 99.9 | 99.9 | 98.3 | 1.6 | 0.1 | 256 | C | 0 | 0 | 1 | 1 |
| braz | Brazil | 1500 | 98.3 | 99.5 | 99.7 | 99.7 | 99.8 | 99.8 | 99.1 | 0.7 | 0.3 | 425,724 | C | 8 | 1 | -2 | 1 |
| brit | Britain | 61 | 99.9 | 99.5 | 98.2 | 98.1 | 98.1 | 97.7 | 76.1 | 22.0 | 1.9 | 1,116,976 | C | 101 | 0 | -3 | 0 |
| briz | British Virgin Is | 1648 | 100.0 | 99.8 | 99.7 | 99.6 | 99.6 | 99.5 | 79.7 | 19.9 | 0.4 | 90 | C | 0 | 0 | -2 | 0 |
| brun | Brunei | c1600 | 6.0 | 40.2 | 42.1 | 44.2 | 45.1 | 52.1 | 13.8 | 31.3 | 54.9 | 180,020 | A | 0 | 0 | -5 | -1 |
| bulg | Bulgaria | c90 | 90.7 | 75.0 | 92.3 | 93.4 | 94.5 | 95.7 | 88.2 | 6.3 | 5.5 | 454,079 | C | 1 | 0 | 3 | 1 |
| burk | Burkina Faso | 1900 | 0.0 | 44.7 | 55.5 | 59.0 | 63.1 | 72.1 | 24.5 | 38.6 | 36.9 | 4,406,314 | B | 0 | 5 | 23 | 1 |
| buru | Burundi | 1879 | 0.1 | 98.0 | 98.9 | 99.0 | 99.2 | 99.5 | 86.9 | 12.3 | 0.8 | 54,611 | C | 0 | 2 | 2 | 1 |
| camb | Cambodia | 1555 | 7.0 | 25.0 | 38.0 | 44.9 | 49.1 | 60.7 | 6.2 | 42.9 | 50.9 | 5,685,563 | A | 0 | 1 | 32 | -1 |
| came | Cameroon | 1845 | 15.7 | 65.0 | 78.0 | 78.4 | 79.9 | 83.9 | 60.3 | 19.6 | 20.1 | 3,027,138 | B | 1 | 1 | 12 | 1 |
| cana | Canada | 1534 | 99.0 | 99.5 | 98.0 | 97.9 | 97.8 | 96.5 | 74.5 | 23.3 | 2.2 | 688,856 | C | 11 | 0 | -4 | 0 |
| cape | Cape Verde | 1462 | 99.9 | 100.0 | 100.0 | 100.0 | 100.0 | 99.9 | 98.8 | 1.2 | 0.1 | 202 | C | 0 | 0 | 0 | 0 |
| caym | Cayman Islands | 1670 | 100.0 | 99.9 | 98.3 | 98.1 | 98.1 | 97.7 | 77.2 | 20.9 | 2.0 | 749 | C | 0 | 0 | -2 | 0 |
| cent | Central African Rep | 1894 | 0.2 | 78.4 | 81.6 | 82.5 | 84.0 | 87.7 | 53.6 | 30.4 | 16.0 | 578,728 | B | 0 | 2 | 5 | 1 |
| chad | Chad | 1663 | 0.0 | 45.0 | 48.1 | 49.0 | 50.1 | 54.0 | 24.4 | 25.7 | 49.9 | 3,818,667 | B | 0 | 40 | -1 | -2 |
| chan | Channel Islands | c550 | 100.0 | 99.9 | 99.7 | 99.6 | 99.5 | 99.3 | 75.9 | 23.6 | 0.5 | 719 | C | 0 | 0 | -10 | 0 |
| chil | Chile | 1541 | 98.5 | 99.6 | 99.6 | 99.6 | 99.6 | 99.7 | 97.2 | 2.4 | 0.4 | 61,134 | C | 0 | 0 | -1 | 1 |
| chin | China | 578 | 18.0 | 20.0 | 53.0 | 57.0 | 64.8 | 70.6 | 13.8 | 51.0 | 35.2 | 444,210,082 | B | 8 | 35 | 31 | 2 |
| colo | Colombia | 1512 | 83.0 | 99.1 | 99.7 | 99.7 | 99.7 | 99.7 | 99.3 | 0.4 | 0.3 | 119,613 | C | 0 | 0 | 0 | 1 |
| como | Comoros | 1517 | 1.0 | 20.2 | 35.0 | 36.1 | 37.4 | 44.4 | 4.3 | 33.1 | 62.7 | 371,333 | A | 0 | 2 | 24 | 0 |
| cong | Congo-Brazzaville | 1491 | 13.9 | 93.0 | 98.8 | 98.9 | 99.0 | 99.4 | 89.0 | 10.0 | 1.0 | 28,634 | C | 0 | 0 | 0 | 1 |
| conz | Congo-Zaire | 1482 | 17.0 | 93.0 | 98.7 | 98.9 | 99.1 | 99.5 | 96.9 | 2.2 | 0.9 | 461,513 | C | 0 | 0 | 1 | 1 |
| cook | Cook Islands | 1823 | 100.0 | 99.9 | 99.9 | 100.0 | 100.0 | 99.9 | 99.3 | 0.7 | 0.1 | 10 | C | 0 | 0 | -2 | 0 |
| cost | Costa Rica | 1514 | 100.0 | 99.9 | 99.9 | 99.9 | 99.9 | 99.8 | 98.7 | 1.2 | 0.1 | 4,553 | C | 2 | 0 | -1 | 1 |
| croa | Croatia | c80 | 99.0 | 97.0 | 98.0 | 98.7 | 99.2 | 99.3 | 97.7 | 1.5 | 0.8 | 33,972 | C | 0 | 1 | 1 | 1 |
| cuba | Cuba | 1512 | 99.8 | 65.0 | 97.7 | 98.7 | 99.1 | 99.2 | 52.1 | 47.0 | 0.9 | 100,633 | B | 0 | 0 | 7 | -1 |
| cypr | Cyprus | 42 | 100.0 | 99.5 | 99.8 | 99.8 | 99.8 | 99.9 | 99.0 | 0.8 | 0.2 | 1,086 | C | 1 | 1 | -2 | -1 |
| czec | Czech Republic | 828 | 99.8 | 95.0 | 99.0 | 99.3 | 99.4 | 99.7 | 56.1 | 43.3 | 0.6 | 59,480 | B | 3 | 0 | 18 | 1 |
| denm | Denmark | 826 | 100.0 | 100.0 | 99.4 | 99.3 | 99.2 | 98.7 | 98.3 | 0.9 | 0.8 | 41,131 | C | 2 | 0 | -3 | 0 |
| djib | Djibouti | 1862 | 5.0 | 35.0 | 40.0 | 43.0 | 45.8 | 51.3 | 9.0 | 36.8 | 54.2 | 345,336 | A | 0 | 0 | -8 | -2 |
| domi | Dominica | 1642 | 100.0 | 99.9 | 99.9 | 99.9 | 99.9 | 99.9 | 99.0 | 0.9 | 0.1 | 62 | C | 0 | 0 | -2 | 1 |
| domr | Dominican Republic | 1494 | 99.8 | 99.9 | 99.9 | 99.9 | 99.9 | 99.9 | 99.7 | 0.2 | 0.1 | 6,278 | C | 0 | 0 | -1 | 0 |
| ecua | Ecuador | 1526 | 90.0 | 99.3 | 99.5 | 99.5 | 99.4 | 99.3 | 99.1 | 0.3 | 0.6 | 71,415 | C | 1 | 0 | -1 | 1 |
| egyp | Egypt | 33 | 34.0 | 48.0 | 73.0 | 75.1 | 77.7 | 81.2 | 22.5 | 55.2 | 22.4 | 15,303,820 | B | 9 | 11 | -5 | 0 |
| elsa | El Salvador | 1525 | 99.5 | 99.8 | 99.9 | 99.9 | 99.9 | 99.9 | 99.7 | 0.2 | 0.1 | 6,319 | C | 0 | 0 | -1 | 1 |
| equa | Equatorial Guinea | 1445 | 16.7 | 96.0 | 98.3 | 98.4 | 98.6 | 98.9 | 95.4 | 3.2 | 1.4 | 6,462 | C | 0 | 1 | 1 | 0 |
| erit | Eritrea | c1800 | 35.0 | 68.0 | 70.3 | 71.8 | 73.6 | 77.6 | 57.5 | 16.1 | 26.4 | 1,017,551 | B | 0 | 1 | 1 | 1 |
| esto | Estonia | c1250 | 99.8 | 90.0 | 93.6 | 96.1 | 98.1 | 98.6 | 47.1 | 51.0 | 1.9 | 26,919 | B | 0 | 3 | 11 | 1 |
| ethi | Ethiopia | c39 | 51.0 | 76.0 | 81.1 | 83.0 | 84.5 | 89.6 | 58.7 | 25.8 | 15.5 | 9,707,024 | B | 1 | 5 | 3 | 0 |
| faer | Faeroe Islands | c750 | 100.0 | 100.0 | 100.0 | 99.9 | 99.9 | 99.9 | 99.9 | 0.0 | 0.1 | 30 | C | 0 | 0 | -1 | 0 |
| fiji | Fiji | 1804 | 95.0 | 75.0 | 84.4 | 86.1 | 88.8 | 90.9 | 62.4 | 26.4 | 11.2 | 91,621 | B | 0 | 1 | -1 | 1 |
| finl | Finland | c1100 | 100.0 | 99.9 | 99.8 | 99.7 | 99.7 | 99.5 | 98.5 | 1.2 | 0.3 | 14,982 | C | 0 | 0 | -2 | 0 |
| fran | France | c80 | 99.9 | 98.0 | 96.4 | 96.4 | 96.3 | 95.1 | 79.1 | 17.2 | 3.7 | 2,188,393 | C | 19 | 0 | -4 | 0 |
| freg | French Guiana | 1598 | 97.1 | 97.5 | 98.2 | 98.5 | 98.8 | 99.0 | 90.5 | 8.3 | 1.2 | 2,240 | C | 0 | 1 | -2 | 1 |
| frep | French Polynesia | 1659 | 99.9 | 98.0 | 98.5 | 98.6 | 98.6 | 98.8 | 91.0 | 7.6 | 1.4 | 3,191 | C | 0 | 0 | -2 | 0 |
| gabo | Gabon | 1673 | 23.0 | 97.0 | 97.8 | 97.9 | 98.1 | 98.5 | 94.1 | 4.0 | 1.9 | 23,478 | C | 0 | 0 | -1 | 1 |
| gamb | Gambia | 1651 | 17.0 | 25.0 | 39.1 | 42.4 | 44.1 | 53.5 | 8.8 | 35.3 | 55.9 | 730,102 | A | 0 | 3 | -1 | -1 |
| geor | Georgia | c150 | 95.9 | 65.0 | 87.9 | 88.2 | 88.6 | 91.1 | 69.5 | 19.1 | 11.4 | 565,806 | C | 0 | 10 | 8 | 1 |
| germ | Germany | c150 | 99.7 | 96.0 | 97.2 | 97.3 | 97.6 | 97.2 | 81.1 | 16.5 | 2.4 | 1,942,922 | C | 31 | 0 | -3 | 0 |
| ghan | Ghana | 1471 | 23.0 | 70.0 | 82.6 | 83.4 | 84.6 | 89.2 | 51.8 | 32.8 | 15.4 | 3,106,004 | B | 0 | 0 | 8 | 1 |
| gibr | Gibraltar | c200 | 99.9 | 94.0 | 94.6 | 94.6 | 94.6 | 94.4 | 88.0 | 6.6 | 5.4 | 1,359 | C | 0 | 0 | -4 | 0 |
| gree | Greece | c40 | 93.4 | 99.0 | 98.5 | 98.5 | 98.4 | 98.0 | 96.6 | 1.8 | 1.6 | 165,750 | C | 8 | 0 | -1 | 0 |
| grel | Greenland | c990 | 97.4 | 99.8 | 99.7 | 99.7 | 99.7 | 99.6 | 80.1 | 19.6 | 0.3 | 166 | C | 0 | 0 | -1 | 0 |
| gren | Grenada | c1650 | 99.9 | 99.9 | 100.0 | 100.0 | 100.0 | 100.0 | 99.2 | 0.8 | 0.0 | 28 | C | 0 | 0 | -1 | 0 |
| guad | Guadeloupe | 1523 | 99.8 | 99.8 | 99.9 | 99.9 | 99.9 | 99.9 | 99.3 | 0.6 | 0.1 | 434 | C | 0 | 0 | -1 | 1 |
| guam | Guam | 1668 | 100.0 | 99.7 | 99.2 | 99.0 | 99.0 | 98.6 | 97.3 | 1.7 | 1.0 | 1,708 | C | 0 | 0 | 0 | 0 |
| guat | Guatemala | 1524 | 99.9 | 99.9 | 99.9 | 99.9 | 99.9 | 100.0 | 98.7 | 1.2 | 0.1 | 7,929 | C | 0 | 0 | -1 | 1 |
| guin | Guinea | 1877 | 6.6 | 12.0 | 35.7 | 38.5 | 41.6 | 45.6 | 7.8 | 33.8 | 58.4 | 4,337,014 | A | 0 | 5 | 17 | -1 |
| gunb | Guinea-Bissau | 1445 | 7.5 | 29.9 | 45.0 | 46.6 | 48.2 | 52.2 | 19.9 | 28.3 | 51.8 | 628,702 | A | 0 | 0 | 15 | -1 |
| guya | Guyana | 1548 | 61.8 | 75.0 | 76.1 | 78.9 | 81.3 | 85.7 | 51.9 | 29.4 | 18.8 | 161,535 | B | 0 | 1 | -5 | 0 |
| hait | Haiti | 1493 | 100.0 | 99.9 | 99.9 | 99.9 | 99.9 | 99.9 | 99.9 | 0.0 | 0.1 | 5,934 | C | 0 | 0 | -1 | 0 |
| hond | Honduras | 1524 | 99.0 | 99.9 | 99.9 | 99.9 | 99.9 | 99.9 | 99.6 | 0.3 | 0.1 | 6,422 | C | 0 | 0 | -1 | 1 |
| hung | Hungary | c200 | 99.8 | 94.0 | 99.2 | 99.2 | 99.4 | 99.4 | 96.9 | 2.5 | 0.7 | 65,545 | C | 1 | 1 | 4 | 1 |
| icel | Iceland | c740 | 100.0 | 99.9 | 100.0 | 100.0 | 100.0 | 99.9 | 99.7 | 0.3 | 0.1 | 154 | C | 0 | 0 | -1 | 0 |
| indi | India | 52 | 15.0 | 35.1 | 53.0 | 56.6 | 59.3 | 66.2 | 12.5 | 46.8 | 40.7 | 412,122,495 | B | 16 | 32 | 20 | 2 |
| indo | Indonesia | c650 | 24.0 | 50.0 | 56.5 | 59.3 | 62.9 | 68.9 | 18.6 | 44.3 | 37.2 | 78,805,877 | B | 3 | 33 | 20 | 1 |
| iran | Iran | 48 | 13.0 | 25.0 | 31.6 | 34.5 | 37.2 | 44.4 | 3.3 | 33.9 | 62.8 | 42,507,292 | A | 2 | 31 | 22 | -1 |
| iraq | Iraq | c50 | 22.0 | 30.0 | 42.5 | 45.0 | 48.4 | 56.1 | 7.8 | 40.6 | 51.6 | 11,916,962 | A | 0 | 4 | -3 | -2 |
| irel | Ireland | c250 | 100.0 | 99.8 | 99.8 | 99.8 | 99.7 | 99.7 | 98.6 | 1.1 | 0.3 | 10,277 | C | 8 | 0 | -1 | 1 |
| isle | Isle of Man | 442 | 99.9 | 99.9 | 99.7 | 99.7 | 99.6 | 99.5 | 76.2 | 23.4 | 0.4 | 292 | C | 0 | 0 | -4 | 0 |
| isra | Israel | 33 | 23.8 | 40.0 | 52.2 | 54.6 | 56.0 | 68.2 | 10.7 | 45.3 | 44.0 | 2,252,726 | B | 30 | 9 | 19 | -1 |
| ital | Italy | 33 | 100.0 | 99.5 | 99.3 | 99.3 | 99.2 | 98.7 | 91.8 | 7.4 | 0.8 | 436,987 | C | 39 | 2 | -3 | 0 |
| ivor | Ivory Coast | 1637 | 5.0 | 50.0 | 66.9 | 69.3 | 72.8 | 78.6 | 37.2 | 35.6 | 27.3 | 4,029,608 | B | 0 | 1 | 9 | 1 |
| jama | Jamaica | 1509 | 99.9 | 98.0 | 98.7 | 98.8 | 98.9 | 99.0 | 52.5 | 46.4 | 1.1 | 27,592 | B | 2 | 0 | -4 | 0 |
| japa | Japan | 1542 | 20.0 | 40.0 | 62.0 | 65.0 | 66.9 | 75.2 | 8.7 | 58.2 | 33.1 | 41,890,821 | B | 6 | 0 | 15 | 0 |
| jord | Jordan | 33 | 16.0 | 35.0 | 48.1 | 51.2 | 54.3 | 63.5 | 9.6 | 44.7 | 45.8 | 3,051,282 | B | 1 | 2 | 29 | 1 |
| kaza | Kazakhstan | c360 | 14.3 | 40.0 | 59.0 | 61.0 | 64.3 | 68.9 | 21.3 | 43.0 | 35.8 | 5,799,212 | B | 0 | 18 | -7 | -1 |
| keny | Kenya | 1498 | 6.9 | 85.0 | 93.0 | 93.6 | 94.2 | 96.2 | 83.5 | 10.7 | 5.8 | 1,742,085 | C | 8 | 6 | 3 | 1 |
| kirg | Kirgizstan | c1180 | 10.3 | 25.0 | 40.8 | 45.3 | 47.4 | 52.4 | 13.7 | 33.7 | 52.6 | 2,473,100 | A | 0 | 19 | -29 | -1 |
| kiri | Kiribati | 1837 | 100.0 | 99.9 | 99.9 | 99.9 | 99.9 | 99.9 | 99.8 | 0.1 | 0.1 | 60 | C | 0 | 0 | -2 | 0 |
| kuwa | Kuwait | c100 | 6.7 | 34.8 | 50.0 | 55.0 | 64.5 | 68.1 | 19.0 | 45.5 | 35.5 | 700,639 | B | 0 | 1 | 9 | 1 |
| laos | Laos | 1630 | 4.0 | 30.0 | 43.4 | 45.5 | 47.6 | 49.8 | 7.5 | 40.1 | 52.5 | 2,849,470 | A | 0 | 1 | 18 | -2 |
| latv | Latvia | c1050 | 99.9 | 94.0 | 98.7 | 98.9 | 99.0 | 99.4 | 76.8 | 22.2 | 1.0 | 22,603 | C | 1 | 5 | 16 | 1 |
| leba | Lebanon | 33 | 82.0 | 80.0 | 89.2 | 90.3 | 91.9 | 93.2 | 62.0 | 29.9 | 8.1 | 266,666 | B | 0 | 0 | -4 | -1 |
| leso | Lesotho | 1833 | 29.5 | 97.9 | 99.6 | 99.6 | 99.6 | 99.5 | 77.1 | 22.5 | 0.4 | 8,139 | C | 0 | 0 | 3 | 1 |
| libe | Liberia | 1822 | 27.1 | 45.1 | 69.8 | 71.3 | 72.5 | 76.7 | 37.9 | 34.6 | 27.5 | 867,108 | B | 0 | 0 | 10 | 0 |
| liby | Libya | 33 | 6.3 | 13.9 | 43.4 | 45.0 | 46.1 | 49.1 | 7.9 | 38.2 | 53.9 | 3,019,596 | A | 0 | 7 | 8 | -2 |
| liec | Liechtenstein | c450 | 100.0 | 99.9 | 98.8 | 98.6 | 98.4 | 98.1 | 92.3 | 6.1 | 1.6 | 538 | C | 0 | 1 | -3 | 0 |
| lith | Lithuania | 1251 | 100.0 | 94.9 | 99.5 | 99.5 | 99.6 | 99.6 | 96.2 | 3.4 | 0.4 | 14,620 | C | 0 | 5 | 6 | 1 |
| luxe | Luxembourg | c250 | 100.0 | 99.7 | 99.5 | 99.3 | 99.1 | 98.9 | 98.5 | 0.6 | 0.9 | 3,931 | C | 0 | 0 | -1 | 0 |
| mace | Macedonia | 60 | 95.0 | 91.0 | 87.1 | 87.5 | 88.1 | 88.9 | 72.6 | 15.5 | 12.0 | 241,781 | C | 0 | 0 | -3 | 1 |
| mada | Madagascar | 1540 | 55.0 | 75.0 | 79.4 | 80.9 | 83.0 | 86.2 | 56.8 | 26.2 | 17.0 | 2,712,337 | B | 0 | 2 | 5 | 1 |
| mala | Malawi | 1561 | 16.9 | 85.0 | 95.1 | 95.3 | 96.1 | 97.5 | 74.1 | 22.0 | 4.0 | 431,511 | C | 0 | 2 | 3 | 1 |
| malb | Malaysia | 1511 | 11.9 | 40.0 | 57.7 | 59.1 | 63.7 | 70.9 | 14.3 | 49.4 | 36.3 | 8,081,332 | B | 2 | 9 | 19 | 0 |

| COUNTRY | | EVANGELIZATION | | | | | | | | | | | | | STRATEGIES | | FUTURES | |
|---|---|---|---|---|---|---|---|---|---|---|---|---|---|---|---|---|---|---|
| | | when begun | status of evangelization, E | | | | | | source of E | | unevangelized | | | | | | | |
| code | short name | year begun | 1900 | 1970 | 1990 | 1995 | 2000 | 2025 | internal | external | U | total | world | | plans | target | growth | prospect |
| 1 | 2 | 152 | 153 | 154 | 155 | 156 | 157 | 158 | 159 | 160 | 161 | 162 | 163 | | 164 | 165 | 166 | 167 |
| mald | Maldives | 1887 | 0.0 | 8.7 | 19.0 | 19.3 | 19.6 | 21.2 | 3.2 | 16.4 | 80.4 | 230,137 | A | | 0 | 1 | 24 | -2 |
| mali | Mali | 1895 | 3.9 | 25.0 | 40.1 | 42.0 | 43.6 | 49.8 | 7.2 | 36.4 | 56.4 | 6,340,283 | A | | 0 | 10 | 11 | -1 |
| malt | Malta | 60 | 100.0 | 100.0 | 100.0 | 100.0 | 99.9 | 99.9 | 99.2 | 0.7 | 0.1 | 220 | C | | 1 | 0 | -1 | 1 |
| mars | Marshall Islands | 1529 | 78.0 | 98.7 | 99.9 | 99.9 | 99.9 | 100.0 | 99.0 | 0.9 | 0.1 | 42 | C | | 0 | 0 | 0 | 0 |
| mart | Martinique | c1550 | 100.0 | 99.9 | 99.9 | 99.9 | 99.9 | 99.8 | 99.2 | 0.7 | 0.1 | 507 | C | | 0 | 0 | -1 | 0 |
| maur | Mauritania | 1448 | 1.0 | 8.0 | 26.5 | 29.2 | 31.9 | 37.1 | 1.6 | 30.3 | 68.1 | 1,818,258 | A | | 0 | 13 | -35 | -2 |
| maus | Mauritius | 1598 | 44.4 | 64.8 | 69.2 | 71.0 | 74.9 | 80.4 | 38.7 | 36.2 | 25.1 | 290,720 | B | | 0 | 0 | 9 | -1 |
| mayo | Mayotte | 1517 | 1.0 | 20.0 | 35.0 | 37.5 | 40.7 | 46.5 | 5.0 | 35.7 | 59.3 | 60,252 | A | | 0 | 2 | 20 | -2 |
| mexi | Mexico | 1518 | 99.8 | 99.8 | 99.8 | 99.8 | 99.9 | 99.9 | 99.3 | 0.6 | 0.2 | 147,917 | C | | 3 | 0 | -1 | 1 |
| micr | Micronesia | 1526 | 90.0 | 99.5 | 99.5 | 99.5 | 99.6 | 99.6 | 97.0 | 2.6 | 0.4 | 441 | C | | 0 | 0 | 0 | 0 |
| mold | Moldavia | c130 | 99.9 | 90.0 | 93.0 | 93.7 | 94.2 | 95.7 | 73.5 | 20.7 | 5.8 | 252,923 | C | | 0 | 5 | 19 | 1 |
| mona | Monaco | c100 | 99.9 | 99.8 | 99.0 | 98.9 | 98.8 | 98.8 | 96.6 | 2.2 | 1.2 | 392 | C | | 0 | 0 | -2 | 0 |
| mong | Mongolia | c650 | 3.8 | 16.0 | 32.3 | 36.5 | 42.8 | 49.0 | 6.8 | 36.0 | 57.2 | 1,522,030 | A | | 1 | 2 | 33 | 1 |
| mont | Montserrat | 1632 | 100.0 | 99.9 | 99.9 | 99.9 | 99.9 | 99.9 | 99.4 | 0.5 | 0.1 | 7 | C | | 0 | 0 | -2 | 0 |
| moro | Morocco | c150 | 7.7 | 28.0 | 40.1 | 41.5 | 42.2 | 47.6 | 5.0 | 37.2 | 57.8 | 16,314,645 | A | | 0 | 8 | 4 | -1 |
| moza | Mozambique | 1506 | 11.0 | 60.0 | 73.0 | 75.0 | 77.0 | 82.0 | 41.6 | 35.4 | 23.0 | 4,521,300 | B | | 0 | 2 | 11 | 1 |
| myan | Myanmar | c920 | 19.6 | 35.0 | 53.1 | 56.9 | 60.9 | 69.0 | 14.0 | 46.9 | 39.1 | 17,852,271 | B | | 1 | 3 | 33 | 1 |
| nami | Namibia | 1805 | 13.4 | 97.0 | 97.6 | 97.7 | 97.7 | 97.9 | 87.5 | 10.2 | 2.3 | 39,161 | C | | 0 | 0 | -2 | 1 |
| naur | Nauru | 1888 | 50.0 | 90.0 | 95.0 | 95.5 | 96.4 | 96.6 | 81.6 | 14.8 | 3.6 | 410 | C | | 0 | 0 | -2 | 0 |
| nepa | Nepal | 1715 | 0.0 | 23.8 | 37.9 | 42.2 | 46.2 | 52.4 | 7.7 | 38.5 | 53.8 | 12,866,777 | A | | 0 | 45 | 66 | 2 |
| neth | Netherlands | c270 | 99.5 | 98.0 | 97.7 | 97.7 | 97.6 | 96.9 | 74.9 | 22.7 | 2.4 | 373,557 | C | | 13 | 0 | -4 | -1 |
| nets | Netherlands Antilles | c1550 | 100.0 | 99.8 | 99.4 | 99.3 | 99.3 | 98.8 | 95.2 | 4.1 | 0.7 | 1,547 | C | | 0 | 0 | -1 | 0 |
| newc | New Caledonia | 1831 | 79.9 | 99.5 | 98.8 | 98.7 | 98.6 | 98.3 | 84.5 | 14.1 | 1.4 | 2,965 | C | | 1 | 0 | -2 | 0 |
| newz | New Zealand | 1785 | 99.8 | 99.5 | 99.1 | 99.1 | 99.1 | 98.5 | 76.2 | 22.9 | 0.9 | 35,988 | C | | 1 | 0 | -3 | 1 |
| nica | Nicaragua | 1517 | 99.0 | 99.9 | 99.9 | 99.9 | 99.9 | 99.8 | 99.0 | 0.9 | 0.1 | 7,125 | C | | 1 | 1 | -1 | 1 |
| niga | Niger | c650 | 0.0 | 15.0 | 38.2 | 40.4 | 42.1 | 47.4 | 4.1 | 38.0 | 57.9 | 6,208,244 | A | | 0 | 12 | 5 | -1 |
| nige | Nigeria | 1487 | 16.7 | 57.8 | 75.2 | 77.3 | 79.8 | 84.6 | 52.1 | 27.7 | 20.2 | 22,559,535 | B | | 9 | 7 | 2 | 1 |
| nork | North Korea | c1000 | 15.0 | 21.1 | 45.5 | 47.2 | 50.0 | 60.0 | 8.1 | 41.9 | 50.0 | 12,026,315 | A | | 0 | 0 | 132 | -2 |
| norl | Northern Cyprus | 42 | 4.3 | 20.1 | 50.6 | 53.3 | 56.0 | 63.9 | 15.1 | 40.9 | 44.0 | 81,374 | B | | 0 | 0 | 4 | 0 |
| norm | Northern Mariana Is | 1521 | 80.0 | 99.5 | 98.6 | 98.8 | 98.9 | 99.0 | 91.9 | 7.0 | 1.1 | 836 | C | | 0 | 0 | -2 | 0 |
| norw | Norway | c900 | 100.0 | 99.6 | 98.8 | 98.7 | 98.6 | 98.0 | 96.7 | 1.9 | 1.4 | 61,076 | C | | 6 | 0 | -2 | 0 |
| oman | Oman | 1508 | 0.0 | 13.0 | 40.6 | 43.9 | 47.0 | 55.2 | 9.9 | 37.1 | 53.0 | 1,347,866 | A | | 0 | 4 | 22 | -1 |
| paki | Pakistan | c750 | 9.6 | 35.0 | 42.5 | 44.3 | 46.8 | 50.5 | 7.4 | 39.4 | 53.2 | 83,307,766 | A | | 0 | 21 | 15 | -1 |
| pala | Palau | 1543 | 84.4 | 99.9 | 99.9 | 99.9 | 99.9 | 99.9 | 99.2 | 0.7 | 0.1 | 11 | C | | 0 | 0 | -2 | 0 |
| pale | Palestine | 33 | 31.9 | 47.7 | 60.9 | 67.1 | 70.6 | 75.8 | 15.3 | 55.3 | 29.4 | 650,425 | B | | 1 | 1 | 5 | -1 |
| pana | Panama | 1513 | 99.0 | 98.5 | 98.4 | 98.4 | 98.4 | 97.5 | 92.7 | 5.7 | 1.7 | 47,114 | C | | 0 | 0 | -3 | 1 |
| papu | Papua New Guinea | c1800 | 17.0 | 95.0 | 97.5 | 97.5 | 97.5 | 98.0 | 91.7 | 5.8 | 2.5 | 113,957 | C | | 0 | 0 | 1 | 1 |
| para | Paraguay | 1524 | 98.0 | 99.5 | 99.8 | 99.8 | 99.8 | 99.8 | 98.9 | 0.9 | 0.2 | 10,063 | C | | 0 | 0 | 0 | 1 |
| peru | Peru | 1532 | 97.0 | 99.0 | 99.7 | 99.7 | 99.7 | 99.7 | 99.0 | 0.7 | 0.3 | 68,433 | C | | 3 | 2 | -1 | 1 |
| phil | Philippines | 1521 | 93.0 | 97.0 | 94.6 | 94.5 | 94.4 | 94.6 | 90.7 | 3.7 | 5.6 | 4,222,787 | C | | 6 | 2 | -1 | 2 |
| pola | Poland | c950 | 99.0 | 98.0 | 99.9 | 99.9 | 100.0 | 100.0 | 99.8 | 0.2 | 0.0 | 16,713 | C | | 0 | 1 | 1 | 2 |
| port | Portugal | c150 | 100.0 | 99.5 | 99.6 | 99.6 | 99.6 | 99.5 | 98.8 | 0.8 | 0.4 | 35,999 | C | | 0 | 0 | -2 | 0 |
| puer | Puerto Rico | 1509 | 100.0 | 99.8 | 99.9 | 99.9 | 99.9 | 99.9 | 99.4 | 0.5 | 0.1 | 3,864 | C | | 0 | 0 | -1 | 0 |
| qata | Qatar | c210 | 2.0 | 34.8 | 48.5 | 54.7 | 56.4 | 61.5 | 15.9 | 40.5 | 43.6 | 261,389 | B | | 0 | 1 | 16 | -1 |
| reun | Reunion | 1649 | 60.0 | 98.5 | 97.4 | 97.3 | 97.2 | 96.9 | 92.6 | 4.6 | 2.8 | 19,656 | C | | 0 | 0 | -3 | -1 |
| roma | Romania | c120 | 99.0 | 95.0 | 99.1 | 99.2 | 99.3 | 99.3 | 97.8 | 1.5 | 0.7 | 162,918 | C | | 1 | 1 | 3 | 2 |
| russ | Russia | c300 | 90.1 | 85.0 | 91.0 | 92.2 | 93.3 | 95.3 | 66.3 | 27.0 | 6.8 | 9,923,477 | B | | 3 | 32 | 21 | 2 |
| rwan | Rwanda | 1889 | 0.2 | 90.0 | 98.2 | 98.4 | 98.9 | 99.0 | 91.7 | 7.2 | 1.1 | 88,387 | C | | 0 | 1 | 5 | -1 |
| saha | Sahara | c200 | 4.0 | 49.0 | 20.0 | 23.0 | 24.6 | 31.9 | 2.3 | 22.3 | 75.4 | 221,118 | A | | 0 | 6 | -10 | -2 |
| saih | Saint Helena | 1561 | 100.0 | 99.9 | 99.9 | 99.9 | 99.9 | 99.8 | 94.7 | 5.2 | 0.1 | 9 | C | | 0 | 0 | -1 | 1 |
| saik | Saint Kitts & Nevis | 1623 | 100.0 | 100.0 | 100.0 | 99.9 | 99.9 | 99.8 | 98.1 | 1.8 | 0.1 | 28 | C | | 0 | 0 | -2 | 0 |
| sail | Saint Lucia | 1648 | 99.8 | 99.8 | 99.1 | 99.1 | 99.0 | 98.8 | 98.4 | 0.6 | 1.0 | 1,573 | C | | 0 | 0 | -1 | 0 |
| saip | Saint Pierre & Miquelon | 1604 | 100.0 | 100.0 | 100.0 | 100.0 | 99.9 | 99.9 | 99.7 | 0.2 | 0.1 | 4 | C | | 0 | 0 | -2 | 1 |
| saiv | Saint Vincent | c1650 | 99.9 | 99.8 | 98.9 | 98.9 | 98.8 | 97.9 | 78.6 | 20.2 | 1.2 | 1,389 | C | | 0 | 0 | -5 | 0 |
| samo | Samoa | 1827 | 100.0 | 99.9 | 99.9 | 99.9 | 99.9 | 99.9 | 99.7 | 0.2 | 0.1 | 113 | C | | 1 | 0 | -1 | 1 |
| sanm | San Marino | 301 | 100.0 | 99.8 | 99.9 | 99.9 | 99.9 | 99.8 | 99.3 | 0.6 | 0.1 | 31 | C | | 0 | 0 | -2 | 0 |
| saot | Sao Tome & Principe | 1485 | 14.0 | 99.5 | 99.9 | 99.9 | 99.9 | 99.9 | 99.3 | 0.6 | 0.1 | 142 | C | | 0 | 0 | -1 | -1 |
| saud | Saudi Arabia | 100 | 2.0 | 18.0 | 40.0 | 46.3 | 54.9 | 62.5 | 8.9 | 46.0 | 45.1 | 9,735,310 | B | | 1 | 4 | 29 | -2 |
| sene | Senegal | 1445 | 10.0 | 35.0 | 42.8 | 44.2 | 46.0 | 49.9 | 9.0 | 37.0 | 54.0 | 5,118,446 | A | | 0 | 6 | 13 | -1 |
| seyc | Seychelles | 1742 | 99.9 | 99.9 | 99.6 | 99.6 | 99.6 | 99.5 | 98.6 | 1.0 | 0.5 | 348 | C | | 0 | 1 | -1 | -1 |
| sier | Sierra Leone | 1785 | 17.6 | 50.0 | 54.9 | 56.4 | 59.2 | 62.9 | 17.5 | 41.7 | 40.8 | 1,981,739 | B | | 0 | 0 | 16 | -2 |
| sing | Singapore | 1511 | 20.0 | 48.1 | 65.2 | 69.6 | 72.7 | 78.4 | 18.2 | 54.5 | 27.3 | 974,057 | B | | 12 | 1 | 29 | 2 |
| slok | Slovakia | 828 | 99.0 | 95.0 | 98.8 | 99.4 | 99.5 | 99.6 | 90.3 | 9.2 | 0.5 | 25,349 | C | | 0 | 0 | 3 | 1 |
| slov | Slovenia | c200 | 100.0 | 96.0 | 99.8 | 99.8 | 99.8 | 99.9 | 97.5 | 2.3 | 0.2 | 3,933 | C | | 0 | 0 | 2 | 1 |
| solo | Solomon Islands | 1845 | 24.0 | 99.5 | 99.8 | 99.8 | 99.9 | 99.9 | 97.5 | 2.4 | 0.1 | 471 | C | | 0 | 0 | 1 | 1 |
| soma | Somalia | 1881 | 1.0 | 5.8 | 33.0 | 38.3 | 43.8 | 46.2 | 4.9 | 38.9 | 56.2 | 4,080,364 | A | | 0 | 11 | -47 | -2 |
| somi | Somaliland | c1890 | 0.0 | 10.0 | 40.0 | 42.0 | 44.7 | 47.8 | 3.3 | 41.4 | 55.3 | 1,566,720 | A | | 0 | 1 | 0 | -2 |
| soua | South Africa | 1501 | 52.0 | 94.9 | 97.7 | 97.8 | 98.1 | 97.5 | 87.3 | 10.8 | 1.9 | 781,832 | C | | 1 | 1 | 0 | 1 |
| souk | South Korea | 1592 | 16.0 | 85.0 | 98.4 | 98.6 | 98.8 | 99.0 | 48.8 | 50.0 | 1.2 | 560,817 | B | | 20 | 0 | 6 | 2 |
| spai | Spain | 63 | 100.0 | 99.8 | 99.7 | 99.7 | 99.7 | 99.5 | 99.3 | 0.4 | 0.3 | 125,103 | C | | 11 | 1 | -2 | 1 |
| span | Spanish North Africa | c400 | 97.0 | 95.0 | 93.7 | 93.4 | 93.4 | 92.1 | 85.0 | 8.4 | 6.6 | 8,550 | C | | 0 | 0 | -4 | 0 |
| sril | Sri Lanka | c100 | 30.0 | 48.0 | 60.0 | 62.0 | 64.6 | 70.0 | 15.4 | 49.2 | 35.4 | 6,670,591 | B | | 0 | 3 | 1 | -1 |
| suda | Sudan | 36 | 4.0 | 25.0 | 49.0 | 52.0 | 53.8 | 60.9 | 22.1 | 31.7 | 46.2 | 13,620,937 | B | | 0 | 65 | 10 | -2 |
| suri | Suriname | 1580 | 57.9 | 75.0 | 83.5 | 83.6 | 83.8 | 88.6 | 50.2 | 33.6 | 16.2 | 67,699 | B | | 0 | 1 | 4 | 1 |
| swaz | Swaziland | 1825 | 10.0 | 95.0 | 99.3 | 99.3 | 99.4 | 99.6 | 77.5 | 21.9 | 0.6 | 6,491 | C | | 0 | 0 | 3 | 1 |
| swed | Sweden | 829 | 99.9 | 99.8 | 98.6 | 98.5 | 98.4 | 97.8 | 77.1 | 21.3 | 1.6 | 140,311 | C | | 5 | 0 | -2 | 1 |
| swit | Switzerland | c200 | 100.0 | 99.9 | 98.4 | 98.3 | 98.2 | 97.5 | 95.1 | 3.1 | 1.8 | 130,557 | C | | 21 | 0 | -2 | 1 |
| syri | Syria | 33 | 37.1 | 46.0 | 57.5 | 60.0 | 62.2 | 68.8 | 14.4 | 47.8 | 37.8 | 6,092,966 | B | | 6 | 0 | -1 | 0 |
| taiw | Taiwan | 1621 | 12.5 | 40.0 | 65.0 | 67.0 | 68.9 | 76.7 | 11.5 | 57.4 | 31.2 | 6,977,716 | B | | 1 | 2 | 5 | 1 |
| taji | Tajikistan | c280 | 2.0 | 23.5 | 39.0 | 42.0 | 44.1 | 49.2 | 5.5 | 38.6 | 55.9 | 3,457,770 | A | | 0 | 18 | -33 | -2 |
| tanz | Tanzania | 1502 | 18.4 | 60.0 | 76.4 | 79.5 | 81.4 | 87.1 | 55.4 | 26.0 | 18.6 | 6,227,819 | B | | 0 | 2 | 11 | 1 |
| thai | Thailand | 1554 | 13.9 | 35.0 | 51.8 | 54.5 | 56.8 | 65.6 | 7.9 | 48.9 | 43.2 | 26,509,177 | B | | 4 | 4 | 9 | 1 |
| timo | Timor | 1511 | 20.8 | 42.0 | 98.0 | 98.4 | 98.8 | 99.1 | 95.4 | 3.4 | 1.2 | 10,692 | C | | 0 | 0 | 3 | 0 |
| togo | Togo | c1860 | 9.6 | 56.0 | 71.8 | 73.9 | 75.8 | 81.1 | 46.7 | 29.1 | 24.2 | 1,118,285 | B | | 0 | 0 | 15 | 1 |
| tong | Tonga | 1797 | 100.0 | 100.0 | 99.9 | 99.9 | 99.9 | 99.9 | 99.5 | 0.4 | 0.1 | 91 | C | | 0 | 0 | -2 | 0 |
| trin | Trinidad & Tobago | 1513 | 90.0 | 82.0 | 89.3 | 90.5 | 91.6 | 93.3 | 70.9 | 20.7 | 8.5 | 109,423 | C | | 0 | 0 | -7 | 0 |
| tuni | Tunisia | c80 | 18.0 | 25.0 | 43.6 | 47.0 | 48.9 | 55.6 | 5.0 | 43.9 | 51.1 | 4,897,282 | A | | 2 | 9 | 16 | -1 |
| turk | Turkey | c35 | 46.1 | 20.0 | 41.0 | 45.8 | 48.6 | 54.3 | 4.3 | 44.3 | 51.4 | 34,243,536 | A | | 6 | 13 | -12 | -1 |
| turm | Turkmenistan | c300 | 6.1 | 20.1 | 29.1 | 32.9 | 34.5 | 39.6 | 5.2 | 29.3 | 65.5 | 2,918,902 | A | | 0 | 16 | -35 | -2 |
| turs | Turks & Caicos Is | 1750 | 100.0 | 100.0 | 99.7 | 99.8 | 99.8 | 99.8 | 89.1 | 10.7 | 0.2 | 35 | C | | 0 | 0 | -1 | 0 |
| tuva | Tuvalu | 1861 | 100.0 | 100.0 | 99.9 | 99.9 | 99.8 | 99.9 | 93.1 | 6.7 | 0.2 | 20 | C | | 0 | 0 | -2 | 0 |
| ugan | Uganda | 1875 | 23.8 | 92.0 | 98.5 | 98.7 | 99.1 | 99.5 | 93.8 | 5.3 | 0.9 | 195,502 | C | | 0 | 2 | 4 | 1 |
| ukra | Ukraine | c200 | 99.8 | 90.0 | 98.0 | 98.2 | 98.5 | 98.8 | 92.5 | 6.0 | 1.5 | 752,837 | C | | 0 | 13 | 6 | 2 |
| unia | United Arab Emirates | c400 | 1.0 | 24.7 | 50.6 | 54.8 | 57.9 | 63.5 | 16.9 | 41.0 | 42.1 | 1,028,415 | B | | 0 | 1 | 7 | 1 |
| usa | USA | 1526 | 99.9 | 99.5 | 98.6 | 98.6 | 98.5 | 97.8 | 78.7 | 19.8 | 1.5 | 4,084,367 | C | | 334 | 1 | -5 | 1 |
| uuay | Uruguay | 1616 | 89.1 | 95.0 | 98.4 | 98.6 | 98.7 | 99.0 | 74.6 | 24.1 | 1.3 | 43,093 | C | | 0 | 0 | -1 | 0 |
| uzbe | Uzbekistan | c280 | 6.8 | 20.0 | 38.0 | 44.0 | 48.4 | 54.0 | 6.2 | 42.2 | 51.6 | 12,558,682 | A | | 0 | 23 | -31 | -1 |
| vanu | Vanuatu | 1830 | 39.0 | 94.0 | 99.0 | 99.2 | 99.3 | 99.4 | 96.1 | 3.2 | 0.7 | 1,304 | C | | 0 | 0 | 2 | 0 |
| vene | Venezuela | 1513 | 97.1 | 99.0 | 99.3 | 99.3 | 99.4 | 99.5 | 97.9 | 1.5 | 0.6 | 149,477 | C | | 3 | 1 | -1 | 1 |
| viet | Viet Nam | 1530 | 26.8 | 52.0 | 60.0 | 63.0 | 66.8 | 74.9 | 15.2 | 51.6 | 33.2 | 26,516,153 | B | | 0 | 0 | 27 | 1 |
| virg | Virgin Is of the US | 1648 | 100.0 | 100.0 | 99.7 | 99.6 | 99.6 | 99.5 | 96.6 | 3.0 | 0.4 | 390 | C | | 0 | 0 | -2 | 0 |
| wall | Wallis & Futuna Is | 1836 | 98.0 | 99.5 | 99.9 | 100.0 | 100.0 | 99.9 | 99.8 | 0.2 | 0.0 | 5 | C | | 0 | 0 | 0 | 0 |
| yeme | Yemen | 342 | 4.9 | 20.0 | 37.0 | 43.0 | 46.6 | 53.1 | 3.3 | 43.3 | 53.4 | 9,673,610 | A | | 0 | 2 | -8 | -1 |
| yugo | Yugoslavia | c70 | 94.8 | 87.6 | 91.2 | 92.2 | 93.4 | 96.1 | 74.3 | 19.1 | 6.6 | 702,914 | C | | 1 | 0 | 7 | 1 |
| zamb | Zambia | 1885 | 2.7 | 90.0 | 97.8 | 98.4 | 98.8 | 99.2 | 86.7 | 12.1 | 1.2 | 113,566 | C | | 0 | 0 | 7 | 1 |
| zimb | Zimbabwe | 1561 | 16.0 | 94.0 | 97.4 | 97.8 | 98.2 | 99.2 | 69.1 | 29.1 | 1.8 | 207,516 | B | | 1 | 0 | 10 | 1 |
| | 11 minicountries | 40 | 88.7 | 90.9 | 90.6 | 91.1 | 91.7 | 93.2 | 68.7 | 23.0 | 8.3 | 1,924 | C | | 37 | 1 | 0 | 0 |
| | Africa | 33 | 20.6 | 60.8 | 74.0 | 75.8 | 77.5 | 81.4 | 49.9 | 27.6 | 22.5 | 176,794,822 | B | | 34 | 278 | 6 | 0 |
| | Antarctica | 1957 | 0.0 | 90.0 | 93.9 | 94.4 | 94.6 | 96.5 | 85.6 | 9.0 | 5.4 | 243 | C | | 0 | 0 | 6 | 0 |
| | Asia | 33 | 18.3 | 32.2 | 53.7 | 57.0 | 61.3 | 66.7 | 14.4 | 46.9 | 38.7 | 1,423,824,293 | B | | 128 | 447 | 16 | 1 |
| | Europe | 33 | 97.6 | 93.9 | 96.3 | 96.7 | 97.1 | 97.2 | 82.4 | 14.7 | 2.9 | 21,474,187 | C | | 318 | 78 | 3 | 1 |
| | Latin America | 1493 | 97.3 | 98.3 | 99.5 | 99.6 | 99.6 | 99.6 | 97.2 | 2.4 | 0.4 | 1,944,600 | C | | 26 | 11 | -1 | 1 |
| | Northern America | 990 | 99.8 | 99.5 | 98.5 | 98.5 | 98.5 | 97.6 | 78.3 | 20.2 | 1.5 | 4,773,514 | C | | 345 | 2 | -5 | 1 |
| | Oceania | 1521 | 82.1 | 98.3 | 98.2 | 98.1 | 98.1 | 97.8 | 79.8 | 18.4 | 1.9 | 563,298 | C | | 9 | 2 | -2 | 0 |
| | **World A** | **33** | **17.3** | **29.8** | **39.9** | **42.3** | **44.8** | **44.4** | **5.9** | **38.9** | **55.2** | **334,256,241** | **A** | | **13** | **382** | **15** | **-1** |
| | **World B** | **33** | **53.2** | **76.8** | **59.2** | **62.1** | **66.2** | **69.1** | **19.8** | **46.4** | **33.8** | **1,269,343,426** | **B** | | **141** | **348** | **20** | **2** |
| | **World C** | **33** | **98.0** | **98.3** | **98.4** | **98.4** | **98.5** | **98.2** | **89.4** | **9.1** | **1.5** | **25,775,290** | **C** | | **706** | **88** | **0** | **1** |
| | **GLOBAL TOTAL** | **33** | **45.7** | **55.6** | **68.4** | **70.4** | **73.1** | **76.4** | **37.9** | **35.2** | **26.9** | **1,629,374,957** | **B** | | **860** | **818** | **1** | **1** |

| COUNTRY | | COUNTRY TRENDS IN THE YEAR AD 2025 | | | | | | | | | | | |
|---|---|---|---|---|---|---|---|---|---|---|---|---|---|
| | | DEMOGRAPHIC TRENDS | | | EVANGELIZATION TRENDS | | | CHRISTIAN TRENDS | | | | | |
| code | short name | pop 2025 | npop | increase p.a. | evangelized | E | outreach | Christians | C% | G% | increase p.a. | gains p.a. | losses p.a. |
| 1 | 2 | 168 | 169 | 170 | 171 | 172 | 173 | 174 | 175 | 176 | 177 | 178 | 179 |
| afgh | Afghanistan | 44,934,122 | 2.77 | 1,242,553 | 15,727,122 | 35.0 | 1,106.54 | 14,200 | 0.0 | 2.83 | 401 | 590 | 189 |
| alba | Albania | 3,819,763 | 0.82 | 31,368 | 3,469,763 | 90.8 | 1.07 | 1,680,000 | 44.0 | 1.70 | 28,624 | 52,396 | 23,772 |
| alge | Algeria | 46,610,551 | 1.58 | 738,037 | 25,610,551 | 54.9 | 160.07 | 159,000 | 0.3 | 2.26 | 3,593 | 4,729 | 1,137 |
| amer | American Samoa | 142,680 | 3.00 | 4,285 | 141,830 | 99.4 | 0.04 | 136,600 | 95.7 | 3.00 | 4,099 | 5,400 | 1,300 |
| ando | Andorra | 154,335 | 2.77 | 4,272 | 152,335 | 98.7 | 0.08 | 140,950 | 91.3 | 2.67 | 3,768 | 6,329 | 2,561 |
| ango | Angola | 25,106,861 | 2.71 | 679,492 | 24,979,161 | 99.5 | 0.02 | 24,441,100 | 97.3 | 2.85 | 695,828 | 948,793 | 252,965 |
| angu | Anguilla | 10,984 | 1.12 | 123 | 10,929 | 99.5 | 0.11 | 9,870 | 89.9 | 1.05 | 104 | 217 | 113 |
| anti | Antigua | 75,080 | 0.42 | 318 | 74,880 | 99.7 | 0.08 | 69,500 | 92.6 | 0.37 | 254 | 1,052 | 798 |
| arge | Argentina | 47,150,313 | 0.97 | 458,032 | 46,650,313 | 98.9 | 0.08 | 43,311,300 | 91.9 | 0.93 | 400,927 | 913,300 | 512,373 |
| arme | Armenia | 3,946,381 | 0.46 | 18,110 | 3,904,381 | 98.9 | 0.07 | 3,659,500 | 92.7 | 0.86 | 31,382 | 77,309 | 45,927 |
| arub | Aruba | 250,376 | 3.63 | 9,081 | 248,876 | 99.4 | 0.04 | 239,800 | 95.8 | 3.60 | 8,628 | 11,782 | 3,153 |
| aust | Australia | 23,090,790 | 0.81 | 186,730 | 22,550,790 | 97.7 | 0.30 | 17,364,000 | 75.2 | 0.59 | 103,216 | 350,479 | 247,263 |
| ausz | Austria | 8,185,725 | -0.01 | -990 | 8,003,025 | 97.8 | 0.12 | 7,123,630 | 87.0 | -0.14 | -9,685 | 127,089 | 136,774 |
| azer | Azerbaijan | 9,402,570 | 0.78 | 73,761 | 3,902,570 | 41.5 | 9.68 | 365,300 | 3.9 | 0.08 | 297 | 4,359 | 4,062 |
| baha | Bahamas | 414,631 | 1.22 | 5,040 | 412,831 | 99.6 | 0.10 | 375,500 | 90.6 | 1.13 | 4,261 | 8,230 | 3,969 |
| bahr | Bahrain | 858,368 | 1.33 | 11,399 | 558,368 | 65.0 | 4.76 | 97,000 | 11.3 | 1.65 | 1,598 | 2,606 | 1,008 |
| bang | Bangladesh | 178,751,214 | 1.31 | 2,338,795 | 110,751,214 | 62.0 | 71.96 | 1,518,000 | 0.8 | 1.96 | 29,793 | 44,882 | 15,089 |
| barb | Barbados | 296,753 | 0.37 | 1,104 | 293,753 | 99.0 | 0.03 | 284,200 | 95.8 | 0.33 | 932 | 4,649 | 3,717 |
| belg | Belgium | 9,917,861 | -0.10 | -9,610 | 9,640,861 | 97.2 | 0.14 | 8,478,570 | 85.5 | -0.22 | -19,057 | 147,208 | 166,265 |
| beli | Belize | 370,035 | 1.73 | 6,420 | 360,035 | 97.3 | 0.08 | 332,900 | 90.0 | 1.69 | 5,628 | 8,301 | 2,673 |
| belo | Belorussia | 9,495,683 | -0.30 | -28,479 | 9,418,683 | 99.2 | 0.16 | 8,107,000 | 85.4 | 0.48 | 38,971 | 205,002 | 166,031 |
| beni | Benin | 11,109,357 | 2.43 | 269,879 | 8,859,357 | 79.7 | 1.30 | 3,850,000 | 34.7 | 3.31 | 127,517 | 162,629 | 35,112 |
| berm | Bermuda | 75,613 | 0.63 | 478 | 75,413 | 99.7 | 0.09 | 69,110 | 91.4 | 0.55 | 381 | 1,319 | 938 |
| bhut | Bhutan | 3,903,897 | 2.46 | 96,217 | 953,897 | 24.4 | 64.79 | 14,500 | 0.4 | 1.64 | 238 | 354 | 116 |
| boli | Bolivia | 13,131,183 | 1.84 | 241,329 | 13,088,183 | 99.7 | 0.08 | 12,153,700 | 92.6 | 1.77 | 215,307 | 337,938 | 122,631 |
| bosn | Bosnia-Herzegovina | 4,323,818 | 0.34 | 14,711 | 3,223,818 | 74.6 | 1.90 | 1,110,000 | 25.7 | -0.90 | -9,968 | 11,666 | 21,634 |
| bots | Botswana | 2,241,857 | 1.30 | 29,199 | 2,151,857 | 96.0 | 0.45 | 1,487,700 | 66.4 | 1.72 | 25,533 | 42,211 | 16,677 |
| boug | Bougainville | 286,097 | 1.47 | 4,214 | 285,897 | 99.9 | 0.04 | 273,800 | 95.7 | 1.51 | 4,138 | 7,298 | 3,160 |
| braz | Brazil | 217,929,781 | 1.00 | 2,169,941 | 217,496,781 | 99.8 | 0.11 | 195,848,000 | 89.9 | 0.93 | 1,813,307 | 4,241,822 | 2,428,515 |
| brit | Britain | 59,960,856 | 0.08 | 45,677 | 58,560,856 | 97.7 | 0.22 | 47,904,500 | 79.9 | -0.06 | -26,850 | 878,545 | 905,395 |
| briz | British Virgin Is | 36,663 | 2.18 | 800 | 36,463 | 99.5 | 0.17 | 31,130 | 84.9 | 2.11 | 657 | 971 | 313 |
| brun | Brunei | 458,972 | 1.35 | 6,205 | 238,972 | 52.1 | 6.13 | 33,500 | 7.3 | 1.15 | 385 | 698 | 314 |
| bulg | Bulgaria | 7,023,064 | -0.63 | -44,241 | 6,723,064 | 95.7 | 0.14 | 5,888,200 | 83.8 | -0.49 | -29,079 | 101,050 | 130,129 |
| burk | Burkina Faso | 23,321,336 | 2.72 | 633,214 | 16,821,336 | 72.1 | 2.53 | 4,760,000 | 20.4 | 3.55 | 169,135 | 216,735 | 47,600 |
| buru | Burundi | 11,568,648 | 2.21 | 255,882 | 11,508,648 | 99.5 | 0.06 | 10,851,000 | 93.8 | 2.31 | 250,164 | 371,586 | 121,423 |
| camb | Cambodia | 16,526,449 | 1.58 | 261,133 | 10,026,449 | 60.7 | 42.39 | 231,100 | 1.4 | 2.70 | 6,250 | 8,741 | 2,491 |
| came | Cameroon | 26,484,402 | 2.28 | 603,040 | 22,214,402 | 83.9 | 0.38 | 16,043,000 | 60.6 | 2.73 | 438,637 | 590,885 | 152,248 |
| cana | Canada | 37,896,497 | 0.79 | 298,509 | 36,571,497 | 96.5 | 0.27 | 28,864,000 | 76.2 | 0.62 | 177,521 | 661,859 | 484,338 |
| cape | Cape Verde | 670,931 | 1.82 | 12,191 | 670,231 | 99.9 | 0.05 | 637,450 | 95.0 | 1.81 | 11,551 | 15,656 | 4,105 |
| caym | Cayman Islands | 77,938 | 2.87 | 2,241 | 76,138 | 97.7 | 0.29 | 59,000 | 75.7 | 2.77 | 1,637 | 2,230 | 594 |
| cent | Central African Rep | 5,703,795 | 1.84 | 104,984 | 5,003,795 | 87.7 | 0.23 | 4,066,000 | 71.3 | 2.05 | 83,213 | 127,247 | 44,035 |
| chad | Chad | 13,908,122 | 2.42 | 336,487 | 7,511,122 | 54.0 | 1.38 | 3,150,000 | 22.6 | 2.39 | 75,249 | 108,607 | 33,359 |
| chan | Channel Islands | 173,400 | 0.50 | 875 | 172,200 | 99.3 | 0.28 | 134,130 | 77.4 | 0.08 | 103 | 2,638 | 2,535 |
| chil | Chile | 19,547,916 | 1.01 | 197,116 | 19,487,916 | 99.7 | 0.13 | 17,246,000 | 88.2 | 0.97 | 166,514 | 367,430 | 200,916 |
| chin | China | 1,462,931,461 | 0.59 | 8,645,236 | 1,032,431,461 | 70.6 | 6.64 | 135,190,000 | 9.2 | 1.68 | 2,276,195 | 3,916,049 | 1,639,855 |
| colo | Colombia | 59,757,874 | 1.39 | 830,397 | 59,547,874 | 99.6 | 0.03 | 57,713,500 | 96.6 | 1.38 | 798,015 | 1,402,852 | 604,837 |
| como | Comoros | 989,515 | 2.07 | 20,492 | 439,515 | 44.4 | 28.60 | 14,850 | 1.5 | 2.94 | 437 | 545 | 108 |
| cong | Congo-Brazzaville | 5,689,140 | 2.67 | 151,953 | 5,653,140 | 99.4 | 0.10 | 5,160,000 | 90.7 | 2.65 | 136,798 | 179,988 | 43,189 |
| conz | Congo-Zaire | 104,787,601 | 2.87 | 3,007,238 | 104,237,601 | 99.5 | 0.03 | 100,935,700 | 96.3 | 2.91 | 2,938,636 | 3,766,309 | 827,673 |
| cook | Cook Islands | 23,736 | 0.78 | 186 | 23,716 | 99.9 | 0.04 | 22,750 | 95.8 | 0.70 | 160 | 377 | 217 |
| cost | Costa Rica | 5,928,508 | 1.56 | 92,641 | 5,918,508 | 99.8 | 0.04 | 5,683,500 | 95.9 | 1.53 | 87,154 | 141,942 | 54,789 |
| croa | Croatia | 4,193,413 | -0.26 | -10,798 | 4,163,413 | 99.3 | 0.03 | 4,031,000 | 96.1 | -0.22 | -8,854 | 75,353 | 84,208 |
| cuba | Cuba | 11,798,235 | 0.21 | 24,554 | 11,698,235 | 99.2 | 1.09 | 5,600,000 | 47.5 | 0.47 | 26,163 | 107,867 | 81,704 |
| cypr | Cyprus | 687,811 | 0.54 | 3,745 | 686,811 | 99.9 | 0.08 | 635,800 | 92.4 | 0.47 | 2,982 | 10,955 | 7,973 |
| czec | Czech Republic | 9,512,292 | -0.30 | -28,162 | 9,482,292 | 99.7 | 0.34 | 7,102,000 | 74.7 | 0.38 | 27,086 | 170,972 | 143,887 |
| denm | Denmark | 5,238,499 | -0.04 | -2,178 | 5,168,499 | 98.7 | 0.11 | 4,674,000 | 89.2 | -0.15 | -6,788 | 88,281 | 95,069 |
| djib | Djibouti | 1,026,235 | 1.92 | 19,722 | 526,235 | 51.3 | 11.53 | 42,000 | 4.1 | 1.56 | 656 | 1,107 | 452 |
| domi | Dominica | 73,442 | 0.15 | 111 | 73,362 | 99.9 | 0.08 | 68,070 | 92.7 | 0.06 | 41 | 822 | 781 |
| domr | Dominican Republic | 11,164,412 | 1.10 | 122,680 | 11,155,412 | 99.9 | 0.06 | 10,484,350 | 93.9 | 1.05 | 109,632 | 220,032 | 110,400 |
| ecua | Ecuador | 17,796,101 | 1.38 | 244,859 | 17,676,101 | 99.3 | 0.03 | 17,231,300 | 96.8 | 1.34 | 231,664 | 415,695 | 184,030 |
| egyp | Egypt | 95,615,454 | 1.34 | 1,285,774 | 77,615,454 | 81.2 | 4.66 | 13,710,000 | 14.3 | 1.13 | 155,272 | 268,654 | 113,382 |
| elsa | El Salvador | 9,062,331 | 1.48 | 134,160 | 9,051,331 | 99.9 | 0.03 | 8,755,150 | 96.6 | 1.44 | 126,190 | 214,267 | 88,077 |
| equa | Equatorial Guinea | 794,724 | 2.28 | 18,095 | 785,924 | 98.9 | 0.11 | 708,600 | 89.2 | 2.31 | 16,371 | 23,876 | 7,504 |
| erit | Eritrea | 6,680,653 | 2.23 | 148,888 | 5,180,653 | 77.5 | 0.52 | 3,400,000 | 50.9 | 2.26 | 76,919 | 106,465 | 29,546 |
| esto | Estonia | 1,131,222 | -0.84 | -9,482 | 1,115,222 | 98.6 | 0.39 | 800,300 | 70.7 | -0.41 | -3,270 | 14,249 | 17,519 |
| ethi | Ethiopia | 115,382,091 | 2.48 | 2,859,623 | 103,382,091 | 89.6 | 0.51 | 68,488,000 | 59.4 | 2.59 | 1,776,330 | 2,484,495 | 708,166 |
| faer | Faeroe Islands | 36,604 | -0.62 | -227 | 36,564 | 99.9 | 0.03 | 35,400 | 96.7 | -0.68 | -240 | 480 | 720 |
| fiji | Fiji | 1,104,141 | 1.21 | 13,388 | 1,004,141 | 90.9 | 0.62 | 621,000 | 56.2 | 1.18 | 7,302 | 14,331 | 7,030 |
| finl | Finland | 5,253,863 | 0.06 | 3,149 | 5,227,463 | 99.5 | 0.09 | 4,780,600 | 91.0 | -0.02 | -916 | 91,062 | 91,979 |
| fran | France | 61,661,804 | 0.17 | 105,599 | 58,641,804 | 95.1 | 0.40 | 41,807,000 | 67.8 | 0.00 | 843 | 760,476 | 759,633 |
| freg | French Guiana | 416,191 | 3.38 | 14,065 | 412,191 | 99.0 | 0.19 | 346,480 | 83.3 | 3.31 | 11,482 | 15,636 | 4,154 |
| frep | French Polynesia | 324,439 | 1.30 | 4,209 | 320,439 | 98.8 | 0.15 | 279,200 | 86.1 | 1.21 | 3,371 | 6,478 | 3,107 |
| gabo | Gabon | 1,981,233 | 1.94 | 38,396 | 1,951,233 | 98.5 | 0.10 | 1,775,900 | 89.6 | 1.89 | 33,641 | 52,820 | 19,180 |
| gamb | Gambia | 2,150,833 | 2.02 | 43,395 | 1,150,833 | 53.5 | 13.03 | 82,000 | 3.8 | 1.96 | 1,608 | 2,642 | 1,034 |
| geor | Georgia | 5,178,116 | 0.17 | 8,605 | 4,718,116 | 91.1 | 0.36 | 3,471,000 | 67.0 | 0.47 | 16,159 | 64,024 | 47,865 |
| germ | Germany | 80,238,159 | -0.10 | -78,291 | 77,988,159 | 97.2 | 0.32 | 59,150,000 | 73.7 | -0.21 | -123,623 | 1,087,769 | 1,211,392 |
| ghan | Ghana | 36,876,215 | 2.43 | 897,647 | 32,876,215 | 89.2 | 0.49 | 22,097,200 | 59.9 | 2.76 | 609,270 | 774,999 | 165,729 |
| gibr | Gibraltar | 21,393 | -0.63 | -136 | 20,193 | 94.4 | 0.14 | 17,730 | 82.9 | -0.79 | -140 | 195 | 335 |
| gree | Greece | 9,862,572 | -0.30 | -30,062 | 9,665,372 | 98.0 | 0.04 | 9,251,900 | 93.8 | -0.34 | -31,779 | 159,180 | 190,959 |
| grel | Greenland | 59,634 | 0.24 | 144 | 59,384 | 99.6 | 0.05 | 56,700 | 95.1 | 0.19 | 106 | 1,259 | 1,153 |
| gren | Grenada | 104,647 | 0.44 | 463 | 104,617 | 99.9 | 0.04 | 100,490 | 96.0 | 0.40 | 402 | 1,620 | 1,218 |
| guad | Guadeloupe | 569,216 | 0.89 | 5,088 | 568,436 | 99.9 | 0.06 | 535,360 | 94.1 | 0.84 | 4,500 | 10,646 | 6,146 |
| guam | Guam | 227,634 | 1.23 | 2,807 | 224,434 | 98.6 | 0.05 | 213,250 | 93.7 | 1.21 | 2,588 | 5,162 | 2,574 |
| guat | Guatemala | 19,816,134 | 2.24 | 444,168 | 19,808,134 | 99.9 | 0.03 | 19,203,500 | 96.9 | 2.21 | 424,032 | 599,168 | 175,136 |
| guin | Guinea | 12,496,941 | 2.10 | 262,613 | 5,696,941 | 45.6 | 8.82 | 580,000 | 4.6 | 2.74 | 15,880 | 22,643 | 6,763 |
| gunb | Guinea-Bissau | 1,946,020 | 1.91 | 37,137 | 1,016,020 | 52.2 | 2.44 | 295,000 | 15.2 | 2.48 | 7,314 | 11,473 | 4,160 |
| guya | Guyana | 1,044,669 | 0.77 | 8,095 | 894,669 | 85.6 | 0.77 | 506,800 | 48.5 | 0.57 | 2,911 | 8,988 | 6,077 |
| hait | Haiti | 11,988,232 | 1.52 | 182,206 | 11,979,532 | 99.9 | 0.05 | 11,373,200 | 94.9 | 1.48 | 168,471 | 300,514 | 132,043 |
| hond | Honduras | 10,656,044 | 2.01 | 213,774 | 10,645,344 | 99.9 | 0.04 | 10,270,000 | 96.4 | 1.98 | 203,271 | 295,701 | 92,430 |
| hung | Hungary | 8,900,388 | -0.48 | -42,634 | 8,843,388 | 99.4 | 0.09 | 8,078,200 | 90.8 | -0.33 | -26,275 | 149,022 | 175,297 |
| icel | Iceland | 328,356 | 0.63 | 2,053 | 328,106 | 99.9 | 0.04 | 314,850 | 95.9 | 0.57 | 1,797 | 6,696 | 4,899 |
| indi | India | 1,330,448,707 | 1.09 | 14,551,460 | 880,448,707 | 66.2 | 7.97 | 98,200,000 | 7.4 | 1.83 | 1,801,150 | 2,870,548 | 1,069,398 |
| indo | Indonesia | 273,442,120 | 1.02 | 2,792,303 | 188,342,120 | 68.9 | 3.38 | 43,000,000 | 15.7 | 1.76 | 756,526 | 1,204,586 | 448,060 |
| iran | Iran | 94,462,501 | 1.34 | 1,266,980 | 41,962,501 | 44.4 | 66.68 | 620,000 | 0.7 | 2.16 | 13,415 | 18,605 | 5,189 |
| iraq | Iraq | 41,013,588 | 2.32 | 951,603 | 23,013,588 | 56.1 | 17.11 | 1,270,500 | 3.1 | 2.18 | 27,714 | 37,395 | 9,681 |
| irel | Ireland | 4,403,843 | 0.67 | 29,340 | 4,388,943 | 99.7 | 0.04 | 4,227,400 | 96.0 | 0.62 | 26,134 | 92,546 | 66,412 |
| isle | Isle of Man | 100,891 | 0.97 | 983 | 100,391 | 99.5 | 0.16 | 86,420 | 85.7 | 0.82 | 713 | 2,346 | 1,633 |
| isra | Israel | 6,926,755 | 1.21 | 84,157 | 4,726,755 | 68.2 | 8.85 | 480,000 | 6.9 | 1.94 | 9,296 | 14,255 | 4,958 |
| ital | Italy | 51,269,528 | -0.44 | -227,473 | 50,599,528 | 98.7 | 0.24 | 40,959,000 | 79.9 | -0.55 | -225,141 | 653,429 | 878,571 |
| ivor | Ivory Coast | 23,345,116 | 1.84 | 430,405 | 18,345,116 | 78.6 | 1.27 | 8,076,000 | 34.6 | 2.19 | 176,649 | 253,614 | 76,964 |
| jama | Jamaica | 3,244,840 | 0.92 | 29,765 | 3,212,390 | 99.0 | 0.22 | 2,630,000 | 81.1 | 0.77 | 20,278 | 46,735 | 26,458 |
| japa | Japan | 121,150,001 | -0.18 | -217,414 | 91,150,001 | 75.2 | 17.23 | 5,000,000 | 4.1 | 0.37 | 18,476 | 102,926 | 84,450 |
| jord | Jordan | 12,062,895 | 2.40 | 289,361 | 7,662,895 | 63.5 | 10.97 | 640,000 | 5.3 | 3.45 | 22,101 | 26,440 | 4,339 |
| kaza | Kazakhstan | 17,698,360 | 0.35 | 61,747 | 12,198,360 | 68.9 | 3.44 | 2,750,000 | 15.5 | 0.06 | 1,613 | 34,311 | 32,698 |
| keny | Kenya | 41,755,990 | 1.32 | 551,397 | 40,155,990 | 96.2 | 0.17 | 34,222,400 | 82.0 | 1.45 | 497,317 | 877,528 | 380,211 |
| kirg | Kirgizstan | 6,096,197 | 1.05 | 63,791 | 3,196,197 | 52.4 | 6.10 | 450,000 | 7.4 | -0.33 | -1,466 | 2,850 | 4,316 |
| kiri | Kiribati | 119,324 | 1.44 | 1,723 | 119,224 | 99.9 | 0.08 | 110,110 | 92.3 | 1.35 | 1,490 | 2,819 | 1,329 |
| kuwa | Kuwait | 2,974,454 | 1.66 | 49,328 | 2,024,454 | 68.1 | 3.94 | 410,000 | 13.8 | 2.01 | 8,224 | 11,701 | 3,477 |
| laos | Laos | 9,652,526 | 2.33 | 224,471 | 4,802,526 | 49.8 | 19.32 | 236,400 | 2.4 | 3.01 | 7,118 | 9,389 | 2,272 |
| latv | Latvia | 1,936,009 | -0.78 | -15,161 | 1,923,509 | 99.4 | 0.27 | 1,509,000 | 77.9 | -0.18 | -2,691 | 30,582 | 33,273 |
| leba | Lebanon | 4,399,649 | 1.18 | 51,892 | 4,099,649 | 93.2 | 0.83 | 2,246,000 | 51.0 | 1.03 | 23,136 | 44,159 | 21,023 |
| leso | Lesotho | 3,506,420 | 1.97 | 69,109 | 3,490,420 | 99.5 | 0.06 | 3,303,400 | 94.2 | 2.11 | 69,703 | 99,863 | 30,160 |
| libe | Liberia | 6,617,526 | 3.01 | 199,093 | 5,077,526 | 76.7 | 0.78 | 2,848,000 | 43.0 | 3.39 | 96,440 | 116,917 | 20,477 |
| liby | Libya | 8,646,769 | 1.75 | 151,269 | 4,246,769 | 49.1 | 13.53 | 292,300 | 3.4 | 2.06 | 6,027 | 8,047 | 2,020 |
| liec | Liechtenstein | 41,252 | 0.92 | 378 | 40,467 | 98.1 | 0.09 | 37,040 | 89.8 | 0.78 | 287 | 979 | 691 |
| lith | Lithuania | 3,398,950 | -0.31 | -10,425 | 3,384,950 | 99.6 | 0.07 | 3,158,000 | 92.9 | -0.07 | -2,217 | 61,985 | 64,202 |
| luxe | Luxembourg | 463,356 | 0.29 | 1,360 | 458,356 | 98.9 | 0.06 | 430,400 | 92.9 | 0.25 | 1,073 | 9,023 | 7,949 |
| mace | Macedonia | 2,257,977 | 0.44 | 9,921 | 2,007,977 | 88.9 | 0.43 | 1,400,000 | 62.0 | 0.33 | 4,663 | 28,113 | 23,450 |
| mada | Madagascar | 28,963,663 | 2.42 | 700,098 | 24,963,663 | 86.2 | 0.66 | 15,000,000 | 51.8 | 2.60 | 390,440 | 505,940 | 115,500 |
| mala | Malawi | 19,958,349 | 2.44 | 486,898 | 19,458,349 | 97.5 | 0.23 | 15,770,900 | 79.0 | 2.56 | 403,351 | 581,562 | 178,211 |
| malb | Malaysia | 30,968,453 | 1.33 | 412,616 | 21,968,453 | 70.9 | 6.20 | 3,050,000 | 9.8 | 2.03 | 61,812 | 89,384 | 27,572 |

| COUNTRY | | COUNTRY TRENDS IN THE YEAR AD 2025 | | | | | | | | | | | |
|---|---|---|---|---|---|---|---|---|---|---|---|---|---|
| | | DEMOGRAPHIC TRENDS | | | EVANGELIZATION TRENDS | | | CHRISTIAN TRENDS | | | | | |
| code | short name | pop 2025 | npop | increase p.a. | evangelized | E | outreach | Christians | C% | G% | increase p.a. | gains p.a. | losses p.a. |
| 1 | 2 | 168 | 169 | 170 | 171 | 172 | 173 | 174 | 175 | 176 | 177 | 178 | 179 |
| mald | Maldives | 501,456 | 2.27 | 11,375 | 106,456 | 21.2 | 132.07 | 800 | 0.2 | 3.14 | 25 | 31 | 6 |
| mali | Mali | 21,295,460 | 2.59 | 551,822 | 10,595,460 | 49.8 | 21.31 | 475,000 | 2.2 | 3.03 | 14,373 | 18,890 | 4,517 |
| malt | Malta | 429,847 | 0.40 | 1,740 | 429,447 | 99.9 | 0.02 | 419,570 | 97.6 | 0.38 | 1,576 | 9,044 | 7,468 |
| mars | Marshall Islands | 127,147 | 2.77 | 3,522 | 127,107 | 99.9 | 0.04 | 122,800 | 96.6 | 2.77 | 3,400 | 4,882 | 1,482 |
| mart | Martinique | 450,094 | 0.52 | 2,340 | 449,194 | 99.8 | 0.04 | 430,040 | 95.5 | 0.46 | 1,984 | 7,501 | 5,517 |
| maur | Mauritania | 4,766,399 | 2.35 | 111,811 | 1,766,399 | 37.1 | 232.03 | 7,580 | 0.2 | 0.57 | 44 | 114 | 70 |
| maus | Mauritius | 1,377,463 | 0.70 | 9,668 | 1,107,463 | 80.4 | 1.26 | 490,000 | 35.6 | 1.05 | 5,157 | 10,327 | 5,170 |
| mayo | Mayotte | 186,507 | 2.46 | 4,585 | 86,507 | 46.4 | 16.65 | 4,900 | 2.6 | 3.21 | 157 | 193 | 36 |
| mexi | Mexico | 130,196,156 | 1.11 | 1,440,707 | 129,996,156 | 99.8 | 0.05 | 123,979,000 | 95.2 | 1.06 | 1,318,449 | 2,617,749 | 1,299,300 |
| micr | Micronesia | 189,609 | 1.89 | 3,586 | 188,909 | 99.6 | 0.07 | 175,800 | 92.7 | 1.87 | 3,294 | 5,416 | 2,122 |
| mold | Moldavia | 4,546,842 | 0.15 | 6,784 | 4,351,842 | 95.7 | 0.17 | 3,726,500 | 82.0 | 0.85 | 31,768 | 99,106 | 67,338 |
| mona | Monaco | 40,692 | 0.77 | 313 | 40,192 | 98.8 | 0.08 | 37,100 | 91.2 | 0.68 | 253 | 927 | 674 |
| mong | Mongolia | 3,708,989 | 1.34 | 49,535 | 1,818,989 | 49.0 | 27.92 | 62,900 | 1.7 | 2.50 | 1,573 | 2,146 | 572 |
| mont | Montserrat | 10,658 | 0.01 | 1 | 10,643 | 99.9 | 0.06 | 10,000 | 93.8 | -0.08 | -8 | 107 | 115 |
| moro | Morocco | 38,529,890 | 1.25 | 482,888 | 18,329,890 | 47.6 | 72.91 | 248,000 | 0.6 | 1.39 | 3,458 | 5,529 | 2,071 |
| moza | Mozambique | 30,611,842 | 1.78 | 545,732 | 25,111,842 | 82.0 | 0.93 | 13,000,000 | 42.5 | 2.20 | 285,509 | 463,089 | 177,580 |
| myan | Myanmar | 58,120,485 | 0.97 | 566,196 | 40,120,485 | 69.0 | 5.29 | 6,382,000 | 11.0 | 2.12 | 135,573 | 206,924 | 71,351 |
| nami | Namibia | 2,337,592 | 1.22 | 28,541 | 2,287,592 | 97.9 | 0.08 | 2,121,800 | 90.8 | 1.15 | 24,506 | 52,046 | 27,541 |
| naur | Nauru | 17,821 | 1.76 | 314 | 17,221 | 96.6 | 0.31 | 13,100 | 73.5 | 1.68 | 220 | 378 | 158 |
| nepa | Nepal | 38,010,174 | 1.87 | 710,044 | 19,910,174 | 52.4 | 12.06 | 1,525,000 | 4.0 | 3.97 | 60,489 | 74,290 | 13,801 |
| neth | Netherlands | 15,781,965 | 0.00 | -149 | 15,296,965 | 96.9 | 0.25 | 12,199,000 | 77.3 | -0.16 | -19,391 | 214,586 | 233,977 |
| nets | Netherlands Antilles | 258,459 | 0.71 | 1,825 | 255,459 | 98.8 | 0.06 | 240,840 | 93.2 | 0.65 | 1,570 | 4,737 | 3,167 |
| newc | New Caledonia | 285,515 | 1.16 | 3,310 | 280,515 | 98.2 | 0.15 | 244,500 | 85.6 | 1.10 | 2,679 | 5,593 | 2,914 |
| newz | New Zealand | 4,694,964 | 0.78 | 36,826 | 4,621,964 | 98.4 | 0.22 | 3,800,000 | 80.9 | 0.66 | 25,052 | 78,670 | 53,618 |
| nica | Nicaragua | 8,696,054 | 2.18 | 189,417 | 8,680,054 | 99.8 | 0.05 | 8,289,200 | 95.3 | 2.14 | 177,145 | 250,007 | 72,862 |
| niga | Niger | 21,495,434 | 2.82 | 605,769 | 10,195,434 | 47.4 | 81.55 | 123,500 | 0.6 | 3.03 | 3,740 | 5,033 | 1,293 |
| nige | Nigeria | 183,041,179 | 2.00 | 3,665,052 | 154,841,179 | 84.6 | 0.80 | 86,000,000 | 47.0 | 2.10 | 1,807,918 | 2,714,358 | 906,440 |
| nork | North Korea | 29,387,635 | 0.81 | 237,097 | 17,632,635 | 60.0 | 11.37 | 1,425,000 | 4.8 | 4.26 | 60,652 | 76,327 | 15,675 |
| norl | Northern Cyprus | 212,470 | 0.55 | 1,178 | 135,970 | 64.0 | 5.97 | 19,500 | 9.2 | 0.69 | 135 | 380 | 245 |
| norm | Northern Mariana Is | 245,191 | 4.67 | 11,448 | 242,691 | 99.0 | 0.14 | 213,000 | 86.9 | 4.57 | 9,742 | 12,313 | 2,571 |
| norw | Norway | 4,812,063 | 0.30 | 14,602 | 4,717,063 | 98.0 | 0.06 | 4,441,000 | 92.3 | 0.22 | 9,579 | 88,096 | 78,517 |
| oman | Oman | 5,351,885 | 3.02 | 161,798 | 2,951,885 | 55.2 | 8.28 | 318,000 | 5.9 | 3.83 | 12,194 | 14,299 | 2,105 |
| paki | Pakistan | 262,999,723 | 2.10 | 5,519,140 | 132,899,723 | 50.5 | 16.84 | 7,450,000 | 2.8 | 2.68 | 199,295 | 259,267 | 59,973 |
| pala | Palau | 33,228 | 2.17 | 721 | 33,198 | 99.9 | 0.06 | 31,260 | 94.1 | 2.10 | 656 | 1,034 | 377 |
| pale | Palestine | 4,132,562 | 2.53 | 104,357 | 3,132,562 | 75.8 | 7.47 | 370,000 | 9.0 | 2.71 | 10,025 | 12,016 | 1,991 |
| pana | Panama | 3,779,174 | 1.13 | 42,594 | 3,684,174 | 97.5 | 0.14 | 3,231,500 | 85.5 | 1.00 | 32,401 | 67,721 | 35,320 |
| papu | Papua New Guinea | 7,173,798 | 1.79 | 128,139 | 7,028,598 | 98.0 | 0.02 | 6,902,400 | 96.2 | 1.84 | 126,729 | 206,382 | 79,654 |
| para | Paraguay | 9,355,207 | 2.15 | 201,147 | 9,335,207 | 99.8 | 0.02 | 9,118,800 | 97.5 | 2.14 | 195,143 | 277,121 | 81,978 |
| peru | Peru | 35,518,199 | 1.31 | 464,818 | 35,423,199 | 99.7 | 0.03 | 34,227,500 | 96.4 | 1.27 | 435,645 | 798,114 | 362,469 |
| phil | Philippines | 108,251,048 | 1.43 | 1,544,444 | 102,391,048 | 94.6 | 0.06 | 96,610,800 | 89.2 | 1.41 | 1,357,982 | 2,203,326 | 845,345 |
| pola | Poland | 39,069,168 | 0.03 | 12,213 | 39,053,168 | 99.9 | 0.02 | 38,264,000 | 97.9 | 0.05 | 20,374 | 738,972 | 718,598 |
| port | Portugal | 9,348,354 | -0.22 | -20,466 | 9,298,354 | 99.5 | 0.10 | 8,460,300 | 90.5 | -0.30 | -25,411 | 141,088 | 166,499 |
| puer | Puerto Rico | 4,477,962 | 0.59 | 26,277 | 4,472,962 | 99.9 | 0.04 | 4,304,100 | 96.1 | 0.55 | 23,626 | 80,526 | 56,900 |
| qata | Qatar | 778,537 | 1.05 | 8,203 | 478,537 | 61.5 | 4.09 | 94,000 | 12.1 | 1.66 | 1,562 | 2,841 | 1,279 |
| reun | Reunion | 879,761 | 0.92 | 8,111 | 852,761 | 96.9 | 0.13 | 752,300 | 85.5 | 0.82 | 6,148 | 13,024 | 6,876 |
| roma | Romania | 19,945,452 | -0.45 | -89,770 | 19,798,452 | 99.3 | 0.09 | 18,126,000 | 90.9 | -0.32 | -58,046 | 316,799 | 374,846 |
| russ | Russia | 137,932,932 | -0.25 | -348,336 | 131,382,932 | 95.3 | 0.37 | 95,791,000 | 69.4 | 0.51 | 490,512 | 2,497,334 | 2,006,821 |
| rwan | Rwanda | 12,426,835 | 1.92 | 238,035 | 12,301,835 | 99.0 | 0.14 | 10,787,000 | 86.8 | 2.11 | 227,829 | 358,243 | 130,415 |
| saha | Sahara | 469,946 | 1.90 | 8,942 | 149,946 | 31.9 | 213.21 | 700 | 0.1 | 1.46 | 10 | 16 | 6 |
| saih | Saint Helena | 7,756 | 0.84 | 65 | 7,741 | 99.8 | 0.04 | 7,420 | 95.7 | 0.81 | 60 | 163 | 103 |
| saik | Saint Kitts & Nevis | 35,052 | -0.37 | -130 | 34,982 | 99.8 | 0.07 | 32,700 | 93.3 | -0.44 | -142 | 233 | 375 |
| sail | Saint Lucia | 208,093 | 1.20 | 2,501 | 205,593 | 98.8 | 0.03 | 198,950 | 95.6 | 1.18 | 2,348 | 4,632 | 2,284 |
| saip | Saint Pierre & Miquelon | 7,171 | 0.35 | 25 | 7,166 | 99.9 | 0.04 | 6,860 | 95.7 | 0.28 | 19 | 144 | 125 |
| saiv | Saint Vincent | 130,781 | 0.55 | 722 | 128,081 | 97.9 | 0.16 | 110,700 | 84.6 | 0.34 | 382 | 1,653 | 1,271 |
| samo | Samoa | 271,417 | 1.65 | 4,491 | 271,217 | 99.9 | 0.05 | 259,320 | 95.5 | 1.61 | 4,176 | 6,645 | 2,469 |
| sanm | San Marino | 32,392 | 0.80 | 260 | 32,332 | 99.8 | 0.11 | 29,180 | 90.1 | 0.71 | 208 | 834 | 626 |
| saot | Sao Tome & Principe | 217,146 | 1.58 | 3,429 | 216,976 | 99.9 | 0.05 | 205,700 | 94.7 | 1.53 | 3,157 | 5,385 | 2,228 |
| saud | Saudi Arabia | 39,964,965 | 2.49 | 995,331 | 24,964,965 | 62.5 | 12.14 | 1,900,000 | 4.8 | 3.53 | 67,081 | 80,780 | 13,699 |
| sene | Senegal | 16,742,579 | 2.30 | 385,190 | 8,352,579 | 49.9 | 7.03 | 1,040,000 | 6.2 | 2.79 | 29,032 | 38,392 | 9,360 |
| seyc | Seychelles | 97,962 | 0.95 | 926 | 97,492 | 99.5 | 0.04 | 93,950 | 95.9 | 0.91 | 851 | 1,842 | 991 |
| sier | Sierra Leone | 8,085,454 | 2.06 | 166,698 | 5,085,454 | 62.9 | 3.75 | 1,070,000 | 13.2 | 2.66 | 28,415 | 44,187 | 15,772 |
| sing | Singapore | 4,167,756 | 0.62 | 26,048 | 3,267,756 | 78.4 | 3.95 | 660,000 | 15.8 | 1.66 | 10,939 | 19,189 | 8,250 |
| slok | Slovakia | 5,392,691 | 0.00 | 220 | 5,371,191 | 99.6 | 0.13 | 4,770,800 | 88.5 | 0.14 | 6,529 | 96,411 | 89,882 |
| slov | Slovenia | 1,817,953 | -0.35 | -6,402 | 1,816,213 | 99.9 | 0.06 | 1,705,850 | 93.8 | -0.28 | -4,768 | 31,106 | 35,874 |
| solo | Solomon Islands | 816,561 | 2.47 | 20,172 | 815,561 | 99.9 | 0.03 | 789,800 | 96.7 | 2.51 | 19,851 | 26,667 | 6,816 |
| soma | Somalia | 16,227,263 | 3.27 | 530,146 | 7,491,263 | 46.2 | 61.43 | 120,000 | 0.7 | 0.66 | 788 | 2,145 | 1,357 |
| somi | Somaliland | 4,984,017 | 2.29 | 113,924 | 2,384,017 | 47.8 | 160.63 | 14,750 | 0.3 | 2.28 | 336 | 503 | 167 |
| soua | South Africa | 46,015,286 | 0.52 | 241,242 | 44,883,286 | 97.5 | 0.17 | 38,272,500 | 83.2 | 0.53 | 201,506 | 742,296 | 540,790 |
| souk | South Korea | 52,532,789 | 0.46 | 241,394 | 51,982,789 | 99.0 | 1.29 | 22,700,000 | 43.2 | 0.69 | 157,458 | 447,110 | 289,652 |
| spai | Spain | 36,658,293 | -0.31 | -114,109 | 36,478,293 | 99.5 | 0.08 | 33,712,500 | 92.0 | -0.38 | -129,127 | 540,066 | 669,193 |
| span | Spanish North Africa | 140,000 | 0.30 | 416 | 129,000 | 92.1 | 0.19 | 108,000 | 77.1 | 0.14 | 150 | 1,052 | 902 |
| sril | Sri Lanka | 23,546,757 | 0.90 | 211,635 | 16,482,757 | 70.0 | 6.41 | 2,225,000 | 9.4 | 0.93 | 20,780 | 44,254 | 23,474 |
| suda | Sudan | 46,264,179 | 1.82 | 840,910 | 28,164,179 | 60.9 | 2.30 | 8,530,000 | 18.4 | 2.22 | 189,770 | 270,122 | 80,353 |
| suri | Suriname | 524,642 | 0.92 | 4,835 | 464,642 | 88.6 | 0.69 | 275,000 | 52.4 | 1.08 | 2,972 | 5,865 | 2,893 |
| swaz | Swaziland | 1,784,790 | 2.31 | 41,266 | 1,777,290 | 99.6 | 0.12 | 1,592,500 | 89.2 | 2.42 | 38,583 | 50,018 | 11,434 |
| swed | Sweden | 9,096,927 | 0.08 | 7,549 | 8,896,927 | 97.8 | 0.48 | 6,030,000 | 66.3 | -0.01 | -871 | 116,353 | 117,223 |
| swit | Switzerland | 7,586,992 | 0.11 | 8,164 | 7,396,992 | 97.5 | 0.12 | 6,595,200 | 86.9 | 0.04 | 2,730 | 125,797 | 123,066 |
| syri | Syria | 26,291,810 | 1.97 | 519,234 | 18,091,810 | 68.8 | 7.90 | 2,033,000 | 7.7 | 1.92 | 39,099 | 53,879 | 14,780 |
| taiw | Taiwan | 25,730,000 | 0.56 | 142,994 | 19,730,000 | 76.7 | 10.61 | 1,700,000 | 6.6 | 0.75 | 12,751 | 33,372 | 20,621 |
| taji | Tajikistan | 8,856,904 | 1.44 | 127,942 | 4,356,904 | 49.2 | 33.86 | 125,000 | 1.4 | -0.17 | -219 | 839 | 1,058 |
| tanz | Tanzania | 57,918,322 | 2.21 | 1,281,172 | 50,418,322 | 87.1 | 0.55 | 32,500,000 | 56.1 | 2.65 | 862,698 | 1,174,698 | 312,000 |
| thai | Thailand | 72,716,978 | 0.68 | 493,751 | 47,716,978 | 65.6 | 26.02 | 1,766,000 | 2.4 | 1.05 | 18,456 | 38,748 | 20,291 |
| timo | Timor | 1,184,977 | 1.18 | 13,941 | 1,173,977 | 99.1 | 0.04 | 1,128,300 | 95.2 | 1.30 | 14,723 | 29,187 | 14,465 |
| togo | Togo | 8,482,467 | 2.45 | 207,993 | 6,882,467 | 81.1 | 0.66 | 4,150,000 | 48.9 | 3.02 | 125,404 | 161,260 | 35,856 |
| tong | Tonga | 105,126 | 0.26 | 272 | 105,006 | 99.9 | 0.10 | 95,360 | 90.7 | 0.16 | 154 | 1,062 | 908 |
| trin | Trinidad & Tobago | 1,493,418 | 0.57 | 8,542 | 1,393,418 | 93.3 | 0.56 | 896,000 | 60.0 | 0.27 | 2,445 | 13,305 | 10,860 |
| tuni | Tunisia | 12,843,081 | 1.18 | 151,168 | 7,143,081 | 55.6 | 88.29 | 80,000 | 0.6 | 1.77 | 1,418 | 2,093 | 675 |
| turk | Turkey | 87,869,200 | 1.12 | 980,002 | 47,669,200 | 54.3 | 104.93 | 450,000 | 0.5 | 0.59 | 2,641 | 7,240 | 4,599 |
| turm | Turkmenistan | 6,286,522 | 1.38 | 86,952 | 2,486,522 | 39.6 | 25.74 | 93,000 | 1.5 | -0.36 | -330 | 517 | 847 |
| turs | Turks & Caicos Is | 33,769 | 2.84 | 960 | 33,689 | 99.8 | 0.10 | 30,640 | 90.7 | 2.80 | 859 | 1,211 | 352 |
| tuva | Tuvalu | 20,674 | 2.30 | 475 | 20,654 | 99.9 | 0.15 | 18,000 | 87.1 | 2.19 | 395 | 566 | 171 |
| ugan | Uganda | 44,435,310 | 2.89 | 1,285,747 | 44,190,310 | 99.4 | 0.08 | 40,900,000 | 92.0 | 3.05 | 1,245,475 | 1,661,428 | 415,953 |
| ukra | Ukraine | 45,687,963 | -0.40 | -181,052 | 45,147,963 | 98.8 | 0.13 | 40,000,000 | 87.6 | -0.18 | -72,978 | 769,022 | 842,000 |
| unia | United Arab Emirates | 3,283,949 | 1.19 | 39,174 | 2,083,949 | 63.5 | 4.34 | 390,000 | 11.9 | 1.48 | 5,765 | 10,242 | 4,477 |
| usa | USA | 325,572,586 | 0.63 | 2,046,842 | 318,272,586 | 97.8 | 0.22 | 261,348,500 | 80.3 | 0.41 | 1,080,218 | 5,463,033 | 4,382,814 |
| uuay | Uruguay | 3,906,674 | 0.63 | 24,705 | 3,866,374 | 99.0 | 0.53 | 2,520,000 | 64.5 | 0.58 | 14,726 | 46,957 | 32,231 |
| uzbe | Uzbekistan | 33,354,778 | 1.27 | 424,267 | 18,011,478 | 54.0 | 46.40 | 380,000 | 1.1 | -0.22 | -822 | 2,617 | 3,439 |
| vanu | Vanuatu | 319,146 | 2.09 | 6,661 | 317,146 | 99.4 | 0.05 | 301,900 | 94.6 | 2.16 | 6,509 | 9,431 | 2,922 |
| vene | Venezuela | 34,775,110 | 1.47 | 509,749 | 34,601,110 | 99.5 | 0.06 | 32,677,500 | 94.0 | 1.43 | 467,475 | 796,865 | 329,389 |
| viet | Viet Nam | 108,037,101 | 1.22 | 1,315,429 | 80,867,101 | 74.9 | 6.13 | 11,345,000 | 10.5 | 2.20 | 249,471 | 354,412 | 104,941 |
| virg | Virgin Is of the US | 83,559 | -0.43 | -355 | 83,109 | 99.5 | 0.05 | 78,880 | 94.4 | -0.50 | -398 | 507 | 906 |
| wall | Wallis & Futuna Is | 17,500 | 0.75 | 131 | 17,490 | 99.9 | 0.02 | 17,110 | 97.8 | 0.75 | 129 | 291 | 163 |
| yeme | Yemen | 38,985,203 | 3.11 | 1,213,966 | 20,695,203 | 53.1 | 322.36 | 64,000 | 0.2 | 2.79 | 1,784 | 2,252 | 468 |
| yugo | Yugoslavia | 10,844,276 | 0.08 | 8,246 | 10,417,276 | 96.1 | 0.33 | 7,858,000 | 72.5 | 0.34 | 26,454 | 171,356 | 144,902 |
| zamb | Zambia | 15,616,246 | 2.15 | 336,204 | 15,496,246 | 99.2 | 0.13 | 13,703,000 | 87.7 | 2.41 | 330,538 | 458,113 | 127,575 |
| zimb | Zimbabwe | 15,092,435 | 1.03 | 156,106 | 14,967,435 | 99.2 | 0.34 | 11,156,900 | 73.9 | 1.41 | 156,821 | 289,253 | 132,432 |
| | 11 minicountries | 30,666 | 1.14 | 351 | 28,583 | 93.2 | 0.46 | 19,552 | 63.8 | 1.13 | 220 | 497 | 277 |
| | Africa | 1,298,310,949 | 2.04 | 26,431,240 | 1,056,895,534 | 81.4 | 0.67 | 633,803,970 | 48.8 | 2.29 | 14,486,822 | 20,875,883 | 6,389,061 |
| | Antarctica | 10,000 | 3.25 | 325 | 9,650 | 96.5 | 0.21 | 8,000 | 80.0 | 3.48 | 279 | 389 | 111 |
| | Asia | 4,723,140,220 | 1.00 | 47,252,418 | 3,150,655,420 | 66.7 | 5.78 | 464,800,100 | 9.8 | 1.60 | 7,418,889 | 12,438,612 | 5,019,724 |
| | Europe | 702,335,374 | -0.15 | -1,041,706 | 682,880,479 | 97.2 | 0.23 | 554,586,470 | 79.0 | -0.04 | -201,290 | 10,883,450 | 11,084,740 |
| | Latin America | 696,648,086 | 1.18 | 8,244,060 | 694,103,761 | 99.6 | 0.08 | 641,115,950 | 92.0 | 1.16 | 7,405,798 | 14,552,065 | 7,146,267 |
| | Northern America | 363,611,501 | 0.64 | 2,344,888 | 354,986,046 | 97.6 | 0.22 | 290,345,170 | 79.9 | 0.43 | 1,256,890 | 6,126,258 | 4,869,368 |
| | Oceania | 39,647,012 | 1.07 | 423,760 | 38,766,584 | 97.8 | 0.21 | 32,010,392 | 80.7 | 0.98 | 312,417 | 734,806 | 422,389 |
| | **World A** | **328,540,207** | **-2.41** | **-7,933,114** | **145,852,207** | **44.4** | **31.75** | **4,453,680** | **1.4** | **-3.31** | **-147,333** | **-105,254** | **42,079** |
| | **World B** | **5,256,798,339** | **1.35** | **71,220,067** | **3,634,692,389** | **69.1** | **4.25** | **692,361,600** | **13.2** | **1.21** | **8,351,982** | **15,837,135** | **7,485,153** |
| | **World C** | **2,238,364,596** | **1.12** | **25,049,459** | **2,197,752,878** | **98.2** | **0.14** | **1,919,854,772** | **85.8** | **1.06** | **20,285,981** | **47,690,408** | **27,404,427** |
| | **GLOBAL TOTAL** | **7,823,703,142** | **1.03** | **80,610,255** | **5,978,297,474** | **76.4** | **1.28** | **2,616,670,052** | **33.4** | **1.08** | **28,304,583** | **63,236,241** | **34,931,659** |

| COUNTRY | | COUNTRY TRENDS IN THE YEAR AD 2050 | | | | | | | | | | | |
|---|---|---|---|---|---|---|---|---|---|---|---|---|---|
| | | DEMOGRAPHIC TRENDS | | | EVANGELIZATION TRENDS | | | CHRISTIAN TRENDS | | | | | |
| code | short name | pop 2050 | npop | increase p.a. | evangelized | E | outreach | Christians | C% | G% | increase p.a. | gains p.a. | losses p.a. |
| 1 | 2 | 180 | 181 | 182 | 183 | 184 | 185 | 186 | 187 | 188 | 189 | 190 | 191 |
| afgh | Afghanistan | 61,003,536 | 1.23 | 750,616 | 24,401,136 | 40.0 | 912.90 | 26,700 | 0.0 | 2.56 | 683 | 973 | 290 |
| alba | Albania | 4,322,172 | 0.50 | 21,416 | 4,022,172 | 93.1 | 0.90 | 2,121,300 | 49.1 | 0.94 | 19,883 | 55,691 | 35,808 |
| alge | Algeria | 57,731,194 | 0.86 | 496,232 | 34,731,194 | 60.2 | 123.04 | 280,000 | 0.5 | 2.29 | 6,410 | 9,121 | 2,710 |
| amer | American Samoa | 200,546 | 1.37 | 2,750 | 199,146 | 99.3 | 0.04 | 191,300 | 95.4 | 1.36 | 2,595 | 4,816 | 2,221 |
| ando | Andorra | 165,365 | 0.28 | 457 | 162,465 | 98.2 | 0.11 | 145,800 | 88.2 | 0.14 | 197 | 3,124 | 2,926 |
| ango | Angola | 36,901,143 | 1.55 | 572,828 | 36,745,543 | 99.6 | 0.03 | 35,516,100 | 96.2 | 1.51 | 534,911 | 824,723 | 289,811 |
| angu | Anguilla | 12,679 | 0.58 | 73 | 12,579 | 99.2 | 0.12 | 11,190 | 88.3 | 0.50 | 56 | 224 | 167 |
| anti | Antigua | 79,230 | 0.22 | 171 | 78,930 | 99.6 | 0.11 | 71,000 | 89.6 | 0.09 | 61 | 1,122 | 1,061 |
| arge | Argentina | 54,507,329 | 0.58 | 317,049 | 53,847,329 | 98.8 | 0.08 | 50,010,300 | 91.7 | 0.58 | 288,519 | 938,653 | 650,134 |
| arme | Armenia | 3,996,282 | 0.05 | 2,009 | 3,961,282 | 99.1 | 0.06 | 3,725,500 | 93.2 | 0.07 | 2,665 | 60,224 | 57,559 |
| arub | Aruba | 347,207 | 1.32 | 4,571 | 344,907 | 99.3 | 0.04 | 330,400 | 95.2 | 1.29 | 4,263 | 9,407 | 5,144 |
| aust | Australia | 25,752,112 | 0.44 | 112,610 | 25,002,112 | 97.1 | 0.41 | 17,669,460 | 68.6 | 0.07 | 12,330 | 296,808 | 284,478 |
| ausz | Austria | 7,093,615 | -0.57 | -40,515 | 6,907,915 | 97.4 | 0.22 | 5,644,700 | 79.6 | -0.93 | -52,297 | 78,603 | 130,901 |
| azer | Azerbaijan | 9,981,064 | 0.24 | 23,866 | 4,681,064 | 46.9 | 16.27 | 271,000 | 2.7 | -1.19 | -3,218 | 614 | 3,832 |
| baha | Bahamas | 485,358 | 0.63 | 3,067 | 482,658 | 99.4 | 0.12 | 432,400 | 89.1 | 0.57 | 2,447 | 8,116 | 5,669 |
| bahr | Bahrain | 991,570 | 0.58 | 5,738 | 691,570 | 69.7 | 4.96 | 116,000 | 11.7 | 0.72 | 833 | 2,391 | 1,558 |
| bang | Bangladesh | 212,494,917 | 0.69 | 1,474,906 | 139,494,917 | 65.6 | 70.04 | 1,963,500 | 0.9 | 1.03 | 20,315 | 43,465 | 23,150 |
| barb | Barbados | 287,566 | -0.13 | -362 | 283,566 | 98.6 | 0.05 | 269,280 | 93.6 | -0.22 | -580 | 4,251 | 4,831 |
| belg | Belgium | 8,918,152 | -0.42 | -37,821 | 8,628,152 | 96.7 | 0.20 | 7,190,000 | 80.6 | -0.66 | -47,255 | 111,932 | 159,187 |
| beli | Belize | 476,722 | 1.02 | 4,855 | 462,722 | 97.1 | 0.11 | 416,000 | 87.3 | 0.90 | 3,725 | 8,109 | 4,385 |
| belo | Belorussia | 8,329,607 | -0.52 | -43,540 | 8,259,807 | 99.2 | 0.10 | 7,504,000 | 90.1 | -0.31 | -23,164 | 146,651 | 169,816 |
| beni | Benin | 15,619,912 | 1.37 | 214,362 | 12,919,912 | 82.7 | 0.97 | 6,570,000 | 42.1 | 2.16 | 141,963 | 198,202 | 56,239 |
| berm | Bermuda | 81,937 | 0.32 | 264 | 81,637 | 99.6 | 0.13 | 72,220 | 88.1 | 0.18 | 127 | 1,291 | 1,163 |
| bhut | Bhutan | 5,686,652 | 1.52 | 86,207 | 1,666,652 | 29.3 | 91.59 | 18,000 | 0.3 | 0.87 | 156 | 302 | 146 |
| boli | Bolivia | 16,967,196 | 1.03 | 174,837 | 16,906,196 | 99.6 | 0.11 | 15,286,700 | 90.1 | 0.92 | 140,885 | 310,262 | 169,377 |
| bosn | Bosnia-Herzegovina | 3,767,221 | -0.55 | -20,708 | 2,867,221 | 76.1 | 2.14 | 913,000 | 24.2 | -0.78 | -7,107 | 14,074 | 21,182 |
| bots | Botswana | 2,797,722 | 0.89 | 24,898 | 2,717,722 | 97.1 | 0.39 | 1,951,000 | 69.7 | 1.09 | 21,273 | 44,177 | 22,905 |
| boug | Bougainville | 412,360 | 1.47 | 6,074 | 412,210 | 99.9 | 0.04 | 397,000 | 96.3 | 1.50 | 5,944 | 10,907 | 4,963 |
| braz | Brazil | 244,229,876 | 0.46 | 1,115,613 | 243,743,376 | 99.8 | 0.14 | 213,509,000 | 87.4 | 0.35 | 738,651 | 3,883,638 | 3,144,988 |
| brit | Britain | 56,666,891 | -0.23 | -127,927 | 55,066,891 | 97.2 | 0.30 | 42,405,000 | 74.8 | -0.49 | -206,336 | 668,055 | 874,391 |
| briz | British Virgin Is | 45,764 | 0.89 | 408 | 45,514 | 99.5 | 0.19 | 38,120 | 83.3 | 0.81 | 310 | 805 | 494 |
| brun | Brunei | 527,548 | 0.56 | 2,947 | 327,548 | 62.1 | 6.44 | 44,000 | 8.3 | 1.10 | 482 | 1,031 | 548 |
| bulg | Bulgaria | 5,672,973 | -0.85 | -48,238 | 5,472,973 | 96.5 | 0.15 | 4,748,700 | 83.7 | -0.86 | -40,679 | 75,522 | 116,201 |
| burk | Burkina Faso | 35,491,174 | 1.69 | 601,166 | 27,491,174 | 77.5 | 2.14 | 8,768,000 | 24.7 | 2.47 | 216,880 | 288,515 | 71,635 |
| buru | Burundi | 15,570,744 | 1.20 | 186,144 | 15,510,744 | 99.6 | 0.05 | 14,770,000 | 94.9 | 1.24 | 183,296 | 329,962 | 146,666 |
| camb | Cambodia | 20,699,517 | 0.90 | 187,260 | 13,699,517 | 66.2 | 37.32 | 357,500 | 1.7 | 1.76 | 6,294 | 10,330 | 4,036 |
| came | Cameroon | 37,289,932 | 1.38 | 513,885 | 32,289,932 | 86.6 | 0.26 | 25,649,000 | 68.8 | 1.89 | 485,960 | 717,826 | 231,867 |
| cana | Canada | 42,310,864 | 0.44 | 186,893 | 40,618,864 | 96.0 | 0.31 | 31,020,000 | 73.3 | 0.29 | 89,512 | 672,378 | 582,866 |
| cape | Cape Verde | 869,051 | 1.04 | 9,041 | 867,851 | 99.9 | 0.05 | 824,150 | 94.8 | 1.03 | 8,512 | 16,003 | 7,492 |
| caym | Cayman Islands | 102,335 | 1.10 | 1,121 | 99,835 | 97.6 | 0.33 | 75,100 | 73.4 | 0.97 | 728 | 1,702 | 974 |
| cent | Central African Rep | 7,688,812 | 1.20 | 92,397 | 6,988,812 | 90.9 | 0.27 | 5,505,000 | 71.6 | 1.22 | 67,126 | 122,176 | 55,050 |
| chad | Chad | 19,693,151 | 1.40 | 275,884 | 11,423,151 | 58.0 | 1.69 | 4,250,000 | 21.6 | 1.21 | 51,224 | 88,667 | 37,443 |
| chan | Channel Islands | 172,707 | -0.02 | -28 | 171,107 | 99.1 | 0.30 | 131,470 | 76.1 | -0.08 | -105 | 2,606 | 2,711 |
| chil | Chile | 22,215,116 | 0.51 | 113,948 | 22,135,116 | 99.6 | 0.15 | 19,185,200 | 86.4 | 0.43 | 81,949 | 347,280 | 265,331 |
| chin | China | 1,456,900,737 | -0.02 | -240,711 | 1,136,400,737 | 78.0 | 5.74 | 168,655,000 | 11.6 | 0.89 | 1,498,704 | 4,182,005 | 2,683,301 |
| colo | Colombia | 71,549,506 | 0.72 | 517,271 | 71,299,506 | 99.7 | 0.04 | 68,588,000 | 95.9 | 0.69 | 475,243 | 1,350,426 | 875,183 |
| como | Comoros | 1,234,481 | 0.89 | 10,971 | 614,481 | 49.8 | 28.54 | 20,800 | 1.7 | 1.36 | 282 | 451 | 168 |
| cong | Congo-Brazzaville | 8,596,804 | 1.67 | 143,140 | 8,552,804 | 99.5 | 0.12 | 7,668,000 | 89.2 | 1.60 | 122,465 | 182,506 | 60,040 |
| conz | Congo-Zaire | 160,359,506 | 1.72 | 2,752,565 | 159,701,506 | 99.6 | 0.03 | 154,854,700 | 96.6 | 1.73 | 2,673,959 | 3,813,689 | 1,139,731 |
| cook | Cook Islands | 28,335 | 0.71 | 201 | 28,310 | 99.9 | 0.07 | 26,500 | 93.5 | 0.61 | 162 | 470 | 308 |
| cost | Costa Rica | 7,194,768 | 0.78 | 55,927 | 7,179,768 | 99.8 | 0.07 | 6,725,750 | 93.5 | 0.68 | 45,451 | 127,102 | 81,651 |
| croa | Croatia | 3,672,619 | -0.53 | -19,429 | 3,652,619 | 99.5 | 0.03 | 3,541,000 | 96.4 | -0.52 | -18,310 | 60,584 | 78,893 |
| cuba | Cuba | 11,095,349 | -0.25 | -27,227 | 11,015,349 | 99.3 | 0.93 | 5,700,000 | 51.4 | 0.07 | 4,037 | 112,565 | 108,528 |
| cypr | Cyprus | 669,537 | -0.11 | -721 | 668,537 | 99.9 | 0.11 | 600,000 | 89.6 | -0.23 | -1,389 | 7,323 | 8,712 |
| czec | Czech Republic | 7,829,309 | -0.78 | -60,741 | 7,809,309 | 99.7 | 0.24 | 6,314,800 | 80.7 | -0.47 | -29,605 | 120,750 | 150,355 |
| denm | Denmark | 4,793,255 | -0.35 | -17,000 | 4,708,255 | 98.2 | 0.15 | 4,088,400 | 85.3 | -0.53 | -21,833 | 66,109 | 87,941 |
| djib | Djibouti | 1,345,928 | 1.09 | 14,679 | 745,928 | 55.4 | 13.21 | 52,500 | 3.9 | 0.90 | 471 | 984 | 513 |
| domi | Dominica | 78,854 | 0.28 | 225 | 78,754 | 99.9 | 0.11 | 70,790 | 89.8 | 0.16 | 111 | 1,169 | 1,058 |
| domr | Dominican Republic | 12,264,704 | 0.38 | 46,199 | 12,252,704 | 99.9 | 0.09 | 11,190,400 | 91.2 | 0.26 | 29,210 | 181,400 | 152,189 |
| ecua | Ecuador | 21,190,075 | 0.70 | 148,470 | 21,030,075 | 99.2 | 0.05 | 20,076,000 | 94.7 | 0.61 | 123,078 | 380,653 | 257,575 |
| egyp | Egypt | 114,844,248 | 0.74 | 844,866 | 96,344,248 | 83.9 | 4.79 | 16,650,000 | 14.5 | 0.78 | 129,898 | 300,227 | 170,330 |
| elsa | El Salvador | 11,237,022 | 0.86 | 97,095 | 11,222,022 | 99.9 | 0.06 | 10,608,100 | 94.4 | 0.77 | 81,773 | 206,525 | 124,751 |
| equa | Equatorial Guinea | 1,122,095 | 1.39 | 15,590 | 1,112,095 | 99.1 | 0.11 | 998,800 | 89.0 | 1.38 | 13,809 | 22,738 | 8,929 |
| erit | Eritrea | 9,085,343 | 1.24 | 112,420 | 7,385,343 | 81.3 | 0.57 | 4,690,000 | 51.6 | 1.29 | 60,733 | 102,052 | 41,319 |
| esto | Estonia | 927,258 | -0.79 | -7,345 | 915,258 | 98.7 | 0.28 | 716,000 | 77.2 | -0.44 | -3,181 | 14,411 | 17,592 |
| ethi | Ethiopia | 169,446,494 | 1.55 | 2,624,772 | 156,446,494 | 92.3 | 0.56 | 100,593,000 | 59.4 | 1.55 | 1,558,769 | 2,434,934 | 876,165 |
| faer | Faeroe Islands | 33,510 | -0.35 | -118 | 33,460 | 99.9 | 0.05 | 32,000 | 95.5 | -0.40 | -129 | 559 | 688 |
| fiji | Fiji | 1,310,187 | 0.69 | 8,998 | 1,210,187 | 92.4 | 0.59 | 760,000 | 58.0 | 0.81 | 6,165 | 16,395 | 10,230 |
| finl | Finland | 4,897,665 | -0.28 | -13,734 | 4,869,265 | 99.4 | 0.13 | 4,305,300 | 87.9 | -0.42 | -17,996 | 71,683 | 89,679 |
| fran | France | 59,882,882 | -0.12 | -70,079 | 56,382,882 | 94.2 | 0.50 | 37,564,500 | 62.7 | -0.43 | -160,439 | 593,481 | 753,920 |
| freg | French Guiana | 580,953 | 1.34 | 7,802 | 576,453 | 99.2 | 0.22 | 473,400 | 81.5 | 1.26 | 5,947 | 13,105 | 7,158 |
| frep | French Polynesia | 387,742 | 0.72 | 2,774 | 383,542 | 98.9 | 0.17 | 327,100 | 84.4 | 0.64 | 2,078 | 6,484 | 4,406 |
| gabo | Gabon | 2,682,170 | 1.22 | 32,696 | 2,652,170 | 98.9 | 0.12 | 2,378,200 | 88.7 | 1.17 | 27,944 | 50,204 | 22,260 |
| gamb | Gambia | 2,773,273 | 1.02 | 28,339 | 1,673,273 | 60.3 | 14.57 | 107,500 | 3.9 | 1.09 | 1,171 | 2,357 | 1,187 |
| geor | Georgia | 5,179,911 | 0.00 | 72 | 4,829,911 | 93.2 | 0.34 | 3,600,000 | 69.5 | 0.15 | 5,259 | 60,699 | 55,440 |
| germ | Germany | 73,303,294 | -0.36 | -264,568 | 71,153,294 | 97.1 | 0.39 | 51,179,400 | 69.8 | -0.58 | -295,451 | 866,833 | 1,162,284 |
| ghan | Ghana | 51,801,802 | 1.37 | 709,019 | 47,301,802 | 91.3 | 0.46 | 32,352,800 | 62.5 | 1.54 | 497,161 | 751,778 | 254,617 |
| gibr | Gibraltar | 17,807 | -0.73 | -130 | 16,607 | 93.3 | 0.18 | 14,050 | 78.9 | -0.93 | -130 | 160 | 290 |
| gree | Greece | 8,233,168 | -0.72 | -59,254 | 8,043,168 | 97.7 | 0.06 | 7,570,000 | 91.9 | -0.80 | -60,509 | 119,051 | 179,560 |
| grel | Greenland | 63,418 | 0.25 | 156 | 63,118 | 99.5 | 0.06 | 59,300 | 93.5 | 0.18 | 106 | 1,382 | 1,276 |
| gren | Grenada | 114,829 | 0.37 | 427 | 114,799 | 99.9 | 0.06 | 107,920 | 94.0 | 0.29 | 308 | 1,992 | 1,684 |
| guad | Guadeloupe | 601,120 | 0.22 | 1,313 | 600,220 | 99.9 | 0.08 | 556,200 | 92.5 | 0.15 | 850 | 9,165 | 8,315 |
| guam | Guam | 266,430 | 0.63 | 1,682 | 261,930 | 98.3 | 0.07 | 244,500 | 91.8 | 0.55 | 1,341 | 4,764 | 3,423 |
| guat | Guatemala | 27,164,748 | 1.27 | 344,907 | 27,154,748 | 99.9 | 0.04 | 26,068,800 | 96.0 | 1.23 | 320,670 | 578,490 | 257,820 |
| guin | Guinea | 16,348,142 | 1.08 | 176,611 | 8,348,142 | 51.1 | 7.79 | 950,000 | 5.8 | 1.99 | 18,937 | 28,551 | 9,614 |
| gunb | Guinea-Bissau | 2,685,384 | 1.30 | 34,816 | 1,535,384 | 57.2 | 2.41 | 450,000 | 16.8 | 1.70 | 7,665 | 12,467 | 4,802 |
| guya | Guyana | 1,165,809 | 0.44 | 5,128 | 1,025,809 | 88.0 | 0.88 | 546,900 | 46.9 | 0.31 | 1,668 | 9,938 | 8,269 |
| hait | Haiti | 15,174,441 | 0.95 | 143,733 | 15,162,241 | 99.9 | 0.08 | 14,014,900 | 92.4 | 0.84 | 117,577 | 284,214 | 166,637 |
| hond | Honduras | 13,920,440 | 1.07 | 149,597 | 13,906,440 | 99.9 | 0.05 | 13,264,700 | 95.3 | 1.03 | 136,464 | 277,467 | 141,004 |
| hung | Hungary | 7,487,699 | -0.69 | -51,586 | 7,441,699 | 99.4 | 0.08 | 6,871,200 | 91.8 | -0.65 | -44,335 | 114,802 | 159,137 |
| icel | Iceland | 340,669 | 0.15 | 502 | 340,369 | 99.9 | 0.05 | 323,400 | 94.9 | 0.11 | 347 | 6,223 | 5,876 |
| indi | India | 1,528,853,081 | 0.56 | 8,524,195 | 1,088,853,081 | 71.2 | 7.69 | 125,300,000 | 8.2 | 0.98 | 1,227,421 | 2,840,032 | 1,612,611 |
| indo | Indonesia | 311,856,857 | 0.53 | 1,644,116 | 229,856,857 | 73.7 | 2.77 | 61,000,000 | 19.6 | 1.41 | 859,199 | 1,630,849 | 771,650 |
| iran | Iran | 114,947,360 | 0.79 | 905,987 | 55,727,360 | 48.5 | 60.92 | 900,000 | 0.8 | 1.50 | 13,517 | 23,453 | 9,936 |
| iraq | Iraq | 54,915,732 | 1.17 | 644,946 | 32,915,732 | 59.9 | 17.29 | 1,800,000 | 3.3 | 1.40 | 25,259 | 41,369 | 16,110 |
| irel | Ireland | 4,710,111 | 0.27 | 12,684 | 4,690,111 | 99.6 | 0.06 | 4,443,800 | 94.3 | 0.20 | 8,883 | 87,671 | 78,789 |
| isle | Isle of Man | 104,067 | 0.12 | 129 | 103,407 | 99.4 | 0.20 | 86,400 | 83.0 | 0.00 | -1 | 1,781 | 1,782 |
| isra | Israel | 7,774,380 | 0.46 | 35,983 | 5,774,380 | 74.3 | 8.17 | 630,000 | 8.1 | 1.09 | 6,890 | 14,519 | 7,629 |
| ital | Italy | 41,196,579 | -0.87 | -358,883 | 40,566,579 | 98.5 | 0.27 | 31,823,000 | 77.2 | -1.00 | -319,646 | 480,702 | 800,348 |
| ivor | Ivory Coast | 30,469,744 | 1.07 | 326,356 | 25,319,744 | 83.1 | 1.23 | 11,378,000 | 37.3 | 1.38 | 157,083 | 268,815 | 111,732 |
| jama | Jamaica | 3,801,233 | 0.64 | 24,140 | 3,763,223 | 99.0 | 0.26 | 2,977,800 | 78.3 | 0.50 | 14,831 | 53,453 | 38,622 |
| japa | Japan | 104,920,961 | -0.57 | -601,865 | 84,920,961 | 80.9 | 14.44 | 5,500,000 | 5.2 | 0.38 | 21,008 | 120,063 | 99,055 |
| jord | Jordan | 16,546,809 | 1.27 | 210,519 | 12,046,809 | 72.8 | 10.61 | 1,038,000 | 6.3 | 1.95 | 20,274 | 29,221 | 8,948 |
| kaza | Kazakhstan | 18,664,590 | 0.21 | 39,728 | 13,664,590 | 73.2 | 3.88 | 2,800,000 | 15.0 | 0.07 | 2,019 | 39,483 | 37,464 |
| keny | Kenya | 51,034,193 | 0.81 | 411,255 | 49,734,193 | 97.5 | 0.13 | 43,872,000 | 86.0 | 1.00 | 438,078 | 950,941 | 512,864 |
| kirg | Kirgizstan | 7,374,583 | 0.76 | 56,372 | 4,374,583 | 59.3 | 8.72 | 450,000 | 6.1 | 0.00 | 0 | 5,126 | 5,126 |
| kiri | Kiribati | 154,678 | 1.04 | 1,614 | 154,548 | 99.9 | 0.09 | 141,420 | 91.4 | 1.01 | 1,423 | 3,403 | 1,980 |
| kuwa | Kuwait | 3,526,891 | 0.68 | 24,115 | 2,526,891 | 71.6 | 3.79 | 527,000 | 14.9 | 1.01 | 5,319 | 11,463 | 6,145 |
| laos | Laos | 13,343,594 | 1.30 | 173,959 | 6,943,594 | 52.0 | 18.69 | 352,700 | 2.6 | 1.61 | 5,690 | 9,023 | 3,333 |
| latv | Latvia | 1,628,441 | -0.69 | -11,230 | 1,618,941 | 99.4 | 0.20 | 1,352,000 | 83.0 | -0.44 | -5,928 | 26,087 | 32,015 |
| leba | Lebanon | 5,168,901 | 0.65 | 33,423 | 4,868,901 | 94.2 | 0.90 | 2,560,000 | 49.5 | 0.52 | 13,435 | 45,000 | 31,565 |
| leso | Lesotho | 4,765,606 | 1.23 | 58,849 | 4,745,606 | 99.6 | 0.05 | 4,538,600 | 95.2 | 1.28 | 58,038 | 98,886 | 40,847 |
| libe | Liberia | 10,009,934 | 1.67 | 167,086 | 8,009,934 | 80.0 | 0.69 | 4,750,000 | 47.5 | 2.07 | 98,191 | 133,009 | 34,818 |
| liby | Libya | 11,004,724 | 0.97 | 106,660 | 5,804,724 | 52.7 | 13.70 | 395,000 | 3.6 | 1.21 | 4,786 | 8,341 | 3,555 |
| liec | Liechtenstein | 41,558 | 0.03 | 12 | 40,608 | 97.7 | 0.13 | 36,040 | 86.7 | -0.11 | -39 | 768 | 807 |
| lith | Lithuania | 2,966,545 | -0.54 | -16,102 | 2,953,545 | 99.6 | 0.06 | 2,787,000 | 93.9 | -0.50 | -13,897 | 49,061 | 62,958 |
| luxe | Luxembourg | 429,777 | -0.30 | -1,291 | 424,277 | 98.7 | 0.11 | 383,700 | 89.3 | -0.46 | -1,759 | 6,357 | 8,115 |
| mace | Macedonia | 2,302,042 | 0.08 | 1,780 | 2,062,042 | 89.6 | 0.46 | 1,414,000 | 61.4 | 0.04 | 563 | 27,005 | 26,442 |
| mada | Madagascar | 40,437,551 | 1.34 | 543,406 | 35,937,551 | 88.9 | 0.53 | 23,500,000 | 58.1 | 1.81 | 425,825 | 614,060 | 188,235 |
| mala | Malawi | 29,008,369 | 1.51 | 437,153 | 28,508,369 | 98.3 | 0.19 | 24,000,000 | 82.7 | 1.69 | 406,496 | 628,496 | 222,000 |
| malb | Malaysia | 36,988,821 | 0.71 | 263,774 | 28,288,821 | 76.5 | 5.90 | 4,100,000 | 11.1 | 1.19 | 48,807 | 95,547 | 46,740 |

| COUNTRY | | COUNTRY TRENDS IN THE YEAR AD 2050 | | | | | | | | | | | |
|---|---|---|---|---|---|---|---|---|---|---|---|---|---|
| | | *DEMOGRAPHIC TRENDS* | | | *EVANGELIZATION TRENDS* | | | *CHRISTIAN TRENDS* | | | | | |
| *code* | *short name* | *pop 2050* | *npop* | *increase p.a.* | *evangelized* | *E* | *outreach* | *Christians* | *C%* | *G%* | *increase p.a.* | *gains p.a.* | *losses p.a.* |
| *1* | *2* | *180* | *181* | *182* | *183* | *184* | *185* | *186* | *187* | *188* | *189* | *190* | *191* |
| mald | Maldives | 680,458 | 1.23 | 8,359 | 157,458 | 23.1 | 135.92 | 1,150 | 0.2 | 1.46 | 17 | 27 | 10 |
| mali | Mali | 31,352,573 | 1.56 | 488,862 | 17,352,573 | 55.3 | 21.11 | 785,000 | 2.5 | 2.03 | 15,934 | 22,308 | 6,374 |
| malt | Malta | 420,549 | -0.09 | -368 | 419,949 | 99.9 | 0.04 | 404,840 | 96.3 | -0.14 | -578 | 7,336 | 7,915 |
| mars | Marshall Islands | 181,681 | 1.44 | 2,612 | 181,641 | 99.9 | 0.04 | 174,000 | 95.8 | 1.40 | 2,443 | 4,879 | 2,436 |
| mart | Martinique | 456,679 | 0.06 | 265 | 455,379 | 99.7 | 0.06 | 428,780 | 93.9 | -0.01 | -50 | 6,802 | 6,852 |
| maur | Mauritania | 6,585,473 | 1.30 | 85,710 | 2,985,473 | 45.3 | 330.72 | 9,000 | 0.1 | 0.69 | 62 | 141 | 79 |
| maus | Mauritius | 1,437,803 | 0.17 | 2,468 | 1,197,803 | 83.3 | 1.18 | 550,000 | 38.3 | 0.46 | 2,547 | 10,060 | 7,513 |
| mayo | Mayotte | 342,300 | 2.46 | 8,416 | 177,300 | 51.8 | 16.73 | 10,000 | 2.9 | 2.89 | 289 | 370 | 81 |
| mexi | Mexico | 146,645,333 | 0.48 | 699,547 | 146,395,333 | 99.8 | 0.06 | 138,100,000 | 94.2 | 0.43 | 597,138 | 2,439,392 | 1,842,254 |
| micr | Micronesia | 254,042 | 1.18 | 2,990 | 253,142 | 99.6 | 0.08 | 234,000 | 92.1 | 1.15 | 2,692 | 5,968 | 3,276 |
| mold | Moldavia | 4,506,222 | -0.04 | -1,617 | 4,352,222 | 96.6 | 0.16 | 3,760,000 | 83.4 | 0.04 | 1,346 | 74,967 | 73,621 |
| mona | Monaco | 40,549 | -0.01 | -6 | 39,949 | 98.5 | 0.11 | 35,900 | 88.5 | -0.13 | -47 | 673 | 721 |
| mong | Mongolia | 4,397,543 | 0.68 | 30,056 | 2,397,543 | 54.5 | 25.94 | 89,000 | 2.0 | 1.40 | 1,244 | 2,313 | 1,069 |
| mont | Montserrat | 11,323 | 0.24 | 27 | 11,303 | 99.8 | 0.12 | 10,100 | 89.2 | 0.04 | 4 | 155 | 151 |
| moro | Morocco | 45,284,285 | 0.65 | 293,530 | 22,634,285 | 50.0 | 67.80 | 329,000 | 0.7 | 1.14 | 3,741 | 7,360 | 3,619 |
| moza | Mozambique | 42,923,153 | 1.36 | 584,304 | 36,923,153 | 86.0 | 0.91 | 19,300,000 | 45.0 | 1.59 | 307,484 | 515,152 | 207,668 |
| myan | Myanmar | 64,889,762 | 0.44 | 286,592 | 48,889,762 | 75.3 | 4.31 | 9,215,000 | 14.2 | 1.48 | 136,405 | 264,310 | 127,904 |
| nami | Namibia | 3,023,017 | 1.03 | 31,253 | 2,973,017 | 98.3 | 0.10 | 2,706,700 | 89.5 | 0.98 | 26,488 | 58,319 | 31,831 |
| naur | Nauru | 23,649 | 1.14 | 269 | 22,949 | 97.0 | 0.37 | 16,750 | 70.8 | 0.99 | 165 | 400 | 235 |
| nepa | Nepal | 49,319,974 | 1.05 | 516,552 | 29,319,974 | 59.4 | 11.26 | 2,392,000 | 4.8 | 1.82 | 43,459 | 67,236 | 23,776 |
| neth | Netherlands | 14,156,272 | -0.43 | -61,424 | 13,631,272 | 96.3 | 0.31 | 10,385,200 | 73.4 | -0.64 | -66,654 | 165,974 | 232,628 |
| nets | Netherlands Antilles | 266,607 | 0.12 | 331 | 262,607 | 98.5 | 0.08 | 243,420 | 91.3 | 0.04 | 104 | 3,894 | 3,790 |
| newc | New Caledonia | 331,798 | 0.60 | 2,000 | 325,198 | 98.0 | 0.18 | 276,600 | 83.4 | 0.49 | 1,368 | 5,282 | 3,914 |
| newz | New Zealand | 5,247,730 | 0.45 | 23,416 | 5,142,730 | 98.0 | 0.23 | 4,173,500 | 79.5 | 0.38 | 15,681 | 81,664 | 65,983 |
| nica | Nicaragua | 11,599,933 | 1.16 | 134,465 | 11,575,933 | 99.8 | 0.06 | 10,955,600 | 94.4 | 1.12 | 122,904 | 237,718 | 114,815 |
| niga | Niger | 32,029,434 | 1.61 | 515,050 | 16,954,434 | 52.9 | 78.60 | 213,000 | 0.7 | 2.20 | 4,695 | 6,461 | 1,766 |
| nige | Nigeria | 244,310,581 | 1.16 | 2,837,940 | 214,310,581 | 87.7 | 0.86 | 115,258,000 | 47.2 | 1.18 | 1,357,958 | 2,487,486 | 1,129,528 |
| nork | North Korea | 30,770,264 | 0.18 | 56,638 | 21,539,264 | 70.0 | 6.09 | 3,040,000 | 9.9 | 3.08 | 93,545 | 138,415 | 44,870 |
| norl | Northern Cyprus | 243,960 | 0.55 | 1,352 | 176,960 | 72.5 | 7.04 | 22,000 | 9.0 | 0.48 | 106 | 426 | 319 |
| norm | Northern Mariana Is | 401,927 | 2.00 | 8,025 | 398,127 | 99.1 | 0.15 | 345,200 | 85.9 | 1.95 | 6,732 | 11,565 | 4,833 |
| norw | Norway | 4,751,521 | -0.05 | -2,406 | 4,636,521 | 97.6 | 0.09 | 4,265,000 | 89.8 | -0.16 | -6,893 | 75,933 | 82,826 |
| oman | Oman | 8,309,910 | 1.78 | 147,549 | 5,159,910 | 62.1 | 6.93 | 651,000 | 7.8 | 2.91 | 18,926 | 23,575 | 4,648 |
| paki | Pakistan | 345,483,897 | 1.10 | 3,790,467 | 190,483,897 | 55.1 | 15.69 | 11,410,000 | 3.3 | 1.72 | 196,221 | 304,045 | 107,825 |
| pala | Palau | 45,443 | 1.26 | 573 | 45,393 | 99.9 | 0.07 | 42,260 | 93.0 | 1.21 | 513 | 1,104 | 592 |
| pale | Palestine | 6,436,795 | 1.79 | 115,111 | 5,286,795 | 82.1 | 7.47 | 624,000 | 9.7 | 2.11 | 13,183 | 16,964 | 3,781 |
| pana | Panama | 4,262,872 | 0.48 | 20,586 | 4,137,872 | 97.1 | 0.18 | 3,511,500 | 82.4 | 0.33 | 11,691 | 59,974 | 48,283 |
| papu | Papua New Guinea | 9,102,764 | 0.96 | 87,125 | 8,918,264 | 98.0 | 0.02 | 8,785,500 | 96.5 | 0.97 | 85,185 | 195,003 | 109,819 |
| para | Paraguay | 12,564,804 | 1.19 | 149,126 | 12,537,304 | 99.8 | 0.03 | 12,138,000 | 96.6 | 1.15 | 139,657 | 266,378 | 126,721 |
| peru | Peru | 42,291,500 | 0.70 | 296,297 | 42,186,500 | 99.8 | 0.05 | 40,261,500 | 95.2 | 0.65 | 262,335 | 779,696 | 517,360 |
| phil | Philippines | 130,893,326 | 0.76 | 998,208 | 124,018,326 | 94.7 | 0.07 | 115,615,300 | 88.3 | 0.72 | 833,467 | 2,083,269 | 1,249,801 |
| pola | Poland | 36,255,656 | -0.30 | -108,225 | 36,235,856 | 99.9 | 0.02 | 35,622,700 | 98.3 | -0.29 | -101,773 | 649,866 | 751,639 |
| port | Portugal | 8,137,217 | -0.55 | -45,037 | 8,077,217 | 99.3 | 0.14 | 7,087,900 | 87.1 | -0.71 | -50,004 | 111,955 | 161,959 |
| puer | Puerto Rico | 4,709,523 | 0.20 | 9,507 | 4,703,823 | 99.9 | 0.05 | 4,475,700 | 95.0 | 0.16 | 7,005 | 74,006 | 67,001 |
| qata | Qatar | 844,094 | 0.32 | 2,734 | 569,094 | 67.4 | 4.37 | 106,000 | 12.6 | 0.48 | 511 | 1,921 | 1,411 |
| reun | Reunion | 958,612 | 0.34 | 3,297 | 927,612 | 96.8 | 0.17 | 795,800 | 83.0 | 0.23 | 1,791 | 11,444 | 9,653 |
| roma | Romania | 16,418,923 | -0.78 | -127,287 | 16,293,923 | 99.2 | 0.09 | 14,984,000 | 91.3 | -0.76 | -113,664 | 252,695 | 366,359 |
| russ | Russia | 121,255,733 | -0.51 | -623,420 | 116,255,733 | 95.9 | 0.27 | 91,642,000 | 75.6 | -0.18 | -162,169 | 1,928,185 | 2,090,354 |
| rwan | Rwanda | 16,007,698 | 1.02 | 162,957 | 15,847,698 | 99.0 | 0.12 | 14,151,000 | 88.4 | 1.09 | 154,485 | 310,146 | 155,661 |
| saha | Sahara | 591,409 | 0.92 | 5,463 | 231,409 | 39.1 | 209.37 | 1,100 | 0.2 | 1.82 | 20 | 31 | 11 |
| saih | Saint Helena | 9,564 | 0.84 | 80 | 9,544 | 99.8 | 0.07 | 8,950 | 93.6 | 0.75 | 67 | 207 | 140 |
| saik | Saint Kitts & Nevis | 36,185 | 0.13 | 46 | 36,085 | 99.7 | 0.09 | 33,020 | 91.3 | 0.04 | 13 | 507 | 494 |
| sail | Saint Lucia | 241,611 | 0.60 | 1,448 | 238,611 | 98.8 | 0.04 | 230,400 | 95.4 | 0.59 | 1,357 | 4,801 | 3,444 |
| saip | Saint Pierre & Miquelon | 7,690 | 0.28 | 22 | 7,675 | 99.8 | 0.08 | 7,110 | 92.5 | 0.14 | 10 | 153 | 143 |
| saiv | Saint Vincent | 140,293 | 0.28 | 395 | 137,093 | 97.7 | 0.24 | 110,700 | 78.9 | 0.00 | 0 | 1,655 | 1,655 |
| samo | Samoa | 350,786 | 1.03 | 3,618 | 350,486 | 99.9 | 0.05 | 332,880 | 94.9 | 1.00 | 3,342 | 7,206 | 3,865 |
| sanm | San Marino | 30,032 | -0.30 | -91 | 29,942 | 99.7 | 0.16 | 25,860 | 86.1 | -0.48 | -125 | 526 | 650 |
| saot | Sao Tome & Principe | 297,077 | 1.26 | 3,748 | 296,847 | 99.9 | 0.06 | 279,830 | 94.2 | 1.24 | 3,466 | 6,264 | 2,798 |
| saud | Saudi Arabia | 54,461,025 | 1.25 | 678,379 | 36,461,025 | 66.9 | 10.08 | 3,290,000 | 6.0 | 2.22 | 73,052 | 100,853 | 27,801 |
| sene | Senegal | 23,135,040 | 1.30 | 301,213 | 12,485,040 | 54.0 | 6.54 | 1,655,000 | 7.2 | 1.88 | 31,043 | 45,011 | 13,968 |
| seyc | Seychelles | 114,561 | 0.63 | 720 | 113,981 | 99.5 | 0.04 | 109,330 | 95.4 | 0.61 | 665 | 2,158 | 1,493 |
| sier | Sierra Leone | 10,994,234 | 1.24 | 135,977 | 7,494,234 | 68.2 | 3.36 | 1,720,000 | 15.6 | 1.92 | 32,969 | 52,250 | 19,281 |
| sing | Singapore | 4,015,382 | -0.15 | -5,978 | 3,265,382 | 81.3 | 3.30 | 760,000 | 18.9 | 0.57 | 4,301 | 17,175 | 12,874 |
| slok | Slovakia | 4,836,424 | -0.43 | -21,016 | 4,821,924 | 99.7 | 0.10 | 4,382,500 | 90.6 | -0.34 | -14,857 | 80,638 | 95,495 |
| slov | Slovenia | 1,486,518 | -0.80 | -11,920 | 1,485,048 | 99.9 | 0.05 | 1,409,320 | 94.8 | -0.76 | -10,724 | 23,889 | 34,613 |
| solo | Solomon Islands | 1,129,692 | 1.31 | 14,763 | 1,128,192 | 99.9 | 0.03 | 1,098,800 | 97.3 | 1.33 | 14,609 | 25,872 | 11,263 |
| soma | Somalia | 23,066,119 | 1.42 | 326,761 | 11,380,119 | 49.3 | 88.61 | 127,000 | 0.6 | 0.23 | 288 | 1,368 | 1,080 |
| somi | Somaliland | 8,769,240 | 2.29 | 200,446 | 4,319,240 | 49.3 | 183.19 | 23,450 | 0.3 | 1.87 | 439 | 638 | 199 |
| soua | South Africa | 52,513,528 | 0.53 | 278,210 | 51,163,528 | 97.4 | 0.17 | 43,682,100 | 83.2 | 0.53 | 231,615 | 859,763 | 628,149 |
| souk | South Korea | 51,274,663 | -0.10 | -49,693 | 50,774,663 | 99.0 | 1.19 | 23,200,000 | 45.2 | 0.09 | 20,227 | 405,579 | 385,352 |
| spai | Spain | 30,226,200 | -0.77 | -232,365 | 30,036,200 | 99.4 | 0.11 | 27,073,500 | 89.6 | -0.87 | -236,464 | 425,753 | 662,218 |
| span | Spanish North Africa | 150,000 | 0.28 | 415 | 138,000 | 92.0 | 0.21 | 113,800 | 75.9 | 0.21 | 238 | 1,490 | 1,252 |
| sril | Sri Lanka | 25,922,770 | 0.39 | 99,874 | 19,442,770 | 75.0 | 6.82 | 2,485,000 | 9.6 | 0.44 | 11,010 | 43,836 | 32,827 |
| suda | Sudan | 59,175,868 | 0.99 | 585,513 | 39,005,868 | 65.9 | 2.22 | 12,100,000 | 20.4 | 1.41 | 170,403 | 288,136 | 117,733 |
| suri | Suriname | 588,300 | 0.46 | 2,701 | 531,500 | 90.3 | 0.71 | 310,500 | 52.8 | 0.49 | 1,512 | 5,809 | 4,297 |
| swaz | Swaziland | 2,436,261 | 1.25 | 30,513 | 2,428,261 | 99.7 | 0.10 | 2,211,000 | 90.8 | 1.32 | 29,212 | 47,409 | 18,197 |
| swed | Sweden | 8,661,396 | -0.20 | -16,981 | 8,421,396 | 97.2 | 0.50 | 5,605,000 | 64.7 | -0.29 | -16,362 | 100,166 | 116,528 |
| swit | Switzerland | 6,744,512 | -0.47 | -31,680 | 6,544,512 | 97.0 | 0.15 | 5,690,100 | 84.4 | -0.59 | -33,499 | 93,960 | 127,458 |
| syri | Syria | 34,490,111 | 1.09 | 376,486 | 25,090,111 | 72.7 | 8.82 | 2,556,000 | 7.4 | 0.92 | 23,513 | 47,693 | 24,180 |
| taiw | Taiwan | 27,981,079 | 0.34 | 94,030 | 22,981,079 | 82.1 | 11.42 | 1,850,000 | 6.6 | 0.34 | 6,268 | 35,701 | 29,434 |
| taji | Tajikistan | 11,292,803 | 0.98 | 110,287 | 6,292,803 | 55.7 | 51.44 | 120,000 | 1.1 | -0.16 | -196 | 1,029 | 1,225 |
| tanz | Tanzania | 80,583,921 | 1.33 | 1,071,626 | 72,583,921 | 90.1 | 0.50 | 48,500,000 | 60.2 | 1.61 | 782,879 | 1,231,019 | 448,140 |
| thai | Thailand | 74,187,913 | 0.08 | 59,452 | 51,537,913 | 69.5 | 24.14 | 2,050,000 | 2.8 | 0.60 | 12,265 | 45,003 | 32,739 |
| timo | Timor | 1,387,351 | 0.63 | 8,778 | 1,377,451 | 99.3 | 0.03 | 1,335,800 | 96.3 | 0.68 | 9,051 | 26,243 | 17,192 |
| togo | Togo | 12,103,866 | 1.43 | 173,358 | 10,303,866 | 85.1 | 0.69 | 6,100,000 | 50.4 | 1.55 | 94,712 | 146,074 | 51,362 |
| tong | Tonga | 109,783 | 0.17 | 191 | 109,633 | 99.9 | 0.13 | 96,800 | 88.2 | 0.06 | 58 | 1,182 | 1,124 |
| trin | Trinidad & Tobago | 1,543,088 | 0.13 | 2,021 | 1,463,088 | 94.8 | 0.68 | 871,500 | 56.5 | -0.11 | -966 | 12,629 | 13,595 |
| tuni | Tunisia | 14,983,165 | 0.62 | 92,655 | 9,033,165 | 60.3 | 74.28 | 120,000 | 0.8 | 1.64 | 1,962 | 3,311 | 1,349 |
| turk | Turkey | 100,664,064 | 0.55 | 548,860 | 59,664,064 | 59.3 | 118.33 | 500,000 | 0.5 | 0.42 | 2,112 | 8,537 | 6,425 |
| turm | Turkmenistan | 7,714,890 | 0.82 | 63,443 | 3,464,890 | 44.9 | 37.50 | 90,000 | 1.2 | -0.13 | -118 | 890 | 1,008 |
| turs | Turks & Caicos Is | 44,233 | 1.09 | 480 | 44,113 | 99.7 | 0.13 | 39,070 | 88.3 | 0.98 | 382 | 966 | 584 |
| tuva | Tuvalu | 27,596 | 1.16 | 321 | 27,566 | 99.9 | 0.16 | 23,850 | 86.4 | 1.13 | 270 | 547 | 277 |
| ugan | Uganda | 64,850,498 | 1.52 | 988,122 | 64,585,498 | 99.6 | 0.06 | 60,866,200 | 93.9 | 1.60 | 975,626 | 1,508,814 | 533,188 |
| ukra | Ukraine | 39,301,745 | -0.60 | -235,989 | 38,981,745 | 99.2 | 0.07 | 36,284,000 | 92.3 | -0.39 | -141,236 | 689,668 | 830,904 |
| unia | United Arab Emirates | 3,615,235 | 0.39 | 13,925 | 2,465,235 | 68.2 | 4.42 | 455,000 | 12.6 | 0.62 | 2,814 | 8,775 | 5,961 |
| usa | USA | 349,317,531 | 0.28 | 985,007 | 340,317,531 | 97.4 | 0.26 | 269,522,000 | 77.2 | 0.12 | 332,205 | 5,377,656 | 5,045,452 |
| uuay | Uruguay | 4,362,137 | 0.44 | 19,284 | 4,326,937 | 99.2 | 0.54 | 2,805,850 | 64.3 | 0.43 | 12,085 | 50,638 | 38,552 |
| uzbe | Uzbekistan | 40,564,971 | 0.79 | 318,795 | 23,934,971 | 59.0 | 57.95 | 406,000 | 1.0 | 0.27 | 1,076 | 5,546 | 4,470 |
| vanu | Vanuatu | 427,541 | 1.18 | 5,030 | 425,261 | 99.5 | 0.05 | 405,000 | 94.7 | 1.18 | 4,787 | 9,247 | 4,459 |
| vene | Venezuela | 42,151,686 | 0.77 | 325,605 | 42,026,686 | 99.7 | 0.07 | 39,226,000 | 93.1 | 0.73 | 287,639 | 767,766 | 480,126 |
| viet | Viet Nam | 126,793,428 | 0.64 | 814,512 | 101,293,428 | 79.9 | 5.33 | 16,009,000 | 12.6 | 1.39 | 222,049 | 417,679 | 195,630 |
| virg | Virgin Is of the US | 85,914 | 0.11 | 96 | 85,414 | 99.4 | 0.08 | 78,850 | 91.8 | 0.00 | -1 | 1,178 | 1,179 |
| wall | Wallis & Futuna Is | 20,838 | 0.70 | 146 | 20,823 | 99.9 | 0.04 | 20,080 | 96.4 | 0.64 | 129 | 362 | 233 |
| yeme | Yemen | 58,801,132 | 1.66 | 974,630 | 34,201,132 | 58.2 | 314.22 | 108,500 | 0.2 | 2.13 | 2,315 | 3,155 | 840 |
| yugo | Yugoslavia | 10,547,870 | -0.11 | -11,686 | 10,327,870 | 97.9 | 0.23 | 8,414,000 | 79.8 | 0.27 | 23,040 | 189,133 | 166,092 |
| zamb | Zambia | 21,203,651 | 1.23 | 261,009 | 21,093,651 | 99.5 | 0.11 | 19,087,000 | 90.0 | 1.33 | 254,696 | 435,450 | 180,754 |
| zimb | Zimbabwe | 18,138,923 | 0.74 | 133,897 | 18,018,923 | 99.3 | 0.28 | 14,108,800 | 77.8 | 0.94 | 133,100 | 313,411 | 180,310 |
| | 11 minicountries | 38,681 | 0.93 | 361 | 36,556 | 94.5 | 0.48 | 24,732 | 63.9 | 0.94 | 234 | 624 | 391 |
| | Africa | 1,766,082,480 | 1.24 | 21,871,238 | 1,489,130,790 | 84.3 | 0.65 | 903,205,240 | 51.1 | 1.43 | 12,888,063 | 21,266,795 | 8,378,732 |
| | Antarctica | 15,000 | 1.64 | 245 | 14,600 | 97.3 | 0.19 | 12,300 | 82.0 | 1.74 | 213 | 398 | 185 |
| | Asia | 5,268,450,631 | 0.44 | 23,076,142 | 3,771,831,331 | 71.6 | 5.45 | 584,715,650 | 11.1 | 0.92 | 5,392,833 | 13,231,088 | 7,838,255 |
| | Europe | 627,691,297 | -0.45 | -2,814,829 | 609,982,657 | 97.2 | 0.24 | 492,725,530 | 78.5 | -0.47 | -2,325,490 | 8,687,162 | 11,012,652 |
| | Latin America | 808,894,884 | 0.60 | 4,848,057 | 805,983,034 | 99.6 | 0.10 | 734,436,790 | 90.8 | 0.55 | 4,003,080 | 13,757,269 | 9,754,189 |
| | Northern America | 391,781,440 | 0.30 | 1,171,107 | 381,088,825 | 97.3 | 0.27 | 300,680,630 | 76.7 | 0.14 | 420,985 | 6,051,885 | 5,630,899 |
| | Oceania | 46,179,707 | 0.61 | 282,603 | 45,011,812 | 97.5 | 0.26 | 35,782,200 | 77.5 | 0.45 | 160,055 | 684,449 | 524,394 |
| | **World A** | **285,544,967** | **-0.56** | **-1,597,533** | **132,263,567** | **46.3** | **71.78** | **1,817,200** | **0.6** | **-3.52** | **-64,006** | **-43,628** | **20,378** |
| | **World B** | **6,113,031,553** | **0.61** | **37,010,002** | **4,508,377,063** | **73.8** | **3.97** | **907,121,890** | **14.8** | **1.09** | **9,856,190** | **20,656,339** | **10,800,149** |
| | **World C** | **2,510,518,919** | **0.46** | **11,549,159** | **2,462,402,419** | **98.1** | **0.15** | **2,142,625,252** | **85.3** | **0.44** | **9,429,581** | **41,748,359** | **32,318,779** |
| | **GLOBAL TOTAL** | **8,909,095,439** | **0.52** | **46,417,409** | **7,103,043,049** | **79.7** | **1.33** | **3,051,564,342** | **34.3** | **0.62** | **18,825,172** | **61,964,477** | **43,139,305** |

# Part 13

# MONITORING

Monitoring global Christianity and world evangelization

*What I say to you, I say to everyone: 'Watch!'*
—Mark 13:37, New International Version

*The immemorial experience of mankind, that new knowledge can only be won through breaking a taboo, that all autonomous thinking is accompanied by a consciousness of guilt, has been a fundamental experience of my own life.*
—Paul Tillich, systematic theologian (1886-1977)

Becoming up-to-date, and keeping up-to-date on new Christian information of every kind is essential for any realistic understanding of the global situation. Part 13 describes 70 new areas of knowledge, how this survey's methodology works, what are the right questions to ask, how to monitor new developments, and how to become proficient in this whole subject of keeping abreast of the overwhelming mass of new data available day by day.

An analysis is provided of a monthly and quarterly publication, the *AD 2000 Global Monitor*, begun in 1990 to track the progress of global mission. A consolidated volume of the first 40 issues was published in 1995 as *AD 2000 Global Monitor: keeping track of world evangelization, 1990-1994* (William Carey Library, 1995). Examples from this book are shown here in a number of grey-screened boxes.

# Monitoring global Christianity and world evangelization

## What is monitoring?

Monitoring in our context takes on two complementary meanings. The first meaning is 'to observe, supervise, or keep under review; to measure or test at intervals' (OED). There is a great deal of this kind of monitoring taking place every day all around us. Traffic lights are monitored, stocks and bonds are monitored, seismic activity is monitored, school children are monitored, and hearts, kidneys, and lungs are monitored. In most every case the latest technology and a large amount of time and money are expended. In some instances it is necessary to monitor activities to save time and money. In others it is a matter of life and death. Regardless, monitoring (in this sense of supervising, observing and measuring) appears to be a fundamental human activity.

In world evangelization, observing, supervising, and measuring are necessary to properly track progress and to take appropriate action where it is warranted. Examples of subjects under review in world evangelization are the growth of the church, the extent of evangelization in peoples, cities, and countries, and the status of translation of Scripture. In each of these cases raw data are available but they must be collected, collated, analyzed, supplemented, interpreted, and the like before true monitoring can take place.

The second meaning of the word 'monitor' is equally important in our context. The root word from Latin is *monere* which means 'to advise, warn, or admonish' (OED). Thus a monitor is 'one who admonishes or gives advice or warning to another as to his conduct' (OED). Consequently, the measurements which are made under our first definition are then analyzed and interpreted to warn or advise. This follows a logical pattern: data are collected through observation, measurements are made, and conclusions relevant to action to be taken are made. The monitoring process thus is often a comprehensive attempt at problem solving.

This can be illustrated by the UN publication *World population monitoring 1989: special report: the population situation in the least developed countries* (New York: United Nations, 1990). Though many statistics describing the status of least developed countries are presented here the stated purpose of the report is 'to review the population concerns of those countries as they strive to develop, though with only the most severely limited social and economic resources at their disposal' (p. 5). The report accomplishes the first aspect of monitoring by observation, data gathering, and measuring. But it goes a step further by using the data to admonish, advise, and warn. The dual aspects of monitoring provide an effective tool for planners and strategists to deal with national and international problems.

In world evangelization this aspect of monitoring is particularly important. What is observed and measured concerning the extent of evangelization, for example, often contains implicit warnings about what must be done. Mission agencies and churches need to be advised and admonished to take action appropriate to various situations in world evangelization.

## A brief history of monitoring world evangelization

Monitoring world evangelization had its genesis in *The Acts of the Apostles* (AD 66). This led to a long chain of world surveys of which the most illustrious were Cosmos Indicopleustes' *Topographia Christiana* in 12 volumes (AD 535), and *The travels of Marco Polo* (AD 1477). The first survey to report world statistics was William Carey's *An enquiry into the obligations of Christians to use means for the conversion of the heathens* (1792). Carey built a foundation for monitoring by collecting data from many sources and bringing it together into a single global survey. Carey used observation and measurements to provide a comprehensive picture of the world in light of the availability of the

gospel. This task was so difficult in the 1790s that no further updates were attempted. Thus he was able to outline the situation just once.

Over the next one hundred years there were various attempts to update Carey's work, primarily in the new genre of Cyclopedias, single-volume sources of data and information which were precursors of the modern annual almanacs. However, the data in these volumes was sketchy and inconsistent from volume to volume.

In the late nineteenth and early twentieth centuries a series of surveys on various aspects of world evangelization were published. E. Bliss' *Encyclopedia of missions* (1891) offered an A-Z approach on the missionary enterprise, including many statistics in text and tables. James Dennis offered equally comprehensive information in his *Centennial volume* (1900). And John R. Mott provided a massive amount of different types of survey material, guided by an interpretative missiological overview, in his classic *The evangelization of the world in this generation* (1900). These were then updated in a series of atlases and statistical volumes: *Statistical atlas of Christian missions* (1910), *World atlas of Christian missions* (1911), *Atlas hierarchicus* (1913), *World statistics of Christian missions* (1916) and *International missionary atlas* (1925). Each of these took the approach of listing agencies (either mainly Catholic or mainly Protestant) and their workers but with no reference to countries, peoples, or languages where no Christians were working. In essence they only monitored certain Christian efforts, not the global status of world evangelization.

The most successful monthly monitor in this period was the *Missionary review of the world* published monthly from 1877 until 1939. Royal Wilder founded it and Arthur T. Pierson carried on the tradition from 1887 until his death in 1911. This review published 80 pages a month commenting not only on existing Christian efforts but on countries and peoples that were not yet targeted. Nonetheless it would have been extremely difficult to piece together a complete global survey from these monthly reports. Instead the missionary review provided a constant source of observations, measurements, warnings, advice, and admonitions on world evangelization.

## World Dominion series

In the early 1920s S.J.W. Clark, Roland Allen, and Thomas Cochrane formed the Survey Application Trust (SAT) in England with the express purpose of surveying and mapping out some of the least evangelized areas of the world. Many of these were published by the World Dominion Press under the able leadership of Alexander McLeish. Top missionaries like Mildred Cable of the China Inland Mission wrote definitive works on unoccupied fields such as her *The challenge of Central Asia* (1938).

## World Christian handbook/encyclopedia

In 1948 the first in a series of *World Christian handbooks* was published. This handbook surveyed the Christian situation at a time when Christian unity was becoming a key issue in the newly-emerging global Christian community. It did not attempt to deal with the unevangelized world. In 1982 the handbook series was continued in a greatly enlarged and more comprehensive format, and published with the title *World Christian encyclopedia*.

## The AD 2000 Series

Using the *World Christian encyclopedia* as a foundation, ongoing research on world evangelization was published in a series of volumes by New Hope Press from 1985 to 1990 entitled 'Global Evangelization Movement: The AD 2000 Series'.

## AD 2000 Global Monitor

By November 1990, rapid developments in the analy-

sis of missions data, as exemplified by the computerized formulae of the World Evangelization Database, warranted a monthly update entitled *AD 2000 Global Monitor*. Most missionary publications did not qualify as 'monitors' because they did not canvas a broad enough range of sources in compiling a comprehensive analysis.

## An ombudsman's role

As we pointed out in the *Monitor* No. 9 (July 1991), page 2, there was a need for ombudsmen in the realm of world evangelization. An ombudsman would scan new stories and missions reports, looking for internal consistency and sense. The *Monitor* itself attempted to serve in this role in relation to the many conflicting reports on world evangelization published in various periodicals and books.

## NEW MONITORING OF WORLD EVANGELIZATION

The *AD 2000 Global Monitor* was begun in 1990 as a monthly trends newsletter, and from 1994 as a quarterly one, on the subject of world evangelization. In January 1995 it was renamed *AD 2025 Global Monitor* to reflect a more realistic event horizon. As such it kept track of, followed, studied, analyzed, and described developments in this subject, and then notified the reader, advised, warned, and published conclusions.

Each issue restricted itself to 4 pages only. Each page dealt with one fixed approach or aspect of monitoring—scanning, research, graphic representation, or documentation and technology.

The contents of this newsletter are therefore described below under these 4 subject areas: new scanning, new research, new global diagrams, and new technology & documentation. Each of these is then divided into some 3 or 4 fixed major subjects, shown below in boldface type, each surrounded by a dozen or more minor subjects, shown listed below in italic type. The whole material can thus be catalogued and analyzed under 14 major subjects and under some 70 subjects in total. These now will be numbered and described in order, with brief descriptions or comments on each.

Note in particular that we illustrate this analysis with a number of examples taken from specific issues of the *Monitor*. These examples are all shown here in screened and dated gray boxes.

## NEW SCANNING

### 1. New Editorial.

From time to time, and not necessarily in every issue, it was necessary to begin with an editorial paragraph emphasizing the purpose of the newsletter and any new directions it might be moving in with regard to the overall health and progress of the Christian world mission.

Example from *Monitor* July 1991:1

*A new menace in missions—innumeracy*
Innumeracy is the inability to understand numbers, to see the importance of numbers, and to handle numbers in everyday life. Basically it's an inability to deal comfortably with the fundamental notions of numbers and chance—which is a malady that often strikes otherwise knowledgeable people. Innumerate people characteristically have a strong tendency to personalize—to be misled by their own experiences, or by the media's focus on individuals and drama.

*Casinos and world evangelization*
We start with a quotation from a very important re-

cent book dealing with innumeracy. 'There is a strong tendency to filter out the bad and the failed and to focus on the good and the successful. Casinos encourage this tendency by making sure that every quarter that is won in a slot machine causes lights to blink and makes its own little tinkle in the metal tray. Seeing all the lights and hearing all the tinkles, it is not hard to get the impression that everyone is winning. Losses or failures are silent' (*Innumeracy: mathematical illiteracy and its consequences*, John Allen Paulos, 1988). Similarly, mission agencies and churches are not anxious to report failures or even mundane results. Instead, the fantastic and positive are highlighted, giving the impression that things are much better than they actually are.

A parallel situation is that international news is usually worse than national news which is worse than state news which is worse than local news. At the international level there is such a huge pool of events that abnormal or catastrophic events are usually highlighted.

If unusual or catastrophic events are highlighted in mission, the overall picture is obscured and distorted. What overall progress is being made is seldom apparent from selective reporting of either spectacular success or spectacular failure.

*Mathematical illiterates are preventing missiological analysis*
How do innumerates frustrate missionary outreach? Consider the global missions situation. Every year, the world's 23,500 denominations and 4,000 Great Commission mission agencies instruct some 10 million Christian leaders—pastors, clergy, bishops, catechists, evangelists, lay officers—to fill out and return detailed statistical questionnaires. This has become the world's biggest single annual enumeration, with enormous potential for creating new outreach. Enter innumerate bureaucrats. We've investigated what happens to the accumulated mountains of paper after they arrive at all these headquarters. The short answer is—nothing. Apart from publishing simple totals, little or no statistical analysis of any kind is done with these statistics. The *AD 2000 Global Monitor* exists to encourage Christians to undertake such analysis and to tap this unique goldmine of annual data.

## 2. New Commentary.
The contents of a number of issues revolved around a certain single subject or theme, usually with surprising or unexpected conclusions. Commentary then focused on these conclusions and made comments and suggestions arising therefrom.

Example from *Monitor* August 1992:1

*Research is more than data collection*
For many the challenge of understanding and monitoring the numbers of reached and unreached peoples is simply a matter of amassing large amounts of data in a central location. Here the emphasis is on the collection tools, particularly those on the field. Since missionaries and nationals are right on the scene, they are looked to for the primary source of information. Once data has been secured from these sources it is brought together nationally and then ported to an international collection center. There it sits in a central computer database for anyone who wants to see it. That, for many, is the end of the process of monitoring.

But data collection is only the beginning of the research process. Once data has been collected it must be analyzed and interpreted. Most of the time it is necessary not only to go back to the original source but to check the data with other sources. Only then can one be somewhat sure of its accuracy. Much has to be considered simply wrong or misleading. After this, data has to be integrated into larger scenarios that provide context and meaning. For this to happen, the person sitting at the end of the data collection process must be a committed researcher, not merely an administrator or a computer whiz (who are not confident monkeying with figures). When one looks at the unreached peoples movement both presently and historically it is surprising that this type of person is difficult to find. Administrators, mobilizers, writers, preachers, computer experts, and others abound but researchers and analysts are in short supply. This is certainly a major cause of the Christ-

ian world's present inability to make sense of both numbers and monitoring in the unreached peoples sphere.

## 3. New Sources.
This brings us to the major philosophy steering the *Monitor*. If one wishes to track and monitor world evangelization it must be based on the deliberate scanning of a large variety of sources. These include periodicals dealing with subjects touching on major subjects, serials, new books, news services, telephone contacts, fax contacts, notes and notices, databases, e-mail, and mail correspondence. These were deliberately invoked and organized to deliver a large and regular supply of new information each month. Thus on average the editors scanned a hundred periodicals regularly (usually monthly); at times the total number scanned rose to 300. Throughout these sources, what we were looking for were new items of information, new reports, new subjects, new developments, new illustrations, new concepts, new issues, and anything else that might throw light on our overall subject.

## 4. New Periodicals.
The major ongoing role in scanning that is being played by periodicals (journals, magazines, newspapers, newsletters, other serials) is noted frequently in the *Monitor* by the source notation in parentheses at the close of any item involving quotation.

Example from *Monitor* October 1991:4

*Scanning the world month by month*
The relentless pursuit of world evangelization has this month led us to scan some 50 current journals. Most include urban items. To illustrate where our sources come from, we list 24 of them here.
*Asiaweek*, Vol. 17, No. 22, May 31, 1991.
*Booklist*, Vol. 87, Nos. 18, 19, 20, May 15, June 1, 15, 1991.
*Bridging peoples*, Vol. 10, No. 3, July 1991.
*Charisma*, Vol. 16, No. 12, July 1991.
*Choice*, Vol. 28, No. 10, June 1991.
*Context*, Vol. 23, No. 9, May 1, 1991.
*EP News Service*, Vol. 40, Nos. 22, 25, May 31, June 21, 1991.
*Ecumenical Press Service*, June 11-20, 21-30, 1991.
*Evangelical missions quarterly*, Vol. 27, No. 3, July 1991.
*The futurist*, Vol. 25, No. 4, July/August 1991.
*India church growth quarterly*, Vol. 12, No. 4, Oct-Dec 1990.
*International Fides Service*, Nos. 3779, 3780, June 26, July 3, 1991.
*John Naisbitt's trend letter*, Vol. 10, No. 12, June 6, 1991.
*Library journal*, Vol. 116, Nos. 9, 10, May 15, June 1, 1991.
*Macworld*, Vol. 8, No. 8, August 1991
*New York Times book review*, June 16, 23, 30, July 7, 14, 1991.
*PPRC emerging trends*, Vol. 13, No. 5, May 1991.
*Scientific American*, Vol. 265, No. 1, July 1991.
*Science news*, Vol. 139:24, Vol. 140:1, June 15, July 6, 1991.
*Technology review*, Vol. 94, No. 5, July 1991.
*Utne reader*, No. 46, July/August 1991.
*World pulse*, Vol. 26, No. 9, May 10, 1991.
*World watch*, Vol. 4, No. 4, July/August 1991.

## 5. New Events.
This third regular major subject in the *Monitor* covers the first main category of new information we need—news items about anything new that's happened relevant to world evangelization. The next 11 subject categories in this listing describe what we searched for. Major concrete advances in scanning and monitoring grow out of this systematic reading of events and the separating out of the significant from the vast mass of news items reported daily, weekly, and monthly in the media.

## 6. New Evangelism.
New items directly reporting on any variety of evangelistic endeavor are a first priority in monitoring. Each item was then reported in the *Monitor*, with identification of agency, activity, title, place, date, duration, attendees, other statistics, sponsors, results. A sentence of evaluation or comment was usually necessary too.

Example from *Monitor* May/June 1996:4

*Africans encounter Christ*
Over 8 million Africans have seen the English language gospel film 'Sabina's Encounter', particularly effective among Muslims. Cinema vans of the Evangelical Lutheran Church of Tanzania will be used to show it to 50 million more in Swahili. The International Christian Media Commission says 'Language dubbing is an effective way to use expensive Christian films to reach Africans for Christ' (*Pulse*, 3/22/96). This is a good example of applying the success of other programs (e.g. the 'Jesus' Film) to new, innovative projects.

## 7. New Mission.
Major new events relating to world mission are scanned and condensed into short paragraphs, with the same concrete descriptors—agency, activity, title, place, date, duration, attendees, other statistics, results.

Example from *Monitor* July-September 1994:1

*Russia's foreign missions zeal reawakens*
In the year 1900, Russians made up the world's largest single ethnolinguistic people, and fielded a vast worldwide network of Christian foreign missions. All that was destroyed under Communism. But now since 1992, some 30 million former Russian atheists have converted to Christ, and zeal for foreign missions is reawakening. Hong Kong pastor Dennis Balcombe reports that many churches in Russia are taking up a serious interest in mission to China. Money is being given for Bibles. Conferences are being held to train Russian Christians in China ministry methods (*NNI*).

This is exactly the type of ministry that can turn a stagnant World A situation into an opportunity. When believers catch a vision for those without the gospel they participate in the Great Commission life of the church.

## 8. New Campaigns.
Formally-organized weekend/one-week/two-week/one-month evangelistic campaigns are especially significant.

Example from *Monitor* January/February 1997:3

*High-energy devotion to Bibles for China*
The Global Strategy Mission Association (La., 504-536-3000) has announced a high-energy motto for its plan to place Bibles in China: 'Every church, everyone, every week'. It refers to their goal of having every member of every church in their network give at least $1.00 towards the printing and placement of Chinese Bibles on a weekly basis. Each Bible regularly costs $3.50, but due to a program of matching funds through partner organizations, the actual cost of GSMA donors is just $1.17. This program shows the kind of high-energy commitment to World A that is possible with a measurable, achievable goal. It could easily be reproduced in any church in the United States.

## 9. New Conferences.
Details of all global, continental, regional, national, confessional, or denominational conferences on our subject matter were regularly scanned and reported. We observed that all such conferences contain sweeping promises, glowing goals, and most conclude with a stirring communique or press release determined to reach the whole world—but one or 2 years later, most have forgotten the promises. The entire Christian world seems to be event-oriented: as soon as such a conference concludes, organizers begin to plan for its successor, or for the next.

Example from *Monitor* August 1993:1

*Major conference on 'Evangelizing mission'*
The theme of the Second National Conference of the Pontifical Mission Societies held from March 29-April 2, 1993 at Ashirbhavan, Kochi in Kerala, India, was the 'Evangelizing Mission of the Church.' Papers were given on various aspects of the central theme of evangelization, studied in the light of *Redemptoris Missio*, John Paul II's mission encyclical. There were talks on the need to involve the laity in missionary

activity, on basic Christian communities, and the importance of adequate training for missions for seminarians, priests, and members of the various orders (*International Fides service*, May 8, 1993:NE150).

## 10. New Scriptures.

Every year some 40 new languages receive Scripture translations for the first time. Such events are of major significance for the societies involved.

Example from *Monitor* December 1992:1

*A World-A poet's saga with Koran and New Testament*
The government of Kirghizia has announced a five-year plan to replace Russian with Kirghiz as the official language. 53% of the country's 4.7 million citizens are ethnic Kirghiz. Recently, a well-known Kirghiz poet, Ernest Tursunov, published his own translation of the Koran in Kirghiz. However, Tursunov could not read Classical Arabic and so did the translation from a Russian edition of the Koran. A leader of the Muslim community has now said Tursunov distorted the sacred text by using poor grammar and syntax, and by giving an excessively free interpretation of the Koran. Others have said he was wrong to even translate it since it is only considered inspired in the original Arabic text. Local Christians also complained that Tursunov next set out to translate the New Testament before learning of a secret 15-year project begun by the Institute for Bible Translation (Stockholm, Sweden) and now completed. As he began work on the New Testament he commented that the contrast between the Koran and the New Testament was like darkness and light. This infuriated local Muslims who issued death threats (later withdrawn) against the well-meaning poet (*News network international*, August 21, 1992:6-8).

## 11. New Distribution.

Like a monster jigsaw puzzle, each piece of the thousands of items describing circulation of the Scriptures across the world is being carefully assembled. Results include (a) a global overview of how many scriptures are in fact distributed each year, (b) the history of annual distribution over the past century, (c) assessment of the current deployment/placement/ density of scriptures today in every country, city, and people, (d) the overall influence of these scriptures over the years, and (e) the results in terms of church plantings and church growth in every population on Earth.

Example from *Monitor* May 1991:1

*Cuba opens to the Bible*
The United Bible Societies has obtained the Cuban government's permission to provide 51,600 Bibles, 20,000 New Testaments, 30,000 Bible portions, and one million Bible selections. This and other recent evangelistic activity in Cuba is rapidly lifting the country from the category World B into World C (*Ecumenical Press Service*, 91.03.20).

## 12. New Inventions.

Current science and technology are resulting in extraordinary fertility of ideas leading to numerous new inventions every year. A majority of these have obvious and immediate application to the Christian world mission. Example: the fax revolution.

Example from *Monitor* Nov/Dec 1996:8

*YWAM uses video technology to forge 'electronic classroom'*
Project Genesis (Global Electronic Networking Educating, Serving and Informing Students) is using a two-way video link to create an 'electronic classroom' connecting missionary students in Budapest, Hungary and Lausanne, Switzerland. The groups will share instructors who will speak from and interact with students at both sites. The system will be used globally to train and equip YWAM workers in remote areas who could not otherwise receive the training they need. YWAM is looking forward to 1,000 University of the Nations locations, but until now this ambitious goal has been hampered by the logistical difficulties in dealing with even the current 200 sites. With the video link, instructors no longer have to travel to global locations, thus eliminating both time and expense.

## 13. New Initiatives.

One immediate result is that churches, missions, and individual Christians are continually setting out new proposals and new initiatives.

Example from *Monitor* February 1993:2

*The CoMission: a large-scale cooperative venture*
At least 56 different Christian organizations are joining together in a large-scale cooperative mission project targeting the former states of the Soviet Union and Eastern Europe. The CoMission strategy involves organizing video Bible studies in each of the 120,000 local public schools of the former Soviet Union, using one-year volunteer workers from the U.S.A. These Bibles studies will be formed from students whose interest is aroused through a new school curriculum entitled, 'Christian ethics and morality: a foundation for society' and from showings of the 'Jesus' film. The Bible studies may last for up to three years. It is hoped that thousands of new Evangelical churches will be formed.

## 14. New Ministries.

Before long these new initiatives crystallize out as new organized ministries, complete with personnel, premises, plants, and programs.

Example from *Monitor* October 1992:2

*Sending missionaries directly from local churches on the rise*
There is a difference between what local churches might accomplish in direct sending of missionaries and a rationale fro doing this. Advocates of local-church sending go too far in taking an adversarial approach to the work of mission agencies. I think he could have effectively backed up the opportunity presented to this church without pitting it against the work of existing agencies.

Direct sending of missionaries from local churches is a new trend that will not go away. Our attitude toward these churches and their efforts should be one of openness and acceptance. There is no reason to oppose them since they are going to attempt to send missionaries regardless. Many people opposed short-term missions when it was first attempted. We can't spend time discussing the philosophical issue of which is better, more effective, more biblical, etc. Our approach should be pragmatic—let's wait and see what the fruit of such ventures is.

One interesting aspect of this trend is that in many cases churches bypass agencies because they want to work in fields beyond existing work. This should be a red flag for the agencies. If they do not get interested in frontier missions they may find the churches bypassing them. This is the ultimate irony when a local church has to take the initiative in frontier mission because their own agencies commissioned to reach the world have become bogged down and trapped into working primarily among reached peoples.

## 15. New Methods.

Again, the plethora of new inventions and ministries leads to quite new methods being evolved.

Example from *Monitor* September/October 1996:4

*Reconciliation march making progress*
Lynn Green, head of YWAM in Harpenden, England and one of the initiators of the 'Reconciliation Walk' following the route of the Crusades, reports that the march is making good progress. 'Our message is well received wherever we go. An imam who received the team in his mosque in Cologne had promised to send the message to 350 associated mosques. When we again visited him, he told us that he had sent it to 600 others. One YWAM member was in a park in Austria, where between 3,000 and 4,000 Moslems were meeting. She heard a speaker saying 'Christians visited our mosque in Cologne to ask for forgiveness for the Crusades. The time has come for us to also admit and ask forgiveness for our historical mistakes.'' (DAWN *FridayFax*).

## 16. New Martyrs.

Since 'Evangelism is the most dangerous business' (Walter Hollenweger), the task of world evangelization has always resulted in a steady stream of Christian martyrs and martyrdom situations. In the 1990s martyrdoms are occurring at an average rate of 500 every day. Most remain unknown and undocumented to the outside world for months or even years. Monitoring these tragic but brilliant flashes of faith has become easier with the invention of e-mail and fax.

Example from *Monitor* May/June 1996:2

*Rwandan Christian martyrs: tens of thousands*
In one of the most horrible eruptions of violence in our century, 500,000 Rwandans were killed from April to June of 1994. Most of the murderers were Hutu militia, and almost all of the victims were Tutsi civilians. A large number of those killed can be counted as Christian martyrs. This has been confirmed by an extensive, carefully-researched report, 'Rwanda: death, despair and defiance,' released by the London-based human rights group, African Rights. 'More Rwandans died in Catholic and Protestant church and parish buildings than anywhere else during the killing frenzy.' This was not merely because all kinds of people fled to church properties. Priests, pastors, nuns, lay church staff, and seminarians were special targets. The killers deliberately desecrated church buildings, another sign of their severe anti-Christian hostility. As the report stated, 'Many of Rwanda's finest priests and nuns died...[The killers attacked] the moral and spiritual fabric of the community. The aim was annihilation.' The report praised the moral courage of many priests, pastors, and nuns who stood against the genocide. Some Christian leaders hid the hunted, cared for the wounded, fed the hungry, and confronted the authorities. Others did not. The report exposes church leaders who could have played a stronger role in stopping the killing, but remained silent. And at the worst of it, some clerics and nuns actively participated in the killing of Tutsis (*Christian century*, 8 November 1995:1041-1042).

## 17. New World A Data.

Perhaps the major achievements of this scanning were to find completely new and unexpected data on World A peoples, languages, and countries. As these data emerged and were amassed they enabled us to appreciate the magnitude of World A as a hitherto unrecognized phenomenon.

Example from *Monitor* Nov/Dec 1996:5

*Uighurs of China*
The Uighur have an organized and violent separatist movement. One organization, based in Kazakhstan, is called the United National Revolutionary Front (and may serve as the umbrella organization for several groups). Another group is called the Movement for the Freedom of Uygurstan. Small clashes and raids have resulted in several deaths, both of Uighurs and of Chinese government soldiers. The government, as might be expected, is cracking down with speed, strength and vigor (*CNCR*, 6/14/96, 7/26/96).

## 18. New Evangelization.

All the data and information in the *Monitor* each month were then examined in order to obtain an idea of progress. To achieve this, ways of forming an index were needed.

Example from *Monitor* August 1993:1

*Extensive evangelization in India*
Over the past few years Samuel Video-Production, founded by Sheila Samuel and her colleagues in India, has been producing fifteen-minute documentaries, musical films and dramas that have shown on Indian national television (Doordarshan) on Christian holy days. The first production was a Christmas special that highlighted John 3:16. In 1991 they produced 'The Cross and the Victory' for Good Friday and Easter. The broadcasting of 'The Birthday of Jesus Christ' on Christmas 1992 was very successful (ICMC *Catalyst*, vol. 7, no. 1:14). Tens of millions, possibly hundreds of millions of Indians have been evangelized through these broadcasts—they have heard (and seen) the gospel and had an adequate opportunity to respond to it.

## 19. New Index.

A precise monthly index of progress was computed

as follows. Each month's *Monitor* was divided into distinct subjects described or analyzed therein. Each was characterized as indicating progress in world evangelization, or decline or failure. The index was then computed as the percentage of all subjects which indicated progress. This is the fourth major subject regularly presented each month in the *Monitor*.

Example from *Monitor* August 1993:1

*A monthly index of progress in world evangelization*
This index monitors progress by measuring the developments, both positive and negative, reported on these 4 pages monthly.

| **GLOBAL MONITOR INDEX**   Month: August 1993 | | |
|---|---|---|
| An index of rate of progress in world evangelization | | |
| PROGRESS | | |
| 1. Developments as reported in this issue:  positive | | UP 55% |
| negative | | DOWN 45% |
| 2. Development trend this month | | UP 10% |
| 3. Global growth of E this month (% of world) | | +0.05% |

## NEW RESEARCH

### 20. New Statistics.
This fifth major subject may be seen as the primary new discovery of the *Monitor*. Two conclusions emerge. Firstly, (1) the vast annual output of new statistics about the Christian world and its secular and religious contexts are a veritable goldmine of new information and data unparalleled in the long history of human enumeration. But secondly, (2) no one is yet analyzing these with any sophistication except for occasional simple totalings. The 10 million or so statistical questionnaires returned to church and mission headquarters every year are selectively read for good quotes, illustrations, and sermon material, before being moved permanently to the archives, there to remain out of reach of researchers until the 20- or 50- or even 100-year rules eventually permit.

### 21. New Censuses.
Governments take major population censuses around the end of every decade. They then take 3 to 5 years before the complete data are published. Half of all the nations in the world still include the religion question ('What is your religion?'). These data every 10 years enable growth rates to be calculated.

Example from *Monitor* April/June 1994:2

*Census enumerates religion in Canada*
From the 1991 Canadian census: 82% Christians (47% Catholics, 35% Protestants), 3.7% other religious affiliation, 13% no religious affiliation, 1.3% atheists or agnostics.

### 22. New Densities.
In reporting new statistics we attempted to put them in context by computing their per capita values. The 1993 distribution total of 1.4 billion scriptures with 6 billion pages is difficult to visualize or comprehend. Turn it into a 'density'—1.1 pages per capita (per inhabitant)—and it becomes easier to evaluate its significance.

Example from *Monitor* December 1992:2

*Lawyers proliferate globally*
The number of lawyers in the world has doubled since 1960 to more than 2 million. Though the number tripled in the U.S.A. in the same period to more than 780,000, the U.S.A. does not have the highest number per capita. That dubious honor goes to Pakistan with 46,000 lawyers or 508.4 per 100,000 population. Singapore's 990 lawyers give it the second highest rate at 396 per 100,000 population. The U.S. is third at 312 per 100,000 population. Though India has 247,373 lawyers it ranks fairly low at only 34.4 per 100,000. The legal industry in the U.S.A. alone has risen to over $100 billion last year (*The economist*, July 18, 1992:3-4).

### 23. New Coverage.
Nowadays it is possible to measure almost any clearly-defined feature, attribute, or activity. The Monitor attempted such coverage of items never previously enumerated.

Example from *Monitor* January 1993:2

*A billion images of Christ*
In 1940 artist Warner Sallman (1892-1968) painted the *Head of Christ*. It has become one of the most endearing images of Jesus in both American and global Christianity. 'Perhaps this is because Sallman's version of Christ—an image found in other popular Sallman works such as the ones featuring Christ guiding the young helmsman, Christ knocking at heart's door, and Christ the good shepherd—has appeared in so many different media of devotional life: Bibles, Sunday-school literature, calendars, posters, church bulletins, clocks lamps, wallet-sized photos, pins and stickers.' Indeed, Sallman's *Head of Christ* has been reproduced over 500 million times. If Sallman's other images are included his total reaches one billion. What is the influence of such images on the massive audience familiar with them? (*The Christian century*, October 7, 1992:868-870). Sallman is an example of what the *Monitor* means by a 'Great Commission Christian'. And as a first approximation, his one billion can be said to have given the world one billion 'offers' or disciple-opportunities'. In practice, of course, untold numbers of individual items among his reproductions will have each been seen by tens, hundreds, or even thousands of different persons.

### 24. New Trends.
This sixth major monthly subject looks for trends in the situation, either short-term or long-term. It draws attention to new trends at the first moment they emerge and reveal themselves.

Example from *Monitor* July/August 1996:4

*Regional conflicts and human suffering*
A new study reveals 42 million people worldwide are threatened by disease and starvation due to regional conflicts. 'Global Humanitarian Emergencies 1996' catalogs more than 20 emergencies caused by countries' internal conflicts or repressive government policies. Countries topping the list are Afghanistan, Sudan, Bosnia, Ethiopia, Angola, Rwanda, Sierra Leone, Liberia, Iraq, Haiti, Eritrea, Somalia, and Tajikistan. These countries need international aid to combat disease and starvation. At the same time, their citizens become refugees, provoking widespread hunger, stress on resources, environmental deterioration, and economic, social, and political collapse. For a copy of this important report contact the U.S. Mission to the United Nations at (212)415-4275 (*Population today*, May 1996:8).

### 25. New Critiques.
Discovery of a new trend leads immediately to the need for evaluation. Is this trend welcome or unwelcome, good or bad? Will it increase World A's prospects of hearing the gospel, or reduce them? A critique should be an objective, fairminded analysis of the situation.

Example from *Monitor* March/April 1996:4

*Population growth and extinction of species*
Population growth is a cause of worldwide biodiversity loss according to the Global Biodiversity Assessment, a report prepared by 1,500 experts and published by UNEP (United Nations Environment Programme). Accelerating demands on resources, economic development, and overconsumption are some of the factors behind a threefold increase in extinctions since 1810 (shortly before the world reached 1 billion in population), compared to the period 1600 to 1810.
    According to the report, biodiversity loss jeopardizes supplies of food, wood, medicine, and energy, as well as decimating the ecology (reported in Population today, Feb 1996:8). This trend should be disturbing to Christians, and particularly to World A advocates, because most of the least-evangelized world stands to lose their few remaining resources as a result.

### 26. New Criticism.
Sometimes our brief critiques indicated that some part of the worldwide church appeared to have erred or to be seriously in error. Inasmuch as we Christians have agreed to live under the command of the Great Commission, any failures need to be brought to people's notice. Naturally this is not a pleasant role for anyone involved; but no mission monitor need be afraid of articulating such criticism.

Example from *Monitor* July 1992:1

*The frontiers of new movements*
When a relatively new charismatic movement like the Vineyard (founded 1978, now led by North American pastor John Wimber) talks about missions they often start from scratch when it comes to strategy. The Vineyard recently acquired 190 Brazilian churches started by a Mennonite missionary that sought a charismatic covering, saying 'We're getting the message. God is calling us to Latin America in a big way.' This comes at a time when a significant part of the world ('World A') has never heard the gospel even once. Though the Vineyard and hundreds of other similar movements have the right to minister anywhere they please, this type of strategy consistently results in an oversaturation of Christian resources in the most heavily-evangelized places in the world (*National & international religion report*, Nov 4, 1991:4).

### 27. New Global Plans.
A seventh major subject concerns the continual formulation and announcement of new global plans for the world's population, usually highlighting the year AD 2000. Any new Christian plans were described in this section. Also covered were major secular AD 2000 plans. A notorious one was the World Health Organization's 'Promise to Children', that by the millennial year all childhood killer diseases would be eradicated. The majority of these rash promises are most unlikely to be fulfilled. For Christians, such broken promises are cruel, unethical, and unacceptable.

Example from *Monitor* March/April 1996:4

*Global plan slogans and mottos*
The history of global plans to evangelize the world was presented in Barrett and Reapsome's *Seven hundred plans to evangelize the world: the rise of a global evangelization movement* (New Hope, 1988). Our statistical table in the January 1996 issue of the *International bulletin of missionary research*, page 25, shows that by mid-1996 the number of global plans is expected to reach 1,190 (and on to 3,000 by AD 2025!). Many of these plans have made use of succinct slogans packed full of meaning. Below is a selection of some of the more prominent ones:

| | |
|---|---|
| 1806 | We Can if We Will |
| 1880 | The Evangelization of the World in This Generation |
| 1889 | To Every Creature |
| 1889 | Make Jesus King |
| 1910 | The Whole Church taking the Whole Gospel to the Whole World |
| 1933 | Evangelize to a Finish to Bring Back the King |
| 1959 | Two Thousand Tongues to Go |
| 1964 | Each One Teach and Win One |
| 1974 | Let the Earth Hear His Voice |
| 1980 | A Church for Every People by the Year 2000 |

The one troubling feature of all these slogans is that they all contained a solemn and sacred promise to the world's population at that time, but that the promises were all broken for the vast majority alive then. The promise was: 'to bring to you during your lifetime the life-giving Good News about Jesus Christ and His salvation, which we believe is essential to your eternal welfare.'
    With each slogan, enthusiasm subsided within 10 years, the plan fizzled out within 20, and the promise became completely forgotten within 30 as that generation died off, unsaved and unevangelized. No Christian leader of those plans has ever been on record as apologizing or even acknowledging that the solemn promise was broken.

## 28. New Case Studies.
Where possible these mini-analyses would be as complete as possible in a few sentences, describing the new trend or plan or concept in just enough detail to show its significance for world evangelization.

Example from *Monitor* November 1992:2

*An informal global plan to worship and praise coalesces*
In 1988, 55,000 Christians marched in London, in a procession of visible praise and worship, displaying unity and solidarity. This was the March for Jesus to the Heart of the nation. Since 1988 a March for Jesus movement has spread to many other countries. On May 23, 1992, 550,000 marchers were involved in 26 countries with the largest march in Berlin (70,000). Larger global events are scheduled for June 12, 1993 (with 1 million marchers in 1,500 cities expected) and June 25, 1994 (in conjunction with the AD 2000 Movement's Day of Prayer). The strategy is outlined in founder Graham Kendrick's new book *Public praise: celebrating Jesus on the streets of the world* (Creation House, 1992, 194 pp., $6.99) where the philosophical and biblical basis for the marches is expounded as well as practical tips on how to organize a march. Some view the marches from local perspective, but the focus is global, including *all* peoples—Worlds A, B, and C.

## 29. New Diagrammatics.
The eighth major subject leads into our monthly visual product, always on page 3. So beforehand, in a few paragraphs on page 2 a new global diagram would be introduced, examined, and its significance briefly explained.

Example from *Monitor* April 1993:2

*Comments on Global Diagram 58* (in *WCT*=GD 55)
In recent times many philosophers and social scientists have predicted the imminent collapse and disappearance of religion on the world scene. In social scientist Burnham Beckwith's *The next 500 years* (1967), the fourth major trend was 'The decline of religion and superstition'. Even today many professional futurists still anticipate this inevitable decline, echoing the slogan 'Religion: it's hard to kill' (Coates and Jarratt, *What futurists believe*, 1989).

What nobody anticipated, as we now know, was the total collapse of Marxism as an ideology in the period 1960-1990. This has been followed by the sudden disappearance of atheistic Communism from 1991 onwards. The resulting surge in religion—mainly in Christianity and Islam—has staggered everyone. As one example, from 1991-1992, 90% of all Russians sat through the 125-minute 'Jesus' Film (based on Luke's Gospel) for the first time. Religion has returned with a vengeance—it's just too hard to kill!

As one result, it is now much easier to draw up sensible future scenarios for Christianity and religion. This is done in the table and graph opposite. Perhaps the most astounding single figure is that Christians—who have trebled in numbers since 1900—are likely again to at least double to 4 billion within 100 years. Has anyone come to terms with the enormous implications of this 300-year numerical explosion? Many churches and agencies today see only the apparent successes revealed in the vast annual increases in their own constituencies. Scarcely anyone has begun to grapple with the enormous problems already being raised at the global level by such growth.

It would be wise, therefore, for any denomination or agency hoping to be around in the 21st century to appoint immediately a '21st Century Task Force' to at least begin the process of speculation and planning. Will there be a steady reservoir of new recruits? How will present sources of income stand up to future inflation and patterns of giving? What will their own organization look like in 25 years' time? and so on.

## 30. New Horizons.
Often these explanations would lead to horizons new to many Christians. Thus Global Diagrams 52-58 described the future of global demography and pushed forward to the year AD 2200 our knowledge of possible futures for youth, women, and the elderly and aged.

Example from *Monitor* November 1992:2

*Comments on Global Diagram 55* (in *WCT*=GD 48)
What are presented in the new diagram on page 3 opposite are the salient facts and figures describing a startling series of 48 trend segments. 22 of these describe the basic background; but 26 present an appalling picture. Anyone previously unfamiliar with these statistics must surely agree that here is a new frontier for the world Christian mission to come to grips with.

Basically what the diagram is portraying is a shocking situation in which the female half of the world's population is heavily disadvantaged—denied full rights and equality, owning almost nothing, paid a pittance, condemned for the next 200 years (on our present scenario) to rancid urban slums, poor, exploited, abused, battered, sick, illiterate, abandoned, homeless, refugees.

The facts of the matter are scarcely in doubt. The literature and documentation supporting this diagram are enormous. But what we are chiefly concerned about is what Christians who take Christ's Great Commission seriously ('Great Commission Christians' in our terminology, now numbering in 1993 some 616 million believers) can do to impact for Christ these 48 200-year trend segments.

An answer we would like to propose now can be expressed in the one word: *Targeting* (see Un sourcebook opposite). By this we mean that Christian individuals or couples, and especially those involved in the world Christian mission, might be encouraged to choose one very specific, clearcut, bite-sized segment (one alarming trend) and might then accept that their vocation from the Lord is to see that that segment becomes radically changed within a realistic time-frame (the next 10 or 20 or 30 years).

Take, for example, the shocking segment or statistic that female urban slumdwellers are likely to soar to 2.2 billion by AD 2200. This is, for Christians, a totally unacceptable situation. So why not appoint a missionary or couple who will deliberately target this one segment of reality, will become world experts on the subject through first-hand knowledge and research, and who will aim to uncover the basic underlying causes of this phenomenon and begin to get these causes radically altered one by one?

Readers familiar with the nonresidential missionary strategy will recognize that the sheer size of such a target is of little consequence. We now have proof of numerous cases where one single missionary or couple have selected as a target a huge previously-unevangelized ethnolinguistic people of 10 or 20 million population, and have made a decisive difference within 3 years. Remember David and Goliath? Targeting is easy when we specify a target exactly.

### NEW GLOBAL DIAGRAMS

## 31. New Diagram.
This ninth regular major subject covered a whole range of subjects. Virtually every topic and concept relevant to world evangelization have been illustrated in these diagrams. See example at bottom of page.

## 32. New Exegesis.
Every new diagram led to new findings, new facts, and new figures. Studying these and placing them in the biblical context surrounding the Great Commission enabled us to produce new exegesis—new meanings discovered in the Scriptures, the timeless Word of God.

## 33. New Concepts.
Often the diagrams permitted us to describe completely new concepts in world mission and evangelization.

Example from *Monitor* July 1992:2

*Comments on Global Diagram 51* (in *WCT*=GD 74)
This month's diagram on page 3 traces the possible evolution of global Christianity in terms of that modern 20th century phenomenon—Christian monoliths. These are independent, autonomous, standalone agencies each with its own separate funding and administration, each controlling some 50 distinct aspects of organized life and outreach. A megamonolith is an enormous monolith with measurements in the millions. A gigamonolith is one whose decadal budget exceeds $1 billion. These have all been described earlier in Global Diagram 47 (in *WCT*=GD 14).

The sequence of minidiagrams 1-5 opposite shows how an outside observer—secular or religious, Muslim or Hindu—sees current global Christianity. At first it seems to be a single huge monolith enjoying an annual budget of $180 billion. As he looks closer, he perceives structure, differentiation, duplication, contradiction, conflict. Eventually he realizes the monoliths can be grouped into 7 rival blocs encompassing 160 related ecclesiastical traditions or fami-

---

Example from *Monitor* November 1990:3 (Note: in this *WCT* volume, this Global Diagram is renumbered as GD 6).

### Global Diagram 2a. CHRIST'S GREAT COMMISSION ANALYZED INTO 2 MINICOMMISSIONS AND 7 MANDATES: 7-P EVANGELIZATION CALLING FOR 7-P EVANGELISM.

The diagram analyzes the words used in the 6 New Testament narratives of Christ's Great Commission given to his followers in AD 33 (Matthew 28:18-20, Mark 16:15-18, Luke 24:45-49, John 20:21-23, John 21:5-22, Acts 1:4-8).

To understand the Commission, it is first divided into 2 **Minicommissions** "Evangelize!" and "Disciple!", and then into 7 **Mandates** described in 12 columns.

Meanings of the 12 columns, including 2 giving statistics of usages (word frequency), are as follows. For meanings of all Greek words, see Table 1.

*Column 1.* **Mandate imperative.** Lines 1-7 give the Big Seven—the 7 Mandates of the Great Commission—in English Bible usage. These are given here as imperatives: Receive (the Holy Spirit)! Go (into all the world)! Witness! Proclaim (the gospel)! Disciple (the nations)! Baptize! Train! Note that what we are calling the overall imperative Evangelize! (Greek, *euangelizo*) does not occur in the Great Commission accounts although its cognate noun *euangelion* (the Good News) does (in Mark 16:15).

*Column 2.* **Greek keyword.** Greek verbs or derivatives central to the Great Commission narratives are given in lines 1-7.

*Column 3.* **Usages.** Each Greek word is followed in this column by a figure which is the number of usages of the word, and its immediate cognates (adjectives or nouns) in the Greek New Testament.

*Column 4.* **Mandate.** This defines the 7 Mandates using a 7-P format to describe the spectrum of 7 generic types of evangelization.

*Column 5.* **Characteristics.** The phrases here describe the differentia of the various Mandates.

*Column 6.* **Human role.** A second set in 7-P format, this time describing the spectrum of 7 generic types of evangelism, the latter term covering the church's human role that these Mandates entail.

*Column 7.* **Sub-types.** The lists here (suggestive, not watertight or exclusive) give sub-types or varieties of evangelism or ministry for the stylized types in column 6.

*Column 8.* **Other keywords.** Keywords (related key nouns) from the Greek or Latin ("L") New Testaments which support or illustrate each Mandate.

*Column 9.* **Usages.** The first figure gives the number of Greek or Latin New Testament usages of the exact noun opposite it in column 8; the second figure gives the total usages of the word and its immediate cognates (adjectives, nouns, or verbs).

*Column 10.* **Dimensions.** The total number of dimensions of "evangelize" related to each Mandate, namely major English synonyms which each contribute something unique to the full-orbed meaning of "evangelize"; divided here under each of the 7 Mandates.

*Column 11.* **Key dimensions.** The column lists a small alphabetized selection of examples of the previous column's total of dimensions of "evangelize", given in imperative mood as constituent commands under the Mandate.

*Column 12.* **Facets.** The final column gives the total of all English verbs which are distinct aspects or facets (or synonyms or near-synonyms or part-synonyms or dimensions) of "evangelize", arranged under each of the 7 Mandates.

lies. The monoliths seem to be all powerful.

What does the future hold for this remarkable power structure? Of the many possible futures, here we report three (developed in more detail in Global Diagrams 29-32, which in *WCT* are numbered 70-73). Future I (Diagram 6 in *WCT* Global Diagram 74) shows the monoliths forced by internal logic (hi-tech, multimedia, artificial intelligence, etc.) and by external pressures (secular scorn, hostile government edicts) to coalesce into one single supermonolith. Future II (Diagram 7 in *WCT* GD 74) shows all monoliths replaced by numbers of massive unorganized ethnic blocs of spontaneous charismatic youths. And Future III (Diagram 8 in *WCT* GD 74) follows one line of thought from the Book of Revelation—the brutal world system finally liquidates not only all the monoliths but also the whole church on Earth, which thus follows its Master to martyrdom.

### 34. New Definitions.

As throughout, we have stressed the importance of quoting and utilizing statistical totals only in conjunction with exact definitions. These have to include an exact time reference (e.g. 'mid-1992') for categories which vary over time; an exact geographical reference (e.g. 'China including Hong Kong, Macao, and Taiwan'); and precise definition of the category in all cases where ambiguities exist.

*See example at bottom of page.*

### 35. New Enumeration.

These global diagrams presented an enumeration of the factors and variables making up each subject. 'Enumeration' has 2 dictionary definitions: (a) numbering with statistics, and (b) listing components one by one.

Example from *Monitor* January 1992:2

*Quantifying hours spent by evangelizers (columns 3-5)*
With these definitions, we can now enumerate the situation of a people, a city, or other population. We therefore ask: How many hours or minutes of evangelizing contact with Christianity, Christ, and the gospel has this population had? And, how many such hours does this population have each day, and how many per capita per year? To understand our method and our results, study Table 1 as you read on below.

Let's assume the average Christian's conscious day is 16 hours (during the day's other 8 hours we're all asleep). That's 5,840 waking hours a year. In these, the Christian is expected to live as a disciple of Jesus, in 3 modes: to be (1) firstly, a Christian *presence*, incarnating his Lord and Master, actively in contact with people (we call the time he spends 'presence-hours' because they are a passive form of witness or evangelizing); (2) secondly as a Great Commission Christian to be *martyrs* (a witness to Jesus and his Resurrection, spending active 'witness-hours'); and (3) thirdly as an evangelist or an evangelizer, actively spreading the *Good News* and passing on the gospel of Christ ('evangelism-hours').

Let's assume next that the average Christian's ac-

tively witnessing day is 4 hours in contact with other people, and his actively evangelistic day is 30 minutes. The 5,840 waking presence-hours thus include 1,460 active witness-hours a year, and this includes 182 evangelism-hours a year.

Now let's quantify this for the entire Christian world. There are 1.8 billion Christians across the globe. Together they spend 10.5 trillion presence-hours a year. Dividing by the total world population of 5.3 billion, this becomes 1,980 Christian presence-hours expended per inhabitant of the globe per year (5.4 presence-hours a day). Dividing instead by the world's 3.5 billion non-Christians, this is 3,000 presence-hours per non-Christian per year. Dividing by the 1,254 million unevangelized, this is 8,380 presence-hours per World A inhabitant per year. This should be enough to ensure evangelizing the world! Like the global supply of food and water, it's entirely adequate—if it's properly shared.

### 36. New Numbers.

The first definition of 'enumerate' in Webster's *New World dictionary of the American language* is: 'To determine the number of; count'. So counting, regularly and with precision, becomes a central activity for the monitoring process.

Example from *Monitor* October 1993:2

**Our Globe's 12,000 Ethnolinguistic Peoples in Worlds A, B, & C,**
half of the page describes one of the globe's 272 countries. Its column "Peoples" gives the total number of ethnolinguistic peoples. columns divide this total into the number of World A peoples, World B peoples, and World C peoples. Note that certain totals at the anomalies such as certain de facto countries being claimed as parts of other countries.

| Peoples | A | B | C | Ref Country | Peoples |
|---|---|---|---|---|---|

### 37. New Tables.

Where 2 or more data variables were available, or one variable and also the time variable (year), they could be presented in the form of compact tables (sometimes also called 'charts'). This makes monitoring easier for the average reader to see what is happening.

Example from *Monitor* August 1991:3

*Mission response from 145 World C countries*
Key to numbers
N=national/citizen home
S=citizen foreign missionaries sent abroad per million
M=foreign missionaries from abroad per million

Key for top 78 mission-sending countries
a=21 donating countries (S>M) (in bold italics)
b=20 draining countries (S<M, M<350)
c=37 looting countries (S<M, M>350)

1. Exemplary response (S>350)

| Ireland | a | 7244 | 3229 | 82 |
|---|---|---|---|---|
| Malta | a | 10966 | 2248 | 55 |
| Samoa | c | 7915 | 1149 | 3603 |
| Belgium | a | 5375 | 969 | 133 |
| Spain | a | 3795 | 826 | 48 |
| Netherlands | a | 3223 | 797 | 136 |
| Portugal | a | 1518 | 489 | 41 |
| Canada | a | 3718 | 475 | 235 |

| Italy | a | 4042 | 473 | 175 |
|---|---|---|---|---|
| Liechtenstein | c | 660 | 472 | 1085 |
| France | a | 2783 | 448 | 272 |
| Switzerland | a | 2633 | 448 | 171 |
| New Zealand | c | 2411 | 421 | 730 |
| Norway | a | 635 | 376 | 155 |

2. Adequate response (350>S.150)

| Bolivia | c | 314 | 337 | 570 |
|---|---|---|---|---|
| Tonga | c | 5430 | 326 | 3721 |
| Australia | a | 2583 | 317 | 227 |
| USA | a | 3294 | 279 | 82 |
| Germany | a | 1993 | 278 | 90 |
| Solomons | c | 6202 | 276 | 1963 |
| Luxembourg | a | 6726 | 265 | 94 |
| Austria | a | 2887 | 249 | 103 |
| Panama | c | 368 | 243 | 623 |

### 38. New Graphics.

Experiments were next made with a wide variety of new graphical methods of conveying information and data.

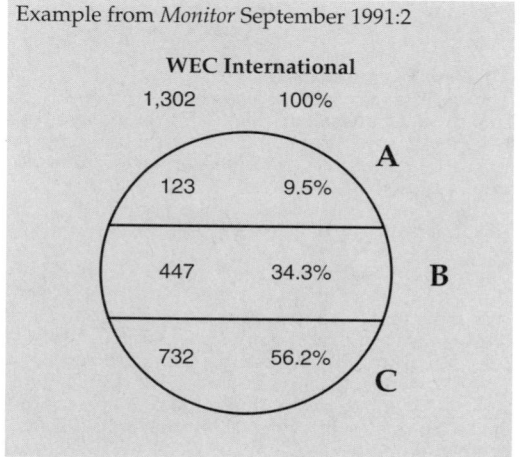

Example from *Monitor* September 1991:2

**WEC International**

1,302          100%

123     9.5%     A

447     34.3%     B

732     56.2%     C

### 39. New Analysis.

With all the above data before us, the *Monitor* then moved on to analyze them in order to bring out new and hitherto unknown or unanticipated aspects and findings.

*Comments on Global Diagram 44 (in WCT=GD 58)*
What this diagram also shows is that the potential in these 23 large countries (each over 10 million in population by AD 2000) is enormous, far greater than at present realized. Assist these countries to reach the modest but entirely reachable adequate level ('S=100) and they will have added 70,000 more missionaries by the end of this decade.

---

Example from *Monitor* August 1992:2 (Note: in this *WCT* volume, this Global Diagram is renumbered as GD 46).

**Global Diagram 52. THE DEMOGRAPHIC FUTURE OF OUR GLOBE:** SEVEN SCENARIOS OF POSSIBLE ALTERNATE FUTURES, AD 1950-2200.

Table 1 below sets out the UN's global population estimates at 11 points over the period AD 1950-2200. Seven alternate scenarios are set out (columns 1-7) based on a wide range of assumed future trends in human fertility. The basic, most-probable case is the UN's long-used Medium (medium fertility) variant (column 4). This assumes that fertility will ultimately stabilize at the replacement level—a fertility rate of 2.05 children per woman (the average number a woman has in her lifetime). The Low variant (column 1) assumes a rate of 1.6 children, the High variant (column 6) 2.5 children. The Instant-Replacement variant (column 3) assumes fertility reached replacement level (2.06) in 1990 and stays at that level thereafter. The Constant-Fertility variant (column 7) is the most frightening; it assumes human obstinacy keeps fertility at the same bloated level as today (4.3 children) from 1990-2150, producing by AD 2150 a population density 160 times today's!

The graphic in the center analyzes a single one of the asso-

ciated secular characteristics—age, in years. The number of people aged over 65 rises from 318 millions in 1990 to 2,780 millions—*a ninefold increase of the elderly.* From today's planet of children, we are headed inexorably for a planet of the aged.

Lastly, Table 2 at the bottom then takes the Medium variant totals (shown in its column 2) for the period AD 1800-2200 and adds a few variables illustrating the Christian world mission. By 2200, non-Christians reach 7 billion, and the total non-Christians ever—since AD 33—have soared to 44 billion. Since the churches claim direct responsibility in their salvation, these are awesome figures indeed.

The good news is contained in columns 5 and 6. Foreign missionaries then are likely to have reached one million—mainly Chinese, Latin Americans, Bantu, Arabs, and South Indians.

# MONITORING 441

### 40. New Profile.

The tenth major subject dealt with targeting the world's unreached ethnolinguistic peoples. From May 1992 several issues of the *Monitor* switched to giving brief monthly single-sheet 2-page miniprofiles of the world's major unevangelized megapeoples—the toughest or most intractable cases. These included: the Qashqai (Iran), Komering (Indonesia), Somali (Somalia), Lampungese (Indonesia), Tajik (Afghanistan), Rejang (Indonesia), Manchu (China), and Turkmen (Turkmenistan). Each profile followed a standard pattern. Each began with a text describing 8 minitopics: location, history, identity, language, political situation, customs, religion, Christianity. The first page carried a map locating the people, a photograph, and a globe depicting its Worlds A/B/C populations. The back page detailed statistics of the country, and of this people—then described ministry options, prayer topics, and bibliography for further reading.

This project, called EthnoScan, aimed to illustrate our profiling process by publishing a few detailed profiles out of a possible 13,000 profiles completed in 1994 and residing in the World Evangelization Database, for later publication in the *World Christian encyclopedia*, Second Edition.

It should be pointed out that, in correct English usage, a 'profile' is a brief sketch only. Synonymous for it are 'outline', or 'silhouette.' Police mug shots of wanted criminals show the wanted person viewed from the side, with a minimum of detail—but enough for the purpose of alerting police sleuths everywhere and tracking him down.

In the electronic version of the WCE-2, each people is fully described by means of 50 or so statistical or descriptive indicators or categories. The reader wanting a profile can select from a range of 6 varieties of profile, from minimal listing to detailed narrative. He then creates the profile he requires, in the detail he needs.

Example from *Monitor* September/October 1996:4

The Amdo of China, profiled on the page opposite, pose many questions about the seriousness with which Christians, Western Christians in particular, take Christ's Great Commission as a *command*, something to be immediately obeyed.

One hundred years ago, the China Inland Mission reported several missionary forays into the mountainous Amdo territory, foothills to the great Tibetan plateau. Friendships were begun, witness was made, promises of future evangelization were given. Then—a hundred years of waiting, and silence; then the entire Amdo population alive in 1896 gradually died off.

One hundred years later, here we Christians are again, professing to obey Christ's commission immediately, consulting literature, poring over maps. But we are doing less for the Amdo than they had 100 years ago. There are still no Scriptures, no evangelists, no house churches, no promised gospel (and no promises yet).

Our story is thus a shameful one—a hundred years of disobedience to the Great Commission. But now, with an entirely new generation of Amdo in existence, the Christian church has yet another opportunity to obey.

### 41. New Map.

An eleventh major subject dealt with diagrammatic maps. Most of the new data evolved by the *Monitor* were amenable to global mapping. Occasionally such a map was included in place of a new diagram. Thus *Monitor* No. 3 (Global Map 1, which in this *WCT* volume is renumbered as Global Diagram 35) depicted the outer boundary of World A and showed how the world's unevangelized megapeoples all live contiguously (next door to each other) within this one continuous boundary. And No. 9 (Global Map 2, or *WCT*=GD 36, shown at right) extended this coverage to depict the boundaries and locations of both World B and World C.

### 42. New Listings.

The second definition of 'enumerate' in Webster's is: 'To name one by one; specify, as in a list'. So listing items—churches, missions, denominations, peoples, cities, countries—is essential at every stage of the monitoring process. As with counting, listing is es-

sential also because it builds credibility. A researcher can say 'There are 4,000 unreached peoples in the world'; but many will not believe him unless he can produce a list of the 4,000 complete with other documentation and proofs.

---

Example from *Monitor* January-March 1994:2

## Our Globe's 211 Least Evangelized Megapeoples

Peoples over 1 million in population in the year 2000 and 50% or less evangelized, forming the heart of World A.

The following list represents the core of the huge, ongoing Ethnoscan project (which is now almost completed). It represents an update of our previous list (*IJFM*, October 1990). Information in this list is based on the World Evangelization Database, soon to be published on disk. All of these peoples represent primary targets for world evangelization if closure is to be achieved, or even attempted, by AD 2000, or AD 2010, or AD 2025.

*Meaning of columns*
1. *Name of people*, anglicized, with any additional or alternate names; together with (in bold capital italics) name of country in which they reside. Identical people names refer to peoples speaking different mother tongues (see column 2).
2. *Autoglossonym*: this people's own name, in their own

language, for their mother tongue; how the people term their own language. Note that virtually all people spell their own language names with a lower-case first letter. English is the only language in the world which capitalizes its autoglossonym (and also, in fact, *all* language names). Names in parentheses are alternates; these are only capitalized if they are anglicized names.
3. *Population of this people in mid-1995* (based on *World population prospects 1992*, United Nations).
4. *Population of this people in mid-2000* (ibid). The enormous population explosion in almost all the countries and peoples listed means that for many this final column is likely to double after a further 30 years. Any mission agency planning logistics of ministry must avoid being caught expecting too few millions in the future. We need millions of seats, millions of tracts, millions of Bibles, millions of hymnsheets—millions of everything!

---

### 43. New Discoveries.

Sometimes this whole process led to truly startling or remarkable findings. A major one was that World A megapeoples—long considered resistant to the gospel—were in fact the most responsive peoples in the world when exact measurements were taken. Thus the Turkmen of Turkmenistan were found to be 50 times as responsive to one hour of evangelism as European peoples throughout Latin America.

Example from *Monitor* October-December 1994:4

5. *Missionaries are encouraged to go to 'harvestable' fields first.*
Our study of evangelism and response has revealed a shocking fallacy on the part of those who espouse a 'harvest' theology. They neglect to factor in the number of 'evangelism-hours' that go into a particular harvest field. Therefore they fail to examine the actual response *per evangelism-hour*. For example, the current enormous harvest in Argentina has to be weighed in light of the millions of evangelism-hours invested. Argentina's responsiveness is surprisingly small when measured in this fashion. Conversely, fields that are considered 'unready for harvest' are that way because they receive little or no evangelistic input. If the same millions of evangelism-hours invested in Argentina were suddenly aimed at a World A country like Turkmenistan the response would be enormous. Our data reveal that Turkmenistan, considered by many to be an 'unripe' field, is actually 50 times more responsive to one hour of evangelism than Argentina!

### 44. New Predictions.

Where data relating to future years had been presented, it was possible, with suitable caution, to launch into new predictions about the future of world evangelization. Care was taken to do this not as one

single prediction but as a series or range or spectrum of possible alternate future scenarios, usually 3 in number.

Example from *Monitor* December 1992:3

*Global Diagram 56* (in *WCT*=GD 49). The accelerating collapse of the global youth explosion: population under 15 for the globe, AD 1900-2200.
By the year 1970, Christianity's major denominations and agencies had recognized the reality of the global youth explosion. This had begun in the 19th century and accelerated in Third-World countries in the 20th century. Churches then began paying special attention to the needs of youth aged 15-24. Five-year plans anticipated growing numbers of applicants as full-time Christian workers.

What was not known then, nor widely recognized subsequently, is that this explosion peaked in 1970 when the global youth population (under 15s) had risen to 37.5% of the world. A 200-year decline then began, as documented in Table 1 below and shown in Graph I. The bold line in each depicts the United Nations' Medium Variant scenario for the future. It is surrounded on both sides by 6 other UN variants. These represent together 7 possible future scenarios based on differing possible fertility patterns.

These new data show that over the next 200 years, youth are expected to decline by half to only 17% of the world. This is clearly a momentous development that the churches need to think about and plan for immediately.

---

Example from *Monitor* July 1991:3

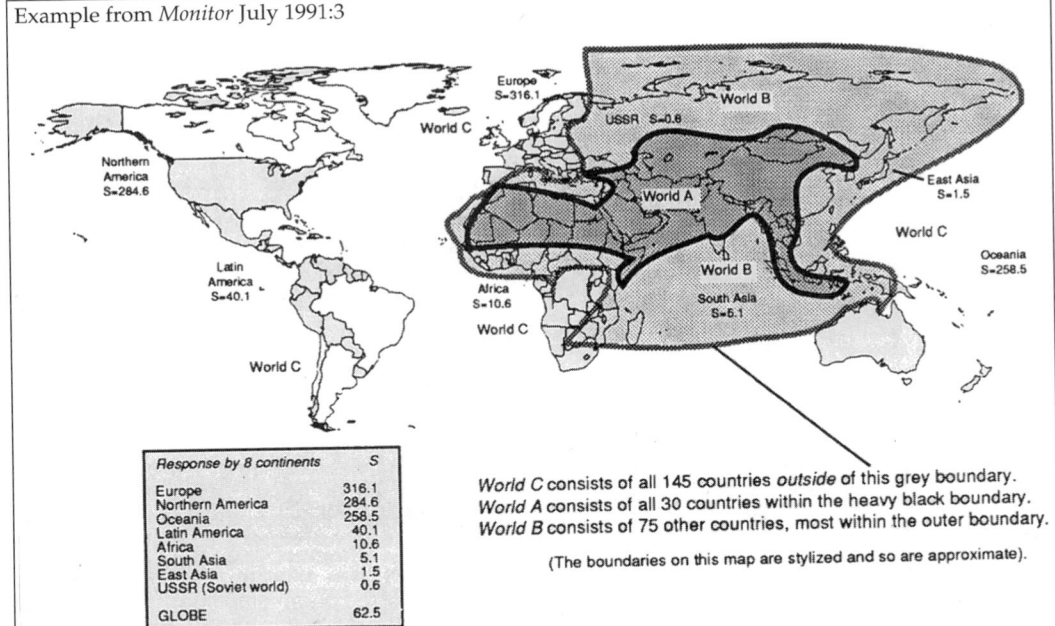

| Response by 8 continents | S |
|---|---|
| Europe | 316.1 |
| Northern America | 284.6 |
| Oceania | 258.5 |
| Latin America | 40.1 |
| Africa | 10.6 |
| South Asia | 5.1 |
| East Asia | 1.5 |
| USSR (Soviet world) | 0.6 |
| GLOBE | 62.5 |

*World C* consists of all 145 countries *outside* of this grey boundary.
*World A* consists of all 30 countries within the heavy black boundary.
*World B* consists of 75 other countries, most within the outer boundary.

(The boundaries on this map are stylized and so are approximate).

Mission agencies likely to be most impacted are those committed to youth-oriented workers who are themselves young (YWAM, OM, World Horizons, Young Life, JOC, et alia). But all church bodies will see an average 50% reduction in new recruits solely due to this one demographic factor.

### 45. New Futurism.

Finally, the various discoveries and predictions enabled us to construct a picture of future possibilities sufficiently firm for us to regard the process as producing a new futurism—a new way of studying and interpreting the future.

Example from *Monitor* August 1992:3

**Table 2. GLOBAL POPULATIONS AND NON-CHRISTIANS SEEN AS THE CHURCH'S RESPONSIBILITY, AD 1800-2200.**

*Notes. Source of column 2: Medium variant in Long-range world population projections: two centuries of population growth, 1950-2150 (New York: United Nations, 1992). Source of columns 3-8: Our globe and how to reach it (1990:128).*

| Year | Population | Non-Christians | Daily increase in non-Christians | Foreign missionaries | Non-Christians per missionary | Cumulative non-Christians since 1800 | Cumulative non-Christians since AD 33 |
|---|---|---|---|---|---|---|---|
| 1 | 2 | 3 | 4 | 5 | 6 | 7 | 8 |
| 1800 | 903 million | 694 million | 76,000 | 7,000 | 99,100 | 0 | 17,736 million |
| 1900 | 1,620 million | 1,062 million | 116,000 | 62,000 | 17,100 | 3,626 million | 21,362 million |
| 1950 | 2,516 million | 1,650 million | 149,000 | 120,000 | 13,700 | 6,103 million | 23,839 million |
| 1970 | 3,684 million | 2,467 million | 216,000 | 240,000 | 10,280 | 7,338 million | 25,074 million |
| 1980 | 4,453 million | 3,020 million | 262,000 | 249,000 | 12,100 | 8,082 million | 25,818 million |
| 1990 | 5,292 million | 3,533 million | 292,000 | 285,000 | 12,400 | 8,881 million | 26,617 million |
| 1991 | 5,385 million | 3,589 million | 295,000 | 290,000 | 12,400 | 8,969 million | 26,705 million |
| 1992 | 5,478 million | 3,649 million | 297,000 | 295,000 | 12,300 | 9,054 million | 26,790 million |
| 1995 | 5,766 million | 3,820 million | 302,000 | 320,000 | 11,900 | 9,311 million | 27,047 million |
| 2000 | 6,261 million | 4,121 million | 292,000 | 400,000 | 10,300 | 9,743 million | 27,479 million |
| 2025 | 8,504 million | 5,419 million | 266,000 | 500,000 | 10,800 | 11,990 million | 29,726 million |
| 2050 | 10,019 million | 6,300 million | 250,000 | 700,000 | 9,000 | 14,075 million | 31,811 million |
| 2100 | 11,186 million | 7,200 million | 220,000 | 800,000 | 9,000 | 18,451 million | 36,187 million |
| 2150 | 11,543 million | 7,043 million | 193,000 | 900,000 | 7,800 | 22,664 million | 40,400 million |
| 2200 | 11,600 million | 6,960 million | 180,000 | 1,000,000 | 6,960 | 26,164 million | 43,900 million |

### NEW TECHNOLOGY AND DOCUMENTATION

### 46. New Books.

We come now to the twelfth regular major subject, and one of the most important: monitoring, listing, and briefly describing the latest new books every month which have something to contribute to the understanding of world evangelization. Of every month's 200-250 new book titles of interest to our subject, the *Monitor* selected the 20 or so most interesting. They were then named, with full bibliographical details including cost, and a brief sentence or two of annotation was added to each.

*See large gray box on next page.*

### 47. New Annotations.

Writing these short notes proved to be very revealing for the editors. We began to see new dimensions of world mission and evangelization. This led to new possibilities for ministry, new possibilities in the ongoing attempt to find solutions to the overall problem of how to implement world evangelization.

To develop a thorough understanding of how people communicate in non-Western societies see *Communication in personal relationships across cultures* edited by William B. Gudykunst, Stella Ting-Toomey, & Tsukasa Nishida (Sage, 1996, 296p, $22.95). Chapters focus on China, Japan, Korea, Mexico, Brazil, Iran, and African countries.

### 48. New Reviews.

Occasionally a major book would call for a lengthier review. Or the reader would be informed of an already existing review in another journal.

Example from *Monitor* July/August 1996:6

*Afghanistan bibliography*
The *Arthur Paul Afghanistan Collection: Pashto and Dari Titles* compiled by Shaista Wahab (1996) is a bibliography based on the Afghanistan materials available in the Arthur Paul Afghanistan Collection. The purpose of this bibliography is to make this unique collection of Afghanistan materials known to scholars interested in the subject area. The Collection has six thousand titles covering aspects of Afghan life and culture from the prehistoric period to the present in more than twenty different languages.

Volume I contains over 800 titles and will be available for $20 each plus shipping and handling. Since the Library consistently adds Afghanistan materials to the collection, an update or a supplement is planned for the future to include those titles that the Library has acquired but have not been listed in this volume. Work on volume II of the *Arthur Paul Afghanistan Collection Bibliography: English and Other European Languages* has been started and will be available for publication late in 1996.

Contact: University of Omaha Library Administrative Office.

### 49. New Bibliographies.

One of the most fruitful sources of new material reported in the *Monitor* on page 4 each month is contained in standard bibliographical listings, reports, or reviews of newly published works. Issue by issue we scanned the *Library journal, Choice, Booklist, New York Times book review, American libraries*, etc.

### 50. New Encyclopedias.

Each year a surprising number of completely new encyclopedias emerges. A number have been described in the *Monitor*. Many of their subjects illuminate world mission.

Example from *Monitor* July/August 1996:6
*The encyclopedia of global industries* (Gale, 1996, 1,034p, $395.00) covers the size of the industry, how it functions, and its history and development for 115 industry groupings worldwide.

### 51. New Atlases.

Likewise with the surprising number of new atlases each year: many have been very helpful for the understanding of Christian mission in the modern world.

Example from *Monitor* April 1991:4
*The atlas of South America* by Moshe Brawerf (New York: Simon and Schuster, 1990, 144 pp., $65.00) is a complete visual introduction to South America, with more than 100 maps and illustrations covering the region and each individual country.

### 52. New Biographies.

In recent months several significant figures in the history of world evangelization have been the subject of biographies, always illuminating. These were monitored.

Example from *Monitor* Nov/Dec 1995:6
*A dictionary of Evangelical biography* edited by Donald Lewis (Blackwell, 1995, 1201 pp., $150.00) covers figures of historical, literary or religious significance who lived between 1730 and 1860 and were associated with the Evangelical Movement in the English-speaking world.

### 53. New Chronologies.

A dozen or more recent histories of Christianity have contained sizeable chronologies on their period.

Example from *Monitor* October 1991:4
*The atlas of the Crusades* by Jonathan Riley-Smith (Facts on File, 1990, 192 pp., $40.00) contains over 100 colorful maps, a detailed chronology from 1095 to 1789, an index, and a glossary of terms.

### 54. New Histories.

Not only are entirely new subjects being written up; time-honored subjects are having their history reexamined, altered, and rewritten.

Example from *Monitor* October 1991:4
Mathematics has a rich history in non-Western cultures such as China, the Arab world, Egypt, Mesopotamia, and India according to George Gheverghese Joseph in *The crest of the peacock: non-European roots of mathematics* (B. Tauris and Co., distributed by St. Martin's, 1991, 384 pp., $29.50).

### 55. New Futures.

As with the past, so with the future—serious studies are proliferating.

Example from *Monitor* September/October 1996:6
How will the postmodern age affect the science of ethnography? Norman K. Denzin examines this question in *Interpretive ethnography: ethnographic practices for the 21st century* (Sage, 1996, 320p, $22.95).

### 56. New Sci-Fi.

A very significant part of literature on the future is science fiction. A more accurate title for this genre would be future fiction.

Example from *Monitor* August 1993:4
British science fiction laureate Arthur C. Clarke tells the tale of the struggle to avert an asteroid on course to collide with Earth in the near future in *The hammer of God* (Bantam, 1993, 226 pp., $19.95).

### 57. New Articles.

For this thirteenth major subject the *Monitor* has had to be extremely selective. Out of thousands of articles on missions in journals and magazines each year, a handful have been selected in the Monitor for their unique coverage of some new development in our subject.

Example from *Monitor* September 1993:4

*China commemorates four Western foreign missionaries*
The *China daily*, which is China's official English daily newspaper, included in its May 19 edition a two-page report on plans by Hualong International Conservation Park in Beijing to set up memorial halls to commemorate four of the renowned Catholic missionaries who lived in China during the 17th and 18th centuries. The four Jesuits to be honored include Matteo Ricci and Giuseppe Castiglione from Italy, Adam Schall from Germany, and Ferdinand Verbiest from Belgium. They are commended as 'Westerners who have contributed in promoting East-West cultural exchanges.' The *China daily* feature, which was replete with biographies of the four and color illustrations, concluded with these words: 'In commemorating our friends from the West who made unforgettable contributions in promoting East-West cultural exchanges, we earnestly hope more and more Westerners devoted to the same cause will come to China.' *China news and church report*, June 11, 1993). What an invitation!

### 58. New Missiology.

Dozens of new books in the realm of missiology—the scientific study of the missionary enterprise—appear each year. One can only monitor all the titles briefly, but his effort at total coverage is always rewarding. It is a quite different approach to concentrating on just a few books which happen to come to our notice.

Example from *Monitor* May/June 1996:6

*The missionary movement in Christian history: studies in the transmission of faith* by Andrew F. Walls (Orbis Books, 1996, 250p, $20.00) makes available for the first time Wall's ideas on missionary expansion with special emphasis on African Christianity.

### 59. New Computerization.

The fourteenth and final major subject in the *Monitor* deals with this surge of new developments now affecting virtually all branches of Christianity. Christians today own and operate over 332 million general-purpose computers. Regular computer news is therefore an essential feature of any serious monitoring of Christian progress in the 1990s. Major developments in hardware, software, and applications come thick and fast every month.

Example from *Monitor* January/February 1997:6

*Recent titles with bearing on our monitoring purpose*

*The Falashas: a short history of the Jews of Ethiopia* by David Kessler (Frank Cass Publishers, 1996, 216p, $19.50 pb) offers a glimpse at a significant people in current African and Middle Eastern history.

*Foreign aid towards the year 2000: experiences and challenges* edited by Olav Stokke (Frank Cass Publishers, 1996, 368p, $22.50 pb) outlines some recent trends that set the stage for the 21st century.

How is technology impacting North Africa? Girma Zawdie and Abdelkader Djeflat edit the contributions of several experts in *Technology and transition: the Maghreb at the crossroads* (Frank Cass Publishers, 1996, 200p, $18.50 pb).

Up-to-date information on the status of Jews around the world can be found in *Jewish year book 1997* edited by Stephen Massil (Valentine Mitchell, 1996, $30.00).

*The international encyclopedia of secret societies and fraternal orders* by Alan Alexrod (Facts on File, 1997, $40.00) is a comprehensive reference that profiles social, ethnic, religious, and political private organizations. For the impact of secret societies in European history see David MacKensie's *Violent solutions: revolutions, nationalism, and secret societies in Europe to 1918* (University Press of America, 1996, 332p, $34.50).

Dilip Hiro's *A dictionary of the Middle East* (St. Martin's Press, 1996, 500p, $30.00) offers a quick reference guide to this volatile region. More comprehensive is Reeva S. Simon's (editor) *Encyclopedia of the modern Middle East* (Macmillan, 1996, 4 volumes, 2,182p, $350.00). On the future of the Persian Gulf see *The Persian Gulf region in the twenty first century: stability and change* by Nozar Alaolmolki (University Press of America, 1996, 226p, $34.00).

*Placenames of the world: origins and meanings for over 2,000 natural features, countries, capitals, territories, cities, and historic sites* by Adrian Room (McFarland, 1997) gives insight into why places carry interesting names. In a similar vein see *People's names: a cross-cultural reference guide to the proper use of over 40,000 personal and familial names in over 100 cultures* by Holly Ingraham (McFarland, 1996, 624p, $65.00).

*Catholicism on the Net* by Thomas C. Fox (Holt, 1996, $16.95) and *Judaism on the Net* by Irving Green (Holt, 1996, $16.95) illustrate how Christians and Jews are utilizing electronic media.

Three new books for 1997 highlight the significance of peoples in world context: (1) *Encyclopedia of immigrant cultures* by David Levinson (Macmillan, 2 volumes, $165.00); (2) *Ethnic groups of nations* by David Levinson (Oryx, $44.50); and (3) *Peoples of Africa* (Facts on File, 6 volumes, $125.00).

Slated for release in November 1997 is John Middleton's *Encyclopedia of Sub-Saharan Africa* (Scribner, 4 volumes, $400.00).

The troubles of Afghanistan are outlined in the *Dictionary of Afghan wars, revolutions, and insurgencies* by Ludwig W. Adamec (Scarecrow, 1996, $48.00).

Solid Central Asia research is found in the second edition of Stephen and Sandra Batalden's *The newly independent states of Eurasia* (1996, $34.95).

*The South-East Asian handbook* edited by Christopher Hudson (Fitzroy Dearborn, 1997, $55.00) offers good information on this important region in the current global context.

C. Bawa Yamba has written an engaging book on the lives of third, fourth, and fifth-generation pilgrims from Nigeria who have "temporarily" settled in Sudan. See *Permanent pilgrims: the role of pilgrimage in the lives of West African Muslims in Sudan* (Smithsonian Institution Press, 1996, 237p, $45.00).

*The Berbers* by Michael Brett and Elizabeth Fentress (Blackwell, 1996, 350p, $45.95) is an overarching survey from prehistoric to modern times of this significant cluster of World A peoples in North Africa. For background information on the region see Dirk Vandewalle's (editor) *North Africa: development and reform in a changing global economy* (St. Martin's Press, 1996, 286p, $49.95).

Five inner Asian cities are examined in Piper Rae Gaubatz's *Beyond the Great Wall: urban form and transformation on the Chinese frontiers* (Stanford, 1996, 378p, $49.50).

*The state of women in the world atlas: an international atlas* by Joni Seager (Penguin, 1996) is available in an updated second edition. Other updated Penguin atlases include *The state of war and peace atlas* by Dan Smith and *The state of the world atlas*, fifth edition by Michael Kidron and Ronald Segal.

*Religion in the megacity: Catholic and Protestant portraits from Latin America* by Philip Berryman (Orbis, 1996, 205p, $18.00) offers an upclose look at different Christian traditions in Sao Paulo, Brazil and Caracas, Venezuela.

No germs allowed! *How to avoid infectious diseases at home and on the road* by Winkler G. Weinberg, M.D. (Rutgers University Press, 1996, $16.95) tells you how to decrease your chances of picking up viruses and disease.

*Sustainable development in Third World countries: applied and theoretical perspectives* edited by Valentine Udoh James (Praeger, 1996, 264p, $69.50) shows how sustainable development requires a successful agricultural base, good conservation and preservation, sound health practices, and socioeconomic planning.

*The globalization of capitalism in Third World countries* by Priyatosh Maitra (Praeger, 1996, 256p, $65.00) challenges traditional views regarding population growth, demographic transitions, and technological transfer in economic development.

*The peoples of Africa: an ethnohistorical dictionary* by James S. Olson (Greenwood, 1996, 681p, $99.50) includes references on 1,800 ethnic groups, a chronology, and a selected bibliography.

*World guide to religious and spiritual organizations* edited by the Union of International Associations (K.G. Saur, 1996, 471p, $375.00) contains 3,495 entries arranged alphabetically including organization's name, main address, date of founding, its aims, objectives, and structure, number of staff, source of finances, activities, publications, countries containing members, and the like.

Richard D. Lewis, one of Britain's foremost linguists, offers informative and practical advice on working and communicating across cultures in *When cultures collide: managing successfully across cultures* (Nicholas Brealey, 1996, 331p, $28.00).

*Mappa Mundi: the Hereford world map* by P.D.A. Harvey (Toronto, 1996, 58p, $20.00 pb) describes this 13th-century British map which put Jerusalem at the top with Christ sitting in judgment above.

*The music and dance of the world's religions: a comprehensive, annotated bibliography of materials in the English language* by E. Gardner Rust (Greenwood, 1996, 504p, $89.50) is a monumental reference work for ethnomusicologists and others interested in music, culture, and religion.

*Muslim women throughout the world: a bibliography* by Michelle Kimball and Barbara R. von Schlegell (Lynne Rienner, 1997, 285p, $75.00) covers 3,000 English-language books and articles and includes a 50 "most highly recommended" books and articles.

A broad range of contributors and unusually broad coverage make *Muslim communities in the new Europe* edited by Gerd Nonneman, Tim Niblock, and Bogdan Szajkowski (Ithaca Press, 1996, 346p, $75.00) an extremely important source of information.

The heart of World A is examined in Richard N. Fyre's *The heritage of Central Asia: from antiquity to the Turkish expansion* (Markus Wiener, 1996, 264p, $16.95).

*The Oxford dictionary of world religions* edited by John Bowker (Oxford University Press, 1997, 1104p, $45.00) contains 8,200 alphabetical entries written by eighty contributors from all around the world, representing the full spectrum of religious experience.

For one of the clearest presentations of the role of women in the church see Rebecca Merrill Groothuis' *Good news for women: a biblical picture of gender equality* (Baker, 1997, $16.99).

*The reconciliation of peoples: challenge to the churches* edited by Gregory Baum and Harold Wells (Orbis Books, 1997, 220p, $18.00) is a collection of fifteen essays on church-based strategies to foster reconciliation between former combatants in contexts like Rwanda, Bosnia, and Sri Lanka.

*Inside the Vatican: the politics and organization of the Catholic Church* by Thomas J. Reese (Harvard University Press, 1997, 317p, $24.95) offers a social scientific analysis of the complexities of the Holy See.

In case you missed it, a monumental study of worship for Christians is *The complete library of Christian worship*, 8 volumes edited by Robert E. Webber (Hendrikson/Star Song, 1995, 3426p, $199.80 (discount price, see http://www.christianbook.com).

Example from *Monitor* Nov/Dec 1996:8

*Samsung develops working prototype of 1GB DRAM*
Samsung (Korea) claims it is the world's first to succeed in developing a fully working die for the 1GB DRAM chip. It would be capable of storing 100,000 double-spaced pages of typewritten text, or 16 hours of audio data. It is expected to be in use commercially in 2002 or 2003.

**60. New Software.**
In the Western world, almost every denomination, church headquarters, agency, institution, and even every parish and local church owns and operates its own computer system. But the quality of the software employed, and the programming being undertaken, are far lower than is the case in the secular world. Often the church official in charge of the computer operation is not professionally trained and does not take or read any of the essential publications reporting new software and products being announced week by week. Many of these announcements in fact have immediate value and application to the church's work.

Example from *Monitor* January/February 1996:8

*Watching history unfold*
Centennia by Clockwork Software is a wonderful application of CD-ROM capabilities to the unfolding story of historical geography. The user can click boxes and watch the nations and empires of Europe wax and wane over the years and centuries. Maps of Asia, the Americans, and the rest of the globe are planned ($89 for DOS, Mac, and Windows; also available at http://www.clockwk.com).

**61. New Databases.**
While almost all Christian agencies now compile their own inhouse databases, these are usually startlingly humdrum—names, addresses, donors, budgets, accounts, stock, personnel files, and so on. Few so far have seen the enormous significance of modern database applications to the implementing of global mission.

Example from *Monitor* February 1993:4
*World resources, 1992-93: a guide to the Global Environment, Database Diskette.* The 1992-93 World Resources Database produced by the World Resources Institute has been revised to accompany their printed report. It covers a wide range of 483 variables—from trade to health to demographics and the environment for countries,f regions, and the world. In addition to the variables included in the printed version, the database includes time series for several variables (Johns Hopkins University Press, 1992, $119.95).

**62. New Technologies.**
As part of this discipline, the *Monitor* staff have systematically scanned, read, and extracted relevant data on new technologies from a variety of scientific publications including *Science News* and *Scientific American*.

Example from *Monitor* September/October 1996:8

*Improving Africa's telecommunications infrastructure*
The whole continent of Africa has fewer telephones than the city of Tokyo. The average wait time for a new line tops eight years. More governments, however, are beginning to understand the importance of telecommunications. Many services are being privatized in order to attract private investment to build infrastructure. Eight African nations have created some form of telecommunications authority to provide information to private investors. Regulatory authorities are also being set up. some countries are investigating establishing cellular phone networks instead, in order to skip the high cost of laying telephone cable.

Advances in telecommunications will be a boon to mission workers in such countries, enabling the better scheduling of training, city-wide crusades, and the work of indigenous workers. Mission agencies repeatedly complain about the extreme difficulty of placing calls to any country in Africa, and improvements here will make vastly easier the building of mission partnerships between the West and African agencies.

**63. New Hypertext.**
This is a long-established method and as such has been described at several points in the *Monitor*. See Index for actual instances.

Example from *Monitor* October 1991:4

*Electronic encyclopedias*
Two new encyclopedias (Franklin's based on the 1989 *Concise Columbia Encyclopedia, Second Edition* with 15,000 entries; and SelecTronics based on the *Random*

*House Encyclopedia New Revised Edition* with 20,000 entries) are now available in picket *Revised Edition* with 20,000 entries) are now available in pocket size 12-ounce computers both utilizing hypertext methods for searching. They both employ text-compression techniques to squeeze these works onto three megabyte ROM chips. The SelecTronics encyclopedia even includes a chronology from 4000 BC to the present. As memory becomes cheaper, larger works will be in the palm of one's hand—far below the current $400 price tag (*Popular science*, September 1991:47-48).

### 64. New Hyperfiction.
This new variety of compilation is explained in the *Monitor* No. 36, page 4.

Example from *Monitor* October 1993:4

*Hyperfiction: a new narrative art form*
'Hyperfiction is a new narrative art form, readable only on the computer, and made possible by the developing technology of hypertext and hypermedia.' Though many adults are not familiar with hypertext, most children are, as it forms the basic interface for most computer games. Hypertext goes beyond electronic storage, however. While many shorter books are now available on diskettes or CD-ROM, most are there for quick search techniques or because a large printed volume takes up little space on electronic media. Hypertext introduces purpose and design into the world of electronic text primarily through 'linking' text beyond that of the left to right, page to page. The reader can navigate through the work in any fashion utilizing the links. For example, there might be a choice of possible endings for a novel that would meet with where the reader feels the work should go—choose the proper link and you are there. Hypermedia goes a step further by adding the dimension of graphics, photographs, sound, music, animation, and film. Any of these can be found in place of the links to enhance the electronic text. These are usually published on CD-ROM due to the enormous size of the files. While the number of titles utilizing this new technology is small, observers expect this media to take off in the next five years (*NY Times book review*, August 29, 1993:1,8-12).

### 65. New Systems.
As each major new computer development occurs, such as laptops, palmtops, PDAs (personal digital assistants), we have endeavored to assess the implications for assisting all persons working for world missions.

Example from *Monitor* July/August 1996:8

*The book of the future?*
Imagine a book of about 200 thin pages that contains the entire text of over 200 books. Joseph Jacobson of MIT Media Laboratory is working on what could be the book of the future, an electronic device that looks and feels like a regular book but contains a microprocessor and a mini CD-ROM drive. Each page is a flat display with thousands of pixels that can represent a page from a book (with text in a font and size that suits the reader). These pages would access data on a CD so that one could sit and read any of 200 books in this single volume. This technology has many advantages over current CD-ROM compilations which require heavy and expensive computer systems that are difficult on the eyes. Jacobson's greatest challenges: screen resolution and power (*Technology review*, May/June 1996:12-13) Uses for a Christian audience or for evangelization are limitless: great Christian works in a single volume, evangelistic or discipleship materials at the fingertips, etc.

### 66. New Artificial Intelligence.
Although contemporary industry now employs hundreds of expert systems, hardly any applications to churches or missions have emerged so far.

### 67. New Applications.
Nevertheless, the enormous variety and number of new computer products and concepts produced every month is having a profound effect on Christians and the computers they own and operate.

Example from *Monitor* July/August 1996:8

*Bringing information to remote areas*
**Ghana.** The country's leaders have signed an agreement with a company that will bring video, radio and limited computer technology to people all over the country. The system is called WorldSpace, and utilizes stationary satellites over Africa, Latin America and Asia which beam signals to special compact radios fitted with videoscreens that allow limited computer data transfer. These radios are solar-powered and about the size of a book, and could provide high-quality sound and computer imagesto over 4 billion people once the system is online in 1999. The radio will cost about $50.

### 68. New Disks & CDs.
Not only are versions of the Bible available now on CD-ROM, but so also are standard tools across the whole area of Christian studies.

Example from *Monitor* January/February 1997:8

*IBS launches Cyberbibles to reach forbidden zones*
The International Bible Society has made the complete Arabic Bible available through the Internet. IBS' Internet host, Gospel Communications Network and its Bible Gateway pages, are among the top 2% of web sites visited in the world, according to *Internet for Christians*. The Bible Gateway offers several Bible versions and a 22,000-topic search function. In 1997 IBS will add the whole Bible in Armenian, Croatian, Indonesian, Latvian, Macedonian, Polish, Romanian, Russian, Serbian, Slovakian, Thai, Ukrainian and Vietnamese to the web site.

### 69. New Monitoring Index.
To illustrate the monitoring process in its global context we produced an exhaustive index of over 13,000 items. Scanning the excerpt below gives one an idea of the breadth of subjects impacting world evangelization.

*See example below.*

### 70. New Overall Assessments.
We conclude this analysis of the Monitor with a handful of assessments in answer to three widely-asked questions.

**1. How is monitoring affecting the goals of the Christian world?**
Monitoring has made agencies and churches aware of the implications of their goals. For many it has provided an outside source of evaluation—a means of tracking progress and decline. This has caused more caution on the part of agencies and churches in setting goals. It has also helped them to be more focused and more detailed. Other agencies and churches have continued on with vague goals that ultimately cannot be measured.

Additionally, as the year for completing a goal rapidly approaches, there is the strong tendency for these same agencies and churches to completely lose sight of their original goals. Oftentimes newer goals and programs effectively supplant earlier ones. The end result is that the original goals and programs associated with them are disowned.

With some of the churches' overarching goals there is the practical need to scale back and restate. In relation to unreached peoples, for example, goals from

a decade ago confidently stated the aim of *reaching* all of them by AD 2000. Closer to AD 2000, the same agencies wrote about *penetrating* each of these with the gospel. Others spoke of *targeting* them by AD 2000. In each case, the goal is pushed back to less demanding objectives. By AD 2000 even targeting goals had not been achieved.

**2. Will World A automatically disappear?**
The central monitoring device in our *Monitor* is the Worlds A, B, C trichotomy which is built on church membership and evangelization statistics. From the standpoint of individuals, the most pressing issue is if and when it is possible for there to be no more World A individuals left in the world (i.e. individuals who have not had an adequate opportunity to hear of and respond to Christianity, Christ, or the gospel). Practically, this entails only two possible outcomes. In the first scenario, everyone would be a Christian (all would be World C individuals). The second, and far more likely scenario, is that a certain percentage of individuals would be Christians and the rest would be World B individuals (i.e. those who have had an adequate opportunity to hear of Christianity, Christ, or the gospel but who have not, or not yet, become Christians).

In order to effectively study this question, the status of the church and evangelization is best analyzed in the context of countries. This is the level where most statistics are gathered—in subjects ranging from population demographics to church membership. From this vantage point we can track the status of Christianity and evangelization among the peoples in a particular country. This helps us to more clearly visualize and implement the missionary task.

Our question then is 'Based on the rate of progress of reaching or evangelizing World A peoples, when are there likely to be no more such groups left?'. The answer is complicated by the fact that while gains are being made by improving communications and transportation, as well as by intentional missionary effort, individuals in World A groups, particularly Muslims, are having more children than most World C groups. So while a certain number of World A groups become more than 50% evangelized every year (thus becoming World B groups), World A probably has sufficient demographic momentum to take it well into the 21st century. That is, the world is not likely to become evangelized soon by present efforts, and hundreds of peoples representing millions of individuals, will remain unreached well past the year AD 2025.

**3. What in retrospect appears to be the overall value of monitoring in world evangelization?**
Monitoring has provided an essential ingredient for world evangelization progress—accountability. This is the factor, more than any other, which has been brought to bear on the church as a whole and on individual denominations, agencies, and churches. Signposts, built on solid data, are clearly marking the path of the churches' efforts in world evangelization. This is true from the broadest level (globally) to the narrowest level (peoples and individuals). Thus, the monitoring process has provided a measuring stick for all agencies, provided they have been willing to apply what is being learned.

As in virtually all other walks of life, the value of detailed monitoring of our pilgrimage through this world has once more been demonstrated.

---

Example from Monitoring Index

Part 14

# MISSIOMETRICS

The science of mission:
counting, measuring, and interpreting global Christianity

*Go and measure the temple of God and the altar, and count the worshipers.*
—Revelation 11:1, Revised English Bible, and New International Version

*We must not despise the science of numbers. That science is of eminent service to the careful interpreter.*
—Augustine of Hippo, AD 400

*Take away number in all things and all things perish. Take calculation from the world and all is enveloped in dark ignorance, nor can he who does not know the way to reckon be distinguished from the rest of the animals.*
—Isidore archbishop of Seville, encyclopedist (c560–636), *Etymologiarum*

The heart of this book and of the whole series *WCE/WCT/WCD* is the science of global mission properly so called. Churches, missions, and agencies here follow the biblical example of the value of measurement through 23 (expanded to 51) of the Bible's related Greek verbs. They thus measure the nature, size, increase, and trends in several thousand variables closely connected with church life, missionary outreach, and evangelization.

Because these 23 or 51 Greek verbs (expanded in Part 23 to 620 English verbs) enable us to measure the phenomena of mission, they therefore are defined here as the major or basic *dimensions* (from the Latin *dimensio*, a measuring) of the science of missiometrics.

Part 14 goes on to describe major areas of secular, religious, Christian, ecclesiastical, and other descriptive measurements. These are then enumerated and analyzed elsewhere in Parts 22 to 25.

A bibliography is drawn up (in Table 14–7) of 600 classics or other books, published throughout the 20 centuries, which impinge on missiometrics and thus help to define the science of global mission. The 600 are each analyzed on 4 missiometric dimensions in order to assess their contribution (from 0% to 100%) to this emerging science.

# The science of mission: counting, measuring, and interpreting global Christianity

## I. BIBLICAL ORIGINS OF MISSIOMETRICS

In his apocalyptic vision, the seer John finds himself faced with the heavenly temple in the New Jerusalem of the future. He is ordered: 'Count the worshipers!' (Revelation 11:1, Revised English Bible). In subsequent centuries, that command has mushroomed into an enormous industry, a whole new science. It enables us to enumerate Christianity and religions and all the myriad facets of life surrounding them.

### The academic study of missions begins
The term 'science of religion' goes back to 1852 when abbé Prosper Leblanc founded it as an autonomous discipline. Soon after, the orientalist Max Muller founded the science of comparative religion by beginning his 51-volume series *The sacred books of the East*. The extension of this description to missions came in 1867 when Protestants founded the first chair of missiology, located at the University of Edinburgh. In the year 1873 the first university chair in the history of religions was founded in Geneva, Switzerland, with others in the science of religion soon after in Holland, France (Paris), Belgium, and Germany (Berlin, Leipzig, Bonn). 1896 saw the first German Protestant chair of missiology when Gustav Warneck (1834-1910) became 'professor of the science of missions' at the University of Halle, Germany. His inaugural lecture included in its title the phrase 'Theological Science'. In 1897 the First International Congress for the Science of Religion was held in Stockholm, Sweden. In 1898 came the journal *Archiv für Religionswissenschaft* (Archives for the Science of Religion), published at Freiburg-im-Breisgau.

The term 'sciences' then became applied to several varieties of the study of religion. 1907 observed the start of a French publishing series, *Encyclopédie des sciences ecclésiastiques*. Then in 1910 came the world's first Roman Catholic chair of missiology, at the University of Münster, Westphalia. Joseph Schmidlin (1876-1944), its first 'professor of missiology' then founded in 1911 the International Institute for Scientific Missionary Research (Internationale Institut für Missionswissenschaftliche Forschungen) and also began publication of the journal *Zeitschrift für Missionswissenschaft*.

### A 'science' of missions is claimed
By 1918 the study of missions had become sufficiently serious and professional for the entire discipline to be regularly labeled a 'science', particularly in German as Missionswissenschaft, usually translated as 'missionary science' or 'the science of missions'. Thus 1918 saw the founding in Berlin of the German Society for the Scientific Study of Missions (Deutsche Gesellschaft für Missionswissenschaft). Its nature was stated as: 'The Society is devoted to the scientific study of missions, both historical and theoretical.' From 1920 on they published a series of volumes called *Missionswissenschaftliche Forschungen* (Researches in the Science of Missions), a series still in progress 80 years later. In Gottingen, Karl Mirbt (1860-1929) raised missiology to the 'full position of a science', especially with regard to his chief interest, missionary statistics. In 1932 the Pontificium Institutum Missionale Scientificum was erected in Rome. In 1951 came the Norwegian missiologist O. G. Myklebust's published proposal *An international institute of scientific missionary research*, a proposal which was never implemented.

From among many further titles one may mention the *Nouvelle revue de science missionnaire* (Switzerland), J. H. Bavinck's *An introduction to the science of missions* (1954), G.F. Vicedom's *The mission of God: an introduction to the science of mission* (1965), and the early work of J. C. Hoekendijk which in 1948 spoke of *Zend-ingswetenschap* (Dutch for 'the science of mission'). This emphasis has continued in Europe and the Americas right up to the present. Thus the South African missiologist M. L. Daneel has recently published some of his extensive eco-theological researches on prophecy and earthkeeping in Zimbabwean independent churches in two German journals, *Zeitschrift für Missionswissenschaft und Religionswissenschaft*, and *Neue Zeitschrift für Missionswissenschaft* (begun back in 1945).

Throughout this period other scholars in other branches of Christian learning were heralding theology itself as 'The queen of the sciences'.

### The term 'science' evolves in meaning
Meanwhile, over this last hundred years the word 'science' has evolved and taken on more precise meaning. A glance at the *Oxford English dictionary*, particularly in its CD-ROM form, will tell us the exact dates in which, year by year since 1850, scores of new sciences have been born and recorded there as neologisms.

What are the essential characteristics of a 'science' today? Back in 1800, 'science' (Latin *scientia*) meant 'knowledge'. But in normal widespread usage over the last two centuries, the term 'science' has moved toward a more specifically empirical meaning, as is shown in *Webster's WNWDAL*: 'Science: systematized knowledge derived from observation, study, and experimentation carried on in order to determine the nature or principles of what is being studied... by experiments and hypothesis'. *Webster's WTNIDEL* is even clearer: science is 'a branch of study that is concerned with observation and classification of facts and especially with the establishment or strictly with the quantitative formulation of verifiable general laws chiefly by induction and hypotheses'.

### Science counts and measures
To be precise, science *measures* things; as the saying goes, 'Science is nothing if it is not metrical'. There is even a science of measurement—metrology, defined as 'the science of weights and measures'. Science therefore must be recognized as clearly not the same as philosophy, nor theology, nor history. Instead, all the sciences are characterized by a close alliance with the central science of mathematics.

### Redefining a 'science' of missions
In the light of this, we must question use of the word 'science' in all those missions titles above. It has certainly indicated a thorough, serious, and professional approach to the study of mission. But it does not correspond to science as understood in secular usage today. It was a correct term back in 1800—it was correct then to extend it to include religious knowledge, biblical knowledge, theological knowledge, historical knowledge, and descriptive knowledge about missions. But in the 20th century this widest approach to the study of missions has been better termed by the more recent term 'missiology' which means 'theology, thought, thinking, and observation about Christian missions'. A fuller definition is: 'the study of the church's mission especially with respect to the nature, purpose, and methods of its missionary activity' (*WTNIDEL*).

From this standpoint, then, missiology as widely understood today should no longer be called, of itself in its entirety, a science. Instead, it is more accurately described as covering a much wider area—the entire area of biblical exegesis, theology of missions, philosophy of missions, history of missions, methodology of missions, biography, bibliography, and contemporary description and analysis of missions. The present book therefore maintains that only a small correction in terms employed is needed. Missiology and missiologists might now be able to recognize that a new component discipline is emerging which can more accurately be called 'the science of missions' because it adapts the contemporary scientific approach (the scientific method, the metrical approach, the empirical emphasis, quantitative compilation, the mathematical foundation) to the phenomena of missions. This new discipline is here given the name missiometrics.

### Mathematics and missions
Mathematical approaches to the subjects of religion, Christianity, and more recently missions have often been published. In 1687 English physicist and mathematician Isaac Newton, greatest scientific genius ever, published *Principia Mathematica* but then retired early to devote himself to its application to the interpretation of the prophecies of Daniel and Revelation. One resulting calculation of his was that the second coming of Christ would not occur until AD 2000. Then in 1699, his disciple John Craige published *Theologiae Christiana Principia Mathematica* (Mathematical Principles of Christian Theology). Two centuries later, Dikran Terzian of Anamasia, Turkey in 1898 published *The mathematics of religion*, in which inter alia he calculated when future persecutions of Armenia's Christians would be likely to end. Despite a wide range of similar publications, most missiologists today perceive little or no connection between missions and mathematics.

There are however many close connections between the two. Let us begin with etymology. The study of missions may be encapsulated in the English verb 'Disciple!', or 'Make disciples!' which translates the Greek New Testament imperative *matheteusate* from the verb *matheteuo*. The cognate noun *mathetes* means 'a learner, pupil, disciple'; it occurs 57 times in the NT. Then there is *mathema* ('what is learned'), and thence the Greek adjective *mathematikos* (with its Latin equivalent, *mathematicus*) which meant and still means 'inclined to learn'. 'Mathematical' in English has subsequently developed the additional meaning 'rigorously exact, precise, accurate, etc'. And so we arrive at today's science of mathematics, defined in *WNWDAL* as 'the group of sciences (including arithmetic, geometry, algebra, calculus, etc) dealing with quantities, magnitudes, and forms, and their relationships, attributes, etc, by the use of numbers and symbols'.

An additional connection comes with the word 'math' itself. In the pre-Christian Sanskrit language, in today's Hindi language, and in today's Indian English, a 'math' is a disciple-training base in Hinduism. These maths or convents of Hindu monks are found in many parts of India, similar in function to Christian monasteries. One of the best-known today is the Hindu missionary organization whose full name is the Ramakrishna Math & Mission. A millennium ago, the Brahman theologian Sankara (AD 788-840) organized these bases under the four great *matha* today, at the four corners of India: at Sringeri (Mysore), Badrinath (Himalayas), Dvaraka (Saurashtra), and Puri (Orissa). These maths control the dogmas, doctrines, ideals, and practices of millions of Saivites across India. By contrast in today's American English, 'math' (British 'maths') and 'the new math' are simply abbreviations widely used for mathematics as currently taught in English-speaking schools in the Western world. But all these usages of 'math' go back to a common origin.

Another word related to 'what is learned' is 'information', which *WNWDAL* defines as 'knowledge

**Table 14–1. Twenty-three major English biblical imperatives outlining the science of missiometrics.**

*Column 1.* Reference number.
*Column 2.* The English verb (in imperative mood, shown in bold type) followed in each case by other exact biblical words in this particular illustration.
*Column 3.* The original Greek verb it translates (shown not in the infinitive tense but in the first person singular indicative), to pinpoint its biblical origin.
*Column 4.* The key Bible reference which uses that English verb to translate that Greek verb, together with initials indicating the Bible version or versions where this English verb occurs.
*Column 5.* A brief comment on some meanings or implications for today.

| 1 | *English verb, example* 2 | *Greek verb* 3 | *Key reference (with version)* 4 | *Comment or recommendation* 5 |
|---|---|---|---|---|
| 1. | **Add** to their number! | *prostithemi* | Acts 2:41, 47, NRSV | 3,000 believers were added on a single day. |
| 2. | **Calculate** the cost! | *psephizo* | Luke 14:28, REB, NAB, NASB | Calculating costs requires detailed work. |
| 3. | **Check** the money! | *etoimazo* | 2 Kings 12:11, REB, JB | Proper accounting procedures are essential. |
| 4. | **Compute** years left! | *syllogizomai* | Leviticus 25:52, NIV | Redemption payments can be complex. |
| 5. | **Count** the worshipers! | *arithmeo* | Revelation 11:1, NIV, REB | One counts to protect, monitor, evangelize. |
| 6. | **Describe** the land! | *diagrapho* | Joshua 18:4, AV/KJV | Describe complex situations item by item. |
| 7. | **Disciple** the nations! | *matheteuo* | Matthew 28:19, The 1911 Bible | This is the central Great Commission command. |
| 8. | **Divide** the property! | *merisasthai* | Luke 12:13-14, GNB | Fair division of resources must be evident. |
| 9. | **Estimate** the cost! | *psephizo* | Luke 14:28, NIV, NRSV | Prior planning is of prime importance. |
| 10. | **List** the names! | *katalego* | 1 Timothy 5:9,11, GNB, NRSV | Listing helps to control vast amounts of data. |
| 11. | **Manage** the property! | *oikonomeo* | Luke 16:1, GNB | Good management depends on knowing facts. |
| 12. | **Measure** the temple! | *metreo* | Revelation 11:1, REB | Measuring is science's main way to create data. |
| 13. | **Multiply** the disciples! | *plethyno* | Acts 6:7, RSV | Churches often grow by compound interest. |
| 14. | **Number** by families! | *arithmeo* | Numbers 1:2, NEB | Numbering family heads gives rapid totals. |
| 15. | **Reckon** the number! | *psephizo* | Revelation 13:18, RSV | Mental arithmetic/reckoning is a vital expertise. |
| 16. | **Register** the world! | *apographo* | Luke 2:1,2,3,5, NRSV | Christians learn from secular enumerations. |
| 17. | **Sum!** (Take the sum!) | *lambano* | Numbers 1:2, AV/KJV | Summaries and summings up depend on sums. |
| 18. | **Survey** the land! | *chorobateo* | Joshua 18:6, REB | Surveys must be thorough, in great detail. |
| 19. | **Take** a census! | *lambano* | Numbers 1:2, NIV, RSV, GNB | The OT is a storehouse of census data. |
| 20. | **Total** up the spoils! | *prostithemi* | Numbers 31:32, NRSV | Regular totalling invariably surprises everyone. |
| 21. | **Weigh** the silver! | *arithmeo* | 2 Kings 12:10, REB | Financial probity demands strict maths. |
| 22. | **Work** out the number! | *psephizo* | Revelation 13:18, REB | Many subjects require lengthy calculations. |
| 23. | **Write** "800"! | *grapho* | Luke 16:7, GNB | Constant writing up of facts and figures is vital. |

acquired in any manner; facts; data; learning', also 'in information theory and computer science, a precise measure of the information content of a message'.

What all this shows is that there is a lengthy chain of meaning from a common origin of the root 'math–', shrouded in the mists of history, through the idea of 'learning' and the concepts of disciples, discipling, and disciple-training, and on to the modern sciences of higher learning, knowledge, informatics, information theory, measurement, and mathematics today. Hence part of the meaning of the Great Commission, for Christian mathematicians at least, is to develop that part of the imperative *Matheteusate!* which depends on and emphasizes information, information sciences, and 'what is learned', making people 'inclined to learn', and certainly developing these burgeoning sciences for the glory of God. The application of that group of sciences to the massive task of obedience to the Great Commission is the area of the new discipline and science called missiometrics.

In what follows below, we analyze the subject and in particular give 6 major shoulder headings (English imperatives in boldface italics in quotation marks) which give exact Scriptural mandates from the newest versions of the English Bible. We are not asserting here that missiometrics has its origin in response to direct New Testament imperatives. Instead it has arisen out of its demonstrable utility in the work of missions. Neither is any one suggesting that these mandates are universally applicable over the centuries, or the exact obligations on today's church, still less on every Christian. Nevertheless, someone somewhere in the churches must certainly be held responsible to take them seriously.

### 1. *'Take a census!'*

We first need to dispel two common misunderstandings. To begin with, many Christians who distrust numbers deny the value of counting, statistics, and censuses in Christian work by quoting king David's sin in ordering up a notorious military census (2 Samuel 24:1-2). However, the sin was not in the census itself, but in the desire for aggrandizement behind it. By contrast, elsewhere the Old Testament is a vast storehouse of censuses and statistical data. In most cases, these appear to have been expressly ordered by God with the recurrent refrain 'Take a census' (Numbers 1:2, NIV, RSV, GNB).

Secondly, another common argument against enumeration of Christian activity goes as follows: 'Never in the New Testament is a Christian leader told to count the churches or individuals under his care, nor those untouched by the gospel,' or 'There is no NT record of counting churches, or of membership rolls.' True. But consider a secular parallel. If you own only the handful of coins in your pocket, you don't need a bank, a bank account, a monthly bank statement, or immediate access to your money through your personal computer. But as your money increases, you need statements showing exact sums, lists of expenditures, and printed balances. Similarly, as long as apostles and presbyters were dealing with relatively small numbers of believers and churches, censuses were unnecessary. But when the hundreds turned to thousands and the thousands to millions, censuses became essential for proper understanding, strategy, management, and outreach.

### 2. *'Count the worshipers!'*

In the Book of Revelation, the seer John was instructed 'Count the worshippers' (11:1, Revised English Bible, 1989, which follows British spelling with two 'p's; also 'Count the worshipers' in New International Version, 1971, which follows American spelling with one 'p'). The English word 'count' comes directly from the Latin *computare*, to compute, and in normal English usage means 'to add up, one by one, by units or groups, so as to get a total' (*WNWDAL*). 'Count' occurs 120 times throughout the Bible (in NIV) and it translates the Greek verb *arithmeo*, which we will examine in more detail below.

Reasons for this command to John are fourfold. Firstly, it could be regarded as preparatory to the restoration and rebuilding of the true temple of God. Secondly, it would be to demonstrate the triumph and magnitude of God's grace toward mankind.

Thirdly, it would be for the protection of God's people against all spiritual and supernatural dangers. Anyone who has shepherded a sizeable group of 20 or more young children around a zoo or a museum knows that the only way to ensure their safety is to count them all every few minutes. Another example would be Jesus' illustration of the man with a hundred sheep (Matthew 18:12-13). The only way that he could find out if any were missing would have been to count up to at least ninety-nine. By counting, he discovered that there was the one missing sheep. A third example comes from the account of Paul's shipwreck off Malta (Acts 27:1-44). In the midst of a major disaster, some eye-witness thought it was sufficiently important at that moment that he counted, or recalled, or recorded the exact number of all on the ship: 'There was a total of 276 of us on board' (Acts 27:37, GNB). Later manuscript copyists saw no significance in the exact number, hence the variant readings 275 and 76. But it's the same as with major catastrophes today—the only way to tell afterwards how many are missing or dead is to have exactly counted them all beforehand.

And fourthly, counting enables monitoring, understanding what is going on, becoming ready to decide what to do next, meeting immediate situations and needs. Counting is one of those basic everyday things all of us do from which many others things can immediately flow.

As with censuses, no one is saying that counting is essential to Christian discipleship. Counting only becomes important when numbers have increased to the point where we cannot grasp what is going on by impressionistic mental arithmetic alone.

### 3. *'List the names!': 23 key English biblical imperatives*

The imperative 'Take a census' in Numbers 1:2 (NIV, RSV) is immediately followed in the Good News Bible by the more specific command 'List the names.' Listing is important throughout the Bible. Lists extend from the genealogy of Adam (Genesis 5:1, GNB: 'This is the list of the descendants of Adam'), to the 72 Gentile nations in the world (Genesis 10), to the unrevealed list in the Lamb's Book of Life (Revelation 20:15). The word 'list' occurs 46 times in GNB, including the very first sentence of the New Testament which proclaims 'This is the list of the ancestors of Jesus Christ'. 'List' in fact translates the very first word of the Greek New Testament, *biblos*. Most Western Christians see little value in that list of 17 verses and 45 names. But for countless Hindus and other non-Christian religionists, that list provides the essential initial authentication of the person of Jesus Christ before they can go on to read and accept the truth of the Gospels.

Further, in addition to 'count' and 'list', the Bible has a whole range of similar verbs or imperatives relating to mathematics, sciences, the information revolution, and the Great Commission. So first of all we ourselves will 'list' these biblical verbs, showing them in Table 14–1 (a brief summary) and then in Table 14–2 (a much more complete listing) before expounding them in more detail. In this table the 5 columns give the English verb (in imperative mood, shown in bold type) followed in each case by other exact biblical words in each particular illustration; next, the original Greek verb it translates (shown not in the infinitive tense but in the first person singular indicative), to pinpoint its biblical origin; then the key Bible reference which uses that English verb to translate that Greek verb, together with initials indicating the Bible version or versions where this English verb occurs; and lastly, a brief comment on some meanings or implications for today. Altogether, this makes a total list of 51 English verbs translating 39 different Greek verbs. Note that usually only the key reference is listed for each verb. For most there are also numerous other direct Scripture references to those precise English verbs, both in the OT and in the NT. In the next paragraphs, these will be interpreted to be the 51 dimensions or basic activities of missiometrics.

#### *Synonyms*

In addition there are a large number of other synonyms or related concepts for the above English verbs which are in the major English Bible versions but are excluded from Table 14–1 in the interests of brevity. These are included in Table 14–2. Many other synonyms not in English Bible use are listed at the end of Table 14–2 under the note 'Synonyms'.

#### *Fifty-one dimensions of missiometrics*

These 51 biblical mandates or mini-mandates together define missiometrics and its arena, its agenda, and its activities. They can be regarded as the 51 dimensions (from the Latin *dimensio*, a measuring) of missiometrics.

Some may surprise the reader, who will ask questions like 'What has the word "bring" got to do with missiometrics or missiology or even evangelization?' Here is a brief threefold answer. (1) "Bring" is a major missiological word because it directly translates the Greek verb *euangelizo* ('evangelize') with the second-highest frequency of all English verbs in New Testament translations (especially RSV, NEB, GNB, NIV, NKJV, NJB, NRSV, REB, and other major English Bibles). (2) 'Bring' plays a significant role in the following sequential chain of 12 synonyms describing the central activity of missionary research, which is the compiling of new data and information: collect, gather, **bring**, put together, compile, compose, write,

**Table 14–2. A full listing of all 51 English biblical imperatives and 27 synonyms delineating 51 dimensions of the science of missiometrics.**

*Column 1.* Reference number. *Column 2.* The English verb (in imperative mood, shown in bold type) followed in each case by other exact biblical words in this particular illustration. *Column 3.* The original Greek verb it translates (shown not in the infinitive tense but in the first person singular indicative), to pinpoint its biblical origin. *Column 4.* The key Bible reference which uses that English verb to translate that Greek verb, together with initials indicating the Bible version or versions where this English verb occurs. *Column 5.* A brief comment on some meanings or implications for today.

| 1 | *English verb, and example* 2 | *Greek verb* 3 | *Key reference (with version)* 4 | *Comment or recommendation* 5 |
|---|---|---|---|---|
| 1. | **Add** to their number! | *prostithemi* | Acts 2:41, 47, NRSV | 3,000 believers were added on a single day. |
| 2. | **Appraise** wisdom! | *exegeomai* | Job 28:27, NIV | Scour existing knowledge to secure wisdom. |
| 3. | **Assess** the silver and gold! | *timographeo* | 2 Kings 23:35, NIV | One should assess quality as well as quantity. |
| 4. | **Bring** your catch! | *enenko* | John 21: 10-11, RSV | Peter then brought and counted 153 large fish. |
| 5. | **Calculate** the cost! | *psephizo* | Luke 14:28, REB, NAB, NASB | Calculating costs requires detailed work. |
| 6. | **Check** the money! | *etoimazo* | 2 Kings 12:11, REB, JB | Proper accounting procedures are essential. |
| 7. | **Classify!** (Class!) | *endrino* | 2 Corinthians 10:12, RSV | Classifying is necessary but with caution. |
| 8. | **Compare** with care! | *synkrino* | 2 Corinthians 10:12, RSV | Comparisons must be done carefully. |
| 9. | **Compute** years left! | *syllogizomai* | Leviticus 25:52, NIV | Redemption payments can be complex. |
| 10. | **Consider** the lilies! | *katamanthano* | Matthew 6:28, RSY, REB | Learn from natural processes of growth. |
| 11. | **Control** 23 towns! | *echo* | 1 Chronicles 2:22, NIV | Control relies on names, facts, figures, totals. |
| 12. | **Count** the worshipers! | *arithmeo* | Revelation 11:1, NIV, REB | One counts to protect, monitor, evangelize. |
| 13. | **Describe** the land! | *diagrapho* | Joshua 18:4, AV/KJV | Describe complex situations item by item. |
| 14. | **Disciple** the nations! | *matheteuo* | Matthew 28:19, The 1911 Bible | This is the central Great Commission command. |
| 15. | **Divide** the property! | *merisasthai* | Luke 12:13-14, GNB | Fair division of resources must be evident. |
| 16. | **Enlist** soldiers! | *stratologeo* | 2 Timothy 2:4, NRSV | Military enlistment demands single-mindedness. |
| 17. | **Enrol** the widows! | *katalego* | 1 Timothy 5:9, 11, RSV | Enrolment necessitates high standards. |
| 18. | **Estimate** the cost! | *psephizo* | Luke 14:28, NIV, NRSV | Prior planning is of prime importance. |
| 19. | **Examine** the fortresses! | *diegeomai* | Psalm 48:13, GNB | Lengthy attention to detail yields results. |
| 20. | **Gather** the pieces! | *synage* | John 6:12, NIV | Amass every scrap of evidence, then collate. |
| 21. | **Inform** people! | *katecheo* | Acts 21:21, AV/KJV | Many catechists today log into the superhighway. |
| 22. | **Inquire** about the sign! | *punthanomai* | 2 Chronicles 32:31, GNB | New meanings emerge as inquiry gathers speed. |
| 23. | **Inspect** the earth! | *episkeptomai* | 1 Samuel 13:15, GNB | Leaders must know their staffs at the grassroots. |
| 24. | **Instruct** others! | *katecheo* | 1 Corinthians 14:19, NRSV | Christians continuously instruct in the faith. |
| 25. | **Investigate** it thoroughly! | *ereunao* | Deuteronomy 13:14, NIV | Close scrutiny leads to startling discoveries. |
| 26. | **Learn** from Me! | *manthano* | Matthew 11:29, REB, AV/KJV | The central aspect of discipleship is learning. |
| 27. | **List** the names! | *katalego* | 1 Timothy 5:9,11, GNB, NRSV | Listing helps to control vast amounts of data. |
| 28. | **Listen** to Solomon! | *akouso* | Luke 11:31, NIV | Research calls on all kinds of wisdom. |
| 29. | **Manage** the property! | *oikonomeo* | Luke 16:1, GNB | Good management depends on knowing facts. |
| 30. | **Measure** the temple! | *metreo* | Revelation 11:1, REB | Measuring is science's main way to create data. |
| 31. | **Multiply** the disciples! | *plethyno* | Acts 6:7, RSV | Churches often grow by compound interest. |
| 32. | **Muster** 400,000! | *episkeptomai* | Judges 20:17, NIV | Strategize when handling huge numbers. |
| 33. | **Number** by families! | *arithmeo* | Numbers 1:2, NEB | Numbering family heads gives rapid totals. |
| 34. | **Observe** man's labor! | *eideo* | Ecclesiastes 8:16, NIV | Scrutinize human behavior for motives. |
| 35. | **Organize** into groups! | *ephemeria* | Nehemiah 12:24, GNB | Jesus seated 5,000 by 50s and 100s. |
| 36. | **Probe** the limits! | *aphikneomai* | Job 11:7, NIV | Probing produces unanticipated new discoveries. |
| 37. | **Reckon** the number! | *psephizo* | Revelation 13:18, RSV | Mental arithmetic/reckoning is a vital expertise. |
| 38. | **Record** his deeds! | *grapho* | John 20:30, NIV, 21:25, NEB | Recording events ensures future audiences. |
| 39. | **Recount** God's praise! | *exangello* | Psalm 79:13, NRSV | Recounting involves multiple repetitions. |
| 40. | **Register** the world! | *apographo* | Luke 2:1,2,3,5, NRSV | Christians learn from secular enumerations. |
| 41. | **Report** God's deeds! | *anangello* | Acts 15:4, NRSV | Formal reporting is necessary at every stage. |
| 42. | **Search** the scriptures! | *ereunao* | John 5:39, 7:52, AV/KJV | Anchor research to biblical revelation. |
| 43. | **Sort** the good from the bad! | *aphorizo* | Matthew 13:47-49, RSV | Sorting leads to ranking, sifting, prioritizing. |
| 44. | **Sum!** (Take the sum!) | *lambano* | Numbers 1:2, AV/KJV | Summaries and summings up depend on sums. |
| 45. | **Survey** the land! | *chorobateo* | Joshua 18:6, REB | Surveys must be thorough, in great detail. |
| 46. | **Take** a census! | *lambano* | Numbers 1:2, NIV, RSV, GNB | The OT is a storehouse of census data. |
| 47. | **Total** up the spoils! | *prostithemi* | Numbers 31:32, NRSV | Regular totalling invariably surprises everyone. |
| 48. | **Value** it good or bad! | *timao* | Leviticus 27:12, RSV | Evaluate quality by means of coded scales. |
| 49. | **Weigh** the silver! | *arithmeo* | 2 Kings 12:10, REB | Financial probity demands strict maths. |
| 50. | **Work** out the number! | *psephizo* | Revelation 13:18, REB | Many subjects require lengthy calculations. |
| 51. | **Write** "800"! | *grapho* | Luke 16:7, GNB | Constant writing up of facts and figures is vital. |

***Synonyms***
In addition there are a large number of other synonyms for the above English verbs which are not included because they do not occur in the major English Bible versions, or do not match the definition of the table. These include: account, analyze, array, audit, balance, buy, catalog, collate, compile, correlate, delineate, digitize, enumerate, evaluate, figure, monitor, pay, quantify, rate, research, scan, symbolize, systematize, tot, weight. These 27 verbs, with the listed 51, make up 78 English verbs which (together with their 40 Greek biblical counterparts) delineate the area in which the science of missiometrics operates.

edit, revise, redact, adapt, rewrite, circulate, publish. (3) Later in this Part 14 it will be shown how the church worldwide is already doing, and doing on a massive scale, precisely this 'bringing' of new data, compiling, and writing in obedience to the Great Commission.

### *To whom do these imperatives apply?*

Each of the imperatives listed in Tables 14–1 and 14–2 originally applied to particular individuals in a particular historical situation. No one is saying they apply to all Christians today, nor even to all persons involved in or organizing missions.

The answer at this point must be the same as the similar query and question often applied to the Great Commission itself. Is it still valid for today's church? Our answer here is Yes, certainly. 'Disciple the nations!' and 'Preach the Good News!' are still valid commands to the entire worldwide church today. Likewise, the 23 imperatives in Table 1 simple expand one aspect of obeying the Great Commission. They can be regarded therefore as further, newer, and perhaps even original or unusual ways in which enterprising missions-minded Christians can promote Christ's world mission. Although they cannot be held obligatory on all Christians, at least somebody in the church should be taking them seriously.

### *From Bible to superhighway*

At this point we note a remarkable new development linking the Bible with the emerging global information superhighway. Of the 78 verbs listed above, some 40 per cent have already become single-word programming commands in scores of computer languages based mainly on English, but also translated into French, German, Spanish, Russian, Chinese, Japanese, Arabic, and 50 other modern languages of wider communication. The most striking example of this is the biblical word 'list'. The foremost language of AI (artificial intelligence, for creating expert systems) is known as LISP, which stands for 'list-programming language'. This unique computer language views the world as a vast series of lists and sublists, and then proceeds to manipulate those lists with commands including 'LIST'. Likewise, 'LIST' is common in the database languages dBase, FoxPro, and many others.

This link between the Bible and the superhighway was not deliberately planned, nor is it even widely recognized yet. But for Christians who believe in God's omniscience and providence, it is of vast significance for communication of the relevance of the Bible in today's world, and hence for evangelization.

The 23 lines in Table 14–1, or the 51 lines in the extended Table 14–2, present the initial biblical raw data supporting the case for a mathematical and scientific approach to missions. To understand this further, we will now investigate 7 of the key Greek verbs involved. They are all related to the fourth biblical imperative being studied here and which is arguably the key concept: Measure!

## 4. *'Measure the temple!'—7 key Greek biblical imperatives*

Since all sciences are characterized by their metrical approach, it is noteworthy that 'measure' is a term much used in English Bibles—136 times in the New International Version, 133 in the New Revised Standard Version, and so on. With usages varying from 'Measure the temple' (Revelation 11:1, REB) and 'Measure Jerusalem' (Zechariah 2:2, NRSV) to the daily sale prices of barley in the town market (2 Kings 7:1, NRSV), the Bible supports a higher level of precision in the lives of God's people than most Christians realize.

The following 7 biblical Greek verbs related to the measuring function are the major ones for understanding the whole complex of the mathematical approach to the science of missions.

### *a. arithmeo.*

The verb means to number, to count, to sum. With its cognate words it is used a large number of times in the Greek Bible: in the Old Testament (the LXX, or Septuagint) the verb is used 43 times, and 3 times in the New Testament. Its related noun *arithmos*, 'a number' is used 141 times in the OT, and 17 times in the NT. Although in the Hebrew Bible the fourth book of Moses was originally called 'In the Desert', from its opening words, in the LXX the Greek title became Arithmoi. Six centuries later, the Latin Vulgate called it Numeri, from which we eventually got the English title 'Numbers'. This word 'number' occurs 134 times in the Good News Bible (314 times, with its cognates, in the New Revised Standard Version). We may further note that there was and is also a Greek noun *arithmetike* which means 'the art of counting'. From all this came the English word 'arithmetic' and the arithmetical sciences.

### *b. grapho.*

Meaning 'describe' or 'write', this verb represents another distinct stage in the scientific treatment of data. Thus in Ezekiel 43:10, NIV we read 'Describe the temple to the people of Israel.' The verb occurs again in Revelation 22: 18,19, as well as a number of other times throughout the Book of Revelation. Writing down the results of what one counts or measures is an essential part of the operation because it renders the impermanent verbal process into a permanent witness to what the situation revealed. 'Writing' in its modern computer meaning of keyboarding our thoughts and findings into the Internet or other global networks vastly multiplies the overall impact of those results.

### *c. katalego.*

Variously translated as 'recount', 'list', 'register', or 'enroll', this verb refers to the important stage of recording membership in a community or population by having one's name written down, which is what enrollment or listing or affiliation usually entails in all societies whether literate or illiterate. Many New Testament churches each maintained a list of needy widows and orphans supported at church expense (1 Timothy 5:9,11, GNB, NRSV).

### *d. metreo.*

With this verb we enter onto the fuller meaning of the prosecution of missions as a science. There are 3 related Greek words here. *Metron* is the noun, meaning an instrument used for measuring, such as the linear measure mentioned in Revelation 21:15. It occurs 80 times in the LXX and 13 times in the Greek New Testament. *Metreo* is the verb, meaning to measure, to take the dimensions of, to judge by a rule or standard, to estimate, or to determine the quantity of things. It occurs 5 times in the LXX and 10 times in the NT. And a third Greek word, the adjective *metrikos*, means 'metrical'. It is not used in the Greek Bible but has been widely used since the origin of science itself on the Greek island of Samos, Ionia in BC 600 with Pythagoras and the origin of mathematics.

We come now to English derivatives. The first English Bible in 1380 had 'Mete the temple!' (Revelation 11:1, Wyclif). Today, the most common derivative is 'meter'. This can be either a basic unit of length (39.37 inches), one thousand of which make one kilometer; or a person who measures; or an instrument or apparatus for measuring (such as an electricity meter, a parking meter, a postage meter). There is also the whole range of specialized measuring instruments which are essential to scientific research: the thermometer (measuring temperature), barometer (pressure), chronometer (for 'exact observation' of time), speedometer (speed in m.p.h. or km.p.h.), odometer (distance), anemometer (wind speed), micrometer (for micromeasurement), and many others.

There is also a large range of adjectives ending in '-metric'. The *Oxford English dictionary*, CD-ROM version, lists over 200.

Another type of derived word current in several sciences ends in the suffix '-metry'. This means the 'action, process or art of measuring' of something which is specified by the initial part of the word. Thus we have telemetry (scientific measurements made at great distances from the observer, being the science of remote sensing), also geometry which is defined as 'the process, art, or science of measuring the world', also anthropometry ('the science of measurement of the human body'). Altogether the *OED* lists and describes 81 nouns ending in '-metry', including such sciences as altimetry, chronometry, iconometry, morphometry, optometry, radiometry, seismometry, sociometry, stylometry, volumetry, and zoometry ('measurement of the dimensions and proportions of the bodies of animals').

Yet another range of sciences is derived using the plural suffix '-metrics'. This refers to a theory of measurement, or a system of measurement. In this category we find econometrics ('the use of mathematical and statistical methods in the field of economics to verify and develop economic theories'), which has just seen the publication of *A dictionary of econometrics* (1994). Then there are many more parallels—jurimetrics, biometrics ('that branch of biology which deals with its data statistically and by quantitative analysis'), dosimetrics (for measuring lethal levels or doses of radiation and the like), cliometrics ('the use of mathematical and statistical methods, and often of computers, in analyzing historical data'), and psychometrics ('the science and technique of mental measurement').

These examples give us the clue we need concerning the location or placement of our new discipline. The relation of missiometrics to missiology is the same as the relation of econometrics to economics, or of jurimetrics to jurisprudence, or of biometrics to biology.

### e. psephizo.

This verb moves us from the comparatively easy task of adding up, counting, and measuring visible objects, to the more difficult task of what to do when hard data that are countable and easy to understand are not available. In the absence of visible data to count, *psephizo* means estimate, reckon, calculate, compute. New Testament usages include Jesus' illustration of the tower-builder who was wise enough to sit down beforehand and 'estimate the cost to see if he has enough' (Luke 14:28, NIV). The NRSV and AT/GB likewise have 'estimate'. The RSV has 'count the cost' there; the Good News Bible and Jerusalem Bible have 'work out'. The Revised English Bible has the builder 'calculating the cost'. Four other major versions also use 'calculate' there (MB, NEB, NAB, NASB). Lastly, the most recent major version, CEV, has 'figure out'.

The most widely-known usage of a number in the Bible may well be in Revelation 13:18, where *psephizo* conveys the exhortation: 'Let him that hath understanding count the number of the Beast'. Note that count in AV/KJV becomes reckon in RSV; work out in NEB, GNB, and REB; figure out in CEV; and calculate in four other major versions (NAB, NASB, NIV, NRSV). In 1594 the Scottish mathematician John Napier did exactly this by inventing the concept of logarithms in order to speed up his calculations of this mystic Number of the Beast, 666.

All these NT usages of *psephizo* are summed up in Thayer's *Greek-English lexicon of the New Testament* (1886/1977:676) as having a range of meaning from 'count with pebbles', and 'vote', to compute, calculate, and reckon, with a preferred usage 'to explain by computing'.

### f. manthano.

As we have seen above, this verb (with its derivative *katamanthano*) means to learn, to be apprised, to increase one's knowledge, to hear, to be informed, to perceive, to find things out from as many sources as possible. It occurs 37 times in the LXX and 25 times in the NT. This imperative (such as 'Consider the lilies of the field, how they grow') takes on a whole new importance with the contemporary arrival of the information superhighway, the Internet, and the flood of hard information on every subject which confronts any serious protagonist for global mission and the

growth of the churches worldwide.

### g. matheteuo.

This last verb takes us back to where we began—to the key imperative in Christ's Great Commission, best translated as 'Disciple the peoples!', as it was in Oxford's *The 1911 Bible*. The Greek verb itself encompasses a range of meanings—to be a disciple, to follow, to make a disciple, to teach, to instruct. It's even linked directly to mathematical calculation in that well-known saying of Jesus: 'No one who does not carry his cross and come with me can be a *disciple* of mine. Would any of you think of building a tower without first sitting down and *calculating* the cost?' (Luke 14:27-28, REB, emphases added). This key saying will now be given further examination, resulting in the fifth of the 6 major English imperatives.

### 5. 'Calculate the cost!'

This Greek verb in our listing of dimensions, *matheteuo*, takes us back to the key imperative in Christ's Great Commission, *matheteusate*. As noted earlier, it has close etymological connections with *mathetes*, *mathema*, and *mathematikos*. This connection helps us to understand Jesus' illustration.

In his saying, Jesus speaks of a serious undertaking requiring one's full attention ('first sitting down'). It presupposes the existence of data requiring to be worked on. One can visualize Jesus observing how builders would work out how much raw materials a new building would require, their cost, cost of transportation, architects' fees, number of workers required, their wages per day, number of days to build, any taxes payable, even possible cost overruns. All these data would result in concrete cost projections. What else can Jesus' illustration tell us? In our analysis of this whole process of disciple-making, we need to evolve some basic unit of measurement. This text provides us with an excellent starting-point.

Let's call this maxim of Jesus a disciple-calculation. Let's define it as a personal occasion in which an individual hears the Good News or is otherwise confronted with the person of Christ, has the opportunity there and then to become a disciple, is made aware of what it might cost him or her, and is told to decide then and there to work out whether to become a disciple or not. Such invitations from Jesus in Palestine could not be deferred till a later or more convenient time; you had only an hour or two to accept, or even only a few minutes. Nicodemus had an hour or two; the Rich Young Ruler perhaps 20 minutes. Blind Bartimeus had only 3 or 4 minutes as Jesus approached and passed by; Matthew seated at the receipt of custom had only a few seconds to make up his mind as Jesus said 'Follow me.'

For our analytical purpose, let's estimate the time that this process takes at an average length of one hour. This 'disciple-calculation' is thus the same unit as one 'evangelism-hour' or one 'disciple-opportunity' or one 'offer' or one 'evangelistic invitation', derived and described in Parts 22-24 of this book.

It thus fits the context to imagine the whole exercise taking the experienced builder at least an hour or so to calculate his prospects. Likewise, presenting the call to discipleship to an individual takes the evangelizer an hour on average—the length of a serious sermon, presentation, or discussion. And it is the same with the exercise about which we read in Acts 19:19, NRSV: 'When the value of these books was calculated, it was found to come to fifty thousand silver coins.' Again, that calculation would have taken at least one hour, or maybe many more hours if it had to be done under adverse circumstances.

Further, like 'list', 'calculate' has now become a key word in millennial information technology. At least 24 of the English verbs tabulated in Table 14–2 above take on greatly enhanced significance in the light of the information and computer revolutions since the 1970s. These verbs are: add, calculate, check, compute, control, count, divide, estimate, examine, inform, instruct, list, measure, multiply, number, record, register, report, sort, sum, total, value, work out, write. For Christians looking for new ways to obey the Commission, or new ways to break up the log jam hindering its obedience, these can all be viewed as imperatives from Christ to his disciples on the information superhighway of the 1990s and 2000s. Whereas Christ spoke of one man doing one calculation in one hour, on this highway today over one billion instructions or calculations (and over one trillion concrete steps) can be done in one single second.

These 24 biblical English verbs above can therefore now be seen to have formidably expanded potential in relation to forwarding Christ's Great Commission.

### 6. 'Work out the number!'

As described above, this sixth English biblical imperative is how the Revised English Bible renders the reference to the mystic number in Revelation 13:18. It leads us to an important clarification at this point. What missiometrics is advocating is numeracy, not numerology (which has the alternate name numerics). Numerology is defined in *WNWDAL* as 'divination by numbers', or 'a system of occultism built around numbers', especially 'birth dates which are the sum of the letters in one's name'. As such it hardly seems to be a legitimate Christian occupation. However, the large literature on this subject includes many items by Christian writers and theologians attempting to harness numerology for the Christian cause. Classics include E.W. Bullinger's *Number in Scripture: its supernatural design and spiritual significance* (1913), and J.J. Davis' *Biblical numerology: a basic study of the use of numbers in the Bible* (1968). The latter has an excellent bibliography of 147 books and 53 articles. Many expound the best-known biblical example, the Number of the Beast itself.

By contrast, missiometrics takes note of numerology but is primarily advocating the distinctly different subject of numeracy (mathematical literacy, facility with numbers). We want Great Commission Christians—especially those in executive, management, or administration positions—to be numerate, which is defined as 'able to understand basic mathematical concepts and operations'. Persons responsible for sending 420,000 foreign missionaries throughout today's volatile and dangerous world should surely be fluent in counting, measuring, checking, listing, estimating, deploying, supporting, protecting, and in the very practical mathematical elements and concepts of probability and chance.

### Essentials for any 'science' of missions

What all of this makes clear is simple: in modern English usage, a 'science' observes, counts, measures, describes, experiments, analyzes, reports. Its scientists must be numerates (mathematical literates). Similarly, missiology is a wide discipline concerned with several billions of people which must therefore have a recognized branch dealing with the science of missions, handling the whole counting, measuring, and statistical aspects of the world Christian mission.

### Is anybody compiling the necessary data?

Any science is powerless unless such data exist. In missions, this is a simple question to answer. Every year, the world's 33,800 denominations and 4,000 Great Commission mission agencies instruct some 10 million Christian leaders—pastors, clergy, bishops, catechists, evangelists, missionaries, lay officers—to fill out and return detailed statistical questionnaires listing and enumerating the year's work and progress. This has become the world's biggest single annual statistical enumeration, with considerable potential for creating new outreach. However, this remarkable census carries a startling postscript. We've investigated what happens to the accumulated mountains of data and paper after they arrive at all these headquarters. The short answer is—nothing. Apart from the publishing of simple totals, and some bold forays by a few executives trained in church growth principles, little or no statistical analysis of any kind is done with any of these statistics. This yawning gap in Christian stewardship should therefore encourage Christians to undertake such analysis and to dig into this unique gold mine of annual data.

### What subjects does missiometrics measure?

The immediate answer is—anything and everything in any way relevant to world mission and global evangelization. At present, churches and missions already regularly measure and report on some 500 variables. Major subject areas include: church membership, church growth, places of worship, church workers, clergy, women workers, home missionaries, foreign missionaries, preachers, evangelists, audiences, catechists, catechumens, converts, baptisms, collections, finances, scripture distribution, literature production, church administration, logistics, broadcasting, computer usage, e-mail volume. A fuller listing of the 180 major variables regularly measured each year by the churches is given in Global Diagram

3 in Part 1 "GeoStatus". These annual series of data provide enough exciting theses for any number of researchers to explore.

### What do Christian statistics mean?
The value of missiometrics may be gauged by considering the usefulness or otherwise of the masses of statistics compiled each year. This raises some fundamental questions: Do these statistics mean anything at all? Are they worth the churches' time and effort involved in collecting them? Do they in any sense assist the churches in realistic planning for mission in the modern world? To answer in a word, such statistics do have three major types of use to the churches: they assist in understanding of the past, in analysis of the present, and in planning for the future. And above all, 'Statistics are signs from God', alerting Christians to the status and predicaments of the world's populations.

### A new way to obey Christ's command
Basically, the church's central problem is that the Great Commission is not being obeyed. Measured by tangible results—such as that disciples numbered 34% of the world in 1900 and they number 34% in AD 2000—20th-century Christians have not yet found the way to implement Christ's command to make disciples of all nations. Only new, fresh, radical interpretations are likely to break the log jam.

This essay suggests that *one* way to obey is to regard the 51 English-Bible dimensions listed in Table 14–2 as component elements of the New Testament imperative *Matheteusate!* and hence of the English mandate 'Disciple the nations!' Under this interpretation, a small number of interested and concerned Great Commission Christians could deliberately adopt these 51 imperatives as legitimate concrete directives of the Great Commission in the world of the 21st century.

In other words, if a few determined disciples would adopt the missiometric method in both its narrower meaning (measuring quantitative data) and its wider meaning (utilizing these data and their interpretation to mobilize obedience to the Commission) then the globe might well see seismic shifts in the overall status of Christ's world mission.

### Summary
Missiometrics is therefore presented here as a new term for a discipline with a lengthy history going back to biblical times. It is concerned to develop an inadequately developed aspect of missiology that can now be termed the science of missions properly so called. This has become a genuine science in that it takes cognizance of the science of mathematics and it analyzes the world by means of survey, measurement, counting, statistics, calculation, computation, and the like. Into this methodology must be inserted 'statistics with a human face', involving biblical exegesis, the history of missions, great historical figures like John Wesley, and every variety of scholarship, as well as the information superhighway, modern computers, compact disks, the Internet, the United Nations Demographic Database (100 variables for 230 countries for each year from 1950 to AD 2050, with 7 alternate future scenarios), and any other relevant new factors immediately as they emerge.

### Prognosis for the 21st century
The kind of contribution that missiometrics supplies can be illustrated by means of the following 3 brief scenarios of past, present, and future—with statistics contrasting yesterday and today with tomorrow.

*Past.* From AD 33 up to today, the grand total of all full-time professional missionaries who have ever served can be computed at 6.3 million foreign missionaries, 36.8 million home missionaries, and 214 million other workers of all Christian confessions. Together these add up to the category that the Roman Catholic Church terms Apostolatus Copiae, the official English translation of which is 'the Workforce for the Apostolate'. The average such missionary in his or her lifetime in the past has produced some 500 disciple-calculations/opportunities/offers/invitations.

*Present.* In the year 2000, the potential impact of all living Great Commission Christians is illustrated by today's 524 million Pentecostals/Charismatics/Neocharismatics in the Renewal in the Holy Spirit. Inter alia they own or operate 85 million general-purpose computers capable together of performing 170 trillion logical/mathematical instructions/calculations per second. By 2000, Renewal members using the Internet numbered some 35 million, increasing by 30,000 a week. The speed and volume of a Great Commission Christian's evangelistic output is now as a result, potentially at least, over 1,000 times greater than in the past. (Example: at Easter 1995, evangelist Billy Graham preached a sermon on the cross of Christ over his Global Mission which was then heard by one billion people worldwide. In our terms, this one sermon generated 1 billion evangelism-hours/offers/invitations/disciple-opportunities/disciple-calculations).

*Future.* Within a generation, by AD 2040 there are likely on present trends to be one billion Pentecostals/Charismatics/Neocharismatics. Inter alia they will own or operate one billion general-purpose computers capable together of performing 100 quadrillion ($10^{17}$) logical/mathematical instructions/ calculations per second. In all likelihood, at least 500 million of these Renewal members will be linked to each other and to all other Christians and to all varieties of global resources via Internet–1 or -2 or -3 or parallel derivatives by a vast array of user-friendly inventions. These will include personal knowbots, which are knowledge robots or gofers that can be sent by you the user anywhere in the world to instantly secure any knowledge or information as needed. Each Christian's potential productivity in mission as a numerate Great Commission Christian, and therefore his or her accountability, might well then have become several million times greater than they are or were in AD 2000.

These scenarios immediately pose a final question. Why would Christians need such staggering powers of calculation? One answer is that the world has become an enormously complex entity—6 billion human beings grouped in 12,600 ethnolinguistic peoples speaking over 13,500 languages. Describing all this complexity results in huge lists. Manipulating such lists requires vast computer memory and prodigious processing power unavailable until the present. Now these powers are becoming available to millions of Christians across the world. The churches need to ensure that world mission benefits from this development. And missiometrics gives them some powerful tools to assist them in obeying their Lord's Commission.

# II. 600 CLASSICS IMPINGING ON THE SCIENCE OF GLOBAL MISSION

This section presents a multilingual chronological bibliography, classification, and database, AD 66–2001. It lists 600 major published works purporting to deal with the whole global phenomenon of Christianity and its purpose and role in the world. This bibliography is given in Table 14–7 and deals with that part of the discipline of missiology which can be called a science in the 20th-21st century understanding of the term. The nature of science has been briefly described at the start of Part 14; it will now be analyzed in much more detail.

The task of science is to observe and explain actual events, processes, or phenomena. Originally the term science was derived from the Latin *scientia*, knowledge. By the 20th century it had become expanded (and at the same time restricted) to systematized knowledge, facts, principles, and methods concerning empirical phenomena whose analysis is dependent on mathematics and numeracy. This covers the whole realm of phenomena and processes, which can be classified and listed as is done below. First, scientific activity can be categorized under a sequence of 10 major stages or cover names as follows:

observing, data-gathering, measuring, mathematics, databasing, analyzing, dimensionizing, theorizing, reporting, applying.

A science starts by observing something previously unexplained, a new phenomenon. It then gathers as much relevant data about it as possible. The phenomenon is measured precisely at various points. At this juncture the role of mathematics as the central science is called in. A database to contain all the available data is now constructed. Analysis begins as certain patterns and regularities and relationships are noted. Before long, certain measurements stand out as exceptionally explanatory and are recognized as major dimensions. Hypotheses are put forward and tested. These are then linked to form a provisional theory or overall explanation. These findings now get written up, reported, and published. Finally, the new discovery is applied to some practical problem or use and new products ensue.

### 118 components of a science today
Second, for any given science those 10 stages cover or include many or even most of the following list of 118 components, arranged here in alphabetical order:

algebra, algorithms, analysis, applications, arithmetic, artificial intelligence, bibliography, calculation, calculus, censuses, chaos, classifications, coding, compilation, computation, computer modeling, concepts, correlation, counting, crosstabulations, cybernetics, data, databases, data-gathering, decimals, deduction, definitions, demographics, descriptions, digitizing, dimensions, empiricism, engineering, enumeration, equations, events, evidence, experimentation, exponentials, extrapolation, factors, facts, figures, findings, formulas, fractals, freeware, futurism, geometry, glossaries, graphics, graphs, hypotheses, indicators, induction, inference, information, instrumentation, instruments, Internet–1 and -2, interpretation, listings, logarithms, logic, maps, mathematics, measurements, methodologies, methods, miniprofiles, monitoring, numbers, numeracy, observations, paradigms, patterns, peer review, personages, phenomena, photographs, pictures, polls, prediction, probability, profiles, programming, projections, publications, quanta, quantification, questionnaires, rates, regularities, remote sensing, reports, robotics, sampling, scales, scanning, software, statistics, surveys, tables, taxonomy, technology, terminology, tests, theories, trends, typologies, variables, variance, websites, and a rapidly increasing number of other scientific aspects or applications.

These 10 and these 118 are shown arranged in logical order in Table 14–3. Each activity's current applications to global mission and world evangelization can be seen from the fact that all 10 and all 118 stages have been extensively employed in the compilation, analysis, and writing of the present volume. Some 10 stages were only partially employed and could be fruitful approaches for specialists in the future: these included numbers 49, 56, 79, 86, 115, 116, 117.

Any and every science is concerned particularly with empirical data (experiment and observation rather than theory), measurement, description, and interpretation and not in the first instance with normative (theoretical, academic) considerations. It creates and uses instruments (defined by *Websters* as: 'measuring devices').

The reader wishing to understand further the term 'science' and its components can be referred to any modern general encyclopedia. Especially illuminating are the following articles in the *New Encyclopaedia Britannica*, 15th edition, 1995: 'History of science' with 75 texts referenced, 'Philosophy of science' with 62 texts listed, 'Theory of measurement', 'Foundations of mathematics', 'Mathematics as a calculatory science', 'Theory of probability', 'Statistics', et alia.

## Table 14–3.  Essential components of a modern science, all with current application to global mission.

| Stages | | Stages | | Stages | | Stages | |
|---|---|---|---|---|---|---|---|
| **OBSERVING** | | 30 | Statistics | 60 | Digitizing | 91 | Interpretation |
| 1 | Observations | 31 | Decimals | 61 | Programming | | **DIMENSIONIZING** |
| 2 | Descriptions | 32 | Censuses | 62 | Software | 92 | Dimensions |
| 3 | Phenomena | 33 | Polls | 63 | Freeware | 93 | Concepts |
| 4 | Events | 34 | Numeracy | 64 | Compilation | 94 | Terminology |
| 5 | Personages | 35 | Demographics | 65 | Coding | 95 | Definitions |
| **DATA-GATHERING** | | 36 | Rates | 66 | Crosstabulations | 96 | Typologies |
| 6 | Data | 37 | Variance | 67 | Extrapolation | 97 | Paradigms |
| 7 | Bibliography | 38 | Variables | 68 | Correlation | 98 | Taxonomy |
| 8 | Literature review | 39 | Indicators | | **ANALYZING** | 99 | Classifications |
| 9 | Evidence | 40 | Instrumentation | 69 | Analysis | 100 | Glossaries |
| 10 | Surveys | 41 | Instruments | 70 | Empiricism | | **THEORIZING** |
| 11 | Questionnaires | 42 | Scales | 71 | Methodologies | 101 | Theories |
| 12 | Monitoring | 43 | Tests | 72 | Calculation | 102 | Deduction |
| 13 | Scanning | | **MATHEMATICS** | 73 | Regularities | 103 | Induction |
| 14 | Facts | 44 | Mathematics | 74 | Patterns | 104 | Futurism |
| 15 | Figures | 45 | Logic | 75 | Chance | 105 | Trends |
| 16 | Information | 46 | Methods | 76 | Intuition | 106 | Projections |
| 17 | Pictures | 47 | Algebra | 77 | Hypotheses | 107 | Prediction |
| 18 | Photographs | 48 | Arithmetic | 78 | Experimentation | | **REPORTING** |
| 19 | Internet-1 | 49 | Geometry | 79 | Cybernetics | 108 | Reports |
| 20 | Internet-2 | 50 | Calculus | 80 | Computation | 109 | Peer review |
| 21 | Profiles | 51 | Formulas | 81 | Remote sensing | 110 | Publications |
| 22 | Miniprofiles | 52 | Exponentials | 82 | Computer modeling | 111 | Abstracts |
| **MEASURING** | | 53 | Equations | 83 | Tables | 112 | Websites |
| 23 | Measurements | 54 | Logarithms | 84 | Graphs | 113 | Reviews |
| 24 | Enumeration | 55 | Algorithms | 85 | Maps | | **APPLYING** |
| 25 | Listings | 56 | Quanta | 86 | Fractals | 114 | Applications |
| 26 | Numbers | 57 | Chaos | 87 | Factors | 115 | Technology |
| 27 | Counting | 58 | Probability | 88 | Findings | 116 | Artificial intelligence |
| 28 | Quantification | | **DATABASING** | 89 | Graphics | 117 | Robotics |
| 29 | Sampling | 59 | Databases | 90 | Inference | 118 | Engineering |

### The proliferation of new sciences

Many new sciences have come into existence in the 20th century. A look at the *Oxford English dictionary*, CD version, shows that some 80 new sciences with names ending in -metrics are now being practiced. In most cases they are part of larger disciplines or subjects but restrict themselves to the purely scientific aspect. Thus economics has created its own scientific branch called econometrics which handles mathematical applications as illustrated in the book *A dictionary of econometrics*, 1994. Other applications peripheral to world mission but offering it assistance include: bibliometrics, cliometrics, biometrics, jurimetrics.

### Naming this new science of global missions

Applied to global mission, this approach results in empirical mission studies, widely understood today by the term 'descriptive missiology'. This has also been called missiography, or missionography. It is composed of one or more of the following empirical subjects: mission history, mission geography, mission education, mission theology, mission literature, missiometrics, exegesis, futuristics, missionary statistics, cartographics, photographics, sociographics, religiometrics, linguametrics, geocommission (the empirical study of Christ's Great Commission), and everything else related to mission.

As far as the content of missiometric materials goes, the most essential component is probably—*missionary statistics*. We should recall at this point the advice of Augustine of Hippo, and of Isidore of Seville (quoted here on the title page of this Part 14). They warn that knowledge can only be advanced by employing numbers and calculation or 'reckoning'. This means the application of the science of numbers.

To unify these various empirical subjects, it would be valuable to coin a single new word. This would have to incorporate recognition of the 'global' dimension. Some scholars have therefore spoken for 30 years or so of this as 'macromissiography'. There are counterparts in other languages: in German *Weltmissionswissenschaft*, in Dutch *Wereldzendingswetenschap*, and in French *science missionaire mondiale*. The most expressive single term in English used here to cover the whole science of global mission is the one that centers on measurement as science's key component: *missiometrics*. This brings together the 3 key ideas—mission, data, measurement, lacking only the global aspect. Adding it produces the somewhat overloaded term *macromissiometrics*. For the present it would seem best to revert back to 'the science of global mission', supported by the methodology of *missiometrics*.

### Components of the science of global mission

Over the years this approach has crystallized out, then, into the science of global mission. Correctly employed, this is that part of the discipline of missiology which adopts the scientific approach described above and directly applies it to the world of mission and its phenomena. This application is described here in Table 14–3, by rearranging the alphabetical listing of 118 components into its 10 major stages. The present volume then contains application of these components to a vast range of phenomena related to global Christianity and global mission.

### Criteria for selection of entries

What follows in the large Table 14–7 is our main listing of major classics or books impinging on missiometrics and thus defining the science of global mission over the 20 centuries of the Christian mission.

In this bibliography, entries are restricted by means of 5 criteria for inclusion, as follows:

1. *Global mission*. Core entries on this subject are mainly books which in some sense illustrate this

## Table 14–4.  Varieties and categories of publications on the science of global mission.

**Categories**

a Atlases (geographies)
b Bibliographies (catalogues, reviews, abstracts)
c Chronologies
d Dictionaries (lexicons, wordbooks)
e Encyclopedias
f Futuristics (futures studies)
g Glossaries (new or unusual or difficult terms)
h Histories
i Biographies (multibiographies, groupings, who's whos)
k Handbooks (compendia, yearbooks, almanacs)
m Mission strategies
n Philosophies
p Periodicals (series)
q Documents
r Encyclicals (or other formal papal documents)
s Surveys
t Theologies
u Directories
w Websites
x Biblical exegesis
y Education
z Art

concept of the Christian global mission or are valuable to it.
2. *The whole world*. Items are only eligible as entries if they represent an overview of the whole world, or most of it.
3. *Global Christianity*. Core items must exhibit an overview of all the branches of Christianity, or most of them or a majority of all Christians.
4. *Substantial length*. All items (with only a few exceptions) must be large, as most world reference books are.
5. *Originality*. Core items must contain substantial quantities of original data, information, and/or concepts, not merely reproducing other books' data or findings.

The term 'mission' is often widely used throughout the missiological literature to mean only either foreign missions or world missions. The term, however, must also be understood to include home mission, cross-cultural missions in Christian countries, local mission, even individual mission (as in biographies). It is necessary therefore to add the adjective 'global' or 'world' to indicate that distinctive meaning of mission that draws attention to its use to describe an overview of the entire mission phenomenon throughout the world and not merely some partial aspect.

Surveys of missions almost always contain a significant volume of systematic statistics making statistical analysis possible. Histories of mission however have often been compiled devoid of statistics; so have several leading dictionaries and even encyclopedias of mission. The present whole listing and analysis is descriptive and non-judgmental, but can only be helpful if it has clear boundaries. Code variables 14, 15, and 16 in Table 14–5 therefore set these boundaries and so assist the reader to locate the most valuable and useful core bibliographical items from the standpoint of constructing and documenting the science of global mission.

### Categories of global mission publications

Entries in Table 14–7 fall under the following listing of 22 categories of publication, as shown in Table 14–4. All are printed books except periodicals (which however become books when a year's issues become bound together) and websites (which offer the user instant printouts up to book length). Each category is coded in Table 14–7's column 9 by the small letter in the first column of Table 14–4. This is then expanded to some 17 variables describing each entry. And in sum, Table 14–7's columns 13, 14, 15, 16, with

## Table 14–5. Descriptive variables, data, and codes describing each book in this bibliography of global mission.

| Column | DESCRIPTORS | Data, values, and codes |
|---|---|---|
| 1 | Reference number | Based on chronological listing in column 2 |
| 2 | Year | Year first published as a book, or year of first of a multivolume work |
| 3 | Author/editor(s) | Initials and surname of first or primary author, and second author if listed, followed by 'ed/eds' if described as editor(s) |
| 4 | Title, subtitle, edition | In original or main language; edition if stated (1st, 2nd, 3rd, etc) |
| 5 | Initials | Initials if widely used to describe this title |
| 6 | Title translated into English | Meaning of title if not in English |
| 7 | Place of publication | City where first published (in local nomenclature) |
| 8 | Volumes | 1 or more (separate books) |
| 9 | Category of publication | a,b,c,d,e,f,g,h,i,k,m,n,p,q,s,t,u,w,x,y,z (as listed above in Table 14–4) |
| 10 | Language of publication | Original or primary language. |
| 11 | Translations | Other language published editions of this material, or (a dash) none. Names may be written in full, as in the list in the text below, or they may be abbreviated either to the first initials or to these 3-letter forms: Eng, Fre, Ger, Dut, Spa, Por, Ita, Lat, Rus, Ukr, Man, Pol, Swe, Nor, Gre, Ara, Kor, Mal, Jap, etc |
| 12 | Ecclesiology | Megabloc of author: O,R,A,P,I,m; a dash (-) signifies secular or non-Christian |

A SCALE OF CONTRIBUTION TO THIS SCIENCE

| | | |
|---|---|---|
| 13 | Empiricism | **5**=entirely empirical/factual/historical/descriptive |
| | | **4**=book mainly empirical or factual |
| | | **3**=both empirical and normative |
| | | **2**=mainly normative |
| | | **1**=normative with occasional empirical material, |
| | | **0**=entirely normative (e.g. theology with no church history) |
| 14 | Statistics | **5**=statistics central to book and its purpose |
| | | **4**=numerous and analyzed |
| | | **3**=numerous but unanalyzed, |
| | | **2**=scattered |
| | | **1**=virtually none |
| | | **0**=none |
| 15 | Total mission content, % | Measured by how many pages or articles or index references are devoted to any and all varieties of 'mission' in general (the whole complex mission/evangelism/conversion/converts/baptism, including home/foreign etc), from any or all megablocs or sources, with 6 types: |
| | | **5**=wholly devoted (>80%) |
| | | **4**=mainly (50-80%) |
| | | **3**=adequately (10-50%) |
| | | **2**=partially (1-10%) |
| | | **1**=marginally (<1% but >0) |
| | | **0**=zero |
| 16 | Global mission content, % | Types as in No. 15 above but refering specifically to 'global mission' or 'world mission', from any or all sources |
| | | **5**=wholly devoted (>80%) |
| | | **4**=mainly (50-80%) |
| | | **3**=adequately (10-50%) |
| | | **2**=partially (1-10%) |
| | | **1**=marginally (<1% but >0) |
| | | **0**=zero |
| 17 | Contribution to science of global mission, % | Sum of 4 columns 13-16, times 5, expressed as a percentage |

their summation in column 17 as a percentage 0-100%, reveal a core of 242 more-involved books indicated by column 17 being equal to 75% or higher surrounded by a periphery of 358 less-involved types.

### Descriptive codes for each book

All entries were now entered, classified, and coded into a relational database, with the following 17 characteristics as shown in Table 14–5. Results—totals of books and percentages—are shown in Table 14–6.

### 414 core books on global mission

All the books entered in this bibliography are, by means of this final variable 16, coded into one of 2 groups. First, those coded 5 or 4 in variable 16 are items strictly on global mission, covering both the whole world or most of it, and also the whole of Christianity or most of it. This is the core of this collection; it consists of items which use the term 'mission' to imply the whole of mission at the global level rather than at local levels only. They are, or contain, overall studies—overviews, worldwide summaries, all-inclusive totals.

### 186 books on background context

Second, by contrast, a fair number of items, shown coded as 3, 2, 1, or 0 in Table 14–6 variable 16 are books not primarily about the scientific aspect of global mission but which nevertheless are important in the study of global mission or useful or even essential as background context. These latter titles are shown here listed not in boldface but in medium type.

A somewhat more subjective criterion when assessing a possible book for inclusion here was: originality. To be included here, a book published after 1900 should contain either an evident quantity of new or original data, or an evident amount of new concepts, new analysis, or new classification. Books which recycle other books' data or concepts or findings are exceedingly numerous and have a valuable function to play within their own constituencies, but have little to contribute to this present investigation of fundamental classics and so are excluded.

### The 4 dimensions of missiometrics

The first 2 questions—Empiricism, and Statistics—define a book's contribution to science.

The last 2 questions—Mission, and Global Mission—define the book's contribution to mission in its widest range of meanings.

The 4 questions therefore describe the book's contribution to the *science of global mission*, and a final figure is calculated—up to 100%—to quantify this contribution.

### A scale of relevance to this new science

The 4 missiometric dimensions may now finally be combined to form one single scale indicating the relevance of each book to the new science of global mission. The code values of the 4 dimensions are added, then multiplied by 5 to produce a percentage figure, as shown in Table 14–6.

The central question is: Does this book contribute *directly* to the *science of mission*? Some 89 of these classics score 90% or more contributing to the *science* of global mission and thus constitute the central core of apologetic literature on the subject. Some 473 are 50% or more contributing, 127 less than 50%.

### Bibliographical entries for the science of global mission

Altogether, there are 600 entries in this bibliography. The entries consist of a core of some 400 books or other large publications, compiled by 500 or so authors, in over 20 major languages: English, French, German, Dutch, Spanish, Portuguese, Italian, Latin, Russian, Ukrainian, Mandarin Chinese, Polish, Swedish, Norwegian, Greek, Arabic, Korean, Tagalog, Malayalam, Japanese, etc. And these 400 are surrounded by another 200 more peripheral books, peripheral, that is, on the margins of the subject of the scientific study of global mission.

In the listing that follows, Table 14–7 lists all entries by chronological year of first publication.

## Table 14–6. 600 books classified by 4 missiometric descriptor dimensions and located on one overall scale of relevance to the science of global mission.

(a) Number of the 600 books for each code on each of 4 descriptors.

| Code | Definition | Empiricism | Statistics | Mission | Global mission |
|---|---|---|---|---|---|
| 0 | Zero | 125 | 136 | 26 | 48 |
| 1 | Occasionally | 5 | 133 | 30 | 22 |
| 2 | Partially | 4 | 161 | 41 | 34 |
| 3 | Half | 146 | 3 | 131 | 82 |
| 4 | Mainly | 19 | 120 | 188 | 126 |
| 5 | Entirely | 301 | 47 | 184 | 288 |
| | **Total** | **600** | **600** | **600** | **600** |

(b) Percentage of the 600 books for each code on each of 4 descriptors.

| Code | Definition | Empiricism | Statistics | Mission | Global mission |
|---|---|---|---|---|---|
| 0 | Zero | 21% | 23% | 4% | 8% |
| 1 | Occasionally | 1% | 22% | 5% | 4% |
| 2 | Partially | 1% | 27% | 7% | 6% |
| 3 | Half | 24% | 1% | 22% | 14% |
| 4 | Mainly | 3% | 20% | 31% | 21% |
| 5 | Entirely | 50% | 8% | 31% | 48% |
| | **Total** | **100%** | **100%** | **100%** | **100%** |

(c) Number and percentage of the 600 books on final overall scale from 0-100%.

| Code | Relevance | Books | Percent |
|---|---|---|---|
| 0 | Nil | 1 | 0.2% |
| 5 | Minimal | 2 | 0.3% |
| 10 | Scattered | 3 | 0.5% |
| 15 | Marginal | 1 | 0.2% |
| 20 | Occasional | 3 | 0.5% |
| 25 | Tangential | 21 | 3.5% |
| 30 | Limited | 28 | 4.7% |
| 35 | Peripheral | 21 | 3.5% |
| 40 | Background | 20 | 3.3% |
| 45 | Partial | 27 | 4.5% |
| 50 | Half | 67 | 11.2% |
| 55 | Useful | 36 | 6.0% |
| 60 | Helpful | 45 | 7.5% |
| 65 | Beneficial | 40 | 6.7% |
| 70 | Necessary | 43 | 7.2% |
| 75 | Core | 60 | 10.0% |
| 80 | Valuable | 43 | 7.2% |
| 85 | Indispensable | 50 | 8.3% |
| 90 | Essential | 48 | 8.0% |
| 95 | Central | 28 | 4.7% |
| 100 | Seminal | 13 | 2.2% |
| | **Total** | **600** | **100.0%** |

**Table 14–7. A bibliographical listing of 600 major classics or books impinging on missiometrics and thus defining the science of global mission, AD 66 – AD 2001.**

| Ref 1 | Year 2 | Authors/editors 3 | Title/subtitle/edition (in original language) 4 | Initials 5 | Title translated into English 6 | Place of publication 7 | Vols 8 | Cat 9 | Language 10 | Translations 11 | Ecc 12 | Em 13 | St 14 | M 15 | GM 16 | % 17 |
|---|---|---|---|---|---|---|---|---|---|---|---|---|---|---|---|---|
| 1 | 66 | Luke | Praxeis ton Hagion Apostolon | AA | The Acts of the Apostles | Roma | 1 | h | Greek | Over 1,500 | R | 5 | 2 | 5 | 5 | 85 |
| 2 | 80 | The Twelve | Didache | | The Teaching of the Twelve Apostles | Damascus | 1 | t | Greek | Latin et al | O | 0 | 0 | 5 | 3 | 40 |
| 3 | 85 | Barnabas | Barnaba Epistole | | The Epistle of Barnabas | Alexandria | 1 | f | Greek | Many | O | 0 | 0 | 5 | 2 | 35 |
| 4 | 96 | John the Divine | Apokalypsis Ioannou tou Theologou | | The Book of Revelation | Ephesus | 1 | f | Greek | Over 1,100 | O | 5 | 2 | 5 | 5 | 85 |
| 5 | 140 | Hermas | Pastor de Hermas | | The Shepherd of Hermas | Roma | 1 | t | Latin | Greek | R | 0 | 0 | 3 | 2 | 25 |
| 6 | 150 | Justin Martyr | Apologia | | Defense | Roma | 1 | t | Latin | Greek | R | 0 | 0 | 5 | 3 | 40 |
| 7 | 197 | Tertullian | Apologia | | In Defense of the Faith | Carthage | 1 | t | Latin | Greek | R | 0 | 0 | 5 | 4 | 45 |
| 8 | 205 | Clement of Alexandria | Protrepticus | | Exhortation to Conversion | Alexandria | 1 | t | Latin | Greek | O | 0 | 0 | 4 | 4 | 40 |
| 9 | 248 | Origen | Contra Celsum | | Against the Teachings of Celsus | Alexandria | 1 | t | Greek | Latin | O | 3 | 0 | 3 | 5 | 55 |
| 10 | 295 | Eusebius of Caesarea | Historia Ecclesiastica | EH | The Ecclesiastical History | Caesarea | 1 | h | Latin | Greek | O | 5 | 1 | 3 | 3 | 60 |
| 11 | 360 | Ephrem | Apostolic Constitutions | | Apostolic Constitutions | Antioch | 8 | k | Greek | Syriac | O | 3 | 0 | 2 | 4 | 45 |
| 12 | 417 | Paulus Orosius | Historia adversus paganos | | A History against Paganism | Sevilla | 7 | h | Latin | Spanish | R | 4 | 0 | 5 | 4 | 65 |
| 13 | 426 | Augustine of Hippo | De Civitate Dei | DCD | The City of God | Carthage | 1 | t | Latin | EFGISP | R | 0 | 0 | 5 | 5 | 50 |
| 14 | 428 | Prosper Tiro | De Vocatione Omnium Gentium | | On the Calling of All Peoples | Marseille | 1 | m | Latin | Italian | R | 4 | 1 | 5 | 5 | 75 |
| 15 | 535 | Cosmas Indicopleustes | Topographia Christiana | TC | The Christian Topography | Alexandria | 12 | s | Latin | | O | 5 | 2 | 3 | 4 | 70 |
| 16 | 594 | Gregory the Great | Dialogi | | Letters and Instructions | Roma | 1 | m | Latin | | R | 3 | 0 | 3 | 4 | 50 |
| 17 | 960 | Adso of Montier-en-Der | De Ortu et Tempore Antichristi | | Letter on the Origin and Time of the Antichrist | Dijon | 1 | f | Latin | Eng,Fre | R | 0 | 0 | 4 | 5 | 45 |
| 18 | 1140 | Bernard of Clairvaux | De consideratione | | On Contemplation | Clairvaux | 5 | m | Latin | Fre,Ger | R | 0 | 0 | 5 | 5 | 50 |
| 19 | 1180 | Joachim of Fiore | Expositio in Apocalypsim | | Exposition on the Apocalypse | Fiore | 1 | f | Latin | Italian | R | 0 | 0 | 5 | 4 | 45 |
| 20 | 1190 | Petrus Comestor | Historia Scholastica | | History of the Bible | Troyes | 1 | h | Latin | Fre,Ita,Spa | R | 5 | 0 | 3 | 2 | 50 |
| 21 | 1265 | Thomas Aquinas | De Aeternitate Mundi contra Murmurantes | DAM | On the Eternity of the World | Paris | 1 | f | Latin | French | R | 0 | 0 | 3 | 4 | 35 |
| 22 | 1272 | Thomas Aquinas | Summa Theologicae | ST | Summary of Theology | Paris | 32 | t | Latin | French | R | 0 | 0 | 3 | 4 | 35 |
| 23 | 1288 | Alexander of Roes | Notitia Seculi | | Secular Knowledge | Koln | 1 | f | Latin | English | R | 3 | 0 | 4 | 5 | 60 |
| 24 | 1294 | Ramon Llull | Petitio Raimundi pro conversione infidelium | | A Petition concerning Conversion of Infidels | Miramar | 1 | m | Latin | Catalan | R | 0 | 0 | 4 | 4 | 40 |
| 25 | 1495 | Girolamo Savonarola | Compendio di Rivelazioni | | The Compendium of Revelations | Firenze | 1 | f | Italian | Latin | R | 4 | 0 | 2 | 1 | 35 |
| 26 | 1498 | Albrecht Durer | Apocalypse | | The Last Times | Nurnberg | 1 | f | German | Eng,Fre | R | 5 | 0 | 3 | 2 | 50 |
| 27 | 1510 | Desiderius Erasmus | Ecclesiastes sive Concionator evangelicus | | Instructions for Preachers of the Gospel | Rotterdam | 1 | m | Latin | Fre,Ger,Ita | R | 0 | 0 | 5 | 4 | 45 |
| 28 | 1516 | Thomas More | Utopia | | Nowhere | London | 1 | f | Latin | English | A | 0 | 0 | 2 | 2 | 20 |
| 29 | 1517 | Leonardo da Vinci | Visiones de Finis Mundi | | Visions of the End of the World | Paris | 1 | f | Latin | Ita,Eng,Fre | R | 0 | 0 | 2 | 5 | 35 |
| 30 | 1536 | John Calvin | Christianae Religionis Institutio | CRI | Institutes of the Christian Religion | Basel | 4 | t | Latin | French | P | 0 | 0 | 5 | 3 | 40 |
| 31 | 1536 | Bartolome de Las Casas | De Unico Vocationis Modo | | The Only Way to Draw All Peoples to the True Religion | Chiapas | 1 | m | Latin | Spanish | R | 0 | 0 | 5 | 5 | 50 |
| 32 | 1544 | Ignatius Loyola | Constitutiones circa Missiones | | Arrangements concerning Missions | Paris | 1 | m | Latin | French | R | 0 | 0 | 5 | 5 | 50 |
| 33 | 1555 | Nostradamus | Centuries | | The Centuries | Lyon | 10 | f | Provencal | Lat,Gre,Ita | R | 5 | 1 | 0 | 0 | 30 |
| 34 | 1574 | Johann Focher | Itinerarium catholicum proficiscentium ad infideles convertendos | | Catholic way | Roma | 1 | m | Latin | Spanish | R | 0 | 0 | 5 | 5 | 50 |
| 35 | 1588 | Jose de Acosta | De Procuranda Indorum Salute | | Finding Salvation for the Heathens | Salamanca | 1 | m | Latin | Spanish | R | 0 | 2 | 5 | 5 | 60 |
| 36 | 1591 | Adrianus Saravia | De diversis ministrorum evangelii gradibus | | The diverse options of ministries of the Gospel | Frankfurt | 1 | m | Latin | Eng,Ger | A | 0 | 1 | 5 | 5 | 55 |
| 37 | 1593 | Anthony Possevin | Bibliotheca selecta de ratione studiorum | | Select Bibliography of Rational Practice | Roma | 1 | m | Latin | Italian | R | 0 | 0 | 5 | 5 | 50 |
| 38 | 1594 | John Napier | Plaine Discovery of the Whole Revelation of Saint John | | — | Edinburgh | 1 | f | English | | P | 5 | 0 | 3 | 3 | 55 |
| 39 | 1601 | Luis de Guzman | Historia de las Missiones | | History of Missions | Alcala | 1 | h | Spanish | | R | 5 | 2 | 4 | 4 | 75 |
| 40 | 1613 | Thomas a Jesu | De Procuranda Salute Omnium Gentium | | Obtaining Salvation for All Peoples | Antwerp | 12 | m | Latin | Spanish | R | 0 | 2 | 5 | 5 | 60 |
| 41 | 1620 | Hieronimus a Matre Dei | Zelus propagationis fidei | | Zeal for the Propagation of the Faith | Koln | 1 | m | Latin | Ger,Ita | R | 0 | 0 | 5 | 5 | 50 |
| 42 | 1622 | Johannes a Jesu | Assertio missionum et rationum adversarum resolutio | | Rational Missionary Assertions against Adversaries | Koln | 1 | m | Latin | German | R | 0 | 0 | 5 | 5 | 50 |
| 43 | 1627 | Joseph Mede | Apocalyptica: Key of the Revelation | | Apocalyptic as the key to Revelation | Cambridge | 1 | f | English | | A | 4 | 1 | 4 | 5 | 70 |
| 44 | 1630 | Francesco Ingoli | Relazione delle Quattro Parti del Mondo | RFPW | Report on the Four Parts of the World | Roma | 1 | s | Italian | Latin | R | 4 | 0 | 5 | 5 | 70 |
| 45 | 1650 | Gisbertus Voetius | De Missionibus Ecclesiasticis | DME | On the Missionary Work of the Church | Utrecht | 1 | m | Latin | Dutch | P | 0 | 1 | 4 | 5 | 50 |
| 46 | 1653 | Raymond Caron | Apostolatus evangelicus Missioneriorum regularium per universum orbem | | Evangelical Apostolate of Regular Missionaries | Antwerp | 1 | m | Latin | Dutch | R | 0 | 2 | 5 | 5 | 60 |
| 47 | 1653 | Alexander Ross | Pansebia: or, A View of All Religions in the World | | — | London | 1 | s | English | | A | 5 | 2 | 3 | 3 | 65 |
| 48 | 1663 | Justinian von Weltz | Appeal to engage in world mission | | — | Nurnberg | 1 | t | Latin | German | P | 0 | 0 | 5 | 3 | 40 |
| 49 | 1672 | P. Erington | Missionarius seu opusculum practicum pro fide propaganda et conservanda | | Missionaries: on Spreading and Conserving the Faith | Roma | 1 | m | Latin | English | R | 0 | 0 | 5 | 5 | 50 |
| 50 | 1675 | Matthias a Corona | Tractatus de Missionibus Apostolicis | | A Tract on Apostolic Missions | Roma | 1 | m | Latin | French | R | 0 | 0 | 5 | 5 | 50 |
| 51 | 1677 | Urbano Cerri | Stato della Religione Cattolica in tutto il Mondo | | State of the Catholic Religion in the World | Roma | 1 | s | Italian | Lat,Eng,Fre | R | 5 | 2 | 5 | 5 | 85 |
| 52 | 1689 | Dominicus de Gubernatis | De Missionibus Antiquis | | On Missions in Earlier Times | Roma | 1 | m | Latin | Ita,Ger,Fre | R | 3 | 2 | 5 | 5 | 75 |
| 53 | 1699 | Isaac Newton | Observations upon the Prophecies of Daniel and the Apocalypse of St John | PDAJ | — | Dublin | 1 | f | English | | A | 5 | 1 | 3 | 3 | 60 |
| 54 | 1699 | John Craige | Theologiae Christianae Principia Mathematica | MPCT | Mathematical Principles of Christian Theology | London | 1 | n | Latin | English | A | 5 | 0 | 2 | 3 | 50 |
| 55 | 1715 | Richard Steele | An Account of the State of the Roman Catholic Religion | | — | London | 1 | s | English | Ita,Fre,Spa | A | 5 | 2 | 5 | 5 | 85 |
| 56 | 1723 | Robert Millar | The History of the Propagation of Christianity, and the Overthrow of Paganism | | — | London | 2 | h | English | | A | 5 | 1 | 4 | 5 | 75 |
| 57 | 1731 | Johann A. Fabricius | Salutaris Lux Evangelii Toti Orbi per Divinam Gratiam Exoriens | | The Gospel, saving Light through Grace to All | Hamburg | 1 | h | Latin | | P | 3 | 1 | 4 | 5 | 65 |
| 58 | 1740 | Nicolaus von Zinzendorf | Instruktion an alle Heydenboten | | Instruction concerning Preaching to Heathens | Herrnhut | 1 | m | German | | P | 0 | 0 | 5 | 5 | 50 |
| 59 | 1742 | Thomas Broughton | An Historical Dictionary of All Religions from the Creation of the World | | — | London | 1 | d | English | | A | 5 | 2 | 4 | 4 | 75 |
| 60 | 1784 | Hannah Adams | Alphabetical Compendium of the Various Sects in the Christian Era | | — | Boston, MA | 1 | s | English | | P | 5 | 2 | 4 | 4 | 75 |
| 61 | 1782 | Andrew Fuller | The Gospel of Christ worthy of all Acceptation | | — | Northampton | 1 | t | English | | P | 0 | 1 | 5 | 5 | 55 |
| 62 | 1792 | William Carey | An Enquiry into the Obligations of Christians to use Means for the Conversion of Heathens | EOC | — | Leicester | 1 | s | English | | P | 3 | 5 | 5 | 5 | 90 |
| 63 | 1795 | Charles F. Dupuis | Origine de tous les cultes, ou religion universelle | | Origin of All Religions, or Universal Religion | Paris | 7 | s | French | | P | 5 | 2 | 2 | 3 | 60 |
| 64 | 1804 | C. F. Staudlin | Kirchliche Geographie und Statistik | KGS | Church Geography and Statistics | Tubingen | 1 | a | German | | P | 5 | 4 | 4 | 4 | 85 |
| 65 | 1806 | C. Meiners | Algemeine kritische Geschichte der Religionen | | Universal Critical History of Religions | Hanover | 2 | h | German | | P | 5 | 2 | 3 | 3 | 65 |
| 66 | 1808 | H. N. Pearson | A Dissertation on the Propagation of Christianity in Different Nations | DPC | — | Oxford | 2 | m | English | | A | 5 | 2 | 3 | 3 | 65 |
| 67 | 1813 | E. Lord | Compendious History of the Principal Protestant Missions to the Heathen | | — | Boston | 2 | h | English | | P | 5 | 2 | 4 | 5 | 80 |
| 68 | 1814 | W. Brown | The History of the Christian Missions of the 16th, 17th, 18th, and 19th Centuries | HCM | — | Edinburgh | 2 | h | English | | P | 5 | 4 | 4 | 5 | 90 |
| 69 | 1815 | Hannah Adams | A Dictionary of All Religions and Religious Denominations, Ancient and Modern | | — | London | 1 | d | English | | P | 5 | 2 | 3 | 4 | 70 |
| 70 | 1815 | CMS | The Spirit of British Missions | | — | London | 1 | t | English | | A | 0 | 0 | 5 | 5 | 50 |
| 71 | 1818 | P. Rho | La fecondita della Sacra Chiesa Romana | | The Expansion of the Holy Roman Church | Brescia | 3 | m | Italian | Latin | R | 3 | 2 | 5 | 5 | 75 |
| 72 | 1818 | G. Hall, S. Newell | The Conversion of the World: or the Claims of 600 Millions | | — | Boston | 1 | m | English | | P | 3 | 5 | 5 | 5 | 90 |
| 73 | 1818 | C. G. Blumhardt | Versuch einer allgemeinen Missionsgeschichte der Kirche Christi | | Attempt at a Universal Missions History of the Church | Basel | 3 | h | German | | P | 3 | 1 | 4 | 5 | 65 |
| 74 | 1819 | M. Winslow | A Sketch of Missions: the Principal Attempts to propagate Christianity among the Heathen | | — | Andover | 1 | s | English | | P | 5 | 2 | 3 | 5 | 75 |
| 75 | 1820 | K. G. Leonhardt | Die gesegnete Ausbreitung des Christentums unter Heyden, Muhammedanern und Juden | | Christendom under Heathens, Muslims, Jews | Dresden | 1 | h | German | | P | 3 | 1 | 4 | 5 | 65 |
| 76 | 1824 | D. Benedict | History of All Religions: Paganism, Mahometism, Judaism, and Christianity | | — | Providence, RI | 1 | h | English | | P | 5 | 2 | 3 | 3 | 65 |
| 77 | 1835 | J. H. Brauer | Beitrage zur Geschichte der Heidenbekehrung | BGH | Toward a History of the Conversion of Heathens | Hamburg | 1 | h | German | | P | 5 | 2 | 3 | 5 | 75 |

| Ref 1 | Year 2 | Authors/editors 3 | Title/subtitle/edition (in original language) 4 | Initials 5 | Title translated into English 6 | Place of publication 7 | Vols 8 | Cat 9 | Language 10 | Translations 11 | Ecc 12 | Em 13 | St 14 | M 15 | GM 16 | % 17 |
|---|---|---|---|---|---|---|---|---|---|---|---|---|---|---|---|---|
| 78 | 1836 | ABCFM | The Duty of the Present Generation to Evangelize the World | | — | Boston | 1 | m | English | | P | 3 | 4 | 5 | 5 | 85 |
| 79 | 1836 | T. S. Skinner | Thoughts on Evangelizing the World | | — | New York | 1 | t | English | | P | 3 | 2 | 4 | 5 | 70 |
| 80 | 1837 | R. Anderson | The Time for the World's Conversion Come | | — | Boston | 1 | t | English | | P | 3 | 2 | 5 | 5 | 75 |
| 81 | 1839 | J. Wyld | An atlas of maps of different parts of the world: stations of Protestant missions | | — | London | 1 | a | English | | A | 5 | 2 | 4 | 4 | 75 |
| 82 | 1841 | G. C. F. Lucke | Missionsstudien oder Beytrage zur Missionswissenschaft | | Mission studies: an attempt at a science of missions | Gottingen | 1 | m | German | | P | 5 | 1 | 4 | 4 | 70 |
| 83 | 1842 | J. A. Huie | History of Christian missions, from the Reformation to the present time, 2nd edition | | — | Edinburgh | 1 | h | English | | P | 5 | 2 | 3 | 5 | 75 |
| 84 | 1842 | J. Wiggers | Kirchliche Statistik oder Darstellung der gesammten christlichen Kirche | | Ecclesiastical statistics of the entire Church | Hamburg | 2 | s | German | | P | 5 | 3 | 4 | 5 | 85 |
| 85 | 1842 | J. Harris | The Great Commission: the church charged to convey the Gospel to the world | | — | Boston | 1 | s | English | | P | 3 | 2 | 5 | 5 | 75 |
| 86 | 1843 | K. A. F. Hinkel | Die Bekehrung der Welt zu Jesus Christus und das christliche Missionswerk | | Conversion of the world to Christ and missions | Berlin | 3 | m | German | | P | 5 | 2 | 5 | 5 | 85 |
| 87 | 1843 | A. Grant | The past and prospective extension of the gospel by missions to the heathen | | — | London | 1 | s | English | | A | 3 | 2 | 3 | 5 | 65 |
| 88 | 1844 | J. N. Brown, ed | Encyclopedia of religious knowledge: Bible, biography, religions, history, missions worldwide | ERK | — | Brattleboro, VT | 1 | e | English | | A | 5 | 2 | 3 | 3 | 65 |
| 89 | 1844 | J. C. Blumhardt | Handbuchlein der Missionsgeschichte und Missionsgeographie | | Handbook on history and geography of missions | Calw | 2 | k | German | | P | 5 | 4 | 4 | 5 | 90 |
| 90 | 1844 | M. R. A. Henrion | Histoire generale des missions catholiques depuis le XIIIe siecle jusqu'a nos jours | | General history of Catholic missions since AD 1200 | Paris | 2 | h | French | Ita,Spa,Ger | R | 5 | 1 | 4 | 5 | 75 |
| 91 | 1844 | O. Corsi | Notizie statistiche delle missioni di tutto il mondo | | Statistical report on missions worldwide | Roma | 1 | s | Italian | | R | 5 | 4 | 3 | 5 | 85 |
| 92 | 1844 | J. P. Migne | Patrologiae cursus completus, seu biblioteca universalis | | A complete library on Patristics | Paris | 221 | q | Latin | French | R | 3 | 1 | 1 | 1 | 30 |
| 93 | 1845 | A. K. Von Heiligen | Die katholische Kirche in ihrer gegenwartigen Ausbreitung auf der Erde | DKK | The present worldwide spread of the Catholic Church | Regensburg | 1 | s | German | | R | 5 | 2 | 5 | 5 | 85 |
| 94 | 1845 | J. Wiggers | Geschichte der evangelischen Mission | | History of Protestant missions | Hamburg | 2 | h | German | | P | 5 | 1 | 4 | 5 | 75 |
| 95 | 1846 | J. C. Blumhardt | Christian missions: a manual of missionary geography and history | | — | London | 2 | a | English | Ger,Fre,Dut | P | 5 | 4 | 4 | 5 | 90 |
| 96 | 1846 | J. Sondermann, ed | Tabellarische Ubersicht uber die protestantischen Missionsgesellschaften | | Tabular overview of Protestant mission agencies | Nurnberg | 1 | s | German | | P | 5 | 4 | 3 | 4 | 80 |
| 97 | 1847 | J. H. Brauer | Das Missionswesen der evangelischen Kirche: Missions-Statistik | | Missions statistics as descriptive of Protestantism | Hamburg | 2 | s | German | | P | 5 | 4 | 3 | 5 | 85 |
| 98 | 1848 | S. E. Morse, ed | The cerographic missionary atlas | | — | New York | 1 | a | English | | P | 5 | 1 | 3 | 5 | 70 |
| 99 | 1849 | R. Vormbaum | Evangelische Missionsgeschichte in Biographien | | Biographies from Protestant mission history | Dusseldorf | 20 | i | German | Swedish | P | 5 | 1 | 5 | 4 | 75 |
| 100 | 1853 | J. Kingsmill | Missions and missionaries: apostolic, Jesuit, and Protestant Christian | | — | London | 1 | i | English | | A | 5 | 1 | 4 | 4 | 70 |
| 101 | 1853 | E. Hawkins | The colonial church atlas, arranged in dioceses, 3rd edition | | — | London | 1 | a | English | | A | 5 | 2 | 3 | 3 | 65 |
| 102 | 1854 | H. Newcomb | A cyclopedia of missions: missionary operations throughout the world, 1st edition | CM | — | New York | 1 | s | English | | P | 3 | 4 | 4 | 5 | 80 |
| 103 | 1854 | J. C. Lowrie | A manual of missions: sketches, maps of Protestant work among unevangelized nations | | — | New York | 1 | k | English | | P | 5 | 4 | 4 | 5 | 90 |
| 104 | 1854 | J. Darling | Cyclopaedia bibliographica: a library manual of theological and general literature | | — | London | 3 | b | English | | A | 4 | 1 | 3 | 3 | 55 |
| 105 | 1854 | J. J. Herzog | Realencyklopadie fur protestantische Theologie und Kirche | RPTK | Encyclopedia of Protestant theology and church | Leipzig | 24 | e | German | | P | 3 | 2 | 3 | 3 | 55 |
| 106 | 1855 | J. Chowanetz | Die Missionen der katholischen Kirche: Begrif, Wesen, Geschichte, Statistik | MKK | Catholic missions: concepts, history, statistics | Neisse | 1 | s | German | | R | 5 | 4 | 4 | 5 | 90 |
| 107 | 1856 | R. Anderson | Outline of missionary policy | | — | New York | 1 | m | English | | P | 0 | 1 | 4 | 5 | 50 |
| 108 | 1857 | H. Hahn | Geschichte der katholischen Missionen seit Jesus Christus bis auf die neueste Zeit | | Catholic mission history from Christ to today | Koln | 5 | h | German | | R | 5 | 1 | 4 | 5 | 75 |
| 109 | 1858 | G. E. Burkhardt | Kleine Missions-Bibliothek der evangelischen Heidenmission | | Bibliography on Protestant missions to heathens | Bielefeld | 5 | b | German | | P | 5 | 4 | 5 | 4 | 90 |
| 110 | 1858 | G. Petri | L'orbe cattolico ossia atlante geografico, storico, ecclesiastico | | Catholic historical ecclesiastical world atlas | Roma | 3 | a | Italian | | R | 5 | 2 | 3 | 3 | 65 |
| 111 | 1859 | CMS | The Church Missionary atlas, 1st edition | CMA | — | London | 1 | a | English | | A | 5 | 2 | 3 | 3 | 65 |
| 112 | 1860 | J. L. Aikman | Cyclopaedia of Christian missions: their rise, progress, and present posiion, 1st edition | CCM | — | London | 1 | e | English | | P | 3 | 4 | 5 | 5 | 85 |
| 113 | 1860 | A. K. Von Heiligen | Statistisches Jahrbuch der Kirche | SJK | Statistical yearbook of the Church | Regensburg | 2 | s | German | | R | 5 | 5 | 3 | 3 | 80 |
| 114 | 1862 | T. W. Marshall | Christian missions: their agents, their methods and their results | | — | London | 3 | s | English | Fre,Ger,Ital | R | 5 | 2 | 4 | 5 | 80 |
| 115 | 1862 | J. L. Aikman | Christ's kingdom in progress: Christian missions, their rise, progress, and present situation | | — | London | 1 | s | English | | P | 3 | 4 | 5 | 5 | 85 |
| 116 | 1862 | H. Venn | The missionary life and labours of Francis Xavier: results of Roman Catholic missions | | — | London | 1 | i | English | German | A | 5 | 2 | 5 | 5 | 85 |
| 117 | 1863 | M. Lacroix, et al | Dictionnaire des missions catholiques | DMC | Dictionary of Catholic missions | Paris | 2 | d | French | | R | 5 | 4 | 5 | 5 | 95 |
| 118 | 1863 | W. B. Boyce, ed | Statistics of Protestant missionary societies | | — | London | 1 | s | English | | A | 5 | 4 | 2 | 3 | 70 |
| 119 | 1864 | S. J. Neher | Kirchliche Geographie und Statistik | KGS | Geography and statistics of the church | Regensburg | 3 | a | German | | R | 5 | 2 | 4 | 3 | 70 |
| 120 | 1866 | J. Hassell | From pole to pole: being the history of Christian missions in all countries of the world | | — | London | 1 | h | English | | A | 5 | 2 | 4 | 4 | 75 |
| 121 | 1867 | P. R. Grundemann, ed | Allgemeiner Missions-Atlas nach Originalquellen | AMA | Universal missions atlas from original sources | Gotha | 4 | a | German | | P | 5 | 2 | 3 | 5 | 75 |
| 122 | 1867 | C. H. C. Plath | Die Erwahlung der Volker im Lichte der Missionsgeschichte | | Election of peoples in light of missions history | Berlin | 1 | h | German | | P | 5 | 2 | 4 | 5 | 80 |
| 123 | 1869 | C. H. C. Plath | Die Missionsgedanken des Freiherrn von Leibnitz | | The missions thinking of Baron von Leibritz | Berlin | 1 | m | German | | P | 0 | 2 | 4 | 4 | 50 |
| 124 | 1869 | R. Anderson | Foreign missions: their relations and claims | | — | New York | 1 | m | English | | P | 0 | 1 | 4 | 5 | 50 |
| 125 | 1872 | W. Moister | The missionary world: an encyclopedia of information in all ages, countries, denominations | MW | — | New York | 1 | e | English | | P | 5 | 2 | 4 | 5 | 80 |
| 126 | 1875 | F. M. Muller | The sacred books of the East | SBE | — | Oxford | 51 | n | English | | P | 5 | 1 | 0 | 0 | 30 |
| 127 | 1877 | W. Smith, ed, H. Wace | Dictionary of Christian biography, literature, sects, and doctrines | DCB | — | London | 4 | i | English | | A | 5 | 2 | 5 | 4 | 80 |
| 128 | 1878 | W. E. Blackstone | Jesus is coming: God's hope for a restless world | | — | Chicago | 1 | f | English | | P | 5 | 0 | 4 | 5 | 70 |
| 129 | 1878 | R. G. Wilder | The missionary review of the world | MRW | — | Princeton, NJ | 20 | p | English | | P | 3 | 4 | 5 | 5 | 85 |
| 130 | 1878 | J. Gall | The science of missions | | — | Edinburgh | 1 | m | English | | P | 5 | 2 | 3 | 3 | 65 |
| 131 | 1879 | J.-J. Gaume | L'evangelisation apostolique du globe, preuve de la divinite du Christianisme | | The missionary evangelization of the globe | Paris | 1 | t | French | | R | 0 | 1 | 2 | 2 | 25 |
| 132 | 1879 | T. Christlieb | Protestant foreign missions: their present state, a universal survey | | — | Gutersloh | 1 | s | English | GDFNS | P | 5 | 4 | 4 | 4 | 85 |
| 133 | 1881 | F. S. Dobbins | A foreign missionary manual: geographical, synoptical, statistical, bibliographical | FMM | — | Philadelphia | 1 | k | English | | P | 3 | 2 | 4 | 4 | 65 |
| 134 | 1882 | W. F. Bainbridge | Around the world tour of Christian missions: a universal survey | | — | Boston | 1 | s | English | | P | 5 | 4 | 4 | 4 | 85 |
| 135 | 1882 | G. Warneck | Outline of a history of Protestant missions from the Reformation to the present time | | — | Leipzig | 1 | h | English | Ger,Dut,Swe | P | 5 | 2 | 4 | 4 | 75 |
| 136 | 1883 | J. Vahl | Missionsatlas: med tilhorende forklaring | | Missions atlas with explanation | Kobenhavn | 4 | a | Danish | | P | 5 | 4 | 4 | 4 | 85 |
| 137 | 1884 | O. Werner | Katholischer Missions-Atlas: neunzehn Karten in Farbendruck | KMA | Catholic missions atlas: 19 maps in color | Freiburg | 1 | a | German | French | R | 5 | 2 | 4 | 5 | 80 |
| 138 | 1884 | C. C. Morrison | The Christian Century/The Christian Oracle (until 1900, refounded 1908) | | — | New York | 15 | p | English | | P | 3 | 1 | 4 | 4 | 60 |
| 139 | 1884 | A. O. Van Lennep, et al | The growth of Christianity during 19 centuries | GC | — | New York | 1 | s | English | | P | 4 | 5 | 5 | 5 | 95 |
| 140 | 1885 | D. L. Moody, A. T. Pierson | An Appeal to Disciples Everywhere | | — | Northfield, MA | 1 | m | English | | P | 0 | 0 | 5 | 5 | 50 |
| 141 | 1886 | J. Johnston | A century of Protestant missions and the increase of the heathen during the hundred years | | — | Edinburgh | 1 | h | English | | P | 5 | 4 | 4 | 4 | 85 |
| 142 | 1886 | A. Fischer | De salute infidelium | | On the salvation of the heathen | Essen | 1 | m | Latin | GFI | R | 0 | 1 | 3 | 5 | 45 |
| 143 | 1886 | A. T. Pierson | The crisis of missions: the voice of the cloud | | — | London | 1 | m | English | Dutch | P | 4 | 4 | 4 | 5 | 85 |
| 144 | 1886 | G. Hagar, ed, A. Rawson | What the world believes: people of all races and nations, rites and ceremonies | | — | New York | 1 | s | English | | P | 5 | 2 | 3 | 3 | 65 |
| 145 | 1886 | P. R. Grundemann | Zur Statistik der evangelischen Mission | ZSM | On Protestant mission statistics | Gutersloh | 1 | s | German | | P | 5 | 4 | 4 | 4 | 85 |
| 146 | 1888 | T. Hogben | God's plan for soul winning | | — | London | 1 | m | English | | P | 0 | 1 | 5 | 4 | 50 |
| 147 | 1888 | E. G. White | The Great Controversy | | — | Battle Creek, MI | 1 | x | English | | P | 5 | 0 | 5 | 5 | 75 |
| 148 | 1889 | J. T. Gracey | A manual of modern missions, historical and statistical accounts of Protestant missions | | — | New York | 1 | k | English | | P | 5 | 4 | 4 | 4 | 85 |
| 149 | 1889 | K. R. Hagenbach | Encyclopadie und Methodologie der theologischen Wissenschaften | EMTW | Encyclopedic methodology of the science of theology | Leipzig | 1 | e | German | | P | 5 | 2 | 2 | 3 | 60 |
| 150 | 1890 | E. Hodder, ed | Conquests of the Cross: a record of missionary work throughout the world | | — | London | 3 | h | English | | A | 5 | 4 | 5 | 5 | 95 |
| 151 | 1890 | P. R. Grundemann | Die Entwickelung der evangelischen Mission im letzten Jahrzehnt (1878-1888) | EMJ | Development of Protestant missions, 1878-1888 | Bielefeld | 1 | s | German | | P | 5 | 5 | 5 | 5 | 100 |
| 152 | 1890 | A. Launay | Histoire generale des missions etrangeres | HGME | General history of foreign missions | Paris | 3 | h | French | | R | 5 | 4 | 5 | 5 | 95 |
| 153 | 1890 | O. Werner | Orbis terrarum catholicus: conspectus geographicus et statisticus | OTC | Geographico-statistical overview of the Catholic world | Freiburg | 1 | a | Latin | | R | 5 | 4 | 4 | 4 | 85 |
| 154 | 1890 | J. G. Frazer | The golden bough: a study in magic and religion | GB | — | London | 12 | n | English | | A | 5 | 0 | 0 | 0 | 25 |
| 155 | 1891 | S. M. Jackson, ed | A bibliography of foreign missions | BFM | — | New York | 1 | b | English | | P | 5 | 1 | 4 | 5 | 75 |
| 156 | 1891 | J. Vahl | Der Stand der evangelischen Heidenmission in den Jahren 1845 und 1890 | | The state of Protestant missions to the heathen | Gutersloh | 1 | s | German | English | P | 3 | 2 | 4 | 4 | 65 |
| 157 | 1891 | G. T. Bettany | Encyclopedia of world religions: a comprehensive popular account | | — | New York | 1 | e | English | | P | 5 | 2 | 3 | 3 | 65 |

| Ref 1 | Year 2 | Authors/editors 3 | Title/subtitle/edition (in original language) 4 | Initials 5 | Title translated into English 6 | Place of publication 7 | Vols 8 | Cat 9 | Language 10 | Translations 11 | Ecc 12 | Em 13 | St 14 | M 15 | GM 16 | % 17 |
|---|---|---|---|---|---|---|---|---|---|---|---|---|---|---|---|---|
| 158 | 1891 | K. Heilmann | Missionskarte der Erde nebst Begleitwort | | World missionary maps with commentary | Gutersloh | 1 | a | German | | P | 5 | 4 | 3 | 4 | 80 |
| 159 | 1891 | E. M. Bliss, ed | The encyclopaedia of missions: descriptive, historical, biographical, statistical, 1st edition | EM-1 | — | New York | 2 | e | English | | P | 3 | 4 | 5 | 4 | 80 |
| 160 | 1891 | A. T. Pierson | The miracles of missions: modern marvels in the history of the missionary enterprise | | — | New York | 4 | h | English | | P | 5 | 1 | 4 | 5 | 75 |
| 161 | 1892 | G. Warneck | Evangelische Missionslehre: ein missionstheoretischer Versuch | EML | Theory of Protestant missions | Gotha | 3 | m | German | | P | 5 | 5 | 3 | 5 | 90 |
| 162 | 1892 | J. Vahl | Missions to the heathen in 1889 and 1890: a statistical review | | — | Kobenhavn | 1 | s | English | | P | 5 | 4 | 4 | 4 | 85 |
| 163 | 1894 | E. M. Bliss | Descriptive catalogue of books on missions and mission lands | | — | Philadelphia | 1 | b | English | | P | 5 | 5 | 5 | 5 | 100 |
| 164 | 1894 | R. N. Cust | Essay on the prevailing methods of the evangelization of the non-Christian world | | — | London | 1 | m | English | | | 5 | 2 | 4 | 5 | 80 |
| 165 | 1894 | P. R. Grundemann | Missions-Studien und Kritiken in Verbindung | | Mission studies and critiques combined | Gutersloh | 2 | m | German | | P | 5 | 5 | 4 | 5 | 95 |
| 166 | 1895 | L. D. Wishard | A new programme of missions: to make colleges in all lands centers of evangelization | | — | New York | 1 | m | English | | P | 0 | 2 | 4 | 5 | 55 |
| 167 | 1895 | E. C. Towne, ed | Rays of light from all lands: Bibles and beliefs of mankind | | — | New York | 1 | s | English | | P | 5 | 2 | 2 | 3 | 60 |
| 168 | 1897 | Leo XIII | Divinum illud munus | | Encyclical 'On the Holy Spirit' | Citta del Vaticano | 1 | r | Latin | EFGSPI | R | 0 | 0 | 4 | 3 | 35 |
| 169 | 1897 | P. Barclay | A survey of foreign missions | SFM | — | Edinburgh | 1 | s | English | | P | 5 | 4 | 4 | 5 | 90 |
| 170 | 1897 | J. S. Dennis | Christian missions and social progress: a sociological study of foreign missions | | — | New York | 3 | s | English | | P | 5 | 5 | 5 | 5 | 100 |
| 171 | 1898 | G. Scurati | Zelo per la conversione degli Infideli, 8th edition | | Zeal for the conversion of the Infidels | Milano | 1 | m | Italian | Latin | R | 3 | 2 | 4 | 5 | 70 |
| 172 | 1899 | R. H. Charles | Eschatology: the doctrine of a future life in Israel, Judaism and Christianity | | — | London | | f | English | | A | 3 | 0 | 3 | 4 | 50 |
| 173 | 1900 | J. R. Mott | The evangelization of the world in this generation | EWTG | — | New York | 1 | m | English | G,F,J,N,Sw | P | 5 | 5 | 5 | 5 | 100 |
| 174 | 1900 | L. C. Barnes | Two thousand years of missions before Carey | | — | Chicago | 1 | h | English | | P | 5 | 2 | 5 | 5 | 85 |
| 175 | 1900 | J. Richter | Vom grossen Missionsfelde: Erzahlungen und Schilderungen | | The wider mission field: connections and descriptions | Gutersloh | 1 | s | German | | P | 5 | 1 | 4 | 5 | 75 |
| 176 | 1901 | A. Schweitzer | Reich Gottes und Christentum | | The mystery of the kingdom of God | Tubingen | 2 | t | German | English | P | 0 | 0 | 4 | 4 | 40 |
| 177 | 1901 | H. P. Beach | A geography and atlas of Protestant missions: their environment, distribution, prospects | | — | New York | 2 | a | English | | P | 5 | 4 | 4 | 4 | 85 |
| 178 | 1901 | P. Pisani | Les missions protestantes a la fin du 19 siecle | | Protestant missions at the end of the 19th century | Paris | 1 | s | French | | P | 5 | 4 | 3 | 4 | 80 |
| 179 | 1901 | A. T. Pierson | The modern mission century | MMC | — | London | 1 | s | English | | P | 5 | 5 | 5 | 5 | 100 |
| 180 | 1901 | A. T. Pierson | The new Acts of the Apostles: the marvels of modern missions | NAA | — | London | 1 | s | English | | P | 5 | 2 | 4 | 5 | 80 |
| 181 | 1902 | J. S. Dennis | Centennial survey of foreign missions: a statistical supplement | CSFM | — | Chicago | 1 | s | English | | P | 5 | 4 | 5 | 5 | 95 |
| 182 | 1902 | A. von Harnack | The mission and expansion of Christianity during the first three centuries | MEC | — | London | 2 | h | English | German | P | 5 | 4 | 4 | 5 | 90 |
| 183 | 1902 | SVMFM | World-wide evangelization, the urgent business of the Church | WWE | — | New York | 1 | m | English | | P | 3 | 2 | 4 | 5 | 70 |
| 184 | 1904 | R. E. Speer | Missions and modern history: missionary aspects of 19th century movements | | — | Chicago | 2 | h | English | | P | 5 | 4 | 4 | 5 | 90 |
| 185 | 1904 | H. O. Dwight, H. A. Tupper | The encyclopedia of missions: descriptive, historical, biographical, statistical, 2nd edition | EM-2 | — | New York | 1 | e | English | | P | 3 | 4 | 5 | 4 | 80 |
| 186 | 1904 | W. E. Blackstone | The Millennium: a discussion of what the Scriptures teach | | — | Chicago | 1 | x | English | | P | 0 | 1 | 4 | 4 | 45 |
| 187 | 1906 | J. Richter | Allgemeine evangelische Missionsgeschichte | AEMG | Universal Protestant missions history | Gutersloh | 5 | h | German | | P | 5 | 4 | 4 | 5 | 90 |
| 188 | 1906 | K. Streit | Katholischer Missionsatlas: die gesamten Missionsgebiete des Erdkreices | KMA | Catholic missions atlas | Steyl | 1 | a | German | French | R | 5 | 5 | 5 | 5 | 100 |
| 189 | 1906 | H. A. Krose | Notices statistiques pour les cartes de l'Atlas des missions catholiques | | Statistical notes on the Catholic missions atlas | Steyl | 1 | a | French | German | R | 5 | 5 | 5 | 5 | 100 |
| 190 | 1906 | K. Streit, ed | Statistische Notizen zum katholischen Missionsatlas | | Statistical notes for Atlas of Catholic missions | Steyl | 1 | a | German | French | R | 5 | 5 | 4 | 5 | 95 |
| 191 | 1907 | F. Cabrol, ed | Dictionnaire d' archeologie chretienne et de liturgie (1907-1953) | | Dictionary of Christian archeology and liturgy | Paris | 15 | d | French | | R | 5 | 2 | 2 | 1 | 50 |
| 192 | 1907 | R. Streit | Die deutsche Missionsliteratur | | German missionary literature | Paderborn | 1 | b | German | | R | 5 | 1 | 5 | 4 | 75 |
| 193 | 1907 | J. W. Bashford | God's missionary plan for the world | | — | New York | 1 | m | English | | P | 0 | 2 | 4 | 5 | 55 |
| 194 | 1908 | J. Hastings, ed | Encyclopaedia of religion and ethics | ERE | — | Edinburgh | 12 | e | English | | P | 3 | 2 | 3 | 1 | 45 |
| 195 | 1908 | H. A. Krose | Katholische Missionstatistik: gegenwartigen Standes der katholischen Heidenmission | KMS | Statistics of Catholic missions among the heathen | Freiburg | 1 | s | German | | R | 5 | 4 | 4 | 5 | 90 |
| 196 | 1908 | E. Pfeiffer | Mission studies: historical survey and outlines of missionary principles and practice | | — | Columbus | 1 | m | English | | P | 5 | 2 | 5 | 5 | 85 |
| 197 | 1908 | W. T. Whitley | Missionary achievement: a survey of world-wide evangelisation | | — | New York | 1 | s | English | | P | 5 | 4 | 5 | 5 | 95 |
| 198 | 1908 | M. Kahler | Schriften zu Christologie und Mission | SCM | Writings on Christology and mission | Munchen | 1 | t | German | | P | 0 | 0 | 3 | 3 | 30 |
| 199 | 1908 | J. L. Barton | The unfinished task of the Christian church:the problem of the world's evangelization | | — | New York | 1 | s | English | | P | 3 | 2 | 5 | 5 | 75 |
| 200 | 1909 | F. Schiele, ed, H. Gunkel | Die Religion in Geschichte und Gegenwart, 1st edition | RGG-1 | Religion in past and present | Tubingen | 6 | e | German | | P | 3 | 4 | 3 | 3 | 65 |
| 201 | 1909 | E. O. Winstedt, ed | The Christian topography of Cosmas Indicopleustes | TC | — | Cambridge | 1 | s | English | | A | 5 | 1 | 3 | 3 | 60 |
| 202 | 1910 | J. R. Mott | Carrying the gospel to all the non-Christian world | CGNW | — | Edinburgh | 1 | m | English | | P | 3 | 4 | 4 | 5 | 80 |
| 203 | 1910 | J. S. Dennis, H. P. Beach | Statistical atlas of Christian missions: directory, missiion stations, maps | SACM | — | Edinburgh | 1 | a | English | | P | 5 | 5 | 5 | 5 | 100 |
| 204 | 1910 | D. W. Myland | The Latter Rain Covenant | | — | Cleveland | 1 | t | English | | P | 3 | 2 | 5 | 5 | 75 |
| 205 | 1910 | J. P. Lilley | The victory of the gospel: a survey of worldwide evangelism | | — | London | 1 | s | English | | A | 5 | 4 | 4 | 5 | 90 |
| 206 | 1911 | H. Wace, ed, W. C. Piercy | A dictionary of Christian biography: literature, sects to AD 700 | | — | London | 1 | I | English | | A | 5 | 0 | 5 | 4 | 70 |
| 207 | 1911 | R. Streit | Fuhrer durch die deutsche katholische Missionsliteratur | | Guide to German Catholic missions literature | Freiburg | 1 | b | German | | R | 5 | 1 | 5 | 4 | 75 |
| 208 | 1911 | F. E. Daubanton | Prolegomena van Protestantsche Zendingswetenschap | | Introduction to Protestant missions | Utrecht | 1 | e | Dutch | | P | 3 | 2 | 3 | 3 | 55 |
| 209 | 1911 | S. M. Zwemer | Unoccupied mission fields of Africa and Asia | UMFAA | — | New York | 1 | s | English | German | P | 5 | 5 | 4 | 5 | 95 |
| 210 | 1912 | J. L. Murray | A selected bibliography of missionary literature | | — | New York | 1 | b | English | | P | 5 | 0 | 4 | 3 | 60 |
| 211 | 1912 | A. Baudrillart, ed | Dictionnaire d'histoire et de geographie ecclesiastiques, editions 1909-1995 | | Historical and geographical church dictionary | Paris | 26 | d | French | | R | 5 | 2 | 3 | 4 | 70 |
| 212 | 1912 | P. Wallenborn | Gehet hin und lehret alle Volker | | Go and teach all peoples | Fulda | 1 | x | German | | R | 0 | 0 | 5 | 5 | 50 |
| 213 | 1912 | J. H. Oldham | International review of missions, 1912-2000 | IRM | — | Geneva | 89 | p | English | | A | 3 | 4 | 4 | 5 | 80 |
| 214 | 1912 | S. M. Zwemer | Missionslose Lander: ungeloste Missionsaufgaben | | Lands without missions, unassigned resources | Basel | 1 | s | German | English | P | 5 | 5 | 4 | 5 | 95 |
| 215 | 1913 | K. Streit | Atlas Hierarchicus, 1st edition | AH-1 | Atlas of Catholic jurisdictions | Paderborn | 1 | a | Latin | | R | 5 | 4 | 4 | 5 | 90 |
| 216 | 1915 | L. J. van Rijckevorsel | Missie en Missieactie | MM | Mission and missionary activity | Nijmegen | 1 | m | Dutch | | R | 3 | 1 | 4 | 4 | 60 |
| 217 | 1916 | R. Streit, ed, J. Dindinger | Biblioteca Missionum, 1916-1974 | BM | Library of missions | Munster | 30 | b | Latin | Italian | R | 3 | 2 | 5 | 2 | 60 |
| 218 | 1916 | P. Heinische | Die Idee der Heidenbekehrung im Alten Testament | | Conversion of the heathen in the Old Testament | Munster | 1 | x | German | | R | 0 | 0 | 5 | 5 | 50 |
| 219 | 1916 | J. H. Oldham | The world and the gospel | | — | London | 1 | m | English | | A | 3 | 4 | 4 | 5 | 80 |
| 220 | 1916 | H. P. Beach, ed | World statistics of Christian missions: missionary societies, statistics, mission stations | WSCM | — | New York | 1 | s | English | | P | 5 | 5 | 5 | 5 | 100 |
| 221 | 1917 | C. Mirbt | Die evangelische Mission: eine Einfuhrung in ihre Geschichte und Eigenart | | Protestant missions: origins and characteristics | Leipzig | 1 | s | German | | P | 5 | 4 | 4 | 4 | 85 |
| 222 | 1917 | J. Schmidlin | Einfuhrung in die Missionswissenschaft, 1st edition, nd 1925 | EMW | Establishing the science of missions | Munster | 1 | m | German | | R | 0 | 4 | 4 | 5 | 65 |
| 223 | 1919 | J. Schmidlin | Katholische Missionslehre im Grundriss | KMLG | Catholic theory of missions | Munster | 1 | t | German | English | R | 0 | 1 | 5 | 5 | 55 |
| 224 | 1919 | Benedict XV | Maximum illud | | Encyclical | Citta del Vaticano | 1 | r | Latin | EFGSPI | R | 0 | 0 | 4 | 5 | 45 |
| 225 | 1919 | E. C. Moore | The spread of Christianity in the modern world | | — | Chicago | 1 | s | English | | P | 5 | 2 | 2 | 3 | 60 |
| 226 | 1920 | P. Charles | Etudes missiologiques | | Missiological studies | Louvain | 1 | m | French | Dutch | R | 0 | 1 | 4 | 4 | 45 |
| 227 | 1920 | J. Richter | Evangelische Missionslehre, 1st edition (2nd 1927) | EML-1 | Protestant theory of missions | Leipzig | 2 | t | German | | P | 3 | 1 | 4 | 3 | 55 |
| 228 | 1920 | J. R. Mott, ed | World survey by the Interchurch World Movement of North America | IWMNA | — | New York | 2 | m | English | | P | 5 | 5 | 5 | 5 | 100 |
| 229 | 1921 | U. Mioni | Manuale di missionologia | | Handbook of missiology | Milano | 1 | k | Italian | | R | 3 | 2 | 3 | 4 | 60 |
| 230 | 1921 | J. E. Lundahl | Varldmissionen | | World missions | Stockholm | 1 | t | Swedish | | P | 5 | 4 | 4 | 5 | 90 |
| 231 | 1922 | Pius XI | Miserimus Redemptor | | Encyclical 'On the Redeemer' | Citta del Vaticano | 1 | r | Latin | EFGSPI | R | 0 | 1 | 4 | 5 | 50 |
| 232 | 1923 | E. A. French | Evangelism in the modern world | | — | London | 1 | m | English | | P | 5 | 2 | 5 | 5 | 85 |
| 233 | 1923 | H. Fischer | Jesu letzter Wille | | Jesus' last will | Steyl | 1 | x | German | | R | 0 | 0 | 5 | 5 | 50 |
| 234 | 1924 | J. Schmidlin | Catholic mission history | CMH | — | Steyl | 1 | h | English | German | R | 5 | 4 | 5 | 5 | 95 |
| 235 | 1924 | W. Garcia | Geografia-atlas de las misiones catolicas | | Atlas of Catholic missions | Burgos | 1 | a | Spanish | | R | 5 | 2 | 3 | 5 | 75 |
| 236 | 1924 | R. H. Glover | The progress of world-wide missions | | — | London | 1 | s | English | | P | 5 | 2 | 4 | 5 | 80 |
| 237 | 1925 | J. Thauren | Atlas der Geschichte der katholischen Missionen | AGKM | Historical atlas of Catholic missions | Steyl | 1 | a | German | | R | 5 | 4 | 4 | 5 | 90 |

| Ref 1 | Year 2 | Authors/editors 3 | Title/subtitle/edition (in original language) 4 | Initials 5 | Title translated into English 6 | Place of publication 7 | Vols 8 | Cat 9 | Language 10 | Translations 11 | Ecc 12 | Em 13 | St 14 | M 15 | GM 16 | % 17 |
|---|---|---|---|---|---|---|---|---|---|---|---|---|---|---|---|---|
| 238 | 1925 | P. R. Pies | Die Heilsfrage der Heiden | | The problem of the salvation of the heathen | Aachen | 1 | x | German | | R | 0 | 0 | 5 | 5 | 50 |
| 239 | 1925 | R. Streit | Die katholische deutsche Missionsliteratur: die geschichtliche Entwicklung | KDML | German Catholic missionary literature | Aachen | 1 | b | German | | R | 5 | 1 | 5 | 4 | 75 |
| 240 | 1925 | J. Schmidlin | Die katholischen Missionen von der Volkerwanderung bis zur Gegenwart | | Catholic missions from migration to the present | Steyl | 1 | h | German | | R | 5 | 4 | 4 | 4 | 85 |
| 241 | 1925 | M. Schlunk | Die Weltmission der Kirche Christi: ein Gang durch neunzehn Jahrhunderte | WMKC | The church's world mission through 19 centuries | Hamburg | 1 | h | German | | P | 5 | 2 | 5 | 5 | 85 |
| 242 | 1925 | Meinertz | Jesus und die Heidenmission | | Jesus and the mission to the heathen | Munster | 1 | x | German | | R | 0 | 0 | 5 | 5 | 50 |
| 243 | 1925 | F. P. Turner | The Foreign Missions Convention at Washington, 1925 | FMC | — | New York | 1 | s | English | | P | 3 | 1 | 5 | 5 | 70 |
| 244 | 1925 | H. P. Beach, C. H. Fahs | World missionary atlas: missionary societies, statistics, maps, mission stations | WMA | — | New York | 1 | a | English | | P | 5 | 5 | 4 | 5 | 95 |
| 245 | 1926 | D. Jenks | A study of world evangelisation | | — | London | 1 | s | English | | P | 5 | 1 | 5 | 5 | 80 |
| 246 | 1926 | Pius XI | Rerum Ecclesiae | | Encyclical on Missions | Citta del Vaticano | 1 | r | Latin | | R | 0 | 0 | 3 | 3 | 30 |
| 247 | 1926 | R. E. Speer | The unfinished task of foreign missions | UTFM | — | New York | 1 | s | English | | P | 3 | 2 | 5 | 5 | 75 |
| 248 | 1927 | A. Henderson, E. Parry | A historical survey of Christian missions from 1st-16th centuries | HSCM | — | London | 1 | h | English | | A | 5 | 1 | 4 | 5 | 75 |
| 249 | 1927 | G. Van Rossum | Missiones Catholicae cura S. C. Propaganda Fide: descriptae, statistica | MC | Catholic missions under S. C. Propaganda: statistics | Citta del Vaticano | 1 | s | Latin | | R | 5 | 5 | 3 | 5 | 90 |
| 250 | 1927 | L. Grammatica | Testo e atlante di geografia ecclesiastia | | Test and atlas of ecclesiastical geography | Bergamo | 1 | a | Italian | | R | 5 | 4 | 3 | 5 | 85 |
| 251 | 1927 | J. Marchant, ed | The future of Christianity | | — | New York | 1 | f | English | | A | 3 | 1 | 4 | 5 | 65 |
| 252 | 1927 | R. Allen | The spontaneous expansion of the Church and the causes which hinder it | SECC | — | London | 1 | m | English | | A | 3 | 2 | 5 | 5 | 75 |
| 253 | 1928 | H. W. Hering, ed | A selected bibliography of recent books on missions and mission problems | | — | New York | 1 | b | English | | P | 5 | 1 | 5 | 5 | 80 |
| 254 | 1928 | R. Streit | Die Weltmission der katholischen Kirche: Zahlen und Zeichen | | World mission of the Catholic church: numbers, signs | Hunfeld | 1 | s | German | | R | 5 | 4 | 4 | 5 | 90 |
| 255 | 1928 | C. H. Fahs | The unfinished evangelistic task | UET | — | London | 1 | s | English | | P | 5 | 5 | 5 | 5 | 100 |
| 256 | 1929 | K. Streit | Atlas Hierarchicus, geographica, statistica, 2nd edition | AH-2 | Atlas of Catholic jurisdictions | Paderborn | 1 | a | Latin | English | R | 5 | 4 | 4 | 5 | 90 |
| 257 | 1929 | K. Streit | Catholic world atlas: geographical, statistical, ethnographic, maps | CWA | — | Paderborn | 1 | a | English | Latin | R | 5 | 4 | 4 | 5 | 90 |
| 258 | 1930 | J. G. Barrow | A bibliography of bibliographies in religion | BBR | — | Ann Arbor, MI | 1 | b | English | | P | 5 | 0 | 0 | 0 | 25 |
| 259 | 1930 | K. Hofmann, M. Buchberger | Lexikon fur Theologie und Kirche, 2nd edition | LThK | Lexicon for theology and church | Freiburg | 12 | d | German | | R | 3 | 2 | 3 | 3 | 55 |
| 260 | 1931 | J. Schmidlin | Catholic mission theory | CMT | — | Techny, IL | 1 | m | English | German | R | 0 | 1 | 5 | 5 | 55 |
| 261 | 1931 | P. Rivet, ed | L'evangile et le Monde: Congres des missions protestantes (9-11 Juin) | | The gospel and the world | Paris | 1 | s | French | | P | 5 | 2 | 4 | 4 | 75 |
| 262 | 1932 | J. Thauren | Atlas der katholischen Missionsgeschichte | AKMG | Atlas of Catholic mission history | Modling | 1 | a | German | | R | 5 | 4 | 4 | 5 | 90 |
| 263 | 1932 | S. J. M. Brown, ed | Bibliographie des missions catholiques | BMC | Bibliography of Catholic missions | Dublin | 1 | b | French | | R | 5 | 0 | 4 | 3 | 60 |
| 264 | 1932 | A. Freitag, H. Ahaus | Het Godsrijk, idee en plannen | | The Kingdom of God: ideas and plans | Steyl | 1 | m | Dutch | | R | 5 | 2 | 4 | 5 | 80 |
| 265 | 1932 | FIDES | Testo-atlante illustrato delle missioni | | Illustrated atlas of missions with text | Roma | 1 | a | Italian | | R | 5 | 4 | 3 | 5 | 85 |
| 266 | 1933 | J. Rommerskirchen, et al | Bibliografia missionaria | BM | Missionary bibliography | Citta del Vaticano | 64 | b | Latin | Italian | R | 3 | 2 | 5 | 2 | 60 |
| 267 | 1933 | G. Van der Leeuw | Phanomenologie der Religion | | Phenomenology of religion | Tubingen | 1 | n | German | Eng,Fre,Ital | P | 0 | 1 | 2 | 2 | 25 |
| 268 | 1933 | G. Kittel, G. Friedrich | Theologisches Worterbuch zum Neuen Testament | TWNT | Theological wordbook of the New Testament | Stuttgart | 10 | d | German | English | P | 5 | 2 | 3 | 2 | 60 |
| 269 | 1934 | A. McLeish | Jesus Christ and world evangelization: missionary principles, Christ's or ours? | JCWE | — | London | 1 | m | English | | P | 5 | 4 | 4 | 3 | 80 |
| 270 | 1935 | H. W. Hering | A worldwide Christian outlook: a selected bibliography for the SVM Convention | WCO | — | New York | 1 | b | English | | P | 5 | 0 | 5 | 5 | 75 |
| 271 | 1935 | A. Cenni | Le missioni cattoliche | MC | Catholic missions | Alba | 1 | s | Italian | | R | 5 | 4 | 4 | 5 | 90 |
| 272 | 1935 | F. J. Montalban | Manuale historiae missionum | | Manual on mission history | Shanghai | 1 | h | Latin | Spanish | R | 5 | 4 | 4 | 5 | 90 |
| 273 | 1935 | H. W. Schomerus | Missionswissenschaft | MW | The science of mission | Leipzig | 1 | m | German | | P | 3 | 2 | 3 | 3 | 55 |
| 274 | 1936 | J. G. K. Harman | Awaiting the light: a survey of the unevangelized areas of the world | | — | London | 1 | s | English | | P | 5 | 5 | 5 | 5 | 100 |
| 275 | 1936 | K. Barth | Die kirchliche Dogmatik | KD | Church dogmatics | Edinburgh | 13 | t | German | English | P | 0 | 0 | 3 | 3 | 30 |
| 276 | 1936 | C. H. Dodd | The apostolic preaching and its developments | APD | — | London | 1 | x | English | Fre,Dut | P | 5 | 0 | 5 | 4 | 70 |
| 277 | 1936 | H. Kraemer | The Christian message in a non-Christian world | CMNW | — | London | 1 | m | English | German | P | 0 | 1 | 5 | 5 | 55 |
| 278 | 1937 | K. S. Latourette | A history of the expansion of Christianity | HEC | — | London | 7 | h | English | German | P | 5 | 4 | 5 | 4 | 90 |
| 279 | 1938 | J. R. Mott | Evangelism for the world today | EWT | — | New York | 1 | s | English | | P | 3 | 2 | 5 | 5 | 75 |
| 280 | 1938 | H. Vieira | Historia das missoes | HM | History of missions | Sao Paulo | 1 | h | Portugese | | R | 5 | 1 | 4 | 5 | 75 |
| 281 | 1938 | J. I. Parker, ed | Interpretative statistical survey of the world mission of the Christian church | ISSWM | — | London | 1 | s | English | | P | 5 | 4 | 4 | 5 | 90 |
| 282 | 1938 | G. Van der Leeuw | Religion in essence and manifestation: a study in phenomenology | | — | London | 1 | n | English | Ger,Fre,Ita | P | 0 | 1 | 2 | 2 | 25 |
| 283 | 1941 | A. T. Houghton | The battle of world evangelisation | BWE | — | London | 1 | m | English | | A | 0 | 1 | 4 | 5 | 50 |
| 284 | 1942 | L. Brierley | 1st World survey of unreached areas: Thy Kingdom come | WSUA | — | London | 1 | s | English | | P | 5 | 5 | 4 | 5 | 95 |
| 285 | 1943 | S. M. Zwemer | Into all the world: the Great Commission | | — | Grand Rapids | 1 | m | English | | P | 0 | 4 | 4 | 5 | 65 |
| 286 | 1943 | C. E. Raven | Science, religion and the future | | — | Cambridge | 1 | f | English | | A | 3 | 0 | 3 | 3 | 45 |
| 287 | 1943 | E. D. Soper | The philosophy of the Christian world mission | | — | Nashville, TN | 1 | n | English | | P | 0 | 0 | 3 | 5 | 40 |
| 288 | 1944 | William Temple | The Church looks forward | | — | London | 1 | f | English | | A | 3 | 0 | 5 | 5 | 65 |
| 289 | 1945 | V. Ferm | An encyclopedia of religion | ER | — | New York | 1 | e | English | | P | 3 | 2 | 1 | 0 | 30 |
| 290 | 1945 | O. G. Myklebust | An international institute of scientific missionary research | | — | Oslo | 1 | m | English | Norwegian | P | 0 | 4 | 4 | 5 | 65 |
| 291 | 1945 | J. Masson | Bibliographie missionnaire moderne: choix cclasse de 1400 titres et notes d'histoire | BMM | Modern missionary bibliography, selected | Tournai | 1 | b | French | | R | 5 | 1 | 5 | 5 | 80 |
| 292 | 1946 | O. Cullman | Christus und die Zeit | CT/CZ | Christ and time | Zurich | 1 | t | German | Eng,Fre,Ital | P | 0 | 0 | 5 | 4 | 45 |
| 293 | 1946 | N. A. Berdyayev | Essai de metaphysique eschatologique | | The beginning and the end | Paris | 1 | f | Russian | Fre,Eng | O | 0 | 0 | 5 | 3 | 40 |
| 294 | 1946 | F. C. Laubach | Prayer: the mightiest force in the world | | — | New York | 1 | m | English | | P | 5 | 1 | 5 | 5 | 80 |
| 295 | 1947 | P. Parente | Euntes docete | | Go and teach | Citta del Vaticano | 40 | p | Latin | English | R | 3 | 2 | 5 | 5 | 75 |
| 296 | 1947 | H. P. Van Dusen | World Christianity: yesterday, today, tomorrow | | — | New York | 1 | f | English | | P | 5 | 2 | 4 | 5 | 80 |
| 297 | 1948 | F. C. Maddox | Set a watchman: a world survey | | — | London | 1 | s | English | | P | 5 | 4 | 5 | 5 | 95 |
| 298 | 1948 | K. S. Latourette, W. R. Hogg | Tomorrow is here: the mission and work of the church | | — | New York | 1 | m | English | | P | 0 | 1 | 5 | 5 | 55 |
| 299 | 1949 | S. M. Paventi | La chiesa missionaria: manuale di missionologia dottrinale e missionografia | CM | The missionary church: missiology and missiography | Roma | 2 | k | Italian | | R | 0 | 1 | 4 | 3 | 40 |
| 300 | 1949 | G. F. Dickerson, ed | Religion index One: periodicals, and Two: multi-author works | | — | Chicago | 12 | p | English | | P | 5 | 1 | 3 | 3 | 60 |
| 301 | 1949 | J. C. Hoekendijk | The evangelization of man in modern mass society | | — | Geneva | 1 | m | English | Fre,Ger | P | 3 | 1 | 4 | 4 | 60 |
| 302 | 1949 | V. R. Edman | The light in dark ages: 18 centuries from the Great Commission to William Carey | | — | Wheaton, IL | 1 | h | English | | P | 5 | 2 | 5 | 5 | 85 |
| 303 | 1949 | K. S. Latourette | The prospect for Christianity | | — | London | 1 | f | English | | P | 0 | 2 | 5 | 5 | 60 |
| 304 | 1949 | K. G. Grubb | World Christian handbook, 1st edition | WCH-1 | — | London | 1 | s | English | | A | 5 | 4 | 3 | 4 | 80 |
| 305 | 1950 | F. C. Laubach | Literacy as evangelism | | — | New York | 1 | m | English | | P | 3 | 4 | 5 | 5 | 85 |
| 306 | 1951 | Pius XII | Evangelii Praecones (Encyclical) | EP | Making the Gospel known | Citta del Vaticano | 1 | r | Latin | EFGISP | R | 0 | 0 | 5 | 5 | 50 |
| 307 | 1951 | M. Schlunk, ed, H. Quiring | Karte der Religionen und Missionen der Erde, 1st edition | | Map of the world's religions and missions | Berne | 1 | a | German | English | P | 5 | 4 | 4 | 5 | 90 |
| 308 | 1951 | J. Despont | Nouvel atlas des missions | NAM | New atlas of missions | Paris | 1 | a | French | | R | 5 | 4 | 3 | 4 | 80 |
| 309 | 1952 | A. McLeish | Christ's hope of the Kingdom | | — | London | 1 | x | English | | P | 5 | 1 | 5 | 5 | 80 |
| 310 | 1952 | A. V. Seumois | Introduction a la Missiologie | | Introduction to missiology | Schoneck | 2 | t | French | Spanish | R | 3 | 2 | 4 | 3 | 60 |
| 311 | 1952 | E. J. Bingle, K. G. Grubb | World Christian handbook, 2nd edition | WCH-2 | — | London | 1 | s | English | | A | 5 | 4 | 3 | 4 | 80 |
| 312 | 1953 | K. S. Latourette | A history of Christianity | | — | London | 1 | h | English | | P | 5 | 4 | 4 | 5 | 90 |
| 313 | 1954 | D. T. Niles | Evangelism: the mission of the Church to those outside her life | | — | Geneva | 1 | m | English | Fre,Ger | P | 3 | 1 | 4 | 4 | 60 |
| 314 | 1954 | J. H. Bavinck | Inleiding in de zendingswetenschap | | Introduction to the science of missions | Kampen | 1 | t | Dutch | English | P | 0 | 1 | 5 | 5 | 55 |
| 315 | 1954 | RCJCLdS | Into all the world: Council of Twelve missionary report | | — | Independence | 1 | s | English | | m | 5 | 1 | 4 | 5 | 75 |
| 316 | 1954 | G. R. Beasley-Murray | Jesus and the future | | — | London | 1 | f | English | | P | 0 | 0 | 4 | 4 | 40 |
| 317 | 1954 | A. M. Chirgwin | The Bible in world evangelism | BWE | — | London | 1 | s | English | French | A | 5 | 1 | 4 | 4 | 70 |

| Ref 1 | Year 2 | Authors/editors 3 | Title/subtitle/edition (in original language) 4 | Initials 5 | Title translated into English 6 | Place of publication 7 | Vols 8 | Cat 9 | Language 10 | Translations 11 | Ecc 12 | Em 13 | St 14 | M 15 | GM 16 | % 17 |
|---|---|---|---|---|---|---|---|---|---|---|---|---|---|---|---|---|
| 318 | 1954 | P. S. Minear | The Christian hope and the Second Coming | | — | Philadelphia | 1 | f | English | | P | 0 | 0 | 4 | 4 | 40 |
| 319 | 1954 | J. Baillie, H.P. Van Dusen | The library of Christian classics | LCC | — | London | 26 | q | English | | P | 3 | 1 | 2 | 2 | 40 |
| 320 | 1954 | J. Bosch | Zendingsvademecum | | Mission handbook | Enschede | 1 | k | Dutch | | P | 0 | 0 | 3 | 4 | 35 |
| 321 | 1955 | J. C. Thiessen | A survey of world missions | SWM | — | Chicago | 1 | s | English | | P | 5 | 4 | 4 | 5 | 90 |
| 322 | 1955 | H. Brunotte, ed, O. Weber | Evangelisches Kirchenlexikon, 1st edition | EKL-1 | Protestant church dictionary | Gottingen | 4 | d | German | | P | 3 | 2 | 3 | 4 | 60 |
| 323 | 1955 | O. G. Myklebust | The study of missions in theological education: the place of world evangelisation | | — | Oslo | 2 | s | English | | P | 3 | 1 | 4 | 4 | 60 |
| 324 | 1955 | L. A. Loetscher, ed | Twentieth century encyclopedia of religious knowledge | TCERK | — | Grand Rapids | 2 | e | English | | P | 3 | 2 | 4 | 4 | 65 |
| 325 | 1956 | D. T. Niles | A monthly letter about evangelism | | — | Geneva | 40 | p | English | Fre,Ger | P | 3 | 1 | 4 | 5 | 65 |
| 326 | 1956 | J. Foster | Beginning from Jerusalem: Christian expansion through 17 centuries | | — | London | 1 | h | English | German | P | 5 | 2 | 5 | 5 | 85 |
| 327 | 1956 | S. Delacroix, ed | Histoire universelle des missions catholiques | HUMC | Universal history of Catholic missions | Paris | 4 | h | French | GISP | R | 5 | 4 | 5 | 5 | 95 |
| 328 | 1956 | L.-J. Suenens | L'Eglise en etat de mission | GEC | The gospel to every creature | Bruges | 1 | m | English | French | R | 0 | 1 | 4 | 5 | 50 |
| 329 | 1956 | A. J. Dain, ed | Mission fields today: a brief world survey | | — | London | 1 | s | English | | A | 5 | 2 | 3 | 5 | 75 |
| 330 | 1956 | H. Kraemer | Religion and the Christian faith | RCF | — | London | 1 | t | English | | P | 0 | 0 | 3 | 4 | 35 |
| 331 | 1956 | T. Ohm | Wichtige daten der Missionsgeschichte | WDMG | Principal dates in the history of missions | Munster | 1 | c | German | French | P | 5 | 4 | 4 | 4 | 85 |
| 332 | 1957 | K. Galling, ed | Die Religion in Geschichte und Gegenwart, 3rd edition: Handworterbuch | RGG-3 | Religion past and present: a handbook | Tubingen | 7 | e | German | | P | 3 | 4 | 3 | 3 | 65 |
| 333 | 1957 | Pius XII | Fidei Donum | | Encyclical on Missions | Citta del Vaticano | 1 | r | Latin | | R | 0 | 0 | 4 | 5 | 45 |
| 334 | 1957 | A. J. M. Mulders | Missiegeschiedenis | | Mission history | Bussum | 1 | h | Dutch | German | R | 5 | 4 | 3 | 4 | 80 |
| 335 | 1957 | F. L. Cross, ed | The Oxford dictionary of the Christian church, 1st edition (also 1974, 1983, 1997) | ODCC | — | Oxford | 1 | d | English | | A | 5 | 2 | 3 | 3 | 65 |
| 336 | 1957 | S. C. Neill | The unfinished task | UT | — | London | 1 | s | English | | A | 3 | 2 | 5 | 5 | 75 |
| 337 | 1957 | E. J. Bingle, K. G. Grubb | World Christian handbook, 3rd edition | WCH-3 | — | London | 1 | s | English | | A | 5 | 4 | 3 | 4 | 80 |
| 338 | 1958 | H. Emmerich, ed | Atlas Missionum a SC de Propaganda Fide dependentium | AM | Atlas of missions under Propaganda Fide | Modling | 1 | a | Latin | | R | 5 | 4 | 4 | 5 | 90 |
| 339 | 1958 | F. van der Meer, et al | Atlas of the early Christian world | AECW | — | London | 1 | a | English | Dutch | P | 5 | 2 | 3 | 4 | 70 |
| 340 | 1958 | G. H. Anderson, ed | Bibliography of the theology of missions in the twentieth century, 1st edition (3rd 1966) | BTM-1 | — | New York | 1 | b | English | | P | 5 | 1 | 5 | 5 | 80 |
| 341 | 1958 | J. Frisque, ed | Bilan du monde, encyclopedie catholique du monde chretien, 1st edition | BM-1 | The world on balance: Catholic world encyclopedia | Louvain | 2 | e | French | | R | 5 | 5 | 4 | 5 | 95 |
| 342 | 1958 | K. S. Latourette | Christianity in a revolutionary age | CRA | — | New York | 5 | h | English | | P | 5 | 4 | 4 | 5 | 90 |
| 343 | 1958 | J. Jeremias | Jesus' promise to the nations | | — | London | 1 | x | English | German | P | 5 | 1 | 4 | 5 | 75 |
| 344 | 1958 | A. Yannoulatos | Porefthendes | | Go ye | Athinai | 9 | p | Greek | | O | 3 | 2 | 4 | 5 | 70 |
| 345 | 1959 | A. Freitag , H. Emmerich | Atlas du monde chretien: l'expansion du christianisme a travers les siecles | AMC | Atlas of the expansion of the Christian world | Brussel | 1 | a | French | Lat,Ger,Dut | R | 5 | 4 | 4 | 5 | 90 |
| 346 | 1959 | E. Molland | Christendom: the Christian churches' doctrines, forms, ways of worship | | — | London | 1 | s | English | Norwegian | P | 5 | 2 | 4 | 4 | 75 |
| 347 | 1959 | P. Teilhard de Chardin | L'avenir de l'homme | | The future of man | Paris | 1 | f | French | English | R | 5 | 1 | 2 | 2 | 50 |
| 348 | 1959 | R. C. Zaehner, ed | The concise encyclopedia of living faiths | CELF | — | New York | 1 | e | English | | R | 3 | 1 | 1 | 1 | 30 |
| 349 | 1959 | A. Freitag, H. Emmerich | The universe atlas of the Christian world: the expansion of Christianity through the centuries | UACW | — | London | 1 | a | English | Lat,Ger,Dut | R | 5 | 4 | 4 | 5 | 90 |
| 350 | 1960 | R. S. Dell | An atlas of Christian history | ACH | — | London | 1 | a | English | | P | 5 | 4 | 4 | 5 | 90 |
| 351 | 1960 | J. H. Bavinck | An introduction to the science of missions | | — | Philadelphia | 1 | m | English | Dutch | P | 0 | 1 | 5 | 5 | 55 |
| 352 | 1960 | L. Vriens, A. Disch | Critical bibliography of missiology | CBM | — | Nijmegen | 1 | b | English | Ger,Fre | R | 3 | 1 | 4 | 3 | 55 |
| 353 | 1960 | J. O. Percy | Facing the unfinished task | | — | Chicago | 1 | s | English | | P | 3 | 2 | 4 | 5 | 70 |
| 354 | 1960 | R. P. Millot | Missions d'aujourd'hui | | Missions in the world today | Paris | 1 | s | French | English,Spa | P | 5 | 4 | 4 | 5 | 90 |
| 355 | 1960 | W. A. Smalley | Selected and annotated bibliography of anthropology for missionaries | | — | New York | 1 | b | English | | P | 5 | 4 | 4 | 4 | 85 |
| 356 | 1960 | J. Foster | To all nations: Christian expansion from 1700 to today | | — | London | 1 | h | English | | P | 5 | 2 | 5 | 5 | 85 |
| 357 | 1960 | F. H. Littell | Weltkirchenlexikon | WKL | World church dictionary | Stuttgart | 1 | d | German | | P | 5 | 2 | 5 | 5 | 85 |
| 358 | 1961 | L. Brierley | 2nd World survey of unreached areas: the challenge of the unachieved | | — | London | 1 | s | English | | P | 5 | 5 | 4 | 5 | 95 |
| 359 | 1961 | John XXIII | Bibliotheca Sanctorum | BS | Bibliography of saints | Roma | 13 | b | Latin | | R | 5 | 1 | 5 | 3 | 70 |
| 360 | 1961 | L. Person, ed | Cumulative list of doctoral dissertations and masters' theses in foreign missions | | — | New York | 1 | b | English | | P | 5 | 1 | 5 | 4 | 75 |
| 361 | 1961 | E. Benz | Kirchengeschichte in okumenischer Sicht | KGOS | Church history from an ecumenical standpoint | Leiden | 1 | h | German | | P | 5 | 4 | 4 | 5 | 90 |
| 362 | 1961 | J. Grundler | Lexikon der christlichen Kirchen und Sekten | LCKS | Lexicon of Christian churches and sects | Wien | 2 | d | German | | P | 5 | 4 | 5 | 3 | 85 |
| 363 | 1961 | A. Santos Hernandez | Misionologia: problemas introductorios y ciencias auxiliares | | Missiology: introductory problems, related sciences | Santander | 1 | m | Spanish | | R | 3 | 4 | 4 | 3 | 70 |
| 364 | 1961 | G. H. Anderson, ed | The theology of the Christian mission | TCM | — | New York | 1 | t | English | | P | 0 | 1 | 5 | 5 | 55 |
| 365 | 1962 | C. Graves, ed | Internationale Okumenische Bibliographie/International Ecumenical Bibliography (IOB/IEB) | IOB/IEB | — | Munchen | 10 | b | English | German | P | 3 | 2 | 3 | 3 | 55 |
| 366 | 1962 | A. Canovesi | La difusione geografica del Christianesimo | | The geographical expansion of Christianity | Torino | 1 | a | Italian | | P | 5 | 4 | 3 | 5 | 85 |
| 367 | 1962 | T. Ohm | Machet zu Jungern alle Volker: Theorie der Mission | | Make disciples of all peoples: theory of mission | Freiburg | 3 | m | German | French | P | 3 | 1 | 4 | 3 | 55 |
| 368 | 1962 | A. J. M. Mulders | Missiologisch bestek: inleiding tot de katholieke missiewetenschap | | Catholic missiological compendium | Hilversum | 1 | t | Dutch | | R | 3 | 2 | 4 | 3 | 60 |
| 369 | 1962 | J. Blauw | The missionary nature of the church: a survey of the biblical theology of mission | | — | New York | 1 | t | English | | P | 0 | 0 | 4 | 5 | 45 |
| 370 | 1962 | A. Martinos, ed | Thriskeutiki kai Ithiki Egyklopaidia | TIE | Religious and ethical encyclopedia | Athinai | 12 | e | Greek | | O | 5 | 4 | 3 | 3 | 75 |
| 371 | 1962 | H. W. Coxill, K. G. Grubb | World Christian handbook, 4th edition | WCH-4 | — | London | 1 | k | English | | P | 5 | 4 | 3 | 4 | 80 |
| 372 | 1962 | H. J. Spaeth, ed | World mission map | | — | Cincinnati | 1 | a | English | | P | 5 | 2 | 3 | 3 | 65 |
| 373 | 1963 | P. Tillich | Christianity and the encounter of the world religions | | — | New York | 1 | t | English | | P | 5 | 0 | 3 | 3 | 55 |
| 374 | 1963 | B. G. M. Sundkler | Missionens varld: missionskundskap och missionshistoria, 1st edition | MV | The world of mission | Stockholm | 1 | s | Swedish | English | P | 3 | 2 | 5 | 5 | 75 |
| 375 | 1963 | P. R. Ackroyd, C. F. Evans | The Cambridge history of the Bible | CHB | — | Cambridge | 3 | h | English | | A | 5 | 5 | 4 | 4 | 90 |
| 376 | 1963 | J. P. Martin | The Last Judgment in Protestant theology from orthodoxy to Ritschl | | — | Grand Rapids | 1 | f | English | | P | 5 | 0 | 2 | 1 | 40 |
| 377 | 1963 | R. E. Coleman | The master plan of evangelism | | — | Grand Rapids | 1 | m | English | | P | 0 | 0 | 5 | 5 | 50 |
| 378 | 1964 | S. C. Neill | A history of Christian missions | HCM | — | Harmondsworth | 1 | h | English | German | A | 5 | 4 | 5 | 5 | 95 |
| 379 | 1964 | J. Frisque, F. Houtart | Bilan du monde: encyclopedie catholique du monde chretien, 2nd edition | BM-2 | The world on balance: Catholic world encyclopedia | Louvain | 2 | e | French | | R | 5 | 5 | 4 | 5 | 95 |
| 380 | 1964 | A. T. van Leeuwen | Christianity in world history: the meeting of the faiths of East and West | CWH | — | Edinburgh | 1 | h | English | Dutch | P | 5 | 2 | 3 | 4 | 70 |
| 381 | 1964 | D. A. McGavran | Church growth bulletin | CGB | — | Pasadena, CA | 15 | p | English | | P | 3 | 2 | 4 | 5 | 70 |
| 382 | 1964 | J. W. Reapsome | Evangelical missions quarterly | EMQ | — | Wheaton, IL | 36 | p | English | | P | 3 | 4 | 4 | 5 | 80 |
| 383 | 1964 | P. Scharpff | Geschichte der Evangelisation: dreihundent Jahre Evangelisation | GE | History of evangelization: the last 300 years | Giessen | 1 | h | German | English | P | 5 | 4 | 3 | 4 | 80 |
| 384 | 1964 | Paul VI | Lumen Gentium: Dogmatic Constitution on the Church | | A light to the Gentiles | Citta del Vaticano | 1 | q | Latin | EFGSPI | R | 0 | 0 | 5 | 5 | 50 |
| 385 | 1964 | A. Freitag, H. Emmerich | The twentieth century atlas of the Christian world | TCACW | — | New York | 1 | a | English | Latin | R | 5 | 4 | 4 | 5 | 90 |
| 386 | 1964 | G. W. Bromiley, ed | Theological dictionary of the New Testament | TDNT | — | Grand Rapids | 9 | d | English | German | P | 5 | 0 | 3 | 4 | 60 |
| 387 | 1964 | J. Moltmann | Theologie der Hoffnung: Untersuchungen zu Begrundung | | Theology of hope: enquiries toward proof | Munchen | 1 | f | German | English | P | 0 | 0 | 3 | 3 | 30 |
| 388 | 1965 | Paul VI | Ad Gentes: Decree on the Church's Missionary Activity | | To all peoples | Citta del Vaticano | 1 | q | Latin | EFGSPI | R | 0 | 0 | 5 | 5 | 50 |
| 389 | 1965 | A. Santos Hernandez | Bibliografia misional | BM | Bibliography of missions | Santander | 2 | b | Spanish | | R | 5 | 1 | 4 | 5 | 75 |
| 390 | 1965 | Paul VI | Gaudium et Spes | | Pastoral Constitution on the Church in Modern World | Citta del Vaticano | 1 | q | Latin | EFGSPI | R | 0 | 0 | 5 | 5 | 50 |
| 391 | 1965 | W. J. Hollenweger | Handbuch der Pfingstbewegung | HPB | Handbook of the Pentecostal movement | Genf | 1 | s | German | English | P | 5 | 4 | 4 | 4 | 85 |
| 392 | 1965 | F. Birkeli, T. Bjerkrheim | Norsk misjonsleksikon | | Lexicon of Norwegian missions | Stavanger | 3 | d | Norwegian | | P | 3 | 2 | 5 | 5 | 75 |
| 393 | 1965 | Paul VI | Nostra Aetate | | Relationship of the Church to Non-Christian Religions | Citta del Vaticano | 1 | q | Latin | EFGSPI | R | 0 | 0 | 5 | 5 | 50 |
| 394 | 1965 | K. Rahner | The Christian of the future | | — | New York | 1 | f | English | German | R | 0 | 0 | 5 | 5 | 50 |
| 395 | 1965 | R. E. Sommerfeld | The church of the 21st century: prospects and proposals | | — | Saint Louis | 1 | f | English | | P | 0 | 0 | 4 | 5 | 45 |
| 396 | 1965 | W. Buhlmann | The coming of the Third Church: an analysis of the present and future of the church | CTC | — | Slough | 1 | f | English | German | R | 3 | 2 | 5 | 5 | 75 |
| 397 | 1965 | B. G. M. Sundkler | The world of mission, 2nd edition | WOM | — | London | 1 | s | English | Swedish | P | 3 | 2 | 5 | 5 | 75 |

| Ref 1 | Year 2 | Authors/editors 3 | Title/subtitle/edition (in original language) 4 | Initials 5 | Title translated into English 6 | Place of publication 7 | Vols 8 | Cat 9 | Language 10 | Translations 11 | Ecc 12 | Em 13 | St 14 | M 15 | GM 16 | % 17 |
|---|---|---|---|---|---|---|---|---|---|---|---|---|---|---|---|---|
| 398 | 1966 | G. F. McLean, ed | Christian philosophy and religious renewal | | — | Washington, DC | 1 | n | English | | R | 1 | 0 | 1 | 0 | 10 |
| 399 | 1966 | P. Scharpff | History of evangelism: 300 years of evangelism in Germany, UK, and USA | HE | — | Grand Rapids | 1 | h | English | German | P | 5 | 4 | 3 | 4 | 80 |
| 400 | 1966 | M. Schlunk, H. Quiring | Map of the world's religions and missions, 4th edition | | — | Stuttgart | 1 | a | English | German | P | 5 | 4 | 4 | 5 | 90 |
| 401 | 1967 | M. Spindler | La Mission, combat pour le salut du monde | | Missions: the fight for the world's salvation | Neuchatel | 1 | t | French | | P | 5 | 1 | 4 | 4 | 70 |
| 402 | 1967 | K. Rahner, C. Ernst | Sacramenturn mundi: an encyclopedia of theology | SM | — | London | 6 | e | English | German | R | 3 | 1 | 1 | 1 | 30 |
| 403 | 1967 | B. L. Goddard, ed | The encyclopedia of modern Christian missions: the agencies | EMCM | — | Camden, NJ | 1 | e | English | | P | 5 | 4 | 5 | 5 | 95 |
| 404 | 1967 | J. Moltmann | Theology of hope: a contemporary Christian eschatology | | — | New York | 1 | t | English | German | P | 0 | 0 | 3 | 3 | 30 |
| 405 | 1967 | H. W. Coxill, K. G. Grubb | World Christian handbook 1968, 5th edition | WCH-5 | — | London | 1 | s | English | | P | 5 | 4 | 3 | 4 | 80 |
| 406 | 1968 | H. Emmerich, ed | Atlas Hierarchicus, 3rd edition | AH-3 | Atlas of Catholic jurisdictions | Modling | 1 | a | Latin | | R | 5 | 5 | 3 | 5 | 90 |
| 407 | 1968 | J. N. B. van den Brink, ed | Bibliographie de cartographie ecclesiastique | BCE | Bibliography of ecclesiastical maps | Leiden | 1 | b | French | | P | 5 | 4 | 3 | 2 | 70 |
| 408 | 1968 | E. Schillebeeckx | God and the future of man | GFM | — | New York | 1 | f | English | German | R | 0 | 0 | 3 | 3 | 30 |
| 409 | 1968 | O. G. Myklebust | International review of missions: index 1912-1966 | IRM | — | Geneva | 1 | b | English | | P | 5 | 0 | 5 | 4 | 70 |
| 410 | 1968 | E. Kirschbaum, ed | Lexikon der christlichen Ikonographie | LCI | Dictionary of Christian iconography | Freiburg | 8 | d | German | | R | 5 | 2 | 2 | 2 | 55 |
| 411 | 1968 | R.-W. Becker | Religion in Zahlen | RZ | Religion in figures | Heidelburg | 1 | s | German | | P | 4 | 5 | 1 | 0 | 50 |
| 412 | 1969 | J. Moltmann | Religion, revolution and the future | RRF | — | New York | 1 | f | English | German | P | 0 | 0 | 3 | 3 | 30 |
| 413 | 1969 | W. Pannenberg | Revelation as history | | — | New York | 1 | t | English | German | P | 3 | 0 | 3 | 3 | 45 |
| 414 | 1969 | A. J. van der Bent | The Christian-Marxist dialogue: an annotated bibliography, 1959-1969 | CMD | — | Geneva | 1 | b | English | French | P | 5 | 0 | 0 | 0 | 25 |
| 415 | 1970 | H. Jedin, K. S. Latourette | Atlas zur Kirchengeschichte: die christlichen Kirchen in Geschichte und Gegenwart | AKG | Atlas of church history past and present | Freiburg | 1 | a | German | | R | 5 | 4 | 3 | 3 | 75 |
| 416 | 1970 | S. C. Neill, G. H. Anderson | Concise dictionary of the Christian world mission | CDCWM | — | London | 1 | d | English | German | A | 3 | 4 | 5 | 4 | 80 |
| 417 | 1970 | J. L. Gonzalez | Historia de las misiones | HM | History of missions | Buenos Aires | 1 | h | Spanish | | R | 5 | 4 | 4 | 5 | 90 |
| 418 | 1970 | G. W. Peters | Saturation evangelism | | — | Grand Rapids | 1 | m | English | | P | 3 | 1 | 4 | 4 | 60 |
| 419 | 1970 | D. Lotz | The evangelization of the world in this generation: Conservative resurgence | | — | Hamburg | 1 | m | English | | P | 5 | 2 | 5 | 5 | 85 |
| 420 | 1970 | A. M. Ramsey , L.-J. Suenens | The future of the Christian church | FCC | — | London | 1 | f | English | | A | 3 | 0 | 3 | 4 | 50 |
| 421 | 1970 | H. Lindsey | The late great planet Earth | | — | Grand Rapids | 1 | f | English | | P | 0 | 0 | 1 | 1 | 10 |
| 422 | 1970 | G. J. Cuming, ed | The mission of the church and the propagation of the faith | | — | Cambridge | 1 | m | English | | A | 0 | 0 | 5 | 5 | 50 |
| 423 | 1970 | J. M. Yinger | The scientific study of religion | SSR | — | New York | 1 | n | English | | | 4 | 4 | 1 | 0 | 45 |
| 424 | 1970 | D. A. McGavran, C. P. Wagner | Understanding church growth | | — | Grand Rapids | 1 | m | English | | P | 0 | 2 | 3 | 5 | 50 |
| 425 | 1971 | H.-W. Gensichen | Glaube fur die Welt: theologische Aspekte der Mission | GW | Faith for the world: theological aspects of mission | Gutersloh | 1 | t | German | | P | 0 | 1 | 4 | 5 | 50 |
| 426 | 1971 | G. L. Alexander | Guide to atlases: world, regional, national, thematic: international listing since 1950 | | — | Metuchen, NJ | 1 | a | English | | — | 4 | 2 | 1 | 0 | 35 |
| 427 | 1971 | J. Metzler, ed | Sacrae Congregationis de Propaganda Fide memoria rerum: 350 Jahre im Weltmission | SCPF | Propaganda Fide: 350 years in world mission | Freiburg | 3 | h | Latin | German | R | 5 | 4 | 4 | 5 | 90 |
| 428 | 1971 | W. J. Danker, W. J. Kang | The future of the Christian world mission | FCWM | — | Grand Rapids | 1 | f | English | | P | 5 | 2 | 5 | 5 | 85 |
| 429 | 1971 | M. A. C. Warren, ed | To apply the Gospel: selections from the writings of Henry Venn | | — | Grand Rapids | 1 | m | English | | A | 1 | 1 | 5 | 5 | 60 |
| 430 | 1972 | G. W. Peters | A biblical theology of missions | BTM | — | Chicago | 1 | t | English | | P | 0 | 1 | 4 | 5 | 50 |
| 431 | 1972 | D. J. Bosch | Missionalia | | — | Pretoria | 28 | p | English | | P | 3 | 2 | 4 | 4 | 65 |
| 432 | 1972 | K. Rahner | Struktur wandel der Kirche als Aufgabe und Chance | | The shape of the church to come | Wien | 1 | f | German | English | R | 1 | 0 | 5 | 4 | 50 |
| 433 | 1972 | P. Eshleman | The Explo story: a plan to change the world | | — | Los Angeles | 1 | m | English | | P | 3 | 2 | 5 | 5 | 75 |
| 434 | 1972 | A. V. Seumois | Theologie missionnaire | TM | Missionary theology | Roma | 1 | t | French | | R | 0 | 0 | 5 | 4 | 45 |
| 435 | 1973 | J. B. Payne | Encyclopedia of biblical prophecy: guide to scriptural predictions and their fulfilment | EBP | — | New York | 1 | e | English | | P | 2 | 1 | 3 | 1 | 35 |
| 436 | 1973 | R. Facelina | Evangelization and mission: international bibliography indexed by computer, 1st edition | | — | Strasbourg | 1 | b | English | French | P | 5 | 1 | 5 | 5 | 80 |
| 437 | 1973 | R.D.Winter et alii | Missiology, 1973-2000 | | — | Pasadena, CA | 28 | p | English | | P | 3 | 2 | 5 | 5 | 75 |
| 438 | 1973 | E. Schillebeeckx | The mission of the church | | — | London | 1 | t | English | Dutch | R | 0 | 0 | 5 | 4 | 45 |
| 439 | 1974 | C. E. Jones | A guide to the study of the Holiness Movement | | — | Metuchen, NJ | 1 | b | English | | P | 5 | 0 | 1 | 0 | 30 |
| 440 | 1974 | I. R. al Faruqi, D. E. Sopher | Historical atlas of the religions of the world | HARW | — | New York | 1 | a | English | | — | 5 | 1 | 0 | 0 | 30 |
| 441 | 1974 | J. Kraus | Missionswissenschaftliche Themen in Festschriften, 1960-1971 | MWTF | Missiological themes in Festschrifts, 1960-1971 | Immensee | 1 | b | German | | R | 3 | 1 | 4 | 4 | 60 |
| 442 | 1974 | P. J. Johnstone | Operation World: day-by-day guide to praying for the world, 1st edition | OW-1 | — | Pasadena, CA | 1 | s | English | | P | 5 | 5 | 4 | 2 | 80 |
| 443 | 1974 | Pontifical Missionary Union | Religious and evangelization of the world: 10th Assembly, Canadian Religious Conf | | — | Ottawa | 1 | m | English | French | R | 3 | 0 | 3 | 5 | 55 |
| 444 | 1974 | G. Muller, G. Krause | Theologische realenzyklopadie | TRE | Encyclopedia of theology | Berlin | 24 | e | German | | P | 0 | 1 | 2 | 2 | 25 |
| 445 | 1974 | A. P. Johnston | World evangelism and the Word of God | | — | Minneapolis | 1 | t | English | | P | 0 | 1 | 4 | 5 | 50 |
| 446 | 1974 | R. R. Bowker | World guide to libraries, 4th edition | | — | New York | 2 | u | English | German | — | 5 | 2 | 0 | 0 | 35 |
| 447 | 1975 | Paul VI | Evangelii Nuntiandi (Apostolic Exhortation) | EN | On announcing the gospel | Citta del Vaticano | 1 | q | Latin | EFGISP | R | 3 | 0 | 5 | 5 | 65 |
| 448 | 1975 | CERDIC | Evangelisation and mission | | — | Strasbourg | 1 | s | English | | P | 0 | 2 | 5 | 4 | 55 |
| 449 | 1975 | S. Pignedoli, ed | Guida delle missioni cattoliche | GMC | Guide to Catholic missions | Citta del Vaticano | 1 | s | Italian | | R | 5 | 5 | 5 | 5 | 100 |
| 450 | 1975 | J. Verkuyl | Inleiding in de nieuwere Zendingswetenschap | | Contemporary missiology: an introduction | Kampen | 1 | t | Dutch | English | P | 3 | 1 | 5 | 5 | 70 |
| 451 | 1975 | S. C. Neill, N. P. Moritzen | Lexikon zur Weltmission | LW | World mission dictionary | Wuppertal | 1 | d | German | English | A | 3 | 4 | 5 | 4 | 80 |
| 452 | 1975 | H. H. Ward | Religion 2101 A.D.: who or what will be God? | | — | Garden City, NY | 1 | f | English | | P | 2 | 1 | 2 | 1 | 30 |
| 453 | 1976 | H. Emmerich, ed | Atlas Hierarchicus, 4th edition | AH-4 | Atlas of Catholic jurisdictions | Modling | 1 | a | Latin | | R | 5 | 5 | 3 | 5 | 90 |
| 454 | 1976 | F. H. Littell | The Macmillan atlas history of Christianity | MAHC | — | New York | 1 | a | English | | P | 5 | 2 | 3 | 3 | 65 |
| 455 | 1977 | H. W. Turner | Bibliography of new religious movements in primal societies | NERMS | — | Boston | 6 | b | English | | P | 5 | 0 | 3 | 3 | 55 |
| 456 | 1978 | J. H. Kane | A concise history of the Christian world mission: a panoramic view, Pentecost to present | CHCWM | — | Grand Rapids | 1 | h | English | | P | 5 | 2 | 3 | 5 | 75 |
| 457 | 1978 | V. T. Istravridis | Bibliografia tes Oikoumenikes Kinesoes, 1960-1970 | BOK | Bibliography of the Ecumenical Movement | Athinai | 1 | b | Greek | | O | 5 | 1 | 2 | 2 | 50 |
| 458 | 1978 | J. Verkuyl | Contemporary missiology: an introduction | CM | — | Grand Rapids | 1 | t | English | Dutch | P | 3 | 1 | 5 | 5 | 70 |
| 459 | 1978 | J. Verkuyl | De onvoltooide taak der wereldzending | | The unfinished task of world missions | Kampen | 1 | | Dutch | | P | 5 | 2 | 5 | 5 | 85 |
| 460 | 1978 | R. R. Bowker | Religious books and serials in print, 1978-1979 | | — | New York | 1 | b | English | | — | 4 | 2 | 2 | 0 | 40 |
| 461 | 1978 | A. P. Johnston | The battle for world evangelism | | — | Wheaton, IL | 1 | m | English | | P | 3 | 1 | 3 | 5 | 60 |
| 462 | 1978 | O. V. Garrison | The encyclopedia of prophecy | EP | — | Secaucus, NJ | 1 | e | English | | P | 0 | 1 | 2 | 1 | 20 |
| 463 | 1978 | J. D. Douglas, ed | The new international dictionary of the Christian Church | NIDCC | — | Exeter, UK | 1 | d | English | | P | 5 | 4 | 5 | 5 | 95 |
| 464 | 1978 | A. Proc, ed | Yearbook of the Orthodox Church | YOC | — | Munchen | 1 | k | English | Ger,Fre | O | 5 | 0 | 1 | 0 | 30 |
| 465 | 1979 | John Paul II | Catechesi Tradendae (Apostolic Exhortation) | | Handing down Catechesis | Citta del Vaticano | 1 | r | Latin | EFGSPI | R | 0 | 0 | 5 | 5 | 50 |
| 466 | 1979 | P. K. Meagher, C. M. Aherne | Encyclopedic dictionary of religion | | — | Washington, DC | 3 | e | English | | R | 3 | 4 | 1 | 0 | 40 |
| 467 | 1979 | G. H. Anderson, J. Bonk | International bulletin of missionary research | IBMR | — | Ventnor, NJ | 21 | p | English | | P | 3 | 2 | 5 | 4 | 70 |
| 468 | 1979 | T. P. Weber | Living in the shadow of the Second Coming: American Premillennialism, 1875-1982 | | — | New York | 1 | f | English | | P | 5 | 0 | 4 | 4 | 65 |
| 469 | 1979 | H. Burkle | Missionstheologie | | Theology of missions | Stuttgart | 1 | t | German | | P | 0 | 2 | 4 | 4 | 50 |
| 470 | 1980 | E. R. Dayton, D. A. Fraser | Planning strategies for world evangelization | | — | Monrovia, CA | 1 | m | English | | P | 0 | 1 | 4 | 5 | 50 |
| 471 | 1981 | M. R. Spindler, ed | Bible and mission: a partially annotated bibliography, 1960-1980 | | — | Leiden | 1 | b | English | | P | 5 | 1 | 4 | 4 | 70 |
| 472 | 1981 | K. Crim | The Abingdon dictionary of living religions | ADLR | — | Nashville, TN | 1 | d | English | | P | 3 | 1 | 2 | 0 | 30 |
| 473 | 1982 | CWME | Mission and evangelism: an ecumenical affirmation | | — | Geneva | 1 | m | English | Fre,Ger | P | 0 | 0 | 5 | 5 | 50 |
| 474 | 1982 | A. Rauch, ed | Orthodoxia | | Orthodoxy | Regensburg | 1 | I | German | | O | 5 | 0 | 4 | 3 | 60 |
| 475 | 1982 | A. Yannoulatos | Panta ta Ethni | | To all peoples | Athinai | 10 | p | Greek | | O | 3 | 2 | 4 | 5 | 70 |
| 476 | 1982 | D. B. Barrett, ed | World Christian encyclopedia: a survey of churches and religions, AD 1900-2000 | WCE-1 | — | Nairobi | 1 | e | English | Japanese | A | 4 | 5 | 5 | 5 | 95 |
| 477 | 1983 | C. E. Jones | A guide to the study of the Pentecostal movement | GSPM | — | Metuchen, NJ | 2 | b | English | | P | 5 | 2 | 3 | 4 | 70 |

| Ref 1 | Year 2 | Authors/editors 3 | Title/subtitle/edition (in original language) 4 | Initials 5 | Title translated into English 6 | Place of publication 7 | Vols 8 | Cat 9 | Language 10 | Translations 11 | Ecc 12 | Em 13 | St 14 | M 15 | GM 16 | % 17 |
|---|---|---|---|---|---|---|---|---|---|---|---|---|---|---|---|---|
| 478 | 1983 | H. Kruger, W. Loser | Okumene Lexikon: Kirchen, Religionen, Bewegungen | OL | Ecumenical dictionary | Frankfurt | 1 | d | German | | P | 3 | 4 | 3 | 2 | 60 |
| 479 | 1984 | J. F. Puglisi, S. J. Voicu | A bibliography of interchurch and interconfessional theological dialogues | | — | Roma | 1 | b | English | | P | 5 | 0 | 3 | 4 | 60 |
| 480 | 1984 | G. Aeschliman | International journal of frontier missions | IJFM | — | Pasadena, CA | 16 | p | English | | P | 3 | 2 | 4 | 5 | 70 |
| 481 | 1984 | M. Lurker | Lexikon der Gotter und Damonen | LGD | Dictionary of gods and demons | Stuttgart | 1 | d | German | English | – | 5 | 1 | 0 | 0 | 30 |
| 482 | 1984 | IAMS | Mission studies, 1984-2000 | IAMS | — | Leiden | 16 | p | English | | P | 3 | 2 | 3 | 4 | 60 |
| 483 | 1984 | J. R. Hinnells, ed | The Facts on File dictionary of religions | FFDR | — | New York | 1 | d | English | | A | 5 | 1 | 1 | 0 | 35 |
| 484 | 1984 | S. M. Burgess | The Holy Spirit: in ancient, Eastern, Medieval Roman Catholic, and Reformation traditions | THS | — | Peabody, MA | 3 | h | English | | P | 3 | 5 | 3 | 3 | 70 |
| 485 | 1984 | J. R. Hinnells, ed | The Penguin dictionary of religions | PDR | — | London | 1 | d | English | | A | 5 | 1 | 1 | 0 | 35 |
| 486 | 1984 | J. E. Kyle, ed | The unfinished task | | — | Ventura, CA | 1 | s | English | | P | 3 | 4 | 3 | 5 | 75 |
| 487 | 1985 | H. Kung | Christentum und Weltreligionen | | Christianity and the world religions | Munchen | 1 | t | German | English | R | 2 | 2 | 2 | 4 | 50 |
| 488 | 1985 | W. A. Meeks, ed | Library of early Christianity | LEC | — | Louisville, KY | 8 | q | English | | P | 5 | 2 | 2 | 2 | 55 |
| 489 | 1985 | A. E. Hurd, P. D. Petersen | Missions and evangelism: a bibliography from the ATLA religion database | | — | Chicago | 1 | b | English | | P | 5 | 0 | 3 | 5 | 65 |
| 490 | 1985 | R. Stark, W. S. Bainbridge | The future of religion: secularization, revival, and cult formation | | — | Berkeley, CA | 1 | f | English | | P | 5 | 2 | 2 | 1 | 50 |
| 491 | 1986 | H. Kung | Christianity and the world religions: paths to dialogue with Islam, Hinduism, Buddhism | CWR | — | Garden City, NY | 1 | t | English | German | R | 3 | 1 | 2 | 4 | 50 |
| 492 | 1986 | C. P. Wagner, ed, W. Arn | Church growth: state of the art | | — | Wheaton, IL | 1 | m | English | | P | 3 | 2 | 4 | 3 | 60 |
| 493 | 1986 | J. J. Stamoolis | Eastern Orthodox mission theology today | | — | New York | 1 | t | English | | O | 3 | 1 | 4 | 3 | 55 |
| 494 | 1986 | E. Fahlbusch, ed | Evangelisches Kirchenlexikon: Internationale theologische Enzyklopadie, 3rd edition | EKL-3 | Protestant church dictionary | Gottingen | 3 | e | German | English | P | 3 | 2 | 2 | 2 | 45 |
| 495 | 1986 | NCCB | Pastoral statement 'To the ends of the Earth' | | — | Washington, DC | 1 | m | English | | R | 3 | 0 | 3 | 5 | 55 |
| 496 | 1986 | M. Takenaka | Sekai kirisuto-kyo hyakka-jiten | SKH | World Christian encyclopedia | Tokyo | 1 | e | Japanese | English | A | 4 | 5 | 5 | 5 | 95 |
| 497 | 1986 | W. Buhlmann | The church of the future: a model for the year 2001 | | — | Slough | 1 | f | English | German | R | 0 | 2 | 5 | 5 | 60 |
| 498 | 1986 | K. P. Yohannan | The coming revolution in world missions: God's Third Wave | | — | Altamonte Sprin | 1 | m | English | | I | 0 | 1 | 3 | 4 | 40 |
| 499 | 1986 | M. Eliade, ed | The encyclopedia of religion | ER | — | New York | 16 | e | English | | O | 3 | 2 | 1 | 0 | 30 |
| 500 | 1987 | H. Chadwick, G. R. Evans | Atlas of the Christian church | ACC | — | London | 1 | a | English | | A | 5 | 4 | 3 | 3 | 75 |
| 501 | 1987 | C. E. Jones | Black Holiness: Black participation in Wesleyan Perfectionist and Pentecostal Movements | | — | Metuchen, NJ | 1 | b | English | | P | 5 | 0 | 1 | 0 | 30 |
| 502 | 1987 | E. Coreth, W. M. Neidl | Christliche Philosophie im katholischen Denken des 19 und 20 Jahrhunderts | CPKD | Philosophy in Catholic thought, 19th-20th centuries | Graz | 3 | n | German | | R | 3 | 0 | 1 | 2 | 30 |
| 503 | 1987 | M. Lurker | Dictionary of gods and goddesses, devils and demons | DGG | — | London | 1 | d | English | German | – | 5 | 1 | 0 | 0 | 30 |
| 504 | 1987 | T. Forrest, ed | Evangelization 2000 | | — | Roma | 8 | p | English | FGSI | R | 3 | 1 | 3 | 5 | 60 |
| 505 | 1987 | D. L. Edwards | Futures of Christianity: historical, contemporary and future trends in the worldwide church | | — | London | 1 | f | English | | A | 3 | 1 | 3 | 3 | 50 |
| 506 | 1987 | T. Yamamori | God's new envoys: strategy for penetrating closed countries | | — | Portland, OR | 1 | m | English | | P | 0 | 1 | 3 | 5 | 45 |
| 507 | 1987 | F. Clark, ed | Interfaith directory | | — | New York | 1 | u | English | | R | 5 | 0 | 0 | 0 | 25 |
| 508 | 1987 | K. Muller, T. Sundermeier | Lexikon missionstheologischer Grundbegriffe | LMG | Dictionary of fundamental principles of missiology | Berlin | 1 | d | German | | R | 3 | 2 | 4 | 3 | 60 |
| 509 | 1987 | H. Kung | Theologie im Aufbruch | | Theology for the future | Munchen | 1 | f | German | English | R | 0 | 1 | 0 | 0 | 5 |
| 510 | 1987 | H. Kung | Theology for the Third Millennium: an ecumenical view | TTM | — | New York | 1 | f | English | German | R | 0 | 1 | 0 | 0 | 5 |
| 511 | 1988 | M. R. Elliott, ed | Christianity and Marxism worldwide: an annotated bibliography | CMW | — | Wheaton, IL | 1 | b | English | | P | 5 | 1 | 2 | 2 | 50 |
| 512 | 1988 | S. M. Burgess, ed, et al | Dictionary of Pentecostal and Charismatic movements | DPCM | — | Grand Rapids | 1 | d | English | | P | 3 | 5 | 5 | 4 | 85 |
| 513 | 1988 | D. B. Barrett, J. W. Reapsome | Seven hundred plans to evangelize the world: the rise of a global evangelization movement | GEM | — | Birmingham, AL | 1 | m | English | | A | 4 | 5 | 5 | 5 | 95 |
| 514 | 1989 | J. Tomko | Guida della missioni cattoliche | GDMC | Guide to Catholic missions | Citta del Vaticano | 1 | s | Italian | | R | 5 | 4 | 4 | 5 | 90 |
| 515 | 1990 | E. Ferguson, ed | Encyclopedia of Early Christianity | | — | New York | 1 | e | English | | P | 5 | 2 | 2 | 0 | 45 |
| 516 | 1990 | E. von Ivanka, ed, J. Tyciak | Handbuch der Ostkirchenkunde, 2nd edition | HO | Handbook of the Eastern churches | Dusseldorf | 1 | k | German | | O | 5 | 2 | 4 | 4 | 75 |
| 517 | 1990 | C. Baladier, ed | Le grand atlas des religions | GAR | Atlas of religions | Paris | 1 | a | French | | R | 5 | 2 | 1 | 1 | 45 |
| 518 | 1990 | D. B. Barrett, T. M. Johnson | Our globe and how to reach it | OG | — | Birmingham, AL | 1 | m | English | | A | 4 | 5 | 5 | 5 | 95 |
| 519 | 1990 | John Paul II | Redemptoris Missio (Encyclical) | RM | The mission of the Redeemer | Citta del Vaticano | 1 | r | Latin | EFGISP | R | 0 | 0 | 5 | 5 | 50 |
| 520 | 1991 | W. J. Chamberlin | Catalogue of English Bible translations: a classified bibliography of versions and editions | CEBT | — | New York | 1 | b | English | | P | 5 | 1 | 0 | 2 | 40 |
| 521 | 1991 | N. Lossky, ed, J. M. Bonino | Dictionary of the ecumenical movement | DEM | — | Geneva | 1 | d | English | | P | 3 | 4 | 2 | 3 | 60 |
| 522 | 1991 | G. Ward | International directory of the world's religions | IDWR | — | Carmel, CA | 1 | u | English | | – | 5 | 0 | 0 | 0 | 25 |
| 523 | 1991 | J. Holm | Keyguide to information sources on world religions | | — | London | 1 | b | English | | P | 5 | 0 | 0 | 0 | 25 |
| 524 | 1991 | G. R. Grimes, ed | Missiological abstracts, 25 years, 1966-1991 | MA | — | Pasadena, CA | 1 | b | English | | P | 3 | 1 | 3 | 4 | 55 |
| 525 | 1991 | J. A. B. Jongeneel | Missiologie | | Missiology | s-Gravenhage | 1 | e | Dutch | English | P | 3 | 4 | 5 | 5 | 85 |
| 526 | 1991 | G. H. Anderson, J. M. Phillips | Mission in the Nineteen Nineties | | — | Grand Rapids | 1 | m | English | | P | 0 | 2 | 4 | 5 | 55 |
| 527 | 1991 | J. D. Douglas, ed | New 20th-century encyclopedia of religious knowledge | NERK | — | Grand Rapids | 1 | e | English | | P | 3 | 2 | 4 | 4 | 65 |
| 528 | 1991 | J. McManners, ed | The Oxford illustrated history of Christianity | OIHC | — | Oxford | 1 | h | English | | A | 5 | 2 | 4 | 4 | 75 |
| 529 | 1991 | D. J. Bosch | Transforming mission: paradigm shifts in theology of mission | TM | — | Maryknoll, NY | 1 | t | English | | P | 3 | 1 | 5 | 4 | 65 |
| 530 | 1992 | Z. Stezycki, ed | Atlas Hierarchicus, 5th edition | AH-5 | Atlas of Catholic jurisdictions | Modling | 1 | a | Latin | | R | 5 | 5 | 3 | 5 | 90 |
| 531 | 1992 | L. H. Hartley | Cities and churches: an international bibliography | CCIB | — | Metuchen, NJ | 3 | b | English | | P | 5 | 0 | 3 | 3 | 55 |
| 532 | 1992 | I. Harris, S. Mews | Contemporary religions: a world guide | CRWG | — | Harlow | 1 | d | English | | A | 3 | 2 | 1 | 1 | 35 |
| 533 | 1992 | J. Comby | Deux milles ans d'evangelisation: histoire de l'expansion chretienne | | 2000 years of evangelization and Christian expansion | Tournai | 1 | h | French | | R | 5 | 2 | 4 | 5 | 80 |
| 534 | 1992 | H. Rzepkowski | Lexikon der Mission: Geschichte, Theologie, Ethnologie | LM | Lexicon of mission: history, theology, ethnology | Graz | 1 | d | German | | R | 3 | 2 | 3 | 3 | 55 |
| 535 | 1992 | T. T. Daniels | Millennialism: an international bibliography | MIB | — | New York | 1 | b | English | | P | 5 | 0 | 0 | 0 | 25 |
| 536 | 1992 | J. A. Scherer, ed, et al | New directions in mission and evangelization: basic statements, 1974-1991 | NDIME | — | Maryknoll, NY | 2 | m | English | | P | 0 | 0 | 3 | 5 | 40 |
| 537 | 1992 | J. A. B. Jongeneel, ed | Pentecost, mission and ecumenism: essays on intercultural theology | | — | Frankfurt am M | 1 | t | English | German | P | 3 | 2 | 5 | 4 | 70 |
| 538 | 1992 | J. R. Hinnells, ed | Who's who of world religions | WWWR | — | New York | 1 | i | English | | A | 5 | 0 | 1 | 0 | 30 |
| 539 | 1993 | W. E. Mills | A bibliography of the nature and role of the Holy Spirit in 20th-century writings | | — | Lewiston, NY | 1 | b | English | | P | 5 | 1 | 4 | 5 | 75 |
| 540 | 1993 | R. Wuthnow | Christianity in the 21st century: reflections on the challenges ahead | | — | New York | 1 | f | English | | P | 0 | 0 | 1 | 1 | 10 |
| 541 | 1993 | I. Hexham | Concise dictionary of religion | | — | Downers Grove | 1 | d | English | | P | 3 | 2 | 2 | 2 | 45 |
| 542 | 1993 | N. Cohn | Cosmos, chaos and the world to come: ancient roots of apocalyptic faith | | — | New Haven | 1 | h | English | | A | 5 | 0 | 0 | 0 | 25 |
| 543 | 1993 | G. A. Mather, L. A. Nichols | Dictionary of cults, sects, religions and the occult | | — | Grand Rapids | 1 | d | English | | P | 5 | 2 | 0 | 0 | 35 |
| 544 | 1993 | P. Poupard, ed | Dictionnaire des religions, 3rd edition | DR | Dictionary of religions | Paris | 2 | d | French | | R | 3 | 2 | 3 | 2 | 50 |
| 545 | 1993 | E. Nunnenmacher, ed | Dizionario di Missiologia | DM | Dictionary of missiology | Bologna | 1 | d | Italian | | R | 0 | 1 | 5 | 5 | 55 |
| 546 | 1993 | M. Jordan | Encyclopedia of gods: over 2,500 deities of the world | EG | — | New York | 1 | e | English | | A | 5 | 0 | 0 | 0 | 25 |
| 547 | 1993 | P. J. Johnstone | Operation World: day-by-day guide to praying for the world, 5th edition | OW-5 | — | Grand Rapids | 1 | s | English | Korean | P | 4 | 3 | 3 | 4 | 70 |
| 548 | 1993 | L. Howe, ed, A. Wain | Predicting the future | | — | Cambridge | 1 | f | English | | A | 3 | 1 | 0 | 0 | 20 |
| 549 | 1993 | A. E. McGrath, ed | The Blackwell encyclopedia of modern Christian thought | BEMCT | — | Oxford | 1 | e | English | | A | 3 | 0 | 2 | 2 | 35 |
| 550 | 1993 | C. Van Engen, D. S. Gilliland | The Good News of the Kingdom: mission theology for the Third Millennium | | — | Maryknoll, NY | 1 | t | English | | P | 0 | 1 | 4 | 5 | 50 |
| 551 | 1993 | J. O'Brien, M. Palmer | The state of religion atlas | | — | London | 1 | a | English | | A | 5 | 5 | 2 | 2 | 70 |
| 552 | 1993 | R. Kirby, E. Brewer | The temples of tomorrow: world religions and the future | | — | London | 1 | f | English | | P | 3 | 2 | 2 | 2 | 45 |
| 553 | 1993 | J. M. Phillips, R. T. Coote | Toward the 21st century in Christian mission: essays in honor of G. H. Anderson | TTCM | — | Grand Rapids | 1 | f | English | | P | 3 | 1 | 5 | 3 | 60 |
| 554 | 1994 | A. Sodano | Annuarium statisticum ecclesiae | ASE | Statistical yearbok of the Church | Citta del Vaticano | 1 | s | Latin | | R | 5 | 5 | 3 | 5 | 90 |
| 555 | 1994 | H. Kung | Christentum: Wesen und Geschichte | | Christianity: essence, history and future | Munchen | 1 | t | German | English | R | 3 | 0 | 0 | 2 | 25 |
| 556 | 1994 | T. Yates | Christian mission in the twentieth century | | — | Cambridge | 1 | h | English | | A | 5 | 1 | 5 | 4 | 75 |
| 557 | 1994 | A. J. van der Bent | Historical dictionary of Ecumenical Christianity | | — | Metuchen, NJ | 1 | d | English | | P | 3 | 1 | 2 | 1 | 35 |

| Ref | Year | Authors/editors | Title/subtitle/edition (in original language) | Initials | Title translated into English | Place of publication | Vols | Cat | Language | Translations | Ecc | Em | St | M | GM | % |
| 1 | 2 | 3 | 4 | 5 | 6 | 7 | 8 | 9 | 10 | 11 | 12 | 13 | 14 | 15 | 16 | 17 |
|---|---|---|---|---|---|---|---|---|---|---|---|---|---|---|---|---|
| 558 | 1994 | J.-M. Berentsen, ed | Missiologi i dag | | Norwegian mission handbook | Oslo | 1 | k | Norwegian | EFGSPI | P | 3 | 2 | 4 | 4 | 65 |
| 559 | 1994 | John Paul II | Tertio Millennio Adveniente (Apostolic Letter) | | On the coming of the Third Millennium | Città del Vaticano | 1 | r | Latin | | R | 0 | 0 | 5 | 5 | 50 |
| 560 | 1994 | M. Pye, ed | The Continuum dictionary of religion | CDR | — | New York | 1 | d | English | | A | 3 | 1 | 1 | 0 | 25 |
| 561 | 1994 | I. Harris, ed | The Longman guide to living religions | LGLR | — | London | 1 | d | English | | — | 3 | 1 | 0 | 0 | 25 |
| 562 | 1994 | M. Pye, ed | The Macmillan dictionary of religion | MDR | — | London | 1 | d | English | | A | 3 | 0 | 0 | 0 | 15 |
| 563 | 1994 | S. Blackburn | The Oxford dictionary of philosophy | ODP | — | Oxford | 1 | t | English | | P | 3 | 1 | 3 | 3 | 0 |
| 564 | 1994 | E. Rommen, ed | Christianity and the religions: a biblical theology of world religions | | — | Pasadena, CA | 1 | q | English | | P | 3 | 0 | 3 | 3 | 50 |
| 565 | 1995 | N. E. Thomas, ed | Classic texts in mission and world Christianity | | — | Maryknoll, NY | 1 | f | English | | P | 5 | 2 | 3 | 4 | 40 |
| 566 | 1995 | Harvey Cox | Fire from heaven: rise of pentecostal spirituality and reshaping of religion in 21st century | FFH | — | Reading, MA | 1 | q | English | | — | 5 | 0 | 1 | 1 | 70 |
| 567 | 1995 | J. H. Billington | Library of Congress subject headings, 18th edition | LCSH | — | Washington, DC | 4 | b | English | | A | 3 | 1 | 0 | | 35 |
| 568 | 1995 | J. R. Hinnells, ed | New dictionary of religions | NDR | — | Oxford | 1 | e | English | Dutch | P | 3 | 4 | 5 | 5 | 25 |
| 569 | 1995 | J. A. B. Jongeneel | Philosophy, science and theology of missions: a missiological encyclopedia | PSTM | — | Frankfurt am M | 2 | b | English | | P | 5 | 2 | 3 | 4 | 85 |
| 570 | 1995 | C. E. Jones | The Charismatic movement: a guide to the study of neo-pentecostalism | CM | — | Metuchen, NJ | 2 | b | English | | P | 5 | 0 | 3 | 1 | 70 |
| 571 | 1995 | E. D. Schandorff | The doctrine of the Holy Spirit: a bibliography showing its chronological development | DHS | — | Lanham, MD | 1 | d | English | | P | 3 | 2 | 1 | 0 | 35 |
| 572 | 1995 | J. Z. Smith, ed | The HarperCollins dictionary of religion | HCDR | — | San Francisco | 1 | e | English | | P | 5 | 4 | 4 | 5 | 30 |
| 573 | 1996 | S. Young, ed | Encyclopedia of women in world religions | EWWR | — | Englewood Cliffs | 2 | d | German | | R | 5 | 0 | 4 | 4 | 35 |
| 574 | 1996 | W. Kasper, H. Bürkle | Lexikon für Theologie und Kirche, 3rd edition | LThK-3 | Lexicon for theology and church | Freiburg | 11 | b | German | | P | 5 | 0 | 2 | 2 | 90 |
| 575 | 1996 | W. M. Johnston | Recent reference books in religion: a guide | RRBR | — | Downers Grove | 1 | h | English | | P | 5 | 5 | 2 | 1 | 45 |
| 576 | 1996 | R. Stark | The rise of Christianity: a sociologist reconsiders history | | — | Princeton, NJ | 1 | d | English | | I | 3 | 2 | 3 | 3 | 65 |
| 577 | 1997 | P. A. Deiros, ed | Diccionario Hispanoamericano de la Misión | DHM | Hispanic American dictionary of mission | Santa Fe | 1 | d | Spanish | | R | 3 | 2 | 4 | 3 | 55 |
| 578 | 1997 | K. Müller, S. B. Bevans | Dictionary of mission: theology, history, perspectives | | — | Maryknoll, NY | 1 | d | English | German | R | 3 | 3 | 4 | 3 | 60 |
| 579 | 1997 | D. J. Hall | The end of Christendom and the future of Christianity | | — | Harrisburg, PA | 1 | f | English | | P | 0 | 0 | 5 | 5 | 70 |
| 580 | 1997 | R. E. Coleman | The Master's way of personal evangelism | | — | Wheaton, IL | 1 | m | English | | A | 3 | 1 | 1 | 0 | 50 |
| 581 | 1997 | J. Bowker, ed | The Oxford dictionary of world religions | ODWR | — | Oxford | 1 | d | English | | P | 5 | 4 | 2 | 2 | 25 |
| 582 | 1997 | P. Brierley, ed | World churches handbook | | — | London | 1 | a | English | | P | 5 | 5 | 4 | 5 | 65 |
| 583 | 1998 | P. Brierley | Atlas of world Christianity | AWC | — | New York | 1 | a | English | | P | 2 | 1 | 3 | 0 | 70 |
| 584 | 1998 | G. H. Anderson, ed | Biographical dictionary of Christian missions | BDCM | — | Edinburgh | 1 | f | English | | P | 5 | 2 | 1 | 0 | 30 |
| 585 | 1998 | P. F. Esler, ed | Christianity for the 21st century | | — | Nashville, TN | 1 | u | English | | P | 1 | 0 | 0 | 0 | 30 |
| 586 | 1998 | J. G. Melton | International directory of the world's religions | IDWR | — | Albany, NY | 12 | f | English | | P | 1 | 0 | 0 | 0 | 25 |
| 587 | 1998 | N. Rescher | Predicting the future: an introduction to the theory of forecasting | | — | Harrisburg, PA | 1 | f | English | | — | 1 | 1 | 5 | 5 | 45 |
| 588 | 1998 | J. Rieger | Remember the poor: the challenge to theology in the twenty-first century | | — | London | 1 | f | English | | P | 1 | 1 | 5 | 5 | 50 |
| 589 | 1998 | J. V. Taylor | The Uncancelled Mandate: Bible studies on mission for the Millennium | UM | — | Oxford | 1 | x | English | | A | 4 | 0 | 3 | 3 | 50 |
| 590 | 1999 | N. Smart | Atlas of the world's religions | AWR | — | Grand Rapids | 5 | a | English | German | A | 4 | 0 | 3 | 3 | 70 |
| 591 | 1999 | E. Fahlbusch, ed | The encyclopedia of Christianity | EC/EKL | — | New York | 1 | e | English | | P | 3 | 5 | 0 | 3 | 25 |
| 592 | 1999 | J. L. Esposito | The Oxford history of Islam | | — | Springfield, MA | 1 | h | English | | — | 5 | 1 | 1 | 0 | 35 |
| 593 | 1999 | W. Doniger, ed | Merriam-Webster's encyclopedia of world religions | MWEWR | — | Dallas, TX | 1 | d | English | | P | 5 | 5 | 3 | 3 | 60 |
| 594 | 2000 | B. F. Grimes | Ethnologue, 14th edition | E-14 | — | Grand Rapids | 1 | d | English | | P | 5 | 3 | 1 | 0 | 60 |
| 595 | 2000 | A. S. Moreau | Evangelical dictionary of world missions | EDWM | — | Hebron, UK | 2 | d | English | | P | 5 | 5 | 3 | 3 | 85 |
| 596 | 2000 | D. Dalby | Linguasphere register | LR-1 | — | Grand Rapids | 1 | d | English | | P | 3 | 5 | 5 | 4 | 85 |
| 597 | 2001 | S. M. Burgess, eds | The new international dictionary of Pentecostal and Charismatic movements | NIDPCM | — | Oxford | 2 | d | English | | A | 4 | 5 | 5 | 5 | 95 |
| 598 | 2001 | D. B. Barrett, T. M. Johnson | World Christian encyclopedia: a survey of churches and religions in the modern world | WCE-2 | — | Pasadena, CA | 2 | e | English | | A | 4 | 5 | 5 | 5 | 95 |
| 599 | 2001 | D. B. Barrett, T. M. Johnson | World Christian trends, AD 30–AD 2200 | WCT | — | Santa Barbara, CA | 1 | d | English | | P | 4 | 4 | 3 | 2 | 65 |
| 600 | 2001 | J. G. Melton, et al, eds | The 21st century encyclopedia of the world's religions | | — | Santa Barbara, CA | 2 | e | English | | P | 4 | 4 | 3 | 2 | 65 |

# III. APPLYING MISSIOMETRICS TO THE CONTEMPORARY GLOBAL SCENE

In this section of the book, we are concerned with explaining how this survey was conducted. In particular we explain how those various aspects of Christianity and religions which can be quantified have in fact been enumerated here. Before we begin on this explanation, though, we must first ask whether such surveys are legitimate or useful or even necessary at all from the Christian standpoint and whether in fact there is any theological justification for such endeavor. Our answer here cannot be termed an adequate theological statement, but only a pointer towards such a theology of enumeration.

## A THEOLOGY OF CHRISTIAN ENUMERATION

### The Great Commission
The background to this survey is the theology of the Christian mission as evidenced in its basic statement and starting-point, the command of the risen Jesus to his disciples recorded in the Gospels: 'Go forth to every part of the world, and proclaim the Good News to the whole creation' (Mark 16:15, NEB). This starting-point is analyzed here in Part 3 "GeoCommission". It is this Great Commission which has inspired Christian missionary endeavor over the centuries since the Apostolic era. It is this mandate also which demands the global perspective utilized throughout the present survey.

### Why do surveys?
From the spiritual and theological standpoints, queries have often been raised concerning the legitimacy of surveying Christian work. Is it right? Is it wrong? Is it compatible with faith? Is it possible? Is it of any value? Is it essential? How can one survey the work of God the Holy Spirit, who is the Evangelizer and Missionary par excellence? What priority if any does such endeavor have for the churches? and so on. A first, immediate answer derives from the Great Commission described here in Part 3. The main justification for surveys of Christianity in its world mission is that they help the followers of Christ to see to what extent they have been faithful to that commission; to perceive the magnitude of their unfinished task; and to discern at what points to commit their resources in order to implement their commission.

### Numbers
The earliest known view of number is the Pythagorean contention that number is the sole inner reality of each thing, e.g. justice is 4, perfection is 10. The article on 'Number' in the *New Catholic encyclopedia* (1967:10.565) continues:

> Number is a way of knowing the quantity, intensity, order, or structure of material reality. With the aid of statistics and probability, number affords scientists the opportunity of predicting and controlling countable or measurable things or events with varying degrees of probability and success.

### Numbers in the Bible
The decimal scale of notation and system of counting were used by the Israelites, Assyrians, Babylonians, Egyptians, Greeks and Romans. They all reckoned by units, tens, hundreds, etc. One book of the Bible is called Numbers (in the Greek Septuagint, 'Arithmoi') because of its emphasis on censuses and enumeration. Numbers occur widely, and are extensively used, elsewhere in the Bible also. There are 3 main usages, as follows.
1. *Exact numbers*. Most usage of numbers in the Bible is simple enumeration, i.e. for simple expression of numerical values. Numbers are used to depict the exact, factual situation, such as the actual number of fighting men available. Such numbers are usually given to the last digit; an example is the 153 fish caught by the Apostles in John 21:11.
2. *Round numbers*. Usage of numbers can also be for rhetorical purposes. As in most languages, bib-

lical Hebrew used 'round numbers', i.e. exact tens, hundreds, thousands, or 20,000 (the highest single number), on the understanding that they were only approximately accurate. Hebrew usage preferred concrete rather than abstract forms of expression, using a definite number when only an approximation was intended. Thus in 1 Corinthians 14:19, Paul says: 'In church I would rather speak five words with my mind than ten thousand words in a tongue'. Numbers are therefore used in the Bible as rhetorical indications of the general order of magnitude, in which case they are given rounded (i.e. with several zeros at the end). In Revelation 9:16, the seer is told the number of mounted troops he sees: 200 million. This is the largest number in the Bible.
3. *Symbolic numbers*. Several numbers developed special meanings of theological significance in the Bible. These included: 1 (unity), 2 (division), 3 (sacred; trinity), 4 (completion), 5 (sufficiency), 8, 10 (a round or complete number), 12 (election), 40 (the average length in years of a generation), 70, 100; et alia. In Revelation 7:4, the total number of the saved is said to be 144,000, which is the number 12 (the number of election), squared, and multiplied by a thousand (an indefinitely large number). It therefore symbolizes the full number of God's saints, the elect. And in Revelation 13:18, the seer calls on his readers to 'work out the meaning of the number of the beast, because the number stands for a man's name. Its number is 666'. The article on 'Numbers' in the *Encyclopedia of religion and ethics* (1916:9,406–417) concludes with the warning:

> It is easy to be led into extravagance in attempting to interpret the significance of numbers; allegorical arithmetic has called forth fantastic absurdities from both Jewish and Christian writers.

### Surveys in the Bible
The Old Testament contains many references to surveys, connected either with the journeyings of the people of Israel; or with the armed forces, military service and military operations; or with religious personnel and the Tabernacle and Temple. Censuses in Egypt are known to have begun as early as BC 2500. Detailed surveys and censuses were made by Moses, as a former Egyptian official, immediately before and after the 40 years' wandering in the wilderness. Later, censuses were taken by Joshua, Saul, David, Joab, Solomon, Ahab, Jehoram, Amaziah, Exra, Nehemiah and other Old Testament prophets, priests and kings. The Old Testament can therefore be seen as a storehouse of census information. The Old Testament narrators are at pains to make it clear that, in so doing, these men were obeying the direct command of the Lord (Yahweh, Jehovah) as part of His evolving plan for His people and for the world: 'The Lord spoke to Moses, saying "Take a census of all the congregation of the people of Israel, by families"' (Numbers 1:1–2, RSV). As the New English Bible version at this point makes clear, this was to be done in great detail: 'The Lord spoke to Moses in these words: "Number the whole community of Israel by families. . .You and Aaron are to make a detailed list of them by their tribal hosts".' Exact counts were to be kept not only of the Israelites but also of prisoners and booty: 'The Lord spoke to Moses and said, "Count all that has been captured, man or beast"' (Numbers 31:26). Exact records of their journeyings were meticulously kept: 'Moses recorded their starting-points stage by stage as the Lord commanded him' (Numbers 33:2). Elsewhere we read of numerous population censuses at different stages in the Israelites journeyings; a survey of the Promised Land (Numbers 13); a census of all aliens resident in Israel (2 Chronicles 2,17); a survey of the houses of Jerusalem (Isaiah 22:10); a survey of the heavenly temple (Ezekiel 40–48); and a variety of other topics in addition to civil, military or religious censuses of the Israelite population. The Old Testament record of the results of all these surveys

runs into many thousands of words.
When we come to the New Testament, we are in the era of the Roman empire, in which official state censuses were taken on average every 5 years. In the reign of Augustus, 3 empire-wide censuses were taken, in BC 28, BC 8 and AD 14.

### Numerical growth in the New Testament
The New Testament records present a healthy interest in numbers, statistics, and their relation to the growth of the church. The Acts of the Apostles records the early history of the church. It is usually recognized that the author Luke, divided his narrative up into 7 parts, at the end of each of which he appended a summary statement of the progress of the gospel to that point. These summaries are: 'The disciples multiplied greatly' (Acts 6:7, RSV), 'The church was multiplied' (9:31), 'The word of the Lord grew and prevailed mightily' (19:20), 'They came in great numbers to Paul... preaching and teaching openly and unhindered.' (28:23, 31).

### Why enumerate or quantify?
The human mind can only comprehend and make sense of a limited number of people, names, populations or situations at any one time. It is usually estimated that the average person can handle at once only up to 500 face-to-face relationships. A pastor can know intimately the names and situations of only 500 parishioners; a bishop can know 500 of his clergy; a headmaster 500 of his pupils; and so on. Exceptional individuals may manage to comprehend more, even up to 1,000; but beyond that number, in order to comprehend the dimensions of their situation, they must resort to enumeration. Christians wanting to understand the numerical dimensions of their task of world evangelization have therefore to come to terms with statistics. Without enumeration, they may be able to comprehend a small community, or a small parish, or a small tribe, or a single-language situation. But for anything larger, as when many communities are involved, or scores of parishes, or numerous peoples, or hundreds of tribes and languages, or thousands of cities and towns, or tens of thousands of Christian denominations, or millions of church personnel or billions of human beings, they must quantify, and quantify with great precision, in order to have even the remotest idea as to what is going on.
Enumeration is defined as spelling-out or describing in detail, listing in order, counting, numbering, often meaning a count or census. Quantification is defined as measuring an item's quantity or number, or transforming qualitative data into quantitative. Together, these 2 procedures can assist the Christian mission by providing a simple way of describing otherwise incomprehensibly-large situations or processes. In so doing they can help us to comprehend the stark realities of a situation.

### Statistics as self-knowledge
One value of surveys to the Christian cause is that they form an application of the principle enunciated by Jesus as one that should guide his disciples' lives: 'You shall know the truth, and the truth will set you free' (John 8:32, NEB). Ignorance cripples; knowledge (especially self-knowledge) liberates. Christians have nothing to fear from the truth, whether it is palatable or unpalatable, exhilarating or alarming. Taking an objective missionary survey may be compared to a person undergoing a routine medical checkup, or receiving a bank statement of his balance of account, or having his car serviced, or having a public-opinion poll conducted into her political party's fortunes. The results are always a valuable corrective to either excessive optimism or undue pessimism, since they tell us with objective precision about a situation where our impressionistic hunches, guesswork and even wishful thinking may be seriously, even dangerously, misleading. Some such thoughts would have been in the mind of pope John XXIII when he addressed the priests of the diocese of Rome during the Roman Synod of 24–31 January 1960 with these words:

Beloved parish priests, pay attention, we beg you, to accurate and well-studied statistics. They are a very important task in governing a parish.

## Wrong use of numbers

A number of Christian traditions refuse to publish their statistics, or even to count their membership. Part of the reason is that the best-known reference to a census in the Bible is a negative case, a classic instance of the wrong use of statistics: king David's numbering of the people in BC 1017 (2 Samuel 24). According to eminent demographers, David's census 'had the effect of delaying the adoption of the census in England and in Christian Europe for many years' (H. Alterman, *Counting people: the census in history*, New York, 1969:26). Against the advice of his senior officers, the king ordered a census of his army and his kingdom. His motives appear to have been, not the glory of God but personal pride, the desire for aggrandizement, the worship of national greatness, through the enforcement of new taxation and forced labor schemes. Although 'The Lord gave him orders that Israel and Judah should be counted' (NEB), the narrative explains that this was in order to teach the king a lesson in spiritual humility. The census was clearly not in the same category as those undertaken by Moses. This case therefore does not prove that, in the Bible, numbering and censuses in themselves are unspiritual activities; it merely indicates that numbering, like most other human activities, can be used for good or ill, and that we should therefore be aware of the possibility of the wrong use, or even deliberate misuse, of such activity.

## The folly of triumphalism

Our present survey, with its massive totals of Christians of many kinds, almost all increasing rapidly every year, is clearly open to the dangers of triumphalism. This is the dogma that large and numerically-expanding churches must necessarily be in themselves good, right, spiritually successful and, in short, what God and the world need most. Instead, these vast totals should have a sobering effect on all Christians: for if the churches are to be effective in serving the rapidly-overpopulating world, they must first of all come to terms with their own staggering population problems.

**'Statistics are signs from God'.** The existence of 340 million handicapped children in the world (like these youngsters at Port Reitz school, Kenya) is both a sign and a call from God to all who seek to serve God and man.

The observer who succumbs to triumphalistic statistical statements taken by themselves is as short-sighted as an advocate of mass megabirths who ignores the resultant problems of overcrowding, infant mortality, undernutrition, scarcity of schools, unemployment and the like. What we are attempting to do here is less ambitious. It is to present an objective and empirical picture of numerical expansion and decline within their total context. The result is an attempt to measure the progress or decline of the churches in so far as progress or decline can be measured by comparative statistics. Subsequent theological assessment and judgment can then later be attempted.

## Statistics as signs from God

In order to serve the world, the church must first discover and comprehend the total environment and total situation in which the peoples of the world find themselves. This gives us as Christians a 3-fold task: (a) to understand the total human situation in which all the peoples of the world corporately live, namely the secular and religious environments surrounding them and conditioning them and often oppressing them; (b) to know who and where these peoples are individually, what their particular secular characteristics and differentia are, and what their individual problems and needs are; and (c) to then interpret these peoples' religious situations (from the standpoints of evangelization, conversion, Christianization, church growth or decline, and so on) in this secular and religious context. In this task, statistical data, and even a single isolated statistical fact (e.g. 'The Turkana tribe is 99% illiterate', or 'This ethnic group has the highest mortality rate in the world') can become for us direct pointers to a peoples' predicament and how they can best be served. In this sense, statistical and other information can alert theologians to new problems as they emerge. It is this spiritual significance of statistical data that prompts the Brothers of Taize to echo their prior Roger Schutz in affirming:

Les chiffres sont les signes de Dieu—Statistics are signs from God.

If this is so, then it both explains and justifies the prodigious amount of effort put into the production of church statistics every year by millions of pastors and congregations, thousands of denominations, hundreds of international Christian organizations, and scores of major confessions and Christian councils around the world. Intuitively in the main, most of them have realized that statistics can be signs from God, in which case enumerating and quantifying are important activities to be taken seriously by all Christians.

## The limits to quantification

Ultimately, it is impossible to quantify the totality of the Christian situation, because numbers usually describe quantity only and cannot normally delineate quality except over a series of clearly-defined gradations. One cannot quantify the faith of a Christian martyr in Albania, or the witness of an imprisoned pastor in Siberia, or the selfless service of relief workers after an earthquake. For this reason it is best to regard statistics only as signs or pointers, or at any rate as concrete starting-points from which qualitative assessments may begin.

But even enumeration pure and simple has its limits: there are some numbers too enormous to be counted at all with any meaning. The Old Testament prophets foresaw a time in the future when the People of God would be too big to be counted; 'The Israelites shall become countless as the sands of the sea which can neither be measured nor numbered' (Hosea 1:10). The same theme recurs right up to the last book of the Bible, where the seer hears the voice of countless angels: 'Myriads upon myriads were, thousands upon thousands...'(Revelation 5:11); he sees 'a vast throng, which no one could count, from every nation, of all tribes, peoples and languages, standing in front of the throne and before the Lamb' (Revelation 7:9); and the hosts of evil also are 'countless as the sands of the sea' (Revelation 20:8).

## STATISTICS IN PROFESSIONAL USAGE

### What are statistics?

Information presented in abstract numerical form is described as statistics. Originally, statistics had nothing to do with numbers. The word originated in German in the 18th century, when Achenwall first coined the term *Statistik* to refer to 'the political science of the several countries', that is, the study of practical politics. The English term first appeared in a 1770 translation from the German (R.A. Bauer, ed, *Social indicators*, 1966:75). 'Statistics' is derived etymologically from the Latin *ratio status* and could well be translated as 'state of the nation'. For several hundred years the primary concern of men who called themselves statisticians was to set up a system of social indicators by which to judge the performance of the society with respect to its norms, values, and goals (Bauer 1966:22). By information as to the 'state' of the nation they meant those statistical measurements that revealed the current situation of the nation, its population and its economy. Today the term has evolved somewhat; the subject of statistics is 'the association and bringing together of those facts which are calculated to illustrate the conditions and prospects of society' (American Statistical Association, 1962). The full definition of the term is: '1. a science dealing with the collection, analysis, interpretation, and presentation of masses of numerical data; 2. a collection of quantitative data' (*Webster's third new international dictionary*, 1971).

With the years the purpose of statistics has sharpened also. In the USA, the decennial census originated as the basis for apportioning representation in the House of Representatives. Statistics in the sense of numbers nowadays are gathered because it is presumed that they will be guides to planning and action.

### Quantification and enumeration

Quantification was not an essential element in the definition of statistics until fairly recently. The term has several meanings; the one we are chiefly interested in is: quantification is 'the transformation of qualitative into quantitative data in scientific methodology' (Webster's 1971). Quantification is sound policy, a necessary corrective, because we cannot really see the dimensions of a complex problem until we quantify it. This process is as helpful as the placing of milestones along a trunk road or continental highway; travellers can immediately assess the progress of their journeying. Enumeration is counting up and totalling with specific and clear treatment of each item. It is defined by Webster as: '1a. The act of listing one after the other; 1b. an itemized list; 2a. the act of counting or numbering; 2b. a count of something (as of a population), a census'.

### Methods of counting

A full description and analysis of methods of counting peoples and of censuses throughout history is given in H. Alterman, *Counting people: the census in history*, 1969. This study begins with the Babylonians, Egyptians, and censuses in the Bible. Censuses usually count heads throughout the whole population, using large numbers of enumerators. Either they count everybody, or they enumerate a small random sample, usually 5%. Where such expensive methods are impossible, estimates are made. There is an interesting parallel here with modern methods of counting large herds of wild animals, which aim to measure total numbers, size and structure of population, distribution and migratory movements. These methods have revealed that counting error increases with counting rate, always in the direction of undercounting: 'It must always be remembered that even highly experienced observers consistently undercount the numbers of animals in a group by as much as 40%' (M. Norton-Griffiths, *Counting animals*, Nairobi, 1975:46). The same error occurs in human demography too: 'All evidence points to universal underenumeration' (H. Alterman, op. cit., 1969:326).

### Statistical indicators

For many of the important topics on which social critics blithely pass judgement, and on which policies are made, there are no yardsticks by which to know whether things are getting better or worse (Bauer 1966:20). This is just as true in the fields of religion and church life. To assist at this point, indicators must be found. Social indicators—statistics, statistical series, and all other forms of evidence—enable us to assess where we stand and are going with respect to our values and goals, and to evaluate specific programs and determine their impact. An information system is needed consisting of 2 parts: (1) regular trend series of social indicators, whereby comparisons from time to time and across societies can be made; and (2) special mechanisms for gathering data on new developments falling outside those regular trend series (ibid, 21).

It must not be imagined that indicators must always be standard types of statistics. Expert judgements by knowledgeable persons can also be valuable indicators. The science of appraising conditions is well organized in welfare, mortgage banking, and other occupational areas.

### Multidimensional definitions and scales
Statistical indicators have often been combined to form 'dimensions' or aspects of religion in people's lives. Multidimensional definitions of religion have been widely accepted in the social scientific study of religion since the work of Allport and of Glock in 1954. Analysts have traced 4, 5 or even up to 13 such dimensions, usually revolving around people's beliefs, credos, behavior, affiliation, and religious profession. In this book, we do not investigate such dimensions in detail, since we are mainly concerned with documenting the basic data upon which such scales can later be built.

### Does Christian work need statistics?
The question is often asked: why do the churches need to bother with statistics at all? From time to time, a handful of theologians attacks any form of preoccupation with numbers in Christian work. One such attempt was H.R. Weber's 'God's arithmetic' (*Frontier*, VI (1963), 298ff). The argument usually revolves around the assertion that one cannot measure God nor his activities or work, which are concerned only with spiritual affairs. Especially in Muslim areas, as an Anglican bishop put it, 'No mission is constituted in its success and none therefore is invalidated by numerical failure. Mission is not a calculus of success but an obligation in love. Statistics do not make it nor can they unmake it' (K. Cragg, *The call of the minaret*, London, 1964:339).

We will shortly be detailing the positive side of the subject. Meanwhile, it should be said that we reject stereotyped statements of the form 'Church statistics are meaningless and notoriously unreliable'. If church statistics have been so in the past, this has been due to error and carelessness on the part of compilers, collators and editors, rather than due to defects in the basic data themselves.

The shortest answer to this question is that virtually every established Christian denomination takes enormous pains, goes to no mean expense, and makes very considerable demands on its overburdened clergy and officers, in order to produce each year such statistics. The most detailed and voluminous statistics of all come annually from the Church of Rome, and from the Evangelical Church of Germany (EKD). Exceptions to this generalization are the new and rapidly-growing pentecostal and other indigenous churches of the Third World, which are too busy expanding to stop and record the fact. In terms of effort and time accorded to this work, though, we can fairly assert that establishing the exact numerical size of its membership is one of the major activities of the empirical Church. This fact alone justifies the present survey and analysis.

### THE VALUE OF CHURCH STATISTICS

### Statistics as objective descriptions
Statistics are valuable in describing a situation because they offer us probably the quickest, most scientific and most objective way of presenting large amounts of highly-condensed and accurate information, and of describing large groupings of peoples and their activities at particular points in time. This term however has 2 usages: (1) it refers to numeral, numerical or quantitative data, or numerical facts systematically collected (*Concise Oxford dictionary*), and (2) it also refers to the science of collecting and classifying numerical data, or that branch of applied mathematics that actually arranges, describes and draws inferences from sets of numerical data. In this book the term is used primarily in the first sense; interested analysts can then move on to the second sense.

### The quality of data
The present volume demonstrates the reliability and value of the large volume of church statistics which it presents and analyzes. To generalize, we regard these statistics on a comparative basis as surprisingly, even remarkably, reliable. For the first time it has now been possible to relate all religious statistics closely to demographic statistics of countries and ethnolinguistic groups, and in particular to government censuses of religion in over half the countries of the world. The result is that religious statistics can be seen to be often more reliable and more detailed than their secular counterparts.

**Statistics with a human face.** Behind the dry bones of all bare statistics are human beings with needs and feelings. *Above.* Child (one of millions of refugees in Africa) awaits milk donated by Swiss Evangelical Churches.

### Putting flesh on the bones
Statistical facts for many people are merely lifeless dry bones. This sparseness, or this cut-and-dried and standardized nature, is indeed one of their values. We go even further in this direction here by standardizing all of our statistical categories so that they have exactly the same definition in every country of the world. However, in each country we put a certain amount of flesh on these bones by supplying, under *WCE* Country Tables 1 and 2, copious and detailed footnotes elaborating on those statistical facts in the tables where such amplification is needed.

### Statistics with a human face
The majority of the statistics reported in this book are statistics of people. People are human beings and not merely cyphers or figures. Statistics may assist us to comprehend certain features about a population, but it should never be forgotten that behind the bare statistics are scores, or hundreds, or thousands, or millions, or billions, of human souls with human needs and feelings. To emphasize this point, we have included a large number of demographic photographs illustrating large crowds of Christians, and of people in general, in various activities across the world. These illustrations assist the data presented here to be seen not merely as 'statistics' but as 'statistics with a human face'.

### One man one religion
There is a considerable ideological overlap, or overlap of belief and culture, between several of the 19 major world religions or philosophies into which we have divided the world in *WCE* Country Tables 1. In Thailand, a Christian may consider himself to be 70% Buddhist also, and vice versa. In India, a Christian may regard himself as also a Hindu. In the USA, Hebrew Christians regard themselves as both Christians and Jews. In Europe, dilettantes may regard themselves as followers of the best aspects of several religions at once. Nevertheless, the overwhelming majority of individuals in the world can be said to have and to profess one single predominant religion or philosophy. In this survey, therefore, we consider every person to be a coherent individual with one single religion or none, or in a small number of cases doubly-professing in 2 distinct religions.

### Statistical compassion
Overall statistics of churches and countries are provided here so that the totality of each situation, and of its human populations and their activities and needs, may be grasped. It is comparatively easy for a local church, or a local mission, or a local group of Christians to show Christian compassion to a few score of needy persons visible and tangible immediately around them; but this is often only a tiny fraction of the total population and of the total need, and there may be thousands of other needy persons who remain invisible and unreached beyond them. The church of Jesus Christ is concerned not just with a favored, visible, minority but with the world's invisible populations in their totality. The statistics in this book have been complied therefore to assist Christians to exercise a world ministry, and to be concerned not only or individuals but also for the world's populations as a whole. To this concern we may give the name 'statistical compassion'.

### Statistics must be read in context
One virtue of statistical facts is that they can stand alone or in isolation and still be correct. However, their value for interpreting a particular situation is considerably enhanced if they are presented and studied, not in isolation, but in a much wider context which we term here the historico-social, photographico-cartographical global context. In other words, statistical facts about people in churches and religions in a particular country need to be read both in the verbal context of a narrative describing history and society in that country, and also in the pictorial or visual context of photographs illustrating concrete statistical situations and maps showing the human environment in which those people live. Further, a country's statistics need to be seen in the light of parallel statistics from other countries and of the total global context. The bigger the numbers of people involved, and the newer or more startling the statistics presented, the more important this wider context is for correctly interpreting the totality of the situation and for convincing readers skeptical of vast numbers and staggering trends. It is for this reason that this survey places its complex statistical tables in this wider historico-socio-photographico-cartographical global context.

### What do church statistics mean?
As already noted, vast efforts are put into the collection of statistics by the over 300 traditions and 33,800 denominations across the world and their 3 million constituent churches and congregations of believers. This raises again the familiar fundamental questions: Do these statistics mean anything at all? Are they worth the churches' time and effort involved in collecting them? Do they in any sense assist the churches in realistic planning for mission in the modern world? After compiling this book, we would wish to answer all 3 questions clearly in the affirmative. We would however point out that, through inadequate analysis by the churches in almost all countries of the world, the true implications of church statistics have almost everywhere not yet even begun to be investigated. Further, proper analysis is only rarely being attempted. This is therefore the place to issue a call to a fresh approach to the collection, use and creative analysis of church statistics. To help churches put the right value on their statistics, and to encourage their proper evaluation, we suggest that such statistics have 3 major types of use to the churches: they assist in understanding of the past, in analysis of the present, and in planning for the future. These can be elaborated as follows.

1. *Understanding the past.* The first use of church statistics, and the most widely employed today, is towards understanding a church's development in the past. Up to the present time, the collection and presentation of church statistics seem to have been of most value to church and mission historians and others writing up the history of the church or denomination concerned; or comparing the church life of a former generation with that of the present; or discussing expansion and other trends from the past to the present. We use statistics ourselves in this way in *WCE's* Country Tables 1 by giving figures of all religions and Christian megablocs in the years 1900 and 2025, thus enabling long-term trends of decline or increase to be detected.

2. *Analyzing the present.* Secondly, statistics are often of considerable contemporary value to church offi-

cials and administrators. This is so in that they enable them to compare the present situation of their church with its immediate past (e.g. the previous year or two), to find out how that situation is changing. For large organizations, it is primarily an urgent or immediate question of logistics (the planning, handling and implementation of large quantities of personnel, material and facilities). The Billy Graham Evangelistic Association, for instance, requires detailed statistics of previous campaigns in order to plan how many chairs, ushers, hymnbooks, etc, are needed for a large campaign, how much literature to produce, how much car parking space needs to be procured, and so on and so forth (their largest single meeting has had 1.1 million physically in attendance). For organized churches and denominations, 3 less immediate but equally profitable areas of analysis are: (1) numerical decline of membership, where this is happening, and the problems it raises (e.g. redundant buildings), (2) numerical growth of membership, where this is happening, and the problems it raises (e.g. inadequate buildings or supplies of hymnbooks), and (3) adult baptisms as an indicator of the impact being made, if any, on the secular or non-Christian world around. By careful analysis of relevant statistics the effectiveness of the churches' organization can be assessed, points of weakness located, and reorganization effected.

There is, however, another and far more valuable type of contemporary analysis which is only rarely being done as yet. This involves relating a church's statistics to current secular statistics concerning the social situation, and social change, in its own country or area. In most parts of the world, a vast amount of secular statistical data is now available. This covers demography, population increase or decline, urban growth, industrialization, migration, age-groups, ethnic groups, social classes, occupational groups, employment, tourism, transportation, mobility, incomes, standards of living, socio-economic status, housing, land use, literacy, publishing, book sales, leisure, radio and TV sets and listening habits, and so on. Much of this is available to the enquirer in printed form, sometimes in the form of pictorial charts, and sometimes in the form of maps. A church or denomination which relates its own statistics to this wealth of secular data can form a realistic appraisal of its own contribution and progress and can gain valuable insights into the present effectiveness of its various ministries.

Such data are widely available both at the international level (published by UN, UNESCO, FAO, WHO, ILO, et alia), and also at the national level (from government census and statistical offices, and national public-opinion and planning organizations). In *WCE* Country Tables 1, we relate church statistics to demographic data at these 2 levels. Moreover, in

many countries, there is also a steady flow of detailed secular data available at subnational levels, namely those of region, province, state, county, municipality, city, district, borough, local authority or ward, down to the secular equivalent of the local church parish or congregation. If a denomination collects and organizes its own data not only at the national level but also broken down by these secular regions and local areas, then immediate comparison and creative analysis at those levels also become possible.

There is a widespread problem here concerning areas of ecclesiastical jurisdiction. In many denominations and in most countries of the world, the boundaries of dioceses, synods, conferences, districts, parishes, presbyteries, circuits and so on bear little or no relation to the local secular or political administrative boundaries within which secular statistics are collected. This means that direct comparisons of church data and secular data are often difficult or impossible. There is a simple remedy, however. By a simple process of adjusting beforehand the areas within which the church collects its statistics, or by totalling or dividing them up to fit the secular boundaries after their collection, church statistical areas can be brought into line with secular areas, and direct comparison is then possible.

3. *Planning for the future.* Using church statistics for strategic forward-planning, i.e. to plan church development and activities in both the immediate future and long-range foreseeable future, is a novel exercise for most denominations. Statistical data about both the church and the environment are indispensable for effective planning. Again, the starting-point is secular planning in the church's locality, region or nation. In many countries, ambitious 5-year or 10-year development plans are being drafted, not only at the national level but also for standard socio-economic planning regions and even for small local areas. The fundamental or base data in all such cases are demographic estimates or projections of the size of the population over the next 5 or 10 years, often divided up into small geographical areas and also by sex (male/female), age-groups, and ethnic or language groups. Such data often include also projections concerning employment trends, literacy, education, leisure patterns, and so on. Population projection into the future is no longer a matter of guesswork or speculation but is now a well-developed science, and in *WCE* Country Tables 1 we use the United Nations Population Division's population projections for all countries of the world for the years 1950-2050. Similarly, a church or group of churches could use regional projections to plan new congregations, manpower deployment, youth ministries, literature evangelism and the like. Another important by-product of such analysis is that churches known

to be making use of secular planning data are often invited by secular authorities to take part themselves in the on-going secular planning process.

The indicators and indexes given here enable interested persons to assess the various purely numerical and hence relatively objective criteria involved in any decision about priorities, and hence to plan realistically for the future.

### Maps and religious geography

Another important aspect of this analysis of the past, present and future is the relating of religious statistics to geography. A church's membership and manpower (past, present, future) can be charted on a map (in particular on government maps with secular data) to provide visual analysis of the church's situation vis-a-vis the secular world, development and social change. The best type of maps to use in this connection are human environment maps, i.e. maps which depict not only topography but also population density, urbanization, political divisions, land resources and land use, communications, transportation and traffic (on air, land and sea), and so on. In this survey we give human environment maps of this type in the GeoAtlas of Christianity and religions (Part 33). On these maps will be found most of the places, areas, regions, ecclesiastical or diocesan headquarters, and so on, referred to in this survey. The geographical location of most churches can be found on them by using addresses in the Directory of global Christianity (*WCE* Part 12). Churches interested in similar maps in their own countries will often find that a wide range is available from their government's department of survey or planning, or from local university departments of geography; or from professional international bodies located elsewhere.

### Improving your church's statistics

With such creative possibilities before us, small improvements in your church's statistical procedures could yield enormous benefits. Churches and denominations, with their administrative officers and planning staff, should therefore realize that their statistics, which are already of considerable value to many other churches and Christian groups of which they themselves may be unaware, could be made of immeasurable greater value, both to themselves, to their sister churches of like tradition, and to the wider Christian world (as well as to the world at large), if the following modifications were made to their procedures.

(1) Each church or denomination should examine the existing statistical categories it uses, and, for the benefit of readers from other churches, confessions or countries, should add to its published figures and reports the fullest definitions of exactly what those categories are measuring, from the standpoints of time (the date the statistics refer to) and geographical area or boundaries. they should make clear which of the following groups are included or excluded in each category: adults and children or infants (defining the ages covered by each group), de jure or de facto members, citizens or aliens, residents or non-residents, immigrants and refugees, Blacks and whites (and all other racial, ethnic and linguistic groups), peasants, farmers, office workers, students (and other occupational groups where known); and so on. When a church official from another country or confession, or any other Christian observer, reads your church's statistical report, the answers to all such queries should be immediately clear to him.

(2) Each church should ensure that the statistics it collects include the following strategic information: (a) some measure of annual decline or growth in membership; (b) some measure of practicing Christians, either weekly or monthly church attenders, or attenders at Easter or Christmas; (c) some measure of the participation or presence of children and infants, i.e. annual baptisms or dedications of infants, and Sunday-school enrolments or weekly attendances; and (d) some measure of conversions from (or losses to) the secular or non-Christian society around, e.g. the year's adult baptisms (indicating from what age it is administered to children), stating in addition what their previous religious backgrounds were (agnostics, atheists, Buddhists, and so on). With this concrete statistical data in hand, your church can then immediately assess its strategic situation.

(3) Each church should consider collecting addi-

**Analyzing the present.** Evangelist Billy Graham preaches at interfaith service in 1970 at Lincoln Memorial, Washington DC (USA). For such meetings, statistics provide answers to questions of logistics, including how many chairs, ushers, hymn sheets, refreshments, etc. are needed.

tional statistics about its membership and its ministries which can be compared directly, for purposes of self-analysis and forward-planning, with the secular or general social statistics regularly collected and published in its own country at national, regional, and local levels, concerning social change in the country and the present and future socioeconomic situations.

(4) Each church should then adjust the boundaries of the areas for which it collects its statistics, so that they coincide with secular or political boundaries at national, regional, and local levels, to enable its statistics to be directly comparable with the secular statistics. No doubt it would cause too great a structural upheaval to alter the actual boundaries of the jurisdictions themselves, which are often hallowed by years, decades or even centuries of existence. There should however be little difficulty in ensuring that the church's statistics are gathered and collated within the boundaries of standard socio-economic planning areas used by local and national governments. Again, all such boundaries implicit in the church's statistical reports need to be clearly described for the benefit of other users.

(5) Each church, finally, might very well consider taking this process to its logical conclusion by redefining and standardizing its own ecclesiastical categories to approach, or even coincide with, some overall worldwide interdenominational or ecumenical system (such as that proposed and followed in this book). This means that it should consider adopting some agreed standardized criteria for enumerating membership and ministry, so that its statistics then become directly comparable both with those of its sister churches of similar denomination, and also with those of other denominations.

A series of standardized questionnaires was in fact evolved to collect data for the present survey, using the major European languages. Each questionnaire asked not only for a denomination's data but also their own exact definitions used, and the relevant date (year). The actual questions asked have resulted in the precise definitions given here in each country's Country Tables 1 and 2 in *WCE*.

## *A MACROECCLESIOGRAPHICAL APPROACH*

### *Macromissiography*

The standpoint or discipline from which the statistical presentation in this book has been compiled may be described as that of missiography (descriptive analysis of the Christian world mission) and ecclesiography (descriptive analysis of the churches). In particular, the discipline followed is that of macromissiography, which is defined here as descriptive and numerical analysis of the entire Christian world mission set in and related to the total global demographic, sociographic, ecological, secular and world religious, non-religious and anti-religious contexts. A parallel term for describing this survey in its totality would be macroecclesiography, the statistical aspect of which could also be termed ecclesiastical macrodemography. Missiography is a new term in English, although for many years the Pontifical Gregorian University in Rome has offered degree courses entitled Missiographia. Though related, all these disciplines are not the same as, and should therefore be distinguished from, either missiology (the science of missions, missionary history, missionary thought and missionary methods) or ecclesiology (the doctrine of the church) or micromissiography (descriptive analysis in detail of a single or a local missionary situation).

### *Research in macroevangelistics*

From another point of view, our approach may be described as research in the science of evangelistics. As described by *Webster's third new international dictionary*, evangelistics is 'the science of the propagation of Christianity'. A science is defined as (a) a branch of study concerned with observation and classification of facts, and (b) accumulated and accepted knowledge that has been systematized and formulated with reference to the discovery of general truths or the operation of general laws (*Webster's*). Research is defined as (a) careful, diligent or close searching, and (b) critical and exhaustive investigation or experimentation having for its aim the discovery of new facts and their correct interpretation or the revision of accepted conclusions (*Webster's*). Our research methodology here has been to collect a vast body of facts and then to evolve from them one particular area in evangelistics, regarded as a science, for which we may coin the term macroevangelistics, meaning the scientific study, at the global level, of the propagation of Christianity. This is initiated here in Part 25 "Macroevangelistics".

### *Range of data available*

Surveying the world in a sentence or two, we find that at least 7 varieties of religious statistics are kept and compiled by churches in one country or another. These are: (1) demographic and sociographic statistics on Christian population in particular areas and peoples; (2) statistics of religious behavior and Christian practice; (3) statistics of ecclesiastical jurisdiction and structures; (4) statistics of church personnel and lay workers; (5) statistics of social and cultural institutions (schools, hospitals, etc); (6) statistics of church prosperity and finance; and (7) statistics of religious psychology, beliefs, motivation and attitudes. Most but not all of these are handled in the present survey.

### *Geopolitico-religious analysis*

When it comes to analyzing the mass of statistical data assembled for this survey, we do so by regarding the world as an aggregate of 238 countries, each of which has certain geographical, socioeconomic, political, cultural and religious characteristics, and which may be classified in various ways, one of which is into the Western (or Capitalist) world, the Communist or formerly Communist or Socialist) world, and the Third (or Non-aligned) World. This process is described here as geopolitico-religiocultural analysis, or, a shorter term, geopolitico-religious analysis.

## *SURVEYING THE GLOBE*

### *A survey of 238 countries*

*WCE* Part 4 contains a survey in a standardized format of the de facto situation in each of the 238 distinct and separate countries in the world in the year 2000, based on the list of countries published quarterly and annually by the United Nations (see *Population and vital statistics report*, UN, 1999, and *UN demographic yearbook*, 1999). This definition of 'country' covers both all sovereign independent nations, and also all nonsovereign dependencies and territories with over 30 inhabitants which do not form a subject, organic or federal part of some larger nation (i.e. dependencies which are self-governing, or governed separately). Because the UN listing is politically conditioned, the listing used in this book differs slightly from it. We attempt a more exact description of the de facto situation by (1) accepting as definitive the divided state of Korea and certain other states; (2) including as distinct and separate countries China (Taiwan), Spanish North Africa, and a small number of other disputed territories with de facto or contested separate existence (Northern Solomons/Bougainville, Palestine, Sahara, Timor), unless the dispute is now over 15 years old and has been settled de facto (e.g. Goa, Sikkim, Kashmir); and (3) excluding certain territories (though listed separately by the UN) on the grounds that each forms part of a larger nation, namely Ascension, Asian Turkey, East Berlin, England, European Turkey, Northern Ireland, Scotland, Tanganyika, Tristan da Cunha, Wales, West Berlin, West Irian, Zanzibar. In this book, the nouns or adjectives 'national' (meaning a citizen as opposed to an alien) are used to mean pertaining to the countries in our listing.

### *Future changes in nation status*

Our present format permits a number of future political changes to be quickly catered for. If 2 of the 238 countries merge, or if a large nation absorbs a smaller territory (such as India absorbing Sikkim), the reader can work out the new Country Tables 1 and 2 for the new entities simply by adding these together for both of the countries involved.

### *Statistics are for one country only*

The statistics given in *WCE* Country Tables 2, as with Country Tables 1, always refer only and exclusively to the country indicated in the table's title. Many churches or dioceses are not found exclusively within the boundaries of a single country, but may spread over into adjacent countries. For such churches or dioceses, the statistics in Country Tables 2 are always divided among the various countries. This may occasion misunderstandings if the reader is familiar with a particular church's statistics but does not realize that the body in question may cover more than one country.

### *Mutually exclusive listings*

The listings of religions and organized churches presented in Country Tables 1 and 2, respectively, are mutually exclusive and non-overlapping, in that the vast majority of persons belong each to only one religion or church, except in Country Table 1 where clearly indicated by indentation of categories. This means that in Country Tables 1 every individual in the world is enumerated only once under only one religion (though he may occur again under an indented category like 'World A individuals' and also in the last line's totals); and in Country Tables 2 every affiliated Christian in the world is enumerated only once, under only one church or denomination (though he may occur again under an indented diocese or other jurisdiction, and also in the last 3 lines' totals, and occasionally also, as explained below, if in the category of doubly-affiliated persons).

### *Major areas and regions*

Traditionally the world has been divided up into 5 or 6 continents. However, this concept has lost much of its significance for modern purposes, since several countries overlap the boundaries of the traditional continents. This survey therefore uses the scheme of regionalization adopted by the United Nations *(World population prospects as assessed in 1998)*. Under this scheme, shown here in Part 16 "GeoCodebook", the world is divided into 7 major areas roughly equivalent to continents, and the 7 are further subdivided into 21 regions for the whole world including 2 undivided major areas. All national statistics obtained in Country Tables 1 and 2 are then summarized by these 7 major areas and 21 regions.

### *Large aggregates mask smaller variations*

This survey demonstrates that, at every level, large aggregate totals can mask or hide significant smaller-scale variations. Consider the question of the expansion of Christianity. At the world level, the totals here in Part 1 show that Christianity is expanding at a rate of 25,210,000 each year. Of this, however, 22,709,000 is natural increase (births minus deaths), and there is a net gain of 2,501,000 by conversions from other religions. But this latter total is itself composed of (a) net continental increases by conversion from other religions of 3,102,000 a year, particularly in Africa and Asia, and (b) net continental decreases or losses to other religions or to irreligion of 619,000 a year, mainly in the Americas and Oceania. Again, the 3,102,000 includes converts to rapidly-growing traditions like the Independents as well as to slower-growing traditions like Lutheranism. Classical Pentecostal growth in its turn consists of areas and nations with remarkable growth (Brazil, Colombia, Romania) and areas of numerical stagnation (Sweden, Britain). National totals in turn often mask great differences from one denomination to the next. And lastly, within a single denomination, there are often great differences in growth from one area to another, from one ethnic group to another, from one social class to another, from one homogeneous group to the next, and from one age group to another; and so on right down to the level of a single congregation or a sub-group within it. In general, further new insights can always be obtained by breaking down large aggregates into their component parts, especially if these latter form each some kind of homogeneous unit either ethnically, racially, linguistically, culturally, socially, politically or geographically.

All of this does not lessen the value of large aggregate totals; it depends on what particular level the reader is interested in. But it does mean that, whatever level is examined and analyzed, that analysis by itself can only tell part of the whole story of massive flux, of ebb and flow, of conversion and defection or apostasy, and of rapid growth here and rapid decline there.

### *Countries as homogeneous units*

This survey attempts to describe the world in terms of homogeneous population units (sometimes also call sub-cultures). These may be defined as population groups, strata, societies or segments of societies within each of which a number of characteristics or interests are held in common by all members, with a common self-consciousness (referring to themselves as 'we', in contrast to others around them as 'they'). It is usual to regard as the clearest example of these groups, strata, societies or segments of societies within each of which a number of characteristics or interests are held in common by all members, with a common self-consciousness (referring to themselves as 'we', in contrast to others around them as 'they'), as the clearest example of these groups the world's 395 ethnocultural families, or even the 12,600 or so smaller ethnolinguistic units (tribes, peoples, languages) that exist in the world today. Other types of homogeneous units are also found in traditional castes, clans or lineages, or in occupational groups such as industrial workers or truck drivers, or in political units or groups (refugees, political prisoners, etc), or in geographical units (cities, districts, regions), or in age-groups, educational groups, socio-economic groups, and so on. Whilst in this survey we accept this position, we must also point out 2 important considerations. (1) Firstly, there is nothing absolute or final about ethnolinguistic or any other types of homogeneous groups, because each of these groups is itself composed of sub-groups, sub-populations and other sub-groups that are even more homogeneous than the parent group. Every homogeneous unit is itself a mosaic of different strata; language groups divided up by dialects, tribes into clans, monolingual populations into social classes or castes, and so on. (2) Secondly, larger units or groupings made up of numbers of these homogeneous units (e.g. nations, countries, continents, the 3 Worlds, and the entire globe itself) may themselves be regarded from one perfectly-valid point of view as homogeneous units, relatively or comparatively speaking. A nation or country, composed as it usually is of a number of homogeneous ethnolinguistic units, itself has a population that is united or unified by all or many of the following 25 shared characteristics held in common: citizenship, patriotism, geographical contiguity, the national name and flag, national territory, national language, national history, a rich heritage of memories, shared historical experience, a common struggle for self-determination (political independence), national consciousness, national traditions, national culture, a joint national inheritance, a national literature, common social institutions, national values, national pride, national economic life, common economic interests, national government, perhaps also a national or state religion. For this reason, throughout this survey we regard countries, treated relatively or comparatively, as homogeneous units. Even a vast country with such disparate ethnic groups as India (and among whom vastly different responses to Christianity have taken place) can still legitimately be regarded as a relatively homogeneous group (unified by the entire spectrum of specifically 'Indian' characteristics) by comparison with France, or Brazil, or Zaire, or any other country. If the reader wishes to conduct a more detailed analysis than we attempt here, the next subdivided level of homogeneous unit is not the 395 ethnocultural families as such (e.g. Bengalis, or Tamils, or Chinese) but these groupings as divided by national boundaries, i.e. ethnolinguistic-peoples-within-national-boundaries (e.g. Chinese in China, Chinese in Japan, Chinese in the USA, etc). In the same way, in the context of God's entire creation of vast numbers of living species, the human population of the globe itself is composed of one single species, Homo Sapiens, members of which by contrast with other species have a large number of unique characteristics in common (physical traits, erect stance, self-consciousness, rational thought, speech and language, ability to read and write, religious consciousness, and so on). From this point of view, therefore, the human population of the world itself composes a single homogeneous unit.

There is theological justification also for the importance we attach to these homogeneous units. In the Bible, the idea and concept of a people carries with it the thought of the solidarity of the community with its leaders and its followers, its rich and its poor, its old and its young, its learned and its ignorant. Particularly in the Old Testament, the people or community is the primary entity, and individuals have no separate importance or existence but derive their being from the larger community. God then deals with people primarily as communities, and only secondarily as isolated individuals.

## Geographical, political and ethnic sub-divisions

The present survey of religions and churches uses as its main unit the country, and the statistical tables each deal only with a single entire country and so give data mainly at the national or country-wide level. However, it is possible for any reader interested in smaller subnational groups to take this analysis further and to use the same method to derive similar tables for those smaller groups; and this analysis further and to use the same method to derive similar tables for those smaller groups; and this paragraph will explain how. As has just been noted, countries' tables mask considerable internal variation. Few if any countries or nations are homogeneous geographically, politically, or ethnically. Most consist of several regions, or provinces, or states, or counties, or ethnic groups, or social classes or strata, or other homogeneous units, or urban and rural areas, or other politically or geographically distinct areas, in which the religious situation may differ widely from one region to the next. In many cases, though, there are sufficient data available in the literature (often that reported at the end of each country's article) to enable new tables in the formats of Country Tables 1 and 2 to be compiled for any subdivision the reader is interested in. Considering Egypt as an example, its census of 22–23.XI.1976 reported population and Christians both at the national level and also divided amongst the country's 25 governorates; thus one could construct a Country Table 1 for each governorate. Considering the United Kingdom (Britain) as a second example, it would be possible to divide Country Tables 1 and 2, as they appear in WCE, into 4 similar pairs of tables analyzing separately the situation in England, Wales, Scotland and Northern Ireland. The same could be done for the city of London, or for Black immigrants in the UK, or for the working classes (70% of the UK population), or for men and women separately, or for young people aged 15–25 years, or for any other groups for which the basic demographic data (the last line in Country Table 1) are readily available from government population census reports or statistical abstracts. Even if exact data on a number of churches and religions were not available divided among the 4 UK regions (for example), each figure in the UK Country Table 1 could be divided among the 4 by making reasonable assumptions and estimates. Once the statistics for the new Tables 1 have been completed using the methodology described below, the reader can begin to analyze and interpret the figures. Clearly, much greater insight into a specific country's situation can be obtained by dividing national totals up by sex, geography, age-groups, social classes, occupations, income-groups, education, literacy, ethnolinguistic groups, and so on. To do this here for all countries is beyond the scope of this book; we therefore give only the country-wide totals in WCE Country Tables 1 and 2.

## THE PRESENT SURVEY

### Two standardized tables

For every country, the survey in WCE Part 4 gives 2 statistical tables, preceded by a section Secular Data which gives the background secular statistical data against which our religious data can be evaluated. Country Table 1, Religious adherents, presents an overview of all adherents of all religions in the country, both organized and unorganized, across the 20th century, in a standardized classification and layout. Country Table 2, Organized churches and denominations, presents an overview of all organized churches in the country and all Christians affiliated to them. These are the national tables from which the world and continental totals in Parts 1 and 10 are derived. These are followed by Part 12, Table 12-1, Geopolitico-religious data and typologies for all countries. In the interests of clarity, the methodology employed in these tables, and all purely methodological considerations, have been kept out of the tables and articles as far as is possible, and are restricted to the present chapter, Part 14. In the pages that follow, we now describe the methodology behind this survey, the sources employed, the layout of the tables, and the classifications, categories and codes used in them. These are then condensed and summarized in 2 quick-reference alphabetical Tables 16-2 and 16-3, in Part 16 "GeoCodebook".

### A ruler is necessary

Country Tables 1 and 2 (also Global Tables and all other tables and charts) are closely printed in order to provide the reader with a complete overview in as compact a space as possible. To get the best use out of these tables, the reader will need to have a straight edge or ruler handy (preferably a transparent ruler) for use in the following ways.

(1) Horizontally. By placing the ruler horizontally under a line across the page, the reader can see at a glance (a) in Country Tables 1, the numerical development or evolution of any religion or Christian megabloc from AD 1900–2025; or (b) in Country Tables 2, the size and characteristics of any organized church or denomination in the 20th century.

(2) Vertically. By placing the ruler vertically up the table, to the right of a column he is interested in, the reader can see at a glance (a) in Country Tables 1, the comparative sizes of all religions and Christian megablocs at any particular year; or (b) in Country Tables 2, comparative sizes or dates of origin for all organized churches and denominations. Also in Country Tables 2, a vertical ruler placed to the right of column 3 (Type) will show the reader at a glance the megablocs and traditions of all churches. For example, if he wants to find Orthodox churches, he can place the ruler to the right of the first (single-letter) subcolumn, and look down the ruler's edge until he finds where these bodies are, coded 'O'. If he wishes to find Methodist bodies, he can move the ruler to the right of the second subcolumn and look down the ruler's edge until he finds the code 'Met'. In the same way, a vertical ruler placed to the immediate right of column 4 (Councils) will show the reader at a glance which churches belong to which Christian councils, if any, for its 5 subcolumns which represent (in order) confessional, international, continental, regional, and national conciliarism. For example, to find which denominations are full members of the World Council of Churches, place the ruler to the immediate right of the 2nd subcolumn and find which denominations have the code W there.

A ruler should also be used for the reader to find his way rapidly around all other large tables in this book.

### Statistics for AD 2000-2025

The tables enable the reader to obtain figures at certain precise points in time during the 20th century, namely the years 1900, mid-1970, mid-1990, the year 2000, and on to 2025 or even 2050 in the Third Millennium. Figures for intermediate years can easily be obtained by extrapolation.

The reader who wants a figure, or figures, for Christians or other religionists in the year 2001, or 2002, etcetera, can obtain them from the appropriate Tables 1 as follows. To get a figure for mid-2001, take the mid-2000 figure shown and simply add the figure under 'Annual change' in the column 'Total'. For mid-2002, add the figure 'Total' twice; for mid-2003, three times; and so on. For mid-1999, subtract 'Total' once. And so on.

From Country Tables 2, the reader can get approximate projections for 2000-2025 by multiplying a denominations' total Christian community by various combinations of the last 3 lines of totals (those for 1995, 2000, and 2025).

### Statistics for after AD 2025

For projections after 2025, one may assume even or linear change in Tables 1. Thus if the reader wants a quick estimate for a figure for AD 2050, he should extrapolate from AD 2000 and 2025.

### Quantifying 80 categories

In this survey we quantify a total of at least 300 different categories for a number of denominations and countries, i.e. for those traditions which produce statistics of them. On the world scale, we quantify some 200 different categories for every nation and denominational tradition. What this all means is because a very substantial part of the entire range of Christian activity in the modern world has been quantified by one tradition or another, it is therefore possible and justifiable for it to be reproduced here.

### We either list or quantify

The principle used throughout this survey is that we attempt to describe the whole spectrum—all religions, all churches and denominations, all parachurch agencies, and all varieties of Christian work and activities.

This we do either by listing by name all significant items present in a particular country, or, where they are too numerous to list, by quantifying and counting them. If any category proves too lengthy, we quantify it and give a statistical total. Thus Country Tables 1 and 2 list most religions and churches in each country, the significant ones at least, but often end their listings with 'Other religionists' (in Tables 1) or 'Other Protestant denominations', 'Other Orthodox churches', etc (in Tables 2). Similarly with other bodies and activities in the footnotes; if these are few, we describe them all by name. but if these are too numerous we always total them, as with seminaries, periodicals, libraries, institutions and agencies.

### *SOURCES*

The sources used in this survey were so numerous and diverse (often a different one for each number in a table) that it has proved impossible to insert them or document them in either the text or the tables. As is documented in Part 31 "Bibliography", the current total of books on Christianity exceeds 4.5 million distinct and separate titles. In most cases, the most authoritative sources, published or unpublished, were available to this book and so were used. The published documentation used is presented in these 3 volumes in the form of 4 separate bibliographies. (a) A 275,500-title *Bibliography of world Christianity* (or, *of the Christian world*) is presented here as a series of select bibliographies appended to the descriptive texts in *WCE* Part 4 for each of the 238 countries, giving descriptive works significant at the national level, i.e. listing for each country the major titles describing Christianity and religions in that country (and restricted to only that one country). (b) A 600-title series of *topical bibliographies* is appended at the ends of half the Parts of this book. (c) A 500-title *World bibliography of Christian directories* (see *WCE* Part 14) lists national, international, confessional, denominational, topical and other types of reference directory significant within their own contexts but not necessarily so at the global level. Lastly, there is (d) the *Selective world bibliography of Christianity* (Part 31).

Most of the materials collected for this survey, however, relate to original and previously unpublished enquiries. A large majority of the data came from field work, unpublished reports, and private communications from the collaborators listed after our title page. The major physical collections of data built up may be summarized here under 12 heads: (1) around 5,000 statistical questionnaires returned by churches and national collaborators over the period 1982-2000; (2) field surveys and interviews on the spot in over 200 countries conducted by the authors, who over the years 1965–2000 visited virtually every country in the world; (3) extensive correspondence over the last 16 years; (4) a mass of unpublished documentation for all countries, collected on the field, including reports, memoranda, facsimiles, photocopies, photographs, maps, statistical summaries and historical documents; (5) a large collection of primary published documents of limited circulation; (6) the collection just described of 600 directories of denominations, Christian councils, confessions and topics; (7) a collection of 4,500 printed contemporary descriptions of the churches, describing denominations, movements, countries and confessions; (8) officially-published reports of 500 government-organized national censuses of population each including the question on religion, in over 120 countries, covering most decades over the period 1900–2000; (9) unpublished reports and data concerning 50 government censuses of population by religion which were unprocessed or had remained incomplete, and which the authors then completed: (10) unpublished computer searches and computerized surveys of 12,000 university doctoral dissertations or master's theses on Christianity and religion, using 40 keywords ('Christian', 'Catholic', 'Protestant', etc): (11) bibliographical listings from searches (including computerized enquiries on key-words) in a number of major libraries including those of the British Library (London), Library of Congress (Washington), Propaganda (Rome), Missionary Research Library (New York), and a score of universities; and (12) a series of in-depth focused interviews with bishops, church leaders, theologians and others (of Catholic, Protestant, Orthodox, Anglican, Independent, and all other traditions), focusing specifically on the meaning, understanding, quantification and interpretation of (a) keywords in use in the propagation of Christianity (evangelization, mission, development, conversion, etc) and (b) the various neologisms evolved here in the course of our survey's statistical analyses (affiliated Christians, crypto-Christians, radio believers, evangelized non-Christians, neocharismatics, postcharismatics, etc).

### *ENUMERATING THE CHRISTIAN WORLD*

***Finding the statistics you want***

Statistics can be useful to the reader in several ways, both specific, general and comparative. Firstly, the reader may want to know the size of one particular figure, for some specific reason (e.g. the number of clergy in the diocese he lives in). Or secondly, he may want a general idea of the size of a particular church (e.g. an overseas denomination he is going to visit). Or thirdly, he may need to compare one church with another, or one set of statistics with another (e.g. which is the largest church in a particular country; or whether the church he supports has more national clergy than expatriate clergy). The statistics in this book attempt to supply these forms of assistance.

***The general order of magnitude***

The main feature of the statistical presentation in this volume is that its primary object is to establish broad areas of magnitude—to give the general order of magnitude of the situation, whether denominational, local, tribal, national, regional, racial, continental or global. From the point of view of the planner, development officer, Bible society executive, broadcaster, journalist or researcher, the important thing is to know (for example) whether Protestants in a particular country number 1,000, or 10,000, or 100,000, or 1 million, or 10 million; the exact size to the last digit may be of interest but is often of little further use. In the same way, many other totals enumerating approximately the entire Christian enterprise have been computed and presented here, such as radio audiences, unevangelized populations, and so on. The word 'approximately' is the operative word in this survey; absolute precision and accuracy are not to be expected, nor in fact are they always necessary for practical working purposes. This means that, although the tables and other statistics may help readers who want specific individual figures, they are mainly designed to give this general-order picture set in the total national and global context. To this end, where detailed local statistics compiled from grass-roots sources have not been available or were incomplete, the tables supply general-order estimates provided by persons familiar with the local statistical situation.

***Comparative statistics***

A second major feature of the statistical presentation is the comparative aspect: statistics of a similar type (e.g. adult membership), if published in a table in a single column, must be comparable from one church to another. Like must be compared with like; and like can only be compared with like. One cannot directly compare Roman Catholic statistics of 'Catholics' with Baptist statistics of 'Baptists', because the former include baptized children and infants and nominal adherents, the latter usually no infants or children but only baptized believing (and usually practicing) adults. To present only such statistics as the churches supply in this way would be frustrating and would merely underline the non-comparability of church statistics from one tradition to another. Ideally, we should collect statistics to the same definitions from all the churches, but for historical reasons it is now virtually impossible to get everybody to use similar definitions. It is, however, possible to adjust a body's figures to make them comparable with those of others. In this book, therefore, the problem is solved (a) by identifying clearly all statistics as applying to either adults only, or to adults plus children; and (b), in cases where a church only enumerates one of these categories, by computing general-order estimates of the other category. Most churches in fact enumerate each year only one type of membership statistics, either the number of adults or communicants on the rolls or records (as do Baptist, Methodists, Pentecostals and other 'gathered' churches) or the total number on the rolls including children and infants (as do Roman Catholics, Orthodox, Lutherans, Reformed, and other traditions with geographical parishes). Relatively few confessions enumerate both adults and total; these include Anglicans, some Reformed and some Lutherans. To make these data comparable from one tradition to another, therefore, the missing figure (adults or total) has been estimated and added either by the churches themselves or by the authors. These latter general-order estimates can usually be spotted by the reader because they are rounded, or more rounded than the church's main aggregated figure which is often given to the last digit. The major case of this method in this book concerns the Roman Catholic Church. Since Catholic statistics never enumerate adult Catholics, we provide general-order estimates of this category throughout by multiplying total affiliated Catholics (baptized plus catechumens) by the national figure for the percentage of the population over 14 years old. This assumption that the age structure of the Catholic Church is similar to that in the country as a whole is reasonably true in the Western (developed) world, although somewhat less accurate in Third-World (developing) countries where proportionately larger numbers of children and young people become Catholics than older people. Our assumption does, however, enable direct numerical comparisons to be made between Catholic statistics and Protestant statistics.

In the same way that comparison can only be made if definitions are like, comparisons of different bodies can only be made for the same point in time. One cannot meaningfully compare Catholics in 1930 with Baptists in 1980; they must be compared for the same year. Likewise it is wrong to add up totals of church memberships for different bodies at different dates, although it may sometimes be satisfactory if one can assume no change took place between the range of dates.

***Reading percentages correctly***

For comparing different quantities we use percentages throughout this survey (e.g. 'Catholics number 70% of the country's population, and Protestants 30%'). However, a single specific religious body or grouping may be quoted in the survey as having several quite different and apparently contradictory percentages attached to it. Thus, in the article on Fiji, we state that Indians who are Roman Catholics form (a) 1.5% of the Indian population of Fiji, (b) 8.9% of all Roman Catholics in Fiji, (c) 0.8% of the whole population of Fiji. All 3 percentages are correct, and consistent, but refer to 3 different ways of expressing the size of Indian Roman Catholics. Throughout this survey, therefore, the reader interested in a particular percentage, or set of percentages, should take care to ascertain precisely how we define them, what larger population is involved, and hence exactly what the percentages mean.

***Accuracy claimed for particular statistics***

Churches and religious bodies do not have at their disposal the vast networks of enumerators and analysts that government censuses and public-opinion polls employ, hence churches' statistics are not able to claim accuracy to the last digit. Similarly, although a government census in 1968 may report the number of Christians to the last digit (e.g. 2,450,793), projections into the future based upon this figure cannot claim complete accuracy but can only be approximations indicating the general order of size of the statistics required. In this book, therefore, the statistics presented fall into 2 categories: general-order estimates, and multi-digit aggregates. General-order estimates can be recognized throughout by their rounded nature, e.g. '5,000', '20,000', '100,000'. Where they occur in a Country Table 2, they usually represent estimates of their own size by the churches themselves; where they occur in a Country Table 1, they represent estimates by persons familiar with the nation, or by the authors as the result of complex computer operations. Multi-digit aggregates can be recognized throughout as figures appearing to claim accuracy to several digits, e.g. '5,291', '21,684', '102,735'. In a number of cases in the book's surveys, a church or diocese returned this kind of statistics rather than rounding it to the nearest hundred or thousand as one would do with a general-order estimate. In such cases Table 2 repeats the unrounded number, for 2 reasons: (1) to indicate the church's claim that the statistic is not a rough guess or general-order estimate but is based on some kind of aggregate or grass-roots roll total or head count, and (2) to enable readers familiar with that church's statistics to recognize the particular figure and hence to know its source and the exact date it applies to, in case more up-to-date or reliable figures later became available. It is remarkable how often such a multi-digit aggregate may be quoted for years after its original computation, and how easily recognizable each one is when it turns up again. Preserving the digits in this way is therefore an aid to the proper use of these statistics; but our practice must not be taken to imply bogus precision or any claim to accuracy to this last digit.

### Choice of best data available

Because our survey has attempted to be comprehensive, in certain countries where no hard statistical data or reliable surveys were available, we have had to rely on the informed estimates of experts in the area and subject. In this volume, we have made no detailed attempt at a critique of each nation's censuses and polls or each church's statistical operations. After examining what is available, we have then selected the best data available until such time as better data come into existence.

### Quantifying inaccessible data

There are a number of areas of church or religious life where it is impossible to obtain accurate statistics, usually because of state opposition to Christianity or religions. Thus it will probably never be possible (nor, perhaps, desirable) to get exact head counts of crypto-Christians, or of isolated radio believers, or of annual conversions to underground churches, and the like. Where such information is necessary to our present survey, we have therefore made reasonable and somewhat conservative estimates.

### Totalling figures of varying accuracy

In each table a number of totals are given at the end. When figures which are multi-digit aggregates (e.g. '102,782') are added together with others which are general-order estimates (e.g. '110,000'), the resulting total (212,783) is printed to the last digit in the interests of consistency and exactness of analysis. However, when such a total is quoted or used outside this survey, it should be rounded (to 210,000), to indicate only the general order of accuracy that it is possible to claim. This avoids the quoting and spreading of totals which appear to claim greater accuracy than is justified.

### Totals for churches with dioceses or other subdivi-
### sions

The same applies to totals for a church with dioceses or other jurisdictions. Figures for a church's dioceses or subdivisions are added and given in Table 2 on its first line to the last digit; but if they are quoted outside this survey they should be rounded.

### Totals and rounding

All our columns of absolute numbers in Country Tables 1 and 2 always add up exactly to the totals and subtotals shown. However, as with all large statistical tables, a column of percentages may not always add up to exactly the total or subtotal indicated, due to rounding. Although in most cases throughout this survey component percentages in fact add up exactly to their respective totals, in a small number of cases this is not so because of the rounding feature. As an example we may total: 0.13%+0.13%+0.13%%=0.39%; when each is rounded to only one place of decimals, the figures become 0.1%+0.1%+0.1%%=0.4%, which introduces a small discrepancy.

### Dates of statistics

It is important, in changing situations, to know the exact date (year, perhaps also month and sometimes day) to which particular statistics apply. This book compares government statistics of religion with churches' statistics; but in doing so, it must be remembered that a government census (or a public-opinion poll) is almost always taken on a single, known day; whereas, by contrast, churches' statistics are compiled over a lengthy period that may amount to 3, 4, 5, 6 or even 7 years from the local grass-roots counting of heads to final compilation of totals by a large denomination or church. Denominational totals published in 1995 therefore probably refer to the situation in 1992, 1991 or even 1990 in the case of very large denominations. This point is important in analyzing religious change and will be elaborated on below.

### Updating a church's statistics

Many of the largest or best-organized churches publish membership statistics annually. This means that the figures given in our Country Tables 2 are not always the latest available for those churches, after the year 1998. It would be inaccurate, however, to describe such figures in Tables 2 as 'out-of-date'; they represent accurately the situation for the year 1995 or 2000. In the case of each such church, the reader wanting the latest available figures should consult the latest edition of that church's yearbook (e.g. *Annuario*

*Pontificio* and *Statistical yearbook of the Church* for the Roman Catholic Church).

### Statistics must be consistent

A major feature of this survey is that care has been taken to make the various statistical categories, the national tables, and the international totals, all fully consistent with each other and without internal statistical discrepancies or contradictions. This means that (1) each statistical category we use has been given a single clear operational definition applicable worldwide and in all countries, churches and religions; and (2) in all complete enumerations in this survey (in Country Tables 1, 2 et alia), all subtotals of absolute numbers add up exactly to the relevant total; and all percentages add up to exactly to 100% (in practice, such totals are sometimes 0.1% or 0.2% out, due to rounding). In particular, in every country the totals of all religious and non-religious populations add up exactly to the countries population, i.e. to exactly 100%. A number of other consistency checks come readily to mind: e.g. in large paedobaptist (infant-baptizing) state churches with few adult conversions each year, the annual number of infant baptisms should be somewhat smaller than the total number of annual births in the country. Vast numbers of new single facts or items of data can be checked in this way before being inputted to the tables. In a few places when data were being collected for this book, different authorities gave, for the same situation, radically divergent data. In most cases the discrepancy was solved and the situation resolved by examining the exact context of the data. It was then found that in almost all cases the differing data referred either to different points in time, or to slightly different geographical areas, or to different definitions of the item in question. As a result this survey is able to give a single figure for every clearly-defined entity at a given point in time. Similarly, where various authorities differ concerning quantifiable matters, we have attempted to present a single statement rather than a series or range of contradictory statements.

## WHO IS A CHRISTIAN?

### Two divergent answers

There are 2 distinct and different ways in which Christians have been enumerated for well over the last 100 years, and in embryo for very much longer. The first is enumeration from the point of view of the state or society at large or the general public, in which individuals are asked in a government census or public-opinion poll to state publicly what religion they adhere to. The second is enumeration from the point of view of the churches, in which congregations or clergy state the total persons that they know are affiliated with them, i.e. whose names and addresses are on their records. These 2 methods almost always in all countries produce significantly different totals. Until now, the usual explanation has been either that governments are prone to over-enumerate or that churches are prone to under-enumerate, or vice versa. It is much more satisfactory to assume that, given their formidable resources and expertise, both are enumerating substantially correctly but that they are enumerating quite different kinds of person; and this assumption is basic to the present survey.

### Who is a Catholic?

The difference becomes sharpest over statistics of Roman Catholics. Africa provides a stark contrast. According to governments and polls organizations, there were 52.8 million Roman Catholics in Africa in 1970, rising to 76.8 million by 1980. According to the Vatican, there were only 45.3 million in 1970, rising to 66.2 million by 1980. Why the discrepancy? The answer is that governments were measuring self-identification (persons who call themselves Roman Catholics), and the Vatican was counting only baptized Catholics and catechumens known to its parishes and priests. Both usages must be accepted and must be taken seriously, since neither is likely to be changed; the best procedure therefore is to qualify these usages of 'Roman Catholics' with 2 different adjectives to distinguish the one from the other. This is done here by use of the terms 'professing Roman Catholics' and 'affiliated Roman Catholics' respectively, defining the latter (in mission countries) to mean all baptized Roman Catholics together with any catechumens, i.e. all persons on the books or records of the Roman Catholic

**The right to profess one's choice.** Census officials (right, center) in Iban/Sea Dayak longhouse in Sarawak (Malaysia) in 1960 ask tattooed Iban (left) what religion he professes.

Church. The latter term then stands for Roman Catholics as enumerated by that church itself.

### Who is a Pentecostal/Charismatic?
Another illustration comes from the above question. According to the 1980 Christianity Today/Gallup poll, 19% of all adults in the USA identified themselves as Pentecostal/Charismatics; yet, according to Gallup, of this 19% only 15% were members affiliated to churches and only 3.5% were regularly active and involved in Pentecostal/Charismatic activities. Why the discrepancy? Our answer to all such problems is that all such data are valid and consistent, but that exact definitions must be used in labeling the results: In this case, 19% of the USA were professing Pentecostals/Charismatics, 15% were Pentecostals/Charismatics affiliated to churches, and 3.5% were regularly-active and involved Pentecostals/Charismatics.

### A new methodology
As a result, this book incorporates a new methodology of enumerating statistics of the Christian world. In the past, certain churches (usually those with a strong link with the state) have quoted, as their membership figures, government census figures of professing adherents; other churches (those with little of no link with the state) have enumerated only those persons regularly or actively participating in church life. These 2 types of statistics are describing quite different entities and therefore cannot properly be compared. Instead, this book divides all statistics of Christians into 4 basic types: professing Christians, affiliated Christians, practicing Christians, and Great Commission Christians (those involved in outreach). These 4 types will now be elaborated on.

### 1. The right to profess one's choice
Our new methodology takes as its starting-point the United Nations 1948 *Universal Declaration of Human Rights*, Article 18: 'Everyone has the right to freedom of thought, conscience and religion; this right includes freedom to change his religion or belief, and freedom, either alone or in community with others and in public or private, to manifest his religion or belief in teaching, practice, worship and observance.' Since its promulgation, this group of phrases has been incorporated into the state constitutions of a large number of countries across the world. This fundamental right also includes the right to claim the religion of one's choice, and the right to be called a follower of that religion and to be enumerated as such. The section on religious freedom in the constitutions of very many nations uses the exact words of the Universal Declaration, and many countries instruct their census personnel to observe this principle. The instructions to enumerators in the 8th Census of Canada (1941) are typical in this respect: 'The religion of each person will be entered according as he or she professes'. This Declaration has however been virtually ignored in the churches and by Christians in general. Almost the first interest in it has been a recent action of the Protestant and Roman Catholic churches in Brazil. In 1978 they published and distributed over one million copies of an ecumenical edition of the Declaration, complete with Bible references and official church pronouncements on the subject.

On this definition in the Declaration, then, 'Christians' means all those who profess to be Christians in government censuses or public-opinion polls, i.e. who declare or identify themselves as Christians, who say 'I am a Christian', 'We are Christians', when asked the question 'What is your religion?' From the biblical point of view, there is justification for the definition in passages such as the word of Jesus in Matthew 10:32 (Good News Bible): 'If anyone declares publicly that he belongs to me, I will do the same for him before my Father in heaven'. A parallel passage is Romans 10:9; a person is a saved Christian 'if you confess with your lips that Jesus is Lord' instead of the required obligatory state-worship formula 'Caesar is Lord'. Another term for professing Christians can therefore be confessing Christians.

Public declaration must therefore be taken seriously when endeavoring to survey the extent of Christianity. This definition covers many categories of Christians including the large numbers of groups and individuals who, while striving to follow Christ and being indisputably Christian, nevertheless refuse to identify themselves with any existing organized Christian church or denomination. Statistics of these

*professing Christians*, or confessing Christians, or declared Christians, or self-identifying Christians, are widely available, published by governments and polls organizations.

Newly baptized members of AICN (Kenya) in 1979 have their names written on printed membership cards in presence of witnesses.

### 2. Affiliated to organized Christianity
By no means all those who profess to be Christians, however, are affiliated to the organized churches and denominations, and so it is necessary to give here also statistics of *affiliated Christians*. We define these as those known to the churches or known to the clergy (usually by names and addresses) and claimed by them in their statistics, i.e. those enrolled on the churches' books or records, with totals which can be substantiated. This usually means all known baptized Christians and their children, and other adherents; it is sometimes termed the total Christian community (because affiliated Christians are those who are not primarily individual Christians but who primarily belong to the corporate community of Christ), or inclusive membership (because affiliated Christians are church members). This definition of 'Christians' is what the churches usually mean by the term, and statistics of such affiliated Christians are what the churches themselves collect and publish. In all countries, it may be assumed with confidence, the churches know better than the state how many Christians are affiliated to them. This therefore gives us a second measure of the total Christians which is quite independent of the first (government census figures of professing Christians).

Newly-baptized infants, Luke and Timothy, are entered into 200-year old parish register in Waterperry, Oxford (England) by Church of England vicar, 1979.

### 3. Religious practice or church attenders
A third definition of membership relates to those who actually practice their religion, i.e. *practicing Christians* who may also be termed active Christians, attending Christians, committed Christians, militant Christians (composing Christ's Church Militant Here on Earth, to quote the Prayer for the Church in the Church of England 1552 Communion Service). Practicing Christians are defined here as those who participate in the ongoing institutional and organized life and pattern of the churches. Using the broadest definition, this covers all affiliated church members who attend church services of public worship a minimum of once a year; and it covers all who fulfil the minimum annual obligation of their church, which may be reception of communion at Easter and/or on other occasions annually. Using a more rigorous definition, this category may be subdivided into

monthly attenders (those who attend church at least once a month) or weekly attenders (those who attend regularly every Sunday). Many churches keep such statistics of practice, and in addition many secular polling organizations provide data on church attendance. Where such data exist, statistics of practice for a denomination or diocese are given in *WCD* Country Table 2, column 10, using the code P (=% practicing); and estimates of practice for the whole country are given in *WCD* Country Table 1. Note that the *percentages* for practicing and non-practicing usually quoted refer to percentages of affiliated Christians, not percentages of the whole country's population. To many persons active in the churches, this definition of 'Christians' is the only one they can use; Christians are those who practice the faith by attending worship regularly within the churches.

### 4. Involvement in the church's outreach
Christians described by types 1, 2, and 3 above are not necessarily activists or zealots or enthusiasts or believers who take their faith seriously enough to practice specifically Christian values. A large number estimated here at 400 millions are church attenders who nevertheless do not live a specifically Christian lifestyle involving obedience to Christ as Lord including involvement in his mandate to outreach and mission. Some 648 millions of Christians do, however, get so involved, taking seriously Christ's final commands to his disciples 'Go', 'Make disciples', 'Baptize', 'Teach'. Because they are aware of these commands and are actively attempting to follow Christ on his mission, this survey terms them *Great Commission Christians*. The totals for every nation are given in Country Tables 1; the methodology for their calculation is set out in Part 21 "GeoPersonnel" and elsewhere.

## CHILDREN ALSO MUST BE INCLUDED

The place of children in Christian enumeration needs critical examination and radical re-emphasis. All churches would agree that the influence and example of parents are the most powerful of all influences. The family is by far the most important instrumentality through which individuals acquire personal, cultural, and social self-identification. In consequence, children of church members are more likely to remain members than those whose parents are not church members. Children of ardent and practicing Christians usually are, to the extent that their years permit, ardent and practicing Christians.

### Children also can practice their faith
Many churches however do not enumerate children of under 15 years. One reason is that it has been widely noted that most conversion crises occur in the 13–20 age group in Christian families or in christianized lands. On this view, therefore, children who have not yet reached 15 (known in Protestant circles as 'the age of decision'), cannot reasonably be expected to be practicing and believing Christians. We here take the opposite view: children and infants also can properly be called Christians, and can actively and regularly (to the extent of their ability) practice the Christian faith. The photographs of practicing Christians shown on this page, and a number of others throughout the book, show children (defined as ages 5–15 years. i.e. the school-age population), infants (defined as under 5 years old, usually termed the pre-school populations) and in several cases new-born babies (see infant baptism services portrayed later) who are present and active or in some way participating in Christian worship and witness. To understand the magnitude of this problem, it is advisable at this point to see just how numerous children are in the Christian world.

### How numerous are children?
Reasonable assumptions on this subject are: (1) in the Christian world the proportions of children and other functional age-groups are (for our own immediate purposes) approximately the same as in their country and in the world at large; (2) children and infants have, in general, the same religion as their parents; and (3) in particular, children and infants of practicing Christians usually practice the faith to the extent that they are able and should therefore also be called practicing Christians too. We then arrive at the conclusion demonstrated in the table below that in

AD 2000 approximately 240 million children and infants in the world can properly be called practicing Christians.

***Enumerate your children and infants***
Since children and infants form in this way over 36% of all professing Christians, and 37% of all affiliated Christians, it stands to reason that in any statistical survey of world Christianity they must not be ignored, whatever a particular confession's answer may be to the questions 'Can an infant be a Christian?' and 'Can an infant be a practicing Christian?'. Churches whose statistical procedures ignore children and infants can now be seen to be seriously underenumerating their own numerical strengths. On the world scale, this situation has given rise to a serious understatement of the size and numerical strength of the Christian community in comparison with the total population, a situation which has often then been rationalized theologically by the assertion that the Body of Christ must always be only the Little Flock, the Saving Remnant, the Gideon's Band (of only 300 persons), in other words only a tiny minority in a non-Christian world.

For a true assessment of the situation, therefore, children and infants must be enumerated. Those world confessions which are Non-Liturgical, such as Baptists, Methodists, Pentecostals and other Protestants whose present procedures enumerate only adult members (15 years and older, i.e. the working-age and old-age population in the table below) should therefore note that these adults probably form only around 63% of their true total community, on their own definition of membership. To arrive at a correct estimate of their true strength vis-a-vis the total population around them they should increase their quoted adult membership figures by dividing them by a factor around 0.63 (63%). The exact procedure by which this has been done in the present survey, for all such denominations in all countries of the world, is explained below in the discussion of the methodology of *WCE* Country Table 2.

It follows that, to ensure comparability from one confession or church to another, it is important to note whether any statistics that one is examining (or quoting) include children and infants. Baptized listings for the Liturgical world confessions—Catholic, Orthodox, Anglicans and some Protestant churches including Lutherans—and also government census figures, do include children and infants; but communicant rolls and other adult listings exclude children and infants and enumerate only adults. Censuses of church attendance often badly under-represent the true situation because attending children and infants are not included among the total of attenders, who are then divided by the total population (which includes children and infants) to arrive at incorrectly-low percentages. A total of adults cannot properly be compared with another total including children, otherwise misleading conclusions may be drawn. In the same way, all public-opinion polls enquiring about affiliation and religious practice enumerate only the adult population. Since the children and infants of religious parents, and of practicing Christians, can also be active attenders, they also must be enumerated to make any accounting complete. In many countries, the religion of children is stated in law to be that of their parents, as in Norway's 1969 law declaring that 'Children born in wedlock belong to the religion of their parents'. It is assumed in this survey therefore that, when such polls data are used, children under 14 have the same characteristics as their parents; i.e. the same religion, and religious practice, as the head of the family; except in rare cases where data to the contrary are available. This means then that all statistics given in Country Tables 1 cover the total community of every religion—men, women and their children and infants.

### *RELIGION DEFINITIONS OF 8 TYPES OF PERSONS, 7 BEING CHRISTIANS*

***Operationalizing our definitions***
We can now proceed to relatively exact definitions of the major variables used in our enumeration of all categories of Christians and other religionists. We can also study how they are quantified and how they are operationalized. The latter term has a specific meaning. 'Operationism or operationalism is the insistence upon the use of operational definitions in science wherever the meaning of a term in quantitative discourse is to be understood' (J. Gould & W.L. Kolb, eds, *A dictionary of the social sciences*; London, 1964:475. See also 'The present state of operationalism', chapter 2 in P.G. Frank (ed), *The validation of scientific theories*, New York, 1954). The value of exact definitions is that different observers or analysts of the same situation should then arrive at similar results. Definitions of simple categories such as 'church personnel', 'institutions', even 'schools', can vary considerably from one user to the next. Our solution here is to formulate definitions which are as precise as possible cross-culturally and cross-nationally, and then to apply these standard definitions for all countries, churches, and religions.

**Children also can practice their faith.** Children and infants who practice the Christian faith (as shown here) number over 240 million, hence deserve proper enumeration. Above. Japanese Christian children pray at Ai Kei Gakuen Community Center, Tokyo.

***Enumerating all categories***
The key to understanding the enumeration of Christians presented in this book lies therefore in grasping the definitions contained in the diagram above, and in the explanation that follows. These definitions arise out of 10 different standpoints or ways of looking at the world and its populations. Table 14–8 sets these out in a comparative format, adding 2 other categories: 'Demography', and 'Evangelization'. To assist in understanding the definitions, we also add global totals for each of the types of Christians and others in the 2 years 1970 and 2000. After giving the diagram, we then explain each of the 10 standpoints.

**1. Demography**
The starting point is the size of the global population in the 2 years 1970 and 2000, as shown on this line.

**2. Religion**
The world may, to start with, be divided into two according to whether or not persons profess any religion. Those who profess no religion (15.2%) may be called either unbelievers or non-believers, or religionists. The term 'religionists' is coming increasingly into use; thus in August 1978 there was held at the Jakko-in Temple Study Centre in Inuyama City, Japan, the Third Conference of Youth Religionists in Japan.

**3. Evangelization**
Secondly, the world is divided into the trichotomy of World A (the unevangelized), World B (evangelized non-Christians), and World C (all Christians).

**4. Christianity**
The world may again be divided into two, into those who are Christians, and those who are non-Christians of all kinds including the non-religious. Christians are defined here as all who call themselves followers of Christ, in public or in private, or who regard themselves as followers of Christ or as part of a Christian community or who claim to be such. As has been explained, this is in accordance with the Universal Declaration of Human Rights, in which every individual has the right to say to what religion he or she belongs and to have this accepted by state and society.

**5. Public profession**
Christians may first be subdivided into 2 main categories—professing, and crypto-Christian—depending on whether or not their faith is publicly known, i.e. known and declared to the public and to the state. Professing Christians are those who profess (declare, state, confess, identify themselves) publicly to be Christians when asked what their religion is, either in government censuses, or in public-opinion polls, or by social scientists or other researchers conducting surveys. Professing Christians are therefore persons known to state or government, and/or to the public at large, and concerning whom statistical totals are known to the state and government and are often published by them or quoted in their dealings with the churches. Such census records constitute a formal declaration or statement to the state revealing one's personal religious preference, and one which may be used by the state against the individual or his family or relatives or associates. Consequently in countries where Christianity is discriminated against, many rightly choose not to reveal this information to the state. These persons, to whom we give the name crypto-Christians, are so important that we should describe them in detail at this point.

*Crypto-Christians*. This grouping is also called secret believers, or non-professing Christians, or Christians not publicly baptized, or clandestine or underground believers. They are those who for reasons of family, personal safety, status, employment or other factors do not declare or reveal their commitment to Christ or expose their faith to public or state scrutiny or enquiry but prefer to keep it private. As a result, they are not enumerated as Christians in government censuses or polls but remain unknown and unenumerated in such public enquiries. For various other reasons also, they remain unknown to governments and unregistered with them, or are overlooked or excluded in government tallies. They are however, usually known to the churches, or join churches openly, or are known by the churches to have been baptized privately, or in fact constitute their own churches. In almost all cases, churches regard them as affiliated, and include them in their own enumerations of affiliation. The churches count them in their statistics, though they often do not record them by name and they take pains to conceal their identity from the state or a hostile populace.

A description of the family background of metropolitan Nikodim of Leningrad (died 1978) provides a good illustration. 'He was born into a party-card-carrying Communist family 49 years ago. His father was a militant atheist. His mother was officially an atheist as well, although privately Nikodim said that she had been a secret believer. He apparently discovered this only after he himself joined the Church, during his teens' (*Religion in Communist lands*, 6, 4 (Winter, 1978), 227).

Another type of secret believer is found in Islamic countries. There are large numbers of Muslims in these countries who are trying to follow Christ whilst remaining in the Muslim community and not breaking with it. The present survey enumerates such persons as 'Hidden Muslim believers in Christ' and estimates their total in the year 1995 at 450,000 in 15 countries.

Secret believers are not necessarily always underground, or persecuted—they are merely unknown to the state or unrecognized by it. Often the state or society at large is completely unaware of the existence of sizeable groups of Christians, especially if they belong to illegal or banned groups (Jehovah's Witnesses, Mormons, New Apostolics, etc.) Certain churches in any case prefer to exist clandestinely, deliberately operating unknown to the state.

Underground Christians may be further characterized as crypto-Protestants, crypto-Catholics, crypto-Orthodox, et alii. Another distinction is that a group may be, for instance, crypto-Witnesses (secret Jehovah's Witnesses) but not crypto-Christians because their religion is officially regarded as Roman Catholic or members of some established or state church.

It will be noticed from *WCE* Country Tables 1 in certain countries that the 'professing' categories are missing for certain 'affiliated' traditions present there. This means that those traditions are in the category of crypto-Christians.

*Safeguarding clandestine Christians*. There is need to preserve the anonymity of crypto-Christians in many countries, due to hostile state apparatus. The data we give in this book are unlikely to harm them because the information usually comes from existing published sources. We mention no persons' names or ad-

# Crypto-Christians

**CRYPTO-CHRISTIANS.** Secret believers in Christ, including those in 'churches of silence' or underground churches, totalled 124 millions in AD 2000. They are defined in this book under the 7 headings given here, for each of which one illustration is given on this page. (1) **Unorganized individuals in legal churches**. Muslim women, including secret believers, leaving Christian Social Centre, Tunis. (2) **Political prisoners or exiles**. Christians being sentenced by people's tribunal, China. In Communist countries, an estimated 8 million Christians were held in prison camps with no fellowship or worship opportunities. (3) **Unregistered Christians**. An underground (illegal) Baptist church near Novosibirsk, Siberia (USSR): (Above) in winter:

(below) in summer, with congregation of 52 believers. (4) **Deliberately-clandestine Christians**. Worship service in Ukrainian forest near Kharkov. In the USSR, there were over 40 highly-organized totally-clandestine denominations, with over 500,000 members. (5) **Anti-state minority sectarians**. Full Gospel Believers Church (Ethiopia), ex-Orthodox converts viciously persecuted by the state from 1972-75 and hence forced underground. (6) **Anti-church believers**. Prayer meeting before crucifix in Subba Rao Movement, India. Members oppose baptism and denominationalism, and call themselves Hindu believers in Christ. (7) **Isolated radio believers**. Convert in Morocco who has begun a network of house radio churches.

dresses. In any case, state files on these groups are greatly more detailed, comprehensive and incriminating than anything we publish here. At the same time, it is necessary to urge Christians in Western countries to be on the alert to avoid any possibility of incrimination of secret believers in such countries.

## 6. Church affiliation

Professing Christians may be subdivided into 2 categories—affiliated, and unaffiliated (often called nominal)—depending on whether or not they are in any sense attached to or associated with organized or institutional Christianity. Affiliated Christians are Christians who are known to or in the churches, who at some time present or past have joined or belonged to one of the churches' categories of membership and affiliation, who hold or have claimed formal membership in a local church, who are known to the churches individually by name and are therefore on the churches' rolls or books at local or grass-roots level. They are therefore Christians with whom the churches are in touch, who are on the records of the institutional churches or organized Christianity, who are not simply individual Christians but are also part of the churches' corporate life, community and fellowship, and who are therefore enumerated by the churches as members or adherents in a form which can be substantiated. Statistics of affiliated Christians, as presented in this book, are always those supplied by the churches themselves, although in a handful of public-opinion polls the question 'Are you a member of any church?' has produced similar data (e.g. AIPO 1954 and 1976, Gallup 1940-2000 in the USA).

In the Western world, affiliated Christians are also professing (known in government censuses), but in Communist countries and in Third-World countries with a dominant non-Christian religion, a sizeable number remain as crypto-Christians. The organized churches, overtly asserting that Jesus is the Christ, are termed by Paul Tillich the manifest church (*Systematic theology*, III, p. 152–382, passim). In cases where 2 churches claim the same people as members (as is widely the case in Latin America with Catholics and Evangelicals), this is shown as a group of doubly-affiliated at the end of *WCE*'s Country Table 2, and in Country Table 1 on the line immediately after all affiliated megablocs, with the negative sign to ensure correct computerized enumeration and addition.

Nominal Christians are defined here as professing Christians who are unaffiliated or unchurched, i.e. not affiliated to churches, nor in contact with them, nor attached to them, nor associated with them, nor

known to them nor on their rolls or books. They are therefore Christians who are outside or have rejected the institutional churches or are otherwise not on the records of organized Christianity, who may individually be Christians but who are not part of the corporate life, community or fellowship of the churches, and who therefore from the churches' point of view are regarded as Christians in name only, whilst at the same time often maintaining Christian beliefs and Christian values. Nominal Christians, in other words, are unaffiliated Christians who, for reasons good or bad, do not belong to the visible and organized community of believers. They are sometimes called the latent church as opposed to the manifest church which unashamedly asserts Jesus as the Christ (Paul Tillich, et alii).

In the Western world (Europe, USA), this term 'nominal' often carries connotations of dishonesty or hypocrisy, and such persons not known to the churches are often regarded as post-Christians forming a penumbra of residual Christianity; though from another point of view they contain large numbers of personally-committed Christians who find themselves indifferent to organized or institutional religion. A full statistical study of this category in one particular nation, the USA, has been undertaken by Gallup International in their poll 'The unchurched American' (June 1978 onwards), whose main finding is: 'A majority of American adults who for one reason or another have rejected the institutional church still adhere to most traditional Christian beliefs and values'. This survey is summarized here in Country Table 1 for the USA. The situation with regard to being 'nominal' is quite different in regions where Christianity is expanding, especially Africa, where this category covers masses of intending or latent Christians who desire to be Christians and regard themselves as followers of Christ but who have not yet been contacted or initiated (catechumenate and baptism) by the churches, because the latter are quite incapable of handling the huge numbers involved. In many Third-World countries where there is a wide difference between Christianity and the local culture or cultures, there is also the serious problem of existing churches being unsuitable for the reception of new converts. A preliminary article written for the 1978 Asian Leadership Conference on Evangelism explains it thus: 'Many who decide for Christ from non-Christian backgrounds do not become members of the Church in the fellowship of believers… There are several factors hindering the new believers from becoming members of the visible church… In certain

cases the new disciples often find it difficult to identify with the existing Christians for social reasons… Uprooting people from their cultures and transposing them into another culture makes it socially difficult for many Asians to become Christians' (George Samuel, 'Nurture the harvest', *Asia's harvest* (ALCOE Newsbulletin), 4 (1978), 1).

Another reason for the existence of large numbers in this category of nominal Christians is that census figures include large numbers of dispersed, or isolated, or scattered Christians, families and groups, including recently-moved or -migrated persons and groups, who are unaffiliated, or not yet affiliated, to churches for a variety of reasons such as a local absence of churches using their own language, or their very recent arrival, and so on.

For all these reasons, the term 'nominal' is therefore used here in its strictly correct or literal sense, i.e. persons who (for whatever reason, good or bad) are at present Christians in name only (viewed from the standpoint of the churches).

Two other variants of affiliation are used in this survey: doubly-affiliated (to 2 denominations at once), and disaffiliated (baptized Christians who have since or recently become professing agnostics or atheists).

'Roll-cleaning' has an important bearing on the size of affiliated membership. Large established or state churches seldom or never 'clean their rolls' (i.e. remove names no longer known to them, or names of members who have left, died, migrated or apostatized). Through not cleaning its rolls regularly and realistically, the Roman Catholic Church in particular has on its rolls vast numbers of names of former Catholics who are now no longer members in any sense. An example is the so-called 'Red Region' of Emilia-Romagna in Italy. Polls have long showed that its population is heavily Communist, 4% being atheists and another 15% agnostics; but *Annuario Pontificio* (1995) still reports that this population, roughly coterminous with the archdiocese of Bologna, is 99% Roman Catholics affiliated to the archdiocese. There is of course truth in this, in that the 99% in all probability were at one time baptized Catholics; now, however, 20% have disaffiliated themselves. We take care of this phenomenon in our tables with the clearly-defined category 'disaffiliated'. A fuller definition will shortly be given.

## 7. Practice

Affiliated Christians may be subdivided into 2 categories—practicing Christians, and non-practicing Christians—depending on whether or not they take

---

**Table 14–8. Definitions of types of persons, religionists, and Christians, with AD 1970-2000 world totals and percentages.**

This table gives the totals of persons in the world, under 10 categories. Each category reports its total for the year AD 1970 in light type, in millions (=m), followed by the year AD 2000 (in millions) in **bold** type. Under each such pair are given the corresponding percentages of the global population at 1970 and 2000.

| Standpoint | Major categories | | | | | |
|---|---|---|---|---|---|---|
| 1. DEMOGRAPHY | GLOBAL POPULATION 3,696 **6,055** millions  100% **100%** | | | | | |
| 2. RELIGION | NONRELIGIONISTS 698 **918** millions 18.9% **15.2%** | RELIGIONISTS 2,998 **5,137** millions 81.1% **84.8%** | | | | Doubly-counted -4 **-14** millions -0.1% **-0.2%** |
| 3. EVANGELIZATION | WORLD A 1,641 **1,629** millions 44.4% **26.9%** | WORLD B 819 **2,426** millions 22.1% **40.1%** | WORLD C 1,236 **2,000** millions 33.5% **33.0%** | | | |
| 4. CHRISTIANITY (to right of double line) | NON-CHRISTIANS 2,460 **4,055** millions 66.5% **67.0%** | CHRISTIANS 1,236 **2,000** millions 33.5% **33.0%** | | | | |
| 5. PUBLIC PROFESSION | PROFESSING CHRISTIANS 1,177 **1,876** millions 31.8% **31.0%** | | | | CRYPTO-CHRISTIANS 59 **124** millions 1.6% **2.0%** | |
| 6. CHURCH AFFILIATION (to right of double dotted line) | DISAFFILIATED -11 **-23** millions -0.3% **-0.4%** | UNAFFILIATED CHRISTIANS 106 **111** millions 2.9% **1.8%** | AFFILIATED CHRISTIANS 1,130 **1,888** millions 30.6% **31.2%** | | Doubly-affiliated -30 **-195** millions -0.8% **-3.2%** | |
| 7. PRACTICE | | | NON-PRACTICING CHRISTIANS 853 **1,350** millions 23.1% **22.5%** | | PRACTICING CHRISTIANS 277 **648** millions 7.5% **10.7%** | |
| 8. CHURCH ATTENDANCE | | | Non-attending members 605 **1,024** millions | Annual attenders 60 **85m** / Occasional attenders 55 **80m** | Radio/TV listeners 50 **100m** / Monthly attenders 120 **200m** | Weekly attenders 240 **400m** |
| 9. BELIEF | | UNCOMMITTED CHRISTIANS 106 **111** millions 2.9% **1.8%** | PARTIALLY-COMMITTED CHRISTIANS 750 **1,388** million 20.2% **22.9%** | | COMMITTED CHRISTIANS Born-again Christians 380 **500** millions | |
| 10. MISSION AND OUTREACH | | LATENT CHRISTIANS 959 **1,352** millions 26.0% **22.3%** | | | GREAT COMMISSION CHRISTIANS 277 **648** millions 7.5% **10.7%** Overt evangelizers / Covert evangelizers | |

any part in the ongoing organized life of the churches. Practicing Christians are affiliated Christians who are involved in or active in or participate in the institutional or organized life of the churches they are affiliated to; or who are regarded by their churches as practicing members because they fulfil their churches' minimum annual attendance obligations or other membership requirements; or who in some way take a recognized part in the churches' ongoing practice of Christianity. Thus in the Church of Scotland 'active communicants' are defined as persons who communicate (receive communion) at least once a year. In 1939 this was 76.8% of all communicants on the rolls, 56.7% in 1943, 72.0% in 1946, and 71.3% in 1959. In the Coptic Orthodox Church (Egypt), a 'practicing Copt' is one who receives communion at least once every 40 days. Sometimes there is a financial connotation; some denominations only count as practicing those adult members who contribute each year to local or central church funds. Certain denominations publish detailed definitions: thus the Christian Church (Disciples of Christ) in the USA explains 'A "participating" member is one who exercises a continuing interest in one or more of the following ways: attendance, giving, activity, spiritual concern for the fellowship of the congregation regardless of the place of residence' (Classification of church membership, General Assembly Resolution No. 57, Detroit 1964). The broadest meaning of the term is of annual church attenders, those who attend a service of public worship (within the ordinary pattern of institutional religion) at least once a year regularly; it excludes those who only attend church on special private family or personal occasions (baptisms, weddings, funerals), or only on civic occasions or state festivals, but it includes all persons who listen to services only over radio and TV (bearing in mind that countless elderly, infirm, sick and handicapped persons who cannot attend church nevertheless listen or view regularly, and that in vast numbers of places where churches are not accessible (e.g. Norway, Africa, oceans) radio/TV services are the only possible form of attendance). In many larger Protestant churches, statistics of affiliated members tend to be close to those of practicing members; in other words, their definition of membership is those who partake of communion at least once a year. Similarly, in many smaller Protestant churches, affiliated members means those who attend regularly or even weekly.

Non-practicing Christians, in contrast, are affiliated Christians who take no part in their churches' ongoing activities, and who are inactive and non-attending or who describe themselves as such. They are sometimes termed dormant Christians, or collectively as the dormant church.

**8. Church attendance**

Practicing Christians may also be termed active, attending, committed or militant Christians, and may be subdivided into several mutually-exclusive categories of attending Christians, as shown in Table 14–3. This information is often obtainable in part from polls data. It covers the 8 main types of attenders shown in the diagram, which may be listed as follows in decreasing order of participation: those who attend church services several times a week (daily attenders); those who attend church church services every Sunday, or Saturday (weekly or Sunday attenders); those who go only twice a month (fortnightly attenders); those who go only once a month (monthly attenders); those who, for reasons of age, infirmity, sickness or in the absence of local churches, in place of church attendance listen regularly to Sunday radio/TV services every week or once a month (radio/TV service listeners); those who attend church on church festivals only (festival attenders); those who attend from time to time or irregularly, i.e. at most 2 or 3 times a year (occasional attenders); and those who attend or take communion once a year only, often at Christmas or Easter only (annual attenders). As explained above, our definition of practicing Christians excludes 2 further categories: civic attenders, i.e. those who attend church services only on civic occasions or state festivals, and private attenders, i.e. those who attend church services only for special private family occasions (baptisms, weddings, funerals). In the Western world, this latter type of attendance is sometimes irreverently termed '4-wheeler religion' because the main participants enter church only when wheeled in prams, wedding cars, or hearses. Care should be taken in examining a poll to see whether its categories are intended to be distinct, mutually-exclusive and non-overlapping (this being the usual situation), or whether they overlap in a cumulative manner; 'annual attenders' in a poll may mean either those who attend only once a year, or the aggregate of all who attend once a year (including those who attend monthly, fortnightly, weekly, daily). On average across the world, Christians attending once a month or more are usually well over half the size of the total of practicing Christians. In this book, 'practicing' percentages always mean % of affiliated Christians (as shown in Country Tables 2 column 10, where P = % practicing every year, and W = % practicing every week, i.e. Sunday attenders); this is because only affiliated Christians can reasonably be expected to practice.

*Attending non-members.* There are 2 further types of church attender that are excluded from our category of practicing Christians. The first are attending non-members, i.e. nominal Christians (who by definition are non-church-members) who occasionally or in some cases regularly attend church services. Such individuals are relatively few in number and are sufficiently negligible in aggregate not to be shown specifically in our Country Tables 1.

*Attending non-Christians.* The second type are attending non-Christians, i.e. persons who attend church services regularly or occasionally, being interested in Christianity, but who are still non-Christians (pagans, Muslims, Hindus, etc). In areas of the world where Christianity is expanding rapidly, large numbers of non-Christians attend church every Sunday as potential converts. This is particularly the case in Black Africa, such as in TEKAN in the Central Belt of Nigeria, in the Tiv Church, and elsewhere in the tropics. All such persons are not included in our category of practicing Christians, and in Country Tables 1 they are included only under their own religions at the times indicated.

**9. Belief**

The foregoing categories of Christians describe the external, visible, observable status of Christianity. However, these categories of themselves can say little or nothing about the inner quality of Christian faith or experience, or about faith and belief. For this reason, several Christian traditions go further and hold that they are only interested in ideal categories like 'believing Christians', 'true believers', 'real Christians', 'committed Christians', 'converted Christians, 'nuclear Christians', 'authentic Christians', 'born-again Christians', and so on.

Unfortunately, virtually no traditions, churches, or agencies actually measure and report such statistics, which means that such categories are useless as variables in any global enumeration. Almost the only example of such statistics on the world level comes from the Assemblies of God, who in their 1998 global report gave for 50 countries figures of members 'Baptized in the Holy Spirit' that totalled to only a fraction of all affiliated members.

It is feasible to define 'Belief' here to include 'Commitment'. Christians may be divided into committed, partially-committed and uncommitted Christians. The term committed can be defined in many different ways; one way, as shown in the diagram, is to regard regular attenders (once a month or more) who profess belief in Christ as Savior and an experience of salvation or conversion, to compose this committed nucleus. Unfortunately, all such categories of commitment are too subjective to enumerate fairly or scientifically, and so they have to be excluded from Country Tables 1 and 2. Attempts have been made, however, to probe deeper and to quantify certain aspects of belief and faith, using public-opinion polls. The most revealingly personal question on belief that has been asked is, perhaps, 'Do you consider that you have been born again (as a Christian)?', and other variants. The experience of new birth is here defined as a turning point in life when one commits oneself to Christ as Savior and Lord. To this question in 1976 in Norway, 18% of all Norwegians replied Yes (27% for all young people), and in the USA 34% of all adults (50% of all professing Protestants, 18% of all professing Catholics) rising to 41% by 1995 (Gallup). Using our definitions of professing, affiliated and practicing Christians. This means that in the USA 49% of all practicing Christians (and 72% of all practicing Protestants) define themselves as born-again Christians. What these figures indicate is that, although statistics of belief and commitment on a world scale are unavailable and not likely to become available, existing statistics of profession, affiliation, practice, attendance, and belief may be taken as a reasonably reliable indicator of the presence of belief and commitment. On the world scale, it is probable that some 40% of all adult practicing Christians would claim this experience of new birth. Children and infants, once again, should be enumerated with their parents, so that one can extend this latter sentence to say that 40% of all practicing Christians of all ages belong to a self-identifying born-again Christian community. Because this and similar questions have only been asked in a handful of nations, all industrialized, these data are not here systematically documented in Country Tables 1, but are given to some extent in *WCE* Part 12 "Dictionary", under the entry 'belief.'

**10. Mission and outreach**

A final typology used here attempts to sum up the previous typologies and to subdivide totals of Christians into those properly termed 'disciples'—all those who take seriously Christ's call to follow him in his mission on Earth—and those other Christians who are not so demarcated, for reasons good or bad. This last typology coins the term 'Great Commission Christians' (alternatively, 'GeoChristians') meaning all who are aware of Christ's final commission, accept it for themselves, and are in some degree involved with Christ in his mission. The opposite category is here termed 'latent Christians'. This whole subject is worked through in Part 21 "GeoPersonnel" where the methodology for measuring Great Commission Christians is derived.

***Pilgrimages***

An important aspect of practicing Christianity is religious tourism, travel and pilgrimages. There are vast numbers of local, national and international shrines and pilgrimage centers across the world, involving huge numbers of persons, and involving Roman Catholic, Orthodox, Anglican, Protestant and indigenous blocs. The total of Christian pilgrims each year is estimated at over 150 million; i.e. 7% of all Christians are on the move as pilgrims every year. A small selection of the major pilgrimage centers described in this book is as follows:

Ankaramalaza (Madagascar),
Aparecida (Brazil; around 1 million a year),
Ars (France),
Bethlehem (Palestine),
Cartago (Costa Rica),
Croagh Patrick (Ireland),
Czestochowa (Poland; 5.5 million a year),
Echmiadzin (Armenia),
Einsiedeln (Switzerland; 150,000 a year in the year 1900),
Ekuphakameni (South Africa),
Farihimena (Madagascar; 1 million from 1947–51),
Fatima (Portugal; 400,000 a year, rising to 1 million in 1967),
Goa (India; 1 million a year),
Guadalupe (Mexico; 2 million a year),
Jerusalem (Palestine; over 300,000 a year),
Kiev (Ukraine; 1.2 million a year in 1886),
Knock (Ireland, since 1879; 1 million a year),
La Salette (France),
Lisieux (France; over 1 million a year),
Lourdes (France; 4.8 million a year, with peak of 8 million in 1958),
Lujan (Argentina; 2 million a year),
Luxembourg (40,000 annually),
Meskuiciai (Hill of Crosses, Lithuania),
Montserrat (Spain; 1.3 million a year),
Morija (South Africa; 4 million a year),
Nineveh (Kenya),
Nkamba-Jerusalem (Zaire),
Palma Sola (Dominican Republic),
Penha (Brazil),
Rome (first Holy Year in AD 1300, 200,000 pilgrims; 1950, 2.5 million; 1975 Holy Year 8,370,000),
Taize (France),
Turin (Italy; 3.3 million visiting Holy Shroud from September-October 1978),
Velankanni (India; over 1 million a year),
Walsingham (Britain),
Zagorsk (Russia),
Zante (Greece).

***Inclusive and exclusive definitions***

From Global Diagram 30's definitions (Part 1), it may be seen that several categories overlap, and several are mutually exclusive. The grand total of all Christians, on this definition, can be counted in 2 main ways: (1) from the state's standpoint, as the total of professing and crypto-Christians, or (2) from the churches' standpoint, as the total of affiliated and unaffiliated (or nominal) Christians. Crypto-Christians are always affiliated (never nominal); and nominal Christians are always professing Christians (never crypto-Christians). Similarly, a professing Christian may at the same time be an affiliated Christian and also a practicing Christian. But a nominal Christian cannot at the same time be an affiliated Christian, nor a practicing Christian; nor indeed can he be a nonpracticing Christian either. To avoid confusion, therefore, great care must be exercised in the exact choice of the terms one wishes to use.

*Mutually-exclusive adherence*

In the same way, this survey uses its terminology for followers of other religions in a mutually-exclusive sense. A person is either a Christian, or a Hindu, or a Muslim, or an atheist, or something else, but he cannot normally be enumerated here as more than one of these at any given time. We recognize that there are many independent individuals who like to think of themselves as having 2, 3, 4 or even more of these labels simultaneously. In reply it should be noted that (1) no government census in any country gives such individuals the option of a multiple choice, (2) such individuals are normally few in number, (3) the vast majority of people in virtually all countries can be clearly described by a single term each, and (4) our survey is a demographic one describing broad populations rather than exceptional individuals. To this extent our use of mutually-exclusive categories is justified.

In one important way, however, this situation is changing. Large numbers of Hindus, and to a smaller extent Buddhists and Muslims, are still calling themselves by those names but are also professing faith in Jesus Christ as Lord, God, and Savior. These persons are categorized here under the generic term 'Other non-Christian believers in Christ', and their statistics are (a) included, together with their myriads of house churches and private mininetworks or even minidenominations, in *WCE* Country Tables 2, and then (b) reconciled in Country Tables 1 by the inclusion of the category 'Doubly-professing religionists' or 'Doubly-counted religionists'.

## QUANTIFYING RELIGIOUS CHANGE

The world religious situation is far from static; change is continual, old religions are waning and new religions are arising. Surges of conversions from one religion to another are constantly taking place; many churches are expanding numerically, others are declining. This survey investigates changes over time in certain quantifiable aspects of church life. It attempts to document this in every country, firstly by compiling statistics for definite years (particularly mid-1970, 1990, 1995, and 2000), and secondly by giving annual rates of increase or decrease for all religions (in Country Tables 1, as described below) and for all individual denominations and churches (in Country Tables 2, column 9, which as explained below gives annual exponential church growth over the 25-year period 1970-1995).

Religion, race and society are in fact not dead mosaics or fixed and unchanging patchworks. They are living and active entities constantly changing in a ceaseless flux of action and reaction. We take account of all this in our survey by incorporating into our texts and tables not only religious change but also indicators of societal, demographic and ethnolinguistic change.

The global situation in AD 2000 is described and analyzed here in Global Diagram 41 'The dynamics of global religious change'.

*Measuring growth rates*

The rates of growth, increase, decrease or decline of membership in many churches can readily be measured from their annually-reported statistics. In this survey this has been done by obtaining the statistics for 2 different years, where possible 5 years apart (to minimize the effects of roll-cleaning and other annual irregularities), usually 1990-1995 and 1995-2000, and working out the average annual growth rate as a percentage. Great care must be taken in such computations to ensure that the statistics used are measuring exactly the same entity (especially geographically) for each of the 2 years concerned. Growth, as per cent increase or decrease per year, must be measured by dividing any annual increase by the identical category of total. Thus a church in a particular country with 500,000 total adherents (including children) in 1995 which grows to 600,000 total adherents (including children) in 2000 shows an increase of 600,000 minus 500,000 = 100,000, which divided by 5 = 20,000 a year, which divided by the mean membership of 550,000 gives an increase rate of 3.64% per year. In practice, this book follows a more accurate method by using the 1970 and 1995 figures for each denomination to arrive at exponential annual rates. Results are set out for every denomination in Country Tables 2 column 9. Values are given to 2 places of decimals. Negative values (e.g. G=-1.03%) indicate that a body is decreasing or declining annually. For each country, the net totals of all such changes in affiliation for the period 1990-2000 were then calculated. Statistics of Christians in the column 'Total' were then compiled under 'Annual change, 1990-2000' in all Country Tables 1. The same was done for non-Christian religions, in most cases by comparing censuses or polls over 5- or 10-year periods. Where no other data were available, for some countries censuses of 1900 and 1970 were available from which century-long trends could be established.

There are several different ways of measuring the growth of a church or body. Firstly, one can measure either adults only, or total community including children; in Country Tables 1 and 2 we always use the latter. Secondly, the growth rate of a church or religious grouping can be measured over a single day, or a month, a year, a decade, or 50 years—and all will yield differing results. In this survey we are concerned primarily to measure long-term rates, i.e. rates over the 25-year period 1970-1995 in Country Tables 2, column 9, and rates over the decade 1990-2000 in Country Tables 1. A growth rate measured for a specific church over a 2- or 3-year period may not be sustained throughout the decade, which explains differences in rates for the same church obtained at different times.

*Checking for plausibility*

A certain amount of religious change or church growth claimed by some bodies may appear unlikely, implausible, exaggerated or even physically impossible. Logarithmic graph paper provides a quick method of checking on the plausibility of any time series of figures of church or population growth. One simply plots the claimed growth figures on a graph (vertical logarithmic axis) against time (horizontal axis). The resulting lines will have to be reasonably linear, or slightly curvilinear, to be credible or plausible. In this sense, log paper is a far more valuable analytical tool than ordinary graph paper.

*Demographic inertia*

Before proceeding to analyze annual change into the 2 major component parts utilized in this survey, we should note an important principle affecting the growth and evolution of populations; large populations only change their basic characteristics gradually or slowly. This demographic inertia is a concept from demography, based on the observable fact that changes in the fertility rate take several decades before they have any effect on the growth rate of a population. In fact, any time-series based on large-scale phenomena, particularly populations in the millions, will behave in a relatively stable manner. This has a useful consequence for missiographers constructing tables describing a country's religious evolution over the decades, in that a study of regular series of government censuses of religion in a country (such as Table 9 and its facing page in *1971 Census of Canada: religious denominations*, p. 9–1, for the years 1921–71) leads to an important generalization: the percentage size of a religious community or population in a country does not change appreciably over the years from one census to the next, even when total population is increasing rapidly, unless (a) large-scale conversions are taking place within the community to or from another religion, or (b) its fertility or biological increase rate is markedly different from the national average, or (c) mass emigration or immigration is under way in the community, or (d) an anti-religious revolution takes place in the country, or (e) religious belief within the community is severely eroded by secularism. In the Western world, the percentage figures for particular religions usually remain unchanged from year to year, or change relatively slowly. In the Communist world, percentages have changed little from one year to the next except as a result of anti-religious revolutions and resulting mass defections or emigrations; and in the Third World, annual increases are gradually taking place in the % Christian of many populations due to mass conversions and long-term missionary activity over the decades.

**Natural change.** Biological change. Claire Elizabeth, infant of 2 Anglican believers, is baptized at All Saints Cathedral, Nairobi in January 1976. All churches experience such biological growth.

*Natural change*

The total annual numerical change (growth or decline) of a religious body or grouping in a particular country is composed of 2 quite different types of change which it is important to identify and to separate. The first is (1) *natural change*, which is change as experienced by the whole population of the country concerned, including all religious bodies, and over which religious bodies have, relatively, little or no control. This natural or demographic change is itself composed of 2 parts, (a) biological change (in UN terminology, 'natural' increase or decrease), which is change due to natural causes properly so called, i.e. the annual net aggregate of births to members of the body minus deaths in it; together with (b) migration change (sometimes termed transfer change), which is the annual net aggregate of immigration into the body (arrival or transfer of members or co-religionists from other countries) minus emigration out of it (departure or transfer of members or co-religionists to other countries). Natural change, consisting of these 2 types together, has been calculated for each country in the world in the biennial UN publication, *World population prospects*, (New York: UN). All churches in all parts of the world experience biological increase nowadays, though rarely are they aware of it as a cause of their growth. All churches also experience on a small scale the continual ebb and flow of migration, as their members move from one country to another, but in only a few cases is the migration change large enough to warrant comparison with biological change. In all Country Tables 1, these net annual changes are shown for all religions as well as countries in the column 'Natural' under 'Annual change, 1990–2000'. When a figure in this column is negative, it means either that deaths are outstripping births, or that nett emigration is outstripping any natural biological increase, or some combination thereof.

*Conversion change*

The natural change just described involves no change in religious allegiance or adherence; from the churches' point of view, it is 'natural' because it represents the state of affairs existing before religious conversions take place. There is therefore a second type of change which occurs when changes in religious allegiance or adherence do take place, i.e. when people leave one religion and join another. Depending on the observer's point of view, this can be called unnatural, non-natural or even supranatural or supernatural change. In this survey, we term it (2) *conversion change*, defined here as consisting entirely of changes in religious allegiance, i.e. the annual nett aggregate of conversions to the body of new adherents from other religions or religious bodies, minus defections (sometimes termed apostasies) from it of former adherents leaving to join other religions or religious bodies, or abandoning religion altogether. A large majority of churches in the Third World are experiencing conversion increase nowadays, whilst in the Western world many older denominations are experiencing conversion decrease as former members withdraw from affiliation, usually into nonreligion. In all Country Tables 1, these net annual changes are shown for all countries and religions in the column 'Conversion' under 'Annual change, 1990-2000'.

It should be carefully noted that our category 'conversions' does not carry here exactly the same theological and evangelistic connotations usually attributed to the term in Christian parlance and scholarship. Rather, our term refers to transfers of allegiance from one religion to another, or from one Christian bloc to another, or or from one type of Christian (e.g. 'affiliated') to another (e.g. 'unaffiliated'), or from religious to nonreligious, and so on. 'Conversion' here includes changes of religious profession due to mixed marriages, one of the commonest causes where Islam and other world religions are involved with Christianity.

### Total = natural + conversion
By asking, then, how much of the total annual change experienced by any particular religious body is due to natural biological causes, how much is due to migration, and how much is due to changes of religious allegiance or adherence, we arrive at the formula for annual change in the body:

**Total change = natural change + conversion change.**

In all Country Tables 1, these 3 types are given for all major religious groupings, giving the totals shown there for all countries and the totals for regions, continents and for the world shown in Part 10 "GeoStatistics".

In order therefore to assess whether a church or religious grouping is expanding by conversions or accretions and not simply by natural causes, we must compare its total growth rate with its biological or natural increase rate.

### Differential fertility, mortality and migration
Because data are rarely available for religious bodies or groupings concerning the actual increase rate due to biological causes (births minus deaths), the assumption has been made in Country Tables 1 that all groups share the same natural increase rate as the national average, unless evidence to the contrary is available. In fact, certain groups have higher fertility than the average (e.g. Irish Roman Catholics in Britain; Blacks in the USA; Roman Catholics in 20th-century Switzerland and Holland; Muslims across Black Africa); and certain Christian bodies in certain countries in certain eras have experienced markedly-reduced mortality compared to that of the general population, due to the introduction of Western medicine (e.g. churches linked to Western missions in India and other developing nations). In general, however, our assumption is adequate for the tables' main purpose of establishing broad areas of magnitude. In the same way, unless specific information is available concerning the migration rate in religious blocs, this is assumed to parallel that of the nation or country. In several countries, however, for churches or blocs where these rates are vastly different from the national averages, higher fertility or different migration rates for certain religious groups have been included in Country Tables 1.

### Hidden changes
An inevitable property of overall compilations of totals such as our Country Tables 1 and 2 is that many smaller internal increases or decreases are hidden or masked. Rapid growth of one body may be hidden in a government census if combined with rapid decline of another body of the same religion or ecclesiastical tradition, or in a different geographical area. Our column 'Annual change' in Country Tables 1 therefore shows not the entire picture of change but only the net losses or gains of each religion or religious bloc.

### All totals are net (nett)
As mentioned at various points above, it must again be remembered that all of our totals of change shown in the tables are net (often spelt 'nett') totals, i.e. gains of all kinds (convesions/births/immigrants) minus loss-es of all kinds (defections/deaths/emigrants).

### Massive increases may be spurious
During our analysis of existing compilations of church

growth data, we have occasionally found apparently large recorded increase rates for specific churches. On investigation these have proved to be spurious, being the results simply of better and more thorough data collection over the years. Such spurious increases have then been amended and replaced in our tables.

### A general idea of conversion
The whole object of the column 'Conversion' in WCE Country Tables 1 is to give a very general idea of the broad order of magnitude of the long-term trends in religious change going on in the country during the decade 1990–2000. The figures given here add up to zero for each country, because conversions to one religion or religious grouping must always mean defections or losses from another religion or religious grouping. By examining this column, it is therefore possible to see where converts are coming from. For example, if Protestants are gaining 100,000 converts a year, and tribal religionists are losing 100,000 a year, and all other groups experience few or no conversions a year, then this is a clear case of a mass movement from tribal religion to Protestantism.

As will shortly be explained, the column 'conversion' was not derived by direct measurement but was derived indirectly by computation. In order to keep the mathematics exact, the figures in the 3 columns under 'Annual change, 1990–2000' are all given to the nearest digit, so that the columns and rows add up exactly; however, this must not be taken to imply any claim to bogus precision. A figure such as '1,937' under 'Conversion', therefore, should be taken to mean, and should be quoted to imply, only that something of the order of 2 thousand people a year are joining that religion or grouping.

### Analyzing annual baptisms
Another way of measuring religious change, this time for a single church or denomination, comes from analyzing statistics of annual baptisms. For a large number of churches, these data are presented in Country Tables 2, column 10, and from them it is possible to see to what extent a church or denomination is keeping up with, or exceeding, or falling behind, the natural population increase (in the case of adult baptisms) and/or the birth rate (in the case of infant baptisms). To do this (for churches practicing only adult baptism), divide the annual number of adult baptisms (coded Y in column 10) by column 6 (adult members); or (for churches practicing infant baptisms (coded y in column 10) by column 8 (total affiliated). The resulting rate, expressed as a % per year, can then be compared with, respectively, either the national natural population increase rate, or the national birth rate. If a church provides only figures for both adult and infant baptisms combined (as is usually the case with the Roman Catholic Church; coded Yy in column 10), and if this rate is appreciably higher than the birth rate in the country, then it means that substantial adult baptisms are taking place. At the national level, the annual religious change indicated by these data on baptisms for all churches is incorporated here in Country Tables 1 in the 2 columns 'Natural' and 'Conversion' increase.

### Statistics of new charismatic movements
In many parts of the world, new Christian movements are beginning and growing rapidly, the largest example being the global neo-pentecostal and charismatic movements within the major older denominations. Such groups have little time or opportunity for self-analysis, and usually keep neither statistics nor exact membership lists. Further, many movements exist within the structures of older denominations, value their close relations with them, and oppose the collecting of statistics as tending to artificially crystallize their identity and to appear to divide charismatics from their non-charismatic fellow-Christians. It must be emphasized here, therefore, that such statistics as we provide in this survey serve merely as an aid to understanding the order of magnitude of the situation and its rapid evolution over the years, and should not be construed as conferring a separate or separatist identity on such movements.

### More elaborate analyses
Our analysis of religious change shown in Country Tables 1 in the 4 columns 'Annual change' gives an overall general idea of the dynamics of change in any country. In this survey, we have not gone into detail further than this. However, by subdividing the first

2 columns into 15 columns, the reader interested in more detailed analysis of any Christian bloc (Roman Catholic, Anglican, etc) can generate more elaborate tables to indicate even more clearly what is going on. In the expanded format shown, our 4 basic columns from Country Tables 1 in this survey are shown as, respectively, the new columns 8, 15, 16 and 17. 'Natural change' as defined in this survey can be divided into (a) 'Biological change' (Births minus 'Deaths') and (b) 'Migration change' or transfer change ('Immigrants' of the same Christian bloc who come into the area or grouping from another country, minus 'Emigrants' who leave the religion or grouping not by defection but by moving or being transferred to another country, these 2 categories encompassing adults, children and infants together). In the same way, Country Table 1's column 'Conversion change' can be divided into 'Converts' (total all individuals gained from other religions) and 'Defections' (total all individuals lost to other religions or to no religion); and 'Converts' can be subdivided into 'Adults' and 'Children and infants'. It is also possible at this point to introduce, with due care, churches' statistics of annual baptisms (both adult and infant), so that one may compare and correlate annual baptisms or conversion figures with the more generalized church growth figures given in Country Tables 1. Normally, infant baptisms relate solely to the infants enumerated in 'Births' below; and adult baptisms relate mainly to persons converted from outside. However, there are 2 major exceptions to this. (1) In the case of a paedobaptist or infant-baptizing church which is making many converts from outside, a number of infant baptisms will be of children of these new converts, which we have located below as column 12. Such a church's statistics of infant baptisms must therefore be apportioned between columns 1 and 12. (2) Likewise, in the case of a church which baptizes adults only (not infants) and which is relatively static, i.e. not making converts from outside, all of its baptisms are of existing church children only, i.e. children of long-standing members, who have grown up in the church over the years, but who were not baptized in infancy; these we have located below in column 10. Such a church's statistics of adult baptisms must therefore be apportioned between columns 9 and 10. This can be done by dividing the total of adult baptisms into the 2 further columns 'Outsiders' i.e. baptisms of persons previously completely outside the Christian bloc in question until their baptism this year, and 'Grown church children' (children of long-standing church members in traditions not practicing infant baptism, who have now reached the age of adult baptism, usually 10–15 years old), These latter should not strictly speaking be termed as 'Converts' but they are included here because 'Adult baptisms' in toto are often so termed.

Other refinements might include investigating differential fertility, mortality and migration, as described above. If these data can be found for each religion and bloc under consideration, the analysis could be made more exact.

In particular countries, the reader may wish to subdivide these columns even further, for instance by sex into males and females, or by age-groups, or by socio-economic groups, or by occupational groups, or by ethnic or linguistic groups, etc. If the data are available, the scope for more elaborate analyses, and therefore for deeper understanding of the whole process, is endless.

### ANALYZING WORLD STATISTICS

Statistics of Christians and of all religions in WCE Part 4 (Country Tables 1 and 2) are arranged and coded in such a way that the reader can follow any or all of 5 main types of worldwide analysis, and 13 sub-types, depending on whichever are of interest or are valid to him, using the geopolitical and religious typologies and data in Table 12-1. The first 2 types below apply only to affiliated Christians in Country Tables 2; the rest apply to both Country Tables 1 and 2. World totals are shown analyzed in these ways in Part 1; regional and continental totals are shown analyzed in Part 10.

### 1. Ecclesiastical analysis
An important part of any description of a church or denomination is what its ecclesiastical tradition is. This information is given for each country for all de-

**Table 14–9. Delineation of the world's 6 major ecclesiastico-cultural megablocs.**

| MEGABLOC or stream of Christianity | CODE | BEGUN AD | WORLD SPIRITUAL HQs | INITIATING OR DOMINANT PEOPLES Peoples | Family | Race | Color | PREDOMINANT WORLDS Political | Developed | Missions |
|---|---|---|---|---|---|---|---|---|---|---|
| 1. Orthodoxy | O | 33 | Constantinople, Moscow, &c | Greeks, Slavs, Russians | Slavic | European | White | Ex-Communist | More | Stagnant |
| 2. Roman Catholicism | R | 33 | Rome | Italians, Latin Americans | Latin | European | White | Western | More | Sending |
| 3. Anglicanism | A | 61 | Canterbury, London | English, British | Germanic | European | White | Western | More | Sending |
| 4. Protestantism | P | 690 | Geneva, New York, &c | Germans, American Whites | Germanic | European | White | Western | More | Sending |
| 5. Independency | I | 1549 | In all globe's capitals | Blacks, Asiatics, Whites, &c | All families | All races | All colors | Third | Less | Receiving |
| 6. Marginal Christianity | m | 1566 | Boston, Brooklyn, Utah, &c | American Whites | Germanic | European | White | Western | More | Sending |

nominations in Country Table 2, column 3 (the last 3 letters). This column lists in coded form some 300 different ecclesiastical traditions (detailed in "GeoCodebook", Part 16), and world statistics of affiliated Christians are analyzed in this way in Part 10.

**2. Conciliar analysis**
In Country Tables 2, column 4, information is given on the membership of the 5 main types of Christian council—confessional, global, continental, regional and national (see GeoCodebook). Christians throughout the world can therefore be analyzed according to the involvement or non-involvement of their churches in the different councils existing across the world; this also is done in Part 10.

**3. Geopolitico-religious analysis**
A major type of analysis is by groups of countries. There are many possible ways of classifying the 238 countries of the world, using geopolitical, or politico-religious, or purely religious typologies. In this book, we employ 10 sub-types of typologies based on 10 subjects; these will shortly be described. The codes used for them are given in the GeoCodebook, and the information describing each country is given in Table 16-1. Using these typologies, Christians are analyzed in the global Tables in Part 10.

**4. Ethnolinguistic analysis**
In analyzing the world's populations, it is important to see people not only as citizens or residents in a particular country, but also to see them as members of the basic homogeneous units to which they belong, and which usually have greater emotional hold over them than the tie of common citizenship. If we can see them thus, they can then more effectively be understood, described, enumerated, approached, reached, known, evangelized and eventually christianized. Such units are people of similar ethnic origin, or of similar race or color, or of similar culture, or of similar language, and so on. We do this in this book by employing an ethnolinguistic typology of homogeneous units, or of families or groupings of homogeneous units. Most of the ethnolinguistic units we employ can themselves be broken down further into yet more meaningful homogeneous units. The right place to do this, however, is not in a global survey such as ours but in detailed studies at the national and local level.

In the same way, Christians also may be classified according to their racial, ethnic, cultural and linguistic as well as national affiliations. This is done in Country Tables 2, column 10, for many individual churches, denominations and dioceses. It is also done for the Christian community as a whole using the classification and code given in WCE Part 8 "Ethnosphere' (Peoples of the World). Parallel data on the total secular population are given at the start of each country's survey article under Secular Data. In consequence, the world's populations, and all Christians, can be analyzed among the world's major ethnolinguistic homogeneous units, its families and peoples.

*SIX MAJOR ECCLESIASTICO-CULTURAL MEGABLOCS*

**5. Ecclesiastico-cultural analysis**
A further, fifth, type of description brings us, finally, to a typology of Christians which is the most widely used by observers and scholars but which is also the least clearly defined. As a result we will now describe it in detail at this point, because we will have to coin and justify certain neologisms which will then be used throughout the book.

It has long been considered useful for many purposes to divide the world's Christians into major his-

torico-cultural ecclesiastical megablocs, coalitions or ongoing or enduring streams, based on historical, ecclesiastical, cultural and phenomenological considerations. Of such major ecclesiastico-cultural megablocs, the most widely recognized and used are the trio (1) *Roman Catholicism*, (2) *Orthodoxy* (both Eastern and Oriental), and (3) *Protestantism*. These are major de facto groupings which have arisen during the course of Christian history among peoples of different cultural areas and nationalities. Although often regarded as worldwide spiritual families, these blocs are not the result of merely religious or theological or spiritual affinities or differences; they incorporate deep nationalistic, ethnic, linguistic and cultural currents as well, as is illustrated from the early history of the Oriental Orthodox churches: 'Adherence to completely incomprehensible dogmas, like the espousal of the Monophysite doctrine by great masses of people in the Orient and in Egypt, was the expression of an anti-imperial and anti-Hellenic separatist nationalism' (Max Weber, *The sociology of religion*, Boston: Beacon, 1963:70–1). These 3 megablocs are in fact differentiated by many such complex factors.

In any comprehensive survey of how Christians regard themselves, however, it soon becomes apparent that there are many large churches and denominations which do not define themselves under any of these 3 terms, and often reject all three. Since they thus cannot be fitted into the simple 3-fold typology, it means that yet other megablocs must exist. Anglicans, for instance, do not regard themselves, as a whole, as either Protestants or Catholics, but regard themselves as forming an intermediate or bridge tradition; Jehovah's Witnesses do not regard themselves as Protestants or as part of main-line Protestantism; and Old Catholics reject any identity with Roman Catholicism. Consequently our survey recognizes the existence of 3 further distinct worldwide megablocs or distinct enduring streams of Christianity: (4) *Anglicanism* (mainly the Anglican Communion and its 700 dioceses, originating in Britain around AD 100 and evolving since the 16th century its distinctive 'bridge' position intermediate between the Protestant and Roman Catholic positions), (5) *Independency*, which refers to the many churches or movements that are independent of historic Christianity (categories 1-4 above), and which are also termed Postdenominationalist, Restorationist, Radical, Neocharismatic movements, also Old Believers and other schisms from Orthodoxy, and Old Catholics and other autocephalous Catholic churches; and (6) *marginal Christians* (para-Christian, quasi-Christian or tangentially-Christian deviations from mainline Christianity claiming a second or supplementary or ongoing source of divine revelation in addition to the Bible, either a new revealed Book, or angelic visitations. or visions; these date from 1566 to the present day and include Unitarians, Jehovah's Witnesses, Christian Scientists, Mormons and vast numbers of other more recent movements).

Between them, these 6 megablocs cover all varieties of Christianity found in the Middle East, Europe, North America, Africa, Asia, Latin America, and Oceania.

*Caucasian-initiated Christianity*
Throughout its history, Christianity as represented by these 6 types or megablocs or streams has been predominantly the religion of the Caucasian or Caucasoid race of peoples, as defined here in our classification Peoples of the World, covering the Semitic, European, Indo-Iranian and related races. Caucasians have always exceeded 85% of all Christians until well into the 20th century, as is tabulated here in Part 1. By 1900 they were still 89%. Furthermore, throughout the last millennium Christianity has been pre-

dominantly the religion of the White peoples, rising from 61% of all Christians in the year 1000 to 93% in 1500 and only gradually falling to 81% by 1900.

In order to better understand and analyze this 6-fold typology of Christians, it is helpful to consider the evolution of Christianity in terms of its indigeneity or indigenousness, i.e. in terms of the main races and peoples among whom it has arisen as an indigenous religious movement. Indigenous churches are those that are native to a people, belonging naturally to the soil as contrasted with churches originating abroad or in an alien culture (*Little Oxford dictionary*). From this point of view, the history of Christianity and the current phenomenon of world Christianity can be described in terms of 3 distinct phases or groupings of indigenous churches, namely those related to Semitic, White, and Non-White peoples respectively. These will now be described in turn.

*1. Indigenous Christianity among Semitic peoples*
Christianity began in the 1st century among the Semitic peoples of the Middle East (defined here as Caucasians of the Middle Eastern geographical race). Four powerful Semitic indigenous church traditions resulted: Syrian Orthodox (later Arab), Coptic Orthodox (later Arab), Ancient Church of the East (Assyrian, later Nestorian), and in the 4th century AD, Ethiopian Orthodox (Amharic). Although dominant at the end of the 1st century AD (70% of all Christians) and numbering 38 million Christians by AD 500, these Semitic traditions later declined drastically to under 5% of all Christians by 1500 and to only 2% by 1650. Today their influence is relatively small (23 million Christians or 1.2% of the world total) and emanates from headquarters in the Arab world (Damascus, Cairo, Beirut, Baghdad) and in the racially-Caucasian Amharic world (Addis Ababa).

Semitic indigenous churches, as currently in existence, may therefore be defined as those original ancient churches among the Semitic peoples dating from the 1st–5th centuries AD which are still in existence today as distinct denominations completely Semitic in membership and leadership (Syrian Orthodox, Coptic Orthodox, Ethiopian Orthodox, Assyrian Orthodox), excluding those originally Semitic churches which have long since become predominantly White in membership and leadership (Catholic, Eastern Orthodox, etc).

*2. Indigenous Christianity among White peoples*
Europeans, the so-called White peoples, were present on the Day of Pentecost in AD 30 (proselytes from Rome, Cretans and others from Asia Minor—Acts 2:10–11). From then on they numbered about 5% of all Christians, rising by AD 100 to around 30% and 38% by AD 500. By AD 1000, Whites numbered 61% of all Christians, and the focus and center of gravity of Christianity's expansion had moved north and northwest into Europe, and it has remained there ever since. As a result, all of the first 4 ecclesiastico-cultural megablocs above are today predominantly European in origin, history, culture, theology, ideology, psychology, ethos, influence, numerical significance, church organization, membership and leadership. From the point of view of race, their members belong predominantly to the European geographical race (including North America). From the point of view of colour, they are predominantly Whites. From the political point of view, all are predominantly centered either in the Western world or in the former Communist world, and have their world spiritual headquarters and centers there. And from the developmental point of view, their main centers are predominantly in the richer and more developed countries.

This European or White Caucasian origin can readily be seen when one considers the origin, and place

# NON-WHITE—INITIATED CHRISTIANITY
### (Non-White indigenous churches)

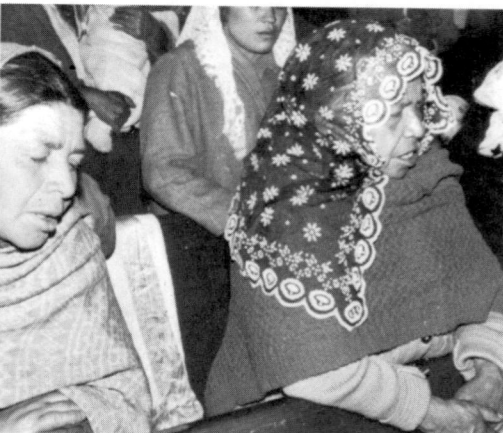

**Amerindian indigenous Christians.** Otomi Indians speaking in tongues in 350,000-strong Independent Pentecostal Christian Church, in Puchuca, Mexico.

**African indigenous Christians.** Pope and cardinals of Maria Legio of Africa (a schism ex Rome) in State House, Nairobi, with Cabinet Minister Hon. Tom Mboya (3rd from left), 1966.

**Latin American indigenous Christians.** Manoel de Mello, founder of 1.5 million-member OBPC (Brazil for Christ), in charismatic blessing of loaves before communion.

**Pacific indigenous Christians.** Member of Ratana Church (also Maori member of parliament) addresses NC-CNZ (National Council of Churches in New Zealand) in Maori meeting house in Christchurch.

**Asian indigenous Christians.** World headquarters of True Jesus Church in Taichung (Taiwan), which sends Chinese missionaries across the world.

*Above* **Caribbean indigenous Christians.** First United Church of Jesus Christ (Apostolic) in Birmingham (UK): members are Jesus-Only pentecostal emmigrants from Jamaica's Bethel Apostolic (Shilo) Church.
*Right* **Black indigenous Christians** (USA). Church of God in Christ (Black pentecostals): District and Field Worker missionaries of Eastern Louisiana (USA) with Supervisor, Mother McGregor Jones, in New Orleans.

and date of origin, of each megabloc, and the ongoing influence exerted by each. These can be rearranged by chronological order of their emergence, as follows. (1) *Orthodoxy* arose as 2 separate branches. Eastern Orthodoxy worldwide traces its origin to the Holy Land itself and in our Country Tables 2 to AD 30; it still looks to Constantinople (the Second Rome) in European Turkey and Moscow (the Third Rome) in European Russia. The smaller grouping of Oriental Orthodoxy, which also traces its origin to AD 30 as shown in Country Tables 2, may be divided into a White part, with the Armenian Apostolic church having its headquarters in Echmiadzin in Armenia; and a Non-White although still Caucasian part, as we have seen above, consisting of the Semitic indigenous churches—the Syrian Orthodox, Coptic Orthodox, Ethiopian Orthodox, and Assyrian traditions with their headquarters in the racially-Caucasian Semitic world (Damascus, Cairo, Addis Ababa, Baghdad, Beirut). Numerically these Non-White traditions are outnumbered 7 to one by the White Orthodox traditions. (2) *Roman Catholicism* worldwide traces its origin to Rome in the 1st century AD (its earliest beginnings being traced in our Country Tables 2 to AD 30) and is still controlled, guided and inspired from its centre in Vatican City, Rome, in Italy. (3) *Anglicanism* worldwide traces its origins (as Country Tables 2 document) to Britain in AD 61, and to this day it still takes its inspiration from Canterbury and London, in England. (4) *Protestantism* worldwide is usually dated back to the 16th-century European Reformation in Geneva and Wittenberg, but, as our Country Tables 2 make clear, its origins in several of the major Protestant churches of Northern Europe go back in unbroken continuity a further 900 years, in fact to at least AD 690; as a bloc it continues to be inspired by German and Scandinavian Lutheranism, by the Dutch and Swiss Reformed traditions, by English Methodism, by the North American Baptist tradition, and a number of other White-initiated traditions. (5) *Independency* traces its origins in part to Old Catholicism in 1724 in the Netherlands and 1863 in Germany, and is still centered on Utrecht in Holland and (Catholic Apostolics) on Zurich in Switzerland; also to Old Believers in Russia; also to many other all-White movements. Lastly, (6) *Marginal Christians* originated in Romania with the Unitarians in 1566, and today it has its major worldwide power centers in the USA (Brooklyn, Boston, Salt Lake City, etc).

Since 1800, and over the last 100 years in particular, these 6 megablocs have all demonstrated their vitality and initiative by expanding out from their bases in Europe and North America across the world to the Non-White races; and the churches begun there are still to a greater or lesser extent under their control or influence. The vitality and initiative of this missionary expansion have been, once again, predominantly from among the White races in European and North American churches.

The historical fact of European or White origin, initiative and ongoing influence must not however be equated with, or construed as, White imperialism or White racism. Non-Whites play important roles in these 6 megablocs, firstly as members of their churches in Europe and North America, secondly as members and leaders of their daughter churches across the world, and thirdly through initiating new movements which remain within those churches (for example, the East African Revival movement within the Anglican and Protestant churches, or the large numbers of new African religious congregations for priests, brothers and sisters begun by Africans within the Roman Catholic Church). Despite all this, however, the overarching ethos remains both European and White; and the Black and Non-White daughter churches which have resulted, although in the case of almost all the largest churches now completely in the hands of local leadership, are still sufficiently close to their parent bodies (and often closely tied to them or controlled by them or influenced by them in theology, ideology, polity and organization) for it to be correct to call them also, as they call themselves, by the terms Roman Catholic, or Protestant, or Anglican, or Orthodox.

In sum, then, the 6 major megablocs described above can still be described as predominantly Caucasian initiatives in origin, predominantly European and North American initiatives in origin, predominantly White initiatives indigenous to the White peoples in origin, predominantly found in the richer and more developed countries, and predominantly based in the Western and formerly Communist worlds of today.

### *3. Indigenous Christianity among Black and Third-World peoples*

As far back as 1549 (Japan) and 1741 (USA), however, new types of Christianity have emerged that do not fit readily into any of the first 4 major megablocs, and since 1900 they have rapidly become numerically increasingly significant on the world scale. These consist of denominations, churches and movements that have been initiated, founded, operated, led, controlled and spread not by Caucasian Whites or Europeans from today's Western or former Communist worlds but by Black, Non-White or Non-European peoples from most of the major geographical races of what is now termed the Third World—Africans, Afro-Americans, American Indians, Asiatics, Mestizos, Northern Indians, Oceanic Negroes—with no dependence on European or North American White initiative, leadership, control, assistance or ties. In most cases these Black or Non-White bodies have been begun as schisms or secessions from, or have otherwise severed their relations with, White denominations belonging to the 4 Europe-initiated megablocs. Of these schisms the vast majority have broken off from Protestantism, although sizeable numbers have split from Roman Catholicism and Anglicanism, with some from the Orthodox megabloc also. The main characteristic common to all these bodies, and that which enables us to see in them a single, coherent new major megabloc or stream parallel to the other 4, is that all were *begun on Black, Non-White or Non-European initiative, in Third-World countries or among Non-White or Non-European* minorit*ies elsewhere*, and since the year 1500. Subsequent to their Black or Third-World origin, they have had their own history; they remain without predominant White or Western control, influence or ties; they have Black or Third-World types of theology; and they have initiated their own foreign missions to many nations. This megabloc or stream covers all Christian movements initiated anywhere by Non-Whites or Non-Europeans, without European assistance, mainly in the Third World but also among Black and Non-White minorities in the Western world. It includes the following: the African indigenous churches (African independent churches movement); similar independent or separatist churches in China, India, Indonesia, Japan, Korea, Latin America, the Philippines, and other Third-World countries; indigenous Christian movements in Oceania; American Indian indigenous churches in North America; Black indigenous churches in the Caribbean; and the Black churches of North America.

The Black churches of North America are particularly interesting in this connection because until recently they have always been classified as a part of North American Protestantism, and sometimes as little more than an unorthodox peripheral fringe around it. An examination of the magnitude of their statistics however suggests that this is an unsatisfactory assessment. In 1970, there were 22,580,000 Blacks (Negroes) in the USA; of these, 95% professed to be Christians (62% Baptists, 17% Methodists, 4% Roman Catholics, 1% Episcopalians, 1% Presbyterians, 1% Lutherans, with 9% independents and others), 1% Jews, 1% Muslims, and 3% non-religious. The total of all Blacks affiliated to churches was about 20,770,000 (92% of the total Black population), of whom only about 8% of all Blacks were in predominantly-White denominations (800,000 Roman Catholics, 500,000 United Methodists, 130,000 SDAs, 95,000 Southern Baptists, 65,000 Episcopalians, etc), and even then were usually found in separate Black churches and denominations which have separated or split from White churches over the preceding 200 years. These Black-led schisms were originally begun to liberate Black Christians from the effects of Protestant White racism, and today they continue as Black initiatives under Black leadership without dependence on White churches, creating their own distinctive forms of Christianity often related to their African religious heritage. The contrast can be expressed thus: White Protestant churches emphasize the literary tradition, formalized theology, and word-oriented or verbalistic worship; the Black churches emphasize emotion, soul, spontaneous non-literary spirituality, Black oral theology, and Black religious music (Negro Spirituals). Although the oldest of these churches (AMEC, AMEZC, NBCUSA, NBCA) have much in common with their White Protestant counterparts, many newer ones (including all Black pentecostals) have very little in common. Rather than being part of Protestantism, the Black pentecostals of the USA 'belong phenomenologically to the non-literary type of communication of the Third World while living in the literary culture of America' (W.J. Hollenweger. *The Black pentecostals' contribution to the church universal*, Geneva: WCC, 1970:11). So then, rather than to continue labeling these Black churches as Protestant, it would be preferable to regard them as sui generis or a new expression of Christianity and to coin a neologism to describe them. Within this new grouping, the AMEC and other older bodies thus would form a Protestant-type wing closer to Protestantism, and the pentecostals an African-type wing closer to their Third-World parallels.

In the same way, although many other Non-European churches in other countries have arisen out of and broken off from world Protestantism, they cannot properly still be called Protestant, and they themselves usually reject the term. Further bodies have broken off from one or other of the 3 other major megablocs, and these also cannot now properly still be called 'Roman Catholic', 'Anglican', 'Orthodox', etc. At the same time, the total adherents of all such bodies have by the year 2000 become numerically so significant (161 million) that they must be taken seriously as a new entity. So far it remains as a somewhat amorphous entity, with as little in common between component parts as is the case with Protestantism itself; and so far there is little awareness of being an entity and no interest as yet in any kind of international meeting together, conferring or organizing. Nevertheless, the fact is that we are faced here with, at least in embryo, and an entirely new historico-cultural major Christian megabloc.

It is important too to note that this megabloc, like the other 5, should not be considered as primarily a racist grouping, although racial in composition. Although Non-White, it is not anti-White. In many ways its churches are open to the White world. A growing number (e.g. the Black churches in Jamaica) send missionaries to White countries, and they and many other (e.g. the South African healing churches) attract sizeable numbers of White members and converts.

The problem arises of what to call this new ecclesiastico-cultural megabloc. Whatever new terminology we attempt tentatively to coin and employ, there will always be critics. In the first place, there is no recognized ethnic or cultural term to refer collectively to the peoples outside Europe and North America, or all peoples other than the White peoples, and so the analyst who needs a single term has to resort (as we have had to above) to the somewhat negative terms 'Non-European' and 'Non-White'. Both these terms are unacceptable in many circles, since they define people negatively in terms of what they are not; to overcome this difficulty, we therefore coin, to parallel them, the somewhat cumbrous term Black/Third-World, referring to peoples native to the Third/World and to the Black race in particular. We will still have occasionally to use the term Non-White in its technically correct descriptive sense, for example when referring collectively to Black and Chinese and Amerindian churches or peoples; for this reason, therefore, we use it capitalized (Non-White). Secondly, we cannot use terms like 'Schismatic', 'Separatist' or 'Secessionist' because many of the movements we are analyzing began de novo as new revival movements without schism or radical break, and also because such terms cannot be applied exclusively to Non-White movements since sizeable numbers of White schisms and secessions take place every year within the European-initiated megablocs. Other terms like Sundkler's South African typology Zionist/Ethiopian/Messianic are not sufficiently general to apply to more than local parts of this bloc.

## *DELINEATING THE INDEPENDENT MEGABLOC*

### *A new multiracial global megabloc emerges*

At this point, a completely new solution has presented itself with the meteoric rise since the 1960s of White-led Postdenominationalist churches and networks across Europe and America. It is now evident that, like the Non-White churches just described, these new bodies are characterized by the same basic term, Independency, which can now be defined as *independent of historic Christianity* whether Orthodox,

Catholic, Anglican, or Protestant. Moreover, it is now widely recognized that these White-led churches are following closely in the paths of the pioneering development of the African indigenous independent churches since 1815, the Asian indigenous independent churches since 1549, the Amerindian indigenous independent churches since 1741, and the Oceanic indigenous independent churches since 1867; as well as the Old Believers since 1666, and the Old Catholics since 1724.

This newly-recognized ecclesiastico-cultural megabloc has now become an immense presence across the world, with over 386 million church members.

*Locally-founded indigenous churches*. Another term widely used in the literature describing these movements is 'indigenous'. Correctly used, this word means 'originating or developing or produced naturally in a particular land or region or environment... not introduced directly or indirectly from the outside' (*Webster's third new international dictionary*, 1971). Indigenous churches may be defined as those originating within a country or race or people, or produced naturally by nationals of that country or members of that race or people, as opposed to churches of foreign or alien origin imported from abroad or introduced from outside the group, such as immigrant churches or mission-related churches. As used and defined here, this term says nothing about whether or not the peoples involved are indigenous to, or the original inhabitants of, the country they happen to be in; the term refers only to the production of Christian movements within their midst. The term also refers, further, only to churches of indigenous tradition; thus if the Roman Catholic or Anglican or Lutheran or Methodist church was begun in a particular country by native evangelists of that country (themselves indigenous to that country), we still term them in this survey Roman Catholic or Anglican or Protestant, etcetera; their resulting churches being of foreign rather than indigenous origin and composition.

Indigenous churches are therefore, and are increasingly called today, locally-founded churches. Indigenous churches as defined thus can, strictly speaking, be either European or non-European, White or Black, although in the literature the predominant tendency has up to now been, for reasons of historical development, to limit the term to the Black and Non-White races. White secessionist churches in many cases regard themselves as having a similar tradition to their parent bodies, albeit purified and reformed; by contrast, Third-World schismatic churches sit loosely to the denominational tradition or bloc of their parent bodies; they regard themselves as no longer Catholic, or Protestant, or Anglican, but as part of a new indigenous and independent bloc. Nevertheless, all of these groups in this new megabloc can properly be called indigenous churches because they were begun in their own countries or among their own peoples by nationals of those countries or members of those peoples. Thus the True Jesus Church is a Chinese indigenous church begun in China by Chinese in 1917; it is strong among Chinese immigrants in Malaysia and in Brazil and in the USA, where it is still correct to call it a Chinese indigenous church.

Similarly, the Black churches of the USA, all of which originated in Black-led schisms from White denominations, can properly be called Black indigenous churches in the sense that they were begun among the black population in the USA by Black people who also happened to be USA nationals. They are indigenous to the Black people of the USA (which has no bearing on the fact that Blacks are not the indigenous peoples or original inhabitants of North America). In particular, USA Black pentecostals represent an indigenous initiative of major significance in that many authorities consider that around the year 1900 they initiated the entire Pentecostal world movement, even though from 1908 onwards in the USA it split into separate Black and White parts. As a result of considerations such as this, we find that we now have several adjectives with which to describe this whole new megabloc: Independent, indigenous, largely Pentecostal/Cha-rismatic/Neocharismatic, Postdenominationalist, Restorationist, Radical, Neo-Apostolic. No one adjective by itself is sufficient, but together the 9 are adequate to differentiate the bloc from the preceding 5 blocs.

In this survey, therefore, we term this new bloc *Independent Christianity*. On our definition, it consists of 2 distinct miniblocs, the first being (1) *Black or Non-White or Non-European churches* begun anywhere in the Third World or among Non-European or Non-White minorities in the Western world. It consists of churches all of which were formed by Non-Europeans since the year 1500, beginning in 1549 in Japan and 1741 in the USA but mostly since 1900, without European assistance or aid and often in the face of European opposition or hostility. It covers and includes African indigenous churches, Amerindian indigenous, Asian indigenous, Black indigenous, Chinese indigenous, Coloured indigenous (in Southern Africa), Filipino indigenous, Indian indigenous (in India), Indonesian indigenous, Japanese indigenous, Korean indigenous, Latin American (Mestizo) indigenous, Oceanic or Pacific indigenous, and other Third-World indigenous churches. It also includes their foreign missions working abroad in other countries.

This new megabloc also consists of (2) *White-led or White-initiated Postdenominationalist churches*, largely begun recently or long after the Non-White movements, rapidly expanding and with missionary links across most countries of the world.

For convenience when discussing these movements in their own contexts we usually refer to them simply as 'Independent churches' in contrast to the Orthodox, Roman Catholic, Anglican, or Protestant churches anywhere which often appear in those contexts as foreign, foreign-originated or foreign-dominated bodies.

In terms of our ethnolinguistic classification Peoples of the World (*WCE* Part 8), this new category of 'indigenous churches' refers to churches formed since AD 1500 and indigenous to any and all peoples and ethnolinguistic groups in any part of the world without exception.

The links between this large variety of new terms, all coined and used in this book, can best be depicted by means of the family tree in Table 16-6, column 3. Almost all these terms are, on our definition, distinct and mutually exclusive categories which do not overlap. However, certain alternative or overlapping terms are sometimes used, such as Bantu indigenous which is part of the wider term African indigenous. Some of this whole range are local ethnic terms, some are geographical, some national, some regional, some continental and one or 2 are global terms. Progressively, these latter terms describe and embrace a range of the former, with at the top our single overall term covering the whole phenomenon.

## SUMMARY CONCERNING MEGABLOCS

### Six basic Christian megablocs
To sum up, when attempting to describe and analyze the Christian world in terms of a handful of major ecclesiastico-cultural megablocs, the best criterion is to ask from whence the major or predominant initiatives and ongoing impulses came, and continue to come, and where they look to for their major or predominant world spiritual headquarters; who the initiating or dominant peoples are, and what ethnolinguistic families, races and color, and what types of world, they belong to. We then arrive at the schema used in this book in Country Tables 1 and given in coded form for all denominations in Country Tables 2, column 3, first letter. With its aid we then obtain the analysis of the world's Christians presented in Parts 1, 10, and elsewhere here.

### Description not evaluation
We should stress again that the object of this survey is primarily descriptive, i.e. to describe as accurately and objectively as possible the actual state of affairs in all significant detail. It is not our purpose here to evaluate the authenticity of particular branches of Christianity. Thus the term 'marginal Christians' coined and defined above contains many movements claiming to be Christian but which, from the standpoint of mainline Catholic, Protestant, Anglican and Orthodox theology are usually considered to be heterodox, unorthodox, quasi-Christian, even pseudo-Christian or heretical, or even not Christian at all. Examples are the many 'New Age cults' that have attained worldwide expansion in the 20th century. In this particular book we are not concerned either to expound their doctrines or to evaluate their Christian commitment, but only to point out that these movements claim to follow Jesus Christ and hence must be included in any objective world survey of the phenomenon called Christianity.

## ECCLESIASTICO-CULTURAL MINOR BLOCS

Within the first 4 of the 6 major ecclesiastico-cultural megablocs just described, there are large numbers of Christians who form distinct and clearly-defined sub-blocs or minor blocs, which in consequence are described and often also enumerated in this book. These will now be described under the 3 headings (a) popular religiosity, (b) popular piety, and (c) Charismatic and Evangelical renewals. The first 2 of these are here collectively termed popular religion, religion of the masses, or religious manifestations of the people, terms which also cover parallel phenomena in non-Christian religions. Among christianized manifestations, term (a) refers to deviant versions of popular religion of Christian background, and term (b) refers to more orthodox or recognizably-Christian versions. These various terms will now be described.

### Non-Christian popular religion
The term popular religion is generally used to cover the universal phenomenon of widespread or popular expressions or varieties of religion, including both Christian forms and also specifically non-Christian forms such as animism, Chinese folk-religion, Bhakti Hinduism, folk Hinduism, Boddhisattva Buddhism, and so on. These varieties are characterized by a deep sense of the presence of God in everything; belief in the extraordinary power of mediators (whether saints or men), rites and prayers; sacred meanings for all happenings; sacred sites and places; and the like. In our survey, we describe non-Christian popular religion in the countries where it occurs, but we give more attention to specifically-Christian or christianized forms, using the 2 terms described in the next few paragraphs.

### Popular religiosity
In numerous countries of the world, there are within the churches unusual or deviant forms of Christianity widely practiced by multitudes who are members of the majority or dominant churches, in particular the Roman Catholic Church. This phenomenon includes several varieties of mass syncretistic folk-Christianity, christo-paganism, spiritist Catholicism, cults of miracles and the miraculous and supernatural, cults of the Virgin Mary or of saints, and other manifestations described in this survey under each of the countries concerned.

These popular expressions of religion, faith, thirst for God, and the desire for worship, miracles and healings, on the part of large masses of people and especially of multitudes of the poor, are here collectively termed popular religiosity. On the negative side, this type of popular religion involves distortions of genuine Christianity through the intrusion of superstition, forms of worship without faith in Christ, marginal sects and cults, syncretism, and non-Christian beliefs and values. Great stress is put on images, medals, relics, statuettes, rosaries, shrines, magical practices and taboos, saints' days, litanies, novenas, processions, pilgrimages, associations and the like. Until recently these manifestations have been regarded only as impure or debased versions or caricatures of Christianity, hence have been despised and attacked by theologians, missionaries and churchmen. To quote Paul VI (*Evangelii Nuntiandi*, section 48), 'Popular religion... is often subject to penetration by many distortions of religion and even superstitions'. Increasingly nowadays, though, they are being reevaluated and seen as valid expressions of people's gropings for God and for genuine experience of Christ, although widely infiltrated with non-Christian forms.

Popular religiosity, then, is the term used here to describe deviant forms of Christian or christianized popular religion. Its clearest and most widespread manifestations are found in the Roman Catholic Church in most countries of Latin America. In Country Tables 1 for those countries, therefore, its followers are enumerated, using the terms Christopagans, and Spiritist Catholics (only in *WCD*).

### Popular piety
The latent Christian values in many types of popular religion are now being discovered by the churches (Roman Catholics in particular), as a result of which they are being seen to be valid expressions of peo-

# Popular religion

**POPULAR RELIGION** (see text overleaf). This world-wide phenomenon occurs in 3 varieties. (1) **Non-Christian popular religion.** *Top left.* Figurines to protect fishermen in front of new Hindu temple in Lima village, Ketam island (Malaysia). *Top right.* Islamic popular religion in Jakarta, Indonesia has 300 syncretistic Muslim sects with 55 million adherents (2) **Popular religiosity** (deviations among Roman Catholics). *Left center.* Christopaganism. Mayan shamans at work with crosses and pagan charms by and in lake Chicabal on top of volcano near Xelu (Central America)                    (continued below)

(3) **Popular piety** (devotion among Roman Catholics). Mass popular devotion to Christ Crucified under various visible representations is widespread. *Left.* (a) An Indian procession in Guatemala. *Above center.* (b) Public enactment of the Crucifixion in Mexico at Easter. *Below.* Enactments of Calvary in Africa (Kenya, 1981) and Solomon Islands.

ple's search for God, although, again, often falling short of fully-Christian doctrine and practice. Particularly notable is widespread popular devotion to the Crucified Christ under various visible representations (in Brazil, 'Senhor Bom Jesus') and other popular expressions of Catholic faith (devotion to the Madonna, etc) including more definitely-Christian versions of the list given in the last but one paragraph above. In *Evangelii Nuntiandi*, Paul VI observed of popular religion: 'It involves an acute awareness of profound attributes of God: fatherhood, providence, loving and constant presence. It engenders interior attitudes rarely observed to the same degree elsewhere: patience, the sense of the Cross in daily life, detachment, openness to others, devotion' (Section 48, 'Popular piety'). A more accurate and positive term for this phenomenon, instead of merely speaking of popular religion, is therefore the title of that section; popular piety. It should also be observed that such manifestations of popular devotion are extremely important in Eastern Europe and other formerly Communist or anti-Christian countries where the churches had long been under constant repressive pressures from the state. In our survey, these manifestations of popular piety are described for numerous countries, but since they often embrace almost the entire Christian community (in Roman Catholic countries especially), they are not separately enumerated or categorized in Country Tables 1.

***Charismatics in Renewal***

In most countries, there have arisen spiritual renewals which have crystallized out into recognizable and measurable movements today. Among older groupings are the Evangelicals (in the English usage of the term), found among Protestants and Anglicans, dating especially from the 18th century Evangelical Revival in the Church of England. Followers are enumerated here in Country Tables 1 for each country under the same term, Evangelicals. Among newer groupings, the best-known is the Charismatic Renewal at present under way since 1960 within (in chronological order of origin) the Anglican, Protestant, Roman Catholic, Old Catholic, and Orthodox traditions. Followers are enumerated here in the notes under Country Tables 1 for each country, using the terms Anglican, Catholic, Orthodox, or Protestant Charismatics.

### *SECULAR DATA FOR AD 2000*

Before every *WCE* Country Table 1, for each country, there is a selection of secular background statistical and other data, in standardized format, concerning items important for evaluating our data that follow on religion, religious change, conversion, church growth, and evangelization. Explanatory notes on most of these data now follow. Numerous sources have been utilized, including UN and UNESCO publications, others referred to below, and this book's own field work and original investigations. All figures refer to the turning point year, AD 2000. Some of the following categories appear only in *WCD*. Most data are known to change little from year to year. Figures absent in a particular country, e.g. TV receivers, or scientific journals, indicate that the item concerned is either zero or negligible in size, or, in a very few cases, of unknown size. Population natural growth rates (totals, births, deaths, migrations) refer to the total de facto (or, present-in-area) resident population, and are taken from the UN computerized population projection model given in *World population prospects, 1970–2000*, (New York: United Nations). Excluded are tourists, visitors, transients, persons in transit, and other temporary individuals or groups. By definition 'natural growth rate', % per year, is equal to the total of 3 components; crude birth rate expressed as % per year, minus crude death rate as % per year, plus nett immigration as % per year (the latter consisting of all de facto immigrants including those who become illegal residents), minus emigrants as % per year. Migration figures are given only in *WCD*.

#### STATE

**Official name**: The full official name in English (as sanctioned by the state for United Nations' usage), followed by that or those in the official languages(s) if not English. Main source: *UN Terminology Bulletin: Country names*. Member countries of the UN have official names in each of the 6 UN official languages (Arabic, Chinese, English, French, Russian, Spanish).
**Short name:** As approved by the country itself for UN usage.
**Unofficial name**: Other names in use for the nation, without official status.
**Alternative name**: Other names in use with official status.
**Earlier name**: Other names still in use unofficially, usually from colonial or pre-Independence days.
**Adjective(s) of nationality**: The officially-sanctioned adjectives, if any ( and occasionally a noun or nouns) agreed by the state and the United Nations for all official, correct usage, firstly in English, and secondly (in parentheses) in the official language of the state if not English (French, German, Italian, Portuguese, Spanish only). Note that in romance languages the adjective is always given with a lower-case first letter. If there is no entry here, there are no officially-approved adjectives, although there may be popular or commonly-used ones. Source: *UN Terminology Bulletin Country names*.
**Flag**: Design officially used as symbol of the nation; verbal description of flag as shown to right of country's name at start of country's survey article.
**Area**: Varying estimates are given by different sources; some include water areas, others do not; some include disputed territories. We give here official figures in square kilometres and in square miles. In several countries it will be noted that the 2 figures are not exactly compatible in which case each has a slightly different definition.
**Description**: A brief comment on any unusual composition, particularly in the case of numerous islands.
**Agricultural land**: Percentage of total area which is of agricultural use: arable land, land under permanent crops, permanent meadows and pastures. Source: *FAO Production yearbook*.
**Government**: Nature of present government or regime in power, with in parentheses brief sketch of historical development.
**Legislature**: Names and sizes of the various legislative chambers.
**Official language(s)**: The majority of languages each have an English name that is phonetic or very close to its own self-appellation. In cases where the English name is quite different it is followed by, in italics in parentheses, the name of the language as used by itself. African languages are given here (only) with their prefixes meaning 'the language of'.
**Monetary unit:** Currency: name of monetary unit, number of smaller units it comprises, value of US$1 (the operational rate of exchange as used by UN et alia, not the official or free rate) showing symbol used for the local currency.
**Chief cities and capital**: Anglicized names are used at this point for all countries; spellings in the national language however are used here in Part 33 "GeoAtlas" and *WCE* Part 10 "MetroScan". Figures for large cities represent the size of the urban agglomeration, where known, and not the size of the city within its official limits.
**Political divisions**: The administrative or political subdivisions into which the country is divided for central and local government purposes.
**Armed forces**: The country's own regular and reserve military forces. Many countries also maintain paramilitary forces as a check on the regular armed forces. Source: *World military and social expeditions 1996*, R.L. Sivard, 16th edition.
**Foreign forces**: Resident military forces from outside the country.
**Dependencies**: Territories politically dependent.

#### DEMOGRAPHY

**Population**: The figure given here is the UN figure for AD 2000.
**Population density**: Given to one decimal place.
**Under 15 years:** The percentage of the population aged 14 years and under.
**Growth rate** (1995–2000): Annual increase in the country's population, divided here into births minus deaths plus the net balance of migration (immigrants minus emigrants). Main source: *World population prospects, 1970–2000, as assessed in 1998* (New York: UN, 1999). Since these figures are projections for 1995–2000, they may differ in places from those in our Tables 1, which refer to the whole decade 1990–2000.
**Mortality:** Infant per 1,000; Maternal per 100,000.
**Life expectancy** at birth, both sexes (1995–2000): Source: UN population database.
**Household size**: The average size of a household in a country (persons sharing the same unit, whether private or collective or institutional) is not the same as that of the average family, being slightly larger due to inclusion of servants, maids, and lodgers, as well as hospitals, homes and other institutions where people live. Household is usually defined on the basis of the arrangements made by persons individually or in groups, for providing themselves with food or other essentials for living. The figures given here are based on the UN medium variant for projections. Source: 'Projections of the number of households and families' (New York: UN Population Division).
**Floor area per person:** A new UN variable, measured as square meters per individual.
**Major languages**: This listing gives the main distinct or separate or mutually unintelligible languages heard or spoken in the country (excluding dialects or variants), listed approximately in order of significance usually numerically (in most cases down to around 1% of the population) but also culturally, politically, commercially, economically, professionally, academically, religiously, and ecclesiastically, etc. Unlike in 'Official languages' above, African languages are here given without prefixes (with prefixes meaning 'the language of' sometimes added in parentheses). In most cases these major languages are followed by a numerical statement indicating the total of all other distinct and separate languages. Sources: government censuses, or own surveys, also here in *WCE* Part 9 "LinguaMetrics".
**Urban dwellers**: Population living in urban areas. taken from the variable 'urbanization' in *World demographic atlas* (UN, 1973 onwards). The exact definition of urban differs from country to country; in most, it covers cities and towns with a population of over 2,000 or 5,000, or even 20,000, or a density of over 1000/sq. km. (See details of all countries' definitions in *UN Demographic yearbook*). In UN statistics, it is usual to tabulate urban population 'as nationally defined', 'corresponding to national concepts', or 'as defined in each country'.
**Urban growth rate p.a.:** Annual increase. Source: *World demographic atlas*.
**Labor force**: Economically active population (both employed and unemployed) as a percentage of total population (excluding students, women at home, retired persons, wholly-dependent persons, et alii). Source: *Year book of labor statistics* (ILO).
**Tourists**: Foreign tourists and visitors from abroad visiting this country during calendar year. Source: *UN Statistical yearbook*.

#### ETHNOLINGUISTIC GROUPS

The percentages refer to the situation in the year 2000, taken from *WCE* Part 8 "EthnoSphere".

#### ECONOMY

**National income per person:** The average per capita annual income, usually derived as GNP (gross national product ) per capita.
**Average annual family income:** Derived by multiplying the national income per person by the average household size.

#### EDUCATION

**Adult literacy**: Percentage of the adult population (15 and over) who can read and write, in any language. Source: *UNESCO Statistical yearbook*. Virtually all the figures given here under SECULAR DATA come from official censuses. Readers should be warned that many other divergent figures are widely quoted in literature elsewhere but that they have no basis in fact. In Table 12-1, we interpolate or extrapolate the official figures to give comparative figures.
**Schools:** Total institutions at the first and second levels (primary and secondary schools), both public and private. This total includes elementary and secondary schools, but excludes pre-primary, post-secondary, technical, vocational, specialized and special schools.
**Universities:** Numbers of distinct universities and degree-granting colleges of all kinds.
**School enrolment (education rate):** Percentage of the school-age population (aged 5–24) who are enrolled in schools. Source: *UNESCO Statistical yearbook*.

#### HEALTH

**Access to health services:** % of population with adequate access.
**Access to safe water:** % of population with adequate access.

**Hospitals**: General and specialized hospitals and other medical establishments with beds (both government and private). Source: *UN Statistical yearbook*.
**Doctors**: Physicians qualified from a medical school, both in private practice and in state service. Source: *UN Statistical yearbook*.

This next section gives, in order to delineate serious societal health problems where they exist, statistics of 8 categories of sick or incapacitated or disadvantaged or handicapped persons, or persons who affect the health of society as a whole, with all of whom Christians and churches have long had a history of compassion, aid and concern: the blind, the deaf, persons murdered, lepers, underweight children, psychotics, drug addicts, and criminals.
**Deaf**: Hearing-impaired persons.
**Murder rate**: Murders per 100,000 per year (Interpol).
**Lepers**: Prevalence (total number of estimated leprosy patients at any given date) followed in parentheses by the prevalence rate (cases per 1,000 population). This item is included here because leprosy is still one of the most dreaded diseases, and one with which Christian missions have long been associated. Although nowadays the term 'leper' is not applied to individuals because of the age-long stigma attached to it, it is useful here for statistical purposes in drawing attention to the magnitude of the problem. Leprosy has a special position because it is the greatest crippler among diseases in the world today, and because of its long duration, relative incurability, high cost of treatment, vast extent (at least 11 million sufferers), and its inexorable persistence (one million new cases every 5 years) as a problem of global magnitude. The figures shown for each country are for estimated cases, registered and unregistered; they are known to change little from year to year. The prevalence rate gives a measure of risk of contagion: countries where it is 0.5 per 1,000 or higher are treated as risk areas by WHO; over 10 per 1,000 are high-risk areas. Data are not given for large Western nations with very small numbers of cases (below 100), or for other nations below 30. Sources: articles, 'The leprosy problem in the world', and 'Further information on the leprosy problem in the world', *Bulletin WHO*.
**Blind**: As in most official censuses, these statistics of blind persons refer to the totally blind. The figures come mostly from the most recent WHO global survey, 'Blindness", in *Epidemiological and vital statistics report* (WHO, Geneva). Complete global surveys of blindness by WHO are underway every 5 years or so.
**Underweight prevalence under 5:** A recent addition to UN-related statistical measures.
**Psychotics** (the mentally ill): The statistics given represent minimum figures for the total number of sufferers from psychoses or other severe mental disorder or disturbance; the mentally ill, or mentally abnormal (which is not the same as mentally retarded or deficient). According to the WHO, 'The per capita incidence of severe or major mental disturbance (psychosis) is much the same in most countries ... One percent of the world are, at any one time, incapacitated by severe mental disorder, and 10% are so affected at some period or other of their lives'. Of these sufferers, about one quarter (at least 0.2% of the population) are schizophrenics (sufferers from schizophrenia). Our category here, with its statistics, does not include the much larger category of sufferers from psychoneurosis, estimated at from 15–25% of the world's populations.
**Drug addicts**: The number of hard-core drug addicts or drug abusers (opium/cannabis/heroin/cocaine/morphine/psychotropic substances (barbiturates, LSD, hallucinogens)/multiple drug abuse). Source: Reports, UN Commission on Narcotic Drugs, et alia. Although statistics are only available for a few countries, drug abuse is serious in many others.
**Criminals**: The total number of distinct criminal offenders detected and identified by the nation's police (but not necessarily arrested or subsequently convicted) during a single year. Source: *International crime statistics* (Saint-Cloud, France: ICPO-Interpol). Comparing these figures from one country to another needs caution because a high coefficient of offenders to population may be due to meticulous record-keeping whilst a low one is often due to poor or sporadic record-keeping.

## LITERATURE
**New book titles**: Annual number of new non-peri-

odical commercial publications (books and pamphlets, including new editions and re-editions but not translations, available to the general public, excluding non-public books or reports) produced, including government publications, university theses, and children's books. Source: *UNESCO Statistical yearbook*, also searches using OCLC (Online Computer Library Catalogue).
**Periodicals**: Number of publications of periodical issue (appearing at regular intervals, each with 2 or more issues a year, excluding annuals and irregular serials, and in any languages), including scientific journals, but excluding non-daily general-interest newspapers (published 3 times a week or less), and excluding daily general-interest newspapers. Source: *UNESCO Statistical yearbook*.
**Scientific journals**: Source: *UNESCO Statistical yearbook*, et al.
**Newspapers**: General-interest newspapers are defined by UNESCO as publications devoted primarily to recording news of current events in public affairs, international affairs, politics, etc. Daily newspapers are defined as those which are published at least 4 times a week. Source: *UNESCO Statistical yearbook*.

## COMMUNICATION
**Phones**: Number of telephones in use, per 1,000 population, percentage mobile in parentheses.
**Radios**: Either estimated number of radio receivers in use (all types including wired receivers), or the number of annual licenses issued or sets declared, per 1,000 population.
**TV sets**: Either estimated number of television receivers in use, or the number of annual licenses issued, per 1,000 population.
**Daily newspaper circulation**: The total circulation, in copies per 1,000 population, of all general-interest daily newspapers.
**Computers**: Number of general-purpose computers in use, per 1,000 population.

## REFUGEES
**Alien refugees from other countries**: Officially-classified refugees entering over the last few years, resettled or not, but excluding labor and other migrants and also returnees (forcibly repatriated deportees), together with others not or not yet officially recognized. Source: *World refugee report* (US Committee for Refugees), annual.
**Citizen refugees in other countries (exiles abroad):** Citizens forced to flee and now temporarily received by the countries of asylum indicated.
**Internal displacement:** Numbers of citizens forced to flee to other areas within their own country.

## HUMAN LIFE AND LIBERTY
The following 4 scales describe socioeconomic states for all countries. The scales give values from 0-100%, with the optimum state being 100%.
**HDI:** Human Development Index.
**HSI:** Human Suffering Index.
**HFI:** Human Freedom Index.
**EFL:** Economic Freedom Level.

### *ENUMERATING ALL RELIGIONS*

The population of an area is usually defined as the total of all inhabitants or residents of that area; in technical terms, this is the de jure population. A strict definition of de jure population in a particular government census may include only legal inhabitants, i.e. long-term, legal residents who are citizens, and may exclude aliens, minorities, nomadic groups, armed forces and other groups. Inhabitants are usually defined as persons who dwell or reside permanently in a place or area, and should be distinguished from the term residents which often implies either a temporary or a relatively short-term period of habitation. By contrast with de jure population measuring inhabitants, however, most government censuses measure the present-in-area or de facto population, which includes illegal residents and all other types of residents, and also non-residents, transients, temporary visitors and sometimes even tourists, at the locations where they slept or spent the night. In practice, strict conformity to either the de jure or de facto definition is rarely achieved in national censuses, and so the United Nations produces its own estimates on its own definitions. Statistics of church membership, by con-

trast, are usually of a modified de jure variety, covering all resident groups but excluding transients, temporary visitors and tourists. In this survey we use the United Nations population definitions, figures and projections, which refer to present-in-area resident populations but excluding non-residents, transients, temporary visitors and tourists, and are therefore more directly comparable with church statistics of membership than either strictly de jure or de facto definitions and figures. In other words, our survey tables here refer to residents rather than to citizens or permanent inhabitants.

The term adherents is therefore used in this book as a general term to refer to the whole present-in-area resident population or inhabitants of all varieties at a particular point in time (excluding transients and temporary visitors) belonging to a particular religion or church—men, women, children, infants, nationals and expatriates (citizens and aliens), native and foreign-born, immigrants, immigrant workers, seasonal immigrants, alien minorities, stateless persons, armed forces stationed in the country (national and foreign, together with their dependents), foreign diplomatic personnel, merchant seamen in port or ashore, aborigines, jungle tribes, nomadic groups, alien displaced persons, internees, returnees, refugees, prisoners, prisoners-of-war, slaves, the hospitalized, the sick, the infirm, the disabled, psychotics, vagrants, and any other national or alien groups resident within the country at the time; together with any of the country's residents (armed forces, diplomats, merchant seamen, civilians) who are normally resident but at the exact time in question are very temporarily out of the country. Excluded are tourists, visitors, transients, persons in transit, and all other very temporary individuals or groups, all of whom are enumerated in this survey under their own countries of residence; and also members of the country's armed forces, diplomats, absentee workers, emigrants and other civilians not permanently resident in their own country at the point of time in question. In many countries, as explained above, this definition of ours would be referred to as the de jure population, although in other countries this term means long-term permanent residents or citizens including residents and armed forces abroad but excluding aliens, immigrant workers, etc. In many countries, also, the de facto population includes tourists, transients and all others physically-present on the census day but excludes citizens and residents temporarily abroad. Our definition of both total population and religious populations thus falls in between the strict de facto and de jure definitions. In cases where the available data on a country's population, for example from population censuses, omit any of the groups we wish to include, the data have been modified here to fit our own definition (usually including all resident alien, minority and underprivileged groups ignored in censuses but known to be present).

### *WCE COUNTRY TABLES 1*

#### *Objects of these tables*
The main object of Country Tables 1 is to show at a glance the overall de facto/de jure religious situation in each country throughout the 20th century, and on into the 21st, and to assist in analysis of the past, understanding of the present, and planning for the future, by providing the following data:
1. the major significant religious and non-religious blocs and groupings in the country, listed as mutually-exclusive categories, and in order of numerical size in AD 2000;
2. a standardized demographic base for every country, giving in the last row of every table the country's population statistics at mid-year for the years 1900 (for the area which comprises the country in 2000), 1970, 1990, 1995, 2000, and 2025, together with annual natural increase for 1990-2000;
3. the religious adherence, or non-adherence, of the entire population (men, women, children and infants);
4. the general order of magnitude of these groupings' adherents, both in absolute numbers and also as percentages of the population, in the years 1900, 1970, 1990, 1995, 2000, 2025;
5. a direct link with Country Tables 2 (depicting organized churches and denominations) by incorporating those tables' totals of affiliated Chris-

tians in all the above years, and the subdivision of these totals into the 6 major ecclesiastico-cultural megablocs;

6. any contemporary major long-term religious trends in the country, expressed as annual changes in religious profession or affiliation over the decade 1990–2000, due either to natural change (biological change or births minus deaths, plus migration change or immigrants minus emigrants), or to conversion change to or from religions (conversions minus defections);

7. the religious situation in the year 1900 (for the country, within present boundaries, i.e. adjusted to include the territory which in 2000 comprises the country);

8. the probable religious situation in the year AD 2025, projected from current trends;

9. footnotes elaborating the basic census and polls data, and any interesting features and additional data concerning particular categories in the table.

## Summary of the 17 columns

The columns are not numbered 1–17 in the tables themselves, but are numbered here to assist in identifying particular columns. This describes all Country Tables 1 in the survey, WCE Part 4; but note that in the Global Tables (Parts 1 and 10), 2 additional columns are added for the year AD 2050.

1. Major religions and subdivisions, listed in AD 2000 order of numerical size
2. Adherents in the year 1900
3. Adherents in 1900 as % total population then
4. Adherents in mid-1970
5. Adherents in mid-1970 as % population then
6. Adherents in mid-1990
7. Adherents in mid-1990 as % population then
8-11. Annual change, 1990–2000, average long-term trend over the decade
8. Annual natural (population) increase among adherents, 1990–2000 (biological increase (births minus deaths) plus net immigration)
9. Annual conversion (or supranatural) increase (+ or -) to adherents, 1990–2000 (measured as col. 10 minus col. 8)
10. total annual increase (+ or -) of adherents, 1990–2000 (= col. 8 plus col. 9) (measured as col. 14 minus col. 4, divided by 10)
11. Rate of change of adherents, 1990–2000, as % per year {[(col. 14 divided by col. 6) ^ (1/10)]-1}x 100
12. Adherents in mid-1995

13. Adherents in mid-1995 as % population then
14. Adherents in mid-2000
15. Adherents in mid-2000 as % population then
16. Adherents in mid-year 2025
17. Adherents in 2025 as % population then

## Degrees of non-Christian religiosity

We have described earlier how the simple category 'Christians' can and should be subdivided in various ways into professing, affiliated, unaffiliated, practicing, nonpractising, and so on. It is important to realize that in exactly the same way all non-Christian religions, and also atheism and non-religion, also contain the whole range of commitment from deeply-religious mystics and proselytizing zealots (even fanatics) down through the indifferent to the nominally-religious or nonpractising doubters. The bulk of the adherents we enumerate in this survey who claim allegiance to Islam, Hinduism, and even to atheism and to no religion, do not practice their profession with any vigor or conviction.

Since this is primarily a survey of the Christian world, our overall statistics of each non-Christian religion are limited to professing adherents only. At the same time the reader should remember throughout that labels like 'Buddhist' include the whole range of degrees of religiosity from devoutly believing and practicing Buddhists to non-believing and non-practicing Buddhists. Where concise data on these degrees of religiosity, practice and commitment are available for the non-Christian religions, they are given briefly in the footnotes under Country Tables 1 for the countries concerned.

## Methodology, sources, and assumptions

Each table has been compiled in a standard format, in approximately the order of compilation now to be described, using the types of source data indicated. Our method of compilation has been to move step by step through a whole chain of logical procedures. The method used is similar to solving a jigsaw puzzle or working out a crossword puzzle, one box at a time, using one position to establish another and one set of data to produce the next, i.e. moving from the known to the unknown (from known figures entered in the table to produce the next, unknown, figure or series of figures) through the following 27 stages.

1. Main religions. First, an alphabetical listing of the major numerically-significant religions and religious blocs in each country was made.

2. Population in 1900. The demographic base line was begun by inserting figures of present-in-area resident population for censuses of the year 1900 published by about 150 countries, summarized in UN Demographic yearbook (1948–53, 1955, 1962) for 110 countries (within their present boundaries, i.e. their areas defined by the frontiers of the year 2000), and supplemented for the remaining countries by extrapolations back to 1900 from Table A 3.8 in World population prospects (1966).

3. Population estimates, 1970–2025. The rest of the demographic base line was now inserted. The most recent census figure is given for each country in SECULAR DATA at the start of each country's article. In Tables 1, however, we use the standardized and comparative mid-year estimates of present-in-area resident population for the years 1970–2025 prepared by the United Nations Population Division and published biennially as World population prospects, (New York: UN). This report gives projections prepared in 4 variants based on differing presuppositions: high, medium, and low; and constant fertility trends. For AD 2025, the high variant gives a world population of 8,379 million, and the constant variant 9,069 million. In Country Tables 1, we have chosen the rather more conservative medium variant projections, which give for AD 2025 a world population of 7,824 million. These UN figures and the projections are, for comparative purposes, more reliable and definitive than the actual population census figures themselves as published by countries, because they incorporate the UN's evaluation and, in particular, adjustments when underenumeration is known to have taken place in a census (as in Mexico 1970), or overenumeration (as in Nigeria 1963), but where the respective governments are reluctant to acknowledge this for internal political reasons. It should be noted in passing that for certain countries (Angola, Colombia, et alia) the Statistical Office of the United Nations still uses church data on baptisms to obtain the estimated number of births and to calculate the crude birth rate (UN Demographic yearbook 1974, p. 252).

4. Annual population increase. At the start of each country's article, SECULAR DATA includes the year 2000 figure for increase, as % per year. This is what we here have called the natural increase,

---

## Table 14–10. Standard terms and codes for 85 categories/varieties/meanings of the term 'Christians', also for 100 categories of non-Christians, and also for 9 major overall totals.

NOTES.

1. This book gives to each distinct religious category a unique alphanumeric code. To assist the user to remember codes useful to him or her, for the most frequently-occurring categories, each code in most cases consists of letters similar to the order of words in the category itself. Thus GCC = Great Commission Christians, AAC = Anglican affiliated Christians, AEAC = Anglican Evangelical affiliated Christians; and so on.

2. Categories and subcategories of Christians are not arranged below in alphabetical order, but in an ecclesiastically logical or chronological order. The 4 major Christian categories or standardized ways of enumerating Christians are shown here and in other tables in boldface type: these are **Christians, professing Christians, affiliated Christians**, and **Great Commission Christians**. By contrast, major categories of non-Christians are however listed alphabetically, but with their

subcategories listed in a logical order.

3. Indented categories form part of, and are included in, the unindented category above them. First indentations (indented once) are in all cases complete; their subcategories always add up to their parent category. Second indentations however, although usually complete, are in several cases selected subgroups not intended as a complete breakdown of their unindented parent subcategory.

4. Certain subcategories are exact repeats, repeated in order to clarify the overall scheme.

5. All other categories are omitted in the published WCE Country Tables 1 where values are zero for the entire period 1900-2025. They all appear, however, in the CD in order to answer search questions like "How many Orthodox Charismatics were there in this country in 1970?" (Answer: "None").

6. All lines have statistics as shown in Country Tables 1, derived as shown in the last column below. Lines with no for-

mulas there receive their totals from outside Country Tables 1 (mostly from censuses or Country Tables 2). Lines with formulas are secondary totals derived from other categories in Country Tables 1 or 2. A few are both, in which case the formulas serve as checks on the accuracy and consistency of the overall tables. Note that all the "doubly-counted", "doubly-affiliated", "disaffiliated", and "doubly-professing" items (2PC, 2AC, xAC, 2RAC, 4ZAC, and 2r) are shown in all tables as negative numbers because they represent a duplication (persons counted, or counting themselves, twice).

7. This whole classification of terms and codes is repeated twice more. Table 16 column 3 lists every single category, and subcategory, alphabetically by code in a listing that covers all variables and codes used in WCE/WCT's tables and in the CD World Christian database.

| ID | Code | Category | Formulas (Definitions) |
|---|---|---|---|
| 1. | C | **Christians** | C = CC + PC = UC + AC = LC + GCC. |
| 2. | | *PROFESSION* | |
| 3. | CC | crypto-Christians | CC = C - PC = SCC + ICC + HCC. |
| 4. | SCC | Secret church members | SCC = CC - ICC - HCC. |
| 5. | BCC | Isolated radio/TV believers | BCC = BIAC. |
| 6. | HCC | Hidden non-Christian believers in Christ | HCC = HHCC + MHCC + BHCC + JHCC + YHCC. |
| 7. | HHCC | Hidden Hindu believers in Christ | HHCC =HHIAC. |
| 8. | MHCC | Hidden Muslim believers in Christ | MHCC = MHIAC. |
| 9. | BHCC | Hidden Buddhist believers in Christ | BHCC = BHIAC. |
| 10. | JHCC | Hidden Jewish believers in Christ | JHCC = JHIAC. |
| 11. | YHCC | Hidden other religionist believers in Christ | YHCC = YHIAC. |
| 12. | PC | **professing Christians** | PC = APC + IPC + mPC + OPC + PPC + RPC + 2PC. |
| 13. | APC | Anglicans | |
| 14. | IPC | Independents | |
| 15. | mPC | Marginal Christians | |
| 16. | OPC | Orthodox | |
| 17. | PPC | Protestants | |
| 18. | PPPC | Popular-religionists | |
| 19. | RPC | Roman Catholics | |
| 20. | SRPC | Spiritist Catholics | |
| 21. | CRPC | Christopagans | |

Continued opposite

*Table 14—10 continued*

| ID | Code | Category | Formulas (Definitions) |
|----|------|----------|------------------------|
| 22. | ERPC | Evangelical Catholics | |
| 23. | PRPC | Popular-religionist Catholics | |
| 24. | 2PC | doubly-professing Christians | 2PC = PC - (APC + IPC + mPC + OPC + PPC + RPC). This sum is always negative. |
| 25. | | *AFFILIATION* | |
| 26. | UC | unaffiliated Christians | UC = C - AC. |
| 27. | AC | **affiliated Christians (church members)** | AC = AAC + IAC + mAC + OAC + PAC + RAC + 2AC + xAC. |
| 28. | pAC | practising church members | pAC = GCC = eAC. |
| 29. | xpAC | nonpracticing church members | xpAC = AC - pAC. |
| 30. | AAC | Anglicans | |
| 31. | EAAC | Anglican Evangelicals | |
| 32. | CAAC | Anglican Charismatics | CAAC = AV2ZAC + Ax2ZAC. |
| 33. | IAC | Independents/Postdenominationalists/Neo-Apostolics | IAC = NIAC + WIAC + OIAC + RIAC + AIAC + PIAC + BIAC + HIAC + MIAC. |
| 34. | EIAC | Independent Evangelicals | EIAC = IEAC |
| 35. | NIAC | Non-White indigenous Christians | NIAC = N3ZAC. |
| 36. | WIAC | White-led Postdenominationalists | WIAC = W3ZAC. |
| 37. | OIAC | Independent Orthodox | |
| 38. | RIAC | Independent Catholics | |
| 39. | AIAC | Independent Anglicans | |
| 40. | PIAC | Independent Protestants | |
| 41. | BIAC | Isolated radio/TV believers | BIAC = B3ZAC + BBIAC. |
| 42. | BBIAC | Non-charismatic radio churches | BBIAC = I-rad. |
| 43. | HIAC | Hidden non-Christian believers in Christ | HIAC = HHIAC + MHIAC + BHIAC + JHIAC + YHIAC. |
| 44. | HHIAC | Hidden Hindu believers in Christ | HHIAC = I-Hin. |
| 45. | MHIAC | Hidden Muslim believers in Christ | MHIAC = I-Mus. |
| 46. | BHIAC | Hidden Buddhist believers in Christ | BHIAC = I-Bud. |
| 47. | JHIAC | Hidden Jewish believers in Christ | JHIAC = I-Jew. |
| 48. | YHIAC | Hidden other religionist believers in Christ | YHIAC = I-rel. |
| 49. | MIAC | Nonhistorical Independents | |
| 50. | CIAC | Charismatic Independents | CIAC = 3ZAC |
| 51. | mAC | Marginal Christians | |
| 52. | EmAC | Marginal Evangelicals | |
| 53. | CmAC | Marginal Charismatics | |
| 54. | OAC | Orthodox | |
| 55. | EOAC | Orthodox Evangelicals | |
| 56. | COAC | Orthodox Charismatics | |
| 57. | PAC | Protestants | |
| 58. | EPAC | Evangelicals | |
| 59. | 1ZAC | Pentecostals | |
| 60. | CPAC | Protestant Charismatics | CPAC = PV2ZAC + Px2ZAC. |
| 61. | RAC | Roman Catholics | |
| 62. | ERAC | Catholic Evangelicals | |
| 63. | CRAC | Catholic Charismatics | CRAC = RV2ZAC + Rx2ZAC. |
| 64. | 2RAC | doubly-counted Catholics | 2RAC = RAC minus the sum of all members enumerated separately by dioceses. Sum is always negative. |
| 65. | 2AC | doubly-affiliated | 2AC = AC - (AAC + IAC + mAC + OAC + PAC + RAC + xAC). This total is always negative. |
| 66. | xAC | disaffiliated | Former Christians (still on church rolls) who now regard themselves as non-Christians or are dead. Negative. |
| 67. | | *Trans-megabloc groupings (also included above):* | |
| 68. | eAC | evangelicals | eAC = GCC = pAC. |
| 69. | EAC | Evangelicals | EAC = CEAC + NEAC + LEAC + IEAC + mEAC. |
| 70. | CEAC | Conservative Evangelicals | 100% of the denomination is Evangelical |
| 71. | NEAC | Neo-Evangelicals | 50-99% of the denomination is Evangelical |
| 72. | LEAC | Conciliar Evangelicals | LEAC = ALEAC + OLEAC + PLEAC + RLEAC. |
| 73. | ALEAC | Anglican Evangelicals | |
| 74. | OLEAC | Orthodox Evangelicals | |
| 75. | PLEAC | Protestant Conciliar Evangelicals | 0-49% of the denomination is Evangelical |
| 76. | RLEAC | Catholic Evangelicals | |
| 77. | FEAC | Fundamentalists | FEAC occurs in CEAC, NEAC and PLEAC. |
| 78. | IEAC | Independent Evangelicals | |
| 79. | mEAC | Marginal Evangelicals | |
| 80. | ZC | Renewal believers | ZC = ZAC + QZAC + ZUC |
| 81. | QZAC | Peripheral Quasi-pentecostals | QZAC = 0QZAC + 1QZAC |
| 82. | 0QZAC | Prepentecostals | |
| 83. | 1QZAC | Postpentecostals | |
| 84. | ZAC | Pentecostals/Charismatics/Neocharismatics | ZAC = 1ZAC + 2ZAC + 3ZAC + 4ZAC. |
| 85. | 1ZAC | Pentecostals (First-Wavers) | 1ZAC = P1ZAC (= members of bodies in Country Tables 2 whose column 3 code begins 'P-Pe'). |
| 86. | P1ZAC | Denominational Pentecostals (White) | P1ZAC = CP1ZAC + OP1ZAC. |
| 87. | CP1ZAC | Classical Pentecostals | CP1ZAC = Original, Trinitarian, largely-White bodies, whose column 3 code begins 'P-Pe' but excludes 'P-Pe1'. |
| 88. | 3CP1ZAC | Holiness Pentecostals | |
| 89. | 2CP1ZAC | Baptistic Pentecostals | |
| 90. | ACP1ZAC | Apostolic Pentecostals | |
| 91. | 1P1ZAC | Oneness Pentecostals | OP1ZAC = Original, 'Jesus Only', largely-White bodies, whose column 3 code = 'P-Pe1'. |
| 92. | 2ZAC | Charismatics (Second-Wavers) | 2ZAC = V2ZAC + x2ZAC = A2ZAC + R2ZAC + O2ZAC + P2ZAC + m2ZAC. |
| 93. | V2ZAC | Mainline active Charismatics | V2ZAC = AV2ZAC + RV2ZAC + mV2ZAC + OV2ZAC + PV2ZAC. |
| 94. | AV2ZAC | Anglican Charismatics (active) | |
| 95. | RV2ZAC | Catholic Charismatics (active) | |
| 96. | mV2ZAC | Marginal Charismatics (active) | |
| 97. | OV2ZAC | Orthodox Charismatics (active) | |
| 98. | PV2ZAC | Protestant Charismatics (active) | |
| 99. | x2ZAC | Mainline Postcharismatics | x2ZAC = Ax2ZAC + Px2ZAC + Rx2ZAC. |
| 100. | Ax2ZAC | Anglican Postcharismatics | Ax2ZAC = CAAC - AV2ZAC. |
| 101. | Px2ZAC | Protestant Postcharismatics | Px2ZAC = CPAC - PV2ZAC. |
| 102. | Rx2ZAC | Catholic Postcharismatics | Rx2ZAC = CRAC - RV2ZAC. |
| 103. | A2ZAC | Anglican Charismatics | A2ZAC = CAAC. |
| 104. | R2ZAC | Catholic Charismatics | R2ZAC = CRAC. |
| 105. | O2ZAC | Orthodox Charismatics | O2ZAC = COAC. |
| 106. | P2ZAC | Protestant Charismatics | P2ZAC = CPAC. |
| 107. | m2ZAC | Marginal Charismatics | |
| 108. | 3ZAC | Neocharismatics (Third-Wavers) | 3ZAC = N3ZAC + O3ZAC + A3ZAC + P3ZAC + R3ZAC + W3ZAC + I3ZAC + r3ZAC + H3ZAC. |
| 109. | N3ZAC | Non-White indigenous Neocharismatics | N3ZAC = bodies whose column 3 begins 'I-3', ends with capital A to V, Y, or Z; plus individual Neocharismatics. |
| 110. | | *Last code letter, A to Z:* | |
| 111. | AN3ZAC | African indigenous pentecostals/charismatics | A |
| 112. | UN3ZAC | Afro-Caribbean indigenous pentecostals/charismatics | U |
| 113. | SN3ZAC | Arab/Assyrian/Semitic neocharismatics | S |
| 114. | DN3ZAC | Black American independent charismatics | D |
| 115. | BN3ZAC | Black American indigenous pentecostals | B |
| 116. | ON3ZAC | Black American Oneness Apostolics | O |
| 117. | YN3ZAC | Brazilian/Portuguese grassroots neocharismatics | Y |
| 118. | NN3ZAC | Colored/Mixed-race indigenous charismatics | N |
| 119. | EN3ZAC | Ethnic (Monoethnic) pentecostal churches | E |
| 120. | FN3ZAC | Filipino indigenous pentecostals/charismatics | F |
| 121. | CN3ZAC | Han Chinese indigenous pentecostals/charismatics | C |
| 122. | IN3ZAC | Indian indigenous pentecostals/charismatics | I |
| 123. | GN3ZAC | Indonesian indigenous pentecostals | G |
| 124. | QN3ZAC | Japanese indigenous pentecostals | Q |
| 125. | KN3ZAC | Korean indigenous pentecostals/charismatics | K |

*Continued overleaf*

*Table 14–10 continued*

| ID | Code | Category | Formulas (Definitions) |
|---|---|---|---|
| 126. | LN3ZAC | Latino-Hispanic grassroots believers | L |
| 127. | HN3ZAC | Messianic Hindu believers in Christ | H |
| 128. | JN3ZAC | Messianic Jewish believers in Christ | J |
| 129. | MN3ZAC | Messianic Muslim believers in Christ | M |
| 130. | PN3ZAC | Pacific/Oceanic indigenous charismatics | P |
| 131. | RN3ZAC | Red Indian/Amerindian neopentecostals | R |
| 132. | VN3ZAC | Vietnamese indigenous neocharismatics | V |
| 133. | ZN3ZAC | other Asian indigenous neocharismatics | Z |
| 134. | TN3ZAC | other Messianic non-Christian believers in Christ | T |
| 135. | W3ZAC | White-led Independent Postdenominationalists | W3ZAC = bodies whose column 3 begins 'I-3', ends with W or X; plus individuals in noncharismatic bodies. |
| 136. | WW3ZAC | European/American White-led Neo-Apostolics | W |
| 137. | XW3ZAC | European White-led New Apostolics | X |
| 138. | O3ZAC | Independent Orthodox neocharismatics | |
| 139. | R3ZAC | Independent Catholic neocharismatics | |
| 140. | A3ZAC | Independent Anglican neocharismatics | |
| 141. | P3ZAC | Independent Protestant neocharismatics | |
| 142. | I3ZAC | Nonhistorical Independent neocharismatics | |
| 143. | B3ZAC | Isolated radio/TV neocharismatics | |
| 144. | H3ZAC | Hidden non-Christian believers in Christ | |
| 145. | HH3ZAC | Hidden Hindu neocharismatics | |
| 146. | MH3ZAC | Hidden Muslim neocharismatics | |
| 147. | BH3ZAC | Hidden Buddhist neocharismatics | |
| 148. | JH3ZAC | Hidden Jewish neocharismatics | |
| 149. | YH3ZAC | Hidden other-religionist neocharismatics | |
| 150. | 4ZAC | doubly-counted 1st-/2nd-/3rd-Wavers | 4ZAC = ZAC - (1ZAC + 2ZAC + 3ZAC). This sum is always negative. |
| 151. | UZC | Unaffiliated renewal believers | |
| 152. | | *MISSION* | |
| 153. | LC | latent (inactive) Christians | LC = C - GCC = UC + xpAC. |
| 154. | xpAC | nonpracticing church members | xpAC = AC - pAC. |
| 155. | UC | unaffiliated Christians | UC = LC - xpAC. |
| 156. | GCC | **Great Commission Christians** | |
| 157. | OEC | overt evangelizers | OEC = GCC - CC. |
| 158. | CC | covert evangelizers | |
| 159. | | *CULTURE* | |
| 160. | iC | indigenous Christians | |
| 161. | aIC | alien Christians | |
| 162. | | *GEOSTATUS* | |
| 163. | A-C | World A Christians | A-C = CAA + CBA + CCA. |
| 164. | B-C | World B Christians | B-C = CAB + CBB + CCB. |
| 165. | C-C | World C Christians | C-C = CAC + CBC + CCC. |
| 166. | X | **NON-CHRISTIANS** | |
| 167. | a | Atheists | |
| 168. | L | Baha'is | |
| 169. | OL | Schismatic Baha'is | |
| 170. | AL | Azali Babis | |
| 171. | sL | other Baha'i sectarians | Note: 's' (or 'z') before a code refers to a specific sect of that code's religion |
| 172. | B | Buddhists | B = MB + TB + LB + VB + BB + FB + NB + YB + sB. |
| 173. | MB | Mahayana Buddhists | MB = IMB + CMB + KMB + JMB + TMB + NMB + PMB + ZMB + SMB . |
| 174. | IMB | Indian Buddhists | |
| 175. | CMB | Chinese Buddhists | |
| 176. | KMB | Korean Buddhists | |
| 177. | JMB | Japanese Buddhists | |
| 178. | NJMB | Nichiren Shu Buddhists | |
| 179. | TJMB | Tendaishu Buddhists | |
| 180. | NJMB | Nara Buddhists | |
| 181. | PJMB | Pure Land (Amida) Buddhists | |
| 182. | TPJMB | True Pure Land Buddhists | |
| 183. | ZJMB | Zen Buddhists | |
| 184. | SJMB | Shingon (Tantrists) Buddhists | |
| 185. | TB | Theravada (Hinayana) Buddhists | |
| 186. | NTB | Neo-Buddhists | |
| 187. | LB | Tibetan Buddhists (Lamaists) | |
| 188. | KLB | Kagyudpa Lamaists | |
| 189. | NLB | Nyingmapa Lamaists | |
| 190. | RLB | Rimaypa Lamaists | |
| 191. | SLB | Sakyapa Lamaists | |
| 192. | VB | Vajrayana (Tantrists) Buddhists | |
| 193. | YB | Buddhayana Buddhists | |
| 194. | FB | Folk-Buddhists | |
| 195. | NB | nonreligious Buddhists | |
| 196. | sB | other sectarian Buddhists | |
| 197. | F | Chinese folk-religionists | |
| 198. | G | Confucianists | |
| 199. | NG | Neo-Confucianists | |
| 200. | T | Ethnoreligionists (Tribalists) | T = AT + NT + PT + ST + WT + zT. |
| 201. | AT | Animists | AT = LAT + HAT + IAT + BAT + PAT. |
| 202. | LAT | Primal religionists | |
| 203. | HAT | Hinduized animists | |
| 204. | IAT | Islamized animists | |
| 205. | BAT | Buddhistic animists | |
| 206. | PAT | Polytheistic animists | |
| 207. | ET | Neopagans | |
| 208. | PT | Polytheists | |
| 209. | ST | Shamanists | |
| 210. | KST | Korean folk-religionists | |
| 211. | WT | Witchcraft eradicationists | |
| 212. | zT | other ethnoreligionist sectarians | |
| 213. | H | Hindus | H = HH+ VH + SH + KH + NH + RH +TH + FH + zH. |
| 214. | HH | Vedantists | |
| 215. | VH | Vaishnavites | |
| 216. | SH | Shaivites | |
| 217. | KH | Saktists | |
| 218. | NH | Neo-Hindus | |
| 219. | RH | Reform Hindus | |
| 220. | TH | Tantrists (Tantrist Hindus) | |
| 221. | FH | Folk/Popular Hindus | |
| 222. | zH | other sectarian Hindus | |
| 223. | V | Jains | V = DV + SV + zV. |
| 224. | DV | Digambara Jains | |
| 225. | SV | Svetambara Jains | |
| 226. | zV | other sectarian Jains | |
| 227. | J | Jews | J = AJ + EJ + SJ + +RJ + OJ + CJ + KJ + NJ + TJ + UJ + FJ + zJ. |
| 228. | AJ | Ashkenazis | |

*Continued opposite*

Table 14–10 continued

| ID | Code | Category | Formulas (Definitions) |
|---|---|---|---|
| 229. | EJ | Oriental Jews | |
| 230. | SJ | Sefardis | |
| 231. | RJ | Reformists | |
| 232. | OJ | Orthodox | |
| 233. | CJ | Reconstructionists | |
| 234. | KJ | Karaites | |
| 235. | NJ | Conservative Jews | |
| 236. | TJ | Samaritans | |
| 237. | UJ | Ultra Orthodox | |
| 238. | FJ | Folk-Judaism | |
| 239. | zJ | other Jewish movements | |
| 240. | M | Muslims | M = SM + HM + XM. |
| 241. | SM | Sunnis | SM = HSM + SSM + MSM + BSM + WSM + zSM. |
| 242. | HSM | Hanafites | |
| 243. | SSM | Shafiites | |
| 244. | MSM | Malikites | |
| 245. | BSM | Hanbalites | |
| 246. | WSM | Wahhabites | |
| 247. | zSM | other Sunni sectarians | |
| 248. | UM | Sufis | |
| 249. | RUM | Neo-Sufis | |
| 250. | sUM | other sectarian Sufis | |
| 251. | HM | Shias | HM = AHM + IHM + ZHM + LHM + sHM. |
| 252. | AHM | Ithna-Asharis | |
| 253. | IHM | Ismailis | |
| 254. | BIHM | Bohoras | |
| 255. | MIHM | Mustalis | |
| 256. | ZHM | Zaydis | |
| 257. | LHM | Alawites | |
| 258. | sHM | other Shia sectarians | |
| 259. | XM | Islamic schismatics | XM = AXM + KXM + DXM + BXM + PXM + MXM + NXM + YXM + sXM. |
| 260. | AXM | Ahmadis | |
| 261. | LAXM | Lahoris | |
| 262. | QAXM | Qadianis | |
| 263. | KXM | Kharijites | |
| 264. | IKXM | Ibadis | |
| 265. | DXM | Druzes | |
| 266. | BXM | Black Muslims | |
| 267. | MXM | Sabbateans | |
| 268. | PXM | Mahdists | |
| 269. | NXM | Neo-Fundamentalists | |
| 270. | sXM | other Islamic sectarians | |
| 271. | FM | Folk-Muslims | |
| 272. | N | New-Religionists (Neoreligionists) | N = SN + NN + AN + MN + PN + TN + UN + ON + VN + CN + FN. |
| 273. | SN | Syncretist neoreligionists | |
| 274. | NN | Nonsyncretist neoreligionists | |
| 275. | AN | Astrologists | |
| 276. | MN | Metaphysicalists | |
| 277. | PN | Paganists | |
| 278. | TN | Theosophists | |
| 279. | UN | Secret societies | |
| 280. | ON | Occultists | |
| 281. | VN | Nativistic cultists | |
| 282. | CN | Cargo cultists | |
| 283. | FN | Self-Religionists | |
| 284. | Q | Nonreligious | |
| 285. | PW | Pan-Religionists | PW are also included in other religions |
| 286. | FPW | Folk-religionists | |
| 287. | PPW | Popular religionists | |
| 288. | S | Shintoists | |
| 289. | HS | Shrine Shinto | |
| 290. | TS | Sect Shinto | |
| 291. | FS | Folk-Shintoists | |
| 292. | K | Sikhs | |
| 293. | U | Spiritists | |
| 294. | AU | Afro-American spiritists | |
| 295. | BU | Afro-Brazilian cultists | |
| 296. | CU | Afro-Caribbean religionists | |
| 297. | SU | Afro-Surinamese religionists | |
| 298. | TU | Animistic neocultists | |
| 299. | UU | Afro-Cuban spiritists | |
| 300. | HU | High Spiritists | |
| 301. | D | Taoists | |
| 302. | Z | Zoroastrians | |
| 303. | PZ | Parsis | |
| 304. | Y | Quasireligionists | |
| 305. | BY | Bogomils | |
| 306. | MY | Mandeans | |
| 307. | NY | Quasi-Christians | |
| 308. | QY | Parareligionists | |
| 309. | FQY | Freemasons | |
| 310. | YY | Yezidis | |
| 311. | rY | other minor religionists | |
| 312. | 2W | doubly-counted religionists | 2W = W - (a + L + B + Y + G + T + H + V + J + M + N + Q + S + F + K + U + D + Z). Sum always negative. |
| 313. | | *TOTALS* | |
| 314. | C | **Christians** | Defined as above. |
| 315. | X | **Non-Christians** | X = a + L + B + Y + G + T + H + V + J + M + N + Q + S + F + K + U + D + Z + 2W. |
| 316. | W | **Religionists** | W = C + X - a - Q + 2W = pop - a - Q. |
| 317. | - | Nonreligionists | |
| 318. | pop | population | |
| 319. | Ppop | A people's population | |
| 320. | Npop | Country's population | |
| 321. | Apop | World A population | |
| 322. | Bpop | World B population | |
| 323. | Cpop | World C population | |
| 324. | Gpop | Total global population | |
| 325. | | *EVANGELIZATION* | |
| 326. | EP | Total evangelized persons | |
| 327. | UP | Total unevangelized persons | UP = pop - EP. |
| 328. | | *GEOSTATUS* | |
| 329. | Apop1 | World A individuals | Apop1 = UP. |
| 330. | Bpop1 | World B individuals | Bpop1 = pop - UP - C. |
| 331. | Cpop1 | World C individuals | Cpop1 = C. |

*Continued overleaf*

*Table 14–10 concluded*

| ID | Code | Category | Formulas (Definitions) |
|----|------|----------|------------------------|
| 332. | | *PEOPLES AND COUNTRIES* | |
| 333. | Apop2 | Population of World A peoples | |
| 334. | Bpop2 | Population of World B peoples | |
| 335. | Cpop2 | Population of World C peoples | |
| | | | |
| 336. | Apop3 | Population of World A countries | |
| 337. | Bpop3 | Population of World B countries | |
| 338. | Cpop3 | Population of World C countries | |
| | | | |
| 339. | | *LOCATION OF INDIVIDUALS* | |
| 340. | | First column letter in list below = World A, B, or C individuals (shown by lowercase letter a, b, or c) | |
| 341. | | Second column letter = who are also within World A/B/C peoples (shown by capital letter) | |
| 342. | | Third column letter = who are also within World A/B/C countries (shown by capital letter) | |
| | | | |
| 343. | aAA | World A individuals in World A peoples in World A countries | |
| 344. | aAB | World A individuals in World A peoples in World B countries | |
| 345. | aAC | World A individuals in World A peoples in World C countries | |
| 346. | aBA | World A individuals in World B peoples in World A countries | |
| 347. | aBB | World A individuals in World B peoples in World B countries | |
| 348. | aBC | World A individuals in World B peoples in World C countries | |
| 349. | aCA | World A individuals in World C peoples in World A countries | |
| 350. | aCB | World A individuals in World C peoples in World B countries | |
| 351. | aCC | World A individuals in World C peoples in World C countries | |
| 352. | bAA | World B individuals in World A peoples in World A countries | |
| 353. | bAB | World B individuals in World A peoples in World B countries | |
| 354. | bAC | World B individuals in World A peoples in World C countries | |
| 355. | bBA | World B individuals in World B peoples in World A countries | |
| 356. | bBB | World B individuals in World B peoples in World B countries | |
| 357. | bBC | World B individuals in World B peoples in World C countries | |
| 358. | bCA | World B individuals in World C peoples in World A countries | |
| 359. | bCB | World B individuals in World C peoples in World B countries | |
| 360. | bCC | World B individuals in World C peoples in World C countries | |
| 361. | cAA | World C individuals in World A peoples in World A countries | |
| 362. | cAB | World C individuals in World A peoples in World B countries | |
| 363. | cAC | World C individuals in World A peoples in World C countries | |
| 364. | cBA | World C individuals in World B peoples in World A countries | |
| 365. | cBB | World C individuals in World B peoples in World B countries | |
| 366. | cBC | World C individuals in World B peoples in World C countries | |
| 367. | cCA | World C individuals in World C peoples in World A countries | |
| 368. | cCB | World C individuals in World C peoples in World B countries | |
| 369. | cCC | World C individuals in World C peoples in World C countries | |

i.e. biological increase plus migration increase, i.e. birth rate minus death rate plus immigration rate minus emigration rate. In Tables 1, a similar figure appears on the last line under the column 'Rate' (rate of increase in 2000), though in this case it is the exponential growth rate for the years 1990–2000 estimated from the UN projections.

5. *Migration.* Migration is usually defined (as in the UK) as a declared intention to reside in or leave a country for at least a year. In a handful of countries, international migration (emigration or immigration, expulsions, refugee movements, etc.) during the period 1990–2000 has been significant. Where the numbers involved are large enough to be noticeable in Country Tables 1, they are included with biological increase in the column 'Natural increase'. In particular, where migrations of large numbers from a particular religious bloc have been taking place during this period (e.g. Jews emigrating from Russia), approximate annual figures are included in the columns 'Annual change, 1990–2000' and the situation is described in the footnotes. The data in this book illustrate an often-noted basic principle: migration results in a decline in religious practice, affiliation and even profession. When persons from strongly-religious cultures migrate to distant lands, unless they move into already-established minorities of their own people their religious ties become looser and they tend to become less religious or even nonreligious (e.g. Chinese folk-religionists, European Protestants). An estimate of annual net migration for each country appears under 'Demography' in its section in SECULAR DATA of *WCD*.

6. *Children.* As has been discussed above in the case of Christianity, children and infants must be included in these tables. Our general principle throughout this survey has been that, except in cases where data to the contrary are available, children and infants have the same religious characteristics as their parents. For Country Tables 1, they are therefore assumed to have their parents' religious profession, or absence of it, unless evidence to the contrary is available. Thus a census showing that 80% of a population are Muslims, or a poll showing 80% of adults are Muslims, also indicates that approximately 80% of all children also are Muslims.

7. *Affiliated Christians.* Figures for Christians affiliated to churches in 1995 were next added, divided into the 6 major ecclesiastical megablocs, taken in every case from the figures derived in Country Table 2 for the country. The absolute numbers were inserted first, in all cases as the exact unrounded totals for 1995 obtained in Country Tables 2, then the percentages were worked out. Country Tables 1 and 2 are in fact directly linked numerically at this point, namely the total of all affiliated Christians in mid-1995, and in this total subdivided into the 6 major ecclesiastical megablocs.

8. *Double affiliation.* Under certain circumstances, the same persons get counted twice as affiliated members by 2 distinct churches or denominations, and allowance must be made for this when adding up totals from all denominations. In certain countries with a nearly-universal state or majority church, many members of Free churches also get enumerated as members by the majority church. In such cases, totals were estimated and added to Country Table 1 and then Country Table 2, as negative quantities (with a minus sign) because they represent a duplication in a series of numbers which when added should give the total number of distinct individuals affiliated to all churches.

9. *Religious profession.* Numbers and percentages of professing adherents in 1995 for each religion were added, based for half the world's countries on the percentages in government censuses of religion or public-opinion polls, updated or backdated to mid-1990 from the last available census or poll during the period 1980–1995. As explained earlier, government census figures do not measure church membership or affiliation but measure what we here call professing Christians. In our presentation here of the results for all censuses, we first of all made the results comparable from one country to another and from one census year to the next by removing from the population figure the small numbers of persons in such categories as 'Not available', 'Unspecified', 'No answer', 'Unknown', 'Object to state', 'No information', which are often present in reports of censuses and polls; the results as percentages were then worked out without them. The accuracy of these census data is high because they are based on a total head count at a single point in time by a vast force of trained enumerators.

10. *Hidden affiliation.* A further phenomenon occurs when persons affiliated to minority or illegal or anti-state or persecuted churches hide this affiliation in government censuses (or whose affiliation is ignored by enumerators) and profess another type of Christianity (usually that of the majority church). Thus, in Latin America, persons affiliated to churches regarded by the state as Evangelical (Evangelicas, -os) may profess to be, or be enumerated as, Catholics in the censuses; such persons are therefore termed here Evangelical Catholics. Similarly, in countries where society or the state or the majority church discriminates against or disapproves of a minority denomination (Jehovah's Witnesses, New Apostolics, etc), its members may be put down in the census as professing Roman Catholics or Protestants or whatever the majority church is.

11. *Percentages.* As described in detail earlier under the heading 'Demographic inertia', the percentage size of a religious community in a country does not change appreciably over the years from one census to the next, even when total population is rapidly increasing, unless there are (a) large-scale conversions within the community to or from another religion, (b) fertility or biological increase rates markedly different from the national average, (c) mass emigration or immigration, (d) anti-religious revolutions, or (e) severe erosion of religious belief due to secularism. In the Western world, the percentage figures for particular religions only change slowly from year to year; in the former Communist world, percentages declined slowly due to anti-religious revolutions and mass emigrations; whereas in the Third World, the % Christian often increases from year to year due to mass conversions and missionary activity.

12. *Unaffiliated and crypto-Christians.* In all countries where professing Christians outnumber those affiliated (Western countries and others with a Christian majority), the difference results in (by our definition) unaffiliated or nominal Christians. In countries where affiliated Christians outnumber those professing (countries where Christians are a minority) the difference results in (by our definition) crypto-Christians.

13. *Practicing Christians.* (*WCD* only) In the several countries where nation-wide polls of church attendance have been taken, these figures were noted. In all other countries, the individual percentages of annual practice from the various denominations were examined, and absolute numbers were computed and totalled, producing the final figures shown in Country Tables 2. In almost all cases, absolute numbers have been rounded to the nearest 10, greater exactitude be-

ing meaningless here. It should be noted that the aggregate of those who attend at least once a year is always greater than the attendance on the major annual festival (Easter or Christmas), because inevitably there are many persons including the sick, infirm, handicapped and radio/TV listeners who are unable to attend on any one specific occasion. This means: (a) for Roman Catholics, the total of all who attend at least once annually is usually around 10% larger than the total of Easter communicants, and may be very much higher in Third-World countries where Catholics face long distances, difficulties of travel, and insufficiency of Easter services; and (b) for Anglicans and Protestants with their far less strict attendance requirements, the total of all who attend at least once annually may be much larger and even up to twice the size of Easter communicants or those who attend on a single major annual festival. This almost universal situation is best documented here in the polls data for the United Kingdom of GB & NI presented under Britain's Country Table 1.

14. *Sub-groups of professing Catholics.* (*WCD* only) In a number of countries, mainly Latin or Latin American, analysis of government censuses of religion indicates that there are large numbers of professing Roman Catholics who are mainly oriented to 3 other, non-Catholic, religious systems: Christopaganism, Evangelicalism (a term used in many Latin government censuses to cover mainly Protestantism, but also including Anglicanism, marginal Protestantism, and indigenous churches), and Spiritism. These subgroups, where they exist, are shown in Country Tables 1 under professing Roman Catholics. It should be noted at this point that the term 'Evangelical' is used throughout this survey in 2 distinct and different senses, firstly as used by states and governments and secondly as used within the churches themselves. These may be described as follows: (1) as understood and used by many non-English-speaking states and governments, notably in their population censuses, the term in the various major languages (Evangelische in German, Evangélique in French, Evangelico in Italian, Evangelico in Spanish and Portuguese) is equivalent to the English term Protestant, or non-Catholic; (2) as understood and used by the churches themselves, especially in the English-speaking world, the term refers to the Evangelical movement within the churches, a subdivision within Protestantism and Anglicanism.
15. *Sub-groups of affiliated Christians.* (*WCD* only). In most countries of the world, there are sizeable numbers of affiliated Christians who also belong to widely-known worldwide groupings or movements, which form clearly-recognized entities and which therefore may be enumerated without difficulty. Of these, the 2 best-known are (a) Evangelicals (the term as understood and used by and in the churches themselves; sometimes called Conservative Evangelicals) and (b) Charismatics; and hence they are enumerated here in Country Tables 1. The complete list of these sub-groups is as follows, with the related major ecclesiastical bloc of which they are a part: Catholic Charismatics (who are affiliated Roman Catholics); Anglican Charismatics, and Anglican Evangelicals (both being affiliated Anglicans); Protestant Charismatics (formerly called Neo-pentecostals), and Evangelicals (both being affiliated Protestants); Orthodox pentecostals (being affiliated Orthodox); and Black Evangelicals (a sub-group of affiliated Black indigenous church members, in the USA only).
16. *Other large religious groupings in 1900, 1970, and 2000.* Where data were available, figures were now inserted for the rest of the larger religious groupings or categories in the listing: Buddhists, Hindus, Muslims, et alii.
17. *Other religionists.* In virtually every country of the world, there are at least a few persons belonging to most of the major world religions, usually diplomats, traders, refugees, military, students, foreign residents, immigrants and so on. The censuses reported under Country Tables 1 often show, for instance, 25 Jews in Trinidad, 63 Muslims, 2 Buddhists, etc. In most cases, they number only tens or hundreds and form too negligible a proportion of the population to be included as separate rows for each religion in Country Tables 1. In the same way, on the fringes of all majority or sizeable religious populations, there is very often a rank growth of ephemeral bodies, exotic sects, transient cults, and so on. In countries where all such groupings are individually small, but in aggregate are not insignificant, they are included at the end of Country Table 1 in a single row under the blanket term 'Other religionists'.
18. *Quasireligions.* This term is used by the Protestant theologian Paul Tillich (in *Christianity and the encounter of the world religions*, New York 1963) to describe those secular pseudoreligious systems which have arisen out of the Judeo-Christian tradition and are now assaulting both Christianity and all other religions. These are defined as near-religions and partial-religions, with a lot in common with nonreligious systems such as Atheism, Marxism, Agnosticism, Humanism, Liberal humanism, scientific materialism, dialectical materialism, nationalism, fascism, Nazism, Communism, Maoism, Leninism, Stalinism, Secularism and similar systems. In this survey, quasireligionists (adherents of quasireligions) are enumerated under 2 categories: anti-religious quasireligionists (atheists) and nonreligious quasireligionists (nonreligious agnostics), as will now be explained.
19. *Atheists.* This book provides a first approximation to the problem of quantifying professing atheists throughout the world. Atheists here are defined as either (1) those professing disbelief in God (belief that there is no God and no supernatural), who abstain from religious activities, who have severed all religious affiliation (e.g. by formally withdrawing from state or majority churches), and who are opposed or militantly opposed to all religion, and are often irreligious (hostile to religion) or anti-religious; or (2) dialectical materialists or those professing belief in Marxist-Leninist Communism regarded as a political faith or quasi-religion. Communism is in fact widely regarded as a quasi-religion; Maoism in China, for instance, has been termed a quasi-religion because it can best be understood as a continuation of the humanistic-religious culture of traditional China. Communism elsewhere can be regarded as religious because, like Nazism and Fascism, it is religious in its claims on the ultimate loyalties of men. Marxism-Leninism is a quasi-religion, a secular religion, because it preaches as dogmas the necessity of class warfare, the dictatorship of the proletariat, the abolition of private property and the nationalization of the means of production. The estimates shown in Tables 1 for all countries give the general order of magnitude of the atheistic community, and are based on the following 3 separate kinds of data. (1) Only a few government population censuses have differentiated between atheists (opposed to religion) and agnostics (indifferent to religion); almost all such censuses in the Western world include both under the single category 'No religion'. In many countries, however, public-opinion polls have been taken differentiating between the 2 categories and giving the number of professing atheists as a percentage of the adult population. This percentage is then applied here to the total population of a country to arrive at an approximate figure for the total atheistic community (adults and their children). (2) In countries where no census or polls data are available, a formula was evolved based on a statistical examination of Communist party membership and atheism in several countries where figures are available, and derived as follows. In most countries of the world, there is a clear distinction between Christians and Communists, based on their ideological commitments; it is regarded as not possible to be both a believer and a materialist, and so a Christian cannot be a Communist or vice versa. Hence in all countries of the world, with only 10 exceptions, 'given the clear philosophical bent of Marxism, one may assume members of Communist parties to be overwhelmingly irreligious', which means that around 95% are professing, dedicated or avowed atheists, i.e. anti-religious persons opposed on principle to religion with varying degrees of hostility (N. McInnes, *The Communist parties of Western Europe*, London: OUP, 1975:53). The 10 exceptions are: Italy (where the PCI is a mass party whose members are about 20% atheists, 40% nonreligious, and 40% professing Catholics), France (where 60% of the PCGF are atheists or nonreligious and 40% professing Roman Catholics) and 8 formerly Communist countries with strong religious majorities which were governed by mass Communist parties among which dedicated atheists number only about 15–50% of party members, remaining members being nonreligious with a small number of religious members. These are Bulgaria, Czechoslovakia, German DR, Hungary, Poland, Romania, Viet Nam, and Yugoslavia. In all countries, as well as adult Communists who are avowed atheists, there are often in addition large numbers of youths and children who belong to militantly atheistic or anti-religious movements, such as China's Young Pioneer Corps (Red Scarves; primary schoolchildren), 20 million teenagers aged 14–25 in the Young Communist League (in 1956), and the over 11 million Red Guards in 1967; or up to 1990 the USSR's 14.5 million Octoberists aged 7–9, and 20 million militantly atheistic Pioneers aged 10–15; and there are also many adherents, fellow-travellers, hangers-on, anarchists, criminals and other de facto atheists. Further, in all Western European and most other non-Communist countries, the annual turnover of Communist party membership is extremely high (up to 16% per year), which means that ex-Communists are far more numerous than communists, perhaps 3 times as numerous (McInnes, op. cit., p. 36–39). Most ex-communists, who are still presumably atheists, remain part of the Communist electorate; statistics of those who vote Communist show that most are neither Communists, ex-Communists, nor atheists. All of this means that the total atheistic community in a country is probably at least around 4 times as large as the number of adult atheists in the Communist party (see statistical documentation on the former USSR in Russia's Country Table 1, footnote 'Atheists'). (3) Lastly, there are, especially in the Western world, a number of atheistic organizations which are not Communist in ideology and may even be politically rightist; and there are numerous individuals who are atheistic humanists or the like. The formula used in Country Tables 1 is therefore (where . = multiplied by):

    Total atheistic community in a country = 4. (number of Communist or other Marxist party members). (% of party members who are atheists), plus 4. (adult membership of any non-Communist atheistic groupings).

20. *Nonreligious* (agnostic or indifferent) populations were also added from censuses and polls, usually in the form of persons whose answer to the question 'What is your religion?' is 'None' or 'No religion' or 'Don't know'. Where no government censuses or polls of religion exist, the numbers of adherents were usually estimated first, and the equivalent percentages worked out after, by subtracting all known religious groupings from the total population. This category covers all forms of nonreligion from quasi-religions to nonreligion proper to complete agnosticism to postreligion (abandonment of all religion or quasi-religion).
21. *Disaffiliated persons* were next calculated for Country Tables 1 (in 11 countries including France, Italy, Spain, and Sweden). These are baptized Roman Catholics and others enumerated as affiliated by the Catholic Church or other majority church, but who have disaffiliated themselves and now profess to be agnostics or atheists, i.e. persons who have recently withdrawn from state or majority churches but who are still regarded as members by those churches.
22. *Christians in 1900.* Figures of Christians in the year 1900 were obtained either from government censuses of that period, or from K. Streit, *Statistische Notizen zum Katholischen Missions-atlas* (1906) for Roman Catholic figures, *Statistical atlas of Christian missions* (World Missionary Conference, 1910) for Protestant and Anglican figures, synod

records for the major Orthodox churches, and a variety of other historical records.

23. *Christians in 1970, 1990, 2000.* Projections for these years were derived by estimating the probable changes in percentage size, or by adding the probable annual increase over the period of 5 or 10 years, based on present trends, and checked or augmented or corrected later by later statistics.

24. *Annual religious changes, 1990–2000,* were next worked out. As explained above, annual change is composed of 2 elements: natural change (biological increase plus migration increase) and non-natural (or supranatural, i.e. conversion) change. The biological increase rate (births minus deaths, % per year) of religious adherents is assumed to be the same as that in the country in which they are situated, unless evidence to the contrary was available. Migration increase of religious communities can be considerable; in such cases, the annual figures were added to make the natural increase column. Then, for each religious grouping, total annual change of all types and the corresponding rate (% per year) were measured from time series statistics or graphs of the growth of the number of adherents over a period of years; these data were available either from successive church affiliation series or from successive population censuses (documented in the footnotes to Country Tables 1). In fact, for half of the world's countries, government censuses of religion are available for at least 1950, 1960, 1970, 1980, and 1990, from which long-term religious trends can be identified. The actual method of calculation used for annual change in Country Tables 1 was as follows. Starting from the 1990 value, projections were made to 1995 and 2000. Then, the exponential growth rate from 1990–2000 was obtained dividing the value for AD 2000 by that of 1990, raising it to the power of 1/10, subtracting 1 and multiplying by 100. This average annual growth rate can then be used to calculate annual change. By subtracting natural change from this total annual change, we arrive at our figures for conversion change. The figures shown represent net increase; i.e. for the Christian religion, this means conversions to Christianity from other religions, minus apostasies or defections from Christianity to other religions or to nonreligion. These annual changes were usually calculated from available data for the period 1990–95, taking into account probable trends for the period 1995–2000; they are therefore presented as average indicators of change for the whole decade 1990–2000.

25. *Christians in 2025.* Projections for the year 2025 are necessarily far more tentative, and should be regarded as only a rough guide based on existing long-term trends and the fact that large populations show relative consistency in their growth over years, decades and centuries. The method here was first to examine for each religion and Christian megabloc the trend in the percentage size of its followers over the period 1900–2000; to plot this progression on a graph; to determine what new factors were likely to be at work in the period 2000–2025; and then to make a conservative estimate or graphical extrapolation of the probable percentage size of each religion by the year 2025. These percentages were then multiplied by the population in AD 2025 (UN medium variant) to give projected numbers of adherents by mid-2025.

In making these statistical projections for the future, we must emphasize that they should be regarded as only a guide. They are one possible scenario based on current trends. They can in no way invalidate the central Christian principle that only God the Holy Spirit controls the future. It is always possible (though unlikely, bearing in mind the demographic inertia of large populations) that the long-term trends of 1900–1990 may peter out or disappear during the years 2000–2025. At the same time, no-one can foresee whether the trends of 1990–2000 may not instead be dramatically accelerated in years to come. As an example, our Country Tables 1 envisage phenomenal growth in the number of Catholic Charismatics in South America, rising by AD 2000 to 34 million in Brazil alone (20% of the total population there) and to a projected 57 million by 2025. This projection is based on present trends; but many observers hold it to be distinctly probable that within the next decade or two the trends may be accelerated and the leadership or even the bulk of the laity in Latin American Catholicism may become predominantly Charismatic ('predominantly' means something well over 50%). However, at the same time we give weight to the principle of demographic inertia described above, namely that whole populations (massive populations in particular) can only change and do only change their basic characteristics slowly and over considerable periods of time. The evidence for this in respect of christianization can be seen from (1) Table 7-1 which shows the comparatively slow numerical growth of Christianity over 20 centuries, and (2) Country Tables 1 and their 1900 and 2000 columns, for most nations of the world.

26. *Missing rows.* It will be noted that in many tables a particular row, which the reader may be looking for, is missing; e.g. the row 'crypto-Christians' is not there for France, the row 'unaffiliated Christians' is absent for Egypt, etc, etc. In our methodology, this means that over the period 1900–2000 these categories are entirely absent, i.e. in size are zero or nil, in those countries.

27. *Religions in order of size.* Lastly, the various religious and nonreligious blocs and groupings in each country were then rearranged in order of numerical size in 2000 to form, with their subdivisions, the final Country Tables 1 as given in WCE Part 4.

## DEFINITIONS OF RELIGIOUS CATEGORIES AND BLOCS

Table 14–10 now summarizes the preceding discussion and sets out the entire classification of Christianity and religions. Each term is then defined below in more detail.

Summarizing the Christian terms defined above, the classification defines the major religious groupings in the world as used in Country Tables 1. Unindented categories are all mutually exclusive, and their totals always add up to 100%, allowance being made for small rounding discrepancies. Indented categories are subdivisions of categories less indented: i.e. categories indented 2 spaces after another category are subdivisions of that category.

Note our 3 basic equations concerning definitions of Christians, based on 3 differing standpoints:

(1) From the standpoint of PROFESSION (public acknowledgement or confession of being a Christian)
Total 'Christians' = professing Christians + crypto-Christians
which also = affiliated Christians (church members) + unaffiliated (or nominal) Christians, which also = Great Commission (overt, practicing) Christians + latent (covert, nonpractising) Christians.

(2) From the standpoint of AFFILIATION (church membership)
Total 'affiliated' = affiliated Roman Catholics + affiliated Protestants + affiliated Orthodox + affiliated Anglicans + affiliated marginal Christians + affiliated Non-White and White Independents, minus doubly-affiliated, minus disaffiliated.

(3) From the standpoint of MISSION (Christ's outreach into the world)
Total 'Great Commission Christians' = total overt plus total covert Christians, which means total openly involved in missions and total involved but not doing so openly.

Note also that the first 9 categories below always (in Tables 1) refer to aggregate totals for all denominations of Christians in all 6 major ecclesiastico-cultural megablocs (Roman Catholic, Protestant, etc) in the whole country.

## MAIN DEFINITIONS FROM TABLE 14–10

What follows are notes describing many of the more significant categories listed and classified in Table 14–10. Those listed are described in numerical order of their ID numbers in that table.

### COUNTRY TABLES 1: RELIGIOUS ADHERENTS IN EACH COUNTRY

*Christians*
= total of all Christian adherents: professing and crypto-Christians, which is here equal to unaffiliated (or nominal) plus affiliated.

*crypto-Christians*
= secret believers in Christ not professing publicly, nor publicly baptized, nor enumerated or known in government census or public-opinion poll, hence unknown to the state or the public or society (but usually affiliated and known to churches), including those in 'churches of silence' or underground churches, of 7 distinct types: (1) unorganized individuals secretly affiliated to or attending legal churches, including persons who choose to identify themselves publicly as non-Christians (i.e. as Hindus, Muslims, non-religious, etc); (2) individuals or congregations permanently exiled, deported or in prison or labor camps, including political prisoners, treated as non-religious by the state but who remain believing Christians through deprived of worship and fellowship opportunities; (3) organized believers in unregistered denominations, and unregistered congregations in legal denominations, which are forced to operate illegally or underground by the state's refusal to grant registration (sometimes termed churches); (4) members of organized deliberate-clandestine networks of illegal underground churches; (5) members of minority churches or marginal bodies or sects in certain countries opposed or hostile to the state hence refusing to divulge their affiliation to census enumerators (Jehovah's Witnesses, New Apostolics, et alii); (6) members of organized movements of believers in Christi who choose not to regard or identify themselves publicly or privately as bodies of Christians (but as Hindus, Muslims, non-religious, etc); and (7) isolated radio believers in non-Christian or anti-Christian areas remote from existing legal churches, initially evangelized through radio programs or mail or radiophonic correspondence courses, prevented from contacting existing churches, who therefore organize their own small cells or informal house congregations based on radio and/or mails.

*professing Christians*
= those publicly professing (declaring, stating, confessing, self-identifying) their preference or adherence in a government census or public-opinion poll, hence unknown to the state or the public.

*unaffiliated (or nominal)*
= those professing but not affiliated to churches, i.e. not churches members; unaffiliated or unchurched (sometimes called residual Christians, latent Christians, anonymous Christians, sometimes post-Christians in industrialized countries); Christians not, no longer, or not yet attached to organized Christianity, or having rejected the institutional churches whilst retaining Christian beliefs and values, who may be Christians individually but are not part of the corporate life, community or fellowship of the churches.

*affiliated Christians*
= church members; all persons belonging to or connected with organized churches; those on the churches' books or records, or with whom the churches are in touch, usually known by name and address to the churches at grass-roots or local parish level; i.e. total of all distinct individuals attached to or claimed by the institutional churches and organized Christianity and hence part of their corporate life, community and fellowship, including children, infants, adherents, catechumens, and members under discipline (totals for 1970–95 are obtained from Tables 2); total church membership, or total church member community, or total Christian community,

or inclusive membership; this is the total of affiliated in the 6 major blocs, minus any doubly-affiliated, minus any disaffiliated.

## Anglicans
= persons related to the Anglican Communion, including dissidents in the Western world.

## Anglican Charismatics
= Anglicans in the organized Charismatic Renewal (healings, tongues, prophesying).

## Non-White indigenous Christians
= Black/Third World indigenous Christians in denominations, churches or movements indigenous to Black or Non-White races originating in the Third world (i.e. all races except the White peoples), locally-founded and not foreign-based or Western-imported, begun since AD 1500, Black/Non-White-founded, Black/Non-White-led, forming autonomous bodies independent of Western and Eastern churches, with no Western ties, often schismatic, separatist, anti-establishment, sometimes anti-Western, anti-White or anti-European in reaction to Western influences.

## White-led Independent Christians
= Postdenominationalists among White races who have started their own independent churches.

## marginal Christians
= followers of para-Christian or quasi-Christian Western movements or deviations out of mainline Protestantism (including pseudo-Christian 'New Age' cults), not professing mainstream Protestant christocentric doctrine but claiming a second or supplementary or ongoing source of divine revelation in addition to the Bible (a new Book, angels, visions), but nevertheless centered on Jesus, Christ, the Cross, the Resurrection, and other Christian features.

## Orthodox
= Eastern (Chalcedonian), Oriental (Pre-Chalcedonian, Non-Chalcedonian, Monophysite), Nestorian (Assyrian), and non-historical Orthodox.

## Orthodox Charismatics
= Orthodox active in the organized Charismatic Renewal (healings, tongues, prophesying)

## Protestants
= Christians in churches originating in, or reformulated at the time of, or in communion with Western world's 16th-century Protestant Reformation; in European languages, usually called Évangéliques (French), Evangelische (German), Evangélicos (Italian, Portuguese, Spanish), though not usually Evangelicals (in English); in Spanish, Portuguese and Italian the term Evangélico in government usage also covers Anglicans, marginal Christians, Independents including Black/Third-World indigenous Christians.

## Roman Catholics
= all Christians in communion with the Church of Rome (affiliated Roman Catholics are here defined as baptized Roman Catholics plus catechumens)

## Catholic Charismatics
= Roman Catholics involved in the organized Catholic Charismatic Renewal (CCR, served by ICCRS in Vatican City); Catholic Charismatics (healing, tongues, prophesying).

## Christopagans
= Amerindian Roman Catholics in Latin America who syncretize folk-Catholicism with organized traditional Amerindian pagan religion.

## Evangelical Catholics
= in Latin countries, professing Roman Catholics who also regard themselves as Evangelicos or Evangeliques and are affiliated to churches which the state terms Evangelical (Protestant, Anglican, indigenous or marginal Protestant); in Latin America, Evangelicos who in a census are still regarded as, or profess to be, Roman Catholics.

## Spiritist Catholics
= Roman Catholics active in organized high or low spiritism, including syncretistic spirit-possession cults.

## doubly-affiliated
= persons affiliated to or claimed by 2 denominations at once (especially Evangelical and Catholic churches in Latin Europe and Latin America); because a duplication, they are shown in the tables as a negative quantity (with a minus sign).

## disaffiliated
= dechristianized persons: baptized Roman Catholics (or other Christians) enumerated as affiliated by a majority or state-linked Catholic church (or other majority or state church) but who have recently formally withdrawn or disaffiliated themselves completely from Christianity and now profess to be nonreligious (agnostics) or atheists; i.e. recent withdrawals from state or majority churches still however regarded as members by those churches, although in fact now backsliders, lapsed, or apostates; sometimes termed post-Christians; because a duplication, they are shown in the tables as a negative quantity (with a minus sign).

## Evangelicals
= a subdivision mainly of affiliated Protestants (Protestants affiliated to churches), namely persons calling themselves Evangelicals as distinct from conciliar ecumenical or non-Evangelical Protestants, or persons belonging to Evangelical congregations, churches or denominations; i.e. Evangelicals properly so called, characterized by commitment to personal religion (including new birth or personal conversion experience), reliance on Holy Scripture as the only basis for faith and Christian living, emphasis on preaching and evangelism, and usually on conversion in theology; usually divided into the 3 groupings Conservative Evangelicals, Conciliar Evangelicals, and Fundamentalists, defined as follows. (1) Persons calling themselves Conservative Evangelicals (mostly in the USA), or (in Europe) so called by the Ecumenical Movement, are sometimes also called Non-Conciliar Evangelicals, Neo-Evangelicals, or Neo-Fundamentalists, or (in german) Evangelikale as opposed to Evangelische which correctly translated means simply Protestant. The term Conservative Evangelical is not accepted by a large section of this grouping, particularly in the USA, who consider the adjective 'Conservative' superfluous and redundant, and who object to the popularizing of the term by the conciliar movement (led by the WCC) to describe Evangelical groups and individuals outside the Ecumenical Movement. They are enumerated here as (a) the total communities (including children) affiliated to institutionalized Conservative Evangelicalism, i.e. in Protestant denominations affiliated to national evangelical fellowships or alliances themselves affiliated to the World Evangelical Fellowship (WEF), and (b) the total communities affiliated to all other Protestant denominations which regard themselves, or are generally regarded, as Conservative Evangelical in doctrine and emphasis (including Pentecostals) but which are not linked to the WEF or institutionalized Conservative Evangelicalism. (2) conciliar Evangelicals, sometimes called ecumenical Evangelicals, who usually call themselves simply Evangelicals, are those who remain within and are affiliated to Protestant denominations not regarded as Conservative Evangelical in doctrine or emphasis but which are instead within the Ecumenical Movement affiliated to national ecumenical councils and/or the World Council of churches (WCC), often called conciliar denominations, and (b) other individual Evangelicals in non-Evangelical parishes or congregations in those denominations. Lastly (3) Fundamentalist, moderate or extreme, are those who began in the USA in the 1920s to oppose theological Liberalism and Modernism, and who are defined as those stressing either the 5 or the 7 so-called fundamental doctrines (inerrant verbal inspiration of the Bible, Virgin Birth, miracles of Christ, Resurrection, total depravity of man, substitutionary Atonement, premillennial Second Coming); enumerated here as (a) the total communities affiliated to Protestant denominations of Fundamentalist doctrine and emphasis usually affiliated to national Fundamentalist councils and/or the International Council of Christian Churches (ICCC), (b) the total communities affiliated to Fundamentalist congregations in non-Fundamentalist denominations, and (c) individual Fundamentalists in non-Fundamentalist congregations and parishes in those

denominations. The most detailed enumeration of all these types of Evangelicals for any country in this book will be found in the footnote EVANGELICALS in WCE Country Table 1 for the USA.

## Anglican Evangelicals
= Anglican Evangelicals (sometimes termed either Conciliar or Conservative Evangelicals, and usually including all whose churchmanship is described as either Evangelical, Conservative Evangelical or Low Church, as distinct from High Church or sacrament persuasions, or Central or Broad Church); characterized by commitment to personal religion (including new birth or personal conversion experience) reliance on Scripture as the only basis for faith, preaching and evangelism; enumerated here as the sum of 3 groupings: (1) the total baptized communities (including children) who are affiliated to Anglican dioceses of Evangelical emphasis or persuasion, where the bulk of the parishes also are Evangelical; (2) those who are affiliated to Evangelical parishes in non-Evangelical dioceses; and (3) individual Evangelicals in dioceses and parishes of non-Evangelical or other persuasion, or of mixed persuasions. The most detailed enumeration of the varieties of Anglican Evangelicals in any country, in this book, will be found in the footnote EVANGELICALS in Country Table 1 for Britain. The figures were derived by sending questionnaires polling a variety of Evangelical leaders and other influential Anglicans in the General Synod of the Church of England and in the major Evangelical organizations.

## Non-Christians
= all who are not Christian adherents of any kind, including non-believers (agnostics, or atheists).

## Afro-American spiritists
= followers of Afro-Brazilian, afro-Cuban and other African religious survivals in the Americas; low spiritists, syncretizing Catholicism with African and Amerindian animistic religions; low spiritists as opposed to high (non-Christian) spiritists; also Afro-American syncretistic cults with Christian elements.

## Atheists
= those professing atheism, skepticism, impiety, disbelief or irreligion, or Marxist-Leninist Communism regarded as political faith, or other anti-religious quasi-religions, and who abstain from religious activities and have severed all religious affiliation; and others opposed, hostile or militantly opposed to all religion (anti-religious); dialectical materialists, militant non-believers anti-religious humanists skeptics.

## Baha'is
= followers of the Baha'i World Faith founded by Baha'u'llah (Baha' Allah).

## Buddhists
= followers of (a) Mahayana (Greater Vehicle) or Northern Buddhism (b) Theravada (Teaching of the Elders) or Hinayana Lesser Vehicle) or Southern= Buddhism; or (c) Vajrayana (Mantrayana, Guhyamantrayana, Tantrayana (Esoteric Vehicle). Tantrism or Lamaism); or (d) traditional Buddhist sects, but excluding neo-Buddhist new religions or religious movements.

## religious Buddhists
= Buddhists who profess Buddhism as both a family religion and also a personal religion.

## non-religious Buddhists
= persons whose family religion is Buddhism but who as individuals profess to have no personal religion.

## Chinese folk-religionists
= followers of traditional Chinese religion, with 6 elements: local deities including Taoist ones, ancestor veneration, Confucian ethics, Chinese universism, divination and magic, some Buddhist elements.

## Confucians
= non-Chinese followers of Confucius and Confucianism.

## Ethnoreligionists
= often called tribal religionists, these are followers of what are termed 'local' religions, which means ethnic or tribal religions restricted to members of one tribe or ethnic group; primal or primitive religionists,

animists, spirit-worshippers, shamanists, ancestor-venerators, polytheists, pantheists, traditionalists (in Africa), local or tribal folk-religionists (excluding Chinese as a special case); in some government censuses termed 'pagans', 'heathens' (so termed in Solomon Islands census of 9.II.1970, inter alia), 'fetishists', 'without religion'; including adherents of neo-paganism or non-Christian local or tribal syncretistic or nativistic movements, cargo cults, witchcraft eradication cults, possession healing movements, tribal messianic movements; usually confined each to a single tribe or people, hence 'tribal' or local as opposed to 'universal' (open to any or all peoples).

*Hindus*
= followers of the main Hindu traditions: (a) Vaishnavite or Vishnativite; (b) Saivite or Shivaite; (c) Saktite or Saktist; (d) Arya Samaj and other reformist movements (excluding Jains and Sikhs); and (e) neo-Hindu movements and modern sects arising out of Hinduism.

*Jains*
= followers of Jain reform movement from Hinduism, composed of the Svetambara and Digambara sects.

*Jews*
= followers of the Orthodox, Reformed, or Liberal schools of Judaism; Ashkenazis, Sefardis (Sephardis); also crypto-Jews.

*Karaites*
= Readers of the Scriptures, followers of Qaraism (a Jewish sect).

*Samaritans*
= Children of Israel (Bene-Yisrael) or Shamerim (Observant Ones), a small Jewish sect.

*Mandaeans*
= Gnostics (Mandaiia), followers of 2nd-century AD syncretistic Jewish-Christian fertility religion (Christians of St John, Followers of John the Baptist, Dippers, Sabaeans).

*Muslims*
= followers of Islam, in its 2 main branches (with schools of law, rites or sects): Sunnis or Sunnites (Hanafite, Hanbalite, Malikite, Shafite), and Shias or Shiites (Ismaili, Ithna-Ashari, Alawite and Zaydi versions), and otherwise orthodox sects; reform movements (Wahhabi, Sanusi, Mahdiya), also heterodox sects (Ahmadiya, Druzes, Kharijites (Ibadites), Yazidis), but excluding syncretistic religions with Muslim elements.

*Ahmadis, Druzes, Yazidis*
= followers of heterodox Muslim sects (allegedly heretical or heterodox bodies; shown indented below the entry 'Muslims', and enumerated also in the total statistics of Muslims).

*New-Religionists*
= followers of the so-called Asiatic 20th-century New Religions, New Religious movements, or radical new crisis religions (new Far Eastern or Asiatic indigenous non-Christian syncretistic mass religions, or new religious movements or sects embodying major innovations and religious systems distinct from those of the traditional world religions, founded since 1800 and mostly since 1945) including the Japanese neo-Buddhist and neo-Shinto new religious movements, and Korean, Chinese, Vietnamese and Indonesian syncretistic religions; et alia.

*Nonreligious*
= those professing no religion, or professing unbelief or non-belief, non-believers, doubters, agnostics, free-thinkers, liberal thinkers, non-religious humanists, non-religious quasi-religionists, post-religious; indifferent to both religion and atheism, apathetic, opposed on principle neither to religion nor atheism; sometimes termed secularists or materialists; also post-Christian, de-christianized or de-religionized populations.

*Parsis (Parsees)*
= descendants of Zoroastrians, still called Zoroastri-

ans today, mainly found in Iran and India.

*Shintoists*
= Japanese who profess, or still profess, Shinto as their first or major religion.

*Sikhs*
= followers of the Sikh reform movement out of Hinduism, who look to the Golden Temple in Amritsar, India (sects: Akali, Khalsa, Nanapanthi, Nirmali, Sewapanthi, Udasi).

*Spiritists*
= non-Christian spiritists or spiritualists, or thaumaturgicalists; high spiritists, as opposed to low spiritists (Afro-American syncretists); followers of medium-religions, medium-religionists.

*Other religionists*
= term used here in Country Tables 1 for adherents of all other smaller non-Christian religions, faiths, quasi-religions, pseudo-religions, para-religions, religious systems, religious philosophies, and semi-religious brotherhoods, not included in the above listing (e.g. Gnostic, Occult, Masonic, Mystic religions).

*Country's population*
= total present-in-area resident population or inhabitants of country at a given mid-year date.

All columns headed % in Country Tables 1 refer to percentages of the total population of the country.

## FOOTNOTES TO COUNTRY TABLES 1

CENSUSES. From its historical usage with regard to population counting, the term census is implicitly reserved for total or complete analysis of a population, although several governments now include partial surveys through sampling procedures. In this book, therefore, the term census always refers only and uniquely to an official government population census (usually complete, 100%, enumeration of the whole population). Footnotes under Tables 1 give details of all censuses which have included a religion question (either complete enumeration or on a sample basis), each shown by the date (day, month, year, in the standard United Nations order) on which it was conducted. Each date is printed in bold type, thus: **9.IV.1961**. Although such data are usually available in published form, in a number of recent cases our survey obtained the data before publication from each country's statistical office or from its annual statistical report to the United Nations on the annual Demographic Yearbook Questionnaire. In a number of other cases, the censuses reported here were official government censuses, but the religion data (and sometimes the entire census results) were never published, or were only made available in duplicated (mimeographed) form. In almost all such cases the editors obtained these unpublished data in visits to government statistical offices or by correspondence with them. It should be noted that in this book we make no detailed attempt at a critique of each nation's censuses, but accept them as the best available data on the subject. Because of the large sizes of the populations enumerated and the need for comparativeness from one census to the next, the results are given here as percentages to the first decimal place (e.g. 65.7%); 2 decimal places are avoided because of their claim to a bogus precision. The major problem faced at his point has been the non-standardized and non-comparable terms and categories used from one census to the next and from one country to another. Thus, many censuses omit certain minorities such as tribal peoples, nomads, aliens, refugees, military, etc. As one example of this, in Australia the legally-defined statistical 'population of Australia' until 1967 was the non-Aboriginal population only. This problem has been solved here by recompiling each census' totals using our standard terminology and methodology. The figures for several censuses as shown in the footnotes have been recomputed and rewritten slightly to incorporate the exact terminology we employ in this survey; thus the category 'Protestants', which in several censuses is used loosely to mean all Christians except Roman Catholics, is here shown divided into our usage of Anglicans, Protestants, Orthodox, Black indigenous, etc. These footnotes contain data from practically all those censuses in all countries in

which the religion question has been asked. Consequently, if no census is quoted in a particular country for 1900, or 1960, or 1990, it means that in that year the question on religion was omitted, or not asked, or not processed or never released. It should also be noted that at each decennial census an increasing number of countries abandon the religion question, despite UN prompting, because of the escalating cost of every question in the census schedule and the fact that religion data from past censuses have rarely been of use in government planning.
POLLS. Whereas censuses usually go to and enumerate the entire population, adults plus children, to the last individual, a poll is taken from a very small carefully-constructed sample (usually around 2,500 adults, or 1,500 for Gallup polls) representative of the entire adult population. Because of the additional questions and the care with which they are formulated, accuracy and meaningfulness are often higher than those of censuses. Like censuses, a poll is taken at a single point in time, and if significant this may be indicated in our footnotes thus: 10.IX.1990, or September 1990, or simply: 1990. Because of the small size of samples, however, polls figures are usually given as integers without decimal places. Among specialists their accuracy is regarded as to plus or minus 3% ('Sampling tolerances', *Religion in America 1977–8* Gallup Opinion Index, p. 116–117).

## NOTES ON RELIGIONS

CHRISTIANS (etcetera). Next follow further details elaborating certain of the categories in Country Tables 1, these being listed in alphabetical order. For further details on the composition of Christian totals (e.g. 'Black/Third-World indigenous', 'marginal Christians'), the reader should turn to the country's Table 2.
ATHEISTS. This footnote summarizes the available source data. Together with secularism, agnosticism (non-religion) et alia, atheism is one of a group of anti-Christian or anti-religious movements collectively known as quasi-religions. Since Communism is widely regarded as a quasi-religion, and since the basic philosophy of Marxists and Marxist regimes is atheistic, the footnote enumerates the Communist phenomenon by giving the name(s) of organized Communist parties, the legal status of each, its attitude vis-a-vis the Sino-Soviet dispute (pro-Soviet, or pro-Chinese, or independent, or split), and statistics of members and of all who voted for Communist parties in any recent elections. Other data on atheism (e.g. polls) are available for certain countries. The method whereby the total of atheists is derived from these data has been described earlier.

*Non-Christian use of 'church'*
The English word 'church' is derived, not directly from the New Testament word ekklesia, but from early Christian usage of the Greek word kyriakon meaning 'belonging to the Lord'. Historically, the word 'church' has therefore a specifically Christian origin and has always had this exclusively Christian meaning. In recent times, however, with the growth of knowledge concerning community life and values in non-Christian religions, confusion has arisen through the use in English of the word 'church', either in loose or popular or journalistic conversation, or officially in the names of organizations, to describe its non-Christian counterparts, namely for communities of believers in Islam, Buddhism, Hinduism, New Religions, et alia. Examples of the official use of 'church' by non-Christian bodies in this way are:
Cao Daist Missionary Church (Viet Nam)
Church of World Messianity (Sekai Kyusei-kyo)
Church Universal & Triumphant (USA)
First Church of Voodoo (USA)
Heavenly Virtue Holy Church (T'ien Te Sheng Hui, in Hong Kong and Malaysia)
Perfect Liberty Church (PL Kyodan, in Japan)
Satanic Church
True Church of Nichiren (Soka Gakkai of Japan)
Unification Church International (based on Korea)
United Buddhist Churches of Viet Nam
Vedic Church of East Africa (Arya Samaj)
Yellow Church of Tibet (a semi-official term for Yellow Hat Lamaist Buddhism)
In addition, there are a host of other non-Christian bodies, sects and cults calling themselves 'Church', which have arisen on the fringes of Christianity in

solidly-Christian lands (especially in the USA) out of Christian roots and retaining some Christian elements. Although we here maintain that 'church' is a specifically Christian term and so should be restricted to Christian usage, we have to recognize that it is becoming increasingly popular as a self-appellation in a number of non-Christian religions.

## WCE COUNTRY TABLES 2: ORGANIZED CHURCHES AND DENOMINATIONS IN EACH COUNTRY

After each country's article in *WCE* Part 4, the second table describes organized denominational Christianity. It lists all Christians organized into bodies, i.e. all Christian affiliated to churches, networks, house groups or similar worship centers, and gives de facto (not de jure) statistical and other descriptive information about each autonomous church body (denomination, diocese or other jurisdiction) that they belong to, representing the statistical situation for, on average or approximately, the year 1995, and/or the period 1990–2000, with in many cases notes updating statistics and in all cases totals for the years 1900, 1970, 1990, 1995, 2000, and 2025. In Roman Catholic, Orthodox and Anglican practice, a diocese is an autonomous and self-governing local church, and is therefore regarded here as the proper unit for comparison with a Protestant or indigenous denomination. The practice here then, in order to give a balanced presentation between the world's 2 major Christian blocs (Protestantism and Roman Catholicism) is to include all Roman Catholic and Orthodox dioceses (with a very occasional omission in the interests of avoiding undue length), and to include all Protestant denominations, as their counterpart. Some very large Protestant denominations themselves also consist of several dioceses or equivalent subdivisions, but these are only listed in a few cases for the very largest churches.

### Comparative symbolics
The table includes the basic descriptive material to enable churches and denominations to be classified and compared with one another, and from one country to another. It thus provides basic or initial material for the science of comparative symbolics. This is the term traditionally applied to that branch of theology or ecclesiology which deals with the various Christian churches and confessions, and their doctrines, creeds, constitutions, ways of worship, devotional life and other distinctive features, studied as a whole.

### Objects of Country Table 2
The objects of listing all churches and denominations in a single statistical table are:
1. to provide a complete overview of all organized Christian churches with members and adherents in the country;
2. to show them in comparative ecumenical or interdenominational perspective;
3. to enable information to be located at a glance concerning any particular denomination, or ecclesiastical tradition, or type of church, or confession (world family of churches or denominations), or missionary society or order;
4. to enable meaningful statistical totals to be compiled for the country, for its region and continent, for world confessions, and for the whole world;
5. to provide a direct and exact numerical link with Country Table 1 (which enumerates all religions, and over the period 1900–2025) by expanding Table 1's figures of affiliated Christians in 1900, 1970, 1990, 1995, 2000 and 2025; and
6. to provide basic or initial classificatory and descriptive material for the science of comparative symbolics.

### One line per denomination or diocese
This comparative table stretches across the page, a single line being given to a single church body (denomination or diocese). In the case of churches with several dioceses, jurisdictions or other subdivisions, statistics are given on a single line each for each diocese, and the totals for the church are found above them on the first line, occupied by the title of the church itself followed by a colon (e.g. 'Church of England:').

### Comprehensiveness
The listing attempts to be comprehensive. It includes all major or significant denominations and dioceses known to exist in the country, together with at the end one or more summary lines covering all other bodies too small to be given a separate line each. In countries with very large numbers of small and relatively insignificant denominations (e.g. USA, Philippines, South Africa), it has been necessary to have a numerical cut-off point, above which all bodies are included, and below which most bodies are not included (e.g. USA, 1,000 adherents). Statistics for these remaining bodies are then summarized at the end of the alphabetical listing under the blanket terms 'Other Protestant denominations... Total 150', 'Other indigenous churches... Total 25', 'Other marginal Protestant bodies... Total 10', and so on.

### Descriptive notes on each body
Brief notes in column 10 crystallize the identity of the body concerned, by giving data such as its past and present names, with translation into English where necessary, and brief socioreligious notes of interest to describe the body and to give it a 'personality' that statistics alone cannot confer. Bodies formerly existing in a country, but now defunct or merged or with a new name, may often be found mentioned in column 10.

### Estimating adults and children
We have already noted above that although a number of denominations produce annual figures of all types of membership, covering and including both adults and children, many other denominations only enumerate one of the 2 standard membership categories we require for this survey (Country Tables 2, columns 6 and 8). Either they enumerate adult members only (as do the Non-Liturgical world confessions including most Protestant bodies), or they only enumerate total affiliated community including children and infants (as do the Liturgical world confessions including Roman Catholic, Anglican and Orthodox bodies). To ensure that the statistics in our table are properly comparable from one denomination to another, we have therefore to estimate the missing figure for each such body. The exact procedure for doing this will now be described.

The usual definitions of adults and children, followed in this book, are those employed by the United Nations as shown above. 'Adults' refers to the working-age and old-age populations, namely all persons of 15 years and over (over-14s); 'children' refers to under-15s (0–14 years old), who may be subdivided into school-age children (5–14 years) and pre-school children or infants, who are aged 0–4 (under-5s).

With these definitions, we can draw up another table showing in its first 2 columns, for any countries we are interested in, the relative sizes of (1) the number of children (under-15s) and (2) the number of adults (over-14s) in each country's population. We do this below for a small selection of typical countries across the world. Next we make the assumptions, described earlier, that (a) in any particular denomination the proportions of children and adults are approximately the same as those in its country's total population, and that (b) children and infants have, in general, the same religion and denomination as their parents. We can now derive the last 2 columns in the table; (3) gives the ratio of adults to total affiliated in any denomination, and (4) gives its inverse, namely the ratio of total affiliated to adults. Knowing one of these 2 types of membership figure for a denomination, we can therefore now estimate the other. If a denomination, for example, in the UK has 100,000 total affiliated including children and infants, then we can estimate its adult members at 77,000; if another denomination there reports 100,000 adults, then we can estimate its total affiliated at 130,000.

To estimate the missing figure for a particular body, we must first decide whether its reported membership figure includes, or excludes, children and infants. In general, if infant baptism is practiced by the denomination, infants are enumerated in its membership figure; if adult baptism only is practiced, the membership figure probably covers adults only. Next, we must establish exactly what age-range is covered by the body's reported figure. For most denominations, the issue will be clearcut: either the age-range will be all ages (0-over 65 years), as with all Roman Catholic and Orthodox dioceses, or it will be only adults over 14, as with most Protestant bodies. Protes-

tant practice here needs to be carefully investigated. In the case of the 2 largest Protestant bodies in the USA, for example, the United Methodist Church's 10,622,173 full members (in 1970) were over-14s (full membership commencing at age 15 on average), whilst the Southern Baptist Convention's total in 1970, 11,629,880 baptized members, were over-9s (baptism taking place between the ages of 8 and 10). In the former USSR, membership was prohibited by law for persons under 18 years old. These latter 2 cases are unusual, however; and in this survey all Protestant bodies are assumed to define their adult membership as over 14 unless evidence to the contrary is available. We can now describe our actual estimation procedure, dividing denominations into 5 categories.

1. *Churches with no adult statistics.* Where a body enumerates not adult members but only total affiliated community including children and infants, we can obtain an estimate for adult membership by multiplying this figure by the country's proportion of the total population who are over 14 years of age (column 3 above). This latter information is given in this book for each country in the secular data at the start of its survey article in *WCE* Part 4. In the USA, for example, of the total population 69% are 15 years or older in age, and so a Roman Catholic or Orthodox diocese there reporting 100,000 total affiliated can be estimated to have a total of adult members of 100,000 x 69% = 69,000.

2. *Churches whose adult statistics refer to over-14s.* Where a body enumerates adults only excluding children under 15 and infants, we follow exactly the reverse procedure, dividing this figure by the proportion of the total population in its country who are adults (or, multiplying by its inverse, given below in column 4). In the USA, a denomination reporting 100,000 adult members over 14 would then be estimated to have a total affiliated community of 100,000 ÷ 69% = 145,000.

3. *Churches whose adult statistics include children over 9.* In some Protestant traditions practicing adult baptism and rejecting infant baptism, the minimum age at which baptism is permitted has been gradually reduced over the years. In Southern Baptist (USA) churches it takes place between the ages 8–10 years, and sometimes as young as 7 or even 6 years old. For such denominations, the above tables table cannot be used and instead we have to return to the country's population data to derive a figure for the proportion of the total population who are over 9 years old (10 years and older). For the USA, this figure recently was 81.9%, and so a denomination reporting 100,000 members over 9 would be estimated to have 122,000 total affiliated.

4. *Churches whose adult statistics cover other age-ranges.* If it is known that a denomination's adult statistics cover other ranges of age, such as over-18s only, or over-20s only, or over-12s, then we have to return in the same way to the country's population data again.

5. *Churches whose adult statistics are strictly reduced.* With certain Protestant traditions (Pentecostal, Holiness, independent, smaller Baptist denominations, et alia), a further factor must be taken into account, namely that the figure for adult membership is usually strictly controlled and rolls are regularly 'cleaned' or reduced in size to exclude lapsed or departed members and to include only the church's regularly-attending baptized communicants in good standing. In such cases its figure for total affiliated, which on our definition includes all other kinds of looser affiliation (unbaptized adults, attending sympathizers, irregularly-attending adults, adults under discipline, adherents, catechumens, as well as their children and infants), will often be 2, 3 or even 4 times as large as the adult membership. In such cases, we have evaluated each denomination's situation individually, using the following standard procedure.

For these categories of churches, our procedure when estimating the missing figure for a specific denomination has been as follows. First, we decide in which of the 5 categories it falls. Secondly, if it falls in categories 2–5 we start from whatever adult figure the denomination reports, enter this in Table 2's column 6, and examine exactly what categories of member it covers. If it falls in category 5, we add an estimate for other types of adult membership (catechumens, unbaptized attenders, irregular attenders, et alia) multiply this new total by the appropriate Affiliated/Adults factor to incorporate children and infants, and then see if other statistical evidence covering children is available (e.g. Sunday-school attendance) which would justify increasing the total, as a result of all which we arrive at the final estimate of total affiliated which appears in Country Table 2 as our column 8.

To sum up, the relationship between our 2 columns 6 and 8 in Country Tables 2 is extremely complex, and although we have used the above guiding principles, other evidence in particular cases may modify the procedure we have used.

### Time level of the statistics
It is important, especially with rapidly-growing churches, to specify the time level, i.e. the exact date or time to which particular data supplied by the churches refer. Large churches are not able to be very precise about their data, and there is no standardization amongst the denominations with regard to the time of year when numbers are counted. Most statistics vary somewhat during the year. For example, the number of foreign missionaries in a particular country will fluctuate from month to month as some go on furlough, or new replacements arrive; again, church members are added, lost, or die, from day to day in a continuous process. Our statistics were collected from the churches themselves during the period 1965–2000. However, the delays and drawn-out processes involved in the gathering of statistics within most churches mean that most membership statistics when published reflect in fact the situation several years earlier, though very few large churches acknowledge this and most continue to assume too recent a date. For rough comparative purposes, it may be assumed that taken as a whole the statistics in Tables 2 refer to the situation at mid-1995, updated to mid-2000 and projected to mid–2025. For more exact information in any particular case, the reader should consult annual reports of the churches he is interested in.

### Multiyear time lags
This time lag or delay in statistical reporting for large churches may be illustrated by considering the annual collecting and publishing of global statistics by the world's biggest church and also statistically its best-organized, namely the Roman Catholic Church. On 9 January 1973 its Central Office of Statistics in Rome published its annual directory *Annuario Pontificio 1973*, containing statistics of Catholics for every jurisdiction in the world. These statistics soon became referred to by interested persons, especially in other churches, as 'the 1973 statistics'. But in fact the statistics referred to the situation at a much earlier date. Working backwards in time from the January 1973 publication date, we find that typesetting began the previous autumn 4 months earlier, and that the manuscript was compiled from questionnaires returned to Rome by the other 2,000 jurisdictions during April-June 1972, having been sent out a couple of months before that. The questionnaire asked all bishops to provide statistical totals describing the situation as at 31 December 1971; the bishops gave their latest available figures, but in fact many of their totals had been obtained or were in circulation several months previously, and a number were repetitions of figures sent in the previous year, or 2 or 3 years previously. These diocesan totals in turn had been compiled from parish returns compiled earlier from actual counts at the parish level done still earlier, in many cases during 1970, or 1969, or in some cases during 1968 or even earlier. In sum, the, *AP 1973* published statistics which described the grass-roots situation, approximately and on average, at the very latest at mid-1970. For this reason in Country Tables 2 we use Catholic statistics from *AP 1973* to represent the situation as at mid-1970. Likewise figures from *AP 2000* reflect the situation in 1995, 1996, or at most 1998. The only exception is for the nation in which statistical reporting procedures are the most rapid, namely the USA; in this case statistics from *The official Catholic directory* (1972) were assumed to best represent the mid-1970 situation.

It can be shown likewise that similar time lags of 2, 3, 4, 5, 6, 7 or even 8 years accompany the publication of statistics by the other major churches of the world. This being so, it follows that any survey of all churches in the world must be subject to a similar, cumulative and hence even larger, time lag, of at least

6, 7, 8, 9 or even 10 years. In this book we indicate this phenomenon by stating that Country Tables 2 represent, on average, the situation in the year 1995; Country Tables 1 then place the figures in the wider religious situation in 1990, 1995, 2000 and projected to 2025.

### Overlapping memberships
Although in almost all cases the lists of churches and denominations in Tables 2 are mutually exclusive, with each Christian being enumerated once and once only under only one body, in a few cases there is a significant amount of overlapping or dual membership of individuals. Sometimes this takes place within a large denomination, as with the Southern Baptist Convention where 'non-resident members' counted in Texas may be the same persons counted as resident members in California whither they have migrated. Sometimes the same individuals belong as members to 2 or more local congregations. Sometimes the overlapping may affect several denominations: in the USA a number of congregations affiliate themselves to, and pay quotas to, more than one nation-wide denomination (e.g. Methodist & Presbyterian; or American Baptist & United Church of Christ). Store-front churches among USA Blacks are sometimes claimed by 2 denominations also. Again there is a certain amount of rebaptism, as when Christians from older denominations baptized in infancy join younger denominations who cause them to be baptized again as adults. Nevertheless, all of these varieties of overlapping are in most countries numerically insignificant or even negligible by comparison with the orders of magnitude shown in the tables.

### Double affiliation
There is however one type of country in the world in which very large numbers of church members are counted twice as affiliated to 2 separate churches. This happens widely in Latin American and European countries with overwhelmingly-large Roman Catholic majorities where sizeable numbers of Catholics have recently (within the previous 10 or 20 years) become Evangelicals (Evangélicos) and joined Protestant, Independent, Anglican or marginal Christian churches. They are then counted as affiliated both by their local Roman Catholic church or diocese, because they were baptized as Catholics, and also by their Evangelical church. This state of affairs is most clearly seen in cases where the total of affiliated members claimed by all the churches is greater than the total population of the country. Obviously, in such cases many people are doubly-affiliated, i.e. being counted twice, usually deliberately and knowingly, but often without the individuals realizing it (e.g. as when a congregation affiliates to both the Northern Baptists and the Southern Baptist Convention by decision of pastor and a few advisors only).

In Country Tables 1 and 2 for these countries, the situation is set out clearly so that it is possible to see how double affiliation arises and how it is enumerated. In all such cases, the exact total of these persons thus doubly-affiliated is taken from Table 1 and inserted as a line at the end of Table 2 immediately before the final totals. In order to keep the mathematics correct, these figures of doubly-affiliated persons are expressed in both tables as negative quantities (with minus signs). The number shown 'affiliated' in Tables 1 and 2 is therefore not the sum of the totals claimed by all churches, but this sum minus the quantity shown as negative, which then gives the total number of distinct individuals affiliated, with each individual counted only once.

### Evangelical Catholics
A further complication arises during government censuses, when it is clear that many of these new Evangelicals are still regarded as, or are enumerated as, or still profess publicly to be, or still declare themselves as, Roman Catholics. In many Latin American countries it is plain that the total of Evangelicals is much greater than that recorded in the official government censuses which often enforce the position that every individual must have only one religion, whatever he or she may say. These persons who are affiliated to Evangelical churches but who are enumerated in the censuses as professing Roman Catholics are termed Evangelical Catholics here in Country Tables 1. Their number in a country is in almost all cases less than that of the doubly-affiliated, since many of the latter identify themselves clearly in the censuses as Evan-

gelicals.

### Zero, hyphen (dash), and dot (period) as information
The symbol 0 in tables means zero, as for example in a case where the number of Christians in 1900 was nil. This is a definite piece of information, and does not mean 'No information available'. Likewise, in Country Tables 2, column 4 (Councils), the symbol . (period, fullstop) means 'Not a member of any council'.

Likewise, in Country Tables 2 the symbol - (hyphen, dash) in a numerical column has an exact special meaning—it means 'no figure exists because this body did not exist in the year 1970, but came into existence after then at the year indicated'.

### Totals
At the end of each Country Table 2 will be found totals at the average date applicable to the data in the table (mid-1970 and mid-1995), and projected totals for AD 2000 and 2025, derived from, or in parallel with, Table 1's analysis of church growth data. Tables 1 and 2 are therefore linked by both giving this one exact category ('affiliated' Christians) for the 6 years 1900, 1970, 1990, 1995, 2000, and 2025.

### Languages, spellings, and orthography
In this table, the names of denominations are listed in one of the 6 major European international languages (English, French, German, Italian, Portuguese, Spanish), depending on which one makes the most sense in a global survey; either as the official language, or the dominant one, or the one most widely used; in most cases, it is English. Certain denominations still insist on using for international purposes a minority-language name, untranslated, and occasionally we reproduce them in that language. Certain countries also are bilingual (e.g. Cameroon) or trilingual (e.g Switzerland); in their cases, church names are given in the churches' own major language.

In Table 2's column 1, place names in church names are given in the local spelling and orthography as standardized in atlases. As in the text, place names in column 10 and in the footnotes are anglicized only if widely used (e.g. Rome, Moscow, Copenhagen). It should be noted that different churches in the same country may differ in their usage for spellings, orthography and transliterations of the same words. If this is the case, we follow each church's usage on its own line. In the same way, in the same country 2 churches may spell an ethnic name in different ways; again, we follow each's usage on its own line.

### Alphabetization
1. All lists of names throughout this book are alphabetized in the standard order shown below, with 2 additions before As-Zz and 9 additions after. A blank space in a name comes first (thus 'Church Society' is listed before 'Churches Society'); and '&', then the alphabet, then all other signs, and lastly numerals.

|        |                       |
|--------|-----------------------|
|        | (blank space)         |
| &      | (ampersand)           |
| Aa-Zz  | (letters of alphabet) |
| -      | (hyphen)              |
| ,      | (comma)               |
| ;      | (semicolon)           |
| :      | (colon)               |
| '      | (apostrophe)          |
| (      | (parenthesis)         |
| )      | (parenthesis)         |
| /      | (oblique, slash)      |
| 0–9    | (numerals)            |

2. In the lists of churches in Table 2 for each country, certain frequently-used words (e.g. 'Church', 'Evangelical') are in some cases abbreviated (e.g. to 'Ch', 'Ev') to keep names to a manageable length; these abbreviations are given in the GeoCodebook (Part 16). When alphabetizing, however, the abbreviated forms are alphabetized on their unabbreviated version, to assist the reader to locate them.

3. The abbreviation 'St' (Saint) is likewise alphabetized on the unabbreviated version.

4. A capital letter (A) precedes its lower-case counterpart (a), but only where 2 names are otherwise identical.

In the sections that now follow, we give first the meanings of various columns in the table, and then the various codes employed in columns 1, 3, 4, and 10.

### SUMMARY OF COLUMNS IN TABLES 2

The first 9 columns give data (names, dates, codes, numbers) that are directly comparable from one line to another in the table, i.e. from one denomination or diocese to another. But in addition, there is a lot of church data available which is not comparable in this way. Some churches enumerate their lay workers, others do not; some are aided by foreign missionary societies, others are not; many operate development projects, many do not; and so on. Column 10 therefore serves as a general space where any further significant data available may be summarized, with the aim of identifying each body clearly, sketching its historical development, and giving it an identity that statistics alone cannot convey. The code used is explained later and is summarized in the GeoCodebook.

After this summary of the 10 columns, detailed explanations and codes are given for a few columns.

#### Column 1   Name  = names of bodies
= Official name of church, denomination or diocese in the country's major European language in use (or in English in ambiguous cases), including standardized abbreviations for dioceses, jurisdictions or other sub-divisions. Initials of these church names, if widely used (mainly for Protestant and Anglican churches), are added at the beginning of the notes in Column 8.

#### Column 2   Begun  = year begun
= year (AD) usually given (by historians or officials of the body concerned) as the main or most significant or earliest date of origin of the body in this country, in permanent form, i.e. with subsequent continuity to the present day; i.e. year when body or its predecessors was founded, begun, re-begun, formed, or organized in this country; when evangelization began in this country, or the first evangelists arrived, or the first immigrants of that church came from another country, or the first missionaries arrived from another land (note that in numerous cases a foreign mission society was preceded by nationals or immigrants; or, it built on a previously existing congregation or church); for a diocese or sub-division, year when diocese or sub-division was formally created or formed; for Roman Catholic jurisdictions, date when first created or erected as a distinct and separate jurisdiction; for Roman Catholic local (national) churches (if followed by dioceses and jurisdictions), year when the first specifically Roman Catholic (for Latin or Greek or other Catholic) missionary activity began in the country; for other large churches (followed by several dioceses or sub-divisions), year when first christian activity began in the country. (Note: c = circa, approximately. For the first 15 centuries, AD, a founding date 'in the 5th century' is thus written here 'c 450')

#### Column 3   Type  = megabloc and tradition
= Ecclesiastical type: major ecclesiastico-cultural megabloc (Roman Catholic, Protestant, etc.), followed by ecclesiastical tradition (Latin, Coptic, Reformed, Pentecostal, etc.).

#### Column 4   Councils  = conciliar memberships
= Conciliarism: membership in 5 types of council or conciliar body — respectively: confessional, world, continental, regional, national.

#### Column 5   Congs  = worship centers
= Congregations or worship centers (all distinct organized groups of worshippers, usually measured by: church buildings, chapels, regular worship premises, worship centers, sites, stations, centers, outposts, preaching points); for the Roman Catholic Church, this column almost always gives the total parishes and quasi-parishes although on a few occasions also with churches and missions (for exact breakdown and meaning in a particular diocese, consult *Annuario Pontificio*; numbers of chapels (often very much greater than number of parishes) are not given in *AP*, but for jurisdictions under Propaganda these are given for 1969 in *Guida delle Missioni Cat-*

*toliche 1970*, also 1989 and subsequently). In many Protestant bodies, 'congregation' is a technical term for an organized self-supporting parish, but the statistics shown here use our wider definition just given. Catholic parishes and quasi-parishes tend to be far larger in size and area than Protestant congregations, but each usually centers on one single parish church building; in addition, a Catholic parish often has numerous mass centers, but these are usually less fixed than Protestant centers and are only rarely enumerated. 'Congregation' here has no reference to the Catholic usage meaning a religious institute order community or society; this latter meaning is enumerated in Column 8 (see code 'C' in GeoCodebook).

#### Column 6   Adults  = total in 1995
= Adult church members (communicants, full members, adult believers, also probationary members, baptized adult non-communicants, sometimes unbaptized attending adults) usually those over 14 years of age, on church's books or rolls (many Protestant bodies enumerate only this adult membership); often termed simply communicants (all those eligible for communion) or full members, although probationary members and baptized adult non-communicants are often also included.

#### Column 7   Affiliated = total in 1970
= Total 1970 church membership or total church member community or inclusive membership (often called total Christian community) affiliated to a church or on its books or records in a form which can be substantiated (Christians, adult members, their children, their infants, catechumens, registered enquirers, unbaptized adults, non-member supporters, attending sympathizers, non-member attenders, adherents, followers, members under discipline) as defined by the church concerned; sometimes called total constituency.

#### Column 8   Affiliated = total in 1995
= Total 1995 figure, for direct comparison with the

**OFFICIAL NAMES.** A church's official name reveals its identity, status, origin, affiliation and legitimation, hence should be used by outsiders with care and respect. This selection of noticeboards comes from Anglican indigenous churches in Togo (Divine Healer's Church of Togo), Nigeria (Eternal Sacred Order of Cherubim & Seraphim) and Congo-Zaire (Eglise des Noirs).

previous column's figure for 1970

**Column 9   G% = church growth 1970-95**
= Exponential church growth rate per year for the 25 years 1970-1995, derived in all cases from the previous 2 columns.

**Column 10   Notes   = further data**
= Names, notes and other statistics; descriptive notes, including some or all of these elements: name of body in local language (if not given in column 1), initials of name if used, translation of name in column 1 into English, alternate or former name(s), co-operating foreign missionary societies (M=), brief notes on historical development, ethnic composition of members or adherents, and any other significant statistics or data that are available.

---

### COLUMN 1: NAMES OF BODIES

#### Churches and denominations
A strictly alphabetical listing of all churches and denominations is given here, using the full official name of each body. The main advantage of this method is that any body can be located with a minimum of searching. If names are abbreviated in any way, the alphabetization follows the unabbreviated form of these names. Names indented 2 or more spaces are either dioceses or other subdivisions (see below), or are churches forming part of a larger church or denomination. If a name is followed by a colon alone (:) it indicates that that body is composed of the several smaller bodies shown indented below it, and that its statistics equal the total of their statistics. To assist the reader get an immediate overview of the numerically significant bodies in the nation, we print in boldface type the name of every church with over 10% of the total affiliated Christian population in the country. Most countries have thus from 3 to 6 such names in bold, with a maximum possible number in practice of 9.

The listing gives the names of all denominations existing in the year 1995, with the addition of any further bodies brought into existence during 1995–2000 (as may be seen by inspecting column 2). The statistics, however, refer in all cases to the actual number of persons present in the year 1995. Thus if a denomination suffers a major schism, the schism is shown with its statistics which are then subtracted from the total the parent body had in 1995 to give the reduced total we show here. With regard to denominations or missions which existed in the country at an earlier period, but which had disappeared, withdrawn, or otherwise gone out of existence by 1995, these do not appear in the listing in column 1. They may be mentioned in the text, or they may be listed in column 10 of Table 2 if a foreign mission, but in general our survey does not attempt systematically to list all such former bodies no longer present in 1995.

The languages used for names provide a compromise between (a) the requirements of individual countries, who need the list of churches presented in their own national language, and (b) the requirements of the use of international languages. Our practice here is to give weight to the major languages of Christian scholarship and Christian communication rather than either to local languages or to the 6 official languages of the United Nations (Arabic, Chinese, English, French, Russian, Spanish). Our usage therefore is as follows. (1) For countries using as official or first language any of the 6 major European international languages (English, French, German, Italian, Portuguese, Spanish), the listing in column 1 is in this language. If this first language is not English, translations into English appear at the start of column 10. It should be noted that the meaning of the official name may often be quite different from the official name used in English or other languages. (2) For countries whose official or first language is not one of the above 6, the listing is given in English, with church names in the national language or vernacular then given in column 10. (3) For bilingual or trilingual countries using 2 or 3 of the 6 languages, names are in either language.

The definite article 'The', and its equivalents in other languages, form part of the official name of almost all denominations and dioceses. In the interests of brevity, however, we omit it throughout in column 1 except for a handful of bodies who insist on including 'The' as a part of their title necessary for their full identification (e.g. 'African Church, The' in Nigeria).

It should be noted that in this book we treat names seriously, especially those of smaller denominations and of bodies in developing countries, because they imply a definite identity and often a tenacious self-assertion. A church's official name, however quaint it may appear to others, usually reveals (to the trained observer) its identity, status, origin, affiliation, theological position, ecclesiastical tradition, churchmanship, and also its legitimation. Such names usually imply or involve the existence of a postal address, telephone, premises, bank account, membership rolls, leadership, organization, history, publications, constitution, legal existence, registration, and recognition by government. A church's official name therefore calls for care and respect in its use by outsiders, without misquotation, misspelling or abbreviation.

#### Dioceses, jurisdictions and other subdivisions
In the table in most countries, the largest churches (especially Roman Catholic, Orthodox and Anglican) are subdivided into their component dioceses, synods, conferences, or other geographical or ethnic jurisdictions. Being autonomous bodies, these subdivisions correspond somewhat to Protestant denominations. In the Orthodox world, jurisdictions are often all termed eparchies. The definition of each of these subdivisions is found in WCE Part 12 "Dictionary". The code letters below, when found before a place name in the title of a subdivision, indicate the official title of the jurisdiction concerned, thus: 'D London' (='The Diocese of London').

*Place names* of dioceses are always given in the primary locally-used spelling or transliteration (either the secular name in the national language, or in the language of the particular local church itself). If there is a recognized English or anglicized version, or alternative spelling, this name follows in brackets, thus: Roma (Rome), Moskva (Moscow), München (Munich), Al Qahirah (Cairo). However, in the case of certain ancient Orthodox and Catholic dioceses, the official name may be an archaic one (e.g. Heliopolis), in which case it is usually given first followed in brackets by the contemporary secular name. When English is not the national language, the official title in the language is often given also, in column 10. Thus the Netherlands entry 'D Rotterdam' has in column 10 'Bisdom Rotterdam' as the title in Dutch of the Diocese of Rotterdam. In cases where such a diocese is followed by other similar dioceses, the vernacular titles are given only once and are not repeated.

*Eastern-rite Catholics.* These may be identified from the code in column 3, but also from the name of the rite or sub-rite in italics in parentheses in column 1 after the name of the jurisdiction, thus: (*Melkite*). Where Latin jurisdictions are in a minority in a country, they themselves are usually identified in the same way: (*Latin*). Elsewhere, Latin jurisdictions, because in the vast majority, are not identified in this manner.

*Dioceses extending over more than one country.* Most dioceses (and almost all Roman Catholic jurisdictions) fall completely inside the boundaries of a single country. However, in those cases where a jurisdiction extends over parts of 2 or more countries, it is shown in the original or base country (that with the see city or the major part of the diocese) without parentheses, but in the other countries (with secondary parts of the jurisdiction) it is shown in column 1 in parentheses, thus: (D Gibraltar). This means that the statistics of the diocese in the base country will not include figures for the whole diocese but only that part in the base country.

The listing that follows below, of code letters used for jurisdictions and subdivisions, is given approximately in descending order of size or importance. An alphabetical listing is given in the "GeoCodebook" in Part 16.

#### Code

| | |
|---|---|
| EP | ecumenical patriarchate |
| P | patriarchate, patriarchal diocese |
| C | catholicate (catholicossate), diocese of a catholicos |
| CR | conciliar region (*regione conciliare*) |
| R | region (apostolic or conciliar) |
| RE | ecclesiastical region |
| Pro | province |
| EPr | ecclesiastical province |
| M | metropolitan archdiocese (with suffragan dioceses); metropolia (when superior to D) |
| AD | archdiocese |
| UD | united diocese |
| UDs | united dioceses |
| D | diocese, eparchy |
| CP | church province |
| EC | episcopal commissariat |
| Epi | episcopal area |
| PE | patriarchal exarchate |
| EA | exarchate apostolic |
| E | exarchate |
| VP | patriarchal vicariate |
| VA | vicariate apostolic |
| MV | military vicariate |
| V | vicariate |
| PA | prefecture apostolic |
| AA | apostolic administration |
| PN | prelature (prelacy) nullius |
| AN | abbey nullius |
| O | military ordinariate |
| J | jurisdiction |
| Co | community (*communauté*) (used only in Zaire Table 2) |
| Con | conference |
| S | synod |
| CD | church district |
| EM | exarchical monastery |
| RN | priory nullius |
| m | mission (sui juris) |
| : | at end of a name, this indicates a composite body whose statistics are the totals of component bodies indented under it |
| (…) | jurisdiction based in another country, of which this body is a part |

#### Indenting
Where one of the titles in this column (or a code letter, or a place name) is found indented one space from the jurisdiction on the line above it, it indicates that it is ecclesiastically dependent on the latter, or subject to it, or a component part of it. Thus almost all Roman Catholic dioceses (coded D) are suffragan dioceses to (i.e. dependent on) a metropolitan archdiocese (coded M), although in practice they are virtually autonomous in the conduct of day-to-day affairs.

#### Order for listing Roman Catholic jurisdictions
The aim of each listing in a country is to show at a glance the structure of the church there, yet at the same time to facilitate the finding of a specific jurisdiction by using a standard amount of alphabetization. Jurisdictions are therefore arranged alphabetically by ecclesiastical province and rank. The order used is as follows:

*Patriarchates* (P), in alphabetical order irrespective of rite, each followed by its suffragan dioceses and jurisdictions, in alphabetical order and indented one space from P.

*Metropolitan archdioceses* (M), in alphabetical order irrespective of rite, each followed by its suffragan dioceses and jurisdictions in alphabetical order and indented one space from M.

*Other individual jurisdictions*, not suffragans and so not indented, in order of rank (AD, D, EC, EA, VA, PA, AA, PN, AN, O, RN, m), and alphabetized within each rank.

#### Use of '&' in column 1
In the interests of shortening lengthy names, the ampersand (&) is used in column 1 as follows: (1) in all cases instead of the English word 'and', (2) in all names of dioceses and jurisdictions in all languages, (3) to join other geographical names or initials, and (4) in a few other cases where exceptionally lengthy names have to be shortened. For all other cases, i.e. names of denominations in French, German, Italian, Portuguese or Spanish, the ampersand is not used but the words 'et', 'and', 'und', 'e', 'y', are used instead.

---

### COLUMN 3: ECCLESIASTICAL TYPE
#### (4-letter code)

This classification is not based on historical evolution or doctrinal criteria, but, in keeping with the whole of this book, is a contemporary description of the actual situation in world Christianity today. For this purpose, certain necessary neologisms have been created (e.g. Black/Third-World indigenous, marginal Christians), all of which are fully defined in WCE

Part 12 "Dictionary".

One object of this classification is to facilitate a single world table of all Christians affiliated to churches, divided into megablocs (streams), families or groupings, as shown in Parts 1, 10, and others in this book. The tables there show at a glance the relative strengths of the various kinds of Christians in the world. Also, another object is to facilitate the science of comparative symbolics (comparison of the various Christian churches and confessions).

### Six ecclesiastico-cultural megablocs (a 1-letter code)

The first letter in this column locates the body concerned in the following mutually-exclusive broad classification. The rationale for this 6-fold typology has already been given above, and full definitions have been given in the discussion on Country Tables 1 above. Three of these blocs are usually called Liturgical (O, R, A) and the remaining 3 are partly Non-Liturgical (P, I, m). The Liturgical blocs are pedobaptists (paedobaptists, i.e. practicing infant baptism) emphasizing ordered worship, with fixed or written liturgies; the Non-Liturgical blocs are partly Baptist, i.e. they practice adult or believer's baptism only, and they emphasize free or spontaneous worship without fixed or written forms. The exceptions to this twofold typology are a few Protestant traditions (Lutheran, Methodist, Reformed) which are not Baptist but are both Liturgical and pedobaptist; a few marginal Christian traditions which baptize infants (Mormons, et alii); and a large number of Independent indigenous churches and bodies which are both Liturgical and pedobaptist.

### Code (in order ORAPIm)

O    Orthodox (Eastern, Oriental, or Assyrian)
R    Roman Catholic
A    Anglican (Episcopalian)
P    Protestant (often called Evangelical)
I    Independent/Postdenominationalist/Neo-Apostolic/Neocharismatic (Non-White or Black/Third-World indigenous, or White-led); independent of historic Christianity
m    marginal Christian (para-Christian, quasi-Christian)

### Ecclesiastical tradition (3-letter code)

The last 3 letters in column 3 describe the ecclesiastical tradition or family (rite, liturgical language, confession, communion, denomination, churchmanship, historical evolution, network, etc) with which each body is most closely connected historically. This does not necessarily imply formal connection with any world confessional family, which is dealt with later under column 4a, 'Confessional conciliarism.' For the purposes of this classification, an ecclesiastical tradition or family is defined as a number of denominations or churches which share a common heritage (allegiance to a historical tradition), a common thought world (theology, worldview) and a similar lifestyle (attitudes to money, property, discipline, moral imperatives, etc). It must be emphasized that this coding is purely descriptive, and almost always self-descriptive in that this is how the church or diocese described itself on the survey questionnaire. It should be taken to imply the best features of the traditions cited, and must not be taken as a stereotype of any bad connotations of the terms used. The categories as used here are all mutually exclusive; where a given body could be described by more than one of them, the most apt or descriptive has been chosen here.

The following classification by tradition or family was derived from our data on denominations gathered during the present survey. A thorough exposition of this idea of a typology of family groups, with a survey of all other types of classification proposed by sociologists and scholars of religion, is given in J.G. Melton, *A directory of religious bodies in the United States* (New York: Garland, 1977, based on 18 family groups present in the USA), and its long subsequent series up to Melton's 6th edition of the *Encyclopedia of American religions*, 1998. Our global typology of 300 families covers many additional groups not found in the USA nor in the Western world. Below, they are set out in systematic fashion, dealing with the 6 megablocs in the order in which they have been introduced and discussed above. For a single complete alphabetical listing, see the "GeoCodebook" in Part 16.

### ORTHODOX (megabloc code O)

The term Orthodox as defined here refers to those churches in Eastern Christendom which claim to hold 'orthodoxy' (right belief, the true faith) as contrasted with heretical beliefs. The code describes the liturgical language used by each church, and/or that traditionally used by its mother church; in addition, there are 5 smaller schismatic traditions. This classification demonstrates the traditional liturgical origins or links of each church. Note that several 3-letter codes are also used to describe Roman Catholic jurisdictions or rites.

### Eastern Orthodox (Chalcedonian, Dyophysite, Byzantine)

The Chalcedonian churches (Eastern churches which accepted the Council of Chalcedon in AD 451, and a total of 7 Ecumenical Councils, and now consider themselves to be in communion (canonical relationship) with the Ecumenical Patriarchate of Constantinople) may be grouped under 2 main families: Greek-speaking (those using Old or Byzantine Greek) and Slavonic-speaking (those using Church Slavonic, sometimes called Old Slavic). A number of churches now use their national language (e.g. Japanese) in their liturgy as well as Greek or Slavonic, even though these national languages such as Japanese cannot yet properly be called their liturgical languages.

#### Code

Alb    Albanian/Greek
Ara    Arabic/Greek (Arabophone, Arab Greek Orthodox)
Bul    Bulgarian/Slavonic
Bye    Byelorussian (White Russian)/Slavonic
Cze    Czech/Slavonic
Est    Estonian/Slavonic
Fin    Finnish/Slavonic
Geo    Georgian/Slavonic
Gre    Greek (New Calendar)
Hun    Hungarian/Slavonic
Lav    Latvian/Slavonic
Mac    Macedonian/Slavonic
Mol    Moldavian/Slavonic
Pol    Polish/Slavonic
Rum    Romanian
Rus    Russian/Slavonic
Ser    Serbian/Slavonic
Slo    Slovak/Slavonic
Ukr    Ukrainian/Slavonic

### Oriental Orthodox (Pre-Chalcedonian, Non-Chalcedonian, Monophysite)

The Oriental churches broke with the Western and Eastern churches at the Council of Chalcedon in AD 451, and only accept 4 of the Ecumenical Councils. Their liturgical languages are as follows (with in parentheses the name of each's church).

#### Code

Arm    Armenian (Armenian Apostolic)
Cop    Coptic & Arabic (Coptic Orthodox)
Eth    Ge'ez/Old Ethiopian (Ethiopian Orthodox)
Syr    Syriac & Arabic (Syrian Orthodox, West Syrian, Jacobite)
SyM    Syriac & Malayalam (Orthodox Syrian, in India)

### Nestorian (Assyrian, East Syrian, Syro-Chaldean; Dyophysite)

The Ancient Church of the East, the original church of Mesopotamia, broke with the Western and Eastern churches at the Council of Ephesus, AD 433. It does not regard itself as part of the Orthodox world, but it is here classified as a third branch of Orthodoxy because its theology, long called Nestorian, was similar to that of the Greek Orthodox patriarch of Constantinople, Nestorius.

#### Code

Nes    Assyrian, East Syrian (Messihaye), Chaldean (Syriac)-speaking, Nestorian, Syro-Chaldean.

### ROMAN CATHOLIC (megabloc code R)

The term Roman Catholic refers to all churches and

persons in communion with the Holy See and the Church of Rome. The code here describes the rite or ethnic sub-rite used in each church or jurisdiction. Catholic jurisdictions in communion with Roman use either the Latin rite, or one of 5 major rites known as Oriental or Eastern Catholic rites. These, together with their 22 ethnic subdivisions, and the liturgical language each uses, are as set out below. Most of these now combine the ancient liturgical languages with their own national language in their liturgies. The Oriental churches are sometimes called Uniate, especially in Eastern Europe. The codes given here to these rites and sub-rites are set out in the left hand column.

| Code | Rite or sub-rite | Liturgical language |
|---|---|---|
| Lat | LATIN RITE | Latin |

ORIENTAL (EASTERN) RITES:

| | | |
|---|---|---|
| | *Alexandrian (Egyptian) rite:* | |
| Cop | Coptic | Coptic & Arabic |
| Eth | Ethiopic | Ge'ez (Old Ethiopian) |
| | *Antiochian (Western Syrian) rite:* | |
| Mal | Syro-Malankara | Malayalam |
| Mar | Maronite | Syriac & Arabic |
| Syr | Syrian | Syriac & Arabic |
| Arm | *Armenian rite* | Old Armenian |
| | *Byzantine (Constantinopolitan) rite:* | |
| Alb | Albanian | Albanian & Old Greek |
| Bul | Bulgarian | Church Slavonic |
| Bye | Byelorussian | Slavonic |
| Geo | Georgian | Georgian |
| Gre | Greek | Old Greek (Byzantine) |
| Hun | Hungarian | Church Slavonic |
| IAb | Italo-Albanian | Old Greek & Albanian |
| Mel | Melkite | Old Greek & Arabic |
| Rum | Romanian | Romanian & Slavonic |
| Rus | Russian | Church Slavonic |
| Rut | Ruthenian | Church Slavonic |
| Slo | Slovak | Church Slavonic |
| Ukr | Ukrainian | Church Slavonic |
| Yug | Yugoslav | Church Slavonic |
| | *Chaldean (Eastern Syrian) rite:* | |
| Cha | Chaldean | Syriac & Arabic |
| SyM | Syro-Malabarese | Malayalam |
| | *Additional codes used here:* | |
| LEr | jurisdiction for both Latin and Eastern-rite Catholics | |
| Ori | jurisdiction for all or several Byzantine rites | |

### ANGLICAN (megabloc code A)

The term Anglican refers to churches of the Anglican Communion and their members, whether they call themselves Protestants, Catholics, Evangelicals, or Episcopalians, and which trace their origin back to the Church of England in the 6th century and the Celtic Church of the 2nd century AD. These churches accepted the Catholic or Roman tradition up to AD 1540, and thereafter a reformed Anglican tradition. The term also applies to schisms from the Anglican Communion in the Western world, originally among European peoples, which claim to remain authentically Anglican, and which retain or claim to retain either apostolic succession of bishops, or Anglican polity, or Anglican orders, or the word Anglican in their title. The code indicates the type of churchmanship recognized by diocesan offices as prevalent in influence or numerically predominant in the church or diocese, or on the part of bishop or clergy, in cases where a clear tradition can be recognized. It is important to realize that this typology should not be related to outmoded party disputes, but is purely descriptive, being a positive and contemporary self-description as viewed from diocesan offices of the actual practice in a church or diocese with regard to liturgy, ritual and churchmanship. In most cases this self-description was returned by diocesan officers on the book's questionnaire to dioceses.

#### Codes

ACa    Anglo-Catholic (formerly called Tractarian)

# Traditions

**Anglican Evangelical.** Consecration in Khartoum Cathedral in 1971 of 2 new Sudanese bishops (on either side of Archbishop in Jerusalem (in mitre), with other bishops from Kenya, Iran, and Egypt.

**Arab Orthodox**. Arab parish priest in Antioch (Turkey) near border with Syria.

**Armenian Apostolic** (Gregorian). Armenian Catholicos Vasken (left).

**Baptist.** Russian Baptist choir at central church in Moscow.

**Catholic Apostolic.** One of many new, ultra-modern, buildings of New Apostolic Church (in Worms, FR Germany)

**Catholic Apostolic.** Its interior, with NAC symbol of Cross over Rising Sun.

**Chaldean**. Archbishop Youhannan S. Issayi of Tehran (former Nestorians now united to Rome) meets Shah in Iran, 1974.

**Coptic Orthodox.** Pope Shenouda III (left) with his Bishop of Ecumenical Affairs, in Cairo.

**Conservative Catholic.** About 21% of all RCs in Europe and North America are traditionalists who prefer the Tridentine (Latin) mass and support Archbishop M. Lefebvre (*pictured*), suspended by Pope Paul VI in 1976. Small groups in several countries have formed schismatic churches.

**Episcopi Vagantes** (Bishops -at-large). The Catholicate of the West, a miniscule unrecognized autocephalous church, was begun in Britain in 1944 by (*pictured*) His Sacred Beatitude Mar Georgius I (H. G. de Willmott Newman).

**Ethiopian Orthodox**. *Left*. Clergy during Timkat (Epiphany) in Addis Ababa. *Right*. Cathedrals new (center) and old (to right), with obelisks, in Aksum.

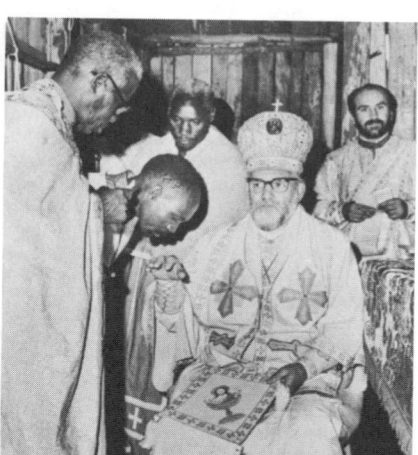

**Greek Orthodox**. Greek Patriarch of Alexandria (center, while serving as Archbishop in East Africa).

**Jehovah's Witnesses** (Russellite). Mass public baptism in Ruislip Lido (UK).

**Liberal Catholic.** Founder (in 1915) and First Presiding Bishop of the Liberal Catholic Church, the Right Rev. J. I. Wedgwood, a leading English Theosophist.

**Lutheran**. Liturgy in Westman Islands, Iceland: first service for population returning after 1973 volcanic eruption disaster.

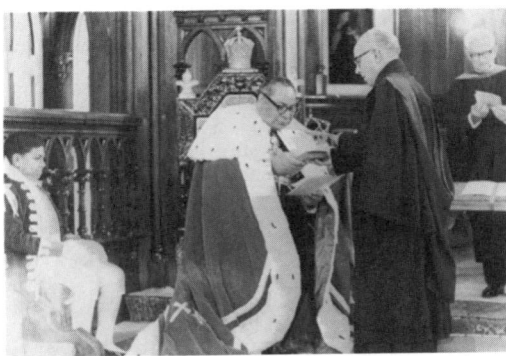

**Methodist.** King of Tonga (a Methodist) receives Bible from Methodist President-General C. F. Gribble during 1967 Coronation.

**Nestorian**. Assyrian world hierarchy led by Catholicos-Patriarch Mar Dinkha IV (center).

**Non-White pentecostal**. Apostle/Preacher/Evangelist of African Apostolic Church of Johane Maranke, Zimbabwe.

**Old Believers**. Flavian, Old Ritualist (Old Believer) Archbishop of Moscow and All Russia (1879-1960), speaking in Zagorsk in 1952.

**Pentecostal**. Italian Pentecostals in Palermo under text 'We preach Christ the power and wisdom of God'.

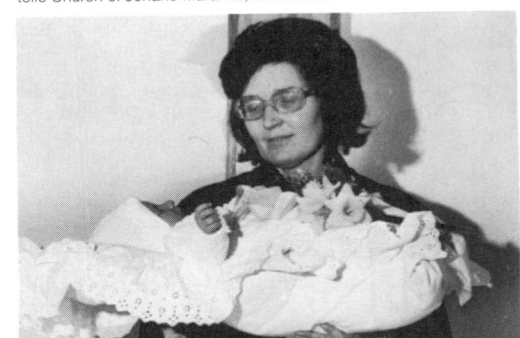

**Reformed Catholic**. Woman minister performs infant baptism in Czechoslovak Hussite Church, Prague.

**Russian Orthodox**. Late Patriarch Alexei during liturgy in Trinity Church, Zagorsk.

**Salvationist**. Jeshi la Wokofu/Salvation Army officers (Captains and Sisters), Kenya Territory, with band.

**Syro-Malabarese**. Liturgy in Diocese of Quilon, Orthodox Syrian Church of the East.

Cen     Central or broad Church (Prayer Book, Liberal, Comprehensive, New Synod Group)
Ecu     local multidenominational Ecumenical (Anglican/Protestant/Catholic) joint parishes
Eva     Evangelical (Anglican Evangelical, or conciliar Evangelical Anglican)
Hig     High Church (Prayer Book Catholic)
Low     Low Church (Conservative Evangelical)
plu     no dominant single tradition; plural or mixed traditions across the whole spectrum of churchmanship

### PROTESTANT (megabloc code P)

The term Protestant (or Evangelical in French, German, Italian, Portuguese and Spanish: respectively, Évangélique, Evangelische, Evangélico, Evangélico, Evangélico) refers primarily to Western Protestant bodies originating in Europe or North America, which trace their origin or definitive reformulation either to the 16th-century European Protestant Reformation or subsequently (including state churches in Germany and Scandinavia and elsewhere which originated as early as AD 90 (West Germany) but which subsequently identified themselves with the Protestant Reformation); and to churches elsewhere throughout the world which are related to them, controlled by them, or in communion with them. The 3-letter code indicates the major denominational, confessional or ecclesiastical tradition followed, evolved, adopted, or claimed, or which best describes objectively the group concerned. Definitions and descriptions of each are given in *WCE* Part 12 "Dictionary". With regard to Pentecostal bodies, note in particular that in this book, proper names of churches excepted, the capitalized terms Pentecostal and Pentecostalism always refer to Classical Pentecostalism and Oneness Pentecostalism among White races and their worldwide related churches and missions, in their varied forms (coded below PeA, Pen, Pe1, Pe2, Pe3, Pe4). By contrast, the non-capitalized forms 'pentecostal' and 'pentecostalism' are reserved for forms of pentecostalism other than White Classical, namely the 2 major streams of Independent renewal here termed (1) Non-White or Black/Third-World indigenous pentecostalism (and its variants as coded below after the 2 characters I-3), and (2) White-led Independent/Postdenominationalist/Neocharismatic movements. In titles or proper names of churches of both kinds, of course, the adjective Pentecostal is always capitalized. This distinction between Pentecostal and pentecostal is made here to make it clear that these are 2 separate ecclesiastical traditions. Non-White or Black/Third-World pentecostalism has arisen, outside the USA, quite independently of Classical Pentecostalism; and within the USA itself, Black pentecostalism has some claim to have preceded White Pentecostalism in time, to be a phenomenon distinct and separate from it, and to itself be regarded as the classical tradition.

These 37 categories as used here are mutually exclusive; where a given body could be described by more than one of them, the most apt or descriptive has been chosen in its Country Table 2.

In English, as explained above, the term Evangelical has a more specialized meaning than in the other European languages, delineating a subgroup or movement within Protestantism and Anglicanism.

The codes that now follow are therefore, in this book, defined as making up the entire spectrum of contemporary Protestantism.

*Codes*

Adv     Adventist (Millerite)
Ang     schism from Anglicanism or Episcopalianism, in Protestant direction rejecting Anglicanism (i.e. without claiming or retaining Anglican name, orders, apostolic succession, et alia)
Bap     Baptist
CBr     Christian Brethren (Plymouth Brethren; Open Brethren only, not Exclusive); independent/open fundamentalist/dispensationalist
com     community church or union congregation (formed by 2 or more denominations), open to all denominations and races
Con     Congregational, Congregationalist
Dis     Disciple, Restorationist, Restorationist Baptist, Christian (Restoration Movement, Campbellites, Disciples, Churches of Christ)
Dun     Dunker (Tunker), Dipper, German Baptist, Brethren (baptism by 3-fold immersion)
EBr     Exclusive Brethren (Plymouth Brethren, Closed, Strict; Darbyites); exclusive fundamentalist/dispensationalist
Fun     Fundamentalist (holding to 5, 7, 9, or 21 Fundamental doctrines or dogmas)
Hol     Holiness (Conservative Methodist, Wesleyan, Free Methodist, non-Pentecostal Perfectionist) (2-experience: conversion, entire sanctification); differing from mainline Methodism only in teaching on sanctification
ind     independent Evangelical, unrelated to other Protestant or indigenous traditions, and at least 2 generations old being begun before the year 1945, and now regarding itself as a denomination within Protestantism and the Protestant world.
Int     Interdenominational Evangelical Protestant (unaffiliated to any denomination, unrelated to any major tradition, or specifically interdenominational); or, church originating from one of the interdenominational Evangelical missionary societies (often called faith missions)
Jew     Messianic, Jewish-Christian, or Jewish crypto-Christian
LuR     Lutheran/Reformed united church or joint mission
Lut     Lutheran, Confessional Lutheran
mar     marginal Protestant (partially embracing unorthodox dogma or practices)

Men     Mennonite, Anabaptist (Left-Wing or Radical Reformation), including other communal Anabaptist sects
Met     Methodist (mainline Methodist, United Methodist); English-speaking Pietist
Mor     Moravian (Continental Pietist)
Non     Nondenominational (no-church or anti-church groups rejecting being described as a church or denomination, or being classed or linked with other churches or denominations)
Ort     schism from Orthodoxy, in Protestant direction (without claiming to retain full historical Orthodoxy)
PeA     Apostolic or Pentecostal Apostolic (differing from other Pentecostals in stress on complex hierarchy of living apostles, prophets and other charismatic officials)
Pen     Pentecostal (Classical Pentecostal of unspecified type); charismatic, healing; the sub-types PeA, Pe2, Pe3, are also termed Classical Pentecostal (as contrasted with Oneness Pentecostal or Independent pentecostal)
Pe1     Oneness-Pentecostal or Unitarian Pentecostal: 'Jesus Only', sometimes called Unitarian (Jesus being regarded as the same as the Holy Spirit, also the Father), or non- or anti-Trinitarian; baptism in name of Jesus only.
Pe2     Baptistic-Pentecostal or Keswick-Pentecostal: 2-crisis-experience (conversion, baptism of the Spirit); Trinitarian
Pe3     Holiness-Pentecostal: 3-crisis-experience (conversion, sanctification, baptism of the Spirit)
Qua     Friends (Quakers, Religious Society of Friends)
rad     isolated radio churches, i.e. unorganized isolated house congregations brought into being by radio evangelism, or mail or radiophonic correspondence courses, and unrelated to other denominations; small cells or groups of isolated radio believers
Ref     Reformed, Presbyterian (the latter term originating in English-speaking areas, the former in continental Europe)
Rom     schism from Roman Catholic Church, in Protestant direction (without claiming to retain full Roman Catholic identity)
Sal     Salvationist (Salvation Army)
sin     single congregation(s): one single autonomous congregation, completely independent and unaffiliated to any denomination or grouping, nor claiming to be a denomination; or a de facto unstructured grouping of such congregations
tel     TV (television) para-denomination, organized solely around regular worship telecasts
Uni     United church, formally constituted by several divergent Protestant and Anglican denominations from different confessions, with voluntary or involuntary (enforced by state) union or merger of bodies of different ecclesiastical tradition
Wal     Waldensian

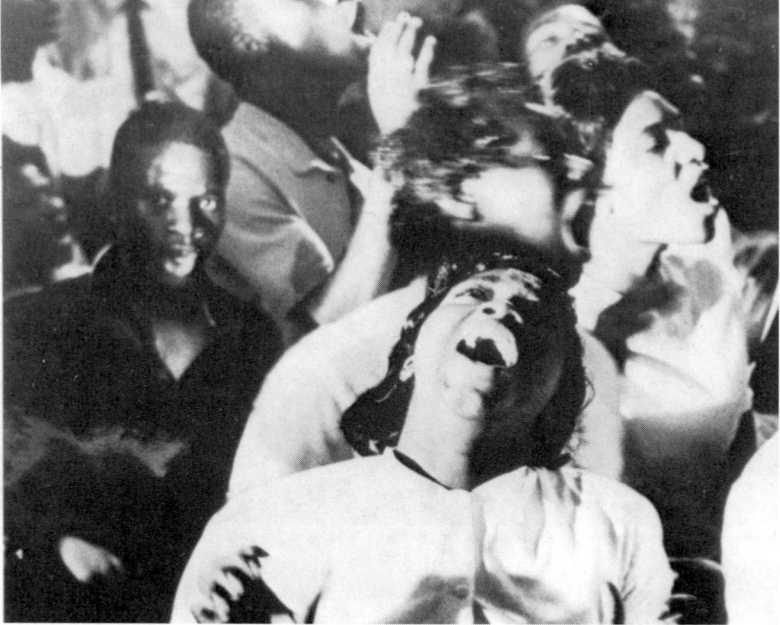

**LITURGICAL/NON-LITURGICAL.** All Christian denominations and traditions may be classified under this 2-fold typology. (1) **Liturgical traditions** (those with ordered worship). *Left*. Roman Catholics in Westminster Cathedral, London. (2) **Non liturgical traditions** (those with spontaneous or free worship). *Right*. Black pentecostals in the USA.

### INDEX (megabloc code I)

**INDEPENDENT (megabloc code I)**

As described at length earlier, this term Independent was first used to describe Christian movements and churches originating not among the White races indigenous mainly to the Western world, nor in the Western or Eastern churches which have arisen there, but originating since AD 1500 among the Black or Non-White races indigenous to the Third World, including Black or Non-White minorities in the Western world, i.e. among any race or people other than the European geographical race as defined here in *WCE* Part 8 "EthnoSphere". The term at first covered movements indigenous to Black or Non-White peoples without foreign origin (i.e. foreign to them); seceding from or asserting their independence from Western or Eastern bodies, and often rejecting the terms 'Protestant', 'Catholic', 'Anglican' and 'Orthodox'; not related to nor controlled by Western Protestant, Catholic, Anglican or Orthodox bodies, but completely independent of them; indigenous as opposed to foreign, alien imported or immigrant tradition, with no foreign ties; local, nationalistic, often separatist, schismatic, anti-Western, of contested orthodoxy; founded, led and supported by Blacks or Non-Whites independently of and without assistance from White churches or missionaries, though sometimes subsequently assisted by Western or Eastern church bodies.

By the 1960s, however, large numbers of similar Independent churches and denominations were recognized among the White races also. The codes used, which include elements of those for Protestant, Catholic, Anglican and Orthodox bodies as listed above, indicate the main Western, Eastern, or indigenous denominational tradition followed, evolved, adopted, claimed, or from which a schism broke. In many cases a new body follows or parallels no clearcut Western or Eastern tradition. The listing that follows below shows this tradition grouped into the Western or Eastern blocs from which these movements have separated or out of which they have sprung.

Some 74% of Christians classified here as 'Independents' also belong to the Pentecostal/Charismatic/Neocharismatic Renewal in the Holy Spirit; they are here termed Third-Wavers or Neocharismatics. This derivation and terminology is described in detail in Part 6 "Independency". Their codes are set out and fully defined in Table 6-5. They all share the common first 2 characters of the codes—'I-3', to enable the reader to examine any list of denominations and networks in Country Tables 2 and to see immediately which are Third-Wavers/Neocharismatics.

Independent denominations can be grouped for convenience under 9 varieties as follows (see extended description in Part 6 "Independency"). Statistics of each are given in Table 10-9 and elsewhere.

**1. Non-White indigenous churches**
The origin of these movements in Africa from 1815 onwards is well known. By AD 2000 their followers were to be found worldwide.

**2. Independent Orthodox schisms**
Recent movements out of historical Orthodoxy, or other schisms from mainstream Orthodoxy have become increasingly frequent. Most claim to retain full historical Orthodoxy but are not recognized as canonical by the bulk of Orthodox churches. Their codes cover most of the codes listed above under Orthodoxy but are preceded not by 'O-' but by 'I-'. Additional codes are as follows.

*Code*

OBe    Old Believers, Old Ritualists (Russians, using Old Slavonic)
OCd    Old Calendarist (or Authentic) Greek Orthodox
ReO    Reformed Orthodox (uncanonical reform movement out of Orthodoxy, retaining Orthodox claims)
sub    sub-Orthodox Russian sect reflecting Orthodox ritual
Tru    True Orthodox (devoutly conservative Russian Orthodox)

**3. Independent Catholic schisms**
The above term as defined in this survey covers a vast range of disparate ecclesiastical phenomena originating in the Western world. These are the mass of over 100 large and small episcopal and non-episcopal autocephalous schismatic churches which exist in the penumbra between Roman Catholicism and Protestantism, and between Roman Catholicism and Anglicanism. They have all broken in recent times (since 1500, and almost all since 1800) either from Rome to introduce Protestant features (married priests, lay leadership, women ministers, individual faith, etc), or from Protestantism to introduce Catholic features (sacraments, authority, episcopacy, hierarchy, the historic succession of the episcopate (apostolic succession), apostolic autocracy, ritual, liturgy, etc), or from Anglicanism to introduce Roman features. Numerically, they fall into 2 classes: (a) sizeable schisms, defined here as those which involve over 100 persons each, and (b), miniscule schisms, begun by a single founder (usually a new episcopus vagans, bishop-at-large), with 100 or under others and often with under 10.

Ecclesiastically, from the point of view of ecclesiastical tradition, the whole range may be divided into the following 6 types, starting at the Catholic end of the spectrum and moving to the Protestant end. Their respective codes are listed after this description.

**(a) *Old Catholic churche*s.** These are a number of traditionally Catholic churches in Europe which have separated in recent times from the church of Rome (especially in 1702, Jansenism; 1724, Church of Utrecht; 1870, Old Catholics; and 1897, Polish National Catholics), opposing recent Roman dogmas including papal infallibility and the immaculate conception and assumption of the Virgin, retaining traditionally conservative Catholic faith and practice and the apostolic succession of bishops, and remaining in communion with and recognized by large parts of historic Christianity (usually Anglicanism and Orthodoxy).

**(b) *Conservative Catholic churches*.** These are other recent sizeable secessions from the Church of Rome in a conservative or reactionary direction protesting against liberal, updating, or modernizing trends in Roman Catholicism, retaining episcopacy but without the Old Catholic or other undisputed historic succession of the episcopate.

**(c) *Minuscule unrecognized autocephalous episcopal churches under bishops-at-large*** (episcopi vagantes). These bodies (listed in Table 6-10) amount to over 130 distinct autocephalous churches schismatic from the Church of Rome or out of communion with it, some with 100 or under or even few or no lay members, claiming to be Catholic, Apostolic, Orthodox, and with valid episcopal orders (almost all in the Ferrette, Vilatte or Mathew successions), which, since the movement's origin in Britain in 1866, have proliferated in Europe, North America and Australasia and also to several Third-World countries, and which although not recognized by historic Christianity nevertheless retain traditional Catholic faith and practice and claim to be reviving primitive Christianity and to be inaugurating a new and final reunion of divided Christendom.

**(d) *Liberal Catholic churches*.** These consist of sizeable episcopal churches of unrecognized succession which have formally embraced various liberal or deviant Catholic views including Theosophical, Masonic, Gnostic, magic or occult dogmas and practices.

**(e) *Latin-rite Independent Catholic churches*.** These represent Latin-rite churches which are historically Catholic and pro-Rome but which have been forced by local circumstances to take a label independent of Rome, e.g. Catholic church in China.

**(f) *Reformed Catholic churches*.** These are recent sizeable secessions from the Church of Rome in a distinctively reformed or Protestant direction, radically altering Catholic faith and practice, usually rejecting (initially at least) the apostolic succession of bishops, and usually not in communion with historic Christianity (Anglicanism or Orthodoxy).

Lastly, is an ecclesiastical family, the Catholic Apostolic churches, which although with some Catholic features has strong pentecostal features also and so is better classified here as a White-led Neocharismatic apostolic family (see code I-3aX). This is a series of non-episcopal secessions out of Protestantism, beginning in Britain in 1832, introducing and combining charismatic manifestations together with the Catholic concepts of the unified church, sacramentarianism, ritual, liturgy, and authority, but rejecting the apostolic succession of bishops and substituting for it a claimed return to apostolic church government through a hierarchy or college of living apostles, in a successional apostolate headed by a chief apostle with quasi-papal powers regarded as the successor of the Apostle Peter and the visible representative or incarnation of Christ on earth.

The 6 Western types are shown coded here below. Similar movements among Third-World peoples, including schisms from the Church of Rome, may be classified here as in this Catholic (non-Roman) family but may be classified as in the Non-White indigenous ecclesiastical tradition; however, the codes are the same as shown here below. For a tabular listing of all episcopal autocephalous churches with claimed (but disputed) apostolic succession, both in the Western world and in the Third World, see Table 6-10 'Autocephalous Episcopal churches with disputed apostolic succession, AD 1650-2000', in Part 6.

Codes for Independent Catholics include the following.

*Code*

CCa    Conservative Catholic (recent schism out of Church of Rome in conservative or reactionary direction, rejecting authority of pope, with or without apostolic succession, protesting against up-dating or liberal trends); Tridentinist, Traditional Catholic
Epi    episcopi-vagantes Catholic, in miniscule unrecognized autocephalous episcopal church under bishops-at-large (episcopi vagantes), with disputed apostolic succession; or (in Third World) linked with such Western bodies; with 100 or under members only
Lat    Latin rite churches which are historically Catholic but have taken an independent label
Lib    Liberal Catholic (church under bishops-at-large holding liberal or deviant Catholic views usually including Theosophical, Masonic, Gnostic, Magical or Occult dogmas and practices)
OCa    Old Catholic (schism out of Church of Rome retaining recognized Old Catholic apostolic succession of bishops; especially schisms of 1702, 1724, 1870, 1897)
ReC    Reformed Catholic (recent schism out of Church of Rome in reformed or Protestant direction)

Some of these codes (especially Epi) could equally well be placed under the brief Anglican section and discussion next, but this would not affect their coding or any subsequent analysis.

**4. Independent Anglican schisms**
There is wide variety in secessions or splits from Anglicanism. The main descriptive traditions are as follows:

*Code*

ACa    Anglo-Catholic (formerly called Tractarian)
ARo    Anglo-Roman (recent schism out of Anglicanism in a Roman Catholic direction, claiming to retain Anglican name, orders, apostolic succession, et alia
Eva    Evangelical (Anglican Evangelical, or conciliar Evangelical, or Evangelical Anglican)
ReA    Reformed Anglican (recent schism or reform movement out of historical Anglicanism, claiming full historical orders and apostolic succession)
TrA    Traditional Anglican

Schisms from Anglicanism which do not claim to remain authentically Anglican and which claim neither Anglican ethos nor apostolic succession, but which may nevertheless retain certain Anglican features (e.g. liturgy, polity, vestments), may be found here classified either under Catholic (non-Roman), or Protestant, or Black/Third-World indigenous categories, and may be given the code Ang or ARo.

**5. Independent Protestant denominations**
Almost all the traditions whose codes are shown under Protestantism above can be found too under the Independency megabloc. For this reason the codes belong at this point also, although they are not repeated here because superfluous.

# MARGINAL CHRISTIANS

This major ecclesiastico-cultural megabloc is described on the opposite page.

*Left.* **Christian Scientists.** Christian Science Center, Boston (USA), world headquarters of Church of Christ, Scientist; Small church at upper right of pool=Original Edifice of the Mother Church, built 1894; abutting it, domed 4,000 seat Mother Church Extension, 1905; long colonnaded building to right=Publishing Society (Monitor), 1933; alongside pool, right, 5-storey Church Colonnade (radio/TV etc); top end of pool, 1,100-seat Sunday School, 1971; left, 29-storey Church Administration, 1975.

*Right.* **Unitarians.** Service held by Czechoslovak Unitarian Association, Prague. Unitarians were the earliest marginal Protestants, begun in Hungary in 1566, but have been declining worldwide since 1900. World headquarters are now in Boston (USA).

*Above.* **Jehovah's Witnesses.** Mass baptism of new converts 'accepting Jehovah God as their new owner', in Ruislip Lido. Middlesex (UK) in 1969, in which year 5,563 were baptized in Britain. World headquarters are in Brooklyn, NY (USA).

*Right.* **Mormons.** World headquarters of Church of Jesus Christ of Latter-day Saints in Salt Lake City, Utah (USA). In foreground, Salt Lake Temple, finished 1893 which is used not for public worship but as school for esoteric teaching, baptism for the dead, and marriage for eternity; center left. Mormon Tabernacle (1863-67) seating 10,000, with 10,000-pipe organ, home of 375 member Salt Lake Tabernacle Choir, possibly foremost choir on Earth.

### 6. Nonhistorical Independents

These are independent bodies with no clear or obvious confessional linkages, past or present, and which have no interest whatever in the 4 megablocs—Orthodox, Catholic, Anglican, or Protestant.—and which are not themselves pentecostal/charismatic.

### 7. Independent White-led Postdenominationalist bodies

The origin of these movements in Europe and America is found mainly in the second half of the 20th century. The numerous varieties of category are all listed in Part 16 "GeoCodebook".

### 8. Isolated radio/TV believers

This category, coded 'I-rad' or 'I-3r', covers believers in areas with Christian broadcasting but no churches or missions.

### 9. Hidden non-Christian believers in Christ.

This very significant category describes NBBCs (nonbaptized believers in Christ) in Hindu, Muslim, or Buddhist countries.

### MARGINAL CHRISTIAN (megabloc code m)

Marginal Christian (para-Christian of Western origin) is a non-judgmental descriptive term coined by this survey and used here to describe those religious systems, churches, bodies, sects or cults, which have arisen out of, or are located on the fringes or margins of, mainline organized Christianity, but which do not identify themselves with it, often describing themselves as only marginally related to mainstream organized Christianity which is regarded as apostate. They are mostly deviations claiming to be Christian and containing major elements derived from Christianity, but not professing mainstream Trinitarian christocentric doctrine and usually being either noncredal or anti-credal; generally originating in a theophany and affirming a second or supplementary or ongoing source of divine revelation in addition to the Bible. 'Marginal' is therefore used here in contrast to 'mainline', and as such it is widely used in the literature (e.g. J.I. Zaretsky & M.P. Leone, eds, *Religious movements in contemporary America* (1974), which is concerned entirely with marginal religious movements). Subsequent to the origin of these movements on the metaphorical periphery, margin or fringes of Western Christian orthodoxy, several of these systems have since expanded across the world to many countries.

This category includes only those recognizably Christian bodies among the many which belong to the corpus of the whole vast range of contemporary metaphysical movements. The Christian bodies can be divided into 2 major wings: (a) occult bodies (Christian branches of Spiritualism, Theosophy, psychic movements), and (b) healing bodies (Christian Science, Divine Science, New Thought, Religious Science, Unity School of Christianity).

Most occult metaphysical bodies such as Spiritualism, Theosophy and its offshoot Rosicrucianism are not properly speaking Christian movements at all, although they embody Christian elements. In this survey they are therefore classified as non-Christian religions or cults, and are enumerated in Country Tables 1 either under 'Other religionists' or under any relevant category such as 'Hindus', 'Spiritists', etc.

*Code   Marginal Christian bodies*

| | |
|---|---|
| Ade | Christadelphian (Unitarian-Adventist) |
| Apo | Apocalyptic, Eschatological |
| BrI | British-Israelite |
| Gno | Gnostic, Esoteric, Anthroposophical |
| Jeh | Jehovah's Witnesses (Russellites; self-appellation, Jehovah's Christian Witnesses), including Bible Student movement (IBSA), and other schismatics or dissidents |
| Jew | Jewish-Christian (incorporating Jewish teachings or practices); or, Jewish crypto-Christians |
| LdS | Latter-day Saints (Mormons), including in over 80 schismatic or dissident bodies |
| Sci | Metaphysical Science, Divine Science, Religious Science, Christian Science, New Thought, magnetic healing, Unity School |
| Spi | Spiritualist, Spiritist (Thaumaturgical), Psychic, Psychical, Occult, mediumistic, psychedelic of specifically Christian type. |

| | |
|---|---|
| Swe | Swedenborgian (Church of the New Jerusalem, New Church, spiritualistic) |
| The | Theosophist, Theosophical, or synthesist (combining philosophy and religions) |
| Unt | Unitarian, Universalist, Free Christian, Liberal Christian |

All of these 3-letter codes are included in one single alphabetized listing of the over 300 traditions or families or varieties in Part 16 "GeoCodebook".

---

### COLUMN 4: CONCILIARISM, COLLEGIALITY, CONSULTATION AND CHURCH ORGANIZATION
### (5-letter code)

This column in Country Tables 2 describes, in 5 letters, the membership of all denominations in councils and organizations, including the confessional structure of the churches, involvement in the conciliar or interdenominational movement, commitment to the conciliar or consultative principle, involvement in collegiality, consultation and co-responsibility, and formal relationships to national and international councils, conferences, orders, congregations, organizations, and associations of churches.

This classification serves the following purposes: (a) for any particular church, denomination or diocese, to indicate its formal relationships to other churches in its own country and beyond; (b) for Roman Catholic local (nation-wide) churches, to indicate the present extent of the participation of the whole people of God in worldwide collegiality, consultation and co-responsibility; (c) in the case of a missionary jurisdiction of the Roman Catholic Church, to elaborate on this relationship by indicating the personnel, order or congregation responsible for staffing the jurisdiction; (d) for all other denominations, to list each's confessional, international, continental, regional, and national conciliar involvement including the interconfessional (crossdenominational) councils to which each belongs; (e) to enable the reader to locate at a glance members belonging to a particular council or internal grouping in any particular country; (f) to give the reader an immediate overview of the extent and nature of interdenominationalism, conciliarism, ecumenism, confessionalism, collegiality, consultation and church organization in a given country; and (g) to enable the reader to assess a particular body's attitude to conciliarism and consultation or to involvement in the conciliar movement. The symbol . in any of these 5 columns indicates that the body concerned has no such relationships (as known at mid-2000). If subsequently it joins any council, the reader can change the dot (.) to the appropriate letter. Bodies with 5 dots (.....) have no interdenominational or conciliar or wider structural ties and so can be termed non-conciliar.

Membership of councils shown in these tables is usually, but not always, all-inclusive; all the member churches present in each country are shown. In a few cases only, a council may have other member churches too small to have been listed in the table, but which are included under the listing 'Other Protestant denominations' or 'Other indigenous churches'.

Again, denominations may have joined a council, then later pulled out, even later rejoined. Others prefer to participate but keep their distance through 'observer' status or 'unofficial membership'. It is best, therefore, to regard this whole column 4 as a 'portrait in oils' rather than an exact photographic image at 30 June 2000.

A further factor is that there exist a number of Christian councils which have individuals or individual congregations as members but not denominations. National councils or alliances or fellowships of this type are listed in the footnotes 'Other national councils' under Country Tables 2.

The basic problem faced by this column and its coding is that it is extremely difficult to compare Roman Catholicism and Protestantism in detail, because whilst the Roman Catholic Church has a highly centralized structure, Protestantism has either a federal structure or no overall structure at all. Nevertheless, the task is attempted in column 4.

The Roman Catholic Church is a special case here in that, as a result of the Ecumenical Council of 1962–5 (Vatican II), all local (nation-wide) churches, all dio-

ceses and all other jurisdictions have belonged to, or are represented on, various types of inter-church and inter-jurisdiction Catholic conciliar body: national episcopal conferences, regional and continental conferences, and, at the apex, the Synod of Bishops. (A further type, provincial episcopal councils for all bishops in an ecclesiastical province, existed from the Council of Trent in 1545–63 up to Vatican II but has now disappeared completely, the last being one in

**World conciliarism.** 1979 Conference of Secretaries of Christian World Communions/CWCs (until 1979, World Confessional Families/WCFs) in Athens, Greece: including Anglican, Protestant, Roman Catholic, and Orthodox leaders.

Belgium up to 1936). Unlike Protestant conciliarism, however, membership in these Catholic councils is not optional and so all dioceses are part of this structure of councils. The representatives on these councils are always the bishops or ordinaries of the dioceses concerned, and the whole structure represents collegiality—government of the church by the whole college of bishops sitting together. However, an additional obligation since Vatican II has been that all dioceses and jurisdictions begin to involve priests, religious personnel, and laity in the whole process of consultation known as co-responsibility, and in particular that they form both diocesan priests' councils and also diocesan pastoral councils (for the whole people of God—bishops, priests, religious personnel, and laity). This requirement, however, has not been universally implemented although a majority of dioceses now have a priests' council, and a majority also have a pastoral council (at least on paper). In a number of countries, the process of co-responsibility has gone a stage further, and national priests' councils and even national pastoral councils had been set up until in 1973 the Vatican clarified that such national organizations were forbidden and could not be accepted in the official structure of the church. All such bodies have therefore become unofficial pressure groups seeking to assert the involvement of priests, religious, and laity in the government of the church.

For dioceses and jurisdictions, column 4 does not reiterate this participation in nation-wide councils (except in the case of a handful of Protestant federations of which the component parts are virtually the same as autonomous denominations). Instead, the column after the first letter indicates, for Roman Catholics, the extent to which the diocese or jurisdiction is under either local or international influence, by showing whether it is staffed by local diocesan (secular) clergy or (for missionary jurisdictions under Propaganda) by an international missionary order or congregation whose initials are then shown.

Most of the international bodies listed below have official names in 2 or more major international languages. If these are English, French or German they are given below (in that order), followed by their initials if widely used.

#### 1st letter: CONFESSIONAL CONCILIARISM, COLLEGIALITY, & CONSULTATION

A confession is a large family of distinct or different autonomous churches or denominations around the world which are linked by similar ecclesiastical tradition, history, polity and name, and usually by some informal or formal organization. Confessions include: Anglicanism, Greek Orthodoxy, Lutheranism, Methodism, Roman Catholicism, and over 230 others (listed here with each's statistics in Table 5-2). Most confessions have councils or permanent organizations and secretariats linking them. Confessional councils as listed here are worldwide in the sense that each is not restricted to any particular geographical or political part of the world.

The code as listed in the GeoCodebook indicates either membership in a Protestant confessional body (linking many denominations of similar tradition), or in a confessional consultative body (for consultation or fellowship only), or in an ecclesiastical family under an Orthodox patriarchate, or in the internal church organization of the largest communion, the Roman Catholic Church. It thus indicates a body's relationship to its own wider communion or confession.

In addition to the world confessional bodies thus listed, there exist a large number of other smaller international bodies. Further, there are a number of continental and regional confessional bodies (e.g. European Baptist Federation, Caribbean Assembly of Reformed Churches). These however are not dealt with or mentioned in column1 nor in column 4 except for a handful of the more significant bodies, which are listed in the GeoCodebook under Continental and Regional Conciliarism.

Table 5-2 sets out the entire range of some 250 confessional councils with each's one-letter code, arranged by attitude to conciliarism. The entire listing is alphabetized by code in Part 16 "GeoCodebook", Table 16-5.

## 2nd letter: WORLD CONCILIARISM , COLLEGIALITY, AND CONSULTATION

The code indicates, for the denomination or diocese concerned, the degree of involvement in, or commitment to, or attitude to, the world interdenominational or ecumenical movement in the widest sense of the term, worldwide consultation between church leaders and clergy and laity, the worldwide conciliar movement (the proliferation of working and planning through councils), and the conciliar principle ('Without counsel plans go wrong; where counsellors are many, plans succeed'—Proverbs 15:22, RSV/Jerusalem). In Protestantism this movement began well over a century ago on the mission fields of Asia and Africa; in the Roman Catholic Church, it has only gained momentum since Vatican II. Conciliarism aims to guide church affairs through the co-operation of denominations, dioceses, hierarchies, church leaders, clergy and laity, in councils—whether ecumenical, confessional, inter-denominational, or intra-denominational (i.e. within a large denomination).

There is a difference of emphasis, in this conciliar involvement, between Protestantism and Roman Catholicism. Protestantism consists of large numbers of autonomous national churches and denominations each run more or less on the conciliar principle internally (consultation between clergy and laity at all levels), but relatively out of touch with each other; hence the growth of conciliarism has meant primarily the establishing of national and international interdenominational councils. The Roman Catholic Church, by contrast, is highly centralized and has long had a worldwide administrative structure and bureaucracy, but has lacked both collegiality (government by all bishops together) and also internal consultation between bishops, clergy and laity. Hence Vatican II initiated major internal conciliar reforms by calling for (a) worldwide collegiality (the whole structure of national and regional episcopal conferences, with the Synod of Bishops at the apex), involving all bishops and ordinaries (but not priests, religious or laity); and (b) consultation and co-responsibility, involving priests, religious personnel and laity as well as bishops, by creating, for the first time, diocesan priests' councils or senates, and diocesan pastoral councils (with religious and lay diocesan pastoral councils (with religious and lay participation). Certain Roman Catholic local (nationwide) churches have gone further in co-responsibility than Vatican II required by establishing national priests' councils and national pastoral councils; but in 1973 the Vatican prohibited their formation as official organs of the church, thus relegating them to unofficial status. Nevertheless, their existence indicates in which countries the movement towards co-responsibility is strongest, liberalism more to the fore than conservatism, and lay and priestly initiatives more pronounced.

Our code here thus portrays how far a denomination or a Roman Catholic local church has progressed along this worldwide road to conciliarism, co-re-

sponsibility and consultation.

### a. Protestant, Anglican, Orthodox, Independent (world conciliarism, i.e. membership in world councils or international associations linking quite different denominations and confessions)

The code indicates membership in, or relation to, an international or world association of denominations of different ecclesiastical traditions. There are 4 categories.

*1. Ecumenical (or conciliar)*
*Code*

W   = World Council of Churches (WCC)/Conseil Oecuménique des Eglises (COE)/Okümenischer Rat der Kirchen (ORK)/Consiglio Ecumenico delle Chiese (CEC); this code indicates a member of the WCC in its own right; for a member church spread over several countries, the code W is given to the headquarters branch, and also to all other branches whose countries are listed in the member's official title; other parts or branches are given the code w

u   = associate member of WCC (small churches, in principle under 10,000 in membership)

w   = related to WCC; not a member in its own right in its own country, but related (e.g. as a foreign diocese or branch) to some larger WCC member-church or grouping based in a different country; or, part of a member-church but whose country is not listed in the member's official title

v   = application for membership made to WCC (either formal or preliminary), but either withdrawn, rejected, delayed indefinitely, or not accepted by 1980, 1990, or 2000

*Notes.* (1) In a number of Western nations, foreign missionary societies of denominations in the ecumenical movement have been in the past, and still are in a handful of cases, linked in national missionary councils whose scope has been international by virtue of their worldwide activities. However, these councils are not used here as indicators of world conciliar membership because both the home denominations and, usually, the national churches they have founded overseas belong to the World Council of Churches. (2) The Roman Catholic Church is not a member of the WCC but has observer status in it. But by AD 2000 the Roman Catholic Church had joined as a full member the national council of churches in over 130 countries, with an additional 40 national councils of churches in which the Roman Catholic Church had not yet obtained membership but with which it had a good working relationship.

*2. Evangelical (partly conciliar)*
Denominations of Evangelical (mainly Conservative Evangelical) emphasis are linked through membership or affiliation with the World Evangelical Fellowship (WEF). Many other denominations and missionary societies reject all interdenominational, ecumenical or formal conciliar links. However, numerous WEF member churches in Britain and America link the missionary churches they have founded in countries across the world into de facto international Christian consultative bodies or councils. Many of the resulting national churches belong to continental, regional or national Evangelical councils, alliances or fellowships affiliated to WEF, which before 1951 was the World Evangelical Alliance, WEA as described below under National Conciliarism.

*Code*

F   = World Evangelical Fellowship (WEF) through links with EFMA, EAGB, NAE, EMA, or other Evangelical alliances

q   = church related to EFMA, but which has also applied to WCC for membership

*3. Fundamentalist (or anti-conciliar)*
Western denominations and missionary societies of strongly Evangelical emphasis often describe themselves by the term Fundamental or Fundamentalist, or nonconciliar, anti-conciliar or anti-ecumenical. A number of such missions in the USA, including several major faith missions, belong to the IFMA which

is a de facto world Christian consultative body or council linking only nondenominational (or faith) missions. A more Fundamentalist body is the ICCC, which is specifically anti-ecumenical (separatist).

*Code*

M   = church or mission related to Interdenominational Foreign Mission Association, USA (IFMA)

N   = church or mission related to both IFMA and EFMA

r   = church related to IFMA, but which has also applied to WCC for membership

T   = International Council of Christian Churches (ICCC)/Conseil Internationale des Eglises Chrétiennes/Internationaler Rat Christlicher Kirchen (IRCK), and The Associated Missions (TAM)

t   = former member of ICCC, or linked with it, but now withdrawn

*4. Non-conciliar*

.   = not a member of or related to any world or international council or association

### b. Roman Catholic (worldwide collegiality and consultation)

All Roman Catholic churches and dioceses are represented at the worldwide Synod of Bishops/Sinodo dei Vescovi/Synodus Episcoporum (every 3 years in Rome, with permanent secretariat) and (in 1962–5) at the worldwide Ecumenical Council (Vatican II). Because all participate, this fact is not here shown in coded form. What is shown in this column in *WCE Country Table 2* requires some explanation of 2 major concepts in Roman Catholic church structure. (1) *Collegiality* is collaboration between the bishops and Rome, and means government through national, regional and continental bishops' conferences, with at the apex the 2 worldwide expressions of collegiality, the Synod of Bishops and the Ecumenical Council. All Catholic local (nation-wide) churches are represented on these 2 bodies by their bishops. This process of worldwide collegiality, however, involves directly only the bishops; it does not involve the rest of the people of God—priests, religious personnel, laity—who do not participate directly. The second concept is (2) *Consultation*, through which the whole people of God—bishops, priests, religious personnel and laity—are involved in the structure and affairs of the church. Officially, consultation by priests, religious personnel and laity must take place only at the diocesan level, through a diocese's pastoral council and its priests' senate; it may also take place at the parish level, though this is not mandatory. At the national level, however, national or nation-wide pastoral councils, and also national priests' councils or senates, have been forbidden by Rome since 1973. Consequently, in many countries priests, religious personnel, laity, and sometimes their bishops, have organized unofficial or unrecognized national priests' organizations and national consultative pastoral bodies.

The code shows where these 2 latter bodies exist in a Catholic local (nation-wide) church, and therefore indicates the extent to which the whole people of God participate in world collegiality and consultation, i.e. the extent to which priests, religious personnel and laity in the local church are attempting to participate in the process of worldwide consultation. The data reflect the situation as at 1995–98.

## 3rd letter: CONTINENTAL CONCILIARISM, COLLEGIALITY, AND CONSULTATION

The code indicates membership in a continent-wide association of different denominations and/or dioceses, or of Roman Catholic national episcopal conferences.

The 6 councils marked + below are affiliated to the WCC as regional conferences and hence are often called ecumenical councils. The Pacific Conference of Churches is included here as a continental conference because it represents Oceania, but the smaller Catholic CEPAC (a member of the PCC) is placed under Regional Conciliarism below. Similarly, the Caribbean is reckoned here as a quasi-continent and so the Caribbean Conference of Churches is included, whereas its smaller member body the Catholic AEC is placed under Regional Conciliarism.

There are in addition several confessional or denominational councils continent-wide in name which are included not here but below under Regional Conciliarism.

Although the Roman Catholic councils here cover each a continent, several are in Catholic usage termed regional conferences because they are each composed of several national episcopal conferences (codes B,F,S).

Corresponding lower-case letters (a,c,e,o,p,u) indicate that a body belongs to the council concerned, not in its own right, but by belonging as a small part (e.g. as a small foreign diocese or branch) to some larger confessional or ecclesiastical grouping based in a different country.

*Code*

A = All Africa Conference of Churches (AACC)/ Conference des Eglises de Toute l'Afrique (CETA)+

a = small foreign part of full member of AACC

B = Consilium Conferentiarum Episcopalium Europae (CCEE) (Council of European Bishops' Conferences)

C = Conference of European Churches (CEC)/Conference des Eglises Europeennes (CEE)/Konferenz Europaischer Kirchen (KEK)+

c = observer status in CEC (Armenian, Bulgarian and Serbian Orthodox Churches); or, small foreign part of a full member of CEC

D = related to European Evangelical Alliance (EEA) through membership in affiliated national fellowship or council or alliance

E = Christian Conference of Asia (CCA) (until 1972, East Asian Christian Conference, EACC)+

e = small foreign part of full member of CCA

F = Federation of Asian Bishops' Conferences (FABC)

G = related to Association of Evangelicals of Africa (AEA; formerly AEAM 'and Madagascar') (member of WEF) through membership in affiliated national fellowship or council

g = associate/special member of AEAM (for isolated denominations)

H = related to Evangelical Association of the Caribbean (EAC) through membership in affiliated national fellowship or council

i = member of AACC through membership in OAIC

L = Consejo Episcopal Latinoamericano (CELAM) (Latin American Episcopal Council)

M = Caribbean Conference of Churches (CCC)+

N = member of Caribbean Conference of Churches (CCC) and also of CELAM

O = Standing Conference of Canonical Orthodox Bishops in the Americas (SCOBA)

o = small foreign part of full member of SCOBA

P = Pacific Conference of Churches (PCC)/Conference des Eglises du Pacifique+

p = small foreign part of full member of PCC

Q = member of CCC, also related to EAC

S = Symposium of Episcopal Conferences of Africa and Madagascar/(SECAM)/Symposium des Conférences Episcopales d'Afrique et de Madagascar (SCEAM)

T = continental council affiliated to ICCC (Latin American Alliance of Christian Churches (LAACC), Far Eastern Council of Christian Churches (FECCC), ICCC European Alliance, Caribbean Council of Christian Churches)

U = Latin American Council of Churches (CLAI), replacing in 1978 Movimiento pro Unidad Evangélica Latinoamericana (UNELAM)

u = indirect member of CLAI through membership in a CLAI-affiliated national council

V = Caribbean Conference of Churches (CCC) and also member of CLAI

X = member of CEC, also related to EEA

x = related to EEA, also observer status in CEC

Y = related to both Evangelical Association of the Caribbean (EAC) and ICCC

. = not a member of nor related to any continental council

4th letter: *REGIONAL CONCILIARISM, COLLEGIALITY, AND CONSULTATION*

The code indicates membership in a council covering a region, which is defined here as a small number of countries (3 or more) within a continent (e.g. Western Asia (Middle East), or South Pacific, or Eastern Africa). A number are regional councils of churches of a single denominational tradition (Roman Catholic, Anglican, Reformed, Lutheran, Pentecostal, etc); and some are continent-wide in name but in practice are only regional because that denomination's presence is not universal or continent-wide. There are several other smaller confessional or denominational councils not included here (see listing in GeoCodebook). The Middle East Council of Churches is an affiliated regional conference of the WCC. For Roman Catholic councils, it should be noted that using our definition of region this code includes 2 kinds of council: (a) regional councils properly so called as defined by the Catholic Church, each composed of a number of national episcopal conferences (codes B,D,E,F,G below); and (b) multi-national conferences, each composed not of episcopal conferences but directly of bishops of dioceses (H,L,M,Q,S,Y,Z).

*Code*

A = Council of the Church in East Asia (CCEA) (until 1975, CCSEA)

B = Association des Conferences Episcopales du Congo/RCA/Tchad (ACECCT) (formerly ACEACCAM)

C = Consejo Anglicano Sud Americano (CASA)/Anglican Council for South America (mainly southern region of continent)

D = Secretariado Episcopal de America Central y Panama (SEDAC) (a regional section of CELAM)

E = Association of Member Episcopal Conferences in Eastern Africa (AMECEA)

F = Conférence Episcopale Regionale de l'Afrique Occidentale Francophone (CERAO) (Regional Episcopal Conference of French-speaking West Africa)

G = Association of Episcopal Conferences of English-speaking West Africa (AECEWA)

H = Conférence Episcopale d'Afrique du Nord/Episcopal Conference of North Africa

I = regional council of Black/Third-World/Non-White indigenous churches

J = Asociación Regional Episcopal del Norte de Sud America (ARENSA) (Anglican; part of CASA)

K = South Pacific Anglican Council (SPAC)

L = Conference des Evêques Latins dans les Regions Arabes (CELRA)

M = Antilles Episcopal Conference (AEC)

N = Middle East Council of Churches (MECC/CEMO) (until 1974, Near East Council of Churches (NECC)/Conseil des Eglises Chrétiennes du Proche-Orient (CEPO)/Majma' al Kan'is fi al Sharq al Adna.)

O = regional council of Orthodox churches

P = attached or partially attached to one of the 6 RC non-Latin Patriarchal Synods (Armenian, Chaldean, Coptic, Maronite, Melkite, Syrian)

Q = Nordic Bishops' Conference (Scandinavian Bishops' Conference/Nordiske Bispekonferanse)

R = Anglican Council of North America and the Caribbean (ACNAC)

S = Interterritorial (Inter-Regional) Meeting of Bishops in Southern Africa (IMBISA) (formerly Southern Africa Catholic Bishops' Conference)

T = regional council affiliated to ICCC (Middle East Bible Council, Central Africa Christian Council, West Africa Council of Christian Churches (WACCC), Australasian Alliance of Bible Believing Christian Churches, Scandinavian Evangelical Council)

U = member of both MECCA and CAPA

V = Conference of the Anglican Provinces of Africa (CAPA) (until 1977, Conference of Archbishops of Anglican Provinces in Africa)

W = member of both AMECEA and CELRA

X = Pentecostal Fellowship of North America (PFNA) until replaced in 1996 by Pentecostal/Charismatic Churches of North America (PCCNA)

Y = Conférence des Evêques du Pacifique (CEPAC)/Episcopal Conference of the Pacific

Z = Regional Conference of Chinese Bishops (Chung Kuo Chu-chiao Tuan)

. = not a member of any regional council

5th letter: *NATIONAL OR PLURINATONAL CONCILIARISM, COLLEGIALITY, AND CONSULTATION*

The code indicates the extent to which a church is involved in national (country-wide) interdenominational or ecumenical conciliarism—i.e. membership in national associations of denominations and/or dioceses. In a few cases, such councils cover 2 countries (or very occasionally, 3) and so can be called plurinational. In a number of cases, too, the Roman Catholic Church is a member, or an associate member, of a national council of churches. All national councils are fully identified by name under each country's Table 2. In addition to such national councils, there are a large number of other national councils which do not have denominations as members; they are therefore not coded in column 4, but they are listed in footnotes 'Other national councils' under Country Tables 2.

*Code*

a = member of 2 national councils, one WCC-related and one Evangelical (WEF- or AEA- or EAC-related)

b = member of 2 national councils, one WCC-related and one Black/Third-World or Non-White indigenous

C = national council (Protestant, Western) with no formal external international affiliations

c = associate member of C (preceding line), or related for certain functions

d = member of 2 national councils, one WCC-related and one unaffiliated (Protestant, Western)

E = national Evangelical alliance or council, affiliated to WEF (World Evangelical Fellowship) and also to one of its regional associations or continental counterparts (AEAM, EAC, EEA, et alia) where existing

e = national Evangelical alliance or council, affiliated to EEA (European Evangelical Alliance)

F = national council including Roman Catholic, Protestant, Anglican and Indigenous churches, but with no formal external international affiliations

f = formerly in the major national council, but has recently withdrawn

G = national Evangelical council affiliated to AEA

H = national council of Pentecostal churches (Protestant, Western)

h = member of some other council (incompletely recorded in Country Table 2, though name and membership are given below it)

I = national council of Black/Third-World or Non-White indigenous churches (run by them, or predominantly of them)

i = member of I (preceding line) and also of H

J = national council of Black/Third-World or Non-White indigenous churches (different to I)

K = national council of churches, or Christian council, in working relationship with WCC but not affiliated to it

k = associate member of K (preceding line), or affiliated for certain services; or permanent (not occasional) observer or consultative member of K

L = national Evangelical council affiliated to EAC (Evangelical Association of the Caribbean)

l = as L, but also affiliated to ICCC

M = national council of foreign missionary societies (church represented through one or more of its mission bodies)

N = national council of churches, or Christian council, affiliated to CWME or WCC (formerly to IMC)

n = associate member of N (preceding line), or affiliated for certain services; or permanent (not occasional) observer member of N

O = national council or liaison committee of Orthodox churches

P = plurinational Roman Catholic episcopal or bishops' conference (covering 2 or 3 countries included in conference's name)

Q  = member of plurinational RC episcopal conference, also full member of national council
related to WCC
q  = as Q, but only observer or associate member
of national council related to WCC
R  = national Roman Catholic episcopal or bishops' conference
r  = small diocese or church attached to Roman
Catholic national episcopal conference in another country (and so not included in conference's name)
S  = member of national RC episcopal conference,
also full member of national council related
to WCC
s  = as S, but only observer or associate member
of national council related to WCC
T  = national council affiliated, or informally related, to ICCC, now withdrawn
u  = member in temporary or once-only co-oper-
ative national conference of churches in nation where permanent council prohibited by
state
V  = member of national RC episcopal conference,
also full member of national council not related to WCC
v  = as V, but only observer or associate member
of national council not related to WCC
W  = national (ecumenical) council of churches, or
Christian council, formally associated with
WCC (these Associate Councils of the WCC
have been called ecumenical councils since
Davos 1955); in some cases associate councils
are also affiliated to CWME of WCC
w  = associate member of W (preceding line), or
affiliated for certain services; or permanent
(not occasional) observer or guest member of
W; or member of countrywide council associated with W
x  = member of 2 other national councils
y  = some other Black/Third-World or Non-White
indigenous national council (different to I or
J)
Z  = member of 3 national councils
z  = member of 3 national councils, one WCC-related and one Evangelical
.  = not a member of any national council

2nd–5th letters    LOCAL/INTERNATIONAL
STAFFING: for Roman Catholic subdivisions (dioceses and jurisdictions) only:
The code indicates the extent to which a diocese or
jurisdiction is under international, or national, or ex-
tra-diocesan, or local control, by describing its staffing.
Almost all jurisdictions in the Western world are
staffed by secular (diocesan) clergy (with religious
clergy for special functions) and thus can be said to
be under local control; this is indicated by the code s
under the second letter. However, a large number of
jurisdictions in mission areas are operated by religious clergy belonging to internationally-organized
missionary institutes (orders, congregations and societies). Before 1969, under the system Jus Commis-
sionis, SC Propaganda Fide would formally confide
a jurisdiction to the care of a particular institute. This
system is still in force for vicariates and prefectures;
but since 1969 for dioceses it has been replaced by
Propaganda granting a mandate (*mandatum*). This
system has proved so tedious that by 1974 mandates
had been granted in only 15 dioceses, and both institutes and local bishops have circumvented the procedure by a simple signed contract or agreement between a bishop and an institute concerning the supply
of manpower and money. Whichever system is in
force in a jurisdiction, in all cases where an institute
supplies the major services to a diocese or jurisdiction and its bishop, or is effectively in charge of a diocese or jurisdiction (i.e. furnishing clergy required),
these last 4 letters in column 4 give the initials of the
institute concerned.

*Code*

s  = local secular or diocesan clergy
sj  = served by (formerly confided to) Society of
Jesus

All other initials, and their full names, can be identified from the Index of Abbreviations, Acronyms and
Initials (Part 32).

2nd–5th letters: STATUS OF DIOCESE IN INTER-
NAL CONCILIARISM, for dioceses of other large
churches. The code describes any relevant and available data providing a differentium from one diocese
to another.

### Russian and other Orthodox churches
The letter indicates the usual rank of the bishop of a
diocese, and hence provides an approximate indication of the relative importance attached to the diocese by the church's councils, its hierarchy and the
Holy Synod; it is therefore a measure of the influence
of a diocese in internal conciliarism, i.e. in the councils of the church.

*Code*

p  = patriarch, patriarch-catholicos
m  = metropolitan
a  = archbishop
e  = exarch
b  = bishop

---

### COUNTRY TABLE 2, COLUMN 10:
### NAMES, NOTES, AND OTHER STATISTICS

This column serves as a general space where any further data that are available may be summarized. For
certain large churches with consistent patterns of
gathering statistics for their component dioceses, it
has been possible to present data in the form of a subtable at the end of column 10, as explained below. The
absence of any particular statistic for a church in column 10 (e.g. no figure for s, seminaries) means, in descending order of probability, either (a) there are none
of these items (seminaries) in that particular church,
or (b) there is nothing particularly significant to report on that subject, or (c) no information on the subject was available.
   The column gives descriptive notes on each denomination and diocese, including a selection of any
significant data concerning the church's name (in column 1) and also the following elements:
• initials of body if commonly in use (in italics)
• additional parts of name of body, or geographical
   sub-title of the body itself (in italics), with any
   wider geographical ecclesiastical jurisdictions
   or entities (not in italics, but with first letters
   capitalized)
• name of body in major national or local language
   (if not given in column 1) (in italics)
• translation of names in column 1 into English (in
   italics)
• alternate name(s) (in italics) or former name(s) not
   in italics)
• co-operating foreign missionary societies (past
   and/or present), preceded by 'M='
• brief geographical notes (area covered, centers, HQ
   = headquarters)
• brief notes on historical development, e.g., A = year
   when church became autonomous (if significant)
• ethnic or linguistic or national/expatriate (citi-
   zen/alien) composition of members or adherents (Christians), as %; ethnic or linguistic
   groups are always shown here with or without
   %s, in descending order of numerical size; a single ethnic name without a % means that all
   Christians, or almost all, belong to the one
   group; ethnic names in column 10 always refer
   to the Christian population, not to the total population
• and any of the following lengthy listings of statistics that might be available (Note: Personnel are
   always the first statistics shown in this column
   10 in the table, given in the order C,n,x,m,w,f,Yy)

*Code*

C  = Roman Catholic religious institutes (i.e. orders, missions, religious congregations and
societies) permanently present and officially
at work (foreign and local) (the 3 figures given
(e.g. C = 3 + 1 + 15) enumerate the number of
distinct institutes of, respectively, clerics
(*priests* mainly, occasionally also brothers and
seminarians), + *brothers*, + *sisters/nuns*)
PC  = priests' council or senate
lc  = council of laity
sc  = sisters' council (women religious personnel)

d  = monasteries (religious houses for men,
monks, brothers)
de  = monasteries and convents
e  = convents (religious houses for women, nuns,
sisters)
ex  = schism (split, secession, break off) from or out
of church or mission indicated
f  = foreign missionary personnel (aliens, expatriates), as defined by church or mission (lay
and ordained, men and women, often including wives; career missionaries and short-
term; usually including only those active on
the field, or seconded or on furlough, but not
home staff or retired personnel)
H  = hospitals operated by church or mission (including leprosaria and sanatoria)
HQ  = location of headquarters, see city, episcopal
residence, secretariat, denominational offices
(usually only given here if not given in, or if
not the same as, title in column 1)
h  = clinics, dispensaries, maternity centers, hospital outposts, mobile clinics, operated by
church or mission
k  = bookshops run by church or mission
L  = (at head of a sub-column) official language
used
M  = co-operating foreign missionary societies, past
and/or present (listed in full in Index of Abbreviations, Acronyms and Initials, in Part 32),
which have a local or national office and administration (and not simply a few individual missionaries) in the country concerned:
for Protestant and Anglican missions, the
home base's nation usually follows in parentheses (if there are 2 or more nations involved,
they are listed in order of the number of missionaries provided); in the case of Roman
Catholic jurisdictions, a mission shown in this
way in column 10 is offering some assistance,
sometimes in the person of the bishop, but if
the jurisdiction has been confined to or is in
the charge of a missionary institute, this latter is shown in column 4 (2nd–5th letters)
m  = men lay workers, brothers, monks (full-time;
Catholic men, religious brothers (members of
men's religious institutes, both nationals and
expatriates), but not including Catholic lay
catechists; Anglican or Orthodox brothers or
monks, or Protestants and Anglicans recognized as workers in church pastoral or evangelistic work, e.g. full-time lay preachers; usually nationals but not expatriate missionaries.
mw  = total full-time lay workers, men + women (=
m + w)
n  = national (citizen) clergy: ordained ministers,
pastors, priests (secular and religious), deacons, including deaconesses and ordained
women, also including bishops; excluding retired; resident in area (not visiting only)
nm  = total men workers, ordained and lay (= n +
m)
nx  = total clergy or ministers, both national plus
expatriate (= n + x) (1 nx means one of unknown nationality)
P  = practicing Christians, % (those fulfilling their
churches' minimum annual obligations of
church attendance, as % of those affiliated and
eligible to attend; this usually exceeds Easter
communicants) (Roman Catholics: most figures are from 1969 returns to SC Propaganda,
modified to exclude non-communicants under 7 years old)
p  = Bible schools, catechist training schools:
Protestant Bible-training schools or short-term
lay training centers, often for lay church workers, often also for ordained workers but of
lower entrance standard (primary education)
than seminaries (some secondary education);
Roman Catholic catechist training schools, of
primary or secondary level
R  = radio letters (normal annual listeners' letters
received from this country by all Christian radio stations or agencies, home or foreign)
r  = church-related or -operated colleges, teacher-
training colleges, major high or secondary
schools, academies, technical or industrial
schools, or other educational institutions of
higher learning
S  = active BCC students (enrolled in Bible correspondence courses)
SS  = Sunday-school enrolment (pupils)

**Service agencies.** Oldest and best known agency serving the churches. British & Foreign Bible Society, showing Warsaw (Poland) HQ in 1970; (*center*) Catholicos Ephram II of Georgia, aged 92.

**Catechists.** Roman Catholic catechist working for his living in ricefields at Mango (Togo).

s = seminaries for preparation for the ordained ministry (major seminaries, theological colleges with premises, plant and permanent staff; Bible academies, Bible institutes, Bible colleges, officer training schools; usually with entrance requirement of some secondary education; Roman Catholic secular/diocesan major seminaries only (excluding religious/regular seminaries); including university departments of theology only if related to or operated by a church); if a number follows in parentheses, it is of seminaries in training for the ordained ministry

school = primary or middle schools (not a secondary or higher) under church or mission auspices

ST = state: name or zip code abbreviation for secular or civil state or province coterminous, or nearly so, with diocese

T = total accumulated BCC enrolments (students who now or in the past have enrolled in Bible correspondence courses)

t = Sunday-schools, sabbath schools (often called in North American usage church schools, though this term usually means day schools operated by churches, (followed in parentheses by enrolment, which often includes adults)

u = participation in a united seminary (sponsored by 2 or more denominations)

V = BCC or conversions (students enrolled in Bible correspondence courses who have professed conversion to Christ as a result)

v = church-related or -operated universities

W = attending Christians, or weekly church attenders, % (church attenders each Sunday or Saturday or weekend (Roman Catholics; attendance at mass) as % of those affiliated and eligible to attend)

w = women lay workers, sisters, nuns (full-time; nationals plus expatriates; Catholic women religious (members of women's religious institutes) but not including Catholic lay women catechists; Anglican or Orthodox sisters or nuns, Protestants and Anglicans in church pastoral or evangelistic work)

x = expatriate (alien, foreign, non-citizen) clergy (ordained ministers, pastors, priests (secular and religious), deacons, deaconesses, ordained women, bishops, missionaries); active only, excluding retired; resident in area (not simply visiting) (NB: in the Third World, this includes both Western ordained missionaries and also pastors and priests from adjoining or other Third-World countries)

Y, y = annual baptisms (new persons baptized in a recent year), Y = adult baptisms (usually over 7 years), y = infant baptisms (under 7), Yy = adults + infants combined. In the case of churches not practicing water baptism (Salvation Army, Quakers, EJCSK, etc). Y = new adult members admitted. In the case of the Roman Catholic Church, baptisms of infants are as significant as of adults and so *AP* always combines the 2 (shown here as Yy); a

division into adults and infants for each diocese was however given in *AP 1970*

z = catechumens, baptismal candidates (these are always included in columns 6, 7, and 8; hence for the Roman Catholic Church, the number of baptized Catholics = column 8 minus catechumens)

( ) = number of students, monks, nuns, Sunday-school scholars, or pupils in the institutions immediate referred to (e.g. 2s(20) means 2 seminaries with 20 seminarians training for the ordained ministry)

% = percentages followed by names are of 2 kinds: (1) % ethnic groups = % of the Christian community who belong to each tribal or ethnic group. (2) % Muslim, % pagan, % Catholic (%RC) = % of the total population in the area or diocese (information only included where significant or unusual compared to other jurisdictions)

### Subtables in column 10

For the Roman Catholic and Orthodox churches, and a few other large churches with several dioceses, column 10 often ends with a sub-table of 5 columns setting out for each diocese the numbers of national and expatriate clergy, men and women religious personnel, and annual baptisms. It should be noted that these figures of personnel represent usually diocesan workers on diocesan staffs; the actual total of all personnel for a church may be somewhat larger because of the presence of non-diocesan staff, personnel seconded to ecumenical or secular agencies, and so on.

*Summary totals for a church with dioceses.* Where a church or denomination has several dioceses indented under it, all statistics on the first line are of grand totals for the whole church, although a full breakdown by dioceses may not be given on the following lines. Thus a church with only one seminary, in one of its dioceses, will show the code '1s' for that diocese, and will also show the total (in this case also '1s') on the line for the whole church. Care must be taken not to construe this repetition as meaning that there are 2 separate seminaries.

*Total affiliated, 1900-2025.* At the end of every Country Table 2 will be found 6 rows entitled 'Churches, members, growth, 1900-2025'. These rows give the total of all the preceding denominations' totals; the last projects the total to AD 2025. The totals of congregations (worship centers) in the bottom 6 rows of column 5 include estimates for all denominations whose total centers are reported above in column 5. *Doubly affiliated.* Persons affiliated to or claimed by 2 denominations at once (as shown defined and described in Tables 1) are also shown in Tables 2.

### NOTES ON TABLE ABOVE.

NATIONAL COUNCILS. The last of the 5 letters in column 4 shows what generic types of national councils of churches exist in the country, and the footnote gives the name of each body in its official language(s), these being separated by slashes, followed by (if Eng-

lish is not official) English translation in parentheses. Also given are the names of any other national councils linking the churches, and totals of any local Christian councils or councils of churches. If this footnote does not appear under a country's Table 2, it indicates that there are no national councils in that country.
OTHER PROTESTANT DENOMINATIONS. In addition to bodies tabulated in Country Table 2, there is in most countries a number of small or very small bodies too numerous for each to be described. A selection of all such bodies which have congregations and some sort of organization (i.e. not unorganized individual persons) are listed in this footnote, with a summary statistical line at the end of the Table. In parentheses after the names there are often given (1) the year of the body began in the nation, (2) the country of origin, (3) the major ethnic group involved, (4) current statistics of membership.
OTHER INDIGENOUS CHURCHES. Additional small Black, Third-World or Non-White indigenous churches are summarized in a line at the end of Country Tables 2 and a selection of names is given in the footnote, sometimes with in brackets data on year begun, ethnic group, and size of current membership.
OTHER CHURCHES. Likewise, other groupings of small bodies (Orthodox, Catholic) may have a summary line at the end of Country Table 2 and a footnote elaborating.
OTHER MARGINAL BODIES. Additional Western marginal bodies are sometimes summarized in a line at the end of Country Tables 2 and listed in the footnote.

---

### COUNTRYTRENDS

### Table *12-1: GEOPOLITICO-RELIGIOUS DATA FOR ALL COUNTRIES*

The table in *WCT* Part 12 "CountryTrends", Table 12-1, provides a mass of comparative data for all countries, with totals for continents and the world.

### Object of Table 12-1

The object of this global table is to present, in comparative format for all the world's 238 countries, with summaries for the world and its 7 continents with their 21 regions, (1) major geopolitical, politico-religious, and purely religious typologies of countries, which means different ways of describing and dividing up the world's countries; and (2) columns of religious and statistical data relating to Christian resources and activities, namely organizations; personnel; the international sharing of personnel (foreign missionary personnel); religious books, periodicals and libraries; scripture distribution; Christian broadcasting; and evangelization.

These typologies and national variables can be used for a variety of analyses attempting to correlate them with the secular data and variables given in *WCE* Part 4 before each country's descriptive text (or with the 55 secular variables given in C.L. Taylor & M.C. Hudson, *World handbook of political and social indicators,* 2nd edition, 1972) and many subsequent

**State Religion or Philosophy**. On this page and opposite are illustrated further aspects of how states officially see themselves, vis-a-vis religion.

**Religious/Christian**. UK (Britain) (a Christian state with 2 established churches): As Head of the Church of England, Her Majesty Queen Elizabeth II (*top*) is crowned by Archbishop of Canterbury in 1953, and (*center*) opens 1975-1980 General Synod in Church House, Westminister.

# Church & State
Some vistas

**Religious/Non-Christian**. *Right*. Egypt (an Islamic state): During 1978 negotiations between Pope Shenouda III (on right) and President Sadat (left) concerning anti-Christian rioting, noon approached and all agreed to pray, with the Egyptian Cabinet (left, all Muslims) falling to their knees.

**Secular.** USA (state separated from church and religion, but maintaining good relations). President Lyndon Johnson addresses religious leaders (Protestant, Catholic, Jewish) in East Room of White House in 1964.

**Atheistic.** China, 1967 (then an atheistic state attempting to destroy religion). During Cultural Revolution militantly atheistic Red Guards surge through Peking streets destroying churches, temples, Scriptures and everything religious.

**Atheistic.** USSR (secular state, but promoting irreligion): Official Soviet anti-religious propaganda attacking pope, patriarchs, bishops, monks, priests, rabbis, mullahs, et alii (dated 1940).

**Graph 14–1.     Sending and receiving of missionaries in World C countries with populations greater than 10,000 in AD 2000.**

see discussion on adjacent page (International sharing of personnel), also Global Diagram 45, and Global Map 8 (in color)

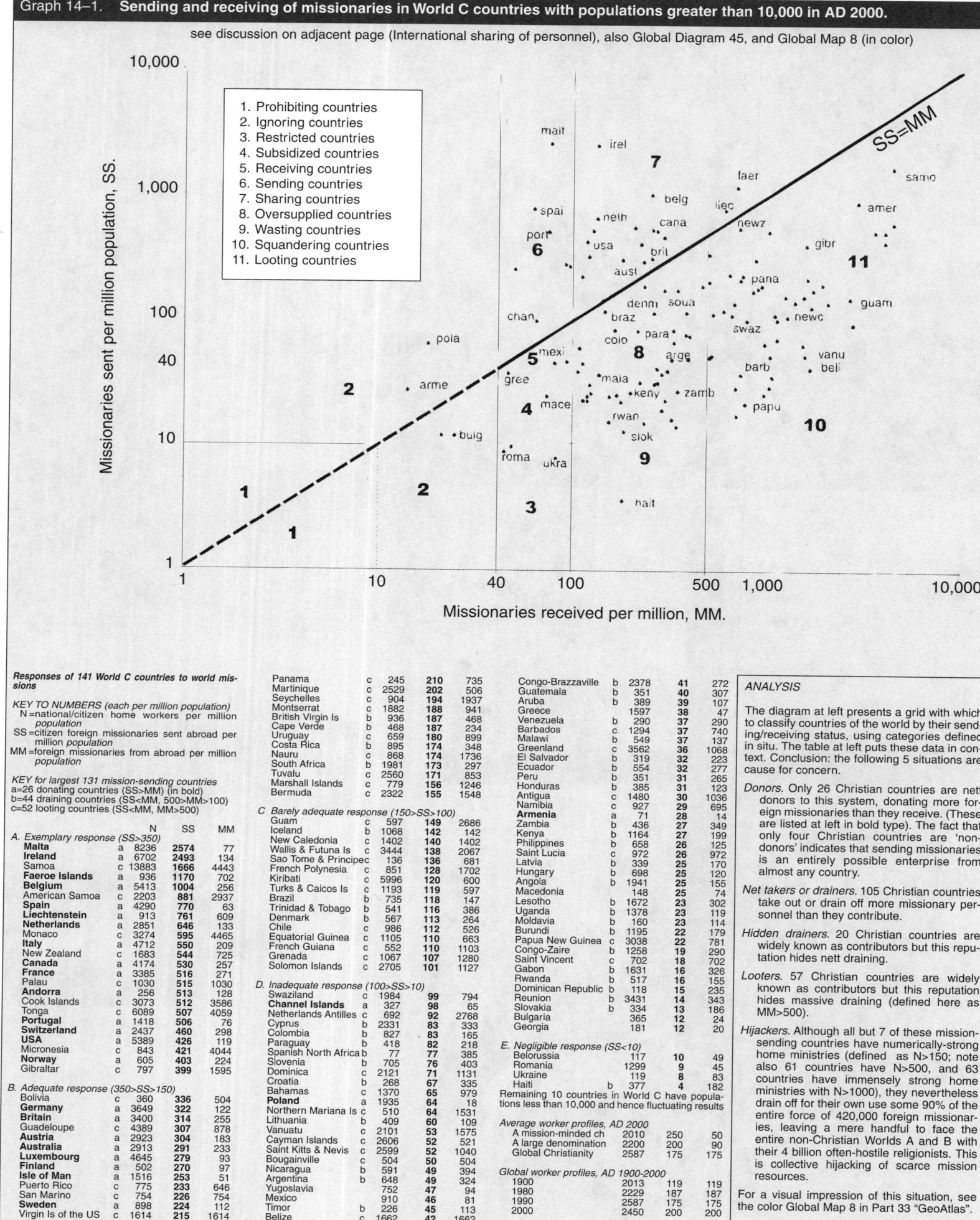

1. Prohibiting countries
2. Ignoring countries
3. Restricted countries
4. Subsidized countries
5. Receiving countries
6. Sending countries
7. Sharing countries
8. Oversupplied countries
9. Wasting countries
10. Squandering countries
11. Looting countries

*Missionaries sent per million population, SS.*

*Missionaries received per million, MM.*

---

*Responses of 141 World C countries to world missions*

*KEY TO NUMBERS (each per million population)*
N = national/citizen home workers per million *population*
SS = citizen foreign missionaries sent abroad per million *population*
MM = foreign missionaries from abroad per million *population*

*KEY for largest 131 mission-sending countries*
a = 26 donating countries (SS>MM) (in bold)
b = 44 draining countries (SS<MM, 500>MM>100)
c = 52 looting countries (SS<MM, MM>500)

|  |  | N | SS | MM |
|---|---|---|---|---|
| **A. Exemplary response (SS>350)** | | | | |
| **Malta** | a | 8236 | **2574** | 77 |
| **Ireland** | a | 6702 | **2493** | 134 |
| Samoa | c | 13883 | **1666** | 4443 |
| **Faeroe Islands** | a | 936 | **1170** | 702 |
| **Belgium** | a | 5413 | **1004** | 256 |
| American Samoa | c | 2203 | **881** | 2937 |
| **Spain** | a | 4290 | **770** | 63 |
| **Liechtenstein** | a | 913 | **761** | 609 |
| **Netherlands** | a | 2851 | **646** | 133 |
| Monaco | c | 3274 | **595** | 4465 |
| **Italy** | a | 4712 | **550** | 209 |
| New Zealand | a | 1683 | **544** | 725 |
| **Canada** | a | 4174 | **530** | 257 |
| **France** | a | 3385 | **516** | 271 |
| Palau | c | 1030 | **515** | 1030 |
| **Andorra** | a | 256 | **513** | 128 |
| Cook Islands | c | 3073 | **512** | 3586 |
| Tonga | c | 6089 | **507** | 4059 |
| **Portugal** | a | 1418 | **506** | 76 |
| **Switzerland** | a | 2437 | **460** | 298 |
| **USA** | a | 5389 | **426** | 119 |
| Micronesia | c | 843 | **421** | 4044 |
| **Norway** | a | 605 | **403** | 224 |
| Gibraltar | c | 797 | **399** | 1595 |
| **B. Adequate response (350>SS>150)** | | | | |
| Bolivia | c | 360 | **336** | 504 |
| **Germany** | a | 3649 | **322** | 122 |
| **Britain** | a | 3400 | **314** | 255 |
| Guadeloupe | c | 4389 | **307** | 878 |
| **Austria** | a | 2923 | **304** | 183 |
| **Australia** | a | 2913 | **291** | 233 |
| **Luxembourg** | a | 4645 | **279** | 93 |
| **Finland** | a | 502 | **270** | 97 |
| **Isle of Man** | a | 1516 | **253** | 51 |
| Puerto Rico | c | 775 | **233** | 646 |
| San Marino | c | 754 | **226** | 754 |
| **Sweden** | a | 898 | **224** | 112 |
| Virgin Is of the US | c | 1614 | **215** | 1614 |

| | | | | |
|---|---|---|---|---|
| Panama | c | 245 | **210** | 735 |
| Martinique | c | 2529 | **202** | 506 |
| Seychelles | c | 904 | **194** | 1937 |
| Montserrat | c | 1882 | **188** | 941 |
| British Virgin Is | b | 936 | **187** | 468 |
| Cape Verde | c | 468 | **187** | 234 |
| Uruguay | c | 659 | **180** | 899 |
| Costa Rica | b | 895 | **174** | 348 |
| Nauru | c | 868 | **174** | 1736 |
| South Africa | b | 1981 | **173** | 297 |
| Tuvalu | c | 2560 | **171** | 853 |
| Marshall Islands | c | 779 | **156** | 1246 |
| Bermuda | c | 2322 | **155** | 1548 |
| **C. Barely adequate response (150>SS>100)** | | | | |
| Guam | c | 597 | **149** | 2686 |
| Iceland | c | 1068 | **142** | 142 |
| New Caledonia | c | 1402 | **140** | 1402 |
| Wallis & Futuna Is | c | 3444 | **138** | 2067 |
| Sao Tome & Principe | c | 136 | **136** | 681 |
| French Polynesia | c | 851 | **128** | 1702 |
| Kiribati | c | 5996 | **120** | 600 |
| Turks & Caicos Is | c | 1193 | **119** | 597 |
| Brazil | b | 735 | **118** | 147 |
| Trinidad & Tobago | c | 541 | **116** | 386 |
| Denmark | b | 567 | **113** | 264 |
| Chile | b | 986 | **112** | 526 |
| Equatorial Guinea | c | 1105 | **110** | 663 |
| French Guiana | c | 552 | **110** | 1103 |
| Grenada | c | 1067 | **107** | 1280 |
| Solomon Islands | c | 2705 | **101** | 1127 |
| **D. Inadequate response (100>SS>10)** | | | | |
| Swaziland | c | 1984 | **99** | 794 |
| **Channel Islands** | a | 327 | **98** | 65 |
| Netherlands Antilles | c | 692 | **92** | 2768 |
| Cyprus | b | 2331 | **83** | 333 |
| Colombia | b | 827 | **83** | 165 |
| Paraguay | b | 418 | **82** | 218 |
| Spanish North Africa | b | 77 | **77** | 385 |
| Slovenia | b | 705 | **76** | 403 |
| Dominica | c | 2121 | **71** | 1131 |
| Croatia | b | 268 | **67** | 335 |
| Bahamas | c | 1370 | **65** | 979 |
| **Poland** | a | 1935 | **64** | 18 |
| Northern Mariana Is | c | 510 | **64** | 1531 |
| Lithuania | b | 409 | **60** | 109 |
| Vanuatu | c | 2101 | **53** | 1575 |
| Cayman Islands | c | 2606 | **52** | 521 |
| Saint Kitts & Nevis | c | 2599 | **52** | 1040 |
| Bougainville | c | 504 | **50** | 504 |
| Nicaragua | b | 591 | **49** | 394 |
| Argentina | b | 648 | **49** | 324 |
| Yugoslavia | | 752 | **47** | 94 |
| Mexico | | 910 | **46** | 81 |
| Timor | b | 226 | **45** | 113 |
| Belize | c | 1662 | **42** | 1662 |

| | | | | |
|---|---|---|---|---|
| Congo-Brazzaville | b | 2378 | **41** | 272 |
| Guatemala | b | 351 | **40** | 307 |
| Aruba | b | 389 | **39** | 107 |
| Greece | | 1597 | **38** | 47 |
| Venezuela | b | 290 | **37** | 290 |
| Barbados | c | 1294 | **37** | 740 |
| Malawi | b | 549 | **37** | 137 |
| Greenland | c | 3562 | **36** | 1068 |
| El Salvador | b | 319 | **32** | 223 |
| Ecuador | b | 554 | **32** | 277 |
| Peru | b | 351 | **31** | 265 |
| Honduras | b | 385 | **31** | 123 |
| Antigua | c | 1480 | **30** | 1036 |
| Namibia | | 927 | **29** | 695 |
| **Armenia** | a | 71 | **28** | 14 |
| Zambia | b | 436 | **27** | 349 |
| Kenya | b | 1164 | **27** | 199 |
| Philippines | b | 658 | **26** | 125 |
| Saint Lucia | c | 972 | **26** | 972 |
| Latvia | b | 339 | **25** | 170 |
| Hungary | b | 698 | **25** | 120 |
| Angola | b | 1941 | **25** | 155 |
| Macedonia | | 148 | **25** | 74 |
| Lesotho | b | 1672 | **23** | 302 |
| Uganda | b | 1378 | **23** | 119 |
| Moldavia | b | 160 | **23** | 114 |
| Burundi | b | 1195 | **22** | 179 |
| Papua New Guinea | c | 3038 | **22** | 781 |
| Congo-Zaire | b | 1258 | **19** | 290 |
| Saint Vincent | c | 702 | **18** | 702 |
| Gabon | b | 1631 | **16** | 326 |
| Rwanda | b | 517 | **16** | 155 |
| Dominican Republic | b | 118 | **15** | 235 |
| Reunion | b | 3431 | **14** | 343 |
| Slovakia | b | 334 | **13** | 186 |
| Bulgaria | | 365 | **12** | 24 |
| Georgia | | 181 | **12** | 12 |
| **E. Negligible response (SS<10)** | | | | |
| Belorussia | b | 117 | **10** | 49 |
| Romania | | 1299 | **9** | 45 |
| Ukraine | b | 119 | **8** | 83 |
| Haiti | b | 377 | **4** | 182 |

Remaining 10 countries in World C have populations less than 10,000 and hence fluctuating results

*Average worker profiles, AD 2000*
| A mission-minded ch | 2010 | 250 | 50 |
|---|---|---|---|
| A large denomination | 2200 | 200 | 90 |
| Global Christianity | 2587 | 175 | 175 |

*Global worker profiles, AD 1900-2000*
| 1900 | 2013 | 119 | 119 |
|---|---|---|---|
| 1980 | 2229 | 187 | 187 |
| 1990 | 2587 | 175 | 175 |
| 2000 | 2450 | 200 | 200 |

---

*ANALYSIS*

The diagram at left presents a grid with which to classify countries of the world by their sending/receiving status, using categories defined in situ. The table at left puts these data in context. Conclusion: the following 5 situations are cause for concern.

*Donors.* Only 26 Christian countries are nett donors to this system, donating more foreign missionaries than they receive. (These are listed at left in bold type). The fact that only four Christian countries are 'non-donors' indicates that sending missionaries is an entirely possible enterprise from almost any country.

*Net takers or drainers.* 105 Christian countries take out or drain off more missionary personnel than they contribute.

*Hidden drainers.* 20 Christian countries are widely known as contributors but this reputation hides nett draining.

*Looters.* 57 Christian countries are widely known as contributors but this reputation hides massive draining (defined here as MM>500).

*Hijackers.* Although all but 7 of these mission-sending countries have numerically-strong home ministries (defined as N>150; note also 61 countries have N>500, and 63 countries have immensely strong home ministries with N>1000), they nevertheless drain off for their own use some 90% of the entire force of 420,000 foreign missionaries, leaving a mere handful to face the entire non-Christian Worlds A and B with their 4 billion often-hostile religionists. This is collective hijacking of scarce mission resources.

For a visual impression of this situation, see the color Global Map 8 in Part 33 "GeoAtlas".

databases.

The full codes used are given in Part 16 "GeoCodebook". Here, we describe only the methodology used in deriving certain of the typologies and other data which employ codes or coded values. For the full listing of Table 12-1's variables, see the first page of Part 12. For any other codes involved, see the GeoCodebook.

## COUNTRIES

*Column 1. Country's code*
This first column identifies all countries, each in alphabetical order being assigned a 4-character code usually the first 4 letters of the country's name.

*Column 2.*
Country's short name in English.

*Column 3. Continent and region*
The simplest and most objective classifications are geographical ones, in which the world's countries are divided up by continents and regions. Unfortunately, 'continent' is too vague a term for every purpose. It usually refers to the larger continuous masses of land, larger than islands such as Greenland; seen thus, the continents are, in order of size: Eurasia, Africa, Northern America, South America, Antarctica, Australasia. According to Webster, a continent is 'a continuous extent or mass of land; one of the great divisions of land on the globe'. The best statement is that there are 7 continents: Africa, Antarctica, Asia, Europe, Latin America, Northern America, Oceania. For our more precise enumerative purposes, we use here the United Nations standardized classification of countries into 7 'major areas' (continents), subdivided into 21 'geographic subdivisions' or 'regions' (see GeoCodebook). A world analysis of Christians in this manner is given in Part 10 "GeoStatistics". And for a detailed listing showing which countries fall under each of these areas or regions, see the first page of Table 7-2.

## LANGUAGES

*Column 18. Official state language*
Countries may be classified according to their countrywide official language or languages (excluding national languages which are not also official), in the year 2000. These languages are shown in the order usually given (if a country has over 3 official languages, only the first 3 are given). Names and codes are given in the GeoCodebook for all official languages. Using this criterion, Christians are analyzed in Part 10, Table 10-4, and also in the color map Global Map 1.

## RELIGIOUS LIBERTY OR PERSECUTION

*Column 56. Religious liberty, AD 2000*
The actual or de facto situation in a country with regard to religious freedom as experienced by the churches usually differs considerably from the de jure situation, in which full freedom of religion is guaranteed on paper by the constitution in virtually every country throughout the world except for Albania from 1950 to 1990. An analogous situation exists with regard to all other types of human rights. In 1998, 50 years after the United Nations promulgated its *Universal Declaration of Human Rights*, detailing 39 economic, social, cultural, civil and political rights, UN members—a majority of all nations— continue to ignore many of them. Full freedom or liberty or toleration of religion is defined in this book along similarly comprehensive lines. It does not mean merely freedom of inner belief and conscience for individuals (as in fact many countries interpret it), but also a whole range of over 30 closely-related other freedoms or rights: freedom of public worship indoors or outdoors, freedom of assembly, freedom of self-government, freedom of association, freedom to organize religious bodies, freedom to organize Bible study circles, freedom to run Christian libraries and bookshops, freedom to collect money and to disburse it, freedom for churches to own buildings or property, freedom to organize credit unions for the benefit of members, freedom to offer medical care where wanted, freedom to engage in mission at home and abroad, freedom to send abroad or receive from abroad foreign missionaries, freedom of Christian political expression, freedom to teach religion and to be taught, freedom for children to join religious associations and to receive Christian instruction, freedom to change one's religion or be converted, freedom of propagation, freedom to travel on religious business within the country and abroad and to return, freedom to listen to radio religious broadcasts from any country, freedom to send and receive religious mail and literature uncensored both inland and abroad; freedom to use national press and broadcasting (radio and TV) facilities; freedom to write, print, publish, mail, broadcast, circulate scriptures, buy and sell literature, distribute, evangelize, proselytize, and baptize. It also includes freedom for minority churches as well as majority churches. Any country which lacks many or most of these freedoms can therefore fairly be said to be deficient in religious liberty. These items can all be arranged as a scale and the status of religious liberty in a country can accordingly be given a numerical value. Countries are here therefore classified by this de facto criterion, describing the situation over the period 1990-2000, which varies from substantial state assistance and genuine promotion (as opposed to control) of Christianity (1–3 below), through complete de facto non-intervention or religious toleration or disinterest (4–5), to ambiguous or ambivalent situations where state interference or obstruction may be accompanied by massive subsidies for purposes of surveillance and control (6–8), and lastly to state hostility or total suppression (9–10). This 10-stage typology, which is based on the documentation given here in our texts on CHURCH AND STATE for each nation, is given in Part 10, and Christians are analyzed by it there.

*Code.    Stage of liberty experienced by churches*
1. State exists solely for promotion of Christianity.
2. State makes sizeable to massive subsidies to promote (but not control) churches (clergy salaries, new buildings).
3. State aids churches (without implying control) with special but limited privileges (tax exemption, legal aid, radio/TV slots, etc).
4. State makes subsidies not to churches but to church schools and/or church medical/social services.
5. State non-interference; churches receive no privileges or aid, nor interference nor obstruction.
6. State imposes on all churches limited or occasional restrictions (e.g. on political activity).
7. State discriminates against or severely obstructs minority churches or churches of citizens (but not those of expatriates).
8. State interference, obstruction, discrimination or repression against all churches; proselytism, broadcasting, publishing, all are prohibited.
9. State hostility, antagonism, or harassment: prohibition of evangelism, missionaries, conversion.
10. State suppression or elimination: no religious activity tolerated.

*Column 57. Christian Safety Index, CSI*
The index measures the degree of safety in the lives of ordinary church members in the country—how safe it is for any Christian citizen to live in his or her own country. It is measured by a formula with 3 components: (a) religious liberty r (column 56, inverted to 10-r, multiplied by 10 to change to a percentage, then weighted by multiplying by 3); (b) plus murder rate p.a. (column 43 divided by 1000 to produce a percentage, inverted to 100-(m/1000); plus (c) Human Suffering Index (column 22, inverted to 100-HSI). CSI then = (the sum of these 3) divided by 5.

## CHURCH/STATE RELATIONS

*Columns 60–63. State religion or philosophy (de jure), 1900–2000*
This next classification is based on the official religion or philosophy of the state, i.e. on how sovereign or nonsovereign states or ruling regimes or colonial governments officially see themselves (or, saw themselves in 1900, 1970, 1990, and 2000) in their formal relation to religion, religions and the churches (as defined in their state constitutions, party constitutions, manifestos and other definitive legal declarations), to what extent they formally acknowledge or recognize or approve of religions and churches. The following 3-fold typology of state religion or philosophy results. After each definition below, an expanded definition follows in parentheses, and then the type is further defined with statements each of which characterizes the situation in several or many (but not necessarily all) countries of that type. This typology is given, describing the situation in each country as at the 4 years 1900, 1970, 1990, and 2000. In Part 10, Christians are analyzed accordingly in Table 10-12.

| Code | Type | Definition and characteristics |
|---|---|---|
| R | Religious | *State identifies itself with religion and its promotion* |

State identified with, or formally linked with, or heavily involved with, or joined in law with, religion or religions or churches and their promotion; state formally proclaims or identifies itself explicitly either as religious (believing in or recognizing the supremacy or existence of God) or as belonging to one particular religion or church; state proclaims or recognizes or favors a state religion or church (legislatively and financially controlled by the state), or an official religion, or a national church or one or more established churches, or recognizes state churches in a majority of the nation's component provinces or parts; state ceremonial and government procedure closely linked with religion or churches; usually no formal or institutional separation of church and state, though separation can co-exist with a state's specifically religious self-identification; a concordat guaranteeing a special or privileged church relationship with the state is in force or in existence; state formally and actively organizes and promotes religion or subsidizes its promotion, or on a formal and permanent basis claims the right of intervention and patronage.

| S | Secular | *State is secular, promoting neither religion nor irreligion* |
|---|---|---|

State separated in law from religion, all religions and all churches and their promotion or suppression, and ignores religion in identifying itself and its role; state neither affirms nor denies any religious, irreligious or philosophical belief, nor shows in its constitution any acknowledgement of the existence of God; state proclaims ideal of complete non-involvement and non-intervention in matters of religion or irreligion, and formally renounces state control over them; separation of religion and politics ordered in constitution.

| A | Atheistic | *State is secular, but formally promotes irreligion* |
|---|---|---|

State identified with Marxist-Leninist atheism, or Marxist (not necessarily Communist) regime almost always with atheistic basic philosophy, formally separated from all religions and churches, but linked for ideological reasons with irreligion and opposed on principle to all religion; de jure freedom of religious belief asserted to be guaranteed, but right of state claimed to oppose religion by discrimination, obstruction or even suppression; state subsidies or financial aid occasionally given, not for promotion of religion but for purposes of surveillance and control.

*Expanded code.* Several states regard themselves as religious in general, or as believing in God, without specifying a particular religion. However, many other religious states identify themselves (or did so in past years) with a single religion or church, and so in this table they have a second code letter added, as shown below. The full code is therefore as follows:

*Code*

| | |
|---|---|
| R | Religious (unspecified) |
| RA | Anglican |
| RB | Buddhist |
| RC | Roman Catholic |
| RD | Adventist |
| RG | Confucian |
| RH | Hindu |
| RI | Islamic |
| RJ | Jewish |
| RL | Lutheran |
| RM | Methodist |
| RO | Orthodox |
| RR | Reformed/Presbyterian |
| RS | Shinto |
| RT | Tribal religionist/Ethnoreligionist |
| RX | Christian (unspecified) |

## INTERNATIONAL SHARING OF PERSONNEL

*Columns 109-112. Citizen and alien foreign missionaries*
These columns document the contributions of all countries to the international sending and receiving of full-time long-term Christian workers, in the context of the foreign mission situation categorized in columns 111-112. The global total of all foreign missionaries in AD 2000, at 420,000, is shown as the last line in both columns 109 and 111.

Another way of classifying countries is from the standpoint of the Christian foreign missionary enterprise, namely the sending and receiving of foreign missionaries and foreign personnel, defined above in detail under the category Global Mission Sharing. Under this concept of mission, the ultimate ideal for a country is no longer that it should be first and foremost a mission-sending country, but is instead that it should both freely send and freely receive substantial numbers of such personnel. 'Missionaries should flow ever more freely from and to all 6 continents in a spirit of humble service' (*Lausanne Covenant*, 1974, paragraph 9). From the point of view of maximum international co-operation and effectiveness in evangelization, the ideal for countries in the future may well be the seventh category in the typology below, namely sharing in large-scale sending and receiving of foreign missionaries and personnel.

To evolve this typology, we prepare the scatter diagram shown in Graph 14–1. On this there are first plotted the total of missionaries received by a country per million of the population, against missionaries sent by that country per million: then we divide the space up into 10 areas, which produces the following 10-fold classification for the world's 238 countries. Note these variables involved: MM = foreign missionaries received from abroad per million population (column 111), and SS = foreign missionaries sent abroad per million population (not given as such in any column, but the reader can work it out from col. 109 divided by country's population). Note: column 110 does not show SS, but the different variable S which is missionaries sent abroad *per million affiliated*, which is a measure of the sending church's commitment to mission.

*Code*

1. *Prohibiting countries* (totalling 17), ie. those closed to foreign mission (but not necessarily closed to internal mission), are defined here as (a) countries which, due to state opposition or societal or communal hostility to Christianity, tolerate neither the sending nor the receiving of foreign missionaries, although in practice up to 10 personnel per million may get in or be sent out without being termed missionaries, usually serving as chaplains or in secular occupations; together with (b) a small number of miniscule territories down to 40 persons in population which are too tiny to be interested in or concerned with the sending or receiving of foreign personnel. Formula: SS≤10, MM≤10.
2. *Ignoring countries* (totalling 28) are defined as those which are not fully closed to foreign mission, but in which foreign personnel received are limited in number to under 40 per million, either by means of government control, or by societal or communal pressure, or as a result of other means. Formula: 40>MM>10, plus 10>MM≥0 where SS>10.
3. *Restricted countries* (totalling 17) are those in which, although they are not closed or partially-closed countries, the numbers of personnel received number 40 or over per million but are restricted somewhat to under 100 per million, and personnel sent out are restricted to under 10 per million, again either by government control, societal or communal pressure, economic forces, or other factors. Formula: 100>MM≥40, SS<10.
4. *Subsidized countries* (totalling 6) are defined here as those which place no restrictions on numbers of missionaries, and in which those received or sent remain small. Formula: SS<40, 100>SS≥10 and 100>MM>40.
5. *Receiving countries* (totalling 2) are defined here as those which place no restrictions on numbers of missionaries, and in which those sent are less than those received. Formula: SS<MM, 100>SS≥40 and 100>MM>40.
6. *Sending countries* (totalling 8) are those in which missionaries sent out number 40 or more per million, and outnumber those received which are limited to between 40–99 per million; these are countries which have traditionally concentrated on foreign missions as a sending operation only. Formula: SS≥MM, 100>MM≥40.
7. *Sharing countries* (totalling 25) are those which embody the fullest development of the idea of the international sharing of personnel, encouraging both the sending and receiving of large numbers of personnel among and within the same churches; and are defined here as countries in which large numbers of foreign missionaries and personnel are both sent and received, each being 100 or more per million, although those sent out always at present substantially outnumber those received. Formula: SS≥MM, MM≥100.
8. *Oversupplied countries* (totalling 22) are defined as those in which missionaries sent out number 40 or more per million, but at the same time missionaries received are always substantially larger in number than those sent out (and usually from quite different churches). Formula: MM>SS, SS≥40, 500>MM≥100.
9. *Wasting countries* (totalling 51) absorb large numbers of mission personnel but waste them on unwise or unnecessary projects. Formula: 500>MM≥100, 40≥SS.
10. *Squandering countries* (totalling 7) take large amounts of mission personnel but use them unwisely. Formula: 40>SS, MM≥500.
11. *Looting countries* (totalling 54) are those which take out far more mission personnel than they need. Formula: SS<MM, MM≥500, SS≥40.

Using this typology, the world situation is analyzed diagramatically in Global Diagram 45, Global Map 8, et alia.

## CHRISTIAN BROADCASTING

*Columns 147-149. Radio/TV audiences*
This section attempts to quantify to some extent the total effect on each country of all Christian religious radio/TV broadcasting (international and national (local radio), shortwave and mediumwave and by all denominations), and in particular to estimate approximately the general order of magnitude of audience listening regularly (at least monthly) to Christian broadcast programs, or viewing them. In column 91 we tabulate the number of radio and TV sets per 100 of the population, to the nearest 1%.

*Two types of listeners*
Listeners to Christian programs can be divided into 2 distinct types: (1) those listening to Christian radio or TV stations, situated either within their own country or, in the case of international radio/TV stations, abroad; and (2) those listening to Christian programs broadcast by state or secular or commercial radio/TV stations, usually within their own country. Naturally, these two overlap to a greater or lesser extent in many countries. In some countries, they represent 2 distinct audiences (differentiated perhaps culturally, or linguistically, or denominationally); in others, they are virtually the same persons.

## EVANGELIZATION, 1900–2025

*Column 152. Year evangelization was begun*
(first resident Christians or missionaries, whether or not subsequently removed). These data can also be used as a typology of countries by dividing the period AD 30–2025 into 2, 3, 4 or more historical periods, as required.

*Columns 153-158. E, as % population evangelized*
The quantification of evangelization is a major subject worked out for the first time in this book. Its methodology is described in Parts 22, 23, 24, and 25.

*Column 163. World*
This reports our Worlds A, B, and C trichotomy where World A countries are those with E<50%; World B, E≥50% and AC<60%; and World C, AC≥60%.

## CHRISTIAN FUTURES

*Column 166. Growth index*
A measure of future church growth relative to the country's future demographic growth utilizing the following formula:
$$((Chr2025/(Chr2000*(Pop2025/Pop2000))) * 100)-100)$$
which compares the number Christians in 2025 (Chr2025) with the number which would have resulted purely from Christian demographic growth (Chr2000*(Pop2025/Pop2000)), then converts this ratio into an index by multiplying by 100 and substracting 100. The index gives the relative difference expressed as a whole number (0 means no difference between projected figure and demographic calculation).

*Column 167. Prospects*
A measure of the future prospects for Christianity in a country, ranging from Bright (+2) to Bleak (-2). This is also illustrated in cartographic form in Global Map 16 (see Part 33 "GeoAtlas").

*Columns 168-191. The future*
Country trends for AD 2025 and AD 2050 were derived with as starting points the extensive UN projections for these 2 years, for every country and for some 100 demographic variables, and for 7 alternate, different future scenarios.

# Part 15

# INSTRUMENTATION

Great Commission Instrument Panels for
the world's 77 largest countries

*Thou hast ordered all things by measure and number and weight.*
—Wisdom of Solomon 11:20, New English Bible

*Use stringed instruments, with 8 strings.*
—Instructions to liturgical musicians for Psalm 6, Contemporary English Version

*In my vision the LORD took me closer, and I saw a man who was sparkling like polished bronze. He was standing near one of the gates and was holding a tape measure in one hand and a measuring stick in the other.*
—Ezekiel 40:3, Contemporary English Version

For modern science and technology, 'instruments' are simply measuring devices. They tell us something definite about ourselves and our activities that we could not otherwise know.

This Part 15 shows that the Christian world has been measuring its vital characteristics over the centuries up to the present point where every day Christians are employing some 2,056 instruments. These are listed here in Table 15–2, with notes on where to find them elsewhere in *WCE/WCT/WCD*.

The start of the Third Millenium enables Christians to assess how useful this sphere of instrumentation has been, and even more important what future role it can play. On this point, a valuable parallel exists between the world of aviation—flight, flight situations, flight controls—and the world of mission. Graphic 15-1 sets out these 2 worlds side by side for the past, the present, and the future—the latter describing a proposal that could go a long way toward helping the Christian mission fulfill its obligations.

# Great Commission Instrument Panels for the world's 77 largest countries

Measurement plays a large part at many levels in the implementation of the Christian operation, agenda, and planning. One thinks, in the first place, of the huge sum of money—US $810 million each year—spent by organized Christianity on professional audits of its finances worldwide. Most Christians agree that this regular and detailed accounting of their monies to the last cent is essential, even if only to deter would-be embezzlers from escalating their predations from their present modest 6% level (US$16 billion each year).

But most Christians are unaware that regular and detailed measurement by the churches goes far beyond the merely financial. In fact, it covers human resources of every kind. This Part discusses the role of instrumentation and documents the 2,056 different instruments that churches and agencies have created and employed in the past—often going back 20 centuries—up to the present, and will continue to employ in the future.

## Instruments are measuring devices

The word 'instrument' has several different meanings—a legal document, a political decision, a musical device—but its most widespread usage is in the worlds of science, technology, and their applications to all human activity.

The simplest definition, and that followed here, is straightforward: an instrument is a measuring device. In the photographic collage overleaf, we illustrate a handful of secular instruments and also a handful of religious instruments in widespread use. These latter may not yet resemble the instruments of the hard or Earth sciences (dials, pointers, physical operation, computerized data recording). But the fact is that the telephone interviews, religious questionnaires, or database variables are all devices producing precise measurements in numeric form. In this role they all qualify for the description 'instruments'.

## Instruments are omnipresent

Almost every area of life employs specialized instruments essential to its proper functioning. Every mode of transportation needs measures of time, distance, speed, position, direction, fuel status. These have tended over the years to crystallize out into a small, standard number of essential instruments, usually six or thereabouts. Automobiles have a driver's panel of speedometer, odometer (mileage), fuel status, engine function (rpm, temperature), oil pressure, time. Aircraft have long had a standard recognizable central panel of 6 conventional flight instruments essential for the pilot to control his craft: airspeed, altitude, attitude (artificial horizon, turn and bank indicator), heading (gyrocompass, magnetic compass direction), vertical speed, fuel supply. Others sometimes included are time, engine status (rpm, temperature, oil pressure), position of flaps. The larger the aircraft, the vaster the number of instruments present to assist the pilot and any specialized flight crew.

## Secular instruments are universal

Space shuttles, submarines, battleships, ocean liners, nuclear aircraft carriers with 6,000 specialized crew aboard are all controlled by a handful of instruments in the cockpit or on the bridge. Another major development has been remote sensing, in which instruments out in space take complex measurements on command from controllers on Earth and transmit the results back.

## Secular instruments often produce religious data

Such instrumentation requires considerable expense. Understandably, churches and religions do not produce their own instrumentation where secular operations exist. Thus churches rely on secular sources for the whole range of demography—counting populations, age cohorts, ethnic and linguistic diversity, and the like. The United Nations' agencies operate a number of databases containing secular measurements of immediate value to churches and religions—literacy, life expectancy, household size, access to health services, telephones, human development indexes, and so on.

Secular instrumentation can also be used to produce religious measurements directly. One can distinguish two modes of operation here: (1) in the decennial population censuses encouraged by the United Nations, half of all countries still direct their national statistical offices to include in their census forms the question 'What is your religion/denomination?' and then publish the results, as in the Swaziland census pictured overleaf; and (2) many secular polling and market research organizations allow churches to append, for a scale of fees, one or more religion questions in political or economic surveys. The first mode loses every year a few countries who remove the religion question as unnecessary because of the high cost of every additional question in a national census. But at the same time, several countries who have never had a religion question in the national census have recently without apology introduced it, as Britain did in its 2000 census because of its value in identifying immigrant communities.

## Sources for Christian instruments

Ten different varieties of instruments (defined as devices which produce measurements) can be described as main producers of Christian data. They are illustrated in the photographic collage overleaf, and are as follows.

*1. Questionnaires.* Most large denominations, missions, and agencies employ printed questionnaires to get large-scale comparative data about their current work, achievements, and status. This present volume estimates that every year 10 million questionnaires are sent out by Christian bodies to their clergy and lay workers, requiring them to reply with all figures requested within 2 or 3 months or so. Most are far too lengthy running on to 10 pages or more, resulting in sizable percentages of failure to return completed replies to headquarters.

A much better practice is to keep the length of a questionnaire to the absolute limit. One good example was the questionnaire which produced the 4-page minisurvey here on the Catholic Charismatic Renewal, CCR (in Part 5 "GeoRenewal", Table 5-5). Its Vatican office faxed the one-page, one-side only questionnaire with only 7 concise questions, to the CCR coordinator in each country. Replies were quickly faxed back, thence to the authors of this volume who then analyzed and tabulated them.

The longest ecclesiastical questionnaire, and the toughest, is the one sent each year by the Vatican to the world's 3,500 Roman Catholic bishops (see Table 15–1, overleaf). Its title in the Latin version is: *Universalis Ecclesiae Annuus Census 2000*; in the English version, it is *Annual General Statistical Questionnaire*. It is 21 pages long in Latin and the 10 other versions in the major lingua francas. In addition to descriptive questions, it asks each bishop 141 separate statistical questions about the work of his diocese in the past year. First and second reminders are sent, where necessary, and a commendable 96% return rate is achieved. Most of this mass of data is then published each January in *Annuario Pontificio*, but little or no scholarly analysis is ever undertaken or published.

A similar fate attends the annual questionnaire

from several thousand denominations worldwide. Their workers laboriously answer the questions and return them. In most cases no analysis ever takes place. Replies are received, read through, then archived, and nothing more is heard of them. Since the total cost to the churches for this annual mega-census is US$1.1 billion, some attempt to learn from all this material seems called for.

One could call a questionnaire such as the one for bishops a single 'instrument'. But is more realistic to follow the practice of this volume, as set out in Table 15–2, and to describe that questionnaire as consisting of 141 statistical instruments arranged either as one single instrument panel, or to be more exact as 20 or so panels labeled after the major subjects dealt with.

**Public-opinion polls.** Here, a worker with Gallup International in USA (*right*) asks question 'What is your religious preference—Protestant, Roman Catholic, Jewish, etc.?'

*2. Interviews by poll.* Many agencies specializing in conducting public opinion polls regularly include religion questions. Several of these specialize in major religion surveys and analyses. The bibliography to this Part lists several of the publications of Gallup International. The actual instrument is a focused interview avoiding vague questions (such as 'Do you go to church?') and instead asking carefully prepared questions (e.g. 'Did you, yourself, happen to attend church or synagogue in the last 7 days?')

*3. Extracting data from secular censuses.* The Swaziland census enumerator in the illustration overleaf is asking 'What is your religion?' and gets the answer from the chief and his wife who state 'We are Zionist Christians'.

*4. Annual statistical reports from agencies.* Most larger denominations, mission boards, and agencies with worldwide work produce sizable statistics of their activities, by country. The United Bible Societies has done this throughout its 54 years of operation. Most agencies have, however, never analyzed their materials.

*5. Online Computer Library Catalogue.* This secular

**Table 15–1. First 2 pages of 21-page annual questionnaire sent by the Vatican to all Catholic Churches in communion with the See of Rome, containing 141 statistical questions as well as other descriptive enquiries.**

1

*Trinae paginae simul sunt in scriptoriam machinulam inserendae, ut suapte natura exempla transcribantur.*

SECRETARIA STATUS

GENERALE ECCLESIAE RATIONARIUM

## Universalis Ecclesiae Annuus Census

### A) DICIONIS ECCLESIASTICAE DESCRIPTIO [1]

Nomen dicionis ecclesiasticae _____ Natio _____

⇩ **Designa congruentem appellationem**

- ☐ Patriarchatus
- ☐ Archidioecesis Metropolita
- ☐ Archidioecesis directo subdita Sanctae Sedi
- ☐ Dioecesis vel Eparchia directo subdita Sanctae Sedi
- ☐ Archidioecesis vel Eparchia propria Patriarchae loci

- ☐ Archidioecesis suffraganea de _____
- ☐ Dioecesis vel Eparchia suffraganea de _____
- ☐ Praelatura Territorialis directo subdita Sanctae Sedi
- ☐ Praelatura Territorialis suffraganea de _____
- ☐ Abbatia Territorialis directo subdita Sanctae Sedi
- ☐ Abbatia Territorialis suffraganea de _____

- ☐ Ordinariatus vel Exarchatus ritus orientalis directo subditus Sanctae Sedi
- ☐ Ordinariatus vel Exarchatus ritus orientalis suffraganeus de _____
- ☐ Ordinariatus Militaris
- ☐ Vicariatus Apostolicus
- ☐ Praefectura Apostolica
- ☐ Administratio Apostolica
- ☐ Missio « sui iuris »
- ☐ Vicariatus Patriarchalis

---

1

⇨ Insert each set of sheets in the typewriter without carbon paper: the special paper used will provide the copies. ⇦

SECRETARIAT OF STATE

CENTRAL STATISTICS OFFICE OF THE CHURCH

## Annual General Statistical Questionnaire

### A) IDENTITY OF THE ECCLESIASTICAL TERRITORY [1]

Diocese: _____ Country: _____

⇩ **Mark + in the appropriate box**

- ☐ Patriarchate
- ☐ Metropolitan archdiocese
- ☐ Archdiocese immediately subject to the Holy See
- ☐ Diocese or eparchy immediately subject to the Holy See
- ☐ Archdiocese or eparchy of the patriarch of _____
- ☐ Archdiocese, suffragan of _____
- ☐ Diocese or eparchy, suffragan of _____
- ☐ Territorial Prelature immediately subject to the Holy See
- ☐ Territorial Prelature, suffragan of _____

- ☐ Territorial Abbacy immediately subject to the Holy See
- ☐ Territorial Abbacy, suffragan of _____
- ☐ Ordinariate or exarchate of Eastern Rite immediately subject to the Holy See
- ☐ Ordinariate or exarchate of Eastern Rite, suffragan of _____
- ☐ Military Ordinariate
- ☐ Apostolic Vicariate
- ☐ Apostolic Prefecture
- ☐ Apostolic Administration
- ☐ Independent mission
- ☐ Patriarchal vicariate

### B) STATISTICS
*(Situation on 31 december)*

| No. | Item | | | Data (figures) |
|---|---|---|---|---|
| 1 | **Area of the territory** | *a)* in square kilometres . . . . . . . . . | | |
| | | *b)* or in square miles . . . . . . . . . | | |
| 2 | **Total population** . . . . . . . . . | | | |
| 3 | **Catholics** (excluding catechumens and those of another rite under a different jurisdiction) . . . . | | | |
| 4 | **Parishes** (territorial or personal) (Include only pastoral centres which have been *canonically erected* as parishes) | whith resident pastor | *a)* under direction of diocesan clergy . | |
| | | | *b)* under direction of religious priests . . | |
| | | whithout pastor (Cfr. Can. 517 § 2) | *c)* administered by priests . . . . . | |
| | | | *d)* in the care of permanent deacons . . | |
| | | | *e)* in the care of professed men religious other than priests or permanent deacons . | |
| | | | *f)* in the care of professed women religious . | |
| | | | *g)* in the care of lay people . . . . . | |
| | | | *h)* completely vacant . . . . . . | |
| | | *Total of parishes* . . . . . . . . . | | |
| 5 | **Other pastoral centres** with permanent assistance . . . . . . . . . | | | |
| 6 | **Bishops** (all those resident in the diocese, including the ordinary) . . . . . . . . . | | | |

agency based in Ohio holds a database with the entire catalogues of the 50,000 or so largest libraries in the world. The user accesses this on his own home computer and makes enquiries by entering any subject or keyword or country name or combination thereof. He or she is then given the total of all such books and any refinements including downloads or printouts needed.

*6. Media, newspapers, broadcasting.* The considerable archives held by these agencies contain vast quantities of data on religions, Christianity in particular.

*7. Measuring evangelism.* Almost any subject such as this is amenable to measurement, quantification, and analysis. Part 22 of this volume examines evangelism under 45 headings or ministries. Many Christian agencies utilize instruments. Thus Campus Crusade for Christ asks its workers how many hours a month they spend on evangelism.

*8. Film attendances.* Since 1978 the 'Jesus' Film Project has held movie showings using the 'Jesus' Film in its 650 different language versions. Detailed records of this activity are kept.

*9. Databases.* These are very numerous and often have data available relevant to Christian mission and evangelism.

*10. Other collections of data.* In this volume, Part 12 "CountryTrends" holds measurements on 191 different instruments, divided into 16 major collections and then into 50 instrument panels averaging 4 instruments each.

**Government censuses.** Here, Swaziland government census enumerator (in hat) explains census question 'What is your religion?' to Chief Mbetse and wife. The reply 'We are Zionist Christians' is then recorded, tabulated and printed in the government census report.

### Organizing data from Christian instruments

With such a wide variety of sources producing Christian data, it is not surprising that they result in a grand total of 2,056 different and distinct Christian instruments, i.e. devices each measuring some different aspect of the Christian world. In Table 15–2 they are shown under 5 major varieties of instrumentation which assist the reader in locating their data either in *WCT* or *WCE* or *WCD*.

### Offering a range of 2,056 instruments

The instruments thus offered in the present series of volumes can be described as follows.

(1) First are country instruments, alerting the user to the values of the major measurable variables in any country he or she is concerned with. The instrumentation analogy is at its clearest here describing how any country can develop a standardized 'Great Commission Instrument Panel' of 6 instruments similar to the handful on an automobile's panel of speedometer, fuel gauge, odometer, tachometer, voltmeter, clock. An aircraft pilot likewise has that small panel with the conventional 6 flight instruments in front of him or her. Our standard panel shows the 6 measurements likely to be of most assistance to Christians wanting to pursue Great Commission initiatives in a country they are unfamiliar with. Table 15-2 goes on to explain where some 479 different instruments, arranged to resemble 83 instrument panels, may be seen in this series' pages to offer further measurements about that country.

(2) Second, there is a series of 74 global diagrams which function as global instruments, though more complex and sophisticated and with far more variables than the usual type of instrument.

(3) Third is a series of topical instruments consist-

**Graphic 15–1. Navigating on global mission, with parallels from aviation: global Christianity's 3 displays, 260 maps, 74 diagrams, 340 screens, 2,056 instruments, 16,000 trends.**

The diagram displays a parallel between pilots of modern aircraft and executives of foreign mission agencies. In the left-hand half of the page below, 20th-century practice forced pilots to face a chaos of separate instruments, constantly monitoring up to 100 instruments facing the pilot's seat, even above (as in Boeing 767 airliner shown).

A similar situation faces Christian executives and decision makers: they face a chaos of some 2,056 separate instruments (listed in the following Table 15–2), including some 5 million separate · and distinct books (titles) describing Christianity and 100,000 of them on mission.

For the 21st century, however, 2 major electronic aids are being developed, as shown in the bottom 3 layers below.

| INSTRUMENTATION IN AVIATION | INSTRUMENTATION IN MISSION |
|---|---|

### DURING THE 20TH CENTURY

A pilot has 100 separate instruments to monitor continuously

Chinese compass

Airspeed

Vertical speed

Wing flaps

### DURING THE 20TH CENTURY—2,056 separate instruments available

Multiple separate and independent sources of data

5 million Christian books

Censuses: 'What is your religion?'

Polls: 'Do you believe in Jesus Christ?'

### IN AD 2000

Current state of the art (left, Boeing 757 and 767; below, Gotha aircraft): pilot has standard 6-instrument panel but must constantly monitor 90 other dials.

Boeing 757/767 Panel

### IN AD 2000

State of the art currently available: (right) annual Vatican questionnaire to bishops asking 141 statistical questions; (below) our Great Commission Instrument Panel with 6 major descriptors.

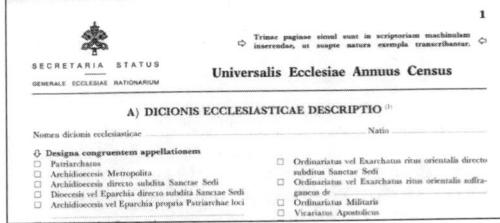

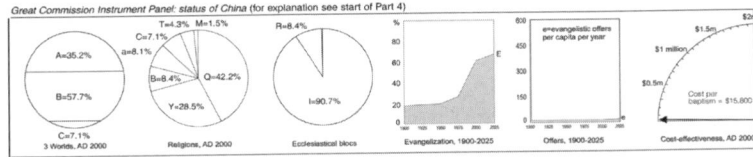

### FOR THE 21st CENTURY

For complete situational awareness, pilots and researchers have produced **EFIS-2000.**
(Electronic Flight Information System) This is a single 7 inch wide screen (full-color multifunction display) with 3 choices:

*First choice* (by touching a button):
(Left) EFIS-1, **Primary Flight Display:** airspeed, vertical speed, altitude, attitude, heading, 30 parameters.

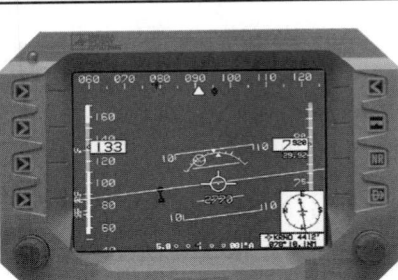

### FOR THE 21st CENTURY

For complete situational awareness, missiologists are proposing **EMIN-2001**
(Electronic Mission Information Navigator) This is any user's home or office computer screen, with 3 choices:

*First choice*:
(Right) EMIN-1, **Global Maps:** 16 full-color global maps, black and white maps, color maps of 238 countries, all with zooming, magnifying, and printout capabilities.

*Second choice*:
(Left) EFIS-2, **Navigation Display:** By touching a tactile button, a pilot can switch from Primary Flight Display to this detailed moving map with GPS (Global Positioning System), flight plan, weather, cloud, crosswinds, storms, traffic, restricted space, terrain modeling, obstacles continually updated: 30 parameters, with voice warnings when boundaries are approached.

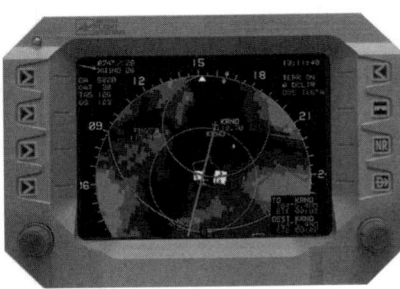

*Second choice*:
(Right) EMIN-2, **Global Diagrams:** 74 diagrams each on one subject including past, present, and future.

This provides users with a Global Navigator or a Country Navigator, as follows:
Overview—4 screens
Past history—13 screens
Present status—28 screens
Future scenarios—24 screens
Long-term futures—5 screens

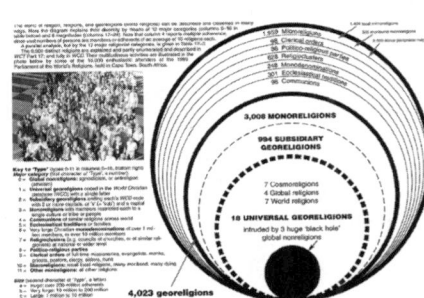

*Third choice*:
(Left) EFIS-3, **Engine Display:** digital monitoring of 40 parameters concerning engine(s) power and condition, with voice warnings when boundaries are approached.

In practice, pilots would need to check this display far less often than the other displays above.

*Third choice*:
(Right) EMIN-3, **Global Chronographics:** invoking the whole 2,000-year history of Christianity, continent by continent and region by region, with large variety of numerical statements, trends, tables, or graphics to user's requirements.

Vertical axis = any instrument or measure

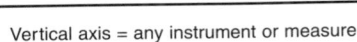
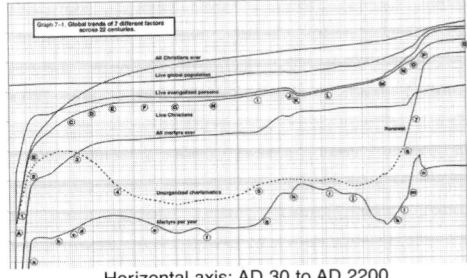

Horizontal axis: AD 30 to AD 2200

ing of 350 statistical tables offering information not on a single country but each on a single topic.

(4) Fourth are 202 database instruments in 6 lengthy printouts giving measurements for the 270 largest of the world's 9,900 different religions, all its 12,600 ethnolinguistic peoples, 13,500 languages, 7,000 metropolises, 3,030 major civil divisions (MCDs, often called provinces of a country), and a name and address directory for 82 topics.

(5) Fifth is a series of 14 visual instruments in the shape of 14 categories with 1,650 photographs selected to support the other ranges of instruments, as the table explains.

In sum, this instrumentation totals some 471 separate panels offering 2,056 instruments giving 4,784,880 measurements in this print series *WCE* and *WCT*. This is complex but hardly excessive. It is the kind of complex instrumentation that one would find in many scientific or commercial parallels—in the pilots' cockpit of a space shuttle, or on the bridge of a nuclear aircraft carrier.

To assist readers to follow the instrumentation analogy, they should consult the verso (the back) of each of the 33 Parts' title pages. There they will find a series of brief comments describing the instrumentation available, and the trends thereby perceived, on the subject of each of the Parts.

***77 Great Commission Instrument Panels***

The parallel this analysis is drawing, between navigating in aviation and navigating on the global Christian mission, is at its clearest in its grouping of 6 instruments to form one Great Commission Instrument Panel for each country in the world. These can be seen in the context of each country's detailed article on Christianity and religions in WCE Part 4 "Countries".

In addition to helping the reader to understand the status of mission in any country, this panel has direct comparative value when the 2 panels of 2 countries are examined alongside each other. This is done here in Table 15–3 which sets out the GCIPs of the globe's 77 largest countries all of which are over 10 million in population each.

This comparative listing has a number of other potential uses. For instance, a mission agency may be looking for new countries in which to begin work and specify the kind of values of 2 or more of the 6 instruments that the agency could undertake to work within. Or the agency might have a ceiling in cost-effectiveness—no more than US $500,000 per new baptized convert. Or only countries where World A is over 50% of the population. Or countries where Independent/Postdenominationalists/Neocharis-matics are at least 10% of all Christians. Or countries where there is no ongoing extensive evangelism under way, i.e. a ceiling measured as e<100 offers per capita per year. And so on.

## *USING CHRISTIAN DATA FOR NAVIGATING*

***Comparing mission with aviation***

The parallel between the use of electronic information in aviation, and in mission, can now be elaborated on. This is set out in detail in Global Diagram 31, and in an abbreviated form here in Graphic 15-1.

On this graphic, a central vertical double-line divider separates the illustrations taken from aviation, which are on the left, from the illustrations taken from mission, which are on the right. This material is then divided by horizontal double lines into 3 distinct time periods: first, at the top, the practice in the 20th century; second, the state of the art in the year 2000; and third, at the bottom, what is now emerging for the 21st century, at the start of the Third Millennium.

***Instrumentation in the 20th century***

1. *The world of aviation* has perfected flight aids for pilots to the point where every aircraft pilot from nuclear bombers to light aircraft relies on a range of from 6 to 300 cockpit instruments, each positioned close to the pilot and each measuring one parameter only. The 4 illustrated are, from left to right, a Chinese compass indicating heading (direction of travel), airspeed, vertical speed, and position of flaps used to slow down aircraft for landing.

2. *The world of mission* does not measure physical or chemical properties but instead it measures variables which are largely social or sociological or sociorelігious. Thus its instruments depend largely on human counting of persons, practices, activities, events, writings, publications, books, polls, sample surveys, censuses, institutions. Some of these variables have been measured annually for up to a century or two. Since the 1930s in America, the Gallup Poll has measured church attendance, beliefs, and activities using nationwide samples of around 2,000 persons. Further to the illustrations on the previous page, the one below shows a Gallup-focused interview at which the enumerator (at left) is asking a basic question about belief: 'Do you believe that Jesus Christ is the Son of God?'

The photograph in Graphic 15-1 depicts the world's largest Christian library, the Biblioteca Apostolica Vaticana (Vatican Apostolic Library) in Rome. It has 1.6 million books and manuscripts. The world's total of books on Christianity is at least 4.5 million. All are available to readers on the shelves of the world's 50,000 largest libraries. Most can be borrowed through libraries for 2 to 4 weeks at a time, including by mail across the world through Interlibrary loan. Many of these books have numbers and statistics on our key subjects. A book can therefore be considered either as a single instrument, or one yielding multiple readings, or as a whole instrument panel itself.

**Belief.** 'Do you believe that Jesus Christ is the Son of God?' Gallup Poll interviewer (left) conducts one of 1,500 detailed interviews on which biennial *Religion in America* (Gallup Opinion Index) is based.

***State of the art instrumentation by AD 2000***

1. *The world of aviation* by the end of the 20th century had perfected instrumentation for pilots in which every pilot had to be familiar with scores or even hundreds of separate instrument dials. His eyes would have to flick constantly from one dial to another. The interior of a pilot's cockpit, shown at left for the newest Boeing 757 and 767 airliners, had by 2000 become a state-of-the-art panorama requiring lengthy cockpit checks before takeoff and becoming a nightmare if anything went wrong. Even attempts at neatness, as for the Gotha airliner shown, required constant training and formidable expertise to comprehend.

2. *The world of mission* operates with several thousand different questionnaires sent out by some 10,000 different agencies in 2,000 different languages. The ultimate state of the art here shown in brief in the right-hand column in Graphic 15-1 and more fully illustrated in Table 15–1, is the Vatican's annual multilingual questionnaire for all its 3,500 dioceses and jurisdictions worldwide. It is entitled in Latin, *Universalis Ecclesiae Annuus Census*, or in English, *Annual General Statistical Questionnaire*. This instructs every bishop to answer 141 precise statistical questions concerning his work in the previous 12 months. Results are then published every January in *Annuario Pontificio*, for every diocese but with no totals or analyses. Some totalling is done every 2 years in *Annuarium Statisticum Ecclesiae* (Statistical Yearbook of the Church), but all the returned questionnaires are promptly archived without further research or analysis.

The second line of 6 instruments shown here in Graphic 15-1 is what WCT/WCE is terming a Great Commission Instrument Panel. It features a conventional array of the 6 instruments of most use to executives, clergy, missionaries and other church workers wishing to navigate across this sea of ecclesiastical data.

## *INSTRUMENTATION FOR THE 21ST CENTURY*

***1. The world of aviation.***

The world of piloting aircraft has recently introduced EMIS-2000. This is a revolutionary rethinking of the role of instruments as aids to pilots. In place of the vast arrays of scores or hundreds of separate instrument dials, Sierra Flight Systems now offers a single 6.5-inch color screen. This serves as a full-color MFD (multi-function display), named EFIS-2000 (Electronic Flight Information System 2000) offering immediate situational awareness in the cockpit at every point of the journey. The pilot uses tactile (by feel) buttons to summon one of 3 MFDs: (1) *Primary Flight Display* (showing aircraft attitude plus 30 standard parameters: airspeed, altitude, etc.), (2) *Navigation Display* (showing a moving/GPS map with 30 parameters including the pilot's flight plan, weather, cloud, crosswinds, storms, traffic around, special use airspace (restricted, firing ranges), terrain modeling, obstacles, all with voice warnings when dangerous levels are reached), or (3) *Engine Display* (digital monitoring of 40 parameters, onscreen trends, again with voice warnings).

This radical new system is designed to serve the entire range of aircraft including experimental vehicles. Under FAA regulations, all American airliners must fly at all times under IFR (Instrument Flight Rules, usually in force for bad weather or night flying). But pilots describe EFIS as Virtual VFR, meaning that even under IFR, pilots experience simulated external visibility, similar to that under Visual Flight Rules (in clear daytime weather).

***2. The world of mission***

The world of Christian ministry through foreign mission can be similarly served by a system named EMIN-2001. This offers, to executives and workers who want to navigate on world mission, situational awareness through the user's single desktop computer screen. (1) EMIN (Electronic Mission Information Navigator) is a CD-based program with 3 alternate screens.

(1) EMIN-1 consists of some 20 full-color *Global Maps* with 220 country maps offering 340 screens with 1,200 parameters, all with zooming and magnifying capability on all maps.

(2) EMIN-2 consists of a *Global Navigator* assisting those wanting to navigate over oceans of data, incorporating 74 Global Diagrams (1-screen or 1-sheet pages) with Globalistics alphabetical index to all data; also including a Country Navigator. All data are divided into 5 presentations: (a) overview (4 diagrams or screens), (b) historical past (13 screens), (c) present (28 screens), (d) future (24 screens), (e) long-term futures (5 screens).

(3) Lastly, EMIN-3 *Global Chronographics* has special reference to 2,000-year trends and events and the whole 20-century history of Christianity, continent by continent and region by region.

## *BIBLIOGRAPHY*

The subject of instrumentation covers a vast area of technical expertise. A search across the world's 50,000 largest libraries reveals that on their shelves they have 44,000 distinct book titles on this subject. The whole range of the sciences, human, social, and hard sciences, is involved. Rather than give a full bibliography, below are given 7 typical titles in social science applications. All offer application in the study of religions. For more detailed lists, use the OCLC catalogue.


*Directorate for Biological, Behavioral, and Social Sciences.* Instrumentation and Instrument Development. National Science Foundation. Washington D.C. 1988.

*Epistemología e instrumentación en ciencias humanas.* J.P. Pourtois. Barcelona: Herder, 1992.

*Epistémologie et instrumentation en sciences humaines.* J.P. Pourtois. Liège: P.Mardaga, 1988. (French translation of item 2 above).

*Instrumentation in education: an anthology.* L.K. Bishop and P.E. Lester. New York: Garland, 1993.

*La recherche-action: ses fonctions, ses fondements et son instrumentation.* G. Goyette. Sillery: Université du Québec, 1987.

*Threshold of intelligibility/comprehensibility of rapid connected speech method and instrumentation.* H.J. deHaan. Alexandria, Va.: U.S. Army Research Institute for the Behavioral and Social Sciences, 1978.

*Truth, method, and measurement: the hermeneutic of instrumentation and the Rasch model.* W.P. Fisher. 1988.

**Table 15–2.  Five varieties of instrumentation in *WCT*, *WCE*, and *WCD*, with 2,056 instruments, to enable orientation while navigating across the globe on the Christian world mission.**

This table describes the whole spectrum of instrumentation derived from the churches' regular measurements of their activities throughout the world. The largest variety, labeled A below, consists of country instruments—measuring activities at the country level.

Then are shown 4 other categories of instrumentation (B, C, D, and E). Second largest is D, database instruments. Lastly, the final line sums and summarizes the 5 categories into the overall instrumentation available in 2 publications: *WCT* (the present volume, *World Christian trends*) and *WCE* (*World Christian encyclopedia* 2001). Readers needing electronic access to these data can find it in the forthcoming online or CD product, *World Christian database, AD 30–AD 2200.*

All these varieties are described below under 10 column headings including 5 statistical columns which extend right down the page as follows: 1 = a reference number; 2 = *WCT*'s or *WCE*'s Part dealing with each; 3 = the Part's title; 4 = subtitle of variety; 5 = groupings of instruments into what are here, for ease of understanding, termed 'varieties of instrument panels'; 6 = number of distinct types of instruments (measuring devices used by churches); 7 = component parts or lines of data per instrument shown in this survey; 8 = number of measurements shown here, either per country or (9) for the whole globe; and 10 = brief explanation.

| Ref | WCT/WCE Part number | Title | Subtitle | Panels | Instruments | Data | Records (a) per country | Records (b) global | Measurements | Notes and comments |
|---|---|---|---|---|---|---|---|---|---|---|
| 1 | 2 | 3 | 4 | 5 | 6 | 7 | 8 | 9 | 10 | |

**A. COUNTRY INSTRUMENTS**

Some 473 of this survey's 2,056 different and separate instruments (devices for measuring any and all measurable aspects of global Christianity), and 83 of its 471 instrument panels, deal with countries as basic unit. These occupy the major part of this table because the globe's 6 billion inhabitants live in countries, and the Christian world is organized primarily by country.

The major significant collection of instruments here is found in *WCT* Part 12 "CountryTrends" and Part 15. This describes 191 measuring devices and lists their measurements for all 238 countries, the 7 continents, and the whole globe. This is summarized in the first line below. Smaller collections are described in the 5 Parts on the lines 2 to 6 that follow. Then comes the major collection, presented in *WCE* Part 4 "Countries"; these are listed below on 13 lines that follow.

Central is line number 13, the standardized **Great Commission Instrument Panel**, with 6 instruments each averaging 4 records (a record being a component line of data, e.g. a denomination, a people, a city), and so 24 measurements for each country. This Panel appears in every country's article in *WCE* Part 4, and for the 77 countries over 10 million in size in *WCT* Part 15 "Instrumentation".

| Ref | Part | Title | Subtitle | Panels | Instruments | Data | per country | global | Notes and comments |
|---|---|---|---|---|---|---|---|---|---|
| 1 | *WCT* Part 12 | "CountryTrends" | Countries | 50 | 191 | 1 | 191 | 45,090 | Data on 270 countries, regions, continents, worlds |
| 2 | *WCE* Part 8 | "EthnoSphere" | Peoples | 1 | 38 | 54 | 2,000 | 540,000 | Data on 12,600 peoples (with 28 detailed profiles) |
| 3 | *WCT* Part 33 | "GeoAtlas" | Global Trends Maps | 1 | 16 | 2 | 30 | 8,100 | 8 pages with 16 global maps |
| 4 | | | Human Environment | 1 | 40 | 1 | 40 | 10,080 | 16 pages of geographical maps covering world |
| 5 | *WCE* Part 10 | "MetroScan" | Metropolises | 1 | 7 | 33 | 230 | 62,100 | Data on 7,000 cities |
| 6 | *WCE* Part 11 | "ProvinceScan" | Provinces | 1 | 9 | 12 | 108 | 29,160 | Data on 3,030 major civil divisions |
| 7 | *WCE* Part 4 | "Countries" | Identification | 1 | 3 | 1 | 3 | 714 | Data on 238 countries: map, name, flag |
| 8 | | | Secular data | 14 | 61 | 1 | 61 | 14,500 | 61 facts or statistics for AD 2000 |
| 9 | | | Country Table 1 | 1 | 16 | 300 | 4,800 | 1,296,000 | Religions and growth rates, AD 1900–2025 |
| 10 | | | Footnotes/censuses | 1 | 10 | 2 | 20 | 5,400 | Detailed data on religions above |
| 11 | | | Country status | 1 | 1 | 4 | 4 | 1,080 | Brief depicting of country's character |
| 12 | | | Narrative text | 1 | 20 | 2 | 40 | 8,100 | Rights, religions, churches, radio/TV, prospects |
| 13 | | | Country summary | 3 | 21 | 4 | 84 | 22,680 | Peoples, Cities, Provinces by Worlds A, B, C |
| 14 | | | Photographs | 1 | 2 | 2 | 4 | 1,080 | Descriptive, analytical photographs of a country |
| 15 | | | Bibliography | 1 | 6 | 10 | 60 | 16,200 | Books, articles, on Christianity in one country |
| 16 | | | Country Table 2 | 1 | 20 | 35 | 700 | 189,000 | Denominations, churches, growth |
| 17 | | | Conciliarism | 1 | 1 | 3 | 3 | 700 | Councils, alliances, fellowships at 5 levels |
| 18 | | | 125-year church growth | 1 | 11 | 6 | 66 | 17,820 | Growth from 1900 to 2025 |
| 19 | *WCT* Part 15 | "Instrumentation" | **Great Commission Instrument Panel** | 1 | 6 | 10 | 60 | **16,200** | 1,620 minidiagrams showing the Top Six instruments |
| 20 | | | **Country instrumentation** | 83 | 479 | 19 | 8,423 | 2,284,000 | Totals of all instrumentation for all countries |

**B. GLOBAL INSTRUMENTS**

All country instruments can be totaled to produce global totals. In addition, however, there are a large number of other global instruments not derived from country measurements. Of these latter, the major ones are the 74 one-page global diagrams shown in *WCT* Part 1 "GeoStatus". These can be interpreted as 20 distinct panels (shown and named in Table 1-3) with 74 complex and sophisticated global instruments. This gives the totals summarized in the following line.

| Ref | Part | Title | Subtitle | Panels | Instruments | Data | per country | global | Notes and comments |
|---|---|---|---|---|---|---|---|---|---|
| 21 | *WCT* Part 1 | "GeoStatus" | Global Diagrams | 20 | 74 | — | | 72,000 | X-rays and CAT-scans of religion's inner workings |
| 22 | *WCT* GD 3 | Denominations | Megacensus | 180 | 360 | 1 | 1,500 | 540,000 | Churches measure 180 major subjects/panels |
| 23 | *WCT* Part 7 | "GeoTrends" | Graphs | 28 | 572 | 1 | 16,016 | 154,400 | Measuring trends at global and local levels |
| 24 | **WCT** | | **Global data** | 228 | 1,006 | — | 17,516 | 766,400 | Totals of all global instrumentation |

**C. TOPICAL INSTRUMENTS**

A number of other instruments measure items not originating via country statistics. This situation is summarized in the following single line. A typical instrument is *WCT* Table 31–3 which describes the world's current literature of 5 million books on Christianity by means of 148 different topics. Of the *WCT/WCE* total of 1,070 statistical tables, 715 are country tables describing the situation country by country, and hence already enumerated above in lines 9, 14, and 17. However, the remaining 355 are key topical tables, covering these 148 subjects like Bible keywords, evangelism, dimensions of 'evangelize', martyrdom, chronology, major developments, postdenominationalism. These topical tables can each be regarded as a separate instrument, often a complex one involving numerous measurements.

| Ref | Part | Title | Subtitle | Panels | Instruments | Data | per country | global | Notes and comments |
|---|---|---|---|---|---|---|---|---|---|
| 25 | | | **Topical tables** | 148 | 355 | 10 | — | 525,400 | Total of all instrumentation on specific topics |

**D. DATABASE INSTRUMENTS**

In 6 cases in *WCE* the simplest way to present huge masses of data has been to reproduce abbreviated versions of databases compiled during this survey and analysis. These 6 are listed as follows. Note that 3 have already been enumerated above (shown by their reference numbers 2, 5, 6 in column 1); the other 6 (26, 27, 28, 29, 30, 31) are now enumerated and then totaled below.

| Ref | Part | Title | Subtitle | Panels | Instruments | Data | per country | global | Notes and comments |
|---|---|---|---|---|---|---|---|---|---|
| 26 | *WCT* Part 17 | "Religiometrics" | | 1 | 23 | — | 40 | 227,500 | Instrumentation on 9,890 religions |
| 27 | *WCE* Part 8 | "EthnoSphere" | | 1 | 38 | 54 | 2,000 | 540,000 | Instrumentation on 12,600 peoples |
| 28 | *WCE* Part 9 | "LinguaMetrics" | | 1 | 27 | — | — | 287,000 | Instrumentation on 13,500 languages |
| 29 | *WCT* Part 18 | "Ethnolinguistics" | Cultures | 5 | 12 | — | — | 397,700 | Instrumentation on 6,629 cultures |
| 30 | | | Lingua francas | 2 | 20 | — | — | 130,680 | Instrumentation on 2,178 lingua francas |
| 5 | *WCE* Part 10 | "MetroScan" | | 1 | 7 | 33 | 230 | 62,100 | Instrumentation on 7,000 cities |
| 6 | *WCE* Part 11 | "ProvinceScan" | | 1 | 9 | 12 | 108 | 29,160 | Instrumentation on 3,030 major civil divisions |
| 31 | *WCE* Part 14 | "GeoDirectory" | | 1 | 82 | — | 20 | 15,000 | Instrumentation on 15,000 agencies under 82 topics |
| 32 | | | Databases 2, 5, 6 | 3 | 54 | 99 | 2,338 | 631,260 | (Already enumerated above) |
| 33 | | | **Databases** | 11 | 202 | — | 3,918 | 1,057,880 | Total instrumentation on religions, languages, agencies |

**E. VISUAL INSTRUMENTS**

The last variety of instrumentation consists of *WCT*'s and *WCE*'s 1,650 photographs. These have been selected from a wider base of 4,000 available photographs, to support the other instruments by illustrating 14 different instruments based on varieties of subject matter, as follows: backgrounds, situations, numbers, persons, events, themes, descriptions, characteristics, definitions, analyses, findings, trends, futures, prospects. Consider the instrument 'numbers'. The church's huge number of 44 million baptisms a year (120,000 every day) is illustrated and to some extent corroborated by one small photograph of the mass baptism, on a single day in 1992, of 70,000 Xhosas in the Transkei river Tsomo (see Photographic Index in *WCE* Part 15 and *WCT* Part 32).

A lot has been learned from each photograph by asking a standard set of 14 questions: What date or year? What country? Where? What event? What activity? What people? How many (size of crowd)? Any names? Who? What language? What religion? What denomination? What symbols? Meaning of anything unusual? Photography has spawned a range of new sciences, including: macrophotography, photomicrography, photogrammetry, photometry, telemetry, et alia. Their contribution to this project is summed up on the line that follows.

| Ref | Part | Title | Subtitle | Panels | Instruments | Data | per country | global | Notes and comments |
|---|---|---|---|---|---|---|---|---|---|
| 34 | | | **Photographs** | 1 | 14 | — | 40 | 151,200 | Photos corroborating statistics, claims, activities |

**F. TOTAL ALL INSTRUMENTATION**

| Ref | | Title | Subtitle | Panels | Instruments | Data | per country | global | Notes and comments |
|---|---|---|---|---|---|---|---|---|---|
| 35 | | **All WCT and WCE totals** | | 471 | 2,056 | 20 | 17,720 | 4,784,880 | **471 instrument panels with 2,056 types of instruments** |

## Table 15–3. A comparative listing of 6-instrument Great Commission Instrument Panels for the globe's 77 largest countries each with over 10 million population.

**Nations and countries compared**
The table on the 10 following pages lists the globe's 77 largest countries each with population over 10 million in AD 2000. These countries are then compared by means of a line of 6 minidiagrams. Each measures a different aspect of the country's religious, ecclesiastical, missionary, and evangelistic situations.

**The 6 standardized instruments**
These standard globes or graphs quantify and illustrate 6 new concepts evolved in this *WCE/WCT/WCD* series of surveys. The 6 are as follows. (1) Sizes of *World's A, B, and C*, with each's population as %. (2) Sizes of main *religions*, as % population (code letters as in Part 16 "GeoCodebook"). (3) *Ecclesiastical megablocs*, as % all affiliated Christians in country. (4) Current state of *evangelization*, E, being total of all evangelized persons, as % population. (5) Ongoing *evangelism* in country as e, evangelistic offers per capita per annum. (6) *Cost-effectiveness* of mission in country, being cost in US dollars of each person newly baptized.

**The GCIP for each country**
The panel enables the reader to quickly grasp the religious and missionary situation in any country. The actual numbers involved in these minidiagrams—either of persons, offers, or finance—can be rapidly obtained by multiplying a country's population (given at left under country name) by the percentages in the first 4, the per capita figure in the 5th, and the total of baptisms (of all Christian denominations) in the 6th. Resulting figures will almost always be startlingly high, because these 77 countries have large, even huge, populations.

**The 77 panels as a comparative aid in navigation**
The greatest value fo the GCIP panels can be obtained by moving one's eye up and down vertically, comparing one country with another. Agencies or boards wanting to either initiate work in countries new to them, or to expand their existing work, will all have differing criteria, conditions, and requirements that affect where they are able to minister. The panels thus assist them as they initiate the process in partic-

ular parts of the world.

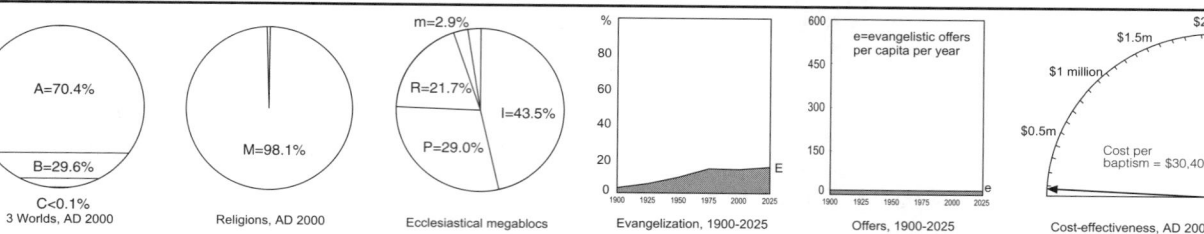

**Afghanistan**

Population: 22,720,000.
Area: 652,225 sq. km.
(251,825 sq. mi.).
Political divisions: 29 provinces.

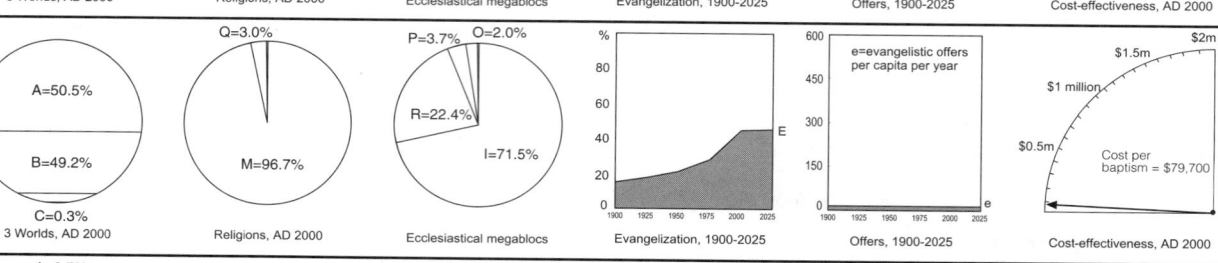

**Algeria**

Population: 31,471,000.
Area: 2,381,741 sq. km.
(919,595 sq. mi.).
Political divisions: 48 provinces.

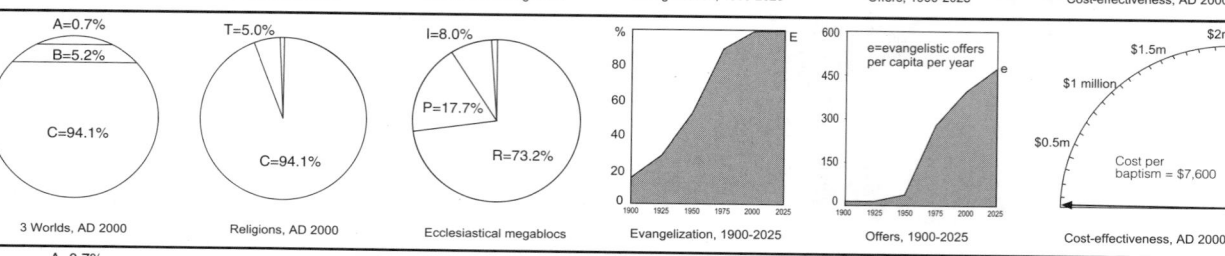

**Angola**

Population: 12,878,000.
Area: 1,246,700 sq. km.
(481,354 sq. mi.).
Political divisions: 18 provinces.

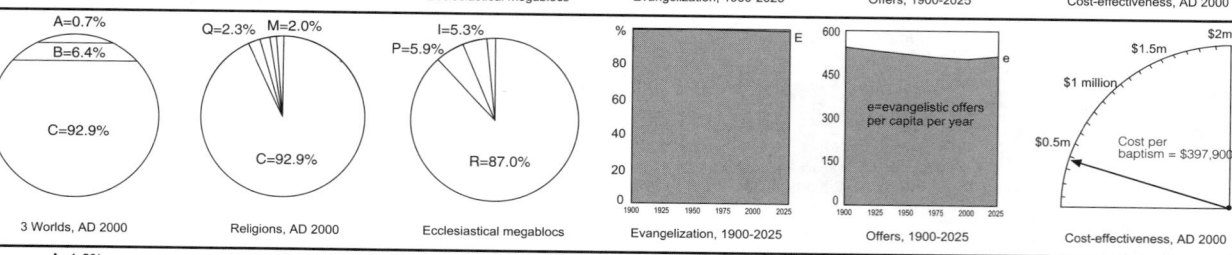

**Argentina**

Population: 37,027,000.
Area: 2,780,400 sq. km.
(1,073,518 sq. mi.).
Political divisions: 24 provinces.

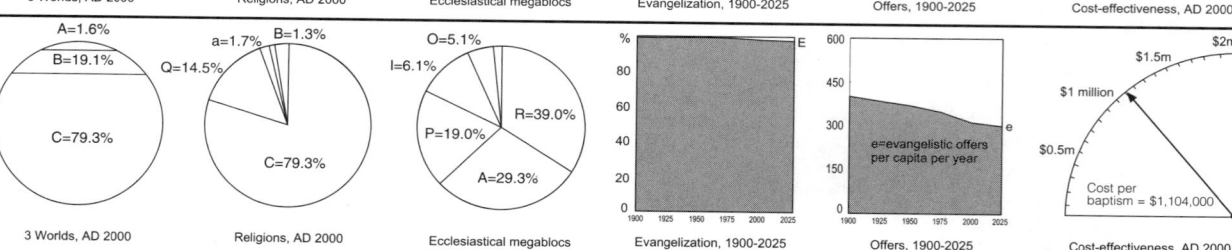

**Australia**

Population: 18,880,000.
Area: 7,682,300 sq. km.
(2,966,200 sq. mi.).
Political divisions: 8 provinces
(6 States and 2 Territories).

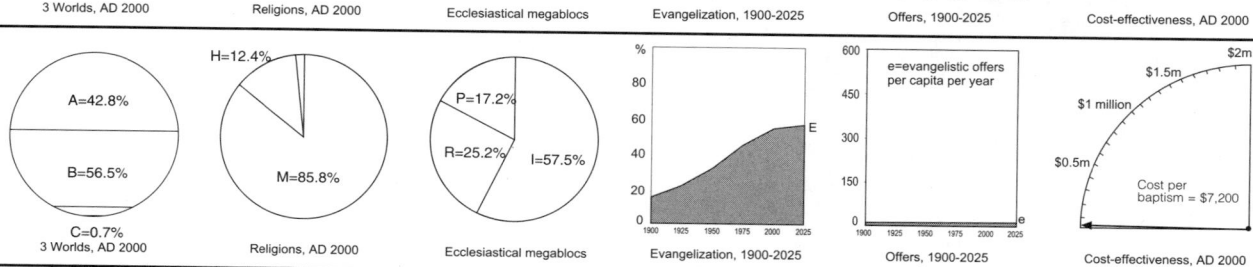

**Bangladesh**

Population: 129,155,000.
Area: 147,570 sq. km. (56,977 sq. mi.).
Political divisions: 6 provinces.

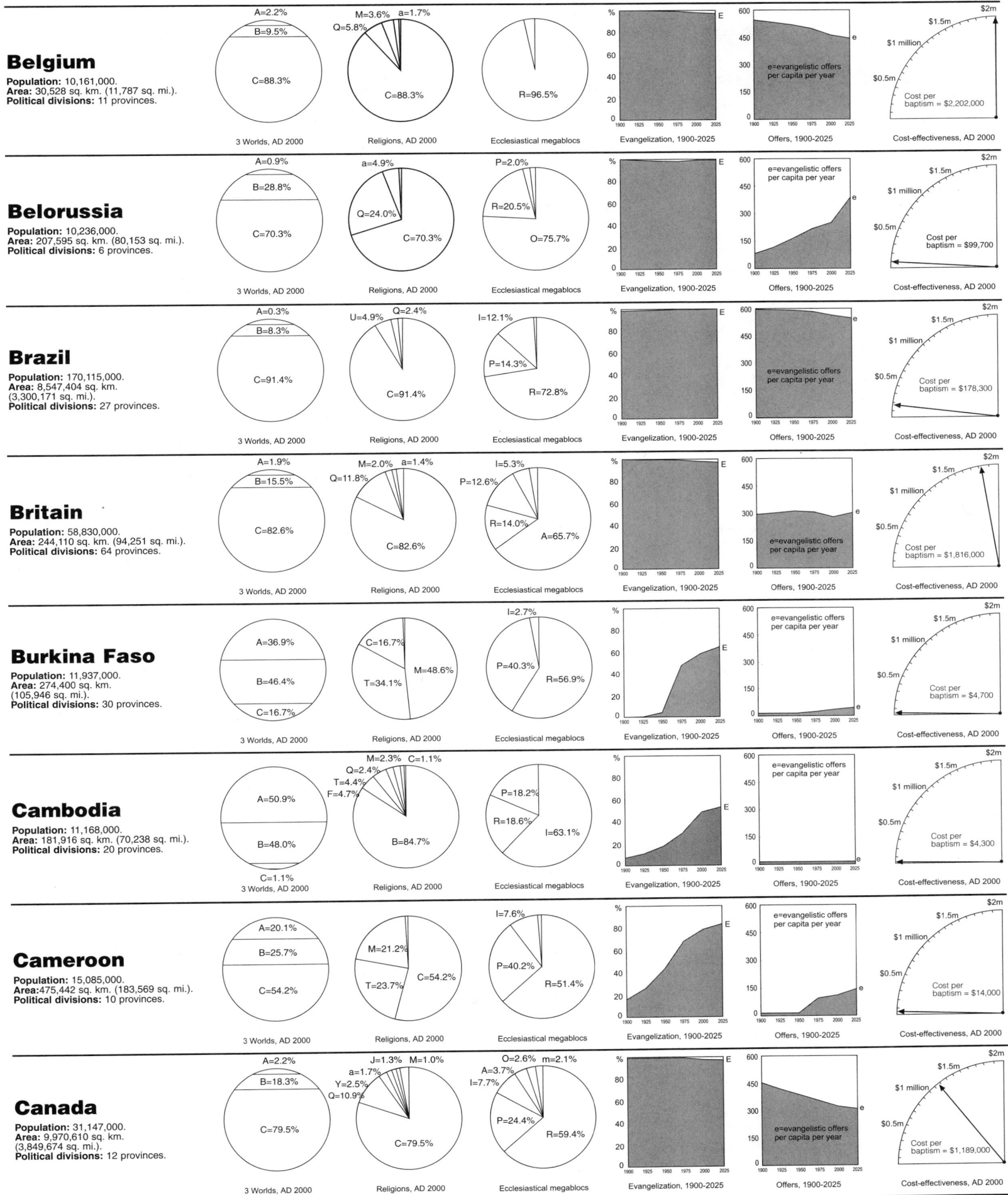

## Belgium

**Population:** 10,161,000.
**Area:** 30,528 sq. km. (11,787 sq. mi.).
**Political divisions:** 11 provinces.

A=2.2%
B=9.5%
C=88.3%

M=3.6% a=1.7%
Q=5.8%
C=88.3%

R=96.5%

3 Worlds, AD 2000 | Religions, AD 2000 | Ecclesiastical megablocs | Evangelization, 1900-2025 | Offers, 1900-2025 | Cost-effectiveness, AD 2000

e=evangelistic offers per capita per year

Cost per baptism = $2,202,000

## Belorussia

**Population:** 10,236,000.
**Area:** 207,595 sq. km. (80,153 sq. mi.).
**Political divisions:** 6 provinces.

A=0.9%
B=28.8%
C=70.3%

a=4.9%
Q=24.0%
C=70.3%

P=2.0%
R=20.5%
O=75.7%

e=evangelistic offers per capita per year

Cost per baptism = $99,700

## Brazil

**Population:** 170,115,000.
**Area:** 8,547,404 sq. km. (3,300,171 sq. mi.).
**Political divisions:** 27 provinces.

A=0.3%
B=8.3%
C=91.4%

U=4.9% Q=2.4%
C=91.4%

I=12.1%
P=14.3%
R=72.8%

e=evangelistic offers per capita per year

Cost per baptism = $178,300

## Britain

**Population:** 58,830,000.
**Area:** 244,110 sq. km. (94,251 sq. mi.).
**Political divisions:** 64 provinces.

A=1.9%
B=15.5%
C=82.6%

M=2.0% a=1.4%
Q=11.8%
C=82.6%

I=5.3%
P=12.6%
R=14.0%
A=65.7%

e=evangelistic offers per capita per year

Cost per baptism = $1,816,000

## Burkina Faso

**Population:** 11,937,000.
**Area:** 274,400 sq. km. (105,946 sq. mi.).
**Political divisions:** 30 provinces.

A=36.9%
B=46.4%
C=16.7%

C=16.7%
M=48.6%
T=34.1%

I=2.7%
P=40.3%
R=56.9%

e=evangelistic offers per capita per year

Cost per baptism = $4,700

## Cambodia

**Population:** 11,168,000.
**Area:** 181,916 sq. km. (70,238 sq. mi.).
**Political divisions:** 20 provinces.

A=50.9%
B=48.0%
C=1.1%

M=2.3% C=1.1%
Q=2.4%
T=4.4%
F=4.7%
B=84.7%

P=18.2%
R=18.6%
I=63.1%

e=evangelistic offers per capita per year

Cost per baptism = $4,300

## Cameroon

**Population:** 15,085,000.
**Area:** 475,442 sq. km. (183,569 sq. mi.).
**Political divisions:** 10 provinces.

A=20.1%
B=25.7%
C=54.2%

M=21.2%
T=23.7%
C=54.2%

I=7.6%
P=40.2%
R=51.4%

e=evangelistic offers per capita per year

Cost per baptism = $14,000

## Canada

**Population:** 31,147,000.
**Area:** 9,970,610 sq. km. (3,849,674 sq. mi.).
**Political divisions:** 12 provinces.

A=2.2%
B=18.3%
C=79.5%

J=1.3% M=1.0%
a=1.7%
Y=2.5%
Q=10.9%
C=79.5%

O=2.6% m=2.1%
A=3.7%
I=7.7%
P=24.4%
R=59.4%

e=evangelistic offers per capita per year

Cost per baptism = $1,189,000

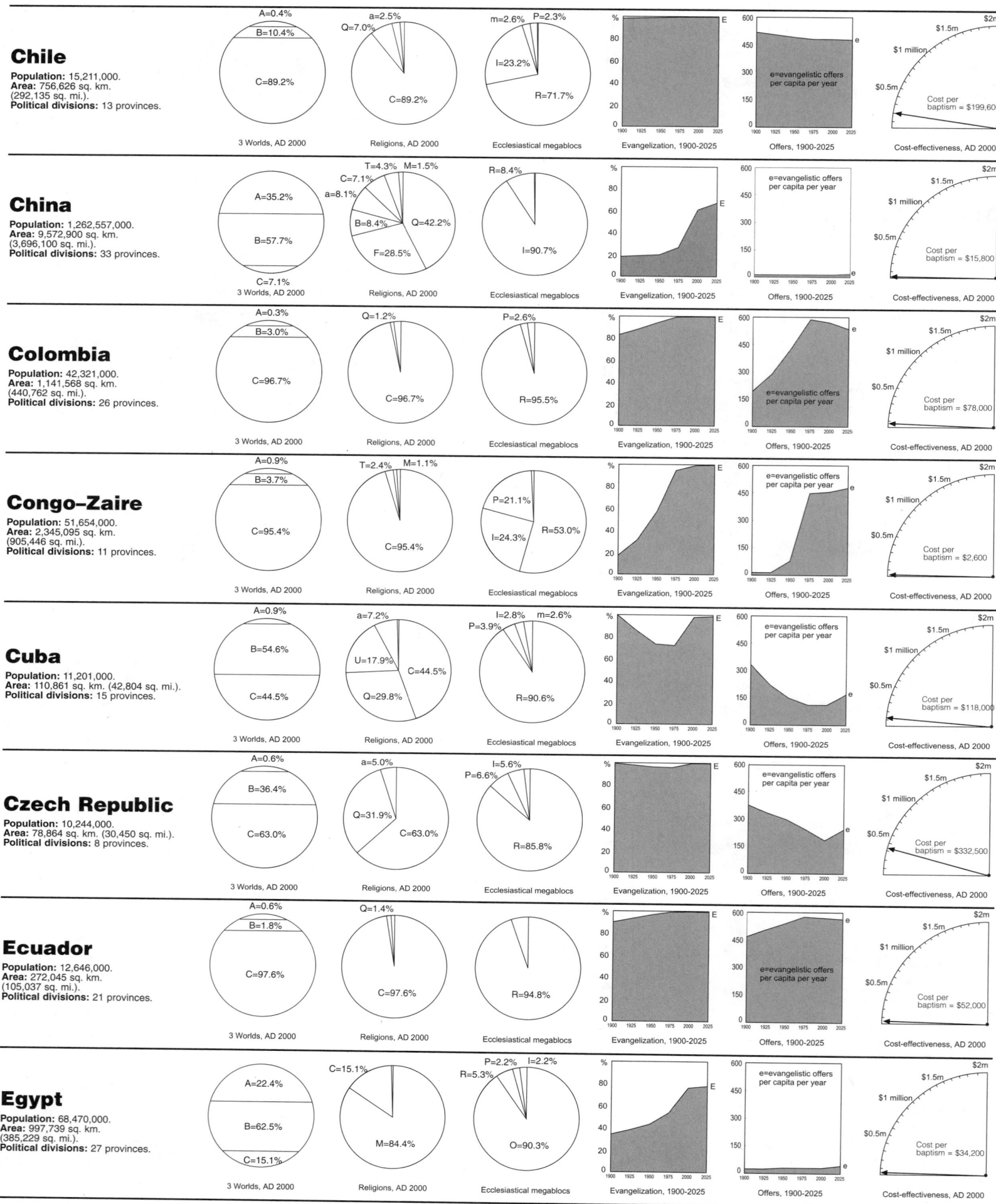

**Chile**
Population: 15,211,000.
Area: 756,626 sq. km.
(292,135 sq. mi.).
Political divisions: 13 provinces.

A=0.4%
B=10.4%
C=89.2%
3 Worlds, AD 2000

a=2.5%
Q=7.0%
C=89.2%
Religions, AD 2000

m=2.6%  P=2.3%
I=23.2%
R=71.7%
Ecclesiastical megablocs

Evangelization, 1900-2025

e=evangelistic offers per capita per year
Offers, 1900-2025

$2m
$1.5m
$1 million
$0.5m
Cost per baptism = $199,600
Cost-effectiveness, AD 2000

**China**
Population: 1,262,557,000.
Area: 9,572,900 sq. km.
(3,696,100 sq. mi.).
Political divisions: 33 provinces.

A=35.2%
B=57.7%
C=7.1%
3 Worlds, AD 2000

T=4.3%  M=1.5%
C=7.1%
a=8.1%
B=8.4%  Q=42.2%
F=28.5%
Religions, AD 2000

R=8.4%
I=90.7%
Ecclesiastical megablocs

Evangelization, 1900-2025

e=evangelistic offers per capita per year
Offers, 1900-2025

$2m
$1.5m
$1 million
$0.5m
Cost per baptism = $15,800
Cost-effectiveness, AD 2000

**Colombia**
Population: 42,321,000.
Area: 1,141,568 sq. km.
(440,762 sq. mi.).
Political divisions: 26 provinces.

A=0.3%
B=3.0%
C=96.7%
3 Worlds, AD 2000

Q=1.2%
C=96.7%
Religions, AD 2000

P=2.6%
R=95.5%
Ecclesiastical megablocs

Evangelization, 1900-2025

e=evangelistic offers per capita per year
Offers, 1900-2025

$2m
$1.5m
$1 million
$0.5m
Cost per baptism = $78,000
Cost-effectiveness, AD 2000

**Congo–Zaire**
Population: 51,654,000.
Area: 2,345,095 sq. km.
(905,446 sq. mi.).
Political divisions: 11 provinces.

A=0.9%
B=3.7%
C=95.4%
3 Worlds, AD 2000

T=2.4%  M=1.1%
C=95.4%
Religions, AD 2000

P=21.1%
I=24.3%
R=53.0%
Ecclesiastical megablocs

Evangelization, 1900-2025

e=evangelistic offers per capita per year
Offers, 1900-2025

$2m
$1.5m
$1 million
$0.5m
Cost per baptism = $2,600
Cost-effectiveness, AD 2000

**Cuba**
Population: 11,201,000.
Area: 110,861 sq. km. (42,804 sq. mi.).
Political divisions: 15 provinces.

A=0.9%
B=54.6%
C=44.5%
3 Worlds, AD 2000

a=7.2%
U=17.9%
C=44.5%
Q=29.8%
Religions, AD 2000

I=2.8%  m=2.6%
P=3.9%
R=90.6%
Ecclesiastical megablocs

Evangelization, 1900-2025

e=evangelistic offers per capita per year
Offers, 1900-2025

$2m
$1.5m
$1 million
$0.5m
Cost per baptism = $118,000
Cost-effectiveness, AD 2000

**Czech Republic**
Population: 10,244,000.
Area: 78,864 sq. km. (30,450 sq. mi.).
Political divisions: 8 provinces.

A=0.6%
B=36.4%
C=63.0%
3 Worlds, AD 2000

a=5.0%
Q=31.9%
C=63.0%
Religions, AD 2000

I=5.6%
P=6.6%
R=85.8%
Ecclesiastical megablocs

Evangelization, 1900-2025

e=evangelistic offers per capita per year
Offers, 1900-2025

$2m
$1.5m
$1 million
$0.5m
Cost per baptism = $332,500
Cost-effectiveness, AD 2000

**Ecuador**
Population: 12,646,000.
Area: 272,045 sq. km.
(105,037 sq. mi.).
Political divisions: 21 provinces.

A=0.6%
B=1.8%
C=97.6%
3 Worlds, AD 2000

Q=1.4%
C=97.6%
Religions, AD 2000

R=94.8%
Ecclesiastical megablocs

Evangelization, 1900-2025

e=evangelistic offers per capita per year
Offers, 1900-2025

$2m
$1.5m
$1 million
$0.5m
Cost per baptism = $52,000
Cost-effectiveness, AD 2000

**Egypt**
Population: 68,470,000.
Area: 997,739 sq. km.
(385,229 sq. mi.).
Political divisions: 27 provinces.

A=22.4%
B=62.5%
C=15.1%
3 Worlds, AD 2000

C=15.1%
M=84.4%
Religions, AD 2000

P=2.2%  I=2.2%
R=5.3%
O=90.3%
Ecclesiastical megablocs

Evangelization, 1900-2025

e=evangelistic offers per capita per year
Offers, 1900-2025

$2m
$1.5m
$1 million
$0.5m
Cost per baptism = $34,200
Cost-effectiveness, AD 2000

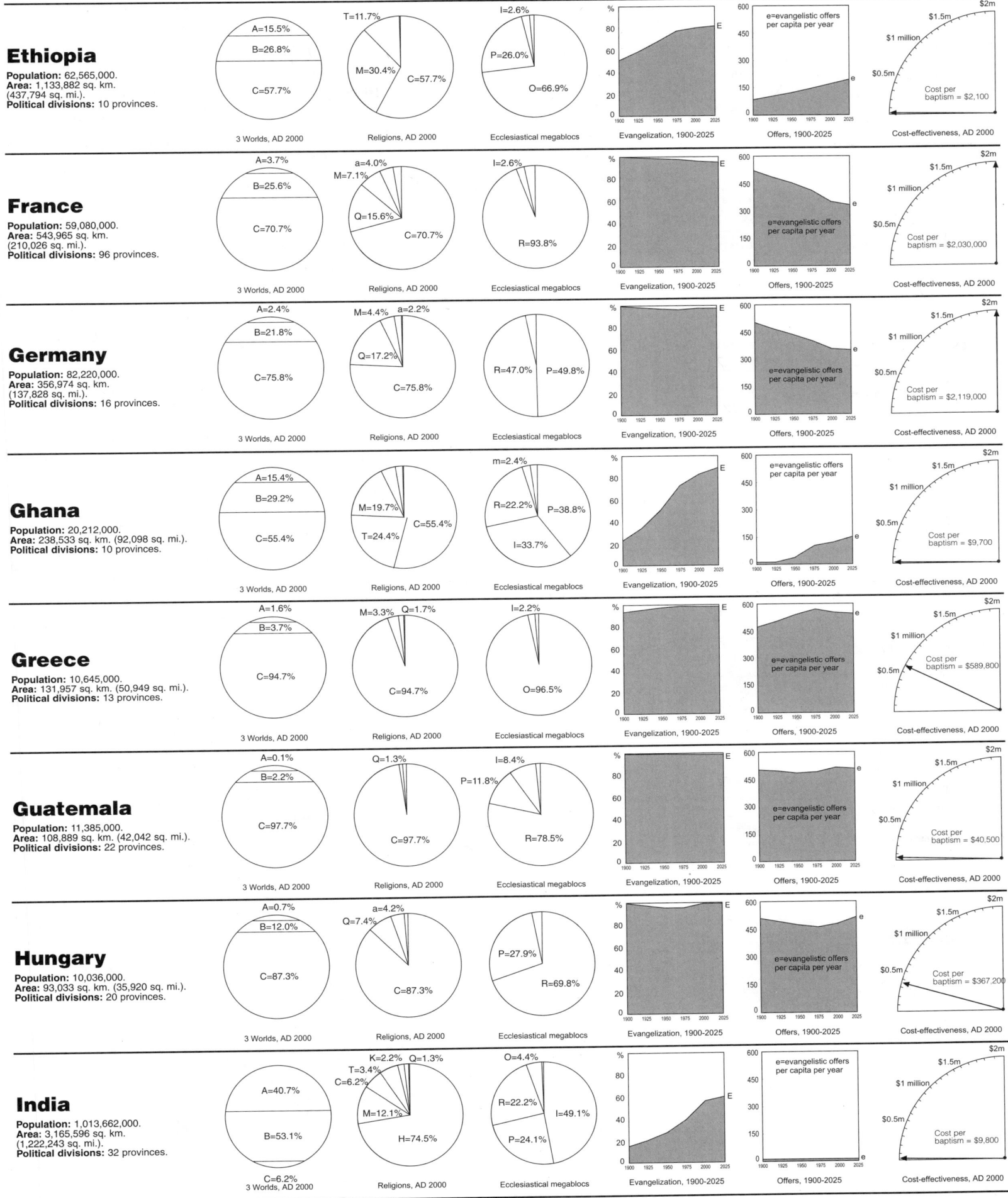

## Ethiopia
**Population:** 62,565,000.
**Area:** 1,133,882 sq. km.
(437,794 sq. mi.).
**Political divisions:** 10 provinces.

A=15.5% B=26.8% C=57.7% — 3 Worlds, AD 2000
T=11.7% M=30.4% C=57.7% — Religions, AD 2000
I=2.6% P=26.0% O=66.9% — Ecclesiastical megablocs
Evangelization, 1900-2025
Offers, 1900-2025 — e=evangelistic offers per capita per year
Cost-effectiveness, AD 2000 — Cost per baptism = $2,100

## France
**Population:** 59,080,000.
**Area:** 543,965 sq. km.
(210,026 sq. mi.).
**Political divisions:** 96 provinces.

A=3.7% B=25.6% C=70.7% — 3 Worlds, AD 2000
a=4.0% M=7.1% Q=15.6% C=70.7% — Religions, AD 2000
I=2.6% R=93.8% — Ecclesiastical megablocs
Evangelization, 1900-2025
Offers, 1900-2025 — e=evangelistic offers per capita per year
Cost-effectiveness, AD 2000 — Cost per baptism = $2,030,000

## Germany
**Population:** 82,220,000.
**Area:** 356,974 sq. km.
(137,828 sq. mi.).
**Political divisions:** 16 provinces.

A=2.4% B=21.8% C=75.8% — 3 Worlds, AD 2000
M=4.4% a=2.2% Q=17.2% C=75.8% — Religions, AD 2000
R=47.0% P=49.8% — Ecclesiastical megablocs
Evangelization, 1900-2025
Offers, 1900-2025 — e=evangelistic offers per capita per year
Cost-effectiveness, AD 2000 — Cost per baptism = $2,119,000

## Ghana
**Population:** 20,212,000.
**Area:** 238,533 sq. km. (92,098 sq. mi.).
**Political divisions:** 10 provinces.

A=15.4% B=29.2% C=55.4% — 3 Worlds, AD 2000
M=19.7% T=24.4% C=55.4% — Religions, AD 2000
m=2.4% R=22.2% P=38.8% I=33.7% — Ecclesiastical megablocs
Evangelization, 1900-2025
Offers, 1900-2025 — e=evangelistic offers per capita per year
Cost-effectiveness, AD 2000 — Cost per baptism = $9,700

## Greece
**Population:** 10,645,000.
**Area:** 131,957 sq. km. (50,949 sq. mi.).
**Political divisions:** 13 provinces.

A=1.6% B=3.7% C=94.7% — 3 Worlds, AD 2000
M=3.3% Q=1.7% C=94.7% — Religions, AD 2000
I=2.2% O=96.5% — Ecclesiastical megablocs
Evangelization, 1900-2025
Offers, 1900-2025 — e=evangelistic offers per capita per year
Cost-effectiveness, AD 2000 — Cost per baptism = $589,800

## Guatemala
**Population:** 11,385,000.
**Area:** 108,889 sq. km. (42,042 sq. mi.).
**Political divisions:** 22 provinces.

A=0.1% B=2.2% C=97.7% — 3 Worlds, AD 2000
Q=1.3% C=97.7% — Religions, AD 2000
I=8.4% P=11.8% R=78.5% — Ecclesiastical megablocs
Evangelization, 1900-2025
Offers, 1900-2025 — e=evangelistic offers per capita per year
Cost-effectiveness, AD 2000 — Cost per baptism = $40,500

## Hungary
**Population:** 10,036,000.
**Area:** 93,033 sq. km. (35,920 sq. mi.).
**Political divisions:** 20 provinces.

A=0.7% B=12.0% C=87.3% — 3 Worlds, AD 2000
a=4.2% Q=7.4% C=87.3% — Religions, AD 2000
P=27.9% R=69.8% — Ecclesiastical megablocs
Evangelization, 1900-2025
Offers, 1900-2025 — e=evangelistic offers per capita per year
Cost-effectiveness, AD 2000 — Cost per baptism = $367,200

## India
**Population:** 1,013,662,000.
**Area:** 3,165,596 sq. km.
(1,222,243 sq. mi.).
**Political divisions:** 32 provinces.

A=40.7% B=53.1% C=6.2% — 3 Worlds, AD 2000
K=2.2% Q=1.3% T=3.4% C=6.2% M=12.1% H=74.5% — Religions, AD 2000
O=4.4% R=22.2% I=49.1% P=24.1% — Ecclesiastical megablocs
Evangelization, 1900-2025
Offers, 1900-2025 — e=evangelistic offers per capita per year
Cost-effectiveness, AD 2000 — Cost per baptism = $9,800

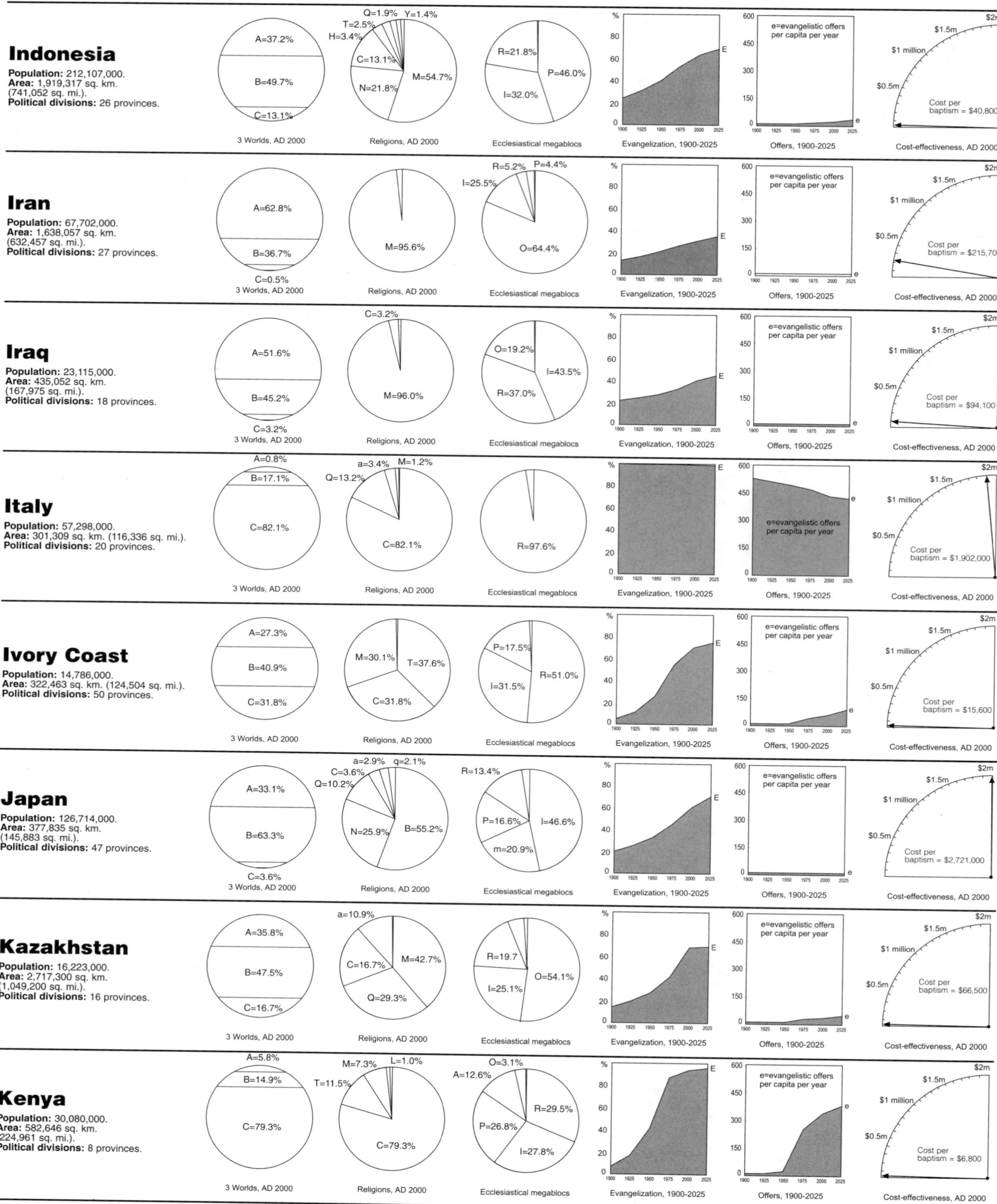

**Indonesia**
Population: 212,107,000.
Area: 1,919,317 sq. km.
(741,052 sq. mi.).
Political divisions: 26 provinces.

3 Worlds, AD 2000: A=37.2%, B=49.7%, C=13.1%
Religions, AD 2000: Q=1.9%, Y=1.4%, T=2.5%, H=3.4%, C=13.1%, M=54.7%, N=21.8%
Ecclesiastical megablocs: R=21.8%, P=46.0%, I=32.0%
Cost per baptism = $40,800

**Iran**
Population: 67,702,000.
Area: 1,638,057 sq. km.
(632,457 sq. mi.).
Political divisions: 27 provinces.

3 Worlds, AD 2000: A=62.8%, B=36.7%, C=0.5%
Religions, AD 2000: M=95.6%
Ecclesiastical megablocs: R=5.2%, P=4.4%, I=25.5%, O=64.4%
Cost per baptism = $215,700

**Iraq**
Population: 23,115,000.
Area: 435,052 sq. km.
(167,975 sq. mi.).
Political divisions: 18 provinces.

3 Worlds, AD 2000: A=51.6%, B=45.2%, C=3.2%
Religions, AD 2000: C=3.2%, M=96.0%
Ecclesiastical megablocs: O=19.2%, I=43.5%, R=37.0%
Cost per baptism = $94,100

**Italy**
Population: 57,298,000.
Area: 301,309 sq. km. (116,336 sq. mi.).
Political divisions: 20 provinces.

3 Worlds, AD 2000: A=0.8%, B=17.1%, C=82.1%
Religions, AD 2000: a=3.4%, M=1.2%, Q=13.2%, C=82.1%
Ecclesiastical megablocs: R=97.6%
Cost per baptism = $1,902,000

**Ivory Coast**
Population: 14,786,000.
Area: 322,463 sq. km. (124,504 sq. mi.).
Political divisions: 50 provinces.

3 Worlds, AD 2000: A=27.3%, B=40.9%, C=31.8%
Religions, AD 2000: M=30.1%, T=37.6%, C=31.8%
Ecclesiastical megablocs: P=17.5%, R=51.0%, I=31.5%
Cost per baptism = $15,600

**Japan**
Population: 126,714,000.
Area: 377,835 sq. km.
(145,883 sq. mi.).
Political divisions: 47 provinces.

3 Worlds, AD 2000: A=33.1%, B=63.3%, C=3.6%
Religions, AD 2000: a=2.9%, q=2.1%, C=3.6%, Q=10.2%, N=25.9%, B=55.2%
Ecclesiastical megablocs: R=13.4%, P=16.6%, I=46.6%, m=20.9%
Cost per baptism = $2,721,000

**Kazakhstan**
Population: 16,223,000.
Area: 2,717,300 sq. km.
(1,049,200 sq. mi.).
Political divisions: 16 provinces.

3 Worlds, AD 2000: A=35.8%, B=47.5%, C=16.7%
Religions, AD 2000: a=10.9%, C=16.7%, M=42.7%, Q=29.3%
Ecclesiastical megablocs: R=19.7, O=54.1%, I=25.1%
Cost per baptism = $66,500

**Kenya**
Population: 30,080,000.
Area: 582,646 sq. km.
(224,961 sq. mi.).
Political divisions: 8 provinces.

3 Worlds, AD 2000: A=5.8%, B=14.9%, C=79.3%
Religions, AD 2000: M=7.3%, L=1.0%, T=11.5%, C=79.3%
Ecclesiastical megablocs: O=3.1%, A=12.6%, R=29.5%, P=26.8%, I=27.8%
Cost per baptism = $6,800

Labels for all rows: 3 Worlds, AD 2000 | Religions, AD 2000 | Ecclesiastical megablocs | Evangelization, 1900-2025 | Offers, 1900-2025 (e=evangelistic offers per capita per year) | Cost-effectiveness, AD 2000

# Madagascar

**Population:** 15,942,000.
**Area:** 587,041 sq. km.
(226,658 sq. mi.).
**Political divisions:** 6 provinces.

A=17.0%
B=33.5%
C=49.5%

3 Worlds, AD 2000

M=2.0%
T=48.0%    C=49.5%

Religions, AD 2000

A=3.7%
I=5.9%
R=42.5%    P=47.5%

Ecclesiastical megablocs

Evangelization, 1900-2025

e=evangelistic offers per capita per year

Offers, 1900-2025

$2m
$1.5m
$1 million
$0.5m
Cost per baptism = $5,300

Cost-effectiveness, AD 2000

# Malawi

**Population:** 10,925,000.
**Area:** 118,484 sq. km. (45,747 sq. mi.).
**Political divisions:** 24 provinces.

A=4.0%
B=19.2%
C=76.8%

3 Worlds, AD 2000

T=7.8%
M=14.8%
C=76.8%

Religions, AD 2000

A=3.3%
I=26.0%    R=38.4%
P=30.4%

Ecclesiastical megablocs

Evangelization, 1900-2025

e=evangelistic offers per capita per year

Offers, 1900-2025

$2m
$1.5m
$1 million
$0.5m
Cost per baptism = $4,300

Cost-effectiveness, AD 2000

# Malaysia

**Population:** 22,244,000.
**Area:** 330,442 sq. km.
(127,584 sq. mi.).
**Political divisions:** 15 provinces.

A=36.3%
B=55.4%
C=8.3%

3 Worlds, AD 2000

T=3.4%  F=1.4%
B=6.7%
H=7.3%
C=8.3%    M=47.7%
F=24.1%

Religions, AD 2000

I=9.9%
A=10.6%
R=44.9%
P=34.2%

Ecclesiastical megablocs

Evangelization, 1900-2025

e=evangelistic offers per capita per year

Offers, 1900-2025

$2m
$1.5m
$1 million
$0.5m
Cost per baptism = $129,000

Cost-effectiveness, AD 2000

# Mali

**Population:** 11,234,000.
**Area:** 1,248,574 sq. km.
(482,077 sq. mi.).
**Political divisions:** 8 provinces.

A=56.4%
B=41.6%
C=2.0%

3 Worlds, AD 2000

C=2.0%
T=16.0%
M=81.9%

Religions, AD 2000

I=7.3%
P=36.5%    R=56.0%

Ecclesiastical megablocs

Evangelization, 1900-2025

e=evangelistic offers per capita per year

Offers, 1900-2025

$2m
$1.5m
$1 million
$0.5m
Cost per baptism = $5,700

Cost-effectiveness, AD 2000

# Mexico

**Population:** 98,881,000.
**Area:** 1,958,201 sq. km.
(756,066 sq. mi.).
**Political divisions:** 32 provinces.

A=0.2%
B=3.5%
C=96.3%

3 Worlds, AD 2000

Q=3.1%
C=96.3%

Religions, AD 2000

I=2.9%
P=3.2%
m=1.9%
R=91.7%

Ecclesiastical megablocs

Evangelization, 1900-2025

e=evangelistic offers per capita per year

Offers, 1900-2025

$2m
$1.5m
$1 million
$0.5m
Cost per baptism = $147,100

Cost-effectiveness, AD 2000

# Morocco

**Population:** 67,702,000.
**Area:** 1,638,057 sq. km.
(632,457 sq. mi.).
**Political divisions:** 27 provinces.

A=57.8%
B=41.6%
C=0.6%

3 Worlds, AD 2000

M=98.3%

Religions, AD 2000

P=2.3%
R=12.7%
I=84.3%

Ecclesiastical megablocs

Evangelization, 1900-2025

e=evangelistic offers per capita per year

Offers, 1900-2025

$2m
$1.5m
$1 million
$0.5m
Cost per baptism = $45,300

Cost-effectiveness, AD 2000

# Mozambique

**Population:** 19,680,000.
**Area:** 812,379 sq. km.
(313,661 sq. mi.).
**Political divisions:** 11 provinces.

A=23.0%
B=38.6%
C=38.4%

3 Worlds, AD 2000

M=10.5%
C=38.4%    T=50.4%

Religions, AD 2000

I=22.0%    R=48.1%
P=27.1%

Ecclesiastical megablocs

Evangelization, 1900-2025

e=evangelistic offers per capita per year

Offers, 1900-2025

$2m
$1.5m
$1 million
$0.5m
Cost per baptism = $1,400

Cost-effectiveness, AD 2000

# Myanmar

**Population:** 45,611,000.
**Area:** 676,577 sq. km.
(261,228 sq. mi.).
**Political divisions:** 14 provinces.

A=39.1%
B=52.6%
C=8.3%

3 Worlds, AD 2000

H=2.0%  y=1.5%
M=2.4%
C=8.3%
T=12.6%
B=72.7%

Religions, AD 2000

I=15.4%
R=15.8%
P=67.1%

Ecclesiastical megablocs

Evangelization, 1900-2025

e=evangelistic offers per capita per year

Offers, 1900-2025

$2m
$1.5m
$1 million
$0.5m
Cost per baptism = $61,100

Cost-effectiveness, AD 2000

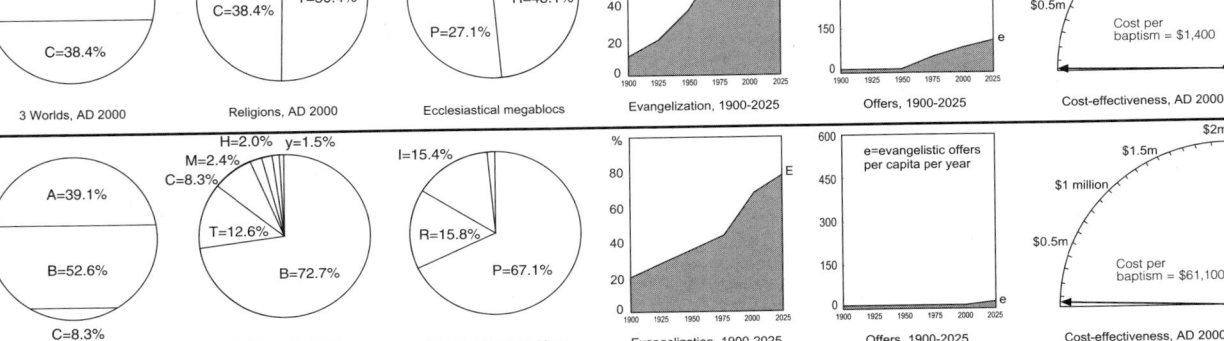

## Nepal

**Population:** 23,930,000.
**Area:** 147,181 sq. km. (56,827 sq. mi.).
**Political divisions:** 14 provinces.

A=53.8%
B=43.8%
C=2.4%

3 Worlds, AD 2000

M=3.9%    C=2.4%
B=8.2%
T=9.4%
H=76.7%

Religions, AD 2000

P=2.5%
I=95.6%

Ecclesiastical megablocs

Evangelization, 1900-2025

e=evangelistic offers per capita per year

Offers, 1900-2025

Cost per baptism = $3,700

Cost-effectiveness, AD 2000

## Netherlands

**Population:** 15,786,000.
**Area:** 41,526 sq. km. (16,033 sq. mi.).
**Political divisions:** 12 provinces.

A=2.4%
B=17.2%
C=80.4%

3 Worlds, AD 2000

M=3.8%    a=1.3%
Q=12.9%
C=80.4%

Religions, AD 2000

I=4.8%
P=41.2%    R=53.0%

Ecclesiastical megablocs

Evangelization, 1900-2025

e=evangelistic offers per capita per year

Offers, 1900-2025

Cost per baptism = $1,832,000

Cost-effectiveness, AD 2000

## Niger

**Population:** 10,730,000.
**Area:** 1,287,000 sq. km.
(496,900 sq. mi.).
**Political divisions:** 7 provinces.

A=57.9%
B=41.5%
C=0.6%

3 Worlds, AD 2000

T=8.7%
M=90.7%

Religions, AD 2000

P=22.3%
I=42.9
R=33.8%

Ecclesiastical megablocs

Evangelization, 1900-2025

e=evangelistic offers per capita per year

Offers, 1900-2025

Cost per baptism = $4,500

Cost-effectiveness, AD 2000

## Nigeria

**Population:** 111,506,000.
**Area:** 923,768 sq. km.
(356,669 sq. mi.).
**Political divisions:** 31 provinces.

A=20.2%
B=33.9%
C=45.9%

3 Worlds, AD 2000

T=9.8%
C=45.9%
M=43.9%

Religions, AD 2000

R=18.6%    I=33.3%
P=19.5%
A=27.8%

Ecclesiastical megablocs

Evangelization, 1900-2025

e=evangelistic offers per capita per year

Offers, 1900-2025

Cost per baptism = $6,400

Cost-effectiveness, AD 2000

## North Korea

**Population:** 24,039,000.
**Area:** 122,762 sq. km. (47,399 sq. mi.).
**Political divisions:** 13 provinces.

A=50.0%
B=47.9%
C=2.1%

3 Worlds, AD 2000

C=2.1%    B=1.5%
T=12.3%
N=12.9%    Q=55.6%
a=15.6%

Religions, AD 2000

P=2.0%
R=11.0%
I=86.4%

Ecclesiastical megablocs

Evangelization, 1900-2025

e=evangelistic offers per capita per year

Offers, 1900-2025

Cost per baptism = $38,400

Cost-effectiveness, AD 2000

## Pakistan

**Population:** 156,483,000.
**Area:** 796,095 sq. km. (307,374 sq. mi.)
**Political divisions:** 6 provinces.

A=53.2%
B=44.3%
C=2.5%

3 Worlds, AD 2000

C=2.5%    H=1.2%
M=96.1%

Religions, AD 2000

I=22.3%    P=47.1%
R=30.6%

Ecclesiastical megablocs

Evangelization, 1900-2025

e=evangelistic offers per capita per year

Offers, 1900-2025

Cost per baptism = $12,100

Cost-effectiveness, AD 2000

## Peru

**Population:** 25,662,000.
**Area:** 1,285,216 sq. km.
(496,225 sq. mi.).
**Political divisions:** 14 provinces.

A=0.3%
B=2.5%
C=97.2%

3 Worlds, AD 2000

Q=1.2%
C=97.2%

Religions, AD 2000

P=5.5%
R=91.5%

Ecclesiastical megablocs

Evangelization, 1900-2025

e=evangelistic offers per capita per year

Offers, 1900-2025

Cost per baptism = $99,300

Cost-effectiveness, AD 2000

## Philippines

**Population:** 75,967,000.
**Area:** 300,076 sq. km. (115,860 sq. mi.).
**Political divisions:** 16 provinces.

A=5.6%
B=4.7%
C=89.7%

3 Worlds, AD 2000

T=2.7%
M=6.2%
C=89.7%

Religions, AD 2000

P=4.6%
I=17.6%
R=76.8%

Ecclesiastical megablocs

Evangelization, 1900-2025

e=evangelistic offers per capita per year

Offers, 1900-2025

Cost per baptism = $38,000

Cost-effectiveness, AD 2000

## Poland

**Population:** 38,765,000.
**Area:** 312,685 sq. km.
(120,728 sq. mi.).
**Political divisions:** 49 provinces.

A=0.1%
B=2.6%
C=97.4%

*3 Worlds, AD 2000*

Q=2.2%
C=97.4%

*Religions, AD 2000*

O=2.7%
R=95.3%

*Ecclesiastical megablocs*

*Evangelization, 1900-2025* — E

*Offers, 1900-2025* — e=evangelistic offers per capita per year — e

*Cost-effectiveness, AD 2000* — $2m / $1.5m / $1 million / $0.5m / Cost per baptism = $225,200

## Romania

**Population:** 22,327,000.
**Area:** 237,500 sq. km. (91,699 sq. mi.).
**Political divisions:** 41 provinces.

A=0.7%
B=11.3%
C=88.0%

*3 Worlds, AD 2000*

a=3.3%   M=1.3%
Q=7.4%
C=88.0%

*Religions, AD 2000*

P=9.5%
R=12.9%
O=75.8%

*Ecclesiastical megablocs*

*Evangelization, 1900-2025* — E

*Offers, 1900-2025* — e=evangelistic offers per capita per year — e

*Cost-effectiveness, AD 2000* — $2m / $1.5m / $1 million / $0.5m / Cost per baptism = $143,500

## Russia

**Population:** 146,934,000.
**Area:** 17,075,400 sq. km.
(6,592,800 sq. mi.).
**Political divisions:** 21 provinces.

A=6.8%
B=35.8%
C=57.4%

*3 Worlds, AD 2000*

a=5.2%
M=7.6%
Q=27.5%   C=57.4%

*Religions, AD 2000*

I=9.0%
O=87.2%

*Ecclesiastical megablocs*

*Evangelization, 1900-2025* — E

*Offers, 1900-2025* — e=evangelistic offers per capita per year — e

*Cost-effectiveness, AD 2000* — $2m / $1.5m / $1 million / $0.5m / Cost per baptism = $129,900

## Saudi Arabia

**Population:** 21,607,000.
**Area:** 2,248,000 sq. km.
(868,000 sq. mi.).
**Political divisions:** 5 provinces.

A=45.1%
B=51.2%
C=3.7%

*3 Worlds, AD 2000*

C=3.7%   H=1.1%
M=93.7%

*Religions, AD 2000*

O=4.6%
P=4.8%
I=10.8%
R=79.5%

*Ecclesiastical megablocs*

*Evangelization, 1900-2025* — E

*Offers, 1900-2025* — e=evangelistic offers per capita per year — e

*Cost-effectiveness, AD 2000* — $2m / $1.5m / $1 million / $0.5m / Cost per baptism = $186,100

## South Africa

**Population:** 40,377,000.
**Area:** 1,223,201 sq. km.
(472,281 sq. mi.).
**Political divisions:** 9 provinces.

A=1.9%
B=15.0%
C=83.1%

*3 Worlds, AD 2000*

M=2.4%   Q=2.4%
H=2.4%
T=8.4%
C=83.1%

*Religions, AD 2000*

A=7.1%
R=9.0%
I=49.7%
P=33.3%

*Ecclesiastical megablocs*

*Evangelization, 1900-2025* — E

*Offers, 1900-2025* — e=evangelistic offers per capita per year — e

*Cost-effectiveness, AD 2000* — $2m / $1.5m / $1 million / $0.5m / Cost per baptism = $82,900

## South Korea

**Population:** 46,844,000.
**Area:** 99,274 sq. km. (38,330 sq. mi.).
**Political divisions:** 15 provinces.

A=1.2%
B=58.0%
C=40.8%

*3 Worlds, AD 2000*

Q=1.5%
G=11.1%
N=15.2%   C=40.8%
B=15.3%
T=15.6%

*Religions, AD 2000*

m=4.0%
R=17.4%   P=41.8%
I=36.3%

*Ecclesiastical megablocs*

*Evangelization, 1900-2025* — E

*Offers, 1900-2025* — e=evangelistic offers per capita per year — e

*Cost-effectiveness, AD 2000* — $2m / $1.5m / $1 million / $0.5m / Cost per baptism = $525,700

## Spain

**Population:** 39,630,000.
**Area:** 504,783 sq. km.
(194,898 sq. mi.).
**Political divisions:** 17 provinces.

A=0.3%
B=6.1%
C=93.6%

*3 Worlds, AD 2000*

Q=4.6%   a=1.1%
C=93.6%

*Religions, AD 2000*

R=98.3%

*Ecclesiastical megablocs*

*Evangelization, 1900-2025* — E

*Offers, 1900-2025* — e=evangelistic offers per capita per year — e

*Cost-effectiveness, AD 2000* — $2m / $1.5m / $1 million / $0.5m / Cost per baptism = $1,321,000

## Sri Lanka

**Population:** 18,827,000.
**Area:** 65,610 sq. km. (25,332 sq. mi.).
**Political divisions:** 25 provinces.

A=35.4%
B=55.2%
C=9.4%

*3 Worlds, AD 2000*

Q=1.8%
M=9.0%
C=9.4%
H=11.3%
B=68.4%

*Religions, AD 2000*

A=3.1%
P=5.8%
I=18.9%
R=71.8%

*Ecclesiastical megablocs*

*Evangelization, 1900-2025* — E

*Offers, 1900-2025* — e=evangelistic offers per capita per year — e

*Cost-effectiveness, AD 2000* — $2m / $1.5m / $1 million / $0.5m / Cost per baptism = $40,700

## Sudan
**Population:** 29,490,000.
**Area:** 2,503,890 sq. km.
(966,757 sq. mi.).
**Political divisions:** 9 provinces.

A=46.2%
B=37.1%
C=16.7%
3 Worlds, AD 2000

T=11.9%
C=16.7%
M=70.3%
Religions, AD 2000

O=2.4% I=2.3%
P=12.1%
R=47.9%
A=35.3%
Ecclesiastical megablocs

Evangelization, 1900-2025

e=evangelistic offers per capita per year
Offers, 1900-2025

Cost per baptism = $23,600
Cost-effectiveness, AD 2000

## Syria
**Population:** 16,125,000.
**Area:** 185,180 sq. km. (71,498 sq. mi.).
**Political divisions:** 14 provinces.

A=37.8%
B=54.4%
C=7.8%
3 Worlds, AD 2000

C=7.8%
M=89.3%
Religions, AD 2000

I=8.0%
R=25.8%
O=63.5%
Ecclesiastical megablocs

Evangelization, 1900-2025

e=evangelistic offers per capita per year
Offers, 1900-2025

Cost per baptism = $46,100
Cost-effectiveness, AD 2000

## Taiwan
**Population:** 22,401,000.
**Area:** 36,179 sq. km. (13,969 sq. mi.).
**Political divisions:** 23 provinces.

A=31.2%
B=62.5%
C=6.3%
3 Worlds, AD 2000

Q=4.2%
C=6.3%
N=6.8%
D=10.2%
F=50.7%
B=20.9%
Religions, AD 2000

m=2.3%
R=25.4%
I=38.2%
P=33.9%
Ecclesiastical megablocs

Evangelization, 1900-2025

e=evangelistic offers per capita per year
Offers, 1900-2025

Cost per baptism = $791,000
Cost-effectiveness, AD 2000

## Tanzania
**Population:** 33,517,000.
**Area:** 942,799 sq. km.
(364,017 sq. mi.).
**Political divisions:** 25 provinces.

A=18.6%
B=31.0%
C=50.4%
3 Worlds, AD 2000

T=16.1%
C=50.4%
M=31.8%
Religions, AD 2000

I=3.7%
A=15.5%
R=48.3%
P=32.3%
Ecclesiastical megablocs

Evangelization, 1900-2025

e=evangelistic offers per capita per year
Offers, 1900-2025

Cost per baptism = $2,500
Cost-effectiveness, AD 2000

## Thailand
**Population:** 61,399,000.
**Area:** 513,115 sq. km. (198,115 sq. mi.).
**Political divisions:** 7 provinces.

A=43.2%
B=54.6%
C=2.2%
3 Worlds, AD 2000

T=2.1% Q=2.0%
C=2.2%
M=6.8%
B=85.3%
Religions, AD 2000

R=19.0%
I=57.9%
P=22.5%
Ecclesiastical megablocs

Evangelization, 1900-2025

e=evangelistic offers per capita per year
Offers, 1900-2025

Cost per baptism = $127,500
Cost-effectiveness, AD 2000

## Turkey
**Population:** 66,591,000.
**Area:** 779,452 sq. km.
(300,948 sq. mi.).
**Political divisions:** 8 provinces.

A=51.4%
B=48.0%
C=0.6%
3 Worlds, AD 2000

M=97.2%
Religions, AD 2000

R=8.2%
P=8.7%
I=20.9%
O=61.0%
Ecclesiastical megablocs

Evangelization, 1900-2025

e=evangelistic offers per capita per year
Offers, 1900-2025

Cost per baptism = $228,800
Cost-effectiveness, AD 2000

## Uganda
**Population:** 21,778,000.
**Area:** 241,040 sq. km. (93,070 sq. mi.).
**Political divisions:** 38 provinces.

A=0.9%
B=10.4%
C=88.7%
3 Worlds, AD 2000

T=4.4%
M=5.2%
C=88.7%
Religions, AD 2000

I=4.3% P=3.1%
A=44.8% R=47.7%
Ecclesiastical megablocs

Evangelization, 1900-2025

e=evangelistic offers per capita per year
Offers, 1900-2025

Cost per baptism = $5,000
Cost-effectiveness, AD 2000

## Ukraine
**Population:** 50,456,000.
**Area:** 603,700 sq. km.
(233,100 sq. mi.).
**Political divisions:** 25 provinces.

A=1.5%
B=15.5%
C=83.0%
3 Worlds, AD 2000

a=4.0% M=1.7%
Q=10.9%
C=83.0%
Religions, AD 2000

P=3.1%
R=13.0%
I=19.8%
O=63.8%
Ecclesiastical megablocs

Evangelization, 1900-2025

e=evangelistic offers per capita per year
Offers, 1900-2025

Cost per baptism = $115,400
Cost-effectiveness, AD 2000

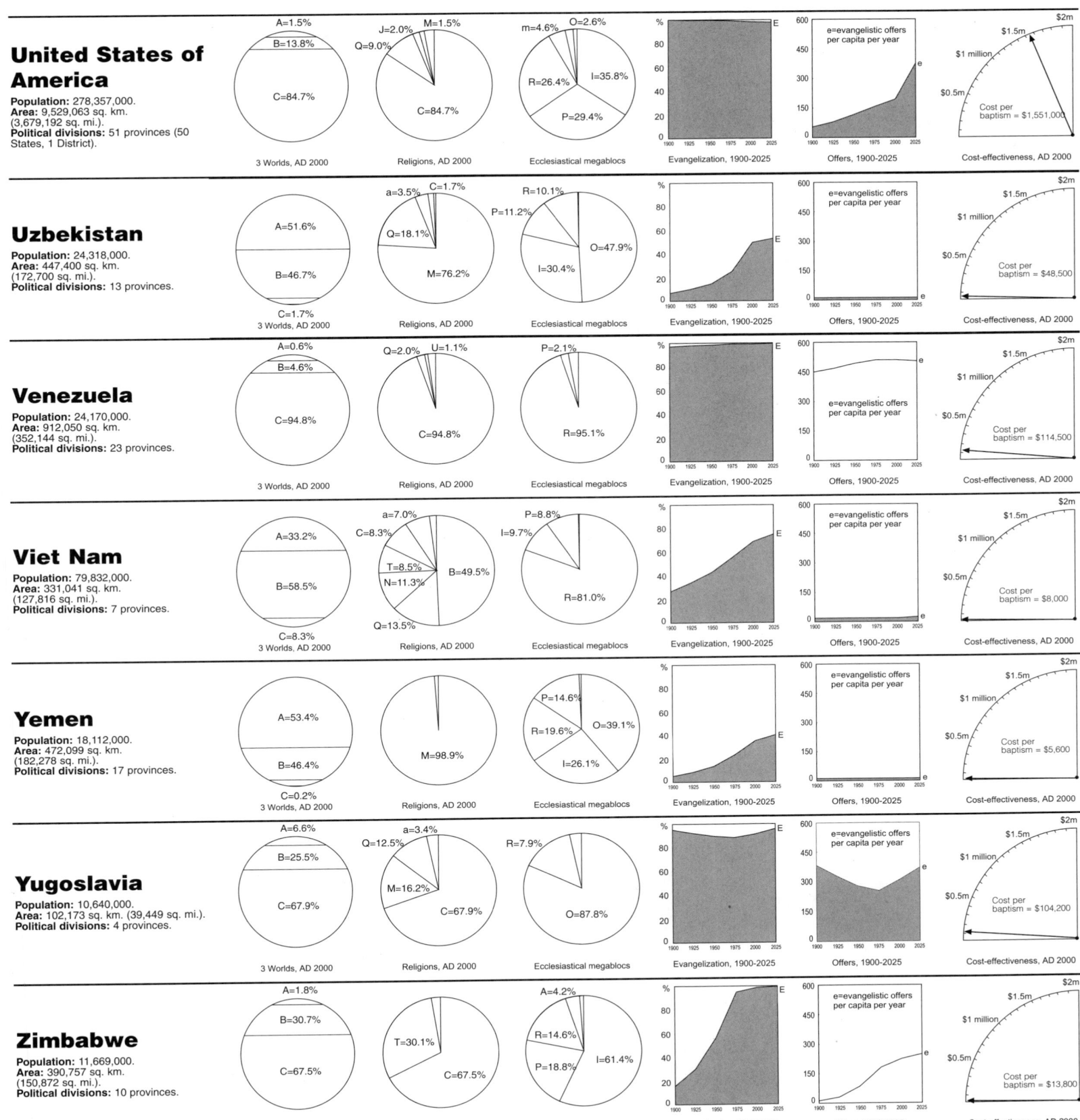

## United States of America

**Population:** 278,357,000.
**Area:** 9,529,063 sq. km.
(3,679,192 sq. mi.).
**Political divisions:** 51 provinces (50 States, 1 District).

A=1.5%
B=13.8%
C=84.7%
*3 Worlds, AD 2000*

M=1.5%
J=2.0%
Q=9.0%
C=84.7%
*Religions, AD 2000*

m=4.6%
O=2.6%
I=35.8%
R=26.4%
P=29.4%
*Ecclesiastical megablocs*

*Evangelization, 1900-2025*

e=evangelistic offers per capita per year
*Offers, 1900-2025*

$2m
$1.5m
$1 million
$0.5m
Cost per baptism = $1,551,000
*Cost-effectiveness, AD 2000*

## Uzbekistan

**Population:** 24,318,000.
**Area:** 447,400 sq. km.
(172,700 sq. mi.).
**Political divisions:** 13 provinces.

A=51.6%
B=46.7%
C=1.7%
*3 Worlds, AD 2000*

a=3.5%
C=1.7%
Q=18.1%
M=76.2%
*Religions, AD 2000*

R=10.1%
P=11.2%
O=47.9%
I=30.4%
*Ecclesiastical megablocs*

*Evangelization, 1900-2025*

e=evangelistic offers per capita per year
*Offers, 1900-2025*

$2m
$1.5m
$1 million
$0.5m
Cost per baptism = $48,500
*Cost-effectiveness, AD 2000*

## Venezuela

**Population:** 24,170,000.
**Area:** 912,050 sq. km.
(352,144 sq. mi.).
**Political divisions:** 23 provinces.

A=0.6%
B=4.6%
C=94.8%
*3 Worlds, AD 2000*

Q=2.0%
U=1.1%
C=94.8%
*Religions, AD 2000*

P=2.1%
R=95.1%
*Ecclesiastical megablocs*

*Evangelization, 1900-2025*

e=evangelistic offers per capita per year
*Offers, 1900-2025*

$2m
$1.5m
$1 million
$0.5m
Cost per baptism = $114,500
*Cost-effectiveness, AD 2000*

## Viet Nam

**Population:** 79,832,000.
**Area:** 331,041 sq. km.
(127,816 sq. mi.).
**Political divisions:** 7 provinces.

A=33.2%
B=58.5%
C=8.3%
*3 Worlds, AD 2000*

a=7.0%
C=8.3%
T=8.5%
N=11.3%
Q=13.5%
B=49.5%
*Religions, AD 2000*

P=8.8%
I=9.7%
R=81.0%
*Ecclesiastical megablocs*

*Evangelization, 1900-2025*

e=evangelistic offers per capita per year
*Offers, 1900-2025*

$2m
$1.5m
$1 million
$0.5m
Cost per baptism = $8,000
*Cost-effectiveness, AD 2000*

## Yemen

**Population:** 18,112,000.
**Area:** 472,099 sq. km.
(182,278 sq. mi.).
**Political divisions:** 17 provinces.

A=53.4%
B=46.4%
C=0.2%
*3 Worlds, AD 2000*

M=98.9%
*Religions, AD 2000*

P=14.6%
O=39.1%
R=19.6%
I=26.1%
*Ecclesiastical megablocs*

*Evangelization, 1900-2025*

e=evangelistic offers per capita per year
*Offers, 1900-2025*

$2m
$1.5m
$1 million
$0.5m
Cost per baptism = $5,600
*Cost-effectiveness, AD 2000*

## Yugoslavia

**Population:** 10,640,000.
**Area:** 102,173 sq. km. (39,449 sq. mi.).
**Political divisions:** 4 provinces.

A=6.6%
B=25.5%
C=67.9%
*3 Worlds, AD 2000*

a=3.4%
Q=12.5%
M=16.2%
C=67.9%
*Religions, AD 2000*

R=7.9%
O=87.8%
*Ecclesiastical megablocs*

*Evangelization, 1900-2025*

e=evangelistic offers per capita per year
*Offers, 1900-2025*

$2m
$1.5m
$1 million
$0.5m
Cost per baptism = $104,200
*Cost-effectiveness, AD 2000*

## Zimbabwe

**Population:** 11,669,000.
**Area:** 390,757 sq. km.
(150,872 sq. mi.).
**Political divisions:** 10 provinces.

A=1.8%
B=30.7%
C=67.5%
*3 Worlds, AD 2000*

T=30.1%
C=67.5%
*Religions, AD 2000*

A=4.2%
R=14.6%
P=18.8%
I=61.4%
*Ecclesiastical megablocs*

*Evangelization, 1900-2025*

e=evangelistic offers per capita per year
*Offers, 1900-2025*

$2m
$1.5m
$1 million
$0.5m
Cost per baptism = $13,800
*Cost-effectiveness, AD 2000*

Part 16

# GEOCODEBOOK

Quick-reference codebook for all statistical tables and diagrams

*All real science rests on classification.*
—Comparative philologist F. Max Müller, father of the history of religion, 1860

Part 16 gives all codes and meanings used throughout this volume and the *World Christian encyclopedia,* with 2 exceptions. (1) The databases shown in *WCE* Parts 7, 8, 9, 10, and 11 give their own codes in their own Parts immediately before the data appears. (2) So likewise does Part 33 "Geoatlas".

The pages that follow set out alphabetically or systematically, for quick reference, the meaning of the mainly mutually-exclusive classifications, categories, columns, codes, and abbreviations used in this volume's statistical tables and in their related *World Christian database.* These summary tables of codes are as follows:

1. Table 16–1 lists countries and country codes used in many tables to save space.

2. Table 16–2 lists global codes used throughout, listed alphabetically by code.

3. Table 16–3 lists global codes used throughout, listed alphabetically by name.

4. Table 16–4 lists standard terms and codes for 85 categories of 'Christians' and 100 varieties of 'non-Christians'.

These are followed by detailed codes used in the 2 main tables describing religions and denominations for every country, which are shown in the main survey articles under *WCE* Part 4 "Countries". These are arranged as follows:

5. Table 16–5 interprets *WCE **Country Tables 1:*** Religion adherents in each country, AD 1900-2025.

6. Table 16–6 explains *WCE **Country Tables 2:*** Organized churches and denominations in each country.

7. Table 16–7 gives codes for ***Part 12 "CountryTrends", Table 12-1:*** Geopolitico-religious data and typologies for all countries and continents, AD 1900-2050.

A listing of all 191 variables is given here, but only those with codes are listed in detail.

8. *WCE **Parts 7, 8, 9, 10, 11.*** These 5 Parts reproduce very large numbers of pages from source databases enumerating respectively the titles Religiometrics, EthnoSphere, Linguametrics, MetroScan, ProvinceScan.

Meanings of all columns and codes that they employ are given each within its Part immediately before its table of data. They are not therefore repeated here in this present GeoCodebook.

***Part 33 "GeoAtlas".*** All scales, codes, symbols, and meanings used on the 16 Global Maps are explained each on its map's Key and under the map's title. Likewise the 18 Human Environment topographical maps that follow have each within it its detailed key with meanings.

# Quick-reference codebook for all statistical tables and diagrams

## 1. COUNTRIES LISTED BY CODE.

**Table 16–1** Standard short names for all 238 countries in the world, expanded official names (anglicized, after UN usage), and 4-letter codes.

|  |  |
|------|---------|
| afgh | **AFGHANISTAN,** The Islamic State of |
| alba | **ALBANIA,** The Republic of |
| alge | **ALGERIA,** The People's Democratic Republic of |
| amer | **AMERICAN SAMOA,** The Territories of |
| ando | **ANDORRA,** The Principality of |
| ango | **ANGOLA,** The Republic of |
| angu | **ANGUILLA,** The Dependency of |
| anta | **ANTARCTICA,** The Continent of |
| anti | **ANTIGUA & BARBUDA,** The Realm of |
| arge | **ARGENTINA;** The Argentine Republic |
| arme | **ARMENIA,** The Republic of |
| arub | **ARUBA,** The Territory of |
| aust | **AUSTRALIA,** The Commonwealth of |
| ausz | **AUSTRIA,** The Republic of |
| azer | **AZERBAIJAN;** The Azerbaijani Republic |
| baha | **BAHAMAS,** The Commonwealth of the |
| bahr | **BAHRAIN,** The State of |
| bang | **BANGLADESH,** The People's Republic of |
| barb | **BARBADOS,** The Realm of |
| belg | **BELGIUM,** The Kingdom of |
| beli | **BELIZE,** The Realm of |
| belo | **BELORUSSIA;** The Republic of Belarus |
| beni | **BENIN,** The Republic of |
| berm | **BERMUDA;** The Colony of the Bermuda Islands |
| bhut | **BHUTAN,** The Kingdom of |
| boli | **BOLIVIA,** The Republic of |
| bosn | **BOSNIA & HERCEGOVINA,** The Republic of |
| bots | **BOTSWANA,** The Republic of |
| boug | **BOUGAINVILLE,** The Republic of |
| braz | **BRAZIL,** The Federative Republic of |
| brit | **BRITAIN;** The United Kingdom of Great Britain and Northern Ireland (UK of GB & NI) |
| briy | **BRITISH INDIAN OCEAN TERRITORY,** The Crown Colony of the |
| briz | **BRITISH VIRGIN ISLANDS,** The Territory of the |
| brun | **BRUNEI,** The State of Brunei Darussalam |
| bulg | **BULGARIA,** The Republic of |
| burk | **BURKINA FASO,** The Democratic Republic of |
| buru | **BURUNDI,** The Republic of |
| camb | **CAMBODIA,** The Kingdom of |
| came | **CAMEROON,** The Republic of |
| cana | **CANADA,** The Dominion of |
| cape | **CAPE VERDE,** The Republic of |
| caym | **CAYMAN ISLANDS,** The Crown Colony of the |
| cent | **CENTRAL AFRICAN REPUBLIC,** The |
| chad | **CHAD,** The Republic of |
| chan | **CHANNEL ISLANDS,** The Crown Dependency of the |
| chil | **CHILE,** The Republic of |
| chin | **CHINA,** The People's Republic of |
| chri | **CHRISTMAS ISLAND,** The Territory of |
| coco | **COCOS (KEELING) ISLANDS,** The Territory of |
| colo | **COLOMBIA,** The Republic of |
| como | **COMOROS,** The Islamic Federal Republic of the |
| cong | **CONGO (BRAZZAVILLE);** The Republic of the Congo |
| conz | **CONGO-ZAIRE;** The Democratic Republic of Congo |
| cook | **COOK ISLANDS,** The Territory Overseas of the |
| cost | **COSTA RICA,** The Republic of |
| croa | **CROATIA,** The Republic of |
| cuba | **CUBA,** The Republic of |
| cypr | **CYPRUS,** The Republic of |
| czec | **CZECH REPUBLIC,** The |
| denm | **DENMARK,** The Kingdom of |
| djib | **DJIBOUTI,** The Republic of |
| domi | **DOMINICA,** The Commonwealth of |
| domr | **DOMINICAN REPUBLIC,** The |
| ecua | **ECUADOR,** The Republic of |
| egyp | **EGYPT,** The Arab Republic of |
| elsa | **EL SALVADOR,** The Republic of |
| equa | **EQUATORIAL GUINEA,** The Republic of |
| erit | **ERITREA,** The State of |
| esto | **ESTONIA,** The Republic of |
| ethi | **ETHIOPIA,** The Federal Democratic Republic of |
| faer | **FAEROE ISLANDS,** The |
| falk | **FALKLAND ISLANDS,** The Crown Colony of the |
| fiji | **FIJI;** The Sovereign Democratic Republic of the Fiji Islands |
| finl | **FINLAND,** The Republic of |
| fran | **FRANCE,** The French Republic |
| freg | **FRENCH GUIANA,** The Department of |
| frep | **FRENCH POLYNESIA,** The Overseas Territory of |
| gabo | **GABON,** The Gabonese Republic |
| gamb | **GAMBIA,** The Republic of the |
| geor | **GEORGIA,** The Republic of |
| germ | **GERMANY,** The Federal Republic of |
| ghan | **GHANA,** The Republic of |
| gibr | **GIBRALTAR,** The Colony of |
| gree | **GREECE;** The Hellenic Republic |
| grel | **GREENLAND** |
| gren | **GRENADA,** The Realm of |
| guad | **GUADELOUPE,** The Department of |
| guam | **GUAM,** The United States Territory of |
| guat | **GUATEMALA,** The Republic of |
| guin | **GUINEA,** The Republic of |
| gunb | **GUINEA-BISSAU,** The Republic of |
| guya | **GUYANA,** The Co-operative Republic of |
| hait | **HAITI,** The Republic of |
| holy | **HOLY SEE,** The (Vatican City State) |
| hond | **HONDURAS,** The Republic of |
| hung | **HUNGARY,** The Republic of |
| icel | **ICELAND,** The Republic of |
| indi | **INDIA,** The Republic of |
| indo | **INDONESIA,** The Republic of |
| iran | **IRAN,** The Islamic Republic of |
| iraq | **IRAQ,** The Republic of |
| irel | **IRELAND,** The Republic of |
| isle | **ISLE OF MAN,** The Crown Dependency of the |
| isra | **ISRAEL,** The State of |
| ital | **ITALY;** The Italian Republic |
| ivor | **IVORY COAST;** The Republic of Côte d'Ivoire |
| jama | **JAMAICA,** The Realm of |
| japa | **JAPAN** |
| jord | **JORDAN,** The Hashemite Kingdom of |
| kaza | **KAZAKHSTAN,** The Republic of |
| keny | **KENYA,** The Republic of |
| kirg | **KIRGIZSTAN;** The Kyrgyz Republic (Kyrgyzstan) |
| kiri | **KIRIBATI,** The Republic of |
| kuwa | **KUWAIT,** The State of |
| laos | **LAOS;** The Lao People's Democratic Republic |
| latv | **LATVIA,** The Republic of |
| leba | **LEBANON;** The Lebanese Republic |
| leso | **LESOTHO,** The Kingdom of |
| libe | **LIBERIA,** The Republic of |
| liby | **LIBYA;** The Libyan Arab Jamahiriya |
| liec | **LIECHTENSTEIN,** The Principality of |
| lith | **LITHUANIA,** The Republic of |
| luxe | **LUXEMBOURG,** The Grand Duchy of |
| mace | **MACEDONIA,** The Republic of |
| mada | **MADAGASCAR,** The Republic of |
| mala | **MALAWI,** The Republic of |
| malb | **MALAYSIA,** The Federation of |
| mald | **MALDIVES,** The Republic of |
| mali | **MALI,** The Republic of |
| malt | **MALTA,** The Republic of |
| mars | **MARSHALL ISLANDS,** The Republic of the |
| mart | **MARTINIQUE,** The Department of |
| maur | **MAURITANIA,** The Islamic Republic of |
| maus | **MAURITIUS,** The Republic of |
| mayo | **MAYOTTE,** The Territorial Collectivity of |
| mexi | **MEXICO;** The United Mexican States |
| micr | **MICRONESIA,** The Federated States of |
| mold | **MOLDAVIA;** The Republic of Moldova |
| mona | **MONACO,** The Principality of |
| mong | **MONGOLIA,** The State of |
| mont | **MONTSERRAT,** The Crown Colony of |
| moro | **MOROCCO,** The Kingdom of |
| moza | **MOZAMBIQUE,** The Republic of |
| myan | **MYANMAR,** The Union of |
| nami | **NAMIBIA,** The Republic of |
| naur | **NAURU,** The Republic of |
| nepa | **NEPAL,** The Kingdom of |
| neth | **NETHERLANDS,** The Kingdom of the |
| nets | **NETHERLANDS ANTILLES,** The |
| newc | **NEW CALEDONIA,** The Overseas Territory of |
| newz | **NEW ZEALAND,** The Dominion of |
| nica | **NICARAGUA,** The Republic of |
| niga | **NIGER,** The Republic of the |
| nige | **NIGERIA,** The Federal Republic of |
| niue | **NIUE ISLAND,** The Overseas Territory of |
| norf | **NORFOLK ISLAND,** The Territory of |
| nork | **NORTH KOREA;** The Democratic PR of Korea |
| norl | **NORTHERN CYPRUS,** The Turkish Republic of |
| norm | **NORTHERN MARIANA ISLANDS,** The Commonwealth of the |
| norw | **NORWAY,** The Kingdom of |
| oman | **OMAN,** The Sultanate of |
| paki | **PAKISTAN,** The Islamic Republic of |
| pala | **PALAU;** The Republic of Belau |
| pale | **PALESTINE;** The Palestine Authority |
| pana | **PANAMA,** The Republic of |
| papu | **PAPUA NEW GUINEA,** The Independent State of |
| para | **PARAGUAY,** The Republic of |
| peru | **PERU,** The Republic of |
| phil | **PHILIPPINES,** The Republic of the |
| pitc | **PITCAIRN ISLANDS,** The Colony of the |
| pola | **POLAND,** The Republic of |
| port | **PORTUGAL;** The Portuguese Republic |
| puer | **PUERTO RICO,** The Commonwealth of |
| qata | **QATAR,** The State of |
| reun | **REUNION,** The Department of |
| roma | **ROMANIA,** The Republic of |
| russ | **RUSSIA;** The Russian Federation |
| rwan | **RWANDA;** The Rwandese Republic |
| saha | **SAHARA;** The Sahara Arab Democratic Republic |
| saih | **SAINT HELENA,** The Colony of |
| saik | **SAINT KITTS & NEVIS,** The Federation of |
| sail | **SAINT LUCIA,** The Realm of |
| saip | **SAINT PIERRE & MIQUELON,** The Territorial Collectivity of |
| saiv | **SAINT VINCENT & THE GRENADINES,** The Realm of |
| samo | **SAMOA,** The Independent State of |
| sanm | **SAN MARINO,** The Republic of |
| saot | **SAO TOME & PRINCIPE,** The Democratic Republic of |
| saud | **SAUDI ARABIA,** The Kingdom of |
| sene | **SENEGAL,** The Republic of |
| seyc | **SEYCHELLES,** The Republic of |
| sier | **SIERRA LEONE,** The Republic of |
| sing | **SINGAPORE,** The Republic of |
| slok | **SLOVAKIA;** The Slovak Republic |
| slov | **SLOVENIA,** The Republic of |
| solo | **SOLOMON ISLANDS,** The Realm of the |
| soma | **SOMALIA;** The Somali Democratic Republic |
| somi | **SOMALILAND;** The Somaliland Republic |
| soua | **SOUTH AFRICA,** The Republic of |
| souk | **SOUTH KOREA;** The Republic of Korea |
| spai | **SPAIN,** The Kingdom of |
| span | **SPANISH NORTH AFRICA** |
| sril | **SRI LANKA,** The Democratic Socialist Republic of |
| suda | **SUDAN,** The Republic of the |
| suri | **SURINAME,** The Republic of |
| sval | **SVALBARD & JAN MAYEN ISLANDS** |
| swaz | **SWAZILAND,** The Kingdom of |
| swed | **SWEDEN,** The Kingdom of |
| swit | **SWITZERLAND;** The Swiss Confederation |
| syri | **SYRIA,** The Syrian Arab Republic |
| taiw | **TAIWAN;** The Republic of China |
| taji | **TAJIKISTAN,** The Republic of |
| tanz | **TANZANIA,** The United Republic of |
| thai | **THAILAND,** The Kingdom of |
| timo | **TIMOR** |
| togo | **TOGO;** The Togolese Republic |
| toke | **TOKELAU ISLANDS,** The Territory Overseas of |
| tong | **TONGA,** The Kingdom of |
| trin | **TRINIDAD & TOBAGO,** The Republic of |
| tuni | **TUNISIA,** The Republic of |
| turk | **TURKEY,** The Republic of |
| turm | **TURKMENISTAN,** The Republic of |
| turs | **TURKS & CAICOS ISLANDS,** The Crown Colony of the |
| tuva | **TUVALU,** The Realm of |
| ugan | **UGANDA,** The Republic of |
| ukra | **UKRAINE** |
| unia | **UNITED ARAB EMIRATES,** The |
| usa | **UNITED STATES OF AMERICA,** The |
| uuay | **URUGUAY,** The Eastern Republic of |
| uzbe | **UZBEKISTAN,** The Republic of |
| vanu | **VANUATU,** The Republic of |
| vene | **VENEZUELA,** The Republic of |
| viet | **VIET NAM,** The Socialist Republic of |
| virg | **VIRGIN ISLANDS OF THE US,** The |
| wall | **WALLIS & FUTUNA ISLANDS,** The Overseas Territory of |
| yeme | **YEMEN,** The Republic of |
| yugo | **YUGOSLAVIA,** The Federal Republic of |
| zamb | **ZAMBIA,** The Republic of |
| zimb | **ZIMBABWE,** The Republic of |

## 2. GLOBAL CODES LISTED BY CODE.

**Table 16–2. Global codes used throughout *WCT, WCE* and related CD *World Christian database,* alphabetically by code.**

Every distinct alphanumeric code listed below—whether one-letter, or from 2 to 8 characters—has meaning as a distinct variable that is being measured, and for which values, results, and meanings are presented at a variety of places in this Encyclopedia and its related CD, the *World Christian database.*

Each alphanumeric code thus used is a unique *global code* in that, wherever it occurs in this *WCE* or *WCT*'s tables or in the related CD, it has in all cases only the *one global meaning*, as set forth below in this table of all such codes. Note that occasionally a single letter may have different meanings if considered in isolation. Thus 'P' means 'Protestant (Protestants, the Protestant megabloc)', whereas 'P..' means 'This people has portions of Scripture (gospels) in their own language, but no New Testament or Bible.' Hence to avoid ambiguity, the entire code must always be carefully extracted, exactly quoted, accurately keyboarded, interrogated, understood, and used.

Note carefully that this listing is of global variables and their codes, to enable users to locate identities and varieties of data instantly. This listing does not include local codes, by which is meant codes that are applicable to the various values of only one single variable (one global code). These local values or codes can be located at the points where variables are being described.

The table below lists all variables alphabetically by code. Table 16–3 which follows lists the same variables but alphabetically by name.

| | |
|---|---|
| 0QZAC | Prepentecostals |
| 1P1ZAC | Oneness Pentecostals (White) |
| 1QZAC | Postpentecostals |
| 1ZAC | Pentecostals (First-Wavers) |
| 2AC | doubly-affiliated Christians |
| 2b | 2nd-language Bible |
| 2CP1ZAC | Baptistic Pentecostals |
| 2n | 2nd-language NT |
| 2p | 2nd-language gospel |
| 2PC | doubly-professing Christians |
| 2RAC | doubly-counted Catholics |
| 2s | 2nd-language scriptures |
| 2W | doubly-counted religionists |
| 2ZAC | Charismatics (Second-Wavers) |
| 3CP1ZAC | Holiness Pentecostals |
| 3ZAC | Neocharismatics (Third-Wavers) |
| 4ZAC | doubly-affiliated pentecostals |
| a | Atheists |
| a | audio scripture availability |
| A- | Anglican megabloc |
| A-C | Christians in World A countries |
| A-V | audio-visual ministries |
| a1 | Audio gospel, hearings per family |
| a2 | Audio gospel, hearings per adult |
| A2ZAC | Anglican Charismatics |
| a3 | Audio gospel, hearings per capita |
| A3ZAC | Anglican Third-Wavers |
| AA | Audio gospel, hearers p.a. per 100 |
| aAA | World A individuals in A peoples in A countries |
| aAB | World A individuals in A peoples in B countries |
| AAC | Anglicans |
| aAC | World A individuals in A peoples in C countries |
| aBA | World A individuals in B peoples in A countries |
| aBB | World A individuals in B peoples in B countries |
| aBC | World A individuals in B peoples in C countries |
| AC | affiliated Christians (church members) |
| aCA | World A individuals in C peoples in A countries |
| aCB | World A individuals in C peoples in B countries |
| aCC | World A individuals in C peoples in C countries |
| ACinc | personal income of church members, $ p.a. |
| ACP1ZAC | Apostolic Pentecostals |
| ad | adults (over 15) as % population |
| Ad | adults (over 15) in a specific population |
| AHM | Ithna-Asharis |
| AIAC | Independent Anglicans |
| AJ | Ashkenazi Jews |
| AL | Azali Babis |
| alC | alien Christians |
| ALEAC | Anglican Evangelicals |
| AN | Astrologists |
| AN3ZAC | African indigenous pentecostals/charismatics |
| APC | Anglicans (professing) |
| Apop | World A population |
| Apop1 | World A individuals |
| Apop2 | Population of World A peoples |
| Apop3 | Population of World A countries |
| AT | Animists |
| AU | Afro-American spiritists |
| au | audio scriptures |
| AV2ZAC | Anglican Charismatics (active) |
| Ax2ZAC | Anglican Postcharismatics |
| AXM | Ahmadis |
| B | Bible, existence of. (if no statistics present) |
| B | Buddhists |
| b | near-Bible |
| B-activity | earliest/latest Bible publication dates |
| B-C | Christians in World B countries |
| b1 | Bibles in use per family |
| b2 | Bibles in use per adult |
| b3 | Bibles in use per capita |
| B3ZAC | Isolated radio/TV Third-Wavers |
| bAA | World B individuals in A peoples in A countries |
| bAB | World B individuals in A peoples in B countries |
| bAC | World B individuals in A peoples in C countries |
| BAT | Buddhistic animists |
| bBA | World B individuals in B peoples in A countries |
| bBB | World B individuals in B peoples in B countries |
| bBC | World B individuals in B peoples in C countries |
| BBIAC | Non-charismatic radio churches |
| bCA | World B individuals in C peoples in A countries |
| bCB | World B individuals in C peoples in B countries |
| BCC | Isolated radio/TV believers |
| bCC | World B individuals in C peoples in C countries |
| beds | hospital beds, per 10,000 population |
| Begun | year in which entity came into being |
| BH3ZAC | Hidden Buddhist neocharismatics |
| BHCC | Hidden Buddhist believers in Christ |
| BHIAC | Hidden Buddhist believers in Christ |
| BIAC | Isolated radio/TV believers |
| BIHM | Bohoras |
| blind | nonsighted (blind) persons |
| BN3ZAC | Black American indigenous pentecostals |
| bpop | births, % p.a. |
| Bpop | World B population |
| Bpop1 | World B individuals |
| Bpop2 | Population of World B peoples |
| Bpop3 | Population of World B countries |
| br | Braille scriptures for blind |
| Bs | complete Bibles distributed p.a. |
| BSM | Hanbalites |
| BU | Afro-Brazilian cultists |
| BXM | Black Muslims |
| BY | Bogomils |
| C | Christians, % |
| C-C | Christians in World C countries |
| C= | Roman Catholic religious institutes at work (clerics + brothers + sisters) |
| cAA | World C individuals in A peoples in A countries |
| CAAC | Anglican Charismatics |
| cAB | World C individuals in A peoples in B countries |
| cAC | World C individuals in A peoples in C countries |
| cBA | World C individuals in B peoples in A countries |
| CBB | culture barriers, total of |
| cBB | World C individuals in B peoples in B countries |
| cBC | World C individuals in B peoples in C countries |
| cc | congregations per million |
| CC | crypto-Christians |
| cCA | World C individuals in C peoples in A countries |
| cCB | World C individuals in C peoples in B countries |
| cCC | World C individuals in C peoples in C countries |
| ce | cost-effectiveness, $ per baptism |
| CEAC | Conservative Evangelicals |
| CG | century's church growth, AD 1900-2000, p.a. |
| CIAC | Charismatic Independents |
| cit-100 | total cities of over 100,000 |
| cit-50 | total cities of over 50,000 |
| CJ | Reconstructionist Jews |
| CmAC | Marginal Charismatics |
| CMB | Chinese Buddhists |
| CN | Cargo cultists |
| CN3ZAC | Han Chinese indigenous pentecostals/charismatics |
| COAC | Orthodox Charismatics |
| code | 4-letter identification code for a country |
| comp | computers (general purpose) in use |
| cou | total countries involved |
| CP1ZAC | Classical Pentecostals |
| CPAC | Protestant Charismatics |
| Cpop | World C population |
| Cpop1 | World C individuals |
| Cpop2 | Population of World C peoples |
| Cpop3 | Population of World C countries |
| CRAC | Catholic Charismatics |
| CRPC | Christopagans |
| CSI | Christian Safety Index |
| CU | Afro-Caribbean religionists |
| CX | contact of Christians with non-Christians |
| d | discipling stage, % |
| D | Taoists |
| D= | denominations |
| dd | denominations per million |
| deaf | hearing-impaired (deaf) persons |
| dev | more/less/least-developed countries |
| di | dialects |
| DN3ZAC | Black American independent charismatics |
| doct | doctors (physicians, surgeons) |
| dpop | deaths, % p.a. |
| ds | distinctiveness of statistics in totalling |
| DV | Digambara Jains |
| DXM | Druzes |
| E | extent of evangelization (persons evangelized), % |
| e | offers per capita per year |
| EAAC | Anglican Evangelicals |
| EAC | Evangelicals |
| EBB | evangelization barriers, total of |
| educ | rate education rate |
| EFL | Economic Freedom Level |
| EIAC | Independent Evangelicals |
| EJ | Oriental Jews |
| EmAC | Marginal Evangelicals |
| EN3ZAC | Ethnic (Monoethnic) pentecostal churches |
| enu | ethnic non-users as % group's population |
| Enu | ethnic non-users of a language |
| EOAC | Orthodox Evangelicals |
| EP | Total evangelized persons |
| EPAC | Protestant Evangelicals |
| ERAC | Catholic Evangelicals |
| ERPC | Evangelical Catholics |
| ET | Neopagans |
| Ev | Evangelicals, % of AC |
| ev | evangelicals, % of country |
| ext | extent or number of countries involved |
| F | Chinese folk-religionists |
| F= | Founder (if a name) |
| fam | families (households) |
| FB | Folk-Buddhists |
| FEAC | Fundamentalists |
| FH | Folk/Popular Hindus |
| FJ | Folk-Judaism |
| FM | Folk-Muslims |
| FN | Self-Religionists |
| FN3ZAC | Filipino indigenous pentecostals/charismatics |
| FPW | Folk-religionists |
| FQY | Freemasons |
| FS | Folk-Shintoists |
| G | Confucianists |
| g | growth of new Christians, % p.a. |
| G | numerical church growth, % p.a. |
| GCC | Great Commission Christians, % country |
| GCCinc | personal income of GCCs, $ p.a. |
| GN3ZAC | Indonesian indigenous pentecostals |
| GNPpc | gross national product, US$ p.a.p.c. |
| Gpop | Total global population |
| h | hearing-impaired scripture availability |
| H | Hindus |
| H3ZAC | Hidden non-Christian believers in Christ |
| HAT | Hinduized animists |
| HCC | Hidden non-Christian believers in Christ |
| HDI | Human Development Index |
| HFI | Human Freedom Index |
| HH | Vedantists |
| HH3ZAC | Hidden Hindu neocharismatics |
| HHCC | Hidden Hindu believers in Christ |
| HHIAC | Hidden Hindu believers in Christ |
| hi | hearing impaired/deaf/signed scriptures |
| HIAC | Hidden non-Christian believers in Christ |
| HM | Shias |
| HN3ZAC | Messianic Hindu believers in Christ |
| hom | households (homes, families) |
| home | household size (persons) |
| hosp | hospitals |
| HS | Shrine Shinto |
| HSI | Human Suffering Index |
| HSM | Hanafites |
| HU | High Spiritists |
| i | intercessors, intercession |
| I- | Independent megabloc |
| I3ZAC | Isolated non-Christian Neocharismatics |
| IAC | Independents/Postdenominationalists/Neo-Apostolics |
| IAT | Islamized animists |
| iC | indigenous Christians |
| IEAC | Independent Evangelicals |
| IHM | Ismailis |
| IKXM | Ibadis |
| IMB | Indian Buddhists |
| IN3ZAC | Indian indigenous pentecostals/charismatics |
| Inet | Internet users |
| IPC | Independents (professing) |
| J | 'Jesus' film availability |
| J | Jews |
| Jayuh | audiovisual resources (five variables) |
| Jf | 'Jesus' Film |
| JH3ZAC | Hidden Jewish neocharismatics |
| JHCC | Hidden Jewish believers in Christ |
| JHIAC | Hidden Jewish believers in Christ |
| JMB | Japanese Buddhists |
| JN3ZAC | Messianic Jewish believers in Christ |
| K | Sikhs |
| KH | Saktists |
| KJ | Karaites |
| KLB | Kagyudpa Lamaists |
| KMB | Korean Buddhists |
| KN3ZAC | Korean indigenous pentecostals/charismatics |
| KST | Korean folk-religionists |
| KXM | Kharijites |
| L | Baha'is |
| L | literary tradition |
| lang | language code |
| LAT | Primal religionists |
| LAXM | Lahoris |
| LB | Tibetan Buddhists (Lamaists) |
| LBB | language barriers, total of |
| LC | latent (inactive) Christians |
| LEAC | Conciliar Evangelicals |
| lepers | leprosy, sufferers from |
| LHM | Alawites |
| Lit | literacy, % |
| LN3ZAC | Latino-Hispanic grassroots believers |
| loc | main country or location involved |
| M | Muslims |
| M= | mission agencies |
| m- | Marginal Christian megabloc |
| m2ZAC | Marginal Charismatics |
| mAC | Marginal Christians (affiliated) |
| mar-sits | major martyrdom situations across 2,000 years |
| martyrs | martyrs for Christ (witness, hostility, death) |
| MB | Mahayana Buddhists |

*Continued opposite*

*Table 16–2 concluded*

| | |
|---|---|
| me | mass evangelism |
| mEAC | Marginal Evangelicals |
| mega | total megacities (over 1 million each) |
| metro | metrodwellers (in cities over 1 million), % |
| MH3ZAC | Hidden Muslim neocharismatics |
| MHCC | Hidden Muslim believers in Christ |
| MHIAC | Hidden Muslim believers in Christ |
| mi | mission agencies, total (coded 0-5) |
| Mi | number of mission agencies |
| MIAC | Nonhistorical Independents |
| MIHM | Mustalis |
| MM | missionaries received per million population |
| MMM | missionaries received per million affiliated |
| MN | Metaphysicalists |
| MN3ZAC | Messianic Muslim believers in Christ |
| mPC | Marginal Christians (professing) |
| mpop | nett immigrants, % p.a. |
| MSM | Malikites |
| Mts | mother-tongue speakers (native speakers) |
| mts | mother-tongue speakers as % of country |
| murder | murder rate, per 100,000 p.a. |
| mV2ZAC | Marginal Charismatics (active) |
| MXM | Sabbateans |
| MY | Mandeans |
| n | near-NT |
| N | New Testament, existence of |
| N | New-Religionists (Neoreligionists) |
| N-activity | earliest and latest NT publication dates |
| n1 | NTs in use per family |
| n2 | NTs in use per adult |
| n3 | NTs in use per capita |
| N3ZAC | Non-White Third-Wavers |
| NB | nonreligious Buddhists |
| NBB | nationality barriers, total of |
| NEAC | Neo-Evangelicals |
| NG | Neo-Confucians |
| NH | Neo-Hindus |
| NIAC | Non-White indigenous Christians |
| NJ | Conservative Jews |
| NJMB | Nara Buddhists |
| NJMB | Nichiren Shu Buddhists |
| NLB | Nyingmapa Lamaists |
| NN | New Testaments distributed p.a. per 100 |
| NN | Nonsyncretist neoreligionists |
| NN3ZAC | Colored/Mixed-race indigenous charismatics |
| Nns | non-native speakers (2nd-language) |
| nns | non-native speakers as % of country |
| Npop | Country's population |
| npop | natural population increase, % p.a. |
| nr | New Reader Scriptures |
| nrp | New Reader Portions (gospels) |
| nrs | New Reader Selections |
| NTB | Neo-Buddhists |
| NTs | New Testaments distributed p.a. |
| NXM | Muslim Neo-Fundamentalists |
| NY | Quasi-Christians |
| O- | Orthodox megabloc |
| O2ZAC | Orthodox Charismatics |
| O3ZAC | Orthodox Third-Wavers |
| OAC | Orthodox (affiliated) |
| od | total offers p.d. (per day) |
| OEC | overt evangelizers |
| OIAC | Independent Orthodox |
| OJ | Orthodox Jews |
| OL | Schismatic Baha'is |
| OLEAC | Orthodox Evangelicals |
| ON | Occultists |
| ON3ZAC | Black American Oneness Apostolics |
| oo | organizations per million |
| OPC | Orthodox (professing) |
| OV2ZAC | Orthodox Charismatics (active) |
| p | near-portion, near-gospel |
| P | Portion (gospel), existence of |
| P- | Protestant megabloc |
| P-activity | earliest/latest gospel publication dates |
| p.. | near-gospel only, for this people |
| P.. | Portion (Gospel) only |
| p.a. | per annum (per year) |
| p.c. | per capita (per person) |
| p.d. | per diem (per day) |
| p.m. | per million |
| p1 | Portions (gospels) placed per family |
| P1ZAC | Denominational Pentecostals (White) |
| p2 | Portions (gospels) placed per adult |
| P2ZAC | Protestant Charismatics |
| p3 | Portions (gospels) placed per capita |
| P3ZAC | Protestant Third-Wavers |
| PAC | Protestants (affiliated) |
| PAT | Polytheistic animists |

| | |
|---|---|
| PC | professing Christians |
| Peo | peoples in a country |
| people | ethnolinguistic or race code |
| PIAC | Independent Protestants |
| PJMB | Pure Land (Amida) |
| PLEAC | Protestant Conciliar Evangelicals |
| PN | Paganists |
| PN. | gospel & NT only |
| pn. | near-NT only, for this people |
| PN3ZAC | Pacific/Oceanic indigenous charismatics |
| PNB | gospel, NT, Bible |
| pnb | near-Bible only, for this people |
| pop | population |
| pop | population (of a people, city, country, continent, world, globe) |
| PP | Portions (gospels) distributed p.a. per 100 |
| PPC | Protestants (professing) |
| ppop | people as % of pop |
| Ppop | population of an ethnolinguistic people |
| PPPC | Protestant popular-religionists |
| PPW | Popular religionists |
| prAC | practicing church members |
| PRPC | Popular-religionist Catholics |
| Ps | Portions (Gospels) distributed p.a. |
| PT | Polytheists |
| pub | published scriptures |
| PV2ZAC | Protestant Charismatics (active) |
| PW | Pan-Religionists |
| Px2ZAC | Protestant Postcharismatics |
| PXM | Mahdists |
| PZ | Parsis |
| Q | Nonreligious |
| QAXM | Qadianis |
| QN3ZAC | Japanese indigenous pentecostals |
| QY | Pararreligionists |
| QZAC | Peripheral Quasi-pentecostals |
| R | responsiveness: new church members p.a. per million offers |
| R- | Roman Catholic megabloc |
| R2ZAC | Catholic Charismatics |
| R3ZAC | Independent Catholic neocharismatics |
| ra | countries transmitting Christian radio |
| RAC | Roman Catholics (affiliated) |
| RBB | religion barriers, total of |
| re | response (baptisms per million offers) |
| religs | total distinct religions significantly present in country |
| RH | Reform Hindus |
| RIAC | Independent Catholics |
| RJ | Reformist Jews |
| RLB | Rimaypa Lamaists |
| RLEAC | Catholic Evangelicals |
| RN3ZAC | Red Indian/Amerindian neopentecostals |
| RPC | Roman Catholics (professing) |
| Rs | ratio non-native speakers ÷ mother-tongue speakers, % |
| ru | ruralites (country-dwellers), % country |
| RUM | Neo-Sufis |
| rural | ruralites (country-dwellers), % |
| RV2ZAC | Catholic Charismatics (active) |
| Rx2ZAC | Catholic Postcharismatics |
| rY | other minor religionists |
| S | missionaries sent abroad per million affiliated |
| S | Shintoists |
| s. | no scriptures in a second language |
| s1 | Selections sent out per family |
| s2 | Selections sent out per adult |
| s3 | Selections sent out per capita |
| sb | Bible in a second language |
| sB | other sectarian Buddhists |
| SBB | lifestyle barriers, total of |
| sc | script |
| SCC | Secret church members |
| Sel | Selections, existence of |
| SH | Shaivites |
| sHM | other Shia sectarians |
| SJ | Sefardi Jews |
| SJMB | Shingon (Tantrists) Buddhists |
| sL | other Baha'i sectarians |
| SLB | Sakyapa Lamaists |
| SM | Sunnis |
| sn | New Testament in a second language |
| SN | Syncretist neoreligionists |
| SN3ZAC | Arab/Assyrian/Semitic neocharismatics |
| sp | gospel in a second language |
| SRPC | Spiritist Catholics |
| SS | missionaries sent abroad per million population |
| ss | second-language scriptures |
| SSM | Shafiites |

| | |
|---|---|
| sss | circulation of all scriptures, p.a. |
| SSS | Selections (1-8 page leaflets) p.a. per 100 |
| ST | Shamanists |
| SU | Afro-Surinamese religionists |
| sUM | other sectarian Sufis |
| SV | Svetambara Jains |
| sXM | other Islamic movements |
| T | Ethnoreligionists (Tribalists) |
| T- | targeting priority |
| TB | Theravada (Hinayana) Buddhists |
| TBB | total barriers to evangelization |
| TH | Tantrists (Tantrist Hindus) |
| TJ | Samaritans |
| TJMB | Tendaishu Buddhists |
| TN | Theosophists |
| TN3ZAC | other Messianic non-Christian believers in Christ |
| TPJMB | True Pure Land Buddhists |
| TS | Sect Shinto |
| TU | Animistic neocultists |
| Tu | total users of a language (speakers, writers, readers) |
| tu | total users/speakers of a language, % of country |
| ty | type or level of religion |
| u | braille scripture availability |
| U | Spiritists |
| U | unevangelized population, % |
| u | urbanites (city-dwellers), % |
| UC | unaffiliated Christians (nominal), % |
| UJ | Ultra Orthodox |
| UM | Sufis |
| UN | Secret societies |
| UN3ZAC | Afro-Caribbean indigenous pentecostals/charismatics |
| UP | Total unevangelized persons |
| ur | unevangelized remnant, % |
| urban | urbanites (city-dwellers) |
| UU | Afro-Cuban spiritists |
| UZC | Unaffiliated renewal believers |
| V | Jains |
| V | volume of evangelization, % |
| v1 | Visual gospel, viewings per family |
| v2 | Visual gospel, viewings per adult |
| V2ZAC | Mainline active Charismatics |
| v3 | Visual gospel, viewings per capita |
| VB | Vajrayana (Tantrists) |
| VH | Vaishnavites |
| VN | Nativistic cultists |
| VN3ZAC | Vietnamese indigenous neocharismatics |
| VV | Visual gospel, viewers p.a. per 100 |
| W | Total religionists,% |
| w.p.m. | full-time citizen Christian workers p.m.a. |
| W3ZAC | White-led Third-Wavers |
| wa | work among |
| WIAC | White-led Postdenominationalists |
| Wo | World (A, B, C) |
| workers | full-time citizen Christian workers in country |
| WSM | Wahhabites |
| WT | Witchcraft eradicationists |
| WW3ZAC | European/American White-led Neo-Apostolics |
| X | Non-Christians, % |
| x2ZAC | Mainline Postcharismatics |
| xAC | disaffiliated (former) church members |
| xc | cross-cultural mission |
| XM | Islamic schismatics |
| xpAC | nonpracticing church members |
| XW3ZAC | European White-led New Apostolics |
| y | new reader scripture availability |
| Y | Quasireligionists |
| YB | Buddhayana Buddhists |
| YH3ZAC | Hidden other-religionist neocharismatics |
| YHCC | Hidden other religionist believers in Christ |
| YHIAC | Hidden other religionist believers in Christ |
| YN3ZAC | Brazilian/Portuguese grassroots neocharismatics |
| YY | Yezidis |
| Z | GCC as % of AC (affiliated) |
| Z | Zoroastrians |
| ZAC | Pentecostals/Charismatics/Neocharismatics |
| ZC | Renewal believers |
| zH | other sectarian Hindus |
| ZHM | Zaydis |
| zJ | other Jewish movements |
| ZJMB | Zen |
| ZN3ZAC | other Asian indigenous neocharismatics |
| zSM | other Sunni sectarians |
| zT | other ethnoreligionist sectarians |
| zV | other sectarian Jains |

# 3. GLOBAL CODES LISTED BY NAME.

**Table 16–3.  Global codes used throughout *WCT, WCE* and related CD *World Christian database,* alphabetically by name.**

| | |
|---|---|
| J | 'Jesus' film availability |
| 2b | 2nd-language Bible |
| 2p | 2nd-language gospel |
| 2n | 2nd-language NT |
| 2s | 2nd-language scriptures |
| code | 4-letter identification code for a country |
| ad | adults (over 15) as % population |
| Ad | adults (over 15) in a specific population |
| AC | affiliated Christians (church members) |
| AN3ZAC | African indigenous pentecostals/charismatics |
| AU | Afro-American spiritists |
| BU | Afro-Brazilian cultists |
| UN3ZAC | Afro-Caribbean indigenous pentecostals/charismatics |
| CU | Afro-Caribbean religionists |
| UU | Afro-Cuban spiritists |
| SU | Afro-Surinamese religionists |
| AXM | Ahmadis |
| LHM | Alawites |
| alC | alien Christians |
| A2ZAC | Anglican Charismatics |
| CAAC | Anglican Charismatics |
| AV2ZAC | Anglican Charismatics (active) |
| ALEAC | Anglican Evangelicals |
| EAAC | Anglican Evangelicals |
| A- | Anglican megabloc |
| Ax2ZAC | Anglican Postcharismatics |
| A3ZAC | Anglican Third-Wavers |
| AAC | Anglicans |
| APC | Anglicans (professing) |
| TU | Animistic neocultists |
| AT | Animists |
| ACP1ZAC | Apostolic Pentecostals |
| SN3ZAC | Arab/Assyrian/Semitic neocharismatics |
| AJ | Ashkenazi Jews |
| AN | Astrologists |
| a | Atheists |
| AA | Audio gospel, hearers p.a. per 100 |
| a2 | Audio gospel, hearings per adult |
| a3 | Audio gospel, hearings per capita |
| a1 | Audio gospel, hearings per family |
| a | audio scripture availability |
| au | audio scriptures |
| A-V | audio-visual ministries |
| Jayuh | audiovisual resources (five variables) |
| AL | Azali Babis |
| L | Baha'is |
| 2CP1ZAC | Baptistic Pentecostals |
| sb | Bible in a second language |
| B | Bible, existence of. (if no statistics present) |
| b2 | Bibles in use per adult |
| b3 | Bibles in use per capita |
| b1 | Bibles in use per family |
| bpop | births, % p.a. |
| DN3ZAC | Black American independent charismatics |
| BN3ZAC | Black American indigenous pentecostals |
| ON3ZAC | Black American Oneness Apostolics |
| BXM | Black Muslims |
| BY | Bogomils |
| BIHM | Bohoras |
| u | braille scripture availability |
| br | Braille scriptures for blind |
| YN3ZAC | Brazilian/Portuguese grassroots neocharismatics |
| YB | Buddhayana Buddhists |
| BAT | Buddhistic animists |
| B | Buddhists |
| CN | Cargo cultists |
| CRAC | Catholic Charismatics |
| R2ZAC | Catholic Charismatics |
| RV2ZAC | Catholic Charismatics (active) |
| ERAC | Catholic Evangelicals |
| RLEAC | Catholic Evangelicals |
| Rx2ZAC | Catholic Postcharismatics |
| CG | century's church growth, AD 1900-2000, p.a. |
| CIAC | Charismatic Independents |
| 2ZAC | Charismatics (Second-Wavers) |
| CMB | Chinese Buddhists |
| F | Chinese folk-religionists |
| CSI | Christian Safety Index |
| A-C | Christians in World A countries |
| B-C | Christians in World B countries |
| C-C | Christians in World C countries |
| C | Christians, % |
| CRPC | Christopagans |
| sss | circulation of all scriptures, p.a. |
| CP1ZAC | Classical Pentecostals |
| NN3ZAC | Colored/Mixed-race indigenous charismatics |
| Bs | complete Bibles distributed p.a. |
| comp | computers (general purpose) in use |
| LEAC | Conciliar Evangelicals |
| G | Confucianists |
| cc | congregations per million |
| CEAC | Conservative Evangelicals |
| NJ | Conservative Jews |
| CX | contact of Christians with non-Christians |
| ce | cost-effectiveness, $ per baptism |
| ra | countries transmitting Christian radio |
| Npop | Country's population |
| xc | cross-cultural mission |
| CC | crypto-Christians |
| CBB | culture barriers, total of |
| dpop | deaths, % p.a. |

| | |
|---|---|
| P1ZAC | Denominational Pentecostals (White) |
| D= | denominations |
| dd | denominations per million |
| di | dialects |
| DV | Digambara Jains |
| xAC | disaffiliated (former) church members |
| d | discipling stage, % |
| ds | distinctiveness of statistics in totalling |
| doct | doctors (physicians, surgeons) |
| 2AC | doubly-affiliated Christians |
| 4ZAC | doubly-affiliated pentecostals |
| 2RAC | doubly-counted Catholics |
| 2W | doubly-counted religionists |
| 2PC | doubly-professing Christians |
| DXM | Druzes |
| N-activity | earliest and latest NT publication dates |
| B-activity | earliest/latest Bible publication dates |
| P-activity | earliest/latest gospel publication dates |
| EFL | Economic Freedom Level |
| EN3ZAC | Ethnic (Monoethnic) pentecostal churches |
| enu | ethnic non-users as % group's population |
| Enu | ethnic non-users of a language |
| people | ethnolinguistic or race code |
| T | Ethnoreligionists (Tribalists) |
| XW3ZAC | European White-led New Apostolics |
| WW3ZAC | European/American White-led Neo-Apostolics |
| ERPC | Evangelical Catholics |
| EAC | Evangelicals |
| Ev | Evangelicals, % of AC |
| ev | evangelicals, % of country |
| EBB | evangelization barriers, total of |
| E | extent of evangelization (persons evangelized), % |
| ext | extent or number of countries involved |
| fam | families (households) |
| FN3ZAC | Filipino indigenous pentecostals/charismatics |
| FH | Folk/Popular Hindus |
| FB | Folk-Buddhists |
| FJ | Folk-Judaism |
| FM | Folk-Muslims |
| FPW | Folk-religionists |
| FS | Folk-Shintoists |
| F= | Founder (if a name) |
| FQY | Freemasons |
| workers | full-time citizen Christian workers in country |
| w.p.m. | full-time citizen Christian workers p.m.a. |
| FEAC | Fundamentalists |
| Z | GCC as % of AC (affiliated) |
| PN. | gospel & NT only |
| sp | gospel in a second language |
| PNB | gospel, NT, Bible |
| GCC | Great Commission Christians, % country |
| GNPpc | gross national product, US$ p.a.p.c. |
| g | growth of new Christians, % p.a. |
| CN3ZAC | Han Chinese indigenous pentecostals/charismatics |
| HSM | Hanafites |
| BSM | Hanbalites |
| hi | hearing impaired/deaf/signed scriptures |
| deaf | hearing-impaired (deaf) persons |
| h | hearing-impaired scripture availability |
| BHCC | Hidden Buddhist believers in Christ |
| BHIAC | Hidden Buddhist believers in Christ |
| BH3ZAC | Hidden Buddhist neocharismatics |
| HHCC | Hidden Hindu believers in Christ |
| HHIAC | Hidden Hindu believers in Christ |
| HH3ZAC | Hidden Hindu neocharismatics |
| JHCC | Hidden Jewish believers in Christ |
| JHIAC | Hidden Jewish believers in Christ |
| JH3ZAC | Hidden Jewish neocharismatics |
| MHCC | Hidden Muslim believers in Christ |
| MHIAC | Hidden Muslim believers in Christ |
| MH3ZAC | Hidden Muslim neocharismatics |
| H3ZAC | Hidden non-Christian believers in Christ |
| HCC | Hidden non-Christian believers in Christ |
| HIAC | Hidden non-Christian believers in Christ |
| YHCC | Hidden other religionist believers in Christ |
| YHIAC | Hidden other religionist believers in Christ |
| YH3ZAC | Hidden other-religionist neocharismatics |
| HU | High Spiritists |
| HAT | Hinduized animists |
| H | Hindus |
| 3CP1ZAC | Holiness Pentecostals |
| beds | hospital beds, per 10,000 population |
| hosp | hospitals |
| home | household size (persons) |
| hom | households (homes, families) |
| HDI | Human Development Index |
| HFI | Human Freedom Index |
| HSI | Human Suffering Index |
| IKXM | Ibadis |
| AIAC | Independent Anglicans |
| R3ZAC | Independent Catholic neocharismatics |
| RIAC | Independent Catholics |
| EIAC | Independent Evangelicals |
| IEAC | Independent Evangelicals |
| I- | Independent megabloc |
| OIAC | Independent Orthodox |
| PIAC | Independent Protestants |
| IPC | Independents (professing) |
| IAC | Independents/Postdenominationalists/Neo-Apostolics |
| IMB | Indian Buddhists |

| | |
|---|---|
| IN3ZAC | Indian indigenous pentecostals/charismatics |
| iC | indigenous Christians |
| GN3ZAC | Indonesian indigenous pentecostals |
| i | intercessors, intercession |
| Inet | Internet users |
| XM | Islamic schismatics |
| IAT | Islamized animists |
| IHM | Ismailis |
| I3ZAC | Isolated non-Christian Neocharismatics |
| BCC | Isolated radio/TV believers |
| BIAC | Isolated radio/TV believers |
| B3ZAC | Isolated radio/TV Third-Wavers |
| AHM | Ithna-Asharis |
| V | Jains |
| JMB | Japanese Buddhists |
| QN3ZAC | Japanese indigenous pentecostals |
| J | Jews |
| KLB | Kagyudpa Lamaists |
| KJ | Karaites |
| KXM | Kharijites |
| KMB | Korean Buddhists |
| KST | Korean folk-religionists |
| KN3ZAC | Korean indigenous pentecostals/charismatics |
| LAXM | Lahoris |
| LBB | language barriers, total of |
| lang | language code |
| LC | latent (inactive) Christians |
| LN3ZAC | Latino-Hispanic grassroots believers |
| lepers | leprosy, sufferers from |
| SBB | lifestyle barriers, total of |
| Lit | literacy, % |
| L | literary tradition |
| MB | Mahayana Buddhists |
| PXM | Mahdists |
| loc | main country or location involved |
| V2ZAC | Mainline active Charismatics |
| x2ZAC | Mainline Postcharismatics |
| mar-sits | major martyrdom situations across 2,000 years |
| MSM | Malikites |
| MY | Mandeans |
| CmAC | Marginal Charismatics |
| m2ZAC | Marginal Charismatics |
| mV2ZAC | Marginal Charismatics (active) |
| m- | Marginal Christian megabloc |
| mAC | Marginal Christians (affiliated) |
| mPC | Marginal Christians (professing) |
| EmAC | Marginal Evangelicals |
| mEAC | Marginal Evangelicals |
| martyrs | martyrs for Christ (witness, hostility, death) |
| me | mass evangelism |
| HN3ZAC | Messianic Hindu believers in Christ |
| JN3ZAC | Messianic Jewish believers in Christ |
| MN3ZAC | Messianic Muslim believers in Christ |
| MN | Metaphysicalists |
| metro | metrodwellers (in cities over 1 million), % |
| M= | mission agencies |
| mi | mission agencies, total (coded 0-5) |
| MMM | missionaries received per million affiliated |
| MM | missionaries received per million population |
| S | missionaries sent abroad per million affiliated |
| SS | missionaries sent abroad per million population |
| dev | more/less/least-developed countries |
| Mts | mother-tongue speakers (native speakers) |
| mts | mother-tongue speakers as % of country |
| murder | murder rate, per 100,000 p.a. |
| NXM | Muslim Neo-Fundamentalists |
| M | Muslims |
| MIHM | Mustalis |
| NJMB | Nara Buddhists |
| NBB | nationality barriers, total of |
| VN | Nativistic cultists |
| npop | natural population increase, % p.a. |
| b | near-Bible |
| pnb | near-Bible only, for this people |
| p.. | near-gospel only, for this people |
| n | near-NT |
| pn. | near-NT only, for this people |
| p | near-portion, near-gospel |
| NTB | Neo-Buddhists |
| 3ZAC | Neocharismatics (Third-Wavers) |
| NG | Neo-Confucianists |
| NEAC | Neo-Evangelicals |
| NH | Neo-Hindus |
| ET | Neopagans |
| RUM | Neo-Sufis |
| mpop | nett immigrants, % p.a. |
| nrp | New Reader Portions (gospels) |
| y | new reader scripture availability |
| nr | New Reader Scriptures |
| nrs | New Reader Selections |
| sn | New Testament in a second language |
| N | New Testament, existence of |
| NTs | New Testaments distributed p.a. |
| NN | New Testaments distributed p.a. per 100 |
| N | New-Religionists (Neoreligionists) |
| NJMB | Nichiren Shu Buddhists |
| s. | no scriptures in a second language |
| BBIAC | Non-charismatic radio churches |
| X | Non-Christians, % |
| MIAC | Nonhistorical Independents |
| Nns | non-native speakers (2nd-language) |
| nns | non-native speakers as % of country |
| xpAC | nonpracticing |

*Continued opposite*

Table 16–3 concluded

| | church members |
| - | Nonreligionists |
| Q | Nonreligious |
| NB | nonreligious Buddhists |
| blind | nonsighted (blind) persons |
| NN | Nonsyncretist neoreligionists |
| NIAC | Non-White indigenous Christians |
| N3ZAC | Non-White Third-Wavers |
| n2 | NTs in use per adult |
| n3 | NTs in use per capita |
| n1 | NTs in use per family |
| Mi | number of mission agencies |
| G | numerical church growth, % p.a. |
| NLB | Nyingmapa Lamaists |
| ON | Occultists |
| e | offers per capita per year |
| 1P1ZAC | Oneness Pentecostals (White) |
| oo | organizations per million |
| EJ | Oriental Jews |
| OAC | Orthodox (affiliated) |
| OPC | Orthodox (professing) |
| COAC | Orthodox Charismatics |
| O2ZAC | Orthodox Charismatics |
| OV2ZAC | Orthodox Charismatics (active) |
| EOAC | Orthodox Evangelicals |
| OLEAC | Orthodox Evangelicals |
| OJ | Orthodox Jews |
| O- | Orthodox megabloc |
| O3ZAC | Orthodox Third-Wavers |
| ZN3ZAC | other Asian indigenous neocharismatics |
| sL | other Baha'i sectarians |
| zT | other ethnoreligionist sectarians |
| sXM | other Islamic movements |
| zJ | other Jewish movements |
| TN3ZAC | other Messianic non-Christian believers in Christ |
| rY | other minor religionists |
| sB | other sectarian Buddhists |
| zH | other sectarian Hindus |
| zV | other sectarian Jains |
| sUM | other sectarian Sufis |
| sHM | other Shia sectarians |
| zSM | other Sunni sectarians |
| OEC | overt evangelizers |
| PN3ZAC | Pacific/Oceanic indigenous charismatics |
| PN | Paganists |
| PW | Pan-Religionists |
| QY | Parareligionists |
| PZ | Parsis |
| 1ZAC | Pentecostals (First-Wavers) |
| ZAC | Pentecostals/Charismatics/Neocharismatics |
| ppop | people as % of country |
| Peo | peoples in a country |
| p.a. | per annum (per year) |
| p.c. | per capita (per person) |
| p.d. | per diem (per day) |
| p.m. | per million |
| QZAC | Peripheral Quasi-pentecostals |
| ACinc | personal income of church members, $ p.a. |
| GCCinc | personal income of GCCs, $ p.a. |
| PAT | Polytheistic animists |
| PT | Polytheists |
| PPW | Popular religionists |
| PRPC | Popular-religionist Catholics |
| pop | population |
| pop | population (of a people, city, country, continent, world, globe) |
| Ppop | population of an ethnolinguistic people |
| Apop3 | Population of World A countries |
| Apop2 | Population of World A peoples |
| Bpop3 | Population of World B countries |
| Bpop2 | Population of World B peoples |
| Cpop3 | Population of World C countries |
| Cpop2 | Population of World C peoples |
| P.. | Portion (Gospel) only |
| P | Portion (gospel), existence of |
| Ps | Portions (Gospels) distributed p.a. |
| PP | Portions (gospels) distributed p.a. per 100 |
| p2 | Portions (gospels) placed per adult |
| p3 | Portions (gospels) placed per capita |

| p1 | Portions (gospels) placed per family |
| 1QZAC | Postpentecostals |
| prAC | practicing church members |
| 0QZAC | Prepentecostals |
| LAT | Primal religionists |
| PC | professing Christians |
| CPAC | Protestant Charismatics |
| P2ZAC | Protestant Charismatics |
| PV2ZAC | Protestant Charismatics (active) |
| PLEAC | Protestant Conciliar Evangelicals |
| EPAC | Protestant Evangelicals |
| P- | Protestant megabloc |
| PPPC | Protestant popular-religionists |
| Px2ZAC | Protestant Postcharismatics |
| P3ZAC | Protestant Third-Wavers |
| PAC | Protestants (affiliated) |
| PPC | Protestants (professing) |
| pub | published scriptures |
| PJMB | Pure Land (Amida) |
| QAXM | Qadianis |
| NY | Quasi-Christians |
| Y | Quasireligionists |
| educ | rate education rate |
| Rs | ratio non-native speakers ÷ mother-tongue speakers, % |
| CJ | Reconstructionist Jews |
| RN3ZAC | Red Indian/Amerindian neopentecostals |
| RH | Reform Hindus |
| RJ | Reformist Jews |
| RBB | religion barriers, total of |
| ZC | Renewal believers |
| re | response (baptisms per million offers) |
| R | responsiveness: new church members p.a. per million offers |
| RLB | Rimaypa Lamaists |
| R- | Roman Catholic megabloc |
| C= | Roman Catholic religious institutes at work (clerics + brothers + sisters) |
| RAC | Roman Catholics (affiliated) |
| RPC | Roman Catholics (professing) |
| rural | ruralites (country-dwellers), % |
| ru | ruralites (country-dwellers), % country |
| MXM | Sabbateans |
| KH | Saktists |
| SLB | Sakyapa Lamaists |
| TJ | Samaritans |
| OL | Schismatic Baha'is |
| sc | script |
| ss | second-language scriptures |
| SCC | Secret church members |
| UN | Secret societies |
| TS | Sect Shinto |
| SJ | Sefardi Jews |
| SSS | Selections (1-8 page leaflets) p.a. per 100 |
| s2 | Selections sent out per adult |
| s3 | Selections sent out per capita |
| s1 | Selections sent out per family |
| Sel | Selections, existence of |
| FN | Self-Religionists |
| SSM | Shafiites |
| SH | Shaivites |
| ST | Shamanists |
| HM | Shias |
| SJMB | Shingon (Tantrists) Buddhists |
| S | Shintoists |
| HS | Shrine Shinto |
| K | Sikhs |
| SRPC | Spiritist Catholics |
| U | Spiritists |
| UM | Sufis |
| SM | Sunnis |
| SV | Svetambara Jains |
| SN | Syncretist neoreligionists |
| TH | Tantrists (Tantrist Hindus) |
| D | Taoists |
| T- | targeting priority |
| TJMB | Tendaishu Buddhists |
| TN | Theosophists |
| TB | Theravada (Hinayana) Buddhists |

| LB | Tibetan Buddhists (Lamaists) |
| TBB | total barriers to evangelization |
| cit-100 | total cities of over 100,000 |
| cit-50 | total cities of over 50,000 |
| cou | total countries involved |
| religs | total distinct religions significantly present in country |
| EP | Total evangelized persons |
| Gpop | Total global population |
| mega | total megacities (over 1 million each) |
| od | total offers p.d. (per day) |
| W | Total religionists,% |
| UP | Total unevangelized persons |
| Tu | total users of a language (speakers, writers, readers) |
| tu | total users/speakers of a language, % of country |
| TPJMB | True Pure Land Buddhists |
| ty | type or level of religion |
| UJ | Ultra Orthodox |
| UC | unaffiliated Christians (nominal), % |
| UZC | Unaffiliated renewal believers |
| U | unevangelized population, % |
| ur | unevangelized remnant, % |
| urban | urbanites (city-dwellers) |
| u | urbanites (city-dwellers), % |
| VH | Vaishnavites |
| VB | Vajrayana (Tantrists) |
| HH | Vedantists |
| VN3ZAC | Vietnamese indigenous neocharismatics |
| VV | Visual gospel, viewers p.a. per 100 |
| v2 | Visual gospel, viewings per adult |
| v3 | Visual gospel, viewings per capita |
| v1 | Visual gospel, viewings per family |
| V | volume of evangelization, % |
| WSM | Wahhabites |
| WIAC | White-led Postdenominationalists |
| W3ZAC | White-led Third-Wavers |
| WT | Witchcraft eradicationists |
| wa | work among |
| Wo | World (A, B, C) |
| Apop1 | World A individuals |
| aAA | World A individuals in A peoples in A countries |
| aAB | World A individuals in A peoples in B countries |
| aAC | World A individuals in A peoples in C countries |
| aBA | World A individuals in B peoples in A countries |
| aBB | World A individuals in B peoples in B countries |
| aBC | World A individuals in B peoples in C countries |
| aCA | World A individuals in C peoples in A countries |
| aCB | World A individuals in C peoples in B countries |
| aCC | World A individuals in C peoples in C countries |
| Apop | World A population |
| Bpop1 | World B individuals |
| bAA | World B individuals in A peoples in A countries |
| bAB | World B individuals in A peoples in B countries |
| bAC | World B individuals in A peoples in C countries |
| bBA | World B individuals in B peoples in A countries |
| bBB | World B individuals in B peoples in B countries |
| bBC | World B individuals in B peoples in C countries |
| bCA | World B individuals in C peoples in A countries |
| bCB | World B individuals in C peoples in B countries |
| bCC | World B individuals in C peoples in C countries |
| Bpop | World B population |
| Cpop1 | World C individuals |
| cAA | World C individuals in A peoples in A countries |
| cAB | World C individuals in A peoples in B countries |
| cAC | World C individuals in A peoples in C countries |
| cBA | World C individuals in B peoples in A countries |
| cBB | World C individuals in B peoples in B countries |
| cBC | World C individuals in B peoples in C countries |
| cCA | World C individuals in C peoples in A countries |
| cCB | World C individuals in C peoples in B countries |
| cCC | World C individuals in C peoples in C countries |
| Cpop | World C population |
| Begun | year in which entity came into being |
| YY | Yezidis |
| ZHM | Zaydis |
| ZJMB | Zen |
| Z | Zoroastrians |

# 4. STANDARD TERMS AND CODES FOR RELIGIONS.

**Table 16–4.   Standard terms and codes for 85 categories/varieties/meanings of the term 'Christians', also for 100 categories of non-Christians, and also for 9 major overall totals.**

NOTES.

1. *WCE* and *WCT* give to each distinct religious category a unique alphanumeric code. The codes themselves are not employed in the print *WCE* or *WCT* but are used on the related *World Christian database* to facilitate rapid retrieval of wanted information. To assist the user to remember codes useful to him or her, for the most frequently-occurring categories each code in most cases consists of letters similar to the order of words in the category itself. Thus GCC = Great Commission Christians, AAC = Anglican affiliated Christians, AEAC = Anglican Evangelical affiliated Christians, and so on.

2. Categories and subcategories of Christians are not arranged below in alphabetical order, but in an ecclesiastically logical or chronological order. The 4 major Christian categories or standardized ways of enumerating Christians are shown here and in all other tables in boldface type: these are **Christians, professing Christians, affiliated Christians,** and **Great Commission Christians.** By contrast, major categories of non-Christians are however listed alphabetically, but with their subcategories listed in a logical order.

3. Indented categories form part of, and are included in, the unindented category above them. First indentations (indented once) are in all cases complete; their subcategories always add up to their parent category. Second indentations however, although usually complete, are in several cases selected subgroups not intended as a complete breakdown of their unindented parent subcategory.

4. A few subcategories are omitted in Country Tables 1 for countries in the print *WCE*, but are included in the total Table of all categories in the CD *World Christian database.* Three of them are exact repeats, repeated in order to clarify the overall scheme.

5. All other categories are omitted in the published Country Tables 1 where values are zero for the entire period 1900-2025. They all appear, however, in the CD in order to answer search questions like 'How many Orthodox Charismatics were there in this country in 1970?' (Answer: 'None').

6. All lines have statistics as shown in Country Tables 1, derived as shown in the last column below. Lines with no formulas there receive their totals from outside Country Tables 1 (mostly from censuses or Country Tables 2). Lines with formulas are secondary totals derived from other categories in Country Tables 1 or 2. A few are both, in which case the formulas serve as checks on the accuracy and consistency of the overall tables. Note that all the 'doubly-counted', 'doubly-affiliated', 'disaffiliated', and 'doubly-professing' items (2PC, 2AC, xAC, 2RAC, 4ZAC, and 2r) are shown in all tables as negative numbers because they represent a duplication (persons counted, or counting themselves, twice).

7. Non-Christian religions are coded into families and subfamilies. A specific sect in one of these may be identified by having the letter 'z' or 's' (for sect) added before the code.

| # | Code | Category | Formula |
|---|---|---|---|
| 1. | C | **Christians** | C = CC + PC = UC + AC + LC + GCC. |
| 2. | | *PROFESSION* | |
| 3. | CC | crypto-Christians | CC = C - PC = SCC + ICC + HCC. |
| 4. | SCC | Secret church members | SCC = CC - ICC - HCC. |
| 5. | BCC | Isolated radio/TV believers | BCC = BIAC. |
| 6. | HCC | Hidden non-Christian believers in Christ | HCC = HHCC + MHCC + BHCC + JHCC + YHCC. |
| 7. | HHCC | Hidden Hindu believers in Christ | HHCC =HHIAC. |
| 8. | MHCC | Hidden Muslim believers in Christ | MHCC = MHIAC. |
| 9. | BHCC | Hidden Buddhist believers in Christ | BHCC = BHIAC. |
| 10. | JHCC | Hidden Jewish believers in Christ | JHCC = JHIAC. |
| 11. | YHCC | Hidden other religionist believers in Christ | YHCC = YHIAC. |
| 12. | PC | **professing Christians** | PC = APC + IPC + mPC + OPC + PPC + RPC + 2PC. |
| 13. | APC | Anglicans | |
| 14. | IPC | Independents | |
| 15. | mPC | Marginal Christians | |
| 16. | OPC | Orthodox | |
| 17. | PPC | Protestants | |
| 18. | PPPC | Popular-religionists | |
| 19. | RPC | Roman Catholics | |
| 20. | SRPC | Spiritist Catholics | |
| 21. | CRPC | Christopagans | |
| 22. | ERPC | Evangelical Catholics | |
| 23. | PRPC | Popular-religionist Catholics | |
| 24. | 2PC | doubly-professing Christians | 2PC = PC - (APC + IPC + mPC + OPC + PPC + RPC). This sum is always negative. |
| 25. | | *AFFILIATION* | |
| 26. | UC | unaffiliated Christians | UC = C - AC. |
| 27. | AC | **affiliated Christians (church members)** | AC = AAC + IAC + mAC + OAC + PAC + RAC + 2AC + xAC. |
| 28. | pAC | practising church members | pAC = GCC + eAC. |
| 29. | xpAC | nonpracticing church members | xpAC = AC - pAC. |
| 30. | AAC | Anglicans | |
| 31. | EAAC | Anglican Evangelicals | |
| 32. | CAAC | Anglican Charismatics | CAAC = AV2ZAC + Ax2ZAC. |
| 33. | IAC | Independents/Postdenominationalists/Neo-Apostolics | IAC = NIAC + WIAC + OIAC + RIAC + AIAC + PIAC + BIAC + HIAC + MIAC. |
| 34. | EIAC | Independent Evangelicals | EIAC = IEAC |
| 35. | NIAC | Non-White indigenous Christians | NIAC = N3ZAC. |
| 36. | WIAC | White-led Postdenominationalists | WIAC = W3ZAC. |
| 37. | OIAC | Independent Orthodox | |
| 38. | RIAC | Independent Catholics | |
| 39. | AIAC | Independent Anglicans | |
| 40. | PIAC | Independent Protestants | |
| 41. | BIAC | Isolated radio/TV believers | BIAC = B3ZAC + BBIAC. |
| 42. | BBIAC | Non-charismatic radio churches | BBIAC = I-rad. |
| 43. | HIAC | Hidden non-Christian believers in Christ | HIAC = HHIAC + MHIAC + BHIAC + JHIAC + YHIAC. |
| 44. | HHIAC | Hidden Hindu believers in Christ | HHIAC = I-Hin. |
| 45. | MHIAC | Hidden Muslim believers in Christ | MHIAC = I-Mus. |
| 46. | BHIAC | Hidden Buddhist believers in Christ | BHIAC = I-Bud. |
| 47. | JHIAC | Hidden Jewish believers in Christ | JHIAC = I-Jew. |
| 48. | YHIAC | Hidden other religionist believers in Christ | YHIAC = I-rel. |
| 49. | MIAC | Nonhistorical Independents | |
| 50. | CIAC | Charismatic Independents | CIAC = 3ZAC |
| 51. | mAC | Marginal Christians | |
| 52. | EmAC | Marginal Evangelicals | |
| 53. | CmAC | Marginal Charismatics | |
| 54. | OAC | Orthodox | |
| 55. | EOAC | Orthodox Evangelicals | |
| 56. | COAC | Orthodox Charismatics | |
| 57. | PAC | Protestants | |
| 58. | EPAC | Evangelicals | |
| 59. | 1ZAC | Pentecostals | |
| 60. | CPAC | Protestant Charismatics | CPAC = PV2ZAC + Px2ZAC. |
| 61. | RAC | Roman Catholics | |
| 62. | ERAC | Catholic Evangelicals | |
| 63. | CRAC | Catholic Charismatics | CRAC = RV2ZAC + Rx2ZAC. |
| 64. | 2RAC | doubly-counted Catholics | 2RAC = RAC minus the sum of all members enumerated separately by dioceses. Sum is always negative. |
| 65. | 2AC | doubly-affiliated | 2AC = AC - (AAC + IAC + mAC + OAC + PAC + RAC + xAC). This total is always negative. |
| 66. | xAC | disaffiliated | Former Christians (still on church rolls) who now regard themselves as non-Christians or are dead. Negative. |
| 67. | | *Trans-megabloc groupings (also included above):* | |
| 68. | eAC | evangelicals | eAC = GCC + pAC. |
| 69. | EAC | Evangelicals | EAC = CEAC + NEAC + LEAC + IEAC + mEAC. |
| 70. | CEAC | Conservative Evangelicals | 100% of the denomination is Evangelical |
| 71. | NEAC | Neo-Evangelicals | 50-99% of the denomination is Evangelical |
| 72. | LEAC | Conciliar Evangelicals | LEAC = ALEAC + OLEAC + PLEAC + RLEAC. |
| 73. | ALEAC | Anglican Evangelicals | |
| 74. | OLEAC | Orthodox Evangelicals | |
| 75. | PLEAC | Protestant Conciliar Evangelicals | 0-49% of the denomination is Evangelical |
| 76. | RLEAC | Catholic Evangelicals | |
| 77. | FEAC | Fundamentalists | FEAC occurs in CEAC, NEAC and PLEAC. |
| 78. | IEAC | Independent Evangelicals | |

*Continued opposite*

*Table 16–4 continued*

|  |  |  | |
|---|------|-------------|---|
| 79. | mEAC | Marginal Evangelicals | |
| 80. | ZC | Renewal believers | ZC = ZAC + QZAC + ZUC |
| 81. | QZAC | Peripheral Quasi-pentecostals | QZAC = 0QZAC + 1QZAC |
| 82. | 0QZAC | Prepentecostals | |
| 83. | 1QZAC | Postpentecostals | |
| 84. | ZAC | Pentecostals/Charismatics/Neocharismatics | ZAC = 1ZAC + 2ZAC + 3ZAC + 4ZAC. |
| 85. | 1ZAC | Pentecostals (First-Wavers) | 1ZAC = P1ZAC (= members of bodies in Country Tables 2 whose column 3 code begins 'P-Pe'). |
| 86. | P1ZAC | Denominational Pentecostals (White) | P1ZAC = CP1ZAC + OP1ZAC. |
| 87. | CP1ZAC | Classical Pentecostals | CP1ZAC = Original, Trinitarian, largely-White bodies, whose column 3 code begins 'P-Pe' but excludes 'P-Pe1'. |
| 88. | 3CP1ZAC | Holiness Pentecostals | |
| 89. | 2CP1ZAC | Baptistic Pentecostals | |
| 90. | ACP1ZAC | Apostolic Pentecostals | |
| 91. | 1P1ZAC | Oneness Pentecostals | OP1ZAC = Original, 'Jesus Only', largely-White bodies, whose column 3 code = 'P-Pe1'. |
| 92. | 2ZAC | Charismatics (Second-Wavers) | 2ZAC = V2ZAC + x2ZAC = A2ZAC + R2ZAC + O2ZAC + P2ZAC + m2ZAC. |
| 93. | V2ZAC | Mainline active Charismatics | V2ZAC = AV2ZAC + RV2ZAC + mV2ZAC + OV2ZAC + PV2ZAC. |
| 94. | AV2ZAC | Anglican Charismatics (active) | |
| 95. | RV2ZAC | Catholic Charismatics (active) | |
| 96. | mV2ZAC | Marginal Charismatics (active) | |
| 97. | OV2ZAC | Orthodox Charismatics (active) | |
| 98. | PV2ZAC | Protestant Charismatics (active) | |
| 99. | x2ZAC | Mainline Postcharismatics | x2ZAC = Ax2ZAC + Px2ZAC + Rx2ZAC. |
| 100. | Ax2ZAC | Anglican Postcharismatics | Ax2ZAC = CAAC - AV2ZAC. |
| 101. | Px2ZAC | Protestant Postcharismatics | Px2ZAC = CPAC - PV2ZAC. |
| 102. | Rx2ZAC | Catholic Postcharismatics | Rx2ZAC = CRAC - RV2ZAC. |
| 103. | A2ZAC | Anglican Charismatics | A2ZAC = CAAC. |
| 104. | R2ZAC | Catholic Charismatics | R2ZAC = CRAC. |
| 105. | O2ZAC | Orthodox Charismatics | O2ZAC = COAC. |
| 106. | P2ZAC | Protestant Charismatics | P2ZAC = CPAC. |
| 107. | m2ZAC | Marginal Charismatics | |
| 108. | 3ZAC | Neocharismatics (Third-Wavers) | 3ZAC = N3ZAC + O3ZAC + A3ZAC +P3ZAC + R3ZAC + W3ZAC + I3ZAC + r3ZAC + H3ZAC. |
| 109. | N3ZAC | Non-White indigenous Neocharismatics | N3ZAC = bodies whose column 3 begins 'I-3', ends with capital A to V, Y, or Z; plus individual Neocharismatics. |
| 110. | | *Last code letter, A to Z:* | |
| 111. | AN3ZAC | African indigenous pentecostals/charismatics | A |
| 112. | UN3ZAC | Afro-Caribbean indigenous pentecostals/charismatics | U |
| 113. | SN3ZAC | Arab/Assyrian/Semitic neocharismatics | S |
| 114. | DN3ZAC | Black American independent charismatics | D |
| 115. | BN3ZAC | Black American indigenous pentecostals | B |
| 116. | ON3ZAC | Black American Oneness Apostolics | O |
| 117. | YN3ZAC | Brazilian/Portuguese grassroots neocharismatics | Y |
| 118. | NN3ZAC | Colored/Mixed-race indigenous charismatics | N |
| 119. | EN3ZAC | Ethnic (Monoethnic) pentecostal churches | E |
| 120. | FN3ZAC | Filipino indigenous pentecostals/charismatics | F |
| 121. | CN3ZAC | Han Chinese indigenous pentecostals/charismatics | C |
| 122. | IN3ZAC | Indian indigenous pentecostals/charismatics | I |
| 123. | GN3ZAC | Indonesian indigenous pentecostals | G |
| 124. | QN3ZAC | Japanese indigenous pentecostals | Q |
| 125. | KN3ZAC | Korean indigenous pentecostals/charismatics | K |
| 126. | LN3ZAC | Latino-Hispanic grassroots believers | L |
| 127. | HN3ZAC | Messianic Hindu believers in Christ | H |
| 128. | JN3ZAC | Messianic Jewish believers in Christ | J |
| 129. | MN3ZAC | Messianic Muslim believers in Christ | M |
| 130. | PN3ZAC | Pacific/Oceanic indigenous charismatics | P |
| 131. | RN3ZAC | Red Indian/Amerindian neopentecostals | R |
| 132. | VN3ZAC | Vietnamese indigenous neocharismatics | V |
| 133. | ZN3ZAC | other Asian indigenous neocharismatics | Z |
| 134. | TN3ZAC | other Messianic non-Christian believers in Christ | T |
| 135. | W3ZAC | White-led Independent Postdenominationalists | W3ZAC = bodies whose column 3 begins 'I-3', ends with W or X; plus individuals in noncharismatic bodies. |
| 136. | WW3ZAC | European/American White-led Neo-Apostolics | W |
| 137. | XW3ZAC | European White-led New Apostolics | X |
| 138. | O3ZAC | Independent Orthodox neocharismatics | |
| 139. | R3ZAC | Independent Catholic neocharismatics | |
| 140. | A3ZAC | Independent Anglican neocharismatics | |
| 141. | P3ZAC | Independent Protestant neocharismatics | |
| 142. | I3ZAC | Nonhistorical Independent neocharismatics | |
| 143. | B3ZAC | Isolated radio/TV neocharismatics | |
| 144. | H3ZAC | Hidden non-Christian believers in Christ | |
| 145. | HH3ZAC | Hidden Hindu neocharismatics | |
| 146. | MH3ZAC | Hidden Muslim neocharismatics | |
| 147. | BH3ZAC | Hidden Buddhist neocharismatics | |
| 148. | JH3ZAC | Hidden Jewish neocharismatics | |
| 149. | YH3ZAC | Hidden other-religionist neocharismatics | |
| 150. | 4ZAC | doubly-counted 1st-/2nd-/3rd-Wavers | 4ZAC = ZAC - (1ZAC + 2ZAC + 3ZAC). This sum is always negative. |
| 151. | UZC | Unaffiliated renewal believers | |
| 152. | | *MISSION* | |
| 153. | LC | latent (inactive) Christians | LC = C - GCC = UC + xpAC. |
| 154. | xpAC | nonpracticing church members | xpAC = AC - pAC. |
| 155. | UC | unaffiliated Christians | UC = LC - xpAC. |
| 156. | GCC | **Great Commission Christians** | |
| 157. | OEC | overt evangelizers | OEC = GCC - CC. |
| 158. | CC | covert evangelizers | |
| 159. | | *CULTURE* | |
| 160. | iC | indigenous Christians | |
| 161. | aIC | alien Christians | |
| 162. | | *GEOSTATUS* | |
| 163. | A-C | World A Christians | A-C = CAA + CBA + CCA. |
| 164. | B-C | World B Christians | B-C = CAB + CBB + CCB. |
| 165. | C-C | World C Christians | C-C = CAC + CBC + CCC. |
| 166. | X | **NON-CHRISTIANS** | |
| 167. | a | Atheists | |
| 168. | L | Baha'is | |
| 169. | OL | Schismatic Baha'is | |
| 170. | AL | Azali Babis | |
| 171. | sL | other Baha'i sectarians | Note: 's' (or 'z') before a code refers to a specific sect of that code's religion |
| 172. | B | Buddhists | B = MB + TB + LB + VB + BB + FB + NB + YB + sB. |
| 173. | MB | Mahayana Buddhists | MB = IMB + CMB + KMB + JMB + TMB + NMB + PMB + ZMB + SMB . |
| 174. | IMB | Indian Buddhists | |
| 175. | CMB | Chinese Buddhists | |
| 176. | KMB | Korean Buddhists | |
| 177. | JMB | Japanese Buddhists | |
| 178. | NJMB | Nichiren Shu Buddhists | |
| 179. | TJMB | Tendaishu Buddhists | |
| 180. | NJMB | Nara Buddhists | |
| 181. | PJMB | Pure Land (Amida) Buddhists | |
| 182. | TPJMB | True Pure Land Buddhists | |
| 183. | ZJMB | Zen Buddhists | |

*Continued overleaf*

*Table 16-4 continued*

| | | | |
|---|---|---|---|
| 184. | SJMB | Shingon (Tantrists) Buddhists | |
| 185. | TB | Theravada (Hinayana) Buddhists | |
| 186. | NTB | Neo-Buddhists | |
| 187. | LB | Tibetan Buddhists (Lamaists) | |
| 188. | KLB | Kagyudpa Lamaists | |
| 189. | NLB | Nyingmapa Lamaists | |
| 190. | RLB | Rimaypa Lamaists | |
| 191. | SLB | Sakyapa Lamaists | |
| 192. | VB | Vajrayana (Tantrists) Buddhists | |
| 193. | YB | Buddhayana Buddhists | |
| 194. | FB | Folk-Buddhists | |
| 195. | NB | nonreligious Buddhists | |
| 196. | sB | other sectarian Buddhists | |
| 197. | F | Chinese folk-religionists | |
| 198. | G | Confucianists | |
| 199. | NG | Neo-Confucianists | |
| 200. | T | Ethnoreligionists (Tribalists) | $T = AT + NT + PT + ST + WT + zT.$ |
| 201. | AT | Animists | $AT = LAT + HAT + IAT + BAT + PAT.$ |
| 202. | LAT | Primal religionists | |
| 203. | HAT | Hinduized animists | |
| 204. | IAT | Islamized animists | |
| 205. | BAT | Buddhistic animists | |
| 206. | PAT | Polytheistic animists | |
| 207. | ET | Neopagans | |
| 208. | PT | Polytheists | |
| 209. | ST | Shamanists | |
| 210. | KST | Korean folk-religionists | |
| 211. | WT | Witchcraft eradicationists | |
| 212. | zT | other ethnoreligionist sectarians | |
| 213. | H | Hindus | $H = HH + VH + SH + KH + NH + RH + TH + FH + zH.$ |
| 214. | HH | Vedantists | |
| 215. | VH | Vaishnavites | |
| 216. | SH | Shaivites | |
| 217. | KH | Saktists | |
| 218. | NH | Neo-Hindus | |
| 219. | RH | Reform Hindus | |
| 220. | TH | Tantrists (Tantrist Hindus) | |
| 221. | FH | Folk/Popular Hindus | |
| 222. | zH | other sectarian Hindus | |
| 223. | V | Jains | $V = DV + SV + zV.$ |
| 224. | DV | Digambara Jains | |
| 225. | SV | Svetambara Jains | |
| 226. | zV | other sectarian Jains | |
| 227. | J | Jews | $J = AJ + EJ + SJ + + RJ + OJ + CJ + KJ + NJ + TJ + UJ + FJ + zJ.$ |
| 228. | AJ | Ashkenazis | |
| 229. | EJ | Oriental Jews | |
| 230. | SJ | Sefardis | |
| 231. | RJ | Reformists | |
| 232. | OJ | Orthodox | |
| 233. | CJ | Reconstructionists | |
| 234. | KJ | Karaites | |
| 235. | NJ | Conservative Jews | |
| 236. | TJ | Samaritans | |
| 237. | UJ | Ultra Orthodox | |
| 238. | FJ | Folk-Judaism | |
| 239. | zJ | other Jewish movements | |
| 240. | M | Muslims | $M = SM + HM + XM.$ |
| 241. | SM | Sunnis | $SM = HSM + SSM + MSM + BSM + WSM + zSM.$ |
| 242. | HSM | Hanafites | |
| 243. | SSM | Shafiites | |
| 244. | MSM | Malikites | |
| 245. | BSM | Hanbalites | |
| 246. | WSM | Wahhabites | |
| 247. | zSM | other Sunni sectarians | |
| 248. | UM | Sufis | |
| 249. | RUM | Neo-Sufis | |
| 250. | sUM | other sectarian Sufis | |
| 251. | HM | Shias | $HM = AHM + IHM + ZHM + LHM + sHM.$ |
| 252. | AHM | Ithna-Asharis | |
| 253. | IHM | Ismailis | |
| 254. | BIHM | Bohoras | |
| 255. | MIHM | Mustalis | |
| 256. | ZHM | Zaydis | |
| 257. | LHM | Alawites | |
| 258. | sHM | other Shia sectarians | |
| 259. | XM | Islamic schismatics | $XM = AXM + KXM + DXM + BXM + PXM + MXM + NXM + YXM + sXM.$ |
| 260. | AXM | Ahmadis | |
| 261. | LAXM | Lahoris | |
| 262. | QAXM | Qadianis | |
| 263. | KXM | Kharijites | |
| 264. | IKXM | Ibadis | |
| 265. | DXM | Druzes | |
| 266. | BXM | Black Muslims | |
| 267. | MXM | Sabbateans | |
| 268. | PXM | Mahdists | |
| 269. | NXM | Neo-Fundamentalists | |
| 270. | sXM | other Islamic sectarians | |
| 271. | FM | Folk-Muslims | |
| 272. | N | New-Religionists (Neoreligionists) | $N = SN + NN + AN + MN + PN + TN + UN + ON + VN + CN + FN.$ |
| 273. | SN | Syncretist neoreligionists | |
| 274. | NN | Nonsyncretist neoreligionists | |
| 275. | AN | Astrologists | |
| 276. | MN | Metaphysicalists | |
| 277. | PN | Paganists | |
| 278. | TN | Theosophists | |
| 279. | UN | Secret societies | |
| 280. | ON | Occultists | |
| 281. | VN | Nativistic cultists | |
| 282. | CN | Cargo cultists | |
| 283. | FN | Self-Religionists | |
| 284. | Q | Nonreligious | |
| 285. | PW | Pan-Religionists | PW are also included in other religions |
| 286. | FPW | Folk-religionists | |
| 287. | PPW | Popular religionists | |
| 288. | S | Shintoists | |
| 289. | HS | Shrine Shinto | |
| 290. | TS | Sect Shinto | |
| 291. | FS | Folk-Shintoists | |
| 292. | K | Sikhs | |

*Continued opposite*

*Table 16–4 concluded*

| 293. | U | Spiritists |
|---|---|---|
| 294. | AU | Afro-American spiritists |
| 295. | BU | Afro-Brazilian cultists |
| 296. | CU | Afro-Caribbean religionists |
| 297. | SU | Afro-Surinamese religionists |
| 298. | TU | Animistic neocultists |
| 299. | UU | Afro-Cuban spiritists |
| 300. | HU | High Spiritists |
| 301. | D | Taoists |
| 302. | Z | Zoroastrians |
| 303. | PZ | Parsis |
| 304. | Y | Quasireligionists |
| 305. | BY | Bogomils |
| 306. | MY | Mandeans |
| 307. | NY | Quasi-Christians |
| 308. | QY | Parareligionists |
| 309. | FQY | Freemasons |
| 310. | YY | Yezidis |
| 311. | rY | other minor religionists |

| 312. | 2W | doubly-counted religionists | $2W = W - (a + L + B + Y + G + T + H + V + J + M + N + Q + S + F + K + U + D + Z)$. Sum always negative. |
|---|---|---|---|

|  |  | **TOTALS** |  |
|---|---|---|---|
| 313. |  |  | Defined as above. |
| 314. | C | **Christians** | $X = a + L + B + Y + G + T + H + V + J + M + N + Q + S + F + K + U + D + Z + 2W$. |
| 315. | X | **Non-Christians** | $W = C + X - a - Q + 2W = pop - a - Q$. |
| 316. | W | **Religionists** |  |
| 317. | - | Nonreligionists |  |
| 318. | pop | population |  |
| 319. | Ppop | A people's population |  |
| 320. | Npop | Country's population |  |
| 321. | Apop | World A population |  |
| 322. | Bpop | World B population |  |
| 323. | Cpop | World C population |  |
| 324. | Gpop | Total global population |  |

|  |  | **EVANGELIZATION** |  |
|---|---|---|---|
| 325. |  |  |  |
| 326. | EP | Total evangelized persons |  |
| 327. | UP | Total unevangelized persons | $UP = pop - EP$. |

|  |  | **GEOSTATUS** |  |
|---|---|---|---|
| 328. |  |  | $Apop1 = UP$. |
| 329. | Apop1 | World A individuals | $Bpop1 = pop - UP - C$. |
| 330. | Bpop1 | World B individuals | $Cpop1 = C$. |
| 331. | Cpop1 | World C individuals |  |

|  |  | **PEOPLES AND COUNTRIES** |
|---|---|---|
| 332. |  |  |
| 333. | Apop2 | Population of World A peoples |
| 334. | Bpop2 | Population of World B peoples |
| 335. | Cpop2 | Population of World C peoples |

| 336. | Apop3 | Population of World A countries |
|---|---|---|
| 337. | Bpop3 | Population of World B countries |
| 338. | Cpop3 | Population of World C countries |

|  |  | **LOCATION OF INDIVIDUALS** |
|---|---|---|
| 339. |  |  |
| 340. |  | First column letter in list below = World A, B, or C individuals (shown by lowercase letter a, b, or c) |
| 341. |  | Second column letter = who are also within World A/B/C peoples (shown by capital letter) |
| 342. |  | Third column letter = who are also within World A/B/C countries (shown by capital letter) |

| 343. | aAA | World A individuals in World A peoples in World A countries |
|---|---|---|
| 344. | aAB | World A individuals in World A peoples in World B countries |
| 345. | aAC | World A individuals in World A peoples in World C countries |
| 346. | aBA | World A individuals in World B peoples in World A countries |
| 347. | aBB | World A individuals in World B peoples in World B countries |
| 348. | aBC | World A individuals in World B peoples in World C countries |
| 349. | aCA | World A individuals in World C peoples in World A countries |
| 350. | aCB | World A individuals in World C peoples in World B countries |
| 351. | aCC | World A individuals in World C peoples in World C countries |
| 352. | bAA | World B individuals in World A peoples in World A countries |
| 353. | bAB | World B individuals in World A peoples in World B countries |
| 354. | bAC | World B individuals in World A peoples in World C countries |
| 355. | bBA | World B individuals in World B peoples in World A countries |
| 356. | bBB | World B individuals in World B peoples in World B countries |
| 357. | bBC | World B individuals in World B peoples in World C countries |
| 358. | bCA | World B individuals in World C peoples in World A countries |
| 359. | bCB | World B individuals in World C peoples in World B countries |
| 360. | bCC | World B individuals in World C peoples in World C countries |
| 361. | cAA | World C individuals in World A peoples in World A countries |
| 362. | cAB | World C individuals in World A peoples in World B countries |
| 363. | cAC | World C individuals in World A peoples in World C countries |
| 364. | cBA | World C individuals in World B peoples in World A countries |
| 365. | cBB | World C individuals in World B peoples in World B countries |
| 366. | cBC | World C individuals in World B peoples in World C countries |
| 367. | cCA | World C individuals in World C peoples in World A countries |
| 368. | cCB | World C individuals in World C peoples in World B countries |
| 369. | cCC | World C individuals in World C peoples in World C countries |

# 5. COUNTRY TABLES 1.

## Table 16–5.    Meanings of *WCE* Country Tables 1.  Religious adherents in each country, AD 1900-2025.

The term adherents refers to the whole de facto (present-in-area) resident population—men, women, children and infants, nationals and expatriates (citizens and aliens), armed services, alien troops, nomadic groups, refugees and so on.

### Brief summary of the 17 columns
The columns are not numbered 1–17 in the tables themselves, but are numbered below here to assist in identifying particular columns. In the Table 1-1 (Part 1), 2 additional columns are added for the year AD 2050, and another for number of countries involved.
1. Major religions, listed in order of numerical size in AD 2000, with indented subdivisions
2. Adherents in the year 1900
3. Adherents in 1900 as % total population then
4. Adherents in mid-1970
5. Adherents in mid-1970 as % total population then
6. Adherents in mid-1990
7. Adherents in mid-1990 as % total population then
8-11. Annual change, 1990-2000; average long-term trend over the decade
8. Annual natural population increase among adherents, 1990-2000 (biological increase (births minus deaths) plus net immigration)
9. Annual conversion (or supranatural) increase (+ or -) to adherents, 1990-2000 (computed as col. 10 minus col. 8)
10. Total annual increase (+ or -) of adherents, 1990-2000 (= col. 8 plus col. 9) (computed as col. 14 minus col. 6, divided by 10)
11. Rate of change of adherents, 1990-2000, as % per year (= col. 14 divided by col. 6, raised to the power of 1/10, minus 1, times 100)
12. Adherents in mid-1995
13. Adherents in mid-1995 as % total population then
14. Adherents in mid-2000
15. Adherents in mid-2000 as % total population then
16. Adherents in the year 2025 (assuming current trends continue)

17. Adherents in 2025 as % total population then

### Definitions of various religious categories
Indented categories, in the listing below and in the tables, are sub-divisions of categories less indented.

Note our 3 basic equations concerning definitions of Christians:
(1) Total 'Christians' = professing Christians + crypto-Christians,
    which also     = affiliated Christians + unaffiliated Christians
(2) Total 'affiliated'  = affiliated Roman Catholics + affiliated Protestants + affiliated Orthodox + affiliated Anglicans + affiliated marginal Christians + affiliated Independents, *minus* doubly-affiliated, *minus* disaffiliated.
(3) Total 'affiliated'  = total practising Christians + non-practising Christians.

Note also that the first 9 categories below always (in Tables 1) refer to aggregate totals for all denominations of Christians (in all 6 major ecclesiastico-cultural megablocs: Roman Catholic, Protestant, etc) in the whole country.

**Percentages.** All columns headed % in Country Tables 1 refer to percentages of the total population of the country.
**Footnotes.** The notes below Country Tables 1 consist of (1) a note on columns and rows, (2) source data from any national population censuses of religion or public-opinion polls, and (3) NOTES ON RELIGIONS elaborating on, or giving additional data on, various categories in the table, these being listed in alphabetical order. If no footnote is given for a particular Christian category (e.g. 'Marginal Christians', 'Black/Third-World indigenous'), details of how the totals are arrived at may be studied in Country Table 2 for the country.

# 6. COUNTRY TABLES 2.

## Table 16–6.    Meanings of *WCE* Country Tables 2.  Organized churches and denominations in each country.

### Brief summary of the 10 columns
In all Country Tables 2, the columns are always numbered 1-10.

Column:

| | | |
|---|---|---|
| 1. | Name | Official name of church, denomination or diocese; names in boldface (heavy) type are churches each with over 10% of the country's affiliated Christians. |
| 2. | Begun | Year when body was begun (or re-begun) permanently in this country (major significant date usually given). |
| 3. | Type | Ecclesiastical type: major ecclesiastico-cultural megabloc, followed after hyphen by ecclesiastical tradition. |
| 4. | Councils | Conciliarism: membership in councils (confessional, international, continental, regional, national). |
| 5. | Congs | Congregations (places of regular worship), 1995 or latest available date. |
| 6. | Adults | Adult church members (over 15 years) on rolls (communicants or full members, often with probationary or baptized non-communicant members), 1995. |
| 7. | Aff 1970 | Total affiliated church membership in 1970. |
| 8. | Affiliated | Total church membership in 1995 (on average) or latest available date; total church member community, or inclusive membership, or total constituency (adults, children, infants, catechumens, adherents, members under discipline, etc) on the church's books or records, or known to the church (this column always includes those in column 6). |
| 9. | G% | Church growth rate, % per year, over 25-year period 1970-1995, on exponential assumption. |
| 10. | Notes | Names, notes and other statistics, covering descriptive data as available. |

The following sections on 4 pages are the codes and abbreviations used in columns 1, 3, 4 and 10. The codes and statistics used in columns 3-7 are all mutually exclusive (i.e. each body belongs to only the type of council shown, and not to others; and individual congregations and Christians are enumerated only once in each Country Table 2, under a single body; in those cases where Christians are affiliated to 2 or more bodies, this is corrected by including them also in Doubly-affiliated).

*Continued opposite*

Table 16–6 continued

## COLUMN 1: NAMES OF BODIES

*(1) Abbreviations in names of bodies*

In order to reduce names to a manageable length, the following standard abbreviations are used when necessary in the lists. In addition, the 3-letter abbreviations in column 3 may sometimes be employed (e.g. Bap, Met, Ref). All names are alphabetized in the listings on their unabbreviated versions.

| | | | | | |
|---|---|---|---|---|---|
| Adv | Adventist | Epis | Episcopal | Luth | Lutheran, Lutherische(e), Luthérien(ne) |
| Apost, Ap | Apostolic, Apostolica | Ev | Evangelical, Evangélique(s), Evangelische(e,-er), Evangélica(s, -o, -os) | Meth | Methodist |
| Asoc | Asociación | | | Min | Ministries, Ministerial |
| Assem | Assemblies | Ex | Exarchate | Miss, Mis | Mission, Misión |
| Assoc, As | Association | Fed | Federation, Federcion | Nac | Nacional |
| Autonom | Autonomous | Fell | Fellowship | Orth | Orthodox(e) |
| Bapt | Baptist | Herm | Hermanos | Patr | Patriarchate |
| Cath | Catholic | Ig, Igl(s) | Igreja, Iglesia(s) (=Church(es)) | Pente | Pentecostal |
| Ch | Church (in Italian, Chiesa) | Indep | Independent, Independiente(s) | Presb | Presbyterian, Presbiteriana |
| Chr | Christian, Chrétien(ne), Christliche | Int | International | Ref | Reformed |
| Chs | Churches | Intern(at) | International(e) | Soc | Society |
| Conf | Conference | I(s) | Island(s); occasionally (in Spanish or Portuguese) Iglesia, Igreja | Syn | Synod |
| Cong(r,s) | Congregation, Congregación | | | Syna | Synagogue(s) |
| Conv | Convention, Convención | JC, J-C, CJ | Jesus Christ, Jésus-Christ, Jesu Cristo, Jesucristo, Cristo Jesus | Un | Union, Unión |
| Cri | Cristiana | | | | |
| E, Egl(s) | Eglise(s) (=Church(es)) | K | Kirche (Church) | | |

Other initials in names of bodies refer either to the country concerned (A = Austria, B = Belgium, etc), or to details explained at the end of the church's line in the table or in the notes beneath the table.

*(2) Dioceses, jurisdictions and other sub-divisions.*

| | | | | | |
|---|---|---|---|---|---|
| AA | apostolic administration | EP | ecumenical patriarchate | R | region (apostolic or conciliar) |
| AD | archdiocese | EPr | ecclesiastical province | RN | priory nullius |
| AN | abbey nullius | EPi | episcopal area | S | synod |
| C | catholicate (catholicossate), diocese of catholicos | J | jurisdiction | UD | united diocese |
| CD | church district | M | metropolitan archdiocese or see; metropolia (when superior to D) | UDs | united dioceses |
| Co | Community (communauté) (used only in Zaire Table 2) | | | V | vicariate |
| | | MV | military vicariate or ordinariate | VA | vicariate apostolic |
| Con | conference | m | mission (sui juris) | VP | patriarchal vicariate |
| CR | conciliar region (regione conciliare) | O | ordinariate | : | (at end of a name) composite body whose statistics are the total of its components shown below it |
| D | diocese, eparchy | P | patriarchate, patriarchal diocese | | |
| E | exarchate | PA | prefecture apostolic | | |
| EA | exarchate apostolic | PE | patriarchal exarchate | ( ) | jurisdiction based in another country, of which this body is a part |
| EC | episcopal commissariat | PN | prelature (prelacy) nullius | | |
| EM | exarchical monastery | Pro | province | | |

## COLUMN 3: ECCLESIASTICAL TYPE (4 letter code)

1st letter: Megabloc (Stream) (definitions are given in *WCT* Part 30 or *WCE* Part 12): A, O, R = Liturgical Pedobaptist (infant-baptizing); I, P, m = partly Non-Liturgical, partly Baptist (adult baptism only).

| | |
|---|---|
| A | Anglican (Episcopalian) |
| I | Independent/Postdenominationalist/Neo-Apostolic (Non-White or Black/Third-World indigenous, White-led Postdenominationalist) |
| m | Marginal Christian (para-Christian of Western origin) |
| O | Orthodox (Eastern, Oriental, or Nestorian/Assyrian) |
| P | Protestant (sometimes called Evangelical) |
| R | Roman Catholic |

2nd–4th letters (last 3 letters of column): Tradition (*major or dominant description*). (Note 1. Most of these codes are prefaced separately by only one megabloc code, but a number can be prefaced by 2 (such as P or I, or R or O). Note 2. All codes beginning '3' refer to Neocharismatic/Third-Wave paradenominations or networks, described separately by the last 2 letters of each: last letter = ethnic origin, middle letter = location on pentecostal/charismatic ecclesiastical spectrum).

| | |
|---|---|
| ACa | Anglo-Catholic |
| Ade | Christadelphian (Adelphoi, Brothers of Christ, Unitarian Adventist) |
| Adv | Adventist |
| Alb | Albanian/Greek-speaking (Byzantine or Orthodox) |
| Ang | schism ex Anglicanism or Episcopalianism, in Protestant direction |
| Apo | apocalyptic, eschatological |
| Ara | Arabic- or Arabic/Greek-speaking (Orthodox) |
| Arm | Armenian (Orthodox (Gregorian) or Eastern-rite Catholic) |
| ARo | Anglo-Roman (schism ex Anglicanism in Roman direction) |
| Bap | Baptist |
| Brl | British-Israelite |
| Bud | Hidden Buddhist believers in Christ |
| Bul | Bulgarian (Orthodox or Byzantine rite) |
| Bye | Byelorussian/Belorussian (White Russian/White Ruthenian) (Orthodox or Byzantine) |
| Byz | Byzantine-rite (jurisdiction for more than one ethnic group) |
| Cat | other Independent Catholic bodies |
| CBr | Christian Brethren (Plymouth Brethren; Open only, not Exclusive); independent/fundamentalist/dispensationalist |
| CCa | Conservative Catholic (schism ex Rome, protesting liberal or updating trends) |
| Cel | Celtic (British) |
| Cen | Central or Broad Church Anglican (Prayer Book Liberal, Comprehensive, New Synod Group) |
| Cha | Chaldean (Eastern Syrian rite) |
| com | community church or union congregation (formed by 2 or more denominations, open to all denominations and races |
| Con | Congregational, Congregationalist |
| Cop | Coptic (Orthodox or Alexandrian-rite) |
| Cze | Czech/Slavonic-speaking (Orthodox) |
| Dis | Disciple, Restorationist, Restorationist Baptist, Christian (Restoration Movement Campbellites, Disciples, Churches of Christ) |
| Div | Divine Science |
| Don | Donatist |
| Dun | Dunker (Tunker), Dipper, German Baptist, Brethren (baptism by 3-fold immersion) |
| EBr | Exclusive Brethren (Plymouth Brethren, Closed, Strict; Darbyites); exclusive fundamentalist/dispensationalist |
| Ecu | Ecumenical (Anglican/Protestant/Orthodox joint parishes) |
| Epi | episcopi-vagantes (bishops-at-large) (only those with 100 or under members) |

| | |
|---|---|
| Est | Estonian (Independent Orthodox) |
| eth | ethnic denomination, monoethnic |
| Eth | Ethiopic, Ethiopian Orthodox, Ge'ez-speaking, Alexandrian |
| Eva | Anglican Evangelical, Protestant Evangelical, Independent Evangelical |
| Fin | Finnish/Slavonic-speaking (Orthodox) |
| Fun | Fundamentalist |
| Gay | Gay/Lesbian homosexual tradition |
| Geo | Georgian Orthodox or Byzantine-rite Roman Catholic |
| Gno | Gnostic, esoteric, anthroposophical |
| Gre | Greek (Orthodox or Byzantine, Greek-speaking) (New Calendar) |
| Hig | High Church Anglican (Prayer Book Catholic) |
| Hin | Hidden Hindu believers in Christ |
| Hol | Holiness (Conservative Methodist, Wesleyan, Free Methodist, non-Pentecostal Perfectionist), 2-experience: conversion, entire sanctification; mainly schisms out of mainline Methodism differing chiefly on sanctification |
| HSA | Holy Spirit Association (Moon) |
| Hun | Hungarian/Slavonic-speaking (Byzantine or Orthodox) |
| IAb | Italo-Albanian (Byzantine) |
| ind | independent evangelical, often fundamentalist (dispensationalist), unrelated to other indigenous traditions, usually regarding itself as a denomination |
| Int | interdenominational evangelical Protestant (unaffiliated to any denomination, unrelated to any major tradition, or specifically interdenominational); faith mission |
| Ita | Italian (Byzantine) |
| Jeh | Jehovah's Witnesses (Jehovah's Christian Witnesses; Russellites) including Bible Student movement and other schismatics or dissidents |
| Jew | Messianic, Jewish-Christian, or Jewish crypto-Christian |
| Lat | Latin-rite Catholics |
| Lav | Latvian Orthodox |
| LdS | Latter-day Saints (Mormons), including Mormon schismatics or dissidents |
| LEr | jurisdiction for both Latin-rite and Eastern-rite Catholics |
| Lib | Liberal Catholic (deviant, Theosophical, Masonic, Gnostic) |
| Low | Low Church Anglican (Conservative Evangelical) |
| LuR | Lutheran/Reformed united church or joint misssion |
| Lut | Lutheran |
| Mac | Macedonian Orthodox |
| Mal | Malankara (Syro-Antiochian, Eastern Syrian), Syro- |

| | |
|---|---|
| | Malankarese |
| Mar | Maronite (Syro-Antiochian, Western Syrian) |
| mar | marginal (Black/Third-World indigenous churches, and Catholic schisms, of unorthodox or syncretistic christology, claiming a second or supplementary source of revelation in addition to the Bible) |
| Mel | Melkite (Byzantine, Greek Catholic; Arabic-speaking) |
| Men | Mennonite, Anabaptist (Left Wing or Radical Reformation), including other communal Anabaptist sects |
| Met | Methodist (mainline Methodist, United Methodist); English-speaking Pietist |
| Mol | Moldavian Orthodox |
| Mon | Montenegrin Orthodox |
| Mor | Moravian (Continental Pietist) |
| Mus | Hidden Muslim believers in Christ |
| NoC | No-Church movement |
| Nes | Assyrian or Nestoran (East Syrian, Messihaye (Christians), Syro-Chaldean; Dyophysite), including dissidents |
| Non | Nondenominational (no church or anti-church groups rejecting being described as a church) |
| Pau | Paulician/Bogomil |
| OBe | Old Believer, Old Ritualist |
| OCa | Old Catholic |
| OCd | Old Calendarist, Authentic Orthodox |
| Ori | plural Oriental (Roman Catholic jurisdiction for all or several Eastern rites together) |
| Ose | Orthodox sect/sectarian |
| Ort | schism from Orthodoxy, in Protestant direction |
| PeA | Apostolic, or Pentecostal Apostolic (stress on complex hierarchy of living apostles, prophets and other charismatic officials); White-originated or -led |
| Pen | Pentecostal (Protestant; Classical Pentecostal of unspecific type); charismatic, faithhealing (Classical Pentecostal sub-types include PeA, Pe1, Pe2, Pe3, Pe4) |
| Pe1 | Oneness-Pentecostal or Unitarian-Pentecostal: 'Jesus only', sometimes unitarian, non- or anti-trinitarian; White-led |
| Pe2 | Baptistic-Pentecostal or Keswick-Pentecostal: 2-crisis-experience (conversion, baptism of the Spirit); White-led, Classical |
| Pe3 | Holiness-Pentecostal: 3-crisis-experience (conversion, sanctification, baptism of the Spirit); White-led, Classical |
| plu | Anglican, of plural or mixed traditions (no single tradition) |

*Continued overleaf*

*Table 16–6 continued*

| Code | Description |
|---|---|
| Pol | Polish/Slavonic-speaking (Orthodox) |
| Pro | ex-Protestant Catholic (movement out of Protestantism in a Catholic direction, receiving episcopacy and apostolic succession) |
| Qua | Friends (Quakers) |
| rad | isolated radio churches (unorganized isolated house congregations or cells of isolated radio believers brought into being by radio, mail and/or radiophonic evangelism) |
| ReA | Reformed Anglican |
| ReC | Reformed Catholic, retaining Roman Catholic claims |
| Ref | Reformed, Presbyterian (the latter originating in English-speaking areas, the former in continental Europe) |
| ReO | Reformed Orthodox (uncanonical reform movement out of Orthodoxy, retaining Orthodox claims) |
| Rum | Romanian (Orthodox or Byzantine) |
| Rus | Russian (Orthodox or Byzantine) |
| Rut | Ruthenian (Byzantine) |
| sAC | Anglican schism of Anglo-Catholic type, retaining Anglicans claims |
| Sal | Salvationist (Salvation Army) |
| Sci | metaphysical science, Divine Science, Religious Science, Christian Science, New Thought, magnetic healing, psychedelic |
| Ser | Serbian/Slavonic-speaking (Orthodox) |
| sin | single congregation(s): one single autonomous congregation, completely independent and unaffiliated to any denomination, nor claiming to be a denomination; or a defacto unstructured grouping of such congregations |
| Sla | Slavonic, Slavonic-speaking (Orthodox), members of several ethnic traditions |
| Slo | Slovak (Byzantine) |
| smi | Anglican schism of mixed types of churchmanship, retaining Anglican claims |
| Spi | Spiritualist, Spiritist (thaumaturgical), psychic, psychical, occult, mediumistic, of specifically Christian type |
| sub | sub-Orthodox Russian sect rejecting Orthodox ritual |
| Swe | Swedenborgian (Church of the New Jerusalem; spiritualistic) |
| SyM | Syro-Malabarese (Eastern Syrian), Syriac/Malayalam-speaking, Orthodox Syrian |
| Syr | Syrian, Syriac-speaking (Orthodox or Syro-Antiochian, West Syrian, Jacobite) |
| tel | TV (television) paradenomination, organized around regular worship telecasts |
| TrA | Traditional Anglican, Traditionalist |
| The | Theosophist, Theosophical, synthesist (combining philosophy and religions) |
| Tru | True Orthodox (devoutly conservative Russian Orthodox) |
| Ukr | Ukrainian (Orthodox or Byzantine) |
| Uni | United church (voluntary or involuntary unions of bodies of different traditions) |
| Unt | Unitarian, Universalist, Free Christian, Liberal Christian |
| Wal | Waldensian |
| Yug | Yugoslav (Byzantine) |
| *All codes beginning '3' = Third-Wavers* | |
| 3aA | African Independent Apostolic |
| 3aB | Black American Apostolic |
| 3aF | Filipino Apostolic |
| 3aK | Korean Apostolic |
| 3aI | Indian Apostolic |
| 3aL | Latin American Apostolic |
| 3aO | Black American Oneness Apostolic |
| 3aP | Pacific Apostolic |
| 3aS | Arab Apostolic |
| 3aU | Afro-Caribbean Apostolic |
| 3aW | White-led Apostolic |
| 3aX | New Apostolic, Catholic Apostolic (Irvingite) or Old Apostolic; sacramentalist, hierarchical |
| 3cA | African Independent charismatic |
| 3cB | Black American charismatic |
| 3cC | Chinese charismatic |
| 3cD | Black American Independent charismatic |
| 3cE | Monoethnic charismatic |
| 3cF | Filipino charismatic |
| 3cI | Indian charismatic |
| 3cK | Korean charismatic |
| 3cL | Latin American charismatic |
| 3cP | Pacific charismatic |
| 3cQ | Japanese charismatic |
| 3cS | Arab charismatic |
| 3cU | Afro-Caribbean charismatic |
| 3cW | White-led charismatic |
| 3cY | Brazilian/Portuguese charismatic |
| 3cZ | other Asian charismatic |
| 3dW | White-led neocharismatic mainliners |
| 3dZ | other Asian doubly-affiliated mainliners |
| 3fA | African Independent Full Gospel |
| 3fB | Black American Full Gospel |
| 3fC | Chinese Full Gospel |
| 3fD | Black American charismatic Full Gospel |
| 3fF | Filipino Full Gospel |
| 3fG | Indonesian Full Gospel |
| 3fI | Indian Full Gospel |
| 3fK | Korean Full Gospel |
| 3fL | Latin American Full Gospel |
| 3fP | Pacific Full Gospel |
| 3fW | White-led Full Gospel |
| 3fY | Brazilian/Portuguese Full Gospel |
| 3fZ | other Asian Full Gospel |
| 3gL | Latin American grassroots |
| 3gU | Afro-Caribbean grassroots |
| 3gY | Brazilian grassroots |
| 3hA | African house-church network |
| 3hE | Monoethnic house-church network |
| 3hG | Indonesian house-church network |
| 3hI | Indian house-church network |
| 3hL | Latin American house-church network |
| 3hP | Pacific house-church network |
| 3hS | Arab house-church network |
| 3hW | White-led house-church network |
| 3hZ | other Asian house-church network |
| 3hV | Vietnamese house-church network |
| 3hK | Korean house-church network |
| 3jA | African healing network |
| 3jW | White-led healing network |
| 3kA | African cell-based network |
| 3kB | Black American cell-based network |
| 3kC | Chinese cell-based network |
| 3kK | Korean cell-based network |
| 3kL | Latin American cell-based network |
| 3kW | White-led cell-based network |
| 3kZ | other Asian cell-based network |
| 3mA | Messianic African Independent |
| 3mC | Messianic Chinese |
| 3mH | Messianic Hindu temples or individuals |
| 3mJ | Messianic Jewish synagogues or individuals |
| 3mM | Messianic Muslim mosques or individuals |
| 3nA | African Independent neocharismatic |
| 3nB | Black American neocharismatic |
| 3nC | Chinese neocharismatic |
| 3nE | Monoethnic neocharismatic |
| 3nF | Filipino neocharismatic |
| 3nG | Indonesia neocharismatic |
| 3nI | Indian neocharismatic |
| 3nL | Latin American neocharismatic |
| 3nN | Creole neocharismatic |
| 3nP | Pacific neocharismatic |
| 3nS | Arab neocharismatic |
| 3nU | Afro-Caribbean neocharismatic |
| 3nW | White-led neocharismatic |
| 3nZ | other Asian neocharismatic |
| 3oA | African Oneness pentecostal |
| 3oC | Chinese Oneness pentecostal |
| 3oF | Filipino Oneness pentecostal |
| 3oG | Indonesian Oneness pentecostal |
| 3oI | Indian Oneness pentecostal |
| 3oL | Latin American Oneness pentecostal |
| 3oO | Black American Oneness pentecostal |
| 3oQ | Japanese Oneness pentecostal |
| 3oU | Afro-Caribbean Oneness pentecostal |
| 3oW | White-led Oneness pentecostal |
| 3oY | Brazilian/Portuguese Oneness pentecostal |
| 3oZ | other Asian Oneness pentecostal |
| 3pA | African Independent pentecostal |
| 3pB | Black American pentecostal |
| 3pC | Chinese pentecostal |
| 3pE | Monoethnic pentecostal |
| 3pF | Filipino pentecostal |
| 3pG | Indonesian pentecostal |
| 3pI | Indian pentecostal |
| 3pK | Korean pentecostal |
| 3pL | Latin American pentecostal |
| 3pN | Creole pentecostal |
| 3pP | Pacific pentecostal |
| 3pQ | Japanese pentecostal |
| 3pR | Amerindian pentecostal |
| 3pS | Arab pentecostal |
| 3pU | Afro-Caribbean pentecostal |
| 3pW | White-led pentecostal |
| 3pY | Brazilian/Portuguese pentecostal |
| 3pZ | other Asian pentecostal |
| 3rA | African radio/TV believers |
| 3rC | Chinese radio/TV believers |
| 3rG | Indonesian radio/TV believers |
| 3rI | Indian radio/TV believers |
| 3rK | Korean radio/TV believers |
| 3rL | Latin American radio/TV network |
| 3rQ | Japanese radio/TV believers |
| 3rS | Arab radio/TV network |
| 3rV | Vietnamese radio/TV believers |
| 3rW | European White radio/TV believers |
| 3rY | Brazilian/Portuguese radio/TV believers |
| 3rZ | other Asian radio/TV believers |
| 3sA | African Independent Spiritual |
| 3sU | Afro-Caribbean Spiritual |
| 3sW | White-led signs and wonders |
| 3tW | White-led restorationist |
| 3vA | African Independent deliverance |
| 3vB | Black American deliverance pentecostal |
| 3vW | White-led deliverance pentecostal |
| 3wA | African Word of Faith/Prosperity |
| 3wF | Filipino Word of Faith/Prosperity |
| 3wP | Pacific Word-of-Faith/Prosperity |
| 3wW | White-led Word of Faith/Prosperity |
| 3xK | Korean pentecostal of mixed traditions |
| 3xL | Latin American neocharismatic of mixed tradtions |
| 3xW | European charismatic of mixed traditions |
| 3zA | Zionist African Independent |
| 3zU | Afro-Caribbean Zionist |

**COLUMN 4: CONCILIARISM, COLLEGIALITY, CONSULTATION, AND CHURCH ORGANIZATION** (5-letter code)

*Note on names.* Most international bodies have official names in 2 or more major international languages. Almost all of these are given in *WCE* Parts 2, 12, or 14, but in the interests of brevity names are given below only once in English (for international bodies with official names in several languages), or in the major European language in use followed by an English translation if widely used. Where a body uses varying sets of initials in its various languages, these are all given below in brackets separated by slashes.

*Conference of Secretaries of Christian World Communions (until 1979 known as World Confessional Families).* The 15 international confessional councils below followed by an asterisk* (making a total of 24 asterisks including duplications) are represented on this conference, begun in 1957; in addition, the following non-confessional international denominational bodies are participants: Church of the Brethren, Salvation Army, General Conference of Seventh-day Adventists, World Convention of Churches of Christ (Disciples).

| *Code* | *Name of communion in English* |
|---|---|
| A | Anglican Consultative Council (ACC)/Lambeth Conference/Anglican Primates Committee* |
| a | Anglican Consultative Council: non-autonomous body* |
| B | Sacred Congregation for Bishops* |
| b | immediately subject to Holy See (under Sacred Congregation for Bishops)* |
| C | canonical relationship with Ecumenical Patriarchate of Constantinople (also the other 3 Greek-speaking Orthodox patriarchates, and Panorthodox conference)* |
| c | claimed but disputed relationship to Ecumenical Patriarchate of Constantinople |
| D | canonical relationship with Syrian Orthodox (Jacobite) Patriarchate of Antioch (Damascus) |
| E | Armenian Catholicate of Echmiadzin |
| e | International Lutheran Conference (ILC) |
| F | member of both WARC and RES (World Alliance of Reformed Churches, and Reformed Ecumenical Synod)* |
| G | Mennonite World Conference (MWC)* |
| I | Organization of African Instituted Churches (OAIC) |
| i | International New Thought Alliance (INTA) |
| J | Reformed Ecumenical Synod (RES)* |
| K | International Federation of Free Evangelical Churches (IFFEC) |
| L | Lutheran World Federation (LWF/FLM/LWB) (member, or congregation formally recognized by LWF)* |
| l | permanent observer (but not member) relationship to Lutheran World Federation (LWF)* |
| M | canonical relationship with Patriarchate of Moscow (in preference to Constantinople)* |
| N | Coptic Orthodox Patriarchate of Alexandria |
| O | Sacred Congregation for the Eastern Churches* |
| o | immediately subject to Holy See (under Sacred Congregation for the Eastern Churches)* |
| P | Sacred Congregation for the Evangelization of Peoples (Propaganda)* |
| p | immediately subject to Holy See (under Propaganda)* |
| Q | Friends World Committee for Consultation (FWCC)* |
| R | World Alliance of Reformed Churches (Presbyterian and Congregational) (WARC)* |
| S | Armenian Catholicate of Cilicia (Sis) |
| T | Baptist World Alliance (BWA/ABM/BWB)* |
| U | International Old Catholic Bishops Conference (Union of Utrecht)* |
| V | World Methodist Council (WMC)* |
| W | member of both WMC and WARC (World Methodist Council, and World Alliance of Reformed Churches)* |
| X | Ukrainian Orthodox Church of the Free World |
| x | quasi-confession (or non-confessional international denominational body), usually with world missionary outreach or, non-canonical Orthodox communion |
| Y | canonical relationship with Ancient Assyrian Church of the East, Patriarchate of the East (Tehran) (Mar Dinkha IV) |
| y | canonical relationship with Ancient Assyrian Church of the East, Patriarchate of Baghdad (Mar Addai) |
| Z | Pentecostal World Conference (PWC) |
| C+M | Great and Holy Council of the Orthodox Church* |
| D + E + N + S | Oriental Orthodox Churches conference |
| . | not a member of any confessional council, nor in communion with historical Orthodox/Anglican/Old Catholic/Roman Catholic churches; no international confessional links or membership of any kind. |

*Continued opposite*

*Table 16–6 continued*

*Other international confessional councils, not coded here.* 20 other non- or antitrinitarian heterodox communions, 20 schismatic communions ex Anglicanism, 25 Conservative networks hostile to historic confessions, 30 other meganetworks White-led Neo-Apostolic, 40 Independent Neocharismatic minicommunions, 50 major Protestant global denominations, African Apostolic Church of Johane Maranke (AACJM), Alliance World Fellowship (AWF), Ancient Assyrian Patriarchate of the East, Anglican Episcopal Council of Churches, Anglican Orthodox Communion, Apostolic World Christian Fellowship (AWCF), Assembly Hall Churches (Local Churches, Little Flock), Baptist Bible Fellowship International (BBFI), Brazil for Christ Evangelical Pentecostal Church (OBPC), Brazilian Catholic Apostolic Church (ICAB), Catholic Charismatic Renewal (CCR), Chaplaincy of Full Gospel Churches (CFGC), Christian Congregation of Brazil (CCB), Christian Holiness Association (CHA), Church of the Brethren, Church of Christ (Manalista), Church of Christ, Scientist, Church of God in Christ (CoGiC), Church of Jesus Christ of Latter-day Saints (CJCLdS), Coalition of Spirit-filled Churches (CSC), Consultation on Uniting and United Churches (CUUC), Confessional Lutheran Synod, Czechoslovak Hussite Church (CCH/CHC), Deeper Life Bible Church (DLBC), Disciples Ecumenical Committee for Consultation (DECC), Ethiopian Orthodox Patriarchate of Addis Ababa, Fellowship of French Evangelical and Reformed Churches (CEVAA) (a worldwide body), General Conference of Seventh-day Adventists (SDA), Gypsy Pentecostal Churches, India Pentecostal Church of God (IPCG), International Association for Religious Freedom (IARF), International Baptist Fellowsip, International Charismatic Consultation on World Evangelization (ICCOWE), International Communion of Charismatic Churches (ICCC), International Communion of the Charismatic Episcopal Church (ICCEC), International Conference of Reformed Churches (ICRC), International Congregational Fellowship (ICF), International Council of Unitarians and Universalists (ICUU), International Evangelical Congregational Union, International Fellowship of Charismatic Churches (IFCC), International League for Apostolic Faith and Order (ILAFO), International Moravian Church in Unity of Brethren, International Reformed Fellowship (IRF), Jehovah's Christian Witnesses, Ligue Oecuménique pour l'Unité Chrétienne, Malankara Orthodox Syrian Catholicossate of the East, Manna Church International, Mar Thoma Syrian Church of Malabar, New Apostolic Church (NAC/NAK), Old Ritualist Churches (Old Believers, Old Calendarists), Philippine Independent Church (IFI/PIC), Reformed Ecumenical Council (REC), Salvation Army (SA), True Jesus Church (TJC), Unification Church (Holy Spirit Association for Unification of World Christianity), Union of Messianic Jewish Congregations (UMJC), Universal Church of the Kingdom of God (UCKG/IURD), Willow Creek Association of Churches (WCAC), World Assemblies of God Fellowship (WAGF), World Convention of Churches of Christ (WCCC), World Fellowship of Reformed Churches (WFRC).

The codes for the next 4 letters apply to all denominations and churches including Roman Catholic local (nation-wide) churches, but not to dioceses or jurisdictions indented under churches (see code for 2nd-5th letters below).

### *2nd letter: World Conciliarism, Collegiality, and Consultation*

F = related or linked to World Evangelical Fellowship (WEF): church or mission related to Evangelical Foreign Missions Association (EFMA), hence tyo NAE (USA), hence to WEF
G = church or mission related to Evangelical Missionary Alliance, UK (EMA), but not to EFMA or IFMA or WEF
H = church or mission related to Australian Evangelical Alliance, but not to EFMA or IFMA or WEF
M = church or mission related to Interdenominational Foreign Misssion Association (IFMA), but not to EFMA
N = church or mission related to both IFMA and EFMA
q = church related to EFMA, which has also applied to WCC for membership
r = church related to IFMA, which has also applied to WCC for membership
s = (diocese staffed by secular clergy: see under 2nd-5th letters, below)
T = International Council of Christian Churches (ICCC), and The Associated Missions (TAM)
t = former member of ICCC, or linked with it, but now withdrawn
u = associate member of WCC (small churches in principle under 10,000 in membership)
v = application for membership or enquiry made to WCC, but either withdrawn, rejected, delayed indefinitely, or otherwise not accepted by 2000
W = World Council of Churches (WCC/COE/ORK)
w = not a member of WCC in own right, but participating (e.g. as a foreign diocese or branch) through some larger confessional or ecclesiastical member grouping based in a different country
x = Roman Catholic local (nation-wide) church with both a national consultative pastoral body, and also a national priests' organization
y = Roman Catholic local (nation-wide) church with a national consultative pastoral body, but with no national priests' organization
z = Roman Catholic local (nation-wide) church with a national priests' organization, but with no national consultative pastoral body
. = (Protestant, Anglican, Orthodox) not a member of nor related to any world or international council; or (Roman Catholic) local church with neither a national priests' organization nor a naitonal consultative pastoral body

### *2nd letter (only for Roman Catholic and Orthodox dioceses and jurisdictions)* STATUS AND STAFFING

a = Orthodox diocese under an archbishop
b = Orthodox diocese under a bishop
e = Orthodox diocese under an exarch
m = Orthodox diocese under a metropolitan
p = Orthodox diocese under a patriarch or catholicos
s = Roman Catholic diocese staffed by secular (diocesan) clergy (usually nationals and not expatriates)

### *2nd-5th letters: LOCAL/INTERNATIONAL STAFFING (only for Roman Catholic dioceses and jurisdictions)*

*sj* and all other initials given here indicate the major Catholic religious or secular missionary institute serving a missionary jurisdiction (formerly, confided to the order). All may be identified from the Index of Abbreviations, Acronyms and Initials (Part 32).

### *3rd letter: Continental Conciliarism, Collegiality, and Consultation*

A = All Africa Conference of Churches (AACC/CETA)
a = small foreign part of full member of AACC
B = Consilium Conferentiarum Episcopalium Europae (CCEE) (Council of European Bishops' Conferences)
C = Conference of European Churches (CEC/CEE/KEK)
c = observer status in CEC; or, small foreign part of full member of CEC
D = related to European Evangelical Alliance (EEA) through membership in affiliated national fellowship or council or alliance
E = Christian Conference of Asia (CCA) (until 1973 East Asian Christian Conference, EACC)
e = small foreign part of full member of CCA
F = Federation of Asian Bishops' Conferences (FABC)
G = related to Association of Evangelicals of Africa (AEA) through membership in affiliated national fellowship or council
g = associate/special member of AEA
H = related to Evangelical Association of the Caribbean (EAC) through membership in affiliated national fellowship or council
I = Organization of African Independent churches (OAJC)
i = member of OAIC, also member of AACC
L = Consejo Episcopal Latinoamericano (CELAM) (LatinAmerican Ep[iscopal Council)
M = Caribbean Conference of Churches (CCC)
N = Caribbean Conference of Churches (CCC) and also member of CELAM
O = Standing conference of Canonical Orthodox Bishops in the Americas (SCOBA)
o = small foreign part of full member of SCOBA
P = Pacific Conference of Churches (PCC)
p = small foreign part of full member of PCC
Q = member of CCC, also related to EAC
S = Symposium of Episcopal Conferences of Africa and Madagascar (SECAM/SCEAM)
T = continental council affiliated to ICCC (Latin American Alliance of Christian Churches (LAACC), Far Eastern Council of Christian Churches (FECCC), ICCC European Alliance, Caribbean Council of Christian Churches)
U = Movimiento pro Unidad Evangelica Latinoamericana, (UNELAM) replaced from 1978 by Latin American Council of Churches (in formation) (CLAI)
u = indirect member of UNELAM/CLAI through membership in a UNELAM/CLAI affiliated national council
V = Caribbean Conference of Churches (CCC) and also member of UNELAM/CLAI
X = member of CEC, also related to EEA
x = related to EEA, also observer status in CEC
Y = related to both Evangelical Association of the Caribbean (EAC) and ICCC
. = not a member of nor related to any continental council

*Other continental councils.* These are numerous: e.g. Confraternidad Latinoamericana de Iglesias Reformadas (CLIR). There are also many other councils which are not coded here either because in formation only or because their members are not denominations but are national councils most of whom have members who in turn are not denominations but are local congregations or individuals. These include:Evangelical Fellowship of Asia (Association of Asian Evangelical Fellowships), and South East Asia Evangelical Alliance (in formation; both related to World Evangelical Fellowship, WEF).

*Lower-case letters* (a, c, e, o, p, u) indicate that a body belongs to the council concerned (A, C, E, O, P, U), not in its own right, but by belonging as a small part (e.g. as a small foreign diocese or branch) to some larger confessional or ecclesiastical grouping based in a different country; or, if listed above, observer status.

### *4th letter: Regional Conciliarism, Collegiality, and Consultation*

A = Council of the Church in East Asia (CCEA) (until 1975, CCSEA)
B = Association des Conférences Episcopales du Congo/Republique Centrafricaine/Tchad (ACECCT) (formerly ACEACCAM)
C = Consejo Anglicano Sud Americano (CASA) (Anglican Council for South America)
D = Secretariado Episcopal de America Central y Panama (SEDAC)
E = Association of Member Episcopal Conferences in Eastern Africa (AMECEA)
e = regional fellowship or council of Evangelical churches (Fellowship of Middle East Evangelical Churches (FMEEC), Evangelical Fellowship/Alliance of the South Pacific (EFSP), Latin American Evangelical Fellowship (CONELA), North American Council of WEF)
F = Conference Episcopale Regionale de l'Afrique Occidentale Francophone (CERAO) (Regional Episcopal Conference of French-speaking West Africa)
G = Association of Episcopal Conferences of English-speaking West Africa (AECEWA)
H = Conference Episcopale d'Afrique du Nord
I = regional council of Black/Third-World or Non-White indigenous churches
J = Asociacion Regional Episcopal del Norte de Sud America (ARENSA) (Anglican; part of CASA)
K = South Pacific Anglican Council (SPAC)
L = Conference des Evêques Latins dans les Regions Arabes (CELRA)
M = Antilles Episcopal Conference (AEC)
N = Middle East Council of Churches (MECC/CEMO) (until 1974 Near East Council of Churches, NECC/CEPO)
O = regional council of Orthodox churches
P = attached or partially attached to one of the 6 RC non-Latin Patriarchal Synods (Armenian, Chaldean, Coptic, Maronite, Melkite, Syrian)
Q = Nordic Bishops' Conference (Scandinavian Bishops' Conference) (Nordiske Bispekonferanse)
R = Anglican Council of North America and the Caribbean (ACNAC)
S = Interterritorial (Inter-Regional) Meeting of Bishops in Southern Africa (IMBISA) (formerly Southern Africa Catholic Bishop' Conference)
T = regional council affiliated to ICCC (Middle East Bible Council, Central Africa Christian of Bible Believing Christian Churches, Scandinavian Evangelical Council)
U = member of both MECC and CAPA
V = Conference/Council of the Anglican Provinces of Africa (CAPA)
W = member of both AMECEA and CELRA
X = Pentecostal Fellowship of North America (PENA)
Y = Conference des Eveques du Pacifique (CEPAC) (Episcopal Conference of the Pacific)
Z = Regional Conference of Chinese Bishops (Chung Kuo Chu-chiao T'uan)
. = not a member of any regional council

*Other regional councils, not coded here.* These are confessional or denominational councils covering a region, together with a number whose names cover a continent but which in practice are only regional because that denomination's presence is not universal there . These include: Anglican Council of Latin America (CALA), Caribbean Assembly of Reformed Churches, Community of Latin American Evangelical Ministries, Conseil Methodiste de l'Quest/Council of the Methodist Church in West Africa, Council of Evangelical Methodist Churches in Latin America (CIEMAL), Council of Reformed Churches in Central Africa, European Baptist Federation (EBF), European Pentecostal Fellowship (EPF), Federation of Evangelical Lutheran Churches of Southern Africa (FELCSA), Fellowship of Evangelical Baptist Churches in Europe, Methodist Consultative Council of the Pacific (MCCP), North America Presbyterian and Reformed Council (NAPARC).

*Continued overleaf*

*Table 16–6 concluded*

***5th letter: National or Plurinational Conciliarism, Collegiality, and Consultation***

All national (country-wide) councils are identified by name in the footnote under each country's Table 2, which also lists other national councils which do not have denominations as members.

a = member of 2 national councils, one WCC-related and one Evangelical (WEF or AEAM or EAC)
b = member of 2 national councils, one WCC-related and one Black/Third-World or Non-White indigenous
C = national council (Protestant or Western) with no formal external international affiliations
c = associate member of C (preceding line), or related for certain functions
d = member of 2 national councils, one WCC-related and one unaffiliated (Protestant or Western)
E = national Evangelical alliance or council, affiliated to WEF (World Evangelical Fellowship) and also to one of its regional associations or continental counterparts (AEAM, EAC, EEA, et alia) where existing
e = national Evangelical alliance or council, affiliated to EEA (European Evangelical Alliance)
F = national council including Roman Catholic, Protestant, Anglican and Independent churches, but with no formal external international affiliations
f = formerly in the major national council, but has recently withdrawn
G = national Evangelical council affiliated to AEAM but not to WEF
H = national council of Pentecostal churches (Protestant)
h = member of some other council (incompletely recorded in Table 2, though name and membership are given below it)
I = national council of Black/Third-World or Non-White indigenous churches (predominantly)
i = member of I (preceding line) and also of H
J = national council of Black/Third-World or Non-White indigenous churches (different to I)
K = national council of churches, or Christian council, in working relationship with WCC but not affiliated to it
k = associate member of K (preceding line), or affiliated for certain services; or permanent observer member of K
L = national Evangelical council affiliated to Evangelical Association of the Caribbean but not (in 1978) to WEF
l = as L, but also affiliated to ICCC
M = national council of foreign missionary societies (church represented through one or more of its mission bodies)
N = national council of churches, or Christian council, affiliated to CWME or WCC (formerly to IMC)
n = associate member of N (preceding line), or affiliated for certain services; or permanent observer member of N
O = national council or liaison committee or Orthodox churches
P = plurinational Roman Catholic episcopal or bishops' conferemce (covering 2 or 3 countries included in conference's name)
Q = member of plurinational RC episcopal conference, also full membre of national council related to WCC
q = as Q, but only observer or associate member of national council related to WCC
R = national Roman Catholic episcopal or bishops' conference
r = small diocese or church attached to RC national episcopal conference in another country (and so not included in conference's name)
S = member of national RC episcopal conference, also full member of national council related to WCC
s = as S, but only observer or associate member of national council related to WCC
T = national council affiliated, or informally related, to ICCC
t = former member of T (preceding line), now withdrawn; or, member of council formerly affiliated to ICCC, now withdrawn
u = member in temporary or once-only national conference of churches in country where permanent council prohibited
V = member of national RC episcopal conference, also full member of national council not related to WCC.
v = As V, but only observer or associate member of national council not related to WCC
W = national (ecumenical) council of churches, or Christian council, formally an associate council of WCC
w = associate member of W (preceding line), or affiliated for certain services; or permanent observer member of W; or member of country-wide council associated with W
x = member of 2 other national councils
y = some other Black/Third-World or Non-White indigenous national council (different to I and J)
Z = member of 3 national councils
z = member of 3 national councils (one WCC-related, one Evangelical)
▪ = not a member of any national council

**COLUMN 10: NAMES, NOTES, AND OTHER STATISTICS**

These descriptive notes include a selection of any significant data concerning some of the following elements (all items in italics are current initials, names, translations or expanded titles of the church's name in column 1): name in major national or local language (in italics), preceded by initials if commonly used (in italics), then geographical sub-title of the body if any (in italics), and wider geographical jurisdictions or entities to which the body belongs (not in italics), translation into English (in italics), alternate name(s) (in italics), former names (not in italics), foreign missionary society(ies) past and/or present, brief geographical or historical notes, ethnic or linguistic or national/expatriate (citizen/alien) composition of members (Christians) as % (in descending order of numerical size, or (single name) dominant ethnic or linguistic group), and any other statistics available.

Italicized abbreviations and initials (in italics) in column 10 are either (a) first initial of the country concercerned (A for Austria, B for Belgium, etc), or (b) local-language words in titles (e.g. in Indonesia, G = Gereja, church) identified in the notes under the table. Non-italicized letters are either (c) initials of co-operating missionary societies (listed in full in Index of Abbreviations, Acronyms and Initials), (d) jurisdictions, as listed above under column 1, or (e) abbreviations and codes common to all countries as set out below. In the listings of statistics in this column in the table, personnel are the first statistics shown, in the order C, n, x, m, w, Yy.

A = year when church became autonomous (if significant)
B = (at head of a sub-column) location in province or state
b = parishes (as defined by the church concerned, if different from column 5)
bc = Roman Catholic diocesan brothers' council
C = Roman Catholic religious institutes (i.e. orders, congregations and societies) officially at work (foreign and local); the 3 figures given (e.g. C = 3 + 1 + 15) enumerate the number of distinct institutes of, respectively, *clerics* (priests mainly, occasionally also with some brothers and seminarians), + *brothers*, + *sisters*
D = Roman Catholic diocesan councils of post-conciliar (Vatican II) type (Synod, PC, pc, bc, lc, se)
d = monasteries (religious houses for men, monks, brothers)
de = monasteries and convents
dec = numerical decline or decrease in recent years compared to earlier larger following
e = convents (religious houses for women, nuns, sisters)
esp = especially
et al = et alia (and other things), et alii (and other people)
ex = schism (split, secession, breakoff) from or out of church or mission indicated
f = foreign missionary personnel (aliens, expatriates), as defined by church or mission (lay and ordained, men and women, usually including only those active on the field, seconded or on furlough)
G = annual growth rate of membership, % pa (% per year), over 25-year period 1970-1995 (G = 0 means zero growth; minus means decline)
H = hospitals operated by church or mission (including leprosaria, sanatoria)
HQ = location of headquarters, see city, episcopal residence, secretariat, denominational offices (usually only given here if not given in, or if not the same as, any location in title in column 1)
h = clinics, dispensaries, maternity centres, mobile clinics, operated by church or mission
i = mission stations (of foreign missionary societies)
j = printing presses or publishing houses operated by church or mission
k = bookshops run by church or mission
L = (at head of a sub-column) official language used
lc = Roman Catholic diocesan council of laity
M = co-operating foreign missionary societies (with a local or national administration) in the past and/or present
MS = Missionary Society (part of title or name)
m = men lay workers, lay preachers, brothers, monks (full-time; nationals plus expatriates; Roman Catholic men religious (brothers as well as priests; members of men's religious institutes, nationals and expatriates) but excluding Roman Catholic lay catechists; Anglican or Orthodox brothers or monks, Protestants and Anglicans in church pastoral or evangelistic work (including nationals but not usually expatriates)
mw = total full-time lay workers (Protestants, Anglicans, Orthodox), or (Roman Catholics) religious men plus women (= m + w)
N = priests prevented from functioning by atheistic state
n = national (citizen) clergy (ordained ministers, pastors, priests (secular and religious), deacons, deaconesses, ordained women, bishops); active only, excluding retired
nm = total men workers, ordained and lay (= n + m)
nx = total clergy or ministers, national plus expatriate (= n + x)
P = practising Christians, % (those fulfilling their churches' minimum annual obligations of church attendance (e.g. Easter attenders or communicants), as % of affiliated Christians eligible to attend)
PC = Roman Catholic diocesan pastoral council, for laity, religious, and clergy, with total members in parentheses ( ); if followed by 2 numbers in parentheses, these = priests/religious members, and lay members
p = Bible schools, catechist training schools: Protestant Bible-training schools, usually for lay church workers, sometimes also for ordained; Roman Catholic catechist training schools, of primary or secondary level
pc = Roman Catholic diocesan priests' council or senate, with total members in parentheses ( ); if followed by 3 numbers in parentheses, these = members nominated by bishop, members ex officio, and members elected by all priests
pp = part-time preachers (unsalaried but officially-accredited volunteer spare-time local preachers, lay preachers, lay readers)
q = religious seminaries (not secular or diocesan; Roman Catholic major seminaries for religious clergy)
qv = quod vide, which see (i.e. refer elsewhere to the item just mentioned)
R = radio letters (normal annual listeners' letters received from this country by all Christian radio stations or agencies, home or foreign)
r = church-related or -operated colleges, teacher training colleges, major high or secondary schools, academies, technical or industrial schools, or other educational institutions of higher learning
RE = Roman Catholic ecclesiastical region (in the USA only)
S = active BCC students (enrolled in Bible correspondence courses)
s = seminaries for preparation for the ordained ministry (major seminaries, theological colleges, Bible academies, Bible institutes, Bible colleges, officers' training schools, church-operated university faculties of theology; Roman Catholic secular/diocesan (but not religious/regular) major seminaries); sometimes followed in parentheses by number of seminarians (in training for the ordained ministy)
sc = Roman Catholic diocesan sisters' council
school = primary or middle schools (not secondary or higher)
SS = Sunday-school enrolment
ST = state: name or zip code abbreviation for secular or civil state or province co-terminous, or nearly so, with diocese
Synod = Roman Catholic diocesan synod (climax of internal ecumenism)
T = total or accumulated BCC enrolments (students in Bible correspondence courses now or in past)
t = Sunday-schools, sabbath schools
u = participation in a united seminary (sponsored by 2 or more denominations)
V = BCC conversions (students enrolled in Bible correspondence courses who have professed conversion as a result)
v = church-related or -operated universities
W = attending Christians, or weekly church attenders, % (attenders each Sunday or Saturday as % of affiliated Christians eligible to attend)
w = women lay workers, sisters, nuns (full-time; nationals plus expatriates; Roman Catholic women religious (members of women's religious institutes) but excluding Catholic lay women catechists; Anglican or Orthodox sisters or nuns, Protestants and Anglicans in church pastoral or evangelistic work)
x = expatriate (alien, foreign, non-citizen) clergy (ordained ministers, pastors, priests (secular and religious), deacons, deaconesses, ordained women, bishops); active only, not retired
Y, y = annual baptisms (new persons baptized in a recent year around 1995-2000); Y = adult baptisms, y = infant baptisms, Yy = adults + infants combined (or, if baptism not practised, Y = new adult members admitted)
z = catechumens, baptismal candidates (these are always included in column 7; hence for the Roman Catholic Church, the number of baptized Catholics = column 7 minus catechumens)
( ) = number of students, monks, nuns, Sunday-school scholars, or pupils in the institutions referred to (e.g. 2s(20) means 2 seminaries with 20 seminarians training for the ordained ministry)
% eth = percentage of Christian population belonging to various ethnic groups
% RC = percentage of total population, in the area of a jurisdiction, who are RCs, Muslims, pagans, etc.

SUBTABLES IN COLUMN 10. For certain large denominations, almost always only the Roman Catholic Church, a subtable for all its dioceses may be given in column 10.

TOTALS FOR A CHURCH WITH DIOCESES. Statistics in column 10 for the first line of a denomination with indented component dioceses under it always include whatever statistics are shown for the dioceses below. Often the totals on the first line are greater than the totals of those below because the dioceses only show part of the breakdown and do not include non-diocesan staff.

DOUBLY-AFFILIATED. These are persons affiliated to or claimed by 2 denominations at once (as shown, defined and described in Country Tables 1; always a negative quantity).

DISAFFILIATED. Former Christians recently withdrawn from state or majority churches (as shown, defined and described in Tables 1); or, still on the churches rolls as members, but now dead.

# 7. PART 12 "COUNTRYTRENDS"

## Table 16–7. Meanings of Table 12-1. Geopolitico-religious data and typologies.

Up to this point, the Codebook has dealt with Country Tables 1 and 2 in *WCE* Part 4. The same codes apply to several other Tables elsewhere in the volume. The Codebook now deals with Table 12-1, labelled here as Table 16–7.

Table 12-1 has 191 columns of data for each of the 238 countries. The entire listing is shown below, followed by the 20 variables with coded values. If no code is given, the column reports statistics of the item described in the title.

| Column | Heading | Subject |
|---|---|---|
| **COUNTRY** | | |
| 1. | *code* | 4-letter country code |
| 2. | *short name* | as in *WCE* Part 4 |
| 3. | *UN* | UN major area and region |
| 4. | *prov* | major civil divisions (provinces, states) |
| **DEMOGRAPHICS** | | |
| 5. | *pop 2000* | population, mid-AD 2000 |
| 6. | *pop 2010* | population, mid-AD 2010 |
| 7. | *pop 2025* | population, mid-AD 2025 |
| 8. | *adults* | population age 15 and over |
| 9. | *apop* | adults as % population |
| 10. | *bpop* | birth rate, % per year |
| 11. | *dpop* | death rate, % per year |
| 12. | *npop* | natural increase, % per year |
| 13. | *life* | life expectancy, years |
| 14. | *hom* | household size (adults, children) |
| 15. | *spac* | floor area per person, sq. meters |
| 16. | *den* | density of population per sq. kilometer |
| 17. | *peop* | total ethnolinguistic peoples |
| 18. | *langs* | official and national state language(s) |
| **GEOPOLITICAL TYPOLOGIES** | | |
| 19. | *dev* | more/less/least-developed |
| 20. | *HDI* | human development index |
| 21. | *HFI* | human freedom index |
| 22. | *HSI* | human suffering index |
| 23. | *liter* | literacy as % population over 15 |
| 24. | *literates* | adult literates (over 15) |
| **SOCIETY** | | |
| ECONOMICS | | |
| 25. | *GNP* | gross national product p.a. per capita |
| 26. | *EFL* | economic freedom level |
| URBANIZATION | | |
| 27. | *rural* | ruralites, country-dwellers (millions) |
| 28. | *urban* | urbanites, town/city dwellers (millions) |
| 29. | *metro* | metropolitan urbanites (millions) |
| METROSCAN | | |
| 30. | *cit50* | cities over 50,000 persons |
| 31. | *cit100* | cities over 100,000 persons |
| 32. | *mega* | megacities over 1 million persons |
| HEALTH | | |
| 33. | *access* | people's access to health services, % |
| 34. | *water* | people's access to safe water, % |
| 35. | *mat-m* | maternal mortality, per 100,000 births |
| 36. | *inf-m* | infant mortality, per 1000 live births |
| 37. | *hosp* | hospitals |
| 38. | *beds* | beds, per 10,000 population |
| 39. | *doct* | doctors |
| 40. | *blind* | nonsighted persons |
| 41. | *deaf* | hearing-impaired persons |
| 42. | *lepers* | persons with leprosy |
| 43. | *murder* | murders per 100,000 per year |
| EDUCATION | | |
| 44. | *educ* | rate % school enrolments, female/male |
| 45. | *schools* | elementary, secondary, high |
| 46. | *univs* | degree-granting colleges, universities |
| COMMUNICATION | | |
| 47. | *news* | daily newspaper copies per 1000 persons |
| 48. | *radios* | radio sets per 1000 persons |
| 49. | *TVs* | TV sets per 1000 persons |
| 50. | *fones* | telephones per 1000 persons |
| 51. | *faxes* | fax machines per 1000 persons |
| 52. | *computers* | general-purpose computers in use |
| 53. | *Internet* | users of Internet, e-mail, www |
| **RELIGIOUS RELATIONS** | | |
| RELIGIONS | | |
| 54. | *religs* | total major religions in country |
| 55. | *indig* | ethnoreligions indigenous to this country |
| RELIGIOUS PERSECUTION | | |
| 56. | *liberty* | religious liberty or persecution |
| 57. | *CSI* | Christian Safety Index, 0-100 |
| 58. | *martyrs* | martyrs ever (less background martyrs) |
| 59. | *martyrs p.a.* | annual average, 1950-2000 |
| CHURCH/STATE RELATIONS: state religion or philosophy | | |
| 60. | *1900* | situation in 1900 |
| 61. | *1970* | situation in 1970 |
| 62. | *1990* | situation in 1990 |
| 63. | *2000* | situation in AD 2000 |
| BIBLIOGRAPHY | | |
| 64. | *items listed* | listed in *WCE* Part 4 after each country's text |
| **CHRISTIANITY** | | |
| CHURCH MEMBERS | | |
| 65. | *affiliated* | affiliated church members |
| 66. | *AC* | affiliated church members, % |
| **FOUR MEGATYPOLOGIES OF RENEWAL** | | |
| 1. THE GREAT COMMISSION | | |
| 67. | *GCCs* | Great Commission Christians |
| 68. | *GCC* | Great Commission Christians, % country |
| 2. ECCLESIASTICAL RENEWAL: 6 MEGABLOCS | | |
| 69. | *Megabloc O* | Orthodox, affiliated |
| 70. | *Megabloc R* | Roman Catholics, affiliated |
| 71. | *Megabloc A* | Anglicans, affiliated |
| 72. | *Megabloc P* | Protestants, affiliated |
| 73. | *Megabloc I* | Independents, affiliated |
| 74. | *Megabloc m* | Marginal Christians, affiliated |
| 3. EVANGELICAL RENEWAL | | |
| 75. | *Evangelicals* | Evangelicals (linked to Ev councils) |
| 76. | *evangelicals* | evangelicals (all varieties) |
| 4. PENTECOSTAL/CHARISMATIC RENEWAL | | |
| 77. | *1st-Wavers* | Pentecostals (Classical denominations) |
| 78. | *2nd-Wavers* | Charismatics (in non-Pentecostal churches) |
| 79. | *3rd-Wavers* | Neocharismatics (Independents) |
| **CHURCHES** | | |
| STRUCTURES | | |
| 80. | *denom* | denominations |
| 81. | *p.m.* | denominations per million |
| 82. | *worship* | worship centers (churches, congregations) |
| 83. | *p.m.* | worship centers per million |
| FINANCE, US$ | | |
| 84. | *personal* | personal income p.a. of all affiliated |
| 85. | *church* | churches' income per year |
| 86. | *parachurch* | parachurch income per year |
| 87. | *ecc crime* | ecclesiastical crime p.a. (embezzlements) |
| **MISSION** | | |
| STATUS OF MISSIONS | | |
| 88. | *stat* | current status of foreign missions, 1-7 |
| 89. | *misags* | foreign mission agencies present |
| 90. | *all orgs* | all service agencies |
| 91. | *p.m.* | all organizations per million |
| MISSION INSTITUTIONS | | |
| 92. | *major* | major institutions |
| 93. | *p.m.* | major institutions per million |
| 94. | *minor* | minor institutions |
| 95. | *p.m.* | minor institutions per million |
| RESPONSE/GROWTH | | |
| 96. | *CG%* | annual church growth 1900-2000, % p.a. |
| 97. | *g%* | new Christians per year, % |
| 98. | *bapt p.a.* | newly baptized persons per year |
| 99. | *resp R* | responsiveness to evangelism |
| 100. | *cost-eff, $* | cost-effectiveness: $ cost per baptism |
| WORLDS A, B, and C | | |
| 101. | *A-individuals* | World A individuals, 2000 |
| 102. | *B-individuals* | World B individuals, 2000 |
| 103. | *C-individuals* | World C individuals, 2000 |
| MINISTRIES | | |
| 104. | *peo-ags* | total agencies-in-peoples |
| **CHRISTIAN PERSONNEL** | | |
| ALL WORKERS | | |
| 105. | *workers* | full-time Christian workers in country |
| 106. | *w.p.m.* | Christian workers per million population |
| CITIZENS | | |
| 107. | *workers* | citizen Christian workers in country |
| 108. | *citw p.m.* | citizen Christian workers per million |
| **GLOBAL MISSION SHARING** | | |
| CITIZENS SENT ABROAD | | |
| 109. | *total* | citizen missionaries working abroad |
| 110. | *p.m.a.* | citizen missionaries abroad, p.m. affiliated |
| ALIENS RECEIVED FROM ABROAD | | |
| 111. | *total* | aliens at work as missionaries |
| 112. | *p.m.* | aliens at work as missionaries, p.m. |
| **CHRISTIAN LITERATURE** | | |
| LIBRARIES | | |
| 113. | *total* | Christian or religious libraries |
| 114. | *p.m.* | Christian or religious libraries, p.m. |
| BOOKS ON CHRISTIANITY IN EACH COUNTRY | | |
| 115. | *total* | all books describing this country's Christians |
| 116. | *1970-99* | such books published since 1970 |
| 117. | *p.a.* | books published per year in AD 2000 |
| PERIODICALS | | |
| 118. | *total* | Christian periodicals |
| 119. | *p.m.* | Christian periodicals, per million |
| **SCRIPTURES** | | |
| BIBLE DISTRIBUTION | | |
| 120. | *goal* | goal for all Bibles in place |
| 121. | *goal p.a.* | required Bibles distributed p.a. |
| 122. | *UBS p.a.* | UBS Bibles distributed p.a. |
| 123. | *other p.a.* | all other Bibles distributed p.a. |
| 124. | *total p.a.* | total all Bibles distributed p.a. |
| 125. | *T/G%* | ratio Bible total (col 124) to goal (col 121), % |
| NEW TESTAMENT DISTRIBUTION | | |
| 126. | *goal* | goal for all NTs in place |
| 127. | *goal p.a.* | required NTs distributed p.a. |
| 128. | *UBS p.a.* | UBS NTs distributed p.a. |
| 129. | *other p.a.* | all other NTs distributed p.a. |
| 130. | *duplicates* | NTs distributed via Bibles p.a. |
| 131. | *total p.a.* | total all NTs distributed p.a. |
| 132. | *T/G%* | ratio NT total (col 131) to goal (col 127), % |
| PORTIONS DISTRIBUTION (GOSPELS) | | |
| 133. | *goal* | goal for all gospels in place |
| 134. | *goal p.a.* | required gospels distributed p.a. |
| 135. | *UBS p.a.* | UBS portions (gospels) distributed p.a. |
| 136. | *other p.a.* | all other gospels distributed p.a. |
| 137. | *duplicates* | gospels distributed via Bibles & NTs p.a. |
| 138. | *total p.a.* | total all gospels distributed p.a. |
| 139. | *T/G %* | ratio gospel total (col 138) to goal (col 134),% |
| SELECTIONS DISTRIBUTION | | |
| 140. | *goal* | goal for all selections in place |
| 141. | *goal p.a.* | required selections distributed p.a. |
| 142. | *UBS p.a.* | UBS selections distributed p.a. |
| 143. | *other p.a.* | all other selections distributed p.a. |
| 144. | *duplicates* | selections distributed via gospels,N or B p.a. |
| 145. | *total p.a.* | total all selections distributed p.a. |
| 146. | *T/G %* | ratio selection total (col 145) to goal (col 141),% |
| **BROADCASTING** | | |
| RADIO/TV AUDIENCES | | |
| 147. | *cb aud* | regular audience for Christian programs, % |
| 148. | *cstat* | audience via Christian stations, % |
| 149. | *secstat* | audience via secular stations, % |
| **EVANGELISM** | | |
| OFFERS VIA 45 MINISTRIES | | |
| 150. | *q per day* | offers (disciple-opportunities) per day |
| 151. | *e p.a.p.c.* | offers per year per capita |
| **EVANGELIZATION** | | |
| WHEN BEGUN | | |
| 152. | *year begun* | year first Christians resident |
| STATUS OF EVANGELIZATION, E | | |
| 153. | *1900* | E (% population evangelized), 1900 |
| 154. | *1970* | E (% population evangelized), 1970 |
| 155. | *1990* | E (% population evangelized), 1990 |
| 156. | *1995* | E (% population evangelized), 1995 |
| 157. | *2000* | E (% population evangelized), 2000 |
| 158. | *2025* | E (% population evangelized), 2025 |
| SOURCE OF E IN AD 2000 | | |
| 159. | *internal* | evangelized by population's Christians |
| 160. | *external* | evangelized by Christians from outside |
| UNEVANGELIZED, AD 2000 | | |
| 161. | *U* | U, % population unevangelized |
| 162. | *total* | unevangelized persons |
| STRATEGIES | | |
| 163. | *World* | 3-fold trichotomy: A, B, C |
| 164. | *plans* | plans to evangelize globe (less 'other plans') |
| 165. | *target* | total top priority target peoples (T=1) |
| FUTURES (CHRISTIAN FUTURISTICS) | | |
| 166. | *growth index* | growth relative to demographics |
| 167. | *prospects* | outlook during 21st century (+2 to -2) |
| **COUNTRY TRENDS IN AD 2025** | | |
| DEMOGRAPHIC TRENDS | | |
| 168. | *pop 2025* | population in AD 2025 |
| 169. | *npop* | natural increase, % per year |
| 170. | *increase p.a.* | total increase per year |
| EVANGELIZATION TRENDS | | |
| 171. | *evangelized* | persons now evangelized |
| 172. | *E* | % of population evangelized |
| 173. | *outreach* | outreach per Christian = (E-C)/C |
| CHRISTIAN TRENDS | | |
| 174. | *Christians* | total all Christians |
| 175. | *C%* | Christians, % |
| 176. | *G%* | Christian growth rate, % p.a., AD 2000-2025 |
| 177. | *increase p.a.* | nett new Christians, p.a. (= 178 minus 179) |
| 178. | *gains p.a.* | Christian births + converts, p.a. |
| 179. | *losses p.a.* | Christian deaths + defectors, p.a. |
| **COUNTRY TRENDS IN AD 2050** | | |
| DEMOGRAPHIC TRENDS | | |
| 180. | *pop 2050* | population in AD 2050 |
| 181. | *npop* | natural increase, % per year |
| 182. | *increase p.a.* | total increase per year |
| EVANGELIZATION TRENDS | | |
| 183. | *evangelized* | persons now evangelized |
| 184. | *E* | % of population evangelized |
| 185. | *outreach* | outreach per Christian = (E-C)/C |
| CHRISTIAN TRENDS | | |
| 186. | *Christians* | total all Christians |
| 187. | *C%* | Christians, % |
| 188. | *G%* | Christian growth rate, % p.a., AD 2025-2050 |
| 189. | *increase p.a.* | nett new Christians, p.a. (= 190 minus 191) |
| 190. | *gains p.a.* | Christian births + converts, p.a. |
| 191. | *losses p.a.* | Christian deaths + defectors, p.a. |

### *NON-STATISTICAL DATA AND TYPOLOGIES*

***COUNTRY***

Column 1 Country's code
Column 3 Continent and region, as defined by UN

| Code | Continent and Region |
|---|---|
| A | Africa |
| A1 | Eastern Africa |
| A2 | Middle Africa |
| A3 | Northern Africa |
| A4 | Southern Africa |
| A5 | Western Africa |
| B | Antarctica |
| C | Asia |
| C1 | Eastern Asia |
| C2 | South-central Asia |
| C3 | South-eastern Asia |
| C4 | Western Asia |
| E | Europe |
| E1 | Eastern Europe |
| E2 | Northern Europe |
| E3 | Southern Europe |
| E4 | Western Europe |
| L | Latin America |
| L1 | Caribbean |
| L2 | Central America |
| L3 | South America |
| N1 | Northern America |
| P | Oceania |
| P1 | Australia-New Zealand |
| P2 | Melanesia |
| P3 | Micronesia |
| P4 | Polynesia |

***GEOPOLITICAL TYPOLOGIES***

Column 19 Development

| Code | |
|---|---|
| 1 | more developed (Europe, NAmerica, Aust-NZ, Japan, Russia, Temperate SAmerica) |
| 2 | less developed |
| 3 | least developed |

*Continued overleaf*

*Table 16–7 concluded*

## DEMOGRAPHICS

Column 18    Official state language(s), AD 2000: Languages are coded here as one-character variables, and include only those which are countrywide, i.e. official throughout their whole country. These are given in 2 listings: (1) at left below, a listing alphabetically by code, and (2) at right below, alphabetically by language.

### Code  Language

| Code | Language | Code | Language | Code | Language |
|---|---|---|---|---|---|
| A | Arabic | t | Tamil | l | Latin |
| B | Bengali | u | Sinhalese | m | Malay |
| C | Chinese (Mandarin) | v | Somali | n | Nauruan |
| D | Dutch | w | Sotho | o | Maltese |
| E | English | x | Sango | p | Palauan |
| F | French | y | Rundi | q | Tigrinya |
| G | German | z | Dzongkha | r | Rwandese |
| H | Hindi | | | s | Seselwa |
| I | Italian | A | Azerbaijani | t | Tok Pisin |
| J | Japanese | B | Belorussian | u | Slovak |
| K | Korean | C | Croatian | v | Chamorro |
| L | Amharic | D | Dari | w | Samoan |
| M | Afrikaans | E | Estonian | x | Swazi |
| N | Persian | F | Catalan | y | Aymara |
| O | Filipino | G | Georgian | z | Tongan |
| P | Portuguese | H | Greenlandic | | |
| Q | Serbo-Croatia | I | Maori | | |
| R | Russian | J | Faeroese | | |
| S | Spanish | K | Kazakh | | |
| T | Turkish | L | Latvian | | |
| U | Urdu | M | Macedonian | | |
| V | Vietnamese | N | Tahitian | | |
| W | Burmese | O | Luxemburgish | | |
| X | Indonesian | P | Pushtu | | |
| Y | Polish | Q | Moldavian | | |
| Z | Thai | R | Romanian | | |
| | | S | Swahili | | |
| a | Albanian | T | Tajik | | |
| b | Bulgarian | U | Ukrainian | | |
| c | Czech | V | Turkmen | | |
| d | Danish | W | Slovenian | | |
| e | Hebrew | X | Tswana | | |
| f | Finnish | Y | Serbian | | |
| g | Greek | Z | Uzbek | | |
| h | Hungarian | | | | |
| i | Irish | a | Armenian | | |
| j | Norwegian | b | Monokutuba | | |
| k | Khmer | c | Chewa | | |
| l | Lao | d | Marshallese | | |
| m | Malagasy | e | Lithuanian | | |
| n | Nepali | f | Divehi | | |
| o | Mongolian | g | Guarani | | |
| p | Bislama | h | Haitian Creol | | |
| q | Quechua | i | Icelandic | | |
| r | Romansch | j | Comorian | | |
| s | Swedish | k | Kirghiz | | |

### Language  Code

| Language | Code | Language | Code | Language | Code |
|---|---|---|---|---|---|
| Afrikaans | M | Kirghiz | k | Tamil | t |
| Albanian | a | Korean | K | Thai | Z |
| Amharic | L | Lao | l | Tigrinya | q |
| Arabic | A | Latin | l | Tok Pisin | t |
| Armenian | a | Latvian | L | Tongan | z |
| Aymara | y | Lithuanian | e | Tswana | X |
| Azerbaijani | A | Luxemburgish | O | Turkish | T |
| Belorussian | B | Macedonian | M | Turkmen | V |
| Bengali | B | Malagasy | m | Ukrainian | U |
| Bislama | p | Malay | m | Urdu | U |
| Bulgarian | b | Maltese | o | Uzbek | Z |
| Burmese | W | Maori | I | Vietnamese | V |
| Catalan | F | Marshallese | d | | |
| Chamorro | v | Moldavian | Q | | |
| Chewa | c | Mongolian | o | | |
| Chinese (Mandarin) | C | Monokutuba | b | | |
| Comorian | j | Nauruan | n | | |
| Croatian | C | Nepali | n | | |
| Czech | c | Norwegian | j | | |
| Danish | d | Palauan | p | | |
| Dari | D | Persian | N | | |
| Divehi | f | Polish | Y | | |
| Dutch | D | Portuguese | P | | |
| Dzongkha | z | Pushtu | P | | |
| English | E | Quechua | q | | |
| Estonian | E | Romanian | R | | |
| Faeroese | J | Romansch | r | | |
| Filipino | O | Rundi | y | | |
| Finnish | f | Russian | R | | |
| French | F | Rwandese | r | | |
| Georgian | G | Samoan | w | | |
| German | G | Sango | x | | |
| Greek | g | Serbian | Y | | |
| Greenlandic | H | Serbo-Croatia | Q | | |
| Guarani | g | Seselwa | s | | |
| Haitian Creol | h | Sinhalese | u | | |
| Hebrew | e | Slovak | u | | |
| Hindi | H | Slovenian | W | | |
| Hungarian | h | Somali | v | | |
| Icelandic | i | Sotho | w | | |
| Indonesian | X | Spanish | S | | |
| Irish | i | Swahili | S | | |
| Italian | I | Swazi | x | | |
| Japanese | J | Swedish | s | | |
| Kazakh | K | Tahitian | N | | |
| Khmer | k | Tajik | T | | |

## RELIGIOUS PERSECUTION

Column 56 Religious liberty

1. State propagates Christianity
2. Massive state subsidies to churches
3. Limited state subsidies to churches
4. State subsidizes schools only
5. Complete state non-interference
6. Limited political restrictions
7. Minorities discriminated against
8. State interference and obstruction
9. State hostility and prohibition
10. State suppression or eradication

Column 57 Christian Safety Index (CSI) computed as follows:  $[AC + (2 \times HSI) + (5 \times (100 - (10 \times \text{Religious liberty code}))) + (2 \times (100 - \text{Murder Rate}))]/10$
Data in this column are percentages. Their meaning is illustrated here from the key of Global Map 7.
*RELIGIOUS LIBERTY*
Very safe (CSI > 85%)
Safe (CSI 80-85%)
Marginally safe (CSI 70-79%)
*RELIGIOUS PERSECUTION*
Some obstruction, harassment (CSI 60-69%)
Some persecution (CSI 50-59%)
*MARTYRDOM SITUATIONS*
Dangerous (CSI 40-49%)
Highly dangerous (CSI under 40%)

## CHURCH/STATE RELATIONS

Columns 60-63
Global Christianity
State religion or philosophy

*Code*

| | | | | | |
|---|---|---|---|---|---|
| A | Atheistic | RH | Hindu | RC | Roman Catholic |
| S | Secular | RI | Islamic | RS | Shinto |
| R | Religious | RJ | Jewish | RT | Ethnoreligionist |
| RD | Adventist | RL | Lutheran | RX | Christian (unspecified) |
| RA | Anglican | RM | Methodist | R | Religious (unspecified) |
| RB | Buddhist | RO | Orthodox | | |
| RG | Confucian | RR | Reformed | | |

## MISSIONS

Column 88. Current status of foreign missions.

| | | | |
|---|---|---|---|
| 7 | sharing | 3 | restricted |
| 6 | sending | 2 | partially-closed |
| 5 | receiving/sending | 1 | closed |
| 4 | receiving | | |

## FUTURES

Column 167. Prospects during 21st century.
*Code*

2 bright
1 fair
0 static
-1 dull
-2 bleak

# 9. PART 33 "GEOATLAS"

The 16 Global Maps in this section utilize data and typologies from Table 12-1 and elsewhere, as indicated on each map under its title. In the process the exact definitions used on the maps differ in a few cases from those in Table 12-1. Thus Global Map 8 creates a more developed scale of foreign missions to utilize the explanatory potential of the mapping procedure. No contradictions are implied, but the reader should note that the scales and meanings of each key on a handful of global maps (especially Global Map 8) are not the same as those in the data in Table 12-1 (in this case, column 88).

Human Environment maps are explained on the verso of Part 33.

Part 17

# RELIGIOMETRICS

Analysis of miniprofiles of 9,900 distinct religions worldwide

*Great beyond all question is the mystery of our religion.*
—Apostle Paul (I Timothy 3:16, Revised English Bible)

The academic disciplines of theology, church history, comparative religion, religious studies, and the like have all been pursued without serious attention to the sciences of missiometrics or religiometrics. Since 5,137 million people on Earth—85% of the world—are religionists who live their lives and livelihood in this context of billions of fellow-believers in some 9,900 different religions, descriptive demographic and numerical analyses of their welfare and their activities are long overdue.

The 2 main Tables 17-5 and 17-6 give one descriptive line of 10 columns to each of the 2,800 largest or most significant religions. Emphasis throughout these miniprofiles is on description of the followers themselves and not primarily on their beliefs or dogmas.

# Analysis of miniprofiles of 9,900 distinct religions worldwide

The usual way in which the world of religions is described numerically is by means of a listing of the 7 largest or best-known world religions each followed by a number enumerating its followers. The familiar form in which this is done is naming the followers of the 7 as shown in Table 17–1, which is itself a shorter version of this volume's Table 1-2.

While valuable as a succinct global summary, if not expanded further such listings become a gross oversimplification of what is in fact a vast global complex of at least 10,000 distinct and different religions across the world. What is needed is a comprehensive global survey, description, typology and classification of all religions.

With this in mind, there are many different ways in which religions can be defined, described, and classified. They are usually defined by their beliefs, systems of belief, dogmas, doctrines, philosophy, origins, history, founders, and current personalities. Such a comparative approach is intensely interesting and valuable for the understanding of religion that it provides. But this approach often ignores statistical enumeration as of little value in understanding religious issues.

### *Defining not 'religion' but 'a religion'*

The difference depends on whether one is studying the abstract category 'religion' or the more specific category 'a religion'. For any scientific study of the latter, concrete aspects such as size, language, race, ethnicity, location, age, and relation to other religions are just as important as the more philosophical aspects.

This part of the survey therefore attempts to present a relational database in which all religions can be listed with comparable variables that can be contrasted, listed, ranked, added, and totaled to give the overall global situation. For this purpose, a religion is defined here in a new and unusual way—in the first instance not by its dogmas, beliefs, or practices, but primarily by its followers or believers or **adherents**, also termed here religionists.

### *Defining a religion by its adherents/followers*

Neither religion nor Christianity can be fully understood without serious attention being given to 5,137 million persons—85% of the world's population—who are religionists, which means followers or adherents or members of the globe's 9,891 different and distinct organized religions.

A religion therefore is defined here as a religious community of believers or followers or adherents who hold there to be something unique in their beliefs, and who give their primary religious allegiance and loyalty to that religion. What this means is that the basic unit of study and analysis here is a specific religion with its religionists, with a short list of features that can be described and measured. Note also that although our preferred terms for those belonging to a religion are (in this order) followers, believers, or adherents, these terms are used here as exact synonyms with wide use of 'adherents' as a slightly more technical sociological term.

A distinct religion is defined here by its adherents' loyalty to it. They accept it as in some sense unique and superior to all other religions, even those closely related to it. In practice, adherents ignore other religions, not necessarily wilfully or deliberately. In practice they can get along without depending on the existence of any or all other religions or their adherents.

Likewise a religion's global significance, its impact and influence in the wider world, can be measured by its adherents' size and other attributes. In the database, some 21 attributes—14 being numerical and 7 descriptive—are tabulated for every religion. Further attributes are added in the table's final column 10,

**Table 17–1. Global status of religions, AD 2000: a minimal statement.**

The following table demonstrates the minimal statistical information typically offered in global comparative studies of religion. Though useful for those wanting a succinct statement, it represents an oversimplification that calls for a far more complex elaboration. (Source of numbers: Table 1-2 in Part 1 "GeoStatus".)

| Name<br>*1* | Followers<br>*2* |
|---|---|
| *Religionists* | *5,137,000,000* |
| Christians | 1,999,564,000 |
| Muslims | 1,188,243,000 |
| Hindus | 811,336,000 |
| Buddhists | 359,982,000 |
| Ethnoreligionists | 228,367,000 |
| Sikhs | 23,258,000 |
| Jews | 14,434,000 |
| *Nonreligionists* | *918,249,000* |
| Agnostics (nonreligious) | 768,159,000 |
| Atheists (Anti-religionists) | 150,090,000 |

**Table 17–2. A typology of 12 varieties of the globe's 10,000 distinct religions in AD 2000, with each's global significance, its range of descriptive attributes, and its current contact with Christians and Christianity.**

***Definition of a religion***
A religion is defined in this survey in the first instance not by its dogmas but primarily by its followers/believers/adherents. This means that a religion is defined by its adherents' loyalty to it; by their acceptance of it as unique and superior to all other religions, which they in practice ignore (though not necessarily deliberately), even those closely related in beliefs; by its relative autonomy (freedom to manage its own affairs); by its use of its own language, culture, customs, property; and by its adherents' ability in practice to get along without depending on any other religions or their adherents. Similarly, a religion's global significance—its significance in the wider world—is measured by its adherents' size and other attributes. These are defined and measured in particular by any distinctive or unique features among 21 of the religion's attributes or properties. Ten of these are tabulated in the 10 columns in Tables 17-5 and 17-6, and are listed here below as columns 1, 2, 3, 4, 5, 6, 7, 8, 9, 10. Note that other columns with a letter (4a, 7a, 8a, 10a-h) are not shown in Tables 17-5 and 17-6 but are available via the related CD.

1. The uniqueness of its **name** or identity, being distinct and distinctive with both collective and individual meanings. Names are given in this column in 4 forms depending on which are best known: (1) either in their own language, or in English usage; and (2) either the name of the religion, or of its religionists (adherents).
2. Any shared **pedigree** or relationship to existing religions, religious movements, or families or clusters of religions, as shown by a code which indicates each religion's relation vertically and horizontally to other religions (see Part 16 "GeoCodebook" and the database version of *WCE* Country Tables 1).
3. Its **type** or layer or level (religion, family of religions, macroreligion, etc.) as measured by a scale 0-11 followed by an indicator of order of magnitude (a to h).
4. Its history, as illustrated in particular by its year of origin (year **begun**).

4a. Size: the numerical size globally of its followers. This is almost universally known and stated, in one form or another. For many religions the meaningful figure is adult members, which refers to persons over 15 years old. The variable in this column enumerates **adult members** in AD 2000. Their figures are given on the related CD, *World Christian database*, but are not given in the tables below.

5. The more common usage is for a religion to compile and quote a larger category than adults, namely the religion's total followers or believers or **adherents** or total community. This is often called the demographic or census or total population figure. It is defined as the total of its adult members plus their children and infants, and all other varieties of followers. Of these 2 statistics (in columns 4a and 5) the more detailed one is the main one reported by the religion, and the less detailed one, or the more obviously rounded one (rounded to the nearest 100 or 1,000 or 10,000 or 100,000) is an estimate computed here from adult/child ratios in the countries concerned.
6. Its **extent**, measured as the number of countries worldwide where it is significantly present.
7. Its geographical **location** expressed as its main or major **country** (shown in its 4-letter coded form), with sometimes (in the end column) a note on where its HQ is.

7a. Its adherents' identity as a **people:** who and what ethnolinguistic people are in the majority in this religion, or what language the majority speak, as indicated by their 6-character ethnic code and/or 8-character language code as used in *WCT* or *WCE*.

8. Its predominant missiological **World** (A, B, or C), being a measure of its context in its major country or ethnolinguistic people and its evangelization.

8a. The number of its adherents who can be said to be evangelistically **unreached** or unevangelized. As with variable 4a above, this variable 8a is not shown in the database table printed below but is accessible on the related CD, *World Christian database.*

9. The current extent of its **contact** with global Christianity and its world mission, or one of its branches, using code 0 = no contact, 1 = sparse or occasional contact, 2 = limited contact, 3 = moderate contact, 4 = extensive contact everywhere, 5 = universal or total contact, with widespread dialogue literature. (See analysis of this variable in Part 28, Table 28-6).
10. Notes, covering initials and translation of name into English, descriptions, examples, name for God, background religions of ethnic group, D = Christian denominations present, M = Christian missions present.

*Typology of basic types of religions*

| *Type* | TWELVE LAYERS OR LEVELS OF RELIGIONS | *Global total of religions* |
|---|---|---|
| 0 | Global nonreligions | 3 |
| 1 | Universal georeligions | 18 |
| 2 | Subsidiary georeligions | 994 |
| 3 | Monoreligions | 3,008 |
| 4 | Communions | 98 |
| 5 | Ecclesiastical traditions | 301 |
| 6 | Monodenominations | 248 |
| 7 | Religioclusters | 628 |
| 8 | Politico-religious parties | 36 |
| 9 | Clerical orders | 98 |
| 10 | Microreligions | 1,959 |
| 11 | Other minor religions | 2,500 |
| — | 'Religion' = each of the above categories | 9,891 |

***Additional names, notes, data, beliefs***

10a. Its **beliefs** and belief system involving the divine or the supernatural, the origin of life, human role on earth, and/or related dogmas; names for Jesus in its language.
10b. Its related **behavior**, customs and experiential phenomena.
10c. Its degree of **independence** from other related religions or religious movements, and the separateness of its traditions.
10d. Its variety of autonomy of **institutions** whether few or many.
10e. Its **leadership**, whether lay or ordained, male or female, religious or nonreligious, absolute or localized, hierarchical or democratic, visible or invisible.
10f. Its literature and **bibliography** of descriptive books and articles.
10g. Its **self-understanding** as a unique religion, with unique validity, self-sufficient, claiming to be superior to several, many, most, or even all other religions, hence claiming completeness and needing no religious input from any other religion.
10h. Its **access to the Christian Scriptures** (a scale 0-5: 0 = no contact, up to 5 = Bible available in main language and in wide use).

***Enumerating attributes***
For each religion listed in the main table below, the first 10 attributes as described above are presented in the 10 columns of the table, in the same order. Additional attributes are measured or further described in the final columns 10a-h, showing a selection of data illustrating each religion.

***Twelve levels of religion*** (column 3, *Type*)
All religions are classified here by *Type* in column 3. Using a 12-point scale, this describes each religion in terms of the various layers or levels composing religions in general and the many ways in which they relate or can be grouped and classified.

Note that the global total of all religions in each *Type* category 0-11, shown in the end column of the minitable immediately below, adds up to the total of all religions. Thus 2 religions may be correctly spoken of as 2 distinct religions even though there may be overlap in adherents, or even with one simply a part of the other. Thus Islam (Muslims) is properly described as a distinct religion; but so also is its excommunicated sect Ahmadiya.

The codes 0-11 shown under *Type* in the large table have the meanings shown in the minitable at left.

**Table 17–3.** The globe's population enumerated by 22 major family pedigrees, by 11 major religionist categories, and by 8 orders of magnitude of followers/adherents, AD 2000.

| Pedigree family | Religionist family | Distinct religions | Followers | 0 | 1 | 2 | 3 | 4 | 5 | 6 | 7 | 8 | 9 | 10 | 11 | a | b | c | d | e | f | g | h |
|---|---|---|---|---|---|---|---|---|---|---|---|---|---|---|---|---|---|---|---|---|---|---|---|
| – | Nonreligionists | 3 | 1,836,497,000 | 3 | — | — | — | — | — | — | — | — | — | — | — | 2 | 1 | — | — | — | — | — | — |
| B | Buddhists | 274 | 1,986,033,000 | — | 1 | 235 | — | — | — | — | 21 | — | — | 17 | — | 3 | 21 | 46 | 73 | 131 | — | — | — |
| C | Christians | 1,331 | 28,722,195,000 | — | 1 | 97 | — | 84 | 301 | 248 | 516 | — | — | 72 | 12 | 24 | 184 | 492 | 296 | 323 | 11 | 1 | — |
| D | Taoists | 10 | 4,725,000 | — | 1 | 6 | — | — | — | — | 3 | — | — | — | — | 1 | — | 2 | 5 | 3 | — | — | — |
| F | Chinese folk-religionists | 1 | 384,807,000 | — | — | 1 | — | — | — | — | — | — | — | — | — | 1 | — | — | — | — | — | — | — |
| G | Confucianists | 2 | 6,399,000 | — | 1 | 1 | — | — | — | — | — | — | — | — | — | — | — | 1 | 1 | — | — | — | — |
| H | Hindus | 90 | 3,356,415,000 | — | 1 | 74 | — | — | — | — | 1 | 6 | 7 | 1 | — | 6 | 6 | 18 | 18 | 41 | 1 | — | — |
| J | Jews | 63 | 79,092,000 | — | 1 | 37 | — | 1 | — | — | 15 | 8 | — | 1 | — | — | 3 | 12 | 14 | 33 | 1 | — | — |
| K | Sikhs | 21 | 29,037,000 | — | 1 | 14 | — | — | — | — | 4 | 1 | — | 1 | — | — | 1 | 1 | 5 | 14 | — | — | — |
| L | Baha'is | 4 | 7,120,000 | — | 1 | 3 | — | — | — | — | — | — | — | — | — | — | 1 | — | — | 3 | — | — | — |
| M | Muslims | 269 | 5,261,498,000 | — | 1 | 178 | — | — | 12 | — | 51 | 21 | 1 | 5 | — | 8 | 22 | 47 | 62 | 125 | 5 | — | — |
| N | New-Religionists | 160 | 902,473,000 | — | 1 | 155 | — | — | — | — | 1 | — | — | 3 | — | — | 14 | 23 | 40 | 80 | 3 | — | — |
| S | Shintoists | 147 | 155,143,000 | — | 1 | 138 | — | — | — | — | 2 | — | — | 6 | — | — | 2 | 9 | 25 | 105 | 5 | 1 | — |
| T | Ethnoreligionists | 4,937 | 864,307,000 | — | 1 | — | 3,008 | — | — | — | — | — | — | 1,928 | — | 2 | 5 | 50 | 332 | 2,620 | 1,375 | 491 | 62 |
| U | Spiritists | 36 | 108,185,000 | — | 1 | 32 | — | — | — | — | 2 | — | — | 1 | — | — | 3 | 6 | 13 | 13 | — | — | — |
| V | Jains | 16 | 8,886,000 | — | 1 | 14 | — | — | — | — | — | — | — | 1 | — | — | — | 3 | 4 | 8 | 1 | — | — |
| W | Religionists | 16 | 1,438,940,000 | — | 1 | 2 | — | 1 | — | — | 12 | — | — | — | — | 3 | — | 4 | 1 | 8 | — | — | — |
| X | Non-Christians | 1 | 4,055,485,000 | — | — | — | — | — | — | — | — | — | — | — | — | 1 | — | — | — | — | — | — | — |
| Y | Quasireligionists | 8 | 137,245,000 | — | 1 | 6 | — | — | — | — | — | — | — | 1 | — | — | 2 | 2 | — | 2 | 1 | — | — |
| Z | Zoroastrians | 2 | 2,794,000 | — | 1 | 1 | — | — | — | — | — | — | — | — | — | — | — | 1 | 1 | — | — | — | — |
| | Other peripheral religionists | 2,000 | 20,000,000 | — | — | — | — | — | — | — | — | — | — | — | 2,000 | — | — | — | — | — | — | — | — |
| | Other hidden religionists | 500 | 1,000,000 | — | — | — | — | — | — | — | — | — | — | — | 500 | — | — | — | — | — | — | — | — |
| | Total non-Christian adherence | 8,560 | 20,646,081,000 | 3 | 17 | 897 | 3,008 | 14 | 301 | 248 | 112 | 36 | 26 | 1,947 | — | 26 | 80 | 226 | 595 | 3,186 | 1,393 | 492 | 62 |
| | Total all religionist adherence | 9,891 | 49,368,276,000 | 3 | 18 | 994 | 3,008 | 98 | 301 | 248 | 628 | 36 | 98 | 1,959 | 2,500 | 50 | 264 | 718 | 891 | 3,509 | 1,404 | 493 | 62 |
| | Multi-counted adherence | | -43,313,227,000 | — | — | — | — | — | — | — | — | — | — | — | — | — | — | — | — | — | — | — | — |
| | Religionists worldwide | 9,888 | 5,136,800,500 | 0 | 18 | 994 | 3,008 | 98 | 301 | 248 | 628 | 36 | 98 | 1,959 | 2,500 | 48 | 263 | 718 | 891 | 3,509 | 1,404 | 493 | 62 |
| | Nonreligionists worldwide | 3 | 918,248,500 | 3 | — | — | — | — | — | — | — | — | — | — | — | 2 | 1 | — | — | — | — | — | — |
| | **Global population** | **9,891** | **6,055,049,000** | 3 | 18 | 994 | 3,008 | 98 | 301 | 248 | 628 | 36 | 98 | 1,959 | 2,500 | 50 | 264 | 718 | 891 | 3,509 | 1,404 | 493 | 62 |

*Column group headers:* UNIVERSAL GEORELIGIONS AND FOLLOWERS / RELIGIONS BY TYPE — Religions by major category (0–11) — Religion by size of adherents/followers (a–h).

where any additional numerical data are added when available for particular religions. All these attributes are listed, defined, and described at the beginning of Table 17–2. Meanwhile, the scale measuring type and magnitude should now be given.

### Key to type and order of magnitude
Column 3 in the full tables that follow (Tables 17-5 and 17-6) gives, for every religion, two components of the indicator 'type'. These 2 scales have the following meanings.

*Major category* (first character of 'Type', a number):
0 = **Global nonreligions:** agnosticism, or antireligion (atheism)
1 = **Universal georeligions** coded in the *World Christian database (WCD)* with a single letter
2 = **Subsidiary georeligions** ending each's *WCD* code with 2 or more capitals, or 's' (= 'sub') and a capital
3 = **Monoreligions** with members restricted each to a single culture or tribe or people
4 = **Communions** of similar religions across world
5 = **Ecclesiastical traditions** or families
6 = Very large Christian **monodenominations** of over 1 million members, or over 10 million members
7 = **Religioclusters** (e.g. councils of churches, or of similar religionists) at national or wider level
8 = **Politico-religious parties**
9 = **Clerical orders** of full-time missionaries, evangelists, monks, priests, pastors, clergy, sisters, nuns
10 = **Microreligions:** small local religions, many moribund, many dying
11 = **Other minireligions:** all other religions

*Size* (second character of 'Type', a letter)
a = Huge: over 200 million adherents
b = Very large: 10 million to 200 million
c = Large: 1 million to 10 million
d = Small: 100,000 to 1 million
e = Very small: 1,000 to 100,000
f = Minuscule: 100 to 1,000
g = Microscopic: 10 to 100
h = Defunct: under 10 adherents, down to zero (extinct)

### How many religions are there?
The answer proposed here depends on the role of the followers of religions. If religion is defined as primarily an entity with a clearly-stated system of beliefs, then it would make sense to recognize the existence of only a handful of distinct religions. Christianity, for example, could in this sense be spoken of as one single religion; likewise with Islam, Hinduism, Buddhism, Judaism, et alia. But if we define a religion by its followers, we find multiple separate entries—in the case of Christianity, as will shortly be demonstrated, one finds over 1,330 separate communities of followers who in practice have nothing to do with each other, who each regard their community as the true (or truest) religion. It thus makes sense to speak of 1,330 separate religions if we make clear that 'separate' means organizationally and without implying hostility or conflict.

### Eleven levels of religions
Among students and scholars of religion, the term 'religion' is employed at widely different levels. Buddhism is usually thought of by most as a religion; others however regard it as a group of religions; yet others insist that it is in fact a whole family of different religions. Likewise Islam is a religion, but so also is its heretical sect Ahmadiyya; and this in turn consists of 2 rival religions, Qadianis and Lahoris. In order to make sense of statistics of their adherents, and to obtain national, regional, continental, and eventually global statistics of each and every religion that can be directly related to demographic populations, it is therefore necessary to clearly define the various levels to avoid double or multiple counting and similar misunderstandings.

All religions are thus classified in column 3 of Table 17–5 and 17-6, using the 10-point scale defined in Tables 17-2 and 17-4. The basic unit, *a religion* is there given a technical description meaning that it is a small measurable building block in this study of religions, in much the same way as the molecule, or the atom, or now the quark, has been so regarded in the study of physics.

This basic unit can appear as various larger entities in the following ascending ranking of complexity: a *religion* can take any of 10 forms, sizes, or shapes: a *local religion* (a tribal religion closed to outsiders), a *cluster of related religions*, a *tradition*, a *megadenomination*, a *macrodenomination*, a *communion* (confession, a family of religions), a *megacommunion* (megatradition), a *megareligion* (a family of megatraditions), a *macroreligion* (a global religion or family of megareligions), and even finally a *cosmoreligion* (universal religion open to all, gigareligion, a huge global macrofamily of macroreligions).

For any specific religion, therefore, all of its complexity as described above can be rapidly pinpointed by means of this single digit describing type together with a 2-, 3-, 4-, or 5- character code as listed in the second column of Table 17-2, 17-4, 17-5, or 17-6.

### A coded pedigree for each religion
Religions are related to other religions in varying degrees which can then be reduced to a simple code representing its pedigree. This is presented and listed in Tables 17-2 and 17-4 for all values of the code. This code can be regarded as the first or primary identifying feature of any religion. The code describes the religion's pedigree or relationship to other existing religions, religious movements, or clusters or families of religions. The code thus indicates each religion's relation vertically and horizontally to other religions. Meanings of these codes are shown here in Part 16 "GeoCodebook", Table 16-3.

The order of letters in the codes used here is designed to assist the user in memorizing codes that represent complex names. An initial letter 's' before capitals indicates a specific sect or example or case in a wider category. Thus Japan's Shinshu Ōtani is coded sTPMB meaning that this religion is a sect of True Pure Land Mahayana Buddhism. Such wider categories may themselves be sects, but still be wide enough to justify a capital letter; thus the Wahhabite school of Sunni Muslims, mainly in Saudi Arabia, is coded WSM. This order of code letters means that to measure the closeness of any 2 religions, the user compares each character in the code, reading from right to left: the final righthand letter first, then the last but one, and so on. This procedure provides an estimate of distance or religious barriers between 2 populations.

### DEFINING 12 MAJOR CATEGORIES OF RELIGION

Each of the major categories from 0 to 11 can now be described and its definition justified.

### 0. Global nonreligions
Before the great religious categories are listed, note must be taken of the existence of 3 huge global nonreligions: atheism with 150 million adherents, agnosticism with 768 million nonreligious or secularist persons, with their combined total of 918 millions whom we term nonreligionists or nonbelievers. These systems have arisen from only 3 million adherents in the year 1900 and have since engulfed the formerly Christian heartlands of Europe, Russia, and North America. They intrude like a monstrous cosmological black hole growing larger every year.

### 1. Universal georeligions
These are the largest religions proper: Christianity, Islam, Hinduism, Buddhism, and 14 others. They encompass the whole world (*gaia* or *geo-* being Greek and Latin for the Earth); and they are universal in the sense that any persons anywhere can become members. They are open to all of any race or background.

Table 17–4. **A classification system of major types of religion in AD 2000.**

| *Code* 1 | *Major category* 2 | *Total* 3 | *Type* 4 | *Type of religion* 5 | *Total* 6 | *Adherents* 7 | *Definition of type of religion incorporating magnitude of adherents/followers* 8 |
|---|---|---|---|---|---|---|---|
| 0 | Global nonreligions | 3 | 0-a | Agnosticism | 2 | 1,686,407,000 | A huge 'black hole,' arising since 1900, engulfing formerly Christian populations |
| | | | 0-b | Atheism | 1 | 150,090,000 | A vast number of organized and unorganized militantly antireligious atheists |
| 1 | Universal georeligions | 18 | 1-a | Cosmoreligion | 7 | 9,362,976,000 | A universal religion (= open to all of any race or background), with over 200 million persons |
| | | | 1-b | Global religion | 4 | 152,382,000 | A universal religion with adherents from 10 million to 200 million adherents |
| | | | 1-c | World religion | 7 | 26,651,000 | A universal religion, worldwide, and with 1 million to 10 million adherents |
| 2 | Subsidiary georeligions | 994 | 2-a | Gigageoreligion | 30 | 17,603,274,000 | A huge megabloc or other segment of a universal georeligion, with over 200 million adherents |
| | | | 2-b | Macrogeoreligion | 87 | 4,403,557,000 | Smaller than a gigageoreligion, but still very large with from 10 million to 200 million adherents |
| | | | 2-c | Megageoreligion | 152 | 490,846,000 | Smaller still, but still large with from 1 million to 10 million adherents |
| | | | 2-d | Minigeoreligion | 232 | 78,680,000 | A small georeligion, with 100,000–1 million adherents |
| | | | 2-e | Quasigeoreligion | 493 | 10,005,000 | A very small georeligion, with 1,000–100,000 adherents |
| 3 | Monoreligions | 3,008 | 3-a | Gigamonoreligion | 1 | 216,161,000 | A huge religion restricted to one culture or people with over 200 million adherents |
| | | | 3-b | Macromonoreligion | 5 | 168,835,000 | A very large religion restricted to one culture or people (10 million to 200 millions) |
| | | | 3-c | Megamonoreligion | 50 | 109,991,000 | A large religion restricted to one culture or people (1 million to 10 millions) |
| | | | 3-d | Minimonoreligion | 332 | 95,740,000 | A small religion restricted to one culture or people (100,000 to 1 million) |
| | | | 3-e | Quasimonoreligion | 2,620 | 44,630,000 | A very small religion restricted to one culture or people (1,000 to 100,000) |
| 4 | Communions | 98 | 4-a | Gigacommunion | 1 | 901,000,000 | A huge global association of similar denominations or religions over 200 million |
| | | | 4-b | Macrocommunion | 24 | 1,327,447,000 | A very large gathering of like-minded denominations or religions, 10 million to 200 million |
| | | | 4-c | Megacommunion | 41 | 151,851,000 | A large association of like-minded denominations or religions, with 1 million to 10 millions |
| | | | 4-d | Minicommunion | 20 | 8,786,000 | A small association of like-minded denominations or religions, with 100,000–1 million |
| | | | 4-e | Quasicommunion | 12 | 202,000 | A very small association of like-minded denominations or religions, with 1,000 to 100,000 |
| 5 | Ecclesiastical traditions | 301 | 5-a | Gigatradition | 1 | 1,043,106,000 | A huge ecclesiastical family or tradition (over 200 million) |
| | | | 5-b | Macrotradition | 27 | 736,497,000 | A very large ecclesiastical family or tradition (10 million to 200 millions) |
| | | | 5-c | Megatradition | 84 | 293,554,000 | A large ecclesiastical family or tradition (1 million to 10 millions) |
| | | | 5-d | Minitradition | 93 | 33,694,000 | A small ecclesiastical family or tradition (100,000 to 1 million) |
| | | | 5-e | Quasitradition | 96 | 2,984,000 | A very small ecclesiastical family or tradition (1,000 to 100,000) |
| 6 | Monodenominations | 248 | 6-b | Macrodenomination | 34 | 1,201,232,000 | A very large monolithic Christian denomination (over 10 million affiliated members) |
| | | | 6-c | Megadenomination | 195 | 609,896,000 | A large denomination (from 1 million to 10 millions) |
| | | | 6-d | Minidenomination | 6 | 1,465,000 | Any small unusual Christian denomination (100,000–1 million) with prominent features |
| | | | 6-e | Quasidenomination | 13 | 323,000 | Any very small unusual denomination (1,000–100,000) with prominent features |
| 7 | Religioclusters | 628 | 7-a | Gigareligiocluster | 8 | 4,223,279,000 | A huge council or association of dissimilar religions (over 200 millions) |
| | | | 7-b | Macroreligiocluster | 78 | 3,327,581,000 | A very large council or association of dissimilar religions (from 10 million to 200 millions) |
| | | | 7-c | Megareligiocluster | 182 | 647,550,000 | A large council or association of dissimilar religions (from 1 million to 10 millions) |
| | | | 7-d | Minireligiocluster | 189 | 66,568,000 | A small council or association of dissimilar religions (from 100,000 to 1 million) |
| | | | 7-e | Quasireligiocluster | 171 | 5,164,000 | A very small council or association of dissimilar religions (from 1,000 to 100,000) |
| 8 | Politico-religious parties | 36 | 8-b | Macropoliticoreligion | 4 | 140,000,000 | A very large political organization or party based on one religion (10 million to 200 millions) |
| | | | 8-c | Megapoliticoreligion | 6 | 15,394,000 | A large political organization or party based on one religion (1 million to 10 millions) |
| | | | 8-d | Minipoliticoreligion | 12 | 4,697,000 | A small political organization or party based on one religion (from 100,000 to 1 million) |
| | | | 8-e | Quasipoliticoreligion | 14 | 388,000 | A very small political organization or party based on one religion (from 1,000 to 100,000) |
| 9 | Clerical orders | 98 | 9-c | Megaclerical order | 1 | 1,500,000 | A large order/congregation/institute/society of full-time workers (over 1 million) |
| | | | 9-d | Miniclerical order | 7 | 1,570,000 | A religious order/congregation/institute/society of full-time workers (100,000 to 1 million) |
| | | | 9-e | Microclerical order | 90 | 725,000 | A small religious order/congregation/institute/society of full-time workers (1,000 to 100,000) |
| 10 | Microreligions | 1,959 | 10-f | Local microreligion | 1,404 | 570,000 | A minuscule organized local religion with from 100 to 1,000 adherents |
| | | | 10-g | Moribund microreligion | 493 | 24,200 | A very small organized local religion, rapidly declining with only 10–100 adherents |
| | | | 10-h | Dying microreligion | 62 | 320 | An all but extinct local religion with less than 10 adherents |
| 11 | Other minor religions | 2,500 | 11-e | Other peripheral religions | 2,000 | 20,000,000 | 2,000 peripheral religions, on the periphery of our definition of religion |
| | | | 11-e | Other hidden religions | 500 | 1,000,000 | 500 clandestine minor religious systems, often illegal or subversive. |
| | Total all religions | 9,891 | | | 9,891 | 49,368,272,520 | Total adherents/followers includes multiple membership/adherence |
| | Multi-counted adherence | | | | | -43,313,223,520 | Persons classified by themselves or by others as in an average of 10 different religions |
| | Religionists worldwide | | | | | 5,136,800,500 | Total individual religionists in world at mid-2000 (85%) |
| | Nonreligionists worldwide | | | | | 918,248,500 | Total individual nonreligionists in world at mid-2000 (15%) |
| | **Global population** | | | | | **6,055,049,000** | **Total individuals at mid-2000** |

In this analysis we subdivide them by size into 7 cosmoreligions, 4 global religions, and 7 world religions (see Table 17–4 for exact definitions).

### 2. *Subsidiary georeligions*

The universal georeligions are mostly vast macrofamilies of smaller religions. This second category refers to the major subdivisions within the universal georeligions. These are mostly huge megablocs, national religions, schools of law, or other large segments. We divide these georeligions (and all the subsequent categories too) by size of their adherents into generic names beginning giga- (1 billion or thereabouts), macro- (around 200 millions), mega- (around 10 millions), mini- (under 1 million), micro- (under 1,000).

### 3. *Monoreligions*

This is the largest number of related but distinct and separate religions.The largest single specific family of religions in the world today is what this survey is calling ethnoreligions. These are religions each confined to members of one single ethnolinguistic people, tribe, or culture. No persons outside the tribe may join; no members may leave (although in this present analysis members who have joined another religion, e.g. Christianity or Islam, are no longer enumerated in an ethnoreligion's demographic totals). In most cases an ethnoreligion has a unique name for God, Creator, or a complex of names for God or of gods (see *WCE* Table 9-12, 'Names for God in 900 languages'). An ethnoreligion is also likely to have unique Creation and Flood and related stories, unique ethics and practices, and usually its own unique language which functions to exclude aliens from other tribes or races. Table 17–6 lists all 388 ethnoreligions each with over 100,000 adherents. Its database records that the total of all ethnoreligions with no restriction due to size is 4,936 different religions. All of these latter are listed with their data on the CD, *World Christian database*.

### *Christianity as a macrofamily of macroreligions*

The next 3 categories apply almost entirely to Christianity and its multitude of religious subdivisions. This is therefore the place to explain the unique place of Christianity and its present fragmentation.

The application of these coding levels to Christianity is complex but provides a rich typology. Clearly Christianity may correctly be termed a single religion; but its adherents would argue that Christians are also composed of many other religions. Roman Catholics are sufficiently different and distinct and separated from Russian Orthodox or Anglicans or Baptists or Pentecostals or Seventh-day Adventists or Jehovah's Witnesses for us to agree that all 7 of these are, in practice, 7 distinct and separate religions. Southern Baptists practice their faith with little or no religious contact with Classical Pentecostals; and so on. In this classification the largest Christian macrodenominations are defined as distinct and separate religions when their adherents each number over 10 million; and those from 1 to 10 million as megadenominations. Macrodenominations (level 6) are included in Tables 17-5 and 17-6, column 3, by the type value 6.

The case for categorizing Christianity as over 1,300 distinct religions can best be made in the next 4 major categories. The phenomenon of global Christianity forms a de facto hierarchy with, at the top, 6 ecclesiastico-cultural megablocs that have arisen over the last 20 centuries. These are, in chronological order of evolution: Orthodox, Roman Catholic, Anglican, Protestant, Independent, and Marginal Christian (see Part 5 "GeoRenewal" for full description). Adherents of these megablocs share the basic beliefs of the Christian faith and religion, but the vast majority live entirely within their megabloc with no contact with the other five. Indeed, there is marked suspicion and even hostility between any 2 of them which is not erased by the many contacts by individuals at church leadership levels and common task levels. Members of these 6 megablocs therefore function as separate religions. Here, they are defined into major category 2 each as a subsidiary georeligion.

The same is true of the 6 megablocs' compartmentalization into 250 distinct and separate communions. Some 98 of these consist of highly-organized alliances each of which shares with its members doctrinal, historical, cultural, linguistic, and other common ground. Their influence is such that we can define them here as separate religions. Another 150 smaller communions have much less influence and so are not counted here as separate religions. Most of the larger communions each usually encompasses from one to 20 common ecclesiastical traditions. In turn, each tradition is supported by from a dozen to hundreds or even thousands of denominations. And these in turn create and belong to and operate a huge variety of geographical clusters that serve as councils or fellowships or alliances at local, national, regional, continental, and global levels.

This de facto hierarchy—communions, traditions, denominations, clusters or councils—does not have the unifying role one might at first expect. The vast majority of members or adherents live within their category and have little or nothing to do with other communions, traditions, denominations, or clusters. They do not need each other's existence, and get along well without it. On our definition, therefore, they are all distinct religions—which is not to say that bad relations exist between them all.

### 4. *Communions*

Of the 250 communions making up Christianity, some 98 are sufficiently different and distinct from others for them each to be within the present definition of a

# Non-Christians: a selection of non-Christian religionists.

**Afro-American spiritists.** Woman priest of Macumba (Brazil's major Afro-Brazilian cult) at Sta Barbara center whose ceremonies last over 4 hours each.

**Ahmadis.** Large crowd of Ahmadis at prayers in Saltpond (Ghana) led by world leader of Ahmadiya Movement in Islam. Hazrat Hafiz Mirza Nasir Ahmad, Khalifat-ul-Massih III (center, white turban).

**Atheists.** Militantly anti-religious Red Guards in Peking (August 1966) hold up Mao's Little Red Book prior to destroying churches and temples.

**Baha'is.** Brazilian children at Instituto Baha'i de Gravatai, Rio Grande do Sul.

**Black Muslims.** USA Black women of World Community of Al-Islam in the West/America, formerly Nation of Islam.

**Buddhists.** World's largest Buddhist monument, a stone polyhedron in Borobudur, Central Java (Indonesia), built AD 800, to which come 500,000 visitors a year. Upper circular terraces hold 72 stupas each containing a Buddha. The whole stupa complex with its 500 Buddhas is a mandala (ritual diagram) or allegory of the universe, representing ascending stages of enlightenment towards nirvana (spiritual freedom).

**Hindus.** Spiritual head of Hindu religion worldwide, Swami Satya Mitra Nandgiri, from 1960-74 His Holiness Swami Jagatguru Shankar Acharya, Head of Dandi Sanyasis, Head of Central India Math (Bhanpur, Ujjain).

Hindu festival Vijay Dashmi, celebrated annually (here, in Nairobi, Kenya).

Tamil woman imploring Hindu god Subrahmanya for help during festival procession in Saidapet district, Madras (India). At top left are the god's musicians.

**Chinese folk-religionists.** In See Yeah Temple (Malaysia), Chap Goh Meh (15th Night) is celebrated with glitter, pomp and gaiety, in a blending of Confucianism, Taoism, Buddhism and worship of local deities.

**Jains.** 25-yearly ceremony of anointing colossal 57 ft. statue of Digambara saint Bahubali (rain god Gomatesvara) with milk, curds and ghee, at Sravana-Belgola, Mysore (India).

**Jews.** Four UK Jewish leaders are interviewed on BBC-1 television, including Editor of *Jewish Chronicle* (second left) and Chief Rabbi Jakobovits of United Hebrew Congregation of the Commonwealth (right).

**Muslims.** Orthodox (Sunni) Muslims at Great Prayer of Thursday before ancient mud mosque in Mopti (Mali), during which all streets are closed.

**Sufi** mosque seating 150 in Cape Town, South Africa. The domes represent the various levels of man's conscience.

**Parsis.** Zoroastrian or Parsi priests in Fire Temple worship spirit of goodness and light, Ahura Mazda, under form of continually-burning sacred fire. Adherents are declining because no converts are accepted.

**Neo-Hindus.** Largest neo-Hindu movement is the Divine Light Mission. Here, 20% of its 5 million followers attend annual Hans Jayanti celebration in Delhi commemorating Guru's late father's birthday.

Center of DLM's devotion is Guru Maharaj Ji (born 1958), worshipped as Lord of the Universe, Divine Incarnation, who became Perfect Master in 1966 at age 8.

**Reform Hindus.** Official opening of new center in Pretoria by Swami Nisreyasananda (left) of the Ramakrishna Mission in Zimbabwe.

**New-Religionists.** Modern Asiatic syncretistic religions with Christian elements (and over 102 million adherents). (1) *Above.* Viet Nam: *Cao Daist Missionary Church* (Doctrine of the Third Revelation of God), worshippers facing altar and Divine Eye inside Holy See Great Divine Temple.

(2) Japan: *Rissho-koseikai* (Society for Establishment of Righteousness), with worshippers in Great Sacred Hall, Tokyo, facing 10-foot gold image of Sakyamuni Buddha on main altar.

(3) USA: *Nichiren Shoshu of America, NSA* (True Church of Nichiren/Soka Gakkai/Value Creation Society): 20,000 NSA conventioneers in Los Angeles in 1972 stage Salute to America.

**Shamanists.** North American Indian shaman of Tlingit tribe (northern British Columbia coast), in spirit helper's headdress, attempts with drum (left) and rattle to effect a cure.

**Shintoists.** In Shinto festival in Japan, young men carry shrines down public street.

**Sikhs.** Five Sikh swordsmen guarding the Granth Sahib (Holy Scriptures) process through Nairobi.

religion. These will therefore be found in the alphabetical listing of religions in Table 17–5 and in the listing by pedigree in Table 17–6.

### 5. Ecclesiastical traditions
By the year 1900 Christianity could be said to consist of only 70 or so separate ecclesiastical traditions. The 20th century introduced a huge variety of newcomers, so that by AD 2000 the total had risen to over 300. These all appear in the 2 full-length listings of 9,900 distinct religions.

### 6. Monodenominations
It would be incorrect to say that all Christian denominations function as distinct religions. Most do not. It is largely a question of size. The bigger a denomination gets, the more self-sufficient it becomes, and the less interest its adherents have for contact with other denominations, even those with similar or identical central beliefs about God, Christ, salvation. The central tenet of this survey's definition of 'a religion' is, it will be remembered, whether or not its organized form is evidenced by adherents' loyalty to it, and by their acceptance of it as unique and superior to all other religions, even those with similar beliefs.

After numerous experiments the present methodology settled on 2 categories. The 34 largest denominations, those each with over 10 million church members, were termed distinct religions in the category macrodenominations. Without claiming to be distinct or separate, in practice they operate as monolithic standalone organizations. And the 195 denominations over 1 million in size but under 10 million were termed distinct religions in the category megadenominations. The term to describe these 2 types together is monodenominations, emphasizing their monolithic and exclusivist nature. Lastly, a handful of even smaller denominations are included in this survey because of unusual prominent features.

### 7. Religioclusters
In this category are 628 clusters of religions or councils of denominations. Of these, 516 have as members Christian denominations, 51 are Muslim, 22 Buddhist, 15 are Jewish, and so on. Because of the wide religious differences (for example, Britain's Standing Conference of Christians, Jews, and Muslims), the fact that they belong to a joint body constitutes it as itself a distinct religion. Especially is this true of Christian clusters. The fact that 10 or 20 or 30 Christian macrodenominations and megadenominations—themselves distinct religions having little or nothing to do with all other denominations—willingly get together in an ongoing organization can be seen to comprise a new religious entity or achievement.

### 8. Politico-religious parties
Muslims, Jews, and Hindus have produced a total of 36 of these entities. They are primarily political parties but with a clearcut religious orientation of activist and radical character.

### 9. Clerical orders
These organized groupings of religious workers group together priests, monks, nuns in ongoing organizations with very specific religious orientation. Most (72) are specifically Christian missionary orders or societies; 17 are Buddhist, and 7 are Hindu. Each sees itself as virtually an autonomous entity; each fits our profile of a distinct religion with dedicated members composing it.

### 10. Microreligions
The listing of all religions by size tapers away to 1,960 smaller bodies each with under 1,000 adherents. Many wield influence out of all proportion to their size.

### 11. Other minor religions
The final category in this typology of religions is a collection of all other types of religion not catered for under categories 0 to 10. Numbering 2,500 distinct and separate religions, it consists of parareligions, pseudoreligions, peripheral religions (on the periphery of our definition of a religion), minor religions well under 100,000 in size, and other lesser varieties.

### COMPILING A RELIGIOMETRIC DATABASE

Using the typology and method described above, a database was then designed and constructed. The first table opposite, Table 17–5, presents a selection of some 2,800 religions most with over 100,000 adherents each, giving each religion one single line in order to facilitate comparative study and analysis. Table 17–5 lists its data alphabetically by name.

Attention also needs to be made to the comparative interest and value of the earlier 2-page collage of photographs illustrating a representative group of today's non-Christian religions.

Lastly, the identical material in Table 17–5 is reordered in Table 17–6 to be ranked by religious pedigree or relationship. Thus all the Buddhist family of religions appear as a single bloc sharing degrees of closeness between the various schools and sects; and so on.

A far larger selection of data on the grand total of 9,900 or so distinct religions is available on the forthcoming CD series *World Christian database*. It is envisaged that scholars and interested persons will continue to augment these data for some time to come.

---

### BIBLIOGRAPHY

For detailed bibliographies on the subject of religion and religions, readers are referred to Part 31 "Bibliography", which gives 1,380 titles in its Selective World Bibliography of Christianity and Religion; and to the 500 titles describing Christianity and religion each in the context of a single, named, ethnolinguistic people, given at the end of Part 18 "Ethnolinguistics".

**Table 17–5. Global survey of 9,900 religions and parareligions in AD 2000, with 2,800 that have significant organization or identity being given a line each, listed alphabetically by name.**

| *Name of religion/religionists* 1 | *Pedigree* 2 | *Type* 3 | *Begun* 4 | *Adherents* 5 | *Ext* 6 | *Coun* 7 | *W* 8 | *X* 9 | *E. g. = examples; name for God, other religions present, D=denominations, M=missions.* 10 |
|---|---|---|---|---|---|---|---|---|---|
| A des Egl et Oeuvres Prot en Algerie | C-nC | 7-e | 1964 | 2,500 | 1 | alge | A | 5 | ADEOPA. A=Assoc. Association of Protestant Churches and Activities in Algeria. |
| A Francophone des PE du Quebec | E-nC | 7-d | 1964 | 500,000 | 1 | cana | C | 5 | A=Alliance. EFFC. Ev Fellowship of Francophone Canada. PE=Protestants Evangéliques. |
| Aboriginal Cult of Maria Lionza | sAU | 2-d | c1860 | 200,000 | 2 | vene | C | 5 | Goddess of water, vegetation. Blacks, Zambos. Syncretistic cult in Yaracuy. Seances, healings. |
| Acoemetae | sO-oC | 9-e | c450 | 30,000 | 4 | iran | A | 5 | SO. Sleepless Ones. Orthodox ascetics/monks, especially of rule of Basil. |
| Ad Dharm | sK | 2-e | 1907 | 10,000 | 1 | paki | A | 0 | 'Original Religion'. F=Ravidas (AD 1450, Sikh). 1907 Ravidasis (Chamar leatherworkers caste). |
| Adhyatma | zV | 2-e | 1620 | 20,000 | 1 | indi | B | 2 | Jain movement for cultivation of inner self to reach supreme truth. F=Banarsidas. |
| Adi ethnoreligionists | sPAT | 3-d | | 478,000 | 1 | indi | A | 2 | God=Ishor. Northern hills, Assam. Also in Tibet, China. Animists/polytheists 98%. D=3. M=4. |
| Adja ethnoreligionists | sAT | 3-d | | 283,000 | 2 | beni | B | 3 | Mono and Atlantique Provinces. Animists 60%, Muslims 20%. D=7. M=3. |
| Advaita Vedanta | sHH | 2-d | c700 | 300,000 | 1 | indi | B | 1 | F=Sankara. Oldest of 6 major schools of Vedism. Monistic. Shiva as atman of the universe. |
| Adventists | P-Adv-tC | 5-b | 1844 | 12,375,000 | 199 | braz | C | 5 | E.g. SDAs. E,N,SBrazil. 10 launches, 2 planes. 306nx,56f,4H,6h,2s,2099t(177230),17036Y. |
| affiliated Christians (church members) | AC | 2-a | 30 | 1,888,439,000 | 238 | usa | C | 5 | All Christians enrolled by name in churches; baptized church members. |
| Affliction cultists | sAT | 3-d | | 400,000 | 20 | zamb | C | 4 | Cults, ritual drumming, in face of affliction, disease. Found among animists across world. |
| Africa Independent Churches Assoc | I-nC | 7-c | c1950 | 2,500,000 | 1 | soua | C | 5 | AICA. Members: over 600 indigenous denominations. Affiliated to SACC, OAIC. |
| Africa Inland Church | P-Non-AC | 6-c | 1895 | 1,740,000 | 1 | keny | C | 5 | M=AIM. 33% Kamba, 27% Kalenjin, 20% Kikuyu. 80n,50x,226f,4H,30h,5p,1s,W=65%,2000Y. |
| African Apost Ch of J Maranke | I-3aA-AC | 6-c | 1932 | 1,040,000 | 1 | zimb | B | 5 | AACJM. VaPostori (Apostles). Ex USA Methodists. Manyika, Zezuru; across Zimbabwe. |
| African Apostolic Ch of J.Maranke | j-fC | 4-c | 1932 | 1,400,000 | 25 | zimb | B | 4 | AACJM. Present in 25 countries, mostly across tropical Africa since 1950 expansion. |
| African Assembs (Back to God) | I-3pA-AC | 6-c | 1943 | 1,714,000 | 1 | soua | C | 5 | Rapidly-expanding Nicholas Bhengu pentecostal movement. 1959, ex AoG(USA). Xhosa, Zulu. |
| African cell-based networks | I-3kA-tC | 5-e | c1970 | 54,000 | 1 | ivor | B | 5 | E.g. Celestial Ch of Christ. Large Nigerian indigenous church. Yoruba elites. In 11 countries. |
| African ethnoreligionists | sLAT | 3-b | | 96,805,000 | 70 | nige | B | 3 | African Traditional Religion (ATR). |
| African Full Gospelers | I-3fA-tC | 5-d | 1920 | 589,000 | 12 | ethi | B | 5 | Indigenous; Swedish & Finnish aid. 1972-75 severe persecution, 300 imprisoned. 200n. |
| African healing networks | I-3jA-tC | 5-e | 1939 | 47,100 | 3 | ghan | B | 5 | E.g. Ex Methodists. Healing herbs, shea-butter, soap. Akan, Ga, Ewe. 9n,3m,600Y. |
| African house-church networks | I-3hA-tC | 5-e | c1970 | 14,400 | 2 | conz | C | 5 | E.g. Christ Groups. Home churches for isolated converts after nationwide EHC campaign. |
| African Indep charismatics | I-3cA-tC | 5-c | 1864 | 2,302,000 | 30 | moza | B | 5 | Total over 20, Foreign missions: huge Rhema Bible Ch, Word of Life World Outreach, &c. |
| African Indep deliverance chs | I-3vA-tC | 5-e | c1980 | 25,200 | 2 | ethi | B | 5 | E.g. In Addis Ababa. Full Gospel theology. |
| African Indep Pente Ch of Africa | I-Ref-AC | 6-c | 1925 | 1,341,000 | 1 | keny | C | 5 | AIPC. 4 Dioceses. Persecution 1939-57; 1964, massive rural growth. Kikuyu. 136n,1p,6000Y. |
| African Independ pentecostals | I-3pA-tC | 5-b | 1907 | 21,820,000 | 41 | nige | B | 5 | Total over 1,500 (see partial list below), including CMF. |
| African Independent Apostolics | I-3aA-tC | 5-b | 1912 | 15,836,000 | 24 | nige | B | 5 | E.g. Heavenly Christianity. Begun Dahomey 1947. Yoruba elites. Rapid growth in 24 countries. |
| African Independent Churches' Conf | I-nC | 7-c | c1960 | 3,400,000 | 1 | zimb | B | 5 | AICC. Fambidzano Yamakereke Avatema, formalized in 1972 with 20 AICs. |
| African Independent Spirituals | I-3sA-tC | 5-c | 1914 | 1,329,000 | 8 | keny | C | 5 | RCC schisms in Africa. 90% Luo. 9 Dioceses, 7 cardinals, pope. Charismatics. 500n. |
| African indig pente/charismatics | AN3ZAC | 2-b | 1864 | 65,911,000 | 60 | zimb | B | 5 | Most AICs are Zionist, Apostolic, Spiritual: ZCC, CCC, AICN, DLBC, AACJM, EJCSK. D=9,300. |
| African Meth Episcopal Ch | I-Met-AC | 6-c | 1787 | 3,654,000 | 1 | usa | C | 5 | AMEC. Black. 13 Districts in USA. 20 bps. Many new megachurches. Africa, W Indies. 7089n. |
| African Meth Episcopal Zion Ch | I-Met-AC | 6-c | 1796 | 1,109,000 | 1 | usa | C | 5 | AMEZC. Black. 10 bishops in Americas, Europe, 2 in Africa. 5500n,1j,6r. |
| African neocharismatics | I-3nA-tC | 5-c | 1920 | 9,708,000 | 13 | conz | C | 5 | E.g. EJCSK. Ch of Christ on Earth thru Prophet Simon Kimbangu. 1H,1s(82),W=44%,36747Y. |
| African neocharismatics | I-3xA-tC | 5-c | | 1,630,000 | 1 | soua | C | 5 | Total around 3,000 more bodies (see below), most with under 50 adults each. |
| African Oneness pentecostals | I-3oA-tC | 5-d | 1919 | 832,000 | 15 | soua | C | 5 | E.g. Oneness Pentecostal. Reformed Ch. HQ Durban. Member of AWCF. |
| African radio/TV believers | I-3rA-tC | 5-d | 1960 | 178,000 | 11 | suda | B | 5 | Isolated Black and Arab radio believers, mainly aged 12-25. R=400(TWR,RVOG&c). |
| African Word of Faith/Prosperity | I-3wA-tC | 5-d | 1980 | 999,000 | 3 | nige | B | 5 | Prosperity gospel teaching, elements of traditional medicine. |
| Afro-American spiritists | AU | 2-c | | 5,649,000 | 20 | jama | B | 5 | Wide range of religions across Caribbean and Latin America. Mostly Blacks. |
| Afro-Brazilian cultists | BU | 2-b | c1800 | 40,000,000 | 1 | braz | C | 5 | Candomble, Xango (Shango), Macumba, Qimbanda, Batuque. |
| Afro-Caribbean Apostolics | I-3aU-tC | 5-e | 1964 | 18,900 | 2 | usa | C | 5 | FCJCA. Mainly Haitians (with some Jamaicans). Abroad: 27 chs (Haiti 20, Jamaica 4). |
| Afro-Caribbean charismatics | I-3cU-tC | 5-e | 1980 | 4,700 | 3 | virg | C | 5 | In about 4 loose networks. |
| Afro-Caribbean grassroots chs | I-3gU-tC | 5-e | | 5,600 | 1 | domr | C | 5 | Total about 10 (see below), mostly from Puerto Rico, Jamaica, Trinidad et alia. |
| Afro-Caribbean indig pente/charis | UN3ZAC | 2-d | 1783 | 736,000 | 38 | trin | C | 5 | West Indies chs of African origin: Spiritual Baptists/Shouters, Revival Zion, NESBC. D=420. |
| Afro-Caribbean neocharismatics | I-3nU-tC | 5-e | c1970 | 2,400 | 2 | mont | C | 5 | Total about 6, from neighboring Caribbean islands. |
| Afro-Caribbean Oneness chs | I-3oU-tC | 5-d | 1955 | 131,000 | 7 | brit | C | 5 | Total 10, mostly immigrating recently from Caribbean. |
| Afro-Caribbean pentecostals | I-3pU-tC | 5-d | 1894 | 524,000 | 19 | brit | C | 5 | Total over 100 more bodies. |
| Afro-Caribbean religionists | CU | 2-d | | 260,000 | 20 | jama | B | 5 | Large numbers across the Caribbean, also in UK, USA, Canada, et alia. |
| Afro-Caribbean Spirituals | I-3sU-tC | 5-e | c1860 | 12,000 | 4 | trin | C | 5 | Shouters. Banned 1917-51. Cathedral in Gonzales. Many former RCs and Anglicans. |
| Afro-Caribbean Zionists | I-3zU-tC | 5-e | 1783 | 37,200 | 1 | jama | B | 5 | 1861-62, Great Christian Revival. Charismatics similar to Shouters, Shakers. |
| Afro-Cuban spiritists | UU | 2-c | c1800 | 2,300,000 | 3 | cuba | B | 5 | Followers of Santeria (Lucumis, Yoruban), Na, Ganga. |
| Afro-Surinamese religionists | SU | 2-e | | 18,000 | 2 | suri | B | 4 | Mainly followers of Winti, Obeah, Voodoo. |
| Afro-West Indian United Coun of Chs | I-nC | 7-d | 1977 | 800,000 | 1 | brit | C | 5 | Afro-Caribbean United Church Council. Members: 30 out of 130 Black denominations in UK. |
| Agama Islam Jawa | sVN | 2-b | | 23,755,000 | 1 | indo | B | 3 | Abangan. Nominal Javanese Muslims in mystical movements classified as New Religions. |
| Aghoris | sSH | 2-e | c1600 | 5,000 | 1 | indi | B | 1 | Successors to defunct ascetic Kapalikas. Tantrist Shaivites. Varanasi. |
| Agonshu | sSN | 2-d | 1978 | 580,000 | 10 | japa | B | 3 | Veneration of Buddhist Agama Sutras. F=Kiriyama Seiyu. Annual mass fire ceremony, Kyoto. |
| Agudat Israel | qOJ | 8-c | 1912 | 1,600,000 | 15 | isra | B | 2 | Orthodox, Zionists political party, Ashkenazi-Hasidic-dominated. |
| Ahir ethnoreligionists | sPAT | 3-d | | 647,000 | 1 | indi | A | 0 | Bhils. In Maharashtra and Gujarat States. Animists/polytheists 79%, Hindus 20%. |
| Ahl al-Dawa | sNXM | 2-e | | 1,000 | 1 | alge | A | 0 | People of the Call. Algerian branch of Muslim Brotherhood. |
| Ahmadis | AXM | 2-c | 1889 | 7,950,000 | 75 | paki | A | 3 | Ahmadiyah Muslim Mission. F=Mirza Ghulam Ahmad, proclaimed as Mahdi. |
| Aidarusiya | ssUM | 2-e | | 20,000 | 4 | yeme | A | 1 | Sub-branch of Hadrami Alawiya Sufis, responsible for spread to South Asia and Indonesia. |
| Aisyiyah | zSM | 2-c | c1920 | 2,000,000 | 3 | indo | B | 3 | Aisiah. Women's auxiliary (one of world's most dynamic) within Muhammadiyah; Javanese. |
| Aizo ethnoreligionists | sAT | 3-d | | 168,000 | 1 | beni | B | 3 | Mono and Atlantique Provinces. Animists 80%. D=RCC. M=SIM,FMB. |
| Ajivakas | zV | 2-e | BC c600 | 10,000 | 1 | indi | B | 1 | Heterodox Jain sect. F=Makkhali Gosala. Free will denied. |
| Akali Dal | qK | 8-e | 1920 | 30,000 | 1 | indi | B | 1 | The Immortal Party. Militantly anti-British, then anti-Indian government. Split by factionalism. |
| Akha ethnoreligionists | sAT | 3-d | | 213,000 | 5 | myan | B | 2 | God=Miyeh. Kengtung Shan State. Animists 50%, Theravada Buddhists 35%. D=4. M=3. |
| Akhand Kirtani Jatha | sK | 2-d | c1950 | 500,000 | 5 | brit | C | 3 | A major Khalsa-based movement for reconversion of Patit (lapsed) Sikhs. |
| Akshar Purushottam Sanstha | sVH | 2-e | | 40,000 | 11 | indi | B | 2 | The major schism ex Swaminarayans, reverencing first disciple Gunatitananda. |
| Al Firmawiya | sNXM | 2-e | c1980 | 30,000 | 1 | egyp | B | 3 | Exclusive militants, clandestine, virtually unknown. |
| Al Hidayah Dawa Movement | fM | 4-e | 1982 | 30,000 | 1 | soua | C | 5 | AHDM. Missionary movement with headquarters in Western Cape. |
| Al Jamiya al Islamiya li al Dawa | sNXM | 2-d | | 100,000 | 1 | egyp | B | 3 | Body sympathetic to Muslim Brotherhood; in Asyut. |
| Al Qutbiyun | ssNXM | 2-e | c1960 | 30,000 | 1 | egyp | B | 3 | Offshoot of Muslim Brotherhood. Leading theoretician Sayyid Qutb sentenced to death in 1965. |
| Alawites | LHM | 2-c | c950 | 1,631,000 | 15 | syri | B | 2 | Nusayris. A Shiite group in Syria. |
| Alawiya Darqawi | sUM | 2-e | 1918 | 10,000 | 1 | alge | A | 0 | Offshoot of the Darqawiya at Mostaganem. Very traditional. F=Ahmad ibn al-Alawi. |
| Alawiya Hadrami | sUM | 2-e | c1220 | 50,000 | 20 | yeme | A | 1 | F=Muhammad ibn Ali. Spread to Indonesia, India, East Africa (Kenya, Zanzibar). |
| Albanian Encouragement Project | C-nC | 7-e | 1991 | 12,000 | 1 | alba | B | 5 | Activist grouping aiming to renew country after 50 years of Communism. |
| Albanian Evangelical Alliance | E-nC | 7-e | 1892 | 3,000 | 1 | alba | B | 5 | AEA. Roots reaching back to F=G. Qiriazi, an Evangelical Brotherhood preacher. |
| Albanian/Greek-speaking Orth | O-Alb-tC | 5-d | 1908 | 605,000 | 4 | alba | B | 5 | E.g. Suppressed 1967, restored 1991. 4 Eparchies: Tirana, Berat, Gjirokastër, Korçë. Tosks. |
| Alevis | sSN | 2-d | c1700 | 500,000 | 15 | turk | A | 1 | Ali-ilahi. Aliani. Qizilbash syncretic religion: Islam, Zoroastrianism, Christianity. |
| al-Hizb al-Islami | sNXM | 2-e | | 5,000 | 1 | tuni | A | 0 | Islamic Party. Local relation to Muslim Brotherhood. |
| Alia Bohoras | ssHM | 2-e | 1621 | 1,000 | 1 | indi | B | 2 | Aliyas. Subsect of Daudis (branch of Mustalis). |
| Alianca Evangelica de Angola | E-nC | 7-d | 1922 | 100,000 | 1 | ango | C | 5 | Evangelical Alliance of Angola (EAA). |
| Alianca Evangelica Portuguesa | E-nC | 7-d | 1935 | 130,000 | 1 | port | C | 5 | AEP. Portuguese Evangelical Christian Alliance. |
| Alianza de Evangelicos | E-nC | 7-d | c1970 | 100,000 | 1 | vene | C | 5 | AEV. Alliance of Evangelicals. |
| Alianza de Igls Presb y Ref de Mexico | C-nC | 7-c | | 1,300,000 | 1 | mexi | C | 5 | AIPREM. Association of Presbyterian & Reformed Churches of Mexico. |
| Alianza Evangelica Costarricense | E-nC | 7-d | 1951 | 280,000 | 1 | cost | C | 5 | AEC. Costa Rican Evangelial Alliance. 14 member denominations. |
| Alianza Evangelica de Guatemala | E-nC | 7-c | 1953 | 1,300,000 | 1 | guat | C | 5 | AEG. Evangelical Alliance of Guatemala. United forum for 17 member churches. In CONELA. |
| Alianza Evangelica de Panama | C-nC | 7-d | 1941 | 128,000 | 1 | pana | C | 5 | AEP. Panama Evangelical Alliance. 5 member denominations. |
| Alianza Evangelica Espanola | E-nC | 7-e | 1887 | 30,000 | 1 | spai | C | 5 | AEE. Spanish Evangelical Alliance. 5 denominations. |
| Aligarh Movement | fM | 4-e | 1865 | 5,000 | 1 | indi | B | 2 | F=S.A. Khan. Educational institution for Indian Muslims, and a few Hindus. |
| Aliran Kebatinan | sIAT | 3-e | | 10,000 | 1 | indo | B | 3 | Mystical sects across Indonesian: Sufi elements. |
| Aliran Kepercayaan | sVN | 2-c | c1500 | 2,000,000 | 1 | indo | B | 2 | 'Faith', official term for all Kebatinan mystical sects. Vast expansion in 1980s, into 400 varieties. |
| All Africa Conference of Churches | A-cC | 7-b | 1963 | 95,000,000 | 70 | keny | C | 5 | AACC/CETA. HQ Nairobi. 130 member denominations and councils. |
| All Ceylon Buddhist Congress | nB | 7-b | 1918 | 12,500,000 | 5 | sril | B | 3 | Theravadins. Leadership of YMBA. |
| All Indonesia Fed of Buddhist Orgs | nB | 7-c | 1978 | 2,000,000 | 2 | indo | B | 3 | Acronym WALUBI. Represents all Buddhist sects to government. |
| All Japan Federation of Buddhist Sects | nB | 7-b | | 81,300,000 | 3 | japa | B | 3 | Nihon Bukkyo Kai. 60 sects, 60 other organizations. |
| Alleanza Evangelica Italiana | E-nC | 7-d | 1974 | 120,000 | 1 | ital | C | 5 | AEI. Italian Evangelical Alliance (IEA). |
| Alliance Ev Francophone de Belgique | E-nC | 7-e | 1981 | 5,000 | 1 | belg | C | 5 | Evangelical Alliance of French-speaking Belgium. |
| Alliance Evangelique du Rwanda | E-nC | 7-d | 1992 | 400,000 | 1 | rwan | C | 5 | AER. |
| Alliance Evangelique du Zaire | E-nC | 7-d | c1960 | 500,000 | 1 | conz | C | 5 | AEZ. Alliance of Zaire. |
| Alliance Evangelique Francaise | E-nC | 7-e | | 6,000 | 1 | fran | C | 5 | AEF. French Evangelical Alliance. |
| Alliance Israelite Universelle | wJ | 7-e | 1860 | 20,000 | 10 | isra | B | 3 | First modern Jewish organization. Secularist. |
| Alliance World Fellowship | r-fC | 4-c | 1955 | 1,820,000 | 45 | usa | C | 5 | AWF. In 45 countries with 10,500 Christian & Missionary Alliance chs. M=CMA. |
| All-India Ecumenical Coordinating Body | nC | 7-b | c1980 | 28,000,000 | 1 | indi | B | 5 | AECB. Project envisaging a future NCCI including the Catholic Ch in India. |

*Continued overleaf*

*Table 17–5 continued*

| *Name of religion/religionists* 1 | *Pedigree* 2 | *Type* 3 | *Begun* 4 | *Adherents* 5 | *Ext* 6 | *Coun* 7 | *W* 8 | *X* 9 | *E. g. = examples; name for God, other religions present, D=denominations, M=missions.* 10 |
|---|---|---|---|---|---|---|---|---|---|
| All-India Fed of National Churches | nC | 7-c | c1980 | 7,000,000 | 1 | indi | B | 5 | AIFNC. Numerous Independent churches, aiming to create an indigenous national Ch of India. |
| All-India Muslim Coalition | nM | 7-c | 1963 | 1,000,000 | 1 | indi | B | 2 | Majlis-i Mushawarat. Coalition of Muslim political parties and agencies. |
| All-India Muslim League | nM | 7-b | 1906 | 101,000,000 | 3 | indi | B | 2 | To safeguard Muslim interests in India. |
| All-India Pentecostal Fellowship | H-nC | 7-c | 1957 | 1,100,000 | 1 | indi | B | 5 | AIPF. |
| All-Malaysia Muslim Welfare Assoc | zSM | 2-b | 1960 | 10,100,000 | 1 | malb | B | 3 | PERKIM. Pertubuham Kebajikan Islam SeMalaysia. 120,000 converts to Islam. |
| All-Nepal Anjuman Islah Samiti | nM | 7-d | | 800,000 | 2 | nepa | A | 1 | Main Muslim organization active in Nepal, with 3 other rival bodies. |
| Alpha Movement | fC | 4-c | 1979 | 1,000,000 | 77 | brit | C | 5 | Anglican evangelistic movement via 10,000 11-week courses in 77 countries and most cities. |
| Altaic ethnoreligionists | sST | 3-c | | 3,000,000 | 4 | russ | B | 5 | Shamanist religions across central/east Russia, Mongolia, China et alia. |
| al-Takfir wal-Hijra | sNXM | 2-e | 1965 | 50,000 | 4 | egyp | B | 3 | Atonement & Flight from Sin Society. (In Algeria, Repentance & Flight). Clandestine extremists. |
| Amal | rHM | 2-e | 1975 | 20,000 | 5 | leba | B | 5 | 'Hope'=acronym for Lebanese Resistance Detachments, to reform Lebanon without violence. |
| Amarapura Nikaya | sTB | 2-e | c1850 | 50,000 | 3 | myan | B | 3 | One of 3 main Theravada divisions, in Amarapura, Burma. 1,000 monasteries, 3,000 monks. |
| American Baptist Chs in USA | P-Bap-AC | 6-c | 1639 | 2,316,000 | 1 | usa | C | 5 | Formerly American Baptist Convention. 8222n,9s(1090),W=34%,3456Y. |
| American Christian Action Council | T-nC | 7-d | c1970 | 230,000 | 1 | usa | C | 4 | ACAC. Fundamentalists, affiliated to ICCC. |
| American Council of Christian Chs | nC | 7-d | c1950 | 420,000 | 1 | usa | C | 4 | ACCC. Fundamentalists related to ICCC until 1968 withdrawal. |
| American Muslim Mission | sBXM | 2-c | 1913 | 1,100,000 | 1 | usa | C | 4 | Mainstream Black Muslims, now Sunnis. F=Elijah Muhammad. |
| Amerindian ethnoreligionists | sPAT | 3-d | | 300,000 | 1 | braz | C | 4 | Traditional animism, fetishism. |
| Amerindian neopentecostals | RN3ZAC | 2-d | 1870 | 535,000 | 3 | mexi | C | 5 | Amerindian neopentecostals: UIEI, Halleluja Church. D=4. |
| Amerindian pentecostals | I-3pR-tC | 5-d | 1923 | 535,000 | 3 | mexi | C | 5 | E.g. Union of Ev Indep Chs. Igl Cristiana Indep Pentecostés. Otomi Indians. HQ Pachuca. |
| Amiris | sMIHM | 2-e | c1600 | 39,000 | 5 | indi | B | 2 | Ismaili subdivision related to Daudis, Mustalis, and Sulaymanis. |
| Amon ethnoreligionists | sBAT | 3-d | | 123,000 | 1 | nige | A | 1 | Plateau State, Bassa LGA; Kaduna State, Saminaka LGA. Animists 60%, Muslims 20%. |
| Ana ethnoreligionists | sAT | 3-d | | 103,000 | 3 | beni | B | 4 | Zou Province. Half in Togo. Animists 70%. D=Yoruba churches from Nigeria. |
| Anagarika | v-oB | 9-e | BC 800 | 30,000 | 1 | indi | B | 2 | Organized Buddhist homeless ascetics who do not enter the sangha. |
| Ananaikyo | sSN | 2-d | 1949 | 218,000 | 1 | japa | B | 3 | Aim to induce kami-possession. Millenarian. Syncretism from all religions. |
| Ananda Marga | sTH | 2-c | 1955 | 2,500,000 | 7 | indi | B | 4 | Self-development Hindu Yoga. F= Anandamurtiji. Also in Europe, USA. |
| Ancient & Mystical Order RC | sON | 2-e | 1915 | 2,000 | 10 | usa | C | 4 | AMORC. RC=Rosae Crucis. Rosicrucians. F=H.Spencer-Lewis. HQ California. |
| Ancient Assyrian Patr of the East | Y-fC | 4-d | c50 | 500,000 | 17 | iraq | A | 5 | Nestorians across Asia from AD 635 on; but by 1402, Tamerlane destroys 12 million believers. |
| Angkatan Democratic Liberal Sabah | nM | 7-d | | 500,000 | 1 | malb | B | 3 | ADIL. Based in Sabah and intended to attract Malay Muslims. |
| Anglican Charismatics | A2ZAC | 2-b | 1907 | 17,562,000 | 163 | brit | C | 5 | Total Anglicans in Renewal, past and present, including children and infants. D=165. |
| Anglican Church of Australia | A-plu-AC | 6-c | 1788 | 4,093,000 | 1 | aust | C | 5 | Ch of England in Australia. 23 Dioceses. 3528n; M=USPG,MTS,NZCMS. |
| Anglican Church of Kenya | A-Eva-AC | 6-c | 1844 | 3,123,000 | 1 | keny | C | 5 | ICK/CPK. Kanisa la Jimbo la Kenya. 26 Dioceses. M=CMS,BCMS. Big losses to ICCEC, NAC. |
| Anglican Church of Nigeria | A-Low-AC | 6-b | 1842 | 20,412,000 | 1 | nige | B | 5 | In CPWA until 1979 when ACN formed. Mushrooming to 63 Dioceses. M=CMS(UK).68f,1p,1s. |
| Anglican Co of North America and C | R-rC | 7-c | | 3,779,000 | 15 | usa | C | 5 | ACNAC. C=Caribbean. |
| Anglican Consultative Council | A-fC | 4-b | 1969 | 80,187,000 | 120 | brit | C | 5 | ACC. HQ London. |
| Anglican Evangelicals | EAAC | 2-b | 1738 | 30,000,000 | 161 | brit | C | 5 | The Evangelical Revival dates from John Wesley's conversion. Now aided by EFAC. |
| Anglican schismatics | I-Ang-tC | 5-c | 1880 | 1,577,000 | 14 | keny | C | 5 | E.g. CCA. Schism of 40% D Maseno. 8 Dioceses. 81% Luo, 10% Luhya. 81n,1p,2400Y,8640y. |
| Anglicans | AAC | 2-b | 61 | 79,650,000 | 166 | brit | C | 5 | 102 million professing, 80 million affiliated to Anglican Communion. |
| Anglo-Catholics | A-ACa-tC | 5-c | 1050 | 2,073,000 | 39 | brit | C | 5 | Rural Church of England, in 494 parishes; also in 37 countries. |
| Anglo-Romans | I-ARo-tC | 5-e | 1897 | 79,000 | 13 | zimb | B | 5 | M=AO(USA). Ex Anglicans. Registered 1924: 1972 Rhodesian African bishop. Ndebele. |
| Anguilla Christian Council | C-nC | 7-e | | 4,800 | 1 | angu | C | 5 | ACC. Formerly part of St Kitts-Nevis bodies. |
| Animists | AT | 3-a | | 216,161,000 | 142 | beni | B | 3 | Belief in spiritual beings, mountains, rocks, trees, rivers. |
| Ansar | sPXM | 2-d | 1885 | 300,000 | 1 | suda | B | 2 | 'Helpers'. Originally, Mahdism. Powerful political party in Sudan. Crushed 1970 by army. |
| Ansar al Sunna al Muhammadiya | sPXM | 2-e | | 30,000 | 1 | egyp | B | 3 | In Port Said and Suhag. Islamic movements hostile to government. |
| Ansaru Allah Community | sPXM | 2-e | 1970 | 4,000 | 1 | usa | C | 5 | Black Muslims. F=Isa Muhammad, regarded as Mahdi. Influenced by Black Power movement. |
| Antaimoro ethnoreligionists | sAT | 3-d | | 281,000 | 1 | mada | B | 4 | Superficially islamized. Animists 50%, Muslims 2%, Baha'is 0.2%(increasing fast). D=1. M=2. |
| Antaisaka ethnoreligionists | sAT | 3-d | | 679,000 | 1 | mada | B | 3 | Southeast coastal strip. Animists 72%, Baha'is 0.1%. D=RCC(D-Farafangana). M=CM. |
| Antandroy ethnoreligionists | sAT | 3-d | | 563,000 | 1 | mada | B | 3 | Extreme south coast of island and inland. Animists 80%. D=RCC(D-Fort-Dauphin). M=CM. |
| Antanosy ethnoreligionists | sAT | 3-d | | 176,000 | 1 | mada | B | 5 | Superficially islamized. Animists 45%, Muslims 2%. D=RCC(D-Fort-Dauphin). M=CM. |
| Anthroposophical Society | ssTN | 2-e | 1912 | 25,000 | 10 | germ | C | 4 | Anthroposophy. Wisdom of Humanity. F=Rudolf Steiner. Ex Theosophy. HQ in Switzerland. |
| Antigua Christian Council | K-nC | 7-e | | 41,000 | 1 | anti | C | 5 | ACC. |
| Antilles Episcopal Conference | M-rC | 7-b | 1975 | 22,556,000 | 20 | trin | C | 5 | AEC. HQ St James. |
| Anuvrata Movement | sSV | 2-e | 1948 | 70,000 | 1 | indi | B | 2 | Modern lay moral revival spreading Jain values. 5 Vows. F=Acharya Tulsi. |
| Anyi ethnoreligionists | sAT | 3-d | | 371,000 | 2 | ivor | B | 5 | God=Nyamiapbili. Many in Ghana. Animists 45%, Muslims 1%. D=6. M=6. |
| apocalyptic chs | I-Apo-tC | 5-e | 1923 | 4,900 | 2 | ukra | C | 5 | Apokalipsisty. Begun Vinnitsa by Catholic priest, spread to Far East; underground. |
| Apostolic Pentecostals | ACP1ZAC | 2-c | 1904 | 1,776,000 | 29 | ghan | B | 5 | Denominations emphasizing Pentecostal church government by living apostles: ACG. D=30. |
| Apostolic World Christian Fellowship | O-fC | 4-c | 1970 | 1,500,000 | 45 | usa | C | 2 | AWCF. Communion based on Oneness Pentecostalism. Largely Black. 170 denominations. |
| Arab Apostolics | I-3aS-tC | 5-e | c1980 | 4,300 | 2 | unia | B | 5 | M=Network International(HQ TX, USA). Social and evangelistic ministries. |
| Arab charismatics | I-3cS-tC | 5-e | 1948 | 71,400 | 9 | isra | B | 5 | In around 20 very loose geographical networks or associations. |
| Arab house-church networks | I-3hS-tC | 5-e | c1950 | 21,400 | 1 | saud | B | 5 | Saudi Arab believers organized into private house meetings; no foreign contacts. |
| Arab neocharismatics | I-3nS-tC | 5-e | c1980 | 12,000 | 1 | iraq | A | 5 | 1,000 attenders a week; public baptisms; wide scripture distribution. |
| Arab pentecostals | I-3pS-tC | 5-e | 1909 | 23,800 | 7 | egyp | B | 5 | E.g. M=World-Wide Missions (USA). 1993, pentecostalized, merged with M=PHC. |
| Arab radio/TV networks | I-3rS-tC | 5-c | 1958 | 1,131,000 | 19 | iraq | A | 5 | Isolated Arab radio believers (students &c). Vast increase after 1985. |
| Arab/Assyrian/Semitic neocharis | SN3ZAC | 2-c | 1909 | 1,264,000 | 40 | iraq | A | 5 | Arabic/Aramaean/Assyrian/Berber/Semitic charismatic chs: Tree of Life Chs, GPC. D=130. |
| Arabic/Greek-speaking Orth | O-Ara-tC | 5-c | 1920 | 1,501,000 | 29 | usa | C | 5 | Former Syrian Antiochian Orth AD NY & NA. In Greek P Antioch. 95% Arab. 110n. |
| Arakan Rohingya Islamic Front | fM | 4-e | | 2,000 | 2 | myan | B | 1 | ARIF. Moderate Muslim guerrilla groups. |
| Arakanese ethnoreligionists | sBAT | 3-d | | 336,000 | 3 | myan | A | 1 | Also in India, Bangladesh. Theravada Buddhists 80%, animists 17%, Muslims 2%. D=3. M=1. |
| Argentina Consultative Com of ICCC | T-nC | 7-e | c1965 | 4,000 | 1 | arge | C | 4 | ACCICCC. |
| Argentine Alliance of Ev Chs | E-nC | 7-d | 1982 | 400,000 | 1 | arge | C | 5 | ACIERA. Alianza Cristiana de Igls Ev de la Rep A. 2,000 member congregations. |
| Ari ethnoreligionists | sAT | 3-d | | 106,000 | 2 | ethi | B | 2 | Gamo Gofa Province. Bilinguals in Amharic and Gofa(Wolayta). Animists 80%. 90 churches. |
| Armenian (Eastern-rite Catholic) | R-Arm-tC | 5-d | 1605 | 163,000 | 15 | usa | C | 5 | E.g. US Armenian rite. |
| Armenian Apostolic C of Echmiadzin | E-fC | 4-c | c35 | 5,593,000 | 28 | arme | C | 5 | C=Catholicossate |
| Armenian Apostolic Church | O-Arm-AC | 6-c | 35 | 2,950,000 | 1 | arme | C | 5 | Catholicate of Echmiadzin. 72 bishops. Charismatic renewal: Brotherhood of Lovers of the Ch. |
| Armenian Apostolic Orthodox | O-Arm-tC | 5-c | 1440 | 6,197,000 | 47 | arme | C | 5 | C of Echmiadzin. 72 bishops. Charismatic renewal: Brotherhood of Lovers of the Church. |
| Arusa Maasai ethnoreligionists | sAT | 3-d | | 174,000 | 1 | tanz | B | 3 | Near Arusha town. Related to Maasai, but agriculturalists. Animists 70%. D=5. M=7. |
| Arusi Galla ethnoreligionists | sAT | 3-d | | 218,000 | 1 | ethi | B | 2 | God=Wagayon. South. Pastoralists. Muslims 85%(Shafi Sunnis), animists 12%. D=6. M=4. |
| Arya Samaj | sRH | 2-c | 1875 | 2,500,000 | 40 | indi | B | 4 | F=Dayananda Sarasvati. Fighting against caste, idol worship, injustice. Worldwide. |
| As des Conf Epis de la Region de AC | B-rC | 7-c | 1989 | 6,297,000 | 7 | cent | B | 5 | ACERAC. AC=l'Afrique Centrale. Covers Cameroon, Chad, CAR, Congo, Equatorial Guinea. |
| As des Confs Epis de l'Afrique Centrale | rC | 7-b | 1985 | 34,069,000 | 5 | conz | C | 5 | ACEAC. Covers Burundi, Rwanda, Congo-Zaire. HQ Kinshasa. |
| As des Patriarches et Eveques Cath L | R-nC | 7-c | c1960 | 1,395,000 | 1 | leba | B | 5 | L=Liban. Assembly of Catholic Patriarchs and Bishops of Lebanon. |
| As of Believers in One Supreme God | sVN | 2-c | c1960 | 3,500,000 | 1 | indo | B | 3 | ABOSG. As=Association. Umbrella organization for 20 Kepercayaan sects. |
| Asali Nirankaris | sK | 2-e | | 5,000 | 1 | indi | B | 2 | True (Sikh-derived) Nirankaris. |
| Asambleas de Dios | P-Pe2-AC | 6-c | 1910 | 1,083,000 | 1 | arge | C | 5 | Assemblies of God. M=SFM(Sweden),NPY(Norway), Elim(Denmark). 65n,1500Y,600z. |
| Ashanti ethnoreligionists | sAT | 3-d | | 227,000 | 3 | ghan | B | 5 | God=Onyankopon. Muslims 28% (massive Ahmadi conversions), animists 6%. D=26. M=10. |
| Ashkenazic Hasidism | sAJ | 2-c | | 2,500,000 | 20 | isra | B | 2 | Strict Jewish dogmas. Yiddish. From Eastern Europe. |
| Ashkenazis | AJ | 2-b | | 11,080,000 | 120 | isra | B | 2 | Yiddish-speaking Judaism. From Germany; Poland, Russia, Ukraine. |
| Asoc Cristiana de Igls Ev de Uruguay | E-nC | 7-e | 1988 | 50,000 | 1 | uuay | C | 5 | ACIERU. Member of CONELA. |
| Asoc Fraternal de Igls Pentecostales | I-nC | 7-d | | 850,000 | 1 | mexi | C | 5 | AFIPM. Pentecostal Fraternal Assoc of Mexico. Many large indigenous denominations. |
| Asoc Pro-Indigenas de Colombia | h-nC | 7-e | | 10,000 | 1 | colo | C | 5 | Association for the Indians of Colombia. |
| Asoc Reg Epis del Norte de Sud Am | J-rC | 7-b | c1980 | 100,000,000 | 6 | arge | C | 5 | ARENSA. |
| Asociacion de Pastores del Paraguay | E-nC | 7-e | c1965 | 3,000 | 1 | para | C | 5 | APP. |
| Asociacion Nacional de Ev de Bolivia | E-nC | 7-d | 1966 | 450,000 | 1 | boli | C | 5 | ANDEB. National Association of Evangelicals of Bolivia. Member of CONELA. |
| Ass of Cath Bishops of Hungary | R-nC | 7-c | 1990 | 6,330,000 | 1 | hung | C | 5 | MPKK. Magyar Puspoki Kar Konferencija. HQ Budapest. |
| Assem de la Hierarchie Cath en Syrie | R-nC | 7-d | | 325,000 | 1 | syri | B | 5 | Assembly of Bishops in the Syrian Arab Republic. |
| Assemblea degli Ordinari Cattolici di TS | nC | 7-d | 1992 | 168,000 | 1 | pale | B | 5 | AOCTS. TS=Terra Santa. Bishops' Conference in the Holy Land. |
| Assembleias de Deus | P-Pe2-AC | 6-b | 1910 | 25,600,000 | 1 | braz | C | 5 | Assemblies of God. 1934,M=AoG,SFM,NPY,FFFM. 30000n,27000mw,20f. |
| Assemblies of God DFM | aog-oC | 9-e | 1914 | 1,800 | 130 | usa | C | 5 | AOGDFM (Division of Foreign Missions). |
| Assemblies of God in Nigeria | P-Pe2-AC | 6-c | 1939 | 1,410,000 | 1 | nige | B | 5 | M=AoG(USA). A=1960. 48% Ibo, 8% Ishan. 667n,31x,8f,3h,1j,5s(296),W=50%,2593Y. |
| Assemblies of God USA | P-Pe2-AC | 6-c | 1906 | 2,294,000 | 1 | usa | C | 5 | General Conference. 95% White. 12037n,1j,4r,13s9200t(1078332),20864Y. |
| Assembly Hall Churches | I-3nC-AC | 6-c | 1922 | 1,434,000 | 1 | chin | B | 5 | Chu Hui So. Little Flock. F=Watchman Nee. 1949: 636 churches, 70,000 members. Jiangxi. |
| Assembly Hall Churches | t-fC | 4-c | 1922 | 2,100,000 | 52 | chin | B | 2 | Local Churches, Little Flock. |
| Asso des Eglises Ev Centrafricaines | E-nC | 7-d | 1973 | 450,000 | 1 | cent | B | 5 | AEEC. Association of Central African Evangelical Churches. |
| Assoc des Egl Chretiennes du Togo | I-nC | 7-e | 1940 | 30,000 | 1 | togo | B | 5 | AECT. Association of Christian Churches in Togo. Independent indigenous AICs. |
| Assoc des Egl et Miss Ev de Guine | E-nC | 7-e | c1980 | 59,000 | 1 | guin | A | 5 | AEMEG. |
| Assoc des Egl et Miss Prot du Mali | G-nC | 7-e | 1963 | 75,000 | 1 | mali | A | 5 | AGEMPEM. Association of Evangelical Protestant Churches & Missions in Mali. |
| Assoc des Musulmans de N Caledonie | nM | 7-e | 1975 | 5,800 | 1 | newc | C | 4 | NCMA. New Caledonia Muslim Association. Schools, imams. |
| Assoc for Research & Enlightenment | sFN | 2-d | 1931 | 100,000 | 1 | usa | C | 5 | ARE. Edgar Cayce. New Age conferences. 12 million books sold. |
| Assoc Interconfess du Luxembourg | h-nC | 7-d | 1965 | 390,000 | 1 | luxe | C | 5 | AIL/LIA. Mutual understanding with Catholics, Protestants, and Jews. |

*Continued opposite*

*Table 17–5 continued*

| Name of religion/religionists 1 | Pedigree 2 | Type 3 | Begun 4 | Adherents 5 | Ext 6 | Coun 7 | W 8 | X 9 | E. g. = examples; name for God, other religions present, D=denominations, M=missions. 10 |
|---|---|---|---|---|---|---|---|---|---|
| Assoc of Episcopal Confs of AWA | G-rC | 7-b | | 15,675,000 | 6 | libe | B | 5 | AECEWA. AWA=Anglophone West Africa. HQ Monrovia. |
| Assoc of Evangelicals of Liberia | E-nC | 7-d | 1968 | 140,000 | 1 | libe | B | 5 | AEL. Begun as Liberian Evangelical Fundamental Fellowship (LEFF), 1974 renamed. |
| Assoc of Evangelicals of Swaziland | nC | 7-e | c1960 | 50,000 | 1 | swaz | C | 5 | AES, member of AEA. |
| Assoc of Member Epis Confs in EA | E-rC | 7-b | 1989 | 33,979,000 | 15 | keny | C | 5 | AMECEA. EA=Eastern Africa. HQ Nairobi. |
| Assoc of Muslims of Southern Sudan | nM | 7-d | 1982 | 100,000 | 2 | suda | B | 2 | AMSS. Mainly Nuba Muslims. |
| Assoc of Reform Zionists of America | RJ | 2-c | 1810 | 3,000,000 | 10 | usa | C | 4 | ARZA. Reform Judaism (Progressive). 1810 Germany then USA, UK, Argentina, NZ, Australia. |
| Assoc pour la Sauvegarde du Quran | fM | 4-e | 1970 | 20,000 | 1 | tuni | A | 1 | Quranic Preservation Society (QPS). Government-backed. |
| Associacao Ev de Mocambique | E-nC | 7-c | | 1,100,000 | 1 | moza | B | 5 | AEM. Evangelical Association of Mozambique. |
| Associacao Evangelica Brasileira | C-nC | 7-b | 1991 | 30,000,000 | 1 | braz | C | 5 | AEB. |
| Associated Christian Chs of Kenya | C-nC | 7-e | | 30,000 | 1 | keny | C | 5 | ACCK. |
| Associated Gospel Churches | nC | 7-c | 1939 | 4,000,000 | 10 | usa | C | 5 | AGC. Service agency for 2-million member Fundamentalist denominations. |
| Associated Pentecostal Chs of NZ | H-nC | 7-e | 1975 | 27,100 | 1 | newz | C | 5 | NZ=New Zealand. |
| Association of Ev Chs of Colombia | E-nC | 7-d | 1948 | 300,000 | 1 | colo | C | 5 | AIEC. Confederacion Evangelica de Colombia. CEDECOL. |
| Association of Ev Chs of Indonesia | E-nC | 7-c | 1970 | 3,000,000 | 1 | indo | B | 5 | PII. Persekutuan Injili Indonesia. Formerly DGGII. 100 denominations. |
| Association of Ev Chs of St Vincent-G | E-nC | 7-e | | 5,000 | 1 | saiv | C | 5 | AECSVG. God=Grenadines |
| Association of Evangelicals of Africa | G-cC | 7-b | 1966 | 19,500,000 | 45 | keny | C | 5 | AEA. Founded as AEAM (M=Madagascar). |
| Association of Independent Chs | I-nC | 7-c | c1960 | 1,100,000 | 1 | zamb | C | 5 | AIC. Initially with 10 member AIC denominations. |
| Association of Indian Clergy | zSM | 2-e | 1919 | 20,000 | 1 | indi | B | 2 | Jamiat ul-Ulama-i Hind. Reformist ulama. HQ Delhi. |
| Association of Light | zSM | 2-e | 1925 | 30,000 | 1 | turk | A | 0 | Nurcus, or Nurcular Camaati, a Turkish Muslim renewal. |
| Association of Muslim Brothers | sXM | 2-e | | 3,000 | 1 | alge | A | 0 | Jammat al-Ikhwan al-Muslimun. |
| Association of Shinto Sects | nS | 7-c | | 6,850,000 | 14 | japa | B | 3 | Coordinating body for Kyoha Shinto Rengo Kai; 12 of the 13 Sects. 1970, Tenrikyo leaves. |
| Association of Shinto Shrines | nS | 7-b | 1946 | 58,512,000 | 25 | japa | B | 3 | Jinja Honcho. 26,000 priests. 98% of all Shrine Shinto organizations. Gradual decline. |
| Assumptionists | aa-oC | 9-e | 1845 | 1,000 | | ital | C | 5 | AA. |
| Assyrian Orthodox | O-Nes-tC | 5-d | 1814 | 268,000 | 18 | iraq | A | 5 | Assyrian Ch. Nestorians. 3 Dioceses. Patriarch Mar Dinkha IV lives in USA. 26n. |
| Astrologists | AN | 2-b | BC 1000 | 10,000,000 | 60 | indi | B | 2 | Stars, planets affect human lives; widespread use of horoscopes, divination. |
| Atheists | a- | 0-b | BC 1000 | 150,090,000 | 161 | chin | B | 3 | Militantly nonreligious and antireligious secularists and communists. |
| Atlanteans | sHU | 10-f | 1957 | 500 | 1 | usa | C | 5 | Philosophical society under spirit guide Helio-Arcanophus. |
| Augustinians | osa-oC | 9-e | 1244 | 3,000 | 60 | ital | C | 5 | OSA. |
| Aurobindo Ashram | zH | 2-e | 1910 | 40,000 | 2 | indi | B | 2 | Purna-Yoga (Integral Yoga (Integral Yoga). HQ Auroville under The Mother. |
| Australian Aboriginal religionists | sAT | 3-e | | 50,000 | 1 | aust | C | 5 | Aboriginal population, including those of mixed race, who still claim to follow own religion. |
| Australian Catholic Bishops' Conf | S-nC | 7-c | 1979 | 5,400,000 | 1 | aust | C | 5 | ACBC. HQ. Canberra. |
| Australian Christian Churches | nC | 7-d | 2000 | 170,000 | 1 | aust | C | 5 | National Alliance of Pentecostal and Charismatic Churches: AoG, Apostolic Chs, et alia. |
| Australian Consultative Co of ICCC | T-nC | 7-d | c1950 | 100,000 | 1 | aust | C | 3 | ACCC. Co=Council. |
| Australian Evangelical Alliance | E-nC | 7-c | 1972 | 1,800,000 | 1 | aust | C | 5 | AEA. |
| Australian Fed of Islamic Councils | nM | 7-d | 1975 | 224,000 | 1 | aust | C | 5 | AFIC. To organize Islam on geographic not sectarian base. HQ Victoria. Turks, Arabs, Serbs. |
| Australian Pentecostal Ministers' Fell | h-nC | 7-d | | 130,000 | 1 | aust | C | 5 | Fellowship of the leaders of Pentecostal denominations in Australia. |
| Azali Babism | AL | 2-e | 1844 | 3,000 | 1 | iran | A | 1 | Remnant opposed to mainstream Bahai. Followers of Bab since 1850. F=Subh-i Azol. Decline. |
| Azamiyah Shadhiliyah | sRUM | 2-d | 1915 | 300,000 | 1 | suda | B | 2 | Reform of Sufi practices. F=Muhammad Madi Abu al-Azaim. |
| Badawiya | sUM | 2-c | c1240 | 1,500,000 | 20 | egyp | B | 3 | Major Sufi order in Egypt, HQ Tanta; one million pilgrims every autumn. Mysticism, miracles. |
| Bagri ethnoreligionists | sAT | 3-c | | 1,865,000 | 1 | indi | A | 0 | In Punjab, Rajasthan, Pakistan. Nomads across India-Pakistan borders. Animists 99%. |
| Baha'is | L | 1-c | 1863 | 7,106,000 | 218 | iran | A | 5 | Acceptance of all religions under mission of Bahaiullah. In 218 countries. |
| Bahamas Christian Council | N-nC | 7-d | 1948 | 210,000 | 1 | baha | C | 5 | BCC. |
| Bahnar ethnoreligionists | sAT | 3-d | | 116,000 | 1 | viet | B | 3 | God=Bok Kei-Dei. Montagnards. Gia Lai-Cong Tum Province. Also in USA. Animists 79%. D=3. |
| Bai ethnoreligionists | sPAT | 3-c | | 1,158,000 | 2 | chin | A | 1 | Yunnan, Sichuan, Guizhou. Polytheists 65%, Buddhists 30%. D=TSPM,RCC. M=7. |
| Bakkaiyah | ssUM | 2-d | c1500 | 500,000 | 1 | mali | A | 0 | Part of Qadiriya, in West Africa in origin. |
| Balanta ethnoreligionists | sAT | 3-d | | 347,000 | 4 | gunb | A | 2 | Animists 81%(strong ancestor cult), Muslims 11%. D=4. M=6. |
| Balinese ethnoreligionists | sHAT | 3-d | | 166,000 | 1 | indo | A | 1 | Shaivite Hindus 80% (15,000 village temples, also ISKCON), syncretists 15%. D=3. M=9. |
| Balmikis | sSN | 2-d | c1880 | 300,000 | 6 | indi | B | 2 | Keshderi Sikhs. F=Valmikis. Chuhra (Sweepers) caste combining Hinduism, Sikhism. |
| Bambara ethnoreligionists | sAT | 3-d | | 669,000 | 10 | mali | B | 3 | God=Alla. Muslims 85%(Maliki Sunnis,with Wahhabis; Tijaniyya,Qadiriyya). D=5. M=9. |
| Bangladesh Muslim League | nM | 7-c | | 6,000,000 | 1 | bang | B | 2 | BML. Denounces advocates of Bengali nationalism. |
| Bangladesh National Council of Chs | N-nC | 7-d | 1954 | 100,000 | 1 | bang | B | 5 | BNCC. Founded as East Pakistan Christian Council. |
| Baptist Bible Fellowship Internat | I-Bap-AC | 6-c | 1950 | 1,560,000 | 1 | usa | C | 5 | BBFI. Ex SBC et alia. 1.7 million by 1976. Whites. In 48 countries. 1s. |
| Baptist Bible Fellowship Internat | b-fC | 4-c | 1950 | 2,500,000 | 50 | usa | C | 5 | BBFI. Schism ex Southern Baptist Convention and others. In 50 countries. |
| Baptist World Alliance | B-fC | 4-b | 1905 | 67,943,000 | 171 | usa | C | 5 | BWA. HQ Maclean, Washington, DC. |
| Baptistic Pentecostals | 2CP1ZAC | 2-b | 1906 | 54,973,000 | 210 | arge | C | 5 | Teaching 2-fold Pentecostal experience of conversion, Spirit-baptism: AoG, ICFG. D=390. |
| Baptistic Pentecostals | P-Pe2-tC | 5-b | 1892 | 56,890,000 | 174 | braz | C | 5 | E.g. Assemblies of God. 1934,M=AoG,SFM,NPY,FFFM. 30000n,27000mw,20f. |
| Baptists | P-Bap-tC | 5-b | 1611 | 52,179,000 | 163 | usa | C | 5 | E.g. SBC. 1845 ex North. 99% White. (1970) 31000n,2H,6s,W=39%,409659Y. (1990) 63352n. |
| Bara ethnoreligionists | sAT | 3-d | | 268,000 | 1 | mada | B | 4 | Large inland area in south of island. Animists 50%. D=1. M=3. |
| Barabaig ethnoreligionists | sAT | 3-d | | 189,000 | 1 | tanz | A | 1 | Close to Taturu. Semi-nomadic pastoralists. Animists 97%. D=4. M=2. |
| Barbados Christian Council | C-nC | 7-d | c1990 | 140,000 | 1 | barb | C | 5 | BCC. |
| Barbados Council of Evangelical Chs | E-nC | 7-e | 1972 | 20,000 | 1 | barb | C | 5 | BCEC. |
| Bariba ethnoreligionists | sAT | 3-d | | 305,000 | 4 | beni | B | 2 | God=Gusune. Also in Nigeria, Togo. Animists 60%, Muslims 32%(growing slowly). D=5. M=4. |
| Basmachis | sUM | 2-e | c1880 | 1,000 | 5 | uzbe | A | 0 | 'Bandits'. Central Asian rebels against Russian imperialism. Crushed by USSR, 1924. |
| Bassa ethnoreligionists | sAT | 3-d | | 194,000 | 3 | libe | B | 5 | God=Nyambe. Grand Bassa County. Animists 32%. Vast numbers of Bassa AIC schisms. D=10. |
| Bassari ethnoreligionists | sAT | 3-d | | 206,000 | 6 | ghan | B | 2 | Also in Togo. 20 clans. Braille Scripture in progress. Animists 73%, Muslims 12%. D=4. M=2. |
| Bata ethnoreligionists | sAT | 3-d | | 118,000 | 2 | nige | A | 1 | Adamaawa State; also in Cameroon. Largely animists 70%, Muslims 20%. Y=1913. D=5. M=1. |
| Batak Christian Protestant Ch | P-Lut-AC | 6-c | 1861 | 2,791,000 | 1 | indo | B | 5 | HKBP. Huria Kristen Batak Protestan. Toba Bataks. 298n,25x,1v,W=45%,1657Y,40928y. |
| Bathalismo | I-mar-AC | 6-d | c1400 | 150,000 | 1 | phil | C | 2 | God Mysterious Mother. Inang Mahiwaga. Rizalists. HQ Nueva Ecija. God=Bathala. |
| Batiniya | sXM | 2-e | 891 | 5,000 | 10 | syri | B | 0 | Several Muslim sects seeking secret esoteric meanings of the Quran. |
| Batuque | sBU | 2-d | c1800 | 900,000 | 1 | braz | C | 5 | Afro-Brazilian spiritists in Belem and central regions of Brazil. Much brazilianized. |
| Bauddha Dharmankur Sabha | sB | 2-d | 1892 | 500,000 | 2 | indi | B | 2 | Begun in Calcutta, reviving West Bengal Buddhism. |
| Baule ethnoreligionists | sAT | 3-d | | 786,000 | 1 | ivor | B | 5 | God=Nyamie. Literates 10%. Animists 44%, Muslims 3%. D=RCC,EPEC,EPC,AoG,AICs. M=7. |
| Bauls | sSN | 2-e | c1900 | 5,000 | 1 | indi | B | 2 | 'Madmen'. Vaishnava/Sufi Hindu/Muslim singing amalgam. |
| Bayramiye | sUM | 2-e | c1430 | 1,000 | 1 | turk | A | 1 | Bairamiyah. Turkish Sufi order widespread in Balkans until banned in 1925; traces still exist. |
| Bayudaya | zJ | 2-e | 1919 | 1,000 | 1 | ugan | C | 2 | Propagation of Judaism, Moses Synagogue. Ex CMS, ex Bamaloki. Ganda. |
| Bedwardites | m-mar-AC | 10-f | 1891 | 200 | 1 | jama | B | 3 | F=Alexander Bedward; self-proclaimed Christ. 1921 violence. |
| Bektashiya | sUM | 2-e | c1300 | 2,000 | 8 | alba | B | 4 | Turkish Sufi order. Checkered history of Ottoman and Communist persecution. Secrecy. Shia. |
| Belize Christian Council | K-nC | 7-d | 1957 | 180,000 | 1 | beli | C | 5 | BCC. Protestants, Anglicans and (since 1969) Roman Catholics. |
| Belorussian Orth Ch: D Minsk | O-Bye-AC | 6-c | 1793 | 4,860,000 | 1 | belo | C | 5 | D Minsk and Byelorussia. Now 10 Dioceses, 10 bishops under P Moscow. 13% Russians. |
| Belz Hasidism | qOJ | 8-e | c1820 | 50,000 | 10 | isra | B | 3 | Holocaust survivors from East Europe. Orthodox, Zionist. Centers across Europe, N America. |
| Benedictines | osb-oC | 9-e | c520 | 8,900 | 40 | ital | C | 5 | OSB. F=Benedict of Nursia. Cenobitical. 1408, first Benedictine congregation. |
| Beshara | sNN | 2-e | c1970 | 1,000 | 2 | brit | C | 5 | A mystical esoteric Sufi order begun in Britain repudiating Islam. |
| Beta Israel | zJ | 2-e | BC c700 | 28,000 | 2 | isra | B | 2 | House of Israel. Falashas (Ethiopian Jews) airlifted to Israel 1984-92. |
| Betsileo ethnoreligionists | sAT | 3-d | | 127,000 | 1 | mada | C | 5 | South center of island. Animists 7%, Baha'is 0.2%(increasing fast). Early Revival center. D=6. |
| Betsimisaraka ethnoreligionists | sAT | 3-c | | 1,584,000 | 2 | mada | B | 3 | Revival center. Animists 77%. D=RCC(2 Dioceses). Eglise du Reveil,FMTA,MET,AICs. M=3. |
| Bhagavatas | sVH | 2-e | c1000 | 30,000 | 10 | indi | B | 1 | Devotees. of Bhagavan (God concerned for human well-being). Many movements. |
| Bhakti | sKH | 2-c | BC c500 | 1,000,000 | 50 | indi | B | 3 | One of the 3 forms of Hindu devotion: Vaisnavas, Saivas, Saktas; also Krsnas. |
| Bharata Janata Parishad | qH | 8-b | 1984 | 50,000,000 | 1 | indi | B | 2 | BJP. Political party advancing Hindu identity. |
| Bharatiya Buddha Mahasabha | wB | 7-d | | 400,000 | 1 | indi | B | 3 | Indian council for guiding Buddhist affairs. |
| Bhatras | sK | 2-e | c1500 | 3,000 | 2 | indi | B | 1 | North Indian pedlar community claiming Brahmin descent. Many Sikhs, now in UK. |
| Bhilala ethnoreligionists | sAT | 3-d | | 644,000 | 1 | indi | A | 0 | Bhils. In Gujarat, Madhya Pradesh, Maharashtra, Karnataka, Rajasthan. Animists 99%. |
| Bimoba ethnoreligionists | sAT | 3-d | | 226,000 | 3 | togo | B | 3 | Also in Burkina Faso. Animists 80%. D=6. M=7. |
| Birifor ethnoreligionists | sAT | 3-d | | 126,000 | 2 | burk | B | 3 | Southwestern area. Many monolinguals. Animists 86%, Muslims 1%. D=3. M=6. |
| Bisapanthis | sDV | 2-d | | 100,000 | 1 | indi | B | 1 | Digambara Jain subsect in southwest India. Liberal. |
| Bishops' Assembly of Egypt | S-nC | 7-d | 1983 | 225,000 | 1 | egyp | B | 5 | Assemblea della Gerarchia Cattolica d'Egitto. |
| Bishops' Conf of England & Wales | s-nC | 7-c | 1987 | 4,228,000 | 1 | brit | C | 5 | HQ London. |
| Bishops' Conference of Scotland | nC | 7-d | 1986 | 766,000 | 1 | brit | C | 5 | BCS. HQ Glasgow. |
| Bishops' Conference of Slovakia | nC | 7-c | 1991 | 3,660,000 | 1 | slok | C | 5 | BKS Biskupska Konferencia Slovenska. HQ Bratislava. |
| Bishops' Conference of Sri Lanka | R-nC | 7-c | 1988 | 1,260,000 | 1 | sril | B | 5 | BCSL. Lanka Raja Guru Sammelanaya. HQ Colombo. |
| Bissa ethnoreligionists | sAT | 3-d | | 233,000 | 1 | burk | B | 2 | South central. Also in Ghana, Ivory Coast. Animists 51%, Muslims 30%. D=2. M=6. |
| Biyo ethnoreligionists | sPAT | 3-d | | 109,000 | 1 | chin | A | 0 | Yunnan Province, near the Hani. Polytheists 98%, a few Buddhists. |
| Black Amer deliverance pente | I-3vB-tC | 5-d | 1960 | 115,000 | 1 | usa | C | 5 | Black Americans stressing deliverance ministry. |
| Black Amer Oneness Apostolics | ON3ZAC | 2-c | 1886 | 2,961,000 | 10 | usa | C | 5 | PAOW, AWCF, Bible Way Churches of Our Lord Jesus Christ WW, COLJCAF. D=150. |
| Black American Apostolics | I-3aB-tC | 5-e | 1925 | 34,400 | 2 | usa | C | 5 | Black Trinitarian Apostolics. Eastern USA, HQ Baltimore. Overseas work in Ghana, Liberia. |
| Black American Apostolics | I-3aO-tC | 5-c | 1886 | 2,164,000 | 3 | usa | C | 5 | E.g. PAOW. Black pentecostals. 600n,1s. Missions:Caribbean, India, Israel, Nigeria; 1,000 chs. |
| Black American cell-based chs | I-3kB-tC | 5-e | 1969 | 28,200 | 1 | usa | C | 5 | WFFM. Cell-based churches. Abroad: 5,000 members in 74 chs (Africa 58, Pakistan 16). |

*Continued overleaf*

*Table 17–5 continued*

| *Name of religion/religionists* 1 | *Pedigree* 2 | *Type* 3 | *Begun* 4 | *Adherents* 5 | *Ext* 6 | *Coun* 7 | *W* 8 | *X* 9 | *E. g. = examples; name for God, other religions present, D=denominations, M=missions.* 10 |
|---|---|---|---|---|---|---|---|---|---|
| Black American charismatics | I-3cB-tC | 5-d | 1964 | 584,000 | 1 | usa | C | 5 | E.g. IEC. Churches: Africa 430, USA 70, South America 50, Italy 20, Jamaica 1. |
| Black American charismatics | I-3cD-tC | 5-d | 1955 | 152,000 | 2 | usa | C | 5 | Black Charismatics arising over last 45 years as separate denominations. |
| Black American Full Gospelers | I-3fB-tC | 5-e | 1978 | 18,000 | 1 | usa | C | 5 | EMCI. Full Gospel theology. Schism ex CoGiC. HQ Arkansas. Abroad: 700 in 1 ch in Japan. |
| Black American Full Gospelers | I-3fD-tC | 5-c | 1993 | 1,320,000 | 1 | usa | C | 5 | FGBCF. F=bp Paul Morton. Black. Ex NBCA, NBCUSA. Missions: Bahamas, S Africa, Russia. |
| Black American indep charis | DN3ZAC | 2-c | 1955 | 1,472,000 | 4 | usa | C | 5 | African American independent charismatic bodies: Full Gospel Baptist Chs Fellowship. D=10. |
| Black American indig pentecostals | BN3ZAC | 2-c | 1889 | 7,635,000 | 20 | usa | C | 5 | Black Pentecostalism: Church of God in Christ, UHCA, Full Gospel Catholic Ch. D=90. |
| Black American neocharismatics | I-3nB-tC | 10-f | | 920 | 1 | sail | C | 5 | Several bodies including Spiritual Baptists (Shouters, Shakers). |
| Black American Oneness chs | I-3oO-tC | 5-d | 1916 | 797,000 | 2 | usa | C | 5 | WW=World Wide. Black Oneness pentecostals. Ex COLJCAF. 360n,4p,W=95%,1000Y. |
| Black American pentecostals | I-3pB-tC | 5-c | 1889 | 6,940,000 | 18 | usa | C | 5 | E.g. Church of God in Christ. HQ Memphis (TN). (1970) 5000n. (1990) 33593n. |
| Black Arabs | zSM | 2-c | | 1,705,000 | 2 | came | B | 3 | Shuwa Muslims in north of country. |
| Black Bobo ethnoreligionists | sAT | 3-d | | 170,000 | 2 | burk | B | 3 | Also in Mali. Animists 50%, Muslims 25%. D=2. M=3. |
| Black Jews | zJ | 2-e | 1920 | 5,000 | 3 | usa | C | 3 | Israelite cults originating in Harlem, New York. Old Testament doctrines. |
| Black Karen ethnoreligionists | sAT | 3-d | | 161,000 | 2 | myan | B | 4 | God=Pa-ra-pyin-zowk. Shan State. Black dress. Buddhists 42%, animists 22%, Baha'is. D=5. |
| Black Muslims | BXM | 2-c | 1913 | 1,650,000 | 5 | usa | C | 5 | Three distinct and separate bodies from original founded by Elijah Muhammad. |
| Black Tai ethnoreligionists | sAT | 3-d | | 711,000 | 6 | viet | A | 1 | Red and Black rivers; Thailand, 3,000 in USA, France, Laos, China. Animists 95%. D=3. M=3. |
| Bnai Brith International | wJ | 7-d | 1843 | 500,000 | 50 | usa | C | 5 | Jewish fraternal organization. B'Nai B'rith. HQ New York. Works through local lodges. |
| Bobova Hasidism | qOJ | 8-e | | 20,000 | 1 | isra | B | 2 | Contemporary Hasidic group, with own rules and regulations. |
| Bodo ethnoreligionists | sHAT | 3-d | | 740,000 | 2 | indi | B | 3 | God=Ishôra. Hinduized animists 93%. D=Goalpara Boro Baptist Ch,NBB,RCC,CNI,ICI. M=7. |
| Bogomils | BY | 10-f | 864 | 500 | 3 | bulg | C | 5 | Manichaeism, Paulicianism, Catharism, Dualist sect. |
| Bohras | BIHM | 2-d | c1150 | 900,000 | 10 | indi | B | 2 | Ismaili sect overlapping with Daudis and Mustalis. |
| Bokkos ethnoreligionists | sAT | 3-d | | 123,000 | 1 | nige | B | 4 | Plateau State, Barakin Ladi and Mangu LGAs. Animists 40%, Muslim 10%. M=NBTT. |
| Bondoukou Kulango ethnoreligionists | sAT | 3-d | | 155,000 | 2 | ivor | A | 0 | Eastern Department, Bondoukou Subprefecture. In Ghana. Animists 92%, Muslims 4%. D=2. |
| Bonpos | sST | 3-e | BC 700 | 40,000 | 1 | chin | B | 3 | Neo-Buddhists of Bon Faith (pre-Buddhism). Tibet, China. Till 1959 330 monasteries. |
| Bornean ethnoreligionists | sAT | 3-c | | 1,500,000 | 1 | indo | B | 3 | Many Kalimantan tribes are still predominantly animists. |
| Botswana Christian Council | W-nC | 7-e | 1966 | 70,000 | 1 | bots | B | 5 | BCC. Lekgotla la Sekeresete la Botswana. |
| Botswana Spiritual Council of Chs | I-nC | 7-d | | 450,000 | 1 | bots | B | 5 | BSCC. |
| Bougists | I-mar-AC | 6-e | 1953 | 45,000 | 1 | cong | C | 2 | Lassyism. Mission de Dieu du Bougie. God of the Candle. |
| Bouna Kulango ethnoreligionists | sAT | 3-d | | 180,000 | 2 | ivor | A | 1 | Eastern Department, Nassian Subprefecture. In Ghana. Animists 90%, Muslims 6%. D=2. M=1. |
| Brahma Kumaris | sNH | 2-d | 1937 | 250,000 | 20 | indi | B | 2 | World Spiritual University (a UN NGO). Run by unmarried women. Millennialist. |
| Brahmanism | sHH | 2-d | BC 2000 | 500,000 | 2 | indi | B | 2 | Earliest Vedic period. Sacrifice and ritual under control of the Brahmins. |
| Brahmasampradaya | sH-oH | 9-e | c1300 | 50,000 | 1 | indi | B | 1 | One of 4 Vaishnava teaching/monastic traditions. Dualistic; Vishnu supreme. Mainly Karnataka. |
| Branch Davidians | m-Adv-AC | 6-e | 1929 | 2,000 | 1 | usa | C | 3 | Cult ex SDA centered in Waco, TX. Destroyed in fire in FBI assault, with 78 killed. |
| Bratslav Hasidism | sOJ | 2-e | 1798 | 4,800 | 1 | slok | C | 4 | Bratslaver. F=rabbi Nahman. |
| Brazil for Christ Ev Pentecostal Ch | e-fC | 4-c | 1955 | 2,000,000 | 10 | braz | C | 5 | OBPC. O Brasil Para Cristo. 5,000 churches. |
| Brazilian Catholic Apostolic Church | B-fC | 4-c | 1945 | 3,000,000 | 20 | braz | C | 5 | ICAB. Igreja Catolica Apostolica Brasileira. Schism ex RCC. 12 dioceses, 25 bishops. |
| Brazilian charismatics | I-3cY-tC | 5-d | 1960 | 773,000 | 2 | braz | C | 5 | National Baptist Convention. Igreja do Renovação. Split ex Brazilian Baptist Convention. |
| Brazilian Full Gospelers | I-3fY-tC | 5-e | 1977 | 36,000 | 1 | braz | C | 5 | E.g. Full Gospel Peace Churches. Amazon. M=Vineyard Chs, GSMA(USA). |
| Brazilian grassroots chs | I-3gY-tC | 5-c | 1970 | 3,600,000 | 1 | braz | C | 5 | Grassroots (GR) churches: Rio has 984 GR chs, São Paulo 1,468 chs with 650,000; NNCM. |
| Brazilian Oneness chs | I-3oY-tC | 5-e | c1960 | 14,900 | 1 | braz | C | 5 | E.g. National Independent Church of Brazil. |
| Brazilian pentecostals | I-3pY-tC | 5-b | 1910 | 18,581,000 | 6 | braz | C | 5 | E.g. Universal Ch of the Kingdom of God. IURD/UCKG. 2000n. In 50 countries (Portugal &c). |
| Brazilian radio/TV believers | I-3rY-tC | 5-e | c1950 | 17,600 | 1 | braz | C | 5 | Isolated radio believers in remote jungle areas. R=49700 (HCJB,TWR,FEBC,Radio Vatican). |
| Brazilian/Portu grassroots neochar | YN3ZAC | 2-b | 1910 | 23,023,000 | 20 | braz | C | 5 | OBPC (Brazil for Christ Ev Ch), IURD/UCKG, CCB, IPF, IPDA. D=460. |
| British Council of Prot Christian Chs | T-nC | 7-e | | 3,000 | 1 | brit | C | 3 | BCPCC. |
| British Evangelical Council | C-nC | 7-e | | 40,000 | 1 | brit | C | 5 | BEC. |
| British Israelites | m-BrI-AC | 6-e | c1830 | 99,000 | 1 | brit | C | 2 | Members believe Anglo-Saxon race have descended from 10 Lost Tribes of Israel. |
| British Pentecostal Fellowship | H-nC | 7-d | 1948 | 200,000 | 1 | brit | C | 5 | BPF. |
| British Wheel of Yoga | zH | 2-e | 1963 | 4,000 | 2 | brit | C | 5 | BWY. Registered charity to propagate yoga. 1,000 certified teachers. |
| British-Israelites | I-BrI-tC | 5-e | 1930 | 77,000 | 5 | usa | C | 3 | Radio Ch of God. Ex CoG(SD). Doctrinal realignments. Schisms 1974. In 124 countries. 400n. |
| Broad Church Anglicans | A-Cen-tC | 5-c | 1078 | 9,109,000 | 32 | brit | C | 5 | Large industrial areas, vast overspill areas. |
| Brotherhood of Cross and Star | I-3nA-AC | 6-c | 1956 | 1,223,000 | 1 | nige | B | 4 | Vast expanding movement with numerous churches abroad. F=Olumba Olumba Obu. |
| Brothers of Christian Instruction | ficp-oC | 9-e | 1817 | 1,300 | | ital | C | 5 | FICP. |
| Brothers of Schools | fsc-oC | 9-e | 1680 | 7,700 | | ital | C | 5 | FSC. |
| Buddhayana | YB | 2-c | 1954 | 1,930,000 | 20 | indo | B | 3 | Syncretistic amalgam of Mahayana, Theravada, with Kasogatan (local Javanese Buddhism). |
| Buddhist Association of Thailand | nB | 7-b | 1934 | 52,382,000 | 2 | thai | B | 3 | 75 provincial associations (14 Chinese). |
| Buddhist believers in Christ | I-Bud-tC | 5-c | c1970 | 2,194,000 | 8 | chin | B | 2 | Hidden Buddhists converted to Christ but remaining within Buddhism as a witness. |
| Buddhist Churches of America | sPJMB | 2-d | 1899 | 120,000 | 10 | usa | C | 5 | Jodoshinshu. Japanese Americans. |
| Buddhist Federation of Australia | nB | 7-d | c1970 | 241,000 | 3 | aust | C | 4 | Huge Nan Tien Temple is part of a Taiwan-based 110 monastery network. |
| Buddhist Publication Society | vB | 9-d | 1958 | 300,000 | 3 | sril | B | 3 | BPS. HQ Kandy. Mission to the West. |
| Buddhist Society of Great Britain and I | nB | 7-e | 1907 | 3,000 | 3 | brit | C | 5 | I=Ireland. All traditions taught. |
| Buddhist Society of India | nB | 7-c | 1951 | 6,000,000 | 1 | indi | B | 2 | Neo-Buddhism of BR Ambedkar; mass conversion of Dalits, 1956. Marathi. |
| Buddhist Sunday Schools Movement | sB | 2-c | 1958 | 3,000,000 | 4 | thai | B | 2 | Many schools around Bangkok. |
| Buddhistic New-Religionists | SN | 2-b | c1850 | 25,000,000 | 3 | japa | B | 3 | New Religions with strong Buddhist elements, influence, dogmas, claims. |
| Buddhists | B | 1-a | | 359,982,000 | 126 | japa | B | 2 | Buddha-dharma. Followers of the Buddha in several hundred schools and sects. |
| Budi Setia | sSN | 2-e | c1960 | 30,000 | 1 | indo | B | 3 | Javanese et alia mystical sect. |
| Bukkyo Shinshu | sPJMB | 2-e | | 5,500 | 2 | japa | B | 3 | HQ Kumamoto-ken. |
| Bukusu ethnoreligionists | sAT | 3-d | | 115,000 | 1 | keny | C | 5 | Bungoma District, Western Province. Animists 15%. D=7. M=6. |
| Bulgarian (Byzantine rite) | R-Bul-tC | 5-e | 1926 | 22,600 | 1 | bulg | C | 5 | Uniates. Catholics of Byzantino-Slav rite. M=AA. |
| Bulgarian Catholic Bishops' Conf | R-nC | 7-e | | 90,000 | 1 | bulg | C | 5 | MEKB. Mejduritualnata Episcopska Konferenzia vav Balgaria. HQ Sofia. |
| Bulgarian Evangelical Alliance | E-nC | 7-d | 1990 | 120,000 | 1 | bulg | C | 5 | BEA. |
| Bulgarian Orthodox | O-Bul-tC | 5-c | 1186 | 6,523,000 | 20 | bulg | C | 5 | Balgarskata Pravoslavna Crkva. 23 bps. 1785n,123de(200m,360w),1j,2s(330),W=13%. |
| Bulgarian Orthodox Church | O-Bul-AC | 6-c | 150 | 6,100,000 | 1 | bulg | C | 5 | Balgarskata Pravoslavna Crkva. 23 bps. 1785n,123de(200m,360w),1j,2s(330),W=13%. |
| Bulgyohwoi | sKMB | 2-d | 1975 | 563,000 | 10 | souk | B | 2 | SGI Hankuk-Bulgyohwoi/Korean Buddhist Council. Emphasis upon world peace. |
| Bulsa ethnoreligionists | sAT | 3-d | | 193,000 | 2 | ghan | A | 2 | God=Nawen. Sandema District. Also in Burkina Faso. Animists 92%, Muslims 1%. D=10. M=5. |
| Bulu Fang ethnoreligionists | sAT | 3-d | | 121,000 | 1 | came | C | 5 | God=Zambe. Covers Ntem, Dja, & Lobo Divisions. Decline. Animists 20%. D=5. M=UBS. |
| Bund Pfingstlicher Gemeinden | H-nC | 7-e | 1961 | 51,000 | 1 | swit | C | 5 | Federation of Pentecostal Churches. |
| Bungan | sVN | 2-e | 1942 | 50,000 | 1 | indo | B | 3 | Renewal movement among Kenyah and Kayan (Borneo). Declining after rapid spread in 1950s. |
| Burmese Theravadins | sTB | 2-b | | 32,000,000 | 32 | myan | B | 1 | Theravada heavily influenced by animism, nats, Hinduism. |
| Busansi ethnoreligionists | sAT | 3-d | | 146,000 | 3 | ghan | B | 2 | Bilinguals in Moore, Hausa, Kusaal, Mampruli. Literates 7%. Animists 67%, Muslims 25%. D=3. |
| Bussho Gonenkai Kyodan | sNJMB | 2-d | | 913,000 | 1 | japa | B | 1 | HQ Minato-ku, Tokyo. |
| Buzan-ha | sSJMB | 2-c | | 1,372,000 | 4 | japa | B | 2 | Larger of 2 main branches of Shingon Buddhism (Shingonshu). |
| Bwiti | I-mar-AC | 6-d | c1890 | 125,000 | 1 | gabo | C | 1 | Eglise des Banzie. Church of the Initiates. Fang members. |
| Byelorussian Orthodox | O-Bye-tC | 5-c | 1793 | 4,920,000 | 6 | belo | C | 5 | White Russians 90%. Now 10 Dioceses, 10 bishops under P Moscow. 13% Russians. |
| Byzantine-rite | R-Byz-tC | 5-d | 1777 | 147,000 | 3 | usa | C | 5 | E.g. PA III. Formerly Ruthenian-rite. |
| C Episcopatuum Communitatis E | cC | 7-a | 1980 | 200,000,000 | 40 | belg | C | 5 | C=Commissio, E=Europaeae. COM.E.CE. HQ Brussels. Covers European Community. |
| C Fundamentalista de Igl Ev de Chile | T-nC | 7-e | c1960 | 37,000 | 1 | chil | C | 3 | CFEC. Confederation of Evangelical Fundamentalist Churches of Chile. 10 denominations. |
| C of Fundamental Ev Chs of Bolivia | T-nC | 7-e | | 2,000 | 1 | boli | C | 3 | CIEFB. Confederacion das Iglesias Fundamentalistas Evangelicas de Bolivia. |
| Cambodian Buddhism | sTB | 2-c | AD 400 | 9,500,000 | 2 | camb | A | 1 | 2 orders in 1970: Mahanikay (3,230 monasteries: 62,700 monks), Thomayat (139: 2,300). |
| Cameroonian Creole ethnoreligionists | sAT | 3-d | | 110,000 | 2 | came | C | 5 | Major lingua franca (50% of country). Animists 12%. D=4. M=UBS. |
| Camillians | mi-oC | 9-e | 1582 | 1,000 | | ital | C | 5 | MI. |
| Campus Crusade for Christ | ccci-oC | 9-e | 1951 | 1,000 | 110 | usa | C | 5 | CCCI. |
| Canadian Council of Ev Prot Chs | T-nC | 7-e | | 50,000 | 1 | cana | C | 4 | CCEPC. |
| Candomble | sBU | 2-c | 1810 | 1,000,000 | 1 | braz | C | 5 | Spiritists in Bahia, Maranhao, Pernambuco. 10,000 centers. Women mediums, dances. Legal. |
| Canossians | fcc-oC | 9-e | 1831 | 3,700 | 20 | ital | C | 5 | FCC. |
| Cao Dai Missionary Church | sSN | 2-c | 1919 | 3,200,000 | 50 | viet | B | 4 | Dai Dao Tam Ky Pho Do (Great Way of the 3 Epochs of Salvation). Catholic syncretism. |
| Capuchins | ofmcap-oC | 9-e | 1525 | 11,700 | | ital | C | 5 | OFMCap. |
| Cargo cultists | CN | 2-e | 1893 | 3,000 | 10 | papu | C | 5 | Over 130 distinct non-Christian cargo cults since 1893. |
| Caribbean Conference of Churches | N-cC | 7-b | 1973 | 15,000,000 | 15 | barb | C | 5 | CCC, also member of CELAM. HQ Bridgetown, Barbados. |
| Carmelites | ocarm-oC | 9-e | | 2,100 | | ital | C | 5 | OCarm. HQ Roma. |
| Carmelites of Mary | cmi-oC | 9-e | 1856 | 1,900 | | indi | B | 5 | CMI. |
| Carthusians | ocart-oC | 10-f | 1084 | 360 | | fran | C | 5 | OCart. F=Bruno. Now 394 monks and 86 nuns, committed to solitude and unbroken silence. |
| Cath Bishops' Conf of the Philippines | R-nC | 7-b | 1988 | 62,570,000 | 1 | phil | C | 5 | CBCP. HQ Manila. |
| Cath Ch in China (Clandestine) | R-Lat-AC | 6-c | 1298 | 7,900,000 | 1 | chin | B | 5 | Tien Chu Chiao Hui. Illegal, loyal to pope, but cooperating with state. Strong in Hebei, Fujian. |
| Cath Ch in China (Underground) | I-Lat-AC | 6-c | 1979 | 1,320,000 | 1 | chin | B | 5 | More organized, confrontational, aggressive, militant part of pro-Rome loyalists. Gansu, Shanxi. |
| Cath Ch in Papua New Guinea | R-Lat-AC | 6-c | 1847 | 1,336,000 | 1 | papu | C | 5 | Many institutions. C=12+8+31. 97H,3q,3s. |
| Catholic Bishops' Conf of Bangladesh | R-nC | 7-d | 1978 | 235,000 | 1 | bang | B | 5 | CBCB. HQ Dhaka. |
| Catholic Bishops' Conf of Japan | R-nC | 7-d | 1973 | 460,000 | 1 | japa | B | 5 | CBCJ. HQ Tokyo. |

*Continued opposite*

*Table 17–5 continued*

| Name of religion/religionists 1 | Pedigree 2 | Type 3 | Begun 4 | Adherents 5 | Ext 6 | Coun 7 | W 8 | X 9 | E. g. = examples; name for God, other religions present, D=denominations, M=missions. 10 |
|---|---|---|---|---|---|---|---|---|---|
| Catholic Bishops' Conf of Malaysia | P-rC | 7-d | 1980 | 870,000 | 3 | malb | B | 5 | CBCMSB or BCMSB. Also covers Singapore, Brunei. HQ Shah Alam (Malaysia). |
| Catholic Bishops' Conf of PNG & SI | rC | 7-c | 1983 | 1,473,000 | 2 | papu | C | 5 | CBCPNGSI. SI=Solomon Islands. HQ Waigani (PNG). |
| Catholic Bishops' Conference of India | R-nC | 7-b | 1976 | 15,500,000 | 1 | indi | B | 5 | CBCI. HQ New Delhi. |
| Catholic Bishops' Conference of Korea | nC | 7-c | 1973 | 3,700,000 | 1 | souk | B | 5 | CBCK. Hanguk Jukyo Hweoi. HQ Seoul. |
| Catholic Ch in Belarus | R-Lat-AC | 6-c | 1600 | 1,400,000 | 1 | belo | C | 5 | 33,000 Uniates. 1995, 100 Polish priests expelled. |
| Catholic Ch in England & Wales | R-LEr-AC | 6-c | 678 | 4,246,000 | 1 | brit | C | 5 | C=55+12+352. P=75%,5s,W=43%. 50% Irish; 7% converts. |
| Catholic Ch in the Czech Rep | R-Lat-AC | 6-c | 828 | 3,756,000 | 1 | czec | B | 5 | Katolicka Cirkev. 1,621 unstaffed parishes. 332de. |
| Catholic Ch in the Netherlands | R-Lat-AC | 6-c | 650 | 5,516,000 | 1 | neth | C | 5 | Rooms-Katholieke Kerk. C=36+16+128. 7q,5s. |
| Catholic Ch in the Philippines | R-Lat-AC | 6-b | 1521 | 61,762,000 | 1 | phil | C | 5 | Iglesia Catolica. C=34+3+66. |
| Catholic Charismatic Renewal | r-fC | 4-b | 1967 | 120,000,000 | 233 | holy | C | 5 | HQ Vatican City. M=ICCRS/ICCRO. |
| Catholic Charismatics | R2ZAC | 2-b | 1967 | 119,912,000 | 234 | braz | C | 5 | Total baptized RCs in CCR, past and present, including children and infants. D=236. |
| Catholic Church in Australia | R-LEr-AC | 6-c | 1803 | 5,445,000 | 1 | aust | C | 5 | From Italy, Poland, Croatia. C=29+8+67. W=61%. |
| Catholic Church in Croatia | R-Lat-AC | 6-c | 250 | 3,950,000 | 1 | croa | C | 5 | 750-year-old church, strong traditions. |
| Catholic Church in Ghana | R-Lat-AC | 6-c | 1481 | 1,813,000 | 1 | ghan | B | 5 | C=4+7+20. (1970)113n,237x. |
| Catholic Church in Hungary | R-LEr-AC | 6-c | 250 | 6,411,000 | 1 | hung | C | 5 | Római Katolikus Egyház. C=3+0+1. |
| Catholic Church in India | R-LEr-AC | 6-b | 1319 | 15,456,000 | 1 | indi | B | 5 | Catholic workers: C=35+15+122. |
| Catholic Church in Indonesia | R-Lat-AC | 6-c | 650 | 5,885,000 | 1 | indo | B | 5 | Gereja Katolik I. C=19+9+70. |
| Catholic Church in Ireland | R-Lat-AC | 6-c | 350 | 3,151,000 | 1 | irel | C | 5 | Eaglais Chaitliceach Rómhánach. C=34+11+104. |
| Catholic Church in Kenya | R-Lat-AC | 6-c | 1498 | 6,989,000 | 1 | keny | C | 5 | Kanisa Katholiki. C=9+11+40. |
| Catholic Church in Korea | R-Lat-AC | 6-c | 1592 | 4,025,000 | 1 | souk | B | 5 | Ch'onju Kyohwe. C=14+2+32. 2p,2s(709),W=63%. |
| Catholic Church in Lebanon | R-LEr-AC | 6-c | 300 | 2,055,000 | 1 | leba | B | 5 | Al-Kanissa al-Kathoulikiah. C=21+2+53. |
| Catholic Church in Lithuania | R-Lat-AC | 6-c | 1251 | 3,331,000 | 1 | lith | C | 5 | Violently persecuted throughout 20th century, especially 1939-1990. |
| Catholic Church in Malawi | R-Lat-AC | 6-c | 1561 | 2,621,000 | 1 | mala | C | 5 | C=4+3+10. (1970) 70n,235x,37143Yy. (1990) |
| Catholic Church in Nigeria | R-Lat-AC | 6-b | 1487 | 13,249,000 | 1 | nige | B | 5 | C=11+4+23. 5p,4s(546). |
| Catholic Church in Pakistan | R-Lat-AC | 6-c | 1594 | 1,142,000 | 1 | paki | A | 5 | Romai Katholik Kalisia. C=9+6+18. (1970) 74n,159x. |
| Catholic Church in Poland | R-Lat-AC | 6-b | 950 | 36,261,000 | 1 | pola | C | 5 | Kosciól Rzymsko-katolicki. C=35+7+99. 26q,24s. |
| Catholic Church in Romania | R-Lat-AC | 6-c | 1000 | 3,366,000 | 1 | roma | C | 5 | Biserica Catolica Romana. 68% Hungarian. C=1+0+0. |
| Catholic Church in Russia | R-LEr-AC | 6-c | 1084 | 1,573,000 | 1 | russ | B | 5 | Rimsko-Katolicheskaya Tserkov. (1970) 12n,45Yy. (1995) 31n,64x,30m,109w,1900Yy. |
| Catholic Church in Slovakia | R-Lat-AC | 6-c | 828 | 3,675,000 | 1 | slok | C | 5 | Formerly in Czechoslavakia. |
| Catholic Church in Slovenia | R-Lat-AC | 6-c | 500 | 1,689,000 | 1 | slov | C | 5 | Majority church now freed of politics. |
| Catholic Church in South Africa | R-Lat-AC | 6-c | 1501 | 3,352,000 | 1 | soua | C | 5 | 72% Bantu, 16% Wh, 10% Col. C=32+7+74. 1q,2s. |
| Catholic Church in Sri Lanka | R-Lat-AC | 6-c | 1517 | 1,261,000 | 1 | sril | B | 5 | Romanu Katolike Sabhava. C=7+6+24,1p,3q,1s. |
| Catholic Church in Tanzania | R-Lat-AC | 6-c | 1449 | 8,264,000 | 1 | tanz | B | 5 | Kanisa Katoliki. C=13+4=39. 12p,4s(389). |
| Catholic Church in the Sudan | R-Lat-AC | 6-c | 1842 | 3,199,000 | 1 | suda | B | 5 | Catholikiyya. 950 Greek Catholics. C=1+2+3. |
| Catholic Church in the Ukraine | R-LEr-AC | 6-c | 1084 | 6,344,000 | 1 | ukra | C | 5 | Rimsko-Katolicheskaya Tserkov. Survived, 1944-91. |
| Catholic Church in the USA | R-LEr-AC | 6-b | 1526 | 58,397,000 | 1 | usa | C | 5 | Strongly developed, often clashing with Vatican. |
| Catholic Church in Uganda | R-Lat-AC | 6-c | 1879 | 8,840,000 | 1 | ugan | C | 5 | Eklezia Enkatoliki. C=6+3+17. 11p,4s(254). |
| Catholic Church in Viet Nam | R-Lat-AC | 6-c | 1530 | 5,146,000 | 1 | viet | B | 5 | Cong Giao. C=11+10+12. (1970) 84781Yy. (1990) |
| Catholic Church in Zambia | R-Lat-AC | 6-c | 1889 | 3,028,000 | 1 | zamb | C | 5 | C=6+4+15 M=WF, SMA, OFM. |
| Catholic Church in Zimbabwe | R-Lat-AC | 6-c | 1561 | 1,115,000 | 1 | zimb | B | 5 | 92% Black, 6% White. C=8+3+21. 1p,1s(64). |
| Catholic Church of Canada | R-LEr-AC | 6-b | 1534 | 13,072,000 | 1 | cana | C | 5 | Eglise Catholique. C=63+17+196. 11q,15s. |
| Catholic Evangelicals | ERAC | 2-c | 1960 | 7,800,000 | 11 | brit | C | 5 | Catholics who become Evangelicals also, by conviction. |
| Catimbo | sBU | 2-d | c1800 | 350,000 | 1 | braz | C | 5 | Afro-Brazilian spiritists in central Brazil, also in northeast. Italian origins. |
| Celestial Church of Christ | I-3aA-AC | 6-c | 1952 | 3,689,000 | 1 | nige | B | 4 | Heavenly Christianity. Begun Dahomey 1947. Yoruba elites. Rapid growth also in 20 countries. |
| Central Bhil ethnoreligionists | sAT | 3-c | | 4,449,000 | 1 | indi | A | 1 | Polytheists/animists 95%. D=RCC(D-Ajmer-Jaipur),CNI(D-Jabalpur),DNC,MCSA,CMA,M=11. |
| Central Conf of American Rabbis | cJ | 7-d | 1889 | 100,000 | 2 | usa | C | 3 | Founding by Reform rabbinate opposing Orthodox and secularizing trends. |
| Central Gond ethnoreligionists | sPAT | 3-c | | 1,721,000 | 1 | indi | B | 2 | God=Parameshwar. Mainly in MP. Hindus 70%, animists 30%. D=Methodists,MPELC. M=12. |
| Central Guere ethnoreligionists | sAT | 3-d | | 264,000 | 1 | ivor | B | 3 | Bilingualism in French and Jula. Literates 10%. Animists 75%, Muslims 10%. D=4. M=5. |
| Central Khmer ethnoreligionists | sBAT | 3-d | | 287,000 | 2 | camb | A | 1 | Theravada Buddhists 94%(1970: 2,826 monasteries, 68,145 monks), animists 3%. D=3. M=7. |
| Central Shona ethnoreligionists | sAT | 3-d | | 886,000 | 3 | zimb | C | 4 | God=Mwari. Main Shona dialect. Animists 33%. D=11. M=3. |
| Central West Gurage ethnoreligionists | sAT | 3-d | | 220,000 | 1 | ethi | B | 4 | Southwestern Shoa Province. Animists 27%, Muslims 30%. D=4. M=3. |
| Central Yi ethnoreligionists | sPAT | 3-d | | 495,000 | 1 | chin | A | 1 | A separate language in Yi official nationality. Polytheists/animists 98%. D=TSPM, RCC. |
| Centre Islamique et Culturel de B | nM | 7-d | 1969 | 200,000 | 3 | belg | C | 5 | ICCB. CICB. Islamic and Cultural Centre of Belgium. Government sponsored. |
| Ch of God Mission International | I-3aA-AC | 6-c | 1968 | 1,430,000 | 1 | nige | B | 5 | Miracle Centre, Benin City. International seminary, led by archbishop B. Idahosa. |
| Ch of JC of Latter-day Saints | m-LdS-AC | 6-c | 1830 | 4,879,000 | 1 | usa | C | 2 | Mormons. HQ Utah. Also 700,000 overseas. (1970) 17272n,91237Y. (1990) 28962n. |
| Ch of Jesus Christ of LdS | m-fC | 4-c | 1830 | 8,650,000 | 116 | usa | C | 3 | CJCLdS. LdS=Latter-day Saints. Mormons. In 116 countries. |
| Ch of the Province of S Africa | A-Hig-AC | 6-c | 1806 | 2,669,000 | 1 | soua | C | 5 | CPSA. 16 Dioceses in SA, 6 abroad. 56% Black, 24% White. 511b,18de,18H,96h,12r,4s(81). |
| Ch of the Province of Tanzania | A-plu-AC | 6-c | 1864 | 2,683,000 | 1 | tanz | B | 5 | CPT. Kanisa la Jimbo la Tanzania (KJT). 16 Dioceses. 160f,3s(55),305n,43x,8629Y,16200y. |
| Chaldean (Eastern Syrian rite) | R-Cha-tC | 5-d | 1553 | 318,000 | 9 | iraq | C | 5 | E.g. Patriarchate,1553. Rapid Catholic influx from north. |
| Chan Buddhism | sZJMB | 2-c | c500 | 1,000,000 | 2 | chin | B | 3 | Form of Zen meditation rooted in Indian Buddhism and developed in China and Japan. |
| Changa ethnoreligionists | sAT | 3-d | | 120,000 | 1 | moza | B | 4 | God=Mngari. Coastal Ndau. Animists 61%. D=AACJM,RCC,AC/CPSA,many other AICs. M=2. |
| Chaplaincy of Full Gospel Churches | F-fC | 4-c | 1984 | 6,500,000 | 6 | usa | C | 5 | CFGC. Full gospel agency credentialing USA military and civilian chaplains. |
| Charan Dasis | sKH | 2-d | c1770 | 150,000 | 1 | indi | B | 2 | Krishna devotionism. In north India among mercantile castes. Yellow clothes. F=Charan Das. |
| Charismatics (Second-Wavers) | 2ZAC | 2-b | 1907 | 175,857,000 | 235 | mexi | C | 5 | All who experience Spirit-baptism but remain within nonpentecostal mainline chs. D=6,530. |
| Chaungtha ethnoreligionists | sBAT | 3-d | | 154,000 | 1 | myan | A | 0 | People of the Valley. Related to Lolo, Burmese. Buddhists/animists 99%. |
| Chewa ethnoreligionists | sAT | 3-d | | 282,000 | 4 | zimb | B | 5 | Mainly in Malawi, Zambia; also Tanzania. Animists 30%, many Baha'is. D=many AICs. M=FMB. |
| Chienchiang ethnoreligionists | sPT | 3-d | | 101,000 | 1 | chin | A | 1 | Guizhou Province. Related to Puyi (Bouyei). Polytheists 80%, Buddhists 19%. D=RCC. |
| Chiesa Cattolica in Italia | R-LEr-AC | 6-b | 40 | 58,772,000 | 1 | ital | C | 5 | Strongest national church, with vibrant Catholic Charismatic Renewal. |
| Chikakusan Minshukyo Kyodan | sTS | 2-d | | 195,000 | 1 | japa | B | 1 | HQ Nagano-ken. |
| China Christian Council | K-nC | 7-b | 1949 | 12,193,000 | 1 | chin | B | 5 | CCC. Revived after 1970. Very influential by 1985. |
| China Islamic Association | nM | 7-b | | 19,168,000 | 1 | chin | B | 3 | CIA. Official representative of Muslims before government and Communist Party. |
| Chinese Buddhist Association | nB | 7-b | 1954 | 60,000,000 | 2 | chin | B | 3 | Government-control after virtually destroyed in Cultural Revolution, 1966-1979. |
| Chinese Buddhists | CMB | 2-b | 60 | 90,000,000 | 60 | chin | B | 1 | Violently suppressed in AD 452, 574, and 845. |
| Chinese Cath Bps' Conf on Mainland | R-nC | 7-c | | 7,500,000 | 1 | chin | B | 5 | CBCM. |
| Chinese Catholic Ch (Patriotic) | I-Lat-AC | 6-c | 1957 | 5,518,000 | 1 | chin | B | 5 | Open Ch. Under Ai Guo Hui (Chinese Catholic Patriotic Association, CCPA). Set up by regime. |
| Chinese cell-based networks | I-3kC-tC | 5-e | 1986 | 27,600 | 1 | sing | B | 5 | E.g. FCBC. Schism ex Singapore Baptist Convention. F=Lawrence Khong. Large, cell-based. |
| Chinese folk-religionists | F | 2-a | BC 1000 | 384,807,000 | 89 | chin | B | 1 | Popular religion: Buddhism, Confucianism, Taoism, universism, ancestor veneration, local gods. |
| Chinese Full Gospelers | I-3fC-tC | 5-e | 1982 | 18,000 | 1 | usa | C | 5 | CFGFI. HQ Houston, TX. Abroad (HQ Kowloon, Hong Kong): 100 chs, 200 ministers. |
| Chinese Mongolian ethnoreligionists | sST | 3-c | | 1,368,000 | 1 | chin | A | 1 | God=Borhan. Nonreligious 50%, shamanists 40%, Lamaists 10%. D=RCC,house churches. |
| Chinese neocharismatics | I-3cC-tC | 5-b | 1963 | 42,930,000 | 3 | chin | B | 5 | 500 Regional Councils, 5,000 Pastoral Districts. M=Taiwanese/Diaspora short-termers; CCRC. |
| Chinese neocharismatics | I-3nC-tC | 5-c | 1921 | 2,337,000 | 57 | chin | B | 5 | Chu Hui So. Little Flock. F=Watchman Nee. 1949: 636 churches, 70,000 members. Jiangxi. |
| Chinese Oneness pentecostals | I-3oC-tC | 5-c | 1917 | 1,287,000 | 12 | chin | B | 5 | Chen Ye-su Chiao Hui. 1949: 1,000 churches. Now with global diaspora. (HQ Taipei, Taiwan). |
| Chinese pentecostals | I-3pC-tC | 5-d | 1905 | 130,000 | 3 | indo | B | 5 | E.g. G Kristus. Chinese pentecostal church in West Java. HQ Jakarta. 12n,W=70%. |
| Chinese radio/TV believers | I-3rC-tC | 5-c | 1933 | 3,020,000 | 2 | chin | B | 5 | Isolated radio believers, mostly students and youths. R=FEBC,Radio Vatican,et alia. |
| Chinese Regional Bishops Conf | rC | 7-b | 1991 | 17,200,000 | 10 | taiw | B | 5 | CRBC. HQ Taipei. |
| Chinese secret societies | sUN | 2-c | c1700 | 1,000,000 | 30 | chin | B | 3 | Mimi Shehui. Unlawful religious associations, pursuing healing and salvation. |
| Chinese Taoist Association | nD | 7-d | | 350,000 | 1 | chin | B | 0 | CTA. Government-controlled. 200 monasteries and temples. |
| Chintaku Reifu Shinkyo | sTS | 2-e | | 10,000 | 1 | japa | B | 1 | Ex Shinrikyo. HQ Daito-shi, Osaka-fu. |
| Chinzei | sPJMB | 2-e | | 7,000 | 2 | japa | B | 3 | A school of Jodo (Pure Land) Buddhism. |
| Chishtiyah | sUM | 2-c | c1210 | 1,000,000 | 1 | afgh | A | 1 | Most widespread and popular Sufi order in South Asia. |
| Chisumphi cultists | sVN | 2-d | c1850 | 200,000 | 2 | mala | C | 2 | Mediumistic ancestor cult among the Northern Chewa. Formerly highly developed. |
| Chittagong Buddhist Association | wB | 7-e | 1887 | 30,000 | 1 | myan | B | 3 | Buddhist welfare organization representing Buddhists in Burma. |
| Chizan-ha | sSJMB | 2-c | | 1,101,000 | 5 | japa | B | 2 | One of the 2 main branches of Shingon Buddhism. |
| Chodhari Bhil ethnoreligionists | sAT | 3-d | | 237,000 | 1 | indi | A | 1 | Gujarat State, Maharashtra, Karnataka, Rajasthan. Animists 95%. M=3. |
| Chogye Chong | sKMB | 2-c | 372 | 7,001,000 | 18 | souk | B | 1 | Daihan-Bulgyo-Chongyejong strict Korean Son (Zen) Buddhism (Chongye), unified 1935. |
| Chokwe ethnoreligionists | sAT | 3-d | | 214,000 | 3 | ango | C | 5 | God=Zambi. Traditional religionists(animists) 70%. Y=1884. D=6. M=4. |
| Chongwhajong | sKMB | 2-d | 1969 | 712,000 | 1 | souk | B | 0 | Daihan-Bulgyo-Chongwhajong (Korean Buddhist Sect of Chongwha; Mahayana). |
| Chontaijong | sKMB | 2-c | 594 | 1,182,000 | 1 | souk | B | 2 | Daihan-Bulgyo-Chontaijong (Korean Buddhist Sect of Chontai; Mahayana). |
| Chopi ethnoreligionists | sAT | 3-d | | 352,000 | 1 | moza | B | 3 | God=Nkulukumba. Southern coast. 57 dialects. Literates 10%. Animists 65%. D=7. M=8. |
| Choseikyo | sTS | 2-e | | 4,500 | 1 | japa | B | 0 | HQ Kochi-ken. Ex Shinrikyo. |
| Christ Apostolic Church | I-3aA-AC | 6-c | 1917 | 1,480,000 | 1 | nige | B | 5 | CAC(1942). 1920 Faith Tabernacle. 39 Districts. 74% Yoruba. 281n,1224m,284,2s,12630Y. |
| Christadelphians | m-Ade-tC | 5-e | 1800 | 66,300 | 20 | brit | C | 3 | E.g. Birmingham Central Basis of Fellowship. 342 ecclesias in 1970. Pacifist. Declining. |
| Christian & Missionary Alliance | cma-oC | 9-e | 1887 | 1,100 | 52 | usa | C | 5 | C&MA. |
| Christian Association of Nigeria | F-nC | 7-b | 1976 | 36,000,000 | 1 | nige | B | 5 | CAN, with as members CCN plus RCC and indigenous churches. |
| Christian Brethren | cb-oC | 9-e | 1828 | 1,400 | 86 | brit | C | 5 | M=Christian Missions in Many Lands (CMML). HQ Britain. |
| Christian Brethren | P-CBr-tC | 5-c | 1827 | 3,051,000 | 113 | russ | B | 5 | Open Brethren with links to Britain and Europe. |

*Continued overleaf*

*Table 17–5 continued*

| Name of religion/religionists 1 | Pedigree 2 | Type 3 | Begun 4 | Adherents 5 | Ext 6 | Coun 7 | W 8 | X 9 | E. g. = examples; name for God, other religions present, D=denominations, M=missions. 10 |
|---|---|---|---|---|---|---|---|---|---|
| Christian Brothers of Schools | fsc-oC | 9-e | 1802 | 2,000 | | ital | C | 5 | FSC. |
| Christian Chs & Chs of Christ | I-Dis-AC | 6-c | 1935 | 1,156,000 | 1 | usa | C | 5 | Church of Christ (Instrumental). Schism ex Disciples. 7312n,40s,6012t(1243445). |
| Christian Chs/Chs of Christ | cc-oC | 9-e | 1930 | 1,200 | | usa | C | 5 | CCCC. |
| Christian Conference of Asia | E-cC | 7-b | 1957 | 150,000,000 | 50 | chin | B | 5 | CCA. HQ Hong Kong. Formerly East Asia Christian Conference. 100 member denominations. |
| Christian Congregation of Brazil | C-fC | 4-c | 1910 | 3,120,000 | 35 | braz | C | 5 | CCB. Congregacao Crista do Brasil. Italian origins. 15,294 churches. |
| Christian Council of Ghana | W-nC | 7-c | 1929 | 3,100,000 | 1 | ghan | B | 5 | CCG. Christian Council of the Gold Coast until 1957. 14 denominations. |
| Christian Council of Lesotho | K-nC | 7-d | | 360,000 | 1 | leso | C | 5 | CCL. Lekhotla la Likereke la Lesotho. |
| Christian Council of Malawi | N-nC | 7-c | 1939 | 1,726,000 | 1 | mala | C | 5 | CCM. Member denominations 15. |
| Christian Council of Nigeria | K-nC | 7-b | 1930 | 23,000,000 | 1 | nige | B | 5 | CCN. 9 member denominations. |
| Christian Council of St Kitts | C-nC | 7-e | | 31,100 | 1 | saik | C | 5 | CCSK. |
| Christian Council of St Vincent | K-nC | 7-e | 1969 | 42,200 | 1 | saiv | C | 5 | CCSV. |
| Christian Council of Tanzania | K-nC | 7-c | 1936 | 6,250,000 | 1 | tanz | B | 5 | CCT. Jumuiya ya Makanisa ya Tanzania. |
| Christian Council of Togo | C-nC | 7-d | 1980 | 320,000 | 1 | togo | B | 5 | CCT. |
| Christian Council of Trinidad and T | N-nC | 7-d | 1966 | 630,000 | 1 | trin | C | 5 | CCTT. T=Tobago. 12 denominations including RCC. |
| Christian Council of Zambia | nC | 7-c | 1945 | 1,918,000 | 1 | zamb | C | 5 | CCZ. 13 member denominations. 1974, withdrawal of SDAs and Wesleyans. |
| Christian Holiness Association | h-fC | 4-c | 1867 | 5,000,000 | 150 | usa | C | 5 | CHA. 22 denominations holding Wesleyan-Arminian theology. |
| Christian Interconfessional ConsCom | K-nC | 7-b | | 60,000,000 | 1 | russ | B | 5 | CICC. (for CIS & Baltic countries). ConsCom=Consultative Committee. |
| Christians | C | 1-a | AD 30 | 1,999,564,000 | 238 | usa | C | 5 | Followers of Jesus Christ, Son of God, Savior, in 238 countries. D=34,000. |
| Christopagans | CRPC | 2-b | | 22,000,000 | 25 | mexi | C | 5 | Latin American Roman Catholics who also practice pre-Columbian animism. |
| Chs of Christ (Non-Instrumental) | I-Dis-AC | 6-c | 1870 | 1,217,000 | 1 | usa | C | 5 | Conservative anti-organ split ex Disciples. 10% Black. 10000n,22s,130000Y. |
| Chungchia ethnoreligionists | sPT | 3-d | | 250,000 | 1 | chin | A | 0 | Guizhou, Guangxi Provinces. Dialect of Northern Zhuang. In Puyi nationality. Polytheists 99%. |
| Church Army | A-oC | 10-f | 1881 | 480 | 13 | brit | C | 5 | Lay and ordained evangelists in Anglican churches. Foreign missions in 13 countries. |
| Church in Wales | A-Hig-AC | 6-c | 300 | 1,360,000 | 1 | brit | C | 5 | Eglwys yng Nghymru. State church until 1920. 6 Dioceses. 2s(50),1000Y. (1995) 671n. |
| Church of Christ (Manalista) | I-3nF-AC | 6-c | 1913 | 1,800,000 | 1 | phil | C | 4 | INC. Iglesia ni Cristo (Manalista). 35 cathedrals, 2 radio stations. Not charismatic. 1902n. |
| Church of Christ (Manalista) | M-fC | 4-c | 1913 | 1,750,000 | 7 | phil | C | 3 | Iglesia ni Cristo (Manalista) F=F. Manalo. 35 cathedrals, 8,400 chs, 3 radio stations. Unitarian. |
| Church of Christ, Scientist | v-fC | 4-c | 1879 | 2,500,000 | 63 | usa | C | 3 | Christian Science. In 63 countries, declining steadily. |
| Church of England | A-plu-AC | 6-b | 100 | 23,860,000 | 1 | brit | C | 5 | Reformed 1558. 1960, Charismatic Renewal, now 12%. 100x,308m,2358w,23s (950). |
| Church of Essential Science | sMN | 2-e | 1964 | 5,000 | 1 | usa | C | 3 | Metaphysical body: Spiritual Frontiers Fellowship. |
| Church of God in Christ | I-3pB-AC | 6-c | 1895 | 6,280,000 | 1 | usa | C | 5 | Black. Largest pentecostal church in USA. HQ Memphis (TN). (1970) 5000n. (1990) 33593n. |
| Church of God in Christ | c-fC | 4-b | 1895 | 10,000,000 | 40 | usa | C | 5 | CoGiC. HQ Memphis, TN. Original black pentecostals. |
| Church of Greece | O-Gre-AC | 6-c | 50 | 9,374,000 | 1 | gree | C | 5 | Ekklesia tes Hellados. 95 bps,7530n,7184b,144d(891m),163e(1709w). |
| Church of North India | P-Uni-AC | 6-c | 1612 | 1,444,000 | 1 | indi | B | 5 | CNI. 1970 union. 24 Dioceses. 60% Harijan (Chamar, Sweepers). 4s,1u. |
| Church of Norway | P-Lut-AC | 6-c | 900 | 3,932,000 | 1 | norw | C | 5 | Norske Kirke, reformed 1536. Now 11 Dioceses. 1280n,65012Yy. |
| Church of Pakistan | P-Uni-AC | 6-c | 1850 | 1,342,000 | 1 | paki | A | 5 | 1970 union:CIPBC, UCNIP(part), MCSA(UMC), Pakistan Lutheran Ch. 8 Dioceses. 600n,128f. |
| Church of Perfect Liberty | sNN | 2-c | 1946 | 1,473,000 | 1 | japa | B | 3 | PLK. PL Kyodan. Formerly Tokumitsukyo. Humans are divine. Life=art, sports, clubs. |
| Church of Scientology | sNN | 2-e | 1954 | 25,000 | 85 | usa | C | 5 | Dianetics, a quasi-religio-therapeutic system. Expensive trainings. |
| Church of South India | P-Uni-AC | 6-c | 1640 | 3,228,000 | 1 | indi | B | 5 | CSI. 70% former Harijans. 21 Dioceses. M=CWMCMS. 56x,1s,3u(142). |
| Church of Sweden | P-Lut-AC | 6-c | 829 | 7,568,000 | 1 | swed | C | 5 | Svenska Kyrkan. Begun 600 years before Reformation. 13 Dioceses. Women clergy. 3350n. |
| Church of the Brethren | i-fC | 4-d | 1719 | 208,000 | 12 | usa | C | 5 | A minuscule grouping regarding self as a Christian World Communion. HQ Elgin, Illinois. |
| Church of the Lord (Aladura) | I-3pA-AC | 6-c | 1930 | 1,674,000 | 1 | nige | B | 5 | Aladura=Praying (Yoruba). Revival ex CMS. In 17 West African nations, also UK, USA, &c). |
| Church of Uganda | A-Eva-AC | 6-c | 1875 | 8,624,000 | 1 | ugan | C | 5 | 27 Dioceses. Balokole Revival. Schisms to new AICs. M=CMS,RCMS,AIM(UK). 142f,8H. |
| Church Universal and Triumphant | sFN | 2-e | 1958 | 18,000 | 20 | usa | C | 4 | 1958, origins in Insight, MSIA, Summit Lighthouse. Under Ascended Masters. F=M.L. Prophet. |
| Churches of Christ | cs-oC | 9-e | 1930 | 1,000 | | usa | C | 5 | No central missions HQ. Non-instrumental Restoration Movement. |
| Churches Together in England | W-nC | 7-b | 1937 | 32,000,000 | 1 | brit | C | 5 | CTE. Preceded by: CCIFSR (1937), BCC (1942). Associated local councils of churches: 750. |
| Churches Together in Man | C-nC | 7-e | c1980 | 48,000 | 1 | isle | C | 5 | CTM. More recent and inclusive body than IOMCC. |
| Chushinkai | sNN | 2-e | | 25,800 | 1 | japa | B | 2 | HQ Ota-ku, Tokyo. |
| Chwabo ethnoreligionists | sAT | 3-d | | 757,000 | 1 | moza | B | 3 | Around Quelimane. Animists 76%, Muslims 7%. D=RCC,SDA. M=UBS. |
| Cistercians | ocist-oC | 9-e | 1098 | 1,300 | | fran | C | 5 | OCist. Founded with Citeaux abbey. 1115, F=Bernard of Clairvaux. |
| Classical Pentecostals | CP1ZAC | 2-b | 1906 | 63,065,000 | 220 | usa | C | 5 | Self-designation of older White denominations, usually excluding Black Pentecostals. D=660. |
| Clergy Society of Hadith People | sWSM | 2-e | c1880 | 40,000 | 1 | paki | A | 0 | Jamiat ul-Ulama-i Ahl-i Hadith. Avoids politics. Pakistani Sunnis, strict so called Wahhabis. |
| Co of Anglican Provinces of Africa | V-rC | 7-b | 1975 | 38,192,000 | 30 | keny | C | 5 | CAPA. Loose committee offering liaison between Anglicans in West, East, and Southern Africa. |
| Co of Ev Chs in Equatorial Guinea | C-nC | 7-e | | 11,200 | 1 | equa | C | 5 | CIEGE. Co=Council. |
| Co of Free Chr and Chs in Finland | C-nC | 7-e | | 5,000 | 1 | finl | C | 5 | CFCCF. Co=Council. Suomen Vapaitten Kristittyjen ja Kirkkokuntien Neuvosto. |
| Co of Muslim Communities of Canada | nM | 7-d | 1972 | 317,000 | 1 | cana | C | 5 | CMCC. Co=Council. Representing all Muslims (70% Sunnis) including Ismailis and Druzes. |
| Coalition of Spirit-filled Churches | f-fC | 4-d | 1997 | 500,000 | 3 | usa | C | 5 | CSC. Agency credentialing USA military and other chaplains. Split ex CFGC. |
| Coastal Makhuwa ethnoreligionists | sAT | 3-d | | 271,000 | 1 | moza | B | 3 | Coast from Moma to Mozambique Island. Animists 60%, Muslims 20%. D=CPSA,RCC. |
| Cochin Jews | zJ | 2-e | 80 | 2,000 | 2 | indi | B | 2 | In Cochin city, Kerala (Malayalam-speaking). |
| Colanaikans | sLAT | 10-f | | 500 | 1 | indi | B | 2 | Only remaining cave-dwelling tribe in India. In Kerala. |
| Colored indig charismatics | NN3ZAC | 2-d | 1931 | 235,000 | 4 | nami | C | 5 | Colored, Métis, mixed-race charismatics: Members in Christ Ch, Christen Gemeente. D=70. |
| Com Miss de l'Egl Prot Unie de Belg | N-nC | 7-e | | 2,000 | 1 | belg | C | 5 | Missionary Commission of the United Protestant Church of Belgium. |
| Combonians | mcci-oC | 9-e | 1867 | 2,300 | | ital | C | 5 | MCCI. |
| Comision Coordinadora Ev de Para | C-nC | 7-e | c1970 | 80,000 | 1 | para | C | 5 | CCEP. Evangelical Co-ordinating Commission of Paraguay. 5 member denominations. |
| Comite Espanol de Coop Entre Igls | K-nC | 7-e | | 67,000 | 1 | spai | C | 5 | CECI. Spanish Committee of Cooperation between the Churches. |
| Comite Ev Pro-Ayuda al Desarrollo | C-nC | 7-d | 1972 | 420,000 | 1 | nica | C | 5 | CEPAD. Evangelical Committee for Development Aid. 30 Evangelical denominations. |
| Comite Interepiscopal Orth de France | O-nC | 7-d | | 300,000 | 1 | fran | C | 5 | Orthodox Interepiscopal Liaison Committee of France. |
| Comite Interreligieux Mauricien | h-nC | 7-c | c1970 | 1,100,000 | 1 | maus | B | 5 | Mauritius Inter-Religious Committee (World Fraternal Solidarity). 17 chs, Hindus, Muslims. |
| Comm of Christian Chs in Suriname | C-nC | 7-d | c1960 | 149,000 | 1 | suri | B | 5 | CCCS. Comite Christelijke Kerken. Moravians, Catholics, Lutherans, Reformed. |
| Commis of Covenanted Chs in Wales | nC | 7-d | 1930 | 600,000 | 1 | brit | C | 5 | 1955 Council of Churches for Wales (Cyngor Eglwysi Cymru). |
| Communio e Liberazione | LRAC | 2-d | 1967 | 120,000 | 30 | ital | C | 5 | Communion & Liberation. Secular lay RC order, loyal to pope. |
| Communion of Chs in Indonesia | W-nC | 7-b | 1950 | 10,000,000 | 1 | indo | B | 5 | DGI/PGI/CCI. Dewan Gereja-Gereja di Indonesia. Major council, with 60 denominations. |
| community churches | I-com-tC | 10-f | | 220 | 1 | nets | C | 5 | Small independent congregation on Aruba, mainly European and other expatriates. |
| Compassion Society | sSN | 2-e | 1949 | 15,000 | 1 | taiw | B | 3 | Tzu Hui Tang. Mediumistic. Many texts. Spirit writing. 600 groups. |
| Comunidades de Base | sRAC | 2-c | c1960 | 4,000,000 | 100 | braz | C | 5 | Basic Christian Communities. 200,000 groups in Catholic parishes across Latin America. |
| Concile des Eglises Ev d'Haiti | E-nC | 7-c | | 1,100,000 | 1 | hait | C | 5 | CEEH. Council of Evangelical Churches of Haili. |
| Concilio Evangelico de Puerto Rico | N-nC | 7-d | 1954 | 500,000 | 1 | puer | C | 5 | CEPR. Evangelical Council of Puerto Rico. |
| Concilio Nacional Ev del Peru | E-nC | 7-d | 1940 | 560,000 | 1 | peru | C | 5 | CNEP. National Evangelical Council of Peru. 53 member denominations (plus 22 associated). |
| Conf de Obispos Catolicos de Cuba | R-nC | 7-c | 1993 | 4,367,000 | 1 | cuba | B | 5 | COCC. Bishops' Conference of Cuba. HQ La Habana. |
| Conf del Episcopado Dominicano | R-nC | 7-c | 1985 | 7,522,000 | 1 | domr | C | 5 | CED. Conference of the Dominican Episcopate. HQ Santo Domingo. |
| Conf del Episcopado Mexicano | R-nC | 7-b | 1979 | 92,770,000 | 1 | mexi | C | 5 | CEM. Conference of the Mexican Episcopate. HQ Cuautitlan Izcalli. |
| Conf des Eveques Cath du Burundi | R-nC | 7-c | 1980 | 3,827,000 | 1 | buru | C | 5 | CECAB. Catholic Bishops' Conference of Burundi. HQ Bujumbura. |
| Conf des Eveques Cath du Canada | R-nC | 7-b | 1986 | 12,400,000 | 1 | cana | C | 5 | CECC. Canadian Conference of Catholic Bishops. HQ Ottawa. |
| Conf des Eveques de Burkina Faso | P-nC | 7-c | 1978 | 1,129,000 | 1 | burk | B | 5 | CEBFN. Bishops' Conference of Burkina Faso & Niger. HQ Ouagadougou. |
| Conf des Eveques du Pacifique | Y-cC | 7-c | 1974 | 2,123,000 | 23 | fiji | B | 5 | CEPAC. Episcopal Conference of the Pacific. Conferentia Episcopalis Pacifici. HQ Suva (Fiji). |
| Conf des Eveques du Senegal, M, CV | T-rC | 7-c | 1973 | 1,007,000 | 4 | cape | C | 5 | Bishops' Conference of S, M (Mauritanie), CV (Cape Verde), GB (Guinea Bissau). |
| Conf des Eveques Latins dans les RA | L-rC | 7-c | 1986 | 1,235,000 | 12 | isra | B | 5 | CELRA. RA=Regions Arabes. HQ Jerusalem. |
| Conf Epis Portuguesa da Metropole | R-nC | 7-c | 1985 | 8,970,000 | 1 | port | C | 5 | CEPM. Portuguese Metropolitan Episcopal Conference. HQ Lisbon. |
| Conf Epis Reg du Nord de l'Afrique | H-rC | 7-d | 1985 | 319,000 | 8 | alge | A | 5 | CERNA. HQ Algiers. |
| Conf Epis Regionale de l'AOF | F-rC | 7-c | | 6,593,000 | 9 | ivor | B | 5 | CERAO. AOF=Afrique Occidentale Francophone/French-speaking West Africa. |
| Conf Episcopal de Guinea Ecuatorial | R-nC | 7-d | 1984 | 391,000 | 1 | equa | C | 5 | CEGE. Episcopal Conference of Equatorial Guinea. HQ Malabo. |
| Conf Episcopal de Mocambique | E-nC | 7-c | 1982 | 3,110,000 | 1 | moza | B | 5 | CEM. Episcopal Conference of Mozambique. HQ Maputo. |
| Conf Episcopal Puertorriquena | R-nC | 7-c | 1986 | 2,900,000 | 1 | puer | C | 5 | CEP. Puerto Rico Episcopal Conference. HQ San Juan. |
| Conf Episcopale de la Cote d'Ivoire | R-nC | 7-c | 1973 | 2,182,000 | 1 | ivor | B | 5 | CECI. Episcopal Conference of the Ivory Coast. HQ Abidjan. |
| Conf Episcopale de l'Ocean Indien | rC | 7-d | 1990 | 991,000 | 6 | maus | B | 5 | CEDOI. HQ Port-Louis (Mauritius). |
| Conf Episcopale de Madagascar | S-nC | 7-c | 1969 | 3,662,000 | 1 | mada | B | 5 | CEM. Episcopal Conference of Madagascar. HQ Antananarivo. |
| Conf Episcopale du Congo-Zaire | R-nC | 7-b | 1981 | 26,300,000 | 1 | conz | C | 5 | CEZ. Episcopal Conference of Congo-Zaire. HQ Kinshasa-Gombe. |
| Conf Episcopale Nat du Cameroun | R-nC | 7-c | 1989 | 3,989,000 | 1 | came | B | 5 | CENC. Episcopal Conference of Cameroon. |
| Conf of Catholic Bps of India/Latin R | R-nC | 7-b | 1994 | 10,740,000 | 1 | indi | B | 5 | CCBI-LR. HQ. New Delhi. Latin Rite Bishops Conference. |
| Conf of Chs in Aotearoa/New Zealand | W-nC | 7-c | 1941 | 1,557,000 | 1 | newz | C | 5 | CCANZ. 1941 National Council of Churches of New Zealand (NCCONZ). 10 denominations. |
| Confe Nacional dos Bispos do Brasil | R-nC | 7-b | 1986 | 153,000,000 | 1 | braz | C | 5 | CNBB. HQ Brasilia. |
| Confed das Ig Ev Fundamentalistas | T-nC | 7-e | | 25,000 | 1 | braz | C | 3 | CIEF. Evangelical Federation of Fundamental Churches of Brazil. |
| Confederacao Evangelico Brasileira | C-nC | 7-e | | 35,000 | 1 | braz | C | 5 | CEB. Evangelical Federation of Brazil. |
| Confederacao Pentecostal do Brasil | I-nC | 7-b | 1959 | 25,200,000 | 1 | braz | C | 5 | CPB. Brazil Pentecostal Federation. Over 20 member denominations. |
| Confederacion Ev de Colombia | E-nC | 7-d | 1950 | 400,000 | 1 | colo | C | 5 | CEC. Evangelical Confederation of Colombia. Members: 20 major denominations. |
| Conference des Eveques de France | R-nC | 7-b | 1975 | 48,600,000 | 1 | fran | C | 5 | CEF. Episcopal Conference of France. HQ Paris. |
| Conference des Eveques Suisses | S-nC | 7-c | 1975 | 3,260,000 | 1 | swit | C | 5 | CES. Schweizerische Bischofskonferenz/Conferenza di Vescovi Svizzeri. HQ Fribourg. |
| Conference Episcopale Centrafricaine | R-nC | 7-d | 1982 | 664,000 | 1 | cent | B | 5 | CECA. Bishops Conference of the CAR. HQ Bangui. |

*Continued opposite*

*Table 17–5 continued*

| Name of religion/religionists 1 | Pedigree 2 | Type 3 | Begun 4 | Adherents 5 | Ext 6 | Coun 7 | W 8 | X 9 | E. g. = examples; name for God, other religions present, D=denominations, M=missions. 10 |
|---|---|---|---|---|---|---|---|---|---|
| Conference Episcopale de Belgique | R-nC | 7-c | 1984 | 8,222,000 | 1 | belg | C | 5 | Episcopal Conference of Belgium. HQ Brussels. |
| Conference Episcopale de Haiti | R-nC | 7-c | 1987 | 6,520,000 | 1 | hait | C | 5 | CEH. Episcopal Conference of Haiti. HQ Port-au-Prince. |
| Conference Episcopale de la Guinee | R-nC | 7-d | c1990 | 117,000 | 1 | guin | A | 5 | CEG. HQ Conakry. |
| Conference Episcopale du Benin | R-nC | 7-c | | 1,266,000 | 1 | beni | B | 5 | CEB. HQ Cotonou. |
| Conference Episcopale du Congo | V-nC | 7-c | 1992 | 1,451,000 | 1 | cong | C | 5 | CEC. Episcopal Conference of the Congo. HQ Brazzaville. |
| Conference Episcopale du Gabon | R-nC | 7-d | 1989 | 745,000 | 1 | gabo | C | 5 | CEG. Episcopal Conference of Gabon. HQ Oyem. |
| Conference Episcopale du Laos et C | P-nC | 7-e | 1971 | 54,000 | 1 | camb | A | 5 | CELAC. HQ Thakhek, Laos. Bishops' Conference of Laos & Cambodia. |
| Conference Episcopale du Mali | R-nC | 7-d | 1973 | 126,000 | 1 | mali | A | 5 | CEM. Episcopal Conference of Mali. HQ Bamako. |
| Conference Episcopale du Rwanda | P-nC | 7-c | 1980 | 3,942,000 | 1 | rwan | C | 5 | CER. Bishops' Conference of Rwanda. |
| Conference Episcopale du Tchad | R-nC | 7-d | 1991 | 502,000 | 1 | chad | B | 5 | CET. Chad Episcopal Conference. HQ N'Djamena. |
| Conference Episcopale du Togo | R-nC | 7-c | 1979 | 1,122,000 | 1 | togo | B | 5 | CET. Episcopal Conference of Togo. HQ Lome. |
| Conference Episcopale du Viet Nam | nC | 7-c | 1980 | 5,320,000 | 1 | viet | B | 5 | CEVN. Bishops Conference of Viet Nam. HQ Toa Giam Muc, Xuan Loc. |
| Conference of European Churches | C-cC | 7-a | 1957 | 505,000,000 | 45 | swit | C | 5 | CEC/CEE/KEK. 120 member denominations. HQ Geneva. |
| Conference of the Chs of Indonesia | R-nC | 7-c | 1973 | 5,752,000 | 1 | indo | B | 5 | KWI. Konperensi Waligereja Indonesia. HQ Jakarta. Formerly Bishops' Conf of Indonesia. |
| Conferencia Epis de Angola e ST | P-rC | 7-c | 1981 | 8,100,000 | 2 | ango | C | 5 | CEAST. Episcopal Conference of Angola & Sao Tome. HQ Luanda. |
| Conferencia Episcopal Argentina | R-nC | 7-b | 1987 | 31,750,000 | 1 | arge | C | 5 | Argentina Episcopal Conference (CEA). HQ Buenos Aires. |
| Conferencia Episcopal Boliviana | R-nC | 7-c | 1989 | 7,350,000 | 1 | boli | C | 5 | CEB. Episcopal Conference of Bolivia. HQ La Paz. |
| Conferencia Episcopal de Chile | R-nC | 7-b | 1994 | 11,900,000 | 1 | chil | C | 5 | CECH. Episcopal Conference of Chile. HQ Santiago. |
| Conferencia Episcopal de Colombia | R-nC | 7-b | 1990 | 40,670,000 | 1 | colo | C | 5 | CEC. Episcopal Conference of Colombia. HQ Bogota. |
| Conferencia Episcopal de Costa Rica | R-nC | 7-c | 1977 | 3,660,000 | 1 | cost | C | 5 | CECOR. Episcopal Conference of Costa Rica. HQ San Jose. |
| Conferencia Episcopal de El Salvador | R-nC | 7-c | 1982 | 5,723,000 | 1 | elsa | C | 5 | CEDES. Episcopal Conference of El Salvador. HQ San Salvador. |
| Conferencia Episcopal de Guatemala | R-nC | 7-c | 1973 | 9,600,000 | 1 | guat | C | 5 | CEG. Episcopal Conference of Guatemala. HQ Guatemala City. |
| Conferencia Episcopal de Honduras | R-nC | 7-c | 1987 | 5,590,000 | 1 | hond | C | 5 | CEH. HQ Tegucigalpa. |
| Conferencia Episcopal de Nicaragua | R-nC | 7-c | 1987 | 4,320,000 | 1 | nica | C | 5 | CEN. Episcopal Conference of Nicaragua. HQ Managua. |
| Conferencia Episcopal de Panama | R-nC | 7-c | 1986 | 2,210,000 | 1 | pana | C | 5 | CEP. Episcopal Conference of Panama. HQ Panama City. |
| Conferencia Episcopal Ecuatoriana | R-nC | 7-b | 1985 | 11,900,000 | 1 | ecua | C | 5 | Ecuador Episcopal Conference. HQ Quito. |
| Conferencia Episcopal Espanola | R-nC | 7-b | 1991 | 38,080,000 | 1 | spai | C | 5 | CEE. Spanish Episcopal Conference. HQ Madrid. |
| Conferencia Episcopal Paraguaya | R-nC | 7-c | 1984 | 4,950,000 | 1 | para | C | 5 | CEP. Paraguay Episcopal Conference. HQ Asuncion. |
| Conferencia Episcopal Peruana | R-nC | 7-b | 1992 | 24,550,000 | 1 | peru | C | 5 | CEP. Peru Episcopal Conference. HQ Lima. |
| Conferencia Episcopal Uruguaya | R-nC | 7-c | 1990 | 2,608,000 | 1 | uuay | C | 5 | CEU. Uruguay Episcopal Conference. HQ Montevideo. |
| Conferencia Episcopal Venezolana | R-nC | 7-b | 1985 | 22,816,000 | 1 | vene | C | 5 | CEV. Venezuela Episcopal Conference. HQ Caracas. |
| Conferentia Episcopalis Lettoniae | R-nC | 7-d | | 490,000 | 1 | latv | C | 5 | CEL. Latvian Episcopal Conference. HQ Riga. |
| Conferentia Episcopalis Lituaniae | R-nC | 7-c | 1992 | 3,105,000 | 1 | lith | C | 5 | CEL. Episcopal Conference of Lithuania. HQ Vilnius. |
| Conferentia Episcopalis Scandiae | rC | 7-d | 1985 | 262,000 | 4 | norw | C | 5 | CES. Scandinavian Bishops' Conference. HQ Oslo (Norway). |
| Conferentia Episcopolis Graeciae | R-nC | 7-e | 1967 | 62,000 | 1 | gree | C | 5 | CEG. Episcopal Conference of Greece. HQ Athens. |
| Conferenza Episcopale dell'Albania | R-nC | 7-d | | 492,000 | 1 | alba | B | 5 | Episcopal Conference of Albania. HQ Shkodre. |
| Conferenza Episcopale Italiana | R-nC | 7-b | 1985 | 55,680,000 | 1 | ital | C | 5 | CEI. Italian Episcopal Conference. HQ Roma. |
| Conferenza Episcopale Ucraina | nC | 7-c | 1992 | 5,578,000 | 1 | ukra | C | 5 | CEU. Ukraine Bishops' Conference. HQ Lviv. |
| Confraternidad Cristiana de Iglesias | K-nC | 7-e | c1970 | 10,000 | 1 | chil | C | 5 | CCI. Christian Fellowship of Churches in Chile (CFCC). |
| Confraternidad Ev de Chile | E-nC | 7-e | 1916 | 25,000 | 1 | chil | C | 5 | CEC. Evangelical Fellowship of Chile. 10 member denominations. |
| Confraternidad Ev de Honduras | E-nC | 7-d | 1945 | 240,000 | 1 | hond | C | 5 | CEH. Formerly Alianza Evangelica Hondurena (AEH), renamed 1990. |
| Confraternidad Ev Ecuatoriana | E-nC | 7-d | 1964 | 250,000 | 1 | ecua | C | 5 | CEE. Ecuador Evangelical Fellowship. |
| Confraternidad Ev Mexicana | E-nC | 7-c | 1982 | 1,700,000 | 1 | mexi | C | 5 | CONEMEX. Mostly related to WEF. |
| Confraternidad Ev Panamena | E-nC | 7-e | 1982 | 30,000 | 1 | pana | C | 5 | CEP. Panamanian Evangelical Confraternity. |
| Confraternidad Ev Salvadorena | E-nC | 7-d | | 400,000 | 1 | elsa | C | 5 | CES. CONESAL. Member of CONELA. |
| Confucianists | G | 1-c | BC 500 | 6,299,000 | 15 | chin | B | 2 | Ju-chia. F= Confucius. Highly organized in South Korea, also Japan, Viet Nam. |
| Congo-Zaire Council of ICCC | T-nC | 7-e | c1960 | 15,000 | 1 | conz | C | 3 | CCICCC. |
| Congregação Cristã do Brasil | I-3pY-AC | 6-c | 1910 | 3,544,000 | 1 | braz | C | 5 | Christian Congregation of B. Italian origins. States: 53% in SPaulo, 30% Paraná. |
| Congregationalists | P-Con-tC | 5-c | 1618 | 2,547,000 | 55 | soua | C | 5 | E.g. UCCSA. 1967 union CUSA,CCA,UCMS,LMS. 50% Colored,40% Bantu,10% White.153n. |
| Conseil Canadien des Eglises | W-nC | 7-c | 1944 | 4,000,000 | 1 | cana | C | 5 | CCE. Canadian Council of Churches. |
| Conseil Chretien des Egls a Madaga | N-nC | 7-c | 1958 | 3,400,000 | 1 | mada | B | 5 | CCEM. Christian Council of Churches in Madagascar. |
| Conseil des Eglises du Maroc | K-nC | 7-e | 1977 | 26,000 | 1 | moro | A | 5 | Morocco Council of Christian Churches: Catholics, Orthodox, Protestants, Anglicans. |
| Conseil Interconf Prot du Benin | C-nC | 7-d | | 110,000 | 1 | beni | B | 5 | Protestant Interconfessional Council of Benin. |
| Conseil National des Egls du Burundi | K-nC | 7-c | | 1,100,000 | 1 | buru | C | 5 | CNEB. National Council of Churches of Burundi. |
| Conseil Oecu des Egls du Congo | K-nC | 7-d | 1943 | 400,000 | 1 | cong | C | 5 | Oecu=Oecumenique. |
| Conseil Protestant du Rwanda | K-nC | 7-c | 1935 | 1,075,000 | 1 | rwan | C | 5 | CPR. Protestant Council of Rwanda. |
| Conseil Superieur des Sac EUJ-C | I-nC | 7-c | c1950 | 1,000,000 | 1 | conz | C | 5 | COSSEUJCA. Eglises-Unies de Jesus-Christ. Supreme Council of Priests/Sacrificateurs. |
| Conseil Supreme des Egls Ev au LS | C-nC | 7-e | c1965 | 53,200 | 1 | leba | B | 5 | Supreme Council of Evangelical Churches in Lebanon & Syria. |
| Consejo Anglicano Sud Americano | C-rC | 7-c | c1970 | 1,100,000 | 6 | chil | C | 5 | CASA. Anglican Council for South America. |
| Consejo de Iglesias de Cuba | N-nC | 7-e | 1941 | 80,000 | 1 | cuba | B | 5 | CIC. Council of Churches of Cuba. |
| Consejo Episcopal Latinoamericano | L-cC | 7-a | 1974 | 461,220,000 | 21 | colo | C | 5 | CELAM. Latin American Episcopal Council. HQ Bogota. |
| Consejo Evangelico de Venezuela | E-nC | 7-d | 1958 | 145,000 | 1 | vene | C | 5 | CEV. Venezuela Council of Churches. 22 member denominations (plus 15 indigenous ones). |
| Consejo Nacional Ev de Nicaragua | E-nC | 7-d | 1966 | 100,000 | 1 | nica | C | 5 | CNEN. |
| Conselho Cristao de Mocambique | C-nC | 7-c | | 1,450,000 | 1 | moza | B | 5 | CCM. Christian Council of Mozambique. |
| Conselho de Igr Cristas em Angola | W-nC | 7-c | 1977 | 1,500,000 | 1 | ango | C | 5 | Council of Christian Churches in Angola. |
| Conselho Nac de Ig Cristas do Brasil | W-nC | 7-b | | 35,000,000 | 1 | braz | C | 5 | CONIC. National Council of Christian Churches in Brazil. |
| Conselho Portugues de Igs Cristas | d-nC | 7-d | | 130,000 | 1 | port | C | 5 | COPIC. Portuguese Council of Christian Churches. |
| Conservative Catholics | I-CCa-tC | 5-c | 1549 | 4,901,000 | 30 | braz | C | 5 | E.g. ICAB. Schism ex Rome by bp of Botucatu. 12 Dioceses, 25 bps. c1990 NNCM splits off. |
| Conservative confessional networks | y-fC | 4-c | | 9,000,000 | 100 | usa | C | 5 | 25 networks or quasiconfessions hostile to historic confessions. |
| Conservative Evangelicals | CEAC | 2-b | 1750 | 83,000,000 | 174 | usa | C | 5 | Evangelicals holding conservative doctrines especially on plenary inspiration of Bible. |
| Conservative Judaism | NJ | 2-c | 1845 | 2,000,000 | 10 | germ | C | 3 | Split ex Reform Judaism. Masorati. Begun Germany: USA 1900; opposing neglect of Halakhah. |
| Consiglio della Chiesa Siro-Malankarese | cC | 7-d | c1980 | 310,000 | 3 | indi | B | 5 | Council of the Syro-Malankarese Church in India. 3 dioceses in south, with 885 parishes. |
| Consilio Latino Americano de Iglesias | cC | 7-b | 1982 | 11,000,000 | 30 | ecua | C | 5 | CLAI. Latin American Council of Churches. Founded in Peru. HQ Quito. 110 member churches. |
| Consilium Conferentiarum Epis E | B-cC | 7-a | 1981 | 287,459,000 | 42 | swit | C | 5 | E=Episcopalium, E=Europae. CCEE. Council of European Bishops' Conferences. HQ St Gallen. |
| Consolata | imc-oC | 9-e | 1901 | 1,000 | | ital | C | 5 | IMC. |
| Consul Council of Indonesian Muslims | qM | 8-d | 1943 | 200,000 | 1 | indo | B | 3 | Masjumi. Majlis Sjuro Muslimin Indonesia. Political party for all factions; 1970 phased out. |
| Consult on Uniting and United Chs | U-fC | 4-b | 1947 | 65,000,000 | 54 | swit | C | 5 | CUUC. Ecumenical conferences sponsored by WCC. |
| Convenção Batista Brasileira | P-Bap-AC | 6-c | 1881 | 1,518,000 | 1 | braz | C | 5 | Brazilian Baptist Conv. M=SBC,BMS. Germans, Japanese. 1382n,320f,1H,77h,1j,30p,29690Y. |
| Conventual Franciscans | ofmconv-oC | 9-e | | 4,400 | | ital | C | 5 | OFMConv. |
| Convince | sCU | 2-e | | 4,000 | 1 | jama | B | 5 | Small ancestral Afro-Protestant cult in East Jamaica. |
| Coptic (Alexandrian rite) | R-Cop-tC | 5-d | 1895 | 207,000 | 1 | egyp | C | 5 | Egyptians, Coptic rite. Patriarch lives in Cairo. M=CM. |
| Coptic Orthodox | O-Cop-tC | 5-c | 1150 | 9,845,000 | 24 | egyp | B | 5 | Al-Kanisah al-Kebtiah al-Orthodoxiah. 42 Dioceses worldwide, 77 bps,5e(200),1500n,5s(200). |
| Coptic Orthodox Church | O-Cop-AC | 6-c | 33 | 9,214,000 | 1 | egyp | B | 5 | Al-Kanisah al-Kebtiah al-Orthodoxiah. 42 Dioceses worldwide, 77 bps,5e(200),1500n,5s(200). |
| Coptic Orthodox Patri of Alexandria | N-fC | 4-c | 33 | 9,797,000 | 27 | egyp | B | 5 | Worldwide diaspora now with 42 dioceses, due to 20 centuries of persecution. |
| Council for Co-operation of Chs in E | K-nC | 7-b | 1978 | 27,000,000 | 1 | ethi | B | 5 | CCCE. E=Ethiopia. Begun by 9 of Ethiopia's largest denominations. |
| Council of African & Allied Chs in UK | J-nC | 7-d | 1979 | 100,000 | 1 | brit | C | 5 | CAAC. Some 20 Black denominations. |
| Council of Bapt Chs in NE India | P-Bap-AC | 6-c | 1836 | 1,743,000 | 1 | indi | B | 5 | CBCNEI. M=ABFMS(USA). Doubled 1950-70. 97n,1x,5704m,54w,9f,6H,12p,1s(110),16363Y. |
| Council of Ch of Christ in Thailand | N-nC | 7-e | 1930 | 85,000 | 1 | thai | B | 5 | CCT. Begun 1930 as Siam National Christian Council. |
| Council of Christian Chs in Germany | W-nC | 7-b | 1948 | 34,000,000 | 1 | germ | C | 5 | CCCG. ACKD. Arbeitsgemeinschaft Christlicher Kirchen in Deutschland. United with East 1991. |
| Council of Christian Chs in India | T-nC | 7-d | c1960 | 250,000 | 1 | indi | B | 4 | CCCI. Originally founded as India Bible Christian Council. |
| Council of Christian Chs in Luxembourg | nC | 7-d | 1997 | 396,000 | 1 | luxe | C | 5 | Ecumenical council of churches (Catholic/Protestant/Orthodox) to resolve issues. |
| Council of Christian Chs in Slovenia | W-nC | 7-e | | 20,000 | 1 | slov | C | 5 | CCCS. |
| Council of Chs in the Netherlands | W-nC | 7-c | 1946 | 8,306,000 | 1 | neth | C | 5 | CCN. Raad van Kerken in Nederland. Replaces 1946-68 Ecumenical Council of Chs. |
| Council of Churches in Kuwait | C-nC | 7-d | 1960 | 155,000 | 1 | kuwa | B | 5 | CCK. Includes wide spectrum of older churches. |
| Council of Churches of Malaysia | W-nC | 7-d | 1948 | 470,000 | 1 | malb | B | 5 | CCM. Until 1975 'CCM and Singapore'. 10 regional councils. Mainly Chinese. |
| Council of Ev Churches of Guatemala | F-nC | 7-d | | 200,000 | 1 | guat | C | 5 | CIEDEG. |
| Council of Free Chs in Hungary | C-nC | 7-e | 1938 | 50,000 | 1 | hung | C | 5 | CFCH. Magyarorszagi Szabadegyhazak Tanacsa. |
| Council of Free Churches | C-nC | 7-e | | 15,000 | 1 | denm | C | 5 | CFC. Evangelisk Frikirkerad. |
| Council of Indonesian Muslim Assoc | qnM | 8-c | 1943 | 6,000,000 | 1 | indo | B | 2 | MASYUMI. Sumatra-based. Banned 1960, revived 1968 as PARMUSI. |
| Council of Swaziland Churches | C-nC | 7-d | 1967 | 140,000 | 1 | swaz | C | 5 | CSC. Begun in expectation of replacing rival SCC. Now related to WCC. RCs members. |
| Council of the Ch of South East Asia | A-rC | 7-d | c1970 | 230,000 | 15 | sing | B | 5 | CCEA, CCSEA. Anglicans from China to Malaysia and Indonesia in the 1980s. Defunct. |
| Council of Torah Sages | sOJ | 2-d | c1920 | 200,000 | 2 | isra | B | 2 | Ger Hasidism. |
| Creole neocharismatics | I-3nN-tC | 5-e | | 74,400 | 2 | nami | C | 5 | E.g. Afrikaans Protestant Ch (S Africa). Total over 30 mainly migrant Coloured groups. |
| Creole pentecostals | I-3pN-tC | 5-d | 1931 | 160,000 | 3 | soua | C | 5 | E.g. Christen Gemeente. 80% Coloured. N&W Cape, Natal, also SWA. 178n. |
| Croatian Episcopal Conference | R-nC | 7-c | 1993 | 3,960,000 | 1 | croa | C | 5 | HBK. Hrvatska Biskupska Konferencija. HQ Zagreb. |
| Crypto-Christians | CC | 2-b | | 123,726,000 | 85 | chin | B | 5 | All secret believers in Christ unknown to state, society, or hostile religions. |

*Continued overleaf*

*Table 17–5 continued*

| *Name of religion/religionists* 1 | *Pedigree* 2 | *Type* 3 | *Begun* 4 | *Adherents* 5 | *Ext* 6 | *Coun* 7 | *W* 8 | *X* 9 | *E. g. = examples; name for God, other religions present, D=denominations, M=missions.* 10 |
|---|---|---|---|---|---|---|---|---|---|
| Crypto-Jews | JCC | 2-d | 650 | 300,000 | 40 | spai | C | 3 | Secretly practising Jews but baptized Christians: Conversos, Marranos ('Swine'), since 1491. |
| Cyprus Evangelical Alliance | E-nC | 7-e | c1970 | 1,000 | 1 | cypr | C | 5 | CEA. |
| Czech Bishops' Conference | R-nC | 7-c | 1993 | 4,135,000 | 1 | czec | B | 5 | CBK. Ceska Biskupska Konference. HQ Prague. |
| Czech Evangelical Alliance | E-nC | 7-e | 1991 | 90,000 | 1 | czec | B | 5 | CEA. |
| Czech Orthodox | O-Cze-tC | 5-e | 1863 | 48,000 | 1 | czec | B | 5 | Církev Pravoslavná v Ceskoslovenská. Mainly Slovaks in east. A=1951. 4 bps,137n,1s. |
| Czechoslovak Hussite Church | H-fC | 4-d | 1920 | 185,000 | 6 | czec | B | 5 | CCH/CHC. Split ex RCC. |
| Dadu Panthis | sSN | 2-e | c1580 | 10,000 | 1 | indi | B | 2 | Hindu-Muslim devotional movement. F=Dadu Dayal. HQ Rajasthan. |
| Dafla ethnoreligionists | sAT | 3-d | | 269,000 | 1 | indi | A | 1 | Assam, Darrang, Arunachal Pradesh. Animists 98%. D=2. M=3. |
| Dagaaba ethnoreligionists | sAT | 3-d | | 458,000 | 2 | ghan | B | 4 | Northwest corner. Also in Burkina Faso. Animists 46%, Muslims 3%. D=2. M=7. |
| Dagomba ethnoreligionists | sAT | 3-d | | 234,000 | 2 | ghan | A | 1 | God=Naawuni. Also in Togo. Literates 2%. Muslims 60%(Sunnis,Ahmadis), animists 37%. D=8. |
| Dai Nihon Daidokyo | sNS | 2-d | | 143,000 | 1 | japa | B | 1 | HQ Fukushima-ken. |
| Daidokyo | sTS | 2-e | | 57,600 | 1 | japa | B | 1 | HQ Fukushima-ken. |
| Daiekai Kyodan | sNJMB | 2-e | | 29,900 | 1 | japa | B | 1 | HQ Osaka-fu. |
| Daigenkyo | sNS | 2-e | | 1,400 | 1 | japa | B | 2 | HQ Okayama-ken. |
| Daihizenkyo | sNS | 2-e | | 3,100 | 1 | japa | B | 0 | HQ Shinjuku-ku, Tokyo. |
| Daihongenkyo Kyodan | sNS | 2-d | | 150,000 | 1 | japa | B | 0 | HQ Nagano-ken. |
| Daijokyo | sNJMB | 2-d | | 410,000 | 3 | japa | B | 1 | HQ Nagoya-shi. |
| Daireido | sNS | 2-e | | 16,900 | 1 | japa | B | 1 | HQ Ishikawa-ken. |
| Daishinkai Kyodan | sNS | 2-e | | 4,500 | 1 | japa | B | 2 | HQ Soraku-gun, Kyoto-fu. |
| Daishizen Tenchi Hi no Okamikyo | sNN | 2-e | | 14,100 | 1 | japa | B | 3 | HQ Toyono-gun, Osaka-fu. |
| Daiuchukyo | sNS | 2-e | | 4,100 | 1 | japa | B | 2 | HQ Adachi-ku, Tokyo. |
| Daiwa Kyodan | sNS | 2-e | | 52,700 | 1 | japa | B | 1 | HQ Sendai-shi, Miyagi-ken. |
| Damdani Taksal | sK | 2-e | c1980 | 5,000 | 1 | indi | B | 2 | Militant anti-moderate Sikh religious school. F=Sant Bhindranwale. |
| Dan ethnoreligionists | sAT | 3-d | | 677,000 | 3 | ivor | B | 3 | Half in Liberia. Animists 62%, Muslims 10%(ongoing conversions to Islam). D=2. M=5. |
| Dancing Religion | sNN | 2-d | 1945 | 325,000 | 1 | japa | B | 2 | Tensho Kotai Jingukyo. F=Kitamura Sayo, claims God appointed her World Savior. Apocalyptic. |
| Dandarawiyah | sUM | 2-e | 1880 | 50,000 | 5 | thai | B | 2 | Spread across Egypt, Malaysia, Thailand, Indonesia, out of Idrisiyah. |
| Dang Tharu ethnoreligionists | sAT | 3-d | | 286,000 | 1 | nepa | A | 0 | West of Bhairawa-Butwal, north of India border. Agropastoralists. Animists 80%, Hindus 20%. |
| Dangs Bhil ethnoreligionists | sPAT | 3-d | | 130,000 | 1 | indi | A | 2 | Gujarat State, Dangs District. Lingua franca. Animists/polytheists 90%. D=CNI. M=2. |
| Dar al-Quran | sUM | 2-e | | 20,000 | 2 | jord | B | 2 | Modern branch of Shadhiliya Sufi order. |
| Darqawiya | sUM | 2-e | c1850 | 30,000 | 4 | moro | A | 1 | Popular traditional-style Sufi order. Wandering mendicants. In UK. |
| Darul Arqam | sXM | 2-e | | 5,000 | 1 | indo | B | 3 | Controversal Muslim renewal organization. |
| Darul Islam | fM | 4-e | 1949 | 10,000 | 1 | indo | B | 0 | Abode of Islam. Revolutionary movement to establish an Islamic state; defeated 1965. W.Java. |
| Dasanami Order | sH-oH | 9-e | c800 | 20,000 | 1 | indi | B | 0 | Wandering Monks. 'The 10 Names' (of Hindu Shaivite ascetic castes). F=Shankara. |
| Daudis | sMIHM | 2-d | 1591 | 300,000 | 15 | indi | B | 2 | Daudiyah. Most also termed Bohras in India. Main Mustali sect. |
| Dawa Party | sHM | 2-e | 1957 | 30,000 | 10 | iraq | A | 1 | Hizb al-Dawa al-Islamiya. Strong in Iraq, Iran. Violently attacked by Baath regime. |
| De Jiao | sSN | 2-e | 1939 | 10,000 | 6 | chin | B | 3 | Tak Kaau (in Cantonese). Religion of Virtue. South China, Hong Kong. |
| Deeper Life Bible Church | d-fC | 4-c | 1973 | 9,000,000 | 45 | nige | B | 5 | DLBC. F=W.F. Kumuyi. HQ church, Lagos, has 150,000 members, 5,000 cells. In 45 countries. |
| Degel Hatorah | qUJ | 8-e | 1988 | 50,000 | 2 | isra | B | 2 | Torah Flag. Ultra-Orthodox Haredi organization, split ex Agudat Israel. |
| Dehonians of the Sacred Heart | sci-oC | 9-e | 1878 | 2,500 | | ital | C | 5 | SCI. |
| Denominational Pente (White) | PIZAC | 2-b | 1910 | 65,833,000 | 225 | cana | C | 5 | White members in the older, larger, more traditional Pentecostal denominations. D=740. |
| Deobandis | zSM | 2-d | c1850 | 200,000 | 1 | indi | B | 2 | Attempt to be Muslim with no involvement with political regimes. 10,000 schools. |
| Deokri Tharu ethnoreligionists | sAT | 3-d | | 119,000 | 1 | nepa | A | 0 | On eastern border with India. Agriculturalists, pastoralists. Animists 95%, Hindus 5%. |
| Deutsche Bischofskonferenz | R-nC | 7-b | 1992 | 28,700,000 | 1 | germ | C | 5 | HQ Bonn/Berlin. Member of ACKD/CCCG. |
| Deutsche Evangelische Allianz | E-nC | 7-c | 1857 | 1,323,000 | 1 | germ | C | 5 | DEA. German Evangelical Alliance. |
| Deutscher Caritasverband | vC | 9-d | 1887 | 220,000 | 40 | germ | C | 5 | Caritas. Founded in Freiburg. Roman Catholic medical care system; 36,000 centers. |
| Dev Samaj | zH | 2-e | 1917 | 1,000 | 4 | indi | B | 2 | F=Agnihotri. Ex Brahmo Samaj. Strict morals, vegetarianism, women's education. |
| Devotees of Islam | sHM | 2-e | 1945 | 5,000 | 1 | iran | A | 0 | Fada'iyan-i Islam. A ruthless terrorist group. Underground, now in decline. |
| Devotees of Islam | qM | 8-e | 1946 | 1,000 | 1 | iran | A | 0 | Fedayeen-i-Islam. Organized Shia political activity. |
| Dhahabiya | ssUM | 2-e | c1450 | 7,000 | 1 | iran | A | 1 | Ex Kubrawiya; revived c 1850. HQ Shiraz. Shia Sufis. |
| Dhammadana Association | sTB | 2-e | c1940 | 3,000 | 1 | thai | B | 2 | Modernizing urban grouping attacking superstition. |
| Dhammarakkhitavamsa | sT-oB | 9-e | c1900 | 5,000 | 1 | sril | B | 3 | Prominent monastic grouping within Amarapura Nikaya. |
| Dhammayut Nikaya | sT-oB | 9-c | c1870 | 1,500,000 | 2 | thai | B | 2 | Thammayut. Theravada monastic community with 1,500 monasteries. |
| Dharmadasis | sSN | 2-e | c1600 | 10,000 | 1 | indi | B | 2 | Subsect of Kabir Panthis. HQ Chattisgarh. Merchants. A Hindu/Muslim/Sikh amalgam. |
| Dhodia ethnoreligionists | sPAT | 3-d | | 128,000 | 1 | indi | A | 1 | Maharashtra, Gujarat, MP, Karnataka, Rajasthan. Bhils. Animists/polytheists 95%. M=ZBM. |
| Dhul-Riyasatayn | ssUM | 2-e | | 10,000 | 1 | iran | A | 0 | Branch of Iranian Nimatullahi Sufi order. |
| Digambara Jains | DV | 2-c | BC 200 | 2,000,000 | 10 | indi | B | 2 | Sky-clad' Jainas (65 monks who go naked). In Maharashtra, Karnataka, and all major cities. |
| Discalced Carmelites | ocd-oC | 9-e | 1562 | 12,500 | | ital | C | 5 | OCD. |
| Disciples | P-Dis-tC | 5-c | 1809 | 1,812,000 | 18 | usa | C | 5 | Liberal wing, Restoration Movement. Schisms, 6886n,4s(348),W=39%,24481Y. |
| Disciples Ecumenical Com for Cons | D-fC | 4-c | | 1,500,000 | 30 | usa | C | 5 | DECC. DE Committee for Consultation. Declining. |
| Dispensationalists | tC | 5-e | c1840 | 30,000 | 160 | brit | C | 5 | Protestants. Millennial schema of biblical interpretation. History as 7 dispensations from God. |
| Divine Life Mission | sHH | 2-e | 1936 | 30,000 | 35 | indi | B | 2 | F=Shivananda, a Tamil doctor. Advaita basis, Hatha yoga. Branches worldwide. |
| Divine Light Mission | sFH | 2-c | 1960 | 1,200,000 | 7 | indi | B | 2 | Begun India, 1971 USA (ashrams in 24 cities); 1982 schism, decline to 30,000 in UK, USA. |
| Divine Science chs | m-Div-tC | 5-e | 1987 | 1,200 | 1 | usa | C | 2 | Divine Science. Metaphysical, New Thought. Aggressive church-planting in CA, ID, BC/Canada. |
| Divine Science Federation Internat | sMN | 2-e | 1888 | 4,000 | 10 | usa | C | 3 | Metaphysical. In INTA. Christ Method of Healing. HQ Denver. In New Zealand, South Africa. |
| Doenmeh | zJ | 2-e | c1650 | 3,000 | 2 | turk | A | 1 | 'Apostates' (in Turkish). Sabbateans following 17th century messiah. Shabbetai Zevi. |
| Dogon ethnoreligionists | sAT | 3-d | | 211,000 | 3 | mali | B | 2 | God=Ama. Agriculturalists, caste system. Animists 48%, Muslims 30%. Secret societies strong. |
| Dolma | sSLB | 2-e | | 1,000 | 1 | chin | B | 0 | Subgroup within Sakyapa Lamaism. |
| Dominica Association of Ev Chs | E-nC | 7-e | | 3,000 | 1 | domi | C | 5 | DAEC. HQ Roseau. 5 member denominations. |
| Dominica Christian Council | C-nC | 7-e | | 60,000 | 1 | domi | C | 5 | DCC. |
| Dominican Association of Ev Chs | E-nC | 7-d | 1983 | 150,000 | 1 | domr | C | 5 | DAEC. Confraternidad Evangelica Dominicana. CONEDO. |
| Dominicans | op-oC | 9-e | 1216 | 51,500 | | fran | C | 5 | OP. Order of Preachers. 6,618 friars (4,913 priests, 1,705 brethren), 4,500 nuns, 40,000 sisters. |
| Drigung Kagyudpa | sKLB | 2-e | c1180 | 4,000 | 6 | chin | B | 1 | Third largest of surving Kagyudpa Lamaism. Many monasteries in Ladakh. |
| Drukpa Kagyudpa | sKLB | 2-e | c1170 | 50,000 | 7 | chin | B | 1 | Dragon Kagyudpa. Tibet, and Bhutan state religion. |
| Druzes | DXM | 2-d | 1017 | 834,000 | 15 | leba | B | 5 | Quasi-Muslims (messianic Ismaili Shias). Lebanon, Syria, Jordan, Israel, Palestine, diaspora. |
| Dunkers | P-Dun-tC | 5-d | 1723 | 603,000 | 15 | germ | C | 5 | Tunkers, Dippers. German Baptists: baptism by 3-fold immersion. |
| Duruma ethnoreligionists | sAT | 3-d | | 109,000 | 1 | keny | B | 4 | God=Mulungu. W Kwale District. Literates in Swahili 13%. Animists 40%, Muslims 25%. D=3. |
| Dvaita-vedanta | sHH | 2-d | 1250 | 100,000 | 1 | indi | B | 2 | F=Madhva. 3rd of 6 classical schools of Vedism. Hindu philosophy and religious attitude. |
| Dwara Nikaya | sT-oB | 9-e | c1850 | 3,000 | 2 | myan | B | 3 | Small Burmese Theravada monastic fraternity. Rationalist. |
| East Africa Christian Alliance | T-nC | 7-d | 1965 | 520,000 | 1 | keny | C | 4 | EACA. Kenya Fundamentalists, affiliated to ICCC, with CCA as largest denomination. |
| East African Revival | fC | 4-c | 1927 | 3,000,000 | 20 | rwan | C | 5 | Rwanda Revival. Balokole (Saved Ones). Pietists. Biennial conventions of 50,000 or so. |
| East Gbari ethnoreligionists | sAT | 3-d | | 139,000 | 1 | nige | C | 5 | God=Shekwohi. States: Niger,Plateau,Kaduna,Kwara. Animists 20%, Muslims 5%. D=4.M=10. |
| Eastern Bete ethnoreligionists | sAT | 3-d | | 115,000 | 1 | ivor | B | 3 | Subprefecture of Gagnoa. Animists 60%. D=RCC,AICs. M=FMB. |
| Eastern Bhil ethnoreligionists | sPAT | 3-c | | 2,676,000 | 1 | indi | A | 1 | Polytheists 95%. D=CMA,CNI,RCC. M=IEM,CGMM,BFI,UPM,YWAM. |
| Eastern Bru ethnoreligionists | sAT | 3-d | | 114,000 | 2 | laos | A | 1 | Savannehkhet Province. Also Thailand, USA. Montagnards. Animists 99%. D=1. M=2. |
| Eastern Kusasi ethnoreligionists | sAT | 3-d | | 434,000 | 1 | ghan | B | 2 | Northeast corner, Bawku District. Literates 2%. Animists 75%, Muslims 5%. D=6. M=6. |
| Eastern Magar ethnoreligionists | sAT | 3-d | | 292,000 | 2 | nepa | A | 1 | Also in Sikkim, Bhutan, India. Some bilinguals in Nepali. Animists 90%, Hindus 10%. D=1. M=2. |
| Eastern Meo ethnoreligionists | sPAT | 3-c | | 1,473,000 | 1 | chin | B | 2 | Northeast Yunnan, Guizhou, Guangxi; Thailand, Viet Nam. Polytheists 94%. D=Chinese Ch. |
| Eastern Nuer ethnoreligionists | sAT | 3-d | | 856,000 | 2 | suda | B | 3 | Nomadic animists 79%, highly resistant to Islam. D=5. M=2. |
| Eastern Tamang ethnoreligionists | sAT | 3-d | | 168,000 | 2 | nepa | B | 2 | Animists 38%, Hindus 27%, Buddhists 23%. 1974, widespread revival. D=NCF. M=3. |
| Eastern Yi ethnoreligionists | sPAT | 3-d | | 861,000 | 1 | chin | A | 1 | Southeastern Yi. Guizhou, Weining Autonomous Region. Polytheists 98%. D=TSPM,RCC. |
| Eckankar | sFN | 2-e | 1965 | 50,000 | 8 | usa | C | 5 | Secret wisdom enabling travel to higher spiritual realms. Eck=Spirit. Pantheist. Maharaj. |
| Ecumenical Advisory Council for CSE | K-nC | 7-c | | 8,995,000 | 1 | egyp | B | 5 | EACCSE. CSE=Church Service in Egypt. |
| Ecumenical Assoc of Chs in Romania | K-nC | 7-b | 1974 | 19,100,000 | 1 | roma | C | 5 | AEBRom. Romanian Council of Churches. |
| Ecumenical Co of Chs in Slovakia | W-nC | 7-d | | 575,000 | 1 | slok | C | 5 | ECCS. |
| Ecumenical Conference of Russia | nC | 7-b | | 77,104,000 | 1 | russ | B | 5 | Recent attempt to give smaller denominations a hearing in front of Orthodox Church's claims. |
| Ecumenical Council of Chs in Austria | W-nC | 7-d | | 505,000 | 1 | ausz | C | 5 | ECCA. Okumenischer Rat der Kirchen in Osterreich |
| Ecumenical Council of Chs in the CR | W-nC | 7-d | 1955 | 560,000 | 1 | czec | B | 5 | ECC-CSR. Ekumenicka Rada Cirkvi v Ceske Republice. (Czech Republic). |
| Ecumenical Council of Denmark | W-nC | 7-c | 1939 | 4,700,000 | 1 | denm | C | 5 | Okumeniske Faellesrad i Danmark. |
| Ecumenical Council of Hungarian Chs | nC | 7-c | 1948 | 2,630,000 | 1 | hung | C | 5 | ECHC. Magyarorszagi Egyhazak Okumenikus Tanaksa MEOT. |
| Ecumenical parishes | A-Ecu-tC | 5-d | | 144,000 | 1 | brit | C | 5 | Growing by 1994 to over 900 Local Ecumenical Partnerships (multidenominational). |
| Ecumenical Patr of Constantinople | C-fC | 4-b | 38 | 46,630,000 | 93 | turk | A | 5 | 20,000 under direct control in Turkey, others nominally so (Bulgarian, Serbian, Russian). |
| EdeJC sur la Terre par Proph SK | I-3nA-AC | 6-c | 1921 | 8,300,000 | 1 | conz | C | 5 | EJCSK. Ch of Christ on Earth thru Prophet Simon Kimbangu. 1H,1s(82),W=44%,36747Y. |
| Edo ethnoreligionists | sAT | 3-d | | 219,000 | 1 | nige | C | 5 | God=Osanobua. Bendel State. Nominal Christians 30%. Animists 20%. M=4. |
| Egl de Jesus-Christ sur la Terre par P | N-nC | 7-c | | 7,500,000 | 1 | conz | C | 5 | Church of Jesus Christ on Earth through the Prophet Simon Kimbangu. |
| Eglise Cath au Cameroun | R-Lat-AC | 6-c | 1883 | 3,812,000 | 1 | came | B | 5 | Catholic Ch. C=14+8+65. 5p,2s(92). |
| Eglise Cath au Congo-Zaire | R-Lat-AC | 6-b | 1482 | 25,620,000 | 1 | conz | C | 5 | Catholic Ch. C=37+23+162. 11p,1q,9x(472). |

*Continued opposite*

*Table 17–5 continued*

| Name of religion/religionists 1 | Pedigree 2 | Type 3 | Begun 4 | Adherents 5 | Ext 6 | Coun 7 | W 8 | X 9 | E. g. = examples; name for God, other religions present, D=denominations, M=missions. 10 |
|---|---|---|---|---|---|---|---|---|---|
| Eglise Cath au Madagascar | R-Lat-AC | 6-c | 1540 | 3,441,000 | 1 | mada | B | 5 | Eglizy Katolika. C=14+5+55. (1975) 61345Yy. (1990) |
| Eglise Cath en Burkina Faso | R-Lat-AC | 6-c | 1900 | 1,083,000 | 1 | burk | B | 5 | Catholic Ch in BF. M=FSC,WF,CSSR. C=4+4+19. |
| Eglise Cath en Côte d'Ivoire | R-Lat-AC | 6-c | 1637 | 2,261,000 | 1 | ivor | B | 5 | C=15+2+17. (1970) 60n,320x,19821Yy. (1990). |
| Eglise Catholique au Bénin | R-Lat-AC | 6-c | 1680 | 1,243,000 | 1 | beni | B | 5 | Catholic Ch. Mainly south. C=2+2+20. 4p,1s(18). |
| Eglise Catholique au Burundi | R-Lat-AC | 6-c | 1879 | 3,891,000 | 1 | buru | C | 5 | Catholic Ch. C=9+6+30. 3p,1s(51). |
| Eglise Catholique au Congo | R-Lat-AC | 6-c | 1883 | 1,431,000 | 1 | cong | C | 5 | Catholic Ch in Congo. C=5+4+16. 3p,1s(19). |
| Eglise Catholique au Haïti | R-Lat-AC | 6-c | 1493 | 6,455,000 | 1 | hait | C | 5 | Catholic Ch in Haiti. C=8+3+21. (1970) 150n. (1990). |
| Eglise Catholique au Rwanda | R-Lat-AC | 6-c | 1889 | 3,895,000 | 1 | rwan | C | 5 | C=6+8+29. (1970) 142n,245x, 766w,110587Yy. (1990) |
| Eglise Catholique au Togo | R-Lat-AC | 6-c | 1871 | 1,062,000 | 1 | togo | B | 5 | C=4+5+15. (1970) 87n,53x,257w,15509Yy,2p.(1990) |
| Eglise Catholique de Belgique | R-Lat-AC | 6-c | 200 | 8,159,000 | 1 | belg | C | 5 | Katholieke Kerk. C=41+14+350. 7p,11q,13s(619). |
| Eglise Catholique de France | R-LEr-AC | 6-b | 80 | 48,761,000 | 1 | fran | C | 5 | Catholic Ch in F. C=71+9+397. 4p,11q,39s. |
| Eglise Catholique Traditionalle | I-CCa-AC | 6-c | 1976 | 1,080,000 | 1 | fran | C | 5 | Schism under abp M. Lefebvre (died 1991). In Germany, Switzerland, UK, USA, 250n. |
| Eglise de Jésus-Christ à Madag | P-Uni-AC | 6-c | 1818 | 2,824,000 | 1 | mada | B | 5 | FJKM. 1968 union of FKM, FPM. M=CCWM,PEMS,FSC. 830n,75r(61000),4s,1u,W=34%. |
| Eglise Deimatiste | I-mar-AC | 6-d | 1922 | 140,000 | 1 | ivor | B | 2 | Church of Ashes of Purification. Bete schism ex RCC led by female pope Lalou. |
| Eglise du Christ au Congo-Zaire | P-Uni-AC | 6-b | 1924 | 10,186,000 | 1 | conz | C | 5 | ECZ. Ch of Christ in Z. 1924, CPC; 1970, united ch. 2538n,10044m,1710f,180000z. |
| Eglise du Christ au Zaire | K-nC | 7-c | 1924 | 9,260,000 | 1 | conz | C | 5 | ECZ. Church of Christ in Zaire. |
| Eglise Ev du Cameroun | P-Ref-AC | 6-c | 1845 | 1,367,000 | 1 | came | B | 5 | EEC. M=PEMS. 33% Bamileke. 91n,9x,911m,62w,67f,1s,1u,W=57%,8944Y,11832y,11098z. |
| Eglise Neo-Apostolique | I-3aX-AC | 6-c | 1970 | 1,706,000 | 1 | conz | C | 5 | NAC. New Apostolic Church. M=Neuapostolische Kirche (HQ Zurich, Switzerland). |
| Ekidokyo | sNN | 2-e | | 1,300 | 1 | japa | B | 3 | HQ Shibuya-ku, Tokyo. |
| Elan Vital | sNH | 2-d | 1935 | 130,000 | 10 | indi | B | 3 | Until 1982, Divine Light Mission, then schism under Maharaj Ji. Growing in UK, USA. |
| Embu ethnoreligionists | sAT | 3-d | | 118,000 | 1 | keny | C | 5 | Embu District. Bilingual in Kikuyu, and some in Swahili. Animists 25%. D=7, many AICs. M=4. |
| Emin Foundation | sFN | 2-e | 1973 | 1,000 | 1 | brit | C | 5 | F=Raymond Armin. HQ London. Self-improvement by group activity. |
| English Sangha Trust | sTB | 2-d | | 150,000 | 3 | brit | C | 5 | Supporting Britain-based monks. |
| Enjoshu | sTJMB | 2-e | | 16,300 | 1 | japa | B | 1 | Sect of Tendai Buddhism. HQ Kyoto-shi. |
| Ennokyo | sNN | 2-d | 1931 | 238,000 | 1 | japa | B | 3 | F=Fukada Ichi. Mystical. Large range of activities. HQ Hyogoken. |
| Entente des Egl et Missions Ev au T | E-nC | 7-d | c1928 | 720,000 | 1 | chad | B | 5 | EEMET. T=Chad/Tchad. |
| Epis Conf of Bosnia-Herzegovina | R-nC | 7-d | | 681,000 | 1 | bosn | B | 5 | BKBIH. Biskupska Konferencija Bosne i Hercegovine. |
| Episcopal Ch of the Sudan | A-Eva-AC | 6-c | 1899 | 2,460,000 | 1 | suda | B | 5 | 12 Dioceses. M=CMS(UK),BCMS. Bari, Azande, Moru. 91n,2x,500m,14f,1h,2r,20000Yy. |
| Episcopal Church in the USA | A-plu-AC | 6-c | 1578 | 2,295,000 | 1 | usa | C | 5 | ECUSA. (1970) 8 US Provinces, 109 Dioceses. 11272n,14s,6370Y,62814y. (1990) 14878n. |
| Episcopal Conference of Ireland | P-rC | 7-c | 1991 | 3,159,000 | 2 | irel | C | 5 | ECI/IEC. Irish Episcopal Conference. HQ Armagh. |
| Episcopal Conference of Malawi | R-nC | 7-c | 1969 | 2,697,000 | 1 | mala | C | 5 | ECM. HQ Lilongwe. |
| Episcopal Conference of Thailand | R-nC | 7-d | 1969 | 255,000 | 1 | thai | B | 5 | Sapa Sangkharat Heng Prathet Thai. Bishops' Conference of Thailand. HQ Bangkok. |
| Episcopal Conference of Turkey | R-nC | 7-e | 1978 | 25,000 | 1 | turk | A | 5 | Conferenza Episcopale della Turchia. |
| episcopi vagantes churches | I-Epi-tC | 5-e | 1970 | 3,500 | 4 | brit | C | 3 | Small bodies (mostly under 100 followers) under bishops-at-large. HQ Glasgow. |
| Er-Ramaniya | sXM | 2-c | 1972 | 3,000,000 | 6 | fran | C | 5 | North African Arabs now in France as citizens; in Marseilles. |
| est | sFN | 2-d | 1971 | 100,000 | 1 | usa | C | 5 | Erhard Seminar Training (screaming abuse at others). In Human Potential Movement. |
| Estonian Council of Churches | K-nC | 7-e | | 40,000 | 1 | esto | B | 5 | ECC. |
| Estonian Evangelical Alliance | E-nC | 7-e | | 60,000 | 1 | esto | B | 5 | EEA. |
| Estonian Orthodox | O-Est-tC | 5-d | 1842 | 196,000 | 5 | esto | B | 5 | Formerly Russian OC (D-Tallinin & Estonia); 1996, placed under EP Constantinople. 11n. |
| Eternal Sacred Order of Ch & S | I-3aA-AC | 6-c | 1925 | 1,140,000 | 1 | nige | B | 5 | Original main body of Cherubim & Seraphim. Many schisms, lawsuits. HQ Ebute-Meta. |
| Ethiopian Episcopal Conference | S-nC | 7-d | 1966 | 450,000 | 1 | ethi | B | 5 | EEC. Consiglio della Chiesa Etiopica. HQ Addis Ababa. (Roman Catholic). |
| Ethiopian Orthodox | O-Eth-tC | 5-b | 1172 | 23,896,000 | 15 | ethi | B | 5 | Ecclesiastical tradition based in Ethiopia, with members in 15 countries. |
| Ethiopian Orthodox Church | O-Eth-AC | 6-b | 332 | 22,087,000 | 1 | ethi | B | 5 | EOC. Ethiopia Tewahido Bete-Cristian. 20 Dioceses. 53 bps, 250000n. 200,000 Charismatics. |
| Ethiopian Orthodox P of Addis Ababa | H-fC | 4-b | 332 | 20,250,000 | 9 | ethi | B | 5 | P=Patriarchate. Now worldwide communion with churches in 9 countries. |
| Ethiopic, Alexandrian rite | R-Eth-tC | 5-d | 1930 | 151,000 | 2 | erit | C | 5 | Katholikawi Membre Pepesenna. Tigrai, Mensa. |
| Ethnic pentecostal churches | EN3ZAC | 2-c | 1890 | 1,536,000 | 20 | chin | B | 5 | Yi Churches, Miao Churches, Nagaland Christian Revival Chs, Gypsy Ev Movement. D=20. |
| Ethnoreligionists | T | 1-a | | 228,367,000 | 142 | nige | B | 2 | 5,000 tribalist religions; local religions open only to members of tribe or ethnopeople. |
| Eur/Amer White-led Neo-Apostolics | WW3ZAC | 2-b | 1805 | 40,457,000 | 200 | usa | C | 5 | AIGA, AVC, CEEC, COTRI, FCFI, IAOGI, ICCC, ICCEC, ICFCM, RBC, VFM, &c. D=3,510. |
| European charismatics | I-3xW-tC | 5-e | 1942 | 70,800 | 1 | brit | C | 5 | E.g. Ch of the Great Shepherd/Pyramid Ch. In Chard, Bradford. M=CGM(USA). Strong in Yorks. |
| European Evangelical Alliance | D-cC | 7-b | 1952 | 16,000,000 | 20 | germ | C | 5 | EEA. HQ Kassel. 20 national Evangelical associations. |
| European radio/TV believers | I-3rW-tC | 5-c | 1939 | 5,834,000 | 11 | russ | B | 5 | Isolated radio believers. R=6000(2800 SGA,415 HCJB,300 FEBC,60 TWR,RVatican,BBC,&c). |
| European White-led New Apos | XW3ZAC | 2-c | 1832 | 9,609,000 | 180 | germ | C | 5 | Neuapostolische Kirche, begun as Universal Catholic Ch, and 30 schismatic bodies. D=190. |
| Ev Alliance of South Pacific Islands | E-nC | 7-d | 1989 | 420,000 | 1 | papu | C | 5 | EASPI. 20 chs in PNG plus SSEC (Solomons). Close relations with Melanesian Council of Chs. |
| Ev Alliance of the Netherlands | E-nC | 7-d | 1979 | 200,000 | 1 | neth | C | 5 | Evangelische Alliantie. Dutch Evangelical Alliance. 2 member denominations. |
| Ev Association of the Caribbean | Y-cC | 7-c | 1977 | 1,000,000 | 9 | barb | C | 5 | EAC. HQ Christ Church (Barbados). 9 member national associations. |
| Ev Churches Fellowship of Ethiopia | E-nC | 7-c | 1972 | 8,133,000 | 1 | ethi | B | 5 | ECFE. |
| Ev Fellowship of New Zealand | E-nC | 7-d | 1985 | 300,000 | 1 | newz | C | 5 | EFNZ. |
| Ev Fellowship of Sierra Leone | E-nC | 7-e | 1959 | 52,200 | 1 | sier | B | 5 | EFSL/SLEF. Members: 5 denominations (all also in UCCSL). |
| Ev Kirche in Deutschland | P-Uni-AC | 6-b | 1946 | 28,363,000 | 1 | germ | C | 5 | EKD. 20 Landeskirchen, 8 other denominations. 300p,39s,P=26%,W=6%. |
| Ev Lutheran Ch in America | P-Lut-AC | 6-c | 1623 | 5,118,000 | 1 | usa | C | 5 | 1987 Union of American Lutheran Ch and Lutheran Church in America. (1990) 17416n. |
| Ev Lutheran Ch in Tanzania | P-Lut-AC | 6-c | 1886 | 2,522,000 | 1 | tanz | B | 5 | ELCT. KKKT(Swahili). A=1963. 10 Dioceses and Synods. M=TAC. 1641m,1s(126),W=75%. |
| Ev Lutheran Ch of Finland | P-Lut-AC | 6-c | 1100 | 4,495,000 | 1 | finl | C | 5 | Suomen Evankelis-Luterilainen Kirkko. 8 Dioceses. 1300n,17p,2s(1400),71575Yy. |
| Evangelical Alliance Mission | eam-oC | 9-e | 1890 | 1,000 | 34 | brit | C | 5 | TEAM. |
| Evangelical Alliance of Algeria | E-nC | 10-f | c1980 | 500 | 1 | alge | A | 5 | EAA. |
| Evangelical Alliance of Cameroon | E-nC | 7-d | | 620,000 | 1 | came | B | 5 | EAC. |
| Evangelical Alliance of Denmark | E-nC | 7-d | | 200,000 | 1 | denm | C | 5 | EAD. Evangelisk Alliance i Danmark |
| Evangelical Alliance of Flanders | E-nC | 7-e | c1970 | 10,000 | | belg | C | 5 | Evangelische Alliantie Vlaanderen. For Flemish-speaking Belgium. |
| Evangelical Alliance of Lesotho | E-nC | 7-e | | 40,000 | 1 | leso | C | 5 | EAL. |
| Evangelical Alliance of Puerto Rico | E-nC | 7-e | c1960 | 70,000 | 1 | puer | C | 5 | EAPR. |
| Evangelical Alliance of Slovakia | E-nC | 7-e | 1905 | 30,000 | 1 | slok | C | 5 | EAS. Evanjelicka Aliancia v Slovenskej Republike. |
| Evangelical Alliance of South Africa | E-nC | 7-c | 1973 | 4,500,000 | 1 | soua | C | 5 | EASA. |
| Evangelical Alliance of Sri Lanka | E-nC | 7-e | c1945 | 70,000 | 1 | sril | B | 5 | EASL. |
| Evangelical Alliance of the UK | E-nC | 7-c | 1846 | 3,000,000 | 1 | brit | C | 5 | EAUK. 20 member denominations. HQ London. Large number of programs and outreach. |
| Evangelical Anglicans | A-Eva-tC | 5-b | 1765 | 17,344,000 | 12 | ugan | C | 5 | 27 Dioceses. Balokole Revival. Schisms to new AICs. M=CMS,RCMS,AIM(UK). 142f,8H. |
| Evangelical Association of Belize | C-nC | 7-e | | 5,000 | 1 | beli | C | 5 | EAB. Including Assemblies of God (which was in BCC until its withdrawal in 1968). |
| Evangelical Catholics | ERPC | 2-b | | 79,900,000 | 150 | irel | C | 5 | Baptized Roman Catholics who also profess to be Protestants or Evangelicals. |
| Evangelical Ch Mekane Yesus | P-Lut-AC | 6-c | 1880 | 2,475,000 | 1 | ethi | B | 5 | ECMY. Dwelling of Jesus. A=1958. (1970) 675n,61x,239f,4H,2s,2872Y,5871y. (1990) 450n. |
| Evangelical Chs of West Africa | P-Eva-AC | 6-c | 1893 | 2,900,000 | 1 | nige | B | 5 | ECWA. M=SIM. A=1956. 800n,500m,50w,672f,3H,88h,31k,22p(692),1s,W=80%,2000Y. |
| Evangelical Fell of the South Pacific | e-rC | 7-d | | 250,000 | 10 | aust | C | 5 | EFSP. HQ Fortitude Valley, Australia. |
| Evangelical Fellowship of Asia | E-cC | 7-b | 1983 | 16,933,000 | 16 | indi | B | 5 | EFA. 18 member national Evangelical Associations/Fellowships. HQ Hyderabad, India. |
| Evangelical Fellowship of Botswana | E-nC | 7-e | 1973 | 10,000 | 1 | bots | B | 5 | EFB. |
| Evangelical Fellowship of Burundi | E-nC | 7-d | | 200,000 | 1 | buru | C | 5 | EFB. |
| Evangelical Fellowship of Cambodia | E-nC | 7-e | | 11,000 | 1 | camb | A | 5 | EFC. |
| Evangelical Fellowship of Canada | E-nC | 7-e | 1964 | 90,000 | 1 | cana | C | 5 | EFC. 29 member denominations, 762 congregations. EFFC for Francophone Canada. |
| Evangelical Fellowship of Eritrea | E-nC | 7-e | | 12,000 | 1 | erit | B | 5 | EFE. |
| Evangelical Fellowship of Fiji | E-nC | 7-e | | 90,000 | 1 | fiji | B | 5 | EFF. |
| Evangelical Fellowship of India | E-nC | 7-c | 1950 | 6,000,000 | 1 | indi | B | 5 | EFI. For both conciliar and nonconciliar Evangelicals. 120 member denominations. |
| Evangelical Fellowship of Kenya | E-nC | 7-d | 1973 | 500,000 | 1 | keny | C | 5 | EFK. |
| Evangelical Fellowship of Malawi | E-nC | 7-d | 1964 | 300,000 | 1 | mala | C | 5 | EFM. Formerly Evangelical Association of Malawi (EAM). |
| Evangelical Fellowship of Pakistan | E-nC | 7-d | 1956 | 140,000 | 1 | paki | A | 5 | EFP. Small body with 5 denominations. |
| Evangelical Fellowship of Palestine | E-nC | 7-e | c1970 | 5,000 | 1 | pale | B | 5 | EFP. |
| Evangelical Fellowship of Singapore | E-nC | 7-e | 1980 | 40,000 | 1 | sing | B | 5 | EFOS. |
| Evangelical Fellowship of Taiwan | E-nC | 7-d | 1953 | 100,000 | 1 | taiw | B | 5 | EFT. Also termed: China Evangelical Fellowship. |
| Evangelical Fellowship of Thailand | E-nC | 7-e | 1969 | 60,000 | 1 | thai | B | 5 | EFT. United Christian Fellowship. 27 foreign mission agencies, 11 Thai agencies, 100 congs. |
| Evangelical Fellowship of the Gambia | E-nC | 7-e | | 3,200 | 1 | gamb | A | 5 | EFG. |
| Evangelical Fellowship of Uganda | E-nC | 7-c | c1960 | 1,000,000 | 1 | ugan | C | 5 | EFU. Loose collaboration between earliest missions. |
| Evangelical Fellowship of Viet Nam | nC | 7-d | c1960 | 100,000 | 1 | viet | B | 5 | EFVN. Evangelicals very active up to 1975, then in decline under persecution. |
| Evangelical Fellowship of Zambia | E-nC | 7-d | 1964 | 900,000 | 1 | zamb | C | 5 | EFZ. Member denominations: 18 Conservative Evangelicals, in AEA. |
| Evangelical Fellowship of Zimbabwe | E-nC | 7-d | 1963 | 171,000 | 1 | zimb | B | 5 | EFZw. Conservative Evangelicals, member of Association of Evangelicals in Africa. |
| Evangelical Missionary Alliance UK | G-wC | 7-d | 1958 | 250,000 | 70 | brit | C | 5 | EMA. |
| Evangelicals | EAC | 2-a | 1520 | 211,000,000 | 237 | usa | C | 5 | Church members affiliated to Evangelical denominations, councils, or agencies. |
| Ewe ethnoreligionists | sAT | 3-d | | 471,000 | 7 | ghan | C | 5 | God=Mawu. Also in Togo. Animists 15%. D=many AICs. M=Bremen Mission(1847-1914),SVD. |
| Ewondo ethnoreligionists | sAT | 3-d | | 220,000 | 1 | came | C | 5 | Centre Province, South Province. Lingua franca. Animists 18%. D=2. M=9. |
| Exclusive Brethren | P-EBr-tC | 5-d | 1838 | 218,000 | 18 | brit | C | 5 | Kelly-Continental; Continuing Tunbridge Wells; Raven-Taylor; Glanton. Darbyites. |
| Falashas | zJ | 2-e | | 84,200 | 2 | ethi | B | 4 | Long-time Ethiopians suddenly air-lifted en mass to Israel. |
| Falun Gong | sCMB | 2-b | | 30,000,000 | 20 | chin | B | 1 | A Buddhist motivation-based sect. 1999 clashes with Communist regime. |

*Continued overleaf*

*Table 17–5 continued*

| Name of religion/religionists 1 | Pedigree 2 | Type 3 | Begun 4 | Adherents 5 | Ext 6 | Coun 7 | W 8 | X 9 | E. g. = examples; name for God, other religions present, D=denominations, M=missions. 10 |
|---|---|---|---|---|---|---|---|---|---|
| Farazis | fM | 4-e | 1818 | 30,000 | 1 | indi | B | 0 | Attempt to bring Islam to all India's societies, rejecting syncretism with Hinduism. |
| Fed Council of Dutch Ref Chs | P-Ref-AC | 6-c | 1652 | 2,893,000 | 1 | soua | C | 5 | Federale Raad van Nederduitse Gereformeerde Kerke. NGK. A family of 4 racial churches. 9x. |
| Fed des Assocs Islamiques du Senegal | nM | 7-c | | 8,306,000 | 1 | sene | A | 1 | FAIS. Federation of Islamic Associations in Senegal. Government-sponsored coordinating body. |
| Fed des Egl et Missions Ev du Benin | E-nC | 7-d | | 170,000 | 1 | beni | B | 5 | Federation of Churches and Missions in Benin. |
| Fed des Egl et Missions Ev du BF | E-nC | 7-d | 1961 | 750,000 | 1 | burk | B | 5 | FEMEBF. Federation of Evangelical Churches and Missions in BF (Burkina Faso). |
| Fed des Egl Indep de Madagascar | I-nC | 7-d | c1960 | 340,000 | 1 | mada | B | 5 | FFKMMT. Federation of Independent Chs of Madagascar. |
| Fed des Eglises Prot de Madagascar | C-nC | 7-d | 1913 | 300,000 | 1 | mada | B | 5 | FFPM. |
| Fed des Egls Chretiennes du Congo | C-nC | 7-c | 1970 | 2,100,000 | 1 | cong | C | 5 | FECC. Federation of Christian Churches in the Congo. Members: SA, EJCSK, Evs; later, RCC. |
| Fed des Egls et Mis Ev du Cameroun | K-nC | 7-d | 1970 | 800,000 | 1 | came | B | 5 | FEMEC. Federation of Protestant Churches & Missions in Cameroon. |
| Féd des Egls Prot de la Suisse | P-Ref-AC | 6-c | 1920 | 2,861,000 | 1 | swit | C | 5 | FEPS. Schweizerischer Ev Kirchenbund (Swiss Federation of Prot Chs). 1697n. |
| Fed Entitades Relig Ev de Espana | C-nC | 7-e | 1992 | 85,000 | 1 | spai | C | 5 | FEREDE. |
| Fed Evangelique de la Cote d'Ivoire | G-nC | 7-d | | 370,000 | 1 | ivor | B | 5 | FECI. Evangelical Federation of the Ivory Coast. |
| Fed Nationale des Musulmans de F | nM | 7-c | 1985 | 4,176,000 | 2 | fran | C | 5 | FNMF. National Federation of French Muslims. 2 rivals: UOIF, Paris Mosque (Algerian). |
| Fed of Asian Bishops' Conferences | F-cC | 7-b | 1972 | 110,480,000 | 30 | chin | B | 5 | FABC. HQ Hong Kong. |
| Fed of Cath Bishops' Confs of Oceania | cC | 7-c | 1992 | 8,227,000 | 35 | newz | C | 5 | FCBCO. HQ Wellington. |
| Fed of Islamic Assoc of Canada & USA | cM | 7-c | 1952 | 1,000,000 | 2 | usa | C | 5 | FIA (formerly IMS). 70% Sunnis, 20% Ismailis. Internal feuding. Decline. |
| Fed of Islamic Assocs of NZ | nM | 7-e | 1979 | 7,200 | 1 | newz | C | 5 | FIANZ. NZ=New Zealand. Fijian Indians, with a few Muslims from Europe. |
| Fed of Islamic Communities of Surinam | nM | 7-e | 1929 | 74,400 | 1 | suri | B | 4 | FIGS. Federatie Islamitsche Gemeenten in Surinam. |
| Fed of Muslim Orgs in the Netherlands | nM | 7-d | 1974 | 594,000 | 1 | neth | C | 5 | FMON. Begun by Dutch converts to Islam. Dissolved 1981; regrouped under MIC. |
| Fed of Non-White Pent Chs in Africa | J-nC | 7-d | | 200,000 | 1 | soua | C | 5 | Federasie Pinkster Sending Kerke in South Africa. |
| Fed of Reconstructionist Congs | cJ | 7-e | 1968 | 50,000 | 6 | usa | C | 5 | 60 congregations worldwide, in USA, Canada, Curacao. |
| Federacion Argentina de Iglesias Ev | N-nC | 7-d | 1950 | 900,000 | 1 | arge | C | 5 | Argentina Federation of Evangelical Churches. |
| Federacion de Igls Ev del Uruguay | N-nC | 7-e | 1956 | 30,000 | 1 | uuay | C | 5 | FIEU. Federation of Evangelical Churches of Uruguay. 10 denominations. |
| Federacion Evangelica de Mexico | N-nC | 7-c | 1927 | 2,000,000 | 1 | mexi | C | 5 | FEM. Evangelical (Protestant) Federation of Mexico. Related to WCC. 13 denominations. |
| Federal Council of African Churches | I-nC | 7-e | | 60,000 | 1 | leso | C | 5 | FCAC. |
| Federation Evangelique de France | C-nC | 7-d | 1967 | 210,000 | 1 | fran | C | 5 | Evangelical Federation of France. Includes 40 single congregations. |
| Federation of Buddhists of Thailand | nB | 7-b | 1975 | 52,000,000 | 1 | thai | B | 2 | FBT. Begun by Mahanikaya monks. |
| Federation of Ev Churches of India | C-nC | 7-c | c1970 | 1,000,000 | 1 | indi | B | 5 | FECI. Members must have no non-Evangelical conciliar ties; 40 denominations. |
| Federation of Mosques in Belgium | nM | 7-d | 1985 | 360,000 | 1 | belg | C | 5 | FMICAB. Fed des Mosquees et Assoc Culturelles Islamiques en B. Formed to counter ICCB. |
| Federation of Synagogues in Britain | cJ | 7-d | 1887 | 301,000 | 1 | brit | C | 5 | F=Lord Swaythling. Oriented toward Eastern European Orthodoxy. |
| Federation Protestante de France | K-nC | 7-d | 1913 | 700,000 | 1 | fran | C | 5 | FPF. Protestant Federation of France. |
| Federazione delle Chiese Ev in Italia | K-nC | 7-e | | 49,000 | 1 | ital | C | 5 | FCEI. Federation of Protestant Churches in Italy. |
| Fell of Chs of Christ of Nigeria | P-Uni-AC | 6-c | 1904 | 2,651,000 | 1 | nige | B | 5 | TEKAN. 1955 Federation, in north, of 8 major denominations (UK, USA origins). 140f,6H,177h. |
| Fell of Ev Pentecostal Chs in Italy | H-nC | 7-e | | 80,000 | 1 | ital | C | 5 | FEPCI. |
| Fellowship of Christ in India | nC | 7-c | c1970 | 2,000,000 | 1 | indi | B | 5 | FCI. Many Independent churches. |
| Fellowship of Evangelicals in Egypt | C-nC | 7-c | 1966 | 1,100,000 | 1 | egyp | B | 5 | FEE. Members: 7 denominations. |
| Fellowship of Gospel Preaching Chs | E-nC | 7-e | | 2,000 | 1 | sail | C | 5 | Evangelical Alliance of St Lucia. |
| Fellowship of Isis | sPN | 2-e | c1930 | 50,000 | 1 | nige | B | 4 | Neo-Pagan movement dedicated to worship of female deities, witches. |
| Fethullahcilar | zSM | 2-e | c1985 | 5,000 | 1 | turk | A | 1 | F=Fethullah Gulen. Appeal to educated youths. |
| Fiji Council of Churches | K-nC | 7-d | 1964 | 350,000 | 1 | fiji | B | 5 | FCC. |
| Fiji Muslim League | nM | 7-e | 1926 | 56,000 | 1 | fiji | B | 4 | FML. Organizes Muslim education, provision of imams. |
| Filipino Apostolics | I-3aF-tC | 5-e | 1965 | 1,100 | 1 | phil | C | 5 | Indigenous pentecostals. All members Ilocanos. 6n,1p,W=25%,80Y. |
| Filipino charismatics | I-3cF-tC | 5-c | 1987 | 1,546,000 | 2 | phil | C | 5 | Including Association of Vineyard Chs (1 ch). |
| Filipino Full Gospelers | I-3fF-tC | 5-c | 1936 | 2,458,000 | 4 | phil | C | 5 | E.g. JILF. Philippines for Jesus. Mass movement. F=E. Villanueva. In 25 countries. |
| Filipino indig pente/charismatics | FN3ZAC | 2-c | 1913 | 6,777,000 | 25 | phil | C | 5 | Jesus is Lord Fellowship, CDCC, March of Faith, Ecclesiae Dei. D=380. |
| Filipino neocharismatics | I-3nF-tC | 5-c | 1913 | 2,105,000 | 2 | phil | C | 5 | E.g. INC. Iglesia ni Cristo (Manalista). 35 cathedrals, 2 radio stations. Not pentecostal. 1902n. |
| Filipino Oneness pentecostals | I-3oF-tC | 5-d | 1948 | 118,000 | 1 | phil | C | 5 | Total about 30, including Philippines Apostolic Christian Fellowship. |
| Filipino pentecostals | I-3pF-tC | 5-d | 1933 | 518,000 | 5 | phil | C | 5 | E.g. Iglesia ti Dios a Sibibiag. Revival Fellowship. Daily radio ministry. 126n,2p. |
| Filipino Word of Faith chs | I-3wF-tC | 5-e | c1975 | 30,000 | 1 | phil | C | 5 | Filipinos teaching Word of Faith/Prospering Gospel. |
| Finnish Ecumenical Council | W-nC | 7-c | 1950 | 4,300,000 | 1 | finl | C | 5 | FEC. Suomen Ekumeeninen Neuvosto. Members: 10 major churches of Finland. |
| Finnish Orthodox | O-Fin-tC | 5-e | 1925 | 66,400 | 2 | finl | C | 5 | Suomen Ortodoksinen Kirkko. 3 Dioceses. Autonomous 1923. Karelians. 5 bps,64n. |
| Finno-Ugric religionists | sST | 3-d | | 500,000 | 2 | finl | C | 5 | Shamanist remnants across Northern and Arctic Europe. |
| Flowery Meo ethnoreligionists | sPT | 3-d | | 254,000 | 3 | viet | B | 2 | Flowered Meo. Northwestern Tonkin Province. Also in China, Laos. Polytheists 88%. D=RCC. |
| Focolare Movement | sLRAC | 2-c | 1943 | 2,000,000 | 13 | ital | C | 5 | Based on John 17:21, lay renewal: youth, families. F=Chiara Lubich. RCs, some Anglicans. |
| Folk-Buddhists | FB | 2-b | | 10,000,000 | 5 | japa | B | 0 | Popularized religion mixing Buddhist elements with local deities or cults. |
| Folk-Hindus | FH | 2-a | | 500,000,000 | 65 | indi | B | 0 | Vast masses who combine Hinduism with local folk religions and deities. |
| Folk-Judaism | FJ | 2-d | | 500,000 | 40 | isra | B | 2 | Popular religious interpretation of Judaism. |
| Folk-Muslims | FM | 2-b | | 80,000,000 | 5 | indo | B | 2 | Large numbers of nominal Muslims who merge Islam with local folk religion and gods. |
| Folk-religionists | FPW | 2-a | | 200,000,000 | 180 | chin | B | 3 | Mixtures of all world religions with local gods and goddesses, popularized. |
| Folk-Shintoists | FS | 2-c | | 1,600,000 | 3 | japa | B | 1 | Minzoku Shinto. Minkan Shinto. Magico-religious rituals, taboos, divination. |
| Followers of Christ Assoc of Malawi | J-nC | 7-d | c1970 | 400,000 | 1 | mala | C | 5 | FCAM. Independent indigenous churches. |
| Fon ethnoreligionists | sAT | 3-c | | 1,015,000 | 5 | beni | B | 5 | Animists 62%(260 fetish monasteries), Muslims 5%. D=RCC(D-Abomey),EPMB,AoG. M=20. |
| Franciscan Clarissians | cmf-oC | 9-e | 1849 | 5,900 | | ital | C | 5 | CMF. Claretians. |
| Franciscans | ofm-oC | 9-e | 1209 | 25,000 | 210 | ital | C | 5 | OFM. F=Francis of Assisi. 3 orders. Friars and priests in over 210 countries. |
| Fraternite Evangelique du Senegal | E-nC | 7-e | 1964 | 2,000 | 1 | sene | A | 5 | FES. Evangelical Fraternity of Senegal. |
| Freemasons | FQY | 2-c | 1714 | 5,900,000 | 37 | brit | C | 5 | Largest worldwide secret society. Members men only. In USA, UK, France. |
| Freie Bahai | sL | 2-e | c1940 | 1,000 | 1 | germ | C | 5 | Bahais Under Provisions of the Covenant. |
| Friends | P-Qua-tC | 5-d | 1652 | 413,000 | 43 | keny | C | 5 | E.g. EAYM. M=FUM. Largest Quaker ch after USA. 99% Luhya. 130n,2x,16f,3H,1s,W=50%. |
| Friends World Comm for Consultation | Q-fC | 4-d | | 403,000 | 43 | brit | C | 5 | FWCC. Comm=Committee. |
| Front Islamique du Salut | qM | 8-d | c1980 | 100,000 | 1 | alge | A | 1 | FIS. Islamic Salvation Front. Fundamentalist. Electoral victory 1990s, then suppressed by army. |
| Fruit of Wisdom | sVN | 2-e | c1850 | 30,000 | 2 | myan | B | 3 | Telakhon. Karen millennialism. Ancient prophecies unfulfilled, so Bibles rejected. Civil war. |
| Fudokyo | sSJMB | 2-e | | 3,800 | 1 | japa | B | 0 | HQ Nakoya-shi. |
| Fudoshu | sNJMB | 2-c | | 1,707,000 | 2 | japa | B | 2 | HQ Okayama-ken. |
| Fuji Goho | sTS | 10-f | | 720 | 1 | japa | B | 1 | HQ Shizuoka-ken. |
| Fuji Honkyo | sTS | 2-e | | 2,400 | 1 | japa | B | 1 | HQ Taito-ku, Tokyo. |
| Fujifuse | sNJMB | 2-e | c1600 | 20,000 | 1 | japa | B | 1 | A Nichiren branch of secret believers until 1874 state recognition. HQ Okayama. |
| Fujikyo | sTS | 2-e | | 1,800 | 1 | japa | B | 0 | HQ Shizuoka-ken. |
| Fukudenkai | sB | 2-e | | 2,500 | 1 | japa | B | 3 | HQ Okayama-shi. |
| Full Gospel Baptist Ch Fell | I-3fD-AC | 6-c | 1993 | 1,320,000 | 1 | usa | C | 5 | FGBCF. F=bp Paul Morton. Black. Ex NBCA, NBCUSA. Missions: Bahamas, S Africa, Russia. |
| Fullness/Praise Network of Chs | I-3cW-AC | 6-c | 1978 | 3,960,000 | 1 | usa | C | 5 | Network of Southern Baptist charismatic churches, many expelled from SBC. |
| Fumyokai Kyodan | sNN | 2-e | | 23,500 | 1 | japa | B | 2 | HQ Kohoku-ku, Yokohama-shi. |
| Fundamentalist Islamic Front | qM | 8-d | 1941 | 600,000 | 20 | paki | A | 0 | Jamaat-i Islami. F=S.A.A.Maududi. Highly organized and successful political party. HQ Lahore. |
| Fundamentalists | FEAC | 2-b | 1909 | 100,000,000 | 80 | usa | C | 5 | Christians holding affirmation of 5, 7, 9, or 21 non-negotiable doctrines. |
| Fundamentalists | P-Fun-tC | 5-d | 1890 | 240,000 | 14 | phil | C | 4 | E.g. Doane Baptists. M=ABWE(Regular Baptists) (USA). Growing very rapidly. 76f,3h,2s. |
| Fusokyo | sTS | 2-d | 1875 | 144,000 | 1 | japa | B | 2 | Mountain worship group based on Mount Fuji. In Sect Shinto. HQ Setagaya, Tokyo. |
| Gabriallists | sg-oC | 9-e | 1910 | 1,200 | | ital | C | 5 | SG. Brothers of Christian Instruction of St gabriel. |
| Gaccha | sSV | 2-e | 1228 | 5,000 | 1 | indi | B | 1 | Breakaway Svetambara Jain sects: Tapa Gaccha, Kharatara Gaccha. |
| Gambia Christian Council | W-nC | 7-e | 1963 | 38,000 | 1 | gamb | A | 5 | GCC. Anglicans, Methodists, Catholics. |
| Gamo ethnoreligionists | sAT | 3-d | | 448,000 | 1 | ethi | A | 1 | Gemu-Gofa Province. Near Lake Abaya. Animists 80%. D=WLEC. M=SIM. |
| Gamti ethnoreligionists | sPAT | 3-d | | 239,000 | 1 | indi | A | 1 | Gujarat State, Broach, Surat. Well-educated Bhils. Animists/polytheists 98%. D=4. M=2. |
| Ganapatyas | sFH | 2-c | 1651 | 1,000,000 | 5 | indi | B | 0 | Popular Hindu devotional movement, worshiping Ganesh. Maharashtra. |
| Garo ethnoreligionists | sAT | 3-d | | 455,000 | 3 | indi | B | 5 | West Assam, Garo Hills, West Bengal, Tripura. Animists 62%. D=3. M=2. |
| Gaudiya Vaisnava Mission | sVH | 2-e | 1870 | 3,000 | 30 | indi | B | 1 | Bengali Hindu Missionary Society. F=Bhaktivinoda Thakura. Devotion of Krishna. |
| Gaudiya-sampradaya | sVH | 2-e | 1520 | 60,000 | 2 | indi | B | 2 | Bengali devotionalism. F=Sri Chaitanya. 1870, revival leading to ISKCON. |
| Gay/Lesbian homosexual chs | I-Gay-tC | 5-d | 1968 | 179,000 | 2 | usa | C | 4 | E.g. UFMCC. MCCs=Metropolitan Community Chs. Gays and lesbians. In 17 nations. 500n. |
| Gedatsukai | sNN | 2-d | 1929 | 500,000 | 10 | japa | B | 3 | Shingon. Honor to rising Sun each day. F=Eizo Okano. HQ Tokyo. Veneration of Kami deities. |
| Gedatsuko | sB | 2-d | | 234,000 | 1 | japa | B | 3 | HQ Shimogyo-ku, Kyoto-shi. |
| Gelugpas | GL-oB | 9-d | c1450 | 100,000 | 30 | chin | B | 3 | Virtuous Ones. Yellow Hat Lamaist monastic order (Dalai Lama's sect); emphasis scholarship. |
| Georgian Orth Ch: C Mtskheta | O-Geo-AC | 6-c | 150 | 2,760,000 | 1 | geor | C | 5 | Catholicate of Mtskheta & Tiflis. 15 Dioceses, 26 bishops. |
| Georgian Orthodox | O-Geo-tC | 5-c | c1100 | 2,853,000 | 9 | geor | C | 5 | Catholicate of Mtskheta & Tiflis. 15 Dioceses, 26 bishops. |
| German Dhammaduta Society | sTB | 2-e | 1957 | 84,000 | 2 | germ | C | 5 | German wing of Buddhist world mission. |
| Getambe Group | sTB | 2-e | 1980 | 1,000 | 1 | sril | B | 3 | Lay meditation society. F=P. Sorada. |
| Ghana Bishops' Conference | R-nC | 7-c | 1993 | 1,925,000 | 1 | ghan | B | 5 | GBC. HQ Accra. |
| Ghana Council of United Churches | C-nC | 7-d | | 700,000 | 1 | ghan | B | 5 | GCUC. Mostly Pentecostal denominations. |
| Ghana Pentecostal Council | H-nC | 7-d | c1985 | 850,000 | 1 | ghan | B | 5 | GPC. Grouping of older Pentecostal bodies with 66 member chs, led by AoG, CoP, AC, CAC. |
| Ghawthiyah | ssUM | 2-d | c1490 | 300,000 | 3 | indi | B | 2 | Begun and continued as part of Qadiriya order, in South Asia. |

*Continued opposite*

*Table 17–5 continued*

| Name of religion/religionists 1 | Pedigree 2 | Type 3 | Begun 4 | Adherents 5 | Ext 6 | Coun 7 | W 8 | X 9 | E. g. = examples; name for God, other religions present, D=denominations, M=missions. 10 |
|---|---|---|---|---|---|---|---|---|---|
| Gideo ethnoreligionists | sAT | 3-d | | 570,000 | 1 | ethi | B | 3 | Animists 69%, Muslims 1%. D=ECMY,WLEC,FGBC,Light of Life Ch,AIC. M=10. |
| Gio ethnoreligionists | sAT | 3-d | | 116,000 | 1 | libe | A | 1 | Dialect of Dan. Animists 90%, Muslims 5%. Ongoing conversions to Islam. D=6. M=3. |
| Giriama ethnoreligionists | sAT | 3-d | | 214,000 | 1 | keny | B | 4 | God=Mulungu. Mijikenda. Bilingual in Swahili. Animists 45%, Muslims 8.5%(Shafi Sunnis). D=6. |
| Gisamjang ethnoreligionists | sAT | 3-d | | 107,000 | 1 | tanz | A | 1 | Semi-nomadic. Pastoralists. Close to Barabaig; dialect of Taturu. Animists 97%. D=2. M=LCA. |
| Gnostics | m-Gno-tC | 5-e | 1842 | 74,000 | 3 | germ | C | 1 | Sonnenwesen/Being Anthroposophical Society. 7 sacraments. HQ Stuttgart. 150n. |
| Godianism | sSN | 2-d | 1945 | 200,000 | 1 | nige | B | 3 | Cult of Aruosa. Founded by Oba of Benin, Akenzua II, using Bini ethnoreligion. |
| God's Kingdom Society | sSN | 2-e | 1934 | 2,500 | 1 | nige | B | 3 | Sabbatarian body combining Catholic, Jehovah's Witnesses, Jewish elements. Polygamous. |
| Goemai ethnoreligionists | sAT | 3-d | | 248,000 | 1 | nige | A | 1 | Plateau State. Lingua franca: Hausa. Animists 89%, Muslims 11%. Mainly RCs. D=4. M=3. |
| Gofa ethnoreligionists | sAT | 3-d | | 130,000 | 1 | ethi | B | 3 | God=Tsosa. Dialect of Wolaytta. Southwest Lake Abaya area. Animists 70%. D=WLEC. M=SIM. |
| Golden Lotus | sD | 2-e | 1150 | 20,000 | 1 | chin | B | 0 | Pure Yang. Chuan-chen Tao (Way of Realizing Truth). |
| Gormati ethnoreligionists | sHAT | 3-c | | 2,161,000 | 1 | indi | B | 2 | God=Devadu. AP,MP,HP,TN, 5 other States. Hindus/polytheists 99%. D=20. M=30. |
| Gospel Faith Mission | I-3aA-AC | 6-c | 1953 | 1,422,000 | 1 | nige | B | 5 | GFM. Schism ex CAC. HQ Ibadan, Benin. M=CAM. Kambari, Ibo, Yoruba, Gongola. 3859Y. |
| Grail Foundation Movement | sSN | 2-d | 1919 | 100,000 | 30 | ausz | C | 5 | Gralsbewegung. Crossbearers. F=O. E. Bernhardt. Reincarnation. HQ Vomperberg. Global. |
| Great Commission Christians | GCC | 2-a | 33 | 647,821,000 | 237 | usa | C | 5 | All church members aware of Christ's Commission and involved in His global mission. |
| Greek (Byzantine rite) | R-Gre-tC | 5-e | 1911 | 2,200 | 2 | gree | C | 5 | Byzantine-rite Catholics. HQ Athens. |
| Greek Orth AD of N&S America | O-Gre-AC | 6-c | 1864 | 1,960,000 | 1 | usa | C | 5 | AD in 1922. In EP Constantinople. 11 Dioceses, 15 bps. 700n,14r,1s(120),W=30%,12650Yy. |
| Greek Orthodox | O-Gre-tC | 5-b | 1083 | 15,439,000 | 72 | gree | C | 5 | Ekklesia tes Hellados. 95 bps,7530n,7184b,144d(891m),163e(1709w). |
| Grenada Inter-Church Council for SW | C-nC | 7-e | 1974 | 83,000 | 1 | gren | C | 5 | 1950 Conference of Chs in Grenada. 1974 Grenada Christian Council. SW=Social Welfare |
| Guajiro ethnoreligionists | sAT | 3-d | | 208,000 | 2 | colo | B | 3 | Many in Venezuela. Pastoralists. Animists 70%. Mass conversions to Baha'i World Faith. D=4. |
| Guardians of the City | sUJ | 2-d | 1935 | 100,000 | 3 | isra | B | 2 | Neturei Karta. Extreme Ultra-Orthodox Jews. Anti-Zionists, breaking from Agudat Israel. |
| Gugan Shinshu | sPJMB | 2-e | | 1,500 | 1 | japa | B | 2 | HQ Fukui-shi. |
| Gumuz ethnoreligionists | sAT | 3-d | | 101,000 | 2 | ethi | A | 1 | Half in Sudan. Animists 86%, Muslims 4%. D=3. M=1. |
| Gun ethnoreligionists | sAT | 3-d | | 126,000 | 3 | beni | B | 5 | God=Jiwheyewhe. Animists 50%, Muslims 10%(Sunnis and Ahmadis, spreading rapidly). D=9. |
| Gunabadi | ssUM | 2-e | | 25,000 | 1 | iran | A | 1 | Branch of Nimatullahi Sufi order. |
| Gurdjieffian Groups | sFN | 2-e | c1920 | 4,000 | 20 | fran | C | 5 | F=G. I. Gurdjieff. Influenced Human Potential Movement. New Age synthesis. |
| Gurenne ethnoreligionists | sAT | 3-d | | 593,000 | 2 | ghan | B | 2 | Animists 83%, Muslims 5%. M=SIL,SIM,WF,WEC. |
| Gurma ethnoreligionists | sAT | 3-d | | 315,000 | 5 | burk | B | 2 | Also in Benin, Niger, Togo. Animists 53%, Muslims 40%. D=2. M=6. |
| Guro ethnoreligionists | sAT | 3-d | | 277,000 | 1 | ivor | B | 3 | God=Ball. West Central Department. Literates 25%. Animists 75%, Muslims 6%. D=3. M=4. |
| Gurunsi ethnoreligionists | sAT | 3-d | | 134,000 | 1 | ghan | B | 2 | Part of Gurenne people. Animists 81%, Muslims 1%. D=5. M=3. |
| Gush Emunim | qUJ | 8-e | 1974 | 2,000 | 2 | isra | B | 2 | Bloc of the Faithful. Major extra-parliamentary force. |
| Guyana Council of Churches | K-nC | 7-e | 1937 | 95,000 | 1 | guya | B | 5 | GCC. 15 member denominations and 4 autonomous regional councils. |
| Guyana Council of the ICCC | T-nC | 7-e | | 1,700 | 1 | guya | B | 4 | GCICCC. |
| Guyana Evangelical Fellowship | E-nC | 7-e | | 50,000 | 1 | guya | B | 5 | GEF. |
| Guze Kannon Shu | sSJMB | 2-e | | 11,700 | 1 | japa | B | 0 | HQ Wakayama-shi. |
| Gypsy Pentecostal Churches | G-fC | 4-d | 1950 | 200,000 | 18 | spai | C | 5 | IEF. Iglesia Evangelica Filadelfia. Pentecostals. Strong also in France, Portugal. |
| Habad Hasidism | sOJ | 2-e | | 25,000 | 1 | isra | B | 2 | Chabad. |
| Hachidai Ryuo Daishizen Aishin K | sNN | 2-d | | 102,000 | 1 | japa | B | 2 | K=Kyodan. HQ Iwamizawa-shi, Hokkaido. |
| Hadiyya ethnoreligionists | sAT | 3-d | | 275,000 | 1 | ethi | B | 3 | Southern Shoa Province. Animists 20%, Muslims 50% and growing. D=3. M=2. |
| Hairy Ishans | sUM | 2-e | | 40,000 | 1 | uzbe | A | 0 | Radical offshoot of Yasawiya Sufi (Ishanism) order, Kirghistan, Uzbekistan. Clandestine, urban. |
| Halveti-Cerrahis | sUM | 2-e | | 3,000 | 1 | turk | A | 1 | Turkish Sufi order in Istanbul, Germany, USA. |
| Hamadsha | sUM | 2-e | c1700 | 2,000 | 1 | moro | A | 0 | Socially despised Sufi order in northern Morocco. |
| Hamalliyah | ssUM | 2-e | 1910 | 30,000 | 9 | maur | A | 0 | Sufi order, offshoot of Tijaniya, in Mauritania and Morocco to Nigeria. Modernizing. |
| Hamas | zSM | 2-e | 1990 | 10,000 | 5 | alge | A | 0 | Al-Haraqa li Mujtama Islami (Movement for Islamic Society). |
| Hamidiya Shadhiliya | ssUM | 2-e | | 15,000 | 1 | egyp | B | 3 | Egyptian branch of notable Sufi order, Shadhiliya. |
| Han charismatic house chs | I-3cC-AC | 6-b | 1950 | 35,686,000 | 1 | chin | B | 5 | 500 Regional Councils, 5,000 Pastoral Districts. M=Taiwanese/Diaspora short-termers; CCRC. |
| Han Chinese indig pente/charis | CN3ZAC | 2-b | 1905 | 49,749,000 | 58 | chin | B | 5 | True Jesus Church, NBM/BAM, AHC(Little Flock), Han Chinese house churches. D=180. |
| Han Chinese Three-Self Chs | I-Uni-AC | 6-b | 1807 | 12,560,000 | 1 | chin | B | 5 | TSPM. 1950, all non-RCs forcibly united. 1966-79, all churches closed. Now 40% registered. |
| Han unregistered house chs | I-AC | 6-b | 1950 | 11,812,000 | 1 | chin | B | 5 | Hundreds of small illegal networks, many isolated, mostly noncharismatic. Rural persecutions. |
| Hanafites | HSM | 2-a | c750 | 531,418,000 | 135 | turk | A | 1 | Oldest and largest of the 4 Sunni schools of law. India, Pakistan, Turkey, C Asia, China, Egypt. |
| Hanbalites | BSM | 2-c | 850 | 2,325,000 | 25 | saud | B | 2 | F=Ahmad ibn Hanbal. Strictest of the 4 Sunni schools of law, officially accepted in Saudi Arabia. |
| Handsome Lake | I-mar-AC | 6-e | 1799 | 5,000 | 1 | cana | C | 2 | Longhouse Religion. Iroquois Indians in Ontario, Quebec, New York state. |
| Hani ethnoreligionists | sPAT | 3-c | | 1,495,000 | 4 | chin | A | 1 | Yunnan, Viet Nam, Laos, Burma. Polytheists (animists, ancestor veneration) 95%. D=TSPM. |
| Hasidism | sOJ | 2-e | 1790 | 50,000 | 5 | pola | C | 4 | Jewish enthusiastic religious movement. Destroyed by Nazis, now only in Israel, USA. |
| Haskalah | sOJ | 2-e | | 20,000 | 1 | isra | B | 2 | Schools of Jewish thought constantly in turmoil or opposition. |
| Hasshukengaku Shinshukyo | sSJMB | 2-e | | 15,900 | 1 | japa | B | 0 | HQ Kumamoto-shi. |
| Hathayoga | sHH | 2-e | c1700 | 20,000 | 1 | indi | B | 0 | Vaishnavas in North India. Inward discipline rejecting external rituals. A Nath cult. |
| Havurat Judaism | zJ | 2-e | 1967 | 5,000 | 1 | isra | B | 2 | Jewish New-Agers, stressing Kabbalah and Hasidism. |
| Heavenly Virtue Holy Church | sSN | 2-d | | 250,000 | 7 | malb | B | 3 | Tien Te Sheng Hui. Chinese, across Southeast Asia. |
| Hermetic Order of the Golden Dawn | sON | 2-e | 1888 | 5,000 | 10 | brit | C | 4 | The most influential Western magical organization; revival of interest in the Occult. |
| Hi no Oshie | sTS | 2-e | | 2,100 | 1 | japa | B | 2 | Mountain worship. HQ Shinguku-ku, Tokyo. |
| Hibtias | ssMIHM | 10-f | 1761 | 500 | 1 | indi | B | 0 | Hibatis, Hiptiyas. Split ex Daudi Ismailis. |
| Hidden Buddhist neocharismatics | BH3ZAC | 2-c | 1950 | 2,194,000 | 15 | myan | B | 2 | Buddhist believers in Christ (NBBCs) who have pentecostal/charismatic gifts. D=15. |
| Hidden Hindu believers in Christ | I-Hin-tC | 5-b | 1857 | 11,964,000 | 7 | indi | B | 2 | Numerous movements but mostly isolated believers and families witnessing within Hinduism. |
| Hidden Hindu neocharismatics | HH3ZAC | 2-c | 1800 | 9,715,000 | 4 | nepa | A | 2 | Hindu believers in Christ (NBBCs) who have pentecostal/charismatic gifts. D=10. |
| Hidden Jewish neocharismatics | JH3ZAC | 2-d | 1896 | 250,000 | 15 | isra | B | 2 | Jewish believers in Christ who have pentecostal/charismatic gifts. D=50. |
| Hidden Muslim neocharismatics | MH3ZAC | 2-d | 1930 | 418,000 | 15 | turk | A | 2 | Muslim believers in Christ (NBBCs) who have pentecostal/charismatic gifts. D=15. |
| Hidden non-Christian believers in C | H3ZAC | 2-b | 1800 | 13,676,000 | 70 | indi | B | 2 | Hindu, Muslim, Buddhist, Jewish, Sikh, Baha'i, New-Religion converts who stay hidden. D=290. |
| Hidden other-relig neocharismatics | YH3ZAC | 2-c | 1980 | 1,100,000 | 50 | japa | B | 2 | Other religionist hidden believers in Christ who have pentecostal/charismatic gifts. D=200. |
| High Church Anglicans | A-Hig-tC | 5-c | 1072 | 7,964,000 | 30 | soua | C | 5 | 16 Dioceses in SA, 6 abroad. 56% Black, 24% White. 511b,18de,18H,96h,12r,4s(81). |
| High Spiritists | HU | 2-c | | 3,750,000 | 30 | fran | C | 5 | Kardecism and other European non-Christian forms without African features. |
| High-caste Hindu believers in C | I-Hin-AC | 6-c | 1800 | 2,800,000 | 1 | indi | B | 2 | Isolated Brahmin believers in Christ as Lord who choose to remain in Hindu society and family. |
| Highland Nung ethnoreligionists | sPAT | 3-d | | 958,000 | 3 | viet | A | 1 | Lang Son, Bac Giang.Also in China, Laos. Polytheists 98%(ancestor worship). |
| Highland Yao ethnoreligionists | sPT | 3-d | | 386,000 | 3 | viet | A | 1 | Across northern Tonkin; Banmethuot. Most in China; Laos. Polytheists 99%. D=RCC. M=2. |
| Hikawa Kamiichijo | sTS | 2-e | | 6,500 | 1 | japa | B | 1 | HQ Osaka-fu. |
| Hikawakyo | sTS | 2-e | | 5,000 | 1 | japa | B | 1 | HQ Osaka-fu. |
| Himalayan ethnoreligionists | sAT | 3-c | | 5,000,000 | 5 | nepa | A | 0 | Many scattered peoples, with animistic religions (2,200,000 in Nepal). |
| Himpunan Penghayat Kepercayaan | cVN | 2-b | 1955 | 60,000,000 | 1 | indo | B | 3 | HPK. Umbrella body for Kebatinan mystical religions. Name changed 1970 and 1979. |
| Hindu fundamentalists | zH | 2-b | | 10,000,000 | 3 | indi | B | 0 | Hindu activists fighting Christians and Muslims to win back Dalits (former Outcastes). |
| Hindu Mahasabha | qH | 8-d | | 800,000 | 1 | indi | B | 0 | Ultra-Orthodox Hindu political group. |
| Hindu Tantrists | TH | 2-c | 400 | 1,000,000 | 15 | indi | B | 0 | Hindu tradition based on Tantras instead of Vedas. Usually Shaktas. Nepal, Bengal, Assam. |
| Hinduized animists | HAT | 3-b | | 20,000,000 | 1 | indi | B | 2 | Animists heavily penetrated by dominant Hindu beliefs and culture. |
| Hindus | H | 1-a | | 811,336,000 | 114 | indi | B | 2 | Based on the Vedas, now with many varieties. |
| Hinomoto Kyodan | sNS | 2-e | | 1,600 | 1 | japa | B | 1 | HQ Hiroshima-ken. |
| Hinomoto Shinseiko | sTS | 2-e | | 2,300 | 1 | japa | B | 1 | HQ Nerima-ku, Tokyo. |
| Hinomotokyo | sTS | 2-e | | 65,100 | 1 | japa | B | 2 | Mountain worship. Ex Shinrikyo. HQ Hiroshima-shi, and Hyogo-ken. |
| Hizbollah | qHM | 8-e | 1982 | 80,000 | 20 | leba | B | 5 | Hezbollah. Party of God. Iran-supported Shia militants. Radical, violent fundamentalists. |
| Hngettwin Nikaya | sT-oB | 9-e | c1850 | 1,000 | 1 | myan | B | 3 | Smallest monastic fraternity in Burma; around Mandalay. |
| Ho ethnoreligionists | sAT | 3-d | | 783,000 | 2 | indi | A | 2 | God=Ishwar. Bihar; Orissa, WB. Also in Bangladesh. Animists 69%, Hindus 30%. D=2. M=7. |
| Hoa Hao | sSN | 2-c | 1939 | 2,050,000 | 10 | viet | B | 2 | Buo Son Ky Hong. Millennialist. F=Huyan Phu So, regarded as the Emergent Buddha. |
| Hoguk Sungdan | v-oB | 9-e | c1950 | 20,000 | 2 | souk | B | 5 | Monks Militia for National Defence (Chogye order). |
| Hokkaido Jinja Kyokai | sHS | 2-e | | 15,000 | 1 | japa | B | 1 | HQ Kami Iso-gun, Hokkaido. |
| Hokke Nichirenshu | sNJMB | 2-e | | 25,500 | 1 | japa | B | 1 | HQ Osaka-shi. |
| Hokke Shinshu | sNJMB | 2-e | | 3,100 | 1 | japa | B | 1 | HQ Shinagawa-ku, Tokyo. |
| Hokkeshu Honmonryu | sNJMB | 2-d | | 369,000 | 1 | japa | B | 1 | HQ Toshima-ku, Tokyo. |
| Hokkeshu Jinmonryu | sNJMB | 2-d | | 146,000 | 1 | japa | B | 1 | HQ Toshima-ku, Tokyo. |
| Hokkeshu Shinmonryu | sNJMB | 2-e | | 64,600 | 1 | japa | B | 1 | HQ Kamigyo-ku, Kyoto-shi. |
| Holiness | P-Hol-tC | 5-c | 1767 | 8,041,000 | 117 | souk | B | 5 | E.g. Kidokyo Tae-Han Songkyol Kyohwei. M=OMS. 354n,14f,3s(500),W=65%,1567Y. |
| Holiness Pentecostals | 3CP1ZAC | 2-c | 1886 | 6,316,000 | 170 | chil | C | 5 | Those holding 3-fold Wesleyan experience of conversion, sanctification, infilling: IPHC. D=240. |
| Holiness Pentecostals | P-Pe3-tC | 5-c | 1886 | 6,317,000 | 118 | usa | C | 5 | First US Pentecostal body. 95% White. In 118 countries. 7359n,1j,30,1s,5266t(478984). |
| Holy Cross | csc-oC | 9-e | 1837 | 1,800 | 15 | ital | C | 5 | CSC. |
| Holy Spirit Associationists | m-HSA-tC | 5-c | 1954 | 1,020,000 | 8 | souk | B | 2 | T'ongil Kyohoe. Unification Ch. Missions to USA, Japan, 120 nations. HQ Seoul. 1013n. |
| Hommon Butsuryu | sSN | 2-d | 1857 | 500,000 | 2 | japa | B | 3 | Lay movement in Kyoto. Ex Buddhism. Main feature: Lotus Sutra. |
| Hong Kong Christian Council | W-nC | 7-d | | 186,000 | 1 | chin | B | 5 | HKCC. |
| Hong Kong Evangelical Fellowship | E-nC | 7-e | 1967 | 90,000 | 1 | chin | B | 5 | HKEF. |
| Hong Kong ICCC-related Council | T-nC | 7-e | | 7,000 | 1 | chin | B | 4 | HKICCC. |
| Honke Myoshu Renmei | sNJMB | 2-e | | 1,400 | 1 | japa | B | 0 | HQ Kanagawa-ken. |

*Continued overleaf*

*Table 17–5 continued*

| Name of religion/religionists 1 | Pedigree 2 | Type 3 | Begun 4 | Adherents 5 | Ext 6 | Coun 7 | W 8 | X 9 | E. g. = examples; name for God, other religions present, D=denominations, M=missions. 10 |
|---|---|---|---|---|---|---|---|---|---|
| Honke Nichirenshu | sNJMB | 2-e | | 2,500 | 1 | japa | B | 2 | One of numerous Nichiren adaptations. |
| Honmon Butsuryushu | sNJMB | 2-d | 1857 | 447,000 | 3 | japa | B | 2 | HQ Kamigyo-ku. No priesthood. Lay-run. |
| Honmon Hokkeshu | sNJMB | 2-d | | 251,000 | 2 | japa | B | 1 | HQ Kamigyo-ku, Kyoto-shi. |
| Honmon Kyooshu | sNJMB | 2-e | | 6,700 | 1 | japa | B | 1 | HQ Chogu-shi, Tokyo. |
| Honpa Nichirenshu | sNJMB | 2-e | | 45,600 | 1 | japa | B | 1 | HQ Osaka-fu. |
| Horaisan Seishinkai | sNN | 2-e | | 5,000 | 1 | japa | B | 3 | HQ Morioka-shi, Iwate-ken. |
| Hospitallers of St John of God | oh-oC | 9-e | 1537 | 1,500 | | ital | C | 5 | OH, FBF. |
| Hosshikai Kyodan | sNJMB | 2-d | | 142,000 | 1 | japa | B | 0 | HQ Iwate-ken. |
| Hossoshu | sNJMB | 2-d | 661 | 600,000 | 4 | japa | B | 2 | One of 6 Nara sects of Japanese Buddhism. 40 temples. 1945, 57,042 adherents. HQ Nara-shi. |
| House of Growth | sSN | 2-c | 1930 | 2,415,000 | 2 | japa | B | 3 | Seicho no Ie. Ex Omotokyo. Positive thinking; denial of evil; all are gods. Literature, lectures. |
| Hre ethnoreligionists | sAT | 3-d | | 107,000 | 1 | viet | B | 2 | Montagnards. Gia Lai-Cong Tum Province. Closest to Sedang. Animists 74%. M=WEC. |
| Hua-yen | sCMB | 2-c | 690 | 3,000,000 | 20 | chin | B | 1 | Kegon (Flower Adornment), a major school of Chinese Buddhism. F=Fa-tsang. |
| Hujjatiyah | sAHM | 2-e | 1953 | 2,000 | 1 | iran | A | 1 | Charitable Hojjatiyah Society of Mahdi. Anti-Bahai anti ayatollah Khomeini after 1978 coup. |
| Human Potential Movement | sFN | 2-d | 1957 | 500,000 | 10 | usa | C | 5 | Consciousness-raising. F=Alan Watts (Esalen Institute). |
| Hungarian (Byzantine rite) | R-Hun-tC | 5-d | 1912 | 283,000 | 1 | hung | C | 5 | Hungarian-speaking. Ruthenian parishes. 1s. |
| Hungarian Evangelical Alliance | E-nC | 7-d | 1936 | 400,000 | 1 | hung | C | 5 | MEA. Magyar Evangeliumi Aliansz. |
| Hungarian Orthodox | O-Hun-tC | 5-e | c1200 | 52,000 | 1 | hung | C | 5 | Autonomous, under P Moscow. Greek/Serbian/Romanian. Many refugees since 1989. 8n. |
| Hurutshe Tswana ethnoreligionists | sAT | 3-d | | 125,000 | 2 | soua | B | 5 | Also in Botswana. Animists 20%, Muslims, Baha'is. Nominal Christians 40%. D=10. M=2. |
| Hutu ethnoreligionists | sAT | 3-d | | 846,000 | 5 | rwan | C | 5 | God=Imana. Small-stature Ruandese. Animists 8%, Muslims 8%(Shafi Sunnis). D=7. M=7. |
| Ibadiya | IKXM | 2-c | c661 | 1,636,000 | 10 | oman | A | 2 | Early Kharijites (630-1100), puritanical; now termed Ibadites. Isolated tribes (Mzab, Omani). |
| IC of Charismatic Episcopal Church | a-fC | 4-d | 1993 | 100,000 | 60 | usa | C | 5 | ICCEC. IC=International Communion. |
| IC of Unitarians and Universalists | u-fC | 4-d | 1570 | 352,000 | 27 | usa | C | 2 | International Council of UU. Begun in Hungary and Romania, 1566 denying Trinitarian doctrine. |
| Ichibata Yakushi Kyodan | sZJMB | 2-d | | 110,000 | 1 | japa | B | 2 | HQ Shimane-ken. |
| Ichigen no Miya | sNS | 2-e | | 4,400 | 1 | japa | B | 1 | HQ Osaka-shi. |
| Identity Christianity | fC | 4-d | 1925 | 500,000 | 10 | usa | C | 3 | Identification of Anglo-Saxon-European Whites with 10 Lost Tribes of Israel. Violent rhetoric. |
| Idrisiyah | ssUM | 2-e | c1800 | 10,000 | 3 | liby | A | 0 | A branch of Sufi order Shadhiliya (Morocco, Libya, et al). Strongest in Egypt. |
| Ig Católica Apostólica Brasileira | I-CCa-AC | 6-c | 1945 | 3,200,000 | 1 | braz | C | 5 | ICAB. Schism by RC ex-bishop of Botucatu. 12 Dioceses, 25 bishops. c1990 NNCM splits off. |
| Ig Católica en Rep Dominicana | R-Lat-AC | 6-c | 1494 | 7,593,000 | 1 | domr | C | 5 | Catholic Ch. C=19+1+32. 5p,2q,2s(55). |
| Ig Ev Pente 'O Brasil para Cristo' | I-3pY-AC | 6-c | 1955 | 2,200,000 | 1 | braz | C | 5 | OBPC. Brazil for Christ. Ex AoG, ex WCC. Church seating 40,000 in São Paulo. In Costa Rica. |
| Ig Universal do Reino de Deus | I-3pY-AC | 6-c | 1977 | 4,800,000 | 1 | braz | C | 4 | Universal Ch of the Kingdom of God. IURD/UCKG. 2000n. In 50 countries (Portugal, Angola). |
| Igala ethnoreligionists | sAT | 3-d | | 280,000 | 1 | nige | B | 5 | God=Ojo. States: Benue, Bendel, Anambra. Animists 32%, Muslims 10%. D=10. M=10. |
| Igbirra ethnoreligionists | sAT | 3-d | | 311,000 | 1 | nige | B | 3 | God=Hinegbau. Kwara State. Literates 25%. Muslims 50%, animists 26%. D=6. M=9. |
| Igbo ethnoreligionists | sAT | 3-d | | 168,000 | 6 | nige | C | 5 | God=Chineke. In 4 States. Animists 1%. Nominal Christians 33%. M=OP,WF,CSSp,LCMS. |
| Igesia Católica en España | R-Lat-AC | 6-b | 63 | 38,949,000 | 1 | spai | C | 5 | Catholic Ch in Spain. C=62+9+244. 114q,48s. |
| Igl Nacional Presb de México | P-Ref-AC | 6-c | 1872 | 1,416,000 | 1 | mexi | C | 5 | IPNM. National Presb Ch. M=PCUS,UPUSA,RCA. Many Indians. 8 synods,700n,85f. |
| Iglesia Católica en Bolivia | R-Lat-AC | 6-c | 1537 | 6,969,000 | 1 | boli | C | 5 | Catholic Ch in Bolivia. C=30+3+69. 6q,1s(121). |
| Iglesia Católica en Chile | R-Lat-AC | 6-b | 1541 | 11,690,000 | 1 | chil | C | 5 | Catholic Ch in Chile. C=49+4+136. 1090x,12p,3s. |
| Iglesia Católica en Colombia | R-Lat-AC | 6-b | 1512 | 40,115,000 | 1 | colo | C | 5 | Catholic Ch. C=46+2+128. 5p,38q,15s(1378),W=63%. |
| Iglesia Católica en Costa Rica | R-Lat-AC | 6-c | 1514 | 3,561,000 | 1 | cost | C | 5 | Catholic Ch in CR. C=8+5+23. (1970) 225n,1p,1q,1s. |
| Iglesia Católica en Cuba | R-Lat-AC | 6-c | 1512 | 4,412,000 | 1 | cuba | B | 5 | Catholic Ch. C=13+1+15. Low practice: W=2%. |
| Iglesia Católica en el Ecuador | R-Lat-AC | 6-b | 1534 | 11,795,000 | 1 | ecua | C | 5 | Catholic Ch in E. C=20+2+37. |
| Iglesia Católica en el Paraguay | R-Lat-AC | 6-c | 1524 | 4,771,000 | 1 | para | C | 5 | Catholic Ch in Paraguay. C=17+1+29. 1p,2q,1s(218). |
| Iglesia Católica en el Perú | R-Lat-AC | 6-b | 1536 | 26,319,000 | 1 | peru | C | 5 | Catholic Ch. 9 Zones. C=40+6+110. 10p,4q,9x(115). |
| Iglesia Católica en El Salvador | R-Lat-AC | 6-c | 1525 | 6,503,000 | 1 | elsa | C | 5 | Catholic Ch. C=18+1+29. 1s(122) (closed in 1973). |
| Iglesia Católica en el Uruguay | R-Lat-AC | 6-c | 1616 | 2,593,000 | 1 | uuay | C | 5 | Catholic Ch in Uruguay. C=34+1+51. 1s,W=18%. |
| Iglesia Católica en Guatemala | R-Lat-AC | 6-c | 1524 | 9,212,000 | 1 | guat | C | 5 | Catholic Ch in Guatemala. C=14+2+27. |
| Iglesia Católica en Honduras | R-Lat-AC | 6-c | 1550 | 5,378,000 | 1 | hond | C | 5 | Catholic Ch in Honduras. C=11+1+23. 2p,1s(19). |
| Iglesia Católica en la Argentina | R-LEr-AC | 6-b | 1539 | 35,478,000 | 1 | arge | C | 5 | C=60+8+170. (1970: 5326nx,12486w,470504Yy). (1990) |
| Iglesia Católica en México | R-Lat-AC | 6-b | 1518 | 128,190,000 | 1 | mexi | C | 5 | Catholic Ch. C=37+3+146. |
| Iglesia Católica en Nicaragua | R-Lat-AC | 6-c | 1522 | 4,679,000 | 1 | nica | C | 5 | Catholic Ch in N. Shortage of vocations. C=5+1+9. |
| Iglesia Católica en Panamá | R-Lat-AC | 6-c | 1513 | 2,194,000 | 1 | pana | C | 5 | C=13+3+22. (1970) 44n,221x,470w,3223Yy, (1990). |
| Iglesia Católica en Puerto Rico | R-Lat-AC | 6-c | 1509 | 2,845,000 | 1 | puer | C | 5 | Catholic Ch in Puerto Rico. C=24+3+75. 2q,2s. |
| Iglesia Católica en Venezuela | R-Lat-AC | 6-b | 1513 | 22,914,000 | 1 | vene | C | 5 | Catholic Church. C=31+3+78. 1q,5s(101),W=10%. |
| Igr Ev da Confissão Lut no Brasil | P-Lut-AC | 6-c | 1823 | 1,014,000 | 1 | braz | C | 5 | IECLB. Lutheran Confession, Germans. M=ALC. 183n,106x,34f,1s(90),14012Yy. |
| Igreja Adventista do Sétimo Dia | P-Adv-AC | 6-c | 1894 | 1,020,000 | 1 | braz | C | 5 | SDAs. E,N,SBrazil. 10 launches, 2 planes. 306nx,56f,4H,6h,1j,8r,2s,2099t(177230),17036Y. |
| Igreja Católica em Angola | R-Lat-AC | 6-c | 1491 | 7,567,000 | 1 | ango | C | 5 | Catholic Ch in Angola. C=12+4+30. |
| Igreja Católica em Moçambique | R-Lat-AC | 6-c | 1506 | 3,010,000 | 1 | moza | B | 5 | C=15+2+32. (1970) 27n,548x,204m,1224w,44591Yy. 39n,290x,409m,561w,125150Yy. |
| Igreja Católica em Portugal | R-Lat-AC | 6-c | 150 | 9,977,000 | 1 | port | C | 5 | Catholic Ch. C=23+3+63. 6q,9x(312). |
| Igreja Católica no Brasil | R-LEr-AC | 6-b | 1500 | 162,292,000 | 1 | braz | C | 5 | C=101+14+329. |
| Igreja Pedra Fundamental | I-3pY-AC | 6-c | 1970 | 2,880,000 | 1 | braz | C | 5 | Cornerstone Gospel Ch. 7th largest in Brazil (after RCC,AoG,CCB, IURD,ICAB, God is Love). |
| Igreja Pentecostal Deus e Amor | I-3pY-AC | 6-c | | 3,194,000 | 1 | braz | C | 5 | God is Love Pentecostal Ch. Huge in big cities: drab. Many chs abroad (Cape Verde, USA, &c). |
| Igrejas Ev da Guinea-Bissau | E-nC | 7-e | c1990 | 8,500 | 1 | gunb | A | 5 | IEGB. |
| I-kuan Tao | sSN | 2-c | 1928 | 3,000,000 | 20 | taiw | B | 1 | Yi Guan Dao. Unity Way. Begun China. Buddhist/Taoist/Christian elements. 2 major rival sects. |
| Ikwere ethnoreligionists | sAT | 3-d | | 211,000 | 1 | nige | B | 3 | Rivers State, 3 LGAs. Animists 60%. D=2. M=3. |
| Ilkwando | sSN | 2-d | 1948 | 844,000 | 1 | souk | B | 4 | Kukje-Dodug Hyophwoi-Ilkwando (Unified Truth Principle); claiming unity of Buddhism, Taoism. |
| Imam-Shahis | sIHM | 2-e | c1200 | 3,000 | 1 | indi | B | 1 | Close to Satpanthis. Small subgroup of Nizari Khojas in India. |
| Inari Shinkyo | sNS | 2-e | | 2,800 | 1 | japa | B | 0 | HQ Kita-ku, Kyoto-shi. |
| Inarikyo | sTS | 2-e | | 12,100 | 1 | japa | B | 1 | HQ Hiroshima-ken. |
| Indep Anglican neocharismatics | A3ZAC | 2-c | 1925 | 1,716,000 | 80 | brit | C | 5 | Neocharismatics within non-pentecostal/charismatic Independent Anglican bodies. D=130. |
| Indep Bulgarian Orthodox | I-Bul-tC | 5-d | 1992 | 600,000 | 1 | bulg | C | 5 | Massive schism ex BOC by disaffected bishops and clergy. |
| Indep Christian Brethren | I-CBr-tC | 5-d | 1856 | 368,000 | 24 | indi | B | 5 | F=Brother Bakht Singh. Chaubra/Sikh converts. Strong in AP; also abroad. M=WEC. 30f. |
| Indep Hungarian Orthodox | I-Hun-tC | 10-f | 1933 | 520 | 1 | hung | C | 5 | E.g. Greek Oriental HOC. Split begun by Serbian P Belgrade. Jacobite succession. Also USA. |
| Indep Latin-rite Catholics | I-Lat-tC | 5-c | 1957 | 6,991,000 | 1 | chin | B | 5 | Open Ch. Under Ai Guo Hui (Chinese Catholic Patriotic Association, CCPA). Set up by regime. |
| Indep Macedonian Orthodox | I-Mac-tC | 5-e | | 1,200 | 1 | aust | C | 5 | Macedonian Orthodox immigrants in Fitzroy (Victoria). Slavs. 1 Bulgarian priest. |
| Indep Moldavian Orthodox | I-Mol-tC | 5-d | 1993 | 756,000 | 1 | mold | C | 5 | Schism of 33% of Orthodox Church from P Moscow, aided by P Bucharest. 25n. |
| Indep Nondenominationalists | I-Non-tC | 5-c | 1741 | 2,314,000 | 71 | chin | B | 5 | Agnostics converted to Christ but remaining in agnostic organizations as a witness. |
| Indep Pentecostal Council of Austria | H-nC | 7-e | | 20,000 | 1 | ausz | C | 5 | IPCA. |
| Indep Romanian Orthodox | I-Rum-tC | 5-d | 1904 | 119,000 | 3 | usa | C | 5 | E.g. Schism rejecting P Bucharest. Now under Orth Ch in America. 50n,39t(1693). |
| Indep Ukrainian Orthodox | I-Ukr-tC | 5-c | 1918 | 7,456,000 | 18 | ukra | C | 5 | Anti-Russian schism, forming own Patriarchate. Huge start, then decline. 36 bps. |
| Indepen Korean pentecostals | I-3xK-tC | 5-d | | 162,000 | 1 | souk | B | 5 | Total about 150 (see list below), including Chinese Ch of Christ. |
| Independent Adventists | I-Adv-tC | 5-d | 1920 | 152,000 | 19 | peru | C | 5 | Ex Israelite Ch of the New Covenant. Cabañistas (Tabernaclers). Schism ex SDAs. |
| Independent Anglo-Catholics | I-ACa-tC | 5-e | 1840 | 16,400 | 2 | aust | C | 5 | ACCA. Schism ex C of E in A rejecting ordination of women, begun with 7 parishes. |
| Independent Assyrians | I-Nes-tC | 5-e | 1967 | 82,900 | 3 | indi | B | 5 | Schism ex Shimun XXIII (USA) supporting rival patriarch Addai (Iraq). 27n. |
| Independent Baptists | I-Bap-tC | 5-b | 1695 | 29,616,000 | 95 | usa | C | 5 | NBC. 1915 split from NBC America. Black. HQ Nashville. (1970) 27500n,1s. (1990) 32832n. |
| Independent Byzantine-rite chs | I-Byz-tC | 5-e | 1984 | 7,200 | 1 | usa | C | 5 | Independent Catholics. Membership abroad: 250,000 in Europe, Africa, Latin America. |
| Independent Cath neocharismatics | R3ZAC | 2-c | 1724 | 1,315,000 | 30 | neth | C | 5 | Neocharismatics within non-pentecostal/charismatic Independent Catholic bodies. D=70. |
| Independent Congregationalists | I-Con-tC | 5-d | 1829 | 980,000 | 22 | conz | C | 5 | E.g. CEUM. Ev Ch in U-M. Ex CECU(EFCA), supported by M=ECCA. HQ Gemena. 50n,50f. |
| Independent Disciples | I-Dis-tC | 5-c | 1820 | 3,930,000 | 96 | usa | C | 5 | Conservative anti-organ split ex Disciples. 10% Black. 10000n,22s,130000Y. |
| Independent Dunkers | I-Dun-tC | 5-d | 1881 | 124,000 | 1 | usa | C | 5 | NFBC (Winona Lake). Grace Brethren. Ex Ashland. 404n,1s,226t(40326),W=86%,2275Y. |
| Independent Estonian Orthodox | I-Est-tC | 5-e | c1940 | 9,600 | 2 | brit | C | 5 | London parishes. Estonian refugees. Under archbishop of Great Britain & Sweden. |
| Independent Evangelicals | EIAC | 2-b | 1800 | 27,000,000 | 191 | usa | C | 5 | Members of Independent/Postdenominationalist churches who affiliate with Evangelicalism. |
| Independent Evangelicals | I-Eva-tC | 5-c | 1833 | 1,536,000 | 48 | usa | C | 5 | E.g. Seeker Churches. F=Bill Hybels. Abroad: 1,500 chs, 70 denominations, 48 countries. |
| independent evangelicals | I-ind-tC | 5-d | 1955 | 395,000 | 2 | phil | C | 5 | E.g. Dispensationalists. Expansion until 1970. HQ Pangasinan. 60% Ilocano. 200n, 3000Y. |
| Independent Friends | I-Qua-tC | 5-e | 1965 | 36,800 | 2 | usa | C | 5 | Quakers. Until 1968: Ev Friends Alliance. 4 YMs: Ev Friends Ch, Kansas, Rocky M, Northwest. |
| Independent Fundamentalists | I-Fun-tC | 5-c | 1894 | 2,029,000 | 31 | brit | C | 5 | Large de facto grouping. Expanding. Healing, foreign missions. 2000n. |
| Independent Greek Orthodox | I-Gre-tC | 5-e | c1950 | 16,600 | 1 | aust | C | 5 | Ex Greek OC (AD Australia) by laity opposing hierarchy. In NSW, SA, Victoria. |
| Independent Holiness | I-Hol-tC | 5-c | 1852 | 1,527,000 | 39 | souk | B | 5 | E.g. Yesukyo Tae-Han Songkyol-kyohwei. HQ Seoul. 185n,1p(140),W=95%,617Y. |
| Independent Lutherans | I-Lut-tC | 5-c | 1830 | 1,848,000 | 20 | indo | B | 5 | E.g. GKPI. GK Protestan I. N Sumatra. Ex HKBP. Batak. 79n,1x,1s,W=55%,7634Yy. |
| Independent Mennonites | I-Men-tC | 5-d | 1812 | 141,000 | 7 | ukra | C | 5 | E.g. AUCECB 1963. German-speaking. Siberia, Frunze, Karaganda; rapid growth in Ukraine. |
| Independent Methodists | I-Met-tC | 5-c | 1787 | 7,293,000 | 46 | usa | C | 5 | E.g. AMEC. Black. 13 USA Districts. 20 bps. Many new megachurches. Africa, W Indies. 7089n. |
| Independent Moravians | I-Mor-tC | 10-f | | 200 | 1 | hond | C | 5 | Unity of the Brethren. Small indigenous split ex Moravian Church. |
| Independent Orth neocharismatics | O3ZAC | 2-d | 1666 | 584,000 | 20 | russ | B | 5 | Neocharismatics within non-pentecostal/charismatic Independent Orthodox bodies. D=90. |
| Independent Prot neocharismatics | P3ZAC | 2-b | 1920 | 20,489,000 | 180 | nige | B | 5 | Neocharismatics within non-pentecostal/charismatic Independent Protestant bodies. D=800. |
| Independent Reformed | I-Ref-tC | 5-c | 1743 | 8,936,000 | 51 | souk | B | 5 | E.g. Tae-Han Yesukyo Changno-hwei (Hap Dong). NAE. Anti-ecumenical schism |
| Independent Russian Orthodox | I-Rus-tC | 5-c | 1617 | 1,062,000 | 30 | ukra | C | 5 | Russian Orthodox Church Outside of Russia. M=ROCOR(until 1990, in exile in USA). |
| Independent Salvationists | I-Sal-tC | 5-d | 1938 | 145,000 | 5 | cong | C | 5 | E.g. Ch of God of the Candle. Vili messiah Zepherin Lassy. Ex SA. Declining. |

*Continued opposite*

*Table 17–5 continued*

| Name of religion/religionists 1 | Pedigree 2 | Type 3 | Begun 4 | Adherents 5 | Ext 6 | Coun 7 | W 8 | X 9 | E. g. = examples; name for God, other religions present, D=denominations, M=missions. 10 |
|---|---|---|---|---|---|---|---|---|---|
| Independent Serbian Orthodox | I-Ser-tC | 5-e | 1766 | 37,300 | 5 | aust | C | 5 | Dissident Yugoslavs rejecting P Belgrade. USA links. One bishop, 9 priests. |
| Independent Spiritualists | I-Spi-tC | 5-d | 1904 | 115,000 | 1 | phil | C | 2 | E.g. Union Espiritista Cristiana de Filipinas. Spiritualist body. HQ Malabon, Rizal. |
| Independent United churches | I-Uni-tC | 5-b | 1807 | 12,781,000 | 3 | chin | B | 5 | E.g. TSPM. 1950, all non-RCs forcibly united. 1966-79, all chs closed. Now 40% registered. |
| Independent Witnesses | I-Jeh-tC | 5-d | 1908 | 365,000 | 7 | conz | C | 4 | Ch of the Watchtower. Ex Jehovah's Witnesses. 1950s, ruthlessly suppressed. In NE. |
| Independents/Postdenominationalists | IAC | 2-a | 1549 | 385,745,000 | 221 | chin | B | 5 | Non-White indigenous Christians; Postdenominationalists, Neocharismatics. |
| India Pentecostal Church of God | n-fC | 4-d | 1924 | 900,000 | 10 | indi | B | 2 | IPCG. Ex CPM, AoG. 80% Malayali. |
| Indian Apostolics | I-3aI-tC | 5-e | 1948 | 58,500 | 2 | indi | B | 5 | ACA. Strong appeal to Hindus; HQ Madras (12,000 in mother church). |
| Indian Buddhists | IMB | 2-c | 1956 | 7,249,000 | 1 | indi | B | 2 | Reformed Buddhism reintroduced by B.R.Ambedkar for Dalits (Untouchables). |
| Indian charismatics | I-3cI-tC | 5-c | 1945 | 1,163,000 | 5 | indi | B | 5 | Including SIWA (450 chs), HBI (816 chs). |
| Indian Ecumenical Conference | fPW | 4-d | 1970 | 600,000 | 3 | usa | C | 5 | Spiritual renewal among Amerindians: Bahai, NAC, RCC, Handsome Lake, &c. |
| Indian Full Gospelers | I-3fI-tC | 5-d | 1911 | 751,000 | 1 | indi | B | 5 | Indigenous chs in Andhra Pradesh. Telugus. Welsh missionary aid. M=Mana Igreja(Portugal). |
| Indian house-church networks | I-3hI-tC | 5-d | c1970 | 365,000 | 3 | indi | B | 5 | M=EHC. Literature distribution campaigns, visiting 4.6 million homes across India every year. |
| Indian indig pente/charismatics | IN3ZAC | 2-b | 1911 | 16,613,000 | 25 | indi | B | 5 | Indian Pentecostal Ch of God, Believers' Chs of India, Christ Groups, IPA, MFGCM. D=580. |
| Indian neocharismatics | I-3nI-tC | 5-d | 1974 | 753,000 | 2 | indi | B | 5 | Based on indigenous ministry M=Gospel for Asia (GFA). F=K.P. Yohanan. 8,500 Indian workers. |
| Indian Oneness pentecostals | I-3oI-tC | 5-d | | 277,000 | 1 | indi | B | 5 | Total 40 bodies, with many USA connections. |
| Indian pentecostals | I-3pI-tC | 5-c | 1918 | 2,553,000 | 12 | indi | B | 5 | E.g. IPC. Ex CPM, AoG. 80% Malayali; congregations throughout India. Abroad: in 12 countries. |
| Indian radio/TV believers | I-3rI-tC | 5-b | 1952 | 10,693,000 | 4 | indi | B | 5 | Radio believers (youths &c). (1970) R=75000 (FEBA,RVOG),T=2810000 (ICI,TEAM,EHC,&c). |
| Indian Shaker Church | sSN | 2-e | 1882 | 2,000 | 3 | cana | C | 4 | Syncretists ex RCC Indians in British Columbia and northwest USA. 25 churches. |
| Indonesian Buddhayana Council | nB | 7-c | 1954 | 1,930,000 | 1 | indo | B | 3 | Majelis Buddhayana Indonesia (MBI). Java. |
| Indonesian Council of Christian Chs | T-nC | 7-e | | 50,000 | 1 | indo | B | 3 | ICCC. |
| Indonesian ethnoreligionists | sIAT | 3-d | | 194,000 | 1 | indo | B | 3 | Mother-tongue speakers of national language, Muslims 75% (Shafi). D=1. M=6. |
| Indonesian Full Gospelers | I-3fG-tC | 5-d | 1970 | 713,000 | 2 | indo | B | 5 | E.g. GBIS. GB Injil Sepenuh. 50% Chinese. Ex GBI(Gbis) retaining name. 450n,1p. |
| Indonesian house-churches | I-3hG-tC | 5-e | c1970 | 24,000 | 1 | indo | B | 5 | Home churches for isolated converts after nationwide EHC campaign. |
| Indonesian indig pentecostals | GN3ZAC | 2-c | 1920 | 6,761,000 | 5 | indo | B | 5 | Indonesia Pentecostal Church (GPI), GBI, GBIS, GPPS, GBT, GUP. D=170. |
| Indonesian Islamic Army | nM | 7-c | 1948 | 1,000,000 | 1 | indo | B | 3 | Tentera Islam Indonesia, or Darul Islam (DI). Insurgents in West Java (Sunda). |
| Indonesian neocharismatics | I-3nG-tC | 5-d | | 377,000 | 1 | indo | B | 5 | Persekutuan Jajasan Kristen. Unregistered Javanese autonomous congregations. |
| Indonesian Oneness chs | I-3oG-tC | 5-c | 1920 | 1,336,000 | 1 | indo | B | 5 | GPI,GPdI. G Pantekosta di Indonesia. 25% Chinese. Many splits, including GBIS. 1500n,3s. |
| Indonesian pentecostals | I-3pG-tC | 5-c | 1923 | 3,724,000 | 2 | indo | B | 5 | Total over 100 (see list below). |
| Indonesian radio/TV believers | I-3rG-tC | 5-d | 1952 | 587,000 | 1 | indo | B | 5 | Isolated radio believers (youths &c). (1970) R=15000 (FEBC,&c), T=55000 (ICI,FEBC,&c). |
| Inibaloi ethnoreligionists | sAT | 3-d | | 144,000 | 1 | phil | A | 1 | Benguet Province, western Nueva Vizcaya Province, Luzon. Animists 92%. D=RCC. M=4. |
| Insight | sFN | 2-e | 1978 | 10,000 | 2 | usa | C | 5 | Insight Transformational Seminars. F=J.-R. Hinkins. HQ Santa Monica. 1979, spreads in UK. |
| Int Charismatic Consultation on WE | K-fC | 4-b | | 50,000,000 | 180 | brit | C | 5 | ICCOWE. WE=World Evangelization. All major renewal bodies. Many congresses. |
| Int Christian Committee in Jerusalem | C-nC | 7-e | c1970 | 3,000 | 1 | pale | B | 5 | ICCJ. |
| Int Communion of Charismatic Chs | d-fC | 4-c | | 6,000,000 | 20 | nige | B | 5 | ICCC. One of several attempts to unite independent churches everywhere. |
| Int Moravian Ch in Unity of Brethren | g-fC | 4-d | 1457 | 582,000 | 27 | brit | C | 5 | Origin in Moravia. |
| Int Spiritual and United IAC | J-nC | 7-c | | 1,000,000 | 1 | keny | C | 5 | IAC=Indigenous African Churches. |
| Inter-Church Council of Tunisia | C-nC | 10-f | 1964 | 500 | 1 | tuni | A | 5 | ICCT. |
| Interdenom Foreign Mission Assoc | M-wC | 7-e | 1917 | 6,000 | | usa | C | 5 | IFMA. 50 foreign mission societies; Fundamentalist and Conservative Evangelical. |
| Internat Christian Committee in Israel | C-nC | 7-e | c1970 | 5,000 | 1 | isra | B | 5 | ICCI. |
| Internat Council of Christians & Jews | wPW | 7-e | | 40,000 | 10 | brit | C | 5 | ICCJ. 12 branches abroad. HQ London. |
| Internat Fed of Free Evangelical Chs | k-fC | 4-d | | 581,000 | 19 | swed | C | 5 | IFFEC. HQ Stockholm. |
| Internat Fell of Charismatic Chs | c-fC | 4-c | c1980 | 2,000,000 | 40 | usa | C | 5 | IFCC. An attempt to unite large numbers of independent congregations. |
| Internat General Assoc of Spiritualists | wU | 7-d | | 120,000 | 4 | usa | C | 5 | Non-Christian churches and temples. Many splits. |
| Internat Network of Engaged Buddhists | wB | 7-c | 1989 | 1,500,000 | 26 | thai | B | 4 | INEB. Social activist stance. |
| Internat Old Catholic Bishops Conf | J-fC | 4-c | | 9,000,000 | 21 | neth | C | 5 | IOCBC. HQ Utrecht. In 21 countries. |
| Internat Union of Gospel Missions | fC | 4-c | 1913 | 7,000,000 | 2 | usa | C | 5 | IUGM. 250 rescue missions serving 7 million homeless in USA, Canada. HQ Kansas. |
| International Council of Christian Chs | T-wC | 7-c | 1948 | 3,000,000 | 30 | neth | C | 4 | ICCC. Fundamentalist, anti-ecumenical. HQ Garderen. 100 member denominations, declining. |
| International Federation of Religions | wPW | 7-e | 1975 | 10,000 | 30 | thai | B | 4 | To promote world peace and fraternity. F=Suchart Kosolkitiwong. Buddhist origins. |
| International Lutheran Council | e-fC | 4-c | | 3,000,000 | 20 | usa | C | 5 | ILC. Body espousing Conservative Lutheranism. |
| International New Thought Alliance | sMN | 2-c | 1914 | 3,000,000 | 30 | usa | C | 5 | INTA. First attempt to unite the plethora of metaphysical movements since 1850. |
| International Sikh Federation | wK | 7-e | 1986 | 1,000 | 1 | indi | B | 2 | Militant radicals. HQ Amritsar. F=Jasbir Singh, masterminder in assassination of Indira Gandhi. |
| Inter-Religious Org of Trinidad & Tobago | nPW | 7-c | 1970 | 1,205,000 | 1 | trin | C | 5 | IROTT. Members: 10 Christian denominations (4 indigenous), 5 Hindu bodies, 4 Muslim. |
| Inter-Rite Bishops' Meeting in Iraq | R-nC | 7-d | c1970 | 268,000 | 1 | iraq | A | 5 | Riunione Interrituale dei Vescovi dell'Iraq. |
| Inter-Territorial Epis Conf of G,L,SL | P-nC | 7-d | 1983 | 350,000 | 1 | sier | B | 5 | ITEC of the Gambia, Liberia and Sierra Leone. HQ Freetown. |
| Interterritorial Meeting of Bps of SA | S-rC | 7-b | 1993 | 16,510,000 | 7 | zimb | B | 5 | IMBISA. SA=Southern Africa. HQ Harare. |
| Inuit ethnoreligionists | sST | 3-e | | 10,000 | 4 | grel | C | 5 | Eskimo religionists from Alaska to Greenland. Hunter-gatherers. Animal rituals. |
| Iramba ethnoreligionists | sAT | 3-d | | 181,000 | 1 | tanz | B | 3 | God=Nzua. Ilamba. Near Singida. Animists 30%, Muslims 35%(Shafi Sunnis). D=2. M=TAC. |
| Iran Council of Churches | K-nC | 7-e | 1951 | 4,500 | 1 | iran | A | 5 | ICC. Shovraye Kelissye Iran. |
| Iranian Episcopal Conference | R-nC | 7-e | 1977 | 16,400 | 1 | iran | A | 5 | Conferenza Episcopale Iraniana. |
| Iraqw ethnoreligionists | sAT | 3-d | | 333,000 | 1 | tanz | B | 3 | God=Mungu. Mbulu District, south of Lake Eyasi. Animists 72%, Muslims 1%. D=4. M=4. |
| Irish Council of Churches | K-nC | 7-d | 1922 | 152,000 | 1 | irel | C | 5 | ICC. Serves both Eire and Northern Ireland (UK). 10 local councils. |
| Isawiyah | sUM | 2-e | | 20,000 | 1 | moro | A | 0 | Sufi order active in Morocco. Branch of Shadhiliya. |
| Ishizuchi Honkyo | sHS | 2-d | | 802,000 | 1 | japa | B | 0 | HQ Saijo-shi, Ehime-ken. |
| Ishizuchikyo | sTS | 2-e | | 11,800 | 1 | japa | B | 1 | HQ Osaka-fu. |
| Ishizuchisan Shingonshu | sSJMB | 2-e | | 94,600 | 1 | japa | B | 0 | HQ Ehime-ken. |
| Ishizuchishu | sTJMB | 2-e | | 10,000 | 1 | japa | B | 0 | Sect of Tendai Buddhism. HQ Ehime-ken. |
| Ishraqiyah | ssUM | 10-f | 1180 | 200 | 1 | syri | B | 3 | Illuminationist school of philosophy. F=Suhrawardi. |
| Ishvara | sFH | 2-e | c1982 | 5,000 | 3 | brit | C | 2 | Also called Lifewaves. An offshoot of Divina Light Mission. |
| ISKCON/Hare Krishna | sKH | 2-d | 1965 | 800,000 | 23 | indi | B | 3 | International Society for Krishna Consciousness. F=A. C. Bhaktivedanta. 100 temples. |
| Islam in Africa Organization | fC | 4-e | 1991 | 3,000 | 5 | nige | B | 4 | HQ Abuja. General Council with 70 members. |
| Islami Hareket | sNXM | 2-e | 1980 | 5,000 | 1 | turk | A | 0 | Islamic Movement (Turkish). Extremist. |
| Islamic Association of the Netherlands | nM | 7-e | 1981 | 63,000 | 1 | neth | C | 5 | Turkish Muslims, based in The Hague. Support of 87 local Turkish organizations. |
| Islamic Call Party | qHM | 8-e | 1957 | 10,000 | 5 | iraq | A | 1 | Hizb al-Da'wah al-Islamiyah. Major Shia activist party. |
| Islamic Call Society | nM | 7-d | 1980 | 300,000 | 2 | liby | A | 0 | Ad Daawa al Islamiya. Missionary organization established by government. Weekly newspaper. |
| Islamic Council of Europe | cM | 7-b | 1973 | 31,566,000 | 30 | brit | C | 5 | HQ London. Coordinating body for Islam in the West. Collaborates with OIC/ICO (Jeddah). |
| Islamic Council of Mozambique | nM | 7-c | | 2,068,000 | 1 | moza | B | 3 | Representing Sunni Muslims, along with Islamic Congress of Mozambique. |
| Islamic Council of Nigeria | nM | 7-b | 1973 | 48,000,000 | 1 | nige | B | 3 | One of several national councils claiming to represent all Nigerian Muslims. |
| Islamic Council of South Africa | qnM | 8-d | 1975 | 947,000 | 2 | soua | C | 5 | ICSA. A moderate Muslim political organization. |
| Islamic Council of the South Pacific | fM | 4-d | 1984 | 150,000 | 20 | fiji | B | 4 | ICSF. Represents Muslims from Australia, NZ, PNG, Fiji, NC, Tonga. HQ Suva. |
| Islamic Jihad al-Bait al-Muqaddas | sNXM | 2-e | | 2,000 | 1 | jord | B | 2 | 'Holy House' (=Jerusalem). Based Amman. Radical Palestinian Islamic group. Suicide attacks. |
| Islamic Liberation Organization | sNXM | 2-e | 1971 | 20,000 | 1 | egyp | B | 3 | Munazzamat al-Tahrir al-Islami. Ex ILP. 1976 leaders executed. |
| Islamic Liberation Party | qSM | 8-e | 1952 | 30,000 | 2 | jord | B | 2 | Hizb al Tahrir al-Islami. No legal status. Radicals focused on seizing power. |
| Islamic Liberation Party | sNXM | 2-e | 1952 | 4,000 | 4 | pale | B | 3 | Hizb al-Tahrir al-Islami. Violence. Jordan, Palestine, Lebanon, Libya. Clandestine. |
| Islamic Modernists South Asia | qSM | 8-b | c1850 | 20,000,000 | 3 | indi | B | 2 | Elite intellectuals implementing social agendas in India and Pakistan. F=Sir S.A. Khan. |
| Islamic Progressive Movement | nM | 7-e | 1980 | 50,000 | 1 | tuni | A | 1 | MPI. Harakat al-Taqaddum al-Islami. Radicals. |
| Islamic Republican Party | qHM | 8-e | c1970 | 5,000 | 1 | iran | A | 0 | Powerful, revolutionary, until 1987 dissolution by Khomieni. |
| Islamic Resistance Movement | sXM | 2-e | c1970 | 50,000 | 2 | pale | B | 3 | Hamas. Harakat al-Muqawama al-Islamiya |
| Islamic schismatics | XM | 2-b | | 14,950,000 | 110 | iraq | A | 0 | A large number of splits or secessions from major schools of Islamic law. |
| Islamic Society of North America | cM | 7-d | 1982 | 400,000 | 2 | usa | C | 5 | ISNA. Umbrella organization for several Muslim professional groups. HQ Plainfield, IN. |
| Islamic Society of Papua New Guinea | nM | 7-e | 1978 | 1,200 | 1 | papu | C | 5 | ISPANG. Represents and organizes Muslims in PNG. |
| Islamic Tendency Movement | sNXM | 2-d | 1988 | 100,000 | 1 | tuni | A | 1 | Leading Muslim fundamentalist religious organization in Tunisia. |
| Islamic Union of Afghan Mujaheddin | zSM | 2-d | 1985 | 100,000 | 1 | afgh | A | 1 | IUAM. Ittehad-i Islami Afghan Mujaheddin. Alliance of 7 Sunni factions. |
| Islamic Unitarianism | sWSM | 2-c | 1909 | 1,000,000 | 1 | saud | B | 2 | Muwahhidun movement. 20th century struggles over Saudi Arabia. |
| Islamic Unity (Unification) Movement | sNXM | 2-e | | 4,000 | 1 | leba | B | 5 | Harakat al-Tawhid al-Islami. Sunni militants. Fundamentalist. |
| Islamized animists | IAT | 3-c | | 3,000,000 | 8 | indo | B | 3 | Animists heavily penetrated by dominant Muslim beliefs and culture. |
| Isle of Man Council of Churches | K-nC | 7-e | | 41,000 | 1 | isle | C | 5 | IOMCC. Associate member of Council of Churches for Britain & Ireland (CCBI, formerly BCC). |
| Ismailis | IHM | 2-b | 909 | 23,772,000 | 45 | indi | B | 2 | Seveners, Khojas, Batiniya, Nizaris, Daudis, Mustalis, Bohras. Most under Aga Khan. |
| Isolated radio believers | ICC | 2-b | 1925 | 17,548,000 | 69 | chin | B | 5 | Scattered individuals and groups across 69 non-Christian countries. |
| isolated radio churches | I-rad-tC | 5-d | 1939 | 356,000 | 7 | pola | C | 2 | Isolated believers in non-religious families. R=9600(SGA, TWR, Radio Vatican, &c). |
| Isolated radio/TV neocharismatics | t3ZAC | 2-d | 1930 | 188,000 | 30 | chin | B | 5 | Neocharismatics among non-pentecostal/charismatic Independent radio believers. D=30. |
| Issaishu | sSJMB | 2-d | | 156,000 | 1 | japa | B | 1 | HQ Yamaguchi-ken. |
| Isson Kyodan | sZJMB | 2-e | | 1,600 | 1 | japa | B | 2 | HQ Ishikawa-ken. |
| Isuzukyo | sTS | 2-e | | 35,400 | 1 | japa | B | 1 | HQ Oka-ku, Tokyo. |
| Italo-Albanian (Byzantine rite) | R-IAb-tC | 5-e | 1919 | 60,400 | 1 | ital | C | 5 | Eastern-rite (Oriental) Albanians living in southern Italy. HQ Lungro. |
| Ithna-Asharis | AHM | 2-b | 680 | 136,655,000 | 70 | iran | A | 1 | Twelvers. Imamis. |
| Ittu ethnoreligionists | sAT | 3-d | | 163,000 | 1 | ethi | B | 3 | God=Waqake. Eastern Oromo, Harar. Muslims 70%(Shafi Sunnis), animists 5%. D=3. M=2. |

*Continued overleaf*

*Table 17–5 continued*

| Name of religion/religionists 1 | Pedigree 2 | Type 3 | Begun 4 | Adherents 5 | Ext 6 | Coun 7 | W 8 | X 9 | E. g. = examples; name for God, other religions present, D=denominations, M=missions. 10 |
|---|---|---|---|---|---|---|---|---|---|
| Ivorian Malinke ethnoreligionists | sAT | 3-d | | 413,000 | 1 | ivor | B | 2 | God=Alla. Traders. Many speak Jula, Bambara. Muslims 67%(Maliki), animists 31%. D=3. M=2. |
| Izumo Hi no Misaki Daijingukyo | sHS | 2-e | | 80,500 | 1 | japa | B | 2 | HQ Hikawa-gun, Shimane-ken. |
| Izumo Kannabikyo | sHS | 2-e | | 1,000 | 1 | japa | B | 1 | HQ Izumo-shi, Shimane-ken. |
| Izumo Oyashirokyo | sTS | 2-c | 1873 | 1,456,000 | 2 | japa | B | 1 | Revivalist Shinto group, one of 13 Kyoha sects. God=Okuninushi, Amaterasu. |
| Izumo Shinto Yakumokyo Shinjinkai K | sNN | 2-e | | 2,800 | 1 | japa | B | 3 | K=Kyodan. HQ Sumiyoshi-ku, Osaka-shi. |
| Izumokyo | sHS | 2-d | | 626,000 | 1 | japa | B | 2 | HQ Hikawa-gun, Shimane-ken. |
| Izumo-taishakyo | sSN | 2-c | 1873 | 2,261,000 | 20 | japa | B | 3 | One of largest Shinko Shukyo (New Religions). Based on Shinto. HQ Taisha, Izumo shrine. |
| Jabriya | sXM | 2-e | | 2,000 | 1 | moro | A | 0 | Muslim sect emphasizing Allah's control, power, and authority. Ex Qadariya. |
| Jafaris | sHM | 2-e | c750 | 50,000 | 1 | iran | A | 1 | Attempt to claim a fifth Islamic law school: Shia Twelver. |
| Jains | V | 1-c | BC 550 | 4,218,000 | 40 | indi | B | 2 | Jainas. 2 sects since AD 79. 6,150 ascetics (4,200 nuns), monasteries. Ahimsa (Nonviolence). |
| Jalaliya | ssUM | 2-d | c1250 | 200,000 | 3 | paki | A | 0 | Sufi, Shia, ex Suhrawardiya. In Afghanistan, Deccan. |
| Jamaa | R2ZAC | 2-e | 1952 | 50,000 | 5 | conz | C | 2 | Family of God. Charismatic movement among African RCs in Katanga. Banned 1974. |
| Jamaat al'Islamiyah | sNXM | 2-e | c1973 | 40,000 | 1 | egyp | B | 3 | About 20 Neo-fundamentalist clandestine splinter groups. |
| Jamaat-i Islami of Bangladesh | nM | 7-e | c1970 | 20,000 | 1 | bang | B | 0 | JIB. Islamic Society. Fundamentalists. HQ Dacca. |
| Jamaat-i Islami of India | nM | 7-d | 1941 | 300,000 | 30 | indi | B | 0 | Fundamentalists. Highly organized. Little political influence. |
| Jamaica Association of Ev Chs | E-nC | 7-e | | 20,000 | 1 | jama | B | 5 | JAEC. Mainly Fundamentalist churches. 13 member denominations. |
| Jamaica Council of Churches | N-nC | 7-d | 1939 | 600,000 | 1 | jama | B | 5 | JCC. Originally only Protestant; 1971 Anglicans and Catholics join. |
| Jamiat ul-Ulama-i Islam | zSM | 2-e | 1945 | 40,000 | 1 | paki | A | 0 | JUI. Pakistan wing of Jamiat ul-Ulama-i Hind. |
| Jamiat ul-Ulama-i Pakistan | qsSM | 8-b | c1930 | 20,000,000 | 2 | paki | A | 1 | Organizational part in Pakistan of Barelvi movement in South Asian Islam. |
| Japan Bible Christian Council | T-nC | 7-e | 1951 | 10,000 | 1 | japa | B | 3 | JBCC. |
| Japan Evangelical Association | E-nC | 7-e | 1968 | 35,000 | 1 | japa | B | 5 | JEA. |
| Japanese Buddhists | JMB | 2-b | | 71,000,000 | 37 | japa | B | 3 | Mainly Mahayana, but many varieties. Total Buddhist sects in Japan: 180. |
| Japanese charismatics | I-3cQ-tC | 5-e | 1946 | 32,500 | 1 | japa | B | 5 | Sei Iesu Kai. |
| Japanese indigenous pentecostals | QN3ZAC | 2-c | 1930 | 1,160,000 | 15 | japa | B | 5 | Spirit of Jesus Church, Primitive Gospel Ch, Holy Ecclesia of Jesus, JJCC. D=50. |
| Japanese Oneness chs | I-3oQ-tC | 5-d | 1937 | 509,000 | 2 | japa | B | 5 | Iesu no Mitama Kyokai Kyodan. Ex AoG. Missions to USA. Brazil. 185n (94 women). |
| Japanese pentecostals | I-3pQ-tC | 5-e | 1930 | 54,200 | 1 | japa | B | 5 | E.g. Genshi Fukuin. Primitive Gospel Ch. Makuya. Split ex Mukyokai. 160n,W=34%,1000Y. |
| Japanese Pure Land Buddhists | sPJMB | 2-b | c1180 | 20,942,000 | 20 | japa | B | 4 | F=Honen. Several rival sects. God=Amitabha/Amida, a god presiding over Western Paradise. |
| Japanese radio/TV believers | I-3rQ-tC | 5-d | 1952 | 567,000 | 1 | japa | B | 5 | Isolated radio believers; mostly students and youths. R=164400,T=850000. |
| Javanese ethnoreligionists | sIAT | 3-c | | 2,000,000 | 2 | indo | B | 3 | Animists in Java with some Islamic elements but still strong animists. |
| Jehovah's Witnesses | m-Jeh-AC | 6-c | 1872 | 2,512,000 | 1 | usa | C | 2 | Watch Tower. World HQ Brooklyn. In USA, 22% Blacks (1975) 25740n,40814Y. (1995) 43663Y. |
| Jehovah's Witnesses | w-fC | 4-b | 1872 | 13,000,000 | 219 | usa | C | 3 | Jehovah's Christian Witnesses. JWs. IBRA. Watch Tower. |
| Jehovah's Witnesses | m-Jeh-tC | 5-b | 1872 | 12,757,000 | 212 | usa | C | 2 | Watch Tower. World HQ Brooklyn. In USA, 22% Blacks (1975) 25740n,40814Y. (1995) 43663Y. |
| Jersey Council of Churches | w-nC | 7-e | c1931 | 60,000 | 1 | chan | C | 5 | JCC. Guernsey Council of Churches (GCC). |
| Jesuits | sj-oC | 9-e | 1540 | 22,600 | 200 | ital | C | 5 | SJ. Society of Jesus. F=Ignatius Loyola. 2,000 universities, colleges, and schools. |
| Jesus Army | I-3.W-AC | 6-e | 1805 | 4,000 | 1 | brit | C | 5 | Bugbrooke Community. Jesus Fellowship. Shepherding controversy. |
| Jesus Assembly of God of Korea | P-Pe2-AC | 6-c | 1952 | 2,380,000 | 1 | souk | B | 5 | Tae-Han Kidokyo Hananim-e Song-Hwei. M=AoG. 205n,19f,1s(300),W=77%,700Y. |
| Jesus is Lord Fellowship | I-3fF-AC | 6-c | 1978 | 2,400,000 | 1 | phil | C | 5 | JILF. Philippines for Jesus. Mass movement. F=E. Villanueva. In 25 countries. |
| Jesus is Lord Fellowship | f-fC | 4-c | 1978 | 2,000,000 | 8 | phil | C | 5 | JILF. Philippine youth movement. Many overseas branches. |
| Jesus People | I-3.W-AC | 6-d | c1960 | 600,000 | 1 | usa | C | 5 | Jesus Movement. Street Christians. Many Prepentecostal groupings over 500 years. |
| Jeungsando | sFN | 2-d | 1911 | 767,000 | 1 | souk | B | 5 | Total Transformation. Folk religion seeking and believing total change-transformation. |
| Jews | J | 1-b | | 14,434,000 | 134 | isra | B | 2 | Practitioners of Judaism in 5 main branches. Centered in Israel, USA, Argentina. |
| Ji Buddhism | sPJMB | 2-d | 1270 | 100,000 | 5 | japa | B | 4 | Ji='Time', a sect of Pure Land Buddhism. F=Ippen. Wandering preachers. |
| Jihad Movement | sNXM | 2-e | c1650 | 1,000 | 1 | maur | A | 0 | Origins in religious fervour sweeping the Maghreb. |
| Jihad Organization | sNXM | 2-d | c1975 | 400,000 | 1 | egyp | B | 3 | Tanzim al-Jihad (Holy War). Deadliest assassinations in 1981-1991. |
| Jihad-i Sazandigi | nHM | 2-e | 1979 | 30,000 | 3 | iran | A | 0 | Reconstruction Crusade; youths aged 20-30 taking Iran Revolution to countryside. Non-military. |
| Jikkokyo | sTS | 2-d | 1882 | 150,000 | 1 | japa | B | 2 | Jikokyo. Japanese mountain worship based on Mount Fuji. HQ Saitama-ken. |
| Jilliwhoi | sNN | 2-c | 1925 | 4,630,000 | 1 | souk | B | 2 | Daisoon Jilliwhoi (Great & Genuine Truth Assembly). |
| Jingukyo | sHS | 2-d | | 107,000 | 1 | japa | B | 0 | HQ Taki-gun, Hyogo-ken. |
| Jinja Honkyo | sHS | 2-d | | 728,000 | 1 | japa | B | 0 | HQ Higashiyama-ku, Kyoto-shi. |
| Jinja Ubusunakyo | sHS | 2-e | | 95,100 | 1 | japa | B | 1 | HQ Mihara-shi, Hiroshima-ken. |
| Jishu | sPJMB | 2-e | | 87,400 | 2 | japa | B | 0 | HQ Kanagawa-ken. |
| Jita ethnoreligionists | sAT | 3-d | | 149,000 | 1 | tanz | B | 5 | God=Nyamuanga. Southeastern shore of Lake Victoria. Animists 50%. D=4. M=3. |
| Jitsugetsukyo | sTS | 2-e | | 18,100 | 1 | japa | B | 2 | Mountain worship. HQ Meguro-ku, Tokyo. |
| Jodo Shinshu Dobo Kyodan | sTPJMB | 2-e | | 1,200 | 1 | japa | B | 2 | HQ Ishikawa-ken. |
| Jodo Shinshu Honganjiha | sTPJMB | 2-c | 1220 | 6,662,000 | 5 | japa | B | 2 | F=Shinran. Major subgroup in True Pure Land. Nishi (Western). 10,000 temples (HQ Kyoto). |
| Jodo Shinshu Kenkoinha | sTJMB | 2-e | | 15,000 | 1 | japa | B | 1 | Sect of Tendai Buddhism. HQ Kyoto-shi. |
| Jodo Shinshu Otaniha | sTPJMB | 2-c | 1220 | 6,715,000 | 10 | japa | B | 4 | True Pure Land Sect. Eastern Temple. 16,890 clergy, 9,980 temples. HQ Shimogyo-ku, Kyoto. |
| Jodo Shu | sPJMB | 2-c | c1180 | 5,778,000 | 5 | japa | B | 3 | Original parent Pure Land Buddhism. F=Honen. |
| Jodoshu Seizan Fukakusaha | sPJMB | 2-e | | 81,300 | 2 | japa | B | 1 | HQ Kyoto-shi. |
| Jodoshu Seizan Zenrinjiha | sPJMB | 2-d | | 157,000 | 2 | japa | B | 1 | HQ Kyoto-shi. |
| Jodoshu Shaseiha | sPJMB | 2-e | | 4,200 | 1 | japa | B | 1 | HQ Higashiyama-ku, Kyoto-shi. |
| John Frum cargo cults | sCN | 2-e | 1939 | 1,000 | 2 | vanu | C | 5 | Cargo cult 1939-40, Tanna. Remnants still believe, practice, await arrival of goods by air or sea. |
| Jordanites | sSN | 2-e | 1895 | 4,500 | 2 | guya | B | 4 | White-Robed Army. West Evangelist Millennial Pilgrim Ch. Hindu/occult/Jewish/African. |
| Kabbalah | sON | 2-d | BC 500 | 300,000 | 10 | isra | B | 2 | Qabalah. Esoteric mystical occult materials, part Jewish. 1890, magic revival as Golden Dawn. |
| Kabir Chaura | sSN | 2-e | c1600 | 5,000 | 1 | indi | B | 2 | One of 12 original subgroupings of Kabir Panthis. HQ Benares. |
| Kabir Panthis | sSN | 2-e | c1480 | 20,000 | 1 | indi | B | 2 | F=Indian guru Kabir. Hindu/Muslim/Sikh. 12 subgroups. |
| Kabre ethnoreligionists | sAT | 3-d | | 461,000 | 3 | togo | B | 3 | God=Eso. Also in Benin, Ghana. Animists 65%, Muslims 10%. D=5. M=8. |
| Kachin ethnoreligionists | sPT | 3-d | | 207,000 | 2 | myan | C | 5 | Kachin State; also India, China. Polytheists 30%, Buddhists 10%. R=FEBC. |
| Kado ethnoreligionists | sPT | 3-d | | 250,000 | 4 | myan | A | 0 | Also in China (south Yunnan) and Laos. Polytheists 85%, Buddhists 10%. D=1. |
| Kagyudpas | KLB | 2-c | c1030 | 9,000,000 | 15 | chin | B | 1 | Followers of the Oral Teaching Lineages. One of 4 main Lamaist orders/sects. In Europe, USA. |
| Kalanga ethnoreligionists | sAT | 3-d | | 150,000 | 2 | bots | B | 5 | God=Ndzimu. Northeast border with Zimbabwe. ResistsTswana culture. Animists 40%. M=6. |
| Kalikulas | sHAT | 3-d | c1600 | 500,000 | 1 | indi | B | 1 | Hindu, Shaktas worshiping terror goddess Kali. |
| Kamba ethnoreligionists | sAT | 3-d | | 177,000 | 4 | keny | C | 5 | God=Ngai. Eastern Province. Animists 5%, Muslims 2%, Baha'is 1%, some Hindus. D=6. M=7. |
| Kambata ethnoreligionists | sAT | 3-d | | 228,000 | 1 | ethi | C | 5 | Southern Shoa Province. Animists 15%, Muslims 5%(many converting to ECMY). D=6. M=2. |
| Kaminomichibikikyo | sTS | 2-e | | 10,300 | 1 | japa | B | 1 | HQ Osaka-shi. |
| Kamwe ethnoreligionists | sAT | 3-d | | 192,000 | 2 | nige | B | 4 | God=Hyalatamwa. Adamawa State, Michika LGA. Animists 57%, Muslims 3%. D=8. M=3. |
| Kandori Konkokyo | sTS | 2-e | | 7,300 | 1 | japa | B | 0 | HQ Okayama-ken. |
| Kanji Panthis | sDV | 2-d | c1900 | 600,000 | 40 | indi | B | 2 | Kanji Swami's reinterpretation attracts large Digambara following. Global following. |
| Kankanaey ethnoreligionists | sAT | 3-d | | 107,000 | 1 | phil | B | 3 | Northern Benguet Province, southwestern Mountain Province, Luzon. Animists 60%. D=7. M=4. |
| Kannagarakyo | sTS | 2-e | | 23,500 | 1 | japa | B | 1 | HQ Nagoya-shi. |
| Kannagarakyo (New) | sNS | 2-e | | 35,400 | 1 | japa | B | 1 | HQ Kagoshima-shi. |
| Kannon Shu | sSJMB | 2-d | | 490,000 | 3 | japa | B | 1 | HQ Osaka-shi. |
| Kapalikas | sSH | 10-f | | 100 | 1 | indi | B | 0 | Defunct ascetic Shaivite tradition held by cremation-ground dwellers. |
| Kara ethnoreligionists | sAT | 3-d | | 100,000 | 4 | tanz | B | 2 | Southeastern shore of Lake Victoria. Many bilinguals in Swahili. Animists 83%. D=1. |
| Karaites | KJ | 2-e | BC c950 | 24,100 | 5 | russ | B | 2 | Readers of the Scriptures. Jewish sect partially accepted in state of Israel. |
| Karakash | zJ | 2-e | | 2,000 | 1 | turk | A | 1 | Artisans and workers, related to the Donmeh ('Apostates'). |
| Karamojong ethnoreligionists | sAT | 3-d | | 113,000 | 1 | ugan | C | 5 | God=Akuj. Karamoja District. Cattle-rustling gangs with machine-guns. Animists 29%.D=5,M=2. |
| Karanga ethnoreligionists | sAT | 3-d | | 587,000 | 5 | zimb | C | 5 | God=Wedenga. Southernmost Shona. Animists 30%. M=SMB,SJ,CMM. |
| Kardecism | sHU | 2-d | 1850 | 700,000 | 10 | braz | C | 5 | Kardecismo. F=Allan Kardec. From France in 1850. 5,000 assocs, 31 hospitals, 435 schools. |
| Karlin-Stolin Hasidism | sOJ | 2-e | c1800 | 6,600 | 1 | lith | C | 4 | Lithuanian Orthodox Jews named after 2 towns. |
| Karmapas | sKLB | 2-c | c1150 | 6,000,000 | 10 | chin | B | 1 | Karma Kagyudpas, largest surviving Tibetan Lamaist Kagyudpa schools. Black Hats. |
| Kasem ethnoreligionists | sAT | 3-d | | 106,000 | 1 | burk | A | 1 | Majority in Ghana. Animists 80%, Muslims 10%. D=AoG. M=FMB,SIL. |
| Kasogatan | sFB | 2-e | c1500 | 30,000 | 1 | indo | B | 1 | Javanese local variety of Buddhism; with Mahayana, Theravada, forms amalgam Buddhayana. |
| Kath Kirche Deutschlands | R-LEr-AC | 6-b | 90 | 28,583,000 | 1 | germ | C | 5 | Catholic Ch in G. C=44=15=302. 10q,20s(1895). |
| Kath Kirche in der Schweiz | R-Lat-AC | 6-c | 200 | 3,265,000 | 1 | swit | C | 5 | Eglise Catholique. Catholic Ch. C=27+2+50. |
| Katholische Kirche Österreichs | R-LEr-AC | 6-c | 174 | 6,032,000 | 1 | ausz | C | 5 | Catholic Ch of Austria. C=47+3+65. 3q,7s. |
| Kaulas | sTH | 2-e | 400 | 15,000 | 3 | indi | B | 2 | Hindi Tantric tradition tracing back to cremation grounds of Kashnir and Swat. |
| Kavi Panthis | zV | 2-e | 1924 | 10,000 | 1 | indi | B | 2 | Modern Jain lay reform movement to reconcile the 2 main Jain sects. Gujarat. |
| Kawruh Bedja | sSN | 2-e | c1960 | 20,000 | 1 | indo | B | 3 | Mystical sect, a Javanese and related language New Religion. |
| Kayah ethnoreligionists | sAT | 3-d | | 187,000 | 1 | myan | B | 3 | Kayah and Karen States. Also in Thailand. Related to Bwe Karen. Animists 75%. D=BBC. |
| Kebatinan | sVN | 2-b | c1800 | 62,359,000 | 3 | indo | B | 3 | Golongan-golongan Kebatinan. Over 300 Javanese mystical new religious movements. |
| Kegon | sNJMB | 2-d | 736 | 705,000 | 3 | japa | B | 2 | Mutual identity of phenomena and great Buddha Dainichi (AD 749). HQ Nara-shi. 1945: 50,915. |
| Kegon Shu | sNJMB | 2-e | 740 | 70,500 | 2 | japa | B | 2 | Nara sect. Name in Chinese: Hua Yen. 60 temples, 900 clergy. HQ Nara-shi. |
| Keh-deo Meo ethnoreligionists | sPT | 3-d | | 126,000 | 1 | chin | A | 1 | A tribe and dialect of Eastern Meo. In southwest, Guizhou Province. Polytheists 97%. M=CSI. |
| Kelao ethnoreligionists | sPT | 3-d | | 495,000 | 2 | chin | A | 0 | In Yunnan, Guizhou, Guangxi, Hunan; Viet Nam. Only 1.4% speak Gelo. Polytheists 99%. |
| Kendayan Dayak ethnoreligionists | sAT | 3-d | | 114,000 | 1 | indo | B | 3 | Kalimantan Barat. Near Bengkayang, also jungle. Few bilinguals in Indonesian. Animists 55%. |

*Continued opposite*

*Table 17–5 continued*

| *Name of religion/religionists* 1 | *Pedigree* 2 | *Type* 3 | *Begun* 4 | *Adherents* 5 | *Ext* 6 | *Coun* 7 | *W* 8 | *X* 9 | *E. g. = examples; name for God, other religions present, D=denominations, M=missions.* 10 |
|---|---|---|---|---|---|---|---|---|---|
| Kenjoshu | sTJMB | 2-e | | 4,900 | 1 | japa | B | 1 | Sect of Tendai Buddhism. HQ Hiroshima-ken. |
| Kenya Episcopal Conference | R-nC | 7-c | 1976 | 7,000,000 | 1 | keny | C | 5 | KEC. HQ Nairobi. |
| Keshdari Sikhs | sK | 2-d | 1700 | 300,000 | 5 | indi | B | 1 | Less committed Sikhs not properly initialed as Khalsa Sikhs. |
| Kettaniyah | sUM | 2-e | | 10,000 | 1 | moro | A | 0 | Sufi order, active in Morocco, associated with Alawiya order. |
| Khalidiyah | ssUM | 2-e | c1850 | 50,000 | 3 | syri | B | 3 | Offshoot of Mujaddidiya Sufi order; widespread to India et al. |
| Khalkha Mongol ethnoreligionists | sST | 3-d | | 507,000 | 1 | mong | A | 0 | God=Borgan. Lamaists 30%, shamanists 30%, nonreligious 28% atheists 10%, Muslims 1%. |
| Khalsa Sikhs | sK | 2-c | 1699 | 4,000,000 | 20 | indi | B | 2 | Pure Ones. Sikh inner-circle created by F=Guru Gobind Singh. |
| Khalwatiyah | sUM | 2-e | c1350 | 5,000 | 20 | leba | B | 5 | Persian, Kurdish, Turkish, Albanian, Syrian origins. |
| Khandeshi ethnoreligionists | sAT | 3-c | | 1,162,000 | 1 | indi | A | 0 | Maharashtra, Gujarat. Dialects: Ahirani, Dangri, Kunbi, Rangari. Animists 70%, Hindus 30%. |
| Kharijites | KXM | 2-c | c630 | 1,636,000 | 10 | iraq | A | 0 | 'Exiters' 3rd main sect of Islam (after Sunnis, Shias). Only Ibadis remain. HQ Basra. |
| Khasi ethnoreligionists | sAT | 3-d | | 546,000 | 2 | indi | B | 5 | God=Blei. Tribals in Assam, Jammu, Kashmir, Manipur, Punjab. UP. Animists 50%. D=4. M=6. |
| Khmu ethnoreligionists | sAT | 3-d | | 714,000 | 5 | laos | A | 2 | Scattered across north. Also Thailand, Burma, USA, France, China. Animists 94%. D=2. M=5. |
| Khoisan ethnoreligionists | sAT | 3-e | | 90,000 | 9 | bots | B | 5 | Khoi Hottentots, San Bushmen. |
| Khulusiyah | ssUM | 2-e | | 10,000 | 1 | turk | A | 1 | Sufi suborder of Qadiriya, shut down by Kemal Ataturk in 1924. |
| Kikueikai Kyodan | sNN | 2-e | | 3,500 | 1 | japa | B | 3 | HQ Kita Kawachi-gun, Osaka-fu. |
| Kinga ethnoreligionists | sAT | 3-d | | 106,000 | 1 | tanz | B | 4 | God=Unguve. Livingston Mountains, shores of Lake Malawi. Animists 40%. D=2. M=2. |
| Kinpusan Shugen Honshu | sTJMB | 2-d | 1945 | 255,000 | 1 | japa | B | 1 | Sect of Tendai Buddhism. HQ Nara-ken. Mountain worship, magical rituals. |
| Kipsigis ethnoreligionists | sAT | 3-d | | 171,000 | 1 | keny | C | 5 | God=Jehovah. In Kalenjin cluster, Rift Valley and west. Animists 20%. D=13. M=4. |
| Kishanganjia ethnoreligionists | sHAT | 3-d | | 101,000 | 1 | indi | A | 0 | In Bihar State, a Bengali-Assamese language. Hinduized animists 99%. |
| Kiso Ontake Honkyo | sHS | 2-d | | 231,000 | 1 | japa | B | 1 | HQ Kiso-gun, Nagano-ken. |
| Kissi ethnoreligionists | sAT | 3-d | | 276,000 | 1 | guin | B | 2 | Also in Sierra Leone. Animists 77%, Muslims 13%. Resistant to advance of Islam. D=4. M=3. |
| Klausenberg-Zanz Hasidism | sOJ | 2-e | | 10,000 | 1 | isra | B | 2 | One of major contemporary Hasidic parties in Israel. |
| Kodo Kyodan | sTJMB | 2-d | 1948 | 391,000 | 1 | japa | B | 1 | Sect of Tendai Buddhism. HQ Yokohama-shi. F=Okano Shodo and wife Kimiko. |
| Kofyar ethnoreligionists | sAT | 3-d | | 141,000 | 1 | nige | A | 1 | Plateau State, 3 LGAs: Shendam, Mangu. Many dialects. Animists 80%, Muslims 10%. D=2. |
| Kokawa Kannon Shu | sTJMB | 2-e | | 18,600 | 1 | japa | B | 2 | Sect of Tendai Buddhism. HQ Wakayama-ken. |
| Kokuchukai | sNJMB | 2-e | | 28,700 | 1 | japa | B | 1 | HQ Edogawa-ku, Tokyo. |
| Komi-Zyrian ethnoreligionists | sST | 3-d | | 161,000 | 2 | russ | B | 3 | God=Jen. North Komi. West of Vogul peoples. Pastoralists, hunters. Shamanists 45%. D=1. |
| Komyo Shingonshu | sSJMB | 2-d | | 102,000 | 1 | japa | B | 0 | HQ Wakayama-ken. |
| Kongoshu | sTJMB | 2-d | | 142,000 | 1 | japa | B | 0 | Sect of Tendai Buddhism. HQ Ehime-ken. |
| Konkomba ethnoreligionists | sAT | 3-d | | 391,000 | 2 | ghan | B | 3 | Northeast. Also in Togo. Animists 79%, Muslims 1%(Sunnis,Ahmadis). M=SVD,WEC,WF. |
| Kono ethnoreligionists | sAT | 3-d | | 182,000 | 4 | sier | B | 2 | God=Yataa. Northeast. Wealthy diamond-mining area. Animists 78%, Muslims 10%.D=11.M=7. |
| Konpirakyo | sTS | 2-e | | 10,000 | 1 | japa | B | 1 | HQ Kagoshima-shi. |
| Konso ethnoreligionists | sAT | 3-d | | 195,000 | 2 | ethi | B | 2 | South of Lake Ciamo. Agriculturalists. Animists 80%. D=ECMY,WLEC. M=SIM. |
| Kopu ethnoreligionists | sPT | 3-d | | 375,000 | 1 | chin | A | 0 | A Lolo language of the Northern Yi. Northern Yunnan Province, Luchuan area. Polytheists 99%. |
| Korea Baptist Convention | P-Bap-AC | 6-c | 1890 | 1,138,000 | 1 | souk | B | 5 | Hankuk Chimnehwei Yonmaeng. East Asia Ch. 1950,M=FMB-SBC. 365n,72f,1H,1s,3122Y. |
| Korea Evangelical Fellowship | E-nC | 7-c | 1953 | 3,700,000 | 1 | souk | B | 5 | KEF. |
| Korean Apostolics | I-3aK-tC | 5-e | 1982 | 8,400 | 1 | usa | C | 5 | 154 missionaries in 38 countries: Russia 670 chs, China 600 chs, Viet Nam 280 chs. |
| Korean Buddhists | KMB | 2-c | 372 | 7,100,000 | 20 | souk | B | 2 | Mahayana Buddhism. |
| Korean cell-based networks | I-3kK-tC | 5-c | 1958 | 1,315,000 | 1 | souk | B | 5 | E.g. YFGC. Adult members: (1961) 800. 100 staff, 50,000 cells. Since 1985 part of AoG. |
| Korean charismatics | I-3cK-tC | 5-e | c1980 | 85,400 | 1 | souk | B | 5 | Based in Anyang city. Several satellite churches. |
| Korean Christian Federation | C-nC | 7-e | 1970 | 12,000 | 1 | nork | A | 5 | KCF. Grouping recognized as official by government regime. |
| Korean ethnoreligionists | sST | 3-c | | 1,619,000 | 26 | chin | B | 3 | God=Hananim. Hyanbian District. Shamanists 55%, Mahayana Buddhists 35%. D=3. M=2. |
| Korean Ev Council of Christian Chs | T-nC | 7-c | c1950 | 3,300,000 | 1 | souk | B | 4 | KECCC, also called NAE (National Association of Evangelicals). Fundamentalists. |
| Korean Full Gospelers | I-3fK-tC | 5-d | 1963 | 369,000 | 5 | usa | C | 5 | KFGCA. M=FGC of Seoul, Korea. Many independent Korean churches in USA. |
| Korean house-church networks | I-3hK-tC | 5-d | 1970 | 804,000 | 2 | chin | B | 5 | Inner Mongolia, Jilin, Liaoning. Most TSPM but vast house networks. M=25 agencies(S Korea). |
| Korean indig pente/charismatics | KN3ZAC | 2-c | 1910 | 3,339,000 | 30 | souk | B | 5 | Yoido FGC, Grace & Truth Ch, FGIGM, Korea Full Gospel Chs of America. D=170. |
| Korean Methodist Church | P-Met-AC | 6-c | 1884 | 1,413,000 | 1 | souk | B | 5 | KMC. Kidokyo Tae-Han Kamni-hwei. M=UMC. 914n,51f,2s(375),W=89%,1850Yy,85000z. |
| Korean New-Religionists | zN | 2-c | c1800 | 7,121,000 | 6 | souk | B | 2 | Over 200 distinct and separate new religious bodies, syncretist and nonsyncretist. |
| Korean pentecostals | I-3pK-tC | 5-d | 1945 | 499,000 | 5 | souk | B | 5 | Independent pentecostals. |
| Korean radio/TV believers | I-3rK-tC | 5-e | | 94,400 | 1 | nork | A | 5 | Isolated radio believers (students, youths). FEBC is heard 2.5 hours per day. |
| Koreri cargo cultists | sCN | 2-e | 1855 | 40,000 | 1 | indo | B | 3 | Golden Age. In West Irian, scores of Konoors (prophets) announcing cargo. |
| Koro ethnoreligionists | sAT | 3-d | | 216,000 | 2 | nige | A | 1 | Kaduna State, Kachia LGA. Animists 70%, Muslims 20%. D=3. M=3. |
| Koshinto Senbokyo | sNS | 2-e | | 23,500 | 1 | japa | B | 1 | HQ Osaka-shi. |
| Kotia ethnoreligionists | sHAT | 3-d | | 253,000 | 1 | indi | A | 1 | Andhra Pradesh, Araku Valley. Lingua franca. Animists/Hindus 99%. D=3. M=6. |
| Kotohira Honkyo | sTS | 2-d | | 136,000 | 1 | japa | B | 0 | HQ Kagawa-ken. |
| Koya ethnoreligionists | sAT | 3-d | | 272,000 | 1 | indi | A | 2 | God=Devudu. In AP, MP. Aborigines in Hyderabad. Animists 78%, Hindus 20%. D=1. M=7. |
| Koyasan Shingonshu | sSJMB | 2-c | 815 | 4,876,000 | 5 | japa | B | 0 | HQ Wakayama-ken. Oldest sect of Tantric Buddhism in Japan. |
| Kpelle ethnoreligionists | sAT | 3-d | | 262,000 | 1 | libe | B | 3 | Resistant to Islam. Animists 43%, Muslims 25%. D=8 (including several AICs). M=5. |
| Krama | sTH | 2-e | 400 | 50,000 | 1 | nepa | A | 0 | Tantric Hindu cult originating in Swat cremation-ground cults. |
| Krio ethnoreligionists | sAT | 3-d | | 223,000 | 1 | sier | B | 5 | Muslims 12%(Maliki Sunnis). 35 Christian denominations including many AICs. M=6. |
| Krishnaists | zH | 2-c | | 5,000,000 | 4 | indi | B | 3 | Worshipers of Krishna via numerous sects including ISKCON. |
| Kubrawiyah | sUM | 2-e | c900 | 3,000 | 1 | turm | A | 1 | Spiritual center of Sufi brotherhood. A major Junayli Sufi order. |
| Kuga Sorta | sSN | 2-e | c1872 | 5,000 | 1 | russ | B | 5 | Big Candle. Cheremis syncretism in Mari ASSR. Christ greatest prophet. Persecuted by ROC. |
| Kui ethnoreligionists | sAT | 3-d | | 584,000 | 4 | indi | A | 2 | Orissa, Udayagiri area; AP, MP, Tamil Nadu. Hindus 54%, animists 45%. D=5. M=5. |
| Kumina | sCU | 2-e | c1700 | 1,000 | 1 | jama | B | 5 | Cumina. Small African ancestor cult similar to Convince. 3 ranks of zombie (gods). |
| Kurama Kokyo | sTJMB | 2-e | | 7,400 | 1 | japa | B | 1 | Sect of Tendai Buddhism. HQ Kyoto-shi. |
| Kuranko ethnoreligionists | sAT | 3-d | | 183,000 | 1 | sier | A | 1 | God=Alla. Also in Guinea. Literates 1%. Animists 68%, Muslims 30%(Maliki Sunnis). D=3. M=4. |
| Kurfei ethnoreligionists | sAT | 3-d | | 194,000 | 1 | niga | A | 1 | God=Allah. Animists 95%, Muslims 5%. Resistant to Islam and Christianity. D=ECWA. M=2. |
| Kuria ethnoreligionists | sAT | 3-d | | 147,000 | 2 | tanz | B | 5 | East of Lake Victoria; many in Kenya. Animists 27%. D=6. M=3. |
| Kurku ethnoreligionists | sAT | 3-d | | 312,000 | 1 | indi | A | 1 | God=Bhagwan. Southern MP, Betul District; Maharashtra. Animists 62%, Hindus 28%. D=2. |
| Kurotani Jodoshu | sPJMB | 2-d | | 407,000 | 2 | japa | B | 1 | HQ Kyoto-shi. |
| Kurozumi-kyo | sTS | 2-d | 1814 | 574,000 | 2 | japa | B | 3 | Sect Shinto. Faith healing thru sun goddess Amaterasu. F=Kurozumi Munetada (1780-1850). |
| Kuruba ethnoreligionists | sAT | 3-d | | 708,000 | 1 | indi | A | 1 | Animists 80%, Hindus 19%. D=Gospel in Action,Brethren,RCC,CSI,UELCI. M=IEM,IBT,QCI. |
| Kurumba ethnoreligionists | sAT | 3-d | | 143,000 | 2 | burk | A | 1 | Yatenga Province. Animists 81%, Muslims 8%. D=2. M=5. |
| Kwanka ethnoreligionists | sAT | 3-d | | 138,000 | 1 | nige | A | 0 | Plateau State (Mangu LGA), Bauchi State. Animists 60%, Muslims 37%. |
| Kwanumjong | sKMB | 2-d | 1940 | 618,000 | 1 | souk | B | 0 | Daihan-Bulgyo-Kwanumjong (Korean Buddhist Sect of Sattva). |
| Kyuseishukyo | sNN | 2-d | | 128,000 | 1 | japa | B | 2 | HQ Beppu-shi, Oita-ken. |
| Laachi | ssUM | 2-e | | 2,000 | 1 | kirg | A | 0 | Highly politicized branch of Yasawiya Sufi order, Kirghizia. |
| Laestadianism | P-Lut-AC | 6-d | 1844 | 200,000 | 1 | swed | C | 5 | Revival among Lapps across Scandinavia. F=L. L. Laestadius. |
| Lahoris | LAXM | 2-d | c1920 | 900,000 | 30 | paki | A | 1 | Ahmadi sect, closest to main Islam. Mosque. |
| Lahu ethnoreligionists | sAT | 3-d | | 263,000 | 3 | chin | B | 5 | God=Guisha. Southwest Yunnan, also in Burma, Thailand, Laos. Animists 50%, Buddhists 10%. |
| Lakota ethnoreligionists | sAT | 3-e | | 2,200 | 1 | usa | C | 5 | Remnants of Amerindian religion of Sioux (Dakotas). |
| Lamaists | LB | 2-b | 640 | 21,490,000 | 30 | chin | B | 1 | Tibet. Worldwide diaspora. Mantra 'Om mani padmi hum'. 1959, 6,000 monasteries destroyed. |
| Lamba ethnoreligionists | sAT | 3-d | | 138,000 | 3 | togo | B | 2 | Region of Kande; also in Benin. Literates 20%. Animists 49%, Muslims 34%. D=2. M=6. |
| Lanka Vipassana Bhavana Samitiya | sTB | 2-e | 1952 | 1,000 | 1 | sril | B | 3 | Lanka Insight Meditation Society. Lay meditation. |
| Lao ethnoreligionists | sBAT | 3-d | | 407,000 | 6 | laos | B | 2 | Monolinguals 100%. Theravada Buddhists 80%(1,900 pagodas), animists 10%. Y=1630. D=2. |
| Lao United Buddhists Association | nB | 7-c | 1977 | 2,650,000 | 2 | laos | A | 1 | LUBA. 7,000 monks, 10,000 novices, in 2,800 monasteries. |
| Laotian Theravada Buddhism | sTB | 2-c | | 2,500,000 | 2 | laos | A | 1 | State religion until 1975. |
| latent (inactive) Christians | LC | 2-a | | 1,351,743,000 | 238 | fran | C | 2 | Numbers fluctuate over 20 centuries. 90% of all Christians throughout the Dark Ages. |
| Latin- & Eastern-rite jurisdiction | R-LEr-tC | 5-c | 1084 | 1,497,000 | 9 | braz | C | 5 | E.g. C=101+14+329. |
| Latin American Apostolics | I-3aL-tC | 5-d | 1929 | 316,000 | 6 | colo | C | 5 | Panamerican Mission. Run by Colombians. Rapid growth. Medellin, Bogota. |
| Latin American cell-based chs | I-3kL-tC | 5-d | c1965 | 282,000 | 2 | elsa | C | 5 | E.g. Elim Christian Mission. Massive evangelism, church growth. 116,000 in 600 weekly calls. |
| Latin American charismatics | I-3cL-tC | 5-d | 1957 | 322,000 | 8 | mexi | C | 5 | E.g. Association of Vineyard Chs (13 chs), Tree of Life Ch (42 chs), house chs everywhere. |
| Latin American Ev Fellowship | K-cC | 7-c | 1982 | 1,500,000 | 18 | arge | C | 5 | CONELA. HQ Buenos Aires (Argentina). Rival to CLAI, with 98 member bodies. |
| Latin American Full Gospelers | I-3fL-tC | 5-d | 1958 | 108,000 | 2 | mexi | C | 5 | E.g. Miracle Revival Crusade Chs. M=MRC,GSMA(USA). |
| Latin American grassroots chs | I-3gL-tC | 5-c | 1928 | 2,657,000 | 15 | chil | C | 5 | Vast numbers of bodies in 15 countries. Including Association of Vineyard Chs (3 chs). |
| Latin American house-churches | I-3hL-tC | 5-e | 1963 | 60,000 | 3 | mexi | C | 5 | E.g. Centers of Christian Love. Christian Fellowship Chs. S.Mexico among Mixtecs. M=MRC. |
| Latin American neocharismatics | I-3nL-tC | 5-e | 1960 | 4,800 | 2 | colo | C | 5 | E.g. IBC. Bible Ch of Colombia. M=BALL World Missions (USA). School, clinic. |
| Latin American neocharismatics | I-3xL-tC | 5-e | 1976 | 22,600 | 1 | hond | C | 5 | E.g. Living Love Christian Organization. Cell-based, with 1,000 house cells. |
| Latin American Oneness chs | I-3oL-tC | 5-c | 1911 | 1,270,000 | 14 | mexi | C | 5 | Light of the World Ch. Messiah Aaron, died 1964. Vast tabernacle Guadalajara. 1h. |
| Latin American pentecostals | I-3pL-tC | 5-c | 1909 | 6,780,000 | 22 | chil | C | 5 | E.g. IMP. Pentecostal Meth Ch. Split ex Methodists; 20 schisms since. 1967, M=IPHC. 120n,1u. |
| Latin American radio/TV chs | I-3rL-tC | 5-e | 1931 | 92,200 | 7 | cuba | B | 5 | Isolated radio believers (students &c). R=480(279 HCJB, 92 FEBC, TWR, Radio Vatican). |
| Latino-Hisp grassroots believers | LN3ZAC | 2-b | 1909 | 11,916,000 | 24 | mexi | C | 5 | Autochthonous grassroots (GR) churches, IMPC, IPP, IOAP, IEMP, IEPC. D=990. Hispanic. |
| Latin-rite Catholics | R-Lat-tC | 5-a | 1491 | 1,043,106,000 | 229 | mexi | C | 5 | E.g. Catholic Ch of Mexico. C=37+3+146. |
| Latter-day Saints | m-LdS-tC | 5-c | 1830 | 8,960,000 | 102 | usa | C | 2 | Mormons. HQ Utah. Also 700,000 overseas. (1970) 17272n,91237Y. (1990) 28962n. |
| Latvian Orthodox | O-Lav-tC | 5-d | c1130 | 260,000 | 1 | latv | C | 5 | Before 1990, 67% Russians, Ukrainians, and other Slavs, 33% Latvians. |

*Continued overleaf*

*Table 17–5 continued*

| Name of religion/religionists 1 | Pedigree 2 | Type 3 | Begun 4 | Adherents 5 | Ext 6 | Coun 7 | W 8 | X 9 | E. g. = examples; name for God, other religions present, D=denominations, M=missions. 10 |
|---|---|---|---|---|---|---|---|---|---|
| Lazarists | cm-oC | 9-e | 1625 | 4,100 | | ital | C | 5 | CM. |
| League of African Chs in Swaziland | I-nC | 7-d | 1937 | 380,000 | 1 | swaz | C | 5 | LACS. Inhlanganl Yamabandla Enkola Esizwe. Serves 30 African indigenous AICs. |
| Legionaires of Christ | lc-oC | 9-e | 1941 | 1,400 | | ital | C | 5 | LC. |
| Lele ethnoreligionists | sAT | 3-d | | 325,000 | 5 | burk | A | 1 | Sangui Province. Animists 85%, Muslims 5%. D=RCC,AoG,EBBF. M=SIL,NBC,FMB. |
| Lesotho Catholic Bishops' Conf | S-nC | 7-d | 1980 | 806,000 | 1 | leso | C | 5 | LCBC. HQ Maseru. |
| Li ethnoreligionists | sPAT | 3-c | | 1,235,000 | 1 | chin | A | 1 | Tropical mountains in Hainan. Polytheists (animists) 100%. D=TSPM. M=5. |
| Liberal Catholic Gnostics | m-Lib-tC | 5-e | 1953 | 37,300 | 1 | fran | C | 1 | E.g. Apostolic Gnostic Ch. Closed groups protecting Gospel from world. Belgium, Brazil, Italy. |
| Liberal Catholics | I-Lib-tC | 5-d | 1915 | 109,000 | 18 | phil | C | 3 | E.g. Iglesia Watawat ng Lahi. Ex RCC. Catholic-type hierarchy. Rizalist, spiritist. |
| Liberian Council of Churches | K-nC | 7-d | | 270,000 | 1 | libe | B | 5 | LCC. |
| Liborismo | sCU | 2-e | 1900 | 70,000 | 1 | domr | C | 5 | Afro-Caribbean spiritists. F=Liborio. 90% are baptized RCs. |
| Lingayats | sSH | 2-c | c1150 | 1,000,000 | 1 | indi | B | 0 | Virashaivas. Saivite sect worshiping linga. Kannada-speaking (Karnataka). |
| Lobi ethnoreligionists | sAT | 3-d | | 476,000 | 3 | burk | A | 1 | Also in Ivory Coast, a few in Ghana. Animists 98%, Muslims 1%. D=2. M=2. |
| Lo-Bos Yali Movement | sCN | 10-f | 1946 | 200 | 1 | papu | C | 3 | Law Boss. Letub Cargo cult among Tangu on Rai coast, New Guinea. F=Yali Singina. |
| Loma ethnoreligionists | sAT | 3-d | | 101,000 | 2 | libe | B | 3 | God=Gala. Loffa County, also Guinea. Resists Islam. Animists 60%, Muslims 25%. D=3. M=5. |
| Lomwe ethnoreligionists | sAT | 3-d | | 857,000 | 2 | moza | B | 4 | Zambezia Province. Also in Malawi. Animists 65%, Muslims 7%. D=7. M=5. |
| Losso ethnoreligionists | sAT | 3-d | | 111,000 | 1 | togo | B | 3 | Doufelgou Prefecture. Animists 75%. D=RCC,EET,AoG. M=OFM,SMA,FSCJ,SIL,FMB. |
| Lotuko ethnoreligionists | sAT | 3-d | | 159,000 | 1 | suda | B | 4 | God=Hollum. Torit District. Animists 58%, Muslims 4%(Sunnis). Highly resistant to Islam. D=3. |
| Lovedu ethnoreligionists | sAT | 3-d | | 101,000 | 1 | soua | B | 3 | Ritual of Rain Queen. Close to Venda, Shona. Animists 50%. Nominal Christians 26%. D=AICs. |
| Low Church Anglicans | A-Low-tC | 5-b | 1091 | 23,207,000 | 15 | nige | B | 5 | In Australia, Nigeria. Mushrooming to 63 Dioceses. M=CMS(UK). 68f,1p,1s,1u. |
| Low-caste Hindu believers in C | I-Hin-AC | 6-c | 1800 | 8,400,000 | 1 | indi | B | 2 | Numerous movements but mostly isolated believers and families witnessing within Hinduism. |
| Lu ethnoreligionists | sPT | 3-d | | 467,000 | 5 | chin | A | 1 | South Yunnan. Also Burma, Laos, Thailand. Viet Nam. Polytheists 80%, Buddhists 18%. M=1. |
| Lubavich Hasidim | sOJ | 2-e | c1800 | 5,000 | 1 | isra | B | 2 | Hasidic movement stressing intellect. Strong work in former USSR. |
| Lui-ists | sSN | 2-d | | 900,000 | 1 | taiw | B | 3 | One of 2 major sects within modern Taiwanese I-kuan Tao (Unity). |
| Lutheran Ch-Missouri Synod | P-Lut-AC | 6-c | 1847 | 2,542,000 | 1 | usa | C | 5 | LCMS. German origin. 1976 schism: AELC. 7041n,16s(1041),5552t(815522),W=45%,94363Yy. |
| Lutheran World Federation | L-fC | 4-b | | 80,000,000 | 150 | swit | C | 5 | LWF. HQ Geneva. |
| Lutheran/Reformed united ch | I-LuR-tC | 5-e | c1970 | 1,400 | 1 | indi | B | 5 | E.g. Fundamentalist split ex CSI, D North Kerala (United Basel Mission Ch). HQ Calicut. |
| Lutheran/Reformed united ch | P-LuR-tC | 5-b | 1517 | 14,345,000 | 22 | neth | C | 5 | E.g. VPKN. 1995, merger of NHK, GKN, and ELKN under way, aiming to finish by AD 2000. |
| Lutherans | P-Lut-tC | 5-b | 1517 | 61,894,000 | 122 | swed | C | 5 | E.g. Svenska Kyrkan. Begun 600 years before Reformation. 13 Diocs. Women clergy. 3350n. |
| Lwena ethnoreligionists | sAT | 3-d | | 121,000 | 3 | zamb | B | 5 | Northwestern, Western Provinces. Mainly in Angola, also in Zaire. Animists 40%. D=11. M=6. |
| Maasai ethnoreligionists | sAT | 3-d | | 557,000 | 2 | keny | B | 5 | God=engAi. Kajiado, Narok; Tanzania. Animists 55%. D=RCC,EFMK,CPK,LCK,AIC. M=18. |
| Macedonian Orthodox | O-Mac-tC | 5-c | 1018 | 1,285,000 | 5 | mace | C | 5 | 1919 integrated into Serbian Orthodox Ch, 1967 declared its independence. 7 bishops. |
| Macedonian Orthodox Church | O-Mac-AC | 6-c | 60 | 1,216,000 | 1 | mace | C | 5 | 1919 integrated into Serbian Orthodox Ch, 1967 declared its independence. 7 bishops. |
| Macumba | sBU | 2-d | c1800 | 100,000 | 1 | braz | C | 5 | Afro-Brazilian spiritists in Rio, Sao Paulo. Magic. More violent and close to Voodoo. |
| Madariya | sUM | 2-c | c1410 | 4,000,000 | 25 | indi | B | 2 | Similar to Hindu holy men; Bengal, north India, also in Nepal. Mostly widespread across S Asia. |
| Madhva Gaudiya Vairagins | sVH | 2-e | | 4,000 | 1 | indi | B | 1 | Order of Vaishnava ascetics prevalent in Orissa state. |
| Mafdal | qOJ | 8-d | 1904 | 100,000 | 1 | isra | B | 2 | National Religious Party. Founded as religio-political Orthodox party. Zionist. |
| Magico-religionists | VN | 2-e | | 10,000 | 5 | brit | C | 5 | Practitioners of magic, wizardry, spells, curses. |
| Maguzawa ethnoreligionists | sAT | 3-d | | 100,000 | 1 | nige | B | 3 | God=Allah. `Pagan Hausa' in North. A tribe of Hausa, 90% animists. Y=1920. D=4. M=3. |
| Maha Bodhi Society | sTB | 2-b | 1900 | 10,000,000 | 20 | sril | B | 4 | MBS. Great Enlightenment Society. Worldwide missions. |
| Mahafaly ethnoreligionists | sAT | 3-d | | 180,000 | 1 | mada | B | 3 | Small area along southwest coast of island. Animists 75%. D=RCC(D-Tulear). M=AA. |
| Mahanikaya | sT-oB | 9-d | c1700 | 200,000 | 2 | thai | B | 2 | Largest Theravada fraternity in Thailand: 95% of 28,000 monasteries, with 200,000 monks. |
| Mahanubhavs | sVH | 2-e | | 5,000 | 1 | indi | B | 1 | Manbhavs. Vaishnava devotional movement in Maharashtra. |
| Mahayanists | MB | 2-a | | 202,233,000 | 115 | japa | B | 1 | Greater Vehicle of Salvation. Family of lineages. Main cultures: Tibeto-Mongol, Sino-Japanese. |
| Mahdavis | sXM | 2-e | 1480 | 2,000 | 1 | indi | B | 2 | Began with a mahdi Sayyid Ahmad in 1480. Very few groups today, mainly Hyderabad, Gujarat. |
| Mahdibaghwalas | sMIHM | 10-f | 1897 | 300 | 1 | indi | B | 0 | Subsect of Daudis. |
| Mahdiyah | sPXM | 2-d | 1881 | 600,000 | 1 | suda | B | 2 | F=Muhammad Ahmad (a Sufi shaykh). Rebels until 1989. Term for all Mahdi-led movements. |
| Mainline active Charismatics | V2ZAC | 2-b | 1960 | 114,029,000 | 225 | phil | C | 5 | All in nonpentecostal churches regularly attending Renewal activities. D=6,500. |
| Mainline Postcharismatics | x2ZAC | 2-b | 1973 | 61,827,000 | 150 | fran | C | 5 | Those who no longer attend Renewal activities but still call selves Charismatics. D=3,540. |
| Maitili ethnoreligionists | sHAT | 3-c | | 1,575,000 | 1 | indi | A | 2 | Tirahutia. In Bihar, MP, WB; Nepal. Educated high-caste Hindus 95%. D=RCC,CNI. M=10. |
| Majelis Upasaka Pandita Agama BI | nB | 7-d | c1975 | 500,000 | 1 | indo | B | 3 | MUABI. Council of Buddhist Lay Spiritual Advisors of Indonesia. Married, no monastic rules. |
| Makoto no Jodo Shinshu Jokojiha | sPJMB | 2-d | | 169,000 | 2 | japa | B | 0 | HQ Fukuoka-shi. |
| Makoto no Michi | sNN | 2-e | | 7,100 | 1 | japa | B | 3 | HQ Setagaya-ku, Tokyo. |
| Makoto no Michikyo | sTS | 2-e | | 10,500 | 1 | japa | B | 3 | In Sect Shinto organization. HQ Ehime-ken. |
| Makua ethnoreligionists | sAT | 3-c | | 1,329,000 | 9 | moza | B | 3 | Animists 59%, Muslims 18%(Shafi Sunnis). D=3. M=14. |
| Makuana ethnoreligionists | sAT | 3-c | | 1,775,000 | 1 | moza | B | 3 | Nampula, south of Meeto area. Animists 59%, Muslims 20%. D=RCC. |
| Malangs | ssUM | 2-e | | 8,000 | 1 | indi | B | 2 | Sufi male religious mendicants (Punjab, Deccan) who totally ignore world, society. Use hashish. |
| Malankara Orth Syrian C of the East | q-fC | 4-c | c52 | 2,197,000 | 20 | indi | B | 5 | C=Catholicossate. Malankara OSCE. Syrians. 10 dioceses, 22 bishops, 1,458 chs, 950 clergy. |
| Malankara rite | R-Mal-tC | 5-d | 1932 | 332,000 | 1 | indi | C | 5 | Kerala. Malayalam, Tamil. 1p. |
| Malayic Dayak ethnoreligionists | sAT | 3-d | | 573,000 | 1 | indo | B | 2 | Kalimantan. West central, to Delang in south. Animists 80%. D=NTM. |
| Malaysia Council of Christian Chs | T-nC | 7-e | | 5,000 | 1 | malb | B | 4 | MCCC. |
| Maldevidan cultists | sSN | 2-e | c1800 | 10,000 | 2 | mart | C | 5 | Syncretistic Hindu/RC mix (Vishnu=Christ). Originally Tamil coolies from India, now Creoles. |
| Malikites | MSM | 2-a | c790 | 221,900,000 | 65 | nige | B | 3 | One of the 4 major schools of law. North, West, and Central Africa, Upper Egypt. Traditionalists. |
| Malinke ethnoreligionists | sAT | 3-d | | 165,000 | 10 | ghan | A | 1 | God=Alla. In 10 West African countries. Animists 65%, Muslims 30%(Sunnis). |
| Malta Episcopal Conference | R-nC | 7-d | 1971 | 368,000 | 1 | malt | C | 5 | MEC. Konferenza Episkopali Maltija. KEM. HQ Floriana. |
| Mamara Senufo ethnoreligionists | sAT | 3-d | | 254,000 | 1 | mali | A | 2 | Northern Senufo. Animists 43%, Muslims 55%. Many fetish houses (temples). D=2. M=5. |
| Mambwe ethnoreligionists | sAT | 3-d | | 130,000 | 2 | zamb | B | 5 | Northeastern Northern Province. Also in Tanzania. Animists 50%. D=5. M=1. |
| Mamprusi ethnoreligionists | sAT | 3-d | | 247,000 | 2 | ghan | A | 1 | Also in Togo. Animists 81%, Muslims 14%(Sunnis,Ahmadis). D=8. M=5. |
| Man Cao Lan ethnoreligionists | sPT | 3-d | | 137,000 | 2 | viet | A | 0 | Moncay Province, North Viet Nam/China border. Also in China. Polytheists 99%. |
| Manchu ethnoreligionists | sST | 3-c | | 2,188,000 | 1 | chin | B | 2 | God=Shang-ti. Folk-religionists 70%, shamanists 20%, Buddhists 10%. D=TSPM. |
| Mandeans | MY | 2-e | AD c20 | 39,000 | 2 | iraq | A | 1 | Sabeans. Subbas. Gnostic beliefs, Palestinian/Syrian origin. Own vast literature. Decline. |
| Mandinka ethnoreligionists | sAT | 3-d | | 112,000 | 3 | gamb | A | 1 | God=Yau. Also Senegal. Muslims 89%(Maliki Sunnis, some Ahmadis),animists 10%. D=4. M=4. |
| Mandyak ethnoreligionists | sAT | 3-d | | 223,000 | 5 | gunb | A | 1 | Also Senegal, Gambia, France. Animists 79%(strong ancestor cult), Muslims 13%. D=3. M=3. |
| Manggarai ethnoreligionists | sAT | 3-d | | 270,000 | 1 | indo | A | 1 | Nusa Tenggara, Flores. Close to Riung. 43 dialects. Muslims 50%, animists 46%. D=RCC. |
| Manipuri ethnoreligionists | sAT | 3-d | | 106,000 | 3 | indi | B | 2 | God=Ishwar. Assam, Manipur. Hindus 85%, animists 7%, Muslims 6.5%. M=4. |
| Manji Kyodan | sSJMB | 2-d | | 276,000 | 1 | japa | B | 0 | HQ Fukuoka-ken. |
| Manna Church International | k-fC | 4-d | 1980 | 200,000 | 35 | port | C | 5 | Mana-Igreja Crista. Cell-based megachurch in Lisbon Tents. Abroad: in 35 countries. |
| Mano ethnoreligionists | sAT | 3-d | | 221,000 | 2 | libe | A | 1 | God=Wala. Nimba County; also Guinea. Animists 95%. D=6. M=2. |
| Manseren cargo cultists | sCN | 2-e | 1855 | 50,000 | 1 | indo | B | 3 | 'The Lord Himself'. Since Dutch arrival in West Irian many prophets foretell coming of cargo. |
| Manyika ethnoreligionists | sAT | 3-d | | 353,000 | 2 | zimb | C | 5 | God=Mwari. Manicaland Province, Umtali; also in Mozambique. Animists 30%. D=10. M=6. |
| Maori Council of Churches | I-nC | 7-d | | 250,000 | 1 | newz | C | 5 | MCC. |
| Mao-shan | sD | 2-d | 364 | 100,000 | 1 | chin | B | 0 | One of Taoism's 86 major sects. Meeting on Mount Mao to receive Scriptures. |
| Mappillas | zSM | 2-d | | 100,000 | 2 | indi | B | 2 | Malayalam-speaking Muslims of Kerala. |
| Mapuche ethnoreligionists | sPT | 3-d | | 122,000 | 2 | chil | C | 5 | God=Ngünemapun. Polytheists 20%, Baha'is 1%. D=5. M=5. |
| Mar Thoma Syrian Ch of Malabar | v-fC | 4-d | 1843 | 875,000 | 25 | indi | B | 5 | Reform ex Orthodox Syrian Church of the East. 6 dioceses, 300 clergy. |
| Marba ethnoreligionists | sAT | 3-d | | 125,000 | 1 | chad | B | 3 | Southwest, Logone district. 20% urban. Animists 79%, a few Muslims. D=2. M=3. |
| Marenje ethnoreligionists | sAT | 3-d | | 435,000 | 1 | moza | B | 3 | Related to Makua. Closest to Chwabo. Animists 73%, Muslims 7%. D=RCC. |
| Marginal Charismatics | m2ZAC | 2-e | 1980 | 15,000 | 15 | usa | C | 3 | Total marginal Christians in Renewal, past and present, including children and infants. D=130. |
| Marginal Christians | MAC | 2-b | 1566 | 26,060,000 | 215 | usa | C | 3 | Unitarians, CJCLdS, JWs, and bodies placing selves on periphery of mainline Christianity. |
| Marginal Evangelicals | EmAC | 2-d | c1900 | 200,000 | 10 | usa | C | 3 | Members of marginal bodies (e.g. JWs, CJCLdS) who regard themselves as Evangelicals. |
| marginal independent Christians | I-mar-tC | 5-c | 1769 | 1,183,000 | 48 | usa | C | 2 | E.g. Native American Ch NAC. 23 Chapters. In all US Indian tribes. Strict ethics; peyote eating. |
| marginal Orthodox | m-Ort-tC | 5-e | 1899 | 87,700 | 2 | russ | B | 2 | Emigrations to Canada, then returns. Villages: Caucasus, Georgia, Siberia, CAsia. |
| Mariamites | sm-oC | 9-e | 1817 | 1,800 | | ital | C | 5 | SM. |
| Marian Brothers (Schools) | fms-oC | 9-e | 1817 | 5,500 | | ital | C | 5 | FMS. |
| Marianists | sm-oC | 9-e | 1816 | 1,500 | | ital | C | 5 | SM. |
| Marka ethnoreligionists | sAT | 3-d | | 151,000 | 1 | burk | A | 1 | Animists 60%, Muslims 28%. D=RCC(D-Nouna-Dedougou),ECEBF. M=CMA,WF,CSSR. |
| Maronite rite | R-Mar-tC | 5-c | 1353 | 3,365,000 | 11 | arge | C | 5 | E.g. Arab Christians from Lebanon. |
| Maru ethnoreligionists | sPAT | 3-d | | 112,000 | 1 | myan | A | 0 | Kachin State, north Burma. Also in China. Related to Kachin. Polytheists/animists 90%. M=2. |
| Maruyamakyo | sTS | 2-e | | 13,500 | 1 | japa | B | 0 | HQ Kanagawa-ken. |
| Masa ethnoreligionists | sAT | 3-d | | 231,000 | 2 | came | B | 2 | God=Alauna. Far North Province. Densely settled. Animists 55%, Muslims 25%. D=2. M=2. |
| Masorati | sOJ | 2-e | | 1,000 | 2 | brit | C | 3 | 'Traditional Movement', close to Conservative Judaism in Israel. |
| Matengo ethnoreligionists | sAT | 3-d | | 104,000 | 2 | tanz | B | 3 | Northeast Lake Nyasa; some in Malawi and Mozambique. Animists 50%. D=1. M=OSB. |
| Maturidiyah | sHM | 2-e | c920 | 20,000 | 1 | iran | A | 1 | Rival to Ashariya school's lack of personal assurance. |
| Mauri ethnoreligionists | sAT | 3-d | | 357,000 | 1 | niga | A | 1 | God=Allah. Animists 99%. Resistant to Islam as well as to Christianity. D=ECWA. M=SIM,EMS. |
| Mawlawiyah | sUM | 2-e | c1250 | 6,000 | 10 | turk | A | 1 | Whirling Dervishes. Mevlevis. Wealthy, urban, artistocratic. Also in Eastern Europe. |
| M'Bona cult | sVN | 2-d | c1900 | 300,000 | 1 | mala | C | 2 | Tribal cult among southern Chewa in Malawi. |
| Meher Baba movement | zH | 2-d | 1924 | 600,000 | 8 | indi | B | 1 | F=Baba as silent miracle-working final avatar of God (after Rama, Jesus, &c). HQ Meherabad.. |

*Continued opposite*

*Table 17–5 continued*

| Name of religion/religionists 1 | Pedigree 2 | Type 3 | Begun 4 | Adherents 5 | Ext 6 | Coun 7 | W 8 | X 9 | E. g. = examples; name for God, other religions present, D=denominations, M=missions. 10 |
|---|---|---|---|---|---|---|---|---|---|
| Meiji Kyodan | sTS | 2-e | | 5,400 | 1 | japa | B | 1 | HQ Osaka-shi. |
| Meijikyo | sTS | 2-d | | 167,000 | 1 | japa | B | 1 | HQ Nagasaki-ken. |
| Meisan Shingonshu | sSJMB | 2-e | | 12,800 | 1 | japa | B | 1 | HQ Wakayama-shi. |
| Meiseikyo | sTS | 2-e | | 94,700 | 1 | japa | B | 1 | HQ Higashi Osaka-shi. |
| Melanesian Council of Churches | K-nC | 7-c | 1965 | 3,000,000 | 1 | papu | C | 5 | MCC. Covers PNG and SI (Solomon Islands). 1971, Catholics join. |
| Melanesian ethnoreligionists | sAT | 3-d | | 100,000 | 10 | papu | C | 5 | Remnants of animistic traditional religions among many peoples and tribes. |
| Melkite rite | R-Mel-tC | 5-c | 1683 | 1,269,000 | 12 | braz | C | 5 | M=SMSP. |
| Mende ethnoreligionists | sAT | 3-d | | 542,000 | 2 | sier | B | 3 | God=Ngewo. Also Liberia. Animists 42%, Muslims 42%(Maliki; 10,000 Ahmadis). D=11. M=9. |
| Mennonite World Conference | G-fC | 4-c | | 1,960,000 | 43 | fran | C | 5 | MWC. |
| Mennonites | P-Men-tC | 5-c | 1525 | 2,187,000 | 59 | indi | B | 5 | E.g. M=Menonnite Brethren Ch of NAmerica. 99% Telugu. 175n,14f,3H,3h,9p,100Y. |
| Merina ethnoreligionists | sAT | 3-d | | 556,000 | 2 | mada | C | 5 | Animists 12%, Muslims 1%, Baha'is 0.2%. D=70% Protestants,RCC,AICs. M=20. |
| Meru ethnoreligionists | sAT | 3-d | | 186,000 | 2 | keny | C | 5 | God=Murungu. Meru District. Animists 10%, Muslims 1%, Baha'is 1%. D=7, many AICs. M=8. |
| Mesmerism | sFN | 2-e | 1766 | 5,000 | 2 | ausz | C | 4 | F=Franz Mesmer, astrologist, hypnotist. Today, part of New Thought (Positive Thinking). |
| Mesoamerican ethnoreligionists | sPAT | 3-e | | 90,000 | 5 | mexi | C | 4 | Remnants of pre-Columbian polytheist animistic religions throughout Central America. |
| Messianic African Independents | I-3mA-tC | 5-e | 1941 | 1,400 | 1 | cong | C | 5 | E.g. ENAC. Ch of the Black Race. Kaki Ch. Founder patriarch Simon Mpadi, Zaire. Ex SA. |
| Messianic Chinese chs | I-3mC-tC | 10-f | c1980 | 180 | 1 | swit | C | 5 | E.g. a number of Local Churches. Chinese. Begun in China. |
| Messianic Hindu believers in C | HN3ZAC | 2-d | 1875 | 163,000 | 2 | indi | B | 3 | Messianic temples, organized Hindu-Christian chs: Hindu Ch of the Lord Jesus, SRM. D=5. |
| Messianic Hindu temples | I-3mH-tC | 5-d | 1875 | 163,000 | 1 | indi | B | 5 | High-caste Hindus. Anti-churches, anti-baptism. Massive healing crusades. Telugu. |
| Messianic Jewish believers in C | JN3ZAC | 2-d | 1894 | 161,000 | 14 | isra | B | 3 | Messianic Jewish synagogues, Fellowship of Messianic Congs, UMJC, IAMCS, JFJ. D=20. |
| Messianic Jewish Christians | I-Jew-tC | 5-e | 1896 | 26,000 | 1 | usa | C | 5 | Black Jews (Jewish observances). Black members. Also Africa, West Indies. |
| Messianic Jews | I-3mJ-tC | 5-d | 1894 | 161,000 | 9 | russ | B | 5 | After 1995 St Petersburg campaigns, 50,000 Russian/Ukrainian/Byelorussian Jews convert. |
| Messianic Muslim believers in C | MN3ZAC | 2-d | 1981 | 126,000 | 2 | bang | B | 3 | Messianic Muslim mosques: Jesus Mosques, Jamaat. D=3. |
| Messianic Muslim mosques | I-3mM-tC | 5-d | 1981 | 126,000 | 2 | bang | B | 5 | Jesus Mosques. M=Global Partners for Development. Most members joined 1982-1991. |
| metaphysical Christians | m-Sci-tC | 5-c | 1879 | 1,074,000 | 55 | usa | C | 2 | E.g. Christian Science. Healing ministry. HQ Mother Church, Boston. Decline 2%pa. 5848n. |
| Methodist Ch of Great Britain | P-Met-AC | 6-c | 1795 | 1,040,000 | 1 | brit | C | 5 | 1795, ex CofE. 34 Districts. Declining 1.8%pa. 4167n,20652pp,1p,4s(141),43423Yy. |
| Methodist Ch of Southern Africa | P-Met-AC | 6-c | 1806 | 2,811,000 | 1 | soua | C | 5 | British origin. 77% Black, 17% White, 5% Coloured. 1000n,4H,1j,5r,2s(60),2400t,2u. |
| Methodist Church in India | P-Met-AC | 6-c | 1856 | 1,140,000 | 1 | indi | B | 5 | SAsia CC, UMC(USA). 11 Annual Conferences. 80% Harijan (Madiga). 20H,4s,735n. |
| Methodist Church, Nigeria | P-Met-AC | 6-c | 1842 | 1,768,000 | 1 | nige | B | 5 | M=MMS(UK). 25% Yoruba, 23% Ibibio, 20% Ijebu, 20% Ibo. 40f,15H,33r,1u,4435Y,6401y. |
| Methodists | P-Met-tC | 5-b | 1747 | 23,095,000 | 108 | usa | C | 5 | E.g. UMC. 1968, EUB merger. 96% White, 4% Black. 81 Confs. 34974n,13s,W=36%. |
| Mexico native ethnoreligionists | sPT | 3-e | | 72,400 | 1 | mexi | C | 5 | Pre-Columbian religious survivals among monolingual Amerindians. |
| Micronesian Council of United CC | C-nC | 7-e | 1958 | 50,000 | 1 | mars | C | 5 | MCUCC. CC=Churches of Christ. |
| Micronesian ethnoreligionists | sPT | 3-e | | 6,200 | 6 | micr | C | 5 | Polytheists in Federated States of Micronesia, also in many other islands. |
| Middle East Council of Churches | N-rC | 7-b | 1927 | 17,574,000 | 19 | cypr | C | 5 | MECC/CEMO. Formerly, Near East Council of Churches; 1974, present name adopted. |
| Milli Gorus | qHSM | 8-e | c1970 | 10,000 | 2 | turk | A | 1 | 'National View'. Conservative religio-political body; also in Germany. |
| Milli Jamiat ul-Ulama-i Hind | ssSM | 2-e | 1988 | 2,000 | 1 | indi | B | 2 | Split from Jamiat ul-Ulama-i Hind. |
| Mina ethnoreligionists | sAT | 3-c | | 1,086,000 | 3 | indi | A | 1 | Aborigines in Rajasthan, Madhya Pradesh. Animists 98%(Hindu elements). M=4. |
| Minetaka Inari Taishakyo | sTS | 2-e | | 4,100 | 1 | japa | B | 0 | HQ Gifu-shi. |
| Mirghaniya | sUM | 2-d | 1830 | 100,000 | 1 | suda | B | 2 | Also termed Khatmiya. Sufi order in Sudan. |
| Misenkyo | sTS | 2-e | | 3,600 | 1 | japa | B | 1 | HQ Yamaguchi-ken. |
| Misogikyo | sTS | 2-d | 1875 | 119,000 | 1 | japa | B | 2 | A purification sect in Kyoha Shinto. HQ Taito-ku, Tokyo. |
| Missionaries of Charity | mc-oC | 9-e | | 4,000 | | indi | B | 5 | MC. |
| Missionaries of the SH of Jesus | msc-oC | 9-e | 1854 | 2,400 | | ital | C | 5 | MSC. SH=Sacred Heart. |
| Missionary Society | zSM | 2-d | 1923 | 100,000 | 30 | indi | B | 2 | Tablighi Jamaat. Faith Movement, Dini Dawat, Major Islamic reformers operating worldwide. |
| Mitajong | sKMB | 2-c | 1943 | 1,026,000 | 1 | souk | B | 1 | Daihan-Bulgyo-Mitajong (Korean Buddhist Sect of Sattva). |
| Mitake-kyo | sTS | 2-c | | 1,648,000 | 2 | japa | B | 2 | Mountain-worship. Shinto sect focused on Mount Ontake, a major religious center. |
| Mitamakyo | sTS | 2-e | | 55,000 | 1 | japa | B | 2 | Mountain worship. HQ Chiba-ken. |
| Mizuhokyo | sTS | 2-e | | 60,000 | 1 | japa | B | 1 | HQ Aomori-ken. |
| Mobilization of the Oppressed | rHM | 2-c | 1980 | 2,000,000 | 1 | iran | A | 0 | Bassij-i Mostazafin. Boy warriors/martyrs forced into combat with Iraq; 1 million killed. |
| Mofa ethnoreligionists | sAT | 3-d | | 286,000 | 1 | came | A | 1 | God=Zhikle. Far North Province; a few Nigeria. Animists 76%, Muslims 20%. Y=1950. D=4. |
| Molao ethnoreligionists | sAT | 3-d | | 103,000 | 1 | chin | A | 2 | North Guangxi. Mulao is unwritten; Agriculturalists. Animists 58%, Buddhists 40%. D=2. |
| Moldavian Orthodox | O-Mol-tC | 5-c | c1975 | 1,334,000 | 3 | mold | C | 5 | Ethnic Moldavians, Romanians under Russian P Moscow; autonomy 1992. 4 Dioceses, 4 bps. |
| Moldovan Orth Ch: D Chisinau | O-Mol-AC | 6-c | | 1,330,000 | 1 | mold | C | 5 | Ethnic Moldavians & Romanians under Russian P Moscow; autonomy 1992. 4 Dioceses, 4 bps. |
| Mon ethnoreligionists | sAT | 3-d | | 792,000 | 1 | myan | A | 1 | God=Kyaik. Animists 75%, Buddhists 20%. D=Ch of Christ,BBC(Mon Baptist Churches Union). |
| Mongolian Buddhism | zLB | 2-d | | 600,000 | 5 | mong | A | 1 | Viciously suppressed by Stalinists from 1917 to 1990. Now revived. |
| Monoethnic charismatics | I-3cE-tC | 5-e | 1965 | 4,800 | 1 | indi | B | 5 | Work begun first among Ho tribe. 70 Indian home missionaries. M=CAM. |
| monoethnic denominationalists | I-eth-tC | 5-c | c1880 | 1,301,000 | 2 | chin | B | 5 | E.g. Large ethnic ch, White and Black Lisu. M=CIM/OMF. Wide cross-cultural evangelism. |
| Monoethnic house churches | I-3hE-tC | 5-e | c1900 | 1,900 | 1 | chin | B | 5 | In 15 Provinces (Liaoning, Hebei). M=SJ,CSI,PRI,JENSCO,CCRC. Korea churches. |
| Monoethnic neocharismatics | I-3nE-tC | 5-e | 1956 | 69,100 | 1 | viet | B | 5 | Co-Duc-Truyen-Giao-Hoi. M=UWM(USA),WEC(1958-68). Among 14 Montagnard tribes. |
| Monoethnic pentecostals | I-3pE-tC | 5-c | 1892 | 1,460,000 | 15 | chin | B | 5 | Widespread ethnic churches among Black, Flowery, Northern, Red, Western Meo. M=AoG. |
| Montifontani | smm-oC | 9-e | 1705 | 1,100 | | ital | C | 5 | SMM. |
| Montoshu Ichimiha | sPJMB | 2-e | | 2,700 | 1 | japa | B | 0 | HQ Kitami-shi, Hokkaido. |
| Montserrat Council for Social Action. | C-nC | 7-e | | 6,100 | 1 | mont | C | 5 | MCSA. |
| Moral Re-Armament | sSN | 2-e | 1920 | 50,000 | 90 | swit | C | 5 | MRA. Oxford Group (until 1938). Began Evangelical, now panreligious. HQ Caux. |
| Moravians | P-Mor-tC | 5-d | 1457 | 603,000 | 27 | tanz | B | 5 | E.g. 2 Provinces: Western (Nyamwezi), Southern (Nyakyusa). M=MBG. 72n,5x,21f,4H,5h,1s. |
| Moriscos | sXM | 2-e | 711 | 5,000 | 1 | arge | C | 5 | Spanish Moors originally from Spain (forced to become Christians but all expelled in 1614). |
| Moslem Bosnjak Organization | qnM | 8-c | 1990 | 1,100,000 | 1 | bosn | B | 3 | MBO. Muslim Bosniacs: Hanafites. Liberals split from Party for Democratic Action. |
| Mossi ethnoreligionists | sAT | 3-c | | 1,203,000 | 9 | burk | B | 4 | Formerly imperial rulers. Animists 16%, Muslims 61%(Maliki Sunnis). D=6. M=8. |
| Mouvement Croix-Koma | I-ReC-AC | 6-e | 1964 | 16,000 | 1 | cong | C | 4 | Nailed to the Cross Movement. In RCC until 1980. |
| Mouvement de la Nahda Islamique | sXM | 2-e | 1974 | 50,000 | 1 | alge | A | 1 | Islamic Renaissance Movement. Radical, appeal to intellectuals. |
| Mouvement du Renouveau Islamique | fM | 4-e | 1978 | 5,000 | 2 | tuni | A | 1 | Movement for the Renewal of Islam. Offshoot of QPS. |
| Mov pro Unidad Ev Latinoamericana | U-cC | 7-c | 1965 | 5,000,000 | 14 | uuay | C | 5 | UNELAM. Founded in Puerto Rico as ecumenical council in formation; 1982, becomes CLAI. |
| Movement for Islamic Revolution | fM | 4-e | | 20,000 | 1 | afgh | A | 1 | Harakat-i Ingilab-i Islami. Moderates. Member of IUAM. |
| Movement of Spirit Inner Awareness | sFN | 2-e | 1967 | 5,000 | 2 | usa | C | 5 | Church of Movement of Spiritual Inner Awareness. MSIA. F=J. R. Hinkins. Related to Insight. |
| Muhammadiyah | zSM | 2-c | 1912 | 9,000,000 | 1 | indo | B | 3 | Followers of Muhammad. Javanese. Modernist reformers, welfare work. |
| Muhammad's Army | zSM | 2-e | | 20,000 | 1 | jord | B | 2 | Jaysh Muhammad. No legal status. Attempts made to overthrow regime and monarchy. |
| Mujaddidiya | ssUM | 2-d | 1650 | 150,000 | 10 | indi | B | 2 | Begun Damascus by Kurdish shaikh. Formerly branch of Naqshabandiya, now own Sufi order. |
| Mujahids | sWSM | 2-e | 1952 | 50,000 | 1 | indi | B | 2 | Reform movement among Mappila Muslims in Kerala. |
| Mukhtariyah | ssUM | 2-c | c1900 | 2,000,000 | 1 | maur | A | 0 | A Qadiriya Sufi order prominent at start of French colonial rule. |
| Mulavamsa | s-oB | 9-e | c1900 | 12,000 | 1 | sril | B | 3 | Prominent monastic grouping within Amarapura Nikaya. |
| Mumuye ethnoreligionists | sAT | 3-d | | 348,000 | 2 | nige | B | 2 | Taraba State. In Cameroon. Literates 5%. Animists (reviving) 81%, Muslims 9%. Y=1932. D=8. |
| Munda ethnoreligionists | sAT | 3-d | | 352,000 | 3 | indi | B | 3 | God=Parameswar. Bihar, Assam; Nepal, Bangladesh. Hindus 53%, animists 20%. D=7. M=9. |
| Mundang ethnoreligionists | sAT | 3-d | | 132,000 | 2 | chad | B | 3 | God=Masing. Also in Cameroon. Animists 45%, Muslims 7%. D=EFLT,AIC. M=UBS,LBWM. |
| Muong ethnoreligionists | sAT | 3-c | | 1,058,000 | 2 | viet | A | 2 | Mostly in mountains of north; also near Banmethuot in south. Animists 94%. D=RCC. M=SIL. |
| Muridiyah | sUM | 2-d | c1900 | 300,000 | 5 | sene | A | 1 | Innovative Sufis. Ex Qadiriya in Mauritania. HQ holy city Touba. Peanut prosperity. |
| Murtipujakas | sSV | 2-e | | 1,000 | 1 | indi | B | 0 | 'Image worshipers'. Pujeras, subsect of Svetambara Jains. |
| Musar Movement | sOJ | 2-e | c1880 | 5,000 | 1 | lith | C | 3 | Orthodox Jews, Lithuania strictness, self-examination. |
| Muslim Association of Nigeria | nM | 7-b | | 30,000,000 | 1 | nige | B | 3 | MAN. Moderate national organization; mobilizes youth, fosters Muslim/Christian relations. |
| Muslim believers in Christs | I-Mus-tC | 5-d | c1950 | 537,000 | 15 | paki | A | 2 | Converted Muslims who remain in Islam to witness there for Christ. |
| Muslim Brotherhood | sNXM | 2-c | 1928 | 1,500,000 | 10 | egyp | B | 3 | al-Ikhwan al-Muslimun. Neo-fundamentalists. Violence 1945-1965. Outlawed in Egypt, 1954. |
| Muslim Sisters | sNXM | 2-d | c1940 | 200,000 | 1 | egyp | B | 3 | Women's movement parallel to Muslim Brotherhood, to restore Islamic women's status. |
| Muslim World League | wM | 7-a | 1962 | 300,600,000 | 80 | saud | B | 2 | MWL. Rabitat al-Alam al-Islami. HQ Mecca. Replacing WMC (Pakistan), Wahhabi leadership. |
| Muslims | M | 1-a | | 1,188,243,000 | 204 | paki | A | 2 | Islam (active submission to the will of Allah). |
| Mustalis | MIHM | 2-d | 1094 | 360,000 | 20 | yeme | A | 0 | Tayibis. Sulaymanis. Smaller of the 2 Ismaili sects. |
| Myanmar Baptist Convention | P-Bap-AC | 6-c | 1813 | 1,940,000 | 1 | myan | B | 5 | BBC, organized 1865. M=ABFMS. 16 Conferences. 19p(827),P=75%,4s,1300t. |
| Myanmar Catholic Bishops Conf | R-nC | 7-d | 1982 | 590,000 | 1 | myan | B | 5 | MCBC. HQ Yangon. |
| Myanmar Council of Churches | W-nC | 7-c | 1949 | 2,150,000 | 1 | myan | B | 5 | MCC. 1914 in NCCI; 1949 Burma Christian Council; renamed 1975. 15 regional councils. |
| Myanmar Evangelical Christian Fell | E-nC | 7-d | 1981 | 500,000 | 1 | myan | B | 5 | MECF. |
| Myochikai Kyodan | sNJMB | 2-d | | 670,000 | 3 | japa | B | 1 | HQ Shibuya-ku, Tokyo. |
| Myodokai Kyodan | sNJMB | 2-d | | 155,000 | 1 | japa | B | 1 | HQ Osaka-shi. |
| Myohoshu | sNJMB | 2-e | | 4,900 | 1 | japa | B | 2 | HQ Nara-ken. |
| Myokenshu | sTJMB | 2-d | | 227,000 | 1 | japa | B | 1 | Sect of Tendai Buddhism. HQ Osaka-fu. |
| Nabulusiyah | ssUM | 2-d | | 300,000 | 1 | turk | A | 0 | Suborder of Sufi Qadiriya, banned in 1924 by Ataturk. |
| Nadvat-ul-Mujahideen | sWSM | 2-e | 1952 | 40,000 | 1 | indi | B | 2 | Formal Islamic reform movement among Mappila of Kerala. |
| Nagas | sS-oH | 9-e | c500 | 6,000 | 1 | indi | B | 1 | A semi-military ascetic Shaivite order. Sky-clad (naked). |
| Nago | sBU | 2-d | c1800 | 300,000 | 1 | braz | C | 5 | Afro-Brazilian Candomble spiritists in Maranhao and Pajelanca. |
| Nagoshias | sMIHM | 10-f | 1789 | 500 | 1 | indi | B | 1 | Nagushis. Small subsect of Daudis. Vegetarians. |

*Continued overleaf*

*Table 17–5 continued*

| *Name of religion/religionists* 1 | *Pedigree* 2 | *Type* 3 | *Begun* 4 | *Adherents* 5 | *Ext* 6 | *Coun* 7 | *W* 8 | *X* 9 | *E. g. = examples; name for God, other religions present, D=denominations, M=missions.* 10 |
|---|---|---|---|---|---|---|---|---|---|
| Nakayama Kojin Hoonkai | sNS | 2-e | | 3,700 | 1 | japa | B | 1 | HQ Okayama-ken. |
| Nakayama Myoshu | sNJMB | 2-d | | 566,000 | 1 | japa | B | 0 | HQ Chiba-ken. |
| Nakayama Shingo Shoshu | sSJMB | 2-d | 1921 | 457,000 | 2 | japa | B | 0 | HQ Saga-ken. |
| Nakhi ethnoreligionists | sPT | 3-d | | 276,000 | 1 | chin | A | 1 | Yunnan. Dongbaists 80%(polytheists),Buddhists 10%,Taoists 9%,shamanists widespread.D=1. |
| Namdharis | sK | 2-d | 1840 | 400,000 | 2 | indi | B | 2 | Also called Kukas. Sikh-related reform movement. HQ Baini. |
| Namibia Evangelical Fellowship | E-nC | 7-e | c1985 | 20,000 | 1 | nami | C | 5 | NEF. |
| Namibian Council of Churches | K-nC | 7-d | 1978 | 930,000 | 1 | nami | C | 5 | NCC. |
| Nanaksar Movement | sK | 2-e | c1930 | 5,000 | 1 | indi | B | 2 | F=Bhai Mani Singh. Meditation, vegetarianism, celibacy. HQ Punjab. |
| Naniguismo | sUU | 2-e | 1834 | 50,000 | 2 | cuba | B | 5 | Afro-Cuban spiritist cult. Propagates African rituals. Secret societies. |
| Naobikyo | sTS | 2-e | | 2,000 | 1 | japa | B | 1 | Mountain worship. HQ Hyogo-ken. |
| Naqshabandiya | sUM | 2-b | c1150 | 50,000,000 | 30 | uzbe | A | 1 | Great Sufi order (most-widespread after Qadiriya) strong in Central Asia, India, West Europe. |
| Nara Buddhists | NJMB | 2-c | c550 | 2,262,000 | 4 | japa | B | 2 | Nara sects were first forms of Buddhism in Japan. Now 7 distinct Nara sects. |
| Nat Co of Chs of American Samoa | W-nC | 7-e | c1970 | 5,000 | 1 | amer | C | 5 | NCCAS. Co=Council. Includes Roman Catholics and nearly all Protestant denominations. |
| Nat Primitive Baptist Convention | I-Bap-AC | 6-c | 1865 | 1,159,000 | 1 | usa | C | 5 | Black. Formerly Colored Primitive Baptists. HQ Tallahassee (FL). 597n,2150t(32200). |
| Nat Spiritual Baptist Council of Chs | I-nC | 7-e | c1950 | 11,000 | 1 | trin | C | 5 | NSBCC. |
| Nath cultists | sS-oH | 9-e | 1200 | 25,000 | 1 | indi | B | 0 | Kanphatas: order of high-caste Shaivite yogis. Monasteries (some Vaishnavite) across India. |
| Nation of Islam | sBXM | 2-d | 1978 | 400,000 | 1 | usa | C | 3 | Split ex-Black Muslims. F=L. Farrakhan. |
| National Association of Evangelicals | E-nC | 7-b | 1942 | 27,000,000 | 1 | usa | C | 5 | NAE. Members 48 denominations with 42,500 congregations. |
| National Association of Evs of Ghana | E-nC | 7-c | 1977 | 1,400,000 | 1 | ghan | B | 5 | NAEG. Founded by 12 organizations. |
| National Bapt Conv of America | I-Bap-AC | 6-c | 1880 | 4,464,000 | 1 | usa | C | 5 | NBC. Part of first major Black Baptist body; NBCUSA split off in 1915. 28574n,1s. |
| National Baptist Conv, USA | I-Bap-AC | 6-b | 1773 | 10,007,000 | 1 | usa | C | 5 | NBC. 1915 split from NBC America. Black. HQ Nashville. (1970) 27500n,1s. (1990) 32832n. |
| National Black Evangelical Association | nC | 7-c | 1963 | 1,000,000 | 6 | usa | C | 5 | NBEA. Formerly NNEA (N=Negro). HQ Portland, OR. |
| National Christian Co of Sri Lanka | W-nC | 7-e | 1923 | 98,000 | 1 | sril | B | 5 | NCCSL. |
| National Christian Council in Japan | W-nC | 7-d | 1911 | 360,000 | 1 | japa | B | 5 | NCCJ. Nippon Kirisutokyo Kyogikai. |
| National Christian Fell of Bangladesh | E-nC | 7-e | 1980 | 3,000 | 1 | bang | B | 5 | NCFB. |
| National Chs Fellowship of Nepal | E-nC | 7-e | 1959 | 80,000 | 1 | nepa | A | 5 | NCFN. |
| National Church of Denmark | P-Lut-AC | 6-c | 826 | 4,508,000 | 1 | denm | C | 5 | Evangelisk-lutherske Folkekirke i Danmark. 10 Dioceses. 99 Deaneries. 1824n,P=40%,2s. |
| National Church of Nigeria | sSN | 2-e | 1948 | 20,000 | 1 | nige | B | 3 | F=K. O. K. Onyioha. Ibo religion with Christian elements. |
| National Co of Chs in the Philippines | W-nC | 7-c | 1963 | 4,520,000 | 1 | phil | C | 5 | NCCP. Sangguniang Pambansa ng mga Simbahan sa Pilipinas. |
| National Co of Chs of Christ in USA | W-nC | 7-b | 1908 | 49,700,000 | 1 | usa | C | 5 | NCCCUSA. 1908, Federal Council of CCNA. Member denominations: 40. |
| National Conf of Catholic Bishops | R-nC | 7-b | 1981 | 61,000,000 | 1 | usa | C | 5 | NCCB. HQ Washington DC. 2001, with USCC forms US Conf of Catholic Bps (USCCB). |
| National Conf of Christians and Jews | nPW | 7-c | 1927 | 9,000,000 | 1 | usa | C | 5 | NCCJ. 61 regional offices in USA, 2,800 trustees. |
| National Council of Chs in Australia | W-nC | 7-c | 1946 | 5,100,000 | 1 | aust | C | 5 | NCCA. |
| National Council of Chs in Korea | N-nC | 7-c | 1919 | 4,300,000 | 1 | souk | B | 5 | NCCK. Hankuk Kidokyo Yonhap-hui. Present name 1946. |
| National Council of Chs in Lithuania | K-nC | 7-d | | 150,000 | 1 | lith | C | 5 | NCCL. |
| National Council of Chs in Pakistan | N-nC | 7-c | 1923 | 1,600,000 | 1 | paki | A | 5 | NCCP. 1923 Punjab Christian Council; subequent name changes 1949, 1971, 1976. |
| National Council of Chs in Taiwan | K-nC | 7-d | | 630,000 | 1 | taiw | B | 5 | NCCT. |
| National Council of Chs of Kenya | K-nC | 7-c | 1918 | 8,521,000 | 1 | keny | C | 5 | NCCK. 1943, Christian Council of Kenya. 30 member denominations. |
| National Council of Chs of Singapore | W-nC | 7-d | 1948 | 125,000 | 1 | sing | B | 5 | NCCS. |
| National Council of Churches in India | W-nC | 7-b | 1953 | 12,500,000 | 1 | indi | B | 5 | NCCI. Origin in 1912 Missionary Council, 1921 National Christian Council. 20 denominations. |
| National Council of Ev Chs of PNG | E-nC | 7-d | 1964 | 375,000 | 1 | papu | C | 5 | Formerly Ev Alliance of Papua New Guinea. |
| National Council of Hindu Temples | nH | 7-d | c1980 | 429,000 | 2 | brit | C | 5 | Major Hindu coordinating body in Britain. |
| National Council of Pentecostal Chs | H-nC | 7-d | 1979 | 220,000 | 1 | papu | C | 5 | NCPC. |
| National Episcopal Conf of Nigeria | V-nC | 7-b | 1976 | 13,400,000 | 1 | nige | B | 5 | NECN. Catholic Bishops' Conference of Nigeria. HQ Lagos. |
| National Ev Christian Fell of Malaysia | E-nC | 7-d | 1983 | 500,000 | 1 | malb | B | 5 | Persaudaraan Kristian Evangelikal Nasional, Malaysia. |
| National Fraternal Council of Chs | J-nC | 7-c | 1929 | 6,175,000 | 1 | usa | C | 5 | NFCC. 1929, Negro (now Black) denominations. |
| National Missionary Bapt Conv | I-Bap-AC | 6-c | 1988 | 3,600,000 | 1 | usa | C | 5 | NMBCA. Split ex NBCA over control of publishing; claims 89% of all members. HQ Nashville. |
| National Patriotic Catholic Assoc | C-nC | 7-c | | 4,600,000 | 1 | chin | B | 5 | NPCA. |
| National Taoist Assoc of Rep of China | nD | 7-e | | 50,000 | 1 | taiw | B | 2 | Coordinating body for well-organized Taoist council. |
| Native American ethnoreligionists | sPT | 3-d | | 410,000 | 2 | usa | C | 5 | Rediscovery of Amerindian traditional religions. |
| Nativistic cultists | VN | 2-b | c1500 | 130,000,000 | 30 | indo | B | 3 | Mystical new religious movements combining local gods with world religions. |
| Ndau ethnoreligionists | sAT | 3-d | | 319,000 | 3 | zimb | B | 5 | God=Mngari. Also in Mozambique, with many as refugees in Zimbabwe. Animists 50%. M=2. |
| Ndebele ethnoreligionists | sAT | 3-d | | 559,000 | 3 | zimb | B | 5 | Animists 36%. Heavily christianized. D=30 large denominations, many AICs. |
| Negrito ethnoreligionists | sAT | 3-e | | 12,000 | 2 | phil | C | 5 | Agta, Onge, Semang and other Australoid peoples. 80% animists; complex religions. |
| Nenpo Shinkyo | sTJMB | 2-d | 1925 | 511,000 | 1 | japa | B | 1 | Sect of Tendai Buddhism. HQ Osaka-shi. |
| Neo-Buddhism | NTB | 2-c | 1951 | 6,000,000 | 3 | indi | B | 2 | Conversion of 4 million Outcastes: Buddhism of social protest (B. R. Ambedkar, Maharashtra). |
| neocharismatic mainliners | I-3dW-tC | 5-e | 1996 | 18,000 | 1 | usa | C | 5 | E.g. Southern Baptist charismatic congregations. Based Fort Worth, TX. No work abroad. |
| Neocharismatic minicommunions | x-fC | 4-b | | 50,000,000 | 160 | usa | C | 5 | 50 Independent paracommunions or quasicommunions. |
| Neocharismatics (Third-Wavers) | 3ZAC | 2-a | 1549 | 295,405,000 | 225 | chin | B | 5 | All baptised in the Holy Spirit in new churches independent of historic Christianity. D=18,810. |
| Neo-Confucianism | NG | 2-d | c1050 | 100,000 | 2 | chin | B | 1 | Confucian response to teaching of Taoism, yin-yang, Five Elements. |
| Neo-Evangelicals | NEAC | 2-b | 1948 | 34,000,000 | 231 | usa | C | 5 | Term coined after World War II for evangelicals distancing themselves from Fundamentalism. |
| Neo-Hasidism | sOJ | 2-d | c1950 | 150,000 | 10 | isra | B | 2 | Contemporary non-Hasidic Jews and Jewish New-Agers. |
| Neo-Hindus | NH | 2-b | | 17,385,000 | 65 | indi | B | 3 | Large variety of new religions based on revivals of Hinduism. |
| Neo-Kabbalah | sON | 2-d | BC 500 | 200,000 | 20 | isra | B | 2 | Jewish New-Agers influenced by occult Kabbalistic practices. |
| Neo-Orthodoxy | zJ | 2-d | c1920 | 300,000 | 8 | isra | B | 2 | German, Polish, Lithuanian and other supporters of Agudat Israel. |
| Neo-Paganism | PN | 2-d | c1850 | 400,000 | 30 | brit | C | 5 | Modern revival of European pre-Christian paganism; worship of Earth Goddess. |
| Neopagans | ET | 3-c | | 4,500,000 | 20 | brit | C | 5 | Followers of modern revivals of ancient pagan religions (Wicca, &c): UK, Iceland, et alia. |
| Neo-Sufism | RUM | 2-b | c1920 | 10,000,000 | 20 | russ | B | 5 | Reform-oriented Sufi orders without excesses of ecstatic activities. Modernizing tendencies. |
| Nepal Christian Fellowship | C-nC | 7-d | | 100,000 | 1 | nepa | A | 5 | NCF. |
| Netherlands Bishops' Conference | S-nC | 7-c | 1986 | 5,450,000 | 1 | neth | C | 5 | Nederlandse Bisschoppen Konferentie. HQ Utrecht. |
| New Age Judaism | zJ | 2-e | | 30,000 | 2 | isra | B | 2 | Close to Havurat Judaism. Renewal communities. |
| New Apostolic Church | n-fC | 4-b | 1863 | 11,000,000 | 80 | swit | C | 3 | NAC/NAK. Neuapostolische Kirche. HQ Zurich. |
| New Apostolic Church, India | I-3aX-AC | 6-c | 1969 | 1,734,000 | 1 | indi | B | 4 | Canada Bezirk. HQ Zurich. Rapid growth. 1973 mission in Kenya, Africa. |
| New Apostolic Church, Kenya | I-3aX-AC | 6-c | 1973 | 1,214,000 | 1 | keny | C | 4 | M=NAC(World HQ Zurich). Begun from Bombay, India. Phenomenal growth. |
| New Apostolics | I-3aX-tC | 5-c | 1832 | 9,637,000 | 149 | indi | B | 5 | Global body. E.g. Canada Bezirk. HQ Zurich. Rapid growth. 1973 mission in Kenya, Africa. |
| New Birth Movement | I-3cC-AC | 6-c | 1980 | 4,800,000 | 1 | chin | B | 5 | NBM, or Born Again Movement (BAM) One branch of the whole house church movement. |
| New Caledonia ethnoreligionists | sPAT | 10-f | | 270 | 1 | newc | C | 5 | Remnants of once strong animistic culture. |
| New Guinea ethnoreligionists | sAT | 3-e | | 80,000 | 1 | papu | C | 5 | Sizeable numbers of animists are still found among several hundred tribes. |
| New Islamic Mission | qM | 8-d | 1945 | 500,000 | 1 | suda | B | 1 | al-Hizb al-Jumhari. Republican Brothers. Party, banned 1969. F=M.M. Taha, hanged 1985. |
| New Life Movement | sSN | 2-e | 1934 | 5,000 | 1 | chin | B | 3 | Constructed religion for political unity. F=Chiang kai-shek. |
| New Sect Shintoists | NS | 2-c | 1945 | 1,837,000 | 30 | japa | B | 3 | Consists of over 47 new Sect Shinto organisations. |
| New Sudan Council of Churches | C-nC | 7-d | | 250,000 | 1 | suda | B | 5 | NSCC. |
| New Thought | sFN | 2-c | c1850 | 1,000,000 | 20 | usa | C | 5 | Positive Thinking. F=P. P. Quimby. Health, happiness, prosperity. |
| New Tribes Mission | ntm-oC | 9-e | 1942 | 1,500 | 25 | usa | C | 5 | NTM. |
| New Zealand Episcopal Conference | R-nC | 7-d | 1974 | 495,000 | 1 | newz | C | 5 | NZEC. HQ Wellington. |
| New-Agers | sFN | 2-b | c1870 | 12,000,000 | 41 | usa | C | 4 | Self-religiosity in 300 diverse forms. Bookshops, spiritual therapy centers. Celtic revivals. |
| New-Religionists | N | 1-b | | 102,356,000 | 60 | japa | B | 4 | Neoreligionists. 200 recent new non-Christian religions, many syncretizing Christianity & others. |
| Ngaju Dayak ethnoreligionists | sAT | 3-d | | 138,000 | 1 | indo | C | 5 | God=Hatalla. Kalimantan. Kapuas, 3 other rivers in south. Lingua franca. Animists 40%. D=2. |
| Ngoni ethnoreligionists | sAT | 3-d | | 252,000 | 4 | mala | C | 5 | Speakers originally spoke Zulu. Animists 13%. D=5. M=5. |
| Ngorba | sSLB | 2-d | 1429 | 500,000 | 2 | chin | B | 1 | Branch of Sakyapa tradition of Tibetan Buddhism. Monasteries across Tibet. |
| Ngwato Tswana ethnoreligionists | sAT | 3-d | | 151,000 | 2 | bots | B | 5 | God=Modimo. Animists 36%. D=UCCSA, RCC(D-Gaborone),CPCA, many AICs. M=20. |
| Nhang ethnoreligionists | sPT | 3-d | | 262,000 | 2 | chin | A | 1 | Yunnan Province; also Viet Nam (official community), USA, France, Laos. Polytheists 97%. |
| Nichiren Hokkeshu | sNJMB | 2-e | | 14,000 | 1 | japa | B | 1 | HQ Fukushima-shi. |
| Nichiren Honshu | sNJMB | 2-e | | 34,800 | 1 | japa | B | 1 | HQ Sakyo-ku, Kyoto-shi. |
| Nichiren Komonshu | sNJMB | 2-e | | 26,600 | 1 | japa | B | 1 | HQ Okayama-ken. |
| Nichiren Shu | sNJMB | 2-c | c1260 | 2,100,000 | 10 | japa | B | 3 | 'Sun Lotus'. The original movement begun by monk Nichiren (1222-1282). HQ Ota-ku, Tokyo. |
| Nichirenshu Fujufuseha | sNJMB | 2-e | c1610 | 16,700 | 1 | japa | B | 1 | HQ Okayama-ken. |
| Nichirenshu Saijokyo | sNJMB | 2-e | | 7,000 | 1 | japa | B | 0 | HQ Okayama-ken. |
| Nichirenshugi Butsuryuko | sNJMB | 2-e | | 2,000 | 1 | japa | B | 1 | HQ Aichi-ken. |
| Nigeria Association of Aladura Chs | I-nC | 7-c | 1960 | 2,100,000 | 1 | nige | B | 5 | NAAC. Isokan Ijo Aladura Nigeria (IIAN). HQ Ibadan. Powerful; 200 member AICs. |
| Nigeria Evangelical Fellowship | G-nC | 7-c | 1966 | 8,000,000 | 1 | nige | B | 5 | NEF. 10 member churches. |
| Nigerian Baptist Convention | P-Bap-AC | 6-c | 1850 | 1,440,000 | 1 | nige | B | 5 | NBC(1914). M=FMB-SBC(USA). Yoruba, Gude, Fali, Kamberi. 780n,187f,5H,3s,7852Y. |
| Nigerian Christian Fellowship | I-3pA-AC | 6-c | | 1,067,000 | 1 | nige | B | 5 | A loosely-organized grouping of pentecostal bodies in eastern Nigeria. HQ Uyo. |
| Nihangs | s-oK | 9-d | 1700 | 200,000 | 2 | indi | B | 2 | Sikh warriors, fighting force created by Guru Gobind Singh; a warrior group of Khalsa Sikhs. |
| Nihon Ehoba Kyodan | sNN | 2-e | | 11,400 | 1 | japa | B | 2 | HQ Meguro-ku, Tokyo. |
| Nihon Jingu Honcho | sHS | 2-e | | 79,100 | 1 | japa | B | 1 | HQ Obihiro-shi, Hokkaido. |

*Continued opposite*

*Table 17–5 continued*

| *Name of religion/religionists* 1 | *Pedigree* 2 | *Type* 3 | *Begun* 4 | *Adherents* 5 | *Ext* 6 | *Coun* 7 | *W* 8 | *X* 9 | *E. g. = examples; name for God, other religions present, D=denominations, M=missions.* 10 |
|---|---|---|---|---|---|---|---|---|---|
| Nihon Jinja Honcho | sHS | 2-e | | 19,600 | 1 | japa | B | 2 | HQ Obihiro-shi, Hokkaido. |
| Nihon Jinja Kyodan | sHS | 2-e | | 2,600 | 1 | japa | B | 0 | HQ Yuki-gun, Ibaraki-ken. |
| Nihon Keishin Suso Jishudan | sNN | 2-e | | 11,000 | 1 | japa | B | 1 | HQ Iizaka-machi, Fukushima-shi. |
| Nihonzan Myohoji Daisanga | sNJMB | 2-e | | 24,300 | 1 | japa | B | 2 | HQ Shibuya-ku, Tokyo. |
| Nimatullahiya | ssUM | 2-d | 1370 | 350,000 | 6 | iran | A | 1 | One of the few Shia Sufi orders. Missions in Europe and America. |
| Nimbaraka Vairagins | sV-oH | 9-e | | 30,000 | 1 | indi | B | 0 | An order of Hindu Vaishnavite ascetics. |
| Ningen Zen Kyodan | sZJMB | 2-e | | 5,200 | 1 | japa | B | 2 | HQ Chiba-ken. |
| Nipponzan Myohoji | sNJMB | 2-d | 1917 | 200,000 | 12 | japa | B | 4 | Wondrous Law of the Lotus Sutra. Global fame for 'peace pagodas'. 1,500 ascetics. |
| Nirankaris | sK | 2-e | c1820 | 30,000 | 1 | paki | A | 0 | Sikh-derived reform movement. F=Baba Dayal Das. God=Nirankar. |
| Nishkam Sevak Jatha | sK | 2-e | c1950 | 20,000 | 3 | brit | C | 5 | F=Kerichowale Baba (a Kenyan Sikh). Sikh reform movement. Vegetarians. |
| Nizamiyah | ssUM | 2-d | c1320 | 800,000 | 1 | indi | B | 2 | One of 2 branches of Chishtiyah Sufis. Revived c 1750. |
| Nizaris | sIHM | 2-b | 950 | 20,000,000 | 12 | indi | B | 1 | Assassins (users of hashish). Loyal to Aga Khan IV. Major Ismaili sect, Tanzania,Syria,India. |
| Njushi-ryu | zLB | 2-d | | 100,000 | 1 | chin | B | 0 | Tibetan. Variety of Lamaism. |
| No-Church movement | I-NoC-tC | 5-e | 1900 | 3,500 | 2 | japa | B | 4 | E.g. Mukyokai. Small Bible study groups. No buildings, no clergy, unorganized. |
| Non-Christians | X | 1-a | | 4,055,485,000 | 238 | chin | B | 2 | Total Non-Christians of all kinds, either religionists or nonreligionists. |
| Nondenominationalists | P-Non-tC | 5-c | 1685 | 3,943,000 | 76 | keny | C | 5 | E.g. M=AIM. 33% Kamba, 27% Kalenjin, 20% Kikuyu. 80n,50x,226f,4H,30h,5p,1s,2000Y. |
| Nonhistorical Indep neocharismatics | I3ZAC | 2-c | 1549 | 3,500,000 | 62 | phil | C | 2 | Neocharismatics in other nonpentecostal Independent chs: PIC/IFI, NBCA. D=300. |
| Nonreligionists | - | 0-a | | 918,248,000 | 236 | chin | B | 2 | All who are not religious or religionists; agnostics (nonreligious) plus atheists (militants). |
| Nonreligious | Q- | 0-a | | 768,159,000 | 236 | chin | B | 2 | Agnostics, secularists, materialists, with no religion but not militantly antireligious or atheists. |
| nonreligious Buddhists | NB | 2-b | c1950 | 54,408,000 | 35 | japa | B | 2 | Persons with Buddhism as family religion but professing no personal religion. |
| Nonsyncretist Neoreligionists | NN | 2-b | 1838 | 53,000,000 | 40 | japa | B | 3 | New Religions with little or no Buddhist/Hindu/Christian elements. |
| Non-White indig Neocharismatics | N3ZAC | 2-a | 1783 | 203,870,000 | 210 | chin | B | 5 | Spirit-baptized Non-Whites in 26 varieties of indigenous, apostolic churches. D=13,425. |
| Nordic Bishops' Conference | Q-rC | 7-d | | 236,000 | 4 | denm | C | 5 | Nordiske Bispekonferanse (Scandinavian Bishops' Conference). |
| North Korean ethnoreligionists | sST | 3-c | | 2,952,000 | 1 | nork | B | 2 | Nonreligious 55%, atheists 16%,New-Religionists 13%,shamanists 12%,Buddhists 1.5%.D=6. |
| Northeastern Dinka ethnoreligionists | sAT | 3-d | | 110,000 | 1 | suda | C | 5 | God=Nhialic. White Nile Dinka. Nomadic animists 90%, Muslims 1%. Resists Islam. D=5. M=4. |
| Northeastern Tai ethnoreligionists | sAT | 3-d | | 163,000 | 1 | thai | B | 2 | Lao. Bangkok. Theravada Buddhists 98%, animists 1%. D=6. M=12. |
| Northern Gond ethnoreligionists | sAT | 3-d | | 385,000 | 1 | indi | A | 1 | God=Parameshwar. Betul and other Districts, MP. Hindus 55%, animists 45%. D=2. M=9. |
| Northern Meo ethnoreligionists | sPAT | 3-d | | 828,000 | 1 | chin | A | 1 | West Hunan. Agriculturalists. Polytheists 96%. D=Chinese CR, RCC, TSPM. M=3. |
| Northern Samo ethnoreligionists | sAT | 3-d | | 167,000 | 1 | burk | B | 2 | Sourou Province. Animists 54%, Muslims 30%. D=2. M=2. |
| Northern Tung ethnoreligionists | sPAT | 3-c | | 2,240,000 | 1 | chin | A | 1 | Guizhou. Polytheists(animists) 80%, Buddhists 20%. D=RCC,TSPM. M=IMB, SIL, TELL, FEBC. |
| Northern Yi ethnoreligionists | sPAT | 3-c | | 1,582,000 | 1 | chin | A | 1 | Northern Nosu. Yunnan, Laos, Viet Nam. Polytheists(animists) 90%, Buddhists 5%. D=2. M=22. |
| Northern Zhuang ethnoreligionists | sPAT | 3-b | | 10,237,000 | 1 | chin | A | 2 | Polytheists 80%, Buddhists 19%. D=TSPM(300 churches),RCC,TJC. M=25. |
| Northwestern Maninka ethnoreligionists | sAT | 3-d | | 201,000 | 2 | mali | A | 1 | Wasulunka. Also in Senegal, Guinea. Muslims 67%(Maliki Sunnis), animists 30%. D=3. M=7. |
| Northwestern Tamang ethnoreligionists | sAT | 3-d | | 107,000 | 1 | nepa | B | 2 | Animists 35%, Hindus 25%, Buddhists 23%. 1974, widespread revival begins. D=3. M=5. |
| Norwegian Evangelical Alliance | E-nC | 7-d | 1858 | 100,000 | 1 | norw | C | 5 | NEA. Evangeliske Allianse i Norge. |
| Norwegian Free Church Council | C-nC | 7-d | | 150,000 | 1 | norw | C | 5 | Norske Frikirkerad. Several non-established Protestant denominations. |
| Nsenga ethnoreligionists | sAT | 3-d | | 181,000 | 3 | zamb | B | 5 | God=Mlungu. East and Central Provinces. Animists 30%, Baha'is. D=7. M=4. |
| Nunuma ethnoreligionists | sAT | 3-d | | 194,000 | 1 | burk | A | 1 | Over 100 villages in Sissili Province. Animists 62%, Muslims 25%. D=3. M=8. |
| Nusairis | sSN | 2-c | 950 | 1,100,000 | 5 | syri | B | 3 | Alawis. Quasi-Muslim extremist sect. Gnostic, Ismaili, and Christian teachings. God=Ali. |
| Nyanja ethnoreligionists | sAT | 3-d | | 195,000 | 3 | moza | B | 5 | God=Mulungu. Animists 42%. D=6; many AICs. M=USPG. |
| Nyiha ethnoreligionists | sAT | 3-d | | 299,000 | 2 | tanz | B | 3 | God=Mulungu. South of Lake Rukwa, on Zambia border. Also in Malawi. Animists 70%. D=4. |
| Nyingmapas | NLB | 2-c | c790 | 7,000,000 | 4 | chin | B | 1 | Red Hat lamas. Followers of the Ancient Teachings. Tibet's oldest Buddhist order; unreformed. |
| Nyoraikyo | sZJMB | 2-e | | 33,400 | 1 | japa | B | 2 | HQ Nagoya-shi. |
| Nyungwe ethnoreligionists | sAT | 3-d | | 320,000 | 3 | moza | B | 3 | Banks of Zambezi. Some in Malawi. Closely related to Sena. Animists 75%. D=3. M=2. |
| NZ Consultative Co of ICCC | T-nC | 7-e | | 5,000 | 1 | newz | C | 4 | NZCCC. Co=Council. NZ=New Zealand. Related to ICCC (USA) |
| Obaku Shu | sZJMB | 2-d | 1650 | 245,000 | 1 | japa | B | 3 | One of 3 schools of Zen in Japan. F=Ingen. 460 temples. HQ Kyoto-fu. |
| Obeah | sCU | 2-e | c1600 | 50,000 | 2 | jama | B | 5 | Secret cult of Ashanti origin (Ghana), for harmful magic. |
| Oblates of Mary Immaculate | omi-oC | 9-e | 1816 | 5,200 | | ital | C | 5 | OMI. |
| Occultists | ON | 2-c | c1700 | 1,500,000 | 50 | usa | C | 2 | Hidden and secret practices. Kabbalah used. c1880, Golden Dawn. |
| Oceanic ethnoreligionists | sPT | 3-d | | 267,000 | 20 | fiji | B | 4 | Decline from 1,300,000 in 1900 in many polytheistic religions. |
| Oecumenische Raad van Kerken | K-nC | 7-e | 1962 | 11,500 | 1 | nets | C | 5 | Curacao Ecumenical Council of Churches. |
| Ohi no Motokyo | sTS | 2-e | | 10,700 | 1 | japa | B | 1 | HQ Shinjuku-ku, Tokyo. |
| Oirat ethnoreligionists | sST | 3-d | | 131,000 | 3 | chin | A | 0 | God=Borhan. Xinjiang Mongolian. Shamanists 60%, Lamaist Buddhists 30%, nonreligious 8%. |
| Okinawan ethnoreligionists | sPAT | 3-e | | 6,000 | 1 | japa | B | 3 | Varieties of animism, shamanism, polytheism on Okinawa. |
| Old Calendarist Orthodox | I-OCd-tC | 5-d | 1924 | 270,000 | 4 | gree | C | 5 | E.g. Paleohemerologites. Old Calendar Greek OC. Ex Ch of G. In USA, Canada. 250n,1100w. |
| Old Catholics | I-OCa-tC | 5-d | 1724 | 910,000 | 19 | usa | C | 5 | E.g. Immigrants from Poland, where church began in 1893. Archbishop, 2 bps, 48n,30w,10m. |
| Old Ritualist Churches | Q-fC | 4-c | 1666 | 1,957,000 | | russ | B | 5 | Old Believers, Old Calendarists. |
| Old Ritualists | I-OBe-tC | 5-c | 1634 | 1,822,000 | 19 | russ | B | 5 | Old Believers. Raskolniki. (Schismatics). Vast extent from Baltic across Siberia. |
| Olive Tree Church | I-mar-AC | 6-e | 1955 | 7,000 | 1 | souk | B | 2 | Chondokwon. F=Pak Tae-son. Name=Revelation 11:4. Vast properties. 1970: 700,550. |
| OMF International | omf-oC | 9-e | 1888 | 1,100 | 28 | brit | C | 5 | Formerly Overseas Missionary Fellowship. Formerly CIM. (China Inland Mission). |
| Omisorakyo | sTS | 2-e | | 10,500 | 1 | japa | B | 1 | HQ Shinagawa-ku, Tokyo. |
| Omiwako | sTS | 2-e | | 12,300 | 1 | japa | B | 0 | HQ Nara-ken. |
| Omiwakyo | sTS | 10-f | | 700 | 1 | japa | B | 0 | HQ Nara-ken. |
| Oneness Pentecostals | 1P1ZAC | 2-c | 1914 | 2,768,000 | 130 | colo | C | 5 | Denominations emphasizing baptism in name of 'Jesus Only'; anti-trinitarian: UPCI. D=80. |
| Oneness Pentecostals | P-Pe1-tC | 5-c | 1914 | 2,768,000 | 74 | usa | C | 4 | E.g. 1945 union PAJC, PC. White. (1970) 4800n. (1990) 7512n. Missions in 74 countries. (83n). |
| Ongbe ethnoreligionists | sBAT | 3-d | | 324,000 | 1 | chin | A | 1 | North coast of Hainan. Most are Han Chinese or Zhuang. Bilinguals. Buddhists/polytheists 99%. |
| Ontakekyo | sTS | 2-d | 1882 | 654,000 | 1 | japa | B | 2 | Japanese mountain worship sect (Mount Ontake). God=3 great Kamis. HQ Nara-ken. |
| Ontakekyo Shuseiha | sTS | 2-e | | 7,400 | 1 | japa | B | 2 | Mountain worship sect. HQ Niigata-ken. |
| Ontakesan Soma Honkyo | sTS | 2-e | | 9,000 | 1 | japa | B | 1 | Mountain worship. HQ Aichi-ken. |
| Ontakesan Taikyo | sTS | 2-e | | 87,500 | 1 | japa | B | 2 | Mountain worship. HQ Shinjuku-ku, Tokyo. |
| Oomoto | sNN | 2-c | 1892 | 1,500,000 | 15 | japa | B | 3 | 'Great Origin' Omotokyo. Omoto. F=peasant woman, Deguchi Nao. Extensive mass media use. |
| Opus Dei | LR-oC | 9-e | 1928 | 76,000 | 80 | ital | C | 5 | Roman Catholic religious order: 1,000 priests. Secrecy, high finance. |
| Oraon ethnoreligionists | sAT | 3-d | | 388,000 | 3 | indi | B | 4 | Bihar, MP. Hindus 37%, animists 20%. D=7. M=3. |
| Order of Buddhist Contemplatives | w-oB | 9-e | 1970 | 2,000 | 1 | usa | C | 5 | OBC. Order in Soto Zen. Abbeys in UK, USA, Canada. |
| Order of Ethiopia | I-Ang-AC | 6-e | 1900 | 50,000 | 1 | soua | C | 5 | Xhosa section in CPSA (Anglican Ch). 1983, first Xhosa bishop after 80 years of promises. |
| Order of the Cross | SN | 2-e | 1904 | 1,000 | 10 | brit | C | 4 | F=J. T. Ferrier, proclaiming unity of all religions. |
| Org of African Indep Chs of Kenya | I-nC | 7-c | | 4,000,000 | 1 | keny | C | 5 | OAICK. |
| Organization of African Instituted Chs | I-fC | 4-b | 1978 | 40,000,000 | 50 | keny | C | 5 | OAIC. HQ Nairobi. |
| Organization of Islamic Action | sHM | 2-e | 1963 | 10,000 | 10 | iraq | A | 1 | Munazzamat al-Amal al-Islami. Shia. Founded in Karbala opposing Baath regime. |
| Organization of the Islamic Conf | qwM | 8-b | 1971 | 50,000,000 | 52 | saud | B | 2 | OIC. al-Mutamar al-Islami. Education, universities. 8 Heads of State summits. HQ Jeddah. |
| Organization of the Islamic Jihad | fM | 4-d | 1971 | 230,000 | 5 | leba | B | 5 | Munazzamat al-Jihad al-Islami. Related to Hizbollah. Assassinations. Outlawed 1973 to 1987. |
| Oriental Jews | EJ | 2-c | | 2,378,000 | 25 | isra | B | 2 | Immigrants from Eastern states. |
| Oriental Orthodox Chs Conference | fC | 4-b | 1965 | 41,600,000 | 70 | ethi | B | 5 | Patriarchates: Armenian, Coptic, Ethiopian, Malankara, Syrian. |
| Original Way of Heavenly Truth | sTS | 2-d | 1925 | 277,000 | 1 | japa | B | 1 | Honmichi. State persecution 1926-1939. God=10 Kamis. |
| Orthodox | OAC | 2-a | 33 | 215,129,000 | 135 | russ | B | 5 | Eastern Orthodox (HQ Constantinople/Istanbul), Oriental Orthodox (5 communions). |
| Orthodox Bahai Faith | OL | 2-e | 1957 | 10,000 | 3 | usa | C | 5 | Largest of several splits ex-Bahai on death of Shoghi Effendi. |
| Orthodox Charismatics | O2ZAC | 2-c | 1970 | 3,167,000 | 87 | arme | C | 5 | Total Orthodox in Renewal, past and present, including children and infants. D=219. |
| Orthodox Church in America | O-Rus-AC | 6-c | 1792 | 2,244,000 | 1 | usa | C | 5 | OCA. Formerly Russian Orth Gk-Cath Ch. A=1970. 7 US Dioceses, 15 bps. 792n,33x,2s(150). |
| Orthodox Church of Eritrea | O-Eth-AC | 6-c | 1955 | 1,598,000 | 1 | erit | B | 5 | Related to Ethiopian OC. 9 Dioceses and bps. 9% urban. Tigre and others. |
| Orthodox Church of Poland | O-Pol-AC | 6-c | 990 | 1,095,000 | 1 | pola | C | 5 | Autokefaliczny Kosciol Prawoslawny. 1939, 4 million. 6 bps. (1970) 216n,216b,1d,1e,1s,1u. |
| Orthodox Evangelicals | EOAC | 2-c | c1900 | 2,000,000 | 4 | russ | B | 5 | Scattered individuals of Evangelical conviction throughout the 20th century. |
| Orthodox Judaism | OJ | 2-c | | 2,500,000 | 110 | isra | B | 2 | Reaction against modernizing and secularizing tendencies in Judaism. |
| Orthodox Patr of Moscow | M-fC | 4-b | 988 | 131,055,000 | 49 | russ | B | 5 | Long missionary tradition, shattered 1917 by Communism, now arising again. |
| Orthodox schismatics | I-Ort-tC | 5-d | 1866 | 111,000 | 7 | kaza | B | 5 | Total about 6, including: ROCOR, UAOC, Byelorussian AOC. |
| Orthodox sectarians | I-Ose-tC | 5-d | 1765 | 114,000 | 3 | russ | B | 5 | Total about 20 (see list below), underground, organized, nationwide. |
| Orthodox Syrian Ch of the East | O-SyM-AC | 6-c | 52 | 2,354,000 | 1 | indi | B | 5 | Malankara OSC, Catholicate of the East. Syrians. 22 bps,942n,1s(85),W=55%,7820Yy. |
| Osterreichische Bischofskonferenz | S-nC | 7-c | 1979 | 6,129,000 | 1 | ausz | C | 5 | Bishops' Conference of Austria. HQ Vienna. |
| Osterreichische Evangelische Allianz | E-nC | 7-e | | 50,000 | 1 | ausz | C | 5 | OEA. |
| Ot Danum ethnoreligionists | sAT | 3-d | | 110,000 | 1 | indo | A | 2 | Kalimantan. South of Schwaner Range. Animists 99%. D=3. M=4. |
| other antitrinitarian communions | m-fC | 4-c | c1500 | 2,000,000 | 20 | usa | C | 4 | Separate communions e.g. International New Thought Alliance (INTA),IARF,IACT,IGAS. |
| other Asian mainliners | I-3dZ-tC | 5-e | c1970 | 12,000 | 2 | sing | B | 5 | Centres in UK, Zambia, Malaysia, Brunei, USA, and 7 other countries. Nominally in AoG. |
| other Asian cell-based networks | I-3kZ-tC | 5-e | 1980 | 43,200 | 1 | thai | B | 5 | E.g. Hope of Bangkok/Thailand. Converted Buddhists. 40 chs in 19 countries (Asia, Europe). |
| other Asian charismatics | I-3cZ-tC | 5-d | 1974 | 113,000 | 6 | uzbe | A | 5 | Including Word of Life Movement. |
| other Asian Full Gospelers | I-3fZ-tC | 5-e | 1978 | 32,400 | 4 | malb | B | 5 | Mainly Chinese members, a few Indians. |
| other Asian house-churches | I-3hZ-tC | 5-e | c1965 | 2,500 | 2 | kaza | B | 5 | Home churches for isolated converts after nationwide EHC campaign. |
| other Asian indig neocharismatics | ZN3ZAC | 2-c | 1948 | 1,153,000 | 40 | thai | B | 5 | Other Asian churches: Hope of God Churches of Thailand, Latter Rain Ch of Malaysia. D=130. |

*Continued overleaf*

*Table 17–5 continued*

| *Name of religion/religionists* 1 | *Pedigree* 2 | *Type* 3 | *Begun* 4 | *Adherents* 5 | *Ext* 6 | *Coun* 7 | *W* 8 | *X* 9 | *E. g. = examples; name for God, other religions present, D=denominations, M=missions.* 10 |
|---|---|---|---|---|---|---|---|---|---|
| other Asian neocharismatics | I-3nZ-tC | 5-d | 1974 | 196,000 | 5 | thai | B | 5 | New Life Chs. Begun in northeast Thailand after screenings of 'Jesus' Film. M=CCCI-JFP. |
| other Asian Oneness chs | I-3oZ-tC | 10-f | c1970 | 340 | 1 | bang | B | 5 | E.g. Mukti Bani Sangsta. M=American Evangelistic Association. All Namasudras. 35nm. |
| other Asian pentecostals | I-3pZ-tC | 5-e | 1948 | 58,700 | 10 | sril | B | 5 | E.g. Svenska Fria Mission. M=SFM(Sweden). HQ Colombo 6, also Nugegoda. 10f. |
| other Asian radio/TV believers | I-3rZ-tC | 5-d | 1952 | 695,000 | 13 | thai | B | 5 | Isolated Thais and Chinese, mainly aged 12-25. R=16000 (FEBC),T=166000 (FEBC,ICI,&c). |
| other Messianic non-Chr believers | TN3ZAC | 2-d | 1950 | 200,000 | 15 | myan | B | 5 | Organized believers staying in Buddhism, Baha'i, Sikhism, &c. D=20. |
| other Neo-Apostolic meganetworks | X-fC | 4-b | | 25,000,000 | 20 | usa | C | 5 | White-led postdenominationalists. |
| Owari Koyasan | sTJMB | 2-e | | 72,100 | 1 | japa | B | 0 | Sect of Tendai Buddhism. HQ Aichi-ken. |
| Oxford Movement | fC | 4-d | 1660 | 500,000 | 40 | brit | C | 5 | High Church renewal within Church of England. 1850, F=Keble, Pusey, Newman. |
| Oyamatokyo | sNS | 2-e | | 20,000 | 1 | japa | B | 0 | HQ Nara-shi. |
| Pacific Apostolics | I-3aP-tC | 5-e | 1988 | 6,000 | 1 | fiji | B | 5 | AGOFI. Indigenous body with apostolic government. Ex AoG, but now 80% ex-Methodists. |
| Pacific charismatics | I-3cP-tC | 5-e | 1978 | 76,900 | 6 | papu | C | 5 | Many varieties of Neocharismatics in several larger Pacific countries. |
| Pacific Conference of Churches | P-cC | 7-b | 1966 | 16,000,000 | 20 | fiji | B | 5 | PCC. One of WCC's 7 regional councils. |
| Pacific Full Gospelers | I-3fP-tC | 5-e | 1962 | 14,300 | 3 | aust | C | 5 | E.g. Associated Full Gospel Chs. Gospel Light Ministry. Split ex AoG. Many Aborigines. |
| Pacific house-church networks | I-3hP-tC | 5-e | c1980 | 62,400 | 3 | fiji | B | 5 | Isolated home churches for converts after nationwide EHC campaign. |
| Pacific neocharismatics | I-3nP-tC | 5-e | 1960 | 11,300 | 2 | solo | C | 5 | Etoism (followers of prophet Eto). Schism ex Methodist Ch on New Georgia. W=90%. |
| Pacific pentecostals | I-3pP-tC | 5-e | 1917 | 38,500 | 11 | papu | C | 5 | E.g. Port Moresby. Pentecostals. Very rapid growth: 35% pa. 10n,4x,W=99%,21Y. |
| Pacific Word-of-Faith chs | I-3wP-tC | 5-e | 1940 | 5,200 | 2 | usa | C | 5 | A network of cell-based churches, most in Pennsylvania. |
| Pacific/Oceanic indig charismatics | PN3ZAC | 2-d | 1917 | 215,000 | 20 | solo | C | 5 | Pacific indigenous churches: Christian Fellowship Ch, AGCFI, Samoan FGC. D=70. |
| Pagan Pathfinders | sPN | 2-e | 1973 | 1,000 | 2 | brit | C | 4 | Neo-Pagan movement; occult techniques, altered states of consciousness. |
| Pajelanca | sBU | 2-d | c1900 | 900,000 | 1 | braz | C | 5 | Spiritist movement related to Candomble, in central Brazil, in Amazonia. |
| Pakistan Council of Christian Chs | T-nC | 7-e | c1955 | 90,000 | 1 | paki | A | 3 | PCCC. Fundamentalists, with 5 member denominations. |
| Pakistan Episcopal Conference | s-nC | 7-c | 1976 | 1,165,000 | 1 | paki | A | 5 | PEC. Catholic Bishops' Conference of Pakistan CBCP. HQ Lahore. |
| Palace of Sacred Peace | sSN | 2-e | | 1,000 | 1 | taiw | B | 2 | Splinter group ex Compassion Society. |
| Pallotinas | sac-oC | 9-e | 1835 | 2,200 | 50 | ital | C | 5 | SAC. |
| Pangestu | sSN | 2-d | 1932 | 100,000 | 1 | indo | B | 3 | Paguyuban Ngesti Tunggal. F=Pakde Nanto. |
| Panhellenic Evangelical Alliance | E-nC | 7-e | 1977 | 12,300 | 1 | gree | C | 5 | PEA. Greek Evangelical Alliance. |
| Pan-Indian Ecumenical Assoc of USA | I-rC | 7-d | c1960 | 500,000 | 2 | cana | C | 5 | Association to assist Amerindian religious groups in USA and Canada. |
| Pan-Islamists | qM | 8-d | c1870 | 100,000 | 1 | egyp | B | 3 | First of many attempts to unite Islam against Western cultural and religious encroachments. |
| Panj Pir cultists | sFH | 2-d | c1500 | 300,000 | 1 | indi | B | 1 | Popularist Hindu-Muslim cult. Devotees from 53 castes choose 5 deities each. |
| Pan-Malaysian Islamic Party | qnM | 8-d | 1951 | 300,000 | 1 | malb | B | 3 | PAS. Parti Islam SaMalaysia. Right-wing Conservative Malay Muslims. |
| Pan-Religionists | PW | 1-a | | 720,000,000 | 238 | indi | B | 4 | Persons holding that all religions are valid and true, or bodies taking this position. |
| Papua New Guinea Council of Chs | C-nC | 7-c | 1970 | 2,900,000 | 1 | papu | C | 5 | PNGCC. |
| Parareligionists | QY | 2-b | | 80,000,000 | 20 | fran | C | 5 | Most members (e.g. Masons) belong also to mainline religions, or deny being a religion. |
| Parsees | PZ | 2-d | c950 | 250,000 | 4 | indi | B | 2 | Zoroastrians fleeing Persian persecution settle in Gujarat. Now wide diaspora in Africa, Europe. |
| Particular Baptists | P-Bap-AC | 6-e | 1620 | 19,000 | 1 | brit | C | 5 | Schism from first Baptist church, in London. National Strict Baptist Assembly. |
| Parvezis | sNXM | 2-e | 1940 | 2,000 | 2 | paki | A | 1 | Followers of Ghulam Ahmad Parvez, expositor of Ahl-i Quran. HQ London. |
| Pasdaran | qM | 8-d | 1979 | 450,000 | 1 | iran | A | 0 | IRGC. Islamic Revolutionary Guards Corps. Uniformed. |
| Passionists | cp-oC | 9-e | 1720 | 1,500 | | ital | C | 5 | CP. |
| Path of Religion | zSM | 2-d | 1968 | 150,000 | 1 | mald | A | 0 | Dheenuge Magu. Supported by a government ministry, for Muslims only. |
| Paulicians | m-Pau-tC | 5-e | c 250 | 6,300 | 2 | bulg | C | 2 | A few communities, speaking Palityan (near Bulgarian). Also in Hungary. Dualist, rejecting OT. |
| Paulists | ssp-oC | 9-e | 1914 | 1,200 | | ital | C | 5 | SSP. |
| Pawari Bhil ethnoreligionists | sAT | 3-d | | 310,000 | 1 | indi | A | 1 | Maharashtra. Animists 98%. D=1. M=5. |
| Pedi ethnoreligionists | sAT | 3-d | | 192,000 | 3 | soua | C | 5 | God=Modimo. Transvaal. Animists 5%, Muslims, Baha'is. Many nominal Christians. D=9. M=8. |
| Peli Association | I-mar-AC | 6-e | 1971 | 5,000 | 1 | papu | C | 2 | Hawk Association. East Sepik. 1972, 200,000 members. M=New Apostolic Ch (Canada). |
| Pente Assemblies of the World | I-3aO-AC | 6-c | 1906 | 1,512,000 | 1 | usa | C | 5 | PAOW. Black pentecostals.600n.Missions in Caribbean, India, Israel, Nigeria; over 1,000 chs. |
| Pentecostal Apostolics | P-PeA-tC | 5-c | 1904 | 1,776,000 | 30 | nige | B | 5 | E.g. TAC. M=ACMM(UK). 1931, invited to assist Aladura churches. Southeast. 6 Areas. 5f,3s. |
| Pentecostal Association of Ghana | J-nC | 7-d | c1980 | 500,000 | 1 | ghan | B | 5 | PAG. 89 member Spiritual denominations. |
| Pentecostal Ch of Indonesia | I-3oG-AC | 6-c | 1920 | 1,336,000 | 1 | indo | B | 5 | GPI,GPdI. G Pantekosta di Indonesia. 25% Chinese. Many splits, including GBIS. 1500n,3s. |
| Pentecostal Council of Chile | N-nC | 7-c | c1950 | 1,812,000 | 1 | chil | C | 5 | PCC. |
| Pentecostal Fell Union of Liberia | H-nC | 7-d | | 111,000 | 1 | libe | B | 5 | PFUL. |
| Pentecostal Fellowship of Malawi | H-nC | 7-d | | 120,000 | 1 | mala | C | 5 | PFM. |
| Pentecostal Fellowship of Zimbabwe | nC | 7-d | c1960 | 170,000 | 1 | zimb | B | 5 | PFZ. An unusually large variety of over 20 Western-related Pentecostal denominations. |
| Pentecostal Methodist Ch of Chile | s-fC | 4-d | 1909 | 720,000 | 7 | chil | C | 5 | IMPC. |
| Pentecostal World Conference | Z-fC | 4-b | 1947 | 68,159,000 | 155 | swit | C | 5 | PWC. No HQ. World conferences every 3 years since 1st in Zurich in 1947. |
| Pentecostal/Charismatic Chs of NA | X-rC | 7-b | | 17,000,000 | 3 | usa | C | 5 | PCCNA. NA=North America. |
| Pentecostals (First-Wavers) | 1ZAC | 2-b | 1886 | 65,833,000 | 225 | braz | C | 5 | Chs of White origin (now 70% Non-White) requiring initial evidence of tongue. D=740. |
| Pentecostals/Charis/Neocharismatics | ZAC | 2-a | 1549 | 523,778,000 | 236 | usa | C | 5 | Total all church members in the Pentecostal/Charismatic/Neocharismatic Renewal. D=21,080. |
| People of the Quran | sNXM | 2-e | 1880 | 5,000 | 1 | indi | B | 0 | Ahl al-Quran. Split ex Ahl al-Hadith. |
| People of the Tradition | sNXM | 2-d | c1700 | 100,000 | 30 | indi | B | 2 | Ahl al-Hadith. Puritanical, mystics, reform. Branches in all major European/UK cities. |
| People of the Truth | sSN | 2-d | c1050 | 507,000 | 4 | iran | A | 1 | Ahl-i-Haqq. Ethnic, tribal groups, mostly Kurdish. Sufi/Zoroastrian/Christian elements. |
| People's Organization churches | I-3cC-AC | 6-c | 1995 | 2,400,000 | 1 | chin | B | 5 | Churches begun with full approval of local authorities, because no TSPM or foreign links. |
| Peripheral Quasi-pentecostals | QZAC | 2-b | 1739 | 17,800,000 | 110 | usa | C | 2 | Prepentecostals and postpentecostals. Renewal believers but not renewal members. D=2,700. |
| Philippine Co of Fundamental Ev Chs | T-nC | 7-d | c1960 | 140,000 | 1 | phil | C | 4 | PCFEC. Co=Council. |
| Philippine Council of Evangelical Chs | E-nC | 7-d | c1950 | 380,000 | 1 | phil | C | 5 | PCEC. 50 member denominations. |
| Philippine Indep Catholic Ch | I-ReC-AC | 6-c | 1981 | 2,400,000 | 1 | phil | C | 5 | PICC. Iglesia Filipina Catolica Independiente. Schism of 40% of ICI by primate M.V.Ga. |
| Philippine Independent Church | I-ReC-AC | 6-c | 1890 | 2,660,000 | 1 | phil | C | 5 | PIC. Iglesia Filipina Independiente, IFI. Ex RCC. Many breakoffs. 470n. |
| Philippine Independent Church | F-fC | 4-c | 1890 | 2,800,000 | 10 | phil | C | 5 | IFI/PIC. Large schism ex RCC. Became Unitarian; now Anglican relations. |
| Philippines for Jesus Movement | I-nC | 7-c | 1983 | 1,100,000 | 1 | phil | C | 5 | PJM. Umbrella organization for 4,300 independent charismatic fellowships and churches. |
| Phu Thai ethnoreligionists | sAT | 3-d | | 133,000 | 1 | laos | A | 1 | Many also in Thailand; some in north Viet Nam. Agriculturalists. Animists 98%. |
| Phuntsok | sSLB | 2-e | c1960 | 1,000 | 1 | chin | B | 1 | Subgroup of Tibetan Buddhist Sakyapa school. |
| Phuthai ethnoreligionists | sAT | 3-d | | 166,000 | 2 | viet | B | 2 | North Viet Nam. Majority in Laos; some in Thailand. Agriculturalists. Animists 95%. M=SIL. |
| Picpus | sscc-oC | 9-e | 1800 | 1,300 | | ital | C | 5 | SSCC. |
| plural Oriental rites | R-Ori-tC | 5-d | 1954 | 280,000 | 3 | pola | C | 5 | Ordinariate for all Eastern-rite Catholics (Melkite, Armenian, et alia). |
| Pluralist Anglicans | A-plu-tC | 5-b | 1075 | 20,104,000 | 41 | brit | C | 5 | 1960, Charismatic Renewal, now 12%. 100x,308m,2358w,23s (950). |
| Pocomania | sCU | 2-e | c1910 | 60,000 | 2 | jama | B | 5 | 'Little Madness'. Afro-Caribbean cult in Jamaica. |
| Pokot ethnoreligionists | sAT | 3-d | | 279,000 | 2 | keny | B | 2 | God=Tororut. Also in Uganda. Semi-nomadic. Animists 84%. Y=1927(BCMS). D=7. M=6. |
| Polish Ecumenical Council | W-nC | 7-c | 1945 | 1,260,000 | 1 | pola | C | 5 | PRE. Polska Rada Ekumeniczna. |
| Polish Episcopal Conference | R-nC | 7-b | 1987 | 35,743,000 | 1 | pola | C | 5 | KEP. Konferencja Episkopatu Polski. HQ Warsaw. |
| Polish Orthodox | O-Pol-tC | 5-c | 1370 | 1,116,000 | 2 | pola | C | 5 | Autokefaliczny Kosciol Prawoslawny. 1939, 4 million. 6 bps. (1970) 216n,216b,1d,1e,1s,1u. |
| Polynesian ethnoreligionists | sPT | 3-d | | 100,000 | 8 | frep | C | 5 | Remnants of once-strong polytheistic religions on numerous islands. |
| Polytheistic animists | PAT | 3-c | | 4,000,000 | 20 | chin | B | 3 | Animists who have a large pantheon of deities, gods, goddesses. |
| Polytheists | PT | 3-c | | 3,000,000 | 30 | indi | B | 2 | Gradual decline but still strong in the Americas, Polynesia, Oceania, India. |
| Popsong | sKMB | 2-c | | 1,000,000 | 3 | souk | B | 1 | Korean version of Mahayana Buddhism. Zen elements. 1935, unified as Chogye Chong. |
| Popular religionists | PPW | 2-a | | 500,000,000 | 150 | fran | C | 5 | Mainly christianized but popular expressions of religion. On every continent. |
| Pormalim | sSN | 2-e | 1907 | 5,000 | 1 | indo | B | 3 | 'The Independents'. Messianic religion among Bataks of Sumatra. |
| Poro | ssT | 3-e | | 40,000 | 1 | sier | B | 2 | West African Mande-speaking secret society for male initiation. |
| Possessed Ones | sUM | 2-e | | 2,000 | 3 | kaza | B | 3 | Divana. Irregular mendicant Sufis across Central Asia. |
| Postpentecostals | 1QZAC | 2-b | 1950 | 10,500,000 | 80 | usa | C | 5 | Former Denominational Pentecostals who have left to join nonpentecostal churches. D=509. |
| Pr C (Reunited Anti-Ecumenical) | I-Ref-AC | 6-c | 1951 | 2,480,000 | 1 | souk | B | 5 | Tae-Han Yesukyo Changno-hwei. (Hap Dong) NAE. Anti-ecumenical schism. 2096n,1s(850). |
| Prarthana Samaj | sRH | 2-e | 1867 | 50,000 | 1 | indi | B | 1 | The Prayer Society. F=R.G. Bhandarkar. Reformist Hindu movement in Maharashtra. |
| Pratyabhijna | sSH | 2-e | c1920 | 10,000 | 1 | indi | B | 2 | 'Recognition'. Philosophical school of Kashmir Shaivism. Strict monism. |
| Premonstratensionists | opraem-oC | 9-e | 1120 | 1,300 | | ital | C | 5 | OPraem. |
| Prepentecostals | 0QZAC | 2-c | 1739 | 7,300,000 | 100 | brit | C | 5 | Charismatic groups not officially in Renewal: numerous Salvationists, Wesleyans. D=2,600. |
| Presb Ch in Korea (Tonghap) | P-Ref-AC | 6-c | 1884 | 2,406,000 | 1 | souk | B | 5 | PCK Tae-Han Yesukyo Changno-hwei. (T'ong-hap). 1303n,109f,6H,15p,3s,16240Yy. |
| Presbyterian Church (USA) | P-Ref-AC | 6-c | 1706 | 3,311,000 | 1 | usa | C | 5 | PCUSA. 1983 merger of UPUSA, PCUS. 1973, 8% lost in schism. 4595n. Missions: 9 nations. |
| Presbyterian Church of Africa | I-Ref-AC | 6-c | 1898 | 1,052,000 | 1 | soua | C | 5 | African Presbyterian Ch. Zulu schism ex UFCSM(UK). Declining. SS=86000,8000z. |
| Presbyterians | P-Ref-tC | 5-b | 1520 | 46,074,000 | 141 | usa | C | 5 | E.g. PCUSA. 1983 merger of UPUSA, PCUS. 1973, 8% lost in schism. 4595n,4s. In 9 nations. |
| Primal religionists | LAT | 3-b | | 15,000,000 | 20 | chin | B | 3 | Original ethnoreligionists with little or no acculturation or syncretism. |
| Primal Therapy | sFN | 2-e | c1960 | 10,000 | 1 | usa | C | 5 | In Human Potential Movement: members aim at 'emitting primal scream'. |
| professing Christians | PC | 2-a | | 1,875,827,000 | 238 | braz | C | 5 | All persons who openly profess or confess to being followers of Christ. |
| Progressive National Bapt Conv | I-Bap-AC | 6-c | 1961 | 3,473,000 | 1 | usa | C | 5 | PNBC. Black. Schism ex NBCUSA, over elections. 863n. Share NBC seminary. |
| Protestant Charismatics | P2ZAC | 2-b | 1959 | 35,200,000 | 231 | aust | C | 5 | Total Protestants in Renewal, past and present, including children and infants. D=5,780. |
| Protestant Chs in Tuvalu & Kiribati | C-nC | 7-e | c1970 | 49,000 | 1 | tuva | C | 5 | PCTK. Cooperation between the 2 dominant churches. |
| Protestant Church in Indonesia | P-Ref-AC | 6-c | 1615 | 2,803,000 | 1 | indo | B | 5 | GPI. Gereja Protestan Indonesia. Former state-controlled Church of the Indies. 770n. |
| Protestant Ev Council in Croatia | E-nC | 7-e | 1992 | 10,000 | 1 | croa | C | 5 | PECC. HQ Osijek. |
| Protestant Evangelicals | PLEAC | 2-b | 1520 | 27,000,000 | 150 | germ | C | 5 | From days of Luther, self-identifying label. Strongest in USA, Germany, UK. |

*Continued opposite*

*Table 17–5 continued*

| Name of religion/religionists 1 | Pedigree 2 | Type 3 | Begun 4 | Adherents 5 | Ext 6 | Coun 7 | W 8 | X 9 | E. g. = examples; name for God, other religions present, D=denominations, M=missions. 10 |
|---|---|---|---|---|---|---|---|---|---|
| Protestant Evangelicals | P-Eva-tC | 5-c | 1840 | 6,214,000 | 89 | nige | B | 5 | E.g. ECWA. M=SIM. A=1956. 800n,500m,50w,672f,3H,88h,31k,22p(692),1s,W=80%,2000Y. |
| Protestant Federation of Haiti | C-nC | 7-c | | 1,000,000 | 1 | hait | C | 5 | PFH. |
| Protestant global denominations | x-fC | 4-b | | 18,000,000 | 210 | usa | C | 5 | 50 major world organisations, paraconfessional or quasiconfessional. |
| Protestants | PAC | 2-a | 1517 | 342,002,000 | 233 | usa | C | 5 | Vast fragmented sphere of denominations in 150 traditions or communions. |
| Providentialists | fdp-oC | 9-e | 1903 | 1,100 | | ital | C | 5 | FDP. |
| Punu ethnoreligionists | sPAT | 3-d | | 555,000 | 3 | chin | A | 1 | Guangxi. Polytheists (animists) 99%, including ancestor worship. |
| Pure Land Buddhists | PJMB | 2-b | c380 | 21,000,000 | 31 | chin | B | 4 | Ching-Tu. Begun China (F=Hui-yuan), then Japan (Jodo Shy). Now almost all in Japan. |
| Pushtimarga | sVH | 2-c | 1510 | 2,000,000 | 1 | indi | B | 2 | Vallabhasampradaya. 'Way of Grace'. Vaishnava devotional sect. Bombay, Gujarat, Rajasthan. |
| Puyi ethnoreligionists | sPAT | 3-c | | 2,269,000 | 2 | chin | A | 2 | Guizhou, Yunnan. 40 dialects. Polytheists 80%, Buddhists 10%, Taoists 8%. D=1. M=12. |
| Qadianis | QAXM | 2-c | c1920 | 9,000,000 | 60 | paki | A | 1 | Main Ahmadiyah sect, regarded as heretical by Sunnis, with Ghulam as final prophet. |
| Qadiriya | sUM | 2-b | c1120 | 20,000,000 | 50 | syri | B | 3 | Oldest Sufi order, widespread in 50 countries from Senegal to Malaysia. Miracles claimed. |
| Qalandars | sUM | 2-e | c1300 | 5,000 | 1 | indi | B | 2 | One of many irregular Sufi orders: mendicant holy beggars who invoke curses on nonpayers. |
| Qarmatians | sIHM | 10-f | 899 | 200 | 1 | bahr | B | 1 | Qaramitah. Dissident group ex Ismailis. F=Hamden al Qarmat. Now virtually only an influence. |
| Qimbanda | sBU | 2-e | | 50,000 | 1 | braz | C | 5 | Malevolent variety of Macumba and Umbanda involving evil spirits, magical practices, wizardry. |
| Qizilbash | sSN | 2-d | c1450 | 204,000 | 10 | afgh | A | 1 | Ethnic group of warriors. Melange of Islam/Zoroastrianism/Christianity. |
| Quasi-Christians | NY | 2-b | | 50,000,000 | 50 | indi | B | 2 | Large number of bodies that are near-Christian or partially-Christian. |
| Quasireligionists | Y | 1-c | | 1,067,000 | 78 | usa | C | 3 | Other religionists, near-religionists, partial-religionists. |
| Rabha ethnoreligionists | sAT | 3-d | | 227,000 | 1 | indi | A | 1 | West Assam State, Garo Hills, Nagaland. Animists 90%, Hindus 6%. D=3. M=4. |
| Radhasoami Satsang | zH | 2-e | 1861 | 90,000 | 1 | indi | B | 0 | In north India. Now 2 rival movements. F=Soamiji Maharaj. |
| Rahmaniyah | sUM | 2-d | 1760 | 400,000 | 20 | alge | A | 0 | Sufi order, ex Khalwatiya. F=Muhammad bin Abd al-Rahman. 1871, led revolt against French. |
| Rajneesh Foundation | sSN | 2-e | 1974 | 4,000 | 2 | indi | B | 2 | F=Bhagwan Shree Rajneesh. Ashram in Oregon, USA, expelled 1985, returned to Poona. |
| Ram Rajya Parishad | qVH | 8-e | 1948 | 30,000 | 1 | indi | B | 3 | F=Swami Karapetri. Hindu political party. |
| Ramakrishna Vedanta Mission | sHH | 2-c | 1886 | 3,000,000 | 25 | indi | B | 2 | F=Swami Vivekananda. 140 maths and centers in India, 50 others across world. |
| Ramanandis | sV-oH | 9-e | c1450 | 40,000 | 1 | indi | B | 1 | Largest Vaishnava ascetic order. F=Ramananda. |
| Ramanna Nikaya | sT-oB | 9-e | 1865 | 2,000 | 1 | sril | B | 3 | One of 3 main divisions of Theravada monks. |
| Ramdasis | sVH | 2-e | c1650 | 20,000 | 2 | indi | B | 1 | Vaishnava devotional movement, with 40 flourishing maths (monasteries). |
| Ramraiyas | sK | 2-e | c1650 | 2,000 | 1 | indi | B | 1 | Schism by Ram Rai, son of Sikh Guru. Other movements are not allowed to associate. |
| Rana Thakur Tharu ethnoreligionists | sAT | 3-d | | 301,000 | 1 | nepa | A | 0 | On eastern border with India. Agriculturalists, pastoralists. Animists 99%. |
| Rashtriya Swayamsevak Sangh | qH | 8-c | 1925 | 3,000,000 | 10 | indi | B | 1 | RSS. Hindu fundamentalists organizing an extremist self-defence militia. |
| Rastafarians | sCU | 2-d | 1930 | 150,000 | 15 | jama | B | 5 | Dreads. Christianity rejected as White man's religion. Messianic, political. |
| Razzaqiyah | ssUM | 2-e | c1830 | 2,000 | 1 | afgh | A | 0 | Suborder of Sufi Qadiriya. In Herat. |
| Recollect Augustinians | oar-oC | 9-e | 1588 | 1,300 | | ital | C | 5 | OAR. |
| Reconstructionist Jews | CJ | 2-e | 1968 | 50,000 | 5 | usa | C | 5 | F=M. M. Kaplan. Opposed to Chosenness, messianism, Zionism, return to Israel. |
| Red Bobo ethnoreligionists | sAT | 3-d | | 339,000 | 3 | burk | B | 3 | Animists 62%, Muslims 10%. D=3. M=8. |
| Red Meo ethnoreligionists | sPT | 3-d | | 204,000 | 3 | viet | A | 1 | Northwest Tonkin Province. Also in China, Thailand. Polytheists 88%. D=RCC. |
| Red Tai ethnoreligionists | sAT | 3-d | | 154,000 | 2 | viet | A | 1 | Viet Nam and Laos in the area of Thanh Hoa Province. Some in USA. Animists 95%. D=RCC. |
| Redeemed Christian Ch of God | I-3aA-AC | 6-c | 1952 | 2,520,000 | 1 | nige | B | 5 | Ex C&S. Abortive aid: 1957, M=AFM(SAfrica), 1963 Velberter M(Germany). 1p. 18 chs in USA. |
| Redemptorists | cssr-oC | 9-e | 1732 | 6,000 | | ital | C | 5 | CSSR. |
| Reform Hindus | RH | 2-c | | 4,460,000 | 30 | indi | B | 2 | Arya Samaj, et alia. Modern attempts to revitalize Hindus and win back converts. |
| Reformed Anglicans | I-ReA-tC | 5-d | 1844 | 179,000 | 10 | soua | C | 5 | Ch of Sobantu (Colenso). Evangelical. Churches: 150 Zulu, 17 White, 2 Coloured. 100n. |
| Reformed Catholics | I-ReC-tC | 5-c | 1881 | 5,292,000 | 11 | phil | C | 5 | E.g. PIC. Iglesia Filipina Independiente, IFI. Ex RCC. Many breakoffs. 470n. |
| Reformed Church of Hungary | P-Ref-AC | 6-c | 1530 | 2,058,000 | 1 | hung | C | 5 | Magyarországi Reformàtus Egyház. 4 Districts & bishops. 85% farmers. 1650n,1j,2s. |
| Reformed Ecumenical Council | s-fC | 4-c | | 5,000,000 | 18 | usa | C | 5 | REC. |
| Reformed Indep Chs Assoc of Malawi | I-nC | 7-d | c1970 | 350,000 | 1 | mala | C | 5 | RICAM. |
| Reformed Ogboni Fraternity | sNY | 2-e | 1914 | 12,000 | 1 | nige | B | 3 | Christian Ogboni Society until 1933. F=J. A. T. Ogunbiyi(Masonic). Yorubas. |
| Reformed Orthodox | I-ReO-tC | 5-c | 1771 | 1,144,000 | 15 | indi | B | 5 | Reform ex Orthodox Syrian Ch. Syrians. 6 Dioceses. 272n,6H,30r,2s,575t,W=37%. |
| Reformiertie Bund | h-nC | 7-c | | 2,000,000 | 1 | germ | C | 5 | Federation of Reformed Churches. 1,000 congregations, mostly in EKD or United bodies. |
| Regional Conf of Chinese Bishops | Z-rC | 7-d | | 250,000 | 10 | chin | B | 5 | Chung Kuo Chu-chiao T'uan. HQ Hong Kong. |
| Regional Islamic Dawa Council SE | cM | 7-b | 1980 | 136,000,000 | 17 | malb | B | 3 | RIDCSEAP. Represents Muslims in SE=Southeast Asia and Pacific. HQ Kuala Lumpur. |
| Religion of Golden Light | sTS | 2-d | 1859 | 683,000 | 2 | japa | B | 2 | Konko-kyo. F=Kawate Bunjiro (1814-1883). Shinto faith-healing. Nationwide. |
| Religion of Heavenly Wisdom | sNN | 2-c | 1838 | 2,990,000 | 40 | japa | B | 4 | Tenrikyo. Faith-healing.17,000 churches, 20,000 mission stations worldwide. Global mission. |
| Religion of the Heavenly Way | sSN | 2-c | 1860 | 1,200,000 | 15 | souk | B | 4 | Chondogyo. Tonghak. Eastern Learning. Confucian/Taoist/Shamanist elements. 4,700 clergy. |
| Religious Advisory Council of the CI | K-nC | 7-e | | 12,000 | 1 | cook | C | 5 | CI=Cook Islands. |
| Religious Science International | sMN | 2-e | 1949 | 12,000 | 8 | usa | C | 4 | Churches: USA 103, Canada 5, UK, Jamaica, South Africa, Barbados. |
| Religious Zionism | zJ | 2-e | | 20,000 | 2 | isra | B | 3 | Religious aspects and parties committed to political Zionists. |
| Renascence Party | qSM | 8-d | 1988 | 500,000 | 1 | tuni | A | 1 | Hizb al-Nahda (Islamic Tendency, MTI). Largest politico-religious movement in Tunisia. |
| Renewal believers | ZC | 2-a | 1549 | 619,906,000 | 236 | usa | C | 5 | Total all renewal believers alive at mid-year. D=25,780 |
| Renewal Movement | zSM | 2-e | c1970 | 2,000 | 1 | indo | B | 3 | Gerakan Pembaharuan (liberal, modernist). |
| Renshindo Kyodan | sNS | 2-e | | 3,400 | 1 | japa | B | 1 | HQ Nerima-ku, Tokyo. |
| Repose & Meditation | sNXM | 2-e | | 20,000 | 1 | egyp | B | 3 | Al Tawaqufwa al Tabayun. 1977, absorbs at-Tafkir. Assassinations. |
| Republic of China Co of Christian Chs | T-nC | 7-e | c1960 | 11,000 | 1 | taiw | B | 4 | RCCCC. Co=Council. Fundamentalists related to ICCC. |
| Restorationism | I-3pW-AC | 6-d | 1970 | 250,000 | 1 | brit | C | 5 | New Churches movement in Britain, labelled R-1, R-2. Neocharismatics. |
| Revival Zion | I-3zU-AC | 6-e | 1783 | 36,800 | 1 | jama | B | 5 | 1861, Great Christian Revival. Neocharismatics similar to Shouters, Shakers. |
| Riang ethnoreligionists | sHAT | 3-d | | 133,000 | 3 | indi | A | 0 | God=Isawr. In Assam, central Tripura. Close to Tripuri. Hinduized animists 90%, Muslims 4%. |
| Rifaiyah | sUM | 2-e | c1150 | 60,000 | 20 | iraq | A | 1 | Gurzmar. Oldest Sufi order. Ecstatics. Also Syria, Yugoslavia, East Africa, India, Europe, USA. |
| Rimaypas | RLB | 2-d | c1860 | 600,000 | 7 | chin | B | 2 | Eclectic Movement. Nonsectarian, spiritual/cultural renaissance, unify the many Lamaist sects. |
| Rinzai Zen Buddhists | sZJMB | 2-c | 1191 | 3,000,000 | 10 | japa | B | 4 | Japanese Zen. F=Lin Chi (Chinese). Overall aim to reproduce Enlightenment experience. |
| Rinzaishu Buttsujiha | sZJMB | 2-e | 1395 | 98,500 | 1 | japa | B | 2 | HQ Kyoto-shi. |
| Rinzaishu Daitokujiha | sZJMB | 2-e | 1324 | 14,700 | 1 | japa | B | 2 | HQ Kita-ku, Kyoto-shi. |
| Rinzaishu Eigenjiha | sZJMB | 2-e | 1361 | 13,600 | 1 | japa | B | 2 | HQ Shiga-ken. |
| Rinzaishu Enkakujiha | sZJMB | 2-d | 1282 | 178,000 | 4 | japa | B | 2 | HQ Kanagawa-ken. |
| Rinzaishu Hokojiha | sZJMB | 2-d | 1384 | 589,000 | 5 | japa | B | 2 | HQ Shizuoka-ken. |
| Rinzaishu Kenchojiha | sZJMB | 2-e | 1253 | 89,400 | 1 | japa | B | 2 | HQ Kanagawa-ken. |
| Rinzaishu Kenninjiha | sZJMB | 2-e | 1202 | 24,000 | 1 | japa | B | 2 | F=Myoan-Eisai (1141-1218) |
| Rinzaishu Kogakujiha | sZJMB | 2-e | 1380 | 30,100 | 1 | japa | B | 2 | HQ Yamanashi-ken. |
| Rinzaishu Kokutaijiha | sZJMB | 2-e | 1327 | 2,300 | 1 | japa | B | 2 | HQ Toyama-ken. |
| Rinzaishu Koshojiha | sZJMB | 2-e | | 3,100 | 1 | japa | B | 2 | HQ Kamigyo-ku, Kyoto-shi. |
| Rinzaishu Myoshinjiha | sZJMB | 2-c | 1337 | 1,628,000 | 22 | japa | B | 4 | Largest Rinzai sect in Japan. 3,000 temples. Declining. HQ Kyoto. Members in USA, Mexico. |
| Rinzaishu Nanzenjiha | sZJMB | 2-e | 1291 | 91,200 | 1 | japa | B | 2 | HQ Kyoto-shi. |
| Rinzaishu Shokokujiha | sZJMB | 2-e | 1382 | 53,800 | 1 | japa | B | 2 | HQ Kyoto-shi. |
| Rinzaishu Tenryujiha | sZJMB | 2-e | 1339 | 82,600 | 1 | japa | B | 2 | HQ Ukyo-ku, Kyoto-shi. |
| Rinzaishu Tofukujiha | sZJMB | 2-e | 1239 | 5,000 | 1 | japa | B | 2 | HQ Kyoto-shi. |
| Rissho Koseikai | sSN | 2-c | 1938 | 5,000,000 | 40 | japa | B | 3 | Society for Establishing Righteousness & Harmony. Ex Reiyukai. HQ Tokyo. Aim: Buddhahood. |
| Risshu | sNJMB | 2-e | 754 | 23,300 | 1 | japa | B | 2 | One of 6 Nara sects of Japanese Buddhism. Strict monasticism. HQ Nara-shi. F=Ganjin/Ching. |
| Ritsu | sNJMB | 2-d | | 500,000 | 3 | japa | B | 2 | Emphasis on Buddhist monastic precepts. |
| Rizalistas | sSN | 2-d | 1896 | 400,000 | 1 | phil | C | 5 | Nationalist movements honoring, as returning Messiah, Jose Rizal y Mercado. Mainly rural. |
| Roman Catholics | RAC | 2-a | 33 | 1,057,328,000 | 235 | braz | C | 5 | All local (national) churches in communion with Holy See (Vatican, Rome). |
| Romanian Byzantine rite | R-Rum-tC | 5-c | 1721 | 2,107,000 | 2 | roma | C | 5 | 1948-90 suppressed, forced into ROC. |
| Romanian Catholic Episcopal Conf | S-nC | 7-c | 1993 | 3,237,000 | 1 | roma | C | 5 | CER. Conferinte Episcopala Romania. |
| Romanian Evangelical Alliance | E-nC | 7-d | 1990 | 400,000 | 1 | roma | C | 5 | REA. Aliantja Evanghelica din Romania. |
| Romanian Orthodox | O-Rum-tC | 5-b | 1359 | 20,012,000 | 23 | roma | C | 5 | Biserica Ortodoxa Romana. The Lord's Army (300,000) is in Evang. Alliance. 20 bps,8545n. |
| Romanian Orthodox Ch | O-Rum-AC | 6-b | 100 | 20,506,000 | 1 | roma | C | 5 | Biserica Ortodoxa Romana 20bps, 8545n. The Lord's Army (300,000) in Evangelical Alliance. |
| Ronga ethnoreligionists | sAT | 3-d | | 146,000 | 2 | moza | C | 5 | God=Sikwembu. South, coastal areas. Also in South Africa. Animists 20%. D=5. M=6. |
| Rosicrucians | sON | 2-d | c1410 | 700,000 | 50 | germ | C | 4 | Secret worldwide esoteric brotherhood. 1915 includes AMORC. Correspondence courses. |
| Rudrasampradaya | sVH | 2-e | c1520 | 15,000 | 1 | indi | B | 2 | Bhakti approach to Vaishnavism. F=Vallabha. |
| Rumiyah | ssUM | 2-e | | 50,000 | 1 | turk | A | 0 | One of many Sufi Qadiri suborders banned by Ataturk in 1924. |
| Rungi ethnoreligionists | sAT | 3-d | | 125,000 | 1 | tanz | B | 5 | Central Bantu. Southeast shore of Lake Tanganyika. Animists 55%. D=RCC,ELCT. |
| Russian (Byzantine rite) | R-Rus-tC | 5-e | 1917 | 11,400 | 1 | russ | C | 5 | For all Russians of Byzantine rite. |
| Russian Orth Ch: D Almaty | O-Rus-AC | 6-c | | 1,890,000 | 1 | kaza | B | 5 | Russians, Ukrainians, Byelorussians, Chuvash, Mordvinians. Mass emigration from 1991. |
| Russian Orthodox | O-Rus-tC | 5-b | 988 | 88,227,000 | 51 | russ | B | 5 | ROC. Russkaya Pravoslavnaya Tserkov. 93 Dioceses, 103 bps, 14000n,60de(5000),82s. |
| Russian Orthodox Church | O-Rus-AC | 6-b | 988 | 81,582,000 | 1 | russ | B | 5 | ROC. Russkaya Pravoslavnaya Tserkov. 93 Dioceses, 103 bps, 14000n,60de(5000),82s. |
| Russian Unified Fell of CEF | I-3pW-AC | 6-c | 1913 | 1,340,000 | 1 | russ | B | 5 | CEF=Christians of the Evangelical Faith. Formerly in AUCECB. 65 churches in Moscow. |
| Ruthenian (Byzantine rite) | R-Rut-tC | 5-d | 1771 | 444,000 | 2 | ukra | C | 5 | Ruthenians. 1949, forced into Orth D Mukachevo. |
| Ruthenian Catholics | R-Rut-tC | 5-d | 1771 | 391,000 | 7 | ukra | C | 5 | Little Russians. Catholic Slavs. In Ukraine, Poland, Hungary, Slovakia. |
| Ryobu Shinto | sS | 2-c | | 1,000,000 | 1 | japa | B | 2 | 'Dual' Shinto. Pattern of Shinto-Buddhist syncretic coexistence. Kamis=historical Buddhas. |
| Ryosenji Shingonshu | sSJMB | 2-e | | 16,100 | 1 | japa | B | 0 | HQ Nara-shi. |

*Continued overleaf*

*Table 17–5 continued*

| Name of religion/religionists 1 | Pedigree 2 | Type 3 | Begun 4 | Adherents 5 | Ext 6 | Coun 7 | W 8 | X 9 | E. g. = examples; name for God, other religions present, D=denominations, M=missions. 10 |
|---|---|---|---|---|---|---|---|---|---|
| Sabbateans | MXM | 2-e | c1600 | 2,000 | 1 | turk | A | 0 | Donmeh (Apostates). Remnant followers of Jewish messiah Shabetai Zevi (1626-1676). |
| Sabillillah Movement | zSM | 2-e | | 20,000 | 1 | thai | B | 2 | One of many Thai Muslim miliant separatist organizations. |
| Sabiriya | ssUM | 2-d | c1350 | 100,000 | 1 | afgh | A | 1 | One of 2 branches of Chishtiya Sufis. |
| Sabiya | sIHM | 2-e | 909 | 2,000 | 1 | syri | B | 2 | Shia Seveners, a sect of Ismailis: only first 7 Imans were legitimate. |
| Sacramentalists | sss-oC | 9-e | 1856 | 1,100 | | ital | C | 5 | SSS. |
| Sacred Cong for the Ev of Peoples | p-fC | 4-b | 1622 | 181,396,000 | 158 | holy | C | 5 | Vatican dicastery administering all Roman Catholic foreign missions across the world. |
| Sacred Cong for the Oriental Chs | o-fC | 4-c | 1862 | 3,700,000 | 37 | holy | C | 5 | Vatican dicastery administering all RC dioceses not based on Latin rite. |
| Sacred Congregation for Bishops | b-fC | 4-a | 1588 | 901,000,000 | 80 | holy | C | 5 | Vatican dicastery for administering dioceses, bishops, new appointments. |
| Sacred Heart Brothers | sc-oC | 9-e | 1821 | 1,600 | | ital | C | 5 | SC. |
| Sadahnm Mithuru Samuluwa | sVB | 2-c | 1962 | 1,000,000 | 2 | sril | B | 3 | Saddhamma Friends Society (SFS). Reformed Theravada. |
| Sadama ethnoreligionists | sAT | 3-d | | 192,000 | 1 | ethi | B | 4 | Northeast of Lake Abaya. Animists 10%, Muslims 37%(Sunnis). D=5. M=SIM. |
| Saddhammavamsa | sT-oB | 9-e | | 6,000 | 1 | sril | B | 3 | Monastic grouping within Amarapura Nikaya. |
| Safi 'Ali Shahi | ssUM | 2-e | | 5,000 | 1 | iran | A | 0 | A branch of Iranian Nimatullahi Sufi order. |
| Safwa ethnoreligionists | sAT | 3-d | | 169,000 | 1 | tanz | B | 2 | In south, around Mbeya town. Animists 78%. D=RCC(D-Mbeya),CPT,Moravian Ch. |
| Sahaja Yoga | sSN | 2-e | c1960 | 20,000 | 1 | indi | B | 2 | F=Nirmala Devi, known as Divine Mother. Energy within. |
| Sahajdhari Sikhs | sK | 2-d | 1699 | 250,000 | 10 | indi | B | 2 | Nanak Panth. Non-Khalsa Sikhs. Independent grouping of Sikhs, cutting one's hair, etc. |
| Sahajiya | sVH | 2-e | c800 | 10,000 | 1 | indi | B | 2 | Sect of Tantrism in Bengal, later becoming Erotic Vaishnavism. Stresses spontaneity in religion. |
| Saharia ethnoreligionists | sPAT | 3-d | | 225,000 | 1 | indi | A | 0 | Tribals in Madhya Pradesh (Shivpuri, Morena, Guna Districts), and Rajasthan. Polytheists 99%. |
| Saijo Inarikyo | sNJMB | 2-d | | 232,000 | 1 | japa | B | 0 | HQ Okayama-ken. |
| Saiva Siddantins | sSH | 2-e | c350 | 20,000 | 1 | indi | B | 1 | Dualists holding plurality of souls eternally distinct from Shiva. Tamils. Bhakti-oriented. |
| Sakalava ethnoreligionists | sAT | 3-d | | 574,000 | 6 | mada | B | 4 | Strongest Muslim presence among Malagasy peoples. Animists 59%, Muslims 7.5%. D=1. M=7. |
| Saktists | KH | 2-b | | 25,720,000 | 35 | indi | B | 1 | Shaktas (Sakti=Power of Shiva). Durga Hinduism. |
| Sakyapas | SLB | 2-c | 1073 | 5,000,000 | 8 | chin | B | 1 | Grey Earth School. One of 4 major sects of Tibet Lamaism. Logicians, debaters, philosophers. |
| Salafiyah | zSM | 2-d | c1900 | 300,000 | 20 | alge | A | 1 | Islamic Modernists reform movement. First Muslim emancipation of women. Anti-Sufi. |
| Salesians | sdb-oC | 9-e | 1859 | 17,600 | | ital | C | 5 | SDB. |
| Salihiyah | sUM | 2-e | c1880 | 50,000 | 1 | soma | A | 1 | Sufi order from Idrisiyah (Saudi Arabia). Widespread in Somalia under 'Mad Mullah'. |
| Salimiya | sS-oM | 9-e | 860 | 2,000 | 1 | saud | B | 2 | Muslim theological school based on '1,000 sayings' of F=Sahl al-Tustari, theologian and mystic. |
| Salvation Army | S-fC | 4-c | 1865 | 2,300,000 | 90 | brit | C | 5 | SA, also in CHA. 923 branches in UK. Evangelistic work, huge social/poverty programs. |
| Salvationists | P-Sal-tC | 5-c | 1865 | 2,275,000 | 84 | usa | C | 5 | E.g. Territories: Central, Eastern, Southern, Western. 38 Divisions. 3735n,33H,4s. |
| Salvatorians | sds-oC | 9-e | 1881 | 1,200 | | ital | C | 5 | SDS. |
| Samaritans | TJ | 10-f | BC 300 | 500 | 5 | isra | B | 2 | Split from Judaism, centered in Tel Aviv suburb Holon, and Shechem (Nablus). |
| Samavesam of Telugu Bapt Chs | P-Bap-AC | 6-c | 1836 | 1,316,000 | 1 | indi | B | 5 | Samavesam of TBC. M=ABFMS. 99% Mala,Madiga. 418n,2s(120),W=40%,4091Y. |
| Samawiyah | sNXM | 2-e | 1980 | 3,000 | 1 | egyp | B | 3 | Subversive Islamic militants prosecuted by government in 1986. |
| Samaya | sTH | 2-d | c400 | 500,000 | 1 | indi | B | 2 | One of the 2 major divisions within Hindu Tantrism. |
| Samburu ethnoreligionists | sAT | 3-d | | 138,000 | 1 | keny | B | 2 | Samburu District. Pastoralists. Related to Maasai. Animists 86%. D=7. M=10. |
| Sammaniyah | ssUM | 2-e | 1760 | 10,000 | 10 | indo | B | 3 | Suborder of Khalwatiya Sufis, from Egypt to Sudan and Sumatra. |
| Samnak Paw Sawan | sTU | 2-e | 1972 | 3,000 | 1 | thai | B | 2 | 'The Abode of Heavenly Fathers'. Urban, spirit exorcisms, mediums. F=Kloom Vajroban. |
| Samoa Council of Churches | C-nC | 7-d | 1964 | 139,000 | 1 | samo | C | 5 | SCC. |
| Samoan Evangelical Fellowship | E-nC | 7-e | | 8,000 | 1 | samo | C | 5 | SEF. |
| Sanakasampradaya | sVH | 2-d | c1350 | 500,000 | 1 | indi | B | 1 | One of 4 contemporary Vaishnava traditions. Brahman is Krishna. |
| Sanatanists | zH | 2-a | BC 1000 | 740,000,000 | 90 | indi | B | 1 | Old Path Hindus. Popularly called Idol-Worshipers. 9 million priests, 15 million sadhus. |
| Sanbo Kyodan | sZJMB | 2-e | | 2,700 | 1 | japa | B | 2 | HQ Kanagawa-ken. |
| San-chiao | sSN | 2-b | BC 500 | 106,000,000 | 2 | chin | B | 3 | Three Ways. Amalgam of Confucian, Taoist, and Buddhist religions in each's entirety. |
| Sande | ssT | 3-e | | 50,000 | 1 | sier | B | 2 | West African Mande-speaking secret society for female initiation. |
| Sant | sVH | 2-d | c1600 | 100,000 | 1 | indi | B | 0 | Based on Vaishnava Bhakti tradition, Nath cultists, et alia. |
| Sant Nirankari Mandal | sK | 2-e | 1945 | 2,000 | 1 | indi | B | 1 | Sikh movement, also known as Nakali Nirankaris (False Nirankaris). |
| Santal ethnoreligionists | sAT | 3-c | | 1,482,000 | 4 | indi | B | 2 | God=Isor. Hindus 78%, animists 21%. M=MMS,ABFMS,LBI,TOR,SDB,SJ,CSM. |
| Santeria | sUU | 2-d | c1550 | 400,000 | 3 | cuba | B | 5 | Way of the Saints. Lucumis. Yoruban. Afro-Cuban-Catholic image-worship. Strong in USA. |
| Santi Asok | sTB | 2-e | 1975 | 30,000 | 1 | thai | B | 3 | This-worldly TV moral reformists in urban 'dhamma families'. Use of Buddha images rejected. |
| Sanusiyah | sRUM | 2-d | 1856 | 500,000 | 3 | liby | A | 1 | F=Grand Sanusi Muhammad Ali. N Africa, Sahara (Tuaregs, Tubus). Qadiriya mysticism. |
| Saora ethnoreligionists | sHAT | 3-d | | 227,000 | 1 | indi | B | 3 | God=Gaddel. Ganjam District, Orissa, AP, MP. Hindus/animists 75%. D=2. M=5. |
| Sapta Darma | sNN | 2-d | 1952 | 100,000 | 1 | indo | B | 3 | Sevenfold Teaching. New Javanese mystical religion. |
| Sara Gambai ethnoreligionists | sAT | 3-d | | 153,000 | 2 | chad | B | 4 | God=Allah. Some in Cameroon. Muslims 26%, animists 20%. D=5. M=7. |
| Sarvodaya Sramadana | sTB | 2-c | 1958 | 2,400,000 | 3 | sril | B | 4 | Buddhist model of social development, reaching 20% of Ceylon's villages. F=A. T. Ariyaratna. |
| Satanism | sON | 2-e | c1800 | 10,000 | 40 | usa | C | 3 | Devil worship. Occult. Desecration of Christian symbols. In Europe, USA, Middle East. |
| Satmar Hasidism | sOJ | 2-e | c1850 | 40,000 | 3 | hung | C | 3 | Transylvanian origins. Anti-Zionist, anti-Israel. HQ New York. |
| Satpanthis | sIHM | 2-e | c1550 | 3,000 | 1 | indi | B | 2 | 'Those who follow the True Path'. Nizari Khojas. HQ Ahmadabad. Many revert to Hinduism. |
| Satya Sai Baba Satsang | zH | 2-d | c1900 | 500,000 | 22 | indi | B | 1 | Sai-Baba (died 1918) as miracle worker avatar, with reincarnation form 1926. Global. |
| Satya Samaj | zV | 10-f | 1964 | 700 | 1 | indi | B | 2 | Modern Jain sect. F=Swami Satyabhakta. Opposes caste system. |
| Sauras | sHAT | 3-c | c1250 | 1,000,000 | 1 | indi | B | 1 | Hindu worshipers of Sun God, Surya. Temples now neglected except Temple of Sun, Konarak. |
| Scheutists | cicm-oC | 9-e | 1862 | 1,400 | | ital | C | 5 | CICM. Decline from 1,946 in 1967. Missionaries of Scheut. |
| schismatic Anglican communions | a-fC | 4-c | 1844 | 7,600,000 | 40 | usa | C | 5 | Over 40 new denominations (REC, ICCEC, AOC, & c). |
| School of the Magic Jewel | sD | 2-c | c300 | 1,000,000 | 1 | chin | B | 1 | Ling-pao Pai. Tao religious branch; Longmen/Dragon Gate (1,300 Caves). |
| Schweizerische Evangelische Allianz | E-nC | 7-d | 1846 | 200,000 | 1 | swit | C | 5 | SEA. Swiss Evangelical Alliance. 24 member denominations. |
| Scolopians | sp-oC | 9-e | 1617 | 2,600 | | ital | C | 5 | SP. Piarists. |
| Scottish Churches Council | nC | 7-c | 1964 | 2,600,000 | 1 | brit | C | 5 | Ecumenical council with Church of Scotland as largest member. |
| Sea Dayak ethnoreligionists | sAT | 3-d | | 359,000 | 3 | malb | B | 5 | Sarawak, Brunei, Indonesia. Animists 51%, Baha'is 4%(mass conversions from 1962). D=4. |
| Sec Epis de America Centr y Panama | D-rC | 7-b | 1970 | 117,020,000 | 8 | pana | C | 5 | SEDAC. HQ Panama City. 8 mainland countries from Panama to Mexico. |
| Secret societies | sUN | 2-c | c1700 | 4,000,000 | 60 | chin | B | 1 | Secular or religious unorthodox brotherhoods, often criminal; such as the many Triads. |
| Sect Shintoists | TS | 2-c | 1882 | 6,000,000 | 20 | japa | B | 3 | Kyoha Shinto. 85 sects (13 being major). No shrines. Served by Association of Sect Shinto. |
| Sefardis | SJ | 2-d | | 952,000 | 80 | arge | C | 4 | Sephardim. Spanish, Portuguese Jews and descendants, now only in USA, Lat America, Israel. |
| Seigikai Kyodan | sNJMB | 2-e | | 36,400 | 1 | japa | B | 0 | HQ Chiba-ken. |
| Seikokyo | sNS | 2-e | | 7,600 | 1 | japa | B | 1 | HQ Higashi Nada-ku, Kobe-shi. |
| Seikyokai | sNN | 2-e | c1960 | 20,000 | 1 | japa | B | 3 | HQ Tsukubo-gun, Okayama-ken. |
| Seiseikyo | sTS | 2-e | | 15,400 | 1 | japa | B | 1 | HQ Aichi-ken. |
| Seishin Myoshokai | sHS | 2-e | | 70,000 | 1 | japa | B | 0 | HQ Fukuyama-shi, Hiroshima-ken. |
| Seishoin Kyodan | sTS | 2-e | | 10,000 | 1 | japa | B | 1 | HQ Kita-ku, Tokyo. |
| Seizan Jodoshu | sPJMB | 2-d | | 131,000 | 2 | japa | B | 1 | HQ Kyoto-fu. |
| Seizanshu | sTJMB | 2-e | | 4,000 | 1 | japa | B | 1 | Sect of Tendai Buddhism. HQ Kyoto-shi. |
| Sekai Heiwa Kyodan | sNN | 2-e | | 23,600 | 1 | japa | B | 3 | HQ Minami-ku, Osaka-shi. |
| Sekai Shindokyo | sTS | 2-e | | 81,800 | 1 | japa | B | 1 | HQ Aichi-ken. |
| Sekishinkai | sNS | 2-e | | 3,200 | 1 | japa | B | 1 | HQ Hiroshima-ken. |
| Selako Dayak ethnoreligionists | sAT | 3-d | | 135,000 | 1 | indo | A | 1 | Kalimantan. Northwest, around Pemangkat. Animists 98%. D=GKE. M=BEM. |
| Selale ethnoreligionists | sAT | 3-d | | 131,000 | 1 | ethi | B | 3 | Central area. Dialect of South Central Oromo. Muslims 85%, animists 5%. D=2. M=SIM. |
| Self-Realization Fellowship | sFN | 2-e | 1920 | 10,000 | 2 | usa | C | 5 | SRF. Hindu-oriented. F=Paramahansa Yogananda. HQ Los Angeles. Monks, nuns, yoga. |
| Self-Realization Order | sFN | 10-f | | 300 | 1 | usa | C | 3 | Monastic grouping within Self Realization Fellowship. |
| Self-Religionists | FN | 2-d | c1850 | 400,000 | 40 | usa | C | 5 | One's self seen as divine. New Age, Human Potential Movement, Insight, Silva. |
| Sena ethnoreligionists | sAT | 3-c | | 1,053,000 | 3 | moza | B | 4 | God=Mulungu. Also in Malawi. Animists 60%, Muslims 1%. M=FF(South Africa),FIFM. |
| Senshin Kyodan | sZJMB | 2-e | | 36,600 | 1 | japa | B | 2 | HQ Mie-gun, Mie-ken. |
| Senshinkyo | sTS | 2-e | | 28,500 | 1 | japa | B | 0 | HQ Hyogo-ken. Ex Shinrikyo. |
| Sephardi Torah Guardians' Party | qUJ | 8-e | 1984 | 60,000 | 2 | isra | B | 2 | Shas. Political party, to counter Ashkenazi domination of Agudat Israel. |
| Serbian Evangelical Alliance | E-nC | 7-e | | 5,000 | 1 | yugo | C | 5 | SEA. |
| Serbian Orthodox | O-Ser-tC | 5-c | 1219 | 7,486,000 | 21 | yugo | C | 5 | Srpska Pravoslavna Crkva. P since AD 1346. 13 Dioceses, 36 bishops,1j,6s. |
| Serbian Orthodox Church | O-Ser-AC | 6-c | 150 | 5,621,000 | 1 | yugo | C | 5 | Srpska Pravoslavna Crkva. P since AD 1346. 13 Dioceses, 36 bishops,1j,6s. |
| Servants of Mary | osm-oC | 9-e | 1233 | 1,100 | | ital | C | 5 | OSM. |
| Servants of the Light | sON | 2-e | c1960 | 5,000 | 2 | usa | C | 3 | Occultist school offering Kabbalistic training. |
| Servicio Social de Igls Dominicanas | K-nC | 7-d | 1962 | 300,000 | 1 | domr | C | 5 | SSID. Social Organization of the Domican Churches. Members: 20 denominations. |
| Sevener Shiites | sIHM | 2-c | 909 | 3,000,000 | 20 | indi | B | 2 | Ismailis. Main body in India, under Aga Khan IV. |
| Seventh-day Adventist Church | P-Adv-AC | 6-c | 1844 | 1,008,000 | 1 | usa | C | 5 | SDA. 9 Unions. 18% Black. 3365n, 42H,5j,88r,3s,3315t(375031),W=88%,24575Y. |
| Seventh-day Adventist Church | V-fC | 4-b | 1844 | 25,000,000 | 200 | usa | C | 5 | SDA, General Conference. HQ Washington D.C. |
| Sgaw Karen ethnoreligionists | sAT | 3-c | | 1,021,000 | 2 | myan | B | 5 | God=Ywa. Animists 49%, Baha'is. D=BBC(Karen),RCC,CPB,SSKBC,AoG,NAC,SDA. M=10. |
| Shadhiliyah | sUM | 2-c | 1230 | 1,000,000 | 30 | egyp | B | 3 | Sunni Sufi order from Morocco to Egypt to Syria. F=al-Shadhili. Wide influence beyond Islam. |
| Shafiites | SSM | 2-a | 810 | 239,900,000 | 105 | malb | B | 3 | Shafi school of Islamic law. Popular in Southeast Asia, East Africa, Arabia, Egypt, S/C Asia. |
| Shaivites | SH | 2-a | BC 2000 | 216,260,000 | 60 | indi | B | 1 | Saivas, devotees of supreme god Shiva and consort Parvati. More ascetic than Vaishnavas.. |
| Shamanists | ST | 3-b | | 26,793,000 | 15 | russ | B | 5 | Trained shamans utilizing sacred power; one of oldest religious practices. |
| Shattariyah | sUM | 2-e | c1450 | 70,000 | 10 | indi | B | 2 | Sufi order across north India and Bengal. Entered from Iran. Mystical scholarship prominent. |

*Continued opposite*

Table 17–5 continued

| Name of religion/religionists 1 | Pedigree 2 | Type 3 | Begun 4 | Adherents 5 | Ext 6 | Coun 7 | W 8 | X 9 | E. g. = examples; name for God, other religions present, D=denominations, M=missions. 10 |
|---|---|---|---|---|---|---|---|---|---|
| Shaykhis | sAHM | 2-e | c1810 | 1,000 | 3 | iran | A | 0 | Kashfiya. Quasi-heterodox school of Twelvers rejecting excesses of Sufism. Iran, southern Iraq. |
| She ethnoreligionists | sDAT | 3-d | | 491,000 | 1 | chin | A | 1 | Fujian. 1,000 speak She; rest Hakka. Animists 70%, Taoists 19%, Buddhists 10%. D=RCC. |
| Shias | HM | 2-b | 680 | 170,100,000 | 75 | syri | B | 3 | Shiites. Followers of Ali, cousin of Mohammed. In Iran, Iraq, Lebanon, India, Pakistan. |
| Shidaido | sNS | 2-e | | 4,600 | 1 | japa | B | 0 | HQ Ishikawa-ken. |
| Shigisan Shingonshu | sSJMB | 2-d | c1000 | 496,000 | 1 | japa | B | 1 | HQ Nara-ken. |
| Shiite Sufis | sUM | 2-b | | 15,000,000 | 30 | iran | A | 1 | A small number of Sufi orders are Shia, though most are Sunni. |
| Shilluk ethnoreligionists | sAT | 3-d | | 142,000 | 1 | suda | B | 5 | God=Jwok. Upper Nile Province. Nomadic animists 72%, highly resistant to Islam. D=3. M=4. |
| Shin Bukkyo Kukaishu | sSJMB | 2-e | | 30,000 | 1 | japa | B | 1 | HQ Hyogo-ken. |
| Shin Shingonshu | sSJMB | 2-e | | 4,200 | 1 | japa | B | 1 | HQ Higashi Osaka-shi. |
| Shinboku Kyodan | sNS | 2-d | | 158,000 | 1 | japa | B | 2 | HQ Toshima-ku, Tokyo. |
| Shingi Shingonshu | sSJMB | 2-d | | 213,000 | 1 | japa | B | 2 | HQ Taito-ku, Tokyo. |
| Shingi-Shingonshu Yudonosanpa | sSJMB | 2-e | | 20,000 | 1 | japa | B | 0 | HQ Yamagata-ken. |
| Shingon Birushana Shu | sSJMB | 2-e | | 4,900 | 1 | japa | B | 1 | HQ Higashi Osaka-shi. |
| Shingon Buddhists | SJMB | 2-b | 810 | 11,000,000 | 6 | japa | B | 3 | True Word. F=Kukai. Tantric Buddhism; 45 sects. God=Great Sun Buddha. HQ Kyoto. |
| Shingon Kyodan | sSJMB | 2-e | | 4,400 | 1 | japa | B | 0 | HQ Tochigi-ken. |
| Shingon Misshu | sSJMB | 2-e | | 22,000 | 1 | japa | B | 0 | HQ Toyama-ken. |
| Shingon Risshu | sNJMB | 2-d | c1250 | 444,000 | 2 | japa | B | 2 | A subgroup of Risshu; 90 temples. HQ Nara-shi. F=Eizon. |
| Shingon Sanboshu | sSJMB | 2-d | | 156,000 | 1 | japa | B | 0 | HQ Huogo-ken. |
| Shingon Shotenshu | sSJMB | 2-e | | 4,400 | 1 | japa | B | 0 | HQ Hyogo-ken. |
| Shingon Shu | sSJMB | 2-d | | 283,000 | 2 | japa | B | 2 | A broader form of modified Shingon. |
| Shingonshu Buzanha | sSJMB | 2-d | 1580 | 879,000 | 3 | japa | B | 2 | HQ Bunkyo-ku, Tokyo. |
| Shingonshu Chizanha | sSJMB | 2-c | 1585 | 1,205,000 | 3 | japa | B | 3 | Based on 'New Interpretation of Shingon' with Pure Land elements. |
| Shingonshu Daigoha | sSJMB | 2-d | | 354,000 | 1 | japa | B | 1 | HQ Kyoto-shi. |
| Shingonshu Daikakujiha | sSJMB | 2-e | | 38,000 | 1 | japa | B | 1 | HQ Kyoto-shi. |
| Shingonshu Dainichiha | sSJMB | 2-e | | 15,000 | 1 | japa | B | 0 | HQ Tochigi-ken. |
| Shingonshu Gochi Kyodan | sSJMB | 2-e | | 10,000 | 1 | japa | B | 0 | HQ Aichi-ken. |
| Shingonshu Hokakujiha | sSJMB | 2-e | | 15,000 | 1 | japa | B | 1 | HQ Nara-ken. |
| Shingonshu Inunakiha | sSJMB | 2-e | | 21,400 | 1 | japa | B | 1 | HQ Osaka-fu. |
| Shingonshu Ishitetsuha | sSJMB | 2-e | | 8,000 | 1 | japa | B | 0 | HQ Ehime-ken. |
| Shingonshu Kazan'inha | sSJMB | 2-e | | 6,100 | 1 | japa | B | 0 | HQ Hyogo-ken. |
| Shingonshu Kojinha | sSJMB | 2-e | | 5,100 | 1 | japa | B | 1 | HQ Hyogo-ken. |
| Shingonshu Kokubunjiha | sSJMB | 2-e | | 81,600 | 1 | japa | B | 2 | HQ Osaka-shi. |
| Shingonshu Kongoinha | sSJMB | 2-e | | 42,200 | 1 | japa | B | 0 | HQ Hyogo-ken. |
| Shingonshu Kyushu Kyodan | sSJMB | 2-e | | 9,800 | 1 | japa | B | 1 | HQ Fukuoka-shi. |
| Shingonshu Murojiha | sSJMB | 2-e | | 27,500 | 1 | japa | B | 1 | HQ Nara-ken. |
| Shingonshu Omuroha | sSJMB | 2-d | | 142,000 | 1 | japa | B | 1 | HQ Kyoto-shi. |
| Shingonshu Reiunjiha | sSJMB | 2-e | | 6,700 | 1 | japa | B | 0 | HQ Bunkyo-ku. |
| Shingonshu Senyujiha | sSJMB | 2-e | | 39,200 | 1 | japa | B | 1 | HQ Kyoto-shi. |
| Shingonshu Shugenha | sSJMB | 2-e | | 62,200 | 1 | japa | B | 0 | HQ Kobe-shi. |
| Shingonshu Sumaderaha | sSJMB | 2-e | | 49,600 | 1 | japa | B | 1 | HQ Kobe-shi. |
| Shingonshu Tojiha | sSJMB | 2-e | | 56,500 | 1 | japa | B | 1 | HQ Kyoto-shi. |
| Shingonshu Yamashinaha | sSJMB | 2-e | | 53,700 | 1 | japa | B | 1 | HQ Kyoto-shi. |
| Shinjinkyo | sNS | 2-e | | 20,900 | 1 | japa | B | 2 | HQ Hyogo-ken. |
| Shinko Shukyo | zN | 2-b | | 32,827,000 | 4 | japa | B | 3 | Japanese New Religions. |
| Shinmeikyo | sNS | 2-e | | 2,000 | 1 | japa | B | 1 | HQ Kochi-ken. |
| Shin-nyo En | sSJMB | 2-c | | 2,100,000 | 2 | japa | B | 2 | 'Garden of the Truth of Buddha'. Lay movement with 500 workers. Focuses on Nirvana Sutra. |
| Shinnyoen | sSJMB | 2-d | 1935 | 191,000 | 1 | japa | B | 1 | HQ Tachikawa-shi, Tokyo. |
| Shinreikai Kyodan | sNS | 2-d | | 137,000 | 1 | japa | B | 1 | HQ Minato-ku, Tokyo. |
| Shinreikyo | sNN | 2-d | | 144,000 | 1 | japa | B | 3 | HQ Nishinomiya-shi, Hyogo-ken. |
| Shinrikyo | sTS | 2-d | 1894 | 588,000 | 2 | japa | B | 3 | Revivalist Shinto group in Kyoha Shinto. Ex Ontakekyo. God=3 deities, Amaterasu. |
| Shinsei Mutsumi Kyodan | sNS | 2-e | | 2,700 | 1 | japa | B | 1 | HQ Edogawa-ku, Tokyo. |
| Shinseikai | sNN | 2-e | | 64,700 | 1 | japa | B | 3 | HQ Ashigara Shimo-gun, Kanagawa-ken. |
| Shinseikyo | sNS | 2-e | | 33,500 | 1 | japa | B | 0 | HQ Aichi-ken. |
| Shinsen Reidokyo | sNN | 2-e | | 37,000 | 1 | japa | B | 3 | HQ Takatsuki-shi, Osaka-fu. |
| Shinsenkyo | sTS | 2-e | | 12,500 | 1 | japa | B | 3 | Mountain worship. HQ Osaka-fu. |
| Shinshu Bukkojiha | sTJMB | 2-d | | 138,000 | 1 | japa | B | 1 | HQ Kyoto-shi. |
| Shinshu Choseiha | sPJMB | 2-e | | 1,100 | 1 | japa | B | 2 | HQ Yokohama-shi. |
| Shinshu Izumojiha | sPJMB | 2-e | | 12,000 | 2 | japa | B | 0 | HQ Fukui-ken. |
| Shinshu Jokojiha | sPJMB | 2-e | | 25,100 | 2 | japa | B | 1 | HQ Niigata-ken. |
| Shinshu Kita Honganjiha | sPJMB | 2-e | | 9,200 | 1 | japa | B | 0 | HQ Otaru-shi, Hokkaido. |
| Shinshu Koshoha | sPJMB | 2-d | | 146,000 | 2 | japa | B | 1 | HQ Shimogyo-ku, Kyoto-shi. |
| Shinshu Sanmontoha | sPJMB | 2-e | | 19,000 | 2 | japa | B | 0 | HQ Fukui-shi. |
| Shinshu Shojojiha | sPJMB | 2-e | | 21,500 | 2 | japa | B | 0 | HQ Fukui-ken. |
| Shinshu Takadaha | sPJMB | 2-d | | 262,000 | 8 | japa | B | 1 | Largest Pure Land sect in Japan, with 600 temples. HQ Mie-ken. |
| Shinshu Yamamotoha | sPJMB | 2-e | | 4,000 | 1 | japa | B | 0 | HQ Fukui-ken. |
| Shinshukyo | sTS | 2-d | 1880 | 531,000 | 1 | japa | B | 3 | Japanese purification movement in Kyoha Shinto. God=Honchi Taishin, Amaterasu. |
| Shinsokyo | sTS | 2-e | | 2,200 | 1 | japa | B | 0 | HQ Aichi-ken. |
| Shinto Ishikirikyo | sHS | 2-d | | 196,000 | 1 | japa | B | 1 | HQ Higashi Osaka-shi. |
| Shinto Ishizuchiha | sNS | 2-e | | 1,200 | 1 | japa | B | 0 | HQ Ehime-ken. |
| Shinto Kanshinkyo | sTS | 2-e | | 35,400 | 1 | japa | B | 0 | HQ Higashi Psaka-shi. |
| Shinto Kokuseikyo | sTS | 2-e | | 6,300 | 1 | japa | B | 2 | Mountain worship sect. HQ Nakaro-ku, Tokyo. |
| Shinto Kotohirakyo | sTS | 2-e | | 37,300 | 1 | japa | B | 1 | HQ Chibu-ken. |
| Shinto Kotokukyo | sNS | 10-f | | 150 | 1 | japa | B | 1 | HQ Hino-shi, Tokyo. |
| Shinto Kyodan | sNS | 2-e | | 10,000 | 1 | japa | B | 1 | HQ Fukuchiyama-shi, Kyoto-fu. |
| Shinto of Grace and Protection | sS | 2-e | 1660 | 5,000 | 2 | japa | B | 3 | Suika Shinto. Influenced by Neo-Confucianism. |
| Shinto Shindokyo | sTS | 2-e | | 4,600 | 1 | japa | B | 1 | HQ Kyogo-ken. |
| Shinto Shinkyo | sNS | 2-e | | 9,400 | 1 | japa | B | 0 | HQ Kochi-ken. |
| Shinto Shinshinkyo | sTS | 2-e | | 21,800 | 1 | japa | B | 0 | HQ Hyogo-ken. |
| Shinto Shuseiha | sTS | 2-e | 1873 | 51,200 | 1 | japa | B | 3 | A Confucian-oriented Japanese movement in Kyoha Shinto. God=Amaterosu. |
| Shinto Taikyo | sTS | 2-e | 1886 | 68,800 | 1 | japa | B | 3 | A Japanese revivalist Shinto group in Kyoha Shinto. No founder. HQ Minato-ku, Tokyo. |
| Shinto Taiseikyo | sTS | 2-d | 1868 | 179,000 | 1 | japa | B | 3 | Confucian-oriented movement in Kyoha Shinto. F=Hirayama Shosai. |
| Shinto Tenkokyo | sTS | 2-e | | 6,100 | 1 | japa | B | 1 | HQ Yamaguchi-ken. |
| Shinto Yamatokyo | sNS | 2-e | | 10,000 | 1 | japa | B | 1 | HQ Ise-shi, Mie-ken. |
| Shintoists | S | 1-c | | 2,762,000 | 8 | japa | B | 1 | 'The Way of the Kami (Gods)'. 150 sects, 80,000 shrines in Japan. |
| Shintoku Kyodan | sTS | 2-e | | 20,100 | 1 | japa | B | 2 | Mountain worship. HQ Setagaya-ku, Tokyo. |
| Shiromani Gurdwara Prabandhak Com | nK | 7-e | 1920 | 1,000 | 1 | indi | B | 2 | Com=Committee. SGPC. Moderate Sikh religious body. |
| Shisei Mahashirakyo | sTS | 2-e | | 5,800 | 1 | japa | B | 0 | HQ Saitama-ken. |
| Shishinkai | sNJMB | 2-e | | 70,200 | 1 | japa | B | 1 | HQ Kita-ku, Tokyo. |
| Shiva Sena | qSH | 8-e | 1966 | 10,000 | 1 | indi | B | 1 | Army of Sivaji. Marathi Hindu nationalist political party in Maharashtra. Militant. |
| Shizen Shindo | sNS | 2-e | | 6,400 | 1 | japa | B | 1 | HQ Shizuoka-ken. |
| Shizensha | sTS | 2-e | | 19,600 | 1 | japa | B | 1 | HQ Osaka-shi. |
| Shobo Hokkeshu | sNJMB | 2-e | | 18,700 | 1 | japa | B | 1 | HQ Kita-ku, Kyoto-shi. |
| Shobokai | sNJMB | 2-e | | 12,600 | 1 | japa | B | 1 | HQ Shinagawa-ku, Tokyo. |
| Shotoku Shu | sNJMB | 2-e | 1950 | 12,800 | 1 | japa | B | 2 | A modern form of Japanese Mahayana. 1950, ex Hossoshu. HQ Nara-ken. |
| Shrine Shintoists | HS | 2-b | 1946 | 62,000,000 | 40 | japa | B | 2 | Jinja Honcho, Jinja Shinto. 26,000 priests, 77,000 shrines. |
| Shugendo | sTJMB | 2-d | c1050 | 104,000 | 1 | japa | B | 2 | Way to control central power. Lay, hostile to clergy. 180 temples. |
| Shugendokyo | sTS | 2-e | | 9,200 | 1 | japa | B | 2 | HQ Tokyo. |
| Shugenshu | sTJMB | 2-e | | 91,000 | 1 | japa | B | 0 | Sect of Tendai. HQ Kamagawa-ken. |
| Shui ethnoreligionists | sPAT | 3-d | | 383,000 | 1 | chin | A | 1 | Guizhou, Guangxi. Official nationality. Agriculturalists. Polytheists/animists 99%. Y=c1880. D=5. |
| Shukyo Hojin Shinto | sTS | 2-e | | 10,000 | 1 | japa | B | 0 | HQ Otaru-shi, Hokkaido. |
| Shuyodan Hoseikai | sNS | 2-e | | 15,800 | 1 | japa | B | 2 | HQ Toshima-ku, Tokyo. |
| Shwegyin Nikaya | sT-oB | 9-e | c1850 | 50,000 | 1 | myan | B | 4 | Smaller school: 50,000 monks. Strict, puritanical. |
| Siddha Yoga | sSH | 2-e | c400 | 14,000 | 10 | indi | B | 3 | Kashmir Shaivite teaching. HQ Ganeshpuri. 40 ashrams in Mexico, Japan, New York. |
| Siddha Yoga Dham | zH | 2-e | 1976 | 40,000 | 60 | usa | C | 4 | F=Swami Muktananda. Kundalini yoga. Daily meditation, vegetarianism. |
| Sierra Leone Muslim Congress | nM | 7-c | c1960 | 2,229,000 | 1 | sier | B | 2 | SLMC. National organization representing all Muslims. HQ Freetown. |
| Sihanaka ethnoreligionists | sAT | 3-d | | 261,000 | 1 | mada | B | 3 | North central, east of Merina. Animists 72%. D=3. M=OSST. |

Continued overleaf

*Table 17–5 continued*

| Name of religion/religionists 1 | Pedigree 2 | Type 3 | Begun 4 | Adherents 5 | Ext 6 | Coun 7 | W 8 | X 9 | E. g. = examples; name for God, other religions present, D=denominations, M=missions. 10 |
|---|---|---|---|---|---|---|---|---|---|
| Sikh Dharma of the W Hemisphere | cK | 7-e | 1969 | 10,000 | 8 | usa | C | 5 | W=Western. Also known as Happy, Healthy & Holy Organization (3HO). |
| Sikhs | K | 1-b | c1500 | 23,258,000 | 34 | indi | B | 2 | Monotheistic revelation to F=Guru Nanak (1469-1539). HQ Amiritsar. |
| Silva Mind Control | sFN | 2-d | 1966 | 200,000 | 1 | mexi | C | 5 | F=Jose Silva. Dynamic meditation to increase mind power. |
| SIM International | sim-oC | 9-e | 1893 | 1,500 | 40 | brit | C | 5 | Formerly Sudan Interior Mission. |
| Singapore Council of Christian Churches | nC | 7-e | c1960 | 15,000 | 1 | sing | B | 5 | SCCC. Fundamentalists related to ICCC. |
| Singh Sabha Movement | nK | 7-e | 1873 | 5,000 | 1 | indi | B | 2 | To promote Sikhism. Many Khalsa colleges accross north India. |
| single congregation(s) | I-sin-tC | 5-c | 1920 | 2,138,000 | 7 | usa | C | 5 | In over 100 noncharismatic single congregations (Moody Bible Institute 8,000 members). |
| Sino-American Buddhist Association | cB | 7-d | 1968 | 800,000 | 5 | usa | C | 4 | SABA. Chinese Buddhist polity. Strict standards. |
| Sisters of Adoration | sabs-oC | 9-e | | 3,700 | | indi | B | 5 | SABS. Blessed Sacrament Sisters. |
| Siyam Nikaya | sT-oB | 9-e | 1753 | 12,000 | 1 | sril | B | 3 | Oldest fraternity of Theravada monks in Ceylon. Strict hierarchy. |
| Siyane Vipassana Bhavana Samitiya | sTB | 2-e | 1955 | 3,000 | 1 | sril | B | 3 | Modern Sri Lankan lay meditation society. |
| Slovak (Byzantine rite) | R-Slo-tC | 5-d | 1818 | 285,000 | 2 | slok | C | 5 | Church of Srlence, liquidated 1945-50. |
| Slovak Orthodox | O-Slo-tC | 5-e | 1863 | 16,000 | 1 | slok | C | 5 | Cirkev Pravoslavna. |
| Slovenia Bishops' Conference | nC | 7-c | 1993 | 1,659,000 | 1 | slov | C | 5 | SSK. Slovenska Skofovska Konferenca. HQ Ljubljana. |
| Smartas | sHH | 2-e | | 60,000 | 1 | indi | B | 2 | South Indian orthodox brahmin community. Strict standards. Syncretistic. |
| Sociedade Mussulmana de Chile | nM | 7-e | c1970 | 4,800 | 1 | chil | C | 5 | Muslim Society of Chile. Operates one Islamic Centre. |
| Society for African Missions | sma-oC | 9-e | 1856 | 1,000 | 15 | ital | C | 5 | SMA. Societas Missionum ad Africa. |
| Society for Social Reform | zSM | 2-c | | 1,600,000 | 1 | kuwa | B | 3 | Jamiyat al-Islah al-Ijtimai. Sunni body based in Kuwait. |
| Society for the Victory of Islam | fM | 4-c | 1961 | 1,000,000 | 1 | nige | B | 3 | Jamaatu Nasril Islam. Fundamentalist, but also reformist organization. |
| Society of Companions of the Spirits | sNN | 2-c | 1922 | 4,260,000 | 10 | japa | B | 2 | Reiyukai Kyodan. Nichirenshu, family values, lay. F=Kubo Ka. HQ Minato-ku. |
| Society of Militant Clergy | sHM | 2-e | 1976 | 5,000 | 1 | iran | A | 1 | Jamiat-i Ruhaniyun-i Mobariz. Shia, conservative. |
| Society of Muslims | nM | 7-e | 1985 | 10,000 | 1 | trin | C | 2 | Jamaat al-Muslimeen. Radical Black Muslim guerrillas whose 1990 attempted coup failed. |
| Soka Gakkai International | sSN | 2-b | 1937 | 18,000,000 | 115 | japa | B | 3 | Value Creation. 1975 SGI; 1990 Lay split ex Nichiren Shoshu. World conversion dropped. |
| Solomon Islands Christian Association | K-nC | 7-d | | 310,000 | 1 | solo | C | 5 | SICA. |
| Solomon Islands ethnoreligionsists | sPT | 3-e | | 13,700 | 1 | solo | C | 5 | Animistic religions mostly on Malaita, with 500 on Guadacanal. |
| Soninke ethnoreligionists | sAT | 3-d | | 352,000 | 7 | mali | A | 0 | Muslims 80%(Sunnis, most in Sufi Tijaniyya and in Hamali sect), animists 20%. M=2. |
| Sons of Israel | zJ | 2-e | BC 200 | 30,000 | 4 | indi | B | 2 | Bene Israel. Largest Jewish body in India; Marathi-speaking. Bombay, Calicut. 12,000 in Israel. |
| Soshindo Honcho | sNS | 2-e | | 18,400 | 1 | japa | B | 1 | HQ Fukuoka-shi. |
| Sotho ethnoreligionists | sAT | 3-d | | 113,000 | 3 | soua | C | 5 | God=Modimo. Also in Lesotho. Animists 5%, Muslims, Baha'is. M=OMI,CSSp,SCJ,OFM,LM. |
| Soto Shu | sZJMB | 2-c | c1240 | 6,842,000 | 15 | japa | B | 3 | Zen Buddhism with temples, priests, rites. China origin. F=Dogen. Popular Buddhist teaching. |
| South African Council of Churches | W-nC | 7-b | 1904 | 12,146,000 | 1 | soua | C | 5 | SACC. 1904, South African General Missionary Conference; 1936, SACC. 16 local councils. |
| South American ethnoreligionists | sPT | 3-c | | 1,250,000 | 10 | braz | C | 5 | Remnant of many Amerindian tribal religions, especially in Amazon basin. |
| South Central Dinka ethnoreligionists | sAT | 3-d | | 128,000 | 1 | suda | C | 5 | God=Nialic. West of White Nile. Animists 39%, Muslims 1%; highly resistant to Islam. D=2. M=2. |
| South Central Gond ethnoreligionists | sAT | 3-d | | 288,000 | 1 | indi | A | 2 | Adilabad District, northern Andhra Pradesh. Hindus 60%, animists 40%. D=2. M=6. |
| South Korean ethnoreligionists | sST | 3-c | | 7,325,000 | 1 | souk | B | 5 | Shamanists 16%, Buddhists 15%, New-Religionists 15%, Confucianists 11%. D=100. M=300. |
| South Toraja ethnoreligionists | sAT | 3-d | | 115,000 | 1 | indo | C | 5 | God=Poeang Mato. Sulawesi. Rantepao is prestige dialect. Animists 20%, Muslims 15%. D=4. |
| Southeast Asian ethnoreligionists | sPAT | 3-c | | 2,000,000 | 15 | thai | B | 2 | Montagnards and other peoples of animistic/polytheistic faith and culture. |
| Southeast Gond ethnoreligionists | sAT | 3-d | | 283,000 | 1 | indi | A | 1 | God=Devudu. Strongly influenced by Telugu, in AP. Hindus 60%, animists 40%. D=2. M=2. |
| Southern Baptist Convention | P-Bap-AC | 6-b | 1845 | 22,960,000 | 1 | usa | C | 5 | SBC. 1845 ex North. 99% White. (1970) 31000n,2H,6s,W=39%,409659Y. (1990) 63352n. |
| Southern Baptist IMB | imb-oC | 9-e | 1845 | 4,200 | 150 | usa | C | 5 | IMB = International Mission Board. Formerly Foreign MB. |
| Southern Bhil ethnoreligionists | sPAT | 3-c | | 1,260,000 | 1 | indi | A | 2 | Polytheists 95%. D=CMA,MCSA,CNI,RCC,AoG. M=IEM,COUNT,CGMM,BFI,UPM,WVI. |
| Southern Kissi ethnoreligionists | sAT | 3-d | | 150,000 | 2 | libe | B | 2 | Lofa County, northwest. Also in Sierra Leone. Literates 15%. Animists 79%, Muslims 10%. D=6. |
| Southern Lisu ethnoreligionists | sPT | 3-d | | 157,000 | 2 | chin | C | 5 | Flowery Lisu(Hwa Lisu), Western Lisu. West Yunnan, Sichuan; Burma. Polytheists 20%. D=3. |
| Southern Maninka ethnoreligionists | sAT | 3-c | | 1,127,000 | 1 | guin | A | 1 | God=Alla. Also in Guinea Bissau, Liberia. Animists 59%, Muslims 39%. D=RCC,EEP. M=10. |
| Southern Ndebele ethnoreligionists | sAT | 3-d | | 163,000 | 1 | soua | C | 5 | God=Nkulunkulu. Transvaal Ndebele(Laka/Black Ndebele & Manala tribes). Animists 20%.D=7. |
| Southern Senufo ethnoreligionists | sAT | 3-d | | 622,000 | 1 | ivor | B | 2 | Animists 65%, Muslims 30%. D=RCC(D-Korhogo),ANBC,EPC. M=WEC,CBFMS,BGC. |
| Southern Yi ethnoreligionists | sPAT | 3-d | | 835,000 | 1 | chin | A | 1 | Eastern Yi, Southern Yi. Black Yi. Yunnan, Guizhou, Sichuan. Polytheists 95%. D=RCC,TSPM. |
| Southern Zhuang ethnoreligionists | sPAT | 3-c | | 4,009,000 | 1 | chin | A | 1 | Southwest Guangxi. Polytheists 90%, some Buddhists. D=TSPM,RCC. M=CSI,YWAM,SIL. |
| Spanda | sSH | 2-e | c850 | 5,000 | 1 | indi | B | 2 | 'Vibration'. One of 3 philosophical schools of Kashmir Shaivism. |
| Spiritans | cssp-oC | 9-e | 1703 | 3,200 | | ital | C | 5 | CSSP. |
| Spiritist Catholics | SRPC | 2-b | 1850 | 82,000,000 | 30 | braz | C | 3 | Baptized RCs either (a)High Spiritists (mainly Umbanda) or (b)Afro-American Low Spiritism. |
| Spiritists | U | 1-b | | 12,334,000 | 55 | braz | C | 5 | Widespread. Adherents here omit 82 millions who are baptized Roman Catholics. |
| Spiritual Unity of Nations Assoc | wPW | 7-e | c1970 | 10,000 | 2 | soua | C | 5 | SUNA. For better relations between religions, especially Christians and Jews. HQ Somerset. |
| Spiritualists | m-Spi-tC | 5-d | 1852 | 131,000 | 10 | usa | C | 2 | E.g. Ecclesiastical Council. Spiritualists ex Christian Science. Mainly NY state. 40n. |
| Spiritualists National Union | nU | 7-e | | 30,000 | 3 | brit | C | 5 | Non-Christian as well as Christian members. |
| Sri Chinmoy Centre | zH | 2-e | 1964 | 3,000 | 5 | usa | C | 4 | F=Chinmoy Kumar Ghose, Hindu guru from Bengal. HQ New York. UN connections as an NGO. |
| Sri Lanka Muslim Congress | qnM | 8-c | 1980 | 1,694,000 | 1 | sril | B | 3 | SLMC. Eastern Province base; a national party since 1986. |
| Sri Lankan Dharmadhuta Society | nB | 7-c | 1952 | 2,000,000 | 1 | sril | B | 3 | Begun from World Fellowship of Buddhists for Theravada missions worldwide. |
| Sri Shankaradeva Sangha | sRH | 2-c | c1500 | 3,500,000 | 5 | indi | B | 1 | Vaishnava reform movement in Assam. F=Shankaradeva (c1500). Reorganised 1933. |
| Sri Vidya | sTH | 2-e | c500 | 10,000 | 1 | indi | B | 2 | South Indian Hindu Tantrism, worshiping goddess Tripurasundari. |
| St Croix Ev Ministerial Association | E-nC | 7-e | | 5,000 | 1 | virg | C | 5 | SCEMA. |
| St Kitts Evangelical Association | E-nC | 7-e | | 3,000 | 1 | saik | C | 5 | SKEA. |
| St Lucia Inter-Church Council | C-nC | 7-d | | 113,000 | 1 | sail | C | 5 | SLICC. |
| St Thomas Inter-Church Council | C-nC | 7-e | | 32,000 | 1 | virg | C | 5 | VIICC. Members: 6 denominations. |
| Standing Co of Canonical Orth Bps | O-cC | 7-c | | 4,000,000 | 12 | usa | C | 5 | SCOBA. Co=Conference. in Americas. All Orthodox bishops in canonical communion. |
| Standing Conf of Jews, Chr & Muslims | cPW | 7-e | 1971 | 10,000 | 20 | brit | C | 5 | Chr=Christians. SCJCME. (E=in Europe) HQ London. |
| Sthanakavasis | sSV | 2-e | | 1,000 | 1 | indi | B | 1 | Dhundiyas. Reformed subgroup within Svetambara Jainas. |
| Strict Brethren | I-EBr-tC | 5-e | 1869 | 44,000 | 5 | egyp | B | 5 | Schism ex American M (Coptic Ev Ch), now large Egyptian-run denominations. |
| Strict Koranic Muslims | sSSM | 2-b | 1272 | 92,266,000 | 1 | indo | B | 3 | Agama Islam Santri. Sunnis of Shafiite rite; mostly coastal peoples on Sumatra. |
| Subud | sNN | 2-d | 1933 | 330,000 | 70 | indo | B | 3 | Susila Buddhi Dharma. Inner force. F=Bapak. Vast properties, banks. UK 2,000, USA 80 cities. |
| Sudan Council of Churches | K-nC | 7-c | 1965 | 5,700,000 | 1 | suda | B | 5 | SCC. Maglis al Kanayis fi Sudan. 10 denominations including RCC. |
| Sudan Episcopal Conference | S-nC | 7-c | 1971 | 3,148,000 | 1 | suda | B | 5 | SEC, SCBC. Sudan Catholic Bishops' Conference. HQ Khartoum. |
| Sudanese Ev Christian Association | E-nC | 7-d | 1973 | 100,000 | 1 | suda | B | 5 | SECA. |
| Sufi Order in the West | sUM | 2-e | 1910 | 30,000 | 3 | brit | C | 5 | Begun in London. F=Hazrat Inyat Khan, from Baroda. Holds 'universal worship'. |
| Sufis | UM | 2-a | c 800 | 237,400,000 | 204 | moro | A | 1 | Mass mystical orders/brotherhoods (70 in Egypt) Morocco to Indonesia; mostly Sunni, few Shia. |
| Suhrawardiyah | ssUM | 2-d | 1180 | 800,000 | 4 | paki | A | 0 | South Asian Shia Sufi order. HQ Multan. Also Afghanistan, India (Deccan, Punjab, Sind). |
| Sukuma ethnoreligionists | sAT | 3-c | | 1,047,000 | 1 | tanz | B | 4 | God=Mulungu. Animists 33%, Muslims 30%. D=RCC,AIC,SDA,CPT,BCT,PCSAT. AICs. M=20. |
| Sukyo Mahikari | sNN | 2-e | 1974 | 7,000 | 1 | japa | B | 3 | Subsect ex Sekai Mahikari Bunmei Kyodan. |
| Sulaymanis | sMIHM | 2-e | c1590 | 40,000 | 1 | indi | B | 2 | Split ex Daudis (Bohras), Ismaili sect. |
| Suleymancis | sUM | 2-e | 1930 | 8,000 | 15 | turk | A | 1 | Turkish renewal movement resisting secular state control. Strong in Germany. HQ Cologne. |
| Sumarah | sNN | 2-e | 1935 | 10,000 | 1 | indo | B | 3 | 'Total surrender to God'. F=Sukino. East and Central Java cities. |
| Sumbwa ethnoreligionists | sAT | 3-d | | 139,000 | 1 | tanz | B | 3 | West of the Sukuma. Animists 53%, Muslims 19%(Shafi Sunnis). D=RCC(M-Tabora). |
| Sumerakyo | sNS | 2-d | | 173,000 | 1 | japa | B | 1 | HQ Shizuoka-ken. |
| Sumerakyo Honinha | sNS | 2-d | | 450,000 | 1 | japa | B | 1 | HQ Fukuoka-shi. |
| Sundanese ethnoreligionists | sIAT | 3-d | | 225,000 | 1 | indo | B | 2 | God=Allah. Muslims 50%(strict Shafi, mosque attenders 55%), New-Religionists 48%. D=7. |
| Sunists | sSN | 2-c | | 1,000,000 | 1 | taiw | B | 3 | One of the 2 major sects out of modern I-kuan Tao (Unity). |
| Sunnis | SM | 2-a | | 1,002,543,000 | 195 | paki | A | 2 | Main body of Islam. Ahl al-Sunna wal-jamaa. The True Muslims. Non-Shia Muslims. |
| Sup As for Islamic Revolution in Iraq | nM | 7-e | 1982 | 30,000 | 1 | iraq | A | 0 | SAIRI. Sup As= Supreme Assembly. Shias under violent persecution by Baath regime. |
| Suppire Senufo ethnoreligionists | sAT | 3-d | | 275,000 | 2 | mali | A | 1 | Around Sikasso; also in Ivory Coast. Animists 50%, Muslims 48%. D=RCC. M=2. |
| Supreme Council for Ghana Pent Chs | I-nC | 7-c | c1970 | 2,550,000 | 1 | ghan | B | 5 | SCGPC (formerly Council of Indep Chs of Ghana, or NCSC, GCLC). 500 Spiritual bodies. |
| Supreme Council for Islamic Affairs | nM | 7-b | 1977 | 48,900,000 | 1 | nige | B | 3 | Major officially-sponsored Muslim organization. |
| Supreme Council of Kenya Muslims | nM | 7-c | 1976 | 2,187,000 | 1 | keny | C | 5 | SUPKEM. Founded as a federation of over 100 Muslim organizations. |
| Supreme Islamic Shii Council | nM | 7-c | 1967 | 1,300,000 | 5 | leba | B | 5 | SISC. Main focus of action for the Shia intelligentsia. |
| Supreme Truth Movement | sSN | 2-d | c1985 | 150,000 | 20 | japa | B | 3 | Aum Shinrikyo. Ex Shinrikyo. Terrorist attacks in Tokyo. Buddhist/Hindu. Big in Russia. |
| Surinamese Islamic Council | nM | 7-e | 1978 | 10,000 | 1 | suri | B | 4 | Surinaamse Islamitsche Organizatie. Split from FIGS. Six branches. |
| Susu ethnoreligionists | sAT | 3-d | | 144,000 | 4 | guin | A | 1 | God=Alla. Muslims 85%(Maliki, since 1600; strongly syncretistic Islam), animists 15%. D=3. |
| Svetambara Jains | SV | 2-c | 79 | 1,500,000 | 20 | indi | B | 2 | 'White-clothed' Jainas. Concentrations: Punjab, Rajasthan, Gujarat. 1,650 monks, 4,400 nuns. |
| Swaminarayan Hindu Mission | w-oH | 9-d | c1900 | 100,000 | 32 | brit | C | 2 | Worldwide missionary arm, especially to USA, UK; well-organized. |
| Swaminarayans | sVH | 2-c | 1801 | 5,000,000 | 33 | indi | B | 3 | In India, UK, Kenya, USA. HQ Gujarat. F= Sahajananda Swami (1781-1830), later deified. |
| Swazi ethnoreligionists | sAT | 3-d | | 351,000 | 4 | soua | C | 5 | Also in Swaziland. Animists 25%. Y=1880. D=5. M=5. |
| Swaziland Conference of Churches | E-nC | 7-d | 1929 | 125,000 | 1 | swaz | C | 5 | SCC. Conciliar membership, from Catholics to AICs. In practice rivals CSC. |
| Swedenborgians | m-Swe-tC | 5-e | 1783 | 28,300 | 15 | soua | C | 3 | New Jerusalem Ch. M=Gen Conf NC(UK). 1961 merged with Ethiopian Cath Ch in Zion; 5n. |
| Swedish Ecumenical Council | W-nC | 7-c | 1932 | 5,900,000 | 1 | swed | C | 5 | SEC. Svenska Ekumeniska Namnden. |
| Swedish Evangelical Alliance | E-nC | 7-d | 1853 | 400,000 | 1 | swed | C | 5 | SEA. Evangeliska Alliansens Svenska Avdelning |
| Swedish Free Church Council | C-nC | 7-d | | 270,000 | 1 | swed | C | 5 | SFCC. Sveriges Frikyrkorad. Council of Free Churches. 85 local Christian councils. |
| Swiss Christian Council of Churches | K-nC | 7-c | | 6,100,000 | 1 | swit | C | 5 | ACKS. Arbeitsgemeinschaft Christlicher Kirchen in der Schweiz. |

*Continued opposite*

*Table 17–5 continued*

| Name of religion/religionists 1 | Pedigree 2 | Type 3 | Begun 4 | Adherents 5 | Ext 6 | Coun 7 | W 8 | X 9 | E. g. = examples; name for God, other religions present, D=denominations, M=missions. 10 |
|---|---|---|---|---|---|---|---|---|---|
| Symposium of Episcopal Confs of AM | S-cC | 7-b | | 103,500,000 | 55 | ghan | B | 5 | AM= Africa & Madagascar. SECAM/SCEAM. HQ Accra. |
| Synagogue Council of America | cJ | 7-c | 1926 | 5,000,000 | 1 | usa | C | 5 | Umbrella body representing major rabbinical organizations (Orthodox, Conservative, Reform). |
| Synanon Church | sFN | 2-e | 1958 | 3,000 | 1 | usa | C | 5 | F=C. E. Dederich. Therapeutic, reforming alcoholism. Vast properties. |
| Syncretist New-Religionists | SN | 2-b | 950 | 160,000,000 | 3 | japa | B | 3 | New Religions which combine substantial elements from Buddhism, Christianity, or others. |
| Syrian Orthodox | O-Syr-tC | 5-c | 1895 | 1,180,000 | 24 | indi | B | 5 | Reassertion by P-Antioch of authority over Malankara OSC (India) and other areas. |
| Syrian Orthodox Patr of Antioch | D-fC | 4-c | 33 | 3,587,000 | 26 | syri | B | 5 | Only 150,000 left in Syria, due to heavy emigration to 26 countries. |
| Syro-Antiochian Rite | R-Syr-tC | 5-d | 1633 | 118,000 | 7 | iraq | C | 5 | Al-Sourian al-Kathoulik (Syrian Catholics). |
| Syro-Malabarese | O-SyM-tC | 5-c | 1876 | 2,417,000 | 12 | indi | B | 5 | Malankara OSC, Catholicate of the East. Syrians. 22 bps,942n,1s(85),W=55%,7820Yy. |
| Syro-Malabarese Rite | R-SyM-tC | 5-c | 1887 | 3,262,000 | 1 | indi | C | 5 | Kerala. Malayalam. |
| Taego Chong | sKMB | 2-c | 1356 | 3,133,000 | 4 | souk | B | 1 | Hankuk-Bulgyo-Taigojong (Korean Buddhist Sect of Taigo). Liberal, rivaling traditionalists. |
| Tai (Shinto Honkyoku) | sTS | 2-c | | 1,091,000 | 2 | japa | B | 1 | Shintokyo. |
| Taidokyo | sTS | 2-e | | 6,800 | 1 | japa | B | 2 | HQ Suginami-ku, Tokyo. |
| Taiwashu | sTJMB | 2-d | | 105,000 | 1 | japa | B | 0 | Sect of Tendai Buddhism. HQ Iwate-ken. |
| Taizenkyo | sNS | 10-g | | 90 | 1 | japa | B | 1 | HQ Itabashi-ku, Tokyo. |
| Taklung Kagyudpa | sKLB | 2-e | c1190 | 50,000 | 2 | chin | B | 0 | Smallest of 4 surviving Kagyudpa schools of Tibetan Buddhism. |
| Tambor de Mina | sBU | 2-d | | 300,000 | 1 | braz | C | 5 | Name for Candomble used in Marenhas. |
| Tanala ethnoreligionists | sAT | 3-d | | 504,000 | 1 | mada | B | 3 | East of Betsileo. Animists 80%. D=RCC(M-Fianarantsoa),ERSM, and other AICs. M=SJ. |
| Tanzania Episcopal Conference | R-nC | 7-c | 1980 | 8,283,000 | 1 | tanz | B | 5 | TEC. HQ Dar-es-Salaam. |
| Tanzania Evangelical Fellowship | E-nC | 7-c | | 3,100,000 | 1 | tanz | B | 5 | TEF. |
| Tao of Unity | sD | 2-d | c1350 | 300,000 | 1 | chin | B | 1 | Cheng-i Tao. Major form or sect of Taoism, utilizing amulets, talismans. |
| Taoists | D | 1-c | | 2,655,000 | 15 | chin | B | 1 | Tao-chiao/Daoists. Separate religion in Taiwan. 86 major sects. In many syncretic religions also. |
| Taranapanthis | sDV | 2-d | 100 | 200,000 | 1 | indi | B | 1 | Samaiya Panthis. Subsect of Digambara Jainas, opposed to image worship. |
| Taro cultists | sCN | 10-f | 1914 | 200 | 1 | papu | C | 2 | Spirited movement, Spirit possession. F=Buninia. |
| Taturu ethnoreligionists | sAT | 3-d | | 163,000 | 1 | tanz | A | 1 | South of the Iraqw. Semi-nomadic pastoralists. Animists 97%. D=3. M=2. |
| Tembu ethnoreligionists | sAT | 3-d | | 151,000 | 1 | soua | C | 5 | Rich cultural history. Xhosa dialect. Animists 25%. Y=1830. Nominal Christians 5%. D=4. M=2. |
| Temne ethnoreligionists | sAT | 3-d | | 415,000 | 2 | sier | B | 2 | God=Kuru. Muslims 60%(Maliki; 2,000 Ahmadis), animists 34%(Poro Secret Society). D=11. |
| Temple of Islam | sBXM | 2-d | 1934 | 600,000 | 1 | usa | C | 5 | F=Wallace D. Ford. |
| Tenchi Mamori Kyodan | sNS | 2-e | | 5,100 | 1 | japa | B | 1 | HQ Osaka-shi. |
| Tenchi no Taikyo | sNN | 2-e | | 8,100 | 1 | japa | B | 3 | HQ Higashi-ku, Osaka-shi. |
| Tenchikyo | sTS | 2-e | | 10,000 | 1 | japa | B | 1 | HQ Kyoto-shi. |
| Tendai Buddhists | TJMB | 2-c | c550 | 5,000,000 | 2 | japa | B | 1 | Tendaishu. Introduced from China. Rationalist monastic order, ascetic, meditative. 20 sects. |
| Tendai Jimonshu | sTJMB | 2-d | c850 | 400,000 | 2 | japa | B | 1 | Schism ex Tendai by F=Enchin. HQ Shiga-ken. Esoteric. Many schisms and sects. |
| Tendai Shinseishu | sTJMB | 2-e | | 74,700 | 1 | japa | B | 1 | HQ Shiga-ken. |
| Tengenkyo | sTS | 2-e | | 10,900 | 1 | japa | B | 2 | HQ Shinagawa-ku, Tokyo. |
| Tenjokyo | sTS | 2-e | | 23,900 | 1 | japa | B | 2 | Mountain worship. HQ Hyogo-ken. |
| Tenkalai | sVH | 2-a | c600 | 240,000,000 | 5 | indi | B | 2 | 'Southern Culture'. South Indian Sri Vaishnava sect, holding divine grace must be earned. |
| Tenonkyo | sNS | 2-e | | 1,600 | 1 | japa | B | 1 | HQ Kita-ku, Kyoto-shi. |
| Tenreikyo | sNS | 2-e | | 11,400 | 1 | japa | B | 0 | HQ Kagawa-ken. |
| Tensha Tsuchimikado Shinto Honcho | sNN | 2-e | | 40,000 | 1 | japa | B | 2 | HQ Onyu-gun, Fukui-ken. |
| Tensha Yamakage Shinto Aishinkai | sNS | 2-e | | 4,700 | 1 | japa | B | 1 | HQ Nakano-ku, Tokyo. |
| Tenshindo Kyodan | sNS | 2-e | | 75,000 | 1 | japa | B | 1 | HQ Bunkyo-ku, Tokyo. |
| Tenshinkyo | sNS | 10-f | | 140 | 1 | japa | B | 1 | HQ Kyoto-fu. |
| Tenshokyo | sTS | 2-e | | 8,900 | 1 | japa | B | 1 | HQ Kamigyo-ku, Kyoto-shi. |
| Tenshu | sSJMB | 2-e | | 20,000 | 1 | japa | B | 2 | One of many Shingon sects with differentiated practices. |
| Tenshukyo | sTS | 2-e | | 7,900 | 1 | japa | B | 1 | HQ Saitama-ken. |
| Tenso Kokyo | sNN | 2-e | | 37,100 | 1 | japa | B | 1 | HQ Moriyama-ku, Nagoya-shi. |
| Tenzenkyo | sTS | 2-e | | 10,100 | 1 | japa | B | 0 | HQ Shimane-ken. |
| Terapanthis/Sky-clad | sDV | 2-d | 1000 | 100,000 | 1 | indi | B | 1 | Subsect of Digambara Jainas in southwest India. Non-mendicants rejected. |
| Testigos de Jehová | m-Jeh-AC | 6-c | 1893 | 1,420,000 | 1 | mexi | C | 2 | Jehovah's Witnesses. Mass literature from 1929. (1975) 5683Y. (1995) 37454Y. |
| Thammakaai Religious Foundation | sTB | 2-c | 1970 | 1,000,000 | 1 | thai | B | 2 | Media, prosperity, flaunting of wealth. Lay asceticism. Conservative. |
| The Family | I-mar-AC | 6-e | 1965 | 12,000 | 1 | usa | C | 3 | Children of God. F=D. Berg. Communes: 185 by 1975, 800 by 1995, 267 million letters sent. |
| The Lord's Army | O2ZAC | 2-d | 1923 | 300,000 | 1 | roma | C | 5 | Lay evangelists body in Romanian Orthodox Church. |
| The Religious Land | sNN | 2-e | 1972 | 3,000 | 4 | thai | B | 3 | Hooppha Sawan. HQ International Fed of Religions (for world peace), 80 miles from Bangkok. |
| The True Sunnis | sHSM | 2-a | c1850 | 230,000,000 | 70 | indi | B | 1 | Ahl-i Sunnat wa Jamaat. F=Ahmad Riza Khan. Barelvis Movement. Massive populist support. |
| Theosophical Society | sTN | 2-e | 1875 | 60,000 | 80 | indi | B | 2 | F=Helena Blavatsky. Wisdom of Tibetan Hidden Masters. 1,223 lodges in 80 countries. |
| Theosophical Society International | wTN | 2-e | 1891 | 34,000 | 20 | usa | C | 4 | F=W. Q. Judge. Ex Theosophical Society. HQ Pasadena, California. |
| Theosophists | m-The-tC | 5-e | 1904 | 5,100 | 3 | germ | C | 2 | E.g. Nature Philosophy Union. Theocratic, messianic. HQ Vomperberg/Tyrol. In 8 nations. |
| Theravadins | TB | 2-b | BC c250 | 136,259,000 | 30 | sril | B | 3 | Theravada, 'Way of the Elders'. Also termed Hinayana (Lesser Vehicle of Salvation). |
| Tho ethnoreligionists | sPAT | 3-c | | 2,246,000 | 5 | viet | A | 1 | God=Duc Chua Ph. Tung Nghia. Also in China, Laos, USA, France. Polytheists 99%. D=2. M=2. |
| Thomayat | sT-oB | 9-e | | 2,300 | 2 | camb | A | 1 | Order of the Law. Close to Thai Thammayut. Destroyed 1975, restored 1991. 104 monasteries. |
| Thuddama Nikaya | sT-oB | 9-d | 1780 | 450,000 | 2 | myan | B | 3 | 80% of monastic fraternity in Burma. 250,000 ordained monks. |
| Tiddim Chin ethnoreligionists | sAT | 3-d | | 156,000 | 2 | myan | C | 5 | God=Pasian. Chin Hills, Tiddim. Also India (Assam), Bhutan. Lingua franca. Animists 40%. D=4. |
| Tijaniyah | sUM | 2-d | 1785 | 600,000 | 16 | alge | A | 1 | Major Sufi order across North and East Africa, Sudan, Turkey, Indonesia. |
| Tiv ethnoreligionists | sAT | 3-d | | 126,000 | 1 | nige | C | 5 | God=Aôndo. Nominal Christians 43%, animists 4%. Y=1911. D=Tiv Ch,RCC. M=SUM,NGK. |
| Tlhaping Tswana ethnoreligionists | sAT | 3-d | | 116,000 | 2 | soua | B | 5 | God=Modimo. North, Botswana border. Animists 40%; many nominal Christians. Y=1821. D=2. |
| Tlharu Tswana ethnoreligionists | sAT | 3-d | | 113,000 | 1 | soua | B | 5 | Some in Botswana. Animists 25%. Nominal Christians widespread. D=many AICs. |
| Tokumitsukyo | sTS | 2-e | 1912 | 22,900 | 1 | japa | B | 3 | 1935 members 600,000 but crushed by state, reforming 1946 as movement PL Kyodan. |
| Tokushinkyo | sTS | 10-f | | 630 | 1 | japa | B | 2 | Mountain worship sect. HQ Osaka-shi. |
| Toma ethnoreligionists | sAT | 3-d | | 121,000 | 1 | guin | A | 1 | Distinct from Loma of Liberia. Animists 67%,Muslims 25%. Resistant barrier to Islam.D=4.M=3. |
| Tonga Council of Churches | K-nC | 7-e | 1968 | 69,500 | 1 | tong | C | 5 | TCC. 1968, Inter-Church Committee; 1973 name changed. |
| Tonga ethnoreligionists | sAT | 3-d | | 197,000 | 3 | moza | B | 5 | God=Chiuta. South, Inhambane area. Animists 50%. D=AC/CPSA,RCC,AICs. M=USPG,UBS. |
| Tonga Evangelical Union | E-nC | 7-e | c1970 | 2,000 | 1 | tong | C | 5 | TEU. |
| Traditionalist Anglicans | I-TrA-tC | 5-e | 1996 | 12,000 | 1 | brit | C | 5 | Anglican Traditionalists, ex C of E over ordination of women. 1,100 clergy. |
| Transcendental Meditation | sNH | 2-c | c1955 | 4,000,000 | 33 | usa | C | 3 | TM. Spiritual Regeneration Movement. In USA, UK (100,000 practicing), India. |
| Trappists | ocso-oC | 9-e | 1098 | 2,600 | | ital | C | 5 | OCSO. |
| Tridharma | sSN | 2-e | 1938 | 6,000 | 2 | indo | B | 3 | Samkauw Hwee (3 Religions): Buddha, Confucius, Lao Tzu. Member of WALUBI. |
| Trika | sSH | 2-e | c750 | 1,000 | 1 | indi | B | 0 | 'Threefold'. One of 3 philosophical schools of Kashmir Shaivism. Ritual, cosmology: Moribund. |
| Trinidad & Tobago Council of Ev Chs | E-nC | 7-e | c1940 | 40,000 | 1 | trin | C | 5 | TTCEC. 15 member Evangelical denominations. |
| Tripuri ethnoreligionists | sHAT | 3-d | | 673,000 | 2 | indi | A | 1 | Assam, eastern Tripura. Many in Bangladesh. Hinduized animists 92%, Muslims 6.5%. D=4. |
| True Jesus Church | I-3oC-AC | 6-c | 1917 | 1,199,000 | 1 | chin | B | 4 | Chen Ye-su Chiao Hui. 1949: 1,000 churches. Now with global diaspora. (HQ Taipei, Taiwan). |
| True Jesus Church | t-fC | 4-c | 1917 | 1,400,000 | 50 | chin | B | 3 | TJC. Chen Yesu Chiao Hui. Chinese Oneness pentecostal church in 50 countries. HQ Taipei. |
| True Nichiren School | sSN | 2-c | 1930 | 1,000,000 | 50 | japa | B | 3 | Nichiren Shoshu. International; this-worldly appeal. 1992, Soka Gakkai splits off. |
| True Orthodox | I-Tru-tC | 5-d | 1927 | 377,000 | 4 | russ | B | 5 | IPTS. Istinno-Pravoslavnaya Tserkov. Remnants of underground church smashed by KGB. |
| True Pure Land Buddhists | TPJMB | 2-b | c1270 | 14,000,000 | 20 | japa | B | 4 | Jodo Shinshu. Also termed Shin Buddhism. Many monks. c1650, splits in 2 sects. |
| Tsao-tung | sZJMB | 2-d | 1108 | 800,000 | 3 | chin | B | 3 | Chan (Zen) school of Buddhism in China. Soto (Japanese). The 5 Ranks/Ways. |
| Tsharpa | sSLB | 2-d | c1540 | 500,000 | 2 | chin | B | 1 | One of 2 rival branches of Sakyapa tradition of Tibetan Buddhism. |
| Tsimihety ethnoreligionists | sAT | 3-d | | 950,000 | 1 | mada | B | 3 | God=Jañahary. Animists 85%. D=RCC(3 Dioceses),ERSM,FMTA, and other AICs. M=4. |
| Tsonga ethnoreligionists | sAT | 3-d | | 634,000 | 4 | soua | C | 5 | God=Sikwembu Nkulukumba. 180,000 refugees. Animists 30%, Muslims, Baha'is. D=5. M=5. |
| Tswa ethnoreligionists | sAT | 3-d | | 978,000 | 3 | moza | B | 3 | God=Nungungulu. Animists 79%. D=UCCSA(ICUM),IMU,RCC,IML,CPSA, many AICs. M=7. |
| Tuburi ethnoreligionists | sAT | 3-d | | 102,000 | 1 | came | B | 3 | Far North Province. Densely settled. Farmers, stockraisers. Animists 60%. D=2. M=2. |
| Tujia ethnoreligionists | sPAT | 3-c | | 6,327,000 | 1 | chin | A | 1 | Northwest Hunan. Unwritten language. Polytheists/animists 99%. D=TSPM,RCC. R=TWR. |
| Tulama ethnoreligionists | sAT | 3-d | | 469,000 | 1 | ethi | B | 5 | Central. Shoa Province. Animists 10%, Muslims 35%(Shafi Sunnis). D=5. M=3. |
| Tulu ethnoreligionists | sAT | 3-d | | 102,000 | 2 | indi | A | 1 | God=Dever. In AP, Kerala, Tamil Nadu, Maharashtra, Karnataka. Hindus 90%. D=CSI. M=1. |
| Tumulung Sisala ethnoreligionists | sAT | 3-d | | 107,000 | 1 | ghan | B | 2 | North central, Tumu District. Animists 68%, Muslims 20%. D=5. M=6. |
| Tunguz religionists | sST | 3-e | | 27,000 | 2 | russ | B | 5 | Shamanists among the Evenki language group. |
| Tunkers | P-Dun-tC | 5-d | 1719 | 631,000 | 7 | cent | B | 5 | E.g. EEF. Brethren Ch. M=NFBC(USA). 70% Baya, 20% Mandja, 10% Karre. 56f,1H,16h,1r,2s. |
| Turkana ethnoreligionists | sAT | 3-d | | 326,000 | 3 | keny | B | 3 | God=Akuj. Lake Turkana. Nomads, pastoralists in semi-arid desert. Animists 87%. D=9. M=6. |
| Turks & Caicos Inter-Ch Committee | C-nC | 7-e | c1970 | 8,000 | 1 | turs | C | 5 | TCICC. Members: Anglicans, Baptists, Catholics, Methodists. |
| Twa ethnoreligionists | sAT | 3-d | | 193,000 | 3 | rwan | B | 3 | God=Imana. Jungle-dwellers. Animists 92%. D=RCC,Anglican Ch/EAR. M=RCMS,WF,FSC. |
| Twelver Khojas | sIHM | 2-d | c1300 | 250,000 | 2 | indi | B | 2 | 14th-century converts from Hinduism to Islam (Shias). Not under Aga Khan IV. |
| Uchu Kyodan | sNS | 2-e | | 9,100 | 1 | japa | B | 2 | HQ Yokohama-shi. |
| Uchu Motohajime Shinkyo | sNN | 2-d | | 106,000 | 1 | japa | B | 3 | HQ Suita-shi, Osaka-fu. |
| Udasis | zH | 2-e | c1600 | 5,000 | 1 | indi | B | 2 | One of 12 subgroups of Kabir Panthis (Hindu/Muslim/Sikh syncretism), now mainstream Hindu. |
| Udmurt ethnoreligionists | sST | 3-d | | 333,000 | 9 | russ | B | 5 | God=Inan. Udmurtia. Orthodox; many pagans. Shamanists 45%, Muslim elements. M=IBT. |
| Uganda Association of Evangelicals | G-nC | 7-d | c1970 | 290,000 | 1 | ugan | C | 5 | UAE. Unofficial body weathering vicious persecution under Amin regime. |
| Uganda Episcopal Conference | S-nC | 7-c | 1974 | 9,130,000 | 1 | ugan | C | 5 | UEC. HQ Kampala. |

*Continued overleaf*

*Table 17–5 continued*

| *Name of religion/religionists* 1 | *Pedigree* 2 | *Type* 3 | *Begun* 4 | *Adherents* 5 | *Ext* 6 | *Coun* 7 | *W* 8 | *X* 9 | *E. g. = examples; name for God, other religions present, D=denominations, M=missions.* 10 |
|---|---|---|---|---|---|---|---|---|---|
| Uganda Joint Christian Council | K-nC | 7-b | 1963 | 15,500,000 | 1 | ugan | C | 5 | UJCC. Effective close cooperation: members Anglicans, Catholics, Orthodox. |
| Uganda Muslim Supreme Council | nM | 7-c | 1965 | 1,137,000 | 1 | ugan | C | 5 | 1965 NAAM, replaced 1972 by UMSC. |
| UK Islamic Mission | fM | 4-c | 1962 | 1,100,000 | 1 | brit | C | 5 | Arising from Pakistan-based Jamaati Islami. 50 centers in south England. |
| Ukrainian Byzantine rite | R-Ukr-tC | 5-c | 1087 | 5,513,000 | 10 | ukra | C | 5 | MM=Great/Major Archdiocese(1 of only 2 in world). |
| Ukrainian Orth Ch (P Moscow) | O-Ukr-AC | 6-b | 991 | 27,497,000 | 1 | ukra | C | 5 | Russian Orthodox Church, Exarchate of the Ukraine, under P Moscow. 37 bishops. |
| Ukrainian Orthodox | O-Ukr-tC | 5-b | 1775 | 27,608,000 | 9 | ukra | C | 5 | Russian Orthodox Church, Exarchate of the Ukraine, under P Moscow. 37 bishops. |
| Ukrainian Orthodox Ch: P Kiev | I-Ukr-AC | 6-c | 1990 | 1,320,000 | 1 | russ | B | 5 | Ukrainians resident in Russia, but loyal to schismatic P-Kiev. |
| Ukrainian Orthodox Ch: P Kiev | I-Ukr-AC | 6-c | 1991 | 4,560,000 | 1 | ukra | C | 5 | Anti-Russian schism, forming own Patriarchate. Huge start, then decline. 36 bps. |
| Ultra Orthodox Judaism | UJ | 2-d | c1750 | 400,000 | 3 | isra | B | 2 | Haredi. Dissociate selves from Orthodox, Neo-Orthodox. Hasidism, Lithuanians. |
| Umbanda | sBU | 2-b | c1900 | 31,000,000 | 22 | braz | C | 5 | Afro-Brazilian spiritists. Uses Kardecismo. Many Whites. Displacing Candomble and Macumba. |
| unaffiliated Christians | UC | 2-b | c1700 | 111,125,000 | 236 | usa | C | 5 | Christians with no affiliation to organized Christianity. |
| unaffiliated Renewal believers | UZC | 2-b | 1950 | 78,328,000 | 230 | usa | C | 5 | Individual believers experiencing Holy Spirit gifts but remaining not in Renewal bodies. D=2,000 |
| unclassified Pentecostals | P-Pen-tC | 5-e | c1970 | 3,600 | 1 | norw | C | 5 | Total about 6 including International Pente Holiness Ch, UPC (USA). |
| Unification Church | h-fC | 4-c | 1936 | 1,020,000 | 120 | souk | B | 4 | HSAUWC. Holy Spirit Assoc for Unifi of World Christianity. Tongil Kyohoe. 1013n. |
| Unified Vietnamese Buddhist Church | nB | 7-b | 1963 | 39,000,000 | 3 | viet | B | 3 | United Buddhist Association, uniting Theravadins and Mahayanists. |
| union congregations | P-com-tC | 5-e | 1908 | 20,400 | 18 | indi | B | 5 | Begun for all Protestants in major new steel city Bhilai (MP). Steel, mines. 3n. |
| Union de Missions Pente Libres | I-nC | 7-e | c1975 | 15,000 | 1 | chil | C | 5 | UMPL. Union of Free Pentecostal Missions and Churches. 40 member denominations. |
| Union des Egl Ev de Pentecote Belge | H-nC | 7-e |  | 12,000 | 1 | belg | C | 5 | Union of Belgian Pentecostal Churches. Vereniging van der Evangelisch Pinkster Kerken in. |
| Union des Orgs Islamiques de France | nM | 7-c | c1980 | 4,100,000 | 2 | fran | C | 5 | UOIF. 1,300 associations. 3 rivals; FNMF, and Paris Mosque (Algeria government control). |
| Union of American Hebrew Congs | cJ | 7-c | 1873 | 2,700,000 | 2 | usa | C | 5 | UAHC. Reform congregations. HQ New York. |
| Union of Evangelical Churches | C-nC | 7-e | 1965 | 3,000 | 1 | turk | A | 5 | UEC. An unofficial loose grouping in Istanbul. |
| Union of Messianic Jewish Congs | j-fC | 4-e | 1979 | 15,000 | 5 | usa | C | 5 | UMJC. |
| Union of Moroccan Muslim Orgs in the N | nM | 7-d | 1978 | 100,000 | 2 | neth | C | 5 | UMMON. N=Netherlands. Federation of 40 local Moroccan bodies. |
| Union of Muslim Orgs of UK and Eire | nM | 7-c | 1970 | 1,200,000 | 2 | brit | C | 5 | Failure to unite British Muslims; 200 local centers. |
| Union of Muslim Teachers | sXM | 2-c | 1926 | 7,000,000 | 1 | indo | B | 3 | Nahdatul Ulama. Traditionalist rival of Muhammadiyah. |
| Union of New Religious Orgs of Japan | snN | 7-b | 1962 | 32,000,000 | 1 | japa | B | 3 | Shin Nihon Shukyo Dantai Rengo Kai. 170 member denominations. |
| Union of Orth Congs of America | cJ | 7-d | 1898 | 800,000 | 1 | usa | C | 5 | Represents over 700 congregations. |
| Union of Orthodox Hebrew Congs | cJ | 7-c | 1926 | 1,000,000 | 2 | usa | C | 5 | F=rabbi Victor Schonfeld, to unite Western Orthodoxy. |
| Union of Tradit Conservative Judaism | fJ | 4-e | 1985 | 20,000 | 1 | usa | C | 5 | Later renamed Institute for Traditional Judaism. |
| Unitarians | m-Unt-tC | 5-d | 1566 | 360,000 | 26 | usa | C | 3 | E.g. 1961 merger of Unitarian Ch, Universalist Chs. Declining. 886n,2s(150). |
| United Church of Zambia | P-Uni-AC | 6-c | 1884 | 1,190,000 | 1 | zamb | C | 5 | UCZ. 1958/65 unions M=PEMS,LMS,MMS,CSM. Lozi,Bemba. 57n,28x,87f,3H,7h,5r,1s.9160Yy. |
| United Bible Societies | wC | 7-a | 1946 | 1,650,000,000 | 210 | brit | C | 5 | UBS. 1804 British & Foreign Bible Society. (1990) HQ Reading, UK. |
| United Ch in Papua New Guinea | P-Uni-AC | 6-c | 1871 | 1,158,000 | 1 | papu | C | 5 | 1968 union: Papua Ekalesia (M=LMS), 4 Methodist areas. 276n,58x,5p,2s(80),19138z. |
| United Ch of Christ in the Phil | P-Uni-AC | 6-c | 1899 | 1,040,000 | 1 | phil | C | 5 | UCCP. 1948 union 4 bodies. M=P Interboard Comm (USA). 342n,47f,10H,16r,2s,1u,1v. |
| United Chr Council of Sierra Leone | N-nC | 7-d | 1924 | 172,000 | 1 | sier | B | 5 | UCCSL. Members: 12 denominations. |
| United Christian Council in Israel | K-nC | 7-e | 1956 | 11,000 | 1 | isra | B | 5 | UCCI. |
| United Christian Council in Palestine | K-nC | 7-e | 1957 | 6,000 | 1 | pale | B | 5 | UCCP. Originated in, and still related to UCCI (Israel). |
| United Church of Canada | P-Uni-AC | 6-c | 1765 | 3,256,000 | 1 | cana | C | 5 | 1925 union, declining since 1960. 11 Conferences. 4p,6s,W=35%. |
| United Church of Christ | P-Uni-AC | 6-c | 1620 | 1,856,000 | 1 | usa | C | 5 | UCC. 1957 union. 1% Black. Missions in 8 Caribbean, West African countries. 9478n,13s. |
| United Church of Religious Science | sMN | 2-e | 1917 | 90,000 | 20 | usa | C | 4 | Metaphysical. Member of INTA. 270 churches. |
| United churches | P-Uni-tC | 5-b | 1612 | 23,997,000 | 45 | germ | C | 5 | E.g. EKD. 20 Landeskirchen, 8 other denominations. 300p,39s,P=26%,W=6%. |
| United Ev Assoc of Antigua-Barbuda | E-nC | 7-e |  | 5,000 | 1 | anti | C | 5 | UEAAB. United Evangelical Association of Antigua & Barbuda. |
| United Ev Lutheran Chs in India | P-Lut-AC | 6-c | 1706 | 1,642,000 | 1 | indi | B | 5 | UELCI. Formed 1975. 9 ELCs. Large % Harijan. Missions to Malaysia, Burma, Tanzania |
| United Lodge of Theosophists | ssTN | 2-e | 1909 | 12,000 | 12 | usa | C | 4 | Schismatic offshoot of original Theosophical Society. Hindu-Buddhist occult mysticism. |
| United Methodist Church | P-Met-AC | 6-b | 1766 | 10,439,000 | 1 | usa | C | 5 | UMC. 1968, EUB merger. 96% White, 4% Black. 81 Confs. 34974n,13s,W=36%. |
| United Muslim Community of Sweden | nM | 7-d | 1948 | 202,000 | 1 | swed | C | 5 | UMCS. 1948 Islamic Union of Sweden, renamed 1975. |
| United Pent Full Gospel Chs of I | I-nC | 7-c | c1950 | 2,100,000 | 1 | indo | B | 5 | UPFGCI. Alamat Jemaat-Jemaat Dari Gereja-Gereja Injil Penuh. I=Indonesia. |
| United Protestant Ch in the N | P-LuR-AC | 6-c | 1995 | 3,395,000 | 1 | neth | C | 5 | VPKN. 1995, merger of NHK, GKN, and ELKN under way, aiming to finish by AD 2000. |
| United Synagogue in Greater London | cJ | 7-e | 1870 | 50,000 | 1 | brit | C | 5 | Ashkenazi Jewish congregations. Supports all who recognize UK chief rabbi. |
| United Synagogue of America | cJ | 7-c | 1913 | 1,250,000 | 1 | usa | C | 4 | Conservative Jewish. F=Solomon Schachter. Many agencies. 830 congs, 1,200 rabbis. |
| United Torah Judaism | qJ | 8-d | 1992 | 100,000 | 5 | isra | B | 3 | UTJ. Non-Zionist Israeli political party. |
| Uniting Aboriginal and Islander CC | I-nC | 7-e |  | 20,000 | 1 | aust | C | 5 | UAICC. CC=Christian Congress. |
| Uniting Church of Australia | P-Uni-AC | 6-c | 1809 | 1,426,000 | 1 | aust | C | 5 | UCA. 1977 union of Cong Union of A, Methodist Ch of A, Presbyterian Ch of A. 10H. |
| Uniting Reformed Ch in SA | P-Uni-AC | 6-c | 1994 | 1,446,000 | 1 | soua | C | 5 | Merger of 2 DRC Churches: NGK in Africa (Bantu Ch) and NG Sendingskerk (Coloured). 850n. |
| Universal Ch of the Kingdom of God | u-fC | 4-c | 1977 | 4,500,000 | 55 | braz | C | 3 | UCKG/IURD. Igreja Universal do Reino de Deus. 10,000 churches, radio/TV, foreign missions. |
| Universal Shaiva Trust | sSH | 2-e | c1980 | 3,000 | 2 | usa | C | 5 | Based in California. Contemporary version of monistic Kashmir Shaivism. |
| Universal World Harmony TS | HU | 2-e | 1961 | 5,000 | 20 | brit | C | 2 | TS="Through Service". UWH/World Council of Service. HQ Plymouth, UK. Esoteric, mediumist. |
| Usipi ethnoreligionists | sHAT | 3-d |  | 110,000 | 2 | indi | A | 0 | In Tripura; Bangladesh. Close to Riang, Tripuri. Hinduized animists 90%, Muslims 6%. D=1. |
| Usuliya | NXM | 2-c | c1150 | 1,000,000 | 2 | iran | A | 1 | Jurisprudence. School of Islamic law almost universally accepted by Shias. Neo-fundamentalist. |
| Vaikhanasas | sVH | 2-e | BC 200 | 12,000 | 1 | indi | B | 2 | Hindu Vaishnava community in South India: Tamilnad, AP, Karnataka. |
| Vaishnava Sahajiyas | sVH | 2-e |  | 20,000 | 1 | indi | B | 0 | Esoteric Bengali cult; illegal practices. |
| Vaishnavites | VH | 2-a | c550 | 549,583,000 | 90 | indi | B | 2 | Sri Vaishnavas, bhakti devotees of god Vishnu and consort Lakshmi. 108 major temples. |
| Vajrayana Buddhism | VB | 2-c | 400 | 1,000,000 | 3 | chin | B | 3 | Thunderbolt Vehicle. Esoteric Buddhism, based on Tibetan-language Vajrayana tradition. |
| Vanuatu Christian Council | K-nC | 7-d | 1967 | 140,000 | 1 | vanu | C | 5 | VCC. 1967. New Hebrides Christian Council founded with 4 member denominations. |
| Vanuatu ethnoreligionists | sPAT | 3-e |  | 6,600 | 1 | vanu | C | 5 | Popularly known as Custom. Melanesian traditional religion, mainly on Tanna and Aniwa. |
| Varkari Panthis | sKH | 2-d | c1250 | 500,000 | 1 | indi | B | 1 | Warkaris, Hindu devotional movement in Maharashtra. F=Jnanesvar. |
| Vasava ethnoreligionists | sPAT | 3-d |  | 392,000 | 1 | indi | A | 1 | Gujarat State, Maharashtra. Bhil subgroup. Animists/polytheists 99%. M=4. |
| Vatakalai | ssVH | 2-b | c 600 | 110,000,000 | 1 | indi | B | 2 | 'Northern Culture'. Subsect of Sri Vaishnavas, holding that divine grace is free, not earned. |
| Vedanta Society | sHH | 2-c | 1896 | 1,400,000 | 2 | indi | B | 3 | 'End of the Vedas'. Western branch (in New York) of Ramakrishna Math (monastery). |
| Vedism | HH | 2-c |  | 5,000,000 | 30 | indi | B | 1 | Emphasis or return to centrality of the Vedas body of Hindu sacred knowledge. |
| Venda ethnoreligionists | sAT | 3-d |  | 573,000 | 2 | soua | B | 4 | God=Mudzimu. Animists 65%. D=DRCA,AoG,CPSA,WC,RCC,CBCSA,ZCC,other AICs. M=15. |
| Verband Unabhangiger Ev Kirchen KS | C-nC | 7-e |  | 75,000 | 1 | swit | C | 5 | KS=Korperschaften der Schweiz. Aarauer Verband. |
| Verbites | svd-oC | 9-e | 1875 | 5,700 |  | ital | C | 5 | SVD. |
| Vereinigte Ev-L Kirche Deutschlands | d-nC | 7-b | 1948 | 12,500,000 | 1 | germ | C | 5 | VELKD. Ev-L=Evangelisch-Lutherische. United Evangelical Lutheran Church in Germany. |
| Vietnamese Buddhists | sSB | 2-b | c50 | 39,533,000 | 10 | viet | B | 3 | Theravadin and Mahayanist from early stage. |
| Vietnamese ethnoreligionists | sAT | 3-d |  | 477,000 | 18 | viet | B | 3 | God=Duc Chua Troi. Mahayana Buddhists 54%, New-Religionists 13%(CDMC), atheists 8%. |
| Vietnamese house-churches | I-3hV-tC | 5-d | 1988 | 114,000 | 1 | viet | B | 5 | Rapid growth: 60,000 converts in 1991. Many tribal churches from 62 tribes. Healings. |
| Vietnamese indig neocharismatics | VN3ZAC | 2-d | 1952 | 231,000 | 2 | viet | B | 5 | Vietnamese churches: Good News house church movement. D=3. |
| Vietnamese radio/TV believers | I-3rV-tC | 5-d | 1952 | 117,000 | 1 | viet | B | 5 | Radio believers in mountains, mostly youths and students. R=4500,T=39000(ICI). |
| Vinaya Vardhana Society | sTB | 2-e | 1932 | 5,000 | 1 | sril | B | 3 | Association for the Protection of Buddhist Discipline. Anticlerical. |
| Vishishtadvaita | sHH | 2-d | 1100 | 100,000 | 1 | indi | B | 2 | F=Ramanuja. Second of 6 classical schools of Vedism. School of qualified non-duality. |
| Vishwa Hindu Parishad | qH | 8-c |  | 2,000,000 | 40 | indi | B | 2 | VHP. World Hindu Organization. Extremist political body giving Hinduism a systematic ideology. |
| Visitandine | f-oC | 9-e |  | 3,100 |  | ital | C | 5 | Visitation Nuns. Drastic decline: (1973) 6,500 in 190 convents, (1996) 2,913 in 154 convents. |
| Vizhitz Hasidism | sOJ | 2-e | 1854 | 20,000 | 2 | isra | B | 2 | Hasidic movement, F=M. M. ben Hayyim Hager (in Austria). |
| Voodoo | sCU | 2-c | c1600 | 5,983,000 | 12 | hait | C | 5 | Vodun. Mix of African traditional religion and Catholicism. |
| Wa ethnoreligionists | sAT | 3-d |  | 366,000 | 1 | myan | B | 2 | God=Siyeh. Shan State. Also in China. Animists 60%, Buddhists 30%. D=4. M=OMF. |
| Wachi ethnoreligionists | sAT | 3-d |  | 348,000 | 2 | togo | B | 2 | Main centers Vogan, Tabligbo; also in Benin. Animists 65%, Muslims 20% (Maliki Sunnis). D=7. |
| Wagdi ethnoreligionists | sPAT | 3-c |  | 1,692,000 | 1 | indi | A | 0 | Udaipur, Rajasthan, Gujarat. Bhils. Second language Hindi. Animists/polytheists 99%. |
| Wahhabites | WSM | 2-c | c1750 | 7,000,000 | 10 | saud | B | 2 | Strict ultra-conservative, puritannical, fundamentalist form of Sunni, through Hanbali school. |
| Walamo ethnoreligionists | sAT | 3-c |  | 1,007,000 | 1 | ethi | B | 4 | Animists 35%. D=WLEC(strong),ECMY(20%), EOC,FGBC,RCC,SDA,AICs. M=12. |
| Waldensian Church | W-fC | 4-e | 1184 | 42,000 | 4 | ital | C | 5 | United with Methodists. |
| Waldensians | P-Wal-tC | 5-e | 1173 | 42,200 | 2 | ital | C | 5 | Waldensian-Methodists. 75n,8x,1p,1s(6),W=40%,320Yy,4135z. |
| Wallega ethnoreligionists | sAT | 3-d |  | 902,000 | 2 | ethi | B | 5 | God=Wagayo. Muslims 40%, animists 25% D=30%: EOC(D-Wallega),BECE,ECMY,SDA. M=3. |
| Washu | sTJMB | 2-c | 1949 | 2,016,000 | 2 | japa | B | 3 | Largest of the 20 sects of Tendai Buddhism. HQ Osaka-shi. |
| Waslatiyah | ssUM | 2-e |  | 40,000 | 1 | turk | A | 0 | Suborder of Sufi Qadiriya, closed down by Ataturk in 1924. |
| Waxianghua ethnoreligionists | sPAT | 3-d |  | 300,000 | 1 | chin | A | 1 | Related to Miao. Western Hunan province. Wuling mountains. Polytheists (animistic) 95%. |
| Way of Man Society | sSN | 2-e |  | 10,000 | 1 | japa | B | 2 | Hito no Michi Kyodan. New religion, now part of PL Kyodan. F=Miki Tokuharu. |
| Way of the Supreme One | sD | 2-d | 1150 | 100,000 | 1 | chin | B | 0 | Tai-i Tao. A school of religious Taoism. F=Hsiao Pao-chen. |
| Wazzaniyah | sUM | 2-e |  | 30,000 | 1 | alge | A | 0 | Ouezzaniyah. In desert villages, most adult males are members. |
| WEC International | wec-oC | 9-e | 1913 | 1,500 | 55 | brit | C | 5 | Weccers. Formerly Worldwide Evangelization Crusade. |
| West Central Limba ethnoreligionists | sAT | 3-d |  | 117,000 | 1 | sier | B | 3 | God=Kanu. Makeni. Also in Guinea. Muslims 52%(conversion begun 1880), animists 34%. D=6. |
| West Gbari ethnoreligionists | sAT | 3-d |  | 119,000 | 1 | nige | B | 3 | Western Gbagyi, in Niger and Plateau States. Animists 40%, Muslims 25%. D=3. M=7. |
| West Makua ethnoreligionists | sAT | 3-d |  | 642,000 | 1 | moza | B | 3 | Niassa Province. Animists 60%, Muslims 20%. D=CPSA,RCC. |
| Western Buddhist Order | nB | 7-d | 1967 | 500,000 | 7 | brit | C | 5 | Friends of the Western Buddhist Order (WBO). Quasi-monastic. F=Venerable Sangharakshita. |
| Western Dinka ethnoreligionists | sAT | 3-d |  | 205,000 | 1 | suda | C | 5 | Southwestern Dinka. Far west of White Nile. Nomadic animists 30%. D=4. M=3. |
| Western Magar ethnoreligionists | sAT | 3-d |  | 168,000 | 1 | nepa | A | 0 | West of Pokhara. Bheri & Koshi Zones. Some bilinguals in Nepali. Animists 70%, Hindus 30%. |

*Continued opposite*

*Table 17–5 continued*

| Name of religion/religionists 1 | Pedigree 2 | Type 3 | Begun 4 | Adherents 5 | Ext 6 | Coun 7 | W 8 | X 9 | E. g. = examples; name for God, other religions present, D=denominations, M=missions. 10 |
|---|---|---|---|---|---|---|---|---|---|
| Western Manchu ethnoreligionists | sST | 3-d | | 193,000 | 1 | chin | A | 0 | Ili region of Xinjiang Province, also Jilin. Xibe spoken by 15%. Shamanists 100%. M=1. |
| Western Meo ethnoreligionists | sAT | 3-c | | 3,492,000 | 1 | chin | B | 2 | Guizhou, Guangxi, Sichuan, Yunnan; Viet Nam, Laos. Polytheists 94%. D=6. M=20. |
| Western Mongol ethnoreligionists | sST | 3-d | | 121,000 | 1 | mong | A | 0 | God=Borgan. Sart-Kalmyk. Ethnic group in Khalkha Mongol. Nonreligious, shamanists. M=3. |
| Western Nuer ethnoreligionists | sAT | 3-d | | 282,000 | 1 | suda | B | 3 | Jikany Cien.Pastoralists. Animists 75%, highly resistant to Islam. D=5. M=2. |
| Western Yi ethnoreligionists | sPT | 3-d | | 303,000 | 1 | chin | A | 1 | Yi nationality. 65% preliterate. Polytheists 92%, some Mahayana Buddhists. D=2. M=CSI. |
| White deliverance pentecostals | I-3vW-tC | 5-d | 1976 | 231,000 | 3 | usa | C | 5 | E.g. VFM. HQ Tulsa, OK. Members abroad: 15,000 in 8 churches in Russia, 45 countries. |
| White Eagle Lodge | sHU | 2-e | | 5,000 | 2 | brit | C | 5 | Spiritism via Native American spirit guide, White Eagle, projecting Cosmic Christ Star. |
| White Fathers | wf-oC | 9-e | 1868 | 2,400 | | ital | C | 5 | WF(PB). Missionaries of Africa (M.Afr.) |
| White Karen ethnoreligionists | sAT | 3-d | | 996,000 | 2 | myan | B | 5 | God=Ywa. Animists 65%, Baha'is. D=BBC,SSKBMS,CPB(D-Yangon),AoG,SDA,NAC. M=10. |
| White Lotus School | sPJMB | 2-e | 402 | 10,000 | 2 | chin | B | 3 | School of Celestial Platform/Pure Land: Pai-lien Tsung, Tien-Tai (in Japan, Tendai). F=Hui-yuan. |
| White Lotus Society | sSN | 2-e | c1050 | 5,000 | 2 | chin | B | 3 | Chinese folk movement, plagued by complex of Buddhist/Taoist/millenarian secret societies. |
| White Meo ethnoreligionists | sPT | 3-d | | 345,000 | 5 | viet | B | 3 | Striped Meo. Tonkin Province. Also in Laos, France, China. Polytheists 80%. D=RCC. M=1. |
| White Tai ethnoreligionists | sAT | 3-d | | 268,000 | 4 | viet | A | 1 | Along Red, Black rivers. Also in Laos, China, France, USA. Animists 60%, Buddhists 35%. D=1. |
| White-clad Terapanthis | sSV | 2-e | c1750 | 50,000 | 1 | indi | B | 0 | Subsect of Sthanakavasis Svetambara Jainas. |
| White-led Apostolics | I-3aW-tC | 5-d | 1938 | 235,000 | 4 | usa | C | 5 | ACM. 45n,10 apostles. Abroad: 62 networks in 42 countries, 4100 chs. |
| White-led cell-based networks | I-3kW-tC | 5-e | 1971 | 93,600 | 2 | port | C | 5 | E.g. Manna Christian Ch. Huge cell-based megachurch in Lisbon. In Europe, Africa, S America. |
| White-led charismatics | I-3cW-tC | 5-b | 1805 | 20,864,000 | 43 | usa | C | 5 | 1,500 smaller networks and 20,000 autonomous single congregations: El Shaddai, &c. |
| White-led Full Gospelers | I-3fW-tC | 5-c | 1895 | 2,941,000 | 6 | usa | C | 5 | Including 1,500 unattached congregations participating in Chaplaincy of Full Gospel Churches. |
| White-led healing networks | I-3jW-tC | 5-d | 1928 | 188,000 | 2 | usa | C | 5 | E.g. Branhamites. Voice of God Recordings. 300,000 worldwide. |
| White-led house churches | I-3hW-tC | 5-e | 1965 | 14,700 | 5 | russ | B | 5 | Isolated home churches after EHC (Every Home for Christ) campaign across Russia. |
| White-led neocharismatics | I-3nW-tC | 5-e | 1656 | 7,500 | 3 | port | C | 5 | Lusitanian Ch. Schism ex Ch of Rome by 11 RC priests. 16n,2s,W=45%,32Yy. |
| White-led Oneness chs | I-3oW-tC | 5-d | 1845 | 929,000 | 8 | usa | C | 5 | Mostly White Charismatics. 1971, assisted by M=CMI (Calvary Ministries International). |
| White-led pentecostals | I-3pW-tC | 5-c | 1974 | 7,406,000 | 55 | russ | B | 5 | E.g. CEF=Christians of the Evangelical Faith. Formerly in AUCECB. 65 churches in Moscow. |
| White-led Postdenominationalists | W3ZAC | 2-b | 1805 | 50,066,000 | 210 | brit | C | 5 | Spirit-baptized Whites in non-Pentecostal/Charismatic apostolic networks. D=3,700. |
| White-led restorationists | I-3tW-tC | 5-d | 1968 | 336,000 | 1 | brit | C | 5 | E.g. F=Terry Virgo. South Coast. Shepherding controversy. R-1 type. NFI missions abroad. |
| White-led signs & wonders chs | I-3sW-tC | 5-e | c1980 | 7,200 | 3 | soua | C | 5 | E.g. Assisted by M=AVC(USA). |
| White-led Word of Faith chs | I-3wW-tC | 5-c | 1953 | 1,323,000 | 6 | nige | B | 5 | Prosperity gospel message. M=Rhema Bible Churches (USA). |
| Wicca | sON | 2-d | BC 300 | 700,000 | 20 | iraq | A | 3 | Witchcraft. Craft. Old Religion. Gardnerianism. Pre-Celtic wisdom, worship of Earth Goddess. |
| Willow Creek Association of Chs | w-fC | 4-d | 1975 | 500,000 | 50 | usa | C | 5 | WCAC. |
| Winti | sSU | 2-e | c1800 | 43,000 | 2 | suri | B | 4 | Afkodre (Idolatry). Folk-religion of Surinamese Creoles. Spirit-possession. Many in Holland. |
| Witchcraft eradicationists | WT | 3-e | 1910 | 20,000 | 30 | keny | C | 5 | Movements primarily in Africa to eradicate witch suspects and magical practices. |
| Wobe ethnoreligionists | sAT | 3-d | | 123,000 | 1 | ivor | B | 3 | Western Department. Animists 71%, Muslims 1%. D=3. M=5. |
| Won Buddhism | sKMB | 2-d | 1916 | 600,000 | 8 | souk | B | 3 | Won Bulgyo (Round Circle). Modernized Zen/Taoism/Confucianism/Chondogyo/Christianity. |
| Woni ethnoreligionists | sPT | 3-d | | 108,000 | 1 | chin | A | 0 | Yunnan, near the Hani. Under Hani official nationality. Polytheists 97%. |
| Word of Life | I-3wW-AC | 6-e | 1983 | 22,500 | 1 | swed | C | 5 | Livets Ord. Faith Movement. Charismatic ministry, HQ Uppsala. 100 churches. |
| Word of Life Evangelical Ch | P-Bap-AC | 6-c | 1927 | 4,700,000 | 1 | ethi | B | 5 | WLEC. M=SIM. 1438n,100x,600m,332f,6H,25h,50p,2s(25),W=85%,10000Y,40000z. |
| World A Christians | A-C | 2-b | 33 | 10,329,000 | 38 | paki | A | 5 | Christians living in World A countries (those under 50% evangelized (E |
| World Alliance of Reformed Chs | P-fC | 4-b | | 60,000,000 | 210 | swit | C | 5 | WARC. HQ Geneva. |
| World Assemblies of God Fellowship | z-fC | 4-b | | 43,000,000 | 140 | souk | B | 5 | WAGF. HQ Seoul, Korea. Also part of PWC. |
| World B Christians | B-C | 2-a | 33 | 513,034,000 | 59 | chin | B | 5 | Christians living in World B countries (under 60% Christian but E>50%). |
| World Buddhist Sangha Council | wB | 7-c | 1966 | 5,000,000 | 70 | sril | B | 4 | WBSC. HQ Colombo. To assist Theravada bhikkhu mendicant missions around world. |
| World C Christians | C-C | 2-a | 33 | 1,476,204,000 | 141 | usa | C | 5 | Christians living in World C countries (60% or more Christian). |
| World Conf on Religion and Peace | wPW | 7-c | 1970 | 3,000,000 | 40 | japa | B | 5 | For all faiths, 7 major conferences. HQ New York, as an UN NGO. |
| World Cong of Chr Fundamentalists | wC | 7-c | c1970 | 2,200,000 | 30 | brit | C | 4 | Based on inerrant infallible Bible. Congresses 1980, 1986, 1990. |
| World Congress of Faiths | wPW | 7-e | 1936 | 2,000 | 31 | brit | C | 5 | F=F. Younghusband. Search for a shared global ethic. HQ London. Branches in 31 countries. |
| World Convention of Chs of Christ | T-fC | 4-b | | 10,000,000 | 130 | usa | C | 5 | WCCC. |
| World Council of Biblical Chs | wC | 7-d | 1980 | 100,000 | 10 | usa | C | 4 | WCBC. Fundamentalists excluding all linked to WCC, WEF, RCC, ICCC, Pentecostals. |
| World Council of Churches | wC | 7-a | 1948 | 460,000,000 | 150 | swit | C | 5 | WCC/COE/ORK. HQ Geneva. |
| World Council of Mosques | wM | 7-c | 1975 | 1,000,000 | 30 | saud | B | 2 | Offshoot of Muslim World League. |
| World Council of Synagogues | wJ | 7-c | 1959 | 2,000,000 | 10 | usa | C | 5 | Represents Conservative Judaism. USA, Argentina, Israel. |
| World Evangelical Fellowship | wC | 7-b | 1846 | 150,000,000 | 100 | sing | B | 5 | WEF. HQ Singapore. Origins in 1846's World's Evangelical Alliance. |
| World Fellowship of Buddhists | wB | 7-a | 1950 | 359,000,000 | 50 | thai | B | 4 | F=Malalasekera (Ceylon). Centralized. HQ Bangkok. 1969 Ninth General Conference. |
| World Fellowship of Religions | wPW | 7-e | 1954 | 50,000 | 30 | indi | B | 2 | WFR. Founded in New Delhi, to foster interreligious toleration and cooperation. |
| World Islamic Call Society | wM | 7-c | 1970 | 4,000,000 | 35 | liby | A | 5 | Jamiat al-Dawa al-Islami al-Alamiya. Militant rival of Saudi-based Muslim World League. |
| World Islamic Council for Propag & R | wM | 7-e | 1988 | 10,000 | 20 | saud | B | 2 | al-Majlis al-Alami al-Islami lil-Dawah wa-al-Ighathah. R=Relief. 17 founder organizations. |
| World Jewish Congress | wJ | 7-b | 1936 | 16,053,000 | 70 | swit | C | 5 | Representatives from 70 countries. Research institute in London. |
| World Methodist Council | W-fC | 4-b | | 70,226,000 | 113 | usa | C | 5 | WMC. HQ Lake Junaluska, NC. |
| World Muslim Congress | wM | 7-d | 1926 | 500,000 | 60 | paki | A | 1 | WMC. Mutamar al-Alam al-Islami. HQ Karachi, 5 regional offices. Losing to Saudi-based MWL. |
| World Red Swastika Society | wD | 7-e | | 50,000 | 4 | chin | B | 1 | Chinese secret society with criminal reputation. |
| World Renewal religionists | sPAT | 3-e | c1600 | 50,000 | 1 | usa | C | 5 | Among California Amerindians; one of several major cults. |
| World Spiritual Council | wPW | 7-e | 1946 | 2,500 | 10 | brit | C | 5 | WSC. Founded in Ashford, Kent to establish contacts between the great world religions. |
| World True Light Civilization | sNN | 2-d | 1959 | 100,000 | 10 | japa | B | 3 | Sekai Mahikari Bunmei Kyodan. Japan center of Universe (at Shizuoka). Ex Sekai Kyuseikyo. |
| World True Religion | sNN | 2-d | 1957 | 621,000 | 1 | souk | B | 4 | Segyejunggyo. Folk religion seeking world peace, realization of human ideals (Utopia). |
| World Union | wPW | 7-e | 1958 | 10,000 | 3 | indi | B | 2 | WU. Inaugurated in Pondicherry; dedicated to search for uniting of mankind on spiritual values. |
| World Union for Progressive Judaism | wJ | 7-c | 1926 | 6,000,000 | 50 | isra | B | 3 | Liberal or Progressive Judaism. |
| World Zionist Organization | wJ | 7-d | 1897 | 300,000 | 80 | isra | B | 2 | F=T. Herzl. Political movement for a Jewish state in Palestine. |
| World's Parliament of Religions | wPW | 7-c | 1893 | 5,000,000 | 140 | chin | B | 5 | Chicago 1893 and 1993. No interest in a World Council of Religions, but Global Ethic popular. |
| Wrekin Trust | sFN | 2-e | 1942 | 1,000 | 1 | brit | C | 3 | New Age movement (astrology, healing, conferences). F=G.Trevelyan, 'alternative spirituality'. |
| Wu-tou-mi Tao | sD | 2-d | c150 | 100,000 | 1 | chin | B | 1 | '5 Pecks of Rice'. Cheng-yi. One of the 2 religious branches of Taoism. |
| Wycliffe Bible Translators | wbt-oC | 9-e | 1934 | 6,300 | 65 | usa | C | 5 | WBT, SIL. |
| Xango | sBU | 2-c | c1800 | 1,000,000 | 1 | braz | C | 5 | Shango (Yoruba god of thunder). Afro-Brazilian spiritists in Pernambuco state. |
| Xhosa ethnoreligionists | sAT | 3-d | | 380,000 | 4 | soua | C | 5 | God=uThixo. Southwest Cape, Transkei. Animists 6%, Muslims. Y=1799(LMS). D=14. M=3. |
| Yakut ethnoreligionists | sST | 3-d | | 132,000 | 2 | russ | B | 5 | God=Tanara. Siberia. Lingua franca. 60% use Russian. Hunters. Shamanists 30%. D=1. M=1. |
| Yali cargo cultists | sCN | 2-e | c1960 | 1,000 | 3 | papu | C | 4 | Wok belong Yali. Cargo-cult churches. |
| Yamatokai | sTS | 2-e | | 4,800 | 1 | japa | B | 1 | HQ Toda-shi, Saitama-ken. |
| Yamatokyo | sHS | 2-e | | 66,200 | 1 | japa | B | 1 | HQ Shiogama-shi, Miyagi-ken. |
| Yan Tatsine | zSM | 2-e | 1960 | 10,000 | 1 | nige | B | 3 | Maitatsine ('He Who Curses', in Hausa). Millenarian sect. 1980-5 violence, rioting; 4,000 killed. |
| Yao ethnoreligionists | sPAT | 3-c | | 2,415,000 | 6 | chin | A | 1 | 53% speak Yao. Polytheists/animists(ancestor-worship) 99%. D=RCC,TSPM,TJC. M=10. |
| Yasawiyah | sUM | 2-d | 1950 | 100,000 | 5 | kaza | B | 3 | Sufi order in Kirghizia, Kazakhstan, Uzbekistan. Offshoot: Laachi. |
| Yemma ethnoreligionists | sAT | 3-d | | 241,000 | 1 | ethi | B | 4 | Youth bilingual in Amharic, older persons in Oromo. Animists 40%, Muslims 10%. D=WLEC. |
| Yezidis | YY | 2-d | c100 | 226,000 | 10 | iraq | A | 1 | Anti-dualistic Kurdish sect. Western Iran, Iraq, Syria, Turkey, Germany, Armenia, Georgia. |
| Yoga | sHH | 2-b | 200 | 30,000,000 | 40 | indi | B | 2 | Best known of 6 orthodox Hindu philosophical systems. F=Yajnavalka. Many current varieties. |
| Yogacara | yJMB | 2-e | c350 | 10,000 | 1 | indi | B | 2 | Yoga-practice. Vijnanavada. Philosophical school 'Mind Only' of Mahayana Buddhism. |
| Yoido Full Gospel Churches | I-3kK-AC | 6-c | 1958 | 1,075,000 | 1 | souk | B | 5 | YFGC. Adult members: (1961) 800. 100 staff, 50,000 cells. Since 1985 part of AoG. |
| Yoruba ethnoreligionists | sAT | 3-d | | 856,000 | 10 | nige | B | 5 | God=Olorun. Muslims 37%(Malikis,Sufis,Ahmadis), animists 4%. Y=1841. D=13. M=8. |
| Youth With A Mission | ywam-oC | 9-e | 1960 | 7,100 | 110 | usa | C | 5 | YWAM. YWAMers. |
| Yugoslav Ecumenical Council | K-nC | 7-c | 1968 | 5,400,000 | 1 | yugo | C | 5 | Ecumenical Council of Churches in Yugoslavia (ECCY). |
| Yugoslav Islamic Community | nM | 7-c | 1882 | 1,722,000 | 1 | yugo | C | 5 | YIC. Rijaset Islamske Zajednice. Coordination, administration. |
| Yunnanese Shan ethnoreligionists | sBAT | 3-d | | 217,000 | 1 | chin | A | 1 | God=Pra Pinsau. Chinese Tai. Yunnan, Sichuan; Thailand. Buddhists 80%(Hinayana). D=2. |
| Yuzu Nenbutsu Shu | sPJMB | 2-d | | 101,000 | 1 | japa | B | 2 | HQ Osaka-shi. |
| Zaike Nichirenshu Jofukai | sNJMB | 2-e | | 24,600 | 1 | japa | B | 1 | HQ Shinjuku-ku, Tokyo. |
| Zambezi Tonga ethnoreligionists | sAT | 3-d | | 137,000 | 2 | zamb | C | 5 | God=Leza. Valley Tonga. Animists 20%. D=12 plus many AICs. M=3. |
| Zambia Christian C for Development | C-nC | 7-c | 1970 | 3,877,000 | 1 | zamb | C | 5 | ZCCD. C=Commission. 30 member denominations including RCC and several AICs. |
| Zambia Episcopal Conference | V-nC | 7-c | 1984 | 3,070,000 | 1 | zamb | C | 5 | ZEC. HQ Lusaka. |
| Zande ethnoreligionists | sAT | 3-d | | 137,000 | 3 | suda | C | 5 | God=Mbori. Mostly in Zaire, also CAR. Animists 15%. D=4. M=3. |
| Zar cultists | sTU | 2-d | | 100,000 | 8 | ethi | B | 4 | Zar (sar)=spirits possessing women only. Nile area:Egypt, Sudan, Ethiopia, Somalia, E.Africa. |
| Zarruquyah | ssUM | 2-e | | 20,000 | 1 | niga | A | 0 | Sufi order based on Maradi in Niger. |
| Zaydis | ZHM | 2-c | c730 | 8,042,000 | 10 | yeme | A | 1 | Smallest Shia branch. Fiver Shiites. Strongest in Yemen. |
| Zen Buddhists | ZJMB | 2-b | 1191 | 13,000,000 | 30 | japa | B | 3 | Brought to Japan from China. Now 22,000 temples in Japan. |
| Zenrinkai | sNN | 2-d | 1947 | 386,000 | 1 | japa | B | 3 | Association for Doing Good to One's Neighbors. Retreats for spiritual training. HQ Fukuoka. |
| Zerma ethnoreligionists | sAT | 3-d | | 300,000 | 5 | niga | A | 1 | God=Ircouei. Also in Nigeria. Muslims 80%(Maliki Sunnis), animists 20%. Talking drums. D=3. |
| Zezuru ethnoreligionists | sAT | 3-d | | 580,000 | 2 | zimb | C | 5 | Animists 28%. Heavily Christianized. AICs particularly strong. D=13. M=6. |
| Zimbabwe Catholic Bishops' Conf | s-nC | 7-c | 1981 | 1,120,000 | 1 | zimb | B | 5 | ZCBC. HQ Harare. |
| Zimbabwe Christian Conference | C-nC | 7-c | 1903 | 1,146,000 | 1 | zimb | B | 5 | ZCC built on 1903 Southern Rhodesia Christian Conference. |
| Zimbabwe Council of Churches | W-nC | 7-c | 1964 | 2,025,000 | 1 | zimb | B | 5 | ZCC or CCZ. Christian Council of Zimbabwe. |
| Zion Christian Ch, South Africa | I-3zA-AC | 6-c | 1914 | 8,400,000 | 1 | soua | C | 5 | ZCC. Ex AFM. Colors green, yellow. Pedi. Abroad: 9 countries (Malawi, Namibia, Mozambique). |

*Continued overleaf*

*Table 17–5 concluded*

| Name of religion/religionists 1 | Pedigree 2 | Type 3 | Begun 4 | Adherents 5 | Ext 6 | Coun 7 | W X 8 9 | E. g. = examples; name for God, other religions present, D=denominations, M=missions. 10 |
|---|---|---|---|---|---|---|---|---|
| Zion Christian Ch, Zimbabwe | I-3zA-AC | 6-c | 1923 | 1,248,000 | 1 | zimb | B 5 | ZCC. Begun by Bishop Mutendi from South Africa. Holy cities. HQ Bikita, Karanga. |
| Zionist African Independents | I-3zA-tC | 5-b | 1909 | 11,968,000 | 6 | soua | C 5 | E.g. ZCC. Ex AFM. Colors green, yellow. Pedi. In 9 countries:Malawi to Namibia, Mozambique. |
| Zoe | z-oC | 10-g | 1907 | 50 | 4 | gree | C 5 | 'Life'. Oldest and most influential lay Orthodox reform movement. Semi-monastic. |
| Zoroastrians | Z | 1-c BC | 1200 | 2,544,000 | 24 | iran | A 2 | Ancient monotheist religion of Persia. God=Ahura Mazda. Iran 1,903,000, Afghanistan 304,000. |
| Zulu ethnoreligionists | sAT | 3-d | | 383,000 | 7 | soua | C 5 | God=Nkulunkulu. Animists 3%;  Muslims(10,000 converts; 1982: Quran in Zulu). D=40 AICs. |
| **Other religions not listed above** | | | | 161,953,000 | 150 | | B 2 | Summaries of types of religions not included above. |
| Other lesser ethnoreligions | | | | 140,953,000 | 110 | nige | B 2 | 4,550 ethnoreligions with less than 100,000 adherents in AD 2000 |
| Other peripheral religions | | | | 20,000,000 | 40 | | A 2 | 2,000 peripheral religions, on the periphery of our definition of religion |
| Other hidden religions | | | | 1,000,000 | 80 | | B 1 | 500 clandestine minor religious systems, often illegal or subversive. |
| **Totals** | | | | | | | | |
| Total all adherents listed above | | | | 49,368,273,000 | 238 | | | 9,891 distinct religions whose total adherents/followers include multiple adherence |
| Multi-counted adherence | | | | -43,313,224,000 | 150 | | | Persons classified by themselves or by others as in an average of 10 different religions |
| Religionists worldwide | | | | 5,136,801,000 | 238 | usa | | Total individual religionists in world at mid-2000 (85%) |
| Nonreligionists worldwide | | | | 918,249,000 | 236 | chin | | Total individual nonreligionists in world at mid-2000 (15%) |
| **Global population** | | | | **6,055,049,000** | **238** | | | **Total individuals at mid-2000** |

**Table 17–6.  Global survey of 9,900 religions and parareligions in AD 2000, with 2,800 that have significant organization or identity being given a line each, listed by pedigree.**

| Name of religion/religionists 1 | Pedigree 2 | Type 3 | Begun 4 | Adherents 5 | Ext 6 | Coun 7 | W 8 | X 9 | E. g. = examples; name for God, other religions present, D=denominations, M=missions. 10 |
|---|---|---|---|---|---|---|---|---|---|
| **Nonreligionists** | - | 0-a | | 918,248,000 | 236 | chin | B | | All who are not religious or religionists; agnostics (nonreligious) plus atheists (militants). |
| Atheists | a- | 0-b | BC 1000 | 150,090,000 | 161 | chin | B | 3 | Militantly nonreligious and antireligious secularists and communists. |
| Nonreligious | Q- | 0-a | | 768,159,000 | 236 | chin | B | 2 | Agnostics, secularists, materialists, with no religion but not militantly antireligious or atheists. |
| **Buddhists** | B | 1-a | | 359,982,000 | 126 | japa | B | 2 | Buddha-dharma. Followers of the Buddha in several hundred schools and sects. |
| Sino-American Buddhist Association | cB | 7-d | 1968 | 800,000 | 5 | usa | C | 4 | SABA. Chinese Buddhist polity. Strict standards. |
| Folk-Buddhists | FB | 2-b | | 10,000,000 | 5 | japa | B | 0 | Popularized religion mixing Buddhist elements with local deities or cults. |
| Kasogatan | sFB | 2-e | c1500 | 30,000 | 1 | indo | B | 1 | Javanese local variety of Buddhism; with Mahayana, Theravada, forms amalgam Buddhayana. |
| Lamaists | LB | 2-b | 640 | 21,490,000 | 30 | chin | B | 1 | Tibet. Worldwide diaspora. Mantra 'Om mani padmi hum'. 1959, 6,000 monasteries destroyed. |
| Kagyudpas | KLB | 2-c | c1030 | 9,000,000 | 15 | chin | B | 1 | Followers of the Oral Teaching Lineages. One of 4 main Lamaist orders/sects. In Europe, USA. |
| Drigung Kagyudpa | sKLB | 2-e | c1180 | 4,000 | 6 | chin | B | 1 | Third largest of surving Kagyudpa Lamaism. Many monasteries in Ladakh. |
| Drukpa Kagyudpa | sKLB | 2-e | c1170 | 50,000 | 7 | chin | B | 1 | Dragon Kagyudpa. Tibet, and Bhutan state religion. |
| Karmapas | sKLB | 2-c | c1150 | 6,000,000 | 10 | chin | B | 1 | Karma Kagyudpas, largest surviving Tibetan Lamaist Kagyudpa schools. Black Hats. |
| Taklung Kagyudpa | sKLB | 2-e | c1190 | 50,000 | 2 | chin | B | 0 | Smallest of 4 surviving Kagyudpa schools of Tibetan Buddhism. |
| Nyingmapas | NLB | 2-c | c790 | 7,000,000 | 4 | chin | B | 1 | Red Hat lamas. Followers of the Ancient Teachings. Tibet's oldest Buddhist order; unreformed. |
| Rimaypas | RLB | 2-d | c1860 | 600,000 | 7 | chin | B | 2 | Eclectic Movement. Nonsectarian, spiritual/cultural renaissance, unify the many Lamaist sects. |
| Sakyapas | SLB | 2-c | 1073 | 5,000,000 | 8 | chin | B | 1 | Grey Earth School. One of 4 major sects of Tibet Lamaism. Logicians, debaters, philosophers. |
| Dolma | sSLB | 2-e | | 1,000 | 1 | chin | B | 0 | Subgroup within Sakyapa Lamaism. |
| Ngorba | sSLB | 2-d | 1429 | 500,000 | 2 | chin | B | 1 | Branch of Sakyapa tradition of Tibetan Buddhism. Monasteries across Tibet. |
| Phuntsok | sSLB | 2-e | c1960 | 1,000 | 1 | chin | B | 1 | Subgroup of Tibetan Buddhist Sakyapa school. |
| Tsharpa | sSLB | 2-d | c1540 | 500,000 | 2 | chin | B | 1 | One of 2 rival branches of Sakyapa tradition of Tibetan Buddhism. |
| Mongolian Buddhism | zLB | 2-d | | 600,000 | 5 | mong | A | 1 | Viciously suppressed by Stalinists from 1917 to 1990. Now revived. |
| Njushi-ryu | zLB | 2-d | | 100,000 | 1 | chin | B | 0 | Tibetan. Variety of Lamaism. |
| Mahayanists | MB | 2-a | | 202,233,000 | 115 | japa | B | 1 | Greater Vehicle of Salvation. Family of lineages. Main cultures: Tibeto-Mongol, Sino-Japanese. |
| Chinese Buddhists | CMB | 2-b | 60 | 90,000,000 | 60 | chin | B | 1 | Violently suppressed in AD 452, 574, and 845. |
| Falun Gong | sCMB | 2-b | | 30,000,000 | 20 | chin | B | 1 | A Buddhist motivation-based sect. 1999 clashes with Communist regime. |
| Hua-yen | sCMB | 2-c | 690 | 3,000,000 | 20 | chin | B | 1 | Kegon (Flower Adornment), a major school of Chinese Buddhism. F=Fa-tsang. |
| Indian Buddhists | IMB | 2-c | 1956 | 7,249,000 | 1 | indi | B | 2 | Reformed Buddhism reintroduced by B.R.Ambedkar for Dalits (Untouchables). |
| Japanese Buddhists | JMB | 2-b | | 71,000,000 | 37 | japa | B | 3 | Mainly Mahayana, but many varieties. Total Buddhist sects in Japan: 180. |
| Nara Buddhists | NJMB | 2-c | c550 | 2,262,000 | 4 | japa | B | 2 | Nara sects were first forms of Buddhism in Japan. Now 7 distinct Nara sects. |
| Bussho Gonenkai Kyodan | sNJMB | 2-d | | 913,000 | 1 | japa | B | 1 | HQ Minato-ku, Tokyo. |
| Daiekai Kyodan | sNJMB | 2-e | | 29,900 | 1 | japa | B | 1 | HQ Osaka-fu. |
| Daijokyo | sNJMB | 2-d | | 410,000 | 3 | japa | B | 1 | HQ Nagoya-shi. |
| Fudoshu | sNJMB | 2-c | | 1,707,000 | 2 | japa | B | 2 | HQ Okayama-ken. |
| Fujifuse | sNJMB | 2-e | c1600 | 20,000 | 1 | japa | B | 1 | A Nichiren branch of secret believers until 1874 state recognition. HQ Okayama. |
| Hokke Nichirenshu | sNJMB | 2-e | | 25,500 | 1 | japa | B | 1 | HQ Osaka-shi. |
| Hokke Shinshu | sNJMB | 2-e | | 3,100 | 1 | japa | B | 1 | HQ Shinagawa-ku, Tokyo. |
| Hokkeshu Honmonryu | sNJMB | 2-d | | 369,000 | 1 | japa | B | 1 | HQ Toshima-ku, Tokyo. |
| Hokkeshu Jinmonryu | sNJMB | 2-d | | 146,000 | 1 | japa | B | 1 | HQ Toshima-ku, Tokyo. |
| Hokkeshu Shinmonryu | sNJMB | 2-e | | 64,600 | 1 | japa | B | 1 | HQ Kamigyo-ku, Kyoto-shi. |
| Honke Myoshu Renmei | sNJMB | 2-e | | 1,400 | 1 | japa | B | 0 | HQ Kanagawa-ken. |
| Honke Nichirenshu | sNJMB | 2-e | | 2,500 | 1 | japa | B | 2 | One of numerous Nichiren adaptations. |
| Honmon Butsuryushu | sNJMB | 2-d | 1857 | 447,000 | 3 | japa | B | 2 | HQ Kamigyo-ku. No priesthood. Lay-run. |
| Honmon Hokkeshu | sNJMB | 2-e | | 251,000 | 2 | japa | B | 1 | HQ Kamigyo-ku, Kyoto-shi. |
| Honmon Kyooshu | sNJMB | 2-e | | 6,700 | 1 | japa | B | 1 | HQ Chogu-shi, Tokyo. |
| Honpa Nichirenshu | sNJMB | 2-e | | 45,600 | 1 | japa | B | 1 | HQ Osaka-fu. |
| Hosshikai Kyodan | sNJMB | 2-d | | 142,000 | 1 | japa | B | 0 | HQ Iwate-ken. |
| Hossoshu | sNJMB | 2-d | 661 | 600,000 | 4 | japa | B | 2 | One of 6 Nara sects of Japanese Buddhism. 40 temples. 1945, 57,042 adherents. HQ Nara-shi. |
| Kegon | sNJMB | 2-d | 736 | 705,000 | 3 | japa | B | 2 | Mutual identity of phenomena and great Buddha Dainichi (AD 749). HQ Nara-shi. 1945: 50,915. |
| Kegon Shu | sNJMB | 2-e | 740 | 70,500 | 2 | japa | B | 2 | Nara sect. Name in Chinese: Hua Yen. 60 temples, 900 clergy. HQ Nara-shi. |
| Kokuchukai | sNJMB | 2-e | | 28,700 | 1 | japa | B | 1 | HQ Edogawa-ku, Tokyo. |
| Myochikai Kyodan | sNJMB | 2-d | | 670,000 | 3 | japa | B | 1 | HQ Shibuya-ku, Tokyo. |
| Myodokai Kyodan | sNJMB | 2-d | | 155,000 | 1 | japa | B | 1 | HQ Osaka-shi. |
| Myohoshu | sNJMB | 2-e | | 4,900 | 1 | japa | B | 2 | HQ Nara-ken. |
| Nakayama Myoshu | sNJMB | 2-d | | 566,000 | 1 | japa | B | 0 | HQ Chiba-ken. |
| Nichiren Hokkeshu | sNJMB | 2-e | | 14,000 | 1 | japa | B | 1 | HQ Fukushima-shi. |
| Nichiren Honshu | sNJMB | 2-e | | 34,800 | 1 | japa | B | 1 | HQ Sakyo-ku, Kyoto-shi. |
| Nichiren Komonshu | sNJMB | 2-e | | 26,600 | 1 | japa | B | 1 | HQ Okayama-ken. |
| Nichiren Shu | sNJMB | 2-c | c1260 | 2,100,000 | 10 | japa | B | 3 | 'Sun Lotus'. The original movement begun by monk Nichiren (1222-1282). HQ Ota-ku, Tokyo. |
| Nichirenshu Fujufuseha | sNJMB | 2-e | c1610 | 16,700 | 1 | japa | B | 1 | HQ Okayama-ken. |
| Nichirenshu Saijokyo | sNJMB | 2-e | | 7,000 | 1 | japa | B | 0 | HQ Okayama-ken. |
| Nichirenshugi Butsuryuko | sNJMB | 2-e | | 2,000 | 1 | japa | B | 1 | HQ Aichi-ken. |
| Nihonzan Myohoji Daisanga | sNJMB | 2-e | | 24,300 | 1 | japa | B | 2 | HQ Shibuya-ku, Tokyo. |
| Nipponzan Myohoji | sNJMB | 2-d | 1917 | 200,000 | 12 | japa | B | 4 | Wondrous Law of the Lotus Sutra. Global fame for 'peace pagodas'. 1,500 ascetics. |
| Risshu | sNJMB | 2-e | 754 | 23,300 | 1 | japa | B | 2 | One of 6 Nara sects of Japanese Buddhism. Strict monasticism. HQ Nara-shi. F=Ganjin/Ching. |
| Ritsu | sNJMB | 2-d | | 500,000 | 3 | japa | B | 2 | Emphasis on Buddhist monastic precepts. |
| Saijo Inarikyo | sNJMB | 2-d | | 232,000 | 1 | japa | B | 0 | HQ Okayama-ken. |
| Seigikai Kyodan | sNJMB | 2-e | | 36,400 | 1 | japa | B | 0 | HQ Chiba-ken. |
| Shingon Risshu | sNJMB | 2-d | c1250 | 444,000 | 2 | japa | B | 2 | A subgroup of Risshu; 90 temples. HQ Nara-shi. F=Eizon. |
| Shishinkai | sNJMB | 2-e | | 70,200 | 1 | japa | B | 1 | HQ Kita-ku, Tokyo. |
| Shobo Hokkeshu | sNJMB | 2-e | | 18,700 | 1 | japa | B | 1 | HQ Kita-ku, Kyoto-shi. |
| Shobokai | sNJMB | 2-e | | 12,600 | 1 | japa | B | 1 | HQ Shinagawa-ku, Tokyo. |
| Shotoku Shu | sNJMB | 2-e | 1950 | 12,800 | 1 | japa | B | 2 | A modern form of Japanese Mahayana. 1950, ex Hossoshu. HQ Nara-ken. |
| Zaike Nichirenshu Jofukai | sNJMB | 2-e | | 24,600 | 1 | japa | B | 1 | HQ Shinjuku-ku, Tokyo. |
| Pure Land Buddhists | PJMB | 2-b | c380 | 21,000,000 | 31 | chin | B | 4 | Ching-Tu. Begun China (F=Hui-yuan), then Japan (Jodo Shy). Now almost all in Japan. |
| Buddhist Churches of America | sPJMB | 2-d | 1899 | 120,000 | 10 | usa | C | 5 | Jodoshinshu. Japanese Americans. |
| Bukkyo Shinshu | sPJMB | 2-e | | 5,500 | 2 | japa | B | 3 | HQ Kumamoto-ken. |
| Chinzei | sPJMB | 2-e | | 7,000 | 2 | japa | B | 3 | A school of Jodo (Pure Land) Buddhism. |
| Gugan Shinshu | sPJMB | 2-e | | 1,500 | 2 | japa | B | 2 | HQ Fukui-shi. |
| Japanese Pure Land Buddhists | sPJMB | 2-b | c1180 | 20,942,000 | 20 | japa | B | 4 | F=Honen. Several rival sects. God=Amitabha/Amida, a god presiding over Western Paradise. |
| Ji Buddhism | sPJMB | 2-d | 1270 | 100,000 | 5 | japa | B | 4 | Ji='Time', a sect of Pure Land Buddhism. F=Ippen. Wandering preachers. |
| Jishu | sPJMB | 2-e | | 87,400 | 2 | japa | B | 0 | HQ Kanagawa-ken. |
| Jodo Shu | sPJMB | 2-c | c1180 | 5,778,000 | 5 | japa | B | 3 | Original parent Pure Land Buddhism. F=Honen. |
| Jodoshu Seizan Fukakusaha | sPJMB | 2-e | | 81,300 | 2 | japa | B | 1 | HQ Kyoto-shi. |
| Jodoshu Seizan Zenrinjiha | sPJMB | 2-d | | 157,000 | 2 | japa | B | 1 | HQ Kyoto-shi. |
| Jodoshu Shaseiha | sPJMB | 2-e | | 4,200 | 1 | japa | B | 1 | HQ Higashiyama-ku, Kyoto-shi. |
| Kurotani Jodoshu | sPJMB | 2-d | | 407,000 | 2 | japa | B | 1 | HQ Kyoto-shi. |
| Makoto no Jodo Shinshu Jokojiha | sPJMB | 2-d | | 169,000 | 2 | japa | B | 0 | HQ Fukuoka-shi. |
| Montoshu Ichimiha | sPJMB | 2-e | | 2,700 | 1 | japa | B | 0 | HQ Kitami-shi, Hokkaido. |
| Seizan Jodoshu | sPJMB | 2-d | | 131,000 | 2 | japa | B | 1 | HQ Kyoto-fu. |
| Shinshu Choseiha | sPJMB | 2-e | | 1,100 | 1 | japa | B | 2 | HQ Yokohama-shi. |
| Shinshu Izumojiha | sPJMB | 2-e | | 12,000 | 2 | japa | B | 0 | HQ Fukui-ken. |
| Shinshu Jokojiha | sPJMB | 2-e | | 25,100 | 2 | japa | B | 1 | HQ Niigata-ken. |
| Shinshu Kita Honganjiha | sPJMB | 2-e | | 9,200 | 1 | japa | B | 0 | HQ Otaru-shi, Hokkaido. |
| Shinshu Koshoha | sPJMB | 2-d | | 146,000 | 2 | japa | B | 1 | HQ Shimogyo-ku, Kyoto-shi. |
| Shinshu Sanmontoha | sPJMB | 2-e | | 19,000 | 2 | japa | B | 0 | HQ Fukui-shi. |
| Shinshu Shojojiha | sPJMB | 2-e | | 21,500 | 2 | japa | B | 0 | HQ Fukui-ken. |
| Shinshu Takadaha | sPJMB | 2-d | | 262,000 | 8 | japa | B | 1 | Largest Pure Land sect in Japan, with 600 temples. HQ Mie-ken. |
| Shinshu Yamamotoha | sPJMB | 2-e | | 4,000 | 1 | japa | B | 0 | HQ Fukui-ken. |
| White Lotus School | sPJMB | 2-e | 402 | 10,000 | 2 | chin | B | 3 | School of Celestial Platform/Pure Land: Pai-lien Tsung, Tien-Tai (in Japan, Tendai). F=Hui-yuan. |
| Yuzu Nenbutsu Shu | sPJMB | 2-d | | 101,000 | 1 | japa | B | 2 | HQ Osaka-shi. |
| True Pure Land Buddhists | TPJMB | 2-b | c1270 | 14,000,000 | 20 | japa | B | 4 | Jodo Shinshu. Also termed Shin Buddhism. Many monks. c1650, splits in 2 sects. |
| Jodo Shinshu Dobo Kyodan | sTPJMB | 2-e | | 1,200 | 1 | japa | B | 2 | HQ Ishikawa-ken. |

*Continued opposite*

*Table 17–6 continued*

| Name of religion/religionists 1 | Pedigree 2 | Type 3 | Begun 4 | Adherents 5 | Ext 6 | Coun 7 | W X 8 9 | E. g. = examples; name for God, other religions present, D=denominations, M=missions. 10 |
|---|---|---|---|---|---|---|---|---|
| Jodo Shinshu Honganjiha | sTPJMB | 2-c | 1220 | 6,662,000 | 5 | japa | B 2 | F=Shinran. Major subgroup in True Pure Land. Nishi (Western). 10,000 temples (HQ Kyoto). |
| Jodo Shinshu Otaniha | sTPJMB | 2-c | 1220 | 6,715,000 | 10 | japa | B 4 | True Pure Land Sect. Eastern Temple. 16,890 clergy, 9,980 temples. HQ Shimogyo-ku, Kyoto. |
| Shingon Buddhists | SJMB | 2-b | 810 | 11,000,000 | 6 | japa | B 3 | True Word. F=Kukai. Tantric Buddhism; 45 sects. God=Great Sun Buddha. HQ Kyoto. |
| Buzan-ha | sSJMB | 2-c | | 1,372,000 | 4 | japa | B 2 | Larger of 2 main branches of Shingon Buddhism (Shingonshu). |
| Chizan-ha | sSJMB | 2-c | | 1,101,000 | 5 | japa | B 2 | One of the 2 main branches of Shingon Buddhism. |
| Fudokyo | sSJMB | 2-e | | 3,800 | 1 | japa | B 0 | HQ Nakoya-shi. |
| Guze Kannon Shu | sSJMB | 2-e | | 11,700 | 1 | japa | B 0 | HQ Wakayama-shi. |
| Hasshukengaku Shinshukyo | sSJMB | 2-e | | 15,900 | 1 | japa | B 0 | HQ Kumamoto-shi. |
| Ishizuchisan Shingonshu | sSJMB | 2-e | | 94,600 | 1 | japa | B 0 | HQ Ehime-ken. |
| Issaishu | sSJMB | 2-d | | 156,000 | 1 | japa | B 1 | HQ Yamaguchi-ken. |
| Kannon Shu | sSJMB | 2-d | | 490,000 | 3 | japa | B 1 | HQ Osaka-shi. |
| Komyo Shingonshu | sSJMB | 2-d | | 102,000 | 1 | japa | B 0 | HQ Wakayama-ken. |
| Koyasan Shingonshu | sSJMB | 2-c | 815 | 4,876,000 | 5 | japa | B 0 | HQ Wakayama-ken. Oldest sect of Tantric Buddhism in Japan. |
| Manji Kyodan | sSJMB | 2-d | | 276,000 | 1 | japa | B 0 | HQ Fukuoka-ken. |
| Meisan Shingonshu | sSJMB | 2-e | | 12,800 | 1 | japa | B 1 | HQ Wakayama-shi. |
| Nakayama Shingo Shoshu | sSJMB | 2-d | 1921 | 457,000 | 2 | japa | B 0 | HQ Saga-ken. |
| Ryosenji Shingonshu | sSJMB | 2-e | | 16,100 | 1 | japa | B 0 | HQ Nara-shi. |
| Shigisan Shingonshu | sSJMB | 2-d | c1000 | 496,000 | 1 | japa | B 1 | HQ Hyogo-ken. |
| Shin Bukkyo Kukaishu | sSJMB | 2-e | | 30,000 | 1 | japa | B 1 | HQ Higashi Osaka-shi. |
| Shin Shingonshu | sSJMB | 2-e | | 4,200 | 1 | japa | B 1 | HQ Nara-ken. |
| Shin-nyo En | sSJMB | 2-c | | 2,100,000 | 2 | japa | B 2 | 'Garden of the Truth of Buddha'. Lay movement with 500 workers. Focuses on Nirvana Sutra. |
| Shingi Shingonshu | sSJMB | 2-d | | 213,000 | 1 | japa | B 2 | HQ Taito-ku, Tokyo. |
| Shingi-Shingonshu Yudonosanpa | sSJMB | 2-e | | 20,000 | 1 | japa | B 0 | HQ Yamagata-ken. |
| Shingon Birushana Shu | sSJMB | 2-e | | 4,900 | 1 | japa | B 1 | HQ Higashi Osaka-shi. |
| Shingon Kyodan | sSJMB | 2-e | | 4,400 | 1 | japa | B 0 | HQ Tochigi-ken. |
| Shingon Misshu | sSJMB | 2-e | | 22,000 | 1 | japa | B 0 | HQ Toyama-ken. |
| Shingon Sanboshu | sSJMB | 2-d | | 156,000 | 1 | japa | B 0 | HQ Huogo-ken. |
| Shingon Shotenshu | sSJMB | 2-e | | 4,400 | 1 | japa | B 0 | HQ Hyogo-ken. |
| Shingon Shu | sSJMB | 2-d | | 283,000 | 2 | japa | B 2 | A broader form of modified Shingon. |
| Shingonshu Buzanha | sSJMB | 2-d | 1580 | 879,000 | 3 | japa | B 2 | HQ Bunkyo-ku, Tokyo. |
| Shingonshu Chizanha | sSJMB | 2-c | 1585 | 1,205,000 | 3 | japa | B 3 | Based on 'New Interpretation of Shingon' with Pure Land elements. |
| Shingonshu Daigoha | sSJMB | 2-d | | 354,000 | 1 | japa | B 1 | HQ Kyoto-shi. |
| Shingonshu Daikakujiha | sSJMB | 2-e | | 38,000 | 1 | japa | B 1 | HQ Kyoto-shi. |
| Shingonshu Dainichiha | sSJMB | 2-e | | 15,000 | 1 | japa | B 0 | HQ Tochigi-ken. |
| Shingonshu Gochi Kyodan | sSJMB | 2-e | | 10,000 | 1 | japa | B 0 | HQ Aichi-ken. |
| Shingonshu Hokakujiha | sSJMB | 2-e | | 15,000 | 1 | japa | B 1 | HQ Nara-ken. |
| Shingonshu Inunakiha | sSJMB | 2-e | | 21,400 | 1 | japa | B 1 | HQ Osaka-fu. |
| Shingonshu Ishitetsuha | sSJMB | 2-e | | 8,000 | 1 | japa | B 0 | HQ Ehime-ken. |
| Shingonshu Kazan'inha | sSJMB | 2-e | | 6,100 | 1 | japa | B 0 | HQ Hyogo-ken. |
| Shingonshu Kojinha | sSJMB | 2-e | | 5,100 | 1 | japa | B 1 | HQ Hyogo-ken. |
| Shingonshu Kokubunjiha | sSJMB | 2-e | | 81,600 | 1 | japa | B 2 | HQ Osaka-shi. |
| Shingonshu Kongoinha | sSJMB | 2-e | | 42,200 | 1 | japa | B 0 | HQ Hyogo-ken. |
| Shingonshu Kyushu Kyodan | sSJMB | 2-e | | 9,800 | 1 | japa | B 1 | HQ Fukuoka-shi. |
| Shingonshu Murojiha | sSJMB | 2-e | | 27,500 | 1 | japa | B 1 | HQ Nara-ken. |
| Shingonshu Omuroha | sSJMB | 2-d | | 142,000 | 1 | japa | B 1 | HQ Kyoto-shi. |
| Shingonshu Reiunjiha | sSJMB | 2-e | | 6,700 | 1 | japa | B 0 | HQ Bunkyo-ku. |
| Shingonshu Senyujiha | sSJMB | 2-e | | 39,200 | 1 | japa | B 1 | HQ Kyoto-shi. |
| Shingonshu Shugenha | sSJMB | 2-e | | 62,200 | 1 | japa | B 0 | HQ Kogawa-ken. |
| Shingonshu Sumaderaha | sSJMB | 2-e | | 49,600 | 1 | japa | B 1 | HQ Kobe-shi. |
| Shingonshu Tojiha | sSJMB | 2-e | | 56,500 | 1 | japa | B 1 | HQ Kyoto-shi. |
| Shingonshu Yamashinaha | sSJMB | 2-e | | 53,700 | 1 | japa | B 1 | HQ Kyoto-shi. |
| Shinnyoen | sSJMB | 2-d | 1935 | 191,000 | 1 | japa | B 1 | HQ Tachikawa-shi, Tokyo. |
| Tenshu | sSJMB | 2-e | | 20,000 | 1 | japa | B 2 | One of many Shingon sects with differentiated practices. |
| Tendai Buddhists | TJMB | 2-c | c550 | 5,000,000 | 2 | japa | B 1 | Tendaishu. Introduced from China. Rationalist monastic order, ascetic, meditative. 20 sects. |
| Enjoshu | sTJMB | 2-e | | 16,300 | 1 | japa | B 1 | Sect of Tendai Buddhism. HQ Kyoto-shi. |
| Ishizuchishu | sTJMB | 2-e | | 10,000 | 1 | japa | B 0 | Sect of Tendai Buddhism. HQ Ehime-ken. |
| Jodo Shinshu Kenkoinha | sTJMB | 2-e | | 15,000 | 1 | japa | B 1 | Sect of Tendai Buddhism. HQ Kyoto-shi. |
| Kenjoshu | sTJMB | 2-e | | 4,900 | 1 | japa | B 1 | Sect of Tendai Buddhism. HQ Hiroshima-ken. |
| Kinpusan Shugen Honshu | sTJMB | 2-d | 1945 | 255,000 | 1 | japa | B 1 | Sect of Tendai Buddhism. HQ Nara-ken. Mountain worship, magical rituals. |
| Kodo Kyodan | sTJMB | 2-d | 1948 | 391,000 | 1 | japa | B 1 | Sect of Tendai Buddhism. HQ Yokohama-shi. F=Okano Shodo and wife Kimiko. |
| Kokawa Kannon Shu | sTJMB | 2-e | | 18,600 | 1 | japa | B 2 | Sect of Tendai Buddhism. HQ Wakayama-ken. |
| Kongoshu | sTJMB | 2-d | | 142,000 | 1 | japa | B 0 | Sect of Tendai Buddhism. HQ Ehime-ken. |
| Kurama Kokyo | sTJMB | 2-e | | 7,400 | 1 | japa | B 1 | Sect of Tendai Buddhism. HQ Kyoto-shi. |
| Myokenshu | sTJMB | 2-d | | 227,000 | 1 | japa | B 1 | Sect of Tendai Buddhism. HQ Osaka-fu. |
| Nenpo Shinkyo | sTJMB | 2-d | 1925 | 511,000 | 1 | japa | B 1 | Sect of Tendai Buddhism. HQ Osaka-shi. |
| Owari Koyasan | sTJMB | 2-e | | 72,100 | 1 | japa | B 0 | Sect of Tendai Buddhism. HQ Aichi-ken. |
| Seizanshu | sTJMB | 2-e | | 4,000 | 1 | japa | B 1 | Sect of Tendai Buddhism. HQ Kyoto-shi. |
| Shinshu Bukkojiha | sTJMB | 2-d | | 138,000 | 1 | japa | B 1 | HQ Kyoto-shi. |
| Shugendo | sTJMB | 2-d | c1050 | 104,000 | 1 | japa | B 1 | Way to control central power. Lay, hostile to clergy. 180 temples. |
| Shugenshu | sTJMB | 2-e | | 91,000 | 1 | japa | B 0 | Sect of Tendai. HQ Kamagawa-ken. |
| Taiwashu | sTJMB | 2-e | | 105,000 | 1 | japa | B 0 | Sect of Tendai. HQ Iwate-ken. |
| Tendai Jimonshu | sTJMB | 2-d | c850 | 400,000 | 2 | japa | B 1 | Schism ex Tendai by F=Enchin. HQ Shiga-ken. Esoteric. Many schisms and sects. |
| Tendai Shinseishu | sTJMB | 2-e | | 74,700 | 1 | japa | B 1 | HQ Shiga-ken. |
| Washu | sTJMB | 2-c | 1949 | 2,016,000 | 2 | japa | B 3 | Largest of the 20 sects of Tendai Buddhism. HQ Osaka-shi. |
| Yogacara | yJMB | 2-e | c350 | 10,000 | 1 | indi | B 2 | Yoga-practice. Vijnanavada. Philosophical school 'Mind Only' of Mahayana Buddhism. |
| Zen Buddhists | ZJMB | 2-b | 1191 | 13,000,000 | 30 | japa | B 3 | Brought to Japan from China. Now 22,000 temples in Japan. |
| Chan Buddhism | sZJMB | 2-c | c500 | 1,000,000 | 2 | chin | B 3 | Form of Zen meditation rooted in Indian Buddhism and developed in China and Japan. |
| Ichibata Yakushi Kyodan | sZJMB | 2-d | | 110,000 | 1 | japa | B 2 | HQ Shimane-ken. |
| Isson Kyodan | sZJMB | 2-e | | 1,600 | 1 | japa | B 2 | HQ Ishikawa-ken. |
| Ningen Zen Kyodan | sZJMB | 2-e | | 5,200 | 1 | japa | B 2 | HQ Chiba-ken. |
| Nyoraikyo | sZJMB | 2-e | | 33,400 | 1 | japa | B 2 | HQ Nagoya-shi. |
| Obaku Shu | sZJMB | 2-d | 1650 | 245,000 | 1 | japa | B 3 | One of 3 schools of Zen in Japan. F=Ingen. 460 temples. HQ Kyoto-fu. |
| Rinzai Zen Buddhists | sZJMB | 2-c | 1191 | 3,000,000 | 10 | japa | B 4 | Japanese Zen. F=Lin Chi (Chinese). Overall aim to reproduce Enlightenment experience. |
| Rinzaishu Buttsujiha | sZJMB | 2-e | 1395 | 98,500 | 1 | japa | B 2 | HQ Kyoto-shi. |
| Rinzaishu Daitokujiha | sZJMB | 2-e | 1324 | 14,700 | 1 | japa | B 2 | HQ Kita-ku, Kyoto-shi. |
| Rinzaishu Eigenjiha | sZJMB | 2-e | 1361 | 13,600 | 1 | japa | B 2 | HQ Shiga-ken. |
| Rinzaishu Enkakujiha | sZJMB | 2-d | 1282 | 178,000 | 4 | japa | B 2 | HQ Kanagawa-ken. |
| Rinzaishu Hokojiha | sZJMB | 2-d | 1384 | 589,000 | 5 | japa | B 2 | HQ Shizuoka-ken. |
| Rinzaishu Kenchojiha | sZJMB | 2-e | 1253 | 89,400 | 1 | japa | B 2 | HQ Kanagawa-ken. |
| Rinzaishu Kenninjiha | sZJMB | 2-e | 1202 | 24,000 | 1 | japa | B 2 | F=Myoan-Eisai (1141-1218) |
| Rinzaishu Kogakujiha | sZJMB | 2-e | 1380 | 30,100 | 1 | japa | B 2 | HQ Yamanashi-ken. |
| Rinzaishu Kokutaijiha | sZJMB | 2-e | 1327 | 2,300 | 1 | japa | B 2 | HQ Toyama-ken. |
| Rinzaishu Koshojiha | sZJMB | 2-e | | 3,100 | 1 | japa | B 2 | HQ Kamigyo-ku, Kyoto-shi. |
| Rinzaishu Myoshinjiha | sZJMB | 2-c | 1337 | 1,628,000 | 22 | japa | B 4 | Largest Rinzai sect in Japan. 3,000 temples. Declining. HQ Kyoto. Members in USA, Mexico. |
| Rinzaishu Nanzenjiha | sZJMB | 2-e | 1291 | 91,200 | 1 | japa | B 2 | HQ Kyoto-shi. |
| Rinzaishu Shokokujiha | sZJMB | 2-e | 1382 | 53,800 | 1 | japa | B 2 | HQ Kyoto-shi. |
| Rinzaishu Tenryujiha | sZJMB | 2-e | 1339 | 82,600 | 1 | japa | B 2 | HQ Ukyo-ku, Kyoto-shi. |
| Rinzaishu Tofukujiha | sZJMB | 2-e | 1239 | 5,000 | 1 | japa | B 2 | HQ Kyoto-shi. |
| Sanbo Kyodan | sZJMB | 2-e | | 2,700 | 1 | japa | B 2 | HQ Kanagawa-ken. |
| Senshin Kyodan | sZJMB | 2-e | | 36,600 | 1 | japa | B 2 | HQ Mie-gun, Mie-ken. |
| Soto Shu | sZJMB | 2-c | c1240 | 6,842,000 | 15 | japa | B 3 | Zen Buddhism with temples, priests, rites. China origin. F=Dogen. Popular Buddhist teaching. |
| Tsao-tung | sZJMB | 2-d | 1108 | 800,000 | 3 | chin | B 3 | Chan (Zen) school of Buddhism in China. Soto (Japanese). The 5 Ranks/Ways. |
| Korean Buddhists | KMB | 2-c | 372 | 7,100,000 | 20 | souk | B 2 | Mahayana Buddhism. |
| Bulgyohwoi | sKMB | 2-d | 1975 | 563,000 | 10 | souk | B 2 | SGI Hankuk-Bulgyohwoi/Korean Buddhist Council. Emphasis upon world peace. |
| Chogye Chong | sKMB | 2-c | 372 | 7,001,000 | 18 | souk | B 1 | Daihan-Bulgyo-Chongyejong strict Korean Son (Zen) Buddhism (Chongye), unified 1935. |
| Chongwhajong | sKMB | 2-d | 1969 | 712,000 | 1 | souk | B 0 | Daihan-Bulgyo-Chongwhajong (Korean Buddhist Sect of Chongwha; Mahayana). |

*Continued opposite*

*Table 17–6 continued*

| Name of religion/religionists 1 | Pedigree 2 | Type 3 | Begun 4 | Adherents 5 | Ext 6 | Coun 7 | W 8 | X 9 | E. g. = examples; name for God, other religions present, D=denominations, M=missions. 10 |
|---|---|---|---|---|---|---|---|---|---|
| Chontaijong | sKMB | 2-c | 594 | 1,182,000 | 1 | souk | B | 2 | Daihan-Bulgyo-Chontaijong (Korean Buddhist Sect of Chontai; Mahayana). |
| Kwanumjong | sKMB | 2-d | 1940 | 618,000 | 1 | souk | B | 0 | Daihan-Bulgyo-Kwanumjong (Korean Buddhist Sect of Sattva). |
| Mitajong | sKMB | 2-c | 1943 | 1,026,000 | 1 | souk | B | 1 | Daihan-Bulgyo-Mitajong (Korean Buddhist Sect of Sattva). |
| Popsong | sKMB | 2-c | | 1,000,000 | 3 | souk | B | 1 | Korean version of Mahayana Buddhism. Zen elements. 1935, unified as Chogye Chong. |
| Taego Chong | sKMB | 2-c | 1356 | 3,133,000 | 4 | souk | B | 1 | Hankuk-Bulgyo-Taigojong (Korean Buddhist Sect of Taigo). Liberal, rivaling traditionalists. |
| Won Buddhism | sKMB | 2-d | 1916 | 600,000 | 8 | souk | B | 3 | Won Bulgyo (Round Circle). Modernized Zen/Taoism/Confucianism/Chondogyo/Christianity. |
| nonreligious Buddhists | NB | 2-b | c1950 | 54,408,000 | 35 | japa | B | 2 | Persons with Buddhism as family religion but professing no personal religion. |
| All Ceylon Buddhist Congress | nB | 7-b | 1918 | 12,500,000 | 5 | sril | B | 3 | Theravadins. Leadership of YMBA. |
| All Indonesia Fed of Buddhist Orgs | nB | 7-c | 1978 | 2,000,000 | 2 | indo | B | 3 | Acronym WALUBI. Represents all Buddhist sects to government. |
| All Japan Federation of Buddhist Sects | nB | 7-b | | 81,300,000 | 3 | japa | B | 3 | Nihon Bukkyo Kai. 60 sects, 60 other organizations. |
| Buddhist Association of Thailand | nB | 7-b | 1934 | 52,382,000 | 2 | thai | B | 3 | 75 provincial associations (14 Chinese). |
| Buddhist Federation of Australia | nB | 7-d | c1970 | 241,000 | 3 | aust | C | 4 | Huge Nan Tien Temple is part of a Taiwan-based 110 monastery network. |
| Buddhist Society of Great Britain and I | nB | 7-e | 1907 | 3,000 | 3 | brit | C | 5 | I=Ireland. All traditions taught. |
| Buddhist Society of India | nB | 7-c | 1951 | 6,000,000 | 1 | indi | B | 2 | Neo-Buddhism of BR Ambedkar; mass conversion of Dalits, 1956. Marathi. |
| Chinese Buddhist Association | nB | 7-b | 1954 | 60,000,000 | 2 | chin | B | 3 | Government-control after virtually destroyed in Cultural Revolution, 1966-1979. |
| Federation of Buddhists of Thailand | nB | 7-b | 1975 | 52,000,000 | 1 | thai | B | 2 | FBT. Begun by Mahanikaya monks. |
| Indonesian Buddhayana Council | nB | 7-c | 1954 | 1,930,000 | 1 | indo | B | 3 | Majelis Buddhayana Indonesia (MBI). Java. |
| Lao United Buddhists Association | nB | 7-c | 1977 | 2,650,000 | 2 | laos | A | 1 | LUBA. 7,000 monks, 10,000 novices, in 2,800 monasteries. |
| Majelis Upasaka Pandita Agama BI | nB | 7-d | c1975 | 500,000 | 1 | indo | B | 3 | MUABI. Council of Buddhist Lay Spiritual Advisors of Indonesia. Married, no monastic rules. |
| Sri Lankan Dharmadhuta Society | nB | 7-c | 1952 | 2,000,000 | 1 | sril | B | 3 | Begun from World Fellowship of Buddhists for Theravada missions worldwide. |
| Unified Vietnamese Buddhist Church | nB | 7-b | 1963 | 39,000,000 | 3 | viet | B | 3 | United Buddhist Association, uniting Theravadins and Mahayanists. |
| Western Buddhist Order | nB | 7-d | 1967 | 500,000 | 7 | brit | C | 5 | Friends of the Western Buddhist Order (WBO). Quasi-monastic. F=Venerable Sangharakshita. |
| Gelugpas | GL-oB | 9-d | c1450 | 100,000 | 30 | chin | B | 3 | Virtuous Ones. Yellow Hat Lamaist monastic order (Dalai Lama's sect); emphasis scholarship. |
| Mulavamsa | s-oB | 9-e | c1900 | 12,000 | 1 | sril | B | 3 | Prominent monastic grouping within Amarapura Nikaya. |
| Dhammarakkhitavamsa | sT-oB | 9-e | c1900 | 5,000 | 1 | sril | B | 3 | Prominent monastic grouping within Amarapura Nikaya. |
| Dhammayut Nikaya | sT-oB | 9-c | c1870 | 1,500,000 | 2 | thai | B | 2 | Thammayut. Theravada monastic community with 1,500 monasteries. |
| Dwara Nikaya | sT-oB | 9-e | c1850 | 3,000 | 2 | myan | B | 3 | Small Burmese Theravada monastic fraternity. Rationalist. |
| Hngettwin Nikaya | sT-oB | 9-e | c1850 | 1,000 | 1 | myan | B | 3 | Smallest monastic fraternity in Burma; around Mandalay. |
| Mahanikaya | sT-oB | 9-d | c1700 | 200,000 | 2 | thai | B | 2 | Largest Theravada fraternity in Thailand: 95% of 28,000 monasteries, with 200,000 monks. |
| Ramanna Nikaya | sT-oB | 9-e | 1865 | 2,000 | 1 | sril | B | 3 | One of 3 main divisions of Theravada monks. |
| Saddhammavamsa | sT-oB | 9-e | | 6,000 | 1 | sril | B | 3 | Monastic grouping within Amarapura Nikaya. |
| Shwegyin Nikaya | sT-oB | 9-e | c1850 | 50,000 | 1 | myan | B | 4 | Smaller school: 50,000 monks. Strict, puritanical. |
| Siyam Nikaya | sT-oB | 9-e | 1753 | 12,000 | 1 | sril | B | 3 | Oldest fraternity of Theravada monks in Ceylon. Strict hierarchy. |
| Thomayat | sT-oB | 9-e | | 2,300 | 2 | camb | A | 1 | Order of the Law. Close to Thai Thammayut. Destroyed 1975, restored 1991. 104 monasteries. |
| Thuddama Nikaya | sT-oB | 9-d | 1780 | 450,000 | 2 | myan | B | 3 | 80% of monastic fraternity in Burma. 250,000 ordained monks. |
| Anagarika | v-oB | 9-e | BC 800 | 30,000 | 1 | indi | B | 2 | Organized Buddhist homeless ascetics who do not enter the sangha. |
| Hoguk Sungdan | v-oB | 9-e | c1950 | 20,000 | 2 | souk | B | 5 | Monks Militia for National Defence (Chogye order). |
| Order of Buddhist Contemplatives | w-oB | 9-e | 1970 | 2,000 | 1 | usa | C | 5 | OBC. Order in Soto Zen. Abbeys in UK, USA, Canada. |
| Bauddha Dharmankur Sabha | sB | 2-d | 1892 | 500,000 | 2 | indi | B | 2 | Begun in Calcutta, reviving West Bengal Buddhism. |
| Buddhist Sunday Schools Movement | sB | 2-c | 1958 | 3,000,000 | 4 | thai | B | 2 | Many schools around Bangkok. |
| Fukudenkai | sB | 2-e | | 2,500 | 1 | japa | B | 3 | HQ Okayama-shi. |
| Gedatsuko | sB | 2-d | | 234,000 | 1 | japa | B | 3 | HQ Shimogyo-ku, Kyoto-shi. |
| Vietnamese Buddhists | sSB | 2-b | c50 | 39,533,000 | 10 | viet | B | 3 | Theravadin and Mahayanist from early stage. |
| Theravadins | TB | 2-b | BC c250 | 136,259,000 | 30 | sril | B | 3 | Theravada, 'Way of the Elders'. Also termed Hinayana (Lesser Vehicle of Salvation). |
| Neo-Buddhism | NTB | 2-c | 1951 | 6,000,000 | 3 | indi | B | 2 | Conversion of 4 million Outcastes: Buddhism of social protest (B. R. Ambedkar, Maharashtra). |
| Amarapura Nikaya | sTB | 2-e | c1850 | 50,000 | 3 | myan | B | 3 | One of 3 main Theravada divisions, in Amarapura, Burma. 1,000 monasteries, 3,000 monks. |
| Burmese Theravadins | sTB | 2-b | | 32,000,000 | 32 | myan | B | 1 | Theravada heavily influenced by animism, nats, Hinduism. |
| Cambodian Buddhism | sTB | 2-c | AD 400 | 9,500,000 | 2 | camb | A | 1 | 2 orders in 1970: Mahanikay (3,230 monasteries: 62,700 monks), Thomayat (139: 2,300). |
| Dhammadana Association | sTB | 2-e | c1940 | 3,000 | 1 | thai | B | 2 | Modernizing urban grouping attacking superstition. |
| English Sangha Trust | sTB | 2-d | | 150,000 | 3 | brit | C | 5 | Supporting Britain-based monks. |
| German Dhammaduta Society | sTB | 2-e | 1957 | 84,000 | 2 | germ | C | 5 | German wing of Buddhist world mission. |
| Getambe Group | sTB | 2-e | 1980 | 1,000 | 1 | sril | B | 3 | Lay meditation society. F=P. Sorada. |
| Lanka Vipassana Bhavana Samitiya | sTB | 2-e | 1952 | 1,000 | 1 | sril | B | 3 | Lanka Insight Meditation Society. Lay meditation. |
| Laotian Theravada Buddhism | sTB | 2-c | | 2,500,000 | 2 | laos | A | 1 | State religion until 1975. |
| Maha Bodhi Society | sTB | 2-b | 1900 | 10,000,000 | 20 | sril | B | 4 | MBS. Great Enlightenment Society. Worldwide missions. |
| Santi Asok | sTB | 2-e | 1975 | 30,000 | 1 | thai | B | 3 | This-worldly TV moral reformists in urban 'dhamma families'. Use of Buddha images rejected. |
| Sarvodaya Sramadana | sTB | 2-c | 1958 | 2,400,000 | 3 | sril | B | 4 | Buddhist model of social development, reaching 20% of Ceylon's villages. F=A. T. Ariyaratna. |
| Siyane Vipassana Bhavana Samitiya | sTB | 2-e | 1955 | 3,000 | 1 | sril | B | 3 | Modern Sri Lankan lay meditation society. |
| Thammakaai Religious Foundation | sTB | 2-c | 1970 | 1,000,000 | 1 | thai | B | 2 | Media, prosperity, flaunting of wealth. Lay asceticism. Conservative. |
| Vinaya Vardhana Society | sTB | 2-e | 1932 | 5,000 | 1 | sril | B | 3 | Association for the Protection of Buddhist Discipline. Anticlerical. |
| Vajrayana Buddhism | VB | 2-c | 400 | 1,000,000 | 3 | chin | B | 3 | Thunderbolt Vehicle. Esoteric Buddhism, based on Tibetan-language Vajrayana tradition. |
| Buddhist Publication Society | vB | 9-d | 1958 | 300,000 | 3 | sril | B | 3 | BPS. HQ Kandy. Mission to the West. |
| Sadahnm Mithuru Samuluwa | sVB | 2-c | 1962 | 1,000,000 | 2 | sril | B | 3 | Saddhamma Friends Society (SFS). Reformed Theravada. |
| Bharatiya Buddha Mahasabha | wB | 7-d | | 400,000 | 1 | indi | B | 3 | Indian council for guiding Buddhist affairs. |
| Chittagong Buddhist Association | wB | 7-e | 1887 | 30,000 | 1 | myan | B | 3 | Buddhist welfare organization representing Buddhists in Burma. |
| Internat Network of Engaged Buddhists | wB | 7-c | 1989 | 1,500,000 | 26 | thai | B | 4 | INEB. Social activist stance. |
| World Buddhist Sangha Council | wB | 7-c | 1966 | 5,000,000 | 70 | sril | B | 4 | WBSC. HQ Colombo. To assist Theravada bhikkhu mendicant missions around world. |
| World Fellowship of Buddhists | wB | 7-a | 1950 | 359,000,000 | 50 | thai | B | 4 | F=Malalasekera (Ceylon). Centralized. HQ Bangkok. 1969 Ninth General Conference. |
| Buddhayana | YB | 2-c | 1954 | 1,930,000 | 20 | indo | B | 3 | Syncretistic amalgam of Mahayana, Theravada, with Kasogatan (local Javanese Buddhism). |
| **Christians** | C | 1-a | AD 30 | 1,999,564,000 | 238 | usa | C | 5 | Followers of Jesus Christ, Son of God, Savior, in 238 countries. D=34,000. |
| World A Christians | A-C | 2-b | 33 | 10,329,000 | 38 | paki | A | 5 | Christians living in World A countries (those under 50% evangelized (E |
| World B Christians | B-C | 2-a | 33 | 513,034,000 | 59 | chin | B | 5 | Christians living in World B countries (under 60% Christian but E>50%). |
| World C Christians | C-C | 2-a | 33 | 1,476,204,000 | 141 | usa | C | 5 | Christians living in World C countries (60% or more Christian). |
| affiliated Christians (church members) | AC | 2-a | 30 | 1,888,439,000 | 238 | usa | C | 5 | All Christians enrolled by name in churches; baptized church members. |
| Anglican Church of Kenya | A-Eva-AC | 6-c | 1844 | 3,123,000 | 1 | keny | C | 5 | ICK/CPK. Kanisa la Jimbo la Kenya. 26 Dioceses. M=CMS,BCMS. Big losses to ICCEC, NAC. |
| Church of Uganda | A-Eva-AC | 6-c | 1875 | 8,624,000 | 1 | ugan | C | 5 | 27 Dioceses. Balokole Revival. Schisms to new AICs. M=CMS,RCMS,AIM(UK). 142f,8H. |
| Episcopal Ch of the Sudan | A-Eva-AC | 6-c | 1899 | 2,460,000 | 1 | suda | B | 5 | 12 Dioceses. M=CMS(UK),BCMS. Bari, Azande, Moru. 91n,2x,500m,14f,1h,2r,20000Yy. |
| Ch of the Province of S Africa | A-Hig-AC | 6-c | 1806 | 2,669,000 | 1 | soua | C | 5 | CPSA. 16 Dioceses in SA, 6 abroad. 56% Black, 24% White. 511b,18de,18H,96h,12r,4s(81). |
| Church in Wales | A-Hig-AC | 6-c | 300 | 1,360,000 | 1 | brit | C | 5 | Eglwys yng Nghymru. State church until 1920. 6 Dioceses. 2s(50),1000Y. (1995) 671n. |
| Anglican Church of Nigeria | A-Low-AC | 6-b | 1842 | 20,412,000 | 1 | nige | B | 5 | In CPWA until 1979 when ACN formed. Mushrooming to 63 Dioceses. M=CMS(UK).68f,1p,1s. |
| Anglican Church of Australia | A-plu-AC | 6-c | 1788 | 4,093,000 | 1 | aust | C | 5 | Ch of England in Australia. 23 Dioceses. 3528n; M=USPG,MTS,NZCMS. |
| Ch of the Province of Tanzania | A-plu-AC | 6-c | 1864 | 2,683,000 | 1 | tanz | B | 5 | CPT. Kanisa la Jimbo la Tanzania (KJT). 16 Dioceses. 160f,3s(55),305n,43x,8629Y,16200y. |
| Church of England | A-plu-AC | 6-b | 100 | 23,860,000 | 1 | brit | C | 5 | Reformed 1558. 1960, Charismatic Renewal, now 12%. 100x,308m,2358w,23s (950). |
| Episcopal Church in the USA | A-plu-AC | 6-c | 1578 | 2,295,000 | 1 | usa | C | 5 | ECUSA. (1970) 8 US Provinces, 109 Dioceses. 11272n,14s,6370Y,62814y. (1990) 14878n. |
| Han unregistered house chs | I-AC | 6-b | 1950 | 11,812,000 | 1 | chin | B | 5 | Hundreds of small illegal networks, many isolated, mostly noncharismatic. Rural persecutions. |
| Jesus Army | I-3.W-AC | 6-e | 1805 | 4,000 | 1 | brit | C | 5 | Bugbrooke Community. Jesus Fellowship. Shepherding controversy. |
| Jesus People | I-3.W-AC | 6-d | c1960 | 600,000 | 1 | usa | C | 5 | Jesus Movement. Street Christians. Many Prepentecostal groupings over 500 years. |
| African Apost Ch of J Maranke | I-3aA-AC | 6-c | 1932 | 1,040,000 | 1 | zimb | B | 5 | AACJM. VaPostori (Apostles). Ex USA Methodists. Manyika, Zezuru; across Zimbabwe. |
| Celestial Church of Christ | I-3aA-AC | 6-c | 1952 | 3,689,000 | 1 | nige | B | 4 | Heavenly Christianity. Begun Dahomey 1947. Yoruba elites. Rapid growth also in 20 countries. |
| Ch of God Mission International | I-3aA-AC | 6-c | 1968 | 1,430,000 | 1 | nige | B | 5 | Miracle Centre, Benin City. International seminary, led by archbishop B. Idahosa. |
| Christ Apostolic Church | I-3aA-AC | 6-c | 1917 | 1,480,000 | 1 | nige | B | 5 | CAC(1942). 1920 Faith Tabernacle. 39 Districts. 74% Yoruba. 281n,1224m,284,2s,12630Y. |
| Eternal Sacred Order of Ch & S | I-3aA-AC | 6-c | 1925 | 1,140,000 | 1 | nige | B | 5 | Original main body of Cherubim & Seraphim. Many schisms, lawsuits. HQ Ebute-Meta. |
| Gospel Faith Mission | I-3aA-AC | 6-c | 1953 | 1,422,000 | 1 | nige | B | 5 | GFM. Schism ex CAC. HQ Ibadan, Benin. M=CAM. Kambari, Ibo, Yoruba, Gongola. 3859Y. |
| Redeemed Christian Ch of God | I-3aA-AC | 6-c | 1952 | 2,520,000 | 1 | nige | B | 5 | Ex C&S. Abortive aid: 1957, M=AFM(SAfrica), 1963 Velberter M(Germany). 1p. 18 chs in USA. |
| Pente Assemblies of the World | I-3aO-AC | 6-c | 1906 | 1,512,000 | 1 | usa | C | 5 | PAOW. Black pentecostals.600n.Missions in Caribbean, India, Israel, Nigeria; over 1,000 chs. |
| Eglise Neo-Apostolique | I-3aX-AC | 6-c | 1970 | 1,706,000 | 1 | conz | C | 5 | NAC. New Apostolic Church. M=Neuapostolische Kirche (HQ Zurich, Switzerland). |
| New Apostolic Church, India | I-3aX-AC | 6-c | 1969 | 1,734,000 | 1 | indi | B | 4 | Canada Bezirk. HQ Zurich. Rapid growth. 1973 mission in Kenya, Africa. |
| New Apostolic Church, Kenya | I-3aX-AC | 6-c | 1973 | 1,214,000 | 1 | keny | C | 4 | M=NAC(World HQ Zurich). Begun from Bombay, India. Phenomenal growth. |
| Han charismatic house chs | I-3cC-AC | 6-b | 1950 | 35,686,000 | 1 | chin | B | 5 | 500 Regional Councils, 5,000 Pastoral Districts. M=Taiwanese/Diaspora short-termers; CCRC. |
| New Birth Movement | I-3cC-AC | 6-c | 1980 | 4,800,000 | 1 | chin | B | 5 | NBM, or Born Again Movement (BAM) One branch of the whole house church movement. |
| People's Organization churches | I-3cC-AC | 6-c | 1995 | 2,400,000 | 1 | chin | B | 5 | Churches begun with full approval of local authorities, because no TSPM or foreign links. |
| Fullness/Praise Network of Chs | I-3cW-AC | 6-c | 1978 | 3,960,000 | 1 | usa | C | 5 | Network of Southern Baptist charismatic churches, many expelled from SBC. |
| Full Gospel Baptist Ch Fell | I-3fD-AC | 6-c | 1993 | 1,320,000 | 1 | usa | C | 5 | FGBCF. F=bp Paul Morton. Black. Ex NBCA, NBCUSA. Missions: Bahamas, S Africa, Russia. |
| Jesus is Lord Fellowship | I-3fF-AC | 6-c | 1978 | 2,400,000 | 1 | phil | C | 5 | JILF. Philippines for Jesus. Mass movement. F=E. Villanueva. In 25 countries. |
| Yoido Full Gospel Churches | I-3kK-AC | 6-c | 1958 | 1,075,000 | 1 | souk | B | 5 | YFGC. Adult members: (1961) 800. 100 staff, 50,000 cells. Since 1985 part of AoG. |

*Continued overleaf*

*Table 17-6 continued*

| Name of religion/religionists 1 | Pedigree 2 | Type 3 | Begun 4 | Adherents 5 | Ext 6 | Coun 7 | W 8 | X 9 | E. g. = examples; name for God, other religions present, D=denominations, M=missions. 10 |
|---|---|---|---|---|---|---|---|---|---|
| Brotherhood of Cross and Star | I-3nA-AC | 6-c | 1956 | 1,223,000 | 1 | nige | B | 4 | Vast expanding movement with numerous churches abroad. F=Olumba Olumba Obu. |
| EdeJC sur la Terre par Proph SK | I-3nA-AC | 6-c | 1921 | 8,300,000 | 1 | conz | C | 5 | EJCSK. Ch of Christ on Earth thru Prophet Simon Kimbangu. 1H,1s(82),W=44%,36747Y. |
| Assembly Hall Churches | I-3nC-AC | 6-c | 1922 | 1,434,000 | 1 | chin | B | 5 | Chu Hui So. Little Flock. F=Watchman Nee. 1949: 636 churches, 70,000 members. Jiangxi. |
| Church of Christ (Manalista) | I-3nF-AC | 6-c | 1913 | 1,800,000 | 1 | phil | C | 4 | INC. Iglesia ni Cristo (Manalista). 35 cathedrals, 2 radio stations. Not charismatic. 1902n. |
| True Jesus Church | I-3oC-AC | 6-c | 1917 | 1,199,000 | 1 | chin | B | 4 | Chen Ye-su Chiao Hui. 1949: 1,000 churches. Now with global diaspora. (HQ Taipei, Taiwan). |
| Pentecostal Ch of Indonesia | I-3oG-AC | 6-c | 1920 | 1,336,000 | 1 | indo | B | 5 | GPI,GPdI. G Pantekosta di Indonesia. 25% Chinese. Many splits, including GBIS. 1500n,3s. |
| African Assembs (Back to God) | I-3pA-AC | 6-c | 1943 | 1,714,000 | 1 | soua | C | 5 | Rapidly-expanding Nicholas Bhengu pentecostal movement. 1959, ex AoG(USA). Xhosa, Zulu. |
| Church of the Lord (Aladura) | I-3pA-AC | 6-c | 1930 | 1,674,000 | 1 | nige | B | 5 | Aladura=Praying (Yoruba). Revival ex CMS. In 17 West African nations, also UK, USA, &c). |
| Nigerian Christian Fellowship | I-3pA-AC | 6-c |  | 1,067,000 | 1 | nige | B | 5 | A loosely-organized grouping of pentecostal bodies in eastern Nigeria. HQ Uyo. |
| Church of God in Christ | I-3pB-AC | 6-c | 1895 | 6,280,000 | 1 | usa | C | 5 | Black. Largest pentecostal church in USA. HQ Memphis (TN). (1970) 5000n. (1990) 33593n. |
| Restorationism | I-3pW-AC | 6-d | 1970 | 250,000 | 1 | brit | C | 5 | New Churches movement in Britain, labelled R-1, R-2. Neocharismatics. |
| Russian Unified Fell of CEF | I-3pW-AC | 6-c | 1913 | 1,340,000 | 1 | russ | B | 5 | CEF=Christians of the Evangelical Faith. Formerly in AUCECB. 65 churches in Moscow. |
| Congregação Cristã do Brasil | I-3pY-AC | 6-c | 1910 | 3,544,000 | 1 | braz | C | 5 | Christian Congregation of B. Italian origins. States: 53% in SPaulo, 30% Paraná. |
| Ig Ev Pente 'O Brasil para Cristo' | I-3pY-AC | 6-c | 1955 | 2,200,000 | 1 | braz | C | 5 | OBPC. Brazil for Christ. Ex AoG, ex WCC. Church seating 40,000 in São Paulo. In Costa Rica. |
| Ig Universal do Reino de Deus | I-3pY-AC | 6-c | 1977 | 4,800,000 | 1 | braz | C | 4 | Universal Ch of the Kingdom of God. IURD/UCKG. 2000n. In 50 countries (Portugal, Angola). |
| Igreja Pedra Fundamental | I-3pY-AC | 6-c | 1970 | 2,880,000 | 1 | braz | C | 5 | Cornerstone Gospel Ch. 7th largest in Brazil (after RCC,AoG,CCB, IURD,ICAB, God is Love). |
| Igreja Pentecostal Deus e Amor | I-3pY-AC | 6-c |  | 3,194,000 | 1 | braz | C | 5 | God is Love Pentecostal Ch. Huge in big cities: drab. Many chs abroad (Cape Verde, USA, &c). |
| Word of Life | I-3wW-AC | 6-e | 1983 | 22,500 | 1 | swed | C | 5 | Livets Ord. Faith Movement. Charismatic ministry, HQ Uppsala. 100 churches. |
| Zion Christian Ch, South Africa | I-3zA-AC | 6-c | 1914 | 8,400,000 | 1 | soua | C | 5 | ZCC. Ex AFM. Colors green, yellow. Pedi. Abroad: 9 countries (Malawi, Namibia, Mozambique). |
| Zion Christian Ch, Zimbabwe | I-3zA-AC | 6-c | 1923 | 1,248,000 | 1 | zimb | B | 5 | ZCC. Begun by Bishop Mutendi from South Africa. Holy cities. HQ Bikita, Karanga. |
| Revival Zion | I-3zU-AC | 6-e | 1783 | 36,800 | 1 | jama | B | 5 | 1861, Great Christian Revival. Neocharismatics similar to Shouters, Shakers. |
| Order of Ethiopia | I-Ang-AC | 6-e | 1900 | 50,000 | 1 | soua | C | 5 | Xhosa section in CPSA (Anglican Ch). 1983, first Xhosa bishop after 80 years of promises. |
| Baptist Bible Fellowship Internat | I-Bap-AC | 6-c | 1950 | 1,560,000 | 1 | usa | C | 5 | BBFI. Ex SBC et alia. 1.7 million by 1976. Whites. In 48 countries. 1s. |
| Nat Primitive Baptist Convention | I-Bap-AC | 6-c | 1865 | 1,159,000 | 1 | usa | C | 5 | Black. Formerly Colored Primitive Baptists. HQ Tallahassee (FL). 597n,2150t(32200). |
| National Bapt Conv of America | I-Bap-AC | 6-c | 1880 | 4,464,000 | 1 | usa | C | 5 | NBC. Part of first major Black Baptist body; NBCUSA split off in 1915. 28574n,1s. |
| National Baptist Conv, USA | I-Bap-AC | 6-b | 1773 | 10,007,000 | 1 | usa | C | 5 | NBC. 1915 split from NBC America. Black. HQ Nashville. (1970) 27500n,1s. (1990) 32832n. |
| National Missionary Bapt Conv | I-Bap-AC | 6-c | 1988 | 3,600,000 | 1 | usa | C | 5 | NMBCA. Split ex NBCA over control of publishing; claims 89% of all members. HQ Nashville. |
| Progressive National Bapt Conv | I-Bap-AC | 6-c | 1961 | 3,473,000 | 1 | usa | C | 5 | PNBC. Black. Schism ex NBCUSA, over elections. 863n. Share NBC seminary. |
| Eglise Catholique Traditionalle | I-CCa-AC | 6-c | 1976 | 1,080,000 | 1 | fran | C | 5 | Schism under abp M. Lefebvre (died 1991). In Germany, Switzerland, UK, USA, 250n. |
| Ig Católica Apostólica Brasileira | I-CCa-AC | 6-c | 1945 | 3,200,000 | 1 | braz | C | 5 | ICAB. Schism by RC ex-bishop of Botucatu. 12 Dioceses, 25 bishops. c1990 NNCM splits off. |
| Christian Chs & Chs of Christ | I-Dis-AC | 6-c | 1935 | 1,156,000 | 1 | usa | C | 5 | Church of Christ (Instrumental). Schism ex Disciples. 7312n,40s,6012t(1243445). |
| Chs of Christ (Non-Instrumental) | I-Dis-AC | 6-c | 1870 | 1,217,000 | 1 | usa | C | 5 | Conservative anti-organ split ex Disciples. 10% Black. 10000n,22s,130000Y. |
| High-caste Hindu believers in C | I-Hin-AC | 6-c | 1800 | 2,800,000 | 1 | indi | B | 2 | Isolated Brahmin believers in Christ as Lord who choose to remain in Hindu society and family. |
| Low-caste Hindu believers in C | I-Hin-AC | 6-c | 1800 | 8,400,000 | 1 | indi | B | 2 | Numerous movements but mostly isolated believers and families witnessing within Hinduism. |
| Cath Ch in China (Underground) | I-Lat-AC | 6-c | 1979 | 1,320,000 | 1 | chin | B | 5 | More organized, confrontational, aggressive, militant part of pro-Rome loyalists. Gansu, Shanxi. |
| Chinese Catholic Ch (Patriotic) | I-Lat-AC | 6-c | 1957 | 5,518,000 | 1 | chin | B | 5 | Open Ch. Under Ai Guo Hui (Chinese Catholic Patriotic Association, CCPA). Set up by regime. |
| Bathalismo | I-mar-AC | 6-d | c1400 | 150,000 | 1 | phil | C | 2 | God Mysterious Mother. Inang Mahiwaga. Rizalists. HQ Nueva Ecija. God=Bathala. |
| Bougists | I-mar-AC | 6-e | 1953 | 45,000 | 1 | cong | C | 2 | Lassyism. Mission de Dieu du Bougie. God of the Candle. |
| Bwiti | I-mar-AC | 6-d | c1890 | 125,000 | 1 | gabo | C | 1 | Eglise des Banzie. Church of the Initiates. Fang members. |
| Eglise Deimatiste | I-mar-AC | 6-d | 1922 | 140,000 | 1 | ivor | B | 2 | Church of Ashes of Purification. Bete schism ex RCC led by female pope Lalou. |
| Handsome Lake | I-mar-AC | 6-e | 1799 | 5,000 | 1 | cana | C | 2 | Longhouse Religion. Iroquois Indians in Ontario, Quebec, New York state. |
| Olive Tree Church | I-mar-AC | 6-e | 1955 | 7,000 | 1 | souk | B | 2 | Chondokwon. F=Pak Tae-son. Name=Revelation 11:4. Vast properties. 1970: 700,550. |
| Peli Association | I-mar-AC | 6-e | 1971 | 5,000 | 1 | papu | C | 2 | Hawk Association. East Sepik. 1972, 200,000 members. M=New Apostolic Ch (Canada). |
| The Family | I-mar-AC | 6-e | 1965 | 12,000 | 1 | usa | C | 3 | Children of God. F=D. Berg. Communes: 185 by 1975, 800 by 1995, 267 million letters sent. |
| African Meth Episcopal Ch | I-Met-AC | 6-c | 1787 | 3,654,000 | 1 | usa | C | 5 | AMEC. Black. 13 Districts in USA. 20 bps. Many new megachurches. Africa, W Indies. 7089n. |
| African Meth Episcopal Zion Ch | I-Met-AC | 6-c | 1796 | 1,109,000 | 1 | usa | C | 5 | AMEZC. Black. 10 bishops in Americas, Europe, 2 in Africa. 5500n,1j,6r. |
| Mouvement Croix-Koma | I-ReC-AC | 6-e | 1964 | 16,000 | 1 | cong | C | 4 | Nailed to the Cross Movement. In RCC until 1980. |
| Philippine Indep Catholic Ch | I-ReC-AC | 6-c | 1981 | 2,400,000 | 1 | phil | C | 5 | PICC. Iglesia Filipina Catolica Independiente. Schism of 40% of ICI by primate M.V.Ga. |
| Philippine Independent Church | I-ReC-AC | 6-c | 1890 | 2,660,000 | 1 | phil | C | 5 | PIC. Iglesia Filipina Independiente, IFI. Ex RCC. Many breakoffs. 470n. |
| African Indep Pente Ch of Africa | I-Ref-AC | 6-c | 1925 | 1,341,000 | 1 | keny | C | 5 | AIPC. 4 Dioceses. Persecution 1939-57; 1964, massive rural growth. Kikuyu. 136n,1p,6000Y. |
| Pr C (Reunited Anti-Ecumenical) | I-Ref-AC | 6-c | 1951 | 2,480,000 | 1 | souk | B | 5 | Tae-Han Yesukyo Changno-hwei. (Hap Dong) NAE. Anti-ecumenical schism. 2096n,1s(850). |
| Presbyterian Church of Africa | I-Ref-AC | 6-c | 1898 | 1,052,000 | 1 | soua | C | 5 | African Presbyterian Ch. Zulu schism ex UFCSM(UK). Declining. SS=86000,8000z. |
| Ukrainian Orthodox Ch: P Kiev | I-Ukr-AC | 6-c | 1990 | 1,320,000 | 1 | russ | B | 5 | Ukrainians resident in Russia, but loyal to schismatic P-Kiev. |
| Ukrainian Orthodox Ch: P Kiev | I-Ukr-AC | 6-c | 1991 | 4,560,000 | 1 | ukra | C | 5 | Anti-Russian schism, forming own Patriarchate. Huge start, then decline. 36 bps. |
| Han Chinese Three-Self Chs | I-Uni-AC | 6-b | 1807 | 12,560,000 | 1 | chin | B | 5 | TSPM. 1950, all non-RCs forcibly united. 1966-79, all churches closed. Now 40% registered. |
| Branch Davidians | m-Adv-AC | 6-e | 1929 | 2,000 | 1 | usa | C | 3 | Cult ex SDA centered in Waco, TX. Destroyed in fire in FBI assault, with 78 killed. |
| British Israelites | m-BrI-AC | 6-e | c1830 | 99,000 | 1 | brit | C | 2 | Members believe Anglo-Saxon race have descended from 10 Lost Tribes of Israel. |
| Jehovah's Witnesses | m-Jeh-AC | 6-c | 1872 | 2,512,000 | 1 | usa | C | 2 | Watch Tower. World HQ Brooklyn. In USA, 22% Blacks (1975) 25740n,40814Y. (1995) 43663Y. |
| Testigos de Jehová | m-Jeh-AC | 6-c | 1893 | 1,420,000 | 1 | mexi | C | 2 | Jehovah's Witnesses. Mass literature from 1929. (1975) 5683Y. (1995) 37454Y. |
| Ch of JC of Latter-day Saints | m-LdS-AC | 6-c | 1830 | 4,879,000 | 1 | usa | C | 2 | Mormons. HQ Utah. Also 700,000 overseas. (1970) 17272n,91237Y. (1990) 28962n. |
| Bedwardites | m-mar-AC | 10-f | 1891 | 200 | 1 | jama | B | 3 | F=Alexander Bedward; self-proclaimed Christ. 1921 violence. |
| Armenian Apostolic Church | O-Arm-AC | 6-c | 35 | 2,950,000 | 1 | arme | C | 5 | Catholicate of Echmiadzin. 72 bishops. Charismatic renewal: Brotherhood of Lovers of the Ch. |
| Bulgarian Orthodox Church | O-Bul-AC | 6-c | 150 | 6,100,000 | 1 | bulg | C | 5 | Balgarskata Pravoslavna Crkva. 23 bps. 1785n,123de(200m,360w),1j,2s(330),W=13%. |
| Belorussian Orth Ch: D Minsk | O-Bye-AC | 6-c | 1793 | 4,860,000 | 1 | belo | C | 5 | D Minsk and Byelorussia. Now 10 Dioceses, 10 bishops under P Moscow. 13% Russians. |
| Coptic Orthodox Church | O-Cop-AC | 6-c | 33 | 9,214,000 | 1 | egyp | B | 5 | Al-Kanisah al-Kebtiah al-Orthodoxiah. 42 Dioceses worldwide, 77 bps,5e(200),1500n,5s(200). |
| Ethiopian Orthodox Church | O-Eth-AC | 6-b | 332 | 22,087,000 | 1 | ethi | B | 5 | EOC. Ethiopia Tewahido Bete-Cristian. 20 Dioceses. 53 bps, 250000n. 200,000 Charismatics. |
| Orthodox Church of Eritrea | O-Eth-AC | 6-c | 1955 | 1,598,000 | 1 | erit | B | 5 | Related to Ethiopian OC. 9 Dioceses and bps. 9% urban. Tigre and others. |
| Georgian Orth Ch: C Mtskheta | O-Geo-AC | 6-c | 150 | 2,760,000 | 1 | geor | C | 5 | Catholicate of Mtskheta & Tiflis. 15 Dioceses, 26 bishops. |
| Church of Greece | O-Gre-AC | 6-c | 50 | 9,374,000 | 1 | gree | C | 5 | Ekklesia tes Hellados. 95 bps,7530n,7184b,144d(891m),163e(1709w). |
| Greek Orth AD of N&S America | O-Gre-AC | 6-c | 1864 | 1,960,000 | 1 | usa | C | 5 | AD in 1922. In EP Constantinople. 11 Dioceses, 15 bps. 700n,14r,1s(120),W=30%,12650Yy. |
| Macedonian Orthodox Church | O-Mac-AC | 6-c | 60 | 1,216,000 | 1 | mace | C | 5 | 1919 integrated into Serbian Orthodox Ch, 1967 declared its independence. 7 bishops. |
| Moldovan Orth Ch: D Chisinau | O-Mol-AC | 6-c |  | 1,330,000 | 1 | mold | C | 5 | Ethnic Moldavians & Romanians under Russian P Moscow; autonomy 1992. 4 Dioceses, 4 bps. |
| Orthodox Church of Poland | O-Pol-AC | 6-c | 990 | 1,095,000 | 1 | pola | C | 5 | Autokefaliczny Kosciol Prawoslawny. 1939, 4 million. 6 bps. (1970) 216n,216b,1d,1e,1s,1u. |
| Romanian Orthodox Ch | O-Rum-AC | 6-b | 100 | 20,506,000 | 1 | roma | C | 5 | Biserica Ortodoxa Romana 20bps, 8545n. The Lord's Army (300,000) in Evangelical Alliance. |
| Orthodox Church in America | O-Rus-AC | 6-c | 1792 | 2,244,000 | 1 | usa | C | 5 | OCA. Formerly Russian Orth Gk-Cath Ch. A=1970. 7 US Dioceses, 15 bps. 792n,33x,2s(150). |
| Russian Orth Ch: D Almaty | O-Rus-AC | 6-c |  | 1,890,000 | 1 | kaza | B | 5 | Russians, Ukrainians, Byelorussians, Chuvash, Mordvinians. Mass emigration from 1991. |
| Russian Orthodox Church | O-Rus-AC | 6-b | 988 | 81,582,000 | 1 | russ | B | 5 | ROC. Russkaya Pravoslavnaya Tserkov. 93 Dioceses, 103 bps, 14000n,60de(5000),82s. |
| Serbian Orthodox Church | O-Ser-AC | 6-c | 150 | 5,621,000 | 1 | yugo | C | 5 | Srpska Pravoslavna Crkva. P since AD 1346. 13 Dioceses, 36 bishops,1j,6s. |
| Orthodox Syrian Ch of the East | O-SyM-AC | 6-c | 52 | 2,354,000 | 1 | indi | B | 5 | Malankara OSC, Catholicate of the East. Syrians. 22 bps,942n,1s(85),W=55%,7820Yy. |
| Ukrainian Orth Ch (P Moscow) | O-Ukr-AC | 6-b | 991 | 27,497,000 | 1 | ukra | C | 5 | Russian Orthodox Church, Exarchate of the Ukraine, under P Moscow. 37 bishops. |
| Igreja Adventista do Sétimo Dia | P-Adv-AC | 6-c | 1894 | 1,020,000 | 1 | braz | C | 5 | SDAs. E,N,SBrazil. 10 launches, 2 planes. 306nx,56f,4H,6h,1j,8r,2s,2099t(177230),17036Y. |
| Seventh-day Adventist Church | P-Adv-AC | 6-c | 1844 | 1,008,000 | 1 | usa | C | 5 | SDA. 9 Unions. 18% Black. 3365n, 42H,5j,88r,3s,3315t(375031),W=88%,24575Y. |
| American Baptist Chs in USA | P-Bap-AC | 6-c | 1639 | 2,316,000 | 1 | usa | C | 5 | Formerly American Baptist Convention. 8222n,9s(1090),W=34%,3456Y. |
| Convenção Batista Brasileira | P-Bap-AC | 6-c | 1881 | 1,518,000 | 1 | braz | C | 5 | Brazilian Baptist Conv. M=SBC,BMS. Germans, Japanese. 1382n,320f,1H,77h,1j,30p,29690Y. |
| Council of Bapt Chs in NE India | P-Bap-AC | 6-c | 1836 | 1,743,000 | 1 | indi | B | 5 | CBCNEI. M=ABFMS(USA). Doubled 1950-70. 97n,1x,5704m,54w,9f,6H,12p,1s(110),16363Y. |
| Korea Baptist Convention | P-Bap-AC | 6-c | 1890 | 1,138,000 | 1 | souk | B | 5 | Hankuk Chimnehwei Yonmaeng. East Asia Ch. 1950,M=FMB-SBC. 365n,72f,1H,1s,3122Y. |
| Myanmar Baptist Convention | P-Bap-AC | 6-c | 1813 | 1,940,000 | 1 | myan | B | 5 | BBC, organized 1865. M=ABFMS. 16 Conferences. 19p(827),P=75%,4s,1300t. |
| Nigerian Baptist Convention | P-Bap-AC | 6-c | 1850 | 1,440,000 | 1 | nige | B | 5 | NBC(1914). M=FMB-SBC(USA). Yoruba, Gude, Fali, Kamberi. 780n,187f,5H,3s,7852Y. |
| Particular Baptists | P-Bap-AC | 6-e | 1620 | 19,000 | 1 | brit | C | 5 | Schism from first Baptist church, in London. National Strict Baptist Assembly. |
| Samavesam of Telugu Bapt Chs | P-Bap-AC | 6-c | 1836 | 1,316,000 | 1 | indi | B | 5 | Samavesam of TBC. M=ABFMS. 99% Mala,Madiga. 418n,2s(120),W=40%,4091Y. |
| Southern Baptist Convention | P-Bap-AC | 6-b | 1845 | 22,960,000 | 1 | usa | C | 5 | SBC. 1845 ex North. 99% White. (1970) 31000n,2H,6s,W=39%,409659Y. (1990) 63352n. |
| Word of Life Evangelical Ch | P-Bap-AC | 6-c | 1927 | 4,700,000 | 1 | ethi | B | 5 | WLEC. M=SIM. 1438n,100x,600m,332f,6H,25h,50p,2s(25),W=85%,10000Y,40000z. |
| Evangelical Chs of West Africa | P-Eva-AC | 6-c | 1893 | 2,900,000 | 1 | nige | B | 5 | ECWA. M=SIM. A=1956. 800n,500m,50w,672f,3H,88h,31k,22p(692),1s,W=80%,2000Y. |
| United Protestant Ch in the N | P-LuR-AC | 6-c | 1995 | 3,395,000 | 1 | neth | C | 5 | VPKN. 1995, merger of NHK, GKN, and ELKN under way, aiming to finish by AD 2000. |
| Batak Christian Protestant Ch | P-Lut-AC | 6-c | 1861 | 2,791,000 | 1 | indo | B | 5 | HKBP. Huria Kristen Batak Protestan. Toba Bataks. 298n,25x,1v,W=45%,1657Y,40928y. |
| Church of Norway | P-Lut-AC | 6-c | 900 | 3,932,000 | 1 | norw | C | 5 | Norske Kirke, reformed 1536. Now 11 Dioceses. 1280n,65012Yy. |
| Church of Sweden | P-Lut-AC | 6-c | 829 | 7,568,000 | 1 | swed | C | 5 | Svenska Kyrkan. Begun 600 years before Reformation. 13 Dioceses. Women clergy. 3350n. |
| Ev Lutheran Ch in America | P-Lut-AC | 6-c | 1623 | 5,118,000 | 1 | usa | C | 5 | 1987 Union of American Lutheran Ch and Lutheran Church in America. (1990) 17416n. |
| Ev Lutheran Ch in Tanzania | P-Lut-AC | 6-c | 1886 | 2,522,000 | 1 | tanz | B | 5 | ELCT. KKKT(Swahili). A=1963. 10 Dioceses and Synods. M=TAC. 1641m,1s(126),W=75%. |
| Ev Lutheran Ch of Finland | P-Lut-AC | 6-c | 1100 | 4,495,000 | 1 | finl | C | 5 | Suomen Evankelis-Luterilainen Kirkko. 8 Dioceses. 1300n,17p,2s(1400),71575Yy. |
| Evangelical Ch Mekane Yesus | P-Lut-AC | 6-c | 1880 | 2,475,000 | 1 | ethi | B | 5 | ECMY. Dwelling of Jesus. A=1958. (1970) 675n,61x,239f,4H,2s,2872Y,5871y. (1990) 450n. |
| Igr Ev da Confissão Lut no Brasil | P-Lut-AC | 6-c | 1823 | 1,014,000 | 1 | braz | C | 5 | IECLB. Lutheran Confession, Germans. M=ALC. 183n,106x,34f,1s(90),14012Yy. |
| Laestadianism | P-Lut-AC | 6-d | 1844 | 200,000 | 1 | swed | C | 5 | Revival among Lapps across Scandinavia. F=L. L. Laestadius. |
| Lutheran Ch-Missouri Synod | P-Lut-AC | 6-c | 1847 | 2,542,000 | 1 | usa | C | 5 | LCMS. German origin. 1976 schism: AELC. 7041n,16s(1041),5552t(815522),W=45%,94363Yy. |
| National Church of Denmark | P-Lut-AC | 6-c | 826 | 4,508,000 | 1 | denm | C | 5 | Evangelisk-lutherske Folkekirke i Danmark. 10 Dioceses. 99 Deaneries. 1824n,P=40%,2s. |
| United Ev Lutheran Chs in India | P-Lut-AC | 6-c | 1706 | 1,642,000 | 1 | indi | B | 5 | UELCI. Formed 1975. 9 ELCs. Large % Harijan. Missions to Malaysia, Burma, Tanzania |

*Continued opposite*

*Table 17–6 continued*

| Name of religion/religionists 1 | Pedigree 2 | Type 3 | Begun 4 | Adherents 5 | Ext 6 | Coun 7 | W 8 | X 9 | E. g. = examples; name for God, other religions present, D=denominations, M=missions. 10 |
|---|---|---|---|---|---|---|---|---|---|
| Korean Methodist Church | P-Met-AC | 6-c | 1884 | 1,413,000 | 1 | souk | B | 5 | KMC. Kidokyo Tae-Han Kamni-hwei. M=UMC. 914n,51f,2s(375),W=89%,1850Yy,85000z. |
| Methodist Ch of Great Britain | P-Met-AC | 6-c | 1795 | 1,040,000 | 1 | brit | C | 5 | 1795, ex CofE. 34 Districts. Declining 1.8%pa. 4167n,20652pp,1p,4s(141),43423Yy. |
| Methodist Ch of Southern Africa | P-Met-AC | 6-c | 1806 | 2,811,000 | 1 | soua | C | 5 | British origin. 77% Black, 17% White, 5% Coloured. 1000n,4H,1j,5r,2s(60),2400t,2u. |
| Methodist Church in India | P-Met-AC | 6-c | 1856 | 1,140,000 | 1 | indi | B | 5 | SAsia CC, UMC(USA). 11 Annual Conferences. 80% Harijan (Madiga). 20H,4s,735n. |
| Methodist Church, Nigeria | P-Met-AC | 6-c | 1842 | 1,768,000 | 1 | nige | B | 5 | M=MMS(UK). 25% Yoruba, 23% Ibibio, 20% Ijebu, 20% Ibo. 40f,15H,33r,1u,4435Y,6401y. |
| United Methodist Church | P-Met-AC | 6-b | 1766 | 10,439,000 | 1 | usa | C | 5 | UMC. 1968, EUB merger. 96% White, 4% Black. 81 Confs. 34974n,13s,W=36%. |
| Africa Inland Church | P-Non-AC | 6-c | 1895 | 1,740,000 | 1 | keny | C | 5 | M=AIM. 33% Kamba, 27% Kalenjin, 20% Kikuyu. 80n,50x,226f,4H,30h,5p,1s,W=65%,2000Y. |
| Asambleas de Dios | P-Pe2-AC | 6-c | 1910 | 1,083,000 | 1 | arge | C | 5 | Assemblies of God. M=SFM(Sweden),NPY(Norway), Elim(Denmark). 65n,1500Y,600z. |
| Assembleias de Deus | P-Pe2-AC | 6-b | 1910 | 25,600,000 | 1 | braz | C | 5 | Assemblies of God. 1934,M=AoG,SFM,NPY,FFFM. 30000n,27000mw,20f. |
| Assemblies of God in Nigeria | P-Pe2-AC | 6-c | 1939 | 1,410,000 | 1 | nige | B | 5 | M=AoG(USA). A=1960. 48% Ibo, 8% Ishan. 667n,31x,8f,3h,1j,5s(296),W=50%,2593Y. |
| Assemblies of God USA | P-Pe2-AC | 6-c | 1906 | 2,294,000 | 1 | usa | C | 5 | General Conference. 95% White. 12037n,1j,4r,13s9200t(1078332),20864Y. |
| Jesus Assembly of God of Korea | P-Pe2-AC | 6-c | 1952 | 2,380,000 | 1 | souk | B | 5 | Tae-Han Kidokyo Hananim-e Song-Hwei. M=AoG. 205n,19f,1s(300),W=77%,700Y. |
| Eglise Ev du Cameroun | P-Ref-AC | 6-c | 1845 | 1,367,000 | 1 | came | B | 5 | EEC. M=PEMS. 33% Bamileke. 91n,9x,911m,62w,67f,1s,1u,W=57%,8944Y,11832y,11098z. |
| Fed Council of Dutch Ref Chs | P-Ref-AC | 6-c | 1652 | 2,893,000 | 1 | soua | C | 5 | Federale Raad van Nederduitse Gereformeerde Kerke. NGK. A family of 4 racial churches. 9x. |
| Féd des Egls Prot de la Suisse | P-Ref-AC | 6-c | 1920 | 2,861,000 | 1 | swit | C | 5 | FEPS. Schweizerischer Ev Kirchenbund (Swiss Federation of Prot Chs). 1697n. |
| Igl Nacional Presb de México | P-Ref-AC | 6-c | 1872 | 1,416,000 | 1 | mexi | C | 5 | IPNM. National Presb Ch. M=PCUS,UPUSA,RCA. Many Indians. 8 synods,700n,85f. |
| Presb Ch in Korea (Tonghap) | P-Ref-AC | 6-c | 1884 | 2,406,000 | 1 | souk | B | 5 | PCK Tae-Han Yesukyo Changno-hwei. (T'ong-hap). 1303n,109f,6H,15p,3s,16240Yy. |
| Presbyterian Church (USA) | P-Ref-AC | 6-c | 1706 | 3,311,000 | 1 | usa | C | 5 | PCUSA. 1983 merger of UPUSA, PCUS. 1973, 8% lost in schism. 4595n. Missions: 9 nations. |
| Protestant Church in Indonesia | P-Ref-AC | 6-c | 1615 | 2,803,000 | 1 | indo | B | 5 | GPI. Gereja Protestan Indonesia. Former state-controlled Church of the Indies. 770n. |
| Reformed Church of Hungary | P-Ref-AC | 6-c | 1530 | 2,058,000 | 1 | hung | C | 5 | Magyarorzsági Reformàtus Egyház. 4 Districts & bishops. 85% farmers. 1650n,1j,2s. |
| Church of North India | P-Uni-AC | 6-c | 1612 | 1,444,000 | 1 | indi | B | 5 | CNI. 1970 union. 24 Dioceses. 60% Harijan (Chamar, Sweepers). 4s,1u. |
| Church of Pakistan | P-Uni-AC | 6-c | 1850 | 1,342,000 | 1 | paki | A | 5 | 1970 union:CIPBC, UCNIP(part), MCSA(UMC), Pakistan Lutheran Ch. 8 Dioceses. 600n,128f. |
| Church of South India | P-Uni-AC | 6-c | 1640 | 3,228,000 | 1 | indi | B | 5 | CSI. 70% former Harijans. 21 Dioceses. M=CWMCMS. 56x,1s,3u(142). |
| Eglise de Jésus-Christ à Madag | P-Uni-AC | 6-c | 1818 | 2,824,000 | 1 | mada | B | 5 | FJKM. 1968 union of FKM, FPM. M=CCWM,PEMS,FSC. 830n,75r(61000),4s,1u,W=34%. |
| Eglise du Christ au Congo-Zaire | P-Uni-AC | 6-b | 1924 | 10,186,000 | 1 | conz | C | 5 | ECZ. Ch of Christ in Z. 1924, CPC; 1970, united ch. 2538n,10044m,1710f,180000z. |
| Ev Kirche in Deutschland | P-Uni-AC | 6-b | 1946 | 28,363,000 | 1 | germ | C | 5 | EKD. 20 Landeskirchen, 8 other denominations. 300p,39s,P=26%,W=6%. |
| Fell of Chs of Christ of Nigeria | P-Uni-AC | 6-c | 1904 | 2,651,000 | 1 | nige | B | 5 | TEKAN. 1955 Federation, in north, of 8 major denominations (UK, USA origins). 140f,6H,177h. |
| United Church of Zambia | P-Uni-AC | 6-c | 1884 | 1,190,000 | 1 | zamb | C | 5 | UCZ. 1958/65 unions M=PEMS,LMS,MMS,CSM. Lozi,Bemba. 57n,28x,87f,3H,7h,5r,1s.9160Yy. |
| United Ch in Papua New Guinea | P-Uni-AC | 6-c | 1871 | 1,158,000 | 1 | papu | C | 5 | 1968 union: Papua Ekalesia (M=LMS), 4 Methodist areas. 276n,58x,5p,2s(80),19138z. |
| United Ch of Christ in the Phil | P-Uni-AC | 6-c | 1899 | 1,040,000 | 1 | phil | C | 5 | UCCP. 1948 union 4 bodies. M=P Interboard Comm (USA). 342n,47f,10H,16r,2s,1u,1v. |
| United Church of Canada | P-Uni-AC | 6-c | 1765 | 3,256,000 | 1 | cana | C | 5 | 1925 union, declining since 1960. 11 Conferences. 4p,6s,W=35%. |
| United Church of Christ | P-Uni-AC | 6-c | 1620 | 1,856,000 | 1 | usa | C | 5 | UCC. 1957 union. 1% Black. Missions in 8 Caribbean, West African countries. 9478n,13s. |
| Uniting Church of Australia | P-Uni-AC | 6-c | 1809 | 1,426,000 | 1 | aust | C | 5 | UCA. 1977 union of Cong Union of A, Methodist Ch of A, Presbyterian Ch of A. 10H. |
| Uniting Reformed Ch in SA | P-Uni-AC | 6-c | 1994 | 1,446,000 | 1 | soua | C | 5 | Merger of 2 DRC Churches: NGK in Africa (Bantu Ch) and NG Sendingskerk (Coloured). 850n. |
| Cath Ch in China (Clandestine) | R-Lat-AC | 6-c | 1298 | 7,900,000 | 1 | chin | B | 5 | Tien Chu Chiao Hui. Illegal, loyal to pope, but cooperating with state. Strong in Hebei, Fujian. |
| Cath Ch in Papua New Guinea | R-Lat-AC | 6-c | 1847 | 1,336,000 | 1 | papu | C | 5 | Many institutions. C=12+8+31. 97H,3q,3s. |
| Catholic Ch in Belarus | R-Lat-AC | 6-c | 1600 | 1,400,000 | 1 | belo | C | 5 | 33,000 Uniates. 1995, 100 Polish priests expelled. |
| Catholic Ch in the Czech Rep | R-Lat-AC | 6-c | 828 | 3,756,000 | 1 | czec | B | 5 | Katolicka Cirkev. 1,621 unstaffed parishes. 332de. |
| Catholic Ch in the Netherlands | R-Lat-AC | 6-c | 650 | 5,516,000 | 1 | neth | C | 5 | Rooms-Katholieke Kerk. C=36+16+128. 7q,5s. |
| Catholic Ch in the Philippines | R-Lat-AC | 6-b | 1521 | 61,762,000 | 1 | phil | C | 5 | Iglesia Catolica. C=34+3+66. |
| Catholic Church in Croatia | R-Lat-AC | 6-c | 250 | 3,950,000 | 1 | croa | C | 5 | 750-year-old church, strong traditions. |
| Catholic Church in Ghana | R-Lat-AC | 6-c | 1481 | 1,813,000 | 1 | ghan | B | 5 | C=4+7+20. (1970)113n,237x. |
| Catholic Church in Indonesia | R-Lat-AC | 6-c | 650 | 5,885,000 | 1 | indo | B | 5 | Gereja Katolik I. C=19+9+70. |
| Catholic Church in Ireland | R-Lat-AC | 6-c | 350 | 3,151,000 | 1 | irel | C | 5 | Eaglais Chaitliceach Rómhánach. C=34+11+104. |
| Catholic Church in Kenya | R-Lat-AC | 6-c | 1498 | 6,989,000 | 1 | keny | C | 5 | Kanisa Katholiki. C=9+11+40. |
| Catholic Church in Korea | R-Lat-AC | 6-c | 1592 | 4,025,000 | 1 | souk | B | 5 | Ch'onju Kyohwe. C=14+2+32. 2p,2s(709),W=63%. |
| Catholic Church in Lithuania | R-Lat-AC | 6-c | 1251 | 3,331,000 | 1 | lith | C | 5 | Violently persecuted throughout 20th century, especially 1939-1990. |
| Catholic Church in Malawi | R-Lat-AC | 6-c | 1561 | 2,621,000 | 1 | mala | C | 5 | C=4+3+10. (1970) 70n,235x,37143Yy. (1990) |
| Catholic Church in Nigeria | R-Lat-AC | 6-b | 1487 | 13,249,000 | 1 | nige | B | 5 | C=11+4+23. 5p,4s(546). |
| Catholic Church in Pakistan | R-Lat-AC | 6-c | 1594 | 1,142,000 | 1 | paki | A | 5 | Romai Katholik Kalisia. C=9+6+18. (1970) 74n,159x. |
| Catholic Church in Poland | R-Lat-AC | 6-b | 950 | 36,261,000 | 1 | pola | C | 5 | Kosciól Rzymsko-katolicki. C=35+7+99. 26q,24s. |
| Catholic Church in Romania | R-Lat-AC | 6-c | 1000 | 3,366,000 | 1 | roma | C | 5 | Biserica Catolica Romana. 68% Hungarian. C=1+0+0. |
| Catholic Church in Slovakia | R-Lat-AC | 6-c | 828 | 3,675,000 | 1 | slok | C | 5 | Formerly in Czechoslavakia. |
| Catholic Church in Slovenia | R-Lat-AC | 6-c | 500 | 1,689,000 | 1 | slov | C | 5 | Majority church now freed of politics. |
| Catholic Church in South Africa | R-Lat-AC | 6-c | 1501 | 3,352,000 | 1 | soua | C | 5 | 72% Bantu, 16% Wh, 10% Col. C=32+7+74. 1q,2s. |
| Catholic Church in Sri Lanka | R-Lat-AC | 6-c | 1517 | 1,261,000 | 1 | sril | B | 5 | Romanu Katolike Sabhava. C=7+6+24,1p,3q,1s. |
| Catholic Church in Tanzania | R-Lat-AC | 6-c | 1449 | 8,264,000 | 1 | tanz | B | 5 | Kanisa Katoliki. C=13+4=39. 12p,4s(389). |
| Catholic Church in the Sudan | R-Lat-AC | 6-c | 1842 | 3,199,000 | 1 | suda | B | 5 | Catholikiyya. 950 Greek Catholics. C=1+2+3. |
| Catholic Church in Uganda | R-Lat-AC | 6-c | 1879 | 8,840,000 | 1 | ugan | C | 5 | Eklezia Enkatoliki. C=6+3+17. 11p,4s(254). |
| Catholic Church in Viet Nam | R-Lat-AC | 6-c | 1530 | 5,146,000 | 1 | viet | B | 5 | Cong Giao. C=11+10+12. (1970) 84781Yy. (1990) |
| Catholic Church in Zambia | R-Lat-AC | 6-c | 1889 | 3,028,000 | 1 | zamb | C | 5 | C=6+4+15 M=WF, SMA, OFM. |
| Catholic Church in Zimbabwe | R-Lat-AC | 6-c | 1561 | 1,115,000 | 1 | zimb | B | 5 | 92% Black, 6% White. C=8+3+21. 1p,1s(64). |
| Eglise Cath au Cameroun | R-Lat-AC | 6-c | 1883 | 3,812,000 | 1 | came | B | 5 | Catholic Ch. C=14+8+65. 5p,2s(92). |
| Eglise Cath au Congo-Zaire | R-Lat-AC | 6-b | 1482 | 25,620,000 | 1 | conz | C | 5 | Catholic Ch. C=37+23+162. 11p,1q,9x(472). |
| Eglise Cath au Madagascar | R-Lat-AC | 6-c | 1540 | 3,441,000 | 1 | mada | B | 5 | Eglizy Katolika. C=14+5+55. (1975) 61345Yy. (1990) |
| Eglise Cath en Burkina Faso | R-Lat-AC | 6-c | 1900 | 1,083,000 | 1 | burk | B | 5 | Catholic Ch in BF. M=FSC,WF,CSSR. C=4+4+19. |
| Eglise Cath en Côte d'Ivoire | R-Lat-AC | 6-c | 1637 | 2,261,000 | 1 | ivor | B | 5 | C=15+2+17. (1970) 60n,320x,19821Yy. (1990). |
| Eglise Catholique au Bénin | R-Lat-AC | 6-c | 1680 | 1,243,000 | 1 | beni | B | 5 | Catholic Ch. Mainly south. C=2+2+20. 4p,1s(18). |
| Eglise Catholique au Burundi | R-Lat-AC | 6-c | 1879 | 3,891,000 | 1 | buru | C | 5 | Catholic Ch. C=9+6+30. 3p,1s(51). |
| Eglise Catholique au Congo | R-Lat-AC | 6-c | 1883 | 1,431,000 | 1 | cong | C | 5 | Catholic Ch in Congo. C=5+4+16. 3p,1s(19). |
| Eglise Catholique au Haïti | R-Lat-AC | 6-c | 1493 | 6,455,000 | 1 | hait | C | 5 | Catholic Ch in Haiti. C=8+3+21. (1970) 150n. (1990). |
| Eglise Catholique au Rwanda | R-Lat-AC | 6-c | 1889 | 3,895,000 | 1 | rwan | C | 5 | C=6+8+29. (1970) 142n,245x, 766w,110587Yy. (1990) |
| Eglise Catholique au Togo | R-Lat-AC | 6-c | 1871 | 1,062,000 | 1 | togo | B | 5 | C=4+5+15. (1970) 87n,53x,257w,15509Yy,2p.(1990) |
| Eglise Catholique de Belgique | R-Lat-AC | 6-c | 200 | 8,159,000 | 1 | belg | C | 5 | Katholieke Kerk. C=41+14+350. 7p,11q,13s(619). |
| Ig Católica en Rep Dominicana | R-Lat-AC | 6-c | 1494 | 7,593,000 | 1 | domr | C | 5 | Catholic Ch. C=19+1+32. 5p,2q,2s(55). |
| Iglesia Católica en España | R-Lat-AC | 6-b | 63 | 38,949,000 | 1 | spai | C | 5 | Catholic Ch in Spain. C=62+9+244. 114q,48s. |
| Iglesia Católica en Bolivia | R-Lat-AC | 6-c | 1537 | 6,969,000 | 1 | boli | C | 5 | Catholic Ch in Bolivia. C=30+3+69. 6q,1s(121). |
| Iglesia Católica en Chile | R-Lat-AC | 6-b | 1541 | 11,690,000 | 1 | chil | C | 5 | Catholic Ch in Chile. C=49+4+136. 1090x,12p,3s. |
| Iglesia Católica en Colombia | R-Lat-AC | 6-b | 1512 | 40,115,000 | 1 | colo | C | 5 | Catholic Ch. C=46+2+128. 5p,38q,15s(1378),W=63%. |
| Iglesia Católica en Costa Rica | R-Lat-AC | 6-c | 1514 | 3,561,000 | 1 | cost | C | 5 | Catholic Ch in CR. C=8+5+23. (1970) 225n,1p,1q,1s. |
| Iglesia Católica en Cuba | R-Lat-AC | 6-c | 1512 | 4,412,000 | 1 | cuba | B | 5 | Catholic Ch. C=13+1+15. Low practice: W=2%. |
| Iglesia Católica en el Ecuador | R-Lat-AC | 6-b | 1534 | 11,795,000 | 1 | ecua | C | 5 | Catholic Ch in E. C=20+2+37. |
| Iglesia Católica en el Paraguay | R-Lat-AC | 6-c | 1524 | 4,771,000 | 1 | para | C | 5 | Catholic Ch in Paraguay. C=17+1+29. 1p,2q,1s(218). |
| Iglesia Católica en el Perú | R-Lat-AC | 6-b | 1536 | 26,319,000 | 1 | peru | C | 5 | Catholic Ch. 9 Zones. C=40+6+110. 10p,4q,9x(115). |
| Iglesia Católica en El Salvador | R-Lat-AC | 6-c | 1525 | 6,503,000 | 1 | elsa | C | 5 | Catholic Ch. C=18+1+29. 1s(122) (closed in 1973). |
| Iglesia Católica en el Uruguay | R-Lat-AC | 6-c | 1616 | 2,593,000 | 1 | uuay | C | 5 | Catholic Ch in Uruguay. C=34+1+51. 1s,W=18%. |
| Iglesia Católica en Guatemala | R-Lat-AC | 6-c | 1524 | 9,212,000 | 1 | guat | C | 5 | Catholic Ch in Guatemala. C=14+2+27. |
| Iglesia Católica en Honduras | R-Lat-AC | 6-c | 1550 | 5,378,000 | 1 | hond | C | 5 | Catholic Ch in Honduras. C=11+1+23. 2p,1s(19). |
| Iglesia Católica en México | R-Lat-AC | 6-b | 1518 | 128,190,000 | 1 | mexi | C | 5 | Catholic Ch. C=37+3+146. |
| Iglesia Católica en Nicaragua | R-Lat-AC | 6-c | 1522 | 4,679,000 | 1 | nica | C | 5 | Catholic Ch in N. Shortage of vocations. C=5+1+9. |
| Iglesia Católica en Panamá | R-Lat-AC | 6-c | 1513 | 2,194,000 | 1 | pana | C | 5 | C=13+3+22. (1970) 44n,221x,470w,3223Yy, (1990). |
| Iglesia Católica en Puerto Rico | R-Lat-AC | 6-c | 1509 | 2,845,000 | 1 | puer | C | 5 | Catholic Ch in Puerto Rico. C=24+3+75. 2q,2s. |
| Iglesia Católica en Venezuela | R-Lat-AC | 6-b | 1513 | 22,914,000 | 1 | vene | C | 5 | Catholic Church. C=31+3+78. 1q,5s(101),W=10%. |
| Igreja Católica em Angola | R-Lat-AC | 6-c | 1491 | 7,567,000 | 1 | ango | C | 5 | Catholic Ch in Angola. C=12+4+30. |
| Igreja Católica em Moçambique | R-Lat-AC | 6-c | 1506 | 3,010,000 | 1 | moza | B | 5 | C=15+2+32. (1970) 27n,548x,204m,1224w,44591Yy. 39n,290x,409m,561w,125150Yy. |
| Igreja Católica em Portugal | R-Lat-AC | 6-c | 150 | 9,977,000 | 1 | port | C | 5 | Catholic Ch. C=23+3+63. 6q,9x(312). |
| Kath Kirche in der Schweiz | R-Lat-AC | 6-c | 200 | 3,265,000 | 1 | swit | C | 5 | Eglise Catholique. Catholic Ch. C=27+2+50. |
| Catholic Ch in England & Wales | R-LEr-AC | 6-c | 678 | 4,246,000 | 1 | brit | C | 5 | C=55+12+352. P=75%,5s,W=43%. 50% Irish; 7% converts. |
| Catholic Church in Australia | R-LEr-AC | 6-c | 1803 | 5,445,000 | 1 | aust | C | 5 | From Italy, Poland, Croatia. C=29+8+67. W=61%. |
| Catholic Church in Hungary | R-LEr-AC | 6-c | 250 | 6,411,000 | 1 | hung | C | 5 | Római Katolikus Egyház. C=3+0+1. |
| Catholic Church in India | R-LEr-AC | 6-b | 1319 | 15,456,000 | 1 | indi | B | 5 | Catholic workers: C=35+15+122. |
| Catholic Church in Lebanon | R-LEr-AC | 6-c | 300 | 2,055,000 | 1 | leba | B | 5 | Al-Kanissa al-Kathoulikiah. C=21+2+53. |
| Catholic Church in Russia | R-LEr-AC | 6-c | 1084 | 1,573,000 | 1 | russ | B | 5 | Rimsko-Katolicheskaya Tserkov. (1970) 12n,45Yy. (1995) 31n,64x,30m,109w,1900Yy. |
| Catholic Church in the Ukraine | R-LEr-AC | 6-c | 1084 | 6,344,000 | 1 | ukra | C | 5 | Rimsko-Katolicheskaya Tserkov. Survived, 1944-91. |
| Catholic Church in the USA | R-LEr-AC | 6-b | 1526 | 58,397,000 | 1 | usa | C | 5 | Strongly developed, often clashing with Vatican. |
| Catholic Church of Canada | R-LEr-AC | 6-b | 1534 | 13,072,000 | 1 | cana | C | 5 | Eglise Catholique. C=63+17+196. 11q,15s. |

*Continued overleaf*

*Table 17–6 continued*

| Name of religion/religionists 1 | Pedigree 2 | Type 3 | Begun 4 | Adherents 5 | Ext 6 | Coun 7 | W 8 | X 9 | E. g. = examples; name for God, other religions present, D=denominations, M=missions. 10 |
|---|---|---|---|---|---|---|---|---|---|
| Chiesa Cattolica in Italia | R-LEr-AC | 6-b | 40 | 58,772,000 | 1 | ital | C | 5 | Strongest national church, with vibrant Catholic Charismatic Renewal. |
| Eglise Catholique de France | R-LEr-AC | 6-b | 80 | 48,761,000 | 1 | fran | C | 5 | Catholic Ch in F. C=71+9+397. 4p,11q,39s. |
| Iglesia Católica en la Argentina | R-LEr-AC | 6-b | 1539 | 35,478,000 | 1 | arge | C | 5 | C=60+8+170. (1970: 5326nx,12486w,470504Yy). (1990) |
| Igreja Católica no Brasil | R-LEr-AC | 6-b | 1500 | 162,292,000 | 1 | braz | C | 5 | C=101+14+329. |
| Kath Kirche Deutschlands | R-LEr-AC | 6-b | 90 | 28,583,000 | 1 | germ | C | 5 | Catholic Ch in G. C=44=15=302. 10q,20s(1895). |
| Katholische Kirche Österreichs | R-LEr-AC | 6-c | 174 | 6,032,000 | 1 | ausz | C | 5 | Catholic Ch of Austria. C=47+3+65. 3q,7s. |
| Anglicans | AAC | 2-b | 61 | 79,650,000 | 166 | brit | C | 5 | 102 million professing, 80 million affiliated to Anglican Communion. |
| Anglican Evangelicals | EAAC | 2-b | 1738 | 30,000,000 | 161 | brit | C | 5 | The Evangelical Revival dates from John Wesley's conversion. Now aided by EFAC. |
| Evangelicals | EAC | 2-a | 1520 | 211,000,000 | 237 | usa | C | 5 | Church members affiliated to Evangelical denominations, councils, or agencies. |
| Conservative Evangelicals | CEAC | 2-b | 1750 | 83,000,000 | 174 | usa | C | 5 | Evangelicals holding conservative doctrines especially on plenary inspiration of Bible. |
| Fundamentalists | FEAC | 2-b | 1909 | 100,000,000 | 80 | usa | C | 5 | Christians holding affirmation of 5, 7, 9, or 21 non-negotiable doctrines. |
| Protestant Evangelicals | PLEAC | 2-b | 1520 | 27,000,000 | 150 | germ | C | 5 | From days of Luther, self-identifying label. Strongest in USA, Germany, UK. |
| Neo-Evangelicals | NEAC | 2-b | 1948 | 34,000,000 | 231 | usa | C | 5 | Term coined after World War II for evangelicals distancing themselves from Fundamentalism. |
| Independents/Postdenominationalists | IAC | 2-a | 1549 | 385,745,000 | 221 | chin | B | 5 | Non-White indigenous Christians; Postdenominationalists, Neocharismatics. |
| Independent Evangelicals | EIAC | 2-b | 1800 | 27,000,000 | 191 | usa | C | 5 | Members of Independent/Postdenominationalist churches who affiliate with Evangelicalism. |
| Marginal Christians | MAC | 2-b | 1566 | 26,060,000 | 215 | usa | C | 3 | Unitarians, CJCLdS, JWs, and bodies placing selves on periphery of mainline Christianity. |
| Marginal Evangelicals | EmAC | 2-d | c1900 | 200,000 | 10 | usa | C | 3 | Members of marginal bodies (e.g. JWs, CJCLdS) who regard themselves as Evangelicals. |
| Orthodox | OAC | 2-a | 33 | 215,129,000 | 135 | russ | B | 5 | Eastern Orthodox (HQ Constantinople/Istanbul), Oriental Orthodox (5 communions). |
| Orthodox Evangelicals | EOAC | 2-c | c1900 | 2,000,000 | 4 | russ | B | 5 | Scattered individuals of Evangelical conviction throughout the 20th century. |
| Protestants | PAC | 2-a | 1517 | 342,002,000 | 233 | usa | C | 5 | Vast fragmented sphere of denominations in 150 traditions or communions. |
| Roman Catholics | RAC | 2-a | 33 | 1,057,328,000 | 235 | braz | C | 5 | All local (national) churches in communion with Holy See (Vatican, Rome). |
| Catholic Evangelicals | ERAC | 2-c | 1960 | 7,800,000 | 11 | brit | C | 5 | Catholics who become Evangelicals also, by conviction. |
| Communio e Liberazione | LRAC | 2-d | 1967 | 120,000 | 30 | ital | C | 5 | Communion & Liberation. Secular lay RC order, loyal to pope. |
| Focolare Movement | sLRAC | 2-c | 1943 | 2,000,000 | 13 | ital | C | 5 | Based on John 17:21, lay renewal: youth, families. F=Chiara Lubich. RCs, some Anglicans. |
| Comunidades de Base | sRAC | 2-c | c1960 | 4,000,000 | 100 | braz | C | 5 | Basic Christian Communities. 200,000 groups in Catholic parishes across Latin America. |
| Pentecostals/Charis/Neocharismatics | ZAC | 2-a | 1549 | 523,778,000 | 236 | usa | C | 5 | Total all church members in the Pentecostal/Charismatic/Neocharismatic Renewal. D=21,080. |
| Pentecostals (First-Wavers) | 1ZAC | 2-b | 1886 | 65,833,000 | 225 | braz | C | 5 | Chs of White origin (now 70% Non-White) requiring initial evidence of tongue. D=740. |
| Denominational Pente (White) | P1ZAC | 2-b | 1910 | 65,833,000 | 225 | cana | C | 5 | White members in the older, larger, more traditional Pentecostal denominations. D=740. |
| Oneness Pentecostals | 1P1ZAC | 2-c | 1914 | 2,768,000 | 130 | colo | C | 5 | Denominations emphasizing baptism in name of 'Jesus Only'; anti-trinitarian: UPCI. D=80. |
| Classical Pentecostals | CP1ZAC | 2-b | 1906 | 63,065,000 | 220 | usa | C | 5 | Self-designation of older White denominations, usually excluding Black Pentecostals. D=660. |
| Baptistic Pentecostals | 2CP1ZAC | 2-b | 1906 | 54,973,000 | 210 | arge | C | 5 | Teaching 2-fold Pentecostal experience of conversion, Spirit-baptism: AoG, ICFG. D=390. |
| Holiness Pentecostals | 3CP1ZAC | 2-c | 1886 | 6,316,000 | 170 | chil | C | 5 | Those holding 3-fold Wesleyan experience of conversion, sanctification, infilling: IPHC. D=240. |
| Apostolic Pentecostals | ACP1ZAC | 2-c | 1904 | 1,776,000 | 29 | ghan | B | 5 | Denominations emphasizing Pentecostal church government by living apostles: ACG. D=30. |
| Charismatics (Second-Wavers) | 2ZAC | 2-b | 1907 | 175,857,000 | 235 | mexi | C | 5 | All who experience Spirit-baptism but remain within nonpentecostal mainline chs. D=6,530. |
| Anglican Charismatics | A2ZAC | 2-b | 1907 | 17,562,000 | 163 | brit | C | 5 | Total Anglicans in Renewal, past and present, including children and infants. D=165. |
| Marginal Charismatics | m2ZAC | 2-e | 1980 | 15,000 | 15 | usa | C | 3 | Total marginal Christians in Renewal, past and present, including children and infants. D=130. |
| Orthodox Charismatics | O2ZAC | 2-c | 1970 | 3,167,000 | 87 | arme | C | 5 | Total Orthodox in Renewal, past and present, including children and infants. D=219. |
| The Lord's Army | O2ZAC | 2-d | 1923 | 300,000 | 1 | roma | C | 5 | Lay evangelists body in Romanian Orthodox Church. |
| Protestant Charismatics | P2ZAC | 2-b | 1959 | 35,200,000 | 231 | aust | C | 5 | Total Protestants in Renewal, past and present, including children and infants. D=5,780. |
| Catholic Charismatics | R2ZAC | 2-b | 1967 | 119,912,000 | 234 | braz | C | 5 | Total baptized RCs in CCR, past and present, including children and infants. D=236. |
| Jamaa | R2ZAC | 2-e | 1952 | 50,000 | 5 | conz | C | 2 | Family of God. Charismatic movement among African RCs in Katanga. Banned 1974. |
| Mainline active Charismatics | V2ZAC | 2-b | 1960 | 114,029,000 | 225 | phil | C | 5 | All in nonpentecostal churches regularly attending Renewal activities. D=6,500. |
| Mainline Postcharismatics | x2ZAC | 2-b | 1973 | 61,827,000 | 150 | fran | C | 5 | Those who no longer attend Renewal activities but still call selves Charismatics. D=3,540. |
| Neocharismatics (Third-Wavers) | 3ZAC | 2-a | 1549 | 295,405,000 | 225 | chin | B | 5 | All baptised in the Holy Spirit in new churches independent of historic Christianity. D=18,810. |
| Indep Anglican neocharismatics | A3ZAC | 2-c | 1925 | 1,716,000 | 80 | brit | C | 5 | Neocharismatics within non-pentecostal/charismatic Independent Anglican bodies. D=130. |
| Hidden non-Christian believers in C | H3ZAC | 2-b | 1800 | 13,676,000 | 70 | indi | B | 2 | Hindu, Muslim, Buddhist, Jewish, Sikh, Baha'i, New-Religion converts who stay hidden. D=290. |
| Hidden Buddhist neocharismatics | BH3ZAC | 2-c | 1950 | 2,194,000 | 15 | myan | B | 2 | Buddhist believers in Christ (NBBCs) who have pentecostal/charismatic gifts. D=15. |
| Hidden Hindu neocharismatics | HH3ZAC | 2-c | 1800 | 9,715,000 | 4 | nepa | A | 2 | Hindu believers in Christ (NBBCs) who have pentecostal/charismatic gifts. D=10. |
| Hidden Jewish neocharismatics | JH3ZAC | 2-d | 1896 | 250,000 | 15 | isra | B | 2 | Jewish believers in Christ who have pentecostal/charismatic gifts. D=50. |
| Hidden Muslim neocharismatics | MH3ZAC | 2-d | 1930 | 418,000 | 15 | turk | A | 2 | Muslim believers in Christ (NBBCs) who have pentecostal/charismatic gifts. D=15. |
| Hidden other-relig neocharismatics | YH3ZAC | 2-c | 1980 | 1,100,000 | 50 | japa | B | 2 | Other religionist hidden believers in Christ who have pentecostal/charismatic gifts. D=200. |
| Nonhistorical Indep neocharismatics | I3ZAC | 2-c | 1549 | 3,500,000 | 62 | phil | C | 2 | Neocharismatics in other nonpentecostal Independent chs: PIC/IFI, NBCA. D=300. |
| Non-White indig Neocharismatics | N3ZAC | 2-a | 1783 | 203,870,000 | 210 | chin | B | 5 | Spirit-baptized Non-Whites in 26 varieties of indigenous, apostolic churches. D=13,425. |
| African indig pente/charismatics | AN3ZAC | 2-b | 1864 | 65,911,000 | 60 | zimb | B | 5 | Most AICs are Zionist, Apostolic, Spiritual: ZCC, CCC, AICN, DLBC, AACJM, EJCSK. D=9,300. |
| Black American indig pentecostals | BN3ZAC | 2-c | 1889 | 7,635,000 | 20 | usa | C | 5 | Black Pentecostalism: Church of God in Christ, UHCA, Full Gospel Catholic Ch. D=90. |
| Han Chinese indig pente/charis | CN3ZAC | 2-b | 1905 | 49,749,000 | 58 | chin | B | 5 | True Jesus Church, NBM/BAM, AHC(Little Flock), Han Chinese house churches. D=180. |
| Black American indep charis | DN3ZAC | 2-c | 1955 | 1,472,000 | 4 | usa | C | 5 | African American independent charismatic bodies: Full Gospel Baptist Chs Fellowship. D=10. |
| Ethnic pentecostal churches | EN3ZAC | 2-c | 1890 | 1,536,000 | 20 | chin | B | 5 | Yi Churches, Miao Churches, Nagaland Christian Revival Chs, Gypsy Ev Movement. D=20. |
| Filipino indig pente/charismatics | FN3ZAC | 2-c | 1913 | 6,777,000 | 25 | phil | C | 5 | Jesus is Lord Fellowship, CDCC, March of Faith, Ecclesiae Dei. D=380. |
| Indonesian indig pentecostals | GN3ZAC | 2-c | 1920 | 6,761,000 | 5 | indo | B | 5 | Indonesia Pentecostal Church (GPI), GBI, GBIS, GPPS, GBT, GUP. D=170. |
| Messianic Hindu believers in C | HN3ZAC | 2-d | 1875 | 163,000 | 2 | indi | B | 3 | Messianic temples, organized Hindu-Christian chs: Hindu Ch of the Lord Jesus, SRM. D=5. |
| Indian indig pente/charismatics | IN3ZAC | 2-b | 1911 | 16,613,000 | 25 | indi | B | 5 | Indian Pentecostal Ch of God, Believers' Chs of India, Christ Groups, IPA, MFGCM. D=580. |
| Messianic Jewish believers in C | JN3ZAC | 2-d | 1894 | 161,000 | 14 | isra | B | 3 | Messianic Jewish synagogues, Fellowship of Messianic Congs, UMJC, IAMCS, JFJ. D=20. |
| Korean indig pente/charismatics | KN3ZAC | 2-c | 1910 | 3,339,000 | 30 | souk | B | 5 | Yoido FGC, Grace & Truth Ch, FGIGM, Korea Full Gospel Chs of America. D=170. |
| Latino-Hisp grassroots believers | LN3ZAC | 2-b | 1909 | 11,916,000 | 24 | mexi | C | 5 | Autochthonous grassroots (GR) churches, IMPC, IPP, IOAP, IEMP, IEPC. D=990. Hispanic. |
| Messianic Muslim believers in C | MN3ZAC | 2-d | 1981 | 126,000 | 2 | bang | B | 3 | Messianic Muslim mosques: Jesus Mosques, Jamaat. D=3. |
| Colored indig charismatics | NN3ZAC | 2-d | 1931 | 235,000 | 4 | nami | C | 5 | Colored, Métis, mixed-race charismatics: Members in Christ Ch, Christen Gemeente. D=70. |
| Black Amer Oneness Apostolics | ON3ZAC | 2-c | 1886 | 2,961,000 | 10 | usa | C | 5 | PAOW, AWCF, Bible Way Churches of Our Lord Jesus Christ WW, COLJCAF. D=150. |
| Pacific/Oceanic indig charismatics | PN3ZAC | 2-d | 1917 | 215,000 | 20 | solo | C | 5 | Pacific indigenous churches: Christian Fellowship Ch, AGCFI, Samoan FGC. D=70. |
| Japanese indigenous pentecostals | QN3ZAC | 2-c | 1930 | 1,160,000 | 15 | japa | B | 5 | Spirit of Jesus Church, Primitive Gospel Ch, Holy Ecclesia of Jesus, JJCC. D=50. |
| Amerindian neopentecostals | RN3ZAC | 2-d | 1870 | 535,000 | 3 | mexi | C | 5 | Amerindian neopentecostals: UIEI, Halleluja Church. D=4. |
| Arab/Assyrian/Semitic neocharis | SN3ZAC | 2-c | 1909 | 1,264,000 | 40 | iraq | A | 5 | Arabic/Aramaean/Assyrian/Berber/Semitic charismatic chs: Tree of Life Chs, GPC. D=130. |
| other Messianic non-Chr believers | TN3ZAC | 2-d | 1950 | 200,000 | 15 | myan | B | 5 | Organized believers staying in Buddhism, Baha'i, Sikhism, &c. D=20. |
| Afro-Caribbean indig pente/charis | UN3ZAC | 2-d | 1783 | 736,000 | 38 | trin | C | 5 | West Indies chs of African origin: Spiritual Baptists/Shouters, Revival Zion, NESBC. D=420. |
| Vietnamese indig neocharismatics | VN3ZAC | 2-d | 1952 | 231,000 | 2 | viet | B | 5 | Vietnamese churches: Good News house church movement. D=3. |
| Brazilian/Portu grassroots neochar | YN3ZAC | 2-b | 1910 | 23,023,000 | 20 | braz | C | 5 | OBPC (Brazil for Christ Ev Ch), IURD/UCKG, CCB, IPF, IPDA. D=460. |
| other Asian indig neocharismatics | ZN3ZAC | 2-c | 1948 | 1,153,000 | 40 | thai | B | 5 | Other Asian churches: Hope of God Churches of Thailand, Latter Rain Ch of Malaysia. D=130. |
| Independent Orth neocharismatics | O3ZAC | 2-d | 1666 | 584,000 | 20 | russ | B | 5 | Neocharismatics within non-pentecostal/charismatic Independent Orthodox bodies. D=90. |
| Independent Prot neocharismatics | P3ZAC | 2-b | 1920 | 20,489,000 | 180 | nige | B | 5 | Neocharismatics within non-pentecostal/charismatic Independent Protestant bodies. D=800. |
| Independent Cath neocharismatics | R3ZAC | 2-c | 1724 | 1,315,000 | 30 | neth | C | 5 | Neocharismatics within non-pentecostal/charismatic Independent Catholic bodies. D=70. |
| Isolated radio/TV neocharismatics | t3ZAC | 2-d | 1930 | 188,000 | 30 | chin | B | 5 | Neocharismatics among non-pentecostal/charismatic Independent radio believers. D=30. |
| White-led Postdenominationalists | W3ZAC | 2-b | 1805 | 50,066,000 | 210 | brit | C | 5 | Spirit-baptized Whites in non-Pentecostal/Charismatic apostolic networks. D=3,700. |
| Eur/Amer White-led Neo-Apostolics | WW3ZAC | 2-b | 1805 | 40,457,000 | 200 | usa | C | 5 | AIGA, AVC, CEEC, COTRI, FCFI, IAOGI, ICCC, ICCEC, ICFCM, RBC, VFM, &c. D=3,510. |
| European White-led New Apos | XW3ZAC | 2-c | 1832 | 9,609,000 | 180 | germ | C | 5 | Neuapostolische Kirche, begun as Universal Catholic Ch, and 30 schismatic bodies. D=190. |
| Peripheral Quasi-pentecostals | QZAC | 2-b | 1739 | 17,800,000 | 110 | usa | C | 2 | Prepentecostals and postpentecostals. Renewal believers but not renewal members. D=2,700. |
| Prepentecostals | 0QZAC | 2-c | 1739 | 7,300,000 | 100 | brit | C | 5 | Charismatic groups not officially in Renewal: numerous Salvationists, Wesleyans. D=2,600. |
| Postpentecostals | 1QZAC | 2-b | 1950 | 10,500,000 | 80 | usa | C | 5 | Former Denominational Pentecostals who have left to join nonpentecostal churches. D=509. |
| Crypto-Christians | CC | 2-b | | 123,726,000 | 85 | chin | B | 5 | All secret believers in Christ unknown to state, society, or host religions. |
| C Episcopatuum Communitatis E | cC | 7-a | 1980 | 200,000,000 | 40 | belg | C | 5 | C=Commissio, E=Europaeae. COM.E.CE. HQ Brussels. Covers European Community. |
| Consiglio della Chiesa Siro-Malankarese | cC | 7-d | c1980 | 310,000 | 3 | indi | B | 5 | Council of the Syro-Malankarese Church in India. 3 dioceses in south, with 885 parishes. |
| Consilio Latino Americano de Iglesias | cC | 7-b | 1982 | 11,000,000 | 30 | ecua | C | 5 | CLAI. Latin American Council of Churches. Founded in Peru. HQ Quito. 110 member churches. |
| Fed of Cath Bishops' Confs of Oceania | cC | 7-c | 1992 | 8,227,000 | 35 | newz | C | 5 | FCBCO. HQ Wellington. |
| All Africa Conference of Churches | A-cC | 7-b | 1963 | 95,000,000 | 70 | keny | C | 5 | AACC/CETA. HQ Nairobi. 130 member denominations and councils. |
| Consilium Conferentiarum Epis E | B-cC | 7-a | 1981 | 287,459,000 | 42 | swit | C | 5 | E=Episcopalium, E=Europae. CCEE. Council of European Bishops' Conferences. HQ St Gallen. |
| Conference of European Churches | C-cC | 7-a | 1957 | 505,000,000 | 45 | swit | C | 5 | CEC/CEE/KEK. 120 member denominations. HQ Geneva. |
| European Evangelical Alliance | D-cC | 7-b | 1952 | 16,000,000 | 20 | germ | C | 5 | EEA. HQ Kassel. 20 national Evangelical associations. |
| Christian Conference of Asia | E-cC | 7-b | 1957 | 150,000,000 | 50 | chin | B | 5 | CCA. HQ Hong Kong. Formerly East Asia Christian Conference. 100 member denominations. |
| Evangelical Fellowship of Asia | E-cC | 7-b | 1983 | 16,933,000 | 16 | indi | B | 5 | EFA. 18 member national Evangelical Associations/Fellowships. HQ Hyderabad, India. |
| Fed of Asian Bishops' Conferences | F-cC | 7-b | 1972 | 110,480,000 | 30 | chin | B | 5 | FABC. HQ Hong Kong. |
| Association of Evangelicals of Africa | G-cC | 7-b | 1966 | 19,500,000 | 45 | keny | C | 5 | AEA. Founded as AEAM (M=Madagascar). |
| Latin American Ev Fellowship | K-cC | 7-c | 1982 | 1,500,000 | 18 | arge | C | 5 | CONELA. HQ Buenos Aires (Argentina). Rival to CLAI, with 98 member bodies. |
| Consejo Episcopal Latinoamericano | L-cC | 7-a | 1974 | 461,220,000 | 21 | colo | C | 5 | CELAM. Latin American Episcopal Council. HQ Bogota. |
| Caribbean Conference of Churches | N-cC | 7-b | 1973 | 15,000,000 | 15 | barb | C | 5 | CCC, also member of CELAM. HQ Bridgetown, Barbados. |
| Standing Co of Canonical Orth Bps | O-cC | 7-c | | 4,000,000 | 12 | usa | C | 5 | SCOBA. Co=Conference. in Americas. All Orthodox bishops in canonical communion. |
| Pacific Conference of Churches | P-cC | 7-b | 1966 | 16,000,000 | 20 | fiji | B | 5 | PCC. One of WCC's 7 regional councils. |
| Symposium of Episcopal Confs of AM | S-cC | 7-b | | 103,500,000 | 55 | ghan | B | 5 | AM= Africa & Madagascar. SECAM/SCEAM. HQ Accra. |

*Continued opposite*

*Table 17–6 continued*

| Name of religion/religionists 1 | Pedigree 2 | Type 3 | Begun 4 | Adherents 5 | Ext 6 | Coun 7 | W 8 | X 9 | E. g. = examples; name for God, other religions present, D=denominations, M=missions. 10 |
|---|---|---|---|---|---|---|---|---|---|
| Mov pro Unidad Ev Latinoamericana | U-cC | 7-c | 1965 | 5,000,000 | 14 | uuay | C | 5 | UNELAM. Founded in Puerto Rico as ecumenical council in formation; 1982, becomes CLAI. |
| Conf des Eveques du Pacifique | Y-cC | 7-c | 1974 | 2,123,000 | 23 | fiji | B | 5 | CEPAC. Episcopal Conference of the Pacific. Conferentia Episcopalis Pacifici. HQ Suva (Fiji). |
| Ev Association of the Caribbean | Y-cC | 7-c | 1977 | 1,000,000 | 9 | barb | C | 5 | EAC. HQ Christ Church (Barbados). 9 member national associations. |
| Great Commission Christians | GCC | 2-a | 33 | 647,821,000 | 237 | usa | C | 5 | All church members aware of Christ's Commission and involved in His global mission. |
| Isolated radio believers | ICC | 2-b | 1925 | 17,548,000 | 69 | chin | B | 5 | Scattered individuals and groups across 69 non-Christian countries. |
| Crypto-Jews | JCC | 2-d | 650 | 300,000 | 40 | spai | C | 3 | Secretly practising Jews but baptized Christians: Conversos, Marranos ('Swine'), since 1491. |
| Alpha Movement | fC | 4-c | 1979 | 1,000,000 | 77 | brit | C | 5 | Anglican evangelistic movement via 10,000 11-week courses in 77 countries and most cities. |
| East African Revival | fC | 4-c | 1927 | 3,000,000 | 20 | rwan | C | 5 | Rwanda Revival. Balokole (Saved Ones). Pietists. Biennial conventions of 50,000 or so. |
| Identity Christianity | fC | 4-d | 1925 | 500,000 | 10 | usa | C | 3 | Identification of Anglo-Saxon-European Whites with 10 Lost Tribes of Israel. Violent rhetoric. |
| Internat Union of Gospel Missions | fC | 4-c | 1913 | 7,000,000 | 2 | usa | C | 5 | IUGM. 250 rescue missions serving 7 million homeless in USA, Canada. HQ Kansas. |
| Islam in Africa Organization | fC | 4-e | 1991 | 3,000 | 5 | nige | B | 4 | HQ Abuja. General Council with 70 members. |
| Oxford Movement | fC | 4-d | 1660 | 500,000 | 40 | brit | C | 5 | High Church renewal within Church of England. 1850, F=Keble, Pusey, Newman. |
| Oriental Orthodox Chs Conference | fC | 4-b | 1965 | 41,600,000 | 70 | ethi | B | 5 | Patriarchates: Armenian, Coptic, Ethiopian, Malankara, Syrian. |
| Anglican Consultative Council | A-fC | 4-b | 1969 | 80,187,000 | 120 | brit | C | 5 | ACC. HQ London. |
| schismatic Anglican communions | a-fC | 4-c | 1844 | 7,600,000 | 40 | usa | C | 5 | Over 40 new denominations (REC, ICCEC, AOC, & c). |
| IC of Charismatic Episcopal Church | a-fC | 4-d | 1993 | 100,000 | 60 | usa | C | 5 | ICCEC. IC=International Communion. |
| Baptist World Alliance | B-fC | 4-b | 1905 | 67,943,000 | 171 | usa | C | 5 | BWA. HQ Maclean, Washington, DC. |
| Sacred Congregation for Bishops | b-fC | 4-a | 1588 | 901,000,000 | 80 | holy | C | 5 | Vatican dicastery for administering dioceses, bishops, new appointments. |
| Brazilian Catholic Apostolic Church | B-fC | 4-c | 1945 | 3,000,000 | 20 | braz | C | 5 | ICAB. Igreja Catolica Apostolica Brasileira. Schism ex RCC. 12 dioceses, 25 bishops. |
| Baptist Bible Fellowship Internat | b-fC | 4-c | 1950 | 2,500,000 | 50 | usa | C | 5 | BBFI. Schism ex Southern Baptist Convention and others. In 50 countries. |
| Ecumenical Patr of Constantinople | C-fC | 4-b | 38 | 46,630,000 | 93 | turk | A | 5 | 20,000 under direct control in Turkey, others nominally so (Bulgarian, Serbian, Russian). |
| Church of God in Christ | c-fC | 4-b | 1895 | 10,000,000 | 40 | usa | C | 5 | CoGiC. HQ Memphis, TN. Original black pentecostals. |
| Christian Congregation of Brazil | C-fC | 4-c | 1910 | 3,120,000 | 35 | braz | C | 5 | CCB. Congregacao Crista do Brasil. Italian origins. 15,294 churches. |
| Internat Fell of Charismatic Chs | c-fC | 4-c | c1980 | 2,000,000 | 40 | usa | C | 5 | IFCC. An attempt to unite large numbers of independent congregations. |
| Syrian Orthodox Patr of Antioch | D-fC | 4-c | 33 | 3,587,000 | 26 | syri | B | 5 | Only 150,000 left in Syria, due to heavy emigration to 26 countries. |
| Deeper Life Bible Church | d-fC | 4-c | 1973 | 9,000,000 | 45 | nige | B | 5 | DLBC. F=W.F. Kumuyi. HQ church, Lagos, has 150,000 members, 5,000 cells. In 45 countries. |
| Disciples Ecumenical Com for Cons | D-fC | 4-c | | 1,500,000 | 30 | usa | C | 5 | DECC. DE Committee for Consultation. Declining. |
| Int Communion of Charismatic Chs | d-fC | 4-c | | 6,000,000 | 20 | nige | B | 5 | ICCC. One of several attempts to unite independent churches everywhere. |
| Armenian Apostolic C of Echmiadzin | E-fC | 4-c | c35 | 5,593,000 | 28 | arme | C | 5 | C=Catholicossate |
| Brazil for Christ Ev Pentecostal Ch | e-fC | 4-c | 1955 | 2,000,000 | 10 | braz | C | 5 | OBPC. O Brasil Para Cristo. 5,000 churches. |
| International Lutheran Council | e-fC | 4-c | | 3,000,000 | 20 | usa | C | 5 | ILC. Body espousing Conservative Lutheranism. |
| Chaplaincy of Full Gospel Churches | F-fC | 4-c | 1984 | 6,500,000 | 6 | usa | C | 5 | CFGC. Full gospel agency credentialing USA military and civilian chaplains. |
| Coalition of Spirit-filled Churches | f-fC | 4-d | 1997 | 500,000 | 3 | usa | C | 5 | CSC. Agency credentialing USA military and other chaplains. Split ex CFGC. |
| Philippine Independent Church | F-fC | 4-c | 1890 | 2,800,000 | 10 | phil | C | 5 | IFI/PIC. Large schism ex RCC. Became Unitarian; now Anglican relations. |
| Jesus is Lord Fellowship | f-fC | 4-c | 1978 | 2,000,000 | 8 | phil | C | 5 | JILF. Philippine youth movement. Many overseas branches. |
| Mennonite World Conference | G-fC | 4-c | | 1,960,000 | 43 | fran | C | 5 | MWC. |
| Int Moravian Ch in Unity of Brethren | g-fC | 4-d | 1457 | 582,000 | 27 | brit | C | 5 | Origin in Moravia. |
| Gypsy Pentecostal Churches | G-fC | 4-d | 1950 | 200,000 | 18 | spai | C | 5 | IEF. Iglesia Evangelica Filadelfia. Pentecostals. Strong also in France, Portugal. |
| Ethiopian Orthodox P of Addis Ababa | H-fC | 4-b | 332 | 20,250,000 | 9 | ethi | B | 5 | P=Patriarchate. Now worldwide communion with churches in 9 countries. |
| Christian Holiness Association | h-fC | 4-c | 1867 | 5,000,000 | 150 | usa | C | 5 | CHA. 22 denominations holding Wesleyan-Arminian theology. |
| Czechoslovak Hussite Church | H-fC | 4-d | 1920 | 185,000 | 6 | czec | B | 5 | CCH/CHC. Split ex RCC. |
| Unification Church | h-fC | 4-c | 1936 | 1,020,000 | 120 | souk | B | 4 | HSAUWC. Holy Spirit Assoc for Unifi of World Christianity. Tongil Kyohoe. 1013n. |
| Organization of African Instituted Chs | I-fC | 4-b | 1978 | 40,000,000 | 50 | keny | C | 5 | OAIC. HQ Nairobi. |
| Church of the Brethren | i-fC | 4-d | 1719 | 208,000 | 12 | usa | C | 5 | A minuscule grouping regarding self as a Christian World Communion. HQ Elgin, Illinois. |
| Internat Old Catholic Bishops Conf | J-fC | 4-c | | 9,000,000 | 21 | neth | C | 5 | IOCBC. HQ Utrecht. In 21 countries. |
| Union of Messianic Jewish Congs | j-fC | 4-e | 1979 | 15,000 | 5 | usa | C | 5 | UMJC. |
| African Apostolic Ch of J.Maranke | j-fC | 4-c | 1932 | 1,400,000 | 25 | zimb | B | 4 | AACJM. Present in 25 countries, mostly across tropical Africa since 1950 expansion. |
| Int Charismatic Consultation on WE | K-fC | 4-b | | 50,000,000 | 180 | brit | C | 5 | ICCOWE. WE=World Evangelization. All major renewal bodies. Many congresses. |
| Manna Church International | k-fC | 4-d | 1980 | 200,000 | 35 | port | C | 5 | Mana-Igreja Crista. Cell-based megachurch in Lisbon Tents. Abroad: in 35 countries. |
| Internat Fed of Free Evangelical Chs | k-fC | 4-d | | 581,000 | 19 | swed | C | 5 | IFFEC. HQ Stockholm. |
| Lutheran World Federation | L-fC | 4-b | | 80,000,000 | 150 | swit | C | 5 | LWF. HQ Geneva. |
| Orthodox Patr of Moscow | M-fC | 4-b | 988 | 131,055,000 | 49 | russ | B | 5 | Long missionary tradition, shattered 1917 by Communism, now arising again. |
| other antitrinitarian communions | m-fC | 4-c | c1500 | 2,000,000 | 20 | usa | C | 4 | Separate communions e.g. International New Thought Alliance (INTA),IARF,IACT,IGAS. |
| Church of Christ (Manalista) | M-fC | 4-c | 1913 | 1,750,000 | 7 | phil | C | 3 | Iglesia ni Cristo (Manalista) F=F. Manalo. 35 cathedrals, 8,400 chs, 3 radio stations. Unitarian. |
| Ch of Jesus Christ of LdS | m-fC | 4-c | 1830 | 8,650,000 | 116 | usa | C | 3 | CJCLdS. LdS=Latter-day Saints. Mormons. In 116 countries. |
| Coptic Orthodox Patri of Alexandria | N-fC | 4-c | 33 | 9,797,000 | 27 | egyp | B | 5 | Worldwide diaspora now with 42 dioceses, due to 20 centuries of persecution. |
| New Apostolic Church | n-fC | 4-b | 1863 | 11,000,000 | 80 | swit | C | 3 | NAC/NAK. Neuapostolische Kirche. HQ Zurich. |
| India Pentecostal Church of God | n-fC | 4-d | 1924 | 900,000 | 10 | indi | B | 2 | IPCG. Ex CPM, AoG. 80% Malayali. |
| Apostolic World Christian Fellowship | O-fC | 4-c | 1970 | 1,500,000 | 45 | usa | C | 2 | AWCF. Communion based on Oneness Pentecostalism. Largely Black. 170 denominations. |
| Sacred Cong for the Oriental Chs | o-fC | 4-c | 1862 | 3,700,000 | 37 | holy | C | 5 | Vatican dicastery administering all RC dioceses not based on Latin rite. |
| Old Ritualist Churches | o-fC | 4-c | 1666 | 1,957,000 | | russ | B | 5 | Old Believers, Old Calendarists. |
| World Alliance of Reformed Chs | P-fC | 4-b | | 60,000,000 | 210 | swit | C | 5 | WARC. HQ Geneva. |
| Sacred Cong for the Ev of Peoples | p-fC | 4-b | 1622 | 181,396,000 | 158 | holy | C | 5 | Vatican dicastery administering all Roman Catholic foreign missions across the world. |
| Friends World Comm for Consultation | Q-fC | 4-d | | 403,000 | 43 | brit | C | 5 | FWCC. Comm=Committee. |
| Malankara Orth Syrian C of the East | q-fC | 4-c | c52 | 2,197,000 | 20 | indi | B | 5 | C=Catholicossate. Malankara OSCE. Syrians. 10 dioceses, 22 bishops, 1,458 chs, 950 clergy. |
| Catholic Charismatic Renewal | r-fC | 4-b | 1967 | 120,000,000 | 233 | holy | C | 5 | HQ Vatican City. M=ICCRS/ICCRO. |
| Alliance World Fellowship | r-fC | 4-c | 1955 | 1,820,000 | 45 | usa | C | 5 | AWF. In 45 countries with 10,500 Christian & Missionary Alliance chs. M=CMA. |
| Salvation Army | S-fC | 4-c | 1865 | 2,300,000 | 90 | brit | C | 5 | SA, also in CHA. 923 branches in UK. Evangelistic work, huge social/poverty programs. |
| Reformed Ecumenical Council | s-fC | 4-c | | 5,000,000 | 18 | usa | C | 5 | REC. |
| Pentecostal Methodist Ch of Chile | s-fC | 4-d | 1909 | 720,000 | 7 | chil | C | 5 | IMPC. |
| World Convention of Chs of Christ | T-fC | 4-b | | 10,000,000 | 130 | usa | C | 5 | WCCC. |
| True Jesus Church | t-fC | 4-c | 1917 | 1,400,000 | 50 | chin | B | 3 | TJC. Chen Yesu Chiao Hui. Chinese Oneness pentecostal church in 50 countries. HQ Taipei. |
| Assembly Hall Churches | t-fC | 4-c | 1922 | 2,100,000 | 52 | chin | B | 2 | Local Churches, Little Flock. |
| Consult on Uniting and United Chs | U-fC | 4-b | 1947 | 65,000,000 | 54 | swit | C | 5 | CUUC. Ecumenical conferences sponsored by WCC. |
| Universal Ch of the Kingdom of God | u-fC | 4-c | 1977 | 4,500,000 | 55 | braz | C | 3 | UCKG/IURD. Igreja Universal do Reino de Deus. 10,000 churches, radio/TV, foreign missions. |
| IC of Unitarians and Universalists | u-fC | 4-d | 1570 | 352,000 | 27 | usa | C | 2 | International Council of UU. Begun in Hungary and Romania, 1566 denying Trinitarian doctrine. |
| Seventh-day Adventist Church | V-fC | 4-b | 1844 | 25,000,000 | 200 | usa | C | 5 | SDA, General Conference. HQ Washington D.C. |
| Mar Thoma Syrian Ch of Malabar | v-fC | 4-d | 1843 | 875,000 | 25 | indi | B | 5 | Reform ex Orthodox Syrian Church of the East. 6 dioceses, 300 clergy. |
| Church of Christ, Scientist | v-fC | 4-c | 1879 | 2,500,000 | 63 | usa | C | 3 | Christian Science. In 63 countries, declining steadily. |
| World Methodist Council | W-fC | 4-b | | 70,226,000 | 113 | usa | C | 5 | WMC. HQ Lake Junaluska, NC. |
| Jehovah's Witnesses | w-fC | 4-b | 1872 | 13,000,000 | 219 | usa | C | 3 | Jehovah's Christian Witnesses. JWs. IBRA. Watch Tower. |
| Waldensian Church | W-fC | 4-e | 1184 | 42,000 | 4 | ital | C | 5 | United with Methodists. |
| Willow Creek Association of Chs | w-fC | 4-d | 1975 | 500,000 | 50 | usa | C | 5 | WCAC. |
| other Neo-Apostolic meganetworks | X-fC | 4-b | | 25,000,000 | 20 | usa | C | 5 | White-led postdenominationalists. |
| Protestant global denominations | x-fC | 4-b | | 18,000,000 | 210 | usa | C | 5 | 50 major world organisations, paraconfessional or quasiconfessional. |
| Neocharismatic minicommunions | x-fC | 4-b | | 50,000,000 | 160 | usa | C | 5 | 50 Independent paracommunions or quasicommunions. |
| Ancient Assyrian Patr of the East | Y-fC | 4-d | c50 | 500,000 | 17 | iraq | A | 5 | Nestorians across Asia from AD 635 on; but by 1402, Tamerlane destroys 12 million believers. |
| Conservative confessional networks | y-fC | 4-c | | 9,000,000 | 100 | usa | C | 5 | 25 networks or quasiconfessions hostile to historic confessions. |
| Pentecostal World Conference | Z-fC | 4-b | 1947 | 68,159,000 | 155 | swit | C | 5 | PWC. No HQ. World conferences every 3 years since 1st in Zurich in 1947. |
| World Assemblies of God Fellowship | z-fC | 4-b | | 43,000,000 | 140 | souk | B | 5 | WAGF. HQ Seoul, Korea. Also part of PWC. |
| latent (inactive) Christians | LC | 2-a | | 1,351,743,000 | 238 | fran | C | 2 | Numbers fluctuate over 20 centuries. 90% of all Christians throughout the Dark Ages. |
| All-India Ecumenical Coordinating Body | nC | 7-b | c1980 | 28,000,000 | 1 | indi | B | 5 | AECB. Project envisaging a future NCCI including the Catholic Ch in India. |
| All-India Fed of National Churches | nC | 7-c | c1980 | 7,000,000 | 1 | indi | B | 5 | AIFNC. Numerous Independent churches, aiming to create an indigenous national Ch of India. |
| American Council of Christian Chs | nC | 7-d | c1950 | 420,000 | 1 | usa | C | 4 | ACCC. Fundamentalists related to ICCC until 1968 withdrawal. |
| Assemblea degli Ordinari Cattolici di TS | nC | 7-d | 1992 | 168,000 | 1 | pale | B | 5 | AOCTS. TS=Terra Santa. Bishops' Conference in the Holy Land. |
| Assoc of Evangelicals of Swaziland | nC | 7-e | c1960 | 50,000 | 1 | swaz | C | 5 | AES, member of AEA. |
| Associated Gospel Churches | nC | 7-c | 1939 | 4,000,000 | 10 | usa | C | 5 | AGC. Service agency for 2-million member Fundamentalist denominations. |
| Australian Christian Churches | nC | 7-d | 2000 | 170,000 | 1 | aust | C | 5 | National Alliance of Pentecostal and Charismatic Churches: AoG, Apostolic Chs, et alia. |
| Bishops' Conference of Scotland | nC | 7-d | 1986 | 766,000 | 1 | brit | C | 5 | BCS. HQ Glasgow. |
| Bishops' Conference of Slovakia | nC | 7-c | 1991 | 3,660,000 | 1 | slok | C | 5 | BKS Biskupska Konferencia Slovenska. HQ Bratislava. |
| Catholic Bishops' Conference of Korea | nC | 7-c | 1973 | 3,700,000 | 1 | souk | B | 5 | CBCK. Hanguk Jukyo Hweoi. HQ Seoul. |
| Christian Council of Zambia | nC | 7-c | 1945 | 1,918,000 | 1 | zamb | C | 5 | CCZ. 13 member denominations. 1974, withdrawal of SDAs and Wesleyans. |
| Commis of Covenanted Chs in Wales | nC | 7-d | 1930 | 600,000 | 1 | brit | C | 5 | 1955 Council of Churches for Wales (Cyngor Eglwysi Cymru). |
| Conference Episcopale du Viet Nam | nC | 7-c | 1980 | 5,320,000 | 1 | viet | B | 5 | CEVN. Bishops Conference of Viet Nam. HQ Toa Giam Muc, Xuan Loc. |
| Conferenza Episcopale Ucraina | nC | 7-c | 1992 | 5,578,000 | 1 | ukra | C | 5 | CEU. Ukraine Bishops' Conference. HQ Lviv. |
| Council of Christian Chs in Luxembourg | nC | 7-d | 1997 | 396,000 | 1 | luxe | C | 5 | Ecumenical council of churches (Catholic/Protestant/Orthodox) to resolve issues. |

*Continued overleaf*

*Table 17–6 continued*

| Name of religion/religionists 1 | Pedigree 2 | Type 3 | Begun 4 | Adherents 5 | Ext 6 | Coun 7 | W 8 | X 9 | E. g. = examples; name for God, other religions present, D=denominations, M=missions. 10 |
|---|---|---|---|---|---|---|---|---|---|
| Ecumenical Conference of Russia | nC | 7-b | | 77,104,000 | 1 | russ | B | 5 | Recent attempt to give smaller denominations a hearing in front of Orthodox Church's claims. |
| Ecumenical Council of Hungarian Chs | nC | 7-c | 1948 | 2,630,000 | 1 | hung | C | 5 | ECHC. Magyarorszagi Egyhazak Okumenikus Tanaksa MEOT. |
| Evangelical Fellowship of Viet Nam | nC | 7-d | c1960 | 100,000 | 1 | viet | B | 5 | EFVN. Evangelicals very active up to 1975, then in decline under persecution. |
| Fellowship of Christ in India | nC | 7-c | c1970 | 2,000,000 | 1 | indi | B | 5 | FCI. Many Independent churches. |
| National Black Evangelical Association | nC | 7-c | 1963 | 1,000,000 | 6 | usa | C | 5 | NBEA. Formerly NNEA (N=Negro). HQ Portland, OR. |
| Pentecostal Fellowship of Zimbabwe | nC | 7-d | c1960 | 170,000 | 1 | zimb | B | 5 | PFZ. An unusually large variety of over 20 Western-related Pentecostal denominations. |
| Scottish Churches Council | nC | 7-c | 1964 | 2,600,000 | 1 | brit | C | 5 | Ecumenical council with Church of Scotland as largest member. |
| Singapore Council of Christian Churches | nC | 7-e | c1960 | 15,000 | 1 | sing | B | 5 | SCCC. Fundamentalists related to ICCC. |
| Slovenia Bishops' Conference | nC | 7-c | 1993 | 1,659,000 | 1 | slov | C | 5 | SSK. Slovenska Skofovska Konferenca. HQ Ljubljana. |
| A des Egl et Oeuvres Prot en Algerie | C-nC | 7-e | 1964 | 2,500 | 1 | alge | A | 5 | ADEOPA. A=Assoc. Association of Protestant Churches and Activities in Algeria. |
| Albanian Encouragement Project | C-nC | 7-e | 1991 | 12,000 | 1 | alba | B | 5 | Activist grouping aiming to renew country after 50 years of Communism. |
| Alianza de Igls Presb y Ref de Mexico | C-nC | 7-c | | 1,300,000 | 1 | mexi | C | 5 | AIPREM. Association of Presbyterian & Reformed Churches of Mexico. |
| Alianza Evangelica de Panama | C-nC | 7-d | 1941 | 128,000 | 1 | pana | C | 5 | AEP. Panama Evangelical Alliance. 5 member denominations. |
| Anguilla Christian Council | C-nC | 7-e | | 4,800 | 1 | angu | C | 5 | ACC. Formerly part of St Kitts-Nevis bodies. |
| Associacao Evangelica Brasileira | C-nC | 7-b | 1991 | 30,000,000 | 1 | braz | C | 5 | AEB. |
| Associated Christian Chs of Kenya | C-nC | 7-e | | 30,000 | 1 | keny | C | 5 | ACCK. |
| Barbados Christian Council | C-nC | 7-d | c1990 | 140,000 | 1 | barb | C | 5 | BCC. |
| British Evangelical Council | C-nC | 7-e | | 40,000 | 1 | brit | C | 5 | BEC. |
| Christian Council of St Kitts | C-nC | 7-e | | 31,100 | 1 | saik | C | 5 | CCSK. |
| Christian Council of Togo | C-nC | 7-d | 1980 | 320,000 | 1 | togo | B | 5 | CCT. |
| Churches Together in Man | C-nC | 7-e | c1980 | 48,000 | 1 | isle | C | 5 | CTM. More recent and inclusive body than IOMCC. |
| Co of Ev Chs in Equatorial Guinea | C-nC | 7-e | | 11,200 | 1 | equa | C | 5 | CIEGE. Co=Council. |
| Co of Free Chr and Chs in Finland | C-nC | 7-e | | 5,000 | 1 | finl | C | 5 | CFCCF. Co=Council. Suomen Vapaitten Kristittyjen ja Kirkkokuntien Neuvosto. |
| Comision Coordinadora Ev de Para | C-nC | 7-e | c1970 | 80,000 | 1 | para | C | 5 | CCEP. Evangelical Co-ordinating Commission of Paraguay. 5 member denominations. |
| Comite Ev Pro-Ayuda al Desarrollo | C-nC | 7-d | 1972 | 420,000 | 1 | nica | C | 5 | CEPAD. Evangelical Committee for Development Aid. 30 Evangelical denominations. |
| Comm of Christian Chs in Suriname | C-nC | 7-d | c1960 | 149,000 | 1 | suri | B | 5 | CCCS. Comite Christelijke Kerken. Moravians, Catholics, Lutherans, Reformed. |
| Confederacao Evangelico Brasileira | C-nC | 7-e | | 35,000 | 1 | braz | C | 5 | CEB. Evangelical Federation of Brazil. |
| Conseil Interconf Prot du Benin | C-nC | 7-d | | 110,000 | 1 | beni | B | 5 | Protestant Interconfessional Council of Benin. |
| Conseil Supreme des Egls Ev au LS | C-nC | 7-e | c1965 | 53,200 | 1 | leba | B | 5 | Supreme Council of Evangelical Churches in Lebanon & Syria. |
| Conselho Cristao de Mocambique | C-nC | 7-c | | 1,450,000 | 1 | moza | B | 5 | CCM. Christian Council of Mozambique. |
| Council of Churches in Kuwait | C-nC | 7-d | 1960 | 155,000 | 1 | kuwa | B | 5 | CCK. Includes wide spectrum of older churches. |
| Council of Free Chs in Hungary | C-nC | 7-e | 1938 | 50,000 | 1 | hung | C | 5 | CFCH. Magyarorszagi Szabadegyhazak Tanacsa. |
| Council of Free Churches | C-nC | 7-e | | 15,000 | 1 | denm | C | 5 | CFC. Evangelisk Frikirkerad. |
| Council of Swaziland Churches | C-nC | 7-d | 1967 | 140,000 | 1 | swaz | C | 5 | CSC. Begun in expectation of replacing rival SCC. Now related to WCC. RCs members. |
| Dominica Christian Council | C-nC | 7-e | | 60,000 | 1 | domi | C | 5 | DCC. |
| Evangelical Association of Belize | C-nC | 7-e | | 5,000 | 1 | beli | C | 5 | EAB. Including Assemblies of God (which was in BCC until its withdrawal in 1968). |
| Fed des Eglises Prot de Madagascar | C-nC | 7-d | 1913 | 300,000 | 1 | mada | B | 5 | FFPM. |
| Fed des Egls Chretiennes du Congo | C-nC | 7-c | 1970 | 2,100,000 | 1 | cong | C | 5 | FECC. Federation of Christian Churches in the Congo. Members: SA, EJCSK, Evs; later, RCC. |
| Fed Entitades Relig Ev de Espana | C-nC | 7-e | 1992 | 85,000 | 1 | spai | C | 5 | FEREDE. |
| Federation Evangelique de France | C-nC | 7-d | 1967 | 210,000 | 1 | fran | C | 5 | Evangelical Federation of France. Includes 40 single congregations. |
| Federation of Ev Churches of India | C-nC | 7-c | c1970 | 1,000,000 | 1 | indi | B | 5 | FECI. Members must have no non-Evangelical conciliar ties; 40 denominations. |
| Fellowship of Evangelicals in Egypt | C-nC | 7-c | 1966 | 1,100,000 | 1 | egyp | B | 5 | FEE. Members: 7 denominations. |
| Ghana Council of United Churches | C-nC | 7-d | | 700,000 | 1 | ghan | B | 5 | GCUC. Mostly Pentecostal denominations. |
| Grenada Inter-Church Council for SW | C-nC | 7-e | 1974 | 83,000 | 1 | gren | C | 5 | 1950 Conference of Chs in Grenada. 1974 Grenada Christian Council. SW=Social Welfare |
| Int Christian Committee in Jerusalem | C-nC | 7-e | c1970 | 3,000 | 1 | pale | B | 5 | ICCJ. |
| Inter-Church Council of Tunisia | C-nC | 10-f | 1964 | 500 | 1 | tuni | A | 5 | ICCT. |
| Internat Christian Committee in Israel | C-nC | 7-e | c1970 | 5,000 | 1 | isra | B | 5 | ICCI. |
| Korean Christian Federation | C-nC | 7-e | 1970 | 12,000 | 1 | nork | A | 5 | KCF. Grouping recognized as official by government regime. |
| Micronesian Council of United CC | C-nC | 7-e | 1958 | 50,000 | 1 | mars | C | 5 | MCUCC. CC=Churches of Christ. |
| Montserrat Council for Social Action. | C-nC | 7-e | | 6,100 | 1 | mont | C | 5 | MCSA. |
| National Patriotic Catholic Assoc | C-nC | 7-c | | 4,600,000 | 1 | chin | B | 5 | NPCA. |
| Nepal Christian Fellowship | C-nC | 7-d | | 100,000 | 1 | nepa | A | 5 | NCF. |
| New Sudan Council of Churches | C-nC | 7-d | | 250,000 | 1 | suda | B | 5 | NSCC. |
| Norwegian Free Church Council | C-nC | 7-d | | 150,000 | 1 | norw | C | 5 | Norske Frikirkerad. Several non-established Protestant denominations. |
| Papua New Guinea Council of Chs | C-nC | 7-c | 1970 | 2,900,000 | 1 | papu | C | 5 | PNGCC. |
| Protestant Chs in Tuvalu & Kiribati | C-nC | 7-e | c1970 | 49,000 | 1 | tuva | C | 5 | PCTK. Cooperation between the 2 dominant churches. |
| Protestant Federation of Haiti | C-nC | 7-c | | 1,000,000 | 1 | hait | C | 5 | PFH. |
| Samoa Council of Churches | C-nC | 7-d | 1964 | 139,000 | 1 | samo | C | 5 | SCC. |
| St Lucia Inter-Church Council | C-nC | 7-d | | 113,000 | 1 | sail | C | 5 | SLICC. |
| St Thomas Inter-Church Council | C-nC | 7-e | | 32,000 | 1 | virg | C | 5 | VIICC. Members: 6 denominations. |
| Swedish Free Church Council | C-nC | 7-d | | 270,000 | 1 | swed | C | 5 | SFCC. Sveriges Frikyrkorad. Council of Free Churches. 85 local Christian councils. |
| Turks & Caicos Inter-Ch Committee | C-nC | 7-e | c1970 | 8,000 | 1 | turs | C | 5 | TCICC. Members: Anglicans, Baptists, Catholics, Methodists. |
| Union of Evangelical Churches | C-nC | 7-e | 1965 | 3,000 | 1 | turk | A | 5 | UEC. An unofficial loose grouping in Istanbul. |
| Verband Unabhangiger Ev Kirchen KS | C-nC | 7-e | | 75,000 | 1 | swit | C | 5 | KS=Korperschaften der Schweiz. Aarauer Verband. |
| Zambia Christian C for Development | C-nC | 7-c | 1970 | 3,877,000 | 1 | zamb | C | 5 | ZCCD. C=Commission. 30 member denominations including RCC and several AICs. |
| Zimbabwe Christian Conference | C-nC | 7-c | 1903 | 1,146,000 | 1 | zimb | B | 5 | ZCC built on 1903 Southern Rhodesia Christian Conference. |
| Conselho Portugues de Igs Cristas | d-nC | 7-d | | 130,000 | 1 | port | C | 5 | COPIC. Portuguese Council of Christian Churches. |
| Vereinigte Ev-L Kirche Deutschlands | d-nC | 7-b | 1948 | 12,500,000 | 1 | germ | C | 5 | VELKD. Ev-L=Evangelisch-Lutherische. United Evangelical Lutheran Church in Germany. |
| A Francophone des PE du Quebec | E-nC | 7-d | 1964 | 500,000 | 1 | cana | C | 5 | A=Alliance. EFFC. Ev Fellowship of Francophone Canada. PE=Protestants Evangéliques. |
| Albanian Evangelical Alliance | E-nC | 7-e | 1892 | 3,000 | 1 | alba | B | 5 | AEA. Roots reaching back to F=G. Qiriazi, an Evangelical Brotherhood preacher. |
| Alianca Evangelica de Angola | E-nC | 7-d | 1922 | 100,000 | 1 | ango | C | 5 | Evangelical Alliance of Angola (EAA). |
| Alianca Evangelica Portuguesa | E-nC | 7-d | 1935 | 130,000 | 1 | port | C | 5 | AEP. Portuguese Evangelical Christian Alliance. |
| Alianza de Evangelicos | E-nC | 7-d | c1970 | 100,000 | 1 | vene | C | 5 | AEV. Alliance of Evangelicals. |
| Alianza Evangelica Costarricense | E-nC | 7-d | 1951 | 280,000 | 1 | cost | C | 5 | AEC. Costa Rican Evangelial Alliance. 14 member denominations. |
| Alianza Evangelica de Guatemala | E-nC | 7-c | 1953 | 1,300,000 | 1 | guat | C | 5 | AEG. Evangelical Alliance of Guatemala. United forum for 17 member churches. In CONELA. |
| Alianza Evangelica Espanola | E-nC | 7-e | 1887 | 30,000 | 1 | spai | C | 5 | AEE. Spanish Evangelical Alliance. 5 denominations. |
| Alleanza Evangelica Italiana | E-nC | 7-d | 1974 | 120,000 | 1 | ital | C | 5 | AEI. Italian Evangelical Alliance (IEA). |
| Alliance Ev Francophone de Belgique | E-nC | 7-e | 1981 | 5,000 | 1 | belg | C | 5 | Evangelical Alliance of French-speaking Belgium. |
| Alliance Evangelique du Rwanda | E-nC | 7-d | 1992 | 400,000 | 1 | rwan | C | 5 | AER. |
| Alliance Evangelique du Zaire | E-nC | 7-d | c1960 | 500,000 | 1 | conz | C | 5 | AEZ. Alliance of Zaire. |
| Alliance Evangelique Francaise | E-nC | 7-e | | 6,000 | 1 | fran | C | 5 | AEF. French Evangelical Alliance. |
| Argentine Alliance of Ev Chs | E-nC | 7-d | 1982 | 400,000 | 1 | arge | C | 5 | ACIERA. Alianza Cristiana de Igls Ev de la Rep A. 2,000 member congregations. |
| Asoc Cristiana de Igls Ev de Uruguay | E-nC | 7-e | 1988 | 50,000 | 1 | uuay | C | 5 | ACIERU. Member of CONELA. |
| Asociacion de Pastores del Paraguay | E-nC | 7-e | c1965 | 3,000 | 1 | para | C | 5 | APP. |
| Asociacion Nacional de Ev de Bolivia | E-nC | 7-d | 1966 | 450,000 | 1 | boli | C | 5 | ANDEB. National Association of Evangelicals of Bolivia. Member of CONELA. |
| Asso des Eglises Ev Centrafricaines | E-nC | 7-d | 1973 | 450,000 | 1 | cent | B | 5 | AEEC. Association of Central African Evangelical Churches. |
| Assoc des Egl et Miss Ev de Guine | E-nC | 7-e | c1980 | 59,000 | 1 | guin | A | 5 | AEMEG. |
| Assoc of Evangelicals of Liberia | E-nC | 7-d | 1968 | 140,000 | 1 | libe | B | 5 | AEL. Begun as Liberian Evangelical Fundamental Fellowship (LEFF), 1974 renamed. |
| Associacao Ev de Mocambique | E-nC | 7-c | | 1,100,000 | 1 | moza | B | 5 | AEM. Evangelical Association of Mozambique. |
| Association of Ev Chs of Colombia | E-nC | 7-d | 1948 | 300,000 | 1 | colo | C | 5 | AIEC. Confederacion Evangelica de Colombia. CEDECOL. |
| Association of Ev Chs of Indonesia | E-nC | 7-c | 1970 | 3,000,000 | 1 | indo | B | 5 | PII. Persekutuan Injili Indonesia. Formerly DGGII. 100 denominations. |
| Association of Ev Chs of St Vincent-G | E-nC | 7-e | | 5,000 | 1 | saiv | C | 5 | AECSVG. God=Grenadines |
| Australian Evangelical Alliance | E-nC | 7-c | 1972 | 1,800,000 | 1 | aust | C | 5 | AEA. |
| Barbados Council of Evangelical Chs | E-nC | 7-e | 1972 | 20,000 | 1 | barb | C | 5 | BCEC. |
| Bulgarian Evangelical Alliance | E-nC | 7-d | 1990 | 120,000 | 1 | bulg | C | 5 | BEA. |
| Concile des Eglises Ev d'Haiti | E-nC | 7-c | | 1,100,000 | 1 | hait | C | 5 | CEEH. Council of Evangelical Churches of Haili. |
| Concilio Nacional Ev del Peru | E-nC | 7-d | 1940 | 560,000 | 1 | peru | C | 5 | CNEP. National Evangelical Council of Peru. 53 member denominations (plus 22 associated). |
| Conf Episcopal de Mocambique | E-nC | 7-c | 1982 | 3,110,000 | 1 | moza | B | 5 | CEM. Episcopal Conference of Mozambique. HQ Maputo. |
| Confederacion Ev de Colombia | E-nC | 7-d | 1950 | 400,000 | 1 | colo | C | 5 | CEC. Evangelical Confederation of Colombia. Members: 20 major denominations. |
| Confraternidad Ev de Chile | E-nC | 7-e | 1916 | 25,000 | 1 | chil | C | 5 | CEC. Evangelical Fellowship of Chile. 10 member denominations. |
| Confraternidad Ev de Honduras | E-nC | 7-d | 1945 | 240,000 | 1 | hond | C | 5 | CEH. Formerly Alianza Evangelica Hondurena (AEH), renamed 1990. |
| Confraternidad Ev Ecuatoriana | E-nC | 7-d | 1964 | 250,000 | 1 | ecua | C | 5 | CEE. Ecuador Evangelical Fellowship. |
| Confraternidad Ev Mexicana | E-nC | 7-c | 1982 | 1,700,000 | 1 | mexi | C | 5 | CONEMEX. Mostly related to WEF. |
| Confraternidad Ev Panamena | E-nC | 7-e | 1982 | 30,000 | 1 | pana | C | 5 | CEP. Panamanian Evangelical Confraternity. |
| Confraternidad Ev Salvadorena | E-nC | 7-d | | 400,000 | 1 | elsa | C | 5 | CES. CONESAL. Member of CONELA. |
| Consejo Evangelico de Venezuela | E-nC | 7-d | 1958 | 145,000 | 1 | vene | C | 5 | CEV. Venezuela Council of Churches. 22 member denominations (plus 15 indigenous ones). |

*Continued opposite*

*Table 17–6 continued*

| Name of religion/religionists 1 | Pedigree 2 | Type 3 | Begun 4 | Adherents 5 | Ext 6 | Coun 7 | W 8 | X 9 | E. g. = examples; name for God, other religions present, D=denominations, M=missions. 10 |
|---|---|---|---|---|---|---|---|---|---|
| Consejo Nacional Ev de Nicaragua | E-nC | 7-d | 1966 | 100,000 | 1 | nica | C | 5 | CNEN. |
| Cyprus Evangelical Alliance | E-nC | 7-e | c1970 | 1,000 | 1 | cypr | C | 5 | CEA. |
| Czech Evangelical Alliance | E-nC | 7-e | 1991 | 90,000 | 1 | czec | B | 5 | CEA. |
| Deutsche Evangelische Allianz | E-nC | 7-c | 1857 | 1,323,000 | 1 | germ | C | 5 | DEA. German Evangelical Alliance. |
| Dominica Association of Ev Chs | E-nC | 7-e | | 3,000 | 1 | domi | C | 5 | DAEC. HQ Roseau. 5 member denominations. |
| Dominican Association of Ev Chs | E-nC | 7-d | 1983 | 150,000 | 1 | domr | C | 5 | DAEC. Confraternidad Evangelica Dominicana. CONEDO. |
| Entente des Egl et Missions Ev au T | E-nC | 7-d | c1928 | 720,000 | 1 | chad | B | 5 | EEMET. T=Chad/Tchad. |
| Estonian Evangelical Alliance | E-nC | 7-e | | 60,000 | 1 | esto | B | 5 | EEA. |
| Ev Alliance of South Pacific Islands | E-nC | 7-d | 1989 | 420,000 | 1 | papu | C | 5 | EASPI. 20 chs in PNG plus SSEC (Solomons). Close relations with Melanesian Council of Chs. |
| Ev Alliance of the Netherlands | E-nC | 7-d | 1979 | 200,000 | 1 | neth | C | 5 | Evangelische Alliantie. Dutch Evangelical Alliance. 2 member denominations. |
| Ev Churches Fellowship of Ethiopia | E-nC | 7-c | 1972 | 8,133,000 | 1 | ethi | B | 5 | ECFE. |
| Ev Fellowship of New Zealand | E-nC | 7-d | 1985 | 300,000 | 1 | newz | C | 5 | EFNZ. |
| Ev Fellowship of Sierra Leone | E-nC | 7-e | 1959 | 52,200 | 1 | sier | B | 5 | EFSL/SLEF. Members: 5 denominations (all also in UCCSL). |
| Evangelical Alliance of Algeria | E-nC | 10-f | c1980 | 500 | 1 | alge | A | 5 | EAA. |
| Evangelical Alliance of Cameroon | E-nC | 7-d | | 620,000 | 1 | came | B | 5 | EAC. |
| Evangelical Alliance of Denmark | E-nC | 7-d | | 200,000 | 1 | denm | C | 5 | EAD. Evangelisk Alliance i Danmark |
| Evangelical Alliance of Flanders | E-nC | 7-e | c1970 | 10,000 | | belg | C | 5 | Evangelische Alliantie Vlaanderen. For Flemish-speaking Belgium. |
| Evangelical Alliance of Lesotho | E-nC | 7-e | | 40,000 | 1 | leso | C | 5 | EAL. |
| Evangelical Alliance of Puerto Rico | E-nC | 7-e | c1960 | 70,000 | 1 | puer | C | 5 | EAPR. |
| Evangelical Alliance of Slovakia | E-nC | 7-e | 1905 | 30,000 | 1 | slok | C | 5 | EAS. Evanjelicka Aliancia v Slovenskej Republike. |
| Evangelical Alliance of South Africa | E-nC | 7-c | 1973 | 4,500,000 | 1 | soua | C | 5 | EASA. |
| Evangelical Alliance of Sri Lanka | E-nC | 7-e | c1945 | 70,000 | 1 | sril | B | 5 | EASL. |
| Evangelical Alliance of the UK | E-nC | 7-c | 1846 | 3,000,000 | 1 | brit | C | 5 | EAUK. 20 member denominations. HQ London. Large number of programs and outreach. |
| Evangelical Fellowship of Botswana | E-nC | 7-e | 1973 | 10,000 | 1 | bots | B | 5 | EFB. |
| Evangelical Fellowship of Burundi | E-nC | 7-d | | 200,000 | 1 | buru | C | 5 | EFB. |
| Evangelical Fellowship of Cambodia | E-nC | 7-e | | 11,000 | 1 | camb | A | 5 | EFC. |
| Evangelical Fellowship of Canada | E-nC | 7-e | 1964 | 90,000 | 1 | cana | C | 5 | EFC. 29 member denominations, 762 congregations. EFFC for Francophone Canada. |
| Evangelical Fellowship of Eritrea | E-nC | 7-e | | 12,000 | 1 | erit | B | 5 | EFE. |
| Evangelical Fellowship of Fiji | E-nC | 7-e | | 90,000 | 1 | fiji | B | 5 | EFF. |
| Evangelical Fellowship of India | E-nC | 7-c | 1950 | 6,000,000 | 1 | indi | B | 5 | EFI. For both conciliar and nonconciliar Evangelicals. 120 member denominations. |
| Evangelical Fellowship of Kenya | E-nC | 7-d | 1973 | 500,000 | 1 | keny | C | 5 | EFK. |
| Evangelical Fellowship of Malawi | E-nC | 7-d | 1964 | 300,000 | 1 | mala | C | 5 | EFM. Formerly Evangelical Association of Malawi (EAM). |
| Evangelical Fellowship of Pakistan | E-nC | 7-d | 1956 | 140,000 | 1 | paki | A | 5 | EFP. Small body with 5 denominations. |
| Evangelical Fellowship of Palestine | E-nC | 7-e | c1970 | 5,000 | 1 | pale | B | 5 | EFP. |
| Evangelical Fellowship of Singapore | E-nC | 7-e | 1980 | 40,000 | 1 | sing | B | 5 | EFOS. |
| Evangelical Fellowship of Taiwan | E-nC | 7-d | 1953 | 100,000 | 1 | taiw | B | 5 | EFT. Also termed: China Evangelical Fellowship. |
| Evangelical Fellowship of Thailand | E-nC | 7-e | 1969 | 60,000 | 1 | thai | B | 5 | EFT. United Christian Fellowship. 27 foreign mission agencies, 11 Thai agencies, 100 congs. |
| Evangelical Fellowship of the Gambia | E-nC | 7-e | | 3,200 | 1 | gamb | A | 5 | EFG. |
| Evangelical Fellowship of Uganda | E-nC | 7-c | c1960 | 1,000,000 | 1 | ugan | C | 5 | EFU. Loose collaboration between earliest missions. |
| Evangelical Fellowship of Zambia | E-nC | 7-d | 1964 | 900,000 | 1 | zamb | C | 5 | EFZ. Member denominations: 18 Conservative Evangelicals, in AEA. |
| Evangelical Fellowship of Zimbabwe | E-nC | 7-d | 1963 | 171,000 | 1 | zimb | B | 5 | EFZw. Conservative Evangelicals, member of Association of Evangelicals in Africa. |
| Fed des Egl et Missions Ev du Benin | E-nC | 7-d | | 170,000 | 1 | beni | B | 5 | Federation of Churches and Missions in Benin. |
| Fed des Egl et Missions Ev du BF | E-nC | 7-d | 1961 | 750,000 | 1 | burk | B | 5 | FEMEBF. Federation of Evangelical Churches and Missions in BF (Burkina Faso). |
| Fellowship of Gospel Preaching Chs | E-nC | 7-e | | 2,000 | 1 | sail | C | 5 | Evangelical Alliance of St Lucia. |
| Fraternite Evangelique du Senegal | E-nC | 7-e | 1964 | 2,000 | 1 | sene | A | 5 | FES. Evangelical Fraternity of Senegal. |
| Guyana Evangelical Fellowship | E-nC | 7-e | | 50,000 | 1 | guya | B | 5 | GEF. |
| Hong Kong Evangelical Fellowship | E-nC | 7-e | 1967 | 90,000 | 1 | chin | B | 5 | HKEF. |
| Hungarian Evangelical Alliance | E-nC | 7-d | 1936 | 400,000 | 1 | hung | C | 5 | MEA. Magyar Evangeliumi Aliansz. |
| Igrejas Ev da Guinea-Bissau | E-nC | 7-e | c1990 | 8,500 | 1 | gunb | A | 5 | IEGB. |
| Jamaica Association of Ev Chs | E-nC | 7-e | | 20,000 | 1 | jama | B | 5 | JAEC. Mainly Fundamentalist churches. 13 member denominations. |
| Japan Evangelical Association | E-nC | 7-e | 1968 | 35,000 | 1 | japa | B | 5 | JEA. |
| Korea Evangelical Fellowship | E-nC | 7-c | 1953 | 3,700,000 | 1 | souk | B | 5 | KEF. |
| Myanmar Evangelical Christian Fell | E-nC | 7-d | 1981 | 500,000 | 1 | myan | B | 5 | MECF. |
| Namibia Evangelical Fellowship | E-nC | 7-e | c1985 | 20,000 | 1 | nami | C | 5 | NEF. |
| National Association of Evangelicals | E-nC | 7-b | 1942 | 27,000,000 | 1 | usa | C | 5 | NAE. Members 48 denominations with 42,500 congregations. |
| National Association of Evs of Ghana | E-nC | 7-c | 1977 | 1,400,000 | 1 | ghan | B | 5 | NAEG. Founded by 12 organizations. |
| National Christian Fell of Bangladesh | E-nC | 7-e | 1980 | 3,000 | 1 | bang | B | 5 | NCFB. |
| National Chs Fellowship of Nepal | E-nC | 7-e | 1959 | 80,000 | 1 | nepa | A | 5 | NCFN. |
| National Council of Ev Chs of PNG | E-nC | 7-d | 1964 | 375,000 | 1 | papu | C | 5 | Formerly Ev Alliance of Papua New Guinea. |
| National Ev Christian Fell of Malaysia | E-nC | 7-d | 1983 | 500,000 | 1 | malb | B | 5 | Persaudaraan Kristian Evangelikal Nasional, Malaysia. |
| Norwegian Evangelical Alliance | E-nC | 7-d | 1858 | 100,000 | 1 | norw | C | 5 | NEA. Evangeliske Allianse i Norge. |
| Osterreichische Evangelische Allianz | E-nC | 7-e | | 50,000 | 1 | ausz | C | 5 | OEA. |
| Panhellenic Evangelical Alliance | E-nC | 7-e | 1977 | 12,300 | 1 | gree | C | 5 | PEA. Greek Evangelical Alliance. |
| Philippine Council of Evangelical Chs | E-nC | 7-d | c1950 | 380,000 | 1 | phil | C | 5 | PCEC. 50 member denominations. |
| Protestant Ev Council in Croatia | E-nC | 7-e | 1992 | 10,000 | 1 | croa | C | 5 | PECC. HQ Osijek. |
| Romanian Evangelical Alliance | E-nC | 7-d | 1990 | 400,000 | 1 | roma | C | 5 | REA. Aliantja Evanghelica din Romania. |
| Samoan Evangelical Fellowship | E-nC | 7-e | | 8,000 | 1 | samo | C | 5 | SEF. |
| Schweizerische Evangelische Allianz | E-nC | 7-d | 1846 | 200,000 | 1 | swit | C | 5 | SEA. Swiss Evangelical Alliance. 24 member denominations. |
| Serbian Evangelical Alliance | E-nC | 7-e | | 5,000 | 1 | yugo | C | 5 | SEA. |
| St Croix Ev Ministerial Association | E-nC | 7-e | | 5,000 | 1 | virg | C | 5 | SCEMA. |
| St Kitts Evangelical Association | E-nC | 7-e | | 3,000 | 1 | saik | C | 5 | SKEA. |
| Sudanese Ev Christian Association | E-nC | 7-d | 1973 | 100,000 | 1 | suda | B | 5 | SECA. |
| Swaziland Conference of Churches | E-nC | 7-d | 1929 | 125,000 | 1 | swaz | C | 5 | SCC. Conciliar membership, from Catholics to AICs. In practice rivals CSC. |
| Swedish Evangelical Alliance | E-nC | 7-d | 1853 | 400,000 | 1 | swed | C | 5 | SEA. Evangeliska Alliansens Svenska Avdelning |
| Tanzania Evangelical Fellowship | E-nC | 7-c | | 3,100,000 | 1 | tanz | B | 5 | TEF. |
| Tonga Evangelical Union | E-nC | 7-e | c1970 | 2,000 | 1 | tong | C | 5 | TEU. |
| Trinidad & Tobago Council of Ev Chs | E-nC | 7-e | c1940 | 40,000 | 1 | trin | C | 5 | TTCEC. 15 member Evangelical denominations. |
| United Ev Assoc of Antigua-Barbuda | E-nC | 7-e | | 5,000 | 1 | anti | C | 5 | UEAAB. United Evangelical Association of Antigua & Barbuda. |
| Christian Association of Nigeria | F-nC | 7-b | 1976 | 36,000,000 | 1 | nige | B | 5 | CAN, with as members CCN plus RCC and indigenous churches. |
| Council of Ev Churches of Guatemala | F-nC | 7-d | | 200,000 | 1 | guat | C | 5 | CIEDEG. |
| Assoc des Egl et Miss Prot du Mali | G-nC | 7-e | 1963 | 75,000 | 1 | mali | A | 5 | AGEMPEM. Association of Evangelical Protestant Churches & Missions in Mali. |
| Fed Evangelique de la Cote d'Ivoire | G-nC | 7-d | | 370,000 | 1 | ivor | B | 5 | FECI. Evangelical Federation of the Ivory Coast. |
| Nigeria Evangelical Fellowship | G-nC | 7-c | 1966 | 8,000,000 | 1 | nige | B | 5 | NEF. 10 member churches. |
| Uganda Association of Evangelicals | G-nC | 7-d | c1970 | 290,000 | 1 | ugan | C | 5 | UAE. Unofficial body weathering vicious persecution under Amin regime. |
| All-India Pentecostal Fellowship | H-nC | 7-c | 1957 | 1,100,000 | 1 | indi | B | 5 | AIPF. |
| Asoc Pro-Indigenas de Colombia | h-nC | 7-e | | 10,000 | 1 | colo | C | 5 | Association for the Indians of Colombia. |
| Assoc Interconfess du Luxembourg | h-nC | 7-d | 1965 | 390,000 | 1 | luxe | C | 5 | AIL/LIA. Mutual understanding with Catholics, Protestants, and Jews. |
| Associated Pentecostal Chs of NZ | H-nC | 7-e | 1975 | 27,100 | 1 | newz | C | 5 | NZ=New Zealand. |
| Australian Pentecostal Ministers' Fell | h-nC | 7-d | | 130,000 | 1 | aust | C | 5 | Fellowship of the leaders of Pentecostal denominations in Australia. |
| British Pentecostal Fellowship | H-nC | 7-d | 1948 | 200,000 | 1 | brit | C | 5 | BPF. |
| Bund Pfingstlicher Gemeinden | H-nC | 7-e | 1961 | 51,000 | 1 | swit | C | 5 | Federation of Pentecostal Churches. |
| Comite Interreligieux Mauricien | h-nC | 7-c | c1970 | 1,100,000 | 1 | maus | B | 5 | Mauritius Inter-Religious Committee (World Fraternal Solidarity). 17 chs, Hindus, Muslims. |
| Fell of Ev Pentecostal Chs in Italy | H-nC | 7-e | | 80,000 | 1 | ital | C | 5 | FEPCI. |
| Ghana Pentecostal Council | H-nC | 7-d | c1985 | 850,000 | 1 | ghan | B | 5 | GPC. Grouping of older Pentecostal bodies with 66 member chs, led by AoG, CoP, AC, CAC. |
| Indep Pentecostal Council of Austria | H-nC | 7-e | | 20,000 | 1 | ausz | C | 5 | IPCA. |
| National Council of Pentecostal Chs | H-nC | 7-d | 1979 | 220,000 | 1 | papu | C | 5 | NCPC. |
| Pentecostal Fell Union of Liberia | H-nC | 7-d | | 111,000 | 1 | libe | B | 5 | PFUL. |
| Pentecostal Fellowship of Malawi | H-nC | 7-d | | 120,000 | 1 | mala | C | 5 | PFM. |
| Reformiertie Bund | h-nC | 7-c | | 2,000,000 | 1 | germ | C | 5 | Federation of Reformed Churches. 1,000 congregations, mostly in EKD or United bodies. |
| Union des Egl Ev de Pentecote Belge | H-nC | 7-e | | 12,000 | 1 | belg | C | 5 | Union of Belgian Pentecostal Churches. Vereniging van der Evangelisch Pinkster Kerken in. |
| Africa Independent Churches Assoc | I-nC | 7-c | c1950 | 2,500,000 | 1 | soua | C | 5 | AICA. Members: over 600 indigenous denominations. Affiliated to SACC, OAIC. |
| African Independent Churches' Conf | I-nC | 7-c | c1960 | 3,400,000 | 1 | zimb | B | 5 | AICC. Fambidzano Yamakereke Avatema, formalized in 1972 with 20 AICs. |
| Afro-West Indian United Coun of Chs | I-nC | 7-d | 1977 | 800,000 | 1 | brit | C | 5 | Afro-Caribbean United Church Council. Members: 30 out of 130 Black denominations in UK. |
| Asoc Fraternal de Igls Pentecostales | I-nC | 7-d | | 850,000 | 1 | mexi | C | 5 | AFIPM. Pentecostal Fraternal Assoc of Mexico. Many large indigenous denominations. |
| Assoc des Egl Chretiennes du Togo | I-nC | 7-e | 1940 | 30,000 | 1 | togo | B | 5 | AECT. Association of Christian Churches in Togo. Independent indigenous AICs. |
| Association of Independent Chs | I-nC | 7-c | c1960 | 1,100,000 | 1 | zamb | C | 5 | AIC. Initially with 10 member AIC denominations. |

*Continued overleaf*

*Table 17–6 continued*

| Name of religion/religionists 1 | Pedigree 2 | Type 3 | Begun 4 | Adherents 5 | Ext 6 | Coun 7 | W 8 | X 9 | E. g. = examples; name for God, other religions present, D=denominations, M=missions. 10 |
|---|---|---|---|---|---|---|---|---|---|
| Botswana Spiritual Council of Chs | I-nC | 7-d | | 450,000 | 1 | bots | B | 5 | BSCC. |
| Confederacao Pentecostal do Brasil | I-nC | 7-b | 1959 | 25,200,000 | 1 | braz | C | 5 | CPB. Brazil Pentecostal Federation. Over 20 member denominations. |
| Conseil Superieur des Sac EUJ-C | I-nC | 7-c | c1950 | 1,000,000 | 1 | conz | C | 5 | COSSEUJCA. Eglises-Unies de Jesus-Christ. Supreme Council of Priests/Sacrificateurs. |
| Fed des Egl Indep de Madagascar | I-nC | 7-d | c1960 | 340,000 | 1 | mada | B | 5 | FFKMMT. Federation of Independent Chs of Madagascar. |
| Federal Council of African Churches | I-nC | 7-e | | 60,000 | 1 | leso | C | 5 | FCAC. |
| League of African Chs in Swaziland | I-nC | 7-d | 1937 | 380,000 | 1 | swaz | C | 5 | LACS. Inhlanganl Yamabandla Enkola Esizwe. Serves 30 African indigenous AICs. |
| Maori Council of Churches | I-nC | 7-d | | 250,000 | 1 | newz | C | 5 | MCC. |
| Nat Spiritual Baptist Council of Chs | I-nC | 7-e | c1950 | 11,000 | 1 | trin | C | 5 | NSBCC. |
| Nigeria Association of Aladura Chs | I-nC | 7-c | 1960 | 2,100,000 | 1 | nige | B | 5 | NAAC. Isokan Ijo Aladura Nigeria (IIAN). HQ Ibadan. Powerful; 200 member AICs. |
| Org of African Indep Chs of Kenya | I-nC | 7-c | | 4,000,000 | 1 | keny | C | 5 | OAICK. |
| Philippines for Jesus Movement | I-nC | 7-c | 1983 | 1,100,000 | 1 | phil | C | 5 | PJM. Umbrella organization for 4,300 independent charismatic fellowships and churches. |
| Reformed Indep Chs Assoc of Malawi | I-nC | 7-d | c1970 | 350,000 | 1 | mala | C | 5 | RICAM. |
| Supreme Council for Ghana Pent Chs | I-nC | 7-c | c1970 | 2,550,000 | 1 | ghan | B | 5 | SCGPC (formerly Council of Indep Chs of Ghana, or NCSC, GCLC). 500 Spiritual bodies. |
| Union de Missions Pente Libres | I-nC | 7-e | c1975 | 15,000 | 1 | chil | C | 5 | UMPL. Union of Free Pentecostal Missions and Churches. 40 member denominations. |
| United Pent Full Gospel Chs of I | I-nC | 7-c | c1950 | 2,100,000 | 1 | indo | B | 5 | UPFGCI. Alamat Jemaat-Jemaat Dari Gereja-Gereja Injil Penuh. I=Indonesia. |
| Uniting Aboriginal and Islander CC | I-nC | 7-e | | 20,000 | 1 | aust | C | 5 | UAICC. CC=Christian Congress. |
| Council of African & Allied Chs in UK | J-nC | 7-d | 1979 | 100,000 | 1 | brit | C | 5 | CAAC. Some 20 Black denominations. |
| Fed of Non-White Pent Chs in Africa | J-nC | 7-d | | 200,000 | 1 | soua | C | 5 | Federasie Pinkster Sending Kerke in South Africa. |
| Followers of Christ Assoc of Malawi | J-nC | 7-d | c1970 | 400,000 | 1 | mala | C | 5 | FCAM. Independent indigenous churches. |
| Int Spiritual and United IAC | J-nC | 7-c | | 1,000,000 | 1 | keny | C | 5 | IAC=Indigenous African Churches. |
| National Fraternal Council of Chs | J-nC | 7-c | 1929 | 6,175,000 | 1 | usa | C | 5 | NFCC. 1929, Negro (now Black) denominations. |
| Pentecostal Association of Ghana | J-nC | 7-d | c1980 | 500,000 | 1 | ghan | B | 5 | PAG. 89 member Spiritual denominations. |
| Antigua Christian Council | K-nC | 7-e | | 41,000 | 1 | anti | C | 5 | ACC. |
| Belize Christian Council | K-nC | 7-d | 1957 | 180,000 | 1 | beli | C | 5 | BCC. Protestants, Anglicans and (since 1969) Roman Catholics. |
| China Christian Council | K-nC | 7-b | 1949 | 12,193,000 | 1 | chin | B | 5 | CCC. Revived after 1970. Very influential by 1985. |
| Christian Council of Lesotho | K-nC | 7-d | | 360,000 | 1 | leso | C | 5 | CCL. Lekhotla la Likereke la Lesotho. |
| Christian Council of Nigeria | K-nC | 7-b | 1930 | 23,000,000 | 1 | nige | B | 5 | CCN. 9 member denominations. |
| Christian Council of St Vincent | K-nC | 7-e | 1969 | 42,200 | 1 | saiv | C | 5 | CCSV. |
| Christian Council of Tanzania | K-nC | 7-c | 1936 | 6,250,000 | 1 | tanz | B | 5 | CCT. Jumuiya ya Makanisa ya Tanzania. |
| Christian Interconfessional ConsCom | K-nC | 7-b | | 60,000,000 | 1 | russ | B | 5 | CICC. (for CIS & Baltic countries). ConsCom=Consultative Committee. |
| Comite Espanol de Coop Entre Igls | K-nC | 7-e | | 67,000 | 1 | spai | C | 5 | CECI. Spanish Committee of Cooperation between the Churches. |
| Confraternidad Cristiana de Iglesias | K-nC | 7-e | c1970 | 10,000 | 1 | chil | C | 5 | CCI. Christian Fellowship of Churches in Chile (CFCC). |
| Conseil des Eglises du Maroc | K-nC | 7-e | 1977 | 26,000 | 1 | moro | A | 5 | Morocco Council of Christian Churches: Catholics, Orthodox, Protestants, Anglicans. |
| Conseil National des Egls du Burundi | K-nC | 7-c | | 1,100,000 | 1 | buru | C | 5 | CNEB. National Council of Churches of Burundi. |
| Conseil Oecu des Egls du Congo | K-nC | 7-d | 1943 | 400,000 | 1 | cong | C | 5 | Oecu=Oecumenique. |
| Conseil Protestant du Rwanda | K-nC | 7-c | 1935 | 1,075,000 | 1 | rwan | C | 5 | CPR. Protestant Council of Rwanda. |
| Council for Co-operation of Chs in E | K-nC | 7-b | 1978 | 27,000,000 | 1 | ethi | B | 5 | CCCE. E=Ethiopia. Begun by 9 of Ethiopia's largest denominations. |
| Ecumenical Advisory Council for CSE | K-nC | 7-c | | 8,995,000 | 1 | egyp | B | 5 | EACCSE. CSE=Church Service in Egypt. |
| Ecumenical Assoc of Chs in Romania | K-nC | 7-b | 1974 | 19,100,000 | 1 | roma | C | 5 | AEBRom. Romanian Council of Churches. |
| Eglise du Christ au Zaire | K-nC | 7-c | 1924 | 9,260,000 | 1 | conz | C | 5 | ECZ. Church of Christ in Zaire. |
| Estonian Council of Churches | K-nC | 7-e | | 40,000 | 1 | esto | B | 5 | ECC. |
| Fed des Egls et Mis Ev du Cameroun | K-nC | 7-d | 1970 | 800,000 | 1 | came | B | 5 | FEMEC. Federation of Protestant Churches & Missions in Cameroon. |
| Federation Protestante de France | K-nC | 7-d | 1913 | 700,000 | 1 | fran | C | 5 | FPF. Protestant Federation of France. |
| Federazione delle Chiese Ev in Italia | K-nC | 7-e | | 49,000 | 1 | ital | C | 5 | FCEI. Federation of Protestant Churches in Italy. |
| Fiji Council of Churches | K-nC | 7-d | 1964 | 350,000 | 1 | fiji | B | 5 | FCC. |
| Guyana Council of Churches | K-nC | 7-e | 1937 | 95,000 | 1 | guya | B | 5 | GCC. 15 member denominations and 4 autonomous regional councils. |
| Iran Council of Churches | K-nC | 7-e | 1951 | 4,500 | 1 | iran | A | 5 | ICC. Shovraye Kelissye Iran. |
| Irish Council of Churches | K-nC | 7-d | 1922 | 152,000 | 1 | irel | C | 5 | ICC. Serves both Eire and Northern Ireland (UK). 10 local councils. |
| Isle of Man Council of Churches | K-nC | 7-e | | 41,000 | 1 | isle | C | 5 | IOMCC. Associate member of Council of Churches for Britain & Ireland (CCBI, formerly BCC). |
| Liberian Council of Churches | K-nC | 7-d | | 270,000 | 1 | libe | B | 5 | LCC. |
| Melanesian Council of Churches | K-nC | 7-c | 1965 | 3,000,000 | 1 | papu | C | 5 | MCC. Covers PNG and SI (Solomon Islands). 1971, Catholics join. |
| Namibian Council of Churches | K-nC | 7-d | 1978 | 930,000 | 1 | nami | C | 5 | NCC. |
| National Council of Chs in Lithuania | K-nC | 7-d | | 150,000 | 1 | lith | C | 5 | NCCL. |
| National Council of Chs in Taiwan | K-nC | 7-d | | 630,000 | 1 | taiw | B | 5 | NCCT. |
| National Council of Chs of Kenya | K-nC | 7-c | 1918 | 8,521,000 | 1 | keny | C | 5 | NCCK. 1943, Christian Council of Kenya. 30 member denominations. |
| Oecumenische Raad van Kerken | K-nC | 7-e | 1962 | 11,500 | 1 | nets | C | 5 | Curacao Ecumenical Council of Churches. |
| Religious Advisory Council of the CI | K-nC | 7-e | | 12,000 | 1 | cook | C | 5 | CI=Cook Islands. |
| Servicio Social de Igls Dominicanas | K-nC | 7-d | 1962 | 300,000 | 1 | domr | C | 5 | SSID. Social Organization of the Domican Churches. Members: 20 denominations. |
| Solomon Islands Christian Association | K-nC | 7-d | | 310,000 | 1 | solo | C | 5 | SICA. |
| Sudan Council of Churches | K-nC | 7-c | 1965 | 5,700,000 | 1 | suda | B | 5 | SCC. Maglis al Kanayis fi Sudan. 10 denominations including RCC. |
| Swiss Christian Council of Churches | K-nC | 7-c | | 6,100,000 | 1 | swit | C | 5 | ACKS. Arbeitsgemeinschaft Christlicher Kirchen in der Schweiz. |
| Tonga Council of Churches | K-nC | 7-e | 1968 | 69,500 | 1 | tong | C | 5 | TCC. 1968, Inter-Church Committee; 1973 name changed. |
| Uganda Joint Christian Council | K-nC | 7-b | 1963 | 15,500,000 | 1 | ugan | C | 5 | UJCC. Effective close cooperation: members Anglicans, Catholics, Orthodox. |
| United Christian Council in Israel | K-nC | 7-e | 1956 | 11,000 | 1 | isra | B | 5 | UCCI. |
| United Christian Council in Palestine | K-nC | 7-e | 1957 | 6,000 | 1 | pale | B | 5 | UCCP. Originated in, and still related to UCCI (Israel). |
| Vanuatu Christian Council | K-nC | 7-d | 1967 | 140,000 | 1 | vanu | C | 5 | VCC. 1967. New Hebrides Christian Council founded with 4 member denominations. |
| Yugoslav Ecumenical Council | K-nC | 7-c | 1968 | 5,400,000 | 1 | yugo | C | 5 | Ecumenical Council of Churches in Yugoslavia (ECCY). |
| Bahamas Christian Council | N-nC | 7-d | 1948 | 210,000 | 1 | baha | C | 5 | BCC. |
| Bangladesh National Council of Chs | N-nC | 7-d | 1954 | 100,000 | 1 | bang | B | 5 | BNCC. Founded as East Pakistan Christian Council. |
| Christian Council of Malawi | N-nC | 7-c | 1939 | 1,726,000 | 1 | mala | C | 5 | CCM. Member denominations 15. |
| Christian Council of Trinidad and T | N-nC | 7-d | 1966 | 630,000 | 1 | trin | C | 5 | CCTT. T=Tobago. 12 denominations including RCC. |
| Com Miss de l'Egl Prot Unie de Belg | N-nC | 7-e | | 2,000 | 1 | belg | C | 5 | Missionary Commission of the United Protestant Church of Belgium. |
| Concilio Evangelico de Puerto Rico | N-nC | 7-d | 1954 | 500,000 | 1 | puer | C | 5 | CEPR. Evangelical Council of Puerto Rico. |
| Conseil Chretien des Egls a Madaga | N-nC | 7-c | 1958 | 3,400,000 | 1 | mada | B | 5 | CCEM. Christian Council of Churches in Madagascar. |
| Consejo de Iglesias de Cuba | N-nC | 7-e | 1941 | 80,000 | 1 | cuba | B | 5 | CIC. Council of Churches of Cuba. |
| Council of Ch of Christ in Thailand | N-nC | 7-e | 1930 | 85,000 | 1 | thai | B | 5 | CCT. Begun 1930 as Siam National Christian Council. |
| Egl de Jesus-Christ sur la Terre par P | N-nC | 7-c | | 7,500,000 | 1 | conz | C | 5 | Church of Jesus Christ on Earth through the Prophet Simon Kimbangu. |
| Federacion Argentina de Iglesias Ev | N-nC | 7-d | 1950 | 900,000 | 1 | arge | C | 5 | Argentina Federation of Evangelical Churches. |
| Federacion de Igls Ev del Uruguay | N-nC | 7-e | 1956 | 30,000 | 1 | uuay | C | 5 | FIEU. Federation of Evangelical Churches of Uruguay. 10 denominations. |
| Federacion Evangelica de Mexico | N-nC | 7-c | 1927 | 2,000,000 | 1 | mexi | C | 5 | FEM. Evangelical (Protestant) Federation of Mexico. Related to WCC. 13 denominations. |
| Jamaica Council of Churches | N-nC | 7-d | 1939 | 600,000 | 1 | jama | B | 5 | JCC. Originally only Protestant; 1971 Anglicans and Catholics join. |
| National Council of Chs in Korea | N-nC | 7-c | 1919 | 4,300,000 | 1 | souk | B | 5 | NCCK. Hankuk Kidokyo Yonhap-hui. Present name 1946. |
| National Council of Chs in Pakistan | N-nC | 7-c | 1923 | 1,600,000 | 1 | paki | A | 5 | NCCP. 1923 Punjab Christian Council; subequent name changes 1949, 1971, 1976. |
| Pentecostal Council of Chile | N-nC | 7-c | c1950 | 1,812,000 | 1 | chil | C | 5 | PCC. |
| United Chr Council of Sierra Leone | N-nC | 7-d | 1924 | 172,000 | 1 | sier | B | 5 | UCCSL. Members: 12 denominations. |
| Comite Interepiscopal Orth de France | O-nC | 7-d | | 300,000 | 1 | fran | C | 5 | Orthodox Interepiscopal Liaison Committee of France. |
| Conf des Eveques de Burkina Faso | P-nC | 7-c | 1978 | 1,129,000 | 1 | burk | B | 5 | CEBFN. Bishops' Conference of Burkina Faso & Niger. HQ Ouagadougou. |
| Conference Episcopale du Laos et C | P-nC | 7-e | 1971 | 54,000 | 1 | camb | A | 5 | CELAC. HQ Thakhek, Laos. Bishops' Conference of Laos & Cambodia. |
| Conference Episcopale du Rwanda | P-nC | 7-c | 1980 | 3,942,000 | 1 | rwan | C | 5 | CER. Bishops' Conference of Rwanda. |
| Inter-Territorial Epis Conf of G,L,SL | P-nC | 7-d | 1983 | 350,000 | 1 | sier | B | 5 | ITEC of the Gambia, Liberia and Sierra Leone. HQ Freetown. |
| As des Patriarches et Eveques Cath L | R-nC | 7-c | c1960 | 1,395,000 | 1 | leba | B | 5 | L=Liban. Assembly of Catholic Patriarchs and Bishops of Lebanon. |
| Ass of Cath Bishops of Hungary | R-nC | 7-c | 1990 | 6,330,000 | 1 | hung | C | 5 | MPKK. Magyar Puspoki Kar Konferencija. HQ Budapest. |
| Assem de la Hierarchie Cath en Syrie | R-nC | 7-d | | 325,000 | 1 | syri | B | 5 | Assembly of Bishops in the Syrian Arab Republic. |
| Bishops' Conference of Sri Lanka | R-nC | 7-c | 1988 | 1,260,000 | 1 | sril | B | 5 | BCSL. Lanka Raja Guru Sammelanaya. HQ Colombo. |
| Bulgarian Catholic Bishops' Conf | R-nC | 7-e | | 90,000 | 1 | bulg | C | 5 | MEKB. Mejduritualnata Episcopska Konferenzia vav Balgaria. HQ Sofia. |
| Cath Bishops' Conf of the Philippines | R-nC | 7-b | 1988 | 62,570,000 | 1 | phil | C | 5 | CBCP. HQ Manila. |
| Catholic Bishops' Conf of Bangladesh | R-nC | 7-d | 1978 | 235,000 | 1 | bang | B | 5 | CBCB. HQ Dhaka. |
| Catholic Bishops' Conf of Japan | R-nC | 7-d | 1973 | 460,000 | 1 | japa | B | 5 | CBCJ. HQ Tokyo. |
| Catholic Bishops' Conference of India | R-nC | 7-b | 1976 | 15,500,000 | 1 | indi | B | 5 | CBCI. HQ New Delhi. |
| Chinese Cath Bps' Conf on Mainland | R-nC | 7-c | | 7,500,000 | 1 | chin | B | 5 | CBCM. |
| Conf de Obispos Catolicos de Cuba | R-nC | 7-c | 1993 | 4,367,000 | 1 | cuba | B | 5 | COCC. Bishops' Conference of Cuba. HQ La Habana. |
| Conf del Episcopado Dominicano | R-nC | 7-c | 1985 | 7,522,000 | 1 | domr | C | 5 | CED. Conference of the Dominican Episcopate. HQ Santo Domingo. |
| Conf del Episcopado Mexicano | R-nC | 7-b | 1979 | 92,770,000 | 1 | mexi | C | 5 | CEM. Conference of the Mexican Episcopate. HQ Cuautitlan Izcalli. |
| Conf des Eveques Cath du Burundi | R-nC | 7-c | 1980 | 3,827,000 | 1 | buru | C | 5 | CECAB. Catholic Bishops' Conference of Burundi. HQ Bujumbura. |
| Conf des Eveques Cath du Canada | R-nC | 7-b | 1986 | 12,400,000 | 1 | cana | C | 5 | CECC. Canadian Conference of Catholic Bishops. HQ Ottawa. |
| Conf Epis Portuguesa da Metropole | R-nC | 7-c | 1985 | 8,970,000 | 1 | port | C | 5 | CEPM. Portuguese Metropolitan Episcopal Conference. HQ Lisbon. |

*Continued opposite*

*Table 17–6 continued*

| Name of religion/religionists 1 | Pedigree 2 | Type 3 | Begun 4 | Adherents 5 | Ext 6 | Coun 7 | W 8 | X 9 | E. g. = examples; name for God, other religions present, D=denominations, M=missions. 10 |
|---|---|---|---|---|---|---|---|---|---|
| Conf Episcopal de Guinea Ecuatorial | R-nC | 7-d | 1984 | 391,000 | 1 | equa | C | 5 | CEGE. Episcopal Conference of Equatorial Guinea. HQ Malabo. |
| Conf Episcopal Puertorriquena | R-nC | 7-c | 1986 | 2,900,000 | 1 | puer | C | 5 | CEP. Puerto Rico Episcopal Conference. HQ San Juan. |
| Conf Episcopale de la Cote d'Ivoire | R-nC | 7-c | 1973 | 2,182,000 | 1 | ivor | B | 5 | CECI. Episcopal Conference of the Ivory Coast. HQ Abidjan. |
| Conf Episcopale du Congo-Zaire | R-nC | 7-b | 1981 | 26,300,000 | 1 | conz | C | 5 | CEZ. Episcopal Conference of Congo-Zaire. HQ Kinshasa-Gombe. |
| Conf Episcopale Nat du Cameroun | R-nC | 7-c | 1989 | 3,989,000 | 1 | came | B | 5 | CENC. Episcopal Conference of Cameroon. |
| Conf of Catholic Bps of India/Latin R | R-nC | 7-b | 1994 | 10,740,000 | 1 | indi | B | 5 | CCBI-LR. HQ. New Delhi. Latin Rite Bishops Conference. |
| Confe Nacional dos Bispos do Brasil | R-nC | 7-b | 1986 | 153,000,000 | 1 | braz | C | 5 | CNBB. HQ Brasilia. |
| Conference des Eveques de France | R-nC | 7-b | 1975 | 48,600,000 | 1 | fran | C | 5 | CEF. Episcopal Conference of France. HQ Paris. |
| Conference Episcopale Centrafricaine | R-nC | 7-d | 1982 | 664,000 | 1 | cent | B | 5 | CECA. Bishops Conference of the CAR. HQ Bangui. |
| Conference Episcopale de Belgique | R-nC | 7-c | 1984 | 8,222,000 | 1 | belg | C | 5 | Episcopal Conference of Belgium. HQ Brussels. |
| Conference Episcopale de Haiti | R-nC | 7-c | 1987 | 6,520,000 | 1 | hait | C | 5 | CEH. Episcopal Conference of Haiti. HQ Port-au-Prince. |
| Conference Episcopale de la Guinee | R-nC | 7-d | c1990 | 117,000 | 1 | guin | A | 5 | CEG. HQ Conakry. |
| Conference Episcopale du Benin | R-nC | 7-c | | 1,266,000 | 1 | beni | B | 5 | CEB. HQ Cotonou. |
| Conference Episcopale du Gabon | R-nC | 7-d | 1989 | 745,000 | 1 | gabo | C | 5 | CEG. Episcopal Conference of Gabon. HQ Oyem. |
| Conference Episcopale du Mali | R-nC | 7-d | 1973 | 126,000 | 1 | mali | A | 5 | CEM. Episcopal Conference of Mali. HQ Bamako. |
| Conference Episcopale du Tchad | R-nC | 7-d | 1991 | 502,000 | 1 | chad | B | 5 | CET. Chad Episcopal Conference. HQ N'Djamena. |
| Conference Episcopale du Togo | R-nC | 7-c | 1979 | 1,122,000 | 1 | togo | B | 5 | CET. Episcopal Conference of Togo. HQ Lome. |
| Conference of the Chs of Indonesia | R-nC | 7-c | 1973 | 5,752,000 | 1 | indo | B | 5 | KWI. Konperensi Waligereja Indonesia. HQ Jakarta. Formerly Bishops' Conf of Indonesia. |
| Conferencia Episcopal Argentina | R-nC | 7-b | 1987 | 31,750,000 | 1 | arge | C | 5 | Argentina Episcopal Conference (CEA). HQ Buenos Aires. |
| Conferencia Episcopal Boliviana | R-nC | 7-c | 1989 | 7,350,000 | 1 | boli | C | 5 | CEB. Episcopal Conference of Bolivia. HQ La Paz. |
| Conferencia Episcopal de Chile | R-nC | 7-b | 1994 | 11,900,000 | 1 | chil | C | 5 | CECH. Episcopal Conference of Chile. HQ Santiago. |
| Conferencia Episcopal de Colombia | R-nC | 7-b | 1990 | 40,670,000 | 1 | colo | C | 5 | CEC. Episcopal Conference of Colombia. HQ Bogota. |
| Conferencia Episcopal de Costa Rica | R-nC | 7-c | 1977 | 3,660,000 | 1 | cost | C | 5 | CECOR. Episcopal Conference of Costa Rica. HQ San Jose. |
| Conferencia Episcopal de El Salvador | R-nC | 7-c | 1982 | 5,723,000 | 1 | elsa | C | 5 | CEDES. Episcopal Conference of El Salvador. HQ San Salvador. |
| Conferencia Episcopal de Guatemala | R-nC | 7-c | 1973 | 9,600,000 | 1 | guat | C | 5 | CEG. Episcopal Conference of Guatemala. HQ Guatemala City. |
| Conferencia Episcopal de Honduras | R-nC | 7-c | 1987 | 5,590,000 | 1 | hond | C | 5 | CEH. HQ Tegucigalpa. |
| Conferencia Episcopal de Nicaragua | R-nC | 7-c | 1987 | 4,320,000 | 1 | nica | C | 5 | CEN. Episcopal Conference of Nicaragua. HQ Managua. |
| Conferencia Episcopal de Panama | R-nC | 7-c | 1986 | 2,210,000 | 1 | pana | C | 5 | CEP. Episcopal Conference of Panama. HQ Panama City. |
| Conferencia Episcopal Ecuatoriana | R-nC | 7-b | 1985 | 11,900,000 | 1 | ecua | C | 5 | Ecuador Episcopal Conference. HQ Quito. |
| Conferencia Episcopal Espanola | R-nC | 7-b | 1991 | 38,080,000 | 1 | spai | C | 5 | CEE. Spanish Episcopal Conference. HQ Madrid. |
| Conferencia Episcopal Paraguaya | R-nC | 7-c | 1984 | 4,950,000 | 1 | para | C | 5 | CEP. Paraguay Episcopal Conference. HQ Asuncion. |
| Conferencia Episcopal Peruana | R-nC | 7-b | 1992 | 24,550,000 | 1 | peru | C | 5 | CEP. Peru Episcopal Conference. HQ Lima. |
| Conferencia Episcopal Uruguaya | R-nC | 7-c | 1990 | 2,608,000 | 1 | uuay | C | 5 | CEU. Uruguay Episcopal Conference. HQ Montevideo. |
| Conferencia Episcopal Venezolana | R-nC | 7-b | 1985 | 22,816,000 | 1 | vene | C | 5 | CEV. Venezuela Episcopal Conference. HQ Caracas. |
| Conferentia Episcopalis Lettoniae | R-nC | 7-d | | 490,000 | 1 | latv | C | 5 | CEL. Latvian Episcopal Conference. HQ Riga. |
| Conferentia Episcopalis Lituaniae | R-nC | 7-c | 1992 | 3,105,000 | 1 | lith | C | 5 | CEL. Episcopal Conference of Lithuania. HQ Vilnius. |
| Conferentia Episcopolis Graeciae | R-nC | 7-e | 1967 | 62,000 | 1 | gree | C | 5 | CEG. Episcopal Conference of Greece. HQ Athens. |
| Conferenza Episcopale dell'Albania | R-nC | 7-d | | 492,000 | 1 | alba | B | 5 | Episcopal Conference of Albania. HQ Shkodre. |
| Conferenza Episcopale Italiana | R-nC | 7-b | 1985 | 55,680,000 | 1 | ital | C | 5 | CEI. Italian Episcopal Conference. HQ Roma. |
| Croatian Episcopal Conference | R-nC | 7-c | 1993 | 3,960,000 | 1 | croa | C | 5 | HBK. Hrvatska Biskupska Konferencija. HQ Zagreb. |
| Czech Bishops' Conference | R-nC | 7-c | 1993 | 4,135,000 | 1 | czec | B | 5 | CBK. Ceska Biskupska Konference. HQ Prague. |
| Deutsche Bischofskonferenz | R-nC | 7-b | 1992 | 28,700,000 | 1 | germ | C | 5 | HQ Bonn/Berlin. Member of ACKD/CCCG. |
| Epis Conf of Bosnia-Herzegovina | R-nC | 7-d | | 681,000 | 1 | bosn | B | 5 | BKBIH. Biskupska Konferencija Bosne i Hercegovine. |
| Episcopal Conference of Malawi | R-nC | 7-c | 1969 | 2,697,000 | 1 | mala | C | 5 | ECM. HQ Lilongwe. |
| Episcopal Conference of Thailand | R-nC | 7-d | 1969 | 255,000 | 1 | thai | B | 5 | Sapa Sangkharat Heng Prathet Thai. Bishops' Conference of Thailand. HQ Bangkok. |
| Episcopal Conference of Turkey | R-nC | 7-e | 1978 | 25,000 | 1 | turk | A | 5 | Conferenza Episcopale della Turchia. |
| Ghana Bishops' Conference | R-nC | 7-c | 1993 | 1,925,000 | 1 | ghan | B | 5 | GBC. HQ Accra. |
| Inter-Rite Bishops' Meeting in Iraq | R-nC | 7-d | c1970 | 268,000 | 1 | iraq | A | 5 | Riunione Interrituale dei Vescovi dell'Iraq. |
| Iranian Episcopal Conference | R-nC | 7-e | 1977 | 16,400 | 1 | iran | A | 5 | Conferenza Episcopale Iraniana. |
| Kenya Episcopal Conference | R-nC | 7-c | 1976 | 7,000,000 | 1 | keny | C | 5 | KEC. HQ Nairobi. |
| Malta Episcopal Conference | R-nC | 7-d | 1971 | 368,000 | 1 | malt | C | 5 | MEC. Konferenza Episkopali Maltija. KEM. HQ Floriana. |
| Myanmar Catholic Bishops Conf | R-nC | 7-d | 1982 | 590,000 | 1 | myan | B | 5 | MCBC. HQ Yangon. |
| National Conf of Catholic Bishops | R-nC | 7-b | 1981 | 61,000,000 | 1 | usa | C | 5 | NCCB. HQ Washington DC. 2001, with USCC forms US Conf of Catholic Bps (USCCB). |
| New Zealand Episcopal Conference | R-nC | 7-d | 1974 | 495,000 | 1 | newz | C | 5 | NZEC. HQ Wellington. |
| Polish Episcopal Conference | R-nC | 7-b | 1987 | 35,743,000 | 1 | pola | C | 5 | KEP. Konferencja Episkopatu Polski. HQ Warsaw. |
| Tanzania Episcopal Conference | R-nC | 7-c | 1980 | 8,283,000 | 1 | tanz | B | 5 | TEC. HQ Dar-es-Salaam. |
| Australian Catholic Bishops' Conf | S-nC | 7-c | 1979 | 5,400,000 | 1 | aust | C | 5 | ACBC. HQ. Canberra. |
| Bishops' Assembly of Egypt | S-nC | 7-d | 1983 | 225,000 | 1 | egyp | B | 5 | Assemblea della Gerarchia Cattolica d'Egitto. |
| Bishops' Conf of England & Wales | s-nC | 7-c | 1987 | 4,228,000 | 1 | brit | C | 5 | HQ London. |
| Conf Episcopale de Madagascar | S-nC | 7-c | 1969 | 3,662,000 | 1 | mada | B | 5 | CEM. Episcopal Conference of Madagascar. HQ Antananarivo. |
| Conference des Eveques Suisses | S-nC | 7-c | 1975 | 3,260,000 | 1 | swit | C | 5 | CES. Schweizerische Bischofskonferenz/Conferenza di Vescovi Svizzeri. HQ Fribourg. |
| Ethiopian Episcopal Conference | S-nC | 7-d | 1966 | 450,000 | 1 | ethi | B | 5 | EEC. Consiglio della Chiesa Etiopica. HQ Addis Ababa. (Roman Catholic). |
| Lesotho Catholic Bishops' Conf | S-nC | 7-d | 1980 | 806,000 | 1 | leso | C | 5 | LCBC. HQ Maseru. |
| Netherlands Bishops' Conference | S-nC | 7-c | 1986 | 5,450,000 | 1 | neth | C | 5 | Nederlandse Bisschoppen Konferentie. HQ Utrecht. |
| Osterreichische Bischofskonferenz | S-nC | 7-c | 1979 | 6,129,000 | 1 | ausz | C | 5 | Bishops' Conference of Austria. HQ Vienna. |
| Pakistan Episcopal Conference | s-nC | 7-c | 1976 | 1,165,000 | 1 | paki | A | 5 | PEC. Catholic Bishops' Conference of Pakistan CBCP. HQ Lahore. |
| Romanian Catholic Episcopal Conf | S-nC | 7-c | 1993 | 3,237,000 | 1 | roma | C | 5 | CER. Conferinte Episcopala Romania. |
| Sudan Episcopal Conference | S-nC | 7-c | 1971 | 3,148,000 | 1 | suda | B | 5 | SEC, SCBC. Sudan Catholic Bishops' Conference. HQ Khartoum. |
| Uganda Episcopal Conference | S-nC | 7-c | 1974 | 9,130,000 | 1 | ugan | C | 5 | UEC. HQ Kampala. |
| Zimbabwe Catholic Bishops' Conf | s-nC | 7-c | 1981 | 1,120,000 | 1 | zimb | B | 5 | ZCBC. HQ Harare. |
| American Christian Action Council | T-nC | 7-d | c1970 | 230,000 | 1 | usa | C | 4 | ACAC. Fundamentalists, affiliated to ICCC. |
| Argentina Consultative Com of ICCC | T-nC | 7-e | c1965 | 4,000 | 1 | arge | C | 4 | ACCICCC. |
| Australian Consultative Co of ICCC | T-nC | 7-d | c1950 | 100,000 | 1 | aust | C | 3 | ACCC. Co=Council. |
| British Council of Prot Christian Chs | T-nC | 7-e | | 3,000 | 1 | brit | C | 3 | BCPCC. |
| C Fundamentalista de Igl Ev de Chile | T-nC | 7-e | c1960 | 37,000 | 1 | chil | C | 3 | CFEC. Confederation of Evangelical Fundamentalist Churches of Chile. 10 denominations. |
| C of Fundamental Ev Chs of Bolivia | T-nC | 7-e | | 2,000 | 1 | boli | C | 3 | CIEFB. Confederacion das Iglesias Fundamentalistas Evangelicas de Bolivia. |
| Canadian Council of Ev Prot Chs | T-nC | 7-e | | 50,000 | 1 | cana | C | 4 | CCEPC. |
| Confed das Ig Ev Fundamentalistas | T-nC | 7-e | | 25,000 | 1 | braz | C | 3 | CIEF. Evangelical Federation of Fundamental Churches of Brazil. |
| Congo-Zaire Council of ICCC | T-nC | 7-e | c1960 | 15,000 | 1 | conz | C | 3 | CCICCC. |
| Council of Christian Chs in India | T-nC | 7-d | c1960 | 250,000 | 1 | indi | B | 4 | CCCI. Originally founded as India Bible Christian Council. |
| East Africa Christian Alliance | T-nC | 7-d | 1965 | 520,000 | 1 | keny | C | 4 | EACA. Kenya Fundamentalists, affiliated to ICCC, with CCA as largest denomination. |
| Guyana Council of the ICCC | T-nC | 7-e | | 1,700 | 1 | guya | B | 4 | GCICCC. |
| Hong Kong ICCC-related Council | T-nC | 7-e | | 7,000 | 1 | chin | B | 4 | HKICCC. |
| Indonesian Council of Christian Chs | T-nC | 7-e | | 50,000 | 1 | indo | B | 3 | ICCC. |
| Japan Bible Christian Council | T-nC | 7-e | 1951 | 10,000 | 1 | japa | B | 3 | JBCC. |
| Korean Ev Council of Christian Chs | T-nC | 7-c | c1950 | 3,300,000 | 1 | souk | B | 4 | KECCC, also called NAE (National Association of Evangelicals). Fundamentalists. |
| Malaysia Council of Christian Chs | T-nC | 7-e | | 5,000 | 1 | malb | B | 4 | MCCC. |
| NZ Consultative Co of ICCC | T-nC | 7-e | | 5,000 | 1 | newz | C | 4 | NZCCC. Co=Council. NZ=New Zealand. Related to ICCC (USA) |
| Pakistan Council of Christian Chs | T-nC | 7-e | c1955 | 90,000 | 1 | paki | A | 3 | PCCC. Fundamentalists, with 5 member denominations. |
| Philippine Co of Fundamental Ev Chs | T-nC | 7-d | c1960 | 140,000 | 1 | phil | C | 4 | PCFEC. Co=Council. |
| Republic of China Co of Christian Chs | T-nC | 7-e | c1960 | 11,000 | 1 | taiw | B | 4 | RCCCC. Co=Council. Fundamentalists related to ICCC. |
| Conference Episcopale du Congo | V-nC | 7-c | 1992 | 1,451,000 | 1 | cong | C | 5 | CEC. Episcopal Conference of the Congo. HQ Brazzaville. |
| National Episcopal Conf of Nigeria | V-nC | 7-b | 1976 | 13,400,000 | 1 | nige | B | 5 | NECN. Catholic Bishops' Conference of Nigeria. HQ Lagos. |
| Zambia Episcopal Conference | V-nC | 7-c | 1984 | 3,070,000 | 1 | zamb | C | 5 | ZEC. HQ Lusaka. |
| Botswana Christian Council | W-nC | 7-e | 1966 | 70,000 | 1 | bots | B | 5 | BCC. Lekgotla la Sekeresete la Botswana. |
| Christian Council of Ghana | W-nC | 7-c | 1929 | 3,100,000 | 1 | ghan | B | 5 | CCG. Christian Council of the Gold Coast until 1957. 14 denominations. |
| Churches Together in England | W-nC | 7-b | 1937 | 32,000,000 | 1 | brit | C | 5 | CTE. Preceded by: CCIFSR (1937), BCC (1942). Associated local councils of churches: 750. |
| Communion of Chs in Indonesia | W-nC | 7-b | 1950 | 10,000,000 | 1 | indo | B | 5 | DGI/PGI/CCI. Dewan Gereja-Gereja di Indonesia. Major council, with 60 denominations. |
| Conf of Chs in Aotearoa/New Zealand | W-nC | 7-c | 1941 | 1,557,000 | 1 | newz | C | 5 | CCANZ. 1941 National Council of Churches of New Zealand (NCCONZ). 10 denominations. |
| Conseil Canadien des Eglises | W-nC | 7-c | 1944 | 4,000,000 | 1 | cana | C | 5 | CCE. Canadian Council of Churches. |
| Conselho de Igr Cristas em Angola | W-nC | 7-c | 1977 | 1,500,000 | 1 | ango | C | 5 | Council of Christian Churches in Angola. |
| Conselho Nac de Ig Cristas do Brasil | W-nC | 7-b | | 35,000,000 | 1 | braz | C | 5 | CONIC. National Council of Christian Churches in Brazil. |
| Council of Christian Chs in Germany | W-nC | 7-b | 1948 | 34,000,000 | 1 | germ | C | 5 | CCCG. ACKD. Arbeitsgemeinschaft Christlicher Kirchen in Deutschland. United with East 1991. |
| Council of Christian Chs in Slovenia | W-nC | 7-e | | 20,000 | 1 | slov | C | 5 | CCCS. |
| Council of Chs in the Netherlands | W-nC | 7-c | 1946 | 8,306,000 | 1 | neth | C | 5 | CCN. Raad van Kerken in Nederland. Replaces 1946-68 Ecumenical Council of Chs. |
| Council of Churches of Malaysia | W-nC | 7-d | 1948 | 470,000 | 1 | malb | B | 5 | CCM. Until 1975 'CCM and Singapore'. 10 regional councils. Mainly Chinese. |

*Continued overleaf*

Table 17–6 continued

| Name of religion/religionists 1 | Pedigree 2 | Type 3 | Begun 4 | Adherents 5 | Ext 6 | Coun 7 | W 8 | X 9 | E. g. = examples; name for God, other religions present, D=denominations, M=missions. 10 |
|---|---|---|---|---|---|---|---|---|---|
| Ecumenical Co of Chs in Slovakia | W-nC | 7-d | | 575,000 | 1 | slok | C | 5 | ECCS. |
| Ecumenical Council of Chs in Austria | W-nC | 7-d | | 505,000 | 1 | ausz | C | 5 | ECCA. Okumenischer Rat der Kirchen in Osterreich |
| Ecumenical Council of Chs in the CR | W-nC | 7-d | 1955 | 560,000 | 1 | czec | B | 5 | ECC-CSR. Ecumenicka Rada Cirkvi v Ceske Republice. (Czech Republic). |
| Ecumenical Council of Denmark | W-nC | 7-c | 1939 | 4,700,000 | 1 | denm | C | 5 | Okumeniske Faellesrad i Danmark. |
| Finnish Ecumenical Council | W-nC | 7-c | 1950 | 4,300,000 | 1 | finl | C | 5 | FEC. Suomen Ekumeeninen Neuvosto. Members: 10 major churches of Finland. |
| Gambia Christian Council | W-nC | 7-e | 1963 | 38,000 | 1 | gamb | A | 5 | GCC. Anglicans, Methodists, Catholics. |
| Hong Kong Christian Council | W-nC | 7-d | | 186,000 | 1 | chin | B | 5 | HKCC. |
| Jersey Council of Churches | w-nC | 7-e | c1931 | 60,000 | 1 | chan | C | 5 | JCC. Guernsey Council of Churches (GCC). |
| Myanmar Council of Churches | W-nC | 7-c | 1949 | 2,150,000 | 1 | myan | B | 5 | MCC. 1914 in NCCI;  1949 Burma Christian Council; renamed 1975. 15 regional councils. |
| Nat Co of Chs of American Samoa | W-nC | 7-e | c1970 | 5,000 | 1 | amer | C | 5 | NCCAS. Co=Council. Includes Roman Catholics and nearly all Protestant denominations. |
| National Christian Co of Sri Lanka | W-nC | 7-e | 1923 | 98,000 | 1 | sril | B | 5 | NCCSL. |
| National Christian Council in Japan | W-nC | 7-d | 1911 | 360,000 | 1 | japa | B | 5 | NCCJ. Nippon Kirisutokyo Kyogikai. |
| National Co of Chs in the Philippines | W-nC | 7-c | 1963 | 4,520,000 | 1 | phil | C | 5 | NCCP. Sangguniang Pambansa ng mga Simbahan sa Pilipinas. |
| National Co of Chs of Christ in USA | W-nC | 7-b | 1908 | 49,700,000 | 1 | usa | C | 5 | NCCCUSA. 1908, Federal Council of CCNA. Member denominations: 40. |
| National Council of Chs in Australia | W-nC | 7-c | 1946 | 5,100,000 | 1 | aust | C | 5 | NCCA. |
| National Council of Chs of Singapore | W-nC | 7-d | 1948 | 125,000 | 1 | sing | B | 5 | NCCS. |
| National Council of Churches in India | W-nC | 7-b | 1953 | 12,500,000 | 1 | indi | B | 5 | NCCI. Origin in 1912 Missionary Council, 1921 National Christian Council. 20 denominations. |
| Polish Ecumenical Council | W-nC | 7-c | 1945 | 1,260,000 | 1 | pola | C | 5 | PRE. Polska Rada Ekumeniczna. |
| South African Council of Churches | W-nC | 7-b | 1904 | 12,146,000 | 1 | soua | C | 5 | SACC. 1904, South African General Missionary Conference; 1936, SACC. 16 local councils. |
| Swedish Ecumenical Council | W-nC | 7-c | 1932 | 5,900,000 | 1 | swed | C | 5 | SEC. Svenska Ekumeniska Namnden. |
| Zimbabwe Council of Churches | W-nC | 7-c | 1964 | 2,025,000 | 1 | zimb | B | 5 | ZCC or CCZ. Christian Council of Zimbabwe. |
| Church Army | A-oC | 10-f | 1881 | 480 | 13 | brit | C | 5 | Lay and ordained evangelists in Anglican churches. Foreign missions in 13 countries. |
| Assumptionists | aa-oC | 9-e | 1845 | 1,000 | | ital | C | 5 | AA. |
| Assemblies of God DFM | aog-oC | 9-e | 1914 | 1,800 | 130 | usa | C | 5 | AOGDFM (Division of Foreign Missions). |
| Christian Brethren | cb-oC | 9-e | 1828 | 1,400 | 86 | brit | C | 5 | M=Christian Missions in Many Lands (CMML). HQ Britain. |
| Christian Chs/Chs of Christ | cc-oC | 9-e | 1930 | 1,200 | | usa | C | 5 | CCCC. |
| Campus Crusade for Christ | ccci-oC | 9-e | 1951 | 1,000 | 110 | usa | C | 5 | CCCI. |
| Scheutists | cicm-oC | 9-e | 1862 | 1,400 | | ital | C | 5 | CICM. Decline from 1,946 in 1967. Missionaries of Scheut. |
| Lazarists | cm-oC | 9-e | 1625 | 4,100 | | ital | C | 5 | CM. |
| Christian & Missionary Alliance | cma-oC | 9-e | 1887 | 1,100 | 52 | usa | C | 5 | C&MA. |
| Franciscan Clarissians | cmf-oC | 9-e | 1849 | 5,900 | | ital | C | 5 | CMF. Claretians. |
| Carmelites of Mary | cmi-oC | 9-e | 1856 | 1,900 | | indi | B | 5 | CMI. |
| Passionists | cp-oC | 9-e | 1720 | 1,500 | | ital | C | 5 | CP. |
| Churches of Christ | cs-oC | 9-e | 1930 | 1,000 | | usa | C | 5 | No central missions HQ. Non-instrumental Restoration Movement. |
| Holy Cross | csc-oC | 9-e | 1837 | 1,800 | 15 | ital | C | 5 | CSC. |
| Spiritans | cssp-oC | 9-e | 1703 | 3,200 | | ital | C | 5 | CSSP. |
| Redemptorists | cssr-oC | 9-e | 1732 | 6,000 | | ital | C | 5 | CSSR. |
| Evangelical Alliance Mission | eam-oC | 9-e | 1890 | 1,000 | 34 | brit | C | 5 | TEAM. |
| Visitandine | f-oC | 9-e | | 3,100 | | ital | C | 5 | Visitation Nuns. Drastic decline: (1973) 6,500 in 190 convents, (1996) 2,913 in 154 convents. |
| Canossians | fcc-oC | 9-e | 1831 | 3,700 | 20 | ital | C | 5 | FCC. |
| Providentialists | fdp-oC | 9-e | 1903 | 1,100 | | ital | C | 5 | FDP. |
| Brothers of Christian Instruction | ficp-oC | 9-e | 1817 | 1,300 | | ital | C | 5 | FICP. |
| Marian Brothers (Schools) | fms-oC | 9-e | 1817 | 5,500 | | ital | C | 5 | FMS. |
| Brothers of Schools | fsc-oC | 9-e | 1680 | 7,700 | | ital | C | 5 | FSC. |
| Christian Brothers of Schools | fsc-oC | 9-e | 1802 | 2,000 | | ital | C | 5 | FSC. |
| Southern Baptist IMB | imb-oC | 9-e | 1845 | 4,200 | 150 | usa | C | 5 | IMB = International Mission Board. Formerly Foreign MB. |
| Consolata | imc-oC | 9-e | 1901 | 1,000 | | ital | C | 5 | IMC. |
| Legionaires of Christ | lc-oC | 9-e | 1941 | 1,400 | | ital | C | 5 | LC. |
| Opus Dei | LR-oC | 9-e | 1928 | 76,000 | 80 | ital | C | 5 | Roman Catholic religious order: 1,000 priests. Secrecy, high finance. |
| Missionaries of Charity | mc-oC | 9-e | | 4,000 | | indi | B | 5 | MC. |
| Combonians | mcci-oC | 9-e | 1867 | 2,300 | | ital | C | 5 | MCCI. |
| Camillians | mi-oC | 9-e | 1582 | 1,000 | | ital | C | 5 | MI. |
| Missionaries of the SH of Jesus | msc-oC | 9-e | 1854 | 2,400 | | ital | C | 5 | MSC. SH=Sacred Heart. |
| New Tribes Mission | ntm-oC | 9-e | 1942 | 1,500 | 25 | usa | C | 5 | NTM. |
| Recollect Augustinians | oar-oC | 9-e | 1588 | 1,300 | | ital | C | 5 | OAR. |
| Carmelites | ocarm-oC | 9-e | | 2,100 | | ital | C | 5 | OCarm. HQ Roma. |
| Carthusians | ocart-oC | 10-f | 1084 | 360 | | fran | C | 5 | OCart. F=Bruno. Now 394 monks and 86 nuns, committed to solitude and unbroken silence. |
| Discalced Carmelites | ocd-oC | 9-e | 1562 | 12,500 | | ital | C | 5 | OCD. |
| Cistercians | ocist-oC | 9-e | 1098 | 1,300 | | fran | C | 5 | OCist. Founded with Citeaux abbey. 1115, F=Bernard of Clairvaux. |
| Trappists | ocso-oC | 9-e | 1098 | 2,600 | | ital | C | 5 | OCSO. |
| Franciscans | ofm-oC | 9-e | 1209 | 25,000 | 210 | ital | C | 5 | OFM. F=Francis of Assisi. 3 orders. Friars and priests in over 210 countries. |
| Capuchins | ofmcap-oC | 9-e | 1525 | 11,700 | | ital | C | 5 | OFMCap. |
| Conventual Franciscans | ofmconv-oC | 9-e | | 4,400 | | ital | C | 5 | OFMConv. |
| Hospitallers of St John of God | oh-oC | 9-e | 1537 | 1,500 | | ital | C | 5 | OH, FBF. |
| OMF International | omf-oC | 9-e | 1888 | 1,100 | 28 | brit | C | 5 | Formerly Overseas Missionary Fellowship. Formerly CIM. (China Inland Mission). |
| Oblates of Mary Immaculate | omi-oC | 9-e | 1816 | 5,200 | | ital | C | 5 | OMI. |
| Dominicans | op-oC | 9-e | 1216 | 51,500 | | fran | C | 5 | OP. Order of Preachers. 6,618 friars (4,913 priests, 1,705 brethren), 4,500 nuns, 40,000 sisters. |
| Premonstratensionists | opraem-oC | 9-e | 1120 | 1,300 | · | ital | C | 5 | OPraem. |
| Augustinians | osa-oC | 9-e | 1244 | 3,000 | 60 | ital | C | 5 | OSA. |
| Benedictines | osb-oC | 9-e | c520 | 8,900 | 40 | ital | C | 5 | OSB. F=Benedict of Nursia. Cenobitical. 1408, first Benedictine congregation. |
| Servants of Mary | osm-oC | 9-e | 1233 | 1,100 | | ital | C | 5 | OSM. |
| Sisters of Adoration | sabs-oC | 9-e | | 3,700 | | indi | B | 5 | SABS. Blessed Sacrament Sisters. |
| Pallotinas | sac-oC | 9-e | 1835 | 2,200 | 50 | ital | C | 5 | SAC. |
| Sacred Heart Brothers | sc-oC | 9-e | 1821 | 1,600 | | ital | C | 5 | SC. |
| Dehonians of the Sacred Heart | sci-oC | 9-e | 1878 | 2,500 | | ital | C | 5 | SCI. |
| Salesians | sdb-oC | 9-e | 1859 | 17,600 | | ital | C | 5 | SDB. |
| Salvatorians | sds-oC | 9-e | 1881 | 1,200 | | ital | C | 5 | SDS. |
| Gabriallists | sg-oC | 9-e | 1910 | 1,200 | | ital | C | 5 | SG. Brothers of Christian Instruction of St gabriel. |
| SIM International | sim-oC | 9-e | 1893 | 1,500 | 40 | brit | C | 5 | Formerly Sudan Interior Mission. |
| Jesuits | sj-oC | 9-e | 1540 | 22,600 | 200 | ital | C | 5 | SJ. Society of Jesus. F=Ignatius Loyola. 2,000 universities, colleges, and schools. |
| Mariamites | sm-oC | 9-e | 1817 | 1,800 | | ital | C | 5 | SM. |
| Marianists | sm-oC | 9-e | 1816 | 1,500 | | ital | C | 5 | SM. |
| Society for African Missions | sma-oC | 9-e | 1856 | 1,000 | 15 | ital | C | 5 | SMA. Societas Missionum ad Africa. |
| Montifontani | smm-oC | 9-e | 1705 | 1,100 | | ital | C | 5 | SMM. |
| Acoemetae | sO-oC | 9-e | c450 | 30,000 | 4 | iran | A | 5 | SO. Sleepless Ones. Orthodox ascetics/monks, especially of rule of Basil. |
| Scolopians | sp-oC | 9-e | 1617 | 2,600 | | ital | C | 5 | SP. Piarists. |
| Picpus | sscc-oC | 9-e | 1800 | 1,300 | | ital | C | 5 | SSCC. |
| Paulists | ssp-oC | 9-e | 1914 | 1,200 | | ital | C | 5 | SSP. |
| Sacramentalists | sss-oC | 9-e | 1856 | 1,100 | | ital | C | 5 | SSS. |
| Verbites | svd-oC | 9-e | 1875 | 5,700 | | ital | C | 5 | SVD. |
| Wycliffe Bible Translators | wbt-oC | 9-e | 1934 | 6,300 | 65 | usa | C | 5 | WBT, SIL. |
| WEC International | wec-oC | 9-e | 1913 | 1,500 | 55 | brit | C | 5 | Weccers. Formerly Worldwide Evangelization Crusade. |
| White Fathers | wf-oC | 9-e | 1868 | 2,400 | | ital | C | 5 | WF(PB). Missionaries of Africa (M.Afr.) |
| Youth With A Mission | ywam-oC | 9-e | 1960 | 7,100 | 110 | usa | C | 5 | YWAM. YWAMers. |
| Zoe | z-oC | 10-g | 1907 | 50 | 4 | gree | C | 5 | 'Life'. Oldest and most influential lay Orthodox reform movement. Semi-monastic. |
| professing Christians | PC | 2-a | | 1,875,827,000 | 238 | braz | C | 5 | All persons who openly profess or confess to being followers of Christ. |
| Christopagans | CRPC | 2-b | | 22,000,000 | 25 | mexi | C | 5 | Latin American Roman Catholics who also practice pre-Columbian animism. |
| Evangelical Catholics | ERPC | 2-b | | 79,900,000 | 150 | irel | C | 5 | Baptized Roman Catholics who also profess to be Protestants or Evangelicals. |
| Spiritist Catholics | SRPC | 2-b | 1850 | 82,000,000 | 30 | braz | C | 3 | Baptized RCs either (a)High Spiritists (mainly Umbanda) or (b)Afro-American Low Spiritism. |
| As des Confs Epis de l'Afrique Centrale | rC | 7-b | 1985 | 34,069,000 | 5 | conz | C | 5 | ACEAC. Covers Burundi, Rwanda, Congo-Zaire. HQ Kinshasa. |
| Catholic Bishops' Conf of PNG & SI | rC | 7-c | 1983 | 1,473,000 | 2 | papu | C | 5 | CBCPNGSI. SI=Solomon Islands. HQ Waigani (PNG). |
| Chinese Regional Bishops Conf | rC | 7-b | 1991 | 17,200,000 | 10 | taiw | B | 5 | CRBC. HQ Taipei. |
| Conf Episcopale de l'Ocean Indien | rC | 7-d | 1990 | 991,000 | 6 | maus | B | 5 | CEDOI. HQ Port-Louis (Mauritius). |
| Conferentia Episcopalis Scandiae | rC | 7-d | 1985 | 262,000 | 4 | norw | C | 5 | CES. Scandinavian Bishops' Conference. HQ Oslo (Norway). |
| Council of the Ch of South East Asia | A-rC | 7-d | c1970 | 230,000 | 15 | sing | B | 5 | CCEA, CCSEA. Anglicans from China to Malaysia and Indonesia in the 1980s. Defunct. |
| As des Conf Epis de la Region de AC | B-rC | 7-c | 1989 | 6,297,000 | 7 | cent | B | 5 | ACERAC. AC=l'Afrique Centrale. Covers Cameroon, Chad, CAR, Congo, Equatorial Guinea. |

Continued opposite

*Table 17–6 continued*

| Name of religion/religionists 1 | Pedigree 2 | Type 3 | Begun 4 | Adherents 5 | Ext 6 | Coun 7 | W 8 | X 9 | E. g. = examples; name for God, other religions present, D=denominations, M=missions. 10 |
|---|---|---|---|---|---|---|---|---|---|
| Consejo Anglicano Sud Americano | C-rC | 7-c | c1970 | 1,100,000 | 6 | chil | C | 5 | CASA. Anglican Council for South America. |
| Sec Epis de America Centr y Panama | D-rC | 7-b | 1970 | 117,020,000 | 8 | pana | C | 5 | SEDAC. HQ Panama City. 8 mainland countries from Panama to Mexico. |
| Assoc of Member Epis Confs in EA | E-rC | 7-b | 1989 | 33,979,000 | 15 | keny | C | 5 | AMECEA. EA=Eastern Africa. HQ Nairobi. |
| Evangelical Fell of the South Pacific | e-rC | 7-d | | 250,000 | 10 | aust | C | 5 | EFSP. HQ Fortitude Valley, Australia. |
| Conf Epis Regionale de l'AOF | F-rC | 7-c | | 6,593,000 | 9 | ivor | B | 5 | CERAO. AOF=Afrique Occidentale Francophone/French-speaking West Africa. |
| Assoc of Episcopal Confs of AWA | G-rC | 7-b | | 15,675,000 | 6 | libe | B | 5 | AECEWA. AWA=Anglophone West Africa. HQ Monrovia. |
| Conf Epis Reg du Nord de l'Afrique | H-rC | 7-d | 1985 | 319,000 | 8 | alge | A | 5 | CERNA. HQ Algiers. |
| Pan-Indian Ecumenical Assoc of USA | I-rC | 7-d | c1960 | 500,000 | 2 | cana | C | 5 | Association to assist Amerindian religious groups in USA and Canada. |
| Asoc Reg Epis del Norte de Sud Am | J-rC | 7-b | c1980 | 100,000,000 | 6 | arge | C | 5 | ARENSA. |
| Conf des Eveques Latins dans les RA | L-rC | 7-c | 1986 | 1,235,000 | 12 | isra | B | 5 | CELRA. RA=Regions Arabes. HQ Jerusalem. |
| Antilles Episcopal Conference | M-rC | 7-b | 1975 | 22,556,000 | 20 | trin | C | 5 | AEC. HQ St James. |
| Middle East Council of Churches | N-rC | 7-b | 1927 | 17,574,000 | 19 | cypr | C | 5 | MECC/CEMO. Formerly, Near East Council of Churches; 1974, present name adopted. |
| Catholic Bishops' Conf of Malaysia | P-rC | 7-d | 1980 | 870,000 | 3 | malb | B | 5 | CBCMSB or BCMSB. Also covers Singapore, Brunei. HQ Shah Alam (Malaysia). |
| Conferencia Epis de Angola e ST | P-rC | 7-c | 1981 | 8,100,000 | 2 | ango | C | 5 | CEAST. Episcopal Conference of Angola & Sao Tome. HQ Luanda. |
| Episcopal Conference of Ireland | P-rC | 7-c | 1991 | 3,159,000 | 2 | irel | C | 5 | ECI/IEC. Irish Episcopal Conference. HQ Armagh. |
| Nordic Bishops' Conference | Q-rC | 7-d | | 236,000 | 4 | denm | C | 5 | Nordiske Bispekonferanse (Scandinavian Bishops' Conference). |
| Anglican Co of North America and C | R-rC | 7-c | | 3,779,000 | 15 | usa | C | 5 | ACNAC. C=Caribbean. |
| Interterritorial Meeting of Bps of SA | S-rC | 7-b | 1993 | 16,510,000 | 7 | zimb | B | 5 | IMBISA. SA=Southern Africia. HQ Harare. |
| Conf des Eveques du Senegal, M, CV | T-rC | 7-c | 1973 | 1,007,000 | 4 | cape | C | 5 | Bishops' Conference of S, M (Mauritanie), CV (Cape Verde), GB (Guinea Bissau). |
| Co of Anglican Provinces of Africa | V-rC | 7-b | 1975 | 38,192,000 | 30 | keny | C | 5 | CAPA. Loose committee offering liaison between Anglicans in West, East, and Southern Africa. |
| Pentecostal/Charismatic Chs of NA | X-rC | 7-b | | 17,000,000 | 3 | usa | C | 5 | PCCNA. NA=North America. |
| Regional Conf of Chinese Bishops | Z-rC | 7-d | | 250,000 | 10 | chin | B | 5 | Chung Kuo Chu-chiao T'uan. HQ Hong Kong. |
| Dispensationalists | tC | 5-e | c1840 | 30,000 | 160 | brit | C | 5 | Protestants. Millennial schema of biblical interpretation. History as 7 dispensations from God. |
| Anglo-Catholics | A-ACa-tC | 5-c | 1050 | 2,073,000 | 39 | brit | C | 5 | Rural Church of England, in 494 parishes; also in 37 countries. |
| Broad Church Anglicans | A-Cen-tC | 5-c | 1078 | 9,109,000 | 32 | brit | C | 5 | Large industrial areas, vast overspill areas. |
| Ecumenical parishes | A-Ecu-tC | 5-d | | 144,000 | 1 | brit | C | 5 | Growing by 1994 to over 900 Local Ecumenical Partnerships (multidenominational). |
| Evangelical Anglicans | A-Eva-tC | 5-b | 1765 | 17,344,000 | 12 | ugan | C | 5 | 27 Dioceses. Balokole Revival. Schisms to new AICs. M=CMS,RCMS,AIM(UK). 142f,8H. |
| High Church Anglicans | A-Hig-tC | 5-c | 1072 | 7,964,000 | 30 | soua | C | 5 | 16 Dioceses in SA, 6 abroad. 56% Black, 24% White. 511b,18de,18H,96h,12r,4s(81). |
| Low Church Anglicans | A-Low-tC | 5-b | 1091 | 23,207,000 | 15 | nige | B | 5 | In Australia, Nigeria. Mushrooming to 63 Dioceses. M=CMS(UK). 68f,1p,1s,1u. |
| Pluralist Anglicans | A-plu-tC | 5-b | 1075 | 20,104,000 | 41 | brit | C | 5 | 1960, Charismatic Renewal, now 12%. 100x,308m,2358w,23s (950). |
| African Independent Apostolics | I-3aA-tC | 5-b | 1912 | 15,836,000 | 24 | nige | B | 5 | E.g. Heavenly Christianity. Begun Dahomey 1947. Yoruba elites. Rapid growth in 24 countries. |
| Black American Apostolics | I-3aB-tC | 5-e | 1925 | 34,400 | 2 | usa | C | 5 | Black Trinitarian Apostolics. Eastern USA, HQ Baltimore. Overseas work in Ghana, Liberia. |
| Filipino Apostolics | I-3aF-tC | 5-e | 1965 | 1,100 | 1 | phil | C | 5 | Indigenous pentecostals. All members Ilocanos. 6n,1p,W=25%,80Y. |
| Indian Apostolics | I-3aI-tC | 5-e | 1948 | 58,500 | 2 | indi | B | 5 | ACA. Strong appeal to Hindus; HQ Madras (12,000 in mother church). |
| Korean Apostolics | I-3aK-tC | 5-e | 1982 | 8,400 | 1 | usa | C | 5 | 154 missionaries in 38 countries: Russia 670 chs, China 600 chs, Viet Nam 280 chs. |
| Latin American Apostolics | I-3aL-tC | 5-d | 1929 | 316,000 | 6 | colo | C | 5 | Panamerican Mission. Run by Colombians. Rapid growth. Medellin, Bogota. |
| Black American Apostolics | I-3aO-tC | 5-c | 1886 | 2,164,000 | 3 | usa | C | 5 | E.g. PAOW. Black pentecostals. 600n,1s. Missions:Caribbean, India, Israel, Nigeria; 1,000 chs. |
| Pacific Apostolics | I-3aP-tC | 5-e | 1988 | 6,000 | 1 | fiji | B | 5 | AGOFI. Indigenous body with apostolic government. Ex AoG, but now 80% ex-Methodists. |
| Arab Apostolics | I-3aS-tC | 5-e | c1980 | 4,300 | 2 | unia | B | 5 | M=Network International(HQ TX, USA). Social and evangelistic ministries. |
| Afro-Caribbean Apostolics | I-3aU-tC | 5-e | 1964 | 18,900 | 2 | usa | C | 5 | FCJCA. Mainly Haitians (with some Jamaicans). Abroad: 27 chs (Haiti 20, Jamaica 4). |
| White-led Apostolics | I-3aW-tC | 5-d | 1938 | 235,000 | 4 | usa | C | 5 | ACM. 45n,10 apostles. Abroad: 62 networks in 42 countries, 4100 chs. |
| New Apostolics | I-3aX-tC | 5-c | 1832 | 9,637,000 | 149 | indi | B | 5 | Global body. E.g. Canada Bezirk. HQ Zurich. Rapid growth. 1973 mission in Kenya, Africa. |
| African Indep charismatics | I-3cA-tC | 5-c | 1864 | 2,302,000 | 30 | moza | B | 5 | Total over 20, Foreign missions: huge Rhema Bible Ch, Word of Life World Outreach, &c. |
| Black American charismatics | I-3cB-tC | 5-d | 1964 | 584,000 | 1 | usa | C | 5 | E.g. IEC. Churches: Africa 430, USA 70, South America 50, Italy 20, Jamaica 1. |
| Chinese neocharismatics | I-3cC-tC | 5-b | 1963 | 42,930,000 | 3 | chin | B | 5 | 500 Regional Councils, 5,000 Pastoral Districts. M=Taiwanese/Diaspora short-termers; CCRC. |
| Black American charismatics | I-3cD-tC | 5-d | 1955 | 152,000 | 2 | usa | C | 5 | Black Charismatics arising over last 45 years as separate denominations. |
| Monoethnic charismatics | I-3cE-tC | 5-e | 1965 | 4,800 | 1 | indi | B | 5 | Work begun first among Ho tribe. 70 Indian home missionaries. M=CAM. |
| Filipino charismatics | I-3cF-tC | 5-c | 1987 | 1,546,000 | 2 | phil | C | 5 | Including Association of Vineyard Chs (1 ch). |
| Indian charismatics | I-3cI-tC | 5-c | 1945 | 1,163,000 | 5 | indi | B | 5 | Including SIWA (450 chs), HBI (816 chs). |
| Korean charismatics | I-3cK-tC | 5-e | c1980 | 85,400 | 1 | souk | B | 5 | Based in Anyang city. Several satellite churches. |
| Latin American charismatics | I-3cL-tC | 5-d | 1957 | 322,000 | 8 | mexi | C | 5 | E.g. Association of Vineyard Chs (13 chs), Tree of Life Ch (42 chs), house chs everywhere. |
| Pacific charismatics | I-3cP-tC | 5-e | 1978 | 76,900 | 6 | papu | C | 5 | Many varieties of Neocharismatics in several larger Pacific countries. |
| Japanese charismatics | I-3cQ-tC | 5-e | 1946 | 32,500 | 1 | japa | B | 5 | Sei Iesu Kai. |
| Arab charismatics | I-3cS-tC | 5-e | 1948 | 71,400 | 9 | isra | B | 5 | In around 20 very loose geographical networks or associations. |
| Afro-Caribbean charismatics | I-3cU-tC | 5-e | 1980 | 4,700 | 3 | virg | C | 5 | In about 4 loose networks. |
| White-led charismatics | I-3cW-tC | 5-b | 1805 | 20,864,000 | 43 | usa | C | 5 | 1,500 smaller networks and 20,000 autonomous single congregations: El Shaddai, &c. |
| Brazilian charismatics | I-3cY-tC | 5-d | 1960 | 773,000 | 2 | braz | C | 5 | National Baptist Convention. Igreja do Renovação. Split ex Brazilian Baptist Convention. |
| other Asian charismatics | I-3cZ-tC | 5-d | 1974 | 113,000 | 6 | uzbe | A | 5 | Including Word of Life Movement. |
| neocharismatic mainliners | I-3dW-tC | 5-e | 1996 | 18,000 | 1 | usa | C | 5 | E.g. Southern Baptist charismatic congregations. Based Fort Worth, TX. No work abroad. |
| other Asian mainliners | I-3dZ-tC | 5-e | c1970 | 12,000 | 2 | sing | B | 5 | Centres in UK, Zambia, Malaysia, Brunei, USA, and 7 other countries. Nominally in AoG. |
| African Full Gospelers | I-3fA-tC | 5-d | 1920 | 589,000 | 12 | ethi | B | 5 | Indigenous; Swedish & Finnish aid. 1972-75 severe persecution, 300 imprisoned. 200n. |
| Black American Full Gospelers | I-3fB-tC | 5-e | 1978 | 18,000 | 1 | usa | C | 5 | EMCI. Full Gospel theology. Schism ex CoGiC. HQ Arkansas. Abroad: 700 in 1 ch in Japan. |
| Chinese Full Gospelers | I-3fC-tC | 5-e | 1982 | 18,000 | 1 | usa | C | 5 | CFGFI. HQ Houston, TX. Abroad (HQ Kowloon, Hong Kong): 100 chs, 200 ministers. |
| Black American Full Gospelers | I-3fD-tC | 5-c | 1993 | 1,320,000 | 1 | usa | C | 5 | FGBCF. F=bp Paul Morton. Black. Ex NBCA, NBCUSA. Missions: Bahamas, S Africa, Russia. |
| Filipino Full Gospelers | I-3fF-tC | 5-c | 1936 | 2,458,000 | 4 | phil | C | 5 | E.g. JILF. Philippines for Jesus. Mass movement. F=E. Villanueva. In 25 countries. |
| Indonesian Full Gospelers | I-3fG-tC | 5-d | 1970 | 713,000 | 2 | indo | B | 5 | E.g. GBIS. GB Injil Sepenuh. 50% Chinese. Ex GBI(Gbis) retaining name. 450n,1p. |
| Indian Full Gospelers | I-3fI-tC | 5-d | 1911 | 751,000 | 1 | indi | B | 5 | Indigenous chs in Andhra Pradesh. Telugus. Welsh missionary aid. M=Mana Igreja(Portugal). |
| Korean Full Gospelers | I-3fK-tC | 5-d | 1963 | 369,000 | 5 | usa | C | 5 | KFGCA. M=FGC of Seoul, Korea. Many independent Korean churches in USA. |
| Latin American Full Gospelers | I-3fL-tC | 5-d | 1958 | 108,000 | 2 | mexi | C | 5 | E.g. Miracle Revival Crusade Chs. M=MRC,GSMA(USA). |
| Pacific Full Gospelers | I-3fP-tC | 5-e | 1962 | 14,300 | 3 | aust | C | 5 | E.g. Associated Full Gospel Chs. Gospel Light Ministry. Split ex AoG. Many Aborigines. |
| White-led Full Gospelers | I-3fW-tC | 5-c | 1895 | 2,941,000 | 6 | usa | C | 5 | Including 1,500 unattached congregations participating in Chaplaincy of Full Gospel Churches. |
| Brazilian Full Gospelers | I-3fY-tC | 5-e | 1977 | 36,000 | 1 | braz | C | 5 | E.g. Full Gospel Peace Churches. Amazon. HQ Santarem. M=Vineyard Chs, GSMA(USA). |
| other Asian Full Gospelers | I-3fZ-tC | 5-e | 1978 | 32,400 | 4 | malb | B | 5 | Mainly Chinese members, a few Indians. |
| Latin American grassroots chs | I-3gL-tC | 5-c | 1928 | 2,657,000 | 15 | chil | C | 5 | Vast numbers of bodies in 15 countries. Including Association of Vineyard Chs (3 chs). |
| Afro-Caribbean grassroots chs | I-3gU-tC | 5-e | | 5,600 | 1 | domr | C | 5 | Total about 10 (see below), mostly from Puerto Rico, Jamaica, Trinidad et alia. |
| Brazilian grassroots chs | I-3gY-tC | 5-c | 1970 | 3,600,000 | 1 | braz | C | 5 | Grassroots (GR) churches: Rio has 984 GR chs, São Paulo 1,468 chs with 650,000; NNCM. |
| African house-church networks | I-3hA-tC | 5-e | c1970 | 14,400 | 2 | conz | C | 5 | E.g. Christ Groups. Home churches for isolated converts after nationwide EHC campaign. |
| Monoethnic house churches | I-3hE-tC | 5-e | c1900 | 1,900 | 1 | chin | B | 5 | In 15 Provinces (Liaoning, Hebei). M=SJ,CSI,PRI,JENSCO,CCRC. Korea churches. |
| Indonesian house-churches | I-3hG-tC | 5-e | c1970 | 24,000 | 1 | indo | B | 5 | Home churches for isolated converts after nationwide EHC campaign. |
| Indian house-church networks | I-3hI-tC | 5-d | c1970 | 365,000 | 3 | indi | B | 5 | M=EHC. Literature distribution campaigns, visiting 4.6 million homes across India every year. |
| Korean house-church networks | I-3hK-tC | 5-d | 1970 | 804,000 | 2 | chin | B | 5 | Inner Mongolia, Jilin, Liaoning. Most TSPM but vast house networks. M=25 agencies(S Korea). |
| Latin American house-churches | I-3hL-tC | 5-e | 1963 | 60,000 | 3 | mexi | C | 5 | E.g. Centers of Christian Love. Christian Fellowship Chs. S.Mexico among Mixtecs. M=MRC. |
| Pacific house-church networks | I-3hP-tC | 5-e | c1980 | 62,400 | 3 | fiji | B | 5 | Isolated home churches for converts after nationwide EHC campaign. |
| Arab house-church networks | I-3hS-tC | 5-e | c1950 | 21,400 | 1 | saud | B | 5 | Saudi Arab believers organized into private house meetings; no foreign contacts. |
| Vietnamese house-churches | I-3hV-tC | 5-d | 1988 | 114,000 | 1 | viet | B | 5 | Rapid growth: 60,000 converts in 1991. Many tribal churches from 62 tribes. Healings. |
| White-led house churches | I-3hW-tC | 5-e | 1965 | 14,700 | 5 | russ | B | 5 | Isolated home churches after EHC (Every Home for Christ) campaign across Russia. |
| other Asian house-churches | I-3hZ-tC | 5-e | c1965 | 2,500 | 2 | kaza | B | 5 | Home churches for isolated converts after nationwide EHC campaign. |
| African healing networks | I-3jA-tC | 5-e | 1939 | 47,100 | 3 | ghan | B | 5 | E.g. Ex Methodists. Healing herbs, shea-butter, soap. Akan, Ga, Ewe. 9n,3m,600Y. |
| White-led healing networks | I-3jW-tC | 5-d | 1928 | 188,000 | 2 | usa | C | 5 | E.g. Branhamites. Voice of God Recordings. 300,000 worldwide. |
| African cell-based networks | I-3kA-tC | 5-e | c1970 | 54,000 | 1 | ivor | B | 5 | E.g. Celestial Ch of Christ. Large Nigerian indigenous church. Yoruba elites. In 11 countries. |
| Black American cell-based chs | I-3kB-tC | 5-e | 1969 | 28,200 | 1 | usa | C | 5 | WFFM. Cell-based churches. Abroad: 5,000 members in 74 chs (Africa 58, Pakistan 16). |
| Chinese cell-based networks | I-3kC-tC | 5-e | 1986 | 27,600 | 1 | sing | B | 5 | E.g. FCBC. Schism ex Singapore Baptist Convention. F=Lawrence Khong. Large, cell-based. |
| Korean cell-based networks | I-3kK-tC | 5-c | 1958 | 1,315,000 | 1 | souk | B | 5 | E.g. YFGC. Adult members: (1961) 800. 100 staff, 50,000 cells. Since 1985 part of AoG. |
| Latin American cell-based chs | I-3kL-tC | 5-d | c1965 | 282,000 | 2 | elsa | C | 5 | E.g. Elim Christian Mission. Massive evangelism, church growth. 116,000 in 600 weekly calls. |
| White-led cell-based networks | I-3kW-tC | 5-e | 1971 | 93,600 | 2 | port | C | 5 | E.g. Manna Christian Ch. Huge cell-based megachurch in Lisbon. In Europe, Africa, S America. |
| other Asian cell-based networks | I-3kZ-tC | 5-e | 1980 | 43,200 | 1 | thai | B | 5 | E.g. Hope of Bangkok/Thailand. Converted Buddhists. 40 chs in 19 countries (Asia, Europe). |
| Messianic African Independents | I-3mA-tC | 5-e | 1941 | 1,400 | 1 | cong | C | 5 | E.g. ENAC. Ch of the Black Race. Kaki Ch. Founder patriarch Simon Mpadi, Zaire. Ex SA. |
| Messianic Chinese chs | I-3mC-tC | 10-f | c1980 | 180 | 1 | swit | C | 5 | E.g. a number of Local Churches. Chinese. Begun in China. |
| Messianic Hindu temples | I-3mH-tC | 5-d | 1875 | 163,000 | 1 | indi | B | 5 | High-caste Hindus. Anti-churches, anti-baptism. Massive healing crusades. Telugu. |
| Messianic Jews | I-3mJ-tC | 5-d | 1894 | 161,000 | 9 | russ | B | 5 | After 1995 St Petersburg campaigns, 50,000 Russian/Ukrainian/Byelorussian Jews convert. |
| Messianic Muslim mosques | I-3mM-tC | 5-d | 1981 | 126,000 | 2 | bang | B | 5 | Jesus Mosques. M=Global Partners for Development. Most members joined 1982-1991. |
| African neocharismatics | I-3nA-tC | 5-c | 1920 | 9,708,000 | 13 | conz | C | 5 | E.g. EJCSK. Ch of Christ on Earth thru Prophet Simon Kimbangu. 1H,1s(82),W=44%,36747Y. |
| Black American neocharismatics | I-3nB-tC | 10-f | | 920 | 1 | sail | C | 5 | Several bodies including Spiritual Baptists (Shouters, Shakers). |
| Chinese neocharismatics | I-3nC-tC | 5-c | 1921 | 2,337,000 | 57 | chin | B | 5 | Chu Hui So. Little Flock. F=Watchman Nee. 1949: 636 churches, 70,000 members. Jiangxi. |
| Monoethnic neocharismatics | I-3nE-tC | 5-e | 1956 | 69,100 | 1 | viet | B | 5 | Co-Duc-Truyen-Giao-Hoi. M=UWM(USA),WEC(1958-68). Among 14 Montagnard tribes. |
| Filipino neocharismatics | I-3nF-tC | 5-c | 1913 | 2,105,000 | 2 | phil | C | 5 | E.g. INC. Iglesia ni Cristo (Manalista). 35 cathedrals, 2 radio stations. Not pentecostal. 1902n. |

*Continued overleaf*

*Table 17–6 continued*

| Name of religion/religionists 1 | Pedigree 2 | Type 3 | Begun 4 | Adherents 5 | Ext 6 | Coun 7 | W 8 | X 9 | E. g. = examples; name for God, other religions present, D=denominations, M=missions. 10 |
|---|---|---|---|---|---|---|---|---|---|
| Indonesian neocharismatics | I-3nG-tC | 5-d | | 377,000 | 1 | indo | B | 5 | Persekutuan Jajasan Kristen. Unregistered Javanese autonomous congregations. |
| Indian neocharismatics | I-3nI-tC | 5-d | 1974 | 753,000 | 2 | indi | B | 5 | Based on indigenous ministry M=Gospel for Asia (GFA). F=K.P. Yohanan. 8,500 Indian workers. |
| Latin American neocharismatics | I-3nL-tC | 5-e | 1960 | 4,800 | 2 | colo | C | 5 | E.g. IBC. Bible Ch of Colombia. M=BALL World Missions (USA). School, clinic. |
| Creole neocharismatics | I-3nN-tC | 5-e | | 74,400 | 2 | nami | C | 5 | E.g. Afrikaans Protestant Ch (S Africa). Total over 30 mainly migrant Coloured groups. |
| Pacific neocharismatics | I-3nP-tC | 5-e | 1960 | 11,300 | 2 | solo | C | 5 | Etoism (followers of prophet Eto). Schism ex Methodist Ch on New Georgia. W=90%. |
| Arab neocharismatics | I-3nS-tC | 5-e | c1980 | 12,000 | 1 | iraq | A | 5 | 1,000 attenders a week; public baptisms; wide scripture distribution. |
| Afro-Caribbean neocharismatics | I-3nU-tC | 5-e | c1970 | 2,400 | 2 | mont | C | 5 | Total about 6, from neighboring Caribbean islands. |
| White-led neocharismatics | I-3nW-tC | 5-e | 1656 | 7,500 | 3 | port | C | 5 | Lusitanian Ch. Schism ex Ch of Rome by 11 RC priests. 16n,2s,W=45%,32Yy. |
| other Asian neocharismatics | I-3nZ-tC | 5-d | 1974 | 196,000 | 5 | thai | B | 5 | New Life Chs. Begun in northeast Thailand after screenings of 'Jesus' Film. M=CCCI-JFP. |
| African Oneness pentecostals | I-3oA-tC | 5-d | 1919 | 832,000 | 15 | soua | C | 5 | E.g. Oneness Pentecostal. Reformed Ch. HQ Durban. Member of AWCF. |
| Chinese Oneness pentecostals | I-3oC-tC | 5-c | 1917 | 1,287,000 | 12 | chin | B | 5 | Chen Ye-su Chiao Hui. 1949: 1,000 churches. Now with global diaspora. (HQ Taipei, Taiwan). |
| Filipino Oneness pentecostals | I-3oF-tC | 5-d | 1948 | 118,000 | 1 | phil | C | 5 | Total about 30, including Philippines Apostolic Christian Fellowship. |
| Indonesian Oneness chs | I-3oG-tC | 5-c | 1920 | 1,336,000 | 1 | indo | B | 5 | GPI,GPdI. G Pantekosta di Indonesia. 25% Chinese. Many splits, including GBIS. 1500n,3s. |
| Indian Oneness pentecostals | I-3oI-tC | 5-d | | 277,000 | 1 | indi | B | 5 | Total 40 bodies, with many USA connections. |
| Latin American Oneness chs | I-3oL-tC | 5-c | 1911 | 1,270,000 | 14 | mexi | C | 5 | Light of the World Ch. Messiah Aaron, died 1964. Vast tabernacle Guadalajara. 1h. |
| Black American Oneness chs | I-3oO-tC | 5-d | 1916 | 797,000 | 2 | usa | C | 5 | WW=World Wide. Black Oneness pentecostals. Ex COLJCAF. 360n,4p,W=95%,1000Y. |
| Japanese Oneness chs | I-3oQ-tC | 5-d | 1937 | 509,000 | 2 | japa | B | 5 | Iesu no Mitama Kyokai Kyodan. Ex AoG. Missions to USA. Brazil. 185n (94 women). |
| Afro-Caribbean Oneness chs | I-3oU-tC | 5-d | 1955 | 131,000 | 7 | brit | C | 5 | Total 10, mostly immigrating recently from Caribbean. |
| White-led Oneness chs | I-3oW-tC | 5-d | 1845 | 929,000 | 8 | usa | C | 5 | Mostly White Charismatics. 1971, assisted by M=CMI (Calvary Ministries International). |
| Brazilian Oneness chs | I-3oY-tC | 5-e | c1960 | 14,900 | 1 | braz | C | 5 | E.g. National Independent Church of Brazil. |
| other Asian Oneness chs | I-3oZ-tC | 10-f | c1970 | 340 | 1 | bang | B | 5 | E.g. Mukti Bani Sangsta. M=American Evangelistic Association. All Namasudras. 35nm. |
| African Independ pentecostals | I-3pA-tC | 5-b | 1907 | 21,820,000 | 41 | nige | B | 5 | Total over 1,500 (see partial list below), including CMF. |
| Black American pentecostals | I-3pB-tC | 5-c | 1889 | 6,940,000 | 18 | usa | C | 5 | E.g. Church of God in Christ. HQ Memphis (TN). (1970) 5000n. (1990) 33593n. |
| Chinese pentecostals | I-3pC-tC | 5-d | 1905 | 130,000 | 3 | indo | B | 5 | E.g. G Kristus. Chinese pentecostal church in West Java. HQ Jakarta. 12n,W=70%. |
| Monoethnic pentecostals | I-3pE-tC | 5-c | 1892 | 1,460,000 | 15 | chin | B | 5 | Widespread ethnic churches among Black, Flowery, Northern, Red, Western Meo. M=AoG. |
| Filipino pentecostals | I-3pF-tC | 5-d | 1933 | 518,000 | 5 | phil | C | 5 | E.g. Iglesia ti Dios a Sibibiag. Revival Fellowship. Daily radio ministry. 126n,2p. |
| Indonesian pentecostals | I-3pG-tC | 5-c | 1923 | 3,724,000 | 2 | indo | B | 5 | Total over 100 (see list below). |
| Indian pentecostals | I-3pI-tC | 5-c | 1918 | 2,553,000 | 12 | indi | B | 5 | E.g. IPC. Ex CPM, AoG. 80% Malayali; congregations throughout India. Abroad: in 12 countries. |
| Korean pentecostals | I-3pK-tC | 5-d | 1945 | 499,000 | 5 | souk | B | 5 | Independent pentecostals. |
| Latin American pentecostals | I-3pL-tC | 5-c | 1909 | 6,780,000 | 22 | chil | C | 5 | E.g. IMP. Pentecostal Meth Ch. Split ex Methodists; 20 schisms since. 1967, M=IPHC. 120n,1u. |
| Creole pentecostals | I-3pN-tC | 5-d | 1931 | 160,000 | 3 | soua | C | 5 | E.g. Christen Gemeente. 80% Coloured. N&W Cape, Natal, also SWA. 178n. |
| Pacific pentecostals | I-3pP-tC | 5-e | 1917 | 38,500 | 11 | papu | C | 5 | E.g. Port Moresby. Pentecostals. Very rapid growth: 35% pa. 10n,4x,W=99%,21Y. |
| Japanese pentecostals | I-3pQ-tC | 5-e | 1930 | 54,200 | 1 | japa | B | 5 | E.g. Genshi Fukuin. Primitive Gospel Ch. Makuya. Split ex Mukyokai. 160n,W=34%,1000Y. |
| Amerindian pentecostals | I-3pR-tC | 5-d | 1923 | 535,000 | 3 | mexi | C | 5 | E.g. Union of Ev Indep Chs. Igl Cristiana Indep Pentecostés. Otomi Indians. HQ Pachuca. |
| Arab pentecostals | I-3pS-tC | 5-e | 1909 | 23,800 | 7 | egyp | B | 5 | E.g. M=World-Wide Missions (USA). 1993, pentecostalized, merged with M=PHC. |
| Afro-Caribbean pentecostals | I-3pU-tC | 5-d | 1894 | 524,000 | 19 | brit | C | 5 | Total over 100 more bodies. |
| White-led pentecostals | I-3pW-tC | 5-c | 1974 | 7,406,000 | 55 | russ | B | 5 | E.g. CEF=Christians of the Evangelical Faith. Formerly in AUCECB. 65 churches in Moscow. |
| Brazilian pentecostals | I-3pY-tC | 5-b | 1910 | 18,581,000 | 6 | braz | C | 5 | E.g. Universal Ch of the Kingdom of God. IURD/UCKG. 2000n. In 50 countries (Portugal &c). |
| other Asian pentecostals | I-3pZ-tC | 5-e | 1948 | 58,700 | 10 | sril | B | 5 | E.g. Svenska Fria Mission. M=SFM(Sweden). HQ Colombo 6, also Nugegoda. 10f. |
| African radio/TV believers | I-3rA-tC | 5-d | 1960 | 178,000 | 11 | suda | B | 5 | Isolated Black and Arab radio believers, mainly aged 12-25. R=400(TWR,RVOG&c). |
| Chinese radio/TV believers | I-3rC-tC | 5-c | 1933 | 3,020,000 | 2 | chin | B | 5 | Isolated radio believers, mostly students and youths. R=FEBC,Radio Vatican,et alia. |
| Indonesian radio/TV believers | I-3rG-tC | 5-d | 1952 | 587,000 | 1 | indo | B | 5 | Isolated radio believers (youths &c). (1970) R=15000 (FEBC,&c), T=55000 (ICI,FEBC,&c). |
| Indian radio/TV believers | I-3rI-tC | 5-b | 1952 | 10,693,000 | 4 | indi | B | 5 | Radio believers (youths &c). (1970) R=75000 (FEBA,RVOG),T=2810000 (ICI,TEAM,EHC,&c). |
| Korean radio/TV believers | I-3rK-tC | 5-e | | 94,400 | 1 | nork | A | 5 | Isolated radio believers (students, youths). FEBC is heard 2.5 hours per day. |
| Latin American radio/TV chs | I-3rL-tC | 5-e | 1931 | 92,200 | 7 | cuba | B | 5 | Isolated radio believers (students &c). R=480(279 HCJB, 92 FEBC, TWR, Radio Vatican). |
| Japanese radio/TV believers | I-3rQ-tC | 5-d | 1952 | 567,000 | 1 | japa | B | 5 | Isolated radio believers; mostly students and youths. R=164400,T=850000. |
| Arab radio/TV networks | I-3rS-tC | 5-c | 1958 | 1,131,000 | 19 | iraq | A | 5 | Isolated Arab radio believers (students &c). Vast increase after 1985. |
| Vietnamese radio/TV believers | I-3rV-tC | 5-d | 1952 | 117,000 | 1 | viet | B | 5 | Radio believers in mountains, mostly youths and students. R=4500,T=39000(ICI). |
| European radio/TV believers | I-3rW-tC | 5-c | 1939 | 5,834,000 | 11 | russ | B | 5 | Isolated radio believers. R=6000(2800 SGA,415 HCJB,300 FEBC,60 TWR,RVatican,BBC,&c). |
| Brazilian radio/TV believers | I-3rY-tC | 5-e | c1950 | 17,600 | 1 | braz | C | 5 | Isolated radio believers in remote jungle areas. R=49700 (HCJB,TWR,FEBC,Radio Vatican). |
| other Asian radio/TV believers | I-3rZ-tC | 5-d | 1952 | 695,000 | 13 | thai | B | 5 | Isolated Thais and Chinese, mainly aged 12-25. R=16000 (FEBC),T=166000 (FEBC,ICI,&c). |
| African Independent Spirituals | I-3sA-tC | 5-c | 1914 | 1,329,000 | 8 | keny | C | 5 | RCC schisms in Africa. 90% Luo. 9 Dioceses, 7 cardinals, pope. Charismatics. 500n. |
| Afro-Caribbean Spirituals | I-3sU-tC | 5-e | c1860 | 12,000 | 4 | trin | C | 5 | Shouters. Banned 1917-51. Cathedral in Gonzales. Many former RCs and Anglicans. |
| White-led signs & wonders chs | I-3sW-tC | 5-e | c1980 | 7,200 | 3 | soua | C | 5 | E.g. Assisted by M=AVC(USA). |
| White-led restorationists | I-3tW-tC | 5-d | 1968 | 336,000 | 1 | brit | C | 5 | E.g. F=Terry Virgo. South Coast. Shepherding controversy. R-1 type. NFI missions abroad. |
| African Indep deliverance chs | I-3vA-tC | 5-e | c1980 | 25,200 | 2 | ethi | B | 5 | E.g. In Addis Ababa. Full Gospel theology. |
| Black Amer deliverance pente | I-3vB-tC | 5-d | 1960 | 115,000 | 1 | usa | C | 5 | Black Americans stressing deliverance ministry. |
| White deliverance pentecostals | I-3vW-tC | 5-d | 1976 | 231,000 | 3 | usa | C | 5 | E.g. VFM. HQ Tulsa, OK. Members abroad: 15,000 in 8 churches in Russia, 45 countries. |
| African Word of Faith/Prosperity | I-3wA-tC | 5-d | 1980 | 999,000 | 3 | nige | B | 5 | Prosperity gospel teaching, elements of traditional medicine. |
| Filipino Word of Faith chs | I-3wF-tC | 5-e | c1975 | 30,000 | 1 | phil | C | 5 | Filipinos teaching Word of Faith/Prospering Gospel. |
| Pacific Word-of-Faith chs | I-3wP-tC | 5-e | 1940 | 5,200 | 2 | usa | C | 5 | A network of cell-based churches, most in Pennsylvania. |
| White-led Word of Faith chs | I-3wW-tC | 5-c | 1953 | 1,323,000 | 6 | nige | B | 5 | Prosperity gospel message. M=Rhema Bible Churches (USA). |
| African neocharismatics | I-3xA-tC | 5-c | | 1,630,000 | 1 | soua | C | 5 | Total around 3,000 more bodies (see below), most with under 50 adults each. |
| Indepen Korean pentecostals | I-3xK-tC | 5-d | | 162,000 | 1 | souk | B | 5 | Total about 150 (see list below), including Chinese Ch of Christ. |
| Latin American neocharismatics | I-3xL-tC | 5-e | 1976 | 22,600 | 1 | hond | C | 5 | E.g. Living Love Christian Organization. Cell-based, with 1,000 house cells. |
| European charismatics | I-3xW-tC | 5-e | 1942 | 70,800 | 1 | brit | C | 5 | E.g. Ch of the Great Shepherd/Pyramid Ch. In Chard, Bradford. M=CGM(USA). Strong in Yorks. |
| Zionist African Independents | I-3zA-tC | 5-b | 1909 | 11,968,000 | 6 | soua | C | 5 | E.g. ZCC. Ex AFM. Colors green, yellow. Pedi. In 9 countries:Malawi to Namibia, Mozambique. |
| Afro-Caribbean Zionists | I-3zU-tC | 5-e | 1783 | 37,200 | 1 | jama | B | 5 | 1861-62, Great Christian Revival. Charismatics similar to Shouters, Shakers. |
| Independent Anglo-Catholics | I-ACa-tC | 5-e | 1840 | 16,400 | 2 | aust | C | 5 | ACCA. Schism ex C of E in A rejecting ordination of women, begun with 7 parishes. |
| Independent Adventists | I-Adv-tC | 5-d | 1920 | 152,000 | 19 | peru | C | 5 | Ev Israelite Ch of the New Covenant. Cabañistas (Tabernaclers). Schism ex SDAs. |
| Anglican schismatics | I-Ang-tC | 5-c | 1880 | 1,577,000 | 14 | keny | C | 5 | E.g. CCA. Schism of 40% D Maseno. 8 Dioceses. 81% Luo, 10% Luhya. 81n,1p,2400Y,8640y. |
| apocalyptic chs | I-Apo-tC | 5-e | 1923 | 4,900 | 2 | ukra | C | 5 | Apokalipsisty. Begun Vinnitsa by Catholic priest, spread to Far East; underground. |
| Anglo-Romans | I-ARo-tC | 5-e | 1897 | 79,000 | 13 | zimb | B | 5 | M=AO(USA). Ex Anglicans. Registered 1924: 1972 Rhodesian African bishop. Ndebele. |
| Independent Baptists | I-Bap-tC | 5-b | 1695 | 29,616,000 | 95 | usa | C | 5 | NBC. 1915 split from NBC America. Black. HQ Nashville. (1970) 27500n,1s. (1990) 32832n. |
| British-Israelites | I-BrI-tC | 5-e | 1930 | 77,000 | 5 | usa | C | 3 | Radio Ch of God. Ex CoG(SD). Doctrinal realignments. Schisms 1974. In 124 countries. 400n. |
| Buddhist believers in Christ | I-Bud-tC | 5-c | c1970 | 2,194,000 | 8 | chin | B | 2 | Hidden Buddhists converted to Christ but remaining within Buddhism as a witness. |
| Indep Bulgarian Orthodox | I-Bul-tC | 5-d | 1992 | 600,000 | 1 | bulg | C | 5 | Massive schism ex BOC by disaffected bishops and clergy. |
| Independent Byzantine-rite chs | I-Byz-tC | 5-e | 1984 | 7,200 | 1 | usa | C | 5 | Independent Catholics. Membership abroad: 250,000 in Europe, Africa, Latin America. |
| Indep Christian Brethren | I-CBr-tC | 5-d | 1856 | 368,000 | 24 | indi | B | 5 | F=Brother Bakht Singh. Chaubra/Sikh converts. Strong in AP; also abroad. M=WEC. 30f. |
| Conservative Catholics | I-CCa-tC | 5-c | 1549 | 4,901,000 | 30 | braz | C | 5 | E.g. ICAB. Schism ex Rome by bp of Botucatu. 12 Dioceses, 25 bps. c1990 NNCM splits off. |
| community churches | I-com-tC | 10-f | | 220 | 1 | nets | C | 5 | Small independent congregation on Aruba, mainly European and other expatriates. |
| Independent Congregationalists | I-Con-tC | 5-d | 1829 | 980,000 | 22 | conz | C | 5 | E.g. CEUM. Ev Ch in U-M. Ex CECU(EFCA), supported by M=ECCA. HQ Gemena. 50n,50f. |
| Independent Disciples | I-Dis-tC | 5-c | 1820 | 3,930,000 | 96 | usa | C | 5 | Conservative anti-organ split ex Disciples. 10% Black. 10000n,22s,130000Y. |
| Independent Dunkers | I-Dun-tC | 5-d | 1881 | 124,000 | 1 | usa | C | 5 | NFBC (Winona Lake). Grace Brethren. Ex Ashland. 404n,1s,226t(40326),W=86%,2275Y. |
| Strict Brethren | I-EBr-tC | 5-e | 1869 | 44,000 | 5 | egyp | B | 5 | Schism ex American M (Coptic Ev Ch), now large Egyptian-run denominations. |
| episcopi vagantes churches | I-Epi-tC | 5-e | 1970 | 3,500 | 4 | brit | C | 3 | Small bodies (mostly under 100 followers) under bishops-at-large. HQ Glasgow. |
| Independent Estonian Orthodox | I-Est-tC | 5-e | c1940 | 9,600 | 2 | brit | C | 5 | London parishes. Estonian refugees. Under archbishop of Great Britain & Sweden. |
| monoethnic denominationalists | I-eth-tC | 5-c | c1880 | 1,301,000 | 2 | chin | B | 5 | E.g. Large ethnic ch, White and Black Lisu. M=CIM/OMF. Wide cross-cultural evangelism. |
| Independent Evangelicals | I-Eva-tC | 5-c | 1833 | 1,536,000 | 48 | usa | C | 5 | E.g. Seeker Churches. F=Bill Hybels. Abroad: 1,500 chs, 70 denominations, 48 countries. |
| Independent Fundamentalists | I-Fun-tC | 5-c | 1894 | 2,029,000 | 31 | brit | C | 5 | Large de facto grouping. Expanding. Healing, foreign missions. 2000n. |
| Gay/Lesbian homosexual chs | I-Gay-tC | 5-d | 1968 | 179,000 | 2 | usa | C | 4 | E.g. UFMCC. MCCs=Metropolitan Community Chs. Gays and lesbians. In 17 nations. 500n. |
| Independent Greek Orthodox | I-Gre-tC | 5-e | c1950 | 16,600 | 1 | aust | C | 5 | Ex Greek OC (AD Australia) by laity opposing hierarchy. In NSW, SA, Victoria. |
| Hidden Hindu believers in Christ | I-Hin-tC | 5-b | 1857 | 11,964,000 | 7 | indi | B | 2 | Numerous movements but mostly isolated believers and families witnessing within Hinduism. |
| Independent Holiness | I-Hol-tC | 5-c | 1852 | 1,527,000 | 39 | souk | B | 5 | E.g. Yesukyo Tae-Han Songkyol-kyohwei. HQ Seoul. 185n,1p(140),W=95%,617Y. |
| Indep Hungarian Orthodox | I-Hun-tC | 10-f | 1933 | 520 | 1 | hung | C | 5 | E.g. Greek Oriental HOC. Split begun by Serbian P Belgrade. Jacobite succession. Also USA. |
| independent evangelicals | I-ind-tC | 5-d | 1955 | 395,000 | 2 | phil | C | 5 | E.g. Dispensationalists. Expansion until 1970. HQ Pangasinan. 60% Ilocano. 200n, 3000Y. |
| Independent Witnesses | I-Jeh-tC | 5-d | 1908 | 365,000 | 7 | conz | C | 4 | Ch of the Watchtower. Ex Jehovah's Witnesses. 1950s, ruthlessly suppressed. In NE. |
| Messianic Jewish Christians | I-Jew-tC | 5-e | 1896 | 26,000 | 1 | usa | C | 5 | Black Jews (Jewish observances). Black members. Also Africa, West Indies. |
| Indep Latin-rite Catholics | I-Lat-tC | 5-c | 1957 | 6,991,000 | 1 | chin | B | 5 | Open Ch. Under Ai Guo Hui (Chinese Catholic Patriotic Association, CCPA). Set up by regime. |
| Liberal Catholics | I-Lib-tC | 5-d | 1915 | 109,000 | 18 | phil | C | 3 | E.g. Iglesia Watawat ng Lahi. Ex RCC. Catholic-type hierarchy. Rizalist, spiritist. |
| Lutheran/Reformed united ch | I-LuR-tC | 5-e | c1970 | 1,400 | 1 | indi | B | 5 | E.g. Fundamentalist split ex CSI, D North Kerala (United Basel Mission Ch). HQ Calicut. |
| Independent Lutherans | I-Lut-tC | 5-c | 1830 | 1,848,000 | 20 | indo | B | 5 | E.g. GKPI. GK Protestan I. N Sumatra. Ex HKBP. Batak. 79n,1x,1s,W=55%,7634Yy. |
| Indep Macedonian Orthodox | I-Mac-tC | 5-e | | 1,200 | 1 | aust | C | 5 | Macedonian Orthodox immigrants in Fitzroy (Victoria). Slavs. 1 Bulgarian priest. |
| marginal independent Christians | I-mar-tC | 5-c | 1769 | 1,183,000 | 48 | usa | C | 2 | E.g. Native American Ch NAC. 23 Chapters. In all US Indian tribes. Strict ethics; peyote eating. |
| Independent Mennonites | I-Men-tC | 5-d | 1812 | 141,000 | 7 | ukra | C | 5 | E.g. AUCECB 1963. German-speaking. Siberia, Frunze, Karaganda; rapid growth in Ukraine. |
| Independent Methodists | I-Met-tC | 5-c | 1787 | 7,293,000 | 46 | usa | C | 5 | E.g. AMEC. Black. 13 USA Districts. 20 bps. Many new megachurches. Africa, W Indies. 7089n. |

*Continued opposite*

*Table 17–6 continued*

| *Name of religion/religionists* 1 | *Pedigree* 2 | *Type* 3 | *Begun* 4 | *Adherents* 5 | *Ext* 6 | *Coun* 7 | *W* 8 | *X* 9 | *E. g. = examples; name for God, other religions present, D=denominations, M=missions.* 10 |
|---|---|---|---|---|---|---|---|---|---|
| Indep Moldavian Orthodox | I-Mol-tC | 5-d | 1993 | 756,000 | 1 | mold | C | 5 | Schism of 33% of Orthodox Church from P Moscow, aided by P Bucharest. 25n. |
| Independent Moravians | I-Mor-tC | 10-f | | 200 | 1 | hond | C | 5 | Unity of the Brethren. Small indigenous split ex Moravian Church. |
| Muslim believers in Christs | I-Mus-tC | 5-d | c1950 | 537,000 | 15 | paki | A | 2 | Converted Muslims who remain in Islam to witness there for Christ. |
| Independent Assyrians | I-Nes-tC | 5-e | 1967 | 82,900 | 3 | indi | B | 5 | Schism ex Shimun XXIII (USA) supporting rival patriarch Addai (Iraq). 27n. |
| No-Church movement | I-NoC-tC | 5-e | 1900 | 3,500 | 2 | japa | B | 4 | E.g. Mukyokai. Small Bible study groups. No buildings, no clergy, unorganized. |
| Indep Nondenominationalists | I-Non-tC | 5-c | 1741 | 2,314,000 | 71 | chin | B | 5 | Agnostics converted to Christ but remaining in agnostic organizations as a witness. |
| Old Ritualists | I-OBe-tC | 5-c | 1634 | 1,822,000 | 19 | russ | B | 5 | Old Believers. Raskolniki. (Schismatics). Vast extent from Baltic across Siberia. |
| Old Catholics | I-OCa-tC | 5-d | 1724 | 910,000 | 19 | usa | C | 5 | E.g. Immigrants from Poland, where church began in 1893. Archbishop, 2 bps, 48n,30w,10m. |
| Old Calendarist Orthodox | I-OCd-tC | 5-d | 1924 | 270,000 | 4 | gree | C | 5 | E.g. Paleohemerologites. Old Calendar Greek OC. Ex Ch of G. In USA, Canada. 250n,1100w. |
| Orthodox schismatics | I-Ort-tC | 5-d | 1866 | 111,000 | 7 | kaza | B | 5 | Total about 6, including: ROCOR, UAOC, Byelorussian AOC. |
| Orthodox sectarians | I-Ose-tC | 5-d | 1765 | 114,000 | 3 | russ | B | 5 | Total about 20 (see list below), underground, organized, nationwide. |
| Independent Friends | I-Qua-tC | 5-e | 1965 | 36,800 | 2 | usa | C | 5 | Quakers. Until 1968: Ev Friends Alliance. 4 YMs: Ev Friends Ch, Kansas, Rocky M, Northwest. |
| isolated radio churches | I-rad-tC | 5-d | 1939 | 356,000 | 7 | pola | C | 2 | Isolated believers in non-religious families. R=9600(SGA, TWR, Radio Vatican, &c). |
| Reformed Anglicans | I-ReA-tC | 5-d | 1844 | 179,000 | 10 | soua | C | 5 | Ch of Sobantu (Colenso). Evangelical. Churches: 150 Zulu, 17 White, 2 Coloured. 100n. |
| Reformed Catholics | I-ReC-tC | 5-c | 1881 | 5,292,000 | 11 | phil | C | 5 | E.g. PIC. Iglesia Filipina Independiente, IFI. Ex RCC. Many breakoffs. 470n. |
| Independent Reformed | I-Ref-tC | 5-c | 1743 | 8,936,000 | 51 | souk | B | 5 | E.g. Tae-Han Yesukyo Changno-hwei (Hap Dong). NAE. Anti-ecumenical schism |
| Reformed Orthodox | I-ReO-tC | 5-c | 1771 | 1,144,000 | 15 | indi | B | 5 | Reform ex Orthodox Syrian Ch. Syrians. 6 Dioceses. 272n,6H,30r,2s,575t,W=37%. |
| Indep Romanian Orthodox | I-Rum-tC | 5-d | 1904 | 119,000 | 3 | usa | C | 5 | E.g. Schism rejecting P Bucharest. Now under Orth Ch in America. 50n,39t(1693). |
| Independent Russian Orthodox | I-Rus-tC | 5-c | 1617 | 1,062,000 | 30 | ukra | C | 5 | Russian Orthodox Church Outside of Russia. M=ROCOR(until 1990, in exile in USA). |
| Independent Salvationists | I-Sal-tC | 5-d | 1938 | 145,000 | 5 | cong | C | 5 | E.g. Ch of God of the Candle. Vili messiah Zepherin Lassy. Ex SA. Declining. |
| Independent Serbian Orthodox | I-Ser-tC | 5-e | 1766 | 37,300 | 5 | aust | C | 5 | Dissident Yugoslavs rejecting P Belgrade. USA links. One bishop, 9 priests. |
| single congregation(s) | I-sin-tC | 5-c | 1920 | 2,138,000 | 7 | usa | C | 5 | In over 100 noncharismatic single congregations (Moody Bible Institute 8,000 members). |
| Independent Spiritualists | I-Spi-tC | 5-d | 1904 | 115,000 | 1 | phil | C | 2 | E.g. Union Espiritista Cristiana de Filipinas. Spiritualist body. HQ Malabon, Rizal. |
| Traditionalist Anglicans | I-TrA-tC | 5-e | 1996 | 12,000 | 1 | brit | C | 5 | Anglican Traditionalists, ex C of E over ordination of women. 1,100 clergy. |
| True Orthodox | I-Tru-tC | 5-d | 1927 | 377,000 | 4 | russ | B | 5 | IPTS. Istinno-Pravoslavnaya Tserkov. Remnants of underground church smashed by KGB. |
| Indep Ukrainian Orthodox | I-Ukr-tC | 5-c | 1918 | 7,456,000 | 18 | ukra | C | 5 | Anti-Russian schism, forming own Patriarchate. Huge start, then decline. 36 bps. |
| Independent United churches | I-Uni-tC | 5-b | 1807 | 12,781,000 | 3 | chin | B | 5 | E.g. TSPM. 1950, all non-RCs forcibly united. 1966-79, all chs closed. Now 40% registered. |
| Christadelphians | m-Ade-tC | 5-e | 1800 | 66,300 | 20 | brit | C | 3 | E.g. Birmingham Central Basis of Fellowship. 342 ecclesias in 1970. Pacifist. Declining. |
| Divine Science chs | m-Div-tC | 5-e | 1987 | 1,200 | 1 | usa | C | 2 | Divine Science. Metaphysical, New Thought. Aggressive church-planting in CA, ID, BC/Canada. |
| Gnostics | m-Gno-tC | 5-e | 1842 | 74,000 | 3 | germ | C | 1 | Sonnenwesen/Being Anthroposophical Society. 7 sacraments. HQ Stuttgart. 150n. |
| Holy Spirit Associationists | m-HSA-tC | 5-c | 1954 | 1,020,000 | 8 | souk | B | 2 | T'ongil Kyohoe. Unification Ch. Missions to USA, Japan, 120 nations. HQ Seoul. 1013n. |
| Jehovah's Witnesses | m-Jeh-tC | 5-b | 1872 | 12,757,000 | 212 | usa | C | 2 | Watch Tower. World HQ Brooklyn. In USA, 22% Blacks (1975) 25740n,40814Y. (1995) 43663Y. |
| Latter-day Saints | m-LdS-tC | 5-c | 1830 | 8,960,000 | 102 | usa | C | 2 | Mormons. HQ Utah. Also 700,000 overseas. (1970) 17272n,91237Y. (1990) 28962n. |
| Liberal Catholic Gnostics | m-Lib-tC | 5-e | 1953 | 37,300 | 1 | fran | C | 1 | E.g. Apostolic Gnostic Ch. Closed groups protecting Gospel from world. Belgium, Brazil, Italy. |
| marginal Orthodox | m-Ort-tC | 5-e | 1899 | 87,700 | 2 | russ | B | 2 | Emigrations to Canada, then returns. Villages: Caucasus, Georgia, Siberia, CAsia. |
| Paulicians | m-Pau-tC | 5-e | c 250 | 6,300 | 2 | bulg | C | 2 | A few communities, speaking Palityan (near Bulgarian). Also in Hungary. Dualist, rejecting OT. |
| metaphysical Christians | m-Sci-tC | 5-c | 1879 | 1,074,000 | 55 | usa | C | 2 | E.g. Christian Science. Healing ministry. HQ Mother Church, Boston. Decline 2%pa. 5848n. |
| Spiritualists | m-Spi-tC | 5-d | 1852 | 131,000 | 10 | usa | C | 2 | E.g. Ecclesiastical Council. Spiritualists ex Christian Science. Mainly NY state. 40n. |
| Swedenborgians | m-Swe-tC | 5-e | 1783 | 28,300 | 15 | soua | C | 3 | New Jerusalem Ch. M=Gen Conf NC(UK). 1961 merged with Ethiopian Cath Ch in Zion; 5n. |
| Theosophists | m-The-tC | 5-e | 1904 | 5,100 | 3 | germ | C | 2 | E.g. Nature Philosophy Union. Theocratic, messianic. HQ Vomperberg/Tyrol. In 8 nations. |
| Unitarians | m-Unt-tC | 5-d | 1566 | 360,000 | 26 | usa | C | 3 | E.g. 1961 merger of Unitarian Ch, Universalist Chs. Declining. 886n,2s(150). |
| Albanian/Greek-speaking Orth | O-Alb-tC | 5-d | 1908 | 605,000 | 4 | alba | B | 5 | E.g. Suppressed 1967, restored 1991. 4 Eparchies: Tirana, Berat, Gjirokastër, Korçë. Tosks. |
| Arabic/Greek-speaking Orth | O-Ara-tC | 5-c | 1920 | 1,501,000 | 29 | usa | C | 5 | Former Syrian Antiochian Orth AD NY & NA. In Greek P Antioch. 95% Arab. 110n. |
| Armenian Apostolic Orthodox | O-Arm-tC | 5-c | 1440 | 6,197,000 | 47 | arme | C | 5 | C of Echmiadzin. 72 bishops. Charismatic renewal: Brotherhood of Lovers of the Church. |
| Bulgarian Orthodox | O-Bul-tC | 5-c | 1186 | 6,523,000 | 20 | bulg | C | 5 | Balgarskata Pravoslavna Crkva. 23 bps. 1785n,123de(200m,360w),1j,2s(330),W=13%. |
| Byelorussian Orthodox | O-Bye-tC | 5-c | 1793 | 4,920,000 | 6 | belo | C | 5 | White Russians 90%. Now 10 Dioceses, 10 bishops under P Moscow. 13% Russians. |
| Coptic Orthodox | O-Cop-tC | 5-c | 1150 | 9,845,000 | 24 | egyp | B | 5 | Al-Kanisah al-Kebtiah al-Orthodoxiah. 42 Dioceses worldwide, 77 bps,5e(200),1500n,5s(200). |
| Czech Orthodox | O-Cze-tC | 5-e | 1863 | 48,000 | 1 | czec | B | 5 | Církev Pravoslavná v Ceskoslovenská. Mainly Slovaks in east. A=1951. 4 bps,137n,1s. |
| Estonian Orthodox | O-Est-tC | 5-d | 1842 | 196,000 | 5 | esto | B | 5 | Formerly Russian OC (D-Tallinn & Estonia); 1996, placed under EP Constantinople. 11n. |
| Ethiopian Orthodox | O-Eth-tC | 5-b | 1172 | 23,896,000 | 15 | ethi | B | 5 | Ecclesiastical tradition based in Ethiopia, with members in 15 countries. |
| Finnish Orthodox | O-Fin-tC | 5-e | 1925 | 66,400 | 2 | finl | C | 5 | Suomen Ortodoksinen Kirkko. 3 Dioceses. Autonomous 1923. Karelians. 5 bps,64n. |
| Georgian Orthodox | O-Geo-tC | 5-c | c1100 | 2,853,000 | 9 | geor | C | 5 | Catholicate of Mtskheta & Tiflis. 15 Dioceses, 26 bishops. |
| Greek Orthodox | O-Gre-tC | 5-b | 1083 | 15,439,000 | 72 | gree | C | 5 | Ekklesia tes Hellados. 95 bps,7530n,7184b,144d(891m),163e(1709w). |
| Hungarian Orthodox | O-Hun-tC | 5-e | c1200 | 52,000 | 1 | hung | C | 5 | Autonomous, under P Moscow. Greek/Serbian/Romanian. Many refugees since 1989. 8n. |
| Latvian Orthodox | O-Lav-tC | 5-d | c1130 | 260,000 | 1 | latv | C | 5 | Before 1990, 67% Russians, Ukrainians, and other Slavs, 33% Latvians. |
| Macedonian Orthodox | O-Mac-tC | 5-c | 1018 | 1,285,000 | 5 | mace | C | 5 | 1919 integrated into Serbian Orthodox Ch, 1967 declared its independence. 7 bishops. |
| Moldavian Orthodox | O-Mol-tC | 5-c | c1975 | 1,334,000 | 3 | mold | C | 5 | Ethnic Moldavians, Romanians under Russian P Moscow; autonomy 1992. 4 Dioceses, 4 bps. |
| Assyrian Orthodox | O-Nes-tC | 5-d | 1814 | 268,000 | 18 | iraq | A | 5 | Assyrian Ch. Nestorians. 3 Dioceses. Patriarch Mar Dinkha IV lives in USA. 26n. |
| Polish Orthodox | O-Pol-tC | 5-c | 1370 | 1,116,000 | 2 | pola | C | 5 | Autokefaliczny Kosciol Prawoslawny. 1939, 4 million. 6 bps. (1970) 216n,216b,1d,1e,1s,1u. |
| Romanian Orthodox | O-Rum-tC | 5-b | 1359 | 20,012,000 | 23 | roma | C | 5 | Biserica Ortodoxa Romana. The Lord's Army (300,000) is in Evang. Alliance. 20 bps,8545n. |
| Russian Orthodox | O-Rus-tC | 5-b | 988 | 88,227,000 | 51 | russ | B | 5 | ROC. Russkaya Pravoslavnaya Tserkov. 93 Dioceses, 103 bps, 14000n,60de(5000),82s. |
| Serbian Orthodox | O-Ser-tC | 5-c | 1219 | 7,486,000 | 21 | yugo | C | 5 | Srpska Pravoslavna Crkva. P since AD 1346. 13 Dioceses, 36 bishops,1j,6s. |
| Slovak Orthodox | O-Slo-tC | 5-e | 1863 | 16,000 | 1 | slok | C | 5 | Cirkev Pravoslavna. |
| Syro-Malabarese | O-SyM-tC | 5-c | 1876 | 2,417,000 | 12 | indi | B | 5 | Malankara OSC, Catholicate of the East. Syrians. 22 bps,942n,1s(85),W=55%,7820Yy. |
| Syrian Orthodox | O-Syr-tC | 5-c | 1895 | 1,180,000 | 24 | indi | B | 5 | Reassertion by P-Antioch of authority over Malankara OSC (India) and other areas. |
| Ukrainian Orthodox | O-Ukr-tC | 5-b | 1775 | 27,608,000 | 9 | ukra | C | 5 | Russian Orthodox Church, Exarchate of the Ukraine, under P Moscow. 37 bishops. |
| Adventists | P-Adv-tC | 5-b | 1844 | 12,375,000 | 199 | braz | C | 5 | E.g. SDAs. E,N,SBrazil. 10 launches, 2 planes. 306nx,56f,4H,6h,2s,2099t(177230),17036Y. |
| Baptists | P-Bap-tC | 5-b | 1611 | 52,179,000 | 163 | usa | C | 5 | E.g. SBC. 1845 ex North. 99% White. (1970) 31000n,2H,6s,W=39%,409659Y. (1990) 63352n. |
| Christian Brethren | P-CBr-tC | 5-c | 1827 | 3,051,000 | 113 | russ | B | 5 | Open Brethren with links to Britain and Europe. |
| union congregations | P-com-tC | 5-e | 1908 | 20,400 | 18 | indi | B | 5 | Begun for all Protestants in major new steel city Bhilai (MP). Steel, mines. 3n. |
| Congregationalists | P-Con-tC | 5-c | 1618 | 2,547,000 | 55 | soua | C | 5 | E.g. UCCSA. 1967 union CUSA,CCA,UCMS,LMS. 50% Colored,40% Bantu,10% White.153n. |
| Disciples | P-Dis-tC | 5-c | 1809 | 1,812,000 | 18 | usa | C | 5 | Liberal wing, Restoration Movement. Schisms, 6886n,4s(348),W=39%,24481Y. |
| Dunkers | P-Dun-tC | 5-d | 1723 | 603,000 | 15 | germ | C | 5 | Tunkers, Dippers. German Baptists: baptism by 3-fold immersion. |
| Tunkers | P-Dun-tC | 5-d | 1719 | 631,000 | 7 | cent | B | 5 | E.g. EEF. Brethren Ch. M=NFBC(USA). 70% Baya, 20% Mandja, 10% Karre. 56f,1H,16h,1r,2s. |
| Exclusive Brethren | P-EBr-tC | 5-d | 1838 | 218,000 | 18 | brit | C | 5 | Kelly-Continental; Continuing Tunbridge Wells; Raven-Taylor; Glanton. Darbyites. |
| Protestant Evangelicals | P-Eva-tC | 5-c | 1840 | 6,214,000 | 89 | nige | B | 5 | E.g. ECWA. M=SIM. A=1956. 800n,500m,50w,672f,3H,88h,31k,22p(692),1s,W=80%,2000Y. |
| Fundamentalists | P-Fun-tC | 5-d | 1890 | 240,000 | 14 | phil | C | 4 | E.g. Doane Baptists. M=ABWE(Regular Baptists) (USA). Growing very rapidly. 76f,3h,2s. |
| Holiness | P-Hol-tC | 5-c | 1767 | 8,041,000 | 117 | souk | B | 5 | E.g. Kidokyo Tae-Han Songkyol Kyohwei. M=OMS. 354n,14f,3s(500),W=65%,1567Y. |
| Lutheran/Reformed united ch | P-LuR-tC | 5-b | 1517 | 14,345,000 | 22 | neth | C | 5 | E.g. VPKN. 1995, merger of NHK, GKN, and ELKN under way, aiming to finish by AD 2000. |
| Lutherans | P-Lut-tC | 5-b | 1517 | 61,894,000 | 122 | swed | C | 5 | E.g. Svenska Kyrkan. Begun 600 years before Reformation. 13 Diocs. Women clergy. 3350n. |
| Mennonites | P-Men-tC | 5-c | 1525 | 2,187,000 | 59 | indi | B | 5 | E.g. M=Menonnite Brethren Ch of NAmerica. 99% Telugu. 175n,14f,3H,3h,9p,100Y. |
| Methodists | P-Met-tC | 5-b | 1747 | 23,095,000 | 108 | usa | C | 5 | E.g. UMC. 1968, EUB merger. 96% White, 4% Black. 81 Confs. 34974n,13s,W=36%. |
| Moravians | P-Mor-tC | 5-d | 1457 | 603,000 | 27 | tanz | B | 5 | E.g. 2 Provinces: Western (Nyamwezi), Southern (Nyakyusa). M=MBG. 72n,5x,21f,4H,5h,1s. |
| Nondenominationalists | P-Non-tC | 5-c | 1685 | 3,943,000 | 76 | keny | C | 5 | E.g. M=AIM. 33% Kamba, 27% Kalenjin, 20% Kikuyu. 80n,50x,226f,4H,30h,5p,1s,2000Y. |
| Oneness Pentecostals | P-Pe1-tC | 5-c | 1914 | 2,768,000 | 74 | usa | C | 4 | E.g. 1945 union PAJC, PC. White. (1970) 4800n. (1990) 7512n. Missions in 74 countries. (83n). |
| Baptistic Pentecostals | P-Pe2-tC | 5-b | 1892 | 56,890,000 | 174 | braz | C | 5 | E.g. Assemblies of God. 1934,M=AoG,SFM,NPY,FFFM. 30000n,27000mw,20f. |
| Holiness Pentecostals | P-Pe3-tC | 5-c | 1886 | 6,317,000 | 118 | usa | C | 5 | First US Pentecostal body. 95% White. In 118 countries. 7359n,1j,30,1s,5266t(478984). |
| Pentecostal Apostolics | P-PeA-tC | 5-c | 1904 | 1,776,000 | 30 | nige | B | 5 | E.g. TAC. M=ACMM(UK). 1931, invited to assist Aladura churches. Southeast. 6 Areas. 5f,3s. |
| unclassified Pentecostals | P-Pen-tC | 5-e | c1970 | 3,600 | 1 | norw | C | 5 | Total about 6 including International Pente Holiness Ch, UPC (USA). |
| Friends | P-Qua-tC | 5-d | 1652 | 413,000 | 43 | keny | C | 5 | E.g. EAYM. M=FUM. Largest Quaker ch after USA. 99% Luhya. 130n,2x,16f,3H,1s,W=50%. |
| Presbyterians | P-Ref-tC | 5-b | 1520 | 46,074,000 | 141 | usa | C | 5 | E.g. PCUSA. 1983 merger of UPUSA, PCUS. 1973, 8% lost in schism. 4595n,4s. In 9 nations. |
| Salvationists | P-Sal-tC | 5-c | 1865 | 2,275,000 | 84 | usa | C | 5 | E.g. Territories: Central, Eastern, Southern, Western. 38 Divisions. 3735n,33H,4s. |
| United churches | P-Uni-tC | 5-b | 1612 | 23,997,000 | 45 | germ | C | 5 | E.g. EKD. 20 Landeskirchen, 8 other denominations. 300p,39s,P=26%,W=6%. |
| Waldensians | P-Wal-tC | 5-e | 1173 | 42,200 | 2 | ital | C | 5 | Waldensian-Methodists. 75n,8x,1p,1s(6),W=40%,320Yy,4135z. |
| Armenian (Eastern-rite Catholic) | R-Arm-tC | 5-d | 1605 | 163,000 | 15 | usa | C | 5 | E.g. US Armenian rite. |
| Bulgarian (Byzantine rite) | R-Bul-tC | 5-e | 1926 | 22,600 | 1 | bulg | C | 5 | Uniates. Catholics of Byzantino-Slav rite. M=AA. |
| Byzantine-rite | R-Byz-tC | 5-d | 1777 | 147,000 | 3 | usa | C | 5 | E.g. PA III. Formerly Ruthenian-rite. |
| Chaldean (Eastern Syrian rite) | R-Cha-tC | 5-d | 1553 | 318,000 | 9 | iraq | C | 5 | E.g. Patriarchate,1553. Rapid Catholic influx from north. |
| Coptic (Alexandrian rite) | R-Cop-tC | 5-d | 1895 | 207,000 | 1 | egyp | C | 5 | Egyptians, Coptic rite. Patriarch lives in Cairo. M=CM. |
| Ethiopic, Alexandrian rite | R-Eth-tC | 5-d | 1930 | 151,000 | 2 | erit | C | 5 | Katholikawi Membre Pepesenna. Tigrai, Mensa. |
| Greek (Byzantine rite) | R-Gre-tC | 5-e | 1911 | 2,200 | 2 | gree | C | 5 | Byzantine-rite Catholics. HQ Athens. |
| Hungarian (Byzantine rite) | R-Hun-tC | 5-d | 1912 | 283,000 | 1 | hung | C | 5 | Hungarian-speaking. Ruthenian parishes. 1s. |
| Italo-Albanian (Byzantine rite) | R-IAb-tC | 5-e | 1919 | 60,400 | 1 | ital | C | 5 | Eastern-rite (Oriental) Albanians living in southern Italy. HQ Lungro. |
| Latin-rite Catholics | R-Lat-tC | 5-a | 1491 | 1,043,106,000 | 229 | mexi | C | 5 | E.g. Catholic Ch of Mexico. C=37+3+146. |
| Latin- & Eastern-rite jurisdiction | R-LEr-tC | 5-c | 1084 | 1,497,000 | 9 | braz | C | 5 | E.g. C=101+14+329. |
| Malankara rite | R-Mal-tC | 5-d | 1932 | 332,000 | 1 | indi | C | 5 | Kerala. Malayalam, Tamil. 1p. |

*Continued overleaf*

*Table 17–6 continued*

| Name of religion/religionists 1 | Pedigree 2 | Type 3 | Begun 4 | Adherents 5 | Ext 6 | Coun 7 | W 8 | X 9 | E. g. = examples; name for God, other religions present, D=denominations, M=missions. 10 |
|---|---|---|---|---|---|---|---|---|---|
| Maronite rite | R-Mar-tC | 5-c | 1353 | 3,365,000 | 11 | arge | C | 5 | E.g. Arab Christians from Lebanon. |
| Melkite rite | R-Mel-tC | 5-c | 1683 | 1,269,000 | 12 | braz | C | 5 | M=SMSP. |
| plural Oriental rites | R-Ori-tC | 5-d | 1954 | 280,000 | 3 | pola | C | 5 | Ordinariate for all Eastern-rite Catholics (Melkite, Armenian, et alia). |
| Romanian Byzantine rite | R-Rum-tC | 5-c | 1721 | 2,107,000 | 2 | roma | C | 5 | 1948-90 suppressed, forced into ROC. |
| Russian (Byzantine rite) | R-Rus-tC | 5-e | 1917 | 11,400 | 1 | russ | C | 5 | For all Russians of Byzantine rite. |
| Ruthenian (Byzantine rite) | R-Rut-tC | 5-d | 1771 | 444,000 | 2 | ukra | C | 5 | Ruthenians. 1949, forced into Orth D Mukachevo. |
| Ruthenian Catholics | R-Rut-tC | 5-d | 1771 | 391,000 | 7 | ukra | C | 5 | Little Russians. Catholic Slavs. In Ukraine, Poland, Hungary, Slovakia. |
| Slovak (Byzantine rite) | R-Slo-tC | 5-d | 1818 | 285,000 | 2 | slok | C | 5 | Church of Srlence, liquidated 1945-50. |
| Syro-Malabarese Rite | R-SyM-tC | 5-c | 1887 | 3,262,000 | 1 | indi | C | 5 | Kerala. Malayalam. |
| Syro-Antiochian Rite | R-Syr-tC | 5-d | 1633 | 118,000 | 7 | iraq | C | 5 | Al-Sourian al-Kathoulik (Syrian Catholics). |
| Ukrainian Byzantine rite | R-Ukr-tC | 5-c | 1087 | 5,513,000 | 10 | ukra | C | 5 | MM=Great/Major Archdiocese(1 of only 2 in world). |
| unaffiliated Christians | UC | 2-b | c1700 | 111,125,000 | 236 | usa | C | 5 | Christians with no affiliation to organized Christianity. |
| Deutscher Caritasverband | vC | 9-d | 1887 | 220,000 | 40 | germ | C | 5 | Caritas. Founded in Freiburg. Roman Catholic medical care system; 36,000 centers. |
| United Bible Societies | wC | 7-a | 1946 | 1,650,000,000 | 210 | brit | C | 5 | UBS. 1804 British & Foreign Bible Society. (1990) HQ Reading, UK. |
| World Cong of Chr Fundamentalists | wC | 7-c | c1970 | 2,200,000 | 30 | brit | C | 4 | Based on inerrant infallible Bible. Congresses 1980, 1986, 1990. |
| World Council of Biblical Chs | wC | 7-d | 1980 | 100,000 | 10 | usa | C | 4 | WCBC. Fundamentalists excluding all linked to WCC, WEF, RCC, ICCC, Pentecostals. |
| World Council of Churches | wC | 7-a | 1948 | 460,000,000 | 150 | swit | C | 5 | WCC/COE/ORK. HQ Geneva. |
| World Evangelical Fellowship | wC | 7-b | 1846 | 150,000,000 | 100 | sing | B | 5 | WEF. HQ Singapore. Origins in 1846's World's Evangelical Alliance. |
| Evangelical Missionary Alliance UK | G-wC | 7-d | 1958 | 250,000 | 70 | brit | C | 5 | EMA. |
| Interdenom Foreign Mission Assoc | M-wC | 7-e | 1917 | 6,000 | | usa | C | 5 | IFMA. 50 foreign mission societies; Fundamentalist and Conservative Evangelical. |
| International Council of Christian Chs | T-wC | 7-c | 1948 | 3,000,000 | 30 | neth | C | 4 | ICCC. Fundamentalist, anti-ecumenical. HQ Garderen. 100 member denominations, declining. |
| Renewal believers | ZC | 2-a | 1549 | 619,906,000 | 236 | usa | C | 5 | Total all renewal believers alive at mid-year. D=25,780 |
| unaffiliated Renewal believers | UZC | 2-b | 1950 | 78,328,000 | 230 | usa | C | 5 | Individual believers experiencing Holy Spirit gifts but remaining not in Renewal bodies. D=2,000 |
| **Taoists** | D | 1-c | | 2,655,000 | 15 | chin | B | 1 | Tao-chiao/Daoists. Separate religion in Taiwan. 86 major sects. In many syncretic religions also. |
| Chinese Taoist Association | nD | 7-d | | 350,000 | 1 | chin | B | 0 | CTA. Government-controlled. 200 monasteries and temples. |
| National Taoist Assoc of Rep of China | nD | 7-e | | 50,000 | 1 | taiw | B | 2 | Coordinating body for well-organized Taoist council. |
| Golden Lotus | sD | 2-e | 1150 | 20,000 | 1 | chin | B | 0 | Pure Yang. Chuan-chen Tao (Way of Realizing Truth). |
| Mao-shan | sD | 2-d | 364 | 100,000 | 1 | chin | B | 0 | One of Taoism's 86 major sects. Meeting on Mount Mao to receive Scriptures. |
| School of the Magic Jewel | sD | 2-c | c300 | 1,000,000 | 1 | chin | B | 1 | Ling-pao Pai. Tao religious branch; Longmen/Dragon Gate (1,300 Caves). |
| Tao of Unity | sD | 2-d | c1350 | 300,000 | 1 | chin | B | 1 | Cheng-i Tao. Major form or sect of Taoism, utilizing amulets, talismans. |
| Way of the Supreme One | sD | 2-d | 1150 | 100,000 | 1 | chin | B | 0 | Tai-i Tao. A school of religious Taoism. F=Hsiao Pao-chen. |
| Wu-tou-mi Tao | sD | 2-d | c150 | 100,000 | 1 | chin | B | 1 | '5 Pecks of Rice'. Cheng-yi. One of the 2 religious branches of Taoism. |
| World Red Swastika Society | wD | 7-e | | 50,000 | 4 | chin | B | 1 | Chinese secret society with criminal reputation. |
| **Chinese folk-religionists** | F | 2-a | BC 1000 | 384,807,000 | 89 | chin | B | 1 | Popular religion: Buddhism, Confucianism, Taoism, universism, ancestor veneration, local gods. |
| **Confucianists** | G | 1-c | BC 500 | 6,299,000 | 15 | chin | B | 2 | Ju-chia. F= Confucius. Highly organized in South Korea, also Japan, Viet Nam. |
| Neo-Confucianism | NG | 2-d | c1050 | 100,000 | 2 | chin | B | 1 | Confucian response to teaching of Taoism, yin-yang, Five Elements. |
| **Hindus** | H | 1-a | | 811,336,000 | 114 | indi | B | 2 | Based on the Vedas, now with many varieties. |
| Folk-Hindus | FH | 2-a | | 500,000,000 | 65 | indi | B | 0 | Vast masses who combine Hinduism with local folk religions and deities. |
| Divine Light Mission | sFH | 2-c | 1960 | 1,200,000 | 7 | indi | B | 2 | Begun India, 1971 USA (ashrams in 24 cities); 1982 schism, decline to 30,000 in UK, USA. |
| Ganapatyas | sFH | 2-c | 1651 | 1,000,000 | 5 | indi | B | 0 | Popular Hindu devotional movement, worshiping Ganesh. Maharashtra. |
| Ishvara | sFH | 2-e | c1982 | 5,000 | 3 | brit | C | 2 | Also called Lifewaves. An offshoot of Divina Light Mission. |
| Panj Pir cultists | sFH | 2-d | c1500 | 300,000 | 1 | indi | B | 1 | Popularist Hindu-Muslim cult. Devotees from 53 castes choose 5 deities each. |
| Vedism | HH | 2-c | | 5,000,000 | 30 | indi | B | 1 | Emphasis or return to centrality of the Vedas body of Hindu sacred knowledge. |
| Advaita Vedanta | sHH | 2-d | c700 | 300,000 | 1 | indi | B | 1 | F=Sankara. Oldest of 6 major schools of Vedism. Monistic. Shiva as atman of the universe. |
| Brahmanism | sHH | 2-d | BC 2000 | 500,000 | 2 | indi | B | 2 | Earliest Vedic period. Sacrifice and ritual under control of the Brahmins. |
| Divine Life Mission | sHH | 2-e | 1936 | 30,000 | 35 | indi | B | 2 | F=Shivananda, a Tamil doctor. Advaita basis, Hatha yoga. Branches worldwide. |
| Dvaita-vedanta | sHH | 2-d | 1250 | 100,000 | 1 | indi | B | 2 | F=Madhva. 3rd of 6 classical schools of Vedism. Hindu philosophy and religious attitude. |
| Hathayoga | sHH | 2-e | c1700 | 20,000 | 1 | indi | B | 0 | Vaishnavas in North India. Inward discipline rejecting external rituals. A Nath cult. |
| Ramakrishna Vedanta Mission | sHH | 2-c | 1886 | 3,000,000 | 25 | indi | B | 2 | F=Swami Vivekananda. 140 maths and centers in India, 50 others across world. |
| Smartas | sHH | 2-e | | 60,000 | 1 | indi | B | 2 | South Indian orthodox brahmin community. Strict standards. Syncretistic. |
| Vedanta Society | sHH | 2-c | 1896 | 1,400,000 | 2 | indi | B | 3 | 'End of the Vedas'. Western branch (in New York) of Ramakrishna Math (monastery). |
| Vishishtadvaita | sHH | 2-d | 1100 | 100,000 | 1 | indi | B | 2 | F=Ramanuja. Second of 6 classical schools of Vedism. School of qualified non-duality. |
| Yoga | sHH | 2-b | 200 | 30,000,000 | 40 | indi | B | 2 | Best known of 6 orthodox Hindu philosophical systems. F=Yajnavalka. Many current varieties. |
| Saktists | KH | 2-b | | 25,720,000 | 35 | indi | B | 1 | Shaktas (Sakti=Power of Shiva). Durga Hinduism. |
| Bhakti | sKH | 2-c | BC c500 | 1,000,000 | 50 | indi | B | 3 | One of the 3 forms of Hindu devotion: Vaisnavas, Saivas, Saktas; also Krsnas. |
| Charan Dasis | sKH | 2-d | c1770 | 150,000 | 1 | indi | B | 2 | Krishna devotionism. In north India among mercantile castes. Yellow clothes. F=Charan Das. |
| ISKCON/Hare Krishna | sKH | 2-d | 1965 | 800,000 | 23 | indi | B | 3 | International Society for Krishna Consciousness. F=A. C. Bhaktivedanta. 100 temples. |
| Varkari Panthis | sKH | 2-d | c1250 | 500,000 | 1 | indi | B | 1 | Warkaris, Hindu devotional movement in Maharashtra. F=Jnanesvar. |
| Neo-Hindus | NH | 2-b | | 17,385,000 | 65 | indi | B | 3 | Large variety of new religions based on revivals of Hinduism. |
| National Council of Hindu Temples | nH | 7-d | c1980 | 429,000 | 2 | brit | C | 5 | Major Hindu coordinating body in Britain. |
| Brahma Kumaris | sNH | 2-d | 1937 | 250,000 | 20 | indi | B | 2 | World Spiritual University (a UN NGO). Run by unmarried women. Millennialist. |
| Elan Vital | sNH | 2-d | 1935 | 130,000 | 10 | indi | B | 3 | Until 1982, Divine Light Mission, then schism under Maharaj Ji. Growing in UK, USA. |
| Transcendental Meditation | sNH | 2-c | c1955 | 4,000,000 | 33 | usa | C | 3 | TM. Spiritual Regeneration Movement. In USA, UK (100,000 practicing), India. |
| Brahmasampradaya | sH-oH | 9-e | c1300 | 50,000 | 1 | indi | B | 1 | One of 4 Vaishnava teaching/monastic traditions. Dualistic; Vishnu supreme. Mainly Karnataka. |
| Dasanami Order | sH-oH | 9-e | c800 | 20,000 | 1 | indi | B | 0 | Wandering Monks. 'The 10 Names' (of Hindu Shaivite ascetic castes). F=Shankara. |
| Nagas | sS-oH | 9-e | c500 | 6,000 | 1 | indi | B | 1 | A semi-military ascetic Shaivite order. Sky-clad (naked). |
| Nath cultists | sS-oH | 9-e | 1200 | 25,000 | 1 | indi | B | 0 | Kanphatas: order of high-caste Shaivite yogis. Monasteries (some Vaishnavite) across India. |
| Nimbaraka Vairagins | sV-oH | 9-e | | 30,000 | 1 | indi | B | 0 | An order of Hindu Vaishnavite ascetics. |
| Ramanandis | sV-oH | 9-e | c1450 | 40,000 | 1 | indi | B | 1 | Largest Vaishnava ascetic order. F=Ramananda. |
| Swaminarayan Hindu Mission | w-oH | 9-d | c1900 | 100,000 | 32 | brit | C | 2 | Worldwide missionary arm, especially to USA, UK; well-organized. |
| Bharata Janata Parishad | qH | 8-b | 1984 | 50,000,000 | 1 | indi | B | 2 | BJP. Political party advancing Hindu identity. |
| Hindu Mahasabha | qH | 8-d | | 800,000 | 1 | indi | B | 0 | Ultra-Orthodox Hindu political group. |
| Rashtriya Swayamsevak Sangh | qH | 8-c | 1925 | 3,000,000 | 10 | indi | B | 1 | RSS. Hindu fundamentalists organizing an extremist self-defence militia. |
| Vishwa Hindu Parishad | qH | 8-c | | 2,000,000 | 40 | indi | B | 2 | VHP. World Hindu Organization. Extremist political body giving Hinduism a systematic ideology. |
| Reform Hindus | RH | 2-c | | 4,460,000 | 30 | indi | B | 2 | Arya Samaj, et alia. Modern attempts to revitalize Hindus and win back converts. |
| Arya Samaj | sRH | 2-c | 1875 | 2,500,000 | 40 | indi | B | 4 | F=Dayananda Sarasvati. Fighting against caste, idol worship, injustice. Worldwide. |
| Prarthana Samaj | sRH | 2-e | 1867 | 50,000 | 1 | indi | B | 1 | The Prayer Society. F=R.G. Bhandarkar. Reformist Hindu movement in Maharashtra. |
| Sri Shankaradeva Sangha | sRH | 2-c | c1500 | 3,500,000 | 5 | indi | B | 1 | Vaishnava reform movement in Assam. F=Shankaradeva (c1500). Reorganised 1933. |
| Shaivites | SH | 2-a | BC 2000 | 216,260,000 | 60 | indi | B | 1 | Saivas, devotees of supreme god Shiva and consort Parvati. More ascetic than Vaishnavas.. |
| Shiva Sena | qSH | 8-e | 1966 | 10,000 | 1 | indi | B | 1 | Army of Sivaji. Marathi Hindu nationalist political party in Maharashtra. Militant. |
| Aghoris | sSH | 2-e | c1600 | 5,000 | 1 | indi | B | 1 | Successors to defunct ascetic Kapalikas. Tantrist Shaivites. Varanasi. |
| Kapalikas | sSH | 10-f | | 100 | 1 | indi | B | 0 | Defunct ascetic Shaivite tradition held by cremation-ground dwellers. |
| Lingayats | sSH | 2-c | c1150 | 1,000,000 | 1 | indi | B | 0 | Virashaivas. Saivite sect worshiping linga. Kannada-speaking (Karnataka). |
| Pratyabhijna | sSH | 2-e | c1920 | 10,000 | 1 | indi | B | 2 | 'Recognition'. Philosophical school of Kashmir Shaivism. Strict monism. |
| Saiva Siddantins | sSH | 2-e | c350 | 20,000 | 1 | indi | B | 1 | Dualists holding plurality of souls eternally distinct from Shiva. Tamils. Bhakti-oriented. |
| Siddha Yoga | sSH | 2-e | c400 | 14,000 | 10 | indi | B | 3 | Kashmir Shaivite teaching. HQ Ganeshpuri. 40 ashrams in Mexico, Japan, New York. |
| Spanda | sSH | 2-e | c850 | 5,000 | 1 | indi | B | 2 | 'Vibration'. One of 3 philosophical schools of Kashmir Shaivism. |
| Trika | sSH | 2-e | c750 | 1,000 | 1 | indi | B | 0 | 'Threefold'. One of 3 philosophical schools of Kashmir Shaivism. Ritual, cosmology: Moribund. |
| Universal Shaiva Trust | sSH | 2-e | c1980 | 3,000 | 2 | usa | C | 5 | Based in California. Contemporary version of monistic Kashmir Shaivism. |
| Hindu Tantrists | TH | 2-c | 400 | 1,000,000 | 15 | indi | B | 0 | Hindu tradition based on Tantras instead of Vedas. Usually Shaktas. Nepal, Bengal, Assam. |
| Ananda Marga | sTH | 2-c | 1955 | 2,500,000 | 7 | indi | B | 4 | Self-development Hindu Yoga. F= Anandamurtiji. Also in Europe, USA. |
| Kaulas | sTH | 2-e | 400 | 15,000 | 3 | indi | B | 2 | Hindi Tantric tradition tracing back to cremation grounds of Kashnir and Swat. |
| Krama | sTH | 2-e | 400 | 50,000 | 1 | nepa | A | 0 | Tantric Hindu cult originating in Swat cremation-ground cults. |
| Samaya | sTH | 2-d | c400 | 500,000 | 1 | indi | B | 2 | One of the 2 major divisions within Hindu Tantrism. |
| Sri Vidya | sTH | 2-e | c500 | 10,000 | 1 | indi | B | 2 | South Indian Hindu Tantrism, worshiping goddess Tripurasundari. |
| Vaishnavites | VH | 2-a | c550 | 549,583,000 | 90 | indi | B | 2 | Sri Vaishnavas, bhakti devotees of god Vishnu and consort Lakshmi. 108 major temples. |
| Ram Rajya Parishad | qVH | 8-e | 1948 | 30,000 | 1 | indi | B | 3 | F=Swami Karapetri. Hindu political party. |
| Akshar Purushottam Sanstha | sVH | 2-e | | 40,000 | 11 | indi | B | 2 | The major schism ex Swaminarayans, reverencing first disciple Gunatitananda. |
| Bhagavatas | sVH | 2-e | c1000 | 30,000 | 10 | indi | B | 1 | Devotees. of Bhagavan (God concerned for human well-being). Many movements. |
| Gaudiya Vaisnava Mission | sVH | 2-e | 1870 | 3,000 | 30 | indi | B | 1 | Bengali Hindu Missionary Society. F=Bhaktivinoda Thakura. Devotion of Krishna. |
| Gaudiya-sampradaya | sVH | 2-e | 1520 | 60,000 | 2 | indi | B | 2 | Bengali devotionalism. F=Sri Chaitanya. 1870, revival leading to ISKCON. |
| Madhva Gaudiya Vairagins | sVH | 2-e | | 4,000 | 1 | indi | B | 1 | Order of Vaishnava ascetics prevalent in Orissa state. |

*Continued opposite*

*Table 17–6 continued*

| Name of religion/religionists 1 | Pedigree 2 | Type 3 | Begun 4 | Adherents 5 | Ext 6 | Coun 7 | W 8 | X 9 | E. g. = examples; name for God, other religions present, D=denominations, M=missions. 10 |
|---|---|---|---|---|---|---|---|---|---|
| Mahanubhavs | sVH | 2-e | | 5,000 | 1 | indi | B | 1 | Manbhavs. Vaishnava devotional movement in Maharashtra. |
| Pushtimarga | sVH | 2-c | 1510 | 2,000,000 | 1 | indi | B | 2 | Vallabhasampradaya. 'Way of Grace'. Vaishnava devotional sect. Bombay, Gujarat, Rajasthan. |
| Ramdasis | sVH | 2-e | c1650 | 20,000 | 2 | indi | B | 1 | Vaishnava devotional movement, with 40 flourishing maths (monasteries). |
| Rudrasampradaya | sVH | 2-e | c1520 | 15,000 | 1 | indi | B | 2 | Bhakti approach to Vaishnavism. F=Vallabha. |
| Sahajiya | sVH | 2-e | c800 | 10,000 | 1 | indi | B | 1 | Sect of Tantrism in Bengal, later becoming Erotic Vaishnavism. Stresses spontaneity in religion. |
| Sanakasampradaya | sVH | 2-d | c1350 | 500,000 | 1 | indi | B | 1 | One of 4 contemporary Vaishnava traditions. Brahman is Krishna. |
| Sant | sVH | 2-d | c1600 | 100,000 | 1 | indi | B | 0 | Based on Vaishnava Bhakti tradition, Nath cultists, et alia. |
| Swaminarayans | sVH | 2-c | 1801 | 5,000,000 | 33 | indi | B | 3 | In India, UK, Kenya, USA. HQ Gujarat. F= Sahajananda Swami (1781-1830), later deified. |
| Tenkalai | sVH | 2-a | c600 | 240,000,000 | 5 | indi | B | 2 | 'Southern Culture'. South Indian Sri Vaishnava sect, holding divine grace must be earned. |
| Vaikhanasas | sVH | 2-e | BC 200 | 12,000 | 1 | indi | B | 2 | Hindu Vaishnava community in South India: Tamilnad, AP, Karnataka. |
| Vaishnava Sahajiyas | sVH | 2-e | | 20,000 | 1 | indi | B | 0 | Esoteric Bengali cult; illegal practices. |
| Vatakalai | ssVH | 2-b | c 600 | 110,000,000 | 1 | indi | B | 2 | 'Northern Culture'. Subsect of Sri Vaishnavas, holding that divine grace is free, not earned. |
| Aurobindo Ashram | zH | 2-e | 1910 | 40,000 | 2 | indi | B | 2 | Purna-Yoga (Integral Yoga) (Integral Yoga). HQ Auroville under The Mother. |
| British Wheel of Yoga | zH | 2-e | 1963 | 4,000 | 2 | brit | C | 5 | BWY. Registered charity to propagate yoga. 1,000 certified teachers. |
| Dev Samaj | zH | 2-e | 1917 | 1,000 | 4 | indi | B | 2 | F=Agnihotri. Ex Brahmo Samaj. Strict morals, vegetarianism, women's education. |
| Hindu fundamentalists | zH | 2-b | | 10,000,000 | 3 | indi | B | 0 | Hindu activists fighting Christians and Muslims to win back Dalits (former Outcastes). |
| Krishnaists | zH | 2-c | | 5,000,000 | 4 | indi | B | 3 | Worshipers of Krishna via numerous sects including ISKCON. |
| Meher Baba movement | zH | 2-d | 1924 | 600,000 | 8 | indi | B | 1 | F=Baba as silent miracle-working final avatar of God (after Rama, Jesus, &c). HQ Meherabad.. |
| Radhasoami Satsang | zH | 2-e | 1861 | 90,000 | 1 | indi | B | 0 | In north India. Now 2 rival movements. F=Soamiji Maharaj. |
| Sanatanists | zH | 2-a | BC 1000 | 740,000,000 | 90 | indi | B | 1 | Old Path Hindus. Popularly called Idol-Worshipers. 9 million priests, 15 million sadhus. |
| Satya Sai Baba Satsang | zH | 2-d | c1900 | 500,000 | 22 | indi | B | 1 | Sai-Baba (died 1918) as miracle worker avatar, with reincarnation form 1926. Global. |
| Siddha Yoga Dham | zH | 2-e | 1976 | 40,000 | 60 | usa | C | 4 | F=Swami Muktananda. Kundalini yoga. Daily meditation, vegetarianism. |
| Sri Chinmoy Centre | zH | 2-e | 1964 | 3,000 | 5 | usa | C | 4 | F=Chinmoy Kumar Ghose, Hindu guru from Bengal. HQ New York. UN connections as an NGO. |
| Udasis | zH | 2-e | c1600 | 5,000 | 1 | indi | B | 2 | One of 12 subgroups of Kabir Panthis (Hindu/Muslim/Sikh syncretism), now mainstream Hindu. |
| **Jews** | J | 1-b | | 14,434,000 | 134 | isra | B | 2 | Practitioners of Judaism in 5 main branches. Centered in Israel, USA, Argentina. |
| Ashkenazis | AJ | 2-b | | 11,080,000 | 120 | isra | B | 2 | Yiddish-speaking Judaism. From Germany; Poland, Russia, Ukraine. |
| Ashkenazic Hasidism | sAJ | 2-c | | 2,500,000 | 20 | isra | B | 2 | Strict Jewish dogmas. Yiddish. From Eastern Europe. |
| Reconstructionist Jews | CJ | 2-e | 1968 | 50,000 | 5 | usa | C | 5 | F=M. M. Kaplan. Opposed to Chosenness, messianism, Zionism, return to Israel. |
| Central Conf of American Rabbis | cJ | 7-d | 1889 | 100,000 | 2 | usa | C | 3 | Founding by Reform rabbinate opposing Orthodox and secularizing trends. |
| Fed of Reconstructionist Congs | cJ | 7-e | 1968 | 50,000 | 6 | usa | C | 5 | 60 congregations worldwide, in USA, Canada, Curacao. |
| Federation of Synagogues in Britain | cJ | 7-d | 1887 | 301,000 | 1 | brit | C | 5 | F=Lord Swaythling. Oriented toward Eastern European Orthodoxy. |
| Synagogue Council of America | cJ | 7-c | 1926 | 5,000,000 | 1 | usa | C | 5 | Umbrella body representing major rabbinical organizations (Orthodox, Conservative, Reform). |
| Union of American Hebrew Congs | cJ | 7-c | 1873 | 2,700,000 | 2 | usa | C | 5 | UAHC. Reform congregations. HQ New York. |
| Union of Orth Congs of America | cJ | 7-d | 1898 | 800,000 | 1 | usa | C | 5 | Represents over 700 congregations. |
| Union of Orthodox Hebrew Congs | cJ | 7-c | 1926 | 1,000,000 | 2 | usa | C | 5 | F=rabbi Victor Schonfeld, to unite Western Orthodoxy. |
| United Synagogue in Greater London | cJ | 7-e | 1870 | 50,000 | 1 | brit | C | 5 | Ashkenazi Jewish congregations. Supports all who recognize UK chief rabbi. |
| United Synagogue of America | cJ | 7-c | 1913 | 1,250,000 | 1 | usa | C | 4 | Conservative Jewish. F=Solomon Schachter. Many agencies. 830 congs, 1,200 rabbis. |
| Oriental Jews | EJ | 2-c | | 2,378,000 | 25 | isra | B | 2 | Immigrants from Eastern states. |
| Folk-Judaism | FJ | 2-d | | 500,000 | 40 | isra | B | 2 | Popular religious interpretation of Judaism. |
| Union of Tradit Conservative Judaism | fJ | 4-e | 1985 | 20,000 | 1 | usa | C | 5 | Later renamed Institute for Traditional Judaism. |
| Karaites | KJ | 2-e | BC c950 | 24,100 | 5 | russ | B | 2 | Readers of the Scriptures. Jewish sect partially accepted in state of Israel. |
| Conservative Judaism | NJ | 2-c | 1845 | 2,000,000 | 10 | germ | C | 3 | Split ex Reform Judaism. Masorati. Begun Germany: USA 1900; opposing neglect of Halakhah. |
| Orthodox Judaism | OJ | 2-c | | 2,500,000 | 110 | isra | B | 2 | Reaction against modernizing and secularizing tendencies in Judaism. |
| Agudat Israel | qOJ | 8-c | 1912 | 1,600,000 | 15 | isra | B | 2 | Orthodox, Zionists political party, Ashkenazi-Hasidic-dominated. |
| Belz Hasidism | qOJ | 8-e | c1820 | 50,000 | 10 | isra | B | 3 | Holocaust survivors from East Europe. Orthodox, Zionist. Centers across Europe, N America. |
| Bobova Hasidism | qOJ | 8-e | | 20,000 | 1 | isra | B | 2 | Contemporary Hasidic group, with own rules and regulations. |
| Mafdal | qOJ | 8-d | 1904 | 100,000 | 1 | isra | B | 2 | National Religious Party. Founded as religio-political Orthodox party. Zionist. |
| Bratslav Hasidism | sOJ | 2-e | 1798 | 4,800 | 1 | slok | C | 4 | Bratslaver. F=rabbi Nahman. |
| Council of Torah Sages | sOJ | 2-d | c1920 | 200,000 | 2 | isra | B | 2 | Ger Hasidism. |
| Habad Hasidism | sOJ | 2-e | | 25,000 | 1 | isra | B | 2 | Chabad. |
| Hasidism | sOJ | 2-e | 1790 | 50,000 | 5 | pola | C | 4 | Jewish enthusiastic religious movement. Destroyed by Nazis, now only in Israel, USA. |
| Haskalah | sOJ | 2-e | | 20,000 | 1 | isra | B | 2 | Schools of Jewish thought constantly in turmoil or opposition. |
| Karlin-Stolin Hasidism | sOJ | 2-e | c1800 | 6,600 | 1 | lith | C | 4 | Lithuanian Orthodox Jews named after 2 towns. |
| Klausenberg-Zanz Hasidism | sOJ | 2-e | | 10,000 | 1 | isra | B | 2 | One of major contemporary Hasidic parties in Israel. |
| Lubavich Hasidim | sOJ | 2-e | c1800 | 5,000 | 1 | isra | B | 2 | Hasidic movement stressing intellect. Strong work in former USSR. |
| Masorati | sOJ | 2-e | | 1,000 | 2 | brit | C | 3 | 'Traditional Movement', close to Conservative Judaism in Israel. |
| Musar Movement | sOJ | 2-e | c1880 | 5,000 | 1 | lith | C | 3 | Orthodox Jews, Lithuania strictness, self-examination. |
| Neo-Hasidism | sOJ | 2-d | c1950 | 150,000 | 10 | isra | B | 2 | Contemporary non-Hasidic Jews and Jewish New-Agers. |
| Satmar Hasidism | sOJ | 2-e | c1850 | 40,000 | 3 | hung | C | 3 | Transylvanian origins. Anti-Zionist, anti-Israel. HQ New York. |
| Vizhitz Hasidism | sOJ | 2-e | 1854 | 20,000 | 2 | isra | B | 2 | Hasidic movement, F=M. M. ben Hayyim Hager (in Austria). |
| United Torah Judaism | qJ | 8-d | 1992 | 100,000 | 5 | isra | B | 3 | UTJ. Non-Zionist Israeli political party. |
| Assoc of Reform Zionists of America | RJ | 2-c | 1810 | 3,000,000 | 10 | usa | C | 4 | ARZA. Reform Judaism (Progressive). 1810 Germany then USA, UK, Argentina, NZ, Australia. |
| Sefardis | SJ | 2-d | | 952,000 | 80 | arge | C | 4 | Sephardim. Spanish, Portuguese Jews and descendants, now only in USA, Lat America, Israel. |
| Samaritans | TJ | 10-f | BC 300 | 500 | 5 | isra | B | 2 | Split from Judaism, centered in Tel Aviv suburb Holon, and Shechem (Nablus). |
| Ultra Orthodox Judaism | UJ | 2-d | c1750 | 400,000 | 3 | isra | B | 2 | Haredi. Dissociate selves from Orthodox, Neo-Orthodox. Hasidism, Lithuanians. |
| Degel Hatorah | qUJ | 8-e | 1988 | 50,000 | 2 | isra | B | 2 | Torah Flag. Ultra-Orthodox Haredi organization, split ex Agudat Israel. |
| Gush Emunim | qUJ | 8-e | 1974 | 2,000 | 2 | isra | B | 2 | Bloc of the Faithful. Major extra-parliamentary force. |
| Sephardi Torah Guardians' Party | qUJ | 8-e | 1984 | 60,000 | 2 | isra | B | 2 | Shas. Political party, to counter Ashkenazi domination of Agudat Israel. |
| Guardians of the City | sUJ | 2-d | 1935 | 100,000 | 3 | isra | B | 2 | Neturei Karta. Extreme Ultra-Orthodox Jews. Anti-Zionists, breaking from Agudat Israel. |
| Alliance Israelite Universelle | wJ | 7-e | 1860 | 20,000 | 10 | isra | B | 3 | First modern Jewish organization. Secularist. |
| Bnai Brith International | wJ | 7-d | 1843 | 500,000 | 50 | usa | C | 5 | Jewish fraternal organization. B'Nai B'rith. HQ New York. Works through local lodges. |
| World Council of Synagogues | wJ | 7-c | 1959 | 2,000,000 | 10 | usa | C | 5 | Represents Conservative Judaism. USA, Argentina, Israel. |
| World Jewish Congress | wJ | 7-b | 1936 | 16,053,000 | 70 | swit | C | 5 | Representatives from 70 countries. Research institute in London. |
| World Union for Progressive Judaism | wJ | 7-c | 1926 | 6,000,000 | 50 | isra | B | 3 | Liberal or Progressive Judaism. |
| World Zionist Organization | wJ | 7-d | 1897 | 300,000 | 80 | isra | B | 2 | F=T. Herzl. Political movement for a Jewish state in Palestine. |
| Bayudaya | zJ | 2-e | 1919 | 1,000 | 1 | ugan | C | 2 | Propagation of Judaism, Moses Synagogue. Ex CMS, ex Bamaloki. Ganda. |
| Beta Israel | zJ | 2-e | BC c700 | 28,000 | 2 | isra | B | 2 | House of Israel. Falashas (Ethiopian Jews) airlifted to Israel 1984-92. |
| Black Jews | zJ | 2-e | 1920 | 5,000 | 3 | usa | C | 3 | Israelite cults originating in Harlem, New York. Old Testament doctrines. |
| Cochin Jews | zJ | 2-e | 80 | 2,000 | 2 | indi | B | 2 | In Cochin city, Kerala (Malayalam-speaking). |
| Doenmeh | zJ | 2-e | c1650 | 3,000 | 2 | turk | A | 1 | 'Apostates' (in Turkish). Sabbateans following 17th century messiah. Shabbetai Zevi. |
| Falashas | zJ | 2-e | | 84,200 | 2 | ethi | B | 4 | Long-time Ethiopians suddenly air-lifted en masse to Israel. |
| Havurat Judaism | zJ | 2-e | 1967 | 5,000 | 1 | isra | B | 2 | Jewish New-Agers, stressing Kabbalah and Hasidism. |
| Karakash | zJ | 2-e | | 2,000 | 1 | turk | A | 1 | Artisans and workers, related to the Donmeh ('Apostates'). |
| Neo-Orthodoxy | zJ | 2-d | c1920 | 300,000 | 8 | isra | B | 2 | German, Polish, Lithuanian and other supporters of Agudat Israel. |
| New Age Judaism | zJ | 2-e | | 30,000 | 2 | isra | B | 2 | Close to Havurat Judaism. Renewal communities. |
| Religious Zionism | zJ | 2-e | | 20,000 | 2 | isra | B | 3 | Religious aspects and parties committed to political Zionists. |
| Sons of Israel | zJ | 2-e | BC 200 | 30,000 | 4 | indi | B | 2 | Bene Israel. Largest Jewish body in India; Marathi-speaking. Bombay, Calicut. 12,000 in Israel. |
| **Sikhs** | K | 1-b | c1500 | 23,258,000 | 34 | indi | B | 2 | Monotheistic revelation to F=Guru Nanak (1469-1539). HQ Amiritsar. |
| Sikh Dharma of the W Hemisphere | cK | 7-e | 1969 | 10,000 | 8 | usa | C | 5 | W=Western. Also known as Happy, Healthy & Holy Organization (3HO). |
| Shiromani Gurdwara Prabandhak Com | nK | 7-e | 1920 | 1,000 | 1 | indi | B | 2 | Com=Committee. SGPC. Moderate Sikh religious body. |
| Singh Sabha Movement | nK | 7-e | 1873 | 5,000 | 1 | indi | B | 2 | To promote Sikhism. Many Khalsa colleges accross north India. |
| Nihangs | s-oK | 9-d | 1700 | 200,000 | 2 | indi | B | 2 | Sikh warriors, fighting force created by Guru Gobind Singh; a warrior group of Khalsa Sikhs. |
| Akali Dal | qK | 8-e | 1920 | 30,000 | 1 | indi | B | 1 | The Immortal Party. Militantly anti-British, then anti-Indian government. Split by factionalism. |
| Ad Dharm | sK | 2-e | 1907 | 10,000 | 1 | paki | A | 0 | 'Original Religion'. F=Ravidas (AD 1450, Sikh). 1907 Ravidasis (Chamar leatherworkers caste). |
| Akhand Kirtani Jatha | sK | 2-d | c1950 | 500,000 | 5 | brit | C | 3 | A major Khalsa-based movement for reconversion of Patit (lapsed) Sikhs. |
| Asali Nirankaris | sK | 2-e | | 5,000 | 1 | indi | B | 2 | True (Sikh-derived) Nirankaris. |
| Bhatras | sK | 2-e | c1500 | 3,000 | 2 | indi | B | 1 | North Indian pedlar community claiming Brahmin descent. Many Sikhs, now in UK. |
| Damdani Taksal | sK | 2-e | c1980 | 5,000 | 1 | indi | B | 2 | Militant anti-moderate Sikh religious school. F=Sant Bhindranwale. |
| Keshdari Sikhs | sK | 2-d | 1700 | 300,000 | 5 | indi | B | 1 | Less committed Sikhs not properly initialed as Khalsa Sikhs. |
| Khalsa Sikhs | sK | 2-c | 1699 | 4,000,000 | 20 | indi | B | 2 | Pure Ones. Sikh inner-circle created by F=Guru Gobind Singh. |
| Namdharis | sK | 2-d | 1840 | 400,000 | 2 | indi | B | 2 | Also called Kukas. Sikh-related reform movement. HQ Baini. |
| Nanaksar Movement | sK | 2-e | c1930 | 5,000 | 1 | indi | B | 2 | F=Bhai Mani Singh. Meditation, vegetarianism, celibacy. HQ Punjab. |
| Nirankaris | sK | 2-e | c1820 | 30,000 | 1 | paki | A | 0 | Sikh-derived reform movement. F=Baba Dayal Das. God=Nirankar. |
| Nishkam Sevak Jatha | sK | 2-e | c1950 | 20,000 | 3 | brit | C | 5 | F=Kerichowale Baba (a Kenyan Sikh). Sikh reform movement. Vegetarians. |

*Continued overleaf*

*Table 17–6 continued*

| *Name of religion/religionists* 1 | *Pedigree* 2 | *Type* 3 | *Begun* 4 | *Adherents* 5 | *Ext* 6 | *Coun* 7 | *W* 8 | *X* 9 | *E. g. = examples; name for God, other religions present, D=denominations, M=missions.* 10 |
|---|---|---|---|---|---|---|---|---|---|
| Ramraiyas | sK | 2-e | c1650 | 2,000 | 1 | indi | B | 1 | Schism by Ram Rai, son of Sikh Guru. Other movements are not allowed to associate. |
| Sahajdhari Sikhs | sK | 2-d | 1699 | 250,000 | 10 | indi | B | 2 | Nanak Panth. Non-Khalsa Sikhs. Independent grouping of Sikhs, cutting one's hair, etc. |
| Sant Nirankari Mandal | sK | 2-e | 1945 | 2,000 | 1 | indi | B | 1 | Sikh movement, also known as Nakali Nirankaris (False Nirankaris). |
| International Sikh Federation | wK | 7-e | 1986 | 1,000 | 1 | indi | B | 2 | Militant radicals. HQ Amritsar. F=Jasbir Singh, masterminder in assassination of Indira Gandhi. |
| **Baha'is** | L | 1-c | 1863 | 7,106,000 | 218 | iran | A | 5 | Acceptance of all religions under mission of Bahaiullah. In 218 countries. |
| Azali Babism | AL | 2-e | 1844 | 3,000 | 1 | iran | A | 1 | Remnant opposed to mainstream Bahai. Followers of Bab since 1850. F=Subh-i Azol. Decline. |
| Orthodox Bahai Faith | OL | 2-e | 1957 | 10,000 | 3 | usa | C | 5 | Largest of several splits ex-Bahai on death of Shoghi Effendi. |
| Freie Bahai | sL | 2-e | c1940 | 1,000 | 1 | germ | C | 5 | Bahais Under Provisions of the Covenant. |
| **Muslims** | M | 1-a | | 1,188,243,000 | 204 | paki | A | 2 | Islam (active submission to the will of Allah). |
| Fed of Islamic Assoc of Canada & USA | cM | 7-c | 1952 | 1,000,000 | 2 | usa | C | 5 | FIA (formerly IMS). 70% Sunnis, 20% Ismailis. Internal feuding. Decline. |
| Islamic Council of Europe | cM | 7-b | 1973 | 31,566,000 | 30 | brit | C | 5 | HQ London. Coordinating body for Islam in the West. Collaborates with OIC/ICO (Jeddah). |
| Islamic Society of North America | cM | 7-d | 1982 | 400,000 | 2 | usa | C | 5 | ISNA. Umbrella organization for several Muslim professional groups. HQ Plainfield, IN. |
| Regional Islamic Dawa Council SE | cM | 7-b | 1980 | 136,000,000 | 17 | malb | B | 3 | RIDCSEAP. Represents Muslims in SE=Southeast Asia and Pacific. HQ Kuala Lumpur. |
| Folk-Muslims | FM | 2-b | | 80,000,000 | 5 | indo | B | 2 | Large numbers of nominal Muslims who merge Islam with local folk religion and gods. |
| Al Hidayah Dawa Movement | fM | 4-e | 1982 | 30,000 | 1 | soua | C | 5 | AHDM. Missionary movement with headquarters in Western Cape. |
| Aligarh Movement | fM | 4-e | 1865 | 5,000 | 1 | indi | B | 2 | F=S.A. Khan. Educational institution for Indian Muslims, and a few Hindus. |
| Arakan Rohingya Islamic Front | fM | 4-e | | 2,000 | 2 | myan | B | 1 | ARIF. Moderate Muslim guerrilla groups. |
| Assoc pour la Sauvegarde du Quran | fM | 4-e | 1970 | 20,000 | 1 | tuni | A | 1 | Quranic Preservation Society (QPS). Government-backed. |
| Darul Islam | fM | 4-e | 1949 | 10,000 | 1 | indo | B | 0 | Abode of Islam. Revolutionary movement to establish an Islamic state; defeated 1965. W.Java. |
| Farazis | fM | 4-e | 1818 | 30,000 | 1 | indi | B | 0 | Attempt to bring Islam to all India's societies, rejecting syncretism with Hinduism. |
| Islamic Council of the South Pacific | fM | 4-d | 1984 | 150,000 | 20 | fiji | B | 4 | ICSF. Represents Muslims from Australia, NZ, PNG, Fiji, NC, Tonga. HQ Suva. |
| Mouvement du Renouveau Islamique | fM | 4-e | 1978 | 5,000 | 2 | tuni | A | 1 | Movement for the Renewal of Islam. Offshoot of QPS. |
| Movement for Islamic Revolution | fM | 4-e | | 20,000 | 1 | afgh | A | 1 | Harakat-i Ingilab-i Islami. Moderates. Member of IUAM. |
| Organization of the Islamic Jihad | fM | 4-d | 1971 | 230,000 | 5 | leba | B | 5 | Munazzamat al-Jihad al-Islami. Related to Hizbollah. Assassinations. Outlawed 1973 to 1987. |
| Society for the Victory of Islam | fM | 4-c | 1961 | 1,000,000 | 1 | nige | B | 3 | Jamaatu Nasril Islam. Fundamentalist, but also reformist organization. |
| UK Islamic Mission | fM | 4-c | 1962 | 1,100,000 | 1 | brit | C | 5 | Arising from Pakistan-based Jamaati Islami. 50 centers in south England. |
| Shias | HM | 2-b | 680 | 170,100,000 | 75 | syri | B | 3 | Shiites. Followers of Ali, cousin of Mohammed. In Iran, Iraq, Lebanon, India, Pakistan. |
| Ithna-Asharis | AHM | 2-b | 680 | 136,655,000 | 70 | iran | A | 1 | Twelvers. Imamis. |
| Hujjatiyah | sAHM | 2-e | 1953 | 2,000 | 1 | iran | A | 1 | Charitable Hojjatiyah Society of Mahdi. Anti-Bahai anti ayatollah Khomeini after 1978 coup. |
| Shaykhis | sAHM | 2-e | c1810 | 1,000 | 3 | iran | A | 0 | Kashfiya. Quasi-heterodox school of Twelvers rejecting excesses of Sufism. Iran, southern Iraq. |
| Ismailis | IHM | 2-b | 909 | 23,772,000 | 45 | indi | B | 2 | Seveners, Khojas, Batiniya, Nizaris, Daudis, Mustalis, Bohras. Most under Aga Khan. |
| Bohras | BIHM | 2-d | c1150 | 900,000 | 10 | indi | B | 2 | Ismaili sect overlapping with Daudis and Mustalis. |
| Mustalis | MIHM | 2-d | 1094 | 360,000 | 20 | yeme | A | 0 | Tayibis. Sulaymanis. Smaller of the 2 Ismaili sects. |
| Amiris | sMIHM | 2-e | c1600 | 39,000 | 5 | indi | B | 2 | Ismaili subdivision related to Daudis, Mustalis, and Sulaymanis. |
| Daudis | sMIHM | 2-d | 1591 | 300,000 | 15 | indi | B | 2 | Daudiyah. Most also termed Bohras in India. Main Mustali sect. |
| Mahdibaghwalas | sMIHM | 10-f | 1897 | 300 | 1 | indi | B | 0 | Subsect of Daudis. |
| Nagoshias | sMIHM | 10-f | 1789 | 500 | 1 | indi | B | 1 | Nagushis. Small subsect of Daudis. Vegetarians. |
| Sulaymanis | sMIHM | 2-e | c1590 | 40,000 | 1 | indi | B | 2 | Split ex Daudis (Bohras), Ismaili sect. |
| Hibtias | ssMIHM | 10-f | 1761 | 500 | 1 | indi | B | 0 | Hibatis, Hiptiyas. Split ex Daudi Ismailis. |
| Imam-Shahis | sIHM | 2-e | c1200 | 3,000 | 1 | indi | B | 1 | Close to Satpanthis. Small subgroup of Nizari Khojas in India. |
| Nizaris | sIHM | 2-b | 950 | 20,000,000 | 12 | indi | B | 1 | Assassins (users of hashish). Loyal to Aga Khan IV. Major Ismaili sect, Tanzania,Syria,India. |
| Qarmatians | sIHM | 10-f | 899 | 200 | 1 | bahr | B | 1 | Qaramitah. Dissident group ex Ismailis. F=Hamden al Qarmat. Now virtually only an influence. |
| Sabiya | sIHM | 2-e | 909 | 2,000 | 1 | syri | B | 2 | Shia Seveners, a sect of Ismailis: only first 7 Imans were legitimate. |
| Satpanthis | sIHM | 2-e | c1550 | 3,000 | 1 | indi | B | 2 | 'Those who follow the True Path'. Nizari Khojas. HQ Ahmadabad. Many revert to Hinduism. |
| Sevener Shiites | sIHM | 2-c | 909 | 3,000,000 | 20 | indi | B | 2 | Ismailis. Main body in India, under Aga Khan IV. |
| Twelver Khojas | sIHM | 2-d | c1300 | 250,000 | 2 | indi | B | 2 | 14th-century converts from Hinduism to Islam (Shias). Not under Aga Khan IV. |
| Alawites | LHM | 2-c | c950 | 1,631,000 | 15 | syri | B | 2 | Nusayris. A Shiite group in Syria. |
| Jihad-i Sazandigi | nHM | 2-e | 1979 | 30,000 | 3 | iran | A | 0 | Reconstruction Crusade; youths aged 20-30 taking Iran Revolution to countryside. Non-military. |
| Hizbollah | qHM | 8-e | 1982 | 80,000 | 20 | leba | B | 5 | Hezbollah. Party of God. Iran-supported Shia militants. Radical, violent fundamentalists. |
| Islamic Call Party | qHM | 8-e | 1957 | 10,000 | 5 | iraq | A | 1 | Hizb al-Da'wah al-Islamiyah. Major Shia activist party. |
| Islamic Republican Party | qHM | 8-e | c1970 | 5,000 | 1 | iran | A | 0 | Powerful, revolutionary, until 1987 dissolution by Khomieni. |
| Amal | rHM | 2-e | 1975 | 20,000 | 5 | leba | B | 5 | 'Hope'=acronym for Lebanese Resistance Detachments, to reform Lebanon without violence. |
| Mobilization of the Oppressed | rHM | 2-c | 1980 | 2,000,000 | 1 | iran | A | 0 | Bassij-i Mostazafin. Boy warriors/martyrs forced into combat with Iraq; 1 million killed. |
| Dawa Party | sHM | 2-e | 1957 | 30,000 | 10 | iraq | A | 1 | Hizb al-Dawa al-Islamiya. Strong in Iraq, Iran. Violently attacked by Baath regime. |
| Devotees of Islam | sHM | 2-e | 1945 | 5,000 | 1 | iran | A | 0 | Fada'iyan-i Islam. A ruthless terrorist group. Underground, now in decline. |
| Jafaris | sHM | 2-e | c750 | 50,000 | 1 | iran | A | 1 | Attempt to claim a fifth Islamic law school: Shia Twelver. |
| Maturidiyah | sHM | 2-e | c920 | 20,000 | 1 | iran | A | 1 | Rival to Ashariya school's lack of personal assurance. |
| Organization of Islamic Action | sHM | 2-e | 1963 | 10,000 | 10 | iraq | A | 1 | Munazzamat al-Amal al-Islami. Shia. Founded in Karbala opposing Baath regime. |
| Society of Militant Clergy | sHM | 2-e | 1976 | 5,000 | 1 | iran | A | 1 | Jamiat-i Ruhaniyun-i Mobariz. Shia, conservative. |
| Alia Bohoras | ssHM | 2-e | 1621 | 1,000 | 1 | indi | B | 2 | Aliyas. Subset of Daudis (branch of Mustalis). |
| Zaydis | ZHM | 2-c | c730 | 8,042,000 | 10 | yeme | A | 1 | Smallest Shia branch. Fiver Shiites. Strongest in Yemen. |
| All-India Muslim Coalition | nM | 7-c | 1963 | 1,000,000 | 1 | indi | B | 2 | Majlis-i Mushawarat. Coalition of Muslim political parties and agencies. |
| All-India Muslim League | nM | 7-b | 1906 | 101,000,000 | 3 | indi | B | 2 | To safeguard Muslim interests in India. |
| All-Nepal Anjuman Islah Samiti | nM | 7-d | | 800,000 | 2 | nepa | A | 1 | Main Muslim organization active in Nepal, with 3 other rival bodies. |
| Angkatan Democratic Liberal Sabah | nM | 7-d | | 500,000 | 1 | malb | B | 3 | ADIL. Based in Sabah and intended to attract Malay Muslims. |
| Assoc des Musulmans de N Caledonie | nM | 7-e | 1975 | 5,800 | 1 | newc | C | 4 | NCMA. New Caledonia Muslim Association. Schools, imams. |
| Assoc of Muslims of Southern Sudan | nM | 7-d | 1982 | 100,000 | 2 | suda | B | 2 | AMSS. Mainly Nuba Muslims. |
| Australian Fed of Islamic Councils | nM | 7-d | 1975 | 224,000 | 1 | aust | C | 5 | AFIC. To organize Islam on geographic not sectarian base. HQ Victoria. Turks, Arabs, Serbs. |
| Bangladesh Muslim League | nM | 7-c | | 6,000,000 | 1 | bang | B | 2 | BML. Denounces advocates of Bengali nationalism. |
| Centre Islamique et Culturel de B | nM | 7-d | 1969 | 200,000 | 3 | belg | C | 5 | ICCB. CICB. Islamic and Cultural Centre of Belgium. Government sponsored. |
| China Islamic Association | nM | 7-b | | 19,168,000 | 1 | chin | B | 3 | CIA. Official representative of Muslims before government and Communist Party. |
| Co of Muslim Communities of Canada | nM | 7-d | 1972 | 317,000 | 1 | cana | C | 5 | CMCC. Co=Council. Representing all Muslims (70% Sunnis) including Ismailis and Druzes. |
| Fed des Assocs Islamiques du Senegal | nM | 7-c | | 8,306,000 | 1 | sene | A | 1 | FAIS. Federation of Islamic Associations in Senegal. Government-sponsored coordinating body. |
| Fed Nationale des Musulmans de F | nM | 7-c | 1985 | 4,176,000 | 2 | fran | C | 5 | FNMF. National Federation of French Muslims. 2 rivals: UOIF, Paris Mosque (Algerian). |
| Fed of Islamic Assocs of NZ | nM | 7-e | 1979 | 7,200 | 1 | newz | C | 5 | FIANZ. NZ=New Zealand. Fijian Indians, with a few Muslims from Europe. |
| Fed of Islamic Communities of Surinam | nM | 7-e | 1929 | 74,400 | 1 | suri | B | 4 | FIGS. Federatie Islamitsche Gemeenten in Surinam. |
| Fed of Muslim Orgs in the Netherlands | nM | 7-d | 1974 | 594,000 | 1 | neth | C | 5 | FMON. Begun by Dutch converts to Islam. Dissolved 1981; regrouped under MIC. |
| Federation of Mosques in Belgium | nM | 7-d | 1985 | 360,000 | 1 | belg | C | 5 | FMICAB. Fed des Mosquees et Assoc Culturelles Islamiques en B. Formed to counter ICCB. |
| Fiji Muslim League | nM | 7-e | 1926 | 56,000 | 1 | fiji | B | 4 | FML. Organizes Muslim education, provision of imams. |
| Indonesian Islamic Army | nM | 7-c | 1948 | 1,000,000 | 1 | indo | B | 3 | Tentera Islam Indonesia, or Darul Islam (DI). Insurgents in West Java (Sunda). |
| Islamic Association of the Netherlands | nM | 7-e | 1981 | 63,000 | 1 | neth | C | 5 | Turkish Muslims, based in The Hague. Support of 87 local Turkish organizations. |
| Islamic Call Society | nM | 7-d | 1980 | 300,000 | 2 | liby | A | 0 | Ad Daawa al Islamiya. Missionary organization established by government. Weekly newspaper. |
| Islamic Council of Mozambique | nM | 7-c | | 2,068,000 | 1 | moza | B | 3 | Representing Sunni Muslims, along with Islamic Congress of Mozambique. |
| Islamic Council of Nigeria | nM | 7-b | 1973 | 48,000,000 | 1 | nige | B | 3 | One of several national councils claiming to represent all Nigerian Muslims. |
| Islamic Progressive Movement | nM | 7-e | 1980 | 50,000 | 1 | tuni | A | 1 | MPI. Harakat al-Taqaddum al-Islami. Radicals. |
| Islamic Society of Papua New Guinea | nM | 7-e | 1978 | 1,200 | 1 | papu | C | 5 | ISPANG. Represents and organizes Muslims in PNG. |
| Jamaat-i Islami of Bangladesh | nM | 7-e | c1970 | 20,000 | 1 | bang | B | 0 | JIB. Islamic Society. Fundamentalists. HQ Dacca. |
| Jamaat-i Islami of India | nM | 7-d | 1941 | 300,000 | 30 | indi | B | 0 | Fundamentalists. Highly organized. Little political influence. |
| Muslim Association of Nigeria | nM | 7-b | | 30,000,000 | 1 | nige | B | 3 | MAN. Moderate national organization; mobilizes youth, fosters Muslim/Christian relations. |
| Sierra Leone Muslim Congress | nM | 7-c | c1960 | 2,229,000 | 1 | sier | B | 2 | SLMC. National organization representing all Muslims. HQ Freatown. |
| Sociedade Mussulmana de Chile | nM | 7-e | c1970 | 4,800 | 1 | chil | C | 5 | Muslim Society of Chile. Operates one Islamic Centre. |
| Society of Muslims | nM | 7-e | 1985 | 10,000 | 1 | trin | C | 2 | Jamaat al-Muslimeen. Radical Black Muslim guerrillas whose 1990 attempted coup failed. |
| Sup As for Islamic Revolution in Iraq | nM | 7-e | 1982 | 30,000 | 1 | iraq | A | 0 | SAIRI. Sup As= Supreme Assembly. Shias under violent persecution by Baath regime. |
| Supreme Council for Islamic Affairs | nM | 7-b | 1977 | 48,900,000 | 1 | nige | B | 3 | Major officially-sponsored Muslim organization. |
| Supreme Council of Kenya Muslims | nM | 7-c | 1976 | 2,187,000 | 1 | keny | C | 5 | SUPKEM. Founded as a federation of over 100 Muslim organizations. |
| Supreme Islamic Shii Council | nM | 7-c | 1967 | 1,300,000 | 5 | leba | B | 5 | SISC. Main focus of action for the Shia intelligentsia. |
| Surinamese Islamic Council | nM | 7-e | 1978 | 10,000 | 1 | suri | B | 4 | Surinaamse Islamitsche Organizatie. Split from FIGS. Six branches. |
| Uganda Muslim Supreme Council | nM | 7-c | 1965 | 1,137,000 | 1 | ugan | C | 5 | 1965 NAAM, replaced 1972 by UMSC. |
| Union des Orgs Islamiques de France | nM | 7-c | c1980 | 4,100,000 | 2 | fran | C | 5 | UOIF. 1,300 associations. 3 rivals; FNMF, and Paris Mosque (Algeria government control). |
| Union of Moroccan Muslim Orgs in the N | nM | 7-d | 1978 | 100,000 | 2 | neth | C | 5 | UMMON. N=Netherlands. Federation of 40 local Moroccan bodies. |
| Union of Muslim Orgs of UK and Eire | nM | 7-c | 1970 | 1,200,000 | 2 | brit | C | 5 | Failure to unite British Muslims; 200 local centers. |
| United Muslim Community of Sweden | nM | 7-d | 1948 | 202,000 | 1 | swed | C | 5 | UMCS. 1948 Islamic Union of Sweden, renamed 1975. |
| Yugoslav Islamic Community | nM | 7-c | 1882 | 1,722,000 | 1 | yugo | C | 5 | YIC. Rijaset Islamske Zajednice. Coordination, administration. |
| Council of Indonesian Muslim Assoc | qnM | 8-c | 1943 | 6,000,000 | 1 | indo | B | 2 | MASYUMI. Sumatra-based. Banned 1960, revived 1968 as PARMUSI. |

*Continued opposite*

*Table 17–6 continued*

| Name of religion/religionists 1 | Pedigree 2 | Type 3 | Begun 4 | Adherents 5 | Ext 6 | Coun 7 | W 8 | X 9 | E. g. = examples; name for God, other religions present, D=denominations, M=missions. 10 |
|---|---|---|---|---|---|---|---|---|---|
| Islamic Council of South Africa | qnM | 8-d | 1975 | 947,000 | 2 | soua | C | 5 | ICSA. A moderate Muslim political organization. |
| Moslem Bosnjak Organization | qnM | 8-c | 1990 | 1,100,000 | 1 | bosn | B | 3 | MBO. Muslim Bosniacs: Hanafites. Liberals split from Party for Democratic Action. |
| Pan-Malaysian Islamic Party | qnM | 8-d | 1951 | 300,000 | 1 | malb | B | 3 | PAS. Parti Islam SaMalaysia. Right-wing Conservative Malay Muslims. |
| Sri Lanka Muslim Congress | qnM | 8-c | 1980 | 1,694,000 | 1 | sril | B | 3 | SLMC. Eastern Province base; a national party since 1986. |
| Salimiya | sS-oM | 9-e | 860 | 2,000 | 1 | saud | B | 2 | Muslim theological school based on '1,000 sayings' of F=Sahl al-Tustari, theologian and mystic. |
| Consul Council of Indonesian Muslims | qM | 8-d | 1943 | 200,000 | 1 | indo | B | 3 | Masjumi. Majlis Sjuro Muslimin Indonesia. Political party for all factions; 1970 phased out. |
| Devotees of Islam | qM | 8-e | 1946 | 1,000 | 1 | iran | A | 0 | Fedayeen-i-Islam. Organized Shia political activity. |
| Front Islamique du Salut | qM | 8-d | c1980 | 100,000 | 1 | alge | A | 1 | FIS. Islamic Salvation Front. Fundamentalist. Electoral victory 1990s, then suppressed by army. |
| Fundamentalist Islamic Front | qM | 8-d | 1941 | 600,000 | 20 | paki | A | 0 | Jamaat-i Islami. F=S.A.A.Maududi. Highly organized and successful political party. HQ Lahore. |
| New Islamic Mission | qM | 8-d | 1945 | 500,000 | 1 | suda | B | 1 | al-Hizb al-Jumhari. Republican Brothers. Party, banned 1969. F=M.M. Taha, hanged 1985. |
| Pan-Islamists | qM | 8-d | c1870 | 100,000 | 1 | egyp | B | 3 | First of many attempts to unite Islam against Western cultural and religious encroachments. |
| Pasdaran | qM | 8-d | 1979 | 450,000 | 1 | iran | A | 0 | IRGC. Islamic Revolutionary Guards Corps. Uniformed. |
| Sunnis | SM | 2-a |  | 1,002,543,000 | 195 | paki | A | 2 | Main body of Islam. Ahl al-Sunna wal-jamaa. The True Muslims. Non-Shia Muslims. |
| Hanbalites | BSM | 2-c | 850 | 2,325,000 | 25 | saud | B | 2 | F=Ahmad ibn Hanbal. Strictest of the 4 Sunni schools of law, officially accepted in Saudi Arabia. |
| Hanafites | HSM | 2-a | c750 | 531,418,000 | 135 | turk | A | 1 | Oldest and largest of the 4 Sunni schools of law. India, Pakistan, Turkey, C Asia, China, Egypt. |
| Milli Gorus | qHSM | 8-e | c1970 | 10,000 | 2 | turk | A | 1 | 'National View'. Conservative religio-political body; also in Germany. |
| The True Sunnis | sHSM | 2-a | c1850 | 230,000,000 | 70 | indi | B | 1 | Ahl-i Sunnat wa Jamaat. F=Ahmad Riza Khan. Barelvis Movement. Massive populist support. |
| Malikites | MSM | 2-a | c790 | 221,900,000 | 65 | nige | B | 3 | One of the 4 major schools of law. North, West, and Central Africa, Upper Egypt. Traditionalists. |
| Islamic Liberation Party | qSM | 8-e | 1952 | 30,000 | 2 | jord | B | 2 | Hizb al Tahrir al-Islami. No legal status. Radicals focused on seizing power. |
| Islamic Modernists South Asia | qSM | 8-b | c1850 | 20,000,000 | 3 | indi | B | 2 | Elite intellectuals implementing social agendas in India and Pakistan. F=Sir S.A. Khan. |
| Renascence Party | qSM | 8-d | 1988 | 500,000 | 1 | tuni | A | 1 | Hizb al-Nahda (Islamic Tendency, MTI). Largest politico-religious movement in Tunisia. |
| Shafiites | SSM | 2-a | 810 | 239,900,000 | 105 | malb | B | 3 | Shafi school of Islamic law. Popular in Southeast Asia, East Africa, Arabia, Egypt, S/C Asia. |
| Jamiat ul-Ulama-i Pakistan | qsSM | 8-b | c1930 | 20,000,000 | 2 | paki | A | 1 | Organizational part in Pakistan of Barelvi movement in South Asian Islam. |
| Milli Jamiat ul-Ulama-i Hind | ssSM | 2-e | 1988 | 2,000 | 1 | indi | B | 2 | Split from Jamiat ul-Ulama-i Hind. |
| Strict Koranic Muslims | sSSM | 2-b | 1272 | 92,266,000 | 1 | indo | B | 3 | Agama Islam Santri. Sunnis of Shafiite rite; mostly coastal peoples on Sumatra. |
| Wahhabites | WSM | 2-c | c1750 | 7,000,000 | 10 | saud | B | 2 | Strict ultra-conservative, puritannical, fundamentalist form of Sunni, through Hanbali school. |
| Clergy Society of Hadith People | sWSM | 2-e | c1880 | 40,000 | 1 | paki | A | 0 | Jamiat ul-Ulama-i Ahl-i Hadith. Avoids politics. Pakistani Sunnis, strict so called Wahhabis. |
| Islamic Unitarianism | sWSM | 2-c | 1909 | 1,000,000 | 1 | saud | B | 2 | Muwahhidun movement. 20th century struggles over Saudi Arabia. |
| Mujahids | sWSM | 2-e | 1952 | 50,000 | 1 | indi | B | 2 | Reform movement among Mappila Muslims in Kerala. |
| Nadvat-ul-Mujahideen | sWSM | 2-e | 1952 | 40,000 | 1 | indi | B | 2 | Formal Islamic reform movement among Mappila of Kerala. |
| Aisyiyah | zSM | 2-c | c1920 | 2,000,000 | 3 | indo | B | 3 | Aisiah. Women's auxiliary (one of world's most dynamic) within Muhammadiyah; Javanese. |
| All-Malaysia Muslim Welfare Assoc | zSM | 2-b | 1960 | 10,100,000 | 1 | malb | B | 3 | PERKIM. Pertubuham Kebajikan Islam SeMalaysia. 120,000 converts to Islam. |
| Association of Indian Clergy | zSM | 2-e | 1919 | 20,000 | 1 | indi | B | 2 | Jamiat ul-Ulama-i Hind. Reformist ulama. HQ Delhi. |
| Association of Light | zSM | 2-e | 1925 | 30,000 | 1 | turk | A | 0 | Nurcus, or Nurcular Camaati, a Turkish Muslim renewal. |
| Black Arabs | zSM | 2-c |  | 1,705,000 | 2 | came | B | 3 | Shuwa Muslims in north of country. |
| Deobandis | zSM | 2-d | c1850 | 200,000 | 1 | indi | B | 2 | Attempt to be Muslim with no involvement with political regimes. 10,000 schools. |
| Fethullahcilar | zSM | 2-e | c1985 | 5,000 | 1 | turk | A | 1 | F=Fethullah Gulen. Appeal to educated youths. |
| Hamas | zSM | 2-e | 1990 | 10,000 | 5 | alge | A | 0 | Al-Haraqa li Mujtama Islami (Movement for Islamic Society). |
| Islamic Union of Afghan Mujaheddin | zSM | 2-d | 1985 | 100,000 | 1 | afgh | A | 1 | IUAM. Ittehad-i Islami Afghan Mujaheddin. Alliance of 7 Sunni factions. |
| Jamiat ul-Ulama-i Islam | zSM | 2-e | 1945 | 40,000 | 1 | paki | A | 0 | JUI. Pakistan wing of Jamiat ul-Ulama-i Hind. |
| Mappillas | zSM | 2-d |  | 100,000 | 2 | indi | B | 2 | Malayalam-speaking Muslims of Kerala. |
| Missionary Society | zSM | 2-d | 1923 | 100,000 | 30 | indi | B | 2 | Tablighi Jamaat. Faith Movement, Dini Dawat, Major Islamic reformers operating worldwide. |
| Muhammad's Army | zSM | 2-e |  | 20,000 | 1 | jord | B | 2 | Jaysh Muhammad. No legal status. Attempts made to overthrow regime and monarchy. |
| Muhammadiyah | zSM | 2-c | 1912 | 9,000,000 | 1 | indo | B | 3 | Followers of Muhammad. Javanese. Modernist reformers, welfare work. |
| Path of Religion | zSM | 2-d | 1968 | 150,000 | 1 | mald | A | 0 | Dheenuge Magu. Supported by a government ministry, for Muslims only. |
| Renewal Movement | zSM | 2-e | c1970 | 2,000 | 1 | indo | B | 3 | Gerakan Pembaharuan (liberal, modernist). |
| Sabilillah Movement | zSM | 2-e |  | 20,000 | 1 | thai | B | 2 | One of many Thai Muslim miliant separatist organizations. |
| Salafiyah | zSM | 2-d | c1900 | 300,000 | 20 | alge | A | 1 | Islamic Modernists reform movement. First Muslim emancipation of women. Anti-Sufi. |
| Society for Social Reform | zSM | 2-c |  | 1,600,000 | 1 | kuwa | B | 3 | Jamiyat al-Islah al-Ijtimai. Sunni body based in Kuwait. |
| Yan Tatsine | zSM | 2-e | 1960 | 10,000 | 1 | nige | B | 3 | Maitatsine ('He Who Curses', in Hausa). Millenarian sect. 1980-5 violence, rioting; 4,000 killed. |
| Sufis | UM | 2-a | c 800 | 237,400,000 | 204 | moro | A | 1 | Mass mystical orders/brotherhoods (70 in Egypt) Morocco to Indonesia; mostly Sunni, few Shia. |
| Neo-Sufism | RUM | 2-b | c1920 | 10,000,000 | 20 | russ | B | 5 | Reform-oriented Sufi orders without excesses of ecstatic activities. Modernizing tendencies. |
| Azamiyah Shadhiliyah | sRUM | 2-d | 1915 | 300,000 | 1 | suda | B | 2 | Reform of Sufi practices. F=Muhammad Madi Abu al-Azaim. |
| Sanusiyah | sRUM | 2-d | 1856 | 500,000 | 3 | liby | A | 1 | F=Grand Sanusi Muhammad Ali. N Africa, Sahara (Tuaregs, Tubus). Qadiriya mysticism. |
| Alawiya Darqawi | sUM | 2-e | 1918 | 10,000 | 1 | alge | A | 0 | Offshoot of the Darqawiya at Mostaganem. Very traditional. F=Ahmad ibn al-Alawi. |
| Alawiya Hadrami | sUM | 2-e | c1220 | 50,000 | 20 | yeme | A | 1 | F=Muhammad ibn Ali. Spread to Indonesia, India, East Africa (Kenya, Zanzibar). |
| Badawiya | sUM | 2-c | c1240 | 1,500,000 | 20 | egyp | B | 3 | Major Sufi order in Egypt, HQ Tanta; one million pilgrims every autumn. Mysticism, miracles. |
| Basmachis | sUM | 2-e | c1880 | 1,000 | 5 | uzbe | A | 0 | 'Bandits'. Central Asian rebels against Russian imperialism. Crushed by USSR, 1924. |
| Bayramiye | sUM | 2-e | c1430 | 1,000 | 1 | turk | A | 1 | Bairamiyah. Turkish Sufi order widespread in Balkans until banned in 1925; traces still exist. |
| Bektashiya | sUM | 2-e | c1300 | 2,000 | 8 | alba | B | 4 | Turkish Sufi order. Checkered history of Ottoman and Communist persecution. Secrecy. Shia. |
| Chishtiyah | sUM | 2-c | c1210 | 1,000,000 | 1 | afgh | A | 1 | Most widespread and popular Sufi order in South Asia. |
| Dandarawiyah | sUM | 2-e | 1880 | 50,000 | 5 | thai | B | 2 | Spread across Egypt, Malaysia, Thailand, Indonesia, out of Idrisiyah. |
| Dar al-Quran | sUM | 2-e |  | 20,000 | 2 | jord | B | 3 | Modern branch of Shadhiliya Sufi order. |
| Darqawiya | sUM | 2-e | c1850 | 30,000 | 4 | moro | A | 1 | Popular traditional-style Sufi order. Wandering mendicants. In UK. |
| Hairy Ishans | sUM | 2-e |  | 40,000 | 1 | uzbe | A | 0 | Radical offshoot of Yasawiya Sufi (Ishanism) order, Kirghistan, Uzbekistan. Clandestine, urban. |
| Halveti-Cerrahis | sUM | 2-e |  | 3,000 | 1 | turk | A | 1 | Turkish Sufi order in Istanbul, Germany, USA. |
| Hamadsha | sUM | 2-e | c1700 | 2,000 | 1 | moro | A | 0 | Socially despised Sufi order in northern Morocco. |
| Isawiyah | sUM | 2-e |  | 20,000 | 1 | moro | A | 0 | Sufi order active in Morocco. Branch of Shadhiliya. |
| Kettaniyah | sUM | 2-e |  | 10,000 | 1 | moro | A | 0 | Sufi order, active in Morocco, associated with Alawiya order. |
| Khalwatiyah | sUM | 2-e | c1350 | 5,000 | 20 | leba | B | 5 | Persian, Kurdish, Turkish, Albanian, Syrian origins. |
| Kubrawiyah | sUM | 2-e | c900 | 3,000 | 1 | turm | A | 1 | Spiritual center of Sufi brotherhood. A major Junayli Sufi order. |
| Madariya | sUM | 2-c | c1410 | 4,000,000 | 25 | indi | B | 2 | Similar to Hindu holy men; Bengal, north India, also in Nepal. Mostly widespread across S Asia. |
| Mawlawiyah | sUM | 2-e | c1250 | 6,000 | 10 | turk | A | 1 | Whirling Dervishes. Mevlevis. Wealthy, urban, artistocratic. Also in Eastern Europe. |
| Mirghaniya | sUM | 2-d | 1830 | 100,000 | 1 | suda | B | 2 | Also termed Khatmiya. Sufi order in Sudan. |
| Muridiyah | sUM | 2-d | c1900 | 300,000 | 5 | sene | A | 1 | Innovative Sufis. Ex Qadiriya in Mauritania. HQ holy city Touba. Peanut prosperity. |
| Naqshabandiya | sUM | 2-b | c1150 | 50,000,000 | 30 | uzbe | A | 1 | Great Sufi order (most-widespread after Qadiriya) strong in Central Asia, India, West Europe. |
| Possessed Ones | sUM | 2-e |  | 2,000 | 3 | kaza | B | 3 | Divana. Irregular mendicant Sufis across Central Asia. |
| Qadiriya | sUM | 2-b | c1120 | 20,000,000 | 50 | syri | B | 3 | Oldest Sufi order, widespread in 50 countries from Senegal to Malaysia. Miracles claimed. |
| Qalandars | sUM | 2-e | c1300 | 5,000 | 1 | indi | B | 2 | One of many irregular Sufi orders: mendicant holy beggars who invoke curses on nonpayers. |
| Rahmaniyah | sUM | 2-d | 1760 | 400,000 | 20 | alge | A | 0 | Sufi order, ex Khalwatiya. F=Muhammad bin Abd al-Rahman. 1871, led revolt against French. |
| Rifaiyah | sUM | 2-e | c1150 | 60,000 | 20 | iraq | A | 1 | Gurzmar. Oldest Sufi order. Ecstatics. Also Syria, Yugoslavia, East Africa, India, Europe, USA. |
| Salihiyah | sUM | 2-e | c1880 | 50,000 | 1 | soma | A | 1 | Sufi order from Idrisiyah (Saudi Arabia). Widespread in Somalia under 'Mad Mullah'. |
| Shadhiliyah | sUM | 2-c | 1230 | 1,000,000 | 30 | egyp | B | 3 | Sunni Sufi order from Morocco to Egypt to Syria. F=al-Shadhili. Wide influence beyond Islam. |
| Shattariyah | sUM | 2-e | c1450 | 70,000 | 10 | indi | B | 2 | Sufi order across north India and Bengal. Entered from Iran. Mystical scholarship prominent. |
| Shiite Sufis | sUM | 2-b |  | 15,000,000 | 30 | iran | A | 1 | A small number of Sufi orders are Shia, though most are Sunni. |
| Sufi Order in the West | sUM | 2-e | 1910 | 30,000 | 3 | brit | C | 5 | Begun in London. F=Hazrat Inyat Khan, from Baroda. Holds 'universal worship'. |
| Suleymancis | sUM | 2-e | 1930 | 8,000 | 15 | turk | A | 1 | Turkish renewal movement resisting secular state control. Strong in Germany. HQ Cologne. |
| Tijaniyah | sUM | 2-d | 1785 | 600,000 | 16 | alge | A | 1 | Major Sufi order across North and East Africa, Sudan, Turkey, Indonesia. |
| Wazzaniyah | sUM | 2-e |  | 30,000 | 1 | alge | A | 0 | Ouezzaniyah. In desert villages, most adult males are members. |
| Yasawiyah | sUM | 2-d | 1950 | 100,000 | 5 | kaza | B | 3 | Sufi order in Kirghizia, Kazakhstan, Uzbekistan. Offshoot: Laachi. |
| Aidarusiya | ssUM | 2-e |  | 20,000 | 4 | yeme | A | 1 | Sub-branch of Hadrami Alawiya Sufis, responsible for spread to South Asia and Indonesia. |
| Bakkaiyah | ssUM | 2-d | c1500 | 500,000 | 1 | mali | A | 0 | Part of Qadiriya, in West Africa in origin. |
| Dhahabiya | ssUM | 2-e | c1450 | 7,000 | 1 | iran | A | 1 | Ex Kubrawiya; revived c 1850. HQ Shiraz. Shia Sufis. |
| Dhul-Riyasatayn | ssUM | 2-e |  | 10,000 | 1 | iran | A | 0 | Branch of Iranian Nimatullahi Sufi order. |
| Ghawthiyah | ssUM | 2-d | c1490 | 300,000 | 3 | indi | B | 2 | Begun and continued as part of Qadiriya order, in South Asia. |
| Gunabadi | ssUM | 2-e |  | 25,000 | 1 | iran | A | 1 | Branch of Nimatullahi Sufi order. |
| Hamalliyah | ssUM | 2-e | 1910 | 30,000 | 9 | maur | A | 0 | Sufi order, offshoot of Tijaniya, in Mauritania and Morocco to Nigeria. Modernizing. |
| Hamidiya Shadhiliya | ssUM | 2-e |  | 15,000 | 1 | egyp | B | 3 | Egyptian branch of notable Sufi order, Shadhiliya. |
| Idrisiyah | ssUM | 2-e | c1800 | 10,000 | 3 | liby | A | 0 | A branch of Sufi order Shadhiliya (Morocco, Libya, et al). Strongest in Egypt. |
| Ishraqiyah | ssUM | 10-f | 1180 | 200 | 1 | syri | B | 3 | Illuminationist school of philosophy. F=Suhrawardi. |
| Jalaliya | ssUM | 2-d | c1250 | 200,000 | 3 | paki | A | 0 | Sufi, Shia, ex Suhrawardiya. In Afghanistan, Deccan. |
| Khalidiyah | ssUM | 2-e | c1850 | 50,000 | 3 | syri | B | 3 | Offshoot of Mujaddidiya Sufi order; widespread to India et al. |
| Khulusiyah | ssUM | 2-e |  | 10,000 | 1 | turk | A | 1 | Sufi suborder of Qadiriya, shut down by Kemal Ataturk in 1924. |
| Laachi | ssUM | 2-e |  | 2,000 | 1 | kirg | A | 0 | Highly politicized branch of Yasawiya Sufi order, Kirghizia. |
| Malangs | ssUM | 2-e |  | 8,000 | 1 | indi | B | 2 | Sufi male religious mendicants (Punjab, Deccan) who totally ignore world, society. Use hashish. |
| Mujaddidiya | ssUM | 2-d | 1650 | 150,000 | 10 | indi | B | 2 | Begun Damascus by Kurdish shaikh. Formerly branch of Naqshabandiya, now own Sufi order. |

*Continued overleaf*

*Table 17–6 continued*

| Name of religion/religionists 1 | Pedigree 2 | Type 3 | Begun 4 | Adherents 5 | Ext 6 | Coun 7 | W 8 | X 9 | E. g. = examples; name for God, other religions present, D=denominations, M=missions. 10 |
|---|---|---|---|---|---|---|---|---|---|
| Mukhtariyah | ssUM | 2-c | c1900 | 2,000,000 | 1 | maur | A | 0 | A Qadiriya Sufi order prominent at start of French colonial rule. |
| Nabulusiyah | ssUM | 2-d | | 300,000 | 1 | turk | A | 0 | Suborder of Sufi Qadiriya, banned in 1924 by Ataturk. |
| Nimatullahiya | ssUM | 2-d | 1370 | 350,000 | 6 | iran | A | 1 | One of the few Shia Sufi orders. Missions in Europe and America. |
| Nizamiyah | ssUM | 2-d | c1320 | 800,000 | 1 | indi | B | 2 | One of 2 branches of Chishtiyah Sufis. Revived c 1750. |
| Razzaqiyah | ssUM | 2-e | c1830 | 2,000 | 1 | afgh | A | 0 | Suborder of Sufi Qadiriya. In Herat. |
| Rumiyah | ssUM | 2-e | | 50,000 | 1 | turk | A | 0 | One of many Sufi Qadiri suborders banned by Ataturk in 1924. |
| Sabiriya | ssUM | 2-d | c1350 | 100,000 | 1 | afgh | A | 1 | One of 2 branches of Chishtiya Sufis. |
| Safi 'Ali Shahi | ssUM | 2-e | | 5,000 | 1 | iran | A | 0 | A branch of Iranian Nimatullahi Sufi order. |
| Sammaniyah | ssUM | 2-e | 1760 | 10,000 | 10 | indo | B | 3 | Suborder of Khalwatiya Sufis, from Egypt to Sudan and Sumatra. |
| Suhrawardiyah | ssUM | 2-d | 1180 | 800,000 | 4 | paki | A | 0 | South Asian Shia Sufi order. HQ Multan. Also Afghanistan, India (Deccan, Punjab, Sind). |
| Waslatiyah | ssUM | 2-e | | 40,000 | 1 | turk | A | 0 | Suborder of Sufi Qadiriya, closed down by Ataturk in 1924. |
| Zarruquyah | ssUM | 2-e | | 20,000 | 1 | niga | A | 0 | Sufi order based on Maradi in Niger. |
| Muslim World League | wM | 7-a | 1962 | 300,600,000 | 80 | saud | B | 2 | MWL. Rabitat al-Alam al-Islami. HQ Mecca. Replacing WMC (Pakistan), Wahhabi leadership. |
| World Council of Mosques | wM | 7-c | 1975 | 1,000,000 | 30 | saud | B | 2 | Offshoot of Muslim World League. |
| World Islamic Call Society | wM | 7-c | 1970 | 4,000,000 | 35 | liby | A | 1 | Jamiat al-Dawa al-Islami al-Alamiya. Militant rival of Saudi-based Muslim World League. |
| World Islamic Council for Propag & R | wM | 7-e | 1988 | 10,000 | 20 | saud | B | 2 | al-Majlis al-Alami al-Islami lil-Dawah wa-al-Ighathah. R=Relief. 17 founder organizations. |
| World Muslim Congress | wM | 7-d | 1926 | 500,000 | 60 | paki | A | 1 | WMC. Mutamar al-Alam al-Islami. HQ Karachi, 5 regional offices. Losing to Saudi-based MWL. |
| Organization of the Islamic Conf | qwM | 8-b | 1971 | 50,000,000 | 52 | saud | B | 2 | OIC. al-Mutamar al-Islami. Education, universities. 8 Heads of State summits. HQ Jeddah. |
| Islamic schismatics | XM | 2-b | | 14,950,000 | 110 | iraq | A | 0 | A large number of splits or secessions from major schools of Islamic law. |
| Ahmadis | AXM | 2-c | 1889 | 7,950,000 | 75 | paki | A | 3 | Ahmadiyah Muslim Mission. F=Mirza Ghulam Ahmad, proclaimed as Mahdi. |
| Lahoris | LAXM | 2-d | c1920 | 900,000 | 30 | paki | A | 1 | Ahmadi sect, closest to main Islam. Mosque. |
| Qadianis | QAXM | 2-c | c1920 | 9,000,000 | 60 | paki | A | 1 | Main Ahmadiyah sect, regarded as heretical by Sunnis, with Ghulam as final prophet. |
| Black Muslims | BXM | 2-c | 1913 | 1,650,000 | 5 | usa | C | 5 | Three distinct and separate bodies from original founded by Elijah Muhammad. |
| American Muslim Mission | sBXM | 2-c | 1913 | 1,100,000 | 1 | usa | C | 4 | Mainstream Black Muslims, now Sunnis. F=Elijah Muhammad. |
| Nation of Islam | sBXM | 2-d | 1978 | 400,000 | 1 | usa | C | 3 | Split ex-Black Muslims. F=L. Farrakhan. |
| Temple of Islam | sBXM | 2-d | 1934 | 600,000 | 1 | usa | C | 5 | F=Wallace D. Ford. |
| Druzes | DXM | 2-d | 1017 | 834,000 | 15 | leba | B | 5 | Quasi-Muslims (messianic Ismaili Shias). Lebanon, Syria, Jordan, Israel, Palestine, diaspora. |
| Kharijites | KXM | 2-c | c630 | 1,636,000 | 10 | iraq | A | 0 | 'Exiters' 3rd main sect of Islam (after Sunnis, Shias). Only Ibadis remain. HQ Basra. |
| Ibadiya | IKXM | 2-c | c661 | 1,636,000 | 10 | oman | A | 2 | Early Kharijites (630-1100), puritanical; now termed Ibadites. Isolated tribes (Mzab, Omani). |
| Sabbateans | MXM | 2-e | c1600 | 2,000 | 1 | turk | A | 0 | Donmeh (Apostates). Remnant followers of Jewish messiah Shabetai Zevi (1626-1676). |
| Usuliya | NXM | 2-c | c1150 | 1,000,000 | 2 | iran | A | 1 | Jurisprudence. School of Islamic law almost universally accepted by Shias. Neo-fundamentalist. |
| Ahl al-Dawa | sNXM | 2-e | | 1,000 | 1 | alge | A | 0 | People of the Call. Algerian branch of Muslim Brotherhood. |
| Al Firmawiya | sNXM | 2-e | c1980 | 30,000 | 1 | egyp | B | 3 | Exclusive militants, clandestine, virtually unknown. |
| Al Jamiya al Islamiya li al Dawa | sNXM | 2-d | | 100,000 | 1 | egyp | B | 3 | Body sympathetic to Muslim Brotherhood; in Asyut. |
| al-Hizb al-Islami | sNXM | 2-e | | 5,000 | 1 | tuni | A | 0 | Islamic Party. Local relation to Muslim Brotherhood. |
| al-Takfir wal-Hijra | sNXM | 2-e | 1965 | 50,000 | 4 | egyp | B | 3 | Atonement & Flight from Sin Society. (In Algeria, Repentance & Flight). Clandestine extremists. |
| Islami Hareket | sNXM | 2-e | 1980 | 5,000 | 1 | turk | A | 0 | Islamic Movement (Turkish). Extremist. |
| Islamic Jihad al-Bait al-Muqaddas | sNXM | 2-e | | 2,000 | 1 | jord | B | 2 | 'Holy House' (=Jerusalem). Based Amman. Radical Palestinian Islamic group. Suicide attacks. |
| Islamic Liberation Organization | sNXM | 2-e | 1971 | 20,000 | 1 | egyp | B | 3 | Munazzamat al-Tahrir al-Islami. Ex ILP. 1976 leaders executed. |
| Islamic Liberation Party | sNXM | 2-e | 1952 | 4,000 | 4 | pale | B | 3 | Hizb al-Tahrir al-Islami. Violence. Jordan, Palestine, Lebanon, Libya. Clandestine. |
| Islamic Tendency Movement | sNXM | 2-d | 1988 | 100,000 | 1 | tuni | A | 1 | Leading Muslim fundamentalist religious organization in Tunisia. |
| Islamic Unity (Unification) Movement | sNXM | 2-e | | 4,000 | 1 | leba | B | 5 | Harakat al-Tawhid al-Islami. Sunni militants. Fundamentalist. |
| Jamaat al'Islamiyah | sNXM | 2-e | c1973 | 40,000 | 1 | egyp | B | 3 | About 20 Neo-fundamentalist clandestine splinter groups. |
| Jihad Movement | sNXM | 2-e | c1650 | 1,000 | 1 | maur | A | 0 | Origins in religious fervour sweeping the Maghreb. |
| Jihad Organization | sNXM | 2-d | c1975 | 400,000 | 1 | egyp | B | 3 | Tanzim al-Jihad (Holy War). Deadliest assassinations in 1981-1991. |
| Muslim Brotherhood | sNXM | 2-c | 1928 | 1,500,000 | 10 | egyp | B | 3 | al-Ikhwan al-Muslimun. Neo-fundamentalists. Violence 1945-1965. Outlawed in Egypt, 1954. |
| Muslim Sisters | sNXM | 2-d | c1940 | 200,000 | 1 | egyp | B | 3 | Women's movement parallel to Muslim Brotherhood, to restore Islamic women's status. |
| Parvezis | sNXM | 2-e | 1940 | 2,000 | 2 | paki | A | 1 | Followers of Ghulam Ahmad Parvez, expositor of Ahl-i Quran. HQ London. |
| People of the Quran | sNXM | 2-e | 1880 | 5,000 | 1 | indi | B | 0 | Ahl al-Quran. Split ex Ahl al-Hadith. |
| People of the Tradition | sNXM | 2-d | c1700 | 100,000 | 30 | indi | B | 2 | Ahl al-Hadith. Puritanical, mystics, reform. Branches in all major European/UK cities. |
| Repose & Meditation | sNXM | 2-e | | 20,000 | 1 | egyp | B | 3 | Al Tawaqufwa al Tabayun. 1977, absorbs at-Tafkir. Assassinations. |
| Samawiyah | sNXM | 2-e | 1980 | 3,000 | 1 | egyp | B | 3 | Subversive Islamic militants prosecuted by government in 1986. |
| Al Qutbiyun | ssNXM | 2-e | c1960 | 30,000 | 1 | egyp | B | 3 | Offshoot of Muslim Brotherhood. Leading theoretician Sayyid Qutb sentenced to death in 1965. |
| Ansar | sPXM | 2-d | 1885 | 300,000 | 1 | suda | B | 2 | 'Helpers'. Originally, Mahdism. Powerful political party in Sudan. Crushed 1970 by army. |
| Ansar al Sunna al Muhammadiya | sPXM | 2-e | | 30,000 | 1 | egyp | B | 3 | In Port Said and Suhag. Islamic movements hostile to government. |
| Ansaru Allah Community | sPXM | 2-e | 1970 | 4,000 | 1 | usa | C | 5 | Black Muslims. F=Isa Muhammad, regarded as Mahdi. Influenced by Black Power movement. |
| Mahdiyah | sPXM | 2-d | 1881 | 600,000 | 1 | suda | B | 2 | F=Muhammad Ahmad (a Sufi shaykh). Rebels until 1989. Term for all Mahdi-led movements. |
| Association of Muslim Brothers | sXM | 2-e | | 3,000 | 1 | alge | A | 0 | Jammat al-Ikhwan al-Muslimun. |
| Batiniya | sXM | 2-e | 891 | 5,000 | 10 | syri | B | 0 | Several Muslim sects seeking secret esoteric meanings of the Quran. |
| Darul Arqam | sXM | 2-e | | 5,000 | 1 | indo | B | 3 | Controversal Muslim renewal organization. |
| Er-Ramaniya | sXM | 2-c | 1972 | 3,000,000 | 6 | fran | C | 5 | North African Arabs now in France as citizens; in Marseilles. |
| Islamic Resistance Movement | sXM | 2-e | c1970 | 50,000 | 2 | pale | B | 3 | Hamas. Harakat al-Muqawama al-Islamiya |
| Jabriya | sXM | 2-e | | 2,000 | 1 | moro | A | 0 | Muslim sect emphasizing Allah's control, power, and authority. Ex Qadariya. |
| Mahdavis | sXM | 2-e | 1480 | 2,000 | 1 | indi | B | 2 | Began with a mahdi Sayyid Ahmad in 1480. Very few groups today, mainly Hyderabad, Gujarat. |
| Moriscos | sXM | 2-e | 711 | 5,000 | 1 | arge | C | 5 | Spanish Moors originally from Spain (forced to become Christians but all expelled in 1614). |
| Mouvement de la Nahda Islamique | sXM | 2-e | 1974 | 50,000 | 1 | alge | A | 1 | Islamic Renaissance Movement. Radical, appeal to intellectuals. |
| Union of Muslim Teachers | sXM | 2-c | 1926 | 7,000,000 | 1 | indo | B | 3 | Nahdatul Ulama. Traditionalist rival of Muhammadiyah. |
| **New-Religionists** | N | 1-b | | 102,356,000 | 60 | japa | B | 4 | Neoreligionists. 200 recent new non-Christian religions, many syncretizing Christianity & others. |
| Astrologists | AN | 2-b | BC 1000 | 10,000,000 | 60 | indi | B | 2 | Stars, planets affect human lives; widespread use of horoscopes, divination. |
| Cargo cultists | CN | 2-e | 1893 | 3,000 | 10 | papu | C | 5 | Over 130 distinct non-Christian cargo cults since 1893. |
| John Frum cargo cults | sCN | 2-e | 1939 | 1,000 | 2 | vanu | C | 5 | Cargo cult 1939-40, Tanna. Remnants still believe, practice, await arrival of goods by air or sea. |
| Koreri cargo cultists | sCN | 2-e | 1855 | 40,000 | 1 | indo | B | 3 | Golden Age. In West Irian, scores of Konoors (prophets) announcing cargo. |
| Lo-Bos Yali Movement | sCN | 10-f | 1946 | 200 | 1 | papu | C | 3 | Law Boss. Letub Cargo cult among Tangu on Rai coast, New Guinea. F=Yali Singina. |
| Manseren cargo cultists | sCN | 2-e | 1855 | 50,000 | 1 | indo | B | 3 | 'The Lord Himself'. Since Dutch arrival in West Irian many prophets foretell coming of cargo. |
| Taro cultists | sCN | 10-f | 1914 | 200 | 1 | papu | C | 2 | Spirited movement, Spirit possession. F=Buninia. |
| Yali cargo cultists | sCN | 2-e | c1960 | 1,000 | 3 | papu | C | 4 | Wok belong Yali. Cargo-cult churches. |
| Self-Religionists | FN | 2-d | c1850 | 400,000 | 40 | usa | C | 5 | One's self seen as divine. New Age, Human Potential Movement, Insight, Silva. |
| Assoc for Research & Enlightenment | sFN | 2-d | 1931 | 100,000 | 1 | usa | C | 5 | ARE. Edgar Cayce. New Age conferences. 12 million books sold. |
| Church Universal and Triumphant | sFN | 2-e | 1958 | 18,000 | 20 | usa | C | 4 | 1958, origins in Insight, MSIA, Summit Lighthouse. Under Ascended Masters. F=M.L. Prophet. |
| Eckankar | sFN | 2-e | 1965 | 50,000 | 8 | usa | C | 5 | Secret wisdom enabling travel to higher spiritual realms. Eck=Spirit. Pantheist. Maharaj. |
| Emin Foundation | sFN | 2-e | 1973 | 1,000 | 1 | brit | C | 5 | F=Raymond Armin. HQ London. Self-improvement by group activity. |
| est | sFN | 2-d | 1971 | 100,000 | 1 | usa | C | 5 | Erhard Seminar Training (screaming abuse at others). In Human Potential Movement. |
| Gurdjieffian Groups | sFN | 2-e | c1920 | 4,000 | 20 | fran | C | 5 | F=G. I. Gurdjieff. Influenced Human Potential Movement. New Age synthesis. |
| Human Potential Movement | sFN | 2-d | 1957 | 500,000 | 10 | usa | C | 5 | Consciousness-raising. F=Alan Watts (Esalen Institute). |
| Insight | sFN | 2-e | 1978 | 10,000 | 2 | usa | C | 5 | Insight Transformational Seminars. F=J.-R. Hinkins. HQ Santa Monica. 1979, spreads in UK. |
| Jeungsando | sFN | 2-d | 1911 | 767,000 | 1 | souk | B | 5 | Total Transformation. Folk religion seeking and believing total change-transformation. |
| Mesmerism | sFN | 2-e | 1766 | 5,000 | 2 | ausz | C | 4 | F=Franz Mesmer, astrologist, hypnotist. Today, part of New Thought (Positive Thinking). |
| Movement of Spirit Inner Awareness | sFN | 2-e | 1967 | 5,000 | 2 | usa | C | 5 | Church of Movement of Spiritual Inner Awareness. MSIA. F=J. R. Hinkins. Related to Insight. |
| New Thought | sFN | 2-c | c1850 | 1,000,000 | 20 | usa | C | 5 | Positive Thinking. F=P. P. Quimby. Health, happiness, prosperity. |
| New-Agers | sFN | 2-b | c1870 | 12,000,000 | 41 | usa | C | 4 | Self-religiosity in 300 diverse forms. Bookshops, spiritual therapy centers. Celtic revivals. |
| Primal Therapy | sFN | 2-e | c1960 | 10,000 | 1 | usa | C | 5 | In Human Potential Movement: members aim at 'emitting primal scream'. |
| Self-Realization Fellowship | sFN | 2-e | 1920 | 10,000 | 2 | usa | C | 5 | SRF. Hindu-oriented. F=Paramahansa Yogananda. HQ Los Angeles. Monks, nuns, yoga. |
| Self-Realization Order | sFN | 10-f | | 300 | 1 | usa | C | 3 | Monastic grouping within Self Realization Fellowship. |
| Silva Mind Control | sFN | 2-d | 1966 | 200,000 | 1 | mexi | C | 5 | F=Jose Silva. Dynamic meditation to increase mind power. |
| Synanon Church | sFN | 2-e | 1958 | 3,000 | 1 | usa | C | 5 | F=C. E. Dederich. Therapeutic, reforming alcoholism. Vast properties. |
| Wrekin Trust | sFN | 2-e | 1942 | 1,000 | 1 | brit | C | 3 | New Age movement (astrology, healing, conferences). F=G.Trevelyan, 'alternative spirituality'. |
| Church of Essential Science | sMN | 2-e | 1964 | 5,000 | 1 | usa | C | 3 | Metaphysical body: Spiritual Frontiers Fellowship. |
| Divine Science Federation Internat | sMN | 2-e | 1888 | 4,000 | 10 | usa | C | 3 | Metaphysical. In INTA. Christ Method of Healing. HQ Denver. In New Zealand, South Africa. |
| International New Thought Alliance | sMN | 2-c | 1914 | 3,000,000 | 30 | usa | C | 5 | INTA. First attempt to unite the plethora of metaphysical movements since 1850. |
| Religious Science International | sMN | 2-e | 1949 | 12,000 | 8 | usa | C | 4 | Churches: USA 103, Canada 5, UK, Jamaica, South Africa, Barbados. |
| United Church of Religious Science | sMN | 2-e | 1917 | 90,000 | 20 | usa | C | 4 | Metaphysical. Member of INTA. 270 churches. |
| Nonsyncretist Neoreligionists | NN | 2-b | 1838 | 53,000,000 | 40 | japa | B | 3 | New Religions with little or no Buddhist/Hindu/Christian elements. |
| Beshara | sNN | 2-e | c1970 | 1,000 | 2 | brit | C | 5 | A mystical esoteric Sufi order begun in Britain repudiating Islam. |
| Church of Perfect Liberty | sNN | 2-c | 1946 | 1,473,000 | 1 | japa | B | 3 | PLK. PL Kyodan. Formerly Tokumitsukyo. Humans are divine. Life=art, sports, clubs. |
| Church of Scientology | sNN | 2-e | 1954 | 25,000 | 85 | usa | C | 5 | Dianetics, a quasi-religio-therapeutic system. Expensive trainings. |

*Continued opposite*

*Table 17–6 continued*

| Name of religion/religionists 1 | Pedigree 2 | Type 3 | Begun 4 | Adherents 5 | Ext 6 | Coun 7 | W 8 | X 9 | E. g. = examples; name for God, other religions present, D=denominations, M=missions. 10 |
|---|---|---|---|---|---|---|---|---|---|
| Chushinkai | sNN | 2-e | | 25,800 | 1 | japa | B | 2 | HQ Ota-ku, Tokyo. |
| Daishizen Tenchi Hi no Okamikyo | sNN | 2-e | | 14,100 | 1 | japa | B | 3 | HQ Toyono-gun, Osaka-fu. |
| Dancing Religion | sNN | 2-d | 1945 | 325,000 | 1 | japa | B | 2 | Tensho Kotai Jingukyo. F=Kitamura Sayo, claims God appointed her World Savior. Apocalyptic. |
| Ekidokyo | sNN | 2-e | | 1,300 | 1 | japa | B | 3 | HQ Shibuya-ku, Tokyo. |
| Ennokyo | sNN | 2-d | 1931 | 238,000 | 1 | japa | B | 3 | F=Fukada Ichi. Mystical. Large range of activities. HQ Hyogoken. |
| Fumyokai Kyodan | sNN | 2-e | | 23,500 | 1 | japa | B | 2 | HQ Kohoku-ku, Yokohama-shi. |
| Gedatsukai | sNN | 2-d | 1929 | 500,000 | 10 | japa | B | 3 | Shingon. Honor to rising Sun each day. F=Eizo Okano. HQ Tokyo. Veneration of Kami deities. |
| Hachidai Ryuo Daishizen Aishin K | sNN | 2-d | | 102,000 | 1 | japa | B | 2 | K=Kyodan. HQ Iwamizawa-shi, Hokkaido. |
| Horaisan Seishinkai | sNN | 2-e | | 5,000 | 1 | japa | B | 3 | HQ Morioka-shi, Iwate-ken. |
| Izumo Shinto Yakumokyo Shinjinkai K | sNN | 2-e | | 2,800 | 1 | japa | B | 3 | K=Kyodan. HQ Sumiyoshi-ku, Osaka-shi. |
| Jilliwhoi | sNN | 2-c | 1925 | 4,630,000 | 1 | souk | B | 2 | Daisoon Jilliwhoi (Great & Genuine Truth Assembly). |
| Kikueikai Kyodan | sNN | 2-e | | 3,500 | 1 | japa | B | 3 | HQ Kita Kawachi-gun, Osaka-fu. |
| Kyuseishukyo | sNN | 2-d | | 128,000 | 1 | japa | B | 2 | HQ Beppu-shi, Oita-ken. |
| Makoto no Michi | sNN | 2-e | | 7,100 | 1 | japa | B | 3 | HQ Setagaya-ku, Tokyo. |
| Nihon Ehoba Kyodan | sNN | 2-e | | 11,400 | 1 | japa | B | 2 | HQ Meguro-ku, Tokyo. |
| Nihon Keishin Suso Jishudan | sNN | 2-e | | 11,000 | 1 | japa | B | 1 | HQ Iizaka-machi, Fukushima-shi. |
| Oomoto | sNN | 2-c | 1892 | 1,500,000 | 15 | japa | B | 3 | 'Great Origin' Omotokyo. Omoto. F=peasant woman, Deguchi Nao. Extensive mass media use. |
| Religion of Heavenly Wisdom | sNN | 2-c | 1838 | 2,990,000 | 40 | japa | B | 4 | Tenrikyo. Faith-healing.17,000 churches, 20,000 mission stations worldwide. Global mission. |
| Sapta Darma | sNN | 2-d | 1952 | 100,000 | 1 | indo | B | 3 | Sevenfold Teaching. New Javanese mystical religion. |
| Seikyokai | sNN | 2-e | c1960 | 20,000 | 1 | japa | B | 3 | HQ Tsukubo-gun, Okayama-ken. |
| Sekai Heiwa Kyodan | sNN | 2-e | | 23,600 | 1 | japa | B | 3 | HQ Minami-ku, Osaka-shi. |
| Shinreikyo | sNN | 2-d | | 144,000 | 1 | japa | B | 3 | HQ Nishinomiya-shi, Hyogo-ken. |
| Shinseikai | sNN | 2-e | | 64,700 | 1 | japa | B | 3 | HQ Ashigara Shimo-gun, Kanagawa-ken. |
| Shinsen Reidokyo | sNN | 2-e | | 37,000 | 1 | japa | B | 3 | HQ Takatsuki-shi, Osaka-fu. |
| Society of Companions of the Spirits | sNN | 2-c | 1922 | 4,260,000 | 10 | japa | B | 2 | Reiyukai Kyodan. Nichirenshu, family values, lay. F=Kubo Ka. HQ Minato-ku. |
| Subud | sNN | 2-d | 1933 | 330,000 | 70 | indo | B | 2 | Susila Buddhi Dharma. Inner force. F=Bapak. Vast properties, banks. UK 2,000, USA 80 cities. |
| Sukyo Mahikari | sNN | 2-e | 1974 | 7,000 | 1 | japa | B | 3 | Subsect ex Sekai Mahikari Bunmei Kyodan. |
| Sumarah | sNN | 2-e | 1935 | 10,000 | 1 | indo | B | 3 | 'Total surrender to God'. F=Sukino. East and Central Java cities. |
| Tenchi no Taikyo | sNN | 2-e | | 8,100 | 1 | japa | B | 3 | HQ Higashi-ku, Osaka-shi. |
| Tensha Tsuchimikado Shinto Honcho | sNN | 2-e | | 40,000 | 1 | japa | B | 2 | HQ Onyu-gun, Fukui-ken. |
| Tenso Kokyo | sNN | 2-e | | 37,100 | 1 | japa | B | 1 | HQ Moriyama-ku, Nagoya-shi. |
| The Religious Land | sNN | 2-e | 1972 | 3,000 | 4 | thai | B | 3 | Hooppha Sawan. HQ International Fed of Religions (for world peace), 80 miles from Bangkok. |
| Uchu Motohajime Shinkyo | sNN | 2-d | | 106,000 | 1 | japa | B | 3 | HQ Suita-shi, Osaka-fu. |
| Union of New Religious Orgs of Japan | snN | 7-b | 1962 | 32,000,000 | 1 | japa | B | 3 | Shin Nihon Shukyo Dantai Rengo Kai. 170 member denominations. |
| World True Light Civilization | sNN | 2-d | 1959 | 100,000 | 10 | japa | B | 3 | Sekai Mahikari Bunmei Kyodan. Japan center of Universe (at Shizuoka). Ex Sekai Kyuseikyo. |
| World True Religion | sNN | 2-d | 1957 | 621,000 | 1 | souk | B | 4 | Segyejunggyo. Folk religion seeking world peace, realization of human ideals (Utopia). |
| Zenrinkai | sNN | 2-d | 1947 | 386,000 | 1 | japa | B | 3 | Association for Doing Good to One's Neighbors. Retreats for spiritual training. HQ Fukuoka. |
| Occultists | ON | 2-c | c1700 | 1,500,000 | 50 | usa | C | 2 | Hidden and secret practices. Kabbalah used. c1880, Golden Dawn. |
| Ancient & Mystical Order RC | sON | 2-e | 1915 | 2,000 | 10 | usa | C | 4 | AMORC. RC=Rosae Crucis. Rosicrucians. F=H.Spencer-Lewis. HQ California. |
| Hermetic Order of the Golden Dawn | sON | 2-e | 1888 | 5,000 | 10 | brit | C | 4 | The most influential Western magical organization; revival of interest in the Occult. |
| Kabbalah | sON | 2-d | BC 500 | 300,000 | 10 | isra | B | 2 | Qabalah. Esoteric mystical occult materials, part Jewish. 1890, magic revival as Golden Dawn. |
| Neo-Kabbalah | sON | 2-d | BC 500 | 200,000 | 20 | isra | B | 2 | Jewish New-Agers influenced by occult Kabbalistic practices. |
| Rosicrucians | sON | 2-d | c1410 | 700,000 | 50 | germ | C | 4 | Secret worldwide esoteric brotherhood. 1915 includes AMORC. Correspondence courses. |
| Satanism | sON | 2-e | c1800 | 10,000 | 40 | usa | C | 3 | Devil worship. Occult. Desecration of Christian symbols. In Europe, USA, Middle East. |
| Servants of the Light | sON | 2-e | c1960 | 5,000 | 2 | usa | C | 3 | Occultist school offering Kabbalistic training. |
| Wicca | sON | 2-d | BC 300 | 700,000 | 20 | iraq | A | 3 | Witchcraft. Craft. Old Religion. Gardnerianism. Pre-Celtic wisdom, worship of Earth Goddess. |
| Neo-Paganism | PN | 2-d | c1850 | 400,000 | 30 | brit | C | 5 | Modern revival of European pre-Christian paganism; worship of Earth Goddess. |
| Fellowship of Isis | sPN | 2-e | c1930 | 50,000 | 1 | nige | B | 4 | Neo-Pagan movement dedicated to worship of female deities, witches. |
| Pagan Pathfinders | sPN | 2-e | 1973 | 1,000 | 2 | brit | C | 4 | Neo-Pagan movement; occult techniques, altered states of consciousness. |
| Buddhistic New-Religionists | SN | 2-b | c1850 | 25,000,000 | 3 | japa | B | 3 | New Religions with strong Buddhist elements, influence, dogmas, claims. |
| Order of the Cross | SN | 2-e | 1904 | 1,000 | 10 | brit | C | 4 | F=J. T. Ferrier, proclaiming unity of all religions. |
| Syncretist New-Religionists | SN | 2-b | 950 | 160,000,000 | 3 | japa | B | 3 | New Religions which combine substantial elements from Buddhism, Christianity, or others. |
| Agonshu | sSN | 2-d | 1978 | 580,000 | 10 | japa | B | 3 | Veneration of Buddhist Agama Sutras. F=Kiriyama Seiyu. Annual mass fire ceremony, Kyoto. |
| Alevis | sSN | 2-d | c1700 | 500,000 | 15 | turk | A | 1 | Ali-ilahi. Aliani. Qizilbash syncretic religion: Islam, Zoroastrianism, Christianity. |
| Ananaikyo | sSN | 2-d | 1949 | 218,000 | 1 | japa | B | 3 | Aim to induce kami-possession. Millenarian. Syncretism from all religions. |
| Balmikis | sSN | 2-d | c1880 | 300,000 | 6 | indi | B | 2 | Keshderi Sikhs. F=Valmikis. Chuhra (Sweepers) caste combining Hinduism, Sikhism. |
| Bauls | sSN | 2-e | c1900 | 5,000 | 1 | indi | B | 2 | 'Madmen'. Vaishnava/Sufi Hindu/Muslim singing amalgam. |
| Budi Setia | sSN | 2-e | c1960 | 30,000 | 1 | indo | B | 3 | Javanese et alia mystical sect. |
| Cao Dai Missionary Church | sSN | 2-c | 1919 | 3,200,000 | 50 | viet | B | 4 | Dai Dao Tam Ky Pho Do (Great Way of the 3 Epochs of Salvation). Catholic syncretism. |
| Compassion Society | sSN | 2-e | 1949 | 15,000 | 1 | taiw | B | 3 | Tzu Hui Tang. Mediumistic. Many texts. Spirit writing. 600 groups. |
| Dadu Panthis | sSN | 2-e | c1580 | 10,000 | 1 | indi | B | 2 | Hindu-Muslim devotional movement. F=Dadu Dayal. HQ Rajasthan. |
| De Jiao | sSN | 2-e | 1939 | 10,000 | 6 | chin | B | 3 | Tak Kaau (in Cantonese). Religion of Virtue. South China, Hong Kong. |
| Dharmadasis | sSN | 2-e | c1600 | 10,000 | 1 | indi | B | 2 | Subsect of Kabir Panthis. HQ Chattisgarh. Merchants. A Hindu/Muslim/Sikh amalgam. |
| God's Kingdom Society | sSN | 2-e | 1934 | 2,500 | 1 | nige | B | 3 | Sabbatarian body combining Catholic, Jehovah's Witnesses, Jewish elements. Polygamous. |
| Godianism | sSN | 2-d | 1945 | 200,000 | 1 | nige | B | 3 | Cult of Aruosa. Founded by Oba of Benin, Akenzua II, using Bini ethnoreligion. |
| Grail Foundation Movement | sSN | 2-d | 1919 | 100,000 | 30 | ausz | C | 5 | Gralsbewegung. Crossbearers. F=O. E. Bernhardt. Reincarnation. HQ Vomperberg. Global. |
| Heavenly Virtue Holy Church | sSN | 2-d | | 250,000 | 7 | malb | B | 3 | Tien Te Sheng Hui. Chinese, across Southeast Asia. |
| Hoa Hao | sSN | 2-c | 1939 | 2,050,000 | 10 | viet | B | 2 | Buo Son Ky Hong. Millennialist. F=Huyan Phu So, regarded as the Emergent Buddha. |
| Hommon Butsuryu | sSN | 2-d | 1857 | 500,000 | 2 | japa | B | 3 | Lay movement in Kyoto. Ex Buddhism. Main feature: Lotus Sutra. |
| House of Growth | sSN | 2-c | 1930 | 2,415,000 | 2 | japa | B | 3 | Seicho no Ie. Ex Omotokyo. Positive thinking; denial of evil; all are gods. Literature, lectures. |
| I-kuan Tao | sSN | 2-c | 1928 | 3,000,000 | 20 | taiw | B | 1 | Yi Guan Dao. Unity Way. Begun China. Buddhist/Taoist/Christian elements. 2 major rival sects. |
| Ilkwando | sSN | 2-d | 1948 | 844,000 | 1 | souk | B | 4 | Kukje-Dodug Hyophwoi-Ilkwando (Unified Truth Principle); claiming unity of Buddhism, Taoism. |
| Indian Shaker Church | sSN | 2-e | 1882 | 2,000 | 3 | cana | C | 4 | Syncretists ex RCC Indians in British Columbia and northwest USA. 25 churches. |
| Izumo-taishakyo | sSN | 2-c | 1873 | 2,261,000 | 20 | japa | B | 3 | One of largest Shinko Shukyo (New Religions). Based on Shinto. HQ Taisha, Izumo shrine. |
| Jordanites | sSN | 2-e | 1895 | 4,500 | 2 | guya | B | 4 | White-Robed Army. West Evangelist Millennial Pilgrim Ch. Hindu/occult/Jewish/African. |
| Kabir Chaura | sSN | 2-e | c1600 | 5,000 | 1 | indi | B | 2 | One of 12 original subgroupings of Kabir Panthis. HQ Benares. |
| Kabir Panthis | sSN | 2-e | c1480 | 20,000 | 1 | indi | B | 2 | F=Indian guru Kabir. Hindu/Muslim/Sikh. 12 subgroups. |
| Kawruh Bedja | sSN | 2-e | c1960 | 20,000 | 1 | indo | B | 3 | Mystical sect, a Javanese and related language New Religion. |
| Kuga Sorta | sSN | 2-e | c1872 | 5,000 | 1 | russ | B | 5 | Big Candle. Cheremis syncretism in Mari ASSR. Christ greatest prophet. Persecuted by ROC. |
| Lui-ists | sSN | 2-d | | 900,000 | 1 | taiw | B | 3 | One of 2 major sects within modern Taiwanese I-kuan Tao (Unity). |
| Maldevidan cultists | sSN | 2-e | c1800 | 10,000 | 2 | mart | C | 5 | Syncretistic Hindu/RC mix (Vishnu=Christ). Originally Tamil coolies from India, now Creoles. |
| Moral Re-Armament | sSN | 2-e | 1920 | 50,000 | 90 | swit | C | 5 | MRA. Oxford Group (until 1938). Began Evangelical, now panreligious. HQ Caux. |
| National Church of Nigeria | sSN | 2-e | 1948 | 20,000 | 1 | nige | B | 3 | F=K. O. K. Onyioha. Ibo religion with Christian elements. |
| New Life Movement | sSN | 2-e | 1934 | 5,000 | 1 | chin | B | 3 | Constructed religion for political unity. F=Chiang kai-shek. |
| Nusairis | sSN | 2-c | 950 | 1,100,000 | 5 | syri | B | 3 | Alawis. Quasi-Muslim extremist sect. Gnostic, Ismaili, and Christian teachings. God=Ali. |
| Palace of Sacred Peace | sSN | 2-e | | 1,000 | 1 | taiw | B | 2 | Splinter group ex Compassion Society. |
| Pangestu | sSN | 2-d | 1932 | 100,000 | 1 | indo | B | 3 | Paguyuban Ngesti Tunggal. F=Pakde Nanto. |
| People of the Truth | sSN | 2-d | c1050 | 507,000 | 4 | iran | A | 1 | Ahl-i-Haqq. Ethnic, tribal groups, mostly Kurdish. Sufi/Zoroastrian/Christian elements. |
| Pormalim | sSN | 2-e | 1907 | 5,000 | 1 | indo | B | 3 | 'The Independents'. Messianic religion among Bataks of Sumatra. |
| Qizilbash | sSN | 2-d | c1450 | 204,000 | 10 | afgh | A | 1 | Ethnic group of warriors. Melange of Islam/Zoroastrianism/Christianity. |
| Rajneesh Foundation | sSN | 2-e | 1974 | 4,000 | 2 | indi | B | 2 | F=Bhagwan Shree Rajneesh. Ashram in Oregon, USA, expelled 1985, returned to Poona. |
| Religion of the Heavenly Way | sSN | 2-c | 1860 | 1,200,000 | 15 | souk | B | 4 | Chondogyo. Tonghak. Eastern Learning. Confucian/Taoist/Shamanist elements. 4,700 clergy. |
| Rissho Koseikai | sSN | 2-c | 1938 | 5,000,000 | 40 | japa | B | 3 | Society for Establishing Righteousness & Harmony. Ex Reiyukai. HQ Tokyo. Aim: Buddhahood. |
| Rizalistas | sSN | 2-d | 1896 | 400,000 | 1 | phil | C | 5 | Nationalist movements honoring, as returning Messiah, Jose Rizal y Mercado. Mainly rural. |
| Sahaja Yoga | sSN | 2-e | c1960 | 20,000 | 1 | indi | B | 2 | F=Nirmala Devi, known as Divine Mother. Energy within. |
| San-chiao | sSN | 2-b | BC 500 | 106,000,000 | 2 | chin | B | 3 | Three Ways. Amalgam of Confucian, Taoist, and Buddhist religions in each's entirety. |
| Soka Gakkai International | sSN | 2-b | 1937 | 18,000,000 | 115 | japa | B | 3 | Value Creation. 1975 SGI; 1990 Lay split ex Nichiren Shoshu. World conversion dropped. |
| Sunists | sSN | 2-c | | 1,000,000 | 1 | taiw | B | 3 | One of the 2 major sects out of modern I-kuan Tao (Unity). |
| Supreme Truth Movement | sSN | 2-d | c1985 | 150,000 | 20 | japa | B | 3 | Aum Shinrikyo. Ex Shinrikyo. Terrorist attacks in Tokyo. Buddhist/Hindu. Big in Russia. |
| Tridharma | sSN | 2-e | 1938 | 6,000 | 2 | indo | B | 3 | Samkauw Hwee (3 Religions): Buddha, Confucius, Lao Tzu. Member of WALUBI. |
| True Nichiren School | sSN | 2-c | 1930 | 1,000,000 | 50 | japa | B | 3 | Nichiren Shoshu. International; this-worldly appeal. 1992, Soka Gakkai splits off. |
| Way of Man Society | sSN | 2-e | | 10,000 | 1 | japa | B | 2 | Hito no Michi Kyodan. New religion, now part of PL Kyodan. F=Miki Tokuharu. |
| White Lotus Society | sSN | 2-e | c1050 | 5,000 | 2 | chin | B | 3 | Chinese folk movement, plagued by complex of Buddhist/Taoist/millenarian secret societies. |
| Theosophical Society | sTN | 2-e | 1875 | 60,000 | 80 | indi | B | 2 | F=Helena Blavatsky. Wisdom of Tibetan Hidden Masters. 1,223 lodges in 80 countries. |
| Anthroposophical Society | ssTN | 2-e | 1912 | 25,000 | 10 | germ | C | 4 | Anthroposophy. Wisdom of Humanity. F=Rudolf Steiner. Ex Theosophy. HQ in Switzerland. |
| United Lodge of Theosophists | ssTN | 2-e | 1909 | 12,000 | 12 | usa | C | 4 | Schismatic offshoot of original Theosophical Society. Hindu-Buddhist occult mysticism. |

*Continued overleaf*

Table 17–6 continued

| Name of religion/religionists 1 | Pedigree 2 | Type 3 | Begun 4 | Adherents 5 | Ext 6 | Coun 7 | W 8 | X 9 | E. g. = examples; name for God, other religions present, D=denominations, M=missions. 10 |
|---|---|---|---|---|---|---|---|---|---|
| Theosophical Society International | wTN | 2-e | 1891 | 34,000 | 20 | usa | C | 4 | F=W. Q. Judge. Ex Theosophical Society. HQ Pasadena, California. |
| Chinese secret societies | sUN | 2-c | c1700 | 1,000,000 | 30 | chin | B | 3 | Mimi Shehui. Unlawful religious associations, pursuing healing and salvation. |
| Secret societies | sUN | 2-c | c1700 | 4,000,000 | 60 | chin | B | 1 | Secular or religious unorthodox brotherhoods, often criminal; such as the many Triads. |
| Magico-religionists | VN | 2-e |  | 10,000 | 5 | brit | C | 5 | Practitioners of magic, wizardry, spells, curses. |
| Nativistic cultists | VN | 2-b | c1500 | 130,000,000 | 30 | indo | B | 3 | Mystical new religious movements combining local gods with world religions. |
| Himpunan Penghayat Kepercayaan | cVN | 2-b | 1955 | 60,000,000 | 1 | indo | B | 3 | HPK. Umbrella body for Kebatinan mystical religions. Name changed 1970 and 1979. |
| Agama Islam Jawa | sVN | 2-b |  | 23,755,000 | 1 | indo | B | 3 | Abangan. Nominal Javanese Muslims in mystical movements classified as New Religions. |
| Aliran Kepercayaan | sVN | 2-c | c1500 | 2,000,000 | 1 | indo | B | 2 | 'Faith', official term for all Kebatinan mystical sects. Vast expansion in 1980s, into 400 varieties. |
| As of Believers in One Supreme God | sVN | 2-c | c1960 | 3,500,000 | 1 | indo | B | 3 | ABOSG. As=Association. Umbrella organization for 20 Kepercayaan sects. |
| Bungan | sVN | 2-e | 1942 | 50,000 | 1 | indo | B | 3 | Renewal movement among Kenyah and Kayan (Borneo). Declining after rapid spread in 1950s. |
| Chisumphi cultists | sVN | 2-d | c1850 | 200,000 | 2 | mala | C | 2 | Mediumistic ancestor cult among the Northern Chewa. Formerly highly developed. |
| Fruit of Wisdom | sVN | 2-e | c1850 | 30,000 | 2 | myan | B | 3 | Telakhon. Karen millennialism. Ancient prophecies unfulfilled, so Bibles rejected. Civil war. |
| Kebatinan | sVN | 2-b | c1800 | 62,359,000 | 3 | indo | B | 3 | Golongan-golongan Kebatinan. Over 300 Javanese mystical new religious movements. |
| M'Bona cult | sVN | 2-d | c1900 | 300,000 | 1 | mala | C | 2 | Tribal cult among southern Chewa in Malawi. |
| Korean New-Religionists | zN | 2-c | c1800 | 7,121,000 | 6 | souk | B | 2 | Over 200 distinct and separate new religious bodies, syncretist and nonsyncretist. |
| Shinko Shukyo | zN | 2-b |  | 32,827,000 | 4 | japa | B | 3 | Japanese New Religions. |
| **Shintoists** | S | 1-c |  | 2,762,000 | 8 | japa | B | 1 | 'The Way of the Kami (Gods)'. 150 sects, 80,000 shrines in Japan. |
| Folk-Shintoists | FS | 2-c |  | 1,600,000 | 3 | brit | B | 1 | Minzoku Shinto. Minkan Shinto. Magico-religious rituals, taboos, divination. |
| Shrine Shintoists | HS | 2-b | 1946 | 62,000,000 | 40 | japa | B | 2 | Jinja Honcho, Jinja Shinto. 26,000 priests, 77,000 shrines. |
| Hokkaido Jinja Kyokai | sHS | 2-e |  | 15,000 | 1 | japa | B | 1 | HQ Kami Iso-gun, Hokkaido. |
| Ishizuchi Honkyo | sHS | 2-d |  | 802,000 | 1 | japa | B | 0 | HQ Saijo-shi, Ehime-ken. |
| Izumo Hi no Misaki Daijingukyo | sHS | 2-e |  | 80,500 | 1 | japa | B | 2 | HQ Hikawa-gun, Shimane-ken. |
| Izumo Kannabikyo | sHS | 2-e |  | 1,000 | 1 | japa | B | 1 | HQ Izumo-shi, Shimane-ken. |
| Izumokyo | sHS | 2-d |  | 626,000 | 1 | japa | B | 2 | HQ Hikawa-gun, Shimane-ken. |
| Jingukyo | sHS | 2-d |  | 107,000 | 1 | japa | B | 0 | HQ Taki-gun, Hyogo-ken. |
| Jinja Honkyo | sHS | 2-d |  | 728,000 | 1 | japa | B | 0 | HQ Higashiyama-ku, Kyoto-shi. |
| Jinja Ubusunakyo | sHS | 2-e |  | 95,100 | 1 | japa | B | 1 | HQ Mihara-shi, Hiroshima-ken. |
| Kiso Ontake Honkyo | sHS | 2-d |  | 231,000 | 1 | japa | B | 1 | HQ Kiso-gun, Nagano-ken. |
| Nihon Jingu Honcho | sHS | 2-e |  | 79,100 | 1 | japa | B | 1 | HQ Obihiro-shi, Hokkaido. |
| Nihon Jinja Honcho | sHS | 2-e |  | 19,600 | 1 | japa | B | 2 | HQ Obihiro-shi, Hokkaido. |
| Nihon Jinja Kyodan | sHS | 2-e |  | 2,600 | 1 | japa | B | 0 | HQ Yuki-gun, Ibaraki-ken. |
| Seishin Myoshokai | sHS | 2-e |  | 70,000 | 1 | japa | B | 0 | HQ Fukuyama-shi, Hiroshima-ken. |
| Shinto Ishikirikyo | sHS | 2-d |  | 196,000 | 1 | japa | B | 1 | HQ Higashi Osaka-shi. |
| Yamatokyo | sHS | 2-e |  | 66,200 | 1 | japa | B | 1 | HQ Shiogama-shi, Miyagi-ken. |
| Association of Shinto Sects | nS | 7-c |  | 6,850,000 | 14 | japa | B | 3 | Coordinating body for Kyoha Shinto Rengo Kai; 12 of the 13 Sects. 1970, Tenrikyo leaves. |
| Association of Shinto Shrines | nS | 7-b | 1946 | 58,512,000 | 25 | japa | B | 3 | Jinja Honcho. 26,000 priests. 98% of all Shrine Shinto organizations. Gradual decline. |
| New Sect Shintoists | NS | 2-c | 1945 | 1,837,000 | 30 | japa | B | 3 | Consists of over 47 new Sect Shinto organisations. |
| Dai Nihon Daidokyo | sNS | 2-d |  | 143,000 | 1 | japa | B | 1 | HQ Fukushima-ken. |
| Daigenkyo | sNS | 2-e |  | 1,400 | 1 | japa | B | 2 | HQ Okayama-ken. |
| Daihizenkyo | sNS | 2-e |  | 3,100 | 1 | japa | B | 0 | HQ Shinjuku-ku, Tokyo. |
| Daihongenkyo Kyodan | sNS | 2-d |  | 150,000 | 1 | japa | B | 0 | HQ Nagano-ken. |
| Daireido | sNS | 2-e |  | 16,900 | 1 | japa | B | 1 | HQ Ishikawa-ken. |
| Daishinkai Kyodan | sNS | 2-e |  | 4,500 | 1 | japa | B | 2 | HQ Soraku-gun, Kyoto-fu. |
| Daiuchukyo | sNS | 2-e |  | 4,100 | 1 | japa | B | 2 | HQ Adachi-ku, Tokyo. |
| Daiwa Kyodan | sNS | 2-e |  | 52,700 | 1 | japa | B | 1 | HQ Sendai-shi, Miyagi-ken. |
| Hinomoto Kyodan | sNS | 2-e |  | 1,600 | 1 | japa | B | 1 | HQ Hiroshima-ken. |
| Ichigen no Miya | sNS | 2-e |  | 4,400 | 1 | japa | B | 1 | HQ Osaka-shi. |
| Inari Shinkyo | sNS | 2-e |  | 2,800 | 1 | japa | B | 0 | HQ Kita-ku, Kyoto-shi. |
| Kannagarakyo (New) | sNS | 2-e |  | 35,400 | 1 | japa | B | 1 | HQ Kagoshima-shi. |
| Koshinto Senbokyo | sNS | 2-e |  | 23,500 | 1 | japa | B | 1 | HQ Osaka-shi. |
| Nakayama Kojin Hoonkai | sNS | 2-e |  | 3,700 | 1 | japa | B | 1 | HQ Okayama-ken. |
| Oyamatokyo | sNS | 2-e |  | 20,000 | 1 | japa | B | 0 | HQ Nara-shi. |
| Renshindo Kyodan | sNS | 2-e |  | 3,400 | 1 | japa | B | 1 | HQ Nerima-ku, Tokyo. |
| Seikokyo | sNS | 2-e |  | 7,600 | 1 | japa | B | 1 | HQ Higashi Nada-ku, Kobe-shi. |
| Sekishinkai | sNS | 2-e |  | 3,200 | 1 | japa | B | 1 | HQ Hiroshima-ken. |
| Shidaido | sNS | 2-e |  | 4,600 | 1 | japa | B | 0 | HQ Ishikawa-ken. |
| Shinboku Kyodan | sNS | 2-d |  | 158,000 | 1 | japa | B | 2 | HQ Toshima-ku, Tokyo. |
| Shinjinkyo | sNS | 2-e |  | 20,900 | 1 | japa | B | 2 | HQ Hyogo-ken. |
| Shinmeikyo | sNS | 2-e |  | 2,000 | 1 | japa | B | 1 | HQ Kochi-ken. |
| Shinreikai Kyodan | sNS | 2-d |  | 137,000 | 1 | japa | B | 1 | HQ Minato-ku, Tokyo. |
| Shinsei Mutsumi Kyodan | sNS | 2-e |  | 2,700 | 1 | japa | B | 1 | HQ Edogawa-ku, Tokyo. |
| Shinseikyo | sNS | 2-e |  | 33,500 | 1 | japa | B | 1 | HQ Aichi-ken. |
| Shinto Ishizuchiha | sNS | 2-e |  | 1,200 | 1 | japa | B | 0 | HQ Ehime-ken. |
| Shinto Kotokukyo | sNS | 10-f |  | 150 | 1 | japa | B | 1 | HQ Hino-shi, Tokyo. |
| Shinto Kyodan | sNS | 2-e |  | 10,000 | 1 | japa | B | 1 | HQ Fukuchiyama-shi, Kyoto-fu. |
| Shinto Shinkyo | sNS | 2-e |  | 9,400 | 1 | japa | B | 0 | HQ Kochi-ken. |
| Shinto Yamatokyo | sNS | 2-e |  | 10,000 | 1 | japa | B | 1 | HQ Ise-shi, Mie-ken. |
| Shizen Shindo | sNS | 2-e |  | 6,400 | 1 | japa | B | 1 | HQ Shizuoka-ken. |
| Shuyodan Hoseikai | sNS | 2-e |  | 15,800 | 1 | japa | B | 2 | HQ Toshima-ku, Tokyo. |
| Soshindo Honcho | sNS | 2-e |  | 18,400 | 1 | japa | B | 1 | HQ Fukuoka-shi. |
| Sumerakyo | sNS | 2-d |  | 173,000 | 1 | japa | B | 1 | HQ Shizuoka-ken. |
| Sumerakyo Honinha | sNS | 2-d |  | 450,000 | 1 | japa | B | 1 | HQ Fukuoka-shi. |
| Taizenkyo | sNS | 10-g |  | 90 | 1 | japa | B | 1 | HQ Itabashi-ku, Tokyo. |
| Tenchi Mamori Kyodan | sNS | 2-e |  | 5,100 | 1 | japa | B | 1 | HQ Osaka-shi. |
| Tenonkyo | sNS | 2-e |  | 1,600 | 1 | japa | B | 1 | HQ Kita-ku, Kyoto-shi. |
| Tenreikyo | sNS | 2-e |  | 11,400 | 1 | japa | B | 0 | HQ Kagawa-ken. |
| Tensha Yamakage Shinto Aishinkai | sNS | 2-e |  | 4,700 | 1 | japa | B | 1 | HQ Nakano-ku, Tokyo. |
| Tenshindo Kyodan | sNS | 2-e |  | 75,000 | 1 | japa | B | 1 | HQ Bunkyo-ku, Tokyo. |
| Tenshinkyo | sNS | 10-f |  | 140 | 1 | japa | B | 1 | HQ Kyoto-fu. |
| Uchu Kyodan | sNS | 2-e |  | 9,100 | 1 | japa | B | 1 | HQ Yokohama-shi. |
| Ryobu Shinto | sS | 2-c |  | 1,000,000 | 1 | japa | B | 2 | 'Dual' Shinto. Pattern of Shinto-Buddhist syncretic coexistence. Kamis=historical Buddhas. |
| Shinto of Grace and Protection | sS | 2-e | 1660 | 5,000 | 2 | japa | B | 3 | Suika Shinto. Influenced by Neo-Confucianism. |
| Sect Shintoists | TS | 2-c | 1882 | 6,000,000 | 20 | japa | B | 3 | Kyoha Shinto. 85 sects (13 being major). No shrines. Served by Association of Sect Shinto. |
| Chikakusan Minshukyo Kyodan | sTS | 2-d |  | 195,000 | 1 | japa | B | 1 | HQ Nagano-ken. |
| Chintaku Reifu Shinkyo | sTS | 2-e |  | 10,000 | 1 | japa | B | 1 | Ex Shinrikyo. HQ Daito-shi, Osaka-fu. |
| Choseikyo | sTS | 2-e |  | 4,500 | 1 | japa | B | 0 | HQ Kochi-ken. Ex Shinrikyo. |
| Daidokyo | sTS | 2-e |  | 57,600 | 1 | japa | B | 1 | HQ Fukushima-ken. |
| Fuji Goho | sTS | 10-f |  | 720 | 1 | japa | B | 1 | HQ Shizuoka-ken. |
| Fuji Honkyo | sTS | 2-e |  | 2,400 | 1 | japa | B | 1 | HQ Taito-ku, Tokyo. |
| Fujikyo | sTS | 2-e |  | 1,800 | 1 | japa | B | 0 | HQ Shizuoka-ken. |
| Fusokyo | sTS | 2-d | 1875 | 144,000 | 1 | japa | B | 2 | Mountain worship group based on Mount Fuji. In Sect Shinto. HQ Setagaya, Tokyo. |
| Hi no Oshie | sTS | 2-e |  | 2,100 | 1 | japa | B | 2 | Mountain worship. HQ Shinguku-ku, Tokyo. |
| Hikawa Kamiichijo | sTS | 2-e |  | 6,500 | 1 | japa | B | 1 | HQ Osaka-fu. |
| Hikawakyo | sTS | 2-e |  | 5,000 | 1 | japa | B | 1 | HQ Osaka-fu. |
| Hinomoto Shinseiko | sTS | 2-e |  | 2,300 | 1 | japa | B | 1 | HQ Nerima-ku, Tokyo. |
| Hinomotokyo | sTS | 2-e |  | 65,100 | 1 | japa | B | 2 | Mountain worship. Ex Shinrikyo. HQ Hiroshima-shi, and Hyogo-ken. |
| Inarikyo | sTS | 2-e |  | 12,100 | 1 | japa | B | 1 | HQ Hiroshima-ken. |
| Ishizuchikyo | sTS | 2-e |  | 11,800 | 1 | japa | B | 1 | HQ Osaka-fu. |
| Isuzukyo | sTS | 2-e |  | 35,400 | 1 | japa | B | 1 | HQ Oka-ku, Tokyo. |
| Izumo Oyashirokyo | sTS | 2-c | 1873 | 1,456,000 | 2 | japa | B | 1 | Revivalist Shinto group, one of 13 Kyoha sects. God=Okuninushi, Amaterasu. |
| Jikkokyo | sTS | 2-d | 1882 | 150,000 | 1 | japa | B | 2 | Jikokyo. Japanese mountain worship based on Mount Fuji. HQ Saitama-ken. |
| Jitsugetsukyo | sTS | 2-e |  | 18,100 | 1 | japa | B | 2 | Mountain worship. HQ Meguro-ku, Tokyo. |
| Kaminomichibikikyo | sTS | 2-e |  | 10,300 | 1 | japa | B | 1 | HQ Osaka-shi. |
| Kandori Konkokyo | sTS | 2-e |  | 7,300 | 1 | japa | B | 0 | HQ Okayama-ken. |
| Kannagarakyo | sTS | 2-e |  | 23,500 | 1 | japa | B | 1 | HQ Nagoya-shi. |

Continued opposite

*Table 17–6 continued*

| Name of religion/religionists 1 | Pedigree 2 | Type 3 | Begun 4 | Adherents 5 | Ext 6 | Coun 7 | W 8 | X 9 | E. g. = examples; name for God, other religions present, D=denominations, M=missions. 10 |
|---|---|---|---|---|---|---|---|---|---|
| Konpirakyo | sTS | 2-e | | 10,000 | 1 | japa | B | 1 | HQ Kagoshima-shi. |
| Kotohira Honkyo | sTS | 2-d | | 136,000 | 1 | japa | B | 0 | HQ Kagawa-ken. |
| Kurozumi-kyo | sTS | 2-d | 1814 | 574,000 | 2 | japa | B | 3 | Sect Shinto. Faith healing thru sun goddess Amaterasu. F=Kurozumi Munetada (1780-1850). |
| Makoto no Michikyo | sTS | 2-e | | 10,500 | 1 | japa | B | 3 | In Sect Shinto organization. HQ Ehime-ken. |
| Maruyamakyo | sTS | 2-e | | 13,500 | 1 | japa | B | 0 | HQ Kanagawa-ken. |
| Meiji Kyodan | sTS | 2-e | | 5,400 | 1 | japa | B | 1 | HQ Osaka-shi. |
| Meijikyo | sTS | 2-d | | 167,000 | 1 | japa | B | 1 | HQ Nagasaki-ken. |
| Meiseikyo | sTS | 2-e | | 94,700 | 1 | japa | B | 1 | HQ Higashi Osaka-shi. |
| Minetaka Inari Taishakyo | sTS | 2-e | | 4,100 | 1 | japa | B | 0 | HQ Gifu-shi. |
| Misenkyo | sTS | 2-e | | 3,600 | 1 | japa | B | 1 | HQ Yamaguchi-ken. |
| Misogikyo | sTS | 2-d | 1875 | 119,000 | 1 | japa | B | 2 | A purification sect in Kyoha Shinto. HQ Taito-ku, Tokyo. |
| Mitake-kyo | sTS | 2-c | | 1,648,000 | 2 | japa | B | 2 | Mountain-worship. Shinto sect focused on Mount Ontake, a major religious center. |
| Mitamakyo | sTS | 2-e | | 55,000 | 1 | japa | B | 2 | Mountain worship. HQ Chiba-ken. |
| Mizuhokyo | sTS | 2-e | | 60,000 | 1 | japa | B | 1 | HQ Aomori-ken. |
| Naobikyo | sTS | 2-e | | 2,000 | 1 | japa | B | 1 | Mountain worship. HQ Hyogo-ken. |
| Ohi no Motokyo | sTS | 2-e | | 10,700 | 1 | japa | B | 1 | HQ Shinjuku-ku, Tokyo. |
| Omisorakyo | sTS | 2-e | | 10,500 | 1 | japa | B | 1 | HQ Shinagawa-ku, Tokyo. |
| Omiwako | sTS | 2-e | | 12,300 | 1 | japa | B | 0 | HQ Nara-ken. |
| Omiwakyo | sTS | 10-f | | 700 | 1 | japa | B | 0 | HQ Nara-ken. |
| Ontakekyo | sTS | 2-d | 1882 | 654,000 | 1 | japa | B | 2 | Japanese mountain worship sect (Mount Ontake). God=3 great Kamis. HQ Nara-ken. |
| Ontakekyo Shuseiha | sTS | 2-e | | 7,400 | 1 | japa | B | 2 | Mountain worship sect. HQ Niigata-ken. |
| Ontakesan Soma Honkyo | sTS | 2-e | | 9,000 | 1 | japa | B | 1 | Mountain worship. HQ Aichi-ken. |
| Ontakesan Taikyo | sTS | 2-e | | 87,500 | 1 | japa | B | 2 | Mountain worship. HQ Shinjuku-ku, Tokyo. |
| Original Way of Heavenly Truth | sTS | 2-d | 1925 | 277,000 | 1 | japa | B | 1 | Honmichi. State persecution 1926-1939. God=10 Kamis. |
| Religion of Golden Light | sTS | 2-d | 1859 | 683,000 | 2 | japa | B | 2 | Konko-kyo. F=Kawate Bunjiro (1814-1883). Shinto faith-healing. Nationwide. |
| Seiseikyo | sTS | 2-e | | 15,400 | 1 | japa | B | 1 | HQ Aichi-ken. |
| Seishoin Kyodan | sTS | 2-e | | 10,000 | 1 | japa | B | 1 | HQ Kita-ku, Tokyo. |
| Sekai Shindokyo | sTS | 2-e | | 81,800 | 1 | japa | B | 1 | HQ Aichi-ken. |
| Senshinkyo | sTS | 2-e | | 28,500 | 1 | japa | B | 0 | HQ Hyogo-ken. Ex Shinrikyo. |
| Shinrikyo | sTS | 2-d | 1894 | 588,000 | 2 | japa | B | 3 | Revivalist Shinto group in Kyoha Shinto. Ex Ontakekyo. God=3 deities, Amaterasu. |
| Shinsenkyo | sTS | 2-e | | 12,500 | 1 | japa | B | 3 | Mountain worship. HQ Osaka-fu. |
| Shinshukyo | sTS | 2-d | 1880 | 531,000 | 1 | japa | B | 3 | Japanese purification movement in Kyoha Shinto. God=Honchi Taishin, Amaterasu. |
| Shinsokyo | sTS | 2-e | | 2,200 | 1 | japa | B | 0 | HQ Aichi-ken. |
| Shinto Kanshinkyo | sTS | 2-e | | 35,400 | 1 | japa | B | 0 | HQ Higashi Psaka-shi. |
| Shinto Kokuseikyo | sTS | 2-e | | 6,300 | 1 | japa | B | 2 | Mountain worship sect. HQ Nakaro-ku, Tokyo. |
| Shinto Kotohirakyo | sTS | 2-e | | 37,300 | 1 | japa | B | 1 | HQ Chibu-ken. |
| Shinto Shindokyo | sTS | 2-e | | 4,600 | 1 | japa | B | 1 | HQ Kyogo-ken. |
| Shinto Shinshinkyo | sTS | 2-e | | 21,800 | 1 | japa | B | 0 | HQ Hyogo-ken. |
| Shinto Shuseiha | sTS | 2-e | 1873 | 51,200 | 1 | japa | B | 3 | A Confucian-oriented Japanese movement in Kyoha Shinto. God=Amaterosu. |
| Shinto Taikyo | sTS | 2-e | 1886 | 68,800 | 1 | japa | B | 3 | A Japanese revivalist Shinto group in Kyoha Shinto. No founder. HQ Minato-ku, Tokyo. |
| Shinto Taiseikyo | sTS | 2-d | 1868 | 179,000 | 1 | japa | B | 3 | Confucian-oriented movement in Kyoha Shinto. F=Hirayama Shosai. |
| Shinto Tenkokyo | sTS | 2-e | | 6,100 | 1 | japa | B | 1 | HQ Yamaguchi-ken. |
| Shintoku Kyodan | sTS | 2-e | | 20,100 | 1 | japa | B | 2 | Mountain worship. HQ Setagaya-ku, Tokyo. |
| Shisei Mahashirakyo | sTS | 2-e | | 5,800 | 1 | japa | B | 0 | HQ Saitama-ken. |
| Shizensha | sTS | 2-e | | 19,600 | 1 | japa | B | 1 | HQ Osaka-shi. |
| Shugendokyo | sTS | 2-e | | 9,200 | 1 | japa | B | 2 | HQ Tokyo. |
| Shukyo Hojin Shinto | sTS | 2-e | | 10,000 | 1 | japa | B | 0 | HQ Otaru-shi, Hokkaido. |
| Tai (Shinto Honkyoku) | sTS | 2-c | | 1,091,000 | 2 | japa | B | 1 | Shintokyo. |
| Taidokyo | sTS | 2-e | | 6,800 | 1 | japa | B | 2 | HQ Suginami-ku, Tokyo. |
| Tenchikyo | sTS | 2-e | | 10,000 | 1 | japa | B | 1 | HQ Kyoto-shi. |
| Tengenkyo | sTS | 2-e | | 10,900 | 1 | japa | B | 2 | HQ Shinagawa-ku, Tokyo. |
| Tenjokyo | sTS | 2-e | | 23,900 | 1 | japa | B | 2 | Mountain worship. HQ Hyogo-ken. |
| Tenshokyo | sTS | 2-e | | 8,900 | 1 | japa | B | 1 | HQ Kamigyo-ku, Kyoto-shi. |
| Tenshukyo | sTS | 2-e | | 7,900 | 1 | japa | B | 1 | HQ Saitama-ken. |
| Tenzenkyo | sTS | 2-e | | 10,100 | 1 | japa | B | 0 | HQ Shimane-ken. |
| Tokumitsukyo | sTS | 2-e | 1912 | 22,900 | 1 | japa | B | 3 | 1935 members 600,000 but crushed by state, reforming 1946 as movement PL Kyodan. |
| Tokushinkyo | sTS | 10-f | | 630 | 1 | japa | B | 2 | Mountain worship sect. HQ Osaka-shi. |
| Yamatokai | sTS | 2-e | | 4,800 | 1 | japa | B | 1 | HQ Toda-shi, Saitama-ken. |
| **Ethnoreligionists** | T | 1-a | | 228,367,000 | 142 | nige | B | 2 | 5,000 tribalist religions; local religions open only to members of tribe or ethnopeople. |
| Animists | AT | 3-a | | 216,161,000 | 142 | beni | B | 3 | Belief in spiritual beings, mountains, rocks, trees, rivers. |
| Amon ethnoreligionists | sBAT | 3-d | | 123,000 | 1 | nige | A | 1 | Plateau State, Bassa LGA; Kaduna State, Saminaka LGA. Animists 60%, Muslims 20%. |
| Arakanese ethnoreligionists | sBAT | 3-d | | 336,000 | 3 | myan | A | 1 | Also in India, Bangladesh. Theravada Buddhists 80%, animists 17%, Muslims 2%. D=3. M=1. |
| Central Khmer ethnoreligionists | sBAT | 3-d | | 287,000 | 2 | camb | A | 1 | Theravada Buddhists 94%(1970: 2,826 monasteries, 68,145 monks), animists 3%. D=3. M=7. |
| Chaungtha ethnoreligionists | sBAT | 3-d | | 154,000 | 1 | myan | A | 0 | People of the Valley. Related to Lolo, Burmese. Buddhists/animists 99%. |
| Lao ethnoreligionists | sBAT | 3-d | | 407,000 | 6 | laos | B | 2 | Monolinguals 100%. Theravada Buddhists 80%(1,900 pagodas), animists 10%. Y=1630. D=2. |
| Ongbe ethnoreligionists | sBAT | 3-d | | 324,000 | 1 | chin | A | 1 | North coast of Hainan. Most are Han Chinese or Zhuang. Bilinguals. Buddhists/polytheists 99%. |
| Yunnanese Shan ethnoreligionists | sBAT | 3-d | | 217,000 | 1 | chin | A | 1 | God=Pra Pinsau. Chinese Tai. Yunnan, Sichuan; Thailand. Buddhists 80%(Hinayana). D=2. |
| She ethnoreligionists | sDAT | 3-d | | 491,000 | 1 | chin | A | 1 | Fujian. 1,000 speak She; rest Hakka. Animists 70%, Taoists 19%, Buddhists 10%. D=RCC. |
| Hinduized animists | HAT | 3-b | | 20,000,000 | 1 | indi | B | 2 | Animists heavily penetrated by dominant Hindu beliefs and culture. |
| Balinese ethnoreligionists | sHAT | 3-d | | 166,000 | 1 | indo | A | 1 | Shaivite Hindus 80% (15,000 village temples, also ISKCON), syncretists 15%. D=3. M=9. |
| Bodo ethnoreligionists | sHAT | 3-d | | 740,000 | 2 | indi | B | 3 | God=Ishôra. Hinduized animists 93%. D=Goalpara Boro Baptist Ch,NBB,RCC,CNI,ICI. M=7. |
| Gormati ethnoreligionists | sHAT | 3-c | | 2,161,000 | 1 | indi | B | 2 | God=Devadu. AP,MP,HP,TN, 5 other States. Hindus/polytheists 99%. D=20. M=30. |
| Kalikulas | sHAT | 3-d | c1600 | 500,000 | 1 | indi | B | 1 | Hindu, Shaktas worshiping terror goddess Kali. |
| Kishanganjia ethnoreligionists | sHAT | 3-d | | 101,000 | 1 | indi | A | 0 | In Bihar State, a Bengali-Assamese language. Hinduized animists 99%. |
| Kotia ethnoreligionists | sHAT | 3-d | | 253,000 | 1 | indi | A | 1 | Andhra Pradesh, Araku Valley. Lingua franca. Animists/Hindus 99%. D=3. M=6. |
| Maitili ethnoreligionists | sHAT | 3-c | | 1,575,000 | 1 | indi | A | 2 | Tirahutia. In Bihar, MP, WB; Nepal. Educated high-caste Hindus 95%. D=RCC,CNI. M=10. |
| Riang ethnoreligionists | sHAT | 3-d | | 133,000 | 3 | indi | A | 0 | God=Isawr. In Assam, central Tripura. Close to Tripuri. Hinduized animists 90%, Muslims 4%. |
| Saora ethnoreligionists | sHAT | 3-d | | 227,000 | 1 | indi | B | 3 | God=Gaddel. Ganjam District, Orissa, AP, MP. Hindus/animists 75%. D=2. M=5. |
| Sauras | sHAT | 3-c | c1250 | 1,000,000 | 1 | indi | B | 1 | Hindu worshipers of Sun God, Surya. Temples now neglected except Temple of Sun, Konarak. |
| Tripuri ethnoreligionists | sHAT | 3-d | | 673,000 | 2 | indi | A | 1 | Assam, eastern Tripura. Many in Bangladesh. Hinduized animists 92%, Muslims 6.5%. D=4. |
| Usipi ethnoreligionists | sHAT | 3-d | | 110,000 | 2 | indi | A | 0 | In Tripura; Bangladesh. Close to Riang, Tripuri. Hinduized animists 90%, Muslims 6%. D=1. |
| Islamized animists | IAT | 3-c | | 3,000,000 | 8 | indo | B | 3 | Animists heavily penetrated by dominant Muslim beliefs and culture. |
| Aliran Kebatinan | sIAT | 3-e | | 10,000 | 1 | indo | B | 3 | Mystical sects across Indonesian: Sufi elements. |
| Indonesian ethnoreligionists | sIAT | 3-d | | 194,000 | 1 | indo | B | 3 | Mother-tongue speakers of national language, Muslims 75% (Shafi). D=1. M=6. |
| Javanese ethnoreligionists | sIAT | 3-c | | 2,000,000 | 2 | indo | B | 3 | Animists in Java with some Islamic elements but still strong animists. |
| Sundanese ethnoreligionists | sIAT | 3-d | | 225,000 | 1 | indo | B | 2 | God=Allah. Muslims 50%(strict Shafi, mosque attenders 55%), New-Religionists 48%. D=7. |
| Primal religionists | LAT | 3-b | | 15,000,000 | 20 | chin | B | 3 | Original ethnoreligionists with little or no acculturation or syncretism. |
| African ethnoreligionists | sLAT | 3-b | | 96,805,000 | 70 | nige | B | 3 | African Traditional Religion (ATR). |
| Colanaikans | sLAT | 10-f | | 500 | 1 | indi | B | 2 | Only remaining cave-dwelling tribe in India. In Kerala. |
| Polytheistic animists | PAT | 3-c | | 4,000,000 | 20 | chin | B | 3 | Animists who have a large pantheon of deities, gods, goddesses. |
| Adi ethnoreligionists | sPAT | 3-d | | 478,000 | 1 | indi | A | 2 | God=Ishor. Northern hills, Assam. Also in Tibet, China. Animists/polytheists 98%. D=3. M=4. |
| Ahir ethnoreligionists | sPAT | 3-d | | 647,000 | 1 | indi | A | 0 | Bhils. In Maharashtra and Gujarat States. Animists/polytheists 79%, Hindus 20%. |
| Amerindian ethnoreligionists | sPAT | 3-d | | 300,000 | 1 | braz | C | 4 | Traditional animism, fetishism. |
| Bai ethnoreligionists | sPAT | 3-c | | 1,158,000 | 2 | chin | A | 1 | Yunnan, Sichuan, Guizhou. Polytheists 65%, Buddhists 30%. D=TSPM,RCC. M=7. |
| Biyo ethnoreligionists | sPAT | 3-d | | 109,000 | 1 | chin | A | 0 | Yunnan Province, near the Hani. Polytheists 98%, a few Buddhists. |
| Central Gond ethnoreligionists | sPAT | 3-c | | 1,721,000 | 1 | indi | B | 2 | God=Parameshwar. Mainly in MP. Hindus 70%, animists 30%. D=Methodists,MPELC. M=12. |
| Central Yi ethnoreligionists | sPAT | 3-d | | 495,000 | 1 | chin | A | 1 | A separate language in Yi official nationality. Polytheists/animists 98%. D=TSPM, RCC. |
| Dangs Bhil ethnoreligionists | sPAT | 3-d | | 130,000 | 1 | indi | A | 2 | Gujarat State, Dangs District. Lingua franca. Animists/polytheists 90%. D=CNI. M=2. |
| Dhodia ethnoreligionists | sPAT | 3-d | | 128,000 | 1 | indi | A | 1 | Maharashtra, Gujarat, MP, Karnataka, Rajasthan. Bhils. Animists/polytheists 95%. M=ZBM. |
| Eastern Bhil ethnoreligionists | sPAT | 3-c | | 2,676,000 | 1 | indi | A | 1 | Polytheists 95%. D=CMA,CNI,RCC. M=IEM,CGMM,BFI,UPM,YWAM. |
| Eastern Meo ethnoreligionists | sPAT | 3-c | | 1,473,000 | 1 | chin | B | 2 | Northeast Yunnan, Guizhou, Guangxi; Thailand, Viet Nam. Polytheists 94%. D=Chinese Ch. |
| Eastern Yi ethnoreligionists | sPAT | 3-d | | 861,000 | 1 | chin | A | 1 | Southeastern Yi. Guizhou, Weining Autonomous Region. Polytheists 98%. D=TSPM,RCC. |
| Gamti ethnoreligionists | sPAT | 3-d | | 239,000 | 1 | indi | A | 1 | Gujarat State, Broach, Surat. Well-educated Bhils. Animists/polytheists 98%. D=4. M=2. |
| Hani ethnoreligionists | sPAT | 3-c | | 1,495,000 | 4 | chin | A | 1 | Yunnan, Viet Nam, Laos, Burma. Polytheists (animists, ancestor veneration) 95%. D=TSPM. |
| Highland Nung ethnoreligionists | sPAT | 3-d | | 958,000 | 3 | viet | A | 1 | Lang Son, Bac Giang.Also in China, Laos. Polytheists 98%(ancestor worship). |

*Continued overleaf*

*Table 17–6 continued*

| Name of religion/religionists 1 | Pedigree 2 | Type 3 | Begun 4 | Adherents 5 | Ext 6 | Coun 7 | W 8 | X 9 | E. g. = examples; name for God, other religions present, D=denominations, M=missions. 10 |
|---|---|---|---|---|---|---|---|---|---|
| Li ethnoreligionists | sPAT | 3-c | | 1,235,000 | 1 | chin | A | 1 | Tropical mountains in Hainan. Polytheists (animists) 100%. D=TSPM. M=5. |
| Maru ethnoreligionists | sPAT | 3-d | | 112,000 | 1 | myan | A | 0 | Kachin State, north Burma. Also in China. Related to Kachin. Polytheists/animists 90%. M=2. |
| Mesoamerican ethnoreligionists | sPAT | 3-e | | 90,000 | 5 | mexi | C | 4 | Remnants of pre-Columbian polytheist animistic religions throughout Central America. |
| New Caledonia ethnoreligionistists | sPAT | 10-f | | 270 | 1 | newc | C | 5 | Remnants of once strong animistic culture. |
| Northern Meo ethnoreligionists | sPAT | 3-d | | 828,000 | 1 | chin | A | 1 | West Hunan. Agriculturalists. Polytheists 96%. D=Chinese CR, RCC, TSPM. M=3. |
| Northern Tung ethnoreligionists | sPAT | 3-c | | 2,240,000 | 1 | chin | A | 1 | Guizhou. Polytheists(animists) 80%, Buddhists 20%. D=RCC,TSPM. M=IMB, SIL, TELL, FEBC. |
| Northern Yi ethnoreligionists | sPAT | 3-c | | 1,582,000 | 1 | chin | A | 1 | Northern Nosu. Yunnan, Laos, Viet Nam. Polytheists(animists) 90%, Buddhists 5%. D=2. M=22. |
| Northern Zhuang ethnoreligionists | sPAT | 3-b | | 10,237,000 | 1 | chin | A | 2 | Polytheists 80%, Buddhists 19%. D=TSPM(300 churches),RCC,TJC. M=25. |
| Okinawan ethnoreligionists | sPAT | 3-e | | 6,000 | 1 | japa | B | 3 | Varieties of animism, shamanism, polytheism on Okinawa. |
| Punu ethnoreligionists | sPAT | 3-d | | 555,000 | 3 | chin | A | 1 | Guangxi. Polytheists (animists) 99%, including ancestor worship. |
| Puyi ethnoreligionists | sPAT | 3-c | | 2,269,000 | 2 | chin | A | 2 | Guizhou, Yunnan. 40 dialects. Polytheists 80%, Buddhists 10%, Taoists 8%. D=1. M=12. |
| Saharia ethnoreligionists | sPAT | 3-d | | 225,000 | 1 | indi | A | 0 | Tribals in Madhya Pradesh (Shivpuri, Morena, Guna Districts), and Rajasthan. Polytheists 99%. |
| Shui ethnoreligionists | sPAT | 3-d | | 383,000 | 1 | chin | A | 1 | Guizhou, Guangxi. Official nationality. Agriculturalists. Polytheists/animists 99%. Y=c1880. D=5. |
| Southeast Asian ethnoreligionists | sPAT | 3-c | | 2,000,000 | 15 | thai | B | 2 | Montagnards and other peoples of animistic/polytheistic faith and culture. |
| Southern Bhil ethnoreligionists | sPAT | 3-c | | 1,260,000 | 1 | indi | A | 2 | Polytheists 95%. D=CMA,MCSA,CNI,RCC,AoG. M=IEM,COUNT,CGMM,BFI,UPM,WVI. |
| Southern Yi ethnoreligionists | sPAT | 3-d | | 835,000 | 1 | chin | A | 1 | Eastern Yi, Southern Yi. Black Yi. Yunnan, Guizhou, Sichuan. Polytheists 95%. D=RCC,TSPM. |
| Southern Zhuang ethnoreligionists | sPAT | 3-c | | 4,009,000 | 1 | chin | A | 1 | Southwest Guangxi. Polytheists 90%, some Buddhists. D=TSPM,RCC. M=CSI,YWAM,SIL. |
| Tho ethnoreligionists | sPAT | 3-c | | 2,246,000 | 5 | viet | A | 1 | God=Duc Chua Ph. Tung Nghia. Also in China, Laos, USA, France. Polytheists 99%. D=2. M=2. |
| Tujia ethnoreligionists | sPAT | 3-c | | 6,327,000 | 1 | chin | A | 1 | Northwest Hunan. Unwritten language. Polytheists/animists 99%. D=TSPM,RCC. R=TWR. |
| Vanuatu ethnoreligionists | sPAT | 3-e | | 6,600 | 1 | vanu | C | 5 | Popularly known as Custom. Melanesian traditional religion, mainly on Tanna and Aniwa. |
| Vasava ethnoreligionists | sPAT | 3-d | | 392,000 | 1 | indi | A | 1 | Gujarat State, Maharashtra. Bhil subgroup. Animists/polytheists 99%. M=4. |
| Wagdi ethnoreligionists | sPAT | 3-c | | 1,692,000 | 1 | indi | A | 0 | Udaipur, Rajasthan, Gujarat. Bhils. Second language Hindi. Animists/polytheists 99%. |
| Waxianghua ethnoreligionists | sPAT | 3-d | | 300,000 | 1 | chin | A | 1 | Related to Miao. Western Hunan province. Wuling mountains. Polytheists (animistic) 95%. |
| World Renewal religionists | sPAT | 3-e | c1600 | 50,000 | 1 | usa | C | 5 | Among California Amerindians; one of several major cults. |
| Yao ethnoreligionists | sPAT | 3-c | | 2,415,000 | 6 | chin | A | 1 | 53% speak Yao. Polytheists/animists(ancestor-worship) 99%. D=RCC,TSPM,TJC. M=10. |
| Adja ethnoreligionists | sAT | 3-d | | 283,000 | 2 | beni | B | 3 | Mono and Atlantique Provinces. Animists 60%, Muslims 20%. D=7. M=3. |
| Affliction cultists | sAT | 3-d | | 400,000 | 20 | zamb | C | 4 | Cults, ritual drumming, in face of affliction, disease. Found among animists across world. |
| Aizo ethnoreligionists | sAT | 3-d | | 168,000 | 1 | beni | B | 3 | Mono and Atlantique Provinces. Animists 80%. D=RCC. M=SIM,FMB. |
| Akha ethnoreligionists | sAT | 3-d | | 213,000 | 5 | myan | B | 2 | God=Miyeh. Kengtung Shan State. Animists 50%, Theravada Buddhists 35%. D=4. M=3. |
| Ana ethnoreligionists | sAT | 3-d | | 103,000 | 3 | beni | B | 4 | Zou Province. Half in Togo. Animists 70%. D=Yoruba churches from Nigeria. |
| Antaimoro ethnoreligionists | sAT | 3-d | | 281,000 | 1 | mada | B | 4 | Superficially islamized. Animists 50%, Muslims 2%, Baha'is 0.2%(increasing fast). D=1. M=2. |
| Antaisaka ethnoreligionists | sAT | 3-d | | 679,000 | 1 | mada | B | 3 | Southeast coastal strip. Animists 72%, Baha'is 0.1%. D=RCC(D-Farafangana). M=CM. |
| Antandroy ethnoreligionists | sAT | 3-d | | 563,000 | 1 | mada | B | 3 | Extreme south coast of island and inland. Animists 80%. D=RCC(D-Fort-Dauphin). M=CM. |
| Antanosy ethnoreligionists | sAT | 3-d | | 176,000 | 1 | mada | B | 5 | Superficially islamized. Animists 45%, Muslims 2%. D=RCC(D-Fort-Dauphin). M=CM. |
| Anyi ethnoreligionists | sAT | 3-d | | 371,000 | 2 | ivor | B | 5 | God=Nyamiapbili. Many in Ghana. Animists 45%, Muslims 1%. D=6. M=6. |
| Ari ethnoreligionists | sAT | 3-d | | 106,000 | 2 | ethi | B | 2 | Gamo Gofa Province. Bilinguals in Amharic and Gofa(Wolayta). Animists 80%. 90 churches. |
| Arusa Maasai ethnoreligionists | sAT | 3-d | | 174,000 | 1 | tanz | B | 3 | Near Arusha town. Related to Maasai, but agriculturalists. Animists 70%. D=5. M=7. |
| Arusi Galla ethnoreligionists | sAT | 3-d | | 218,000 | 1 | ethi | B | 2 | God=Wagayon. South. Pastoralists. Muslims 85%(Shafi Sunnis), animists 12%. D=6. M=4. |
| Ashanti ethnoreligionists | sAT | 3-d | | 227,000 | 3 | ghan | B | 5 | God=Onyankopon. Muslims 28% (massive Ahmadi conversions), animists 6%. D=26. M=10. |
| Australian Aboriginal religionists | sAT | 3-e | | 50,000 | 1 | aust | C | 5 | Aboriginal population, including those of mixed race, who still claim to follow own religion. |
| Bagri ethnoreligionists | sAT | 3-c | | 1,865,000 | 1 | indi | A | 0 | In Punjab, Rajasthan, Pakistan. Nomads across India-Pakistan borders. Animists 99%. |
| Bahnar ethnoreligionists | sAT | 3-d | | 116,000 | 1 | viet | B | 3 | God=Bok Kei-Dei. Montagnards. Gia Lai-Cong Tum Province. Also in USA. Animists 79%. D=3. |
| Balanta ethnoreligionists | sAT | 3-d | | 347,000 | 4 | gunb | A | 2 | Animists 81%(strong ancestor cult), Muslims 11%. D=4. M=6. |
| Bambara ethnoreligionists | sAT | 3-d | | 669,000 | 10 | mali | B | 3 | God=Alla. Muslims 85%(Maliki Sunnis,with Wahhabis; Tijaniyya,Qadiriyya). D=5. M=9. |
| Bara ethnoreligionists | sAT | 3-d | | 268,000 | 1 | mada | B | 4 | Large inland area in south of island. Animists 50%. D=1. M=3. |
| Barabaig ethnoreligionists | sAT | 3-d | | 189,000 | 1 | tanz | A | 1 | Close to Taturu. Semi-nomadic pastoralists. Animists 97%. D=4. M=2. |
| Bariba ethnoreligionists | sAT | 3-d | | 305,000 | 4 | beni | B | 2 | God=Gusune. Also in Nigeria, Togo. Animists 60%, Muslims 32%(growing slowly). D=5. M=4. |
| Bassa ethnoreligionists | sAT | 3-d | | 194,000 | 3 | libe | B | 5 | God=Nyambe. Grand Bassa County. Animists 32%. Vast numbers of Bassa AIC schisms. D=10. |
| Bassari ethnoreligionists | sAT | 3-d | | 206,000 | 6 | ghan | B | 2 | Also in Togo. 20 clans. Braille Scripture in progress. Animists 73%, Muslims 12%. D=4. M=2. |
| Bata ethnoreligionists | sAT | 3-d | | 118,000 | 2 | nige | A | 1 | Adamaawa State; also in Cameroon. Largely animists 70%, Muslims 20%. Y=1913. D=5. M=1. |
| Baule ethnoreligionists | sAT | 3-d | | 786,000 | 1 | ivor | B | 5 | God=Nyamie. Literates 10%. Animists 44%, Muslims 3%. D=RCC,EPEC,EPC,AoG,AICs. M=7. |
| Betsileo ethnoreligionists | sAT | 3-d | | 127,000 | 1 | mada | C | 5 | South center of island. Animists 7%, Baha'is 0.2%(increasing fast). Early Revival center. D=6. |
| Betsimisaraka ethnoreligionists | sAT | 3-c | | 1,584,000 | 2 | mada | B | 3 | Revival center. Animists 77%. D=RCC(2 Dioceses). Eglise du Reveil,FMTA,MET,AICs. M=3. |
| Bhilala ethnoreligionists | sAT | 3-d | | 644,000 | 1 | indi | A | 0 | Bhils. In Gujarat, Madhya Pradesh, Maharashtra, Karnataka, Rajasthan. Animists 99%. |
| Bimoba ethnoreligionists | sAT | 3-d | | 226,000 | 3 | togo | B | 3 | Also in Burkina Faso. Animists 80%. D=6. M=7. |
| Birifor ethnoreligionists | sAT | 3-d | | 126,000 | 2 | burk | B | 3 | Southwestern area. Many monolinguals. Animists 86%, Muslims 1%. D=3. M=6. |
| Bissa ethnoreligionists | sAT | 3-d | | 233,000 | 1 | burk | B | 2 | South central. Also in Ghana, Ivory Coast. Animists 51%, Muslims 30%. D=2. M=6. |
| Black Bobo ethnoreligionists | sAT | 3-d | | 170,000 | 2 | burk | B | 3 | Also in Mali. Animists 50%, Muslims 25%. D=2. M=3. |
| Black Karen ethnoreligionists | sAT | 3-d | | 161,000 | 2 | myan | B | 4 | God=Pa-ra-pyin-zowk. Shan State. Black dress. Buddhists 42%, animists 22%, Baha'is. D=5. |
| Black Tai ethnoreligionists | sAT | 3-d | | 711,000 | 6 | viet | A | 1 | Red and Black rivers; Thailand, 3,000 in USA, France, Laos, China. Animists 95%. D=3. M=3. |
| Bokkos ethnoreligionists | sAT | 3-d | | 123,000 | 1 | nige | B | 4 | Plateau State, Barakin Ladi and Mangu LGAs. Animists 40%, Muslim 10%. M=NBTT. |
| Bondoukou Kulango ethnoreligionists | sAT | 3-d | | 155,000 | 2 | ivor | A | 0 | Eastern Department, Bondoukou Subprefecture. In Ghana. Animists 92%, Muslims 4%. D=2. |
| Bornean ethnoreligionists | sAT | 3-c | | 1,500,000 | 1 | indo | B | 3 | Many Kalimantan tribes are still predominantly animists. |
| Bouna Kulango ethnoreligionists | sAT | 3-d | | 180,000 | 2 | ivor | A | 1 | Eastern Department, Nassian Subprefecture. In Ghana. Animists 90%, Muslims 6%. D=2. M=1. |
| Bukusu ethnoreligionists | sAT | 3-d | | 115,000 | 1 | keny | C | 5 | Bungoma District, Western Province. Animists 15%. D=7. M=6. |
| Bulsa ethnoreligionists | sAT | 3-d | | 193,000 | 2 | ghan | A | 2 | God=Nawen. Sandema District. Also in Burkina Faso. Animists 92%, Muslims 1%. D=10. M=5. |
| Bulu Fang ethnoreligionists | sAT | 3-d | | 121,000 | 1 | came | C | 5 | God=Zambe. Covers Ntem, Dja, & Lobo Divisions. Decline. Animists 20%. D=5. M=UBS. |
| Busansi ethnoreligionists | sAT | 3-d | | 146,000 | 3 | ghan | B | 2 | Bilinguals in Moore, Hausa, Kusaal, Mampruli. Literates 7%. Animists 67%, Muslims 25%. D=3. |
| Cameroonian Creole ethnoreligionists | sAT | 3-d | | 110,000 | 2 | came | C | 5 | Major lingua franca (50% of country). Animists 12%. D=4. M=UBS. |
| Central Bhil ethnoreligionists | sAT | 3-c | | 4,449,000 | 1 | indi | A | 1 | Polytheists/animists 95%. D=RCC(D-Ajmer-Jaipur),CNI(D-Jabalpur),DNC,MCSA,CMA,M=11. |
| Central Guere ethnoreligionists | sAT | 3-d | | 264,000 | 1 | ivor | B | 3 | Bilingualism in French and Jula. Literates 10%. Animists 75%, Muslims 10%. D=4. M=5. |
| Central Shona ethnoreligionists | sAT | 3-d | | 886,000 | 3 | zimb | C | 4 | God=Mwari. Main Shona dialect. Animists 33%. D=11. M=3. |
| Central West Gurage ethnoreligionists | sAT | 3-d | | 220,000 | 1 | ethi | B | 4 | Southwestern Shoa Province. Animists 27%, Muslims 30%. D=4. M=3. |
| Changa ethnoreligionists | sAT | 3-d | | 120,000 | 1 | moza | B | 4 | God=Mngari. Coastal Ndau. Animists 61%. D=AACJM,RCC,AC/CPSA,many other AICs. M=2. |
| Chewa ethnoreligionists | sAT | 3-d | | 282,000 | 4 | zimb | B | 5 | Mainly in Malawi, Zambia; also Tanzania. Animists 30%, many Baha'is. D=many AICs. M=FMB. |
| Chodhari Bhil ethnoreligionists | sAT | 3-d | | 237,000 | 1 | indi | A | 1 | Gujarat State, Maharashtra, Karnataka, Rajasthan. Animists 95%. M=3. |
| Chokwe ethnoreligionists | sAT | 3-d | | 214,000 | 3 | ango | C | 5 | God=Zambi. Traditional religionists(animists) 70%. Y=1884. D=6. M=4. |
| Chopi ethnoreligionists | sAT | 3-d | | 352,000 | 1 | moza | B | 3 | God=Nkulukumba. Southern coast. 57 dialects. Literates 10%. Animists 65%. D=7. M=8. |
| Chwabo ethnoreligionists | sAT | 3-d | | 757,000 | 1 | moza | B | 3 | Around Quelimane. Animists 76%, Muslims 7%. D=RCC,SDA. M=UBS. |
| Coastal Makhuwa ethnoreligionists | sAT | 3-d | | 271,000 | 1 | moza | B | 3 | Coast from Moma to Mozambique Island. Animists 60%, Muslims 20%. D=CPSA,RCC. |
| Dafla ethnoreligionists | sAT | 3-d | | 269,000 | 1 | indi | A | 1 | Assam, Darrang, Arunachal Pradesh. Animists 98%. D=2. M=3. |
| Dagaaba ethnoreligionists | sAT | 3-d | | 458,000 | 2 | ghan | B | 4 | Northwest corner. Also in Burkina Faso. Animists 46%, Muslims 3%. D=2. M=7. |
| Dagomba ethnoreligionists | sAT | 3-d | | 234,000 | 2 | ghan | A | 1 | God=Naawuni. Also in Togo. Literates 2%. Muslims 60%(Sunnis,Ahmadis), animists 37%. D=8. |
| Dan ethnoreligionists | sAT | 3-d | | 677,000 | 3 | ivor | B | 3 | Half in Liberia. Animists 62%, Muslims 10%(ongoing conversions to Islam). D=2. M=5. |
| Dang Tharu ethnoreligionists | sAT | 3-d | | 286,000 | 1 | nepa | A | 0 | West of Bhairawa-Butwal, north of India border. Agropastoralists. Animists 80%, Hindus 20%. |
| Deokri Tharu ethnoreligionists | sAT | 3-d | | 119,000 | 1 | nepa | A | 0 | On eastern border with India. Agriculturalists, pastoralists. Animists 95%, Hindus 5%. |
| Dogon ethnoreligionists | sAT | 3-d | | 211,000 | 3 | mali | B | 2 | God=Ama. Agriculturalists, caste system. Animists 48%, Muslims 30%. Secret societies strong. |
| Duruma ethnoreligionists | sAT | 3-d | | 109,000 | 1 | keny | B | 4 | God=Mulungu. W Kwale District. Literates in Swahili 13%. Animists 40%, Muslims 25%. D=3. |
| East Gbari ethnoreligionists | sAT | 3-d | | 139,000 | 1 | nige | C | 5 | God=Shekwohi. States: Niger,Plateau,Kaduna,Kwara. Animists 20%, Muslims 5%. D=4.M=10. |
| Eastern Bete ethnoreligionists | sAT | 3-d | | 115,000 | 1 | ivor | B | 3 | Subprefecture of Gagnoa. Animists 60%. D=RCC,AICs. M=FMB. |
| Eastern Bru ethnoreligionists | sAT | 3-d | | 114,000 | 2 | laos | A | 1 | Savannehkhet Province. Also Thailand, USA. Montagnards. Animists 99%. D=1. M=2. |
| Eastern Kusasi ethnoreligionists | sAT | 3-d | | 434,000 | 1 | ghan | B | 2 | Northeast corner, Bawku District. Literates 2%. Animists 75%, Muslims 5%. D=6. M=6. |
| Eastern Magar ethnoreligionists | sAT | 3-d | | 292,000 | 2 | nepa | A | 1 | Also in Sikkim, Bhutan, India. Some bilinguals in Nepali. Animists 90%, Hindus 10%. D=1. M=2. |
| Eastern Nuer ethnoreligionists | sAT | 3-d | | 856,000 | 2 | suda | B | 3 | Nomadic animists 79%, highly resistant to Islam. D=5. M=2. |
| Eastern Tamang ethnoreligionists | sAT | 3-d | | 168,000 | 2 | nepa | B | 2 | Animists 38%, Hindus 27%, Buddhists 23%. 1974, widespread revival. D=NCF. M=3. |
| Edo ethnoreligionists | sAT | 3-d | | 219,000 | 1 | nige | C | 5 | God=Osanobua. Bendel State. Nominal Christians 30%. Animists 20%. M=4. |
| Embu ethnoreligionists | sAT | 3-d | | 118,000 | 1 | keny | C | 5 | Embu District. Bilingual in Kikuyu, and some in Swahili. Animists 25%. D=7, many AICs. M=4. |
| Ewe ethnoreligionists | sAT | 3-d | | 471,000 | 7 | ghan | C | 5 | God=Mawu. Also in Togo. Animists 15%. D=many AICs. M=Bremen Mission(1847-1914),SVD. |
| Ewondo ethnoreligionists | sAT | 3-d | | 220,000 | 1 | came | C | 5 | Centre Province, South Province. Lingua franca. Animists 18%. D=2. M=9. |
| Fon ethnoreligionists | sAT | 3-c | | 1,015,000 | 5 | beni | B | 5 | Animists 62%(260 fetish monasteries), Muslims 5%. D=RCC(D-Abomey),EPMB,AoG. M=20. |
| Gamo ethnoreligionists | sAT | 3-d | | 448,000 | 1 | ethi | A | 1 | Gemu-Gofa Province. Near Lake Abaya. Animists 80%. D=WLEC. M=SIM. |
| Garo ethnoreligionists | sAT | 3-d | | 455,000 | 3 | indi | B | 5 | West Assam, Garo Hills, West Bengal, Tripura. Animists 62%. D=3. M=2. |
| Gideo ethnoreligionists | sAT | 3-d | | 570,000 | 1 | ethi | B | 3 | Animists 69%, Muslims 1%. D=ECMY,WLEC,FGBC,Light of Life Ch,AIC. M=10. |
| Gio ethnoreligionists | sAT | 3-d | | 116,000 | 1 | libe | A | 1 | Dialect of Dan. Animists 90%, Muslims 5%. Ongoing conversions to Islam. D=6. M=3. |
| Giriama ethnoreligionists | sAT | 3-d | | 214,000 | 1 | keny | B | 4 | God=Mulungu. Mijikenda. Bilingual in Swahili. Animists 45%, Muslims 8.5%(Shafi Sunnis). D=6. |
| Gisamjang ethnoreligionists | sAT | 3-d | | 107,000 | 1 | tanz | A | 1 | Semi-nomadic. Pastoralists. Close to Barabaig; dialect of Taturu. Animists 97%. D=2. M=LCA. |

*Continued opposite*

*Table 17–6 continued*

| *Name of religion/religionists* 1 | *Pedigree* 2 | *Type* 3 | *Begun* 4 | *Adherents* 5 | *Ext* 6 | *Coun* 7 | *W* 8 | *X* 9 | *E. g. = examples; name for God, other religions present, D=denominations, M=missions.* 10 |
|---|---|---|---|---|---|---|---|---|---|
| Goemai ethnoreligionists | sAT | 3-d | | 248,000 | 1 | nige | A | 1 | Plateau State. Lingua franca: Hausa. Animists 89%, Muslims 11%. Mainly RCs. D=4. M=3. |
| Gofa ethnoreligionists | sAT | 3-d | | 130,000 | 1 | ethi | B | 3 | God=Tsosa. Dialect of Wolaytta. Southwest Lake Abaya area. Animists 70%. D=WLEC. M=SIM. |
| Guajiro ethnoreligionists | sAT | 3-d | | 208,000 | 2 | colo | B | 3 | Many in Venezuela. Pastoralists. Animists 70%. Mass conversions to Baha'i World Faith. D=4. |
| Gumuz ethnoreligionists | sAT | 3-d | | 101,000 | 2 | ethi | A | 1 | Half in Sudan. Animists 86%, Muslims 4%. D=3. M=1. |
| Gun ethnoreligionists | sAT | 3-d | | 126,000 | 3 | beni | B | 5 | God=Jiwheyewhe. Animists 50%, Muslims 10%(Sunnis and Ahmadis, spreading rapidly). D=9. |
| Gurenne ethnoreligionists | sAT | 3-d | | 593,000 | 2 | ghan | B | 2 | Animists 83%, Muslims 5%. M=SIL,SIM,WF,WEC. |
| Gurma ethnoreligionists | sAT | 3-d | | 315,000 | 5 | burk | B | 2 | Also in Benin, Niger, Togo. Animists 53%, Muslims 40%. D=2. M=6. |
| Guro ethnoreligionists | sAT | 3-d | | 277,000 | 1 | ivor | B | 3 | God=Ball. West Central Department. Literates 25%. Animists 75%, Muslims 6%. D=3. M=4. |
| Gurunsi ethnoreligionists | sAT | 3-d | | 134,000 | 1 | ghan | B | 2 | Part of Gurenne people. Animists 81%, Muslims 1%. D=5. M=3. |
| Hadiyya ethnoreligionists | sAT | 3-d | | 275,000 | 1 | ethi | B | 3 | Southern Shoa Province. Animists 20%, Muslims 50% and growing. D=3. M=2. |
| Himalayan ethnoreligionists | sAT | 3-c | | 5,000,000 | 5 | nepa | A | 0 | Many scattered peoples, with animistic religions (2,200,000 in Nepal). |
| Ho ethnoreligionists | sAT | 3-d | | 783,000 | 2 | indi | A | 2 | God=Ishwar. Bihar; Orissa, WB. Also in Bangladesh. Animists 69%, Hindus 30%. D=2. M=7. |
| Hre ethnoreligionists | sAT | 3-d | | 107,000 | 1 | viet | B | 2 | Montagnards. Gia Lai-Cong Tum Province. Closest to Sedang. Animists 74%. M=WEC. |
| Hurutshe Tswana ethnoreligionists | sAT | 3-d | | 125,000 | 2 | soua | B | 5 | Also in Botswana. Animists 20%, Muslims, Baha'is. Nominal Christians 40%. D=10. M=2. |
| Hutu ethnoreligionists | sAT | 3-d | | 846,000 | 5 | rwan | C | 5 | God=Imana. Small-stature Ruandese. Animists 8%, Muslims 8%(Shafi Sunnis). D=7. M=7. |
| Igala ethnoreligionists | sAT | 3-d | | 280,000 | 1 | nige | B | 5 | God=Ojo. States: Benue, Bendel, Anambra. Animists 32%, Muslims 10%. D=10. M=10. |
| Igbirra ethnoreligionists | sAT | 3-d | | 311,000 | 1 | nige | B | 3 | God=Hinegbau. Kwara State. Literates 25%. Muslims 50%, animists 26%. D=6. M=9. |
| Igbo ethnoreligionists | sAT | 3-d | | 168,000 | 6 | nige | C | 5 | God=Chineke. In 4 States. Animists 1%. Nominal Christians 33%. M=OP,WF,CSSp,LCMS. |
| Ikwere ethnoreligionists | sAT | 3-d | | 211,000 | 1 | nige | B | 3 | Rivers State, 3 LGAs. Animists 60%. D=2. M=3. |
| Inibaloi ethnoreligionists | sAT | 3-d | | 144,000 | 1 | phil | A | 1 | Benguet Province, western Nueva Vizcaya Province, Luzon. Animists 92%. D=RCC. M=4. |
| Iramba ethnoreligionists | sAT | 3-d | | 181,000 | 1 | tanz | B | 3 | God=Nzua. Ilamba. Near Singida. Animists 30%, Muslims 35%(Shafi Sunnis). D=2. M=TAC. |
| Iraqw ethnoreligionists | sAT | 3-d | | 333,000 | 1 | tanz | B | 3 | God=Mungu. Mbulu District, south of Lake Eyasi. Animists 72%, Muslims 1%. D=4. M=4. |
| Ittu ethnoreligionists | sAT | 3-d | | 163,000 | 1 | ethi | B | 3 | God=Waqake. Eastern Oromo, Harar. Muslims 70%(Shafi Sunnis), animists 5%. D=3. M=2. |
| Ivorian Malinke ethnoreligionists | sAT | 3-d | | 413,000 | 1 | ivor | B | 2 | God=Alla. Traders. Many speak Jula, Bambara. Muslims 67%(Maliki), animists 31%. D=3. M=2. |
| Jita ethnoreligionists | sAT | 3-d | | 149,000 | 1 | tanz | B | 5 | God=Nyamuanga. Southeastern shore of Lake Victoria. Animists 50%. D=4. M=3. |
| Kabre ethnoreligionists | sAT | 3-d | | 461,000 | 3 | togo | B | 3 | God=Eso. Also in Benin, Ghana. Animists 65%, Muslims 10%. D=5. M=8. |
| Kalanga ethnoreligionists | sAT | 3-d | | 150,000 | 2 | bots | B | 5 | God=Ndzimu. Northeast border with Zimbabwe. ResistsTswana culture. Animists 40%. M=6. |
| Kamba ethnoreligionists | sAT | 3-d | | 177,000 | 4 | keny | C | 5 | God=Ngai. Eastern Province. Animists 5%, Muslims 2%, Baha'is 1%, some Hindus. D=6. M=7. |
| Kambata ethnoreligionists | sAT | 3-d | | 228,000 | 1 | ethi | C | 5 | Southern Shoa Province. Animists 15%, Muslims 5%(many converting to ECMY). D=6. M=2. |
| Kamwe ethnoreligionists | sAT | 3-d | | 192,000 | 2 | nige | B | 4 | God=Hyalatamwa. Adamawa State, Michika LGA. Animists 57%, Muslims 3%. D=8. M=3. |
| Kankanaey ethnoreligionists | sAT | 3-d | | 107,000 | 1 | phil | B | 3 | Northern Benguet Province, southwestern Mountain Province, Luzon. Animists 60%. D=7. M=4. |
| Kara ethnoreligionists | sAT | 3-d | | 100,000 | 4 | tanz | B | 2 | Southeastern shore of Lake Victoria. Many bilinguals in Swahili. Animists 83%. D=1. |
| Karamojong ethnoreligionists | sAT | 3-d | | 113,000 | 1 | ugan | C | 5 | God=Akuj. Karamoja District. Cattle-rustling gangs with machine-guns. Animists 29%.D=5,M=2. |
| Karanga ethnoreligionists | sAT | 3-d | | 587,000 | 5 | zimb | C | 5 | God=Wedenga. Southernmost Shona. Animists 30%. M=SMB,SJ,CMM. |
| Kasem ethnoreligionists | sAT | 3-d | | 106,000 | 1 | burk | A | 1 | Majority in Ghana. Animists 80%, Muslims 10%. D=AoG. M=FMB,SIL. |
| Kayah ethnoreligionists | sAT | 3-d | | 187,000 | 1 | myan | B | 3 | Kayah and Karen States. Also in Thailand. Related to Bwe Karen. Animists 75%. D=BBC. |
| Kendayan Dayak ethnoreligionists | sAT | 3-d | | 114,000 | 1 | indo | B | 3 | Kalimantan Barat. Near Bengkayang, also jungle. Few bilinguals in Indonesian. Animists 55%. |
| Khandeshi ethnoreligionists | sAT | 3-c | | 1,162,000 | 1 | indi | A | 0 | Maharashtra, Gujarat. Dialects: Ahirani, Dangri, Kunbi, Rangari. Animists 70%, Hindus 30%. |
| Khasi ethnoreligionists | sAT | 3-d | | 546,000 | 2 | indi | B | 5 | God=Blei. Tribals in Assam, Jammu, Kashmir, Manipur, Punjab. UP. Animists 50%. D=4. M=6. |
| Khmu ethnoreligionists | sAT | 3-d | | 714,000 | 5 | laos | A | 2 | Scattered across north. Also Thailand, Burma, USA, France, China. Animists 94%. D=2. M=5. |
| Khoisan ethnoreligionists | sAT | 3-e | | 90,000 | 9 | bots | B | 5 | Khoi Hottentots, San Bushmen. |
| Kinga ethnoreligionists | sAT | 3-d | | 106,000 | 1 | tanz | B | 4 | God=Unguve. Livingston Mountains, shores of Lake Malawi. Animists 40%. D=2. M=2. |
| Kipsigis ethnoreligionists | sAT | 3-d | | 171,000 | 1 | keny | C | 5 | God=Jehovah. In Kalenjin cluster, Rift Valley and west. Animists 20%. D=13. M=4. |
| Kissi ethnoreligionists | sAT | 3-d | | 276,000 | 1 | guin | B | 2 | Also in Sierra Leone. Animists 77%, Muslims 13%. Resistant to advance of Islam. D=4. M=3. |
| Kofyar ethnoreligionists | sAT | 3-d | | 141,000 | 1 | nige | A | 1 | Plateau State, 3 LGAs: Shendam, Mangu. Many dialects. Animists 80%, Muslims 10%. D=2. |
| Konkomba ethnoreligionists | sAT | 3-d | | 391,000 | 2 | ghan | B | 3 | Northeast. Also in Togo. Animists 79%, Muslims 1%(Sunnis,Ahmadis). M=SVD,WEC,WF. |
| Kono ethnoreligionists | sAT | 3-d | | 182,000 | 4 | sier | B | 2 | God=Yataa. Northeast. Wealthy diamond-mining area. Animists 78%, Muslims 10%.D=11.M=7. |
| Konso ethnoreligionists | sAT | 3-d | | 195,000 | 2 | ethi | B | 2 | South of Lake Ciamo. Agriculturalists. Animists 80%. D=ECMY,WLEC. M=SIM. |
| Koro ethnoreligionists | sAT | 3-d | | 216,000 | 2 | nige | A | 1 | Kaduna State, Kachia LGA. Animists 70%, Muslims 20%. D=3. M=3. |
| Koya ethnoreligionists | sAT | 3-d | | 272,000 | 1 | indi | A | 2 | God=Devudu. In AP, MP. Aborigines in Hyderabad. Animists 78%, Hindus 20%. D=1. M=7. |
| Kpelle ethnoreligionists | sAT | 3-d | | 262,000 | 1 | libe | B | 3 | Resistant to Islam. Animists 43%, Muslims 25%. D=8 (including several AICs). M=5. |
| Krio ethnoreligionists | sAT | 3-d | | 223,000 | 1 | sier | B | 5 | Muslims 12%(Maliki Sunnis). 35 Christian denominations including many AICs. M=6. |
| Kui ethnoreligionists | sAT | 3-d | | 584,000 | 4 | indi | A | 2 | Orissa, Udayagiri area; AP, MP, Tamil Nadu. Hindus 54%, animists 45%. D=5. M=5. |
| Kuranko ethnoreligionists | sAT | 3-d | | 183,000 | 1 | sier | A | 1 | God=Alla. Also in Guinea. Literates 1%. Animists 68%, Muslims 30%(Maliki Sunnis). D=3. M=4. |
| Kurfei ethnoreligionists | sAT | 3-d | | 194,000 | 1 | niga | A | 1 | God=Allah. Animists 95%, Muslims 5%. Resistant to Islam and Christianity. D=ECWA. M=2. |
| Kuria ethnoreligionists | sAT | 3-d | | 147,000 | 2 | tanz | B | 5 | East of Lake Victoria; many in Kenya. Animists 27%. D=6. M=3. |
| Kurku ethnoreligionists | sAT | 3-d | | 312,000 | 1 | indi | A | 1 | God=Bhagwan. Southern MP, Betul District; Maharashtra. Animists 62%, Hindus 28%. D=2. |
| Kuruba ethnoreligionists | sAT | 3-d | | 708,000 | 1 | indi | A | 1 | Animists 80%, Hindus 19%. D=Gospel in Action,Brethren,RCC,CSI,UELCI. M=IEM,IBT,QCI. |
| Kurumba ethnoreligionists | sAT | 3-d | | 143,000 | 2 | burk | A | 1 | Yatenga Province. Animists 81%, Muslims 8%. D=2. M=5. |
| Kwanka ethnoreligionists | sAT | 3-d | | 138,000 | 1 | nige | A | 0 | Plateau State (Mangu LGA), Bauchi State. Animists 60%, Muslims 37%. |
| Lahu ethnoreligionists | sAT | 3-d | | 263,000 | 3 | chin | B | 5 | God=Guisha. Southwest Yunnan, also in Burma, Thailand, Laos. Animists 50%, Buddhists 10%. |
| Lakota ethnoreligionists | sAT | 3-e | | 2,200 | 1 | usa | C | 5 | Remnants of Amerindian religion of Sioux (Dakotas). |
| Lamba ethnoreligionists | sAT | 3-d | | 138,000 | 3 | togo | B | 2 | Region of Kande; also in Benin. Literates 20%. Animists 49%, Muslims 34%. D=2. M=6. |
| Lele ethnoreligionists | sAT | 3-d | | 325,000 | 5 | burk | A | 1 | Sangui Province. Animists 85%, Muslims 5%. D=RCC,AoG,EBBF. M=SIL,NBC,FMB. |
| Lobi ethnoreligionists | sAT | 3-d | | 476,000 | 3 | burk | A | 1 | Also in Ivory Coast, a few in Ghana. Animists 98%, Muslims 1%. D=2. M=2. |
| Loma ethnoreligionists | sAT | 3-d | | 101,000 | 2 | libe | B | 3 | God=Gala. Loffa County, also Guinea. Resists Islam. Animists 60%, Muslims 25%. D=3. M=5. |
| Lomwe ethnoreligionists | sAT | 3-d | | 857,000 | 2 | moza | B | 4 | Zambezia Province. Also in Malawi. Animists 65%, Muslims 7%. D=7. M=5. |
| Losso ethnoreligionists | sAT | 3-d | | 111,000 | 1 | togo | B | 3 | Doufelgou Prefecture. Animists 75%. D=RCC,EET,AoG. M=OFM,SMA,FSCJ,SIL,FMB. |
| Lotuko ethnoreligionists | sAT | 3-d | | 159,000 | 1 | suda | B | 4 | God=Hollum. Torit District. Animists 58%, Muslims 4%(Sunnis). Highly resistant to Islam. D=3. |
| Lovedu ethnoreligionists | sAT | 3-d | | 101,000 | 1 | soua | B | 3 | Ritual of Rain Queen. Close to Venda, Shona. Animists 50%. Nominal Christians 26%. D=AICs. |
| Lwena ethnoreligionists | sAT | 3-d | | 121,000 | 3 | zamb | B | 5 | Northwestern, Western Provinces. Mainly in Angola, also in Zaire. Animists 40%. D=11. M=6. |
| Maasai ethnoreligionists | sAT | 3-d | | 557,000 | 2 | keny | B | 5 | God=engAi. Kajiado, Narok; Tanzania. Animists 55%. D=RCC,EFMK,CPK,LCK,AIC. M=18. |
| Maguzawa ethnoreligionists | sAT | 3-d | | 100,000 | 1 | nige | B | 3 | God=Allah. `Pagan Hausa' in North. A tribe of Hausa, 90% animists. Y=1920. D=4. M=3. |
| Mahafaly ethnoreligionists | sAT | 3-d | | 180,000 | 1 | mada | B | 3 | Small area along southwest coast of island. Animists 75%. D=RCC(D-Tulear). M=AA. |
| Makua ethnoreligionists | sAT | 3-c | | 1,329,000 | 9 | moza | B | 3 | Animists 59%, Muslims 18%(Shafi Sunnis). D=3. M=14. |
| Makuana ethnoreligionists | sAT | 3-c | | 1,775,000 | 1 | moza | B | 3 | Nampula, south of Meeto area. Animists 59%, Muslims 20%. D=RCC. |
| Malayic Dayak ethnoreligionists | sAT | 3-d | | 573,000 | 1 | indo | B | 2 | Kalimantan. West central, to Delang in south. Animists 80%. D=NTM. |
| Malinke ethnoreligionists | sAT | 3-d | | 165,000 | 10 | ghan | A | 1 | God=Alla. In 10 West African countries. Animists 65%, Muslims 30%(Sunnis). |
| Mamara Senufo ethnoreligionists | sAT | 3-d | | 254,000 | 1 | mali | A | 2 | Northern Senufo. Animists 43%, Muslims 55%. Many fetish houses (temples). D=2. M=5. |
| Mambwe ethnoreligionists | sAT | 3-d | | 130,000 | 2 | zamb | B | 5 | Northeastern Northern Province. Also in Tanzania. Animists 50%. D=5. M=1. |
| Mamprusi ethnoreligionists | sAT | 3-d | | 247,000 | 2 | ghan | A | 1 | Also in Togo. Animists 81%, Muslims 14%(Sunnis,Ahmadis). D=8. M=5. |
| Mandinka ethnoreligionists | sAT | 3-d | | 112,000 | 3 | gamb | A | 1 | God=Yau. Also Senegal. Muslims 89%(Maliki Sunnis, some Ahmadis),animists 10%. D=4. M=4. |
| Mandyak ethnoreligionists | sAT | 3-d | | 223,000 | 5 | gunb | A | 1 | Also Senegal, Gambia, France. Animists 79%(strong ancestor cult), Muslims 13%. D=3. M=3. |
| Manggarai ethnoreligionists | sAT | 3-d | | 270,000 | 1 | indo | A | 1 | Nusa Tenggara, Flores. Close to Riung. 43 dialects. Muslims 50%, animists 46%. D=RCC. |
| Manipuri ethnoreligionists | sAT | 3-d | | 106,000 | 3 | indi | B | 2 | God=Ishwar. Assam, Manipur. Hindus 85%, animists 7%, Muslims 6.5%. M=4. |
| Mano ethnoreligionists | sAT | 3-d | | 221,000 | 2 | libe | A | 1 | God=Wala. Nimba County; also Guinea. Animists 95%. D=6. M=2. |
| Manyika ethnoreligionists | sAT | 3-d | | 353,000 | 2 | zimb | C | 5 | God=Mwari. Manicaland Province, Umtali; also in Mozambique. Animists 30%. D=10. M=6. |
| Marba ethnoreligionists | sAT | 3-d | | 125,000 | 1 | chad | B | 3 | Southwest, Logone district. 20% urban. Animists 79%, a few Muslims. D=2. M=3. |
| Marenje ethnoreligionists | sAT | 3-d | | 435,000 | 1 | moza | B | 3 | Related to Makua. Closest to Chwabo. Animists 73%, Muslims 7%. D=RCC. |
| Marka ethnoreligionists | sAT | 3-d | | 151,000 | 1 | burk | A | 1 | Animists 60%, Muslims 28%. D=RCC(D-Nouna-Dedougou),ECEBF. M=CMA,WF,CSSR. |
| Masa ethnoreligionists | sAT | 3-d | | 231,000 | 2 | came | B | 2 | God=Alauna. Far North Province. Densely settled. Animists 55%, Muslims 25%. D=2. M=2. |
| Matengo ethnoreligionists | sAT | 3-d | | 104,000 | 2 | tanz | B | 3 | Northeast Lake Nyasa; some in Malawi and Mozambique. Animists 50%. D=1. M=OSB. |
| Mauri ethnoreligionists | sAT | 3-d | | 357,000 | 1 | niga | A | 1 | God=Allah. Animists 99%. Resistant to Islam as well as to Christianity. D=ECWA. M=SIM,EMS. |
| Melanesian ethnoreligionists | sAT | 3-d | | 100,000 | 10 | papu | C | 5 | Remnants of animistic traditional religions among many peoples and tribes. |
| Mende ethnoreligionists | sAT | 3-d | | 542,000 | 2 | sier | B | 3 | God=Ngewo. Also Liberia. Animists 42%, Muslims 42%(Maliki; 10,000 Ahmadis). D=11. M=9. |
| Merina ethnoreligionists | sAT | 3-d | | 556,000 | 2 | mada | C | 5 | Animists 12%, Muslims 1%, Baha'is 0.2%. D=70% Protestants,RCC,AICs. M=20. |
| Meru ethnoreligionists | sAT | 3-d | | 186,000 | 2 | keny | C | 5 | God=Murungu. Meru District. Animists 10%, Muslims 1%, Baha'is 1%. D=7, many AICs. M=8. |
| Mina ethnoreligionists | sAT | 3-c | | 1,086,000 | 3 | indi | A | 1 | Aborigines in Rajasthan, Madhya Pradesh. Animists 98%(Hindu elements). M=4. |
| Mofa ethnoreligionists | sAT | 3-d | | 286,000 | 1 | came | A | 1 | God=Zhikle. Far North Province; a few Nigeria. Animists 76%, Muslims 20%. Y=1950. D=4. |
| Molao ethnoreligionists | sAT | 3-d | | 103,000 | 1 | chin | A | 2 | North Guangxi. Mulao is unwritten; Agriculturalists. Animists 58%, Buddhists 40%. D=2. |
| Mon ethnoreligionists | sAT | 3-d | | 792,000 | 1 | myan | A | 1 | God=Kyaik. Animists 75%, Buddhists 20%. D=Ch of Christ,BBC(Mon Baptist Churches Union). |
| Mossi ethnoreligionists | sAT | 3-c | | 1,203,000 | 9 | burk | B | 4 | Formerly imperial rulers. Animists 16%, Muslims 61%(Maliki Sunnis). D=6. M=8. |
| Mumuye ethnoreligionists | sAT | 3-d | | 348,000 | 2 | nige | B | 2 | Taraba State. In Cameroon. Literates 5%. Animists (reviving) 81%, Muslims 9%. Y=1932. D=8. |
| Munda ethnoreligionists | sAT | 3-d | | 352,000 | 3 | indi | B | 3 | God=Parameswar. Bihar, Assam; Nepal, Bangladesh. Hindus 53%, animists 20%. D=7. M=9. |
| Mundang ethnoreligionists | sAT | 3-d | | 132,000 | 2 | chad | B | 3 | God=Masing. Also in Cameroon. Animists 45%, Muslims 7%. D=EFLT,AIC. M=UBS,LBWM. |
| Muong ethnoreligionists | sAT | 3-c | | 1,058,000 | 2 | viet | A | 2 | Mostly in mountains of north; also near Banmethuot in south. Animists 94%. D=RCC. M=SIL. |

*Continued overleaf*

*Table 17–6 continued*

| Name of religion/religionists 1 | Pedigree 2 | Type 3 | Begun 4 | Adherents 5 | Ext 6 | Coun 7 | W 8 | X 9 | E. g. = examples; name for God, other religions present, D=denominations, M=missions. 10 |
|---|---|---|---|---|---|---|---|---|---|
| Ndau ethnoreligionists | sAT | 3-d | | 319,000 | 3 | zimb | B | 5 | God=Mngari. Also in Mozambique, with many as refugees in Zimbabwe. Animists 50%. M=2. |
| Ndebele ethnoreligionists | sAT | 3-d | | 559,000 | 3 | zimb | B | 5 | Animists 36%. Heavily christianized. D=30 large denominations, many AICs. |
| Negrito ethnoreligionists | sAT | 3-e | | 12,000 | 2 | phil | C | 5 | Agta, Onge, Semang and other Australoid peoples. 80% animists; complex religions. |
| New Guinea ethnoreligionists | sAT | 3-e | | 80,000 | 1 | papu | C | 5 | Sizeable numbers of animists are still found among several hundred tribes. |
| Ngaju Dayak ethnoreligionists | sAT | 3-d | | 138,000 | 1 | indo | C | 5 | God=Hatalla. Kalimantan. Kapuas, 3 other rivers in south. Lingua franca. Animists 40%. D=2. |
| Ngoni ethnoreligionists | sAT | 3-d | | 252,000 | 4 | mala | C | 5 | Speakers originally spoke Zulu. Animists 13%. D=5. M=5. |
| Ngwato Tswana ethnoreligionists | sAT | 3-d | | 151,000 | 2 | bots | B | 5 | God=Modimo. Animists 36%. D=UCCSA, RCC(D-Gaborone),CPCA, many AICs. M=20. |
| Northeastern Dinka ethnoreligionists | sAT | 3-d | | 110,000 | 1 | suda | C | 5 | God=Nhialic. White Nile Dinka. Nomadic animists 90%, Muslims 1%. Resists Islam. D=5. M=4. |
| Northeastern Tai ethnoreligionists | sAT | 3-d | | 163,000 | 1 | thai | B | 2 | Lao. Bangkok. Theravada Buddhists 98%, animists 1%. D=6. M=12. |
| Northern Gond ethnoreligionists | sAT | 3-d | | 385,000 | 1 | indi | A | 1 | God=Parameshwar. Betul and other Districts, MP. Hindus 55%, animists 45%. D=2. M=9. |
| Northern Samo ethnoreligionists | sAT | 3-d | | 167,000 | 1 | burk | B | 2 | Sourou Province. Animists 54%, Muslims 30%. D=2. M=2. |
| Northwestern Maninka ethnoreligionists | sAT | 3-d | | 201,000 | 2 | mali | A | 1 | Wasulunka. Also in Senegal, Guinea. Muslims 67%(Maliki Sunnis), animists 30%. D=3. M=7. |
| Northwestern Tamang ethnoreligionists | sAT | 3-d | | 107,000 | 1 | nepa | B | 2 | Animists 35%, Hindus 25%, Buddhists 23%. 1974, widespread revival begins. D=3. M=5. |
| Nsenga ethnoreligionists | sAT | 3-d | | 181,000 | 3 | zamb | B | 5 | God=Mlungu. East and Central Provinces. Animists 30%, Baha'is. D=7. M=4. |
| Nunuma ethnoreligionists | sAT | 3-d | | 194,000 | 1 | burk | A | 1 | Over 100 villages in Sissili Province. Animists 62%, Muslims 25%. D=3. M=8. |
| Nyanja ethnoreligionists | sAT | 3-d | | 195,000 | 3 | moza | B | 5 | God=Mulungu. Animists 42%. D=6; many AICs. M=USPG. |
| Nyiha ethnoreligionists | sAT | 3-d | | 299,000 | 2 | tanz | B | 3 | God=Mulungu. South of Lake Rukwa, on Zambia border. Also in Malawi. Animists 70%. D=4. |
| Nyungwe ethnoreligionists | sAT | 3-d | | 320,000 | 3 | moza | B | 3 | Banks of Zambezi. Some in Malawi. Closely related to Sena. Animists 75%. D=3. M=2. |
| Oraon ethnoreligionists | sAT | 3-d | | 388,000 | 3 | indi | B | 4 | Bihar, MP. Hindus 37%, animists 20%. D=7. M=3. |
| Ot Danum ethnoreligionists | sAT | 3-d | | 110,000 | 1 | indo | A | 2 | Kalimantan. South of Schwaner Range. Animists 99%. D=3. M=4. |
| Pawari Bhil ethnoreligionists | sAT | 3-d | | 310,000 | 1 | indi | A | 1 | Maharashtra. Animists 98%. D=1. M=5. |
| Pedi ethnoreligionists | sAT | 3-d | | 192,000 | 3 | soua | C | 5 | God=Modimo. Transvaal. Animists 5%, Muslims, Baha'is. Many nominal Christians. D=9. M=8. |
| Phu Thai ethnoreligionists | sAT | 3-d | | 133,000 | 1 | laos | A | 1 | Many also in Thailand; some in north Viet Nam. Agriculturalists. Animists 98%. |
| Phuthai ethnoreligionists | sAT | 3-d | | 166,000 | 2 | viet | B | 2 | North Viet Nam. Majority in Laos; some in Thailand. Agriculturalists. Animists 95%. M=SIL. |
| Pokot ethnoreligionists | sAT | 3-d | | 279,000 | 2 | keny | B | 2 | God=Tororut. Also in Uganda. Semi-nomadic. Animists 84%. Y=1927(BCMS). D=7. M=6. |
| Rabha ethnoreligionists | sAT | 3-d | | 227,000 | 1 | indi | A | 1 | West Assam State, Garo Hills, Nagaland. Animists 90%, Hindus 6%. D=3. M=4. |
| Rana Thakur Tharu ethnoreligionists | sAT | 3-d | | 301,000 | 1 | nepa | A | 0 | On eastern border with India. Agriculturalists, pastoralists. Animists 99%. |
| Red Bobo ethnoreligionists | sAT | 3-d | | 339,000 | 3 | burk | B | 3 | Animists 62%, Muslims 10%. D=3. M=8. |
| Red Tai ethnoreligionists | sAT | 3-d | | 154,000 | 2 | viet | A | 1 | Viet Nam and Laos in the area of Thanh Hoa Province. Some in USA. Animists 95%. D=RCC. |
| Ronga ethnoreligionists | sAT | 3-d | | 146,000 | 2 | moza | C | 5 | God=Sikwembu. South, coastal areas. Also in South Africa. Animists 20%. D=5. M=6. |
| Rungi ethnoreligionists | sAT | 3-d | | 125,000 | 1 | tanz | B | 5 | Central Bantu. Southeast shore of Lake Tanganyika. Animists 55%. D=RCC,ELCT. |
| Sadama ethnoreligionists | sAT | 3-d | | 192,000 | 1 | ethi | B | 4 | Northeast of Lake Abaya. Animists 10%, Muslims 37%(Sunnis). D=5. M=SIM. |
| Safwa ethnoreligionists | sAT | 3-d | | 169,000 | 1 | tanz | B | 2 | In south, around Mbeya town. Animists 78%. D=RCC(D-Mbeya),CPT,Moravian Ch. |
| Sakalava ethnoreligionists | sAT | 3-d | | 574,000 | 6 | mada | B | 4 | Strongest Muslim presence among Malagasy peoples. Animists 59%, Muslims 7.5%. D=1. M=7. |
| Samburu ethnoreligionists | sAT | 3-d | | 138,000 | 1 | keny | B | 2 | Samburu District. Pastoralists. Related to Maasai. Animists 86%. D=7. M=10. |
| Santal ethnoreligionists | sAT | 3-c | | 1,482,000 | 4 | indi | B | 2 | God=Isor. Hindus 78%, animists 21%. M=MMS,ABFMS,LBI,TOR,SDB,SJ,CSM. |
| Sara Gambai ethnoreligionists | sAT | 3-d | | 153,000 | 2 | chad | B | 4 | God=Allah. Some in Cameroon. Muslims 26%, animists 20%. D=5. M=7. |
| Sea Dayak ethnoreligionists | sAT | 3-d | | 359,000 | 3 | malb | B | 5 | Sarawak, Brunei, Indonesia. Animists 51%, Baha'is 4%(mass conversions from 1962). D=4. |
| Selako Dayak ethnoreligionists | sAT | 3-d | | 135,000 | 1 | indo | A | 1 | Kalimantan. Northwest, around Pemangkat. Animists 98%. D=GKE. M=BEM. |
| Selale ethnoreligionists | sAT | 3-d | | 131,000 | 1 | ethi | B | 3 | Central area. Dialect of South Central Oromo. Muslims 85%, animists 5%. D=2. M=SIM. |
| Sena ethnoreligionists | sAT | 3-c | | 1,053,000 | 3 | moza | B | 4 | God=Mulungu. Also in Malawi. Animists 60%, Muslims 1%. M=FF(South Africa),FIFM. |
| Sgaw Karen ethnoreligionists | sAT | 3-c | | 1,021,000 | 2 | myan | B | 5 | God=Ywa. Animists 49%, Baha'is. D=BBC(Karen),RCC,CPB,SSKBC,AoG,NAC,SDA. M=10. |
| Shilluk ethnoreligionists | sAT | 3-d | | 142,000 | 1 | suda | B | 5 | God=Jwok. Upper Nile Province. Nomadic animists 72%, highly resistant to Islam. D=3. M=4. |
| Sihanaka ethnoreligionists | sAT | 3-d | | 261,000 | 1 | mada | B | 3 | North central, east of Merina. Animists 72%. D=3. M=OSST. |
| Soninke ethnoreligionists | sAT | 3-d | | 352,000 | 7 | mali | A | 0 | Muslims 80%(Sunnis, most in Sufi Tijaniyya and in Hamali sect), animists 20%. M=2. |
| Sotho ethnoreligionists | sAT | 3-d | | 113,000 | 3 | soua | C | 5 | God=Modimo. Also in Lesotho. Animists 5%, Muslims, Baha'is. M=OMI,CSSp,SCJ,OFM,LM. |
| South Central Dinka ethnoreligionists | sAT | 3-d | | 128,000 | 1 | suda | C | 5 | God=Nialic. West of White Nile. Animists 39%, Muslims 1%; highly resistant to Islam. D=2. M=2. |
| South Central Gond ethnoreligionists | sAT | 3-d | | 288,000 | 1 | indi | A | 2 | Adilabad District, northern Andhra Pradesh. Hindus 60%, animists 40%. D=2. M=6. |
| South Toraja ethnoreligionists | sAT | 3-d | | 115,000 | 1 | indo | C | 5 | God=Poeang Mato. Sulawesi. Rantepao is prestige dialect. Animists 20%, Muslims 15%. D=4. |
| Southeast Gond ethnoreligionists | sAT | 3-d | | 283,000 | 1 | indi | A | 1 | God=Devudu. Strongly influenced by Telugu, in AP. Hindus 60%, animists 40%. D=2. M=2. |
| Southern Kissi ethnoreligionists | sAT | 3-d | | 150,000 | 2 | libe | B | 2 | Lofa County, northwest. Also in Sierra Leone. Literates 15%. Animists 79%, Muslims 10%. D=6. |
| Southern Maninka ethnoreligionists | sAT | 3-c | | 1,127,000 | 1 | guin | A | 1 | God=Alla. Also in Guinea Bissau, Liberia. Animists 59%, Muslims 39%. D=RCC,EEP. M=10. |
| Southern Ndebele ethnoreligionists | sAT | 3-d | | 163,000 | 1 | soua | C | 5 | God=Nkulunkulu. Transvaal Ndebele(Laka/Black Ndebele & Manala tribes). Animists 20%.D=7. |
| Southern Senufo ethnoreligionists | sAT | 3-d | | 622,000 | 1 | ivor | B | 2 | Animists 65%, Muslims 30%. D=RCC(D-Korhogo),ANBC,EPC. M=WEC,CBFMS,BGC. |
| Sukuma ethnoreligionists | sAT | 3-c | | 1,047,000 | 1 | tanz | B | 4 | God=Mulungu. Animists 33%, Muslims 30%. D=RCC,AIC,SDA,CPT,BCT,PCSAT. AICs. M=20. |
| Sumbwa ethnoreligionists | sAT | 3-d | | 139,000 | 1 | tanz | B | 3 | West of the Sukuma. Animists 53%, Muslims 19%(Shafi Sunnis). D=RCC(M-Tabora). |
| Suppire Senufo ethnoreligionists | sAT | 3-d | | 275,000 | 2 | mali | A | 1 | Around Sikasso; also in Ivory Coast. Animists 50%, Muslims 48%. D=RCC. M=2. |
| Susu ethnoreligionists | sAT | 3-d | | 144,000 | 4 | guin | A | 1 | God=Alla. Muslims 85%(Maliki, since 1600; strongly syncretistic Islam), animists 15%. D=3. |
| Swazi ethnoreligionists | sAT | 3-d | | 351,000 | 4 | soua | C | 5 | Also in Swaziland. Animists 25%. Y=1880. D=5. M=5. |
| Tanala ethnoreligionists | sAT | 3-d | | 504,000 | 1 | mada | B | 3 | East of Betsileo. Animists 80%. D=RCC(M-Fianarantsoa),ERSM, and other AICs. M=SJ. |
| Taturu ethnoreligionists | sAT | 3-d | | 163,000 | 1 | tanz | A | 1 | South of the Iraqw. Semi-nomadic pastoralists. Animists 97%. D=3. M=2. |
| Tembu ethnoreligionists | sAT | 3-d | | 151,000 | 1 | soua | C | 5 | Rich cultural history. Xhosa dialect. Animists 25%. Y=1830. Nominal Christians 5%. D=4. M=2. |
| Temne ethnoreligionists | sAT | 3-d | | 415,000 | 2 | sier | B | 2 | God=Kuru. Muslims 60%(Maliki; 2,000 Ahmadis), animists 34%(Poro Secret Society). D=11. |
| Tiddim Chin ethnoreligionists | sAT | 3-d | | 156,000 | 2 | myan | C | 5 | God=Pasian. Chin Hills, Tiddim. Also India (Assam), Bhutan. Lingua franca. Animists 40%. D=4. |
| Tiv ethnoreligionists | sAT | 3-d | | 126,000 | 1 | nige | C | 5 | God=Aôndo. Nominal Christians 43%, animists 4%. Y=1911. D=Tiv Ch,RCC. M=SUM,NGK. |
| Tlhaping Tswana ethnoreligionists | sAT | 3-d | | 116,000 | 2 | soua | B | 5 | God=Modimo. North, Botswana border. Animists 40%; many nominal Christians. Y=1821. D=2. |
| Tlharu Tswana ethnoreligionists | sAT | 3-d | | 113,000 | 1 | soua | B | 5 | Some in Botswana. Animists 25%. Nominal Christians widespread. D=many AICs. |
| Toma ethnoreligionists | sAT | 3-d | | 121,000 | 1 | guin | A | 1 | Distinct from Loma of Liberia. Animists 67%,Muslims 25%. Resistant barrier to Islam.D=4.M=3. |
| Tonga ethnoreligionists | sAT | 3-d | | 197,000 | 3 | moza | B | 5 | God=Chiuta. South, Inhambane area. Animists 50%. D=AC/CPSA,RCC,AICs. M=USPG,UBS. |
| Tsimihety ethnoreligionists | sAT | 3-d | | 950,000 | 1 | mada | B | 3 | God=Jañahary. Animists 85%. D=RCC(3 Dioceses),ERSM,FMTA, and other AICs. M=4. |
| Tsonga ethnoreligionists | sAT | 3-d | | 634,000 | 4 | soua | C | 5 | God=Sikwembu Nkulukumba. 180,000 refugees. Animists 30%, Muslims, Baha'is. D=5. M=5. |
| Tswa ethnoreligionists | sAT | 3-d | | 978,000 | 3 | moza | B | 3 | God=Nungungulu. Animists 79%. D=UCCSA(ICUM),IMU,RCC,IML,CPSA, many AICs. M=7. |
| Tuburi ethnoreligionists | sAT | 3-d | | 102,000 | 1 | came | B | 3 | Far North Province. Densely settled. Farmers, stockraisers. Animists 60%. D=2. M=2. |
| Tulama ethnoreligionists | sAT | 3-d | | 469,000 | 1 | ethi | B | 5 | Central. Shoa Province. Animists 10%, Muslims 35%(Shafi Sunnis). D=5. M=3. |
| Tulu ethnoreligionists | sAT | 3-d | | 102,000 | 2 | indi | A | 1 | God=Dever. In AP, Kerala, Tamil Nadu, Maharashtra, Karnataka. Hindus 90%. D=CSI. M=1. |
| Tumulung Sisala ethnoreligionists | sAT | 3-d | | 107,000 | 1 | ghan | B | 2 | North central, Tumu District. Animists 68%, Muslims 20%. D=5. M=6. |
| Turkana ethnoreligionists | sAT | 3-d | | 326,000 | 3 | keny | B | 3 | God=Akuj. Lake Turkana. Nomads, pastoralists in semi-arid desert. Animists 87%. D=9. M=6. |
| Twa ethnoreligionists | sAT | 3-d | | 193,000 | 3 | rwan | B | 3 | God=Imana. Jungle-dwellers. Animists 92%. D=RCC,Anglican Ch/EAR. M=RCMS,WF,FSC. |
| Venda ethnoreligionists | sAT | 3-d | | 573,000 | 2 | soua | B | 4 | God=Mudzimu. Animists 65%. D=DRCA,AoG,CPSA,WC,RCC,CBCSA,ZCC,other AICs. M=15. |
| Vietnamese ethnoreligionists | sAT | 3-d | | 477,000 | 18 | viet | B | 3 | God=Duc Chua Troi. Mahayana Buddhists 54%, New-Religionists 13%(CDMC), atheists 8%. |
| Wa ethnoreligionists | sAT | 3-d | | 366,000 | 1 | myan | B | 2 | God=Siyeh. Shan State. Also in China. Animists 60%, Buddhists 30%. D=4. M=OMF. |
| Wachi ethnoreligionists | sAT | 3-d | | 348,000 | 2 | togo | B | 2 | Main centers Vogan, Tabligbo; also in Benin. Animists 65%, Muslims 20% (Maliki Sunnis). D=7. |
| Walamo ethnoreligionists | sAT | 3-c | | 1,007,000 | 1 | ethi | B | 4 | Animists 35%. D=WLEC(strong),ECMY(20%), EOC,FGBC,RCC,SDA,AICs. M=12. |
| Wallega ethnoreligionists | sAT | 3-d | | 902,000 | 2 | ethi | B | 5 | God=Wagayo. Muslims 40%, animists 25% D=30%: EOC(D-Wallega),BECE,ECMY,SDA. M=3. |
| West Central Limba ethnoreligionists | sAT | 3-d | | 117,000 | 1 | sier | B | 3 | God=Kanu. Makeni. Also in Guinea. Muslims 52%(conversion begun 1880), animists 34%. D=6. |
| West Gbari ethnoreligionists | sAT | 3-d | | 119,000 | 1 | nige | B | 3 | Western Gbagyi, in Niger and Plateau States. Animists 40%, Muslims 25%. D=3. M=7. |
| West Makua ethnoreligionists | sAT | 3-d | | 642,000 | 1 | moza | B | 3 | Niassa Province. Animists 60%, Muslims 20%. D=CPSA,RCC. |
| Western Dinka ethnoreligionists | sAT | 3-d | | 205,000 | 1 | suda | C | 5 | Southwestern Dinka. Far west of White Nile. Nomadic animists 30%. D=4. M=3. |
| Western Magar ethnoreligionists | sAT | 3-d | | 168,000 | 1 | nepa | A | 0 | West of Pokhara. Bheri & Koshi Zones. Some bilinguals in Nepali. Animists 70%, Hindus 30%. |
| Western Meo ethnoreligionists | sAT | 3-c | | 3,492,000 | 1 | chin | B | 2 | Guizhou, Guangxi, Sichuan, Yunnan; Viet Nam, Laos. Polytheists 94%. D=6. M=20. |
| Western Nuer ethnoreligionists | sAT | 3-d | | 282,000 | 1 | suda | B | 3 | Jikany Cien.Pastoralists. Animists 75%, highly resistant to Islam. D=5. M=2. |
| White Karen ethnoreligionists | sAT | 3-d | | 996,000 | 2 | myan | B | 5 | God=Ywa. Animists 65%, Baha'is. D=BBC,SSKBMS,CPB(D-Yangon),AoG,SDA,NAC. M=10. |
| White Tai ethnoreligionists | sAT | 3-d | | 268,000 | 4 | viet | A | 1 | Along Red, Black rivers. Also in Laos, China, France, USA. Animists 60%, Buddhists 35%. D=1. |
| Wobe ethnoreligionists | sAT | 3-d | | 123,000 | 1 | ivor | B | 3 | Western Department. Animists 71%, Muslims 1%. D=3. M=5. |
| Xhosa ethnoreligionists | sAT | 3-d | | 380,000 | 4 | soua | C | 5 | God=uThixo. Southwest Cape, Transkei. Animists 6%, Muslims. Y=1799(LMS). D=14. M=3. |
| Yemma ethnoreligionists | sAT | 3-d | | 241,000 | 1 | ethi | B | 4 | Youth bilingual in Amharic, older persons in Oromo. Animists 40%, Muslims 10%. D=WLEC. |
| Yoruba ethnoreligionists | sAT | 3-d | | 856,000 | 10 | nige | B | 5 | God=Olorun. Muslims 37%(Malikis,Sufis,Ahmadis), animists 4%. Y=1841. D=13. M=8. |
| Zambezi Tonga ethnoreligionists | sAT | 3-d | | 137,000 | 2 | zamb | C | 5 | God=Leza. Valley Tonga. Animists 20%. D=12 plus many AICs. M=3. |
| Zande ethnoreligionists | sAT | 3-d | | 137,000 | 3 | suda | C | 5 | God=Mbori. Mostly in Zaire, also CAR. Animists 15%. D=4. M=3. |
| Zerma ethnoreligionists | sAT | 3-d | | 300,000 | 5 | niga | A | 1 | God=Iricouei. Also in Nigeria. Muslims 80%(Maliki Sunnis), animists 20%. Talking drums. D=3. |
| Zezuru ethnoreligionists | sAT | 3-d | | 580,000 | 2 | zimb | C | 5 | Animists 28%. Heavily Christianized. AICs particularly strong. D=13. M=6. |
| Zulu ethnoreligionists | sAT | 3-d | | 383,000 | 7 | soua | C | 5 | God=Nkulunkulu. Animists 3%; Muslims(10,000 converts; 1982: Quran in Zulu). D=40 AICs. |
| Neopagans | ET | 3-c | | 4,500,000 | 20 | brit | C | 5 | Followers of modern revivals of ancient pagan religions (Wicca, &c): UK, Iceland, et alia. |
| Polytheists | PT | 3-c | | 3,000,000 | 30 | indi | B | 2 | Gradual decline but still strong in the Americas, Polynesia, Oceania, India. |
| Chienchiang ethnoreligionists | sPT | 3-d | | 101,000 | 1 | chin | A | 1 | Guizhou Province. Related to Puyi (Bouyei). Polytheists 80%, Buddhists 19%. D=RCC. |
| Chungchia ethnoreligionists | sPT | 3-d | | 250,000 | 1 | chin | A | 0 | Guizhou, Guangxi Provinces. Dialect of Northern Zhuang. In Puyi nationality. Polytheists 99%. |

*Continued opposite*

*Table 17–6 continued*

| Name of religion/religionists 1 | Pedigree 2 | Type 3 | Begun 4 | Adherents 5 | Ext 6 | Coun 7 | W 8 | X 9 | E. g. = examples; name for God, other religions present, D=denominations, M=missions. 10 |
|---|---|---|---|---|---|---|---|---|---|
| Flowery Meo ethnoreligionists | sPT | 3-d | | 254,000 | 3 | viet | B | 2 | Flowered Meo. Northwestern Tonkin Province. Also in China, Laos. Polytheists 88%. D=RCC. |
| Highland Yao ethnoreligionists | sPT | 3-d | | 386,000 | 3 | viet | A | 1 | Across northern Tonkin; Banmethuot. Most in China; Laos. Polytheists 99%. D=RCC. M=2. |
| Kachin ethnoreligionists | sPT | 3-d | | 207,000 | 2 | myan | C | 5 | Kachin State; also India, China. Polytheists 30%, Buddhists 10%. R=FEBC. |
| Kado ethnoreligionists | sPT | 3-d | | 250,000 | 4 | myan | A | 0 | Also in China (south Yunnan) and Laos. Polytheists 85%, Buddhists 10%. D=1. |
| Keh-deo Meo ethnoreligionists | sPT | 3-d | | 126,000 | 1 | chin | A | 1 | A tribe and dialect of Eastern Meo. In southwest, Guizhou Province. Polytheists 97%. M=CSI. |
| Kelao ethnoreligionists | sPT | 3-d | | 495,000 | 2 | chin | A | 0 | In Yunnan, Guizhou, Guangxi, Hunan; Viet Nam. Only 1.4% speak Gelo. Polytheists 99%. |
| Kopu ethnoreligionists | sPT | 3-d | | 375,000 | 1 | chin | A | 0 | A Lolo language of the Northern Yi. Northern Yunnan Province, Luchuan area. Polytheists 99%. |
| Lu ethnoreligionists | sPT | 3-d | | 467,000 | 5 | chin | A | 1 | South Yunnan. Also Burma, Laos, Thailand. Viet Nam. Polytheists 80%, Buddhists 18%. M=1. |
| Man Cao Lan ethnoreligionists | sPT | 3-d | | 137,000 | 2 | viet | A | 0 | Moncay Province, North Viet Nam/China border. Also in China. Polytheists 99%. |
| Mapuche ethnoreligionists | sPT | 3-d | | 122,000 | 2 | chil | C | 5 | God=Ngünemapun. Polytheists 20%, Baha'is 1%. D=5. M=5. |
| Mexico native ethnoreligionists | sPT | 3-e | | 72,400 | 1 | mexi | C | 5 | Pre-Columbian religious survivals among monolingual Amerindians. |
| Micronesian ethnoreligionists | sPT | 3-e | | 6,200 | 6 | micr | C | 5 | Polytheists in Federated States of Micronesia, also in many other islands. |
| Nakhi ethnoreligionists | sPT | 3-d | | 276,000 | 1 | chin | A | 1 | Yunnan. Dongbaists 80%(polytheists),Buddhists 10%,Taoists 9%,shamanists widespread.D=1. |
| Native American ethnoreligionists | sPT | 3-d | | 410,000 | 2 | usa | C | 5 | Rediscovery of Amerindian traditional religions. |
| Nhang ethnoreligionists | sPT | 3-d | | 262,000 | 2 | chin | A | 1 | Yunnan Province; also Viet Nam (official community), USA, France, Laos. Polytheists 97%. |
| Oceanic ethnoreligionists | sPT | 3-d | | 267,000 | 20 | fiji | B | 4 | Decline from 1,300,000 in 1900 in many polytheistic religions. |
| Polynesian ethnoreligionists | sPT | 3-d | | 100,000 | 8 | frep | C | 5 | Remnants of once-strong polytheistic religions on numerous islands. |
| Red Meo ethnoreligionists | sPT | 3-d | | 204,000 | 3 | viet | A | 1 | Northwest Tonkin Province. Also in China, Thailand. Polytheists 88%. D=RCC. |
| Solomon Islands ethnoreligionists | sPT | 3-e | | 13,700 | 1 | solo | C | 5 | Animistic religions mostly on Malaita, with 500 on Guadacanal. |
| South American ethnoreligionists | sPT | 3-c | | 1,250,000 | 10 | braz | C | 5 | Remnant of many Amerindian tribal religions, especially in Amazon basin. |
| Southern Lisu ethnoreligionists | sPT | 3-d | | 157,000 | 2 | chin | C | 5 | Flowery Lisu(Hwa Lisu), Western Lisu. West Yunnan, Sichuan; Burma. Polytheists 20%. D=3. |
| Western Yi ethnoreligionists | sPT | 3-d | | 303,000 | 1 | chin | A | 1 | Yi nationality. 65% preliterate. Polytheists 92%, some Mahayana Buddhists. D=2. M=CSI. |
| White Meo ethnoreligionists | sPT | 3-d | | 345,000 | 5 | viet | B | 3 | Striped Meo. Tonkin Province. Also in Laos, France, China. Polytheists 80%. D=RCC. M=1. |
| Woni ethnoreligionists | sPT | 3-d | | 108,000 | 1 | chin | A | 0 | Yunnan, near the Hani. Under Hani official nationality. Polytheists 97%. |
| Shamanists | ST | 3-b | | 26,793,000 | 15 | russ | B | 5 | Trained shamans utilizing sacred power; one of oldest religious practices. |
| Altaic ethnoreligionistists | sST | 3-c | | 3,000,000 | 4 | russ | B | 5 | Shamanist religions across central/east Russia, Mongolia, China et alia. |
| Bonpos | sST | 3-e | BC 700 | 40,000 | 1 | chin | B | 3 | Neo-Buddhists of Bon Faith (pre-Buddhism). Tibet, China. Till 1959 330 monasteries. |
| Chinese Mongolian ethnoreligionists | sST | 3-c | | 1,368,000 | 1 | chin | A | 1 | God=Borhan. Nonreligious 50%, shamanists 40%, Lamaists 10%. D=RCC,house churches. |
| Finno-Ugric religionists | sST | 3-d | | 500,000 | 2 | finl | C | 5 | Shamanist remnants across Northern and Arctic Europe. |
| Inuit ethnoreligionists | sST | 3-e | | 10,000 | 4 | grel | C | 5 | Eskimo religionists from Alaska to Greenland. Hunter-gatherers. Animal rituals. |
| Khalkha Mongol ethnoreligionists | sST | 3-d | | 507,000 | 1 | mong | A | 0 | God=Borgan. Lamaists 30%, shamanists 30%, nonreligious 28% atheists 10%, Muslims 1%. |
| Komi-Zyrian ethnoreligionists | sST | 3-d | | 161,000 | 2 | russ | B | 3 | God=Jen. North Komi. West of Vogul peoples. Pastoralists, hunters. Shamanists 45%. D=1. |
| Korean ethnoreligionists | sST | 3-c | | 1,619,000 | 26 | chin | B | 3 | God=Hananim. Hyanbian District. Shamanists 55%, Mahayana Buddhists 35%. D=3. M=2. |
| Manchu ethnoreligionists | sST | 3-c | | 2,188,000 | 1 | chin | B | 2 | God=Shang-ti. Folk-religionists 70%, shamanists 20%, Buddhists 10%. D=TSPM. |
| North Korean ethnoreligionists | sST | 3-c | | 2,952,000 | 1 | nork | B | 2 | Nonreligious 55%, atheists 16%,New-Religionists 13%,shamanists 12%,Buddhists 1.5%.D=6. |
| Oirat ethnoreligionists | sST | 3-d | | 131,000 | 3 | chin | A | 0 | God=Borhan. Xinjiang Mongolian. Shamanists 60%, Lamaist Buddhists 30%, nonreligious 8%. |
| Poro | ssT | 3-e | | 40,000 | 1 | sier | B | 2 | West African Mande-speaking secret society for male initiation. |
| Sande | ssT | 3-e | | 50,000 | 1 | sier | B | 2 | West African Mande-speaking secret society for female initiation. |
| South Korean ethnoreligionists | sST | 3-c | | 7,325,000 | 1 | souk | B | 5 | Shamanists 16%, Buddhists 15%, New-Religionists 15%, Confucianists 11%. D=100. M=300. |
| Tunguz religionists | sST | 3-e | | 27,000 | 2 | russ | B | 5 | Shamanists among the Evenki language group. |
| Udmurt ethnoreligionists | sST | 3-d | | 333,000 | 9 | russ | B | 5 | God=Inan. Udmurtia. Orthodox; many pagans. Shamanists 45%, Muslim elements. M=IBT. |
| Western Manchu ethnoreligionists | sST | 3-d | | 193,000 | 1 | chin | A | 0 | Ili region of Xinjiang Province, also Jilin. Xibe spoken by 15%. Shamanists 100%. M=1. |
| Western Mongol ethnoreligionists | sST | 3-d | | 121,000 | 1 | mong | A | 0 | God=Borgan. Sart-Kalmyk. Ethnic group in Khalkha Mongol. Nonreligious, shamanists. M=3. |
| Yakut ethnoreligionists | sST | 3-d | | 132,000 | 2 | russ | B | 5 | God=Tanara. Siberia. Lingua franca. 60% use Russian. Hunters. Shamanists 30%. D=1. M=1. |
| Witchcraft eradicationists | WT | 3-e | 1910 | 20,000 | 30 | keny | C | 5 | Movements primarily in Africa to eradicate witch suspects and magical practices. |
| **Spiritists** | U | 1-b | | 12,334,000 | 55 | braz | C | 5 | Widespread. Adherents here omit 82 millions who are baptized Roman Catholics. |
| Afro-American spiritists | AU | 2-c | | 5,649,000 | 20 | jama | B | 5 | Wide range of religions across Caribbean and Latin America. Mostly Blacks. |
| Aboriginal Cult of Maria Lionza | sAU | 2-d | c1860 | 200,000 | 2 | vene | C | 5 | Goddess of water, vegetation. Blacks, Zambos. Syncretistic cult in Yaracuy. Seances, healings. |
| Afro-Brazilian cultists | BU | 2-b | c1800 | 40,000,000 | 1 | braz | C | 5 | Candomble, Xango (Shango), Macumba, Qimbanda, Batuque. |
| Batuque | sBU | 2-d | c1800 | 900,000 | 1 | braz | C | 5 | Afro-Brazilian spiritists in Belem and central regions of Brazil. Much brazilianized. |
| Candomble | sBU | 2-c | 1810 | 1,000,000 | 1 | braz | C | 5 | Spiritists in Bahia, Maranhao, Pernambuco. 10,000 centers. Women mediums, dances. Legal. |
| Catimbo | sBU | 2-d | c1800 | 350,000 | 1 | braz | C | 5 | Afro-Brazilian spiritists in central Brazil, also in northeast. Italian origins. |
| Macumba | sBU | 2-d | c1800 | 100,000 | 1 | braz | C | 5 | Afro-Brazilian spiritists in Rio, Sao Paulo. Magic. More violent and close to Voodoo. |
| Nago | sBU | 2-d | c1800 | 300,000 | 1 | braz | C | 5 | Afro-Brazilian Candomble spiritists in Maranhao and Pajelanca. |
| Pajelanca | sBU | 2-d | c1900 | 900,000 | 1 | braz | C | 5 | Spiritist movement related to Candomble, in central Brazil, in Amazonia. |
| Qimbanda | sBU | 2-e | | 50,000 | 1 | braz | C | 5 | Malevolent variety of Macumba and Umbanda involving evil spirits, magical practices, wizardry. |
| Tambor de Mina | sBU | 2-d | | 300,000 | 1 | braz | C | 5 | Name for Candomble used in Marenhas. |
| Umbanda | sBU | 2-b | c1900 | 31,000,000 | 22 | braz | C | 5 | Afro-Brazilian spiritists. Uses Kardecismo. Many Whites. Displacing Candomble and Macumba. |
| Xango | sBU | 2-c | c1800 | 1,000,000 | 1 | braz | C | 5 | Shango (Yoruba god of thunder). Afro-Brazilian spiritists in Pernambuco state. |
| Afro-Caribbean religionists | CU | 2-d | | 260,000 | 20 | jama | B | 5 | Large numbers across the Caribbean, also in UK, USA, Canada, et alia. |
| Convince | sCU | 2-e | | 4,000 | 1 | jama | B | 5 | Small ancestral Afro-Protestant cult in East Jamaica. |
| Kumina | sCU | 2-e | c1700 | 1,000 | 1 | jama | B | 5 | Cumina. Small African ancestor cult similar to Convince. 3 ranks of zombie (gods). |
| Liborismo | sCU | 2-e | 1900 | 70,000 | 1 | domr | C | 5 | Afro-Caribbean spiritists. F=Liborio. 90% are baptized RCs. |
| Obeah | sCU | 2-e | c1600 | 50,000 | 2 | jama | B | 5 | Secret cult of Ashanti origin (Ghana), for harmful magic. |
| Pocomania | sCU | 2-e | c1910 | 60,000 | 2 | jama | B | 5 | 'Little Madness'. Afro-Caribbean cult in Jamaica. |
| Rastafarians | sCU | 2-d | 1930 | 150,000 | 15 | jama | B | 5 | Dreads. Christianity rejected as White man's religion. Messianic, political. |
| Voodoo | sCU | 2-c | c1600 | 5,983,000 | 12 | hait | C | 5 | Vodun. Mix of African traditional religion and Catholicism. |
| High Spiritists | HU | 2-c | | 3,750,000 | 30 | fran | C | 5 | Kardecism and other European non-Christian forms without African features. |
| Universal World Harmony TS | HU | 2-e | 1961 | 5,000 | 20 | brit | C | 2 | TS="Through Service". UWH/World Council of Service. HQ Plymouth, UK. Esoteric, mediumist. |
| Atlanteans | sHU | 10-f | 1957 | 500 | 1 | usa | C | 5 | Philosophical society under spirit guide Helio-Arcanophus. |
| Kardecism | sHU | 2-d | 1850 | 700,000 | 10 | braz | C | 5 | Kardecismo. F=Allan Kardec. From France in 1850. 5,000 assocs, 31 hospitals, 435 schools. |
| White Eagle Lodge | sHU | 2-e | | 5,000 | 2 | brit | C | 5 | Spiritism via Native American spirit guide, White Eagle, projecting Cosmic Christ Star. |
| Spiritualists National Union | nU | 7-e | | 30,000 | 3 | brit | C | 5 | Non-Christian as well as Christian members. |
| Afro-Surinamese religionists | SU | 2-e | | 18,000 | 2 | suri | B | 4 | Mainly followers of Winti, Obeah, Voodoo. |
| Winti | sSU | 2-e | c1800 | 43,000 | 2 | suri | B | 4 | Afkodre (Idolatry). Folk-religion of Surinamese Creoles. Spirit-possession. Many in Holland. |
| Samnak Paw Sawan | sTU | 2-e | 1972 | 3,000 | 1 | thai | B | 2 | 'The Abode of Heavenly Fathers'. Urban, spirit exorcisms, mediums. F=Kloom Vajroban. |
| Zar cultists | sTU | 2-d | | 100,000 | 8 | ethi | B | 4 | Zar (sar)=spirits possessing women only. Nile area:Egypt, Sudan, Ethiopia, Somalia, E.Africa. |
| Afro-Cuban spiritists | UU | 2-c | c1800 | 2,300,000 | 3 | cuba | B | 5 | Followers of Santeria (Lucumis, Yoruban), Na, Ganga. |
| Naniguismo | sUU | 2-e | 1834 | 50,000 | 2 | cuba | B | 5 | Afro-Cuban spiritist cult. Propagates African rituals. Secret societies. |
| Santeria | sUU | 2-d | c1550 | 400,000 | 3 | cuba | B | 5 | Way of the Saints. Lucumis. Yoruban. Afro-Cuban-Catholic image-worship. Strong in USA. |
| Internat General Assoc of Spiritualists | wU | 7-d | | 120,000 | 4 | usa | C | 5 | Non-Christian churches and temples. Many splits. |
| **Jains** | V | 1-c | BC 550 | 4,218,000 | 40 | indi | B | 2 | Jainas. 2 sects since AD 79. 6,150 ascetics (4,200 nuns), monasteries. Ahimsa (Nonviolence). |
| Digambara Jains | DV | 2-c | BC 200 | 2,000,000 | 10 | indi | B | 2 | Sky-clad' Jainas (65 monks who go naked). In Maharashtra, Karnataka, and all major cities. |
| Bisapanthis | sDV | 2-d | | 100,000 | 1 | indi | B | 1 | Digambara Jain subsect in southwest India. Liberal. |
| Kanji Panthis | sDV | 2-d | c1900 | 600,000 | 40 | indi | B | 2 | Kanji Swami's reinterpretation attracts large Digambara following. Global following. |
| Taranapanthis | sDV | 2-d | 100 | 200,000 | 1 | indi | B | 1 | Samaiya Panthis. Subsect of Digambara Jainas, opposed to image worship. |
| Terapanthis/Sky-clad | sDV | 2-d | 1000 | 100,000 | 1 | indi | B | 1 | Subsect of Digambara Jainas in southwest India. Non-mendicants rejected. |
| Svetambara Jains | SV | 2-c | 79 | 1,500,000 | 20 | indi | B | 2 | 'White-clothed' Jainas. Concentrations: Punjab, Rajasthan, Gujarat. 1,650 monks, 4,400 nuns. |
| Anuvrata Movement | sSV | 2-e | 1948 | 70,000 | 1 | indi | B | 2 | Modern lay moral revival spreading Jain values. 5 Vows. F=Acharya Tulsi. |
| Gaccha | sSV | 2-e | 1228 | 5,000 | 1 | indi | B | 1 | Breakaway Svetambara Jain sects: Tapa Gaccha, Kharatara Gaccha. |
| Murtipujakas | sSV | 2-e | | 1,000 | 1 | indi | B | 0 | 'Image worshipers'. Pujeras, subsect of Svetambara Jains. |
| Sthanakavasis | sSV | 2-e | | 1,000 | 1 | indi | B | 1 | Dhundiyas. Reformed subgroup within Svetambara Jainas. |
| White-clad Terapanthis | sSV | 2-e | c1750 | 50,000 | 1 | indi | B | 0 | Subsect of Sthanakavasis Svetambara Jainas. |
| Adhyatma | zV | 2-e | 1620 | 20,000 | 1 | indi | B | 2 | Jain movement for cultivation of inner self to reach supreme truth. F=Banarsidas. |
| Ajivakas | zV | 2-e | BC c600 | 10,000 | 1 | indi | B | 1 | Heterodox Jain sect. F=Makkhali Gosala. Free will denied. |
| Kavi Panthis | zV | 2-e | 1924 | 10,000 | 1 | indi | B | 2 | Modern Jain lay reform movement to reconcile the 2 main Jain sects. Gujarat. |
| Satya Samaj | zV | 10-f | 1964 | 700 | 1 | indi | B | 2 | Modern Jain sect. F=Swami Satyabhakta. Opposes caste system. |
| **Pan-Religionists** | PW | 1-a | | 720,000,000 | 238 | indi | B | 4 | Persons holding that all religions are valid and true, or bodies taking this position. |
| Standing Conf of Jews, Chr & Muslims | cPW | 7-e | 1971 | 10,000 | 20 | brit | C | 5 | Chr=Christians. SCJCME. (E=in Europe) HQ London. |
| Folk-religionists | FPW | 2-a | | 200,000,000 | 180 | chin | B | 3 | Mixtures of all world religions with local gods and goddesses, popularized. |
| Indian Ecumenical Conference | fPW | 4-d | 1970 | 600,000 | 3 | usa | C | 5 | Spiritual renewal among Amerindians: Bahai, NAC, RCC, Handsome Lake, &c. |
| Inter-Religious Org of Trinidad & Tobago | nPW | 7-c | 1970 | 1,205,000 | 1 | trin | C | 5 | IROTT. Members: 10 Christian denominations (4 indigenous), 5 Hindu bodies, 4 Muslim. |
| National Conf of Christians and Jews | nPW | 7-c | 1927 | 9,000,000 | 1 | usa | C | 5 | NCCJ. 61 regional offices in USA, 2,800 trustees. |

*Continued overleaf*

*Table 17–6 concluded*

| Name of religion/religionists | Pedigree | Type | Begun | Adherents | Ext | Coun | W X | E. g. = examples; name for God, other religions present, D=denominations, M=missions. |
|---|---|---|---|---|---|---|---|---|
| *1* | *2* | *3* | *4* | *5* | *6* | *7* | *8 9* | *10* |
| Popular religionists | PPW | 2-a | | 500,000,000 | 150 | fran | C 5 | Mainly christianized but popular expressions of religion. On every continent. |
| Internat Council of Christians & Jews | wPW | 7-e | | 40,000 | 10 | brit | C 5 | ICCJ. 12 branches abroad. HQ London. |
| International Federation of Religions | wPW | 7-e | 1975 | 10,000 | 30 | thai | B 4 | To promote world peace and fraternity. F=Suchart Kosolkitiwong. Buddhist origins. |
| Spiritual Unity of Nations Assoc | wPW | 7-e | c1970 | 10,000 | 2 | soua | C 5 | SUNA. For better relations between religions, especially Christians and Jews. HQ Somerset. |
| World Conf on Religion and Peace | wPW | 7-c | 1970 | 3,000,000 | 40 | japa | B 5 | For all faiths, 7 major conferences. HQ New York, as an UN NGO. |
| World Congress of Faiths | wPW | 7-e | 1936 | 2,000 | 31 | brit | C 5 | F=F. Younghusband. Search for a shared global ethic. HQ London. Branches in 31 countries. |
| World Fellowship of Religions | wPW | 7-e | 1954 | 50,000 | 30 | indi | B 2 | WFR. Founded in New Delhi, to foster interreligious toleration and cooperation. |
| World Spiritual Council | wPW | 7-e | 1946 | 2,500 | 10 | brit | C 5 | WSC. Founded in Ashford, Kent to establish contacts between the great world religions. |
| World Union | wPW | 7-e | 1958 | 10,000 | 3 | indi | B 2 | WU. Inaugurated in Pondicherry; dedicated to search for uniting of mankind on spiritual values. |
| World's Parliament of Religions | wPW | 7-c | 1893 | 5,000,000 | 140 | chin | B 5 | Chicago 1893 and 1993. No interest in a World Council of Religions, but Global Ethic popular. |
| **Non-Christians** | X | 1-a | | 4,055,485,000 | 238 | chin | B 2 | Total Non-Christians of all kinds, either religionists or nonreligionists. |
| **Quasireligionists** | Y | 1-c | | 1,067,000 | 78 | usa | C 3 | Other religionists, near-religionists, partial-religionists. |
| Bogomils | BY | 10-f | 864 | 500 | 3 | bulg | C 5 | Manichaeism, Paulicianism, Catharism, Dualist sect. |
| Mandeans | MY | 2-e | AD c20 | 39,000 | 2 | iraq | A 1 | Sabeans. Subbas. Gnostic beliefs, Palestinian/Syrian origin. Own vast literature. Decline. |
| Quasi-Christians | NY | 2-b | | 50,000,000 | 50 | indi | B 2 | Large number of bodies that are near-Christian or partially-Christian. |
| Reformed Ogboni Fraternity | sNY | 2-e | 1914 | 12,000 | 1 | nige | B 3 | Christian Ogboni Society until 1933. F=J. A. T. Ogunbiyi(Masonic). Yorubas. |
| Pararel igionists | QY | 2-b | | 80,000,000 | 20 | fran | C 5 | Most members (e.g. Masons) belong also to mainline religions, or deny being a religion. |
| Freemasons | FQY | 2-c | 1714 | 5,900,000 | 37 | brit | C 5 | Largest worldwide secret society. Members men only. In USA, UK, France. |
| Yezidis | YY | 2-d | c100 | 226,000 | 10 | iraq | A 1 | Anti-dualistic Kurdish sect. Western Iran, Iraq, Syria, Turkey, Germany, Armenia, Georgia. |
| **Zoroastrians** | Z | 1-c BC 1200 | | 2,544,000 | 24 | iran | A 2 | Ancient monotheist religion of Persia. God=Ahura Mazda. Iran 1,903,000, Afghanistan 304,000. |
| Parsees | PZ | 2-d | c950 | 250,000 | 4 | indi | B 2 | Zoroastrians fleeing Persian persecution settle in Gujarat. Now wide diaspora in Africa, Europe. |
| Other religions not listed above | | | | 161,953,000 | 150 | | B 2 | Summaries of types of religions not included above. |
| Other lesser ethnoreligions | | | | 140,953,000 | 110 | nige | B 2 | 4,550 ethnoreligions with less than 100,000 adherents in AD 2000 |
| Other peripheral religions | | | | 20,000,000 | 40 | | A 2 | 2,000 peripheral religions, on the periphery of our definition of religion |
| Other hidden religions | | | | 1,000,000 | 80 | | B 1 | 500 clandestine minor religious systems, often illegal or subversive. |
| **Totals** | | | | | | | | |
| Total all adherents listed above | | | | 49,368,273,000 | 238 | | | 9,891 distinct religions whose total adherents/followers include multiple adherence |
| Multi-counted adherence | | | | -43,313,224,000 | 150 | | | Persons classified by themselves or by others as in an average of 10 different religions |
| Religionists worldwide | | | | 5,136,801,000 | 238 | usa | | Total individual religionists in world at mid-2000 (85%) |
| Nonreligionists worldwide | | | | 918,249,000 | 236 | chin | | Total individual nonreligionists in world at mid-2000 (15%) |
| **Global population** | | | | 6,055,049,000 | 238 | | | **Total individuals at mid-2000** |

# ETHNOLINGUISTICS

Integrating the panorama of races, cultures, peoples, languages, lingua francas

*There before me was a great multitude that no one could count, from every nation, tribe, people and language, standing before the throne.*

—Revelation 7:9, New International Version

*I saw another angel. This one was flying across the sky and had the eternal good news to announce to the people of every race, tribe, language, and nation on Earth*

—Revelation 14:6, Contemporary English Version

In Part 18 an attempt is made to unravel and integrate the close relationships of the handful of different categories widely used to describe individuals and populations—race, culture, ethnicity, language. Tables are produced showing the numerical relationships between these categories at the global level as well as at country, region, and continent levels.

One startling finding is that many practitioners of mission draw the language statistics they need for planning purposes from totals of mother-tongue (native) speakers, often dating from censuses 10 or 20 years old. Hardly anybody uses or is aware of the much larger totals including non-native speakers, which are often 2, 3, 4 times bigger. As Global Diagram 27 and Tables 18-8, 18-9, and 18-10 demonstrate, the errors involved in this oversight involving 983 lingua francas are considerable.

# Integrating the panorama of races, cultures, peoples, languages, lingua francas

## I. OVERVIEW COMBINING 3 GLOBAL CLASSIFICATIONS

Every cohesive or homogenous population can be described as having certain common, shared properties or descriptors. For an adequate surveying, listing, describing, analyzing, and in due course classifying of the world's vast number of peoples and populations, observers have coined at least 66 major descriptive terms. These are investigated below in 3 stages using the names of 3 different approaches which may be regarded as, and termed, incipient new sciences.

This volume presents an ethnolinguistic descriptive enumeration of each country's (1) total population, and (2) total of affiliated Christians, throughout the 20th century. In this Part the methodology is explained and the classification itself is given with its codes and full descriptive data on all peoples arranged by country.

This enumeration is built on the taxonomy and classification of race, races, ethnicity, cultures, peoples, families, with physical/geographical/genetic characteristics as set out in *The new Encyclopedia Britanica*, 15th edition, 1975-2001 versions. These annually updated versions contain lengthy expositions, in 1975 entitled 'Races of Mankind', 10 pages with photographs of faces within 16 geographical races and local races. In 2000, the major articles had become 'Human Evolution' (52 pages), 'Modern Human Populations' (11 pages), and 'The Races of Mankind' (6 pages) with scores of new terms and references listed in the volumes' main Index. The 5–page text below, and *WCE* Tables 8–1 and 8–2, are all built on this mass of new data, new understandings, and new concepts.

The inclusion of this analysis by races, peoples, tribes, and cultures is an affirmation of the centrality of indigenous cultures to local expressions of Christianity, of the right to exist of minority tribes and peoples, of their autonomy in their own areas, of their importance from the Christian standpoint vis-a-vis the world's dominant peoples and cultures, and of the need to reduce the imperialistic influence of these latter (especially Western culture) in non-Western local churches and lands. It is also an affirmation of the necessity to view people, not primarily as nationals of a given country, but primarily as members of the natural homogeneous units they belong to, through which they may most effectively be described.

The Bible frequently draws attention to the complex mosaic of peoples who compose the human race. In the Great Commission, the command of Christ is to 'Go and disciple all peoples' (*panta ta ethne*, Matthew 28:19). In attempting to depict this vast diversity of peoples, the Book of Revelation provides descriptive listings at 7 points, each time of 4 entities, as follows (using the RSV text):

1. every tribe and tongue and people and nation (Revelation 5:9);
2. every nation, all tribes and peoples and tongues (7:9);
3. many peoples and nations and tongues and kings (10:11);
4. the peoples and tribes and tongues and nations (11:9);
5. every tribe and people and tongue and nation (13:7);
6. every nation and tribe and tongue and people (14:6);
7. peoples and multitudes and nations and tongues (17:15).

In these 7 listings, 5 points can be noted: (a) 3 of the 4 entities occur in all 7 lists, namely 'nation' (an ethnic term), 'people' (a cultural term), and 'tongue' (a linguistic term); (b) another term, 'tribe' (an ethnocultural term, often with connotations of color or skin pigmentation) occurs in 5 of the lists; (c) another, 'multitudes' illustrates the demographic aspect; (d) a last term, 'kings' (here used to personify 'kingdoms'), invokes the ideas of nationality, citizenship, subject status, and the like; and (e) in other English versions than the RSV, other synonyms emerge such as 'race' for 'nation' in 10:11 (Good News Bible), 'kindred' for 'tribe' (5:9, AV/KJV), 'language' for 'tongue', et alia. The Bible can thus be said to be fully aware of the vast ethnolinguistic diversity of the world and of its importance for the Christian world mission.

From a descriptive or anthropological point of view, therefore, a human population (or an individual) has 6 related but distinct characteristics: race, color, ethnic origin, nationality, culture, and language. Race and color are inherited (passed from generation to generation), whereas culture and language are learned; and ethnic origin is a less clearly-defined characteristic referring to the main name by which a people is usually known. Ethnic groups are often grouped by anthropologists into primary ethnic culture areas. The sixth term, nationality (citizenship), may be inherited or acquired, and unlike the other 5 characteristics may be changed instantaneously and with ease. Of the 5 which cannot be changed, race and language are the clearest-defined concepts, and their worldwide manifestations have been classified by biologists and linguists respectively as follows.

### An identity code

This world ethnocultural ethnolinguistic classification can be seen to give a unique code to every segment of population anywhere in the world. Adding geopolitical codes, a population's code identifies it by ethnic group, language, country, continent, region, province, city, religion, megabloc, denomination, and the whole range of ecclesiastico-cultural descriptors.

The 2 main descriptors, or race and language, will now each be further investigated.

### ETHNOMETRICS: a race and culture code

As the name implies, this first approach measures persons and properties making up each *ethnos* (Greek for ethnic nation or people). It utilizes a scientific perspective called ethnometrics which brings together concepts from anthropology, biology, and culture. This latter term is defined as the shaping of human existence in the world. These concepts produce measurable categories that we are terming race, ethnicity, culture, people. They result in seeing the world divided into 6,600 *cultures* and a larger number of 12,600 *ethnocultural peoples*. This first approach is named 'Cultures of the World' and is described in detail in *WCE* Part 8 "Ethnosphere", Table 8–1. The approach builds on the series of 7 categories labeled

**Table 18–1. Three codes classifying 17 categories of races, cultures, languages, and peoples, with 66 alternate descriptive terms.**

| Category column 1 | Totals 2 | Example 1 3 | Example 2 4 | Example 3 5 |
|---|---|---|---|---|
| **A. RACE CODE (7 categories, 40 descriptors).** | | | | |
| 1. **Race** (stock, biological grouping, culture race, macrorace) | 5 | Mongoloid | Caucasoid | Negroid |
| 2. **Geographic race** (continental race, regional race, megarace) | 13 | Asian | European | African |
| 3. **Culture world** (cultural lifestyle, cultural worldview, culture civilization, stylized color, color pool, biogenetic pool, skin pigmentation) | 7 | Yellow | White | Black |
| 4. **Local race** (culture province, culture net, culture area, culture sphere, local breeding population, nation, national race, reproductive isolate, genetically distinct population) | 71 | Altaic | Germanic | Nilotic |
| 5. **Ethnocultural family** (culture cluster, microrace, culture complex, single breeding population, ethnic family, culture family, large grouping of specific cultures) | 395 | Turkish | British | Dinka |
| 6. **Culture** (people grouping) = one of the several or many names of groups making up an ethnocultural family | 6,629 | Rumelian Turk | English | Padang Dinka |
| 7. **Ethnocultural people** (ethnic group within a single country, people group, tribe, culture-in-country) | 12,000 | Rumelian Turks in Turkey | Britons in Britain | Padang Dinka in Sudan |
| **B. LANGUAGE CODE (9 categories, 24 descriptors)** | | | | |
| 1. **Macrozone** (sector) | 10 | Eurasian | Indo-European | Mandic |
| 2. **Zone** (microzone, phylozone, geozone) | 100 | Transasiatic | Germanic | Nilotic |
| 3. **Set** (language set) | 684 | Turkic | Germanic | West Nilotic |
| 4. **Chain** (language chain) | 1,403 | Turkic | West Germanic | Dinka-Nuer |
| 5. **Net** (network, language net) | 2,684 | Southwest Turkic | Anglo-Saxon | Dinka |
| 6. **Cluster** (outer language, language cluster) | 4,962 | Oghuz | Global English | Northeast Jieng |
| 7. **Language** (inner language, autoglossonym) | 13,510 | osmanli | Standard English | padang |
| 8. **Dialect** (sublanguage) | 30,000 | karamanli | Cockney | paloc |
| 9. **Lingua franca** (non-native usage, language influence) | 1,500 | Turkish | International English | Dinka |
| **C. PEOPLE CODE (1 additional category, 2 descriptors)** | | | | |
| 1. **People** (ethnolinguistic people = a people in one country with a specific language as mother tongue; with unique combined identity code = race code + language code) | 12,583 | Rumelian Turks in Turkey speaking osmanli | Britons in Britain speaking Standard English | Padang Dinka in Sudan speaking padang |

**AUSTRALOID**

Paiwan Aborigine

New Guinea Papuans

**CAUCASOID**

Punjabi laborers

**CAPOID**

Twa pygmies

Kalahari Bushman

Arusi Galla girl

English archbishop

**PEOPLES OF THE WORLD.** A selection illustrating widely-different racial and cultural characteristics. The 5 races (shown in bold capitals on photos delineated by thick rules) are represented here by some 15 peoples (named at lower right of each's photo), shown in the same order as in the classification in Tables 18-3, 18-4, and 18-5.

**MONGOLOID**

Jivaro warrior (Amerindian)

Korean girls

Tibetan (Panchen Lama)

Maori parliamentarian

**NEGROID**

Kabre peasant

Yoruba apostle

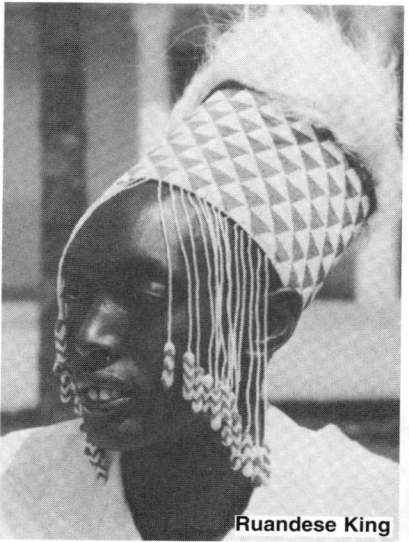

Ruandese King

Kikuyu witchdoctor

18–3 columns 3 – 9, and in Table 18–4 columns 3 – 5, and Table 18–5 columns 3 – 5.

### LINGUAMETRICS: a language code

Second come concepts from a new science dealing not with linguistics but describing itself as geolinguistics (a term coined in Dalby, *The Linguasphere register*, volume 1, pages 97-98). This term is defined as the study of the world's languages and their relationships, including language speakers, language influence, language usage, lingua francas. This produces the second new metric approach called linguametrics, with all languages classified by a LANGUAGE CODE. It results in seeing the world divided among 5,000 different *clusters* (or outer languages) and 13,500 different *languages* (or inner languages). This second approach is here named 'World Language Classification' and is described in detail in *WCE* Part 9 "Linguametrics" and in the 2-volume survey *The Linguasphere register*. Note that the code's first 6 categories below are anglicized cover names. Overall statistics under this approach are shown here in Table 18–5 columns 7 and 8.

| Table 18–2. | The globe's peoples and population classified by 11 people sizes. | |
|---|---|---|
| *Size of people* | *Peoples* | *Population* |
| Over 10 million | 101 | 4,014,806,000 |
| 1 million - 10 million | 453 | 1,307,746,000 |
| 500,000 - 1 million | 337 | 235,524,000 |
| 100,000 - 500,000 | 1,511 | 338,252,000 |
| 50,000 - 100,000 | 992 | 69,721,000 |
| 10,000 - 50,000 | 3,018 | 71,086,000 |
| 1,000 - 10,000 | 4,100 | 17,019,000 |
| 100 - 1,000 | 1,788 | 884,000 |
| under 100 | 232 | 10,800 |
| Zero | 51 | 0 |
| **Totals** | **12,583** | **6,055,048,800** |

### ETHNOLINGUISTICS: a culture/language code

Third, these 2 approaches can be merged and integrated to provide a further new approach involving both race and language, and provisionally termed the new science of ethnolinguistics. This results in a single integrated panorama and listing of a single new spectrum that is here termed *ethnolinguistic peoples*. For simplicity, the present analysis reserves for this category the definitive shorthand term *peoples*. A people is thus defined as an ethnolinguistic entity with a specific race code and a specific language code, with the 2 together constituting a PEOPLE CODE.

This third approach is here labeled 'Peoples of the World' and its 12,600 peoples are printed out in full in *WCE* Part 8 "Ethnosphere". Statistical summaries are given here as Table 18–2, Table 18–3 column 10, Table 18–4 column 6, and Table 18–5 column 6.

### Three examples of the 3 codes

This whole process can be illustrated by means of examples. The first is the Turkish language, with its autoglossonym *osmanli*, and its long list of dialects and closely-related languages (see *The Linguasphere register*, page 2:345). All the 17 category names for both race and language are as shown in column 3 of Table 18–1.

A more complex example is shown in column 4 with its 17 category names. The 'British' or 'Britons' or 'English' are a culture, in 170 countries. In each e.g. 'Britons in Britain' they form one ethnocultural people; but if they have several different languages as mother tongue, each is termed an ethnolinguistic people or for shorthand purposes, simply a people such as 'Britons in Britain speaking Standard English'.

A third example, shown in column 5, comes from Africa, giving the related names for the famed Dinka peoples of the Sudan.

Note that in the actual enumeration (as in Tables 18-2, -3, -4, and -5), we exclude the category 'ethnocultural people' because its replacement by 'ethnolinguistic people' or simply 'people' is close enough but is much more useful and usable. Note also that a 'culture' and/or a 'people', like a 'language', are all concrete realities with proper nouns rather than categories and so do not each need their own separate codes. In other words, these coding systems identify categories or types rather than the individual end products.

The rest of the ethnolinguistic or people code can be taken to be exactly the same as the 2 systems described above, with their categories of anglicized cover names. With ethnolinguistic people, as just described, this makes a grand total of 17 categories altogether, with a total of 66 different descriptors.

### RELATING THE 3 CLASSIFICATIONS

The 3 tables that follow delve stage by stage into the complex relationships that exist between races, cultures, languages, and peoples.

#### Peoples and languages by 5 races
Table 18–3 lists the 5 races of humankind and show how the globe's 71 local races and 393 ethnocultural families are divided among them. By population size, the Caucasoid race has by far the most numerous individuals. By number of cultures, the Mongoloid race is largest. By number of clusters (outer languages), the Australoid race is largest.

#### People-language similarity in names
A new variable in these comparative tables is shown in the final column 'Similarity %'. This refers to the computer-assessed similarity between a people's anglicized name and its autoglossonym. This is highest for the Australoid race, where 66% of all its peoples have names of their autoglossonyms that are recognizably close to their anglicized people names. The reason is that most have no literary tradition enabling different names to evolve. By contrast, the lowest similarity (19%) is found among Caucasoid races in which European authors would employ people names quite different from the peoples' own names for themselves and their languages.

#### Peoples and languages by 71 local races
Table 18–4 lists the 71 local races (culture areas) of humankind and gives the distribution among them of cultures, languages, and peoples. The concentrations of over 1,000 languages for certain local races only— Melanesian, Papuan, Indo-Malay, and Bantu—are striking. Almost all the figures are surprising even to persons long familiar with the languages concerned.

#### Peoples and languages by 395 cultural families
Table 18–5 is the biggest table at this point. It sets out the entire classification by race and culture, totals related cultures, peoples, and languages, and gives short but representative lists of cultures on each line representing one ethnocultural family.

#### Peoples of the world
This whole complex classification can now be illustrated by means of a series of photographs and tables. The 3 illustrations on this page show 3 African peoples exhibiting marked racial, cultural, and language characteristics. The collage of photographs opposite illustrates the 5 conventional races of humankind—Australoid, Capoid, Caucasoid, Mongoloid, and Negroid—and a small selection of 15 of their 6,629 constituent cultures and/or 12,583 constituent peoples. And Table 18–2 above enumerates this latter end product by dividing these peoples into 11 categories of their population sizes.

**Race, culture, language.** Three illustrations from Africa of these separate but related characteristics.
*Top* (1) **Race.** A youth of Negro race, Black skin color, Central Bantoid family, Mossi tribe, speaking the Moré language. In the old Mossi empire, no person with such facial incisions could be made a slave. Race, skin color, even identification scars, are inherited and permanent.
*Center* (2) **Culture.** Bassari singers and dancers in Dakar (Senegal) enact their rich cultural heritage. By individuals, culture is not so much inherited as learned.
*Bottom.* (3) **Language.** Dinka-speaking Nilotic tribesmen in Wau (Sudan) sing traditional Dinka praise songs and perform traditional tribal dance. Language also is not inherited but learned.

RACE CODE in Table 18–1, each followed by the alternate descriptive terms shown in parentheses. Column 2 labelled 'Totals' gives the total number of occurrences of each category. Thus the globe has 5 races, 13 geographic races, 71 local races, and so on.

Note that the first 6 categories are always given in this survey as anglicized cover names. Overall statistics under this approach are shown here in Table

# 2. A WORLD ETHNOCULTURAL CLASSIFICATION (=RACE CODE)

## Race

From the biological or purely physical or genetic or serological (blood-group) point of view, race (or physical type) is a biological concept referring to the taxonomic (classificatory) unit immediately below the species. Thus, the human race today consists of a single surviving species, Homo Sapiens, and 5 surviving subspecies or races or racial stocks (many others having long become extinct): Australoid, Capoid, Caucasoid, Mongoloid and Negroid. Between these are various hybrid races, known as clines (Negroid-Caucasoid, Mongoloid-Caucasoid, etc). Race covers such physical features as skin color, stature, blood group, head shape and hair type. From the point of view of skin color, all can be given a stylized label each in order to permit approximate numerical analysis. For the 5 races, these are, respectively, (1) Grey (a stylized color combining the concepts 'early', 'aboriginal', non-White, non-Black, non-Yellow), (2) also Grey, (3) White, (4) Yellow, (5) Black. Government censuses often enumerate populations in this way, especially in the use of White and Black. In Portuguese, in the 1960 and 1970 censuses of Mozambique, Chinese persons were classified as 'Yellows', defined there as persons with 4 Yellow grandparents; and in the Angola censuses, there were 'Whites' (Brancos), 'Blacks', (Pretos), etc. In Spanish, the 1903 census of the Philippines enumerated people as Moreno (Brown), Amarillo (Yellow), Blanco (White), Negro (Black), etc. In this classification, certain geographical races are labeled Tan, Brown, Red. Tan refers to ochre- or olive- or yellow-brown- or light-brown-skinned peoples. Red is a term traditionally in use for American Indians. The result of all these typologies is a series of possible classifications which vary considerably from scholar to scholar but which approximate to the one given here as Table 18–5 entitled CULTURES OF THE WORLD, especially in the first and third capital letters of each people's coded name.

Where statistics of race are to be gathered, government census and allied bureau often define their terms with great precision. In the USA, employment regulations define the term 'Indian' exactly as (a) members of any recognized Indian tribe now under Federal jurisdiction, (b) descendants of any such members residing within the present boundaries of any Indian reservation, (c) all others of one-half or more of Indian blood of tribes indigenous to the United States, (d) Eskimos and other Aboriginal people of Alaska, and (e) persons of at least one-quarter degree Indian ancestry. In Viet Nam, 'Chinese' are defined as anyone with a Chinese ancestor 5 generations back.

An important extension of race is the concept of geographical race, as popularized and described by *The new Encyclopaedia Britannica* (1975, 2000). (In the 2000 edition the article is virtually unchanged but the actual term has been shortened to 'geographic race'). Geographical race is defined as one of the 13 broad, geographically-delimited races of mankind, a collection of human populations, usually rather similar physically, delimited by some natural boundary, such as an ocean, and tending to have similar heredity, skin color, hair type, language, and the like. Table 18–5 follows these guidelines and in fact utilizes the same nomenclature for the major races.

An important caution needs to be given here. The concept of different races is regarded by many scientists as outdated, for the reasons that the multiple origins of man have not been proven, population movements with resulting interbreeding have been continuous since the origin of man, and that populations today grade into each other to such an extent that no pure stocks exist. There is no such thing as a 'pure' race; instead, there exist almost imperceptible gradations of genetic character from one group of people to the next. For these purposes this classification has some value, it being understood that none of the 5 races and 7 colors are original or pure or isolated stocks and that all overlap to a greater or lesser extent.

## Culture

A people is characterized by a distinctive culture based on a distinctive mother tongue. A culture can be described as a group of people who do things together in a patterned way: sharing beliefs and customs with a worldview at the centre, together with values and standards of judgement and conduct, common institutions, a common language with shared proverbs, myths, folk-tales and arts, a common history, and common land or territory. Classifications of peoples using this criterion usually divide peoples into ethnic culture areas. An example of this may be seen in the map and table 'Primary European ethnic culture areas' in *The new Encyclopaedia Britannica* (1975), which divides Europe into 4 major culture areas, 22 culture provinces, and 158 distinct peoples. A different aspect of culture is that it can cover a whole range of social strata or socio-religious stratification, such as India's over 26,000 castes in the 4 categories of Vedic theory.

### COMPILING THE ETHNOCULTURAL DATABASE

This database can be termed by many adjectives. It is an attempt to describe the world of peoples by various overall taxonomic characteristics—ethnic, racial, biogenetic, cultural, linguistic, ethnolinguistic, ethnocultural. It has been built up country by country from a large variety of sources—government censuses, public-opinion polls, sociological or anthropological research, sociopolitical studies, bibliographies and literature, ecclesiastical enquiries and reports of all kinds. These sources number some 800,000 titles or books on ethnolinguistic names and criteria, available on the shelves of the world's 50,000 leading libraries. A small selection are listed in the bibliography below immediately after this codebook section.

The meaning of the codes and columns in Table 18–5 will now be given.

### Codes for Table 18–5 'Cultures of the world'
This table has 11 columns, as follows.

### Column 1: A multi-character code
This first column consists of a classification of race and culture and ethnic family, shown below as the 4-page Table 18–5. In it, each ethnolinguistic people (or culture, or microrace) is given a 5- or 6-character alphanumeric code (example: CEW19m) defining its race, geographical race, major culture area (stylized color), ethnocultural family (local race), and its own unique code number as a culture or microrace. These 6 codes are composed as follows:

*Subcolumns*
1 *Race (stock, biological grouping)*
   A = Australoid
   B = Capoid
   C = Caucasian (Caucasoid)
   M = Mongolian (Mongoloid)
   N = Negro (Negroid)
2 *Geographic race (continental race, region)*
   A = African
   E = European
   F = Afro-American
   I = American Indian
   L = Latin American
   M = Middle Eastern
   N = Indo-Iranian
   O = Oceanic
   P = Pacific
   R = Arctic Mongoloid
   S = Asian
   U = Austro-Asiatic
   Y = Early African
3 *Culture world (stylized color/skin pigmentation, biogenetic pool)*
   B = Black
   G = Grey
   N = Brown
   R = Red
   T = Tan
   W = White
   Y = Yellow
Note: In the listing in Tables 18-4 and 18-5 this variable 'Culture world' is given in subcolumn 3 and (unlike the other 5 subcolumns) is not given its own separate lines in column 2.
4-5 *Local race (culture net, local breeding population/reproductive isolate, genetically distinct population, nation)*
A 2-digit code numbered 01 to 71 defines each local race uniquely (the 3 preceding letters serve merely to further classify the population by race and culture world/stylized color). The codes for the 71 local races are given below in Tables 18-4 and 18-5 'Cultures of the world' and in the people classification in *WCE* Part 8, Table 8-2, 'Peoples of the world'.
6 *Ethnocultural family (culture cluster, microrace, single breeding population, ethnic group, culture family)*
In numerous cases where a local race is particularly large or important, especially on the Christian scene, its code has been given here a further character subdividing the local race into its major component culture clusters or families or other groupings. When this further character is employed, it is added in the form of lowercase letters (a,b,c,d,e,f, etc), as shown below. The letters x, y and z, when used, refer to any remaining cultures and peoples not covered by the preceding a,b,c... series.

This classification can be greatly extended to encompass all lower levels of subdivisions. This is done in *WCE* Table 8-2 by adding the 8-character language code, as described in *WCE* Part 9 "LinguaMetrics". The resulting variable, termed 'Identity code', then describes subdivisions of each culture cluster, where such exist.

The remainder of the 9 columns of Table 18–5 have the following meanings (Table 18–4 has the same meanings except column 3 = Population in AD 2000, and column 4 = Ethnocultural families):

---

**Table 18–3. The 5 races of humankind with their constituent geographic races, culture worlds, local races, ethnocultural families, cultures, peoples, and languages, AD 2000.**

| Race | Code | Population | Races | Geographic races | Culture worlds | Local races | Ethno-cultural families | Cultures | Peoples | Clusters | Languages | Similarity % | AC |
|---|---|---|---|---|---|---|---|---|---|---|---|---|---|
| *1* | *2* | *3* | *4* | *5* | *6* | *7* | *8* | *9* | *10* | *11* | *12* | *13* | *14* |
| Australoid | A | 69,924,000 | 1 | 2 | 2 | 10 | 32 | 1,693 | 1,839 | 1,828 | 3,933 | 66.2 | 17.8 |
| Capoid | B | 1,154,000 | 1 | 1 | 1 | 2 | 5 | 78 | 113 | 81 | 183 | 33.6 | 36.7 |
| Caucasoid | C | 3,057,303,000 | 1 | 4 | 6 | 24 | 126 | 816 | 3,741 | 263 | 1,115 | 18.6 | 37.6 |
| Mongoloid | M | 2,265,858,000 | 1 | 4 | 5 | 19 | 127 | 2,093 | 3,621 | 1,603 | 4,345 | 44.2 | 14.5 |
| Negroid | N | 648,090,000 | 1 | 2 | 3 | 16 | 105 | 1,949 | 3,030 | 1,187 | 3,933 | 49.6 | 60.6 |
| Other minor peoples | | 12,720,000 | | | | | | | 239 | | | – | 32.4 |
| Totals | | 6,055,049,000 | 5 | 13 | 17 | 71 | 395 | 6,629 | 12,583 | 4,962 | 13,509 | 41.0 | 31.2 |

**Table 18–4.** An overview of the 71 local races (culture areas) of humankind with their constituent ethnocultural families, cultures, peoples, and languages, AD 2000.

| RACE GEOGRAPHIC RACE Local race | | POPULATION | CULTURE | | PEOPLE | LANGUAGE | | Similarity | AC |
|---|---|---|---|---|---|---|---|---|---|
| Code 1 | name 2 | in 2000 3 | Ethno-cultural families 4 | cultures 5 | peoples 6 | clusters 7 | languages 8 | % 9 | % 10 |
| A | **AUSTRALOID** (Archaic White) | 69,924,000 | 32 | 1,693 | 1,839 | 1,828 | 3,933 | 66 | 17.9 |
| AU | AUSTRO-ASIATIC | 60,413,000 | 19 | 316 | 419 | 449 | 1,071 | 52 | 8.7 |
| AUG01 | Ainu/Aborigine | 399,000 | 2 | 17 | 17 | 26 | 109 | 47 | 82.0 |
| AUG02 | Australian Aborigine | 193,000 | 1 | 57 | 59 | 296 | 633 | 54 | 67.9 |
| AUG03 | Mon-Khmer | 20,214,000 | 5 | 121 | 185 | 49 | 148 | 55 | 7.7 |
| AUG04 | Munda-Santal | 11,753,000 | 5 | 26 | 38 | 8 | 25 | 63 | 9.0 |
| AUG05 | Negrito (Oceanic/Asiatic) | 1,554,000 | 1 | 60 | 69 | 59 | 109 | 46 | 73.5 |
| AUG06 | Pre-Dravidian | 26,299,000 | 4 | 34 | 50 | 10 | 46 | 42 | 3.9 |
| AUG07 | Vedda | 380 | 1 | 1 | 1 | 1 | 1 | 0 | 50.0 |
| AO | OCEANIC | 9,511,000 | 13 | 1,377 | 1,420 | 1,379 | 2,862 | 70 | 75.9 |
| AON08 | Fijian | 355,000 | 1 | 8 | 12 | 16 | 74 | 92 | 96.1 |
| AON09 | Melanesian | 4,307,000 | 6 | 514 | 520 | 505 | 1,235 | 65 | 75.5 |
| AON10 | Papuan | 4,849,000 | 6 | 855 | 888 | 858 | 1,553 | 73 | 74.9 |
| B | **CAPOID** (Archaic African) | 1,154,000 | 5 | 78 | 113 | 81 | 183 | 34 | 36.7 |
| BY | EARLY AFRICAN | 1,154,000 | 5 | 78 | 113 | 81 | 183 | 34 | 36.7 |
| BYG11 | Khoisan | 602,000 | 4 | 58 | 81 | 79 | 171 | 31 | 51.7 |
| BYG12 | Pygmy | 552,000 | 1 | 20 | 32 | 2 | 12 | 41 | 20.3 |
| C | **CAUCASIAN** (Caucasoid) | 3,057,303,000 | 126 | 816 | 3,741 | 263 | 1,115 | 19 | 37.6 |
| CE | EUROPEAN | 923,069,000 | 63 | 196 | 1,745 | 79 | 450 | 15 | 74.5 |
| CEW13 | Albanian | 6,225,000 | 1 | 8 | 20 | 2 | 18 | 25 | 34.7 |
| CEW14 | Armenian | 7,467,000 | 1 | 2 | 50 | 1 | 3 | 0 | 83.2 |
| CEW15 | Baltic | 5,587,000 | 2 | 2 | 35 | 2 | 5 | 0 | 87.8 |
| CEW16 | Basque | 3,223,000 | 1 | 5 | 15 | 1 | 12 | 7 | 89.8 |
| CEW17 | Caucasian | 8,500,000 | 4 | 41 | 119 | 20 | 52 | 47 | 28.8 |
| CEW18 | Celtic | 13,383,000 | 5 | 9 | 21 | 4 | 25 | 24 | 80.0 |
| CEW19 | Germanic (Teutonic) | 367,258,000 | 19 | 36 | 557 | 17 | 152 | 6 | 70.8 |
| CEW20 | Greek | 14,188,000 | 1 | 5 | 88 | 2 | 12 | 0 | 96.2 |
| CEW21 | Latin (Romance) | 207,479,000 | 13 | 65 | 484 | 22 | 131 | 29 | 84.0 |
| CEW22 | Slav | 289,759,000 | 16 | 23 | 356 | 8 | 40 | 7 | 72.5 |
| CN | INDO-IRANIAN | 1,414,592,000 | 33 | 332 | 988 | 92 | 390 | 31 | 5.1 |
| CNN23 | Dravidian | 230,789,000 | 5 | 40 | 121 | 19 | 39 | 48 | 17.8 |
| CNT24 | Iranian | 127,263,000 | 8 | 77 | 237 | 28 | 98 | 27 | 0.4 |
| CNN25 | North Indian | 1,056,541,000 | 20 | 215 | 630 | 45 | 253 | 30 | 2.9 |
| CL | LATIN AMERICAN | 362,353,000 | 4 | 10 | 91 | 4 | 19 | 0 | 92.6 |
| CLT26 | Latin-American White (Branco) | 88,232,000 | 1 | 1 | 6 | 1 | 11 | 0 | 91.5 |
| CLT27 | Latin-American White (Blanco) | 87,176,000 | 1 | 3 | 43 | 0 | 0 | 0 | 88.4 |
| CLN28 | Mestiço (Portuguese) | 20,476,000 | 1 | 1 | 3 | 0 | 0 | 0 | 94.8 |
| CLN29 | Mestizo (Spanish) | 166,470,000 | 1 | 5 | 39 | 3 | 8 | 0 | 95.2 |
| CM | MIDDLE EASTERN | 357,289,000 | 26 | 278 | 917 | 88 | 256 | 13 | 15.1 |
| CMT30 | Arab (Arabic) | 228,527,000 | 1 | 36 | 378 | 9 | 42 | 11 | 8.1 |
| CMT31 | Assyrian | 903,000 | 1 | 6 | 33 | 1 | 9 | 9 | 90.3 |
| CMT32 | Berber | 31,619,000 | 12 | 43 | 103 | 5 | 29 | 12 | 0.2 |
| CMT33 | Cushitic | 50,733,000 | 6 | 96 | 149 | 57 | 130 | 36 | 20.6 |
| CMT34 | Ethiopic | 28,272,000 | 4 | 14 | 30 | 10 | 22 | 17 | 80.6 |
| CMT35 | Jewish | 16,672,000 | 1 | 82 | 217 | 5 | 23 | 3 | 3.5 |
| CMT36 | Maltese | 563,000 | 1 | 1 | 7 | 1 | 1 | 0 | 95.0 |
| M | **MONGOLIAN** (Mongoloid, Asiatic) | 2,265,858,000 | 127 | 2,093 | 3,621 | 1,603 | 4,345 | 44 | 14.5 |
| MI | AMERICAN INDIAN | 77,647,000 | 20 | 811 | 1,109 | 713 | 1,746 | 45 | 90.4 |
| MIR37 | Central Amerindian | 32,515,000 | 8 | 258 | 341 | 129 | 402 | 43 | 93.1 |
| MIR38 | Northern Amerindian | 12,335,000 | 3 | 175 | 213 | 174 | 380 | 68 | 76.2 |
| MIR39 | Southern Amerindian | 32,797,000 | 9 | 378 | 555 | 410 | 964 | 38 | 93.1 |
| MR | ARCTIC MONGOLOID | 160,000 | 2 | 13 | 20 | 14 | 35 | 10 | 80.0 |
| MRY40 | Eskimo-Aleut | 160,000 | 2 | 13 | 20 | 14 | 35 | 10 | 80.0 |
| MS | ASIAN | 2,182,415,000 | 85 | 1,190 | 2,347 | 814 | 2,430 | 44 | 11.6 |
| MSY41 | Altaic | 163,992,000 | 15 | 62 | 314 | 17 | 67 | 50 | 1.0 |
| MSY42 | Chinese | 1,222,179,000 | 3 | 38 | 272 | 18 | 75 | 0 | 7.7 |
| MSY43 | Eurasian | 1,858,000 | 1 | 12 | 26 | 0 | 4 | 0 | 47.3 |
| MSY44 | Indo-Malay | 306,458,000 | 20 | 648 | 830 | 543 | 1,595 | 57 | 31.2 |
| MSY45 | Japanese | 130,012,000 | 2 | 12 | 51 | 5 | 25 | 16 | 3.3 |
| MSY46 | Korean | 75,665,000 | 1 | 1 | 36 | 3 | 10 | 0 | 27.9 |
| MSY47 | Miao-Yao | 12,875,000 | 2 | 22 | 46 | 14 | 37 | 17 | 4.6 |
| MSY48 | Paleoasiatic | 36,000 | 1 | 10 | 10 | 7 | 10 | 40 | 12.5 |
| MSY49 | Tai | 90,070,000 | 5 | 51 | 111 | 18 | 95 | 53 | 1.5 |
| MSY50 | Tibeto-Burmese | 82,291,000 | 20 | 287 | 477 | 171 | 449 | 59 | 9.6 |
| MSW51 | Uralian | 25,006,000 | 12 | 35 | 139 | 14 | 51 | 19 | 81.2 |
| MSY52 | Viet-Muong | 71,972,000 | 3 | 12 | 35 | 4 | 12 | 26 | 7.9 |
| MP | PACIFIC | 5,636,000 | 20 | 79 | 145 | 62 | 134 | 48 | 90.5 |
| MPY53 | Euronesian | 3,900,000 | 1 | 17 | 35 | 2 | 12 | 6 | 92.6 |
| MPY54 | Micronesian | 297,000 | 8 | 23 | 34 | 18 | 32 | 62 | 93.3 |
| MPY55 | Polynesian | 1,439,000 | 11 | 39 | 76 | 42 | 90 | 62 | 84.2 |
| N | **NEGROID** (Negro, Equatorial) | 648,090,000 | 105 | 1,949 | 3,030 | 1,187 | 3,933 | 50 | 60.6 |
| NA | AFRICAN | 509,473,000 | 95 | 1,874 | 2,870 | 1,184 | 3,880 | 52 | 53.6 |
| NAB56 | Bantoid | 74,513,000 | 3 | 404 | 574 | 322 | 847 | 46 | 22.5 |
| NAB57 | Bantu | 233,026,000 | 17 | 598 | 955 | 220 | 1,145 | 61 | 72.1 |
| NAN58 | Eurafrican (Coloured) | 10,208,000 | 1 | 32 | 83 | 3 | 24 | 7 | 79.9 |
| NAB59 | Guinean (Kwa) | 78,414,000 | 15 | 185 | 271 | 147 | 527 | 56 | 65.1 |
| NAB60 | Hausa-Chadic | 33,980,000 | 2 | 187 | 247 | 188 | 443 | 55 | 7.3 |
| NAB61 | Kanuri (Saharan) | 6,290,000 | 1 | 11 | 29 | 5 | 10 | 52 | 0.0 |
| NAB62 | Nilotic (Para-Nilotic) | 24,779,000 | 20 | 110 | 168 | 82 | 220 | 41 | 57.5 |
| NAB63 | Nuclear Mande | 17,706,000 | 13 | 48 | 108 | 25 | 86 | 36 | 2.7 |
| NAB64 | Peripheral Mande | 5,208,000 | 11 | 16 | 26 | 10 | 19 | 58 | 16.6 |
| NAB65 | Songhai | 4,599,000 | 3 | 5 | 17 | 4 | 8 | 24 | 0.3 |
| NAB66 | Sudanic | 20,750,000 | 9 | 278 | 392 | 178 | 551 | 54 | 53.7 |
| NF | AFRO-AMERICAN | 138,617,000 | 10 | 75 | 160 | 3 | 53 | 8 | 86.5 |
| NFB67 | Dutch-speaking | 694,000 | 2 | 7 | 14 | 0 | 4 | 0 | 83.7 |
| NFB68 | English-speaking | 41,064,000 | 2 | 47 | 89 | 2 | 36 | 13 | 74.8 |
| NFB69 | French-speaking | 12,386,000 | 2 | 10 | 22 | 1 | 9 | 0 | 91.7 |
| NFB70 | Portuguese-speaking | 56,169,000 | 2 | 4 | 7 | 0 | 1 | 14 | 92.5 |
| NFB71 | Spanish-speaking | 28,304,000 | 2 | 7 | 28 | 0 | 3 | 0 | 89.2 |
| | Other minor peoples | 12,720,000 | | —— | 239 | — | — | — | 32.4 |
| | **GLOBE** | **6,055,049,000** | **395** | **6,629** | **12,583** | **4,962** | **13,509** | **41** | **31.2** |

*Column 2:* Anglicized name of race or family.

*Column 3:* Population in AD 1900.

*Column 4:* Population in AD 2000

*Column 5:* Cultures

*Column 6:* Peoples

*Column 7:* Language clusters (outer languages)

*Column 8:* Languages

*Column 9:* Similarity: the % ratio of all cases where the anglicized name of a people or culture using a language is similar to the autoglossonym of its mother tongue.

*Column 10:* Affiliated Christians, %

*Column 11:* Names of a selection of cultures

### Index of cultures, peoples and languages

A comprehensive index to all names in this classification is given in the related *World Christian database*. This index enables readers immediately to locate any name they come across.

### Statistical analysis

Using the codes above, the ethnolinguistic compositions of each country's population, and of its affiliated Christians, were then quantified. Two procedures were employed. The first was to add a 3-digit number in front of each code, this number being the percentage (to the first 5 places of decimals, from 0.1% to 99.9%, omitting decimal points) of the country's total population, or its total of affiliated Christians, who belong to the people that follow it. Thus if the composition of a country's population was '80.0% Chinese, 20% British', this was converted to the 2 coded elements '800MSY42a, 200CEW19i'.

The second procedure was to calculate, via census statistics where available, the same percentages to 5 places of decimals. These results are then shown in *WCE* Table 8-2, column 3.

### A rule is necessary

The classification as shown in *WCE* Tables 8-1 and 8-2 is closely printed in order to provide the reader with as complete an overview as possible, in as compact a space as possible. Readers should use a ruler or straight edge to find their way around as quickly as they require, both vertically and horizontally.

### Summary description

The following additional points should be noted by way of explanation and summary. (1) Names of the 5 races, 13 geographic races, 7 culture worlds, 71 local races, 395 ethnocultural families, 4,962 language cultures, and 12,600 constituent peoples shown here are given in their usual generally-preferred anglicized form (usually giving the singular form only and not the plural; excluding their forms in other languages; and in almost all cases omitting diacritical marks) in strictly alphabetical order by name. Their codes, accordingly, are not fully in alphabetical order throughout these tables. The local races can then be seen to be numbered 01-71 in numerical sequence. (2) This entire classification gives anglicized (English) names only, together with a handful of non-English terms which have now come into English use also (e.g. Mestizo), or which are necessary here for exact identification or to avoid confusion. Prefixes for Bantu and other peoples (A-, Ama-, Ba-, Ma-, Ovi-, Va-, Wa-, &c) are omitted.

A large number of all these anglicized names have equivalents in French, German, Italian, Portuguese, Spanish and other international languages, in addition to names in use in their own local languages. These names in other languages are too numerous to be included below, but are stored in the longer computerized version. In the same way, derivations and meanings of these anglicized names are not given here but in the computerized version (many in fact mean simply 'people' or 'man'); for a comprehensive reference to meanings, see the *New Encyclopaedia Britannica*. (3) Local races (in the second column below, in boldface type) are subdivided into their component clusters in cases where a local race is particularly large or important, especially on the Christian scene. (4) The European geographic race as defined

## Table 18–5. Cultures of the world: the 395 ethnocultural families (microraces) of humankind with their constituent cultures, peoples, and languages, AD 1900 – AD 2000.

| Code<br>1 | **RACE**<br>GEOGRAPHIC RACE<br>**Local race**<br>Ethnocultural family<br>2 | *Pop 1900*<br>3 | *Pop 2000*<br>4 | *Cultures*<br>5 | *Peoples*<br>6 | *Clusters*<br>7 | *Langs*<br>8 | *Sim*<br>9 | *AC*<br>10 | *A selection of constituent cultures, peoples, tribes, languages, alternative names or synonyms*<br>11 |
|---|---|---|---|---|---|---|---|---|---|---|
| A | **AUSTRALOID** (Archaic White) | 12,257,700 | 69,924,000 | 1,693 | 1,839 | 1,828 | 3,933 | 66 | 17.9 | Australoid (Archaic White, Proto-Caucasoid, Classical Australoid) |
| AU | AUSTRO-ASIATIC | 10,274,100 | 60,413,000 | 316 | 419 | 449 | 1,071 | 52 | 8.7 | Aboriginals in Australasia, Southeast Asia, India; Austro-Asiatic |
| AUG01 | **Ainu/Aborigine** | 58,100 | 399,000 | 17 | 17 | 26 | 109 | 47 | 82.0 | Ainu; also Ainu-like Formosan Aborigine |
| AUG01a | Aborigine | 55,700 | 382,000 | 15 | 15 | 24 | 106 | 53 | 84.6 | Asian Aborigines, Amis, Bunan, Drukai, Gaoshan, Paiwan, Pyuma, Tsou |
| AUG01b | Ainu | 2,400 | 17,000 | 2 | 2 | 2 | 3 | 0 | 22.4 | Ainu |
| AUG02 | **Australian Aborigine** | 41,600 | 193,000 | 57 | 59 | 296 | 633 | 54 | 67.9 | Arunta, Bidjandjara, Gunwingguan, Kariera, Mumgin, Pama-Nyungan, Tiwi, Warramunga |
| AUG03 | **Mon-Khmer** | 3,561,000 | 20,214,000 | 121 | 185 | 49 | 148 | 55 | 7.7 | Mon-Khmer, Australoid peoples with Mongoloid admixture |
| AUG03a | Khasi | 260,000 | 1,216,000 | 2 | 3 | 1 | 3 | 100 | 48.4 | Khasi, Synteng (Pnar) |
| AUG03b | Khmer | 2,340,000 | 11,941,000 | 4 | 11 | 1 | 5 | 0 | 0.6 | Khmer (Cambodian) |
| AUG03c | Mon | 218,000 | 1,166,000 | 4 | 4 | 2 | 7 | 75 | 0.9 | Mon (Peguan), Nyahkur, Talaing |
| AUG03d | Nicobarese | 5,000 | 47,700 | 6 | 7 | 2 | 6 | 57 | 81.1 | Central (Camorta, Kathcall, Nancowry, Trinkat), North (Bompaka, Car, Chowra, Teressa), South; Shompe |
| AUG03z | other Mon-Khmer | 738,000 | 5,843,000 | 105 | 160 | 43 | 127 | 58 | 14.6 | Bahnar, Bo, Boloven, Brao, Cham Re, Katu, Khmu, Ma, Mnong, Oi, Palaung, Pear, Sedang, So, Suai, Wa |
| AUG04 | **Munda-Santal** | 3,523,000 | 11,753,000 | 26 | 38 | 8 | 25 | 63 | 9.0 | Munda (Kherwarl): Northern, Southern, Western |
| AUG04a | Ho | 462,000 | 1,134,000 | 1 | 2 | 0 | 1 | 100 | 0.6 | Ho (Lankakol), Lohara |
| AUG04b | Mundari | 462,000 | 1,652,000 | 3 | 5 | 0 | 2 | 80 | 26.0 | Birhor, Mundari (Kol, Horo) |
| AUG04c | Santal | 1,906,000 | 7,019,000 | 3 | 9 | 1 | 4 | 78 | 3.6 | Karmali (Kohle), Mahili (Mahli), Pahariya (Mal Paharia), Santal (Santali, Satar), Turi |
| AUG04d | Saora | 231,000 | 302,000 | 1 | 1 | 1 | 2 | 0 | 22.5 | Saora (Savara, Sora) |
| AUG04z | other Munda-Santal | 462,000 | 1,646,000 | 18 | 21 | 6 | 16 | 52 | 18.2 | Asuri, Bhumij, Chenchu, Gadaba (Gutob), Geta, Juang, Kharia, Koda, Korku, Korwa, Nahari, Remo, Turi |
| AUG05 | **Negrito (Oceanic/Asiatic)** | 77,900 | 1,554,000 | 60 | 69 | 59 | 109 | 46 | 73.5 | Aeta, Andamanese, Malaccan (Aslian), New Guinea Pygmy (Aiome), Ekari (Kapauku), Semang, Senoi |
| AUG06 | **Pre-Dravidian** | 3,007,300 | 26,299,000 | 34 | 50 | 10 | 46 | 42 | 3.9 | Proto-Australoid (Pre-Dravidian Aboriginal) |
| AUG06a | Bhil | 1,154,000 | 13,870,000 | 18 | 22 | 3 | 32 | 45 | 0.4 | Bhil (Bhili), Gamti, Pawari Bhil, Tadvi Bhil |
| AUG06b | Gond | 1,385,000 | 8,997,000 | 7 | 16 | 2 | 4 | 13 | 0.5 | Gond (Gondi): Adilalad, Betul, Bisonhom Maria, Chhindwara, Hill Maria, Koya, Mandla, Muria |
| AUG06c | Oraon | 462,000 | 2,124,000 | 3 | 5 | 1 | 3 | 40 | 43.5 | Oraon (Kurukh, Kurux, Uraon) |
| AUG06z | other Pre-Dravidian | 6,300 | 1,308,000 | 6 | 7 | 4 | 7 | 100 | 1.5 | Kadir, Kandh, Khond (Kui), Kolami, Kolarian, Kurumba, Malto, Naiki, Paniyan |
| AUG07 | **Vedda** | 5,200 | 380 | 1 | 1 | 1 | 1 | 0 | 50.0 | Vedda (Indo-Australoid, Bedda, Veddah, Veddoid, Weddo) |
| AO | OCEANIC | 1,983,600 | 9,511,000 | 1,377 | 1,420 | 1,379 | 2,862 | 70 | 75.9 | Melanesian, Melanesoid, Oceanic Negro, Oceanic Negroid, Papuasian; Heonesian |
| AON08 | **Fijian** | 54,300 | 355,000 | 8 | 12 | 16 | 74 | 92 | 96.1 | Fijian (Bauan), Kadavu, Rotuman |
| AON09 | **Melanesian** | 594,600 | 4,307,000 | 514 | 520 | 505 | 1,235 | 65 | 75.5 | Melanesian (island, coastal) |
| AON09a | New Caledonian | 25,900 | 81,400 | 33 | 34 | 32 | 76 | 38 | 89.3 | New Caledonian: Houailou (Wailu), Lai, Lifu (Lific), Maré (Nengone), Ponérihouen |
| AON09b | New Guinea Melanesian | 227,000 | 838,000 | 225 | 225 | 250 | 591 | 69 | 84.4 | Bwaidoga, Dobu, Graged, Keopara, Kiriwina, Motu, Police Motu, Tuna, Usiai, Yabem |
| AON09c | New Hebridean | 41,600 | 150,000 | 106 | 108 | 91 | 222 | 66 | 88.0 | New Hebridean; Efate, Epi, Malo, Mota, Nguna-Tongoa, Paama, Tanna |
| AON09d | Solomoni Melanesian | 82,800 | 401,000 | 69 | 69 | 64 | 149 | 70 | 92.5 | Solomoni: Bambatana, Bugotu, Kerebuto, Kwaio, Maringe, Nggela, Roviana, Saa, To'abaita, Vaturanga |
| AON09e | Western Melanesian | 210,000 | 2,742,000 | 77 | 79 | 68 | 197 | 65 | 68.9 | Ambonese, Ceramese, Irianese (Bonggo, Sobei, Tobati, Yamna), other Moluccan and South Moluccan |
| AON09f | Neo-Melanesian | 7,300 | 95,300 | 4 | 5 | 0 | 0 | 20 | 84.5 | Half-Melanesian, Melanesian-Papuan, Bislama Creole |
| AON10 | **Papuan** | 1,334,700 | 4,849,000 | 855 | 888 | 858 | 1,553 | 73 | 74.9 | Papuan (Indo-Pacific, Non-Austronesian), Papuasian |
| AON10a | Irianese Papuan | 273,000 | 962,000 | 199 | 211 | 201 | 391 | 65 | 66.7 | Asmat, Bentoeni, Damal, Dani, Djabi, Jali, Marind-Anim, Sentani |
| AON10b | New Guinea Papuan (Eastern) | 874,000 | 3,210,000 | 599 | 620 | 600 | 1,035 | 76 | 83.8 | Awa, Chimbu, Enga, Gadsup, Gahuku, Guhu-Samane, Kiwai, New Britain Papuan, Orokaiva, Wabago |
| AON10c | North Halmaheran | 77,900 | 291,000 | 16 | 16 | 14 | 32 | 69 | 24.8 | Galelos, Ibu, Kau, Loloda, Makian, Modole, Morotai, Papu, Tabaru, Temate, Tidore, Tobelo, Wai |
| AON10d | Solomoni Papuan | 28,200 | 117,000 | 20 | 20 | 23 | 44 | 80 | 94.0 | Solomoni Papuan: Bougainvillian, Rendova, Russell Islander, Santa Cruz, Savosavo, Vella Lavella (Bilua) |
| AON10e | Timorese Papuan | 77,900 | 263,000 | 18 | 18 | 18 | 40 | 78 | 43.7 | Alorese, Kisarese, Timorese Papuan |
| AON10f | Torres Strait Islander | 3,700 | 6,400 | 3 | 3 | 2 | 11 | 0 | 65.6 | Torres Strait Islander: Mabuiag, Mer, Saibai |
| B | **CAPOID** (Archaic African) | 134,000 | 1,154,000 | 78 | 113 | 81 | 183 | 34 | 36.7 | Descendants of Early, Paleolithic or Prehistoric Africans |
| BY | EARLY AFRICAN | 134,000 | 1,154,000 | 78 | 113 | 81 | 183 | 34 | 36.7 | Aboriginal descendants of Bushmanoid, Sangoan Pygmy, Pygmoid |
| BYG11 | **Khoisan** | 49,900 | 602,000 | 58 | 81 | 79 | 171 | 31 | 51.7 | Khoisan (Bushmanoid, Click): Central Khoisan (Khoe), North (Zhu), South (Kwi) |
| BYG11a | Bergdama | 12,500 | 77,700 | 1 | 1 | 0 | 1 | 0 | 90.0 | Bergdama (Damara, Haukoin, Mountain Damara) |
| BYG11b | East African Bushman | 15,200 | 228,000 | 19 | 24 | 10 | 16 | 33 | 39.0 | Boni, Dorobo (Asa, Okiek), Kindiga (Hadzapi, Tindiga), Manjo, Midgan (Ribi), Sandawe, Sanye, Teuso |
| BYG11c | Hottentot | 6,300 | 128,000 | 4 | 6 | 5 | 25 | 50 | 93.8 | Cape Hottentot (Grigriqua), Nama (Namaqua), Gimsbok Nama |
| BYG11d | South African Bushman | 15,900 | 168,000 | 34 | 50 | 64 | 129 | 28 | 19.1 | Dukwe, Gwi, Heikum, Hiechware, Hukwe, Korana, Koroca, Kung, Namib, Naron, Nusan, Ohekwe, Xam |
| BYG12 | **Pygmy** | 84,100 | 552,000 | 20 | 32 | 2 | 12 | 41 | 20.3 | Pygmy (Negrillo, Pygmoid): Binga (Bongo, Koa, Yaga), Gesera (Twa, Zigaba), Mbuti (Aka, Efe, Twides) |
| C | **CAUCASIAN** (Caucasoid) | 842,807,920 | 3,057,303,000 | 816 | 3,741 | 263 | 1,115 | 19 | 37.6 | Caucasian, Caucasoid, Indo-European |
| CE | EUROPEAN | 440,971,120 | 923,069,000 | 196 | 1,745 | 79 | 450 | 15 | 74.5 | European: Alpine, Armenian, Mediterranean, Nordic |
| CEW13 | **Albanian** | 1,434,000 | 6,225,000 | 8 | 20 | 2 | 18 | 25 | 34.7 | Albanian (Shiptar): Gheg (Dukagjin, Malësia), Tosk (Camõvia, Labëria, Myzeqe) |
| CEW14 | **Armenian** | 2,505,000 | 7,467,000 | 2 | 50 | 1 | 3 | 0 | 83.2 | Armenian (Ashksarhik, Hay, Hayq), Thrace-Phrygian, Ermeni |
| CEW15 | **Baltic** | 2,195,000 | 5,587,000 | 2 | 35 | 2 | 5 | 0 | 87.8 | Balt: East Baltic, Baltic-Slavic |
| CEW15a | Latvian | 649,000 | 1,544,000 | 1 | 17 | 1 | 1 | 0 | 80.2 | Latvian (Lett, Lettish), Latgalian |
| CEW15b | Lithuanian | 1,546,000 | 4,043,000 | 1 | 18 | 1 | 4 | 0 | 90.8 | Lithuanian, Samogit |
| CEW16 | **Basque** | 558,000 | 3,223,000 | 5 | 15 | 1 | 12 | 7 | 89.8 | Basque (Euskarian, Navarrese) |
| CEW17 | **Caucasian** | 3,366,000 | 8,500,000 | 41 | 119 | 20 | 52 | 47 | 28.8 | Ibero-Caucasian (Paleocaucasian) |
| CEW17a | Adygo-Abkhazi | 295,000 | 1,471,000 | 5 | 23 | 3 | 6 | 9 | 7.6 | Abazinian, Abkhazian, Adyghe, Circassian (Cherkess, Karbardian), Ubykh |
| CEW17b | Dagestani | 757,000 | 1,922,000 | 27 | 58 | 9 | 30 | 64 | 0.3 | Aguly, Avar, Budukh, Dargin, Dargwa, Khinalug, Kryz, Lakk, Lezgin, Rutul, Tabasaran, Tsakhur, Udi |
| CEW17c | Georgian | 1,809,000 | 3,864,000 | 6 | 23 | 6 | 13 | 9 | 60.4 | Georgian (Kartvelian), Laze (Chan, Laz, Zan), Mingrelian, Svan, Gruzim |
| CEW17d | Nakh | 505,000 | 1,243,000 | 3 | 15 | 2 | 3 | 100 | 0.0 | Veinakh: Bat, Chechen (Kokhchi, Shishan), Ingush (Galgai), Kist |
| CEW18 | **Celtic** | 6,644,720 | 13,383,000 | 9 | 21 | 4 | 25 | 24 | 80.0 | Celtic: Continental (Gaulish), Insular (Brythonic: Breton, Cornish, Welsh; Goidelic: Irish, Manx, Scottish) |
| CEW18a | Breton | 988,000 | 1,920,000 | 2 | 2 | 1 | 6 | 0 | 71.6 | Breton: Comouaille, Léon, Tréguier, Vannes |
| CEW18b | Irish | 4,838,000 | 7,905,000 | 3 | 9 | 1 | 12 | 56 | 81.7 | Irish (Gaelic, Erse), Irish Traveller (Nomad, Shelta) |
| CEW18c | Scottish Gaelic | 76,400 | 93,800 | 1 | 1 | 0 | 1 | 0 | 83.1 | Scottish Gaelic (Gaelic, Gael, Goidel, Scots Gaelic) |
| CEW18d | Welsh | 742,000 | 3,463,000 | 1 | 7 | 1 | 4 | 0 | 80.8 | Welsh (Cymraeg) |
| CEW18z | other Celtic | 320 | 510 | 2 | 2 | 1 | 2 | 0 | 94.1 | Cornish, Manx |
| CEW19 | **Germanic (Teutonic)** | 164,289,400 | 367,258,000 | 36 | 557 | 17 | 152 | 6 | 70.8 | North Germanic (Scandinavian), West Germanic (Afrikaans, Dutch, English, Flemish, Frisian, German) |
| CEW19a | Afrikaner | 476,000 | 3,009,000 | 1 | 10 | 0 | 0 | 0 | 90.6 | Afrikaner (Afrikaans, Boer) |
| CEW19b | Alsatian | 1,111,000 | 1,588,000 | 1 | 1 | 0 | 0 | 0 | 70.0 | Alsatian, Lotharingian, Alemannic |
| CEW19c | Anglo-Australian | 3,183,000 | 14,121,000 | 1 | 16 | 0 | 1 | 100 | 65.8 | Anglo-Australian (English) |
| CEW19d | Anglo-Canadian | 2,422,000 | 15,352,000 | 1 | 6 | 0 | 1 | 100 | 65.8 | Anglo-Canadian (English) |
| CEW19e | Anglo-New Zealander | 650,000 | 2,997,000 | 1 | 9 | 0 | 1 | 100 | 67.1 | Anglo-New Zealander (English), Pakeha |
| CEW19f | Austrian | 6,257,000 | 8,751,000 | 2 | 14 | 1 | 15 | 0 | 86.1 | Austrian (German), Tirolean, Bavarian Austrian |
| CEW19g | Danish | 2,485,000 | 6,968,000 | 1 | 12 | 0 | 1 | 0 | 88.4 | Danish (Dane) |
| CEW19h | Dutch | 5,318,000 | 15,733,000 | 2 | 24 | 1 | 11 | 0 | 67.6 | Dutch (Netherlandic), Groningen Dutch |
| CEW19i | English (British) | 34,913,000 | 57,407,000 | 3 | 177 | 2 | 16 | 1 | 67.7 | British: Briton, English, Scot, Scottish; many regional dialects and peoples |
| CEW19j | Faeroese | 14,600 | 46,800 | 1 | 2 | 0 | 1 | 0 | 93.2 | Faeroese (Faroese, Faeroe Islander) |
| CEW19k | Flemish | 4,232,000 | 6,481,000 | 1 | 11 | 0 | 1 | 0 | 89.2 | Fleming (Flemish, Netherlandic) |
| CEW19l | Frisian | 177,000 | 921,000 | 3 | 5 | 4 | 7 | 0 | 72.0 | Frisian: East, North, West |
| CEW19m | German | 46,183,000 | 91,881,000 | 11 | 116 | 4 | 49 | 0 | 75.1 | German (East Middle, High, Low, West Middle): Bavarian, Franconian, German-Swiss, Saxon, Swabian |
| CEW19n | Icelander | 82,800 | 333,000 | 2 | 5 | 1 | 1 | 0 | 94.9 | Icelander (Icelandic) |
| CEW19o | Luxemburger | 201,000 | 413,000 | 1 | 5 | 0 | 1 | 0 | 93.7 | Luxemburger (Letzeburgesch) |
| CEW19p | Norwegian | 2,488,000 | 8,633,000 | 1 | 13 | 2 | 6 | 0 | 91.8 | Norwegian: New Norwegian (Nynorski, Landsmal), Dano-Norwegian (Bokmal), Russonorsk |
| CEW19q | Swedish | 5,110,000 | 13,356,000 | 1 | 12 | 1 | 22 | 0 | 66.5 | Swedish (Swede), Finlander Swede |
| CEW19r | Ulster Irish | 721,000 | 1,096,000 | 1 | 2 | 0 | 0 | 0 | 91.4 | Ulster Irish (Northern Irish, English-speaking), British Irish |
| CEW19s | USA White | 48,265,000 | 118,170,000 | 1 | 117 | 1 | 18 | 0 | 65.7 | English-speaking USA White (of numerous ethnic backgrounds, but mother tongue now English) |
| CEW20 | **Greek** | 4,033,000 | 14,188,000 | 5 | 88 | 2 | 12 | 0 | 96.2 | Hellenic (Romaic): Demotic Greek, Katharevusa; Cretan, Peloponnesian, Tsakonian; Cypriot, Karakachan |
| CEW21 | **Latin (Romance)** | 113,144,000 | 207,479,000 | 65 | 484 | 22 | 131 | 29 | 84.0 | Latin (Romance, Romanic, Italic), Latin European |
| CEW21a | Catalonian | 3,285,000 | 11,719,000 | 1 | 8 | 1 | 6 | 0 | 94.1 | Catalonian (Catalan): Andorran, Balearic, East Catalan, Valencian, West Catalan |
| CEW21b | French | 35,357,000 | 33,985,000 | 13 | 150 | 2 | 19 | 1 | 76.8 | French, Franco-Swiss, metropolitan French, Monégasque; Bourbonnais, Francien, Gallo, Orléanais |
| CEW21c | French-Canadian | 1,917,000 | 10,872,000 | 2 | 3 | 0 | 1 | 0 | 69.8 | French-Canadian (French), Cajun, Acadian |
| CEW21d | Galician | 1,639,000 | 4,065,000 | 2 | 7 | 0 | 1 | 0 | 95.0 | Galician (Northern Portuguese, Gallego), Fala |
| CEW21e | Italian | 35,268,000 | 64,860,000 | 13 | 74 | 4 | 22 | 85 | 82.7 | Italian, Italo-Swiss, Sanmarinese, Sicilian; Gallo-Italian, Tuscan, Venetan |
| CEW21f | Moldavian | 1,388,000 | 2,687,000 | 1 | 16 | 0 | 0 | 100 | 71.4 | Moldavian (Eastern Daco-Rumanian, Bessarabian) |
| CEW21g | Portuguese | 6,482,000 | 13,805,000 | 2 | 48 | 0 | 2 | 0 | 92.5 | Portuguese: Central, Insular, Northern, Southern |
| CEW21h | Rhaeto-Romanian | 258,000 | 760,000 | 4 | 8 | 3 | 11 | 0 | 84.2 | Rhaeto-Romanian: Friulian, Ladin, Rhaetian, Romansh (Grishun, Rumantsch), Sursilvan, Sutsilvan |
| CEW21i | Romanian | 9,515,000 | 19,843,000 | 3 | 35 | 2 | 6 | 0 | 89.4 | Aromanian (Vlach, Volokh), Romanian (Rumanian): Daco-Rumanian, Transylvanian, Wallachian |
| CEW21j | Sardinian | 729,000 | 1,547,000 | 5 | 5 | 1 | 7 | 60 | 80.5 | Sard (Sardinian, Sardo): dialects Campidanian, Gallurian, Logudorian, Sassarian |
| CEW21k | Spanish | 14,774,000 | 24,896,000 | 8 | 55 | 2 | 15 | 2 | 94.6 | Spaniard Spanish (Castellano, Castillan): Andalusian, Aragonese, Asturias, Leonese |
| CEW21l | Walloon | 2,313,000 | 3,383,000 | 1 | 8 | 1 | 15 | 0 | 84.8 | Walloon (French) |
| CEW21z | other Latin | 219,000 | 15,057,000 | 10 | 67 | 6 | 26 | 84 | 75.9 | Corsican, Franco-Provençal, Gibraltarian, Istriot, Latin, Occitan (Gascon, Languedoc, Provençal) |
| CEW22 | **Slav** | 142,802,000 | 289,759,000 | 23 | 356 | 8 | 40 | 7 | 72.5 | Slav (Slavic, Slavonic): East, South, West |
| CEW22a | Bosnian | 804,000 | 3,106,000 | 1 | 12 | 0 | 0 | 0 | 0.0 | Bosniac (Serbo-Croatian), Muslmani |
| CEW22b | Bulgar | 3,287,000 | 8,067,000 | 2 | 34 | 1 | 1 | 65 | 84.6 | Bulgar (Bulgarian), Palityan: Central, Eastern, Northeastern, Western |
| CEW22c | Byelorussian | 4,687,000 | 10,175,000 | 1 | 26 | 0 | 1 | 0 | 65.7 | Byelorussian (Belorussian, White Russian): Northeastern, Northwestern, Southwestern |
| CEW22d | Croatian | 2,057,000 | 5,820,000 | 1 | 24 | 0 | 1 | 0 | 94.6 | Croatian (Croat), Serbo-Croatian; Cakavian, Kajkavian |
| CEW22e | Czech | 7,842,000 | 11,213,000 | 1 | 20 | 1 | 1 | 0 | 48.8 | Czech: Bohemian, Moravian, Silesian; Hanak, Horak, Yalach, Zahorak |
| CEW22f | Kashubian | 146,000 | 154,000 | 2 | 2 | 0 | 2 | 0 | 90.3 | Kashubian (Pomeranian), Slovincian |
| CEW22g | Macedonian | 699,000 | 1,684,000 | 1 | 10 | 0 | 1 | 0 | 89.5 | Macedonian: Armin (Macedo-Rumanian), Bulgarian Macedonian |
| CEW22h | Montenegrin | 237,000 | 490,000 | 1 | 5 | 0 | 0 | 0 | 66.9 | Montenegrin (Serbo-Croatian) |
| CEW22i | Polish | 25,513,000 | 41,794,000 | 2 | 40 | 1 | 2 | 0 | 95.4 | Polish; Great Polish, Little Polish, Masurich, Mazovian, Silesian |
| CEW22j | Russian | 67,095,000 | 143,111,000 | 1 | 74 | 2 | 5 | 0 | 62.5 | Russian, Great Russian: Central, Northern, Southern |

*Continued overleaf*

*Table 18–5 continued*

| Code 1 | **RACE** GEOGRAPHIC RACE **Local race** Ethnocultural family 2 | *Pop 1900* 3 | *Pop 2000* 4 | *Cultures* 5 | *Peoples* 6 | *Clusters* 7 | *Langs* 8 | *Sim* 9 | *AC* 10 | *A selection of constituent cultures, peoples, tribes, languages, alternative names or synonyms* 11 |
|---|---|---|---|---|---|---|---|---|---|---|
| CEW22k | Ruthenian | 414,000 | 1,475,000 | 3 | 7 | 0 | 1 | 0 | 86.5 | Ruthenian (Carpatho-Russian, Carpatho-Ukrainian, Rusin, Ruthene) |
| CEW22l | Serbian | 4,167,000 | 8,981,000 | 2 | 32 | 1 | 8 | 0 | 78.1 | Serbian (Serb, Serbo-Croatian, Shtokavian); Torlakian |
| CEW22m | Slovak | 3,795,000 | 7,271,000 | 1 | 16 | 0 | 1 | 0 | 79.5 | Slovak: Central, Eastern, Western |
| CEW22n | Slovene | 903,000 | 2,195,000 | 1 | 14 | 1 | 13 | 0 | 89.1 | Slovene (Slovenian): Northwestern, Western |
| CEW22o | Sorb | 185,000 | 269,000 | 2 | 3 | 1 | 2 | 67 | 71.0 | Sorb (Lusatian, Sorabian) Sorbian (East, High, Low), Wendish |
| CEW22p | Ukrainian | 20,971,000 | 43,955,000 | 1 | 37 | 0 | 1 | 0 | 86.9 | Ukrainian: Carpathian, Little Russian, Northern, Podolian, Southeastern, Southwestern, Volhynian |
| CN | INDO-IRANIAN | 302,350,800 | 1,414,592,000 | 332 | 988 | 92 | 390 | 31 | 5.1 | Caucasoid peoples from Iran to Indian subcontinent; Indo-Aryan (Indic), Iranian, Dravidian |
| CNN23 | **Dravidian** | 58,790,000 | 230,789,000 | 40 | 121 | 19 | 39 | 48 | 17.8 | Dravidian (Indo-Dravidian, Paleo-Indian) |
| CNN23a | Kanarese | 12,470,000 | 38,304,000 | 4 | 8 | 3 | 6 | 25 | 5.7 | Kanarese (Kannada): Badaga, Kurumba |
| CNN23b | Malayall | 9,019,000 | 39,079,000 | 2 | 19 | 1 | 1 | 5 | 38.0 | Malabari, Malayali (Malayalam), Paliyan, Panlyan |
| CNN23c | Tamil | 18,784,000 | 72,684,000 | 8 | 39 | 3 | 7 | 67 | 19.5 | Tamil: Ceylon Tamil, Indian Tamil, Kling (SE Asia); Grantha, Vattelluttu |
| CNN23d | Telugu | 18,282,000 | 74,964,000 | 3 | 18 | 3 | 8 | 72 | 13.3 | Andhra, Telugu (Gentoo) |
| CNN23z | other Dravidian | 235,000 | 5,758,000 | 23 | 37 | 9 | 17 | 43 | 0.5 | Brahul (Kur Galli), Ceylon Moor, Coorg, Irula, Koya, Mannan, Parji, Toda, Tulu, Urali |
| CNT24 | **Iranian** | 17,863,800 | 127,263,000 | 77 | 237 | 28 | 98 | 27 | 0.4 | Iranian (Iranic): Afghani, Baluchi, Kurdish, Ossetian, Persian, Tadzhik |
| CNT24a | Afghani | 5,059,000 | 32,327,000 | 5 | 23 | 3 | 9 | 4 | 0.1 | Pathan (Pashtun, Pushtu): Afridi, Durrani, Ghilzal, Mahsud, Mangal, Parachi, Shinwari, Waziri, Yusufzal |
| CNT24b | Baluchi | 897,000 | 8,752,000 | 5 | 17 | 1 | 4 | 6 | 0.0 | Baluchi (Baluch, Baloch): Kechi, Lotuni, Makrani, Rakhshani, Sarawani |
| CNT24c | Kurdish | 2,312,000 | 29,961,000 | 10 | 53 | 2 | 7 | 23 | 0.1 | Kurd (Kurdish): Akre, Amadiyah, Dahuk, Kermanji, Kermanshahi, Sulaimani (Mukri), Zaza |
| CNT24d | Nuristani | 35,800 | 89,100 | 9 | 13 | 6 | 16 | 46 | 0.0 | Nuristani: Ashkun, Kafiri, Kati, Nangalami, Prasun, Tregami, Walgeli, Wai-aia |
| CNT24e | Ossetian | 252,000 | 731,000 | 1 | 15 | 1 | 2 | 0 | 43.9 | Ossetian (Ossete, Ossetin, Ossetic: Digor, Iron, Tagaur, Tual), Jassic |
| CNT24f | Persian | 4,466,000 | 28,943,000 | 12 | 49 | 3 | 13 | 16 | 0.4 | Persian (Dari, Farsi): Gabri, Gazi, Khunsari, Natazi, Sivandi, Sol, Tati, Vafsi |
| CNT24g | Tadzhik | 2,831,000 | 10,735,000 | 5 | 18 | 2 | 5 | 61 | 0.0 | Farsiwan, Mountain Tajik, Pamir Tadzhik (Bartang, Ishkashin, Vakhan, Yazgulem), Selekur, Yaghnobi |
| CNT24z | other Iranian | 2,011,000 | 15,724,000 | 30 | 49 | 10 | 42 | 49 | 0.1 | Bakhtiari, Firozkohi, Galesh, Gilaki, Hazara-Berberi, Jamshidi, Luri, Mazanderani, Shughni, Talysh |
| CNN25 | **North Indian** | 225,697,000 | 1,056,541,000 | 215 | 630 | 45 | 253 | 30 | 2.9 | Indic, Indo-Aryan; Caribbean East Indian, Indo-Mauritian, Indo-Pakistani; subdivided into 30,000 castes |
| CNN25a | Assamese | 6,045,000 | 16,232,000 | 1 | 3 | 0 | 1 | 0 | 1.1 | Assamese Bengali (Eastern, Western), Asami |
| CNN25b | Bengali | 46,676,000 | 199,300,000 | 9 | 31 | 1 | 14 | 71 | 1.1 | Calit-Bhasa, Sadhu-Bhasa: caste Bengali (Arzal, Ashraf), outcaste (Namasudra, Pallya); Rajbansi |
| CNN25c | Bihari | 9,577,000 | 91,881,000 | 14 | 22 | 2 | 11 | 32 | 0.9 | non-tribal Bihari: Bhojpuri, Magahi, Maithill (Tirhutia), Nagpuri (Sadani) |
| CNN25d | Goanese | 464,000 | 10,225,000 | 6 | 14 | 0 | 6 | 21 | 22.3 | Goanese (Konkani, Gomantaki; Bankoti) |
| CNN25e | Gujarati | 11,659,000 | 50,554,000 | 4 | 32 | 2 | 21 | 3 | 2.3 | Gujarati: Barla, Gamadia, Gramya Koll (Kohli), Patidar, Patnuli, Tarimuki, Sourashtra |
| CNN25f | Gypsy | 2,365,000 | 16,564,000 | 42 | 175 | 7 | 19 | 8 | 44.6 | Gypsy (Rom, Romany); tribes: Gitano, Kalderash, Lambadi (Banjuri), Lovara, Manush (Sinti), Tschourara |
| CNN25g | Hindi | 56,015,000 | 230,544,000 | 18 | 96 | 4 | 16 | 30 | 2.2 | Hindi: Eastern (Awadhi, Bagheli, Chhattisgarhi, Kosadi, Kosali), Western (Braj Bhasa, Bundell, Kanauji) |
| CNN25h | Jat | 1,687,000 | 15,857,000 | 7 | 12 | 1 | 4 | 25 | 2.2 | Awan (Lahnda), Jat (Jhat, Jatki, Multani) |
| CNN25i | Kashmiri | 1,974,000 | 6,759,000 | 23 | 35 | 12 | 57 | 54 | 0.0 | Dard: Dogra, Kafiri (Western Dardic), Kho, Khowari (Central Dardic), Kishtwari, Kohistani, Pashai, Shina |
| CNN25j | Marathi | 20,773,000 | 84,291,000 | 10 | 15 | 1 | 11 | 33 | 4.9 | Marathi: Dekini, Desi, Kunbi, Maratha, Poona |
| CNN25k | Nepalese | 3,168,000 | 29,305,000 | 16 | 26 | 3 | 18 | 42 | 1.8 | Chambiali, Garhwali, Gorkhali, Khas-kura, Kulu, Nepali, Pahari (Jaunsari, Kumauni, Palpa), Tarai, Tharu |
| CNN25l | Oriya | 9,233,000 | 33,838,000 | 11 | 13 | 1 | 10 | 38 | 1.4 | Oriya (Ordi, Uriya, Utkali): Bhatri, Halbi, Mughalbandi |
| CNN25m | Parsi | 109,000 | 216,000 | 1 | 4 | 0 | 1 | 100 | 0.1 | Parsi (Parsee) (Gujarati) |
| CNN25n | Punjabi | 25,563,000 | 132,841,000 | 11 | 45 | 1 | 15 | 24 | 3.8 | Punjabi: Western (Lahnda), Gurmukhi, Dogri-Kongri, Majhi |
| CNN25o | Rajasthani | 10,899,000 | 23,256,000 | 19 | 26 | 2 | 21 | 42 | 1.0 | Rajasthani, Rajput, Thakur: Ahirwati, Harauti, Jalpuri, Malvi, Marwari, Mewati, Nimadi |
| CNN25p | Sindhi | 3,913,000 | 21,656,000 | 6 | 16 | 1 | 11 | 56 | 0.2 | Sindhi: Kachchi, Lari, Lasi, Macharia, Saraiki, Sindh, Thareli, Vicholl |
| CNN25q | Sinhalese | 2,601,000 | 14,222,000 | 3 | 16 | 2 | 2 | 0 | 4.5 | Sinhalese (Cingalese: Low-Country, Up-Country or Kandyan), Maldivian (Divehi) |
| CNN25r | Urdu | 12,502,000 | 78,115,000 | 3 | 31 | 1 | 3 | 90 | 0.1 | Urdu (Hindustani, Khari Boli): Bangaru, Deccani (Dakhni), Deswali, Hariani |
| CNN25z | other North Indian | 474,000 | 843,000 | 10 | 17 | 4 | 12 | 47 | 26.2 | Anglo-Indian, Arain, Burusho (Burushaski), Ceylon Burgher, Gujar, Julaha, Lamani (Labhani), Lohar |
| CL | LATIN AMERICAN | 47,778,000 | 362,353,000 | 10 | 91 | 4 | 19 | 0 | 92.6 | Europeans resident in Latin America for over one generation, or partially assimilated, or of mixed race |
| CLT26 | **Latin-American White (Branco)** | 9,591,000 | 88,232,000 | 1 | 6 | 1 | 11 | 0 | 91.5 | Portuguese-speaking White Brazilian of pure Portugese or other European origin |
| CLT27 | **Latin-American White (Blanco)** | 12,149,000 | 87,176,000 | 3 | 43 | 0 | 0 | 0 | 88.4 | Spanish-speaking White of pure Spanish/European origin (Argentinian, Costa Rican, Puerto Rican) |
| CLN28 | **Mestiço (Portuguese)** | 2,167,000 | 20,476,000 | 1 | 3 | 0 | 0 | 0 | 94.8 | Portuguese/Amerindian/African; Caboclo (Portuguese/Amerindian), Mulatto (more White than Black) |
| CLN29 | **Mestizo (Spanish)** | 23,871,000 | 166,470,000 | 5 | 39 | 3 | 8 | 0 | 95.2 | Chicano, Chilote, Cholo, Ladino, Mestizo, Pachuco; mixed Spanish/Amerindian/African Negro |
| CM | MIDDLE EASTERN | 51,708,000 | 357,289,000 | 278 | 917 | 88 | 256 | 13 | 15.1 | Semito-Hamitic (Afrasian, Afro-Asiatic, Erythraic, Erythraen, Hamito-Semitic, Lisramic) |
| CMT30 | **Arab (Arabic)** | 34,064,000 | 228,527,000 | 36 | 378 | 9 | 42 | 11 | 8.1 | Bedouin, Copt, Egyptian, Levantine, Maghreb, Palestinian, Saharan (Baggara, Moor, Shoa), Yemeni |
| CMT31 | **Assyrian** | 124,000 | 903,000 | 6 | 33 | 1 | 9 | 9 | 90.3 | Aissor, Aramaean, Chaldean, Elkoosh: Eastern Neo-Assyrian, Syriac, Neo-Syriac, West Aramaic |
| CMT32 | **Berber** | 3,716,000 | 31,619,000 | 43 | 103 | 5 | 29 | 12 | 0.2 | Berbero-Libyan (Northern Hamite): Kabyle, Rif, Shawiya, Shluh, Tamazigt, Tuareg, Udalan, Zenati |
| CMT32a | Arabized Berber | 494,000 | 8,342,000 | 4 | 14 | 0 | 0 | 0 | 0.1 | Arabized, Arabic-speaking, detribalized Berber, Moor |
| CMT32b | Beraber | 538,000 | 3,917,000 | 1 | 8 | 0 | 1 | 0 | 0.1 | Beraber (Tamazigt): Idrassen, Ndhir, Seri, Serruchen, Yafelman, Zaer, Zayan, Zemmur; Central Shilha |
| CMT32c | Kabyle | 476,000 | 3,487,000 | 2 | 6 | 0 | 2 | 0 | 1.3 | Kabyle (Bergus, Sanhajah, Zouaouah) |
| CMT32d | Oasis Berber | 162,000 | 566,000 | 14 | 15 | 1 | 10 | 20 | 0.0 | Oasis Berber: Figig, Filala, Gadames, Jalo, Jofra, Mzab, Siwa, Tuat, Wargla |
| CMT32e | Rif | 308,000 | 2,492,000 | 4 | 6 | 0 | 3 | 33 | 0.1 | Rif (Riffian): Metalsa, Znassen, Northern Shilha |
| CMT32f | Shawiya | 194,000 | 1,846,000 | 1 | 3 | 0 | 1 | 100 | 0.0 | Shawiya (Chaouyah) |
| CMT32g | Shluh | 580,000 | 4,288,000 | 2 | 6 | 1 | 4 | 0 | 0.1 | Shleuh (Shilha, Masmudah, Tashellhayt): Aghbar, Fruga, Glawa, Massat, Susiua, Southern Shilha |
| CMT32h | Tuareg | 167,000 | 1,919,000 | 3 | 17 | 2 | 3 | 0 | 0.0 | Tuareg (Tamahaq, Tamashek): Ahaggaren, Air, Antessar, Asben, Aulliminden, Azjer, Ifora, Udalan |
| CMT32i | Zenaga | 13,000 | 38,200 | 2 | 4 | 1 | 1 | 25 | 0.0 | Zenaga: Allush, Girganke, Mbarek, Meshduf, Nasser, Sirifou, Tichit |
| CMT32y | other Moor | 552,000 | 4,337,000 | 2 | 9 | 0 | 1 | 11 | 0.0 | White Moor, Black Moor, Maure, Bidan, Nimadi |
| CMT32z | other Berber | 232,000 | 386,000 | 7 | 14 | 0 | 3 | 14 | 0.0 | Atta, Drawa, Guanche, Jerba, Menasser, Nefusa, Uregu, Warain, Zekara |
| CMT33 | **Cushitic** | 5,847,000 | 50,733,000 | 96 | 149 | 57 | 130 | 36 | 20.6 | Cushitic (Eastern Hamite, Hamitic): Eastern Cushitic, Southern Cushitic, West Cushitic (Omotic) |
| CMT33a | Agau | 40,200 | 387,000 | 9 | 11 | 4 | 10 | 27 | 39.0 | Awiya, Awngi, Bilin (Bitin), Bogos, Damot, Falasha (Kaila), Kamta, Kemant (Qemant), Khamir, Kwara |
| CMT33b | Galla | 3,221,000 | 20,687,000 | 13 | 29 | 2 | 11 | 34 | 26.0 | Oromo: Arusi, Bararetta, Boran, Gabbra, Ittu, Kwottu, Macha, Rendille, Salale, Tulama, Wallega, Wallo |
| CMT33c | Iraqw | 64,800 | 463,000 | 1 | 1 | 1 | 1 | 100 | 25.5 | Iraqw (Asa, Erokh, Iraku, Mbulu, Ngomwia) |
| CMT33d | Sidamo | 723,000 | 12,028,000 | 53 | 58 | 34 | 72 | 50 | 39.4 | Bako, Burji, Darasa, Hadya, Janjero, Kaffa, Kambatta, Konso-Geleba, Maji, Ometo, Reshiat, Walamo |
| CMT33e | Somali | 1,368,000 | 13,790,000 | 4 | 24 | 3 | 16 | 8 | 0.0 | Darod, Digil, Dir, Geri, Hawiya, Ishaak, Issa (Esa), Mijertein, Ogaden, Rahanwein, Sab, West Somali |
| CMT33z | other Cushitic | 430,000 | 3,378,000 | 16 | 26 | 13 | 20 | 35 | 1.1 | Beja (Ababda, Amarar, Amer, Bisharin, Bogo, Hadendowa), Burungi, Danakil (Afar), Goroa, Mbugu, Saho |
| CMT34 | **Ethiopic** | 2,868,000 | 28,272,000 | 14 | 30 | 10 | 22 | 17 | 80.6 | Ethiopic (Semitic, Ethiosemitic, African Semitic) |
| CMT34a | Amhara | 2,024,000 | 20,014,000 | 3 | 10 | 2 | 4 | 0 | 88.5 | Amhara (Amharic), Argobba, Harari (Adere); Abyssinian |
| CMT34b | Tigrai | 482,000 | 5,398,000 | 1 | 4 | 1 | 1 | 0 | 76.5 | Tigrai (Tigrinya: Habesha) |
| CMT34c | Tigre | 161,000 | 827,000 | 2 | 6 | 1 | 1 | 33 | 6.1 | Tigre (Hasi, Xassa), Mensa |
| CMT34z | other Ethiopic | 201,000 | 2,033,000 | 8 | 10 | 6 | 16 | 30 | 43.9 | Fuga, Geez (Ethiopic), Gogot (Dobi), Gurage, Maskan, Muher, Soddo |
| CMT35 | **Jewish** | 4,872,000 | 16,672,000 | 82 | 217 | 5 | 23 | 3 | 3.5 | Hebrew: Ashkenazi (Western Jew, Yiddish), Maghreb (Oriental), Sefardi (Judeo-Spanish, Ladino) |
| CMT36 | **Maltese** | 217,000 | 563,000 | 1 | 7 | 1 | 1 | 0 | 95.0 | Maltese |
| M | **MONGOLIAN** (Mongoloid, Asiatic) | 674,015,540 | 2,265,858,000 | 2,093 | 3,621 | 1,603 | 4,345 | 44 | 14.5 | Mongolian (Mongoloid, Asiatic, Oriental) |
| MI | AMERICAN INDIAN | 10,154,900 | 77,647,000 | 811 | 1,109 | 713 | 1,746 | 45 | 90.4 | Amerindian (American Mongoloid, Amerind), including mixed-blood (Métis, Half-Breed) |
| MIR37 | **Central Amerindian** | 5,245,000 | 32,515,000 | 258 | 341 | 129 | 402 | 43 | 93.1 | Meso-American: Azteco-Tanoan, Mayan, Oto-Manguean, Pueblo Indian, Uto-Aztecan |
| MIR37a | Aztec | 896,000 | 2,143,000 | 5 | 19 | 4 | 11 | 58 | 94.4 | Aztec (Nahuatl), Nahua (Mexicano, Mexicanero), Pipil |
| MIR37b | Maya | 1,304,000 | 5,789,000 | 67 | 89 | 30 | 81 | 46 | 89.6 | Chol, Chontal, Chorti, Huastec, Lacandon, Mam, Quiché (Cakchiquel, Kekchi), Tzeltal, Tzotzil, Yucatec |
| MIR37c | Mixtec | 273,000 | 514,000 | 38 | 44 | 12 | 62 | 39 | 90.1 | Amuzgo, Cuicatec, Mixtec, Trique |
| MIR37d | Otomi | 431,000 | 663,000 | 14 | 15 | 8 | 19 | 67 | 92.2 | Chichimec (Jonaz), Ixtenco, Matlatzinca, Mazahua, Mezquital, North & South Pame, Sierra, Tenango |
| MIR37e | Part-Indian | 1,405,000 | 9,717,000 | 1 | 2 | 0 | 0 | 0 | 95.0 | Indian of mixed blood: Half-Indian, Semi-Indian (non-tribal, detribalized) |
| MIR37f | Zapotec | 314,000 | 760,000 | 41 | 63 | 12 | 48 | 33 | 89.1 | Chatino, Zapotec (Juárez, South Mountain, Valley, Villalta): Choapán, Etla, Istmo, Mitia, Rincon |
| MIR37y | Detribalized Amerindian | 301,000 | 10,390,000 | 1 | 1 | 0 | 0 | 0 | 95.0 | Half-Indian, Part-Indian (Spanish-speaking tribal) |
| MIR37z | other Central Amerindian | 321,000 | 2,539,000 | 91 | 108 | 63 | 181 | 44 | 87.1 | Chinantecan, Huichol, Lenca, Mazatec, Miskito, Mixe-Zoque, Tarahumara, Tarascan, Totonac, Yaqui |
| MIR38 | **Northern Amerindian** | 555,300 | 12,335,000 | 175 | 213 | 174 | 380 | 68 | 76.2 | Native Indian (pure Amerindian, registered American Indian); also Indian of mixed blood |
| MIR38a | North American Indian | 308,000 | 1,199,000 | 168 | 204 | 166 | 371 | 70 | 83.0 | Algonkian (Ojibwa), Creek, Cherokee, Sioux, Iroqois, Na-Dene (Athabaskan: Apache, Navajo), Penutian |
| MIR38b | Part-Indian (Métis) | 177,000 | 10,602,000 | 5 | 7 | 8 | 9 | 29 | 75.3 | Indian/White, Indian/French, Métis (Mixed-Blood, Half-Caste), unregistered or non-status Indian; Creole |
| MIR38y | Detribalized Amerindian | 70,300 | 534,000 | 2 | 2 | 0 | 0 | 0 | 78.1 | Half-Indian (English-speaking), Detribalized urbanite |
| MIR39 | **Southern Amerindian** | 4,354,600 | 32,797,000 | 378 | 555 | 410 | 964 | 38 | 93.1 | Andean-Equatorial; Arawakan, Cariban, Macro-Chibchan, Macro-Ge, Quechumaran, Tucanoan, Tuplan |
| MIR39a | Arawak | 22,000 | 545,000 | 57 | 73 | 76 | 164 | 34 | 37.4 | Arawak (Arowak): Bauré, Campa, Goajiro, Machiguenga, Mojo, Wapishana, Wiriná |
| MIR39b | Aymara | 624,000 | 3,431,000 | 4 | 10 | 3 | 5 | 70 | 92.1 | Aymara (Oruro), Cauqui (Jaqaru), Lupaca, Ubina |
| MIR39c | Carib | 25,600 | 263,000 | 41 | 66 | 45 | 112 | 39 | 70.7 | Bakairi, Cannibal, Carib, Cariban, Chocó, Galibi, Guicuru, Island Carib, Makushi, Trio, Waiwai |
| MIR39d | Jungle Amerindian | 128,000 | 415,000 | 113 | 161 | 127 | 313 | 50 | 37.1 | Auca, Chapacura, Jivaro (Achuale, Murato), Pano, Saparo, Taruma, Tucano, Ve, Witoto |
| MIR39e | Lowland Amerindian | 166,000 | 5,436,000 | 92 | 136 | 96 | 213 | 29 | 91.1 | Chibcha (Cayapa, Cuna, Guaymi). Emerillon, Guarani, Lengua, Mataco, Oyampi, Palikur, Toba, Tupi |
| MIR39f | Mapuche | 104,000 | 778,000 | 2 | 3 | 1 | 5 | 100 | 67.7 | Araucanian, Mapuche: Divihet, Huiliche, Manzanero, Mapudungu, Pehuenche, Pichunche, Taluhet |
| MIR39g | Quechua | 3,170,000 | 21,648,000 | 35 | 54 | 19 | 51 | 44 | 97.7 | Quechua: Almaguero, Ancash, Ayachucho, Cajamarca, Huánuco, Junin, Lamano, Ucayall |
| MIR39y | Detribalized Amerindian | 6,000 | 14,600 | 1 | 1 | 0 | 0 | 0 | 28.1 | Part-Indian (Spanish- or Portuguese-speaking) |
| MIR39z | other Southern Amerindian | 109,000 | 267,000 | 33 | 51 | 43 | 101 | 12 | 72.3 | Other tribes and languages unrelated to the 7 major language groups; also Half-Indian |
| MR | ARCTIC MONGOLOID | 14,870 | 160,000 | 13 | 20 | 14 | 35 | 10 | 80.0 | Arctic, Arctic Mongoloid, Eskimoid |
| MRY40 | **Eskimo-Aleut** | 14,870 | 160,000 | 13 | 20 | 14 | 35 | 10 | 80.0 | Aleut, Eskaleut, Eskimo |
| MRY40a | Aleut | 970 | 6,700 | 2 | 4 | 4 | 12 | 25 | 82.1 | Aleut (Unangan): Atka, Attuan, Unalaskan |
| MRY40b | Eskimo | 13,900 | 153,000 | 11 | 16 | 10 | 23 | 6 | 80.4 | Eskimo (Inuit): Greenlander, Inupik (Inuk), Polar Eskimo, Siberian Eskimo (Yuit), Yupik (Yuk) |
| MS | ASIAN | 663,273,970 | 2,182,415,000 | 1,190 | 2,347 | 814 | 2,430 | 44 | 11.6 | Asian, Asiatic (Classical Mongoloid, East Asiatic) |
| MSY41 | **Altaic** | 42,838,000 | 163,992,000 | 62 | 314 | 17 | 67 | 50 | 1.0 | Altaic (Altayan): Mongolian, Tungus-Manchu, Turkic (Karluk, Hunnic, Oghuz) |
| MSY41a | Azerbaijani | 4,207,000 | 21,222,000 | 2 | 21 | 0 | 1 | 5 | 0.0 | Azerbaijani (Azerbaijanian, Azeri): Airym, Aynallu, Karapapakh, Qasqay (Kashkai) |
| MSY41b | Bashkir | 631,000 | 1,488,000 | 1 | 11 | 0 | 1 | 0 | 7.2 | Bashkir: Burzhan, Kuvakan, Yurmaty |
| MSY41c | Chuvash | 883,000 | 1,792,000 | 1 | 12 | 1 | 1 | 100 | 35.0 | Chuvash (Anatri, Viryal) |
| MSY41d | Gagauz | 130,000 | 584,000 | 1 | 7 | 0 | 1 | 86 | 30.0 | Gagauz (Gagauzi) |
| MSY41e | Kazakh | 3,649,000 | 11,812,000 | 1 | 19 | 1 | 1 | 100 | 0.0 | Kazakh (Hasako, Qazag, Qazagi) |
| MSY41f | Khalka-Mongol | 1,781,000 | 5,305,000 | 2 | 10 | 1 | 3 | 10 | 0.5 | Mongolian: Bargu, Chakhar, Dariganga, Khalka-Mongol, Kharchin, Meng, Ordos, Ujumuchin, Urat |
| MSY41g | Kirgiz | 893,000 | 3,323,000 | 1 | 10 | 0 | 1 | 100 | 0.0 | Kirgiz (Kirghiz, Kirghizi, Koerhkossu) |
| MSY41h | Tatar | 3,043,000 | 11,969,000 | 3 | 32 | 1 | 5 | 63 | 1.5 | Tatar (Tartar): Central, Mishar (Western), Uralian, Crimean Tatar, Siberian Tatar (Baraba, Ishim, Tara, Tom) |
| MSY41i | Tungus-Manchu | 1,895,000 | 11,241,000 | 11 | 14 | 5 | 17 | 50 | 0.1 | Amur, Even (Lamut), Manchu, Nanai (Gold, Hoche, Olcha), Orochon, Sibo, Tungus (Evenki, Solon) |
| MSY41j | Turkish | 13,892,000 | 49,479,000 | 3 | 52 | 1 | 3 | 2 | 0.1 | Turkish (Osmanli): Anatolian Turk (including Yuruk), Asian Turk, Black Sea Turk, Rumelian Turk |
| MSY41k | Turkmen | 1,348,000 | 5,782,000 | 2 | 14 | 0 | 2 | 86 | 0.0 | Turkmen (Turkman, Turkoman): Erseri, Kizilbash, Sarak, Tekke |

*Continued opposite*

*Table 18–5 continued*

| Code<br>1 | **RACE**<br>GEOGRAPHIC RACE<br>**Local race**<br>Ethnocultural family<br>2 | Pop 1900<br>3 | Pop 2000<br>4 | Cultures<br>5 | Peoples<br>6 | Clusters<br>7 | Langs<br>8 | Sim<br>9 | AC<br>10 | A selection of constituent cultures, peoples, tribes, languages, alternative names or synonyms<br>11 |
|---|---|---|---|---|---|---|---|---|---|---|
| MSY41l | Uzbek | 6,327,000 | 24,560,000 | 2 | 21 | 1 | 5 | 100 | 0.1 | Uzbek (Uzbeki): Kypchak, Lockhay, Oghuz, Qurama, Sart, Northern & Southern Uzbek |
| MSY41m | Yakut | 126,000 | 448,000 | 2 | 3 | 1 | 2 | 100 | 56.3 | Yakut (Dolgan, Jeko, Sakha) |
| MSY41y | other Mongolian | 299,000 | 2,479,000 | 12 | 30 | 4 | 8 | 57 | 2.3 | Bayat, Buryat, Dahur (Dagur), Darkhat, Kalmyk, Mogul, Oyrat (Altai), Santa, Tu (Mongour), Tunghsiang |
| MSY41z | other Turkic | 3,734,000 | 12,509,000 | 18 | 58 | 1 | 16 | 45 | 0.9 | Afshar, Karaim, Karachay, Kara-Kalpak, Khakas, Khoton, Kumyk, Nogay, Shahseven, Tuvinian, Uighur |
| MSY42 | **Chinese** | 455,861,000 | 1,222,179,000 | 38 | 272 | 18 | 75 | 0 | 7.7 | Chinese (Sinitic), including diaspora Chinese (Totok) and overseas non-Chinese-speaking (Peranakan) |
| MSY42a | Han Chinese | 453,013,000 | 1,212,333,000 | 35 | 259 | 18 | 75 | 0 | 7.8 | Mandarin, Cantonese (Yüeh), Hakka, Hsiang, Kan, Min, Minnan (Amoy-Swatow, Hoklo, Taiwanese), Wu |
| MSY42b | Hui | 2,843,000 | 9,833,000 | 2 | 12 | 0 | 0 | 0 | 0.0 | Hui (Dungan)(Mandarin-speaking): Ho, Hui-tze, Hwei, Khuei, Panghse, Panthay (Panthe) |
| MSY42c | Sino-Burmese | 5,000 | 13,700 | 1 | 1 | 0 | 0 | 0 | 1.0 | Chinese/Burmese mixed races |
| MSY43 | **Eurasian** | 53,800 | 1,858,000 | 12 | 26 | 0 | 4 | 0 | 47.3 | Anglo-Burmese, Anglo-Chinese, Injerto (Latin American White/Chinese or Japanese), Macanese |
| MSY44 | **Indo-Malay** | 48,999,900 | 306,458,000 | 648 | 830 | 543 | 1,595 | 57 | 31.2 | Oceanic & Southern Mongoloid, Western Austronesian, Indonesian, Hesperonesian, Chamic |
| MSY44a | Balinese | 818,000 | 4,210,000 | 1 | 2 | 1 | 4 | 100 | 1.1 | Balinese |
| MSY44b | Batak | 1,130,000 | 8,094,000 | 10 | 11 | 6 | 15 | 91 | 58.9 | Batak: Angkola, Dairi, Karo, Mandalling, Pakpak, Simalungun, Toba |
| MSY44c | Buginese | 1,095,000 | 4,417,000 | 4 | 6 | 4 | 16 | 50 | 0.9 | Buginese (De, Sindjai), Campalagian (Tasing), Luwu, Malimpung |
| MSY44d | Chamorro | 4,000 | 147,000 | 1 | 4 | 1 | 3 | 50 | 98.0 | Chamorro (Guamanian) |
| MSY44e | Iban | 55,200 | 758,000 | 6 | 7 | 3 | 22 | 29 | 43.5 | Iban (Sea Dayak), Birawut, Balau, Millikin, Seberuang |
| MSY44f | Ilocan | 970,000 | 9,025,000 | 1 | 3 | 1 | 2 | 100 | 97.3 | Ilocan (Ilocano, Iloko) |
| MSY44g | Javanese | 16,448,000 | 79,140,000 | 6 | 18 | 3 | 14 | 6 | 11.6 | Javanese (Basa Kedatan, Madhya, Ngoko, Pegon): Banjuwangi, Cheribon, Indramaju, Tegal, Tengger |
| MSY44h | Madurese | 2,727,000 | 15,319,000 | 4 | 5 | 2 | 5 | 40 | 0.3 | Madurese: Bangkalan, Bawean, Pamekasan, Sumenep, Boyanese, Kangean |
| MSY44i | Makassarese | 467,000 | 1,885,000 | 4 | 4 | 4 | 8 | 50 | 0.2 | Makassarese (Tawna): Selajar, Tonthian, Turatea, Kalao, Wotu |
| MSY44j | Malagasy | 2,605,000 | 15,359,000 | 22 | 42 | 7 | 36 | 50 | 48.6 | Antaisaka, Antandroy, Bara, Betsileo, Betsimisaraka, Merina, Sakalava, Sihanaka, Tanala, Tsimihety |
| MSY44k | Malay | 2,667,000 | 44,199,000 | 44 | 87 | 14 | 72 | 48 | 2.1 | Bahasa Indonesia, Cham-Malay, Malay: Baba Malay, Bahasa Malay, Mergui, Pasemah, Pattani, Selung |
| MSY44l | Minahasan | 234,000 | 1,617,000 | 10 | 10 | 10 | 27 | 60 | 64.9 | Menadonese: Mongondow, Ratahan, Tombulu, Tomini, Tondano, Tonsawang, Tontemboan |
| MSY44m | Palawan | 22,800 | 115,000 | 5 | 7 | 7 | 11 | 86 | 8.9 | Babuyan, Batah, Palawan (Palawano), Tagbanwa, Baras |
| MSY44n | Sundanese | 5,298,000 | 29,075,000 | 3 | 3 | 2 | 7 | 67 | 0.3 | Sundanese: Banten, Priangan, Badui |
| MSY44o | Tagalog | 1,679,000 | 19,923,000 | 4 | 28 | 1 | 8 | 11 | 97.0 | Tagalog (Philipino, Pilipino, Filipino) |
| MSY44p | Toraja | 351,000 | 2,056,000 | 28 | 29 | 24 | 91 | 62 | 45.0 | Toraja (Koro, Palu, Poso, Sadang), Galumpang, Kulawi |
| MSY44q | Visayan | 2,136,000 | 27,118,000 | 9 | 9 | 8 | 32 | 67 | 97.5 | Visayan (Bisayan, Cebuano): Constantino, Hillgaynon (Ilongo), Samaran (Waray-Waray), Surigaonon |
| MSY44x | other Filipino | 2,589,000 | 17,710,000 | 113 | 118 | 95 | 265 | 63 | 65.9 | Bicol, Bontoc (Igorot), Ibanag, Ifugao, Magindanao, Maranao, Pampangan, Pangasinan, Sulu-Samal |
| MSY44y | other Indonesian | 7,656,000 | 23,855,000 | 290 | 319 | 274 | 738 | 63 | 15.5 | Achenese, Banjarese, Dayak, Dusun (Kadazan), Kenyah, Lampong, Minangkabau, Nias, Sasak, Timorese |
| MSY44z | other Malaysian | 47,900 | 2,438,000 | 83 | 118 | 76 | 219 | 57 | 23.6 | Bisaya, Cham, Jaral, Kayan, Kedayan, Kelabit, Melanau, Murut, Orang-Laut (Bajau, Moken, Sea Gypsy) |
| MSY45 | **Japanese** | 45,055,000 | 130,012,000 | 12 | 51 | 5 | 25 | 16 | 3.3 | Japanese, Okinawan, Ryukyuan; Eastern Altaic |
| MSY45a | Japanese | 44,650,000 | 128,607,000 | 1 | 38 | 3 | 10 | 0 | 3.3 | Japanese (Nipponese), Japanese-American (Issei, Kibel, Nisel, Sansei): Nan-oo, Hoku-oo, Satsuma |
| MSY45b | Ryukyuan | 405,000 | 1,406,000 | 11 | 13 | 2 | 15 | 62 | 2.9 | Ryukyuan: Central Okinawan, Luchu), Northern (Amami), Southern (Miyako, Sakishima), Hogan |
| MSY46 | **Korean** | 13,430,000 | 75,665,000 | 1 | 36 | 3 | 10 | 0 | 27.9 | Korean (Hangul & Choson Muntcha alphabets): Central, Cheju-do (Southern) |
| MSY47 | **Miao-Yao** | 2,578,000 | 12,875,000 | 22 | 46 | 14 | 37 | 17 | 4.6 | Meo-Yao: Kelao, Lakwa, Lati, Miao (Meo-Hmong, Hmu), She (Sho), Yao |
| MSY47a | Miao | 2,021,000 | 8,436,000 | 13 | 31 | 10 | 29 | 13 | 6.6 | Chi-lao (Kelao), Miao: Black Meo, Blue Meo, Hwa (Flowered) Meo, Red Meo, Striped Meo, White Meo |
| MSY47b | Yao | 557,000 | 4,439,000 | 9 | 15 | 4 | 8 | 27 | 0.7 | Laka, Puna, She (Sho), Yao (Iu Mien, Kim Mien, Lingnan Yao, Man, Yu Mien), Highland Yao |
| MSY48 | **Paleoasiatic** | 20,100 | 36,000 | 10 | 10 | 7 | 10 | 40 | 12.5 | Aboriginal (Paleosiberian, Hyperborean): Chukchi, Gilyak, Itelmen, Kett, Koryak, Nivkh, Yukaghir (Odul) |
| MSY49 | **Tai** | 13,219,000 | 90,070,000 | 51 | 111 | 18 | 95 | 53 | 1.5 | Kam-Tai (Dalc), Thai-Chuang Tai, Tai-Kadal: Central, Northern, Southwestern Tai |
| MSY49a | Zhuang | 5,213,000 | 25,105,000 | 18 | 29 | 6 | 30 | 31 | 1.1 | N & C Tai: Chinese Nung, Chuang, Chungchia, Molao, Thai Nung, Padi, Phula, Puyi, Tho, Tu, Tulao |
| MSY49b | Lao | 2,386,000 | 19,403,000 | 2 | 10 | 1 | 2 | 80 | 1.4 | Lao (Northeastern Thai, Thai Isan, Thai Lao), Nyaw |
| MSY49c | Shan | 746,000 | 3,314,000 | 5 | 8 | 1 | 5 | 75 | 0.6 | Burmese Shan: Eastern Shan (Tai Dau), Khamti (Ahom), Shan-Bama (Nglo), Tal Nul, Tal Yai, Red Shan |
| MSY49d | Thai | 3,335,000 | 29,370,000 | 4 | 20 | 1 | 6 | 75 | 2.1 | Tai (Central Thai, Khon-Thai, Siamese), Northern Thai (Kammyang), Southern Thai |
| MSY49z | other Tai | 1,539,000 | 12,879,000 | 22 | 44 | 9 | 52 | 48 | 1.2 | Be, Black Tai, Gial, Kadai, Kam, Khun, Li, Lu, Nhang, Phutal, Puyl, Red Tai, Sek, Tay, White Tai, Yuan |
| MSY50 | **Tibeto-Burmese** | 17,503,800 | 82,291,000 | 287 | 477 | 171 | 449 | 59 | 9.6 | Tibeto-Burmese (Tibeto-Burman), Gyarung-Mishmi, Himalayan |
| MSY50a | Bhotia | 180,000 | 1,646,000 | 13 | 17 | 6 | 22 | 24 | 0.1 | Bhotia (Bhote, Bhutia, Bhutanese, Dzongkha), Sikkimese (Sikami) |
| MSY50b | Burmese | 7,538,000 | 30,221,000 | 7 | 17 | 2 | 9 | 41 | 0.9 | Burmese: Arakan, Bama, Burman, Maghl, Tenasserim, Danau, Intha, Rohingya, Yangbye |
| MSY50c | Chin | 199,000 | 1,948,000 | 38 | 59 | 25 | 79 | 64 | 50.0 | Asho Chin, Khumi, Kuki Chin (Kukish), Laizo, Mru, Ngawn, Salzang, Teizang, Tiddim, Zo, Zomi, Zotung |
| MSY50d | Garo | 260,000 | 976,000 | 5 | 8 | 2 | 11 | 25 | 40.1 | Deori (Chutiya), Garo (Bodo), Hajang, Koch, Mandi, Migam |
| MSY50e | Gurung | 67,100 | 180,000 | 8 | 10 | 5 | 8 | 30 | 0.1 | Gurung, Gurung Gurkha, Thakali |
| MSY50f | Kachin | 157,000 | 1,305,000 | 9 | 17 | 7 | 14 | 65 | 43.1 | Kachin: Atzi, Maru, Norra, Nung, Rawang, Singpho (Chingpo, Jinghpaw) |
| MSY50g | Karen | 1,126,000 | 4,941,000 | 18 | 24 | 12 | 22 | 63 | 38.9 | Red Karen: Bghai, Kayah, Padaung, Yinbaw, Zayein; White Karen (Pa-O, Taungthu), Pwo, Sgaw Karen |
| MSY50h | Kirati | 108,000 | 462,000 | 14 | 27 | 12 | 25 | 22 | 0.1 | Rai, Kirati, Ral Kirati: Athpare, Chamling, Khaling, Saam, Sampange, Thulunge |
| MSY50i | Lahu | 31,400 | 14,395,000 | 28 | 51 | 14 | 47 | 73 | 4.0 | Hani, Lahu (I, Laku, Musseh, Nakhi (Moso), No), Lolo (Ho, Kopu, Laka, Nosu, Xa), Tuchia, Wu-man |
| MSY50j | Lepcha | 11,300 | 79,600 | 1 | 3 | 1 | 4 | 100 | 2.3 | Lepcha (Rong, Rongke) |
| MSY50k | Limbu | 66,700 | 355,000 | 2 | 4 | 1 | 3 | 100 | 0.1 | Limbu (Chang, Monpa, Subah, Tsong): Fagural, Fedopla, Tamarkholea |
| MSY50l | Lisu | 31,400 | 886,000 | 3 | 7 | 1 | 3 | 71 | 75.3 | Lisu (Hwa (Yawyin), Lasaw, Lishaw): Black Lisu, Flowery Lisu (Southern Lisu), Shisham, White Lisu |
| MSY50m | Lushai | 252,000 | 617,000 | 4 | 8 | 4 | 9 | 88 | 98.7 | Lushai (Mizo), Mara (Lakher, Zao), Shendu |
| MSY50n | Magar | 113,000 | 629,000 | 6 | 9 | 5 | 6 | 89 | 0.0 | Gurkha, Magar, Mangari, Kham-Magar, Maikhoti-Kham |
| MSY50o | Manipuri | 490,000 | 1,511,000 | 2 | 4 | 1 | 2 | 75 | 1.2 | Manipuri: Meithei, & scheduled hill tribes (Empeo, Kabui, Khoirao, Kwoireng, Maram), Ponna |
| MSY50p | Naga | 241,000 | 1,661,000 | 38 | 46 | 29 | 55 | 74 | 73.8 | Angami, Ao, Chakesang, Chakru, Chang, Konyak, Lhota, Tangsa, Rengma, Sema, Zemi-Zeliang, Zheza |
| MSY50q | Sherpa | 32,900 | 56,100 | 1 | 2 | 0 | 1 | 100 | 0.1 | Sherpa (Sharpa Bhotia) |
| MSY50r | Tibetan | 2,369,000 | 12,253,000 | 42 | 98 | 17 | 65 | 48 | 1.2 | Bodic: Central (Lhasa), Northern, Southern, Western: Amdo, Balti, Bod, Kamba, Ladakhi, Lahull, Zargska |
| MSY50s | Tripuri | 808,000 | 2,017,000 | 5 | 11 | 1 | 3 | 64 | 5.0 | Chakma, Magh, Riang, Tipura (Tipera), Tripuri, Usipi, Ushoi |
| MSY50z | other Tibeto-Burmese | 3,422,000 | 6,154,000 | 43 | 55 | 26 | 61 | 73 | 7.8 | Akha, Bawm, Dafla, Hmar, Kachari, Loba, Mung, Nasi, Newarl, Nu, Pai, Palaychi, Sunwar, Tamang, Yi |
| MSW51 | **Uralian** | 13,437,370 | 25,006,000 | 35 | 139 | 14 | 51 | 19 | 81.2 | Uralic race (a Caucasoid/Mongoloid cline): Finno-Ugric, Neoasiatic, Uralic; Magyar, Samoyed |
| MSW51a | Estonian | 556,000 | 1,089,000 | 2 | 21 | 1 | 2 | 0 | 48.5 | Estonian: Setu, Tallinn (Reval), Tartu (Dorpat); Vod, Vodian |
| MSW51b | Finnish | 2,832,000 | 6,017,000 | 1 | 11 | 1 | 6 | 0 | 88.9 | Finnish: Hame, Savo, Suomi |
| MSW51c | Karelian | 126,000 | 257,000 | 4 | 10 | 1 | 4 | 0 | 66.5 | Karelian, Ludic, Olonets, Tver, Ingrian, Luzh, Livvikovian |
| MSW51d | Komi | 252,000 | 516,000 | 2 | 9 | 0 | 2 | 67 | 35.3 | Komi (Zyryan): Komi-Permyak, Yazva |
| MSW51e | Lapp | 21,200 | 37,500 | 8 | 17 | 3 | 9 | 24 | 91.2 | Lapp (Lopari, Saamian): Inari, Kola, Lule, Pite, Ruija, Skolt, Southern, Ume, Samish, Ter |
| MSW51f | Livonian | 970 | 1,300 | 1 | 1 | 0 | 1 | 0 | 70.8 | Livonian (Eastern, Western), Liv, Kurlyad |
| MSW51g | Magyar | 8,342,000 | 14,448,000 | 1 | 25 | 1 | 6 | 0 | 85.1 | Magyar (Hungarian, Ob-Ugric), Csango, Siculi, Szekely |
| MSW51h | Mari | 252,000 | 735,000 | 3 | 10 | 1 | 2 | 50 | 89.8 | Mari (Cheremis): High Mari, Low Mari |
| MSW51i | Mordvin | 631,000 | 1,062,000 | 3 | 16 | 1 | 2 | 13 | 62.7 | Erzya (Erza), Moksha, Mordvin (Mordoff, Mordovian, Mordva, Mordvinian) |
| MSW51j | Samoyed | 20,100 | 42,500 | 5 | 5 | 2 | 6 | 0 | 4.5 | Samoyed: Enets (Yenisei), Kamas, Nenets (Nentsy, Yurak), Nganasan (Tavgi), Selkup (Ostyak-Samoyed) |
| MSW51k | Udmurt | 379,000 | 744,000 | 1 | 9 | 1 | 1 | 100 | 54.0 | Udmurt (Kalmez, Votyak) |
| MSW51z | other Finno-Ugric | 25,100 | 56,900 | 4 | 5 | 2 | 10 | 0 | 35.7 | Ingrian, Khanti (Ostyak), Mansi (Vogul), Ob Ugrian, Veps, Votic |
| MSY52 | **Viet-Muong** | 10,278,000 | 71,972,000 | 12 | 35 | 4 | 12 | 26 | 7.9 | Muong, Vietnamese (Kinh, Tonkinese) |
| MSY52a | Muong | 155,000 | 1,118,000 | 1 | 2 | 1 | 2 | 100 | 5.3 | Muong (Viet-Muong): Pi, Thang, Tong, Wang |
| MSY52b | Vietnamese | 10,113,000 | 70,820,000 | 2 | 23 | 1 | 1 | 0 | 8.0 | Vietnamese (Annamese, Cochinchinese, Ching, Kinh, Quoc-ngu, Tonkinese), Gin, Jhing |
| MSY52z | other Viet-Muong | 10,000 | 34,900 | 9 | 10 | 2 | 9 | 70 | 2.2 | Arem, Hung Khong Kheng, May, Nguon, Sach, Tay Pong, Pakatan, Ruc, Thavung, Yellow Leaf |
| MP | PACIFIC | 571,800 | 5,636,000 | 79 | 145 | 62 | 134 | 48 | 90.5 | Pacific Islander (Eastern Austronesian, Oceanic) |
| MPY53 | **Euronesian** | 258,000 | 3,900,000 | 17 | 35 | 2 | 12 | 6 | 92.6 | European/Austronesian: Bislama, Filipino Mestizo, Hawaiian Pidgin, Neo-Melanesian, Pitcairner |
| MPY54 | **Micronesian** | 53,710 | 297,000 | 23 | 34 | 18 | 32 | 62 | 93.3 | Nuclear Micronesian (Gilbertese, Marshallese, Ponapese, Trukese, Ulithian), Nauruan, Yapese |
| MPY54a | Gilbertese | 21,700 | 96,500 | 1 | 6 | 1 | 4 | 0 | 92.8 | Gilbertese (Kiribertese) |
| MPY54b | Marshallese | 6,800 | 56,900 | 1 | 2 | 1 | 2 | 0 | 95.3 | Marshallese (Ebon; Ralik, Ratak) |
| MPY54c | Nauruan | 810 | 23,400 | 2 | 3 | 2 | 2 | 100 | 92.7 | Nauruan |
| MPY54d | Ponapese | 5,300 | 33,300 | 4 | 4 | 3 | 5 | 75 | 95.8 | Ponapese (Ponapean), Mokilese, Ngatik, Pingilapese |
| MPY54e | Trukese | 10,000 | 44,200 | 7 | 7 | 5 | 10 | 71 | 93.2 | Trukese (Ruk; Falchuk), Mapia, Paafang, Puluwat, Satawalese |
| MPY54f | Ulithian | 1,100 | 5,200 | 2 | 3 | 2 | 2 | 100 | 96.2 | Ulithian (Fals, Ngulu, Sonsoral, Sorol) |
| MPY54g | Yapese | 1,800 | 12,600 | 1 | 1 | 1 | 1 | 100 | 77.8 | Yapese |
| MPY54z | other Micronesian | 6,200 | 25,000 | 5 | 8 | 3 | 6 | 75 | 96.4 | Banaban, Carolinian, Kusalean (Kosraen), Mortlock, Palauan, Wolean |
| MPY55 | **Polynesian** | 260,090 | 1,439,000 | 39 | 76 | 42 | 90 | 62 | 84.2 | Polynesian: Hawaiian, Maori, Marquesan, Samoan, Tahitian, Tongan, Uvean |
| MPY55a | Hawaiian | 76,300 | 239,000 | 2 | 2 | 1 | 2 | 50 | 90.0 | Hawaiian, Neo-Hawaiian, Hawaiian American |
| MPY55b | Maori | 64,800 | 401,000 | 1 | 4 | 1 | 6 | 100 | 67.3 | Maori (New Zealand Maori), Rotorua-Taupo |
| MPY55c | Marquesan | 1,800 | 8,400 | 2 | 2 | 2 | 7 | 100 | 84.5 | Marquesan: Northwest Marquesan, Southeast Marquesan (Fatuhivan) |
| MPY55d | Rarotongan | 10,900 | 50,500 | 3 | 8 | 3 | 9 | 38 | 88.1 | Cook Islands Maori (Atiu, Rarotongan), Manohiki, Mauke, Mitiaro, Pukapukan, Rakahanga, Kuki |
| MPY55e | Samoan | 41,800 | 354,000 | 1 | 8 | 1 | 2 | 100 | 90.7 | Samoan |
| MPY55f | Tahitian | 16,700 | 108,000 | 2 | 5 | 2 | 3 | 100 | 94.4 | Tahitian, Neo-Tahitian, Rurutu, Rapa |
| MPY55g | Tongan | 22,500 | 137,000 | 2 | 8 | 2 | 5 | 88 | 93.4 | Tongan (Tonga-Uvea): Niuafo'ou, Niuatoputapu |
| MPY55h | Tuamotuan | 3,400 | 19,900 | 1 | 1 | 2 | 9 | 0 | 83.9 | Tuamotuan (Pa'umotuan), Napukan |
| MPY55i | Uvean | 5,000 | 25,000 | 1 | 4 | 1 | 3 | 0 | 91.6 | Uvean (Wallisian), East Uvean |
| MPY55j | West Uvean | 490 | 2,800 | 1 | 1 | 1 | 1 | 0 | 96.4 | Loyalty Islander, Haigan, Ouvea, West Uvean |
| MPY55z | other Polynesian | 16,400 | 91,900 | 23 | 33 | 26 | 43 | 52 | 89.0 | Futunan, Niuean, Solomoni (Rennellese, Sikalana, Tikopian), Tokelauan, Tubualan, Tuvaluan |
| N | **NEGROID** (Negro, Equatorial) | 90,411,600 | 648,090,000 | 1,949 | 3,030 | 1,187 | 3,933 | 50 | 60.6 | Negro (Negroid, Equatorial, Black) |
| NA | AFRICAN | 68,086,100 | 509,473,000 | 1,874 | 2,870 | 1,184 | 3,880 | 52 | 53.6 | African: Congold, Nigritic, Niger-Congo, Nilo-Saharan, Macro-Sudanic |
| NAB56 | **Bantoid** | 9,428,000 | 74,513,000 | 404 | 574 | 322 | 847 | 46 | 22.5 | Bantoid (=Bantu-like), Broad Bantu, Benue-Congo |
| NAB56a | Central Bantoid (Voltaic) | 2,564,000 | 23,465,000 | 101 | 159 | 75 | 239 | 27 | 16.9 | Bariba, Birifor, Bobo, Busa, Dagari, Dogon, Grunshi, Gurma, Kabre, Lobi, Moba, Mossi, Senufo, Somba |
| NAB56b | Eastern Bantoid (Benue) | 2,391,000 | 16,445,000 | 239 | 272 | 188 | 464 | 61 | 72.7 | Anyang, Basakomo, Birom, Ekoi, Ibibio (Efik), Jarawa, Jukun, Katab, Tion, Tiv, Yako, Zumper: Semi-Bantu |
| NAB56c | Western Bantoid (Atlantic) | 4,473,000 | 34,604,000 | 64 | 143 | 59 | 144 | 37 | 2.5 | Balante, Bijogo, Bullom, Diola, Fulani, Kissi, Limba, Pepel, Serer, Sherbro, Temne, Tenda, Tukulor, Wolof |
| NAB57 | **Bantu** | 31,200,000 | 233,026,000 | 598 | 955 | 220 | 1,145 | 61 | 72.1 | Bantu-speaking (Benue-Congo); Bantu Proper, Narrow Bantu |
| NAB57a | Cameroon Highland Bantu | 710,000 | 4,043,000 | 52 | 66 | 25 | 86 | 44 | 69.8 | Bamileke, Fungum, Li(Bali), Mum(Bamum), Ndob, Nen, Nsaw(Banso), Nsungli, Tikar, Widekum, Wum |
| NAB57b | Central Bantu | 8,293,000 | 54,572,000 | 100 | 180 | 21 | 154 | 68 | 64.2 | Bemba, Chewa, Chokwe, Kimbundu, Kongo-Kuba, Lomwe, Makonde, Makua, Nyanja, Sena, Vili, Yao |
| NAB57c | Equatorial Bantu | 2,120,000 | 11,302,000 | 97 | 130 | 62 | 247 | 56 | 82.5 | Amba, Babwe, Bangi, Bira, Budu, Dzem, Fang, Kaka, Kota, Kumu, Maka, Ngala, Rega, Sanga, Topoke |
| NAB57d | Interlacustrine Bantu | 5,638,000 | 45,313,000 | 45 | 93 | 7 | 69 | 48 | 84.3 | Chiga, Ganda, Gusii, Ha, Haya, Konjo, Luhya, Nkole, Nyoro, Ruanda, Rundi, Soga, Sonjo, Toro, Zinza |
| NAB57e | Kenya Highland Bantu | 1,518,000 | 15,027,000 | 21 | 29 | 8 | 57 | 38 | 82.6 | Chagga, Embu, Kamba, Kikuyu (Gikuyu), Mbere, Meru, Pare (Asu), Shambala (Sambaa), Taita, Tharaka |
| NAB57f | Luba | 1,116,000 | 8,973,000 | 13 | 16 | 1 | 26 | 81 | 93.9 | Luba (Bena Kalundwe, Bena Kanioka), Lulua, Lunda, Mbagani(Kete), Salampasu, Songe, Yeke |

*Continued overleaf*

*Table 18–5 concluded*

**RACE**
GEOGRAPHIC RACE
**Local race**
Ethnocultural family

| Code 1 | 2 | *Pop 1900* 3 | *Pop 2000* 4 | *Cultures* 5 | *Peoples* 6 | *Clusters* 7 | *Langs* 8 | *Sim* 9 | *AC* 10 | *A selection of constituent cultures, peoples, tribes, languages, alternative names or synonyms* 11 |
|---|---|---|---|---|---|---|---|---|---|---|
| NAB57g | Middle Zambezi Bantu | 222,000 | 2,363,000 | 24 | 37 | 3 | 23 | 84 | 66.1 | East Caprivian, Ila, Koba (Yeye), Lenje, Lozi, Lukolwe, Mashi, Mbukushu, Nkoya, Subia, Tonga, Totela |
| NAB57h | Mongo | 1,452,000 | 8,214,000 | 33 | 36 | 20 | 152 | 72 | 95.0 | Bosaka, Ekonda, Kela, Kutshu, Mbole, Mongo, Ngandu, Ngombe, Nkundo, Songomeno, Tetela |
| NAB57i | Nguni | 2,324,000 | 22,212,000 | 8 | 29 | 1 | 11 | 66 | 82.0 | Angoni (Gomani, Mombera, Mpezeni), Fingo, Laka, Manala, Ndebele, Pondo, Swazi, Tembu, Xhosa, Zulu |
| NAB57j | Northeast Coastal Bantu | 708,000 | 8,800,000 | 42 | 79 | 6 | 60 | 43 | 19.4 | Bajun, Comorian, Digo, Giriama, Hadimu, Pemba, Pokomo, Segeju, Shirazi, Swahili, Zaramo, Zigua |
| NAB57k | Northwestern Bantu | 618,000 | 2,580,000 | 83 | 101 | 46 | 161 | 50 | 78.5 | Bubi, Duala, Duma, Koko, Kossi, Kpe, Kundu, Lumbo, Mpongwe, Ngumba, Puku, Seke, Shogo, Teke |
| NAB57l | Shona | 540,000 | 9,812,000 | 9 | 28 | 1 | 11 | 64 | 58.0 | Kalanga, Karanga (Duma), Korekore, Manyika, Nambya, Ndau, Tawara, Zezuru (Hera, Rozwi) |
| NAB57m | Sotho | 1,162,000 | 8,608,000 | 6 | 13 | 2 | 7 | 85 | 75.4 | Eastern Sotho (Pedi), Northeastern Sotho (Lovedu, Venda), Southern Sotho |
| NAB57n | Southwestern Bantu | 1,390,000 | 6,013,000 | 13 | 23 | 4 | 23 | 83 | 84.4 | Ambo (Ovambo: Kwangali, Ndonga, Okavango), Herero, Mbundu (Ovimbundu), Ngonyelu, Nyaneka |
| NAB57o | Tanganyika Bantu | 1,953,000 | 15,282,000 | 43 | 53 | 11 | 48 | 87 | 53.5 | Bena, Fipa, Gogo, Hehe, Iramba, Iwa, Nyakyusa, Nyamwezi, Safwa, Sagara, Sukuma, Sumbwa, Turu |
| NAB57p | Tsonga | 949,000 | 6,153,000 | 6 | 12 | 2 | 8 | 58 | 53.8 | Tsonga (Shangaan): Chopi, Hlengwe, Lenge, Nwanati, Ronga, Tswa, Tsonga (Thonga, Tonga) |
| NAB57q | Tswana | 487,000 | 3,758,000 | 3 | 30 | 0 | 2 | 83 | 44.0 | Western Sotho: Hurutshe, Kgatla, Kwena, Ngwaketse, Ngwato, Rolong, Tlhaping, Tlharu, Tlokwa |
| NAN58 | **Eurafrican (Coloured)** | 872,000 | 10,208,000 | 32 | 83 | 3 | 24 | 7 | 79.9 | Afro-European: Aku, Americo-Liberian (Kwi), Baster, Caboverdian, Cape Coloured, Krlo, Mulatto, Wescos |
| NAB59 | **Guinean (Kwa)** | 10,218,700 | 78,414,000 | 185 | 271 | 147 | 527 | 56 | 65.1 | Guinean (Kwa) |
| NAB59a | Akan | 1,390,000 | 12,665,000 | 23 | 39 | 23 | 54 | 56 | 51.9 | Volta-Comoe: Akim (Akyem), Akwapim, Anyi-Baule, Ashanti, Attie, Brong, Fanti, Gonja, Guan, Kwahu; Twi |
| NAB59b | Central Togolese | 37,900 | 488,000 | 18 | 23 | 15 | 32 | 30 | 74.0 | Adele, Akebu, Akposo, Avatime, Basila, Buem, Kebu, Krachi, Logba, Nyangbo, Tafi, Tribu (Ntrubo) |
| NAB59c | Edo | 585,000 | 2,282,000 | 22 | 23 | 21 | 52 | 74 | 66.8 | Edo (Bini): Aakwo, Degema, Engenni, Epie, Eruhwa, Ishan (Esa, Isa), Kukuruku (Afenmai), Uhami |
| NAB59d | Ewe | 440,000 | 3,489,000 | 2 | 8 | 1 | 27 | 100 | 77.4 | Anglo, Ewe (Elbe, Ephe, Krepe), Gilidyi, Ho, Hwe |
| NAB59e | Fon | 318,000 | 3,375,000 | 12 | 19 | 4 | 24 | 68 | 29.1 | Fon (Dahomean): Adja, Aizo, Djedj, Fongbe, Hwelanu, Mabi, Wachi, Whydah, Xweda |
| NAB59f | Ga-Adangbe | 183,000 | 1,485,000 | 3 | 5 | 3 | 10 | 40 | 57.2 | Adangbe (Adangme), Anima, Awutu, Ga, Kpone, Krobo, Ningo, Osuduku, Prampram, Se (Shai), Accra |
| NAB59g | Gun | 74,700 | 530,000 | 3 | 5 | 0 | 3 | 80 | 48.3 | Gun: Egun, Tofinu, Wemenu, Alada, Gu, Mahi, Maxi |
| NAB59h | Ibo | 2,881,000 | 16,519,000 | 9 | 15 | 7 | 23 | 60 | 96.5 | Ibo (Igbo): Abriba, Adda, Ekpeye, Ika, Izi, Ngwa, Ngwo, Onitsha, Owerri |
| NAB59i | Ijaw | 325,000 | 1,282,000 | 11 | 12 | 8 | 37 | 50 | 87.4 | Brass (Nembe), Ibani, Ijaw (Ijo), Ikwere, Kabo, Kalabari, Kumbo, Mein, Nkoro, Okurikan |
| NAB59j | Kru | 288,000 | 2,711,000 | 38 | 51 | 31 | 154 | 45 | 40.3 | Bakwe (Krumen), Bassa, Bete, Dida, Grebo, Krahn, Kru (Crau, Krao, Krawi, Nana), Sapo (Pahn), Wobe |
| NAB59k | Lagoon | 90,400 | 1,057,000 | 13 | 14 | 13 | 23 | 43 | 79.9 | Abe, Abure, Ajukru, Alladian (Alagya), Ari, Assini, Avikam, Ebrie, Gwa, Mekyibo, Nzima |
| NAB59l | Popo | 45,700 | 409,000 | 1 | 2 | 1 | 3 | 0 | 70.2 | Popo (Mina): Anecho, Ge, Mina, Peda, Pia |
| NAB59m | Nupe | 325,000 | 2,299,000 | 3 | 3 | 3 | 17 | 33 | 13.8 | Bassange (Nge), Batache, Beni, Dibo, Egagi, Ebe, Gbedye, Igbira, Kakanda, Kupa, Kusopa, Nupe, Zam |
| NAB59n | Yoruba | 3,072,000 | 26,082,000 | 8 | 29 | 4 | 24 | 79 | 60.7 | Ana, Bunu, Egba, Ekiti, Ife, Igala, Igbomina, Ijebu, Ikale, Ilaje, Itsekiri, Nago, Ondo, Owo, Oyo, Yoruba |
| NAB59z | other Guinean | 163,000 | 3,741,000 | 19 | 23 | 13 | 44 | 48 | 63.8 | Gade, Gbari, Idoma, Isoko, Urhobo (Abraka, Agbon, Ewu, Olomu, Sobo, Ughelli, Uwherun), Yala |
| NAB60 | **Hausa-Chadic** | 4,181,000 | 33,980,000 | 187 | 247 | 188 | 443 | 55 | 7.3 | Hausa-speaking Chadic peoples, other Chadic peoples |
| NAB60a | Hausa | 3,218,000 | 24,400,000 | 1 | 25 | 1 | 2 | 84 | 0.1 | Adarawa, Azna, Hausa (Afuno), Kanawa, Katsenawa, Kurfei, Maguzawa, Mauri, Tazarawa, Zazzagawa |
| NAB60b | Plateau Chadic | 963,000 | 9,579,000 | 186 | 222 | 187 | 441 | 51 | 25.7 | Angas, Bura, Kapsiki, Kirdi, Kotoko, Mandara, Margi, Masa, Matakam, Musgum, Tangale, Tuburi, Wurkum |
| NAB61 | **Kanuri (Saharan)** | 1,099,000 | 6,290,000 | 11 | 29 | 5 | 10 | 52 | 0.0 | Beriberi, Berti, Bornu, Bulgeda, Daza, Kanembu, Kanuri (Saharan Negro), Manga, Teda, Tubu, Zagawa |
| NAB62 | **Nilotic (Para-Nilotic)** | 3,816,500 | 24,779,000 | 110 | 168 | 82 | 220 | 41 | 57.5 | Nilo-Hamitic: East Nilotic, Eastern Sudanic, Prenilote, South Nilotic, West Nilotic |
| NAB62a | Acholi | 123,000 | 920,000 | 1 | 2 | 0 | 1 | 100 | 94.6 | Acholi (Gan, Gang, Shuli) |
| NAB62b | Alur | 50,500 | 1,196,000 | 2 | 4 | 2 | 3 | 50 | 90.9 | Alur (Alua, Lur, Luri) |
| NAB62c | Anuak | 38,100 | 127,000 | 2 | 3 | 2 | 5 | 33 | 8.0 | Anuak (Yambo), Pari |
| NAB62d | Barea | 24,100 | 72,500 | 1 | 1 | 1 | 4 | 100 | 5.0 | Barea (Barya, Nera) |
| NAB62e | Bari | 153,000 | 652,000 | 3 | 5 | 2 | 7 | 80 | 81.0 | Bari: Mondari, Nyambara, Nyepu, Pojulu, Kuku, Fajulu |
| NAB62f | Dinka | 604,000 | 1,896,000 | 5 | 6 | 5 | 13 | 0 | 66.9 | Agar, Bor, Dinka (Denkawi, Jang), Gok, Luaich, Maluai, Padang, Rek, Raik, Ruweng, Twij |
| NAB62g | Kalenjin | 294,000 | 2,346,000 | 11 | 11 | 3 | 26 | 45 | 54.7 | Kalenjin: Elgeyo (Keyo), Kipsigis, Marakwet, Nandi, Tatoga, Tugen, Terik, Barabaig, Endo |
| NAB62h | Kunama | 24,100 | 226,000 | 1 | 3 | 2 | 8 | 100 | 20.3 | Kunama (Bazen, Cunama), Dilla |
| NAB62i | Lango | 149,000 | 1,143,000 | 1 | 1 | 1 | 5 | 100 | 93.7 | Lango (Langi, Leb-Lano, Umiro) |
| NAB62j | Luo | 516,000 | 4,760,000 | 2 | 5 | 1 | 2 | 100 | 91.5 | Gaya (Girange, Wagela), Luo (Joluo, Dholuo), Nilotic Kavirondo, Nyifwa, Padhola (Dama, JoPadhola) |
| NAB62k | Maasai | 113,000 | 1,392,000 | 4 | 9 | 3 | 4 | 33 | 27.4 | Arusha, Elmolo, Kwafi, Lumbwa, Maasai, Njemps, Samburu, Baraguyu |
| NAB62l | Mao | 8,100 | 1,300 | 1 | 1 | 1 | 1 | 100 | 4.9 | Mao (Amam, Anfillo, Mau, Mayo), Busasi |
| NAB62m | Nubian | 194,000 | 2,992,000 | 20 | 33 | 9 | 24 | 18 | 0.1 | Anag, Barabra (Danagla, Kenuzi, Maha, Nile Nubian, Nubi), Birked, Dair, Dilling, Midobi, Nyimang, Temein |
| NAB62n | Nuer | 299,000 | 1,565,000 | 3 | 5 | 2 | 11 | 0 | 19.7 | Atwot, Barr, Gaweir, Jalal, Ji Kany Cien, Lak, Lau, Nuer, Nyuong, Thiang |
| NAB62o | Shilluk | 110,000 | 259,000 | 1 | 1 | 1 | 2 | 0 | 44.8 | Shilluk; Dembo (Bwodho), Kapango, Shatt (Thuri), Shilluk Luo |
| NAB62p | Suk | 34,200 | 357,000 | 1 | 2 | 1 | 2 | 100 | 21.6 | Suk (Pokot): Cepleng, Endo, Kimunkon, Upe |
| NAB62q | Teso | 265,000 | 1,764,000 | 3 | 5 | 3 | 7 | 80 | 93.1 | Itesyo, Kumam, Teso (Bakedi, Iteso), Mening |
| NAB62r | Turkana | 55,400 | 402,000 | 1 | 3 | 1 | 1 | 100 | 18.8 | Ngamatak, Nibelai, Nithir, Turkana (Elgume) |
| NAB62y | other Nilotic | 346,000 | 2,161,000 | 28 | 41 | 24 | 49 | 46 | 50.1 | Didinga, Fajulu, Ik, Jie, Jur, Kakwa, Karamojong, Latuka, Murle, Sabaot, Suri, Surma, Tepeth, Topotha |
| NAB62z | other Prenilote | 416,000 | 547,000 | 19 | 27 | 18 | 45 | 26 | 7.8 | Berta (Shangalla), Fung, Gule (Hameg), Gumuz, Ingessana (Tabi), Koma, Meban, Mesongo, Uduk, Ulu |
| NAB63 | **Nuclear Mande** | 1,690,200 | 17,706,000 | 48 | 108 | 25 | 86 | 36 | 2.7 | Mande: Bambara, Bozo, Dialonke, Kasonke, Konyanke, Koranko, Malinke, Soninke, Yalunka |
| NAB63a | Bambara | 456,000 | 4,625,000 | 2 | 12 | 2 | 24 | 0 | 3.1 | Bambara (Bamana), Dyangirte, Gan, Kaiongo, Masasi, Nyamosa, Somono, Toro, Dafi, Marka |
| NAB63b | Bozo | 22,200 | 23,300 | 3 | 4 | 3 | 3 | 50 | 0.0 | Bozo (Sorko, Sorogo), Tieyaxo |
| NAB63c | Dialonke | 31,700 | 27,600 | 1 | 2 | 0 | 0 | 0 | 0.1 | Dialonke (Djalonke, Jallonke, Northern Yalunka) |
| NAB63d | Kagoro | 10,400 | 25,400 | 1 | 1 | 0 | 1 | 0 | 1.0 | Kagoro (Bagane, Logoro) |
| NAB63e | Kasonke | 26,100 | 143,000 | 1 | 2 | 0 | 1 | 0 | 2.7 | Kasonke (Kasson, Khasonke, Xasonke) |
| NAB63f | Konyanke | 19,900 | 336,000 | 2 | 3 | 0 | 2 | 33 | 0.6 | Gyomande, Konyanke (Konianke), Mau |
| NAB63g | Koranko | 58,000 | 416,000 | 2 | 3 | 1 | 3 | 33 | 1.5 | Koranko (Kuranko), Lele |
| NAB63h | Malinke | 645,000 | 7,198,000 | 12 | 29 | 1 | 9 | 45 | 0.6 | Bambugu, Malinke (Mandingo, Mandinka, Maninka, Wangara), Mikifore: Komendi, Konya, Yarse, Jula |
| NAB63i | Nono | 2,600 | 118,000 | 1 | 1 | 1 | 4 | 100 | 0.0 | Djennenke, Nono, Sorogama Bozo |
| NAB63j | Soninke | 139,000 | 1,460,000 | 2 | 12 | 1 | 5 | 75 | 0.0 | Aser, Aswanik, Diawara, Dyakanke, Gadyaga, Marka, Serahuli, Silabe, Soninke (Sarakole), Toubakal |
| NAB63k | Susu | 163,000 | 1,061,000 | 1 | 5 | 1 | 1 | 0 | 0.2 | Susu (Soso) |
| NAB63l | Yalunka | 7,300 | 234,000 | 1 | 3 | 0 | 1 | 100 | 0.2 | Yalunka (Southern Dialonke, Yalun Soso) |
| NAB63z | other Nuclear Mande | 109,000 | 2,038,000 | 19 | 31 | 15 | 32 | 29 | 14.0 | Busansi, Kong Diula (Dyula), Huela, Ligbi, Samo, Sya, Samogho |
| NAB64 | **Peripheral Mande** | 752,600 | 5,208,000 | 16 | 26 | 10 | 19 | 58 | 16.6 | Mande-fu: Dan, Gagu, Gbande, Guro, Kono, Kpelle, Loko, Loma (Toma), Mende, Ngere, Vai |
| NAB64a | Dan | 95,200 | 1,252,000 | 2 | 5 | 1 | 2 | 60 | 22.4 | Dan (Da), Gio (San, Yafuba, Yakuba), Tura |
| NAB64b | Gagu | 6,000 | 40,600 | 1 | 1 | 1 | 1 | 0 | 10.1 | Gagu (Gban) |
| NAB64c | Gbande | 9,400 | 179,000 | 1 | 2 | 0 | 1 | 50 | 6.2 | Belle, Gbande (Bande, Gbassi), Gbundi, Weima |
| NAB64d | Guro | 30,100 | 387,000 | 2 | 2 | 2 | 2 | 0 | 19.3 | Guro (Gwio, Kwendre, Kweni, Lo), Mwa, Nwan, Mona |
| NAB64e | Kono | 49,400 | 227,000 | 1 | 3 | 1 | 4 | 100 | 11.4 | Kono (Kolo, Kondo, Konnoh) |
| NAB64f | Kpelle | 113,000 | 987,000 | 3 | 3 | 2 | 3 | 0 | 29.6 | Kpelle (Gbese, Gerse, Guerze, Kpese, Pessy) |
| NAB64g | Loko | 29,800 | 142,000 | 1 | 2 | 0 | 1 | 100 | 3.7 | Loko (Landro, Landogo) |
| NAB64h | Loma | 50,500 | 348,000 | 2 | 2 | 1 | 2 | 100 | 10.6 | Loma (Balu, Buzi, Domor, Gisima, Jokoi, Loghoma, Toa, Toma, Wuboma) |
| NAB64i | Mende | 318,000 | 1,286,000 | 1 | 2 | 1 | 1 | 100 | 9.4 | Ko (Comende), Kpa, Mende (Boumpe, Hulo, Kossa, Kosso), Sewa |
| NAB64j | Ngere | 26,700 | 235,000 | 1 | 2 | 1 | 1 | 0 | 4.3 | Mano, Ngere, Niadrubu, Zague, Zahon, Maa |
| NAB64k | Vai | 24,500 | 124,000 | 1 | 2 | 0 | 1 | 100 | 0.6 | Vai (By, Galdinas, Gallina, Karo, Nai, Vei) |
| NAB65 | **Songhai** | 311,500 | 4,599,000 | 5 | 17 | 4 | 8 | 24 | 0.3 | Dendi, Songhai, Zerma (Djerma) |
| NAB65a | Dendi | 12,500 | 105,000 | 1 | 4 | 0 | 1 | 100 | 5.1 | Dendi (Dandawa) |
| NAB65b | Songhai | 226,000 | 1,631,000 | 3 | 8 | 2 | 5 | 0 | 0.3 | Gao, Koroboro, Songhai (Sonhrai), Tombmata, Maranse, Belbali |
| NAB65c | Zerma | 73,000 | 2,862,000 | 1 | 5 | 2 | 2 | 0 | 0.1 | Zerma (Adzerma, Djerma, Dyabarma, Zaberma) |
| NAB66 | **Sudanic** | 4,516,600 | 20,750,000 | 278 | 392 | 178 | 551 | 54 | 53.7 | Sudanic (Central & Eastern Nigritic): Adamawa-Eastern/Ubangian, Surma |
| NAB66a | Azande | 713,000 | 1,845,000 | 4 | 7 | 3 | 7 | 100 | 86.6 | Azande (Niam-Niam, Sande, Zande), Bandya, Idio, Barambu, Pambia, Tagbu |
| NAB66b | Banda | 281,000 | 1,413,000 | 29 | 39 | 15 | 65 | 69 | 65.0 | Banda, Belingo, Dakpwa, Langbwasse, Mbanja, Tagbo, Wada, Wasa, Yakwa |
| NAB66c | Baya | 584,000 | 2,635,000 | 41 | 61 | 22 | 97 | 59 | 38.0 | Baya (Baja, Gbaya), Bogoto, Chamba, Duru, Jen, Longuda, Mbum, Mumuye, Vere, Yungur |
| NAB66d | Fur | 292,000 | 1,625,000 | 16 | 23 | 9 | 21 | 17 | 0.1 | Baygo, Dagu (Daju), Dalinga, Forenga, Fur, Kimr, Kungara, Mararit, Sila, Sungor, Tama, Temurka, Shatt |
| NAB66e | Madi | 64,900 | 802,000 | 12 | 19 | 15 | 32 | 37 | 79.9 | Bongo, Kreish, Logo, Madi, Mittu, Olubo |
| NAB66f | Mandja | 55,700 | 242,000 | 1 | 2 | 0 | 1 | 50 | 55.8 | Mandja (Mangia), Manza |
| NAB66g | Moru-Mangbetu | 299,000 | 4,680,000 | 15 | 23 | 11 | 44 | 52 | 86.6 | Moru-Mangbetu: Lendu, Lugbara, Mamvu, Mangbetu, Mayogo, Moru, Okebu, Popoi, Rumbi, Avukaya |
| NAB66h | Nuba | 308,000 | 1,110,000 | 29 | 39 | 25 | 68 | 21 | 20.5 | Kordofanian: Heiban, Kadugli, Katla, Koalib, Krongo, Mesakin, Moro, Otoro, Tagali, Talodi, Tumtum |
| NAB66z | other Sudanic | 1,919,000 | 6,398,000 | 131 | 179 | 78 | 216 | 61 | 40.2 | Bagirmi, Bwaka, Kare, Masalit, Mbai, Mubi, Mundang, Ndogo, Ngama, Nzakara, Sango, Sara, Yakoma |
| NF | AFRO-AMERICAN | 22,325,500 | 138,617,000 | 75 | 160 | 3 | 53 | 8 | 86.5 | Black of African or mixed descent: Antillean, Cafuso, Coloured, Creole, Mulatto, Negro, Preto, Zambo |
| NFB67 | **Dutch-speaking** | 97,500 | 694,000 | 7 | 14 | 0 | 4 | 0 | 83.7 | Dutch-speaking Black of African or mixed descent |
| NFB67a | Black | 12,300 | 38,300 | 3 | 5 | 0 | 2 | 0 | 69.7 | Bush Negro, Dutch-speaking, Negro, Boni, Djuka, Saramaccan |
| NFB67b | Creole | 85,200 | 655,000 | 4 | 9 | 0 | 2 | 0 | 84.6 | Antillean Creole, Mulatto, Papiamento (Spanish/Dutch Creole), Sranan (Taki-Taki), Surinam Creole |
| NFB68 | **English-speaking** | 11,424,000 | 41,064,000 | 47 | 89 | 2 | 36 | 13 | 74.8 | English-speaking Black of African or mixed descent including speakers of English-based Pidgin-Creoles |
| NFB68a | Black (African Negro) | 11,127,000 | 38,863,000 | 23 | 55 | 2 | 27 | 7 | 74.5 | African Negro, Bush Negro, USA Negro/Black (80% Negro/20% White), West Indian Black |
| NFB68b | Mulatto | 297,000 | 2,201,000 | 24 | 34 | 0 | 9 | 24 | 80.0 | Afro-Asian, Afro-Chinese, Black Carib (Garif), Coloured, Creole, Guyanese, Maroon, Mulatto |
| NFB69 | **French-speaking** | 2,073,000 | 12,386,000 | 10 | 22 | 1 | 9 | 0 | 91.7 | French-speaking Black of African or mixed descent |
| NFB69a | Black | 1,444,000 | 8,923,000 | 3 | 8 | 1 | 4 | 0 | 92.7 | Black, Boni, Bush Negro, Noir, Guadeloupian, Haitian Black |
| NFB69b | Creole | 629,000 | 3,464,000 | 7 | 14 | 0 | 5 | 0 | 89.0 | Antillese, Dominican Creole, French (Black) Creole, Mulatto (Mulatre), Haitian Creole |
| NFB70 | **Portuguese-speaking** | 5,960,000 | 56,169,000 | 4 | 7 | 0 | 1 | 14 | 92.5 | Portuguese-speaking Black of African or mixed descent |
| NFB70a | Black | 1,986,000 | 18,713,000 | 1 | 1 | 0 | 0 | 0 | 89.5 | Preto (Black) (African Negro), Brazilian Black |
| NFB70b | Mulato | 3,974,000 | 37,456,000 | 3 | 6 | 0 | 1 | 17 | 94.0 | Cafuso (Negro/Amerindian), Crioulo, Mulato (more Black than Portuguese), Quilombola |
| NFB71 | **Spanish-speaking** | 2,771,000 | 28,304,000 | 7 | 28 | 0 | 3 | 0 | 89.2 | Spanish-speaking Black of African or mixed descent |
| NFB71a | Black | 857,000 | 9,129,000 | 1 | 11 | 0 | 0 | 0 | 84.9 | Negro, Spanish Black, Colombian Black, Mexican Black |
| NFB71b | Mulatto | 1,914,000 | 19,175,000 | 6 | 17 | 0 | 3 | 0 | 91.3 | Chinocholo, Criollo of mixed race, Mulatto, Palenquero, Spanish Creole, Zambo (Negro/Amerindian) |

here, and the term European, include Whites who have emigrated outside Europe and the Western world for the first generation (30 years) only, but exclude Whites of the second or more generations in the Third World if they have intermarried or assimilated with Non-Whites, and who are therefore here considered to have become separate Third-World peoples by then. (5) To illustrate the third subcolumn 'Culture world', another category 'Color', a term from physical anthropology describing biological race characteristics, is defined here and given as a stylized typology of 7 terms. Where 2 or 3 terms are given (e.g. 'White/Tan/Brown'), it means that the culture or people concerned is predominantly White but significant numbers are either Tan or Brown; only the predominant color is included in the code. (6) For each culture cluster, the last column gives a selection of its major constituent cultures, peoples, subpeoples, tribes, languages (on this classification, 13,500 on the world scene) or dialects with, (in parentheses) synonyms or alternative names in use. Slightly different alternate spellings are only given occasionally where necessary for easy identification. (7) Names in the last column are ethnic, or are both ethnic and linguistic. (8) The addition 'et alii' refers to the existence of several others groupings; the addition '&c' refers to the presence of a large number of other smaller groupings.

### Statistics, 1900-2025
For all ethnolinguistic peoples in this classification, statistics are given here in *WCE* Table 8-2, with world summary statistics. Full statistics, for all peoples, of total populations, total Christians, affiliated Christians, unaffiliated Christians, practicing Christians, Great Commission Christians—given both as absolute numbers, as percentages of their total population, and ranked in various ways—are given on the related CD.

### Bibliography
Literature on specific peoples is immense. What is provided here is a bibliography of descriptive and analytical literature, mainly books and scholarly articles. Each deals with one culture or people, usually with one people in one country.

### CODES FOR WCE PART 8 "ETHNOSPHERE" (TABLE 8-2, PEOPLES OF THE WORLD)

Now that *WCT*'s tables have been described above and their codes listed there, the larger database shown in *WCE* as Table 8-2 will be described. These para-

graphs should be regarded as an extension of Part 16 "GeoCodebook". depicting the totality of all these data.

The 230 pages of this lengthy table set out the 12,600 distinct and separate peoples (each being defined as a culture-in-one-country) who inhabit the world's 238 countries, and each's values for 38 columns. Peoples are set out across 2 facing pages in alphabetical order within countries also in alphabetical sequence. Each people therefore is described on one single line (with the same opening reference number) across the 2 facing pages.

### COLUMN
1. ID or reference number (for 1 line on 2 facing pages).
2. Ethnic name of people (people-in-a-country), anglicized.

### POPULATION
3. Persons in each people as % country, 1995-2010.
4. Persons in each people, in 1995.
5. Persons in each people, in 2000.
6. Persons in each people, in 2025.

### IDENTITY CODE
7. Race/ethnic code (6 characters), as in *WCE* Table 8-1.
8. Language code (7 characters), as in *WCE* Table 9-13.

### LANGUAGE
9. Autoglossonym (people's own name for language, in most cases this being an *inner-language*, but sometimes an *outer-language*, this being identified by the word *'cluster'*). Note that accents and other diacritical marks in this column are not explained here and may be technical or phonetic, etc. For exact spelling of any name consult Dalby, *Linguasphere* for the code shown.
10. Users of this language in this country, % (selective), both native speakers and non-native users.

### CHURCH
11. Affiliated Christians, % of this people.
12. Church members (affiliated persons).

### MINISTRY (codes: see WCE Part 9, before Tables 9-12 and 9-13).
13. 'Jesus' Film availability
14. Audio scriptures (a)
15. New Reader Scriptures (y)
16. Braille Scriptures for the blind (u)

17. Hearing-impaired (signed) Scriptures for the deaf (h)
18. Discipleship/discipling (d, 0–10)
19. Work among (agencies at work: wa, 0–10)
20. Cross-cultural mission (xc, 0-16)
21. Mass evangelistic campaigns (mc, 0–5)
22. Mission agencies present (mi, 0–5)

### SCRIPTURE
23. Biblioglossonym (official name of language for any translation done or under way). Note: if an asterisk is added, it means there is also an alternate biblioglossonym (usually from WBT/SIL). See full explanation before *WCE* Table 9-13.

#### Published scriptures:
24. P=Portion (Gospel; 1 Book), p=near-Portion, . =none.
25. N=New Testament (27 Books), n=near-NT, . =none.
26. B=Bible (whole 66 or 80 Books), b=near-Bible, . =none.
27. Second-language scriptures (usable by over 50% of this people's population) (ss)

### EVANGELIZATION
28. Denominations present (with major work among this people, D).
29. Alien Christians (of another culture resident among this people, aC, 0–10)
30. Exponential church growth, % per year, for period AD 1900-2000.
31. Countries broadcasting Christian programs in this language (r, 0–8)
32. E, % of this population now evangelized.
33. U, % of this population unevangelized.
34. Location of this people in World A/B/C trichotomy.

### EVANGELISM
35. Evangelistic offers received per capita per year (e, 0–900)
36. Responsiveness to Christianity (R)
37. Targeting variable (T, 1–10)

### ADDITIONAL DESCRIPTIVE DATA
38. Locations, civil divisions, literacy, other religions, church history, D=actual number of denominations, dioceses, church growth, M=missions at work, parachurch agencies, ministries, movements.

# 3. A WORLD LANGUAGE CLASSIFICATION (=LANGUAGE CODE)

### Language
In this volume, language as a distinct entity separate from race, culture, and ethnicity is described and classified into 10 macrozones and 100 microzones, as shown in Table 18–6. This table enumerates the rest of the categories involved—sets, chains, nets, clusters, languages. The full World Language Classification with its 13,509 distinct languages is given in *WCE* Part 9 "LinguaMetrics". What follows in the paragraphs below is a discussion of language as a distinct part of the ethnolinguistic definition of peoples and cultures.

Language is the principal means of communicating culture (a word which itself commonly embraces the entire way of life of a people). From the linguistic point of view, the world's 13,000 distinct living languages (excluding dead languages and those no longer spoken) as shown in the classification can be classified into 10-16 major linguistic families (or 24 major phyla or groupings or superstocks, or from 40-100 families according to some classifications), with several minor ones consisting each of one language isolate. Languages are usually classified in the first instance genetically (evolution from a common ancestral language), in some cases with the superimposing of further classification typologically (grammatical or lexical similarities in language structure). The total of languages according to different scholars varies widely, and is clearly dependent on how

one differentiates between language and dialect. The index of languages and alternative names in C. F. & F. M. Voegelin's *Classification and index of the world's languages* (New York: Elsevier, 1977, 658p), lists some 28,300 different names. There is considerable variety also in the classifications proposed by linguists, using techniques such as genetic relationship, glottochronology and lexicostatistics, but they all usually include the following families: Indo-European, Hamito-Semitic, Ural-Altaic, Caucasian (Georgian), Sino-Tibetan, Malayo-Polynesian (Austronesian), Dravidian, Amerindian, Nilotic, Sudanese-Guinean, Hottentot-Bushman, and Bantu. A detailed listing of most living languages, with all living dialects and alternate spellings, and also Scripture translation status, is given in *Ethnologue*, ed B. F. Grimes (Wycliffe Bible Translators, 14th edition 2000). This work usually divides living languages into the following 24 phyla: Afro-Asiatic, Austronesian, Austro-Asiatic, Azteco-Tanoan, Australian, Caucasian, Dravidian, Hokan, Indo-European, Indo-European Creole, Kam-Tai, Khoisan, Macro-Algonkian, Macro-Chibchan, Macro-Siouan, Na-Dene, Niger-Kordofanian, Nilo-Saharan, Oto-Manguean, Penutian, Papuan, Paleo-Siberian, Sino-Tibetan, and Ural-Altaic.

There are, therefore, various definitions of language and dialect, some stricter and some looser. For the purposes of *WCE/WCT/WCD*, a distinct language is defined as one which has, or should have, or is

agreed to need to have, its own separate and distinct translation of Holy Scripture, instead of its speakers being satisfied with (or being told by missions or translators to be satisfied with) Scriptures already translated into another tongue which is held to be sufficiently close or comprehensible. In many such cases (2 languages using a single translation), the 2 languages may often be correctly regarded as dialects of each other rather than as separate languages.

In this statistical analysis, the category 'Languages' for a given country is enumerated and quantified here as consisting of mother tongues and lingua francas either (a) native to the country, even if minuscule in size (e.g. Bushmen tribes in Southern Africa with a handful of speakers), or (b) in the case of expatriates, with as speakers a community (not just isolated individuals) numbering at least 0.05% of the country's population, or (c) significant enough for them to be officially listed as languages in use in the country by government censuses or schedules or other similar publications.

### Compiling the linguametric database
Utilizing this classification, data were now added covering all of the church's worldwide ministries that focus on languages. These cover: Scripture translation and distribution, Christian publishing, Christian literature, books and periodicals, broadcasting and telecasting, audiovisual approaches, ministries

to the blind, the deaf, the handicapped, with special reference to children of all ages and also to nonliterates. Of particular interest is *WCE* Table 9-12, Names for God in 900 languages.

This extensive database is available on CDs related to David Dalby's *Linguasphere: register of the world's languages and speech communities*, including the forthcoming CD, *World Christian database*. It is partially reproduced there as *WCE* Table 9-13 which lists all 13,509 languages of the world (but not dialects) together with many of the ministries listed above.

Of many new discoveries that flow from this material, one of the most significant is the relationship between languages with direct ministries (e.g. the Zulu Bible, or the 'Jesus' Film in Hindi) and their thousands of closely related languages. This can be stated in single-sentence form: Every language (also termed 'inner language' or 'narrow language') listed here benefits directly from language ministries in any other language shown as within the same language cluster (also termed 'outer language' or 'broad language'). Thus at the end of *WCE* Table 9-13 it can be seen that a number of languages around Zulu, and within its cluster, in practice have access to the Scriptures. Though termed here 'indirect access', it is nevertheless adequate access. This analysis terms this further by affirming that a language has access to, or understands or uses, a *near-Bible*. This role of near-scriptures—near-Bible, near-New Testament, near-gospel, near-selection, near-'Jesus' Film, near-audio scripture, near-Braille scripture, near-signed scripture, near-broadcast, et alia—clearly revolutionizes the extent to which Gutenberg's original vision in inventing printing with movable type (to see the Holy Scriptures disseminated and available to all the peoples of the world) is being realized today.

## CODEBOOK FOR LINGUAMETRICS TABLE 9-13

The 280 pages in *WCE* Part 9 "LinguaMetrics" set out the 13,500 distinct and separate languages spoken during the 20th century. Data for each language occupies one single line across one page only. Note that the unit 'a language' is a single entity independent of any country or countries it is spoken in. By contrast, the unit 'a people' refers to one ethnocultural ethnolinguistic people residing in one particular country; spread over 10 countries, it would count as 10 peoples.

### Extinct languages

Note that some 1,000 languages spoken in the 20th century are now extinct. This is demonstrated by the firm '0', zero, in the population columns 5 and 6. Some 400 others are either nearly extinct (dying, with under 10 speakers), or endangered (under 100), or moribund (under 1,000).

### Little-known languages

Note also that numerous languages have a blank space in those 2 columns, meaning that no population figure is assigned to them. At this stage in the evolution of this complex database, their populations (mostly unknown or relatively unknown in the literature because as yet unstudied by linguists or anthropologists) are combined with other better-studied and better-known languages within their language cluster. In many cases, also, their situation is one of duplication—their 'speakers' can also be said to be at the same time speakers of other closely-related near-languages.

For full understanding of the origins, compilation from 1975-1999, and rationale for this Linguasphere/World Language Classification's categories and codes, consult the definitive publication by David Dalby, *Linguasphere*. The version employed here is a slightly earlier published version differing only in the codes assigned to a few languages.

### Column and codes

The following brief listing will enable the reader to use the lengthy compilation of data for 13,509 languages that follows. For more explanation, consult *WCE* Part 3 "Codebook".

Note that most languages have several alternate names or spellings; these, together with several thousand dialects, are not given here but are published in Dalby's *Linguasphere*, and on related CDs.

Note also that although almost all reference names here are written out in full, a number as part of their

**Table 18–6. The globe's 10 language macrozones and 100 zones tabulated by sets, nets, clusters, languages, native speakers, % church members, and % evangelized persons, AD 2000.**

| Zone<br>1 | Zone name<br>2 | Sets<br>3 | Chains<br>4 | Nets<br>5 | Clusters<br>6 | Langs<br>7 | Native speakers<br>8 | AC %<br>9 | E %<br>10 |
|---|---|---|---|---|---|---|---|---|---|
| 0 | **AFRICAN** macrozone | 44 | 78 | 137 | 277 | 761 | 69,441,000 | 31.7 | 62.7 |
| 00 | MANDIC zone | 4 | 13 | 25 | 34 | 104 | 22,935,000 | 6.0 | 50.1 |
| 01 | SONGHAIC zone | 1 | 1 | 2 | 5 | 9 | 4,665,000 | 0.3 | 36.1 |
| 02 | SAHARIC zone | 3 | 3 | 4 | 5 | 10 | 6,138,000 | 0.0 | 30.3 |
| 03 | SUDANIC zone | 2 | 6 | 14 | 37 | 147 | 8,124,000 | 68.9 | 90.0 |
| 04 | NILOTIC zone | 3 | 10 | 22 | 45 | 138 | 20,810,000 | 68.2 | 91.1 |
| 05 | NILO-SAHELIC zone | 16 | 24 | 38 | 57 | 140 | 5,727,000 | 5.6 | 25.5 |
| 06 | KORDOFANIC zone | 4 | 6 | 10 | 18 | 51 | 512,000 | 36.7 | 63.5 |
| 07 | RIFTIC zone | 4 | 5 | 7 | 7 | 7 | 125,000 | 73.4 | 95.7 |
| 08 | NAMA-TSHUIC zone | 2 | 3 | 4 | 14 | 85 | 342,000 | 63.9 | 80.3 |
| 09 | KALAHARIC zone | 5 | 7 | 11 | 55 | 70 | 61,300 | 15.1 | 41.1 |
| 1 | **AFROASIAN** macrozone | 43 | 83 | 183 | 278 | 683 | 390,490,000 | 14.3 | 62.6 |
| 10 | TAMAZIC zone | 1 | 1 | 1 | 4 | 29 | 19,734,000 | 0.3 | 33.0 |
| 11 | COPTIC zone | 1 | 1 | 1 | 1 | 1 | 7,200 | 99.0 | 100.0 |
| 12 | SEMITIC zone | 1 | 3 | 10 | 24 | 86 | 279,933,000 | 15.3 | 64.7 |
| 13 | BEJIC zone | 1 | 1 | 1 | 1 | 1 | 2,514,000 | 0.0 | 21.5 |
| 14 | MID CUSHITIC zone | 7 | 10 | 21 | 25 | 70 | 43,004,000 | 18.7 | 66.3 |
| 15 | PARA-CUSHITIC zone | 2 | 4 | 5 | 6 | 8 | 617,000 | 22.8 | 63.4 |
| 16 | OMOTIC zone | 6 | 9 | 24 | 30 | 57 | 5,600,000 | 40.6 | 78.0 |
| 17 | EAST CHADIC zone | 7 | 17 | 34 | 41 | 83 | 1,727,000 | 28.2 | 61.2 |
| 18 | BIUMANDARIC zone | 9 | 17 | 34 | 64 | 196 | 4,566,000 | 23.0 | 57.2 |
| 19 | WEST CHADIC zone | 8 | 20 | 52 | 82 | 152 | 32,788,000 | 2.6 | 59.4 |
| 2 | **AUSTRALASIAN** macrozone | 222 | 476 | 789 | 1,162 | 2,207 | 5,285,000 | 73.9 | 91.8 |
| 20 | WEST IRIANIC zone | 26 | 47 | 70 | 103 | 199 | 540,000 | 56.1 | 78.5 |
| 21 | NORTH IRIANIC zone | 22 | 38 | 59 | 77 | 129 | 198,000 | 45.0 | 68.5 |
| 22 | MADANGIC zone | 23 | 68 | 96 | 101 | 116 | 120,000 | 81.7 | 96.9 |
| 23 | SOUTH IRIANIC zone | 11 | 21 | 39 | 58 | 162 | 247,000 | 84.9 | 99.1 |
| 24 | TRANSIRIANIC zone | 22 | 69 | 136 | 251 | 521 | 3,002,000 | 82.0 | 97.6 |
| 25 | WEST PAPUASIC zone | 25 | 35 | 60 | 76 | 126 | 459,000 | 37.1 | 68.0 |
| 26 | SEPIC zone | 22 | 56 | 74 | 97 | 143 | 358,000 | 79.8 | 96.2 |
| 27 | EAST PAPUIC zone | 26 | 50 | 85 | 101 | 162 | 304,000 | 84.4 | 96.9 |
| 28 | DARWINIC zone | 21 | 38 | 58 | 85 | 119 | 9,900 | 60.1 | 89.0 |
| 29 | PAMA-NYUNGIC zone | 24 | 54 | 112 | 213 | 530 | 47,800 | 59.2 | 88.1 |
| 3 | **AUSTRONESIAN** macrozone | 75 | 203 | 521 | 1,180 | 3,188 | 324,516,000 | 33.1 | 71.3 |
| 30 | FORMOSIC zone | 11 | 17 | 21 | 24 | 106 | 413,000 | 84.9 | 99.7 |
| 31 | HESPERONESIC zone | 21 | 62 | 163 | 463 | 1,369 | 314,332,000 | 32.0 | 70.9 |
| 32 | MESONESIC zone | 5 | 17 | 56 | 136 | 352 | 5,888,000 | 55.9 | 73.3 |
| 33 | HALYAMAPENIC zone | 1 | 4 | 18 | 42 | 108 | 198,000 | 52.8 | 73.8 |
| 34 | NEOGUINEIC zone | 7 | 39 | 92 | 173 | 410 | 642,000 | 83.4 | 99.2 |
| 35 | NEOBRITANNIC zone | 9 | 23 | 52 | 81 | 203 | 481,000 | 86.6 | 99.8 |
| 36 | SOLOMONIC zone | 6 | 17 | 34 | 45 | 89 | 167,000 | 92.4 | 99.9 |
| 37 | NEOCALEDONIC zone | 4 | 9 | 21 | 39 | 96 | 105,000 | 88.1 | 99.9 |
| 38 | WEST PACIFIC zone | 8 | 11 | 42 | 119 | 290 | 612,000 | 92.5 | 99.8 |
| 39 | TRANSPACIFIC zone | 3 | 4 | 22 | 58 | 165 | 1,679,000 | 86.0 | 99.8 |
| 4 | **EURASIAN** macrozone | 36 | 61 | 112 | 210 | 623 | 851,028,000 | 12.2 | 65.7 |
| 40 | EUSKARIC zone | 1 | 1 | 1 | 1 | 12 | 953,000 | 92.6 | 99.9 |
| 41 | URALIC zone | 3 | 4 | 10 | 14 | 52 | 25,627,000 | 81.4 | 98.8 |
| 42 | CAUCASIC zone | 3 | 6 | 12 | 20 | 53 | 8,449,000 | 28.4 | 52.9 |
| 43 | SIBERIC zone | 3 | 4 | 6 | 6 | 8 | 31,000 | 7.9 | 37.7 |
| 44 | TRANSASIATIC zone | 4 | 4 | 5 | 17 | 68 | 156,922,000 | 1.1 | 44.1 |
| 45 | EAST ASIATIC zone | 3 | 3 | 5 | 11 | 40 | 206,388,000 | 12.4 | 73.0 |
| 46 | SOUTH ASIATIC zone | 11 | 23 | 42 | 84 | 219 | 105,162,000 | 8.0 | 64.9 |
| 47 | DAIC zone | 2 | 7 | 13 | 24 | 95 | 96,885,000 | 1.4 | 48.6 |
| 48 | MIENIC zone | 1 | 2 | 2 | 8 | 30 | 12,037,000 | 4.7 | 45.9 |
| 49 | DRAVIDIC zone | 5 | 7 | 16 | 25 | 46 | 238,575,000 | 17.6 | 78.7 |
| 5 | **INDOEUROPEAN** macrozone | 10 | 20 | 46 | 147 | 902 | 2,683,096,000 | 45.6 | 78.2 |
| 50 | CELTIC zone | 1 | 3 | 4 | 5 | 24 | 6,037,000 | 80.6 | 99.8 |
| 51 | ROMANIC zone | 1 | 1 | 4 | 28 | 189 | 709,190,000 | 89.6 | 99.7 |
| 52 | GERMANIC zone | 1 | 2 | 4 | 26 | 228 | 452,850,000 | 70.3 | 98.9 |
| 53 | SLAVONIC zone | 1 | 1 | 1 | 8 | 39 | 292,629,000 | 71.9 | 98.8 |
| 54 | BALTIC zone | 1 | 1 | 2 | 2 | 5 | 5,587,000 | 87.8 | 99.9 |
| 55 | ALBANIC zone | 1 | 1 | 1 | 2 | 18 | 5,767,000 | 30.7 | 80.6 |
| 56 | HELLENIC zone | 1 | 1 | 2 | 2 | 13 | 14,100,000 | 96.2 | 100.0 |
| 57 | ARMENIC zone | 1 | 1 | 1 | 1 | 3 | 6,966,000 | 82.7 | 99.8 |
| 58 | IRANIC zone | 1 | 3 | 11 | 25 | 89 | 123,198,000 | 0.4 | 37.9 |
| 59 | INDIC zone | 1 | 6 | 16 | 48 | 294 | 1,066,772,000 | 2.6 | 53.5 |
| 6 | **NORTH AMERICAN** macrozone | 52 | 108 | 165 | 310 | 805 | 12,754,000 | 89.4 | 99.6 |
| 60 | ARCTIC zone | 1 | 2 | 4 | 14 | 35 | 171,000 | 81.8 | 99.1 |
| 61 | ATHABASKIC zone | 2 | 5 | 11 | 21 | 64 | 307,000 | 75.2 | 99.8 |
| 62 | ALGONKIC zone | 1 | 5 | 10 | 22 | 61 | 436,000 | 86.9 | 98.4 |
| 63 | NORTH PACIFIC zone | 24 | 41 | 51 | 84 | 174 | 161,000 | 88.6 | 99.5 |
| 64 | IROQUO-DAKOTIC zone | 3 | 6 | 11 | 21 | 43 | 207,000 | 79.6 | 98.7 |
| 65 | CIRCUMGOLFIC zone | 8 | 17 | 19 | 23 | 33 | 58,800 | 86.8 | 99.5 |
| 66 | AZTECOTANIC zone | 2 | 8 | 21 | 42 | 105 | 2,462,000 | 91.7 | 99.0 |
| 67 | OTO-MANGIC zone | 1 | 9 | 15 | 40 | 165 | 2,282,000 | 90.6 | 99.9 |
| 68 | MAYANIC zone | 1 | 5 | 12 | 26 | 76 | 5,824,000 | 89.5 | 99.9 |
| 69 | MESOMERIC zone | 9 | 10 | 11 | 17 | 49 | 845,000 | 88.6 | 99.9 |
| 7 | **SINOTIBETAN** macrozone | 21 | 43 | 106 | 187 | 526 | 1,331,775,000 | 7.5 | 65.1 |
| 70 | BODIC zone | 1 | 4 | 10 | 25 | 76 | 13,432,000 | 1.5 | 31.8 |
| 71 | HIMALAYIC zone | 4 | 6 | 16 | 25 | 48 | 2,430,000 | 0.2 | 20.7 |
| 72 | GARIC zone | 2 | 4 | 15 | 23 | 52 | 4,062,000 | 27.4 | 67.3 |
| 73 | KUKIC zone | 4 | 12 | 31 | 49 | 134 | 5,642,000 | 41.9 | 76.0 |
| 74 | MIRIC zone | 1 | 1 | 5 | 5 | 13 | 1,208,000 | 1.6 | 27.7 |
| 75 | KACHINIC zone | 1 | 2 | 3 | 3 | 11 | 1,139,000 | 44.9 | 81.2 |
| 76 | NUNGIC zone | 4 | 4 | 5 | 6 | 18 | 674,000 | 12.3 | 32.6 |
| 77 | LOLO-BURMIC zone | 2 | 8 | 18 | 23 | 80 | 48,155,000 | 3.4 | 50.7 |
| 78 | KARENIC zone | 1 | 1 | 2 | 12 | 22 | 4,941,000 | 38.9 | 89.9 |
| 79 | SINITIC zone | 1 | 1 | 1 | 16 | 72 | 1,250,092,000 | 7.4 | 66.0 |
| 8 | **SOUTH AMERICAN** macrozone | 122 | 189 | 286 | 418 | 975 | 23,006,000 | 91.0 | 98.5 |
| 80 | CARIBIC zone | 1 | 11 | 18 | 37 | 96 | 208,000 | 75.7 | 96.7 |
| 81 | ARAWAKIC zone | 2 | 18 | 31 | 51 | 110 | 530,000 | 37.3 | 74.7 |
| 82 | TUPIC zone | 10 | 14 | 28 | 50 | 129 | 5,872,000 | 94.3 | 99.7 |
| 83 | INTEROCEANIC zone | 16 | 26 | 33 | 47 | 86 | 716,000 | 75.0 | 96.4 |
| 84 | PRE-ANDINIC zone | 20 | 32 | 56 | 73 | 186 | 199,000 | 23.8 | 61.0 |
| 85 | ANDINIC zone | 13 | 14 | 17 | 28 | 72 | 14,301,000 | 95.9 | 99.9 |
| 86 | CHACONIC zone | 10 | 16 | 21 | 26 | 63 | 918,000 | 68.4 | 99.0 |
| 87 | MATOGROSSIC zone | 16 | 18 | 33 | 36 | 86 | 80,900 | 50.4 | 90.9 |
| 88 | AMAZONIC zone | 23 | 28 | 35 | 56 | 125 | 178,000 | 44.6 | 74.4 |
| 89 | BAHIANIC zone | 11 | 12 | 14 | 14 | 22 | 3,900 | 60.9 | 97.3 |
| 9 | **TRANSAFRICAN** macrozone | 59 | 142 | 339 | 793 | 2,839 | 391,502,000 | 61.7 | 88.5 |
| 90 | ATLANTIC zone | 16 | 20 | 36 | 52 | 124 | 27,197,000 | 2.3 | 43.9 |
| 91 | VOLTAIC zone | 8 | 19 | 42 | 76 | 246 | 23,960,000 | 16.7 | 62.6 |
| 92 | ADAMAWIC zone | 3 | 17 | 27 | 60 | 171 | 2,810,000 | 27.3 | 62.3 |
| 93 | UBANGIC zone | 2 | 8 | 18 | 37 | 139 | 6,794,000 | 68.9 | 94.7 |
| 94 | MELIC zone | 2 | 3 | 4 | 7 | 20 | 2,154,000 | 6.3 | 50.2 |
| 95 | KRU-GREBIC zone | 2 | 4 | 4 | 29 | 152 | 2,880,000 | 40.8 | 82.1 |
| 96 | WEST AKANIC zone | 13 | 24 | 37 | 66 | 181 | 23,771,000 | 54.1 | 93.9 |
| 97 | DELTIC zone | 2 | 2 | 6 | 8 | 37 | 1,282,000 | 87.4 | 99.8 |
| 98 | BENUIC zone | 10 | 24 | 76 | 200 | 522 | 63,006,000 | 70.4 | 94.6 |
| 99 | BANTUIC zone | 1 | 21 | 89 | 258 | 1,247 | 237,648,000 | 72.3 | 94.5 |
| | Doubly counted smaller languages | | | | | | -27,844,900 | | |
| | Global total | 684 | 1,403 | 2,684 | 4,962 | 13,509 | 6,055,049,000 | 31.1 | 72.9 |

name end with a capital letter, or occasionally a low-ercase one, and period, with the following meanings:

| | | | |
|---|---|---|---|
| A | = proper | P | = peripheral |
| C | = Central | N | = North |
| E | = East | S | = South |
| F | = formalized, revived | T | = traditional |
| G | = generalized, standard | U | = urban |
| H | = historical | V | = vehicular |
| M | = Middle | W | = West |

### Names for Scripture languages

Column 12 in this table records each language's biblioglossonym, if any exists. This is the official or formal name given as the language's name in connection with its translation of the Christian Scriptures. Usually, it is an anglicized name ('French', 'German', 'Zulu', etc) but in many cases it is named by the speakers themselves who term it in their own language ('français', 'deutsch', 'isiZulu', etc).

The 2 major Scripture translation agencies—United Bible Societies (UBS), and Wycliffe Bible Translators/Summer Institute of Linguistics (WBT/SIL)—often have confusingly different language names for the same autoglossonym (own language). Sometimes it is simply a small difference in spelling, but often it is a completely different name: WBT utilizes anglicized names while UBS uses many vernacular names. In the majority of cases, this database shows the UBS name.

The disadvantage of this difference is that the 2 biblioglossonyms in such cases are incompatible from the standpoint of each other's computers, databases, and hence search capability. Even if the difference is a single letter, ordinary programs will not note that these refer to the identical language.

This distinction is recorded in column 12 by means of an asterisk (*) attached to a biblioglossonym. *Its presence* means: either (a) in addition to this biblioglossonym, there is at least one other biblioglossonym (usually that used by WBT/SIL) not given on this printout; or (b) 2 or more biblioglossonyms are or have been used by one of the 2 agencies; or (c) in addition to the main biblioglossonym shown, one or more of this language's dialects have their own translations (not recorded here) and thus their own distinct biblioglossonyms.

Likewise, the *absence* of an asterisk means either (a) the 2 agencies use an identical biblioglossonym for the language under consideration, or (b) only one agency knows of or uses a biblioglossonym at this point.

### Meanings of columns in WCE Table 9-13
*Column*
   1. Language code

### REFERENCE NAME
   2. Cover-name (in capitals)
      Autoglossonym (own name for language)
   3. Countries where significantly spoken or used
   4. Peoples using this language as mother tongue

### MOTHER-TONGUE (NATIVE) SPEAKERS
   5. In AD 2000
   6. In AD 2025 (assuming current trends)

### MEDIA
   7. Countries broadcasting Christian programs in this language:
*Code   Meaning*
   0  No broadcasts
   1  Local only or in same-cluster language
   2  National, within this country
   3  External broadcasts from this country
   4  International, from one foreign country
   5  Plurinational, from 2–4 countries
   6  Multinational, from 5–9 countries
   7  Multicontinental, from 10-20 countries
   8  Global broadcasts from 20 or more countries

### CHURCH among language's native speakers
   8. Affiliated Christians (AC), % of population
   9. Evangelization, E (% of population evangelized)
   10. Worlds A/B/C: location of most speakers

### SCRIPTURES
   11. Scripture Translation Status (a scale 0-92): see details at end of *WCE* Part 1.
   12. Biblioglossonym (official name of Scripture translation, if published or under way); sometimes the anglicized name is preferred by speakers, sometimes the autoglossonym)
      Note meaning of any asterisk after a biblioglossonym (see detailed explanation above): an asterisk * means: one or more additional biblioglossonyms for this autoglossonym (language reference name) exist
      No asterisk means: biblioglossonym is the only one in use for this autoglossonym.

### PRINT SCRIPTURES

13-15. Scriptures in print (...=none, P..=gospel only, PN.=New Testament, PNB=whole Bible, pnb=near-Bible)
   16. Portion/gospel activity (year of first publication and year of latest, if any)
   17. New Testament activity (year of first publication and year of latest, if any)
   18. Bible activity (year of first publication and year of latest, if any)

### AVAILABILITY OF AUDIOVISUALS
   19. 'Jesus' Film year first published
   20. 'Jesus' Film availability, viewership:
*Code   Meaning*
   0  not available in mother tongue or its cluster of languages
   1  Available in mother tongue (if under 10% of all speakers) or in its cluster
   2  Available, viewers 10–50%
   3  Available, viewers 51–100%
   4  Vast impact in mother tongue (viewers>100%)

   Next 4 lines 21–24: a dot in any of these 4 columns means: Nothing available
   21. Audio scriptures available:

| Code | Item | Value | Meaning |
|---|---|---|---|
| • | nothing | 0 | No audio scriptures available |
| c | materials | 1 | Audio materials available only in same-cluster language |
| s | Selection | 1 | Selections/teaching/music purchasable on cassette |
| r | radio | 2 | Radio audio selections hearable |
| a | Portion | 3 | Audio gospels purchasable |
| A | Testament | 4 | Audio NT purchasable |
| B | Bible | 5 | Audio whole Bible purchasable |

   22. New Reader Scriptures available = y
   23. Braille scriptures available = u
   24. Signed scriptures available = h

### DIALECTS
   25. Reference number: indicating a language's total of *dialects* (not listed here but named only on CD); subtract any language's reference number from the next reference number shown, minus 1 (e.g. 00-AAAA-a mandinka-kango has minus 7 plus 12 minus 1 = 4 dialects).

# 4. AN INTEGRATED GLOBAL ETHNOLINGUISTIC CLASSIFICATION
## (=PEOPLE CODE)

### A single classification
These 3 classifications overlap a good deal, but by no means at all points. There is in fact no precise correlation between race, physical type, color, language and culture. The world distribution of languages does, however, correspond broadly with that of human races. As just noted, the matter is complicated by the fact that, for both race and language, scholars of different nationalities and persuasions have proposed numerous overlapping, often conflicting and even contradictory classifications. For the purposes of WCE/WCT/WCD, however, what is needed is one single stable classification of all living peoples and languages (excluding all now extinct) in which all proper names in use, whether racial, ethnic, national, cultural, linguistic, or pertaining to color, and whether referring to a single people or language or to a major family or grouping, and all their synonyms and alternate names, can be inserted into a single framework which will show the relationships between all names (in their generally-preferred anglicized versions only, excluding forms in other languages), together with population and other data referring to each name. In the main, members of each ethnic group have a similar mother tongue (first language), whatever country they live in or have migrated to. The 3 preceding classifications have therefore been combined, in their various published versions, and have evolved a single classification (here termed ethnolinguistic) of the peoples of the world at 11 progressively more detailed levels: 5 major races (as detailed above, changing the mainly biological ending -oid for the

last 3 races, to obtain Caucasian, Mongolian, and Negro) with 7 skin colors; 13 geographical races and 4 sub-races; 71 ethnolinguistic families (sometimes termed microraces, sometimes local races); 395 peoples (or, sub-families or ethnic culture areas); 12,600 constituent peoples and sub-peoples (13,500 languages); and many thousand additional names ranked in 4 further levels of subdivisions. This classification is based on the various extant schemes of nearness of language plus nearness of racial, ethnic, cultural, and culture-area characteristics.

The full classification also contains several thousand synonyms, alternative names, variant spellings, and names in other languages than English. It contains Bantu names with ethnic prefixes (Ama-, Ba, Ma-, Ovi-, Wa-, etc) and linguistic prefixes (Eki-, Ki, Lo-, Lu-, etc), though these are omitted in the present classification. The grand total of all such names with all variant spellings must be over 70,000. Over 12,000 of these tribes, language groups, nations, clans and other social division are listed in J. G. Leyburn, *Handbook of ethnography* (New Haven: Yale University Press, 1931); and, as noted above, 28,300 names are listed in Voegelin 1977 in English usage (i.e. in anglicized form), with at least a further 50,000 variations and usages in French, German, Spanish, Portuguese, Italian, Russian and the other major languages of world scholarship. In addition many peoples and languages are named with yet other terms by, and unique to, their surrounding peoples and languages. Altogether, the grand total of all ethnolinguistic names must be over 100,000 distinct terms. A reduced version of the

full classification, evolved with special reference to this survey of Christianity, covering the first 6 of the above levels together with codes for the first 5 levels only (races, colors, geographical races, ethnolinguistic families, peoples) is given here in the anglicized listing PEOPLES OF THE WORLD in *WCE* Table 8–2. In it, each ethnolinguistic family, and most of the world's major peoples, are given a code number and are also classified by race, geographical race and color. Most of the ethnic groups it lists may be seen located geographically in the detailed ethnic maps in *Atlas narodov mira* (Atlas of the peoples of the world, Moscow, 1964–1998). Similar maps, but with a different classification, are found in *Peoples of the earth:* Volume 20, *The future of mankind* (Europa Verlag, 1973–1990).

The reader should note that the classification is neither purely 'ethnic' nor 'racial' nor 'linguistic' nor 'cultural', but is ethnocultural and/or ethnolinguistic; and that on this definition an 'ethnolinguistic people' means an ethnic or ethnocultural or racial group speaking its own language or mother tongue. In the 20th century, mass international migration has therefore sometimes involved, over a generation or two, a change in the way an ethnic group is classified. For example, in 1972 in the USA, 2.2 million people (1.1% of the population) were of Russian origin (*Statistical abstract of the United States*, 1973–2001), but only 334,000 (0.2%) spoke Russian as their mother tongue (1970 Census of Population). This means that large numbers of persons of Russian origin (0.9% of the USA population) no longer speak Russian as their mother tongue and so (on this classification) have

## Table 18–7. The globe's 100 largest distinct cultures described by race, countries, peoples, autoglossonyms, Christians, and evangelization, AD 2000–AD 2025.

This table integrates and summarizes the categories involved in this Part 18 (race, culture, nation, people, language, Christians). It lists the 100 largest distinct cultures in descending order of size in AD 2000. Note that a culture can span several countries (column 4) and consist of many peoples in those countries (column 5).

| *Culture (anglicized name)* 1 | *RaceID* 2 | *LangID* 3 | *Ctrys* 4 | *Peops* 5 | *Ppop2000* 6 | *Ppop2025* 7 | *Autoglossonym* 8 | *AC%* 9 | *E%* 10 | *W* 11 | *Major countries, in size order* 12 |
|---|---|---|---|---|---|---|---|---|---|---|---|
| Han Chinese (Mandarin) | MSY42a | 79-AAAB-b | 93 | 96 | 813,348,000 | 943,206,000 | bei-jing-hua (kuoyu) | 7.70 | 70.76 | B | chin; taiw; cana; malb; usa |
| Latin American Mestizo | CLN29 | 51-AABB-h | 25 | 34 | 152,456,000 | 211,215,000 | latino americano | 96.22 | 99.96 | C | mexi; colo; vene; chil; usa |
| Russian | CEW22j | 53-AAAE-d | 73 | 74 | 143,111,000 | 136,387,000 | russkiy | 62.48 | 99.61 | C | russ; ukra; kaza; usa; belo |
| Japanese | MSY45a | 45-CAAA-a | 36 | 38 | 128,607,000 | 124,122,000 | koku-go | 3.30 | 69.60 | B | japa; braz; usa; souk; chin |
| USA White | CEW19s | 52-ABAC-s | 116 | 117 | 118,170,000 | 138,436,000 | General American | 65.70 | 99.66 | C | usa; cana; mexi; brit; pana |
| Central Bengali | CNN25b | 59-AAFT-c | 1 | 1 | 102,112,000 | 141,323,000 | Standard baanglaa | 0.14 | 57.14 | B | bang |
| Han Chinese (Wu) | MSY42a | 79-AAAD | 1 | 2 | 94,859,000 | 109,914,000 | WU cluster | 12.90 | 74.89 | B | chin |
| West Bengali | CNN25b | 59-AAFT-e | 19 | 19 | 90,669,000 | 120,151,000 | West bengali | 2.34 | 62.85 | B | indi; bang; brit; paki; myan |
| Brazilian White (Branco) | CLT26 | 51-AABA-h | 6 | 6 | 88,232,000 | 112,993,000 | General brasileiro | 91.50 | 99.91 | C | braz; port; swed; uuay; boli |
| Latin American White (Blanco) | CLT27 | 51-AABB-h | 34 | 41 | 87,169,000 | 112,821,000 | latino americano | 88.36 | 99.86 | C | arge; mexi; colo; cuba; vene |
| South Korean | MSY46 | 45-AAAA-b | 35 | 36 | 75,665,000 | 87,446,000 | kukŏ | 27.88 | 83.00 | B | souk; nork; chin; usa; japa |
| Maratha (Maharathi) | CNN25j | 59-AAFU-m | 4 | 4 | 75,650,000 | 99,290,000 | deshi-marathi | 5.20 | 65.70 | B | indi; maus; zimb; keny |
| Telugu (Andhra, Tolangan) | CNN23d | 49-DBAB-a | 13 | 15 | 74,010,000 | 97,129,000 | telugu | 13.43 | 71.84 | B | indi; myan; unia; malb; soua |
| Tamil (Madrasi, Tamalsan) | CNN23c | 49-EBEA-b | 28 | 32 | 72,292,000 | 94,619,000 | tamil | 19.47 | 84.54 | B | indi; sril; malb; soua; sing |
| Vietnamese (Kinh) | MSY52b | 46-EBAA-a | 22 | 22 | 70,769,000 | 95,300,000 | viêt | 7.90 | 72.50 | B | viet; usa; fran; camb; aust |
| German (High German) | CEW19m | 52-ABCE-a | 83 | 84 | 70,538,000 | 70,789,000 | Standard hoch-deutsch | 71.70 | 99.72 | C | germ; usa; pola; russ; cana |
| Western Punjabi (Lahnda) | CNN25n | 59-AAFE-e | 2 | 2 | 66,841,000 | 112,327,000 | lahnda | 4.40 | 50.39 | B | paki; indi |
| Han Chinese (Cantonese) | MSY42a | 79-AAAM-a | 48 | 50 | 66,298,000 | 77,422,000 | Central yue | 4.58 | 74.15 | B | chin; malb; viet; usa; sing |
| Urdu (Islami, Undri) | CNN25r | 59-AAFO-d | 29 | 29 | 64,376,000 | 89,045,000 | Standard urdu | 0.13 | 53.26 | B | indi; paki; bang; saud; soua |
| Hindi (High Hindi) | CNN25g | 59-AAFO-c | 1 | 1 | 63,061,000 | 82,769,000 | Standard hindi | 2.10 | 61.60 | B | indi |
| Egyptian Arab | CMT30 | 12-AACF-a | 23 | 26 | 62,819,000 | 88,229,000 | masri | 16.58 | 80.71 | B | egyp; liby; ital; iraq; saud |
| Hindi (Bazaar, Popular) | CNN25g | 59-AAFO-e | 63 | 63 | 58,755,000 | 77,739,000 | General hindi | 1.71 | 57.96 | B | indi; bang; soua; paki; nepa |
| Javanese (Orang Jawa) | MSY44g | 31-PIAA-g | 10 | 11 | 55,104,000 | 71,107,000 | General jawa | 12.86 | 78.36 | B | indo; malb; neth; sing; saud |
| English (British) | CEW19i | 52-ABAC-b | 170 | 174 | 51,798,000 | 54,433,000 | standard English | 66.76 | 99.67 | C | brit; soua; aust; usa; cana |
| Gujarati | CNN25e | 59-AAFH-b | 29 | 29 | 50,142,000 | 66,412,000 | Standard gujaraati | 2.28 | 61.47 | B | indi; paki; brit; tanz; ugan |
| Turk | MSY41j | 44-AABA-a | 45 | 50 | 48,716,000 | 62,727,000 | osmanli | 0.10 | 54.39 | B | turk; germ; bulg; fran; neth |
| Han Chinese (Jinyu) | MSY42a | 79-AAAB-l | 1 | 1 | 47,351,000 | 54,865,000 | hui-zu | 7.00 | 50.00 | A | chin |
| Han Chinese (Min Nan) | MSY42a | 79-AAAJ-i | 12 | 15 | 47,142,000 | 55,083,000 | chao-shan | 8.18 | 73.09 | B | chin; taiw; malb; thai; sing |
| Han Chinese (Hunanese) | MSY42a | 79-AAAE-a | 2 | 2 | 44,288,000 | 51,331,000 | xiang | 2.01 | 38.02 | A | chin; malb |
| Ukrainian | CEW22p | 53-AAAE-b | 37 | 37 | 43,955,000 | 40,762,000 | ukrainskiy | 86.91 | 99.87 | C | ukra; russ; pola; usa; mold |
| Eastern Punjabi (Gurmukhi) | CNN25n | 59-AAFE-c | 28 | 28 | 43,942,000 | 57,791,000 | General panjabi | 3.03 | 62.39 | B | indi; cana; saud; brit; usa |
| Polish (Pole, Silesian) | CEW22i | 53-AAAC-c | 39 | 39 | 41,793,000 | 42,614,000 | polski | 95.36 | 99.95 | C | pola; usa; ukra; belo; germ |
| Malayali (Malabari) | CNN23b | 49-EBEB-a | 17 | 18 | 39,077,000 | 51,351,000 | malayalam | 37.98 | 99.34 | B | indi; unia; kuwa; malb; usa |
| Bhojpuri Bihari (Deswali) | CNN25c | 59-AAFQ-a | 4 | 4 | 38,003,000 | 50,396,000 | bhojpuri | 0.98 | 38.85 | A | indi; nepa; fiji; maus |
| Awadhi (Baiswari, Bagheli) | CNN25g | 59-AAFP-a | 2 | 2 | 37,995,000 | 50,047,000 | awadhi | 2.47 | 34.84 | A | indi; nepa |
| Brazilian Mulato | NFB70b | 51-AABA-h | 3 | 4 | 37,446,000 | 47,973,000 | General brasileiro | 93.99 | 99.94 | C | braz; uuay; freg |
| Kanarese (Canarese) | CNN23a | 49-EBAA-a | 3 | 4 | 37,219,000 | 48,852,000 | kannada | 5.80 | 69.29 | B | indi; malb; sing |
| Han Chinese (Hakka) | MSY42a | 79-AAAG-a | 24 | 25 | 37,068,000 | 43,473,000 | Literary hakka | 2.34 | 57.71 | B | chin; taiw; malb; indo; indi |
| Italian | CEW21e | 51-AABQ-c | 59 | 60 | 35,786,000 | 35,378,000 | Standard italiano | 82.06 | 99.82 | C | ital; usa; arge; fran; germ |
| Maitili (Maithili, Tharu) | CNN25c | 59-AAFQ-b | 2 | 2 | 34,219,000 | 45,625,000 | maithili | 0.96 | 32.85 | A | indi; nepa |
| Syrian-Arabian Arab | CMT30 | 12-AACF-f | 80 | 122 | 33,955,000 | 52,264,000 | syro-palestinian | 20.86 | 77.02 | B | syri; jord; usa; leba; pale |
| Orisi (Utkali, Vadiya) | CNN25l | 59-AAFS-a | 3 | 3 | 33,417,000 | 43,859,000 | odiaa | 1.40 | 58.84 | B | indi; myan; bang |
| USA Black (Afro-American) | NFB68a | 52-ABAE-a | 14 | 16 | 32,741,000 | 38,297,000 | talkin-black | 75.21 | 99.72 | C | usa; cana; germ; brit; mexi |
| French | CEW21b | 51-AABI-d | 132 | 133 | 31,603,000 | 34,102,000 | General français | 76.01 | 99.76 | C | fran; usa; conz; belg; ital |
| Algerian Arab | CMT30 | 12-AACB-b | 14 | 20 | 29,674,000 | 42,466,000 | East maghrebi | 0.31 | 58.40 | B | alge; tuni; liby; fran; iran |
| Braj Bhakha (Antarbedi) | CNN25g | 59-AAFO-i | 1 | 2 | 27,377,000 | 35,932,000 | braj-kannauji | 2.19 | 40.66 | A | indi |
| Persian (Irani) | CNT24f | 58-AACC-c | 32 | 32 | 26,639,000 | 37,640,000 | Standard farsi | 0.37 | 55.15 | B | iran; afgh; turk; usa; iraq |
| Burmese (Myen, Bhama) | MSY50b | 77-AABA-a | 8 | 8 | 25,901,000 | 33,029,000 | bama | 0.86 | 63.71 | B | myan; bang; thai; indi; malb |
| Han Chinese (Kan) | MSY42a | 79-AAAF-a | 1 | 1 | 25,272,000 | 29,283,000 | gan | 6.00 | 43.00 | A | chin |
| Hausa (Hausawa) | NAB60a | 19-HAAB-a | 18 | 25 | 24,400,000 | 41,395,000 | hausa | 0.09 | 60.54 | B | nige; niga; suda; came; ghan |
| Javanese Indonesian | MSY44g | 31-PHAA-c | 1 | 1 | 22,897,000 | 29,518,000 | bahasa-indonesia | 9.00 | 75.50 | B | indo |
| Sundanese (Urang Sunda) | MSY44n | 31-PJAA-a | 1 | 1 | 22,494,000 | 28,998,000 | Central sunda | 0.08 | 54.58 | B | indo |
| Northern Uzbek | MSY41l | 44-AABD-a | 18 | 18 | 22,093,000 | 30,178,000 | Central uzbek | 0.09 | 48.29 | A | uzbe; taji; kirg; turm; kaza |
| Nepalese (Eastern Pahari) | CNN25k | 59-AAFD-b | 6 | 6 | 22,024,000 | 32,713,000 | nepali | 2.29 | 54.65 | B | nepa; indi; bhut; myan; bang |
| Central Thai (Siamese) | MSY49d | 47-AAAB-d | 13 | 13 | 21,863,000 | 25,971,000 | Central thai | 2.48 | 66.36 | B | thai; usa; laos; sing; myan |
| Spaniard | CEW21k | 51-AABB-c | 40 | 41 | 21,369,000 | 20,201,000 | General español | 94.61 | 99.95 | C | spai; fran; germ; usa; braz |
| Yoruba (Oyo, Ekiti, Ijebu | NAB59n | 98-AAAA-a | 12 | 12 | 20,576,000 | 33,938,000 | Standard yoruba | 57.27 | 99.53 | B | nige; beni; ghan; ivor; togo |
| Brazilian Mestico | CLN28 | 51-AABA-h | 3 | 3 | 20,476,000 | 26,236,000 | General brasileiro | 94.82 | 99.95 | C | braz; para; port |
| Sindhi | CNN25p | 59-AAFF-a | 7 | 7 | 20,402,000 | 33,511,000 | Standard sindhi | 0.14 | 45.69 | A | paki; indi; unia; malb; afgh |
| Azerbaijani (Turk) | MSY41a | 44-AABA-f | 20 | 20 | 20,274,000 | 27,233,000 | azeri | 0.01 | 30.30 | A | iran; azer; iraq; turk; russ |
| Amhara | CMT34a | 12-ACBA-b | 8 | 8 | 19,930,000 | 36,762,000 | General amarinya | 88.84 | 99.88 | C | ethi; soma; suda; erit; germ |
| Tagalog (Pilipino) | MSY44o | 31-CKAA-a | 24 | 25 | 19,849,000 | 27,473,000 | Proper tagalog | 97.01 | 99.97 | C | phil; usa; saud; cana; taiw |
| Romanian | CEW21i | 51-AADC-a | 27 | 28 | 19,584,000 | 17,690,000 | limba românească | 89.42 | 99.89 | C | roma; usa; ukra; mold; germ |
| Brazilian Black | NFB70a | 51-AABA-h | 1 | 1 | 18,713,000 | 23,972,000 | General brasileiro | 89.50 | 99.89 | C | braz |
| Colombian Mulatto | NFB71b | 51-AABB-h | 9 | 12 | 18,459,000 | 24,770,000 | latino americano | 91.21 | 99.91 | C | colo; domr; cuba; puer; ecua |
| Pathan (Pukhtun, Afghani) | CNT24a | 58-ABDA-a | 15 | 17 | 17,853,000 | 33,074,000 | pashto | 0.06 | 34.07 | A | afgh; paki; iran; brit; turk |
| Yemeni Arab | CMT30 | 12-AACF-n | 15 | 15 | 16,877,000 | 36,020,000 | yemeni | 0.02 | 43.24 | A | yeme; saud; egyp; somi; soma |
| Northeastern Tai (Isan) | MSY49b | 47-AAAC-a | 1 | 2 | 16,318,000 | 19,326,000 | isan | 1.40 | 56.34 | B | thai |
| Assamese | CNN25a | 59-AAFT-s | 3 | 3 | 16,232,000 | 21,362,000 | axamiyaa | 1.09 | 55.46 | B | indi; bhut; bang |
| Saudi Arab | CMT30 | 12-AACF-k | 9 | 10 | 16,195,000 | 29,889,000 | Central `anazi | 0.47 | 53.43 | B | saud; unia; oman; qata; kuwa |
| Anglo-Canadian | CEW19d | 52-ABAC-r | 6 | 6 | 15,352,000 | 18,615,000 | General Canadian | 65.82 | 99.66 | C | cana; usa; brit; newz; niga |
| Southern Punjabi | CNN25n | 59-AAFE-r | 1 | 2 | 15,351,000 | 25,800,000 | siraiki | 4.30 | 55.27 | B | paki |
| Iraqi Arab | CMT30 | 12-AACF-g | 14 | 15 | 15,160,000 | 26,538,000 | syro-mesopotamian | 0.68 | 52.78 | B | iraq; jord; usa; paki; indi |
| Dutch | CEW19h | 52-ABCA-a | 23 | 23 | 15,141,000 | 15,471,000 | algemeen-nederlands | 67.28 | 99.67 | C | neth; usa; soua; cana; germ |
| Sudanese Arab | CMT30 | 12-AACF-c | 9 | 26 | 15,063,000 | 23,219,000 | sudani | 4.22 | 55.29 | B | suda; egyp; yeme; liby; ethi |
| Bangri (Deswali, Hariani) | CNN25g | 59-AAFO-h | 1 | 1 | 14,900,000 | 19,556,000 | baangaru | 3.60 | 45.10 | A | indi |
| Igbo (Ibo) | NAB59h | 98-FAAA-e | 1 | 1 | 14,828,000 | 24,341,000 | South Central igbo. | 98.00 | 99.98 | C | nige |
| Hungarian (Magyar) | MSW51g | 41-BAAA-a | 25 | 25 | 14,448,000 | 13,545,000 | General magyar | 85.12 | 99.85 | C | hung; roma; usa; slok; yugo |
| Visayan (Bisayan, Cebu) | MSY44q | 31-CKGP-a | 1 | 1 | 14,434,000 | 20,568,000 | Vehicular cebuan | 98.20 | 99.98 | C | phil |
| Eastern Pathan | CNT24a | 58-ABDA-c | 2 | 3 | 14,351,000 | 24,078,000 | pakhto | 0.20 | 46.42 | A | paki; unia |
| Anglo-Australian | CEW19c | 52-ABAC-x | 16 | 16 | 14,121,000 | 17,274,000 | General Australian | 65.74 | 99.66 | C | aust; usa; newz; brit; papu |
| Sinhalese (Singhalese) | CNN25q | 59-ABBA-a | 12 | 12 | 13,908,000 | 17,421,000 | Historical sinhala | 4.60 | 63.51 | B | sril; indi; thai; unia; malb |
| Portuguese | CEW21g | 51-AABA-e | 46 | 47 | 13,795,000 | 14,149,000 | General português | 92.49 | 99.93 | C | port; usa; fran; soua; braz |
| Greek (Hellenic, Dimotiki) | CEW20 | 56-AAAA-c | 80 | 82 | 13,556,000 | 13,458,000 | dhimotiki | 96.43 | 99.96 | C | gree; usa; germ; cypr; aust |
| Swedish (Swede) | CEW19q | 52-AAAD-r | 12 | 12 | 13,356,000 | 14,417,000 | svea-svensk | 66.51 | 99.66 | C | swed; usa; finl; norw; cana |
| USA Mestizo (Chicano) | CLN29 | 51-AABB-k | 1 | 2 | 12,944,000 | 15,139,000 | chicano | 83.13 | 99.83 | C | usa |
| Somali | CMT33e | 14-GAGA-a | 15 | 20 | 12,810,000 | 25,452,000 | af-soomaali | 0.04 | 41.28 | A | soma; ethi; somi; yeme; keny |
| Northern Zhuang (Chwang) | MSY49a | 47-AAAG-n | 1 | 1 | 12,796,000 | 14,827,000 | wu-ming | 1.00 | 39.00 | A | chin |
| Moroccan Arab | CMT30 | 12-AACB-a | 9 | 9 | 12,781,000 | 17,154,000 | West maghrebi | 0.27 | 48.92 | A | moro; fran; belg; alge; neth |
| Deccani | CNN25r | 59-AAFU-m | 1 | 1 | 12,726,000 | 16,703,000 | deshi-marathi | 0.00 | 38.50 | A | indi |
| Han Chinese (Min Pei) | MSY42a | 79-AAAI-c | 4 | 4 | 12,683,000 | 14,701,000 | South min-dong | 10.06 | 73.04 | B | chin; indo; thai; brun |
| Bundelkhandi (Bondili) | CNN25g | 59-AAFO-j | 1 | 2 | 12,594,000 | 16,529,000 | bundeli | 1.49 | 45.88 | A | indi |
| Magadhi Bihari (Maghori) | CNN25c | 59-AAFQ-g | 1 | 4 | 12,352,000 | 16,212,000 | magahi | 1.04 | 28.41 | A | indi |
| Jat (Jati, Bangri) | CNN25h | 59-AAFO-h | 1 | 1 | 12,164,000 | 15,965,000 | baangaru | 2.60 | 45.10 | A | indi |
| Madurese | MSY44h | 31-PHJA | 1 | 1 | 12,090,000 | 15,586,000 | madura | 0.20 | 48.70 | A | indo |
| Chhattisgarhi (Khatahi) | CNN25g | 59-AAFR-a | 1 | 3 | 12,027,000 | 15,785,000 | chhattisgarhi | 1.30 | 41.64 | A | indi |
| Kazakh | MSY41e | 44-AABC-c | 19 | 19 | 11,812,000 | 13,257,000 | kazakh | 0.03 | 41.14 | A | kaza; chin; uzbe; russ; mong |
| Catalonian | CEW21a | 51-AABE-b | 8 | 8 | 11,719,000 | 10,987,000 | català | 94.07 | 99.94 | C | spai; fran; arge; mexi; germ |
| Malay (Melaju, Melayu) | MSY44k | 31-PHAA-b | 22 | 22 | 11,644,000 | 15,764,000 | bahasa-malaysia | 0.44 | 52.94 | B | malb; indo; sing; phil; brit |
| Czech (Bohemian) | CEW22e | 53-AAAD-a | 20 | 20 | 11,213,000 | 10,789,000 | czesky | 48.79 | 99.49 | B | czec; usa; slok; germ; cana |
| Manchu (Man) | MSY41i | 79-AAAB-b | 1 | 1 | 10,938,000 | 12,674,000 | bei-jing-hua (kuoyu) | 0.02 | 50.02 | B | chin |

now become USA Whites (English-speaking), leaving only the 0.2% to be classified here as Russian-speaking Russians. In the same way, millions of Europeans have emigrated to South America over the last century, including Russians and Ukrainians, but after the first generation or so they have tended to lose their original mother tongues and have become assimilated to what is called the Latin American White race (Spanish- or Portuguese-speaking). Similarly, in countries such as the USA, Brazil, France, et alia, it is necessary to distinguish between (e.g.) Polish-speaking Polish immigrants on the one hand, and, on the other, persons of Polish origin who are now assimilated to the dominant race and culture. Likewise, every year millions of individuals and families who migrate to countries of different language and ethnic group are recorded here in those countries by their original mother-tongue ethnic group until such time (usually one generation) as they have changed their mother tongue and become absorbed in the dominant national group (e.g. Italian families who move permanently to Germany and who eventually become Germans linguistically and culturally). A different set of cases concerns peoples who, through emigration, retain a strong identity but change their

mother tongue to a local language (e.g. Chinese who now speak only Indonesian, Mexican Indians who are now monolingual in Spanish only, etc); because such peoples still retain their ethnic identity and culture, they are classified here as still members of their original ethnic group.

The term 'ethnolinguistic people' refers to that group which speaks the language shown as its first or primary or cultural or official language. In France, for instance, 82.0% of the population are French-speaking ethnic Frenchmen. Of these, 13 million (24.6%) speak for everyday purposes Occitan (Gascon, Languedoc, Provençal), a Romance language closer to Catalan than to French, although they use French as their official and cultural language. In this classification, therefore, the 13 million are classified under the ethnolinguistic term 'French', the only persons coded under 'Occitan' being the handful for whom Occitan and not French is their primary or cultural or only language.

In a few cases, it is difficult to be consistent in classification on a global scale because a name has both ethnic, cultural and religious meanings, all closely related, but applied in different countries and their censuses with differing emphases. The major example of

this concerns the Jewish people. In most countries and censuses Jews are regarded as an ethnic group as well as a religious group, and they are treated as such in this survey. In the USA, they are classified not in the general 'USA White' category although they are in fact mostly White and mostly English-speaking, but in the separate category 'Jewish'. The reason is that the main criterion in all ambiguous situations is their answer to the question: 'What is the first, or main, or primary ethnic or ethnolinguistic term by which persons identify themselves, or are identified by people around them?'

*Ethnolinguistic composition of all countries*
A voluminous ethnolinguistic analysis of every country's population is given in the large database printed out here country by country as *WCE* Table 8-2. Readers wanting printouts arranged by any other criteria can obtain these from the related electronic *World Christian database*.

# 5. THE RANGE OF GLOBAL LINGUA FRANCAS

*A survey of lingua francas*
Another product of this series of typologies has been a survey of the world's lingua francas. Originally this term meant 'Frankish language' and referred to a hybrid language (French, Italian, Spanish, English, Arabic, et alia) used by the 13th-century Crusaders and Mediterranean seamen. Nowadays it is best translated as 'Common Language' and refers to any language with large numbers of non-native speakers. Older English dictionaries still give only the 'hybrid' definition, but newer dictionaries define it thus '1. any language widely used as a means of communication among speakers of other languages. 2. The Italian-Provencal jargon formerly widely used in eastern Mediterranean ports.' (*Random House College Dictionary*, revised edition, 1988).

For our survey here, data were collected from a vast variety of sources including demographic censuses and polls. Surprisingly, almost all languages were found to have a penumbra of non-native speakers around their core mother tongue or native speakers. Where censuses were absent, an elaborate formula was then evolved including a language's involvement in politics, education, economics, trade, broadcasting, religion, and a wide range of other factors. Results are tabulated for the whole world in Table 18–8 and 18-9. In Table 18–10 are listed all 407 lingua francas each with over 1 million non-native speakers. And Global Diagram 27 gives an overview of the whole phenomenon including a minidiagram setting out the world's largest 12 and largest 32 outer lingua francas and their internal composition (non-users, monolinguals, translinguals, bilinguals, multilinguals, same-cluster users, different-cluster users).

*Essential definitions to grasp*
In order to grasp the size and significance of this whole phenomenon, readers need to understand the precise definitions employed here (and set out in Part 30 "Glossary" and in Tables 18-8, 18-9, 18-10, and also in Global Diagram 27). These definitions or usages are:
(a) Mother-tongue or native speakers (coded Mts)
(b) Non-native speakers (coded Nns)
(c) Total all users or speakers as the sum of (a) and (b) (coded Tus)
(d) The ratio total speakers over mother-tongue speakers (coded T/M)
(e) The 2 varieties of lingua franca: (1) outer lingua francas, where the name of an entire cluster (or 'outer language') is regarded in popular use as useful, or as a correct term (e.g. 'Global English is a lingua franca', here termed an outer lingua franca); and (2) inner lingua francas, where the name of a single language (or 'inner language') is regarded in popular use as useful, or as a correct term (e.g. 'standard urdu is a lingua franca', here termed an inner lingua franca).

| Table 18–8. The globe's 983 lingua francas each with over 100,000 non-native speakers, and 8,600 smaller lingua francas. | | | | | | | | |
|---|---|---|---|---|---|---|---|---|
| Non-natives 1 | Langs 2 | Peoples 3 | Speakers: Native 4 | Non-native 5 | Total speakers Total speakers 6 | T/M 7 | Christians 8 | AC% 9 |
| *Inner lingua francas* | | | | | | | | |
| Over 10 million | 62 | 1,857 | 3,474,599,000 | 3,542,701,000 | 7,017,300,000 | 2.02 | 2,019,292,000 | 28.8 |
| 1 million - 10 million | 174 | 1,759 | 1,505,315,000 | 554,305,000 | 2,059,620,000 | 1.37 | 690,114,000 | 33.5 |
| 500,000 - 1 million | 101 | 488 | 392,997,000 | 70,403,000 | 463,400,000 | 1.18 | 291,155,000 | 62.8 |
| 100,000 - 500,000 | 270 | 805 | 239,510,000 | 58,447,000 | 297,957,000 | 1.24 | 122,345,000 | 41.1 |
| 50,000 - 100,000 | 180 | 450 | 68,295,000 | 13,104,000 | 81,399,000 | 1.19 | 37,203,000 | 45.7 |
| 10,000 - 50,000 | 610 | 1,095 | 92,695,000 | 15,149,000 | 107,844,000 | 1.16 | 43,179,000 | 40.0 |
| 1,000 - 10,000 | 1,341 | 1,840 | 41,672,000 | 4,690,000 | 46,361,000 | 1.11 | 18,049,000 | 38.9 |
| 100 - 1,000 | 1,471 | 1,692 | 6,919,000 | 603,000 | 7,522,000 | 1.09 | 2,961,000 | 39.4 |
| Under 100 | 1,064 | 1,160 | 532,000 | 35,100 | 567,800 | 1.07 | 317,000 | 55.8 |
| Zero | 3 | 3 | 290,000 | 0 | 290,000 | 1.00 | 157,000 | 54.1 |
| **Total** | **5,276** | **11,149** | **5,822,824,000** | **4,259,437,100** | **10,082,260,800** | **1.73** | **3,224,772,000** | **32.0** |
| *Outer lingua francas* | | | | | | | | |
| Over 10 million | 52 | 2,952 | 4,390,011,000 | 3,878,149,000 | 8,268,160,000 | 1.88 | 2,370,808,000 | 28.7 |
| 1 million - 10 million | 119 | 2,139 | 1,213,154,000 | 397,029,000 | 1,610,183,000 | 1.33 | 716,622,000 | 44.5 |
| 500,000 - 1 million | 46 | 301 | 106,403,000 | 31,248,000 | 137,651,000 | 1.29 | 54,214,000 | 39.4 |
| 100,000 - 500,000 | 159 | 981 | 170,524,000 | 37,189,000 | 207,713,000 | 1.22 | 83,962,000 | 40.4 |
| 50,000 - 100,000 | 128 | 497 | 55,205,000 | 9,085,000 | 64,290,000 | 1.16 | 28,822,000 | 44.8 |
| 10,000 - 50,000 | 380 | 1,092 | 67,120,000 | 9,064,000 | 76,184,000 | 1.14 | 29,323,000 | 38.5 |
| 1,000 - 10,000 | 959 | 1,744 | 33,475,000 | 3,406,000 | 36,881,000 | 1.10 | 14,494,000 | 39.3 |
| 100 - 1,000 | 1,204 | 1,608 | 5,939,000 | 481,000 | 6,420,000 | 1.08 | 2,792,000 | 43.5 |
| Under 100 | 908 | 1,027 | 482,000 | 30,200 | 512,200 | 1.06 | 293,000 | 57.2 |
| Zero | 0 | 0 | 0 | 0 | 0 | 0.00 | 0 | 0.0 |
| **Total** | **3,955** | **12,341** | **6,042,313,000** | **4,365,681,200** | **10,407,994,200** | **1.72** | **3,301,330,000** | **31.7** |
| *All lingua francas* | | | | | | | | |
| Over 10 million | 114 | 4,809 | 7,864,610,000 | 7,420,850,000 | 15,285,460,000 | 1.94 | 4,390,100,000 | 28.7 |
| 1 million - 10 million | 293 | 3,898 | 2,718,469,000 | 951,334,000 | 3,669,803,000 | 1.35 | 1,406,736,000 | 38.3 |
| 500,000 - 1 million | 147 | 789 | 499,400,000 | 101,651,000 | 601,051,000 | 1.20 | 345,369,000 | 57.5 |
| 100,000 - 500,000 | 429 | 1,786 | 410,034,000 | 95,636,000 | 505,670,000 | 1.23 | 206,307,000 | 40.8 |
| 50,000 - 100,000 | 308 | 947 | 123,500,000 | 22,189,000 | 145,689,000 | 1.18 | 66,025,000 | 45.3 |
| 10,000 - 50,000 | 990 | 2,187 | 159,815,000 | 24,213,000 | 184,028,000 | 1.15 | 72,502,000 | 39.4 |
| 1,000 - 10,000 | 2,300 | 3,584 | 75,147,000 | 8,096,000 | 83,242,000 | 1.11 | 32,543,000 | 39.1 |
| 100 - 1,000 | 2,675 | 3,300 | 12,858,000 | 1,084,000 | 13,942,000 | 1.08 | 5,753,000 | 41.3 |
| Under 100 | 1,972 | 2,187 | 1,014,000 | 65,300 | 1,080,000 | 1.07 | 610,000 | 56.5 |
| Zero | 3 | 3 | 290,000 | 0 | 290,000 | 1.00 | 157,000 | 54.1 |
| **Total** | **9,231** | **23,490** | **11,865,137,000** | **8,625,118,300** | **20,490,255,000** | **1.73** | **6,526,102,000** | **31.8** |

*Their global extent*
Table 18–8 has 3 levels of data. The top layer analyzes inner lingua francas as defined above, which are languages as defined in the World Language Classification (as in *WCE*, Part 9 "Linguametrics"). It was found that 4.2 billion persons were speakers of non-native languages. The ratio of total speakers (meaning native plus non-native) to native speakers (mother tongue) varied from 2 down to 1 (column 7, variable T/M).

The second layer of data in Table 18–8 analyzes outer lingua francas as defined above, which are outer languages also called clusters, being groupings of languages all of which within the same cluster speak and

understand 80% or more of basic vocabulary of common human experience.

The third level of data simply combines by addition the 2 previous layers. This method implies considerable overlapping and duplication, but the outcome remains clear: the globe has 407 languages or clusters each used by over 1 million non-native speakers. And it has 983 languages or clusters each used by over 100,000 non-native speakers.

A similar type of analysis results if, instead of classifying lingua francas by number of non-native speakers, we classify them by the total of all speakers—native as well as non-native. Both of these types have their own direct application in the various communication ministries of the Christian world, especially publishing, scripture distribution, and both radio and TV broadcasting.

Table 18–8 has set out the data analyzed by non-native speakers;  Table 18–9 then extends the classification to total all speakers.

### Classifying the largest lingua francas

Table 18–9 presents 2 different but complementary ways of classifying all lingua francas. The first way does this by the range of speakers of non-native languages; the second way by the range of total all speakers.

### A complete listing

The third of these lingua franca tables is the 4-page Table 18–10. This sets out the entire list of these 407 largest lingua francas each spoken by over 1 million non-native speakers. Names in medium type are inner lingua francas shown as languages, using their autoglossonyms (note that all languages except English and American spell their autoglossonym with a lowercase initial letter). Names in bold type, however, are the outer lingua francas termed by their cluster names in anglicized form, where such exist.

### Vast new possibilities in communication

Not only are the data in these 3 tables almost unknown in church circles, they have scarcely begun to be used, even in twos and threes, for the myriad translation and communication needs of global Christianity. With many of the larger languages now coming into use via the Internet, the time has arrived for serious research and implementation of the immense potential they represent.

**Table 18–9.   The globe's largest lingua francas classified by (a) number of non-native speakers, and (b) total number of all speakers.**

### (a)  Classification by non-native speakers

#### 1.  OVERVIEW

Number of lingua francas

| Non-native speakers | Outer | Inner | Total |
|---|---|---|---|
| lingua francas > 100 million non-native speakers | 6 | 6 | 12 |
| lingua francas > 50 million non-native speakers | 15 | 13 | 28 |
| lingua francas > 10 million non-native speakers | 52 | 62 | 114 |
| lingua francas > 1 million non-native speakers | 171 | 236 | 407 |
| lingua francas > 100,000 non-native speakers | 376 | 607 | 983 |

#### 2.  RANGES OF SPEAKERS

| Non-native speakers | Outer | Inner | Total |
|---|---|---|---|
| Over 100 million non-native speakers | 6 | 6 | 12 |
| 50 million - 100 million non-native speakers | 9 | 7 | 16 |
| 10 million - 50 million non-native speakers | 37 | 49 | 86 |
| 1 million - 10 million non-native speakers | 119 | 174 | 293 |
| 500,000 - 1 million non-native speakers | 46 | 101 | 147 |
| 100,000 - 500,000 non-native speakers | 159 | 270 | 429 |

### (b)  Classification by total all speakers

#### 1.  OVERVIEW

Number of lingua francas

| Total all speakers | Outer | Inner | Total |
|---|---|---|---|
| lingua francas > 100 million all speakers | 20 | 21 | 41 |
| lingua francas > 50 million all speakers | 41 | 44 | 85 |
| lingua francas > 10 million all speakers | 107 | 121 | 228 |
| lingua francas > 1 million all speakers | 320 | 454 | 774 |
| lingua francas > 100,000 all speakers | 876 | 1,302 | 2,178 |

#### 2.  RANGES OF SPEAKERS

| Total all speakers | Outer | Inner | Total |
|---|---|---|---|
| Over 100 million all speakers | 20 | 21 | 41 |
| 50 million - 100 million all speakers | 21 | 23 | 44 |
| 10 million - 50 million all speakers | 66 | 77 | 143 |
| 1 million - 10 million all speakers | 213 | 333 | 546 |
| 500,000 - 1 million all speakers | 112 | 189 | 301 |
| 100,000 - 500,000 all speakers | 444 | 659 | 1,103 |

## Table 18–10. **The globe's 407 lingua francas (236 inner and 171 outer) each with over 1 million non-native speakers, ranked by these non-native speakers.**

The table lists all languages each with 1 million or more non-native speakers in addition to their own native (mother-tongue) speakers, in the year 2000. The listing contains 2 varieties of these lingua francas: (1) **inner lingua francas** shown in medium type, with their names in autoglossonym form (own vernacular names), are languages as defined in the World Language Classification, each sharing with its dialects 85% or more basic vocabulary of common human experience (*WCE* Part 9 "Linguametrics"); and (2) **outer lingua francas** shown in bold type, with anglicized names, are language clusters as defined in WLC, outer languages, each containing a small grouping of distinct languages but all mutually intercomprehensive by virtue of sharing 80% basic vocabulary of common human experience. There is a certain amount of overlapping and duplication (e.g. Standard English and General American) largely due to a language being the only 1 or 2 languages in its outer language (cluster).

*Meaning of columns*
1. WLC code (see *WCE* Table 9–13).
2. Name of lingua franca.
3. Native (mother-tongue) speakers.
4. Non-native speakers (with reasonable degree of competence).
5. Total speakers or users.
6. Number of peoples with this language as mother tongue.
7. Ratio total speakers to native speakers.
8. Christians (total speakers who are church members).
9. Church members as % of total speakers.
10. Ministries exercised: 'Jesus' Film, audio scriptures, New Reader Scriptures, Braille scriptures, signed scriptures (see codes at end of *WCT* Part 24).
11. Scriptures published (P, N, B, p, n, b) (see end of Part 24).
12. Scriptures available in a second language used by over 50% of speakers.

| WLC code 1 | Language 2 | Native speakers 3 | Non-native speakers 4 | Total speakers 5 | Peoples 6 | T/M 7 | Christians 8 | AC% 9 | Jayuh 10 | Scrip 11 | SS 12 |
|---|---|---|---|---|---|---|---|---|---|---|---|
| 52-ABAC | **Global English** | 234,031,000 | 1,085,826,000 | 1,319,857,000 | 388 | 5.64 | 555,653,000 | 42.10 | 3Bsuh | PNB | b |
| 52-ABAC-b | Standard English | 53,368,000 | 534,025,000 | 587,393,000 | 196 | 11.01 | 183,565,000 | 31.25 | 3Bsuh | PNB | b |
| 52-ABAC-s | General American | 134,532,000 | 492,079,000 | 626,611,000 | 129 | 4.66 | 320,298,000 | 51.12 | 1Bsuh | PNB | b |
| 79-AAAB | **Mandarin Chinese** | 882,103,000 | 436,493,000 | 1,318,597,000 | 114 | 1.49 | 114,012,000 | 8.65 | 2Bsuh | PNB | b |
| 79-AAAB-b | bei-jing-hua (kuoyu) | 834,678,000 | 415,961,000 | 1,250,638,000 | 109 | 1.50 | 109,237,000 | 8.73 | 2Bsuh | PNB | b |
| 51-AABI | **French** | 48,629,000 | 228,849,000 | 277,478,000 | 171 | 5.71 | 150,981,000 | 54.41 | 4B.uh | PNB | b |
| 59-AAFO | **Hindi-Urdu** | 263,964,000 | 227,863,000 | 491,827,000 | 112 | 1.86 | 17,790,000 | 3.62 | 4Asuh | PNB | b |
| 51-AABB | **Spanish** | 337,010,000 | 206,066,000 | 543,076,000 | 210 | 1.61 | 474,005,000 | 87.28 | 4B.uh | PNB | b |
| 51-AABI-d | general français | 35,830,000 | 204,873,000 | 240,703,000 | 149 | 6.72 | 128,364,000 | 53.33 | 1B.uh | PNB | b |
| 31-PHAA | **Indonesian** | 55,521,000 | 173,718,000 | 229,239,000 | 45 | 4.13 | 24,518,000 | 10.70 | 4Asuh | PNB | b |
| 31-PHAA-c | bahasa-indonesia | 41,103,000 | 145,097,000 | 186,200,000 | 16 | 4.53 | 20,874,000 | 11.21 | 4Asuh | PNB | b |
| 51-AABB-c | general español | 23,159,000 | 119,361,000 | 142,520,000 | 48 | 6.15 | 118,127,000 | 82.88 | 2B.uh | PNB | b |
| 52-ABCE | **High German** | 71,117,000 | 96,117,000 | 167,234,000 | 98 | 2.35 | 111,571,000 | 66.72 | 2B.uh | PNB | b |
| 52-ABCE-a | standard hoch-deutsch | 71,117,000 | 95,978,000 | 167,095,000 | 96 | 2.35 | 111,457,000 | 66.70 | 2B.uh | PNB | b |
| 99-AUSM | **Swahili** | 3,751,000 | 94,128,000 | 97,879,000 | 43 | 26.09 | 66,545,000 | 67.99 | 4Asu. | PNB | b |
| 59-AAFE | **Punjabi** | 136,022,000 | 76,134,000 | 212,157,000 | 52 | 1.56 | 8,129,000 | 3.83 | 2Asu. | PNB | b |
| 59-AAFO-d | standard urdu | 66,314,000 | 70,194,000 | 136,508,000 | 31 | 2.06 | 3,132,000 | 2.29 | 2Asuh | PNB | b |
| 53-AAAE | **Russian** | 200,870,000 | 68,261,000 | 269,131,000 | 154 | 1.34 | 161,537,000 | 60.02 | 4B.uh | PNB | b |
| 79-AAAM-a | central yue | 66,362,000 | 65,492,000 | 131,854,000 | 52 | 1.99 | 7,966,000 | 6.04 | 3A.uh | PNB | b |
| 79-AAAM | **Cantonese** | 66,362,000 | 65,492,000 | 131,854,000 | 52 | 1.99 | 7,966,000 | 6.04 | 3A.uh | PNB | b |
| 52-ABAH | **West Coast Creole** | 2,606,000 | 63,414,000 | 66,020,000 | 21 | 25.33 | 29,337,000 | 44.44 | 4.s.h | PN. | b |
| 51-AABB-h | latino americano | 300,844,000 | 62,474,000 | 363,318,000 | 153 | 1.21 | 331,014,000 | 91.11 | 4B.uh | pnb | b |
| 59-AAFT | **Bengali** | 217,240,000 | 60,681,000 | 277,921,000 | 44 | 1.28 | 6,249,000 | 2.25 | 4Asuh | PNB | b |
| 53-AAAE-d | russkiy | 145,587,000 | 60,472,000 | 206,059,000 | 87 | 1.42 | 111,653,000 | 54.19 | 4B.uh | PNB | b |
| 79-AAAD | **Shanghainese** | 94,898,000 | 57,844,000 | 152,742,000 | 9 | 1.61 | 16,322,000 | 10.69 | 1A... | PNB | b |
| 59-AAFU | **Marathi** | 106,459,000 | 57,247,000 | 163,706,000 | 31 | 1.54 | 9,896,000 | 6.04 | 3Asu. | PNB | b |
| 59-AAFO-e | general hindi | 64,508,000 | 52,745,000 | 117,253,000 | 64 | 1.82 | 4,480,000 | 3.82 | 3Asuh | pnb | b |
| 59-AAFU-m | deshi-marathi | 88,393,000 | 51,121,000 | 139,514,000 | 7 | 1.58 | 7,073,000 | 5.07 | 2Asu. | PNB | b |
| 52-ABAH-e | nigerian-creole | 1,020,000 | 49,994,000 | 51,014,000 | 2 | 50.00 | 23,463,000 | 45.99 | 1.s.h | Pn. | b |
| 59-AAFO-c | standard hindi | 63,061,000 | 49,896,000 | 112,957,000 | 1 | 1.79 | 4,388,000 | 3.88 | 1Asuh | PNB | b |
| 51-AABQ | **Italian** | 36,509,000 | 49,178,000 | 85,687,000 | 68 | 2.35 | 69,345,000 | 80.93 | 2B.uh | PNB | b |
| 51-AABQ-c | standard italiano | 36,319,000 | 48,970,000 | 85,289,000 | 66 | 2.35 | 69,013,000 | 80.92 | 2B.uh | PNB | b |
| 19-HAAB-a | hausa | 29,864,000 | 48,864,000 | 78,728,000 | 26 | 2.64 | 20,187,000 | 25.64 | 4Asu. | PNB | b |
| 19-HAAB | **Hausa** | 29,864,000 | 48,864,000 | 78,728,000 | 26 | 2.64 | 20,187,000 | 25.64 | 4Asu. | PNB | b |
| 59-AAFT-e | west bengali | 90,730,000 | 48,197,000 | 138,926,000 | 20 | 1.53 | 5,199,000 | 3.74 | 1Asuh | PNB | b |
| 31-CKAA-a | proper tagalog | 22,509,000 | 44,857,000 | 67,366,000 | 28 | 2.99 | 60,788,000 | 90.23 | 4Bs.. | PNB | b |
| 31-CKAA | **Filipino** | 22,509,000 | 44,857,000 | 67,366,000 | 28 | 2.99 | 60,788,000 | 90.23 | 4Bs.. | PNB | b |
| 49-DBAB | **Telegu** | 76,204,000 | 43,327,000 | 119,531,000 | 18 | 1.57 | 12,621,000 | 10.56 | 2Asu. | PNB | b |
| 49-DBAB-a | telugu | 76,174,000 | 43,323,000 | 119,497,000 | 16 | 1.57 | 12,620,000 | 10.56 | 2Asu. | PNB | b |
| 49-EBEA | **Tamil** | 72,690,000 | 42,043,000 | 114,733,000 | 35 | 1.58 | 16,950,000 | 14.77 | 2Asu. | PNB | b |
| 49-EBEA-b | tamil | 72,292,000 | 41,987,000 | 114,280,000 | 32 | 1.58 | 16,946,000 | 14.83 | 2Asu. | PNB | b |
| 59-AAFQ | **Bihari** | 89,665,000 | 40,255,000 | 129,920,000 | 20 | 1.45 | 3,331,000 | 2.56 | 1.s.. | PN. | b |
| 59-AAFE-e | lahnda | 66,924,000 | 39,436,000 | 106,360,000 | 4 | 1.59 | 3,903,000 | 3.67 | 1csu. | PNb | b |
| 12-AACF | **Colloquial Arabic** | 174,378,000 | 37,445,000 | 211,823,000 | 300 | 1.21 | 24,019,000 | 11.34 | 4Asuh | PNB | b |
| 99-AUSM-b | standard ki-swahili | 682,000 | 33,632,000 | 34,314,000 | 19 | 50.31 | 22,270,000 | 64.90 | 4Asu. | PNB | b |
| 99-AUIF | **Ngala** | 3,322,000 | 33,492,000 | 36,814,000 | 14 | 11.08 | 33,589,000 | 91.24 | 4asu. | PNB | b |
| 52-ABAC-x | General Australian | 14,378,000 | 32,798,000 | 47,176,000 | 18 | 3.28 | 13,957,000 | 29.59 | 1Bsuh | pnb | b |
| 31-PIAA | **Javanese** | 56,256,000 | 31,993,000 | 88,249,000 | 18 | 1.57 | 11,098,000 | 12.58 | 2As.h | PNB | b |
| 31-PIAA-g | general jawa | 55,104,000 | 31,707,000 | 86,811,000 | 11 | 1.58 | 11,027,000 | 12.70 | 2As.h | PNB | b |
| 58-AACC | **Persian** | 47,594,000 | 30,358,000 | 77,952,000 | 86 | 1.64 | 488,000 | 0.63 | 2Asu. | PNB | b |
| 59-AAFH | **Gujarati** | 50,142,000 | 29,753,000 | 79,895,000 | 29 | 1.59 | 3,145,000 | 3.94 | 2A.u. | PNB | b |
| 59-AAFH-b | standard gujaraati | 50,142,000 | 29,753,000 | 79,895,000 | 29 | 1.59 | 3,145,000 | 3.94 | 2A.u. | PNB | b |
| 12-AACB | **Western Arabic** | 49,874,000 | 28,861,000 | 78,735,000 | 50 | 1.58 | 1,024,000 | 1.30 | 2A.uh | PNB | b |
| 59-AAFE-c | general panjabi | 43,942,000 | 25,673,000 | 69,615,000 | 28 | 1.58 | 3,162,000 | 4.54 | 1Asu. | PNB | b |
| 99-AUSM-z | ki-ngwana | 1,033,000 | 24,543,000 | 25,576,000 | 1 | 24.76 | 23,168,000 | 90.58 | 2Asu. | PNB | . |
| 99-AUIF-b | vehicular lingala | 2,475,000 | 24,368,000 | 26,843,000 | 9 | 10.84 | 24,480,000 | 91.20 | 4asu. | PNB | b |
| 79-AAAJ | **Taiwanese** | 48,925,000 | 24,114,000 | 73,039,000 | 23 | 1.49 | 7,058,000 | 9.66 | 2A..h | PNB | b |
| 59-AAFP | **East Hindi** | 39,144,000 | 23,252,000 | 62,395,000 | 14 | 1.59 | 2,420,000 | 3.88 | 2A.u. | PN. | b |
| 59-AAFP-a | awadhi | 37,995,000 | 22,843,000 | 60,838,000 | 2 | 1.60 | 2,339,000 | 3.84 | 1c.u. | Pn. | b |
| 31-PHAA-b | bahasa-malaysia | 11,644,000 | 22,560,000 | 34,204,000 | 22 | 2.94 | 2,452,000 | 7.17 | 1asuh | PNB | b |
| 58-AACC-c | standard farsi | 30,745,000 | 22,445,000 | 53,190,000 | 35 | 1.73 | 404,000 | 0.76 | 1Asu. | PNB | b |
| 79-AAAJ-i | chao-shan | 47,142,000 | 22,325,000 | 69,467,000 | 15 | 1.47 | 5,419,000 | 7.80 | 1A..h | PNB | b |
| 47-AAAB | **Thai** | 39,481,000 | 21,752,000 | 61,233,000 | 25 | 1.55 | 1,211,000 | 1.98 | 3asuh | PNB | b |
| 59-AAFO-i | braj-kannauji | 27,380,000 | 21,664,000 | 49,044,000 | 3 | 1.79 | 1,930,000 | 3.94 | 4csuh | PNb | b |
| 52-ABAE | **Black English** | 36,427,000 | 21,533,000 | 57,960,000 | 44 | 1.59 | 42,009,000 | 72.48 | 0B.uh | PNB | b |
| 59-AAFO-h | baangaru | 27,064,000 | 21,414,000 | 48,477,000 | 2 | 1.79 | 2,167,000 | 4.47 | 1asuh | pnb | b |
| 49-EBEB | **Malayalam** | 39,208,000 | 21,312,000 | 60,520,000 | 33 | 1.54 | 16,169,000 | 26.72 | 2Asu. | PNB | b |
| 49-EBEB-a | malayalam | 39,147,000 | 21,302,000 | 60,449,000 | 21 | 1.54 | 16,167,000 | 26.75 | 2Asu. | PNB | b |
| 44-AABA | **Turkish** | 87,669,000 | 20,859,000 | 108,529,000 | 117 | 1.24 | 2,050,000 | 1.89 | 3A.u. | PNB | b |
| 79-AAAB-l | hui-zu | 47,426,000 | 20,533,000 | 67,958,000 | 5 | 1.43 | 4,774,000 | 7.03 | 1Asuh | pnb | b |
| 49-EBAA | **Kanarese** | 37,441,000 | 20,481,000 | 57,922,000 | 9 | 1.55 | 3,434,000 | 5.93 | 3Asu. | PNB | b |
| 49-EBAA-a | kannada | 37,219,000 | 20,449,000 | 57,668,000 | 4 | 1.55 | 3,413,000 | 5.92 | 2Asu. | PNB | b |
| 59-AAFS | **Oriya** | 34,210,000 | 20,064,000 | 54,273,000 | 17 | 1.59 | 1,705,000 | 3.14 | 3Asu. | PNB | b |
| 52-ABAE-a | talkin-black | 32,741,000 | 19,961,000 | 52,703,000 | 16 | 1.61 | 38,379,000 | 72.82 | 0B.uh | pnb | b |
| 79-AAAG | **Hakka** | 37,068,000 | 19,845,000 | 56,913,000 | 25 | 1.54 | 2,347,000 | 4.12 | 1A... | PNB | b |
| 79-AAAG-a | literary hakka | 37,068,000 | 19,845,000 | 56,913,000 | 25 | 1.54 | 2,347,000 | 4.12 | 1A... | PNB | b |
| 59-AAFS-a | odiaa | 33,417,000 | 19,666,000 | 53,084,000 | 3 | 1.59 | 1,675,000 | 3.16 | 3Asu. | PNB | b |
| 51-AABB-k | chicano | 12,944,000 | 19,345,000 | 32,288,000 | 2 | 2.49 | 24,091,000 | 74.61 | 1B.uh | pnb | b |
| 58-ABDA | **Pushtu** | 32,313,000 | 18,354,000 | 50,667,000 | 22 | 1.57 | 306,000 | 0.60 | 1As.. | PNB | b |
| 59-AAFQ-a | bhojpuri | 38,005,000 | 18,210,000 | 56,215,000 | 5 | 1.48 | 1,473,000 | 2.62 | 1.s.. | Pn. | b |
| 79-AAAE | **Xiang** | 44,288,000 | 18,139,000 | 62,427,000 | 2 | 1.41 | 2,169,000 | 3.47 | 1.... | ... | b |
| 79-AAAE-a | xiang | 44,288,000 | 18,139,000 | 62,427,000 | 2 | 1.41 | 2,169,000 | 3.47 | 1.... | ... | b |
| 58-AAAA | **Kurdish** | 17,969,000 | 17,764,000 | 35,733,000 | 46 | 1.99 | 369,000 | 1.03 | 3A... | PN. | b |
| 12-AACB-b | east maghrebi | 31,990,000 | 17,400,000 | 49,390,000 | 34 | 1.54 | 769,000 | 1.56 | 2A.uh | PNB | b |
| 12-ACAC-a | tigrinya | 5,466,000 | 16,469,000 | 21,935,000 | 6 | 4.01 | 12,344,000 | 56.28 | 2As.. | PNB | b |
| 12-ACAC | **Tigray** | 5,466,000 | 16,469,000 | 21,935,000 | 6 | 4.01 | 12,344,000 | 56.28 | 2As.. | PNB | b |
| 47-AAAB-d | central thai | 27,933,000 | 15,364,000 | 43,298,000 | 20 | 1.55 | 960,000 | 2.22 | 3asuh | PNB | b |
| 12-ACBA | **Amharic** | 19,977,000 | 15,287,000 | 35,264,000 | 10 | 1.77 | 25,309,000 | 71.77 | 3Asuh | PNB | b |
| 59-AAFQ-b | maithili | 34,219,000 | 15,276,000 | 49,495,000 | 2 | 1.45 | 1,239,000 | 2.50 | 1.s.. | Pn. | b |
| 12-ACBA-b | general amarinya | 19,933,000 | 15,252,000 | 35,185,000 | 9 | 1.77 | 25,287,000 | 71.87 | 3Asuh | PNB | b |

*Continued opposite*

*Table 18–10 continued*

| WLC code 1 | Language 2 | Native speakers 3 | Non-native speakers 4 | Total speakers 5 | Peoples 6 | T/M 7 | Christians 8 | AC% 9 | Jayuh 10 | Scrip 11 | SS 12 |
|---|---|---|---|---|---|---|---|---|---|---|---|
| 90-BAAA | **Pulaar-Fulfulde** | 19,766,000 | 15,145,000 | 34,910,000 | 46 | 1.77 | 5,918,000 | 16.95 | 4As.. | PNB | b |
| 59-AAFD | **East Pahari** | 22,100,000 | 14,664,000 | 36,765,000 | 11 | 1.66 | 1,023,000 | 2.78 | 2Asu. | PNB | b |
| 59-AAFD-b | nepali | 22,088,000 | 14,655,000 | 36,743,000 | 9 | 1.66 | 1,023,000 | 2.78 | 2Asu. | PNB | b |
| 52-ABAC-r | General Canadian | 16,451,000 | 14,201,000 | 30,652,000 | 10 | 1.86 | 19,486,000 | 63.57 | 1Bsuh | pnb | b |
| 51-AABE | **Catalonian** | 11,731,000 | 14,022,000 | 25,753,000 | 9 | 2.20 | 24,132,000 | 93.71 | 2a..h | PNB | b |
| 51-AABE-b | català | 11,719,000 | 14,019,000 | 25,739,000 | 8 | 2.20 | 24,118,000 | 93.70 | 2a..h | PNB | b |
| 99-AUSM-q | ki-unguja | 883,000 | 13,835,000 | 14,717,000 | 6 | 16.68 | 6,367,000 | 43.26 | 1Asu. | pnb | b |
| 98-AAAA | **Yoruba** | 25,111,000 | 13,625,000 | 38,737,000 | 25 | 1.54 | 21,469,000 | 55.42 | 3asu. | PNB | b |
| 51-AABI-i | français nord-américain | 9,738,000 | 13,175,000 | 22,913,000 | 2 | 2.35 | 15,423,000 | 67.31 | 1B.uh | pnb | b |
| 58-AAAA-c | kurdi | 7,094,000 | 13,130,000 | 20,223,000 | 8 | 2.85 | 102,000 | 0.50 | 2c... | PN. | b |
| 31-PJAA | **Sundanese** | 22,494,000 | 12,821,000 | 35,315,000 | 1 | 1.57 | 1,612,000 | 4.56 | 1A... | PNB | b |
| 31-PJAA-a | central sunda | 22,494,000 | 12,821,000 | 35,315,000 | 1 | 1.57 | 1,612,000 | 4.56 | 1A... | PNB | b |
| 59-AAFF | **Sindhi** | 23,030,000 | 12,086,000 | 35,116,000 | 19 | 1.52 | 401,000 | 1.14 | 1as.. | PNB | b |
| 98-AAAA-a | standard yoruba | 20,576,000 | 12,011,000 | 32,587,000 | 12 | 1.58 | 17,240,000 | 52.91 | 3asu. | PNB | b |
| 51-AABA | **Portuguese** | 184,292,000 | 11,856,000 | 196,148,000 | 106 | 1.06 | 176,674,000 | 90.07 | 3Bsuh | PNB | b |
| 44-AABD | **East Turkic** | 34,318,000 | 11,811,000 | 46,129,000 | 50 | 1.34 | 733,000 | 1.59 | 2A.u. | PNB | b |
| 46-EBAA-a | viêt | 72,047,000 | 11,768,000 | 83,814,000 | 23 | 1.16 | 6,876,000 | 8.20 | 1Asu. | PNB | b |
| 46-EBAA | **Vietnamese** | 72,047,000 | 11,768,000 | 83,814,000 | 23 | 1.16 | 6,876,000 | 8.20 | 1Asu. | PNB | b |
| 47-AAAC | **Laotian** | 19,410,000 | 11,681,000 | 31,091,000 | 12 | 1.60 | 547,000 | 1.76 | 2As.. | PNB | b |
| 44-AABA-a | osmanli | 59,476,000 | 11,619,000 | 71,096,000 | 60 | 1.20 | 1,614,000 | 2.27 | 1A.u. | PNB | b |
| 59-AAFF-a | standard sindhi | 20,402,000 | 11,474,000 | 31,876,000 | 7 | 1.56 | 342,000 | 1.07 | 1as.. | PNB | b |
| 12-AACB-a | west maghrebi | 17,567,000 | 11,081,000 | 28,648,000 | 13 | 1.63 | 244,000 | 0.85 | 1A.uh | pnb | b |
| 00-AAAB | **East Mandekan** | 6,536,000 | 10,886,000 | 17,423,000 | 21 | 2.67 | 1,427,000 | 8.19 | 4As.. | PNB | b |
| 58-ABDA-a | pashto | 17,853,000 | 10,582,000 | 28,435,000 | 18 | 1.59 | 85,500 | 0.30 | 1As.. | pnb | b |
| 59-AAFO-j | bundeli | 12,594,000 | 9,965,000 | 22,558,000 | 2 | 1.79 | 800,000 | 3.54 | 1asuh | pnb | b |
| 51-AABA-e | general português | 15,355,000 | 9,921,000 | 25,276,000 | 85 | 1.65 | 18,944,000 | 74.95 | 2Bsuh | PNB | b |
| 99-AURG | **Kongo** | 9,780,000 | 9,703,000 | 19,483,000 | 19 | 1.99 | 17,909,000 | 91.92 | 4as.. | PNB | b |
| 59-AAFT-s | axamiyaa | 16,232,000 | 9,697,000 | 25,930,000 | 3 | 1.60 | 771,000 | 2.98 | 3asuh | PNB | b |
| 79-AAAF | **Gan** | 25,272,000 | 9,603,000 | 34,875,000 | 1 | 1.38 | 2,193,000 | 6.29 | 0.... | ... | b |
| 79-AAAF-a | gan | 25,272,000 | 9,603,000 | 34,875,000 | 1 | 1.38 | 2,193,000 | 6.29 | 0.... | ... | b |
| 77-AABA | **Burmese** | 30,542,000 | 9,480,000 | 40,022,000 | 20 | 1.31 | 1,039,000 | 2.60 | 4Asu. | PNB | b |
| 99-AUSM-i | ki-mvita | 98,400 | 9,421,000 | 9,519,000 | 1 | 96.77 | 7,039,000 | 73.95 | 1Asu. | pnb | b |
| 12-AACF-f | syro-palestinian | 34,259,000 | 9,350,000 | 43,609,000 | 128 | 1.27 | 9,788,000 | 22.45 | 1Asuh | Pnb | b |
| 47-AAAC-a | isan | 16,325,000 | 9,279,000 | 25,604,000 | 4 | 1.57 | 432,000 | 1.69 | 1cs.. | PNB | b |
| 99-AUIF-c | bangala-3 | 842,000 | 9,121,000 | 9,963,000 | 4 | 11.83 | 9,103,000 | 91.37 | 1csu. | PNB | b |
| 12-AACD | **Sahara Bedouin** | 16,947,000 | 9,053,000 | 26,000,000 | 64 | 1.53 | 255,000 | 0.98 | 0a... | PN. | b |
| 12-AACF-c | sudani | 16,499,000 | 8,857,000 | 25,356,000 | 55 | 1.54 | 2,116,000 | 8.35 | 4Asuh | PNb | b |
| 98-FAAA | **Central Igbo** | 15,008,000 | 8,677,000 | 23,686,000 | 6 | 1.58 | 18,658,000 | 78.78 | 2..u. | PNB | b |
| 98-FAAA-e | south central igbo | 14,828,000 | 8,600,000 | 23,428,000 | 1 | 1.58 | 18,463,000 | 78.80 | 1..u. | pnb | . |
| 99-AUTF | **Ngoni** | 20,647,000 | 8,489,000 | 29,137,000 | 26 | 1.41 | 23,674,000 | 81.25 | 4Asu. | PNB | b |
| 31-CKGP-a | vehicular cebuano | 14,434,000 | 8,372,000 | 22,806,000 | 1 | 1.58 | 21,514,000 | 94.33 | 2Asu. | PNB | . |
| 31-CKGP | **Cebuan** | 14,434,000 | 8,372,000 | 22,806,000 | 1 | 1.58 | 21,514,000 | 94.33 | 2Asu. | PNB | . |
| 14-FBAA | **Oromo** | 20,715,000 | 8,161,000 | 28,876,000 | 29 | 1.39 | 9,456,000 | 32.75 | 2As.. | PNB | b |
| 77-AABA-a | bama | 26,230,000 | 8,159,000 | 34,388,000 | 11 | 1.31 | 901,000 | 2.62 | 4Asu. | PNB | b |
| 90-BAAA-q | fula-adamawa | 2,133,000 | 7,837,000 | 9,970,000 | 3 | 4.67 | 4,046,000 | 40.58 | 1cs.. | PNB | b |
| 59-AAFE-r | siraiki | 15,380,000 | 7,828,000 | 23,209,000 | 4 | 1.51 | 851,000 | 3.67 | 2asu. | PNb | b |
| 58-ABDA-c | pakhto | 14,351,000 | 7,755,000 | 22,106,000 | 3 | 1.54 | 220,000 | 1.00 | 1as.. | PNB | b |
| 44-AABC | **Central Turkic** | 15,764,000 | 7,605,000 | 23,369,000 | 37 | 1.48 | 1,068,000 | 4.57 | 4A.u. | PN. | b |
| 44-AABA-f | azeri | 20,658,000 | 7,506,000 | 28,164,000 | 22 | 1.36 | 178,000 | 0.63 | 2a.u. | PNB | b |
| 99-AUSM-d | ki-tikuu | 91,400 | 7,332,000 | 7,424,000 | 3 | 81.20 | 5,336,000 | 71.87 | 1csu. | pnb | b |
| 52-ABCA | **Dutch** | 21,736,000 | 7,325,000 | 29,061,000 | 41 | 1.34 | 21,539,000 | 74.12 | 2Bsuh | PNB | b |
| 52-ABAH-f | cameroonian-creole | 892,000 | 7,235,000 | 8,126,000 | 3 | 9.11 | 4,411,000 | 54.28 | 4.s.h | Pn. | b |
| 51-AABI-m | français-d'afrique | 910,000 | 7,226,000 | 8,135,000 | 6 | 8.94 | 3,553,000 | 43.67 | 1B.uh | pnb | b |
| 59-AAFG | **Rajasthani** | 19,523,000 | 7,154,000 | 26,676,000 | 22 | 1.37 | 663,000 | 2.48 | 4.s.. | PN. | b |
| 79-AAAI-c | south min-dong | 12,683,000 | 7,083,000 | 19,766,000 | 4 | 1.56 | 1,776,000 | 8.98 | 1A... | PNB | b |
| 79-AAAI | **Min-Coastal** | 12,683,000 | 7,083,000 | 19,766,000 | 4 | 1.56 | 1,776,000 | 8.98 | 1A... | PNB | b |
| 47-AAAG | **Huang-Chuang** | 12,922,000 | 6,673,000 | 19,595,000 | 2 | 1.52 | 599,000 | 3.06 | 1r... | P.. | b |
| 47-AAAG-n | wu-ming | 12,796,000 | 6,654,000 | 19,450,000 | 1 | 1.52 | 597,000 | 3.07 | 1r... | P.. | b |
| 12-AACD-a | hassaaniyya | 11,603,000 | 6,320,000 | 17,923,000 | 32 | 1.54 | 40,200 | 0.22 | 0a... | pn. | b |
| 31-PHJA | **Madurese** | 12,116,000 | 6,290,000 | 18,406,000 | 3 | 1.52 | 807,000 | 4.38 | 1.s.. | PNB | b |
| 44-AABD-a | central uzbek | 22,854,000 | 6,278,000 | 29,132,000 | 19 | 1.27 | 208,000 | 0.71 | 1A.u. | PNb | b |
| 59-AAFR | **Chhattisgarhi** | 12,855,000 | 6,231,000 | 19,087,000 | 7 | 1.48 | 539,000 | 2.82 | 2as.. | P.. | b |
| 53-AAAE-b | ukrainskiy | 43,955,000 | 6,171,000 | 50,126,000 | 37 | 1.14 | 41,554,000 | 82.90 | 3A.uh | PNB | b |
| 31-LDAA | **Central Malagasy** | 9,549,000 | 6,164,000 | 15,713,000 | 24 | 1.65 | 8,788,000 | 55.93 | 2Asu. | PNB | b |
| 12-AACF-a | masri | 65,696,000 | 6,160,000 | 71,856,000 | 31 | 1.09 | 11,167,000 | 15.54 | 2Asuh | PNB | b |
| 12-AACF-g | syro-mesopotamian | 16,698,000 | 6,118,000 | 22,816,000 | 18 | 1.37 | 382,000 | 1.67 | 1Asuh | pnb | b |
| 00-AAAB-z | jula-kan | 1,040,000 | 6,105,000 | 7,145,000 | 6 | 6.87 | 1,057,000 | 14.79 | 1cs.. | PNb | b |
| 59-AAFR-a | chhattisgarhi | 12,027,000 | 6,101,000 | 18,128,000 | 3 | 1.51 | 531,000 | 2.93 | 2as.. | P.. | b |
| 31-PHAA-d | malayu-pasar | 2,772,000 | 6,057,000 | 8,829,000 | 5 | 3.18 | 1,192,000 | 13.50 | 1csuh | PNb | b |
| 99-AUSX | **Nyanja-Sena** | 12,034,000 | 5,831,000 | 17,865,000 | 29 | 1.48 | 10,774,000 | 60.31 | 3.su. | PNB | b |
| 44-AABC-c | kazakh | 11,812,000 | 5,800,000 | 17,612,000 | 19 | 1.49 | 897,000 | 5.09 | 4A.u. | PN. | b |
| 53-AAAC | **Lekhitic** | 42,280,000 | 5,480,000 | 47,761,000 | 44 | 1.13 | 44,641,000 | 93.47 | 2A.uh | PNB | b |
| 53-AAAC-c | polski | 42,126,000 | 5,468,000 | 47,594,000 | 42 | 1.13 | 44,489,000 | 93.48 | 2A.uh | PNB | b |
| 59-AAFQ-g | magahi | 12,352,000 | 5,438,000 | 17,790,000 | 4 | 1.44 | 463,000 | 2.60 | 1.s.. | PN. | . |
| 45-CAAA | **Japanese** | 128,987,000 | 5,227,000 | 134,213,000 | 45 | 1.04 | 7,194,000 | 5.36 | 1B.uh | PNB | b |
| 45-CAAA-a | koku-go | 128,987,000 | 5,227,000 | 134,213,000 | 45 | 1.04 | 7,194,000 | 5.36 | 1B.uh | PNB | b |
| 52-ABCF | **South German** | 10,496,000 | 5,182,000 | 15,678,000 | 25 | 1.49 | 13,498,000 | 86.10 | 0B.uh | PN. | b |
| 10-AAAC | **North Tamazigh** | 16,659,000 | 5,147,000 | 21,805,000 | 50 | 1.31 | 281,000 | 1.29 | 4A... | PN. | b |
| 52-ABAC-u | South British African English | 1,103,000 | 5,006,000 | 6,108,000 | 3 | 5.54 | 4,816,000 | 78.84 | 1Bsuh | pnb | b |
| 59-AAFG-h | jaipuri | 10,687,000 | 4,943,000 | 15,630,000 | 3 | 1.46 | 416,000 | 2.66 | 4.s.. | Pn. | b |
| 90-AAAA | **Wolof** | 3,755,000 | 4,889,000 | 8,643,000 | 8 | 2.30 | 255,000 | 2.95 | 4.s.. | PN. | b |
| 59-ABBA | **Singalese** | 13,931,000 | 4,871,000 | 18,803,000 | 15 | 1.35 | 1,093,000 | 5.81 | 2asuh | PNB | b |
| 59-ABBA-a | historical sinhala | 13,908,000 | 4,869,000 | 18,777,000 | 13 | 1.35 | 1,092,000 | 5.82 | 2asuh | PNB | b |
| 90-AAAA-a | vehicular wolof | 3,567,000 | 4,840,000 | 8,407,000 | 7 | 2.36 | 245,000 | 2.92 | 4.s.. | PN. | b |
| 99-AUMA | **Thagicu** | 11,745,000 | 4,750,000 | 16,495,000 | 13 | 1.40 | 13,558,000 | 82.20 | 3as.. | PNB | b |
| 51-AADC | **Moldavian** | 22,995,000 | 4,747,000 | 27,741,000 | 47 | 1.21 | 23,496,000 | 84.70 | 3A.u. | PNB | b |
| 51-AADC-a | limba româneasca | 22,995,000 | 4,747,000 | 27,741,000 | 47 | 1.21 | 23,496,000 | 84.70 | 3A.u. | PNB | b |
| 52-ABCB | **Afro-Nederlands** | 6,550,000 | 4,685,000 | 11,236,000 | 18 | 1.72 | 9,562,000 | 85.11 | 2B.uh | PNB | b |
| 52-ABCC | **North German** | 10,408,000 | 4,684,000 | 15,092,000 | 13 | 1.45 | 12,655,000 | 83.85 | 2A.uh | PNB | b |
| 53-AAAG | **Serbo-Croatian** | 18,333,000 | 4,674,000 | 23,007,000 | 76 | 1.25 | 15,836,000 | 68.83 | 2Asuh | PNB | b |
| 58-AAAA-a | kurmanji | 10,702,000 | 4,610,000 | 15,313,000 | 36 | 1.43 | 267,000 | 1.74 | 3c... | PN. | b |
| 51-AABO | **Gallo-Italian** | 14,806,000 | 4,602,000 | 19,407,000 | 9 | 1.31 | 16,290,000 | 83.94 | 0B... | PN. | b |
| 99-AUSE | **Central Nyanza** | 12,577,000 | 4,469,000 | 17,046,000 | 27 | 1.36 | 14,152,000 | 83.02 | 4Bs.h | PNB | b |
| 58-AACC-f | dari | 7,594,000 | 4,418,000 | 12,012,000 | 6 | 1.58 | 20,100 | 0.17 | 1Asu. | PNb | b |
| 52-AAAD | **East Nordic** | 20,357,000 | 4,381,000 | 24,738,000 | 28 | 1.22 | 18,127,000 | 73.28 | 2B.uh | PNB | b |
| 99-AURG-a | ki-tuba | 3,481,000 | 4,330,000 | 7,811,000 | 3 | 2.24 | 7,164,000 | 91.72 | 4as.. | PNB | b |
| 91-GGAA | **Mossi-Dagaari** | 10,337,000 | 4,292,000 | 14,629,000 | 25 | 1.42 | 3,612,000 | 24.69 | 2A... | PNB | b |
| 99-AUSM-p | zanzibari | 160,000 | 4,278,000 | 4,438,000 | 2 | 27.82 | 2,007,000 | 45.22 | 1csu. | pnb | b |
| 51-AABG | **Oc** | 11,754,000 | 4,277,000 | 16,031,000 | 5 | 1.36 | 11,887,000 | 74.15 | 0A... | PN. | b |
| 44-AABD-d | east uyghur | 8,431,000 | 4,259,000 | 12,690,000 | 14 | 1.51 | 312,000 | 2.45 | 1r.u. | PNB | b |
| 99-AUTE | **Sotho Tswana** | 12,061,000 | 4,236,000 | 16,297,000 | 44 | 1.35 | 11,532,000 | 70.76 | 4Asu. | PNB | b |
| 52-ABCB-a | afrikaans | 6,461,000 | 4,069,000 | 10,530,000 | 16 | 1.63 | 9,012,000 | 85.58 | 2B.uh | PNB | b |
| 99-AUTF-g | i-si-zulu | 8,877,000 | 4,025,000 | 12,901,000 | 7 | 1.45 | 11,262,000 | 87.29 | 3asu. | PNB | b |
| 00-AAAB-a | bamanan-kan | 4,366,000 | 3,973,000 | 8,339,000 | 10 | 1.91 | 318,000 | 3.81 | 4As.. | PNB | b |
| 12-AACE | **Sahel Bedouin** | 5,910,000 | 3,893,000 | 9,803,000 | 28 | 1.66 | 738,000 | 7.53 | 0...h | PN. | b |
| 46-CABA | **Kherwari** | 10,602,000 | 3,824,000 | 14,425,000 | 26 | 1.36 | 1,010,000 | 7.00 | 3as.. | PNB | b |

*Continued overleaf*

*Table 18–10 continued*

| WLC code 1 | Language 2 | Native speakers 3 | Non-native speakers 4 | Total speakers 5 | Peoples 6 | T/M 7 | Christians 8 | AC% 9 | Jayuh 10 | Scrip 11 | SS 12 |
|---|---|---|---|---|---|---|---|---|---|---|---|
| 52-ABCA-g | oostvlaandersch | 6,481,000 | 3,817,000 | 10,298,000 | 11 | 1.59 | 8,981,000 | 87.21 | 1Bsuh | pnb | b |
| 44-AABB | **Northwest Turkic** | 8,845,000 | 3,760,000 | 12,605,000 | 50 | 1.43 | 2,215,000 | 17.58 | 2A.u. | PN. | b |
| 12-AABA-b | ivrit | 1,741,000 | 3,751,000 | 5,492,000 | 6 | 3.15 | 249,000 | 4.53 | 2B.uh | PNB | b |
| 12-AABA | **Hebrew** | 1,741,000 | 3,751,000 | 5,492,000 | 6 | 3.15 | 249,000 | 4.53 | 2B.uh | PNB | b |
| 99-AUTA | **Shona** | 9,812,000 | 3,743,000 | 13,555,000 | 28 | 1.38 | 7,818,000 | 57.68 | 3asuh | PNB | b |
| 53-AAAG-a | standard srpski | 12,513,000 | 3,711,000 | 16,223,000 | 52 | 1.30 | 9,589,000 | 59.10 | 1Asuh | PNB | b |
| 99-AUSY | **Makhua** | 11,386,000 | 3,642,000 | 15,029,000 | 18 | 1.32 | 4,113,000 | 27.37 | 2.s.. | PNB | b |
| 47-AAAB-a | yuan | 6,515,000 | 3,625,000 | 10,140,000 | 2 | 1.56 | 138,000 | 1.36 | 1csuh | PNB | b |
| 51-AABD | **Aragonese** | 1,981,000 | 3,606,000 | 5,588,000 | 1 | 2.82 | 5,256,000 | 94.06 | 0.... | ... | b |
| 51-AABD-b | aragonés | 1,981,000 | 3,606,000 | 5,588,000 | 1 | 2.82 | 5,256,000 | 94.06 | 0.... | ... | b |
| 51-AABR | **Neapolitan** | 12,077,000 | 3,575,000 | 15,652,000 | 2 | 1.30 | 12,734,000 | 81.36 | 0.... | P.. | b |
| 52-ABAH-b | krio | 554,000 | 3,562,000 | 4,115,000 | 5 | 7.43 | 588,000 | 14.28 | 4.s.h | PN. | b |
| 52-AAAD-r | svea-svensk | 13,380,000 | 3,535,000 | 16,916,000 | 14 | 1.26 | 11,341,000 | 67.05 | 1A.uh | PNB | b |
| 52-ABCA-a | algemeen-nederlands | 15,255,000 | 3,508,000 | 18,763,000 | 30 | 1.23 | 12,558,000 | 66.93 | 2Bsuh | PNB | b |
| 99-AUSX-a | nyanja-cewa | 5,813,000 | 3,377,000 | 9,190,000 | 10 | 1.58 | 5,898,000 | 64.18 | 3.su. | PNB | b |
| 59-AAFJ | **North Bhil** | 10,604,000 | 3,360,000 | 13,964,000 | 6 | 1.32 | 231,000 | 1.65 | 1.s.. | PN. | b |
| 31-CBAA-b | vehicular ilocano | 9,025,000 | 3,346,000 | 12,371,000 | 3 | 1.37 | 11,686,000 | 94.46 | 2A.u. | PNB | b |
| 31-CBAA | **Ilocano** | 9,025,000 | 3,346,000 | 12,371,000 | 3 | 1.37 | 11,686,000 | 94.46 | 2A.u. | PNB | b |
| 52-ABCF-q | brazilinien-deutsch | 73,300 | 3,329,000 | 3,402,000 | 1 | 46.45 | 3,106,000 | 91.30 | 0A.uh | pn. | b |
| 91-GGAA-a | moo-re | 8,053,000 | 3,324,000 | 11,378,000 | 10 | 1.41 | 2,821,000 | 24.79 | 2A... | PNB | b |
| 52-ABAI | **Oceanian Creole** | 894,000 | 3,174,000 | 4,068,000 | 21 | 4.55 | 3,360,000 | 82.60 | 4asuh | PNB | b |
| 44-AABB-e | tatar | 6,819,000 | 3,173,000 | 9,993,000 | 21 | 1.47 | 1,783,000 | 17.84 | 2c.u. | Pn. | b |
| 99-AUTF-a | i-si-xhosa | 7,452,000 | 3,153,000 | 10,605,000 | 6 | 1.42 | 8,724,000 | 82.27 | 2Asu. | PNB | b |
| 31-CKGL-e | vehicular hiligay | 7,132,000 | 3,138,000 | 10,270,000 | 1 | 1.44 | 9,734,000 | 94.77 | 2Asu. | PNB | b |
| 31-CKGL | **Hiligay** | 7,132,000 | 3,138,000 | 10,270,000 | 1 | 1.44 | 9,734,000 | 94.77 | 2Asu. | PNB | b |
| 99-AURQ | **Luba-Songye** | 8,920,000 | 3,083,000 | 12,003,000 | 16 | 1.35 | 11,080,000 | 92.31 | 4Asu. | PNB | b |
| 99-AGEH | **Kwa** | 14,200 | 3,003,000 | 3,017,000 | 1 | 212.16 | 1,556,000 | 51.56 | 0.... | ... | . |
| 99-AGEH-b | central kwa | 14,200 | 3,003,000 | 3,017,000 | 1 | 212.16 | 1,556,000 | 51.56 | 0.... | ... | . |
| 99-AGEG-b | northeast ndanda | 15,500 | 3,001,000 | 3,017,000 | 1 | 194.17 | 1,559,000 | 51.67 | 0.... | ... | . |
| 99-AGEG | **Ndanda** | 15,500 | 3,001,000 | 3,017,000 | 1 | 194.17 | 1,559,000 | 51.67 | 0.... | ... | . |
| 99-AGAB | **South Menchum** | 65,600 | 2,951,000 | 3,017,000 | 2 | 45.99 | 1,577,000 | 52.28 | 0.... | ... | . |
| 70-AAAA | **Phöke** | 9,109,000 | 2,912,000 | 12,021,000 | 40 | 1.32 | 278,000 | 2.31 | 0a... | PNB | b |
| 52-ABAI-c | tok-pisin creole | 502,000 | 2,867,000 | 3,368,000 | 6 | 6.71 | 2,759,000 | 81.89 | 3asuh | PNB | b |
| 51-AABB-b | standard castellano | 28,200 | 2,831,000 | 2,859,000 | 1 | 101.32 | 44,600 | 1.56 | 1A.uh | pnb | b |
| 51-AABO-e | lombardo-siculo | 8,798,000 | 2,815,000 | 11,613,000 | 1 | 1.32 | 9,784,000 | 84.25 | 0c... | pn. | b |
| 99-AGEF-b | central fe'fe' | 205,000 | 2,812,000 | 3,017,000 | 1 | 14.75 | 1,615,000 | 53.52 | 0.... | ... | . |
| 99-AGEF | **Fefe** | 205,000 | 2,812,000 | 3,017,000 | 1 | 14.75 | 1,615,000 | 53.52 | 0.... | ... | . |
| 41-BAAA | **Hungarian** | 15,383,000 | 2,810,000 | 18,193,000 | 29 | 1.18 | 15,287,000 | 84.03 | 2A.u. | PNB | b |
| 41-BAAA-a | general magyar | 15,383,000 | 2,810,000 | 18,193,000 | 29 | 1.18 | 15,287,000 | 84.03 | 2A.u. | PNB | b |
| 12-AACF-k | central anazi | 16,195,000 | 2,793,000 | 18,988,000 | 10 | 1.17 | 185,000 | 0.98 | 4Asuh | pnb | b |
| 99-AUIJ | **Mongo** | 1,864,000 | 2,785,000 | 4,649,000 | 3 | 2.49 | 4,358,000 | 93.74 | 4.... | PNB | . |
| 96-FCAA | **Baule** | 1,803,000 | 2,781,000 | 4,584,000 | 1 | 2.54 | 1,702,000 | 37.14 | 4As.. | PNB | . |
| 96-FCAA-a | central baule | 1,803,000 | 2,781,000 | 4,584,000 | 1 | 2.54 | 1,702,000 | 37.14 | 4As.. | PNB | . |
| 59-AAFJ-c | giraasiaa-bhili | 8,826,000 | 2,736,000 | 11,562,000 | 3 | 1.31 | 190,000 | 1.64 | 1.s.. | PN. | . |
| 93-ABBA | **Ngbandi-Sango** | 928,000 | 2,733,000 | 3,661,000 | 11 | 3.95 | 1,857,000 | 50.73 | 4.s.. | PNB | b |
| 99-AGEA | **Ngemba** | 290,000 | 2,727,000 | 3,017,000 | 7 | 10.41 | 1,629,000 | 54.00 | 0.... | ... | . |
| 46-CABA-a | santali | 6,845,000 | 2,695,000 | 9,540,000 | 7 | 1.39 | 409,000 | 4.29 | 2as.. | PNB | b |
| 47-AAAB-f | pak-thai | 4,827,000 | 2,688,000 | 7,515,000 | 1 | 1.56 | 107,000 | 1.43 | 1csuh | pnb | b |
| 99-AGAB-b | ba-ngwe | 59,600 | 2,680,000 | 2,739,000 | 1 | 45.99 | 1,432,000 | 52.29 | 0.... | ... | . |
| 52-ABCD | **Central German** | 7,294,000 | 2,615,000 | 9,909,000 | 9 | 1.36 | 7,317,000 | 73.84 | 0A.uh | ... | b |
| 85-FAAH | **South Quechua** | 7,928,000 | 2,590,000 | 10,519,000 | 13 | 1.33 | 10,203,000 | 97.00 | 3As.. | PNB | b |
| 99-AURR | **Bemba-Lamba** | 5,368,000 | 2,576,000 | 7,945,000 | 30 | 1.48 | 6,951,000 | 87.50 | 4.su. | PNB | b |
| 52-ABAH-c | kroo-english | 78,400 | 2,571,000 | 2,649,000 | 4 | 33.80 | 817,000 | 30.84 | 1.s.h | pn. | b |
| 31-LDAA-a | merina | 3,891,000 | 2,494,000 | 6,385,000 | 5 | 1.64 | 4,405,000 | 68.99 | 2Asu. | PNB | b |
| 59-AAFU-b | varhaadi | 7,559,000 | 2,493,000 | 10,052,000 | 2 | 1.33 | 304,000 | 3.03 | 1csu. | pnb | . |
| 99-AUIJ-c | basi-mongo | 1,668,000 | 2,492,000 | 4,161,000 | 2 | 2.49 | 3,903,000 | 93.80 | 4.... | PNB | . |
| 53-AAAD | **Czechoslovak** | 18,555,000 | 2,480,000 | 21,035,000 | 40 | 1.13 | 13,049,000 | 62.04 | 2Asuh | PNB | b |
| 52-ABCD-j | ostfränkisch | 6,881,000 | 2,461,000 | 9,342,000 | 4 | 1.36 | 6,792,000 | 72.70 | 0A.uh | ... | b |
| 00-AAAA | **West Mandekan** | 5,549,000 | 2,422,000 | 7,971,000 | 25 | 1.44 | 317,000 | 3.98 | 4a... | PN. | b |
| 47-AAAC-b | lao | 3,085,000 | 2,402,000 | 5,487,000 | 8 | 1.78 | 115,000 | 2.10 | 2As.. | PNB | b |
| 58-AABA | **Balochi** | 8,752,000 | 2,401,000 | 11,154,000 | 17 | 1.27 | 58,100 | 0.52 | 3.s.. | P.. | b |
| 04-ACCA | **Luo-Padhola** | 4,853,000 | 2,395,000 | 7,249,000 | 7 | 1.49 | 6,227,000 | 85.90 | 4As.. | PNB | b |
| 99-AGED | **Ngomba-Bagam** | 622,000 | 2,395,000 | 3,017,000 | 5 | 4.85 | 1,753,000 | 58.10 | 0.s.. | PNB | . |
| 96-FCCB | **Akan** | 7,230,000 | 2,392,000 | 9,623,000 | 15 | 1.33 | 4,844,000 | 50.34 | 4ssu. | PNB | b |
| 90-BAAA-n | fula-sokoto | 6,434,000 | 2,356,000 | 8,790,000 | 9 | 1.37 | 869,000 | 9.88 | 1cs.. | PNB | b |
| 59-AAFT-c | standard baanglaa | 102,112,000 | 2,322,000 | 104,433,000 | 1 | 1.02 | 160,000 | 0.15 | 4Asuh | PNB | . |
| 04-ACCA-b | dho-luo | 4,478,000 | 2,310,000 | 6,788,000 | 5 | 1.52 | 5,804,000 | 85.51 | 2As.. | PNB | b |
| 99-AUMA-a | gi-gikuyu | 5,806,000 | 2,309,000 | 8,114,000 | 4 | 1.40 | 7,044,000 | 86.81 | 3as.. | PNB | b |
| 96-MAAA-a | standard ewe | 3,484,000 | 2,300,000 | 5,783,000 | 7 | 1.66 | 3,662,000 | 63.32 | 4Asu. | PNB | b |
| 96-MAAA | **Ewe** | 3,484,000 | 2,300,000 | 5,783,000 | 7 | 1.66 | 3,662,000 | 63.32 | 4Asu. | PNB | b |
| 52-ABAF | **Carib Anglo-Creol** | 7,307,000 | 2,292,000 | 9,598,000 | 60 | 1.31 | 6,959,000 | 72.50 | 1a..h | PN. | b |
| 98-ICBA | **Ibibio-Efik** | 5,076,000 | 2,292,000 | 7,368,000 | 12 | 1.45 | 5,996,000 | 81.38 | 3as.. | PNB | b |
| 58-AACC-j | tajiki | 5,434,000 | 2,277,000 | 7,711,000 | 15 | 1.42 | 51,600 | 0.67 | 2asu. | PNB | b |
| 51-AABC | **Astur-Leones** | 505,000 | 2,230,000 | 2,736,000 | 2 | 5.41 | 2,542,000 | 92.92 | 0B.uh | P.. | b |
| 51-AABC-a | astur | 495,000 | 2,229,000 | 2,725,000 | 1 | 5.50 | 2,531,000 | 92.90 | 0B.uh | P.. | b |
| 46-FBAA | **Khmer** | 11,941,000 | 2,217,000 | 14,158,000 | 11 | 1.19 | 164,000 | 1.16 | 2A... | PNB | b |
| 31-PHBB-a | paranakan | 6,253,000 | 2,208,000 | 8,462,000 | 3 | 1.35 | 2,813,000 | 33.25 | 0A... | ... | b |
| 31-PHBB | **Peranakan** | 6,253,000 | 2,208,000 | 8,462,000 | 3 | 1.35 | 2,813,000 | 33.25 | 0A... | ... | b |
| 99-AGEE | **Ghomala** | 811,000 | 2,206,000 | 3,017,000 | 2 | 3.72 | 1,793,000 | 59.42 | 0.... | P.. | . |
| 99-AGEE-d | southeast ghomala | 811,000 | 2,206,000 | 3,017,000 | 2 | 3.72 | 1,793,000 | 59.42 | 0.... | P.. | . |
| 14-GAGA | **Somali** | 13,690,000 | 2,196,000 | 15,886,000 | 31 | 1.16 | 699,000 | 4.40 | 2A... | PNB | b |
| 56-AAAA | **Greek** | 14,088,000 | 2,191,000 | 16,279,000 | 90 | 1.16 | 15,268,000 | 93.79 | 2B.uh | PNB | b |
| 51-AABR-b | campano-molisano | 7,257,000 | 2,177,000 | 9,434,000 | 1 | 1.30 | 7,589,000 | 80.44 | 0.... | P.. | b |
| 70-AAAA-c | utsang | 5,596,000 | 2,148,000 | 7,744,000 | 22 | 1.38 | 223,000 | 2.88 | 0a... | PNB | b |
| 14-GAGA-a | af-soomaali | 12,883,000 | 2,125,000 | 15,007,000 | 26 | 1.16 | 697,000 | 4.64 | 2A... | PNB | b |
| 56-AAAA-c | dhimotiki | 13,560,000 | 2,089,000 | 15,649,000 | 85 | 1.15 | 14,702,000 | 93.95 | 2B.uh | PNB | b |
| 52-AAAC-e | ny-norsk | 8,636,000 | 2,079,000 | 10,716,000 | 14 | 1.24 | 9,408,000 | 87.80 | 0B.uh | PNB | b |
| 52-AAAC | **West Nordic** | 8,638,000 | 2,079,000 | 10,717,000 | 15 | 1.24 | 9,410,000 | 87.80 | 0B.uh | PNB | b |
| 58-AACE | **Caspian-Persian** | 7,773,000 | 2,070,000 | 9,843,000 | 9 | 1.27 | 29,000 | 0.29 | 1.... | ... | b |
| 31-PHGA | **Minang** | 5,890,000 | 2,053,000 | 7,943,000 | 4 | 1.35 | 253,000 | 3.19 | 2.... | PN. | b |
| 93-ABBA-a | sango | 469,000 | 2,044,000 | 2,513,000 | 5 | 5.36 | 1,167,000 | 46.45 | 4.s.. | PNB | b |
| 99-AUTD | **Tswa-Ronga** | 5,155,000 | 1,974,000 | 7,129,000 | 9 | 1.38 | 3,826,000 | 53.67 | 3.s.. | PNB | b |
| 12-AACE-a | shuwa | 1,706,000 | 1,951,000 | 3,656,000 | 5 | 2.14 | 411,000 | 11.24 | 0...h | PN. | b |
| 99-AUSD | **West Nyanza** | 23,839,000 | 1,915,000 | 25,754,000 | 42 | 1.08 | 21,255,000 | 82.53 | 4Asu. | PNB | b |
| 44-BAAB | **Monghol** | 6,987,000 | 1,894,000 | 8,881,000 | 31 | 1.27 | 287,000 | 3.23 | 3A..h | PNB | b |
| 47-AAAE | **Huang-Nung** | 7,992,000 | 1,893,000 | 9,885,000 | 15 | 1.24 | 222,000 | 2.24 | 0.... | P.. | b |
| 59-AAFU-n | konkan-marathi | 5,754,000 | 1,888,000 | 7,642,000 | 2 | 1.33 | 228,000 | 2.99 | 1csu. | PNb | . |
| 99-AURP | **Cokwe-Lunda** | 4,887,000 | 1,888,000 | 6,775,000 | 23 | 1.39 | 5,646,000 | 83.33 | 0.... | PNB | . |
| 45-AAAA-b | kukö | 75,665,000 | 1,881,000 | 77,546,000 | 36 | 1.02 | 21,902,000 | 28.24 | 2A... | PNB | b |
| 14-FBAA-a | tulema | 4,714,000 | 1,881,000 | 6,596,000 | 5 | 1.40 | 2,826,000 | 42.84 | 1cs.. | pnb | b |
| 45-AAAA | **Korean** | 75,665,000 | 1,881,000 | 77,546,000 | 36 | 1.02 | 21,902,000 | 28.24 | 2A... | PNB | b |
| 53-AAAH | **Bulgarian** | 10,056,000 | 1,878,000 | 11,935,000 | 47 | 1.19 | 9,847,000 | 82.51 | 2A.uh | PNB | b |
| 12-AACE-b | baggaari | 3,998,000 | 1,852,000 | 5,850,000 | 20 | 1.46 | 307,000 | 5.25 | 0...h | pn. | b |
| 99-AURG-b | ki-fiote | 2,325,000 | 1,845,000 | 4,170,000 | 2 | 1.79 | 3,817,000 | 91.54 | 1as.. | PNB | b |
| 51-AACC | **Gallo-Creole** | 14,323,000 | 1,823,000 | 16,146,000 | 59 | 1.13 | 14,168,000 | 87.75 | 3As.. | PNB | b |
| 52-ABCG-a | general schwytzer-tütsch | 4,498,000 | 1,815,000 | 6,314,000 | 8 | 1.40 | 5,719,000 | 90.58 | 0B.uh | PN. | b |

*Continued opposite*

*Table 18–10 concluded*

| WLC code 1 | Language 2 | Native speakers 3 | Non-native speakers 4 | Total speakers 5 | Peoples 6 | T/M 7 | Christians 8 | AC% 9 | Jayuh 10 | Scrip 11 | SS 12 |
|---|---|---|---|---|---|---|---|---|---|---|---|
| 52-ABCG | **Swiss German** | 4,498,000 | 1,815,000 | 6,314,000 | 8 | 1.40 | 5,719,000 | 90.58 | 0B.uh | PN. | b |
| 51-AABH | **Oil** | 4,529,000 | 1,798,000 | 6,328,000 | 10 | 1.40 | 5,256,000 | 83.06 | 0A.uh | P.. | b |
| 51-AABI-a | historical français | 10,100 | 1,788,000 | 1,798,000 | 4 | 178.49 | 491,000 | 27.33 | 1B.uh | pnb | b |
| 79-AAAK-c | wanning | 6,143,000 | 1,780,000 | 7,923,000 | 5 | 1.29 | 158,000 | 1.99 | 1a... | p.. | b |
| 79-AAAK | **Min-Hainan** | 6,143,000 | 1,780,000 | 7,923,000 | 5 | 1.29 | 158,000 | 1.99 | 1a... | P.. | b |
| 14-FBAA-b | mecha | 3,563,000 | 1,777,000 | 5,340,000 | 2 | 1.50 | 2,124,000 | 39.77 | 2cs.. | PNB | b |
| 47-AAAE-a | south huang | 6,965,000 | 1,773,000 | 8,738,000 | 10 | 1.25 | 195,000 | 2.24 | 0.... | P.. | b |
| 46-FBAA-b | khmae | 10,838,000 | 1,769,000 | 12,608,000 | 8 | 1.16 | 151,000 | 1.20 | 2A... | PNB | b |
| 47-AAAA | **Northwest Tai** | 6,012,000 | 1,721,000 | 7,732,000 | 27 | 1.29 | 182,000 | 2.35 | 3.s.. | PNB | b |
| 44-AABC-d | kirghiz | 3,323,000 | 1,715,000 | 5,037,000 | 10 | 1.52 | 169,000 | 3.35 | 2r.u. | PN. | b |
| 02-AAAA | **Kanuri** | 4,989,000 | 1,666,000 | 6,655,000 | 9 | 1.33 | 671,000 | 10.09 | 4.... | PN. | p |
| 99-AUSF | **North Nyanza** | 6,355,000 | 1,664,000 | 8,019,000 | 14 | 1.26 | 6,927,000 | 86.38 | 4.s.. | PNB | b |
| 42-CABB | **East Georgian** | 3,163,000 | 1,663,000 | 4,826,000 | 21 | 1.53 | 3,296,000 | 68.30 | 2A.u. | PNB | b |
| 42-CABB-a | kharthuli | 3,099,000 | 1,647,000 | 4,746,000 | 19 | 1.53 | 3,292,000 | 69.36 | 2A.u. | PNB | b |
| 99-AURG-c | ki-yombe | 1,566,000 | 1,626,000 | 3,191,000 | 4 | 2.04 | 2,965,000 | 92.91 | 1cs.. | Pnb | b |
| 53-AAAD-b | slovensky | 7,334,000 | 1,623,000 | 8,957,000 | 19 | 1.22 | 7,031,000 | 78.50 | 1Asuh | PNB | b |
| 98-ICBA-b | ibibio | 3,463,000 | 1,622,000 | 5,085,000 | 4 | 1.47 | 4,163,000 | 81.86 | 3cs.. | pnb | b |
| 59-AAFA | **Kashmiri** | 4,875,000 | 1,620,000 | 6,495,000 | 5 | 1.33 | 114,000 | 1.76 | 2.... | PNB | . |
| 59-AAFA-e | siraji-kashmiri | 4,833,000 | 1,614,000 | 6,447,000 | 3 | 1.33 | 114,000 | 1.76 | 2.... | PNB | . |
| 99-AUMA-i | ki-kamba | 3,305,000 | 1,584,000 | 4,889,000 | 2 | 1.48 | 3,993,000 | 81.66 | 1cs.. | PNB | b |
| 59-AAFO-b | historical hindi | 2,405,000 | 1,581,000 | 3,987,000 | 2 | 1.66 | 796,000 | 19.96 | 1Asuh | PNB | b |
| 59-AAFC | **Central Pahari** | 5,865,000 | 1,572,000 | 7,437,000 | 7 | 1.27 | 107,000 | 1.44 | 1.... | PN. | b |
| 31-CKDA | **Bicol** | 3,485,000 | 1,568,000 | 5,053,000 | 1 | 1.45 | 4,807,000 | 95.14 | 1A.u. | PNB | b |
| 31-CKDA-b | legaspi | 3,485,000 | 1,568,000 | 5,053,000 | 1 | 1.45 | 4,807,000 | 95.14 | 1A.u. | PNB | b |
| 48-AAAA | **Chuanqiandian** | 4,685,000 | 1,566,000 | 6,251,000 | 16 | 1.33 | 522,000 | 8.35 | 2A... | PN. | b |
| 59-AAFU-o | konkani-gomantaki | 3,772,000 | 1,562,000 | 5,334,000 | 8 | 1.41 | 2,270,000 | 42.56 | 3asu. | PNb | b |
| 96-MAAG | **Fon-Gun** | 2,294,000 | 1,561,000 | 3,855,000 | 13 | 1.68 | 1,269,000 | 32.92 | 2As.. | PNB | b |
| 99-AGED-b | ngyemboong | 404,000 | 1,556,000 | 1,960,000 | 2 | 4.85 | 1,135,000 | 57.89 | 0.s.. | PNB | . |
| 00-AAAA-h | maninka-kan | 3,440,000 | 1,538,000 | 4,978,000 | 8 | 1.45 | 230,000 | 4.63 | 3a... | PN. | b |
| 96-FCCB-c | twi | 4,900,000 | 1,537,000 | 6,437,000 | 12 | 1.31 | 3,347,000 | 51.99 | 4ssu. | PNB | b |
| 99-AURJ | **Umbundu** | 3,267,000 | 1,528,000 | 4,795,000 | 2 | 1.47 | 4,032,000 | 84.09 | 0a... | PNB | . |
| 77-BFAA | **Tujia** | 6,353,000 | 1,525,000 | 7,877,000 | 1 | 1.24 | 133,000 | 1.69 | 0a... | ... | b |
| 77-BFAA-a | tujia | 6,353,000 | 1,525,000 | 7,877,000 | 1 | 1.24 | 133,000 | 1.69 | 0a... | ... | b |
| 99-AURJ-a | u-mbundu | 3,245,000 | 1,525,000 | 4,771,000 | 1 | 1.47 | 4,021,000 | 84.29 | 0a... | PNB | . |
| 59-AAFE-p | hindko | 4,401,000 | 1,496,000 | 5,898,000 | 2 | 1.34 | 80,500 | 1.37 | 1csu. | PNb | b |
| 98-AAAA-c | west yoruba | 4,001,000 | 1,493,000 | 5,494,000 | 10 | 1.37 | 3,691,000 | 67.19 | 1csu. | Pnb | b |
| 52-ABCF-b | donau-bayrisch | 8,755,000 | 1,487,000 | 10,242,000 | 14 | 1.17 | 8,719,000 | 85.13 | 0B.uh | pn. | b |
| 12-AACD-f | west egyptian | 2,563,000 | 1,486,000 | 4,049,000 | 2 | 1.58 | 174,000 | 4.29 | 0c... | PN. | . |
| 90-BAAA-o | fula-bororo | 2,163,000 | 1,472,000 | 3,636,000 | 5 | 1.68 | 686,000 | 18.87 | 1cs.. | pnb | b |
| 48-AAAA-a | hmong-daw | 4,143,000 | 1,462,000 | 5,605,000 | 7 | 1.35 | 405,000 | 7.22 | 2A... | PN. | . |
| 44-BAAB-e | oyrat | 3,822,000 | 1,457,000 | 5,278,000 | 6 | 1.38 | 113,000 | 2.13 | 1a..h | PNb | b |
| 31-PKAA-a | bali | 4,210,000 | 1,430,000 | 5,640,000 | 2 | 1.34 | 222,000 | 3.94 | 1.... | pnb | b |
| 31-PKAA | **Bali** | 4,210,000 | 1,430,000 | 5,640,000 | 2 | 1.34 | 222,000 | 3.94 | 1.... | PNB | b |
| 99-AUSE-f | o-ru-nya-nkore | 3,746,000 | 1,429,000 | 5,176,000 | 8 | 1.38 | 4,863,000 | 93.96 | 3As.h | PNB | b |
| 58-AACA | **Luri-Kumzari** | 6,205,000 | 1,411,000 | 7,616,000 | 5 | 1.23 | 6,600 | 0.09 | 0.... | ... | b |
| 58-AACA-a | luri-bakhtiari | 6,202,000 | 1,410,000 | 7,612,000 | 4 | 1.23 | 6,600 | 0.09 | 0.... | ... | . |
| 53-AAAE-c | bielorusskiy | 10,175,000 | 1,409,000 | 11,583,000 | 26 | 1.14 | 7,198,000 | 62.14 | 3A.uh | PNB | b |
| 51-AABH-f | wallon | 3,383,000 | 1,399,000 | 4,782,000 | 8 | 1.41 | 4,040,000 | 84.48 | 0A.uh | P.. | b |
| 85-JABA | **Aymara** | 3,011,000 | 1,399,000 | 4,410,000 | 8 | 1.46 | 4,066,000 | 92.20 | 2.s.. | PNB | b |
| 51-AABR-e | east central siciliano | 4,820,000 | 1,398,000 | 6,218,000 | 1 | 1.29 | 5,145,000 | 82.75 | 0.... | P.. | b |
| 31-LDAA-c | north betsimisaraka | 2,140,000 | 1,388,000 | 3,528,000 | 2 | 1.65 | 1,199,000 | 33.99 | 1Asu. | pnb | . |
| 47-AAAA-e | shan | 4,291,000 | 1,368,000 | 5,659,000 | 5 | 1.32 | 139,000 | 2.46 | 3.s.. | PNB | b |
| 99-AUSA | **Nyiha-Fipa** | 5,133,000 | 1,367,000 | 6,500,000 | 20 | 1.27 | 2,815,000 | 43.30 | 4.... | PNB | b |
| 99-AUTE-e | se-sotho | 4,019,000 | 1,363,000 | 5,382,000 | 5 | 1.34 | 4,267,000 | 79.28 | 3asu. | PNB | b |
| 82-AAIF | **Guaraní** | 5,705,000 | 1,360,000 | 7,065,000 | 21 | 1.24 | 6,684,000 | 94.61 | 3As.. | PNB | b |
| 10-AAAC-a | ta-shelhit | 4,549,000 | 1,357,000 | 5,906,000 | 6 | 1.30 | 12,800 | 0.22 | 4c... | Pn. | b |
| 44-AABA-e | turkmen | 5,398,000 | 1,346,000 | 6,745,000 | 12 | 1.25 | 24,400 | 0.36 | 3c.u. | PNb | b |
| 02-AAAA-b | yerwa | 4,027,000 | 1,339,000 | 5,365,000 | 6 | 1.33 | 586,000 | 10.91 | 4.... | PN. | . |
| 82-AAIF-b | vehicular aba-ñeeme | 5,587,000 | 1,327,000 | 6,914,000 | 3 | 1.24 | 6,579,000 | 95.16 | 1a... | pnb | b |
| 99-AURR-h | i-ci-bemba | 2,287,000 | 1,327,000 | 3,613,000 | 6 | 1.58 | 3,099,000 | 85.75 | 4.su. | PNB | b |
| 99-AUSO | **Shambala-Sagara** | 5,388,000 | 1,310,000 | 6,697,000 | 16 | 1.24 | 2,691,000 | 40.18 | 0a... | PNB | b |
| 99-AURQ-l | vehicular ci-luba | 3,203,000 | 1,310,000 | 4,513,000 | 2 | 1.41 | 4,190,000 | 92.84 | 4csu. | PNB | b |
| 31-QBBA | **Buginese** | 3,951,000 | 1,300,000 | 5,250,000 | 3 | 1.33 | 196,000 | 3.74 | 2.... | PNB | b |
| 50-ABAA | **Welsh** | 3,522,000 | 1,292,000 | 4,814,000 | 8 | 1.37 | 3,717,000 | 77.21 | 2A.uh | PNB | b |
| 50-ABAA-b | standard cymraeg | 3,522,000 | 1,292,000 | 4,814,000 | 8 | 1.37 | 3,717,000 | 77.21 | 2A.uh | PNB | b |
| 10-AAAC-b | ta-mazight | 3,917,000 | 1,282,000 | 5,199,000 | 8 | 1.33 | 25,500 | 0.49 | 1a... | Pn. | b |
| 51-AABA-b | galego | 4,054,000 | 1,276,000 | 5,330,000 | 6 | 1.31 | 5,038,000 | 94.52 | 1csuh | PNB | b |
| 14-FBAA-e | qottu | 3,253,000 | 1,269,000 | 4,522,000 | 1 | 1.39 | 1,445,000 | 31.96 | 1cs.. | PNb | n |
| 99-AUTD-c | shi-shangana | 3,094,000 | 1,263,000 | 4,357,000 | 4 | 1.41 | 2,827,000 | 64.87 | 3.s.. | PNB | b |
| 52-ABAE-i | Oceanian English | 2,788,000 | 1,254,000 | 4,042,000 | 3 | 1.45 | 2,813,000 | 69.60 | 0B.uh | pnb | b |
| 99-AUSE-r | o-lu-ganda | 3,076,000 | 1,251,000 | 4,326,000 | 3 | 1.41 | 3,285,000 | 75.93 | 3Bs.h | PNB | b |
| 96-MAAD | **Gen** | 409,000 | 1,250,000 | 1,659,000 | 2 | 4.06 | 713,000 | 43.01 | 0.... | PN. | . |
| 99-AUTA-a | standard chi-shona | 3,016,000 | 1,246,000 | 4,261,000 | 5 | 1.41 | 2,583,000 | 60.62 | 3csuh | PNB | b |
| 59-AAFE-l | dogri | 3,506,000 | 1,235,000 | 4,741,000 | 4 | 1.35 | 88,600 | 1.87 | 1asu. | PNb | . |
| 04-CAAD | **Nandi-Kipsigis** | 1,773,000 | 1,235,000 | 3,008,000 | 6 | 1.70 | 2,149,000 | 71.44 | 4As.. | PNB | b |
| 99-AUTE-d | se-pedi | 3,046,000 | 1,231,000 | 4,277,000 | 3 | 1.40 | 3,670,000 | 85.80 | 2asu. | PNB | b |
| 90-BAAA-d | futa-jalon | 3,169,000 | 1,221,000 | 4,390,000 | 5 | 1.39 | 42,900 | 0.98 | 2as.. | Pnb | . |
| 31-NAAA | **Aceh** | 3,389,000 | 1,220,000 | 4,609,000 | 1 | 1.36 | 152,000 | 3.30 | 2A... | PN. | . |
| 31-CKGK | **Samarenyo** | 3,566,000 | 1,212,000 | 4,779,000 | 1 | 1.34 | 4,586,000 | 95.98 | 2a.u. | PNB | . |
| 85-JABA-a | central aymara | 2,470,000 | 1,209,000 | 3,679,000 | 7 | 1.49 | 3,391,000 | 92.17 | 2.s.. | PNB | b |
| 52-ABAC-i | Irish English | 5,202,000 | 1,175,000 | 6,377,000 | 9 | 1.23 | 5,549,000 | 87.01 | 1Asuh | pnb | . |
| 99-AIAA | **Tikari** | 33,000 | 1,174,000 | 1,207,000 | 1 | 36.62 | 607,000 | 50.32 | 0.... | PN. | . |
| 31-LDAA-j | betsileo | 1,808,000 | 1,173,000 | 2,980,000 | 1 | 1.65 | 2,221,000 | 74.51 | 1Asu. | pnb | . |
| 96-MAAG-a | standard fon | 1,675,000 | 1,158,000 | 2,833,000 | 5 | 1.69 | 876,000 | 30.91 | 2as.. | PNb | b |
| 53-AAAH-b | bulgarski | 8,302,000 | 1,145,000 | 9,447,000 | 35 | 1.14 | 7,817,000 | 82.74 | 2A.uh | PNB | b |
| 99-AUTE-g | se-tswana | 3,689,000 | 1,145,000 | 4,834,000 | 26 | 1.31 | 2,407,000 | 49.80 | 4Asu. | PNB | b |
| 51-AABG-b | lengadocian | 2,818,000 | 1,143,000 | 3,961,000 | 2 | 1.41 | 2,928,000 | 73.91 | 0c... | Pn. | b |
| 99-AURI | **Mbundu-Songo** | 3,122,000 | 1,099,000 | 4,221,000 | 6 | 1.35 | 3,538,000 | 83.82 | 0.... | PNB | . |
| 99-AGEA-e | proper n-gemba | 116,000 | 1,089,000 | 1,205,000 | 1 | 10.41 | 646,000 | 53.62 | 0.... | ... | . |
| 31-PECA | **South Batak** | 4,282,000 | 1,088,000 | 5,370,000 | 5 | 1.25 | 2,795,000 | 52.05 | 2.s.. | PNB | b |
| 51-AABI-f | français-suisse | 1,273,000 | 1,081,000 | 2,353,000 | 2 | 1.85 | 2,018,000 | 85.76 | 1B.uh | pnb | b |
| 99-AURI-a | ki-mbundu | 2,992,000 | 1,074,000 | 4,066,000 | 2 | 1.36 | 3,423,000 | 84.17 | 0.... | PNB | . |
| 99-AUSA-k | i-ci-fipa | 3,473,000 | 1,069,000 | 4,543,000 | 3 | 1.31 | 1,916,000 | 42.18 | 1.... | PNB | . |
| 99-ABAA | **Tiv** | 2,868,000 | 1,061,000 | 3,929,000 | 1 | 1.37 | 3,198,000 | 81.40 | 4s... | PNB | . |
| 99-ABAA-a | dzwa-tiv | 2,868,000 | 1,061,000 | 3,929,000 | 1 | 1.37 | 3,198,000 | 81.40 | 4s... | PNB | . |
| 44-AABD-b | south uzbek | 2,467,000 | 1,054,000 | 3,521,000 | 3 | 1.43 | 6,500 | 0.18 | 1c.u. | pnb | b |
| 93-BAAA | **Zande** | 1,795,000 | 1,049,000 | 2,844,000 | 7 | 1.58 | 2,431,000 | 85.48 | 4As.. | PNB | b |
| 99-AUSQ | **Makonde-Yao** | 3,929,000 | 1,046,000 | 4,975,000 | 13 | 1.27 | 1,186,000 | 23.85 | 4.s.. | PNB | b |
| 93-BAAA-a | pa-zande | 1,740,000 | 1,038,000 | 2,778,000 | 4 | 1.60 | 2,379,000 | 85.64 | 4As.. | PNB | b |
| 58-AABA-a | east balochi | 3,060,000 | 1,037,000 | 4,097,000 | 3 | 1.34 | 25,400 | 0.62 | 1.s.. | P.. | b |
| 85-FAAH-e | potosí | 4,074,000 | 1,034,000 | 5,109,000 | 2 | 1.25 | 4,949,000 | 96.88 | 2as.. | PNB | b |
| 58-AACE-a | mazandarani | 3,445,000 | 1,033,000 | 4,478,000 | 1 | 1.30 | 4,800 | 0.11 | 1.... | ... | b |
| 59-ACBA | **Southeast Rom** | 4,673,000 | 1,032,000 | 5,705,000 | 76 | 1.22 | 43,400 | 0.24 | 1A... | PN. | b |
| 12-AACF-n | yemeni | 16,957,000 | 1,017,000 | 17,974,000 | 18 | 1.06 | 43,400 | 0.24 | 1Asuh | pnb | b |
| 99-AURG-f | central ki-koongo | 1,180,000 | 1,000,000 | 2,181,000 | 4 | 1.85 | 1,986,000 | 91.06 | 4as.. | PNB | b |

### *BIBLIOGRAPHY: PEOPLES AND THEIR RELIGIONS*

Every human race, culture, people, language has extensive coverage of their religions in serious literature and research publications. We estimate the total of such distinct books at 850,000.

This bibliography is only a selection from a huge literature. It highlights the wealth of data, information, knowledge, and analysis that exists for individual or particular cultures, languages, and ethnolinguistic peoples, in most cases dealing with their religion. In most cases an item refers to only one such people. Available bibliographies on any or all peoples and languages may be obtained online via OCLC (Online Computer Library Catalog), which utilizes the names and classification scheme of the USA Library of Congress. Readers using this system should enter as keywords not only the anglicized name of the people or language being investigated; enter also the French name, German name, Spanish name, and any other alternate spellings and names.


*A bibliography of the Hmong (Miao) of Southeast Asia and the Hmong refugees in the United States.* D. P. Olney. 2nd ed. *Southeast Asian refugee studies, Occasional papers*, no. 1. Minneapolis, MN: Center for Urban and Regional Affairs, University of Minnesota, 1983. 75p.

'A brief history and development factors of the Karen Baptist Church of Burma (Myanmar).' S. D. Say. Th.M. thesis, Fuller Theological Seminary, Pasadena, CA, 1990. 206p.

*A century of growth: the Kachin Baptist Church of Burma.* H. G. Tegenfeldt. South Pasadena, CA: William Carey Library, 1974. 512p.

*A church in the wilds: the remarkable story of the establishment of the South American mission amongst the hitherto savage and intractable natives of the Paraguayan Chaco.* W. B. Grubb. London: Seeley Service, Dutton, 1914. 287p.

'A comparative survey of Eskimo–Aleut religion,' G. H. Marsh, *Anthropological papers of the University of Alaska*, 3, 1 (1954), 21–36.

'A comparison of Tamil and Chinese Lutheran churches in peninsular Malaysia and Singapore.' D. W. Vierow. D.Miss. thesis, Fuller Theological Seminary, Pasadena, CA, 1976. 283p.

'A cross–cultural communication of Biblical truth in Grebo villages of Maryland County, Liberia.' R. J. Martin. D.Min. thesis, Southeastern Baptist Theological Seminary, Wake Forest, NC, 1990. 130p.

*A decade with the Basotho.* H. Sleath. Ed., T. Coggin. Johannesburg: Dept. of Public Relations and Communication of the Methodist Church of Southern Africa, 1988. 127p.

*A glossary of the tribes and castes of the Punjab and North–West Frontier Province.* D. Ibbetson, E. Maclagan & H. A. Rose. Reprint, New Delhi: Rima, 1985. 3 vols.

*A history of Christianity in the Balkans: a study in the spread of Byzantine culture among the Slavs.* M. Spinka. *Studies in church history*, 1. Chicago: American Society of Church History, 1933. 202p.

'A history of church growth among the Yalunka tribe of Sierra Leone (1951–1983).' S. M. Harrigan. M.A. thesis, Columbia Graduate School of Bible and Missions, Columbia, SC, 1985. 110p.

*A history of the Arab peoples.* A. Hourani. Cambridge, MA: Harvard University Press, 1991. 532p.

*A history of the Jews in Macedonia.* A. Matkovski. Skopje, Macedonia: Madeconian Review Editions, 1982. 223p.

'A history of the Turkman people,' V. V. Barthold, in *Four studies of the history of Central Asia.* Leiden: E. J. Brill, 1962.

*A maternal religion: the rôle of women in Tetum myth and ritual.* D. Hicks. *Monograph series on Southeast Asia, Special Report*, no. 22. De Kalb, IL: Northern Illinois University, Center for Southeast Asian Studies, 1984. 141p.

'A missiological strategy for the evangelization of lowland Laotian refugees in the United States.' C. T. Wright. Ph.D. dissertation, Southwestern Baptist Theological Seminary, Fort Worth, TX, 1988. 2 vols.

*A Pacific bibliography: printed matter relating to the native peoples of Polynesia, Melanesia and Micronesia.* C. R. H. Taylor. 2nd ed. Oxford, UK: Clarendon Press, 1965. 692p.

'A people divided: the tame Nosu of Yunnan and the wild Nosu of Sichuan,' R. R. Covell, chapter 9 in *The liberating gospel in China: the Christian faith among China's minority peoples.* Grand Rapids, MI: Baker, 1995.

'A select bibliography of works on the Tamangs of Nepal,' A. Höfer, *Bulletin of the Nepal Studies Association*, 10 (1976), 34–36.

*A Solomon Island society: kinship and leadership among the Siuai of Bougainville.* D. L. Oliver. Cambridge, MA: Harvard University Press, 1955.

'A strategy for planting churches in Java through the Sangkakala Mission: with special emphasis on the Javanese and Chinese people.' A. Sutanto. Ph.D. dissertation, Fuller Theological Seminary, Pasadena, CA, 1986. 211p.

'A study of Karen Baptist Church growth in Myanmar.' L. Zan. Th.M. thesis, Fuller Theological Seminary, Pasadena, CA, 1993. 115p.

'A study of the growth of the church of Christ among the Tonga tribe of Zambia.' J. S. Shewmaker. M.A. thesis, Fuller Theological Seminary, Pasadena, CA, 1969. 278p.

'A study of the religious customs and practices of the Rajbangshis of North Bengal.' R. H. Clark. Ph.D. dissertation, Hartford Seminary Foundation, Hartford, CT, 1969. 598p.

*A Zuni atlas.* T. J. Ferguson & E. R. Hart. Norman, OK: University of Oklahoma, 1990. 240p.

'About the original religion of the Creoles in Suriname.' J. Schoffelmeer. *Mededelingen van het Surinaams Museum*, no. 38 (December 1982) 6-48; no. 39 (April 1983) 4-65.

*Adat, Islam and Christianity in a Batak homeland.* S. R. Siregar. *Papers in international studies, Southeast Asian series*, no. 57. Athens, OH: Ohio University Center for International Studies, Southeast Asia Program, 1981. 108p.

*African and African American studies.* Middletown, CT: Choice, 1993. 148p. (Bibliographic work with 754 titles).

'Aging, religion, and mastery style among the Quechua of Pocona, Bolivia.' T. L. Schemper. Ph.D. dissertation, Northwestern University, Evanston, IL, 1987. 176p.

*Aladura: a religious movement among the Yoruba.* J. D. Y. Peel. London: Oxford University Press for the International African Institute, 1968. 338p.

*Allons faire le tour du ciel et de la terre: le chamanisme des Hmong vu dans les textes.* J. Mottin. Bangkok: White Lotus, 1982. 559p.

*Ambivalence et culte de possession: contribution à l'étude du Bori hausa.* J. Monfouga-Nicolas. Paris: Anthropos, [1972]. 403p.

*Among the Bantu nomads: a record of forty years spent among the Bechuana, a numerous and famous branch of the Central South African Bantu, with the first full description of their ancient customs, manners, and beliefs.* J. T. Brown. London: Seeley, Service & Co., 1926. 272p. (Treats religion).

*Among the primitive Bakongo: a record of thirty years close intercourse with the Bakongo and other tribes of equatorial Africa, with a description of their habits, customs, and religious beliefs.* J. H. Weeks. London: Seely, Service & Co., 1914. 318p.

*An African trail.* J. K. Mackenzie. West Medford, MA: Central Committee on the United Study of Foreign Missions, 1917. 222p. (Religion of Bulu of Cameroon).

*An analytical guide to the bibliographies on modern Egypt and the Sudan.* C. L. Geddes. *Bibliographic series*, no. 2. Denver, CO: American Institute of Islamic Studies, 1972. 78p. (Deals with Muslim peoples in Egypt and Sudan).

'An annotated bibliography of the Thakalis,' M. Vinding & K. B. Bhattachan, *Contributions to Nepalese studies*, 12, 3 (1985), 1–24. (140 titles).

'An ethnic geography of Kuwait: a study of eight ethnic groups.' A. B. Al-Ostad. Ph.D. dissertation, Kent State University, Kent, OH, 1986. 257p.

'An ethnography of the Mahorais (Mayotte, Comoro Islands).' J. Breslar. Ph.D. dissertation, University of Pittsburgh, Pittsburgh, PA, 1981. 3 vols

'An eye in the sky, one deep in the earth: elements of Zaose religion,' A. Roberts, in *Ethnologies: hommage à Marcel Griaule*, p.291–306. S. Ganay et al (ed). Paris: Hermann, 1987.

*An inquiry into the animism and folk–lore of the Guiana Indians.* W. E. Roth. 1915; reprint, New York: Johnson Reprint Corp., [1970]. 453p.

*An outline of Dahomean religious belief.* M. J. Herskovits & F. S. Herskovits. *Memoirs of the American Anthropological Association*, no. 41. 1933; reprint, New York: Kraus, 1976. 77p.

'Animisme, religion caduque: étude qualitative et quantitative sur les opinions et la pratique religieuse en Basse–Casamance (pays diola),' L. Thomas, *Bulletin de l'IFAN*, 27 (B), 1-2 (1965), 1–41.

*Anthropological bibliography of aboriginal Nicaragua.* J. A. Lines, E. M. Shook & M. D. Olien. *Tropical Science Center occasional paper*, no. 3. San Jose: Tropical Science Center, 1965. 98p.

*Anthropology and ethnography of the peoples of Somalia.* N. Puccioni. New Haven, CT: Human Relations Area Files, 1960. 205p. (Translated from Italian).

*Anthropology in Indonesia, a bibliographical review.* R. M. Koentjaraningrat. *Koninklijk Instituut voor Taal-, Land- en Volenkunde, Bibliographical series*, no. 8. The Hague: Martinus Nijhoff, 1975. 343p.

*Approche de la religion des Birifor.* A. Erbs. Paris: Musée de l'Homme, 1975. 75p.

'Arte Nalu,' A. Augusto da Silva, *Boletim Cultural da Guiné Portuguesa*, 11, 44 (1956), 27–47. (Art and religion).

'Asante Catholicism: ritual communication of the Catholic faith among the Akan of Ghana.' J. P. Obeng. Ph.D. dissertation, Boston University, Boston, 1991. 327p.

*Asen, iron altars of the Fon people of Benin: October 2–December 21, 1985, Emory University, Museum of Art and Archaeology, Michael C. Carlos Hall, Emory University, Atlanta, Georgia.* E. G. Bay. Atlanta: The Museum, 1985. 48p.

*Atlas narodov mira (Atlas of the peoples of the world).* Moscow: Akademia, 1964.

*Atlas of modern Jewish history.* E. Friesel. New York: Oxford University Press, 1990. 159p.

*Atlas of world cultures: a geographical guide to ethnographic literature.* D. H. Price. Newbury Park, CA and London: Sage Publications, 1990. 156p.

*Australian Aboriginal religion.* R. M. Berndt. *Iconography of religions*, section 5: Australia. Leiden: E. J. Brill, 1974. 4 vols.

'Bakuu: possessing spirits of witchcraft on the Tapanahony,' D. Vernon, *Nieuwe West–Indische Gids*, 54, 1 (1980), 1–38.

*Balinese temple festival.* C. Hooykaas. *Bibliotheca Indonesica*, no. 15. The Hague: Martinus Nijhoff, 1977. 109p.

*Bantu philosophy of life in the light of the Christian message: a basis for an African vitalistic theology.* D. R. K. Nkurunziza. Frankfurt: Lang, 1989. 307p.

*Banyarwanda et Barundi.* R. Bourgeois. Brussels: Institut Royal Colonial Belge, 1954–58. 4 vols. (Vol.1 treats "ethnology," vol. 2 "custom," and vol. 3 "religion and magic").

*Basotho religion and Western thought.* L. B. B. Machobane. Edinburgh: Centre of African Studies, Edinburgh University, 1995. 57p.

*Batek negrito religion: the world–view and rituals of a hunting and gathering people of Peninsular Malaysia.* K. Endicott. Oxford, UK: Clarendon Press, 1979. 234p.

'Belize: Black Caribs,' N. L. S. González, in *Witchcraft and sorcery of the American native peoples*, p.279–93. D. E. Walker Jr. (ed). Moscow, ID: University of Idaho Press, 1989.

*Bemba–speaking women of Zambia in a century of religious change (1892–1992).* H. F. Hinfelaar. Leiden: E. J. Brill, 1994. 238p. (Revision of author's Ph.D. dissertation, University of London, 1989).

'Biblical basis of church growth and its application to the Kachin Baptist church of Burma.' H. Naw. D.Miss. thesis, Trinity Evangelical Divinity School, Deerfield, IL, 1990. 209p.

*Bibliografía antropológica aborigen de Costa Rica.* J. A. Lines, E. M. Shook & M. D. Olien. *Occasional papers*, no. 7. San José: Tropical Science Center, 1967. 196p.

'Bibliografía antropológica de Costa Rica,' M. E. B. de Wille, *Boletín bibliográfico de antroplogía Americana*, 38, 47 (1976), 63–82.

*Bibliographie ethno–sociologique de la Tunisie.* A. Louis. *Publications de l'Institut des belles lettres arabes*, 31. Tunis: N. Bascone, 1977. 448p.

'Bibliography of bibliographies on the Inuit,' I. Kleivan, in *Artica 1978: 7th Northern Libraries Colloquy, 19–23 September 1978*, p.39–41. S. Devers (ed). Paris: Éditions du Centre National de la Recherche Scientifique, 1982.

*Bibliography of the Ewes.* R. Arkaifie. Cape Coast, Ghana: University of Cape Coast, 1976. 81p. (Large section on Christianity).

*Bibliography of the peoples and cultures of mainland Southeast Asia.* J. F. Embree & L. O. Dotson. New Haven, CT: Yale University, 1950. 821p.

'Bibliography on peoples of Zimbabwe.' M. F. C. Bourdillon & A. Cheater. Computer database and printout, University of Zimbabwe, Harare, Zimbabwe, 1983.

*Body of power, spirit of resistance: the culture and history of a South African people.* J. Comaroff. Chicago: University of Chicago Press, 1985. 276p. (Treats Barolong boo Ratshidi people and Zion Christian Church).

*Breve estudio sobre las tribus moras de Mauritania.* A. C. de Laiglesia. *Primer informe*, 10. Madrid: Instituto Hispano-Arabe de Cultura, [1985]. 120p.

*Buddhist traditions and culture of the Kathmandu valley (Nepal).* K. Vaidya. Kathmandu: Sajha, 1986. 299p.

'Buryat religion and society,' L. Krader, *Southwestern journal of anthropology*, 10, 3 (1954), 322–51.

*Bwiti: an ethnography of the religious imagination in Africa.* J. W. Fernandez. Princeton, NJ: Princeton University Press, 1982. 731p. (Religion of the Fang).

'Campa cosmology,' G. Weiss, *Ethnology*, 11, 2 (1972), 157–72.

*Catholics, peasants, and Chewa resistance in Nyasaland, 1889–1939.* I. Linden & J. Linden. Berkeley, CA: University of California Press, 1974. 235p.

*China's minority nationalities.* M. Yin (ed). Beijing: Foreign Languages Press, 1989. 455p.

'Christ in tribal culture: a study of the interaction between Christianity and Semai society of peninsular Malaysia in the context of the history of the Methodist Mission (1930–1983).' H. P. Shastri. Thesis, Universität Heidelberg, 1989. 213p.

'Christian education among the Ovambo people: the house as the center of transmitting culture and tradition.' B. Haileka. S.T.M. thesis, Lutheran Theological Seminary at Gettysburg, Gettysburg, PA, 1994. 245p.

*Christian Indians and Indian nationalism, 1885–1950: an interpretation in historical and theological perspectives.* G. Thomas. Frankfurt: Lang, 1979. 271p.

*Christian response to change in East African traditional societies.* G. G. Brown. *Woodbrooke occasional papers*, 4. London: Friends Home Service Committee for Woodbrooke College, 1973. 55p.

'Christianity and culture in Kenya: an encounter between the African Inland Mission and the Marakwet belief systems and culture.' S. K. Elolia. Ph.D. dissertation, Toronto School of Theology, Toronto, 1992. 2 vols.

*Christianity and native traditions: indigenization and syncretism among the Inuit and Dene of the western Arctic.* A. R. Gualtieri. Notre Dame, IN: Cross Roads Books, 1984. 186p.

*Christianity and the Eastern Slavs.* B. Gasparov & O. Raevsky-Hughes. *California Slavic studies*, vol. 16. Berkeley, CA: University of California Press, 1993.

*Christianity and the Shona.* M. W. Murphree. London: Athlone Press, 1969. 200p.

*Christianity in northern Malawi: Donald Fraser's missionary methods and Ngoni culture.* T. J. Thompson. *Studies in Christian mission*, vol. 15. New York: E. J. Brill, 1995.

'Christianity in South–west Arabia,' J. S. Trimingham, chapter 8 in *Christianity among the Arabs in pre–Islamic times*, p.287–308. London: Longman, 1979.

'Christianity in the Batak culture: the making of an indigenous church.' G. P. Harahap. M.S.T. thesis, Trinity Lutheran Seminary, Columbus, OH, 1982. 196p.

'Christianity, politics, and the Manyika: a study of the influence of religious attitudes and loyalties on political values and activities of Africans in Rhodesia.' N. E. Thomas. Thesis, Boston University, Boston, 1968. 396p.

'Christianizing the Karen.' K. M. Dettmer. M.A. thesis, Arizona State University, Tempe, AZ, 1987. 113p.

*Church, state, and people in Mozambique: an historical study with special emphasis on Methodist developments in the Inhambane Region.* A. Helgesson. *Studia missionalia Upsaliensia*, 54. Uppsala: Uppsala University Swedish Institute of Missionary Research, 1994. 455p.

*Cities and caliphs: on the genesis of Arab Muslim urbanism.* N. Al Sayyad. New York: Greenwood Press, 1991. 207p.

*Coastal Bantu of the Cameroons.* E. Ardener. London: International African Institute, 1956. 116p.

'Communicating the Gospel among the Iban: a resource manual for new cross–cultural missionaries.' J. A. Fowler. D.Min. thesis, Southern Methodist University, Dallas, TX, 1976. 148p.

*Consultation of Lutheran Churches on work in West Africa among Fulani speaking people: Dakar, Senegal, January 14–21, 1979.* R. Lehtonen (ed). Geneva: Lutheran World Federation, 1979. 108p.

'Contact between the Kipsigis traditional religion and world view and Christianity.' C. C. Cheruiyot. S.T.M. thesis, Drew University, Madison, NJ, 1985. 118p.

'Contribution á l'étude du comportement religieux des Wodaabe

Dageeja du Nord–Cameroun,' R. Labatut, *Journal des Africanistes*, 48, 2 (1978), 63–92.
'Conversion to Protestantism and social change in a Bolivian Aymara community.' D. C. Knowlton. M.A. thesis, University of Texas, Austin, TX, 1982. 261p.
*Cosmology and social life: ritual exchange among the Mambai of East Timor.* E. G. Traube. Chicago: University of Chicago Press, 1986. 273p.
'Crossing religious frontiers: Christianity and the transformation of Bulu society, 1892–1925.' P. R. Dekar. Ph.D. dissertation, University of Chicago, Chicago, IL, 1978. 392p.
*Croyances et pratiques religieuses traditionelles des Mossi.* P. Ilboudo. *Etudes sur l'histoire et l'archéologie du Burkina Faso*, vol. 3. Stuttgart: Franz Steiner, 1990. 160p.
*Cultural anthropology of the Middle East: a bibliography.* R. Strijp. Leiden: E. J. Brill, 1992–. (Multivolume work in progress).
*Cultural atlas of China.* C. Blunden & M. Elvin. New York: Facts on File, 1983.
*Cultural patterns and economic change (anthropological study of Dhimals of Nepal).* R. R. Regmi. Delhi: Motilal Banarsidass, 1985. 218p.
*Curse, retribution, enmity as data in natural religion, especially in Timor, confronted with scripture.* P. Middlekoop. Amsterdam: Jacob van Campen, 1960. 168p.
'Cutting the ancient cords: the Lahu and Wa are liberated from demons,' R. R. Covell, chapter 10 in *The liberating gospel in China: the Christian faith among China's minority peoples.* Grand Rapids, MI: Baker, 1995.
*Das Exil der Götter: Geschichte und Vorstellungswelt einer afrokubanischen Religion.* S. Palmié. Frankfurt am Main: P. Lang, 1991. 527p.
*Deep Mende: religious interactions in a changing African rural society.* D. Reeck. *Studies on religion in Africa*, 4. Leiden: E. J. Brill, 1976. 102p.
'De–westernizing Christianity among the Krobo of Ghana.' D. K. Tei-Kwabla. D.Miss. thesis, Fuller Theological Seminary, Pasadena, CA, 1983. 460p.
'Diaspora Indians: church growth among Indians in West Malaysia.' C. D. Thomas. D.Miss. thesis, Fuller Theological Seminary, Pasadena, CA, 1976. 337p.
*Dictionary of Celtic religion and culture.* B. Maier. Trans., C. Edwards. Woodbridge, UK and Rochester, NY: Boydell Press, 1997. 346p.
*Dictionary of Himalayan people.* J. C. Regmi & S. Shiwakothi. *Nepal Antiquary*, nos. 50-55. Kathmandu: Office of the Nepal Antiquary, 1983. 220p.
*Die Religionen des Hindukusch.* K. Jettmar with contributions by S. Jones and M. Klimburg. *Die Religionen der Menschheit*, vol. 4, no. 1. Stuttgart, West Germany: Verlag W. Kohlhammer, 1975. 525p.
*Die Toura: zwischen Geisterglaube und Evangelium.* I. Bearth-Braun. *Telos-Taschenbucher*, Nr. 7615. Neuheusen-Stuttgart: Hänssler, 1993. 99p.
'Dieux souverains et rois dévots dans l'ancienne royauté de la vallée du Népal,' G. Toffin, *L'homme*, 26, 3 (1986), 71–95. (Deals with Newar kingship).
*Disinheriting the Jews: Abraham in early Christian controversy.* J. S. Siker. Louisville, KY: Westminster John Kox Press, 1991. 296p.
*Divinity and experience: the religion of the Dinka.* G. Lienhardt. Oxford, UK: Clarendon, 1961. 328p.
*Doing theology with the Maasai.* D. Priest Jr. Pasadena, CA: William Carey Library, 1990. 248p.
'Drugs and mysticism: the Bwiti of the Fang,' J. Binet, *Diogènes* (Paris), 86 (Summer 1974), 31–54.
*Du Mvett: essai sur la dynastie Ekang Nna.* D. A. Ndoutombe. Paris: L'Harmattan, 1986. 184p. (Deals with religion of the Fang).
*Eastern European national minorities, 1919–80: a handbook.* S. M. Horak. Littleton, CO: Libraries Unlimited, 1985. 353p.
*El cristianismo aymara: inculturación o culturización.* L. Jolicoeur. Cochabamba: Universidad Católica Boliviana, 1994. 465p.
*El judío en Costa Rica.* J. Schifter, L. Gudmundson & M. S. Castro. *Serie estudios sociopolíticos*, no. 4. San José: Editorial Universidad Estatal a Distancia, 1979. 385p.
*El monte: igbo–finda, ewe orisha, vititi nfinda: notas sobre las religiones, la magia, las supersticiones y el folklore de los negros criollos y el pueblo de Cuba.* L. Cabrera. 7th ed. Miami: Ediciones Universal, 1992. 589p.
*El nacimiento y la muerte entre los bribris.* M. E. B. Wille. San José: Editorial Universidad de Costa Rica, 1979. 264p.
*El sistema religioso de los afrocubanos.* R. Lachatañeré. Havana: Editorial de Ciencias Sociales, 1992. 450p.
*Elements of Southeastern Indian religion.* No. 1 of section 10, *North America*, of *Iconography of religions.* C. Hudson. Leiden: E. J. Brill, 1984. 36p.
*Encyclopaedia of peoples of the world.* S. Gonen. New York: Holt, Henry, 1993. 704p.
*Encyclopaedic dictionary of demography.* D. Valentei. New York: State Mutual Book and Periodical Service, 1985. 608p.
*Encyclopedia of Jewish history: events and eras of the Jewish people.* J. Alpher (ed). New York: Facts on File, 1986. 288p.
*Encyclopedia of Native American biography: six hundred life stories of important people.* D. A. Grindle. New York: Holt, Henry, 1996. 512p.
*Encyclopedia of Native American ceremonies.* M. A. Pesantubbee. Santa Barbara, CA: ABC-CLIO, 1996.
*Encyclopedia of Native American tribes.* C. Waldman. New York: Facts on File, 1987. 308p.
*Encyclopedia of North American Indian tribes.* B. Yenne. New York: Random House, 1988.
*Encyclopedia of North American Indians.* F. E. Hoxie (ed). HM, forthcoming. 11 vols.
*Encyclopedia of the Holocaust.* I. Gutman (ed). New York: Macmillan, 1989–1996. 5 vols.
*Encyclopedia of the Indians of the Americas.* H. Waldman (ed). St. Clair Shores, MI: Scholarly Press, 1981. 7 vols.
*Encyclopedia of world cultures.* D. Levinson (ed). New York: Macmillan, 1995. 10 vols.; 6,500p.
*Encyclopedia Yiddishanica.* E. Markowitz. Fredericksburg, VA: Haymark, 1980. 450p.
*Eskimos: Greenland and Canada.* No. 2 of section 8: *Arctic peoples*, of *Iconography of religions.* I. Kleivan & B. Sonne. Leiden: E. J. Brill, 1985. 52p.
*Ethnic groups of insular Southeast Asia.* F. M. LeBar et al. New Haven, CT: Human Relations Area Files Press, 1964.
*Ethnic groups of mainland Southeast Asia.* F. M. LeBar, G. C. Hickey & J. K. Musgrave. New Haven, CT: Human Relations Area Files Press, 1964. 288p.
*Ethnic minorities in Belize: Mopan, Kekchi and Garifuna.* R. Wilk & M. Chapin. Belize City: SPEAR, 1990. 43p.
*Ethnic minorities in Vietnam.* D. N. Van, C. T. Son & L. Hung. Hanoi: Foreign Languages Publishing House, 1984. 305p.
*Ethnicity and nationality in Singapore.* C. S. Foon. *Southeast Asia series*, no. 78. Athens, OH: Ohio University Monographs in International Studies, 1987. 229p.
*Ethnographic atlas.* G. P. Murdock. Pittsburgh, PA: University of Pittsburgh, 1967.
*Ethnographic bibliography of North America, 4th edition. Supplement 1973–1987.* M. M. Martin & T. J. O'Leary. New Haven, CT: Human Relations Area Files Press, 1990. 3 vols. (Previously published as *Ethnographic bibliography of North America* . G. P. Murdock, 1960, 1975.).
'Ethnographic notes on the Tamangs of Nepal,' C. von Fürer–Haimendorf, *Eastern anthropologist*, 9 (3–4 March 1956), 166–77.
*Ethnographical survey of the Miskito and Sumu Indians of Honduras and Nicaragua.* E. Conzemius. Washington, DC: Bureau of American Ethnology, 1932. Bulletin no. 106. 191p.
*Ethnography, North Africa (Tunisia, Algeria).* R. Herzog. Berlin: Gebrüder Borntraeger, 1981. 46p. (Summaries in English and French).
*Ethnologie religieuse des Kuta, mythologie et folklore.* E. Andersson. Uppsala: Almquist & Wiksell, 1987. 164p.
'Evangelism on the perpendicular among the Lisu people of Yunnan,' R. R. Covell, chapter 6 in *The liberating gospel in China: the Christian faith among China's minority peoples.* Grand Rapids, MI: Baker, 1995.
*Eyes of the night: witchcraft among a Senegalese people.* W. S. Simmons. Boston: Little, Brown & Co., 1971. 169p. (Treats Badyaranke).
*Faith and the Intifada: Palestinian Christian voices.* N. S. Ateek, M. H. Ellis & R. Radford Ruether (eds). Maryknoll, NY: Orbis Books, 1992. 204p.
*Festivals, religious practices, and traditions of Telugus in Mauritius.* R. Sokappadu. N.p., 1992. 64p.
*First fruits of the forest: amongst the Tharus of North India.* B. Pritchard. London: Regions Beyond Missionary Union, 1962. 14p.
'Folk religion among the Chinese in Singapore and Malaysia.' L. Tjandra. D.Miss. thesis, Fuller Theological Seminary, Pasadena, CA, 1988. 392p. (Text in Chinese with extended summary in English).
*For the land and the Lord: Jewish fundamentalism in Israel.* I. S. Lustick. New York: Council on Foreign Relations, 1988. 227p.
*Girkaa: une cérémonie d'initiation au culte de possession bòorii des Hausa de la région de Maradi (Niger).* V. Erlmann & H. Magagi. Berlin: Dietrich Reimer Verlag, 1989. 173p.
*God: ancestor or creator? Aspects of traditional beliefs in Ghana, Nigeria and Sierra Leone.* H. Sawyerr. London: Longman, 1970. 118p.
*Good magic in Ovambo.* M. Hiltunen. Helsinki: Suomen Antropologinen Seura, 1993. 234p.
*Gourmantche ethnoanthropology: a theory of human being.* R. A. Swanson. Lanham, MD: University Press of America, 1985. 464p.
'Growth of the Church of God through Ushirika groups among the Luhya in Nairobi, Kenya.' R. E. Edwards. D.Miss. thesis, Fuller Theological Seminary, Pasadena, CA, 1989. 377p.
*Guérisseurs et magiciens du Sahel.* J. Gibbal. Paris: Presses universitaires de France, 1984. 160p.
*Gurkhas.* C. J. Morris. 2nd ed. *Handbooks for the Indian Army.* Delhi: Government of India, 1936; reprint, B. R. Publishing, 1985. 182p.
*Gypsies: Indians in exile.* D. P. Singhal. *Kirpa Dai series in folklore and anthropology*, 5. Berkeley, CA: Folklore Institute, 1982. 170p.
*Handbook of Middle American Indians.* R. Wauchope et al (ed). Austin, TX: University of Texas Press, 1964–86. 16 vols, plus 4 supplemental vols.
*Handbook of South American Indians.* J. H. Steward (ed). Washington, DC: Smithsonian Institution, Bureau of American Ethnology, 1946–59. 7 vols.
*Harmony ideology: justice and control in a Zapotec mountain village.* L. Nader. Stanford, CA: Stanford University Press, 1990. 343p.
*Harvard encyclopedia of American ethnic groups.* S. Thernstrom (ed). Cambridge, MA: Harvard University Press, 1980.
*Hausa studies: a selected bibliography of B.A., M.A., and Ph.D. papers available in Northern Nigerian universities.* E. L. Powe. 2nd ed. Kano, Nigeria: Bayero University, 1983. 29p. (330 items; religion is a main heading).
*Hausa women in the twentieth century.* C. Coles & B. Mack (eds). Madison, WI: University of Wisconsin Press, 1991. 308p.
*Hawks of the sun: Mapuche morality and its ritual attributes.* L. C. Faron. Pittsburgh, PA: University of Pittsburgh Press, 1964. 220p.
*Headhunters about themselves: an ethnographic report from Irian Jaya, Indonesia.* J. H. M. Boelaars. *Koninklijk Instituut voor Taal–, Land– en Volkenkunde, Verhandelingen*, no. 92. The Hague: Martinus Nijhoff, 1981. 296p. (Study of Jaqaj tribe by missionary).
*Heart drum: spirit possession in the Garifuna communities of Belize.* B. Foster. 2nd rev. ed. Belize: Cubola Productions, 1994. 59p.
*Hegemony and culture: politics and religious change among the Yoruba.* D. D. Laitin. Chicago: University of Chicago, 1986. 252p.
'Hinduism and Buddhism in the Kathmandu Valley (Nepal),' D. N. Gellner, in *The world's religions*, p.739–55. S. Sutherland et al (eds). London: Croom Helm, 1988. (Deals with Newars).
*History of the American Baptist Chin Mission: a history of the introduction of Christianity into the Chin Hills of Burma by missionaries of the American Baptist Foreign Mission Society during the years 1899 to 1966.* R. G. Johnson. Valley Forge, PA: R. G. Johnson, 1988. 2 vols
'History of the Methodist Church in its Rotuman setting,' J. Langi, in *Island churches: challenge and change*, p.1–73. C. W. Foreman (ed). Suva, Fiji: University of the South Pacific, Institute of Pacific Studies, 1992.
'Hmong ethnohistory: an historical study of Hmong culture and its implications for ministry.' J. Davidson. D.Miss. thesis, Fuller Theological Seminary, Pasadena, CA, 1993. 230p.
*Hopi Indian altar iconography.* No. 5 of section 10, *North America*, of *Iconography of religions.* A. W. Geertz. Leiden: E. J. Brill, 1987. 39p.
*Horses, musicians, & gods: the Hausa cult of possession–trance.* F. E. Besmer. South Hadley, MA: Bergin & Garvey, 1983. 290p.
*Hunters and herders of Southern Africa: a comparative ethnography of the Khoisan peoples.* A. Barnard. Cambridge, UK: Cambridge University Press, 1992. 349p. (Treats religion).
*Iconography of New Zealand Maori religion.* No. 1 of section 2, *New Zealand*, of *Iconography of religions.* D. R. Simmons. Leiden: E. J. Brill, 1986. 33p.
'Identity conflict and ceremonial events in a Sereer community of Saalum, Senegal.' K. M. Marcoccio. Ph.D. dissertation, Brandeis University, Waltham, MA, 1987. 347p.
*Imperialism, evangelism, and the Ottoman Armenians, 1878–1896.* J. Salt. London: Frank Cass and Co., 1993. 198p.
*In search of China's minorities.* Z. Weiwen & Z. Qingnan. Beijing: New World Press, 1993. 354p.
'In search of the Karen king: a study in Karen identity with special reference to 19th century Karen evangelism in Northern Thailand.' A. P. Hovemyr. Doctoral dissertation, University of Uppsala, Uppsala, Sweden, 1989. 207p.
*In sorcery's shadow: a memoir of apprenticeship among the Songhay of Niger.* P. Stoller & C. Olkes. Chicago: University of Chicago Press, 1987. 252p.
*In the wake of martyrs: a modern saga in ancient Ethiopia.* A. E. Brant. Langley, British Columbia: Omega Publications, 1992. 300p.
'Inculturation of rites of Christian initiation of the Kewabi people of Papua New Guinea.' M. T. Dwan. M.T.S. thesis, Catholic Theological Union, Chicago, 1993. 81p.
*Indianen en kerken in Suriname: identiteit en autonomie in het binnenland.* J. Vernooij. Paramaribo: Stichting Wetenschappelijke Informatie, 1989. 178p.
*Indians of Northeastern North America.* No. 7 of section 10, *North America*, of *Iconography of religions.* A. W. Geertz. Leiden: E. J. Brill, 1986. 50p.
'Innocent pioneers and their triumphs in a foreign land: a critical look at the work of the American Baptist Mission in the Chin Hills, 1899–1966 in Burma from a missiological perspective.' Cung Lian Hup. Th.D. thesis, Lutheran School of Theology, Chicago, 1993. 204p.
*Introduction au wanzanisme ou au culte ancestral.* B. Lala. Bangui, C.A.R.: B. Lala, 1991. 19p.
*Inventaire ethnique du Sud–Cameroon.* I. Dugast. *Populations*, no. 1. Yaoundé, Cameroon: l'Institut Français d'Afrique Noire, 1949. 159p.
*Islam in tribal societies: from the Atlas to the Indus.* A. S. Ahmed & D. M. Hart. London: Routledge & Kegan Paul, 1984. 350p.
*Islam in tropical Africa.* I. M. Lewis (ed). 2nd ed. London: International African Institute in association with Indiana University, 1988. ("Studies presented and discussed at the Fifth International African Seminar, Ahmadu Bello University, Zaria, January 1964").
*Islamic Britain: religion, politics and identity among British Muslims.* P. Lewis. London and New York: I. B. Tauris, 1994. 256p.
*Islamic peoples of the Soviet Union: an historical and statistical handbook.* S. Akiner. 2nd ed. London: KPI, 1986. 462p.
*Jewish life in Muslim Libya: rivals and relatives.* H. E. Goldberg. Chicago: University of Chicago Press, 1990. 197p.
*Jewish–American history and culture: an encyclopedia.* J. Fischel & S. Pinsker. New York: Garland, 1991.
*Jews in the Soviet Union since 1917: paradox of survival.* N. Levin. New York: New York University Press, 1988. 2 vols.
*Jews of Arab and Islamic countries: history, problems, solutions.* H. M. Haddad. New York: Shengold, 1984. 158p.
*Kinkirsi, Boghoba, Saba: das Weltbild der Nyonyosi in Burkina Faso.* A. Schweeger-Hefel. Vienna: A. Schendl, 1986. 436p.
*Kpele lala: Ga religious songs and symbols.* M. Kilson. Cambridge, MA: Harvard University, 1971. 313p.
*Kunst und Religion der Lobi.* P. Meyer. Zurich: Museum Rietberg, 1981. 184p.
*Kurdish ethnonationalism.* N. Entessar. Boulder, CO: L. Rienner, 1992. 216p.
'La dimension thérapeutique du culte des rab: Ndop, tuuru et samp.,' A. Zempleni, *Psychopathologie Africaine*, 2, 3 (1966), 295–439.
*La naissance à l'envers: essai sur le rituel du Bwiti Fang au Gabon.* A. Mary. Paris: L'Harmattan, 1983. 384p.
*La poésie populaire et les chants religieux du Gabon.* S. Swiderski and M.–L. Girou–Swiderski. Ottawa: Editions de l'Université d'Ottawa, 1981. 290p. (Summary in English, French, German, Italian, Polish, and Spanish).
*La religion Bouiti.* S. Swiderski. *Série culture du Gabon.* Ottawa: Legas, 1989–. In progress to 5 vols. (Summaries in English, Italian, German, Spanish, and Polish).
'La religion musulmane: facteur d'intégration ou d'identification ethnique. Le cas des yarsé du Burkina Faso,' A. Kouanda, in *Les ethnies ont une histoire*, p.125–34. J. P. Chrétien & G. Prunier (eds). Paris: Karthala, 1989.

*La religiosidad contemporánea maya–kekchí.* L. Pacheco. Quito, Ecuador: Ediciones Abya–Yala, 1992. 225p.

*La secta del Bwiti en la Guinea Española.* A. de V. Vilaldach. Madrid: Instituto de Estudios Africanos, 1958. 63p.

*La structure socio–politique et son articulation avec la pensée religieuse chez les Aja–Tado du Sud–est Togo.* K. E. Kossi. *Arbeiten aus dem Seminar für Völkerkunde der Johann Wolfgang Goethe-Universität Frankfurt am Main,* vol. 21. Stuttgart: F. Steiner, 1990. 325p.

*La tierra no da así nomás: los ritos agrícolas en la religión de los aymara–cristianos.* H. van den Berg. La Paz: HISBOL, 1990. 352p.

*L'Angola traditionelle: une introduction aux problèmes magico–religieux.* M. L. Rodrigues de Areia. Coimbra, Portugal: Tipografia de Atlántida, 1974.

*Language, religion, and ethnic assertiveness: the growth of Sinhalese nationalism in Sri Lanka.* K. N. O. Dharmadasa. Ann Arbor, MI: University of Michigan, 1993. 384p.

*Le ginnili devin, poète et guerrier afar (Ethiopie et République de Djibouti).* D. Morin. *Langues et cultures africaines,* 16. Paris: Peeters, 1991. 146p. (Summaries in English and Afar).

'Le Harrisme et le Bwiti: deux réactions Africaines à l'impact Chrétien,' R. Bureau, *Recherches de Sciences Religieuses,* 63, 1 (1975), 83–100.

*Le Noir du Yatenga: pays Mossi et Gourounsi.* L. Tauxier. Paris: Larose, 1912. 796p. (Mossi, Gurunsi, and Fulani peoples, including their religion).

*Le paysan limbu, sa maison et ses champs.* P. Sagant. *Le monde d'outre mer passé et présent,* 1st series, 41. Paris: Mouton with Ecole des Hautes Etudes en Sciences Sociales, 1976. 404p.

*Le pouvoir du Bangré: enquête initiatique à Ouagadougou.* K. Fidaali. Paris: Presses de la Renaissance, 1987. 222p.

'Le sens des limites: maladie, sorcellerie, religion et pouvoir chez les Winye, Gourounsi du Burkina Faso.' J. Jacob. Doctoral dissertation, Université de Neuchâtel, 1988. 384p.

*Le symbolisme religieux dans l'ethnie Ngambay: approche culturelle de la religion.* L. Draman Odial. St.–Paul, Ottawa: Université St.–Paul, 1975–1976. 100p.

*Le système religieux des Evhé.* A. de Surgy. Paris: L'Harmattan, 1988. 343p.

*Le vodu en Afrique de l'Ouest: rites et traditions: le cas des sociétés Guen–Mina (Sud–Togo).* I. de La Torre. *Collection anthropologie—Connaissance des hommes.* Paris: L'Harmattan, 1991. 179p.

*Lepcha, my vanishing tribe.* A. R. Foning. Delhi: Sterling, 1987. 314p. (Treats religion).

'Les activités religieuses des jeunes enfants chez les Bobo,' G. L. Moal, *Journal des Africanistes* (Paris), 51, 1–2 (1981), 235–50.

'Les Bandas de l'Oubangui–Chari (Afrique Equatoriale Française),' R. P. J. Daigre, *Revue internationale d'ethnologie et de linguistiques anthrôpos,* 26 (1932) 647–95, and 27 (1933) 151–81.

*Les Bobo: nature et fonction des masques.* G. Le Moal. *Travaux et documents de l'ORSTOM,* no. 121. Paris: ORSTOM, 1980. 545p.

*Les chemins de Nya: culte de possession au Mali.* J. P. Colleyn. *Anthropologie visuelle,* 1. Paris: Editions de l'Ecole des Hautes Etudes en Sciences Sociales, 1988. 221p.

*Les Diola: essai d'analyse fonctionelle sur une population de Basse–Casamance.* L. Thomas. *Mémoire,* 55. Dakar: IFAN, 1959. 2 vols.

*Les êtres surnaturels dans la religion populaire khmère.* Ang Chouléan. Paris: Cedorek, 1986. 369p.

*Les Gbaya.* J. Hilberth. *Studia Ethnographica Upsaliensia,* 19. Uppsala: Studia Ethnographica Upsaliensia, 1962. 142p.

*Les Gurungs—une population himalayenne du Népal.* B. Pignède. Ed., L. Dumont. *Le monde d'outre mer passé et present,* 3rd series, 21. Paris: Mouton, 1966. 414p.

*Les hommes qui cueillent la vie: les Imragen.* F. Pelletier. *L'Aventure vécue.* Paris: Flammarion, 1986. 246p.

'Les peuples de la République démocratique du Congo, du Rwanda et du Burundi,' A. Dorsinfang-Smets, in *Ethnologie régionale,* p.566–661, vol. I. J. Poirier (ed). Paris: Gallimard, 1972.

'Les populations de la côte française des Somalis,' R. Muller, in *Mer Rouge Afrique orientale, études sociologiques et linguistiques: préhistoire—explorations—perspectives d'avenir,* p.45–102. M. Albospeyre et al (ed). *Cahiers de l'Afrique et l'Asie,* no. 5. Paris: J. Peyronnet, 1959.

*Les populations païennes du Nord–Cameroun et de l'Adamaoua.* B. Lembezat. Paris: Presses Universitaires de France, 1961. 252p.

*Les rites beti au Christ: essai de pastorale liturgique sur quelques rites de nos ancêtres.* I. Tabi. N.p., 1991. 31p.

*Les rites secrets des primitifs de l'Oubangui.* A. Vergiat. Paris: Payot, 1936. 308p.

*Les Senufo et le christianisme.* R. Deniel. Korhogo–Abidjan: Inades, 1979. 67p.

*Les symboles divinatoires: analyse socio–culturelle d'une technique de divination des Cokwe d'Angola (Ngombo ya Cisuka).* M. L. Rodrigues de Areia. Coimbra, Portugal: Instituto de Antropologia, Universidade de Coimbra, 1985. 555p.

*Les Tamangs du Népal—usages et religion.* B. Steinman. Paris: Edition Recherche sur les Civilisations, 1987. 310p.

*L'Habitation des Fali: montagnards du Cameroun septentrional.* J. Lebeuf. Paris: Librairie Hachette, 1961. 607p. (Includes Fali religion).

*Life among the Magars.* G. Shepherd. Kathmandu: Sahayogi, 1982. 269p.

*Like people you see in a dream: first contact in six Papuan societies.* E. L. Schieffelin & R. Crittenden. Stanford, CA: Stanford University Press, 1991. 343p.

*L'intérieur des choses: maladie, divination et reproduction sociale chez les Bisa du Burkina.* S. Fainzang. Paris: L'Harmattan, 1986. 204p.

'L'Islam et les tribus dans la colonie du Niger,' P. Marty, *Revue des études islamiques,* (1930), 333–429.

*Living among the Bedouin Arabs.* A. R. Johnson. New York: Vantage Press, 1985. 99p.

*Llamamiento de Dios al pueblo Gitano.* Terrassa: Adolfo Giménez, 1981.

*Los nicaro y los chorotega según las fuentes históricas.* A. M. Chapman. *Serie historia y geografía,* no. 4. San José: Universidad de Costa Risa, 1960. 115p.

'Maisin Christianity: an ethnography of the contemporary religion of a seaboard Melanesian people.' J. Barker. Ph.D. dissertation, University of British Columbia, 1985. 578p.

*Maîtres et possédés: les dieux, les rites et l'organisation sociale chez les Tharu.* G. Krauskopff. Paris: Editions du Centre Nationale de la Recherche Scientifique, 1989. 276p.

'Mande settlement and the development of Islamic institutions in Sierra Leone,' D. E. Skinner, *International journal of African historical studies,* 11, 1 (1978), 32–62.

*Manding: focus on an African civilization.* International Conference on Manding Studies. London: School of Oriental and African Studies, University of London, 1972. 5 vols.

'Men of the sea: coastal tribes of southern Thailand's west coast,' D. W. Hogan, *Journal of the Siam society,* 60, pt. 1 (1972), 205–234.

*Mende religion: aspects of belief and thought in Sierra Leone.* A. J. Gittins. *Studia Instituti Anthropos,* vol. 41. Nettetal, Germany: Steyler Verlag-Wort und Werk, 1987. 258p.

*Minorities in the Middle East: a history of struggle and self–expression.* M. Nisan. Jefferson, NC: McFarland & Co., 1991. 272p.

*Minority groups in the Republic of Vietnam.* J. L. Schrock et al. Washington, DC: Department of the Army, Pamphlet, no. 550–105, 1966. 1,163p.

'Mission impossible: the unreached Nosu on China's frontier.' R. Covell. Pasadena, CA: Hope Publishing House, 1990. 319p.

*Mission in Burma: the Columban Fathers' forty–three years in Kachin country.* E. Fischer. New York: Seabury, 1980. 164p.

*Missionaries and western education in the Bechuanaland protectorate 1859–1904: the case of the Bangwato.* P. T. Mgadla. *Studies on the church in southern Africa,* no. 2. Gaborone: University of Botswana, 1989. 47p.

*Missionaries, miners, and Indians: Spanish contact with the Yaqui nation of Northwestern New Spain, 1533–1820.* E. H. Hart. Tucson, AZ: University of Arizona Press, 1981. 152p.

*Modern Kongo prophets: religion in a plural society.* W. MacGaffey. *African systems of thought series.* Bloomington, IN: University of Indiana Press, 1983. 285p.

*Moeurs et coutumes des indigènes.* H. Mayet. 52p.

'Monk, householder and priest: Newar Buddhism and its hierarchy of ritual.' D. N. Gellner. D.Phil. dissertation, Oxford University, Oxford, UK, 1987. 586p.

'Mountain spirits and maize: Catholic conversion and renovation of traditions among the Q'eqchi' of Guatemala.' R. Wilson. Ph.D. dissertation, University of London, 1990. 382p.

*Muslim Chinese: ethnic nationalism in the People's Republic.* D. C. Gladney. *Harvard East Asian Monographs,* 149. Cambridge, MA and London: Council on East Asian Studies at Harvard University, and Harvard University Press, 1991. 499p. (Treats the Chinese government's response to rising ethnic nationalism among the Hui).

*Muslim peoples: a world ethnographic survey.* R. V. Weekes (ed). 2nd ed. Westport, CT: Greenwood Press, 1984. 2 vols.

*Muslims in Central Asia: expressions of identity and change.* J. Gross (ed). Durham, NC: Duke University Press, 1992. 238p.

*Muslims of the Soviet Union: a guide.* A. Bennigsen & S. E. Wimbush. London: Hurst, 1985. 294p.

*Muslims through discourse: religion and ritual in Gayo society.* J. R. Bowen. Princeton, NJ: Princeton University Press, 1993. 370p.

'Myths and rituals of the Ethiopian Bertha,' A. Triulzi, in *Peoples and cultures of Ethio–Sudan borderlands.* M. L. Bender (ed). *Committee on Northeast African Studies,* no. 10. East Lansing, MI: African Studies Center, Michigan State University Press, 1981. 214p.

'National minorities in Albania, 1919–1980,' S. M. Horak, in *East European national minorities: 1919–1980: a handbook,* p.309–313. S. M. Horak (ed). Littleton, CO: Libraries Unlimited, 1985.

*Native American religions: a geographical survey.* J. J. Collins. Lewiston, NY: E. Mellen Press, 1991. 411p.

*Native American religions: North America.* L. E. Sullivan (ed). *Encyclopedia of religion series.* New York: Macmillan, 1989.

*Native American religious action: a performance approach to religion.* S. D. Gill. *Studies in comparative religion.* Columbia, SC: University of South Carolina Press, 1987. 199p.

*Native American studies.* Middletown, CT: Choice, 1993. 54p. (Bibliographic work with 278 titles).

*Native peoples of South America.* J. H. Steward & L. C. Faron. New York: McGraw Hill, 1959. 479p.

*Native peoples of the Russian far north.* N. Vakhtin. London: Minority Rights Group, 1992. 38p.

*Ndebele religion and customs.* W. Bozongwana. Gweru, Zimbabwe: Mambo Press in association with the Literature Bureau, 1983. 56p.

*Nepal et ses populations.* M. Gaborieau. *Pays et Populations.* Brussels: Editions Complexe, 1978. 308p.

'Newar Buddhist initiation rites,' J. K. Locke, *Contributions to Nepalese studies,* 2, 2 (1975), 1–23.

*Ngaju religion: the conception of God among a south Borneo people.* H. Schärer. Trans., R. Needham. *Koninklijk Instituut voor Taal-, Land- en Volkenkunde, Translation series,* no. 6. The Hague, Netherlands: Martinus Nijhoff, 1963. 229p. (By missionary).

*Nigerian studies, or the religious and political system of the Yoruba.* R. E. Dennett. *Cass library of African studies, General studies,* no. 48. 1910; reprint, London: Frank Cass, 1968. 235p.

*Nomad: a year in the life of a Qashqa'i tribesman in Iran.* L. Beck. Berkeley, CA: University of California Press, 1991. 503p.

*Nomads of the world.* R. L. Breeden (ed). Washington, DC: National Geographic Society, 1971. 200p.

*Nomads of western Tibet: the survival of a way of life.* M. C. Goldstein & C. M. Beall. Berkeley, CA: University of California Press, 1990. 191p.

'Nomination, réincarnation et/ou ancêtre tutélaire? Un mode de survie: l'example des Sérèr Ndout (Sénégal),' M. Dupire, *L'Homme,* 22, 1 (1982), 5–31.

'Norway's Gypsy minority,' U. Jørstad, *Scandinavian review,* 58, 2 (1970), 129–37.

*Nyabingi: the social history of an African divinity.* J. Freedman. Tervuren, Belgium: Musée Royal de l'Afrique Centrale, 1984. 119p.

'Obstructions and strategizing in church planting among the Tamil Hindus in Sri Lanka.' V. Chandy. D.Miss thesis, Fuller Theological Seminary, Pasadena, CA, 1984. 276p.

*Of water and the spirit: ritual, magic, and initiation in the life of an African shaman.* M. P. Somé. New York: Putnam, 1994. 311p.

*Old and new in Southern Shona independent churches.* M. L. Daneel. *Monographs under the auspices of the Afrika–Studiecentrum, Leiden.* The Hague: Mouton Atlantic Highlands, 1971–88. 3 vols.

*Olódùmarè: god in Yoruba belief.* E. B. Idowu. New York: Praeger, 1963. 222p.

*One Europe—100 nations.* R. N. Pedersen. Clevedon, UK: Channel View Books, 1992. 170p.

*One God—two temples: schismatic process in a Kekchi village.* J. Schackt. *Occasional papers,* no. 13. Oslo: University of Oslo, 1986. 206p. (Treats cargo system).

*Option für die Anderen: Kirche und ursprüngliche Religionen am Beispiel der Kuna–Indianer.* A. Wagua. Lucerne, Switzerland: Romero-Haus, 1992. 18p.

*Orisha: the gods of Yorubaland.* J. Gleason. New York: Atheneum, 1971. 122p.

*Ottomans, Turks and the Jewish polity: a history of the Jews of Turkey.* W. F. Weiker. Lanham, MD: University Press of America, 1992. 386p.

*Outline of world cultures.* G. P. Murdock. 3rd ed. New Haven, CT: Human Relations Area Files, 1963.

*Oxford illustrated encyclopedia of peoples and cultures.* R. Hoggart (ed). Oxford, UK and New York: Oxford University Press, 1992. 399p.

*People movements in Southern Polynesia: studies in the dynamics of church–planting and growth in Tahiti, New Zealand, Tonga, and Samoa.* A. R. Tippett. Chicago: Moody Press, 1971. 288p.

*Peoples and cultures.* A. Rogers. Oxford, UK: Oxford University Press, 1992. 256p.

*Peoples and cultures of Ethio–Sudan borderlands.* M. L. Bender (ed). *Committee on Northeast African Studies,* no. 10. East Lansing, MI: African Studies Center, Michigan State University Press, 1981. 214p.

*Peoples and cultures of Kenya.* A. Fedders. Nairobi: Transafrica, 1979.

*Peoples and cultures of the Middle East.* A. Shiloh (ed). New York: Random House, 1969. 506p.

*Peoples and cultures of the Middle East: an anthropological reader.* L. E. Sweet (ed). Garden City, NY: Natural History Press, 1970. 2 vols.

*Peoples and cultures of the Pacific: an anthropological reader.* A. P. Vayda (ed). Garden City, NY: Natural History Press, 1968.

*Peoples, languages and migrations in Central Asia: a century of Russian rule.* C. H. Minges. New York: Columbia University Press, 1967.

*Peoples of Africa.* J. Middleton. New York: Arco Publishing, 1978. 200p.

*Peoples of Central Asia.* L. Krader. Bloomington, IN: University of Indiana Press, 1963. 319p.

*Peoples of Sierra Leone.* M. McCulloch. *Ethnographic survey of Africa: Western Africa,* part 2. 1950; reprinted with supplementary bibliography, London: International African Institute, 1964. 102p.

*Peoples of South Asia.* C. Maloney. New York: Holt, Rinehart and Winston, 1974. 584p.

*Peoples of the earth.* E. Evans–Pritchard (ed). Danbury: Grolier, 1973. 20 vols.

*Peoples of the Golden Triangle: six tribes in Thailand.* P. W. Lewis & E. Lewis. London: Thames and Hudson, 1984. 300p. (Deals with Karen, Hmong, Mien, Akha, Lahu, and Lisu).

*Peoples of the Horn of Africa: Somali, Afar and Saho.* I. M. Lewis. London: International African Institute, 1969.

*Peoples of the world: Africans south of the Sahara: the culture, geographical setting, and historical background of 34 African peoples.* J. Moss & G. Wilson. Detroit, MI: Gale Research, 1991. 461p. (For young readers).

*Perpetual dilemma: Jewish religion in the Jewish state.* S. Z. Abramov. Cranbury, NJ: Associated University Presses, 1976. 432p.

'Perseverance of African beliefs in the religious ideas of the Bosnegers in Surinam,' B. E. Bekier, *Hemispheres,* no. 1 (1985), 93–108.

'Personhood, possession and the law in Ewe gorovodu culture.' J. V. Rosenthal. Ph.D. dissertation, Cornell University, Ithaca, NY, 1993. 389p.

*Philippine ethnography: a critically annotated and selected bibliography.* S. Saito. *East–West bibliographic series,* no. 2. Honolulu, HI: University Press of Hawaii, 1972. 512p.

'Philosophy, initiation and myths of the Indians of Guiana and adjacent countries,' C. H. de Goeje, in *Internationales Archiv für Ethnographie,* p.1–136, vol. 44. W. D. van Nieuwenhuis et al (eds). Leiden: E. J. Brill, 1943.

*Pilgrims in a strange land: Hausa communities in Chad.* J. A. Works. New York: Columbia University Press, 1976. 294p.

*Polish Jewry: history and culture.* M. Fuks et al. Trans., B. Piotrowska & L. Petrowicz. Warsaw: Interpress, 1982. 196p.

*Prairie and plains Indians.* No. 2 of section 10, *North America,* of *Iconography of religions.* Å. Hultkrantz. Leiden: E. J. Brill, 1973. 46p.

*Pratique de la tradition religieuse et reproduction sociale chez les Guen/Mina du Sud–est du Togo.* E. Adjakly. Geneva: Institut Universitaire d'Études du Développement, 1985. 150p.

'Process of departure of the Uzbek population from religion,' S. M. Mirhasilov, in *Secularization in multi–religious societies: Indo–Soviet perspectives: papers presented at the Indo–Soviet Symposium on Problems of Secularization in Multi–Religious Societies, Tashkent, 1978*, p.241–57. S. C. Dube & V. N. Basilov (ed). New Delhi: Indian Council of Social Science Research, 1983.

*Publications in languages of the Micronesian Islands from the libraries of Bernice P. Bishop Museum and Hawaiian Mission Children's Society, Honolulu, Hawaii.* P. T. Mochida. Honolulu, 1977. 53p. (Microfilm; chiefly biblical and other religious works in Gilbertese, Kusaie, Marshallese, Mortlock, Nauru and Ponape languages).

*Pueblo cultures.* No. 4 of section 10, *North America*, of *Iconography of religions.* B. Wright. Leiden: E. J. Brill, 1986. 29p.

*Race and culture: a world view.* T. Sowell. New York: Basic Books, 1994. 347p.

*Rainmaking rites of Tswana tribes.* I. Schapera. Cambridge, UK: African Studies Centre, 1971. 144p.

*Reference encyclopedia of the American Indian.* B. T. Klein. 6th ed. New York: Todd Publications, 1993. 681p.

*Religion among the Bantu in South Africa.* B. L. Ellis. Johannesburg: University of the Witwatersrand Library, 1968. (Contains bibliography).

'Religion and authority in a Korekore community,' M. F. C. Bourdillon, *Africa* (London), 49, 2 (1979), 172–81.

*Religion and custom in a Muslim society: the Berti of Sudan.* L. Holy. *Cambridge studies in social and cultural anthropology*, 78. Cambridge, UK: Cambridge University Press, 1991. 239p.

'Religion and ethnicity in the arts of a Limba chiefdom,' S. Ottenberg, *Africa*, 58, 4 (1988), 437–65.

*Religion and healing in Mandari.* J. Buxton. Oxford, UK: Clarendon Press, 1973. 443p.

*Religion and political culture in Kano.* J. N. Paden. Berkeley, CA and Los Angeles: University of California Press, 1973. 461p.

'Religion and social organization among a West African Muslim people: the Susu of Sierra Leone.' J. S. Thayer. Ph.D. dissertation, University of Michigan, Ann Arbor, MI, 1981. 386p.

*Religion and society among the Tagbanuwa of Palawan Island, Philippines.* R. B. Fox. *Monograph series*, no. 9. Manila: National Museum, 1982. 262p.

*Religion and society in Arab Sind.* D. N. Maclean. *Monographs and theoretical studies in sociology and anthropology*, no. 25. Leiden: E. J. Brill, 1989. 201p.

*Religión de los Nicaraos: análisis y comparación de tradiciones culturales Nahuas.* M. León–Portilla. *Universidad Autónoma de México.* Mexico City: UNAM, 1972. 116p.

'Religion in a Fante town of Southern Ghana.' H. D. Hornsey. Ph.D. dissertation, University of London, 1979. 354p.

*Religion in a Tswana chiefdom.* B. A. Pauw. London: Oxford University Press for the International African Institute, 1960. 258p.

*Religion in an African society: a study of the religion of the Kono people of Sierra Leone in its social environment with special reference to the function of religion in that society.* R. T. Parsons. Leiden: E. J. Brill, 1964. 245p.

*Religion in native North America.* C. Vecsey (ed). Moscow, ID: University of Idaho Press, 1990. 208p.

*Religion in New Zealand.* C. Nichol & J. Veitch (eds). 2nd ed. Wellington, NZ: Victoria University, 1983. 313p.

*Religion, morality and the person: essays on Tallensi religion.* M. Fortes. *Cambridge paperback library. Essays in social anthropology.* Cambridge, UK: Cambridge University Press, 1987. 347p.

'Religion traditionnelle et techniques thérapeutiques des Lébou du Sénégal,' O. Silla, *Bulletin de l'IFAN*, 30 (B) (1968), 1566–80.

*Religión y magia entre los indios de Costa Rica de origen sureño.* C. H. A. Piedra. *Publicaciones de la Universidad de Costa Rica, Serie historia y geografía*, no. 6. San José: Universidad de Costa Rica, 1965. 83p.

*Religious practices of the Guji Oromo.* J. Van de Loo. Addis Ababa, 1991. 153p.

'Revival Christianity among the Urat of Papua New Guinea: some possible motivational and perceptual antecedents.' S. L. Eyre. Ph.D. dissertation, University of California, San Diego, 1988. 300p.

*Rhythms of a Himalayan village.* H. R. Downs. San Francisco: Harper & Row, 1980. 228p. (Deals with Sherpa religion).

'Rites d'initiation et vie en société chez les Sérèrs du Sénégal,' H. Gravrand, *Afrique documents* (Dakar), 52 (1960), 129–44.

'Ritual paradoxes in Nepal: comparative perspectives on Tamang religion,' D. Holmberg, *Journal of Asian studies*, 43 (August 1984), 197–222.

'Ritual systems in Cuban Santería.' J. M. Murphy. Ph.D. dissertation, Temple University, Philadelphia, 1981. 396p.

*Sacrifice and sharing in the Philippine highlands: religion and society among the Buid of Mindoro.* T. Gibson. *London School of Economics monographs in social anthropology*, no. 57. London: Athlone, 1986. 262p.

*Sacrifice in Ibo religion.* F. A. Arinze. Ed., J. S. Boston. Ibadan, Nigeria: Ibadan University, 1970. 129p.

*Samoan village: then and now.* L. D. Holmes & E. R. Holmes. 2nd ed. *Case studies in cultural anthropology.* Fort Worth, TX: Harcourt Brace Jovanovich College Publishers, 1992. 176p.

*Secret societies and the church: an evaluation of the Poro and Sande secret societies and the missionary among the Mano of Liberia.* P. J. Harrington. Rome: Pontificia Universitas Gregoriana, Facultas Scientiarum Socialium, 1975. 71p.

'Shadow and substance: a Mopan Maya view of human existence,' A. E. Fink, *Canadian journal of native studies*, 7, 2 (1987), 399–414.

*Shamanism and the art of the eastern Tukanoan Indians.* No. 1 of section 9, *South America*, of *Iconography of religions.* G. Reichel-Dolmatoff. Leiden: E. J. Brill, 1987. 25p.

*Sherpas through their rituals.* S. Ortner. *Cambridge studies in cultural systems*, no. 2. Cambridge, UK: Cambridge University Press, 1978. 195p.

'Shona independent churches and ancestor worship,' M. L. Daneel, in *African initiatives in religion*, p.160–70. D. B. Barrett (ed). *21 studies from Eastern and Central Africa.* Nairobi: East African Publishing House, 1971.

*Sincretismo religioso de los indigenas de Bolivia.* J. Esch-Jakob. La Paz, Bolivia: HISBOL, 1994. 132p.

*Sixteen cowries: Yoruba divination from Africa to the New World.* W. Bascom. Bloomington, IN: Indiana University, 1980. 790p.

*Sketches from the Karen hills.* A. Bunker. New York: Revell, 1910. 215p. (American Baptist missionary work).

'Social organizational aspects of religious change among Basotho.' D. Bosko. Ph.D. dissertation, New York University, New York, 1983. 368p.

*Société et religion chez les Newar du Népal.* G. Toffin. Paris: Centre Nationale de la Recherche Scientifique, 1984. 668p.

'Some developments in Bemba religious history,' D. Werner, *Journal of religion in Africa*, 4 (1971), 1–24.

*Songs of life: an introduction to Navajo religious culture.* No. 3 of section 10, *North America*, of *Iconography of religions.* S. D. Gill. Leiden: E. J. Brill, 1979. 31p.

*Soo Thah: a tale of the making of the Karen nation.* A. Bunker. London: Anderson & Ferrier, 1902. 280p. (Deals with a Karen convert to Christianity).

'Sorcery and witchcraft in Bechuanaland,' I. Schapera, *African affairs*, 51, 202 (1952), 41–50. (On Tswana religion).

'Sorcery and witchcraft with the Bayei and Hambukushu: a cross cultural comparison,' T. J. Larson, *South African journal of ethnology*, 12, 4 (1989), 131–36.

*Sorcery in its social setting: a study of the Northern Rhodesia Cewa.* M. G. Marwick. Manchester, UK: Manchester University Press, 1965. 339p.

*South African Jewry: a contemporary survey.* M. Arkin. Cape Town: Oxford University Press, 1984. 212p.

'South Asia: the Baluch frontier tribes of Pakistan,' R. G. Wirsing, in *Protection of ethnic minorities: comparative perspectives*, p.277–312. R. G. Wirsing (ed). New York: Pergamon Press, 1981.

'South West Africa and its indigenous people,' O. Levinson, *South Africa International*, 3 (1972), 19–27.

*Southeast Asian tribes, minorities, and nations.* P. Kunstadter (ed). Princeton, NJ: Princeton University Press, 1967. 2 vols.

*Soviet empire: the Turks of Central Asia and Stalinism.* O. K. Caroe. New York: St. Martin's Press, 1953.

'Space, motion and symbol in Tetum,' D. Hicks, In *Indonesian religions in transition*, p.35–47. R. S. Kipp & S. Rodgers (ed). Tucson, AZ: University of Arizona Press, 1987.

*Spanish Jesuit churches in Mexico's Tarahumara.* P. M. Roca. Tuscon, AZ: University of Arizona Press, 1979. 369p.

*Spider divination in the Cameroons.* P. Gebauer. *Publications in anthropology*, no. 10. Milwaukee, WI: Milwaukee Public Museum, 1964. 157p.

'Spirit possession and deprivation cults,' I. M. Lewis, *Man*, 1, 3 (1966), 307–329.

*Spirit possession and personhood among the Kel Ewey Tuareg.* S. J. Rasmussen. Cambridge, UK: Cambridge University Press, 1995. 189p.

*Spirits of protest: spirit–mediums and the articulation of consensus among the Zezuru of Southern Rhodesia (Zimbabwe).* P. Fry. *Cambridge studies in social anthropology*, no. 14. Cambridge, UK: Cambridge University Press, 1976. 145p.

'Spirituality of the Basotho: the values of the reign of God.' M. R. A. Khiba. M.T.S. thesis, Catholic Theological Union, Chicago, 1991. 97p.

'Split–level Christianity in Africa: a study of the persistence of traditional religious beliefs and practices among the Akan Methodists of Ghana.' M. K. Forson. D.Miss. thesis, Asbury Theological Seminary, Wilmore, KY, 1993. 337p.

*Tamang ritual texts, I: preliminary studies in the folk–religion of an ethnic minority in Nepal.* A. Höfer. *Beiträge zur Südasienforschung*, vol. 65. Wiesbaden, Germany: Franz Steiner, 1981. 184p.

*Taming the wind of desire: psychology, medicine, and aesthetics in Malay shamanistic performance.* C. Laderman. *Comparative studies of health systems and medical care.* Berkeley, CA and Los Angeles: University of California Press, 1991. 382p.

'Teach them unto your children: contextualization of Basanga puberty rites in the United Methodist Church.' D. N. Persons. Ph.D. dissertation, Fuller Theological Seminary, Pasadena, CA, 1990. 344p.

'Tharus of Dang: rites de passage and festivals,' D. P. Rajaure, *Kailash*, 9, 2–3 (1982), 177–258.

'Tharus of Dang: Tharu religion,' D. P. Rajaure, *Kailash*, 9, 1 (1982), 61–96.

'Tharus of Dang: the people and the social context,' D. P. Rajaure, *Kailash*, 8, 3–4 (1981), 155–82.

'The adoption and diffusion of Christianity amongst the Khumi–Chin people of the Upper Kaladan river area of Arakan, North–West Burma from 1900 to 1966 (with an appendix up–date to 1988).' A. N. Nason. M.A. thesis, University of Warwick, Coventry, UK, 1988. 170p.

*The Akan doctrine of God: a fragment of Gold Coast ethics and religion.* J. B. Danquah. 2nd ed. *Cass library of African studies, Africana modern library*, no. 2. 1944; reprint, London: Frank Cass, 1968. 206p.

*The Arab Christian: a history in the Middle East.* K. Cragg. London: Mowbray, 1992. 303p.

*The Armenians in history and the Armenian question.* E. Uras. Istanbul: Documentary Publications, 1988. 1064p.

*The atlas of mankind.* L. Clarke (ed). London: Mitchell Beazley & Rand McNally, 1982. 208p.

*The Azerbaijani Turks: power and identity under Russian rule.* A. L. Altstadt. Stanford, CA: Hoover Press, 1992. 330p.

*The Baluchis and the Pathans.* R. G. Wirsing. London: Minority Rights Group, 1981. 23p.

*The Bambara.* No. 2 of section 7, *Africa*, of *Iconography of religions.* D. Zahan. Leiden: E. J. Brill, 1974. 32p.

*The ban of the bori: demons and demon–dancing in West and North Africa.* A. J. N. Tremearne. London: Heath Cranton & Ouseley, 1914. 497p.

*The Bantu–speaking peoples of Southern Africa.* W. D. Hammond-Tooke (ed). London: Routledge & Kegan Paul, 1974. 525p.

*The Barbarians of Asia: the peoples of the Steppes from 1600 B.C.* S. Legg. 1970; New York: Dorset Press, 1990. 350p.

*The Bassa of Liberia: a study of culture, historical development, and indigenization of the Gospel.* L. Vanderaa. N.p., 1982. 138p.

*The Bauls of Bangladesh: a study of an obscure religious cult.* A. S. M. Anwarul Karim. Kushtia: Lalan Academy, 1980. 212p.

*The Bedouin of Cyrenaica: studies in personal and corporate power.* E. L. Peters. Ed., J. Goody & E. Marx. *Cambridge studies in social and cultural anthropology*, no. 72. Cambridge, UK: Cambridge University Press, 1990. 329p.

*The Beja tribes of the Sudan.* A. Paul. Cambridge, UK: Cambridge University Press, 1954.

*The Cape Malays: history, religion, traditions, folk tales: the Malay quarter.* I. D. du Plessis. 3rd ed. Cape Town: Balkema, 1972. 97p.

*The Cherokees: a population history.* R. Thornton. Lincoln, NE: University of Nebraska Press, 1990. 253p.

'The church in Ghana: towards a redemptive African ecclesiology.' R. B. Otchere. D.Min. thesis, Wesley Theological Seminary, Washington, DC, 1990. 157p.

*The Church of Christ in The Sudan Among the Tiv: a sociological perspective.* A. Dzurgba. Ibadan, Nigeria: Dept. of Religious Studies, University of Ibadan, 1992. 145p.

'The claim of Maori identity on the cultural structure of church and society in New Zealand.' C. B. Turley. D.Min. thesis, School of Theology at Claremont, Claremont, CA, 1977. 141p.

*The clash of cultures: Christian missionaries and the Shona of Rhodesia.* G. Z. Kapenzi. Washington, DC: University Press of America, 1979. 104p.

*The Cossacks.* P. Longworth. London: Constable, 1969. 409p.

*The countries and tribes of the Persian Gulf.* S. B. Miles. 2nd ed. London: Cass, 1966. 643p.

*The Crimean Tartars.* A. Fisher. Stanford, CA: Hoover Institution Press, 1978. 264p.

*The cult of Ifá among the Yoruba. Vol. 1: folk practice and the art.* E. M. McClelland. London: Ethnographica, 1982. 125p.

'The cultural politics of religious change: a study of the Kpelle of Liberia.' R. Stakeman. Ph.D. dissertation, Stanford University, Stanford, CA, 1982. 355p.

'The curse on Ham's descendants: its missiological impact on Zairian Mbala Mennonite Brethren.' N. U. Lumeya. Ph.D. dissertation, Fuller Theological Seminary, Pasadena, CA, 1988. 238p.

*The Dani of Irian Jaya before and after conversion.* D. J. Hayward. Sentani, Irian Jaya, Indonesia: Regions Press, 1980. 233p.

'The despised serfs of southwest China: liberation in Christ of the Miao,' R. R. Covell, chapter 4 in *The liberating gospel in China: the Christian faith among China's minority peoples.* Grand Rapids, MI: Baker, 1995.

'The divining basket of the Ovimbundu,' L. Tucker, *Journal of the Royal Anthropological Institute*, 70, 2 (1940), 171–201.

*The drums of affliction: a study of religious processes among the Ndembu of Zambia.* V. W. Turner. Oxford, UK: Clarendon Press, 1968. 326p.

'The dual legacy: government authority and mission influence among the Glebo of eastern Liberia, 1834–1910.' J. J. Martin. Ph.D. dissertation, Boston University, Boston, 1978. 479p.

*The early years of a Dutch colonial mission: the Karo field.* R. S. Kipp. Ann Arbor, MI: University of Michigan Press, 1990. 272p.

'The emergence of a Diola Christianity,' R. M. Baum, *Africa*, 60, 3 (1990), 370–98.

*The encyclopedia of the peoples of the world.* A. Gonen (ed). New York: Holt, Henry, 1993. 703p.

*The Ewe–speaking peoples of the Slave Coast of West Africa, their religion, manners, customs, laws, languages, &c.* A. B. Ellis. London: Chapman & Hall, 1890. 331p.

'The expansion of Islam among the Bambara under French rule, 1890–1940.' S. A. Harmon. Ph.D. dissertation, University of California, Los Angeles, 1988. 562p.

*The family of man.* London: Marshall Cavendish, 1974. 7 vols.

*The Gaia atlas of first peoples: a future for the indigenous world.* J. Burger et al. New York and London: Anchor Books of Doubleday, 1990. 191p.

'The Gbaya naming of Jesus: an inquiry into the contextualization of soteriological themes among the Gbaya of Cameroon.' T. G. Christensen. Th.D. thesis, Lutheran School of Theology, Chicago, 1984. 484p.

*The Gurkhas.* B. Farwell. New York: W. W. Norton, 1984. 317p.

*The Gurungs of Nepal.* D. A. Messerschmidt. Warminster, UK: Aris & Philips, 1976. 151p.

*The Gypsies.* A. Fraser. Oxford, UK: Blackwell, 1992. 370p.

*The Gypsies in Poland: history and customs.* J. Ficowski. Trans., E. Healey. Warsaw: Interpress, 1989. 303p.

*The gypsies of Eastern Europe.* D. Crowe & J. Kolsti (eds). Armonk, NY and London: M. E. Sharpe, 1991. 200p.

'The Gypsy population of Yugoslavia,' T. P. Vukanovic, *Journal of the Gypsy Lore Society*, 42, 1/2 (1963), 10–27.

*The Hausa people: a bibliography.* F. A. Salamone with the assistance of J. A. McCain. New Haven, CT: Human Relations Area Files, 1983. 2 vols.

'The history and development of the Church among the Bawm tribe and the future plan for the evangelization of other tribes in Bangladesh.' P. B. Tlung. M.Div. thesis, Asian Center for Theological Studies and Mission, Seoul, Korea, 1987. 194p.

'The history and growth of the churches in Chin State, Myanmar (Burma).' Khuang Nawni. Th.M. thesis, Fuller Theological Seminary, Pasadena, CA, 1990. 184p.

'The history of the Thakaalis according to the Thakaali tradition,' S. Gauchan & M. Vinding, *Kailash*, 5, 2 (1977), 97–184.

*The Hmong: an annotated bibliography, 1983–1987.* J. C. Smith. *Southeast Asian refugee studies, Occasional papers*, no. 7. Minneapolis, MN: Center for Urban and Regional Affairs, University of Minnesota, 1988. 67p.

*The Holy Ghost Fathers and Catholic worship among the Igbo people of eastern Nigeria.* D. E. O. Ogudo. Paderborn, Germany: Verlag Bonifatius-Druckerei, 1988. 331p.

*The House of Phalo: a history of the Xhosa people in the days of their independence.* J. B. Peires. Johannesburg: Ravan Press, 1981. 281p. (Treats Xhosa religion and response to Christianity).

*The image of god among the Sotho–Tswana.* G. M. Setiloane. Rotterdam, Netherlands: A. A. Balkema, 1976. 298p. (Treats Christianity among Sotho-Tswana).

*The impact of Christianity on the tribes of Northeast India.* S. Karotemprel. Shillong, India: Sacred Heart Theological College, 1994. 63p.

*The Indians of Central and South America: an ethnohistorical dictionary.* J. S. Olson. Westport, CT: Greenwood Press, 1991. 504p.

*The influence of Islam on a Sudanese religion.* J. Greenberg. *Monographs of the American Ethnological Society*, no. 10. Seattle, WA: University of Washington, 1966. 73p.

'The influence of Islam on the Afar.' K. Shehim. Ph.D. dissertation, University of Washington, Seattle, WA, 1982. 230p.

'The influence of Western Christianity on the African culture: the Abaluyia of Western Kenya.' L. N. Shamalla. M.T.S. thesis, Emory University, Atlanta, 1995. 99p.

'The Javanese in Surinam: ethnicity in an ethnically plural society.' P. Suparlan. Ph.D. dissertation, University of Illinois, Urbana–Champaign, 1976. 390p.

*The Jews of Arab lands: a history and source book.* N. A. Stillman. Philadelphia: Jewish Publication Society of America, 1979. 427p.

*The Jews of Islam.* B. Lewis. Princeton, NJ: Princeton University Press, 1984. 257p.

*The Jews of the Middle East 1860–1972.* H. J. Cohen. Jerusalem: Israel Universities Press, 1973. 197p.

*The Jews of the Ottoman Empire and the Turkish Republic.* S. J. Shaw. New York: New York University Press, 1991. 393p.

*The Jews of the Soviet Union: the history of a national minority.* B. Pinkus. Cambridge, UK: Cambridge University Press, 1988. 397p.

*The Kachins: religion and custom.* C. Gilhodes. Calcutta: Catholic Orphan Press, 1922. 304p.

*The Kachins: their customs and traditions.* O. Hanson. 1913; reprint, New York: AMS, 1982. 225p.

*The Kalunga concept in Ovambo religion from 1870 onwards.* T. Aarni. Stockholm: Almquist & Wicksell, 1982. 166p.

*The Kavango peoples.* G. D. Gibson, T. J. Larson & C. R. McGurk. Wiesbaden, Germany: Franz Steiner Verlag, 1981. 275p. (Treats religion).

'The Kavango: the country, its people and history,' K. F. R. Budack, *Namib und Meer*, 7 (1976), 29–42.

'The Kikuyu, Christianity and the Africa Inland Mission.' D. P. Sandgren. Ph.D. dissertation, University of Wisconsin, Madison, WI, 1976. 427p.

*The Kurds: a concise history and fact book.* M. Izady. Washington, DC: Crane Russak, 1991. 285p.

*The Kurds: a contemporary overview.* P. G. Kreyenbroek & S. Sperl (eds). London: Routledge, 1992. 262p.

*The Kurds of Iraq: tragedy and hope.* M. M. Gunter. New York: St. Martin's Press, 1992. 185p.

'The land as body: an essay on the interpretation of ritual among the Manjaks of Guinea–Bissau,' W. V. Binsbergen, *Medical anthropology quarterly*, 2, 4 (1988), 386–401. (Treats religious rituals).

*The Lapps.* R. Bosi. *Ancient people and places.* London: Thames & Hudson, 1960. 220p. (Discusses Lapp religion).

*The Lebanese in the world: a century of emigration.* A. Hourani & N. Shehadi (eds). London: Center for Lebanese Studies/I. B. Tauris, 1993. 741p.

*The liberating gospel in China: the Christian faith among China's minority peoples.* R. R. Covell. Grand Rapids, MI: Baker, 1995. 288p.

*The listening ebony: moral knowledge, religion, and power among the Uduk of Sudan.* W. James. Oxford, UK: Clarendon Press, 1988. 391p.

*The making of Bamana sculpture: creativity and gender.* S. C. Brett-Smith. *RES monographs in anthropology and aesthetics.* Cambridge, UK: Cambridge University Press, 1994. 372p.

'The making of Christianity in a southern African kingdom: GammaNgwato, ca. 1870 to 1940.' P. S. Landau. Ph.D. dissertation, University of Wisconsin, Madison, WI, 1992. 589p.

'The Maya evangelical church in Guatemala.' A. J. Lloret. Th.D. thesis, Dallas Theological Seminary, Dallas, TX, 1976. 357p.

'The Mayahac of the Kekchi Belizeans,' J. Cayetano, *Belizean studies*, 10, 2 (1982), 1–8.

'The Mecca pilgrimage by West African pastoral nomads,' J. S. Birks, *Journal of modern African studies*, 15, 1 (1977), 47–58.

*The Mexican Kikapoo Indians.* F. A. Latorre & D. L. Latorre. *Texas Pan–American series.* Austin, TX: University of Texas Press, 1976. 401p.

*The minorities of northern China: a survey.* H. Schwartz. Bellingham, WA: Western Washington University Press, 1984.

*The modern Uzbeks: from the fourteenth century to the present: a cultural history.* E. A. Allworth. Stanford, CA: Hoover Institution Press, 1990. 424p.

*The myth of ritual: a native's ethnography of Zapotec life–crisis rituals.* F. E. Gundi & A. H. Jiménez. Tucson, AZ: University of Arizona Press, 1986. 147p.

*The Naron: a Bushman tribe of the central Kalahari.* D. F. Bleek. Cambridge, UK: University of Cape Town, Publications of the School of African Life and Language, 1928. 67p.

*The native tribes of South West Africa.* C. H. L. Hahn. Cape Town: Cape Times, 1928. 214p.

'The new people of God: the Christian community in the African Orthodox Church (Karing'a) and the Arathi (Agikuyu spirit churches).' F. K. Githieya. Ph.D. dissertation, Emory University, Atlanta, 1992. 405p.

'The Orang Asli: an outline of their progress in modern Malaya,' A. Jones, *Journal of Southeast Asian history*, 9, 2 (1968), 286–305.

*The other Jews: the Sephardim today.* D. J. Elazar. New York: Basic Books, 1989. 248p.

'The Ovambo sermon: a study of the preaching of the Evangelical Lutheran Ovambo–Kavango Church in South West Africa.' S. Löytty. Tampereen Keskuspaino thesis, University of Helsinki, Tampere, Finland, 1971. 175p.

'The Paramacca Maroons: a study in religious acculturation.' J. D. Lenoir. Ph.D. dissertation, New School for Social Research, New York, 1973. 213p.

*The Penguin atlas of diasporas.* G. Chaliand & J. Rageau. Trans., A. M. Berret. New York and London: Viking Penguin, 1995. 204p. (Originally published as Atlas des Diasporas. Editions Odile Jacob, 1991).

*The people of Nepal.* D. B. Bista. 5th ed. Kathmandu: Ratna Pustak Bhandar, 1987. 210p.

*The people of the stones: the Chepangs of central Nepal.* N. Rai. Kathmandu: Centre for Nepal and Asian Studies, 1985. 125p.

*The people of Tibet.* C. Bell. Oxford, UK: Clarendon Press, 1928. 319p.

*The peoples of Africa: an ethnohistorical dictionary.* J. S. Olson. Westport, CT: Greenwood press, 1996. 689p.

*The peopling of Southern Africa.* R. Inskeep. Cape Town: Philip, 1978. 160p.

*The pool that never dries up.* R. Wynne. London: USPG, 1988. 129p. (Christian missions among the Hambukushu).

'The position of women in the Sisala divination cult,' E. L. Mendonsa, in *The new religions of Africa*, p.57–66. B. Jules–Rosette (ed). Norwood, NJ: Ablex Publishing, 1979.

*The possessed and the dispossessed: spirits, identity, and power in a Madagascar migrant town.* L. A. Sharp. *Comparative studies of health systems and medical care*, no. 37. Berkeley, CA: University of California Press, 1993. 364p.

'The presence of Islam among the Akan of Ghana: a bibliographic essay,' R. A. Silverman & D. Owusu–Ansah, *History in Africa*, 16 (1989), 325–39.

'The prime mover and fear in Inuit religion: a discussion of "native views",' J. G. Oosten, in *Continuity and identity in native America: essays in honor of Benedikt Hartmann*, p.69-83. M. Jansen et al (eds). Leiden: E. J. Brill, 1988.

'The problem of a female deity in translation,' R. Venberg, *Bible Translator*, 35, 4 (October 1984), 415–417. (Translating the Bible for the Pévé tribe, southwestern Chad. Reprinted from *Bible Translator*, April 1971).

'The Qashqa'i,' R. Weekes, in *Muslim peoples*, p.631–37, vol. 2. Westport, CT: Greenwood Press, 1984. (Lists 25 books and articles on the Qashqa'i).

*The Qashqa'i nomads of Fars.* P. Oberling. The Hague: Mouton, 1974. 277p.

*The Qashqa'i of Iran.* L. Beck. New Haven, CT: Yale University Press, 1986. 400p.

'The Raute: notes on a nomadic hunting and gathering tribe of Nepal,' J. Reinhard, *Kailash*, 2, 4 (1974), 233–71.

*The rise and fall of the Black Caribs of St. Vincent.* I. E. Kirby & C. I. Martin. Kingstown, St. Vincent: St. Vincent Archaeological and Historical Society, 1972. 65p.

*The sacred mountain of Colombia's Kogi Indians.* No. 2 of section 9, *South America*, of *Iconography of religions.* G. Reichel-Dolmatoff. Leiden: E. J. Brill, 1990. 38p.

*The Samaritans.* A. D. Crown (ed). Tübingen, Germany: Mohr, 1989. 813p.

'The Seleka–Rolong and the Wesleyan Methodist missionaries, 1823–1884.' R. L. Watson. Ph.D. dissertation, Boston University, Boston, 1974. 237p.

*The Sherpas of Nepal—Buddhist highlanders.* C. von Fürer–Haimendorf. 1972; reprint, New Delhi: Sterling, 1979. 298p.

*The Shona and the Ndebele of Southern Rhodesia.* H. Kuper, A. J. B. Hughes & J. van Velsen. London: International African Institute, 1954. 131p.

*The Shona peoples: an ethnography of the contemporary Shona, with special reference to their religion.* M. F. C. Bourdillon. 3rd ed. Gwelo, Zimbabwe: Mambo Press, 1987. 359p.

*The Slovene minority of Carinthia.* T. M. Barker with the collaboration of A. Moritsch. *East European Monographs*, no. 169. Boulder, CO: East European Monographs, 1984. 415p.

'The social structure of the Pokot and its implications for church planting: a new paradigm for strategic African missions.' R. G. Lewis. D. Miss. thesis, Biola University, La Mirada, CA, 1991. 260p.

'The southern Methodists and the Atetela: the history of the Methodist Episcopal Church, South, in the central Congo, 1912–1960.' Okenge Owandji Kasongo. Ph.D. dissertation, University of Kentucky, Lexington, KY, 1982. 230p.

*The spirits and their cousins: some aspects of belief, ritual, and social organization in a rural Hausa village in Niger.* R. H. Faulkingham. Amherst, MA: Dept. of Anthropology, University of Massachusetts, 1975. 57p.

*The springs of Mende belief and conduct: a discussion of the influence of the belief in the supernatural among the Mende.* W. T. Harris & H. Sawyerr. Freetown: Sierra Leone University Press, 1968. 152p.

'The supernatural world of the Badyaranké of Tonghia (Senegal),' W. Simmons, *Journal des africanistes*, 37, 1 (1967), 41–72.

'The Tajik of Afghanistan,' D. B. Barrett, *International journal of frontier missions*, 10 (April 1993), 93–94.

*The Talaings.* R. Halliday. Rangoon: Superintendent, Government Printing, 1917. 164p. (Treats religion).

*The timetables of Jewish history: a chronology of the most important people and events in Jewish history.* J. Gribetz et al. New York: Simon & Schuster, 1993. 752p.

*The Tshi–speaking peoples of the Gold Coast of West Africa: their religion, manners, customs, laws, language, etc.* A. B. Ellis. 1887; reprint, Chicago: Benin Press, 1964. 343p.

'The Tshwa response to Christianity: a study of the religious and cultural impact of Protestant Christianity on the Tshwa of Southern Mocambique.' A. Helgesson. M.A. thesis, University of the Witwatersrand, Johannesburg, 1971. 296p.

*The Tswana.* I. Schapera. 2nd ed. London: International African Institute, 1976. 93p.

'The Turkmen in the age of imperialism: a study of the Turkmen people and their incorporation into the Russian Empire.' M. Saray. University Society Printing House, 1989.

'The Uighurs of Xinjiang,' A. al–Hada (pseudonym), *International journal of frontier missions*, 2, 4 (1985), 373–83.

'The Uzbeks and their ideas of ultimate reality and meaning,' H. R. Battersby, *Ultimate reality and meaning*, 8, 3 (1985), 172–95.

'The Uzbeks in Afghanistan,' E. Naby, *Central Asian Survey*, 3, 1 (1984), 1–21.

*The victim and its masks: an essay on sacrifice and masquerade in the Maghreb.* A. Hammoudi. Chicago: University of Chicago Press, 1993. 214p. (Also in French).

*The Vlachs: the history of a Balkan people.* T. J. Winnifrith. London: Duckworth, 1987. 180p.

*The Volga Tatars: a profile in national resilience.* A. A. Rorlich. Stanford, CA: Hoover Institution Press, 1986. 288p.

*The Yaka and Suku.* No. 1 of section 7, *Africa*, of *Iconography of religions.* A. P. Bourgeois. Leiden: E. J. Brill, 1985. 26p

*Tibet: Bon religion: a death ritual of the Tibetan Bonpos.* No. 13 of section 12, *East and Central Asia*, of *Iconography of religions.*H. P. Kvaerne. Leiden: E. J. Brill, 1985. 34p.

'Tierce, Eglise, ma Mère: ou, la conversion d'une Communauté païenne au Christ.' A. T. Sanon. Thesis, Institut Catholique de Paris, 1970. 294p.

*Tin mosques and Ghanatowns: a history of Afghan camel drivers in Australia.* C. Stevens. Melbourne: Oxford University Press, 1989. 400p.

*Tonga Christianity.* S. Shewmaker. South Pasadena, CA: William Carey Library, 1970. 215p.

'Toward a new missionary impulse of the Karen Baptist Church of Myanmar.' S. D. Say. D. Miss. thesis, Fuller Theological Seminary, Pasadena, CA, 1993. 276p.

'Towards an Aymara church.' D. Llanque Chana. M.Th. thesis, St. John's Seminary, 1979. 146p.

'Tradition and change among the pastoral Harasiis in Oman,' D. Chatty, in *Anthropology and development in North Africa and the Middle East.* Boulder, CO: Westview Press, 1990.

*Tradition and Christianity in the Bakossi society: a lecture delivered in the Presbyterian Theological College, Nyasoso, 6 Jan. 1976.* S. N. Ejedepang–Koge. N.p., 1976. 23p.

'Traditional religion in Nigeria with particular reference to the Yoruba,' E. A. Odumuyinwa, in *Nigerian life and culture: a book of readings.* O. Y. Oyeneye & M. O. Shoremi (eds). Ago–Iwoye, Nigeria: Ogun State University, 1985.

*Tribes, government, and history in Yemen.* P. Dresch. Oxford, UK: Clarendon Press, 1989. 440p.

*Tribes in Oman.* J. R. L. Carter. London: Peninsular, 1982. 176p.

*Tribus, ethnies et pouvoir en Mauritanie.* P. Marchesin. Paris: Karthala, 1992. 437p.

'Turkmen,' W. G. Irons, in *Muslim peoples: a world ethnographic survey.* 2nd ed. Westport, CT: Greenwood Press, 1984. Ed. R. V. Weekes.

'Ukrainian Catholics and Orthodox in Poland,' A. Sorokowski, *Religion in Communist lands*, 14, 3 (1986), 244–61.

*Un cycle oral hagiographique dans le Moyen–Atlas marocain.* J. Drouin. *Série Sorbonne*, 2. Paris: Publications de la Sorbonne, 1975. 270p.

'Un exemple d'indépendence et de résistance religieuse: les hommes et les dieux Lobi,' M. Cros, *Mondes et Développement* (Paris), 17, 65 (1989), 59–65.

'Un système philosophique sénégalais: la cosmologie des Diola,' L. V. Thomas, *Présence africaine*, 32/33 (1960), 64–76.

*Unreached peoples: clarifying the task.* H. Schreck & D. B. Barrett (ed). Monrovia, CA: MARC; Birmingham, AL: New Hope, 1987. 310p.

'Varieties of religion and religious specialists among the Susu of Sierra Leone,' J. S. Thayer, in *Sierra Leone studies at Birmingham, 1983: proceedings of the third Birmingham Sierra Leone Studies Symposium, 15th-17th July 1983, Fircroft College, Birmingham.* P. K. Mitchell & A. Jones (eds). Birmingham, UK: University of Birmingham, Centre of West African Studies, 1984.

*Virgin Islands English creoles.* G. Sprave. *Microstate studies*, vol. 1. N.p.: Caribbean Research Institute, 1977, p.8–28.

*Wind, sand, and silence: travels with Africa's last nomads.* V. Englebert. San Francisco: Chronicle Books, 1992. 181p. (Descriptions of Tuareg, Bororo, Danakil, and Turkana).

'Witchcraft among the Akamba and Africa Inland Church, Kenya.' J. M. Mbuva. M.A. thesis, Fuller Theological Seminary, Pasadena, CA, 1992. 177p.

'Witchcraft among the Tapanahoni Djuka,' W. van Wetering, in *Maroon societies: rebel slave communities in the Americas*, p.370–88. R. Price (ed). Garden City, NY: Anchor Press/Doubleday, 1973.

*Witchcraft and sorcery in Ovambo.* M. Hiltunen. Helsinki: Finnish Anthropological Society, 1986. 178p.

*Witchcraft, oracles and magic among the Azande.* E. E. Evans–Pritchard. Oxford, UK: Clarendon, 1937. 558p.

'Women, ecology and Islam in the making of modern Hausa cultural history.' M. W. Bivins. Ph.D. dissertation, Michigan State University, East Lansing, MI, 1994. 265p.

*Women of fire and spirit: history, faith and gender in Roho religion in Nyanza.* C. H. Hoehler–Fatton. New York: Oxford University Press, 1995.

'Words and blessings: Batak Catholic discourses in North Sumatra.' B. Sutanto. Ph.D. dissertation, Cornell University, Ithaca, NY, 1989. 369p.

*World cultures encyclopedia.* Human Relations Area Files. New Haven, CT: Yale University with G. K. Hall, 1991–94. 10 vols.

'Yao religion and society,' J. Lemoine, in *Highlanders of Thailand*, p.195–211. J. McKinnon & W. Bhruksasri (eds). Kuala Lumpur, Malaysia: Oxford University Press, 1983.

*Yoruba beliefs and sacrificial rites.* J. O. Awolalu. London: Longman, 1979. 203p.

*Yoruba religion and medicine in Ibadan.* G. E. Simpson. Ibadan, Nigeria: Ibadan University, 1980. 195p.

'Yoruba religion in Trinidad: transfer and reinterpretation,' M. W. Lewis, *Caribbean quarterly*, 24, 3–4 (1978), 18–32.

*Yoruba religious carving: pagan and Christian sculpture in Nigeria and Dahomey.* K. Carroll. London: G. Chapman, 1967. 184p.

*Zimbabwe.* D. Potts. 2nd ed. *World bibliographical series*, vol. 4. Oxford, UK: CLIO Press, 1993. 402p. (See especially 'Religion,' p.99–109).

Part 19

# GEOSCRIPTURES

Global distribution and density of Christian scriptures, AD 30-AD 2025

*The Scriptures say, 'The message was told everywhere on Earth. It was announced all over the world.'*

—Romans 10:18, Contemporary English Version

*The Scriptures train God's servants to do all kinds of good deeds.*

—2 Timothy 3:17, Contemporary English Version

The Christian mandate is to spread the Good News of the Holy Scriptures throughout the world. Part 19 examines how well this is being undertaken today. Using the detailed statistics published annually by over 200 Bible societies, it compares actual achievement in scripture translation, distribution, and density (copies in place per population) with the long-term goals set and announced by those agencies.

# Global distribution and density of Christian scriptures, AD 30-AD 2025

## THE GLOBAL PICTURE

For Christians, the Bible represents the ultimate riches, the definitive presentation about God, Christ, the Holy Spirit, salvation, discipleship, and God's plans for the future. Christians have always recognized their obligation to pass these riches on to the entirety of peoples, populations, and languages throughout the world. Table 19–1 below summarizes where our globe's populations are today in this respect.

In its overall survey, Table 19–1 lists in its column 1 ten varieties of access to the Christian Scriptures. Columns 2 to 5 then divide the world impressionistically into a simple dichotomy: (1) the *fortunates* (persons with access to scriptures), and (2) the *unfortunates* (persons without such access). Christians recognize that they have thereby consigned those populations in column 5 to a fate described under 10 predicaments in column 6. The present Part 19 "Geo-Scriptures" attempts to analyze this situation in more detail.

## A BRIEF HISTORY OF PERSONAL SCRIPTURES

### Living and dying without personal scriptures
In the first century of the Apostolic era, very few Christians had personal copies of any parts of the Christian scriptures. The idea itself of there being a definitive collection of inspired writings to add to the Hebrew and Greek Old Testaments took over 330 years in coming to fruition. That subject was only finally resolved in the year AD 367 when the canon of the New Testament was finally agreed on as the 27 books listed in Athanasius' Easter Letter for the East, by the Synod of Rome in AD 382 for the West, and by the Synod of Carthage in AD 397 for the entire church. So by this latter date with its 35 million living Christians, some 145 million Christians who had already lived and died on earth had completed their lives of witness and discipleship without owning more than a sheet of two of Holy Scripture for themselves. By this date too, some 2,540,000 Christians had given their lives for Christ as martyrs without the comfort and support of personal copies of Holy Scripture.

The history of this subject of providing Christians with their own scriptures is set out here in Table 19–2. This analysis can now continue as a commentary on the numerical situation there set out.

### Personal scriptures become a possibility
A millennium later the situation had barely changed. By AD 1450 a total of 2.2 billion Christians had lived and died on earth, 17 million of them as martyrs, without personal copies of Scripture. But in that year a momentous event took place. In 1450 came the invention of printing (typography and the printing press) by Johannes Gutenberg (c1395–1468) in Mainz, Germany. He did this in order to implement a bold vision—how to to disseminate Holy Scripture across the world. By 1500, more than 100 printed editions of the Bible had been produced. By that time Europe had 40 printing presses and had produced 15 million printed volumes, a large proportion being Christian works including 98 distinct editions of the Latin Vulgate. In the subsequent centuries it became the norm for the ordinary Christian disciple to obtain and own his own personal copy of at least one book or even a larger part of the Scriptures.

## THE GOAL OF SCRIPTURES FOR ALL

### Scriptures for all on Earth
Gradually the idea germinated of fulfilling literally what Gutenberg had glimpsed in outline—the providing of scriptures to everybody in the entire world.

In May 1833 W.S. Plummer of Virginia made a detailed proposal that the American Bible Society cooperate with other societies to put a Bible in the hands of every family in the world within 20 years. Plummer's plan estimated world population then at 800 million, and the total of families to be supplied at 130 million. He even calculated that this would cost a grand total of US$130 million over the 20 years. Although adopted enthusiastically by several of the Bible societies of Europe and America, the plan eventually fizzled out.

## STRATEGIZING DISTRIBUTION

### The Hakone formula
A handful more of times such global plans with detailed calculations surfaced, only to fizzle out in the same way. Eventually they became the firm policy of the United Bible Societies at the 1963 17th Council Meeting and World Assembly held in Hakone (Japan). There under the new slogan 'God's Word for a New Age', UBS president F.D. Coggan, archbishop of York and (later) Canterbury, lamented the inadequacy of the current 50 million copies of scriptures (Bibles, New Testaments, and Portions/Gospels) then being distributed by Bible societies, and pledged to triple this to 150 million a year within the subsequent 3 years. The UBS formalized this Hakone Formula, as it was named, resolving to provide by 1966:

'A Bible for every Christian home.
At least a New Testament for every Christian.
At least a Portion for all who can read and for every literate'.

Notably absent at that time was any goal referring to the world's 700 million nonliterate adult non-Christians, nor to the 100 million nonliterate adult Christians, nor to the world's 40 million blind persons, nor to the 400 million deaf persons, nor to the whole world of 1.5 billion handicapped persons. Neither did any goal address the needs of the world's 1.6 billion children.

However, as can be seen from the UBS' subsequent annual statistics of circulations achieved, these bold but firm pledges were never honored. The UBS distribution of those 3 basic forms of scriptures rose somewhat by 1966 but even in the following 30 years never exceeded 85 million.

### The fate of the 3 major goals
The Hakone goals should have proved easy to monitor and to implement, at least at the global level. The first two goals were straightforward enough for encouraging results to appear, though no records remain of any attempt to measure their relation to the goals. The third of the 3 goals proved far too ambitious and never exceeded even 15% of its goal. No one had realized the immensity of the populations involved. In 1963 the world had 1,300 million literate adults. To put this number of gospels in each's hands would have required a distribution of 130 million a year for 10 years. Even worse, by AD 2000 literates had grown to 3,256 million requiring a distribution of 326 million a year for 10 years. By contrast, after 1963, subsequent distribution never exceeded 40 million by UBS nor even 50 million by all agencies together. We will shortly analyze the reasons for this.

What subsequently happened is clear. Although detailed statistics of distribution were methodically collected, tabulated, totaled, and published every year since 1950, no one subjected these invaluable data to any serious form of scientific analysis. Instead, the annual listings were given cursory inspection to note and publicize the commendable efforts of those Bible societies in whose countries numerical increases were occurring. Countries showing poor or declining circulations were encouraged to aim for annual increases, often with specific increases of 10% or more being urged. No one answered the question: To what precise extent are the Hakone goals as applied to this country or that actually being met or not?

It is evident now that global evaluation is paradoxical—enormous successes together with startling failures. The situation at the global level is set out in Table 19–1 in brief and 19-2 in detail.

### A new attempt at global distribution
Observing the problem of meeting the goal regarding Portions, in 1967 the UBS inaugurated a new category of scriptures called Selections, being 1-, 2-, 4-,

---

## Table 19–1. Ten global dichotomies depicting adequate and inadequate direct access to Christian scriptures in AD 2000.

There are many and varied reasons why whole populations do not have adequate access to Holy Scripture, or, more specifically, to scriptures (this term with small 's' is defined here as printed copies of Bibles, New Testaments, Portions (gospels), or Selections). Most people on Earth have some access to scriptures, or at least the prospects of access as soon as current translation programs are completed. 'New versions' in this table refers to new translations, or revisions, or new publishing activities in a people's languages.

In this table 10 different ways are shown of dividing the globe with its 6,100 million population into a simple dichotomy of those with direct access (the fortunate ones, being those with adequate access) and those without (the unfortunate ones, being those with inadequate, indirect, or even zero access). These are arranged below in descending order of accessibility.

At this point we define 'direct access' as excluding indirect access via near-scriptures in closely-related languages. The value of near-scriptures is explained 2 pages later, also in *WCT* Parts 24 and 31, and in full detail in *WCE* Parts 8 and 9.

| Criterion | FORTUNATES (persons with direct access) | Persons | UNFORTUNATES (persons without direct access) | Persons | Predicament |
|---|---|---|---|---|---|
| 1 | 2 | 3 | 4 | 5 | 6 |
| 1. Benefit | All using own scriptures regularly | 1,100 million | All not being helped by scriptures | 5,000 million | No benefit |
| 2. Opportunity | Owners of multiple scriptures | 2,000 million | All denied copies because of multiple-copy owners | 4,100 million | No opportunity |
| 3. Copies | Persons with own scripture copies | 3,000 million | All with no scripture copies | 3,100 million | No copies |
| 4. Contact | All in regular contact with scriptures | 3,400 million | All with no contact at all with scriptures | 2,700 million | No contact |
| 5. Literacy | Literates and their children | 4,000 million | Nonliterates and their children | 2,100 million | No literacy |
| 6. Awareness | Persons aware of scriptures | 4,100 million | All persons unaware of scriptures | 2,000 million | No awareness |
| 7. Gospel | Persons aware of Christ and gospel | 4,500 million | All persons unaware of Christ or gospel | 1,600 million | No gospel |
| 8. Translation | All with access to own-language translations | 5,600 million | All with no access to own-language translations | 500 million | No translation |
| 9. Prospects | All with access to ongoing new versions | 5,800 million | All with no current first translating underway | 300 million | No prospects |
| 10. Something | All with some access or prospects | 5,900 million | Neither access, awareness, prospects, nor hope | 200 million | Nothing |

## Table 19–2. Global totals of Bibles and New Testaments needed, distributed per year, in place (density), with percent promises met, AD 400–AD 2025.

This table tracks the number of copies of the complete Bible, and copies of the New Testament, produced, circulated, and put in place across the world at 24 points over Christianity's 2,000-year history. The analysis then compares the numbers needed by the whole world (enumerated by means of the church's goals and promises) with the numbers actually provided. (Note: 'm' means millions). This then produces final percentages (columns 15 and 22) showing the degree to which the church's promises have been kept and met, with 100% recording successful achievements.

*Assumptions*
(a) Christians have usually promised to see a Bible in every literate Christian family, home, or household, and to see a New Testament owned by every literate adult Christian.
(b) These 2 goals are not distinct and unrelated, but the second overlaps the first and is augmented by it. A householder with a Bible counts also as an adult believer with a New Testament. Thus enumeration of the second goal is arrived at by taking the number of NTs distributed per year (column 18) and adding to it the number of Bibles distributed per year (column 11, because they also contain the whole NT), then dividing this total by the number of NTs needed (Column 15), times 100. The resulting % measures either achievement or failure in reaching the goal, using 2 standards: (1) 100% = the goal has actually been achieved numerically (assuming equitable distribution); or (2) 200% = the goal has more certainly been achieved by allowing an extra 100% to cover both waste and inadequate or unfair or inequitable distribution.
(c) Throughout the centuries, copies of both books have lasted an average of 20 years before disintegrating from wear and tear, or becoming lost, wasted, discarded, disintegrated, burned, destroyed, or otherwise out of use or needing to be replaced.

*Meanings of columns*
Note: in all columns, 'm' = millions
1. *Year.*
2. *Persons.* Global population at mid-year.
3. *Homes.* Total families, homes, or households in world, assuming 5 persons per home (2 spouses, 1 adult over 15, 2 children under 15).
4. *Literates* Persons able to read and write, as % all adults.
5. *Christians, %.* Christians of all ages including children and infants, as % world population.
6. Number of all *Christians,* computed as column 2 times column 5 divided by 100.
7. *Christian literates, %* (adults able to read and write).
8. *Christian adults, %.* Christians over 15 years old or older, as %.
9. Number of *literate Christian homes* or families (column 3 x column 5 over 100 x column 7 over 100). This gives the number of copies of the Bible needed in place (owned, in use) in order to meet Hakone Goal 1, the promise of a copy for every literate Christian family, home, or household.
10. *UBS Bibles p.a.* Annual distribution of copies of the whole Bible due to (from AD 1710–1946) Bible societies (first being the Cansteinische Bibelanstalt in Germany in 1710, then 1804 BFBS, ABS, NBSS, et alia), and since 1946 the United Bible Societies. *Note.* Minor discrepancies between this table and Table 12–1 are due to varying discrepant methods of enumerating amounts distributed and amounts needed.
11. Bible societies' (UBS') *distribution of Bibles as %* all distribution.
12. *All Bibles p.a.* Total all means of Bible distribution/sales, being that of Bible societies plus commercial publishers (OUP, Nelson, Collins, et alia), free-distribution agencies (Gideons, since 1900), plus Bible societies not in UBS (IBS, WBT, TBL, TLB, &c).
13. *UBS Bibles in place.* Copies of Bible actually in place (owned, in use) assuming 20-year average life of a copy. Column 13 = 20 times column 10.
14. *All Bibles in place.* Copies of Bibles actually in place due to all means. Column 14 = 20 times column 12.
15. *Promises met: Bibles.* Extent to which the churches' promise of a Bible for every literate Christian home was met at each epoch or year, 100% being the stated goal. Column 15 = column 14 divided by column 9, times 100.
16. Number of *literate adult Christians* in the world, computed as column 2 times column 5 times column 7 times column 8, divided by 1 million. This also gives the number of NT copies (either as NTs or as whole Bibles) needed in place in order to meet Hakone Goal 2, the promise of an NT for every literate adult Christian.
17. *UBS NTs p.a.* Annual distribution of separate NTs (the 27 Books, bound) due to Bible societies or UBS (see details in note 9 above).
18. Bible societies'(UBS') *NT distribution* as % all NT distribution.
19. *All NTs p.a.* Total all means of NT distribution/sales (the 27 Books, bound) (see note 12 above), including duplication (NTs in Bibles); so column 19 = column 17 ÷ 18 x 100 plus column 12.
20. *UBS NTs in place.* Copies of separate NT (the 27 Books) actually in place (owned, in use) due to Bible societies/UBS, but excluding duplication. Column 20 = column 17 x 20.
21. *All NTs in place.* Copies of NT (the 27 Books) actually in place due to all means as in column 19; including duplication (NTs in Bibles); column 21 = column 19 times 20.
22. *Promises met: NTs.* Extent to which the churches' promise of an NT for every literate adult Christian was met at each epoch or year, 100% being the stated goal, 200% the advisable goal. Computed as column 21 divided by column 16, times 100.

| Time | OUR GLOBE: The world's population, homes, adults %, literates %, Christians % and total (m = millions) | | | | | | | BIBLES NEEDED AND PROVIDED: Bibles needed | Bibles distributed p.a. | | | Bibles in place | | Promises met | NEW TESTAMENTS NEEDED AND PROVIDED: NTs needed | NTs distributed p.a. | | | NTs in place | | Promises met |
|---|---|---|---|---|---|---|---|---|---|---|---|---|---|---|---|---|---|---|---|---|---|
| Year 1 | Persons 2 | Homes 3 | % Lit 4 | % Chr 5 | Christians 6 | Chr Lit% 7 | Chr Ad% 8 | Literate Christian homes 9 | UBS 10 | % UBS 11 | All 12 | UBS 13 | All 14 | % met 15 | Literate adult Christians 16 | UBS 17 | % UBS 18 | All 19 | UBS 20 | All 21 | % met 22 |
| 400 | 189m | 38m | 10 | 13 | 25m | 13 | 70 | 0.7m | – | – | 0.04m | – | 0.8m | 121 | 2m | – | – | 0.2m | – | 5m | 209 |
| 1400 | 352m | 70m | 1 | 16 | 57m | 3 | 70 | 0.3m | – | – | 0.08m | – | 1.6m | 473 | 1m | – | – | 0.5m | – | 10m | 806 |
| 1500 | 423m | 85m | 2 | 18 | 76m | 4 | 70 | 0.6m | – | – | 0.2m | – | 4.0m | 654 | 2m | – | – | 0.8m | – | 16m | 750 |
| 1833 | 1,094m | 220m | 12 | 25 | 277m | 40 | 68 | 22.2m | 0.7m | 50 | 1.4m | 14m | 28m | 126 | 75m | 1.4m | 70 | 3.4m | 28m | 68m | 90 |
| 1900 | 1,620m | 300m | 28 | 34 | 558m | 60 | 71 | 61.8m | 3.0m | 56 | 5m | 60m | 108m | 175 | 239m | 4.4m | 60 | 13m | 88m | 254m | 106 |
| 1950 | 2,521m | 500m | 40 | 34 | 856m | 74 | 70 | 125.6m | 2.5m | 30 | 8m | 50m | 166m | 132 | 443m | 6.0m | 30 | 28m | 120m | 564m | 127 |
| 1960 | 3,022m | 600m | 45 | 34 | 1,029m | 76 | 70 | 155.2m | 3.0m | 30 | 10m | 60m | 200m | 129 | 547m | 8.0m | 30 | 37m | 160m | 733m | 134 |
| 1963 | 3,205m | 640m | 50 | 34 | 1,087m | 80 | 69 | 173.7m | 3.3m | 29 | 11m | 66m | 228m | 131 | 600m | 9.0m | 29 | 42m | 180m | 848m | 141 |
| 1964 | 3,270m | 650m | 55 | 34 | 1,107m | 80 | 69 | 176.1m | 3.5m | 28 | 13m | 70m | 250m | 142 | 611m | 10.0m | 28 | 48m | 200m | 964m | 158 |
| 1965 | 3,337m | 670m | 62 | 34 | 1,128m | 82 | 69 | 185.7m | 3.6m | 27 | 13m | 72m | 267m | 144 | 638m | 11.0m | 27 | 54m | 220m | 1,081m | 169 |
| 1966 | 3,406m | 680m | 63 | 34 | 1,149m | 82 | 68 | 188.1m | 3.8m | 26 | 15m | 76m | 292m | 155 | 640m | 12.0m | 26 | 61m | 240m | 1,215m | 190 |
| 1967 | 3,476m | 690m | 63 | 34 | 1,170m | 85 | 68 | 197.4m | 4.0m | 25 | 16m | 80m | 320m | 162 | 676m | 13.0m | 25 | 68m | 260m | 1,360m | 201 |
| 1970 | 3,696m | 740m | 64 | 33 | 1,236m | 88 | 67 | 217.5m | 5.1m | 23 | 22m | 102m | 443m | 204 | 726m | 14.0m | 23 | 83m | 280m | 1,661m | 229 |
| 1974 | 4,000m | 780m | 65 | 33 | 1,333m | 87 | 68 | 226.2m | 5.1m | 20 | 26m | 102m | 510m | 225 | 789m | 15.0m | 20 | 101m | 300m | 2,010m | 255 |
| 1975 | 4,075m | 815m | 65 | 33 | 1,359m | 87 | 68 | 236.4m | 5.5m | 20 | 28m | 110m | 550m | 233 | 804m | 16.0m | 20 | 108m | 320m | 2,150m | 267 |
| 1980 | 4,440m | 890m | 65 | 33 | 1,476m | 87 | 70 | 257.3m | 6.2m | 21 | 30m | 124m | 594m | 231 | 899m | 17.1m | 21 | 112m | 342m | 2,232m | 248 |
| 1984 | 4,755m | 960m | 65 | 33 | 1,578m | 87 | 70 | 277.3m | 9.7m | 22 | 44m | 194m | 880m | 317 | 961m | 20.0m | 22 | 135m | 400m | 2,694m | 280 |
| 1990 | 5,266m | 1,060m | 71 | 33 | 1,748m | 87 | 70 | 304.9m | 16.2m | 25 | 65m | 324m | 1,300m | 426 | 1,061m | 30.0m | 25 | 185m | 600m | 3,707m | 349 |
| 1991 | 5,349m | 1,075m | 72 | 33 | 1,773m | 87 | 71 | 310.0m | 18.3m | 26 | 70m | 366m | 1,408m | 454 | 1,095m | 31.8m | 26 | 193m | 636m | 3,854m | 352 |
| 1992 | 5,430m | 1,090m | 72 | 33 | 1,798m | 87 | 71 | 314.1m | 16.9m | 27 | 63m | 338m | 1,252m | 399 | 1,111m | 30.6m | 27 | 176m | 612m | 3,519m | 317 |
| 1995 | 5,666m | 1,251m | 77 | 33 | 1,877m | 87 | 71 | 317.6m | 18.9 | 35 | 54m | 356m | 1,220m | 372 | 1,154m | 31.0m | 35 | 142m | 620m | 2,836m | 246 |
| 1996 | 5,745m | 1,160m | 72 | 33 | 1,901m | 87 | 71 | 334.0m | 19.4m | 30 | 66m | 388m | 1,315m | 394 | 1,174m | 38.0m | 30 | 195m | 760m | 3,892m | 331 |
| 2000 | 6,055m | 1,211m | 77 | 33 | 2,000m | 87 | 72 | 347.5m | 21.0m | 30 | 70m | 420m | 1,400m | 403 | 1,253m | 40.0m | 30 | 203m | 800m | 4,067m | 325 |
| 2025 | 7,824m | 1,560m | 84 | 33 | 2,617m | 90 | 77 | 467.1m | 40.0m | 35 | 114m | 800m | 2,280m | 488 | 1,792m | 50.0m | 35 | 257m | 1,000m | 5,130m | 286 |

or 8-page illustrated leaflets or booklets, with a selection of from 10 to 100 scripture verses and passages on particular relevant topics in the different countries and languages. These proved to have the mass appeal and circulation being sought, reaching 171 million a year by 1971 and leveling off around 500 million a year from 1980 to 1997. The Bible societies therefore have not approached the more grandiose vision of a complete Bible for every home in the world and instead have settled for giving everyone in the world slightly more than what the Christians of AD 70 or AD 397 or AD 1450 or AD 1833 had, namely everyone on Earth owning a few sheets of paper with some 20 to 100 key verses of Holy Scripture. This can certainly be regarded as at least a personal copy for every one on Earth wanting to own one.

## *MEASURING ADEQUACY OF DENSITY*

### *Developing a precise methodology of monitoring*

Having presented this brief overall review of the difficulties of global distribution of the Scriptures, this survey will now examine in more depth the current situation beginning with the need for precise definitions. Then follow enumeration, analysis of all the major variables involved, and an investigation of the situation at global, continental, and national levels. Meanwhile, Table 19–2 above gives the overall global situation with regard to access to scriptures over the whole range of Christian history from AD 400 to AD 2025.

### *Overall goals*

This Part 19 is not attempting a comprehensive description of the entire Bible movement or the role of the Christian Scriptures throughout the centuries or throughout the world. Instead it is an attempt to examine, measure, and analyze the overall goals of the churches and Bible societies in this respect.

There is universal agreement that their overall task is to work for adequate global coverage and availability of the Scriptures for all peoples, all populations, and all individuals throughout the world. In measuring overall progress with this goal, a major result is that the remaining overall unfinished task of Scripture dissemination can then be clearly and unambiguously delineated.

### *Definitions of Scripture and scriptures*

An important detail of usage should be noted at this point. (a) *Scripture* (with a capital 'S') always here refers to the proper noun Scripture, or its variants Holy Scripture or the Scriptures, which means the Christian Scriptures, the Holy Bible, which is the Christian source book regarded as the Word of God. (b) By contrast, the term a *scripture* or *scriptures* (with lowercase 's') always here refers to mass-produced printed copies of the Scriptures, in whole or in part.

### *Six basic types of scriptures*

Agencies specializing in scripture dissemination keep regular statistics of 6 basic categories of scriptures, suitable for all audiences, represented here in the book's tables and databases by these 6 codes:

(1) B or BB = *Bibles,* meaning copies of the whole or complete Bible with its 66 constituent books, or 80 if the Apocrypha (the Deuterocanonical books) is included. Note: the double letter codes, BB etc, usually means 'distributed per year per 100 population'.

(2) N or NN = *New Testaments,* being copies of the New Testament with its 27 books.

(3) P or PP = *Portions,* which are usually gospels (copies of one of the four Gospels Matthew, Mark, Luke, or John), or copies of other whole books of the Bible.

These 3 products are the church's main priority for dissemination. From AD 33 to AD 1450 this involved copying by hand, a slow and laborious process. Suddenly after the invention of printing in 1450, this was revolutionized and mass printings of Portions, New

## Table 19–3. For 6 types of scripture product, adequacy levels for density in place or in use, and annual new distribution to maintain global adequacy.

The table sets out the minimum figures for scriptures in use, and scriptures newly distributed each year, in order to reach and maintain global adequacy. Actual current distribution by UBS and other sources relates to the period 1995–2000. It varies from oversaturation with some scriptures to falling far short of goals with others.

*Column*
1. *The 6 types of scripture product.* Note that a 'Visual gospel' means a presentation (showing), to one person, of the 3-hour 'Jesus' Film; and an 'Audio gospel' means a broadcast or other audio presentation of one hour of reading Scripture, usually from the Gospel story, this being heard by one listener or one listening family.
ADEQUATE SCRIPTURE DENSITY
2. *Average life of a copy,* or period of adequate coverage

by visual presentation (once every 20 years) or by audio (once every 5 years).
3. Definition of adequacy: *copies per family* (1 Bible for every family on Earth, 3 New Testaments, etc.).
4. Definition of adequacy: *copies per adult* (spouses plus 1 adult child or relative or servant).
5. Definition of adequacy: *copies per capita.*
ANNUAL NEW DISTRIBUTION NEEDED
6. *Minimum annual distribution as % for any type of population* in order to ensure and maintain adequate density in place or in use (for printed scriptures) or adequate hearings (for audio) or viewings (for visual presentations).
7. *Prudent annual distribution as % population.* This is twice column 6 in size, to counter poor or bad distribution due to waste, losses, floods, hostility, seizures, impoundings, failed schemes, multiple ownership of copies by individuals, and the

like. Having stated this caution, the recommended levels in columns 8 and 9 return to the minimal levels of columns 6.
8. *Recommended adequate levels for annual distribution, % population.* These are as stipulated in existing UBS distribution goals modified to this book's proposed new global distribution goals as detailed in this table.
ADEQUATE VERSUS CURRENT LEVELS
9. *Proposed* new adequate global distribution figures, copies per year (or hearings or viewings), as derived here.
10. *Current UBS annual distribution.* (excluding non-UBS scripture distributors, commercial publishers, et alia).
11. *Current global distribution from all sources, p.a.*

| | ADEQUATE DENSITY OF SCRIPTURES IN USE | | | | ANNUAL NEW DISTRIBUTION NEEDED | | | ADEQUATE VERSUS CURRENT LEVELS | | |
|---|---|---|---|---|---|---|---|---|---|---|
| Type | Life (years) | Per family | Per adult | Per capita | For any population | Prudent distribution | Recommended adequate levels | Adequate distribution p.a. | Current distribution p.a. UBS only | All sources |
| 1 | 2 | 3 | 4 | 5 | 6 | 7 | 8 | 9 | 10 | 11 |
| Bible | 20 | 1 | 0.3 | 0.2 | 1% | 2% | 1% of literate Christian population p.a. | 15 million | 21 million | 70 million |
| New Testament | 20 | 3 | 1 | 0.6 | 5% | 10% | 5% of literate adult Christians p.a. | 37 million | 13 million | 110 million |
| Portion/gospel | 10 | 3 | 1 | 0.6 | 10% | 20% | 10% of literate adults p.a. | 265 million | 48 million | 130 million |
| Selection | 2 | 1 | 0.3 | 0.2 | 20% | 40% | 20% of literate population p.a. | 166 million | 550 million | 1,700 million |
| Audio gospel | 5 | 1 | 0.3 | 0.2 | 20% | 40% | 20% of all nonliterates with radio access p.a. | 62 million | 10 million | 300 million |
| Visual gospel | 20 | 3 | 1 | 0.6 | 5% | 10% | 5% of all nonliterates with no radio access p.a. | 12 million | 1 million | 30 million |

Testaments, and Bibles began.

Three additional types of scriptures have recently become widespread:

(4) S or SS = *Selections,* which are 1-, 2-, 4-, or 8-page illustrated leaflets containing from 10 to 100 selected topical Bible verses or passages.

(5) au = *audio gospels* or other scriptures, which are either sound cassettes, tapes, disks, or CDs with recording of a Gospel or other whole book of the Bible, or broadcast (radio) events where Scripture is read out, often at dictation speed, as part of a serious ongoing program of dissemination.

(6) video or film versions that closely follow the biblical narrative and text. There are several outstanding examples of these, the most noteworthy being the 'Jesus' Film, a visual gospel which is a color presentation of the life of Christ as set forth in the Gospel according to Luke. This professional product is available in 700 languages, as a video or an 8mm or 16mm movie.

### Fifteen specialized types of scriptures
In addition to the 6 basic types of scriptures, the churches and Bible societies use and enumerate several other types, coded as follows:

(7) nrp = *New Reader Portions* (illustrated gospels suitable for new literates).
(8) nrs = *New Reader Selections* (always illustrated).
(9) br = *Braille scriptures* for the blind.
(10) hi = hearing impaired/deaf *signed scriptures* for the deaf.
(11) There are also *comic scriptures* (Bible stories presented in pictorial comic form), (12) *electronic scriptures* (computerized or CD-ROM versions), (13) *interactive scriptures,* (14) *children's versions,* (15) *large-print edition versions,* (16) *abridged or shortened versions,* (17) *study Bibles,* (18) *concordances* appended to Bibles, (19) *commentaries* with text of Bible books, and (20) several other types. In fact, every newly-developed medium results, almost as soon as introduced, in a new form of scriptures. Thus in 1996, (21) *whole Bibles* appeared *on the Internet* when the International Bible Society placed the entire Bible online in Arabic, Ukrainian, and 25 other languages.

### Three varieties of distribution
In many countries of the world there are 3 quite different ways in which scriptures are distributed:

1. *Commercial* distribution, in which copies are sold in bookshops by secular or religious publishers at commercially viable prices.
2. *Subsidized* distribution, which is the policy of Bible societies, churches and agencies, in which the larger scriptures (New Testaments, Bibles) are always sold but for a subsidized price somewhat similar to one day's wages for a working man or woman.
3. *Free* distribution, in which all varieties of scripture are systematically given away free of charge; this is the method followed by The Gideons and similar organizations.

### Four kinds of language
This analysis recognizes that scriptures may reach a specific people in 4 different kinds of language:

a. in the *mother-tongue* (here given the name autoglossonym, or autonym for short);

b. in a *near-language* or cluster language; where no mother-tongue scripture translation exists, a people may be reached via a translation in a nearby language within their language cluster (outer language) as defined here in Part 18 "Ethnolinguistics" or more fully in *WCE* Part 9 "LinguaMetrics";

c. in an *intercultural language,* often called a language of wider communication, or lingua franca, or trade language, or market language; and

d. in *any other second language* that the people happen to use or understand.

### Incompatibilities of terminology
Because language users have created different methodologies and different orthographies and different translations over the years, serious contradictions in nomenclature and incompatibilities of terminology are now used and are becoming found in different computer databases. This means it is often impossible to identify particular scriptural languages, termed here biblioglossonyms. Thus the language databases of the American Bible Society, United Bible Societies, and Wycliffe Bible Translators, contain numerous languages under differing names for those same languages, without clarification. Our World Language Classification (see Part 18, or *WCE* Part 9, or the fullest version in the 2-volume *The Linguasphere Register,* 2000) attempts to remove these incompatibilities, and the attendant confusion they spread, by means of a computerized catalog of all alternate names of every kind.

### Some analytical terms
A number of technical terms are utilized in this analysis, having the following specific meanings:
*Access* = the overall situation of how much access a people has to scriptures;
*Adequacy* = the degree to which the supply of scriptures meets the precise goal described above;
*Autoglossonym* (or, autonym) = the name a people uses for its mother tongue in its own idiom;
*Availability* = scriptures which are available in print for immediate use by interested persons;
*Biblioglossonym* = the official name given by scripture providers to a language for its scriptures;
*Circulation* = often used as a synonym for distribution;
*Density* = a precise measure of status after dissemination of scriptures per family, per adult, per capita, and per thousand persons (see Table 19–5);
*Dissemination* = the degree to which scriptures have been placed or exist or are in use in homes, offices, churches, schools, hotels, hospitals, throughout society;
*Distribution* = statistics of scriptures moved, sent,

shipped, delivered, sold, or otherwise circulated per year;
*Durability* = life of a scripture publication before it becomes useless due to wear and tear;
*Existence* = the existence of scripture translations in a people's languages, either mother tongue or lingua franca;
*Near-Bible* = a translation of the Bible in a language within one's own cluster (outer language);
*Near-scripture* = a scripture in a related language within one's own cluster;
*Near-translation* = availability of a translation of scripture in a language in one's own cluster;
*Placement* = the term used by The Gideons for the locating and counting of scriptures among recipients;
*Usage* = a synonym here for density.

In this analysis an attempt is made to define, describe, enumerate, and analyze the adequacy of a people's access to Scripture, leading to the following as its major single term:
*Adequate access* = existence of translation, together with availability of distribution. This results in the following major analysis.

### GLOBAL ADEQUACY OF ACCESS

The Christian starting-point on this subject is that every person on Earth has a basic inalienable human right to direct access to some form of scripture in a language he or she understands.

The overall goal in scripture distribution should therefore be to ensure that everyone has adequate access as defined by announced or agreed global goals. This Part 19 has set out an analysis of the subject that could result in firm and unambiguous methods for measuring whether a particular country, or people, or population of language speakers, or any other population are receiving adequate access.

### Background assumptions—a summary
This analysis has put forward the following 16 assumptions about the average situation at the global level.

1. *Adults* are defined as all persons ages 15 or older. All under 15 are children or infants.
2. *A family* on average consists of 5 persons: 2 spouses, another adult (15 or over), 2 children or infants (under 15).
3. *Literates* are adults (over 15) who can read and write. Children are never included in literacy surveys.
4. *A literate family* is a family of 3 literate adults plus their children and infants.
5. *The literate world* consists of all literate adults plus their children and infants.
6. *Nonliterates* are adults unable to read or write.
7. *A nonliterate family* is a family of nonliterate adults

plus their children and infants.
8. *The nonliterate world* consists of all nonliterate adults plus their children and infants.
9. *Varieties of scriptures* most distributed are fourfold: the whole or complete Bible (all 66 or 80 books), New Testament (27 Books), Portion (one whole Book, usually a Gospel), Selection (1- to 8-page leaflet or booklet of key Scripture verses).
10. *Distribution* is assumed to be fair, even, and to actually get past any opposition to those needing copies.
11. *Average life* of a scripture is governed by use, wear and tear, waste, climate, humidity, termites, and a host of other factors: thus on average a Bible lasts 20 years before needing to be replaced, a New Testament 20 years, a Portion/Gospel 10 years, a Selection 2 years.
12. *Primary adequacy* is the state where distribution of a scripture variety exactly matches the population figures related to its announced goal.
13. *Overall adequacy* of access for a population is the state where all 6 goals are met where relevant subpopulations exist.
14. *Multiple-copy users*, that is persons who each buy or obtain 2, 3, 4 or sometimes more copies of a type of scripture being distributed free or subsidized, even heavily subsidized, are not encouraged but must be reckoned with.
15. *Full or double adequacy*: to allow for unfair or uneven distribution, losses, waste, confiscations, multiple users, and so on, full adequacy is here defined as the range from primary adequacy up to twice that figure, defined here as *prudent distribution*. It may be seen simply as the annual distribution required to provide and maintain an adequate density in place or in use if the assumed life of all scriptures is reduced to exactly half of the years shown in Table 19–3, column 2. Full adequacy can usually be written: 200%.
16. *Superfluous distribution*. If the actual distribution for any variety of scripture is higher than twice the primary adequacy, best specified as 200%, this indicates that there exists a large amount of waste, duplication, or uneven or unnecessary or superfluous distribution of scriptures, or even that the Christian population is saturated or oversaturated with scriptures.

***Defining scripture access***

Basic data for the analysis of adequacy are given in Part 12 "CountryTrends", Table 12-1, columns 120-146. These enable readers to measure the ideal or optimum density of scriptures in place or in use, or of accumulated audiences together with the annual new distribution required to maintain those densities. Clearly, a number of assumptions must be made at various points in an analysis such as this. However, the practical implications for the churches and agencies are that, if they are to be true to their global task, the following totals must be met each year from all sources: 15 million Bibles, 37 million New Testaments, 265 million Portions/gospels, 166 million Selections; and in addition 62 million illiterates must hear an audio gospel by radio or television, and 12 million illiterates and their children without access to radio or TV must view a visual gospel. These goals are entirely possible, and in fact are already being exceeded at a number of points. The one remaining difficulty is fair distribution and deployment. At present, huge quantities of scriptures are piling up in World C, the Christian world, resulting in vast numbers of Christians owning multiple copies of subsidized scriptures. By contrast, 1.6 billion persons in World A, the unevangelized world, get no opportunities whatever to get hold of even one copy of scripture for each individual or even each family.

### *OVERALL SCRIPTURE ACCESS*

The investigation of this subject began earlier with an overall statement of adequate and inadequate access to scriptures as experienced by the world's populations. This was set out in Table 19–1. It is a shocking indictment of global Christianity that the world contains 2 billion persons who remain unaware of the existence of Christian scriptures in any shape or form.

The remainder of the tables in this Part 19 measure different aspects of this situation with increasing degrees of precision.

***Current existence of translations***

The first and most obvious absence of adequate access to Scripture concerns languages with no existing scripture translations in the mother tongue, nor any being planned. This situation is measured here by means of a 93-point scale showing for every language where it is located today in terms of access to translations (see Table 19–7). Data on the number of languages at each point on the scale are given partially in *WCE* Part 9 "LinguaMetrics", and full details and totals are given in the electronic *World Christian database AD 30-2200.*

***Current distribution and usage***

The major compilation of statistics of distribution and density in the present analysis, country by country, for all 7 continents, for Worlds A, B, and C, and for the whole globe, has been placed for convenience here in Part 12 "CountryTrends", Table 12-1, columns 120-146. That table gives up to 7 columns to each of the 4 main varieties of scriptures being distributed—Bibles, New Testaments, Portions/Gospels, and Selections. Each variety's current annual distribution in every country on Earth is then analyzed in accordance with the Hakone/UBS goals with slight modification to avoid ambiguities. The reader wishing to follow this analysis and conclusions step by step should photocopy those 6 pages from Table 12-1 (and also color photocopy Global Map 10 in Part 33 "GeoAtlas") and then read the following narrative explanations below.

### *1. BIBLE DISTRIBUTION GOALS*

This commentary begins with the 6 columns on this subject, columns 120-125, in Table 12-1.

***Column 120: Goal.*** The column operationalizes the goal of seeing a copy of the complete Bible in the hands of every literate Christian family in the country concerned. The computation is similar to that described at the beginning of Table 19–2 above. The column measures the number of Bibles needed in place within the country (the 'scripture density') needed to meet this goal. The total of families (or homes or households) assumes an average of 5 persons per home (2 spouses, 1 adult over 15, 2 children under 15). The number of literate Christian homes or families can therefore be estimated from each country's population divided by 5, times literacy percent divided by 100, times Christian percent divided by 100.

***Column 121: Goal per year.*** To maintain this goal an annual distribution must be set up and maintained, equal to column 120 divided by 20 (the average life of a Bible copy in years).

***Column 122: UBS p.a.*** This is the published annual total distribution.

***Column 123: other p.a.*** Similar distribution by all non-UBS entities (including commercial publishers) are now added. In many countries this number is far greater than the UBS total. In such a case the Bible agency in that country might well be encouraged to save its limited resources for other varieties of distribution.

***Column 124: total p.a.*** This is the total of columns 122 and 123.

***Column 125: T/G % (total p.a. divided by Goal p.a., which is column 124 divided by column 121 times 100).***

This last column is the crucial one for assessing the achievement or failure of any country with regard to reaching the Hakone goals. The figure '100%' in this column means that the country itself has exactly achieved the goal. '50%' means it has only got half way there. '300%' means that distribution is 3 times larger than the goal.

Interpretation of these results is straightforward.'100%' exactly fulfils the stated goal, although complete and perfect distribution across the whole population has to be assumed. If we need to take into account unequal or unbalanced distribution, it might be better to state that the goal has been reached when its achieved figure is twice the perfect percentage, namely '200%'. But vastly higher figures like '454%' for Brazil or '5434%' for Pakistan or '949%' for Singapore immediately raise the question as to why in those countries the Bible societies are distributing vastly more Bibles than the stated goals require. There are always good explanations, and probably also good reasons, why certain countries have these figures so high. But it does immediately pose the major strategic question 'Why then have any goals at all?' if they can thus be far surpassed, because they can only be surpassed at the expense of other goals for other types of scripture, especially when one realizes that Bible societies produce and print expensive scripture materials at heavily subsidized cost.

***Disparity between countries.*** This final column 125 also immediately raises the question of whether Bible distribution in any country should operate solely for the good of its own population or whether all countries should help each other. Examination of column 125 shows that this first Hakone goal is not being met by 53 countries (their percentages being less than 100%) but that the remaining 170 countries are distributing far more than the goal requires (more than 100%). The global situation is clearly depicted here in the color Global Map 10. This would be an ideal situation for central strategic leadership to work out guidelines for harnessing UBS resources cost-effectively.

### *2. NEW TESTAMENT DISTRIBUTION*

The NT analysis is similar to that for the complete Bible, with the exception of a new category termed 'duplicates'. This refers to the obvious fact that when counting the number of New Testaments distributed in a country one must add the UBS total for NTs, secondly the NT totals of all other Bible agencies, and then also the number of complete Bibles already being distributed, all of which, of course, contain the New Testament itself.

The final column 132 measures the total NT distribution divided by the goal. A similar analysis to that for the complete Bible can easily be done by examining column 132. The results indicate 75 countries which fall short of the Hakone goal (under 100%), and 163 which have surpassed the goal. Seven countries have even surpassed the goal by over 1,000%. Again, the color Global Map 10 shows the situation at a glance.

There is a vast field for honest examination and analysis here because it is extremely difficult to guess at how particular countries vary. Who would have guessed, for example, that the original founding country in 1804 of the whole Bible society movement, Britain, is today failing to reach the Hakone goal for New Testaments (88%); or that the country producing the first organized Bible society in 1710, Germany, would be failing to reach the 2 Hakone goals (the Bible 98%, NT 58%); while at the same time impoverished countries like Bangladesh would have exceeded both goals (123% and 199%)? The world record for exceeding a goal goes to another low-income country, to Pakistan, whose Bible distribution holds the global record of 5,434% or 54 times the Hakone goal. In other words, all countries and all Bible agencies could easily fulfill these goals if all were encouraged to take the following three steps.

(1) Take seriously goal achievement and monitor one's countries' progress scientifically;

(2) Aim to exceed the 4 goals by a further 100% to reach 200% to allow for uneven distribution;

(3) Refuse to allow the overkill of any goal exceeding 300%, at which point determined efforts should be made to use the surplus resources for goal-reaching in any other countries reaching less than 100%.

### *3. PORTIONS AND 4. SELECTIONS*

An identical set of procedures will result in similar analyses for Portion (Gospel) distribution (Table 12-1, columns 133-139), and Selection distribution (columns 140-146).

The same Table 12-1 also describes the current situation in the worlds' 7 continents, the 3 missiological Worlds A, B, and C; and also, on a final line, a summary of the global situation. These will now be briefly commented on.

Again, Global Map 10 illustrates the situation at a glance.

## ACHIEVING GOALS BY CONTINENT AND WORLD

Successes and failures to reach the Hakone goals are surprisingly evenly divided across the world. The reader should examine the continental, Worlds A/B/C, and global lines for all 4 varieties of scripture distribution at the end of Table 12-1's columns 120-146, and attempt his or her own interpretations of what, where, and why these figures are being generated.

Here is a brief summary of achievements.

a. *Global*. At the global level, all 4 Hakone goals are being surpassed, and surpassed not only at the 100% level but also at the 200% level that we are suggesting allows for uneven deployment of scripture distribution (Bibles 250%, New Testaments 216%, Portions/Gospels 209%, Selections 7,650%).

b. *Worlds A, B, C*. Almost all varieties show high achievement over 200%. The only total under 100% is of Portions/Gospels in World A with 24%, due to its huge number of unevangelized non-Christians entitled to get a gospel each under Hakone goal 3.

c. *Continents*. Again, of the 28 totals only 3 are under 100%.

d. *Countries*. With 238 countries the situation now becomes extremely complex. The visual presentation in color in Global Map 10 in Part 33 "GeoAtlas" can help rapid scanning of countries. A few interpretations for certain countries (Britain, Germany, Bangladesh, Pakistan) have been made above. Many more are now possible.

e. *Peoples and languages*. This whole analysis could continue down to the level of every ethnolinguistic people, and every language. The major obstacle at present is that, surprisingly, Bible agencies do not collect annual data by those categories. It would be a major step forward if annual totals were always available broken down by language.

### Defining 7 adequacy levels

This whole subject of measuring adequacy can be investigated in a number of other ways. These can only be briefly sketched here. These provide alternative approaches to all-important questions that all persons concerned to get the Scriptures to the world must face.

### Assessing immediate needs

The first approach is via Table 19–4, which asks and answers 7 questions such as: 'How many persons today need or should each immediately get a gospel?' Clearly, the answer depends on the reader's definition of what goal has been set. In this case, the goal is stated as 'One gospel for every person over 5 on Earth, every 10 years'. In the table's Subtable 4 this question is then answered with 98 distinct statistics. Table 19–4's 6 other subtables add a further 364 numerical answers.

### Distributing 6 scripture products

Table 19–5 presents a more theoretical or general approach in detail. It operates through 4 sets of statistics: (1) distribution figures per year as percent of population, (2) density of copies per family, (3) density per adult, and (4) density per capita. Through a step-by-step methodology the table sets out a 7-fold scale of adequacy for the 6 main categories of scriptures and for the 3 kinds of users—families, adults, and individuals.

### Analysis by age, literacy, religion

Table 19–6 is a further approach, which operates separately through, firstly, the basic audience categories of adults, children, and families; secondly, analyzing them further into the 4 worlds of literates, nonliterates, radio nonliterates, and no-radio nonliterates; and thirdly introducing the distinction of being Christians or non-Christians.

### Translations by language

A completely different subject may be investigated beginning with Global Diagram 26, which summarizes the World Language Classification set forth in *WCE* Part 9 "LinguaMetrics". On the diagram will be seen a subtable at the left which gives, for the varieties of speech forms there enumerated, the numbers able to access Bibles, New Testaments, and Portions/Gospels.

### Stategizing translation

The last subject considered in this short survey is a subject separate from scripture distribution—scripture translation, which means producing the text of Scripture in a new language. Table 19–7 sets out the global situation with reference to the world's 13,500 distinct and different languages. It offers a scale of 93 levels of attainment and states where every language is on that scale.

The scale represents a gradual chronological sequence of steps or stages from 0 = no translation in this language or its cluster or its net, right through to 92 = whole Bible available on the Internet with a full range of electronic or web services. Each higher step is an advance on the previous step, in most cases, although a language can bypass a stage or leapfrog over several stages. Also, certain stages, e.g. scriptures in Braille for the blind, may not happen, or always happen, at the designated point.

Although every language's experience is unique and cannot be stereotyped, the cumulative total of how many languages have reached any and every point on the scale does give a realistic impression of how much has been accomplished in Bible translation. It also reminds Christians of how much remains to be done in the still unfinished task of offering the full benefits of Holy Scripture to the globe's populations in the entirety of their linguistic complexity.

---

### BIBLIOGRAPHY—a brief selection

*All about Bibles*. J. R. Ohlenburger. New York: Oxford University Press, 1985. 75p.
*Audio Scriptures handbook*. V. B. Søgaard. Reading, U.K.: United Bible Societies, 1991.
*Bibles across the world*. N. B. Cryer. London: Mowbrays, 1979. 257p.
*Books and readers in the early church: a history of early Christian texts*. H. Y. Gamble. New Haven, CT: Yale University Press, 1995. 349p.
*Catalogue of English Bible translations: a classified bibliography of versions and editions including books, parts, and Old and New Testament Apocrypha and Apocryphal books*. W. J. Chamberlin. *Bibliographies and indexes in religious studies*, 21. New York: Greenwood, 1991. 946p. (The best and most complete for its listing of English Bible translations, 9,000 titles and editions).
*Cheap Bibles: nineteenth–century publishing and the British and Foreign Bible Society*. L. Howsam. Cambridge and New York: Cambridge University Press, 1991.
*Heresy and literacy, 1000–1530*. P. Biller & A. Hudson (eds).

*Cambridge studies in medieval literature*, 23. Cambridge: Cambridge University Press, 1994. 339p.
*Illustrated history of the Bible*. Porter. New York: Oxford University Press.
*Literacy, Bible reading, and church growth through the ages*. M. Watkins. Pasadena, CA: William Carey Library, 1978. 238p.
*Pass the Word: fifty years of Wycliffe Bible Translators*. H. Steven (ed). Huntington Beach, CA: Wycliffe Bible Translators, 1984. 148p.
*Religion and the people, 800–1700*. J. Obelkevich (ed). Chapel Hill: University of North Carolina Press, 1979. 342p.
*Scriptures of the world: a compilation of the 2,018 languages in which at least one book of the Bible has been published since the Bible was first printed by Johann Gutenberg*. L. Lupas & E. F. Rhodes (eds). New York and Reading, UK: United Bible Societies, 1992. 145p. (A series every 2 years since 1960).
*Spreading the Word: the Bible business in nineteenth–century America*. P. J. Wosh. Ithaca, NY and London: Cornell University Press, 1994. 285p.
*Taking the Word to the world: 50 years of the United Bible Societies*. E. H. Robertson. Nashville, TN: Thomas Nelson, 1996. 350p.
*The Bible and Bibles in America*. E. S. Frerichs. Atlanta: Scholars Press, 1988. 232p.
*The book of a thousand tongues*. E. A. Nida (ed). 2nd ed. London: United Bible Societies, 1972. 536p. (Catalogue of 1,399 languages with printed scriptures, giving a scripture passage for each).
*The Cambridge history of the Bible*. P. R. Ackroyd and C. F. Evans (vol. 1), G. W. Lampe (vol. 2), S. L. Greenslade (vol. 3) (eds). Cambridge, UK: Cambridge University Press, 1963–70. 3 vols.
*The literacy of the laity in the Middle Ages*. J. W. Thompson. *Burt Franklin research & source works series*, 2. New York: Burt Franklin, 1960.
'The Scriptures in the Christian world mission: three historical considerations,' W. R. Hogg, *Missiology*, 12, 4 (October 1984), 389–404.
*World translations progress report 1996*. New York and Reading, UK: United Bible Societies, 1996. 128p.
*World translations progress report supplement 1996*. New York and Reading, UK: United Bible Societies, 1996. 124p.

## Table 19–4. Assessing immediate needs for scripture distribution in any or all countries, peoples, or languages on Earth, with goals for AD 2000-AD 2025.

This table describes a method for estimating how many copies of 6 main varieties of scriptures are needed immediately today, or at the very least each year over the next 25 years. It enlarges long-term Christian goals beyond the Hakone goals to the supplying of scriptures not primarily to Christians and their families but to the whole global population in its entirety.

Below are 8 subtables, the first 7 being sequences of related figures answering 7 different questions in each's title by means of one sequence of connected rows per table; and one final overall summary table which is not a sequence but a series of single-line standalone statements combining the 7 previous tables. The overall theme is: *How many copies or numbers of 6 varieties of scriptures, in any language or country, or in the whole world, do the churches need to print and distribute each year?* Each question is answered in a number of different ways, one per line or row, from the standpoint of 52 or so different criteria from among which readers may select definitions they consider the most significant. (See explanations of all criteria at bottom of previous tables). The figures given here below refer to the whole world.

Overall, two distinct and different answers are given here. First, in column 6 are given in bold type the totals of persons of all religions or none (and in column 7 those of them who are Christians) who need to be served and immediately supplied with scriptures *today* (in the next 12 months) if the churches' obligations and promises are to be completely fulfilled at one stroke. In assessing need, it is irrelevant whether or not the churches' cumbersome logistical operations permit it. Starving millions need food immediately; spread over 20 years would be too late.

Second, though, and perhaps more realistically, columns 8-11 give the required annual distribution figures if this task were to be spread over the next 25 years. This would permanently correct the problem, though at the expense of today's scripture-less millions.

Note 2 important features of these tables. First, every category in columns 5 and 6 of Subtables 2 through 7 embodies the criteria of all the other previous categories above it in the subtable. Thus in the row 2-l with criterion "AFFORDABILITY-Bible", persons "Able to pay for a Bible" is referring not to the entire world population but to literate family heads without a Bible or near-Bible but keen to get one. Second, in Subtables 2 through 7, every row is derived logically from the row immediately above it. Thus every figure in column 6 in every row is derived by subtracting its "EXCLUSIONS" figure in column 4 from the previous row's column 6. In other words, each of the Subtables 2 through 7 starts with the entire population of the world in column 6, then item by item removes or excludes populations regarded as non-priority on its stated criterion, which includes all previous criteria.

*Meaning of columns.* These have identical meanings for all 8 subtables, as follows.

1. Reference letter. In Subtable 8, this becomes a numbered sequence with fuller explanations on the previous page.

2. CRITERION. Standpoint, point of departure, or situation from which the question is answered on its line. On each line, the previous line's column 6 is divided into two (its columns 4 and 6).

3–4. EXCLUSIONS. The method here is first to exclude that population which, on each criterion, is not its priority concern. For example, if under "BIBLE USE" we want to find out how many families need a Bible, we must first exclude all families which already possess a Bible. *Column 3* describes the category; *column 4* enumerates it.

5–7. **IMMEDIATE TARGET AUDIENCE**. These are the major columns in the table. ***Column 5*** specifies the exact population being aimed at as priority market. ***Column 6*** (in bold type) enumerates this, giving the number of new scriptures immediately needing to be printed and distributed to each category today, within the next 12 months, if the churches are to meet their stated goals. ***Column 7*** specifies how many of these are Christians (individuals or families), this thereby giving an intermediate first step essential to the whole ongoing process.

8–11. LONG TERM DISTRIBUTION. These columns derive the annual distribution needed in order to reach all the stated goals in 25 years' time, by AD 2025. If instead of immediate provision of need, as shown in column 6, we allow 25 years until AD 2025 to reach that goal, 3 annual components are needed. ***Column 8*** divides column 6 by 25 to spread the bulk of the load year by year over 25 years. It includes or covers annual replacement needs as users' copies wear out or get lost. ***Column 9*** adds an item covering waste in the distribution process, made up of 3 components: (a) wasted, lost, destroyed, spoiled, or undelivered copies which never get into the hands of users, (b) unwise distribution in which saturated populations receive vast new printings whilst unreached peoples get nothing, and (c) multiple purchases in which many individuals own multiple copies thereby depriving millions of potential users who then get none. These 3 components of waste are estimated at 10% p.a. of column 8's figures. ***Column 10*** allows for new annual growth in column 6's figures, estimating this at 2% p.a. of column 6 due largely to demographic increase. For example, the number of families in the world is increasing at present by 24 million new families a year. Adding columns 8,9, and 10 gives a final total in ***column 11.*** This is then the total distribution per year needed in order to reach all goals by AD 2025.

| CRITERION<br>Column 1 | 2 | EXCLUSIONS (i.e. persons regarded as non-priority, on the stated criterion in column 2)<br>Category 3 | Persons 4 | **IMMEDIATE TARGET AUDIENCE OR PRIORITY MARKET** Scriptures needed in place to complete all goals now<br>Category 5 | **Persons** 6 | Christians 7 | Annual new distribution needed to complete all goals by AD 2025<br>Bulk 8 | Waste 9 | Growth 10 | ***Total*** 11 |
|---|---|---|---|---|---|---|---|---|---|---|
| Subtable 1. **How many persons today have either access to scripture, or no access to any variety?** (Goal: access for all 6,100 million persons on Earth). | | | | | | | | | | |
| a. | ACCESS | All with some access to scripture | 5,800 million | All with no access to scripture | **300 million** | | | | | |
| Subtable 2. **How many families today need immediate access to a complete Bible?** (Goal: one Bible in every family/ household on Earth, with 20-year book life). | | | | | | | | | | |
| a. | HUMANITY | Nobody | 0 | Every person on Earth | **6,100 million** | 2,000 m | 290 m | 29 m | 116 m | **435 m** |
| b. | MATURITY | Children (under 15s) | 1,950 million | Adults (over 15s) | **4,150 million** | 1,330 m | 198 m | 20 m | 79 m | **297 m** |
| c. | FAMILIES | Adult family dependents | 1,400 million | Family heads and spouses | **2,750 million** | 890 m | 133 m | 13 m | 53 m | **199 m** |
| d. | HOUSEHOLDS | Spouses | 1,450 million | Household heads (=families) | **1,300 million** | 440 m | 65 m | 6 m | 26 m | **97 m** |
| e. | LITERACY | Nonliterate family heads | 450 million | Literate family heads | **850 million** | 400 m | 43 m | 4 m | 17 m | **64 m** |
| f. | OWN-BIBLE USE | Current own-Bible-using families | 350 million | Literate heads without own-Bible | **500 million** | 260 m | 25 m | 2 m | 10 m | **37 m** |
| g. | NEAR-BIBLE USE | Near-Bible owner families | 50 million | Without own-Bible or near-Bible | **450 million** | 220 m | 23 m | 2 m | 9 m | **34 m** |
| h. | WIDER-BIBLE USE | Wider-Bible owner families | 100 million | Without own/near/wider Bible | **350 million** | 190 m | 18 m | 2 m | 7 m | **27 m** |
| i. | PAST OWNERSHIP | Former Bible-owner families | 30 million | Never had a Bible | **320 million** | 160 m | 16 m | 2 m | 6 m | **24 m** |
| j. | SHAREABILITY | Families able to share a Bible | 10 million | Unable to share a Bible | **310 million** | 140 m | 15 m | 2 m | 6 m | **23 m** |
| k. | DEMAND-Bible | Families uninterested or hostile | 60 million | Keen to get a Bible | **250 million** | 100 m | 13 m | 1 m | 5 m | **19 m** |
| l. | AFFORDABILITY-Bible | Unable to pay for a Bible | 100 million | Able to pay for a Bible | **150 million** | 50 m | 8 m | 1 m | 3 m | **12 m** |
| m. | AVAILABILITY-Bible | Nonbuyers though Bibles in stock | 50 million | Out of stock, worth restocking | **100 million** | 30 m | 5 m | 1 m | 2 m | **8 m** |
| n. | SATISFACTION-Bible | Dissatisfied with existing versions | 50 million | Out of print, worth reprinting | **50 million** | 20 m | 3 m | 0 m | 1 m | **4 m** |
| o. | TRANSLATION-Bible | Translation in progress | 50 million | No translation yet made | **0 million** | 0 m | 0 m | 0 m | 0 m | **0 m** |
| Subtable 3. **How many persons today need or should each immediately get his or her own NT?** (Goal: one NT for every adult on Earth, with 20-year book life). | | | | | | | | | | |
| a. | HUMANITY | Nobody | 0 | Every person on Earth | **6,100 million** | 2,000 m | 290 m | 29 m | 116 m | **435 m** |
| b. | MATURITY | Children (under 15s) | 1,950 million | Adults (over 15s) | **4,150 million** | 1,330 m | 198 m | 20 m | 79 m | **297 m** |
| c. | LITERACY | Nonliterates (over 15s) | 1,300 million | Literates (over 15s) | **2,850 million** | 1,000 m | 122 m | 12 m | 49 m | **183 m** |
| d. | BIBLE USE | Current Bible-users | 1,200 million | Literates without a Bible | **1,650 million** | 500 m | 67 m | 7 m | 27 m | **101 m** |
| e. | OWN-NT USE | Current own-NT-users without Bible | 1,000 million | Literates without own-NT or Bible | **650 million** | 200 m | 23 m | 2 m | 9 m | **34 m** |
| f. | NEAR-NT USE | Near-NT-owners | 110 million | Without own-NT, near-NT, or Bible | **540 million** | 190 m | 22 m | 2 m | 9 m | **33 m** |
| g. | WIDER-NT USE | Wider-NT-owners | 200 million | Without own/near/wider NT | **340 million** | 170 m | 17 m | 2 m | 7 m | **26 m** |
| h. | PAST OWNERSHIP | Former NT-owners | 20 million | Never had any NT or Bible | **320 million** | 160 m | 16 m | 2 m | 6 m | **24 m** |
| i. | DEMAND-NT | Uninterested or hostile | 100 million | Keen to get an NT | **220 million** | 110 m | 11 m | 1 m | 4 m | **16 m** |
| j. | AFFORDABILITY-NT | Unable to pay for a copy | 60 million | Able to pay for an NT | **160 million** | 80 m | 8 m | 1 m | 3 m | **12 m** |
| k. | AVAILABILITY-NT | Nonbuyers though NT in stock | 50 million | Out of stock, worth restocking | **110 million** | 50 m | 6 m | 1 m | 2 m | **9 m** |
| l. | SATISFACTION-NT | Dissatisfied with existing versions | 30 million | Out of print, worth reprinting | **80 million** | 30 m | 4 m | 0 m | 2 m | **6 m** |
| m. | TRANSLATION-NT | Translation in progress | 80 million | No translation yet made | **0 million** | 0 m | 0 m | 0 m | 0 m | **0 m** |
| Subtable 4. **How many persons today need or should each immediately get a gospel?** (Goal: one gospel for every person over 5 on Earth, every 10 years). | | | | | | | | | | |
| a. | HUMANITY | Nobody | 0 | Every person on Earth | **6,100 million** | 2,000 m | 580 m | 58 m | 116 m | **754 m** |
| b. | INFANCY | Infants (under 5s) | 700 million | Adults and children over 5 | **5,400 million** | 1,700 m | 514 m | 51 m | 103 m | **668 m** |
| c. | BIBLE USE | Current Bible-users | 1,200 million | Persons without a Bible | **4,200 million** | 1,300 m | 404 m | 40 m | 81 m | **525 m** |
| d. | NT USE | Current NT-users (including Bibles) | 2,000 million | Persons without Bible or NT | **2.200 million** | 700 m | 204 m | 20 m | 41 m | **265 m** |
| e. | OWN-GOSPEL USE | Own-gospel-owners without B or NT | 390 million | Persons over 5 without own-gospel | **1,810 million** | 600 m | 165 m | 17 m | 33 m | **215 m** |
| f. | NEAR-GOSPEL USE | Near-gospel owners | 400 million | Without own- or near-gospel | **1,410 million** | 450 m | 125 m | 13 m | 25 m | **163 m** |
| g. | WIDER-GOSPEL USE | Wider-gospel owners | 150 million | Without own/near/wider gospel | **1,260 million** | 420 m | 110 m | 11 m | 22 m | **143 m** |
| h. | PAST OWNERSHIP | Former gospel-owners | 160 million | Never had a gospel | **1,100 million** | 400 m | 100 m | 10 m | 20 m | **130 m** |
| i. | NEW READERSHIP-NRP | New Reader Portion literates | 280 million | Never heard of NRP program | **820 million** | 300 m | 82 m | 8 m | 16 m | **106 m** |
| j. | DEMAND-gospel | Uninterested or hostile | 500 million | Keen to get a gospel | **320 million** | 100 m | 32 m | 3 m | 6 m | **41 m** |
| k. | AFFORDABILITY-gospel | Unable to pay for a gospel | 100 million | Able to pay for a gospel | **220 million** | 70 m | 22 m | 2 m | 4 m | **28 m** |
| l. | AVAILABILITY-gospel | Nonbuyers though gospels in stock | 50 million | Out of stock, worth restocking | **170 million** | 60 m | 17 m | 2 m | 3 m | **22 m** |
| m. | SATISFACTION-gospel | Dissatisfied with existing versions | 100 million | Out of print, worth reprinting | **70 million** | 30 m | 7 m | 1 m | 1 m | **9 m** |
| n. | TRANSLATION-gospel | Translation in progress | 70 million | No translation yet made | **0 million** | 0 m | 0 m | 0 m | 0 m | **0 m** |
| Subtable 5. **How many persons today need immediate access to a selection?** (Goal: one selection for every family or household on Earth, every 2 years). | | | | | | | | | | |
| a. | HUMANITY | Nobody | 0 | Every person on Earth | **6,100 million** | 2,000 m | 2,900 m | 290 m | 116 m | **3,306 m** |
| b. | HOUSEHOLDS | Spouses, children, adult dependents | 4,800 million | Household heads (=families) | **1,300 million** | 400 m | 600 m | 60 m | 24 m | **684 m** |
| c. | OWN-SELECTIONS | Families who have own-selections | 640 million | Families not getting own-selections | **660 million** | 220 m | 330 m | 33 m | 13 m | **376 m** |
| d. | NEAR-SELECTIONS | Families with near-selections | 200 million | Without own- or near-selections | **460 million** | 150 m | 230 m | 23 m | 9 m | **262 m** |
| e. | WIDER-SELECTIONS | Families with wider-selections | 300 million | Without own/near/wider selections | **160 million** | 50 m | 80 m | 8 m | 3 m | **91 m** |
| f. | NEW READERSHIP-NRS | New Reader Selection families | 97 million | Never heard of NRS program | **63 million** | 20 m | 32 m | 3 m | 1 m | **36 m** |
| g. | DEMAND-selection | Families uninterested or hostile | 20 million | Keen to get a selection | **43 million** | 15 m | 22 m | 2 m | 1 m | **25 m** |
| h. | SATISFACTION-selection | Dissatisfied with existing versions | 33 million | Out of print, worth reprinting | **10 million** | 5 m | 5 m | 1 m | 0 m | **6 m** |
| i. | TRANSLATION-selection | Translation in progress | 10 million | No translation yet made | **0 million** | 0 m | 0 m | 0 m | 0 m | **0 m** |

*Continued opposite*

*Table 19–4 concluded*

| CRITERION<br>*Col* 1 2 | EXCLUSIONS (i.e. persons regarded as non-priority, on the stated criterion in column 2)<br>*Category* 3 | *Persons* 4 | IMMEDIATE TARGET AUDIENCE OR PRIORITY MARKET<br>New scriptures needed to complete all goals now<br>*Category* 5 | ***Persons*** 6 | *Christians* 7 | Annual new distribution needed to complete all goals by AD 2025<br>*Bulk* 8 | *Waste* 9 | *Growth* 10 | ***Total*** 11 |
|---|---|---|---|---|---|---|---|---|---|
| Subtable 6. **How many persons today need to be immediately shown the 'Jesus' Film?** (Goal: every adult or child on Earth to view it once, every 20 years). | | | | | | | | | |
| a. HUMANITY | Nobody | 0 | Every person on Earth | **6,100 million** | 2,000 m | 290 m | 29 m | 116 m | **435 m** |
| b. CHILDHOOD | Children under 12 | 1,410 million | Adults and children over 12 | **4,690 million** | 1,390 m | 220 m | 22 m | 88 m | **330 m** |
| c. VISUALS | 'Jesus' Film past viewers (over 12s) | 1,100 million | 'Jesus' Film nonviewers over 12 | **3,590 million** | 1,200 m | 180 m | 18 m | 72 m | **270 m** |
| d. GOSPEL USE | Gospel-owners (P, N, or B) | 2,300 million | Nonviewers, no scripture access | **1,290 million** | 430 m | 65 m | 7 m | 26 m | **98 m** |
| e. DEMAND-film | Uninterested or hostile | 500 million | Keen to see film | **790 million** | 260 m | 40 m | 4 m | 16 m | **60 m** |
| f. PLANNING-film | Showings planned and underway | 300 million | No showings planned, but possible | **490 million** | 160 m | 25 m | 3 m | 10 m | **37 m** |
| g. TRANSLATION-film | Translation in progress or envisaged | 490 million | No translation made or planned | **0 million** | 0 m | 0 m | 0 m | 0 m | **0 m** |
| Subtable 7. **How many persons today need immediate access to scripture-based audio or radio/TV broadcasts?** (Goal: access for all over 5s by 2025.) | | | | | | | | | |
| a. HUMANITY | Nobody | 0 | Every person on Earth | **6,100 million** | 2,000 m | 290 m | 29 m | 116 m | **435 m** |
| b. INFANCY | Infants (under 5s) | 700 million | Adults and children over 5 | **5,400 million** | 1,700 m | 257 m | 26 m | 103 m | **386 m** |
| c. BROADCASTING | No broadcasting in own languages | 710 million | Broadcasting in own languages | **4,690 million** | 1,400 m | 222 m | 22 m | 89 m | **333 m** |
| d. RADIO/TV SETS | All without radio/TV sets or access | 3,500 million | Adults with radio/TV sets or access | **1,190 million** | 310 m | 47 m | 5 m | 19 m | **71 m** |
| e. ACCESS | Radio and print scripture access | 450 million | Radios but no print scripture access | **740 million** | 160 m | 24 m | 2 m | 10 m | **36 m** |
| f. DEMAND-radio/TV | Uninterested or hostile | 560 million | Keen to listen or view | **180 million** | 60 m | 9 m | 1 m | 4 m | **14 m** |
| g. PLANNING-radio/TV | Programs planned or underway | 180 million | Nothing planned or envisaged | **0 million** | 0 m | 0 m | 0 m | 0 m | **0 m** |
| Subtable 8. **Summary of all global populations with and without scripture access.** (This is not a sequence, but single-line standalone statements.) | | | | | | | | | |
| 1. HUMANITY | Nobody | 0 | Every person on Earth | **6,100 million** | | | | | |
| 2. INFANCY | Infants (under 5s) | 700 million | Adults and children over 5 | **5,400 million** | | | | | |
| 3. CHILDHOOD | Children under 12 | 1,410 million | Adults and children over 12 | **4,690 million** | | | | | |
| 4. MATURITY | Children (under 15s) | 1,950 million | Adults (over 15s) | **4,150 million** | | | | | |
| 5. FAMILIES | Adult family dependents | 1,400 million | Family heads and spouses | **2,750 million** | | | | | |
| 6. HOUSEHOLDS | Spouses | 1,450 million | Household heads (=families) | **1,300 million** | | | | | |
| 7. YOUTH | Older adults (over 24s) | 2,869 million | Youths (ages 15-24) | **1,055 million** | | | | | |
| 8. ACCESS | All with some access to scripture | 5,800 million | All with no access to scripture | **300 million** | | | | | |
| 9. BROADCASTING | No broadcasting in own languages | 710 million | Broadcasting in own languages | **4,690 million** | | | | | |
| 10. RADIO/TV SETS | All without radio/TV sets or access | 3,500 million | All with radio/TV sets or access | **2,600 million** | | | | | |
| 11. PLANNING-radio/TV | Programs planned or underway | 180 million | Nothing planned or envisaged | **0 million** | | | | | |
| 12. VISUALS | 'Jesus' Film viewers (over 12s) | 1,100 million | 'Jesus' Film nonviewers | **5,000 million** | | | | | |
| 13. PLANNING-film | Showings planned and underway | 300 million | No showings planned but possible | **490 million** | | | | | |
| 14. SELECTIONS | Selections received by families | 1,040 million | Families not getting selections | **660 million** | | | | | |
| 15. GOSPEL USE | Gospel-owners (P, N, or B) | 2,300 million | Persons over 5 without a gospel | **1,810 million** | | | | | |
| 16. NEAR-GOSPEL USE | Near-gospel owners | 400 million | Without a gospel or near-gospel | **1,410 million** | | | | | |
| 17. PAST OWNERSHIP | Former gospel-owners | 160 million | Never had a gospel | **1,100 million** | | | | | |
| 18. LITERACY | Nonliterates (over 15s) | 1,300 million | Literates (over 15s) | **2,850 million** | | | | | |
| 19. YOUTH LITERACY | Literates over 24 years | 2,250 million | Literate youths (15-24) | **850 million** | | | | | |
| 20. DEPENDENCY | Literate dependents | 1,600 million | Literate family heads | **650 million** | | | | | |
| 21. NEW READERSHIP-NRS | New Reader Selection families | 97 million | New literates without NRS | **60 million** | | | | | |
| 22. NEW READERSHIP-NRP | New Reader Portion literates | 280 million | New literates without NRP | **40 million** | | | | | |
| 23. NT USE | Current NT-users (N or B) | 2,200 million | Literates without an NT | **650 million** | | | | | |
| 24. NEAR-NT USE | Near-NT owners | 110 million | Without NT, near-NT, or Bible | **540 million** | | | | | |
| 25. PAST OWNERSHIP | Former NT-owners | 20 million | Never had any NT or Bible | **320 million** | | | | | |
| 26. YOUTH USE | Literate youths with own NT | 300 million | Literate youths without an NT | **550 million** | | | | | |
| 27. BIBLE USE | Current Bible-using families | 1,100 million | Literate heads without a Bible | **500 million** | | | | | |
| 28. NEAR-BIBLE USE | Near-Bible owner families | 300 million | Without a Bible or near-Bible | **450 million** | | | | | |
| 29. PAST OWNERSHIP | Former Bible-owners | 30 million | Never had a Bible | **220 million** | | | | | |
| 30. SHAREABILITY | Able to share a Bible | 150 million | Unable to share a Bible | **310 million** | | | | | |
| 31. FAMILY USE | Literate families with a Bible | 350 million | Literate families without a Bible | **500 million** | | | | | |
| 32. DEMAND-radio/TV | Uninterested or hostile | 560 million | Keen to listen to radio/TV | **180 million** | | | | | |
| 33. DEMAND-film | Uninterested or hostile | 500 million | Keen to see 'Jesus' Film | **790 million** | | | | | |
| 34. DEMAND-selection | Families uninterested or hostile | 20 million | Keen to get a selection | **43 million** | | | | | |
| 35. DEMAND-gospel | Uninterested or hostile | 500 million | Keen to get a gospel | **320 million** | | | | | |
| 36. DEMAND-NT | Uninterested or hostile | 100 million | Keen to get an NT | **220 million** | | | | | |
| 37. DEMAND-Bible | Families uninterested or hostile | 60 million | Keen to get a Bible | **250 million** | | | | | |
| 38. AFFORDABILITY-gospel | Unable to pay for a gospel | 100 million | Able to pay for a gospel | **220 million** | | | | | |
| 39. AFFORDABILITY-NT | Unable to pay for an NT | 60 million | Able to pay for an NT | **160 million** | | | | | |
| 40. AFFORDABILITY-Bible | Unable to pay for a Bible | 100 million | Able to pay for a Bible | **150 million** | | | | | |
| 41. AVAILABILITY-gospel | Non-buyers though gospels in stock | 50 million | Out of stock, worth restocking | **170 million** | | | | | |
| 42. AVAILABILITY-NT | Nonbuyers though NTs in stock | 50 million | Out of stock, worth restocking | **110 million** | | | | | |
| 43. AVAILABILITY-Bible | Nonbuyers though Bibles in stock | 50 million | Out of stock, worth restocking | **100 million** | | | | | |
| 44. SATISFACTION-selection | Dissatisfied with existing versions | 33 million | Out of print, worth reprinting | **10 million** | | | | | |
| 45. SATISFACTION-gospel | Dissatisfied with existing versions | 100 million | Out of print, worth reprinting | **70 million** | | | | | |
| 46. SATISFACTION-NT | Dissatisfied with existing versions | 30 million | Out of print, worth reprinting | **80 million** | | | | | |
| 47. SATISFACTION-Bible | Dissatisfied with existing versions | 50 million | Out of print, worth reprinting | **50 million** | | | | | |
| 48. TRANSLATION-film | Translation in progress or envisaged | 490 million | No translation made or planned | **0 million** | | | | | |
| 49. TRANSLATION-selection | Translation in progress | 10 million | No translation yet made | **0 million** | | | | | |
| 50. TRANSLATION-gospel | Translation in progress | 70 million | No translation yet made | **0 million** | | | | | |
| 51. TRANSLATION-NT | Translation in progress | 80 million | No translation yet made | **0 million** | | | | | |
| 52. TRANSLATION-Bible | Translation in progress | 50 million | No translation yet made | **0 million** | | | | | |

NOTES AND COMMENTARY ON CRITERIA AND ROWS

The following notes provide explanation of the criteria numbered 1-52 in column 2 in Subtable 8 above. The notes also apply to criteria of the same names in Subtables 1-7.

1. HUMANITY. Goal: to reach with scriptures all persons, irrespective of race, gender, age, religion, location, economic level, income, education, health, occupation, interests, demand.
2. INFANCY. Children from birth to 5 years usually do not need their own books.
3. CHILDHOOD. Usually from 0-15 years, sometimes 0-12 years.
4. MATURITY. Adults: those over 15 years.
5. FAMILIES. Global average: 5 related persons—head, spouse, 1 adult dependent over 15, 2 children under 15.
6. HOUSEHOLDS. Includes servants, non-relatives.
7. YOUTH. Persons 15-24 years of age.
8. ACCESS. Availability of scripture in any language people understand.
9. BROADCASTING. Radio or TV reaches only 31% of the world.
10. RADIO/TV SETS. One radio or one TV often serves multiple listeners or viewers.
11. PLANNING-radio/TV. The extent to which current absence of services is likely to change soon.
12. VISUALS. Viewers (Luke's Gospel): 18% of all over 12s.
13. PLANNING-film. the extent to which showings are likely to begin soon.
14. SELECTIONS. 2, 4, 8-page leaflets of topical scripture texts or passages.
15. GOSPEL USE. A Portion is a complete Bible book, usually a Gospel, of up to 40 pages. "Gospel-owners" may or may not include owners of N or B (NT or Bible).
16. NEAR-GOSPEL USE. 'Near-gospel' = gospel in a related same-cluster language and in use as such.
17. PAST OWNERSHIP. Persons who formerly owned a gospel but then lost or mislaid it.
18. LITERACY. Literates are normally defined as % among adult (over-15) population only.
19. YOUTH LITERACY. Literates as % among population ages 15-24 only.
20. DEPENDENCY. Family members not counting family head.
21. NEW READERSHIP-NRS. New Reader Selections are illustrated and assist persons to read or learn to read.
22. NEW READERSHIP-NRP. New Reader Portions are gospels, illustrated, and part of literacy training.
23. NT USE. Number of literates with or without access to and use of NT. Figures may (as here) include, or exclude, owners or users of complete Bible.
24. NEAR-NT USE. 'Near-NT' = NT in a related same-cluster language and in use as such.
25. PAST OWNERSHIP. Persons who formerly owned an NT but then lost or mislaid it.
26. YOUTH USE. Literate youths (ages 15-24) with or without own NT.
27. BIBLE USE. Number of literate families with or without own Bible copy.
28. NEAR-BIBLE USE. 'Near-Bible' = Bible in a related same-cluster language and in use as such.
29. PAST OWNERSHIP. Families who formerly owned a Bible but then lost or mislaid it.
30. SHAREABILITY. Ability to use or share a copy of scripture belonging to others.
31. FAMILY USE. Families able to use their copy of the Bible because literates, excluding nonliterates owning own copy.
32. DEMAND-radio/TV. Interest or disinterest in broadcast scriptures.
33. DEMAND-film. Interest or disinterest in seeing 'Jesus' Film when a showing is announced.
34. DEMAND-selection. Interest or disinterest when families are offered selections or NRS.
35. DEMAND-gospel. Interest or disinterest when offered gospel or NRP.
36. DEMAND-NT. Response when a NT becomes available.
37. DEMAND-Bible. Response when a Bible becomes available.
38. AFFORDABILITY-gospel. Ability to pay when gospels are on sale.
39. AFFORDABILITY-NT. Ability to pay when NTs are on sale.
40. AFFORDABILITY-Bible. Ability to pay when Bibles are on sale.
41. AVAILABILITY-gospel. Gospels may be out of stock, or in stock but without takers.
42. AVAILABILITY-NT. NT may be out of stock, or in stock but without buyers.
43. AVAILABILITY-Bible. Bibles may be out of stock, or in stock but without buyers.
44. SATISFACTION-selection. Net worth reprinting due to dissatisfaction with product.
45. SATISFACTION-gospel. Net worth reprinting due to dissatisfaction with product.
46. SATISFACTION-NT. Net worth reprinting due to dissatisfaction with product.
47. SATISFACTION-Bible. Net worth reprinting due to dissatisfaction with product.
48. TRANSLATION-film. Availability of 'Jesus' Film in a language people understand (only 6% of world's 13,500 languages).
49. TRANSLATION-selection. Availability of translating in a language people understand.
50. TRANSLATION-gospel. Availability of translating in a language people understand (3,000 out of world's 13,500 languages)
51. TRANSLATION-NT. Availability of NT translating in people's own language (1,200 out of 13,500 languages at present).
52. TRANSLATION-Bible. Availability of Bible translating in family's own language (400 out of 13,500 languages at present). If no translation has yet been made or is yet begun, then, obviously, immediate target market is zero.

**Table 19–5.  Six basic scripture products and 7 levels quantifying each's dissemination, distribution, and density for any population (globe, world, continent, country, city, speech community, people), literate or nonliterate, Christian or non-Christian.**

This table sets out ranges of numbers by means of which the adequacy of actual distribution and placement figures may be assessed.

*A scale of distribution level*
The first column, 1, consists of 7 codes describing, for each of the 6 basic scripture products, the 7 levels of adequacy or inadequacy of scripture distribution whose meanings are given in column 2. Column 3 gives the percentage of the population involved (the number of persons being reached). The figures in columns 3 to 6 then give the ranges of numbers applicable to each of the 6 sets of 7 levels.

*Adequacy levels*
The 6 levels of adequate scripture distribution and use are shown by the 6 lines in bold type for code 4 "Adequate". These 6 bold lines represent approximately the ultimate goals of churches and Bible societies. These are the suggested levels by which those goals may be adequately or reasonably or satisfactorily achieved. The period stated (2, 10, or 20 years, or one-time) indicates the average life of copies, or maximum life if treated properly, or reasonable time shares of the church's limited resources.

*Quantifying "adequacy"*
The numerical range or extent of these adequacy levels are enumerated here by means of the sign >, which means "is greater than". So an adequate level of Bible distribution per year is quantified here below as "2>BB>1", which means "New Bibles distributed per year lie between 2% and 1% of total literate Christian population." When investigating adequacy for a specific population, it is essential to compile total annual distribution of all kinds including that of all agencies and sources (free distribution, subsidized distribution, and commercial distribution). The levels are meaningless if less than all sources are enumerated.

*Adequate scripture dissemination*
"Adequate" distribution of the 6 major forms of scripture, for any population (language, people, city, country, continent, or globe), may be defined as any one or more of the following:
a. BIBLE (1,300 pages): One print Bible per literate Christian family every 20 years, which is its average life.
b. NEW TESTAMENT (300 pages): One print NT per literate adult Christian (over 15) every 20 years, which is its average life.
c. PRINT GOSPEL (PORTION) (from 25 to 40 pages): One gospel per literate adult every decade (10 years), which is its average life.
d. SELECTION (1-, 2-, 4-, or 8-page print leaflets with thematic or topical or needs-based scripture passages): One selection per family every 2 years, which is its average life.
e. AUDIO GOSPEL: One one-time hearing of an audio cassette or radio broadcast or other programmed reading or enacting of a gospel, or life of Christ, or scripture readings, for one hour every 5 years per family.
f. VISUAL GOSPEL: One one-time viewing every 20 years of "Jesus" Film (Luke's Gospel, 3 hours), or similar film on Life of Christ, per adult or child.

**(a) BIBLE DISTRIBUTION AND USE** (one Bible per Christian family, with 20-year book life)

| Code 1 | Meaning 2 | Annual distribution BB=new Bibles p.a. % of population 3 | Density (use, placement) $b_1$=Bibles in use per family 4 | $b_2$=Bibles in use per adult 5 | $b_3$=Bibles in use per capita 6 |
|---|---|---|---|---|---|
| | | INADEQUACY | | | |
| 0 | Nil | $BB=0$ | $b_1=0$ | $b_2=0$ | $b_3=0$ |
| 1 | Minimal | $0.1>BB>0$ | $0.1>b_1>0$ | $0.03>b_2>0$ | $0.02>b_3>0$ |
| 2 | Partial | $0.5>BB>0.1$ | $0.5>b_1>0.1$ | $0.1>b_2>0.03$ | $0.1>b_3>0.02$ |
| 3 | Substantial | $1>BB>0.5$ | $1>b_1>0.5$ | $0.3>b_2>0.1$ | $0.2>b_3>0.1$ |
| | ADEQUACY | | | | |
| **4** | **Adequate** | **$2>BB>1$** | **$2>b_1>1$** | **$0.6>b_2>0.3$** | **$0.4>b_3>0.2$** |
| | SUPERFLUITY | | | | |
| 5 | Saturated | $5>BB>2$ | $5>b_1>2$ | $2>b_2>0.6$ | $1>b_3>0.4$ |
| 6 | Oversaturated | $BB>5$ | $b_1>5$ | $b_2>2$ | $b_3>1$ |

**(b) NEW TESTAMENT DISTRIBUTION AND USE** (one NT per adult Christian, with 20-year book life)

| Code 1 | Meaning 2 | Annual distribution NN=new NTs p.a. % of population 3 | Density (use, placement) $n_1$=NTs in use per family 4 | $n_2$=NTs in use per adult 5 | $n_3$=NTs in use per capita 6 |
|---|---|---|---|---|---|
| | | INADEQUACY | | | |
| 0 | Nil | $NN=0$ | $n_1=0$ | $n_2=0$ | $n_3=0$ |
| 1 | Minimal | $1>NN>0$ | $1>n_1>0$ | $0.2>n_2>0$ | $0.2>n_3>0$ |
| 2 | Partial | $2>NN>1$ | $2>n_1>1$ | $0.5>n_2>0.2$ | $0.4>n_3>0.2$ |
| 3 | Substantial | $3>NN>2$ | $3>n_1>2$ | $1>n_2>0.5$ | $0.6>n_3>0.4$ |
| | ADEQUACY | | | | |
| **4** | **Adequate** | **$6>NN>3$** | **$6>n_1>3$** | **$2>n_2>1$** | **$1.2>n_3>0.6$** |
| | SUPERFLUITY | | | | |
| 5 | Saturated | $20>NN>6$ | $20>n_1>6$ | $4>n_2>2$ | $4>n_3>1.2$ |
| 6 | Oversaturated | $NN>20$ | $n_1>20$ | $n_2>4$ | $n_3>4$ |

**(c) PRINT GOSPEL (PORTION) DISTRIBUTION** (one portion per literate adult every 10 years)

| Code 1 | Meaning 2 | Annual distribution PP=new Portions p.a. % of population 3 | Density (use, placement witness) $p_1$=Portions placed per family 4 | $p_2$=Portions placed per adult 5 | $p_3$=Portions placed per capita 6 |
|---|---|---|---|---|---|
| | | INADEQUACY | | | |
| 0 | Nil | $PP=0$ | $p_1=0$ | $p_2=0$ | $p_3=0$ |
| 1 | Minimal | $0.5>PP>0$ | $0.25>p_1>0$ | $0.1>p_2>0$ | $0.05>p_3>0$ |
| 2 | Partial | $2>PP>0.5$ | $1>p_1>0.25$ | $0.3>p_2>0.1$ | $0.2>p_3>0.05$ |
| 3 | Substantial | $6>PP>2$ | $3>p_1>1$ | $1>p_2>0.3$ | $0.6>p_3>0.2$ |
| | ADEQUACY | | | | |
| **4** | **Adequate** | **$12>PP>6$** | **$6>p_1>3$** | **$2>p_2>1$** | **$1.2>p_3>0.6$** |
| | SUPERFLUITY | | | | |
| 5 | Saturated | $30>PP>12$ | $10>p_1>6$ | $4>p_2>2$ | $3>p_3>1.2$ |
| 6 | Oversaturated | $PP>30$ | $p_1>10$ | $p_2>4$ | $p_3>3$ |

**(d) SELECTION DISTRIBUTION** (one selection per family every 2 years)

| Code 1 | Meaning 2 | Annual distribution SS=Selections p.a. % of population 3 | Density (use, notice, witness) $s_1$=Selections in use per family 4 | $s_2$=Selections in use per adult 5 | $s_3$=Selections in use per capita 6 |
|---|---|---|---|---|---|
| | | INADEQUACY | | | |
| 0 | Nil | $SS=0$ | $s_1=0$ | $s_2=0$ | $s_3=0$ |
| 1 | Minimal | $1>SS>0$ | $0.1>s_1>0$ | $0.03>s_2>0$ | $0.02>s_3>0$ |
| 2 | Partial | $5>SS>1$ | $0.5>s_1>0.1$ | $0.1>s_2>0.03$ | $0.1>s_3>0.02$ |
| 3 | Substantial | $10>SS>5$ | $1>s_1>0.5$ | $0.3>s_2>0.1$ | $0.2>s_3>0.1$ |
| | ADEQUACY | | | | |
| **4** | **Adequate** | **$20>SS>10$** | **$2>s_1>1$** | **$0.6>s_2>0.3$** | **$0.4>s_3>0.2$** |
| | SUPERFLUITY | | | | |
| 5 | Saturated | $50>SS>20$ | $5>s_1>2$ | $2>s_2>0.6$ | $1>s_3>0.4$ |
| 6 | Oversaturated | $SS>50$ | $s_1>5$ | $s_2>2$ | $s_3>1$ |

**(e) AUDIO GOSPEL AUDIENCES** (one audio hearing per family every 5 years)

| Code 1 | Meaning AA =Hearers p.a. 2 | Annual audience $a_1$=Hearings % of population 3 | Cumulative audience $a_2$=Hearings per family 4 | $a_3$=Hearings per adult 5 | per capita 6 |
|---|---|---|---|---|---|
| | | INADEQUACY | | | |
| 0 | Nil | $AA=0$ | $a_1=0$ | $a_2=0$ | $a_3=0$ |
| 1 | Minimal | $5>AA>0$ | $0.2>a_1>0$ | $0.02>a_2>0$ | $0.05>a_3>0$ |
| 2 | Partial | $10>AA>5$ | $0.5>a_1>0.2$ | $0.1>a_2>0.02$ | $0.1>a_3>0.05$ |
| 3 | Substantial | $20>AA>10$ | $1>a_1>0.5$ | $0.3>a_2>0.1$ | $0.2>a_3>0.1$ |
| | ADEQUACY | | | | |
| **4** | **Adequate** | **$40>AA>20$** | **$2>a_1>1$** | **$0.6>a_2>0.3$** | **$0.4>a_3>0.2$** |
| | SUPERFLUITY | | | | |
| 5 | Saturated | $60>AA>40$ | $5>a_1>2$ | $2>a_2>0.6$ | $1>a_3>0.4$ |
| 6 | Oversaturated | $AA>60$ | $a_1>5$ | $a_2>2$ | $a_3>1$ |

**(f) VISUAL GOSPEL AUDIENCES** (one viewing per adult or child every 20 years)

| Code 1 | Meaning VV=Viewers p.a. 2 | Annual audience $v_1$=Viewings percent 3 | Cumulative audience $v_2$=Viewings per family 4 | $v_3$=Viewings per adult 5 | per capita 6 |
|---|---|---|---|---|---|
| | | INADEQUACY | | | |
| 0 | Nil | $VV=0$ | $v_1=0$ | $v_2=0$ | $v_3=0$ |
| 1 | Minimal | $1>VV>0$ | $1>v_1>0$ | $0.5>v_2>0$ | $0.2>v_3>0$ |
| 2 | Partial | $2>VV>1$ | $2>v_1>1$ | $1>v_2>0.5$ | $0.5>v_3>0.2$ |
| 3 | Substantial | $5>VV>2$ | $5>v_1>2$ | $2>v_2>1$ | $1>v_3>0.5$ |
| | ADEQUACY | | | | |
| **4** | **Adequate** | **$10>VV>5$** | **$10>v_1>5$** | **$4>v_2>2$** | **$2>v_3>1$** |
| | SUPERFLUITY | | | | |
| 5 | Saturated | $20>VV>10$ | $20>v_1>10$ | $8>v_2>4$ | $4>v_3>2$ |
| 6 | Oversaturated | $VV>20$ | $v_1>20$ | $v_2>8$ | $v_3>4$ |

**Table 19–6.  A comparison of existing and proposed global goals for scripture distribution in AD 2000-AD 2001 with global population analyzed by age, literacy, religion, access to radio, with scripture provision and adequacy of access.**

## Subtable A. Global populations in AD 2000 analyzed by age, literacy, religion, and access to radio.

**Meaning of rows 1-20**
1. AD 2000 GLOBE. These figures apply to the entire world.
2. *Adults.* Persons aged 15 years or older. Literacy statistics always apply only to these adults.
3. *Children.* Persons aged under 15 years, including infants. Literacy statistics never cover or include children under 15.
4. *Families.* Defined as, on average, 5 persons, usually 3 adults (2 spouses, 1 adult over 15) and 2 children. In this Table 13–7, numbers in italics always identify families.
5. LITERATE WORLD. The world of all literate families, i.e. all literate adults plus their dependent children.
9. NONLITERATE WORLD. The world of all nonliterate families, i.e. all nonliterate adults plus their dependent children.
13. RADIO NONLITERATES. The world of nonliterate families but with access to radio or TV broadcasting.
17. NO-RADIO NONLITERATES. The world of nonliterate families who also have no access to radio or TV broadcasting.

**Meaning of columns 1–7**
1. Name of population or segment: adults = 15 years or older, children = under 15s. Family = 5 persons.
2. Size of population in AD 2000.
3. Annual increase in population: due to births p.a.
4. Christians in AD 2000.
5. New Christians or births p.a.
6. Non-Christians in AD 2000.
7. New non-Christians or births p.a.

| Segments 1 | Population 2 | New p.a. 3 | Christians 4 | New p.a. 5 | Non-Christians 6 | New p.a. 7 |
|---|---|---|---|---|---|---|
| 1.AD 2000 GLOBE | 6055m | 133.2m | 2000m | 45.8m | 4055m | 87.4m |
| 2. Adults | 4264m | 93.2m | 1467m | 32.1m | 2797m | 61.1m |
| 3. Children | 1827m | 40.0m | 628m | 13.7m | 1199m | 26.3m |
| 4. *Families* | 1218m | 26.6m | 419m | 9.2m | 799m | 17.4m |
| 5.LITERATE WORLD | 4312m | 94.3m | 1483m | 32.4m | 2829m | 61.9m |
| 6. Adults | 3256m | 66.0m | 1039m | 22.7m | 1980m | 43.3m |
| 7. Children | 1293m | 28.3m | 445m | 9.7m | 849m | 18.6m |
| 8. *Families* | 862m | 18.8m | 297m | 6.5m | 566m | 12.3m |
| 9.NONLITERATE WORLD | 1779m | 38.9m | 612m | 13.4m | 1167m | 25.5m |
| 10. Adults | 1245m | 27.2m | 428m | 9.4m | 817m | 17.8m |
| 11. Children | 533m | 11.7m | 183m | 4.0m | 350m | 7.7m |
| 12. *Families* | 356m | 7.8m | 122m | 2.7m | 233m | 5.1m |
| 13.RADIO NONLITERATES | 1548m | 33.8m | 532m | 11.7m | 1015m | 22.2m |
| 14. Adults | 1083m | 23.7m | 372m | 8.2m | 711m | 15.5m |
| 15. Children | 464m | 10.2m | 159m | 3.5m | 305m | 6.7m |
| 16. *Families* | 310m | 6.7m | 106m | 2.3m | 203m | 4.4m |
| 17.NO-RADIO NONLITERATES | 231m | 5.1m | 80m | 1.7m | 152m | 3.3m |
| 18. Adults | 162m | 3.5m | 56m | 1.2m | 106m | 2.3m |
| 19. Children | 69m | 1.5m | 24m | 0.5m | 45m | 1.0m |
| 20. *Families* | 46m | 1.0m | 16m | 0.3m | 41m | 0.7m |

## Subtable B. Global scripture provision in AD 2000 for beneficiary populations by type of scripture, and adequacy of annual distribution utilizing existing goals and proposed goals.

**Meaning of rows 1-6 and 1-7**
Each row in this subtable explains and expounds one specific goal of scripture distribution. These are divided into 2 separate lists of 6 goals each, as follows:
(a) **EXISTING GOALS** are goals that are already operative and have in fact been in use for up to 40 years. Goals 1–3 represent the UBS' Hakone Formula (1963); note that in the first 2 goals the word 'literate' was not clearly specified, as it was in Goal 3. Goal 4 refers to the 1967 start of the UBS' Selection program, aimed at the entire world population through its literate families. Goal 5 refers to the global agendas of Christian broadcasting agencies, together with agencies working with scriptures on cassettes, tapes, records, or disks. Goal 6 is the blanket goal announced by the 'Jesus' Film Project and other audiovisual agencies. Often such goals duplicate coverage already provided by Bible societies and denominations.
(b) **PROPOSED GOALS** are a set of 6 goals proposed by this book, with 2 characteristics. (1) Each goal is exactly specified so that its targets/beneficiaries as described in Subtable A are precisely delineated and enumerated, making close monitoring for any and all populations possible; and (2) All unnecessary duplication is removed (for example, there is no reason to give millions of gospels to populations who already have their own copies of the complete Bible or New Testament in their homes). Lastly, Goals 5 and 6 are proposed to concentrate on the nonliterate world and in particular (Goal 6) nonliterates without access to Christian radio or audio scriptures.

**Meaning of columns 1–18**
TARGETS
1. *Goal* number, from 1 to 6.
2. *Beneficiaries* of goal's exact, specified provision.
DEMOGRAPHICS INVOLVED (m=millions)
3. *Persons* in AD 2000 population. Note that a dash instead of a number (in columns 3–8) means that category is not relevant for the goal being described.
4. *Families* in AD 2000. Numbers in italics here always enumerate families (shown in columns 4, 6, 8).
5. *Christians* in AD 2000.
6. *Christian families* in AD 2000.
7. *Non-Christians* in AD 2000.
8. *Non-Christian families* in AD 2000
SCRIPTURE PROVISION (m=millions of copies)
9. *Type* or variety of scripture

10. *Needed*: copies needed in use to fulfil goal
11. *Life:* average life of copies in years
12. *Distribution* per year needed to reach column 10 level
13. *Duplication.* That part of column 12 which is already reached by previous lines (goals).
14. *Unduplicated.* That part of column 12 unreached by previous line (goal). This column therefore presents the final adequate levels being proposed by this analysis.
FORMULAS FOR ADEQUATE LEVELS
15. *Adequate annual distribution level* in order to meet goal precisely: single calculation including any duplication.
16. As column 15 but excluding any duplication in previous line.
OFFERS
17. *e* (evangelistic offers per capita per year) provided by goal to all persons involved.
18. *Offers per copy* (evangelistic scriptural offers) generated by 1 scripture under this goal.

### (a) EXISTING GOALS

| TARGETS Beneficiaries 1  2 | DEMOGRAPHICS INVOLVED (m=millions) Population Persons 3 | Families 4 | Christians Persons 5 | Families 6 | Non-Christians Persons 7 | Families 8 | SCRIPTURE PROVISION (m=millions) Type 9 | Needed in use 10 | Life, years 11 | Dist pa 12 | Dup 13 | Undup 14 | FORMULAS FOR ADEQUATE LEVELS Adequate annual distribution level With duplication 15 | Without 16 | OFFERS e p.c. 17 | 18 |
|---|---|---|---|---|---|---|---|---|---|---|---|---|---|---|---|---|
| 1. All Christian families | – | – | 2095m | 419m | – | – | Bible | 419m | 20 | 21m | 0 | 21m | BB=1% of all Christians | 1 | 150 | 750 |
| 2. All Christian adults | – | – | 1467m | – | – | – | NT | 1467m | 20 | 73m | 21m | 52m | NN=3% of Christians | 3 | 30 | 30 |
| 3. All literate adults | 3019m | – | 1039m | – | 1980m | – | Gospel | 3019m | 10 | 302m | 52m | 250m | PP=6% of literate adults | 8 | 3 | 3 |
| 4. All literate families | 4312m | 862m | 1483m | 297m | 2829m | 566m | Selection | 862m | 2 | 431m | 250m | 181m | SS=10% of literate world | 4 | 1 | 5 |
| 5. All families with radio | 5300m | 1060m | 1823m | 365m | 3477m | 695m | Audio gospel | 1060m | 5 | 212m | 150m | 62m | AA=20% of families with radio | 6 | 1 | 5 |
| 6. All persons on Earth | 6055m | – | 2000m | – | 4055m | – | Visual gospel | 6055m | 20 | 304m | 292m | 12m | VV=5% of Earth's population | 0.2 | 3 | 3 |

### (b) PROPOSED GOALS

| TARGETS Beneficiaries 1  2 | DEMOGRAPHICS INVOLVED (m=millions) Population Persons 3 | Families 4 | Christians Persons 5 | Families 6 | Non-Christians Persons 7 | Families 8 | SCRIPTURE PROVISION (m=millions) Type 9 | Needed in use 10 | Life, years 11 | Dist pa 12 | Dup 13 | Undup 14 | FORMULAS FOR ADEQUATE LEVELS Adequate annual distribution level With duplication 15 | Without 16 | OFFERS e p.c. 17 | 18 |
|---|---|---|---|---|---|---|---|---|---|---|---|---|---|---|---|---|
| LITERATE WORLD | | | | | | | | | | | | | | | | |
| 1. Literate Christian families | – | – | 1,483m | 297m | – | – | Bible | 297m | 20 | 15m | 0 | 15m | BB=1% of literate Christian world | 1 | 30 | 150 |
| 2. Literate Christian adults | – | – | 1039m | – | – | – | NT | 1039m | 20 | 52m | 15m | 37m | NN+BB=5% of literate Christian adults | 3.5 | 30 | 30 |
| 3. All literate adults | 3256m | – | 1039m | – | 1980m | – | Gospel | 3019m | 10 | 302m | 37m | 265m | PP+NN+BB=10% of all literate adults | 9 | 3 | 3 |
| 4. All literate families | 4312m | 862m | 1483m | 297m | 2829m | 566m | Selection | 862m | 2 | 431m | 265m | 166m | SS+PP+NN+BB=10% of literate world | 4 | 1 | 5 |
| NONLITERATE WORLD | | | | | | | | | | | | | | | | |
| 5. All literate world | | | | | | | | | | | | | | | | |
| 6. Radio nonliterate families | 1548m | 310m | 532m | 106m | 1015m | 203m | Audio gospel | 310m | 5 | 62m | 0 | 62m | AA=20% of radio nonliterate families | 20 | 1 | 5 |
| 7. No-radio nonliterates | 231m | 46m | 80m | 16m | 152m | 30m | Visual gospel | 231m | 20 | 12m | 0 | 12m | VV=5% of no-radio nonliterates | 5 | 3 | 3 |

## Table 19–7. Scripture translation status: each language's status in translation, publication, provision, and availability: a chronological sequence of 93 stages giving totals of languages at each status.

The present status of scripture translation and publication into print in the entire world of languages is shown pinpointed below using a mutually-exclusive sequential time scale. On this scale, every language in the world at any given moment in time has one single unique numerical code value. Note that, for specific languages, individual steps or even whole sequences can be and in fact may have been bypassed or leapfrogged. In most cases, placing a language at a certain stage implies that it has passed through, or bypassed, all previous stages. In cases where a language could be construed as being at 2 points on the scale simultaneously, we always choose here the more advanced stage and its code. Where multiple versions or translations or projects exist in a language, the code assigned always refers to this highest stage (most advanced development). The last 16 categories (codes 77–92) represent satisfactory completed Bibles; the last 11 (82–92)

represent the most advanced types of Bible translation available today. Note that 'portions' (complete books of the Bible) here do not include 'selections' (short extracts or parts of complete books), and that 'Bibles' here can either include or (more usually) exclude the Deutero-Canonical Books (Apocrypha). It should further be observed that the values of this variable for a particular biblioglossonym in a specified script are the same whatever countries or contexts it is found in.

The second column of figures gives cumulative totals for each status from 0-92. Interpretation follows these lines: 'Only 30 languages out of 13,509 have reached the highest level (code 92)'; or, '1,943 languages have or can understand and use the whole Bible'; or, '6,638 languages have a portion or gospel they can understand and use'.

Note the 2 major levels describing scripture provision in any

language:
(1) SCRIPTURES ABSENT (21 categories), and
(2) SCRIPTURES PRESENT (72 categories; this latter covers S = selections, P = portion (gospel, book), N = New Testament, and B = Bible.
Onto these 2 levels of availability are built the following 3 stages of translation work in the language:
(a) NO WORK IN PROGRESS (34 categories, describing work needed but not under way or not yet begun; or not needed, or contested; or extinct or obsolete).
(b) WORK IN PROGRESS (37 categories, with phrase 'under way', or 'in production/in press').
(c) WORK (ON NT OR BIBLE) COMPLETED (22 categories, representing a degree of finality or end of the current translation process).

Name of language: . . . . . . . . . . . . . . . . . . . . . . . . . . . . . .
Date for report below: . . . . . . . . . . . . . . . . . . . . . . . . .
Code (sts) = scripture translation status, or status of language's speakers (0–92)
Total = total of languages at each level in AD 2000:
Total 1 = All languages benefitting directly from scriptures in closely-related languages.
Total 2 = Cumulative total of languages in Total 1, starting at the lower end at stage 92 and adding upwards.

| Code | Total languages: 1 | 2 |
|---|---|---|
| **NO SCRIPTURE ACCESS AT ALL** | | |
| 0 = No translations in this language, nor its cluster, nor its net | 1,300 | 13,509 |
| **SCRIPTURES ABSENT** | **5,514** | |
| **NO WORK IN PROGRESS** | **4,159** | |
| 1 = No translations in this language, need for survey stated | 152 | 12,248 |
| 2 = No translations yet, definite need, but nothing under way | 700 | 12,096 |
| 3 = No translations yet, probable need | 234 | 11,396 |
| 4 = No translations yet, possible need | 1,980 | 11,162 |
| 5 = No translations yet, unlikely or undetermined need | 115 | 9,182 |
| 6 = No translations; no need as bilingual in a scripture language | 220 | 9,067 |
| 7 = No translations; bilingual, but need contested | 100 | 8,847 |
| 8 = No translations; speakers nearly extinct, hence no need | 455 | 8,747 |
| 9 = No translations; speakers now extinct | 199 | 8,292 |
| **WORK IN PROGRESS** | **1,355** | |
| 10 = First translating under way, selection (topical Scripture verses) | 100 | 8,093 |
| 11 = First translating of a portion (gospel) under way | 40 | 7,993 |
| 12 = First translating under way, whole of New Testament | 360 | 7,953 |
| 13 = First translating under way, whole of Old Testament | 2 | 7,593 |
| 14 = First translating under way, whole Bible | 6 | 7,591 |
| 15 = First translating under way, whole Bible with Apocrypha | 6 | 7,585 |
| 16 = First translating begun but later placed on hold | 50 | 7,579 |
| 17 = First translating begun but later suspended or dropped | 40 | 7,529 |
| 18 = Work on Braille version for the blind | 117 | 7,489 |
| 19 = Work on signed version for the deaf | 25 | 7,372 |
| 20 = Work on production of Luke's Gospel as 'Jesus' Film | 609 | 7347 |
| **SCRIPTURES PRESENT: SELECTION ONLY** (a few verses) | **100** | |
| 21 = Selections in print, but no complete Book | 100 | 6,738 |
| **SCRIPTURES PRESENT: PORTION** (gospel or complete book) | **1,963** | |
| **NO WORK IN PROGRESS** | **1,691** | |
| 22 = Gospel or portion (complete book) in print (if since 1975) | 242 | 6,638 |
| 23 = Portion in print, but obsolescent (over 25 years ; latest 1951–1975) | 217 | 6,396 |
| 24 = Portion in print, but obsolete (over 50 years ; latest 1950 or earlier) | 528 | 6,179 |
| 25 = Portion in print, definite need for further translating, none under way | 40 | 5,651 |
| 26 = Portion in print, possible need for further translating, none under way | 50 | 5,611 |
| 27 = Portion in print; but speakers/readers now nearly extinct | 24 | 5,561 |
| 28 = Portion in print; but speakers now extinct | 40 | 5,537 |
| 29 = Portions available in Braille for blind persons | 200 | 5,497 |
| 30 = Portions available in sign/signed language for deaf persons | 40 | 5,297 |
| 31 = Audio portions available | 200 | 5,257 |
| 32 = Luke's Gospel available as 'Jesus' Film | 110 | 5,057 |
| **WORK IN PROGRESS** | **272** | |
| 33 = Portion in print, additional portion under way | 34 | 4,947 |
| 34 = Portion in print, but new portion under way in new orthography | 20 | 4,913 |
| 35 = Portion in print, first translation of NT under way | 125 | 4,893 |
| 36 = Portion in print, first translation of OT under way | 3 | 4,768 |
| 37 = Portion in print, first translation of Bible under way | 10 | 4,765 |
| 38 = Portion in print, first translation of Bible with Apocrypha under way | 10 | 4,755 |
| 39 = First NT in production/in press (translated but not yet published) | 50 | 4,745 |
| 40 = First Bible in production/in press (translated but not yet published) | 20 | 4,695 |
| **SCRIPTURES PRESENT: NEW TESTAMENT ONLY** | **2,897** | |
| **NO WORK IN PROGRESS** | **1,220** | |
| 41 = NT in print, being first translation (if latest date is since 1975) | 418 | 4,675 |
| 42 = NT in print, but obsolescent (over 25 years ; latest 1951–1975) | 440 | 4,257 |
| 43 = NT in print, but obsolete (over 50 years ; latest 1950 or earlier) | 177 | 3,817 |

| Code | Total languages: 1 | 2 |
|---|---|---|
| 44 = NT in recent print, revision needed but not under way | 118 | 3,640 |
| 45 = NT in print; but speakers/readers now nearly extinct | 32 | 3,522 |
| 46 = NT in print; but speakers now extinct | 35 | 3,490 |
| **WORK IN PROGRESS** | **412** | |
| 47 = NT in print, revision needed and under way | 20 | 3,455 |
| 48 = NT in print, new translation needed and under way | 22 | 3,435 |
| 49 = NT in revision in production (translated, not yet published) | 60 | 3,413 |
| 50 = NT in new translation in production (translated, not yet published) | 30 | 3,353 |
| 51 = NT in print, first translation of OT under way | 130 | 3,323 |
| 52 = NT in print, first translation of Bible under way | 50 | 3,193 |
| 53 = NT in print, first translation of Bible with Apocrypha under way | 10 | 3,143 |
| 54 = NT in print, first Bible in production (translated, not yet published) | 90 | 3,133 |
| **WORK ON NT COMPLETED** | **1,100** | |
| 55 = NT in print, satisfactory or adequate (literal or formal translation) | 200 | 3,043 |
| 56 = NT in print (popular language translation) | 30 | 2,843 |
| 57 = NT in print (common-language, dynamic equivalent translation) | 600 | 2,813 |
| 58 = NT in Braille available | 100 | 2,213 |
| 59 = NT in special versions (children's NT, comics, etc) available | 90 | 2,113 |
| 60 = Audio NT available | 80 | 2,023 |
| **SCRIPTURES PRESENT: WHOLE BIBLE** (with/without Apocrypha) | **1,943** | |
| **NO WORK IN PROGRESS** | **749** | |
| 61 = Bible in print, being first translation (if since 1975), no further plans | 200 | 1,943 |
| 62 = Bible in print, but obsolescent (over 25 years ; latest 1951–1975) | 120 | 1,743 |
| 63 = Bible in print, but obsolete (over 50 years ; latest 1950 or earlier) | 343 | 1,623 |
| 64 = Bible in print, revision or new translation needed, not under way | 20 | 1,280 |
| 65 = Bible in print; but speakers/readers nearly extinct | 40 | 1,260 |
| 66 = Bible in print; but speakers now extinct | 26 | 1,220 |
| **WORK IN PROGRESS** | **624** | |
| 67 = Bible in print, revision of NT needed and under way | 20 | 1,194 |
| 68 = Bible in print, new translation of NT needed and under way | 59 | 1,174 |
| 69 = Bible in print, revision of OT needed and under way | 5 | 1,115 |
| 70 = Bible in print, new translation of OT needed and under way | 18 | 1,110 |
| 71 = Revision of whole Bible under way | 214 | 1,092 |
| 72 = New translation of whole Bible under way | 233 | 878 |
| 73 = Revision of whole Bible with Apocrypha under way | 20 | 645 |
| 74 = New translation of whole Bible with Apocrypha under way | 10 | 625 |
| 75 = Bible in revision in production (translated, not yet published) | 20 | 615 |
| 76 = Bible in new translation in production (translated, not yet published) | 25 | 595 |
| **WORK ON BIBLE COMPLETED** | **570** | |
| 77 = Bible in print, satisfactory or adequate (literal or formal translation) | 30 | 570 |
| 78 = Bible with Apocrypha in print, satisfactory or adequate | 10 | 540 |
| 79 = Bible in print (Union version), satisfactory or adequate | 10 | 530 |
| 80 = Bible in print (literary language or high-quality new translation) | 15 | 520 |
| 81 = Bible in print (popular language translation) | 5 | 505 |
| 82 = Bible in print (common-language, dynamic equivalent translation) | 100 | 500 |
| 83 = Bible in print (interconfessional CLT/DE translation) | 30 | 400 |
| 84 = Bible in Braille available | 100 | 370 |
| 85 = Bible available for handicapped (deaf, nonliterates, new literates) | 20 | 270 |
| 86 = Bible in print, concordance or dictionary also in print | 40 | 250 |
| 87 = Bible stories available as colored comics, or in children's Bible | 30 | 210 |
| 88 = Bible in print in special versions: study Bible, commentaries | 30 | 180 |
| 89 = Audio Bible available | 20 | 150 |
| 90 = Bible available in video | 5 | 130 |
| 91 = Bible available electronically on Internet | 95 | 125 |
| 92 = Bible available on Internet, full range electronic or web services | 30 | 30 |
| **All languages** | **13,509** | |

# FINANCE

The finances of global Christianity, AD 1900-AD 2001

*Leaders of Israel, the people must bring you one sixtieth of their grain harvests as offer-
ings to me. They will also bring one percent of their olive oil.*
—Ezekiel 45:13-14, Contemporary English Version

*These people think religion is supposed to make you rich.*
—1 Timothy 6:5, CEV

*The love of money causes all kinds of trouble. Some people want money so much that
they have given up their faith and caused themselves a lot of pain.*
—I Timothy 6:10, CEV

*Avoid as you would the plague a clergyman who is also a man of business.*
—Jerome (AD 345-419)

A basic resource in any Christian activity is money—money collected, and money spent. In the Christian world, money is accounted for—raised, collected, counted, banked, audited, published—with more exaction and precision, usually to the last cent, than any other resource.

Part 20 draws on Christian financial statements of several kinds to arrive at one overall statement of annual income and annual expenditure of global Christianity. These exact procedures followed in almost all churches show that huge sums are regularly embezzled by top custodians.

The data also enable analyses of the cost-effectiveness of Christian activity in each country of the world.

# The finances of global Christianity, AD 1900-AD 2001

This Part 20 discusses and analyzes Christian financial resources at the global level and asks how extensive they are today and how effective they are for today's global mission.

## MONEY IN THE BIBLE

### The example of Jesus

An obvious starting point for attempting to assess the role of money in the Bible is the example of Jesus himself. Here we are immediately faced with the stark contrast of Jesus' own lifestyle compared with that of his followers today.

Jesus did not carry money nor own any. He had no silver or gold, no cash income, no property, no stocks or shares, no current account, no savings account, no hedge against inflation, no tax havens, no financial reserves. He had nowhere to lay his head. He was less well off than the foxes or the birds. He lived in poverty. But his impact on the world was enormous. He founded what was largely the original Church of the Poor, a fellowship of the oppressed, the exploited, the politically powerless, the deprived, the dispossessed. He commanded his first followers: 'Do not carry any gold, silver, or copper money in your pockets' (Matthew 10:9, GNB). Today he has 2 billion followers who receive annual incomes totaling US$15.2 trillion and who own two-thirds of the earth's entire resources. On this basis, global Christianity has become overwhelmingly the Church of the Rich. To what extent are its members having any impact on the wider world today?

### The biblical importance of finance

In English translations of the Bible, the word 'money' occurs extensively: 210 times in the Good News Bible, 122 in the New International Version. Often the connotation is of something unspiritual, bad, demonic: 'You cannot serve both God and money' (Luke 16:13, GNB). Jesus propounded several notable parables based on money; he dealt harshly with money-changers and money-lenders. Yet money is a necessary evil for his followers, requiring them to use it but to handle it cautiously.

Two usages of the word 'finance' demonstrate this ambiguity. Firstly, the Apostle Paul writes that its use is inescapable, since every Christian needs support: 'I did not bother you for financial help' (2 Corinthians 12:13, GNB). But secondly, Christian workers must set higher priorities: 'It is not right for us to neglect the preaching of God's word in order to handle finances' (Acts 6:2, GNB).

### Money and the command 'Evangelize!'

There are several financial dimensions to this central mandate. Part 23 'Evangelization' lists and describes some 400 dimensions of euangelizo in English, among which are several financial usages. Exegetes who have carefully examined the list of 51 dimensions relevant to measuring mission and evangelization cannot fail to have noticed that a number of them—38% of the total—refer to the right handling of money. The most explicit are the mandates 'Calculate the cost!' (Luke 14:28, REB, NAB, NASB), 'Check the money!' (2 Kings 12:11, REB, JB), 'Weigh the silver!' (2 Kings 12:10, REB), and 'Total up the spoils!' (Numbers 31:32, NRSV). There are numerous other financial imperatives such as add, calculate, count, estimate, manage, register, sum, write. All of this implies that in order to evangelize, Christians must utilize money accurately, honestly, and disinterestedly for the good of all. The reason, clearly, is that money plays an essential role in the operation of God's work—the human side of the life of the churches, the global human task of world mission.

## TODAY'S GLOBAL STATUS

Not surprisingly, money plays an important role in religion, religions, Christianity, confessions, denominations, churches, missions, and even in evangelism. It therefore occupies a central role in implementing human responsibility for evangelizing today's world. But first, a glance at the wider role of money in secular usage will reveal how widespread the wrong use or misuse of money is.

### The world of billions squandered

Each year in today's world, billions of dollars are, from the Christian standpoint, recklessly wasted. We are all familiar with the appalling global squandering of resources going on around us throughout the twentieth century, in most of which Christians individually and corporately have been deeply involved. These involve the environment and pollution, forests and desertification, oil, coal, minerals and other energy sources. Major resources are the 10 million species on earth (20 % nearing extinction), and, most importantly, the human populations themselves. The total cost of wasteful actions and policies in these areas is enormous.

Then there are the vast annual expenditures on causes to which Christians are either fundamentally opposed, or hostile, or at any rate cool. International and national crime, especially of the organized varieties, is known to involve over US$750 billion each year. Of this, illicit drug traffic accounts for some $250 billion. In the United States the two most lucrative forms of crime cost the following: $25 billion a year on the cocaine industry (1982 figure), and $44 billion a year on white-collar thefts such as fraud and computer crime (1977 figure). Criminal justice to combat these activities costs United States taxpayers over $26 billion in 1979 alone. In addition, several times as much as these sums goes on the less criminal activities of graft, corruption, and embezzlement each year. Further, there are scores of lesser examples of squandering when considered in the total world context. The USA documents its total expenditure in the most detail, hence provides most of the concrete examples and comes under the most scrutiny (and fire). There, dog owners spend $3.2 billion each year on their dogs; tobacco products sold rose from $16.7 billion in 1970 to $20.4 billion in 1980; and alcoholic beverages consumed rose from $22.4 billion to $42.8 billion over the same period. A high percentage of the persons involved are Christians of one persuasion or another.

But the best-documented mass squandering of resources, in the view of many thinking Christians, is the arms race linked with the global military-industrial complex. Worldwide military expenditure rose from $236 billion in 1969 to $480 billion in 1978 and $1 trillion in AD 2000. Of this, 35% was spent by the United States, and 25% by the former U.S.S.R. It is known that some 500,000 scientists (50% of the world's one million), including many Nobel Prize laureates, are involved today in military and defense expenditure, together with 100 million employed citizens working under national ministries of defense. By AD 2000 this expenditure on the arms race reached over $165 a year for every man, woman, and child on earth. Over 60 million Christians—employees, employers, scientists, government leaders—are deeply involved in this issue, since their whole livelihood stems from it.

### The world of billions in poverty

By contrast, some 46% of the world, or 2.8 billion people, live in varying degrees of poverty. They eke out a living in twenty-six countries, each with a per capita income of under $235 per year. This sounds bad enough, but the full picture is much worse. The world today has some 1,090 million persons living in absolute poverty, each with an income of less than $90 a year. This is one-third of the entire developing world, the Third World; to it must be added 150 million on the edge of poverty in China. As defined by the World Bank, absolute poverty is a clearly defined category that represents 'a condition of life so characterized by malnutrition, illiteracy and disease as to be beneath any reasonable definition of human decency.' With each month that passes, these totals increase as the gap between affluence and poverty widens almost everywhere.

Worldwide, absolute poverty is overwhelmingly concentrated in the rural areas of developing countries. It has many dire consequences, centering on a chronic lack of the basic necessities for survival. Among these consequences: 1.3 billion human beings remain without adequate shelter; landlessness and mass unemployment are rampant; 2.2 billion do not have access to adequate water supply; some 50 million are temporarily displaced or permanently unsettled refugees; 991 million adults are illiterate with no access to literature; 1.2 billion have little or no access to schools; 1.5 billion have no access to medical care; 800 million people (20% of the Third World, and up to 33% in several countries) suffer from inadequate and uncertain diet and thus from severe protein-calorie malnutrition; and some 1.2 billion human beings on earth are hungry or malnourished.

This catastrophic state of affairs is to some extent a direct consequence of the blatant misuse of resources sketched in the preceding section. The predicament of the 2 billion 'have-nots' (the poor) is a damning indictment of the diversion or even theft of trillions of dollars over the years by the 2 billion 'haves' (the rich). From another point of view, however, the blame rests on mismanagement and corruption on the part of many Third-World governments. Symptomatic of this is the enormous mushrooming of worldwide national debt, from $100 billion in 1970 to $1.6 trillion by AD 2000, now owed to banks in the Western world by over twenty-five developing and Communist-bloc countries. The great majority of this is owed by solidly Christian countries: Brazil ($100 billion), Mexico ($90 billion, Argentina ($65 billion) Venezuela ($35 billion), Poland ($40 billion), Philippines ($17 billion). In fact, some 87 % of this world debt is owed, corporately or nationally, by Third-World or Communist-world Christians to Western Christians. Servicing these massive debts alone obliges them to pay over $100 billion a year. In comparison with such sums, North-South aid formally given by rich countries to the Third World remains little more than a drop in the bucket.

In this context, let us investigate where the Christian world and its mission stand today. How large are their resources?

### A global table of resources

There are various types of Christian resources. Clearly, the main one is the basic one: people. Human beings won to the service of Christ and their fellow beings are undoubtedly the main Christian resource. Subsidiary resources may be listed as follows: workers (full-time personnel), missionaries, scriptures, books, literature, periodicals, libraries, institutions, service agencies, organizations, broadcasting, et alia. An attempt at tabulating these for each of the continents of the world across the twentieth century was given in Global Table 12 in the 1982 World Christian encyclopedia, with an updated version for AD 2000 given here as Table 20–1.

## THE INCOME OF GLOBAL CHRISTIANITY

In this article we are investigating only one of these resources, finance, and only one aspect of Christian finance, namely, money received and money donated each year by the entire world community of all Chris-

**MONEY-CHANGING HONESTLY**

**EXPELLING SWINDLERS**

**EXPOSING MONEY SCAMS**

**BEGINNING SMALL**

**TITHING SACRIFICIALLY**

**MANAGING STRICTLY**

**SERVING THE NEEDY**

**JOINING 5 MILLION TREASURERS**

**SELLING EFFICIENTLY**

**HANDLING TRANSPARENTLY**

**OPERATING COST-EFFECTIVELY**

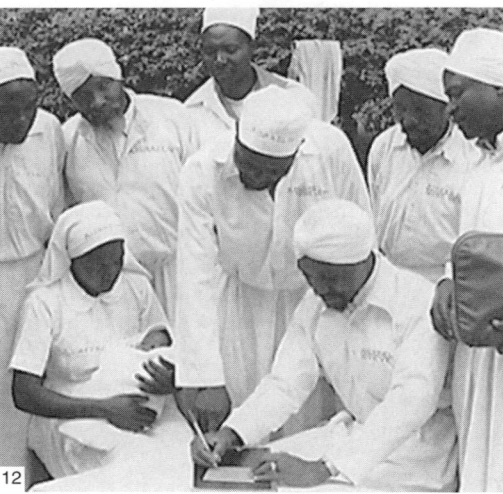

**VERIFYING DOUBLE SIGNATURES**

## Twelve aspects of finance
(see notes on facing page, bottom left)

**Table 20–1. Christian global live income and giving per year, AD 1900-AD 2000, by ecclesiastical megablocs, continents, and Worlds A, B, C.**

| Ref | Globe: Amount (in US$) | AD 1900 Globe | Continents in AD 2000: Africa | Asia | Europe | Latin America | Northern America | Oceania | Worlds in AD 2000: World A | World B | World C | AD 2000 Globe |
|---|---|---|---|---|---|---|---|---|---|---|---|---|
| 1. | Total population, in millions of persons | 1,619.6 | 784.4 | 3,682.6 | 728.9 | 519.1 | 309.6 | 30.4 | 605.3 | 3,755.0 | 1,694.7 | 6,055.0 |
| 2. | Total income: gross national product, billion, US$ pa | 397.1 | 515 | 8,823 | 9,267 | 1,714 | 8,117 | 428 | 886 | 8,577 | 19,401 | 28,865 |
| 3. | Average income per person: GNP per capita, US$ pa | 245.2 | 657 | 2,396 | 12,714 | 3,302 | 26,214 | 14,091 | 1,464 | 2,284 | 11,448 | 4,767 |
| 4. | GLOBAL CHURCH MEMBERSHIP | | | | | | | | | | | |
| 5. | Affiliated church members (millions of persons) | 521.6 | 335.1 | 307.3 | 536.8 | 475.7 | 212.2 | 21.4 | 10.0 | 491.3 | 1,387.1 | 1,888.4 |
| 6. | PERSONAL INCOME OF CHURCH MEMBERS (billion $ pa) | 270.0 | 199.6 | 588.2 | 6,976.6 | 1,574.4 | 5,570.2 | 288.5 | 10.5 | 772.0 | 14,415.2 | 15,197.7 |
| 7. | Orthodox (billion $ pa) | 60.0 | 12.0 | 22.5 | 397.6 | 2.2 | 146.3 | 12.0 | 3.4 | 185.0 | 404.3 | 592.7 |
| 8. | Roman Catholics (billion $ pa) | 138.0 | 46.4 | 152.4 | 4,186.3 | 1,301.1 | 1,601.9 | 106.8 | 2.5 | 136.6 | 7,255.9 | 7,395.0 |
| 9. | Anglicans (billion $ pa) | 15.8 | 16.4 | 5.8 | 485.6 | 3.6 | 72.0 | 81.4 | 0.1 | 11.6 | 653.1 | 664.8 |
| 10. | Protestants (billion $ pa) | 53.3 | 54.8 | 137.9 | 1,684.8 | 132.8 | 1,620.4 | 64.4 | 1.3 | 153.2 | 3,540.6 | 3,695.1 |
| 11. | Independents (billion $ pa) | 4.1 | 68.8 | 232.5 | 164.9 | 114.9 | 1,883.6 | 17.8 | 3.2 | 248.0 | 2,231.4 | 2,482.6 |
| 12. | Marginal Christians (billion $ pa) | 0.5 | 1.2 | 37.1 | 57.4 | 19.9 | 245.9 | 6.0 | 0.0 | 37.6 | 329.9 | 367.6 |
| 13. | Trans-megabloc groupings | | | | | | | | | | | |
| 14. | Evangelicals (billion $ pa) | 37.1 | 31.7 | 130.4 | 367.7 | 141.0 | 1,146.0 | 60.0 | 1.0 | 142.0 | 1,733.8 | 1,876.8 |
| 15. | Pentecostals/Charismatics (billion $ pa) | 0.4 | 99.1 | 243.8 | 497.7 | 496.1 | 2,114.0 | 56.9 | 3.1 | 258.8 | 3,245.6 | 3,507.5 |
| 16. | Great Commission Christians (billion $ pa) | 40.3 | 56.1 | 397.6 | 3,167.2 | 175.8 | 2,906.8 | 146.1 | 6.2 | 492.6 | 6,350.8 | 6,849.6 |
| 17. | POTENTIAL GIVING IF CHRISTIANS TITHED | | | | | | | | | | | |
| 18. | Potential giving | 27.0 | 20.0 | 58.8 | 697.7 | 157.4 | 557.0 | 28.8 | 1.1 | 77.2 | 1,441.5 | 1,519.8 |
| 19. | ACTUAL GIVING BY CHURCH MEMBERS | | | | | | | | | | | |
| 20. | Giving to all causes (billion $ pa) | 8.8 | 3.9 | 11.5 | 136.6 | 30.8 | 109.1 | 5.6 | 0.2 | 15.1 | 282.2 | 297.6 |
| 21. | Giving to secular or non-Christian causes | 0.8 | 0.4 | 1.0 | 12.4 | 2.8 | 9.9 | 0.5 | 0.0 | 1.4 | 25.7 | 27.1 |
| 22. | Giving to Christian causes (billion $ pa) | 8.0 | 3.6 | 10.5 | 124.2 | 28.0 | 99.1 | 5.1 | 0.2 | 13.7 | 256.6 | 270.5 |
| 23. | (a) to churches and denoms (billion $ pa) | 7.0 | 1.4 | 4.2 | 49.5 | 11.2 | 39.5 | 2.0 | 0.1 | 5.5 | 102.3 | 107.9 |
| 24. | (b) to parachurch agencies (billion $ pa) | 1.0 | 2.1 | 6.3 | 74.6 | 16.8 | 59.6 | 3.1 | 0.1 | 8.3 | 154.2 | 162.6 |
| 25. | INCOME OF ORGANIZED CHRISTIANITY | | | | | | | | | | | |
| 26. | Via the 6 megablocs | 8.0 | 3.6 | 10.5 | 124.2 | 28.0 | 99.1 | 5.1 | 0.2 | 13.7 | 256.6 | 270.5 |
| 27. | Orthodox (billion $ pa) | 1.8 | 0.2 | 0.4 | 7.1 | 0.0 | 2.6 | 0.2 | 0.1 | 3.3 | 7.2 | 10.5 |
| 28. | Roman Catholics (billion $ pa) | 4.1 | 0.8 | 2.7 | 74.5 | 23.2 | 28.5 | 1.9 | 0.0 | 2.4 | 129.2 | 131.6 |
| 29. | Anglicans (billion $ pa) | 0.5 | 0.3 | 0.1 | 8.6 | 0.1 | 1.3 | 1.4 | 0.0 | 0.2 | 11.6 | 11.8 |
| 30. | Protestants (billion $ pa) | 1.6 | 1.0 | 2.5 | 30.0 | 2.4 | 28.8 | 1.1 | 0.0 | 2.7 | 63.0 | 65.8 |
| 31. | Independents (billion $ pa) | 0.1 | 1.2 | 4.1 | 2.9 | 2.0 | 33.5 | 0.3 | 0.1 | 4.4 | 39.7 | 44.2 |
| 32. | Marginal Christians (billion $ pa) | 0.0 | 0.0 | 0.7 | 1.0 | 0.4 | 4.4 | 0.1 | 0.0 | 0.7 | 5.9 | 6.5 |
| 33. | Via 3 trans-megabloc groupings: | | | | | | | | | | | |
| 34. | Evangelicals (billion $ pa) | 1.1 | 0.6 | 2.3 | 6.5 | 2.5 | 20.4 | 1.1 | 0.0 | 2.5 | 30.9 | 33.4 |
| 35. | Pentecostals/Charismatics (billion $ pa) | 0.0 | 1.8 | 4.3 | 8.9 | 8.8 | 37.6 | 1.0 | 0.1 | 4.6 | 57.8 | 62.4 |
| 36. | Great Commission Christians (billion $ pa) | 1.2 | 1.0 | 7.1 | 56.4 | 3.1 | 51.7 | 2.6 | 0.1 | 8.8 | 113.0 | 121.9 |
| 37. | RATES OF GIVING TO CHRISTIAN CAUSES | | | | | | | | | | | |
| 38. | Giving per congregation per year ($) | 4,601.2 | 5,886.1 | 9,136.5 | 227,289.2 | 60,678.2 | 156,060.1 | 93,720.4 | 3,339.8 | 9,432.4 | 132,615.8 | 78,459.7 |
| 39. | Giving per congregation per week ($) | 88.5 | 113.2 | 175.7 | 4,370.9 | 1,166.9 | 3,001.2 | 1,802.3 | 64.2 | 181.4 | 2,550.3 | 1,508.8 |
| 40. | Giving per church member per year ($) | 15.3 | 10.6 | 34.1 | 231.3 | 58.9 | 467.3 | 240.2 | 18.7 | 28.0 | 185.0 | 143.3 |
| 41. | Giving per church member per week ($) | 0.3 | 0.2 | 0.7 | 4.4 | 1.1 | 9.0 | 4.6 | 0.4 | 0.5 | 3.6 | 2.8 |
| 42. | GIVING TO GLOBAL FOREIGN MISSIONS | | | | | | | | | | | |
| 43. | Giving to Christian foreign missions (million $ pa) | 200.0 | 197.0 | 580.5 | 6,885.8 | 1,553.9 | 5,497.7 | 284.7 | 10.4 | 761.9 | 14,227.7 | 15,000.0 |
| 44. | Giving to missions per church member per year ($) | $0.38 | $0.59 | $1.89 | $12.83 | $3.27 | $25.91 | $13.32 | $1.04 | $1.55 | $10.26 | $7.94 |
| 45. | Giving to missions per church member per week ($) | $0.01 | $0.01 | $0.04 | $0.25 | $0.06 | $0.50 | $0.26 | $0.02 | $0.03 | $0.20 | $0.15 |

***Methodological notes***

*a. Limits of the above table.* This table deals, not with static wealth but with the annual movement of Christian financial resources by individual Christians and their churches and agencies. It refers mainly to the first, or initial, level of Christian finance, i.e., to live Christian stewardship, which means ongoing financial resources in the pockets of today's Christians and the amounts that they donate each year. The table includes endowments, bequests, state support, political support, business support, and other forms of Christian income and the secondary and subsequent levels of Christian finances such as the activities of funding bodies that circulate or otherwise spend the money donated by Christians.

*b. Variables shown.* The 40 variables shown from line 6 down are suggestive and selective rather than comprehensive.The full listing of all financial variables likely to be useful to mission strategists approaches 100 or more. The fuller computerized version of this table incorporates the second and subsequent levels of giving. *Definitions of financial variables.* These largely follow World Bank usage.

*c. Continents.* Our usage here follows that of United Nations agencies, which divide the world's 238 countries into 6 'major areas' (equivalent to continents) and 21 'regions'. The UN does not include Antarctica; we do, but not in this particular table. Our terms ('Africa', etc.) are therefore defined as in UN publications. Note that continental comparisons are complicated by conflicting definitions: e.g., the World Bank defines Turkey as in Europe, and Indonesia with Oceania, whereas UN agencies define both countries as in Asia The UN defines Azerbaijan and Armenia as in Western Asia; the *Ethnologue* (WBT/SIL) defines them as in Europe. This kind of idiosyncratic usage means that no one uses, or can use, the others' databases.

*d. Amounts of money.* All amounts are given either as billions of US dollars per year or as millions of US dollars per year, or as dollars per year or per week. Numbers follow USA usage: a billion is 1,000 million (in German, French, and British English: 1 Milliarde, or milliard) and 1,000 billion is a trillion (in German, 1 Billion; in French and British English, 1 billion).

*e. Constituencies involved.* The first 3 lines refer to the total population of the whole world. All remaining lines, where unindented, refer to the totals of or for all affiliated Christians (church members) of all confessions. Lines indented refer to subdivisions (e.g., Roman Catholics, Protestants).

*f. Giving.* This term refers here mainly to 'live giving', i.e., money given or donated per year or per week by living Christians (though it includes bequests). Christian giving to secular causes is included only in nos. 20 and 21. In all other lines, Christian giving refers exclusively to giving to specifically Christian causes, which means to churches, denominations, parachurch agencies, or to individual Christian workers or groups or causes.

*g. Tithing.* 'Potential' Christian giving (line 18) refers to what would be given if all Christians tithed (gave 10% of all personal income). Several communions do this strictly.

*h. Past giving to missions.* The global total of giving to Protestant and Anglican foreign missions in the year 1800 is estimated to have been US $75,000, and in the year 1900 to have been US $19,100,000 (both at 1900 values of the dollar). In terms of AD 2000 dollars (each worth only 6 cents of the 1900 dollar) these sums are respectively $2 million and $320 million.

*i. Surveys of giving.* The most exact annual surveys of giving come from the USA. Total official or publicly recognized giving to charities there—secular and religious—has risen steadily each year from $6 billion in 1955 to $39.6 billion in 1978, of which 46.5% ($18.4 billion) was then classified as giving to 'Religion' (*Giving USA: Annual Reports,* American Association of Fundraising Counsel, New York). In 1982 the total rose to $60 billion, and by 2000 to $80 billion. Of all giving to charities, 81% is by individuals. These well-defined and thorough annual surveys do not however cover the total extent of Christian giving, omitting as they do much anonymous or private or secret or unheralded giving, or unofficial or spontaneous or unplanned or one-time acts of charity to individuals in need, beggars, family members, or acquaintances, et alia. *Polls.* The Princeton Religion Research Center (Gallup) and *Christianity Today* publish poll results covering percentage of income donated in the USA. Thus 16% of USA residents give 10% or more to all causes, 13% give between 5–9%, 33% less than 4%, and 26% give nothing. *Denominational giving.* Total donations from their own church members are published annually by many denominations (see *Yearbook of American and Canadian Churches,* annually).

tians. Starting with United Nations and World Bank data, it has been possible to build up a computerized global table of Christian financial resources.This table is given in detail for all countries in the *World Christian database, AD 30-2200.* We shall now comment on some of the figures there, at the same time showing how further figures can be derived by simple arithmetic, depending on what the reader is interested in. Numbers in parentheses following the headings below refer to numbered rows in the listing shown here as Table 20–1.

### *Christians' personal income and lifestyle (nos. 3,6)*

The first three lines of the table show the world distribution of population, total income and income per person. Average income at the world level is around $4,770 per person each year. Because Christians are concentrated in the Western world, their average income (no. 6 divided by no. 5) is far higher at $8,050. Non-Christians average only $3,280 (subtract no. 6 from no. 2, then divide by the sum of no. 1 minus no. 5). Since lifestyle depends on income, Christians across the world can be seen to live on average at a level about 2.5 times higher than non-Christians.

**TWELVE ASPECTS OF FINANCE—captions for photos opposite**

These illustrations show aspects of the church's daily encounter with money. Details of each are as follows.

1. Money-changing challenges Christians to observe total honesty. ('The Money Changers', stained glass in Le Mans Cathedral, AD 1240).
2. 'Christ driving the Traders from the Temple', El Greco (1541-1614).
3. From the movie rock opera 'Jesus Christ Superstar'; a modern version of Christ evicting the money-changers.
4. Founding of the Baptist Missionary Society, 1792: Andrew Fuller passes his snuff box and raises £13-2s-6d ($20).
5. Children's church procession in Rwanda, offering money, tithes, other valuables, teaching stewardship of money and possessions.
6. First annual board meeting of newly-formed Bible Society of Eritrea, in Asmara, 1992.
7. Switzerland postage stamp honoring Salvation Army for its work as major fund-raiser for Christian social services.
8. Church treasurers worldwide number 5 million; here, new treasurer (left) poses with pastor of Life Messengers Mission, Uganda.
9. Brisk sales in Bible House, Manila, Philippines, moving 14 million scriptures each year.
10. In huge Kimbanguist openair service in Congo-Zaire, ushers line up to carefully empty offertory baskets into larger bowls; all aspects of handling monies are observed by many officials and witnesses at every stage.
11. Bibles printed at Amity Press are shipped out of Hefei Distribution Center, China, with vastly cheaper transport costs than in Western world.
12. Most large churches and agencies require 2 signatures on bank checks; in Nairobi, witnesses in AICN watch signing process.

### *260 million Christians in absolute poverty*

So much for the averages. There is a further factor, however: income distribution is so unequal that, whereas 52 % of all Christians live in affluence and a further 35 % are comparatively well off, 13 % live in absolute poverty.

The degradation and agony of absolute poverty are thus shared by millions of our fellow Christians. Some 100 million Christians live in the world's twenty-six poorest countries. In all developing countries, Christians living in absolute poverty number some 260 million. This is 24% of the world's 1,090 million absolutely poor, as well as 13% of all Christians. Of these, half live in Latin America, a third in Africa, the rest in South and Southeast Asia. This is what we usually mean by the 'Church of the Poor'. By the world's standards, they have nothing. Today a vast literature has been building up on their predicament from the theological and biblical standpoints.

How 'poor' is the Church of the Poor? Here we meet a strange paradox. On the one hand, the answer is: shockingly, appallingly, scandalously, outrageously poor. It is surely outrageous that 1,040 million affluent Christians can continue to allow 260 million brethren in Christ to exist in abject poverty year after year, or even worse to starve to death in full view. But from another point of view, the answer, surprisingly, is that this church is largely financially self-supporting, and that it has huge potential financial resources right there amid its membership. The personal income of the 260 million looks bad enough when expressed as an average of $100 per person per year, but in aggregate it amounts to the huge sum of $26 billion each year. Their churches operate on income of well over $300 million a year, enough to run major relief programs of all kinds.

Again, the major problem is that distribution is grossly unfair. In the 'churches of the poor,' that is, in the actual denominations to which the 260 million belong, they exist in close proximity to some 30 million relatively affluent co-citizen, elite, fellow Christians above them. These include the hierarchies of church leaders who control the churches, few of whom are poor and a number of whom have become very rich since taking office. Regrettably, these 30 million show less concern for the poor than many of their co-religionists in the Western world.

Yet another side of the paradox is that this Church of the Poor is poor only in material goods. They are far from being spiritual paupers. Spiritually, it is the Church of the Rich. Some of the richest and most dynamic forms of Christianity today, and the most rapid church growth, are to be found in these areas of material poverty and destitution. Within this Church of the Poor we count the 50 millions involved in the Charismatic and Neocharismatic Renewal throughout India and South Asia; the 466,000 base ecclesial communities (or, the Iglesia Popular) in Latin America; and the entire 80-million-strong African Indigenous Churches movement among Africa's lowest social classes. This Church of the Poor is the only part of global Christianity whose lifestyle is similar to that of Jesus on earth. They are the only Christians who are able with complete accuracy to proclaim, with the apostle Peter (Acts 3:6): 'Silver and gold have I none; but such as I have give I thee: in the name of Jesus Christ of Nazareth, rise up and walk!'

### *CHRISTIAN FINANCIAL RESOURCES*

***Personal income of Christians***

What about total resources? How much in aggregate are the world's 1.9 billion church members worth each year on the world scene, considering here only the aspect of financial income? The answer is easy to compute, but startling to comprehend: $15.2 trillion. The largest slice of this (46%) goes to Europe, the next (37%) to North America. The influential worldwide community of Evangelicals alone have personal income totaling just under $1 trillion a year. All this looks impressive. It looks less satisfactory when its uses are expressed in percentage terms, as we shall shortly do.

***Stewardship and tithing (nos. 17-36)***

So much for the individual and aggregate personal income of Christians. How much do they give away each year? In theory, many confessions and communions assert that Christians should tithe, which means give away 10 percent of their income. If all did this, the total would be $1,520 billion a year. In practice, they give a third of this—something like $320 billion, if we include every kind of Christians. But it makes more sense here to restrict the definition of 'Christians' to all affiliated church members. In this case, their annual donations total $298 billion. Forty-six percent of this comes from Europe, 37 percent from North America. Africa contributes a mere 1.3 percent, Asia 3.9 percent.

***Where does all this money go? (nos. 19-24)***

Now we examine what happens to those massive sums.

Who are the immediate beneficiaries of all this wealth? A few percentages can answer this question. Though Christians number only 33% of the world population, they receive 53% of the entire world's annual income—and spend 98% of it on themselves. Put this way, it is shocking. Put another way, each year North American and European church members spend $12.5 trillion on themselves personally and on their families. The Church of the Rich (the 'Middle-class Church') is at heart a selfish and a self-serving church.

Of the remaining 2% of Christians' income, a meager 0.2%, or $27 billion a year, is given or donated to secular or non-Christian causes and charities; and about 1.8%, or $270 billion a year, is given or donated directly to Christian causes. This latter sum forms the vast bulk of what the churches and parachurch agencies across the world receive to run the worldwide Christian church and its annual operations.

***Giving to secular causes (no. 21)***

These figures in the preceding paragraph can be rearranged to convey a much more favorable perspective. Christians support their own religion financially, as one would expect; but they also give 10% as much again to secular charities (famine relief, hospitals, handicapped programs, cancer research, etc.) or even to non-Christian causes. Christians are heavily involved in financial support of social and development programs in the world beyond or outside the boundaries of the churches. This is surely greatly to their credit.

The actual breakdown by category is instructive. In the United States, some 14% of all giving by Christians goes to secular education, 13.4% to health and secular hospitals, 9.9% to social welfare, 6.2% to arts and the humanities, 2.8% to civic and public services, and 7.1% to other secular causes. The remaining 46.4% is spent directly on religion and religious causes, which in the United States context means largely Christian causes.

***Giving to Christian causes (nos. 22-24)***

Before the year 1900, over 90% of Christian giving was channeled through the churches and denominations. A modest 10 percent supported the Bible societies and missionary societies. But the twentieth century has seen the emergence on a massive scale of over 40,000 distinct new parachurch agencies whose finances are independent of the churches. This ought to be regarded by older denominations and agencies, not with envy or jealousy but simply as the latest development in the long history of where Christian wealth is concentrated. Unfortunately their attitude often resembles that of the older brother in the parable of the Prodigal son (see Luke 15). Be that as it may, in 1980 36% of all Christian giving to Christian causes was regularly bypassing the churches and denominations; by 1995 this had risen to 60%. In consequence, giving to denominations in many countries is declining at an alarming rate. One major example and cause of this that springs to mind is Christian broadcasting. Nonexistent in 1900, by 1977 religious broadcasting in the United States alone accounted for $500 million as the cost of broadcast time. On the world scale the total cost of Christian broadcasting is over three times larger, around $2 billion in 1982, skyrocketing to some $6 billion by AD 2000.

***Giving to denominations (no. 23)***

All this is bad news for the world's 33,800 Christian denominations. Their once unchallenged hold on their members' giving, and their appeal as worthy causes are dwindling. While their members do not reach the widely taught stewardship target of tithing (giving 10% of personal income), nevertheless they do average 2% of income. But a tenth of this is given to secular causes, and another 55% to parachurch organizations, leaving only a third for the operation of the denominations and local churches themselves. And their third is rapidly declining.

***Individual giving (nos. 37-45)***

These huge sums of money become more intelligible when reduced to what the average individual contributes. On the world level, the average church member gives $143 a year (which is $2.75 a week). As one would expect, individual giving is highest in the strongholds of the Church of the Rich (the affluent West)—$466 a year in North America; is much lower in the strongholds of the Church of the Poor in Asia ($34 a year) and in Latin America ($59 a year); and is lowest of all ($11 a year) in the Church of the Absolutely Poor in the continent with the lowest per-capita income of all, Africa.

### *THE INCOME OF ORGANIZED GLOBAL CHRISTIANITY*

The sheer magnitude of money available to Christians and their churches and agencies is starkly revealed in Table 20–2. This ranks all countries of the world by the personal income of Great Commission Christians (column 8).

As will be seen from Table 20–2, huge figures result when we compute any large country's or church's income. Contrary to popular stereotype, many denominations in the Third World, even in areas of abject poverty and neglect, generate vast annual income. Thus the Kimbanguist Church of Zaire ((EJCSK) has (using AD 2000 figures) 9.5 million members handling $2 billion in personal annual income, of which they donate over $20 million to their denomination annually. In South Africa, Zion Christian Church's 7.2 million members have personal income of $21 billion, from which the ZCC gets a church income of $200 million. The largest Third-World denomination, the Assemblies of God in Brazil, has 19 million members, personal income of $57 billion, and church income averages $1 billion a year. Lastly, China's 89 million Christians have personal income of $49 billion of which $2 billion is donated to and used by their churches.

Let us now analyze this income for organized global Christianity, and see how it is expended.

### *A GLOBAL BALANCE SHEET*

It is possible here to give a simplified annual balance sheet, or overall budget, listing the main expenditures on the part of global Christianity. The current cost of items is approximately as follows shown in Table 20–3.

***Enough silver and gold to tackle any task***

Altogether, it is not surprising that aggregate totals turn out to be staggeringly high. Table 20–3 shows that the annual income of organized global Christianity reaches $270 billion. Of this, denominations and churches receive $108 billion. But even this monumental sum is surpassed by what the paradenominational bodies and service agencies receive: $162 billion.

The moral is clear. Christians have enough money to implement even their wildest dreams of worldwide ministry and global evangelization.

### *THE EXPENDITURES OF ORGANIZED GLOBAL CHRISTIANITY*

Examination of the expenditures on the balance sheet in Table 20–3, from 3 distinct and different standpoints, reveals a large number of surprises and disturbing comparisons. Here we deal only with a few issues.

***First standpoint: global priorities need changing***

This point of view classifies expenditures in terms of the Christian global apostolate. Some 82% of expenditure is spent on the home pastoral ministries of the churches in their home countries, the heartlands of the Christian faith—Europe, the Americas, and the rest of the 141 World C countries. Another 12% is spent on home missions in those same countries. This leaves only 5.6% to operate foreign missions. This miniscule sum, exemplified in the pitiful fraction of 0.1% directed toward the unevangelized world (World A), goes a long way toward explaining why global Christianity, which numbered 34% of the globe's population in AD 1900, numbers 33% in AD 2000.

***Second standpoint: Christian funds are entirely adequate***

By identifying who the donors are and who the beneficiaries are, we see that the 6 major ecclesiastico-cul-

**Table 20–2. Countries ranked by personal annual income of each's total of Great Commission Christians in AD 2000: (1) the Top 11 countries each with over $100 billion, (2) the Top 34 countries each with over $10 billion, and (3) the Top 83 countries each with over $1 billion.**

| Code | Country | Pop 2000 | GNPpc $ | AC 2000 | AC income $ | GCC | GCC Income $ | GCC % |
|---|---|---|---|---|---|---|---|---|
| 1 | 2 | 3 | 4 | 5 | 6 | 7 | 8 | 9 |
| usa | USA | 278,357,141 | 26,980 | 191,827,627 | 5,175,509,376,460 | 98,662,079 | 2,661,902,891,420 | 35.44 |
| germ | Germany | 82,220,490 | 27,510 | 58,783,222 | 1,617,126,437,220 | 26,146,513 | 719,290,572,630 | 31.80 |
| fran | France | 59,079,709 | 24,990 | 41,116,959 | 1,027,512,805,410 | 24,539,680 | 613,246,603,200 | 41.54 |
| ital | Italy | 57,297,886 | 19,020 | 46,922,140 | 892,459,102,800 | 24,220,748 | 460,678,626,960 | 42.27 |
| brit | Britain | 58,830,160 | 18,700 | 39,053,151 | 730,293,923,700 | 21,120,856 | 394,960,007,200 | 35.90 |
| cana | Canada | 31,146,639 | 19,380 | 20,237,778 | 392,208,137,640 | 12,604,889 | 244,282,748,820 | 40.47 |
| spai | Spain | 39,629,775 | 13,580 | 37,073,672 | 503,460,465,760 | 17,132,496 | 232,659,295,680 | 43.23 |
| neth | Netherlands | 15,785,699 | 24,000 | 10,282,853 | 246,788,472,000 | 6,515,668 | 156,376,032,000 | 41.28 |
| souk | South Korea | 46,843,989 | 9,700 | 18,681,876 | 181,214,197,200 | 13,329,255 | 129,293,773,500 | 28.45 |
| japa | Japan | 126,714,220 | 39,640 | 3,436,881 | 136,237,962,840 | 3,116,536 | 123,539,487,040 | 2.46 |
| aust | Australia | 18,879,524 | 18,720 | 12,587,959 | 235,646,592,480 | 6,485,759 | 121,413,408,480 | 34.35 |
| belg | Belgium | 10,161,164 | 24,710 | 8,518,696 | 210,496,978,160 | 4,675,333 | 115,527,478,430 | 46.01 |
| swit | Switzerland | 7,385,708 | 40,630 | 6,445,548 | 261,882,615,240 | 2,541,157 | 103,247,208,910 | 34.41 |
| braz | Brazil | 170,115,463 | 3,640 | 155,475,609 | 565,931,216,760 | 24,207,478 | 88,115,219,920 | 14.23 |
| russ | Russia | 146,933,847 | 2,240 | 83,618,357 | 187,305,119,680 | 29,373,498 | 65,796,635,520 | 19.99 |
| swed | Sweden | 8,910,214 | 23,750 | 6,000,356 | 142,508,455,000 | 2,499,326 | 59,358,992,500 | 28.05 |
| chin | China | 1,262,556,787 | 620 | 88,955,347 | 55,152,315,140 | 81,352,742 | 50,438,700,040 | 6.44 |
| ausz | Austria | 8,210,520 | 26,890 | 6,909,670 | 185,801,026,300 | 1,722,957 | 46,330,313,730 | 20.98 |
| port | Portugal | 9,874,853 | 9,740 | 9,080,231 | 88,441,449,940 | 3,570,189 | 34,773,640,860 | 36.15 |
| norw | Norway | 4,461,033 | 31,250 | 4,201,262 | 131,289,437,500 | 1,074,638 | 33,582,437,500 | 24.09 |
| irel | Ireland | 3,730,239 | 14,710 | 3,355,446 | 49,358,610,660 | 1,805,772 | 26,562,906,120 | 48.41 |
| soua | South Africa | 40,376,579 | 3,160 | 31,800,789 | 100,490,493,240 | 7,717,095 | 24,386,020,200 | 19.11 |
| newz | New Zealand | 3,861,905 | 14,340 | 2,562,219 | 36,742,220,460 | 1,541,611 | 22,106,701,740 | 39.92 |
| arge | Argentina | 37,027,297 | 8,030 | 33,985,872 | 272,906,552,160 | 2,739,882 | 22,001,252,460 | 7.40 |
| finl | Finland | 5,175,743 | 20,580 | 4,579,451 | 94,245,101,580 | 1,033,772 | 21,275,027,760 | 19.97 |
| denm | Denmark | 5,293,239 | 29,890 | 4,751,110 | 142,010,677,900 | 682,522 | 20,400,582,580 | 12.89 |
| indi | India | 1,013,661,777 | 340 | 62,243,546 | 21,162,805,640 | 50,364,266 | 17,123,850,440 | 4.97 |
| mexi | Mexico | 98,881,289 | 3,320 | 93,806,927 | 311,438,997,640 | 5,123,454 | 17,009,867,280 | 5.18 |
| indo | Indonesia | 212,107,385 | 980 | 26,364,858 | 25,837,560,840 | 14,599,219 | 14,307,234,620 | 6.88 |
| taiw | Taiwan | 22,401,000 | 12,400 | 1,179,743 | 14,628,813,200 | 820,752 | 10,177,324,800 | 3.66 |
| czec | Czech Republic | 10,244,177 | 3,870 | 4,819,136 | 18,650,056,320 | 2,591,316 | 10,028,392,920 | 25.30 |
| ukra | Ukraine | 50,455,980 | 1,630 | 41,669,097 | 67,920,628,110 | 6,110,588 | 9,960,258,440 | 12.11 |
| chil | Chile | 15,211,294 | 4,160 | 13,358,340 | 55,570,694,400 | 2,222,359 | 9,245,013,440 | 14.61 |
| pola | Poland | 38,765,085 | 2,790 | 37,498,059 | 104,619,584,610 | 2,958,523 | 8,254,279,170 | 7.63 |
| sing | Singapore | 3,566,614 | 26,730 | 402,936 | 10,770,479,280 | 292,499 | 7,818,498,270 | 8.20 |
| egyp | Egypt | 68,469,695 | 790 | 10,320,466 | 8,153,168,140 | 8,196,488 | 6,475,225,520 | 11.97 |
| vene | Venezuela | 24,169,722 | 3,020 | 22,735,834 | 68,662,218,680 | 1,861,728 | 5,622,418,560 | 7.70 |
| malb | Malaysia | 22,244,062 | 3,890 | 1,771,189 | 6,889,925,210 | 1,355,307 | 5,272,144,230 | 6.09 |
| colo | Colombia | 42,321,361 | 1,910 | 40,935,888 | 78,187,546,080 | 2,673,679 | 5,106,726,890 | 6.32 |
| uuay | Uruguay | 3,337,058 | 5,170 | 2,161,729 | 11,176,138,930 | 891,482 | 4,608,961,940 | 26.71 |
| belo | Belorussia | 10,236,181 | 2,070 | 6,584,077 | 13,629,039,390 | 2,162,574 | 4,476,528,180 | 21.13 |
| hung | Hungary | 10,035,568 | 4,120 | 8,749,732 | 36,048,895,840 | 1,066,779 | 4,395,129,480 | 10.63 |
| puer | Puerto Rico | 3,868,602 | 7,800 | 3,722,291 | 29,033,869,800 | 544,610 | 4,247,958,000 | 14.08 |
| phil | Philippines | 75,966,500 | 1,050 | 66,600,057 | 69,930,059,850 | 3,915,959 | 4,111,756,950 | 5.15 |
| myan | Myanmar | 45,611,177 | 1,790 | 3,741,464 | 6,697,220,560 | 2,257,465 | 4,040,862,350 | 4.95 |
| cuba | Cuba | 11,200,684 | 1,300 | 4,822,909 | 6,269,781,700 | 2,584,208 | 3,359,470,400 | 23.07 |
| thai | Thailand | 61,399,249 | 2,740 | 1,345,167 | 3,685,757,580 | 1,187,923 | 3,254,909,020 | 1.93 |
| luxe | Luxembourg | 430,615 | 41,210 | 402,674 | 16,594,195,540 | 75,421 | 3,108,099,410 | 17.51 |
| isra | Israel | 5,121,683 | 15,920 | 294,078 | 4,681,721,760 | 192,425 | 3,063,406,000 | 3.76 |
| saud | Saudi Arabia | 21,606,691 | 7,040 | 786,985 | 5,540,374,400 | 417,623 | 2,940,065,920 | 1.93 |
| nige | Nigeria | 111,506,095 | 260 | 50,965,002 | 13,250,900,520 | 11,252,805 | 2,925,729,300 | 10.09 |
| kuwa | Kuwait | 1,971,634 | 17,390 | 247,535 | 4,304,633,650 | 163,948 | 2,851,055,720 | 8.32 |
| yugo | Yugoslavia | 10,640,150 | 2,000 | 6,885,557 | 13,771,114,000 | 1,398,890 | 2,797,780,000 | 13.15 |
| roma | Romania | 22,326,502 | 1,480 | 19,627,363 | 29,048,497,240 | 1,857,773 | 2,749,504,040 | 8.32 |
| pale | Palestine | 2,215,393 | 14,584 | 188,289 | 2,746,006,776 | 169,540 | 2,472,571,360 | 7.65 |
| unia | United Arab Emirates | 2,441,436 | 17,400 | 262,745 | 4,571,763,000 | 137,255 | 2,388,237,000 | 5.62 |
| slok | Slovakia | 5,387,191 | 2,950 | 4,324,186 | 12,756,348,700 | 761,996 | 2,247,888,200 | 14.14 |
| peru | Peru | 25,661,669 | 2,310 | 24,702,049 | 57,061,733,190 | 968,929 | 2,238,225,990 | 3.78 |
| came | Cameroon | 15,084,969 | 650 | 7,761,501 | 5,044,975,650 | 3,388,574 | 2,202,573,100 | 22.46 |
| slov | Slovenia | 1,985,557 | 8,200 | 1,736,806 | 14,241,809,200 | 264,345 | 2,167,629,000 | 13.31 |
| gree | Greece | 10,644,744 | 8,210 | 10,061,020 | 82,600,974,200 | 262,176 | 2,152,464,960 | 2.46 |
| malt | Malta | 388,544 | 12,000 | 371,381 | 4,456,572,000 | 170,064 | 2,040,768,000 | 43.77 |
| kaza | Kazakhstan | 16,222,563 | 1,330 | 2,591,803 | 3,447,097,990 | 1,443,467 | 1,919,811,110 | 8.90 |
| leba | Lebanon | 3,281,787 | 2,660 | 1,734,821 | 4,614,623,860 | 720,781 | 1,917,277,460 | 21.96 |
| paki | Pakistan | 156,483,155 | 460 | 3,812,245 | 1,753,632,700 | 3,520,938 | 1,619,631,480 | 2.25 |
| zimb | Zimbabwe | 11,669,029 | 540 | 6,917,360 | 3,735,374,400 | 2,934,675 | 1,584,724,500 | 25.15 |
| ghan | Ghana | 20,212,495 | 390 | 8,666,976 | 3,380,120,640 | 3,925,064 | 1,530,774,960 | 19.42 |
| suda | Sudan | 29,489,719 | 800 | 4,874,391 | 3,899,512,800 | 1,910,208 | 1,528,166,400 | 6.48 |
| boli | Bolivia | 8,328,665 | 800 | 7,786,232 | 6,228,985,600 | 1,724,676 | 1,379,740,800 | 20.71 |
| ivor | Ivory Coast | 14,785,832 | 660 | 4,353,882 | 2,873,562,120 | 2,035,544 | 1,343,459,040 | 13.77 |
| viet | Viet Nam | 79,831,650 | 240 | 6,567,922 | 1,576,301,280 | 5,597,118 | 1,343,308,320 | 7.01 |
| cost | Costa Rica | 4,023,422 | 2,610 | 3,870,161 | 10,101,120,210 | 514,542 | 1,342,954,620 | 12.79 |
| guat | Guatemala | 11,385,295 | 1,340 | 10,684,153 | 14,316,765,020 | 974,549 | 1,305,895,660 | 8.56 |
| pana | Panama | 2,855,683 | 2,750 | 2,457,064 | 6,756,926,000 | 445,061 | 1,223,917,750 | 15.59 |
| bots | Botswana | 1,622,220 | 3,020 | 751,073 | 2,268,240,460 | 384,089 | 1,159,948,780 | 23.68 |
| trin | Trinidad & Tobago | 1,294,958 | 3,770 | 795,865 | 3,000,411,050 | 287,827 | 1,085,107,790 | 22.23 |
| latv | Latvia | 2,356,508 | 2,270 | 1,576,425 | 3,578,484,750 | 471,566 | 1,070,454,820 | 20.01 |
| keny | Kenya | 30,080,372 | 280 | 22,477,365 | 6,293,662,200 | 3,693,709 | 1,034,238,520 | 12.28 |
| sril | Sri Lanka | 18,827,054 | 700 | 1,755,120 | 1,228,584,000 | 1,402,374 | 981,661,800 | 7.45 |
| ethi | Ethiopia | 62,564,875 | 100 | 31,161,159 | 3,116,115,900 | 9,745,644 | 974,564,400 | 15.58 |
| jama | Jamaica | 2,582,577 | 1,510 | 1,121,713 | 1,693,786,630 | 635,819 | 960,086,690 | 24.62 |
| ecua | Ecuador | 12,646,068 | 1,390 | 12,307,787 | 17,107,823,930 | 646,048 | 898,006,720 | 5.11 |
| cypr | Cyprus | 600,506 | 13,420 | 551,594 | 7,402,391,480 | 66,156 | 887,813,520 | 11.02 |
| syri | Syria | 16,124,618 | 1,120 | 1,257,709 | 1,408,634,080 | 791,510 | 886,491,200 | 4.91 |
| esto | Estonia | 1,396,158 | 2,860 | 529,875 | 1,515,442,500 | 292,255 | 835,849,300 | 20.93 |
| elsa | El Salvador | 6,276,023 | 1,610 | 6,098,022 | 9,817,815,420 | 510,916 | 822,574,760 | 8.14 |
| lith | Lithuania | 3,670,269 | 1,900 | 3,213,397 | 6,105,454,300 | 429,935 | 816,876,500 | 11.71 |
| mold | Moldavia | 4,380,492 | 920 | 2,798,558 | 2,574,673,360 | 836,487 | 769,568,040 | 19.10 |
| icel | Iceland | 280,969 | 24,950 | 265,259 | 6,618,212,050 | 30,470 | 760,226,500 | 10.84 |
| croa | Croatia | 4,472,600 | 3,250 | 4,256,386 | 13,833,254,500 | 233,171 | 757,805,750 | 5.21 |
| para | Paraguay | 5,496,453 | 1,690 | 5,173,602 | 8,743,387,380 | 429,463 | 725,792,470 | 7.81 |
| domr | Dominican Republic | 8,495,338 | 1,460 | 8,026,705 | 11,718,989,300 | 496,611 | 725,052,060 | 5.85 |
| ugan | Uganda | 21,778,450 | 240 | 18,944,173 | 4,546,601,520 | 3,019,984 | 724,796,160 | 13.87 |
| tanz | Tanzania | 33,517,014 | 120 | 15,722,778 | 1,886,733,360 | 5,627,411 | 675,289,320 | 16.79 |
| bulg | Bulgaria | 8,225,045 | 1,330 | 6,657,950 | 8,855,073,500 | 493,299 | 656,087,670 | 6.00 |
| ango | Angola | 12,878,188 | 410 | 10,934,238 | 4,483,037,580 | 1,545,888 | 633,814,080 | 12.00 |
| iran | Iran | 67,702,199 | 4,700 | 313,990 | 1,475,753,000 | 129,374 | 608,057,800 | 0.19 |
| papu | Papua New Guinea | 4,608,145 | 1,160 | 3,785,528 | 4,391,212,480 | 523,096 | 606,791,360 | 11.35 |
| liby | Libya | 5,604,722 | 6,510 | 170,352 | 1,108,991,520 | 93,153 | 606,426,030 | 1.66 |
| guad | Guadeloupe | 455,687 | 9,200 | 432,948 | 3,983,121,600 | 65,752 | 604,918,400 | 14.43 |
| zamb | Zambia | 9,168,700 | 400 | 7,052,084 | 2,820,832,000 | 1,506,682 | 602,672,800 | 16.43 |

*Continued overleaf*

Table 20–2 continued

| Code | Name | Pop 2000 | GNPpc $ | AC 2000 | AC income $ | GCC | GCC Income $ | GCC % |
|------|------|----------|---------|---------|-------------|-----|--------------|-------|
| 1 | 2 | 3 | 4 | 5 | 6 | 7 | 8 | 9 |
| nami | Namibia | 1,725,868 | 2,000 | 1,349,211 | 2,698,422,000 | 295,226 | 590,452,000 | 17.11 |
| mada | Madagascar | 15,941,727 | 230 | 7,629,263 | 1,754,730,490 | 2,487,601 | 572,148,230 | 15.60 |
| turk | Turkey | 66,590,940 | 2,780 | 373,155 | 1,037,370,900 | 198,054 | 550,590,120 | 0.30 |
| frep | French Polynesia | 235,061 | 16,940 | 198,725 | 3,366,401,500 | 32,345 | 547,924,300 | 13.76 |
| chan | Channel Islands | 152,898 | 12,000 | 100,781 | 1,209,372,000 | 40,543 | 486,516,000 | 26.52 |
| baha | Bahamas | 306,529 | 11,940 | 266,851 | 3,186,200,940 | 40,536 | 483,999,840 | 13.22 |
| conz | Congo-Zaire | 51,654,496 | 120 | 47,151,525 | 5,658,183,000 | 3,898,238 | 467,788,560 | 7.55 |
| liec | Liechtenstein | 32,843 | 33,000 | 27,051 | 892,683,000 | 14,173 | 467,709,000 | 43.15 |
| nork | North Korea | 24,039,193 | 950 | 500,213 | 475,202,350 | 468,670 | 445,236,500 | 1.95 |
| ando | Andorra | 77,985 | 16,200 | 70,205 | 1,137,321,000 | 26,551 | 430,126,200 | 34.05 |
| mart | Martinique | 395,362 | 10,000 | 373,372 | 3,733,720,000 | 42,790 | 427,900,000 | 10.82 |
| libe | Liberia | 3,154,001 | 770 | 932,060 | 717,686,200 | 542,686 | 417,868,220 | 17.21 |
| mala | Malawi | 10,925,238 | 170 | 7,032,260 | 1,195,484,200 | 2,457,034 | 417,695,780 | 22.49 |
| alba | Albania | 3,113,434 | 670 | 1,070,390 | 717,161,300 | 614,345 | 411,611,150 | 19.73 |
| nets | Netherlands Antilles | 216,775 | 10,400 | 184,912 | 1,923,084,800 | 38,128 | 396,531,200 | 17.59 |
| iraq | Iraq | 23,114,884 | 2,000 | 724,662 | 1,449,324,000 | 196,953 | 393,906,000 | 0.85 |
| leso | Lesotho | 2,152,553 | 770 | 1,445,329 | 1,112,903,330 | 510,738 | 393,268,260 | 23.73 |
| cong | Congo-Brazzaville | 2,943,464 | 680 | 2,332,878 | 1,586,357,040 | 567,743 | 386,065,240 | 19.29 |
| beni | Benin | 6,096,559 | 370 | 1,684,195 | 623,152,150 | 1,004,584 | 371,696,080 | 16.48 |
| berm | Bermuda | 64,590 | 31,870 | 55,675 | 1,774,362,250 | 11,327 | 360,991,490 | 17.54 |
| gabo | Gabon | 1,226,127 | 3,490 | 1,085,756 | 3,789,288,440 | 102,629 | 358,175,210 | 8.37 |
| qata | Qatar | 599,065 | 11,600 | 59,635 | 691,766,000 | 30,261 | 351,027,600 | 5.05 |
| burk | Burkina Faso | 11,936,823 | 230 | 1,984,078 | 456,337,940 | 1,521,822 | 350,019,060 | 12.75 |
| jord | Jordan | 6,669,341 | 1,510 | 273,522 | 413,018,220 | 228,157 | 344,517,070 | 3.42 |
| guam | Guam | 167,556 | 20,300 | 156,656 | 3,180,116,800 | 16,931 | 343,699,300 | 10.10 |
| barb | Barbados | 270,449 | 6,560 | 196,858 | 1,291,388,480 | 49,919 | 327,468,640 | 18.46 |
| geor | Georgia | 4,967,561 | 440 | 3,008,814 | 1,323,878,160 | 742,337 | 326,628,280 | 14.94 |
| newc | New Caledonia | 214,029 | 8,000 | 161,679 | 1,293,432,000 | 40,236 | 321,888,000 | 18.80 |
| sanm | San Marino | 26,514 | 24,700 | 23,779 | 587,341,300 | 12,895 | 318,506,500 | 48.63 |
| swaz | Swaziland | 1,007,895 | 1,170 | 680,841 | 796,583,970 | 271,534 | 317,694,780 | 26.94 |
| maus | Mauritius | 1,156,498 | 3,380 | 369,432 | 1,248,680,160 | 88,727 | 299,897,260 | 7.67 |
| arme | Armenia | 3,519,569 | 730 | 2,953,693 | 2,156,195,890 | 395,380 | 288,627,400 | 11.23 |
| brun | Brunei | 328,080 | 15,800 | 24,592 | 388,553,600 | 18,199 | 287,544,200 | 5.55 |
| togo | Togo | 4,629,218 | 310 | 1,749,095 | 542,219,450 | 917,794 | 284,516,140 | 19.83 |
| moza | Mozambique | 19,680,456 | 80 | 6,460,533 | 516,842,640 | 3,554,815 | 284,385,200 | 18.06 |
| isle | Isle of Man | 79,166 | 10,800 | 52,438 | 566,330,400 | 25,633 | 276,836,400 | 32.38 |
| cent | Central African Rep | 3,615,266 | 340 | 1,608,999 | 547,059,660 | 811,638 | 275,956,920 | 22.45 |
| oman | Oman | 2,541,739 | 4,820 | 121,916 | 587,635,120 | 55,517 | 267,591,940 | 2.18 |
| fiji | Fiji | 816,905 | 2,440 | 459,745 | 1,121,777,800 | 105,120 | 256,492,800 | 12.87 |
| freg | French Guiana | 181,313 | 10,580 | 152,736 | 1,615,946,880 | 23,745 | 251,222,100 | 13.10 |
| hond | Honduras | 6,485,445 | 600 | 6,057,600 | 3,634,560,000 | 414,293 | 248,575,800 | 6.39 |
| reun | Reunion | 699,406 | 4,300 | 607,104 | 2,610,547,200 | 56,272 | 241,969,600 | 8.05 |
| uzbe | Uzbekistan | 24,317,851 | 970 | 394,334 | 382,503,980 | 244,386 | 237,054,420 | 1.00 |
| mona | Monaco | 33,597 | 25,000 | 31,101 | 777,525,000 | 8,786 | 219,650,000 | 26.15 |
| grel | Greenland | 56,156 | 15,500 | 39,350 | 609,925,000 | 12,438 | 192,789,000 | 22.15 |
| buru | Burundi | 6,695,001 | 160 | 5,152,841 | 824,454,560 | 1,144,771 | 183,163,360 | 17.10 |
| mace | Macedonia | 2,023,580 | 860 | 1,287,192 | 1,106,985,120 | 212,563 | 182,804,180 | 10.50 |
| sene | Senegal | 9,481,161 | 600 | 467,291 | 280,374,600 | 300,623 | 180,373,800 | 3.17 |
| faer | Faeroe Islands | 42,749 | 15,000 | 39,590 | 593,850,000 | 11,794 | 176,910,000 | 27.59 |
| rwan | Rwanda | 7,733,127 | 180 | 6,336,822 | 1,140,627,960 | 960,617 | 172,911,060 | 12.42 |
| bahr | Bahrain | 617,217 | 7,840 | 62,698 | 491,552,320 | 21,414 | 167,885,760 | 3.47 |
| erit | Eritrea | 3,850,388 | 570 | 1,934,358 | 1,102,584,060 | 286,321 | 163,202,970 | 7.44 |
| kirg | Kirghizia | 4,699,337 | 700 | 465,665 | 325,965,500 | 225,162 | 157,613,400 | 4.79 |
| bang | Bangladesh | 129,155,152 | 240 | 931,740 | 223,617,600 | 639,011 | 153,362,640 | 0.49 |
| virg | Virgin Is of the US | 92,954 | 11,740 | 86,159 | 1,011,506,660 | 11,931 | 140,069,940 | 12.84 |
| hait | Haiti | 8,222,025 | 250 | 7,639,424 | 1,909,856,000 | 535,309 | 133,827,250 | 6.51 |
| chad | Chad | 7,650,982 | 180 | 1,438,014 | 258,842,520 | 718,153 | 129,267,540 | 9.39 |
| moro | Morocco | 28,220,843 | 1,110 | 174,476 | 193,668,360 | 109,745 | 121,816,950 | 0.39 |
| nica | Nicaragua | 5,074,194 | 380 | 4,857,432 | 1,845,824,160 | 307,306 | 116,776,280 | 6.06 |
| bosn | Bosnia-Herzegovina | 3,971,813 | 300 | 1,385,885 | 415,765,500 | 368,217 | 110,465,100 | 9.27 |
| nepa | Nepal | 23,930,490 | 200 | 576,061 | 115,212,200 | 543,340 | 108,668,000 | 2.27 |
| alge | Algeria | 31,471,278 | 1,600 | 90,877 | 145,403,200 | 65,098 | 104,156,800 | 0.21 |
| samo | Samoa | 180,073 | 1,120 | 169,129 | 189,424,480 | 85,350 | 95,592,000 | 47.40 |
| guin | Guinea | 7,430,346 | 550 | 231,322 | 127,227,100 | 169,775 | 93,376,250 | 2.28 |
| span | Spanish North Africa | 130,000 | 8,000 | 104,324 | 834,592,000 | 11,344 | 90,752,000 | 8.73 |
| arub | Aruba | 102,747 | 15,890 | 95,241 | 1,513,379,490 | 5,402 | 85,837,780 | 5.26 |
| anta | Antarctica | 4,500 | 80,000 | 3,400 | 272,000,000 | 1,000 | 80,000,000 | 29.40 |
| anti | Antigua | 67,560 | 7,690 | 53,713 | 413,052,970 | 10,329 | 79,430,010 | 15.29 |
| amer | American Samoa | 68,089 | 2,600 | 55,240 | 143,624,000 | 30,261 | 78,678,600 | 44.44 |
| beli | Belize | 240,709 | 2,630 | 197,139 | 518,475,570 | 28,865 | 75,914,950 | 11.99 |
| norm | Northern Mariana Is | 78,356 | 10,500 | 69,260 | 727,230,000 | 7,226 | 75,873,000 | 9.22 |
| sier | Sierra Leone | 4,854,383 | 180 | 510,494 | 91,888,920 | 389,099 | 70,037,820 | 8.02 |
| tuni | Tunisia | 9,585,611 | 1,820 | 50,503 | 91,915,460 | 36,504 | 66,437,280 | 0.38 |
| suri | Suriname | 417,130 | 880 | 172,334 | 151,653,920 | 70,952 | 62,437,760 | 17.01 |
| guya | Guyana | 861,334 | 590 | 374,036 | 220,681,240 | 104,650 | 61,743,500 | 12.15 |
| seyc | Seychelles | 77,435 | 6,620 | 71,795 | 475,282,900 | 9,236 | 61,142,320 | 11.93 |
| azer | Azerbaijan | 7,734,015 | 480 | 357,802 | 171,744,960 | 126,853 | 60,889,440 | 1.64 |
| norl | Northern Cyprus | 185,045 | 12,402 | 16,106 | 199,746,612 | 4,479 | 55,548,558 | 2.42 |
| saiv | Saint Vincent | 113,954 | 2,280 | 78,439 | 178,840,920 | 24,080 | 54,902,400 | 21.13 |
| solo | Solomon Islands | 443,643 | 910 | 403,203 | 366,914,730 | 59,890 | 54,499,900 | 13.50 |
| cape | Cape Verde | 427,724 | 960 | 406,880 | 390,604,800 | 55,921 | 53,684,160 | 13.07 |
| mali | Mali | 11,233,821 | 250 | 224,365 | 56,091,250 | 200,207 | 50,051,750 | 1.78 |
| briz | British Virgin Is | 21,366 | 8,000 | 14,892 | 119,136,000 | 6,229 | 49,832,000 | 29.15 |
| tong | Tonga | 98,546 | 1,630 | 89,688 | 146,191,440 | 27,926 | 45,519,380 | 28.34 |
| micr | Micronesia | 118,689 | 2,010 | 108,662 | 218,410,620 | 22,442 | 45,108,420 | 18.91 |
| turm | Turkmenistan | 4,459,293 | 920 | 98,883 | 90,972,360 | 48,002 | 44,161,840 | 1.08 |
| caym | Cayman Islands | 38,371 | 5,000 | 25,820 | 129,100,000 | 7,430 | 37,150,000 | 19.36 |
| laos | Laos | 5,433,036 | 350 | 112,563 | 39,397,050 | 100,576 | 35,201,600 | 1.85 |
| vanu | Vanuatu | 190,417 | 1,200 | 170,054 | 204,064,800 | 28,820 | 34,584,000 | 15.14 |
| sail | Saint Lucia | 154,366 | 3,370 | 144,339 | 486,422,430 | 9,556 | 32,203,720 | 6.19 |
| camb | Cambodia | 11,167,719 | 270 | 118,398 | 31,967,460 | 103,375 | 27,911,250 | 0.93 |
| timo | Timor | 884,541 | 644 | 815,391 | 525,111,804 | 39,435 | 25,396,140 | 4.46 |
| saip | Saint Pierre & Miquelon | 6,567 | 11,000 | 6,388 | 70,268,000 | 2,251 | 24,761,000 | 34.28 |
| gunb | Guinea-Bissau | 1,213,111 | 250 | 155,645 | 38,911,250 | 97,900 | 24,475,000 | 8.07 |
| mont | Montserrat | 10,629 | 12,527 | 10,170 | 127,399,590 | 1,946 | 24,377,542 | 18.31 |
| equa | Equatorial Guinea | 452,661 | 380 | 394,698 | 149,985,240 | 63,372 | 24,081,360 | 14.00 |
| boug | Bougainville | 198,495 | 1,400 | 185,331 | 259,463,400 | 16,167 | 22,633,800 | 8.14 |
| gren | Grenada | 93,717 | 2,980 | 90,745 | 270,420,100 | 6,456 | 19,238,880 | 6.89 |
| naur | Nauru | 11,519 | 8,070 | 8,341 | 67,311,870 | 2,187 | 17,649,090 | 18.99 |
| taji | Tajikistan | 6,188,201 | 340 | 129,612 | 44,068,080 | 50,711 | 17,241,740 | 0.82 |
| sval | Svalbard & Jan Mayen | 3,676 | 16,000 | 1,749 | 27,984,000 | 1,066 | 17,056,000 | 29.00 |
| domi | Dominica | 70,714 | 2,990 | 66,757 | 199,603,430 | 5,057 | 15,120,430 | 7.15 |
| gibr | Gibraltar | 25,082 | 6,600 | 21,368 | 141,028,800 | 2,285 | 15,081,000 | 9.11 |
| pala | Palau | 19,426 | 5,000 | 18,371 | 91,855,000 | 2,814 | 14,070,000 | 14.49 |
| mars | Marshall Islands | 64,220 | 1,890 | 60,103 | 113,594,670 | 7,300 | 13,797,000 | 11.37 |
| saik | Saint Kitts & Nevis | 38,473 | 5,170 | 36,000 | 186,120,000 | 2,098 | 10,846,660 | 5.45 |

Continued opposite

Table 20–2  concluded

| Code | Name | Pop 2000 | GNPpc $ | AC 2000 | AC income $ | GCC | GCC Income $ | GCC % |
|------|------|----------|---------|---------|-------------|-----|--------------|-------|
| 1 | 2 | 3 | 4 | 5 | 6 | 7 | 8 | 9 |
| saih | Saint Helena | 6,293 | 9,000 | 5,332 | 47,988,000 | 1,167 | 10,503,000 | 18.54 |
| djib | Djibouti | 637,634 | 850 | 28,194 | 23,964,900 | 11,995 | 10,195,750 | 1.88 |
| gamb | Gambia | 1,305,363 | 320 | 47,198 | 15,103,360 | 30,607 | 9,794,240 | 2.34 |
| niga | Niger | 10,730,102 | 220 | 58,270 | 12,819,400 | 44,186 | 9,720,920 | 0.41 |
| kiri | Kiribati | 83,387 | 920 | 77,331 | 71,144,520 | 10,228 | 9,409,760 | 12.27 |
| holy | Holy See | 1,000 | 20,000 | 980 | 19,600,000 | 461 | 9,220,000 | 46.10 |
| mong | Mongolia | 2,662,020 | 310 | 33,393 | 10,351,830 | 29,582 | 9,170,420 | 1.11 |
| wall | Wallis & Futuna Is | 14,517 | 4,654 | 14,021 | 65,253,734 | 1,885 | 8,772,790 | 12.98 |
| turs | Turks & Caicos Is | 16,760 | 2,172 | 13,262 | 28,805,064 | 3,513 | 7,630,236 | 20.96 |
| saot | Sao Tome & Principe | 146,775 | 350 | 132,103 | 46,236,050 | 21,628 | 7,569,800 | 14.74 |
| soma | Somalia | 7,264,500 | 500 | 98,583 | 49,291,500 | 13,606 | 6,803,000 | 0.19 |
| yeme | Yemen | 18,112,066 | 260 | 30,656 | 7,970,560 | 23,012 | 5,983,120 | 0.13 |
| falk | Falkland Islands | 2,255 | 7,000 | 1,783 | 12,481,000 | 757 | 5,299,000 | 33.57 |
| cook | Cook Islands | 19,522 | 2,000 | 18,492 | 36,984,000 | 2,521 | 5,042,000 | 12.91 |
| bhut | Bhutan | 2,123,970 | 420 | 9,649 | 4,052,580 | 8,666 | 3,639,720 | 0.41 |
| afgh | Afghanistan | 22,720,416 | 600 | 6,897 | 4,138,200 | 4,081 | 2,448,600 | 0.02 |
| briy | British Indian Ocean | 2,000 | 5,000 | 900 | 4,500,000 | 480 | 2,400,000 | 24.00 |
| angu | Anguilla | 8,309 | 2,000 | 7,186 | 14,372,000 | 1,098 | 2,196,000 | 13.21 |
| maur | Mauritania | 2,669,547 | 460 | 6,526 | 3,001,960 | 3,914 | 1,800,440 | 0.15 |
| tuva | Tuvalu | 11,719 | 800 | 9,745 | 7,796,000 | 2,240 | 1,792,000 | 19.11 |
| como | Comoros | 592,749 | 470 | 7,061 | 3,318,670 | 3,558 | 1,672,260 | 0.60 |
| norf | Norfolk Island | 2,075 | 2,500 | 1,353 | 3,382,500 | 595 | 1,487,500 | 28.67 |
| toke | Tokelau Islands | 1,500 | 3,000 | 1,368 | 4,104,000 | 283 | 849,000 | 18.87 |
| niue | Niue Island | 1,876 | 2,500 | 1,736 | 4,340,000 | 329 | 822,500 | 17.54 |
| mayo | Mayotte | 101,621 | 600 | 1,866 | 1,119,600 | 929 | 557,400 | 0.91 |
| somi | Somaliland | 2,832,677 | 155 | 8,381 | 1,299,055 | 3,120 | 483,600 | 0.11 |
| mald | Maldives | 286,223 | 990 | 358 | 354,420 | 300 | 297,000 | 0.10 |
| chri | Christmas Island | 3,424 | 1,000 | 442 | 442,000 | 247 | 247,000 | 7.21 |
| pitc | Pitcairn Islands | 47 | 12,000 | 42 | 504,000 | 19 | 228,000 | 40.43 |
| saha | Sahara | 293,357 | 207 | 487 | 100,809 | 284 | 58,788 | 0.10 |
| coco | Cocos (Keeling) Is | 726 | 900 | 123 | 110,700 | 63 | 56,700 | 8.68 |

**Regions (UN definitions)**

| Code | Name | Pop 2000 | GNPpc $ | AC 2000 | AC income $ | GCC | GCC Income $ | GCC % |
|------|------|----------|---------|---------|-------------|-----|--------------|-------|
| A1 | Eastern Africa | 246,968,897 | 235 | 138,014,308 | 33,352,047,275 | 37,607,187 | 8,014,913,490 | 15.23 |
| A2 | Middle Africa | 95,652,928 | 317 | 72,839,712 | 21,563,965,180 | 11,117,863 | 4,485,291,810 | 11.62 |
| A3 | Northern Africa | 173,265,225 | 1,237 | 15,785,876 | 14,427,352,289 | 10,422,824 | 8,993,039,768 | 6.02 |
| A4 | Southern Africa | 46,885,115 | 2,959 | 36,027,243 | 107,366,643,000 | 9,178,682 | 26,847,384,020 | 19.58 |
| A5 | Western Africa | 221,672,874 | 332 | 72,448,611 | 22,907,989,660 | 22,493,698 | 7,727,880,180 | 10.15 |
| B | Antarctica | 4,500 | 80,000 | 3,400 | 272,000,000 | 1,000 | 80,000,000 | 29.40 |
| C1 | Eastern Asia | 1,485,217,209 | 4,417 | 112,787,453 | 387,718,842,560 | 99,117,537 | 313,903,692,300 | 6.67 |
| C2 | South-central Asia | 518,540,013 | 1,444 | 107,864,537 | 126,372,334,514 | 29,467,075 | 40,524,766,950 | 5.68 |
| C3 | South-eastern Asia | 1,490,777,681 | 572 | 73,329,903 | 30,258,758,250 | 58,624,078 | 22,977,499,990 | 3.93 |
| C4 | Western Asia | 188,015,190 | 3,502 | 13,306,415 | 43,800,351,748 | 4,681,655 | 20,220,113,468 | 2.49 |
| E1 | Eastern Europe | 306,990,068 | 2,233 | 216,346,515 | 481,407,916,750 | 48,212,833 | 109,334,271,660 | 15.71 |
| E2 | Northern Europe | 94,383,021 | 19,044 | 67,720,290 | 1,309,921,336,340 | 29,520,148 | 560,580,679,180 | 31.28 |
| E3 | Southern Europe | 144,173,517 | 13,008 | 120,246,992 | 1,617,389,945,420 | 48,489,396 | 739,505,825,340 | 33.63 |
| E4 | Western Europe | 183,340,345 | 26,774 | 132,517,774 | 3,567,872,737,870 | 66,239,688 | 1,757,813,667,310 | 36.13 |
| L1 | Caribbean | 38,138,906 | 2,335 | 28,306,571 | 72,422,368,954 | 5,416,634 | 13,311,155,868 | 14.20 |
| L2 | Central America | 135,222,060 | 2,798 | 128,028,498 | 358,430,484,020 | 8,318,986 | 22,146,477,100 | 6.15 |
| L3 | South America | 345,777,082 | 3,605 | 319,323,831 | 1,143,577,060,150 | 38,565,828 | 140,322,061,550 | 11.15 |
| N1 | Northern America | 309,631,093 | 26,214 | 212,166,818 | 5,570,172,069,350 | 111,292,984 | 2,906,764,181,730 | 35.94 |
| P1 | Australia-New Zealand | 22,747,654 | 17,971 | 15,152,096 | 272,392,748,140 | 8,028,275 | 143,521,901,420 | 35.29 |
| P2 | Melanesia | 6,471,634 | 1,539 | 5,165,540 | 7,636,865,210 | 773,329 | 1,296,889,860 | 11.95 |
| P3 | Micronesia | 543,153 | 8,930 | 498,724 | 4,469,663,480 | 69,128 | 519,606,570 | 12.73 |
| P4 | Polynesia | 630,950 | 7,365 | 558,186 | 3,964,623,154 | 183,159 | 785,220,570 | 29.03 |

**Continents (UN definitions)**

| Code | Name | Pop 2000 | GNPpc $ | AC 2000 | AC income $ | GCC | GCC Income $ | GCC % |
|------|------|----------|---------|---------|-------------|-----|--------------|-------|
| A | Africa | 784,445,039 | 656 | 335,115,750 | 199,617,997,404 | 90,820,254 | 56,068,509,268 | 11.58 |
| B | Antarctica | 4,500 | 80,000 | 3,400 | 272,000,000 | 1,000 | 80,000,000 | 29.40 |
| C | Asia | 3,682,550,093 | 2,395 | 307,288,308 | 588,150,287,072 | 191,890,345 | 397,626,072,708 | 5.21 |
| E | Europe | 728,886,951 | 12,714 | 536,831,571 | 6,976,591,936,380 | 192,462,065 | 3,167,234,443,490 | 26.40 |
| L | Latin America | 519,138,048 | 3,301 | 475,658,900 | 1,574,429,913,124 | 52,301,448 | 175,779,694,518 | 10.07 |
| N | North America | 309,631,093 | 26,214 | 212,166,818 | 5,570,172,069,350 | 111,292,984 | 2,906,764,181,730 | 35.94 |
| P | Oceania | 30,393,391 | 14,090 | 21,374,546 | 288,463,899,984 | 9,053,891 | 146,123,618,420 | 29.79 |

**Mission worlds**

| Code | Name | Pop 2000 | GNPpc $ | AC 2000 | AC income $ | GCC | GCC Income $ | GCC % |
|------|------|----------|---------|---------|-------------|-----|--------------|-------|
| | World A | 605,303,996 | 1,464 | 10,026,564 | 10,548,883,544 | 7,281,018 | 6,171,095,548 | 1.20 |
| | World B | 3,755,011,992 | 2,284 | 491,326,295 | 771,979,359,808 | 279,101,242 | 492,625,350,728 | 7.43 |
| | World C | 1,694,733,127 | 11,447 | 1,387,086,434 | 14,415,169,859,962 | 361,438,727 | 6,350,800,073,858 | 21.33 |
| | **Global totals** | **6,055,049,115** | **4,767** | **1,888,439,293** | **15,197,698,103,314** | **647,820,987** | **6,849,596,520,134** | **10.70** |

tural blocs of Christians each contributes and spends vast sums each year. Two of the largest and most dynamic of these global forces—Evangelicals, and the Pentecostal/Charismatic/Neocharismatic Renewal—each raise over $60 billion annually. But the evidence shows that these 2 groupings only directly utilize or control the expenditure of some 20% of the income they supply. The rest is swallowed up in maintaining the vast ongoing machinery of the rest of institutionalized global Christianity. Rightly managed, a single one of these groupings could change the world.

The most intriguing figure is that our new category of Great Commission Christians—all those determined to take seriously Christ's mandate to the church—raises $164 billion every year but directly controls the expenditure of less than 20%. Again, if they could somehow get themselves mobilized and organized, this huge trans-bloc grouping could alter the fortunes of Worlds A and B within a few months.

### Third standpoint: 6 specific items need comment
By itemizing some 40 separate expenditure items, this more detailed part of the balance sheet permits closer scrutiny and raises questions for the churches to pursue. Here are 6 issues in particular.

1. *Administration* (line 68). This accounts for 29% of the total expenditure of the Christian world. To some observers this will appear reasonable, to others inevitable, but to others a shockingly large waste of resources.

2. *Censuses* (line 76). Every year the Christian world's churches, agencies, and institutions require their employees—bishops, clergy, pastors, lay leaders, missionaries, evangelists, teachers, administrators, et alii—to fill out a total of 10 million annual statistical reports. This is the world's largest single annual enumeration. Its total cost is $1.1 billion. This annual gold mine of new data on the progress of global Christianity is, however, virtually unanalyzed from one year to the next. Most of these returns get archived within a few weeks of receipt at headquarters. Great Commission Christians could insist on a proper analysis and accounting of these materials.

3. *Earthkeeping* (line 61). A huge new movement within the churches has sprung up around the world emphasizing Christian responsibility for protecting and nurturing all aspects of the natural environment. At an estimated $3 billion, this is one of the most positive new expenditures. The major initiatives to date have come from within the 80-million-member African Independent Churches, especially in Southern Africa.

4. *Ecclesiastical crime* (line 79). This item describes theft of Christian funds (embezzlement) by directly-responsible church officials or treasurers appointed to handle churches' and agencies' monies. It will be enlarged upon shortly below.

5. *Audits* (line 71). Professional financial audits are estimated to cost the Christian world $810 million a year. (See comment 'Cost of audits' below).

6. *Computers* (line 88). A last comment concerns the mushrooming costs, to the Christian world, of computer hardware, software, personnel, and online charges. It is estimated that Christians now own and operate 350 million general-purpose computers that cost them $400 billion to purchase—a staggering diversion of traditional church and other Christian monies.

### Rich and Poor contrasted
A more generalized comment concerns how compartmentalized and unconnected the Christian world is. Thus although 260 million Christians in Third-World countries are living and dying in absolute poverty, many local churches in Europe and North

America continue to spend 7-figure sums on new organs, sanctuary extensions, and the like. In the Western church, denominational spending on property increases year by year. Thus the value of new construction of religious buildings in the United States (again, the best-documented country) rose from $0.9 billion in 1970 to $1.6 billion in 1980 and to well over $5 billion by AD 2000. There, certainly, we see overwhelmingly the Church of the Rich. Yet, again paradoxically, the Church of the Poor exists in parallel in the United States, mostly as a Black or a Hispanic urban phenomenon. Even here, though, 'Church of the Poor' is a relative term, since the poor as officially defined in the United States have per-capita incomes over sixty times greater than the absolutely poor in the Third World.

### Global foreign mission (lines 23-26)
It is in its global religious outreach that the Christian world seems least certain of itself and of its mission. Only 5.6% of global Christian giving ($15 billion a year) goes to support the Christian world mission. Outreach, foreign service, evangelism among non-Christians, conversion, new and experimental types of mission and ministry, translation of the Scriptures into non-Christian languages—these attract the least money. The remaining 95% of global Christian giving ($255 billion a year) goes on the home church and its ministries at home. The average church member, donating his $2.75 a week, gives out of this only $0.15 (fifteen American cents) to support Christian foreign missions. This indicates a very low level of commitment to the Great Commission of the Lord Jesus Christ: 'Make disciples of all nations.' In this respect, the entire Christian world is a Church of the Poor—poor in spiritual dynamic and in missionary vision and obedience.

## MANAGING GLOBAL CHRISTIAN MONIES

Some further comments on budget items in Table 20–3 can now be made.

### Accountability
The Christian world today has around 5 million church treasurers, of whom some 2% are full-time salaried officers. Most larger denominations, agencies, and institutions have long since instituted strict accountability, accounting, accounts, accountants, audits, procedures, financial reports, and balance sheets that report their financial situation to their constituencies of church members, donors, treasurers, and law officers. Churches which relax this vigilance soon pay dearly for their negligence.

### Embezzlement (line 79)
As described in Table 20–4, the annual total of $16 billion embezzled exceeds the worldwide church's foreign missions' expenditures of $15 billion. Probably 80% of all cases are kept private or swept under the carpet, but each year a rash of megathefts (over $1 million each) is uncovered and publicized in the secular media. A sampling from 1994-6: Salvation Army (UK), $13 million; Episcopal Church in the USA, $2.2 million; Catholic Diocese of Brooklyn, New York, $1.2 million; Evangelical Lutheran Church of America (New England) $1.1 million; Mississippi Baptist College, $3 million stolen by its president. A different type of case is the loss of $354 million by a large number of Evangelical agencies in the USA who had placed funds with New Era which went bankrupt in 1995.

Many cases share a number of strange similarities. Culprits are usually caught red-handed, are often trusted national treasurers or even bishops or other denominational heads, and have usually been siphoning off monies for 5-10 years or more, before being detected. In many cases the first rumors are categorically denied by church leaders. When the first newspaper story appears it often contains an appeal by the bishop or denominational head urging the immediate Christian grace of compassion and forgiveness toward the embezzler. This suggests to readers that the leaders concerned may well have been involved themselves in the theft, or are concerned for their own reputations as managers. Another recurring feature is that often the body concerned is fortunate enough to recover the loss through insurance, seizure of cars and houses. In such cases, as when the Salvation Army (UK) actually recovered $13.2 mil-

lion, instead of being a dire warning of tragic loss it becomes a success story of smart action by administrators after the event.

One way or another, Christians need to tighten up the scrutinizing of all funds holding their monies and to insist on all the accepted safeguards and controls and on all the strictest procedures.

### Cost of audits (line 71)
Professional financial audits are estimated to cost the Christian world $810 million a year. On learning that this figure is 3 times the cost of Christianity's 2,500 evangelistic mass campaigns a year (line 60), and almost exceeds the entire cost of circulating the Scriptures throughout the globe (line 64), many Christian leaders are appalled at the imbalance. On reflection, however, they soon realize that if audit costs were reduced by one half, then in all probability current embezzlements would double to $32 billion annually. Conversely, if tougher and stricter audits were introduced costing twice those at present, it is probable that embezzlements would fall drastically, saving the Christian world at least $5 billion a year.

### Insisting on financial controls
Two of the basic rules for safeguarding public monies are (1) there must always be 2 signatories on all checks and documents, that of the finance officer and that of the ecclesiastical head (bishop, moderator, etc), and (2) receipt of income must be handled by separate staff to those making expenditures. In most cases of mega-embezzlement it soon becomes apparent that the normal strict controls were ignored at some juncture. Often busy church leaders about to depart on extended travels will sign a number of blank checks. The most blatant invitation to theft occurred in a large denomination whose presiding bishop permitted the national treasurer to sign on his behalf and hence to provide both the required signatures herself.

Huge sums can be saved by insisting on these control procedures being exactly followed.

### Money gets tighter
In recent years most Christian organizations have tightened up on beneficiaries and boundaries within which disbursements of their budget are permissible. Usually 95% of all denominational/agency money is spent, and can only be spent, on denominational/agency causes, projects, and personnel. Certain time-honored obligations outside the strict denominational and confessional boundaries may be continued without being questioned—e.g. a denomination's annual donation to the American Bible Society, emergencies, disasters, refugees, famine relief. However, support or donations for countless small projects or personnel outside the boundaries have been becoming harder and harder and in many cases have dried up completely.

### The absence of global sharing
From these trends it can be deduced that organized global Christianity is still a long way from any form of global sharing of resources. Its vast array of global monoliths still reserve their money virtually exclusively to themselves.

### Transdenominational giving or support
Particularly hard hit have been the following. First, multidenominational causes directly and obviously benefitting the donor agency are nevertheless being cut out (note the difficulties of financing the WCC, WEF, UBS, similar to that of financing the United Nations). Second, smaller interdenominational causes or appeals are simply excised or ignored without explanation or reply. And thirdly, outright donations have been reduced to virtually nothing even in cases where senior executives' promises and pleas have been insistent.

### The role of research and development (line 62)
One reason for this dismal state of affairs with regard to global mission is the absence of sufficient serious research on the subject. Research is essential to the prosecution of all large enterprises in the modern secular world. Most countries recognize this by allocating massive financial resources to research, averaging some 2.1% of their gross national product. Many commercial and industrial enterprises allocate 5% of their total income, some as high as 10%. In 1980, the total national research-and-development expenditure on the sciences was 2.33% of GNP in the United States

($61 billion), 2.3% in Europe ($76 billion), and 3.47% in the Soviet Union ($38 billion). The world total spent on research and development in 1980 was $210 billion. Well over 90% of this is spent in, and therefore primarily benefits, the techno-economic colossi in the North of the planet (the Western world and the European Communist world). The South (the Third World) benefits only indirectly, if at all.

The result of this recognition of research is that vast sums are available to experiment in numerous new directions at once. This is an essential element in research, since in scientific or industrial applications any new line of research has only a 1:8000 chance of success. A typical case is the chemical multinational Hoechst UK. In 1982 it spent $240 million on pharmaceuticals research. In 1983 it spent UK £1 million a day on agrochemical and related health and nutrition research, employing 13,000 people in fifteen different countries on its research program. One concrete result of this area of research is that average human male life expectancy in Britain has increased from 41 years in the year 1870 to 70 years today.

The Norwegian missiologist Olav Myklebust once said: 'What theology is to the church, missionary research is to the task of world evangelization'. In other words, it is fundamentally essential. Without adequate research, the global work of Christ and in particular its mission and outreach have often floundered in ignorance or error.

How extensive is Christian research today? Until the 1950s research has always been almost completely decentralized, relying on the voluntary and unorganized labors of thousands of scholars in all disciplines. Between them nowadays they produce some 110,000 new scholarly research books on the Christian faith every year.

Together with these individual scholars, there has grown up since 1950 a vast, loose network of 950 Christian or church-related research centers across the world. These undertake research on the entire range of Christian issues, from biblical archeology and biblical exegesis to human rights and futurological topics. Yet, since 1970 these 950 centers have been seriously undermined by drastically curtailed funding. The vast majority of denominational centers, and some 90% of all church researchers since 1970, have subsequently collapsed or otherwise gone into oblivion. Their total budgets with those of all other Christian research activity have fallen to some $81 million a year. For global Christianity, a global organization with an annual budget of $270 billion, this is an exceptionally small proportion: only 0.03%. Such a low outlay is shortsighted in the extreme by contemporary standards. And only a small fraction of this goes to research on global mission.

So then, we are faced with yet another shocking paradox: church members in many countries pay out of their own pockets more for secular and military research ($300 billion a year) than they pay to support organized Christianity in all its forms worldwide ($270 billion a year). The world's 1.9 billion church members pay for secular research (including that to advance the arms race) to the tune of some 2.2% of their incomes each year (involuntarily no doubt, via government taxes), yet at the same time they pay less than 0.0003% of their incomes for Christian or church-related research. In fact, Christians pay out of their pockets 7,000 times as much for secular research, including nuclear-weapons research, as they pay for specifically Christian research to advance the kingdom of God.

This therefore represents an urgent call to all organizations professing to support the world Christian mission to immediately include in their annual budgets a fixed percentage of between 5% as a maximum and 1% as a minimum, specifically for research. While this would cover research on all subjects of primary concern to the particular mission of each, it should also contain an element for genuinely international, interdenominational, interconfessional, multidisciplinary research on global mission and world evangelization. If these organizations followed the example of well-run and efficient secular bodies who have discovered that to spend 1% per year on research brings rich dividends, then each year there would be $2 billion available for all varieties of Christian and church-related research, and $105 million for research specifically on global mission. These are the sensible sums to spend on research for such a complex global operation.

## Table 20–3. Current annual income and expenditures of both unorganized and organized global Christianity, with the latter viewed and analyzed under 3 standpoints, AD 2000.

| Line 1 | Category or item 2 | % 3 | Amount, US$ 4 |
|---|---|---|---|
| 1. | **GLOBAL CHRISTIANITY** | | |
| 2. | a. **GLOBAL INCOME per year** .......................... | 100.0 | 15,300 billion |
| 3. | Personal income of all church members (unorganized) .................... | 95.7 | 14,642 billion |
| 4. | Personal income of all unaffiliated Christians .......................... | 4.0 | 612 billion |
| 5. | Institutional income from secular sources (state, industry, etc) | 0.3 | 46 billion |
| 6. | b. **GLOBAL EXPENDITURES per year** ...................... | 100.0 | 15,300 billion |
| 7. | Personal and family expenditures of all church members (unorganized) ........ | 94.04 | 14,418 billion |
| 8. | Personal and family expenditures of unaffiliated Christians .................... | 4.0 | 612 billion |
| 9. | Personal donations of Christians to secular or nonreligious causes .......... | 0.2 | 29 billion |
| 10. | Collective expenditures of **organized global Christianity** ................... | 1.76 | **270 billion** |
| 11. | A. **MINISTRY AND MISSION of organized global Christianity** | | |
| 12. | This first standpoint views income and expenditures in terms of the Christian global apostolate. | | |
| 13. | a. **INCOME per year** ............................................ | 100.0 | **270 billion** |
| 14. | Direct regular live Christian income (donations from Christians, tithes, etc) .... | 70.0 | 189 billion |
| 15. | Indirect income from past Christians (legacies, endowments, etc) ............ | 20.0 | 54 billion |
| 16. | Institutional investments (funds, properties) .............................. | 7.0 | 19 billion |
| 17. | Secular income from investments, state/political/business/commercial support . | 3.0 | 8 billion |
| 18. | b. **EXPENDITURES per year** ...................................... | 100.0 | **270 billion** |
| 19. | Home pastoral ministry ..................................... | 82.4 | 223 billion |
| 20. | Home missions ........................................ | 12.0 | 32 billion |
| 21. | Monocultural home missions .............................. | 9.0 | 24 billion |
| 22. | Cross-cultural home missions ............................. | 3.0 | 8 billion |
| 23. | Foreign missions ........................................ | 5.6 | 15 billion |
| 24. | 1. Pastoral ministry in World C contexts ...................... | 4.8 | 13 billion |
| 25. | 2. Evangelistic ministry in World B contexts ................... | 0.7 | 1.75 billion |
| 26. | 3. Outreach in World A contexts ............................ | 0.1 | 0.25 billion |
| 27. | B. **DONORS AND BENEFICIARIES in organized global Christianity** | | |
| 28. | This second standpoint begins to identify the populations involved. | | |
| 29. | a. **INCOME per year** (sums donated by individual Christians to churches, agencies) | 100.0 | **270 billion** |
| 30. | (1) By Christians in these 6 major ecclesiastico-cultural megablocs: | | |
| 31. | Anglicans ......................................... | 3.6 | 10 billion |
| 32. | Independents/Postdenominationalists ........................... | 16.3 | 44 billion |
| 33. | Marginal Christians .................................. | 2.7 | 7 billion |
| 34. | Orthodox .......................................... | 11.4 | 31 billion |
| 35. | Protestants ........................................ | 20.0 | 54 billion |
| 36. | Roman Catholics .................................... | 45.9 | 124 billion |
| 37. | (2) Or, in these 3 trans-bloc groupings (overlapping with the 6 megablocs): | | |
| 38. | Evangelicals ....................................... | 23.0 | 62 billion |
| 39. | Pentecostals/Charismatics/Neocharismatics ................. | 25.7 | 69 billion |
| 40. | Great Commission Christians .......................... | 60.7 | 164 billion |
| 41. | b. **EXPENDITURES** per year (recipients, who are thus the major beneficiaries) ... | 100.0 | **270 billion** |
| 42. | 1. Funds spent on Christians (World C persons) .................. | 96.8 | 261 billion |
| 43. | 2. Funds spent on Evangelized non-Christians (World B persons) .......... | 2.9 | 7.8 billion |
| 44. | 3. Funds spent on Unevangelized non-Christians (World A persons) ......... | 0.3 | 0.81 billion |
| 45. | C. **CATEGORIES AND ITEMS within organized global Christianity** | | |
| 46. | This third standpoint itemizes expenditures under specific recognized categories. | | |
| 47. | a. **INCOME per year** ............................................ | 100.0 | **270 billion** |
| 48. | Denominations' and churches' income .......................... | 36.0 | 108 billion |
| 49. | Parachurch/service agencies' income ............................ | 64.0 | 162 billion |
| 50. | b. **EXPENDITURES per year:** | 100.0 | **270 billion** |
| 51. | Ministry salaries: | | |
| 52. | 5 million full-time Christian workers in full-time ministry .............. | 15.1 | 41 billion |
| 53. | Workers in World C contexts ............................. | 14.9 | 40 billion |
| 54. | Ordained clergy and pastors ......................... | 1.4 | 4 billion |
| 55. | Workers in World B contexts ............................. | 0.13 | 0.35 billion |
| 56. | Workers in World A contexts ............................. | 0.01 | 0.027 billion |
| 57. | Pensions, retirement plans .................................... | 0.3 | 0.81 billion |
| 58. | Ministry expenses (pastoralia, equipment, secretarial) ................ | 3.0 | 8 billion |
| 59. | Ministry programs: | 5.0 | 14 billion |
| 60. | Evangelistic mass campaigns (2,500 a year) ................. | 0.1 | 0.27 billion |
| 61. | Earthkeeping (environmentalism) ......................... | 1.0 | 3 billion |
| 62. | Research ........................................ | 0.03 | 0.081 billion |
| 63. | Academic scholarship (theology, Bible, history, religion) ........ | 0.01 | 0.027 billion |
| 64. | Scriptures (translation, printing, distribution) ................ | 0.4 | 1.1 billion |
| 65. | Films, audiovisuals ................................. | 1.0 | 3 billion |
| 66. | Other ministries ................................... | 2.46 | 7 billion |
| 67. | Ministry training: 1 million seminarians (4,600 seminaries) ............. | 4.0 | 11 billion |
| 68. | Administration: | 29.0 | 78 billion |
| 69. | Honorary personnel (including 5 million unpaid or partly-paid treasurers) ... | 0.5 | 1 billion |
| 70. | Accounting and finance (loans, interest, fees, taxes) ................... | 5.0 | 14 billion |
| 71. | Annual audits ................................... | 0.3 | 0.81 billion |
| 72. | Administrative salaries: 1 million accountants, accounts clerks ........ | 1.8 | 4.8 billion |
| 73. | Property (buildings, plant, rents, taxes, fees) ................ | 2.0 | 5 billion |
| 74. | New property (construction, new buildings) ................ | 3.0 | 8 billion |
| 75. | Maintenance (upkeep, insurance, repairs) ................ | 3.0 | 8 billion |
| 76. | Annual censuses .................................... | 0.4 | 1.1 billion |
| 77. | Legal affairs, litigation ................................ | 2.5 | 7 billion |
| 78. | Losses due to mismanagement ......................... | 3.0 | 8 billion |
| 79. | Ecclesiastical crime (embezzlements) ..................... | 6.0 | 16 billion |
| 80. | Other administrative expenses ......................... | 1.8 | 4.8 billion |
| 81. | Education (partial support): ................................. | 14.0 | 38 billion |
| 82. | Adult education .................................... | 1.0 | 3 billion |
| 83. | Health services (partial support): ............................ | 3.3 | 9 billion |
| 84. | Medical missions ................................... | 0.1 | 0.27 billion |
| 85. | Health plans ....................................... | 0.9 | 2.4 billion |
| 86. | Communications (publishing, publications, media, advertising): ............. | 7.3 | 20 billion |
| 87. | Broadcasting ...................................... | 2.7 | 7 billion |
| 88. | Computers (hardware, software, updates, personnel) ................ | 4.5 | 12 billion |
| 89. | Conferences, meetings ................................ | 2.8 | 8 billion |
| 90. | Travel ............................................. | 2.3 | 6 billion |
| 91. | Miscellaneous ministry expenses ......................... | 5.2 | 14 billion |

### Notes

This table describes and analyzes primarily the origins and usages of the sum of **US$270 billion**, which is the total collective income and expenditures of organized global Christianity each year, with particular reference to the year AD 2000. Of the table's 4 sections below, the first sets the background to the total amount of money circulating at the disposal of the Christian world, unorganized as well as organized into churches and agencies.

The remaining 3 sections analyze the $270 billion from 3 different standpoints: (A) ministry and mission, (B) donors and beneficiaries, and (C) categories and items widely used to track the flow of monies.

Column 3 shows the magnitude of all items, all expressed as percentages of the $270 billion. Groupings of these figures add to broader categories unindented above them. Column 4 then gives these magnitudes in billions of dollars.

### Notes on specific lines

1. Defined as the total empirical Christian world of individuals, members, churches, denominations, agencies, and institutions.
2. Total amount of money circulating annually in the Christian world or available for Christian uses, or passing through Christians' hands and pockets each year.
3. Income of all church members, unorganized meaning before parts become organized by Christian churches or agencies.
4. Unaffiliated or nominal Christians are mostly unknown to the churches and have little or no financial interaction with them.
5. Income raised by Christian institutions from secular sources.
7. Church members on average donate 1.3% of their incomes to churches or agencies. The other 98.7% covers personal or family needs and activities.
8. Unaffiliated Christians spend income on personal and family interests, with little or nothing spent on organized Christian bodies.
9. Christians in the USA donate each year some $8 billion to secular or nonreligious causes (hospitals, schools, charities).
10. This is the major sum analyzed in this table. It does not follow exactly the format of a balance sheet since it deals only with annual income and expenditures and does not cover assets. These latter can however be estimated as follows: (1) global assets of individual Christians (total nett worth), $140,000 billion ($140 trillion); (2) global assets of Christian institutions and organizations, $2,700 billion ($2.7 trillion).

11. **MINISTRY AND MISSION**
12. Analysis from the standpoint of the Christian vocation to mission and ministry.
13. This total sum is handled through over 20 million separate and unrelated bank accounts, with no overall control, oversight, reporting, or even awareness.
14. Direct consequence of committed stewardship of money.
15. The figures represent current income from giving by Christians now dead, in the form of legacies, bequests, trusts, endowments, investments, stocks, foundations, and the like. Almost entirely in Europe and Northern America.
16. Income generated by Christian institutions themselves.
17. Many governments subsidize Christian schools, hospitals, broadcasting, and other Christian ministries.
20. All denominations with over a million members organize separate home and foreign mission agencies (the latter in line 23).

27. **DONORS AND BENEFICIARIES**
28. Who gives and who gets these sums of money? This second standpoint identifies the populations involved.
30. These 6 basic megablocs are as shown in *WCE* Part 4, Country Tables 1 & 2.
37. These 3 trans-bloc groupings are as defined in Part 14 "Missiometrics" and shown in all Country Tables 1.
39. The Renewal is regarded as composed of 3 distinct waves (First, Second, Third), as described in Part 5 "GeoRenewal".
42. This line states that 96.8% of the entire income of all Christian organizations is spent on, and primarily benefits, other Christians at home or abroad.

45. **CATEGORIES AND ITEMS**
46. This third analysis lists the specific categories and items of payment each year. Most are widely understood and used in the churches' and agencies' own accounting.
48. This item has been declining in percentage annually since 1900 when it stood at 88%.
49. This item has been increasing in percentage annually since its 1900 value of 12%, and massively so since 1990.
61. This item is a recent and rapidly-growing aspect of global Christian concern, especially among African independent churches and in the worldwide ecumenical movement.
71. At 0.3% of income, this is the average cost of professional audits carried out by Christian bodies of all kinds.
74. The value of new construction of religious buildings in the USA alone rose from $900 million in 1970 to $5,000 million in AD 2000.
76. Every year Christian agencies and denominations instruct 10 million workers to fill out and return 10 million questionnaires detailing work and achievements in the previous year. These censuses cost on average $90 per questionnaire to compile, complete, return, process, analyze, report, and circulate or publish.
78. Mismanagement is here defined as losses due to incompetence and carelessness, rather than to criminal corruption. A recent example: in 1996 the Church Commissioners for England admitted losing £800 million of the Church of England's funds due to bad investments.
79. Embezzlement, defined here as criminal theft by treasurers or other top officials responsible for Christian monies, has risen markedly since 1900 and now stands at 6% of income. Although alarming, it represents a level of corruption considerably smaller than that existing in the secular worlds of national and international industry, commerce, business, and government.
81. Organized Christianity operates, but only partially pays for, a worldwide network of 190,000 schools, 1,500 universities and colleges.
83. Churches, mission agencies, and Christian organizations operate, but only partially pay for, 30,000 medical clinics and 5,000 hospitals worldwide.

**Table 20–4. A selection of 24 recent massive 6-, 7-, 8-, and 9-figure embezzlements of Christian funds by top custodians.**

| Year<br>1 | Amount, $<br>2 | Loser or vehicle<br>3 | Alleged culprit<br>4 | Place<br>5 | Country<br>6 | Description<br>7 | Prison sentence<br>8 |
|---|---|---|---|---|---|---|---|
| 1986 | 20,000,000 | PTL/Heritage USA | President | Carolinas | USA | Theft, lavish life-style. | 45 years |
| 1990 | 4,000,000 | Mining land claims in Idaho | Promoter | Idaho | USA | Church investors swindled. | — |
| 1991 | 16,000,000 | Holy Spirit FM, Righteous Radio LP | Legal Director | Georgia | USA | Sonrise Management, for 150 radio stations. | — |
| 1992 | 5,000,000 | Hispanic (Mexican) Apostolate | Treasurer | Los Angeles | USA | Theft, 500 victims. | — |
| 1992 | 22,000,000 | United Church of Christ | Bank officials | New York | USA | Pensions Board swindle. Grand larceny. | 3 years |
| 1992 | 354,000,000 | New Era Philanthropy | Founder | Philadelphia | USA | Consortium of 500 Evangelical agencies. | 12 years |
| 1993 | 3,000,000 | Baptist College, Jackson, MS | President | Jackson | USA | Thefts over 25 years as president. | — |
| 1994 | 8,000,000 | National Council of Churches of Christ | Officials | New York | USA | International fraud of health insurance premiums. | — |
| 1995 | 13,000,000 | Salvation Army | Financial Consultant | London | Britain | Bogus investment scheme. | — |
| 1995 | 5,000,000 | Catholic Archdiocese of La Paz | Treasurer | La Paz | Bolivia | Huge theft over several years unnoticed. | — |
| 1996 | 400,000 | United Methodist Church | Comptroller General | New York | USA | UMC Board of Global Ministries. | 10 years |
| 1996 | 10,000,000 | Evangelical Free Ch, Burbank, CA | Deacon | Burbank | USA | Land investments for 80 church members. | 10 years |
| 1996 | 1,200,000 | Catholic Diocese of Brooklyn, NY | Pensions Manager | Brooklyn | USA | Lay Pension Office; culprit confessed. | — |
| 1996 | 1,100,000 | Ev Lutheran Ch in America | Treasurer | Northeast | USA | New England Synod. Larceny, laundering. | — |
| 1996 | 2,200,000 | Episcopal Ch in the USA | National Treasurer | New York | USA | Female official stole over 5-year period. | 5 years |
| 1997 | 3,000,000 | Chinese 3-Self Churches | Chairman | Guandong | China | Theft of donations from Hong Kong. | 5 years |
| 1998 | 6,000,000 | Church of the Nazarene | Investment Director | Washington | USA | Investment scam in 21 states. | 11 years |
| 1998 | 40,000,000 | Evangelical Friends Church | Investment Manager | Seattle | USA | Biggest pyramid scheme in church history. | 8 years |
| 1998 | 5,200,000 | National Baptist Convention | President | Tampa | USA | Racketeering, grand theft, tax evasion. | 9 years |
| 1998 | 2,025,000 | Ch of Norway/Sweden/Denmark | President, WARC | Cape Town | South Africa | Donations of 9 million rand missing. | Yes |
| 1998 | 3,800,000 | Catholic Archdiocese of Boston | Urban Planning Director | Boston | USA | Church officials lying to real estate developer. | Yes |
| 1999 | 12,000,000 | Sovereign Ministries International | Founder | Orlando | USA | Investment scheme to build churches. | 10 years |
| 1999 | 448,000,000 | Greater Ministries International Church | Pastor | Tampa | USA | Gold in Liberia promised. 18,000 investors. | 12 years |
| 1999 | 500,000,000 | Baptist Foundation of Arizona | President | Phoenix | USA | Related to Arizona Southern Baptist Convention. | — |
| Estimated total of all church or Christian funds embezzled, 1980-2000 | | | $75 billion. | | | | |
| Estimated annual total embezzled, AD 2000 | | | $16 billion. | | | | |

*Note.* The table reports only a small selection of the largest sums embezzled. Cases are known to occur in almost all countries, involving sums from many millions to thousands of smaller amounts. Most cases are never noticed at all by the churches robbed. Most cases reported above are from the USA because that country's secular press and media report such cases in detail whenever they occur. In most other countries, cases of this kind never see the light of day because church authorities gloss over them or sweep them under the carpet without publicity. *Culprits.* Most are never caught. Column 4 above reports the alleged culprits. In only a fraction of all other cases are culprits brought to justice; 95% escape undetected. *Prison sentence.* Outcome after the courts have indicted and convicted the culprits.

## *HOW COST-EFFECTIVE IS CHRISTIANITY?*

How much does it cost, or how much is it costing, to actually achieve what Christians are supposed to be achieving on our globe? If it is possible to measure the extent of this achievement, or failure to achieve it, and the relevant cost involved, then this should surely be a priority duty laid upon every member of the Christian church.

### *Some definitions*

First it is necessary to define exactly our key terms. *Cost* is 'the amount of money, time, effort, etc required to achieve an end.' The verb 'to cost' produces a *costing*, which means 'to estimate the cost of making a product or program, the amount of money spent in producing or manufacturing a commodity' *(Websters' New World dictionary of the American language, 1996).* Further, *cost accounting* is 'a system for recording, analyzing, and allocating production and distribution costs' *(ibid).* Our main adjective *cost-effective* then means 'economical in terms of the goods or services received for the money spent'; the related noun is *cost-effectiveness (American Heritage dictionary* on CD-ROM, 1996).

### *The Christian product sought*

The starting point should therefore be to answer the question: what is the primary responsibility of Christians on the Earth? We can answer as follows. For the moment, we see the church with its 2 billion members, receiving and spending every year a vast sum of money—$15.2 trillion by the year AD 2000. This sum is entrusted to the church, which spends it on a whole vast array of activities—humanitarian, ethical, religious, as well as specifically Christian, missionary, and evangelistic. This establishes *cost*.

We now need a measure of *effect* or effectiveness. The church of Christ's prime responsibility is to obey the head of the church, the Risen and Ascended Christ himself, and in particular to obey his central legacy of command to his followers. This command is, by universal recognition, enshrined in Christ's Great Commission after his resurrection. We may recall again Karl Barth's dictum 'The Great Commission is truly the most genuine utterance of the risen Jesus'. For documentation on its mandate we have the 6 major New Testament passages expounded here in Part 3 "GeoCommission". Of these the clearest and most direct is found in Matthew 28:19, CEV: 'Go to the people of all nations and make them my disciples. *Baptize them'* (emphasis added). The command is to make disciples and the concrete measurable action is to baptize them into his body the church.

In practice, this is virtually the only directly measurable action contained in the many dimensions and facets of the Great Commission narratives. As such, this imperative 'Baptize!' becomes a highly significant indicator and measure of the obedient discipleship of the entire body of all church members.

### *Christian product and Christian cost*

For our purposes here, then, the commodity or end product is newly baptized persons each year, and the cost is the total amount of money Christ's followers expend on everything they do during that year. So 'cost' here cannot be restricted to only the actual visible costs directly involved in the baptizing process itself. Rather, it means the actual cost of *all* aspects of Christian activity including scripture distribution, radio, television, computers, literature, administration, training, and all else the churches engage in.

One measure of Christianity's effectiveness, therefore, in its work in any country, people, language, city, or other grouping, is the number of new persons being baptized. Worldwide today this amounts to 45 millions a year. One measure of comparative cost-effectiveness can thus be obtained by computing the overall cost of each new person baptized. For the globe as a whole, this is $15.2 trillion divided by 45 million, which is $330,000 per newly baptized person.

### *Meanings of this new criterion*

As a global average this is a staggeringly large figure. It has multiple meanings. (1) It clarifies the enormous cost of each individual won for Christ's church. (2) It reminds Christians too critical of past triumphalism that the mandate to win disciples is still central to genuine Christianity. (3) Its numerical value is portrayed here in Table 12-1, column 100, and graphically for every country in the world (in *WCE* Part 4 "Countries", and *WCT* Part 15, Table 15-3) as the last in the standardized strip of 6 minidiagrams under each Country Table 1 which is here termed Great Commission Instrument Panel. There it takes the form of an aeronautical cockpit instrument telling the pilot speed, altitude, distance gone, and the like. (4) Its greatest value is as a comparative index, showing where each country is on the entire spectrum from the most cost-effective church (in Mozambique at $1,360 a baptism) to the least (in Japan at $2.7 million a baptism), as shown in the 2 minidiagrams below. The 10 top countries on this criterion, and the 10 bottom countries, are shown in Part 11 "Listings", Nos. 23-24.

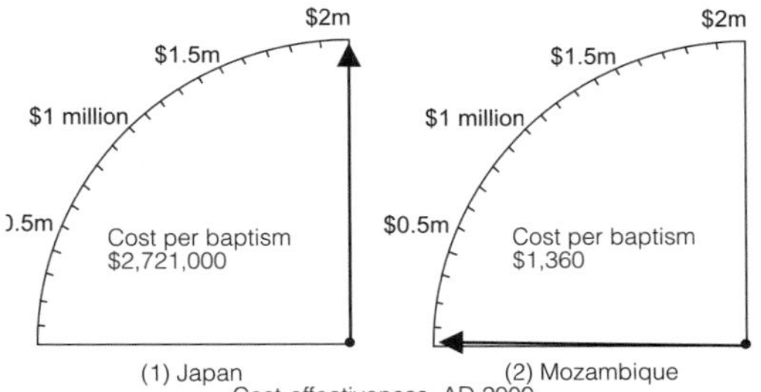


(1) Japan (2) Mozambique
Cost-effectiveness, AD 2000

### *A failure in management*

Often the blame for shortfalls in funding Christian projects is laid by management squarely on the laity, the rank and file of Christians in the churches. To the contrary, our survey has demonstrated that it is ludicrously incorrect to blame the laity who donate $270 billion of their own money every year to support the churches and agencies. What has gone wrong is clearly a failure in management, a failure to use these massive funds wisely, strategically, and cooperatively. There are obviously entirely enough funds to pay for the thousands of worthwhile projects and operations which arise every year but which at present fail to secure proper funding and then collapse.

### *A failure of vision*

A concrete example of this failure in leadership concerns the computer technology known as artificial intelligence (AI). These programs are also called 'expert systems' because they replicate exactly the expertise of an expert in any subject from arranging office staff vacation times to planning landings on the planet Mars. By 1980 several large multinational companies had hundreds of these systems operating cost-effectively, and by 2000 thousands. By AD 2010 it is expected that every business and enterprise will depend on such customized systems at every level.

In 1986 the editors of the *World Christian encyclopedia* carried out a concerted endeavor to persuade foreign mission agencies to adopt this technology. Although spectacular results were being obtained (for example, for matching up mission job opportunities with potential new mission recruits), theological objections were raised to the very idea of 'artificial' intelligence; bureaucrats took over and killed this highly promising new Christian enterprise.

## *CONCLUSION*

From this examination of the money circulating in Christian circles for Christian work each year, several conclusions can be drawn. First, the terms 'Church of the Poor' and 'Church of the Rich' have many complementary and overlapping meanings. The Church of the Rich usually refers to the affluent West. It has enormous material wealth, but contains within it sizable pockets of the Church of the Poor. Spiritually this middle-class Church of the Rich is, from some aspects, a mere pauper itself and so has gradually become

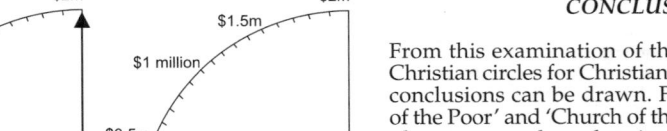

looked down on by Third-World Christians as itself spiritually a Church of the Poor. Likewise, the initial meaning of the term 'Church of the Poor' usually refers to the Third World. It lives largely in absolute material poverty yet has sizable enclaves of the Church of the Rich prospering within it oblivious of the plight of their neighbors. Paradoxically this Church of the Poor has an abundance of charisma and charismata, and so has become spiritually a Church of the Rich.

Second, there is plenty of money available worldwide to meet all reasonable Christian global goals and obligations. There is entirely enough to undertake the effective prosecution of the Christian world mission. There is enough to undertake every type if research essential to the prosecution of the churches' life and mission. there is even enough to enable the Church of the Poor to break out of its vicious environment and bring out the rest of humanity with it. It is simply a question of vision, determination, challenge, mobilization, redistribution, management, internal control, and sharing.

This assessment is not affected by temporary setbacks—world recession, shortfalls in giving to particular relief bodies, escalating inflation, fluctuating oil prices, bankruptcies among Christian in situations, even graft and corruption where they exist in Christian organizations. Even the most radical proposal of all—that Christians unilaterally implement a global redistribution of income—is a practical proposition that could have immense global repercussions. A voluntary 10% cut in income on the part of all church-member Christians in Europe and North America could produce a 93% increase in income on the part of the entire 1.4 billion population of South Asia, or an 82% increase throughout Latin America, or a 158% increase for every soul in Africa.

Third, responsibility to act is not confined to Western Christians in their Church of the Rich. We have noted about that in the Church of the Poor, there is a combination of 30 million relatively affluent Christians on top of 260 million Christians in absolute poverty. This means that if these nouveaux-riches elites, including leadership hierarchies, redistributed their income and their wealth, they would solve much of the imbalance without outside interference or charity from the West.

Unfortunately, mere theorizing or pious exhortations are unlikely to motivate affluent Christians anywhere in this direction. Instead it is a question of research (what actually is the true situation?), then information (get your facts right), then communication (let me tell you the situation), then confrontation (do you know how bad things are?), then education (we are all responsible), then persuasion (do something about it)—and then implementation.

Despite the logic of this situation, it would be unrealistic to expect the Christian community on any continent to be totally obedient to this particular heavenly vision. Eighty-five years ago Samuel Zwemer, apostle to Islam, put it succinctly when contributing to John R. Mott's classic *The Evangelization of the World in This Generation*. Difficult regions like Arabia, he said, and indeed the whole world, 'could easily be evangelized within the next thirty years if it were not for the wicked selfishness of Christians'.

To a large extent, the global sharing by Christians of money, wealth, property, and goods could solve most of these problems, including those of famine, poverty, disease, unemployment, dangerous water supply, and so on. Because this is so, there is a sense in which Christians are to blame for the persistence of the present disastrous state of affairs. Every Christian with an income of over $500 a year ought to be deeply concerned and actively involved in this problem. At the least, each should consider donating 10% of his or her income to Third-World missions or charities, or to studying, preaching, writing, teaching, or researching about the situation. Every Christian who ignores this obligation lies under the solemn judgment of God on this issue.

Several centuries ago a Roman pope who was an avid patron of the arts is said to have surveyed the vast artistic riches he had amassed, and to have gloated: 'No longer can the Church of Jesus Christ now say "Silver and gold have I none"'. 'True, Sire,' a subordinate replied. "but then neither can she now say, "Rise up and walk!"' Material wealth has always carried the risk of attendant spiritual bankruptcy. Today's Church of the Rich, on all its definitions, has vast resources capable of reaching the entire world for Christ. But unless these resources are immediately deployed to that end, this church will ultimately prove to have had minimal spiritual impact upon the world.

### *BIBLIOGRAPHY*


*1992 resource sharing book: Pacific: programmes/projects and services.* Geneva: World Council of Churches, 1991. 871p.

*A comparison of the growth in the United States per capita income and population with the Free Methodist Church budget and membership for the years 1967 and 1982.* J. L. Ronsvalle. Urbana, IL: Empty Tomb, 1987. 11p.

'A ministry of stewardship development through a participatory budgeting process.' D. M. Becker. D.Min. thesis, Southwestern Baptist Theological Seminary, Fort Worth, TX, 1992. 200p.

'A new twist on stewardship: foundational pledge renewals.' S. McCary. Paper, Candler School of Theology National Institute in Church Finance and Administration, Atlanta, 1994. 33p.

'A program to cultivate the practice of financial stewardship in a local Christian Reformed congregation.' R. Heerspink. D.Min. thesis, Trinity Evangelical Divinity School, Deerfield, IL, 1993. 243p.

*A study in giving and stewardship campaigns.* L. H. Adcock. , 1994. 32p. (National Institute in Church Finance and Administration, Candler School of Theology, Emory University, Atlanta. Summer Seminar, 1994).

'A study of fundraising practices in selected parachurch organizations in Nairobi.' A. Dei-Awuku. M.A. thesis, Daystar University College and Wheaton College, Wheaton, IL and Nairobi, Kenya, 1987. 328p.

'An analysis of the variables that affect the financial support of Korea Nazarene Theological College by the Korea Nazarene Church.' M. G. Shin. Ed.D. thesis, Kansas State University, Manhattan, KS, 1988. 166p.

'An empirical analysis of stewardship factors in selected large congregations of the Presbyterian Church (U.S.A.).' G. E. Hollingshead. Th.D. thesis, Eastern Baptist Theological Seminary, Wynnewood, PA, 1986. 254p.

*An estimate of Catholic household contributions to the Sunday offertory collection during 1991.* J. C. Harris. Washington, DC: Life Cycle Institute, Catholic University of America, 1992. 106p.

*An introduction to church finances.* D. R. Pollock. *Christian ministries management library series B Accounting*, vol. 1. Diamond Bar, CA: Christian Ministries Management Association, 1986. 49p.

*Basic accounting for churches: a turnkey manual.* J. A. Henry. Nashville, TN: Broadman & Holman, 1994. 173p.

*Behind the stained glass window: money dynamics in the church.* J. Ronsvalle & S. Ronsvalle. Grand Rapids, MI: Baker, 1996.

'Cash management in the religious non–profit sector: a survey of three major denominations' practices.' J. R. Peirce. M.U.A. thesis, Virginia Polytechnic Institute and State University, Blacksburg, VA, 1994. 100p.

*Catholic contributions: sociology and policy.* A. Greeley & W. McManus. Chicago: Thomas More Press, 1987.

*Christian stewardship in the South Pacific.* J. Sharpe. Madang, Papua New Guinea: Kristen Pres, 1972. 77p.

'Christian stewardship in the Synod of Livingstonia.' O. P. Mazunda. D.Min. thesis, Columbia Theological Seminary, Decatur, GA, 1984. 175p.

'Church finances: chaos to automation.' L. R. Patterson. Paper, National Association of Church Business Administrators, 1985. 54p. (An account of the reorganization of financial procedures at the First Baptist Church, Roanoke, VA, submitted for certification of The National Association of Church Business Administrators).

'Church finances for lean times.' L. Willard. Paper, Candler School of Theology, Emory University, Atlanta, 1992. 37p. (National Institute in Church Finance and Administration, Summer Seminar, 1992).

*Church finances for people who count: a basic handbook for church treasurers, trustees, deacons, and ministry staff.* M. Tennyson. Grand Rapids, MI: Zondervan Academic and Professional Books, 1990. 157p.

*Church financial management handbook.* R. B. Baltz & J. J. Powell III. Jackson, MS: Church Management Institute, School of Management, Millsaps College, 1986. 55p.

*Church financial statistics and related data.* New York: National Council of Churches of Christ in the U.S.A., 1976.

'Congregational vs. denominational giving: an analysis of giving patterns in the Presbyterian Church in the United States and the Reformed Church in America,' R. J. Nemeth & D. A. Luidens, *Review of religious research*, 36, 2 (December 1994), 111–22.

'Current concerns in church finance.' D. J. Christensen. M.A. thesis, Columbia Biblical Seminary and Graduate School of Missions, Columbia, SC, 1987. 103p.

'Determinants of religious giving in American denominations: data from two nationwide surveys,' D. R. Hoge & F. Yang, *Review of religious research*, 36, 2 (December 1994), 123–48.

'Developing church financial policies and procedures.' C. McHorse. Paper, National Association of Church Business Administrators, 1993. 64p. (Submitted for certification of the National Association of Church Business Administrators. Develops financial policies and procedures for St. Luke's Episcopal Church, San Antonio, TX).

*Die Kirche und unser Geld: Daten, Tatsachen, Hintergründe.* H. Herrmann. Hamburg: Rasch und Röhring, 1990. 272p.

*Die Kirchenfinanzierung in Kirche und Staat der Gegenwart: die Kirchensteuer im internationalen Umfeld kirchlicher Abgabensystem und im heutigen Sozial– und Kulturstaat Bundesrepublik Deutschland.* H. Marré. 3 teilweise überarb. und ergänzte Aufl ed. *Münsterischer Kommentar zum Codex Iuris Canonici Beiheft*, 4. Essen: Ludgerus Verlag, 1991. 126p. (German tax law and legislation concerning religious organizations).

'Economic and attitudinal factors in Catholic and Protestant religious giving,' P. A. Zaleski & C. E. Zech, *Review of religious research*, 36, 2 (December 1994).

*Eglise, finance et royauté: la floraison des décimes dans la France du Moyen Age.* B. Causse. Lille Paris: ANRT Aux Amateurs de livres, 1988. 2 vols, 873p.

*El crédito eclesiástico en la Nueva España, siglo XVIII.* G. von Wobeser. México: Universidad Nacional Autónoma de México, Instituto de Investigaciones Históricas, 1994. 275p.

*El Imperio del Vaticano.* N. Lo Bello. Buenos Aires: Editorial Grito Sagrado, 1986. 168p.

*Encyclopedia of fund raising: a three volume work on how to organize fund raising special events.* G. M. Plessner. Arcadia, CA: Fund Raisers, Inc., 1980–1992. 3 vols, 351p. (Volumes 2 and 3 are revised editions).

*Entre idéal et réalité: finances et religion du Moyen–Age ßa l'époque contemporaine.* M. Aubrun. Clermont-Ferrand: Publications de l'Institut d'études du Massif Central, 1994. 419p.

*Excelling in global giving!* D. A. Jensen. Wheaton, IL: Conservative Baptist Foreign Mission Society, 1991. 72p.

*Faith and philanthropy in America.* R. Wuthnow & V. A. Hodgkinson (eds). San Francisco: Jossey–Bass, 1990.

'Financial accountability of religious organizations.' J. R. Johnson. B.G.S. thesis, Texas Tech University, Lubbock, TX, 1994. 37p.

*Financial trends in Christian organisations.* P. W. Brierley. *MARC monograph*, no. 10. Bromley, Kent, UK: MARC Europe, 1988. 39p. (Includes response by Derek Tidball).

*Financing American religion.* M. Chaves & S. L. Miller, eds. London: Sage, 1999.

*Finanz und Finanzpolitik des heiligen Stuhls: römische Kurie und Vatikanstaat seit Papst Paul VI.* H. Benz. *Vierteljahrschrift für Sozial und Wirtschaftsgeschichte Beihefte*, Nr. 108. Stuttgart: Franz Steiner Verlag, 1993. 183p.

*Finanzwissenschaftliche Aspekte von Religionsgemeinschaften: 23. Hochschulkurs des Instituts für Finanzwissenschaft an der Universität Innsbruck. Schriften zur öffentlichen Verwaltung und öffentlichen Wirtschaft*, 117. Baden-Baden: Nomos Verlagsanstalt, 1989. 228p.

*Friends, funds, and freshmen: a manager's guide to Christian college advancement.* W. K. Willmer (ed). Washington, DC: Christian College Coalition, 1990. 126p.

*From belief to commitment: the activities and expenditures of religious congregations in the United States: a summary report.* V. A. Hodgkinson. Washington, DC: Independent Sector, 1988. 27p.

*Funding churches in the future: proceedings of a national symposium on financial support and development in the Catholic Church.* Washington, DC: Foundations and Donors Interested in Catholic Activities, 1988. 76p.

*Funding third world missions: the pursuit of true Christian partnership.* L. Bush. Singapore and Wheaton, IL: World Evangelical Fellowship Missions Commission, 1990. 30p.

*Giving and volunteering in the United States.* V. A. Hodgkinson & M. S. Weitzman. Washington, DC: Independent Sector, 1992.

*Giving USA. Annual Reports.* American Association of Fund-Raising Counsel Trust for Philanthropy. A. E. Kaplan. 40th edition, 1995.

'Guidelines for internal financial controls.' J. Illg. Paper, Saint Paul Seminary School of Divinity of the College of St. Thomas, St. Paul, MN, 1989. 46p. (Paper for the National Association of Church Business Administration).

*Human development report 1996.* New York and Oxford, UK: Oxford University Press, 1996. 239p. (Published annually for the United Nations Development Programme).

*Il caso Marcinkus: le vie del denaro sono infinite.* L. Coen. Milan: A. Mondadori, 1991. 306p.

*Im Namen Gottes?: der mysteriöse Tod des 33–Tage–Papstes, Johannes Paul I: Tatsachen und Hintergründe.* D. A. Yallop. Munich: Knaur, 1988. 464p.

*In God's name: an investigation into the murder of Pope John Paul I.* D. A. Yallop. Toronto and New York: Bantam, 1985. 398p. (Pursues a theory that John Paul I was murdered because he was preparing to expose fraud in the Banco Ambrosiano).

'Increasing congregational mission focus while maintaining congregational financial stability.' W. R. Miles. D.Min. thesis, Garrett-Evangelical Theological Seminary, Evanston, IL, 1993. 130p. (Case study of First Christian Church, Greeley, CO).

*Kirchliche Finanzwirtschaft.* H. D. Hessler. Berlin: Duncker & Humblot, 1990–. 1 vol to date.

*Kirchlicher Finanzausgleich: Kanonistische Aspekte zu einen gesamtkirchlich neu entdecken Mittel kirchlicher Finanzverteilung.* F. Kalde. *Forschungen zur kirchenrechtswissenschaft*, 16. Würzburg: Echter, 1993. 176p.

*La batalla por el tesoro de San Pietro: Ultrafin.* A. Baeza. 2nd ed. Madrid: ABL editor, 1994. 542p.

*Les églises et l'argent: actes du colloque de 1988.* Paris: Presses de l'Université de Paris Sorbonne, 1989. 74p.

*Les finances de l'Église de France.* R. Gaucher. Paris: A. Michel, 1981. 288p.

'Major fund campaigns and their impact on the financial giving pattern of the local church.' F. W. Cassell. D.Min. thesis, San Francisco Theological Seminary, San Anselmo, CA, 1984. 272p.

*Managers with God: continuing the work Christ began.* D. Kauffman. Scottdale, PA: Herald Press, 1990. 196p.

'Managing the church budget by cash flow.' J. W. Perkins. National Association of Church Business Administrators, 1988. 35p. (A study of First Baptist Church, Ferguson, MO, submitted for certification of the National Association of Church Business Administrators).

*Mastering church finances.* R. L. Bergstrom, G. Fenton & W. A. Pohl. *Mastering ministry.* Portland, OR: Multnomah Press Christianity Today, 1992. 166p.

*Money matters: personal giving in American churches.* D. R. Hoge et al. Louisville, KY: Westminster John Knox Press, 1996. 260p.

*Money, motivation, and mission in the small church.* A. Pappas. *Small church in action.* Valley Forge, PA: Judson Press, 1989. 125p.

*Money, power, greed: has the church been sold out?* J. M. Montgomery. Ventura, CA: Regal Books, 1987. 179p.

*Money: who has how much and why.* A. Hacker. New York: Scribner, 1997. 254p.

*More money, new money, big money: creative stratigies for funding today's church.* W. C. Barrett. Nashville, TN: Discipleship Resources, 1992. 154p.

*National directory of philanthropy for Native Americans.* P. A. Meiners (ed). Kansas City, MO: Corporate Resource Consultants, 1992. 148p.

'Optimum church building financing methods.' A. E. Lowder. Paper, George Fox College, Department of Continuing Education, 1991. 45p.

*Origins of church wealth in Mexico: ecclesiastical revenues and church finances, 1523–1600.* J. F. Schwaller. Albuquerque, NM: University of New Mexico Press, 1985. 253p.

*Philanthropy in the world's traditions.* W. F. Ilchman, S. N. Katz & E. L. Queen II (eds). *Philanthropic studies.* Bloomington, IN: Indiana University Press, 1998. 400p.

*Poor Richard's principle.* R. Wuthnow. Princeton, NJ: Princeton University Press, 1996. 448p.

*Por qué murió Albino Luciani?* A. Baeza. 2nd ed. Madrid: ABL Editor, 1994. 387p.

*Raising funds in Kenya: a survey of middle to upper income Nairobi churchgoers: a research project.* D. R. Downes. Nairobi: Daystar University College, 1991. 100p.

*Rankings: church related comprehensive colleges and universities: selected management ratios: handbook for classifying and comparing institutions.* Boulder, CO: John Minter Associates, 1991.

*Reaching out to the World with the word: a report on the gathering of funds by congregations, as of June 30, 1983.* Milwaukee, WI: The Synod, 1983. 64p. (Closing report to the Wisconsin Evangelical Lutheran Synod on the Reaching Out offering.).

*Report of the Task Force on Finances: submitted to the Office of the President, The Lutheran Church—Missouri Synod.* St. Louis, MO: Missouri Synod Lutheran Task Force on Finances, 1993. 16p.

*Research on factors influencing giving to religious bodies.* D. R. Hoge & D. L. Griffin. Indianapolis, IN: Ecumenical Center for Stewardship Studies, 1992.

'Simultaneous determination of church contributions and church attendance,' D. H. Sullivan, *Economic inquiry,* 23 (1985), 309–20.

*Social statistics.* H. M. Blalock Jr. 2nd ed. New York: McGraw-Hill, 1972.

*Statistical abstract of the United States, 1996: the national data book.* Washington, DC: Bureau of the Census, 1996. 1,036p. (Published annually).

'Stewardship practices in Kenya with proposed solutions.' A. N. Birai. D.Min. thesis, Andrews University, Seventh–day Adventist Theological Seminary, Barrien Springs, MI, 1994. 266p.

*Survey of United Methodist opinion: promotion of funds for the United Methodist Church.* Dayton, OH: General Council on Ministries Research Office, United Methodist Church, 1987. 22p.

*Svenska kyrkans finansförmögenhet.* Stockholm: Civildepartementet Allmanna forlaget, Kundtjanst distributor, 1992]. 105p.

'The acts of financial administration by diocesan bishops according to the norms of canon 1277.' T. H. Vowell. D.C.L. thesis, Saint Paul University, Ottowa, Ontario, 1991. 293p.

*The Budget of the Episcopal Church.* N.p.: Episcopal Church Joint Standing Committee on Program, Budget and Finance, 1988. 28 p

*The Catholic philanthropic tradition in America.* M. J. Oates. Bloomington, IN: Indiana University Press, 1995. 252p.

*The complete guide to managing your money: Your finances in changing times; Using your money wisely; Debt–free living.* L. Burkett. New York: Inspirational Press, 1996. 3 vols. in one; 567p.

*The emerging parish: the Notre Dame study of Catholic life since Vatican II.* J. Castelli & J. Gremillion. San Francisco: Harper & Row, 1987.

'The financial relationship of the Catholic elementary school to its parish: burden or blessing.' J. McCauley. Ed.D. thesis, Seattle University, Seattle, WA, 1994. 240p.

*The gospel of good giving: stewardship in Australian churches.* D. McDiarmid. Melbourne: Joint Board of Christian Education, 1990. 64p.

*The mainline church's funding crisis: issues and possibilities.* R. E. Vallet & C. E. Zech. Grand Rapids, MI: Eerdmans; Manlius, NY: Rose Publications, 1995. 195p.

*The Mormon corporate empire.* J. Heinerman & A. D. Shupe. Boston: Beacon Press, 1985. 407p.

'The Receipts and Benevolences of Presbyterian Congregations, 1973–1988,' G. A. Krohn, *Journal for the scientific study of religion,* 34 (March 1995), 17–34.

*The state of church giving through 1992.* J. L. Ronsvalle & S. Ronsvale. Champaign, IL: empty tomb, 1994. (Analyzes data on giving for thirty one denominations in the U.S.).

'The stewardship of money: theological perspectives and pastoral education.' R. S. Bair. D.Min. thesis, Garrett-Evangelical Theological Seminary, Evanston, IL, 1994. 230p.

*The Supreme Court and public funds for religious schools: the Burger years, 1969–1986.* J. E. Bryson & S. H. Houston. Jefferson, NC: McFarland, 1990. 360p. (Covers law and legislation concerning church related schools in the U.S.).

'Through the maze of church accounting and tax regulations.' J. S. Klaerig. Paper, Candler School of Theology, Emory University, Atlanta, 1989. 67p. (A project paper for the National Institute in Church Finance and Administration, August 1989).

*Tithing and other gifts.* G. Burch. Skeld, Shetland: Open Bible Trust, 1993. 17p. (Published in the United States by Grace Publications).

*Together in mission: a series of mini–dramas celebrating the 50th anniversary of Unified Promotion–Basic Mission Finance.* J. R. Ryan. Indianapolis, IN: Church Finance Council, 1985. 15p.

*Tutorial for church financial and membership records: using off–the–shelf commercial software computer programs (MS DOS system).* L. V. Blakley. *Computer software series,* CSS-27. Stillwater, OK: Cooperative Extension Service, Division of Agriculture, Oklahoma State University, 1987. 1 vol.

*Understanding church finances: the economics of the local church.* L. H. Hartley. New York: Pilgrim Press, 1984.

*Wealth and power in American Zion.* A. D. Shupe. Lewiston, NY: E. Mellen Press, 1992. 341p. (Revised and updated edition of *The Mormon corporate empire).*

'Where your treasure is: financial and emotional over–investment in clergy deployment.' H. W. Whitaker. D.Min. thesis, Wesley Theological Seminary, Washington, DC, 1994. 117p. (A study of clergy job stress and church financial management at St. Stephen's Episcopal Church, Earlesville, MD).

'Why strict churches are strong,' L. R. Iannaccone, *American journal of sociology,* 99, 5 (March 1994), 1180–1211.

*World missions handbook: for local churches.* G. LaForge. Springfield, MO: World Missions Service Center, 1984. 89p.

*Your money, mission, ministry: a report on how your money makes mission & ministry possible.* Nashville, TN: United Methodist Communications, 1986. 48p.

'Your money or your life: the influence of endowments upon the local church.' J. A. Simpson. D.Min. thesis, Andover Newton Theological School, Newton Center, MA, 1994. 189p.

# Part 21

# GEOPERSONNEL

Great Commission Christians: workforce for the apostolate

*The devil has an unspeakable dread of the Society of Jesus entering China, but I am confident that Jesus Christ, our Saviour and Redeemer, will disappoint his wishes and make his vain hope void.*

—Francis Xavier's last letter, China coast, 1552

Keeping close track of the numbers of personnel—both the whole body of followers and also its full-time or part-time workers—and their activities is essential in any walk of life. In the case of religions, this includes their vocation, their quality, their selection, their training, their activities, their health, their safety, their probable years of service, their eventual replacement, retirement, and long-term scenarios for the future.

Part 21 provides basic enumeration of all Christian personnel—both full-time workers, part-timers, and laypersons. It then quantifies a new core category: Great Commission Christians, defined as all church members who take seriously Christ's call to follow him in mission to the world.

# Great Commission Christians: workforce for the apostolate

The term 'GeoPersonnel' is used here to describe the totality of persons involved in the world mission of global Christianity. It covers all individuals and groups and agencies and communities who are in some definable sense active with regard to Christ's mission among the human race.

Part 21 therefore ranges over the questions of who, how many, and where are the human resources now in place to undertake this mission. We begin by calling these human resources 'evangelizing Christians', and move on to coining and defining them as 'Great Commission Christians' (GCCs). Part 21 then closes with this survey's methodology for enumerating GCCs for every people and country in the world.

In the course of measuring these human resources, this analysis also highlights the need for evaluation of global Christianity, national Christianity, churches, denominations, agencies, and individual Christians. It derives objective factors to evaluate and enumerate (a) the effectiveness of the discipleship of Christians and their outreach, (b) the individual and collective effectiveness of churches and agencies, and (c) the overall effectiveness of the whole of global Christianity.

## Non-evangelizing Christians

Before describing the whole range of 20 synonyms for Christianity's human resources for mission, we should first describe briefly the rest of global Christianity who are not at present involved in mission in any realistic manner.

It is shown in Part 23 "Evangelization" that all Christians should correctly be regarded as, and termed, evangelized. But whether or not they assist in other people becoming evangelized is quite another matter. In general, we may say that unaffiliated Christians, non-practicing Christians, and also de-christianized persons, although all themselves evangelized, are persons who contribute nothing to the ongoing process of the evangelizing of others, either among their own people and country or among persons and countries beyond. They are Christians who, for one reason or another, good or bad, are unable or unwilling to obey Christ's commission to them to evangelize. We therefore term them, in this survey, 'non-evangelizing Christians' or 'latent Christians' ('dormant Christians' is also used), and we will later be enumerating this category precisely for every country and ethnolinguistic people on Earth.

## SYNONYMS FOR ACTIVE CHRISTIANS

We turn now to list and briefly interpret a range of 20 synonyms and other descriptive terms in current use.

1. *Evangelizing Christians*. As stated above, the normal situation is that all Christians have already become and so are already evangelized persons. But further, in contrast to non-evangelizing Christians, all committed Christians and practicing Christians are persons who are themselves both evangelized, and also evangelizing. Whether deliberately or subconsciously or even unconsciously, they contribute to the ongoing process of the evangelizing of others, both among their own people and country and often also among peoples and countries beyond. Their lives and examples constantly involve outreach to outsiders, those outside the Christian faith; they evangelize others as part of their regular Christian lives. They are Christians who, to varying degrees and according to their ability and opportunity, are attempting to obey some or all of the component parts of Christ's commission to them to evangelize. In this survey, we therefore give them the name 'evangelizing Christians', and we will later be enumerating this category precisely for every country and ethnolin-guistic people on earth.

2. *The People of God.* This phrase is one of the major New Testament terms for Christians and the church that they compose. Its raison d'etre is clear. In Vatican II's 'Decree on the Church's Missionary Activity' (1966), it was stated: 'The whole church is missionary, and the work of evangelization is a basic duty of the People of God.' In other words, the People of God are, or normally are, or are to be, or normally ought to be, evangelizing Christians.

3. *The Body of Christ*. This is another major New Testament term for the church. Christ is often seen nowadays as primarily evangelizing. The WCC Evanston Assembly in 1954 affirmed 'Jesus Christ is the Evangelist.' Among Catholics, referring to 'Christ the Evangelizer' in its opening title, Paul VI's *Evangelii Nuntiandi* (1975) stated: 'Jesus himself, the Good News of God, was the very first and the greatest evangelizer.' As the Body of Christ, therefore, Christians are inescapably bound up with Christ's evangelizing ministry. The Body of Christ consists of evangelizing Christians.

4. *The evangelizing church*. This idea and phrase is a newly-coined one now coming into widespread use. First on the scene with this particular emphasis were the Eastern Orthodox in a 1974 Bucharest consultation. Orthodox understanding of mission emphasizes the ecclesial character of evangelism. The effective evangelizing agency in a particular population is not simply the aggregate of a number of evangelizing individuals but rather the whole fellowship of the faithful acting together. For the Orthodox, 'The chief evangelizer of the Church is the bishop,' and they speak of 'the evangelizing power of the Divine liturgy.' Secondly, Evangelicals in the 1974 ICOWE congress called for 'a strong, powerfully evangelizing church'. Thirdly, the 1974 3rd Synod of Bishops called the Church to be 'faithful to her evangelizing mission,' and their call was elaborated by *Evangelii Nuntiandi* in its chapter I 'From Christ the Evangelizer to the Evangelizing Church.' Lastly, the 1975 WCC Nairobi Assembly stated:

> Evangelism cannot be delegated to either gifted individuals or specialized agencies. It is entrusted to the 'whole church,' the body of Christ, in which the particular gifts and function of all members are but expressions of the life of the whole body.

Increasingly, the church is being seen as basically and primarily an evangelizing community. In 1978 the general secretary of the Netherlands Reformed Church, a former WCC director of communications, wrote: 'The Christian community is an evangelizing community. All it says points to its message; all it does exemplifies its message.' Illustrative of this trend is the series of 12 articles in *Foundations* (1977) describing a USA denomination in these words: 'American Baptist Churches as an evangelizing community.'

Evangelizing Christians are therefore those who belong to the evangelizing Church.

5. *Normal Christians*. Evangelizing Christians are not unusual or strange or deviant varieties of Christians; they are the norm, the normal pattern and purpose of Christian living.

6. *Intentional Christians*. This term is used in several circles to refer to the overall Christian intent to work for the Kingdom of God and to spread the Christian faith.

7. *Authentic Christians*. Active and activist Christians impress non-Christians as the genuine article. Such authenticity is important for sustaining the church's credibility.

8. *Nuclear Christians*. This term emphasizes that evangelizing Christians form the genuine nucleus or core of the Church as it fulfills its primary task of evangelization.

9. *99.5% laity*. It is important to realize that evangelizing Christians, the evangelizing Church, consist almost entirely of lay persons—non-ordained, non-professional Christians, engaged full-time in secular occupations in the secular world. In the vast majority of Christian denominations across the world, the laity number from 99.0% to 99.9% of the entire membership of the church. The global average is 99.7%.

The centrality of the laity in evangelism has always been recognized. In 1954 the WCC's first survey *Evangelism* stated, 'Laymen are on the frontier, served by the ministry whose function it is to equip the people of God for its mission.' Nearly every lay believer meets in his daily work people who are outsiders or even (in many parts of the world) persons who are unevangelized or unreached by the gospel. Anglican bishop of Winchester John V. Taylor wrote in 1968 of 'a truly evangelizing servanthood of the laity in the secular world.' *Evangelii Nuntiandi* also in its section 70 'The Laity' had a great deal to say about 'Gospel-inspired lay people . . . Conscious of their evangelizing role' and their 'very special form of evangelization':

> Their own field of evangelizing activity is the vast and complicated world of politics, society and economics, but also the world of culture, of the sciences and the arts, of international life, of the mass media.

10. *The Workforce for the Apostolate*. The other side of the above is that on average only 0.3% of the whole evangelizing church, of all evangelizing Christians, consists of full-time clerical or lay professional workers. This is a very tiny proportion indeed. Nevertheless, for the Orthodox it is still the professionals who lead:

> The chief evangelizer of the Church is the bishop, with his presbyterion and diaconate as well as the monastic establishment.

Roman Catholic and Anglican usage places similar emphasis upon the bishop's central role in coordinating evangelism. *Evangelii Nuntiandi gives* as its ideal not a group of obscure laity but 'that model evangelizer, the Apostle Paul,' and entitles its chapter VI 'The Workers for Evangelization.' These are those whom the Vatican officially in Latin terms Apostolatus Copiae, whose official translation in English is the Workforce for the Apostolate, or 'the apostolic force,' namely all full-time church workers, bishops, priests, deacons, brothers, monks, nuns, sisters, and lay workers.

Two new Roman Catholic missionary societies or congregations have recently been formed whose titles embody this ideal. An international African missionary society has been founded in Tanzania with 20 novices, the Evangelizing Sisters of Mary. And in Hong Kong, there is a Chinese indigenous religious congregation, Sisters Announcers of the Lord, with initially 24 members. While not denying the importance of the laity's role, these 2 congregations emphasize that professional religious personnel can often be initiators and leaders as evangelizing Christians.

11. *Evangelists*. A number of Christian leaders in the past have attempted to galvanize the laity by pressing slogans such as 'Every baptized Christian an evangelist.' One such was V.S. Azariah, bishop of Dornakal in South India. R. Leavell held the same view:

'No evangelism is complete until the evangelized become evangelists.' The idea behind this is the fully biblical idea that all Christians must be evangelizing Christians. However, as shown in Part 22, the English word 'evangelist' is best used only of professionals, either of church workers whose denominations employ this term for them (usually catechists), or of professional full-time preachers engaged in mass evangelism through public preaching employing the media. Clearly, not all Christians are called to be evangelists in these senses.

12. *Evangelizers.* Evangelizing Christians are evangelizers. This term also has recently come into widespread use. In the *1975 Yearbook of Jehovah's Witnesses*, under the title 'Two million evangelizers world wide!' there is the report that in 1974 'Jehovah's Christian witnesses in the United States have had their finest year in the evangelizing work, with 81,588 being baptized.'

At the other end of the ecclesiastical spectrum, the term has also come into fashion in the Roman Catholic Church. *Evangelii Nuntiandi* commented that 'Finally, the person who has been evangelized goes on to evangelize others.' Paul VI then marveled at the 'multitude of splendid evangelizers all through the Church's history.' He also noted that 'The Christian family . . . becomes the evangelizer of many other families and of the neighborhood of which it forms part.' Over the subsequent 25 years, the same terminology has been carried on by subsequent popes John Paul I and John Paul II: 'In the Church, every one of the faithful is an evangelizer.'

13. *Trained Christians.* Most Christians do not become activists and evangelizers automatically. Training is needed and, in the today's church circles, widely available to all Christians who take this subject seriously.

14. *Mobilized Christians.* Evangelized Christians are mobilized Christians. As far back as 1952, bishop Lesslie Newbigin pointed out:

The challenge is to mobilize the entire forces of the Church for evangelism . . . the enlistment of the whole membership for the task of evangelism.

During the 1970s, Evangelicals developed this concept with their total mobilization campaigns based on the Evangelism-in-Depth movement in Latin American countries during the 1960s.

15. *Militant Christians.* Evangelizing Christians are militants. The latter noun is widely used in the world of trade unions, strikes, labor disputes, picket lines, neofundamentalism, terrorism, and anarchism. Its use in Christian circles has until recently repudiated all manifestations of violence. In English usage, it goes back at least to the 1552 Book of Common Prayer of the Church of England, whose Service of Holy Communion included the exhortation 'Let us pray for the whole estate of Christ's Church Militant Here on Earth.' This concept has the value of underlying that evangelizing Christians have committed themselves, not to a safe or quiet life, but to a dangerous way of life. As the Pentecostal theologian W. Hollenweger has put it, 'Christian witness is *martyria* . . . dangerous. Evangelism is the most risky job'.

16. *Apostolic Christians.* This expression is becoming widespread among the second-largest major ecclesiastico-cultural megabloc, the Independents/Postdenominationalists.

17. *Practicing Christians.* Evangelizing Christians are practicing Christians. This means that they are regular church attenders, that they adhere to Christian standards and values, and participate in the ongoing life of organized Christianity.

18. *The force for evangelism.* The next pair of synonyms that we give for evangelizing Christians are the most recent technical terms to be coined. 'The force for evangelism' was coined in Dayton and Fraser's *Planning strategies for evangelism: a workbook* (1975).

19. *A force for evangelization.* As a related synonym this term came into use among Roman Catholic charismatics from 1977 onwards and was later picked up by North American Evangelicals in the documents for the Consultation on World Evangelization (Thailand) in 1980. In the latter case, it was meant as a renamed version of the previous term. Using our own approach and terminology, it is not as correct as the previous term. In using the term, we and all other users are referring to and measuring the church and its human resources (members, methods, media, etc), for which the more correct term is evangelism.

20. *Great Commission Christians.* In the light of our emphasis on Christ's Great Commission as a call to evangelize, a natural popular term for evangelizing Christians is Great Commission Christians, i.e. Christians who emphasize, obey and live by the Great Commission. A minimum definition would be as follows: Great Commission Christians are all those Christians of any tradition, culture, or nationality who, in some measure and according to their lights, talents and opportunities, are being intentionally obedient to Christ's Great Commission to be active on behalf of his mission on Earth.

We will now construct several scales to measure this obedience.

## MEASURING GREAT COMMISSION OBEDIENCE

A question to be answered first concerns the standard we wish to set. It would be possible to propose

Table 21–1. **A comparative scale of obedience to the Great Commission.**

| Question | Answer Yes No | Comments |
|---|---|---|
| 1. Are you a practicing Christian? | | |
| 2. Can you quote or paraphrase the Great Commission? | | |
| 3. Is this Commission binding on the worldwide Church today? | | |
| 4. Can you give 2 examples of how the Church is obeying it now? | | |
| 5. Is the Commission obligatory on you also today? | | |
| 6. Can you give 2 examples of how you are obeying it now? | | |
| Total of points | _____ | |

The totals obtained will vary from 0 to 6, and can be assessed as follows. A score of zero indicates non-evangelizing Christians. Scores 1–6 indicate evangelizing Christians, of the following 6 varieties:

1 =*minimally-evangelizing Christians*: practicing but unaware of the Great Commission
2 =*partially-evangelizing Christians*: practicing, aware, but uncommitted to it
3 =*semi-evangelizing Christians*: practicing, aware, committed, but uninformed about it
4 =*moderately-evangelizing Christians*: practicing, aware, committed and informed, but uninvolved
5 =*seriously-evangelizing Christians*: practicing, aware, committed, informed, involved, but not actively evangelizing
6 =*fully-evangelizing Christians*: practicing, aware, committed, informed, involved, and actively evangelizing

We may further categorize them in relation to the Commission thus:
1–4 = Christians uninvolved with the Great Commission
5 = Christians involved with the Great Commission
6 = fully-involved Great Commission Christians

a very strict definition of 'obedience,' including perhaps active support for and participation in evangelistic activities and causes, full financial involvement, and possibly even enrollment in training courses, Bible schools, and missionary societies or agencies at home or abroad. Unfortunately, only a tiny proportion of all Christians would qualify to meet such criteria. Also, such a strict definition would favor the professionals in contrast to the laity. Accordingly, it would be preferable to err slightly in the other direction, being as little judgmental as possible, and giving the benefit of the doubt to all persons who are, at any rate, making some effort however slight to evangelize.

The scale we require should measure religious practice (church attendance), awareness of the Great Commission, commitment to it, being informed about it, involvement in it, and actual evangelizing activity.

This scale is intended to be administered by an enumerator, incognito or without prior explanation, to a Christian individual, group, church or congregation, a denomination, or to the Christian community among a population, people group, nation or other homogeneous group. The enumerator asks the questions one at a time, and himself decides and writes down the respondent's scores, especially noting his or her awareness, knowledge, and activity (scoring Yes = 1 in first answer column, or No = 0 in second column of the scale presented in Table 20-1).

## MEASURING THE FORCE FOR EVANGELISM

This phrase has come into widespread use in Evangelical and Roman Catholic circles since 1975. In that year, the LCWE produced their workbook, designed to assist Christians to discover for themselves how best they could evangelize. In Roman Catholic circles 'the apostolic force' refers only to professionals. The laity, however, have recently become massively involved in the Catholic Charismatic Renewal. Speaking of the first National Conference of the Catholic Charismatic Renewal in the Dominican Republic on January 15, 1978, the organizer fr Emiliano Tardif of Canada stated: 'There are now 990 prayer groups in the Dominican Republic . . . which is an extraordinary force for evangelization in the country.' Because this is a visible force, it can be enumerated, measured, and compared from one population to another.

These 2 usages indicate that the concept of 'the force for evangelism' is a corporate and ecclesial one. It does not consist simply of the aggregate of a number of individual evangelizing Christians acting separately, but it includes local church members, local Christian leaders, local church workers and professionals, foreign missionaries, and major denominational leaders both acting separately and acting corporately in church life combined into local prayer and study groups (also know as basic communities), local congregations, local churches, organizations, agencies, sodalities, societies, and any and all other Christian forces and resources at work or available in the particular field or population under consideration.

When attempting to measure the force for evangelism in a given population, it would be as well to make a clear distinction between the actual force for evangelism—what is actually available now—and the potential force for evangelism. The latter equals the former together with all other possible or potential forces, on the spot or elsewhere outside, which might well be mobilized if this was considered desirable, necessary, and feasible.

Table 21–2. **Definition of the actual force for evangelism.**

This force in an area or population consists of the following:
1. The total of all existing evangelizing Christians in, related to, or in contact with, that area or population;
2. Any visiting Christians (visiting relatives, tourists, visiting preachers, visiting professionals, short-term missionaries, etc);
3. The organized local church or churches there;
4. The local Christian leadership, foreign as well as national;
5. Local church organizations and agencies;
6. Other parachurch organizations and agencies working there, at national or international levels; and
7. Other organizations outside the area or population but already contributing to evangelization there.

### The actual force for evangelism
A large number of the photographs in *WCE* and *WCT*

illustrate the actual force for evangelism in virtually all areas of the world. Although it is usual to want to know what the size of this force is in a particular geographical area, or population unit, one can also enumerate the force for occupational or other groupings cutting across geographical entities. One example is the medical world. More people pass through the hospitals of this world than pass through the Christian churches these days. But Christian work in hospitals has been extensive almost everywhere, and today an immense army of Christian medicals—doctors, nurses, technicians, administrators, chaplains—is at work throughout the world. A number of specialized agencies, such as the International Hospitals Christian Fellowship (IHCF), are attempting to coordinate this army and ensure that, as a specialized force

Table 21–3. **The potential force for evangelism.**

This force in an area or population consists of the following:
1. the actual or available force for evangelism;
2. those who are at present non-practicing Christians but who could be mobilized;
3. interested parachurch organizations and agencies outside the area, and not at present involved but known to be interested;
4. other organizations and agencies outside the area and not at present interested, but who could be approached.

for evangelism, it effectively evangelizes the world of medicine.

We may now define this force as in the following table.

### The potential force for evangelism

The force for evangelism as defined above excludes nominal Christians, non-practicing Christians, and Christians unaffiliated to churches. This is not intended to be a judgment on them, or an abandoning of them, but is a purely practical matter. If the churches in a city are planning a citywide rally in 4 weeks' time and want to know the exact size of their available force for evangelism, it would not be very wise or realistic to count on these 3 groups for support or assistance. But in the long term, one group in particular, non-practicing Christians, might very well respond to determined approaches by the churches, and so can be regarded as part of the total potential force for evangelism in a given area or population.

It was with such consideration in mind that the WCC's first survey *Evangelism* in 1954 defined evangelism as a function of the entire organized church: 'Evangelism is the participation of the total Christian community in Christ's mission in the world.' 'Total Christian community' is a technical term meaning the entire membership of organized Christianity, i.e. all persons who are in any way members of or affiliated to the churches. It includes non-practicing Christians (defined as affiliated Christians who are not practicing Christians), but not nominal or unaffiliated Christians.

Others regard the potential force for evangelism as embracing the total Body of Christ, covering all varieties of Christians including non-practicing and also nominal Christians. The great Japanese evangelist of the 1930s, Toyohiko Kagawa, felt that the sheer bulk of the total number of all Christians could have significant evangelistic bearing in a non-Christian country. As reported in 1932 by William Axling, secretary of the National Christian Council of Japan,

Kagawa was convinced that until the Christians of Japan should number one million strong they could not become a creative force mighty enough to fashion the national life according to the Christian pattern.

Because of this conviction, in 1928 Kagawa had launched the Kingdom of God Movement, a comprehensive Japanese-led plan supported by most Protestants.

Another example of massive potential concerns AMEN, acronym for American Military Evangelizing Nations. This was an unusual program of lay evangelism begun in 1976 by the USA denomination, Churches of Christ. The aim was to locate, and enlist in active evangelism, all Christian military personnel in the United States armed forces around the world.

The USA armed forces numbered 2,087,000 men and women in 1978, declining to 1,448,000 by 1998, and practicing Christians among them have always averaged 60% of the total. This has yielded a potential force for evangelism of at least 0.9 million, a vast force indeed. This became widely noticed both in the Desert Storm war for Kuwait (1992) and in Somalia. (1993). Whether it is appropriate, or merely ludicrous, to attempt to undertake global evangelization with heavily-armed military personnel (and with nuclear weaponry) is not under discussion here. We note further that the armed services of many countries across the world—notably Russia, South Korea, and Western European countries—have similar evangelistic networks among their troops.

In general, the force may be defined and rapidly estimated as in Tables 21-1, 21-2, and 21-3.

### Areas for research

Theologically, the actual force for evangelism consists of those called by God to be the active Body of Christ in the world. We need not be surprised if they are unimpressive by sociological criteria. In the Corinthian church, there were 'not many wise, not many powerful, not many of noble birth,' but 'God chose what is weak in the world to shame the strong' (1 Corinthians 1:26–27, RSV). Most early Christians, according to Gibbon's *The History of the Decline and Fall of the Roman Empire* (1776–1788), were from the dregs of society. All of this means that there need be no surprise or dissatisfaction if the available force for evangelism is sociologically inadequate or defective — as, for instance, the Christians of Pakistan who are predominantly of low-caste Hindu origin and therefore despised by the majority in that Islamic nation.

However, the concept of a potential force for evangelism means that Christians should work towards getting the most gifted persons into the existing force for evangelism. This opens up vast areas where research on this subject would be invaluable. Two can be mentioned here. (1) It is well known that, if one is seeking to introduce change or innovation into a society, the best people to approach first are the 6% or so who are known to be those open to change, the innovators and the carriers of change. To locate such persons is a specific research task. (2) Lay Christians are found in employment throughout secular society, and even in non-Christian society, in most parts of the world. We need to tabulate and analyze the pattern of opportunities for evangelization presented by such employment, especially in government, business, commerce, industry, media, academia, and social concerns.

## EVALUATING CHRISTIANS: THE Z-FACTOR

This evaluation can be summed up as posing and then answering the question: 'To what extent has this portion of the Christian church fulfilled the command of Christ to engage in mission and be the Body of Christ, the servant church, following its Master in love, compassion, witness, evangelism, service, and life for others?' To focus our question more concretely, we can relate it to Christ's Great Commission 'Go into all the world, preach the gospel to and make disciples of all nations'. Individuals or churches or agen-

cies who are found to be obeying this command can be defined as, and termed, Great Commission Christians.

Our method consists of first creating (a) a scale from 0–10 evaluating the obedience to the Great Commission of any individual Christian, past, present, or futures; then extending this to (b) a related scale evaluating a denomination within a country; (c) a similar scale evaluating a parachurch or service agency in a country; (d) the same scale evaluating an ecclesiastico-cultural megabloc in a country ('Protestants', 'Orthodox', etc.); (e) the same scale evaluating Christians in each ethnolinguistic people in a country; (f) the same scale evaluating organized Christianity as a whole in each country; and (g) the same scale evaluating global Christianity as a whole. All of these scales from (b) to (g) thus lead to summation at continental and global levels.

We call this evaluation of Christians the Z-factor (similar, perhaps, to the idea of an 'Omega factor') to imply that this is a final or ultimate evaluation based on all the intermediate or temporary or local or confessional or partisan varieties of evaluation that exist at the present. Obviously we are not trying to anticipate the Last Judgment, nor are we producing anything else but our own provisional, surface assessment. As a practical tool for comparative analyses and realistic planning, however, our Z-factor (for collectivities, or z-factor for individuals) might well prove to be widely acceptable as the best objective assessment so far.

The Z-factor therefore attempts to give us the following rapid evaluation of any particular Christian body: a measure of its overall success or failure as the church in mission, the servant church. The Z-factor measures the final analysis, the bottom line, the end product, the ultimate assessment, its degree of advancement of the Christian cause, in furthering progress of the kingdom of God on Earth, faithfulness of the church, obedience to Christ's Great Commission/Great Commandment/Great Proclamation, a verdict on its Christian life on Earth, its usefulness in God's plan. It measures the degree to which your Christian life or that of any other Christian or church or organization counts or has counted as a follower of Christ. Not a measure of your inner sanctity, or your personal holiness, or your private discipleship, but a surface measure of how much use you are, or appear to be, in the Christian enterprise in its life-or-death struggle across the world.

In sum, the Z-factor measures and evaluates Christian servanthood, obedience, effectiveness, quality, achievement, value, accomplishment, life for others, helpfulness to others, faithfulness.

We describe next 3 possible, alternate methods and scales for enumerating Z and arriving at totals of Great Commission Christians for every country and people across the world.

## QUANTIFYING GREAT COMMISSION CHRISTIANS —1

### Evaluating an individual Christian

To help everybody understand our analysis, we begin with the individual Christian. We start by developing this scale, encouraging the reader to apply it

Table 21–4. **Scale 1: Evaluating the discipleship of a Christian individual: the z-factor.**

| Code col. 1 | Sphere 2 | Subject 3 | Question (in quote marks) 4 | Yes/No 5 | %Yes in USA 6 |
|---|---|---|---|---|---|
| | LIFESTYLE | | | | |
| 1 | | Church practice: | 'Have you attended church in the last 7 days?' | | 42 |
| 2 | | Stewardship: | 'Do you donate or spend 10% or more of your salary for Christian causes?' | | 10 |
| 3 | | Commitment to Christ: | 'Would you say you have committed your life to Jesus Christ, or not?' | | 72 |
| 4 | | Great Commission awareness: | 'How much can you quote of the words of Jesus' Great Commission?' | | 10 |
| | LIFE FOR OTHERS | | | | |
| 5 | | Christian work/activity: | 'Do you do any full-time or volunteer Christian work?' | | 39 |
| 6 | | Scripture circulation: | 'Have you read or spread the Bible in the last 7 days?' | | 33 |
| 7 | | Human need involvement: | 'Do you help regularly in aid or relief work?' | | 70 |
| | EVANGELIZATION | | | | |
| 8 | | Personal evangelism: | 'Have you recently led other people to place their faith in Christ?' | | 51 |
| 9 | | Contact with non-Christian religions: | 'Can you name 10 or more World A non-Christians whom you know personally?' | | 3 |
| 10 | | Martyrdom: | 'Was this person killed/martyred for the faith?' | | 1 |
| | OVERALL EVALUATION | | Total 'Yes' out of 10: _____ z-factor as a percentage: _____ | | |
| | | | Z-factor for USA=Total/100, as a %: | | 35.7 |

to himself, his colleagues, and any other Christians he is interested in. Clearly in this volume it would be impossible to work out this factor for large numbers of individuals, but we do include in Part 8 "Who's Who" a listing of the names of 700 Christian leaders prominent in world evangelization from AD 33 to the present. From their biographies it was possible to evaluate each of them to provide a single number from 0–10 which was then expressed as 0–100% in a separate table, becoming what is called here the individual's z-factor. We are not passing final judgment on them. We are simply measuring surface characteristics in order to help us get a better handle on reality and, hopefully, to help the church to plan its human response to Christ's call to mission and to deploy its human resources better for the future.

There are many possible questions with which one could evaluate this discipleship of an individual Christian. Here we select 4 spheres with 10 subjects and cast them as 10 dichotomous Yes/No questions. These derive from 10 subjects or aspects of Christian life shown in column 3 of Table 21–4 with the best, shortest, and simplest form of words for a question (column 4) so that the user can score 'Yes' (which we score as 1) or 'No' (a score of 0) in column 5. Then in order to supply illustration, the final column 6 gives (from actual Gallup and other polls) the percentage of the USA population today (regarded in this instance as a Christian country, a World-C entity comparable to a Christian body) that answer the exact question with a 'Yes'. By way of illustration, too, in 1997 Mother Teresa scored 9 for many years before her death (One is glad she never reached 10, which would have embodied a 'Yes' to question No. 10!)

**'Stand in the Gap' 1997** in Washington DC showing 1.5 million Promise Keepers praying and witnessing (part of the USA's 98 million Great Commission Christians).

### Definition of an individual Great Commission Christian

We can now proceed to exact definition on this subject. A Great Commission Christian, as an individual, is defined here as a Christian who scores 5 or more 'Yes' answers on the 10-point scale above, that is, who scores 50% or more out of a possible score of 100%. His or her z-factor is thus: > 50%.

So what does being a Great Commission Christian mean? Certainly, it means experiencing several of the 10 factors listed above. But it's more than any single one of them.
— It's more than just church attendance
— It's more than just giving money to the church
— It's more than just verbal commitment to Christ
— It's more than just awareness of the Great Commission
— It's more than just being a Christian worker or volunteer
— It's more than just involvement in Scripture dis-

tribution (or just reading it)
— It's more than just good deeds in human need relief
— It's more than just personal witness/personal work/personal evangelism
— It's more than just contact/rubbing shoulders with non-Christians
— It's more than just losing your life as a martyr
— **It's having a total of at least 5 of these. . .**

### A total of at least 5 of these
For a church or other body of Christians, then, the total of its Great Commission Christians is the total of all its individual church members for each of whom z> 50%.

The concept can next be quantified for large populations using 2 different methods by means of an analysis of, firstly, denominations; and secondly, affiliated Christians in a homogenous population such as an ethnolinguistic people. These results can be, and have been, supported by other varieties of evaluation of commitment to Christ's mission.

### QUANTIFYING GREAT COMMISSION CHRISTIANS—2

#### Evaluating a denomination's commitment to mission
A second, completely different method of quantifying Great Commission Christians starts with each individual denomination and evaluates it impressionistically, or by means of a scale, with a rating Z, which represents the percentage of the denomination's members that the observer estimates are likely to be Great Commission Christians. Based on knowledge of the denomination's beliefs and activities, on its awareness of the Great Commission, on its mission programs and interests, and on attitudes to foreign missions, an estimate is made and the people's total of GCCs is arrived at. After all the denominations in a country have been thus evaluated, the country's overall GCC total for the country is obtained, and then the country's overall evaluation Z expressed as a percentage is produced, thus:

$$Z = (GCC/AC)100.$$

This factor Z is a comparative evaluation of the commitment to Christ's mission of the whole body of Christians in a particular country (or region, or continent, or the whole world).

Ideally, the Z-factor for a denomination in a country, or in a continent, or in the whole world would be obtained as the percentage of its affiliated church members who qualify as Great Commission Christians by individually having z> 50%. However, such data would in practice be impossible to get except through expensive sample surveys. What we do instead is to think of the denomination in question, and its detailed circumstances. Then with its detailed statistics if any in front of us, we go through the same 10 questions estimating the average answer on each. For most denominations, GCC is usually around 30%, ranging from 90% for a small denomination to 5% for a very large geopolitical one.

Table 21–5 shows the form these 10 subjects take when applied as a scale to a denomination. For those wanting more precision, another longer-term method would be to draw up a scale of 100 Yes/No questions, most with related numerical levels, dealing with 100 more-detailed subjects useful in the evaluating of a denomination. This would also give a percentage figure.

#### Evaluating an ecclesiastico-cultural megabloc in a country
To evaluate all Roman Catholics, or all Protestants, one proceeds as for the above, adding all the denominations/churches to get totals for Great Commission Christians and thus the megabloc's Z-factor.

#### Evaluating organized Christianity in a country
To do the same for the entire Christian body in any country, proceed as for the above, combining the figures for all the Christian traditions (the ecclesiastico-cultural megablocs) to arrive at, for each country, a single total of Great Commission Christians and thus the country's Z-factor.

#### Evaluating global Christianity
Finally, we can arrive at the global total of Great

---

**Table 21–5.  Scale 2: Evaluating the discipleship of a denomination/church: the Z-factor.**

Name of denomination (or church, or confession, or tradition) . . . . . . . . . . . . . . . . . . . . . . . . . . . . . . . . . . . . . . . . . :

Evaluation: Which of the following 10 subjects strike you the observer as hallmarks, or positive emphases, or obvious characteristics, of this denomination or church in this country? Column 3 gives the numerical criteria (proportion of church members) for answering these 10 expressed as questions leading to a 'Yes' answer.  In column 4, answer each subject with a '1'(=Yes) or a '0'(=No).  Then total this column to get the final evaluation expressed out of a maximum of 10.  Then multiply by 10 to give the final value of Z, which is expressed as a percentage.  Z then gives the percentage of the total church membership of this denomination/church who are defined as Great Commission Christians.

*Coded criteria for a denomination are as follows:*
- W = weekly church attendance, percent of membership;
- i = income donated by members or spent on Christian causes, percent personal income;
- f = estimated proportion of self-professed committed membership (along lines of the Gallup question in No. 3 of the above scale for individuals);
- S = citizen foreign missionaries sent and now supported abroad from this denomination (or country), per million church members or church population;
- N = full-time citizen Christian workers per million church members;
- s = total scriptures distributed per year per church member within this denomination (or per Christian within a country);
- HDI = Human Development Index, expressed as a percentage;
- v = proportion of church members doing personal evangelism;
- c = proportion of church members actually in contact with real non-Christians in non-Christian religions in non-Christian lands in Worlds A or B;
- m = proportion of church members who get killed/martyred for the faith.

| Code | Component | Criterion | Yes/No | Comments |
|------|-----------|-----------|--------|----------|
| col 1 | 2 | 3 | 4 | 5 |
| | *LIFESTYLE* | | | |
| 1 | Church practice | W>50% | | |
| 2 | Stewardship | i>2% | | |
| 3 | Commitment to Christ | f>50% | | |
| 4 | Great Commission awareness | S>100 p.m.a. | | |
| | *LIFE FOR OTHERS* | | | |
| 5 | Christian work/activity | N>150 p.m.a. | | |
| 6 | Scripture circulation | s>1 p.a. | | |
| 7 | Human need involvement | HDI>80% | | |
| | *EVANGELIZATION* | | | |
| 8 | Personal evangelism | v>10% | | |
| 9 | Contact with non-Christian religions | c>10% | | |
| 10 | Martyrdom | m>0.1% | | |
| | OVERALL EVALUATION | | | Total out of 10:_____ |
| | | | | Z-factor, %:_____ |

**Table 21–6.    A rapid-assessment scale of cross-cultural mission (xc) for a people or population.**

| Code col. 1 | Mission situation 2 | Mission-receiving 3 | Mission-sending 4 | Missionaries sent per million, S 5 |
|---|---|---|---|---|
| 0 | No cross-cultural work going on | Absent | Absent | *Comment on codes 0–7:* Although S=0 for these 8 codes, from codes 5–7 zeal for sending out missions becomes higher and becomes a factor in making people into GCCs |
| 1 | Indirect witness only | Rare | Absent | |
| 2 | Indirect ministries from outside | Indirect | Absent | |
| 3 | Occasional visits by evangelists | Occasional | Absent | |
| 4 | One missionary or evangelist resident | Pioneering | Absent | |
| 5 | 2 or more missionaries resident | Ongoing | Absent | |
| 6 | Church-planting well under way | Sizeable | Absent | |
| 7 | Indigenous workers (evangelists, clergy) | Maximum | Absent | |
| 8 | Self-sufficient denominations exist | Declining | Negligible | $S<10$ |
| 9 | Some mission programs exist | Occasional | Sporadic | $20>S>10$ |
| 10 | Over 20 missionaries/million sent out | Sparse | Inadequate | $50>S>20$ |
| 11 | Over 50 missionaries/million sent out | Negligible | Not quite adequate | $100>S>50$ |
| 12 | Over 100 missionaries/million sent out | Superfluous | Barely adequate | $200>S>100$ |
| 13 | Over 200 missionaries/million sent out | Unwanted | Adequate | $400>S>200$ |
| 14 | Over 400 missionaries/million sent out | Unnecessary | Substantial | $600>S>400$ |
| 15 | Over 600 missionaries/million sent out | Repetitive | Exemplary | $800>S>600$ |
| 16 | Over 800 missionaries/million sent out | Counterproductive | Phenomenal | $S>800$ |

Commission Christians, and thus the global Z-factor, by adding the totals for all countries.

## QUANTIFYING GREAT COMMISSION CHRISTIANS—3

### Evaluating a people's commitment to mission

A third approach to quantifying Great Commission Christians starts with ethnolinguistic peoples as the basic units. This is the most detailed method employed in *WCE* and *WCT*, and the most satisfactory since all the necessary data are available. Its results are given in *WCE* Part 8 "EthnoSphere" for all peoples in the world, with each country's totals also being reported in its Country Table 1. The starting-point is a consideration of the variable xc, cross-cultural mission, shown for every people in Ethno-Sphere column 20.

### Cross-cultural mission among a people (variable xc)

This mutually-exclusive scale of 17 code values set out in Tables 21-6 and 21-7 has 3 distinct but complementary meanings: (1) status of cross-cultural mission in this population, both received from outside and sending to outside; (2) status and effectiveness of the resultant evangelism and evangelization; and (3) enumeration of Great Commission Christians as the nucleus of the church active in cross-cultural mission.

### 1. Quantifying cross-cultural mission, xc

Firstly, this variable measures directly the extent of missionary or evangelistic activity among this people (either directed to them or performed by them), involving mission external to this culture (from outside, or to outside, i.e. cross-cultural). It traverses the spectrum from peoples among whom no church exists and no Christian mission of any kind is going on (code 0), through mission-receiving peoples (codes 1–6), through peoples with self-sufficient churches (codes 7–8), to mission-sending peoples involved in active programs sending and supporting their own workers abroad which in practice means to other cultures (codes 9–16). The scale spans a range from the church's relative absence of obedience to the Great Commission (codes 7–11), to adequate obedience (codes 12–16). The codes are given in full in Table 20-7 but for the moment can be arranged under the following schema describing a people's states:

A.  *Cross-cultural mission-receiving is essential* (codes 0–6)
   —but is not yet under way (codes 0–1)
   —but now is under way (codes 2–6)
B.  *Self-sufficiency in church and mission* (cross-cultural receiving is no longer essential) (codes 7–8)
   —since churches now have their own indigenous workers and leaders (code 7)
   —since Christians now have their own organized denominations (code 8)
C.  *Cross-cultural mission-sending develops* (codes 9–11)
   —at first inadequate (codes 9–11), but then
D.  *Adequate obedience to the Great Commission* (codes 12–16)
   —initially, more or less adequate (codes 12–14)
   —then finally, exemplary or phenomenal (codes 15-16).

### 2. Contribution of xc to evangelization scale E

Secondly, as with the discipleship variable, the alien Christians variable, and even the E-scale itself, this mission scale xc has another major meaning. It forms a measure of the past and present influence of the evangelistic impact of cross-cultural mission on this people's population. Code xc is therefore used as part of the formula for constructing E, the comparative scale of demographic evangelization (see Part 24 "Microevangelistics"). In this interpretation, the code number stands for the percentage of the people's population who have become evangelized as a result of cross-cultural mission, both into and out of its own culture. This influence can be seen to vary from 0% to a maximum of 16% of the population.

This variable differs from the variable wa (work among this population segment) which focuses on all varieties of Christian work, both monocultural and cross-cultural, and focuses more on the resulting presence or absence of viable Christian churches of all varieties, their density, and their health and vitality. The xc variable measures directly the presence or absence of cross-cultural mission.

A detailed table of the meaning of each of the 16 codes is set out in Table 20-7. Note that the variable S measures the number of a people's own foreign missionaries sent out from the people per million church members.

### 3. Contribution of xc to measuring Great Commission Christians

Thirdly, the scale has a further meaning as shown by its use in the construction of an additional concept: GCC, the number of all Great Commission Christians among this people's members. In this interpretation, the code number indicates the percentage of the people's population likely to have produced the cross-cultural activity and zeal observed. This can also vary from 0% to 16% of the population.

Summing up all these meanings, we arrive at the following detailed schema and listing of codes.

### Great Commission Christians (GCCs)

This now leads to a major new way to measure the church's obedience to Christ's call to mission. What we need to quantify is the size of the total Christian presence active in mission in any population. Because this means people's obedience to Christ's Great Commission, we have termed this variable GCCs (being the total persons), or GCC (their percentage of the specific people's population), or Z (being their percentage of that people's affiliated church members).

For some years past existing attempts to describe precisely this category have succeeded in enumerating only a part of the whole concept. There is first the whole range of historically-related terms for ecclesiastical families or traditions—Anglican, Baptist,

**Table 21–7.    A detailed explanatory scale of cross-cultural mission, receiving and sending, for a people or population (variable xc).**

**Code**

**CROSS-CULTURAL MISSION-RECEIVING IS ESSENTIAL (few or no churches or Christians yet)**

0 = No cross-cultural or other external or internal Christian work begun or going on among this people in this country

1 = Witness only indirectly via returning residents or visits or letters from friends or relatives in this people's diaspora who have been reached by the gospel abroad (refugees, migrant workers, expatriates, students abroad, tourists abroad)

2 = Only indirect or 'off-the-spot' ministries from outside (aid, radio, literature in this or other languages, occasional visits from or contact with lay Christians)

3 = Occasional or irregular visits by cross-cultural evangelists or missionaries or teams; or, unorganized tent-making ministries in the area (the latter usual when non-indigenous resident church adherents number over 20%, i.e. codes 9 or 10 for the Alien Christianity variable, a

4 = At least one pioneer full-time resident cross-cultural evangelist or missionary working in this language among this culture in this country

5 = Ongoing evangelism by 2 or more cross-cultural evangelists or missionaries with church planting beginning or in early stages

6 = Church planting well under way by cross-cultural evangelists or missionaries, with some or many congregations already formed of or for this people, with considerable or adequate or even saturated churches now existing

**SELF-SUFFICIENCY IN CHURCH AND MISSION (cross-cultural mission-receiving is no longer essential)**

7 = Indigenous workers of this people (ministers, evangelists, catechists, lay readers) formally trained abroad or at home and now serving in churches with this people in them (but few or none serving abroad)

8 = One or more denominations or subdivisions (dioceses, synods, conferences, districts etc) exist predominantly of this people, autonomous and independent of outside cross-cultural or foreign mission; own missionaries sent out are less than 10 per million church members (S<10; negligible sending)

**CROSS-CULTURAL MISSION-SENDING DEVELOPS**

9 = One or more denominations sending out less than 20 missionaries per million (20>S>10 per million; sporadic sending)

10 = One or more denominations sending abroad or to other cultures less than 50 missionaries per million church members (50>S>20; inadequate sending)

11 = Denominations sending out cross-culturally less than 100 missionaries per million (100>S>50; not quite adequate sending)

**ADEQUATE OBEDIENCE TO THE GREAT COMMISSION (defined as S>100)**

12 = Denominations sending out cross-culturally over 100 missionaries per million (200>S>100; barely adequate sending)

13 = Denominations sending out cross-culturally over 200 missionaries per million (400>S>200; adequate sending)

14 = Denominations sending out cross-culturally over 400 missionaries per million (600>S>400; substantial sending)

15 = Denominations sending out cross-culturally over 600 missionaries per million (800>S>600; exemplary sending)

16 = Denominations sending out cross-culturally over 800 missionaries per million (S>800; phenomenal sending)

Lutheran, Methodist, Reformed, and 200 others. None of these adequately describes our 'active in mission' criterion because each such term covers large numbers of non-practicing, latent, or dormant church members who are inactive in mission and remain ignorant of the Great Commission.

Further attempts have been made to define this nucleus active in mission. In the Protestant world, widely-used categories include 'Born-again Christians', 'Real Christians', and the like. Other terms are narrower and more partisan, including 'True believers', and 'Bible-believing Christians'. The problem is: few if any churches or denominations compile grassroots statistics of any of these categories, so they remain subjective and purely theoretical as far as any global survey is concerned.

In the Evangelical world, statistics labeled 'Evangelicals' are widely used as if coterminous with our active GCC category. But 'Evangelicals' is a historical term tracing its origins to the Evangelical Revival in the Church of England 250 years ago under the Wesleys and Whitefield. Today, like 'Methodists' and all the other family labels, 'Evangelicals' covers and includes both committed Christians active in mission, and also millions of persons inactive in mission, ignorant of the Great Commission, and even many who reject the Commission as irrelevant or who relegate its applicability solely to New Testament times.

In the Roman Catholic world, the only membership measure collected globally is of 'baptized Catholics', which includes children and infants. Sometime studies exist of 'Sunday mass-attenders', but adult Catholics, 'real Catholics', or 'true Catholics' are never enumerated on any overall scale. There is, however, a formidable new category on which detailed statistical surveys are now available: Catholic Charismatics both adult and total community.

In the Orthodox world either one is a baptized Orthodox believer, or one is not. The former are always enumerated; the latter never. Variations on these terms do not exist or are not in general use.

### *Defining Great Commission Christians*

This category is here defined as all Christians of any ecclesiastical tradition who believe Christ's Great Commission is binding on all Christians and as a result are themselves intentionally and demonstrably active in that mission both monoculturally and also where possible cross-culturally.

The category of Great Commission Christians is therefore not simply a measure of people's inner acceptance of Christianity; nor of personal or corporate spirituality; nor of commitment to Christianity, church, or even Bible; nor of personal sanctity or holiness; nor of church attendance or religious practice; nor of personal or collective Christian ethics and behavior; nor even of religious zeal in any of its forms. Certainly it requires all of these, but in addition it embraces further essential criteria. In addition to its own identity, its relation to its non-Christian context must be taken into account.

The GCC variable evolved here is in the first instance a measure of (1) awareness among a specific ethnolinguistic people of *the non-Christian target world* around Christians *within their own culture;* (2) awareness of Christianity's basic obligation to serve the non-Christian world as well as the Christian world; (3) acceptance of Christ's Great Commission to make disciples of all peoples and determination to obey that Commission both inside and outside their own territory; and (4) individual and corporate *action, activity, and commitment to Christ's mission* as defined in that Commission, both monoculturally and cross-culturally.

It can be seen, therefore, that 'Great Commission Christians' are not identical with any of the vast range of terms in present use for the inner core or nucleus of committed church members—'believers', 'the faithful', 'disciples', 'real Christians', 'true Christians', 'true believers', 'genuine Christians', 'practicing Christians', 'communicants', 'born-again Christians', 'Bible-believing Christians', 'charismatics', 'Evangelicals', 'Fundamentalists', or the 400 or so other traditions presented in *WCE*'s Country Tables 2, column 3 (see "GeoCodebook" in Part 16).

### *Quantifying a people's GCCs*

There are several ways in which one could derive measures of this category. One such way would start with crypto-Christians (secret believers)—sizable in number in most non-Christian or anti-Christian nations. One could assume that, because the risks in being clandestine or secret believers are relatively high, all crypto-Christians are serious about following Christ and therefore about obeying his last Commission. Great Commission Christians would thus consist of (a) all covert crypto-Christians, and (b) a proportion of the remaining affiliated Christians, who would be overt or open Christians known as such to state and society. However, the data necessary to operationalize these categories do not exist for the 12,600 ethnolinguistic peoples. Churches do not ask for or compile the necessary statistics.

The way followed here takes a different path. The proportion of Great Commission Christians in a specific population, here termed GCC as a percentage of total population, is defined as dependent on 3 properties of that population: X = its non-Christian population as a percentage of the whole; S = the number of foreign or cross-cultural missionaries sent out and supported by this people per million of its affiliated Christians; and xc, the cross-cultural missionary situation of the population. The rationale for this is as follows.

### 1. Non-Christians, X

Their presence among one's own people and language and culture is, for their Christian friends, acquaintances, and relatives, a powerful motive for undertaking Great Commission activities—witnessing, proclaiming, discipling, baptizing. When Christians are very few in number, say AC = 1%, they are surrounded by 99% non-Christians and the need to witness and make disciples among them is obvious and clear. GCCs then form a majority of the Christians. But at the other end of the spectrum, when Christians have expanded to say AC = 99%, the miniscule number of non-Christians ceases to concern the churches weighed down as they are with a multitude of other Christian duties and interests. GCCs then can (and often do) fall to zero.

### 2. Own missionaries per million, S

A major empirical test of a church's Great Commission concern is S, the number of its own members it sends out as full-time foreign cross-cultural missionaries, per million church members. This variable is incorporated in the scale of cross-cultural mission, xc, produced above. The relation between S and xc is shown in the 2 opening rows of Table 21–8.

We are further defining GCCs as consisting of 2 parts: (1) those Christians who are concerned mainly to implement the Commission monoculturally, that is within their own ethnolinguistic people's boundaries, and (2) those Christians concerned mainly to implement the Commission cross-culturally, beyond their own cultural boundaries and on to the ends of the earth. These 2 parts can be separately enumerated as follows.

### 3. Two types of mission, xc

#### *a. Monocultural mission*

It is a legitimate concern to want to see all non-Christians in your own culture evangelized and discipled. The first few converts in any newly-entered people are usually zealous to see their entire people reached. Difficulties arise however much later when AC (affiliated Christians as % of that culture's people) approaches 100%. This approximates to the stage xc = 7. The GCC-related monocultural task gets smaller and smaller until there are no non-Christians there left to evangelize. Interest in the subject then disappears. We can express all this mathematically by 4 propositions, as follows.

a. In anti-Christian or hostile countries or peoples,

**Table 21–8. Estimating for any ethnolinguistic people the value of Z, the percentage of affiliated Christians (AC) who are Great Commission Christians (GCC), for the 3 Worlds A, B, and C; for 3 obedience situations; and for 4 other variables.**

*Notes.*

1.The large outlined box below presents values of Z as percentages of a people's affiliated church members.

2.The formula used here is: **Z = 89–AC + xc + 0.05S**, or **Z = X + xc + 0.05S - 11**, where AC = affiliated Christians as % of this people's population, X = non-Christians as % population, xc = cross-cultural missionary situation of this people (coded 0–16), and S = foreign or cross-cultural missionaries sent out and supported by this people per million affiliated Christians.

3.The double vertical line defines obedience to the Great Commission as the situation of peoples for whom S≥100 per million (or, xc≥12). Situations to the left of this divide show peoples (a) unable to obey (because they have no viable church, or no missionary tradition, or teaching, or no resources); or (b) unwilling to obey (with a sizeable enough church, but unwilling to take the Great Commission seriously); to the right of the divide, peoples are (c) obedient (by sending out their own missionaries in adequate numbers).

4. The white unshaded area between the upper and lower limits defines people situations that are actually possible. No people exists in the shaded areas where Z is negative, and few where Z >100.

5. Note that a more exact statement about X is that for a small minority of the larger or more dominant peoples in democratic countries, a small percentage of Christians are nominal Christians (UC) unaffiliated to the churches, and that the third column below actually represents (X + UC), since total population = 100% = (AC + UC) + X; or, (UC + AC) + X = 100%. For the vast majority of peoples in the world, however, UC is of negligible size for this particular computation.

**Values of Z for the 3 worlds (A, B, C); for 3 obedience situations (a, b, c); and 4 other variables (AC, X, xc, and S).**

| | | | *a. Unable to obey the Great Commission* | | | | | | | *b. Able to obey but disobedient* | | | | | *c. Obedient to the Great Commission* | | | | |
|---|---|---|---|---|---|---|---|---|---|---|---|---|---|---|---|---|---|---|---|
| World | AC | X | xc=0<br>S=0<br>xc + 0.05 S=0 | 1<br>0<br>1 | 2<br>0<br>2 | 3<br>0<br>3 | 4<br>0<br>4 | 5<br>0<br>5 | 6<br>0<br>6 | 7<br>0<br>7 | 8<br>5<br>8 | 9<br>10<br>10 | 10<br>20<br>11 | 11<br>50<br>13 | 12<br>100<br>17 | 13<br>200<br>23 | 14<br>400<br>34 | 15<br>600<br>45 | 16<br>800<br>56 |
| World C | 100 | 0 | -11 | -10 | -9 | -8 | -7 | -6 | -5 | -4 | -3 | -1 | 0 | 2 | 6 | 12 | 23 | 34 | 45 |
| | 99 | 1 | -10 | -9 | -8 | -7 | -6 | -5 | -4 | -3 | -2 | 0 | 1 | 3 | 7 | 13 | 24 | 35 | 46 |
| | 95 | 5 | -6 | -5 | -4 | -3 | -2 | -1 | 0 | 1 | 2 | 4 | 5 | 7 | 11 | 17 | 28 | 39 | 50 |
| | 90 | 10 | -1 | 0 | 1 | 2 | 3 | 4 | 5 | 6 | 7 | 9 | 10 | 12 | 16 | 22 | 33 | 44 | 55 |
| | 80 | 20 | 9 | 10 | 11 | 12 | 13 | 14 | 15 | 16 | 17 | 19 | 20 | 22 | 26 | 32 | 43 | 54 | 65 |
| | 70 | 30 | 19 | 20 | 21 | 22 | 23 | 24 | 25 | 26 | 27 | 29 | 30 | 32 | 36 | 42 | 53 | 64 | 75 |
| | 60 | 40 | 29 | 30 | 31 | 32 | 33 | 34 | 35 | 36 | 37 | 39 | 40 | 42 | 46 | 52 | 63 | 74 | 85 |
| World B | 50 | 50 | 39 | 40 | 41 | 42 | 43 | 44 | 45 | 46 | 47 | 49 | 50 | 52 | 56 | 62 | 73 | 84 | 95 |
| | 40 | 60 | 49 | 50 | 51 | 52 | 53 | 54 | 55 | 56 | 57 | 59 | 60 | 62 | 66 | 72 | 83 | 94 | 105 |
| | 30 | 70 | 59 | 60 | 61 | 62 | 63 | 64 | 65 | 66 | 67 | 69 | 70 | 72 | 76 | 82 | 93 | 104 | 115 |
| | 20 | 80 | 69 | 70 | 71 | 72 | 73 | 74 | 75 | 76 | 77 | 79 | 80 | 82 | 86 | 92 | 103 | 114 | 125 |
| | 10 | 90 | 79 | 80 | 81 | 82 | 83 | 84 | 85 | 86 | 87 | 89 | 90 | 92 | 96 | 102 | 113 | 124 | 135 |
| World A | 5 | 95 | 84 | 85 | 86 | 87 | 88 | 89 | 90 | 91 | 92 | 94 | 95 | 97 | 101 | 107 | 118 | 129 | 140 |
| | 1 | 99 | 88 | 89 | 90 | 91 | 92 | 93 | 94 | 95 | 96 | 98 | 99 | 101 | 105 | 111 | 122 | 133 | 144 |
| | 0.1 | 99.9 | 88.9 | 89.9 | 90.9 | 91.9 | 92.9 | 93.9 | 94.9 | 95.9 | 96.9 | 98.9 | 99.9 | 101.9 | 105.9 | 111.9 | 122.9 | 133.9 | |
| 144.9 | | | | | | | | | | | | | | | | | | | |

especially those in World A, virtually all of the affiliated Christians are GCCs.

b. In the heavily-christianized countries of World C, and in heavily-christianized ethnolinguistic peoples therein (those with AC>95%), non-Christians X become so few in number (<5%) that they generate little or no monocultural Great Commission interest or zeal. This means that as AC approaches 100%, GCCs tend to dwindle to a size similar to the number of non-Christians.

c. Hence the ratio of GCCs to ACs in a people appears empirically to be proportional to the percentage of non-Christians X. Note also that for most peoples X = 100-AC.

d. So therefore this leads to the following formula for GCC's monocultural component (note that the slash / means 'divided by'):

Monocultural GCC/AC = X/100 = 1-AC/100.

or,

Monocultural GCC/AC = 1-0.01 AC

or,

**Monocultural GCC = AC (1- 0.01 AC).**

### b. Cross-cultural mission

This second component covers the fuller meaning of GCCs , which is all those wanting to see the mission of Christ spread across the entirety of the world's 12,600 cultures. At this point we introduce a direct measure of a people's concern for this cross-cultural mission: S, which is defined as the number of their own foreign or cross-cultural missionaries sent out across their borders by an ethnolinguistic people, measured as per million of its affiliated church members. This variable S is built in to the scale measuring cross-cultural mission, variable $xc$ given above (defined and derived above in Table 21–7, or in Part 24 "Microevangelistics", or see Part 16 "GeoCodebook").

This second component means that the larger the percentage of a population who are GCCs, the more this will be reflected in commitment to sending their own members abroad as foreign missionaries. It will be noticed from the list of 16 codes for $xc$ that the code $xc=7$ indicates a level at which no missionaries have yet been sent out, and that for $xc<7$ the flow is the reverse with foreign or cross-cultural missionaries being received *from* other cultures rather being sent out *to* other cultures. Moreover, between $xc = 7$ and $xc = 11$, its own missionaries are being sent out but only in relatively small numbers (S<100). This means that for purposes of measurement and analysis, we can set the level S = 100 as the dividing point between a people's obedience to the Great Commission (defined as S≥100) and its disobedience or absence of obedience to the Great Commission (defined as S<100).

Cross-cultural mission can therefore be seen to depend on 2 related but distinct, measurable elements, each of which can be zero below a certain level of development. (1) The first element is $(xc - 11)$, which means that at the scale level of $xc = 11$ and below, it makes no contribution to the size of GCCs. (2) The second element, directly comparable to the first and to be added to it, is a further, more sophisticated use of S (the direct measurement of a people's zeal for cross-cultural mission), which we express here as the element (0.05 S). Being interpreted, this element means that it only makes a positive or noticeable contribution to the size of GCCs where S exceeds 10 (S > 10).

Adding these 2 elements results in the combined cross-cultural element $(xc + 0.05 S - 11)$.

This whole viewpoint can be expressed mathematically thus:

Cross-cultural GCC = AC (xc + 0.05 S - 11)/100
$$= 0.01 (xc + 0.05 S - 11) AC.$$

that is,

**Cross-cultural GCC = 0.01 (xc + 0.05 S - 11) AC.**

Adding this second component to the first component for monocultural mission, we arrive at the final formula embracing both monocultural and cross-cultural mission:

Total GCC = AC (1–0.01 AC) + 0.01AC (xc +

0.05 S - 11)

which reduces to

Total GCC = AC [1–0.01 AC + 0.01 (xc + 0.05 S - 11)]

or,

**Total GCC = 0.01 AC (89-AC + xc + 0.05 S).**

It is valuable also to express GCC as a percentage of AC, yielding our earlier variable Z defined as Z = 100 (GCC/AC). Thus if all church members in a population are GCCs, then Z = 100. In general, the formula gives

Z = (100-AC) + (xc-11 + 0.05 S),

or,

Z = 89 - AC + xc + 0.05 S,

up to a maximum possible value of 100% (and a minimum possible value of 0%).

This then leads to 3 final formulas, any one of which may be used as the user requires:

**(1) GCC = 0.01 AC (89-AC + xc + 0.05 S),**

or

**(2) Z = 89-AC + xc + 0.05 S,**

or

**(3) Z = X + xc + 0.05 S - 11.**

The relationships between AC, X, and Z can be seen set out in Table 21–8.

Putting all this into words, for any population GCC as a percentage of AC is the numerical total of 2 components: (1) X, the non-Christian percentage, plus (2) $xc + 0.05 S - 11$, which is the distance of the cross-cultural variable $xc$ above or below the 'not quite adequate sending' level where $xc = 11$.

These formulas apply primarily to any single ethnolinguistic people, and to the aggregate of all its Christians together of every confession, to their combined affiliated church member total, and to the combined total of all their missionaries. The formulas are not in the first instance intended to be applied to other varieties of populations—cities, provinces, countries, continents, or the whole world. Nor should they be applied to one single denomination, or to one confession. The total number of GCCs in any larger grouping such as a country can however readily be obtained by summing the totals for each of its component ethnolinguistic peoples.

### Evaluating denominations, churches, congregations, individuals

The above analysis does however provide us with a simple rule of thumb test of any church organization or population or individual or family with regard to eligibility for this adjectival 'Great Commission' status. The dividing line adopted above, S=100 per million (one in 10,000) provides an easy test which can be applied in a few moments. For a church, a worshiping congregation, or a denomination, we need only to estimate the number of foreign or cross-cultural missionaries that the church or organization sends out and/or supports at any given time. First, estimate the organization's size. If it is a church of 10,000 members (including children) it must be relating to—or sending and supporting—at least one foreign or cross-cultural missionary, in order to be rightly called a 'Great Commission' church. If it is a denomination of 1 million members, it would have to send and support 100 such missionaries. And so on.

**Table 21–9. Six scales measuring distance, barriers, and frontiers in evangelistic outreach.**

1. NATIONALITY (based on political frontiers, and citizenship)

   NBB= 0  Of the same nationality, residing in same country
   NBB= 1  Of different nationality but residing in same country
   NBB= 2  Of the same nationality, but residing in different countries
   NBB= 3  Of different nationality, residing in different countries

2. LIFESTYLE (based on comparison of per capita incomes)

   SBB= 0  Of same or similar socioeconomic status
   SBB= 1  Evangelizer gets less than half the income of his hearers
   SBB= 2  Evangelizer gets more than twice the income of his hearers
   SBB= 3  Evangelizer gets over 10 times the income of his hearers

3. CULTURE (based on comparison of 6-character ethnolinguistic codes)

| | | Code |
|---|---|---|
| CBB= 0 | Of the same ethnolinguistic people, i.e. same name | Same 6-character code, same people name |
| CBB= 1 | Of a different ethnolinguistic people but same cluster/subfamily | Same 6-character code, different people name |
| CBB= 2 | Of a different ethnolinguistic cluster/subfamily | Same first 5 characters, different 6th |
| CBB= 3 | Of a different ethnolinguistic family/microrace/local race | Same first 3 letters, different 4th-5th place |
| CBB= 4 | Of a different color (physical type) | Same first 2 letters, different 3rd |
| CBB= 5 | Of a different geographical race | Same first letter, different 2nd |
| CBB= 6 | Of a different race | Different first letter |

4. LANGUAGE (based on comparison of 8-character language codes)

| | | Code |
|---|---|---|
| LBB= 0 | Of the same dialect | Same 8-character code |
| LBB= 1 | Of different dialect but same language | Same characters 1-7, different 8th |
| LBB= 2 | Of different language but same cluster | Same characters 1-6, different 7th |
| LBB= 3 | Of different cluster but same net | Same characters 1-5, different 6th |
| LBB= 4 | Of different net but same chain | Same characters 1-4, different 5th |
| LBB= 5 | Of different chain but same set | Same characters 1-3, different 4th |
| LBB= 6 | Of different set but same glossozone | Same digits 1-2, different 3rd character |
| LBB= 7 | Of different glossozone but same macrozone | Same first digit, different 2nd |
| LBB= 8 | Of different macrozone | Different first digit |

5. RELIGION (based on comparison of religion codes of 1-5 letters)

| | | Code |
|---|---|---|
| RBB= 0 | Of same microreligion, and same exact religion name | Same code, same exact religion name |
| RBB= 1 | Of same microreligion but different exact religion name | Same code, different exact name |
| RBB= 2 | Of different microreligion but same cluster/family of religions | Same last 4 letters, different lefthand letter |
| RBB= 3 | Of different cluster/family but same religious bloc | Same last 3 letters, different 3rd from last |
| RBB= 4 | Of different religious bloc but same category | Same last 2 letters, different 2nd from last |
| RBB= 5 | Of different category but same macroreligion | Same last letter, different 1st from last |
| RBB= 6 | Of different macroreligion or world religion | Different last letter (at extreme right) |

6. EVANGELIZATION (based on Worlds A/B/C trichotomy)

| | | Code |
|---|---|---|
| EBB= 0 | Target population is in a World C people | AC≥60%, E>95% |
| EBB= 1 | Target population is in a World B people | E≥50%, AC<60% |
| EBB= 2 | Target population is in a World A people | E<50% |

**TOTAL DISTANCE/BARRIERS/FRONTIERS**
TBB = sum of the above, ranging 0-28.

A parallel test is to establish the size of the church's foreign missions offerings, collections, and donations for one year. Remembering that the average annual cost of one missionary is US$30,000, to be rightly called a Great Commission church, a church of 10,000 members must raise $30,000 a year specifically for foreign missions. A church of 100 members would have to have a foreign missions budget of $300. And so on.

So then, we arrive at the following quick-reference rules of thumb:
1. *Denominations*. A Great Commission denomination or paradenomination or network of churches is one that sends out over 100 foreign or cross-cultural missionaries per million affiliated church members.
2. *Churches*. A Great Commission church or congregation is one that either sends, supports, or relates to at least one missionary per 10,000 affiliated church members, or raises for foreign missions at least $30,000 per year per 10,000 members.
3. *Individuals*. A Great Commission individual is a Christian church member who, inter alia, deliberately donates specifically to foreign missions at least $3 a year, or 6 US cents a week.

These standards, especially the last, may strike the reader as very conservative levels or very low levels to set. This is true: at those levels obedience to the Great Commission is only what our typology calls 'Barely adequate'. Nevertheless they do provide us with a valuable and meaningful dichotomous benchmark for the adjectival 'Great Commission' term. This is clearly shown if we remember that some two-thirds of the world's 33,800 denominations, 3 million churches and congregations, and 1,900 million church members do not meet even this low level and so cannot here be called 'Great Commission' bodies or individuals. Only one-third of Christianity can. This coincides with the average informed observer's assessment of the actual overall status of global Christianity today.

## BARRIERS TO GREAT COMMISSION CHRISTIANS' OUTREACH

This present review of GeoPersonnel and the role of Great Commission Christians finishes with a review of a major aspect of their work, namely mapping the barriers to their evangelistic ministry that exist in the world of today.

### Distance, barriers, and frontiers
The distances between peoples, and the barriers to communication that exist between them, and hence the frontiers a Great Commission Christian has to cross in order to engage in outreach, can be categorized under 6 heads as follows:

1. **Nationality:** political barriers (citizens/aliens, country boundaries).
2. **Lifestyle:** socioeconomic barriers (differences of per capita income).
3. **Culture:** racial-ethnolinguistic barriers (race, ethnicity, color).
4. **Language:** linguistic barriers (proximity, intercomprehension, mutual unintelligibility).
5. **Religion:** religious barriers (micro, mini, or macro).
6. **Evangelization:** barriers of stages in awareness of Christianity, Christ, and the gospel (Worlds A, B, C).

The resulting barriers to evangelistic outreach between a Great Commission Christian and any other person or homogenous population can be pinpointed and measured by means of the 6 scales. First, we locate the Christian's relationship to the target population on each of the scales; second, we add the barriers from all 6 scales to give an overall measure of the total barriers or distance or frontiers that exist. In the scales set out in Table 21–9, note that '0' = no-frontier or no-barrier; '1' = one-frontier or one-barrier; '2' = two-frontier or two-barrier; etc.

### Measuring distance via 27 barriers
To find out how many barriers exist between a Great Commission Christian and a target population, we add the total of barriers perceived in the 6 scales, thus:

Total distance/barriers/frontiers = TBB,

where

TBB = NBB + SBB + CBB +LBB + RBB + EBB,

where

NBB = nationality barriers (0–3)
SBB = lifestyle barriers (0–3)
CBB = cultural barriers (0–6)
LBB = language barriers (0–8)
RBB = religious barriers (0–6)
EBB = evangelistic barriers (0–2))
and
TBB = total barriers (maximum 28).

Each of these 6 scales is described, with its range of values, in Table 21–9.

Part 22

# EVANGELISM

Numerical analysis
of ongoing evangelism worldwide

*God gives each of us chance after chance to be saved from death and brought into the
light that gives life.*
—Job 33:29-30, Contemporary English Version

Part 22 describes evangelism—the organized propagation of the Christian Good News—under 45 constituent ministries, for each of which churches, missions, and agencies keep detailed records. Ways of measuring are then derived concerning how much evangelism is being received by individuals and thus by countries, peoples, languages, cities and their populations .

# Numerical analysis
# of ongoing evangelism worldwide

In this Part 22, we begin to tackle the toughest nut of all, if we want to measure or monitor frontier mission—how to quantify all the varieties of evangelism and evangelization, organized and unorganized, individual or collective. What follows is an exploration to define the boundaries and to stake out the territory. This exploration extends through 4 closely related sections, Parts 22-25, which the reader should study in sequence as a connected whole.

The first section, Part 22, constructs, compiles, and then interprets the first of 2 closely-related global diagrams in our 25-year ongoing series of 74 or so diagrams. Global Diagram 32 deals with the quantifying of evangelism as an overall concept, under which we have identified and described some 45 different types or varieties of evangelism grouped under the headings of the 7 Mandates of the Great Commission as shown in Global Diagram 6.

This section Part 22 deals with the outreach of Christians beyond the boundaries of the churches. It focuses in on evangelism, usually understood to mean the organized spreading of the Christian message of God's love in Christ to those without it. The subsequent 4 Parts deal with related subjects in a logical sequence, as follows. Part 23 "Evangelization" delineates the wider meaning of the term 'evangelize' and its cognates. Part 24 "Microevangelistics" begins the process of quantifying all aspects of evangelism and evangelization for individuals and for a whole variety of population units, large and small. In the process a major scale is derived and a method evolved from existing data for measuring the status of evangelization for any population. Part 25 "Macroevangelistics" then describes the findings of all these approaches at the macro or global level.

Meanwhile, Part 21 "GeoPersonnel" has enumerated all persons working for, or active in, the Christian world and its global mission—both full-time workers and also all active Christians themselves. Part 26 "GeoResponse" then describes people's response to Christianity, evangelism and evangelization and derives a number of significant measures of church growth, and of responsiveness to evangelism, or of the absence of them.

With these backgrounds and contexts, the first item to be investigated and measured is: *evangelism*.

## Origins of evangelism

Although the theme of God's favor arises at a number of points in the Old Testament, Christian evangelism begins only in the Incarnation—the coming of Jesus, his life and ministry, his commands, his cross, his resurrection, and his ascension. The mandate for evangelism then is encapsulated firstly in the 6 New Testament accounts of Christ's Great Commission, and then secondly in the multiple occurrences of the Greek verb *euangelizo* and its huge number of synonyms. For this reason the starting point for this investigation of evangelism is Global Diagram 6 entitled "GeoCommission", the concept which brings together the 2 strands of biblical emphasis and evidence—Christ's Great Commission, and the richest biblical word 'Evangelize!'—and analyzes them into 2 Minicommissions and 7 Mandates. This diagram has been extensively expounded in Part 3 "GeoCommission". For our analytical purposes in this Part 22, the tabular part of that diagram is reproduced here as Table 22–1. Readers wanting a fuller description are referred to the global diagram itself in Part 1 "GeoStatus", then to Part 3 itself.

## Table 22–1. GeoCommission: the origins of evangelism in (a) Christ's Great Commission, and (b) the richest biblical word Evangelize!

| MANDATE IMPERATIVE English (1) | NT Greek (2) | Usages (3) | DOMINANT CHARACTERISTIC (4) | HUMAN ROLE (5) | SUB-TYPES OF EVANGELISM (6) | RESULTING WORDS (7) | OUTREACH MINISTRIES (8) | OVERVIEW (9) | OTHER KEYWORDS (related nouns) Greek, Latin (L) (10) | Usages (11) | Total (12) | Key dimensions (13) | FACETS English (14) |
|---|---|---|---|---|---|---|---|---|---|---|---|---|---|
| **OVERALL IMPERATIVE:** | | | | | | | | | | | | | |
| **Evangelize!** | euangelizo | 133 | Authoritative | **7-P Evangelism** | Pluriform evangelism<br>Evangelistic work | EVANGELIZING WORDS | 45 | **7-P Evangelization** | euangelion<br>semeia kai terata<br>evangelizatio (L) | 76/133<br>77/84<br>41 | 400 | Evangelize with signs following | 700 |
| **MINICOMMISSION I: EVANGELIZE!**<br>**CONSTITUENT MANDATES:** | | | | | | | | | | | | | |
| 1. **Receive!** | labete<br>verb:<br>**lambano** | 263 | Spirit-dominated | **Prayer evangelism** | Baptism in the Spirit<br>Spirit evangelism<br>Pneumatization<br>Renewal in the Spirit<br>Intercession<br>Power evangelism | HIDDEN WORDS | 2 | **Pneumatic evangelization** | parakletos<br>dynamis<br>pneumatikos<br>exousia | 5/34<br>120/331<br>28/413<br>103/107 | 10 | Accompany, Be filled, Breathe, Cooperate, Follow, Participate, Pneumatize, Pray, Receive power, Stay, Wait | 33 |
| 2. **Go!** | poreuthentes<br>verb:<br>**poreuomai** | 154 | Person-implemented | **Pre-evangelism** | Apostolate<br>Mission<br>Extension<br>Outreach<br>Primary evangelism<br>Visitation evangelism<br>Visual evangelism<br>Audiovisual evangelism | VISUAL WORDS | 11 | **Preparatory evangelization** | apostole<br>missio (L) | 4/255<br>900 | 45 | Act, Contact, Develop, Encounter, Engage, Extend, Go, Help, Impact, Influence, Itinerate, Liberate, Love, Make aware, Occupy, Permeate, Prepare, Reach, Seek, Send, Show, Target, Touch, Transmit, Visit | 101 |
| 3. **Witness!** | martyres<br>verb:<br>**martyreo** | 173 | Unorganized, private | **Personal evangelism** | Person-to-person witness<br>Personal work<br>Individual evangelism<br>Dialogue evangelism<br>Gossiping the gospel<br>Seed-sowing<br>Prophetic evangelism | PERSONAL WORDS<br>Conversational evangelism | 2 | **Presence evangelization** | martyria<br>praesencia (L)<br>justitia (L)<br>pax (L)<br>dialogismos | 57/173<br>120<br>220<br>200<br>14/43 | 60 | Be martyred, Be present, Bring, Carry, Confess, Dialogue, Expose, Gossip, Inform, Propagate, Radiate, Report, Say, Share, Shine, Sow, Spread, Talk, Tell, Testify, Witness | 132 |
| 4. **Proclaim!** | keryxate<br>verb:<br>**kerysso** | 72 | Ordered, public | **Preaching evangelism** | Public evangelism<br>Mass evangelism<br>Demonstration evangelism<br>Deliverance evangelism<br>Incarnational evangelism<br>Saturation evangelism | PROCLAIMED WORDS | 6 | **Proclamation evangelization** | kerygma<br>apologia (L) | 8/72<br>8/18 | 48 | Advertise, Announce, Declare, Demonstrate, Do miracles, Exorcise, Explain, Expound, Give a message, Give opportunity, Herald, Make listen, Preach, Present, Proclaim, Prove, Publish, Read, Reason, Refute, Saturate, Translate | 85 |
| **MINICOMMISSION II: DISCIPLE!** | | | | | | | | | | | | | |
| 5. **Disciple!** | matheteusate<br>verb:<br>**matheteuo** | 266 | Convert-oriented | **Persuasion evangelism** | Paracletic evangelism<br>Harvest evangelism<br>Discipling evangelism<br>Verdict evangelism<br>Decision evangelism<br>Lordship evangelism<br>Healing evangelism<br>Power healing | WRITTEN WORDS | 9 | **Pressure evangelization** | paraklesis<br>therismos<br>mathetes<br>therapeia | 29/34<br>13/36<br>261/266<br>3/47 | 63 | Appeal, Catch, Compel, Confront, Conquer, Convert, Convince, Denounce, Disciple, Exhort, Forgive, Give, Harvest, Heal, Impart, Implore, Invite, Offer, Persuade, Press, Reap, Retain, Urge, Warn, Win | 128 |
| 6. **Baptize!** | baptizontes<br>verb:<br>**baptizo** | 111 | Church-oriented | **Pastoral evangelism** | Baptism<br>Baptizing evangelism<br>Evangelism that results in churches<br>Church planting<br>Incorporation<br>Shepherding<br>Celebration evangelism | PRINTED WORDS | 9 | **Planting evangelization** | baptismos<br>koinonia<br>ekklesia<br>leitourgeia<br>eucharistia<br>katechumenos | 23/111<br>19/59<br>115<br>6/15<br>15/54<br>8 | 35 | Affiliate, Baptize, Bless, Build, Catechize, Confirm, Enroll, Feed, Grow, Incorporate, Initiate, Minister, Multiply, Plant, Praise, Sacramentalize, Serve, Tend, Worship | 70 |
| 7. **Train!** | didaskontes<br>verb:<br>**didasko** | 212 | Ministry-oriented | **Programmed evangelism** | Teaching evangelism<br>Electronic evangelism<br>Broadcasting<br>Radio/TV evangelism | ELECTRONIC WORDS | 6 | **Pedagogical evangelization** | didache<br>diakonia<br>oikodome | 30/212<br>34/101<br>18/59 | 21 | Broadcast, Celebrate, Cultivate, Edify, Educate, Follow-up, Instruct, Mobilize, Nurture, Program, Teach, Train | 43 |

## EVANGELIZE!

## RECEIVE!

## GO!

## WITNESS!

## PROCLAIM!

## DISCIPLE!

## BAPTIZE!

## TRAIN!

**The 7 Modes of Evangelism**

Each Mandate's illustration(s) are within a rectangular border following the related verbal Mandate shown above each photos in capital letters. Evangelism means the following modes (numbers are those in bottom left corner of photos):

1. **Evangelism.** This 4th-century Greek painting entitled 'Evangelismos' meant 'Annunciation'.
2. **Prayer evangelism.** John Wesley at Oxford waited 6 years before conversion in 1738.
3. **Pre-evangelism.** Evangelism begins with 'The Departure of the Apostles'.
4. **Personal evangelism.** Evangelism means naming the Name of Jesus, identifying oneself with him.
5. **Preaching evangelism.** John Wesley preached 40,000 sermons to enormous crowds.
6. Another example: D.L. Moody led 750,000 individuals to Christ.
7. **Persuasion evangelism.** Wycliffe led Lollards to begin small Bible study groups.
8. Another example: In Brazil, pope John Paul II exhorts 1 million Brazilians to be Christ's disciples.
9. **Pastoral evangelism.** Evangelism is baptizing new converts into the church's fellowship.
   Photos 9-11 show South African evangelists baptizing 70,000 Xhosas in one day.
12. Another example: a large baptism of Gypsy Pentecostals in France.
13. **Programmed evangelism.** The 2nd International Conference for Itinerant Evangelists, Amsterdam, stressed training needs (1986).

# The 7 Modes of Evangelism

## Table 22–2. Evangelism described under 7 types/modes of evangelizing words.

| Imperative column 1 | Human role 2 | EVANGELIZING WORDS 3 | Description of 'words' 4 |
|---|---|---|---|
| Receive ! | Prayer evangelism | HIDDEN WORDS | Words **hidden** in **prayer**, uttered in private to God through charismata **received** by Christians. |
| Go ! | Pre-evangelism | VISUAL WORDS | Visible signs **preparing** hearers for the gospel as **Christians go, visit, help, show, live, suffer, even die.** |
| Witness ! | Personal evangelism | PERSONAL WORDS | Words through which individual Christians **witness** about Christ **personally** to non-Christians by their **presence** in word and deed in unstructured situations, even get **martyred.** |
| Proclaim ! | Preaching evangelism | PROCLAIMED WORDS | Words **preached** by professional workers **proclaiming** and **expounding** the gospel in structured situations. |
| Disciple ! | Persuasion evangelism | WRITTEN WORDS | The formal, definitive **written** words of Holy Scripture in 3,500 languages **press** and **persuade** listeners and **offer disciple**-opportunities. |
| Baptize ! | Pastoral evangelism | PRINTED WORDS | **Baptism, church-planting,** and **pastoral** life are surrounded daily by millions of **printed** Christian words. |
| Train ! | Programmed evangelism | ELECTRONIC WORDS | Since 1920, Christians have been **taught** and **trained** by trillions of **electronic**-media **programmed** words. |

### INVESTIGATING EVANGELISM

Jesus is regarded by Christians as not only the Good News (*euangelion*) but also the master Evangelizer and Evangelist bringing that same good news to the human race. Column 7 of Table 22–1 analyzes how he did this in Palestine and how, through his church, he continues to do this today. The words he employed and employs form a typology of 7 distinct types of words corresponding to 7 modes of evangelism. In his Palestinian ministry Jesus employed 5 main modes or points of contact with people through words, which can be listed as follows: (1) *hidden words* (his private hopes and prayers), (2) *visual words* (what people saw of his person, his life, his lifestyle, his deeds, and his actions), (3) *personal words* (face to face meetings with an individual or group), (4) *proclaimed words* (Jesus' preaching and teaching to groups or crowds), (5) *written words* (Jesus' use of scrolls of the Old Testament as the written Word of God). After his resurrection, Jesus delivered 2 further Mandates *Baptize!* and *Train!* After his ascension, Jesus then expanded these latter 2 mandates into 2 completely new things. First, he formally founded his church (in the sense that the Day of Pentecost in Acts 2 records in words 'the birthday of the church') with its church-planting imperative. And second, he formally launched a massive leadership training program selecting, calling out, setting apart, training a whole new age of sevenfold leadership in ministry: disciples, apostles, prophets, evangelists, healers, pastors, teachers. He thus expanded the understanding of his Great Commission which his disciples have later expanded into 2 further categories of evangelizing words: (6) *printed words* (literature, tracts, periodicals, books), and (7) *electronic words* (broadcasting, radio/TV, cassettes, computers, et alia). These 7 types of evangelizing words can be seen in the diagram to be formalized outcomes of, or responses to, the 7 Mandates (column 1) of the Great Commission. It can be analyzed under this category 'words' because words are the main form of human communication.

### Categorizing evangelism as 7-fold
As shown in Global Diagram 6 this analysis divides evangelism into 7 types or modes, as set out in its column 5. The whole schema of the Great Commission can therefore be arranged in terms of these categories. The first 8 columns of the diagram expound the concept evangelism; the remaining columns 9–14 expound the wider concept evangelization which will be investigated in Part 23. These categories are not intended to be watertight or definitive but are simply useful tools for analyzing and understanding this very complex concept. This 7-fold interpretation is further clarified in column 4 of Table 22–2.

### Evangelism as 45 distinct ministries
In Table 22–3 evangelism is described under the 7 categories of Mandate, under the human role each requires, under the type of evangelizing 'words', and then finally under 45 distinct ministries of ministry. This is expanded somewhat in Table 22–3 below with a description of each of the 7 categories of evangelizing words and of the 45 ministries themselves, in the final column of the table.

## Table 22–3. Evangelism described under 7 modes of evangelizing words and 45 distinct outreach ministries.

| Imperative 1 | Human role 2 | EVANGELIZING WORDS / Outreach ministries 3 | Description of 'words' (lines in capitals) and ministries (lines in lowercase) (**bold** type = major keywords in each ministry under one of the 7 Imperatives/Mandates) 4 |
|---|---|---|---|
| Receive! | Prayer evangelism | HIDDEN WORDS<br>1. Intercession<br>2. Inner renewal/spirituality | WORDS **HIDDEN** IN PRIVATE **PRAYER**, CHARISMATA **RECEIVED**.<br>**Continuing** earnestly in **prayer, interceding** for persons and peoples.<br>**Being filled** with the Holy Spirit, **waiting**, then **following** Jesus. |
| Go! | Pre-evangelism | VISUAL WORDS (audiovisuals)<br>3. Christians' lifestyle<br>4. Audiovisual ministries<br>5. Plays/concerts/operas/shows<br>6. 'Jesus' Film shows<br>7. Audio scriptures<br>8. Scripture leaflets/selections<br>9. Every-home campaign visits<br>10. New Reader Scriptures<br>11. Braille scriptures<br>12. Signed/deaf scriptures<br>13. Christian suffering | CHRISTIANS **GO**, HELP, SHOW **VISIBLE** SIGNS **PREPARING** HEARERS.<br>**Going, meeting, bringing the love** of God by Christian **living** and **lives**.<br>**Sending out, speaking out, displaying, showing** words and pictures.<br>**Shows illustrating** Christian doctrine, history, ethics.<br>**Portraying** the **incarnation**, person, **work**, and **ministry** of Jesus.<br>**Making** Scripture **available** to nonliterates, reading aloud, **corresponding**.<br>**Impacting** whole populations with mass **illustrated** leaflets.<br>**Going, seeking, visiting, contacting, touching, encountering, giving**.<br>**Providing** pictorial literacy primers, **supplying** gospels for new literates.<br>**Doing miracles, giving** sight to the blind.<br>**Reaching** deaf persons with the gospel.<br>**Showing** how Christians live through sickness, **suffering**, even death. |
| Witness! | Personal evangelism | PERSONAL WORDS<br>14. Personal evangelism<br>15. Martyrdoms | CHRISTIANS **WITNESS PERSONALLY** BY **PRESENCE**, WORD, **DEED**, DYING.<br>**Telling** others about Jesus, **speaking, gossiping** the gospel, **introducing, informing**.<br>The **witness** of those who lose their lives for Christ and are **martyred**. |
| Proclaim! | Preaching evangelism | PROCLAIMED WORDS<br>16. Full-time home church workers<br>17. Foreign missionaries<br>18. Evangelists<br>19. Short-term missionaries<br>20. Part-time evangelizers<br>21. Mission agencies | WORDS **PREACHED, PROCLAIMING** THE GOSPEL IN STRUCTURED SITUATIONS.<br>**Preaching, stating, reading**.<br>**Translating, interpreting, expounding, saturating**.<br>**Proclaiming, announcing, declaring, heralding, presenting**.<br>**Demonstrating, saturating**.<br>**Giving opportunity** to many others.<br>**Advertising**, enabling workers to **promulgate** the gospel. |
| Disciple! | Persuasion evangelism | WRITTEN WORDS (Scriptures)<br>22. Portions/gospels<br>23. Near-gospels<br>24. New Testaments<br>25. Near-New Testaments<br>26. Bibles<br>27. Near-Bibles<br>28. 2nd-language gospels<br>29. 2nd-language NTs<br>30. 2nd-language Bibles | **WRITTEN** SCRIPTURES **PERSUADING, PRESSING DISCIPLE**-OPPORTUNITIES.<br>**Imparting, forgiving, offering, explaining**.<br>Circulating gospels among related languages with no scriptures.<br>**Persuading, discipling, reaping**.<br>**Distributing** the whole story of Jesus to related languages with no scriptures.<br>**Convincing, winning, converting, healing**.<br>**Offering** the Bible's riches to related languages without it.<br>**Catching, confronting** scripture-less languages through lingua francas.<br>Harvesting scripture-less languages through wider-communication languages.<br>**Making** the Bible's riches **understandable** to all through trade and similar languages. |
| Baptize! | Pastoral evangelism | PRINTED WORDS (literature)<br>31. Denominational materials<br>32. Local church output<br>33. Outside Christian literature<br>34. Church-planting output<br>35. Institutional ministries/records<br>36. Christian books<br>37. Christian periodicals<br>38. Tracts<br>39. Other documentation | **BAPTISM**, CHURCH-**PLANTING**, **PASTORAL** LIFE, **PRINTED** WORDS.<br>**Catechizing, baptizing, confirming, incorporating** new believers, **pastoring**.<br>**Enroling, affiliating, worshiping, blessing**.<br>**Helping, supporting**.<br>**Planting** new churches, **building**, church **growth**.<br>**Serving, ministering**.<br>**Feeding, growing**.<br>**Tending, shepherding**.<br>**Multiplying** individual ministries.<br>**Praising, singing**. |
| Train! | Programmed evangelism | ELECTRONIC WORDS<br>40. Programmed training<br>41. Christian radio programs<br>42. Christian TV programs<br>43. Urban media (cable TV, &c)<br>44. Christian-owned computers<br>45. Internet/networks/e-mail | **TRAINED** BY **ELECTRONIC**-MEDIA **PROGRAMMED** WORDS.<br>**Instructing, teaching, educating, making** people **learn**.<br>**Broadcasting, following-up**.<br>**Telecasting teaching** materials, **cultivating, edifying**.<br>**Working among** all varieties of peoples, especially urban populations, **uniting**.<br>Programming the church's many activities, e-mailing, **faxing**.<br>**Mobilizing** the vast area of Christian resources worldwide; surfing, **training**. |

## QUANTIFYING EVANGELISM

Evangelism is the activity, individual or collective, usually organized, by which Christians set forth and spread the Good News of Jesus Christ so that others may believe and become his disciples in his church. Evangelism means contact with Christ. It means facing or confronting people with the person and work of the Savior. It means giving people an opportunity to follow Christ, to become his disciples. Ultimately, therefore, what the quantification of evangelism boils down to (at the human level) is—measuring the various modes of contact that persons or populations have had with evangelizers, that is with Christian believers and all their varieties of influences. In short, it means enumerating the duration, quality, and intensity of all conversations and awareness resulting from this contact with Christians, Christianity, Christ, and the gospel.

### Two categories of participants

Quantifying evangelism results from monitoring the interactions of 2 quite separate and distinct categories of people or roles. First there are the activities of *Christian evangelizers* themselves, proclaiming the Good News in season and out of season. These activities can be measured as 'witness-hours', or 'evangelism-hours', the number of man-hours or woman-hours spent on varieties of evangelizing. (The exact definitions of all neologisms used here are given in Part 30 "Glossary".). This witness then results in them functioning as *Christian opportunity-givers* (a synonym or sub-role or sub-variety of evangelizers), who give to others numbers of clear, unambiguous, specific opportunities or offers or invitations to become Christ's disciples; these events or occasions can be termed 'disciple-opportunities' or 'offers'.

Second, the recipients of these occasions then become *opportunity-receivers*, or *offer-receivers*. These are all those who willingly or unwillingly find themselves faced with these opportunities to become Christ's disciples, whether knowingly or unwittingly, as well as whether for the first time, second time, or even multiple times. Note carefully that we are not at this point measuring their *response* (which may range from hostility and rejection to interest to approval to acceptance, conversion, and baptism). Measuring response is a separate subject and needs its own separate quantification; we have explored this elsewhere in Global Diagrams 34 et alia.

### How long does it take to evangelize a person?

To understand the process and this terminology better, consider 7 cases in the New Testament where Jesus, the master Evangelizer, gives 7 individuals each one single, individual, personal disciple-opportunity. In descending order of brevity, here they are, with the biblical reference and the amount of time that each encounter took, or takes to read: (a) Nicodemus (John 3:1–21; perhaps an hour or two); (b) Herod (Luke 23:7–12; about an hour); (c) the Samaritan Woman at the Well (John 4:7–29; probably under an hour); (d) Pontius Pilate (John 18:28–19:16; 3 brief interviews—probably half an hour or so); (e) the Rich Young Ruler (Matthew 19:16–22; about 20 minutes or so, although the account of the discussion takes only 40 seconds to read aloud); (f) Blind Bartimeus (Mark 10:46–52; about 3 or 4 minutes); and (g) Matthew the Tax-Gatherer (Matthew 9:9; 'Follow me'—1 second). Here we see Jesus contacting and then evangelizing 7 persons in an hour or less each (under one witness-hour), creating and then giving them 7 disciple-opportunities, and watching as the 7 each receives his or her opportunity or offer or invitation and then reacts to it.

How much time is enough to make such a contact into an adequate disciple-opportunity? This list of 7 brief biblical narratives suggests 15 minutes each may often be enough, everything else being in place. Generalizing to the whole world, across 20 centuries and up to AD 2000, and being very conservative, we could say that one whole hour is needed. During this hour, on average some 5,000 words will be spoken, and heard. To be even more on the safe side, we could elaborate on this to say that before we would consider an individual to have become 'adequately' evangelized, he or she needs to have received at least one clearly-focused evangelism-hour producing one disciple-opportunity, and if possible a variety of other more general evangelizing activities producing up to 10 disciple-opportunities or offers or invitations. Note also that although individuals can avoid contact with

Christ, once confronted by Christ he evangelizes them whether they want to be evangelized or not.

### Decision involves counting the cost

In this process of offering the gospel, a key element is contained in Jesus' own words in the analogy of the tower-builder, as follows:

> No one who does not carry his cross and come with me can be a *disciple* of mine. Would any of you think of building a tower without first sitting down and *calculating* the cost? (Luke 14:27–28, REB, emphases added).

Here the 2 key words, shown italicized, are disciple and calculating. Becoming a disciple, says Jesus, is a serious undertaking requiring one's full attention ('first sitting down'). It presupposes the existence of facts and figures as the builder worked out amounts of raw materials needed, their cost, their transport, dates of delivery, architects' fees, number of workers required, their rates of pay per day, number of days to build, taxes payable, and so on. The whole calculation would take the builder many minutes, perhaps an hour or more.

We may call this whole process as explained by Jesus a disciple-calculation. It can be seen to be simply another term, or another variant, of the basic unit of evangelism we are looking for. Presenting the call to discipleship to an individual takes the evangelizer an hour on average—the length of a sermon, presentation, discussion, counselling, explaining the cost, helping someone count the cost before deciding, and so on.

### Defining the unit of evangelism

We now proceed to answer the question: given the basic unit is one evangelism-hour, what does it constitute or amount to? What is achieved by that hour? Twenty-seven answers from the terminology of Jesus' own Palestinian ministry are set out in Table 22–4.

An example is the word 'chance'. Jesus' ministry involved giving individuals, groups, and whole crowds many chances—one chance after another—to understand the gospel and to become his disciples.

This is the idea also in Elihu's advice to Job in Old Testament days: 'God gives each of us chance after chance to be saved from death and brought into the light that gives life' (Job 33: 29–30, CEV). When Jesus spent an hour of evangelism, therefore, each hearer was receiving a God-given chance to enter on eternal life. This is answer No. 16 in Table 22–4.

All 27 names for this unit shown in the last column of that table shed further light on the subject. All 27 convey some additional meaning for this definition of our unit of measurement. They are all synonymous. But in order to clarify this analysis, we will standardize on 2 terms: (1) Jesus, followed after him by each disciple, creates an *evangelism-hour*, and (2) each of his hearers and those being evangelized thus becomes a beneficiary and receives an *offer* of new life in Christ, which they can then accept or reject, temporarily or permanently.

### Seven varieties of offering disciple-opportunities

In the Palestinian ministry of Jesus, we noted 5 main modes or types of contact through words producing disciple-opportunities. These can be expanded and catalogued as follows, prior to quantifying them:

(1) *hidden words* (his private hopes and prayers): his intercessory words and plans to extend the Good News to those around him; (2) *visual words* (what people saw of his person, his life, his lifestyle, his deeds, his actions): everything implied in the Incarnation of the Word of God; (3) *personal words* (personal evangelism): face-to-face meetings with an individual or a group, with conversation, the spoken word, shared words, dialogue, challenge; (4) *proclaimed words* (public proclamation): Jesus' face-to-face preaching and teaching of the proclaimed word to groups, crowds, even multitudes; and (5) *written words*: use of the written Word of God, in this case Jesus' use of scrolls of the Old Testament (later to become hand-copied scriptures). Two millennia later, disciples of Jesus can add the 2 additional modes: (6) *printed words*: print media, apologetics, and other literature, tracts, magazines, books; and (7) *electronic words*: electronic media, telephones, broadcasting, radio/TV, also via cassettes, compact disks (CD-ROM), computers, Internet, and World Wide Web.

---

## Table 22–4.   Defining a measurable unit of evangelism: 27 alternatives that Jesus used.

To be useful in statistical analysis, a unit by means of which amounts of evangelism can be measured must have a widely-understood name and a precise definition numerically. The basic unit used in this analysis is one evangelism-hour. This table gives 26 other alternative descriptions or synonyms.

In the table below, *column 1* gives a series of 27 verbs describing what Jesus did in Palestinian times, and what he and his English-speaking disciples do today, in order to evangelize his hearer or hearers and to make them his disciples. *Column 2* describes the reaction of the individual recipient to that unit. And *column 3* gives the technical terms for the unit.

(a) *The biblical narratives*

| 1 Jesus the Evangelizer— | 2 The individual recipient— | 3 Name for unit |
|---|---|---|
| 1. —encounters | —is encountered | an encounter |
| 2. —contacts | —is contacted | a contact |
| 3. —meets | —is met | a meeting |
| 4. —reveals his presence | —becomes aware of Jesus | an awareness |
| 5. —reaches out | —is reached | an outreach |
| 6. —touches | —is touched | a touch |
| 7. —converses | —is conversed with | a conversation |
| 8. —sows a seed | —gets a seed | a seed |
| 9. —gives a message | —is given a message | a message |
| 10. —witnesses | —is witnessed to | a witness |
| 11. —tells the Good News | —is told the gospel | a talk |
| 12. —presents | —is presented with | a presentation |
| 13. —declares | —is declared to | a declaration |
| 14. —preaches | —is preached to | a sermon |
| 15. —communicates | —is communicated to | a communication |
| 16. —gives a chance | —is given a chance | a chance |
| 17. —gives an opportunity | —has an opportunity | a disciple-opportunity |
| 18. —calls | —hears Jesus' call | a call |
| 19. —invites | —is invited to follow | an invitation |
| 20. —offers | —is offered Christ | an offer |
| 21. —explains the cost | —has to count the cost | a disciple-calculation |
| 22. —asks for a choice | —has to choose | a choice |
| 23. —challenges | —makes a decision | a decision Yes or No |
| 24. —commands | —obeys or refuses | · a response Yes or No |

(b) *A standardized unit*

| 1 Jesus the Evangelizer— | 2 The individual recipient— | 3 Standardized unit |
|---|---|---|
| 25. —**evangelizes** | —becomes **evangelized** | one **evangelism-hour** |
| 26. —**speaks** as Word of God | —**hears** Jesus' words | 5,000 **evangelism-words** |
| 27. —**creates** an offer | —**receives** an offer | one **evangelistic offer** |

*Definition of unit adopted here.* One unit, termed one evangelism-hour, is the amount of evangelism communicated in either (a) one hour, or (b) 5,000 words, or (c) something much shorter when a rapid response takes place (as with Matthew's call in Matthew 9:9). Normally this unit takes one hour or so in a discussion or presentation or reading or hearing of the gospel taking around 5,000 words, but it can be a shorter period if closure is reached. The context is understood to be one or more varieties of evangelism directed at the individual recipient or recipients.

**Table 22–5. Daily hours of evangelizing ministry by Jesus, the apostles, martyrs, and today's Christians.**

Key to columns:
1 = Names and types of evangelizers
2 = hours = Presence-hours per day
3 = W-hours = Witness-hours per day
4 = E-hours = Evangelism-hours per day
5 = Evangelism-hours per year

| | *Evangelizers* *column 1* | *P-hours* *2* | *W-hours* *3* | *E-hours* *4* | *Hours p.a.* *5* |
|---|---|---|---|---|---|
| 1. | Jesus in Palestine | 24 | 24 | 24 | 8,760 |
| 2. | An apostle (Peter, Paul, The Twelve) | 24 | 24 | 4 | 1,460 |
| 3. | A martyr in AD 1000 | 24 | 24 | 1 | 365 |
| | *In the year AD 2000:* | | | | |
| 4. | An ordained pastor | 16 | 6 | 2 | 730 |
| 5. | A mega-evangelist. | 16 | 6 | 0.5 | 200 |
| 6. | A full-time evangelist | 16 | 4 | 1.4 | 500 |
| 7. | A part-time evangelist | 16 | 2 | 0.3 | 100 |
| 8. | A lay catechist | 16 | 4 | 0.5 | 200 |
| 9. | A career missionary | 16 | 6 | 2 | 730 |
| 10. | A short-term missionary | 16 | 5 | 1 | 365 |
| 11. | A part-time evangelizer | 16 | 4 | 0.8 | 292 |
| 12. | A trained tentmaker | 16 | 4 | 0.7 | 255 |
| 13. | A lone-wolf tentmaker | 12 | 2 | 0.6 | 216 |
| 14. | A GCC layperson | 12 | 2 | 0.25 | 91 |
| 15. | An average Christian | 10 | 0.6 | 0.2 | 73 |
| 16. | An inactive Christian | 8 | 0 | 0 | 0 |

*Footnotes on table above*
**Columns.** The 3 columns 2,3, and 4 give the number of hours each day expended on the 3 basic varieties of evangelizing activity: (a) a Christian's presence, (b) witness and (c) evangelism. Column 5 gives the resulting totals of evangelism-hours produced per year (p.a.).

The reasoning behind the numbers is as follows, line by line.

**Lines.**
1. *Jesus.* As the master Evangelizer, Jesus is here accorded the maximum 24 hours because (a) he was continuously present and influential even when asleep (e.g. during the storm on Galilee, Mark 4:38), (b) he was and is 'The Faithful and True Martys/Witness' (Revelation 3:14, RSV), and (c) he was and is himself the permanent embodiment of the Evangel/Good News.
2. *Apostles.* Peter, the Twelve, and Paul were each martyred for the faith. When in prison, they were watched 24 hours a day, awake or asleep. In life and in death, their witness was continuous.
3. *Martyrs.* As with line 2, all martyrs were and are 'witnesses' (Greek, *martyres*) continuously, day and night. Most have not been free, however, to engage in any continuous organized evangelism.
4. *Pastors, ministers, clergy.* Today's full-time clergy (often regarded, with evangelists and missionaries, as 'religious professionals') balance a multitude of activities and responsibilities, have private or family lives, and regular hours of sleep, hence are here shown with fewer hours than previous lines.
5. *Mega-evangelists.* Full-time professionals with large support teams who concentrate on organized evangelistic presentation of the gospel and who regularly preach to crowds of over 1,000 at a time and occasionally.to over 1 million.
6. *Full-time evangelists.* Professionals who regularly address crowds of several hundred at a time.
7. *Part-time evangelists.* Nonprofessionals who nevertheless regularly conduct smaller campaigns or address numerous meetings.
8. *Lay catechists.* Nonprofessionals who instruct catechumens locally.
9. *Missionaries.* Full-time career foreign missionaries who engage the non-Christian world in cross-cultural ministry.
10. *Short-term missionaries.* Full-time workers who serve abroad for less than one year.
11. *Part-time evangelizers.* Persons in full-time secular employment who give substantial time each week to part-time or volunteer Christian work, specializing in the spreading of the gospel.
12. *Tentmakers.* These are bivocational missionaries who combine the missionary vocation with full-time secular employment.
13. *Lone-wolf tentmakers.* Operating alone rather than in accountability or support teams, untrained lone-wolf operators are limited in that they miss many opportunities for witness and evangelism that teams and mission agencies engender.
14. *Great Commission Christians.* GCC laypersons are all those church members who are active or attempt to be active in the cause of Christ's Great Commission.
15. *Average Christians.* Most Christians devote scant time (6 minutes a day) to actively forwarding Christ's mission; including GCCs, this makes an average per Christian of 12 minutes a day.
16. *Inactive Christians.* Uninterested in or uncommitted to Christ's mission, these Christians (many of whom are church members) are defined as those who avoid witness and evangelism and do not engage in it.

We will shortly quantify these 7 modes of evangelism. But first we will discuss how to enumerate hours spent on evangelizing in general.

### *Three levels of evangelizing activity*

Let us now sharpen enumeration by defining exactly all the terms involved. In Jesus' ministry, he evangelized at 3 levels: (A) by his *presence* (who he was and what he did each day), (B) by his *witness*—mainly unstructured situations as occasion arose (such as that before Pilate), and (C) by his *evangelism*—structured preaching, proclamation, and teaching (such as the Sermon on the Mount, or his parables). In the same way, we can recognize that these 3 modes represent for us as disciples 3 different levels of evangelizing activity: our Christian *presence*, our *witness*, and our *evangelism.* These 3 will then enable us to measure by means of hours and words. The best way to understand all these neologisms is to keep them constantly before us as a series of definitions, as is done at the top of Global Diagram 32. The entire schema of the present analysis, with its statistics, are set out in Table 22–6; the derivation of each ministry's global statistics is done later in this Part 22.

### *Quantifying hours spent by evangelizers (Table 22–5, columns 2–5)*

The first step is to quantify the amount of time that Christians spend each day on evangelizing. This is set out in Table 22–5, 'Daily hours of evangelizing ministry.' This table considers the situation of Jesus in Palestine, the apostles, martyrs, and of 13 varieties of present-day Christians. To enumerate how many disciple-opportunities all this generates, we will first consider the personal evangelism of 5 different varieties of Christians.

#### 1. Normal Christians

Let's begin by examining the situation of the normal Christian—the ordinary Christian, the real Christian, the ideal Christian, the Christian properly so-called who genuinely follows Christ and seeks his guidance in life.

Let's assume the normal Christian's conscious day is 16 hours (during the day's other 8 hours we're all asleep). That's 5,840 waking hours a year (p.a., per annum). In these, the normal Christian is expected to live as a disciple of Jesus, in 3 modes; to be firstly, (1) a Christian *presence,* incarnating his Lord and Master, actively in contact with people (we call the time he spends 'presence-hours' to represent the widest form of witnessing and evangelizing); secondly as a Great Commission Christian to be (2) a *martys* (the Greek New Testament word for a follower who was an eyewitness to Jesus and his Resurrection, spending active 'witness-hours'); and thirdly to be (3) an *evangelizer* or an evangelist, actively spreading the Good News and passing on the gospel of Christ ('evangelism-hours'). Note that, as we are defining them, evangelism-hours are also included in witness-hours (evangelism being a specific form of witness), and both form part of the presence-hours category.

Let's assume next that the average Christian's actively witnessing day (witness by life and by word) is 4 hours in contact with other people, and that his actively evangelistic day is 30 minutes. His 5,840 waking presence-hours thus include 1,460 active witness-hours a year, and both include 182 evangelism-hours a year.

#### 2. Actual Christians

Now let's quantify this for the entire Christian world. There are 2 billion Christians across the globe. These are not, to our regret, all 'normal' Christians—probably only a third are. If all were normal Christians, together they would spend 10.5 trillion presence-hours a year. If we think instead about the actual situation with only a third as 'normal' Christians, this would drop to 3.5 trillion presence-hours a year (see Table 22–6, column 4, under 'Christians', also the bottom 2 rows). Dividing by the total world population of 6 billion, this becomes 580 Christian presence-hours expended per inhabitant of the globe per year (1.6 presence-hours a day). Dividing instead by the world's 4 billion non-Christians, this is 870 presence-hours per non-Christian per year. Dividing instead by the 1,600 million unevangelized, this is 2,180 presence-hours per World A inhabitant per year. This should be enough to ensure evangelizing the world! Like the global supply of food and water, it's entirely adequate—*if it's properly shared and distributed.*

#### 3. Active Christians

Let's sharpen our definitions by talking next about an exact category that we have enumerated. 'Active' Christians are defined here as all Christians who are active with regard to mission, to Christ's world mission, to Christ's command to extend the faith. Using the precise methodology described in Part 21 "GeoPersonnel", we focus now on this category—our globe's 648 million active, committed, Great Commission Christians. They put in 2.8 trillion presence-hours a year, of which 473 billion are Great Commission 'witness-hours' a year (see Table 22–5, columns 1 and 3) which is 79 per global inhabitant a year (0.2 hours a day), or 118 Great Commission witness-hours per non-Christian per year. Specifically on evangelism, these Great Commission Christians each do 91 evangelism-hours a year which totals to 59 billion evangelism-hours a year. This can also be stated as 15 evangelism-hours per global inhabitant a year. Again, adequate—if properly distributed.

#### 4. Full-time workers

An even sharper approach ensues when we consider full-time Christian workers, who number 5 million today (see Table 22–6, row 16). As full-time evangelizers they put in 3.7 billion evangelism-hours a year. This is 37 evangelism-minutes per global inhabitant a year.

#### 5. Foreign missionaries

Finally, let's consider the world's 420,000 foreign missionaries. They put in 2.5 billion presence-hours per year which is 0.6 presence-hours per non-Christian per year. Further, they also engage in 900 million witness-hours per year which is 0.23 witness-hours per non-Christian per year (14 minutes of contact each year, 2 seconds every day, or 14 seconds a week). Lastly, they do 300 million active evangelism-hours per year.

## *THE GLOBAL OUTPUT OF EVANGELISM*

With all these definitions and examples in place, it is now the time to work through the large inventory and summary in Table 22–6 with the intent of measuring the total of all evangelistic activity worldwide. To understand the general order of magnitude involved and the huge numbers that result, we can begin with a short descriptive paragraph describing the USA as the world's leading country for volume of evangelism produced.

### *How much evangelism does a country get?*

To see what this means for a country, consider the world's most-evangelized country, the United States of America with its 170 million church members. These produce 993 billion presence-hours p.a., which is 3,970 hours per USA inhabitant p.a. This includes 1,200 Great Commission witness-hours per USA inhabitant p.a. And in the USA, individual Great Commission Christians by their own personal evangelism also produce the remarkable number of 10.5 billion evangelism-hours p.a., which is 42 evangelism-hours per year for every person in the population. If we now add all the other 44 ministries or types of evangelism, the grand total climbs to 98 evangelism-hours a year. This means that the average USA non-Christian gets multiple repeated opportunities to hear about and follow Christ. But it also means that the average USA Great Commission Christian continues year after year to receive, directed at him and saturating him, 89 additional disciple-opportunities which (because he is already a disciple) he does not need. This is 'chance after chance' with a vengeance. It's exactly analogous to wasted food.

### *Seven modes, 45 ministries, hours spent, media (columns 1-7)*

These 4 categories and measurements are set out in Table 22–6. Column 1 is a reference number. Column 2 lists the 7 modes or types of evangelism in the form of evangelistic words. Column 3 gives the starting data for each line's attempt to quantify its ministry. Columns 4, 5 and 6 measure the 3 types of evangelizing ministry set out above in Table 22–5. And Column 7 introduces a major factor in this drama, namely the effect of the various forms of media.

### *Quantifying hours received by audiences*

These definitions now lead to measurements about

**Table 22–6.  Hours spent evangelizing each year via 45 ministries, hours received by hearers, 7 types/mandates/modes of words disseminated, and offers of discipleship made per year.**

| Ref 1 | 7 MODES, 45 MINISTRIES 2 | ITEMS, AD 2000 3 | HOURS SPENT EVANGELIZING p.a. | | | MEDIA 7 | RECEIVED p.a. 8 | WORDS DISSEMINATED p.a. | | OFFERS p.a. 11 |
|---|---|---|---|---|---|---|---|---|---|---|
| | | | Presence-hours 4 | Witness-hours 5 | Evangelism-hours 6 | | | Witness-words 9 | Evangelism-words 10 | |
| | **1. HIDDEN WORDS** | *Intercessors* | *Presence-hours* | *Witness-hours* | *Evangelism-hours* | *Media* | *Hearer-hours* | *Witness-words* | *Evangelism-words* | *Offers* |
| 1. | Intercession/prayerwalks/campaigns | 200 million | 876 billion | 146 billion | 18.3 billion | 1 | 18.3 billion | 730 trillion | 91 trillion | 18.3 billion |
| 2. | Inner renewal/spirituality | 375 million | 1,506 billion | 137 billion | 19.5 billion | 1 | 19.5 billion | 684 trillion | 98 trillion | 19.5 billion |
| | **2. VISUAL WORDS** (audiovisuals) | *Visuals p.a.* | *Presence-hours* | *Witness-hours* | *Evangelism-hours* | *Media* | *Hearer-hours* | *Witness-words* | *Evangelism-words* | *Offers* |
| 3. | Christians' lifestyle | 100 million | 438 billion | 73 billion | 18.3 billion | 1 | 18.3 billion | 365 trillion | 91 trillion | 18.3 billion |
| 4. | Audiovisual ministries | 50 million | 219 billion | 37 billion | 3.0 billion | 25 | 76.0 billion | 4,563 trillion | 380 trillion | 76.0 billion |
| 5. | Plays/concerts/operas/shows | 20 million | 14.6 billion | 4.9 billion | 2.4 billion | 20 | 48.7 billion | 487 trillion | 243 trillion | 48.7 billion |
| 6. | 'Jesus' Film shows (700 languages) | 3 million | 3.3 billion | 1.1 billion | 548 million | 100 | 54.8 billion | 548 trillion | 274 trillion | 54.8 billion |
| 7. | Audio scriptures | 1 million | 110 million | 37 million | 18 million | 1,000 | 18.3 billion | 183 trillion | 91 trillion | 18.3 billion |
| 8. | Scripture leaflets/selections | 4.1 billion | 16.4 billion | 4 billion | 4.1 billion | 5 | 20.5 billion | 103 trillion | 103 trillion | 20.5 billion |
| 9. | Every-home campaigns/visitations | 160 million | 1.9 billion | 500 million | 160 million | 50 | 8.0 billion | 120 trillion | 40 trillion | 8.0 billion |
| 10. | New Reader Scriptures | 50 million | 1 billion | 200 million | 76 million | 10 | 760 million | 10 trillion | 4 trillion | 760 million |
| 11. | Braille scriptures | 10 million | 20 billion | 6 billion | 2 billion | 5 | 10.0 billion | 150 trillion | 50 trillion | 10.0 billion |
| 12. | Signed/deaf scriptures | 30 million | 6 billion | 2 billion | 600 million | 5 | 3.0 billion | 45 trillion | 15 trillion | 3.0 billion |
| 13. | Christian suffering | 260 million | 2.6 billion | 1 billion | 260 million | 10 | 2.6 billion | 39 trillion | 13 trillion | 2.6 billion |
| | **3. PERSONAL WORDS** | *Persons* | *Presence-hours* | *Witness-hours* | *Evangelism-hours* | *Media* | *Hearer-hours* | *Witness-words* | *Evangelism-words* | *Offers* |
| | Personal evangelism due to: | | | | | | | | | |
| 14. | Great Commission Christians | 648 million | 2,838 billion | 473 billion | 59.1 billion | 3 | 177.4 billion | 7,096 billion | 887 trillion | 177.4 billion |
| 15. | Martyrdoms | 160,000 | 1.4 billion | 58 million | 1.6 billion | 1,000 | 1.6 billion | 292 trillion | 8 trillion | 1.6 billion |
| | **4. PROCLAIMED WORDS** | *Professionals* | *Presence-hours* | *Witness-hours* | *Evangelism-hours* | *Media* | *Hearer-hours* | *Witness-words* | *Evangelism-words* | *Offers* |
| 16. | Full-time home church workers | 5,104,000 | 29.8 billion | 7.5 billion | 3.7 billion | 2 | 7.5 billion | 75 trillion | 37 trillion | 7.5 billion |
| 17. | Foreign missionaries | 420,000 | 2.5 billion | 900 million | 307 million | 20 | 6.1 billion | 92 trillion | 31 trillion | 6.1 billion |
| 18. | Evangelists | 1,230,500 | 7.2 billion | 1.8 billion | 110.5 billion | 100 | 11.1 billion | 898 trillion | 55 trillion | 11.1 billion |
| 19. | Short-term missionaries/workers | 400,000 | 2.3 billion | 700 million | 146 million | 10 | 1.5 billion | 37 trillion | 7 trillion | 1.5 billion |
| 20. | Part-time evangelizers | 20 million | 116.8 billion | 29.2 billion | 5.8 billion | 2 | 11.7 billion | 292 trillion | 58 trillion | 11.7 billion |
| 21. | Mission agencies | 4,000 | 208 million | 62 million | 21 million | 100 | 2.1 billion | 31 trillion | 10 trillion | 2.1 billion |
| | **5. WRITTEN WORDS** (Scriptures) | *Copies p.a.* | *Pages p.a.* | *Witness-hours* | *Evangelism-hours* | *Media* | *Hearer-hours* | *Witness-words* | *Evangelism-words* | *Offers* |
| 22. | Portions/gospels (25 pages) | 323 million | 8.1 billion | 4 billion | 808 million | 6 | 4.8 billion | 121 trillion | 24 trillion | 4.8 billion |
| 23. | Near-gospels | 200 million | 5 billion | 3 billion | 480 million | 6 | 2.9 billion | 75 trillion | 14 trillion | 2.9 billion |
| 24. | New Testaments (300 pages) | 121 million | 36.3 billion | 18 billion | 3.6 billion | 8 | 29 billion | 726 trillion | 145 trillion | 29 billion |
| 25. | Near-NTs | 50 million | 15 billion | 8 billion | 1.4 billion | 8 | 10.8 billion | 300 trillion | 54 trillion | 10.8 billion |
| 26. | Bibles (1,300 pages) | 53.8 million | 69.9 billion | 35 billion | 7 billion | 10 | 69.9 billion | 1,749 trillion | 350 trillion | 69.9 billion |
| 27. | Near-Bibles | 10 million | 13 billion | 7 billion | 1.2 billion | 10 | 12 billion | 325 trillion | 60 trillion | 12 billion |
| 28. | 2nd-language gospels | 100 million | 2.5 billion | 1 billion | 200 million | 3 | 600 million | 19 trillion | 3 trillion | 600 million |
| 29. | 2nd-language NTs | 70 million | 21 billion | 11 billion | 1.4 billion | 4 | 5.6 billion | 210 trillion | 28 trillion | 5.6 billion |
| 30. | 2nd-language Bibles | 30 million | 39 billion | 20 billion | 3 billion | 5 | 15 billion | 488 trillion | 75 trillion | 15 billion |
| | **6. PRINTED WORDS** (literature) | *Pieces p.a.* | *Pages p.a.* | *Witness-hours* | *Evangelism-hours* | *Media* | *Hearer-hours* | *Witness-words* | *Evangelism-words* | *Offers* |
| 31. | Denominational materials | 2.5 billion | 20 billion | 5 billion | 1.9 billion | 1 | 1.9 billion | 25 trillion | 9 trillion | 1.9 billion |
| 32. | Local church output | 200 million | 10 billion | 7 billion | 3.8 billion | 1 | 3.8 billion | 35 trillion | 19 trillion | 3.8 billion |
| 33. | Outside Christian literature | 300 million | 100 billion | 30 billion | 10 billion | 10 | 100 billion | 1,500 trillion | 1 trillion | 100 billion |
| 34. | Church-planting output | 58,000 | 580 million | 170 million | 58 million | 10 | 600 million | 9 trillion | 3 trillion | 600 million |
| 35. | Institutional ministries/records | 481,000 | 17.6 billion | 5 billion | 1.8 billion | 1 | 1.8 billion | 26 trillion | 9 trillion | 1.8 billion |
| 36. | Christian books (100 pages) | 3.5 billion | 350 billion | 58 billion | 35 billion | 2 | 70 billion | 583 trillion | 350 trillion | 70 billion |
| 37. | Christian periodicals (30 pages) | 50 million | 1.5 billion | 500 million | 150 million | 10 | 1.5 billion | 25 trillion | 8 trillion | 1.5 billion |
| 38. | Tracts (2 pages) | 5 billion | 10 billion | 5 billion | 2.5 billion | 1 | 2.5 billion | 25 trillion | 13 trillion | 2.5 billion |
| 39. | Other documentation | 2.5 billion | 10 billion | 3.5 billion | 1.2 billion | 1 | 1.2 billion | 18 trillion | 6 trillion | 1.2 billion |
| | **7. ELECTRONIC WORDS** | *Items* | *Hours a day* | *Witness-hours* | *Evangelism-hours* | *Media* | *Hearer-hours* | *Witness-words* | *Evangelism-words* | *Offers* |
| 40. | Programmed training (TEE, &c) | 60 million | 1 million | 500,000 | 180,000 | 10,000 | 18 billion | 25 trillion | 90 trillion | 18 billion |
| 41. | Christian radio programs | 1,000 | 1 million | 600,000 | 1 million | 50,000 | 50 billion | 150 trillion | 250 trillion | 50 billion |
| 42. | Christian TV programs | 400 | 400,000 | 100,000 | 200,000 | 100,000 | 20 billion | 50 trillion | 100 trillion | 20 billion |
| 43. | Urban media (cable TV, &c) | 3,000 | 1 billion | 300,000 | 450,000 | 12,000 | 5.4 billion | 18 trillion | 27 trillion | 5.4 billion |
| 44. | Christian-owned computers | 332 million | 39.2 billion | 981 million | 98.1 billion | 350 | 34.3 billion | 1,717 trillion | 172 trillion | 34.3 billion |
| 45. | Internet/www/e-mail networks | 65 million | 19.5 billion | 5.9 billion | 2 billion | 30 | 58.5 billion | 878 trillion | 293 trillion | 58.5 billion |
| | **TOTAL HOURS, WORDS, AND OFFERS** | | | | | | | | | |
| | *7 types/modes of evangelizing words:* | *Ministries* | *Presence-hours* | *Witness-hours* | *Evangelism-hours* | *Media* | *Hearer-hours* | *Witness-words* | *Evangelism-words* | *Offers* |
| | Hidden words | 2 | 2,382 billion | 283 billion | 38 billion | 1.0 | 37.8 billion | 1,414 trillion | 189 trillion | 37.8 billion |
| | Visual words | 11 | 723 billion | 129 billion | 31 billion | 8.3 | 260.8 billion | 6,611 trillion | 1,304 trillion | 260.8 billion |
| | Personal words | 2 | 2,840 billion | 473 billion | 59 billion | 3.0 | 179.0 billion | 7,388 trillion | 895 trillion | 179.0 billion |
| | Proclaimed words | 6 | 159 billion | 40 billion | 10 billion | 3.9 | 39.9 billion | 1,424 trillion | 199 trillion | 39.9 billion |
| | Written words | 9 | 210 billion | 105 billion | 19 billion | 7.9 | 150.7 billion | 4,012 trillion | 754 trillion | 150.7 billion |
| | Printed words | 9 | 520 billion | 115 billion | 46 billion | 1.8 | 83.3 billion | 2,246 trillion | 416 trillion | 83.3 billion |
| | Electronic words | 6 | 60 billion | 7 billion | 2 billion | 90.8 | 186.2 billion | 2,837 trillion | 931 trillion | 186.2 billion |
| | **Grand totals per year** | 45 | 6,892 billion | 1,152 billion | 206 billion | 4.6 | 937.6 billion | 25,932 trillion | 4,688 trillion | 937.6 billion |
| | Grand totals per year per global inhabitant | | 1,138 | 190 | 34 | 4.6 | 155 | 4,282,727 | 774,225 | 155 |

the receiving end of evangelism, the effect of the 45 varieties of evangelism on the situation of a people, an ethnic group, a language community, a city, a country, or any other population. We therefore summarize the previous data to produce concrete answers to several questions: How many hours or minutes of evangelizing contact with Christianity, Christ, and the gospel has this population had? And, how many such hours does this population have each day, and how many per capita per year? To understand the method and its results, Table 22–7 (which is also reproduced in Global Diagram 32) provides each stage for each ministry.

### Quantifying hours received by those being evangelized (column 8)

Now comes a staggering increase in order of magnitude, a direct result of the media factor. We can illustrate it from the Argentina Crusade of November 13–17, 1991. For it, evangelist Billy Graham preached the gospel for some 10 hours—that is, he expended 10 of our 'evangelism-hours'. But for 5 nights his words were received by a radio/TV audience of 70 million each night throughout Latin America. So his 10 evangelism-hours instantly became 700 million 'hearer-hours'. It's like Jesus' miracle of Feeding the Five Thousand, with its instantaneous multiplication of the 7 loaves and 5 fishes. The evangelist's 10 evangelism-hours suddenly became, as far as his audience is concerned, 700 million evangelism-hours or hearer-hours or (using our agreed standard terminology) offers. We term this 70-million-fold multiplication the

'media factor'.

Admittedly, this is an unusually massive case. In Table 22–6, column 7 gives the much lower average media factor we use to compute column 8 for all such evangelism in general (=column 6 x column 7).

Of the 45 varieties of evangelism, all have a media factor of at least 1. One factor is as high as 100,000. Another 14 factors are each greater than 10. This is a major characteristic of contemporary evangelism. Properly understood and patiently surveyed and enumerated, this could be the missing key that helps the church to tackle and complete its gargantuan task of evangelizing a world of 6 billion people.

### Quantifying words disseminated (columns 9-10)

Words mean power and action. The city of Washington D.C. is known to produce every day 200 billion official words—spoken, written, telegraphed, faxed, e-mailed, broadcast, or published. That's 72 trillion words p.a. In the same way we can assess the huge effect of evangelization by measuring its output of words.

We return therefore to enumerating words, as a refinement of hours. This results in a somewhat different way of quantifying the amount of evangelism by counting the number of 'witness-words' (our blanket term for all person-words spoken by Christian disciples in both witness and evangelism) and 'evangelism-words'. These are words heard or received by the target individual or population and which then proceed to evangelize them. The totals depend partularly on the different communication modes em-

ployed. Table 22–6 lists the 7 varieties of words (modes of contact) and the 3 levels of evangelizing activity, and then tabulates the number of copies of the various media, number of standardized pages or broadcasts or showings involved, and the equivalent number of 'hearer-hours' (column 8) through which these words reach their targets.

### Quantifying offers made (column 11)

The final column of Table 22–6 refers to the related number of disciple-opportunities. This gives the number of persons who have had an offer of discipleship made to them. It is derived by dividing column 10 by the average number of words required for a disciple-opportunity, earlier defined as 5,000. (By definition, the numbers are identical in size to those in column 8). Continuing our brief illustration above: evangelist Billy Graham preaches for only 10 hours (10 evangelism-hours) in sermons using some 50,000 words, but the 70 million who hear him actually get 3.5 trillion evangelism-words. Altogether these offer his audiences some 700 million disciple-opportunities—700 million offers.

### e as a measure of extent of opportunity

A new variable, e, can now be introduced. The extent to which a people or population has received adequate disciple-opportunities can be easily enumerated by computing e=total all disciple-opportunities received per year, per capita. Allowance has to be made, of course, for uneven distribution and the probability that many persons in the population will have had not one but multiple opportunities. But it's a beginning in precise enumerating and accounting.

### Summary: 'human rights' must include the gospel

This table allows us to make some general observations.

As Christians we affirm the whole range of the human rights of every individual, every people, and every population on Earth. In a plentiful world, everyone has the right to a fair share of food, water, shelter, clothing, energy, electricity, health, literacy, literature, education, money, and also to their spiritual counterparts—salvation in Christ, the Good News, the gospel, scriptures, missions, literature, broadcasts, churches, evangelism, witness, witness-hours, witness-words, evangelism-hours, evangelism-words, disciple-opportunities. Everyone has the fundamental, inalienable, basic right to at least one chance to become a disciple—an absolute minimum of one definitive evangelism-hour and one disciple-opportunity, perhaps 10 times that number as an immediate practical target toward the eventual goal of a fair share, and then an ongoing right to the average global individual share of those 34 evangelism-hours and 155 disciple-opportunities a year per capita.

The basic problem is the same as with world hunger and starvation—the supply is vastly more than adequate but distribution is criminally inadequate. Current distribution of the benefits of Christianity, Christ, and the gospel is uneven, unfair, unplanned, chaotic, counterproductive. This subject will be examined in detail later in Part 25 "Macroevangelistics". Meanwhile, summary statistics of distribution of evangelism to Worlds A, B, and C are shown to the left of the globe in Global Diagram 32. The reader will notice an alarming imbalance. Over a billion Christians in World C get everything Christianity has to offer and 95% of all its tangible benefits; over a billion non-Christians in World A get nothing. Yet we as missionary-minded Christians continue to direct 84% of all our evangelizing activity at other Christians. Who will fight to change this?

### QUANTIFYING VARIETIES OF OUTREACH 20 YEARS AGO

We begin the quantifying of all 45 varieties of evangelism by examining how the churches have enumerated outreach, both in the past (the 1970s) and the present (the start of a new millennium).

It is well-known that the great majority of statistics collected by denominations and churches consist of data about the church's membership itself. However, the scientific study of the growth of the church, or the discipline of church growth studies, can tell us only about the size of the churches themselves, about their rates of growth or decline, and so on. They can tell us nothing about the outreach of this force for evangelism, beyond the very dubious assumption that the only significance in outreach is not in the outreach itself but in the results of that outreach in the form of concrete additions to church membership. That discipline does not utilize, nor analyze statistical data about the outreach of the church among outsiders in the non-Christian world. And this outreach is what evangelism and the Great Commission are all about.

That is a strange lacuna, given the fact that the statistics of many varieties of outreach have long been produced by the churches on a regular basis. A few examples selected from 8 countries or regions, and coming from the decade 1970-1979, will now be given, arranged alphabetically by geographical area.

1. *China (Taiwan) and TV viewers.* In this republic 20 years ago there were some 14,000 Lutherans in 6 denominations, a very small community under 0.1% of the total population in size. In 1977, their sponsored China Lutheran Hour began a 30-minute TV broadcast every Sunday afternoon, which reached 2 million people (12% of the population) regularly. This particular outreach therefore reached an audience about 140 times the size of the sponsoring churches.

2. *Guam and medical outpatients.* On this Pacific island in the 1970s there were 3 Roman Catholic medical centers. One of them alone treated 45,500 outpatients yearly; ignoring repeat visits, this was 45% of the entire population. Strictly speaking, this was not mainly 'outreach' because Guam was already 97% Christian (and 80% Roman Catholic), but this activity was outreach so far as non-Christians and unaffiliated Christians were concerned.

3. *India and campaign attenders.* Evangelistic campaigns in all parts of the world are among the best-documented so far as statistics of outreach are concerned. At the end of 1977, one Billy Graham crusade in Calcutta drew over 100,000 attenders, of whom audience research indicated 40% were Hindus.

4. *Israel, Italy and sailors.* Thirty years ago, the Scandinavian Seamen's Church in Israel had 2 centers, in the ports of Haifa and Ashdod, with about 100 active members out of 500 total Christian community. But each year these centers were visited by 6,000 seamen, an outreach of 60 times the active membership. In Genoa, another tiny body the Missione Norvegese per Marittimi received 10,000 visitors a year to its Seamen's Mission.

5. *Kenya and radio listeners.* The Lutheran Church in Kenya was in 1975 a very small denomination (7,000 adult members, 15,000 total Christian community) but its weekly broadcasts over the state's Voice of Kenya produced a regularly-listening population of over 200,000 in the Kisii and Luo languages. Many very small churches around the world likewise have long had large radio outreach of this order (30 listeners per adult church member).

6. *Korea and listener response.* At that period the Korean Lutheran Church also had only 1,100 members, but its Lutheran Hour broadcasts drew a listener response of over 400,000 pieces of mail at times. Also, over 450 South Koreans enrolled in its Bible correspondence courses.

7. *Middle East and correspondence course enrollments.* In Middle East and North African countries, Pentecostals in 1970 were very small in number. Nevertheless, their International Correspondence Institute (Assemblies of God, USA) at that time had 300,000 enrolled students for its Bible correspondence courses in this area. Of these students 70% were Muslims. A large number too were secondary-school pupils who professed making the decision to follow Christ.

8. *Switzerland and tract distribution.* The Swiss Pentecostal Mission 30 years ago was a small body with 3,172 adult members (in 1970) in 108 churches. In 1977 they reported distribution of 1,340,550 evangelistic tracts and 10,610 evangelistic cassettes (over 400 items per adult member). One result was 366 baptisms (a growth rate of 11.5% per year); but another was that 4,000 times as many persons received a tract setting out the Christian faith and its offer of salvation.

One could multiply such examples literally a thousandfold, because large numbers of small denominations across the world specialize in one or more significant types of outreach, and almost all keep some sort of statistical record.

From these examples in the 1970s we move to a comprehensive survey of all current types of evangelism at the start of the Third Millennium.

### QUANTIFYING 45 DIMENSIONS (MINISTRIES) OF EVANGELISM, AD 2000

With the foregoing assumptions, definitions, and methodology in mind, it is comparatively easy to review the entire spectrum of all activities related to evangelism. As a result we can reduce it to 45 major areas or components. These are the basic dimensions or building blocks of evangelism. These 45 distinct outreach ministries are types or varieties of evangelism. They have been listed in Table 22–3, and in Table 22–6. Here, we label them for shorthand purposes as 'Ministries'. These ministries will now be defined and elaborated on, and examples or illustrations of each with their statistics will be given.

As before, the 45 varieties are classified and arranged under the 7 major modes of evangelizing words. For each ministry below (shown in bold italic type and numbered 1–45), the first paragraph describes and defines that ministry and what it covers. Second and subsequent paragraphs then give one or more specific illustrations each of a current, contemporary ministry, with its relevant statistics. A final paragraph then gives this survey's estimate of the total number of evangelism-hours per annum that this variety of ministry—worldwide and for all Christian confessions—is generating in AD 2000, how the media role multiplies these into many more offers received by persons being targeted, and the number of persons it thus reaches. This is given as the last 3 lines of each ministry's description, in italics in this form:

*Evangelism-hours originated per year.* This is the actual number of hours put in by evangelizers of all Christian confessions, in each type of ministry each year: e.g. a part-time evangelist who preaches for one hour twice a week, each week throughout the year, thus originates 104 evangelism-hours per annum.

*Media factor.* This is a multiplying factor representing the audience benefitting from one hour of each variety of ministry. The factor is needed for use here whenever statistics of these end beneficiaries are not counted, compiled, collected, or available. The meaning of the factor is straightforward: e.g. the evangelist is heard each time by an average audience of 100 people, so media factor = 100.

*Total offers received per year.* The end product is this total, which is the number of person-hours that actually reach, or get through to, and so are received by people each year, being the product of the preceding 2 lines. Note carefully that 'received' says nothing about the recipients' acceptance or rejection of the message. Similarly, the evangelist's end-product is that, from his own 104 hours, people actually receive 10,400 evangelism-hours—which from here on are termed offers/disciple-opportunities—every year. Again, nothing is said or implied about either acceptance or rejection.

### HIDDEN WORDS

This first mode of evangelism has as its Mandate and imperative 'Receive!' This mode refers to evangelizing words not visible to the outside world, especially to words hidden in prayer, uttered in private to God through charismata received by Christians. These ministries are not subject to exact enumeration or the publishing of precise statistics except here and there. Basically the activities are private and hidden—but nonetheless very real. Here we label them Ministries Nos. 1 and 2.

**1. Intercession.** This first variety of outreach ministry is one that Christians exercise by praying for specific, named causes, situations, populations, and persons. In particular, we refer here to prayer—private or public, individual or corporate, occasional or regular, spontaneous or organized—directly related to evangelism. This means prayer primarily directed to the welfare of non-Christians and especially for unreached or unevangelized populations.

The major example of this ministry over the last 18 centuries has been the organized daily intercession that takes place in Christian monasteries, Catholic, Orthodox, Anglican, or Protestant. Today some 7,000 monasteries around the world (including ashrams, convents, abbeys, priories, prayer houses, 'gethsemanes', and a variety of modern counterparts), with 2 million full-time member intercessors, pray continuously—often round the clock, 24 hours a day—for the mission of Christ to the non-Christian world and for that world's conversion to Christ.

Evangelization 2000, based on the Vatican, reports that it is backed up by 4,000 contemplative communities (monasteries, convents, ashrams, abbeys, houses) which now intercede around the clock and around the world. Altogether, linked with this there are at present 36 distinct Protestant or Catholic global prayer networks for world evangelization, 10 million prayer groups, 20 million Christians in full-time prayer ministry, and some 100 million laypersons who have become daily intercessors. In addition to these cooperating networks there are a dozen more distinct and separate worldwide intercessory networks which each either operate alone or with only 2 or 3 other networks. Most of the 50 or so global networks join with the others and are responsible for numerous Protestant, Catholic, and Protestant/Catholic concerts of prayer and other intercession campaigns. In

1994 and subsequent years, Evangelicals organized a campaign 'Praying through the 10/40 Window', in which some 20 million Evangelicals undertook 6 months of daily intercession for the evangelizing of the 1.6 billion unevangelized persons in the main World A countries and peoples.

Surprisingly, many of the larger networks actually collect and publish annual statistics relevant to, if not directly enumerating, this hidden ministry. Thus Every Home for Christ International (formerly World Literature Crusade, or Every Home Crusade) enumerates its prayer materials sent out regularly to its committed intercessors. By 1991 EHC was distributing 2,640,449 prayer bulletins each year in 28 languages for its work in 169 countries. In the first half of 1994 this rate was remaining more or less constant with 1,109,895 bulletins printed in 29 languages. Totalling similar data from all other agencies, whether global networks or smaller entities, shows an annual distribution of evangelistic prayer materials of all kinds approximating 200 million pieces, roughly one for each intercessor.

The grand total of all such Christians is: 200 million daily intercessors. If, on average, each prays for the evangelizing of specific individuals and peoples, by name, for 15 minutes a day, this produces the following totals.

*Evangelism-hours originated per year: 18.3 billion.*
*Media factor: 1.*
*Total offers received per year: 18.3 billion.*

**2. Inner renewal/spirituality.** This phrase here is defined as that eventual state in which a formerly inactive, or moribund, or lethargic, or dormant, or latent church or denomination moves rapidly to being alive, vibrant, enthusiastic, active, and full of life. The lives of its members suddenly become full of meaning and purpose. The phrase also covers other major areas of Christian activity and impact such as spirituality, mysticism, spiritual gifts, charismata, and spiritual warfare.

Almost every part of historic global Christianity is being transformed now by one form of renewal or another. One of the most startling recent cases concerns Albania.

The Albanian Orthodox Church seemed moribund and beyond hope throughout the years of vicious Communist repression in Albania from 1945-1990. But during the Easter season in 1992 unprecedented numbers of Albanians flocked to Orthodox churches, partaking of communion and going to confession. Some 15,000 attended the Easter service in Tirana's Orthodox Church of the Assumption. The entire 3-hour service was broadcast nationwide on both television and radio. The present government has been highly cordial to the churches and a quite new renewal is taking place for Albanians both in the Orthodox church and in others (*Ecumenical Press Service*, 92.05.53). Why must renewal be expected to channel itself only in particular denominations? Renewal in one denomination seems always to be opposed by another; this is one of the more surprising, even bizarre, findings of this volume's global survey.

Many such renewals present in the churches today are described and illustrated in Global Diagram 12. The largest single example is the 20th Century Pentecostal/Charismatic/Neocharismatic Renewal in the Holy Spirit. By AD 2000 it numbered 524 million church members worldwide, and the day-to-day outreach of these members was resulting in growth of over 9 million new members each year.

A number of different measures of prayer and spirituality are used by the various denominations and agencies. The Assemblies of God USA in its annual statistics has a column 'Baptized in the Holy Spirit'; for 1993 this total was 1,078,859 worldwide per year.

In AD 2000 this Renewal's active adult church members numbered 375 million. If on average each member was spending an hour or so every week on his or her internal renewal—attending a prayer meeting for some evangelistic cause—then this would result in the following totals.

*Evangelism-hours originated per year: 19.5 billion.*
*Media factor: 1.*
*Total offers received per year: 19.5 billion.*

## VISUAL WORDS

This second mode of evangelism has as its Mandate and imperative 'Go!'. This mode refers to evangelizing words directly visible or audible to all non-Christians around, especially for nonliterates. They are visible signs preparing hearers for the gospel as Christians go, visit, help, show, live, suffer, even die. This covers Ministries Nos. 3 to 13.

**3. Christians' lifestyle.** The way real Christians live is itself a powerful form of evangelism, commending the gospel by its fruits visible for all to see.

There is a direct parallel here with Jesus' own ministry on Earth. People saw him, heard him, saw his deeds, his lifestyle. They were supremely impressed by 3 aspects in particular: (1) his personal quality of life—honesty, integrity, holiness, personality, concern for others; (2) his supernatural quality of life—divine nature, prophetic stance, intercession with God; and (3) the signs and wonders he demonstrated—healings, exorcisms, miracles. For Jesus, the verb *euangelizo* meant to spread good news with signs following.

In the present era Christian lifestyle can and often does exhibit similar features: (1) the personal quality of life (human qualities) of professed disciples can have vast influence; (2) supernatural features of the Christian community (divine qualities) cause widespread admiration—prayer, intercession, concern for the underprivileged; and (3) signs and wonders (*semeia kai terata* in the Gospels and Acts of the Apostles) have continued throughout the 20 centuries to the present day. Two striking examples out of a vast repertoire of cases can be briefly mentioned.

Firstly, visions of Jesus appearing to non-Christian individuals have become very numerous and have led to the conversion of large numbers of Muslims, Hindus and Buddhists.

Secondly, startling and unexplained phenomena have become common in many parts of the world. One such is fire walking in Zimbabwe, practiced as far as is known by only one Christian movement worldwide, the million-member African Apostolic Church of Johane Maranke (AACJM). Every 3 months or so, most Christian denominations in Zimbabwe—both mainline and African indigenous—hold traditional all-night religious vigils or festivals called in the Shona language, *mpungwe*. These feature night-long prayer and praise, repentance, continuous singing by youth choirs, spiritual preparation, eucharist, and communion. But only one body, the AACJM practices fire walking. A huge bonfire is lit and devotees in white robes walk unharmed through flames, burning logs, and red-hot embers. The practice goes back 68 years to the church's founder himself, Maranke. Today, every member of Zimbabwe's 915,000 Vapostori (Apostles) is expected to undertake this fire walk once in his lifetime. The church's hierarchy of prophets, however, each engage in this practice on multiple occasions. And throughout the night until dawn fervent youth choirs sing continuously.

Contemporary Christian life-style consists of myriads of phenomena of these kinds across the world. It is no wonder they engender vast varieties of evangelism and evangelistic ministries.

Christians demonstrating a genuinely Christ-like lifestyle today probably number at least 100 million. If this is evident to outsiders for half an hour a day, for each Christian, this results in the following totals.

*Evangelism-hours originated per year: 18.3 billion.*
*Media factor: 1.*
*Total offers received per year: 18.3 billion.*

**4. Audiovisual ministries.** Although this descriptive terminology is only a couple of centuries old, the whole vast range of Christian art (paintings, sculpture, tapestry, et alia) has amply fulfilled this ministry over the last 20 centuries. Luther was firmly of the opinion that artistic representation could aid the proclamation of the gospel. Likewise with many other reformers and missionaries. Orthodox art produced works whose content demonstrated not just God's creation but the New Creation in Christ. Four varieties of art, resulting in enormous global circulations, will now be illustrated.

(a) *Icons.* One special form of visual representation of Jesus and his gospel is the icon—stylized religious paintings, especially portraits of Jesus, God, the Trinity, and the saints, revered in liturgical worship in the Orthodox world. Icons have often been called 'windows on eternity', or a 'Bible for the laity', to quote pope Gregory the Great. In modern times, an icon of a recent martyred hero, Oscar Romero is shown here in Part 4. Counting every variety of reproduction (including nowadays the Internet) there must be well over 2 billion copies of icons circulating today. Illustrated here is the most famous Russian icon, Rublev's 'The Holy Trinity', based on Genesis 18:2-8.

(b) *Logos.* A logo or logotype is a graphic symbol or visual representation of an agency's purpose or property. It is a particularly Anglican or Protestant form, often with colophon (motto) attached. A fair number of logos of Christian agencies are illustrated in this volume (see Global Diagrams 6, 12, 13, 22, 28, 32, 34, 42, 61, 65, 67, and many other illustrations such as John Calvin's personal motto, shown in Part 2 "CosmoChronology" next to AD 1536). One of the best-known is that of Oxford University Press (founded in 1478, illustrated here). This contains a colophon from the Latin Vulgate encapsulating the raison d'etre of this venerable Bible press and global publisher: 'Dominus illuminatio mea'—in the long series of English Bibles 'The Lord is my Light' from Psalm 27:1. Or, in the Contemporary English Version, 'You, Lord, are the light that keeps me safe.' This one image with its direct testimony exists around the world in several billion copies today.

(c) *Stamps.* This project *WCE-WCT* reproduces a large number of official state postage stamps that have explicitly Christian themes or illustrations. The one illustrated here is from Italy in 1922: Christ giving his Great Commission. Such stamps with Christian representation circulate in many billions of copies each year.

DOMI MINA
NVS TIO
ILLV MEA

**BILLION-COPY IMAGES**. These images exist today in tens of billions of copies worldwide. *Top left.* **Orthodox**. 'The Holy Trinity' (1422) by monk Andrei Rublev is the most famous of Russian icons (or, 'windows on eternity'). *Top right.* **Anglican**. Logo of Oxford University Press (begun 1478): 'Dominus illuminatio mea' (Psalm 27:1), with 3 crowns of the Trinity. *Lower left.* **Catholic**. Postage stamp (Italy) showing Jesus giving his Great Commission. Many billions of postage stamps carry the story of Christ and the gospel. *Lower right.* **Protestant**. Sallman's 'Head of Christ' (1940), the world's most famous Protestant portrayal of Jesus.

(d) *Paintings.* Christian art of this sort has appeared throughout the 20 centuries of Christian history. The illustration shown here is of one remarkable ministry that centers on one individual Christian whose work has resulted in a billion images of Christ. In 1940 artist Warner Sallman (1892-1968) painted the *Head of Christ*. It has become one of the most endearing images of Jesus in both American and global Christianity. Perhaps this is because Sallman's version of Christ—an image found in other popular Sallman works such as the ones featuring Christ guiding the young helmsman, Christ knocking at heart's door, and Christ the good shepherd—has appeared in so many different media of devotional life: Bibles, Sunday-school literature, calendars, posters, church bulletins, clocks, lamps, wallet-sized photos, pins and stickers. Indeed, Sallman's *Head of Christ* has been reproduced over 500 million times. If Sallman's other images are included his total reaches one billion. What is the influence of such images on the massive audience familiar with them? (*The Christian century*, October 7, 1992:868-870). Sallman is an example of what this Encyclopedia means by a 'Great Commission Christian'. And as a first approximation, his one billion can be said to have given the world one billion 'offers' or 'disciple-opportunities'. In practice, of course, untold numbers of individual items of his reproductions will have each been seen by tens, hundreds, or even thousands of different persons, and for untold hours.

In addition to thousands of works of art illustrating the gospel, there is still another variety—architecture. In England, Canterbury Cathedral has since the Middle Ages depicted the entire Bible story in its stained glass windows (originally to evangelize a non-literate population). Today more tourists and others—over 4 million—visit it each year than the total inhabitants in 14th-century England.

Audiovisual ministries are therefore ministries which employ a large variety of materials reproducing audible or visible versions of the gospel. These include (1) cassette ministries, using standard small audio tapes; (2) the older gramophone records, sometimes powered by mains electricity or by batteries, but often simply by hand spinning of the disk; (3) flash cards, flannelgraphs, posters, photo series; (4) filmstrips usually of between 30 and 100 frames each.

An agency with a vast repertoire is Gospel Recordings (Pasadena, California). Since 1938 GR has been producing records (and lately cassettes, tapes, and disks) with short audio messages or sermons on. Cumulatively, these can be termed evangelistic gospel recordings. Their achievement is to have made these available in 4,679 different languages by 1996.

There are literally hundreds of other audiovisual ministries which should be included and enumerated under this heading. All that can be done at this point is to give a cautious, conservative, low-end estimate as follows, indicating the general order of magnitude of this variety of evangelism.

*Evangelism-hours originated per year: 3 billion.*
*Media factor: 25.*
*Total offers received per year: 76.0 billion.*

**5. Plays/concerts/operas/shows.** This variety of evangelism refers to a whole range of theatrical, cinematic, radio, and television epics or narratives or productions which can be described as clearly evangelistic—presenting Christianity, Christ, and the gospel. The range includes Christian theatre, plays, shows, opera, ballet, musicals, music performances, concerts, as well as films/movies of other Bible or Christian subjects in addition to the depiction of the life of Christ.

The most famous play is undoubtedly the Oberammergau Passion Play. Spared from the plague in 1633, the inhabitants of Oberammergau village in Bavaria vowed to reenact the passion of Christ every 10 years. This they did in 1634 and have subsequently done, since 1680 on the decennial year. Averaging a cast of 700 villagers, the play lasts 8 hours in its specially-built openair theatre. It has become a lucrative community enterprise. In 1970 there were nearly 100 performances before a total audience of 530,000; in 1990, 95 performances from May to September, seen by 460,000 visitors and generating US$5 million for this village of 5,000. The vivid portrayal of Christ's passion is, of course, powerful evangelism; it thus creates some 4 million evangelistic offers every tenth year.

Another typical initiative comes from Finland: the Tampere Theatre's production of the Gospel of Mark.

Possibly the most popular, acceptable, effective, and successful evangelistic presentation of all time has been Handel's oratorio 'Messiah', an artistic masterpiece written in 1741. Its 53 sections of biblical texts are a skillfully crafted statement of Christian doctrine describing the mighty drama of human redemption.

'Messiah' is the most performed major choral work in history, and most likely the single most performed musical work around the world today. It is also the perfect evangelistic tool—professional, popular, participatory, universally-acclaimed, yet all the time biblical, Bible-quoting, Christ-centered, eschatological. Although not deliberately evangelistic, its phenomenal success in Britain is linked with the Evangelical Revival in the Church of England, and with John Wesley's robust doctrine of assurance of salvation.

Its remarkable evangelistic effect is heightened by the absence of the name 'Jesus' (used once only, in section 51 from 1 Corinthians 15:57), and the cautious lowkey use of the name 'Christ'. An example from the formerly atheistic USSR will illustrate the resulting acceptability in a Muslim environment in Russia.

'Messiah's first performance in the Russian language and in Russia itself was held on February 17–18, 1992 in Kazan, Russia, the capital of Tatarstan, among the Kazan Tatars. 1992 was the 250th anniversary of Handel's masterpiece, which was first performed on April 13, 1742 in Dublin, Ireland. It was particularly fitting that the Tatars would be recipients of this message; they are 95% Muslims. The city of Kazan is 50% Muslim and 50% Christian (Russian Orthodox). A crossroads of East and West, it is known as the most Oriental city in Europe and the most European city in the Orient. The translation of the piece into Russian was initiated by two brothers in Seattle, Washington, USA and took over two years to finish. Extensive revisions were required to retain the artistic flavor of the work and remain true to the Russian Bible. A Seattle choir teamed up with the Tatarstan opera to perform the work.

Over the last 250 years, performances of 'Messiah' have taken place at least once a year, usually at Christmas, in almost every Christian city in Britain, America, Canada, Australia, and Ireland—some 3,000 metropolises. Annual performances in the 1990s take place in some 20,000 churches, cathedrals, choirs, clubs, societies, festivals, colleges, et alia, across largely the English-speaking world. Performances have average attendance of 200 persons each and vary in length from 4 hours to an average of 2 hours for abbreviated Christmas versions. Performers vary from 50 to over 5,000 at one time. Altogether these attract 4 million attenders in person every year, and so deliver 8 million evangelistic offers to their audiences.

A second variety of audiences today are those receiving broadcasts over radio or television, or persons listening privately to a multitude of recordings, tapes, or CDs. These are shorter on average, around 1 hour in length. With a worldwide audience of some 50 million each Christmas, 50 million evangelistic offers are produced. The grand total of all offers per year resulting from 'Messiah' is therefore around 58 million.

There are numerous other musical compositions based on the Gospel story. A widely-known one is Bach's 'Saint Matthew Passion' (1729), a Lutheran church musical setting based on chronological facts of the life of Christ.

Going beyond this huge worldwide English-language coverage, there is also a vast coverage of similar musical works composed and presented in French, German, Spanish, Italian, Portuguese, Russian, Polish, Ukrainian, Dutch, and a grand total of 50 other global languages of wider communication.

This category of evangelism also includes thousands of other artistic performances which, whether deliberately or not, do in fact clearly present Jesus Christ and his gospel. Among these are many narratives based on the Bible or church history that have been hugely successful as dramas, theatre plays, musicals, and radio plays ('The Man Born to be King' in 1945). Among the most-viewed movies have been: 'The Ten Commandments', 'The Robe', 'Quo Vadis', 'The Shoes of the Fisherman', and 'Here I Stand'. Altogether, this whole spectrum of works has resulted in the following totals.

*Evangelism-hours originated per year: 2.4 billion.*
*Media factor: 20.*
*Total offers received per year: 48.7 billion.*

**6. 'Jesus' Film shows.** More specifically, there has been a long history of movies portraying the life of Jesus. Here are brief details of 11 such.

1. 'Intolerance' (1916) had a portrayal of Jesus still ranked as one of the most successful ever.
2. 'The King of Kings' (1927), a lavish film in color directed by Cecil DeMille.
3. 'Ben Hur' (1959) included the Nativity, Sermon on the Mount, the Crucifixion.
4. 'King of Kings' (1961) was intended to appeal to younger audiences.
5. 'The Greatest Story Ever Told' (1965) had an all-star cast but was one of the least faithful to the Gospels.
6. 'The Gospel According to St Matthew' (1966) offered a realistic Palestine.
7. 'Godspell' (1973) was a musical of renown depicting Jesus as a clown in modern-day New York City.
8. 'Jesus Christ Superstar' (1973) was based on a rock opera and remains memorable for its musical score.
9. 'Jesus of Nazareth' (1977), directed by Franco Zeffirelli, was a blockbuster miniseries, the most faithful to the Gospels, and still widely watched.
10. 'The Last Temptation of Christ' (1988) was controversial depicting Jesus as consumed with self-doubt and sexual awareness.
11. 'Jesus', the classic spread worldwide by Campus Crusade for Christ.

The latter title represents a unique variety of evangelism. It refers to and covers a multi-language film or tape presentation of the life and ministry of Jesus in the Holy Land from BC 6 to AD 33. By showing visually and visibly the life of Jesus, it offers millions of viewers, in a vivid and unforgettable couple of hours, a visual account of his ministry in Palestine. Such a viewer usually gets a far clearer picture of Jesus, his words and deeds, than anyone present in the crowded scenes in the Galilee and Judea of AD 30–33.

This ministry, the Jesus Film Project, is organized around the professionally-produced movie 'Jesus', a 2 hours 5 minutes film which covers the entire Gospel of Luke. With brief introduction and epilogue, a showing lasts 2.5 hours. The visual film remains unchanged, but it is then produced with 400 different sound tracks translated into the world's 400 major languages. By mid-1999 'Jesus' had been viewed—in churches, schools, cinemas, halls, homes, open-air sites, theatres, and on television—by well over a billion viewers in 550 languages in 200 countries.

This ministry is unique in that 2 levels of media factors need to be considered. First, one operator/evangelist shows the film, and on average 70 persons see it; and second, the audience passes on its message to persons not attending. At the first level, the number of annual showings of this film in AD 2000 was over 3 million. On average each is attended by 70 people, making an annual audience of 219 million persons. At 2.5 hours per show, this results in 548 million evangelism-hours.

Among all the varieties of evangelism, this one perhaps makes the deepest impression on recipients. Far more than those who hear a proclaimed message, or read words of Scripture, or listen to a friend's witness, viewers of the 'Jesus' Film receive a vivid and indelible personal impression that turns them, in many cases, into lifelong personal witnesses themselves.

As a result a further expansion takes place at the second level as the attenders leave the showing and pass on to others what they have vividly seen and witnessed. Each urges yet others to see the film. And a fair number go so far as to purchase their own copy and show it to family and friends. Using our terminology, this results in a second 'media factor' of 100, this being the number of evangelism-hours received by outside beneficiaries for each hour received by the audience who have seen the show. This results in the following totals, which include the other varieties of Life of Christ films.

*Evangelism-hours originated per year: 548 million.*
*Media factor: 100.*
*Total offers received per year: 54.8 billion.*

**7. Audio scriptures.** Another variety that has blossomed in the 20th century hinges on recordings, records, disks, tapes, cassettes of the full texts of Christian Scriptures—gospels, New Testaments, Bibles—in several thousand languages. These can then be circulated, bought, sold, copied, reproduced, translated, and—a most important development—broadcast over radio, either at talking speed (for listeners to tape-record) or at dictation speed (for listeners to write down). All the evidence indicated that hundreds of thousands, and probably millions, of individuals across the world are engaged in precisely this activity.

By 1997, audio scriptures had been prepared and were widely circulating, through the United Bible Societies, Forum of Bible Agencies, Audio Scriptures International, and other specialist agencies, in some 4,600 languages.

In a major development in 1996, the 'Jesus' Film Project, which utilizes 8mm film, 16mm film, and video tapes, began distributing a parallel series of 'Story of Jesus' audio CDs and cassettes of the Gospel of Luke, in 241 languages, for use in broadcasting over radio stations and mainly for countries where videos are either prohibited or too expensive to circulate widely.

*Evangelism-hours originated per year: 18 million.*
*Media factor: 1,000.*
*Total offers received per year: 18.3 billion.*

**8. Scripture leaflets/selections.** Jesus sprinkled his Palestinian teachings with quotations from the Bible (the Septuagint Greek and Hebrew Old Testaments), varying in length from short texts to well-known narratives and exegesis of longer passages. A similar ministry is performed today through the widespread and continuous scattering, in every walk of life, of short Scripture texts and passages in leaflet form.

The UBS has formalized these with its category

'Selections', defined as 4- or 8-page booklets with a number of carefully selected Scripture passages. Often these are topical (family, children, health, government, etc), often related to the Christian year (Advent, Christmas, Lent, Easter), often doctrinal (person or work of Christ, nature of God, faith).

In 1991, the total UBS world distribution of selections was 520,534,736; in 1993, it was 515, 227, 962; in 1994, it was 481,510,705; in 1997 456,517,465. Scores of other agencies also publish large ranges and quantities of similar selections.

The grand total of all such annual productions is some 4.1 billion selections. Assuming each selection is read once in the year, by one person, averaging one hour's reading silently or aloud, the results are as follows.

*Evangelism-hours originated per year: 4.1 billion.*
*Media factor: 5.*
*Total offers received per year: 20.5 billion.*

**9. Every-home campaign visits.** In his itinerations Jesus frequently visited people's homes and there delivered major teaching, healing miracles, or other definitive ministry. House-to-house visiting has always been an important initial stage in evangelistic strategy. Massive programs of nationwide campaigns now make this a leading form of evangelism.

The first attempt by a mission organization to reach systematically every home in an entire nation took place from 1912-1917 in Japan. There the Oriental Missionary Society actually visited its 10,300,000 houses. So successful did they find it that it was then extended to other countries, and then finally to the world.

More recently, the major example is Every Home for Christ International. This organization was begun in Canada in 1946 as the World Literature Crusade (WLC) for radio outreach. It then expanded to systematic tract distribution through Every Home Crusades through (from the first EHC in 1953, to 1985) 1.42 billion printed gospel messages in 103 countries resulting in 14.5 million documented written responses for Christ, to (by 1991) 1.75 billion in 143 nations, to (by 1994) 1.78 billion with 19.1 million responses, and to (by 1996) 1,854,604,130 booklet distributions with 22,239,518 responses over the last 43 years. Since 1953 it has specialized in house-to-house visitation to entire populations of countries. By 1996 the total of all such visits had risen to 10,387,900 in the previous year.

A typical home visit involves 2 EHC workers who spend up to 30 minutes in the home evangelizing the household (whose average size is 5 persons). During this time the gospel is explained, for some 60 worker-minutes, and so one disciple-opportunity is given. Before leaving they present the family with two 8-page booklets in the family's own language or languages, one written for children and the other for adults. Thus this typical unit of visiting works out at 2 workers times 1/2 an hour = 1 evangelism-hour (one disciple-opportunity), plus 2 evangelism-hours for booklets, = 3 evangelism-hours, times 5 recipients in the household, = 15 evangelism-hours per visit. Further, a literate family person present is given 2 response vehicles to later return by mail: (1) any decision statements, and (2) any requests for more information. Those are returned by 10% who then get a followup home visit a few days later, plus Bible correspondence course (4-part scripture booklet). Those making decisions are then linked to local churches; or, if none exist, they are formed into EHC's special creations known as Christ Groups containing 50, 100, or even 1000 converts. Many such Groups then evolve into regular congregations or churches. A final stage in this process is reached when local, regional, and national media publicize the whole campaign. The additional media factor for this final stage may be assessed at 3.

Our basic home visit has thus grown from the single evangelism-hour originated by the 2 workers into: 15x1.1x3=49.5 evangelism-hours received by beneficiaries. Since EHC's annual total of home visits in the 1990s has been averaging 16 million, this totals 16 million evangelism-hours originated, which then become 792 million evangelistic offers received per year, with an overall media factor of 49.5.

In addition to EHC and other major parallel organizations there are thousands of small local church or parish visitation campaigns each year. EHC is therefore only the tip of the iceberg for such campaigns, estimated at only some 10% of the grand total. This yields the following totals for all such endeavors in this home-visitation variety of evangelism.

*Evangelism-hours originated per year: 160 million.*
*Media factor: 50.*
*Total offers received per year: 8.0 billion.*

**10. New Reader Scriptures.** Jesus was a literate himself, accustomed to public reading and exposition of the written Scriptures. He constantly drew attention to them and helped people grapple with them for themselves. He wrote or drew on the ground (John 8:6,8). He challenged skeptics: 'Have you never read in the Scriptures ...' (Matthew 21:42).

In 1967 the United Bible Societies inaugurated a new variety of scriptures, designed especially for the newly literate or potential literates, called NRS (New Reader Scriptures). They consisted of somewhat simplified translations of portions (single books of the Bible), or of selections (smaller collections of Bible passages). These can be analyzed separately.

(a) *New Reader Portions* (NRPs or, with statistics, nrp) usually consist each of one of the Gospels, together with line drawings or illustrations. A series of 5 graded booklets then leads the new reader to the point where he or she can move to the study of the standard New Testament in the language concerned. In 1991, the total UBS world distribution of NRPs was 20,350,609. In 1996 it was 18,928,916; in 1997 14,438,132. With average length at 30 pages offering 3 hours' reading time to readers, this provided during the decade of the 1990s an average of 61 million evangelism-hours a year.

(b) *New Reader Selections* (nrs, with statistics) are usually each arranged around a single topic, or local feature, or event, or date, or time in the Christian year. Easy to read, illustrated, attractively printed, they prove very popular. In 1991, UBS world distribution was 36,937,639 New Reader Selections. In 1996 this had fallen to 27,268,698; in 1997 it rose to 33,462,842. Offering less than 30 minutes' reading time, they provided during the 1990s an average of 15 million evangelism-hours a year. Grand annual totals for both UBS varieties of evangelism: 76 million evangelism-hours, producing 760 million offers.

*Evangelism-hours originated per year: 76 million.*
*Media factor: 10.*
*Total offers received per year: 760 million.*

**11. Braille scriptures.** Jesus illustrated his teachings and his ministry with a judicious smattering of 'signs and wonders'. One of the most dramatic was: restoring sight to blind persons.

In the year 1830, a teacher at a school for the blind named Louis Braille developed a raised dot system which became standard for the English-speaking world. In 1932, Standard English Braille was adopted in the USA.

Braille books are far bulkier than print counterparts. They cover at least 10 times more pages than normal printed books, and to read each page takes 10 times as long. So a Braille New Testament could take its reader 100 times as much time as normal, which thus gives its reader 10 times more disciple-opportunities per day as he or she puzzles over every page.

Nonsighted or totally blind persons worldwide number some 19.3 million in AD 2000. In addition another 30 million are legally blind. Of these 49 million blind, 10 million have access to a Braille scripture in their own language, which on average takes 200 hours to read, equivalent to 200 evangelism-hours. The world total thus amounts to around 2 billion evangelism-hours.

Far more significant numerically, however, is the impact of this 'sign' of Jesus' healing power on normally sighted persons who see what Braille can do for blind people they know. Here we may anticipate a media factor of at least 5—for every blind person's miracle of 'seeing' Jesus, at least a handful of 4 observers or onlookers will take note of Jesus' impact and thus will themselves receive a disciple-opportunity.

*Evangelism-hours originated per year: 2 billion.*
*Media factor: 5.*
*Total offers received per year: 10.0 billion.*

**12. Signed/deaf scriptures.** Jesus performed a second variety of miracle related to his evangelism: restoring hearing to deaf persons.

Sign languages were developed in Europe over 4 centuries ago. In Britain, schools for the deaf were begun in mid-19th century. There are many regional differences in national sign languages. Many in Europe and America have wide TV usage, which assists standardization. The world in AD 2000 contains 365 million deaf (hearing-impaired) persons, of whom 150 million are severely so, and 23 million are totally deaf. Of these about 15 per cent use or understand a sign language.

Parallel to the 'miracle' of a blind person 'seeing' Christ through Braille is the 'miracle' of a deaf person 'hearing' Christ through seeing signed scriptures—Bible passages presented in a sign language such as ASL (American Sign Language) or the quite different systems used in over 60 languages other than English. Of all deaf persons, about 30 million have access to signed scriptures in their own sign language, providing on average some 20 evangelism-hours per person each year. This 'miracle' of the deaf 'hearing' the gospel is then noted by a handful of on average 4 observers and onlookers and thus impacts some 5 times that number.

*Evangelism-hours originated per year: 600 million.*
*Media factor: 5.*
*Total offers received per year: 3.0 billion.*

**13. Christian suffering.** Jesus promised his disciples that theirs would not be a life of ease but a life of hardship, persecution, and suffering. Here are some modern illustrations of this. Of all Christians, 10% live persecuted by society or state, 13% live in absolute poverty, 25% have no access to medical care, 7% live on the verge of starvation, 14% had or have no education, 20% are without adequate shelter, 31% are handicapped (one fifth being children), and at any one time 38% are suffering from disease or sickness.

Jesus also taught his disciples to redeem suffering and use it for the glory of God. The lives of the 260 million Christians who suffer but who at the same time reflect Christ and his suffering are among the most powerful and influential of all modern 'signs' of the gospel. If each one's suffering is observed or noted or reported for an average of an hour each every year, this provides a vast number of examples which are also disciple-opportunities. Word of all this then disseminates widely via a media factor of at least 10—one person tells another and eventually the ripples spread outwards until 10 or so are aware of it.

The impact of this ministry of suffering, as with most other ministries, can be further enhanced if in addition mass media factors are applied, such as television with its media factor of 100,000 (see Tables 22–3 and 22–7, Ministry 42). Thus the sufferings of one Christian would normally (on this method of estimating) be measured as 1 evangelism-hour per year, producing 10 offers per year received by observers. But if now reported over TV for 5 minutes a day for 2 weeks (12 weekdays), these 10 offers would immediately expand to 10 times 100,000 = 1 million offers per year.

The 3 lines below employ only the original media factor without TV.

*Evangelism-hours originated per year: 260 million.*
*Media factor: 10.*
*Total offers received per year: 2.6 billion.*

**PERSONAL WORDS**

The third of the 7 modes of evangelism has as its Mandate and imperative 'Witness!'. This refers to evangelizing words at the grassroots—the day-to-day evangelism of ordinary Christians as they go about their work, home life, and social activities. These are words through which individual Christians witness about Christ personally to non-Christians by their presence in word and deed in unstructured situations, even get martyred. This results in Ministries Nos. 14 and 15.

**14. Personal evangelism.** Sometimes called 'personal work', this is the usually private endeavor of an active Christian to interest or enrol other persons for the faith, usually by means of one-on-one conversation. It is more than personal witness; it contains a presentation of the Good News and of Christ's invitation to accept him and become his disciple. This is one of the distinguishing marks of Great Commission Christians. They are carefully, and constantly, on the lookout in order to create situations for evangelizing and if possible discipling other individuals and groups.

Personal evangelism is regularly monitored in public-opinion polls. In a survey dated December 1982, the Gallup Organization asked a nation-wide representative random sample of Americans the carefully-phrased question: 'Have you ever tried to encourage someone to believe in Jesus Christ or to accept Him as his or her Savior?' Results: 51% of all Americans answered 'Yes', 41% 'No', and 8% 'No opinion/Don't know'. Among those defined by the Gallup Poll as 'spiritually committed' in 3 stages, the 'Yes' answers were 69%, 80%, and 83%.

Based on large quantities of similar data over the years up to the present, we have arrived at a global total in AD 2000 of 648 million Great Commission Christians—active, spiritually committed, averaging half an hour each day in some variety of evangelism. The methods of calculating this total of GCCs, and its division by countries, peoples, languages, denominations, and confessions, are described in Part 21"GeoPersonnel". Results for countries and peoples are shown in *WCE* Part 8 "EthnoSphere".

Personal evangelism is not the easiest of ministries. Some Christians of outgoing personality take to it naturally, 'moving from cooking to Christ in 5 minutes'. Other Christians of more reserved personality find it the hardest of ministries, especially speaking to complete strangers; they therefore work hardest on the other varieties of evangelism. On average, it is likely that 80% of all Great Commission Christians at least attempt it, spending from 5 minutes to 2 hours a day (averaging 15 minutes a day, or 91 hours a year) on personal evangelism. To this must be added a media factor of 3, since multiple persons are often addressed. Below we measure the resulting volume of personal evangelism that results.

*Evangelism-hours originated per year: 59.1 billion.*
*Media factor: 3*
*Total offers received per year: 177.4 billion.*

**15. Martyrdoms.** In his audiovisual presentation of the gospel Jesus often warned that a disciple's commitment to God's work could result in death. This has subsequently been the case throughout church history.

In the 20th century, martyrdoms have become widely known about and recognized as a result of regular and persistent reports in the media, year after year. In the light of 20 centuries of Christian history, it is safe to say that martyrdom has been the single most significant factor leading to the evangelization and christianization of a people or nation.

The grand total of all Christian martyrs since World War II has averaged 300,000 a year. This toll fell dramatically with the collapse of Communist regimes in Eastern Europe and the USSR during 1989–1992. Since 1995 martyrs have averaged 160,000 a year.

To measure a martyr's evangelistic impact, we can envisage him or her facing hostile forces and being in the public glare for some 10 hours or so before being killed. Up to the year 1900 'the public glare' probably averaged 100 persons. But today, with massive print, broadcast, and electronic media coverage, that average audience has increased by at least an order of magnitude (which means 10 times more). Each's martyrdom thus then becomes a 'sign' to 1,000 or so observers of this whole process and the witness to Christ it generated.

*Evangelism-hours originated per year: 1.6 million.*
*Media factor: 1,000.*
*Total offers received per year: 1.6 billion.*

## PROCLAIMED WORDS

This fourth of the 7 modes of evangelism has as its Mandate and imperative 'Proclaim!'. This refers to evangelizing words produced by those Christian professionals and agencies that engage in mission and outreach. These are words preached by professional workers proclaiming and expounding the gospel in structured situations. This covers Ministries Nos. 16 to 21. Specifically this centers on proclamation, the public announcement of the Good News. Such proclamation is initiated by these workers, and is regular to some degree, systematic, repeated, and thorough, utilizing whole varieties of proclamation.

In the Roman Catholic world, this is the major (and in practice the only) overall category enumerated worldwide in annual statistics. It is termed Apostolatus Copiae, officially translated into English as the Workforce for the Apostolate. It includes all pastoral workers, home missionaries, and foreign missionaries. This is fully described in Global Diagram 15.

**16. Full-time home church workers.** Full-time Christian workers are found virtually everywhere. In this analysis we divide them into home workers (dealt with here as No. 16) and foreign workers (No. 17).The term covers all employees of churches, denominations, agencies, and institutions. They may even be self-employed. The category usually covers ongoing employment lasting more than one year, usually long-term and excluding short-term workers (less than one year). The range of vocations covered is vast, from theologians, bishops, clergy at one end to administrators, accountants, secretaries, manual laborers at the other. But all may be considered as part of the church's proclamation of the Christian faith, either by word of mouth, or by writing, or (equally important) by unspoken words reflected in their service and their quality of life.

In the year 1900, full-time home workers numbered some 2,170,000, made up of 434,000 home missionaries and 1,736,000 home pastoral clergy and workers not primarily engaged in outreach.

In the year 2000, full-time Christian home workers, of all confessions, were estimated at 5,100,000 worldwide (see detailed analysis in Global Diagram 11). As one illustration, 120,000 Indians today serve in India as full-time Christian workers; 30,000 of these are home missionaries (mostly cross-cultural), including 3,000 Indian Jesuits. A third of all these personnel are charismatics. If one credits each with an average of 2 hours a day for any of the multitudinous varieties of evangelism, especially pastoral evangelism and public preaching and proclamation, this amounts to 730 evangelizing-hours a year per person. This results in the following totals.

*Evangelism-hours originated per year: 3.7 billion.*
*Media factor: 2.*
*Total offers received per year: 7.5 billion.*

**17. Foreign missionaries.** A foreign missionary is defined here as a full-time Christian worker of any age, race, or occupation, who works in a country in which he or she is not a citizen (or national) but is a foreigner (or alien). In most cases, though not all, he or she works with people of quite different culture, thus meriting the descriptive term 'cross-cultural missionary'. Let us examine the situation in two quite different countries, India and Ireland.

The Catholic Church in India at present sends over 2,000 Indian-citizen men and women as foreign missionaries to other countries; it has 3 Indian missionary institutes or societies (Society of the Missionaries of St Francis Xavier, Indian Missionary Society, and the Heralds of Good News). Adding Protestants, India now sends abroad as foreign missionaries a total of 4,500 of its citizens, serving in 80 countries. And, again, around a third of all these personnel are charismatics.

According to a recent survey by the Irish Missionary Union, there are 4,498 Roman Catholic missionaries working at present in 88 developing countries. This number is 9.39% lower than 1986 and 14.2% lower than 1981. (There are 186 missionaries from other Christian churches in Ireland). 73% of the sisters are in Africa. Of the priests, 786 are in South Africa (though 112 are retired), 480 in Nigeria, 447 in Kenya, 233 in the Philippines, and 195 in Brazil.

The estimated total for AD 2000 of Christian foreign missionaries of all confessions was 420,000. At 730 evangelism-hours per year per missionary, total evangelism originated was 307 million evangelism-hours. With a media factor of 20, this gives the totals that follow.

*Evangelism-hours originated per year: 307 million.*
*Media factor: 20.*
*Total offers received per year: 6.1 billion.*

**18. Evangelists.** Evangelists may be defined here as part-time or full-time Christian workers who specialize in the public or private proclamation of the gospel, structured or unstructured. This can take place through small groups, house meetings, church services, open air meetings, public rallies, broadcasts, up to large highly-publicized evangelistic campaigns over several days.

Terminology varies considerably from one Christian tradition to another. Episcopal churches often term such workers 'catechists', remembering that the biblical verb 'catechize' translates several New Testament Greek synonyms of the verb *euangelizo*. The 2 titles, evangelist and catechist, are thus almost interchangeable and their ministries can be considered together as is done in Table 22–6.

For the Catholic Church, catechists are a missionary function in non-Christian or mission-receiving countries and so are not enumerated nor present in Europe and North America. Exact statistics of Catholic catechists are published each year by the Congregation for the Evangelization of Peoples. The total has risen rapidly from 45,000 in 1970, to 190,000 in 1977, to 370,000 in 1985, to 430,000 in 1992, and to 500,000 by AD 2000. Of these, some 13% are full-time professional missionary catechists; 87% are part-time or volunteer (occasional) catechists. Table 22–6 combines these workers with their Anglican, Protestant, Orthodox, and Independent counterparts.

For the purposes of this survey, therefore, we classify evangelists and catechists by 7 levels of the size of their operations, as follows:

1. *Nonprofessional, part-time evangelists* form the vast bulk of the category, numbering some 700,000 in AD 2000. Many denominations in developing countries employ a rank or category called 'evangelists'. Often no salaries are paid, so evangelists have to work part-time. Average time spent on direct evangelism may be set at around a quarter of an hour each day.

2. *Part-time catechists* number some 460,000 in AD 2000, located mainly in Asia and in Sub-Saharan Africa. Their contribution to evangelization is creating 230 million evangelistic offers each year.

3. *Full-time professional evangelists* have mushroomed since 1950. Usually each has started an independent evangelistic association bearing his (or, very occasionally, her) name, in order to regularize salaries and support. Total in AD 2000: 10,000 evangelists, who personally put in an average of one hour 24 minutes a day on direct evangelism.

4. *Full-time professional missionary catechists* number 60,000 in AD 2000. Often they have graduated from seminaries, Bible schools, or other training establishments. Their labors produce some 1,200 million evangelistic offers a year.

5. *Macroevangelists* is the term that best fits those whose evangelistic organizations have grown large enough to support teams of associate evangelists undertaking multiple campaigns, crusades and macrocrusades. There are at least 500 such macroevangelists, defined here as all those who regularly preach live to crowds of over 1,000 at a time (including radio/TV listeners/viewers). Each's evangelism results in the evangelist personally preaching or talking for an average of around 3 hours a day.

The two charismatic evangelists Charles and Frances Hunter had a vision on March 31, 1990 to 'Take a census of the world.' They felt they were told, 'Honduras will be the first nation on earth where the gospel will be preached to every creature.' In January 1991, in cooperation with most of the Evangelical churches in Honduras they went door-to-door taking a census as well as offering a simple explanation of salvation. Over 1 million new converts (in a country of 5.3 million) are claimed; census results are still being analyzed. Next in line are Costa Rica, Nicaragua, Guatemala, and parts of the United States.

6. *Mega-evangelists* are defined here as those evangelists who from time to time actually preach live to

**Table 22–7. Seven varieties of evangelists and catechists with each's annual contribution to evangelism, AD 2000.**

| Category | Number | Hours p.a. | Evangelism-hours inputted | Media factor | Offers p.a. |
|---|---|---|---|---|---|
| 1. Part-timers: a. evangelists | 700,000 | 100 | 70 million | 10 | 700 million |
| 2. Part-timers: b. catechists | 460,000 | 50 | 23 million | 10 | 230 million |
| 3. Full-timers: a. evangelists | 10,000 | 500 | 5 million | 100 | 500 million |
| 4. Full-timers: b. catechists | 60,000 | 200 | 12 million | 100 | 1,200 million |
| 5. Macroevangelists | 500 | 1,000 | 500,000 | 1000 | 500 million |
| 6. Mega-evangelists | 30 | 200 | 6,000 | 1 million | 6,000 million |
| 7. Global evangelists | 2 | 50 | 100 | 20 million | 2,000 million |
| Overall | 1,230,532 | 90 | 110,506,100 | 100 | 11,130 million |

crowds of over one million (including both face-to-face and over radio/TV). Some 30 well-known evangelists in a variety of cultures across the world are in this category in AD 2000.

German mega-evangelist Reinhard Bonnke recently preached to 1.67 million people who attended 6 evening meetings in Kaduna, Nigeria with 500,000 people at the culminating Saturday meeting held in Muhamed Murtala Square. Note the numerics in the case of this final meeting: an evangelist preaches over a 2-hour period, inputting 2 evangelism-hours; a sophisticated media system transmits his sermon live to 500,000 face-to-face hearers (a 'media factor' of 500,000); who thus receive one million evangelism-hours. During this week response also was measured. More than 200,000 decision cards were signed by Kaduna citizens declaring that they had received Jesus as Savior. The cards were then distributed for follow-up to pastors of 255 local churches who sponsored the meetings. In other words, 12% of all attenders made decisions during that week. By 1996 Bonnke had preached face-to-face to 28,545,000 persons, of whom 6,053,190 registered decisions for Christ.

7. *Global evangelists*: this term is reserved here for any evangelist who in practice has addressed, and still can address, the entire globe at once, or who reaches live an audience of approaching one billion hearers at once (mostly via radio/TV). In AD 2000 only 2 such persons were attaining this. The first is Billy Graham, who preached face-to-face to 180 millions from 1940–1995, and over radio/TV to over a billion during Global Mission 1995. The second is John Paul II who, though not a professional evangelist, fulfilled this function from 1978–1995 by regularly expounding Christianity, Christ, and the gospel to multimillion-hearer audiences. Naturally these two only attempt to do this after exceptionally careful preparation each time and for a relatively small number of hours (50) each year.

The climax of global evangelist Graham's ministry was reached with his 1995 GMBG (Global Mission with Billy Graham). For the 3 days March 16-18, he preached for a total of only 6 hours in Hiram Bithorn Stadium in San Juan, Puerto Rico, but was heard face-to-face by 100,000 people and simultaneously via satellite by up to one billion people at thousands of sites worldwide in 170 countries using 80 languages and 450,000 local Global Mission-trained counselors. Naturally the actual numbers listening varied considerably from one minute to the next as huge numbers tuned in late or exited early, or malfunctions occurred. But for those 6 hours our 'media factor' would certainly for the first time in history have reached 20 million meaning that the total audience would have approached or even passed 1 billion (1,000 million) for a few minutes here and there.

These numbers can be compared and systematized as shown in Table 22–7.

In AD 2000, therefore, the total number of evangelists worldwide is estimated at some 710,000, and catechists at 520,000. Assessing them as spending a daily average of a quarter of an hour on their profession, Table 22–7 yields the following totals.

*Evangelism-hours originated per year: 110.5 million.*
*Media factor: 100.*
*Total offers received per year: 11.1 billion.*

**19. Short-term missionaries.** Short-term Christian workers are usually defined as those who work full-time, or in full-time church or other Christian jobs, for a period of over one month but less than one year in length, and (for short-term missionaries) who work abroad.

This variety of workers has grown prominent since the 1960s. The total of short-term Christian workers serving abroad in the year 2000 and after is estimated at 400,000 at any one time. Applying the average of one hour a day on evangelism, this yields the following totals.

*Evangelism-hours originated per year: 146 million.*
*Media factor: 10.*
*Total offers received per year: 1.5 billion.*

**20. Part-time evangelizers.** This category is defined here as persons who have secular employment but who nevertheless put in a substantial amount of work each week as part-time or volunteer Christian workers, specializing in the spreading of the gospel. This includes Methodist lay preachers, Anglican lay readers, Catholic parish assistants (when not full-time), parish visitors, and a whole variety of roles in almost all denominations. Many are fully organized, as is the Catholic Mission League, a lay missionary association in India with 750,000 members—the largest lay mission association in Asia.

Another most important variety of part-time evangelizers are the world's 250,000 'tentmakers'. A tentmaking ministry usually refers to a self-supporting ministry in which a Christian worker or missionary or minister earns his or her livelihood in some secular occupation. Tentmakers properly so called are defined here as Christians in secular employment in non-Christian, anti-Christian, closed, hostile or otherwise unfriendly countries in Worlds A or B where full-time Christian workers or foreign missionaries are not permitted to operate. Such tentmakers, named after the secular profession practiced by the Apostle Paul and his friends Aquila and Priscilla (Acts 18:2–3), are nowadays widely recognized and served by mission agencies and such events as conferences in 1991, 1992, and 1994, leading up the 2nd International Congress of Tentmakers International Exchange (TIE), held near London, UK in April 1996.

Our estimate here is that this category of part-time evangelizers embraces some 20 million part-time workers engaged in one or other form of evangelism, for a global average of 48 minutes a day.

*Evangelism-hours originated per year: 5.8 billion.*
*Media factor: 2.*
*Total offers received per year: 11.7 billion.*

**21. Mission agencies.** These are agencies which exist to implement Christ's world mission. They undertake foreign missions and outreach and other cross-cultural missions activity. They are organizations engaging full-time in this fourth mode of evangelism. In this Encyclopedia they are termed Great Commission agencies, and they are estimated to number some 4,000.

In addition to the hours of proclamation put in by their employees (already enumerated in Ministries 16–19), agencies produce magazines, news services, audiovisual materials, videos, broadcasts, et alia. On average this can be enumerated as likely to approach 100 hours a week related to evangelism, per agency. This produces a grand total of 20.8 million evangelism-hours a year. And with virtually every such agency nowadays utilizing computers, e-mail, mass-mailing lists, multi-faxing, the Internet and other global networks, virtually every activity has far larger end impact than is immediately apparent. For purposes of analysis, here we divide agencies' activities into 2 distinct categories: non-computer-related, and computer-related. For the first kind, a media factor of at least 100 seems typical, and so is used here to enumerate Ministry No. 21. For the second kind, computerized activities are enumerated later under Ministries Nos. 44 and 45.

Individual agencies often influence vast numbers of non-Christians each. Thus the founder of Operation Mobilisation, George Verwer, states that in India OM has given the gospel to 250–300 million people in the last 30 years. Every Home Crusade is on their third coverage of all the homes in India. Trans World Radio has had remarkable success in beaming the gospel to remote villages. Likewise with 1,750 other agencies. All this evidence indicates that India is becoming rapidly evangelized though lack of response means unreached peoples remain widespread.

An important recent development involving mission agencies is the rise and spread of strategic evangelism partnerships (SEPs) since 1985. These are small fellowships linking, for example, all missionaries, pastors and other workers from every denomination and agency targeting an unreached or unevangelized non-Christian ethnolinguistic people or population. Once trust and fellowship begin among the several workers, entirely new strengths are discovered.

The totals produced by all such ministries are estimated as follows.

*Evangelism-hours originated per year: 21 million.*
*Media factor: 100.*
*Total offers received per year: 2.1 billion.*

## WRITTEN WORDS (scriptures)

This fifth of the 7 modes of evangelism has as its Mandate and imperative 'Disciple!' This refers to evangelizing words produced by, because directly from, the written Word of God, which is the Bible, the Christian Scriptures. The reference is to the way in which the formal, definitive written words of Holy Scripture in 3,500 languages press and persuade listeners and offer them disciple-opportunities. This covers Ministries Nos. 22–30. 'Script' means 'handwriting; written words, letters, or figures', and 'Scripture' means 'anything written, sacred writings, the Old and New Testaments' (*Webster's New World dictionary*). Scriptural texts and passages have always been recognized as having enormous evangelizing power. Jesus himself in his Palestinian ministry constantly quoted the Hebrew and Greek Scriptures, saying 'It is written . . . ', or 'Have you not read . . .'

A more exact and fuller description of this variety of evangelizing words would be 'Spoken and written words of Scripture'. This is because the major way in which Scripture has been communicated down the centuries has been orally—the oral use of Scripture, the reading of texts or passages aloud, the public reading of the Bible, the spoken quoting of it in witness and conversation. Oral Scripture practice thus covers a whole vast area of evangelism and Scripture use, Bible reading, Bible memorization, Bible advertising, Bible quotation, Bible exposition, Bible scholarship, Bible translation, Bible circulation, Bible application.

To this must be added the whole ministry of writing out Scripture verses by hand, especially in person-to-person correspondence, authoring manuscripts, journalism, and even in Bible translation.

To bring more precision to this analysis, we define the term 'scripture' (with small 's') to mean one actual printed (or occasionally handwritten) copy (Bible, NT, gospel, selection) circulated as the result of mass distribution.

The simplest way of measuring this whole impact of the Scriptures is to enumerate the total numbers of new copies of scriptures circulating each year, whether free, subsidized, or commercial. The annual distribution of scriptures in 2,500 languages across the world, and everything flowing from it, is clearly a major ongoing form of evangelism. First, in Ministries Nos. 22–30 we enumerate the 9 basic varieties of scriptures. Second, we assume that the average reader is likely to read, read silently, read aloud, or hear read aloud by others, some 8 scripture pages (5,000 words) in each hour. Third, we then estimate that each such section of 8 printed pages, after being distributed, is by itself likely in its lifetime to give someone one disciple-opportunity, which means it is likely to generate at least one evangelism-hour. In other words, one hour's reading, whether silently or aloud, will cover, read aloud, or hear read aloud, 8 pages and will generate for its reader one evangelism-hour.

These basic assumptions therefore suggest that, for example, the production and circulation of one copy of a printed 300-page New Testament will on average generate some 37 disciple-opportunities in the course of its 20-year lifetime. It's a very reasonable, if very conservative, assumption. This way of assessing the impact of one single distributed scripture is derived by making the assumption that every copy of scripture fulfils the primary purpose in its production and distribution by being read, in full, *once*.

The number of words in the complete English Bible (AV/KJV) is 810, 697, with 800,000 as the average for all English versions (and also in most other languages). For comparison the Hebrew Old Testament (Masoretic Text) has 424,027 words. We can therefore standardize the size of 'typical' scriptures as follows: a Bible in any language contains 1,300 pages, a New Testament 300 pages (190,000 words), a gospel 25 pages (15,000 words). Times to read straight through once at 5,000 words an hour are therefore: Bible 160 hours, NT 38 hours, gospel 3 hours.

We now first make the very conservative assumption that one Bible, once distributed, evangelizes a reader by being read through once, taking 160 hours. On this analysis, a single copy of the Bible thus directly produces, in its lifetime, 160 evangelism-hours. That this is a reasonable, as well as very conservative, assumption is proved by the fact of the market's demand—the huge annual distribution of scriptures continues year after year because billions of people want them and millions of workers supplying them are satisfied that all these copies are adequately fulfilling their purpose.

Now comes a further stage. The evangelistic impact of one copy of the Bible is often far greater than this one reader or once-through reading. Taking into account the vast media use of the Bible, it is reasonable to posit here a media factor of 5, as is shown in

Ministry No. 26 below. This means that one copy of a Bible can be expected to result in, during its lifetime, 160 x 5 = 800 offers (disciple-opportunities).

The same argument applies to distribution of New Testaments (150 offers per copy), gospels (6 offers per copy), and selections. All of these will now be enumerated separately in Ministries Nos. 22–30.

*Indirect-access or secondary-access scriptures*
Faced today with some 7,000 distinct languages with no Scripture translations yet done, translators have long recognized that a people's right of access to the Scriptures may be partially or even adequately met, temporarily or even permanently, if translations exist in either of 2 forms.

The first is (a) *near-scriptures*, which are defined as scriptures in any closely-related language, itself defined here as one within the same language cluster as presented in *WCE* Part 9 "Linguametrics"; the 3 varieties of near-scriptures are here enumerated under Ministries Nos. 23, 25, and 27.

The second form is (b) *second-language scriptures*, which are defined as scriptures in any second language in wide use among the people, especially a trade language, a lingua franca, even a national language provided it is known to most of this people's population.

Using these criteria, the number of peoples with access to Scripture rises dramatically. This may be shown in the form of separate statements, as follows:

(a) Number of languages with complete Bible in them: 400;

(b) Number of languages with only a near-Bible (complete Bible in related language within each's cluster): 1,940.

It will be seen from the table that second-language scripture distribution markedly increases worldwide evangelistic coverage and impact. In fact, it provides as much coverage as distribution in mother tongues does. This duplication means that the same copies of scriptures which are made available to mother tongue speakers, thereby offering them disciple-opportunities, are also made available to secondary speakers. In effect, this is another kind of media factor, a doubling of effectiveness through the medium of publication and distribution.

**22. Portions/gospels (25 pages).** A portion is a single book of the Bible published separately as a booklet by itself. Portions most frequently appearing vary in length from 40 pages long (the Gospel of Luke) to only a page or two (Philemon, 2 John, Jude). Most, however, are gospels. Average length is 25 pages.

Annual distribution of these single books by the UBS in 1991was 31,091,070 scripture portions, plus 20,350,609 NRPs (New Reader Portions). The latter were earlier included here under variety No. 10 to measure their visual impact. They are included again here to measure their contribution to serious Bible reading.

The major distributors of these portions are the world's 180 Bible societies and agencies. However, thousands of other organizations, especially local churches, engage in scripture distribution. These other agencies in 1995 produced some 70 million between them, making a total annual production of scripture portions worldwide of 120 million. By the year 2000, annual distribution from all sources had reached 323 million. At 25 pages per portion, and a reading speed of 10 pages an hour, this results in a grand total of 808 million evangelism-hours per annum.

*Evangelism-hours originated per year: 808 million.*
*Media factor: 6.*
*Total offers received per year: 4.8 billion.*

**23. Near-gospels.** For a language into which no Scripture has yet been translated, a 'near-gospel' is a copy of a gospel in a closely-related language within the same language cluster as shown in *WCE* Part 9 "LinguaMetrics". In the judgment of translators and suppliers of the Scriptures, such as national Bible societies, peoples benefitting from the presence of such near-gospels may be reckoned to be adequately supplied and not in the highest priority of need for a translation in their own mother tongue.

*Evangelism-hours originated per year: 480 million.*
*Media factor: 6.*
*Total offers received per year: 2.9 billion.*

**24. New Testaments (300 pages).** Translation and publication of the New Testament in a new language is not simply a temporary resting-point on the journey to production of the whole Bible. For many agencies, especially the Summer Institute of Linguistics (SIL, also termed Wycliffe Bible Translators, WBT), the NT alone is the sensible end goal for its own workers to aim at. Having completed the NT, WBT's translators then move on to other languages which as yet have nothing at all translated. They leave local translators supported by local churches to continue to translate by moving on to the Old Testament.

In 1994, total New Testaments distributed by all agencies—free, or subsidized, or commercial—amounted to 89,793,000. By AD 2000 this had risen to 121 million a year.

*Evangelism-hours originated per year: 3.6 billion.*
*Media factor: 8.*
*Total offers received per year: 29 billion.*

**25. Near-New Testaments.** This term relates to languages in which no Scripture has yet been translated. A 'near-NT' is a copy in a closely-related language within the same language cluster (see "Linguametrics"). In view of the limited translation resources in national Bible societies, peoples may have to be satisfied with such an NT even though they may prefer or want their own translation.

*Evangelism-hours originated per year: 1.4 billion.*
*Media factor: 8.*
*Total offers received per year: 10.8 billion.*

**26. Bibles (1,300 pages).** Translation and publication of the whole Bible is so complex a process that such translation has been achieved, so far, in only 400 languages—barely 3% of the world's total.

The majority of translations of the Bible taking place are done under the auspices of the United Bible Societies with its 180 Bible societies and agencies. In addition, scores of other organizations from the Gideons (free placements of copies) to commercial publishers record their annual sales. For 1994 the total distribution from all sources was 58,686,000; by AD 2000, 54 million a year.

*Evangelism-hours originated per year: 7 billion.*
*Media factor: 10.*
*Total offers received per year: 69.9 billion.*

**27. Near-Bibles.** Among a people with a mother tongue into which at present no scriptures have been translated or produced, a 'near-Bible' is a translation of the complete Bible into a closely-related language within the same language cluster (see "LinguaMetrics"). This may not be entirely satisfactory to the people concerned but since same-cluster languages share over 80% of common vocabulary, it is certainly better than nothing.

*Evangelism-hours originated per year: 1.2 billion.*
*Media factor: 10.*
*Total offers received per year: 12 billion.*

**28. Second-language gospels.** This category refers to any people who have a published gospel available in a language distant or different from their mother tongue and which is understood by over 50% of that people's population. Usually this is a language of wider communication (international language, lingua franca, trade language, market language, church language), but sometimes it is simply a neighboring or geographically nearby language.

Examples are legion. In Tanzania the government has long attempted to suppress Bible publication in vernaculars, in order to enforce total concentration of meagre church resources on scriptures in the national and official language, Swahili. The whole Swahili Bible has been available since 1891, and 90% of the population of almost all tribes speak Swahili as second language. In view of the overwhelming advantages that such a language has over vernaculars in most countries, the best assessment of its ministry contribution is to reckon that the entire Christian population of a people have 1 evangelistic offer per capita per year as a result of Swahili gospels being in circulation and known to be in circulation.

*Evangelism-hours originated per year: 200 million.*
*Media factor: 3.*
*Total offers received per hour: 600 million.*

**29. Second-language New Testaments.** The category refers to a people with a New Testament available in a language of wider communication understood by over 50% of that people's population. Its ministry contribution may be assessed at 2 offers originated per year per Christian in the people concerned.

*Evangelism-hours originated per year: 1.4 billion.*
*Media factor: 4*
*Total offers received per year: 5.6 billion.*

**30. Second-language Bibles.** This ministry of evangelism is particularly powerful in that national and international languages multiply its influence far more than is usually understood. It refers here to a people with a complete Bible available and circulating in a language of wider communication understood by over 50% of that people's population. Again, national languages and other lingua francas have enormous multiplication and resulting influence. The present assessment is that this ministry contribution to evangelism is an additional 5 offers per year per Christian, as a result of being in circulation and being known to be in circulation.

*Evangelism-hours originated per year: 3.0 billion.*
*Media factor: 5*
*Total offers received per year: 15 billion.*

## PRINTED WORDS (literature)

The sixth of the 7 modes of evangelism has as its Mandate and imperative 'Baptize!'. This refers to evangelizing words other than Scripture produced and circulated in printed form in order to implement a whole further range of ministries based on Christian literature. The Mandate 'Baptize!' encompasses the church's duty to engage in pastoral evangelism, to initiate new believers, to catechize new converts, to plant churches, to train, worship, minister, multiply. That Christians are obeying this Mandate is evident from the current global total of newly baptized persons per year: 40 million. This results in an enormous volume of documentation. Baptism, church-planting, and pastoral life are surrounded daily by millions of printed Christian words. In all of these the vast expansion of printed literature plays a central role. They are enumerated here under 9 main varieties of evangelism, here termed Ministries Nos. 31–39.

**31. Denominational materials.** There are at present some 33,800 denominations in the world. The central offices of at least 10,000 of them produce specialized literature to directly assist their local churches in evangelism and outreach. These cover teaching, catechism, baptism classes, Sunday schools, and the like.

Baptism candidates are particularly well served, with everything from a printed certificate of baptism up to published catechism and Bible study notes. Altogether, a safe minimal estimate would be that this vast mass of denominational materials is read or used by every church member for at least one hour each year.

*Evangelism-hours originated per year: 1.9 billion.*
*Media factor: 1.*
*Total offers received per year: 1.9 billion.*

**32. Local church output.** There are in the world in the year 2000 some 3.4 million local churches (parish churches, congregations, or other places of worship). All of them in open countries (those with complete freedom of writing, publication, printing, and distribution) produce large quantities of printed materials directly supporting the church's evangelism and outreach. Once again, a minimal estimate would show the average church member spending at least two hours each year reading, studying, distributing, using, and explaining these materials. And all of this is done in the local church's own language.

*Evangelism-hours originated per year: 3.8 billion.*
*Media factor: 1.*
*Total offers received per year: 3.8 billion.*

**33. Outside Christian literature.** A quite different form of printed material is experienced through outside languages—literature not produced primarily to benefit this local church in its own language. Some literature comes through alien or foreign or other-culture Christians who live on the people's territory often with their own alien congregations. But most outside literature comes in, incidentally or accidentally, via the major lingua francas. Although not originally intended for this people, the materials are usually avidly read and so have a sizeable media factor here estimated at 10.

*Evangelism-hours originated per year: 10 million.*
*Media factor: 10.*
*Total offers received per year: 100 million.*

**34. Church-planting output.** A vast amount of printed literature is produced and circulated concerning what has since 1960 become a whole new ecclesiastical industry—church planting. Around 2,000 denominations and 3,000 missions agencies now incorporate church growth methodology and have organized departments to promote church planting, both in their home countries and on their mission fields abroad. As one result, by the year 2000 newly-planted churches each year had risen to 58,000. Each one may be assumed to be the result of a large number (at least 1,000) of printed-word pages, or 1,000 evangelism-hours at one hour a page. Hence the annual evaluation is as shown below.

*Evangelism-hours originated per year: 58 million.*
*Media factor: 10.*
*Total offers received per year: 600 million.*

**35. Institutional ministries/records.** In AD 2000, major Christian institutions numbered 105,000. Minor church-related or Christian-related institutions numbered a further 376,000. Every one of these 481,000 institutions is—or is supposed to be—a center of Christian outreach, evangelism, apologetics, training. Each produces a voluminous annual output of literature and documentation. Each is supposed to maintain detailed records. Far from being dry and lifeless, all such materials—especially histories, accounts of ministries, library holdings, apologetical materials—can have direct and persuasive evangelistic value.

The assumption made here, therefore, is that every institution on average produces at least 10 evangelism-hours every day—at least 10 opportunities for others to enter on the life of discipleship.

*Evangelism-hours originated per year: 1.8 billion.*
*Media factor: 1.*
*Total offers received per year: 1.8 billion.*

**36. Christian books (100 pages).** A printed book is defined by UNESCO as one having 48 or more pages. In 1995 the total number of all new titles produced on any subject, secular or religious, reached the astronomical figure of 900,000, and by 2000 it had risen to over 1 million per year. With reprints of older titles this results in the printing of 30 billion copies a year.

Specifically Christian titles and books (excluding Bibles and New Testaments which have been enumerated under Ministries Nos. 24–30) are around 3% of these totals—22,000 new titles a year (or 63,000 including devotional books, hymnbooks, etc) resulting in 3.5 billion copies printed every year. With average length of 100 pages, the reader would read an average Christian book in 10 hours. Assuming initially one reader per copy, this therefore results in 35 billion evangelism-hours.

If finally we envisage every copy of a Christian book being read by an average of 2 readers a year, this gives a media factor of 2.

*Evangelism-hours originated per year: 35 billion.*
*Media factor: 2*
*Total offers received per year: 70 billion.*

**37. Christian periodicals (30 pages).** A most important role is played in outreach, evangelism, and apologetics by Christian periodicals, serials, magazines, journals, newspapers and the like. In the year 2000 the total of all these periodicals in 3,000 languages was 34,500, with circulation of some 50 million. If each issue takes an average 3 hours to read, these produce 150 million evangelism-hours. Each issue would have many more different readers than a book, so a media factor of at least 10 is likely.

*Evangelism-hours originated per year: 150 million.*
*Media factor: 10.*
*Total offers received per year: 1.5 billion.*

**38. Tracts (2 pages).** A tract is a short, concise, self-contained, standalone presentation of the gospel averaging a couple of sides of a small piece of paper. There has been a long and honorable history of Christian outreach through tract distribution. The latter is estimated in AD 2000 to total 5 billion tracts per year. Although taking an average of only 15 minutes to read, every tract is designed to deliver to its reader one disciple-opportunity irrespective of length. At the same time one must take into account the enormous wastage with this approach. Due to the mass distribution techniques employed, at least half the total output will be discarded or trashed without being read. One can expect only 2.5 billion a year to find a reader, and most will not be read by additional persons.

A typical example of the evangelistic creativity tracts make possible comes from Ujjain in north India. At the 1992 Kumbh Mela (Nectar Festival) with 10 million Hindus bathing in a river Ganges confluence, 225 Indian missionary workers distributed one million copies of the Gospel of John and 3 million gospel tracts in 33 days. The tracts would have produced 3 million offers, the former (at 2.5 offers per gospel, as in Ministry No. 22 above) 2.5 million, or 24,000 per missionary worker. On average, each worker distributed one tract every minute.

Utilizing our estimate above of 2.5 billion usable tracts per annum, the following global figures result.

*Evangelism-hours originated per year: 2.5 billion.*
*Media factor: 1*
*Total offers received per year: 2.5 billion.*

**39. Other documentation.** This variety of ministry covers a vast range of activity. One of the most effective is the placing of Christian articles or stories in secular newspapers and magazines. A striking example comes from the former Soviet Union. Since 1990, Christian Agency Good News (ABC) has published evangelistic articles in more than 1.2 billion copies of Russian and Ukrainian newspapers and magazines. If only one person read an article in each copy, and spent 15 minutes reading it, this would represent 300 million evangelism-hours which would have generated 300 million discipleship-offers, amounting to 50 million a year. Similar cases of such initiative from around the world probably yield a total of 500 million offers a year.

All the varieties of printed evangelizing words enumerated above in Ministries Nos. 31–38 refer to organized evangelism, evangelism by organizations, evangelism by corporate bodies or professionals. But in addition there is a huge individual or non-professional counterpart in the millions of letters and other messages written and sent by individual Great Commission Christians. If we assume that 10% of all these individuals type or print and send out each year letters while spending 10 evangelism-hours, this then amounts to a total of 650 million evangelism-hours a year.

*Evangelism-hours originated per year: 1.2 billion.*
*Media factor: 1.*
*Total offers received per year: 1.2 billion.*

## ELECTRONIC WORDS

The seventh and last of the 7 modes of evangelism has as its Mandate and imperative 'Train!' This mode is defined here as evangelizing words created and circulated as electronic words. In the 20th century, Christians have been taught and trained by trillions of electronic-media programmed words. Up to 1836, church training was entirely non-electronic, being only by spoken and written teaching. But since the origin of electric and electronic media, the latter has grown until today measured by sheer volume it is by far the largest proportion. This development has followed some 13 varieties or stages of the evolution of the electronic media—telegraph (since 1836), telephone (1876), movies (1882), radio (1921), television (1936), computers (1945), fax machines (1969), personal computers (1975), answering machines (1975), voice mail (1980), e-mail (1980), CD-ROM (1980), and the Internet (1985). This seventh and final mode thus covers the last of the varieties of evangelism—Ministries Nos. 40–45.

**40. Programmed training (TEE, TEEE, &c).** Systematized Christian teaching on evangelism has followed development of secular communications. Bible correspondence courses followed the Penny Post in Britain, and radiophonic 'schools of the air' came after the invention of broadcasting. After the invention and rapid expansion of distance education from 1945 in Britain and the USA, TEE (Theological Education by Extension) and TEEE (TEE and Evangelism) followed soon after. Origins of the TEE movement were at a Presbyterian seminary in Guatemala in 1963; by 1980 there were over 200 major TEE organizations worldwide with 400 programs and 60,000 extension students in 90 countries. By 1963 only a fraction of all the activities involved had become electronic; by 1980, some 20% had; but by 1995 virtually everything depended on electronics.

Meanwhile by 1966 Bible correspondence courses were mushrooming worldwide. Responses from individuals by then ranged from 110,000 enrolments in a typically hostile anti-Christian country (Morocco) to 4 million a year in the USA (Catholic as well as Protestant courses). One of the largest denominational programs was that of the 8-million-member Seventh-day Adventist Church. In 1986 they had 180 Bible correspondence schools in 77 languages with 520,167 annual enrollments and 281,345 graduating.

In 1967 came the International Correspondence Institute (later, ICI University) in Belgium run by the Assemblies of God, with by 1987 a total of 5,077,014 enrolments in 164 nations. Still later came tape instruction, video packages, then CD-ROMs, then programmed training by e-mail over the Internet and other networks open to anyone across the world.

A conservative estimate for the year 2000 would be that some 60 million persons were receiving some kind of electronic programmed instruction and training in some aspects of evangelism and mission. At 30 hours per person, this would produce an end product of 1.8 billion evangelism-hours a year, the large number being due to the sizeable media factor here and in other broadcast varieties of evangelism.

*Evangelism-hours originated per year: 180,000.*
*Media factor: 10,000.*
*Total offers received per year: 18 billion.*

**41. Christian radio programs.** Christian broadcasting has since its origin in 1921 reached more people for every hour of evangelism than any other variety. In Latin America, the most heard radio evangelist is Maria Miranda, heard by 100 million a day, over 537 stations in 22 countries (1990). Hundreds of other Protestant locally-produced broadcasts are heard daily, generating a vast volume of mail. Even hostile anti-Christian countries benefit: thus 10% of the population of Yemen listens to Christian radio.

In our terms, broadcasting (both radio and TV) has by far the largest 'media factor'. The result in AD 2000 is that the world's 4,000 Christian radio and TV stations reach 510 million persons monthly with Christian programming. And an additional 1,409 million hear Christian programs monthly over secular stations (governmental or commercial). Around two thirds of all this is due to radio and one third to television.

One of the most influential and long-lasting evangelistic ministries has been 'The Lutheran Hour' over radio station KFUO operated by the Lutheran Hour' over radio station KFUO operated by the Lutheran Church—Missouri Synod since 1925. By 1931, 5 million a week heard its brilliant preaching; by 1987, there were 40 million regular listeners in 31 languages around the world.

The non-Christian world has become wide open to this major variety of evangelism. Thus by the year 2000, 85 percent of the Chinese population have become reachable daily by radio and television, according to a Chinese government agency, the Ministry of Radio, Film, and Television. In 1990, China had 639 radio stations and 509 TV stations with coverage reaching 74.7% and 79.5% respectively. The Chinese people own 380 million radios, 178 million TV sets, and the countryside is peppered with more than 82 million loudspeakers. Radio Beijing is now third in the world for its multiplicity of broadcast languages and length of broadcast hours with listeners in more than 140 countries and areas. By AD 2000 China's 80 million Christians were still not yet permitted to broadcast Christian programs over this huge network, but such a goal is certain to be eventually attained, perhaps by AD 2010. The challenge for Christians is twofold: how to broadcast (at present from abroad) material of such quality that this huge audience will tune in, and how to reach the 230 million citizens of China who currently do not have any access at all to radio or TV.

If we make the conservative assumption that regular monthly listeners/viewers of Christian programs receive 1 hour a month of evangelism of one variety or another, this yields the final total below from which we work backwards to the first line.

*Evangelism-hours originated per year: 1 million.*
*Media factor: 50,000.*
*Total offers received per year: 50 billion.*

**42. Christian TV programs.** An American film 'The Bible in the Beginning' was recently shown on Japanese television station NTV and was watched by 13 million Japanese (over 12% of the population). The two and a half hour film (originally 3 hours before being edited by the Japan Bishops Conference) was well received by viewers, many of whom called NTV to express their appreciation for the film. Interest in the Bible in Japan has also led to a new campaign 'The Bible in 100 weeks' which takes the reader through the Old Testament in 60 weeks and 40 weeks for the New Testament.

In October 1990, 3 shows were aired on Argentinian TV by CBN (Christian Broadcasting Network). Over 8 million people saw the programs and 3 million repeated the salvation prayer. Assuming these figures represent reality, then 25% of the population of Argentina saw the broadcast (i.e. were evangelized) and 10% of the population accepted Christ as personal Savior.

Christian television is beginning to reach hitherto closed areas such as the Middle East. Power increases for the transmission of television programs for Europe are now producing expanded signals also for much of North Africa, the Middle East and Turkey. In addition vast changes in satellite use mean that for the first time over 40 million Muslims Arabs and 50 million Turks can be reached via television. So far, Christian mission agencies have been slow to see the new potential.

*Evangelism-hours originated per year: 200,000.*
*Media factor: 100,000.*
*Total offers received per year: 20 billion.*

**43. Urban media (cable TV, &c).** The world's 7,000 metropolises over 50,000 in population (or the 50,000 cities over 10,000 in size), and urban areas in general, inevitably get first opportunity to experience new forms of communication. Rural areas trail a long way behind. Consequently, urban areas and their 2.6 billion urbanites have considerably higher exposure to the newest forms of electronic evangelism. Of these metropolises, every year some 1,400 (20%) hold city-wide evangelistic campaigns featuring radio, TV, relays, satellites, video instruction, computer networks, the Internet, et alia.

Results of recent campaigns are even more striking then those of 20 or 30 years earlier. The Rev. Y. Jeyaraj, general superintendent, Assemblies of God of India, has summed up a recent evangelistic campaign in Madras in startling terms: 'I have never seen so many Moslems and Hindus accept Christ. Conservatively, there were more than 250,000 converted. Never in my life have I seen more miracles. All of Madras was shaken for Jesus' (*Charisma*, December 1992).

A recent new specifically-urban ministry is the phenomenal spread since 1987 of the annual March for Jesus. On a day in June each year, in some 2,500 cities in 200 countries across the world, around 12 million Christians from all the churches march through the city center for 3 or 4 hours with the one aim of collective witness to the person of Jesus. By 1999 the grand total of all persons who had thus marched had reached 100 million.

One new medium of communication is cable television. Hundreds of cities are now being wired for this new service, notable for the large number of TV channels it offers users. A number of these channels accept religious programs. Christian evangelists are far ahead of other Christian workers in their use of this medium.

A reasonable assumption here is that urban media programs featuring evangelism are found in some 3,000 metropolises and cities worldwide, involving on average three hours a week, or 150 hours a year. This produces 450,000 evangelism-hours a year. With a sizeable media factor of 12,000, this results in 5.4 billion offers each year.

*Evangelism-hours originated per year: 450,000.*
*Media factor: 12,000.*
*Total offers received per year: 5.4 billion.*

**44. Christian-owned computers.** The vast and rapidly-growing cacophony of Christian electronic words may be summarized under 2 headings: corporate or professional (the activities of full-time organized agencies), and individual or amateur (largely part-time laypersons). Under this head (No. 44) we are including internal or inhouse word-processing, databasing, donor lists, accounting, desktop publishing—all computer-related activities, except e-mail and other networking activity which are counted here as a separate ministry, No. 45.

(1) *Agencies.* In AD 2000, Christian churches, denominations, agencies, and other organizations owned or operated 5 million general-purpose computers, from huge mainframes to work stations to minicomputers to desktop-publishing computers to word processors. If one assumes that the average such computer produces materials for 30 minutes (2,500 words) a day, then this huge assembly of official, corporate, full-time equipment can be estimated to create, produce, transmit, and disseminate at least 12.5 billion words a day. And of all this, around 3% can be estimated to relate to evangelism, outreach, and mission. This makes 375 million words a day, or 137 billion electronic evangelizing words a year. At the rate of 5,000 words per hour, this is 27.4 million evangelism-hours each year.

(2) *Individuals.* From the start of the personal computer revolution in 1975, there has grown up a vast unorganized, informal, individual, largely lay movement producing millions more evangelizing words every day. In AD 2000, individual Christians owned and operated some 332 million personal computers, including laptops, notebooks, palmtops, and personal digital assistants. With these they write letters, print memos, fax documents, control their bank accounts, create lengthy reports, post notices on bulletin boards, and so on. If the average such computer entered only 100 words a day, for all Christian individual computers this would amount to 11.8 trillion words a year. Of all these words probably only 3% (354 billion words p.a.) relate to some variety of evangelism, mission, or outreach. Nevertheless, in aggregate this still implies a total of 70.7 million evangelism-hours a year.

For both agencies and individuals, these totals can be added, with 27.4 plus 70.7 adding to 98.1 million. To this must be applied a large media factor, estimated at 350.

*Evangelism-hours originated per year: 98.1 million.*
*Media factor: 350.*
*Total offers received per year: 34.3 billion.*

**45. Internet/networks/e-mail.** The latest mega-activity to be added to types of evangelism comes from the enormous expansion of electronic mail and online network activity, particularly over the Internet with its 277 million users in AD 2000 (198 million being Christians). Major networks include: CompuServe, America Online. Thousands of Christian organizations advertise and evangelize via their own home pages on the World Wide Web. The influence of Christians through chat groups, bulletin boards, and through personal and corporate e-mail increases exponentially year by year. Total Great Commission Christians utilizing e-mail in AD 2000 were estimated at 65 million, including 35 million Pentecostals/Charismatics/Neocharismatics. Being conservative we can estimate that each sends messages with evangelistic or mission content of around 500 words in length (transmitting for an average of 6 minutes a day, or 30 hours a year). Christian e-mailers and networkers thus originate 2 billion evangelism-hours a year.

*Evangelism-hours originated per year: 2 billion.*
*Media factor: 30.*
*Total offers received per year: 58.5 billion.*

### *GLOBAL VOLUME OF EVANGELISM, AD 2000*

All the preceding totals for the 7 modes and 45 ministries can now be summarized and assessed to see their overall impact. This is done above in Table 22–6. These same figures are also found in Global Diagram 32, in Part 1, where they are illustrated and explained in a wider context. That diagram should be consulted to understand the definitions and implications of the various factors and figures resulting.

From this table it will be seen that the total amount of evangelism being generated or originated by Christians each year through all 45 varieties of ministries is 206 billion evangelism-hours. This then results in a global grand total of 938 billion hearer-hours received. Using the various synonyms developed earlier in this Part 22, this implies 938 billion offers, invitations, calls, chances, evangelizings, disciple-opportunities, disciple-calculations, reviews, responses, choices, or dichotomous decisions Yes or No.

The significance of this achievement can be seen if we divide by global population. The amount of evangelism received per capita in AD 2000 can then be computed as: 155 evangelism-hours. This means that, given fair distribution of these ministries, every person in the world ought to receive 155 invitations/disciple-opportunities each year. In practice, unfortunately, distribution is anything but fair—absurdly unfair, in fact. In World C, 2.0 billion Christians (including 648 million Great Commission Christians, who do not need any further disciple-opportunities since they are already active disciples) are bombarded with 84% of all evangelism to the tune of 394 new 'invitations' per capita every year. Meanwhile, non-Christians in World B get only 62 per capita (five a month), and the 1.6 billion unfortunates in World A get—by definition—no opportunities at all.

This problem of uneven distribution is further examined in Parts 24 and 25, and is quantified in Part 1's Global Diagram 40.

### *BIBLIOGRAPHY*


'A Biblical evaluation of John Wimber's concept of power evangelism.' D. R. Downs. Th.M. thesis, Dallas Theological Seminary, Dallas, TX, 1989. 143p.

'A critical analysis of power evangelism as an evangelistic methodology of the signs and wonders movement.' D. H. Shepherd. Th.D. thesis, Mid-America Baptist Theological Seminary, Germantown, TN, 1991. 248p.

*A global view of Christian missions: from Pentecost to the present.* J. H. Kane. Grand Rapids, Mich.: Baker Book House, 1971. 602p.

*A gospel to proclaim.* N. McCulloch. London: Darton, Longman and Todd, 1992. 106p.

*A guide to the study of the Holiness Movement.* C. E. Jones. *ATLA bibliography series*, no. 1. Metuchen, N.J.: Scarecrow Press and ATLA, 1974. 946p.

'A historical study of the CCCOWE movement: the first ten years (1976–1986).' T. L. W. Lam. Th.M. thesis, Fuller Theological Seminary, Pasadena, CA, 1988. 125p.

'A manual for open–air field evangelism directed toward church planting.' P. C. Eyster. D.Min. thesis, Mid-America Baptist Theological Seminary, Germantown, TN, 1993. 143p.

*A new workbook on rural evangelism.* C. Napier & J. J. Hamilton-Brown (eds). Blandford Forum: Parish and People, 1994. 100p.

*A people for his name: a church–based missions strategy.* P. A. Beals. Rev. ed. Pasadena, CA: William Carey Library, 1995. 259p.

'A program of evangelism and discipleship of inner–city teenagers in Chicago.' M. Burton. M.A. thesis, Moody Bible Institute, Chicago, 1994. 119p.

*A short account of the historical and present position of Russian Orthodox Missions.* E. Smirnoff. 1903; reprint, Welshpool, UK: Stylite Publishing, 1986. 95p.

*A true and lively faith: evangelical revival in the church of Ireland.* A. R. Acheson. N.p.: Church of Ireland Evangelical Fellowship, 1992. 40p.

*Alaskan missionary spirituality.* M. Oleska (ed). New York: Paulist Press, 1987. (Documents relating to Russian Orthodox missionaries in Alaska and their relationship to colonialism).

'An analysis and critique of evangelism within the Church of God: with implications for the local congregation in America.' C. M. Thornton. D.Min. thesis, Columbia Theological Seminary, Decatur, GA, 1990. 134p.

*An evangelism cookbook.* D. Cook. N.p.: Paternoster, 1988. 128p.

*Anglican cycle of prayer: praying together for persons and places around the world—1996.* London: Church House Publishing; Cincinnati, OH: Forward Movement Publications, 1995. 160p. (Annual publication of the Anglican Communion designed to focus attention on the world of Anglican missions worldwide).

*Anglo–Catholicism: a study in religious ambiguity.* W. S. F. Pickering. London: Routledge, 1989; London: SPCK, 1991. 302p.

*Baptism in the Malankara church: a study on the baptismal ritual of the Malankara church.* M. Elenjikal. *Dharmaram College studies*, 14. Bangalore, India: Dharmaram Publications, 1974. 218p.

*Basic ecclesial communities: the evangelization of the poor.* A. Barreiro. Maryknoll, New York: Orbis Books, 1982.

*Basic ecclesial communities: the evangelization of the poor.* A. Barreiro. Maryknoll, New York: Orbis Books, 1982.

*Bihar: church and people groups.* S. V. Albert (ed). Madras: Church Growth Association of India, 1992. 168p.

'Bishop Festo Kivengere's philosophy of evangelism.' J. M. M. Senyonyi. M.A. thesis, Trinity Evangelical Divinity School, Deerfield, IL, 1992. 146p.

*Bishops and societies: a study of Anglican colonial and missionary expansion, 1698–1850.* H. Cnattingius. London: SPCK, 1952.

*Black Americans and the evangelization of Africa 1877–1900.* W. L. Williams. Madison, Wis. and London: University of Wisconsin Press, 1982. 278p.

*Bryan Green, parson–evangelist.* B. Green. Thame: Bryan Green Society, 1994. 186p.

*Call & response: biblical foundations of a theology of evangelism.* W. Klaiber. Trans., H. Perry-Trauthig & J. A. Dwyer. Nashville, TN: Abingdon Press, 1997.
*Called and empowered: global mission in Pentecostal perspective.* M. Dempster, B. D. Klaus & D. Petersen (eds). Peabody, MA: Hendrickson, 1991.
*C.H. Spurgeon: the pastor evangelist.* M. Nicholls. Didcot: Baptist Historical Society, 1992. 189p.
*Charisms and new evangelization.* P. J. Cordes. N.p.: St Paul Publications, 1992. 171p.
*Charles Grandison Finney 1792–1875: revivalist and reformer.* K. Hardman. N.p.: Evangelical, 1990. 538p.
*Children and evangelism.* P. Frank. London: Marshall Pickering, 1992. 200p.
*Colonial evangelism: a socio–historical study of an East African mission at the grassroots.* T. O. Beidelman. Bloomington, IN: Indiana University Press, 1982.
*Come on in!: sharing the good news through groups: a practical action guide.* M. Parker. London: Methodist Church Home Mission, 1993. 90p.
*Communicating faith in a technological age.* J. McDonnell & F. Trampiets (eds). N.p.: St Paul Publications, 1989. 175p.
*Concise dictionary of the Christian world mission.* S. Neill, G. H. Anderson & J. Goodwin (eds). London: Lutterworth, 1970. 704p.
'Contextualized methodology for crisis evangelism among the poor.' C. E. Young. D.Min. thesis, Westminster Theological Seminary, Chestnut Hill, PA, 1989.
*Creating confidence in evangelism: a master photocopy book to help your church in the decade of evangelism.* J. Young. Warwick: CPAS, 1991. 40p.
*Creating understanding: a handbook for Christian communication across cultural landscapes.* D. K. Smith. Grand Rapids, Mich.: Zondervan, 1992. 382p.
*Creative ideas for youth evangelism.* N. Aiken & M. Brown (eds). London: Marshall Pickering, 1992. 208p.
*Crisis and hope in Latin America: an evangelical perspective.* E. A. Nuñez C. & W. D. Taylor. Rev. ed. Pasadena, Calif.: William Carey Library, 1996. 544p.
*D. James Kennedy: the man and his ministry.* H. L. Williams. Nashville, Tenn.: Thomas Nelson Publishers, 1990. 347p.
*D. L. Moody (Born 1837) and his place in modern evangelism.* J. C. Pollock. *The Evangelical Library Annual lecture*, 1987. London: The Evangelical Library, 1987–1989. 22p.
*David Watson: a biography.* T. Saunders. London: Hodder & Stoughton, 1992. 336p.
*Deaneries, evangelism and unity.* Banbury: Parish and People, 1992. 15p.
'Developing a ministry of evangelism through hospitality at St. Luke's Episcopal Church.' V. M. Sheay. D.Min. project, Drew University, Madison, NJ, 1992. 151p.
*Divided we stand?* G. Coates. Eastbourne, U.K.: Kingsway, 1987. 185p.
*Doing theology with the Maasai.* D. Priest Jr. Pasadena, CA: William Carey Library, 1990. 248p.
*Earthen vessels: American evangelicals and foreign missions, 1880–1980.* J. A. Carpenter & W. R. Shenk (eds). Grand Rapids, MI: Eerdmans, 1990. 368p.
*Effective evangelism.* F. McClung. London: Marshall Pickering, 1988. 64p.
*Encyclopedia of evangelism and church growth.* E. Townes.
'Euangelizomai,' G. Friedrich, in *Theologisches Worterbuch zum Nueun Testament*, p.Vol II, p.707–37. G. Kittel (ed). Stuttgart: Kolhammer, 1932–78.
*Evangelieverkondiging aan die boesmans deur middel van visuele hulpmiddele.* A. H. Le Roux. Potchefstroom: PU vir CHO, Instituut vir Reformatoriese Studie, 1989. 23p.
'Evangelion–Evangelizó, a contextual analysis of their meaning in the New Testament and the Apostolic Fathers.' J. F. Parker. Th.D. thesis, New Orleans Baptist Theological Seminary, 1989. 215p.
'Evangelisation bei Johann Hinrich Wichern und Theodor Christlieb.' A. H. Kuemmerle. Th.M. thesis, Regent College, Vancouver, BC, 1991. 176p.
*Evangelism.* Atlanta: Home Mission Board of the S.B.C, [1988].
*Evangelism 2000: two thousand proclaiming Christ in the 21st century.* Fowler John W. Boise, Idaho: Pacific Press Pub. Association, 1994. 159p.
*Evangelism and church growth: a practical encyclopedia.* E. L. Towns (ed). Ventura, California: Regal Books, 1995. 427p.
*Evangelism and social action: uniting the church to heal a lost and broken world.* R. J. Sider. London: Hodder & Stoughton, 1993. 256p.
*Evangelism and the poor.* V. K. Samuel & C. Sugden. Bangalore, India: Partnership in Mission—Asia, 1983.
*Evangelism and the poor.* V. K. Samuel & C. Sugden. Bangalore, India: Partnership in Mission—Asia, 1983.
*Evangelism and the poor.* V. K. Samuel & C. Sugden (eds). 2nd ed ed. Oxford: Published for Partnership in Mission-Asia by Regnum Books, 1987. 170p.
*Evangelism by fire.* R. Bonnke. Rev. ed ed. Eastbourne, U.K.: Kingsway, 1994. 253p.
*Evangelism: doing justice and preaching grace.* H. M. Conn. Grand Rapids, MI: Zondervan, 1984.
*Evangelism: doing justice and preaching grace.* H. M. Conn. Grand Rapids, Mich.: Zondervan, 1984.
*Evangelism for a new age: creating churches for the next century.* J. W. Drane. London: Marshall Pickering, 1994. 235p.
*Evangelism from the bottom up.* W. E. Pannell. Grand Rapids, MI: Zondervan, 1991.
*Evangelism from the bottom up.* W. E. Pannell. Grand Rapids, Mich.: Zondervan, 1991.
'Evangelism in the African American Presbyterian congregation: equipping the church for growth.' J. H. Logan. Th.M. thesis, Columbia Theological Seminary, Decatur, GA, 1992. 175p.
'Evangelism in the city of Chicago.' E. Brydon. M.A. thesis, Lincoln Christian Seminary, Lincoln, IL, 1986. 123p.
*Evangelism techniques.* Yola, Nigeria: Follow-up Bible Class, Christian Corpers' Fellowship, c1991. 95p.
*Evangelism that really works.* J. Clarke. London: SPCK, 1995. 171p.
*Evangelism through the local church.* M. Green. London: Hodder & Stoughton, 1990. 480p.
*Evangelismo personal.* C. J. Sharp. El Paso, Tex.: Evangelismo Hispano-Americano, [1988?]. 76p.
*Evangelist to the world.* J. Wilson. N.p.: Lutterworth, 1989. 95p.
*Evangelistische Strategie: unter Völkern in der kommunistischen Welt.* H. Hartfeld. Stephanus ed. Uhldingen: Stepahnus, 1986. 72p.
*Evangelization and culture.* A. Shorter. London: G. Chapman, 1994. 175p.
*Evangelization today.* B. Häring. New, revised ed. Slough, U.K.: St. Paul Publications, 1990. 187p.
*Everyday evangelism.* G. Crossley. Welwyn: Evangelical Press, 1987. 224p.
*Explaining evangelism.* S. Bowen. N.p.: Sovereign World, 1991. 71p.
*Fifty ways you can share your faith.* T. Campolo. Eastbourne, U.K.: Kingsway, 1994. 122p.
*Frank Buchman: a life.* G. Lean. London: Constable, 1985. 602p.
*Friendship evangelism.* F. Schneider. N.p.: MARC, 1989. 188p.
*From revival to evangelism or the effects of spiritual renewal.* C. W. Carter. Salem, Ohio: Schmul, 1986. 246p.
*George Whitefield: evangelist of the 18th–century revival.* A. A. Dallimore. London: Wakeman Trust, 1990. 224p.
*Global mission: a story to tell: an interpretation of Southern Baptist foreign missions.* W. Crawley. Nashville: Broadman Press, 1985. 400p.
*Glory!: Billy Bray the King's son.* F. W. Bourne. N.p.: Ambassador/Highway, 1989. 124p.
*Go and evangelise.* A. Owen. N.p.: Harvestime, 1992. 95p.
*Go!: the excitement of personal evangelism.* D. Lehmann. London: Hodder & Stoughton, 1988. 176p.
*God made it grow: historical sketches of TEAM's church planting work.* V. Mortenson. Pasadena, California: William Carey Library, 1994. 1003p.
*Good News and how to share it.* M. Green. Oxford: Bible Reading Fellowship, 1993. 111p.
*He tells us to go: evangelism—sharing good news in a divided world.* I. Coffey. *Foundations Hodder Christian paperbacks.* London: Hodder & Stoughton, 1986. 62p.
*Henry Drummond: 1851–1897: Fellow of the Royal Society, Edinburgh, Fellow of the Geological Society.* Loanhead: F.J. Stewart, 1985. 27p.
*How to share your faith.* L. Samuel. 2nd ed. Welwyn: Evangelical, 1985. 128p.
*IBRA Radio—reaching the world.* E. Johansson. [Niagara Falls, Ontario: IBRA, n.d.]. 107p.
*Icons: windows on eternity: theology and spirituality in colour.* G. Limouris. Geneva: WCC, 1990. 228p.
'Improving the Evangelistic Program of the Calvary Baptist Church, Erwin, Tennessee.' F. M. Womack. D.Min. thesis, Mid-America Baptist Theological Seminary, Germantown, TN, 1991. 144p.
*In search of the Great Commission: what did Jesus really say?* W. L. Banks. Chicago: Moody Press, 1991. 168p.
*In the way: a study of Christian missionary endeavours.* K. Burridge. Vancouver: University of British Columbia Press, 1991. 323p.
*In word and deed: evangelism and social responsibility.* B. Nicholls. Exeter: Paternoster, 1985. 238p. (Published on behalf of the Lausanne Committee for World Evangelization and the World Evangelical Fellowship).
*Jesus is your best mate: evangelism in the inner–city and council estate cultures.* D. Cave. London: Marshalls, 1985. 189p.
*John Wesley and the Anglican evangelicals of the eighteenth century a study in cooperation and separation with special reference to the Calvinistic controversies.* A. Brown-Lawson. Edinburgh: Pentland, 1994. 425p.
*Kingdom evangelism.* J. Wimber. London: Hodder & Stoughton, 1989. 32p.
*Let's tell the world.* W. R. L. Scragg. N.p.: British Union Conference, 1990. 7p.
*Liberal evangelism.* J. Saxbee. London: SPCK, 1994. 127p.
*Life to share: discovering a biblical vision for evangelism.* J. K. Stoner, J. Egli & G. E. Bontrager. Newton, Kans. and Scottdale, Pa.: Faith and Life Press and Mennonite Publishing House, 1991. 112p.
*Liturgical evangelism: worship as outreach and nurture.* R. E. Webber. Harrisburg, PA: Morehouse Publishing, 1986. 126p.
*Local church evangelism: patterns and approaches.* A. H. Gray & D. F. Wright (eds). Edinburgh: Saint Andrew, 1987. 184p.
'Making EE work: the cross–cultural adaption and local application of EEIII International in Lisbon, Portugal.' C. E. Quarterman. D.Min. thesis, Reformed Theological Seminary, Jackson, MS, 1986. 136p.
*Marching to glory: the history of the Salvation Army in the United States, 1880–1992.* E. H. McKinley. 2d ed. Grand Rapids, Mich. and Cambridge, U.K.: Eerdmans, 1995. 471p.
*Mass evangelism.* Atlanta: Home Mission Board of the S.B.C, [1988].
*Media in church and mission: communicating the gospel.* V. Søgaard. Pasadena, California: William B. Carey Library, 1993. 301p.
*Missiological abstracts, 25 years, 1966–1991.* G. R. Grimes (ed). Rev. ed. Pasadena, CA: Fuller Theological Seminary, 1991. 336p. (Abstracts of 720 dissertations, theses, and projects produced at the School of World Mission at Fuller Theological Seminary).
*Mission and evangelism: an ecumenical affirmation.* E. Castro (ed). Geneva: CWME, 1982.
'Mission and evangelism in Urban Rural Mission,' E. Castro, *International review of mission*, 74, 303 (July 1987), 324–330.
*Mission in the nineteen 90s.* G. H. Anderson, J. M. Phillips & R. T. Coote (eds). Grand Rapids, Mich. and New Haven, Connecticut: Eerdmans and Overseas Missions Study Center, 1991. 80P.
*Mission theology: 1948–1975, years of worldwide creative tension, ecumenical, evangelical, and Roman Catholic.* R. C. Bassham. Pasadena, California: William Carey Library, 1979. 452p.
*Mission und Religion in der systematische Theologie der Gegenwart: das Missionsverständnis deutschsprachiger protestantischer Dogmatiker im 20 Jahrhundert.* H. Wrogemann. *Forschungen zur systematischen und ökumenischen Theologie, Bd. 79.* Göttingen: Vanderhoeck & Ruprecht, 1997. 350p. (Originally presented as the author's doctoral thesis at Heidelberg University in 1995).
*Mission work in today's world: insights and outlooks.* J. S. Hofman. Pasadena, CA: William B. Carey Library, 1993. 220p.
*Missionary conquest: the gospel and Native American cultural genocide.* G. E. Tinker. Minneapolis, MN: Fortress Press, 1993.
*Missions and evangelism: a bibliography selected from the ATLA religion database, January, 1985.* A. E. Hurd & P. D. Petersen (eds). Rev. ed. Chicago: American Theological Library Association, Religion Indexes, 1985. 788p.
*Moody blues: D.L.Moody's affect on the Scottish church.* J. S. Salmond. London: Excalibur Press, 1992. 63p.
*New directions in mission and evangelization; vol. 1: basic statements 1974–1991; vol. 2: theological foundations.* J. A. Scherer & S. B. Bevans (eds). *New directions in mission and evangelization*, 1. Maryknoll, NY: Orbis, 1992. 2 vols.
*New wineskins for global mission: a compendium.* S. Stockdale (ed). Pasadena, Calif.: William Carey Library, 1996. 459p. (Reports from a conference sponsored by the Episcopal Church Missionary Community, April 27-May 1, 1994, Ridgecrest, North Carolina).
*Of revelation and revolution: Christianity, colonialism and consciousness in South Africa.* J. Comaroff. Chicago: University of Chicago Press, 1991.
*Open–air evangelism: a practical handbook.* M. Howe (ed). Alresford: Christian Literature Crusade, 1991. 212p.
*Orthodox perspectives on mission.* A. Keshishian (abp). Oxford: Regnum Books, 1992. 138p. (The author, Primate of the Armenian Apostolic Church in Lebanon, explores in this collection of essays and lectures the contribution of the Orthodox tradition to world missions.).
*Papers presented at the symposium on Power Evangelism.* Pasadena, California: Fuller, 1988.
*Partners in the Gospel: the strategic role of partnership in world evangelization.* J. H. Kraakevik & D. Welliver (eds). Wheaton, IL: The Billy Graham Center, Wheaton College. 224p.
*Personal evangelism.* L. Tomczak. *Oasis Bible notes.* Hove Milton Keynes. Frontier Word, 1992. 62p.
*Power evangelism.* J. Wimber. Rev. and updated with study guide ed. London: Hodder & Stoughton, 1992. 269p.
*Power evangelism and the word of God.* D. Bridge. Eastbourne, U.K.: Kingsway, 1987. 249p.
*Power evangelism: signs and wonders today.* J. Wimber. London: Hodder & Stoughton, 1985. 191p.
*Practical ideas in evangelism: a master photocopy book to help your church in the decade of Evangelism.* J. Young. Warwick: CPAS, 1992. 40p.
*Practical lessons for evangelism among Muslims.* V. Stacey. Rev. ed ed. N.p.: Interserve, c1988. 33p.
*Pray TV: televangelism in America.* S. Bruce. London: Routledge, 1990. 224p.
*Proclaiming Christ in Christ's way: studies in integral evangelism: essays presented to Walter Arnold on the occasion of his 60th birthday.* V. Samuel & A. Hauser (eds). Oxford: Regnum Books, 1989. 228p.
*Profane evangelism: taking the gospel into 'unholy places'.* M. Van Houten. Grand Rapids, Mich.: Ministry Resources Library, Zondervan, 1989. p.
*Radical evangelism.* P. Gilbert. *Pioneer perspectives.* Milton Keynes. Word, 1992. 92p.
*Reaching children.* P. Butler. N.p.: Scripture Union, 1992. 160p.
'Reaching the masses with an affordable mini television station.' P. A. Valiente. M.A. thesis, Moody Bible Institute, Chicago, 1994. 97p.
*Reaching the unchurched.* M. Hill. Amersham-on-the-Hill: Scripture Press, 1994. 155p.
'Reaching the unreachable: using a market–sensitive approach to evangelism to reach nominal Christians in Austria.' T. L. Zimmerman. D.Min. thesis, Denver Conservative Baptist Seminary, Denver, CO, 1994. 183p.
*Reaching young families.* J. Wigley. Warwick: CPAS, 1994. 40p.
*Redemptoris missio: encyclical letter of the Supreme Pontiff John Paul II on the permanent validity of the Church's missionary mandate.* John Paul II. *Catholic Truth Society*, No. 601. London: Catholic Truth Society, 1991. 64p.
*Redescribing evangelism.* G. Reid. London: British Council of Churches, 1989. 11p.
'Rethinking evangelism in the local congregation.' D. F. Whiteley. D.Min. thesis, Columbia Theological Seminary, Decatur, GA, 1989. 180p.
*Revival and rebellion in colonial central Africa.* K. E. Fields. Princeton, NJ: Princeton University Press, 1985.
*Sadhu Sundar Singh.* J. Daniel. London: Laymen's Evangelical Fellowship International, c1994. 82p.
*Seamen's missions: their origin and early growth.* R. Kverndal. Pasadena, California: William Carey Library, 1986. 931p.
*Seeking a sanctuary: Seventh–day Adventism and the*

*American dream.* M. Bull & K. Lockhart. New York: Harper & Row, 1989. 335p.

*Selective bibliography on evangelism and evangelization.* D. B. Barrett. Nairobi: Centre for the Study of World Evangelization, 1980. (1,400 items).

*Shape up for evangelism.* P. Neilson. N.p.: Handsel Press and Rutherford House, 1988. 21p.

*Sharing the good news with the poor World Evangelical Fellowship Theological Commission. Outreach and Identity: Evangelical Theological Monographs No. 11.* Seoul, Korea: [WEF Theological Commission], 1993. 38p.

*Small group evangelism.* R. Peace. Downers Grove, Illinois: InterVarsity Press, 1985; London: Scripture Union, 1987. 190p.

*Smith Wigglesworth: a man who walked with God.* G. Stormont. : Sovereign World, 1990. 140p.

*Spirit aflame: Luis Palau's mission to London.* S. Holton. London: Hodder & Stoughton, 1985. 174p.

*T.C. Hammond: Irish Christian: his life and legacy in Ireland and Australia.* W. Nelson. Edinburgh: Banner of Truth Trust, 1994. 197p.

*Telling God's story: Bible theology and narrative.* G. Loughlin. Cambridge: Cambridge University Press, 1996.

*Telling others: the Alpha initiative.* N. Gumbel. Eastbourne, U.K.: Kingsway, 1994. 155p.

*Telling the good news together.* N.p.: British Council of Churches, 1988. 19p.

*The ABC of personal evangelism.* R. Smith. Manila: Christ for Greater Manila, 1988, c1986. 127p.

*The apostolic preaching and its development.* C. H. Dodd. London: Hodder & Stoughton, 1936, 1951. 96p. + chart. (Three lectures in which the author tries to trace the content of the Gospel and it was preached by the Apostles).

*The Bible in world evangelization.* T. Houston. Dublin: National Bible Society of Ireland, 1993. 43p.

*The Billy Graham story.* W. C. Martin. N.p.: Hutchinson, 1992. 735p.

*The churching of America 1776–1990: winners and losers in our religious economy.* R. Finke & R. Stark. New Brunswick, NJ: Rutgers University Press, 1992. 344p.

*The encyclopedia of missions: descriptive, historical, biographical, statistical.* O. Dwight, H. A. Tupper & E. M. Bliss (eds). 2nd ed. New York and London: Funk & Wagnalls, 1904; reprint, Detroit, MI: Gale Research, 1975. 865p.

*The Ethiopian Orthodox church.* A. Wondmagegnehu & J. Motovu (eds). Addis Ababa: The Ethiopian Orthodox Mission, 1970. 195p.

*The evangelism toolkit.* L. Singlehurst (ed). Rev. ed ed. Farnham: CWR, 1993. 92p.

*The flaming tongue: the impact of 20th century revivals.* J. E. Orr. Chicago: Moody Press, 1973. 255p.

*The future of the Christian world mission: studies in honor of R. Pierce Beaver.* W. J. Danker & W. J. Kang (eds). Grand Rapids, Mich.: Eerdmans, 1971. 181p.

*The Gospel and its meaning: a theology for evangelism and church growth.* H. L. Poe. Grand Rapids, MI: Zondervan Publishing House, 1996. 334p.

*The Gospel connection: a study in evangelism for the nineties.* M. Marshall. London: Darton, Longman and Todd, 1991. 224p.

*The great commission: biblical models for evangelism.* M. Arias & A. Johnson. Nashville, TN: Abingdon Press, 1992. 142p.

*The journals of George Whitefield.* R. Backhouse (ed). London: Hodder & Stoughton, 1993. 256p.

*The logic of evangelism.* W. J. Abraham. London: Hodder & Stoughton, 1989. 256p.

*The making and unmaking of an evangelical mind: the case of Edward Carnell.* R. Nelson. Cambridge: Cambridge University Press, 1987. 265p.

*The master plan of evangelism.* R. E. Coleman. Old Tappan, NJ: Revell, 1963. (Published in India as *The Lord's plan to spread the Good News.* Madras: Evangelical Literature Service, 1963).

*The missionary emphasis of Lukan pneumatology.* J. M. Penney. *Journal of Pentecostal theology: supplementary series,* 12. Sheffield, U.K.: Sheffield Academic Press, 1997. 143p.

*The missionary nature of the church: a survey of the biblical theology of mission.* J. Blauw. *Foundations of the Christian mission.* New York: McGraw-Hill, 1962. 182p.

*The new Catholic evangelization.* K. Boyack CSP (ed). New York and Mahwah, NJ: Paulist Press, 1992. 245p.

'The pastor's opportunities VI: evangelism in the city,' L. Newbigin, *The Expository Times,* 98, 12 (September 1987), 355–358.

'The pastor's opportunities VI: evangelism in the city,' L. Newbigin, *The Expository Times,* 98, 12 (September 1987), 355–358.

*The reluctant evangelist.* P. Miller. Eastbourne, U.K.: Kingsway, 1990. 192p.

'The rhetoric of evangelization: a study of pragmatic constraints on organizational systems of rhetoric.' J. C. Swanson. Ph.D. dissertation, University of Texas at Austin, 1989. 463p.

'The significance of dialogue in the cross–cultural evangelism of the apostle Paul.' A. J. Butkovich. M.A. thesis, Capital Bible Seminary, Lanham, MD, 1991. 64p.

*The soul winner.* C. H. Spurgeon. Fearn: Christian Focus, 1992. 255p.

*The story of New Tribes Mission.* K. J. Johnston. Sanford, Fla.: New Tribes Mission, 1985. 299p.

*The witness of the Oriental Orthodox churches.* K. Sarkissian. Beirut: Mesrob Press, 1968. 91p.

*The woman evangelist: the life and times of charismatic evangelist Maria B. Woodworth–Etter.* W. E. Warner. *Studies in evangelicalism,* no. 8. Metuchen, NJ: Scarecrow Press, 1986. 352p.

*This Gospel shall be preached: a history and theology of Assemblies of God foreign missions since 1959.* G. B. McGee. Springfield, Mo.: Gospel Publishing House, 1989. 2 vols., 646p.

*To reach a nation: the challenge of evangelism in a mass–media age.* G. Reid. Hodder Christian paperbacks. London: Hodder & Stoughton, 1987. 185p.

*Turning the world upside down: a century of missionary endeavour.* W. T. Stunt et al. 3d ed. Bath, U.K.: Echoes of Service, 1973. 671p.

*Unreached peoples: clarifying the task.* H. Screck & D. Barrett (eds). Monrovia, CA: MARC; Birmingham, AL: New Hope, 1987. 310p.

*Using the Bible in evangelism.* D. Tidball. Swindon: Bible Society, 1985. 112p.

*Using the Bible in evangelism.* D. Tidball. Rev. ed ed. Swindon: Bible Society, 1993. 109p.

*Videos for evangelism.* K. Jackson. N.p.: Jay, 1992. 24p.

*World survey by the Interchurch World Movement.* New York: Interchurch Press, 1920. 2 vols.

Part 23

# EVANGELIZATION

'Evangelize!' in 420 dimensions:
its historical development

*We wish to remind the entire Church that its first duty is that of evangelization.*
—John Paul I, immediately after his election as pope, 1978

Part 23 contains an extensive examination of the biblical Greek verb *euangelizo,* its 210 Greek synonyms, its English transliteration *evangelize,* and the latter's 420 English-language dimensions (from Latin *dimensio,* a measurement). Many dimensions are each illustrated by a photograph, and then in Table 23–19 all 420 are described with each's source data, from biblical texts to historical usages up to quotations from Christian leaders and theologians today. 'Evangelize!' thus emerges as Christianity's richest single word.

# 'Evangelize!' in 420 dimensions: its historical development

### The evolution of 'evangelize', 'evangelism', and 'evangelization'

It is widely assumed in the English-speaking world that the terms 'evangelism' and 'evangelization' are exact synonyms, with identical meaning. The true situation is vastly more complex. It has been investigated and documented in the 1987 monograph, *Evangelize! a historical survey of the concept*. The present Part 23 will take the discussion 4 stages further. Firstly, it will summarize the historical and current usages of the root word in biblical Greek, *euangelizo*, and its English transliteration 'evangelize'. Secondly, it will explore the differences of meaning between the 2 derived English nouns, 'evangelism' and 'evangelization'. Thirdly, it will describe various typologies of these meanings coined in the recent past by noted Christians—Karl Barth, Donald A. McGavran, pope Paul VI, pope John Paul II, C.P. Wagner. And fourthly, 'evangelize' and 'evangelization' will be analyzed into 420 distinct dimensions, for each of which we then list its usages—biblical, historical, and current.

## SUMMARY OF USAGES AND MEANINGS OF 'EVANGELIZE'

Our survey of usages of the word 'evangelize' and its cognates throughout history can be summarized, and a number of conclusions drawn, under 29 points as follows.

1. *Greek keyword*. The Greek word *euangelizo*, which transliterates into English as 'evangelize', occurs 22 times in the Greek Old Testament (Septuagint) and 56 times in the Greek New Testament, in 12 of its 27 books. Seventeen of the NT usages (30%) refer to events before the Resurrection of Christ and are largely used of divine activity then. Of these, 9 usages or 16%, refer to Jesus' own evangelizing activity during his ministry in Palestine before the Resurrection. By contrast, 39 usages (70%) refer to events after Pentecost and are largely used to describe human, ecclesiastical evangelistic activity.

2. *Greek synonyms*. In addition to *euangelizo*, the Greek New Testament employs a whole range of 210 Greek verbs of extraordinarily rich variety to cover the activities that today are called evangelism and/or evangelization. Of these 210, 10 are very close variants of *euangelizo* itself; 4 are very close synonyms (*kerysso, menuo, homologeo, ereugomai*); 7 are here termed The Big Seven, being the 7 Mandates in Christ's Great Commission; 19 are major synonyms and near-synonyms; 140 are synonyms in varying degree; and 210 are related New Testament Greek verbs overlapping in meaning with *euangelizo*. With nouns and adjectives as well as verbs, these all combine to make a total of 500 close Greek cognates of *euangelizo*.

3. *English keyword*. The Greek word *euangelizo* came to the fore in the 1st century after Christ as Koine Greek was becoming the Mediterranean world's main lingua franca. The English word 'evangelize' was in coined in Wyclif's Bible in the 14th century but did not become prominent until it came to the fore in the 19th century, during and after which English has become the modern world's main lingua franca.

4. *English terms*. The English word 'evangelize' and its cognates ('evangelizing', 'evangelization', 'evangelism', 'evangelized', et alia) have come into widespread use since 1850 in the Protestant and Anglican worlds, and since 1965 in the Roman Catholic world. They are not however used much in biblical translations: instead, *euangelizo* is translated, in the major contemporary English Bible versions, by 40 other English verbs of which the 6 most common are, in order, 'preach', 'bring', 'tell', 'proclaim', 'declare', 'announce'.

5. *Translating Greek*. The Greek verb *euangelizo* is translated in The Top 40 of the 500 versions of the English Bible by 80 biblical near-translations: 44 English verbs directly translating *euangelizo*, 20 translating its 10 close variants, and another 20 translating its 4 closest synonyms (Global Diagram 7 items 3 and 4). Our analysis lists 51 direct translations as 'macrotranslations'.

6. *Translating synonyms*. These 210 Greek synonyms of *euangelizo* translate, using only standard Greek-English lexicons, into over 500 current English verbs with meanings parallel to *euangelizo*. All, both Greek and English, have several cognates each, i.e. derived nouns, participles, and adjectives.

7. *English cognates*. The English verb 'evangelize' is supported by 11 separate but overlapping categories of related words. The Big Ten are the 10 words most frequently used to directly translate *euangelizo* in The Top 40 of the 500 English Bible versions: in order of frequency, these 10 are: preach, bring, tell, proclaim, declare, announce, evangelize, give, spread, make hear. Some 34 other English verbs are also used to translate *euangelizo*. Another 40 are used to translate close synonyms. The Big Seven are synonyms being the 7 Mandates of Christ's Great Commission, as shown here in Graphic 23-1. Another 40 verbs translate the 19 major synonyms and near-synonyms of *euangelizo*.

8. *Correctness*. The question arises: Which of all these 700 English verbs can be said to represent the most 'correct' English usage? The answer can only come from actual usage. Both the most correct present usage, and also the future usage, of 'evangelize' must depend to a large extent on past and present usage, both biblical and non-biblical.

9. *Definitions*. In English, some 500 different definitions of the concept 'evangelize' have been set forth in print, using vastly differing terminology and employing over 620 different synonymous verbs. Some definitions have been claimed to be fully comprehensive, or exclusively true, or all embracing, but are found on examination to be oversimplifications. Many definitions are narrow and exclusivist. Some take the view 'Evangelizing means proclamation only, not winning converts', others the view 'Evangelizing means winning converts, not proclamation only', and each has denounced the other as inadequate or incorrect. Of the 500, our analysis lists the 250 major ones and terms them 'macrodefinitions'.

10. *Chaos*. This proliferation of definitions has in turn been denounced by major Christian organizations and gatherings as a situation of 'bewildering variety', 'almost chaotic confusion', and 'a source of disturbing confusion among Christians'. On closer inspection, however, almost all serious definitions that have been set down in black and white are found to be each reporting on only one or several of the multifold aspects of 'evangelize'. Far from being incompatible, they can now be seen to be mutually compatible, and so collectively to form a vast body of cohesive interpretation on the concept of evangelization.

11. *Complexity*. To 'evangelize' is in fact an immensely complex process made up of a large variety of elements. It is multifaceted, pluriform, inclusive and comprehensive. The term 'evangelize' and its cognates are therefore words of tremendous complexity, like all other words that are rich in meaning.

12. *Dimensions*. In this vast complexity, some 420 elements (verbs, imperatives) stand out as, in biblical and historical usage as well as in contemporary usage, the definitive dimensions of 'evangelize'. Collectively these 420 dimensions (from the Latin *dimensio*, a measuring) describe the whole range of meanings of our concept 'evangelize'.

13. *Exclusiveness*. The 420 dimensions are not necessarily all mutually exclusive in meaning, and in fact there is considerable semantic overlapping or partial overlapping among them.

14. *Total facets*. The 500 definitions with their 620 synonyms of 'evangelize' can be reduced to, and categorized under, both these 420 dimensions and also another 180 less significant levels which we term facets. Together with all the higher levels, this makes a grand total of 620 facets in all. These 620 imperatives related to widely-used terms can be identified as distinct and separate dimensions, activities, concepts, aspects, facets, components, parts, stages, phases, steps, elements, or modes of evangelization.

15. *Biblical and nonbiblical*. All of these 420 terms representing dimensions are biblical in the sense of being present as words used in English translations of the Bible. Of these, 110 are translations of the closest biblical synonyms of *euangelizo*; here, we term these 'key dimensions', or macrocommands because they feature in the New Testament accounts of the Great Commission. A small number of other terms, around 100, are not biblical in this sense (e.g. propagation, saturation, diffusion, dissemination, transmission, permeation, feedback, polarization, etc), although they are in accord with the whole biblical ethos.

16. *2,000 synonyms and cognates*. From this analysis of definitions, we arrive at the conclusion that the concept 'evangelize' can be analyzed under, or into, a grand total of 620 facets, using this term to mean English verbs which directly contribute semantically or conceptually to the full-orbed meaning of the word 'evangelize'. All these facets are synonyms, near-synonyms, part-synonyms, analogous words, similes and metaphors or aspects of 'evangelize' in written or spoken use. Finally, with all cognates (nouns and adjectives) these add up to a grand total of 2,400 English words related to 'evangelize'. Our overall deduction is of the overwhelmingly kaleidoscopic nature of the biblical concept *Evangelize!* It can clearly be regarded as the richest term in the entire Christian vocabulary.

17. *Cognates for beneficiaries*. This vast terminology means that we now have a rich terminology for describing not simply evangelizers—those undertaking evangelism—but also its beneficiaries, which means those persons who benefit from being given the Good News. If there are many numerous and different dimensions of evangelizing, there are therefore at least as many different dimensions of being evangelized, becoming evangelized, or having been evangelized. Altogether, this vast pool of related

terminology adds up to the 2,400 total cognates mentioned above.

18. *Interchanging synonyms.* In official translations of church documents, the interchangeability of many of these terms for dimensions is marked. 'Evangelize' and its cognates are often translated interchangeably with their synonyms as a result of the translation process.

19. *Wider meanings.* Most of these dimensions and synonyms have far wider usage in current English than this purely evangelistic meaning. One definition or synonym is 'Evangelization is communication'; but the latter word also covers a vast range of secular meanings (telecommunications, postal services, correspondence, announcements, publications, satellites, telephony, e-mail, faxing, websites, communicable disease, and so on). 'Evangelization' is therefore only a special case of the wider, general category 'communication'.

20. *Listing.* The 420 dimensions, and the total of 620 facets of all kinds including English synonyms, near-synonyms, part-synonyms, analogous words, similes, and metaphors all contribute something to the study of the full-orbed concept of evangelization. This can be grasped by studying any complete listing of all such words. This is done here by listing on a single page the 400 dimensions in alphabetical order in Table 23–18; or by the fuller detailed listings in Table 23–19.

21. *The 7 Mandates.* All 51 macrotranslations, 110 macrocommands, 250 macrodefinitions, 420 dimensions, 620 facets, and 2,400 cognates can be classified or categorized for convenience under the 7 mandates of the Great Commission, and also under a 3-fold typology of viewpoints: (a) the church's viewpoint as the evangelizers, (b) the world's viewpoint as the evangelized, and (c) God's viewpoint as the Divine Evangelizer.

22. *Summary meaning.* From the standpoint of biblical exegesis, the best brief summary of the overall meaning of 'evangelize' and cognates is probably 'obedience to Christ's Great Commission', this being subdivided into its 7 basic mandates *Receive! Go! Witness! Proclaim! Disciple! Baptize! Train!*

23. *Overall meaning.* The best single overall description, therefore, for the meaning of 'evangelize' and cognates is that they express the totality of meaning contained in the 620 facets surveyed here. 'Evangelize' is best used as equivalent to the whole range of activities involved in obedience to the Great Commission and in the spreading of the gospel.

24. *Global terms.* The phrases 'world evangelization' and 'global evangelization' refer to the presence or effect at the global level of all of these 420 dimensions and 620 facets separately, corporately and in aggregate.

25. *Revaluing terms.* 'Evangelize' and cognates are key words and key concepts in Christian theology. If the terms themselves become, or have become, overused, overexposed, debased, discredited or devalued in any way, in any circles, this does not mean that they should now be abandoned or replaced. Instead, they must be revalued or recredited drawing upon their inherent richness of meaning and usage throughout history.

26. *Selective use.* 'Evangelize' and cognates are not, however, indispensable in the sense that they must be used on every and all occasions. To preserve their value, they should only be used selectively and with discrimination in the context of their vast range of synonyms, which should be used to some extent interchangeably and in all cases where the total meaning conveyed by 'evangelize' is not strictly essential, or meant, or required.

27. *Restricting use.* 'Evangelize' and cognates therefore should, preferably, always and only be used when this total meaning is meant, required or essential.

28. *Two nouns.* All modern European languages except English employ, for the activity of evangelizing, only one noun in practice, namely 'evangelization' (or *evangelisation* in French, *Evangelisation* in German, *evangelizzazione* in Italian; etc) derived from the Latin word *evangelizatio*. English is the only language which gives major employ, for the activity of evangelizing, to 2 nouns, the second being 'evangelism' derived from the Greek word *euangelismos*.

29. *Two key terms.* In English, these 2 nouns 'evangelization' and 'evangelism' are not synonyms, but have clear differentia. 'Evangelism' is usually used only in reference to deliberate, organized, human evangelistic activity. 'Evangelization' refers to the whole range of evangelizing activity, both human and divine, as well as the overall situation and status produced by all such activities.

Table 23–1. **30 pairs of English words ending in -ism and -ization.**

| -ism | -ization |
|---|---|
| alcoholism | alcoholization |
| anglicism | anglicization |
| antagonism | antagonization |
| arabism | arabization |
| cannibalism | cannibalization |
| capitalism | capitalization |
| catechism | catechization |
| colonialism | colonialization |
| communism | communization |
| evangelism | evangelization |
| humanism | humanization |
| idealism | idealization |
| institutionalism | institutionalization |
| legalism | legalization |
| liberalism | liberalization |
| magnetism | magnetization |
| mechanism | mechanization |
| militarism | militarization |
| modernism | modernization |
| moralism | moralization |
| nationalism | nationalization |
| organism | organization |
| radicalism | radicalization |
| rationalism | rationalization |
| realism | realization |
| secularism | secularization |
| socialism | socialization |
| spiritualism | spiritualization |
| symbolism | symbolization |
| terrorism | terrorization |

### EVANGELISM AND EVANGELIZATION ARE NOT SYNONYMS

The last point in the foregoing summary must now be elaborated on. Readers who have worked through our survey of usages in detail here and elsewhere will have noticed that almost all Christian writers or conference statements on this subject in the English language have had 3 characteristics in common. Firstly, (1) they prefer to use as their main substantive *either* the word 'evangelization', *or* the word 'evangelism'; secondly, (2) they then use only the one word, to the almost complete exclusion of the other; and thirdly, (3) they treat the other word as completely synonymous, or virtually so, but as a poor substitute.

The most striking illustration of this is the ecumenical evangelist/statesman John R. Mott. As his copious publications show, he shifted from using 'evangelization' almost exclusively before 1910 to replacing it by 'evangelism' almost exclusively after 1935. Another example we have documented elsewhere is the official Roman Catholic avoidance of the English word 'evangelism' and exclusive use of 'evangelization' except in discussion with non-Catholics. This has been a widespread practice. Statements like 'Evangelism or evangelization means the proclamation of good news' (by a South India Protestant missionary in 1934) are common, as also are cases where the writer quotes an earlier definition but, either deliberately, or unwittingly, changes the particular substantive used to the other of the two.

Some literature treats the distinction as so unimportant as to be barely worth bothering about. Thus,

Engel and Norton's 1975 study had as its title *What's gone wrong with the harvest? a communication strategy for the church and world evangelism* on its paperback cover but printed the last 2 words as 'world evangelization' on its title page a couple of pages later. Likewise many publications quote in print the names of bodies with 'Evangelization' in their titles but misquote it as the word 'Evangelism'. A body formed in 1976, the Chinese Congress on World Evangelization (CCOWE), is frequently misquoted as the Chinese Congress on World Evangelism.

But 'evangelization' and 'evangelism' are emphatically not exact synonyms in the English language. One needs only to compile a brief listing of parallel pairs of English words to see that words ending in -ism (which are derived in most cases from Greek roots) always have different nuances of meaning to their counterparts ending in -ization (which are derived in most cases from Latin roots). Table 23–1 illustrates this.

From this table we may generalize that words ending with -ism tend to represent ideology (as witness Fascism, Nazism, Marxism, Maoism, et alia); and words ending with -ization tend to represent a wider and more inclusive entity, namely the related processes of action or the spreading of some characteristic. Thus 'secularism' refers to 'A concept of the world according to which the latter is self-explanatory, without any need for recourse to God, who thus becomes superfluous and an encumbrance', or 'A view of life based on the premise that religion and religious considerations should be ignored or purposely excluded' (Webster); while 'secularization' refers to 'The act or process of making secular; or of converted to or imbuing with secularism; the condition of being secularized' (Webster). In other words, 'secularism' is an ideology contained within, 'or covered by, or one of the aspects of, the wider entity 'secularization'.'

Evangelization, then, is much more than evangelism. Exactly what the differentia are between the 2 concepts will now be investigated.

### EVANGELISM DEFINED

In Part 22 we investigated thoroughly the term 'evangelism' and how to define and enumerate it. Now we turn our attention for a moment to defining it in greater detail in order to highlight its differentia vis-a-vis 'evangelization'. Here are 4 more or less authoritative definitions.

1. 'Evangelism: performance of the functions of an evangelist' (*Oxford English dictionary*, 1897).

2. 'Evangelism is the participation of the total Christian community in Christ's mission in the world' (*World Council of Churches, Evangelism*, 1954).

3. 'Evangelism is the activity of the Church in telling the Gospel to sinners with intent to bring them to a saving knowledge of Christ' (Macauley & Belton, *Personal evangelism*, 1956).

4. 'Evangelism is what we do to help make the Christian faith, life and mission a live option to undiscipled people, both outside and inside the congregation' (G.G. Hunter, *The contagious congregation*, 1979).

From these definitions, we will list the differentia of this word 'evangelism' and then explain them somewhat. Evangelism is
—human activity
—conscious activity
—deliberate activity
—planned activity
—organized activity
—overt activity
—church activity
—ecclesiastical activity

The English word 'evangelism' has over the centuries come to refer to a distinctly and distinctively human activity on the part of the church or of individual Christians. It is the church's conscious day-to-day raison d'etre and responsibility, and consists of the specific, deliberate activities, approaches, methods and methodologies involved in discharging that responsibility. 'Evangelism' now appears to be one, though only one, of the component parts of the wider entity 'evangelization'. Defined as overt organized activities, evangelism can cease overnight, as for instance in a country when a violently anti-religious Communist military regime has taken power and immediately banned all overt evangelistic activity. In such a case, the *extent* of evangelization may remain completely unchanged or unaffected for several years thereafter. Usually it is the case that evangelism influences evangelization, especially its state or extent, but it is not necessarily the case. Much evangelism is directed only at existing church members, who by definition have already been adequately evangelized, and so produces no further fresh evangelization nor increases the state or extent of evangelization one iota. Some evangelism, if insensitive to local culture and politics, may actually impede, or obstruct, or even harm evangelization.

Evangelism can be regarded as in indicator of the rate of change of the state and extent of evangelization in a population or country. If there is no evangelism going on, the state of evangelization remains virtually static or stagnant or unchanged from one day to the next.

Evangelism, then, is the church's human, conscious, deliberate, planned, organized, overt, church, ecclesiastical, evangelizing activity and activities, approaches, methods, and methodologies involved in the spreading of the gospel.

## EVANGELISM AND EVANGELIZATION: HUMAN AND DIVINE

Another way of understanding these 2 terms is the allocating of human responsibility. Evangelism is human activity, the response of humans (Christians) to the Great Commission. But above it we must always recognize a much wider sphere of evangelizing influence including God's own evangelizing activity. This can be examined in various ways.

### *Christ the Evangelizer*

Our survey in Part 3 and elsewhere has shown that throughout history Christians have recognized the central role in evangelizing activity of Jesus as God the Son. As the Gospel of Matthew puts it, 'He who sows the good seed is the Son of Man'. Christ is the subject of *euangelizo* 9 times out of its 56 New Testament occurrences (this is 16%). Hence, 'evangelizing' is always Christ's own work, in which the church may from time to time be allowed to participate and cooperate. For Protestants, Jesus Christ is therefore the True Witness, the Supreme Missionary, already at work across the world long before his church arrives on the scene. 'The Church must be aware that Christ precedes us in evangelism'. He is the Evangelist (WCC Evanston Assembly, 1954), the Master Evangelist whose methods all should study and follow. The church's role is minor: as Karl Barth has stated, 'The church merely accompanies him in mission, assisting as it can'.

To quote the WCC's 2nd Assembly in 1954: 'We must remember that evangelism is God's work in which we are the agents. It is not our own work.' For Roman Catholics, he is 'Christ the Evangelizer': 'Jesus himself, the Good News of God, was the very first and the greatest evangelizer'; hence 'Evangelization is the actual, operative action of Christ here and now in his Church'.

### *The Spirit of Evangelization*

In the same way, this survey shows that Christians have always recognized the central role of God the Holy Spirit in evangelization. The Holy Spirit, as third person of the Holy Trinity, is Jesus Christ in another form; in Acts 16:7, he is termed 'the Spirit of Jesus'. As noted earlier, in 9 of the 56 occurrences of *euangelizo* in the New Testament, the verb is used in the context of activity on the part of the Holy Spirit ('Messengers announced the Good News (*euangelizo*) by the power of the Holy Spirit', 1 Peter 1:12, GNB). Consequently, for Anglicans, 'The Holy Spirit is *the* communicator; the Church is the medium of communication' (D. Webster 1974:15). For Protestants, as John Mott wrote in 1900, 'Above all, preaching the Gospel involves the accompanying power and work of the Holy Spirit'. Or, in the words of the official radio preacher of The Lutheran Hour, 'Apostolic evangelism is carried out in the power of the Holy Spirit'; and, 'Evangelism depends much on the prevenient work of the Holy Spirit'. For the Eastern Orthodox, 'It is God, through the power of the Holy Spirit, who does the work of evangelistic witness'. For Roman Catholics, 'The Holy Spirit is the principal agent of evangelization'. *Evangelii Nuntiandi* devotes its last chapter, VII, to the subject it entitles 'The Spirit of Evangelization'. An excellent section elaborates on the Holy Spirit's prevenient work of evangelization:

> The Holy Spirit places on every evangelizer's lips the words which he could not find by himself, and at the same time the Holy Spirit predisposes the soul of the hearer to be open and receptive to the Good News and to the Kingdom being proclaimed... It is he who in the depths of consciences causes the word of salvation to be accepted and understood... Through the Holy Spirit the Gospel penetrates to the heart of the world.

### *Two types of evangelizer*

We noted earlier that 70% of occurrences of the word *euangelizo* in the New Testament refer to human activity, which we are also terming ecclesiastical evangelistic activity, whilst 30% refer to divine activity without ecclesiastical evangelistic involvement. From this and the above 2 paragraphs we may observe that in Christian experience there are 2 distinct types of evangelizer involved in the whole process of evangelization: (1) the divine, sinless Evangelizer, whether seen as God or Christ or as his Holy Spirit, and (2) human, ecclesiastical, sinful evangelizers. Further, these latter consist of 4 varieties: (a) witnesses, i.e. the active lay church of ordinary Christians who witness to Christ as opportunity arises, as and where possible in their daily secular avocations; (b) evangelizers proper, referring to ordinary Christians who deliberately make opportunities to pass on to others the Good News; (c) evangelists, i.e. full-time Christian workers dedicated to the work of organized public mass evangelism; and (d) church leaders, this latter as exemplified by the Eastern Orthodox affirmative: 'The chief evangelizer of the Church is the bishop with his presbyterion and diaconate as well as the monastic establishment'.

Historically, this latter is the way it was for hundreds of years. This is the way the Irish bishop Kilian and his 11 companions evangelized in 7th-century Germany. It was dangerous, though—all 12 were soon martyred, as were a long succession of evangelizer-bishops throughout Europe's Dark Ages: Adalbert, Alphege, Boniface, Eskil, Gerard of Csanad, Gottschalk, Henry of Uppsala, Kuno of Trier, Magnus, Stanislaw, Thomas Becket, et alii.

A good biblical illustration of these distinctions comes from the story of Philip and the Ethiopian eunuch in Acts 8: 26-40. The human evangelizer is Philip the Deacon, who was both a church leader (*diakonos*, one of the original diaconate) and also an evangelist (*euangelistes*). On this occasion he was also an ordinary witness (*martys;* see Acts 1:8) on his travels, not expecting in the desert to engage in organized evangelism or evangelistic endeavor (which he had earlier been engaged in at Samaria, verse 5). Suddenly, opportunity arises. In response to the Ethiopian official's request, Philip evangelized him up to the point of baptizing him. But behind all Philip's human activities, in this account we also see clearly a whole chain of events produced directly by the organizing agency and evangelistic influence of the Holy Spirit (see especially 8:29, 39). The Spirit's work in preparation of the ground long before Philip's evangelism began requires a special descriptive term, which we will shortly coin.

### *Evangelization: 3 major types*

As a result, we can now recognize, formalize, and define 2 distinct types of evangelization, depending on whether or not human evangelistic involvement is present. If it is, we can further divide the latter into 2 forms of activity, depending on whether or not this human involvement has been organized and planned, or is unorganized and unplanned. Thus we arrive at the schema below, which can be verbalized in the following sentences.

**Table 23–2. A schema of 3 major types of evangelization.**

| *Characteristic* | *Type 1* | *Type 2* | *Type 3* |
|---|---|---|---|
| Divine involvement | Present | Present | Present in all evangelization |
| Human involvement | Present | Present | Absent (or, not consciously or deliberately present) |
| Human evangelistic activity | Unplanned | Planned | None |
| **Type of evangelization** | **Witness** | **Evangelism** | **Pneumatic Evangelization** (Pneumatization) |

There are 3 main types of evangelization, as shown in Table 23–2. There is divine involvement in all 3 types of evangelization, but there is not necessarily deliberate human involvement. If human evangelistic involvement is also present, we term it 'evangelism'. So then, if it is the unorganized, unplanned, random, individual witnessing activity of Christians, it is termed in some church circles (by no means all) 'witness': or, if it is the organized, planned, deliberate, overt, ecclesiastical evangelistic activity of the church interspersed with individual witness, we term it 'evangelism'. If no conscious or deliberate human evangelistic activity is involved, then only the Spirit of Evangelization is evangelistically involved, and so we will now have to create the neologisms in the schema to describe it. These neologisms will be explained over the next few pages.

### *The evangelism of Jesus*

The evangelistic activity of Jesus himself is in a special category because Jesus was both human and divine, both Son of Man and Son of God. It has become usual in English to describe his evangelizing work during his 3-year ministry in Palestine as 'evangelism', not 'evangelization'. A refinement would be to say that Jesus' evangelism then was part of his wider work of evangelization. Thus literature on his ministry speaks of *The evangelism of Jesus* (E.C. Wareing 1918); *The personal evangelism of Jesus* (F.V. McFatridge 1939): and *The evangelism of Jesus* (M. Stokes 1960); while the best-selling manual by Methodist professor of evangelism R.E. Coleman, *They met the Master* (1973) was subtitled *A study manual on the personal evangelism of Jesus.* His work before the Resurrection was visibly human, hence in our schema it is properly termed evangelism.

## EVANGELIZATION WITHOUT EVANGELISM

We have next to consider what to make of the vast amount of evangelizing activity which is not evangelism as defined above, involving neither the earthly activity of Jesus in Palestine nor human evangelistic activity after Pentecost. What remains is not very prominent in the New Testament—8 occurrences of *euangelizo* out of 56, or 14%—but this is because purely divine activity is not being highlighted on this subject. The 14% is in fact only the tip of the iceberg. If the Holy Spirit, the Divine Evangelizer, is evangelizing through some activity or agency which has no conscious human or ecclesiastical evangelistic involvement, then we need a term or terms to describe it. As shown in the schema in Table 23–2, in this study we coin and use the neologisms 'pneumatic evangelization' or 'pneumatization' for this widespread and significant activity. It will shortly be defined and expounded below, and a number of examples of its 'silent' witness will be described as factors in the Scale of Comparative Demographic Evangelization that will be evolved in Part 24.

## EVANGELIZATION CLASSIFIED UNDER ITS KEYWORDS

A fair number of notable attempts have been made to divide the overall concept 'evangelization' into its major components or keywords or ingredients or basic elements or dimensions. For some scholars this has meant dichotomization into 2 major elements; for others, 3,4,5,6,7,8 or even 9 components were essential. In the 1930s Swiss Reformed theologian Karl Barth analyzed the church's witness in its plurality under the 2 heads 'speech' and 'action', each with 6 subdivisions or dimensions to it, giving 12 basic forms of ministry which, he held, have always characterized the church through the ages. These are shown

| Table 23–3. | **Karl Barth's analysis of the major components of evangelization.** |
| --- | --- |

| Speech | Action |
| --- | --- |
| praise | prayer |
| preaching | cure of souls |
| teaching | production of outstanding Christian examples |
| evangelization | physical and material service |
| foreign missions | prophetic action |
| theology | fellowship |

in Table 23–3.

Others followed with different listings. Mott's anthology of 120 different definitions of 'evangelize' for the Tambaram IMC conference in 1938 contained several such short lists submitted by his correspondents. As one illustration, the agricultural missionary S. Higginbottom listed 5 keywords: 'Evangelism is the *presentation* of the Gospel by *preaching, teaching, healing* and *service*'.

The best way to form a typology has appeared subsequently to many people to be to select the 3 or 4 nouns in New Testament Greek which seem to them to best constitute together the essence of evangelization. The first clear typology of his kind was a 3-fold one which emerged in 1950 with Dutch ecumenist J.C. Hoekendijk's widely-influential article 'The call to evangelism'. Evangelism to be valid, he said, must have 3 complementary components widely used in the Greek New Testament: preaching (*kerygma*), fellowship (*koinonia*), and service (*diakonia*). Throughout the decade of the 1950s, the World Council of Churches continued to debate 'What are the true dimensions of evangelism?' and answered this with Hoekendijk's typology as formalized in the title of Episcopalian canon T.O. Wedel's 1957 study: 'Evangelism's threefold witness: *kerygma, koinonia, diakonia.*'

Inevitably, however, others even within the WCC secretariat perceived different Greek keywords to be the major ones. In 1955 Hoekendijk's successor as WCC Secretary for Evangelism, Ceylonese evangelist D.T. Niles, wrote in his book *An evangelizing church:*

> The methods by which the early church propagated the faith are described in the New Testament as *kerussein* (preaching), *dialegesthai* (discussion), and *didaskein* (teaching).

Others found Hoekendijk's trilogy compelling but inadequate. In a 1959 study, Anglican canon Douglas Webster insisted that in evangelism there were not 3 essential ingredients but 4. The fourth, vital, element, was another Greek noun meaning 'witness':

> These four ingredients—fellowship (*koinonia*), preaching (*kerygma*), witness (*martyria*) and service (*diakonia*)—make up the evangelism of the early Church. They are the permanent and unalterable and indispensable elements of all true evangelism.

Fifteen years later, however, Webster proffered a quite different 3-fold schema:

> Evangelism has three ingredients: knowing the gospel, communicating the Gospel, persuading but not compelling men about the Gospel.

Meanwhile, market researcher J. Engel and American Evangelical colleagues put forward yet another trilogy:

> The Great Commission has three communication mandates: to proclaim, to persuade, and to cultivate the believer (Engel & Norton 1975).

At this time also, Evangelical missiologist C. Peter Wagner coined the phrase '3P Evangelism', defining evangelism in terms of 3 English nouns beginning with the letter P: Presence, Proclamation, and Persuasion. Still others have added further nouns. Surveying earlier attempts, South African missiologist David J. Bosch in 1980 noted that in Western missiological circles 'evangelism' had long been considered synonymous with 'mission'. For 'mission' he proposed the 5-fold typology *martyria, kerygma, koinonia, diakonia, leitourgia,* this latter (meaning worship or

liturgical service) being 'the encounter of the Church with the Lord'. He also added, for good measure, *dialogismos* (dialogue), *oikodome* (edification of members), and the Latin word *praesencia* (presence).

Obviously, each of these typologies is valid, helpful, and illuminating. Our problem is that they are all different.

It is extraordinarily difficult to be fully consistent in this matter. The formal teachings of recent Roman pontiffs on this subject are instructive. In 1975's *Evangelii Nuntiandi,* section 17, Paul VI defined evangelization in terms of 5 elements often identified with it, as shown in Table 23–4 (arranged here with the official English version's terms on the left, with their counterparts from the official Latin version on the right). But in the same document only 7 pages later on, in section 24, he gave an entirely different listing of 7 elements, using the words shown in Table 23–5.

Six years later in the Philippines, his successor John Paul II, a keen admirer and frequent expositor of *Evangelii Nuntiandi,* gave a definitive listing of the 9 'vital dimensions of evangelization'. As Table 23–6 shows, only 3 of these dimensions occur in Paul VI's 2 lists in either the official English or Latin versions.

These 3 papal lists, as can be seen, barely overlap—they might just as well be definitions of 3 entirely different or distinct (though obviously related) concepts. The 3 lists barely overlap either with Karl Barth's 12-fold list above. They also barely overlap with Mott's, or Hoekendijk's, or Wedel's, or Niles', or Webster's, or Wagner's, or Bosch's, or any of the other detailed Protestant, Anglican and Orthodox lists surveyed in the monograph *Evangelize! a historical survey of the concept* (1987). We seem to be faced with contradictory ideas within confessions and even within leading individuals in those confessions.

There is, however, a simple solution. The only way to make sense of all this is to say that each and every one of these elements listed above, or for that matter elsewhere, forms part of the total of all elements or components of evangelization, but that different ex-

| Table 23–4. | **Paul VI's analysis of the 5 major components of evangelization.** |
| --- | --- |

| English | Latin |
| --- | --- |
| proclamation | demonstratio |
| preaching | praedicatio |
| catechesis | catechesis |
| baptism | baptismus |
| sacraments | dispensatio |

| Table 23–5. | **Paul's VI's alternative analysis of the 7 major components of evangelization.** |
| --- | --- |

'Evangelization is made up of various elements:'

| English | Latin |
| --- | --- |
| renewal | renovatio |
| witness | testificatio |
| proclamation | nuntiatio |
| adherence | adhaesio |
| entry | ingressio |
| signs | signa |
| apostolic initiative | opera |

| Table 23–6. | **John Paul II's analysis of the 9 major components of evangelization.** |
| --- | --- |

| English |
| --- |
| proclaiming |
| administering sacraments |
| teaching |
| catechizing |
| caring for the sick |
| assisting the poor and orphans |
| exercising charity |
| serving by prayer and sacrifice |
| building up local communities |

positors under differing circumstances may well need to quote different abbreviated selections for their own immediate purposes.

The approach we therefore adopt in this present analysis takes this thinking a stage further, hopefully to its logical conclusion where all the major elements become included. As we saw above when describing

Global Diagram 7, we can locate in the Greek New Testament not just 3 or 4 keywords closely identified with *euangelizo* and cognates; we can locate at least 210 synonymous Greeks verbs with scores more related cognates including participles, adjectives, and nouns. If we restrict our search for the moment to Greek nouns, 17 major ones often referred to as closely related to *euangelizo* immediately come to light, as shown in Table 23–7.

### EVANGELIZATION CLASSIFIED UNDER SEVEN MANDATES

Having presented a range of proposed typologies, we will now attempt to create one single typology embracing all such meanings. To begin with, we should see whether this listing above can be reduced to a small handful of major keywords, in the interests of understanding the overall picture. From the biblical point of view, the best single overall meaning of 'evangelize' and cognates is probably that utilized by the mission historian K.S. Latourette: the meaning is 'obedience to the Great Commission'. As we discovered in Global Diagram 6, this phrase can be subdivided into 7 essential elements, components, ingredients, stages, or phases, based on the 7 basic Great Com-

| Table 23–7. | **17 New Testament Greek keywords closely related to euangelizo.** |
| --- | --- |

| Greek | English |
| --- | --- |
| euangelion | good news |
| kerygma | proclamation |
| koinonia | fellowship |
| diakonia | service, diaconate |
| martyria | witness, martyrdom |
| didache | teaching, didactic |
| poreuthentes | going, carrying |
| apostole (apostello) | apostolate |
| paraklesis | exhortation, Paraclete |
| apologismos | apologetics |
| pneuma, -tikos | pneumatization |
| leitourgia | liturgy |
| eucharistia | eucharist |
| dialogismos | dialogue |
| therapeia | therapy, healing |
| mathetes | disciple, -ing |
| baptismos | baptism, baptizing |

mission mandates and their keywords: *Receive! Go! Witness! Proclaim! Disciple! Baptize! Train!* The actual words used in the Greek New Testament's account of the formal words of Christ in instituting this 7-fold Great Commission—all usually translated as imperatives in English though 3 are participles in the Greek and one is a noun—are as follows: *labete, poreuthentes, martyres, keruxate, matheteusate, baptizontes, didaskontes.* This gives us a 7-fold typology which we will shortly develop in the tables below.

A classic illustration of this 7-fold sequence may be noted at this point from 2 Pauline passages. In 1 Corinthians 12:28 (dated AD 54), the Apostle lists 8 varieties of ministry: apostles, prophets, teachers, miracle-workers, healers, helpers, administrators, tongues-speakers. A decade later, in Ephesians 4:11-12 (dated AD 63, hence describing a later stage in church organization), he lists only 5 varieties: apostles, prophets, evangelists, pastors, teachers. In this latter passage, Paul is comparing God's gift of the Levites to his people for service in the time of Moses, with God's gift of Christian workers to equip his people for service in the Apostolic era. Quoting from Psalm 68:18, he says of Christ: 'It was he who 'gave gifts to mankind'; he appointed some to be apostles, others to be prophets, others to be evangelists, others to be pastors and teachers' (Ephesians 4:11, GNB).

From the standpoint of evangelization, these 2 Pauline passages may be paraphrased and combined into 7 categories as follows, and as set out in Table 23–8. (1) Christ through the Spirit has given to all receptive followers, or *disciples,* the necessary gifts for successful evangelism. (2) As a result, some were called to be *apostles,* pioneers traveling to distant lands to initiate the work of the gospel. (3) Others would be *prophets,* witnessing to the nations in the power of the Spirit, these being accredited and supported by striking phenomena such as those accompanying tongues-speakers. (4) Others would be *evangelists,* itinerant foreign missionaries like Paul himself, proclaiming the gospel everywhere, often with such

**Table 23–8. Seven ministries or vocations in response to 7 Mandates of the Great Commission.**

| Stage | Text | Keyword | Mandate | Type of evangelism | Type of evangelization |
|-------|------|---------|---------|--------------------|-----------------------|
| 1 | These were his gifts | disciples | 1 Receive! | Prayer evangelism | Pneumatic evangelization |
| 2 | some to be apostles | apostles | 2 Go! | Pre-evangelism | Preparatory evangelization |
| 3 | some to be prophets | prophets | 3 Witness! | Personal evangelism | Presence evangelization |
| 4 | some to be evangelists | evangelists | 4 Proclaim! | Preaching evangelism | Proclamation evangelization |
| 5 | some to be healers | healers | 5 Disciple! | Persuasion evangelism | Pressure evangelization |
| 6 | some to be pastors | pastors | 6 Baptize! | Pastoral evangelism | Planting evangelization |
| 7 | some to be teachers | teachers | 7 Train! | Programmed evangelism | Pedagogical evangelization |

'signs following' as 'demonstrations of mighty powers' given by miracle-workers. (Note in passing that the Contemporary English Version translates Paul's word in Ephesians *evangelistas*, not by 'evangelists' but by 'missionaries'). (5) Others would be *healers*, assisting body and soul to get right with God, persuading hearers to become disciples. (6) Still others would be *pastors* to baptize and shepherd the new converts, building up the church, assisted by such helpers as deacons (providing practical services) and administrators (responsible for finance). Lastly, (7) yet others would be *teachers*, training disciples and

commissioning them in turn to go forth in outreach and mobilizing them for multiplication evangelism.

Using variations of wording in several English New Testament versions, we can therefore arrange the 7 stages described in these passages in Table 23–8. At the same time we add, in a final column, neologisms for 7 types of evangelization ('7-P Evangelization') related to, or parallel to, or incorporating, the 7 types of evangelism ('7-P Evangelism') in the preceding column.

These 2 easily remembered linked phrases for each Mandate of this 7-fold English-language typology—

'7-P Evangelization calling for 7-P Evangelism'—are presented in Global Diagram 6. Each Mandate, and each pair of linked phrases, are fully expounded here in Table 23–19, 'Documenting the 420 dimensions of "evangelize".'

### ANALYZING 'EVANGELIZE' AND 'EVANGELIZATION'

It is now time to link the word 'evangelize' with the wider meaning contained in the noun 'evangelization'. Graphic 23-1, which is further expanded in Part 1 "GeoStatus" as Global Diagram 33, presents 10 levels of analysis. The starting point is the group of actual English verbs used in English Bibles to translate *euangelizo*.

#### Analysis 1: HOW THE TOP 40 ENGLISH BIBLES TRANSLATE EUANGELIZO

In order to discover the whole meaning for today of the English word 'evangelize', the most obvious place

**Graphic 23–1. Ten levels of analysis of 'evangelize' and 'evangelization' in 420 kaleidoscopic dimensions.**

This graphic portrays in abbreviated form relationships and clusterings among English verbs related to the English word 'evangelize'. This verb is portrayed below by the heavy, central circle. Around it are circles depicting the major English synonyms and near-synonyms, almost all of which are used in English Bible versions. Full details of the meaning and background of all terms are set out in Global Diagram 33 in Part 1.

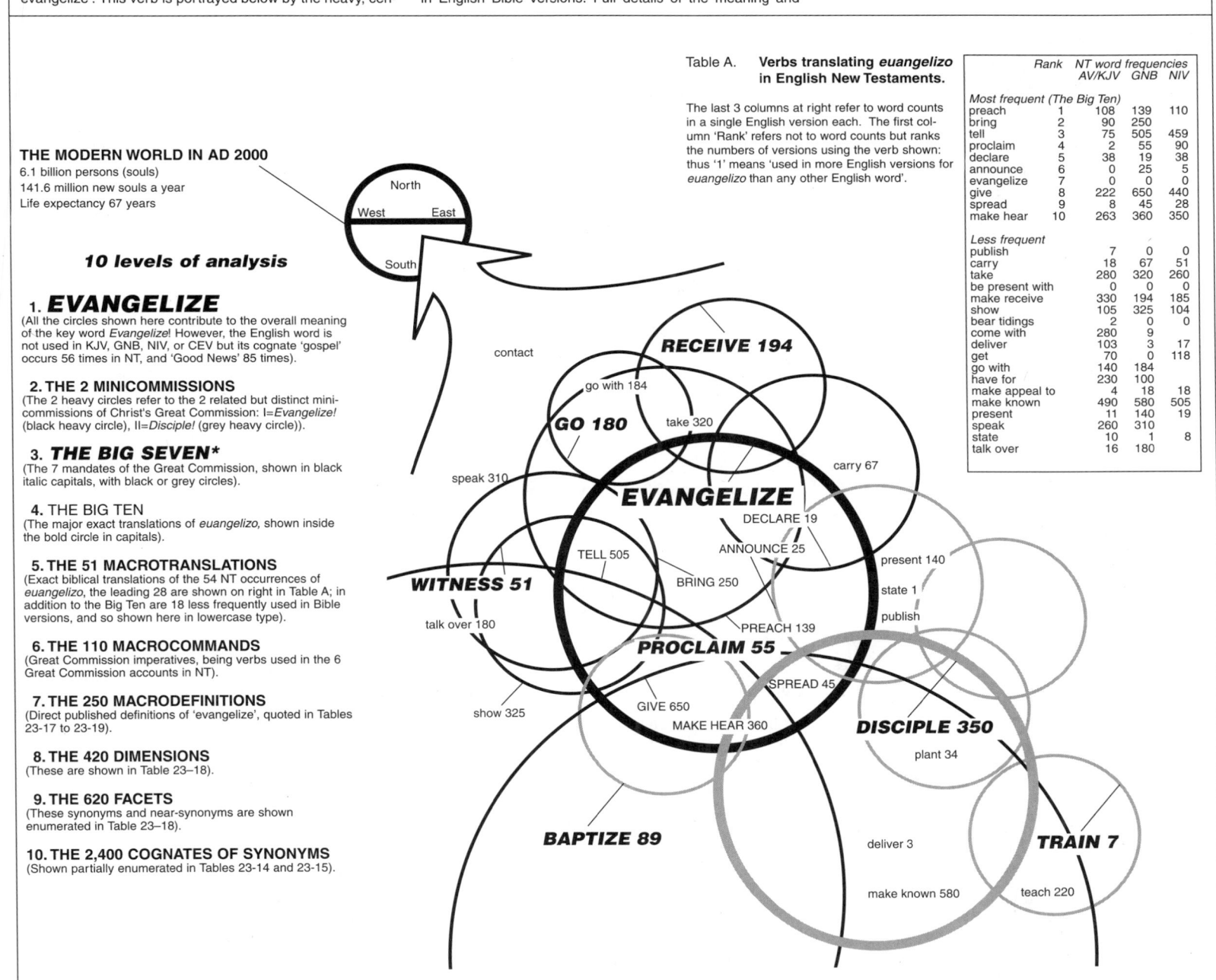

**Table A. Verbs translating *euangelizo* in English New Testaments.**

The last 3 columns at right refer to word counts in a single English version each. The first column 'Rank' refers not to word counts but ranks the numbers of versions using the verb shown: thus '1' means 'used in more English versions for *euangelizo* than any other English word'.

| | Rank | NT word frequencies | | |
|---|------|------|------|------|
| | | AV/KJV | GNB | NIV |
| *Most frequent (The Big Ten)* | | | | |
| preach | 1 | 108 | 139 | 110 |
| bring | 2 | 90 | 250 | |
| tell | 3 | 75 | 505 | 459 |
| proclaim | 4 | 2 | 55 | 90 |
| declare | 5 | 38 | 19 | 38 |
| announce | 6 | 0 | 25 | 5 |
| evangelize | 7 | 0 | 0 | 0 |
| give | 8 | 222 | 650 | 440 |
| spread | 9 | 8 | 45 | 28 |
| make hear | 10 | 263 | 360 | 350 |
| | | | | |
| *Less frequent* | | | | |
| publish | | 7 | 0 | 0 |
| carry | | 18 | 67 | 51 |
| take | | 280 | 320 | 260 |
| be present with | | 0 | 0 | 0 |
| make receive | | 330 | 194 | 185 |
| show | | 105 | 325 | 104 |
| bear tidings | | 2 | 0 | 0 |
| come with | | 280 | 9 | |
| deliver | | 103 | 3 | 17 |
| get | | 70 | 0 | 118 |
| go with | | 140 | 184 | |
| have for | | 230 | 100 | |
| make appeal to | | 4 | 18 | 18 |
| make known | | 490 | 580 | 505 |
| present | | 11 | 140 | 19 |
| speak | | 260 | 310 | |
| state | | 10 | 1 | 8 |
| talk over | | 16 | 180 | |

**THE MODERN WORLD IN AD 2000**
6.1 billion persons (souls)
141.6 million new souls a year
Life expectancy 67 years

*10 levels of analysis*

1. **EVANGELIZE**
(All the circles shown here contribute to the overall meaning of the key word *Evangelize*! However, the English word is not used in KJV, GNB, NIV, or CEV although its cognate 'gospel' occurs 56 times in NT, and 'Good News' 85 times).

2. **THE 2 MINICOMMISSIONS**
(The 2 heavy circles refer to the 2 related but distinct minicommissions of Christ's Great Commission: I=*Evangelize!* (black heavy circle), II=*Disciple!* (grey heavy circle)).

3. **THE BIG SEVEN***
(The 7 mandates of the Great Commission, shown in black italic capitals, with black or grey circles).

4. THE BIG TEN
(The major exact translations of *euangelizo*, shown inside the bold circle in capitals).

5. **THE 51 MACROTRANSLATIONS**
(Exact biblical translations of the 54 NT occurrences of *euangelizo*, the leading 28 are shown on right in Table A; in addition to the Big Ten are 18 less frequently used in Bible versions, and so shown here in lowercase type).

6. **THE 110 MACROCOMMANDS**
(Great Commission imperatives, being verbs used in the 6 Great Commission accounts in NT).

7. **THE 250 MACRODEFINITIONS**
(Direct published definitions of 'evangelize', quoted in Tables 23-17 to 23-19).

8. **THE 420 DIMENSIONS**
(These are shown in Table 23–18).

9. **THE 620 FACETS**
(These synonyms and near-synonyms are shown enumerated in Table 23–18).

10. **THE 2,400 COGNATES OF SYNONYMS**
(Shown partially enumerated in Tables 23-14 and 23-15).

| Date | Initials | Title |
|------|----------|-------|
| | | **Table 23–9. The Top 41 Bibles, being 41 major versions of the complete Bible in English, AD 1382-2000.** |
| 1382 | WB | Wycliffe Bible (First Version) |
| 1535 | CB | Coverdale's Bible |
| 1537 | TB-M | Tyndale Bible (Matthew's) |
| 1539 | GB-C | Great Bible (Coverdale's/Cromwell's/Cranmer's) |
| 1560 | GB | Geneva Bible |
| 1568 | BB | Bishops' Bible |
| 1610 | DRB | Douai-Rheims Bible |
| 1611 | AV/KJV | Authorized Version (King James Version) |
| 1749 | DRCB | Douai-Rheims-Challoner Bible |
| 1885 | RV/ERV | Revised Version (English RV) |
| 1901 | ASV | American Standard Version |
| 1902 | EB-R | Emphasized Bible (Rotherham) |
| 1903 | HBME | Holy Bible in Modern English (The Complete Bible) |
| 1924 | MB | Moffatt Bible |
| 1939 | AT/GB | American Translation (Goodspeed Bible) |
| 1949 | BBE | Basic Bible (Bible in Basic English) |
| 1950 | KB | Knox Bible |
| 1952 | RSV | Revised Standard Version |
| 1957 | HBAEM | Holy Bible from Ancient Eastern Manuscripts (Lamsa) |
| 1959 | MLB/NBV | Modern Language Bible (New Berkeley Version) |
| 1961 | NWT | New World Translation |
| 1961 | NCE/CCD | New Catholic Edition/Confraternity of Christian Doctrine |
| 1964 | AB | Anchor Bible |
| 1965 | AmB | Amplified Bible |
| 1966 | JB | Jerusalem Bible |
| 1970 | NAB | New American Bible |
| 1970 | NEB | New English Bible |
| 1971 | TLB | The Living Bible |
| 1971 | NASB | New American Standard Bible |
| 1976 | GNB/TEV | Good News Bible (Today's English Version) |
| 1978 | NIV | New International Version |
| 1982 | NKJV | New King James Version |
| 1985 | NJB | New Jerusalem Bible |
| 1986 | NLV | New Life Version |
| 1987 | NCV | New Century Version |
| 1988 | CCB | Christian Community Bible (Catholic Pastoral Edition) |
| 1989 | NRSV | New Revised Standard Version |
| 1989 | REB | Revised English Bible |
| 1995 | GW | God's Word to the Nations |
| 1995 | CEV | Contemporary English Version |
| 1996 | NLT | New Living Translation |
| 2004 | CSB | Christian Standard Bible |

to start is the Bible. The Greek verb *euangelizo* occurs 54 times in the Koine Greek New Testament and 50 times in the Septuagint, the first Greek Old Testament. Which English verb or verbs translate it in the English Bible?

The answer is straightforward, but finding it is complex indeed. To start with, there are now over 500 different translations of the complete Bible into English. Some 40 of these are of major significance, and these we have analyzed in detail. Most are well-known by their initials. They are, with first publication date of each's complete Bible, as shown in Table 23–9. The one exception to this dating procedure is the Anchor Bible, which began publication in 1964 with different scholars handling a book each, and is still in progress in 1999.

Tables 23-9 and 23-12 actually list 41 Bible versions (plus 1 more by AD 2004), but the subsequent detailed analysis deals with 40 (including the Anchor Bible, although still not completed 36 years after first publication, but excluding 1996's NLT as close to 1971's TLB). For this reason this list of major English Bibles is here termed either The Top 40 (popular usage) or The Top 41 (more precise), even The Top 42 (by AD 2005).

Let us now proceed to list systematically the words used for *euangelizo* in these Top 40 Bibles. To make the study more precise, we restrict it to words in the Greek New Testament only, excluding the Septuagint. This procedure results in the listings in Table 23–12, which will shortly be analyzed.

In accordance with the best modern translation practice, no complex Greek or Hebrew Bible word is necessarily always translated by the same, single English word. A variety of words may be used, heavily reliant on context. We will not be surprised to discover, therefore, that *euangelizo* is translated in the 40 major English Bibles by, not one, but 44 different English words. If one expands the list to cover as well a dozen less widely-known English versions, including partial versions (usually New Testament only),

the total rises to 60 English words. But first we must examine the leading contenders in influence, those in complete Bible versions.

### Analysis 2:
### THE 2 MINICOMMISSIONS

This analysis of the Great Commission has already begun in Part 3 "GeoCommission" by dividing the Commission into 2 Minicommissions, 'Evangelize!' and 'Disciple!'. The typologies that result are set out in Global Diagram 6, and shown here in abbreviated form in Graphic 23-1.

### Analysis 3:
### THE BIG SEVEN

The 2 Minicommissions are further divided into the 7 Mandates of the Great Commission, set out in Global Diagrams 6 and 33. These are referred to now as the Big Seven, as illustrated in Graphic 23-1.

### Analysis 4:
### THE MOST-USED TRANSLATIONS: THE BIG TEN

A first major line of investigation arises when we ask what are the 'Top Ten' ways to translate *euangelizo*. The first thing the reader notices is that 10 English verbs stand out as more widely used than any of the rest. These are set out in Table 23–10, and are put in wider context in Table 23–13. The actual frequencies are shown in Table 23–12.

Taken together, these 10 imperatives may be regarded as the Bible's answer to the question: Which are the 10 leading meanings of the transliterated verb that is *euangelizo* in Greek?

### Analysis 5:
### 51 MACROTRANSLATIONS OF EUANGELIZO

A second major line of investigation arises when we examine the entire range of words used to directly translate *euangelizo*. To emphasize the significance of the 44 English words used in English complete Bibles to directly translate this word, plus 16 other words used in other New Testaments, we here label them 'macrotranslations'. They have been used, repeated, copied, published, disseminated, commented on, so many times that they have had major formative influence on English-speaking Christianity, and especially on English-speaking home missions, foreign missions, evangelism, and the whole world of influence of the Scriptures and their dissemination.

These macrotranslations are set out in Table 23–12. Vertically, the 54 New Testament locations with usages of *euangelizo* are listed. Horizontally, the 41 leading English complete Bible versions are shown. A numerical analysis of frequency is given under the table on the 2 facing pages, and a further analysis in Table 23–13.

Table 23–13 then lists and analyzes the 51 macrotranslations in 3 ways—alphabetically, by mandate, and by frequency of occurrence in The Top 40 English Bible versions.

### Analysis 6:
### 110 GREAT COMMISSION MACROCOMMANDS

A third major line of investigation arises when we realize the close relation between the word 'evangelize' and Christ's Great Commission. The latter is the English term most frequently used to describe the 6 New Testament narratives in which the Risen Christ imparted his final instructions to his disciples before his Ascension. These 6 narratives are: Matthew 28:18-20, Mark 16:15-20, Luke 24:44-53, John 20:19-31, John 21:4-25, and Acts 1:1-14.

In the Greek originals of these narratives, and in all subsequent English Bibles, the actual verbs *euangelizo* and 'evangelize' themselves do not occur. A cognate, *euangelion* (gospel or good news) does however occur once, in Mark 16:15. But a close relationship between these verbs and the Great Commission exists and has always been understood. The clearest statement has been that made by missions historian

Kenneth Scott Latourette, at the International Missionary Council in 1950: 'By evangelism is meant obedience to the Great Commission'. To evangelize, then, means to obey the Great Commission.

On examining the 6 narratives of the Great Commission, in the translations presented in 30 of the major 20th century English Scripture translations, we find that they contain a large number of component imperatives or commands—in fact, around 110 distinct English verbs. These are listed in Table 23–14 in 3 ways: (1) chronologically by New Testament book, chapter and verse, and version; (2) alphabetically; and (3) by the 7 Mandates of the Great Commission that they relate to most closely.

Most of these 110 English verbs are clearly synonyms of 'evangelize' in one sense or another. The rest can be called near-synonyms of 'evangelize', or its closely-related components or elements.

We have already noted the absence of the actual verbs *euangelizo* and 'evangelize' from the Greek and English narratives of the Commission. Those narratives however record only the tip of the iceberg of all the occasions, discussions, questions and answers, preachings, teachings, amplifications, and reiterations of that Commission by the Risen Christ during the Forty Days. So it is not surprising to also discover that 33 of our 51 macrotranslations likewise do not occur in the English Great Commission accounts. Nevertheless they are authoritative imperatives which we may classify as also macrocommands. The list of these verbs is as follows:

announce, assure, be here with, bear tidings, carry, come with, declare, deliver, encourage, evangelize, explain, extend, get, give, give chance, go with, have for, herald, introduce, make clear, make hear, make learn, make listen, make receive, offer, progress, publish, report, reveal, speak, spread, state, take.

What this means is that this whole listing of Great Commission imperatives and verbs with their extensions provides us with yet another spectrum making up the concept 'evangelize'. 'Evangelize' can thus be seen as a concept made up of 110 elements that we can term Great Commission macrocommands.

### Analysis 7:
### 250 MACRODEFINITIONS OF 'EVANGELIZE'

A fourth major line of investigation arises when published definitions of 'evangelize, evangelism, evangelization' are collected, classified, and analyzed. The present enquiry located over 500 such definitions, mostly widely-circulated, and mostly written by worldwide Christian leaders well-known in mission and evangelism circles. Numerous definitions overlap, but some 250 were sufficiently distinct for them to be classified as 'macrodefinitions'. This neologism refers to all synonyms each defined by any published authority as what the term 'evangelize' means. To be specific, this means synonyms defined by authoritative quotations in print of the kind 'To evangelize means...', 'Evangelism is...', or 'Evangelization is...'

The list of 250 macrodefinitions includes The Big Ten, the 51 macrotranslations, and the 110 macrocommands. The list is given below in Table 23–17, column 5: all words there using the code '4' are macrodefinitions. And each macrodefinition is de-

### Table 23–10. The Big Ten: the 10 verbs used most often in major English Bibles to directly translate *euangelizo*.

In this listing the verbs are given in the imperative and have their universal object, the Good News of Jesus Christ, supplied. From this point on in the present analysis, however, the English verbs themselves will normally be quoted, in the interests of brevity, without this universal object 'the Good News'. It must however always remain understood.

1. *Preach* the Good News!
2. *Bring* the Good News!
3. *Tell* the Good News!
4. *Proclaim* the Good News!
5. *Declare* the Good News!
6. *Announce* the Good News!
7. *Evangelize!*
8. *Give* the Good News!
9. *Spread* the Good News!
10. *Hear* the Good News! Make them *hear!*

## Table 23–11. Macrotranslations used as synonyms for the biblical concept 'evangelize': 51 English verbs translating *euangelizo* in The Top 40 major Bible versions (adding 9 in minor versions), ranked alphabetically, also by Great Commission Mandate, and also by frequency of occurrence.

| (a) Listed alphabetically: | | (b) Listed by Mandate: | | (c) Ranked by frequency of occurrence in The Top 40 versions | |
|---|---|---|---|---|---|
| | Synonym | I. | RECEIVE! | | |
| | | II. | GO! | | |
| 1 | **Announce** | 1 | **Bring** | 1 | **Preach** |
| 2 | Assure | 2 | Carry | 2 | **Bring** |
| 3 | Be here with | 3 | Come | 3 | **Tell** |
| 4 | Bear tidings* | 4 | Extend* | 4 | **Proclaim** |
| 5 | **Bring** | 5 | **Give** | 5 | **Declare** |
| 6 | Carry | 6 | Go with* | 6 | **Announce** |
| 7 | Come | 7 | Reach* | 7 | **Evangelize** |
| 8 | **Declare** | 8 | Send | 8 | **Give** |
| 9 | Deliver | 9 | Show | 9 | **Spread** |
| 10 | Denounce | 10 | Supply | 10 | **Make hear** |
| 11 | Encourage | 11 | Take | 11 | Show |
| 12 | **Evangelize** | III. | WITNESS! | 12 | Make receive |
| 13 | Explain | 12 | Be here with | 13 | Deliver |
| 14 | Extend* | 13 | Bear tidings* | 14 | Make known |
| 15 | Get | 14 | Deliver | 15 | Promise |
| 16 | **Give** | 15 | Get | 16 | Come |
| 17 | Give chance | 16 | Have for | 17 | Take |
| 18 | Go with* | 17 | Introduce | 18 | Have for |
| 19 | Have for | 18 | **Make hear** | 19 | Carry |
| 20 | Herald | 19 | Make known | 20 | Send |
| 21 | Introduce | 20 | Relate | 21 | Explain |
| 22 | Invite* | 21 | Report | 22 | Report |
| 23 | Make clear | 22 | Reveal* | 23 | Say |
| 24 | **Make hear** | 23 | Say | 24 | Offer |
| 25 | Make known | 24 | Speak | 25 | Publish |
| 26 | Make learn* | 25 | **Spread** | 26 | Relate |
| 27 | Make listen* | 26 | Talk | 27 | Speak |
| 28 | Make receive | 27 | **Tell** | 28 | Be here with |
| 29 | Offer | IV. | PROCLAIM! | 29 | Get |
| 30 | **Preach** | 28 | **Announce** | 30 | Present |
| 31 | Present | 29 | **Declare** | 31 | Give chance |
| 32 | **Proclaim** | 30 | Give chance | 32 | Save |
| 33 | Progress | 31 | Herald | 33 | Herald |
| 34 | Promise | 32 | Make clear | 34 | Introduce |
| 35 | Publish | 33 | Make listen* | 35 | Assure |
| 36 | Reach* | 34 | **Preach** | 36 | Encourage |
| 37 | Relate | 35 | Present | 37 | Progress |
| 38 | Report | 36 | **Proclaim** | 38 | Make clear |
| 39 | Return | 37 | Promise | 39 | Denounce |
| 40 | Reveal* | 38 | Publish | 40 | Supply |
| 41 | Save | 39 | State* | 41 | Talk |
| 42 | Say | V. | DISCIPLE! | 42 | Return |
| 43 | Send | 40 | Assure | 43 | Bear tidings* |
| 44 | Show | 41 | Denounce | 44 | Go with* |
| 45 | Speak | 42 | Encourage | 45 | State* |
| 46 | **Spread** | 43 | Explain | 46 | Reach* |
| 47 | State* | 44 | Invite* | 47 | Make listen* |
| 48 | Supply | 45 | Make receive | 48 | Reveal* |
| 49 | Take | 46 | Offer | 49 | Make learn* |
| 50 | Talk | 47 | Return | 50 | Extend* |
| 51 | **Tell** | 48 | Save | 51 | Invite* |
| | | VI. | BAPTIZE! | | |
| | | VII. | TRAIN! | | |
| | | 49 | Make learn* | | |
| | | 50 | Progress | | |
| | | O. | OVERALL IMPERATIVE | | |
| | | 51 | **Evangelize** | | |

Notes: 1. Verbs in bold type are The Big Ten.
2. Verbs with an asterisk (*) = not in The Top 40 major Bible versions but only in minor versions (see Table 23–19).

fined in words in Table 23–19, using the same reference numbers as in Table 23–17.

### Analysis 8:
### 420 DIMENSIONS OF 'EVANGELIZE'

A 'dimension', from the Latin word *dimensio* (a measuring), refers to a component or element or direction which is capable of being measured. A fifth major line of investigation therefore arises when we attempt to establish the major components or dimensions of the English word and concept 'evangelize'. Several theologians have recognized that among the vast number of elements, aspects, synonyms, part-synonyms, or facets of evangelization we ought to be able to locate a number of distinct and separate dimensions. In 1959 D.T. Niles, a Ceylonese missiologist who practiced as a Methodist preacher, wrote of 'different dimensions of witness to the one Lord'; one dimension was preaching, another discussing, while 'On still other occasions the simple presence of a worshiping community or man is the witness.' We have also noted earlier John Paul II's 9-fold listing. This he summed up as: 'All these apostolic activities continue to be vital dimensions of evangelization.'

For our purpose, the concept 'dimension' is a very powerful one. In secular usage, the first meaning and in fact the main meaning of 'dimension' is an aspect or attribute which can be measured. So we are concerned to locate aspects of evangelization which we can then measure.

We must now establish a definitive listing of the dimensions of evangelization—those aspects which are not simply exact synonyms or correspondences but which each have some unique meaning or significant differentia to contribute. While doing this there are 2 dangers to avoid. The first is overelaboration. D.J. Bosch has complained that in Western theology 'evangelism' has degenerated into an umbrella-term for the entire manner by which the gospel becomes a reality in a man's life. By allowing the term to become too all-embracing, we rob it of its distinctive and incisive meaning.

The second danger is oversimplification. 'Evangelize' is a very complex concept and our dimensions should fully demonstrate this richness. To quote the 1947 Whitby conference of the International Missionary Council:

Evangelism is not to be defined in any narrow and exclusive sense. It covers the whole of the wide and multifarious range of missionary activity and includes any act or process by which people are won to acknowledge Christ as their Saviour and King and to give themselves to His service in the fellowship of the Church.

More recently, bishop Yap Kim-Hao has made the same point in his 1974 article 'Evangelism today: multifaceted, pluriform, inclusive and comprehensive'. Evangelism has indeed got numerous facets and di-

mensions. A striking example of this multiplicity, because unintentional, is found in the report of the World Council of Churches' 5th Assembly, in 1975 in Nairobi. A single sentence there contained 22 of these facets or dimensions, all of which (shown below in boldface italic type) are in our listing of 420 dimensions of evangelization:

The *gospel* always includes: the *announcement* of God's Kingdom and *love* through Jesus Christ, the *offer* of grace and *forgiveness* of sins, the *invitation* to *repentance* and faith in Him, the *summons* to *fellowship* in God's Church, and *command* to *witness* to God's *saving* words and *deeds*, the *responsibility* to *participate* in the *struggle* for justice and human dignity, the *obligation* to *denounce* all that hinders human *wholeness*, and a *commitment* to *risk life* itself.

These 22 dimensions, and in fact all 420 dimensions of 'evangelize' as defined in this study are described below in Tables 23–17, 23–18, and 23–19.

### Analysis 9:
### 620 FACETS OF 'EVANGELIZE'

A sixth major line of investigation arises finally as we attempt to understand the huge variety of synonyms that this study has uncovered. In addition to The Big Ten, the 51 macrotranslations, the 110 macrocommands, the 250 macrodefinitions, and the 420 dimensions of 'evangelize', there are around 200 other synonyms or near-synonyms with some degree of closeness to the central concept.

A very thorough listing with analysis of a majority of all these synonyms and near-synonyms of 'evangelize' is given in the *Modern concordance to the New Testament* (1976). Its findings are regrouped and shown in Table 23–15.

The term we apply to this entire range of synonyms is 'facets'. All 620 facets are shown listed and categorized in Table 23–17 below. Meanwhile, a brief table of totals of these 6 varieties of synonym is given here in Table 23–16.

### Analysis 10:
### 2,400 COGNATES OF SYNONYMS

This is by no means the end of the story. Every one of the 420 dimensions and 620 facets of 'evangelize' has its own train of cognates, synonyms, and near-synonyms. There is no room here to explore this further; one should simply note that this analysis of the one English word 'evangelize' results in at least 2,400 synonyms and other words at varying semantic distances. It is a kaleidoscopic concept indeed, hence its characterization as the richest word in the entire Christian vocabulary.

### CLASSIFYING ALL CATEGORIES AND COGNATES OF THE 620 FACETS

#### An overall classification

Lastly, each of the 620 facets can be presented under 4 related or cognate forms (verb, participle, adjective, noun). The main task now therefore is to bring some order into this vast array of 620 different English verbs and the grand total of 2,400 cognates overlapping in meaning with 'evangelize'. This can be done through a series of stages. (1) First these terms are separated into verbs, participles, adjectives, and nouns. (2) Next, they are arranged in approximately logical order, or chronological order—e.g. receiving, going, witnessing, proclaiming, discipling, baptizing, training. (3) They are then each located under one or other of the 7 Mandates of the Great Commission, as explained above. (4) All synonyms which do not appear to contribute anything unique to our understanding of the concept are then removed. (5) Lastly, the list is reduced to its irreducible parts or dimensions. (6) These 420 dimensions are then the essential elements, components, facets, ideas, building blocks, and aspects of the concept of evangelization.

#### Quantifying evangelization

When it shortly becomes necessary to quantify the concept of evangelization, its division into 420 dimensions renders the task much easier. Dimensions,

(continued on page 709)

## Table 23–12. The origin of macrotranslations: 42 English verbs used in 41 major English Bible versions to translate *euangelizo* at its 54 Greek New Testament occurrences.

1. This 2-page table lists the English verbs that translate the Greek verb *euangelizo* in each of its 54 New Testament occurrences (shown in the left-hand column below), and does this for each of the 41 major English translations of the complete Bible from 1382 to the present day. These versions are shown along the top of the table, numbered 1-41, each identified by its initials (spelled out in full in Table 23–9) and its year of publication.

2. A macrotranslation is defined as an English verb translating *euangelizo* in a Bible version. These number 42 different verbs in The Top 40 major Bibles, shown in the table below and listed alphabetically for convenience in Table 23–12. The number increases to 51 if one includes other lesser-known Scripture translations (shown in Table 23–13 and Tables 23-17, 23-18, and 23-19).

3. Certain intransitive verbs ("hear", "receive") are turned into transitive ones in the rest of this analysis (Table 23–13 onward), thus "make hear", "make receive".

4. Below the table is a 13-line numerical analysis, one line for each of The Big Ten macrotranslations. Each line gives for each version 2 figures: (1) the table occurrences, followed by (2) in italics its percentage (rounded to the nearest integer) of the 54 occurrences. The line in bold shows figures relating to the macrotranslation 'Evangelize'.

5. In 17 cases represented below by hyphens (-), *euangelizo* has no direct English verb translating it at that particular occurrence in that particular version.

6. The Anchor Bible (1964 onwards) has 10 cases where no commentary has yet appeared on a biblical book, hence no translation has yet been published. The New Living Translation (1996) is analyzed below and listed as one of the 40 but not included in the detailed analysis in Tables 23-12 and 23-14.

7. A fuller analysis both vertically and horizontally is tabulated in Table 23–12.

| *Bible version* | WB | CB | TB-M | GB-C | GB | BB | DRB | AV/KJV | DRCB | RV/ERV |
|---|---|---|---|---|---|---|---|---|---|---|
| *Year published* | 1382 | 1535 | 1537 | 1539 | 1560 | 1568 | 1610 | 1611 | 1749 | 1885 |
| | *1* | *2* | *3* | *4* | *5* | *6* | *7* | *8* | *9* | *10* |
| *Occurrences* | | | | | | | | | | |
| 1. Matthew 11:5 | preach | preach | preach | receive | receive | preach | preach | preach | preach | preach |
| 2. Luke 1:19 | euangelise | show | show | show | show | show | evangelize | show | bring | bring |
| 3. Luke 2:10 | preach | bring | bring | bring | bring | bring | evangelize | bring | bring | bring |
| 4. Luke 3:18 | euangelise | preach | preach | preach | preach | preach | evangelize | preach | preach | preach |
| 5. Luke 4:18 | preach | preach | preach | preach | preach | preach | evangelize | preach | preach | preach |
| 6. Luke 4:43 | preach | preach | preach | preach | preach | preach | evangelize | preach | preach | preach |
| 7. Luke 7:22 | preach | preach | preach | preach | receive | preach | evangelize | preach | preach | preach |
| 8. Luke 8:1 | euangelise | show | show | show | publish | show | evangelize | show | evangelize | bring |
| 9. Luke 9:6 | preach | preach | preach | preach | preach | preach | evangelize | preach | preach | preach |
| 10. Luke 16:16 | euangelise | preach | preach | preach | preach | preach | evangelize | preach | preach | preach |
| 11. Luke 20:1 | preach | preach | preach | preach | preach | preach | evangelize | preach | preach | preach |
| 12. Acts 5:42 | euangelise | preach | preach | preach | preach | preach | evangelize | preach | preach | preach |
| 13. Acts 8:4 | euangelise | preach | preach | preach | preach | preach | evangelize | preach | preach | preach |
| 14. Acts 8:12 | preach | preach | preach | preach | preach | preach | evangelize | preach | preach | preach |
| 15. Acts 8:25 | preach | preach | preach | preach | preach | preach | evangelize | preach | preach | preach |
| 16. Acts 8:35 | preach | preach | preach | preach | preach | preach | evangelize | preach | preach | preach |
| 17. Acts 8:40 | preach | preach | preach | preach | preach | preach | evangelize | preach | preach | preach |
| 18. Acts 10:36 | show | preach | preach | preach | preach | preach | preach | preach | preach | preach |
| 19. Acts 11:20 | preach | preach | preach | preach | preach | preach | preach | preach | preach | preach |
| 20. Acts 13:32 | show | declare | declare | declare | declare | declare | preach | declare | declare | bring |
| 21. Acts 14:7 | preach | preach | preach | preach | preach | preach | evangelize | preach | preach | preach |
| 22. Acts 14:15 | show | preach | preach | preach | preach | preach | preach | preach | preach | bring |
| 23. Acts 14:21 | euangelise | preach | preach | preach | preach | preach | evangelize | preach | preach | preach |
| 24. Acts 15:35 | euangelise | preach | preach | preach | preach | preach | evangelize | preach | preach | preach |
| 25. Acts 16:10 | preach | preach | preach | preach | preach | preach | evangelize | preach | preach | preach |
| 26. Acts 17:18 | tell | preach | preach | preach | preach | preach | preach | preach | preach | preach |
| 27. Romans 1:15 | preach | preach | preach | preach | preach | preach | evangelize | preach | preach | preach |
| 28. Romans 10:15 | preach | bring | bring | bring | bring | bring | evangelize | bring | preach | bring |
| 29. Romans 15:20 | preach | preach | preach | preach | preach | preach | preach | preach | preach | preach |
| 30. 1 Corinthians 1:17 | preach | preach | preach | preach | preach | preach | evangelize | preach | preach | preach |
| 31. 1 Corinthians 9:16 | preach | preach | preach | preach | preach | preach | evangelize | preach | preach | preach |
| 32. 1 Corinthians 9:16a | preach | preach | preach | preach | preach | preach | evangelize | preach | preach | preach |
| 33. 1 Corinthians 9:18 | preach | preach | preach | preach | preach | preach | preach | preach | preach | preach |
| 34. 1 Corinthians 15:1 | preach | preach | preach | preach | preach | preach | preach | preach | preach | preach |
| 35. 1 Corinthians 15:2 | preach | preach | preach | preach | preach | preach | preach | preach | preach | preach |
| 36. 2 Corinthians 10:16 | preach | preach | preach | preach | preach | preach | evangelize | preach | preach | preach |
| 37. 2 Corinthians 11:7 | preach | preach | preach | preach | preach | preach | evangelize | preach | preach | preach |
| 38. Galatians 1:8 | preach | preach | preach | preach | preach | preach | evangelize | preach | preach | preach |
| 39. Galatians 1:8a | preach | preach | preach | preach | preach | preach | evangelize | preach | preach | preach |
| 40. Galatians 1:9 | preach | preach | preach | preach | preach | preach | evangelize | preach | preach | preach |
| 41. Galatians 1:11 | preach | preach | preach | preach | preach | preach | evangelize | preach | preach | preach |
| 42. Galatians 1:16 | preach | preach | preach | preach | preach | preach | evangelize | preach | preach | preach |
| 43. Galatians 1:23 | preach | preach | preach | preach | preach | preach | evangelize | preach | preach | preach |
| 44. Galatians 4:13 | preach | preach | preach | preach | preach | preach | evangelize | preach | preach | preach |
| 45. Ephesians 2:17 | preach | preach | preach | preach | preach | preach | evangelize | preach | preach | preach |
| 46. Ephesians 3:8 | preach | preach | preach | preach | preach | preach | evangelize | preach | preach | preach |
| 47. 1 Thessalonians 3:6 | tell | show | declare | declare | bring | bring | report | bring | relate | bring |
| 48. Hebrews 4:2 | hear | hear | declare | declare | preach | preach | denounce | preach | declare | preach |
| 49. Hebrews 4:6 | tell | preach | preach | preach | preach | preach | preach | preach | preach | preach |
| 50. 1 Peter 1:12 | preach | preach | preach | preach | preach | preach | evangelize | preach | preach | preach |
| 51. 1 Peter 1:25 | preach | preach | preach | preach | preach | preach | evangelize | preach | preach | preach |
| 52. 1 Peter 4:6 | preach | preach | preach | preach | preach | preach | evangelize | preach | preach | preach |
| 53. Revelation 10:7 | preach | preach | preach | preach | declare | declare | evangelize | declare | declare | declare |
| 54. Revelation 14:6 | preach | preach | preach | preach | preach | preach | evangelize | preach | preach | proclaim |

| *Bible version* | ASV | EB-R | HBME | MB | AT/GB | BBE | KB | RSV | HBAEM | MLB/NB |
|---|---|---|---|---|---|---|---|---|---|---|
| *Year published* | 1901 | 1902 | 1903 | 1924 | 1939 | 1949 | 1950 | 1952 | 1957 | 1959 |
| | *11* | *12* | *13* | *14* | *15* | *16* | *17* | *18* | *19* | *20* |
| *Occurrences* | | | | | | | | | | |
| 1. Matthew 11:5 | preach | tell | give | – | preach | give | preach | preach | give | evangelize |
| 2. Luke 1:19 | bring | deliver | tell | tell | tell | give | bring | bring | bring | announce |
| 3. Luke 2:10 | bring | bring | make known | bring | bring | give | bring | bring | bring | announce |
| 4. Luke 3:18 | preach | tell | evangelise | preach | preach | give | give | preach | preach | preach |
| 5. Luke 4:18 | preach | tell | tell | preach | preach | give | preach | preach | preach | preach |
| 6. Luke 4:43 | preach | tell | preach | preach | preach | give | preach | preach | preach | preach |
| 7. Luke 7:22 | preach | tell | tell | preach | preach | give | preach | preach | give | evangelize |
| 8. Luke 8:1 | bring | deliver | relate | tell | tell | give | spread | bring | give | tell |
| 9. Luke 9:6 | preach | deliver | evangelise | preach | tell | preach | preach | preach | preach | preach |
| 10. Luke 16:16 | preach | proclaim | preach | preach | proclaim | preach | preach | preach | preach | preach |
| 11. Luke 20:1 | preach | tell | evangelise | preach | preach | preach | preach | preach | preach | preach |
| 12. Acts 5:42 | preach | tell | declare | preach | preach | preach | preach | preach | preach | preach |
| 13. Acts 8:4 | preach | tell | preach | preach | preach | preach | spread | preach | preach | preach |
| 14. Acts 8:12 | preach | tell | announce | preach | – | give | preach | preach | preach | tell |
| 15. Acts 8:25 | preach | tell | preach | preach | tell | give | preach | preach | preach | preach |
| 16. Acts 8:35 | preach | tell | tell | preach | tell | give | preach | tell | preach | tell |
| 17. Acts 8:40 | preach | tell | evangelise | preach | tell | preach | preach | preach | preach | bring |
| 18. Acts 10:36 | preach | announce | promise | preach | make known | give | give | preach | preach | make known |
| 19. Acts 11:20 | preach | announce | proclaim | tell | tell | give | preach | preach | preach | preach |
| 20. Acts 13:32 | bring | bring | announce | preach | bring | give | preach | bring | preach | bring |
| 21. Acts 14:7 | preach | announce | evangelise | preach | preach | preach | preach | preach | preach | preach |
| 22. Acts 14:15 | bring | bring | declare | preach | bring | give | preach | bring | preach | bring |
| 23. Acts 14:21 | preach | deliver | evangelise | preach | proclaim | preach | preach | preach | preach | bring |
| 24. Acts 15:35 | preach | tell | preach | preach | preach | preach | preach | preach | preach | preach |
| 25. Acts 16:10 | preach | tell | evangelise | preach | tell | give | preach | preach | preach | tell |
| 26. Acts 17:18 | preach | announce | tell | preach | tell | preach | preach | preach | preach | tell |
| 27. Romans 1:15 | preach | announce | evangelise | preach | preach | give | preach | preach | preach | preach |
| 28. Romans 10:15 | bring | bring | preach | come | bring | give | tell | preach | bring | publish |
| 29. Romans 15:20 | preach | announce | supply | preach | preach | take | preach | preach | preach | preach |
| 30. 1 Corinthians 1:17 | preach | tell | evangelise | preach | preach | preach | preach | preach | preach | preach |
| 31. 1 Corinthians 9:16 | preach | tell | preach | preach | preach | preach | preach | preach | preach | preach |
| 32. 1 Corinthians 9:16a | preach | tell | preach | preach | preach | – | preach | preach | preach | – |
| 33. 1 Corinthians 9:18 | preach | tell | preach | preach | offer | preach | preach | preach | preach | preach |
| 34. 1 Corinthians 15:1 | preach | make known | declare | preach | present | give | preach | preach | preach | preach |
| 35. 1 Corinthians 15:2 | preach | announce | preach | receive | – | give | preach | – | preach | – |
| 36. 2 Corinthians 10:16 | preach | carry | preach | preach | preach | take | preach | preach | preach | evangelize |
| 37. 2 Corinthians 11:7 | preach | announce | preach | preach | preach | give | preach | preach | preach | preach |
| 38. Galatians 1:8 | preach | announce | promise | preach | preach | preach | preach | preach | preach | preach |
| 39. Galatians 1:8a | preach | announce | promise | preach | preach | – | preach | preach | preach | preach |
| 40. Galatians 1:9 | preach | announce | announce | preach | preach | preach | preach | preach | preach | evangelize |
| 41. Galatians 1:11 | preach | announce | preach | preach | preach | preach | preach | preach | preach | preach |
| 42. Galatians 1:16 | preach | announce | preach | preach | preach | give | preach | preach | preach | preach |
| 43. Galatians 1:23 | preach | announce | preach | preach | preach | preach | preach | preach | preach | preach |
| 44. Galatians 4:13 | preach | announce | preach | preach | preach | preach | preach | preach | preach | evangelize |
| 45. Ephesians 2:17 | preach | announce | announce | come | come | preach | – | preach | preach | preach |
| 46. Ephesians 3:8 | preach | announce | proclaim | bring | preach | make clear | make known | preach | preach | preach |
| 47. 1 Thessalonians 3:6 | bring | bring | report | bring | bring | give | tell | bring | bring | bring |
| 48. Hebrews 4:2 | preach | deliver | promise | have for | preach | hear | proclaim | come | preach | preach |
| 49. Hebrews 4:6 | preach | deliver | promise | get | preach | hear | come | receive | preach | receive |
| 50. 1 Peter 1:12 | preach | tell | evangelise | preach | bring | preach | evangelize | preach | preach | preach |
| 51. 1 Peter 1:25 | preach | announce | proclaim | – | bring | give | preach | preach | preach | preach |
| 52. 1 Peter 4:6 | preach | deliver | preach | preach | preach | give | bring | preach | preach | preach |
| 53. Revelation 10:7 | declare | tell | promise | assure | give | give | make known | announce | proclaim | give |
| 54. Revelation 14:6 | proclaim | announce | announce | have for | announce | give | preach | proclaim | preach | proclaim |

*Vertical analysis of the 54 verbs*

| *Words* | WB *Total* | WB *%* | CB | *%* | TB-M | *%* | GB-C | *%* | GB | *%* | BB | *%* | DRB | *%* | AV/KJV | *%* | DRCB | *%* | RV/ERV | *%* |
|---|---|---|---|---|---|---|---|---|---|---|---|---|---|---|---|---|---|---|---|---|
| 1. THE BIG TEN: | 51 | *94* | 51 | *94* | 52 | *96* | 51 | *94* | 50 | *93* | 52 | *96* | 52 | *96* | 52 | *96* | 53 | *98* | 54 | *100* |
| *Preach* | 39 | *72* | 47 | *87* | 47 | *87* | 46 | *85* | 45 | *83* | 47 | *87* | 11 | *20* | 47 | *87* | 47 | *87* | 45 | *83* |
| *Bring* | – | *0* | 2 | *4* | 2 | *4* | 2 | *4* | 3 | *6* | 3 | *6* | – | *0* | 3 | *6* | 2 | *4* | 7 | *13* |
| *Tell* | 3 | *6* | – | *0* | – | *0* | – | *0* | – | *0* | – | *0* | – | *0* | – | *0* | – | *0* | – | *0* |
| *Proclaim* | – | *0* | – | *0* | – | *0* | – | *0* | – | *0* | – | *0* | – | *0* | – | *0* | – | *0* | 1 | *2* |
| *Declare* | – | *0* | 1 | *2* | 3 | *6* | 3 | *6* | 2 | *4* | 2 | *4* | – | *0* | 2 | *4* | 3 | *6* | 1 | *2* |
| *Announce* | – | *0* | – | *0* | – | *0* | – | *0* | – | *0* | – | *0* | – | *0* | – | *0* | – | *0* | – | *0* |
| ***Evangelize*** | **8** | ***15*** | **–** | ***0*** | **–** | ***0*** | **–** | ***0*** | **–** | ***0*** | **–** | ***0*** | **41** | ***76*** | **–** | ***0*** | **1** | ***2*** | **–** | ***0*** |
| *Give* | – | *0* | – | *0* | – | *0* | – | *0* | – | *0* | – | *0* | – | *0* | – | *0* | – | *0* | – | *0* |
| *Spread* | – | *0* | – | *0* | – | *0* | – | *0* | – | *0* | – | *0* | – | *0* | – | *0* | – | *0* | – | *0* |
| *Hear* | 1 | *2* | 1 | *2* | – | *0* | – | *0* | – | *0* | – | *0* | – | *0* | – | *0* | – | *0* | – | *0* |
| 2. *Other verbs* | 3 | *6* | 3 | *6* | 2 | *4* | 3 | *6* | 4 | *7* | 2 | *4* | 2 | *4* | 2 | *4* | 1 | *2* | – | *0* |
| 3. *No translated verb* | – | *0* | – | *0* | – | *0* | – | *0* | – | *0* | – | *0* | – | *0* | – | *0* | – | *0* | – | *0* |

| *Words* | ASV | *%* | EB-R | *%* | HBME | *%* | MB | *%* | AT/GB | *%* | BBE | *%* | KB | *%* | RSV | *%* | HBAEM | *%* | MLB/NB | *%* |
|---|---|---|---|---|---|---|---|---|---|---|---|---|---|---|---|---|---|---|---|---|
| 1. THE BIG TEN: | 54 | *100* | 45 | *83* | 44 | *87* | 45 | *83* | 47 | *87* | 49 | *91* | 50 | *93* | 51 | *94* | 54 | *100* | 49 | *91* |
| *Preach* | 45 | *83* | – | *0* | 17 | *31* | 39 | *72* | 28 | *52* | 20 | *37* | 39 | *72* | 42 | *78* | 46 | *85* | 30 | *56* |
| *Bring* | 7 | *13* | 5 | *9* | – | *0* | 3 | *6* | 7 | *13* | – | *0* | 3 | *6* | 6 | *11* | 4 | *7* | 5 | *9* |
| *Tell* | – | *0* | 20 | *37* | 5 | *9* | 3 | *6* | 8 | *15* | – | *0* | 2 | *4* | 1 | *2* | – | *0* | 5 | *9* |
| *Proclaim* | 1 | *2* | 1 | *2* | 3 | *6* | – | *0* | 2 | *4* | – | *0* | 1 | *2* | 1 | *2* | 1 | *2* | 1 | *2* |
| *Declare* | 1 | *2* | – | *0* | 3 | *6* | – | *0* | – | *0* | – | *0* | – | *0* | – | *0* | – | *0* | – | *0* |
| *Announce* | – | *0* | 19 | *35* | 5 | *9* | – | *0* | 1 | *2* | – | *0* | – | *0* | 1 | *2* | – | *0* | 2 | *4* |
| ***Evangelize*** | **–** | ***0*** | **–** | ***0*** | **10** | ***19*** | **–** | ***0*** | **–** | ***0*** | **–** | ***0*** | **1** | ***2*** | **–** | ***0*** | **–** | ***0*** | **5** | ***9*** |
| *Give* | – | *0* | – | 0 | 1 | *2* | – | *0* | 1 | *2* | 27 | *50* | 2 | *4* | – | *0* | 3 | *6* | 1 | *2* |
| *Spread* | – | *0* | – | – | – | *0* | – | – | – | *0* | – | *0* | 2 | *4* | – | *0* | – | *0* | – | *0* |
| *Hear* | – | *0* | – | *0* | – | *0* | – | – | – | *0* | 2 | *4* | – | *0* | – | *0* | – | *0* | – | *0* |
| 2. *Other verbs* | – | *0* | 9 | *17* | 10 | *19* | 7 | *13* | 5 | *9* | 3 | *6* | 3 | *6* | 2 | *4* | – | *0* | 3 | *6* |
| 3. *No translated verb* | – | *0* | – | *0* | – | *0* | 2 | *4* | 2 | *4* | 2 | *4* | 1 | *2* | 1 | *2* | – | *0* | 2 | *4* |

*Continued opposite*

Table 23–12 concluded

| Bible version | NWT | NCE/CCD | AB | AmB | JB | NAB | NEB | TLB | NASB | GNB/TEV | NIV | NKJV | NJB | NLV | NCV | CCB | NRSV | REB | GW | CEV | NLT |
|---|---|---|---|---|---|---|---|---|---|---|---|---|---|---|---|---|---|---|---|---|---|
| Year published | 1961 | 1961 | 1964 | 1965 | 1966 | 1970 | 1970 | 1971 | 1971 | 1976 | 1978 | 1982 | 1985 | 1986 | 1986 | 1988 | 1989 | 1989 | 1995 | 1995 | 1996 |
| | 21 | 22 | 23 | 24 | 25 | 26 | 27 | 28 | 29 | 30 | 31 | 32 | 33 | 34 | 35 | 36 | 37 | 38 | 39 | 40 | 41 |
| Occurrences | | | | | | | | | | | | | | | | | | | | | |
| 1. Matthew 11:5 | declare | preach | bring | preach | proclaim | preach | hear | preach | preach | preach | preach | preach | proclaim | preach | tell | preach | bring | bring | hear | hear | preach |
| 2. Luke 1:19 | declare | bring | announce | bring | bring | bring | bring | send | bring | tell | tell | bring | bring | bring | tell | bring | bring | bring | tell | tell | bring |
| 3. Luke 2:10 | declare | bring | announce | bring | bring | proclaim | have for | bring | bring | be here with | bring | bring | bring | bring | bring | give | bring | bring | have for | have for | bring |
| 4. Luke 3:18 | declare | preach | preach | preach | announce | preach | announce | announce | preach | preach | preach | preach | proclaim | preach | preach | encourage | proclaim | announce | tell | preach | announce |
| 5. Luke 4:18 | declare | bring | preach | preach | bring | bring | announce | preach | preach | bring | preach | preach | bring | preach | tell | bring | bring | announce | tell | tell | preach |
| 6. Luke 4:43 | declare | proclaim | proclaim | preach | proclaim | announce | give | preach | preach | preach | preach | preach | proclaim | preach | tell | announce | proclaim | give | tell | hear | preach |
| 7. Luke 7:22 | tell | preach | preach | preach | proclaim | preach | hear | hear | preach | preach | preach | preach | proclaim | preach | tell | give | bring | bring | hear | hear | preach |
| 8. Luke 8:1 | declare | proclaim | announce | bring | proclaim | proclaim | proclaim | announce | preach | preach | proclaim | bring | proclaim | tell | tell | preach | bring | proclaim | spread | tell | announce |
| 9. Luke 9:6 | declare | preach | preach | preach | proclaim | spread | tell | preach | preach | preach | preach | preach | proclaim | preach | tell | proclaim | bring | announce | tell | tell | preach |
| 10. Luke 16:16 | declare | preach | x | preach | preach | proclaim | – | introduce | preach | tell | preach | preach | preach | preach | tell | spread | proclaim | proclaim | tell | preach | preach |
| 11. Luke 20:1 | declare | preach | x | preach | proclaim | proclaim | tell | preach | preach | preach | preach | preach | proclaim | preach | tell | proclaim | tell | tell | tell | tell | preach |
| 12. Acts 5:42 | declare | preach | proclaim | proclaim | proclaim | proclaim | tell | preach | preach | preach | proclaim | preach | proclaim | preach | tell | proclaim | proclaim | tell | tell | tell | preach |
| 13. Acts 8:4 | declare | preach | preach | preach | preach | preach | preach | preach | preach | preach | preach | preach | preach | preach | tell | preach | proclaim | preach | spread | tell | preach |
| 14. Acts 8:12 | declare | preach | preach | preach | preach | preach | – | – | preach | proclaim | preach | preach | preach | tell | tell | announce | proclaim | say | spread | say | – |
| 15. Acts 8:25 | declare | preach | preach | proclaim | preach | proclaim | bring | preach | preach | preach | preach | preach | preach | preach | preach | bring | proclaim | bring | spread | tell | preach |
| 16. Acts 8:35 | declare | preach | bring | announce | explain | tell | tell | tell | preach | tell | tell | preach | explain | preach | tell | tell | proclaim | tell | tell | explain | tell |
| 17. Acts 8:40 | declare | preach | preach | preach | proclaim | announce | preach | preach | preach | preach | preach | preach | proclaim | preach | preach | announce | proclaim | preach | spread | tell | preach |
| 18. Acts 10:36 | declare | preach | proclaim | announce | bring | proclaim | give | spread | preach | proclaim | tell | preach | bring | tell | send | proclaim | preach | give | bring | offer | hear |
| 19. Acts 11:20 | declare | preach | preach | proclaim | proclaim | announce | tell | give | preach | tell | tell | preach | proclaim | preach | tell | give | proclaim | tell | spread | tell | preach |
| 20. Acts 13:32 | declare | bring | tell | bring | tell | announce | give | bring | preach | bring | tell | declare | tell | bring | tell | announce | bring | give | tell | tell | bring |
| 21. Acts 14:7 | declare | preach | preach | preach | preach | proclaim | spread | preach | preach | preach | preach | preach | preach | preach | announce | preach | proclaim | spread | spread | preach | preach |
| 22. Acts 14:15 | declare | bring | preach | bring | come | bring | bring | bring | preach | announce | bring | preach | come | preach | bring | tell | bring | bring | spread | – | bring |
| 23. Acts 14:21 | declare | preach | preach | preach | preach | proclaim | bring | preach | preach | preach | preach | preach | preach | preach | tell | proclaim | proclaim | bring | spread | preach | preach |
| 24. Acts 15:35 | declare | preach | preach | proclaim | proclaim | preach | preach | preach | preach | preach | preach | preach | proclaim | preach | preach | preach | proclaim | preach | spread | preach | preach |
| 25. Acts 16:10 | declare | preach | preach | proclaim | bring | proclaim | bring | preach | preach | preach | preach | preach | bring | tell | tell | give | proclaim | take | tell | preach | preach |
| 26. Acts 17:18 | declare | proclaim | preach | preach | preach | speak | preach | tell | preach | preach | preach | preach | preach | preach | tell | speak | tell | preach | tell | talk | tell |
| 27. Romans 1:15 | declare | preach | preach | preach | bring | preach | declare | preach | preach | preach | preach | preach | preach | preach | preach | progress | proclaim | declare | tell | tell | preach |
| 28. Romans 10:15 | declare | preach | preach | preach | bring | announce | spread | bring | bring | bring | bring | preach | preach | bring | bring | bring | bring | spread | tell | preach | bring |
| 29. Romans 15:20 | declare | preach | preach | preach | preach | preach | bring | preach | preach | proclaim | preach | preach | preach | preach | preach | preach | proclaim | take | spread | preach | preach |
| 30. 1 Corinthians 1:17 | declare | preach | proclaim | evangelize | preach | preach | proclaim | preach | preach | tell | preach | preach | preach | preach | tell | proclaim | proclaim | proclaim | spread | tell | preach |
| 31. 1 Corinthians 9:16 | declare | preach | preach | preach | preach | preach | preach | preach | preach | preach | preach | preach | preach | preach | tell | announce | proclaim | preach | spread | preach | preach |
| 32. 1 Corinthians 9:16a | declare | preach | preach | preach | preach | preach | preach | preach | preach | preach | preach | preach | preach | preach | tell | preach | proclaim | preach | spread | preach | – |
| 33. 1 Corinthians 9:18 | declare | preach | preach | preach | preach | preach | preach | preach | preach | preach | preach | preach | preach | preach | tell | announce | proclaim | preach | spread | preach | preach |
| 34. 1 Corinthians 15:1 | declare | preach | proclaim | proclaim | preach | preach | preach | preach | preach | preach | preach | preach | preach | tell | receive | preach | proclaim | preach | tell | preach | preach |
| 35. 1 Corinthians 15:2 | declare | preach | proclaim | preach | preach | preach | preach | save | preach | preach | preach | preach | preach | preach | tell | preach | proclaim | preach | tell | – | save |
| 36. 2 Corinthians 10:16 | declare | preach | preach | preach | carry | preach | carry | preach | preach | preach | preach | preach | preach | preach | tell | bring | proclaim | carry | spread | preach | preach |
| 37. 2 Corinthians 11:7 | declare | preach | preach | preach | preach | preach | preach | preach | preach | preach | preach | preach | preach | preach | preach | give | proclaim | preach | tell | preach | preach |
| 38. Galatians 1:8 | declare | preach | x | preach | preach | preach | preach | preach | preach | preach | preach | preach | preach | preach | preach | preach | proclaim | preach | tell | preach | preach |
| 39. Galatians 1:8a | declare | preach | x | preach | preach | deliver | preach | preach | preach | preach | preach | preach | preach | preach | preach | preach | proclaim | preach | give | – | preach |
| 40. Galatians 1:9 | declare | preach | x | preach | preach | preach | preach | preach | preach | preach | preach | preach | preach | preach | tell | preach | proclaim | preach | tell | preach | preach |
| 41. Galatians 1:11 | declare | preach | x | proclaim | preach | proclaim | hear | preach | preach | preach | preach | preach | preach | preach | preach | preach | proclaim | preach | spread | preach | preach |
| 42. Galatians 1:16 | declare | preach | x | proclaim | preach | spread | proclaim | show | preach | preach | preach | preach | preach | preach | tell | make known | proclaim | proclaim | tell | announce | proclaim |
| 43. Galatians 1:23 | declare | preach | x | proclaim | preach | preach | preach | preach | preach | preach | preach | preach | preach | preach | preach | preach | proclaim | preach | spread | preach | preach |
| 44. Galatians 4:13 | declare | preach | x | preach | preach | bring | bring | bring | preach | preach | preach | preach | preach | preach | preach | announce | announce | bring | bring | preach | bring |
| 45. Ephesians 2:17 | declare | announce | proclaim | preach | bring | announce | proclaim | bring | preach | preach | preach | preach | bring | preach | preach | proclaim | proclaim | proclaim | come | preach | bring |
| 46. Ephesians 3:8 | declare | announce | announce | proclaim | proclaim | preach | proclaim | tell | preach | take | preach | preach | proclaim | preach | tell | announce | bring | proclaim | spread | tell | tell |
| 47. 1 Thessalonians 3:6 | give | make known | x | bring | give | report | bring | bring | bring | bring | bring | bring | give | bring | bring | return | bring | bring | tell | tell | bring |
| 48. Hebrews 4:2 | declare | declare | preach | proclaim | receive | hear | hear | give | preach | hear | preach | preach | receive | hear | preach | hear | hear | preach | hear | hear | announce |
| 49. Hebrews 4:6 | declare | declare | receive | give | hear | announce | hear | have chance | preach | hear | preach | preach | hear | hear | hear | receive | receive | hear | hear | hear | hear |
| 50. 1 Peter 1:12 | declare | preach | proclaim | preach | preach | preach | bring | announce | preach | announce | preach | preach | preach | preach | preach | preach | bring | bring | spread | preach | announce |
| 51. 1 Peter 1:25 | declare | preach | preach | preach | bring | preach | preach | preach | preach | proclaim | preach | preach | bring | preach | preach | bring | announce | preach | tell | – | preach |
| 52. 1 Peter 4:6 | declare | preach | preach | preach | tell | preach | preach | preach | preach | preach | preach | preach | bring | preach | preach | preach | proclaim | preach | tell | preach | preach |
| 53. Revelation 10:7 | declare | declare | announce | announce | announce | announce | promise | announce | preach | announce | announce | declare | announce | tell | tell | proclaim | announce | promise | make known | tell | announce |
| 54. Revelation 14:6 | declare | preach | preach | tell | announce | herald | proclaim | preach | preach | announce | proclaim | preach | announce | preach | preach | proclaim | proclaim | proclaim | spread | announce | preach |

*Vertical analysis of the 54 verbs*

| *Words* | *Total %* | | | | | | | | | | | | | | | | | | | | |
|---|---|---|---|---|---|---|---|---|---|---|---|---|---|---|---|---|---|---|---|---|---|
| 1. THE BIG TEN: | 54 100 | 53 98 | 43 80 | 54 100 | 50 93 | 50 93 | 49 91 | 48 89 | 54 100 | 51 94 | 54 100 | 54 100 | 51 94 | 54 100 | 52 96 | 48 89 | 53 98 | 49 91 | 51 94 | 45 83 | 52 96 |
| *Preach* | – 0 | 40 74 | 27 50 | 31 57 | 23 43 | 23 43 | 16 30 | 30 56 | 50 93 | 33 61 | 41 76 | 48 89 | 26 48 | 41 76 | 18 33 | 16 30 | 1 2 | 18 33 | – 0 | 22 41 | 32 59 |
| *Bring* | – 0 | 5 9 | 2 4 | 6 11 | 9 17 | 4 7 | 9 17 | 7 13 | 4 7 | 4 7 | 4 7 | 4 7 | 8 15 | 5 9 | 4 7 | 6 11 | 13 24 | 10 19 | 2 | 4– 0 | 8 15 |
| *Tell* | 1 2 | – 0 | 1 2 | 1 2 | 2 4 | 1 2 | 5 9 | 3 6 | – 0 | 5 9 | 5 9 | – 0 | 1 2 | 6 11 | 28 52 | 2 4 | 2 4 | 4 7 | 23 43 | 16 30 | 3 6 |
| *Proclaim* | – 0 | 3 6 | 8 15 | 11 20 | 11 20 | 11 20 | 6 11 | – 0 | – 0 | 3 6 | 3 6 | – 0 | 12 22 | – 0 | – 0 | 9 17 | 33 61 | 7 13 | – 0 | – 0 | 1 2 |
| *Declare* | 52 96 | 3 6 | – 0 | – 0 | – 0 | – 0 | 1 2 | – 0 | – 0 | – 0 | – 0 | 2 4 | – 0 | – 0 | – 0 | – 0 | – 0 | 1 2 | – 0 | – 0 | – 0 |
| *Announce* | – 0 | 2 4 | 5 9 | 3 6 | 3 6 | 8 15 | 2 4 | 4 7 | – 0 | 4 7 | 1 2 | – 0 | 2 4 | – 0 | 1 2 | 8 15 | 3 6 | 3 6 | – 0 | 2 4 | 5 9 |
| ***Evangelize*** | **– 0** | **– 0** | **– 0** | **1 2** | **– 0** | **– 0** | **– 0** | **– 0** | **– 0** | **– 0** | **– 0** | **– 0** | **– 0** | **– 0** | **– 0** | **– 0** | **– 0** | **– 0** | **– 0** | **– 0** | **– 0** |
| *Give* | 1 2 | – 0 | – 0 | 1 2 | 1 2 | – 0 | 3 6 | 2 4 | – 0 | – 0 | – 0 | – 0 | 1 2 | – 0 | – 0 | 5 9 | – 0 | 3 6 | 1 2 | – 0 | – 0 |
| *Spread* | – 0 | – 0 | – 0 | – 0 | – 0 | 2 4 | 2 4 | 1 2 | – 0 | – 0 | – 0 | – 0 | – 0 | – 0 | – 0 | 1 2 | – 0 | 2 4 | 21 39 | – 0 | – 0 |
| *Hear* | – 0 | – 0 | – 0 | – 0 | 1 2 | 1 2 | 5 9 | 1 2 | – 0 | 2 4 | – 0 | – 0 | 1 2 | 2 4 | 1 2 | 1 2 | 1 2 | 1 2 | 4 7 | 5 9 | 2 4 |
| 2. *Other verbs* | – 0 | 1 2 | 1 2 | – 0 | 4 7 | 4 7 | 3 6 | 5 9 | – 0 | 3 6 | – 0 | – 0 | 3 6 | – 0 | 2 4 | 6 11 | 1 2 | 5 9 | 3 6 | 5 9 | 1 2 |
| 3. *No translated verb* | – 0 | – 0 | 10 19 | – 0 | – 0 | – 0 | 2 4 | 1 2 | – 0 | – 0 | – 0 | – 0 | – 0 | – 0 | – 0 | – 0 | – 0 | – 0 | – 0 | 4 7 | 2 4 |

## Table 23–13. Frequencies of 42 English macrotranslations of *euangelizo* in its 54 New Testament occurrences, in The Top 40 English Bible versions.

This table takes the list of 54 occurrences shown in the opening column of Table 23–12, and for each occurrence tabulates the number of times each macrotranslation is used in each of The Top 40 English Bible versions. Note 2 additional symbols: (a) hyphens (-) represent occurrences of *euangelizo* where an English translation avoids using a verb at all; and (b) crosses (x) under the Anchor Bible (AB 1964) represent New Testament books as yet unpublished.

1. Data are analyzed under 3 sections. In the first part of the table, the 42 macrotranslations documented at 2,160 NT locations in Table 23–12 are listed and enumerated by overall totals and by percentages. The 10 verbs shown in bold type are The Big Ten macrotranslations.
2. The second section gives total frequencies for each verse. The percentages relate to the 40 Bible versions.
3. The third section gives total frequencies for each of The Top 40 English Bible versions identified by initials (spelled out in full in Table 23–9) and year of publication. The percentages relate to the 54 NT occurrences of *euangelizo*.

*1. Overall frequencies at 54 occurrences in 40 Bible versions*

| *Macrotranslations* | *Total* | *Percent* |
|---|---|---|
| **announce** | 79 | 3.70 |
| assure | 1 | 0.05 |
| be here with | 1 | 0.05 |
| **bring** | 170 | 7.97 |
| carry | 4 | 0.19 |
| come | 8 | 0.38 |
| **declare** | 80 | 3.75 |
| deliver | 9 | 0.42 |
| denounce | 1 | 0.05 |
| encourage | 1 | 0.05 |
| **evangelize** (eu-,-ise) | 67 | 3.10 |
| explain | 3 | 0.14 |
| get | 1 | 0.05 |
| **give** | 53 | 2.48 |
| have chance | 1 | 0.05 |
| have for | 5 | 0.23 |
| **hear** | 30 | 1.41 |
| herald | 1 | 0.05 |
| introduce | 1 | 0.05 |
| make clear | 1 | 0.05 |
| make known | 9 | 0.42 |
| offer | 2 | 0.09 |
| **preach** | 1,231 | 57.71 |
| present | 1 | 0.05 |
| **proclaim** | 129 | 6.05 |
| progress | 1 | 0.05 |
| promise | 8 | 0.38 |
| publish | 2 | 0.09 |
| receive | 12 | 0.56 |
| relate | 2 | 0.09 |
| report | 3 | 0.14 |
| return | 1 | 0.05 |
| save | 1 | 0.05 |
| say | 2 | 0.09 |
| send | 3 | 0.14 |
| show | 16 | 0.75 |
| speak | 2 | 0.09 |
| **spread** | 31 | 1.45 |
| supply | 1 | 0.05 |
| take | 5 | 0.23 |
| talk | 1 | 0.05 |
| **tell** | 153 | 7.08 |
| - (no verb) | 17 | 0.79 |
| x (unpublished) | 10 | 0.46 |
| *Grand totals* | 2,160 | 100.00 |

*2. Frequencies for each NT occurrence in The Top 40*

| | *Total* | *Percent* |
|---|---|---|
| ***Matthew 11:5*** | | |
| bring | 3 | 7.50 |
| declare | 1 | 2.50 |
| evangelize | 1 | 2.50 |
| give | 3 | 7.50 |
| hear | 3 | 7.50 |
| preach | 22 | 55.00 |
| proclaim | 2 | 5.00 |
| receive | 2 | 5.00 |
| tell | 2 | 5.00 |
| - | 1 | 2.50 |
| ***Luke 1:19*** | | |
| announce | 2 | 5.00 |
| bring | 18 | 45.00 |
| declare | 1 | 2.50 |
| deliver | 1 | 2.50 |
| euangelise | 1 | 2.50 |
| evangelize | 1 | 2.50 |
| give | 1 | 2.50 |
| send | 1 | 2.50 |
| show | 6 | 15.00 |
| tell | 8 | 20.00 |
| ***Luke 2:10*** | | |
| announce | 2 | 5.00 |
| be here with | 1 | 2.50 |
| bring | 27 | 67.50 |
| declare | 1 | 2.50 |
| evangelize | 1 | 2.50 |
| give | 2 | 5.00 |
| have for | 3 | 7.50 |
| make known | 1 | 2.50 |
| preach | 1 | 2.50 |
| proclaim | 1 | 2.50 |
| ***Luke 3:18*** | | |
| announce | 4 | 10.00 |
| declare | 1 | 2.50 |
| encourage | 1 | 2.50 |
| euangelise | 1 | 2.50 |
| evangelise | 1 | 2.50 |
| evangelize | 1 | 2.50 |
| give | 2 | 5.00 |
| preach | 25 | 62.50 |
| proclaim | 2 | 5.00 |
| tell | 2 | 5.00 |
| ***Luke 4:18*** | | |
| announce | 2 | 5.00 |
| bring | 7 | 17.50 |
| declare | 1 | 2.50 |
| evangelize | 1 | 2.50 |
| give | 1 | 2.50 |
| preach | 23 | 57.50 |
| tell | 5 | 12.50 |
| ***Luke 4:43*** | | |
| announce | 2 | 5.00 |
| declare | 1 | 2.50 |
| evangelize | 1 | 2.50 |
| give | 3 | 7.50 |
| hear | 1 | 2.50 |
| preach | 24 | 60.00 |
| proclaim | 5 | 12.50 |
| tell | 3 | 7.50 |
| ***Luke 7:22*** | | |
| bring | 2 | 5.00 |
| evangelize | 2 | 5.00 |
| give | 3 | 7.50 |
| hear | 4 | 10.00 |
| preach | 22 | 55.00 |
| proclaim | 2 | 5.00 |
| receive | 1 | 2.50 |
| tell | 4 | 10.00 |
| ***Luke 8:1*** | | |
| announce | 2 | 5.00 |
| bring | 6 | 15.00 |
| declare | 1 | 2.50 |
| deliver | 1 | 2.50 |
| euangelise | 1 | 2.50 |
| evangelize | 2 | 5.00 |
| give | 2 | 5.00 |
| preach | 3 | 7.50 |
| proclaim | 7 | 17.50 |
| publish | 1 | 2.50 |
| relate | 1 | 2.50 |
| show | 5 | 12.50 |
| spread | 2 | 5.00 |
| tell | 6 | 15.00 |
| ***Luke 9:6*** | | |
| announce | 1 | 2.50 |
| bring | 1 | 2.50 |
| declare | 1 | 2.50 |
| deliver | 1 | 2.50 |
| evangelise | 1 | 2.50 |
| evangelize | 1 | 2.50 |
| preach | 25 | 62.50 |
| proclaim | 3 | 7.50 |
| spread | 1 | 2.50 |
| tell | 5 | 12.50 |
| ***Luke 16:16*** | | |
| declare | 1 | 2.50 |
| euangelise | 1 | 2.50 |
| evangelize | 1 | 2.50 |
| introduce | 1 | 2.50 |
| preach | 25 | 62.50 |
| proclaim | 5 | 12.50 |
| spread | 1 | 2.50 |
| tell | 3 | 7.50 |
| - | 1 | 2.50 |
| x | 1 | 2.50 |
| ***Luke 20:1*** | | |
| declare | 1 | 2.50 |
| evangelise | 1 | 2.50 |
| evangelize | 1 | 2.50 |
| preach | 25 | 62.50 |
| proclaim | 4 | 10.00 |
| tell | 7 | 17.50 |
| x | 1 | 2.50 |
| ***Acts 5:42*** | | |
| declare | 2 | 5.00 |
| euangelise | 1 | 2.50 |
| evangelize | 1 | 2.50 |
| preach | 22 | 55.00 |
| proclaim | 8 | 20.00 |
| tell | 6 | 15.00 |
| ***Acts 8:4*** | | |
| declare | 1 | 2.50 |
| euangelise | 1 | 2.50 |
| evangelize | 1 | 2.50 |
| preach | 31 | 77.50 |
| proclaim | 1 | 2.50 |
| spread | 2 | 5.00 |
| tell | 3 | 7.50 |
| ***Acts 8:12*** | | |
| announce | 2 | 5.00 |
| declare | 1 | 2.50 |
| evangelize | 1 | 2.50 |
| give | 1 | 2.50 |
| preach | 23 | 57.50 |
| proclaim | 1 | 2.50 |
| say | 2 | 5.00 |
| send | 1 | 2.50 |
| spread | 1 | 2.50 |
| tell | 4 | 10.00 |
| - | 3 | 7.50 |
| ***Acts 8:25*** | | |
| bring | 3 | 7.50 |
| declare | 1 | 2.50 |
| deliver | 1 | 2.50 |
| evangelize | 1 | 2.50 |
| give | 1 | 2.50 |
| preach | 27 | 67.50 |
| proclaim | 3 | 7.50 |
| spread | 1 | 2.50 |
| tell | 2 | 5.00 |
| ***Acts 8:35*** | | |
| announce | 1 | 2.50 |
| bring | 1 | 2.50 |
| declare | 1 | 2.50 |
| evangelize | 1 | 2.50 |
| explain | 3 | 7.50 |
| give | 1 | 2.50 |
| preach | 17 | 42.50 |
| proclaim | 1 | 2.50 |
| tell | 14 | 35.00 |
| ***Acts 8:40*** | | |
| announce | 2 | 5.00 |
| bring | 1 | 2.50 |
| declare | 1 | 2.50 |
| evangelise | 1 | 2.50 |
| evangelize | 1 | 2.50 |
| preach | 27 | 67.50 |
| proclaim | 3 | 7.50 |
| spread | 1 | 2.50 |
| tell | 3 | 7.50 |
| ***Acts 10:36*** | | |
| announce | 2 | 5.00 |
| bring | 3 | 7.50 |
| declare | 1 | 2.50 |
| give | 4 | 10.00 |
| make known | 2 | 5.00 |
| offer | 1 | 2.50 |
| preach | 17 | 42.50 |
| proclaim | 4 | 10.00 |
| promise | 1 | 2.50 |
| send | 1 | 2.50 |
| show | 1 | 2.50 |
| spread | 1 | 2.50 |
| tell | 2 | 5.00 |
| ***Acts 11:20*** | | |
| announce | 2 | 5.00 |
| declare | 1 | 2.50 |
| give | 3 | 7.50 |
| preach | 20 | 50.00 |
| proclaim | 5 | 12.50 |
| spread | 1 | 2.50 |
| tell | 8 | 20.00 |
| ***Acts 13:32*** | | |
| announce | 3 | 7.50 |
| bring | 12 | 30.00 |
| declare | 9 | 22.50 |
| give | 3 | 7.50 |
| preach | 5 | 12.50 |
| show | 1 | 2.50 |
| tell | 7 | 17.50 |
| ***Acts 14:7*** | | |
| announce | 2 | 5.00 |
| declare | 1 | 2.50 |
| evangelise | 1 | 2.50 |
| evangelize | 1 | 2.50 |
| preach | 30 | 75.00 |
| proclaim | 2 | 5.00 |
| spread | 3 | 7.50 |
| ***Acts 14:15*** | | |
| announce | 1 | 2.50 |
| bring | 15 | 37.50 |
| come | 2 | 5.00 |
| declare | 2 | 5.00 |
| give | 1 | 2.50 |
| preach | 15 | 37.50 |
| show | 1 | 2.50 |
| spread | 1 | 2.50 |
| tell | 1 | 2.50 |
| - | 1 | 2.50 |
| ***Acts 14:21*** | | |
| bring | 3 | 7.50 |
| declare | 1 | 2.50 |
| deliver | 1 | 2.50 |
| euangelise | 1 | 2.50 |
| evangelise | 1 | 2.50 |
| evangelize | 1 | 2.50 |
| preach | 26 | 65.00 |
| proclaim | 4 | 10.00 |
| spread | 1 | 2.50 |
| tell | 1 | 2.50 |
| ***Acts 15:35*** | | |
| declare | 1 | 2.50 |
| euangelise | 1 | 2.50 |
| evangelize | 1 | 2.50 |
| preach | 31 | 77.50 |
| proclaim | 4 | 10.00 |
| spread | 1 | 2.50 |
| tell | 1 | 2.50 |
| ***Acts 16:10*** | | |
| bring | 3 | 7.50 |
| declare | 1 | 2.50 |
| evangelise | 1 | 2.50 |
| evangelize | 1 | 2.50 |
| give | 2 | 5.00 |
| preach | 22 | 55.00 |
| proclaim | 3 | 7.50 |
| take | 1 | 2.50 |
| tell | 6 | 15.00 |
| ***Acts 17:18*** | | |
| announce | 1 | 2.50 |
| declare | 1 | 2.50 |
| preach | 26 | 65.00 |
| proclaim | 1 | 2.50 |
| speak | 2 | 5.00 |
| talk | 1 | 2.50 |
| tell | 8 | 20.00 |
| ***Romans 1:15*** | | |
| announce | 1 | 2.50 |
| bring | 1 | 2.50 |
| declare | 3 | 7.50 |
| evangelise | 1 | 2.50 |
| evangelize | 1 | 2.50 |
| give | 1 | 2.50 |
| preach | 28 | 70.00 |
| proclaim | 1 | 2.50 |
| progress | 1 | 2.50 |
| tell | 2 | 5.00 |
| ***Romans 10:15*** | | |
| announce | 1 | 2.50 |
| bring | 20 | 50.00 |
| come | 1 | 2.50 |
| declare | 1 | 2.50 |
| evangelize | 1 | 2.50 |
| give | 1 | 2.50 |
| preach | 10 | 25.00 |
| publish | 1 | 2.50 |
| spread | 2 | 5.00 |
| tell | 2 | 5.00 |
| ***Romans 15:20*** | | |
| announce | 1 | 2.50 |
| bring | 1 | 2.50 |
| declare | 1 | 2.50 |
| preach | 31 | 77.50 |
| proclaim | 2 | 5.00 |
| spread | 1 | 2.50 |
| supply | 1 | 2.50 |
| take | 2 | 5.00 |
| ***1 Corinthians 1:17*** | | |
| declare | 1 | 2.50 |
| evangelise | 1 | 2.50 |
| evangelize | 2 | 5.00 |
| preach | 26 | 65.00 |
| proclaim | 5 | 12.50 |
| spread | 1 | 2.50 |
| tell | 4 | 10.00 |
| ***1 Corinthians 9:16*** | | |
| announce | 1 | 2.50 |
| declare | 1 | 2.50 |
| evangelize | 1 | 2.50 |
| preach | 33 | 82.50 |
| proclaim | 1 | 2.50 |
| spread | 1 | 2.50 |
| tell | 2 | 5.00 |
| ***1 Corinthians 9:16a*** | | |
| declare | 1 | 2.50 |
| evangelize | 1 | 2.50 |
| preach | 32 | 80.00 |
| proclaim | 1 | 2.50 |
| spread | 1 | 2.50 |
| tell | 2 | 5.00 |
| - | 2 | 5.00 |
| ***1 Corinthians 9:18*** | | |
| announce | 1 | 2.50 |
| declare | 1 | 2.50 |
| offer | 1 | 2.50 |
| preach | 33 | 82.50 |
| proclaim | 1 | 2.50 |
| spread | 1 | 2.50 |
| tell | 2 | 5.00 |
| ***1 Corinthians 15:1*** | | |
| declare | 2 | 5.00 |
| give | 1 | 2.50 |
| make known | 1 | 2.50 |
| preach | 29 | 72.50 |
| present | 1 | 2.50 |
| proclaim | 3 | 7.50 |
| receive | 1 | 2.50 |
| tell | 2 | 5.00 |
| ***1 Corinthians 15:2*** | | |
| announce | 1 | 2.50 |
| declare | 1 | 2.50 |
| give | 1 | 2.50 |
| preach | 27 | 67.50 |
| proclaim | 2 | 5.00 |
| receive | 1 | 2.50 |
| save | 1 | 2.50 |
| tell | 2 | 5.00 |
| - | 4 | 10.00 |
| ***2 Corinthians 10:16*** | | |
| bring | 1 | 2.50 |
| carry | 4 | 10.00 |
| declare | 1 | 2.50 |
| evangelize | 2 | 5.00 |
| preach | 28 | 70.00 |
| proclaim | 1 | 2.50 |
| spread | 1 | 2.50 |
| take | 1 | 2.50 |
| tell | 1 | 2.50 |
| ***2 Corinthians 11:7*** | | |
| announce | 1 | 2.50 |
| declare | 1 | 2.50 |
| evangelize | 1 | 2.50 |
| give | 2 | 5.00 |
| preach | 33 | 82.50 |
| proclaim | 1 | 2.50 |
| tell | 1 | 2.50 |
| ***Galatians 1:8*** | | |
| announce | 1 | 2.50 |
| declare | 1 | 2.50 |
| evangelize | 1 | 2.50 |
| preach | 33 | 82.50 |
| proclaim | 1 | 2.50 |
| promise | 1 | 2.50 |
| tell | 1 | 2.50 |
| x | 1 | 2.50 |
| ***Galatians 1:8a*** | | |
| announce | 1 | 2.50 |
| declare | 1 | 2.50 |
| deliver | 1 | 2.50 |
| evangelize | 1 | 2.50 |
| give | 1 | 2.50 |
| preach | 30 | 75.00 |
| proclaim | 1 | 2.50 |
| promise | 1 | 2.50 |
| - | 2 | 5.00 |
| x | 1 | 2.50 |
| ***Galatians 1:9*** | | |
| announce | 2 | 5.00 |
| declare | 1 | 2.50 |
| evangelize | 2 | 5.00 |
| preach | 31 | 77.50 |
| proclaim | 1 | 2.50 |
| tell | 2 | 5.00 |
| x | 1 | 2.50 |
| ***Galatians 1:11*** | | |
| announce | 1 | 2.50 |
| declare | 1 | 2.50 |
| evangelize | 1 | 2.50 |
| hear | 1 | 2.50 |
| preach | 31 | 77.50 |
| proclaim | 3 | 7.50 |
| spread | 1 | 2.50 |
| x | 1 | 2.50 |

*Continued opposite*

*Table 23–13, concluded*

### Galatians 1:16
| | Total | Percent |
|---|---|---|
| announce | 2 | 5.00 |
| declare | 1 | 2.50 |
| evangelize | 1 | 2.50 |
| give | 1 | 2.50 |
| make known | 1 | 2.50 |
| preach | 25 | 62.50 |
| proclaim | 4 | 10.00 |
| show | 1 | 2.50 |
| spread | 1 | 2.50 |
| tell | 2 | 5.00 |
| x | 1 | 2.50 |

### Galatians 1:23
| | | |
|---|---|---|
| announce | 1 | 2.50 |
| declare | 1 | 2.50 |
| evangelize | 1 | 2.50 |
| preach | 33 | 82.50 |
| proclaim | 2 | 5.00 |
| spread | 1 | 2.50 |
| x | 1 | 2.50 |

### Galatians 4:13
| | | |
|---|---|---|
| announce | 3 | 7.50 |
| bring | 5 | 12.50 |
| declare | 1 | 2.50 |
| evangelize | 2 | 5.00 |
| preach | 28 | 70.00 |
| x | 1 | 2.50 |

### Ephesians 2:17
| | | |
|---|---|---|
| announce | 4 | 10.00 |
| bring | 3 | 7.50 |
| come | 3 | 7.50 |
| declare | 1 | 2.50 |
| evangelize | 1 | 2.50 |
| preach | 22 | 55.00 |
| proclaim | 5 | 12.50 |
| - | 1 | 2.50 |

### Ephesians 3:8
| | | |
|---|---|---|
| announce | 4 | 10.00 |
| bring | 2 | 5.00 |
| declare | 1 | 2.50 |
| evangelize | 1 | 2.50 |
| make clear | 1 | 2.50 |
| make known | 1 | 2.50 |
| preach | 19 | 47.50 |
| proclaim | 6 | 15.00 |
| spread | 1 | 2.50 |
| take | 1 | 2.50 |
| tell | 3 | 7.50 |

### 1 Thessalonians 3:6
| | | |
|---|---|---|
| bring | 22 | 55.00 |
| declare | 2 | 5.00 |
| give | 4 | 10.00 |
| make known | 1 | 2.50 |
| relate | 1 | 2.50 |
| report | 3 | 7.50 |
| return | 1 | 2.50 |
| show | 1 | 2.50 |
| tell | 4 | 10.00 |
| x | 1 | 3 |

### Hebrews 4:2
| | | |
|---|---|---|
| come | 1 | 2.50 |
| declare | 5 | 12.50 |
| deliver | 1 | 2.50 |
| denounce | 1 | 2.50 |
| give | 1 | 2.50 |
| have for | 1 | 2.50 |
| hear | 11 | 27.50 |
| preach | 14 | 35.00 |
| proclaim | 2 | 5.00 |
| promise | 1 | 2.50 |
| receive | 2 | 5.00 |

### Hebrews 4:6
| | | |
|---|---|---|
| announce | 1 | 2.50 |
| come | 1 | 2.50 |
| declare | 2 | 5.00 |
| deliver | 1 | 2.50 |
| get | 1 | 2.50 |
| give | 1 | 2.50 |
| have chance | 1 | 2.50 |
| hear | 10 | 25.00 |
| preach | 15 | 37.50 |
| promise | 1 | 2.50 |
| receive | 5 | 12.50 |
| tell | 1 | 2.50 |

### 1 Peter 1:12
| | | |
|---|---|---|
| announce | 2 | 5.00 |
| bring | 4 | 10.00 |
| declare | 1 | 2.50 |
| evangelize | 1 | 2.50 |
| evangelize | 2 | 5.00 |
| preach | 27 | 67.50 |
| proclaim | 1 | 2.50 |
| spread | 1 | 2.50 |
| tell | 1 | 2.50 |

### 1 Peter 1:25
| | | |
|---|---|---|
| announce | 2 | 5.00 |
| bring | 4 | 10.00 |
| declare | 1 | 2.50 |
| evangelize | 1 | 2.50 |
| give | 1 | 2.50 |
| preach | 26 | 65.00 |
| proclaim | 2 | 5.00 |
| tell | 1 | 2.50 |
| - | 2 | 5.00 |

### 1 Peter 4:6
| | | |
|---|---|---|
| bring | 2 | 5.00 |
| declare | 1 | 2.50 |
| deliver | 1 | 2.50 |
| evangelize | 1 | 2.50 |
| give | 1 | 2.50 |
| preach | 31 | 77.50 |
| proclaim | 1 | 2.50 |
| tell | 2 | 5.00 |

### Revelation 10:7
| | | |
|---|---|---|
| announce | 10 | 25.00 |
| assure | 1 | 2.50 |
| declare | 9 | 22.50 |
| evangelize | 1 | 2.50 |
| give | 3 | 7.50 |
| make known | 2 | 5.00 |
| preach | 5 | 12.50 |
| proclaim | 2 | 5.00 |
| promise | 3 | 7.50 |
| tell | 4 | 10.00 |

### Revelation 14:6
| | | |
|---|---|---|
| announce | 7 | 17.50 |
| declare | 1 | 2.50 |
| evangelize | 1 | 2.50 |
| give | 1 | 2.50 |
| have for | 1 | 2.50 |
| herald | 1 | 2.50 |
| preach | 17 | 42.50 |
| proclaim | 9 | 22.50 |
| spread | 1 | 2.50 |
| tell | 1 | 2.50 |

## 3. Frequencies in The Top 40 English Bibles

| | Total | Percent |
|---|---|---|

### WB 1382
| | | |
|---|---|---|
| euangelise | 8 | 14.81 |
| hear | 1 | 1.85 |
| preach | 39 | 72.22 |
| show | 3 | 5.56 |
| tell | 3 | 5.56 |

### TB-M 1525
| | | |
|---|---|---|
| bring | 2 | 3.70 |
| declare | 3 | 5.56 |
| preach | 47 | 87.04 |
| show | 2 | 3.70 |

### CB 1535
| | | |
|---|---|---|
| bring | 2 | 3.70 |
| declare | 1 | 1.85 |
| hear | 1 | 1.85 |
| preach | 47 | 87.04 |
| show | 3 | 5.56 |

### GB-C 1539
| | | |
|---|---|---|
| bring | 2 | 3.70 |
| declare | 3 | 5.56 |
| preach | 46 | 85.19 |
| receive | 1 | 1.85 |
| show | 2 | 3.70 |

### GB 1560
| | | |
|---|---|---|
| bring | 3 | 5.56 |
| declare | 2 | 3.70 |
| preach | 45 | 83.33 |
| publish | 1 | 1.85 |
| receive | 2 | 3.70 |
| show | 1 | 1.85 |

### BB 1568
| | | |
|---|---|---|
| bring | 3 | 5.56 |
| declare | 2 | 3.70 |
| preach | 47 | 87.04 |
| show | 2 | 3.70 |

### DRB 1610
| | | |
|---|---|---|
| denounce | 1 | 1.85 |
| evangelize | 41 | 75.93 |
| preach | 11 | 20.37 |
| report | 1 | 1.85 |

### AV/KJV 1611
| | | |
|---|---|---|
| bring | 3 | 5.56 |
| declare | 2 | 3.70 |
| preach | 47 | 87.04 |
| show | 2 | 3.70 |

### DRCB 1749
| | | |
|---|---|---|
| bring | 2 | 3.70 |
| declare | 3 | 5.56 |
| evangelize | 1 | 1.85 |
| preach | 47 | 87.04 |
| relate | 1 | 1.85 |

### RV/ERV 1885
| | | |
|---|---|---|
| bring | 7 | 12.96 |
| declare | 1 | 1.85 |
| preach | 45 | 83.33 |
| proclaim | 1 | 1.85 |

### ASV 1901
| | | |
|---|---|---|
| bring | 7 | 12.96 |
| declare | 1 | 1.85 |
| preach | 45 | 83.33 |
| proclaim | 1 | 1.85 |

### EB-R 1902
| | | |
|---|---|---|
| announce | 19 | 35.19 |
| bring | 5 | 9.26 |
| carry | 1 | 1.85 |
| deliver | 7 | 12.96 |
| make known | 1 | 1.85 |
| proclaim | 1 | 1.85 |

### HBME 1903
| | | |
|---|---|---|
| tell | 20 | 37.04 |
| announce | 5 | 9.26 |
| declare | 3 | 5.56 |
| evangelise | 10 | 18.52 |
| give | 1 | 1.85 |
| make known | 1 | 1.85 |
| preach | 17 | 31.48 |
| proclaim | 3 | 5.56 |
| promise | 6 | 11.11 |
| relate | 1 | 1.85 |
| report | 1 | 1.85 |
| supply | 1 | 1.85 |
| tell | 5 | 9.26 |

### MB 1924
| | | |
|---|---|---|
| assure | 1 | 1.85 |
| bring | 3 | 5.56 |
| come | 2 | 3.70 |
| get | 1 | 1.85 |
| have for | 2 | 3.70 |
| preach | 39 | 72.22 |
| receive | 1 | 1.85 |
| tell | 3 | 5.56 |
| - | 2 | 3.70 |

### AT/GB 1939
| | | |
|---|---|---|
| announce | 1 | 1.85 |
| bring | 7 | 12.96 |
| come | 1 | 1.85 |
| deliver | 1 | 1.85 |
| give | 1 | 1.85 |
| make known | 1 | 1.85 |
| offer | 1 | 1.85 |
| preach | 28 | 51.85 |
| present | 1 | 1.85 |
| proclaim | 2 | 3.70 |
| tell | 8 | 14.81 |
| - | 2 | 3.70 |

### BBE 1949
| | | |
|---|---|---|
| give | 27 | 50.00 |
| hear | 2 | 3.70 |
| make clear | 1 | 1.85 |
| preach | 20 | 37.04 |
| take | 2 | 3.70 |
| - | 2 | 3.70 |

### KB 1950
| | | |
|---|---|---|
| bring | 3 | 5.56 |
| come | 1 | 1.85 |
| evangelize | 1 | 1.85 |
| give | 2 | 3.70 |
| make known | 2 | 3.70 |
| preach | 39 | 72.22 |
| proclaim | 1 | 1.85 |
| spread | 2 | 3.70 |
| tell | 2 | 3.70 |
| - | 1 | 1.85 |

### RSV 1952
| | | |
|---|---|---|
| announce | 1 | 1.85 |
| bring | 6 | 11.11 |
| come | 1 | 1.85 |
| preach | 42 | 77.78 |
| proclaim | 1 | 1.85 |
| receive | 1 | 1.85 |
| tell | 1 | 1.85 |
| - | 1 | 1.85 |

### HBAEM 1957
| | | |
|---|---|---|
| bring | 4 | 7.41 |
| give | 3 | 5.56 |
| preach | 46 | 85.19 |

### MLB/NB 1959
| | | |
|---|---|---|
| proclaim | 1 | 1.85 |
| announce | 2 | 3.70 |
| bring | 5 | 9.26 |
| evangelize | 5 | 9.26 |
| give | 1 | 1.85 |
| make known | 1 | 1.85 |
| preach | 30 | 55.56 |
| proclaim | 1 | 1.85 |
| publish | 1 | 1.85 |
| receive | 1 | 1.85 |
| tell | 5 | 9.26 |
| - | 2 | 3.70 |

### NWT 1961
| | | |
|---|---|---|
| declare | 52 | 96.30 |
| give | 1 | 1.85 |
| tell | 1 | 1.85 |

### NCE/CCD 1961
| | | |
|---|---|---|
| announce | 2 | 3.70 |
| bring | 5 | 9.26 |
| declare | 3 | 5.56 |
| make known | 1 | 1.85 |
| preach | 40 | 74.07 |
| proclaim | 3 | 5.56 |

### AB 1964
| | | |
|---|---|---|
| announce | 5 | 9.26 |
| bring | 2 | 3.70 |
| preach | 27 | 50.00 |
| proclaim | 8 | 14.81 |
| receive | 1 | 1.85 |
| tell | 1 | 1.85 |
| x | 10 | 18.52 |

### AmB 1965
| | | |
|---|---|---|
| announce | 3 | 5.56 |
| bring | 6 | 11.11 |
| evangelize | 1 | 1.85 |
| give | 1 | 1.85 |
| preach | 31 | 57.41 |
| proclaim | 11 | 20.37 |
| tell | 1 | 1.85 |

### JB 1966
| | | |
|---|---|---|
| announce | 3 | 5.56 |
| bring | 9 | 16.67 |
| carry | 1 | 1.85 |
| come | 1 | 1.85 |
| explain | 1 | 1.85 |
| give | 1 | 1.85 |
| hear | 1 | 1.85 |
| preach | 23 | 42.59 |
| proclaim | 11 | 20.37 |
| receive | 1 | 1.85 |
| tell | 2 | 3.70 |

### NAB 1970
| | | |
|---|---|---|
| announce | 8 | 14.81 |
| bring | 4 | 7.41 |
| deliver | 1 | 1.85 |
| hear | 1 | 1.85 |
| herald | 1 | 1.85 |
| preach | 23 | 42.59 |
| proclaim | 11 | 20.37 |
| report | 1 | 1.85 |
| speak | 1 | 1.85 |
| spread | 2 | 3.70 |
| tell | 1 | 1.85 |

### NEB 1970
| | | |
|---|---|---|
| announce | 2 | 3.70 |
| bring | 9 | 16.67 |
| carry | 1 | 1.85 |
| declare | 1 | 1.85 |
| give | 3 | 5.56 |
| have for | 1 | 1.85 |
| hear | 5 | 9.26 |
| preach | 16 | 29.63 |
| proclaim | 6 | 11.11 |
| promise | 1 | 1.85 |
| spread | 2 | 3.70 |
| tell | 5 | 9.26 |
| - | 2 | 3.70 |

### TLB 1971
| | | |
|---|---|---|
| announce | 4 | 7.41 |
| bring | 7 | 12.96 |
| give | 2 | 3.70 |
| have chance | 1 | 1.85 |
| hear | 1 | 1.85 |
| introduce | 1 | 1.85 |
| preach | 30 | 55.56 |
| save | 1 | 1.85 |
| send | 1 | 1.85 |
| show | 1 | 1.85 |
| spread | 1 | 1.85 |
| tell | 3 | 5.56 |
| - | 1 | 1.85 |

### NASB 1971
| | | |
|---|---|---|
| bring | 4 | 7.41 |
| preach | 50 | 92.59 |

### GNB/TEV 1976
| | | |
|---|---|---|
| announce | 4 | 7.41 |
| be here with | 1 | 1.85 |
| bring | 4 | 7.41 |
| hear | 2 | 3.70 |
| preach | 33 | 61.11 |
| proclaim | 3 | 5.56 |
| send | 1 | 1.85 |
| take | 1 | 1.85 |
| tell | 5 | 9.26 |

### NIV 1978
| | | |
|---|---|---|
| announce | 1 | 1.85 |
| bring | 4 | 7.41 |
| preach | 41 | 75.93 |
| proclaim | 3 | 5.56 |
| tell | 5 | 9.26 |

### NKJV 1982
| | | |
|---|---|---|
| bring | 4 | 7.41 |
| declare | 2 | 3.70 |
| preach | 48 | 88.89 |

### NJB 1985
| | | |
|---|---|---|
| announce | 2 | 3.70 |
| bring | 8 | 14.81 |
| come | 1 | 1.85 |
| explain | 1 | 1.85 |
| give | 1 | 1.85 |
| hear | 1 | 1.85 |
| preach | 26 | 48.15 |
| proclaim | 12 | 22.22 |
| receive | 1 | 1.85 |
| tell | 1 | 1.85 |

### NLV 1986
| | | |
|---|---|---|
| bring | 5 | 9.26 |
| hear | 2 | 3.70 |
| preach | 41 | 75.93 |
| tell | 6 | 11.11 |

### NCV 1986
| | | |
|---|---|---|
| announce | 1 | 1.85 |
| bring | 4 | 7.41 |
| hear | 1 | 1.85 |
| preach | 18 | 33.33 |
| receive | 1 | 1.85 |
| send | 1 | 1.85 |
| tell | 28 | 51.85 |

### CCB 1988
| | | |
|---|---|---|
| announce | 8 | 14.81 |
| bring | 6 | 11.11 |
| encourage | 1 | 1.85 |
| give | 5 | 9.26 |
| hear | 1 | 1.85 |
| make known | 1 | 1.85 |
| preach | 16 | 29.63 |
| proclaim | 9 | 16.67 |
| progress | 1 | 1.85 |
| receive | 1 | 1.85 |
| return | 1 | 1.85 |
| speak | 1 | 1.85 |
| spread | 1 | 1.85 |
| tell | 2 | 3.70 |

### NRSV 1989
| | | |
|---|---|---|
| announce | 3 | 5.56 |
| bring | 13 | 24.07 |
| hear | 1 | 1.85 |
| preach | 1 | 1.85 |
| proclaim | 33 | 61.11 |
| receive | 1 | 1.85 |
| tell | 2 | 3.70 |

### REB 1989
| | | |
|---|---|---|
| announce | 3 | 5.56 |
| bring | 10 | 18.52 |
| carry | 1 | 1.85 |
| declare | 1 | 1.85 |
| give | 3 | 5.56 |
| hear | 1 | 1.85 |
| preach | 18 | 33.33 |
| proclaim | 7 | 12.96 |
| promise | 1 | 1.85 |
| say | 1 | 1.85 |
| spread | 2 | 3.70 |
| take | 2 | 3.70 |
| tell | 4 | 7.41 |

### GW 1995
| | | |
|---|---|---|
| bring | 2 | 3.70 |
| come | 1 | 1.85 |
| give | 1 | 1.85 |
| have for | 1 | 1.85 |
| hear | 4 | 7.41 |
| make known | 1 | 1.85 |
| spread | 21 | 38.89 |
| tell | 23 | 42.59 |

### CEV 1995
| | | |
|---|---|---|
| announce | 2 | 3.70 |
| explain | 1 | 1.85 |
| have for | 1 | 1.85 |
| hear | 5 | 9.26 |
| offer | 1 | 1.85 |
| preach | 22 | 40.74 |
| say | 1 | 1.85 |
| talk | 1 | 1.85 |
| tell | 16 | 29.63 |
| - | 4 | 7.41 |

**Table 23-14.  110 macrocommands: 80 in 6 New Testament Great Commission narratives, ranked chronologically, alphabetically, and by Mandate, and 30 in related narratives.**

This table lists and analyzes the 80 personal commands from the Risen Christ by means of the 6 major structured Great Commission occasions. The other 30 commands were given during the Forty Days but outside the 6 main occasions.

Each of the 80 personal commands is listed here only once in each of the 3 listings, at its first usage in the order of narrative, chapter, and verse as shown in the first listing below. *Verse.* Each command is followed by the number of the verse where it first occurs, also (in parentheses) the main Bible version where it occurs most significantly. Often it occurs in mul-

tiple versions not shown here. *Mandate.* Shown also is the number, I-VII, of the Great Commission Mandate under which the command is categorized here.

### a. Ranked chronologically by NT verses

| Narrative Command | Verse | | Mandate |
|---|---|---|---|
| **1. Matthew 28:18-20** | | | |
| Go | 19 | (AV) | II |
| Teach | 19 | (AV) | VII |
| Train | 19 | (NTCE) | VII |
| Set forth | 19 | (Rieu) | II |
| Disciple | 19 | (1911 AV) | V |
| Baptize | 19 | (AV) | VI |
| Immerse | 19 | (Rotherham) | VI |
| Observe | 20 | (REB) | II |
| Command | 20 | (REB) | V |
| Do | 20 | (CEV) | II |
| **2. Mark 16:15-20** | | | |
| Go forth | 15 | (NEB) | II |
| Preach | 15 | (CEV) | IV |
| Proclaim | 15 | (REB) | IV |
| Believe | 16 | (CEV) | V |
| Condemn | 16 | (ASV) | V |
| Save | 16 | (AV) | V |
| Perform miracles | 17 | (GNB) | II |
| Bring | 17 | (NEB) | II |
| Cast out | 17 | (AV) | II |
| Expel | 17 | (Weymouth) | II |
| Force | 17 | (CEV) | V |
| Drive out | 17 | (REB) | II |
| Speak in tongues | 17 | (Knox) | III |
| Place hands on | 18 | (GNB) | V |
| Lay hands on | 18 | (REB) | V |
| Make well | 18 | (MB) | V |
| Heal | 18 | (CEV) | V |
| Work | 20 | (AV) | VII |
| Confirm | 20 | (ASV) | VI |
| Attest | 20 | (NEB) | III |
| **3. Luke 24:44-53** | | | |
| Tell | 44 | (CEV) | III |
| Mean | 44 | (NEB) | III |
| Fulfill | 44 | (AV) | O |
| Open | 45 | (AV) | III |
| Enlighten | 45 | (Knox) | V |
| Make understand | 45 | (CEV) | V |
| Continue | 45 | (Williams) | I |
| Forgive | 47 | (Goodspeed) | V |
| Make repent | 47 | (NIV) | V |
| Witness | 48 | (NEB) | III |
| Promise | 49 | (AV) | IV |
| Stay | 49 | (CEV) | I |
| Be clothed | 49 | (ASV) | I |
| Worship | 52 | (CEV) | VI |
| Thank | 53 | (GNB) | VI |
| Praise | 53 | (AV) | VI |
| **4. John 20:19-31** | | | |
| Show | 20 | (AV) | II |
| Send | 21 | (AV) | II |
| Receive | 22 | (GNB) | I |
| Retain | 23 | (AV) | V |
| Reach | 27 | (AV) | II |
| Do miracles | 30 | (Beck) | II |
| Write | 31 | (AV) | VI |
| **5. John 21:4-25** | | | |
| Catch | 5 | (CEV) | V |
| Fish | 5 | (GNB) | V |
| Throw a net | 6 | (NIV) | III |
| Cast a net | 6 | (AV) | III |
| Haul | 6 | (REB) | V |
| Drag | 11 | (CEV) | V |
| Come | 12 | (AV) | II |
| Appear | 14 | (NEB) | III |
| Love | 15 | (REB) | II |
| Feed | 15 | (CEV) | VI |
| Tend | 15 | (NASB) | VI |
| Shepherd | 16 | (ABUV) | VI |
| Make known | 17 | (AV) | III |
| Care | 17 | (NIV) | II |
| Follow | 19 | (GNB) | I |
| Testify | 24 | (NIV) | III |
| Record | 25 | (REB) | II |
| **6. Acts 1:1-14** | | | |
| Instruct | 2 | (NEB) | VII |
| Order | 2 | (NASB) | V |
| Present | 3 | (RSV) | IV |
| Prove | 3 | (CEV) | IV |
| Demonstrate | 3 | (AB) | IV |
| Discuss | 3 | (MB) | III |
| Charge | 4 | (ASV) | V |
| Wait | 4 | (CEV) | I |
| Answer | 7 | (NEB) | III |
| Pray | 14 | (CEV) | I |

### b. Ranked alphabetically

| Command | Verse | | Mandate | Narrative |
|---|---|---|---|---|
| Answer | 7 | (NEB) | III | Acts 1:1-14 |
| Appear | 14 | (NEB) | III | John 21:4-25 |
| Attest | 20 | (NEB) | III | Mark 16:15-20 |
| Baptize | 19 | (AV) | VI | Matthew 28:18-20 |
| Be clothed | 49 | (ASV) | I | Luke 24:44-53 |
| Believe | 16 | (CEV) | V | Mark 16:15-20 |
| Bring | 17 | (NEB) | II | Mark 16:15-20 |
| Care | 17 | (NIV) | II | John 21:4-25 |
| Cast a net | 6 | (AV) | III | John 21:4-25 |
| Cast out | 17 | (AV) | II | Mark 16:15-20 |
| Catch | 5 | (CEV) | V | John 21:4-25 |
| Charge | 4 | (ASV) | V | Acts 1:1-14 |
| Come | 12 | (AV) | II | John 21:4-25 |
| Command | 20 | (REB) | V | Matthew 28:18-20 |
| Condemn | 16 | (ASV) | V | Mark 16:15-20 |
| Confirm | 20 | (ASV) | VI | Mark 16:15-20 |
| Continue | 45 | (Williams) | I | Luke 24:44-53 |
| Demonstrate | 3 | (AB) | IV | Acts 1:1-14 |
| Disciple | 19 | (1911 AV) | V | Matthew 28:18-20 |
| Discuss | 3 | (MB) | III | Acts 1:1-14 |
| Do | 20 | (CEV) | II | Matthew 28:18-20 |
| Do miracles | 30 | (Beck) | II | John 20:19-31 |
| Drag | 11 | (CEV) | V | John 21:4-25 |
| Drive out | 17 | (REB) | II | Mark 16:15-20 |
| Enlighten | 45 | (Knox) | V | Luke 24:44-53 |
| Expel | 17 | (Weymouth) | II | Mark 16:15-20 |
| Feed | 15 | (CEV) | VI | John 21:4-25 |
| Fish | 5 | (GNB) | V | John 21:4-25 |
| Follow | 19 | (GNB) | I | John 21:4-25 |
| Force | 17 | (CEV) | V | Mark 16:15-20 |
| Forgive | 47 | (Goodspeed) | V | Luke 24:44-53 |
| Fulfill | 44 | (AV) | O | Luke 24:44-53 |
| Go | 19 | (AV) | II | Matthew 28:18-20 |
| Go forth | 15 | (NEB) | II | Mark 16:15-20 |
| Haul | 6 | (NIV) | V | John 21:4-25 |
| Heal | 18 | (CEV) | V | Mark 16:15-20 |
| Immerse | 19 | (Rotherham) | VI | Matthew 28:18-20 |
| Instruct | 2 | (NEB) | VII | Acts 1:1-14 |
| Lay hands on | 18 | (REB) | V | Mark 16:15-20 |
| Love | 15 | (REB) | II | John 21:4-25 |
| Make known | 17 | (AV) | III | John 21:4-25 |
| Make repent | 47 | (NIV) | V | Luke 24:44-53 |
| Make understand | 45 | (CEV) | V | Luke 24:44-53 |
| Make well | 18 | (MB) | V | Mark 16:15-20 |
| Mean | 44 | (NEB) | III | Luke 24:44-53 |
| Observe | 20 | (REB) | II | Matthew 28:18-20 |
| Open | 45 | (AV) | III | Luke 24:44-53 |
| Order | 2 | (NASB) | V | Acts 1:1-14 |
| Perform miracles | 17 | (GNB) | II | Mark 16:15-20 |
| Place hands on | 18 | (GNB) | V | Mark 16:15-20 |
| Praise | 53 | (AV) | VI | Luke 24:44-53 |
| Pray | 14 | (CEV) | I | Acts 1:1-14 |
| Preach | 15 | (CEV) | IV | Mark 16:15-20 |
| Present | 3 | (RSV) | IV | Acts 1:1-14 |
| Proclaim | 15 | (REB) | IV | Mark 16:15-20 |
| Promise | 49 | (AV) | IV | Luke 24:44-53 |
| Prove | 3 | (CEV) | IV | Acts 1:1-14 |
| Reach | 27 | (AV) | II | John 20:19-31 |
| Receive | 22 | (GNB) | I | John 20:19-31 |
| Record | 25 | (REB) | II | John 21:4-25 |
| Retain | 23 | (AV) | V | John 20:19-31 |
| Save | 16 | (AV) | V | Mark 16:15-20 |
| Send | 21 | (AV) | II | John 20:19-31 |
| Set forth | 19 | (Rieu) | II | Matthew 28:18-20 |
| Shepherd | 16 | (ABUV) | VI | John 21:4-25 |
| Show | 20 | (AV) | II | John 20:19-31 |
| Speak in tongues | 17 | (Knox) | III | Mark 16:15-20 |
| Stay | 49 | (CEV) | I | Luke 24:44-53 |
| Teach | 19 | (AV) | VII | Matthew 28:18-20 |
| Tell | 44 | (CEV) | III | Luke 24:44-53 |
| Tend | 15 | (NASB) | VI | John 21:4-25 |
| Testify | 24 | (NIV) | III | John 21:4-25 |
| Thank | 53 | (GNB) | VI | Luke 24:44-53 |
| Throw a net | 6 | (NIV) | III | John 21:4-25 |
| Train | 19 | (NTCE) | VII | Matthew 28:18-20 |
| Wait | 4 | (CEV) | I | Acts 1:1-14 |
| Witness | 48 | (NEB) | III | Luke 24:44-53 |
| Work | 20 | (AV) | VII | Mark 16:15-20 |
| Worship | 52 | (CEV) | VI | Luke 24:44-53 |
| Write | 31 | (AV) | VI | John 20:19-31 |

### c. Ranked by Mandate

| Command | Verse | | Mandate | Narrative |
|---|---|---|---|---|
| **I. RECEIVE!** | | | | |
| Be clothed | 49 | (ASV) | I | Luke 24:44-53 |
| Continue | 45 | (Williams) | I | Luke 24:44-53 |
| Follow | 19 | (GNB) | I | John 21:4-25 |
| Pray | 14 | (CEV) | I | Acts 1:1-14 |
| Receive | 22 | (GNB) | I | John 20:19-31 |
| Stay | 49 | (CEV) | I | Luke 24:44-53 |
| Wait | 4 | (CEV) | I | Acts 1:1-14 |
| **II. GO!** | | | | |
| Bring | 17 | (NEB) | II | Mark 16:15-20 |
| Care | 17 | (NIV) | II | John 21:4-25 |
| Cast out | 17 | (AV) | II | Mark 16:15-20 |
| Come | 12 | (AV) | II | John 21:4-25 |
| Do | 20 | (CEV) | II | Matthew 28:18-20 |
| Do miracles | 30 | (Beck) | II | John 20:19-31 |
| Drive out | 17 | (REB) | II | Mark 16:15-20 |
| Expel | 17 | (Weymouth) | II | Mark 16:15-20 |
| Go | 19 | (AV) | II | Matthew 28:18-20 |
| Go forth | 15 | (NEB) | II | Mark 16:15-20 |
| Love | 15 | (REB) | II | John 21:4-25 |
| Observe | 20 | (REB) | II | Matthew 28:18-20 |
| Perform miracles | 17 | (GNB) | II | Mark 16:15-20 |
| Reach | 27 | (AV) | II | John 20:19-31 |
| Record | 25 | (REB) | II | John 21:4-25 |
| Send | 21 | (AV) | II | John 20:19-31 |
| Set forth | 19 | (Rieu) | II | Matthew 28:18-20 |
| Show | 20 | (AV) | II | John 20:19-31 |
| **III. WITNESS!** | | | | |
| Answer | 7 | (NEB) | III | Acts 1:1-14 |
| Appear | 14 | (NEB) | III | John 21:4-25 |
| Attest | 20 | (NEB) | III | Mark 16:15-20 |
| Cast a net | 6 | (AV) | III | John 21:4-25 |
| Discuss | 3 | (MB) | III | Acts 1:1-14 |
| Make known | 17 | (AV) | III | John 21:4-25 |
| Mean | 44 | (NEB) | III | Luke 24:44-53 |
| Open | 45 | (AV) | III | Luke 24:44-53 |
| Speak in tongues | 17 | (Knox) | III | Mark 16:15-20 |
| Tell | 44 | (CEV) | III | Luke 24:44-53 |
| Testify | 24 | (NIV) | III | John 21:4-25 |
| Throw a net | 6 | (NIV) | III | John 21:4-25 |
| Witness | 48 | (NEB) | III | Luke 24:44-53 |
| **IV. PROCLAIM!** | | | | |
| Demonstrate | 3 | (AB) | IV | Acts 1:1-14 |
| Preach | 15 | (CEV) | IV | Mark 16:15-20 |
| Present | 3 | (RSV) | IV | Acts 1:1-14 |
| Proclaim | 15 | (REB) | IV | Mark 16:15-20 |
| Promise | 49 | (AV) | IV | Luke 24:44-53 |
| Prove | 3 | (CEV) | IV | Acts 1:1-14 |
| **V. DISCIPLE!** | | | | |
| Believe | 16 | (CEV) | V | Mark 16:15-20 |
| Catch | 5 | (CEV) | V | John 21:4-25 |
| Charge | 4 | (ASV) | V | Acts 1:1-14 |
| Command | 20 | (REB) | V | Matthew 28:18-20 |
| Condemn | 16 | (AV) | V | Mark 16:15-20 |
| Disciple | 19 | (1911 AV) | V | Matthew 28:18-20 |
| Drag | 11 | (CEV) | V | John 21:4-25 |
| Enlighten | 45 | (Knox) | V | Luke 24:44-53 |
| Fish | 5 | (GNB) | V | John 21:4-25 |
| Force | 17 | CEV) | V | Mark 16:15-20 |
| Forgive | 47 | (Goodspeed) | V | Luke 24:44-53 |
| Haul | 6 | (REB) | V | John 21:4-25 |
| Heal | 18 | (CEV) | V | Mark 16:15-20 |
| Lay hands on | 18 | (REB) | V | Mark 16:15-20 |
| Make repent | 47 | (NIV) | V | Luke 24:44-53 |
| Make understand | 45 | (CEV) | V | Luke 24:44-53 |
| Make well | 18 | (MB) | V | Mark 16:15-20 |
| Order | 2 | (NASB) | V | Acts 1:1-14 |
| Place hands on | 18 | (GNB) | V | Mark 16:15-20 |
| Retain | 23 | (AV) | V | John 20:19-31 |
| Save | 16 | (AV) | V | Mark 16:15-20 |
| **VI. BAPTIZE!** | | | | |
| Baptize | 19 | (AV) | VI | Matthew 28:18-20 |
| Confirm | 20 | (ASV) | VI | Mark 16:15-20 |
| Feed | 15 | (CEV) | VI | John 21:4-25 |
| Immerse | 19 | (Rotherham) | VI | Matthew 28:18-20 |
| Praise | 53 | (AV) | VI | Luke 24:44-53 |
| Shepherd | 16 | (ABUV) | VI | John 21:4-25 |
| Tend | 15 | (NASB) | VI | John 21:4-25 |
| Thank | 53 | (GNB) | VI | Luke 24:44-53 |
| Worship | 52 | (CEV) | VI | Luke 24:44-53 |
| Write | 31 | (AV) | VI | John 20:19-31 |
| **VII. TRAIN!** | | | | |
| Instruct | 2 | (NEB) | VII | Acts 1:1-14 |
| Teach | 19 | (AV) | VII | Matthew 28:18-20 |
| Train | 19 | (NTCE) | VII | Matthew 28:18-20 |
| Work | 20 | (AV) | VII | Mark 16:15-20 |

**OVERALL IMPERATIVE:**
**O. EVANGELIZE!**

| | | | | |
|---|---|---|---|---|
| Fulfill | 44 | (AV) | O | Luke 24:44-53 |

by definition, can be measured. We will then show that these dimensions can be quantified by means firstly of a scale with some 270 dichotomous Yes/No factors; and secondly, by means of a simple formula of 20 numerical variables that can be done in one's head for any population segment by means of mental arithmetic.

### A tabular presentation: Table 23–17

The results of the method just described are given below as a 6-column table. The whole table presents the 420 verbal dimensions of 'evangelize' each with 4 cognate or related terms (verb, participle, adjective, noun), making a total of 420 distinct and separate (though complementary and overlapping) dimensions, placed within the context of the total of 620 facets and the grand total of 2,400 related cognate words. The whole is shown divided up into the 7 Mandates of the Great Commission.

### Four distinct viewpoints

The layout of Table 23–17 also emphasizes 4 different viewpoints. These are 4 distinct ways of seeing, looking at, visualizing, describing, understanding, defining, interpreting, and later quantifying, measuring, analyzing and evaluating evangelization. The first viewpoint (column 1) forms the divine perspective, how God views it as he commands his people (*Evangelize!*); the last 3 viewpoints (columns 2,3,4) form the human perspective, namely how the church reacts (by *evangelizing*), how the world experiences it or looks at it (it becomes *evangelized*), and how the analyst (missiologist) conceptualizes it (he observes *evangelization*). A final pair of columns assess the significance of each facet.

### Meanings of the 6 columns

After the initial reference column which enables the

user to count, find, and navigate through this mass of dimensions and facets, column numbers have the following meanings:

*column*

1. How God (the Great Evangelizer) views it: what imperative (verb) the church has been commanded by the Great Commission to obey. (God says **'Preach!'**).
2. How the church (the evangelizers) views it: what activity (participle) the church is doing or should be doing, in response to God's imperative. (The church is active in **preaching**).
3. How the world (the evangelized) views it: what effect (adjective) on itself the world experiences or perceives in consequence of columns 1 and 2. (The world is **preached** to).
4. How the analyst (the missiologist) views it: what concept (noun) describes this whole dimension and what type of ministry it is trying to accomplish. (Evangelization includes the **preaching** of the gospel).
5. Code (1-6) for which of the main categories this imperative comes under.
6. List of all the categories which describe this imperative.

### Six categories of synonyms

The last 2 columns 5 and 6 in Table 23–17 give the relative significance of all these synonyms of 'evangelize'. What they are coding is exegetical power—the power which each facet is able to muster to assist exegesis of the original Greek *euangelizo* in its English transliteration. The code numbers in column 5 have the following meaning:

| Code | Meaning |
|------|---------|
| 1 | = One of The Big Ten |

| | |
|---|---|
| 2 | = A macrotranslation |
| 3 | = A macrocommand |
| 4 | = A macrodefinition |
| 5 | = A **dimension** |
| 6 | = A facet |

All these numbers 1-6 refer back to the data presented and discussed in the foregoing dozen or so pages. Thus any item whose full code includes the code number 1 is one of *The Big Ten*. All with code 2 identify the *51 macrotranslations* (exact biblical translations) of the word *euangelizo* used in English Bible versions. All with code 3 identify the *110 macrocommands* found in the 6 Great Commission narratives and their extensions. All with code 4 highlight the *250 macrodefinitions* being quoted (published definitions of the form 'Evangelizing is...'). All with code 5 identify the *420 dimensions* themselves, the main focus of this enquiry, each of which is measurable, and each expounded and commented on in words, sentences, and quotations in Table 23–19. And all with code 6 show the complete listing of all synonyms and near-synonyms, the *620 facets*.

Column 6 therefore combines all categories by which each facet can be known. The large-scale overlapping is illustrated by No. 303 'preach'. This facet is at one and the same time a dimension, a macrodefinition, a macrocommand, a macrotranslation, and also one of The Big Ten. These codes are therefore not mutually exclusive nor watertight. They overlap: each category is also an item in all the categories underneath it. Thus one of The Big Ten is also a macrotranslation, also a macrocommand, also a macrodefinition, also a dimension, and also a facet.

Dimension is the central category in this analysis. The last 2 columns in Table 23–17 thus enable the reader to rapidly locate any term or any category, to see the exegetical-explanatory power of any facet, and to see how the facets relate to each other and to the whole family of synonyms, near-synonyms, and cognates.

The grand totals involved in this vast enumeration have already been given in Table 23–16.

The main impression this huge listing conveys is, once again, of the kaleidoscopic nature of our central term, *'Evangelize!'*

After Table 23–17, Table 23–18 provides a one-page alphabetical listing or index of all the dimensions and facets.

### DOCUMENTING THE 420 DIMENSIONS

This analysis now closes with a large reference section. Table 23–19 gives greatly expanded biblical and extra-biblical documentation for published or printed usages of all the dimensions (excluding all facets which are not dimensions). The table looks at each imperative under an etymological microscope and gives detailed but concise information on each dimension of evangelization. The numbering followed is exactly the same as that in Table 23–17. In a systematic and standardized presentation, there will be found the following data.

(a) The major or typical usages of each dimension from any English versions of the Bible, with exact quotations, contexts, and references; for all 4 keywords in this dimension—verb, participle, adjective, noun—any directly-relevant New Testament references are given from the whole range of the 41 leading English Bible translations. Occasionally, Old Testament references are added where they throw additional light on the terms.

(b) A selection may next be given from major usages of the English terms from the Post-Apostolic Age up to the present day. Significant usages in print of any of the 4 keywords in this dimension up to the present are listed in chronological order. Periods (full-stops) separate them into distinct and separate usages. Books or journals employing the keywords in

---

The *Modern concordance to the New Testament* (ed M. Darton, 1976) lists 4,900 Greek keywords (out of the NT's total of 5,600 Greek words) with each's frequency of usage (word count), and 4,700 English keywords, all classified under 341 distinct Greek/English key group-themes and 800 English single-word themes. One of these major keywords is the Greek verb *euangelizo*. This is grouped under the key group-theme 'Tell-Preach-Proclaim' together with 10 variants and 4 other closely-synonymous Greek verbs. An additional 57 other key group-themes set out scores of Greek and English synonyms and near-synonyms to *euangelizo*, with hundreds of other related verbs. The 58 group-themes are given below in alphabetical order in **bold** type, each followed by any immediate synonyms or related verbs in medium type. Each group-theme can be seen derived, documented, expounded, and presented in great detail in the *Modern concordance*.

**accompany-follow**
**accuse-charge-defend**-answer-explain-prosecute
**agree-consent**-acknowledge-accept
**ask-pray**-plead-beg-invite-appeal to-request-urge-demand-implore-beseech
**blame-rebuke-warn**-reprove-refute-remonstrate with-caution
**bless-praise-glory**-commend-recommend-credit
**care-concern-devote**
**catch-seize**-trap-snare-snatch-ambush-take by force-capture-attain-apprehend
**come-arrive**-be present-attain-reach-penetrate-visit
**cut-divide**-allot-share
**disperse-scatter**-spread-strew-give out-litter
**encourage-persuade**-support-dare-comfort-sympathize with-warn-convince-be bold enough-advise-urge-console-help-win over
**farm**-crop-sow-seed-plant-reap-harvest-gather-gather in-sift-winnow-thresh
**fight-struggle**-strive-agonize-exercise-train
**find-happen**-meet-chance on-attain
**firm-confirm-guarantee**-secure-fix-strengthen-affirm-reaffirm-establish-pledge-secure-validate-balance-endorse
**fish**-catch
**free-set free**-discharge
**give**-bestow-offer-proffer-present-hand over-grant-entrust-deliver-supply-provide
**go-pass**-set out-pursue-depart-go about-advance-penetrate-journey-travel
**grow-sprout-bud**-spread-bear fruit-produce crops
**have mercy-pity**-forgive-take pity on
**hear-listen-learn**-receive-heed-note-make disciples
**interpret-explain**-translate-report-tell
**know-understand**-recognize-realize-remember-perceive-grasp-comprehend-consider-reason
**love**-befriend
**make peace-reconcile**
**measure**
**name-call-acclaim**
**obey-submit-subject**
**order-regulate-instruct**-command-enjoin
**press-insist**-make-force
**prophesy**-speak in tongues
**put-set-appoint**-set out-place-put in place-lay out
**quarrel-dispute**-contend-argue
**receive-accept**-get-gain
**remember**-recall-remind

**repent**-change
**rise-raise**-exalt-lift up-lift high
**save-cure**-rescue-deliver-redeem-heal-restore-make well-make whole-set right-put right-recover
**say-tell-speak**-talk-utter-preach-speak in tongues-discuss-shout-reply-forewarn-debate-confer-chatter-gossip-dispute-consult-address-express-give a message-foretell-forewarn-account for-mean-assert-allege-report-spread-describe-respond-answer-make a speech
**seek-pursue**-look for-follow-search-explore-aim at-target-study-research
**send**-send out-commission-fetch-bring-start-write to
**serve-minister**-attend-wait upon-aid-relieve-help-administer-look after
**share-partner**-fellowship
**shepherd-herd**-pastor-tend-look after-care for
**shine-light**-illumine-light up-dazzle
**show-reveal-open**-demonstrate-point out-warn-make clear-clarify-appear-make known-manifest-disclose-indicate-direct-instruct-uncover-unveil-expose-make obvious-make evident-lift the veil-lay bare
**stay-live**-remain-wait-rest-spend time-dwell-persevere-continue-keep-settle-inhabit-be devoted to-be faithful-persist-lodge
**stretch out**-extend-prolong
**take-bring-lead**-capture-collect-get-win-catch-overtake-hand to-carry-bear-introduce
**teach**-instruct-indoctrinate-inform-tell-hear-receive-initiate-ready-disciple-correct-warn-advise-admonish-discipline
**tell-preach-proclaim**-bring-announce-declare-herald-report-recount-give account-acknowledge-profess-publish-distribute-circulate-communicate-praise-glorify-confess-bless-thank-admit-utter-expound-inform-demonstrate-imply-give news-pass news on-confirm-claim-recognize-call-broadcast-disseminate-reckon-regard-cast a net-evangelize-foretell
**touch**
**turn-return**-bring back-convict-win-win over-conquer-defeat-overcome-vanquish-triumph over
**victory-conquer**
**voice-sound**-shout-cry out-sing-chant-cry-roar-thunder-yell-howl-call out-noise abroad
**water-baptize-wash**-dip-soak-saturate-cleanse-pour out-sprinkle
**will-want**-decide-choose
**witness-testify**-bear witness-attest-urge-appeal-submit
**write-read**-register-enrol-note-record-describe-inscribe-enumerate-number-certify

their titles are also listed, in the chronological sequence. Abbreviated references (author and year followed by a colon and then a page number) mean that the book or article concerned will be found in the present book in Part 31 or in the *Selective bibliography on evangelism and evangelization* in Part 22. All authors are given with their initials except in the case of the major collection of definitions and usages which is referred to here simply as 'Mott 1938'. Direct quotations are in some cases condensed in the interests of brevity; where a significant amount is omitted, this is indicated by 3 dots (...).

(c) Finally, and in particular to assist a number of dimensions whose relation to 'evangelize' may not be immediately apparent, these relations are shown in brief systematic closing statements in standardized format in boldface type, showing the exact relation of one or more of the 4 keywords of this dimension and its major synonyms to 'evangelize' or cognates. This standardized form states: 'To evangelize is...', 'Evangelizing is...', 'Being evangelized is...', or 'Evangelization is...'.

Between them these biblical texts, historical notes, more recent quotations, book titles, and closing overall statements cover and include the great majority of all definitions that have been proposed in the history of the concept down to the present day. Together they constitute our own unified definition of the concept, which is followed throughout the present book.

To get a comprehensive, immediate overview of the meaning and usages of 'evangelize' and cognates, therefore, move rapidly through these 420 dimensions as described in this Table 23–19 but read only the short summary statement or statements printed as a brief final paragraph at each's end, immediately above each dimension's closing horizontal rule. For a total bird's-eye view, keep Table 23–17 in mind. For a single-page overview, turn to Table 23–18. For an ultra-short overview, see column 11 on Global Diagram 6. And to locate data on any particular term, find it alphabetically in Table 23–18 then look its reference number up in Table 23–19.

## Table 23–17. 420 dimensions and 620 facets of 'evangelize', 'evangelism', and 'evangelization': or, 585 ways to minister in order to reach the world with the gospel.

All the entries in the table's first column are *facets* of 'evangelize'; they list 585 of the estimated 620 facets which are synonyms or near-synonyms of 'evangelize'. All the entries in **bold** type are *dimensions* of 'evangelize'; they list 407 of its estimated 420 dimensions. All these verbs can be regarded as imperatives embodying different ways for disciples to engage in evangelizing outreach in the world.

Columns 1-4 give the 4 keywords which are cognate to each facet, as follows. Column 1: Imperative (verb): [*Evangelize!* means...]. Column 2: Activity (participle): [*Evangelizing* means...]. Column 3: Effect (adjective): [*Evangelized*

means...]. Column 4: Concept (noun): [*Evangelization* means...]. Dashes (-) mean that no obviously applicable keyword is available in English.

Columns 5-6 code each facet's significance, its highest code, that is, its exegetical power in setting out the biblical meaning of 'evangelize'. Column 6 lists all the descriptive categories each falls under; column 5 gives the major category concerned.

*Dimensions* are all shown in column 5 as 1, 2, 3, 4, or 5; or in column 6 as all items with a 5 in their code.

The numbers in both columns mean: 1 = One of **The Big**

**Ten**, 2 = a *macrotranslation* (word in English Bibles exactly translating *euangelizo*), 3 = a *macrocommand* (verb or command in the 6 Great Commission narratives or extensions), 4 = a *macrodefinition* (with quoted published definition such as 'To evangelize is to...'), 5 = a *dimension* (each being measurable, and each expounded and commented on in words, sentences, and quotations in the following Table 23–19), and 6 = a *facet* of 'evangelize'. Thus, for example, in reference number 303, the entry '123456' means that 'preach' can be described as in all 6 categories.

| | MINICOMMISSION MANDATE Dimension Facet | HUMAN ROLE Type of evangelism | EFFECT ON WORLD Effect of evangelism | STATUS/ACHIEVEMENT Type of evangelization | | Significance Exegetical power | ILLUSTRATIONS |
|---|---|---|---|---|---|---|---|
| Ref col | God's viewpoint Imperative (Verb) 1 | Church's viewpoint Activity (Participle) 2 | World's viewpoint Effect (Adjective) 3 | Analyst's viewpoint Concept (Noun) 4 | Code 5 | Categories Descriptions 6 | From here to the end of this Table 23–17, this end column features 50 photographs or images (postage stamps, paintings) illustrating a selection of major dimensions or facets of 'evangelize', each identified by its initial number in the listing. |

### MINICOMMISSION I: Evangelize! (consisting of Mandates 1,2,3,4 with Dimensions or Facets 1-326)

Component Mandates:

**I.    RECEIVE!    PRAYER EVANGELISM    PNEUMATIC EVANGELIZATION**

| Ref | 1 | 2 | 3 | 4 | 5 | 6 |
|---|---|---|---|---|---|---|
| 1. **accompany** | accompanying | accompanied for | accompaniment | 5 | 56 |
| 2. **be clothed** | being clothed | clothed for | clothing | 3 | 3456 |
| 3. **be filled** | being filled | filled for | fullness | 5 | 56 |
| 4. **commit** | committing | committed to | commitment | 4 | 456 |
| 5. **continue** | continuing | continued for | continuation | 3 | 3456 |
| 6. **cooperate** | cooperating | cooperated for | cooperation | 4 | 456 |
| 7. **expect** | expecting | expected for | expectation | 4 | 456 |
| 8. **follow** | following | followed for | following | 3 | 3456 |
| 9. **intercede** | interceding | interceded for | intercession | 5 | 56 |
| 10. **participate** | participating | participated in | participation | 4 | 456 |
| 11. **persist** | persisting | persisted with | persistence | 5 | 56 |
| 12. **pneumatize** | pneumatizing | pneumatized | pneumatization | 4 | 456 |
| 13. **pray** | praying | prayed for | prayer | 3 | 3456 |
| 14. **receive** | receiving | received for | reception | 3 | 3456 |
| 15. **stay** | staying | stayed for | stay | 3 | 3456 |
| 16. **wait** | waiting | waited for | wait | 3 | 3456 |

**II.    GO!    PRE-EVANGELISM    PREPARATORY EVANGELIZATION**

| Ref | 1 | 2 | 3 | 4 | 5 | 6 |
|---|---|---|---|---|---|---|
| 17. **act** | acting | acted on | action | 4 | 456 |
| 18. **advance** | advancing | advanced into | advance | 4 | 456 |
| 19. **aid** | aiding | aided | aid | 5 | 56 |
| 20. **aim** at | aiming | aimed at | aim | 5 | 56 |
| 21. **apply** | applying | applied | application | 5 | 56 |
| 22. **approach** | approaching | approached | approach | 5 | 56 |
| 23. **arrive** | arriving | arrived at | arrival | 5 | 56 |
| 24. assist | assisting | assisted | assistance | 6 | 6 |
| 25. **bring** | bringing | brought to | bringing | 1 | 123456 |
| 26. **calculate** | calculating | calculated about | calculation | 5 | 56 |
| 27. care | caring | cared for | care | 3 | 3456 |
| 28. **carry** | carrying | carried | carrying | 2 | 23456 |
| 29. **cast out** | casting out | cast out from | casting out | 4 | 456 |
| 30. **come** | coming | come for | come | 2 | 23456 |
| 31. **compute** | computing | computed | computation | 5 | 56 |
| 32. **contact** | contacting | contacted | contact | 4 | 456 |
| 33. correspond | corresponding | corresponded with | correspondence | 6 | 6 |
| 34. **count** | counting | counted | count | 5 | 56 |
| 35. depart | departing | departed for | departure | 6 | 56 |
| 36. **deploy** | deploying | deployed to | deployment | 5 | 56 |
| 37. design | designing | designed | design | 6 | 6 |
| 38. **develop** | developing | developed | development | 4 | 456 |
| 39. **display** | displaying | displayed | display | 5 | 56 |
| 40. **do** | doing | done to | deed | 3 | 3456 |
| 41. **do miracles** | doing miracles | miracles done for | miraculousness | 3 | 3456 |
| 42. **drive out** | driving out | driven out | driving | 3 | 3456 |
| 43. **dwell** | dwelling | dwelled | dwelling-place | 5 | 56 |
| 44. **encounter** | encountering | encountered | encounter | 4 | 456 |
| 45. **engage** | engaging | engaged | engagement | 4 | 456 |
| 46. enumerate | enumerating | enumerated | enumeration | 6 | 6 |
| 47. **estimate** | estimating | estimated | estimation | 5 | 56 |
| 48. **exhibit** | exhibiting | exhibited | exhibition | 5 | 56 |
| 49. exorcize | exorcizing | exorcized | exorcism | 6 | 6 |
| 50. **expel** | expelling | expelled | expulsion | 3 | 3456 |
| 51. **explore** | exploring | explored | exploration | 5 | 56 |
| 52. **extend** | extending | extended | extension | 2 | 23456 |
| 53. focus | focusing | focused | focus | 6 | 6 |
| 54. **free** | freeing | freed | freedom | 5 | 56 |
| 55. **give** | giving | given for | gift | 1 | 123456 |
| 56. **go** | going | gone to | going | 3 | 3456 |
| 57. **go forth** | going forth | gone into | going forth | 3 | 3456 |
| 58. **go with** | going with | gone with | going with | 2 | 23456 |
| 59. **illustrate** | illustrating | illustrated | illustration | 4 | 456 |
| 60. **impact** | impacting | impacted | impact | 4 | 456 |
| 61. implement | implementing | implemented | implementation | 6 | 6 |
| 62. incarnate | incarnating | incarnated | incarnation | 6 | 6 |
| 63. indicate | indicating | indicated | indication | 6 | 6 |
| 64. **inhabit** | inhabiting | inhabited | inhabitation | 5 | 56 |
| 65. **influence** | influencing | influenced | influence | 4 | 456 |
| 66. **inspect** | inspecting | inspected | inspection | 5 | 56 |
| 67. **irradiate** | irradiating | irradiated | irradiation | 5 | 56 |
| 68. **itinerate** | intinerating | intinerated through | intineration | 5 | 56 |
| 69. **journey** | journeying | journeyed to | journeyings | 5 | 56 |
| 70. **liberate** | liberating | liberated | liberation | 4 | 456 |
| 71. **list** | listing | listed | list | 5 | 56 |
| 72. **live** | living | lived for | life | 4 | 456 |
| 73. look for | looking for | looked for | look | 6 | 6 |
| 74. **love** | loving | loved | love | 3 | 3456 |
| 75. **make available** | making available | made available to | availability | 5 | 56 |
| 76. **make see** | making see | seen | sight | 5 | 56 |
| 77. **measure** | measuring | measured | measurement | 5 | 56 |

3. **Be filled!** The Spirit falls at Pentecost.

9. **Intercede!** On hilltop, youths intercede for city of Prizren, Kosovo.

13. **Pray!** Huge prayer meeting in limestone caves, China.

28. **Carry!** Moody's wagon for carrying Bibles and workers, Chicago 1886.

34. **Count!** Oberammergau Passion Play needs detailed daily counting.

39. **Display!** Modern church Ronchamp displays Good News.

59. **Illustrate!** The 'Jesus' Film viewed by huge Russian audience.

68. **Itinerate!** United Church of Canada mobile chapel with evangelists.

74. **Love!** Mother Teresa speaks of Jesus to the dying.

77. **Measure!** Domesday Book, best medieval survey ever (AD 1085).

continued

*Table 23–17 continued*

|  | | | | | | |
|---|---|---|---|---|---|---|
| 78. | **meet** | meeting | met | meeting | 4 | 456 |
| 79. | migrate | migrating | migrated to | migration | 6 | 6 |
| 80. | **missionize** | missionizing | missionized | missionization | 4 | 456 |
| 81. | move | moving | moved | removal | 6 | 6 |
| 82. | note | noting | noted | noting | 6 | 6 |
| 83. | **number** | numbering | numbered | number | 5 | 56 |
| 84. | **observe** | observing | observed | observation | 3 | 3456 |
| 85. | **occupy** | occupying | occupied | occupation | 4 | 456 |
| 86. | paint | painting | painted | painting | 6 | 6 |
| 87. | pay attention | paying attention | paid attention to | attentiveness | 6 | 6 |
| 88. | **penetrate** | penetrating | penetrated | penetration | 4 | 456 |
| 89. | **perform miracles** | performing miracles | performed for | performance | 3 | 3456 |
| 90. | **permeate** | permeating | permeated | permeation | 4 | 456 |
| 91. | pervade | pervading | pervaded | pervasion | 6 | 6 |
| 92. | pity | pitying | pitied | pitying | 6 | 6 |
| 93. | **plan** | planning | planned | plan | 5 | 56 |
| 94. | **point** | pointing | pointed to | pointing | 5 | 56 |
| 95. | **portray** | portraying | portrayed | portrayal | 5 | 56 |
| 96. | **prepare** | preparing | prepared | preparation | 4 | 456 |
| 97. | protest | protesting | protested | protestation | 6 | 6 |
| 98. | **provide** | providing | provided for | provision | 5 | 56 |
| 99. | pursue | pursuing | pursued | pursuance | 6 | 6 |
| 100. | **reach** | reaching | reached | outreach | 2 | 23456 |
| 101. | **record** | recording | recorded | recording | 3 | 3456 |
| 102. | **register** | registering | registered | registration | 5 | 56 |
| 103. | relieve | relieving | relieved | relief | 6 | 6 |
| 104. | research | researching | researched | research | 5 | 56 |
| 105. | **reside** | residing | resided in | residence | 5 | 56 |
| 106. | **risk** | risking | risked for | risk | 4 | 456 |
| 107. | scan | scanning | scanned | scan | 5 | 56 |
| 108. | **search** | searching | searched | searching | 5 | 56 |
| 109. | **seek** | seeking | sought | seeking | 4 | 456 |
| 110. | select | selecting | selected | selection | 6 | 6 |
| 111. | **send** | sending | sent to | sending | 2 | 23456 |
| 112. | send out | sending out | sent out to | sending out | 6 | 6 |
| 113. | **set forth** | setting forth | set forth to | setting forth | 3 | 3456 |
| 114. | **set out** | setting out | set out for | setting out | 5 | 56 |
| 115. | **settle** | settling | settled | settlement | 5 | 56 |
| 116. | **show** | showing | showed | show | 2 | 23456 |
| 117. | **show mercy** | showing mercy | showed mercy | show of mercy | 5 | 56 |
| 118. | **signal** | signaling | signaled | signaling | 5 | 56 |
| 119. | **sort** | sorting | sorted | sort | 5 | 56 |
| 120. | speak out | speaking out | spoke out | speaking out | 6 | 6 |
| 121. | start | starting | started on | start | 6 | 6 |
| 122. | **strategize** | strategizing | strategized | strategy | 5 | 56 |
| 123. | **study** | studying | studied | study | 5 | 56 |
| 124. | **suffer** | suffering | suffered | suffering | 4 | 456 |
| 125. | **sum** | summing | summed | summation | 5 | 56 |
| 126. | **supply** | supplying | supplied | supply | 5 | 56 |
| 127. | **survey** | surveying | surveyed | survey | 5 | 56 |
| 128. | symbolize | symbolizing | symbolized | symbolization | 6 | 6 |
| 129. | **take** | taking | taken | taking | 2 | 23456 |
| 130. | take pity on | taking pity on | taken pity on | pity | 6 | 6 |
| 131. | **target** | targeting | targeted | target | 5 | 56 |
| 132. | **total** | totalling | totalled | totality | 5 | 56 |
| 133. | **touch** | touching | touched | touch | 4 | 456 |
| 134. | tour | touring | toured | tourism | 6 | 6 |
| 135. | **transmit** | transmitting | transmitted | transmittal | 4 | 456 |
| 136. | transport | transporting | transported | transportation | 6 | 6 |
| 137. | **travel** | traveling | traveled to | travel | 5 | 56 |
| 138. | **visit** | visiting | visited | visitation | 5 | 56 |
| 139. | visualize | visualizing | visualized | visualization | 6 | 6 |

### III. WITNESS! — PERSONAL EVANGELISM — PRESENCE EVANGELIZATION

|  | | | | | | |
|---|---|---|---|---|---|---|
| 140. | **acknowledge** | acknowledging | acknowledged | acknowledgment | 4 | 456 |
| 141. | **acquaint** | acquainting | acquainted with | acquaintance | 4 | 456 |
| 142. | **admit** | admitting | admitted | admittance | 5 | 56 |
| 143. | **advocate** | advocating | advocated | advocacy | 5 | 56 |
| 144. | **affirm** | affirming | affirmed | affirmation | 4 | 456 |
| 145. | **answer** | answering | answered | answer | 3 | 3456 |
| 146. | **appear** | appearing | appeared to | appearance | 3 | 3456 |
| 147. | apprise | apprising | apprised | appraisal | 6 | 6 |
| 148. | **assert** | asserting | asserted | assertion | 5 | 56 |
| 149. | asseverate | asseverating | asseverated | asseveration | 6 | 6 |
| 150. | **associate** | associating | associated with | association | 5 | 56 |
| 151. | **attest** | attesting | attested to | attestation | 3 | 3456 |
| 152. | **be here with** | being here with | been here with | being here | 2 | 23456 |
| 153. | **be martyred** | being martyred | martyred in | martyrdom | 3 | 3456 |
| 154. | **be present** | being present | been present to | presence | 4 | 456 |
| 155. | **bear tidings** | bearing tidings | borne to | bearing of tidings | 2 | 23456 |
| 156. | **cast a net** | casting a net | cast a net at | net-casting | 3 | 3456 |
| 157. | chat | chatting | chatted about | chatting | 6 | 6 |
| 158. | chatter | chattering | chattered at | chattering | 6 | 6 |
| 159. | **circulate** | circulating | circulated among | circulation | 5 | 56 |
| 160. | **claim** | claiming | claimed | claim | 5 | 56 |
| 161. | **commend** | commending | commended | commendation | 4 | 456 |
| 162. | **communicate** | communicating | communicated | communication | 4 | 456 |
| 163. | **confess** | confessing | confessed | confession | 4 | 456 |
| 164. | **converse** | conversing | conversed | conversation | 4 | 456 |
| 165. | **convey** | conveying | conveyed | conveyance | 4 | 456 |
| 166. | corroborate | corroborating | corroborated | corroboration | 6 | 6 |
| 167. | **cry** | crying | cried to | cry | 5 | 56 |
| 168. | dazzle | dazzling | dazzled | dazzle | 6 | 6 |
| 169. | **deliver** | delivering | delivered | delivery | 2 | 23456 |
| 170. | depose to | deposing to | deposed to | deposition | 6 | 6 |
| 171. | **describe** | describing | described | description | 4 | 456 |
| 172. | **dialogue** | dialoguing | dialogued with | dialogue | 4 | 456 |
| 173. | **diffuse** | diffusing | diffused | diffusion | 4 | 456 |
| 174. | **disclose** | disclosing | disclosed | disclosure | 5 | 56 |
| 175. | **discuss** | discussing | discussed | discussion | 3 | 3456 |
| 176. | disperse | dispersing | dispersed | dispersion | 6 | 6 |
| 177. | **disseminate** | disseminating | disseminated | dissemination | 4 | 456 |
| 178. | **expose** | exposing | exposed | exposure | 4 | 456 |
| 179. | **express** | expressing | expressed | expression | 5 | 56 |
| 180. | **extol** | extolling | extolled in | extolment | 5 | 56 |
| 181. | **foretell** | foretelling | foretold to | foretelling | 5 | 56 |
| 182. | **forewarn** | forewarning | forewarned | forewarning | 5 | 56 |
| 183. | **further** | furthering | furthered | furtherance | 5 | 56 |
| 184. | **get** | getting | got | getting | 2 | 23456 |

76. **Make see!** Blind Filipino boys prepare to see and find Jesus through the first Braille gospels in their language.

116. **Show!** Spain's National Evangelical Symphonic Orchestra perform Handel's 'Messiah' (composed in 1741) in Spanish.

117. **Show mercy!** 'Caribbean Mercy' one of YWAM's 4-ship Mercy Ships Fleet with 700 doctors, nurses, crews, travelling worldwide.

137. **Travel!** 'Departure of the Apostles' on their worldwide travels, AD 38 (German School, Munich Penakothek).

153. **Be martyred!** Enraged Muslim mob in Java murders 6 young church workers, 1999.

172. **Dialogue!** In Thailand, Buddhist monk talks with WCC officers about God, Jesus, salvation, Bible, prayer.

*continued*

Table 23–17 continued

| | | | | | |
|---|---|---|---|---|---|
| 185. **give account** | giving account | given account of | giving of account | 5 | 56 |
| 186. **give evidence** | giving evidence | given evidence on | giving of evidence | 5 | 56 |
| 187. give out | giving out | given out | giving out | 6 | 6 |
| 188. **gossip** | gossiping | gossiped to | gossiping | 5 | 56 |
| 189. **hand down** | handing down | handed down | handing down | 5 | 56 |
| 190. **hand to** | handing to | handed to | handing to | 5 | 56 |
| 191. **have for** | having for | had for | having for | 2 | 23456 |
| 192. **hold** | holding | held | holding | 5 | 56 |
| 193. howl | howling | howled at | howling | 6 | 6 |
| 194. **illuminate** | illuminating | illuminated | illumination | 4 | 456 |
| 195. imply | implying | implied to | implication | 6 | 6 |
| 196. **inform** | informing | informed on | information | 4 | 456 |
| 197. **introduce** | introducing | introduced | introduction | 2 | 23456 |
| 198. invoke | invoking | invoked for | invocation | 6 | 6 |
| 199. lay bare | laying bare | laid bare | laying bare | 6 | 6 |
| 200. lift the veil | lifting the veil | lifted for | lifting | 6 | 6 |
| 201. light | lighting | lit | lighting | 6 | 6 |
| 202. **maintain** | maintaining | maintained | maintenance | 5 | 56 |
| 203. **make accessible** | making accessible | made accessible to | accessibility | 4 | 456 |
| 204. **make aware** | making aware | aware of | awareness | 4 | 456 |
| 205. **make hear** | making hear | hearing | hearing | 1 | 123456 |
| 206. **make known** | making known | made known to | knowledge | 2 | 23456 |
| 207. manifest | manifesting | manifested to | manifestation | 6 | 6 |
| 208. **mean** | meaning | meant | meaning | 3 | 3456 |
| 209. **mention** | mentioning | mentioned | mentioning | 5 | 56 |
| 210. **name** | naming | named | naming | 4 | 456 |
| 211. **narrate** | narrating | narrated | narration | 4 | 456 |
| 212. noise abroad | noising abroad | noised abroad in | noising | 6 | 6 |
| 213. **open** | opening | opened | opener | 3 | 3456 |
| 214. **pass on** | passing on | passed on | passing on | 5 | 56 |
| 215. place | placing | placed | placement | 6 | 6 |
| 216. **profess** | professing | professed in | profession | 5 | 56 |
| 217. **propagate** | propagating | propagated in | propagation | 4 | 456 |
| 218. **prophesy** | prophesying | prophesied to | prophecy | 4 | 456 |
| 219. **radiate** | radiating | radiated | radiation | 4 | 456 |
| 220. recall | recalling | recalled to | recollection | 6 | 6 |
| 221. **reckon** | reckoning | reckoned with | reckoning | 5 | 56 |
| 222. **recognize** | recognizing | recognized | recognition | 4 | 456 |
| 223. **recommend** | recommending | recommended | recommendation | 5 | 56 |
| 224. **recount** | recounting | recounted | recounting | 5 | 56 |
| 225. **relate** | relating | related to | relation | 2 | 23456 |
| 226. remind | reminding | reminded | reminder | 6 | 6 |
| 227. **reply** | replying | replied to | reply | 5 | 56 |
| 228. **report** | reporting | reported on | reporting | 2 | 23456 |
| 229. **respond** | responding | responded to | response | 5 | 56 |
| 230. **reveal** | revealing | revealed to | revelation | 2 | 23456 |
| 231. roar | roaring | roared at | roaring | 6 | 6 |
| 232. **say** | saying | said | saying | 5 | 56 |
| 233. **scatter** | scattering | scattered | scattering | 5 | 56 |
| 234. scream | screaming | screamed at | screaming | 6 | 6 |
| 235. **share** | sharing | shared | sharing | 4 | 456 |
| 236. **shine** | shining | shined | shining | 4 | 456 |
| 237. shriek | shrieking | shrieked at | shrieking | 6 | 6 |
| 238. sound | sounding | sounded at | sounding | 6 | 6 |
| 239. **sow** | sowing | sowed in | sowing | 4 | 456 |
| 240. **speak** | speaking | spoken to | speaking | 2 | 23456 |
| 241. **speak in tongues** | speaking in tongues | spoken in tongues | tongues-speaking | 3 | 3456 |
| 242. **spread** | spreading | spread over | spreading | 1 | 123456 |
| 243. **story** | storying | storied to | storying | 5 | 56 |
| 244. strew | strewing | strewed over | strewing | 6 | 6 |
| 245. **talk** | talking | talked to | talking | 4 | 456 |
| 246. **tell** | telling | told to | telling | 1 | 123456 |
| 247. **testify** | testifying | testified to | testifying | 3 | 3456 |
| 248. **throw a net** | throwing a net | threw a net over | net-throwing | 3 | 3456 |
| 249. thunder | thundering | thundered at | thundering | 6 | 6 |
| 250. transfer | transferring | transferred | transferral | 6 | 6 |
| 251. uncover | uncovering | uncovered | uncovering | 6 | 6 |
| 252. unveil | unveiling | unveiled | unveiling | 6 | 6 |
| 253. utter | uttering | uttered to | uttering | 6 | 6 |
| 254. **witness** | witnessing | witnessed to | witness | 3 | 3456 |
| 255. yell | yelling | yelled at | yelling | 6 | 6 |
| **IV. PROCLAIM!** | **PREACHING EVANGELISM** | | **PROCLAMATION EVANGELIZATION** | | |
| 256. acclaim | acclaiming | acclaimed | acclamation | 5 | 56 |
| 257. **address** | addressing | addressed | address | 4 | 456 |
| 258. **advertise** | advertising | advertised to | advertising | 5 | 56 |
| 259. **alert** | alerting | alerted | alerting | 5 | 56 |
| 260. **announce** | announcing | announced to | announcement | 1 | 123456 |
| 261. **argue** | arguing | argued with | argument | 5 | 56 |
| 262. **blanket** | blanketing | blanketed | blanketing | 5 | 56 |
| 263. caution | cautioning | cautioned | cautioning | 6 | 6 |
| 264. clarify | clarifying | clarified | clarification | 6 | 6 |
| 265. **confer** | conferring | conferred with | conference | 5 | 56 |
| 266. **contend** | contending | contended with | contention | 5 | 56 |
| 267. credit | crediting | credited to | creditation | 6 | 6 |
| 268. cry out | crying out | cried out to | crying out | 6 | 6 |
| 269. cure | curing | cured | cure | 6 | 6 |
| 270. **debate** | debating | debated with | debate | 5 | 56 |
| 271. **declare** | declaring | declared to | declaration | 1 | 123456 |
| 272. deduce | deducing | deduced | deduction | 6 | 6 |
| 273. **defend** | defending | defended | defense | 4 | 456 |
| 274. **demonstrate** | demonstrating | demonstrated | demonstration | 3 | 3456 |
| 275. depict | depicting | depicted to | depiction | 6 | 6 |
| 276. detail | detailing | detailed | detailing | 6 | 6 |
| 277. **discourse** | discoursing | discoursed | discourse | 5 | 56 |
| 278. **dispute** | disputing | disputed with | dispute | 5 | 56 |
| 279. emphasize | emphasizing | emphasized to | emphasis | 6 | 6 |
| 280. endorse | endorsing | endorsed | endorsement | 6 | 6 |
| 281. entrust | entrusting | entrusted with | entrustment | 6 | 6 |
| 282. **exalt** | exalting | exalted about | exaltation | 5 | 56 |
| 283. **expound** | expounding | expounded to | exposition | 4 | 456 |
| 284. **familiarize** | familiarizing | familiarized with | familiarization | 4 | 456 |
| 285. **fill** | filling | filled | filling | 5 | 56 |
| 286. forbid | forbidding | forbidden | forbiddance | 6 | 6 |
| 287. **give a message** | giving a message | given a message | giving of a message | 5 | 56 |
| 288. **give chance** | giving a chance | given a chance | giving of a chance | 2 | 23456 |
| 289. **give notice** | giving notice | given notice | giving of notice | 5 | 56 |
| 290. **give opportunity** | giving opportunity | given opportunity | giving of an opportunity | 4 | 456 |
| 291. **herald** | heralding | heralded to | heralding | 2 | 23456 |

205. **Make hear!** Teaching signed languages, Burkina Faso Center for Deaf Youths helps hundreds to hear about Jesus.

206. **Make known!** 1987-2000, annual March for Jesus by 100 million Christians in 2,500 cities across world.

210. **Name!** Naming Jesus, procession in Helsinki protests Communist persecution.

239. **Sow!** 'The Sower', Bible societies' symbol.

247. **Testify!** Old-style street preacher with sandwich-board texts and megaphone testifies despite public scorn.

278. **Dispute!** Luther nails to Schlosskirche door his 95 Theses in Latin, starting Protestant Reformation in 1517.

283. **Expound!** Luther opens Scripture in his Wittenberg pulpit.

303. **Preach!** Woman evangelist Rowena Rand (Bahamas).

continued

Table 23–17 continued

| | | | | | |
|---|---|---|---|---|---|
| 292. **interpret** | interpreting | interpreted to | interpretation | 5 | 56 |
| 293. issue | issuing | issued | issuance | 6 | 6 |
| 294. lay out | laying out | laid out | layout | 6 | 6 |
| 295. **lecture** | lecturing | lectured | lecture | 5 | 56 |
| 296. **lift** | lifting | lifted | lifting | 5 | 56 |
| 297. **make a speech** | making a speech | made a speech to | speech-making | 5 | 56 |
| 298. **make clear** | making clear | made clear to | clarification | 2 | 23456 |
| 299. **make evident** | making evident | made evident to | evidence | 5 | 56 |
| 300. **make listen** | making listen | listening | listening | 2 | 23456 |
| 301. make obvious | making obvious | made obvious to | obviousness | 6 | 6 |
| 302. **notify** | notifying | notified | notification | 4 | 456 |
| 303. **preach** | preaching | preached to | preaching | 1 | 123456 |
| 304. **predict** | predicting | predicted to | prediction | 5 | 56 |
| 305. **present** | presenting | presented with | presentation | 2 | 23456 |
| 306. **proclaim** | proclaiming | proclaimed to | proclamation | 1 | 123456 |
| 307. **promise** | promising | promised | promise | 2 | 23456 |
| 308. **promulgate** | promulgating | promulgated in | promulgation | 4 | 456 |
| 309. **prove** | proving | proved | proven | 3 | 3456 |
| 310. publicize | publicizing | publicized | publicity | 6 | 6 |
| 311. **publish** | publishing | published to | publication | 2 | 23456 |
| 312. put before | putting before | put before | putting before | 6 | 6 |
| 313. **read** | reading | read to | reading | 5 | 56 |
| 314. **reason** | reasoning | reasoned with | reasoning | 4 | 456 |
| 315. recite | reciting | recited to | recitation | 6 | 6 |
| 316. **refute** | refuting | refuted | refutation | 5 | 56 |
| 317. repeat | repeating | repeated to | repetition | 6 | 6 |
| 318. resuscitate | resuscitating | resuscitated | resuscitation | 6 | 6 |
| 319. **saturate** | saturating | saturated | saturation | 4 | 456 |
| 320. set before | setting before | set before | setting before | 6 | 6 |
| 321. **shout** | shouting | shouted at | shouting | 5 | 56 |
| 322. show up | showing up | showed up | showing up | 6 | 6 |
| 323. sing | singing | sang to | song | 6 | 6 |
| 324. **state** | stating | stated | statement | 2 | 23456 |
| 325. threaten | threatening | threatened | threatening | 6 | 6 |
| 326. **translate** | translating | translated to | translation | 5 | 56 |

**MINICOMMISSION II:  Disciple!**  *(consisting of Mandates 5,6,7 with Dimensions or Facets 327-579)*

Component Mandates:

| **V. DISCIPLE!** | PERSUASION EVANGELISM | | PRESSURE EVANGELIZATION | | |
|---|---|---|---|---|---|
| 327. **accept** | accepting | accepted | acceptation | 4 | 456 |
| 328. accuse | accusing | accused | accusation | 6 | 6 |
| 329. acquire | acquiring | acquired for | acquisition | 6 | 6 |
| 330. agree | agreeing | agreed with | agreement | 6 | 6 |
| 331. ambush | ambushing | ambushed | ambush | 6 | 6 |
| 332. **appeal** | appealing | appealed to | appeal | 4 | 456 |
| 333. apprehend | apprehending | apprehended | apprehension | 6 | 6 |
| 334. apprentice | apprenticing | apprenticed | apprenticeship | 6 | 6 |
| 335. ask | asking | asked | asking | 6 | 6 |
| 336. **assure** | assuring | assured | assurance | 2 | 23456 |
| 337. **attrac**t | attracting | attracted | attraction | 4 | 456 |
| 338. **beg** | begging | begged | begging | 5 | 56 |
| 339. **believe** | believing | believed | belief | 3 | 3456 |
| 340. **beseech** | beseeching | beseeched | beseeching | 5 | 56 |
| 341. bestow | bestowing | bestowed | bestowal | 6 | 6 |
| 342. blame | blaming | blamed | blame | 6 | 6 |
| 343. bring back | bringing back | brought back | bringing back | 6 | 6 |
| 344. **call** | calling | called to | call | 4 | 456 |
| 345. call out | calling out | called out to | calling out | 6 | 6 |
| 346. capture | capturing | captured | capture | 6 | 6 |
| 347. **catch** | catching | caught | catch | 3 | 3456 |
| 348. cause | causing | caused | causation | 6 | 6 |
| 349. censure | censuring | censured | censure | 6 | 6 |
| 350. **challenge** | challenging | challenged | challenge | 5 | 56 |
| 351. change | changing | changed | change | 6 | 6 |
| 352. **charge** | charging | charged | charge | 3 | 3456 |
| 353. comfort | comforting | comforted | comfort | 6 | 6 |
| 354. **command** | commanding | commanded | command | 3 | 3456 |
| 355. **compel** | compelling | compelled | compulsion | 4 | 456 |
| 356. comprehend | comprehending | comprehended | comprehension | 6 | 6 |
| 357. **condemn** | condemning | condemned | condemnation | 3 | 3456 |
| 358. **confront** | confronting | confronted | confrontation | 4 | 456 |
| 359. **conquer** | conquering | conquered | conquest | 4 | 456 |
| 360. consider | considering | considered | consideration | 6 | 6 |
| 361. **convert** | converting | converted | conversion | 4 | 456 |
| 362. **convince** | convincing | convinced | conviction | 4 | 456 |
| 363. criticize | criticizing | criticized | criticism | 6 | 6 |
| 364. customize | customizing | customized | customization | 6 | 6 |
| 365. dare | daring | dared | daring | 6 | 6 |
| 366. deal with | dealing with | dealt with | deal | 6 | 6 |
| 367. defeat | defeating | defeated | defeat | 6 | 6 |
| 368. demand | demanding | demanded of | demand | 6 | 6 |
| 369. **denounce** | denouncing | denounced | denunciation | 2 | 23456 |
| 370. direct | directing | directed at | direction | 6 | 6 |
| 371. **disciple** | discipling | discipled | discipleship | 3 | 3456 |
| 372. **distribute** | distributing | distributed in | distribution | 5 | 56 |
| 373. **divide** | dividing | divided | dividend | 4 | 456 |
| 374. **drag** | dragging | dragged | dragging | 3 | 3456 |
| 375. embolden | emboldening | emboldened | emboldening | 6 | 6 |
| 376. **encourage** | encouraging | encouraged | encouragement | 2 | 23456 |
| 377. **enjoin** | enjoining | enjoined | enjoining | 5 | 56 |
| 378. **enlighten** | enlightening | enlightened | enlightenment | 3 | 3456 |
| 379. **entreat** | entreating | entreated | entreaty | 5 | 56 |
| 380. excite | exciting | excited | excitement | 6 | 6 |
| 381. **exhort** | exhorting | exhorted | exhortation | 4 | 456 |
| 382. **explain** | explaining | explained | explanation | 2 | 23456 |
| 383. **find** | finding | found | finding | 5 | 56 |
| 384. **fish** | fishing | fished in | fishing | 3 | 3456 |
| 385. **force** | forcing | forced | forceful | 3 | 3456 |
| 386. **forgive** | forgiving | forgiven | forgiveness | 3 | 3456 |
| 387. **gather in** | gathering | gathered | gathering | 4 | 456 |
| 388. grant | granting | granted | grant | 6 | 6 |
| 389. **grasp** | grasping | grasped | grasping | 5 | 56 |
| 390. **guide** | guiding | guided | guidance | 5 | 56 |
| 391. **harvest** | harvesting | harvested | harvest | 4 | 456 |
| 392. **haul** | hauling | hauled | haul | 3 | 3456 |
| 393. **heal** | healing | healed | healing | 3 | 3456 |
| 394. **hunt** | hunting | hunted | hunt | 4 | 456 |

**292. Interpret!** East African Revival Convention rapid-fire sentence-by-sentence preaching to 50,000 in 4 languages (3 interpreting).

**326. Translate!** Amerindian team translates New Testament into Hixkaryana language, northwest Brazil.

347. **Catch!** 'The Miraculous Drought of Fishes' (from John 21) by C. Witz, AD 1444 (the background resembles Lake Geneva).

358. **Confront!** Global evangelist John Paul II challenges Russian president Gorbachev, an atheist, to accept Christ as Lord.

372. **Distribute!** In 1438, Gutenberg (*left*) invents movable-type printing press to evangelize world via scripture distribution (as in Calcutta, *right*).

382. **Explain!** Global evangelist Billy Graham explains faith in Christ to China president Zhemin (*right*).

continued

Table 23–17 continued

| | | | | | |
|---|---|---|---|---|---|
| 395. **impart** | imparting | imparted to | impartation | 4 | 456 |
| 396. **implore** | imploring | implored | imploring | 5 | 56 |
| 397. induce | inducing | induced | induction | 6 | 6 |
| 398. **insist** | insisting | insisted on | insistence | 5 | 56 |
| 399. **invite** | inviting | invited | invitation | 2 | 23456 |
| 400. **involve** | involving | involved in | involvement | 4 | 456 |
| 401. **lay hands on** | laying hands on | laid on | laying-on of hands | 3 | 3456 |
| 402. **lead** | leading | led | leading | 3 | 3456 |
| 403. **make acknowledge** | making acknowledge | acknowledging | acknowledgement | 4 | 456 |
| 404. **make choose** | making choose | choosing | choice | 4 | 456 |
| 405. make concede | making concede | conceding | concession | 6 | 6 |
| 406. **make decide** | making decide | deciding | decision | 4 | 456 |
| 407. **make put** | making put | putting | putting | 5 | 56 |
| 408. **make realize** | making realize | realizing | realization | 4 | 456 |
| 409. **make receive** | making receive | receiving | reception | 2 | 23456 |
| 410. **make repent** | making repent | repenting | repentance | 3 | 3456 |
| 411. **make respond** | making respond | responding | responsiveness | 4 | 456 |
| 412. **make trust** | making trust | trusting | trust | 5 | 56 |
| 413. **make understand** | making understand | understanding | understanding | 3 | 3456 |
| 414. **make well** | making well | made well | wellness | 3 | 3456 |
| 415. **make whole** | making whole | made whole | wholeness | 4 | 456 |
| 416. net | netting | netted | netting | 6 | 6 |
| 417. **oblige** | obliging | obliged | obligation | 5 | 56 |
| 418. **offer** | offering | offered | offering | 2 | 23456 |
| 419. **order** | ordering | ordered | order | 3 | 3456 |
| 420. overcome | overcoming | overcame | overcoming | 6 | 6 |
| 421. overtake | overtaking | overtaken | overtaking | 6 | 6 |
| 422. **perceive** | perceiving | perceived | perception | 4 | 456 |
| 423. **persuade** | persuading | persuaded | persuasion | 4 | 456 |
| 424. **place hands on** | placing hands on | placed hands on | hand placement | 3 | 3456 |
| 425. **plead** | pleading | pleaded with | pleading | 5 | 56 |
| 426. **polarize** | polarizing | polarized | polarization | 6 | 456 |
| 427. prescribe | prescribing | prescribed | prescription | 6 | 6 |
| 428. **press** | pressing | pressed | pressure | 4 | 456 |
| 429. pressurize | pressurizing | pressurized | pressurization | 6 | 6 |
| 430. prevail upon | prevailing upon | prevailed upon | prevalence | 6 | 6 |
| 431. proffer | proffering | proffered | proffering | 6 | 6 |
| 432. prosecute | prosecuting | prosecuted | prosecution | 6 | 6 |
| 433. **put right** | putting right | put right | putting right | 5 | 56 |
| 434. **react** | reacting | reacted | reaction | 4 | 456 |
| 435. **reap** | reaping | reaped in | reaping | 4 | 456 |
| 436. **rebuke** | rebuking | rebuked | rebuking | 5 | 56 |
| 437. **recruit** | recruiting | recruited | recruitment | 4 | 456 |
| 438. **remonstrate with** | remonstrating | remonstrated with | remonstration | 5 | 56 |
| 439. **reprimand** | reprimanding | reprimanded | reprimand | 5 | 56 |
| 440. **reproach** | reproaching | reproached | reproach | 5 | 56 |
| 441. **reprove** | reproving | reproved | reprobation | 5 | 56 |
| 442. **request** | requesting | requested | requisition | 5 | 56 |
| 443. **rescue** | rescuing | rescued | rescue | 5 | 56 |
| 444. **restore** | restoring | restored | restoration | 5 | 56 |
| 445. **retain** | retaining | retained | retention | 3 | 3456 |
| 446. **return** | returning | returned | return | 5 | 56 |
| 447. **save** | saving | saved | salvation | 2 | 23456 |
| 448. seize | seizing | seized | seizure | 6 | 6 |
| 449. **set right** | setting right | set right | setting right | 5 | 56 |
| 450. snare | snaring | snared | ensnarement | 6 | 6 |
| 451. snatch | snatching | snatched | snatching | 6 | 6 |
| 452. submit | submitting | submitted | submission | 6 | 6 |
| 453. **summon** | summoning | summoned | summons | 4 | 456 |
| 454. sympathize with | sympathizing with | sympathized with | sympathy | 6 | 6 |
| 455. **take alive** | taking alive | taken alive | taking alive | 5 | 56 |
| 456. take by force | taking by force | took by force | forcible taking | 6 | 6 |
| 457. **transform** | transforming | transformed | transformation | 5 | 56 |
| 458. trap | trapping | trapped | entrapment | 6 | 6 |
| 459. triumph over | triumphing over | triumphed over | triumph over | 6 | 6 |
| 460. **turn** | turning | turned | turning | 4 | 456 |
| 461. **urge** | urging | urged | urging | 4 | 456 |
| 462. vanquish | vanquishing | vanquished | vanquishing | 6 | 6 |
| 463. **warn** | warning | warned | warning | 4 | 456 |
| 464. **win** | winning | won over | winnings | 4 | 456 |

| VI. **BAPTIZE!** | **PASTORAL EVANGELISM** | | **PLANTING EVANGELIZATION** | | |
|---|---|---|---|---|---|
| 465. **add** | adding | added to | addition | 5 | 56 |
| 466. **administer** | administering | administered | administration | 5 | 56 |
| 467. **affiliate** | affiliating | affiliated | affiliation | 4 | 456 |
| 468. balance | balancing | balanced | balance | 6 | 6 |
| 469. **baptize** | baptizing | baptized | baptism | 3 | 3456 |
| 470. **bear fruit** | bearing fruit | bore fruit | fruit-bearing | 5 | 56 |
| 471. **bless** | blessing | blessed | blessing | 5 | 56 |
| 472. **build** | building | built | building | 5 | 56 |
| 473. **catechize** | catechizing | catechized | catechesis | 4 | 456 |
| 474. chant | chanting | chanted | chanting | 6 | 6 |
| 475. **cleanse** | cleansing | cleansed | cleansing | 5 | 56 |
| 476. **confirm** | confirming | confirmed | confirmation | 5 | 56 |
| 477. congregationalize | congregationalizing | congregationalized | congregationalization | 6 | 6 |
| 478. console | consoling | consoled | consolation | 6 | 6 |
| 479. **dedicate** | dedicating | dedicated | dedication | 5 | 56 |
| 480. dip | dipping | dipped | dipping | 6 | 6 |
| 481. **enlist** | enlisting | enlisted | enlistment | 5 | 56 |
| 482. **enrol** | enroling | enroled | enrolment | 5 | 56 |
| 483. **establish** | establishing | established | establishment | 5 | 56 |
| 484. **feed** | feeding | fed | food | 3 | 3456 |
| 485. **fellowship** | fellowshiping | fellowshiped over | fellowship | 4 | 456 |
| 486. **fix** | fixing | fixed | fixation | 5 | 56 |
| 487. **gain** | gaining | gained | gain | 5 | 56 |
| 488. glorify | glorifying | glorified | glorification | 6 | 6 |
| 489. **grow** | growing | grew | growth | 4 | 456 |
| 490. guarantee | guaranteeing | guaranteed | guarantee | 6 | 6 |
| 491. **help** | helping | helped | help | 4 | 456 |
| 492. herd | herding | herded | herding | 6 | 6 |
| 493. **immerse** | immersing | immersed | immersing | 3 | 3456 |
| 494. implant | implanting | implanted | implantation | 6 | 6 |
| 495. incorporate | incorporating | incorporated | incorporation | 6 | 6 |
| 496. **initiate** | initiating | initiated | initiation | 5 | 56 |
| 497. **live out** | living out | lived out | outliving | 4 | 456 |
| 498. look after | looking after | looked after | looking after | 6 | 6 |
| 499. make attend | making attend | attending | attendance | 6 | 6 |
| 500. **make peace** | making peace | made peace in | peacemaking | 4 | 456 |
| 501. **minister** | ministering | ministered to | ministry | 4 | 456 |

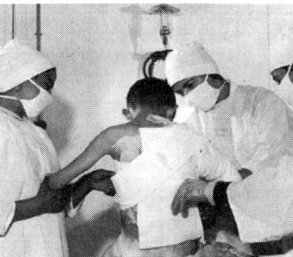

**393. Heal!** Treating burn patient at Il-Maten Methodist hospital (Algeria).

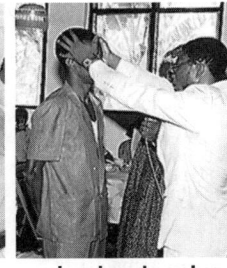

**401. Lay hands on!** Ministering healing in Gambia.

**399. Invite!** Evangelist Moody climaxes sermon with appeal, 1871.

**418. Offer!** 'I offered them Christ': John Wesley uses his preferred idiom.

**423. Persuade!** Mahout in Gujarat gets New Reader gospel.

**467. Affiliate!** Newly-baptized AICN members sign in (Kenya).

**469. Baptize!** Jesus' 6th mandate (1) in a Bangalore village (India), (2) baptizing 70,000 Xhosas at once (South Africa), (3) Gypsy Pentecostal mass baptism (France), and (4) in the True Jesus Church of India.

**476. Confirm!** Bishop confirms new Anglican (Trinidad).

**493. Immerse!** In Myanmar, an ex-Buddhist monk is baptized.

*continued*

*Table 23–17 concluded*

| | | | | | |
|---|---|---|---|---|---|
| 502. **multiply** | multiplying | multiplied | multiplication | 4 | 456 |
| 503. partner | partnering | partnered with | partnership | 6 | 6 |
| 504. **pastor** | pastoring | pastored | pastoralia | 5 | 56 |
| 505. pastoralize | pastoralizing | pastoralized | pastoralization | 6 | 6 |
| 506. **plant** | planting | planted | plantation | 4 | 456 |
| 507. pledge | pledging | pledged | pledge | 6 | 6 |
| 508. pour out | pouring out | poured out | outpouring | 6 | 6 |
| 509. **praise** | praising | praised | praising | 3 | 3456 |
| 510. **produce crop** | producing crop | produced crop | crop production | 4 | 456 |
| 511. reaffirm | reaffirming | reaffirmed | reaffirmation | 6 | 6 |
| 512. **reconcile** | reconciling | reconciled | reconciliation | 4 | 456 |
| 513. regulate | regulating | regulated | regulation | 6 | 6 |
| 514. **remember** | remembering | remembered | remembrance | 5 | 56 |
| 515. **reproduce** | reproducing | reproduced | reproduction | 4 | 456 |
| 516. **sacramentalize** | sacramentalizing | sacramentalized | sacramentalization | 4 | 456 |
| 517. **secure** | securing | secured | security | 4 | 456 |
| 518. **serve** | serving | served | service | 4 | 456 |
| 519. **shepherd** | shepherding | shepherded | shepherding | 3 | 3456 |
| 520. soak | soaking | soaked | soaking | 6 | 6 |
| 521. sprinkle | sprinkling | sprinkled | sprinkling | 6 | 6 |
| 522. sprout | sprouting | sprouted | sprouting | 6 | 6 |
| 523. **strengthen** | strengthening | strengthened | strengthening | 4 | 456 |
| 524. **support** | supporting | supported | support | 4 | 456 |
| 525. **tend** | tending | tended | tending | 3 | 3456 |
| 526. **thank** | thanking | thanked | thanks | 3 | 3456 |
| 527. validate | validating | validated | validation | 6 | 6 |
| 528. wait upon | waiting upon | waited upon | waiting upon | 6 | 6 |
| 529. **wash** | washing | washed | washing | 5 | 56 |
| 530. **welcome** | welcoming | welcomed | welcoming | 4 | 456 |
| 531. **worship** | worshiping | worshiped | worship | 3 | 3456 |
| 532. **write** | writing | written to | writing | 3 | 3456 |

| **VII. TRAIN!** | **PROGRAMMED EVANGELISM** | | **PEDAGOGICAL EVANGELIZATION** | | |
|---|---|---|---|---|---|
| 533. **admonish** | admonishing | admonished | admonition | 4 | 456 |
| 534. advise | advising | advised | advertisement | 6 | 6 |
| 535. agonize | agonizing | agonized | agonizing | 6 | 6 |
| 536. approve | approving | approved | approval | 6 | 6 |
| 537. **ascertain** | ascertaining | ascertained | ascertainment | 5 | 56 |
| 538. **broadcast** | broadcasting | broadcasted to | broadcasting | 5 | 56 |
| 539. **celebrate** | celebrating | celebrated | celebration | 5 | 56 |
| 540. **classify** | classifying | classified | classification | 5 | 56 |
| 541. **commission** | commissioning | commissioned | commissioning | 4 | 456 |
| 542. compare | comparing | compared with | comparison | 6 | 6 |
| 543. conciliate | conciliating | conciliated | conciliation | 6 | 6 |
| 544. conclude | concluding | concluded | conclusion | 6 | 6 |
| 545. contribute | contributing | contributed to | contribution | 6 | 6 |
| 546. correct | correcting | corrected | correction | 6 | 6 |
| 547. **cultivate** | cultivating | cultivated | cultivation | 4 | 456 |
| 548. discipline | disciplining | disciplined | disciplining | 6 | 6 |
| 549. edify | edifying | edified | edification | 6 | 6 |
| 550. **educate** | educating | educated | education | 4 | 456 |
| 551. **exercise** | exercising | exercised | exercising | 4 | 456 |
| 552. **fax** | faxing | faxed to | facsimile | 5 | 56 |
| 553. **followup** | following-up | followed up | followup | 4 | 456 |
| 554. **fight** | fighting | fought over | fighting | 5 | 56 |
| 555. imagine | imagining | imagined over | imagination | 6 | 6 |
| 556. indoctrinate | indoctrinating | indoctrinated | indoctrination | 6 | 6 |
| 557. infer | inferring | inferred | inference | 6 | 6 |
| 558. **instruct** | instructing | instructed | instruction | 3 | 3456 |
| 559. **make learn** | making learn | learning | learning | 2 | 23456 |
| 560. mediate | mediating | mediated to | mediation | 6 | 6 |
| 561. **mobilize** | mobilizing | mobilized | mobilization | 4 | 456 |
| 562. narrowcast | narrowcasting | narrowcasted | narrowcasting | 6 | 6 |
| 563. **nurture** | nurturing | nurtured | nurturance | 4 | 456 |
| 564. **progress** | progressing | progressed | progression | 2 | 23456 |
| 565. prosper | prospering | prospered | prosperity | 6 | 6 |
| 566. **ready** | readying | readied | readiness | 4 | 456 |
| 567. **renew** | renewing | renewed | renewal | 5 | 56 |
| 568. review | reviewing | reviewed | review | 6 | 6 |
| 569. **strive** | striving | strived with | striving | 4 | 456 |
| 570. **struggle** | struggling | struggled with | struggling | 4 | 456 |
| 571. **take note** | taking note | taken note of | notetaking | 4 | 456 |
| 572. **teach** | teaching | taught | teaching | 3 | 3456 |
| 573. telecast | telecasting | telecast to | telecasting | 6 | 6 |
| 574. think | thinking | thought of | thinking | 6 | 6 |
| 575. tolerate | tolerating | tolerated | toleration | 6 | 6 |
| 576. **train** | training | trained | training | 3 | 3456 |
| 577. **unite** | uniting | united | unification | 4 | 456 |
| 578. **work** | working | worked | work | 3 | 3456 |
| 579. **work among** | working among | worked among | work among | 4 | 456 |

**OVERALL IMPERATIVE**

| **O.   EVANGELIZE!** | | | | | |
|---|---|---|---|---|---|
| 580. **discharge** | discharging | discharged | discharge | 4 | 456 |
| 581. **fulfill** | fulfilling | fulfilled | fulfillment | 3 | 3456 |
| 582. **account** | accounting | accounted for | accountability | 4 | 456 |
| 583. **be responsible** | being responsible | been responsible for | responsibility | 4 | 456 |
| 584. **obey** | obeying | obeyed over | obedience | 4 | 456 |
| 585. **evangelize** | evangelizing | evangelized | evangelization | 1 | 123456 |

502. **Multiply!** 6000-character Amity Press word processor mass-produces 4 million Chinese Bibles a year for China's 91 million Christians.

538. **Broadcast!** Evangelist Graham reaches 1 billion at once.

561. **Mobilize!** 1.5 million Christian men at 'Stand in the Gap' 1997.

572. **Teach!** Anglican evangelistic outreach Alpha Course mushrooms from Britain to 10,000 11-week courses in 77 countries worldwide.

576. **Train!** Largest Christian conference ever, EXPLO-74 trains 323,419 Koreans in evangelism for 1 week in 1974 in Seoul.

585. **Evangelize!** This survey ends by returning to the original meaning of the early Greek painting (left) 'Evangelismos', namely 'Annunciation' or telling of the Good News; with (right) Roselli's more modern rendering.

## Table 23–18.  420 dimensions and 620 facets of 'evangelize' listed alphabetically.

This table provides a single alphabetical index to all dimensions of 'evangelize' (shown in bold type), and to words which are facets only (shown in medium type). In front of each word is its reference number in Tables 23–17 and 23–19, where more data and information about its relationship to 'evangelize' may be found.

| No. | Word | No. | Word | No. | Word |
|---|---|---|---|---|---|
| 327 | accept | 4 | **commit** | 380 | **excite** |
| 256 | **acclaim** | 162 | **communicate** | 551 | **exercise** |
| 1 | **accompany** | 542 | compare | 48 | **exhibit** |
| 582 | **account** | 355 | **compel** | 381 | **exhort** |
| 328 | accuse | 356 | comprehend | 49 | exorcize |
| 140 | acknowledge | 31 | **compute** | 7 | **expect** |
| 141 | **acquaint** | 543 | conciliate | 50 | **expel** |
| 329 | acquire | 544 | conclude | 382 | **explain** |
| 17 | **act** | 357 | **condemn** | 51 | **explore** |
| 465 | **add** | 265 | **confer** | 178 | **expose** |
| 257 | **address** | 163 | **confess** | 283 | **expound** |
| 466 | **administer** | 476 | **confirm** | 179 | **express** |
| 142 | **admit** | 358 | **confront** | 52 | **extend** |
| 533 | **admonish** | 477 | congregationalize | 180 | **extol** |
| 18 | **advance** | 359 | **conquer** | 284 | **familiarize** |
| 258 | **advertise** | 360 | consider | 552 | fax |
| 534 | advise | 478 | console | 484 | **feed** |
| 143 | **advocate** | 32 | **contact** | 485 | **fellowship** |
| 467 | **affiliate** | 266 | **contend** | 554 | **fight** |
| 144 | **affirm** | 5 | **continue** | 285 | **fill** |
| 535 | agonize | 545 | contribute | 383 | **find** |
| 330 | agree | 164 | **converse** | 384 | **fish** |
| 19 | **aid** | 361 | **convert** | 486 | **fix** |
| 20 | **aim at** | 165 | **convey** | 53 | focus |
| 259 | alert | 362 | **convince** | 8 | **follow** |
| 331 | ambush | 6 | **cooperate** | 553 | **followup** |
| 260 | **announce** | 546 | correct | 286 | forbid |
| 145 | **answer** | 33 | correspond | 385 | **force** |
| 332 | **appeal** | 166 | corroborate | 181 | **foretell** |
| 146 | **appear** | 34 | **count** | 182 | **forewarn** |
| 21 | **apply** | 267 | credit | 386 | **forgive** |
| 333 | apprehend | 363 | criticize | 54 | **free** |
| 334 | apprentice | 167 | **cry** | 581 | **fulfill** |
| 147 | apprise | 268 | **cry out** | 183 | **further** |
| 22 | **approach** | 547 | **cultivate** | 487 | **gain** |
| 536 | approve | 269 | cure | 387 | **gather** |
| 261 | **argue** | 364 | customize | 184 | **get** |
| 23 | **arrive** | 365 | dare | 55 | **give** |
| 537 | ascertain | 168 | dazzle | 287 | **give a message** |
| 335 | ask | 366 | deal with | 185 | **give account** |
| 148 | **assert** | 270 | **debate** | 288 | **give chance** |
| 149 | asseverate | 271 | **declare** | 186 | **give evidence** |
| 24 | assist | 479 | **dedicate** | 289 | **give notice** |
| 150 | **associate** | 272 | deduce | 290 | **give opportunity** |
| 336 | assure | 367 | defeat | 187 | give out |
| 151 | **attest** | 273 | **defend** | 488 | **glorify** |
| 337 | attract | 169 | **deliver** | 56 | **go** |
| 468 | balance | 368 | demand | 57 | **go forth** |
| 469 | **baptize** | 274 | **demonstrate** | 58 | **go with** |
| 2 | **be clothed** | 369 | **denounce** | 188 | **gossip** |
| 3 | **be filled** | 35 | **depart** | 388 | **grant** |
| 152 | **be here with** | 275 | **depict** | 389 | **grasp** |
| 153 | **be martyred** | 36 | **deploy** | 490 | **guarantee** |
| 154 | **be present** | 170 | depose to | 390 | **guide** |
| 583 | **be responsible** | 171 | **describe** | 189 | **hand down** |
| 470 | bear fruit | 37 | **design** | 190 | **hand to** |
| 155 | **bear tidings** | 276 | **detail** | 391 | **harvest** |
| 338 | beg | 38 | **develop** | 392 | **haul** |
| 339 | **believe** | 172 | **dialogue** | 191 | **have for** |
| 340 | **beseech** | 173 | **diffuse** | 393 | **heal** |
| 341 | bestow | 480 | dip | 491 | **help** |
| 342 | blame | 370 | **direct** | 291 | **herald** |
| 262 | blanket | 371 | **disciple** | 492 | herd |
| 471 | **bless** | 548 | discipline | 192 | **hold** |
| 25 | **bring** | 174 | **disclose** | 193 | howl |
| 343 | bring back | 277 | **discourse** | 394 | **hunt** |
| 538 | **broadcast** | 175 | **discuss** | 194 | **illuminate** |
| 472 | **build** | 176 | disperse | 59 | **illustrate** |
| 26 | calculate | 39 | **display** | 555 | imagine |
| 344 | **call** | 278 | **dispute** | 60 | **impact** |
| 345 | call out | 177 | **disseminate** | 395 | **impart** |
| 346 | capture | 372 | **distribute** | 494 | **implant** |
| 27 | **care** | 373 | **divide** | 61 | **implement** |
| 28 | **carry** | 40 | **do** | 396 | **implore** |
| 156 | **cast a net** | 41 | **do miracles** | 195 | imply |
| 29 | **cast out** | 374 | **drag** | 62 | incarnate |
| 347 | catch | 42 | **drive out** | 495 | incorporate |
| 473 | **catechize** | 43 | **dwell** | 63 | **indicate** |
| 348 | cause | 549 | **edify** | 556 | indoctrinate |
| 263 | caution | 550 | **educate** | 397 | **induce** |
| 539 | **celebrate** | 375 | embolden | 557 | infer |
| 349 | censure | 279 | **emphasize** | 65 | **influence** |
| 350 | **challenge** | 44 | **encounter** | 196 | **inform** |
| 351 | change | 376 | **encourage** | 64 | **inhabit** |
| 474 | chant | 280 | endorse | 496 | **initiate** |
| 352 | **charge** | 45 | **engage** | 398 | **insist** |
| 157 | chat | 377 | **enjoin** | 66 | **inspect** |
| 158 | chatter | 378 | **enlighten** | 558 | **instruct** |
| 159 | **circulate** | 481 | **enlist** | 9 | **intercede** |
| 160 | **claim** | 482 | **enrol** | 292 | **interpret** |
| 264 | clarify | 379 | **entreat** | 197 | **introduce** |
| 540 | **classify** | 281 | entrust | 399 | **invite** |
| 475 | **cleanse** | 46 | enumerate | 198 | invoke |
| 30 | **come** | 483 | **establish** | 400 | **involve** |
| 353 | comfort | 47 | **estimate** | 67 | **irradiate** |
| 354 | **command** | 585 | **evangelize** | 293 | issue |
| 161 | **commend** | 282 | **exalt** | | |
| 541 | **commission** | | | | |

| No. | Word | No. | Word | No. | Word |
|---|---|---|---|---|---|
| 68 | **itinerate** | 94 | **point** | 114 | **set out** |
| 69 | **journey** | 426 | **polarize** | 449 | **set right** |
| 199 | **lay bare** | 95 | **portray** | 115 | **settle** |
| 401 | **lay hands on** | 508 | pour out | 235 | **share** |
| 294 | lay out | 509 | **praise** | 519 | **shepherd** |
| 402 | **lead** | 13 | **pray** | 236 | **shine** |
| 295 | **lecture** | 303 | **preach** | 321 | **shout** |
| 70 | **liberate** | 304 | **predict** | 116 | **show** |
| 296 | **lift** | 96 | **prepare** | 117 | **show mercy** |
| 200 | lift the veil | 427 | prescribe | 322 | show up |
| 201 | light | 305 | **present** | 237 | shriek |
| 71 | **list** | 428 | **press** | 118 | **signal** |
| 72 | **live** | 429 | pressurize | 323 | **sing** |
| 497 | **live out** | 430 | prevail upon | 450 | **snare** |
| 498 | look after | 306 | **proclaim** | 451 | snatch |
| 73 | look for | 510 | **produce crop** | 520 | **soak** |
| 74 | **love** | 216 | **profess** | 119 | **sort** |
| 202 | **maintain** | 431 | proffer | 238 | **sound** |
| 297 | **make a speech** | 564 | **progress** | 239 | **sow** |
| 203 | **make accessible** | 307 | **promise** | 240 | **speak** |
| 403 | **make acknowledge** | 308 | **promulgate** | 241 | **speak in tongues** |
| 499 | make attend | 217 | **propagate** | 120 | speak out |
| 75 | **make available** | 218 | **prophesy** | 242 | **spread** |
| 204 | **make aware** | 432 | prosecute | 521 | sprinkle |
| 404 | **make choose** | 565 | prosper | 522 | sprout |
| 298 | **make clear** | 97 | **protest** | 121 | **start** |
| 405 | make concede | 309 | **prove** | 324 | **state** |
| 406 | **make decide** | 98 | **provide** | 15 | **stay** |
| 299 | **make evident** | 310 | publicize | 243 | story |
| 205 | **make hear** | 311 | **publish** | 122 | **strategize** |
| 206 | **make known** | 99 | pursue | 523 | **strengthen** |
| 559 | **make learn** | 312 | put before | 244 | strew |
| 300 | **make listen** | 433 | **put right** | 569 | **strive** |
| 301 | make obvious | 219 | **radiate** | 570 | **struggle** |
| 500 | **make peace** | 100 | **reach** | 123 | **study** |
| 407 | **make put** | 434 | **react** | 452 | **submit** |
| 408 | **make realize** | 313 | **read** | 124 | **suffer** |
| 409 | **make receive** | 566 | **ready** | 125 | **sum** |
| 410 | **make repent** | 435 | **reap** | 453 | **summon** |
| 411 | **make respond** | 314 | **reason** | 126 | **supply** |
| 76 | **make see** | 436 | **rebuke** | 524 | **support** |
| 412 | **make trust** | 220 | recall | 127 | **survey** |
| 413 | **make understand** | 221 | **reckon** | 128 | **symbolize** |
| 414 | **make well** | 222 | **recognize** | 454 | sympathize with |
| 415 | **make whole** | 223 | **recommend** | 129 | **take** |
| 207 | **manifest** | 512 | **reconcile** | 455 | **take alive** |
| 208 | **mean** | 101 | **record** | 456 | take by force |
| 77 | **measure** | 224 | **recount** | 571 | **take note** |
| 560 | mediate | 437 | **recruit** | 130 | take pity on |
| 78 | **meet** | 316 | **refute** | 245 | **talk** |
| 209 | **mention** | 102 | **register** | 131 | **target** |
| 79 | migrate | 513 | regulate | 572 | **teach** |
| 501 | **minister** | 225 | **relate** | 573 | telecast |
| 80 | **missionize** | 103 | relieve | 246 | **tell** |
| 561 | **mobilize** | 514 | **remember** | 525 | **tend** |
| 81 | **move** | 226 | remind | 247 | **testify** |
| 502 | **multiply** | 438 | **remonstrate with** | 526 | **thank** |
| 210 | **name** | 567 | **renew** | 574 | think |
| 211 | **narrate** | 317 | repeat | 325 | threaten |
| 562 | narrowcast | 227 | **reply** | 248 | **throw a net** |
| 416 | **net** | 228 | **report** | 249 | thunder |
| 212 | noise abroad | 439 | **reprimand** | 575 | tolerate |
| 82 | note | 440 | **reproach** | 132 | **total** |
| 302 | **notify** | 515 | **reproduce** | 133 | **touch** |
| 83 | number | 441 | **reprove** | 134 | **tour** |
| 563 | **nurture** | 442 | **request** | 576 | **train** |
| 584 | **obey** | 443 | **rescue** | 250 | transfer |
| 417 | **oblige** | 104 | research | 457 | **transform** |
| 84 | **observe** | 105 | **reside** | 326 | **translate** |
| 85 | **occupy** | 229 | **respond** | 135 | **transmit** |
| 418 | **offer** | 444 | **restore** | 136 | transport |
| 213 | **open** | 318 | resuscitate | 458 | trap |
| 419 | **order** | 445 | **retain** | 137 | **travel** |
| 420 | **overcome** | 446 | **return** | 459 | triumph over |
| 421 | overtake | 230 | **reveal** | 460 | **turn** |
| 86 | paint | 568 | review | 251 | uncover |
| 10 | **participate** | 106 | **risk** | 577 | **unite** |
| 503 | partner | 231 | roar | 252 | unveil |
| 214 | **pass on** | 516 | **sacramentalize** | 461 | **urge** |
| 504 | **pastor** | 319 | **saturate** | 253 | utter |
| 505 | pastoralize | 447 | **save** | 527 | validate |
| 87 | **pay attention** | 232 | **say** | 462 | vanquish |
| 88 | **penetrate** | 107 | **scan** | 138 | **visit** |
| 422 | **perceive** | 233 | **scatter** | 139 | visualize |
| 89 | **perform miracles** | 234 | scream | 16 | **wait** |
| 90 | **permeate** | 108 | **search** | 528 | wait upon |
| 11 | **persist** | 517 | **secure** | 463 | **warn** |
| 423 | **persuade** | 109 | **seek** | 529 | **wash** |
| 91 | pervade | 448 | seize | 530 | **welcome** |
| 92 | pity | 110 | **select** | 464 | **win** |
| 215 | **place** | 111 | **send** | 254 | witness |
| 424 | **place hands on** | 112 | **send out** | 578 | **work** |
| 93 | **plan** | 518 | **serve** | 579 | **work among** |
| 506 | **plant** | 320 | set before | 531 | **worship** |
| 425 | **plead** | 113 | **set forth** | 532 | **write** |
| 507 | pledge | | | 255 | yell |
| 12 | **pneumatize** | | | | |

## Table 23–19.  Documenting the 420 dimensions of 'evangelize'.

Table 23–17 has listed and classified 620 English verbs which are facets of the verb 'evangelize'. Using that order, the table below now gives documentation and brief explanations for each of the 420 facets which are here termed *dimensions* of evangelization. Each dimension is numbered exactly as in Table 23–17, which means that the numbers shown below are not always consecutive (missing numbers are facets not closely enough related to 'evangelize' to qualify as dimensions). The table is divided at 2 points into Minicommissions I (at the beginning) and II (after facet No. 326); and also divided at 7 points into Mandates 1,2,3,4,5,6, and 7. At each such point a brief explanation is given. For many dimensions, there are opening Scripture references, followed by non-Scripture quotations or usages, including books and articles, many being recent or current. In all this material, where the dimension's name occurs it is shown in bold type (bolder than medium but not as heavy as black).

At the end of each dimension's entry, one or two brief sentences are given, always in italics with the dimension in black, which illustrate the contribution of that dimension to the overall meaning of 'evangelize'. The reader wanting a rapid overview of all 420 dimensions should therefore scan the pages for these closing paragraphs in italics, which italics thus contain definitive or standard usages of 'evangelize'.

### MINICOMMISSION I: EVANGELIZE!

The first half of the Great Commission embraces the first 4 Mandates, which are: RECEIVE! GO! WITNESS! PROCLAIM! These are chronologically the first stages that would-be evangelizers must go through. Of the 326 facets under this Minicommission, 240 are dimensions, 134 are macrodefinitions, 69 are macrocommands, 36 are macrotranslations, and 10 are in The Big Ten. In fact, 9 of The Big Ten are located entirely in this segment. This shows that the major thrust of the word 'evangelize' lies in Minicommission I.

Collectively, these 4 stages deal with receiving the power to evangelize, actually going out, witnessing as opportunity arises, then lastly proclaiming in organized cohesive presentations. Minicommission I is thus named here by its major emphasis: Evangelize!

### I.  RECEIVE!

This first Mandate states the essential prerequisite to all evangelization. Potential evangelizers will get nowhere unless they first ask for and receive God's gifts and God's power. This Mandate can therefore be characterized thus: It is Spirit-dominated. Here this stage is termed: **Pneumatic evangelization** (see detailed documentation under dimension No. 12 below). This essential stage is best stated as: receiving the infilling of the Holy Spirit. Its human counterpart is **Prayer evangelism**.

Of the 16 facets, all are dimensions of 'evangelize', so are listed below; 12 are macrodefinitions (with quoted published definitions like 'To evangelize is...'); 7 are macrocommands (verbs in the 6 Great Commission NT narratives); but none are macrotranslations directly translating *euangelizo*, and none are in The Big Ten.

1.  **Accompany.** This word occurs 24 times in the NRSV (9 of which are in the Apocrypha and Deuterocanonical books). 'Jesus went to a town called Nain, **accompanied** by his disciples' (Luke 7:11, GNB). 'The Lord worked with them and confirmed his word by the signs that **accompanied** it' (Mark 16:20, NIV). 'Paul wanted Timothy to **accompany** him' (Acts 16:3, NRSV). A contemporary theological statement is:'The church merely **accompanies** Christ in mission, assisting as it can' (Karl Barth 1950).
*Evangelizing is* **accompanying** *Christ.*

2.  **Be clothed.** The verb occurs in the 3rd of the 6 Great Commission narratives: 'Until you have **been clothed** with power from on high' (Luke 24:49, NIV).
*Evangelizing is ineffective unless the evangelizers have* **been clothed** *with spiritual power.*

3.  **Be filled.** New Testament usages: 'He will **be filled** with the Holy Spirit' (Luke 1:15, NIV). 'They were all **filled** with the Holy Spirit and began to talk in other languages' (Acts 2:4, GNB). 'Peter, **filled** with the Holy Spirit' (Acts 4:8, NIV). 'Be filled with the Spirit' (Ephesians 5:18, NIV). 'His Spirit **fills** us with power, love' (2 Timothy 1:7, GNB).
*Evangelizers must* **be filled** *with the Spirit before true evangelism can take place.*

4.  **Commit.** Jesus said 'Full authority in heaven and on earth has been **committed** to me. Go forth therefore' (Matthew 28:18, NEB). 'Father, into thy hands I **commit** my spirit' (Luke 23:46, NEB). Paul and Barnabas 'with prayer and fasting **committed** them to the Lord' (Acts 14:23, NEB). 'I **commit** you to God and to the word of his grace' (Acts 20:32, NIV). 'I am simply discharging the trust **committed** to me' (1 Corinthians 9:17, NIV). 'The gospel always includes... a **commitment** to risk life itself' (WCC 5th Assembly, Nairobi 1975).
*To evangelize is to* **commit** *one's life and talents to Christ's mission in the world.*

5.  **Continue.** In the 3rd Great Commission narrative: 'So that they might **continue** to understand' (Luke 24:45, Williams). 'With great power the apostles continued to testify to the resurrection of the Lord Jesus' (Acts 4:33, NIV). 'They **continued** to teach and preach the Good News' (Acts 5:42, GNB). 'Evangelism is the supreme and unique business of **continuing** Christ's task on earth' (G. Baez Camargo in J.R. Mott 1938:63).
*Evangelism is* **continuing** *Christ's work on earth.*

6.  **Cooperate.** 'Evangelism means to me **cooperation** with the Spirit of God in presenting to non-Christians Jesus' Good News' (G. Bowles in J.R. Mott 1938:39). 'Total evangelism demands the **cooperation** of every single Christian' (Whitby IMC in Ranson 1948:218).
*Evangelism is* **cooperation** *with the Holy Spirit.*

7.  **Expect.** '**Expect** great things from God. Attempt great things for God' (William Carey, missionary to India, 1792). 1947: 5th Meeting of International Missionary Council, at Whitby (Canada) coins term '**Expectant** evangelism'. 'To evangelize is to sow and wait in respectful humility and in **expectant** hope' (J.C. Hoekendijk 1950:48).
*Evangelizing is* **expectant** *sowing.*

8.  **Follow.** There are some 400 instances in OT and NT. '**Follow** me' (Luke 9:59, NIV). In the 5th Great Commission narrative, Jesus said to Peter: '**Follow** me '(John 21:19, AV/KJV). 'A few men became **followers** of Paul' (Acts 17:34, NIV). '**Follow** my example' (1 Corinthians 11:1, NIV). 'They **follow** the Lamb wherever he goes' (Revelation 14:13, NIV). The CEV prefers 'followers' for 'disciples'.
*Evangelizing is* **following** *Christ.*

9.  **Intercede.** 'The Spirit himself **intercedes** for us' (Romans 8:26, NIV).
*Evangelization follows* **intercession.**

10.  **Participate.** 'So that through them you may **participate** in the divine nature' (2 Peter 1:4, NIV). 'Evangelism is the **participation** of the total Christian community in Christ's mission in the world' (WCC, *Evangelism,* 1954:59). 'To evangelize is to **participate** in Christ's life and in his ministry to the world' (WCC 2nd Assembly, *Evanston speaks*, 1954:31). 'Evangelism is the church's **participation** in the messianic work of Jesus Christ' (H.J. Margull 1962:280).
*To evangelize involves to* **participate** *in the Holy Spirit. Evangelizing means* **participating** *in the Holy Spirit. Evangelization is* **participation** *in the Spirit's divine action.*

11.  **Persist.** 'To those who by **persistence** in doing good seek glory, honor and immortality' (Romans 2:7, NIV).
*Evangelization requires continual* **persistence** *at every point.*

12.  **Pneumatize.** The Greek word *pneuma* meaning the Spirit (literally: wind, air, spirit, influence, inspiration) occurs 131 times in the New Testament: *Pneuma Hagion* (the Holy Spirit) 83 times; and the derived adjective *pneumatikos* (spiritual, of the Spirit) some 30 times. A large number of derivatives of *pneuma* are listed as English words in *Webster's third new international dictionary* (1971), including **pneumatic** ('spiritual, a spiritual being'), pneumatics (= pneumatology, 'the doctrine of the Holy Spirit', considered a separate branch of philosophy in the 17th century), pneumatological, pneumatography ('descriptive pneumatology'), pneumatomachy ('denial of the deity of the Holy Spirit'), pneumatism ('observable phenomena and exterior signs, frequently interpreted as indicating that one is possessed by the Holy Spirit'), **pneumatize** ('to make pneumatic', also (OED) 'to fan by blowing'), **pneumatized** ('having air-filled cavities'), **pneumatization** ('the presence or development of air-filled cavities'), et alia. Around 1900, St John's Gospel was widely termed 'The Pneumatic Gospel' because of its emphasis on the Spirit. The term is also used in theological German, e.g. 'Die pneumatische Dimension der Eucharistie' (the pneumatic dimension of the Eucharist). These terms, in various European languages, have been widely used in conjunction with 'evangelization' since Vatican II (1962-5), especially as (Latin) *aspectus pneumatologicus evangelizationis*. J. Saraiva Martins, in an article 'Dimensione pneumatologica dell'evangelizzazione' (1979), speaks of 'l'aspetto pneumatico dell'evangelizzazione' (the pneumatic aspect of evangelization), giving 183 footnotes and copious biblical references.
*Being evangelized means being* **pneumatized** *by the Holy Spirit, with Spirit-filled pockets. Evangelization means a population's* **pneumatization** *or action on it by the Holy Spirit, blown across with Spirit-filled pockets.*

13.  **Pray.** This dimension is widespread throughout the Bible. Frequency in the NRSV (with Apocrypha and Deuterocanonical books) is 466 occurrences, made up as follows: **pray** 155, **prayed** 83, **prayer** 142, **prayers** 37, **praying** 33, **prays** 16. After receiving the Great Commission from the Risen Christ, 'They all joined together constantly in **prayer**' (Acts 1:14, NIV). '**Pray** to the Lord for me' (Acts 8:24, NIV). '**Pray** that I may proclaim it clearly' (Colossians 4:4, NIV).
*Evangelism begins in* **prayer.** *Evangelization only follows* **prayer.**

14.  **Receive.** '**Receive** the Holy Spirit' (John 20:22, NIV). 'You will **receive** power when the Holy Spirit comes on you' (Acts 1:8, NIV). 'They **received** their share of the Holy Spirit' (Hebrews 6:4, GNB).
*Evangelizing is not possible until believers* **receive** *the gifts of the Spirit.*

15.  **Stay.** '**Stay** in the city until you have been clothed with power from on high' (Luke 24:49, NIV). 'Go over to that carriage and **stay** close to it' (Acts 8:29, GNB). 'Peter **stayed** on in Joppa for many days' (Acts 9:43, GNB).
*Evangelizing requires a period of* **staying** *in a place until God reveals his instructions.*

16.  **Wait.** '**Wait** for the gift I told you about' (Acts 1:4, GNB). 'To **wait** for the promise of the Father' (Acts 1:4, RSV). 'To evangelize is to sow and **wait** in respectful humility and in expectant hope' (J.C. Hoekendijk 1950:48).
*Evangelizing only follows a period of* **waiting** *for God's personal instruction to proceed.*

### II.  GO!

The second Mandate sees the evangelizer starting out on his task. This is the stage of **Preparatory evangelization.** It is person-implemented. It results in Christians engaging in **Pre-evangelism.**

Of the 123 facets listed in Table 23–17 under this Mandate, 102 are dimensions, and 2 are in The Big Ten (*Bring! Give!*).

17.  **Act.** 'Evangelization is the actual operative **action** of Christ here and now in his Church' (PMB 1976). 'Evangelism is all Christian **acts** done with

intention to transmit the treasure we have in earthen vessels' (D.A. McGavran 1977:66). 'Evangelism: **activity** of a missionary' (*New York Times everyday reader's dictionary of misunderstood, misused, and mispronounced words*, 2nd edition, 1985).

*To evangelize is to* **act** *with intention to pass on the gospel. Evangelization means* **action** *or* **activity** *on Christ's behalf.*

18. **Advance.** 'What has happened to me has really served to **advance** the gospel' (Philippians 1:12, NIV). '...actually only served to **advance** and give a renewed impetus to the spreading of the good news' (Philippians 1:12, Amplified New Testament). R.P. Beaver, *To* **advance** *the gospel: selections from the writings of Rufus Anderson* (1967).

*Evangelizing is* **advancing** *the gospel.*

19. **Aid.** 'Come to our **aid**!' (Psalm 44:26, GNB). 'You are my saviour, O Lord—hurry to my **aid**!' (Psalm 70:5, GNB). 'You sent me **aid** again and again' (Philippians 4:16, NIV).

*To evangelize is to* **aid** *people in finding God.*

20. **Aim at.** 'Aim at those things that bring peace' (Romans 14:19, GNB).

*Evangelizing requires* **aiming** *at God's will.*

21. **Apply.** Used 11 times in GNB ('Lord, does this parable **apply** to us?', Luke 12:41), 14 times in NRSV ('**Apply** your mind to my teaching', Proverbs 22:17; 'I am **applying** it to Christ and the church', Ephesians 5:32). M.A.C. Warren, *To* **apply** *the Gospel: a selection from the writings of Henry Venn* (1971).

*To evangelize is to* **apply** *the gospel. Evangelization requires* **application.**

22. **Approach.** 'As they were on their journey and **approaching** the city' (Acts 10:9, NIV).

*Evangelizing involves* **approaching** *where non-Christians live.*

23. **Arrive.** 'When I **arrived** in Troas to preach the Good News about Christ' (2 Corinthians 2:12, GNB).

*Evangelization begins on* **arrival** *of evangelizers.*

25. **Bring.** 'Bring' directly translates *euangelizo* with the second-highest frequency of English verbs in the NT (DB, RSV, NEB, GNB, JB, BV, BLE, NIV, NJB, NKJV, NRSV, REB). It also translates other NT Greek synonyms of *euangelizo*. 'I **bring** you good news' (Luke 2:10, AV/KJV, RSV, NIV). 'We are here to **bring** the Good News to you' (Acts 13:32, GNB). 'We **bring** you good news' (Acts 14:15, RSV). 'After **bringing** the good news to that town' (Acts 14:21, NEB). 'We came to you **bringing** the Good News about Christ' (2 Corinthians 10:14, GNB). 'Evangelize. To **bring** as good tidings' (*The Century dictionary*, 1889). 'Evangelize. To **bring** good tidings' (*A new English dictionary*, Oxford 1897). '**Bringing** souls to Christ'. Evangelism is: 'to **bring** the Gospel within the reach of every creature' (J.R. Mott 1895), 'the **bringing** of men and women into contact with the Risen Christ' (A.J. Cross in Mott 1938:58), 'the effective **bringing** to men's consciousness of the fact of God's all-wise and active love' (J.S.M. Hooper in Mott 1938:25), 'a conscious desire and longing to **bring** others into contact with Christ' (W.J. Thompson in Mott 1938:52), '**bringing** Christ to the world, and the world to Christ' (M.T. Titus in Mott 1938:35), 'to **bring** all men in touch with the redeeming power of Christ' (G. Baez Camargo in Mott 1938:53), 'the **bringing** of persons to Christ as Saviour and Lord' (WCC 2nd Assembly, *Evanston speaks*, 1954:34), 'to **bring** the unredeemed into vital contact with the Redeemer' (M. Taylor 1974:6). 'To evangelize is to tell or to **bring** good news' (D. Webster 1964:583).

*To evangelize is to* **bring** *the gospel. Evangelizing is* **bringing** *the gospel. Evangelization is the* **bringing** *of the gospel to others and others to Christ.*

26. **Calculate.** Jesus said, '**Calculate** the cost' (Luke 14:28, REB). 'The value of these books was **calculated** '(Acts 19:19, NRSV). 'Let anyone with understanding **calculate**' (Revelation 13:18, NRSV).

*Evangelizing often requires* **calculating** *logistics.*

27. **Care.** The verbs *bosko* and *poimaino* (John 21:15-17) mean: **care, care** for, take **care** of, tend, nourish, nurture, herd, lead to pasture, feed, look after,

shepherd, protect, rule, govern, foster, guide. 'You took **care** of me, in prison and you visited me' (Matthew 25:36, GNB). 'Jesus said, Take **care** of my sheep' (John 21:17, GNB, NIV).

*To evangelize is to* **care**. *Evangelizing is* **caring** *as witness. Evangelization is* **caring** *that demonstrates the gospel.*

28. **Carry.** 'Carry' directly translates *euangelizo* a few times, as in 'We can **carry** the gospel to lands that lie beyond you' (2 Corinthians 10:16, NEB, REB), also on occasion in the Jerusalem Bible's NT. In addition it translates other NT Greek synonyms of *euangelizo*. 'The Lord's message was **carried**' throughout the district (Acts 13:49, TCNT). 'At all times **carry** faith as a shield' (Ephesians 6:16, GNB). *Carrying the Gospel to all the Non-Christian World* (World Missionary Conference, Report of Commission I, Edinburgh 1910). 'We are commissioned to **carry** the gospel to the whole world' (WCC 1976:54).

*To evangelize is to* **carry** *the gospel. Evangelizing is* **carrying** *the gospel. Evangelization is the* **carrying** *of the gospel.*

29. **Cast out.** The current version of this outdated usage is 'drive out', referring to exorcism. Widely employed in AV/KJV: 'In my name shall they **cast out** devils' (Mark 16:17).

*Evangelizing often begins with the* **casting out** *of demons.*

30. **Come.** This term directly translates *euangelizo* in 2 NT versions: 'We have **come** with the Good News' (Acts 14:15, TCNT and NJB). The term also translates other synonyms of *evangelizo*: 'Jesus said to them, **Come** with me, and I will teach you to catch men' (Mark 1:17, GNB). 'We were the first to **come** all the way to you with the gospel' (2 Corinthians 10:14, RSV). The idea of **coming** in evangelism is also conveyed in the Epistle to the Hebrews: 'Good news **came** to us just as to them' (Hebrews 4:2, RSV).

*To evangelize is to* **come** *with the gospel, and to see that the gospel* **comes** *to people.*

31. **Compute.** The verb occurs once in NIV, twice in RSV, not in KJV nor in GNB. 'He is to **compute** that and pay' (Leviticus 25:52, NIV). 'The priest shall **compute** the money-value for it according to the years that remain', '**Compute** the valuation for it' (Leviticus 27:18, 23, RSV). '**Compute**: to determine a number or amount by reckoning' (*Webster's New World dictionary of the American language*, 1984). The role of **compute** in evangelization derives from its meanings 'determine its value' or 'make a reckoning'—to evangelize requires careful, exact assessment of the value of any evangelistic approach, especially where huge numbers of hearers are involved.

*Evangelizing requires* **computing** *numbers and totals to ensure effective communication of the gospel.*

32. **Contact.** 'A hundred thousand souls in Uganda have been brought into close **contact** with the gospel' (G. Pilkington in Mott 1900:89). 'The Gospel is speedily gaining such a rapid diffusion in Manchuria that we may anticipate at no distant date its **contact** with every village and town of the country' (J.R. Mott 1900:83). 'Evangelism is to me the bringing of men and women into **contact** with the Risen Christ' (A.J. Cross in Mott 1938:58, also D. Crommelin in Mott 1938:68). 'Evangelism is a conscious desire and longing to bring others into **contact** with Christ' (W.J. Thompson in Mott 1938:52). 'It is the task of evangelism to bring the unredeemed into vital **contact** with the Redeemer' (M. Taylor 1964:593).

*Evangelizing is* **contacting** *people for Christ. Being evangelized is being* **contacted** *by the gospel. Evangelization means* **contact** *with Christ and the gospel.*

34. **Count.** The word occurs 120 times throughout the Bible (in NIV): '**Counted** and listed' (Numbers 1:22, NIV), '**Count** the money that had been brought' (2 Kings 12:10, NIV). In Revelation 11:1 it is part of God's orders: '**Count** the worshipers' (NIV), 'Measure the temple of God and the altar, and **count** the worshippers' (REB). The word comes from the Latin *computare*, to compute, and in normal English usage means 'to add up, one by one, by units or groups, so as to get a total' (*Webster's New World*

*dictionary of the American language*, 1984).

*Evangelizing crowds or audiences requires* **counting** *people.*

36. **Deploy.** This term is used in English Bibles in reference exclusively to military applications, namely in the strategic or tactical **deployment** of troops. Dictionary definitions are wider: thus to **deploy** means 'to scatter, extend, display, place', 'to extend or place as if **deploying** troops' (*Webster's TNID*); or 'to station or place forces or equipment in accordance with a plan', 'to spread out or place like military troops' (*Webster's NWDAL*).

*Successful evangelizing necessitates the* **deployment** *of evangelists, missionaries, personnel, money, equipment, and whole varieties of other resources.*

*To evangelize involves the* **deploying** *of evangelizers. Evangelization proceeds as the force for evangelism is* **deployed**.

38. **Develop.** 'Evangelization involves an explicit message about peace, justice and **development**' (*Evangelii Nuntiandi* 1975, section 29). 'Between evangelization and human advancement—**development** and liberation—there are in fact profound links' (ibid, section 31). 'The tasks of liberation, **development** and evangelism are all integral parts of mission' (E. Castro 1978).

In normal parlance, we say that property or land has been **developed** when adequate building has taken place on it. This does not mean that every square foot is covered by buildings, but only that the density of building, by contrast with grass, gardens or other unbuilt-on areas, seems to adequately **develop** the property as far as desirable or possible. In Christian work, **development** is now a widely-used term, and many regard it as a distinct part of evangelization: 'As a tangible expression of Christian charity, our **development** aid does automatically present Christ to man, and therefore is a factor to leading men to Christ' (Archbishop D.D. Lourdusamy, Secretary, Congregation for the Evangelization of Peoples, 19 September 1977 in Munich).

*Being evangelized means being* **developed** *by the gospel. Evangelization is* **development** *of and by the gospel.*

39. **Display.** 'The day he **displayed** his miraculous signs' (Psalm 78:43, NIV). 'That Christ Jesus might **display** his unlimited patience as an example for those who would believe' (1 Timothy 1:16, NIV).

*Evangelization involves* **display** *of God's presence and power.*

40. **Do.** Jesus said, 'Teach them to **do** everything I have told you' (Matthew 28:20, CEV). 'Evangelism means living, **doing** and talking for Christ. By **doing,** I refer to work such as medical work, nursing, and social uplift' (S.B. Boon-Itt in Mott 1939:51). 'Evangelism is all Christian acts **done** with intention to transmit the treasure we have in earthen vessels' (D.A. McGavran 1977:66).

*Evangelizing is* **doing** *things for Christ.*

41. **Do miracles.** 'So that your disciples may see the **miracles** you **do**' (John 7:3, NIV). 'His disciples saw Jesus **do** many other **miracles**' (John 20:30, Beck). '**Miraculous** signs were **done** by the apostles' (Acts 2:43, NIV). 'Are all teachers? **Do** all work **miracles**?' (1 Corinthians 12:29, NIV). '**Miracles** were **done** among you' (2 Corinthians 12:12, NIV).

*Evangelizing often sees* **miracles done**.

42. **Drive out.** Jesus 'appointed twelve... with a commission to **drive out** devils' (Mark 3:15,22, NEB). Among the signs authenticating preaching of the Great Commission were exorcisms, the 'casting out' (AV/KJV, ASV) of evil spirits. Believers 'will **drive out** demons in my name' (Mark 16:17, GNB); 'In my name they will **drive out** demons' (NIV).

*Evangelization often results in* **driving out** *of demons.*

43. **Dwell.** 'Let the word of Christ **dwell** in you richly' (Colossians 3:16, NIV).

*Evangelizing requires* **dwelling** *in Christ.*

44. **Encounter.** 'Certain philosophers **encountered** Paul' (Acts 17:18, AV/KJV). Evangelism de-

mands: 'Firstly, there must be **encounter** with the world' (WCC 2nd Assembly, *Evanston speaks*, 1954:35). 'Evangelism is the bringing of persons to Christ... There must be personal **encounter** with Christ' (*Evanston speaks*, 1954:34). 'Evangelism is **encounter**. The outcome of the **encounter** cannot be foretold' (*Lambeth Conference report 1958*). Book by theologian Paul Tillich, *Christianity and the encounter of the world religions* (1963). Evangelism is everything 'from the first **encounter** until baptism' (J. Masson 1968:131f). 'Evangelism includes the word spoken in testimony to all **encountered** in the day's business and pleasure' (R.P. Beaver 1968:13). Books by J.J. Spae: *Christianity encounters Japan* (1968), *The Buddhist-Christian encounter* (1977).

*Being evangelized means being* **encountered** *by the gospel.*

**45. Engage.** 'Evangelism is **engagement**. We are involved in a solidarity with other men' (J. Poulton 1975:10).

*To evangelize is to* **engage** *others for Christ. Evangelizing is* **engaging**. *Evangelization is* **engagement** *in an action.*

**47. Estimate.** 'The priest shall **estimate** the cash value' (Leviticus 27:18, GNB). Jesus said 'First sit down and **estimate** the cost to see if he has enough' (Luke 14:28, NIV, NRSV).

*Evangelizing involves* **estimating** *audiences and logistics.*

**48. Exhibit.** 'Jesus Christ was publicly **exhibited**' (Galatians 3:1, NRSV).

*To evangelize is to* **exhibit** *Christ and his gospel to public scrutiny.*

**50. Expel.** This verb occurs in the Markan version of the Great Commission: 'By my name they shall **expel** demons' (Mark 16:17, Weymouth).

*Evangelizing often results in* **expulsion** *of demons.*

**51. Explore.** The Danites told them 'Go, **explore** the land' (Judges 18:2, NIV).

*To evangelize is to* **explore** *unevangelized territory.*

**52. Extend.** This term is used once to directly translate *euangelizo*: 'The wretched of the earth have God's salvation hospitality **extended** to them' (Luke 7:22, The Message/NTCE). It is also used for the whole purpose of redemption: 'The purpose of this was that the blessing of Abraham should in Christ Jesus be **extended** to the Gentiles' (Galatians 3:14, REB).

One of the 3 main objects of the WSCF (founded 1896, with by 1928 over 3,000 student organizations) has been: 'To enlist students in the work of **extending** the Kingdom of Christ throughout the whole world'. 'Evangelism also must include the **extension** of the Christian tradition through preaching' (Y. Abe in Mott 1938:37). 'By evangelism we mean the **extension** of the Evangel, the Gospel of salvation in Christ' (C.W. Iglehart in Mott 1938:42). 'Evangelism is the **extension** work of the glad tidings of salvation taught in the Gospels' (S. Sato in Mott 1938:45).

*To evangelize is to* **extend** *the gospel to others. Evangelizing is* **extending** *one's experience of Christ to others. Evangelization means* **extension** *of the gospel.*

**54. Free.** 'Everyone who believes in him is set **free** from all the sins' (Acts 13:38, GNB).

*Evangelizing is setting people* **free**.

**55. Give.** 'Give' is used to directly translate *euangelizo* with the 7th highest frequency of English words, as in 'I must **give** the good news of the Kingdom of God to the other towns also' (Luke 4:43, NEB, REB, also Acts 10:36 and 13:32 both in NEB and REB; also NTME, KB, BLE, LB, NJB). It also translates several NT Greek synonyms of *euangelizo*. Other more general usages: 'The message **given** to our ancestors' (Hebrews 2:2, GNB). '**Give** to everyone who asks you' (Luke 6:30, NIV). 'What I have I **give** you' (Acts 3:6, NIV). 'I **give** you this charge: Preach' (2 Timothy 4:1, NIV). 'This grace was **given** us in Christ Jesus' (2 Timothy 1:9, NIV). Evangelization 'means the **giving** to all men an adequate opportunity of knowing Jesus Christ' (J.R. Mott 1900:4-5).

*To evangelize is to* **give** *the gospel. Evangelizing is* **giving** *the gospel. Evangelization is the* **giving** *of the* **gift** *of the gospel to people.*

**56. Go.** Several Greek NT words overlap in meaning with *euangelizo*. *Poreuomai* means to **go**, proceed, travel. *Apostello* means (active) to send, send out, dispatch a message or messenger, or (passive) to go, be sent, depart, or set out. 'Go', 'send', 'sent' and cognates all occur very widely. In the Gospel of John alone, Jesus states some 46 times that the Father has sent him. '**Go** into all the world' (Mark 16:15, RSV). '**Go** quickly and tell' (Matthew 28:7, RSV). '**Go** and proclaim the kingdom of God' (Luke 9:60, GNB). '**Go**, for I will send you far away to the Gentiles' (Acts 22:21, GNB). 'The Holy Spirit said to Philip '**Go**' (Acts 8:29). 1947: founding of a missiological journal, *Euntes docete* (**Go** and teach), begun by the Urbanian University, Rome. 'Evangelism is **going** to the people outside' (W.E.R. Sangster 1948:14). 1959: founding of a journal, *Porefthendes* (**As you go**), begun by the Church of Greece's missionary institute. Other books: *Go! revolutionary New Testament theology* (C.W. Kingsley & G. Delamarter 1965). *Going for God* (B. Macindoe 1972). 'The Great Commission is '*Christlike-***going** ' (K. Koyama, in Anderson & Stransky 1975:70-75).

*To evangelize is to* **go** *at the Lord's command. Evangelizing means* **going** *when commanded.*

**57. Go forth.** This verb is a close variant of 'Go'. Jesus said, '**Go forth** therefore and make all nations my disciples' (Matthew 28:19, NEB).

*Evangelizing is* **going forth** *into action for Christ.*

**58. Go with.** This verb, another close variant of 'Go', directly translates *euangelizo* in one instance: the disciples '**went** from place to place **with** the Good News' (Acts 8:4, TCNT). Other indirect usages: 'He **went** to a city called Nain, and his disciples and a great crowd **went with** him' (Luke 7:11, RSV). 'Jesus' followers turned back and would not **go with** him any more' (John 6:66, GNB). 'Let us all **go with** the Teacher' (John 11:16, GNB). 'The Spirit told me to **go with** them without hesitation' (Acts 11:12, GNB).

*To evangelize is to* **go with** *the gospel. Evangelizing means* **going with** *the gospel.*

**59. Illustrate.** 'This is an **illustration** for the present time' (Hebrews 9:9, NIV). The idea of this dimension is the giving of visual, concrete, tangible support and evidence to the verbal, aural transmission of the gospel. In J.R. Mott's phrase, evangelization is '**illustrating** the Gospel by Christlike ministry' (Mott 1900:7).

*Evangelizing is* **illustrating** *the good news.*

**60. Impact.** 'Essentially evangelism is the instrument whereby the living God through His Holy Spirit makes his **impact** upon the spirits of men' (Tambaram, *Evangelism* 1939:422). *The* **impact** *of Christianity on the non-Christian world* (J.H. Bavinck 1949). 'Evangelism is the **impact** of the whole Christian community upon those who are outside its life' (WCC, *Evangelism* 1954:44); 'Evangelism should be conceived in terms of the **impact** of the Christian community on its total environment' (ibid, 53). 'The word evangelism may indicate the total **impact** of Christians upon the non-Christian world' (Evangelical Alliance of Great Britain, 1968).

*Being evangelized is being* **impacted** *by the gospel. Evangelization is the* **impact** *of the gospel on the world.*

**64. Inhabit.** 'From one man he made every nation of men, that they should **inhabit** the whole earth' (Acts 17:26, NIV).

*Evangelizers must* **inhabit** *regions they wish to evangelize.*

**65. Influence.** 'Evangelization. The action or process of evangelizing, or bringing under the **influence** of the Gospel' (*A new English dictionary*, Oxford 1897). 'Half Manchuria is beyond Christian **influence**' (J.R. Mott 1939:408-9). **Influence** may work at a distance, and is usually invisible, indirect.

*Evangelizing is* **influencing** *others for the gospel. Being evangelized is being* **influenced** *by the gospel. Evangelization is the* **influence** *of the gospel, or* **influence** *by the gospel.*

**66. Inspect.** 'You shall **inspect** your fold' (Job 5:24, NRSV). 'I **inspected** the walls of Jerusalem' (Nehemiah 2:13, NRSV). 'The Lord sent them to go and **inspect** the earth' (Zechariah 1:10, GNB). 'Go and **inspect** the earth!' (Zechariah 6:7, GNB).

*Evangelizing begins with the* **inspecting** *of the audience and their situation.*

**67. Irradiate.** 'The doctrine of the Saviour has **irradiated** the whole Oikumene' (Eusebius, AD 310, *Ecclesiastical history*, 2,3,1, English translation).

*Being evangelized is being* **irradiated** *by the gospel. Evangelization is* **irradiation** *by the gospel.*

**68. Itinerate.** The word means 'to travel from place to place in connection with work'. There is a long history of **itinerant** evangelists in Christian witness and expansion. In 1983 and 1986 some 12,000 evangelists attended the 1st and 2nd International Conferences for Itinerant Evangelists, in Amsterdam.

*To evangelize may require ceaseless* **itineration**.

**69. Journey.** 'Philip set out on a mission **journey**' (Acts 8:40, Rieu). 'In **journeying** oft, in perils' (2 Corinthians 11:26, AV/KJV). 'They set out on their **journey** in the service of Christ' (3 John 7, GNB).

*Evangelizing is ceaseless* **journeying**.

**70. Liberate.** 'The creation itself will be **liberated**' (Romans 8:21, NIV). 'Between evangelization and human advancement—development and **liberation**—there are in fact profound links' (*Evangelii Nuntiandi* 1975, section 31). 'The tasks of **liberation**, development and evangelism are all integral parts of mission' (E. Castro 1978).

*Evangelization includes* **liberation**.

**71. List.** The imperative 'Take a census' in Numbers 1:2 (NIV, RSV) is immediately followed in the Good News Bible by the more specific command '**List** the names'. Moses 'drew up the **lists** as follows in the wilderness of Sinai' (Numbers 1:19, REB). Other usages: 'counted and **listed**' (Numbers 1:22, NIV); 'Make a **list** of their names ' (Numbers 3:40, NIV); 'He **listed** for him the officials' (Judges 8:14, NRSV); 'These are the tribes, **listed** by name' (Ezekiel 48:1, NIV). Prominent **lists** in the Bible include the genealogy of Adam (Genesis 5), the 72 Gentile nations (Genesis 10), Matthew's and Luke's genealogies of Jesus (Matthew 1:1-17, Luke 3:23-38), and the many references in revelation to the unrevealed names **listed** in the Lamb's Book of Life (concluding with 20:15).

**Listing** is important throughout the Bible. In the early church, Timothy was told to 'add any widow to the **list** of widows' (1 Timothy 5:9, GNB), whereby deserving widows were 'put on the **list**' of those devoted to good works (ibid, NRSV). The word '**list**' occurs 46 times in GNB, and the very first sentence of the New Testament proclaims 'This is the **list** of the ancestors of Jesus Christ.' Most Western Christians see little value in that **list**. But for countless Hindus and other non-Christian georeligionists, that **list** provides the essential initial authentication of the person of Jesus Christ before they can go on to accept the truth of the Gospels.

'**List**' is one of many Bible synonyms of 'evangelize' which are widely used in the 1990s as computer programming commands on the information superhighway.

*To evangelize involves* **listing** *persons, resources, documents, times, places, funds, opportunities.*

**72. Live.** 'Evangelism means **living**, doing and talking for Christ' (S.B. Boon-Itt in Mott 1939:51). 'Evangelization must touch **life**' (*Evangelii Nuntiandi* 1975, section 47). 'The gospel always includes... a commitment to risk **life** itself' (WCC 5th Assembly, Nairobi 1975).

*Evangelizing requires the evangelizer's whole* **life**.

**74. Love.** 'This is my command: **Love** each other' (John 15:17, NIV). Simon Peter said: 'Lord, you know I **love** you' (John 21:16, NEB). '**Love** your neighbour as you **love** yourself' (Romans 13:9, GNB).

*To evangelize is to* **love** *the world and its peoples.*

**75. Make available.** To evangelize is to **make available** the gospel, and all other Christian resources, to persons deprived of them.

*Evangelizing is* **making** *the gospel* **available** *to others.*

76. **Make see**. '**See**' is widely used throughout Old and New Testaments (and too numerous for inclusion in the *NIV Complete Concordance*). **Making** people **see** Christ or his miracles is a visual evangelistic influence but not necessarily leading to faith and conversion: 'When they **saw** him, they worshipped him; but some doubted' (Matthew 28:17, RSV). 'They **saw** him, but somehow they did not recognize him' (Luke 24:16, GNB). 'Sir, we wish to **see** Jesus' (John 12:21, RSV). 'Of **making** all people **see** how God's secret plan is' (Ephesians 3:9, GNB). Often however it does imply saving faith, as in the books *Sir, we would see Jesus* (D.T. Niles 1938) and *I just saw Jesus* (Paul Eshleman, Jesus Film Project, 1985).

*To evangelize is to* **make** *people* **see** *Christ.*

77. **Measure.** The Greek verb *metreo* occurs 5 times in the Septuagint and 10 times in the Greek NT. Its derived noun *metron* occurs 80 times in the LXX (Septuagint) and 13 times in the Greek NT. The English verb and its cognates occur 95 times in GNB, especially in Ezekiel (49 times) and in Revelation (7 times). 'The Lord wants weights and **measures** to be honest' (Proverbs 16:11, GNB). 'Go and **measure** the temple of God' (Revelation 11:1, GNB). The English verb means to take the dimensions of, to judge by a rule or standard, to determine the quantity of things, or 'to find out or estimate the extent, dimensions, etc of, especially by a standard' (*Websters NWDAL*). It stands at the center of all sciences and the scientific method.

As a social activity, evangelism depends on **measuring** at a large number of points, from its logistics to its economics to its communication processes. **Measurement** is therefore an important dimension of evangelization.

*Evangelizing requires* **measuring.**

78. **Meet.** 'Certain philosophers **met** Paul' (Acts 17:18, RSV). 'To evangelise means to **meet** the need of the world for Christ' (D.T. Niles, *Sir, we would see Jesus*, 1938:16) 'To evangelize means to **meet** people in situations where the Gospel of Jesus Christ is given the opportunity to change individuals and groups' (M.E. Marty 1975:77).

*Evangelizing is* **meeting** *people.*

80. **Missionize.** A direct translation of *euangelizo* is found in the account where Philip 'set out on a **missionary** journey' (Acts 8:40, Rieu). 'Evangelism is not one of various branches of **missionary** activity, but the whole of it' (G.D. Phillips in Mott 1938:84). *Evangelism: the* **mission** *of the Church to those outside her life* (WCC survey, 1954). 'Evangelism. **Missionary** activity' (*Longmans English Larousse 1968*). 'Evangelism: activity of a **missionary**' (*New York Times everyday reader's dictionary of misunderstood, misused, and mispronounced words*, 2nd edition, 1985).

For Roman Catholics, **mission** = evangelization and planting of the Church (Vatican II 1965); for CWME of WCC, **mission** = liberation, development, humanization, and evangelism (E. Castro 1978).

*Evangelization is one of the components of* **mission.**

83. **Number.** The fourth book in the Old Testament is named ***Numbers*** (in Latin, ***Numeri;*** in Greek Septuagint, *Arithmoi*). '**Number**' is used 134 times in the Good News Bible. The OT is filled with censuses of people, property, land. The NT enumerates the rise and expansion of the Early Church.

*To evangelize starts with* **numbering** *those to be evangelized. Evangelization involves* **enumeration**.

84. **Observe.** In the 1st Great Commission narrative: 'Teaching them to **observe** all things' (Matthew 28:20, AV/KJV). 'Herod feared John and **observed** him' (Mark 6:20, AV/KJV).

*Being evangelized involves* **observing** *Christian witness and teaching. Evangelization involves* **observation** *of witnesses.*

85. **Occupy.** '**Occupy** till I come' (Luke 19:13, AV/KJV).

*To evangelize is to* **occupy** *territory. Evangelizing is* **occupying**. *Evangelization is* **occupation.**

88. **Penetrate.** 'There are still many nations within and outside the empire to which the gospel has not yet **penetrated**' (Origen, AD 200). 'By the end of the 3rd century, there was no area in the Roman Empire which had not been **penetrated** by the Gospel' (S.C. Neill et al 1971). 'We have one task, the **penetration** of the entire world in our generation with the Gospel' (Billy Graham, Berlin 1966:34). 'The goal is the total **penetration** of the world with the gospel of Christ' (W.D. Roberts 1967:97), 'Evangelism is **penetration** of Hindu and other non-Christian cultures by the new humanity in Christ' (M.M. Thomas in Hargreaves 1972:102-3). 'Through the Holy Spirit the Gospel **penetrates** to the heart of the world' (*Evangelii Nuntiandi* 1975, section 75). 'A citywide evangelistic crusade has 3 major phases: Preparation, **Penetration**, and Preservation. **Penetration** involves obvious personal and massive evangelization' (Leighton Ford in Douglas 1975:610). The Asia Christian Communications Fellowship (ACCF) based in Hong Kong 'promotes the use of all available media to **penetrate** and permeate local cultures with the Gospel' (1978). 'The 1978 Bolivia crusade will open up South America for further **penetration** of the gospel to all segments of society' (Luis Palau 1978).

*Being evangelized means being* **penetrated** *by the gospel. Evangelization is* **penetration** *by the gospel.*

89. **Perform miracles.** '**Perform** a **miracle** to show that God approved of him' (Luke 11:16, GNB). 'The Lord worked with them and proved that their preaching was true by the **miracles** that were **performed**' (Mark 16:20, GNB). 'Look at all the **miracles** this man is **performing**' (John 11:47, GNB).

*Evangelizing often sees* **miracles performed.**

90. **Permeate.** 'In nations where the Gospel has not thoroughly **permeated** the society' (Luis Palau in Douglas 1975:607). 'We are commissioned to allow the gospel to **permeate** all realms of human life' (WCC 1976:54). Purpose of the newly-formed ACCF (Asia Christian Communications Fellowship) in Hong Kong, 1977: 'It will promote the use of all available media to penetrate and **permeate** local cultures with the Gospel through relevant programs and products orientated to the needs of Asians'.

*Being evangelized is being* **permeated** *with the gospel. Evangelization is* **permeation** *with or by the gospel.*

93. **Plan.** 'Many times I have **planned** to visit you' (Romans 1:13, GNB). 'Do I make my **plans** in a worldly manner?' (2 Corinthians 1:17, NIV).

*Evangelizing requires prior* **planning.**

94. **Point.** The verb is an exact or precise mode of indicating. '**Point** the way to Zion!' (Jeremiah 4:6, GNB). Jesus '**pointed** to his disciples and said 'Look!' ' (Matthew 12:49, GNB). 'Trying to find out the time and circumstances to which the Spirit of Christ in them was **pointing** when he predicted the sufferings of Christ' (1 Peter 1:11, NIV).

*Evangelizing is* **pointing** *people to Christ.*

95. **Portray.** 'Before your very eyes Jesus Christ was clearly **portrayed** as crucified' (Galatians 3:1, NIV), 'publicly **portrayed**' (RSV).

*Evangelism requires* **portraying** *Christ.*

96. **Prepare.** 'He did this to **prepare** all God's people for the work of Christian service' (Ephesians 4:12, GNB). 'Be **prepared** in season and out of season' (2 Timothy 4:2, NIV). 'A serious **preparation** is needed for all workers for evangelization' (Paul VI, *Evangelii Nuntiandi* 1975, section 73).

*Evangelizers need* **preparation.**

98. **Provide.** '**Provide** him with life-giving water' (John 4:14, GNB). '**Provide** some horses for Paul to ride and get him safely through' (Acts 23:24, GNB).

*To evangelize is to* **provide** *for other evangelizers as well as the unevangelized.*

100. **Reach.** This term is used to directly translate *euangelizo* in one version, the Christian Community Bible (Catholic Pastoral Edition): 'Good news is **reaching** the poor' (Matthew 11:5, CCB). '**Reach**' is used 5 times in AV/KJV, '**reached**' twice. 'The sound of their voice went out to all the world; their words **reached** the ends of the earth' (Romans 10:18, GNB; note that 'went out' and '**reached**' are both *exelthen* in the Greek NT). 'Are you the only ones the word of God has **reached**?' (1 Corinthians 14:36, RSV). 'God's grace **reaches** more and more people' (2 Corinthians 4:15, GNB). 'The Good News which has **reached** you is spreading all over the world' (Colossians 1:6, JB). Justin Martyr (AD 150) claimed that 'The Gospel had **reached** the barbarian tribes' (J. Orr 1899:47). But 'The gospel has not yet **reached** the Chinese or the Ethiopians beyond the river' (Origen, on Matthew 24:14, about AD 220). 'The Gospel can and should be brought within the **reach** of every creature within this generation' (J.R. Mott in *The Student Volunteer*, January 1895). 'Evangelism is every possible way of **reaching** outside the church to bring people to faith in Christ' (G.E. Sweazey 1953, 1976:19). 'Evangelism is the place where the Church discovers itself in its true depth and **outreach**' (WCC 2nd Assembly, *Evanston speaks*, 1954:33). 'No task in the world is more important than **reaching** every person on earth with the Word of God' (UBS, *Scriptures of the world*, 1976:9). 'The astonishing **outreach** of the community to the world is a fact' (K. Barth in Scott 1978:15). 'Jesus is himself the Good News **reaching** out through us' (*Lambeth Conference report* 1978:93-4). In the 1970s, evangelist Leighton Ford launched a series of **Reachout** crusades in the USA, Canada and elsewhere. The word '**Outreach**' occurs in the titles of numerous Christian organizations, e.g. Middle East Christian **Outreach**.

*To evangelize is to* **reach** *people with the gospel, or to bring the gospel within* **reach** *of* **unreached** *people. Evangelizing is* **reaching** *out. Evangelization is* **outreach** *with the gospel.*

101. **Record.** This verb and cognates occur 41 times in NRSV , emphasizing that results need to be written down to become permanent. 'They **recorded** the survey on a scroll, town by town, in seven portions' (Joshua 18:9, REB). 'Jesus did many other miraculous signs... which are not **recorded** in this book' (John 20:30, NIV). 'If it were all to be **recorded** in detail, I suppose the whole world could not hold the books that would be written' (John 21:25, NEB). Much of the value of signs, miracles, and evangelism is when it is written down or **recorded,** thereby reaching a vastly larger set of audiences.

*Evangelizing expands through* **recording** *events.*

102. **Register**. '**Register**' and cognates are used 17 times in NRSV ('**registration**' 3 times). 'They **registered** themselves in their clans' (Numbers 1:18, NRSV), '**registered** by name' (1 Chronicles 4:41, NRSV), 'enrolled in the **register**' (Ezekiel 13:9, NRSV), 'that all the world should be **registered**' (Luke 2:1, NRSV).

'**Register**' is one of the 37 key English biblical imperatives delineating the science of missiometrics.

*Evangelizing may need the dimension of* **registering** *persons. Evangelization involves* **registration.**

105. **Reside.** Where a Christian **resides**, settles, or chooses to live can have major bearing on the area's evangelization. Thus on the Day of Pentecost, '**residents** of Mesopotamia' (Acts 2:8, NIV) were converted in Jerusalem but then immediately returned home to evangelize and plant the church in Mesopotamia.

*Evangelizing springs out of* **residing.**

106. **Risk.** 'Barnabas and Paul—men who have **risked** their lives for the name of our Lord Jesus Christ' (Acts 15:25-26, NIV). 'It was **risky** to go on with the voyage' (Acts 27:9, NEB). 'They **risked** their lives for me' (Romans 16:4, NIV). 'The gospel always includes... a commitment to **risk** life itself' (WCC 5th Assembly, Nairobi 1975).

*Evangelism is* ***risky****. Evangelizers need to be ready for* **risk.**

107. **Scan**. The verb is not a biblical term. In English it means 'to look at closely, to examine in sequence, to check automatically' (*WNWDAL*). It is a dimension of evangelization in that evangelism can be assisted by **scanning** large amounts of information such as mission reports and documentation, new literature on mission, and the like.

*Evangelization arises through **scanning** the entire global context and situation.*

**108. Search.** 'The prophets made careful **search** and investigation' (1 Peter 1:10, GNB).
*To evangelize is to **search** for ways to reach people.*

**109. Seek.** 'Seek' (with 'sought', etc) is used 115 times in AV/KJV, and widely in other versions. 'The Son of Man came to **seek** and to save the lost' (Luke 19:10, GNB). 'Dr. Trumbull rarely quoted Scripture when he was first **seeking** to win men to Christ' (*Taking men alive* 195:86). 'True evangelism is **seeking** to bring men into conversion' (B.S.W. Green 1951:37). Evangelism is 'a shepherd **seeking** a lost sheep' (D. Webster 1959:192). 'Evangelism is **seeking** and finding the lost' (C.P. Wagner in Stott 1971).
*To evangelize is to **seek** people for Christ. Evangelizing is **seeking**. Evangelization is **seeking** people with the gospel.*

**111. Send.** The term occasionally is used to directly translate *euangelizo*: 'It was he who **sent** me to you with this good news!' (Luke 1:19, TLB). Other usages include: 'The Message he **sent** to the children of Israel' (Acts 10:35, The Message/NTCE). 'That he might **send** them out to preach' (Mark 3:14, NIV). 'As the Father has **sent** me, I am **sending** you' (John 20:21, NIV). '**Send** men to Joppa' (Acts 10:5, NIV). 'He has **sent** his message to Israel's descendants, and made the good news of peace known to them through Jesus Christ' (Acts 10:36, AT/GB).'I will **send** you far away to the Gentiles' (Acts 22:21, NIV). '**Send** the book to the churches' (Revelation 1:11, GNB). '**Sent** throughout the whole earth' (Revelation 5:6, GNB). The NT Greek word *apostello* means '**send**', so that ' 'Evangelism' means apostolate' (J.N. Monzo in Mott 1938:65).
Subsequently, the word **sending** (Dutch, Afrikaans) has become the main modern word in those languages to translate 'mission'.
*Evangelizers must be **sent** by God.*

**113. Set forth.** Jesus said, '**Set forth** and make all peoples your disciples' (Matthew 28:19, Rieu).
*To evangelize is to **set forth** with the gospel.*

**114. Set out.** This phrase is used in one paraphrase of Acts to directly translate *euangelizo*—Philip '**set out** on a missionary journey' (Acts 8:40, Rieu).
*Evangelizing involves **setting out** with the gospel.*

**115. Settle.** In its first sense as 'begin to live permanently in a location', this OT verb occurs 93 times in GNB (and none in NT); or 136 times in NIV OT, 14 times in NIV NT. 'Occupy the land and **settle** in it, because I am giving it to you' (Numbers 33:53, GNB).
*Evangelizers must **settle** in order to have the greatest impact.*

**116. Show.** 'Show' has been used in a number of versions to directly translate *euangelizo*. The earliest instance was 600 years ago. Wycliffe's first English Bible, completed in 1382, transliterated the verb and so coined a new English word, 'euangelisen'. But after his death, his disciples decided this was too Catholic, too Roman, too Latin a word, and in their 1395 revised Bible replaced it mainly by 'preche', and less frequently by '**schew**' (today's '**show**'), as in '**schewinge** the Lord Jhesu'.
In Luke 1:19, AV/KJV, *euangelizo* is translated as Gabriel being sent 'to **shew** thee these glad tidings' (GNB and NIV, however, have 'to tell you this good news'); and as '**showing** the glad tidings of the Kingdom of God' (Luke 8:1, AV/KJV); also in Galatians 1:16, LB.
'Show' also translates several NT Greek synonyms of *euangelizo*. 'I will **show** wonders in the heaven' (Acts 2:19, NIV). '**Shewing** by the scriptures that Jesus was Christ' (Acts 18:28, AV/KJV). 'To **show** that God is faithful' (Romans 15:8, GNB). '...he might **show** the incomparable riches of his grace' (Ephesians 2:7, NIV). 'According to the pattern you were **shown** on the mountain' (Hebrews 8:5, GNB). 'This is how God **showed** his love' (1 John 4:9, NIV).'He **showed** me Jerusalem' (Revelation 21:10, GNB).
*To evangelize is to **show** people the gospel.*

**117. Show mercy.** 'You should have had **mercy** on your fellow-servant, just as I had **mercy** on you' (Matthew 18:33, GNB).
*Evangelizing includes **showing mercy** to unfortunates.*

**118. Signal.** 'I will **signal** to the nations' (Isaiah 49:22, GNB). 'Give the **signal** and announce the news!' (Jeremiah 50:2, GNB). 'Give the **signal** to attack!' (Jeremiah 51:27, GNB). 'So they **signalled** their partners' (Luke 5:7, NIV).
*Evangelizing requires **signalling** for help from partners.*

**119. Sort.** The verb is used in Jesus' parable of the Catch of Fish as a synonym for 'divide': 'Men sat down and **sorted** the good into vessels' (Matthew 13:48, RSV). In dictionary usage the verb means 'To arrange according to class or kind' (*WNWDAL*). As a dimension of evangelization, it emphasizes the need for thinking, planning, and prioritizing. Only by **sorting** all possible targets of evangelism can evangelizers determine their optimum courses of action.
*Evangelizing requires **sorting** of priorities and targets.*

**122. Strategize.** 'Devise your **strategy**' (Isaiah 8:10, NIV).
*Evangelization demands **strategic** thinking.*

**123. Study.** '**Study** the Scriptures' (John 7:52, GNB).
*Evangelizing begins with **studying** the people being evangelized.*

**124. Suffer.** 'Take your part in **suffering** for the Good News' (2 Timothy 1:8, GNB), 'Join with me in **suffering** for the gospel ' An essential element in Jesus' ministry was his **suffering**. Likewise, the way Christians face, accept, and endure **suffering**—including loss of loved ones, and even one's own sickness and death—is indispensable to evangelization and has a profound effect on non-Christians who see it.
*To evangelize is to endure **suffering** for the gospel's sake. Evangelization entails **suffering**.*

**125. Sum.** 'Sum' is a basic human activity on which many other activities depend. The English Bible uses the term sparingly but with acknowledgement of the need for precision that the term implies: 'Have him count the entire **sum**' (2 Kings 22:4, NRSV), 'the exact **sum** of money' (Esther 4:7, NRSV), 'It cost me a large **sum** of money' (Acts 22:28, NRSV). In the total monitoring and logistics of evangelism, '**sum**' and '**summing**' clearly form an indispensable, if minor, dimension of evangelization.
*Evangelization requires and involves **summing** and **summation**.*

**126. Supply.** Describing his ministry in Illyricum, Paul states 'I have **supplied** the Good News of Christ' throughout the region (Romans 15:19, HBME).
*Evangelizing requires **supplying** the gospel where it is absent.*

**127. Survey.** 'Go and make a **survey** of the land' (Joshua 18:8, NIV). '**Survey** the land in seven portions' (Joshua 18:6, REB).
*Evangelizing requires **surveys** of surroundings and populations.*

**129. Take.** 'Take' is used occasionally in GNB and other versions to directly translate *euangelizo*, as in 'God had called us to **take** the good news there' (Acts 16:10, REB). 'God gave me the privilege of **taking** to the Gentiles the Good News about the infinite riches of Christ' (Ephesians 3:8, GNB). 'To obey its Lord's commission to **take** the Gospel to all nations' (J.R.W. Stott in Anderson & Stransky 1975:7). 'The uncompleted task of **taking** the message of Jesus Christ into all the world' (S.E. Wirt 1978:9).
*To evangelize is to **take** the gospel somewhere. Evangelizing is **taking** the gospel. Evangelization is the **taking** of the gospel.*

**131. Target.** 'Why have you made me your **target**?' (Job 7:20, NIV). 'God uses me for **target**-practice' (Job 16:12, GNB).

*To evangelize is to **target** whatever keeps people away from God.*

**132. Total.** The word is used twice in the Good News Bible: 'The **total** came to fifty thousand silver coins' (Acts 19:19); 'There was a **total** of 276 of us on board' (Acts 27:37). The usages rise to 18 times in the NRSV Bible, where the phrase 'the **total** enrolment' (of the camp, camps, Levites, etc.) is a refrain in Numbers. 'The booty remaining from the spoil that the troops had taken **totaled** 675,000 sheep, 72,000 oxen, 61,000 donkeys, and 32,000 persons in all' (Numbers 31:32, NRSV).
Obviously in any form of evangelization it is important for the evangelizers to bear in mind the **totality** of their audience. In this sense, **totaling** is an indispensable dimension of evangelization.
*Evangelization requires a continual process of assessment including **totaling**.*

**133. Touch.** 'Touch' is used 56 times in AV/KJV. 'All who **touched** it were made well' (Matthew 14:36, GNB). 'Jesus stretched out his hand and **touched** him' (Luke 5:13, GNB). 'Evangelism signifies the endeavor of the Church to bring all men in **touch** with the redeeming power of Christ' (G. Baez Camargo in Mott 1939:53). '45% of China is still entirely **untouched** by Christian forces' (J.R. Mott 1939:408-9). In the non-Christian world of 1920, 160 million people remained 'utterly **untouched**' by the gospel (Interchurch World Movement of North America, *World Survey*, New York, 1920). 'Evangelization must **touch** life' (*Evangelii Nuntiandi* 1975, section 47). P. Eshleman, *The touch of Jesus* (1995).
*Evangelism must **touch** hearers' lives.*

**135. Transmit.** 'Transmit' translates several NT Greek synonyms of *euangelizo* in some versions, though not used in AV/KJV, GNB, NIV. 'To preach the Gospel is to **transmit** good news' (Mott 1900:6). 'Evangelism also must include the **transmission** and extension of the Christian tradition' (Y. Abe in Mott 1938:37). 'Evangelism is the **transmission** of the Gospel of Christ to the whole world' (A. Ebisawa in Mott 1938:40). '*Dendo*, the equivalent in Japanese of evangelism, means '**transmitting** the way' ' (S. Saito in Mott 1938:44). 'Evangelism is in the first place the **transmission** of God's question to humanity about accepting Jesus Christ' (W.A. Visser't Hooft in Anderson 1975:123). 'Evangelization is not merely the communication of an evangelical message of which we are the **transmitters**' (*PMV* 63, 1976:2). *Evangelii Nuntiandi* (1975, section 73) speaks of 'those who have the mission of **transmitting** the Word of God' (i.e. 'the evangelizers' or 'workers for evangelization') and (section 71) 'The family ought to be a place where the Gospel is **transmitted**'. 'Evangelism is all Christian acts done with intention to **transmit** the treasure we have in earthen vessels' (D.A. McGavran 1977:66).
*Being evangelized is having the gospel **transmitted** to one. Evangelization is **transmission** of the gospel.*

**137. Travel.** Jesus '**travelled** all over Galilee, preaching in the synagogues' (Mark 1:39, GNB). 'Jesus **travelled** through towns and villages, preaching the Good News' (Luke 8:1, GNB). 'Peter **travelled** everywhere' (Acts 9:32, GNB).
*Evangelizing means constant **travelling**.*

**138. Visit.** 'Jesus went round **visiting** all the towns and villages' (Matthew 9:35, GNB). 'You took care of me, in prison and you **visited** me' (Matthew 25:36, GNB). 'Not allowed by his religion to **visit** or associate with Gentiles' (Acts 10:28, GNB).
*Evangelizing starts with **visiting**.*

### III.  WITNESS!

The third Mandate describes the stage where Christians first become involved with attempting to evangelize non-Christians. **Presence evangelization** implies that Christians are right there. Witness is usually unorganized, private, spontaneous; it happens as opportunity arises. It is best known as **Personal evangelism**.
Of its 116 facets, 83 are dimensions, and 3 are in The Big Ten (*Hear! Spread! Tell!*).

**140. Acknowledge.** 'Anyone who **acknowledged**

that Jesus was the Christ would be put out of the synagogue' (John 9:22, NIV). 'If anyone **acknowledges** that Jesus is the Son' (1 John 4:15, NIV). '**Acknowledge** Jesus Christ as coming in the flesh' (2 John 7, NIV).

*To evangelize is to* **acknowledge** *Christ's missionary purpose in life.*

141. **Acquaint.** '**Acquaint**' translates NT Greek synonyms of *euangelizo*; also used in AV/KJV primarily of knowing people. 'Then Felix, who was well **acquainted** with the Way...' (Acts 24:22, NIV). '...not **acquainted** with the teaching about righteousness' (Hebrews 5:13, NIV). 'Evangelism is **acquainting** a non-Christian with the values of a vital contact with God through Christ' (C.R. Watson in Mott 1938:53). 'Evangelize. To make **acquainted** with the Gospel' (*Chambers Twentieth Century dictionary* 1973).

*Being evangelized is being* **acquainted** *with the gospel. Evangelization is* **acquaintance** *with the gospel.*

142. **Admit**. The verb is close to 'confess': 'He **admitted** that the Supreme God controls all human kingdoms' (Daniel 5:21, GNB). 'Many of the believers came, publicly **admitting** and revealing what they had done' (Acts 19:18, GNB). Paul told the crowd in the temple, 'But this I **admit** to you, that . . . I worship the God of our ancestors' (Acts 24:14, NRSV).

*To evangelize is to* **admit** *that one is a follower of Christ, and to* **admit** *others into knowledge of the gospel.*

143. **Advocate.** The Stoic philosophers in Athens explained Paul's evangelizing as 'He seems to be **advocating** foreign gods' (Acts 17:18, NIV).

*Evangelizers are* **advocates** *for the unevangelized.*

144. **Affirm.** 'He **affirms** his covenant with them' (Psalm 25:14, GNB).

*To evangelize is to* **affirm** *Christ and his gospel.*

145. **Answer.** Receiving the Great Commission from the Risen Christ, 'They asked him... He **answered**' (Acts 1:7, NEB). 'Be ready at all times to **answer** anyone who asks you to explain the hope you have in you' (1 Peter 3:15, GNB).

*Evangelizing sees* **answering** *questions as major opportunity.*

146. **Appear.** It is clear from the Resurrection accounts that Jesus' **appearances** were few and far between. They were unpredictable, but just sufficient for faith to respond. Jesus '**appeared** to them from time to time during forty days' (Acts 1:3, TCNT).

*Evangelism is helping others see Jesus* **appearing** *to them.*

148. **Assert.** About an hour later another **asserted**, 'Certainly this fellow was with him, for he is a Galiliean' (Luke 22:59, NIV).

*To evangelize is to* **assert** *the gospel.*

150. **Associate.** 'To **associate** with a Gentile or visit him' (Acts 10:28, NIV).

*Evangelizing begins in* **associating** *with the unevangelized.*

151. **Attest.** 'All Israel... recognized that Samuel was **attested** as a prophet of the Lord' (1 Samuel 3:20, NIV). The Lord confirmed 'the Word by the miracles that **attested** their work' (Mark 16:20, Rieu).

*To evangelize is to* **attest** *the truth of the gospel.*

152. **Be here with.** This term is used to directly translate *euangelizo* in GNB: '**I am here with** good news for you' (Luke 2:10). A similar usage involves the simple verb 'to be': 'Since then, there **is** the good news of the kingdom of God' (Luke 16:16, NEB). Note that GNB does not capitalize 'good news' except in all cases of direct reference to the whole gospel as '*the* Good News'.

*Evangelizing involves* **being** *where people and their needs are.*

153. **Be martyred.** The Greek verb ***martyreo*** (bear witness) and its noun ***martyria*** (witness) in New Testament times meant witnessing about Christ without implying that real witness always and inevitably resulted in death. By the end of the 1st century, however, those words had taken on the additional meaning of 'witness by one's death'. Hints of this later meaning occur in the New Testament, e.g. 'The blood of your **martyr** Stephen was shed' (Acts 22:20, NIV), and in the Apocalypse: 'Antipas was my faithful **martyr**' (Revelation 2:13, AV/KJV), or 'Antipas, my faithful witness, was killed there' (Revelation 2:13, GNB), and 'Jesus Christ, the faithful witness, the first to be raised from death' (Revelation 1:5, GNB). Also the vision of the Harlot 'drunk with the blood of the saints and the blood of the **martyrs** of Jesus ' (Revelation 17:6, RSV).

*Evangelization has always been closely related to, preceded by, and followed with* **martyrs** *and* **martyrdom.**

154. **Be present.** The idea of **presence** is common. 'The power of the Lord was **present** to heal the sick' (Luke 5:17, GNB). 'The power of our Lord Jesus is **present**' (1 Corinthians 5:4, NIV). 'The *koinonia* manifests the *shalom*, as it is **present** among man' (J.C. Hoekendijk 1950:171). 'On still other occasions the simple **presence** of a worshipping community or man is the witness' (D.T. Niles 1959). 'Our Christian **presence** in the world is indispensable to evangelism' (ICOWE, *Lausanne Covenant*, 1974, section 4).

*Evangelizers need to* **be present** *where the unevangelized live.*

155. **Bear tidings.** The phrase is used once in a Scripture version directly translating the use of *euangelizo* in Isaiah 52:7, praising the messengers who '**bear** Glad-**tidings** of peace' (Romans 10:15, Conybeare).

*To evangelize is to* **bear tidings.**

156. **Cast a net.** 'They were **casting a net**' (Matthew 4:18, NIV). '**Cast a net**' is American usage, whereas current British usage is '**throw a net**', as in 'Fishermen **throw their net** out into the lake' (Matthew 13:47, GNB). Jesus said, '**Cast** the **net** on the right side of the ship' (John 21:6, AV/KJV).

*To evangelize is to* **cast** *one's* **net** *as widely as possible.*

159. **Circulate.** 'This story has been widely **circulated** among the Jews' (Matthew 28:15, NIV).

*Evangelizing is* **circulating** *news about Christ.*

160. **Claim.** 'Paul **claims** that he (Jesus) is alive' (Acts 25:19, GNB).

*Evangelizing is* **claiming** *that Christ is alive.*

161. **Commend.** '**Commend**' translates several NT Greek synonyms of *euangelizo.* With cognates it occurs 25 times in AV/KJV. 'God **commendeth** his love toward us' (Romans 5:8, AV/KJV). 'The true medical missionary will constantly **commend** the Gospel to his patients by word as well as by deed' (J.R. Mott 1900:14). Apologetics is defined as 'the reasoned **commendation** of Christianity to persons interested but not yet convinced' (C.H. Dodd 1936:4). W.E.R. Sangster, *Let me* ***commend:*** *the Sam P. Jones Lectures on Evangelism* (Abingdon, 1948). 'The proclamation of the gospel and every argument to **commend** it' (WCC 2nd Assembly, *Evanston speaks*, 1954:40).

*To evangelize is to* **commend** *the gospel. Evangelizing is* **commending** *Christ. Evangelization is* **commendation** *of the gospel.*

162. **Communicate.** This word is used in somewhat archaic fashion 12 times in AV/KJV, and not in later translations. 'I **communicated** unto them that gospel which I preach among the Gentiles' (Galatians 2.2). 'That the **communication** of thy faith may become effectual' (Philemon 6). Since 1900, extra-scriptural usage has become widespread. '**Communicating** a knowledge of Christ and his mission to men' (J.R. Mott 1900:6). 'Evangelism means to me the **communication** of Christ' (G.M. Fisher in Mott 1938:410). 'The **communication** of the good news is evangelism... Evangelism is the **communication** of the special revelation of God in Christ' (G.E. Phillips 1939:89). 'Evangelism is an activity of the mouth or pen by which the Good News of God's redeeming acts is **communicated**' (L. Newbigin 1958:22). 'Evangelism is an act of **communicating** with a view to conversion' (J.I. Packer 1961:85). W. Barclay, ***Communicating*** *the gospel* (The Laird Lectures, 1968). 'Evangelism is effectively **communicating** the Gospel' (C.P. Wagner 1971). 'Evangelistic witness is understood to be restricted to the **communication** of Christ to those who do not consider themselves Christian, wherever these people may be found' (Orthodox Consultation, Bucharest 1974, in Anderson 1975:268). 'Evangelization is the demonstration and **communication** of God's love and salvation' (UTC Bangalore 1974). 'Evangelization is **communicating** the eternal truth of God clearly and understandably to all age groups' (L. Palau in J.D. Douglas 1975:602). 'World evangelism is the **communication** of the good news' (Brazil National Strategy Group, ICOWE, in Douglas 1975:1344-6). By 1977 'Here's Life America had **communicated** the gospel to some 85% of all Americans' (W.R. Bright 1977:32). 'The nature of evangelization is the **communication** of the Good News' (SWG/LCWE 1978).

'To **communicate** is to put your thoughts into words, actions or attitudes in such a way that the person with whom you are **communicating** understands your thoughts in the way you meant them' (L. Brierley 1978:pc). However, in its correct or normal usage, '**communication**' presupposes understanding but not necessarily agreement or acceptance. In the AV/KJV case above (Galatians 2:2), Paul **communicated** but his message was not accepted by a number of his hearers (2:4,5). One can therefore find correct, or adequate, or even full **communication** of the gospel in cases where the gospel is subsequently not accepted but instead is rejected.

Some definers of 'evangelism' see a false dichotomy between '**communication**' and 'proclamation, announcing, preaching', as if the former were in some way superior to the latter, the latter being caricatured as 'mere proclamation' assumed to imply or involve inadequate linguistic or cultural **communication**. Actually, these terms should all have the same meaning; that is, 'proclamation' and related words as used in the New Testament presuppose adequate or satisfactory **communication**.

*To evangelize is to* **communicate** *the gospel. Evangelizing is* **communicating**. *Evangelization is the* **communication** *of the gospel.*

163. **Confess.** '**Confess**' occurs 26 times in AV/KJV (translating *homologeo* 18 times, *exhomologeo* 8); and it is widespread in RSV, NEB, GNB, et alia.
Also, it translates NT Greek synonyms of *euangelizo.* 'Everyone will **confess** that I am God' (Romans 14:11, GNB). 'Every tongue will **confess** that Jesus Christ is Lord' (Philippians 2:11, RSV). 'Christ Jesus who in his testimony before Pontius Pilate made the good **confession**' (1 Timothy 6:13, RSV). 'Your **confession** of the gospel' (2 Corinthians 9:13, NIV). 'The WCC Nairobi Assembly 1975 has as its theme 'Jesus Christ frees and unites', an evangelistic assertion dealt with under the title '**Confessing** Christ today' ' (P.A. Potter to 1974 Synod of Bishops in Rome).

For Christians, evangelizing is '**confessing** Christ today' in the modern world, with conviction. Our use of the term **confession** here, as usually, implies formal **confession.**

*To evangelize is to* **confess** *Christ and the gospel. Evangelizing is* **confessing** *Christ. Evangelization is the* **confession** *of Christ.*

164. **Converse.** The verb 'converse' is not used in NT, and the noun rarely. 'Let your **conversation** be always full of grace' (Colossians 4:6, NIV).

*Evangelizing involves* **conversing** *with all whose paths cross ours.*

165. **Convey.** 'Evangelization is the **conveying** of the offer of salvation' (A.G. Hogg in Mott 1938:21). 'I would define evangelism as the **conveying** to others the true knowledge of God revealed in Christ' (H. Lightbody in Mott 1939:81). To evangelize is 'to **convey** the message of Christ to the whole community' (E. Castro 1977:4).

*Evangelizing is* **conveying** *good news.*

167. **Cry.** A number of near-synonyms of 'evangelize' cover the less-controlled or less-reasonable end of the spectrum of public utterances. The blind man '**cried** out, 'Jesus! Son of David! Take pity on me!' ' (Luke 18:38, GNB).

*To evangelize is to preach, or to tell, or even to* **cry** *out or otherwise cause a disturbance.*

**169. Deliver.** 'Deliver' directly translates *euangelizo* in the Emphasized NT (Rotherham) at 3 points: Luke 8:1 'proclaiming and **delivering** the glad message', Luke 9:6 '**delivering** the glad message' of the Kingdom of God, and Hebrews 4:2; also by Weymouth's NTMS in Acts 8:25 '**delivering** the Lord's Word', and in Galatians 1:8, NAB. '**Deliver**' also translates several NT Greek synonyms of *euangelizo*, including *paradidesthai*, to **deliver**, give up to, transmit, which is used 110 times in the Greek NT. 'After they had given their testimony and **delivered** the Lord's message, they went back to Jerusalem' (Acts 8:25, AT/GB).
*Evangelization is **delivering** a message. Being evangelized means having the gospel **delivered** to one. Evangelization is **delivery** of the gospel.*

**171. Describe.** 'Go up and down and write a **description** of the land' (Joshua 18:8, RSV). 'What parable shall we use to **describe** it?' (Mark 4:30, NIV). Peter '**described** how the Lord had brought him out of prison' (Acts 12:17, NIV). 'Before your very eyes you had a clear **description** of the death of Jesus Christ on the cross!' (Galatians 3:1, GNB).
*Evangelizing includes **describing** how Christ can help people.*

**172. Dialogue.** The NT Greek verb *dialegomai* means to speak alternately or converse in discussion. From its related noun *dialogos* comes the English noun and verb '**dialogue**', which occurs 21 times in AV/KJV. '**Dialogue** is also, implicitly, a proclamation of the Gospel' (Secretariat for Non-Believers, Vatican, 1968:I.1). 'Indispensable to evangelism is that kind of **dialogue** whose purpose is to listen sensitively in order to understand' (*Lausanne Covenant*, 1974, section 4). '**Dialogue** with People of Living Faiths and Ideologies' (WCC sub-unit, meeting in Thailand 1977; see S.J. Samartha (ed), *Faith in the midst of faiths: reflections on dialogue in community*, 1977). ''**Dialogue**' should not be confused with evangelism. But it is also a way by which Christians may share the Good News about Jesus with those who worship God within another faith' (*Report of the Lambeth Conference* 1978:92). 'Religious **dialogue** should be the ideal form of evangelization' (Federation of Asian Bishops' Conferences, Calcutta 1978, in *International Fides service* No. 2928, 24 February 1979:111).
In English, the noun '**dialogue**' has been in use since 1401, and means 'a conversation carried on between 2 or more persons; a colloquy, talk together'; and the related verb 'to discuss' since 1607, meaning 'to hold a **dialogue** or conversation'. There is even a verb 'to dialoguize', dating from 1599, meaning 'to take part in **dialogue**'.
*Evangelizing involves **dialoguing** with others about Christ. Evangelization is **dialogue**.*

**173. Diffuse.** 'The Gospel is speedily gaining such a rapid **diffusion** in Manchuria that we may anticipate at no distant date its contact with every village and town in the country' (J.R. Mott 1900:83). In several modern Italian Bibles, the Italian verb '*diffondevano*' is used in Acts 8:4; according to current Italian-English dictionaries, it means '**diffuse**, give out, shed, spread, propagate, publicize, make known, broadcast, circulate'. 'Several societies for the more general **diffusion** of the gospel' (*Account*, CMS 1799, p.4-5). 'The Gospel is speedily gaining a rapid **diffusion**' throughout Manchuria (J.R. Mott 1900:83). 'Centers of evangelization sufficiently near each other to **diffuse** the gospel over the intervening spaces' (G. Robson in Mott 1900:153). 'To **diffuse** the knowledge of the Gospel throughout the world in a generation' (J.R. Mott 1900:13).
*Being evangelized is having the gospel **diffused** through a population. Evangelization is **diffusion** of the gospel.*

**174. Disclose.** 'The mystery that has been kept hidden for ages and generations, but is now **disclosed** to the saints' (Colossians 1:26, NIV).
*To evangelize is to **disclose** God's plan to others.*

**175. Discuss.** '**Discussing** what "rising from the dead" meant' (Mark 9:10, NIV). 'A teacher of the Law was there who heard the **discussion**' (Mark 12:28, GNB). Jesus appeared to them '**discussing** the affairs of God's realm' (Acts 1:3, MB). Paul 'held dis-

cussions in the synagogue with the Jews and with the Gentiles' (Acts 17:17, GNB), '**discussions** with the Jews' (Acts 18:19, GNB). Paul 'had **discussions** daily in the lecture hall of Tyrannus' (Acts 19:8-9, NIV). The English word '**discuss**' was first recorded in the year 1607. In these 3 verses in Acts it translates the Greek verb *dialegomai*, which is there translated 'dispute' in AV/KJV, 'hold **discussions**' in GNB, and 'argue' in NRSV. **Discuss** is best regarded as a close synonym of the transliterated verb 'dialogue'.
*To evangelize is to **discuss** formally or informally.*

**177. Disseminate.** 'The third great missionary principle: God honors the **dissemination** of His word, and the preaching of Christ, as the chief means of conversion' (Henry Venn, 'A Sermon at the Consecration of Two Bishops', CMS London 1849). 'The printing press has greatly multiplied the power of the Church to **disseminate** Christian truth' (J.R. Mott 1900:113). 'Evangelism (*dendo*) is to **disseminate** news' (S. Saito in Mott 1938:43). 'Evangelism is to **disseminate** the good tidings' (S.H. Wainwright in Mott 1938:47). 'Evangelism: the **dissemination** of the gospel' (*New York Times everyday reader's dictionary of misunderstood, misused, and mispronounced words*, 2nd edition, 1985).
'**Dissemination**' is the process of spreading and dispersing seed on a wide scale. Thus the Parable of the Sower can also be regarded as the Parable of the Seed (emphasizing **dissemination**) or the Parable of the Four Soils (emphasizing where the seed falls): 'Some of the seed fell along the path, some on rocky ground, some among thorn bushes, some in good soil' (Luke 8:5-8, GNB); 'The seed is the word of God' (Luke 8:11, GNB).
*Being evangelized is having the gospel **disseminated** in a population. Evangelization is **dissemination** of the gospel.*

**178. Expose.** 'Expose', 'exposure' are used in RSV, GNB, NIV. 'Every one who does evil hates the light, and does not come to the light, lest his deeds should be **exposed**' (John 3:20, RSV). 'Evangelism means adequate **exposure** to Christ Himself, the Fact of Christ and the facts about Christ' (J.R. Mott 1939:61). During Taiwan's multimedia campaigns of 1975 'Knowing Jesus' and 1977 'The Gospel of Forgiveness', 'millions were **exposed** to the Christian message. Of the 16 million people in Taiwan, it is estimated that at least 10 million were **exposed** to the basic content of the theme'. 1975 research on Islam in Africa asked the question: 'What % of Muslims do you believe have been **exposed** to the gospel?' (G.O. Swank 1977: 1). '**Exposure**' was standard CCCI (Campus Crusade) usage in the 1970s: as a result of Here's Life Canada (1977), '50% of the Canadian population was **exposed**, in some way, to the claims of Christ'; 'We want every Christian to visualize the entire Philippines **exposed** to the claims of Christ by 1980'. 'Our marketing consultant estimated that 175 million people in the USA were **exposed** to the 'I found it!' campaign' (W.R. Bright 1979:172). After the 1979 Billy Graham campaign, 'There is hardly a Chinese in Singapore who has not been **exposed** to a considerable extent to the Gospel' (P.J. Johnstone 1979:pc).
*Being evangelized is being **exposed** to or by the gospel. Evangelization is **exposure** to or by the gospel.*

**179. Express.** 'Not in words taught us by human wisdom but in words taught by the Spirit, **expressing** spiritual truths in spiritual words' (1 Corinthians 2:13, NIV).
*To evangelize is to **express** the nature of the gospel to others.*

**180. Extol.** 'I will **extol** the Lord at all times' (Psalm 34:1, NIV).
*Evangelism should **extol** God's love for the lost and the unevangelized.*

**181. Foretell.** 'Dear friends, remember what the apostles of our Lord Jesus Christ **foretold**' (Jude 17, NIV).
*To evangelize includes **foretelling** the results of one's acceptance or rejection of the gospel.*

**182. Forewarn.** 'Forewarn' occurs only twice in AV/KJV. 'I will forewarn you' (Luke 12:5, AV/KJV).

*Being evangelized includes being **forewarned**. Evangelization involves a **forewarning** for hearers.*

**183. Further.** 'The things which happened unto me have fallen out rather unto the **furtherance** of the gospel' (Philippians 1:12, AV/KJV). 'To the happy **furtherance** of your faith' (Philippians 1:25, Knox). A book by Southern Baptist missiologist W.O. Carver, *The **furtherance** of the Gospel* (1935).
*To evangelize is to **further** the gospel.*

**184. Get.** This verb directly translates *euangelizo* in two NT versions: 'Those who formerly **got** the good news' (Hebrews 4:6, Moffatt); and, the Apostles 'then were right back at it again, **getting** out the Message' (Acts 14:7, The Message/NTCE). It is important for people to first **get** the gospel for themselves, and then to **get** it out to others.
*Evangelizing is **getting** the gospel out to others.*

**185. Give account.** 'Peter **gave** them a complete **account** of what had happened' (Acts 11:4, GNB). 'We must all **give** an **account** of ourselves' (Hebrews 4:13, GNB).
*Evangelization requires **accountability** and **accounting**.*

**186. Give evidence.** The living God 'has always **given evidence** of his existence by the good things he does' (Acts 14:17, GNB).
*To evangelize is to **give** people **evidence** of God's love and salvation.*

**188. Gossip.** This word is used in the Bible only negatively of destructive **gossip**. However, '**Gossip** the gospel' as a synonym for 'evangelize' is used in *Evanston speaks* (WCC 1954:29), and has been widely used subsequently to emphasize the importance of the daily chatting of ordinary Christians in routine situations. This unorganized, even unintentional, witness by the world's 1.9 billion church members may well be a far more potent evangelistic force than the organized proclamation of clergy and other Christian professionals.
*Evangelizing is **gossiping** the good news.*

**189. Hand down.** 'Just as they were **handed down** to us by those who from the first were eyewitnesses' (Luke 1:2, NIV). The Pharisees asked Jesus, 'Why is it that your disciples do not follow the teaching **handed down** by our ancestors?' (Mark 7:5, GNB).
*Evangelization involves the **handing down** of the gospel from one generation to the next.*

**190. Hand to.** Jesus 'took a cup, gave thanks to God, and **handed** it to them' (Mark 14:23, GNB).
*To evangelize is to **hand to** people the opportunity to hear the gospel.*

**191. Have for.** This phrase directly translates *euangelizo* in NEB: 'I **have** good news **for** you' (Luke 2:10, NEB, also CEV).
*Evangelizing is **having** news about God **for** people.*

**192. Hold.** 'You are saved by the gospel if you **hold** firmly to it' (1 Corinthians 15:2, GNB).
*To evangelize involves to **hold** on to essentials.*

**194. Illuminate.** 'After ye were **illuminated**' (Hebrews 10:32, AV/KJV). 'Dominus **illuminatio** mea' ('The Lord is my light', Psalm 27:1, Vulgate Bible, AD 404; motto of Oxford University Press founded in 1478). 'The light of Christ **illuminates** the whole world' (*Liturgy of the Presanctified*, AD 692; deathbed words of Marcarius Glukharev, Apostle to the Altai, 1792-1847). 'It is a general opinion among enlightened Christians, that this world is destined to be **illuminated** by the light of the gospel' (C. Adams 1850:17-19). The Second Vatican Council desired 'that through the preaching of the Gospel all people would be **illuminated** by the light of Christ that shines on the face of the Church' (Pope John Paul II, 13 November 1978).
*Being evangelized means being **illuminated** by the gospel. Evangelization is **illumination** by the gospel.*

**196. Inform.** 'Inform' is used in AV/KJV, RSV, GNB, et al. It also translates several NT Greek synonyms of *euangelizo*. 'The Jews are **informed** that thou teachest all to forsake Moses' (Acts 21:21,

AV/KJV). 'Felix, who was well-**informed** about the Way' (Acts 24:22, GNB).

**Information** is defined as 'something told; news; intelligence', as 'knowledge acquired in any manner; facts; data; 'learning', and as 'in **information** theory and computer science, a precise measure of the **information** content of a message' (WNWDAL). As such it is an important element in and dimension of evangelization.

*Being evangelized is being* **informed** *about the gospel. Evangelization is* **information** *about Christ and the gospel.*

197. **Introduce.** This word is used once to directly translate *euangelizo*, in Luke 16:16, LB: 'John **introduced** the Good News that the Kingdom of God would come soon.'

*Evangelizing is* **introducing** *the gospel to people, and people to the gospel.*

202. **Maintain.** 'For we **maintain** that a man is justified by faith apart from observing the law' (Romans 3:28, NIV).

*To evangelize is to* **maintain** *the truth of the gospel.*

203. **Make accessible.** 'Through Christ we have obtained **access** to this grace in which we stand' (Romans 5:2, RSV). 'The evangelization of the world in this generation involves such a distribution of missionary agencies as will **make** the knowledge of the Gospel **accessible** to all men' (J.R. Mott 1900:4-5). 'Evangelism is the proclaiming of the Gospel Message so that anyone who desires may have **access** to the plan of salvation' (S.A. Moffett in Mott 1938:48). The United Bible Societies 'exist for a single purpose, to **make** the Word of God **accessible** to all mankind' (UBS press release 'The Bible across Frontiers', Nairobi, March 1976).

*Being evangelized means having the gospel* **accessible.** *World evangelization means* **making** *the whole gospel* **accessible** *to the whole world.*

204. **Make aware.** 'I am always **aware** of the Lord's presence' (Psalm 16:8, GNB). 'Are you not **aware** of what the law says?' (Galatians 4:21, NIV). Research on Islam in Africa, 1975, asked the question: 'What % of Muslims do you believe have been exposed to the gospel in some way so that they are **aware** of it?' (G.O. Swank 1977: ). '**Awareness**' is a category frequently measured by CCCI (Campus Crusade): at end of Here's Life America campaign, 80% of the 85.6 million persons who were exposed to the 4-week media campaign became aware of what it referred to: 'At least 70% of the people surveyed in these cities were **aware** that what has been found was new life in Jesus Christ'; 'During the 1978 Here's Life Hong Kong campaign, 85% of the population were found to be **aware** of the 'I found it' phrase' (W.R. Bright 1977:63, et alia).

As a result of proclamation and parallel forms of evangelization, whole populaces become **aware** that the gospel exists and is influencing them and confronting them. Naturally, degrees of **awareness** vary greatly. Faced with the same exposure, some will remain virtually **unaware**, others will become **dimly-aware**, somewhat aware, half aware, or considerably aware, and still others will become **fully aware**. Such **awareness** in varying degrees of the realities of Christianity, Christ and the gospel, gradually extends into other areas too. Populations become **aware** also of the mission of Christ, the existence of disciples, the whole range of evangelizing activity including the making of disciples and the ongoing processes of discipling, baptizing and teaching. They become **aware** of the existence of martyria, kerygma, koinonia, diakonia, and the other key dimensions of evangelization.

In highly-literate and highly-informed non-Christian societies, large numbers of people **make** themselves **aware** of Christianity, Christ and the gospel through their own efforts, in particular through literature. Even anti-Christian polemic, though giving a distorted view, can fulfill this function.

**Awareness** of the existence and message of small groups can be very extensive today, no doubt due primarily to the mass media. Two newspaper polls in the British Isles illustrate this. In 1977 the number of charismatics was less than 1% of the total population. But in Ireland, when asked by a poll if they were **aware** of the Catholic Charismatic Renewal, 86% of the population replied Yes and 7% No; 20% liked it, 17% did not, 35% were undecided. In Britain that year, 82% replied Yes, 17% No; 17% reacted positively, 26% negatively. Under 1% were charismatics, but over 80% were **aware** that charismatics existed and were aware of what they stood for.

**Awareness** of many new forms of evangelization spreads extremely rapidly, sometimes overnight (due to television), throughout modern urbanized, industrialized, secularized populations.

*Evangelizing is* **making** *people* **aware** *of the gospel. Being evangelized is being* **aware,** *or becoming* **aware**, *or being* **made aware** *of the gospel. Evangelization is* **awareness** *of Christianity, Christ, and the gospel.*

205. **Make hear.** '**Hear**' is widely used throughout all versions, as e.g. Romans 10:17, RSV: 'Faith comes from what is **heard**, and what is **heard** comes by the preaching of Christ.' '**Hear**' also translates *euangelizo* and its NT Greek synonyms in NEB (Luke 7:22), GNB (Hebrews 4:2, 6), the latter also in NJB. 'The poor are **hearing** the good news' (Matthew 11:5, NEB). 'We have **heard** the Good News', and 'Those who first **heard** the Good News' (Hebrews 4:2,6, GNB). 'Let the Earth **hear** His Voice' (title of ICOWE, Lausanne 1974). 'There are millions who have never **heard** the good news' (WCC Nairobi, 1976:45). Aim of 1978 Nigeria Congress on Evangelization: 'That everybody may **hear** the Gospel clearly enough to understand sufficiently to make a decision'. 'How shall they **hear**?' (title of COWE, Thailand 1980).

The great Anglican evangelist George Whitefield had a massive 'organ-like' voice unexcelled in history. He could be **heard** miles away. 'Franklin, with customary exactness, computed that Whitefield could be **heard** by 30,000 people in the open air' at any one time. On one occasion Franklin mentally divided the audience by a grid and estimated its size at 35,000.

'**Hearing**' in biblical usage implies more than mere physical **hearing**. Isaiah was told by God, 'Go and say to this people, '**Hear** and **hear**, but do not understand' ' (Isaiah 6:9, RSV). In our contexts it means '**hearing** with understanding', implying a linguistically satisfactory message, with adequate (not necessarily perfect) communication. It also includes reading printed forms of preaching.

*Evangelizing is* **making** *others* **hear** *the gospel. Being evangelized is* **hearing**, *being* **made** *to* **hear**, *or having* **heard,** *the gospel. Evangelization is the* **hearing** *of the gospel.*

206. **Make known.** This term directly translates *euangelizo* 9 times in The Top 40 English versions: 'He **made** the good news of peace **known**' (Acts 10:36, AT/GB); '**making known** to the Gentiles' the unsearchable riches of Christ (Ephesians 3:8, Knox). It also translates several NT Greek synonyms of *euangelizo*; further, it occurs in RSV, GNB, NIV, etc. 'To **make** the word of God fully **known**' (Colossians 1:25, RSV). 'The revelation of the mystery which was kept secret for long ages... is now **made known** to all nations' (Romans 16:25-26, RSV). '...**make known** the gospel's secret' (Ephesians 6:19, GNB). In 1896, 'Half of the adult population of Manchuria **know** that there is a Christian Gospel... A third **know** enough to pronounce Christianity the best religion' (J.R. Mott 1900:83). 'The Church is confronted today with a literally worldwide opportunity to **make** Christ **known**' (World Missionary Conference, Edinburgh 1910.). 'To me evangelism is **making known** to men the good news' (W.M. Miller in Mott 1938:50). 'Evangelism is primarily **making known** the love of God' (P.O. Philip in Mott 1938:32). 'Evangelism means **making known** the love of God in Christ' (Bishop L.H. Roots in Mott 1938:14). 'Evangelism means to let others **know** the way and teachings of Jesus Christ' (S. Saito in Mott 1938:44). 'Evangelism includes all attempts to **make** the message of Christ **known**' (A.B. Van Doren in Mott 1938:35). 'Christ has commanded His Church to **make known** the Gospel and evangelism is obedience to this command' (*Nationwide Initiative in Evangelism*, Britain, 1979).

**Knowledge** is of 2 kinds: **knowledge** about something or someone, and **knowledge** of something or someone. The latter implies personal acquaintance and relationship. The world is moving towards a situation of global total or immediate **knowledge** in many subjects, including evangelization.

*To evangelize is* **to make** *the gospel* **known**. *Evangelizing is* **making** *the gospel* **known**. *Evangelization is* **knowledge** *of and about Christ and the gospel.*

208. **Mean.** Jesus asked the Emmaus road disciples, 'What do you **mean**?', then later said 'This is what I **mean** by saying '(Luke 24:19,44, NEB).

*To evangelize is to explain the* **meaning** *of Christ's sayings.*

209. **Mention.** 'Every time I pray, I **mention** you and give thanks to my God' (Philemon 4, GNB).

*To evangelize is to* **mention** *names for intercession.*

210. **Name.** 'To carry my **name** before the Gentiles' (Acts 9:15, NIV). 'To speak in the **name** of Jesus' (Acts 5:40, NIV). 'They were baptized in the **name** of the Lord Jesus' (Acts 19:5, GNB). Theological works: *No other name* (W.A. Visser't Hooft 1960). The essence of evangelism is '**Naming** the **Name**' of Jesus (Emilio Castro, WCC).

*To evangelize is to* **name** *the* **name** *of Jesus. Evangelizing is* **naming** *the Savior.*

211. **Narrate.** This verb or its cognates are not used in AV/KJV, GNB, NIV, or other versions. RSV has one usage, where Luke as author begins his gospel: 'Inasmuch as many have undertaken to compile a **narrative**' (Luke 1:1); and where NEB and REB have a similar usage 2 verses later where Luke states that he has 'decided to write a connected **narrative** for you' (Luke1:3, NEB), or 'to write an orderly **narrative**' (REB).

*To evangelize is to* **narrate** *the story of Jesus and his Good News.*

213. **Open.** 'Then **opened** he their understanding' (Luke 24:45, AV/KJV). 'You are to **open** their eyes and turn them from the darkness to the light and from the power of Satan to God' (Acts 26:18, GNB). Definition espoused by Emilio Castro, general secretary of the World Council of Churches 1983-92: 'Evangelism is our **opening** up the mystery of God's love to all people' (*A monthly letter about evangelism*, 12 (December 1977)).

*To evangelize is to* **open** *people's eyes.*

214. **Pass on.** To **pass** news **on,** or any other benefits or warnings, is a clear Christian duty. 'You must **pass on** to them the warnings I give you' (Ezekiel 33:7, GNB). 'He received God's living messages to **pass on** to us' (Acts 7:38, GNB). 'I **passed on** to you what I received' (1 Corinthians 15:3, GNB).

*Evangelizing is* **passing on** *the gospel.*

216. **Profess.** 'The gospel of Christ, which you **profess**' (2 Corinthians 9:13, GNB).

*To evangelize is to* **profess** *one's faith to unbelievers.*

217. **Propagate.** '**Propagate**' and cognates do not occur in AV/KJV, GNB, NIV. In 1622, the Sacred Congregation for the **Propagation** of the Faith (**Propaganda** Fide) was founded in Rome. In 1701, the Society for the **Propagation** of the Gospel in Foreign Parts (SPG) was founded in London. 'The **propagation** which keeps God's seed alive on the earth and eventually spreads that seed over the earth and subdues it, is evangelization' (A.T. Pierson 1888:22). '**Propagation** of the Christian faith' (J.R. Mott 1900:15). 'Evangelization is joyful **propaganda** in its best and widest sense, to present Jesus Christ' (P.A. Eakin in Mott 1938:57). 'Evangelism therefore means the **propagation** of the Gospel' (D. Webster 1959:76). Evangelization is '**propagation** of the faith, and also its perennial deepening and vitalization' (B. Haring 1974:43-4). 'Church-centred evangelism is concerned with **propagation** as well as with persuasion' (H.A. Snyder in Douglas 1975:331).

'**Propagating**' conveys the idea of the methods making up organized evangelism. 'The methods by which the early Church **propagated** the faith are described in the NT as kerussein, dialegesthai (discussion), and didaskein' (D.T. Niles 1955:3).

*To evangelize is to* **propagate** *the gospel. Evangelizing is* **propagating** *the gospel. Evangelization is* **propagation** *of the gospel.*

218. **Prophesy.** The term translates several NT Greek synonyms of *euangelizo*. 'My two witnesses shall **prophesy**' (Revelation 11:3, AV/KJV). 'The tes-

timony of Jesus is the spirit of **prophecy**' (Revelation 19:10, AV/KJV). 'To evangelize is more than **prophecy**, more than preaching the gospel. It is preaching the gospel with effect, with signs following' (M.A.C. Warren 1955:23). To prophesy in the New Testament is, primarily, to speak or preach in or under the power or influence of the Holy Spirit, and only secondarily to predict or foretell future events.

*To evangelize is to* **prophesy**. *Evangelizing is* **prophesying**. *Evangelization is* **prophecy**.

**219. Radiate.** 'Radiate' and cognates to not occur in AV/KJV or GNB. Many hymns include this theme: e.g. 'Christ, Whose glory fills the skies, Christ the true, the only Light... Fill me, **Radiancy** Divine... shining to the perfect day'. 'Great is the Lord; the royal city shines on all with **radiant** grace' (Hymn 93, paraphrase of Psalm 48, *Psalm praise*, 1973. 'Christ is the light of all nations. Hence this Synod eagerly desires to shed on all men that **radiance** of His which brightens the countenance of the Church. This it will do by proclaiming the gospel to every creature (cf. Mark 16:15)' (Vatican Council II, *Lumen Gentium* 1964:I.1, ed W.M. Abbott 1966:14-15). 'Christians **radiate** in an altogether simple and unaffected way their faith in values and their hope' (*Evangelii Nuntiandi* 1975, section 21). 'The family ought to be a place from which the Gospel **radiates**' (ibid, section 71).

**Radiation** is the process of emitting electromagnetic energy (heat, light, gamma rays, x-rays, etc). Some **radiation** (e.g. from x-ray machines, or nuclear power plants) can be beneficial to some people (patients, users of electricity) and yet at the same time be harmful, even lethal, to others. Evangelization can be compared to **radiation** and also to **radioactivity**, the property exhibited by certain types of matter that spontaneously emit energy and subatomic particles, which then can penetrate almost anything. Evangelii Nuntiandi speaks of the hidden energy of the Good News as that evangelical force (1975, section 4).

*To evangelize is to* **radiate** *the gospel. Evangelizing is* **radiating**. *Evangelization is* **radiation** *of the gospel.*

**221. Reckon.** Jesus' parable of the Unforgiving Servant begins by portraying the King as 'He began the **reckoning**' (i.e. calculated the sums of money owed to him; Matthew 18:24, NRSV). 'Reckon' is one of several mathematical terms used as near-synonyms around situations centering on evangelization: 'Let him who has understanding **reckon** the number of the beast' (Revelation 13:18, RSV).

*Evangelizing involves* **reckoning** *up the status of logistics, finance and other aspects of the context.*

**222. Recognize.** 'When they **recognize** the grace given' (Galatians 2:9, NIV). 'Recognition' is used in RSV.

The idea behind the statement 'Every tongue will confess that Jesus Christ is Lord' (Philippians 2:11) is not the mass or total conversion of the world to faith, but the mass **recognition** of Christ by the world. In India, for decades vast numbers of Hindus have **recognized** Jesus Christ as in some sense Saviour and Lord, without receiving baptism or becoming Christians. Our use of the term '**recognition**' here implies formal **recognition**.

*Being evangelized is* **recognizing** *Christ. Evangelization is bringing people, or being brought, to* **recognition** *of Christ.*

**223. Recommend.** 'I recommend to you our sister Phoebe' (Romans 16:1, GNB). 'Letters of **recommendation** to you' (2 Corinthians 3:1, NIV).

*Evangelizing is* **recommending** *Christ and his gospel.*

**224. Recount.** 'From generation to generation we will recount your praise' (Psalm 79:13, NRSV, NIV). The Greek verb here, *euangello*, is a near-synonym of *euangelizo*.

*To evangelize is to* **recount** *God's praises.*

**225. Relate.** This word directly translates *euangelizo* in the early Catholic Bible DRCB (1 Thessalonians 3:6), and also in HBME: '**relating** the good news of the kingdom' (Luke 8:1). Other usage: Mary Magdalene '**related** to them what he had told her' (John

20:18, GNB).

*To evangelize is to* **relate** *the story of the gospel.*

**227. Reply.** 'I know how to **reply**' (Job 20:3, GNB). *Evangelizers* **reply** *to requests about faith.*

**228. Report.** This verb is used to directly translate *euangelizo* in HBME (1903) and in 2 Catholic Bibles ( DRB and NAB) in translating 1 Thessalonians 3:6: 'Timothy has returned to us from you **reporting** the good news'. The usual Greek word for '**report**' is *anangello*, which is widely used in the NT interchangeably along with *angello* and *apangello*. The English word '**report**' and cognates are used 80 times in NRSV. With regard to Jesus, 'a **report** about him spread' (Luke 4:14, NRSV). 'They **reported** all that God had done with them' (Acts 15:4, NRSV).

*Evangelizing includes* **reporting** *on one's work. To evangelize is to* **report** *one's own experience of Christ.*

**229. Respond.** 'My people fail to **respond**' (Isaiah 50:2, GNB). 'The Lord opened her heart to **respond** to Paul's message' (Acts 16:14, NIV).

*Evangelizing is a wide-ranging process that includes* **response** *to the gospel.*

**230. Reveal.** 'Reveal' directly translates *euangelizo* in one version: 'All the plans he had **revealed** to his servants, the prophets' (**Revelation** 10:7, The Message/NTCE). It also translates several NT Greek synonyms of *euangelizo*. The word is widely used in AV/KJV, et alia. Indeed, the last book of the Bible is the Book of **Revelation**, in all English versions. 'The gospel **reveals** how God puts people right with himself' (Romans 1:17, GNB). 'Jesus Christ himself **revealed** the gospel to me' (Galatians 1:12, GNB). 'Christian evangelism to me is to allow oneself to be used as the Vehicle whereby the Holy Spirit **reveals** to others that Jesus Christ is the Son of God' (A.J. Elliott in Mott 1938:92). 'The gospel will be **revealed** to all' (WCC 2nd Assembly, *Evanston speaks*, 1954:41).

*To evangelize is to* **reveal** *Christ. Evangelizing is* **revealing** *Christ. Evangelization is* **revelation** *of Christ.*

**232. Say.** 'We are all here in the presence of God, waiting to hear anything that the Lord has instructed you to **say**' (Acts 10:33, GNB).

*To evangelize is to* **say** *to others 'God loves you'.*

**233. Scatter.** In the Parable of the Sower, 'He scattered the seed in the field' (Matthew 13:4, GNB); also, 'You gather crops where you did not **scatter** seed' (Matthew 25:24, GNB).

*Evangelizing is* **scattering** *seed.*

**235. Share.** 'Share' occurs in RSV, though not in AV/KJV. 'This I do for the gospel's sake, in order to **share** '(1 Corinthians 9:23, NIV). '**Sharers** together in the promise in Christ Jesus' (Ephesians 3:6, NIV). 'Evangelism is a passion to **share** Christ with others' (J.S. Ryang in Mott 1938:49). 'I would define evangelism as the **sharing** of one's deepest soul-transforming experiences of Jesus Christ with others' (M.T. Titus in Mott 1938:34, also L.A. Dixon in Mott 1938:91). *Good news to* **share** (D. Webster 1974). 'Evangelism is **sharing** this Gospel with others' (J.R.W. Stott in Anderson 1975:13). 'Evangelism means basically **sharing** the good news' (M. Wright 1976:1). 'Persuasion evangelism involves **sharing** Christ personally with individuals or small groups' (P. Means 1978). R. Pilkington, *How to evangelise the Jesus way: a practical handbook for* **sharing** *your faith* (1979). 'God is love' (1 John 4:16), and love always expresses itself by **sharing**.

*To evangelize is to* **share** *the gospel. Evangelizing is* **sharing** *the gospel. Evangelization is the* **sharing** *of the gospel.*

**236. Shine.** 'Shine' is used 22 times in AV/KJV. 'Your light must **shine** before people' (Matthew 5:16, GNB). 'John was like a lamp, burning and **shining**' (John 5:35, GNB). 'You must **shine** like stars lighting up the sky' (Philippians 2:15, GNB). 'After God's light had **shone** on you' (Hebrews 10:32, GNB). The image of light is widespread: 'I am the light of the world' (John 8:12, GNB). 'Jesus Christ the Light of the World' (title of WCC 3rd Assembly, New Delhi 1961). 'The evil god of the world keeps them from seeing the light **shining** on them, the light that comes from the Good News about the glory of

Christ' (2 Corinthians 4:4, GNB).

*To evangelize is to* **shine** *with the gospel. Evangelizing is* **shining**. *Evangelization means* **shining**.

**239. Sow.** The Parable of the **Sower** (Matthew 13, Mark 4, Luke 8): 'Once there was a man who went out to **sow** corn' (Mark 4:3, GNB); 'The **sower sows** God's message' (Mark 4:14, GNB). 'To evangelize is to **sow** and wait in respectful humility and in expectant hope' (J.C. Hoekendijk 1950:48).

The Parable of the **Sower** is a parable of evangelism, particularly of '**sowing** evangelism'. Since 1896, the figure of 'The **Sower**', taken from H. Thorneycroft's statue 'A **sower**' in Kew Gardens, London, has been used extensively by the British & Foreign Bible Society, and the United Bible Societies, as the leading symbol of their ministries.

*To evangelize is to* **sow** *the word. Evangelizing is* **sowing**. *Evangelization is the* **sowing** *of the gospel.*

**240. Speak.** 'Speak' is used a handful of times to directly translate *euangelizo*: Paul 'was heard to **speak** of 'Jesus' and 'the resurrection' ' (Acts 17:18, NAB). 'I may be bold in **speaking** about the gospel' (Ephesians 6:20, GNB). 'The Lord had **spoken** unto them' (Mark 16:19, AV/KJV).

*Evangelizing is* **speaking** *for Christ.*

**241. Speak in tongues.** Among the signs authenticating the preaching of the Great Commission are that believers 'will **speak in** strange **tongues**' (Mark 16:17, GNB); 'They will **speak in** new **tongues**' (NIV).

*Evangelizing often includes* **speaking in tongues**.

**242. Spread.** 'Spread' is used to directly translate *euangelizo* in NEB and REB (both in Acts 14:7, Romans 10:15), JB, BLE, NAB (Luke 9:6, Galatians 1:16), NTME (Luke 16:16), Knox (Luke 8:1, Acts 8:4), Weymouth (Acts 8:4), TLB (Acts 10:36), et alia. 'Spread' is used most often (21 times out of the NT's 54 uses of *euangelizo*) in the 1995 translation GW (God's Word to the Nations). It also translates other NT Greek synonyms of *euangelizo*. 'Spreading the word' (Acts 8:4, BLE). 'They continued to **spread** the good news' (Acts 14:7, NEB). 'The Good News which has reached you is **spreading** all over the world' (Colossians 1:6, JB). 'To **spread** the gospel' (Philippians 4:3, GNB).

The popes, fathers and scholastics often spoke of the *dilatio* (**spreading**) of the church: see Thomas Aquinas, Comm. in Matth. 16:28. 'Evangelism. Labours to **spread** the gospel' (Funk & Wagnalls Dictionary 1893). '**Spreading** the knowledge of the gospel' (J.R. Mott 1900:13). 'By Japanese Christians, dendo or evangelism is understood to mean **spreading**, making known, explaining the teachings of Jesus Christ' (S. Saito in Mott 1938:44). '**Spreading** the good news of Jehovah's Kingdom' (1960 Yearbook of Jehovah's Witnesses, 1959:46-7). 'Evangelism: the **spreading** of the gospel' (sole meaning given in Penguin English dictionary 1965). 'Evangelize. To **spread** the Christian gospel in' (Longmans English Larousse 1968). 'The ICI goal of **spreading** the gospel 'from all nations to all nations' is becoming a reality' (Assemblies of God USA, 1976). '**Spreading** God's love around the world' (25th anniversary motto, Campus Crusade for Christ International, 1976).

*To evangelize is to* **spread** *the gospel. Evangelizing is* **spreading** *the gospel. Evangelization is the* **spreading** *of the gospel.*

**243. Story.** 'This is the **story** of Noah' (Genesis 6:9, GNB). 'The Book of Kings contains the **stories** of the sons of Joash' (2 Chronicles 24:27, GNB). The swineherds 'went into the town, where they told the whole **story**' (Matthew 8:33, GNB). Except for this last reference, all biblical usages (GNB, NIV) use the word in its negative sense of either gossip, lies, or narratives of doubtful characters.

The relatively new missionary method of '**storying**', or 'telling the **story**', or simply narrating the Bible **story** beginning with Genesis, has gained popularity from 1990 onwards.

*Evangelizing is* **storying**. *Evangelization is telling the* **story** *of God and of Jesus.*

**245. Talk.** Use in the NT is widespread. '**Talk**' is frequently used to directly translate NT Greek synonyms of *euangelizo*. 'Jesus was **talking** to them about the Father' (John 8:27, GNB). 'He **talked** with them about the Kingdom of God' (Acts 1:3, GNB). Saul '**talked** and debated with the Grecian Jews' (Acts 9:29, NIV). 'Felix sent for Paul and listened to him as he **talked** about faith in Christ Jesus' (Acts 24:24, GNB). 'Evangelism means living, doing and **talking** for Christ' (S.B. Boon-Itt in Mott 1939:51).

*Evangelizing is **talking** for Christ.*

---

**246. Tell.** 'Tell' is the 3rd most frequently-used word to directly translate *euangelizo*, used in RSV, NEB, GNB, BLE, NIV, REB, CEV, GW, et alia. '**Telling** the good news' (Acts 5:42, NEB). 'He **told** him the gospel of Jesus' (Acts 8:35, BLE). 'We **tell** you the good news' (Acts 13:32, NIV). Other NT Greek words which are synonyms of *euangelizo* are also translated '**tell**' in AV/KJV, REV (many occurrences), et alia. 'Evangelise. To **tell** good tidings' (*A new English dictionary*, Oxford 1897). 'Evangelism is **telling** others of one's own experience' (S. Saito in Mott 1938:44). 'The fundamental meaning and aim of all evangelism (is) to **tell** the good news of Jesus in such a way as to elicit a response of faith' (D. Webster 1959:152). 'Evangelism is the **telling** of the facts about Jesus Christ and the stating of their implications for each man and for society' (J. Poulton 1973). 'To evangelize is to **tell** or to bring good news' (D. Webster 1974:6). 'Evangelism is the **telling** of what God has done for all men in Christ, in such a way that they will respond to him freely' (ibid:9). 'Evangelism is **telling** the story of Jesus' (Bishop D. Brown 1978:2).

'**Telling**' the gospel suggests ordinary, everyday converse with others, rather than special or formal occasions. It is similar to the phrase 'gossiping the gospel'.

*To evangelize is to **tell** the gospel to others. Evangelizing is **telling** good news. Evangelization is the **telling** of the gospel.*

---

**247. Testify.** 'Testify', 'testimony' and cognates occur 68 times in AV/KJV. 'John **testifies** concerning him' (John 1:15, NIV). 'This is the disciple who **testifies** to these things' (John 21:24, NIV). 'With great power the apostles continued to **testify** to the resurrection of the Lord Jesus' (Acts 4:33, NIV). '**Testifying** to the gift of God's grace' (Acts 20:24, NIV).

*To evangelize is to **testify** about Christ.*

---

**248. Throw a net.** This phrase is British usage; American usage is 'cast a net'. 'Fishermen throw their net out into the lake' (Matthew 13:47, GNB). 'Throw your net out on the right side of the boat, and you will catch some' (John 21:6, GNB).

*To evangelize is to **throw** one's **net** wide.*

---

**254. Witness.** 'Witness' and 'bear **witness**' are widely used, especially in Johannine writings, 60 times in AV/KJV. '**Witness**' also translates NT Greek synonyms of *euangelizo*. The noun *martyria* (**witness**) occurs 37 times in the Greek NT, or 73 times with all its cognates. 'It is you who are the **witnesses** to all this' (Luke 24:48, NEB). 'You will bear **witness** for me' (Acts 1:8, The Translator's NT). 'Having fully borne **witness** and spoken' (Acts 8:25, ENT). A simple translation into modern English would be: *martyreo* means 'to tell at cost'.

There has been widespread use from 13th-20th centuries. *Martyria* is 'the evangelistic **witness** to Christ's nature and significance, which aims at faith (TWNT 1933:IV,500). 'Evangelism is personal **witness**' (A. McLeish in Mott 1938:81). 'Evangelism is **witness** for Christ given by proclamation, fellowship and service' (IMC Willingen 1953). 'In the last analysis evangelism means personal **witness** to Jesus Christ' (D. Webster 1959:79-80). 'Evangelism is **witness** to Christ's saviourhood and lordship' (R.P. Beaver 1968:13). 'Evangelistic **witness** is first of all and primarily a confrontation of many by the message' (Orthodox Consultation, Bucharest, 1975:269). 'To evangelize is first of all to bear **witness**' (Evangelii Nuntiandi 1975, section 26). 'Evangelism is the Church's **witness** to Jesus Christ' (Anglican Consultative Council/ACC-3 Trinidad 1976:51). 'Christian **witness** is martyria... dangerous. Evangelism is the most risky job' (W. Hollenweger 1976:96). 'Evangelism as faithful **witness** to Jesus Christ' (M. Nash 1977:8). A.A. Trites, *The New Testament concept of **witness*** (Cambridge: Cambridge University Press,

1977). *Martyria/mission: the **witness** of the Orthodox churches today* (I. Bria 1980). *Common **witness*** (Joint Working Group RCC/WCC, 1980).

This documentation is major evidence of the shift from a strictly biblical definition of 'evangelize' to the far wider definition current in churches and agencies today.    Thus we note that the English word '**witness**' is not among the 40 macrotranslations of 'evangelize'/'evangelism' found in any of the range of 38 or so major English Bible versions. Nevertheless, many Christian authorities (as documented above) equate the two: 'Evangelism is **witness**', and 'To evangelize is first of all to bear **witness**.'

*To evangelize is to **witness** to Christ. Evangelizing is **witnessing**. Evangelization is **witness**.*

---

## IV. PROCLAIM!

The fourth Mandate covers the stage of organized, public evangelism. **Proclamation evangelization** means ordered, organized, public, professional endeavors to evangelize. For Christians its best-known variety is **Preaching evangelism,** with an organized, methodical sermon or talk or other formal presentation of the Christian gospel.

Of the 71 facets under this Mandate, 4 are in The Big Ten (*Announce! Declare! Preach! Proclaim!*).

---

**256. Acclaim.** Numbers 23:21 portrays Israel as having Yahweh '**acclaimed** as a king among them' (NRSV). The word '**acclaim**' signifies enthusiastic proclamation, 'to greet with loud approval; applaud; to announce or acknowledge with applause; hail' (*Webster's NWDAL*).

*To evangelize is to **acclaim** Christ as Lord.*

---

**257. Address.** Although entirely absent in AV/KJV, GNB-NT, and rarely present in NIV, the verb '**address**' is used on many key occasions in NEB (Matthew 5:2, 9:6, 23:1, 23:7, 28:5, Luke 7:1, 23:20, John 8:12, Acts 2:14, 4:1, 15:7, 19:25, 20:7, 21:40, Romans 3:19, 1 Corinthians 14:28, 34, 35, 2 Corinthians 1:18, 5:11, 7:14, 12:19, Hebrews 12:5, 1 John 5:13), and in most of these also in REB. 'Jesus then **addressed** the crowds' (Matthew 23:1, REB), Peter '**addressed** them' (Acts 2:14, NEB), Paul '**addressed** them in the Jewish language' (Acts 21:40, NEB, REB).

*Evangelizing is **addressing** the crowds with the gospel.*

---

**258. Advertise.** 'I will **advertise** thee' (Numbers 24:14, AV/KJV, also ASV). '**Advertise! Advertise! Advertise** the King and his Kingdom' (J.F. Rutherford, head of Jehovah's Witnesses from 1917–1942, at Cedar Point, Ohio, International convention in 1922).

*To evangelize is to **advertise** the gospel.*

---

**259. Alert.** 'Be **alert**, be on the watch!' (1 Peter 5:8, GNB).

*Evangelizing is **alerting** people to spiritual realities. Evangelism requires being continually on the **alert**.*

---

**260. Announce.** 'Announce' is the 5th most frequently-used word to directly translate *euangelizo* in RSV and GNB; also used in NEB, BLE (but not AV/KJV). '**Announce**' also translates several NT Greek synonyms of *euangelizo*. 'We are here to **announce** the Good News' (Acts 14.15, GNB). 'They **announced** the Good News by the power of the Holy Spirit' (1 Peter 1:12, GNB). 'Another angel... with an eternal message of Good News to **announce** to the peoples of the earth' (Revelation 14:6, GNB).

An early meaning of the Greek word *euangelismos*, and the exclusive meaning of the modern Greek word *evangelismos* today, is for the **Annunciation** of the Virgin Mary by the archangel Gabriel (see Luke 1:28). 'Evangelize. To **announce** the good news' (*The Century dictionary* 1889). 'Evangelize. To **announce** glad tidings to' (*A new English dictionary*, Oxford 1897). 'Evangelism is the **announcement** of the good news' (E.K. Higdon in Mott 1938:56). 'Evangelism is the **announcement** of the Gospel message' (L.G. Paik in Mott 1938:48). 'Evangelism is **announcing** Jesus Christ yesterday, today, and tomorrow' (E. Castro 1968:149). 'True evangelism takes place wherever there is the **announcement** of the good news' (H. Maurier 1968:233). 'The word 'evangelism' should be restricted in meaning to **announcing** the

message of salvation' (Evangelical Alliance of Great Britain, *On the other side*, 1968:61). 1975, Paul VI's Apostolic Exhortation Evangelii Nuntiandi (**Announcing** the Gospel).

To '**announce**' is to declare especially for the first time (D. Webster 1973); it suggests a formal or official occasion.

*To evangelize is to **announce** the gospel. Evangelizing is **announcing** the gospel. Evangelization is the **announcement** of the gospel.*

---

**261. Argue.** On Paul in Jewish synagogues: 'He **argued** with them' (Acts 17:2, RSV, NRSV), he '**argued** persuasively about the kingdom of God' (Acts 19:8-9, NRSV). '**Argue**' is a close synonym of 'discuss' and 'dispute'.

*Evangelizing may with profit engage in **arguing** one's case.*

---

**262. Blanket.** 'During the year 1976, God's message of love and forgiveness **blanketed** Kerala', '**blanketing** Kerala with the claims of Jesus Christ' (W.R. Bright 1977:154).

*Evangelization includes **blanketing** whole populations.*

---

**265. Confer.** This word has 2 distinct shades of meaning. 'He found the army officers in a **conference**' (2 Kings 9:5, GNB). Jesus said, 'I **confer** on you a kingdom' (Luke 22:29, NIV). '**Conferring** with his advisers' (Acts 25:12, GNB). The word normally means (1) give, grant, bestow, or (2) talk, discuss, converse. All of these play a role in evangelization.

*The evangelist **confers** with those he meets in order to, if possible, **confer** faith on them.*

---

**266. Contend.** '**Contend** for the faith' (Jude 3, NIV).

*To evangelize is to **contend** for the faith with any adversaries.*

---

**270. Debate.** Saul '**talked** and **debated** with the Grecian Jews' (Acts 9:29, NIV). 'This brought Paul and Barnabas into sharp dispute and **debate** with them' (Acts 15:2, NIV). Apollos 'vigorously refuted the Jews in public **debate**' (Acts 18:28, NIV).

*Evangelizing includes formal **debating** with opponents.*

---

**271. Declare.** 'Declare' is the 6th most frequently-used direct translation for *euangelizo* in English versions, and is widely used in DB, AV/KJV, RSV, NWT, NEB, et alia. One version, the New World Translation (1961, Jehovah's Witnesses' official Bible) translates 52 of the Greek NT's 54 occurrences of *euangelizo* by the single translation '**declare**'. '**Declare**' also translates other NT Greek synonyms of *euangelizo*. 'We **declare** unto you glad tidings' (Acts 13:32, AV/KJV). 'They **declared** all that God had done with them' (Acts 14:27, RSV). 'Evangelism **declares** that salvation through Christ is available' (J.M. Springer in Mott 1938:62). 'To evangelize is to **declare** this hope to the world until the consummation of the Kingdom and the coming of the King' (WCC 2nd Assembly, *Evanston speaks*, 1954:41).

*To evangelize is to **declare** the gospel. Evangelizing is **declaring** the gospel. Evangelization is **declaration** of the gospel.*

---

**273. Defend.** The key words are *apologia* (Greek for 'defense') and *apologeisthai* ('speak in one's defense'), which occur in Acts 19:33 and 22:1 respectively: Paul said 'Hear ye my **defense**' (Acts 22:1, AV/KJV). 'I was free to **defend** the gospel' (Philippians 1:7, GNB). 'I am put here for the **defense** of the gospel' (Philippians 1:16, NIV) or '**defending** the gospel' (GNB).

There is considerable extra-biblical usage. Apologetics is defined as 'systematic argumentative tactics or discourse in defense of the Christian faith against outside criticism' (Webster's 1971), 'the **defense** of the Christian faith on intellectual grounds' (Oxford dictionary of the Christian Church, 1957). Historically, apologetics 'began with the presentation of the case for Christianity to non-Christians by the 2nd-century Apologists' (ibid). See also *A history of apologetics* (A. Dulles 1971). 'Evangelization must include the willingness to take up the work of apologetics' (K. Hamilton, 'Apologetics and evangelization', in Douglas 1975:1202). 'Apologetics is not the same as evangelism, yet it should not be separated from the evangelistic task' (W.S.C. Tyndale, 'Apologetics in evangelism report', in Douglas 1975:1203).

*To evangelize is to defend the gospel. Evangelization is the defense of the gospel.*

**274. Demonstrate.** Jesus 'showed Himself alive after His passion by many convincing **demonstrations**' (Acts 1:3, AB). '**Demonstration**' has one occurrence in AV/KJV, RSV: 'My speech and my message were in **demonstration** of the Spirit and power' (2 Corinthians 2:4, RSV). 'Christian faith will **demonstrate** its world-conquering power' (J.H. Oldham in *IRM* 1912:8). 'Evangelism means doing for Christ, the work of **demonstration** such as medical work, nursing and social uplift' (S.B. Boon-Itt in Mott 1938:51). 'The emerging pattern of evangelism is: In proclamation, fellowship and service, the Church must **demonstrate** the Gospel in the actual life context of men' (WCC, *Evangelism*, 1954:59). 'The proclamation of the gospel must be accompanied by the **demonstration** of its transforming power' (WCC 2nd Assembly, *Evanston speaks*, 1954:40). 'Evangelization is the **demonstration** and communication of God's love and salvation in Jesus Christ for the wholeness of man and creation' (UTC Bangalore 1974). 'Evangelization is proclamation of the gospel accompanied by **demonstration** of the power of the Holy Spirit in deeds and signs and acts' (D. Watson 1976:26-31, J.C. Hoekendijk 1972).

*To evangelize is to demonstrate the gospel to people. Evangelizing is demonstrating the gospel. Evangelization is the demonstration of the gospel.*

**277. Discourse.** The word implies a lengthy address or addresses. 'When Jesus had finished this **discourse**' (Matthew 7:28, NEB; also 19:1, 26:1). 'But when (Paul's) **discourse** turned to questions of morals, self-control, and the coming judgment, Felix became alarmed' (Acts 24:25, NEB).

*Evangelism often produces lengthy discourses.*

**278. Dispute.** Saul 'also talked and **disputed** with the Greek-speaking Jews' (Acts 9:29, GNB). 'This brought Paul and Barnabas into sharp **dispute** and debate with them' (Acts 15:2, NIV).

*Evangelizing involves disputing where necessary.*

**282. Exalt.** Evangelization requires the **exaltation** of the central Christian verities—God, Christ, sin, the Cross, salvation.

*To evangelize is to exalt God and Christ.*

**283. Expound.** 'He **expounded** all things to his disciples' (Mark 4:34, AV/KJV). 'Peter **expounded** it unto them' (Acts 11:4, AV/KJV). J.R. Mott characterized societies for diffusing Christian literature as '**expounding** the Gospel through a wide range of printed works' (J.R. Mott 1900:122).

*To evangelize is to expound the gospel.*

**284. Familiarize.** 'Evangelism denotes efforts to bring home the gospel to those who are **unfamiliar** with it' (R. Rouse 1967:807). 'Evangelism is the proclamation of the gospel to those who are **unfamiliar** with it' (S.C. Neill 1970:199).

*Being evangelized is becoming familiarized with the gospel. Evangelization is familiarization with the gospel.*

**285. Fill.** Widespread use in NT. 'You have **filled** Jerusalem with your teaching' (Acts 5:28, NIV). 'We are but of yesterday, and we have **filled** every place among you—cities, islands, fortresses, towns, market-places, the very camp, tribes, companies, palace, senate, forum' (Tertullian, *Apology* xxxvii, AD 197). 'It seems entirely possible to **fill** the earth with the knowledge of Christ before the present generation passes away' (J.R. Mott 1900:128); 'to **fill** the whole world with the knowledge of Christ in this generation' (closing phrase of J.R. Mott's *The evangelization of the world in this generation*, 1900:210).

*Evangelization fills the world with the knowledge of God's love.*

**287. Give a message.** 'The same Spirit **gives** a message full of knowledge' (1 Corinthians 12:8, GNB). 'He has **given** us the **message**' (2 Corinthians 5:19, GNB). 'The **message given** to our ancestors by the angels' (Hebrews 2:2, GNB).

*To evangelize is to give a message.*

**288. Give chance.** The idea of **chance** is raised several times in the context of proclaiming the gospel. A clear statement from the Old Testament comes in Elihu's words to Job: 'God **gives** each of us **chance** after **chance** to be saved from death and brought into the light that gives life' (Job 33:29-30, CEV). Also in the New Testament: 'This will be your **chance** to tell the Good News' (Luke 21:13, GNB). 'They did not even have a **chance** to eat' (Mark 6:31, NIV). In one case 'have a **chance**' directly translates *euangelizo* and its meaning: 'Yet the promise remains and some get in—but not those who had the first **chance**, for they disobeyed God' (Hebrews 4:6, TLB). 'Evangelization is an honest endeavor to **give** everyone a **chance** to hear about and to accept Jesus Christ' (Bishop J. Chitamber in Mott 1938:17). 'Evangelism I would define as **giving** the individual a fair **chance** to know and accept for himself Jesus Christ' (A.K. Reischauer in Mott 1938:43). 'Evangelized: to have had a real **chance** to intelligently decide to become responsible members of Christ's Church' (E. Pentecost 1974:xi).

*Evangelizing is giving others a chance to hear of salvation.*

**289. Give notice.** Paul 'went to the temple to **give notice** of the date when the days of purification would end' (Acts 21:26, NIV).

*Evangelists give notice of God's offer of salvation and that it does not extend indefinitely.*

**290. Give opportunity.** '**Opportunity**' is used 5 times in AV/KJV, and more in other versions. '...to **give** the people of Israel the **opportunity** to repent and have their sins forgiven' (Acts 5:31, GNB). 'The whole world is now having an **opportunity** of hearing' (Colossians 1:23, NTME). 'It may be that God will **give** them the **opportunity** to repent and come to know the truth' (2 Timothy 2:25, GNB). 'The evangelization of the world in this generation means the **giving** to all men an adequate **opportunity** of knowing Jesus Christ' (J.R. Mott 1900:4-5). 'To **give** every man the **opportunity** of hearing the Gospel in his own tongue' (J.G.K. Harman 1936:13). 'Evangelism is the work which aims at **giving** men an **opportunity** to know the Gospel of Christ' (L.P. Larsen in Mott 1938:73). 'By 'evangelize' we mean that every soul should have a reasonable **opportunity** of hearing the Gospel' (L. Brierley 1944:35). 'An area is unevangelized when its people have no **opportunity** to hear the gospel' (D.A. McGavran in S.C. Neill et al, *Concise dictionary of the Christian world mission*, 1970:616). 'To evangelize means to meet people in situations where the Gospel of Jesus Christ is **given** the **opportunity** to change individuals and groups' (M.E. Marty 1975:77). The purpose of evangelization is 'to **give** individuals and groups a valid **opportunity** to accept or reject Jesus Christ' (LCWE Bermuda 1978). 'The aim of this campaign is that everyone in our country should have the **opportunity** to become a Christian by the end of 1980' (Operation Good News, Nigeria, 1978-80).

*To evangelize is to give people the opportunity to accept Christ. Evangelization is giving people the opportunity to accept Christ.*

**291. Herald.** Although the word *kerusso* ('herald') is the closest NT Greek synonym to *euangelizo*, '**herald**' is used only rarely in English Scripture, and only as a noun. 'Of this gospel I was appointed a **herald**' (2 Timothy 1:11, NIV). A major classic on the art of public preaching is J.S. Stewart, *Heralds of God*, 1946. On one occasion the word directly translates the verb *euangelizo*: 'I saw another angel flying in midheaven, the **herald** of everlasting good news to the whole world' (Revelation 14:6, NAB).

*To evangelize is to herald the good news. Evangelization is working as a herald.*

**292. Interpret.** 'Another has the gift of ecstatic utterance of different kinds, and another the ability to **interpret** it' (1 Corinthians 12:10, NEB).

*Evangelizing is interpreting the gospel.*

**295. Lecture.** Paul 'had discussions daily in the lecture hall of Tyrannus' (Acts 19:9, NIV).

*Evangelization may include formal lecturing in public.*

**296. Lift.** Jesus 'lifted him to his feet' (Mark 9:27,

NIV). 'The Son of Man must be **lifted up**' (John 3:14, NIV). 'When you have **lifted up** the Son of Man, then you will know that I am the one' (John 8:28, NIV). '**Lift up** their hands in prayer' (1 Timothy 2:8, GNB).

*Evangelization lifts up every aspect of human life.*

**297. Make a speech.**

*Evangelizing involves making speeches as occasion arises.*

**298. Make clear.** The term is used once to directly translate *euangelizo*, in the Basic Bible: 'So that I might **make clear** to the Gentiles the good news of the unending wealth of Christ' (Ephesians 3:8, BBE). Other usages: 'We have **made** this **clear** to you at all times' (2 Corinthians 11:6, GNB). 'To those who were to receive what he promised, God wanted to make it very **clear** that he would never change his purpose' (Hebrews 6:17, GNB).

*Evangelizing is making clear what the gospel is.*

**299. Make evident.** 'At least believe on the **evidence** of the miracles themselves' (John 14:11, NIV). Barnabas 'saw the **evidence** of the grace of God' (Acts 11:23, NIV). 'Let your gentleness be **evident** to all ' (Philippians 4:5, NIV).

*Evangelizing is making the gospel evident.*

**300. Make listen.** '**Listen**' is used to directly translate *euangelizo* in several versions: '**Listening** to him go on about Jesus and the resurrection' (Acts 17:18, The Message/NTCE), also in AV/KJV, GNB, et al. 'Not everyone, of course, **listens** to the Good News' (Romans 10:16, JB). 'Felix sent for Paul and **listened** to him as he talked about faith in Christ Jesus' (Acts 24:24, GNB). **Listening** requires or means more than hearing, since it implies careful attention being given to messenger and message.

*Being evangelized is listening, or having listened, to the gospel. Evangelizers make people listen to the gospel. Evangelization is listening to the gospel.*

**302. Notify.** '**Notify**' translates several NT Greek synonyms of *euangelizo*. '**Notify**' is not used in English NT, but only in OT: 'We **notify** you that it shall not be lawful to impose tribute' (Ezra 7:24, RSV).

One '**notifies**' a person of something when one sends a **notice** of formal communication or legal advice concerning it, as a matter requiring his attention (Webster's 1973:443). The concept '**notification**' here as a dimension of evangelization covers the idea that healings, signs and miracles—whether performed by Jesus in his ministry or by the church after Pentecost—were selective occasions intended to be signs for those in process of being evangelized. The idea is conveyed in Mark 16:20, GNB: 'The Lord worked with them and proved that their preaching was true by the miracles that were performed'.

*Being evangelized is being notified. Evangelization is notification.*

**303. Preach.** In 1382, the first English Bible was produced. It transliterated the NT Greek verb *euangelizo* by means of Wycliffe's neologism 'euangelisen'; but in the revised Bible of 1395, Wycliffe's disciples replaced it everywhere by '**preche**' (**preach**), or occasionally 'schew' (show). Since then '**preach**' has become by far the most widespread single word used in English versions to directly translate *euangelizo*. It also translates its major synonym *kerusso* and a number of other synonyms, in DB, AV/KJV, RSV, NEB, GNB, NIV, et alia. This situation was recognized in 'Evangelize. To **preach** the Gospel' (*A new English dictionary*, Oxford 1897). '**Preach**' is also the first meaning given in the majority of modern dictionaries, and in widespread ecclesiastical usage. 'To me evangelism means the **preaching** of the Gospel' (J.J. Banninga in Mott 1938:16). 'Evangelism is the **preaching** of the Good News' (Bishop F.L. Norris in Mott 1938:14). 'Evangelism is the **preaching** of the Christian Gospel by words' (Bishop C.P. Wang in Mott 1938:16).

British theologian and bishop D. Jenkins (1978:115) has drawn attention to the disadvantages of using the word '**preach**' to translate *euangelizo* in the anti-preaching cultures of Europe where **preaching** is discredited. Elsewhere, this is not the case. For the Coptic Orthodox Church, this method of evangelism dignifies the title of pope Shenouda III's weekly 30,000-copy evangelistic newspaper Mega-let el-Kiraza (literally, The **Preaching** of the Word), based on his Bible studies before 8,000 hearers in St Mark's Cathedral, Cairo, every Friday evening from 1964 into the 1990s. This also illustrates that '**preach**' is not tied to only the spoken word, but includes the written word as well.

*To evangelize is to* **preach** *the gospel. Evangelizing is* **preaching** *the gospel. Evangelization is the* **preaching** *of the gospel.*

**304.  Predict.** 'What the prophet had **predicted** long before' (2 Kings 23:16, GNB). 'Come here and **predict** what will happen' (Isaiah 41:22, GNB). 'Agabus stood up and by the power of the Spirit **predicted** that a severe famine was about to come over all the earth' (Acts 11:28, GNB). The Spirit of Christ '**predicted** the sufferings of Christ and the glories that would follow' (1 Peter 1:11, NIV). 'The Scriptures **predicted** the condemnation they have received' (Jude 4, GNB).

*Evangelizing includes* **predicting** *aspects of the gospel and its reception.*

**305.  Present.** The verb directly translates *euangelizo* on one occasion: 'I **presented** to you the good news' (1 Corinthians 15:1, Goodspeed). The verb 'to **present**' is further used in all NT versions. To his apostles Jesus '**presented** himself alive after his passion by many proofs' (Acts 1:3, RSV). 'May we know what this new teaching is that you are **presenting**?' (Acts 17:19, NIV). In subsequent writing, there has been exceptionally wide recent usage. 'Evangelization is the **presenting** of the Gospel' (SVMU in E. Stock 1899:III.656). 'Preached in such a manner as will constitute an intelligent and intelligible **presentation** of the message' (J.R. Mott 1900:7). 'To evangelise is so to **present** Christ Jesus in the power of the Holy Spirit, that men shall come to put their trust in God through Him' (Archbishops' Inquiry 1918). 'Evangelism signifies to me the art of **presenting** Christ the Redeemer' (A.E. Harper in Mott 1938:18). 'Evangelism is the endeavor to **present** the Gospel' (H. Kramer in Mott 1938:72). 'Evangelism means to me essentially the **presentation** of the Christian message to men and women' (K.S. Latourette in Mott 1938:97). 'The process of **presenting** the challenge of Christ' (E.H. Munson in Mott 1938:13). 'Evangelism involved the **presentation** of the truth about Christ' (Bishop J.W. Pickett in Mott 1938:33). 'Evangelism is the **presentation** of the truth and life of Christianity both by word and by deed' (R.E. Speer in Mott 1938:103). 'To me evangelism is the task of **presenting** the whole Christian Gospel, by word and deed' (Bishop P.L. Tsen in Mott 1938:15). 'Evangelism is the **presentation** of the Evangel' (R.P. Wilder in Mott 1938:105). 'Evangelism is the **presentation** of the Good News of God in Jesus Christ' (IMC Tambaram 1938). 'Evangelism is the proclamation and **presentation** of the good news of God in Jesus Christ' (WCC Geneva 1947, IMC Whitby 1947). 'Evangelism is all the forms of **presenting** Christ and the Church to non-Christian societies from the first encounter until baptism' (J. Masson 1968:131ff). 'There must be **presentation**, penetration and saturation' (G.W. Peters 1970:30). 'Evangelization is the intelligible, attractive, meaningful, purposeful and persuasive **presentation** of the Gospel' (G.W. Peters 1972:210). Evangelization is 'not communication of meaningful information about salvation but its **presentation** by the community of believers through liturgy' (Orthodox Consultation, Bucharest 1974). 'Evangelism is the process of **presenting** the Gospel' (D.A. McGavran 1977:pc). 'At least one out of two persons would receive Christ this very moment if they could hear a simple, clear-cut **presentation** of the gospel' (W.R. Bright 1977:134).

'**Presenting**' the gospel is a very specific act, limited in scope to a particular time, place, evangelizer, group or individual. It is a specific application of 'evangelizing'. Jesus himself sent new believers to give immediate **presentations** of himself and his deeds (such as the blind man sent to the Pharisees).

*To evangelize is to* **present** *the gospel. Evangelizing is* **presenting** *Christ. Evangelization is the* **presentation** *of the gospel.*

**306.  Proclaim.** 'Proclaim' is the 4th most frequently-used word to directly translate *euangelizo* in English NTs. Used twice in AV/KJV, more widely is RSV (41 times), NEB, GNB, NIV. '**Proclaiming** the good news' (Luke 8:1, NEB). 'Go and **proclaim** the kingdom of God' (Luke 9:60, GNB). '**Proclaim**' also translates several NT Greek synonyms of *euangelizo*, notably its major synonym *kerusso*. The verb *kerusso* (herald, **proclaim**) occurs 60 times in the Greek NT, the noun *kerygma* (the preaching or **proclamation**) 8 times, and *kerux* (preacher) 3 times. It is also widespread in more recent usage. 'Evangelize. To **proclaim** the Gospel' (*A new English dictionary*, Oxford 1897). '*Euangelizesthai* is the powerful **proclamation** of the good news' (G. Friedrich in Kittel, *TWNT* 1938, English translation *TDNT* 1964:II.720). 'The **proclamation** of the evangel is evangelism' (Bishop V.S. Azariah in Paton 1938). 'I would define evangelism as a **proclamation** of the Gospel' (Sherwood Eddy in Mott 1938:91). 'Evangelism is the **proclaiming** of the Gospel Message' (S.A. Moffett in Mott 1938:48). 'Evangelism means to me primarily the **proclamation** of the Good News' (D.T. Niles in Mott 1938:32). 'To evangelize is to **proclaim** good news to men in such a way as to elicit the response of acceptance' (M.A.C. Warren 1955:23). 'Evangelism is the **proclaiming** of the Gospel, particularly to those who have not heard it, or who have not understood it, or who have not responded to it, or who have forgotten it' (D. Webster 1974:7). 'Evangelism itself is the **proclamation** of the historical, biblical Christ as Saviour and Lord, with a view to persuading people to come to him' (ICOWE, *Lausanne Covenant* 1974, section 4). 'We are commissioned to **proclaim** the Gospel of Christ to the ends of the earth' (WCC 6th Assembly, Nairobi 1975, Section I).

Proponents of the centrality of '**proclamation**' in evangelism should never be caricatured as interpreting evangelism to mean 'merely the verbal and propositional communication of the gospel.' The concept implies full communication in all its aspects.

*To evangelize is to* **proclaim** *the gospel. Evangelizing is* **proclaiming** *the gospel. Evangelization is* **proclamation** *of the gospel.*

**307.  Promise.** The verb is used to directly translate *euangelizo* 6 times in the 1903 version HBME (see Table 17–6 for locations); and also in Revelation 10:7 in 2 major Bible versions: 'As he **promised** to his servants the prophets' (NEB, REB). The verb also occurs more generally elsewhere: 'He **promised** through his holy prophets long ago' (Luke 1:70, GNB). 'I send the **promise** of my Father upon you' (Luke 24:49, AV/KJV). 'The Good News was **promised** long ago' (Romans 1:2, GNB). 'Sent to proclaim the **promised** life' (2 Timothy 1:1, GNB).

*Evangelizing is* **promising** *hearers that the gospel is for them and applies to them.*

**308.  Promulgate.** 'Evangelism. The **promulgation** of the blessed gospel' (Dr Samuel Johnson's *Dictionary*, 1755).

*To evangelize is to* **promulgate** *the Good News.*

**309.  Prove.** Paul in the synagogue 'held discussions with the people, quoting and explaining the Scriptures and **proving** from them that the Messiah had to suffer' (Acts 17:2-3, GNB). 'The Lord worked with them and **proved** that their preaching was true by the miracles that were performed' (Mark 16:20, GNB). Jesus showed himself alive 'by many infallible **proofs**' (Acts 1:3, AV/KJV). 'With convincing **proof** of the power of God's Spirit' (1 Corinthians 2:4, GNB).

*Evangelizing involves* **proving** *the truth of the gospel.*

**311.  Publish.** The word first appeared as a direct translation of *euangelizo* in the Geneva Bible of AD 1560: 'He himself went through everie citie and towne, preaching, and **publishing** the kingdome of God' (Luke 8:1). '**Publish**' also occurs 7 times in AV/KJV. 'The gospel must first be **published** among all nations' (Mark 13:10, AV/KJV). 'The word of the Lord was **published** throughout all the region' (Acts 13:49, AV/KJV). Also used in ABUV (1863: Acts 11:20), Conybeare (1 Corinthians 1:17), GNB, NIV. '**Publishers**' is the official term used by Jehovah's Witnesses for ordinary, active, baptized church members in their work of evangelistic witness. Detailed statistics are kept of this category and are **published** annually.

*To evangelize is to* **publish** *good news.*

**313.  Read.** Of the Ethiopian eunuch: 'Seated in his chariot, he was **reading** the prophet Isaiah' (Acts 8:28, RSV).

*Evangelizing for many people centers on* **reading** *about, or* **reading** *to others about, the gospel.*

**314.  Reason.** 'Reason' translates several NT Greek synonyms of *euangelizo*, especially *dialegomai, -esthai*, meaning to speak alternately or converse in discussion (from which the Greek noun *dialogos* and the English noun 'dialogue' are derived). The word occurs 21 times in AV/KJV. 'As Paul **reasoned**, Felix trembled' (Acts 24:25, AV/KJV). 'To preach the gospel: to **reason** or discuss' (J.R. Mott 1900:6). 'The methods by which the early Church propagated the faith are described in the NT as *kerussein*, *dialegesthai* (discussion), and *didaskein*' (D.T. Niles 1955:3).

*To evangelize is to* **reason** *with people about the gospel. Evangelization is* **reasoning** *with people about the gospel.*

**316.  Refute.** Apollos 'vigorously **refuted** the Jews in public debate' (Acts 18:28, NIV). An elder/overseer/bishop must '**refute** those who oppose' the gospel (Titus 1:9, NIV).

*Evangelization may involve* **refutation.**

**319.  Saturate.** 'Saturate' is not used in AV/KJV, RSV, GNB, NIV, or other major versions. There is however considerable recent usage in other literature. 'The International Missionary Council believes that every part of the Christian enterprise must be **saturated** with and controlled by the conscious evangelistic purpose' (*Evangelism*, IMC 1939:423). The term '**Saturation** evangelism' came into use in the 1960s together with 'evangelism-in-depth' and 'total mobilization evangelism'. G.W. Peters in *Saturation evangelism* (1970) has a detailed bibliography of 270 books and articles on the subject (covering Evangelism-in-Depth, New Life for All, et alia). '**Saturate**' is mainly used to describe the results of mass-evangelism organizations such as CCCI (Campus Crusade): 'To **saturate** the Philippines with the claims of Christ', 'to **saturate** Burma with the gospel by 1980'. P. Eshleman in 'What is **saturation**?' (CCCI 1974) considers a campus **saturated** when 70% of all staff and students have heard the gospel, 1% have become active disciples, and 0.1% have vocations to full-time service. 'You cannot **saturate** Pakistan or anywhere else with radio with one or two short programs a week... No people of the earth can be **saturated** with the Gospel unless every means is being used' (P. Booth, Radio Worldwide/WEC, 1979).

*To evangelize is to* **saturate** *with the gospel. Evangelizing involves* **saturating.** *Evangelization means* **saturation** *with or by the gospel.*

**321.  Shout.** This word implies a sudden, loud outburst of feeling and emotion, and so occurs throughout the OT and NT (165 times in NRSV, 236 times in GNB, etc). Isaiah 58:1 has these usages, in the 4 versions shown in parentheses: 'The Lord says, '**Shout** as loud as you can!' (GNB), '**Shout** it aloud!' (NIV), **Shout** the message!' (CEV), '**Shout** out, do not hold back!' (NRSV). In the NT, it is used of Jesus' own proclamation of good news: 'Jesus stood up and **shouted**, "If you are thirsty, come to me and drink!"' (John 7:37, also 7:28, CEV). Other NT usages: 'Jesus cried out with a loud **shout**' (Matthew 27:46, GNB), 'Paul **shouted** in a loud voice', Acts 16:28 (NRSV).

*Evangelists often have to* **shout** *the message. Evangelism may involve* **shouting.**

**324.  State.** This root word directly translates *euangelizo* in one version: 'Adhere to my **statement** of' the gospel (1 Corinthians 15:2, Moffatt).

*To evangelize is to* **state** *the gospel in clear terms.*

**326.  Translate.** Evangelizing requires **translating** the unchanging gospel into language and terms that the hearers can understand.

*The evangelizer is a* **translator**, *and a Bible* **translator** *is an evangelizer.*

## MINICOMMISSION II: DISCIPLE!

The second half of the Great Commission now begins. It embraces the final 3 Mandates: DISCIPLE! BAPTIZE! TRAIN! These deal with an advanced stage of evangelization as disciple-making, winning converts, baptizing, planting churches, training.

### V.  DISCIPLE!

The fifth Mandate depicts the stage where evangelizers drive home the Christian message to those who show interest or concern, whether individuals, groups, audiences, or populations. The description **Pressure evangelization** does not imply unethical methods. Certainly, this stage is convert-oriented. But it merely states that people do not become Christians without properly-practiced **Persuasion evangelism**. Note how strong these constituent dimensions are: Challenge! Command! Compel! Confront! Denounce! Disciple! (Make disciples!) Entreat! Force! Implore! Insist! Persuade! Plead! Press! Urge! Of the 138 facets under this Mandate, none are in The Big Ten.

**327.  Accept.** This word occurs in the context of *euangelizo*, and translates its synonyms: 'Accepting another gospel' (Galatians 1:6, GNB). 'To evangelise is... to **accept** Him as their Saviour' (Archbishops' Inquiry 1918).
*Evangelizing is accepting the gospel and helping others to do likewise.*

**332.  Appeal.** 'I appeal to you' (Romans 12:1, GNB). 'God appealing to you through us' (2 Corinthians 5:20, TCNT, Moffatt, Goodspeed). 'The appeal we make does not spring from error' (1 Thessalonians 2:3, NIV).
*To evangelize is to appeal to individuals. Evangelizing is appealing to people to accept the gospel. Evangelization involves bringing an appeal to people.*

**336.  Assure.** The word directly translates *euangelizo* in one translation: 'as he **assured** his servants the prophets' (Revelation 10:7, Moffatt).'I assure you that if you believe' (Matthew 21:21, GNB). 'I assure you that people can be forgiven all their sins' (Mark 3:28, GNB).
*Evangelizing is assuring people about God and his forgiveness.*

**337.  Attract.** 'Make the teaching about God our Savior **attractive**' (Titus 2:10, NIV).
*To evangelize is to attract others by one's words and actions.*

**338.  Beg.** 'I **beg** you be reconciled to God' (2 Corinthians 5:20, C.B. Williams).
*Evangelizing may involve begging others to accept the gospel.*

**339.  Believe.** 'Whoever **believes** and is baptized will be saved' (Mark 16:16, GNB). '**Believe** in the Lord Jesus, and you will be saved' (Acts 16:31, RSV, GNB, NIV). 'Those who do not **believe** the Good News from God' (1 Peter 4:17, GNB). This verb itself has several synonyms, including 'have faith', 'show faith', 'exercise faith', as in 'The people who have faith in me without seeing me' and 'If you have faith in him, you will have true life' (John 20:29, 31, CEV). **Believing**, or having faith in Christ, is an obvious essential prerequisite to successful evangelism.
*Evangelizing necessitates and springs from believing in the gospel.*

**340.  Beseech.** 'We **beseech** you on behalf of Christ, be reconciled to God' (2 Corinthians 5:20, RSV).
*Evangelizing may involve beseeching people to turn to God.*

**344.  Call.** 'Call' directly translates several NT Greek synonyms of *euangelizo*. 'Call' is widely used in AV/KJV et alia. 'I have not come to **call** the righteous, but sinners to repentance' (Luke 5:32, NIV). 'Evangelism means a **call** to a life Christ-controlled throughout' (G.C. Pidgeon in Mott 1938:99). In the early Church, 'To evangelize was to **call** for a decision about God's liberating action in Jesus Christ' (O. Costas 1974:34). 'The evangelistic witness is a **call** to salvation' (Orthodox Consultation, Bucharest 1974, in Anderson 1975:268). 'To evangelize is to **call**

people to personal commitment to Jesus Christ, to baptism and membership of the church' (J.S. Robertson, USPG, 1977:pc). Speaking of Catholic youth today, 'Have they ever been properly evangelised—**called** to a living faith in Jesus Christ?' (*ICCRO Newsletter*, July-August, 1993).
*Being evangelized is being called to faith in Christ. Evangelization is calling people through the gospel.*

**347.  Catch.** 'Catch' is used several times in most Scripture versions. 'Let down your nets for a **catch**' (Luke 5:4, RSV). 'From now on you will be **catching** men' (Luke 5:10, GNB). 'Young men, haven't you **caught** anything?' (John 21:5, GNB). 'Throw your net out on the right side of the boat, and you will **catch** some' (John 21:6, GNB).
In biblical usages, the **catch** or haul is not usually symbolic of believers alone, but of believers and unbelievers together. The Parable of the Net (Matthew 13:47-50) illustrates this: fishermen '**catch** all kinds of fish', then 'divide the fish' and 'the worthless ones are thrown away' (GNB). The latter was normal practice. Smaller fish especially were thrown back to let them grow larger and breed further. But in the Miraculous **Catch** of Fishes in John 21, the **catch** was 100% perfect—153 big fish (John 21:11). According to Jerome, this number—which is the sum of all integers from 1 to 17, and is also the sum of multiplying the prime numbers 17, 3, and 3—signifies the catholicity of the Church, the total number of the elect.
*Being evangelized is being caught through the gospel. Evangelization is being caught by the gospel, a catch for the gospel.*

**350.  Challenge.** 'You people hate anyone who **challenges** injustice' (Amos 5.10, GNB). 'Ten years of **challenging** Africa', R. Gourlae, *A monthly letter about evangelism* (WCC 1961), describing a Nigeria mission.
*To evangelize is to challenge people to respond to the gospel.*

**352.  Charge.** 'I **charge** you to obey carefully' (1 Chronicles 28:8, GNB). Jesus '**charged** them' not to depart from Jerusalem (Acts 1:4, ASV).'In the sight of God... I **charge** you to keep this command' (1 Timothy 6:13, NIV). 'I give you this **charge**: Preach the Word' (2 Timothy 4:1, NIV).
*Evangelizing is charging colleagues to preach the Great Commission.*

**354.  Command.** 'Jesus **commanded** them not to tell anyone of the vision' (Matthew 17:9, REB). Jesus '**commanded** them that they should not depart from Jerusalem' (Acts 1:4, AV/KJV). 'He **commanded** us to preach the gospel to the people' (Acts 10:42, GNB). 'I **command** you in the name of Jesus' (Acts 19:13, GNB). 'God has **commanded** you to obey' (Hebrews 9:20, GNB). '**Command** and teach these things' (1 Timothy 4:11, NIV). 'Christ has **commanded** His church to make known the Gospel and evangelism is obedience to this **command**' (*Nationwide Initiative in Evangelism*, Britain, 1979).
*To evangelize is to obey Christ's command.*

**355.  Compel.** 'Go out to the highways and hedges, and **compel** people to come in' (Luke 14:23, RSV). 'And now, **compelled** by the Spirit' (Acts 20:22, NIV). 'I am **compelled** to preach' (1 Corinthians 9:16, NIV). 'Christ's love **compels** us' (2 Corinthians 5:14, NIV).
In modern everyday usage, '**compelling**' people to do things is frowned on as an infringement of their human rights and their freedom of choice. Scriptural use of this strong term is evidence of the overarching necessity of evangelization.
*Evangelizing is compelling people to enter the Kingdom of God.*

**357.  Condemn.** 'Condemn' is used 31 times in AV/KJV, and '**condemnation**' 12 times; also in modern versions (RSV, NEB, GNB, et alia). 'He that disbelieveth shall be **condemned**' (Mark 16:16, ASV).

'Whoever believes in him is not **condemned**' (John 3:18, NIV). 'By his faith he **condemned** the world' (Hebrews 11:7, NIV).
*Being evangelized includes having one's sinful lifestyle condemned. Evangelization involves condemnation of people's sinful lifestyle.*

**358.  Confront.** 'Confront' is used in RSV and in the OT in NIV and other versions, but not in AV/KJV or GNB. '**Confronting** all thought and all life with the Gospel' (J.H. Oldham in *IRM* 1912:8). Book by J.R. Mott, *Confronting young men with the Living Christ* (1923). 'The most vital and most extensive task of Christian missions is that of **confronting** all men now living with the supreme claims of Jesus Christ' (J.R. Mott 1928:27). 'Evangelism means to me to **confront** men with the Gospel' (W.A. Visser't Hooft in Mott 1938:70). 'Evangelism is to **confront** people with the essential message of the Gospel' (H. Kraemer in Mott 1938:72). 'Evangelism is the decisive **confrontation** of men with the Gospel' (D.T. Niles 1959). 'The heart of evangelism is the initial act of **confronting** someone else with Jesus' (D. Webster 1959:152). 'Evangelism essentially is **confronting** a person with Christ' (Billy Graham in 1952:11). 'To be evangelized is to be **confronted** with the decision: to join or not' (E. Castro 1968:149). 'Evangelistic witness is first of all and primarily a **confrontation** of man by the message of the one holy and undivided Trinity' (Orthodox Consultation, Bucharest 1974, quoted in Anderson 1975:269). 'Evangelization is the **confrontation** of the world with the gospel' (Eastern Europe National Strategy Group, ICOWE, in Douglas 1975:1356).
*To evangelize is to confront people with the gospel. Evangelizing is confronting people. Evangelization is confrontation of people with the gospel.*

**359.  Conquer.** The Rider on a white horse went forth '**conquering** and bent on **conquest**' (Revelation 6:2, NTME). *Conquest for Christ in Africa, 1902-52: a history of the Consolata Fathers in Kenya* (1952). 'The Master disclosed God's strategy of world **conquest**' (R.E. Coleman 1963:18). Church growth expositor Vergil Gerber has said 'Evangelism is 'big game hunting' ' (1976). Many branches of Christianity have been gripped by the vividness of the biblical metaphors concerning warfare, fighting, victory, triumph, and **conquest**. One thinks of the great hymns of militant faith: Luther's 'Ein Feste Burg' ('A mighty fortress is our God'), or 'Onward Christian soldiers, marching as to war'.
Some traditions have totally organized themselves on military lines, as has William Booth's Salvation Army (now a global denomination with 4 million members), Wilson Carlisle's Church Army (Anglican, 320 captains and sisters), or, in Romania, J. Trifa's The Lord's Army, formed within the Romanian Orthodox Church in 1918 and now with 300,000 members including many priests. Many of the 80-million-member African Independent Churches also are organized on strictly military lines.
*Being evangelized means being conquered by the gospel. Evangelization is conquest in the name of Christ.*

**361.  Convert.** 'Except ye be **converted**, ye shall not enter into the kingdom of heaven' (Matthew 18:3, AV/KJV). 'They passed through... reporting the **conversion** of the Gentiles' (Acts 15:3, RSV). There is widespread dictionary usage. 'Evangelization. The state of being **converted** to the Christian faith' (*A new English dictionary*, Oxford 1897, 1933). '**Conversion** is merely the first step in evangelism' (C. Hoffman in Mott 1938:94). 'Evangelism means the **conversion** of people from worldliness to Christ-like godliness' (T. Kagawa in Mott 1938:42). 'Evangelisation: **conversion**' (sole meaning given, Collins *Family dictionary* 1959). In many other dictionary definitions, 'evangelize' is synonymous with '**convert**', 'win', 'christianize', 'recruit'. 'Evangelize. To **convert** by preaching' (*The Century dictionary* 1889). 'Evangelize. To **convert** by preaching' (*Funk & Wagnalls dictionary* 1893). 'Evangelize: to **convert** to

Christianity' (*Webster's third dictionary* 1909). 'Evangelise: to **convert** by preaching the gospel' (sole meaning given, Collins *Family dictionary* 1959). 'Evangelise: **convert** to Christianity' (*Penguin English dictionary* 1965). 'Evangelize. To **convert** to Christianity' (*Random House dictionary* 1966). 'Evangelize. To **convert** to Christianity' (*Heritage illustrated dictionary* 1969). 'Evangelize: **convert** to Christianity' (*Webster's third new international dictionary*, 1971). 'Evangelise: to Christianise' and 'Evangelisation: Christianisation' (*Chambers Twentieth Century dictionary* 1973).

*Being evangelized involves being* **converted** *to or against Christ. Evangelization involves* **conversion** *to, or rejection of, Christ.*

---

362. **Convince.** 'Convince' is used in AV/KJV, elsewhere being translated 'argue with', 'refute', 'condemn', 'lecture'; and also in GNB. 'Some of them were **convinced** and joined Paul and Silas' (Acts 17:4, GNB). 'Trying to **convince** both Jews and Greeks' (Acts 18:2, GNB). 'Paul mightily **convinced** the Jews publicly' (Acts 18:28, AV/KJV) 'Paul has succeeded in **convincing** many people' (Acts 19:26, GNB). 'With **convincing** proof of the power of God's Spirit' (1 Corinthians 2:4, GNB).

Apologetics is defined as 'the reasoned commendation of Christianity to persons interested but not yet **convinced**' (C.H. Dodd 1936:4). 'Evangelization must include the willingness to take up the work of apologetics' (K. Hamilton, 'Apologetics and evangelization', in Douglas 1975:1202). 'Apologetics is not the same as evangelism, yet it should not be separated from the evangelistic task' (W.S.C. Tyndale, 'Apologetics in evangelism report', in Douglas 1975:1203).

*Being evangelized is being* **convinced** *by or about the gospel. Evangelization includes* **conviction.**

---

369. **Denounce.** This verb is used to directly translate *euangelizo* in one version: 'To us also it hath been **denounced**, as also to them' (Hebrews 4:2, Rheims/DRB 1st edition 1582). 'Denounce' also translates several Greek NT synonyms of *euangelizo*. 'Denounce' is not used in AV/KJV although most of its synonyms are (especially 'rebuke' 28 times), but it occurs in modern versions. 'Jesus began to **denounce** the cities' (Matthew 11:20, NIV). 'Evangelism means the **denunciation** of all idols or powers which are opposed to God's purposes for mankind... The announcement of the Gospel implies the **denunciation** of everything that is not in agreement with the Gospel' (J.H. Poulton 1975:4).

*To evangelize is to* **denounce.** *Evangelizing includes* **denouncing.** *Evangelization involves* **denunciation.**

---

371. **Disciple.** Although the more familiar form of this verb is 'make **disciples**', the older form occurs in The 1911 Bible (King James Version, 'The Text carefully corrected and amended by American Scholars', published by Oxford University Press, New York): 'Go ye therefore, and **disciple** all the nations' (Matthew 28:19). In the Greek NT, the verb '**disciple**' (*matheteuo*) occurs 4 times (Matthew 13:52, 27:57, 28:19, Acts 14:21), and the noun '**disciple**' (*mathetes*) 262 times. 'Go, then, to all peoples everywhere and make them my **disciples**' (Matthew 28:19, GNB). 'They won a large number of **disciples**' (Acts 14:21, NIV). The term and its cognates have been widely employed. 'Evangelism involves both a verbal witness and a life of **discipleship**' (WMC Edinburgh 1910). 'Evangelism, in its simplest terms, means to me the winning of men and women to the **discipleship** of Christ' (J.J. Conning in Mott 1938:90). 'Evangelism includes not only preaching but also making **disciples**' (K.S. Latourette & W.R. Hogg 1948:121). 'Evangelism is persuading them to become **disciples**' (C.P. Wagner in Stott 1971).'Evangelism proclaims Christ and persuades men to become His **disciples**' (D.A. McGavran 1972). 'Evangelization for us is in a very real sense synonymous with **discipleship**' (G. Cook, INDEP (1975):7). Essay entitled '**Discipleship** evangelism' (W. Scott in Wirt 1978).

*To evangelize is to* **disciple** *people. Evangelizing is* **discipling.** *Evangelization is extending* **discipleship** *to people.*

---

372. **Distribute.** Jesus 'gave thanks for these and told the disciples to **distribute** them' (Mark 8:7, GNB).

*To evangelize is to* **distribute** *God's gift of grace.*

---

373. **Divide.** 'Divide' is frequent in all Scripture versions. 'When the net is full, they pull it to shore and sit down to **divide** the fish' (Matthew 13:48, GNB). '**Divide** the inheritance' (Luke 2:13, RSV), '**Divide** the property' (Luke 2:13-14, GNB). 'The people of the city were **divided**; some sided with the Jews, and some with the apostles' (Acts 14:4, RSV).

*Evangelizing results in* **dividing** *hearers into those for Christ and those against.*

---

374. **Drag.** On the Sea of Tiberias, the Risen Lord directed the disciples' nets until a massive haul was caught. Hauling it in proved too difficult. Eventually Simon Peter '**dragged** the net ashore' (John 21:11, NIV). The parallel with fishing for souls—evangelism—is that although the catch may be abundant in the shape of large crowds coming forward to register decisions for Christ, there is still heavy work to do: counselling, followup, shepherding, teaching, training, administration, logistics.

*Evangelism involves heavy work* **dragging** *people inexorably on.*

---

376. **Encourage.** The term is used once to directly translate *euangelizo*: 'John **encouraged** the people and raised their hope' (Luke 3:18, CCB); also a synonym in Paul 'went through those regions and **encouraged** the people with many messages' (Acts 20:2, GNB).

*To evangelize is to* **encourage** *people to listen to God's call.*

---

377. **Enjoin.** 'Jesus **enjoined** them not to tell anyone' (Matthew 17:9, NEB).

*To evangelize is to* **enjoin** *decision and action.*

---

378. **Enlighten.** The disciples ate with the Risen Lord, and 'Then he **enlightened** their minds' (Luke 24:45, Knox). 'After you were **enlightened**' (Hebrews 10:32, RSV). 'It is a general opinion among **enlightened** Christians' (C. Adams 1850:17–19).

*Evangelizing is* **enlightening** *hearers.*

---

379. **Entreat.** 'Entreat' translates several NT Greek synonyms of *euangelizo*. 'We **entreat** you in Christ's name' (2 Corinthians 5:20, Knox). 'I **entreat** you... live up to your calling' (Ephesians 4:1, NEB).

*To evangelize is to* **entreat.**

---

381. **Exhort.** 'Exhort' translates several NT Greek synonyms of *euangelizo*. 'John **exhorted** the people' (Luke 3:18, NIV). 'To preach the Gospel is to teach and to **exhort**' (J.R. Mott 1900:6).

*Being evangelized is being* **exhorted** *to accept Christ.*

---

382. **Explain.** 'Explain' directly translates *euangelizo* at one point: 'Philip proceeded to **explain** the good news of Jesus to him' (Acts 8:35, NJB). The verb also translates several NT Greek synonyms of *euangelizo*. 'Explain' is used in RSV, GNB, et alia. 'Philip **explained** the gospel of Jesus to him' (C.H. Rieu's Translation of The Acts of the Apostles, 1957, on Acts 8:35). 'How can I understand unless someone **explains** it to me?' (Acts 8.31, GNB). 'Peter **explained** to them in order' (Acts 11:4, RSV). In the synagogues, Paul 'held discussions with the people, quoting and **explaining** the Scriptures and proving from them that the Messiah had to suffer' (Acts 17:2-3, GNB). 'I **explained** the gospel message that I preach to the Gentiles' (Galatians 2:2, GNB). 'We have evangelism when a truly Christian man **explains** his message' (J. McKenzie in Mott 1938:27). 'By Japanese Christians, *dendo* or evangelism is understood to mean **explaining** the teachings of Jesus Christ' (S. Saito in Mott 1938:44). 'Evangelizing means first and foremost to **explain** the gospel' (G. Peters 1970:31).

*To evangelize is to* **explain** *the gospel. Evangelizing is* **explaining** *the gospel. Evangelization is the* **explanation** *of the gospel.*

---

383. **Find.** Jesus taught: 'Seek and you will **find**' (Luke 11:9, NIV), ' Go after the lost sheep (REB, the one that is missing) until he **finds** it' (Luke 15:4, NIV)). 'At once he **found** his brother Simon and told him 'We have **found** the Messiah' ' (John 1:41, GNB). 'Philip **found** Nathanael and told him (John 1:45,

GNB). Peter '**found** many people gathered' (Acts 10:27, GNB). '**Found** in the gospel' (1 Timothy 1:11, GNB). *Finding men for Christ* (G.F. Dempster 1935), a book on personal evangelism. 'Evangelism is seeking and **finding** the lost' (C.P. Wagner in Stott 1971).

*To evangelize is to* **find** *people for Christ. Being evangelized is being* **found** *by the gospel.*

---

384. **Fish.** 'Follow me, and I will make you **fishers** of men' (Matthew 4:19, RSV). 'Simon Peter said, 'I am going **fishing**' ' (John 21:3, GNB).

**Fishing** is not synonymous with catching; it is casting the net, or line, with the intent of catching. Even experienced **fishermen** can be unsuccessful with a catch, and often are. ('We toiled all night and took nothing', Luke 5:5, RSV). But obedience to the command '**Fish**' must not be judged by success or the lack of it. The whole operation of **fishing** is selective; **fishermen** historically have only caught an infinitesimal proportion of **fish** around them. But the 20th century has seen a totally new situation. The **fishing** industry throughout the world has now reached enormous proportions and has become highly organized. As a direct consequence, in many seas and areas catches approach 100 percent and **fish** are becoming wiped out. The biblical image of **fishing** follows the original, traditional pattern, not the modern one.

*To evangelize is to* **fish** *for men. Evangelizing is* **fishing.** *Evangelization is* **fishing** *for men.*

---

385. **Force.** 'By using my name they will **force** out demons' (Mark 16:17, CEV). '**Force** them to come in' (Luke 14:23, Berkeley). Once again, a very strong English verb is deliberately used (as with 'compel', 'urge', 'press', q.v.) to drive home the seriousness of the evangelistic predicament.

*Evangelizing may often require* **forcing** *out demons (exorcism) or* **forcing** *hearers hesitating about discipleship.*

---

386. **Forgive.** 'Son, your sins are **forgiven**' (Mark 2:5, NIV). Jesus said to them, 'Receive the Holy Spirit. If you **forgive** the sins of any, they are **forgiven;** if you retain the sins of any, they are retained' (John 20:22-3, RSV). 'They will be saved by having their sins **forgiven**' (Luke 1:77, GNB). 'That repentance and **forgiveness** of sins should be preached in his name to all nations' (Luke 24:47, RSV). 'Everyone who believes in him receives **forgiveness** of sins' (Acts 10:43, NIV).

*To evangelize is to proclaim* **forgiving** *and* **forgiveness** *through Christ.*

---

387. **Gather.** 'Gather money to repair' (2 Kings 12:7, RSV). '**Gather** the people' (Joel 2:16, NIV).'He will **gather** his wheat into his barn' (Matthew 3:12, GNB). 'The harvest is large, but there are few workers to **gather** it in' (Matthew 9:37, GNB). '**Gather** where I have not scattered seed' (Matthew 25:26, NIV). 'He who does not **gather** with me, scatters' (Luke 11:23, NIV). '**Gather** the pieces that are left over' (John 6:12, NIV). Evangelism is 'the direct representation of the Gospel, or the **gathering** in of the harvest' (B.S.W. Green 1951:19).

*Evangelizing is* **gathering** *in the crop.*

---

389. **Grasp.** 'They did not **grasp** what he was talking about' (Luke 18:34, NEB). 'Our **grasp** of truth' (2 Corinthians 6:6, NEB).

*To evangelize is to* **grasp** *reality and act accordingly.*

---

390. **Guide.** 'Can one blind man be **guide** to another?' (Luke 6:39, NEB). 'The Lamb who is at the centre of the throne will be their shepherd and will **guide** them to springs of the water of life' (Revelation 7:17, REB).

*To evangelise is to* **guide** *souls toward God.*

---

391. **Harvest.** 'Harvest' has 47 usages in OT, 13 in NT (AV/KJV). 'The crops are now ripe and ready to be **harvested**!' (John 4:35, GNB). 'The time has come; the earth is ripe for the **harvest**!... The earth's **harvest** was reaped' (Revelation 14:15-16, GNB). Evangelism is 'the direct representation of the Gospel, or the gathering in of the **harvest**' (B.S.W. Green 1951:19). P. Beyerhaus, *It is harvest time* (1970). J. Engel & W. Norton, *What's gone wrong with the harvest?* (1975).

**Harvesting** is the culminating element of finality in the whole process of persuasion evangelism. The catch has now been caught, the fishes in the net hauled in, the crops reaped, the wheat gathered in.

*Evangelizing is* **harvesting.** *Being evangelized includes being* **harvested**. *Evangelization includes* **harvest**.

392. **Haul.** After the Risen Lord directed them where to throw their net, 'they were unable to **haul** their net in because of the large number of fish' (John 21:6, NIV).

*Evangelizing is* **hauling** *in the nets.*

393. **Heal.** The Greek words *therapeuein* (to **heal**) and *therapeia* (**healing**), with synonyms, figure prominently in the NT. In English, '**heal**' is widespread in AV/KJV, RSV, NEB, GNB, et alia. 'They will also **heal** sick people' (Mark 16:18, CEV).'The disciples traveled through all the villages, preaching the Good News and **healing** people everywhere' (Luke 9:6, GNB). 'Jesus went about teaching and preaching and **healing**' (Matthew 9:35, RSV). 'Evangelism is the presentation of the Gospel by preaching, teaching, **healing** and service' (S. Higginbottom in Mott 1938:19). In New Testament days, '**Healing** was itself a proclamation of the Gospel... The apostles regarded the ministry of Christian **healing** as part of their evangelistic activity' (D. Webster 1959:83). *Healing evangelism: strengthen your witnessing with effective prayer for the sick* (1995), a lengthy discussion and exposition by Presbyterian evangelist Don Dunkerley.

*To evangelize is to* **heal**. *Evangelizing includes* **healing**. *Evangelization includes* **healings**.

394. **Hunt.** 'May the Lord make you as great a **hunter** as Nimrod!' (Genesis 10:9, GNB). 'Evangelism is 'big game **hunting**' ' (V. Gerber in G.O. Swank 1977:ix).

*Evangelists have to work at* **hunting** *for souls.*

395. **Impart.** '**Impart**' translates several NT Greek synonyms of *euangelizo.* The word occurs 3 times in AV/KJV, as: 'We are willing to have **imparted** unto you, not the gospel of God only, but also our own souls' (1 Thessalonians 2.8, AV/KJV). '*Euangelizesthai* is the **impartation** of *soteria*'... 'To evangelize is to **impart** salvation' (Kittel's *TWNT* II.720, in German 1932, in English 1964). 'Evangelism is the **imparting** of the Christian experience in all its implications from one life to another' (Y. Abe in Mott 1938:37). 'Evangelism is a heart-desire to **impart** the knowledge of Jesus Christ to others' (J.S. Ryang in Mott 1938:49).

*Being evangelized is having the gospel* **imparted** *to one. Evangelization is the* **impartation** *of the gospel.*

396. **Implore.** 'We **implore** you on Christ's behalf: be reconciled to God' (2 Corinthians 5:20, TCNT).

*To evangelize is to* **implore** *people to accept Christ. Evangelizing is* **imploring**. *Evangelization is* **imploring**.

398. **Insist.** 'Jesus **insisted**, 'Children, how hard it is to enter the kingdom of God!' ' (Mark 10:24, NEB). 'I solemnly urge you to preach the message, to **insist** upon proclaiming it (whether the time is right or not)' (2 Timothy 4:2, GNB).

*Evangelizing must* **insist** *on its own centrality and not be diverted.*

399. **Invite.** '**Invite**' is used once to directly translate *euangelizo*: 'Now it's all kingdom of God—the glad news and compelling **invitation** to every man and woman' (Luke 16:16, The Message/NTCE). '**Invite**' also translates several NT Greek synonyms of *euangelizo* in some versions. Neither it nor its cognates occur in AV/KJV, but the usage abounds in later versions. '**Invite** to the banquet anyone you find' (Matthew 22:9, NIV). '**Invite** the poor' (Luke 14:13, NIV). 'Many are **invited**, but few are chosen' (Matthew 22:14, GNB). 'Peter **invited** the men in' (Acts 10:23, GNB). 'Those who have been **invited**' (Revelation 19:9, GNB). More recent usage is also widespread. 'Evangelism means **inviting** everyone to become children of God' (S. Knak in Mott 1938:71). 'The evangelistic proclamation comes in terms of an **invitation** to decision' (E. Castro 1968:149). 'Evangelization is the explicit proclamation of the mystery of Christ and a direct **invitation** to adhere to his gospel' (B. Haring 1974:43-4). In the early Church, 'To evangelize was to **invite** people to confess Jesus Christ' (O. Costas 1974:34). 'Evangelization: **inviting** into the kingdom of grace' (P. Beyerhaus in Douglas 1975:283).

*To evangelize is to* **invite** *people to accept Christ. Evangelizing is* **inviting** *people. Evangelization is an* **invitation** *to accept Christ.*

400. **Involve.** '**Involve**' and cognates are not used in AV/KJV, nor later as synonyms of 'evangelize'. Despite USA mass-evangelism techniques, 'In American history evangelizers have always implied personal **involvement** between themselves and the evangelized' (M.E. Marty 1975:80). 'Evangelization is not a one-way transfer from the person evangelizing to the person being evangelized... People, especially youth, must be actively **involved** in their own evangelization or catechesis' (Pro Mundi Vita 63, 1976).

Evangelization is not simply communication in the sense of a one-way transfer. It involves 2 parties. It is bi-directional, **involving** an outgoing message and incoming feedback. It is communication with **involvement**, with feedback, with answer, with response. According to the Japanese missiologist Kosume Koyama, 'The Great Commission is not 'one-way-traffic' but 'Christlike going', going on the basis of the life and ministry of Jesus Christ; it is intensely two-ways... He gave up his right of way' (K. Koyama in Anderson 1975:72-3). This feedback or response may be negative in the sense of disagreement with the message, or hostility, or rejection. This need for, and requirement of feedback to the evangelizer leads us on into the next of our 5 major types, namely Persuasion Evangelism.

*Being evangelized means being or becoming* **involved** *with the gospel. Evangelization means* **involvement** *with the gospel.*

401. **Lay hands on.** Authenticating the preaching of the Great Commission were healings through **laying on of hands** (in current usage, placing on of hands). 'They shall **lay hands on** the sick, and they shall recover' (Mark 16:18, AV/KJV).

*Evangelizing may include the* **laying on** *of* **hands.**

402. **Lead.** 'Can a blind man **lead** a blind man?' (Luke 6:39, NIV). Jesus '**led** them out of the city as far as Bethany' (Luke 24:50, GNB, REB). 'If you are **led** by the Spirit' (Galatians 5:18, NIV). 'He will **lead** them to springs of living water' (Revelation 7:17, NIV).

*Evangelizers* **lead** *people to Christ.*

403. **Make acknowledge.** '**Acknowledge**' translates several NT Greek synonyms of *euangelizo:* it is also used in AV/KJV: '**Acknowledgement** of the mystery of God' (Colossians 2:2, AV/KJV). 'Never able to **acknowledge** the truth' (2 Timothy 3:7, NIV). 'Evangelism is the winning of men to **acknowledge** Christ as their Saviour and King' (Archbishop W. Temple in Mott 1938:85). 'Let all nations **acknowledge** your saving power' (Church of England, Morning Prayer, Series 3, SPCK 1974).

To **acknowledge** the truth of Christ and the gospel is not necessarily to accept it for oneself. The ultimate Christian goal is the universal **acknowledgment** of the Lordship of Christ: 'At the name of Jesus every knee shall bow, Every tongue confess him King of Glory now'; but this will not signify universal acceptance of the gospel nor universal conversion.

*Being evangelized is* **acknowledging** *the truth of the gospel. Evangelization is* **acknowledgment** *of the gospel.*

404. **Make choose.** Widespread in OT: '**Choose** ye this day whom ye will serve' (Joshua 24:25, AV/KJV), less so in NT. 'He **chose** twelve' (Mark 3:14, GNB). 'If anyone **chooses** to do God's will, he will find out' (John 7:17, NIV).'Evangelism is proclamation which faces humanity with the inescapable **choice** of making a decision' (Anglican Consultative Council/ACC-3 Trinidad 1976:51). 'Evangelism is communication sufficiently understandable for the hearers or readers to make an intelligent **choice** either for or against acceptance of Jesus Christ' (L. Brierley 1976:pc). **Choice** is an essential ingredient of life. Refusing to **choose** is itself a **choice**.

The role of the evangelizer is to help others make the **choice**, **choosing** to follow Christ. This can be accomplished in many ways. One way is to directly urge on them the desired course of action: 'So then, brothers, **choose** seven men among you' (Acts 6:3, GNB).

*Evangelizing is* **making** *persons* **choose** *life in Christ. Being evangelized is* **choosing**. *Evangelization is a* **choice** *for or against the gospel.*

406. **Make decide.** 'The next day Jesus **decided** to leave' (John 1:43, NIV). 'The whole Sanhedrin reached a **decision**' (Mark 15:1, NIV). 'To be evangelized is to be confronted with the **decision**: to join or not' (E. Castro 1968:149).

*Being evangelized means being or becoming* **decided** *concerning the gospel. Evangelization involves* **decision** *for or against the gospel.*

407. **Make put**. The verb **put** is widely used in AV/KJV, GNB, occasionally in NIV. 'He will **put** his angels in charge of you' (Matthew 4:6, NEB). Jesus '**put** his hands on a few sick people' (Mark 6:5, NEB). Jesus 'noticed a poor widow **put** in two tiny coins' (Luke 21:2, NEB). 'He who **puts** his faith in the Son has hold of eternal life' (John 3:36, NEB). Anyone 'who **puts** his trust in him who sent me has hold of eternal life' (John 5:24, NEB). 'When we **put** our trust in the Lord Jesus Christ' (Acts 11:17, NEB). '**Put** in trust with the gospel' (1 Thessalonians 2:4, AV/KJV). To evangelize is therefore to **make** others **put** their trust likewise.

In recent usage, 'To evangelise is so to present Christ Jesus in the power of the Holy Spirit, that men shall come to **put** their trust in God through Him' (Archbishops' Inquiry 1918).

*Evangelizing is* **putting** *one's trust in God and helping to* **make** *others* **put** *theirs also.*

408. **Make realize.** '**Realize**' and cognates are not employed in AV/KJV, but occur in other versions. '...not **realizing** that God's kindness leads you toward repentance?' (Romans 2:4, NIV). 'Evangelism means the process whereby men are caused to **realize** their need of salvation and are persuaded to accept Jesus as Saviour' (H.C. Tucker in Mott 1938:65). Evangelizing means making Jesus Christ **real** to people.

*Being evangelized is* **realizing** *that the gospel is true. Evangelization is* **realization** *of the truth of the gospel.*

409. **Make receive.** '**Receive**' and '**Receive** news' are widely used in most translations, either signifying acceptance of God's gift or initial acceptance followed by rejection. It directly translates *euangelizo* in Hebrews 4:6, RSV: 'Those who formerly **received** the good news failed to enter because of disobedience.' 'The gospel you **received** from us' (2 Corinthians 11:4, GNB).

'**Receive**' is one of many of the synonyms of 'evangelize' which embody either acceptance or rejection of Christ or his message. A head of state may **receive** in audience the ambassador of a hostile state; he may be offered, **receive** and accept a letter from the hostile head of state; but he may then reject the message or any demands or conditions contained therein. **Reception** of a message need not imply agreement or approval.

*To evangelize is to* **make** *people* **receive** *the gospel. Being evangelized is* **receiving** *news of the gospel. Evangelization is* **reception** *of the news about the gospel.*

410. **Make repent.** 'Scripture foretells the sufferings of the Messiah and his rising from the dead on the third day, and declares that in his name **repentance** bringing the forgiveness of sins is to be proclaimed' (Luke 24:46-7, REB).

*Evangelizing means* **making** *the unrepentant* **repent.**

411. **Make respond.** '**Respond**', '**response**' are used in RSV, et alia (not in AV/KJV). 'To evangelize is to proclaim good news to men in such a way as to elicit the **response** of acceptance' (M.A.C. Warren 1955:23). 'Our part in evangelism might be described as bringing about the occasions for men's **response** to Jesus Christ' (WCC Uppsala 1968). 'A people is not evangelized until it has **responded** to the good news of the message' (E. Pentecost 1974:58-9). '80% of the people who heard the Gospel **re-**

**sponded** positively' (Explo 74 in Korea, Campus Crusade 1974). 'Evangelism means basically sharing the good news in such a way as to seek a **response** to Christ and his claims' (M. Wright 1976:1). 'Evangelization means enabling people to **respond** to the claims of Christ on their lives' (*Lambeth Report* 1978:93-4). 'Evangelism is telling the story of Jesus in such a way that people **respond**' (Bishop D. Brown 1978:2). 'Evangelism is the command to **respond**: 'Be reconciled to God' ' (Leighton Ford in Wirt 1978:27).

**Response**, properly so termed, can be either positive or negative. An invitation or an offer entails and produces a **response**, either one of acceptance or one of rejection.

*Being evangelized is* **responding** *to Christ's invitation. Evangelization is* **response** *to the gospel's invitation.*

412. **Make trust**. The term is widely used in most Bible versions, as in '**Trust** in the Lord' (Psalm 27:14, GNB). 'Neither let Hezekiah **make** you **trust** in the Lord' (2 Kings 18:30, AV/KJV).

*To evangelize is* **make** *others* **trust** *in Christ. To be evangelized is to have been* **made** *to* **trust** *in Christ.*

413. **Make understand.** '**Understand**' and cognates are widely used in AV/KJV, RSV, and most other versions. 'Jesus said, 'Listen and **understand**!' ' (Matthew 15:10, GNB). 'Then opened he their **understanding,** that they might **understand** the scriptures' (Luke 24:45, AV/KJV). 'Philip asked him, 'Do you **understand** what you are reading?' The official replied, 'How can I **understand** unless someone explains it to me?' ' (Acts 8:30-31, GNB). 'The rejection of the gospel can be made only with knowledge, and this can be the case only when the announcing has been completely **understood**' (G. Warneck in Mott 1900:9). 'Evangelization is the preaching of Jesus Christ communicating the eternal truth of God clearly and **understandably**' (L. Palau in Douglas 1975:602).

Research on Islam in Africa by G.O. Swank (1977: xiv et passim) using the question 'What %, in your opinion, have **understood** the gospel whether they received it or not?' gave as results Uganda 15%, several others 5%. 'To evangelize is to call people to an **understanding** that God in Christ has reconciled the world to himself' (J.S. Robertson 1977:pc). The aim of Operation Good News (Nigeria 1978-80) was 'that everybody may hear the Gospel clearly enough to **understand** sufficiently to make a decision'.

Being evangelized requires not only hearing, but also listening and **understanding**. Evangelization is 'hearing with **understanding**'. **Understanding** consists of both intellectual **understanding** and emotional **understanding.**

*Being evangelized means* **understanding** *the gospel. Evangelization includes the* **understanding** *of the gospel.*

414. **Make well.** 'They will **make** them **well**' (Mark 16:18, MB). 'This faith has **made** him completely **well**' (Acts 3:16, NEB).

*Evangelizing often sees the sick* **made well.**

415. **Make whole.** 'The crippled **made whole**' (Matthew 15:31, GNB). 'Wilt thou be **made whole**?' (John 5:6, AV/KJV). 'Jesus Christ **maketh** thee **whole**' (Acts 9:34, AV/KJV).

*Evangelizing includes* **making** *people* **whole.**

417. **Oblige.** Paul stated, 'I have an **obligation** to all peoples, to the civilized and to the savage' (Romans 1:14, GNB).

*Evangelizers are* **obliged** *to spread the gospel.*

418. **Offer.** This verb directly translates *euangelizo* on two occasions. The first is: 'In my preaching I can **offer** the good news without cost' (1 Corinthians 9:18, Goodspeed-AT/GB). The second occasion is significant being in the newest Bible, the CEV: God 'sent Jesus Christ the Lord of all, to **offer** peace to them' (Acts 10:36). '**Offer**' also translates several NT Greek synonyms of *euangelizo.* Its usage in English versions is widespread, as: 'God has **offered** us the promise' (Hebrews 4:1, GNB). Also, 'God was in Christ, **offering** peace and forgiveness to the people of this world' (2 Corinthians 5:19, CEV). '**Offer**' was a favourite terminology with John Wesley: 'I **offered** Christ to a crowd of 10,000'. '*Euangelizesthai* is to **offer** salvation' (Kittel, *TWNT*, 1932, English translation 1964:II.720). 'Evangelization is the conveying of the **offer** of salvation' (A.G. Hogg in Mott 1938:21). 'Evangelism means the **offer** of God's Supreme Gift to others' (General Evangeline Booth in Mott 1938:78). 'The evangelizing Church will **offer** this gift of *koinonia* in its preaching and teaching' (WCC 2nd Assembly, *Evanston speaks*, 1954:34). 'Evangelism is the **offering** of Christ to men so that they may accept Him' (A. Skevington Wood 1966; Methodist). 'Evangelism comes to men with a present **offer** based upon Christ's victory on the Cross' (P. Beyerhaus in Douglas 1975:291). 'Evangelization will always contain a clear proclamation that in Jesus Christ salvation is **offered** to all men, as a gift of God's grace and mercy' (*Evangelii Nuntiandi* 1975, section 27). An **offer** entails and produces a response of either acceptance or rejection.

*To evangelize is to* **offer** *Christ. Evangelizing is* **offering** *Christ. Evangelization is the* **offering** *of the gospel to people,* **offering** *discipleship, with distinct* **offers.**

419. **Order.** Christ's relationship with his disciples must be seen in its true light: he is the Kyrios, the Lord; he commissions, he instructs, he commands, he **orders**: 'He gave them **orders**' (Acts 1:4, NT in Basic English; also NASB); 'He gave them this **order**' (GNB).

*Evangelizers are disciples under* **orders.**

422. **Perceive.** '**Perceive**' is widespread in AV/KJV, RSV. 'Sir, I **perceive** that you are a prophet' (John 4:19, RSV). **Perceiving** here means seeing.

*Being evangelized is* **perceiving** *the gospel. Evangelization is* **perception** *of the gospel.*

423. **Persuade.** '**Persuade**' translates several NT Greek synonyms of *euangelizo,* especially *peitho.* '**Persuade**' and cognates occur 26 times in AV/KJV. 'Some of them were **persuaded**, and joined Paul and Silas' (Acts 17: 4, RSV). 'Almost thou **persuadest** me to be a Christian' (Acts 26:28, AV/KJV). 'Knowing the fear of the Lord, we **persuade** men' (2 Corinthians 5:11, RSV). There is widespread recent use. 'Evangelism is the art of **persuading** people to accept Jesus Christ' (S. Higginbottom in Mott 1938:19). 'To me evangelism is making known to men the good news and **persuading** them to yield themselves in Christ' (W.M. Miller in Mott 1938:50, also P.O. Philip in Mott 1938:32). 'Evangelism means to let others know, and **persuade** them to follow and practice, the way and teachings of Jesus Christ' (S. Saito in Mott 1938:43-4). 'Evangelism is the presentation of the truth with a view to **persuading** men to accept it' (R.E. Speer in Mott 1938:103). 'Evangelism is **persuasive** proclamation of the Gospel' (C. Warren 1966:1). 'Evangelism is the proclamation of the Gospel, with the purpose of **persuading** sinners to put their trust in God' (World Congress on Evangelism 1966, in Mooneyham 1967:6). 'Evangelizing means to explain the Gospel to others and **persuade** them to accept' (G.W. Peters 1970:31). 'Evangelism is seeking and finding the lost, effectively communicating the Gospel to them and **persuading** them to become Christ's disciples' (C.P. Wagner in Stott 1971). 'Evangelism proclaims Christ and **persuades** men to become His disciples' (D.A. McGavran 1972:57). '**Persuading** but not compelling men' (D. Webster 1974:21). 'Evangelism is the proclamation of Christ, with a view to **persuading** people to come to him personally' (*Lausanne Covenant* 1974, section 4). The goal of evangelization is 'the **persuading** of men and women to accept Jesus Christ' (LCWE Bermuda 1978). '**Persuasion** evangelism involves sharing Christ personally with individuals or small groups' (P. Means 1978:7).

**Persuasion** is a major enterprise commercially by means of the media. In 1978, Britain spent UK £1,800 million on advertising or **persuading** people to buy products (BBC-TV, 'The **Persuaders**'; V. Packard, *The hidden* ***persuaders***).

*To evangelize is to* **persuade** *people to follow Christ. Evangelizing is* **persuading** *people. Evangelization is the* **persuasion** *of people to accept Christ.*

424. **Place hands on.** Among the signs authenticating the preaching of the Great Commission were healings originated by believers. 'They will **place** their **hands on** sick people, who will get well' (Mark 16:18, GNB, NIV), or 'lay hands on' (AV/KJV, ASV).

*Evangelizing often involves the* **placing** *of* **hands on** *the sick.*

425. **Plead**. 'We **plead** on Christ's behalf: let God change you from enemies into his friends!' (2 Corinthians 5:20, GNB).

*To evangelize is to* **plead** *for the lives of the unconverted.*

426. **Polarize.** There is no biblical usage, but some use outside. 'The final result of evangelism is not the unification of mankind but a growing **polarization** between the Kingdom of God and the kingdom of Satan' (P. Beyerhaus in Douglas 1975:289).

Jesus brought not peace but a dividing sword: faced with his message, it was impossible to serve two masters. Persuasion inevitably results in **polarization.** To '**polarize**' is defined as to divide into 2 opposites, or to divide or to cause to gather or become concentrated about 2 opposite poles or opposing extremes (*Webster's third new international dictionary*, 1971; *Longmans dictionary of contemporary English*, 1978). The Great Commission required that, as the church evangelized, people would be moved or **polarized** into 2 clearcut camps, one for Christ, and one against him. Examples are John 20.23: 'Forgive' some, 'Retain the sins' of others, this incident being described in the Anchor Bible as 'a prognostication of the ways in which the power of forgiveness will divide men'. In Mark 16:16, some will 'believe', others will 'not believe'. Again, in 2 Corinthians 2:15, GNB, the message is 'a fragrance that brings life' to some, but 'a deadly stench' to others.

**Polarization** of the world is therefore an integral part of the mandates conferred in the Great Commission. At the same time, we should note that the dimension '**polarization**' is not a deliberate responsibility given to Christians, nor an activity of the church. It is not the church which **polarizes**; it is the gospel, proclaimed, which **polarizes**. Hence it is the world which **polarizes** itself after contact with Christianity, Christ, and the gospel.

*Being evangelized means becoming* **polarized***. Evangelization means* **polarization** *into those for and those against Christ.*

428. **Press.** '**Press** people to come in' (Luke 14:23, Moffatt). 'I **press** on to take hold' (Philippians 3:12, NIV). 'I face daily the **pressure** of my concern' (2 Corinthians 11:28, NIV). '**Pressing** the claims of Christ upon individuals' (J.R. Mott 1900:7).

*To evangelize is to* **press** *people. Evangelizing is* **pressing** *people to accept the gospel. Evangelization involves bringing* **pressure** *on people.*

433. **Put right.** This phrase occurs 49 times in GNB-NT. 'The person who is **put right** with God through faith shall live' (Romans 1:17, GNB). 'Everyone who believes is **put right** with God' (Romans 10:4, GNB).

*Evangelizing is seeing people* **put right** *with God.*

434. **React.** '**React**' and cognates do not occur in AV/KJV, GNB, NIV, though the idea is present. The presence of Christ evangelizing can be recognized in Rembrandt's paintings 'only by the manner in which those around him **react**' (W.A. Visser't Hooft 1957:35). All genuine evangelism produces or is accompanied by 2 **reactions,** either acceptance or rejection, and 'Where both **reactions** occur it is usually evidence that the Spirit is there' (D. Webster 1959:83).

**Reacting** to Christ always accompanies evangelization. In his masterly volume *Rembrandt and the Gospel* (1957), W.A. Visser't Hooft goes on to describe how the Dutch painter in his later works emphasized the incognito of Christ, showing him not as the Divine Son of God but as an outwardly insignificant son of man.

In fact none of Rembrandt's various representations reveal Christ's personality in a direct way. 'Only by the manner in which those around him **react** is it possible for his presence to be recognized... The terror of the crucifixion is expressed in the faces of the disciples and the women. And in the Emmaus picture we read in the features of the disciples the amazing truth: Christ lives!' (ibid).

*Being evangelized involves **reacting** to Christ. Evangelization involves the **reaction** of people to Christ.*

**435. Reap.** 'You reap harvests where you did not sow' (Matthew 25:24, GNB). 'One man sows, another man reaps' (John 4:37, GNB). 'Use your sickle and reap the harvest!' (Revelation 14:15, GNB). Christ himself, as Son of Man, is the Reaper (Revelation 14:14).

*To evangelize includes to **reap**. Evangelizing involves **reaping**. Evangelization includes **reaping**.*

**436. Rebuke.** 'Rebuke publicly all those who commit sins' (1 Timothy 5:20, GNB).

*Evangelizing involves an element of **rebuking** sin and sinners.*

**437. Recruit.** In the early church, 'To evangelize was to **recruit** people for God's kingdom' (O. Costas 1974:34).

*Evangelizing is **recruiting** people for Christ.*

**438. Remonstrate with.** This verb means 'to say or plead in objecting or protesting' (*Webster's*). It parallels 'argue', 'dispute', 'debate', 'rebuke' in its application to evangelism.

*Evangelizing includes **remonstrating** with recalcitrant or hostile audiences.*

**439. Reprimand.** 'John **reprimanded** Herod, the governor, because he had married Herodias, his brother's wife' (Luke 3:19, GNB).

*Evangelizing includes an element of **reprimanding** flagrant sinners.*

**440. Reproach.** 'The people in the towns where Jesus had performed most of his miracles did not turn from their sins, so he **reproached** those towns. 'How terrible!' ' (Matthew 11:20-1, GNB).

*To evangelize involves to **reproach**.*

**441. Reprove.** Jesus said, 'All whom I love I **reprove** and discipline' (Revelation 3:19, NEB).

*Evangelism may need to include **reproving** people.*

**442. Request.** 'Jesus made his prayers and **requests** with loud cries and tears' (Hebrews 5:7, GNB). 'They came to Philip... with a **request**. 'Sir,' they said, 'we would like to see Jesus ' ' (John 12:21, NIV).

*Evangelism enables seekers to make their **requests**.*

**443. Rescue.** Jesus said, 'I will **rescue** you from your own people and from the Gentiles' (Acts 26:17, NIV).

*Evangelizing includes **rescuing** people.*

**444. Restore.** 'Ananias coming in and laying his hands on him to **restore** his sight' (Acts 9:12, NEB).

*Evangelization includes **restoration**.*

**445. Retain.** Jesus said, 'If you forgive the sins of any, they are forgiven; if you **retain** the sins of any, they are **retained**' (John 20:23, RSV).

*Evangelizers forgive or **retain** sin as hearers wish.*

**446. Return.** This term directly translates *euangelizo* once in the leading English Bibles, in the Christian Community Bible/Catholic Pastoral Edition: 'Timothy has just **returned** with good news of your faith and love' (1 Thessalonians 3:6, CCB).

*Evangelizers **return** with good news, or sometimes disappointment.*

**447. Save.** The term is used to translate a verbal construction embodying *euangelizo* only once, in the Living Bible paraphrase: 'It is this Good News that **saves** you if you still firmly believe it' (1 Corinthians 15:2, LB). 'Whoever believes and is baptized will be **saved**' (Mark 16:16, GNB). 'God has come to **save** his people!' (Luke 7:16, GNB). 'Believe in the Lord Jesus, and you will be **saved**' (Acts 16:31, RSV, GNB, NIV). 'And so be able to **save** some of them' (Romans 11:14, GNB). 'That I may **save** some of them' (1 Corinthians 9:22, GNB). 'You are **saved** by the gospel' (1 Corinthians 15:2, GNB).

*Evangelizing is **saving** people. Evangelization is, or includes, **salvation**.*

**449. Set right.** Evangelizing is **setting** people **right**

with God.

*To evangelize is to **set** people **right** with God.*

**453. Summon.** 'I am about to **summon** all peoples' (Jeremiah 1:15, NIV). Evangelism is '**summoning** men to come to God in Christ' (B.S.W. Green 1951:24).

*Evangelism is a **summons** to people to come to God.*

**455. Take alive.** This is a rare usage, occurring only once in the English NT. It translates the Greek verb *zogreo*. Jesus said to Peter, 'From henceforth thou shalt **take** men **alive**' (Luke 5:10, ERV margin). The usage has been widely popularized by a noted book by C.G. Trumbull, *Taking men alive: studies in the principles and practice of individual soul-winning* (1907, 1957).

*Evangelism is **taking** people **alive** for Christ.*

**457. Transform.** 'Let God **transform** you inwardly' (Romans 12:2, GNB). This verb is one of those which depict what the result of evangelization could be.

*Evangelizing results in God **transforming** people.*

**460. Turn.** 'You are to open their eyes and **turn** them from the darkness to the light and from the power of Satan to God' (Acts 26:18, GNB).

*Evangelizing is the attempt to **turn** people to God.*

**461. Urge.** '**Urge** them to come in' (Luke 14:23, G.M. Lamsa). 'Strongly **urging** upon the Jews' (Acts 18:5, Berkeley Version). This word is yet another in the series of strong words and synonyms for 'persuade' used to describe effective evangelism in certain contexts.

*To evangelize is to **urge** people to accept the gospel.*

**463. Warn.** 'Warn' translates several NT Greek synonyms of *euangelizo*. There is also an element of **warning** in some 7% of all words used to translate synonyms of *euangelizo*, including 'admonish', 'censure', 'criticize', 'rebuke', 'refute', 'show up', et alia. '**Warn**' and cognates have 9 occurrences in the NT. 'Who **warned** you to flee from the wrath to come?' (Matthew 3:7, RSV). 'Wherever people don't welcome you, leave that town and shake the dust off your feet as a **warning** to them' (Luke 9:5, GNB). 'Him we proclaim, **warning** every man and teaching every man in all wisdom' (Colossians 1:28, RSV).

*To evangelize includes to **warn** hearers. Evangelizing involves **warning**. Evangelization involves the **warning** of hearers.*

**464. Win.** 'Win' or 'win over' translates several NT Greek synonyms of *euangelizo*. 'To **win** a single convert' (Matthew 23:15, NIV). 'Evangelize. To **win** over to the Gospel or the Christian faith' (*A new English dictionary*, Oxford 1897, 1933, with the usage 'to **win** over to' first recorded in 1652). 'Evangelism is the **winning** of individual men and women for Jesus Christ' (E.A. French et al 1923:13). 'Evangelism is the work of **winning** men and women to definite, avowed allegiance to Jesus Christ' (C.J.L. Bates in Mott 1938:39). 'Evangelism is the **winning** of men to acknowledge Christ as their Saviour and King' (Archbishop W. Temple in Mott 1938:85). 'Evangelism means the **winning** of men and women to the discipleship of Christ' (J.J. Conning in Mott 1938:90).

*To evangelize is to **win** people for Christ, or to **win** them over. Evangelizing is **winning** souls. Evangelization involves having converts **won**.*

## VI.  BAPTIZE!

The sixth Mandate has progressed to an advanced stage in the whole spectrum of evangelization. **Planting evangelization** is church-oriented; it deals with baptizing, church planting, church organization, and administration. This is the fascinating human sphere of **Pastoral evangelism**.

Of the 68 facets under this Mandate, none are in The Big Ten.

**465. Add.** This term is one of those mathematical verbs close to evangelization and which are essential to its context, logistics, implementation, and success. '**Add**' means 'to combine (numbers) into a sum; calculate the total of' (*Webster's NWDAL*).

In the Bible, the word and cognates occur 89 times in NRSV: 'Three thousand persons were **added**'

(Acts 2:41), 'Day by day the Lord **added** to their number' (Acts 2:47). 'The Lord **added** new converts to their number' (Acts 2:47, REB). '**Add** to the list' (1 Timothy 5:9, GNB).

*Evangelism and evangelization result in **adding** converts to the church.*

**466. Administer.** 'There are differences of **administrations**, but the same Lord' (1 Corinthians 12:5, AV/KJV). '... **administered** by us to the glory of the same Lord' (2 Corinthians 8:19, AV/KJV). 'No one should blame us about this liberal gift which we are **administering**' (2 Corinthians 8:20, RSV). Paul said to Felix, 'For many years you have **administered** justice in this province' (Acts 24:10, NEB).

*Evangelizing involves **administering**. Evangelization has an essential component in **administration**.*

**467. Affiliate.** '**Affiliated**' and cognates are not employed in AV/KJV. However, its synonym 'member' occurs 21 times in AV/KJV, also in RSV et alia . 'You are the body of Christ and individually members of it' (1 Corinthians 12:27, RSV). 'Adoption' is another major theme in Pauline theology (see Romans 8:9, Galatians 4, Ephesians 1). Membership in the church is near the end of the whole spectrum of the Christian's experience covered by the term 'evangelization'. 'To evangelize is to call people to baptism and membership of the church' (J.S. Robertson 1977:pc).

*Being evangelized involves being **affiliated** or refusing to be. Evangelization embraces **affiliation** or its rejection.*

**469. Baptize.** 'Baptize' (in Greek, *baptizo*, *baptizein*) occurs 58 times in AV/KJV, and '**baptism**' 21 times. 'The Pharisees rejected God's purpose for themselves and refused to be **baptized** by John' (Luke 7:30, GNB), 'being not **baptized** of John' (AV/KJV). '**Baptize** them' (Matthew 28:19, GNB). 'Whoever believes and is **baptized** will be saved' (Mark 16:16, GNB). 'Christ did not send me to **baptize** but to preach the gospel' (1 Corinthians 1:17, RSV). '**Baptism** is part of the church's proclamation. Its role is revelatory. It orders man to proclaim publicly his being in Christ. **Baptism** is not only itself a witness, but a commitment of the **baptized** person to further witness' (Karl Barth 1948). Evangelism is everything 'from the first encounter until **baptism**' (J. Masson 1968:131ff). '**Baptism** was not merely an occasion when Christians confessed Christ before men; the rite itself was regarded as setting forth the Gospel' (D. Webster 1974:8). 'To evangelize is to call people to **baptism**' (J.S. Robertson 1977:pc).

**Baptizing** means initiating new believers into the life of the Christian community. Masson's statement of the classical Roman Catholic understanding that evangelizing covers everything 'from the first encounter until **baptism**' is as broad a definition as seems advisable if the word 'evangelizing' is to retain any distinctive meaning. A definition must stop somewhere. This Catholic missionary one stops at **baptism**, leaving *plantatio ecclesiae* (planting of the church and church growth) as the next stage of mission after evangelization.

The command '**Baptize**' sharpens the polarizing effect of evangelism that we have just investigated under the commands 'Persuade' and 'Disciple'. In Luke 7:30, it is clear that the Pharisees had heard the good news from John the **Baptist** and his call to the **baptism** of repentance, but had refused to be **baptized** and chose to remain **unbaptized**. Refusal to be **baptized** is often equivalent to rejection of Christ. Evangelization therefore involves persuading people one way or other, discipling those who will and leaving others who refuse, **baptizing** those who believe and leaving those who reject.

*To evangelize includes to **baptize** or offer **baptism**. Evangelizing includes **baptizing**. Evangelization is extending **baptism** to people.*

**470. Bear fruit.** Jesus said, 'A healthy tree **bears** good **fruit**' (Matthew 7:17, GNB). 'They hear the message, accept it, and **bear fruit**' (Mark 4:20, GNB).

*Evangelizing results in and includes **bearing fruit**.*

**471. Bless.** 'Through you God will **bless** all mankind' (Galatians 3:8, GNB). 'The gospel keeps bringing **blessings** and is spreading throughout the world' (Colossians 1:6, GNB).

*Evangelization brings and spreads* **blessings.**

**472. Build.** 'The church... was left in peace to **build** up its strength' (Acts 9:31, NEB). 'In order to **build** up the body of Christ' (Ephesians 4:12, GNB).
*Evangelizing results in* **building** *the church.*

**473. Catechize.** 'Catechize' translates several NT Greek synonyms of *euangelizo*. 'Catechize' comes from the NT Greek verb *katecheo*, to teach by word of mouth, to instruct, or (passive) to be informed. For early Christian writers, it meant 'to instruct in the elements of religion'. From Apostolic days 'The name of **catechesis** was given to the whole of the efforts within the Church to make disciples, and to educate and instruct them' (John Paul II, *Catechesi Tradendae* 1979, section 1). '**Catechesis** as a stage in evangelization' (ibid, sub-title). '**Catechesis** is one of these moments—a very remarkable one—in the whole process of evangelization' (ibid, section 18).
*Evangelizing includes* **catechizing.**

**475. Cleanse.** A leper said, ' 'Sir, if you want to, you can make me **clean**.' Jesus stretched out his hand and touched him. 'I do want to,' he answered. 'Be **clean**!' ' (Matthew 8:2,3, GNB). 'He has forgotten how he was **cleansed** from his former sins' (2 Peter 1:9, NEB).
*Evangelizing results in* **cleansings.**

**476. Confirm.** 'Whoever accepts his message **confirms** by this that God is truthful' (John 3:33, GNB). The Lord '**confirmed** the message of his grace' (Acts 14:3, NEB, NIV).
*Evangelization includes its own* **confirmation.**

**479. Dedicate.** 'Be in no hurry to lay hands on someone to **dedicate** him to the Lord's service' (1 Timothy 5:22, GNB).
*Evangelizing requires* **dedicating** *the evangelizers.*

**481. Enlist.** Used once in GNB (1 Samuel 14:52) and once in NRSV (2 Timothy 2:4), the word is a close synonym of 'enrol'.
*Evangelizing aims at* **enlisting** *hearers for Christ.*

**482. Enrol.** This verb is used 81 times in NRSV (65 times in the Book of Numbers). 'So he **enrolled** them in the wilderness' (Numbers 1:19, NRSV). 'The total number that Moses **enrolled** by clans at the command of the Lord was 22,000' (Numbers 3:39, GNB).
*Evangelizing results in* **enrollment** *for Christ and in the church.*

**483. Establish.** 'I was free to defend the gospel and **establish** it firmly' (Philippians 1:7, GNB). God 'is able to **establish** you by my gospel and the proclamation of Jesus Christ' (Romans 16:25, NIV).
*Evangelizing is* **establishing** *the gospel.*

**484. Feed.** Jesus said to Peter, '**Feed** my lambs', '**Feed** my sheep' (John 21:15,17, NIV).
*Evangelizing includes* **feeding** *God's flock.*

**485. Fellowship.** Koinonia (**fellowship**) occurs 19 times in the Greek NT, and '**fellowship**' 14 times in AV/KJV. 'They devoted themselves to the apostles' teaching and **fellowship**' (Acts 2:42, RSV). 'To evangelise is... to serve Him as their King in the **fellowship** of His Church' (Archbishops' Inquiry 1918). 'These three aspects, kerygma, koinonia, and diakonia, should be integrated in our work of evangelism' (J.C. Hoekendijk 1950:171). 'Evangelism's threefold witness: kerygma, koinonia, diakonia' (article by T.O. Wedel 1957). 'The four ingredients—koinonia, kerygma, martyria and diakonia (service)—make up the evangelism of the early Church' (D. Webster 1959:84). 'The evangelizing Church will offer this gift of koinonia in its preaching and teaching' (WCC 2nd Assembly, Evanston speaks, 1954:33-4).
  The place of **fellowship**, or community in the church, is very important. 'To evangelize means today as well the demand for Church community. It must become clear that faith in the Christian Message can only be won, kept and practiced in the community of the Church' (S. Knak in Mott 1938:179).
*To evangelize is to offer* **fellowship** *in Christ.*

**486. Fix.** The term indicates deliberate concentra-

tion and focusing on the person or persons being evangelized. 'Peter **fixed** his eyes on him' (Acts 3:4, NEB). 'Paul **fixed** his eyes on the Council' (Acts 23:1, NEB).
*Evangelizing* **fixes** *people's eyes on Jesus.*

**487. Gain.** 'By losing his life for my sake, he will **gain** it' (Matthew 10:39, NEB). 'After bringing the good news to that town, where they **gained** many converts, they returned to Lystra' (Acts 14:21, NEB). 'For the sake of **gaining** Christ' (Philippians 3:8, NEB).
*Evangelizing includes* **gaining** *converts.*

**489. Grow.** 'This gospel is producing fruit and **growing**' (Colossians 1:6, NIV). 'The number of disciples kept **growing**' (Acts 6:1,GNB). 'The whole body **grows**' (Ephesians 4:16, GNB).
*Evangelizing includes churches* **growing.** *Evangelization comes to fruition in church* **growth.**

**491. Help.** 'A centurion came up to ask his **help**' (Matthew 8:5, NEB). 'It is our duty to **help** the weak' (Acts 20:35, NEB). '**Help** those who are in need' (2 Corinthians 8:13, GNB). '**Help** those who are to receive salvation' (Hebrews 1:14, GNB).
*To evangelize is to* **help** *people find God.*

**493. Immerse.** The Emphasized New Testament (J.B. Rotherham) translates the Great Commission mandate 'Baptize' in Matthew 28:19 as '**immersing** them into the name'.
*Evangelizing includes* **immersing** *people in the name of Christ.*

**496. Initiate.** Evangelization leads to and includes **initiation** into the Christian faith, usually through the sacraments of baptism, church membership, and the eucharist.
*Evangelization includes* **initiating** *persons into Christ.*

**497. Live out.** 'Evangelism means **living**, doing and talking for Christ, more by **living** than the other two' (S.B. Boon-Itt in Mott 1939:51). 'Evangelism includes...the quality of **life** seen in Christ's followers' (A.B. Van Doren in Mott 1938:35). 'Still another aspect of evangelism is the attempt to bring people into the full **life** of the Church as expressed in a local congregation' (WCC 2nd Assembly, *Evanston speaks*, 1954:33-4). 'To evangelize is more than to proclaim the Gospel by word. It is to **live** in conformity with it' (D.T. Niles 1959:40). 'Evangelization must touch **life**'(*Evangelii Nuntiandi* 1975, section 47). 'The primary means of evangelistic witness today is the authentic Christian **life**' (Orthodox Consultation, Bucharest 1974, in Anderson & Stransky 1975:275). 'World evangelism is communication reconciling men from all nations to God and integrating them into the **life** of the church' (Brazil National Strategy Group, ICOWE, in Douglas 1975:1344-6).
*To evangelize is to* **live out** *the gospel. Evangelizing is* **living out** *the gospel. Evangelization is* **life** *and* **lifestyle** *manifesting the gospel.*

**500. Make peace.** 'Go at once and **make peace** with your brother' (Matthew 5:24, GNB). Stephen described how Moses 'saw two Israelites fighting, and he tried to **make peace** between them' (Acts 7:26, GNB). 'Christ came and preached the Good News of **peace** to all' (Ephesians 2:17, GNB).
*Evangelizing is* **making peace** *between man and God.*

**501. Minister.** 'Minister', 'ministry' are widely employed in both OT and NT, and in many English versions. 'Evangelization is a complex **ministry**... the most fundamental of all the **ministries**' (E. LaVerdiere 1980:27).
*Evangelizing is the first and most basic* **ministry.**

**502. Multiply.** 'Multiply' and cognates occur 89 times in the Bible (AV/KJV), 11 times in NT. 'God said to them 'Be fruitful and **multiply**, and fill the earth and subdue it; and have dominion' ' (Genesis 1:28, RSV). 'God said to Noah, '**Multiply** upon the earth' ' (Genesis 8:17, 9:7, RSV). 'God said to Jacob, 'Be fruitful and **multiply**' ' (Genesis 35:11, RSV). 'The number of the disciples **multiplied** greatly' (Acts 6:7, RSV). 'The church was **multiplied**' (Acts 9:31, RSV). 'The word of God grew and **multiplied**' (Acts

12:24, RSV). The term '**multiplication** evangelism' has been in use since the early 1950s; a book describing it is *Born to reproduce* (D. Trotman 1955). A different metaphor is expounded in the title *Multiplying the loaves: the Bible in mission and evangelism* (G.H. Wolfensberger 1968). 'Church-centred evangelism is concerned with propagation (in the fundamental sense of reproduction or **multiplication**) as well as with persuasion... The evangelistic task is not really complete until it becomes self-perpetuating' (H.A. Snyder 1975:331,347). 'The connection between discipleship and evangelistic **multiplication**... producing reproducers' (W. Scott in Wirt 1978:112). 'Evangelism **multiplied** through discipleship' (ibid,110).
*Being evangelized leads to seeing other evangelized persons* **multiplied.**

**504. Pastor.** 'He appointed some to be apostles, others to be prophets, others to be evangelists, others to be **pastors** and teachers' (Ephesians 4:11, GNB).
*Evangelizing includes* **pastoring** *and shepherding the flock of Christ.*

**506. Plant.** 'Plant' is used 13 times in AV/KJV, more in later versions. 'I **planted** the seed, Apollos watered it' (1 Corinthians 3:6, NIV). It is also widespread in nonbiblical usage. 'The most suitable persons to **plant** the gospel among the Heathen' (*Account*, CMS 1799:11). 'What hinders the immediate effort to **plant** the Gospel in every nation?' (Judson Smith, 1887, in Mott 1900:139). Evangelization is a lengthy process extending from first proclamation to baptism and to *plantatio ecclesiae* (see J. Masson 1968). 'In its totality, evangelization consists in the **implantation** of the Church' (Paul VI, *Evangelii Nuntiandi* 1975, section 28). 'Evangelization is complete when the Church has been firmly **planted**' (D.A. McGavran 1977:pc). 'Church renewal, church expansion, and new church **planting** must become organic parts of evangelism' (L.F.S. Ford in Wirt 1978:28).
*To evangelize is to* **plant.** *Evangelizing is* **planting.** *Evangelization is the* **implantation** *of the gospel and the church.*

**509. Praise.** 'She straightened up and began to **praise** God' (Luke 13:13, NEB). 'One of them, finding himself cured, turned back **praising** God aloud' (Luke 17:15, NEB). After receiving the Great Commission, the apostles 'spent all their time in the temple **praising** God' (Luke 24:53, NEB).
*Evangelizing is* **praising** *God, and Christ.*

**510. Produce crop.** 'He waits for his land to **produce** precious **crops**' (James 5:7, GNB). 'The earth **produced** its **crops**' (James 5:18, GNB).
*Evangelization results in* **production** *of crops, both material and spiritual.*

**412. Reconcile.** 'Try hard to be **reconciled** to him' (Luke 12:58, NIV). 'Be **reconciled** to God' (2 Corinthians 5:20, NIV).
*To evangelize is to get people* **reconciled** *to God.*

**514. Remember.** 'You **remember** why I preached the Gospel to you the first time' (Galatians 4:13, GNB). '**Remember** Jesus Christ, who was raised from death' (2 Timothy 2:8, GNB).
*Evangelizing is bringing Christ to people's* **remembrance.**

**515. Reproduce.** A book describing the concept 'multiplication evangelism' is *Born to* **reproduce** (D. Trotman 1955). 'Church-centred evangelism is concerned with propagation (in the fundamental sense of **reproduction** or multiplication) as well as with persuasion... The evangelistic task is not really complete until it becomes self-perpetuating' (H.A. Snyder 1975:331,347). 'The connection between discipleship and evangelistic **mutliplication**... producing **reproducers**' (W. Scott in Wirt 1978:112). '**Reproducers**' are defined as Christians who win *and train* one new disciple a year (D. Trotman).
*Being evangelized leads those evangelized being further* **reproduced.** *Evangelization leads to further* **reproduction** *of evangelizers.*

**516. Sacramentalize.** The Greek word *eucharistia*

occurs in the NT 15 times as a noun (thanksgiving) and 38 times as the verb *eucharisteo* (give thanks). The Eucharist (Lord's Supper), which is termed a '**sacrament**' (secret or sacred gift) by some 85% of the entire Christian world, is a major form of Christian proclamation: 'For as often as you eat this bread and drink the cup, you proclaim the Lord's death until he comes' (1 Corinthians 11:26, RSV).

There is considerable later theological development of this theme. 'Christian evangelism to me is to experience through worship, through partaking of the **Sacrament**, and through Bible study, more complete oneness with God' (A.J. Elliott in Mott 1938:92). 'The evangelizing Church will offer koinonia in its worship and **sacraments**' (WCC 2nd Assembly, Evanston speaks, 1954:34). 'The Eucharist shows itself to be the source and the apex of the whole work of preaching the gospel' (Vatican II, 'Decree on the Ministry and Life of Priests', 1965). 'It has been possible to define evangelization in terms of proclaiming Christ, of catechesis, of conferring Baptism and the other **Sacraments**' (Evangelii Nuntiandi 1975, section 17). 'It is a mistake to make a contrast between evangelization and **sacramentalization**... The role of evangelization is to lead each individual Christian to live the **Sacraments** as true **Sacraments** of faith' (Evangelii Nuntiandi 1975, section 47). 'Evangelization and **Sacramental** Life' (chapter 60), and 'Evangelizing Power of the Eucharist' (chapter 7) in J. Hofinger 1976. 'The Eucharist: Centre of Evangelization' (sub-title in cardinal Basil Hume 1978:7). 'The Eucharist proclaims the Lord's death until he comes. The Eucharist can be a public witness' ('Eucharist and Evangelization', CWME/WCC Melbourne 1980).

The importance of the synonym 'liturgy' (NT Greek leitourgeia) is often stressed. 'The liturgy always is... itself a proclamation of the gospel' (D. Webster 1959:83). 'On still other occasions the simple presence of a worshipping community or man is the witness' (D.T. Niles 1959). 'Liturgy is the heart of evangelism', 'the centrality of liturgy to evangelism' (J.A.T. Robinson 1960:5,6). 'I see the evangelistic attraction of the liturgical life of churches in socialist countries' (E. Castro 1977:4).

Our quotations above show that, in the minds of many Christian traditions today, eucharist or liturgy forms an essential dimension of, or even the heart of, evangelization. Mostly these are traditions under fire or pressure in countries hostile to Christianity. Liturgy becomes the most effective form of evangelization in situations where explicit proclamation, public witness and bold mission are prohibited. Eastern Orthodoxy in particular counts on ways of worship to evangelize in the contemporary hostile world.

The closing imperative of the Great Commission in Matthew's Gospel is 'Remember' (Greek, Idou), also translated 'Behold', 'Lo', 'Be assured', and even 'Mind you' (Berkeley Version). 'Remember, I am with you always' recalls the continuing **sacrament** of the Lord's Supper, the Eucharist.

*Being evangelized involves being* **sacramentalized** *by the gospel. Evangelization centers on the eucharistic* **sacrament** *as proclamation of the gospel.*

---

517. **Secure.** The term is frequent in the Bible (71 times in GNB, 60 times in NRSV); mostly in the OT, and in the NT only 3 (GNB) or 7 (NRSV) times. 'The Lord gave Israel **security**' (Joshua 23:1, GNB).

*Evangelizing is* **securing** *souls for the kingdom of heaven. To evangelize is to* **secure** *souls for Christ.*

---

518. **Serve.** '**Serve**', '**service**' and '**servant**' occur some 590 times in the Bible (AV/KJV); '**service**' 15 times in the NT; *diakonia* (service) occurs 34 times in the Greek NT. Nonbiblical usage is as prolific. 'To evangelise is... to **serve** Him as their King in the fellowship of His Church' (Archbishops' Inquiry 1918). 'Evangelism is the preaching of the Christian Gospel by words and by cooperation in social **service** or any other kind of good works' (Bishop C.P. Wang in Mott 1938:16). 'Evangelism includes... activities which are **serviceable** to individuals or communities' (A.B. Van Doren in Mott 1938:35). 'Evangelism is a passion to share Christ with others... through any and all forms of **service**' (J.S. Ryang in Mott 1938:49). 'Evangelism essentially denotes **service**' (H. Scholten in Mott 1938:61). 'Evangelism is the presentation of the Gospel by preaching, teaching, healing and **service**' (S. Higginbottom in Mott 1938:19). 'Evangelism is the winning of men to acknowledge Christ as their Saviour and King, so that they give themselves to His **service**' (Archbishop W. Temple in Mott 1939:53). 'These three aspects, *kerygma, koinonia,* and *diakonia,* should be integrated in our work of evangelism' (J.C. Hoekendijk 1950:171). 'Evangelism's threefold witness: *kerygma, koinonia, diakonia*' (T.O. Wedel 1957). 'Fellowship, preaching, witness and **service** (*diakonia*) are the permanent and unalterable and indispensable elements of all true evangelism', and '**Service** is an essential aspect of evangelism' (D. Webster 1959:84,153). 'Evangelism is **service** and witness' (subheading in T. Vinay 1968:152).

*To evangelize is to* **serve** *God and man in the gospel.*

---

519. **Shepherd.** Jesus said to Peter, '**Shepherd** my sheep' (John 21:16, ABUV-Broadus). 'Be **shepherds** of the church of God' (Acts 20:28, GNB).

*Evangelizing includes* **shepherding** *of converts.*

---

523. **Strengthen.** After healing the cripple at the temple, Peter announced, 'The name of Jesus, by awakening faith, has **strengthened** this man' (Acts 3:16, NEB). The church 'was **strengthened** and grew in numbers' (Acts 9:31, GNB). 'I have the **strength** to face all conditions by the power that Christ gives me' (Philippians 4:13, GNB).

*Evangelizing is* **strengthening** *the churches so that they may grow.*

---

524. **Support.** With regard to the itinerant evangelists, 'We are bound to **support** such men, and so play our part in spreading the truth' (3 John 8, NEB). 'We ought to **support** such people, and so play our part in spreading the truth' (3 John 8, REB).

*Evangelizing involves* **supporting** *other evangelizers.*

---

525. **Tend.** The verbs *bosko* and *poimaino* (John 21:15-17) mean: **tend**, care for, nourish, nurture, herd, lead to pasture, feed, look after, shepherd, protect, rule, govern, foster, guide. '**Tend** my sheep... **Tend** my lambs' (John 21:15-17, NASB, RSV).

*To evangelize is to* **tend** *lost sheep. Evangelizing is* **tending** *as witness. Evangelization is the* **tending** *of lost sheep and thereby demonstrating the gospel.*

---

526. **Thank.** After receiving Christ's Great Commission, the apostles 'spent all their time in the Temple giving **thanks** to God' (Luke 24:53, GNB). 'When the Gentiles heard this, they were overjoyed and **thankfully** acclaimed the word of the Lord' (Acts 13:48, NEB). 'Always give **thanks** for everything' (Ephesians 5:20, GNB). 'Be **thankful** in all circumstances' (1 Thessalonians 5:18, GNB). 'We **thank** you that you have taken your great power and have begun to rule!' (Revelation 11:17, GNB).

*Evangelizing includes giving* **thanks** *to God.*

---

529. **Wash.** Jesus said to the blind man, 'Go and **wash** your face in the Pool of Siloam... So the man went, **washed** his face, and came back seeing' (John 9:7, GNB).

*Evangelizers assist people* **wash** *their sins away.*

---

530. **Welcome.** The Pharisees complained about Jesus, 'This fellow **welcomes** sinners and eats with them' (Luke 15:2, NEB).

*Evangelizing is* **welcoming** *sinners in Christ's name.*

---

531. **Worship.** On the occasion of giving the Great Commission, 'When they saw him, they **worshipped** him' (Matthew 28:17, GNB). 'They **worshipped** him' (Luke 24:52, GNB). If an unbeliever hears the church **worshipping** in glossolalia, 'he will bow down and **worship** God, confessing 'Truly God is here among you!' ' (1 Corinthians 14:25, GNB). 'On still other occasions, the simple presence of a **worshipping** community or man is the witness' (D.T. Niles 1959).

*Evangelizers evangelize as they* **worship** *God.*

---

532. **Write.** 'Those here **written** have been recorded in order that you may hold the faith' (John 20:31, NEB). 'We should **write** a letter telling them' (Acts 15:20, GNB). 'So I **write** to all of you in Rome' (Romans 1:7, GNB). 'We **write** to you about the Word of life' (1 John 1:1, GNB). 'I **write** to you, young men' (1 John 2:13, NIV). 'I had to **write** and urge you' (Jude 3, NIV). '**Write**!' as an imperative occurs 13 times in Revelation (NRSV); with its cognates, '**write**' occurs 419 times in the NRSV Bible.

*Evangelization among literate populations is heavily involved with* **writing.**

---

## VII. TRAIN!

The seventh and final Mandate completes the cycle. The newly-evangelized are now trained to themselves become evangelizers. **Pedagogical evangelization** undertakes to do just this. It is ministry-oriented. Very often it results in **Programmed evangelism**—highly-organized and well-thought-out training courses, teaching syllabuses, tapes, videos, primers, textbooks on evangelism and its methods, and the whole range of electronic approaches: broadcasting, computing, networking.

Of the 47 facets under this Mandate, 27 are dimensions, 20 are macrodefinitions, 6 are macrocommands, and 2 are macrotranslations. None are in The Big Ten.

---

533. **Admonish.** 'Paul **admonished** them' (Acts 27:9, AV/KJV). 'Bring them up in the nurture and **admonition** of the Lord' (Ephesians 6:4, AV/KJV).

*Being evangelized is being* **admonished**. *Evangelization includes* **admonishment/admonition.**

---

537. **Ascertain.** Paul said to Felix, 'You can **ascertain** the facts for yourself' (Acts 24:11, NEB).

*Being evangelized is* **ascertaining** *the truth of the gospel.*

---

538. **Broadcast.** To evangelize is to **broadcast** the gospel message throughout all varieties of media.

*Evangelizers* **broadcast** *the Good News.*

---

539. **Celebrate.** 'I am so happy I found my lost sheep. Let us **celebrate**!' (Luke 15:6, GNB).

*Evangelization results in* **celebration.**

---

540. **Classify.** There is one usage in NRSV: the Apostle Paul wrote 'We do not dare to **classify** or compare ourselves' (2 Corinthians 10:12). The verb is a synonym of '**class**' or 'compare' and means 'To arrange or group in **classes** according to some system or principle' (*Webster's NWDAL*). As such it has an important role to play as a minor dimension of evangelization.

*Evangelizing may require the evangelist to* **classify** *his audience mentally before he can get a hearing.*

---

541. **Commission.** 'He laid his hands on him and **commissioned** him' (Numbers 27: 23, NIV). 'They had been **commissioned** by David' (2 Chronicles 7:6, GNB). Jesus 'appointed twelve... with a **commission** to drive out devils' (Mark 3:15, NEB). 'I have become its servant by the **commission** God gave me to present to you the word of God' (Colossians 1:25, NIV). 'How could anyone spread the news without a **commission** to do so?' (Romans 10:15, NEB). 'We have been entrusted with this **commission**' (2 Corinthians 4:1). 'Paul, an apostle... by **commission** from Jesus Christ' (Galatians 1:1, NEB). 'From Paul, apostle of Christ Jesus **commissioned** by the will of God' (Colossians 1:1, NEB). 'To obey its Lord's **commission** to take the Gospel to all nations' (J.R.W. Stott in Anderson & Stransky 1975:7).

*Evangelizers are believers* **commissioned** *to evangelize.*

---

547. **Cultivate.** 'The desolate land will be **cultivated**' (Ezekiel 36:34, NIV). 'The Jews are like this **cultivated** tree' (Romans 11:24, GNB). 'The Great Commission has three communication mandates: to proclaim, to persuade, and to **cultivate** the believer' (J. Engel & W. Norton 1975).

*Evangelization includes* **cultivation** *of believers.*

---

550. **Educate.** 'Wisdom is a fountain of life to the wise, but trying to **educate** stupid people is a waste of time' (Proverbs 16:22, GNB).

*Evangelizing is* **educating** *in the gospel.*

---

551. **Exercise.** Evangelizing is **exercising** the church's duty to spread the gospel.

*Evangelism is the* **exercise** *of a God-given gift.*

**552. Fax.** This neologism emerged after 1990 to refer to a completely new communication mode, namely sending messages or drawings or photos by telephone. Almost immediately Christians began to evangelize with this medium, spreading the gospel over fax (facsimile) telephone lines.

*Faxing the gospel is evangelizing.*

**553. Followup.** Evangelizing includes **followup** activity and planning.

*Following up is an essential part of evangelism.*

**554. Fight.** 'We are not **fighting** against human beings but against the wicked spiritual forces in the heavenly world, the rulers, authorities, and cosmic powers of this dark age' (Ephesians 6:12, GNB).

*Evangelizing is* **fighting** *spiritual forces enslaving people. Evangelizers are* **fighters** *for the gospel. Evangelism is the* **fight** *to save people's souls.*

**558. Instruct.** 'Instruct' and cognates are widely used in AV/KJV and other versions. 'Instruct' translates several NT Greek synonyms of *euangelizo*. The Risen Christ 'giving **instructions** through the Holy Spirit' (Acts 1:2, NEB). 'I began to **instruct** him [his Amerindian helper Friday] in the knowledge of the true God' (Daniel Defoe, *Robinson Crusoe*, 1719). 'Evangelize. To **instruct** in the gospel, or law of Jesus' (sole usage given in Dr Samuel Johnson's *Dictionary*, 1755). 'Evangelize. To **instruct** in the gospel' (*The Century dictionary* 1889). 'Evangelize. To **instruct** in the gospel' (*Funk and Wagnalls dictionary* 1893). 'Evangelize. To **instruct** in the gospel' (*Webster's third dictionary* 1909).

*Being evangelized is being or having been* **instructed**. *Evangelization is* **instruction** *in the gospel.*

**559. Make learn.** 'Learn' is used once to directly translate *euangelizo*: 'The wretched of the earth **learn** that God is on their side' (Matthew 11:5, The Message/NTCE). Other usage: 'Our people must **learn** to spend their time doing good' (Titus 3:14, GNB).

*Being evangelized is* **learning** *to respond to Christ. Evangelizing is* **making** *others* **learn** *of the gospel.*

**561. Mobilize.** 'The King of Aram **mobilized** his entire army' (2 Kings 6:24, NIV). 'Evangelizing means **mobilizing** men for God' (H. Scholten in Mott 1938:610). 'Evangelism is a conscientious attempt to **mobilize** all the Christians and their resources in a given area' (R. Loren in C.W. Taylor 1969:44).

*Evangelizing includes* **mobilizing**.

**563. Nurture.** 'Bring them up in the **nurture** and admonition of the Lord' (Ephesians 6:4, AV/KJV); '**Nurture** them' (ASV).

The thought here is the need for the believer to be fed, nourished, **nursed**, care for, reared, tended, cherished, succoured, fostered, managed, trained, instructed, educated, disciplined, schooled. 'Bring them up with Christian discipline and instruction' (Ephesians 6:4, TCNT).

*Being evangelized includes being* **nurtured** *through the gospel. Evangelization is* **nurture** *demonstrating the gospel.*

**564. Progress.** The term is used once to directly translate *euangelizo*: 'Hence my eagerness to make the Gospel **progress** also among you Romans' (Romans 1:15, CCB). Other usages: 'The things that have happened to me have really helped the **progress** of the gospel' (Philippians 1:12, GNB). 'Practice these things and devote yourself to them, in order that your **progress** may be seen by all' (1 Timothy 4:15, GNB).

*To evangelize is to see the gospel make* **progress**.

**566. Ready.** This verb and adjective occur 84 times in OT and NT. 'To make **ready** a people prepared for the Lord' (Luke 1:17, NRSV). 'Always be **ready** to make your defense to anyone who demands from you an accounting for the hope that is in you' (1 Peter 3:15, NRSV).

*Evangelizing is* **readying** *persons for the work of the kingdom.*

**567. Renew.** God our Savior 'saved us through the washing of rebirth and **renewal** by the Holy Spirit' (Titus 3:5, NIV).

*Evangelization includes* **renewal**.

**569. Strive.** 'I **strive** always to keep my conscience clear before God and man' (Acts 24:16, NIV). 'It is love, then, that you should **strive** for' (1 Corinthians 14:1, GNB). '**Strive** for perfection' (2 Corinthians 13:11, GNB). '**Strive** for righteousness, godliness, faith, love, endurance' (1 Timothy 6:11, GNB).

*To evangelize is to* **strive** *for the gospel.*

**570. Struggle.** 'Help these women, who shared my **struggles** in the cause of the Gospel' (Philippians 4:3, NEB). Jude decides 'to write at once and appeal to you to join the **struggle** in defence of the faith' (Jude 3, NEB).

*Evangelization is the* **struggle** *to defend and spread the gospel.*

**571. Take note.** 'Take note of what you hear' (Mark 4:24, NEB). '**Take note** of this: the kingdom of God has come close' (Luke 10:11, NEB). 'They **took note** that these men had been with Jesus' (Acts 4:13, NEB).

*Evangelizing requires continual* **taking note** *of others' surroundings and circumstances.*

**572. Teach.** 'Teach' translates several NT Greek synonyms of *euangelizo*; and it is widely used in all English versions, often in parallel with *euangelizo*. The Greek noun *didache* (**teaching**) occurs 30 times in the NT. 'Go ye therefore, and **teach** all nations' (Matthew 28:19, AV/KJV). '**Teaching** them' (*didaskontes*) (Matthew 28:20, RSV). 'As is **taught** in the Good News I preach' (2 Timothy 2:8, GNB). 'To **teach** others also' (2 Timothy 2:2, GNB). '**Teaching** and preaching' (Acts 15:35, AV/KJV). 'Take note of those who **teach** the gospel of Jesus in all lands' (Origen, *Contra Celsum*, VI.LXXIX, AD 248). 'The chief means for the evangelization of the world are the faithful **teaching** and preaching of the pure Gospel of salvation' (A. Duff in *Proceedings of the Union Missionary Convention*, New York 1854:15). 'Evangelism includes not only preaching but also making disciples and **teaching** the observance of the whole range of

the commands of Christ' (K.S. Latourette & W.R. Hogg 1948:121).

In 1959, the Urbanian University (Vatican) founded a missiological journal *Euntes docete* ('Go and **teach**', based on Matthew 28:19, Vulgate/Latin Bible). 'Evangelize. To **teach** Christianity to' (Longman's English Larousse 1968). 'The Church exists in order to evangelize, that is to say in order to preach and **teach**' (*Evangelii Nuntiandi* 1975, section 14). 'Evangelize: to **teach** the Christian religion as an evangelist' (*Longman's dictionary of contemporary English*, 1978).

*To evangelize is to* **teach** *the gospel. Evangelizing is* **teaching**. *Evangelization is the* **teaching** *of the unevangelized, the evangelized, and evangelizers.*

**576. Train.** 'Train' occurs in one Great Commission account: 'Go out and **train** everyone you meet, far and near, in this way of life' (Matthew 28:19, The Message/NTCE). 'Train' translates several NT Greek synonyms of *euangelizo*. It also translates *matheteuein* ('To make disciples') in Matthew 13:52, RSV: 'Every scribe who has been **trained** for the kingdom of heaven'. Other usages: 'The divine **training** that is in faith' (1 Timothy 1.4, RSV). 'The grace of God has appeared for the salvation of all men, **training** us' (Titus 2:11-12, RSV). For a people group, 'Evangelization is complete when the Church has been firmly planted, replete with ministerial **training** methods and institutions' (D.A. McGavran 1977:pc). R. Sisson, *Training for evangelism* (1979). 'The National Initiative in Evangelism (England) exists in part to provide **trainers** to **train** local church people in evangelism' (NIE 1979).

The rationale for **training** is the completion of the entire process of evangelization, from at the start unreached non-Christians to at the end becoming **trained** Great Commission workers. 'No evangelism is complete until the evangelized become evangelists' (R. Leavell 1951:116).

*To evangelize includes to* **train** *evangelizers. Evangelizing involves* **training**. *Evangelization means the* **training** *of the evangelized to become evangelizers.*

**577. Unite.** 'Remain **united** with me' (John 15:4, NEB). 'We were baptized into **union** with Christ Jesus' (Romans 6:3, NEB). 'His gift is eternal life, in **union** with Christ Jesus' (Romans 6:23, NEB). 'That the universe, all in heaven and on earth, might be brought into a **unity** in Christ' (Ephesians 1:10, NEB).

*To evangelize is to* **unite** *people with Christ.*

**578. Work.** After the Great Commission, the disciples 'went forth, and preached every where, the Lord **working** with them' (Mark 16:20, AV/KJV). A major part of that **work** produced miracles: 'The miracles they **worked** proved that their message was true' (Mark 16:20, CEV). Timothy 'has served with me in the **work** of the gospel' (Philippians 2:22, NIV).

*Evangelizing is the* **work** *of the gospel.*

**579. Work among.** '... miracles, portents, and signs, which God **worked among** you through him' (Acts 2:22, NEB). 'Acknowledge those who are **working** so hard **among** you' (1 Thessalonians 5:12, NEB).

## OVERALL IMPERATIVE: EVANGELIZE!

Finally, there are a handful of synonyms of 'evangelize', together with the actual word itself, which sum up all the prior meanings. All 6 of these facets are also

dimensions, all are macrodefinitions, 2 are macrocommands, and one—*Evangelize!* itself—is both a macrotranslation and also one of The Big Ten.

**580. Discharge.** This is a key word related to 'obligation'. It is not used in AV/KJV. 'I am simply **discharging** the trust committed to me' (1 Corinthians 9:17, NIV). 'The evangelization of the world in this generation... describes a period in which Christians should **discharge** their obligation toward an unevangelized world' (J.R. Mott 1900:9). 'The words evangelize and evangelization are used (here) in the sense of a **discharge** of the obligation resting upon the Christian Church to give every man the opportunity of hearing the Gospel' (J.G.K. Harman 1936:13).

There is a host of parallels, synonyms, and allusions here. 'Necessity is laid upon me. Woe to me if I do not preach the gospel!' (1 Corinthians 9:16, RSV); 'Necessity compels me to do that' (ibid, O.M.

Norlie NT); 'I am under orders to do so' (ibid, GNB). 'Duty' is used twice in AV/KJV. Again, 'The Church has no rest so long as she has not done her best to proclaim the Good News of Jesus the Saviour' (Evangelii Nuntiandi 1975, section 53). 'We wish to remind the entire Church that its duty is that of evangelization' (John Paul I immediately after his election as pope, August 1978).

'The obligation is laid upon the Church of Christ to evangelize' (B.S.W. Green 1951:20). 'The whole Church is under obligation to obey its Lord's commission to take the Gospel to all nations' (J.R.W. Stott in Anderson & Stransky 1975:7). To '**discharge**' an obligation is the opposite of to neglect it.

*To evangelize is to* **discharge** *one's obligation. Evangelizing is* **discharging** *an obligation. Evangelization*

*is an obligation to the world that the church must* **discharge**.

**581. Fulfill.** 'Fulfill' (active voice) occurs 13 times in AV/KJV. Jesus said, 'All things must be **fulfilled**' (Luke 24:44, AV/KJV). 'I have **fulfilled** my task in bearing the Glad-tidings of Christ' (Romans 15:19, W.J. Conybeare). '**Fulfill** the law of Christ' (Galatians 6:2, AV/KJV). 'To **fulfill** the word of God' (Colossians 1:25, AV/KJV). '**Fulfill** the royal law' (James 2:8, AV/KJV). '**Fulfilled**' occurs 47 times in AV/KJV. 'The time is **fulfilled**, and the kingdom of God is at hand' (Mark 1:15 AV/KJV). 'What shall be the sign when all these things shall be **fulfilled**?' (Mark 13:4, AV/KJV); 'What will be the sign when the **fulfillment** of all this is at hand?' (NEB). 'God hath put in their hearts to **fulfill** his will... until the words of God shall be **fulfilled**' (Revelation 17:17, AV/KJV). 'Till the thousand years should be **fulfilled**' (Revelation 20:3, AV/KJV). World evangelization is 'the Church **fulfilling** its supreme and biblical responsibility under the direction of the Holy Spirit' (Caribbean National Strategy Group report, ICOWE, in J.D. Douglas 1975:1350). 'The time of evangelism will not last for ever; it will be succeeded by the time of the Kingdom **fulfilled**'; and, to evangelize is 'to declare this hope to the world until the consummation of the Kingdom and the coming of the King' (WCC 2nd Assembly, *Evanston speaks* 1954:41).

*To evangelize is to **fulfill** the church's mission. Evangelizing is **fulfilling** mission. Evangelization is **fulfillment** of the church's mission.*

582. **Account.** 'Account' occurs 17 times in AV/KJV, as well as in other versions. 'Account for the funds!' (2 Kings 12:15, GNB).'On the day of judgment men will render **account**' (Matthew 12:36, RSV). 'Account for your management!' (Luke 16:2, NIV). 'So that the whole world may be held **accountable** to God' (Romans 3:19, RSV). 'Each of us shall give **account** of himself to God' (Romans 14:12, RSV). 'They will give **account** to him who is ready to judge the living and the dead. For this is why the gospel was preached' (1 Peter 4:5, RSV).

In the same way that the Church is **accountable** before God for its obedience or disobedience to the Great Commission, so all persons, once they become evangelized, are now **accountable** before God for how they respond to Christ and his call to them.

*Being evangelized is being made **accountable** before God. Evangelization means **accountability** before God.*

583. **Be responsible.** 'Responsibility' is not used in AV/KJV, though several of its synonyms are. 'This generation will be held **responsible**' (Luke 11:50, NIV). 'Your blood be on your own heads! I am clear of my **responsibility**' (Acts 18:6, NIV). Elsewhere, evangelization is 'the presenting of the Gospel in such a manner to every soul in this world that the **responsibility** for what is done with it shall no longer rest upon the Christian Church, or on any individual Christian, but shall rest on each man's head for himself' (SVMU in E. Stock, *History of the Church Missionary Society*, 1899:III.656). 'Evangelism is the presentation of the Evangel in such a way that the **responsibility** for what is done with it will rest entirely with him who is evangelized' (R.P. Wilder in

Mott 1938:105). 'The **responsibility** to evangelize belongs to the whole body of Christ' (*Lausanne Covenant* 1974, section 8). 'Evangelization constitutes the **responsibility** of each believer and local church in obedience to the great commission' (J.D. Douglas 1975:1344-6). *Evangelism: Church **responsibility** today* (National Student Christian Congress, London, 1978).

*Being evangelized means being made **responsible**. Evangelization means having final **responsibility** for one's own choice.*

584. **Obey.** 'Obey', 'obedience', and cognates occur 53 times in AV/KJV, and widely elsewhere. 'Obey' translates several NT Greek synonyms of *euangelizo*. 'I did not fail to **obey** the heavenly vision' (Acts 26:19, TCNT). 'Who do not **obey** the Good News about our Lord Jesus' (2 Thessalonians 1:8, GNB). 'Those who do not **obey** the gospel' (1 Peter 4:17, NIV). 'By evangelism is meant **obedience** to the Great Commission' (K.S. Latourette in IMC committee, 1950). 'To **obey** its Lord's commission to take the Gospel to all nations' (J.R.W. Stott in Anderson & Stransky 1975:7). 'Christ has commanded His Church to make known the Gospel and evangelism is **obedience** to this command' (*Nationwide Initiative in Evangelism*, Britain, 1979).

*To evangelize is to **obey** the Great Commission. Evangelization is **obeying**. Evangelization is **obedience** to the Great Commission.*

585. **Evangelize.**This English verb was first recorded as coined ('**euangelisen**') in 1382 by John Wycliffe for the first translation of the Bible into English. His disciples replaced most of its occurrences in the 1388 revision by 'preche' and 'schew'. The fate of the English transliteration down to the present day is shown by exact word counts for the 40 major English Bible versions over the centuries; these are given in Table 23–11. 'Evangelize' occurs 67 times in these 40 versions, in its 3 spellings: **euangelise** (Wyclif in AD 1380), **evangelise** (British spelling), and **evangelize** (American English).

All subsequent Anglican and Protestant major English Bibles then avoided '**evangelize**' in favor of 'preach'. As a result, '**evangelize**' has been ignored and so totally absent in all subsequent mainstream or authorized or official English Bibles to the present day—in TB-M (1525), CB (1535), GB-C (1539), GB (1560), BB (1568), AV/KJV (1611), RV/ERV (1885), ASV (1901), MB (1924), AT/GB (1929), RSV (1952), JB (1966), NAB (1970), NEB (1970), TLB

(1971), NASB (1971), GNB/TEV (1976), NIV (1978), NKJV (1982), NJB (1985), NCV (1986), CCB (1988), NRSV (1989), REB (1989), GW (1995), CEV (1995). The most surprising of these omissions are the most popular modern versions: RSV, NEB, TLB, NASB, GNB, NIV, NKJV, NRSV, REB, CEV. The main exception is in Catholic Bibles: the 1582 Rheims New Testament used '**evangelize**' in 41 of the 54 NT occurrences of euangelizo. The 1749 Douay-Challoner revised Bible replaced all these except for one single usage of '**evangelize**' (in Luke 8:1). Of subsequent Catholic Bibles, Knox uses it only once (1 Peter 1:12), while all the modern Catholic versions—JB, NAB, NJB, CCB—omit it altogether.

There is, however, a small handful of other less official usages. (1) In 1903 the Holy Bible in Modern English (Farrar Fenton) translated euangelizo by '**evangelize**' 10 times. (2) The Apostles returned to Jerusalem '**evangelizing**' many Samaritan villages' (Acts 8:25, Helen Montgomery's Centenary Translation, or NTME, 1924). (3) Paul's vision of a call to Macedonia was 'to **evangelize** there' (Acts 16:10, earlier Berkeley Version of the NT). (4) The 1959 revision of MLB/NBV (Berkeley) translates euangelizo by '**evangelize**' 5 times. Paul's goal was 'that we may **evangelize** those beyond you' (2 Corinthians 10:16); also 'The poor are **evangelized**' (Matthew 11:5, also Luke 7:22); 'If anyone **evangelizes** you' (Galatians 1:9); and 'The first time I **evangelized** you' (Galatians 4:13). (5) 'Christ sent me out not to baptize but to **evangelize** by preaching the glad tidings' (1 Corinthians 1:17, AmB). (6) Jehovah's Witnesses use **evangelize** and cognates—verb, participle, adjective, and noun—frequently in their New World Translation, but never to translate euangelizo which is everywhere (with only 2 exceptions) translated by 'declare'. (7) After one isolated occurrence in 1965 (in 1 Corinthians 1:17, AmB) all new translations up to the present day have studiously avoided translating euangelizo by '**evangelize**' anywhere or everywhere. The only partial exception is in NAB (1970) where although euangelizo is absent in the Greek of Philippians 4:15 the English reads 'at the start of my **evangelizing**'.

Since '**evangelize**' is thus a major translation of euangelizo, even being one of The Big Ten in frequency, it is reasonable to expect that future mainline/authorized/official versions of the English Bible may rehabilitate the word, reintroduce it into the Scriptures as a central concept, and thus recognize its major role in contemporary Christianity.

Part 24

# MICROEVANGELISTICS

Enumerating and quantifying the concept of evangelization

*The LORD spoke to Moses..: 'Number the whole community of Israel' (NEB)/'Take a census of all the congregation of the people of Israel' (RSV).*
—Numbers 1:1-2, New English Bible, and Revised Standard Version.

*The angel who spoke to me had a gold measuring stick to measure the city and its gates and its walls.*
—Revelation 21:15, Contemporary English Version

'Evangelistics' is defined in Webster's *Third new international dictionary* as the scientific study of the Christian faith and in particular of its expansion and spread. Part 24 begins the process by reviewing the history and evolution of methods to enumerate empirical Christianity; its followers, and its outreach at the micro level—an individual, a population, a people, a city, a country. Descriptive scales are then derived to select 20 key variables for a formula that quantifies the extent of evangelization among a population—what percentage E of its persons have become evangelized. This leads to a related but significantly different standard measure of ongoing evangelistic activity, e, defined as the number of evangelistic offers now being received per capita, per year.

# Enumerating and quantifying the concept of evangelization

Evangelistics is the science that studies the propagation of Christianity (*Webster's/WTNIDEL*). Microevangelistics is the science that studies this subject starting at the microscopic level—each individual, each component, each word, each factor—and builds up from this detailed study of each aspect to make sense of the whole.

This Part 24 deals with the enumerating and quantifying of evangelization in all its aspects. The history of significant achievements and literature on the subject is reviewed and the methodology behind all scales proposed is set out. A number of scales measuring the personal and organizational status of evangelization are described. Two major current scales implemented in this survey are derived, also 7 major groupings of variables, subdivided into 45 distinct outreach ministries or varieties of evangelism (as explained in Part 22), making a total of 100 variables all of which are then given for all population segments for every country. Finally, a compact formula is derived enabling the reader to compute the status of evangelization in any segment of population using only mental arithmetic applied to the printed pages of the databases.

## A recent attempt to quantify evangelization
By 1985, the history of Christianity had produced some 788 distinct and separate global plans to evangelize the world. All were described, analyzed, and evaluated in the book *Seven hundred plans to evangelize the world* (1988). By AD 2000 that total had risen to some 1,500 distinct global plans. These plans are listed and analyzed here in Part 27 "GeoStrategies".

Around half of these plans included a definite promise to begin by undertaking a comprehensive survey of the state of world evangelization. Only 10 plans eventually produced anything approaching the fulfilment of this promise.

Unfortunately, this subject has never been adequately addressed by any other of these global plans, nor by the various ecclesiastical worlds, nor by the academic world. We need first to ask, therefore, what would be the purpose of any such attempt to enumerate evangelization at the global level.

### REASONS FOR QUANTIFICATION

#### Why enumerate?
An answer to this often-asked question can be brief. The reason for quantifying is to enable persons seriously concerned with a subject to get a grasp on the status quo, to assess the subject's present state, to understand its current progress and its hindrances, to get a handle on the realities of the situation, and to perceive trends from the present into both the short-term and long-term futures. The necessity for enumerating evangelization may be found by glancing at a short list of secular global problem areas parallel to evangelization, and seeing what the international organizations set up to handle those areas do concerning their enumeration. These are set out in Table 24–1 below.

#### A secular parallel
A close parallel to evangelization is literacy. Here is an obvious good characteristic that those who uphold human rights can fight for: the right of every individual to be taught to read and write. Yet at the global level it has long been a problem area. Many observers have suspected that over large areas of the world, literacy has recently been declining, due to literacy efforts being overwhelmed and surpassed by the population explosion. How are planners, strategists and activists to approach this problem?

The first and most essential answer is to obtain annual statistics of how literacy is actually faring, in every nation and thence at the global level. This gathering of statistics has been the responsibility of UNESCO since 1945 and, despite immense technical difficulties, it has published results regularly since. Table 24–1 demonstrates that secular global bodies who are responsible for specific problem areas see part of their task as the regular enumeration and quantification of those areas.

## The objects of quantifying evangelization
It is the same with the religious problem area called evangelization. Because of its global nature involving over 6 billion people, it is too huge an area for the human mind to comprehend without numerical help. The whole objective of enumerating evangelization is therefore to enable concerned persons and organizations to understand the situation and to ask and answer certain types of questions essential for any kind of assessment, evaluation, coordinated action, and equitable distribution of resources. The objects, with examples of the types of questions that can be answered, are as follows.

1. To get a handle on any very large situation (e.g. "Africa is now 80% evangelized, though 25 countries are still under 40% evangelized");
2. To compare evangelization in one populace with that in another populace, in order to be able to make comparative statements (e.g. "The population of South India is very much more evangelized than the population of North India");
3. To compare the present extent or level of evangelization with that in the recent past in order to determine present trends (e.g. "The evangelization of Thailand is increasing rapidly every year");
4. To compare the present extent or level of world evangelization with that in previous eras in order to determine long-term trends (e.g. "The world is now more evangelized than it was in 1800 or 1900"); and
5. To compare the present extent of world evangelization with the ultimate goal of evangelizing the whole world (e.g. "The world is now 70% evangelized").

## What the churches enumerate at present
Up to the present, enumeration in all churches and Christian traditions centers on the criterion of baptism or reception into membership. Most churches measure their total of baptized members, and of new baptisms each year. In addition, many churches measure indicators of Christian practice: communicants, Sunday worship attenders. Many also measure their work force: bishops, priests, deacons, ministers, evangelists, preachers, sisters, monks, and so on. In the comprehensive enumeration of the churches in the 1982 *World Christian encyclopedia*, some 80 different measures of church membership and activity were enumerated. By AD 2000, the total of all distinct measures enumerated each year by church and agencies had risen to 180 subjects; these are listed here in Part 1, Global Diagram 3.

The difficulty is that all of these measures describe only the church, not the outsiders whom the church wants to evangelize. They describe only conversion, christianization, and church life, not outreach or evangelization. To this date, no major church or Christian tradition has attempted to quantify, on a systematic and regular basis, the extent of its evangelizing activity or its other varieties of outreach. The following brief history of the subject will illustrate this.

### HISTORY OF QUANTIFYING EVANGELIZATION, 1792–1938

#### Early attempts at quantification
Missionary statesmen since William Carey (1792) and Henry Venn (1841) have long advocated the regular keeping of statistics of missionary endeavor, but these embraced only church membership statistics. The first attempts to enumerate the full extent of evangelization date from John R. Mott's impact on the scene. His 1900 classic *The evangelization of the world in this generation* contained statements such as these:

> Half of the adult population of Manchuria know that there is a Christian gospel. Dr. Ross said that one-third of the people had heard of Christ, and knew enough to pronounce Christianity the best religion.

But 4 decades later, despite Mott's continuing influence as chairman of the International Missionary Council, systematic enumeration of evangelization had proceeded no further. The IMC survey for its 1938 meeting in Tambaram, South India included only occasional statements such as:

> 45% of China is still entirely untouched by Christian forces. Half of Manchuria is beyond Christian influence.

This latter statement can be inverted to read: By 1938, 55% of China had been touched by Christian forces, and 50% of Manchuria had come under Christian influence. But the handful of statements of this kind was entirely inadequate for assessing the status of the global situation.

### SCALES OF EVANGELIZATION, 1962

From New Testament days, Christians enumerated a range of subjects connected with the church—church membership, new baptisms, number of leaders and workers, number of churches, and so on. Before 1950, however, the subjects of outreach and evangelization were not clear enough concepts in the Christian world, nor defined with the necessary precision to result in their regular and systematic enumeration.

Since the 1950s, several scales have been evolved that indicate an individual's, or a people's, or a country's, or any other population's status and progress with regard to becoming evangelized. These will now be briefly described, dated from the year of their first publication in print.

#### 1962: first scales for (a) state and (b) rate
The first large-scale attempt was begun in 1962 and published in 1965 under the title *The evangelization of West Africa today: a survey across 21 nations and 150 tribes*. This ambitious project was commissioned by the Division of World Mission and Evangelism, World Council of Churches in 1962. It progressed under the leadership of a French Protestant missionary, Pierre Benignus, until his untimely death in an air crash on Mount Cameroon in 1963. All his data, maps, and documentation perished with him. His work was then continued by a 3-man team commissioned by the WCC and now joined by the All Africa Conference of Churches as sponsors. This team consisted of J.S. Lawson (a Togolese; AACC associate general secretary), B.B. Ayam (later a bishop in the Church of Nigeria) and D.B. Barrett (a CMS missionary). From March to June 1965 they travelled across Africa reporting in detail on the situation in 150 ethnolinguistic peoples. Their report contained Barrett's maps of the tribes' locations, and statistical tables measuring the current state, and the present rate of change, of each's evangelization. The current status or state (in French, *état*) of evangelization was represented by the symbol E, which at that time was a 5-point assessment of each people's situation, as shown in Table 24–2.

This variable evolved some 5 years later into E (% evangelized), the eventual indicator of comparative

**Table 24–1.  Global statistics: a range of 100 subjects enumerated by 55 international organizations in their 82 statistical yearbooks.**

The list of organizations in this table is given in 2 parallel forms: first, alphabetically by initials of each organization (given in column 1); and second, alphabetically by each major subject area (given in bold type in column 4).

### I. Organizations ranked alphabetically by initials (in column 1)

| Initials | Organization | Subjects (=all in bold type in columns 3 and 4) | Title of statistical yearbook or encyclopedia |
|---|---|---|---|
| 1 | 2 | 3 | 4 |
| AT&T | AT&T Communications | | The world's **telephones** |
| FAO | **Food** and **Agriculture** Organization | | Yearbook of **agricultural** statistics |
| FAO | **Food** and **Agriculture** Organization | | **Forest fire** statistics |
| FAO | **Food** and **Agriculture** Organization | | FAO **Production** yearbook |
| FAO | **Food** and **Agriculture** Organization | | FAO **Trade** yearbook |
| FAO | **Food** and **Agriculture** Organization | | **Fertilizer** yearbook |
| FAO | **Food** and **Agriculture** Organization | | The state of **food** and **agriculture** |
| FAO | **Food** and **Agriculture** Organization | | Yearbook of **fishery** statistics |
| FAO | **Food** and **Agriculture** Organization | | Yearbook of **forest** products |
| GATT | General Agreement on **Tariffs** & **Trade** | | International **trade** |
| IAEA | International **Atomic Energy** Agency | | International **atomic energy** annual report |
| IATA | International **Air Transport** Association | | World **air transport** statistics |
| IBRD | International Bank for **Reconstruction** & **Development** | | World **development** report |
| IBRD | International Bank for **Reconstruction** & **Development** | | **Commodity** trade and price trends |
| IBRD | International Bank for **Reconstruction** & **Development** | | World **debt** tables |
| IBRD | International Bank for **Reconstruction** & **Development** | | World tables **(economic, social)** |
| ICAC | International **Cotton** Advisory Committee | | **Cotton:** world statistics |
| ICAO | International **Civil Aviation** Organization | | **Civil aviation** statistics of the world |
| ICO | International **Cocoa** Organization | | Quarterly bulletin of **cocoa** statistics |
| IEA | International **Energy** Agency | | **Energy** statistics |
| IEA | International **Energy** Agency | | Annual **oil and gas** statistics |
| IEA-CIS | **Coal** Information System | | **Coal** information |
| IICSR | International Institute for Comparative **Social Research** | | World handbook of **political and social** indicators |
| IISI | International **Iron** and **Steel** Institute | | **Steel** statistical yearbook |
| IISI | International **Iron** and **Steel** Institute | | World **steel** in figures |
| ILO | International **Labour** Organization | | Year book of **labour** statistics |
| ILZSG | International **Lead and Zinc** Study Group | | **Lead** and **zinc** statistics |
| IMF | International **Monetary** Fund | | **Balance of payments** statistics yearbook |
| IMF | International **Monetary** Fund | | Direction of **trade** statistics yearbook |
| IMF | International **Monetary** Fund | | Government **finance** statistics yearbook |
| IMF | International **Monetary** Fund | | International **financial** statistics yearbook |
| INCB | International **Narcotics** Control Board | | Statistics on **narcotic drugs** |
| INCB | International **Narcotics** Control Board | | Statistics on **psychotropic substances** |
| INTERPOL | International **Criminal Police** Organization | | International **crime** statistics |
| IPSA | Houghton Mifflin Company | | Information Please **sports** almanac |
| IRF | International **Road** Federation | | World **road** statistics |
| IRSG | International **Rubber** Study Group | | World **rubber** statistics handbook |
| ISI | International Statistical Institute | | World **fertility** survey |
| ISO | International **Sugar** Organization | | ISO Statistical bulletin **(sugar)** |
| ITC | International **Tea** Committee | | ITC Annual bulletin of statistics **(tea)** |
| ITC | International **Tin** Council | | **Tin** statistics |
| ITMF | International **Textile** Manufacturers Federation | | International **man-made fibre production** statistics |
| ITU | International Telecommunication Union | | Yearbook of common carrier **telecommunication** statistics |
| IUR | International Union of **Railways** | | International **railway** statistics |
| IWC | International **Whaling** Commission | | International **whaling** statistics |
| IWC | International **Wheat** Council | | World **wheat** statistics |
| LRS | Lloyd's Register of **Shipping** | | Statistical tables **(shipping)** |
| MVMA | **Motor Vehicle** Manufacturers Association | | World **motor vehicle** data |
| NBA | National **Basketball** Association | | The official NBA **basketball** encyclopedia |
| NFL | National **Football** League | | Sports encyclopedia: pro **football** |
| NLB | National League **Baseball** | | **Baseball** encyclopedia |
| OECD | Organization for **Economic Cooperation** & Development | | **Economic** outlook |
| OECD | Organization for **Economic Cooperation** & Development | | **Iron** and **steel** industry |
| OECD | Organization for **Economic Cooperation** & Development | | **Pulp** and **paper** quarterly statistics |
| OECD | Organization for **Economic Cooperation** & Development | | **Maritime** transport |
| OPEC | Organization of **Petroleum** Exporting Countries | | OPEC Annual statistical bulletin **(oil)** |
| RCC | **Catholic** Church | | Annuario Pontificio **(jurisdictions)** |
| RCC | Secretariat of State, **Catholic** Church | | Statistical yearbook of **the Church** |
| SCEP | Sacred Congregation for the **Evangelization** of Peoples | | Guida delle **missioni** cattoliche |
| UBS | United **Bible** Societies | | **Scriptures** of the world |
| UBS | United **Bible** Societies | | World **translations** progress report |
| UBS | United Bible Societies | | Book of Two Thousand **Tongues** |
| UN | UN/FAO/ILO/UNESCO/WHO | | Compendium of **social** statistics |
| UN | UN **Population** Commission & UN Statistical Office | | UN **Demographic** yearbook |
| UN | UN **Population** Council | | Induced **abortion:** a world review |
| UN | UN Statistical Office | | Compendium of **housing** statistics |
| UN | UN Statistical Office | | UN Statistical yearbook **(socioeconomic)** |
| UN | UN Statistical Office | | Yearbook of **construction** statistics |
| UN-SITC | Standard International **Trade Classification** | | Yearbook of **international trade** statistics |
| UN/CIA/&c | **World Priorities** | | World **military** and **social** expenditures |
| UNCTAD | UN Conference on **Trade** & **Development** | | Handbook of international **trade** & **development** statistics |
| UNCTAD | UN Conference on **Trade** & **Development** | | **Tungsten** statistics |
| UNECE | **Economic** Commission for Europe | | Bulletin of statistics on **world trade** in engineering products |
| UNESCO | UN **Education, Scientific** & **Cultural** Organization | | UNESCO Statistical yearbook **(social, scientific)** |
| UNHCR | UN High Commission for **Refugees** | | Populations **(refugees)** of concern to UNHCR, annual statistical review |
| UNIDO | UN **Industrial Development** Organization | | Yearbook of **industrial** statistics |
| UNNAS | UN **National Account**s Statistics | | Yearbook of **national accounts** statistics |
| UNSO/WESS | World **Energy** Suppliers System | | Yearbook of **world energy** statistics |
| UPU | Universal **Postal** Union | | **Postal** statistics |
| USACDA | US **Arms** Control & **Disarmament** Agency | | World **military expenditures and arms transfers** |
| WBMS | World Bureau of **Metal** Statistics | | World **metal** statistics |
| WBT | Wycliffe **Bible** Translators | | Ethnologue: **languages** of the world |
| WCC | World Council of **Churches** | | Handbook of member **churches** |
| WERC | World **Evangelization** Research Center | | World **Christian** encyclopedia I & II |
| WHO | World **Health** Organization | | World **health** statistics annual |
| WIPO | World Intellectual **Property** Organization | | Industrial **property** statistics |
| WMO | World **Meteorological** Organization | | WMO **climatological** normals |
| WTO | World **Tourism** Organization | | World **travel** statistics |

Continued opposite

*Table 24–1 concluded*

**II. Organizations ranked alphabetically by major subject area (in bold type in column 4)**

| Initials 1 | Organization 2 | Subjects 3 | Title of statistical yearbook or encyclopedia 4 |
|---|---|---|---|
| UN | UN **Population** Council | | Induced **abortion**: a world review |
| AO | **Food** and **Agriculture** Organization | | Yearbook of **agricultural** statistics |
| IATA | International **Air Transport** Association | | World **air transport** statistics |
| IAEA | International **Atomic Energy** Agency | | International **atomic energy** annual report |
| IMF | International **Monetary** Fund | | **Balance of payments** statistics yearbook |
| NL | National League **Baseball** | | **Baseball** encyclopedia |
| NBA | National **Basketball** Association | | The official NBA **basketball** encyclopedia |
| WERC | World **Evangelization** Research Center | | World **Christian** encyclopedia I & II |
| WCC | World Council of **Churches** | | Handbook of member **churches** |
| ICAO | International **Civil Aviation** Organization | | **Civil aviation** statistics of the world |
| WMO | World **Meteorological** Organization | | WMO **climatological** normals |
| IEA-CIS | **Coal** Information System | | **Coal** information |
| ICO | International **Cocoa** Organization | | Quarterly bulletin of **cocoa** statistics |
| IBRD | International Bank for **Reconstruction** & **Development** | | **Commodity** trade and price trends |
| UN | UN Statistical Office | | Yearbook of **construction** statistics |
| ICAC | International **Cotton** Advisory Committee | | **Cotton**: world statistics |
| INTERPOL | International **Criminal Police** Organization | | International **crime** statistics |
| IBRD | International Bank for **Reconstruction** & **Development** | | World **debt** tables |
| UN | UN **Population** Commission & UN Statistical Office | | UN **Demographic** yearbook |
| IBRD | International Bank for **Reconstruction** & **Development** | | World **development** report |
| OECD | Organization for **Economic Cooperation** & Development | | **Economic** outlook |
| IBRD | International Bank for **Reconstruction** & **Development** | | World tables (**economic, social**) |
| IEA | International **Energy** Agency | | **Energy** statistics |
| ISI | International Statistical Institute | | World **fertility** survey |
| FAO | **Food** and **Agriculture** Organization | | **Fertilizer** yearbook |
| IMF | International **Monetary** Fund | | Government **finance** statistics yearbook |
| IMF | International **Monetary** Fund | | International **financial** statistics yearbook |
| FAO | **Food** and **Agriculture** Organization | | Yearbook of **fishery** statistics |
| FAO | **Food** and **Agriculture** Organization | | The state of **food** and **agriculture** |
| NFL | National **Football** League | | Sports encyclopedia: pro **football** |
| FAO | **Food** and **Agriculture** Organization | | **Forest fire** statistics |
| FAO | **Food** and **Agriculture** Organization | | Yearbook of **forest** products |
| WHO | World **Health** Organization | | World **health** statistics annual |
| UN | UN Statistical Office | | Compendium of **housing** statistics |
| UNIDO | UN **Industrial** Development Organization | | Yearbook of **industrial** statistics |
| UN-SITC | Standard International **Trade** Classification | | Yearbook of **international trade** statistics |
| OECD | Organization for **Economic Cooperation** & Development | | **Iron** and **steel** industry |
| RCC | **Catholic** Church | | Annuario Pontificio (**jurisdictions**) |
| ILO | International **Labour** Organization | | Year book of **labour** statistics |
| WBT | Wycliffe **Bible** Translators | | Ethnologue: **languages** of the world |
| ILZSG | International **Lead and Zinc** Study Group | | **Lead** and **zinc** statistics |
| ITMF | International **Textile** Manufacturers Federation | | International **man-made fibre production** statistics |
| OECD | Organization for **Economic Cooperation** & Development | | **Maritime** transport |
| WBMS | World Bureau of **Metal** Statistics | | World **metal** statistics |
| UN/CIA/&c | **World Priorities** | | World **military** and **social expenditure**s |
| USACDA | US **Arms** Control & **Disarmament** Agency | | World **military** expenditures and arms transfers |
| SCEP | Sacred Congregation for the **Evangelization** of Peoples | | Guida delle **missioni** cattoliche |
| MVMA | **Motor Vehicle** Manufacturers Association | | World **motor vehicle** data |
| INCB | International **Narcotics** Control Board | | Statistics on **narcotic drugs** |
| UNNAS | UN **National Accou**nts Statistics | | Yearbook of **national accounts** statistics |
| OPEC | Organization of **Petroleum** Exporting Countries | | OPEC Annual statistical bulletin (**oil**) |
| IEA | International **Energy** Agency | | Annual **oil and gas** statistics |
| IICSR | International Institute for Comparative **Social Research** | | World handbook of **political and social** indicators |
| UPU | Universal **Postal** Union | | **Postal** statistics |
| FAO | **Food** and **Agriculture** Organization | | FAO **Production** yearbook |
| WIPO | World Intellectual **Property** Organization | | Industrial **property** statistics |
| INCB | International **Narcotics** Control Board | | Statistics on **psychotropic substances** |
| OECD | Organization for **Economic Cooperation** & Development | | **Pulp** and **paper** quarterly statistics |
| IUR | International Union of **Railways** | | International **railway** statistics |
| UNHCR | UN High Commission for **Refugees** | | Populations (**refugees**) of concern to UNHCR, annual statistical review |
| IRF | International **Road** Federation | | World **road** statistics |
| IRSG | International **Rubber** Study Group | | World **rubber** statistics handbook |
| UBS | United **Bible** Societies | | **Scriptures** of the world |
| LRS | Lloyd's Register of **Shipping** | | Statistical tables (**shipping**) |
| UN | UN/FAO/ILO/UNESCO/WHO | | Compendium of **social** statistics |
| UNESCO | UN **Education, Scientific** & **Cultural** Organization | | UNESCO Statistical yearbook (**social, scientific**) |
| UN | UN Statistical Office | | UN Statistical yearbook (**socioeconomic**) |
| IPSA | Houghton Mifflin Company | | Information Please **sports** almanac |
| IISI | International **Iron** and **Steel** Institute | | **Steel** statistical yearbook |
| IISI | International **Iron** and **Steel** Institute | | World **steel** in figures |
| ISO | International **Sugar** Organization | | ISO Statistical bulletin (**sugar**) |
| ITC | International **Tea** Committee | | ITC Annual bulletin of statistics (**tea**) |
| ITU | International **Telecommunication** Union | | Yearbook of common carrier **telecommunication** statistics |
| AT&T | AT&T Communications | | The world's **telephones** |
| RCC | Secretariat of State, **Catholic** Church | | Statistical yearbook of **the Church** |
| ITC | International **Tin** Council | | **Tin** statistics |
| UBS | United **Bible** Societies | | Book of Two Thousand **Tongues** |
| GATT | General Agreement on **Tariffs** & **Trade** | | International **trade** |
| FAO | **Food** and **Agriculture** Organization | | FAO **Trade** yearbook |
| IMF | International **Monetary** Fund | | Direction of **trade** statistics yearbook |
| UNCTAD | UN Conference on **Trade** & **Development** | | Handbook of international **trade** & **development** statistics |
| UBS | United **Bible** Societies | | World **translations** progress report |
| WTO | World **Tourism** Organization | | World **travel** statistics |
| UNCTAD | UN Conference on **Trade** & **Development** | | **Tungsten** statistics |
| IWC | International **Whaling** Commission | | International **whaling** statistics |
| IWC | International **Wheat** Council | | World **wheat** statistics |
| UNSO/WESS | World **Energy** Supplies System | | Yearbook of **world energy** statistics |
| UNECE | **Economic** Commission for Europe | | Bulletin of statistics on **world trade** in engineering products |

**Table 24–2. Evaluation state, E, for a people or population.**

| Code | Meaning |
|---|---|
| 1 = | highly evangelized, with many personnel |
| 2 = | somewhat evangelized, adequate personnel |
| 3 = | inadequately evangelized, personnel needed |
| 4 = | sizeable areas unreached, few workers |
| 5 = | unevangelized, no workers |

demographic evangelization.

The second variable in the 1965 survey measured the current rate of change of response to Protestant missions in each people, using the simple formula:

Evangelization rate = (total Protestant community) divided by (total people's population), divided by (total years since arrival of Protestant missions)

This gave in fact a first approximation to a much later and more sophisticated indicator, e (evangelism-hours per annum per capita), which we have derived and analyzed above in Part 22 "Evangelism".

On the basis of these indicators, the 1965 report divided the 150 West African peoples or tribes into 5 categories of response to evangelization: those with extremely rapid response (30 tribes), moderately high response (33 tribes), below average response (22 tribes), very low response (23 tribes), and negligible response (25 tribes).

This report also listed a whole range of statistical terminology in use in the churches of West Africa for the varieties of Christian enumeration, and defined each of them in terms of some 30 steps or stages of the Christian life. This scale had been continuously revised, and reformulated from time to time. Its eventual published version was as the table 'Terminology of church membership and Christian enumeration', in the *World Christian encyclopedia* (1982:850–1).

***1972: more elaborate scales for E and SE***

Over the period 1965–1972 the West African survey was expanded east, north, and south to become the AACC project 'The Evangelization of Africa Today'. The data and findings were published in 1972 as *Frontier situations for evangelization in Africa, 1972: a survey report*. The basic data were gathered on 500 questionnaires, one for each ethnic or linguistic group or people, entitled 'Studies of Church Growth in Africa'. These were then returned by foreign missionaries, clergy, ministers, scholars, and other observers familiar with the situation among one or more of those peoples. The key question was No. 15, as follows:

> "How far would you say this tribe is now **evangelised**?"

For this survey, this question was deliberately placed with no further explanation or elaboration. The meaning or definition of this term "evangelised" was thus deliberately left unstated. What we wanted to discover was what the term actually meant to practitioners in the day-to-day work of evangelization, especially to those engaged as full-time professionals in foreign missions.

The replies to this question were so new, vivid, and imaginative, with quite a number including a numerical percentage in their replies, that we were able to rank them in the form of a scale, then to enumerate them from 0–100%, and thus to produce 3 new variables or measures: E (Evangelized), U (Unevangelized), and SE (Status of evangelization). These will now be described.

(1) *E (Evangelized).* The 5-point scale of impressionistic judgments in 1965 now became a 12-fold typology built on the actual words of the respondents. Since no-one had yet evolved or was using any scale at that period, replies were impressionistic (they are reproduced below using the European spelling "evangelise"). By the time that some 500 questionnaires had been returned covering 300 peoples of Africa, answers to question No. 15 were assembled, graded and classified divided into 12 stages each representing the percentage of the population which the phrases indicated were likely to have become evangelized. This is set out in Table 24–3.

(2) *U (Unevangelized).* The second variable measured the approximate number of unevangelized persons in each tribe (the unevangelized community, including young children and infants), estimated by multiplying population by 1-E/100. The figure given in this column for each nation was then the total of the figures for each tribe listed below it, i.e. the total unevangelized persons in frontier situations in the nation.

(3) *SE (Status of evangelization).* This index indicated the extent to which the total primary evangelistic task in a tribe (viewed as the twofold one of evangelizing the individuals and families composing the tribe, and of providing the scriptures in a tribe's language, i.e. numerical and cultural evangelisation) had been completed. The index was defined as follows: SE = E x (number of the 3 main types of Scripture translation—gospel, New Testament, whole Bible—available in the tribe's own mother language or widely-used lingua franca such as Hausa, Swahili, English, divided by 3), per cent.

The maximum value of this index, 100%, indicated a fully-evangelized tribe with the complete Bible available in its language; the minimum value (zero) indicated a tribe in which evangelization of people or language or culture had not yet begun.

A selection of tables was appended to the survey report, detailing the situation of a large number of tribes. Overall, the survey reported that of Africa's 1,045 tribes-within-nations (with in 1972 a population of 367 millions), 270 were Muslim or heavily islamized peoples (with a population of 140 millions), 512 were responsive and evangelized peoples (with a population of 180 millions), and 263 were unevangelized peoples (with a population of 47 millions).

**Table 24–3. Descriptive phrases quantifying "evangelised" used on questionnaires by respondents to a 1965 survey.**

The scale below is built on the quoted phrases by which specialists working among specific peoples replied to the central question: "How far would you say this tribe is now evangelised?" Note that, in the 1960s, most missiologists interested in world evangelization used the British spelling with 's' instead of 'z'. This table follows the actual usage of this 1965 global survey.

| *Phrases used* | *E (% evangelised)* |
|---|---|
| "Fully evangelised"; "all areas evangelised", "all have heard the gospel"; "probably none has not heard the gospel at least once" | 100-95 |
| "Mostly evangelised"; "pretty well evangelised; "very few have not heard something of the gospel" | 90 |
| "No region completely unevangelised"; "one relatively small unevangelised area"; "only small marginal unevangelised area's; "only isolated villages unevangelised" | 85 |
| "Several areas unevangelised"; "many people are still unevangelised"; "evangelised, general" | 80 |
| "Fair coverage of evangelisation"; "well evangelised", "extensively evangelised" | 70 |
| "A majority has been evangelised"; "most villages (but not individuals) have been touched" | 60 |
| "About half have been evangelised" | 50 |
| "Partially evangelised"; "evangelisation is under way" | 30 |
| "Still largely unevangelised"; "still virtually pioneer work"; "large areas quite unreached" | 20 |
| "Very little evangelised"; "only slightly evangelised"; "mostly unevangelised"; "very few have heard the Gospel at all", "most areas unreached" | 10 |
| "A very small percentage"; "scarcely evangelised"; "very sparsely evangelised"; "hardly touched by the gospel"; "95% of the territory has no Christian contact of any sort"; "evangelisation has scarcely begun", or "is just beginning" | 5 |
| "Unevangelised"; "unreached"; "under 1% reached so far" | 0 |

Source: *Frontier situations for evangelisation in Africa* (1972).

**Table 24–4. A rapid-calculation scale for the extent of a population's evangelization.**

*Name of country or population:*
*Year:* *Percentage*

| | |
|---|---|
| 1. What percentage are Christians (of any type)? | .. |
| 2.How much awareness of Christ is there among non-Christians? How much evangelism (evangelistic outreach), of all types is going on? Answer by estimating how many non-Christians evangelism has touched, or how many have this awareness (expressed as % population). Select one answer out of the 8 options below and add its figure in the end column; then total the 2 figures in that column, writing the total (up to a maximum of 100% on the end line. | |
| None, or virtually none (0%) | .. |
| A little, a few people (10%) | .. |
| A lot, a number of people (20%) | .. |
| A large amount, many people (30%) | .. |
| A very large amount, very many people (40%) | .. |
| An extremely large amount, extremely large numbers (50%) | .. |
| A vast amount, vast numbers (60%) | .. |
| Complete, virtually everyone (100%) | .. |
| TOTAL EVANGELIZATION, E (maximum 100%) | ___ % |

## *A QUICK-CALCULATION SCALE OF EVANGELIZATION, 1964–70*

***A rapid-calculation scale***

Some users of these data then asked for a way to estimate at short notice the extent of evangelization in a country or people or area or group that they were concerned with, but who found the other scales evolved in this analysis too complex or too tedious to work out. This then resulted in a simplified one, based on the fuller ones and condensed from them, but very much quicker to employ. This results in Table 24–4 above.

The first stage in operating this 1970 scale today would be to estimate what proportion of the population are Christians, of any type, either affiliated (church members) or professing. This figure is tabulated in *WCE* Part 4 "Countries" in its Country Tables 1 for all countries, and in its Part 8 "EthnoSphere" for all ethnolinguistic peoples in the world. In Table 24–4, the user should write this figure down after Question 1. This percentage of the population is already evangelized, as explained earlier. Next, estimate how much awareness of Christianity, Christ and the gospel there is on the part of the non-Christian population. This may be due to personal evangelism, or preaching evangelism, or persuasion evangelism, or pastoral evangelism; or in the absence of any effective evangelism, it may have arisen from influences unconnected with the churches (what we call here pneumatic evangelization). A starting-point for doing this would be to list all known outreach at present going on (of the kinds just given for 8 typical countries or regions), being sure to consider and investigate all the churches present, and all parachurch and other organizations working among this population, of all Christian traditions. Having thus considered all the influences at work, make an impressionistic selection of one of the 8 suggested percentages from 0% to 100%, write it in, then add up to get the final value E. Naturally, this total cannot exceed 100%.

This formula may also be used, in reverse, to give an approximate indication of the amount of awareness of Christ or of evangelism or evangelization or of outreach going on in a country. First obtain our value of E (worked out from the more complex Scale of Comparative Demographic Evangelization) tabulated in this Part 24 shortly. Next, subtract the percentage who are Christians. Then decode the resulting figure using the code we give below (e.g. 40% means that 'a very large amount' of evangelism is going on, or has been going on recently, or it means that "very many people" are aware of Christianity, Christ and the gospel; 0% means no evangelistic outreach, and no awareness of Christ; etc.). The end product is a figure giving the percentage of the total population who are evangelized non-Christians as a result of the churches' evangelistic outreach or similar influences.

## THE JOHNSTONE SCALE OF EVANGELISTIC EXPOSURE, 1964-80

Patrick Johnstone trained as a research chemist in Britain before serving in Southern and Central Africa from 1962–1978 as an evangelist of the Dorothea Mission. He published a number of surveys on evangelization beginning with the 1964 preliminary 32-page *Operation World* describing the prayer needs of 24 countries. In 1965 came a detailed report 'A survey of Mozambique'. In 1972 he produced the first full-volume *Operation World* as a world survey of missions and churches. In 1978 came the second edition of *Operation World*, OW-2. From the beginning of 1980 he began work as international research secretary of WEC International (formerly Worldwide Evangelization Crusade). Subsequently he published OW-3 in 1980, the 4th edition OW-4 in 1985, the 5th edition OW-5 in 1993, and the 6th in 2001.

From 1975–79, Johnstone worked on possible methods of measuring evangelized situations, using computer technology. He then evolved a practical 7-factor scale using only 7 indicators that would be particularly applicable to local church workers and missionaries who could easily enumerate them without having to call in outside technical help. Johnstone's definition of evangelization in his enumerations was as follows:

A person has been evangelized when he has been so presented with the gospel that he sees it relevant to his own need and must make a moral choice for it or against.

Johnstone then established several densities or levels for his 7 indicators, each of which would be equivalent to a population being 100% reached or evangelized. Where a factor reached or exceeded his prescribed density, this meant: '100% of the population has been reached or evangelized by, or has come under the evangelizing influence of, this factor'. Next, the actual densities for each of the 7 factors were computed, added and divided by 7 to obtain a final value R%. This symbol was then interpreted as the percentage of that population who could be said to have been *reached* by the gospel. The densities were as shown in Table 24–5.

### A COMPARISON OF THESE TWO APPROACHES TO SCALES

From 1975 Johnstone and Barrett worked together on the problem of quantifying evangelization, producing a variety of results.

It will be seen that the resulting Johnstone Scale of Evangelistic Exposure differs somewhat from Barrett's earlier scales, also from the 10-factor Scale of Individual Evangelization shortly to be described (Table 24–6), the 12-factor Scale of Corporate Evangelization (Table 24–7), and also from the 276-factor Barrett Scale of Comparative Demographic Evangelization presented in Table 24–8. Johnstone measured the number of persons in a population who could be said to have been personally reached or evangelized, to which he gave the symbol R% (reached). If he got a result of R = 57% for a particular nation or people, this meant that, in all probability, this percentage of the population were likely to have been exposed to the gospel, to have had a chance to hear it, and so to have had the gospel adequately presented to them.

A major feature of the Johnstone scale was that it allowed for segments of the population unlikely to be exposed and subtracted them from the final total.

Each constituent people was assessed by the same model, thus providing a consistent overall methodology with significant comparative power.

By contrast, the Barrett scales concentrated more on measuring the collective or communal or corporate extent of evangelization, which included both the sum total or aggregate of individuals evangelized, and also additional percentages covering the evangelization of their culture, their subconscious, their history, their language, and other societal factors. However, when results for particular countries were compared, it was found that E% for a given population as enumerated on the Barrett scales turned out to be similar in size to, and sometimes identical to R% on the Johnstone scale.

A second difference between the 2 scales was that Johnstone and Barrett each prescribed slightly different densities or levels for evangelized situations. Clearly, the exact levels one chooses are bound to be somewhat arbitrary, and different observers may well prefer differing levels on the basis of their own experiences in evangelism and evangelization. Both scales, however, started with affiliated Christians (who could reasonably or normally be expected to themselves be reached and evangelized persons) and then moved on to add the effect of the other major evangelistic or evangelizing influences.

### The interchangeability of indices

These 2 approaches to measuring evangelization by Johnstone and Barrett were deliberately kept separate and pursued independently of each other as different experimental approaches to a largely unknown task. The fact that results proved to be closely similar simply illustrates the well-known principle in experimental sociology called the 'interchangeability of indices'. This states that (a) when a researcher is measuring any new and complex situation, he is likely to encounter a bewildering array of possible empirical indicators, but that (b) it does not matter much which actual indicators he chooses to study and measure provided they are broadly representative of the concept he is measuring. The end results will be approximately the same.

### OTHER SCALES OF EVANGELIZATION, 1974–1980

#### 1974: the ICOWE dichotomous scale

In 1974, Evangelical missiologist Edward Pentecost published a study *Reaching the unreached*. This began a long period of research under the auspices of the International Congress on World Evangelization (ICOWE) in 1974, then the LCWE from 1974–80, the 1980 COWE consultation in Thailand, and the Manila congress in 1989. Throughout, peoples were placed on a dichotomous scale, defined in 1974 as: 'A people is unreached/unevangelized when less than 20% are professing Christians.' On this basis, the companion volume *Unreached Peoples* was also published in 1974, defining some 700 peoples as unreached or unevangelized. Starting in 1979, this resulted in the first volume of an annual series *Unreached Peoples*. Dayton and Wagner's *Unreached Peoples 1980* dealt with the Muslim world.

From our point of view in the present analysis, the ICOWE dichotomy had 2 shortcomings. First, it confused evangelization and conversion (or, evangelization and christianization) by regarding them as virtually synonymous in practice; and second, it made no distinction between peoples who had never come into contact with the gospel, and those who had contact but who then resisted or rejected the gospel.

#### 1975: an ICOWE 6-stage scale

A more detailed scale was set out in questionnaires circulated from 1975 onwards in another attempt at global data-gathering on evangelization. The question was asked about a specified people group:

'To what extent has this group had an opportunity to hear a clear presentation of the Gospel?' Respondents were given 6 choices and asked to check one:

1  None have heard
2  Very few have heard
3  10–25% have heard
4  25–50% have heard
5  50–75% have heard
6  Practically all have heard

Although large numbers of replies were received, the answers were too subjective to be comparable, and no use of these data was subsequently made.

#### 1975: a scale of openness to evangelization

ICOWE also proposed a scale to measure, not the present status of evangelization among a people, but that people's openness to evangelization or future willingness to receive the gospel if it were to be presented to them. Persons in a given people group were asked to state their openness or attitude to Christianity, by checking one of the following 6 phrases:

1  Very favorable
2  Favorable
3  Indifferent
4  Reluctant
5  Opposed
6  Hostile

Some valuable results were found. In Brazil in 1976, a public opinion poll among students and young employees found that 75% owned their own Bible or New Testament, and 84% stated that they would attend an evangelistic service if invited.

#### 1975: the Engel Scale

Another scale proposed by ICOWE and LCWE was one originally evolved by V. Sogaard, a student at Wheaton College, Illinois, and subsequently elaborated by his tutor, James Engel, who published is in his 1975 book *What's gone wrong with the harvest?*

For 5 years the Engel Scale was widely popularized by LCWE and its supporting agencies, mainly from the USA. In the opinion of many scholars concerned with evangelization and church growth, however, the Engel Scale had certain weaknesses. To those familiar with the psychology of conversion in preliterate societies, the scale placed too much stress on the intellect, especially on an intellectual grasp of Christian truths. The reservations of many were summed up by researcher Johnstone: 'I feel that people respond to the challenge of the person of the Lord Jesus Christ long before they have a clear understanding of the content of the Gospel in many cases, and these people are definitely evangelized.'

The Engel Scale was useful in clarifying people's thoughts somewhat. It was applied to a handful of specific cases of ethnolinguistic peoples. However, its doom was sealed in that it produced no new data describing the actual status of the world's 12,000 peoples; and it resulted in no published literature of analytical or scholarly stature. It remained a theoretical, normative, inspirational approach that was not followed through into usable results.

#### 1977: Swank's analysis in Nigeria

A much more precise and accurate form of research by SIM missionary G.O. Swank and a team of Nigerian researchers produced *Frontier peoples of Central Nigeria and a strategy for outreach* (1977). For each of the peoples and countries he studied, Swank asked the question: 'What percentage of Muslims do you believe have been exposed to the gospel in some way so that they are aware of it?' The answers he obtained included '50%' for Nigeria and Uganda, and an average of '25%' for other countries with sizeable Muslim communities. His second question was: 'What percentage, in your opinion, have understood the gospel whether they received it or not?' The answers that he obtained, for 30 peoples of Central Nigeria, varied from 'All' and 'Almost all', to exact percentages like '75%', down to 'Few' and 'Very few'.

| Table 24–5. **Johnstone Scale of Evangelistic Exposure.** | | | | |
|---|---|---|---|---|
| Factor | Density for 100% reached/evangelized population | | | |
| | Level | | Per million | Yes? |
| 1. Affiliated Christians | 1 per 2 people | | 500,000 | . . |
| 2. Worship Centers (congregations) | 1 per 3,750 people | | 267 | . . |
| 3. Full-time workers | 1 per 1,500 people | | 667 | . . |
| 4. Bible distribution per year | 1 per 100 people | | 10,000 | . . |
| 5. Christian institutions | 1 per 15,000 people | | 67 | . . |
| 6. Service agencies | 1 per 100,000 people | | 10 | . . |
| 7. Radio/TV sets | 1 per 10 people | | 100,000 | —— |
| | | Number of 'Yes' factors present | | . . |
| | | Percent of population reached, R | | ___ % |

**Table 24–6. A Scale of Individual Evangelization: measuring an individual's status with regard to evangelization.**

Please answer each question in column 1 with *Yes* or *No*, in column 2.

| Question | Answer | Answers (% of USA population) | | |
| | | Yes | No | No opinion |
| --- | --- | --- | --- | --- |
| *1* | *2* | *3* | *4* | *5* |
| 1. Do you consider yourself to be a Christian, or not? | .. | 81 | 12 | 7 |
| 2. Are you a member of any church? | .. | 69 | 31 | 0 |
| 3. Do you have a Bible in your home? | .. | 98 | 1 | 1 |
| 4. Is the Bible the inspired Word of God? | .. | 81 | 12 | 7 |
| 5. Is Jesus the divine Son of God? | .. | 85 | 9 | 6 |
| 6. Did Jesus rise again from the Dead? | .. | 80 | 10 | 10 |
| 7. Do you think Jesus will return again? | .. | 79 | 10 | 11 |
| 8. Have you received any Christian training in the past? | .. | 77 | 23 | 0 |
| 9. Does God have a plan for your life? | .. | 80 | 10 | 10 |
| 10. Has Jesus had any impact on your life? | .. | 87 | 7 | 6 |
| Total (0-10) .. | | | | |

*Scoring the respondent's answers*
Calculate a total score for the 10 questions based on: each Yes=1, No=1/2 (one half), No opinion=0. A total score for any one individual can thus vary between 0 and 10.

*Interpreting his or her total score*
A total score of 0-2 can be interpreted as = unevangelized (0 = completely unevangelized, 1 = partially evangelized); 3 or more = adequately evangelized; 6 or more = heavily evangelized; 9 or more = fully evangelized, 10 = discipled (a committed believing Christian).

### *Quantifying Christian outreach*

There are 2 basic elements in an evangelized situation involving a number of people that need to be enumerated before we can quantify the whole. The first is the Christian base from which evangelism is launched. This is the evangelizing church, or evangelizing Christians, or the force for evangelism; and the principles and method for enumerating this have been dealt with in a later section, Part 21 "GeoPersonnel". There now remains the task of enumerating the second element, the church's outreach to the wider population.

### *FURTHER DEVELOPMENT OF SCALES, 1975–1995*

From 1975 on, the various Barrett scales were refined and combined to produce 4 distinct and different scales: (1) a 10-question Scale of Individual Evangelization (given below, and first published in *Seven hundred plans to evangelize the world*, 1988); (2) a 12-factor Scale of Corporate Evangelization (to be derived next); then (3) a 206-factor Scale of Comparative Demographic Evangelization (first published in the 1982 *World Christian encyclopedia*, pages 120–121); and finally (4) the expanded 277-factor Scale of Comparative Demographic Evangelization that follows shortly in this Part 24 as Table 24–8.

To understand the evolution of these scales, a detailed examination of the background to evangelization and the major factors involved will now be undertaken. This process began in 1975 but is written up here in the present tense.

### *WHAT IS AN EVANGELIZED INDIVIDUAL?*

The first question to be resolved starts with the basic unit of any population or situation—the individual person. When does an individual become evangelized, and what are the essential elements that make up or characterize an evangelized individual?

### *Determining an individual's status*

With regard to evangelization, an individual's status can be regarded as having become evangelized when he becomes adequately aware—cognitively, intellectually, emotionally and pragmatically—of God's good news or evangel (*euangelion* in Greek) in Jesus Christ, sees its meaning and relevance for himself, and is able to make some kind of response. We can measure this by measuring his awareness of Christianity, Christ, and the gospel. This has often been done, by means of carefully thought-out, constructed, tested and implemented public-opinion polls. It has been done in various places year by year over the last 50 years, and in 50 different countries of the world.

The greatest amount of expertise in this matter has been amassed by the Gallup Poll. Based on their experience of what questions have been asked, and can be asked in scientific polls, we can draw up the following scale of 10 questions to be put to an individual, anywhere in the world.

The first 4 questions deal directly with awareness of Christianity, the next 3 with awareness of Christ, and the last 3 with awareness of the gospel as a personal factor in this individual's life. The questions can either be asked directly of individuals, or covered discreetly in an interview on wider or other or unrelated topics, or asked by mail, or asked and answered based on an individual's published statements or writings, or can be asked and answered by proxy (for example, we could imagine ourselves in the position of a Muslim in Jakarta, or a Hindu in Bombay, or a Marxist in Peking, and estimate what his answers would be).

Individuals are then asked the questions, and are scored on each either with a Yes, a No or a No Opinion (often called Don't Know). The total score of an individual, as explained under the questions, can be interpreted to give the individual's status with regard to evangelization. Awareness of a particular subject can be either positive or negative. An answer Yes indicates a positive evangelizing influence on his life in respect to a particular question. An answer No means that, although he disagrees with the question's subject, he nevertheless is sufficiently aware of it to deny or reject it; the answer therefore indicates at least partial evangelizing influence. If the answer is No Opinion, it means either that the individual is unaware of the subject and so does not know how to answer (hence that he is unevangelized on that subject), or it can mean that he does in fact understand the question but chooses not to answer even though he could (i.e. there is at least some evangelizing influence on that subject).

By way of illustration, we have superimposed on this scale below percentage figures (the 3 righthand columns) indicating how persons in the USA answer these questions today. They form Gallup's often-repeated findings on these exact questions for the population of the USA as a whole.

### *Evangelization in the USA*

On this scale, the average score for an individual in the USA works out at 8.795 (817 times 1, plus 125 times one half, plus 58 times zero, divided by 100). Interpretation is as follows. The average individual in the USA has become heavily evangelized in the sense that the entire population understands 2 or more of the questions. In numerical terms, some 94.2% of the population (the average of the first 2 columns) understand the 10 questions sufficiently to answer Yes or No, and to that extent are fully evangelized; 5.8% (third column) do not understand all the questions but are nevertheless adequately evangelized; none of the population understands less than 2 questions; a negligible number (under 0.5%) are unevangelized in the sense that they understand none of the 10 questions.

### *WHAT IS AN EVANGELIZED CORPORATE SITUATION?*

Having briefly sketched the historical evolution of earlier scales, and the characteristics of an evange-

lized individual, we move now towards a more detailed and more scientific attempt to compile a composite scale of corporate evangelization. First, we ask what is meant by an evangelized situation, and we examine a short list of 12 factors which, although not themselves evangelistic outreach in the sense of actual activity, are the agents or causes of that activity. Second, we examine and list the entire range of all factors responsible for or involved in the production of evangelized situations. The result is shown as Table 24–7.

### *What factors make up an evangelized situation?*

It is necessary now to attempt to delineate, as precisely as possible, the elements or dimensions of a situation which may properly be regarded as having become evangelized: an evangelized community, an evangelized people, an evangelized population, an evangelized area, an evangelized stratum of society, an evangelized country or nation, an evangelized continent, an evangelized world. As this stage, we use the adjective 'evangelized' by itself; at a later stage we will show that it is possible to introduce degrees of a population being evangelized, up to and including being fully-evangelized. The factors we discuss in the next dozen or so paragraphs should be regarded only as indicators of likelihood; i.e. if they are present, or have been present for a lengthy period of time such as 10 years, then it is likely that the population concerned has become evangelized. We may divide our descriptors or indicators into 2 categories: (1) a large number of non-numerical elements which may be present, and which can be regarded as dichotomous (Yes/No, or Present/Absent) factors, and which in aggregate describe the less readily-quantifiable dimensions of an evangelized situation; and (2) a small number of numerical factors describing the nation-wide or population-wide situation, using readily-available data of the kind gathered for the present survey, which in aggregate add up to describe several more readily-quantifiable dimensions of an evangelized situation.

### *Dichotomous factors*

There are a large number of factors or elements influencing or describing evangelization, namely a series of activities (means, methods, media, modes, agents and agencies) which in a given country may or may not be present. Some of these are causative, producing or advancing evangelization; others are not causative but are the consequences of evangelized situations. As one example, there is the recent phenomenon of mass enrollment in Bible correspondence courses. Over 4 million non-Christians across the world, including 2 million Muslims and Hindus, have taken such courses by mail, involving daily study of the Bible over a period of weeks, months or years. Non-Christians who have taken such courses must certainly be considered to have become evangelized; together with them, there are in addition vast numbers of other non-Christians (relatives, friends, acquaintances) with whom the students have discussed the contents of these courses, many of whom also by thus themselves have become evangelized. One factor or element in an evangelized situation can therefore be an affirmative answer to a question phrased thus: 'Are Bible correspondence courses making a widespread contribution to evangelization in this population?' The rest of 120 similar dichotomous Yes/No factors, considered to be significant by specialists in our subject, can be seen listed below in the larger of the 2 scales now to be described, namely Table 24–8.

### *Quantifiable factors*

A certain number of elements are more amenable to direct quantification. We begin by considering 12 such elements in relation to what we here may consider as the basic unit of society, namely the face-to-face community. The sociological term 'community' has been defined by cultural anthropologist G.P. Murdock as the maximal group of persons who normally reside together in face-to-face association. Such a group is bound together by a complex network of interpersonal relationships; and each such community has a culture of its own. Anthropologists have shown how among aboriginals and in primitive civilizations (nomadic hunting bands, cave dwellers, etc) the local group size is relatively small at 25 persons; but that in advanced civilizations, living in compact villages or settlements or communes or in extended families or lineages or clans, the more complex social forces that exist create normal residential units averaging 500 persons each in size. Even in a massive metropolis like London (population 10 million), in its populous districts 'streets make up a sort of 'village' of 100 to 200 people . . . where few outsiders ever come.' Throughout the world, including in urbanized industrialized societies the popular masses 'live, more often than not, in small, closely-knit communities, as circumscribed in social scale as the village, city quarter, street or popular housing estate.' We may therefore estimate the size of our standard basic community at 500 persons, and, bearing in mind its face-to-face character, we can investigate the effect on it of our 12 evangelistic elements.

a. *The presence of active Christians.* One first factor in evangelization is the presence of ordinary active Christians, i.e. of a number of non-specialized or nonprofessional Christians, going about their normal active Christian lives. How many non-Christians does a force of active Christians evangelize? Putting the question another way, what proportion must active Christians in a community reach before the whole community can be considered to have become evangelized by them? A quarter, a third, a half, three-quarters?

Church growth theologian D.A. McGavran's estimate was 30%:

> Any country where across the board in every homogeneous unit there are congregations of Christians and 30% or more of most homogeneous units are consciously Christian must be classified as evangelized. Examples are the USA, Germany, Britain, Australia, Batakland in Sumatra, the Kikuyu and Kamba tribes in Kenya, in India the Mizos, Nagars and Chamars of Tamil Nadu; etc.

In our standardized basic community where everybody knows everyone else, our own more conservative estimate would be that if 50% of the members are active, believing and practicing Christians (250 persons out of 500), then it is likely that the other 50% have obtained from contact with them some idea of what Christianity, Christ and the gospel are all about, i.e. have become in effect evangelized. We can therefore state our first descriptor: a community may be said to have become evangelized if there is at least one active Christian for every 2 persons in the population.

Next, there are usually present also a number of more specialized professional agents, agencies or centers of evangelization. Eleven of these will now be considered, arranged in order of increasing size of population influenced by one unit.

b. *Radio/TV sets in use.* In countries where Christian radio/TV programs may readily and regularly be heard in the people's own languages, a community may reasonably be said to have become evangelized through radio/TV if there are 100 or more radio/TV sets in use among the 500 population. This represents 20% or 1 in 5 persons, but with many or even most sets reaching multiple audiences the average number of listeners in practice would be 2 or 3 times as many.

c. *Bible distribution.* Scripture distribution is clearly of major importance too. The Bible is usually regarded as the church's major evangelistic instrument. If at least one printed new copy of the Bible is distributed each year in this community, in its own language, then (since the average life of these books is 20 years) in a stable situation it means that 20 copies are probably in circulation (or, one book per 25 persons in the community). So all members literate or preliterate will soon come into contact with the Bible in some shape or form and may be reckoned thereby to have had the opportunity to learn about the gospel, i.e. to have become evangelized.

d. *New Testament distribution.* This factor is similar to the preceding one, with a similar density. It must be noted that all other literature (portions, selections, etc.) are omitted from these 2 basic factors; they will be introduced as a refinement at a later stage when constructing our largest scale.

e. *Worship centers* (parishes, quasi-parishes, church buildings, congregations, house churches, outstations, but omitting weekday house groups) provide the physical bases necessary for evangelistic outreach; indeed, in most parts of the world, the base of evangelization is the local church. In most local churches across the world the gospel is preached every Sunday through sermon, Scripture reading, liturgy, testimony, Bible class, Sunday school, etc. Observers have long realized that the critical factor for an evangelized situation is how widespread such centers are and how close they are to each other. In 1897 Dr George Robson of the United Presbyterian Church of Scotland, and editor of the *Missionary record*, held that if the churches mobilized their resources for world evangelization

> there would be little difficulty, within one generation, in covering the whole open field of heathendom with centers of evangelization sufficiently near each other to diffuse the gospel over the intervening spaces.

The actual densities which obtain in fully-christianized situations across the world are as follows: one Roman Catholic parish/quasi-parish has on average 2,400 Catholics, whereas one Protestant congregation averages 300 total Christian community; this gives an average figure of one Christian worship center for 500 Christians. The density at which we may define a situation as evangelized (though not yet christianized) is considerably lower than this, and we may set it at around one worship center for every 5,000 population or 10 communities. We will shortly estimate that evangelization becomes more possible and likely if the total or secular population density of an area or region exceeds 27 persons per square kilometer (70 per square mile). Our density of one worship center for 5,000 people therefore amounts to one congregation for every 185 square kilometers (72 square miles); which means one congregation linearly every 14 kilometers or 8 miles. Where congregations are nearer together than this, we may say that we have, in all probability, an evangelized situation.

f. *Local personnel* (full-time professionals of local citizenship; nationals, citizens) play a key role too. In Roman Catholic, Orthodox, Lutheran, and Anglican thinking, the number of parishioners to one priest is often used as an index of adequate pastoral care of all individuals. One priest per 1,000 Catholics is considered the ideal, one per 2,000 tolerable, and one per 4,000 the pastoral danger point beyond which the basic pastoral and religious needs of a community cannot be cared for. Adequate pastoral care of all individuals is the ideal in order to have a christianized situation; but in order to have simply an evangelized situation the number of workers can be considerably less dense. In most Christian traditions, a local pastor or catechist or evangelist can probably get to know and evangelize 10 of our basic communities as part of his regular on-going responsibilities. If the ratio of personnel to population exceeds 1:5,000 persons (for example, 1:4,000), then, we may define the communities as evangelized.

g. *Foreign personnel* (missionaries) have an even more direct evangelistic role. Although not able to operate in such depth as local personnel, they usually operate more widely and on larger populations. It has long been reckoned, since the days of John R. Mott and his 1900 classic *The evangelization of the world in this generation*, that a non-Christian territory can be evangelized in due course by a comparatively small number of foreign missionaries, in a fixed proportion to total population. Mott conducted the first professional survey on this subject:

> Leading authorities on all the great mission-fields have been asked to estimate how many missionaries, in addition to native assistants, would be required so to lead the missionary enterprise as to accomplish the evangelization of those countries within a generation.

The numbers returned by mission professionals across the world were startlingly small. The estimates included only 40 more missionaries to complete the task in the great nation of Korea, and 320 in Brazil. The apostle to Islam S.M. Zwemer replied, 'Arabia could be easily be evangelized within the next 30 years if it were not for the wicked selfishness of Christians' (Mott 1900:145). He envisaged the task requiring only 100 students and US$100,000.

The number of native workers required was usually quoted as 10 times the number of foreign workers required. The range of answers to Mott's request concerning the adequate proportion of foreign missionaries to total non-Christian population varied from 1:10,000 heathen to 1:100,000. The average figure quoted was 1:50,000; the most frequently-specified ideal, 1:20,000 (Mott 1900:162).

This last proportion, 1:20,000, is far from excessive, and is in fact extremely modest. The time span involved was not accurately specified by Mott, but by implication he seems to have meant 'over the average missionary's span of foreign service,' namely about 10 years at that time. During their period of this length, thousands of missionaries must have influenced vastly greater numbers. In the same way as George Whitefield in 18th-century England and America often preached to crowds of 30,000 at once in the open air, so in responsive fields missionaries of the 1900 era regularly found themselves addressing crowds of 5,000 or 10,000, with 30,000 on special occasions. Even as late as 1960 in Cameroon, a French missionary was likely to find that his catechism or baptism classes numbered 50,000 a time.

On average, then, we may define an evangelized situation as one in which there is a ratio of at least one foreign missionary for every 10,000 persons in the population, i.e. one for every 20 or so basic communities.

h. *Christian institutions* have, by their presence as well as by their programs, long played a major role in evangelization. One of the major expressions of this has been the vast network of secular schools under church or Christian auspices. In 1980, these numbered some 140,000 elementary or primary schools worldwide, and 40,000 secondary schools. Though of declining importance in the Western world, they are still a major factor in developing countries. The 123 Roman Catholic secondary schools in Hong Kong still produce many converts.

Another significant type of institution are monasteries, which are now recovering their historic role as centers of evangelization, especially in large numbers of recently-renewed charismatic Catholic and Orthodox monasteries across the world. The evangelizing influence of these and of the other major institutions enumerated in this Encyclopedia (hospitals,

**Table 24–7. A Scale of Corporate Evangelization: estimated densities corresponding to an evangelized situation in a population due to 12 independent criteria.**

| | *Density for an evangelized situation in a community of 500* | | | |
|---|---|---|---|---|
| *Evangelizing factor* | *People level* | *Community level* | *Per million* | *Yes?* |
| Active Christians | > 1 per 2 people | 250 per community | >500,000 | . . |
| Radio/TV sets | > 1 per 5 people | 100 per community | >200,000 | . . |
| Annual Bible distribution | > 1 per 500 people | 1 per community | >2,000 | . . |
| Annual NT distribution | > 1 per 500 people | 1 per community | >2,000 | . . |
| Worship centers | > 1 per 5,000 | 1 per 10 communities | >200 | . . |
| Local personnel | > 1 per 5,000 | 1 per 10 communities | >200 | . . |
| Foreign personnel | > 1 per 10,000 | 1 per 20 communities | >100 | . . |
| Institutions | > 1 per 25,000 | 1 per 50 communities | >40 | . . |
| Periodical titles | > 1 per 100,000 | 1 per 200 communities | >10 | . . |
| Service agencies | > 1 per 200,000 | 1 per 400 communities | >5 | . . |
| Religious libraries | > 1 per 250,000 | 1 per 500 communities | >4 | . . |
| Denominations | > 1 per 250,000 | 1 per 500 communities | >4 | . . |
| | | Number of 'Yes' factors present | | ___ |
| | | Percent of population evangelized, E | | ___ % |

monasteries, printing presses, radio stations, seminaries, universities, colleges, secondary (but not primary) schools, research centers, and other centers) may be said to extend to, on average, something like 50 communities each, i.e. 25,000 people. So then if there are more institutions among the population than one per 25,000, the population may be considered likely to have become evangelized.

The foregoing factors may be regarded as causative of an evangelized situation. There are several other possible factors that are less causative, less cause than effect, rather being indicators descriptive of the presence of such a situation. Of these, we select here only 4 more.

i. *Christian periodicals* (newspapers, magazines, journals) arise in situations that have already become somewhat evangelized, the evangelized level being something like one title for 100,000 people (200 communities).

j. *Service agencies* (Bible societies, councils of churches, parachurch agencies, et alia) of significance at the national level have an even wider evangelistic influence, estimated here at 400 communities or 200,000 people to one agency (excluding local branches from this enumeration).

k. *Religious libraries* likewise arise in christianized areas; the general evangelizing influence of one such Christian library may be estimated as extending to around 250,000 people (500 communities).

Lastly, there is one factor very easy to calculate which serves as a general indicator, somewhat rough and ready, but particularly useful if detailed data on all the foregoing factors are not readily available.

l. *Denominations*, by which we mean the total of distinct and separate denominations at work which have churches in this population, are the parent bodies of most of the preceding 11 factors. In the early days among a non-Christian population, the first foreign missionary societies to arrive have usually adopted the principle of comity and have agreed to divide up the population among themselves on geographical, ethnic or linguistic grounds, to avoid overlapping and duplication of effort. An average figure for the size of population that the average-size denomination feels able to evangelize by itself would be a quarter of a million or so (250,000, or 500 of our basic communities). If the number of denominations present in the population or country is less than this level (which is 4 denominations per million), over a period of the

last 10 or so years, then the population is probably, from this one particular point of view, unevangelized; and over 4 denominations per million, it is probably evangelized. At the same time, when the grand total of denominations becomes too large (over 20), rivalry and confusion set in and this constitutes a hindrance to evangelization (as shown by factor No. 257 on the Scale of Comparative Demographic Evangelization).

### Densities for an evangelized situation
To sum up, a population may be said to have become evangelized to the extent that the following quantifiable factors have now reached or surpassed the levels or densities indicated (the symbol ≥ means 'is greater than or equal to'). In Table 24–7, each level is expressed in 3 different ways: first, the number of people evangelized by one unit; second, the number of communities evangelized by one unit, or the number of units needed to evangelize one community; and third, the number of units (i.e. of personnel, institutions, etc.) needed to evangelize each million population. These 12 factors are thus the first elements in producing a well-rounded scale for quantifying corporate or collective evangelization.

### Probability of evangelization
The 12 quantifiable factors just described, and indeed the whole scale with all the other factors which will shortly be evolved here, are best seen not as deterministic factors but as indicators of probability only. If the number of worship centers is over 200 per million population, then it is likely or *probable* that the situation is an evangelized one; if 2 factors are above our specified levels, it is more probable, if 5 are, it is even more probable still; if 10 are, it is highly probable; if 12 are, it is virtually certain. In the same way, the factors are describing only the average situation in a country or population; in practice, distribution of any of them (manpower, centers, agencies, scriptures, etc.) is rarely found spread evenly over the whole country but is concentrated more in certain areas and less in others. For this reason one should only generalize in this way with caution, speaking of probability only.

### 12 separate measures of evangelization
This analysis is possible also in cases where hardly any hard data at all exist. These 12 factors give us 12 different measures of whether or not a situation is evangelized. If we have numerical data for only one of them, say No. 5, worship centers, then this is better than nothing; if the number turns out to be more than one center per 5,000 population, then it is likely we have an evangelized situation.

### Numerous other combination measures
If we had numerical data for only 4 of these factors, these could also be combined into a single percentage measure, by dividing the number of factors that were above the prescribed density by 4, then multiplying by 100. Thus if only one of the 4 was above the prescribed density, then in all probability the situation would be only 25% evangelized. With 12 factors available for combining into pairs, trios, quartets, etc, this gives the user a large number of possible measures.

Further, the 12 factors themselves can be combined to make up one single scale for measuring the degree to which a population is evangelized. One simply adds up the number of factors which are above the prescribed density, divides by 12, and multiplies by 100. Thus if 9 factors are above the prescribed densities, the population is portrayed as 75% evangelized.

## MEASURING COMPARATIVE DEMOGRAPHIC EVANGELIZATION

In the present analysis, this 12-factor scale has not been separately enumerated, because it will now be incorporated into our 276-factor Scale of Comparative Demographic Evangelization, shown on the following pages as Table 24–8. Using this complex scale, we can, and did, enumerate its value for all countries of the world, and for the period 1900-2000. This scale is however far too complex for everyday use. Consequently it will then be condensed into a shorter scale based on a 20-variable formula, which is elsewhere enumerated (in Part 12) for every country and (in *WCE* Part 8) for every ethnolinguistic people across the globe.

The main building-block in Table 24–8 is a series of dichotomous Yes/No questions. Each question deals with one specific subject or dimension of evangelization. If its answer is Yes, the respondent writes '1' in its end column to signify the assumption that the presence of this particular factor or variable influences *an additional* 1% of the population concerned. This assumption is based on a considerable accumulation of quantifiable data. Table 24–8 is as numerical as is attainable in practice: some 71 questions state a precise numerical level. And of these, some 30 state '1%' as their level.

**Table 24–8. A Scale of Comparative Demographic Evangelization: 277 empirical variables effecting a population's status of having become evangelized.**

This scale measures the amount of evangelization that has gone on, and is going on, among a population or segment. In one of its meanings it derives the percentage of that population who individually can be said to have now become evangelized.

Name of this **population** or segment:
Name of this population or segment's **country**:
**Year** of inquiry:

## A. EVANGELIZERS (the force for evangelism)

*(This subject is defined and elaborated in Part 21 "GeoPersonnel")*

1. What percentage of this population are affiliated Christians (baptized church members, of all denominations)?
*(Add in the end column this number, to 1 or 2 places of decimals only if accuracy justifies it. Note that although only church members who are active in mission can properly be termed active evangelizers (for what this survey terms Great Commission Christians), those inactive in mission are still inactive evangelizers and must also be counted as themselves evangelized. See discussion in Parts 22-25).*

## B. EVANGELISM (the church's outreach)

*(Organized below as 7 responses to the 7 Mandates of Christ's Great Commission. For questions 2 through 244, and 265-273, score + 1 in end column for each "Yes" answer, or 0 for "No").*

### *MINICOMMISSION I: Evangelize!*

*(This covers questions Nos. 2-124).*

**PRAYER EVANGELISM (Pneumatic Evangelization): *Receive!***

**INTERCESSION**

2. Are churches elsewhere known to be praying for the evangelization of this population segment specifically?
3. Does printed prayer literature circulate describing this population segment?
4. Have any recent organized concerts of Prayer, or prayer walks, focused in on this population segment?
5. Are national days of prayer, Kirchentags, Bible days, Bible weeks, et alia celebrated?
6. Does the number of intercessors anywhere on Earth, praying for this population, exceed its population?
7. Is this population a megapeople (exceeding 1 million by AD 2000)?

**RENEWAL MOVEMENTS WITHIN THE CHURCHES**

8. Are power encounters, power evangelism, or power christianity known of or practiced within this population?
9. Is the Catholic Charismatic Renewal significant here?
10. Is the Charismatic Renewal significant in the older Protestant, Anglican or Orthodox churches?
11. Is renewal through basic ecclesial communities (small groups) significant?
12. Are other revival or renewal movements within the churches significant?
13. Does the total of all Christians in renewal movements exceed 1% of church membership?

**PRE-EVANGELISM (Preparatory Evangelization): *Go!***

**HISTORY AND CONTEXT**

14. Have Christians been resident here for 100 years or more?
15. Neighboring and surrounding populations: are they evangelized?

**COLLECTIVE LIFESTYLE**

16. Is the overall image of local Christians and their collective way of life attractive?
17. Do local Christians collectively practicing simple, sacrificial, or life-for-others lifestyle exceed 10% of the population?

**PREPARATION**

18. Is "World A" thinking, strategy, research, data compilation, target selection, preparation under way with regard to this population?

**TRAVEL AND MIGRATION**

19. Air travellers on business: are Christians among them 1% annually?
20. Tourists (including Bible smugglers, et alii): are Christians among them over 1% annually?
21. Excursionists (day trippers/visitors/commuters across frontiers): are Christians among them over 1% annually?
22. Are internal tourism and travel major factors?
23. Is internal migration (change of residence) marked within this population?
24. Migrant workers from other countries: are Christians among them over 1%?
25. Recent diaspora immigrants (minorities from other countries): are Christians among them over 1%?
26. Refugees from abroad: are Christians among them over 1%?
27. Expatriate civilians in secular professions (government, industry, commerce): are Christians among them over 1%?
28. Foreign armed forces: are Christians among them over 1%?
29. Foreign students: are Christians among them over 1%?
30. Do non-Christians make professional contacts with Christian countries (via UN, UNESCO, WHO, UPU, FAO, ILO, commerce, science, diplomacy, journalism, etc)?
31. Mail correspondence with relatives, formerly citizens, who are Christians now living in exile or diaspora: is this a factor?
32. In non-Christian countries, are visits noticeable from relatives living abroad or in a diaspora who have recently become Christians?
33. Are there numerous returning citizens who have lived abroad as non-Christians in a Christian country (as students, migrant workers, diplomats, military etc)?
34. Are church- or Christian-sponsored tours, safaris, vacations plentiful?
35. Has initial visitation of non-Christians (home or temple visiting) been widespread and widely noticed?

**DEVELOPMENT**

36. Can this population be described as "more developed" rather than "less developed"?
37. Population density: is it 27/sq. km (70/sq. mile) or more?
38. Are Christians social action, social justice, service, development projects noticeable?
39. Is there relief, emergency or disaster aid by Christian agencies?

**ART, ARTIFACTS, AND ARCHITECTURE: "THE SILENT WITNESS"**

40. Christian architecture: do churches, cathedrals, buildings, massive statues of Christ carry impact?
41. Religious art with Christian themes: are paintings, portraits, murals, icons, sculptures, symbols, popular/mass reproductions, souvenirs widespread?
42. Is there a tradition of Christian symbolism in carpets, saddles, ornamentation?
43. The Christian Year: are Christmas, Easter, Sundays, etc, publicly observed?
44. Place names: do numerous cities have specifically Christian names?
45. The Holy Shroud of Turin, and similar relics: is over 1% of the population aware of them?
46. Are there widely-publicized badges, crests, coats of arms, mottoes, slogans, etc with specific biblical content or witness to Christ?
47. Do Christians make much use of posters, billboards, commercial advertising?
48. State's official postage stamps and coins: have any recently portrayed the Bible or life of Christ?
49. Are Christian exhibitions, displays, tableaux, panoramas frequent?
50. Public auctions of Christian art: are these regular and well-publicized in the media?

**AUDIOVISUALS: THE PERFORMING ARTS**

51. Is there folk media evangelism (traditional performing arts, recitations, poetry, mime, song)?
52. Is there church-produced drama (live theatre, dance, opera, ballet, mystery plays, passion plays, etc)?
53. Are there public media-publicized commercial theatre plays, musicals, show, opera, ballet, on the Bible or life of Christ?
54. Are there church music concerts and organ recitals (especially in post-Christian countries)?
55. Are Christian films and audiovisual media (photographs, filmstrips, slides, etc) widely used in ministry and evangelism?
56. Are there public media-publicized commercial cinema showings of films on the Bible or life of Christ?
57. Is the "Jesus" Film available in the mother tongue?
58. Has the "Jesus" Film in the mother tongue been seen yet by more than 10% of the population?
59. Has the "Jesus" Film in any other language (second language or lingua franca) been seen yet by more than 10% of the population?
60. Have other film shows on the Bible or the life of Christ reached 1% or more of the population?

**OTHER SPECIALIZED MINISTRIES**

61. Is Scripture available or regularly heard in audio form through tapes, cassettes, or broadcasting?
62. Is Scripture widely available by means of mass-distributed, popularized, illustrated, topical leaflets ("Selections")?
63. Have there been one or more united every-home visitation/literature-saturation campaigns?
64. Does modern technology contribute here to evangelism (aviation, helicopters, hovercraft, computers, silicon chips, computerized multilingual hand dictionaries, high-speed presses, telex, satellite TV, etc)?

**SPECIALIZED-GROUP MINISTRIES**

65. Is there specialized evangelism among the exploited and oppressed, the poor, beggars, refugees, squatters, minorities, et alii?
66. Is there evangelism among society's misfits: anarchists, revolutionaries, drug addicts, criminals, delinquents, prisoners, prisoners of war, et alii?
67. Is there specialized evangelism among handicapped and incapacitated populations—cripples, lepers, blind, deaf, sick, suffering, bereaved, psychotics, et alii?
68. Is there evangelism for other special groups: children, orphans, youth migrants, athletes, campers, tourists, seamen, gypsies, et alia?
69. Are New Reader Scriptures (for new literates) available in this language?
70. Are scriptures available in Braille for the blind?
71. Are scriptures available in any signed language for the deaf?
72. Are there any other significant audiovisual ministries at work?

**SIGNS AND POINTERS**

73. Is there or has there been in the last 5 years, widespread social disturbance unrest, upheaval, turmoil, war, disaster, et alia)?
74. Are there widespread and widely-known "signs following" (healings, deliverances, miracles, visions, theophanies, tongues, prophecies)?
75. Have there been recent reported visible appearances of Jesus to individuals or groups?
76. Are there sites of apparitions of Virgin Mary in this population's territory
77. Internal pilgrimages: do Christian pilgrims annually number over 1% of the population?
78. Pilgrims from other countries: are Christians among them over 1% annually?
79. Christian suffering: do believers facing illness, adversity, disaster, even death, provide any ultimate visual sign to unbelievers?

**PERSONAL EVANGELISM (Presence Evangelization): *Witness!***

**UNSTRUCTURED OR IMPROMPTU WITNESSING**

80. Does the total of Great Commission Christians in this population exceed 10%
81. Is Christian presence (witness by quality of life) noteworthy?
82. Christian witness in the secular worlds of politics, industry, commerce, science, arts, media: is this marked?
83. Do adult Christians engaging in active personal witnessing (by word: personal work, small group evangelism) number over 1% of the population?
84. Is there meaningful dialogue with non-Christian religions or quasi-religions (atheism, etc)?
85. Is there an extensive literature on dialogue between Christianity and the local majority religion or quasi-religion?
86. Is personal lifestyle evangelism (an evangelistic life-style explained to others) on the part of Christians noticeable?
87. Are changed lives, character changes, notable among church h members?
88. Is the country's head of state, or its chief executive, a practicing Christian?
89. Are personal Christian names frequently reported in the media?
90. Is there any evangelism using bush telegraph or other tradition media?
91. Is there any wall newspaper (community-produced) evangelism?
92. Are there national mass marches, Marches for Jesus, or other mass processions of witness?
93. Impromptu preaching or witnessing at weddings and funerals (graveyard evangelism) in post-Christian and atheistic states: is this regular?
94. Is telephone evangelism practiced?
95. Is postal evangelism (mail evangelism) employed?
96. Martyrdoms (the ultimate witness): do believers killed for their faith by hostile persons number more than 200 per million church population each year?

**PREACHING EVANGELISM (Proclamation Evangelization): *Proclaim!***

**PROFESSIONAL EVANGELISM**

97. Local personnel (national home church workers); are there 100 per million or more?
98. Do local church workers (clergy, laity, of local citizenship) outnumber foreign church workers here?

*Continued overleaf*

*Table 24–8 continued*

99. Are there local evangelists or catechists (related to a single local church congregation)?
100. Does regular Sunday public preaching (kerygma) in this population's churches spread the gospel effectively?
101. Are there religious orders and personnel (brothers, monks, sisters, nuns), local or foreign?
102. Foreign missionaries and personnel (aliens from abroad): are there 100 per million or more?
103. Are there foreign chaplains and chaplaincies to alien residents?
104. Are there chaplains to armed forces, military chaplains or evangelists?
105. Are there professional itinerant evangelists, itinerant workers, itinerant missionaries, colporteurs?
106. Are there clandestine itinerant evangelists, foreign couriers, et alii?
107. Are there professional speakers, lecturers, and preachers actively spreading the gospel in this population?
108. Are there itinerant musicians, choirs, bands, singing groups, pop groups actively spreading the gospel?
109. Are Christian short-term workers, youth teams, youth vacation workers at work?
110. Are there part-time workers, lay preachers, unpaid evangelists, evangelizers, tentmakers, supplementary clergy, bivocational clergy?
111. Do seminarians or theological students conduct local evangelistic missions?

**AGENCY EVANGELISM**

112. Are there specialized national or international evangelistic associations or agencies or alliances?
113. Are there nation-wide clandestine organized evangelistic networks (in atheistic or anti-Christian states)?
114. Do mission agencies and organizations working among this population exceed 10 per million?
115. Is there significant cross-cultural mission benefiting this population?
116. Are there systematic house-to-house visitation campaigns?
117. House-to-house visitation: have over 1% of all homes been visited recently?

**MASS EVANGELISM**

118. Does organized mass evangelism reach or benefit this population?
119. Mass evangelistic campaigns (indoor, outdoor, tent campaigns, seaside campaigns, crusades, etc): are these frequent?
120. Are there total mobilization campaigns (evangelism-in-depth, follow-through evangelism, lordship evangelism)?
121. Do campaigns feature multiplication evangelism, or saturation evangelism?
122. Are there multimedia (TV/radio/press/literature) campaigns or crusades with followup?
123. Evangelistic campaign attenders or persons reached: is the annual aggregate over 1% of the population?
124. Recorded enquirers or decisions for Christ (all types of campaigns): is the annual aggregate over 1% of the population?

## *MINICOMMISSION II: Disciple!*

*(This covers questions Nos. 125-244).*

**PERSUASION EVANGELISM (Pressure Evangelization): *Disciple!***

**DISCIPLING EVANGELISM**

125. Are there camp evangelism, camp meetings held?
126. Are rural evangelism, village evangelism practiced?
127. Is there organized urban mission, urban evangelism, inner-city ministry?
128. Is there occupational evangelism (industrial mission, labor evangelism, factory evangelism, etc)?
129. Is there student evangelism, campus evangelism, sectional evangelism, school evangelism?
130. Is there any ship evangelism (visits by evangelistic ships MV Logos, MV Doulos, mission boats, etc)?

**SCRIPTURE DISTRIBUTION EVANGELISM**

131. Have any scripture translations been done for over 100 years?
132. Do secular libraries (universities, etc) contain the Bible or Christian literature?
133. Is the Bible taught in state or government schools?
134. Does annual major scripture distribution (Bibles, NTs, portions) exceed 1% of the population?
135. Are scriptures being printed by official state or government presses?
136. Are dynamic equivalence translations available in the main language?
137. Do over 50% of the population have scriptures translated into their mother tongues.
138. Are these translations modern (not more than 25 years since most recent version was published)?
139. Total Bible distribution per year: is it 2,000 per million or more?
140. Total New Testament distribution per year: is it 2,000 per million or more?
141. Are scripture portions (gospels or complete books) widely available in the main language?
142. Are near-gospels (portions in a closely-related language in same cluster) available?
143. Is the New Testament widely available in the main language?
144. Are near-NTs (NTs in a closely-related language in same cluster) available?
145. Is the Bible widely available in the main language?
146. Are near-Bibles (complete Bibles in a closely-related language in same cluster) available?
147. Are colporteurs and bible women active in colportage?
148. Are mailed scriptures widespread (e.g. sent to all telephone subscribers)?
149. Are daily Bible reading materials in these languages widely available?
150. Are Bible correspondence courses widespread?
151. Are there scripture free-distribution campaigns?
152. Is clandestine scripture distribution widespread?
153. Are special versions of the Bible available (children, illustrated, electronic, Internet, media versions, study Bibles, Bible story books, etc)?
154. Are concordances or Scripture commentaries available?
155. Bible correspondence course students: do they exceed 1% of the population?
156. Are scripture verses or phrases used in poster evangelism, professional advertising, billboards, bumper stickers, lapel pins, and the like?
157. Are scripture portions available in any widely-understood second language or lingua franca?
158. Is the New Testament available in any widely-understood second language?
159. Is the whole Bible available in any widely-understood second language?

**PASTORAL EVANGELISM (Planting Evangelization): *Baptize!***

**CONTEXT OF LOCAL CHURCH**

160. Do denominations brought into being among this population, and now working among it, exceed 4 per million?
161. Worship centers (parishes, churches, congregations): are there 80 per million or more?
162. Reachability of churches: is the average distance between churches under 5 km (3 miles)?
163. Are practicing Christians (as defined by denominations) over 50% of all affiliated Christians?
164. Does the Christian community have blood-ties with 10% or more of all non-Christians?
165. Cultural barriers: has the Christian community avoided being a ghetto culturally or linguistically alien to most non-Christians in this country?
166. Do Christians of a different or alien culture live among this population, being over 1% of its size?
167. Is *philadelphia* (brotherly love) a marked characteristic of churches in this population segment?
168. Do Christians project an evident life for others (*diakonia*, service), especially to outsiders?

**LOCAL-CHURCH EVANGELISM**

169. Is current church extension and church-planting (new churches in new areas) significant?
170. Does current church growth (membership increase, % p.a.) exceed demographic increase by 1% or more?
171. Local church converts/baptisms/confirmations: is the annual aggregate for all churches over 1% of the population?
172. Do new church members(% p.a.) exceed the demographic birth rate by 1% or more?
173. Is there an evangelistically-attractive church life (*koinonia*, fellowship?
174. Is there public liturgical worship (daily or weekly *leitourgeia*, liturgy)?
175. Is liturgical preaching (sermons at the eucharist) practiced?
176. Do other weekly local church activities (services, meetings, special groups) advance evangelism?
177. Baptism and other sacraments: do these present any public witness?
178. Are corporate witness and involvement of the laity marked (organized lay ministries, lay apostolate, precinct evangelism, house groups, etc.)?
179. Are there family evangelism, family catechesis, family counseling services linked to evangelistic campaigns?
180. Are there church open-air activities (local preaching or local processions of witness)?
181. Are there local parish or congregational weekend or week-long evangelistic missions?
182. Are there clandestine (illegal, underground) local church activities?

**CHRISTIAN INSTITUTIONS**

183. Christian institutions: are there 40 per million or more?
184. Are ministries of healing through hospitals, clinics, medical services widely known?
185. Christian medicine and public health programs, campaigns, medical workers: are these widespread?
186. Annual medical consultations in Christian hospitals: do they exceed 1% of the population?
187. Do church-operated schools, colleges, universities, seminaries, centers, monasteries, presses, et alia make any impact?
188. Are there clandestine (illegal) schools, colleges, monasteries, presses, etc?
189. Education rate (population aged 5-24 enrolled in schools): is it 50% or over?
190. Does secular education make pupils aware of Christ in any way?
191. Pupils and students in all types of Christian schools and colleges: do they exceed 1% of the population?

**CHRISTIAN LITERATURE (OTHER THAN SCRIPTURES)**

192. Before 1900, did the main language have an extensive literary tradition?
193. Before 1900, did this language have extensive indigenous Christian literature?
194. Is there extensive indigenous Christian literature in this language today?
195. Is this language permeated today by Christian/biblical phraseology and idiom?

**PRINT-MEDIA EVANGELISM**

196. Adult literacy: is it 50% or more?
197. Are literacy campaigns by churches or missions significant?
198. Is a wide range of Christian literature readily available at easy-to-afford prices?
199. Pieces of Christian literature excluding scriptures (tracts, leaflets, books, periodicals): is the annual number distributed or sold more than 1% of the population?
200. Are Christian periodicals effective in evangelization?
201. Do titles of Christian periodicals number 10 per million or more?
202. Are Christian tracts (leaflets) being distributed widely?
203. Are Christian articles, features, photos, or Bible verses often printed in secular newspapers?
204. Are Christian bookshops, or outlets through secular bookshops, widespread?
205. Religious libraries: do they number 4 per million or more?
206. Does clandestine (hand-copied) literature circulate widely?

**UNITED EVANGELISM**

207. Do all major denominations cooperate in evangelism?
208. Is there a citywide or national Christian council of churches (and/or agencies), or alliance or fellowship, which has impacted this population?
209. Have there been one or more united literacy/literature/evangelism campaigns?

**PROGRAMMED EVANGELISM (Pedagogical Evangelization): *Train!***

**TEACHING SCHOOLS/COURSES**

210. Do catechesis/baptism instruction, catechumenate, and any catechetical renewal emphasize evangelism?
211. Do Sunday schools and local children's ministries contribute markedly to evangelism?
212. Sunday-school enrolments: do children and adults enrolled number over 1% of the population?
213. Is there local church training in discipling, evangelism, local courses, schools of evangelism?
214. Are there evangelistic conferences, seminars, house parties, conventions?
215. Are there mass lay-discipleship-leadership-training programs, TEE, etc?
216. Do organized schools of evangelization (such as ACCSE) enrol members of this population?
217. Has any national congress on evangelism been held which has impacted this population?
218. Are there mediated training packages for evangelism?
219. Is there any cassette, tape, videotape, disc (record), or flexidisc evangelism?
220. Are there schools or courses for Christian journalists?

**INDIGENIZATION OF CHRISTIAN OUTREACH AND MISSION**

221. Are there any home (domestic) mission boards or societies with local workers?
222. Is the home ministry produced by this population for missionary outreach stronger than 100 citizen/member workers per million?
223. Are there any indigenous foreign mission boards or societies?
224. Does this people or population send abroad, as foreign missionaries or personnel, more than 100 citizens per million?
225. Is there any indigenous Christian theological writing?
226. Bible study group movements (house groups, school groups, etc): do groups number over 1 per 10,000 population?
227. Are there programs teaching conscientization, humanization, or liberation theology?
228. Is there a corpus of indigenous Christian theological writing?

*Continued opposite*

Table 24–8 concluded

| | |
|---|---|
| 229. Are there indigenously-composed hymns and songs? . . . . . . . . . . . . . . . . . | . . |
| 230. Are there any indigenously-initiated or locally-founded denominations (not imported or foreign-initiated or foreign-related)? . . . . . . . . . . . . . . . . | . . |

**RADIOPHONIC EVANGELISM**
231. Radio/TV receivers: are there 200 per 1,000 population or more? . . . . . . . . . . .  . .
232. Is there regular radio evangelism in the main language? . . . . . . . . . . . . . . .  . .
233. Is there regular radio evangelism in the other major languages? . . . . . . . . . . .  . .
234. Is there regular TV evangelism in the main language? . . . . . . . . . . . . . .  . .
235. Is there regular TV evangelism in the other major languages? . . . . . . . . . . . .  . .
236. Are there any Christian radiophonic schools (radio/TV plus local classes)? . . . .  . .
237. Is there any Christian participatory radio/TV (phone-in, talk-back)? . . . . . . . . .  . .
238. Do urbanites (urban dwellers) in this population number over 50%? . . . . . . . . .  . .
239. Do urban/industrialized media (cable TV, city broadcasting stations, interactive TV) contain Christian material? . . . . . . . . . . . . . . . . . . . . . . . .  . .
240. Are computers used by over 1% of Christians in the population? . . . . . . . . . . . .  . .
241. Do Christians use Internet/e-mail/networks to benefit this population? . . . . . . . .  . .
242. Are there clandestine (illegal) Christian radio stations? . . . . . . . . . . . . . . .  . .
243. Do isolated radio believers number over 1% of the population? . . . . . . . . . . .  . .
244. Regular audience for Christian radio/TV programs: is it over 1% of the population? . . . . . . . . . . . . . . . . . . . . . . . . . . . . . . . . . . . . . . . .  . .

# C. HINDRANCES TO EVANGELIZATION
*(Score -1 (minus 1) in end column for each "Yes" answer, or 0 for "No", for questions Nos. 245-264)*

245. State religion: is the state either Islamic, Hindu, Buddhist, Jewish, or other religious, or atheistic? . . . . . . . . . . . . . . . . . . . . . . . . . . . . . . . . .  . .
246. State opposition: does the state officially prohibit conversion to Christianity, or evangelism or proselytism? . . . . . . . . . . . . . . . . . . . . . . . . . . . . .  . .
247. Religiously persecution or harassment: is religious liberty for all denominations severely obstructed or suppressed? . . . . . . . . . . . . . . . . . . . . . . . . . .  . .
248. Are there systematic state attempts at removing children from Christian parent's influence? . . . . . . . . . . . . . . . . . . . . . . . . . . . . . . . . . . .  . .
249. Is there extensive state jamming of Christian radio from abroad? . . . . . . . . . . .  . .
250. Has the state in recent times deliberately dechristianized most previously Christian-name cities? . . . . . . . . . . . . . . . . . . . . . . . . . . . . . . . . .  . .
251. Spread of quasi-religions (secularism, materialism, agnosticism, atheism): are non-religious persons and atheists over 10% of the population? . . . . . . . . . . .  . .
252. Resurgence among non-Christian religions (Islam, Hinduism, Buddhism, spiritism, et alia): is this occurring? . . . . . . . . . . . . . . . . . . . . . . . . .  . .
253. Popular religiosity or piety (mass syncretistic folk-Christianity, christopaganism, spiritist Catholicism, et alia): are over 10% of the population involved? . . . .  . .
254. Nominal Christianity: do inactive or latent Christians (nominal Christians and non-practicing church members) total over 20% of the population? . . . . . . .  . .
255. Evangelistic distance: are the bulk of Christians separated from non-Christians by more than 5 religious or cultural frontiers? . . . . . . . . . . . .  . .
256. Is there unusual neglect of the Great Commission on the part of the churches? . . . .  . .

257. Multiplicity of rival Christian bodies: are there over 20 separate denominations within this population? . . . . . . . . . . . . . . . . . . . . . . . . . . . . . . . . .  . .
258. Have missionary or evangelistic methods/preaching/communication been poor or even bad (e.g. linguistically inadequate)? . . . . . . . . . . . . . . . . . .  . .
259. Is there extreme racial, tribal, class, or gender tension (apartheid, suppression of women, etc) within the churches? . . . . . . . . . . . . . . . . . . . . . . . . . .  . .
260. Are there other tensions or conflicts within the churches (ideological, political, etc)? . . . . . . . . . . . . . . . . . . . . . . . . . . . . . . . . . . . . . .  . .
261. Mail reliability and censorship: does less than 50% of all Christian mail (internal and external) get through? . . . . . . . . . . . . . . . . . . . . . . . . . .  . .
262. Inflation (rising costs): is it 20% per year or more? . . . . . . . . . . . . . . . . . . .  . .
263. Is extreme poverty, disease or illiteracy widespread? . . . . . . . . . . . . . . . . .  . .
264. Is there extreme exploitation of the poor by landowners, capitalists, multinationals, military-industrial complexes, etc? . . . . . . . . . . . . . . . . . . .  . .

## TOTALS

**OVERALL EVANGELISTIC COVERAGE**
Has this people, city, country, or other population or segment been adequately evangelized from these standpoints:
265.　—major geographical areas? . . . . . . . . . . . . . . . . . . . . . . . . . . . . . .  . .
266.　—all ethnic groups and sub-groups (tribes, languages)? . . . . . . . . . . . . . . .  . .
267.　—all minority groups (immigrants, refugees, aliens, etc)? . . . . . . . . . . . . . .  . .
268.　—all socio-economic classes? . . . . . . . . . . . . . . . . . . . . . . . . . . . . . .  . .
269.　—11 age-groups (infants to old people)? . . . . . . . . . . . . . . . . . . . . . . . .  . .
270.　—the worlds of industry, commerce, government? . . . . . . . . . . . . . . . . . . .  . .
271.　—all non-Christian religious groups? . . . . . . . . . . . . . . . . . . . . . . . . . .  . .
272.　—all other groupings or strata of society? . . . . . . . . . . . . . . . . . . . . . . .  . .
**SPECIAL OR UNUSUAL FACTORS**
273. If there are any additional factors either favoring or hindering evangelization in this city or country, name each, and for each add percentage point (*either plus or minus*) in the end column (*up to a maximum of plus or minus 10*) . . . . . . . . . . . . . . . . . . . . . . . . . . . . .  . .

**TOTAL VOLUME OF EVANGELIZATION EXPERIENCED, V**
274. Subtotal, here termed V, of all above factors 1-273 (*positive minus negative*) . .  . .
275. Value of E derived from V (*score E = V if V<100, or E = 100 if V>100*) . . . . . . . .  . .
276. Closed minorities in an otherwise evangelized population (*express as a negative %*) . . . . . . . . . . . . . . . . . . . . . . . . . . . . . . . . . . . . . . .  . .
277. All other unevangelized holdout individuals in evangelized groupings (*express as a negative %*) . . . . . . . . . . . . . . . . . . . . . . . . . . . . . . .  . .

**COMPARATIVE DEMOGRAPHIC EVANGELIZATION, E**
FINAL VALUE OF E (*score final total for E as: No. 278 = 275 minus 276 and 277*)

278. **Total extent or level, E** (maximum 100%) . . . . . . . . . . . . . . . . . . . . . . . . . .  . .

---

## A brief assessment of Table 24–8

The Scale of Comparative Demographic Evangelization presented in this table covers all the relevant bases but is too complex for everyday practical use on a wide scale. There is first the problem of the unavailability of data concerning most populations: for a large number of its 277 questions, no ready source of data is likely to be found. Nevertheless, for a fair number of populations in different parts of the world, the authors did compile answers to all the questions. The resulting values of V (a measure of the total volume of evangelism) and of E were found to be consistent with the simpler scales described earlier. For practical use in the future, 2 new scales are necessary: (1) we need a simple rapid-use one-variable scale which replaces the 277 questions by a single representative question measuring how adequate or inadequate Christian work among this population is; and (2) we need a formula which represents the 277 questions by means of a much smaller number of 20 or so variables, and which can do this by computer from existing databases. To secure credibility and usefulness, at the same time the results should be obtainable by the general reader via visual inspection of the printed version of the relevant database, using mental arithmetic no more complex than simple addition.

These 2 new scales will now be derived.

### A NEW RAPID-USE MEASURE OF ADEQUACY

#### Secular parallels

There are secular parallels to any attempt to measure adequacy of evangelization. Thus many features of an individual's health and well-being can be exactly measured, and exact boundaries of adequacy promulgated. Some of these parallels are shown in Table 24–9.

An example is the use of radioactivity (radiation) to control human disease such as cancer. A highly-radioactive beam is focused on the diseased part and destroys it. The strength of the beam must fall between exactly-calculated limits. If the beam's energy is lower than the adequate level for therapy, it will have no value to the patient. If it exceeds a known upper adequate level, it may kill the patient.

The simplest and most vivid of these indicators re-

lated to an individual's health is the body-mass index, BMI for short. This is calculated as: (a) in European usage, your body's weight (in kilograms), divided by your height (in meters) squared; or (b) in American usage, your weight (in pounds, lbs), times 704, divided by your height (in inches) squared. Using either usage, for a person weighing 160 lbs who is 5 ft 10 inches tall, his BMI works out at 23.0.

With the BMI, there is recognized to be a clearly-delineated range of values, from 20-27, within which a person's body is seen to be safely or adequately built and distributed. Above 27, there is risk of cardiac and other diseases. Below 20, a person is likely to be undernourished or inadequately structured. So the 160 lb person above whose BMI = 23 turns out to have the optimum figure for a healthy lifestyle.

Again, a person's intake of vitamins can be categorized exactly as Inadequate, Adequate, or Superfluous. It can even be dangerous if he or she takes

more than the adequate amount of, for instance, Vitamin A.

All such examples help us in our own search to establish adequate levels in Christian work.

#### Adequacy levels in Christian work

With these secular parallels in mind, we can now construct the Christian work-among parallel scale. This is done in Table 24–10 entitled 'Adequacy, inadequacy, or superfluity of Christian work and resources among a population (variable wa).' Its 12 columns are explained below the title.

#### Measuring adequacy of existing work and resources (variable wa)

This variable measures the extent of Christian work and resources of all kinds among a population. Essentially it is a quantified and evaluative version of the 'work-among' data reported in WCE Part 8 "Eth-

---

| Table 24–9. | Established levels of adequacy, inadequacy, and superfluity in 15 human situations. | | | | |
|---|---|---|---|---|---|
| Subject *1* | Item being measured (per capita: one person) *2* | INADEQUATE (deficiency) *3* | ADEQUATE (sufficiency) *4* | OPTIMUM *5* | SUPERFLUOUS (waste or toxicity) *6* |
| Money | Annual income, US $ (a) in the USA | <5,000 | 5,000-20,000 | 20,000 | >100,000 |
| | (b) in the world as a whole | <1,000 | 1,000-5,000 | 5,000 | >10,000 |
| Safe water | Water drunk per day, oz | <16 | 16-64 | 64 | >100 |
| Medical care | Visits to doctor per year | 0 | 1-10 | 3 | >10 |
| | Visits to doctor per lifetime | <40 | 40-400 | 100 | >400 |
| Dental care | Fluoride in water per day, mg | <1.5 | 1.5-4.0 | 2 | >4.0 |
| Food | Calories per day | <2,000 | 2,000-2,500 | 2,400 | >2,500 |
| Body energy-1 | Sugar, calories per day | <200 | 200-250 | 200 | >250 |
| Body energy-2 | Fat, calories per day | <600 | 600-750 | 600 | >750 |
| Body energy-3 | Carbohydrates, calories per day | <1,000 | 1,000-1,500 | 1,200 | >1,500 |
| | Cholesterol, mg per day | <250 | 250-350 | 300 | >350 |
| | Salt, grams per day | <4 | 4-6 | 5 | >6 |
| Vitamins | Vitamin A, IU per day | <5,000 | 5,000-50,000 | | >50,000 |
| | B2 (riboflavin), mg per day | <1.2 | 1.2-1.3 | 1.3 | >1.3 |
| Body fat | Body-mass index (BMI) | <20 | 20-27 | 23 | >27 |
| Well-being | Adult body weight, % water in | <55 | 55-65 | 60 | >65 |
| Mission | Agencies, work, resources (see Table 24–10) | Codes 0-4 | Codes 5-7 | Code 7 | Codes 8-10 |

## Table 24–10. Adequacy, inadequacy, or superfluity of Christian work and resources among a population (variable wa).

The 12 columns of this table are as follows:
**1. Code.** The "Work Among" variable wa is quantified as a code, on a scale from 0 to 10, which describes the status of organized Christian work, activity, or coverage among a people or population, measuring the Christian world's interest/concern/contact with or involvement with that people. It measures the overall amount of Christian work going on with regard to that people (that is, the amount of resources now available, in place and in use), originating both within it and from outside it. The emphasis in this variable is thus on how much Christian work is actually going on; it is not primarily a measure of either a people's or population's exposure to the gospel nor of its response to the gospel, although codes 5-10 do include an element of this. In practice, the main way of measuring this variable, in cases where data are available, is by means of column 8, congregations per million.
**2. Types of contact.** The code delineates 3 broad work-among kinds or types of situation: (a) *inadequacy* (inadequate resources, too little work, deficiency), coded as wa=0,1,2,3, or 4; (b) *adequacy* (adequate resources, enough work, sufficiency), coded as wa=5, 6, or 7; and (c) *superfluity* (superfluous resources, too much work, unnecessary duplication, waste, toxicity), coded as wa=8, 9, or 10.The value of wa arrived at here for each population is the largest of the several measures now to be described for columns 4, 6, or 8.
**3. Categories and meanings.** The code produces 11 de-

scriptive work-among categories or adjectives, shown as a single word each, in capitals. Additional phrases follow underneath each, amplifying the meaning.
**4. Denominations.** This variable, with its symbol dd, estimates the number of distinct Christian denominations in or serving this population, per million persons, on average. To this total of denominations we also add all distinct or separate ecclesiastical jurisdictions (dioceses, provinces, synods, etc.). This total is then the basic unit of *denominationalism* among this people. This categorizing is intended only to draw attention to the approximate order of magnitude of the situation. If dd is over 10 per million (as is the case with 46 countries of the world), then this depicts the state of gross oversaturation in those countries—far too many separate, rival, standalone denominations competing with each other for shares of the pie, namely members, money, property, activity, involvement, workers, publicity, recognition, fame, influence, achievement.
**5.** This variable is the same measure as column 4, but inverted to show population per denomination.
**6. Organizations.** This variable, with its symbol oo, estimates the number of Christian organizations of all kinds (mission agencies, service agencies, broadcasting agencies, scripture agencies, institutions, also including denominations and their dioceses or jurisdictions) in or serving this population, per million persons, on average. This is therefore a measure of *organized Christianity* in its totality as experienced by this pop-

ulation.
**7.** This is the same measure as column 6, but inverted to show population per organization.
**8. Congregations.** The next variable, with its symbol cc, is probably the most accurate and detailed measuring instrument on this subject. It estimates the number of congregations or worship centers in or serving this population, per million persons, on average. This is a measure of *the local church* (in Protestant usage), a concept which plays a major role (some would say *the* major role) in Christian outreach.
**9.** This is the same measure as column 8, but inverted to show population per congregation.
**10. Worlds.** This column shows how these work-among types and categories mesh into the 3-world trichotomous schema of the entire globe divided into Worlds A, B, and C. The typing is exact but in some cases approximate because slightly differing results emerge from use of the 3 different variables in columns 4, 6, and 8.
**11. Countries.** The figures show the number of the world's countries in each of the 11 work-among categories.
**12. Peoples.** Finally, the last column gives the number of the world's ethnolinguistic peoples in each of the 11 work-among categories.

| wa Code 1 | 3 TYPES OF CONTACT: see a,b,c below  2    11 categories and meanings 3 | DENOMINATIONS | | ORGANIZATIONS | | CONGREGATIONS | | WORLDS | | |
|---|---|---|---|---|---|---|---|---|---|---|
| | | Denominations per million, dd 4 | Persons per denomination 5 | Organizations per million, oo 6 | Persons per organization 7 | Congregations per million, cc 8 | Persons per congregation 9 | W 10 | Coun 11 | Peoples 12 |
| **a.** | **INADEQUACY** (inadequate resources, too little work, deficiency) | | | | | | | | | |
| 0 | **UNTOUCHED** Nothing. No work, no presence, no attempts of any kind known or detectable. | 0 | -- | 0 | -- | 0 | -- | A | 0 | 14 |
| 1 | **UNCONTACTED** No contact, virtually nothing but very occasional minor influences. | 0-0.1 | >10 million | 0-1 | >1 million | 0-1 | >1 million | A | 0 | 269 |
| 2 | **UNENGAGED** No ongoing regular work, but occasional contact, visits, or activities; first contact planned. | 0.1-0.5 | 2,000,000-10,000,000 | 1-2 | 500,000-1,000,000 | 1-5 | 500,000-1,000,000 | A | 1 | 350 |
| 3 | **UNREACHED** Minimal contact. Very little work, deficient work. Miniscule influence. | 0.5-1 | 1,000,000-2,000,000 | 2.5 | 200,000-500,000 | 5-10 | 100,000-500,000 | A | 4 | 976 |
| 4 | **UNDISCIPLED** Regular but inadequate contact. Sizable but insufficient work. | 1-2 | 500,000-1,000,000 | 5-10 | 100,000-200,000 | 10-80 | 12,500-100,000 | A | 23 | 1,516 |
| **b.** | **ADEQUACY** (adequate resources, enough work, sufficiency) | | | | | | | | | |
| 5 | **PARTIALLY-DISCIPLED** Adequate contact. Sufficient work and workers, but resistance and little or partial response; only a nucleus of church members. | 2-3 | 333,000-500,000 | 10-20 | 50,000-100,000 | 80-200 | 5,000-12,500 | B | 37 | 2,377 |
| 6 | **DISCIPLED** Adequate contact. Sufficient work and workers, widespread response; large numbers of churches and members. | 3-4 | 250,000-333,000 | 20-50 | 20,000-50,000 | 200-500 | 2,000-5,000 | B | 28 | 989 |
| 7 | **CHURCHED** Fully adequate contact, with very large response. More than adequate work. Overlapping activities of all kinds on several topics. | 4-5 | 200,000-250,000 | 50-100 | 10,000-20,000 | 500-1,000 | 1,000-2,000 | C | 60 | 2,388 |
| **c.** | **SUPERFLUITY** (superfluous resources, too much work, waste, toxicity) | | | | | | | | | |
| 8 | **SATURATED** Superfluous contact. Redundant activities. Unnecessary duplication. | 5-10 | 100,000-200,000 | 100-1,000 | 1,000-10,000 | 1,000-2,000 | 500-1,000 | C | 63 | 1,557 |
| 9 | **OVERSATURATED** Multiple, repetitive contact. Massive redundancy, overlapping, waste. | 10-50 | 20,000-100,000 | 1,000-2,000 | 500-1,000 | 2,000-3,000 | 330-500 | C | 20 | 1,684 |
| 10 | **HYPERSATURATED** Repeated excessive contact, work, presence, activities, confusion, lavish waste, even toxicity. | >50 | <20,000 | >2,000 | <500 | >3,000 | <330 | C | 2 | 463 |

noSphere", column 19. Further, column 38 'Additional descriptive data' does this by enumerating all Christian organizations (churches, agencies, denominations) which have significant presence or work among this population, and then classifying their aggregate contribution.

The 'work among' situation can be quantified or measured here in 3 distinct, different, but overlapping ways. We measure it by using a code based on data obtained by computing either (1) the number of Christian denominations at work per million of this people, (variable dd), or (2) the number of Christian

organizations (agencies including denominations) per million (variable oo), or (3) the number of congregations (churches, worship centers) per million population (variable cc). If data are available to measure 2 or even all 3 of these, we take the highest code figure that results. Usually however, one measure will suffice for arriving at the general order of magnitude (which is what the code itself is all about).

*Evaluating adequacy.* Quantifying congregations and organizations in this way gives us the opportunity to evaluate the adequacy or otherwise of Christian activity or coverage among a population, plac-

ing each population on a scale of adequacy ranging from 0 to 10. We need first to set levels of coverage, which may appear arbitrary on first sight, but which seem increasingly right as one gets into the data in detail. We therefore label codes 0-4 to mean *Inadequacy*, or insufficiency, or deficient work. Codes 5-7 mean *Adequacy*, because either dd or oo or cc (or all 3) are within the limits of adequacy defined as shown. Codes 8-10 mean *Superfluity*, by which is meant a situation where a population is the recipient of too much work—unnecessarily large amounts of resources are being poured in, even squandered, resulting in duplication, overlapping, repetition, confusion, waste, redundancy, saturation, even perhaps leading to a dangerous level of toxicity.

### *MEASURING TWO NEW KEY MINISTRIES*

Before the actual formula can be set out in detail, there are 3 key ministries which are not directly enumerated by churches or missions and which must therefore be measured by newly derived variables. these are *personal evangelism, alien Christianity, and adequacy of work among* a population.

***1. Measuring personal evangelism (variable d)***
Since 648 million Great Commission Christians engage in personal evangelism of various kinds, this is a most important ministry. It is measured by means of a discipleship scale, d, which varies from 0 to 10. Its derivation and values are set out in Table 24–11.

***2. Measuring alien Christianity (variable aC)***
Most peoples of the world have on their territory an alien Christian presence in the form of churches of aliens or foreigners or non-indigenous persons, of different cultures to the host ethnolinguistic people. This can have powerful effect on a strongly non-Christian or anti-Christian people, much as a speck of grit inside an oyster. Derivation and values of this factor are set out in Table 24–12.

### *A FORMULA FOR MEASURING EVANGELISM AND EVANGELIZATION*

As described earlier in Part 3 "GeoCommission" and in Global Diagrams 6 and 33, Christ's Great Commission can be understood as consisting of 2 Mini-commissions (*Evangelize!* and *Disciple!*) which cover 7 New Testament mandates (*Receive! Go! Witness! Proclaim! Disciple! Baptize! Train!*). These 7 Mandates define 7 components of the concept 'evangelization' and can be addressed by means of 7 human roles or modes of 'evangelism'. These 7 can in turn be seen to result in 7 different types/modes of words and 7 different kinds of evangelism. To enumerate, measure, and quantify this whole subject, we earlier in Part 22 subdivided the 7 modes into some 45 outreach ministries which are main varieties or spheres of evangelism as set out in Table 22-3 and diagrammatically in Global Diagram 6. These are set out further in Table 24–13.

In order to keep track of these 45 ministries, almost all churches and missions regularly compile statistics on a number of related activities. As a result, we can expand that analysis to measure both the concept of 'evangelism' and the wider concept of 'evangelization' by selecting a small number of representative indicators or variables from each of the 7 component sections of the Scale of Comparative Demographic Evangelization. In order to monitor the situation in each and all of the world's population segments, in this analysis we therefore select 20 such measures and combine them into a basic formula for the quantification of the concept of evangelization—evangelizing, evangelizers, evangelism, evangelized, and evangelization. An important feature of this formula is that it is based only on addition and subtraction, and so is simple enough for the reader to work out in his or her head by mental arithmetic using the printed tables in this volume or in *WCE* Part 8. In this way he or she can microexamine the analysis at any point as it proceeds.

Below are set out the main components in this schema of measurement. First we divide the various evangelistic influences into 2 major divisions:

**A. EVANGELIZERS** (the force for evangelism; clearly, those who engage in evangelism must, normally, themselves also be already evangelized); and

**B. EVANGELISM** (the church's outreach; the 7 main types/modes of evangelizing activity, or "words", that evangelizers and others engage in).

These 7 types of evangelistic words, the 45 ministries which illustrate them here, and the 20 variables and code letters by which those chosen for the formula are represented, can all be seen in Table 24–13. In its column 3 are listed all those varieties enumerated in the typology being evolved here. In the formula for E, however, a few varieties listed in column 3 are represented by variables with slightly different meanings (shown in column 5, which also adds items not in the formula itself).

Column 4 indicates which of the 277 questions on the Scale of Comparative Demographic Evangelization are selected to illustrate and represent each variety of evangelism. Note again that columns 3, 4, 5, and 6 may not always be obviously connected for a particular line, but that they represent a progression of thought on the subject of how to quantify items not quantified regularly by churches and agencies. Column 6 gives the 20 symbols comprising the formula (19 positive representing evangelizers, followed by 18 varieties of evangelism; and one negative (the last one) representing hindrances to evangelism). A

**Table 24–11. Discipleship scale: personal evangelism through local or indigenous Christianity among this people (variable d).**

This mutually-exclusive scale of 11 code values has 2 distinct but complementary meanings: (1) status of discipleship, and (2) status and effectiveness of personal evangelism.

(1) *Discipleship.* Firstly, it forms a discipleship scale in that it measures the extent to which this people has been discipled, or the extent of Christian discipleship among this people, especially for peoples with very few or no Christians at all. It does this by measuring the present size of the total Christian community, of all Christian traditions (Protestant, Anglican, Catholic, Orthodox, Independent), among this people on its own home territory in this country. "Church adherents" here means church members and their children, i.e. total affiliated Christians (affiliated to, or on the rolls of, all organized Christian churches and denominations). It therefore is measuring the present extent of local or indigenous Christianity among this people. "Indigenous" here in this variable means simply "of this people," "culturally indigenous to this people," "relating to the people under immediate consideration"; it does not refer to whether or not a people is or was originally indigenous to its country. Thus the term "indigenous church" in this variable covers, strictly speaking, all churches with members among this people, whether this people is indigenous to the country or is an immigrant or alien minority, and whether their churches are ecclesiastically either indigenous or imported. (This means that this term "indigenous church" is used here in this variable and the next in its widest sense and not in the commonly-used sense whereby it means only those locally-founded independent churches started by indigenous persons as opposed to Western-related or foreign mission-originated churches.) In assigning one code value to each people, we attempt to visualize and include the effect of radio evangelism and literature evangelism, which often result in hidden converts, especially in vast non-Christian populations with high education and easy access to radio and literature. In cases where a people can correctly be categorized by two or more codes, e.g. a people with only one congregation (= code 2) but whose church adherents number 6 percent (as for 60 converts in a tribe of 1,000 people) (= code 7), we always choose the largest code number (= code 7).

| *Code* | |
|---|---|
| 0 = | No known local or indigenous believers of this culture in this people's territory in this country |
| 1 = | A few isolated scattered local or indigenous believers of this culture (numbering less than 0.005%), but no known indigenous congregation (house church or radio church) |
| 2 = | A single known local or indigenous congregation or worship group or center or small unorganized fellowship of believers of this culture (house church, radio church), with believers from 0.005% to under 0.01% of this people's population |
| 3 = | A small unorganized cluster or handful of 2 or more churches or congregations of local or indigenous believers of this culture (fellowships, house churches, radio churches), with believers from 0.01% of this people's population to under 0.05% |
| 4 = | An organized local or indigenous group of churches with believers numbering from 0.05% to under 0.1% of this people's population |
| 5 = | Local or indigenous church adherents of this culture (all traditions) number from 0.1% to under 1.0% |
| 6 = | Local or indigenous church adherents of this culture number from 1% to under 5% |
| 7 = | Local or indigenous church adherents of this culture number from 5% to under 10% |
| 8 = | Local or indigenous church adherents of this culture number from 10% to under 20% |
| 9 = | Local or indigenous church adherents of this culture number from 20% to under 50% |
| 10 = | Local or indigenous church adherents of this culture number from 50% of this people's population to 100% |

(2) *Personal evangelism.* Secondly, this scale has an additional and more significant meaning. It forms a measure of the status, amount, effectiveness, and past and present influence of personal evangelism among this people's population as undertaken by local/indigenous Christians of this people. In this interpretation, the code number stands for the percentage of the people's population who have become evangelized in the recent past and up to the present as a result of local Christians' personal witness and evangelism. To obtain this variable, use the figure arrived at in the previous meaning of the scale Discipleship. The effectiveness of personal evangelism can therefore be seen to vary from 0% to a maximum of 10% of this people's population.

**Table 24–12. Alien or non-indigenous Christianity on this people's home territory (variable aC).**

This mutually-exclusive scale of 11 code values has 2 distinct but complementary meanings: (1) status of resident alien Christianity on this population's territory, and (2) status and effectiveness of personal evangelism by resident aliens (outsiders).

The scale refers to local alien Christian influence, i.e. it measures the degree of Christian presence from outside of this culture by monitoring the effect of surrounding Christians and their local churches (places of worship) on the people under consideration. It refers to the effect on this people (who are here termed indigenous in or to their own culture or area) of Christians and churches who belong to other, different, cultures (here termed alien or non-indigenous peoples or cultures) but who are nevertheless resident within this people's home territory or the area in which they live. This territory or area may be clearly demarcated as originally or de facto the indigenous people's own territory; or, in the case of an immigrant people scattered throughout a city or a country, its "territory" is not primarily its own and may be shared with one or even many other peoples; and it can be as large as a city or even the country itself. Note that the percentages in the code below are obtained by dividing the number of alien or non-indigenous church adherents in the area by the total of this indigenous people's population (not by the non-indigenous population, nor by the total population). This means that there will be many cases where the percentage may be over 100 percent, even 200 percent, 300 percent or even far more; all such cases are covered by the final category, code 10.

| *Code* | |
|---|---|
| 0 = | No known alien or non-indigenous believers of other cultures resident in this people's territory or area |
| 1 = | A few isolated scattered alien or non-indigenous believers, without congregations |
| 2 = | A single alien or non-indigenous congregation or worship group or center or small unorganized fellowship of believers of other cultures, with members from 0.005% to under 0.01% |
| 3 = | A small unorganized cluster or handful of 2 or more alien congregations of non-indigenous believers of other cultures (fellowships, house churches, radio churches) with members from 0.01% to under 0.05% |
| 4 = | An organized alien or non-indigenous church with members from 0.05% to under 0.1% of the size of the indigenous people's population |
| 5 = | Alien or non-indigenous church adherents of other cultures (all traditions) number from 0.1% to under 1.0% of the indigenous people's size |
| 6 = | Alien or non-indigenous church adherents of other cultures number from 1% to under 5% |
| 7 = | Alien or non-indigenous church adherents of other cultures number from 5% to under 10% |
| 8 = | Alien or non-indigenous church adherents of other cultures number from 10% to under 20% |
| 9 = | Alien or non-indigenous church adherents of other cultures number from 20% to under 50% |
| 10 = | Alien or non-indigenous church adherents of other cultures number over 50% (50% or more) of the size of the indigenous people's population |

As with the discipleship variable d, this alien scale has a second meaning. It forms a measure of the past and present influence of the evangelistic impact of alien congregations on the indigenous people's population. In this interpretation, the code number stands for the percentage of the indigenous people's population who have become evangelized in the recent past and up to the present, as a result of alien Christians' presence, witness, and service. This can be seen to vary from 0% to a maximum of 10%.

**Table 24–13.    Elements from 45 outreach ministries in a formula for evangelism and evangelization in a population segment.**

*Meaning of columns:*
1. Number (from 1-7) of the related Great Commission Mandate.
2. Type of words produced under this Mandate.
3. Outreach ministry or variety of evangelism.
4. Number of this ministry in Scale of Comparative Demographic Evangelization (Table 24–8).
5. Variable chosen to represent and enumerate this ministry.
6. Symbol of this ministry in *WCE* Part 8 "EthnoSphere".
7. Column in Part 8 "EthnoSphere".
8. Maximum effect (value) of this variable.

| Mandate | Type of words | Variety of evangelism | Scale No. | Variable in formula | Symbol | Ethno | Max % |
|---|---|---|---|---|---|---|---|
| col 1 | 2 | 3 | 4 | 5 | 6 | 7 | 8 |
| **A. EVANGELIZERS** | | Christians (church members) . . . | 1 | Affiliated, % | AC | 11 | 100 |
| **B. EVANGELISM** via 45 ministries | | | | | | | |
| 1. | HIDDEN WORDS | Intercession . . . . . . . . . . . . . . . | 6 | Intercessors | i | 11 | 5 |
| | | Inner renewal . . . . . . . . . . . . . . | 13 | Charismatics, % | - | - | - |
| 2. | VISUAL WORDS | Christians' lifestyle . . . . . . . . . . | 17 | Lifestylers, % | - | - | - |
| | | Audiovisual ministries . . . . . . . . | 50 | Extent | - | - | - |
| | | Plays/concerts/operas/shows . . . | 53 | Extent | - | - | - |
| | | "Jesus" Film (Luke's Gospel) . . . | 57 | Audiences | Jf | 13 | 7 |
| | | Audio scriptures . . . . . . . . . . . . | 61 | Availability | au | 14 | 5 |
| | | Scripture leaflets/selections . . . . | 62 | Mass distribution | - | - | - |
| | | Every-home visitations . . . . . . . . | 63 | Homes visited | - | - | - |
| | | New Reader Scriptures (NRS) . . . | 69 | Distribution | nr | 15 | 2 |
| | | Braille scriptures . . . . . . . . . . . . | 70 | Availability | br | 16 | 1 |
| | | Signed/deaf scriptures . . . . . . . . | 71 | Availability | hi | 17 | 1 |
| | | Christian suffering . . . . . . . . . . . | 79 | Extent | - | - | - |
| 3. | PERSONAL WORDS | Personal evangelism by: | | | | | |
| | | Great Commission Christians . | 83 | Personal work | d | 18 | 10 |
| | | Martyrdoms . . . . . . . . . . . . . . . . | 96 | Extent | - | - | - |
| 4. | PROCLAIMED WORDS | Full-time home church workers . | 97 | Adequate work among | - | 19 | - |
| | | Foreign missionaries . . . . . . . . | 102 | Cross-cultural mission | xc | 20 | 16 |
| | | Evangelists, catechists . . . . . . . | 105 | Mass evangelism | me | 21 | 5 |
| | | Short-term workers . . . . . . . . . | 109 | Weeks served | - | - | - |
| | | Part-time evangelizers . . . . . . . | 110 | Hours per month | - | - | - |
| | | Mission agencies . . . . . . . . . . . | 114 | Agencies at work | mi | 22 | 5 |
| 5. | WRITTEN WORDS | Portions/gospels (25 pages) . . . | 141 | Distribution | P . . | 24 | 1 |
| | | Near-gospels . . . . . . . . . . . . . . | 142 | Availability | p . . | 24 | 1 |
| | | New Testaments (300p) . . . . . . . | 143 | Distribution | PN . | 25 | 4 |
| | | Near-New Testaments . . . . . . . . | 144 | Availability | pn . | 25 | 2 |
| | | Bibles (1,300p) . . . . . . . . . . . . . | 145 | Distribution | PNB | 26 | 10 |
| | | Near-Bibles . . . . . . . . . . . . . . . . | 146 | Availability | pnb | 26 | 3 |
| | | 2nd-language gospels . . . . . . . . | 157 | Availability | sp | 27 | 1 |
| | | 2nd-language NTs . . . . . . . . . . | 158 | Availability | sn | 27 | 2 |
| | | 2nd-language Bibles . . . . . . . . . | 159 | Availability | sb | 27 | 3 |
| 6. | PRINTED WORDS | Denominational materials . . . . . . | 160 | Denominations | D | 29 | 5 |
| | | Local church output . . . . . . . . . | 161 | Worship centers | - | - | - |
| | | Outside Christian literature . . . . | 166 | Outside Christians | aC | 30 | 10 |
| | | Church-planting output . . . . . . . | 169 | Church growth | - | - | - |
| | | Institutional ministries/records . | 191 | Pupils, students | - | - | - |
| | | Christian books (100p) . . . . . . . | 194 | Sales | - | - | - |
| | | Christian periodicals (30p) . . . . | 201 | Subscriptions | - | - | - |
| | | Tracts (2p) . . . . . . . . . . . . . . . . | 202 | Circulation | - | - | - |
| | | Other documentation . . . . . . . . | 203 | Articles, stories | - | - | - |
| 7. | ELECTRONIC WORDS | Programmed training (TEE, &c) . | 215 | Extent | - | - | - |
| | | Christian radio programs . . . . . . | 232 | Countries transmitting | ra | 31 | 8 |
| | | Christian TV programs . . . . . . . | 234 | Audiences | - | - | - |
| | | Urban media (cable TV, etc) . . . . | 239 | Urbanites | u | - | 4 |
| | | Christian-owned computers . . . . | 240 | Users | - | - | - |
| | | Internet/www/e-mail/networks . . | 241 | Extent | - | - | - |
| **C. HINDRANCES** | | | | | | | |
| | Negative influences | Unevangelized pockets . . . . . . . | 276 | Size of pockets | ur | - | -1 |
| | | Religious liberty . . . . . . . . . . . . . | 246 | Stage | rl | - | -2.5 |
| | | Human Development Index . . . . | 263 | Range | hd | - | -2.5 |
| | | Literacy . . . . . . . . . . . . . . . . . . . | 263 | % of adults | li | - | -2.5 |
| | | Maximum possible % | . . . . . . . . . . . . . . . . . . . . . . . . . . . . | | | | 211 |

hyphen (-) in this column means that that particular variable is not included in our present compact 20-variable formula.

Column 7 shows in what column of the *World Christian database*, as shown in "EthnoSphere", the numerical or coded data will be found for each people. Column 8 gives the maximum possible value of each, as a percentage. When these are added it shows 2 overall maximum possible values. The total volume of evangelization experienced by any population segment, here given the symbol V, is 250. And the maximum value of E is 100%.

All the symbols in column 6 head columns tabulated for all ethnolinguistic peoples. The one exception is the variable 'Urban media', which is tabulated for all countries (Part 12) and all cities (*WCE* Part 10 "MetroScan").

## QUANTIFYING THE TOTAL VOLUME OF EVANGELIZATION, V

This section will now describe the method of monitoring and quantifying 7 related but quite different measures of the status of evangelization, evangelism, and evangelizers in any segment of population. These measures are for a people, a metropolis, a country, a nation, a region, a continent, or the whole world.

Our basic instrument is a formula with the 20 elements described above each measuring a different aspect of evangelism and evangelization. Each element or factor has a code whose value stands for the percentage of the population which that factor is estimated to have caused to become evangelized. These values are deliberately set low or small in order to balance the overlapping or duplication that are inevitable in this type of analysis, because all the variables are interdependent in varying degrees.

The first form of the formula is, in the order of the preceding table and with parentheses around each of the 7 types of evangelism and evangelization:

$$V = AC + (i) + (Jf + au + nr + br + hi) + (d) + (xc + me + mi) + (P + N + B + ss) + (D + aC) + (ra + u) - (rl + hd + li).$$

To help the user to understand the methodology of this sequence and to follow it himself using mental arithmetic, this formula's variables are arranged in the same order as shown in the *World Christian database*, given here as *WCE* Part 8 "EthnoSphere". The user can thus follow the formula across the 2 facing pages he will find there.

The letters shown refer to the titles of columns on printouts. For a specific population, each variable has a code value which is a percentage of the total population; V is then computed as the sum of the 19 values, namely the first figure (affiliated Christians, AC) plus the remaining 18 code values. It can be seen that V has a theoretical maximum possible value of 250, which suggests evangelistic 'overkill' of 150%. In other words, an extra 150% of evangelistic effort has been expended which cannot increase E since E cannot exceed 100%.

What this means is simple: there are all sorts of ways in which a population can reach the maximum figure possible for its evangelized members, namely E=100%. Hardly any of the factors—types or varieties of evangelism—are individually indispensable. If dictators or totalitarian regimes prohibit one variety, the gospel finds other ways to spread.

This variable, V, has already been introduced at the end of the Scale of Comparative Demographic Evangelization (Table 24–8). In the present more compact formula, V will shortly be used to measure the total volume or quantity of all types and varieties of evangelism and evangelization.

### QUANTIFYING THE EXTENT OF EVANGELIZATION, E

The second form of the formula produces the variable E, which measures the status of evangelization in a population—the extent to which the individuals in the population have become evangelized, or the percentage of persons who have become evangelized.

The formula is the same as for V with the addition of one variable, ur (=unevangelized remnant):

$$E = AC + (i) + (Jf + au + nr + br + hi) + (d) + (xc + me + mi) + (P + N + B + ss) + (D + aC) + (ra + u) - (rl + hd + li) - ur.$$

E differs from V in that it has an immovable ceiling, an imposed maximum of 100%. E cannot be greater than 100%, which describes the state in which everyone in the population has become adequately evangelized. At this point in the computer program, therefore, if V>100 then to obtain E, V is first set to 100, and then E is modified by the formula E=100-ur. The last variable ur is a negative one reducing E slightly but only invoked in heavily evangelized peoples, cities, or countries, virtually all of which have small remaining or remnant unevangelized individuals or ethnolinguistic minorities. Thus whenever V adds up to 100 or over, in the present compact formula E is automatically set to 100 and then ur is subtracted from it, yielding our final working value of E.

### CODEBOOK AND METHODOLOGY OF THE FORMULA

#### Codes and values of the 20 variables

This is now the place to give the full codes for those variables, adding methodological comments. The numbers or letters under '*Code*' for all variables below are given as they appear in the printed columns of the peoples and languages databases ("EthnoSphere" and "LinguaMetrics"). In addition, letter codes are given their numerical values required for the enumeration of E and other indexes. The "Value" figure means the percentage of this population (from 0% to 10%) that we estimate to have become evangelized as a result of the presence of this specific ministry. Abbreviated versions of all codes are found in Part 16 "GeoCodebook".

The variable E is a composite obtained by adding the values of the 20 variables whose symbols are shown at left margin in bold type in Table 24–14, followed in italics by their names. These are set out here preceded by 2 large covernames and one lesser one.

## MEASURING EVANGELISTIC OFFERS

### Two approaches to measurement
In Part 22 "Evangelism" we began by enumerating evangelism-hours and evangelistic offers with their per capita per year derivation. This is the comparative variable denoted here by e. In this Part 24 we have enumerated the results of these hours and offers, namely the resulting evangelized state, E, the percent of total population who have become evangelized. These 2 variables can now be derived from each other, providing readers with a way to extend the analysis from ministries to countries, peoples, language groups, and other populations.

### Quantifying total and per capita evangelism-hours or offers, Q and e
Several new variables measure the volume of direct evangelism (ongoing evangelistic endeavor, from both internal and external sources) currently being expended on or experienced by this population segment, expressed as rate of increase per day or per year.

As described in Part 22, Table 22-7, one evangelistic offer made to an individual, or one disciple-opportunity, is defined as an occasion on which some variety of evangelism takes place, lasting one hour of the individual's time. This unit is thus termed an evangelism-hour, or an offer.

As discussed earlier, there are two or three hundred distinct varieties of evangelism, internal and external, many of which have been quantified in the present survey. These have been incorporated in the various formulas and variables: AC, E, U, R, V. They now enable us to create direct measures of the number of evangelism-hours or offers received by a population, measured as Q and e.

These new variables Q and e are as follows.

### Total evangelistic offers per day, Q
This variable measures the total number of evangelistic offers (disciple-opportunities) being directed at, or experienced by, the population on average every day of the year at present (per diem, per day, p.d.). Q is derived as follows:

$$Q = pop(AC)V/10,000$$

where pop = total population, AC = percent affiliated Christian, V = all evangelizing factors (maximum 250), which is the same as E whenever V<100.

### Total offers per capita per year, e
This variable, in this series of quantitative attributes, has 2 related meanings. (a) It measures the total number of evangelism-hours actually heard or received per person per year, on average. Also (b) it measures the present level or total of offers per person (evangelistic disciple-opportunities per capita) being directed at, or experienced by, the population in the course of one year (per annum, p.a.) It is derived by the following formula, expressed in 2 separate forms:

$$e = 365 Q/pop$$

or

$$e = 0.0365 (AC)V$$

### Prioritizing evangelistic work
This variable e is the figure to compare directly with similar figures for other peoples. In Part 28 "GeoTargeting", the range of values of e (from 0 to its theoretical maximum of 912.5) is combined to form an evangelistic targeting variable T. This ranges from code 1 (= top priority, because it stands for e<0.01) to code 10 (= lowest priority, because most of the population are already Great Commission Christians). The scale is shown set out in full in Part 28 "GeoTargeting".

### An interpretation
At the scale's upper end, values of e greater than 365—which means an average, for every person in a population, of one offer every day—surely represent, to quote Job 33:29-30 again, 'chance after chance' taken to extremes. After all, the biblical prophets attacked gross disparities of wealth, property, income, food, water, and other benefits of life. If Jesus' evangelism-hours represent the most valuable of all such benefits, those who are saturated or even sated with huge quantities they cannot use are depriving vast numbers of people elsewhere.

### Other variables
Other ways of measuring evangelism, evangelistic provision, and targetability can be derived by other combinations of data variables. One such, useful for clarifying how much provision non-Christians (X) could get if evangelism were directed mainly at them, would be:

Total offers per non-Christian per year (e/X), obtained by dividing e (offers p.a.) by the total of all non-Christians in the country as a percentage, times 100.

## Table 24–14. Codes and values for quantifying evangelization by means of a 20–variable formula.

### A. EVANGELIZERS (the force for evangelism)

Symbol
AC=**Christians** (church members as percent of population; values range from zero to 100%, i.e. from 0 to 100)

### B. EVANGELISM (the church's outreach)

#### 1. HIDDEN WORDS

Symbol

**i**    **Intercessors** (size of intercessors across the world praying for this people; values 0-5).

This variable is used here as an approximate measure of the relative volume of intercession specifying this people likely to be being generated by virtue of the size (and therefore the importance, fame, notoriety) of the population segment concerned. It is clearly of enormous (though completely unexplored) significance when the number of intercessors from any part of the world, who are praying specifically for a certain people or population, rises to or exceeds the actual number of persons in this population. In practice it is impossible to quantify intercessors accurately, since their work is hidden. From one point of view, it would be reasonable to expect that every church member is likely to pray for the extension of Christ's kingdom at least within his or her own ethnolinguistic people. Our own more conservative and, hopefully, more realistic estimate is 200 million (10% of the world's church members).

At the lower end of the membership scale, we may reasonably assume that the number of intercessors will include the native Christians themselves (e.g Mongolia's newly baptized 2,000 converts are likely to be all praying for their families and friends regularly). As a first approximation here, therefore, this code estimates the total intercessors to be of approximately the same general order of magnitude as the number of Christians.

Thus, of the current world total of 200 million Christian intercessors praying each day for our world, over 50 million (code 5) are likely to know about and pray for the largest people on Earth, China's 1 billion people, with its 77 million Han Chinese Christians. At the other end of the scale, only a handful—perhaps only a few score intercessors (code 0)—have ever heard of the unevangelized Ingessana of the Sudan, an isolated people of only 30,000 population, with no known Christians. This variable is therefore deduced by examining the data column 'Church members', and coding each people 0-5 accordingly.

Values of i for specific peoples are not given in WCE Part 8 "EthnoSphere", in deference to their hidden status. But the computerized formula computes i as indicated above and adds its value to the totals of V and E.

| Code | Intercessors likely to be involved | This people's church members |
|---|---|---|
| 0 | Less than 1,000 intercessors | Christians under 1,000 |
| 1 | Between 1,000-10,000 intercessors | Christians between 1,000-10,000 |
| 2 | Between 10,000-1 million intercessors | Christians between 10,000-1 million |
| 3 | Between 1-20 million intercessors | Christians between 1-20 million |
| 4 | Between 20-50 million intercessors | Christians between 20-50 million |
| 5 | Over 50 million intercessors | Christians over 50 million |

#### 2. VISUAL WORDS

**Jf**    **'Jesus' Film** (values 0-4).

As explained above, the code below means the percentage of this population (from 0% to 4%) likely to have become evangelized through this ministry alone, and which we can add to the effect of other ministries and factors in order to create E% (persons evangelized by all ministries and factors).

| Code | Meaning |
|---|---|
| 0 | Not available in mother tongue or its cluster of languages |
| 1 | Available in mother tongue (if under 10% all speakers) or in its cluster |
| 2 | Available, viewers 10-50% |
| 3 | Available, viewers 50-100% |
| 4 | Vast impact in mother tongue: (viewers >100%) |

**au**    **Audio scriptures** (availability of audio scriptures in mother tongue or its cluster; values 0-5).

Each category in this variable also contains all preceding categories. For this language, the following code indicates what is available. Values 1,3,4,5 involve cassettes that can be purchased.

| Code | Item | Value | Meaning |
|---|---|---|---|
| • | nothing | 0 | No audio scriptures or selections available |
| c | materials | 1 | Audio materials available only in a same-cluster language |
| s | selections | 1 | Selections/teaching/music purchasable on cassette |
| r | radio | 2 | Radio selections: audio selections hearable over radio |
| a | portion | 3 | Audio scriptures purchasable: gospels or other portions |
| A | Testament | 4 | Audio scriptures purchasable: New Testament |
| B | Bible | 5 | Audio scriptures purchasable: complete Bible |

**nr**    **New Reader Scriptures** (for new literates in this mother tongue or its cluster of languages; values 0-1).

NRS publications always contain visual illustrations. A Selection is a booklet under 24 pages long; a Portion is a gospel or other complete book of the Bible of 24 or more pages).

| Code | Value | Meaning |
|---|---|---|
| • | 0 | Nothing available |
| s | 1 | New Reader Scriptures available |

**br**    **Braille scriptures** (for the unsighted/nonsighted or blind, related to mother tongue or its cluster; values 0-1).

| Code | Value | Meaning |
|---|---|---|
| • | 0 | Nothing available |
| u | 1 | Braille scriptures available |

**hi**    **Signed/deaf scriptures** (for the hearing-impaired or deaf, for any people's mother tongue or its cluster of languages; values 0-1).

| Code | Value | Meaning |
|---|---|---|
| • | 0 | Nothing available |
| h | 1 | Signed scriptures available |

#### 3. PERSONAL WORDS

**d**    **Discipling/personal work** (evangelizing influence of local or indigenous disciples; also contains an element of these disciples discipling or making other disciples; values 0-10).

| Code | Meaning |
|---|---|
| 0 | No known local or indigenous believers of this culture |
| 1 | A few scattered local or indigenous believers (numbering less than 0.005%) |
| 2 | A single indigenous congregation or worship center (with members from 0.005% to under 0.01%) |
| 3 | A small unorganized cluster of 2 or more churches (with members from 0.01% to under 0.05%) |
| 4 | Organized believers from 0.05% to under 0.1% |
| 5 | Local church adherents from 0.1% to under 1.0% |
| 6 | Local adherents from 1% to under 5% |
| 7 | Local adherents from 5% to under 10% |
| 8 | Local adherents from 10% to under 20% |
| 9 | Local adherents from 20% to under 50% |
| 10 | Local adherents from 50% to 100% |

#### 4. PROCLAIMED WORDS

**xc**    **Cross-cultural mission** (evangelizing influence of cross-cultural mission and related personnel, including variable S = own foreign or cross-cultural missionaries sent out per million of its affiliated church members; values 0-16).

The highest 5 values reflect extremely high commitment to sending own missionaries, arising out of heavily-evangelized communities. See detailed derivation in Part 21 "Geo-Personnel".

| Code | Meaning |
|---|---|
| | CROSS-CULTURAL MISSION-RECEIVING IS ESSENTIAL |
| 0 | No cross-cultural work going on |
| 1 | Only indirect witness via relatives or returning residents |
| 2 | Only indirect ministries from outside |
| 3 | Occasional visits by evangelists or missionaries or teams |
| 4 | At least one resident full-time missionary or evangelist |
| 5 | Two or more resident missionaries or evangelists at work |
| 6 | Church planting well under way |
| | SELF-SUFFICIENCY IN CHURCH AND MISSION (mission-receiving is no longer essential) |
| 7 | Indigenous workers working here among their own people |
| 8 | One or more denominations mainly of this people, but producing negligible mission personnel (S<10 missionaries per million church members) |
| | CROSS-CULTURAL MISSION-SENDING DEVELOPS |
| 9 | Denominations with sporadic mission-sending programs (under 20 personnel per million): 20>S>10 |
| 10 | Inadequate number of own missionaries sent out per million: 50>S>20 |
| 11 | Not quite adequate own missionaries sent out per million (less than 100): 100>S>50 |
| | ADEQUATE OBEDIENCE TO THE GREAT COMMISSION (defined as S>100) |
| 12 | Barely adequate number of own missionaries sent out per million: 200>S>100 |
| 13 | Adequate own missionaries sent out per million: 400>S>200 |
| 14 | Substantial own missionaries sent out per million: 600>S>400 |
| 15 | Exemplary number of own missionaries sent out per million: 800>S>600 |
| 16 | Phenomenal number of own missionaries sent out per million: S>800 |

**me**    **Mass evangelism** (contact with organized mass evangelism; values 0-5).

| Code | Meaning |
|---|---|
| 0 | None, nothing |
| 1 | Visiting evangelists, witnesses, or minicampaigns |
| 2 | Local one-church evangelistic missions |
| 3 | Leaflet/booklet/scripture distribution campaigns |
| 4 | Denominational evangelistic campaigns (public or clandestine) |
| 5 | Interdenominational mass evangelistic campaigns |

**mi**    **Mission agencies at work** (working among this population; values 0-5). The variable indicates how many organized mission agencies are at work in this country among this people or other segment, with offices and/or assigned personnel in this country. The code indicates what percent influence each category has on E%.

| Code | Meaning |
|---|---|
| 0 | None at work |
| 1 | One mission agency at work |
| 2 | Two mission agencies at work |
| 3 | 3-10 mission agencies at work |
| 4 | 11-20 mission agencies at work |
| 5 | Over 20 mission agencies at work |

#### 5. WRITTEN WORDS

The next 4 variables describe the people's or language community's current access to the official or formal or definitive or standard version of the Word of God, the written or printed Scripture. This access comes via 3 varieties: (a) mother-tongue scriptures, (b) same-cluster scriptures, here termed "near-scripture", and (c) second-language (trade language or lingua france) scriptures. The first 2 varieties, are described for the 3 columns below (describing respectively portion, NT, whole Bible) under varieties (a) and (b); the third variety, (c), is described in the single-column variable that follows. In every case the 4 variables indicate what the highest access is (mother-tongue access being more effective than same-cluster access).

(a) Mother-tongue scriptures (scriptures available in mother tongue, or a related close dialect; total values 0-10).

| Code | Value | Meaning |
|---|---|---|
| • | 0 | Nothing published |
| P | 1 | Portion (gospel) |
| N | 3 | New Testament |
| B | 6 | Bible |

(b) Same-cluster scriptures (if scriptures are absent in the mother tongue, scriptures may nevertheless be available in a related same-cluster language, termed here "near-scriptures" (near-gospel, near-NT, near-Bible); if so, they are indicated here by lower-case letters as shown below; total aggregate values 0-6).

Continued opposite

Table 24–14 concluded

| Code | Value | Meaning |
|------|-------|---------|
| • | 0 | Nothing published |
| p | 1 | Portion (gospel), i.e. a near-gospel |
| n | 2 | New Testament, i.e. a near-NT |
| b | 3 | Bible, i.e. a near-Bible |

Summing up the above 2 sets of codes, we can combine them as follows. Columns 25-27 thus contain 3 variables describing the status of the 3 major varieties of scriptures—portion, New Testament, whole Bible—which may show any of the following symbols, with values and meanings below.

| Code | Value | Meaning |
|------|-------|---------|
| • | 0 | Nothing published (mother-tongue or same-cluster) |
| P | 1 | Portion (gospel) in mother-tongue or dialect |
| N | 3 | NT in mother tongue or dialect |
| B | 6 | Whole Bible in mother tongue or dialect |
| p | 1 | Portion (gospel) only in a same-cluster language (near-gospel) |
| n | 2 | NT only in a same-cluster language (near-NT) |
| b | 3 | Bible only in a same-cluster language (near-Bible) |

This situation for a particular people is indicated by the sum total of whichever of these 7 codes are shown in columns 25 plus 26 plus 27, varying from 0 to 10.

An alternative quick-reference format to assist the reader wanting to utilize the data shown is as follows.

**P..** **Portion (gospel)** (portion in mother tongue or same cluster, values 0-1).

| Code | Value | Meaning |
|------|-------|---------|
| • | 0 | Nothing published (mother-tongue or same-cluster) |
| p | 1 | Portion (gospel) only in a same-cluster language (near-gospel) |
| P | 1 | Portion (gospel) in own mother tongue or dialect |

**PN.** **New Testament** (NT in mother tongue or same cluster; values 0-3).

| Code | Value | Meaning |
|------|-------|---------|
| • | 0 | Nothing published (mother-tongue or same-cluster) |
| n | 2 | NT only in a same-cluster language (near-NT) |
| N | 3 | NT in own mother tongue or dialect |

**PNB** **Bible** (complete Bible in mother tongue or same cluster; values 0-6).

| Code | Value | Meaning |
|------|-------|---------|
| • | 0 | Nothing published (mother-tongue or same-cluster) |
| b | 3 | Whole Bible only in a same-cluster language (near-Bible) |
| B | 6 | Whole Bible in own mother tongue or dialect |

**ss** **Second-language scriptures** (if both mother-tongue or same-cluster scriptures are absent, scriptures may nevertheless be available in an unrelated second or other language understood by a majority (50% or more) of this people, such as a trade language, market language, lingua france, or other language of wider communication; if so, this is indicated here by one lowercase letter; values 0-3).
Note that this variable is a single one-letter column showing a value (. or p, n, or b) once for each people.

| Code | Value | Meaning |
|------|-------|---------|
| • | 0 | No scriptures in any second language (or, monolinguals > 50%) |
| p | 1 | Portions available in a second language |
| n | 2 | NT available in a second language |
| b | 3 | Bible available in a second language |

### 6. PRINTED WORDS

The next 2 variables are regarded here as indicators of the volume and therefore of the evangelizing influence of *Christian literature and printed words* circulating among this people in their mother tongue and in any second language due to (1) organized denominations (with literature produced by their headquarters, parish structures, and other varieties of institutions), and (2) Christians of other outside cultures but residing on this people's territory (with their own varieties of literature).

**D** **Denominations** (total working among this population; values 0-5).
The variable indicates how many denominations are present and working among this people or other kind of segment, not simply as an outside mission agency but with actual church members from among this people. Dioceses and other autonomous jurisdictions are counted here as denominations. The code indicates what percent influence each category, with its corresponding volume of Christian literature and printed words, has on E (% evangelized).

| Code | Meaning |
|------|---------|
| 0 | None present |
| 1 | One denomination present |
| 2 | Two denominations present |
| 3 | 3-10 denominations present |
| 4 | 11-20 denominations present |
| 5 | Over 20 denominations present |

**aC** **Outside Christians** (evangelizing influence of outside or alien or non-indigenous Christianity; values 0-10).
The code indicates what percent influence each category, with its corresponding volume of Christian literature and printed words, has on E (% evangelized).

| Code | Meaning |
|------|---------|
| 0 | No known alien believers on this territory |
| 1 | A few scattered alien believers, without congregations |
| 2 | A single alien congregation or worship center (with members from 0.005% to under 0.01%) |
| 3 | A small unorganized cluster of 2 or more alien churches (with numbers from 0.01% to under 0.05%) |
| 4 | An organized alien church with members from 0.05% to under 0.1% |
| 5 | Alien church members from 0.1% to under 1.0% |
| 6 | Alien church members from 1% to under 5% |
| 7 | Alien church members from 5% to under 10% |
| 8 | Alien church members from 10% to under 20% |
| 9 | Alien church members from 20% to under 50% |
| 10 | Alien church members from 50% to 100% or more |

### 7. ELECTRONIC WORDS

**ra** **Christian broadcasting** (measured by total of countries transmitting by radio in this language; values 0-8).

| Code | Meaning |
|------|---------|
| 0 | None |
| 1 | Local broadcasts only or any broadcast in a same-cluster language |
| 2 | National broadcasts within this country |
| 3 | External broadcasts from this country |
| 4 | International broadcasts from one foreign country |
| 5 | Plurinational broadcasts from 2-4 countries |
| 6 | Multinational broadcasts from 5-9 countries |
| 7 | Multicontinental broadcasts from 10-19 countries |
| 8 | Global worldwide broadcasts from 20 or more countries |

**u** **Urban media** (measured by urbanites as % of country's population; values 1-4).

| Code | Meaning |
|------|---------|
| 0 | Country's urbanites under 10% |
| 1 | Country's urbanites from 10% to under 20% |
| 2 | Country's urbanites from 20% to under 30% |
| 3 | Country's urbanites from 30% to under 50% |
| 4 | Country's urbanites 50% or more |

## C. HINDRANCES

The following codes and values represent hindrances to evangelization. These values are measured and reported in every country in Part 12 "CountryTrends" and applied to peoples in the evangelization formulas on the preceding pages by subtracting the value given in the tables below.

**rl** **religious liberty** (stage of liberty experienced by the churches)

| Code | Value | Meaning |
|------|-------|---------|
| 1 | 0 | State exists solely for promotion of Christianity |
| 2 | 0 | State makes sizable to massive subsidies to promote churches |
| 3 | 0 | State aids churches with special but limited privileges |
| 4 | 0 | State makes subsidies not to churches but to church schools/services |
| 5 | 0 | State non-interference |
| 6 | 0.5 | State imposes on all churches limited or occasional restrictions |
| 7 | 1.0 | State discriminates against minority churches |
| 8 | 1.5 | State interference, obstruction against all churches |
| 9 | 2.0 | State hostility, antagonism, or harassment |
| 10 | 2.5 | State suppression or elimination |

**hd** **human development** (as measured by the United Nations Human Development Index, HDI)

| Range | Value | Meaning |
|-------|-------|---------|
| >75 | 0 | adequate level of human development |
| 75-65 | 0.5 | minimal level of human development |
| 65-55 | 1.0 | low level of human development |
| 55-45 | 1.5 | very low level of human development |
| 45-35 | 2.0 | extremely low level of human development |
| <35 | 2.5 | dangerously low level of human development |

**li** **literacy** (measured below as % of adult population able to read)

| Range | Value | Meaning |
|-------|-------|---------|
| >75 | 0 | adequate level of literacy |
| 75-65 | 0.5 | minimal level of literacy |
| 65-55 | 1.0 | low level of literacy |
| 55-45 | 1.5 | very low level of literacy |
| 45-35 | 2.0 | extremely low level of literacy |
| <35 | 2.5 | dangerously low level of literacy |

**ur** **Unevangelized remnant** (known unevangelized populations or pockets, as % country or people or city; invoked only when preceding %s, which make up V, exceed 100%, in which case the final value of E is obtained by means of the following formula):

$$E = 100 - ur.$$

Since in most cases exact values for ur are not known, the following standardized approximation is here employed throughout:

$$E = 100 - X/100, \text{ shortened to } E = 100 - 0.01X, \text{ where } X = \text{non-Christians as \% population.}$$

Since X = 100 - AC, this formula reduces to:

$$E = 99 + AC/100 = 99 + 0.01 \, AC.$$

Part 25

# MACROEVANGELISTICS

Analyzing world evangelization
as a global phenomenon and goal

*I invite the whole world to turn to me and be saved. I alone am God!*
—Isaiah 45:22, Contemporary English Version

*Paul spoke there everyday for two years, until every Jew and Gentile in Asia had heard the Lord's message.*
—Paul in Ephesus, AD 53-55 (Acts 19:9-10, CEV)

*This is one duty everywhere, to make known among the nations the greatness of God.*
—John Calvin, sermon on Isaiah 12:4-5

Macroevangelistics is the science of the study of Christian activity and outreach at the global level. Part 25 divides the globe's population into the trichotomy of Worlds A, B, and C. World A in particular—the unevangelized world—is described and quantified as the church's main area of poor, bad, or even nonexistent information visibility.

# Analyzing world evangelization as a global phenomenon and goal

This Part 25 begins with a detailed description of the least evangelized world in AD 2000. After this descriptive narrative, the emphasis switches to precise definition of terms, to measurement, and to analysis by means of 3 large statistical tables.

## DESCRIBING WORLD A

### The least evangelized world in AD 2000–2001
The twentieth century is ending with over 1.6 billion individuals completely unaware of Christ, Christianity, or the gospel.

This, despite the fact that Christians from all ecclesiastical traditions announced over 1,250 plans to evangelize the world in the 20th century. These took the form of books, articles, reports, conferences, and slogans. In the latter part of the 20th century these plans began to focus on AD 2000 as a deadline. Today, in AD 2000, over 800 plans are still active but their goals are largely unmet.

This part presents a snapshot of the status of world evangelization at the start of the 21st century. In order to accurately describe the overall situation a threefold trichotomy was developed. The three tiers are World C—the Christian world, that of church members and professing Christians; World B—the non-Christian world that has been evangelized by Christians; and World A—the non-Christian world that has not yet been evangelized by Christians. The focus of this description is World A, the least evangelized world. Note that precise definitions of the measurement of Worlds A, B, and C are found in the text above Table 25–9.

### Background facts and figures on evangelization
Table 25–1 enumerates 22 major findings on evangelization in AD 2000. One is immediately struck by the fact that the churches produce more than enough evangelism to give every person an opportunity to know Jesus Christ. In fact, given the current volume of evangelizing, 155 such opportunities could be given to every man, woman, and child on earth in AD 2000. Furthermore, the peoples most responsive to this message surprisingly are World A peoples. Nonetheless, Christians continue to expend the vast majority of evangelistic resources in the Christian world. This lack of strategic focus and fair distribution of evangelism is at the heart of the church's failure to offer the good news to all peoples.

### Daily changes in the unevangelized
To understand this problem further, Table 25–2 shows changes in the world in a 24-hour period. The over-all impact of evangelism is found at the bottom of the table where it reports that although 206,000 new people are evangelized every day, this only decreases the 1.6 billion unevangelized by 9,900. Within a couple of years, however, that trend is expected to reverse itself slightly, leading to over 1.8 billion unevangelized by AD 2025.

### Major unevangelized concentrations
Tables 25–3 to 25–8 briefly outline the major unevangelized population segments: megacountries, megapeoples, megacities, and major civil divisions (provinces). Global Map 25–1 puts these in context by roughly mapping out their geographic location. These 6 tables must be read with great care for their exact meaning as stated in their titles. Thus 4 tables list, in descending order, the *largest population* units which are World A units (25–2, 25–6, 25–7, 25–8). The other 2 list the *least-evangelized* units (measured by U, percent unevangelized, 25–4, 25–5).

This 'great unevangelized belt' was described in detail in 1911 by Samuel Zwemer (*The unoccupied mission fields of Africa and Asia*), further developed throughout the 20th century, then popularized as the 10/40 Window in the 1990s. Nonetheless, the core of the unevangelized world remains—largely as it was at the beginning of the 20th century.

### Three overviews of Worlds A, B, C
Precise enumerating of Worlds A, B, and C can be done in 3 quite different ways: by the counting of individuals, or by peoples, or by countries.

Tables 25–9 begins by depicting the total situation of Worlds A, B, and C by population segments. First it depicts individuals, then peoples, then countries. This produces a total of 27 different A/B/C contexts. It reveals the worst unevangelized situation as (under the code aAA) those unfortunate peoples in unevangelized peoples in unevangelized countries. At the other end of the spectrum as (under the code cCC) those fortunate enough to be evangelized individuals who are part of evangelized peoples in evangelized countries. Arrows on this table show how all the various totals are derived.

### A closer look at formulas
Table 25–10 now describes 2 main formulas involved in this enumeration. The main one, used throughout *WCE/WCT/WCD*, enumerates past evangelization resulting in the current status of all persons who have become evangelized, measured as E%.

The second one enumerates present, current, ongoing evangelism, measured as e, the total of current evangelizing offers per capita per year.

### The status of cities and provinces
Table 25–11 extends this typology to cover cities and provinces also.

All of these methods and their resulting statistics are listed, with many variables documenting evangelization (and the response to evangelism), in *World Christian encyclopedia*, 2001, Parts 8, 9, 10, and 11.

### Appallingly bad distribution
Table 25–12 now presents the detailed statistical evidence on the distribution of the 45 varieties of evangelistic ministry between the 3 Worlds A, B, and C. Although, obviously, these evangelism resources should as a matter of first priority be extended to World A's populations as the most needy beneficiaries, in practice they scarcely benefit at all. World A gets only 0.2% of this pie—a shocking situation.

Equally clearly, the top priority of top beneficiary should be the 238,962,000 persons classified here in Table 25–9 as code aAA—World A individuals in World A peoples in World A countries.

### Summary lists of unevangelized megapeoples.
Finally, Tables 25–13 and 25–14 list those peoples over one million in size that represent the least evangelized world. These have all appeared on lists throughout the 20th century but have yet to be taken seriously by mission agencies and evangelistic enterprises.

Evangelizing the whole world has always implied that missionaries and evangelists could not limit their efforts to already-won peoples but clearly had to continue entering unreached peoples until all peoples had a viable Christian witness. Nonetheless, a major study in 1990 showed that most agencies still had less than 3% of their missionaries among these least evangelized peoples (who represented over 30% of the world's population). Despite more plans and considerable publicity from 1990 to AD 2000, the 20th century is ending with some 4,000 unevangelized ethnolinguistic peoples (or about 10,000 unreached peoples) Today, as we look back over the entire 20th century, we see that although Christian resources were more than adequate for evangelizing the world, 9 out of every 10 new missionaries sent out went to work among already Christian peoples.

If evangelistic goals at the beginning of the 21st century are to be achieved, then agency leaders will have to understand World A and set it as a top priority. Only then will the least evangelized begin to receive their fair share of global evangelism.

For further documentation and analysis see *World Christian encyclopedia*, 2001.

---

**Table 25–1.  A selection of 22 new facts and figures about evangelism and evangelization in global Christianity today.**

1. Christians produce enough evangelism around the world for every person to hear the gospel for one hour every other day all year long.
2. Despite Christ's command to evangelize, 67% of all humans from AD 30 to the present day have never even heard of his name.
3. Since AD 33, 85% of all Christians have ignored Christ's Great Commission; only 15% have actively sought to obey it.
4. 648 million Christians today are active in Christ's world mission; 1,352 million Christians ignore it.
5. 50% of all Christians today have no contact of any kind with the world's 4 billion non-Christians.
6. The country with the fastest Christian expansion ever is China, now at 10,000 new converts every day.
7. 124 million new souls begin life on Earth each year, but Christianity's 4,000 foreign mission agencies baptize only 4 million new persons a year.
8. 91% of all Christian outreach/evangelism targets other Christians in World C countries, cities, peoples, populations, or situations.
9. 90% of all foreign mission boards target only easy Worlds B and C population targets that promise relatively quick results.
10. 818 unevangelized ethnolinguistic peoples have never been targeted by any Christian agencies ever.
11. 96% of all foreign missionaries work among existing churches; only 4% work where no church exists.
12. 40% of the church's entire foreign mission resources are being deployed to just 10 oversaturated countries already possessing strong citizen-run home ministries.
13. The 3 least cost-effective countries over 1 million in population for Christian outreach are: Japan, Switzerland, Denmark.
14. The 3 most cost-effective countries over 1 million in population for Christian outreach are: Mozambique, Ethiopia, Tanzania.
15. Per hour of ministry, the 5 megapeoples most responsive to Christianity, Christ, and the gospel are: Khandeshi, Awadhi, Magadhi, Bai, Berar Marathi.
16. Per hour of ministry, the 5 megapeoples least responsive to Christianity, Christ, and the gospel are: Swedish, Russian, Lithuanian, Polish, Georgian.
17. It costs Christians 700 times more money to baptize converts in rich World C countries (Switzerland) than in poor World A countries (Nepal).
18. 150 major ethnolinguistic peoples each have over 100,000 unevangelized ethnoreligionists.
19. Each year, 180 million Bibles and NTs are wasted—lost, destroyed, or disintegrated—due to incompetence, hostility, bad planning, or inadequate manufacture.
20. Out of 648 million Great Commission Christians, 70% have never been told about World A's 1.6 billion unevangelized individuals.
21. If current trends of failure in evangelism continue, by 2025 over 1.8 billion people in 3,000 peoples will remain unevangelized.
22. Everywhere on Earth can now easily be targeted with at least 3 of the 45 varieties of effective evangelism.

**Table 25–2.  Our globe each 24 hours: daily worldwide statistical changes.**

Over the next 24-hour period, these average increases will occur. Each item will have its own impact on macroevangelistics in the last 6 lines in this table.

| Category | Amount |
|---|---|
| **WORLD POPULATION** | |
| Births (new persons born) | 340,500 |
| Deaths (new persons dying) | 144,000 |
| Increase in population | 196,000 |
| International migrants | 275,000 |
| Households (families) | 104,100 |
| Literates | 281,000 |
| **URBANIZATION** | |
| Non-Christian urbanites | 129,000 |
| Urban dwellers (urbanites) | 190,400 |
| Urban poor | 77,000 |
| Urban slumdwellers | 38,000 |
| **WORLD RELIGIONS** | |
| New non-Christian religions | 2 |
| *Non-Christians* | *147,000* |
| Atheists | 1,200 |
| Baha'is | 400 |
| Buddhists | 10,600 |
| Chinese folk-religionists | 10,700 |
| Confucianists | 120 |
| Ethnoreligionists | 8,200 |
| Hindus | 37,000 |
| Jains | 100 |
| Jews | 350 |
| Muslims | 68,000 |
| New-Religionists | 2,800 |
| Nonreligious | 16,700 |
| Shintoists | -90 |
| Sikhs | 1,100 |
| Spiritists | 600 |
| Taoists | 70 |
| Zoroastrians | 160 |
| *Christians* | *69,000* |
| **GLOBAL CHRISTIANITY** | |
| New baptized church members | 122,000 |
| Christian deaths | 50,000 |
| Evangelicals | 11,000 |
| Urban Christians | 61,000 |
| Pentecostals/Charismatics/Neocharismatics | 30,000 |
| Great Commission Christians | 25,500 |
| Christian martyrs | 470 |
| **ECCLESIASTICAL MEMBERSHIP** | |
| Anglicans | 3,400 |
| Independents | 26,000 |
| Marginal Christians | 1,200 |
| Orthodox | 3,200 |
| Protestants | 13,300 |
| Roman Catholics | 37,000 |
| **MEMBERSHIP BY CONTINENT** | |
| Africa | 24,500 |
| Asia | 19,400 |
| Europe | 2,200 |
| Latin America | 21,000 |
| Northern America | 5,000 |
| Oceania | 800 |
| **CHRISTIAN ORGANIZATIONS** | |
| Worship centers | 500 |
| **CHRISTIAN WORKERS** | |
| Nationals (citizens) | 300 |
| Aliens (foreign missionaries) | 20 |
| Home missionaries | 30 |
| Short-term missionaries | 50 |
| **CHRISTIAN FINANCE (in US$)** | |
| Personal income of church members | $1.5 billion |
| Giving to Christian causes | $66 million |
| Churches' income | $22 million |
| Parachurch and institutional income | $44 million |
| Ecclesiastical crime (sums embezzled) | $5.5 million |
| Income of global foreign missions | $5 million |
| **NEW TECHNOLOGY** | |
| New Christian computer users | 100,000 |
| Christians joining the Internet | 68,500 |
| **CHRISTIAN LITERATURE** | |
| New books/articles on evangelization | 7 |
| **SCRIPTURE DISTRIBUTION (all sources)** | |
| Bibles | 165,000 |
| New Testaments | 334,000 |
| Gospels | 1,000,000 |
| Selections | 11,200,000 |
| **CHRISTIAN BROADCASTING** | |
| New regular listeners/viewers | 210,000 |
| **CHRISTIAN EVANGELISM** | |
| Evangelism-hours | 500 million |
| Offers | 2.6 billion |
| **WORLD EVANGELIZATION** | |
| Unevangelized persons | -9,900 |
| Evangelized persons | 206,000 |

### UNDERLYING CLARIFICATIONS

The rest of the present survey proceeds to a detailed study of the global trichotomy of evangelization that is here described in the 3 terms World A, World B, and World C.

The subject is a further extension of the little-used but extremely valuable English term 'evangelistics'. This is defined in Webster's *Third new international dictionary* as 'the science of the propagation of Chris-

tianity'. The key words 'evangelize', 'evangelism', and 'evangelization' have already been analyzed in detail here in Parts 22 and 23. Part 24 has taken the subject further into "Microevangelistics", defined as the detailed quantification and measurement of evangelization at the smallest levels of the individual and the ethnic, linguistic, political and other entities that he or she belongs to. Now with the present Part 25 "Macroevangelistics" the focus shifts to the same analysis at the global or world or macro level—the extent to which the entire world of 6 billion persons has been or become evangelized. It leads to the basic trichotomy, to be investigated in more detail below, of Worlds A, B, and C.

This investigation can be begun by examining the question of who Christians are, in relation to evangelization. There is a need to answer a set of basic questions, as follows:

- Are Christians evangelized?
- Are all Christians evangelized?
- If only some varieties are, which ones? or,
- Should the term 'evangelized' be restricted to only certain kinds of Christians? If so, which kinds?
- Can Christians correctly be called evangelizing, evangelized, or evangelizers?

### ARE CHRISTIANS EVANGELIZED?

#### Which are evangelized, which are evangelizing?
The science of microevangelistics requires us to study, define, and delineate the evangelized individual, the unevangelized individual, and the process by which the latter becomes the former. The science of macroevangelistics is simply microevangelistics extended to peoples, cities, countries, and other large populations up to the global level itself. It is now necessary therefore for us to do some clear thinking about the correct, logical relationship of the category 'Christians' to our exactly-defined terms 'evangelized' and 'evangelizing'. We can pose the problem in a more technical question, as follows:

Can we relate 'evangelized' and 'evangelizing' to any of the standard statistical categories employed by the churches across the world in their present or current enumerations of their own Christians?

#### Are all Christians evangelized?
This is the basic question, and it is a most important one. One can safely say that nowhere else is there so much terminological confusion or illogical thought within the churches and their agencies for world mission. The question can further be put in the following extended form: Can, or should, all Christians of all kinds and sorts and categories without exception (professing, nominal, unaffiliated, affiliated, baptized, communicant, practicing, attending, active, inactive, et alii) be correctly said to be, or to have been, or to have become evangelized, i.e. adequately aware of Christianity, Christ, and the gospel?

This question can be answered in terms of the global terminology of Christian enumeration evolved in the 1982 first edition of the *World Christian encyclopedia,* and extended, finalized and summarized here in in Global Diagram 30. There, all Christians (known for shorthand purposes as 'World C') are divided into 3 statistical categories: (a) Great Commission Christians, (b) non-practicing church members, and (c) unaffiliated or nominal Christians. Here, then, are 6 answers.

#### 1. All Great Commission Christians have become evangelized
Great Commission Christians are defined as all those Christians who not only follow Christ but are serious about obeying his Great Commission 'Go into all the world and make disciples of all nations.' They are defined as all Christians who are active in mission. Obviously, they must all be aware of Christianity, Christ, and his gospel—which is our definition of being evangelized. So then, if there are 648 million Great Commission Christians in the world today, there must be at least 648 million evangelized persons in the world.

#### 2. Committed Christians have already become evangelized
Secondly, it is obvious that there need be no argument over a number of other similar varieties of Christians. There are many worldwide varieties of Christians

who are specifically committed to total obedience to Christ and his mission. Although all these persons are virtually the same in definition as 'Great Commission Christians', in many quarters this neologism is not yet in use and other terms and categories are employed. These include (a) mission enthusiasts—the whole world of 420,000 foreign missionaries and the vast network of 4,000 agencies and several hundred million supporters in every country who maintain them, encourage them, pray for them, and pay for them; (b) Pentecostals/Charismatics/Neocharismatics—the whole world of 524 million Pentecostals, Neopentecostals, Charismatics, Catholic Charismatics, Anglican Charismatics, Independent Charismatics, Third-Wavers, and all other varieties of Charismatic Christians; and (c) Evangelicals—the whole world of Protestant and Anglican Evangelicalism, defined as persons strongly committed to the Bible and biblical emphases centering on evangelism. All such specifically-committed Christians are active, practicing, and earnest Christians and are obviously themselves long past the stage of first becoming evangelized.

#### 3. Practicing church members have already become evangelized
Thirdly, it should be equally clear that all practicing church members of all traditions have themselves already become evangelized. They are obviously aware of Christianity, they worship Christ regularly, they read the gospel in the Scriptures, they hear the gospel expounded from the pulpit each week in church. They are correctly termed evangelized because they themselves form the whole of that organized, active, practicing Christianity which features in our definition of demographic evangelization.

#### 4. What about non-practicing church members?
So much for committed and practicing Christians. However, it is on the subject of inactive Christians, nominal Christians, and non-practicing Christians that some clear thinking on our part is required. Since we have given all the terms involved exact operational definitions, this should not be difficult although the results may be surprising to all who have not already faced up to the logic the situation requires.

What then can be said about the status of non-practicing church members? This term is defined here as those who are affiliated church members but who for one reason or another are non-practicing, non-attending, inactive, or dormant. In spite of the fact that they are not fulfilling their membership obligations, such persons are still affiliated to organized Christianity. To that extent they have in the past come and in the present still come into contact with it from time to time, as well as into frequent contact with individual active Christians, with the gospel, and with many varieties of evangelism. Since they are thus, inadvertently or otherwise, in contact with and aware of organized Christianity, Christ, and the gospel, they cannot correctly be termed unevangelized. Instead, they are evangelized persons who are members of the empirical church but who have not, or not yet, accepted Christ's call to active discipleship.

#### 5. What about unaffiliated or nominal Christians?
Nominal or unaffiliated Christians are defined here as those who profess publicly to be Christians (e.g. in censuses or polls), even to be adherents of particular traditions (Catholic, Protestant, Baptist, etc.), but who are not affiliated to any church or denomination, i.e. are not written down on the rolls as church members. They are Christians in name, and often only in name. In Europe and North America, many public-opinion polls have been taken in which such persons state or profess publicly 'I am a Christian,' 'I am a Protestant,' 'I am a Catholic,' 'I am a believer in Christ,' 'I am a follower of Jesus,' et alia. Since they thus publicly profess knowledge of Christianity and Christ, they cannot correctly be termed unevangelized. Instead, they are evangelized persons who profess to have responded to Christ but who have not in fact accepted Christ's call to membership in his church.

#### 6. What about the dechristianized?
Europe and America are well-known for their large dechristianized masses particularly in urban industrial society. How does one define the 'dechristianized'?

It is common to regard the large, secularized, materialist, post-Christian or nominally Christian masses

## Table 25–3. The 10 largest World A countries.
*AC = percent church members    U = percent unevangelized*

| Rank | Country | Population | AC | U | Unevangelized |
|---|---|---|---|---|---|
| 1. | Pakistan | 156,483,000 | 2.4 | 53.2 | 83,312,000 |
| 2. | Iran | 67,702,000 | 0.5 | 62.8 | 42,510,000 |
| 3. | Turkey | 66,591,000 | 0.6 | 51.4 | 34,241,000 |
| 4. | Algeria | 31,471,000 | 0.3 | 50.5 | 15,877,000 |
| 5. | Morocco | 28,221,000 | 0.6 | 57.8 | 16,314,000 |
| 6. | Uzbekistan | 24,318,000 | 1.6 | 51.6 | 12,558,000 |
| 7. | North Korea | 24,039,000 | 2.1 | 50.0 | 12,027,000 |
| 8. | Nepal | 23,930,000 | 2.4 | 53.8 | 12,867,000 |
| 9. | Iraq | 23,115,000 | 3.1 | 51.6 | 11,918,000 |
| 10. | Afghanistan | 22,720,000 | 0.0 | 70.4 | 16,000,000 |

## Table 25–4. The 10 least evangelized megacountries.
*AC = percent church members    U = percent unevangelized*

| Rank | Country | Population | AC | U | Unevangelized |
|---|---|---|---|---|---|
| 1. | Bhutan | 2,124,000 | 0.5 | 79.2 | 1,683,000 |
| 2. | Afghanistan | 22,720,000 | 0.0 | 70.4 | 16,000,000 |
| 3. | Mauritania | 2,670,000 | 0.2 | 68.1 | 1,818,000 |
| 4. | Turkmenistan | 4,459,000 | 2.2 | 65.5 | 2,919,000 |
| 5. | Azerbaijan | 7,734,000 | 4.6 | 63.0 | 4,873,000 |
| 6. | Iran | 67,702,000 | 0.5 | 62.8 | 42,510,000 |
| 7. | Guinea | 7,430,000 | 3.1 | 58.4 | 4,337,000 |
| 8. | Niger | 10,730,000 | 0.5 | 57.9 | 6,208,000 |
| 9. | Morocco | 28,221,000 | 0.6 | 57.8 | 16,314,000 |
| 10. | Mongolia | 2,662,000 | 1.3 | 57.2 | 1,522,000 |

## Table 25–5. The 10 largest World A megapeoples.
*AC = percent church members    U = percent unevangelized*

| Rank | Country | People | Population | AC | U | Unevangelized |
|---|---|---|---|---|---|---|
| 1. | Pakistan | Western Punjabi (Lahnda) | 66,810,000 | 4.4 | 51.6 | 34,474,000 |
| 2. | China | Han Chinese (Jinyu) | 47,351,000 | 7.0 | 53.0 | 25,096,000 |
| 3. | China | Han Chinese (Hunanese) | 44,226,000 | 2.0 | 59.0 | 26,093,000 |
| 4. | India | Awadhi (Baiswari, Bagheli) | 37,352,000 | 2.5 | 66.5 | 24,839,000 |
| 5. | India | Bhojpuri Bihari (Deswali) | 36,071,000 | 1.0 | 60.0 | 21,635,000 |
| 6. | India | Maitili (Maithili, Tharu) | 31,636,000 | 1.0 | 63.0 | 19,924,000 |
| 7. | China | Han Chinese (Kan) | 25,272,000 | 6.0 | 54.0 | 13,647,000 |
| 8. | Uzbekistan | Northern Uzbek | 19,024,000 | 0.1 | 50.9 | 9,683,000 |
| 9. | Pakistan | Sindhi | 18,259,000 | 0.0 | 51.0 | 9,310,000 |
| 10. | India | Braj Bhakha (Antarbedi) | 17,990,000 | 2.5 | 56.5 | 10,165,000 |

## Table 25–6. The 10 least evangelized megapeoples.
*AC = percent church members    U = percent unevangelized*

| Rank | Country | People | Population | AC | U | Unevangelized |
|---|---|---|---|---|---|---|
| 1. | Iran | Bakhtiari | 1,137,000 | 0.0 | 90.0 | 1,023,000 |
| 2. | Turkey | Dimili Kurd (Southern Zaza) | 1,145,000 | 0.0 | 88.0 | 1,008,000 |
| 3. | Indonesia | Banjarese (Banjar Malay) | 2,085,000 | 0.0 | 87.0 | 1,814,000 |
| 4. | Iran | Luri (Lori, Feyli) | 4,870,000 | 0.0 | 84.0 | 4,091,000 |
| 5. | Indonesia | Lampungese (Lamponger) | 2,065,000 | 0.0 | 84.0 | 1,735,000 |
| 6. | Egypt | Bedouin | 1,369,000 | 0.0 | 84.0 | 1,150,000 |
| 7. | India | Khandeshi | 1,660,000 | 0.2 | 82.8 | 1,374,000 |
| 8. | Pakistan | Western Baluch | 1,083,000 | 0.0 | 82.0 | 888,000 |
| 9. | China | Khamba (Khams Bhotia) | 1,707,000 | 0.1 | 81.0 | 1,382,000 |
| 10. | Algeria | Tajakant Bedouin | 1,290,000 | 0.0 | 80.0 | 1,032,000 |

## Table 25–7. The 10 largest World A megacities.
*AC = percent church members    U = percent unevangelized*

| Rank | Country | City | Population | AC | U | Unevangelized |
|---|---|---|---|---|---|---|
| 1. | Iran | TEHRAN (Teheran) | 7,380,000 | 0.9 | 51.4 | 3,790,000 |
| 2. | India | Ahmadabad (Ahmedabad) | 4,154,000 | 1.6 | 55.2 | 2,293,000 |
| 3. | Morocco | Casablanca (Dar el Beida) | 3,535,000 | 0.9 | 52.5 | 1,857,000 |
| 4. | Turkey | ANKARA (Ancyra, Angora) | 3,190,000 | 0.2 | 51.8 | 1,652,000 |
| 5. | Afghanistan | KABOL (Kabul) | 2,716,000 | 0.2 | 63.5 | 1,724,000 |
| 6. | India | Lucknow | 2,565,000 | 0.8 | 61.0 | 1,566,000 |
| 7. | India | Kanpur (Cawnpore) | 2,447,000 | 0.8 | 51.0 | 1,249,000 |
| 8. | Iran | Mashhad (Meshed) | 2,378,000 | 0.2 | 58.1 | 1,381,000 |
| 9. | India | Surat | 2,341,000 | 0.3 | 56.5 | 1,322,000 |
| 10. | India | Jaipur (Jeypore) | 2,143,000 | 0.4 | 61.4 | 1,316,000 |

## Table 25–8. The 10 largest World A major civil divisions, AD 2000.
*AC = percent church members    U = percent unevangelized*

| Rank | Country | Civil division | Population | AC | U | Unevangelized |
|---|---|---|---|---|---|---|
| 1. | Pakistan | Sindh | 35,423,000 | 1.8 | 53.4 | 18,909,000 |
| 2. | Pakistan | North-West Frontier | 20,331,000 | 0.3 | 70.4 | 14,319,000 |
| 3. | India | Haryana | 19,590,000 | 1.1 | 50.7 | 9,932,000 |
| 4. | China | Sinkiang Uighur | 17,314,000 | 0.3 | 61.9 | 10,723,000 |
| 5. | Turkey | ic Anadolu (Central Anatolia) | 15,443,000 | 0.1 | 53.9 | 8,319,000 |
| 6. | Iran | Tehran | 11,172,000 | 1.0 | 52.1 | 5,817,000 |
| 7. | India | Jammu and Kashmir | 9,267,000 | 1.3 | 50.5 | 4,680,000 |
| 8. | Turkey | Dogu Anadolu (East Anatolia) | 8,098,000 | 0.1 | 55.9 | 4,527,000 |
| 9. | Turkey | Karadeniz kiyisi (Black Sea Coast) | 8,051,000 | 0.1 | 53.9 | 4,338,000 |
| 10. | Pakistan | Balochistan | 8,041,000 | 0.5 | 65.2 | 5,241,000 |

## Global Map 25–1. The great unevangelized belt: World A defined in terms of countries and peoples, AD 2000.

This map depicts with a single black boundary the geographical domain of World A, the unevangelized world, defined in terms of ethnolinguistic peoples. Its exact definition is as follows.

*Black line boundary.* Inside this line live virtually every one of the globe's 168 least evangelized megapeoples (each over 1 million in population and less than 50% evangelized, see Table 25–13 for complete listing). It is also the case that inside this line live all 50 of the globe's megapeoples between 50% and 70% evangelized, and numerous smaller peoples. Altogether all these encompass 85% of all the 1.6 billion unevangelized individuals on Earth. Also, the vast majority of the world's 10,000 unreached minipeoples reside within this boundary, making it a prime strategic target for frontier missions.

*Describing World A by segments.* Of the 38 countries defined as in World A, 31 are megacountries (each with population over 1 million) found wholly within the black line boundary depicting World A. The largest are listed in Table 25–3. World A megapeoples are listed in Tables 25–5 and 25–6. World A megacities are listed in Table 25–7 and World A provinces in Table 25–8.

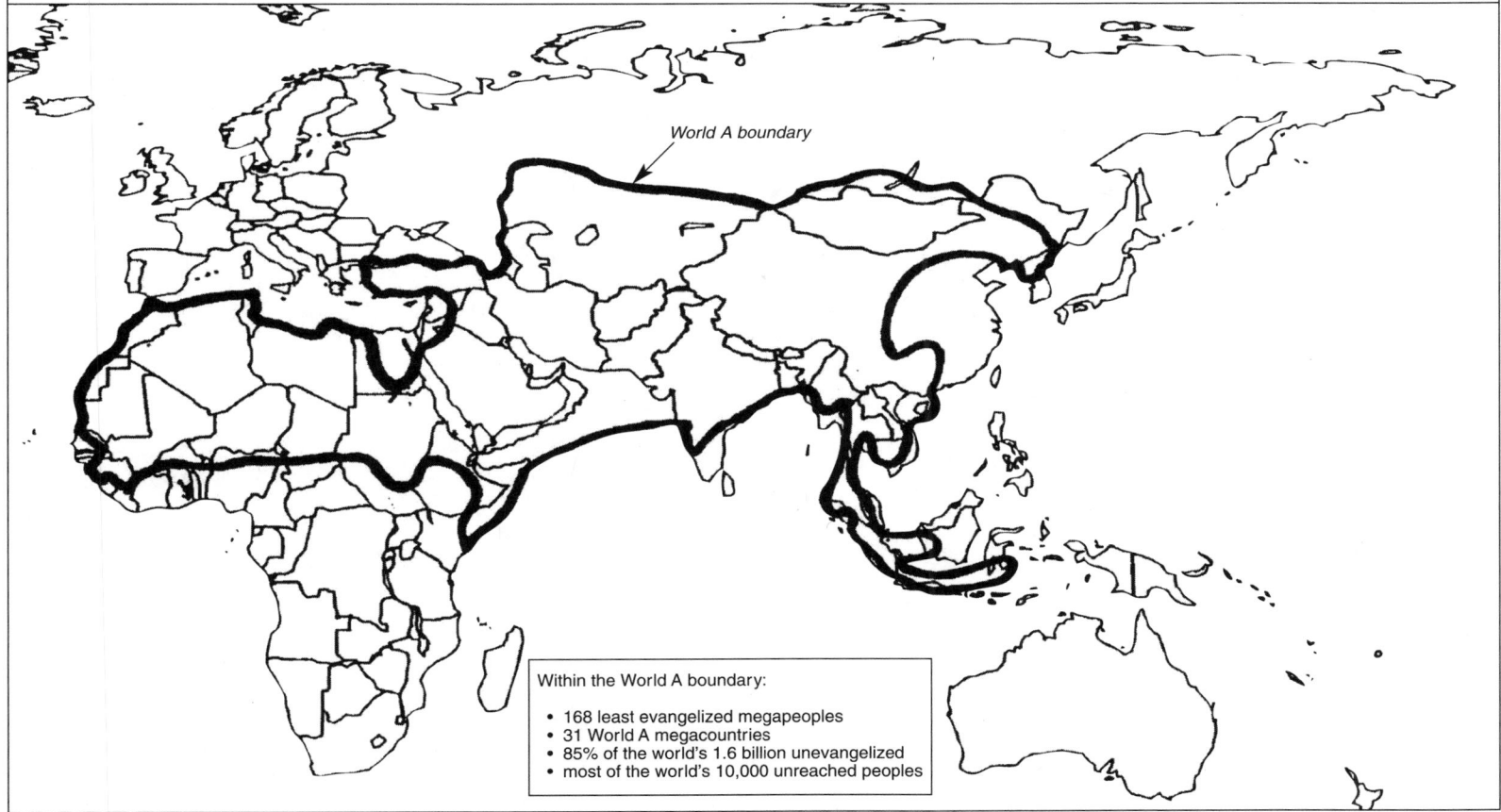

World A boundary

Within the World A boundary:

- 168 least evangelized megapeoples
- 31 World A megacountries
- 85% of the world's 1.6 billion unevangelized
- most of the world's 10,000 unreached peoples

of industrialized Europe and North and Latin America as unevangelized persons whom the churches must re-evangelize all over again. Is this a correct use of terms? Secularized or dechristianized peoples and individuals usually make no Christian profession, or profess to be atheists or agnostics, and regard themselves as non-Christians. However, a vast number of them were baptized into the churches as children or infants, underwent Christian instruction of some kind (Sunday school, baptism or confirmation classes), and are still on those churches' membership rolls. Only recently have they abandoned religion and become dechristianized. Nevertheless, they cannot correctly be termed unevangelized, a term which implies no contact at all with organized Christianity and no knowledge at all of Christianity, Christ, or the gospel. In fact, the vast majority were already evangelized in their earlier days as Christians; and, as we have seen with education, for individuals once evangelized means remaining evangelized for life. Dechristianized persons thus remain evangelized throughout their lifetime.

### Conclusion: all Christians are evangelized

A Christian is defined as a person who is an adherent of Christianity, a follower of Christ, and a person who has to some extent heard and responded to the gospel, either positively or negatively. We therefore conclude that all persons who can correctly be called Christians, of whatever type or tradition or category, can also correctly be termed evangelized. This is the norm. The normal meaning of things is that all Christians have already been or become evangelized and remain evangelized today.

If the norm is that all Christians are evangelized persons, then to call any specific Christians 'unevangelized' is a contradiction in terms. This must be resolved by bringing into line one's usage of terms in a fashion similar to what is being set out here.

Of course, there will always here and there be numbers of individual exceptions to this rule — individuals in heavily-evangelized societies who have managed to remain completely or totally ignorant of Christianity. In such cases, they should not be called 'Christians' either. In any case, they are only a tiny fraction. Where peoples as a whole are concerned, our conclusion is valid.

Despite this caveat, we have arrived at a major conclusion in respect to the quantification of evangelization. If there are 2.0 billion Christians in the world, then there are, at least, 2.0 billion evangelized people in the world.

## MEASURING GLOBAL EVANGELIZATION

Churches and missionaries across the world produce each year voluminous hard data describing the whole range of varieties of evangelistic operations and their effect on the globe's entire population. For any specific people, population, or especially megapopulation, volumes of fresh data are generated year by year but only rarely get tabulated, printed, or published, and regrettably only very rarely get analyzed. The present analysis concentrates its attention on 6 variables at the global level (and then at the level of any of its component populations). These 6 variables ready for measurement are as follows:

a. The 45 different varieties of evangelistic activities, which are enumerated in Table 25–12;

b. The total volume of evangelism, using the symbol V as percentage of the population;

c. The resulting state of evangelization, E, being the percentage of the population which has become evangelized;

d. The current or ongoing amount of evangelism, e, being the number of offers or disciple-opportunities being received per capita and per year;

e. The resulting christianization, using the symbols AC, ZAC, GCC, inter alia, and their rates of increase;

f. The resulting tripartite categorization or trichotomy of Worlds A, B, and C.

## EVOLVING THE WORLDS A/B/C TRICHOTOMY

To recapitulate, the present analysis begins with the merging of 2 straightforward dichotomies: (1) knowledge of, or ignorance of, the evangel (the good news of Christianity, Christ, and the gospel), and (2) acceptance of this evangel, or rejection of it. Merging these 2 produces the 3-part trichotomy of relation to the evangel, applicable to any individual, or any ethnolinguistic people, or any country.

### Three different populations

The 3 parts of this trichotomy divide human populations into 3 kinds of people, as follows:

1. Those persons who know nothing about the evangel, have never heard of Jesus, and are completely unaware of Christianity, Christ, and the gospel. Persons in this huge bloc of humanity are here termed the *unevangelized*, and are given the title World A.

2. Those who are adequately aware of Christianity, Christ, and the gospel but have not, or not yet, accepted Christ as Lord and so remain as non-Christians. Numbering 40% of the globe's population, persons in this vast bloc are here termed *evangelized non-Christians*, and are given the title World B.

3. Those who are aware of the evangel and have responded by becoming followers of Christ, are here termed *Christians*, and are given the title World C.

### 27 different World A/B/C situations

The 3 basic population blocs just defined live in very diverse contexts directly relevant to their situations. An individual is conditioned firstly by the ethnolinguistic people he or she belongs to, and secondly by the country he or she resides in. People live in a whole range of different evangelistic contexts, from extreme World A situations (a World A individual in a World A people in a World A country) to saturated World C situations (a World C individual in a World C people in a World C country). This produces the 27-part typology shown in Table 25–9.

### Two different definitions and formulas

All these situations and magnitudes can now be measured. Two different but related methodologies have been employed and produce 2 different but related formulas, both valid and valuable. These measure (1)

---

**Table 25–9.** **27 varieties of Worlds A, B, and C individuals located in A/B/C contexts (peoples), and thus in A/B/C countries.**

The table is divided horizontally into 3 layers, termed 'World A' (unevangelized), 'World B' (evangelized non-Christians), and 'World C' (Christians). All numbers in this table are totals of *individuals*, except columns 11 and 14 (totals of *peoples*) and 17 (totals of countries) and the grey arrows show how totals are arrived at. Of the 27 × 27 = 729 possible lines, only 12 are shown here.
*Columns*
1. 3-letter code: definitions
Example: aAA = World A individuals in World A peoples in World A countries.
1st letter:

- a = World A individual = an unevangelized person
- b = World B individual = an evangelized non-Christian
- c = World C individual = a Christian

2nd letter:
- A = World A people = one with evangelized persons <50%
- B = World B people = one with E≥50%, AC<60%
- C = World C people = one with AC≥60%

3rd letter:
- A = World A country = one with evangelized persons <50%
- B = World B country = one with E≥50%, AC<60%
- C = World C country = one with AC≥60%

2. Population of each of the 27 varieties of individuals

4. Subtotal of prior lines above in column 2
8. Totals of individuals coded a, b, c
10. Population of each of the 9 peoples. The bold type plus grey arrows leads from bold type in column 2 to illustrate how totals are formed up to column 16
11. Number of peoples involved
13. Subtotal populations of A, B, C peoples above
14. Number of peoples in Worlds A, B, C
16. Population of A, B, C countries. The italic type plus 3 grey arrows leading to 3 italic type in column 8 illustrate how totals are formed
17. Number of countries in Worlds A, B, C

| INDIVIDUALS | | | | | | | | PEOPLES | | | | | | | COUNTRIES | | |
|---|---|---|---|---|---|---|---|---|---|---|---|---|---|---|---|---|---|
| Code 1 | individuals 2 | code 3 | sub-total 4 | Code 5 | sub-total 6 | Code 7 | total 8 | Code 9 | Population 10 | Pple 11 | Code 12 | Population 13 | Pple 14 | Code 15 | Population 16 | Ctrys 17 |
| **World A Individuals** | | | by people | | by country | | | **World A Peoples** | | | | | | **World A Countries** | | |
| aAA | **238,962,484** | | | | | | | AA | **386,073,487** | 1,044 | | | | A | 605,303,985 | 38 |
| aAB | 438,492,144 | | | | | | | AB | 705,422,675 | 2,260 | | | | | | |
| aAC | 9,194,676 | aA- | 686,649,304 | a-A | 334,258,565 | | | AC | 15,269,897 | 529 | A | 1,106,766,059 | 3,833 | | | |
| aBA | 95,288,938 | | | | | | | | | | | | | | | |
| aBB | 829,962,463 | | | | | | | | | | | | | | | |
| aBC | 14,040,679 | aB- | 939,292,080 | a-B | 1,269,343,422 | | | | | | | | | | | |
| aCA | 7,144 | | | | | | | | | | | | | | | |
| aCB | 888,815 | | | | | | | | | | | | | | | |
| aCC | 2,536,162 | aC- | 3,432,120 | a-C | 25,771,517 | a | 1,629,373,504 | | | | | | | | | |
| **World B Individuals** | | | | | | | | | | | | | | | | |
| bAA | **143,412,835** | | | | | | | | | | | | | | | |
| bAB | 253,044,277 | | | | | | | | | | | | | | | |
| bAC | 5,786,219 | bA- | 402,243,331 | b-A | 260,718,570 | | | **World B Peoples** | | | | | | | | |
| bBA | 116,701,898 | | | | | | | BA | 216,126,906 | 206 | | | | | | |
| bBB | 1,654,388,911 | | | | | | | BB | 2,770,158,337 | 1,551 | | | | **World B Countries** | | |
| bBC | 32,394,693 | bB- | 1,803,485,502 | b-B | 1,972,624,235 | | | BC | 62,397,118 | 1,057 | B | 3,048,682,361 | 2,814 | B | 3,755,011,923 | 59 |
| bCA | 603,837 | | | | | | | | | | | | | | | |
| bCB | 65,191,046 | | | | | | | | | | | | | | | |
| bCC | 154,601,187 | bC- | 220,396,070 | b-C | 192,782,099 | b | 2,426,124,903 | | | | | | | | | |
| **World C Individuals** | | | | | | | | | | | | | | | | |
| cAA | **3,698,169** | | | | | | | | | | | | | | | |
| cAB | 13,886,254 | | | | | | | | | | | | | | | |
| cAC | 289,002 | cA- | 17,873,425 | c-A | 10,326,850 | | | | | | | | | | | |
| cBA | 4,136,069 | | | | | | | | | | | | | | | |
| cBB | 285,806,963 | | | | | | | | | | | | | | | |
| cBC | 15,961,747 | cB- | 305,904,779 | c-B | 513,044,266 | | | **World C Peoples** | | | | | | | | |
| cCA | 2,492,612 | | | | | | | CA | 3,103,592 | 198 | | | | | | |
| cCB | 213,351,050 | | | | | | | CB | 279,430,911 | 1,381 | | | | **World C Countries** | | |
| cCC | 1,459,928,861 | cC- | 1,675,772,522 | c-C | 1,476,179,609 | c | 1,999,550,725 | CC | 1,617,066,210 | 4,357 | C | 1,899,600,713 | 5,936 | C | 1,694,733,225 | 141 |
| **Total** | **6,055,049,133** | | 6,055,049,133 | | 6,055,049,133 | | 6,055,049,133 | | 6,055,049,133 | 12,583 | | 6,055,049,133 | 12,583 | | 6,055,049,133 | 238 |

## Table 25–10.  Two different formulas for constructing the World's A/B/C trichotomy.

1. The first of the two is based on E, the percentage of the population who have become evangelized as a result *of past evangelism*.
2. The second of the two is based on e, the number of evangelistic offers being heard or received, per capita per annum, in other words evangelized as a result of *present evangelism*.
   In practice the 2 methods result in a very similar trichotomy,

with the 3 numbers of countries and peoples in the same general order of magnitude. Numbers of population involved can be seen, however, to differ markedly.
   In practice, the present survey utilized the E method throughout; the e method is used primarily for the targeting scale in Part 28.

| Method | World | Definition | Countries number | Population | Peoples number | Population |
|---|---|---|---|---|---|---|
| 1 | 2 | 3 | 4 | 5 | 6 | 7 |
| E-formula | A | E<50% | 38 | 605,304,000 | 3,833 | 1,106,766,000 |
| | B | E≥50%, AC<60% | 59 | 3,755,012,000 | 2,814 | 3,048,682,000 |
| | C | AC≥60% | 141 | 1,694,733,000 | 5,936 | 1,899,601,000 |
| e-formula | A | e<10 | 30 | 865,912,000 | 3,638 | 2,214,813,000 |
| | B | 200>e≥10 | 54 | 3,078,128,000 | 2,949 | 1,897,668,000 |
| | C | e≥200 | 154 | 2,111,009,000 | 5,996 | 1,942,568,000 |

the evangelized status of an individual, people, or country as *a result of all prior evangelistic activity*, and measured for people or country by the symbol E (status of evangelization, per cent of population). E is measured by means of the 23-variable formula derived at the end of Part 24 "Microevangelistics". Based on this, the trichotomy consists of: World A defined by E<50%; World B by E>50% but AC <60%; and World C by AC>60%.

Secondly, there is (2) *the current level of evangelistic activity*, measured by the symbol e (offers per capita per year). e is related to E by the formula e=0.0365(AC)E if 100>E. Based on this, the trichotomy is defined thus: World A is defined by e<10, World B by 200>e>10, and World C by e>200. The results of these 2 methods are shown in Table 25–10 above.

In the present survey, the E formula is used throughout *WCE/WCT/WCD*. The e-formula is used in analysis only in Part 28 "Geotargeting".

### VISUALIZING THE STATE OF THE GLOBE

At this stage a brief summary global table is useful to clarify all the numbers and categories involved. This is done in Table 25–11, repeating the various totals in a slightly different context.

#### Assessing the global situation

The fastest way of assessing the situation is by means of a map, and this is done here in Global Map 25-1, which is itself part of Global Diagram 35 (see Part 1 "GeoStatus"). World A is described there as the central part of the Eurasian-African continent, centered, surprising enough at the very spot where Jesus gave his Great Commission 20 centuries ago. It is ironic that this huge swath of population running from Morocco on the Atlantic Ocean through to China adjacent to the Pacific Ocean should still to this day be the main locus of the unevangelized, with a massive population of 1.6 billion persons who have never heard of Christianity, Christ, or the gospel. These tables and maps present the basic data in compact and summary form.

### WORLDS A, B, C FROM AD 30–AD 2000

It is instructive at this point to examine the fluctuation of population down the centuries in response to the Great Commission and Christians' obedience to it. Global Diagram 8 gives 16 representations of the globe divided into World A, B, and C populations. It can be seen that the size of World A has varied very considerably over the centuries. At the millennial year AD 2000 itself, World A appears to be once again increasing in total numbers of persons although decreasing steadily in proportion to the whole globe.

### DISTRIBUTING EVANGELISM

The first of 2 closely-related diagrams (Global Diagram 32, analyzed in Part 22) has developed the quantification of evangelization, defining the term as consisting of *presence, witness, and evangelism*. Now in a second diagram (Global Diagram 40) it is necessary to zero in for a closer look at the third component, evangelism. By expanding the last column in Global Diagram 32 it becomes possible to produce the detailed analysis by Worlds A, B, and C that is presented here in Global Diagram 40.

With this second diagram, our series of 74 global diagrams shown in Part 1 "GeoStatus" arrives at the heart of the problem confronting world evangelization today—unequal distribution. In a nutshell, this problem has two aspects, the first satisfactory, the second unsatisfactory. These are: (1) The church worldwide is evangelizing—spreading the Good News of Jesus Christ—far and wide, creating every day the startlingly high total of over 2 billion offers or opportunities for others to become Christ's disciples. But, (2) 99.8% of all of this evangelistic effort is directed only at people who have already been evangelized earlier, including 82.9% at people who are Christians and so already are disciples.

This second diagram shows the distribution of all this effort among the 3 worlds of the mission trichotomy, Worlds A, B, and C. Table 25–12 shows the relevant figures, most given per day (per diem, p.d.).

Some figures are surprisingly high. Audiovisuals, especially the 'Jesus' Film, play a dominant role in evangelism in the 21st century. This analysis into 3 worlds (columns 6-14) reveals the following trends.

### WORLD A: LOCAL EVANGELISTS PREDOMINATE

One of the largest one-item percentages of daily offers in the unevangelized world is contributed by local evangelists (such as Palestinian free-lance evangelists across the Arabian peninsula). Such evangelists are responsible for some 9% of all 4.1 million disciple-opportunities each day in World A (see columns 6 and 7). Another leading contribution in size is circulation of complete Bibles and near-Bibles. These give World A dwellers opportunities at the rate of 389,000 a day (column 6). This is much more effective than circulation of scripture selections, portions, or even of New Testaments; it is also far more effective than any other forms of literature.

### WORLD B: PERSONAL EVANGELISM WORKS BEST

Column 9 shows that personal evangelism by Great Commission Christians is the largest single evangelistic mode in World B peoples (24%), who are non-Christian but have already become evangelized even if only at some primary level. Local evangelists are still very important but have fallen to under 2%.

### WORLD C: ELCETRONIC WORDS TOPS THE LIST

Column 12 shows that in the Christian world one of the largest generators of offers comes through electronic words such as radio, TV, and even the Internet. Technology is increasingly important to Christian witness (20%). By contrast, professional circulation of complete Bibles has dropped in effectiveness to less than 10%.

How should one assess these findings? Let's return to our earlier illustration. There is a close parallel with the problem of world hunger today. Enough food is produced every day to feed the whole world. Yet 2 billion persons across the globe are undernourished, 1.2 billion go hungry every night, and 500 million live on the verge of starvation. Agencies distributing food cannot supply every need but must reach a balance involving need, priorities, adequate supply, equal opportunity, fair shares. And the already well-fed should not be allowed to divert such supplies to their own use.

Likewise, Table 25–12 shows that the average Christian in World C receives every day 530 times more invitations than an unevangelized non-Christian in World A. This is clearly an unbalanced situation. Proper balance must mean that at least as much attention is given to the individual in World A as in Worlds B or C.

## Table 25–11.  Worlds A, B, and C by individuals, countries, peoples, cities, and provinces, AD 2000.

The status of world evangelization is outlined in concise form below. The world's population is divided in 5 different segments horizontally, (1) 6 billion individuals, (2) 238 countries, (3) 12,600 peoples, (4) 5,200 cities, and (5) 3,000 provinces. Vertically these segments are divided into three categories related to how evangelized they are, World A, B, and C, and their total.
   Defintions for these are as follows:
   *Individuals*. World A is the unevangelized world—those non-Christians who have never heard the good news of Jesus Christ.
   World B is the evangelized world—those non-Christians who have heard the good news.
   World C is the Christian world—those who have heard the good news and responded by becoming Christians.
   With the remaining four segments (*countries, peoples,*

*cities, provinces*) the trichotomy is measured as follows:
   World A—segments where less than 50% of the population have been evangelized.
   World B—segments where 50% or more of the population have been evangelized but less than 60% are church members.
   World C—segments where 60% or more of the population are church members.

*Analyzing World A by segments.*
   *Countries*. World A countries stretch from Morocco to Indonesia containing the heart of the Muslim, Hindu, and Buddhists worlds. Although some have substantial Christian minorities, they remain largely unevangelized.
   *Peoples*. World A peoples speak thousands of languages and live primarily in World A and B countries. Although scrip-

tures have been translated into many of these languages, they receive the least attention of Bible translators and distribution societies.
   *Cities*. Most urban mission specialists do not even recognize the names of World A megacities. Yet these represent the real challenge in urban missions in the future.
   *Provinces*. Some of the larger World C provinces are more populous than most smaller Christian countries. The scarcity of Christian resources remains an almost intractable problem.
   One can see that although World C is a substantial portion of the world's population, an equally large portion, namely World A, has been overlooked by Christian missionaries and evangelists. If evangelistic goals are to be met in the near future, each of these World A segments will have to be entered soon by the global force of evangelists and missionaries.

| World | Individuals Population | Countries Number | Population | Peoples Number | Population | Cities Number | Population | Provinces Number | Population |
|---|---|---|---|---|---|---|---|---|---|
| A | 1,629,374,000 | 38 | 605,304,000 | 3,833 | 1,106,766,000 | 983 | 239,563,000 | 535 | 550,433,000 |
| B | 2,426,125,000 | 59 | 3,755,012,000 | 2,814 | 3,048,682,000 | 1,858 | 916,674,000 | 769 | 3,614,010,000 |
| C | 1,999,551,000 | 141 | 1,694,733,000 | 5,936 | 1,899,601,000 | 2,384 | 876,113,000 | 1,726 | 1,890,606,000 |
| Total | 6,055,049,000 | 238 | 6,055,049,000 | 12,583 | 6,055,049,000 | 5,225 | 2,032,350,000 | 3,030 | 6,055,049,000 |

What is a 'fair share' for the inhabitants of World A? Numerically, it could be described as just over one fourth of the global whole, since the 1.6 billion unevangelized amount today to some 27% of the globe. This would be some 694 million offers a day given to World A—170 times as large as its present share, which results on average in one offer being made every year for every individual in World A.

But it is not only a question of fair shares or equal distribution of evangelism across the globe. There is the question of why most persons in World C should be getting primary evangelism at all. To serve 3 parallel but different types of analysis, our definition of World C takes 3 alternate forms: (1) all persons or *individuals* who individually are Christian disciples; or (2) all ethnolinguistic *peoples* whose populations are each over 60% Christians and 95% evangelized; or (3) all *countries* over 60% Christians and 95% evangelized. Whichever of the 3 definitions we find most helpful in understanding, it is obvious that persons in World C both are heavily evangelized already and also are mostly Christian disciples already. Why therefore are they still being continuously deluged with 2,155 million opportunities/invitations/offers to become disciples every day?

A personal illustration may help. Every week each of us who is a church member finds himself or herself, as an ordinary Christian disciple, sitting in services or meetings large or small (or listening on radio or television) in which for an hour or so each of us hears a preacher explaining the gospel and inviting his audience to accept Jesus Christ as Lord. If his audience is 200 persons, then, in our terminology, he has produced one evangelism-hour and 450 disciple-opportunities. But we are disciples already; we belong to World C. We do not need such additional offers (we need to be told how to be better disciples, but that is not the issue here). This overlap in resources may be trivial in our case, but it assumes enormous importance when it escalates to its present level of 2 billion such redundant 'wasted' offers every day, as it has done and as it continues to do.

Any serious solution to this problem will depend on deliberate attempts by agencies to increase the abysmally small figures in column 6, or in column 7 the pitifully small percentage of each variety of evangelism which actually gets to World A. In particular, agencies could be challenged to zero in each on one specific low percentage in that column and could determine to double it, treble it, or even quadruple it within the next 12 months.

There are 45 such percentages in that column 7, every one under 1.2%. So it only needs 45 mission agencies to take action, and then this entire situation—stagnant over the last 100 years—could at last begin to be transformed.

## *PROBLEMS OF FAIR DISTRIBUTION*

A number of our Global Diagrams can usefully be studied at this point. Global Diagram 40 highlights the problem at its clearest by showing how the vast mass of today's evangelistic ministry is in fact divided among the populations of Worlds A, B, and C. World A, the world of 1.6 billion persons who have never heard of Jesus and his salvation is still after 20 centuries receiving only a minuscule share.

## *SHARING GLOBES*

Global Diagrams 37 to 39 show in diagrammatic form how the whole range of ministries and their denominations spread their resources at present across the world. With this magnitude of resources, it should surely be possible to complete world evangelization in a year or two if Christians got their abilities and resources together. Just such an opportunity was thought to have arrived in the year 1990, when denominations and confessions around the world each announced world evangelization plans for the 10 years following, labeling this period the Decade of Evangelism. Ten years later, others would evaluate whatever was achieved as commendable but the endeavor as a whole as a massive squandering of opportunity and, to human eyes at least, a total catastrophic failure.

## *THE UNIVERSAL DECADE OF EVANGELISM*

Part 27 "GeoStrategies" describes the multitude of concrete plans launched by the churches for this strategic 10-year period. One heard of '2,000 Plans for AD 2000' with at least a hundred promising to achieve final fulfilment of the Great Commission and completion of the task of world evangelization. This meant a promise to World A to move the globe to-

**Table 25–12. Disciple opportunities offered daily by Christians divided up among recipients/beneficiaries in Worlds A, B, and C, in AD 2000.**

| Ref | 7 MODES, 45 MINISTRIES | OFFERS TO WHOLE WORLD | | | OFFERS TO WORLD A | | | OFFERS TO WORLD B | | | OFFERS TO WORLD C | | |
|---|---|---|---|---|---|---|---|---|---|---|---|---|---|
| | | *Offers p.a.* | *Daily offers* | *%* | *Daily offers* | *%* | *%* | *Daily offers* | *%* | *%* | *Daily offers* | *%* | *%* |
| *1* | *2* | *3* | *4* | *5* | *6* | *7* | *8* | *9* | *10* | *11* | *12* | *13* | *14* |
| **1.** | **HIDDEN WORDS** | | | | | | | | | | | | |
| 1. | Intercession/prayerwalks/campaigns | 18.3 billion | 50,000,000 | 1.9 | 400,000 | 0.8 | 9.8 | 10,000,000 | 20.0 | 2.4 | 39,600,000 | 79.2 | 1.8 |
| 2. | Inner renewal/spirituality | 19.5 billion | 53,425,000 | 2.1 | 53,000 | 0.1 | 1.3 | 8,014,000 | 15.0 | 2.0 | 45,358,000 | 84.9 | 2.1 |
| **2.** | **VISUAL WORDS (audiovisuals)** | | | | | | | | | | | | |
| 3. | Christians' lifestyle | 18.3 billion | 50,000,000 | 1.9 | 100,000 | 0.2 | 2.5 | 9,000,000 | 18.0 | 2.2 | 40,900,000 | 81.8 | 1.9 |
| 4. | Audiovisual ministries | 76.0 billion | 208,333,000 | 8.1 | 208,000 | 0.1 | 5.1 | 41,667,000 | 20.0 | 10.2 | 166,458,000 | 79.9 | 7.7 |
| 5. | Plays/concerts/operas/shows | 48.7 billion | 133,333,000 | 5.2 | 13,000 | 0.0 | 0.3 | 5,333,000 | 4.0 | 1.3 | 127,987,000 | 96.0 | 5.9 |
| 6. | 'Jesus' Film shows (700 languages) | 54.8 billion | 150,000,000 | 5.8 | 1,500,000 | 1.0 | 36.9 | 30,000,000 | 20.0 | 7.3 | 118,500,000 | 79.0 | 5.5 |
| 7. | Audio scriptures | 18.3 billion | 50,000,000 | 1.9 | 50,000 | 0.1 | 1.2 | 2,500,000 | 5.0 | 0.6 | 47,450,000 | 94.9 | 2.2 |
| 8. | Scripture leaflets/selections | 20.5 billion | 56,164,000 | 2.2 | 56,000 | 0.1 | 1.4 | 6,740,000 | 12.0 | 1.6 | 49,368,000 | 87.9 | 2.3 |
| 9. | Every-home campaigns/visitations | 8 billion | 21,918,000 | 0.9 | 66,000 | 0.3 | 1.6 | 3,288,000 | 15.0 | 0.8 | 18,564,000 | 84.7 | 0.9 |
| 10. | New Reader Scriptures | 0.8 billion | 2,055,000 | 0.1 | 4,000 | 0.2 | 0.1 | 206,000 | 10.0 | 0.1 | 1,845,000 | 89.8 | 0.1 |
| 11. | Braille scriptures | 10 billion | 27,397,000 | 1.1 | 5,000 | 0.0 | 0.1 | 1,370,000 | 5.0 | 0.3 | 26,022,000 | 95.0 | 1.2 |
| 12. | Signed/deaf scriptures | 3.0 billion | 8,219,000 | 0.3 | 4,000 | 0.1 | 0.1 | 164,000 | 2.0 | 0.0 | 8,051,000 | 98.0 | 0.4 |
| 13. | Christian suffering | 2.6 billion | 7,123,000 | 0.3 | 36,000 | 0.5 | 0.9 | 712,000 | 10.0 | 0.2 | 6,375,000 | 89.5 | 0.3 |
| **3.** | **PERSONAL WORDS** | | | | | | | | | | | | |
| | Personal evangelism due to: | | | | | | | | | | | | |
| 14. | Great Commission Christians | 177.4 billion | 486,000,000 | 18.9 | 97,000 | 0.0 | 2.4 | 97,200,000 | 20.0 | 23.8 | 388,703,000 | 80.0 | 18.0 |
| 15. | Martyrdoms | 1.6 billion | 4,384,000 | 0.2 | 1,000 | 0.0 | 0.0 | 658,000 | 15.0 | 0.2 | 3,725,000 | 85.0 | 0.2 |
| **4.** | **PROCLAIMED WORDS** | | | | | | | | | | | | |
| 16. | Full-time home church workers | 7.5 billion | 20,416,000 | 0.8 | 41,000 | 0.2 | 1.0 | 3,062,000 | 15.0 | 0.7 | 17,313,000 | 84.8 | 0.8 |
| 17. | Foreign missionaries | 6.1 billion | 16,800,000 | 0.7 | 168,000 | 1.0 | 4.1 | 2,016,000 | 12.0 | 0.5 | 14,616,000 | 87.0 | 0.7 |
| 18. | Evangelists | 11.1 billion | 30,274,000 | 1.2 | 363,000 | 1.2 | 8.9 | 5,510,000 | 18.2 | 1.3 | 24,401,000 | 80.6 | 1.1 |
| 19. | Short-term missionaries/workers | 1.5 billion | 4,000,000 | 0.2 | 20,000 | 0.5 | 0.5 | 600,000 | 15.0 | 0.1 | 3,380,000 | 84.5 | 0.2 |
| 20. | Part-time evangelizers | 11.7 billion | 32,000,000 | 1.2 | 32,000 | 0.1 | 0.8 | 4,480,000 | 14.0 | 1.1 | 27,488,000 | 85.9 | 1.3 |
| 21. | Mission agencies | 2.1 billion | 5,699,000 | 0.2 | 57,000 | 1.0 | 1.4 | 684,000 | 12.0 | 0.2 | 4,958,000 | 87.0 | 0.2 |
| **5.** | **WRITTEN WORDS (Scriptures)** | | | | | | | | | | | | |
| 22. | Portions/gospels (25 pages) | 4.8 billion | 13,274,000 | 0.5 | 27,000 | 0.2 | 0.7 | 2,655,000 | 20.0 | 0.6 | 10,592,000 | 79.8 | 0.5 |
| 23. | Near-gospels | 2.9 billion | 7,890,000 | 0.3 | 15,000 | 0.2 | 0.4 | 1,894,000 | 24.0 | 0.5 | 5,981,000 | 75.8 | 0.3 |
| 24. | New Testaments (300 pages) | 29.0 billion | 79,562,000 | 3.1 | 80,000 | 0.1 | 2.0 | 14,321,000 | 18.0 | 3.5 | 65,161,000 | 81.9 | 3.0 |
| 25. | Near-NTs | 10.8 billion | 29,589,000 | 1.2 | 30,000 | 0.1 | 0.7 | 5,918,000 | 20.0 | 1.4 | 23,641,000 | 79.9 | 1.1 |
| 26. | Bibles (1,300 pages) | 69.9 billion | 191,616,000 | 7.5 | 192,000 | 0.1 | 4.7 | 34,491,000 | 18.0 | 8.4 | 156,933,000 | 81.9 | 7.3 |
| 27. | Near-Bibles | 12.0 billion | 32,877,000 | 1.3 | 197,000 | 0.6 | 4.8 | 7,233,000 | 22.0 | 1.8 | 25,447,000 | 77.4 | 1.2 |
| 28. | 2nd-language gospels | 600 million | 1,644,000 | 0.1 | 10,000 | 0.6 | 0.2 | 411,000 | 25.0 | 0.1 | 1,223,000 | 74.4 | 0.1 |
| 29. | 2nd-language NTs | 5.6 billion | 15,342,000 | 0.6 | 77,000 | 0.5 | 1.9 | 3,682,000 | 24.0 | 0.9 | 11,583,000 | 75.5 | 0.5 |
| 30. | 2nd-language Bibles | 15.0 billion | 41,096,000 | 1.6 | 82,000 | 0.2 | 2.0 | 9,041,000 | 22.0 | 2.2 | 31,973,000 | 77.8 | 1.5 |
| **6.** | **PRINTED WORDS (literature)** | | | | | | | | | | | | |
| 31. | Denominational materials | 1.9 billion | 5,173,000 | 0.2 | 1,000 | 0.0 | 0.0 | 310,000 | 6.0 | 0.1 | 4,862,000 | 94.0 | 0.2 |
| 32. | Local church output | 3.8 billion | 10,345,000 | 0.4 | 1,000 | 0.0 | 0.0 | 828,000 | 8.0 | 0.2 | 9,516,000 | 92.0 | 0.4 |
| 33. | Outside Christian literature | 100 million | 279,000 | 0.0 | 30 | 0.0 | 0.0 | 28,000 | 10.0 | 0.0 | 250,970 | 90.0 | 0.0 |
| 34. | Church-planting output | 600 million | 1,589,000 | 0.1 | 200 | 0.0 | 0.0 | 191,000 | 12.0 | 0.0 | 1,397,800 | 88.0 | 0.1 |
| 35. | Institutional ministries/records | 1.8 billion | 4,810,000 | 0.2 | 500 | 0.0 | 0.0 | 385,000 | 8.0 | 0.1 | 4,424,500 | 92.0 | 0.2 |
| 36. | Christian books (100 pages) | 70.0 billion | 191,781,000 | 7.5 | 19,000 | 0.0 | 0.5 | 19,178,000 | 10.0 | 4.7 | 172,584,000 | 90.0 | 8.0 |
| 37. | Christian periodicals (30 pages) | 1.5 billion | 4,110,000 | 0.2 | 400 | 0.0 | 0.0 | 164,000 | 4.0 | 0.0 | 3,945,600 | 96.0 | 0.2 |
| 38. | Tracts (2 pages) | 2.5 billion | 6,849,000 | 0.3 | 1,000 | 0.0 | 0.0 | 685,000 | 10.0 | 0.2 | 6,163,000 | 90.0 | 0.3 |
| 38. | Other documentation | 1.2 billion | 3,151,000 | 0.1 | 300 | 0.0 | 0.0 | 189,000 | 6.0 | 0.0 | 2,961,700 | 94.0 | 0.1 |
| **7.** | **ELECTRONIC WORDS** | | | | | | | | | | | | |
| 40. | Programmed training (TEE, &c) | 18.0 billion | 49,315,000 | 1.9 | 5,000 | 0.0 | 0.1 | 4,932,000 | 10.0 | 1.2 | 44,378,000 | 90.0 | 2.1 |
| 41. | Christian radio programs | 50.0 billion | 136,986,000 | 5.3 | 27,000 | 0.0 | 0.7 | 27,397,000 | 20.0 | 6.7 | 109,562,000 | 80.0 | 5.1 |
| 42. | Christian TV programs | 20.0 billion | 54,795,000 | 2.1 | 5,000 | 0.0 | 0.1 | 5,480,000 | 10.0 | 1.3 | 49,310,000 | 90.0 | 2.3 |
| 43. | Urban media (cable TV, &c) | 5.4 billion | 14,795,000 | 0.6 | 1,000 | 0.0 | 0.0 | 296,000 | 2.0 | 0.1 | 14,498,000 | 98.0 | 0.7 |
| 44. | Christian-owned computers | 34.3 billion | 94,068,000 | 3.7 | 9,000 | 0.0 | 0.2 | 12,229,000 | 13.0 | 3.0 | 81,830,000 | 87.0 | 3.8 |
| 45. | Internet/www/e-mail networks | 58.5 billion | 160,274,000 | 6.2 | 16,000 | 0.0 | 0.4 | 24,041,000 | 15.0 | 5.9 | 136,217,000 | 85.0 | 6.3 |
| | **TOTAL HOURS, WORDS, AND OFFERS** | | | | | | | | | | | | |
| | *7 types/modes of evangelizing words:* Ministries | | | | | | | | | | | | |
| | Hidden words | 37.8 billion | 103,425,000 | 4.0 | 453,000 | 0.4 | 11.1 | 18,014,000 | 17.4 | 4.4 | 84,958,000 | 82.1 | 3.9 |
| | Visual words | 260.8 billion | 714,542,000 | 27.8 | 2,042,000 | 0.3 | 50.2 | 100,980,000 | 14.1 | 24.7 | 611,520,000 | 85.6 | 28.4 |
| | Personal words | 179.0 billion | 490,384,000 | 19.1 | 98,000 | 0.0 | 2.4 | 97,858,000 | 20.0 | 23.9 | 392,428,000 | 80.0 | 18.2 |
| | Proclaimed words | 39.9 billion | 109,189,000 | 4.3 | 681,000 | 0.6 | 16.7 | 16,352,000 | 15.0 | 4.0 | 92,156,000 | 84.4 | 4.3 |
| | Written words | 150.7 billion | 412,890,000 | 16.1 | 710,000 | 0.2 | 17.4 | 79,646,000 | 19.3 | 19.5 | 332,534,000 | 80.5 | 15.4 |
| | Printed words | 83.3 billion | 228,087,000 | 8.9 | 23,430 | 0.0 | 0.6 | 21,958,000 | 9.6 | 5.4 | 206,105,570 | 90.4 | 9.6 |
| | Electronic words | 186.2 billion | 510,233,000 | 19.9 | 63,000 | 0.0 | 1.5 | 74,375,000 | 14.6 | 18.2 | 435,795,000 | 85.4 | 20.2 |
| | Grand totals per year | 937.6 billion | 2,568,750,000 | 100.0 | 4,070,430 | 0.2 | 100 | 409,183,000 | 15.9 | 100.0 | 2,155,496,570 | 83.9 | 100.0 |
| | Grand totals per inhabitant | 155 p.a. | 0.42 p.d. | | 0.002 p.d. | | | 0.17 p.d. | | | 1.08 p.d. | | |

**Table 25–13. The globe's largest unevangelized peoples, 168 World A megapeoples ranked by total of unevangelized persons, AD 2000.**

The following list represents peoples over 1 million in population in the year 2000 and less than 50% evangelized. All of these peoples represent top priorities for world evangelization if closure is to be achieved, or even attempted, by AD 2010, or AD 2025, or AD 2050. More complete data on all of these peoples can be found in the *World Christian encyclopedia*, Part 8 "Ethnosphere".
*Meaning of columns:*
*1. Name of country, anglicized version.*
*2. Name of people, anglicized, with any additional or alternate names.*
*3. Population of this people in mid-2000.*
*4. Number of evangelized persons in this people.*
*5. Number of unevangelized persons in this people.*

| *Country* | *Name of megapeople* | *Population* | *Evangelized* | *Unevangelized* |
|---|---|---|---|---|
| *1* | *2* | *3* | *4* | *5* |
| Pakistan | Western Punjabi (Lahnda) | 66,810,000 | 32,336,000 | 34,474,000 |
| China | Han Chinese (Hunanese) | 44,226,000 | 18,133,000 | 26,093,000 |
| China | Han Chinese (Jinyu) | 47,351,000 | 22,255,000 | 25,096,000 |
| India | Awadhi (Baiswari, Bagheli) | 37,352,000 | 12,513,000 | 24,839,000 |
| India | Bhojpuri Bihari (Deswali) | 36,071,000 | 14,436,000 | 21,635,000 |
| India | Maitili (Maithili, Tharu) | 31,636,000 | 11,712,000 | 19,924,000 |
| China | Han Chinese (Kan) | 25,272,000 | 11,625,000 | 13,647,000 |
| India | Braj Bhakha (Antarbedi) | 17,990,000 | 7,825,000 | 10,165,000 |
| Uzbekistan | Northern Uzbek | 19,024,000 | 9,341,000 | 9,683,000 |
| Pakistan | Sindhi | 18,259,000 | 8,949,000 | 9,310,000 |
| Yemen | Yemeni Arab | 16,189,000 | 7,612,000 | 8,577,000 |
| India | Magadhi Bihari (Maghori) | 11,941,000 | 3,823,000 | 8,118,000 |
| India | Bangri (Deswali, Hariani) | 14,900,000 | 6,944,000 | 7,956,000 |
| Iran | Azerbaijani (Turk) | 10,762,000 | 2,906,000 | 7,856,000 |
| India | Deccani | 12,726,000 | 5,091,000 | 7,635,000 |
| China | Northern Zhuang (Chwang) | 12,796,000 | 5,374,000 | 7,422,000 |
| Afghanistan | Pathan (Pukhtun, Afghani) | 10,807,000 | 3,784,000 | 7,023,000 |
| India | Chhattisgarhi (Khatahi) | 11,944,000 | 5,411,000 | 6,533,000 |
| India | Jat (Jati, Bangri) | 12,164,000 | 5,668,000 | 6,496,000 |
| Indonesia | Madurese | 12,090,000 | 5,948,000 | 6,142,000 |
| Morocco | Moroccan Arab | 11,739,000 | 5,665,000 | 6,074,000 |
| India | Rajasthani (Marwari) | 10,120,000 | 4,260,000 | 5,860,000 |
| China | Hui (Dungan, Tunya, Huizui) | 9,581,000 | 3,832,000 | 5,749,000 |
| India | Kanauji (Western Hindi) | 9,386,000 | 3,717,000 | 5,669,000 |
| China | Uighur (Kashgar) | 8,035,000 | 2,732,000 | 5,303,000 |
| India | Berar Marathi (Brahmani) | 7,552,000 | 2,568,000 | 4,984,000 |
| Cambodia | Central Khmer (Cambodian) | 9,512,000 | 4,626,000 | 4,886,000 |
| Kazakhstan | Kazakh | 8,672,000 | 3,818,000 | 4,854,000 |
| Azerbaijan | Azerbaijani (Azeri Turk) | 6,627,000 | 2,188,000 | 4,439,000 |
| China | Tujia (Tuchia) | 6,353,000 | 2,059,000 | 4,294,000 |
| Turkey | Northern Kurd (Kermanji) | 5,926,000 | 1,779,000 | 4,147,000 |
| Iran | Luri (Lori, Feyli) | 4,870,000 | 779,000 | 4,091,000 |
| Bangladesh | Sylhetti Bengali | 6,052,000 | 2,003,000 | 4,049,000 |
| Indonesia | Minangkabau (Padang) | 5,347,000 | 1,926,000 | 3,421,000 |
| China | Han Chinese (Hainanese) | 5,682,000 | 2,392,000 | 3,290,000 |
| India | Konkanese | 5,479,000 | 2,191,000 | 3,288,000 |
| India | Central Bhil | 4,683,000 | 1,606,000 | 3,077,000 |
| India | Kashmiri (Keshur) | 4,592,000 | 1,608,000 | 2,984,000 |
| Afghanistan | Afghani Tajik (Tadzhik) | 4,067,000 | 1,139,000 | 2,928,000 |
| Turkey | Crimean Tatar | 4,661,000 | 1,771,000 | 2,890,000 |
| China | Southern Zhuang | 4,455,000 | 1,604,000 | 2,851,000 |
| Pakistan | Western Pathan (Afghani) | 4,851,000 | 2,042,000 | 2,809,000 |
| Turkey | Turkish Kurd | 5,327,000 | 2,611,000 | 2,716,000 |
| China | Central Tibetan (Hsifan) | 5,116,000 | 2,425,000 | 2,691,000 |
| Iran | Mazanderani (Tabri) | 3,445,000 | 793,000 | 2,652,000 |
| Thailand | Southern Tai (Pak Thai) | 4,827,000 | 2,269,000 | 2,558,000 |
| Iran | Iranian Kurd | 4,062,000 | 1,545,000 | 2,517,000 |
| Turkmenistan | Turkmen (Trukhmeny) | 3,532,000 | 1,060,000 | 2,472,000 |
| Iran | Gilaki | 3,445,000 | 982,000 | 2,463,000 |
| Pakistan | Eastern Baluch | 3,046,000 | 640,000 | 2,406,000 |
| Tajikistan | Tajik (Tadzhik) | 4,096,000 | 1,722,000 | 2,374,000 |
| Indonesia | Balinese | 4,205,000 | 1,936,000 | 2,269,000 |
| Indonesia | Achehnese (Aceh, Atjeh) | 3,389,000 | 1,187,000 | 2,202,000 |
| Iran | Southern Kurd (Carduchi) | 3,094,000 | 930,000 | 2,164,000 |
| China | Northern Tung (Dong, Kam) | 2,800,000 | 647,000 | 2,153,000 |
| Nigeria | Yerwa Kanuri (Beriberi) | 3,444,000 | 1,343,000 | 2,101,000 |
| Pakistan | Northern Hindko (Hindki) | 3,301,000 | 1,254,000 | 2,047,000 |
| Pakistan | Southern Baluch | 2,545,000 | 535,000 | 2,010,000 |
| Pakistan | Brahui (Kur Galli, Kalat) | 2,641,000 | 666,000 | 1,975,000 |
| Indonesia | Malay (Coast Malay) | 3,460,000 | 1,523,000 | 1,937,000 |
| China | Puyi (Bouyei, Pu-I) | 2,834,000 | 907,000 | 1,927,000 |
| China | Chinese Mongolian (Mongol) | 3,420,000 | 1,506,000 | 1,914,000 |
| India | Eastern Bhil (Vil) | 2,817,000 | 904,000 | 1,913,000 |
| Kirgizstan | Kirghiz | 2,812,000 | 929,000 | 1,883,000 |
| Indonesia | Sasak (Lombok) | 2,463,000 | 641,000 | 1,822,000 |
| Indonesia | Banjarese (Banjar Malay) | 2,085,000 | 271,000 | 1,814,000 |
| Morocco | Arabized Berber | 3,488,000 | 1,679,000 | 1,809,000 |
| Nepal | Maitili (Tirahutia) | 2,583,000 | 806,000 | 1,777,000 |
| Senegal | Wolof | 3,281,000 | 1,543,000 | 1,738,000 |
| Indonesia | Lampungese (Lamponger) | 2,065,000 | 330,000 | 1,735,000 |
| Indonesia | Buginese (Bugis) | 3,309,000 | 1,588,000 | 1,721,000 |
| Guinea | Fula Jalon (Futa Dyalon) | 2,752,000 | 1,046,000 | 1,706,000 |
| India | Garhwali (Pahari Gashwali) | 2,279,000 | 593,000 | 1,686,000 |
| Algeria | Hamyan Bedouin | 2,197,000 | 550,000 | 1,647,000 |
| Niger | Zerma (Dyerma) | 2,762,000 | 1,134,000 | 1,628,000 |
| Morocco | White Moor (Bidan) | 2,258,000 | 632,000 | 1,626,000 |
| India | Kumaoni (Central Pahari) | 2,204,000 | 604,000 | 1,600,000 |
| Morocco | Southern Shilha (Shleuh) | 2,526,000 | 939,000 | 1,587,000 |
| Indonesia | Riau (Malay) | 2,163,000 | 605,000 | 1,558,000 |
| Myanmar | Burmese Shan (Thai Yai) | 2,975,000 | 1,476,000 | 1,499,000 |
| Ethiopia | Somali | 2,440,000 | 952,000 | 1,488,000 |
| China | Yao (Highland Yao, Man) | 2,377,000 | 896,000 | 1,481,000 |
| India | Kortha Bihari | 2,027,000 | 568,000 | 1,459,000 |
| Tunisia | Sahel Bedouin | 2,051,000 | 595,000 | 1,456,000 |
| India | Nagpuri Bihari (Sadri) | 2,054,000 | 616,000 | 1,438,000 |
| India | Bagri (Bahgri, Bagari) | 1,884,000 | 454,000 | 1,430,000 |
| Afghanistan | Southern Uzbek | 1,838,000 | 441,000 | 1,397,000 |
| India | Dogri (Hindi Dogri) | 2,318,000 | 930,000 | 1,388,000 |
| China | Khamba (Khams Bhotia) | 1,707,000 | 325,000 | 1,382,000 |
| India | Khandeshi | 1,660,000 | 286,000 | 1,374,000 |
| Somaliland | Somali | 2,541,000 | 1,169,000 | 1,372,000 |
| Iraq | Southern Kurd (Sorani) | 1,965,000 | 631,000 | 1,334,000 |
| Japan | Eta | 2,534,000 | 1,204,000 | 1,330,000 |
| Morocco | Central Shilha (Berraber) | 2,087,000 | 775,000 | 1,312,000 |
| Afghanistan | Hazara (Berberi) | 1,848,000 | 536,000 | 1,312,000 |
| India | Tulu (Tullu, Thulu, Tal) | 2,048,000 | 758,000 | 1,290,000 |
| Nepal | Bhojpuri Bihari | 1,879,000 | 602,000 | 1,277,000 |
| Algeria | Shawiya (Chaouia) | 1,649,000 | 379,000 | 1,270,000 |
| Iran | Afghan Persian (Kaboli) | 1,896,000 | 646,000 | 1,250,000 |
| China | Bai (Baizi, Whites) | 1,776,000 | 559,000 | 1,217,000 |
| Pakistan | Central Pathan | 1,721,000 | 518,000 | 1,203,000 |
| India | Wagdi (Wagheri, Vaged) | 1,694,000 | 493,000 | 1,201,000 |
| Myanmar | Arakanese (Maghi, Mogh) | 1,916,000 | 728,000 | 1,188,000 |
| Egypt | Bedouin | 1,369,000 | 219,000 | 1,150,000 |
| Bangladesh | Bihari | 1,937,000 | 794,000 | 1,143,000 |
| China | Northern Yi (I, Lolo) | 1,757,000 | 624,000 | 1,133,000 |
| Guinea | Southern Maninka | 1,904,000 | 787,000 | 1,117,000 |
| Indonesia | Rejang | 1,377,000 | 276,000 | 1,101,000 |
| Indonesia | Makassarese (Macassar) | 1,877,000 | 792,000 | 1,085,000 |
| India | Nimadi (Nimari) | 1,417,000 | 341,000 | 1,076,000 |
| Nigeria | Sokoto Fulani | 1,896,000 | 855,000 | 1,041,000 |
| Nigeria | Western Fulani (Bororo) | 1,673,000 | 637,000 | 1,036,000 |
| Algeria | Tajakant Bedouin | 1,290,000 | 258,000 | 1,032,000 |
| Iran | Bakhtiari | 1,137,000 | 114,000 | 1,023,000 |
| Iraq | Northern Kurd (Kermanji) | 1,502,000 | 481,000 | 1,021,000 |
| Turkey | Dimili Kurd (Southern Zaza) | 1,145,000 | 137,000 | 1,008,000 |
| Algeria | Greater Kabyle (Western) | 1,948,000 | 942,000 | 1,006,000 |
| Indonesia | Low Malay Creole | 1,485,000 | 505,000 | 980,000 |
| Nigeria | Haabe Fulani (Town Fulani | 1,896,000 | 918,000 | 978,000 |
| Morocco | Northern Shilha (Riffian) | 1,647,000 | 694,000 | 953,000 |
| Libya | Tripolitanian Arab | 1,734,000 | 786,000 | 948,000 |
| China | Li (Paoting) | 1,237,000 | 299,000 | 938,000 |
| China | Hani (Uni, Ouni) | 1,397,000 | 459,000 | 938,000 |
| Iraq | Azerbaijani (Azeri Turk) | 1,294,000 | 375,000 | 919,000 |
| Iran | Zott Gypsy (Nawar) | 1,286,000 | 386,000 | 900,000 |
| Mongolia | Khalkha Mongol | 1,691,000 | 800,000 | 891,000 |
| Pakistan | Western Baluch | 1,083,000 | 195,000 | 888,000 |
| China | Kazakh | 1,238,000 | 359,000 | 879,000 |
| Sri Lanka | Ceylon Moor | 1,391,000 | 528,000 | 863,000 |
| Pakistan | Southern Pathan | 1,503,000 | 664,000 | 839,000 |
| Syria | Bedouin Arab | 1,193,000 | 358,000 | 835,000 |
| China | Tho (Tai Tho) | 1,073,000 | 253,000 | 820,000 |
| India | Southern Bhil | 1,326,000 | 509,000 | 817,000 |
| Chad | Shuwa (Chad Arab, Baggara) | 1,258,000 | 441,000 | 817,000 |
| Algeria | Central Shilha (Beraber) | 1,149,000 | 334,000 | 815,000 |
| Viet Nam | Tho (Tai Tho, Tay) | 1,181,000 | 366,000 | 815,000 |
| Libya | Cyrenaican Arab | 1,473,000 | 668,000 | 805,000 |
| Iran | Turkmen (Turkomani) | 1,055,000 | 253,000 | 802,000 |
| Syria | Western Kurd (Kermanji) | 1,182,000 | 391,000 | 791,000 |
| Tajikistan | Northern Uzbek | 1,456,000 | 671,000 | 785,000 |
| Iraq | Bedouin | 1,017,000 | 234,000 | 783,000 |
| Iraq | Iraqi Kurd | 1,387,000 | 611,000 | 776,000 |
| Morocco | Jebala (Rif) | 1,213,000 | 449,000 | 764,000 |
| India | Garhwali (Central Pahari) | 1,014,000 | 254,000 | 760,000 |
| Philippines | Magindanaw (Ilanum) | 1,189,000 | 441,000 | 748,000 |
| Myanmar | Yangbye (Yangye) | 1,025,000 | 282,000 | 743,000 |
| Philippines | Low Malay Creole | 1,139,000 | 398,000 | 741,000 |
| Thailand | Pattani Malay (Thai Islam | 1,152,000 | 415,000 | 737,000 |
| Uzbekistan | Tajik (Tadzhik) | 1,146,000 | 413,000 | 733,000 |
| Egypt | Arabized Berber | 1,369,000 | 645,000 | 724,000 |
| Senegal | Fulakunda (Fula Cunda) | 1,177,000 | 459,000 | 718,000 |
| India | Mina | 1,052,000 | 340,000 | 712,000 |
| Pakistan | Southern Hindko | 1,100,000 | 396,000 | 704,000 |
| Egypt | Halebi Gypsy (Nawari) | 1,096,000 | 406,000 | 690,000 |
| India | Mirpur Punjabi | 1,014,000 | 325,000 | 689,000 |
| India | Rajasthani (Mewari) | 1,014,000 | 326,000 | 688,000 |
| Pakistan | Afghani Tajik (Tadzhik) | 1,203,000 | 518,000 | 685,000 |
| India | Ho | 1,132,000 | 448,000 | 684,000 |
| India | Rajasthani (Bikaneri) | 1,014,000 | 346,000 | 668,000 |
| Viet Nam | Muong (Thang, Wang) | 1,114,000 | 449,000 | 665,000 |
| China | Yunnanese Shan (Dai) | 1,142,000 | 491,000 | 651,000 |
| Indonesia | Gorontalese (Wau, Watia) | 1,056,000 | 406,000 | 650,000 |
| Cameroon | Adamawa Fulani (Fula) | 1,271,000 | 623,000 | 648,000 |
| Philippines | Maranao (Lanao, Ranao) | 1,075,000 | 430,000 | 645,000 |
| India | Malvi (Ujjaini, Malavi) | 1,149,000 | 505,000 | 644,000 |
| Thailand | Northern Khmer (Cambodian) | 1,087,000 | 490,000 | 597,000 |
| Mali | Fula Macina (Niafunke) | 1,077,000 | 485,000 | 592,000 |
| Myanmar | Mon (Talaing, Mun) | 1,056,000 | 484,000 | 572,000 |

wards the final measure where E = 100%. Major mission boards like the Southern Baptist Convention's Foreign Mission Board, since renamed International Mission Board, had since 1976 proclaimed the plan named Bold Mission Thrust with its pledge that by the year 2000 every last person on Earth would have heard the gospel and had the opportunity to become a disciple of Jesus Christ. The official plan of the Roman Catholic Church, Evangelization 2000 was launched by John Paul II in January 1990 with the ambitious goal by AD 2000 of bringing a majority of the human race (51%) to conversion to Christ, and the rest of the world to have heard the gospel. And in 1988 the United Bible Societies had pledged to place a copy of the Holy Scriptures in the hands of every young adult ages 15-24 in the language he or she understood best by the year 2000.

Regrettably, none of these 3 goals had been anywhere near to being reached when the year AD 2000 either arrived or finally closed.

### GOOD INTENTIONS AND THE HARSH REALITY

The observant reader will already have noted the stark contrast between the 1990 goals set forth by the entire Christian world and the basic Christian statistics for AD 2000. This contrast can be stated as follows: the world has remained unchanged at 33% Christian over the entire decade of 1990-2000. Despite massive efforts delivering 937 billion evangelistic offers every year, the total number of unevangelized

## Table 25–14. The globe's largest unevangelized peoples, 168 World A megapeoples ranked alphabetically by country and its peoples, AD 2000.

The following list represents peoples over 1 million in population in the year 2000 and less than 50% evangelized. All of these peoples represent top priorities for world evangelization if closure is to be achieved, or even attempted, by AD 2010, or AD 2025, or AD 2050. More complete data on all of these peoples can be found in the *World Christian encyclopedia*, Part 8 "Ethnosphere".

Meaning of columns:
1. *Name of country, anglicized version.*
2. *Name of people, anglicized, with any additional or alternate names.*
3. *Population of this people in mid-2000.*
4. *Number of evangelized persons in this people.*
5. *Number of unevangelized persons in this people.*

| Country 1 | Name of megapeople 2 | Population 3 | Evangelized 4 | Unevangelized 5 |
|---|---|---|---|---|
| Afghanistan | Afghani Tajik (Tadzhik) | 4,067,000 | 1,139,000 | 2,928,000 |
| Afghanistan | Hazara (Berberi) | 1,848,000 | 536,000 | 1,312,000 |
| Afghanistan | Pathan (Pukhtun, Afghani) | 10,807,000 | 3,784,000 | 7,023,000 |
| Afghanistan | Southern Uzbek | 1,838,000 | 441,000 | 1,397,000 |
| Algeria | Central Shilha (Beraber) | 1,149,000 | 334,000 | 815,000 |
| Algeria | Greater Kabyle (Western) | 1,948,000 | 942,000 | 1,006,000 |
| Algeria | Hamyan Bedouin | 2,197,000 | 550,000 | 1,647,000 |
| Algeria | Shawiya (Chaouia) | 1,649,000 | 379,000 | 1,270,000 |
| Algeria | Tajakant Bedouin | 1,290,000 | 258,000 | 1,032,000 |
| Azerbaijan | Azerbaijani (Azeri Turk) | 6,627,000 | 2,188,000 | 4,439,000 |
| Bangladesh | Bihari | 1,937,000 | 794,000 | 1,143,000 |
| Bangladesh | Sylhetti Bengali | 6,052,000 | 2,003,000 | 4,049,000 |
| Cambodia | Central Khmer (Cambodian) | 9,512,000 | 4,626,000 | 4,886,000 |
| Cameroon | Adamawa Fulani (Fula) | 1,271,000 | 623,000 | 648,000 |
| Chad | Shuwa (Chad Arab, Baggara) | 1,258,000 | 441,000 | 817,000 |
| China | Bai (Baizi, Whites) | 1,776,000 | 559,000 | 1,217,000 |
| China | Central Tibetan (Hsifan) | 5,116,000 | 2,425,000 | 2,691,000 |
| China | Chinese Mongolian (Mongol) | 3,420,000 | 1,506,000 | 1,914,000 |
| China | Han Chinese (Hainanese) | 5,682,000 | 2,392,000 | 3,290,000 |
| China | Han Chinese (Hunanese) | 44,226,000 | 18,133,000 | 26,093,000 |
| China | Han Chinese (Jinyu) | 47,351,000 | 22,255,000 | 25,096,000 |
| China | Han Chinese (Kan) | 25,272,000 | 11,625,000 | 13,647,000 |
| China | Hani (Uni, Ouni) | 1,397,000 | 459,000 | 938,000 |
| China | Hui (Dungan, Tunya, Huizui) | 9,581,000 | 3,832,000 | 5,749,000 |
| China | Kazakh | 1,238,000 | 359,000 | 879,000 |
| China | Khamba (Khams Bhotia) | 1,707,000 | 325,000 | 1,382,000 |
| China | Li (Paoting) | 1,237,000 | 299,000 | 938,000 |
| China | Northern Tung (Dong, Kam) | 2,800,000 | 647,000 | 2,153,000 |
| China | Northern Yi (I, Lolo) | 1,757,000 | 624,000 | 1,133,000 |
| China | Northern Zhuang (Chwang) | 12,796,000 | 5,374,000 | 7,422,000 |
| China | Puyi (Bouyei, Pu-I) | 2,834,000 | 907,000 | 1,927,000 |
| China | Southern Zhuang | 4,455,000 | 1,604,000 | 2,851,000 |
| China | Tho (Tai Tho) | 1,073,000 | 253,000 | 820,000 |
| China | Tujia (Tuchia) | 6,353,000 | 2,059,000 | 4,294,000 |
| China | Uighur (Kashgar) | 8,035,000 | 2,732,000 | 5,303,000 |
| China | Yao (Highland Yao, Man) | 2,377,000 | 896,000 | 1,481,000 |
| China | Yunnanese Shan (Dai) | 1,142,000 | 491,000 | 651,000 |
| Egypt | Arabized Berber | 1,369,000 | 645,000 | 724,000 |
| Egypt | Bedouin | 1,369,000 | 219,000 | 1,150,000 |
| Egypt | Halebi Gypsy (Nawari) | 1,096,000 | 406,000 | 690,000 |
| Ethiopia | Somali | 2,440,000 | 952,000 | 1,488,000 |
| Guinea | Fula Jalon (Futa Dyalon) | 2,752,000 | 1,046,000 | 1,706,000 |
| Guinea | Southern Maninka | 1,904,000 | 787,000 | 1,117,000 |
| India | Awadhi (Baiswari, Bagheli) | 37,352,000 | 12,513,000 | 24,839,000 |
| India | Bagri (Bahgri, Bagari) | 1,884,000 | 454,000 | 1,430,000 |
| India | Bangri (Deswali, Hariani) | 14,900,000 | 6,944,000 | 7,956,000 |
| India | Berar Marathi (Brahmani) | 7,552,000 | 2,568,000 | 4,984,000 |
| India | Bhojpuri Bihari (Deswali) | 36,071,000 | 14,436,000 | 21,635,000 |
| India | Braj Bhakha (Antarbedi) | 17,990,000 | 7,825,000 | 10,165,000 |
| India | Central Bhil | 4,683,000 | 1,606,000 | 3,077,000 |
| India | Chhattisgarhi (Khatahi) | 11,944,000 | 5,411,000 | 6,533,000 |
| India | Deccani | 12,726,000 | 5,091,000 | 7,635,000 |
| India | Dogri (Hindi Dogri) | 2,318,000 | 930,000 | 1,388,000 |
| India | Eastern Bhil (Vil) | 2,817,000 | 904,000 | 1,913,000 |
| India | Garhwali (Central Pahari) | 1,014,000 | 254,000 | 760,000 |
| India | Garhwali (Pahari Gashwali) | 2,279,000 | 593,000 | 1,686,000 |
| India | Ho | 1,132,000 | 448,000 | 684,000 |
| India | Jat (Jati, Bangri) | 12,164,000 | 5,668,000 | 6,496,000 |
| India | Kanauji (Western Hindi) | 9,386,000 | 3,717,000 | 5,669,000 |
| India | Kashmiri (Keshur) | 4,592,000 | 1,608,000 | 2,984,000 |
| India | Khandeshi | 1,660,000 | 286,000 | 1,374,000 |
| India | Konkanese | 5,479,000 | 2,191,000 | 3,288,000 |
| India | Kortha Bihari | 2,027,000 | 568,000 | 1,459,000 |
| India | Kumaoni (Central Pahari) | 2,204,000 | 604,000 | 1,600,000 |
| India | Magadhi Bihari (Maghori) | 11,941,000 | 3,823,000 | 8,118,000 |
| India | Maitili (Maithili, Tharu) | 31,636,000 | 11,712,000 | 19,924,000 |
| India | Malvi (Ujjaini, Malavi) | 1,149,000 | 505,000 | 644,000 |
| India | Mina | 1,052,000 | 340,000 | 712,000 |
| India | Mirpur Punjabi | 1,014,000 | 325,000 | 689,000 |
| India | Nagpuri Bihari (Sadri) | 2,054,000 | 616,000 | 1,438,000 |
| India | Nimadi (Nimari) | 1,417,000 | 341,000 | 1,076,000 |
| India | Rajasthani (Bikaneri) | 1,014,000 | 346,000 | 668,000 |
| India | Rajasthani (Marwari) | 10,120,000 | 4,260,000 | 5,860,000 |
| India | Rajasthani (Mewari) | 1,014,000 | 326,000 | 688,000 |
| India | Southern Bhil | 1,326,000 | 509,000 | 817,000 |
| India | Tulu (Tullu, Thulu, Tal) | 2,048,000 | 758,000 | 1,290,000 |
| India | Wagdi (Wagheri, Vaged) | 1,694,000 | 493,000 | 1,201,000 |
| Indonesia | Achehnese (Aceh, Atjeh) | 3,389,000 | 1,187,000 | 2,202,000 |
| Indonesia | Balinese | 4,205,000 | 1,936,000 | 2,269,000 |
| Indonesia | Banjarese (Banjar Malay) | 2,085,000 | 271,000 | 1,814,000 |
| Indonesia | Buginese (Bugis) | 3,309,000 | 1,588,000 | 1,721,000 |
| Indonesia | Gorontalese (Wau, Watia) | 1,056,000 | 406,000 | 650,000 |
| Indonesia | Lampungese (Lamponger) | 2,065,000 | 330,000 | 1,735,000 |
| Indonesia | Low Malay Creole | 1,485,000 | 505,000 | 980,000 |
| Indonesia | Madurese | 12,090,000 | 5,948,000 | 6,142,000 |
| Indonesia | Makassarese (Macassar) | 1,877,000 | 792,000 | 1,085,000 |
| Indonesia | Malay (Coast Malay) | 3,460,000 | 1,523,000 | 1,937,000 |
| Indonesia | Minangkabau (Padang) | 5,347,000 | 1,926,000 | 3,421,000 |
| Indonesia | Rejang | 1,377,000 | 276,000 | 1,101,000 |
| Indonesia | Riau (Malay) | 2,163,000 | 605,000 | 1,558,000 |
| Indonesia | Sasak (Lombok) | 2,463,000 | 641,000 | 1,822,000 |
| Iran | Afghan Persian (Kaboli) | 1,896,000 | 646,000 | 1,250,000 |
| Iran | Azerbaijani (Turk) | 10,762,000 | 2,906,000 | 7,856,000 |
| Iran | Bakhtiari | 1,137,000 | 114,000 | 1,023,000 |
| Iran | Gilaki | 3,445,000 | 982,000 | 2,463,000 |
| Iran | Iranian Kurd | 4,062,000 | 1,545,000 | 2,517,000 |
| Iran | Luri (Lori, Feyli) | 4,870,000 | 779,000 | 4,091,000 |
| Iran | Mazanderani (Tabri) | 3,445,000 | 793,000 | 2,652,000 |
| Iran | Southern Kurd (Carduchi) | 3,094,000 | 930,000 | 2,164,000 |
| Iran | Turkmen (Turkomani) | 1,055,000 | 253,000 | 802,000 |
| Iran | Zott Gypsy (Nawar) | 1,286,000 | 386,000 | 900,000 |
| Iraq | Azerbaijani (Azeri Turk) | 1,294,000 | 375,000 | 919,000 |
| Iraq | Bedouin | 1,017,000 | 234,000 | 783,000 |
| Iraq | Iraqi Kurd | 1,387,000 | 611,000 | 776,000 |
| Iraq | Northern Kurd (Kermanji) | 1,502,000 | 481,000 | 1,021,000 |
| Iraq | Southern Kurd (Sorani) | 1,965,000 | 631,000 | 1,334,000 |
| Japan | Eta | 2,534,000 | 1,204,000 | 1,330,000 |
| Kazakhstan | Kazakh | 8,672,000 | 3,818,000 | 4,854,000 |
| Kirgizstan | Kirghiz | 2,812,000 | 929,000 | 1,883,000 |
| Libya | Cyrenaican Arab | 1,473,000 | 668,000 | 805,000 |
| Libya | Tripolitanian Arab | 1,734,000 | 786,000 | 948,000 |
| Mali | Fula Macina (Niafunke) | 1,077,000 | 485,000 | 592,000 |
| Mongolia | Khalkha Mongol | 1,691,000 | 800,000 | 891,000 |
| Morocco | Arabized Berber | 3,488,000 | 1,679,000 | 1,809,000 |
| Morocco | Central Shilha (Berraber) | 2,087,000 | 775,000 | 1,312,000 |
| Morocco | Jebala (Rif) | 1,213,000 | 449,000 | 764,000 |
| Morocco | Moroccan Arab | 11,739,000 | 5,665,000 | 6,074,000 |
| Morocco | Northern Shilha (Riffian) | 1,647,000 | 694,000 | 953,000 |
| Morocco | Southern Shilha (Shleuh) | 2,526,000 | 939,000 | 1,587,000 |
| Morocco | White Moor (Bidan) | 2,258,000 | 632,000 | 1,626,000 |
| Myanmar | Arakanese (Maghi, Mogh) | 1,916,000 | 728,000 | 1,188,000 |
| Myanmar | Burmese Shan (Thai Yai) | 2,975,000 | 1,476,000 | 1,499,000 |
| Myanmar | Mon (Talaing, Mun) | 1,056,000 | 484,000 | 572,000 |
| Myanmar | Yangbye (Yangye) | 1,025,000 | 282,000 | 743,000 |
| Nepal | Bhojpuri Bihari | 1,879,000 | 602,000 | 1,277,000 |
| Nepal | Maitili (Tirahutia) | 2,583,000 | 806,000 | 1,777,000 |
| Niger | Zerma (Dyerma) | 2,762,000 | 1,134,000 | 1,628,000 |
| Nigeria | Haabe Fulani (Town Fulani) | 1,896,000 | 918,000 | 978,000 |
| Nigeria | Sokoto Fulani | 1,896,000 | 855,000 | 1,041,000 |
| Nigeria | Western Fulani (Bororo) | 1,673,000 | 637,000 | 1,036,000 |
| Nigeria | Yerwa Kanuri (Beriberi) | 3,444,000 | 1,343,000 | 2,101,000 |
| Pakistan | Afghani Tajik (Tadzhik) | 1,203,000 | 518,000 | 685,000 |
| Pakistan | Brahui (Kur Galli, Kalat) | 2,641,000 | 666,000 | 1,975,000 |
| Pakistan | Central Pathan | 1,721,000 | 518,000 | 1,203,000 |
| Pakistan | Eastern Baluch | 3,046,000 | 640,000 | 2,406,000 |
| Pakistan | Northern Hindko (Hindki) | 3,301,000 | 1,254,000 | 2,047,000 |
| Pakistan | Sindhi | 18,259,000 | 8,949,000 | 9,310,000 |
| Pakistan | Southern Baluch | 2,545,000 | 535,000 | 2,010,000 |
| Pakistan | Southern Hindko | 1,100,000 | 396,000 | 704,000 |
| Pakistan | Southern Pathan | 1,503,000 | 664,000 | 839,000 |
| Pakistan | Western Baluch | 1,083,000 | 195,000 | 888,000 |
| Pakistan | Western Pathan (Afghani) | 4,851,000 | 2,042,000 | 2,809,000 |
| Pakistan | Western Punjabi (Lahnda) | 66,810,000 | 32,336,000 | 34,474,000 |
| Philippines | Low Malay Creole | 1,139,000 | 398,000 | 741,000 |
| Philippines | Magindanaw (Ilanum) | 1,189,000 | 441,000 | 748,000 |
| Philippines | Maranao (Lanao, Ranao) | 1,075,000 | 430,000 | 645,000 |
| Senegal | Fulakunda (Fula Cunda) | 1,177,000 | 459,000 | 718,000 |
| Senegal | Wolof | 3,281,000 | 1,543,000 | 1,738,000 |
| Somaliland | Somali | 2,541,000 | 1,169,000 | 1,372,000 |
| Sri Lanka | Ceylon Moor | 1,391,000 | 528,000 | 863,000 |
| Syria | Bedouin Arab | 1,193,000 | 358,000 | 835,000 |
| Syria | Western Kurd (Kermanji) | 1,182,000 | 391,000 | 791,000 |
| Tajikistan | Northern Uzbek | 1,456,000 | 671,000 | 785,000 |
| Tajikistan | Tajik (Tadzhik) | 4,096,000 | 1,722,000 | 2,374,000 |
| Thailand | Northern Khmer (Cambodian) | 1,087,000 | 490,000 | 597,000 |
| Thailand | Pattani Malay (Thai Islam) | 1,152,000 | 415,000 | 737,000 |
| Thailand | Southern Tai (Pak Thai) | 4,827,000 | 2,269,000 | 2,558,000 |
| Tunisia | Sahel Bedouin | 2,051,000 | 595,000 | 1,456,000 |
| Turkey | Crimean Tatar | 4,661,000 | 1,771,000 | 2,890,000 |
| Turkey | Dimili Kurd (Southern Zaza) | 1,145,000 | 137,000 | 1,008,000 |
| Turkey | Northern Kurd (Kermanji) | 5,926,000 | 1,779,000 | 4,147,000 |
| Turkey | Turkish Kurd | 5,327,000 | 2,611,000 | 2,716,000 |
| Turkmenistan | Turkmen (Trukhmeny) | 3,532,000 | 1,060,000 | 2,472,000 |
| Uzbekistan | Northern Uzbek | 19,024,000 | 9,341,000 | 9,683,000 |
| Uzbekistan | Tajik (Tadzhik) | 1,146,000 | 413,000 | 733,000 |
| Viet Nam | Muong (Thang, Wang) | 1,114,000 | 449,000 | 665,000 |
| Viet Nam | Tho (Tai Tho, Tay) | 1,181,000 | 366,000 | 815,000 |
| Yemen | Yemeni Arab | 16,189,000 | 7,612,000 | 8,577,000 |

persons on Earth, far from decreasing to zero, has remained static each year at 1.6 billion in 1990 and in AD 2000. The reason for this disastrous state of affairs is simply that the churches and missions failed to take into account the population explosion which resulted—among a number of similar unanticipated factors—in the unevangelized world increasing at 13 million each year.

### A CLOSING SUMMARY

The best way to sum up the wide ranging data and concerns in this Part 25 "Macroevangelistics" is to show in 2 final tables, Table 25–13 and 25–14, the actual current status of World A by listing its 168 largest unevangelized megapeoples. The challenge presented by this listing is profound.

## BIBLIOGRAPHY

*A Church for all peoples: missionary issues in a world Church.* E. LaVerdiere (ed). Collegeville, MN: Liturgical Press, 1993. 104p.

*A history of the expansion of Christianity.* K. S. Latourette. New York: Harper, 1937–45. 7 vols.

*Atlas du monde chrétien: l'expansion du Christianisme à travers les siècles.* A. Freitag et al. Paris and Brussels: Elsevier, 1959. 215p. (Maps and photographs. English edition under title, *The twentieth century atlas of the Christian world: the expansion of Christianity through the centuries.* New York: Hawthorn, 1964).

*Believing in the future: toward a missiology of Western culture.* D. J. Bosch. *Christian mission and modern culture.* Valley Forge, PA: Trinity Press International, 1995. 79p.

*Bibliographia missionaria.* 1935–74; Rome: Pontificia Università do Propagande Fide, 1986–. 50 vols. to date. (Annual review of previous year's literature; until 1971, some overlap with *Bibliotheca missionum,* but has now superseded it for current literature).

'Bibliography on world mission and evangelism,' *International review of mission,* (At end of all issues).

*Bibliotheca missionum.* R. Streit. Freiburg: Herder, 1916–71. 28 vols. (The major complete and retrospective Catholic bibliography of missions; discontinued 1971 and superseded by *Bibliographia missionaria*).

*Called and empowered: global mission in Pentecostal perspective.* M. Dempster, B. D. Klaus & D. Petersen (eds). Peabody, MA: Hendrickson, 1991.

*Carrying the gospel to all the non-Christian world.* Edinburgh: Oliphant/Revell, 1910. (World Missionary Conference, Report of Commission I).

*Catholic mission history.* J. Schmidlin. Techny, IL: Mission Press, 1933. 878p. (Translated from the German).

*Catholic mission theory.* J. Schmidlin. Techny, IL: Mission Press, 1931. 559p. (Translation of *Katholische Missionslehre im Grundriss*).

*Christian mission in the twentieth century.* T. Yates. Cambridge, UK: Cambridge University Press, 1994. 291p.

*Christianity and missions, 1450–1800.* J. S. Cummins (ed). *An expanding world: the European impact on world history, 1450–1800,* 28. Brookfield, VT: Ashgate, 1997. 350p.

*Christianity and the religions: a biblical theology of world religions.* E. Rommen & H. Netland (eds). *Evangelical Missiological Society series,* 2. Pasadena, CA: William Carey Library, 1995. 274p.

*Classic texts in mission and world Christianity.* N. E. Thomas (ed). *American Society of Missiology series,* 20. Maryknoll, NY: Orbis, 1995. 366p.

*Concise dictionary of the Christian world mission.* S. Neill, G. H. Anderson & J. Goodwin (eds). London: Lutterworth, 1970. 704p.

*Contemporary missiology: an introduction.* J. Verkuyl. Trans. & ed., D. Cooper. Grand Rapids, MI: Eerdmans, 1978. 428p.

*Critical bibliography of missiology.* L. Vriens. Nijmegen: VSKB Publ, 1960.

*Dictionary catalog of the Missionary Research Library, New York.* Boston: G.K. Hall, 1967. 17 vols., 13,039p. (273,000 entries).

*Dictionary of mission: theology, history, perspectives.* K. Müller et al. (eds). *American Society of Missiology series,* 24. Maryknoll, NY: Orbis, 1997. 544p.

*Encyclopedia of missions: descriptive, historical, biographical, statistical.* H. O. Dwight et al. (eds). 1904. Repr. ed. Detroit, MI: Omnigraphics, 1975.

*Encyclopedia of modern Christian missions: the agencies.* B. L. Goddard (ed). Camden, NJ: T. Nelson, 1967. 762p.

*Errand to the world: American Protestant thought and foreign missions.* W. R. Hutchison. Chicago: University of Chicago Press, 1987. 239p.

*God's call to mission.* D. W. Shenk. Scottdale, PA: Herald Press, 1994. 229p.

*Gospel and mission in the writings of Paul: an exegetical and theological analysis.* P. T. O'Brien. Grand Rapids, MI: Baker, 1993. 175p.

*Histoire universelle des missions catholiques.* S. Delacroix. Paris: Librarie Grund, 1956–58. 4 vols. (Profuse illustrations and maps).

*International review of missions: index 1912–1966.* O. G. Myklebust. Geneva: IRM, 1968. (Bibliography of 1,900 articles).

*Lexikon missionstheologischer grundbegriffe.* K. Müller & T. Sundermeier (eds). Berlin: Dietrich Reiner, 1987.

*Media in church and mission: communicating the gospel.* V. Søgaard. Pasadena, CA: William Carey Library, 1993. 301p.

*Missiological abstracts, 25 years, 1966–1991.* G. R. Grimes (ed). Pasadena, CA: Fuller Theological Seminary, 1991. 336p. (Abstracts of 720 dissertations, theses, and projects produced at the School of World Mission at Fuller Theological Seminary).

*Missiology: an ecumenical introduction: texts and contexts of global Christianity.* F. J. Verstraelen (ed). Grand Rapids, MI: Eerdmans, 1995. 505p.

*Mission trends.* G. H. Anderson & T. F. Stransky C.S.P. (eds). New York: Paulist Press; Grand Rapids, MI: Eerdmans. 5 vols.

*New directions in mission and evangelization; vol. 1: basic statements 1974–1991; vol. 2: theological foundations.* J. A. Scherer & S. B. Bevans (eds). Maryknoll, NY: Orbis, 1992. 2 vols.

*Pentecost, mission and ecumenism: essays on intercultural theology.* J. A. B. Jongeneel et al. (eds). *Studies in the intercultural history of Christianity,* 75. Frankfurt am Main: Peter Lang, 1992. 386p.

*Philosophy, science and theology of mission in the 19th and 20th centuries: a missiological encyclopedia.* J. A. B. Jongeneel (ed). *Studies in the intercultural history of Christianity,* 92, 106. Frankfurt am Main: P. Lang, 1995–1997. 2 vols.

*Re–visioning mission: the Catholic Church and culture in postmodern America.* R. G. Cote. *Isaac Hecker studies in religion and American culture.* Mahwah, NJ: Paulist, 1996. 197p.

*Roots of the great debate in mission: mission in historical and theological perspective.* R. E. Hedlund. *Theological issues series,* 3. Bangalore, India: Theological Book Trust, 1993. 529p.

*Sacrae Congregationis de Propaganda Fide Memoria Rerum.* J. Metzler et al. (eds). Freiburg: Herder, 1972–76. 3 vols., 4,500p. (History of Catholic missions, 1622–1972).

*Spiritual power and missions: raising the issues.* E. Rommen (ed). *Evangelical Missiological Society series,* 3. Pasadena, CA: William Carey Library, 1995. 163p.

*Studies in missions: an index of theses on missions.* Monrovia, CA: MARC, 1974. 73p. (200 theses and dissertations).

*The evangelization of the world in this generation.* J. R. Mott. New York: Student Volunteer Movement for Foreign Missions, 1900. 253p.

*The good news of the kingdom: mission theology for the third millennium.* C. Van Engen, D. S. Gilliland & P. Pierson (eds). Maryknoll, NY: Orbis Books, 1993. 336p.

*The gospel and frontier peoples: a report of a consultation, December 1972.* R. P. Beaver (ed). Pasadena, CA: William Carey Library, 1972. 413p.

*The recovery of mission: beyond the pluralist paradigm.* V. Ramachandra. Grand Rapids, MI: Eerdmans, 1996. 305p.

*Transforming mission: paradigm shifts in theology of mission.* D. J. Bosch. *American Society of Missiology series,* 16. Maryknoll, NY: Orbis, 1991. 597p.

*Wichtige daten der Missionsgeschichte.* T. Ohm. Münster: Aschendorffsche Verlagsbuchhandlung, 1956. (French: *Les principaux faits de l'histoire des missions,* 1961. 162p).

*Write the vision: the Church renewed.* W. R. Shenk. *Christian mission and modern culture.* Valley Forge, PA: Trinity Press International, 1995. 127p.

Part 26

# GEORESPONSE

Church growth, baptism, and responsiveness to Christianity

*Baptize them in the name of the Father, the Son, and the Holy Spirit.*
—the Risen Christ, Matthew 28:19, Contemporary English Version

*Those who accepted what Peter said were baptized, and some three thousand were added to the number of believers that day.*
—Acts of the Apostles 2:14, Revised English Bible

Much of what churches and agencies measure in their annual census relates to the response of peoples and populations to Christian outreach, mission, and evangelism. Part 26 narrates the 7 different varieties of new responses that the churches encounter. An important comparative measure emerges, namely R, responsiveness of a population, defined and quantified as new church members baptized per year, per million evangelism-hours expended per year, or per million evangelistic offers extended per year.

# Church growth, baptism, and responsiveness to Christianity

There are a vast number of ways and methods of observing and measuring response. Virtually all Christian churches and agencies maintain some degree of monitoring, however small—observing, noting, reporting, enumerating, counting, recording, writing down, entering data, totaling the effect of all their activities, circulating the results. This section endeavors to summarize these activities, seen as responses to Christianity, Christ, and the gospel.

## What Christians measure—1

Christians can and do measure the present status quo and whatever changes are going on. They measure—the current position, changes going on now in that position, increase or decrease in that position, rates of change over the last year, or 5 years, 10 years, 30 years, or even 100 years. In particular, they measure new changes at present taking place from one year to the next, measuring these as annual rates.

## What Christians measure—2

Christians can and do measure people, resources, monies, properties, and much more. They measure—
— attenders at worship, new attenders, increase in attenders
— attenders at rallies, at meetings, at new events, at most other activities, increase in activities
— enrolments, new enrolments, increase in enrolments
— sales, new sales, increase in sales
— finance, new finance, increase in finance
— resources, new resources, increase in resources

## What Christians measure—3

Christians can and do measure a large variety of persons and their communities and organizations. Increasingly, they do this using standardized universal categories recognized as important by Christians across the world. They measure—persons, groups (e.g. house meetings, prayer meetings, youth activities), congregations, churches, associations of churches, denominations, councils and conciliarism, confessions, world communions, major ecclesiasticocultural blocs, global megablocs, organized Christianity as a whole, organized and unorganized global Christianity. In the various non-Christian religions, somewhat similar monitoring also goes on, but is nothing like the degree in Christianity. Consequently, Christians also measure the size and strengths of any and all non-Christian religions forming the context around them.

We will now describe the actual practices of the Christian world as churches and agencies measure response. For convenience, these are discussed under the 7 Mandates of Christ's Great Commission. Each of 7 varieties of response can then be seen as responses to the 7 varieties of words which make up evangelism as listed in Global Diagram 6 in Part 1.

## I. NEW SPIRITUALITY
### (responses to hidden words)

A first variety of response relates to the 1st Mandate of the Great Commission: 'Receive!'—receive Christ, receive the Spirit, receive power. These are responses to words hidden in the prayers of millions of believers and intercessors.

It must never be forgotten that Christianity is first and foremost a spiritual phenomenon involving personal faith, hope, love and other hard-to-measure attributes—prayer, intercession, trust, vocation, humility, self-denial, repentance, honesty, obedience. Nevertheless, it is possible to measure most of these characteristics objectively. Many churches and agencies in fact do so, especially polling agencies which ask the public very specific, precise questions on all these topics ('Do you believe Jesus is the Son of God?',

'Do you pray every day?', 'Does the Christian faith influence your business practices?', et alia). The result is a vast amount of statistical data on the spiritual aspects of global Christianity, including revivals and renewal movements of many varieties.

### New intercessors

Among spiritual topics being enumerated today one of the most important concerns the ministry of prayer, especially organized intercession. Statistics are regularly published about: prayer organizations, their membership, prayer meetings, prayer conferences, concerts of prayer, prayer retreats (such as the Korea prayer mountains), circulation of daily prayer guides, sales of books and literature about prayer, numbers of monastic institutions (monasteries, convents, abbeys), monks (priests and brothers), nuns (sisters), services, vigils, worship services, et alia. Most such enumerations are however idiosyncratic to the particular church or agency involved. They do not yet use globally-valid categories or definitions, which makes global totaling and global comparison difficult.

### New power recipients

Numerous attempts have been made, by the 21% of global Christianity involved in the Pentecostal/Charismatic Renewal, to count persons experiencing the power of the Holy Spirit. For many years the Assemblies of God, now with 35 million adherents worldwide, published annual totals of 'Persons filled with the Holy Ghost for the first time', and some of its branches still continue this practice.

### New inner renewal

Overall statistics of those responding to the many varieties of revival and renewal are also compiled. Due attention has to be paid, however, to the difference between visible phenomena which can be objectively measured, and invisible attributes, actions, and attitudes internal to Christian believers and so which can only be described and measured approximately.

## II. NEW OUTREACH
### (responses to visual words)

A second variety of response relates to the 2nd Mandate of the Great Commission: 'Go!' This emphasizes the central role in Christian mission of 3 factors: (1) ceaseless mobility, and (2) organized journeyings, (3) ongoing visibility of the results of such journeyings and the benefits to others of believing in Christ. The responses are usually related to visual words produced through the worldwide Christian community.

### New travels

The movement of Christian workers around the world has increased enormously over the period 1900–2000. Detailed records are kept by most churches and agencies of these itinerations, movements, postings, transfers, travels, and the like. In addition, ordinary church members are more mobile than ever in history. Each year 250 million Christians travel as foreign tourists, and 2,900 million Christians go on domestic tours within their own countries.

### New pilgrims

Each year 150 million Christians—8% of organized global Christianity—are on the move as religious pilgrims visiting recognized pilgrimage sites and shrines. Many sites compile and publish exact and detailed statistics of all such pilgrims each year.

### New contacts

Many agencies are meticulous in listing or cataloging their contacts—persons met (especially non-Christian religious leaders), persons in need, persons en-

quiring, persons interested, persons committing themselves in some way or another. Thus one very large Protestant agency Campus Crusade for Christ enumerates, inter alia, the total number of conversations with non-Christians per month carried out by each worker.

### New recipients

Persons receiving gifts or free offers of various kinds, secular or religious, are also tracked in statistics. These deal with relief, aid, refugee aid, other charity, festival aid. Items received may be a tract, gospel, Bible, tape, video, book, grant, collection, cash, food, clothing, medicine, parcel, crate, or even a whole container.

### New visible signs and wonders

The visibility of the Christian faith is brought vividly before the world year by year in particular by unexpected or surprising or startling events. Large numbers of physical healings are regularly documented in print or on camera (as with the Roman Catholic centers of Lourdes, Medugorje, and hundreds of other shrines). Exorcisms, glossolalia, and other charismata occur in virtually all ecclesiastical traditions nowadays. Frightening developments—such as public martyrdoms of Christians—get media coverage. Other less spectacular audiovisual 'signs' continue day by day: the blind get Braille scriptures, the deaf get signed scriptures, the isolated get audio scriptures, the preliterate get 'Jesus' Film videos, the newly literate get New Reader scriptures. For those prepared to take the trouble to investigate, these signs and wonders of the spread of Christ's good news are startling in their multiplicity.

## III. NEW WITNESS
### (responses to personal words)

A third variety of response relates to the 3rd Mandate of the Great Commission: 'Witness!' These are responses to the personal words of millions of Christians.

### New witnessing events

'Witness' is defined here as the unorganized testimony of a Christian or group of Christians given to another person or persons, as occasion may arise; the person-to-person contact is unstructured, the time and place are not chosen by the Christian. In this it differs from 'evangelism' in which Christians organize or structure their actual presentation of the gospel to specific audiences who are often captive audiences. Nevertheless, large-scale witnessing often requires a measure of organizing. Most churches have processions of witness of one variety or another outside the church building. And at the citywide or nationwide levels, Marches for Jesus have become a major phenomenon, involving annually every May millions of Christians and totaling 100 million for the whole decade of the 1990s.

### New sympathizers

As a result of the contacts of Christians with non-Christians, and due to the witness to Christ thus given, there arises around the churches a whole new category often termed 'sympathizers' (widely used in French, sympatisants), also termed seekers. These are non-Christians who nevertheless are strongly attracted to Christ and Christianity, often to the point of regularly attending Christian worship services. Churches term ministries toward them as evangelization, dialogue, apologetics. At the point where such persons formally apply for Christian initiation (baptism), they are usually then termed enquirers, catechumens, or baptismal candidates. In many of the world's mission fields, such as tropical Africa just below the Sahara, such catechumens actually outnumber already baptized church members.

### New purchasers
The communication of Christianity has become a major industry with huge financial turnovers and profits. It involves Bibles, gospels, Christian books, tapes. In the absence of direct measures of church membership, one can often use such sales figures. One instance comes from South Africa: hymnbook sales enable researchers to estimate the million-plus memberships of the largest African independent churches.

### New personal work
Churches do not enumerate this function, but public-opinion pollsters do. In the USA a national sample of the general population answered the question 'Have you recently attempted to lead someone else to faith in Christ?' as follows: 51% said Yes. Projected to the national population, this means that 135 million Americans claim to be involved in some variety of personal evangelism.

## IV. NEW HEARERS
### (responses to proclaimed words)

A fourth variety of response relates to the 4th Mandate of the Great Commission: 'Proclaim!' In this category are a variety of statistics compiled by churches which enumerate persons who form the regular ongoing audiences for the formal proclamation of the gospel. The responses are responses to the proclaimed words of millions of Christian activists.

With this fourth category we enter the realm of organized, institutionalized Christianity. Anything organized requires the raising of money and the expenditure of money. Anything requiring money results in accounting and auditing. The sums involved are so huge that, as Table 20-3 indicates, Christians have to commission annual audits costing them $810 million. The financial records thus produced then form a major resource for researchers looking for concrete indicators of Christian activity and response of all kinds.

### New listeners
Every day millions of persons listen for the first time to Christian preaching or teaching. Statistics kept include Sunday church attenders, regular attenders, annual attenders, first-time attenders, visitors, Sunday-school attenders, Bible class attenders, communicants (communion attenders), audiences, hearers, viewers. Thus every showing of the 'Jesus' Film has statistics emerging from it, recording inter alia total viewers (=those 'evangelized' by that particular performance).

### New ongoing ministries
Parallel to all these are statistics of days or even hours spent by church workers, especially clergy, preachers and teachers, lay ministers, parish assistants, parish workers, parish visitors, hospital visitors, hospital chaplains, religious personnel, administrators.

### New missionaries and evangelists
These persons are those charged by the churches with the full-time task of verbally presenting the Christian faith to the non-Christian world. Both home missionaries and foreign missionaries, and all their activities, are extensively enumerated each year. New workers in this category amount to some 20% per annum (and a further 20% leave for other spheres of Christian work elsewhere).

### New music outreach
Records are kept of a vast range of musical activities, regular or occasional. Church choirs meet to practice or perform several times a week. Statistics are kept of church concerts, church recitals, church bands, church singing groups, church music broadcasts. Usually these include statistics of audiences. One of the most effective, most significant, and longest-staged is Handel's *Messiah* as expounded in Part 22 "Evangelism".

### New home visitation
Every day Christians pay pastoral or evangelistic visits, organized or unorganized, to at least one million homes or households across the world. Where visits are organized, records are kept. The largest numbers are the daily visits by church pastors and parish clergy from the thousands of organized pastoral denominations on 6 continents. Agencies like Every Home for Christ (formerly Every Home Crusade) keep detailed statistics of visits, persons contacted, literature requested or distributed, languages employed, and so on.

## V. NEW DISCIPLES
### (responses to written words)

A fifth variety of response relates to the 5th Mandate of the Great Commission: 'Disciple!' which means: Make people into My disciples. Responses now become direct responses to the written words of Holy Scripture, God's Word, with its personal challenge to all who hear them.

### New personal responses
This variety monitors the various ways in which people respond personally to the Christian message. Churches and agencies keep a range of counts on such things; most relate to people's openly stated decisions to either start on the Christian life or to do something new in their discipleship.

### New decisions
Such a decision may be: to convert to Christianity, to become a Christian, or a church member, or a regular attender, or a committed Christian, or a better Christian, or a volunteer, or a full-time church worker, or an ordained pastor, or a home missionary, or even a career foreign missionary. One widespread route may be by making a public decision of some kind at a large meeting: walking to the front or to the altar-rail; raising hands/hand/handkerchiefs or standing up; going forward; making appointments to see a minister/evangelist/counselor/worker; signing decision cards (after meetings or services, or by mail as result of a Bible correspondence course, or radio programs). Decisions like these occur throughout the world at a rate of at least 30,000 a day.

### New initiates
A large number of those decisions will lead directly to church affiliation, with a decision to join the church in some tangible form. Usually, this will be by joining a church's regular initiation program. Thus it may be to become a candidate for the catechumenate, or for some other form of instruction.

The most common form of enumeration used by churches and agencies with regard to all such decisions are counts of such persons, often expressed by the signing of decision/convert/commitment cards. For shorthand purposes these are often termed 'decisions' or 'converts', although most churches and workers realize that all such categories will always include persons at very different stages in the process of decision or conversion.

Again, the number of persons being initiated, or catechumens, will depend on the length of the church's period of instruction. Where the period is only a month or two before admission numbers will be relatively small; but where instruction covers 1, 2, or even 5 years, numbers become enormous.

### New student evangelism
Students (school pupils, college students) form a special category requiring different evangelistic approaches that respect children's and young people's rights. Among this type of response are the widespread audiences of school children in non-Christian countries who listen to Christian radio, who then apply for Bible correspondence courses, and who at graduation send in signed decision cards.

### New scripture distribution
Every year some 4.6 billion new copies of the Bible or part of it are circulated by a vast army of Bible society workers, colporteurs, church workers, and ordinary church members. This process is carefully monitored and totals are recorded by country, by language, by type of scripture, and often by denomination or agency. The significance of such careful enumeration of circulation records is that in thousands of cases new Christians attribute their conversion to direct contact with one single copy of the Scriptures— Bible, New Testament, gospel, selection, or other piece of scripture.

## VI. NEW CHURCHES
### (responses to printed words)

A sixth variety of response relates to the 6th Mandate of the Great Commission: 'Baptize!' This is the whole subject of church planting and subsequent church growth. Nowadays this is in most cases inseparably linked with printed words—announcements, posters, advertisements of meetings, programs, schedules, leaflets, hymnsheets, decision cards, letters to pastors, introductions to churches, membership lists, church programs, et alia.

### New baptisms
Baptism is uniquely the Christian world's rite of initiation. Annual totals of baptisms may be regarded as the major indicator of ongoing Christian progress. Most churches and denominations recognize its importance by keeping lists of names of these newly affiliated persons, and compile exact statistics of them whenever they occur. In practice the baptism rate is the same as, or approximates to, the new church member rate.

Not surprisingly, vast numbers are involved, amounting to some 45 million new Christians baptized in each successive year. Baptism services in lakes or rivers at which thousands are baptized over 2 or 3 hours are common; and this survey contains several photographs of such events.

### New institutional responses
Most of the world's 105,000 major Christian institutions and 376,000 minor institutions keep records. Almost all the world's 5,500 Christian hospitals and 30,000 medical centers have records which together add up to 55 million medical consultations a year. Likewise the 400 million pupils enrolled in Christian schools are all regularly enumerated.

### New literature circulated
Another major area of church activity concerns the production and distribution of Christian literature. Some 74,000 new Christian book titles a year are published, with 3.5 billion copies printed. Some 5 billion Christian tracts (leaflets) are circulated each year. All this can readily be analyzed.

### New churches planted
If baptism is the first, the second major indicator of ongoing Christian progress is the planting of new churches, new congregations, or new fellowships into which the newly baptized persons may be organized. This leads to the technical study and analysis of church growth.

### Two kinds of church growth
Church growth is often said to be composed of 2 major categories: (a) *quantitative* growth (measurable, numerical, statistical), and (b) *qualitative* growth (non-measurable), this referring to a church's quality of life, spirituality, maturity, self-support, caring ministries, outreach, evangelism, et alia. The former (a) is easy, because churches count membership, workers, baptisms. The latter (b) however is seldom enumerated by churches. Qualitative aspects can nevertheless be measured by researchers creating their own variables and then compiling their own data. Normally, however, church growth studies deal only with the church's own quantitative data.

### Quantitative church growth, G
Analysis of church growth usually begins with the following basic situation: a church or other grouping of Christians has affiliated church members numbering membership $m_1$ in year $t_1$ which then changes to $m_2$ in year $t_2$. 'Growth' therefore is $m_2-m_1$ members.

The rate of growth per year is best computed by assuming exponential expansion, which will now be briefly explained.

### Exponential church growth
This is an accurate method, similar to growth rates used by demographers, bankers, economists, and many others. It assumes that growth between any 2 points follows an exponential curve. Here it is necessary to use a standard handheld calculator with an exponential key. First we compute $m_2/m_1$, key it in, then enter $t_2-t_1$. The result is shown as $1.0 + G/100$, so this has to be rearranged to give the final figure of church growth G% per year.

예 수 혁 명  ◉ EXPLO'74  엑 스 플 로 '74 성 령 폭 발

민 족 의 가 슴 마 다 그 리 스 도 를 심 어 이 땅 에 성 령 의 계 절 이 오 게 하 자

**Rapid growth in non-Christian countries.** Two countries with very rapid church growth in predominantly non-Christian populations
(1) **South Korea** (still 59% non-Christian). *Above.* Largest Christian conference in history, EXPLO-74 (2nd Training Conference on Evangelism) attracted 323,419 residents for a week in 1974 in Seoul, Korea. In Korea, also, non-conciliarism is widespread; conciliarism attracts little interest.
(2) **Togo** (still 57% non-Christian). *Below.* Festive procession through a Togo village for first mass celebrated by young Roman Catholic priest (center).

## Two ways of analyzing church growth trends

Church growth means the rate of change of the numerical size of the church, the churches, or a church. It is measured as the annual rate of numerical change (increase or decrease, growth or decline) of a congregation, or a denomination, or all in a country. Figures can be expressed as number of persons per year, or churches per year, or as percent age rate. It is usually expressed in formulas by the symbol G, per cent per year.

There are 2 ways in which growth can be analyzed. The first is to divide a church growth quantity into 3 distinct components describing the Christian community concerned:

1. demographic increase (*births* minus *deaths*; also called natural increase)
2. conversion increase (*conversions* minus *defections*)
3. transfer increase (*immigrants* or transfers in, minus *emigrants* or transfers out)

A second way of analyzing church growth is in terms of 2 distinct components only:
1. *entries* into the church, popularly known as 'the front door' into the church; gains in membership, usually measured as new baptisms or receptions; also measured by *births*, plus *conversions* (converts), plus *immigrants* or transfers in.
2. *exits* from the church, popularly known as 'the back door' out of the church; departures or losses, composed of *deaths*, plus *defections* or apostasies (defectors, apostates, lapsees), plus *emigrants* or transfers out.

Let us assign symbols to each of these 8 italicized variables as follows, expressing them as percent rates per year: b = births, d = deaths; c = conversions, a = defections; i = immigrants, u = emigrants; also g = entries (gains), x = exits (losses). The formulas connecting them are:

$$g = b+c+i$$

$$x = d+a+u.$$

Then

G = nett demographic increase + nett conversion increase + nett transfer increase

$$= (b-d) + (c-a) + (i-u)$$

or,

$$G = \text{entries minus exits} = g-x = (b+c+i)-(d+a+u).$$

Of these 8 variables, 3 are usually relatively small or even negligible: these are a, i, and u.

G measures church growth, or church member growth, but we need to find, and so will shortly develop, a variable more directly related to response. This variable will then be able to function as a major indicator or predictor of where response is occurring or where responsiveness is likely to occur.

Note at this point, to avoid confusion of terms, that G is the code primarily describing a particular *denomination's* current annual growth rate (given in *WCE* Part 4, Country Tables 2, column 9). It should not be confused with the similar variable CG which reports the exponential growth rate, % p.a., across the entire century (AD 1900-2000), for every *ethnolinguistic people* in every country (given in *WCE* Part 8 column 30) or for every *country* itself (in *WCT* Part 12 column 96).

## New church member rate, g

This important new variable, g, measures: entries through the front door, ignoring exits through the back door. It stands for the annual rate of *addition* of new church members—the total new church members added to the church's rolls every year, without subtracting losses. It means: new entries, new individuals entering, without subtracting new exits. Using the church growth formula for G above,

since $G = (b-d) + (c-a) + (i-u)$

then g = birth rate + conversion rate+transfer rate
$$= b+c+i$$

or,   g = G+(d+a+u).

In most cases, this formula can be abbreviated to

$$g = G+d.$$

In other words, to find the present rate of growth of new church members being added to the church (which are reported here for every country in Part 12 column 97), take the current church growth rate (given, for every denomination, in *WCE* Part 4, Country Table 2, column 9) and add the death rate to it. This latter rate is tabulated in Part 12 column 11 for every country in the world.

## Measuring church growth across the 20th century

For every ethnolinguistic people, the *World Christian database* gives the number of church members for the years 1900 and AD 2000. The average long-term church growth rate over these 100 years (symbol, CG, measured as % p.a.) is adequately represented by these 2 figures. Our method then uses a calculator or software formula to compute or measure the exponential growth rate CG over this period. The results for global agglomerations can be seen in Table 12-1 column 96 for all countries; and for all ethnolinguistic peoples in *WCE* Part 8 column 30.

### VII. NEW TRAINEES
#### (responses to electronic words)

A seventh variety of response relates to the 7th Mandate of the Great Commission: 'Train!' This relates to all types of teaching ministry. It is especially important with the mushrooming growth of electronic ministries, which now produce just over 200 trillion evangelism-words a year. Responses to these electronic words have become virtually worldwide and continuous; one hears of new responses at every turn.

## New persons in training

The most meaningful categories enumerated by churches and agencies may well be those of trainees— Christians who have committed themselves to serious programs of spiritual teaching, instruction, or training. Statistics compiled include: seminarians, theological students, enrollees in theological education by extension (TEE), short-term workers, graduates, postgraduate students, and students and enrollees in a huge variety of training courses: orientation courses, Bible correspondence courses, distance education, radiophonic courses. Also measured are hours under instruction, semester credits, costs of tuition, number of instructors, et alia.

## New radio/TV audiences

Each year the worldwide audience regularly listening to Christian broadcasting rises by 70 millions (4.3%). By AD 2000 the total listeners and viewers reached 30% of the world (1.8 billions). These totals are analyzed in a variety of ways to study response, especially by audience research centers.

## New isolated radio believers

A small but very significant side effect of Christian broadcasting is the total of 5 million isolated radio believers who have become Christians, and call themselves such, while living scattered at random across vast regions which have no churches or denominations. This mode of response to Christianity results in 400,000 new converts (believers) a year.

## New non-baptized believers in Christ

A related category of respondees is what this analysis is calling non-baptized believers in Christ. These are individuals, families, and small groups in the great world religions of Islam, Hinduism, and Buddhism, who have heard the gospel, have responded with believing faith, have accepted Christ as Lord, but have made the choice of remaining within those religions without joining the churches or becoming baptized, or even without calling themselves Christians. The grand total of all such non-baptized believers in Christ is over 30 millions by AD 2000.

### ASSESSING OVERALL RESPONSIVENESS, R

The most informative type of variable for measuring a population's actual overall response to Christian-

ity, evangelism, or evangelization, would be one that combines information about response with information about the amount of effort that Christians have inputted in order to produce that response. Obviously, if a population receives little or no evangelistic input done by Christians, no one should be surprised if it results in little or no output (new Christians) among that population.

Connecting 'output' with 'input' opens a whole new vista in the understanding of a population's situation with regard to Christianity, mission, and evangelism. At this stage we are not saying that there is a definite, causal connection between the actual amounts of input and output. We are simply defining each, describing each precisely, measuring each, comparing each, and then endeavoring to discover the implications and ultimately each's overall meaning and significance.

## Measuring output

The method of measuring these 2 categories' output and input for a population starts off as follows. 'Output' is the number of new Christians every year. This requires computation of the rate of growth of new Christians—new church members, to be precise. As described earlier, this has 3 elements: demographic increase, conversion increase, and transfer increase. It has already been computed in this analysis as, and labeled as, g % per year. The actual number of new Christians each year in a population of P persons of whom AC % are affiliated Christians is therefore:

New Christians per year = (P.AC/100)(g/100)
$$= \text{P.AC.g}/10,000.$$

## Measuring input

'Input' is the per capita rate of new evangelism—the number of evangelism-hours, or disciple-opportunities, or offers. It has been computed in Part 24 of this analysis as, and labeled as, e per capita per year. Since one evangelism-hour is a very small entity—like a single seed in agricultural planning, or one bit or byte in computing, or one mile in astronomy—we need to define and utilize a much larger evangelistic unit (as with one metric ton per hectare in grain production, or one gigabyte of computer memory, or one a.u.— astronomical unit, being the mean distance between the Earth and Sun, 93 million miles; or the even larger units parsec and light-year).

## Definition of standard evangelistic unit (SEU)

We meet this need here by creating a new standard evangelistic unit (SEU) defined as 1 million evangelism-hours or offers. It is the actual amount of input of evangelism-hours experienced by or reaching a population of P persons divided by 1 million. Its formula is:

New standard evangelistic units per year
$$= \text{Pe}/1,000,000.$$

The general order of magnitude of this unit can readily be visualized as follows in the following 12 one-line definitions. This is then expanded in the much larger analysis shown in Table 26–1.

One standard evangelistic unit (SEU) is the volume of evangelism engendered by any one of the following alternate activities:
- One radio preacher's one-hour sermon heard by an audience of 1 million
- 400,000 people seeing the 'Jesus' Film (2 hours 5 minutes, with 25 minutes local introduction and ending)
- A team of 10 foreign missionaries working with a population for 5 years
- 740 people reading the Bible right through
- 29,000 people each reading privately a printed gospel (35 pages)
- All 5.1 million full-time Christian workers each speaking to 12 persons for 1 minute
- All 648 million Great Commission Christians each witnessing to 1 person for 6 seconds
- 250 workers visiting 1,000 homes (4 persons a home) for an hour each
- A million people witnessing a martyrdom over a hostile regime's TV
- All existing 3.6 billion Christian books each being read by someone for 1 second
- The 5 million New Reader Scriptures printed per year each being read by somebody for 12 min-

## Table 26–1. Multiple ministry options for producing one standard evangelistic unit (one SEU= one million evangelistic offers).

Each line below describes a scenario which, for many peoples of the world, has already been producing the number of new baptisms or converts or new church members shown in *WCE* Part 8 "EthnoSphere", column 33, under the symbol R. Each line below therefore tells the reader how to generate sufficient evangelism to produce the result of one SEU (one million evangelistic offers) in order to generate the value of R (new baptisms per year), for any other people, city, or population anywhere in the world.

The concept *evangelism* is describable under 45 different types or varieties of ministry, as shown in the first 2 columns at left below. These are fully explained in Part 22 "Evangelism".

Several hundred enumerated variables for measuring these ministries are available from churches and missions. There are therefore literally thousands of combinations or activities that would each produce one million evangelistic offers. This exactly-defined variable is thus termed one standard evangelistic unit, or one SEU, equal to one million offers. The table below sets out 67 such activities. The first column gives the number, from 1 to 45, of the ministry being there illustrated. In some cases, 2 or 3 or even 4 lines are given to illustrate a major ministry. The reader wanting to know more of the method used (including the size of media factor employed when the number of end beneficiaries is unknown) can turn to that ministry's number in Part 22. Then in the main column below is set out a numerical scenario to reach one million offers. Each line contains the figures necessary to reach one million by clear thinking and simple multiplication. Each line could be varied in a multitude of ways; one could increase the number of persons involved, which would require a decrease in the unit of activity there described; and so on.

All these lines can be regarded as ministry options—possible ways of pursuing the goal of world evangelization. And they are multiple options indeed.

The value of enumerating the volume of evangelism going on in this way is that it alerts one to the likely size of numerical response in baptisms or conversions. Thus in *WCE* Part 8 "EthnoSphere", column 33 tells the reader the empirical value of R, which is the number of new church members per year in that population which are now being produced by one SEU. Also, in Part 28 "GeoTargeting", Table 28–5 gives a wide range of examples of this. Together, these tables offer mission strategists and missionaries a wealth of flexible tools with which to reach specific clearly-defined target populations.

| *Ministry (number and name)* | *A range of activities needed to each produce one million evangelistic offers (1 SEU)* |
|---|---|
| **HIDDEN WORDS** | |
| 1. Intercession | 200 million intercessors pray for a single specific ethnolinguistic people for 20 seconds. |
| Intercession | A district of 1,000 churches, of 100 members each, prays for unreached peoples for 12 minutes every Sunday morning for a year. |
| Intercession | A local prayer group of 100 intercessors prays for the unreached for 30 minutes every day for one year. |
| 2. Inner renewal | The world's 176 million Charismatics each pray for the unconverted for 20 seconds. |
| **VISUAL WORDS (AUDIOVISUALS)** | |
| 3. Christians' lifestyle | The fact that 100 million Christians demonstrate an attractive Christlike lifestyle is acknowledged in 50 words in a Muslim book. |
| Christians' lifestyle | The world's 2.4 billion evangelized non-Christians each observe the Christlike lifestyle of a Christian individual for 1 second. |
| Christians' lifestyle | A city of 10 million non-Christians reads a 6-minute newspaper account of a local Christian's Christlike behavior. |
| 4. Audiovisual ministries | The 1 billion reproductions of Sallman's *Head of Christ* are each looked at by one person for 3.6 seconds. |
| 5. 'Jesus' Film shows | In three days of viewings, 400,000 people see the 'Jesus' Film (the Gospel of Luke, 2.5 hours including presentation). |
| 'Jesus' Film shows | 1 million unevangelized persons each hear the name of Jesus for the first time. |
| 'Jesus' Film shows | 160 private video showings of the 2.5-hour 'Jesus' Film each attract 50 viewers who then each hold a further showing for 50. |
| 6. Plays/concerts/operas/shows | The 8-hour decennial performances of the Oberammergau Passion Play stun its audience of 530,000 with its climactic last 2 hours. |
| 7. Audio scriptures | Audio scriptures are broadcast at dictation speed to 1,000 listeners for 2.7 hours a day for one year. |
| Audio scriptures | The 1 million audio scriptures produced per year are each heard by somebody for 1 hour. |
| 8. Scripture leaflets/selections | 200 members of a local church each distribute, every Sunday for a year, 200 4-page Scripture selection leaflets. |
| 9. Every-home campaign visits | A church conducts a one-year campaign with 250 pairs of members each making a 30-minute visit to 10 4-person homes a week. |
| Every-home campaign visits | 250 church workers visit 1,000 homes (4 persons a home) for an hour each. |
| 10. New Reader Scriptures | The 5 million New Reader Scriptures printed per year are each read by somebody for 12 minutes. |
| 11. Braille scriptures | 260 nonsighted (blind) persons are enabled to each receive and read a New Testament in Braille (readable in 3,800 hours). |
| 12. Signed/deaf scriptures | 10,000 deaf persons (hearing-impaired) are each enabled to access signed scriptures for 100 hours. |
| 13. Christian suffering | 10 non-Christians observe the sufferings of 1,000 Christians under persecution for 5 hours every weekday for a month. |
| Christian suffering | A city of 1 million non-Christians watches a 5-minute TV news item describing the unjust sufferings of 12 local resident disciples. |
| **PERSONAL WORDS** | |
| 14. Personal evangelism | A local church of 1,000 members each witnesses to one person for one hour every day for 3 years. |
| Personal evangelism | All 648 million Great Commission Christians each witness 'Jesus is Lord' to 1 person for 6 seconds. |
| 15. Martyrdoms | A city of 100,000 non-Christians sees a 5-minute TV report of the martyrdom of 120 worshipers burned to death by fanatics. |
| Martyrdoms | A million people watch a 1-hour rigged martyrdom trial and execution over a hostile regime's TV. |
| **PROCLAIMED WORDS** | |
| 16. Full-time home church workers | A preacher preaches two 1-hour sermons to 1,000 people every Sunday for 10 years. |
| Full-time home church workers | 340 clergy or home church workers minister in pastoral evangelism to 2 persons each for 2 hours a day for 2 years. |
| Full-time home church workers | All 5.1 million full-time Christian workers each speak to 12 persons for 1 minute. |
| 17. Foreign missionaries | 10 foreign missionaries evangelize an ethnic population of 1,000 for 2 hours a day, for 7 weeks. |
| Foreign missionaries | A missionary nurse distributes food and medicines to 1,000 refugees in 4 camps on 21 days a month each for a year. |
| 18. Evangelists | 12 evangelists preach to 100 people for 15 minutes a day or 4 sermons a week for 10 years. |
| Evangelists | A macroevangelist preaches the gospel of Jesus to 1,000 people for 2 hours a night, 5 nights a week for 2 years. |
| Evangelists | A megaevangelist preaches the gospel of Jesus to 1 million people for 1 hour. |
| Evangelists | A global evangelist preaches the gospel of Jesus to 1 billion people for 3.6 seconds, saying 'The risen Lord Jesus Christ loves you.' |
| 19. Short-term missionaries | 270 short-term missionaries each evangelize 10 persons at a rate of one hour a day for one year. |
| Short-term missionaries | 27 short-term missionaries each evangelize 10 persons at a rate of an hour a day for 10 years. |
| 20. Part-time evangelizers | 500 teachers each speak about the Christian faith to a class of 40 pupils for one hour a week for one year. |
| Part-time evangelizers | 1,700 part-time evangelizers spend 48 minutes a day on 2 persons throughout one year. |
| 21. Mission agencies | A Great Commission agency undertakes 200 person-hours to plan a crusade to reach 100,000 abroad. |
| **WRITTEN WORDS** (Scriptures) | |
| 22. Portions/gospels | 330,000 people are each given and read a printed gospel (25 pages each, 3 hours to read). |
| 23. Near-gospels | 10 local church bookstores each sell or distribute 1,100 near-gospels a day (3 hours to read) in a one-month campaign. |
| 24. New Testaments | Using a tricycle, a colporteur distributes 10 New Testaments every weekday for 10 years. |
| 25. Near-New Testaments | A scripture-less tribe of 26,300 adults uses a new near-NT to meet their own needs for one copy each. |
| 26. Bibles | A megachurch of 6,250 Christians each sell or give a Bible to someone who agrees to read it right through and then does so. |
| 27. Near-Bibles | A newly-interested megapeople with no scriptures translated purchases 6,250 near-Bibles for its schools. |
| 28. 2nd-language gospels | A Bible agency mails out 900 second-language gospels every day for a year. |
| 29. 2nd-language NTs | Two colporteurs each distribute in one year 13,000 second-language New Testaments. |
| 30. 2nd-language Bibles | A national Bible society's book van sells 520 second-language Bibles a month for one year. |
| **PRINTED WORDS** (literature) | |
| 31. Denominational materials | A small denomination of 50,000 active members gets each to use or distribute ministry materials for 23 minutes a week for a year. |
| 32. Local church output | A large denomination of 1,000 local churches gets each to distribute evangelistic materials for 1,000 hours every year. |
| 33. Outside Christian literature | 10 foreign Christian books (each of 100 pages, 10 hours to read) are read by 1,000 local Christians monthly for a year. |
| 34. Church-planting output | A denomination plants 200 new churches, each after circulating 100 members with 500 pages of printed church growth materials. |
| 35. Institutional ministries/records | 270 Christian institutions produce or record 10 discipleship challenges/chances/offers each day for a year. |
| 36. Christian books | All existing 3.6 billion Christian books are each read by someone for 1 second. |
| 37. Christian periodicals | 3 issues are published of a 30-page Christian periodical with 1,100 circulation. |
| 38. Tracts | A missionary designs, prints, and gets distributed 2 million 2-page evangelistic tracts. |
| 39. Other documentation | A million Christians each write a letter with evangelistic content to a prisoner/refugee/victim/orphan. |
| **ELECTRONIC WORDS** | |
| 40. Programmed training | 33,000 listeners receive electronic programmed training on evangelism for 30 hours. |
| 41. Christian radio programs | A radio announcer broadcasts brief 5-minute devotions about Jesus each day for 4 months to an audience of 100,000 listeners. |
| Christian radio programs | In a 12-month period, 100,000 radio listeners hear one 1-hour evangelistic program monthly, or two 8-minute programs weekly. |
| 42. Christian TV programs | Ten consecutive nights of one TV preacher's one-hour program are seen by an audience of 100,000. |
| 43. Urban media (cable TV, &c) | In 2 metropolises, a year of urban media programs features electronic evangelism for 10,000 viewers for an hour a week. |
| 44. Christian owned computers | A church outreach network linking 2,740 computers originates 5,000 witness-words (one hour) a day for one year. |
| 45. Internet/networks/e-mail | The 198 million Christians who are Internet users each send somebody one e-mail evangelistic message of 33 words taking 24 seconds to read. |
| Internet/networks/e-mail | 100 Christians arrange to each send evangelistic messages over the Internet to 10 persons for 8 hours a day for 125 days. |
| Internet/networks/e-mail | A Christian information offer on the World Wide Web receives 1 million hits, downloading 5 billion evangelistic or discipling words. |

utes
- The 1 million audio scriptures produced per year each being heard by somebody for 1 hour.

A much more comprehensive listing of 64 definitions of this SEU is set out as Table 26–1.

### Measuring responsiveness, R

A population's actual responsiveness therefore, defined as output per input, is measured here as *new church members per year, per million offers* (disciple-opportunities, or received evangelism-hours) extended to the population and received by them per year. This is done by combining the above 2 formulas, as follows:

Responsiveness R = output/input = new church members per year/million evangelism-hours per year = (P.AC.g/10,000)/(Pe/1,000,000)

So,

R = 100AC.g/e.

Since the formula for e (see Part 24) is

e = 0.0365 AC.V,

this then gives as an alternate formula

R = 2740g/V

where g = new church member growth rate measured as % per year, and V=volume of demographic evangelization, identical with E (% of population evangelized) in all cases where V or E<99. This second formula for R is the simpler of the two to understand and utilize. It is therefore used here to compute values of R throughout this analysis.

### Interpreting global responsiveness to Christianity

For the world as a whole, these figures taken from Table 22-6 show that global Christianity in AD 2000 spent on evangelism a total evangelistic input of 206 billion evangelism-hours resulting in 938 billion disciple-opportunities or offers, or 938,000 standard evangelistic units (SEUs). Together these result in or produce 45 million baptisms or new church members across the world each year. This is a baptism rate of 2.5% per annum, which is virtually identical to the 1990–2000 global birth rate of 2.5%. From this standpoint, at least, organized Christianity is only just keeping up with the population explosion but is making no numerical gains or inroads beyond it.

This growth rate can be inserted in the formula R = 2740g/V, with the global evangelization figure of V =E =70, to give as the value for global responsiveness to Christianity 46 new church members per SEU. The figure is lowest in World C with its heavily christianized populations, higher in World B, but highest of all in World A where values of R rise to over 3000 among some countries and peoples. In World C with its universal value of V≥100 ) (meaning V is greater than or equal to 100), or more precisely 250>V>100 (V lies between 250 and 100), there is a direct relationship between R and g, expressed thus:

R≤27.4g

or more precisely

27.4g>R>10.96g.

This can be verbalized as responsiveness R lies between 11g and 27g. If the global value g = 2.5 is inserted, this produces a global responsiveness of between 68.5 and 27.4. This means that every million offers generated anywhere in World C results on average in from 27 to 68 new baptisms/conversions/responses somewhere on Earth.

By contrast, if the one million offers were generated in World A's unevangelized peoples, where V = E = 10 on average, the result would be a response of 685 new baptisms/conversions/responses.

### Analyzing a large state church

This enables us to understand the growth of the largest or majority church in any country. As an example, the Church of England, the established church in England, numbers within the borders of England 23 million baptized members and adds each year some 300,000 newly baptized persons (g = 1.3% p.a.), slightly lower than Britain's birth rate of 1.35% p.a. At the same time, however, other baptized members are exiting through the back door—mainly through deaths at the national rate of 1.14% p.a. Meanwhile, there is a nett immigration rate of 0.08% p.a.

The result of all this is the following brief analysis. Evangelism in the Church of England is so extensive and so all-pervasive that the variable V has reached its maximum value of 250. As a result, R = 27.4g = 35.6.

Verbalizing, every one million offers of discipleship extended to the English population by the Church of England produces a response of some 36 new persons baptized. Evangelizers wanting to see more results from their labors can be sympathized with if they both want and then attempt to find more responsive populations to work with. Comparative responses for R in different ethnolinguistic populations worldwide can be seen and contrasted in *WCE* Part 8 "EthnoSphere". Country response rates are presented in Table 12-1.

# Part 27

# GEOSTRATEGIES

1,500 global plans to evangelize the world: a kaleidoscopic synthesis

*We humans make plans, but the LORD has the final word.*
—Proverbs 16:1, Contemporary English Version

*This is the LORD's message for his rebellious people: 'You follow your own plans instead of mine; you make treaties without asking me.'*
—Isaiah 30:1, Contemporary English Version

The English world 'strategy' originates in 10 New Testament Greek words relating to, warfare, military service, armies, army divisions, camp, soldiers, magistrates. Parallels with a Christian disciple's service include *strateia* (military service), *stratia* (army), *strateuomai* (to serve in the army), *strategos* (general or military leader, governor, generalship), and *stratologeo* (to enlist for military service).

Part 27 documents and analyzes the Christian world's 1,500 distinct strategies or global plans to evangelize the world, proposed over the last 2,000 years. Despite massive allocation of personnel and money, most of these plans fizzled out within a decade. A kaleidoscopic synthesis building on all these plans is then tentatively proposed here under the name World Christian Global Action Plan (WCGAP).

# 1,500 global plans to evangelize the world: a kaleidoscopic synthesis

## I. ANALYSIS OF GLOBAL PLANS FROM AD 30–AD 2000

### What is a world evangelization plan?

This is a survey and analysis of 1,500 remarkably single minded plans, produced over the 20 centuries of the Christian era from AD 30, up to and including plans that were finally unveiled in the year 2000. These are Great Commission plans proposed by Great Commission Christians who have accepted the obligation to evangelize the world. These are called global plans, or simply plans. Each has attempted to answer the question: How can, or could, or should, or may, or might, or will the world become evangelized by the good news of Jesus Christ?

First, an important point to keep in mind: This is not a list of 1,500 approved or praiseworthy global plans! No one is saying they are all to be commended, or are commendable. This is a broad spectrum survey. On this subject a strictly descriptive—not prescriptive—stance is taken. Plans are reported on and described. They are neither approved or disapproved of. Any group's theology, christology, ecclesiology, or doctrine of Scripture is not being judged. Instead of theological criteria, missiological criteria are employed: What plans claim to be related to Christ's Great Commission and the great events arising out of it? Meanwhile, data are presented in such a way that any reader can easily go through Table 27–21, with a highlighter and draw up his or her own approved list.

Second, the obvious question: What is a plan? English dictionaries define it: 'plan. A scheme, program, outline, or sketch for doing something.' Similarly, the verb to plan means 'to devise a scheme, to have in mind as a project or purpose' (*Webster's New World dictionary of the American language*, 1984).

However, it is crucial for readers to remember that throughout the use of the word 'plan' transcends the standard dictionary definition. Here another obvious question arises: What constitutes a global plan? How concrete or how big does it have to be? How complex, or how comprehensive? How interdenominational? This question is answered by drawing up and applying some precise criteria and then developing an exact definition.

### Criteria for inclusion

1. *Intention*. There needs to be an overarching interest in, or concern for, one, several, or all of 10 major biblical themes: Christ's Great Commission, obedience of The Twelve Apostles, discipling the nations, global mission, worldwide witness and evangelism, world evangelization, the biblical End-times, rise of the Antichrist, Christ's Parousia (Second Advent), the Millennium. Of these, the first one for today's Christians to pay attention to is the Great Commission.

2. *Theological orientation*. Plans here are, or claim to be, broadly Christian, which means they (at least at origin) claim to be based on and centered on (a) the Bible as the Word of God and on Jesus Christ as Savior and Lord, and (b) all, or at least a majority, of the 10 biblical themes enumerated in the previous paragraph. These Great Commission plans are proposed by people who regard themselves at Great Commission Christians—all who claim to be Christians, who profess personal faith in Jesus Christ as Savior and Lord, and who profess to be motivated by Jesus' Great Commission.

   To be as broadly descriptive as possible requires that a handful of plans be included that are usually termed marginal Christian, or quasi-Christian, or pseudo-Christian. Including them indicates how difficult it is to classify religious phenomena in watertight compartments.

   Any other plans in which Christ and the Bible are not central are excluded—non-christocentric plans, partially Christian plans, syncretistic plans with Christian elements, or any based on non-Christian religions (Hinduism, Islam, New Age, et alia), or on interreligious, or multireligious, or interfaith, or quasireligious theological or philosophical positions.

3. *Scope*. A global plan must articulate a clear concern for the whole world. At the least, this implies use of words or phrases like 'world,' 'worldwide,' 'whole world,' 'entire world,' 'globe,' 'global,' 'universal,' 'intercontinental,' 'all nations' (in biblical Greek, *panta ta ethne*). If a plan is concerned only with one continent (such as Africa), or one region (such as the Middle East), or several localities, or a handful of countries (such as those in which an agency happens to have obtained footholds), then here it is not a global plan but is only partially global and so has to be termed primarily a nonglobal plan and thus to be excluded from the main list.

4. *Identity*. A global plan needs to have a recognized or recognizable identity as such, in the eyes of its immediate audience and also of the wider world of missions. This means the plan should have a title of its own, an author or proposer, a constituency or sponsor, a history of sorts, and some kind of documentation of its existence.

5. *Concreteness*. A plan needs to have an element of concreteness about it. It should at least contain one or two elements of the concrete or the definite, rather than being simply a vague or general call to win the world.

6. *Size*. One definition of 'plan' in Webster's, as noted above, is 'a sketch for doing something.' Obviously, the thousands of small, simple sketches that must have been put forward on this subject over 20 centuries are not included here. Extreme brevity or smallness is clearly a criterion for exclusion. But, then, neither is large size of itself a criterion for inclusion. Much depends on the context.

   In earlier centuries, some single sermons, or single documents, or single slogans, have had as much impact and influence as any of today's gargantuan schemes. However, the central plans of major denominations or missions or parachurch agencies which each have work in over 50 nations of the world, or which each have over 5,000 foreign missionary personnel, are included in cases where they have long publicized a clear global Great Commission goal.

7. *Uniqueness*. Each plan must have something unique or different about it. It can't simply repeat earlier attempts or statements.

8. *Complexity*. Plans can vary from very simple to very complex. As with scientific formulas like Einstein's $e=mc^2$, the simplest plans may well be the most profound. But even a simple plan, to be included here, must have inherent complexity within it, like a seed has.

9. *Linkages*. Many plans, especially since the year 1800, are linked with, or even part of, wider plans. A number of the Catholic plans in the 1990s are closely linked, at least in theory. However, as long as each has its own separate identity, name, organization, offices, officers, budget, goals, etc, it is included in the listing. Such linkage therefore need not necessarily exclude plans from the listing, if they clearly have their own separate identity.

10. *Ethics*. Since this is a total listing of all known plans, some will inevitably be questionable. Many plans incorporate unethical elements in them. Several are clearly racist. Plans having a racist or other unethical presupposition are not excluded. This means the list is a listing of all plans good or bad. By compiling this listing plans are neither judged, nor approved, nor legitimized. They are simply reported.

11. *Exclusiveness*. Many plans are exclusive (excluding the rest of the Christian world) giving the impression that they intend to evangelize the world without anyone else's assistance. Many others are inclusive, specifying that the cooperation of other churches and agencies is essential to their vision or plan. So a global plan can be inclusive or exclusive; it can also be monodenominational, or monoconfessional, or it can be interdenominational (controlled by a number of denominations), or ecumenical; or it can be nondenominational, with the issue of church affiliation ignored (sometimes called the parachurch approach). It seems to make little difference to a plan's appeal or clout. In fact, exclusive plans, or plans made by only a single denomination, have often had a clear edge over the rest in cohesiveness, cutting edge, clout, funding, and availability of personnel.

12. *Literature*. All plans have some write-up describing their features—either a few paragraphs, some correspondence, or printed leaflets or brochures, or even a fullscale book or books. Even a brief passing reference in the literature is sufficient to document its existence. These plans are not merely verbal or aural proposals or ideas, but plans which have to some degree, large or small, at least entered the literature and are on record.

13. *Significance*. The ultimate criterion is this: Is this plan sufficiently significant to be included in such a listing? To determine this each plan is carefully considered not only in terms of the above criteria, but also in the context of all the other plans, and of the whole list.

### Varieties of plans

Once the above criteria are satisfied, plans are found to come in a wide variety of forms or formats. The listing includes at least the following 67 varieties, graded from (0) the absence of human plans to (10) massively-detailed master plans. The 67 varieties in 11 groups, are arranged as follows:

0. Visions, scenarios, views, End-time panoramas.
1. Calls, appeals, slogans, mottoes, challenges.
2. Sermons, edicts, encyclicals, charges, letters.
3. Documents, reports, books, treatises, articles, analyzes, surveys, assessments, periodicals, publications.
4. Promises, pledges, intents, proposals, declarations, conferences, conference resolutions.
5. Unorganized attempts, undertakings, movements, campaigns, events, drives, enterprises, networks.
6. Statements by ongoing bodies: organizations, groups, structures, committees, councils, boards, societies.
7. Announcements, outlines, plans, projects, aims, goals.
8. Designs, methods, ways, procedures, processes, formulations, tactics.
9. Detailed schemes, schemas, strategies, programs.
10. Master blueprints, timetables, schedules.

### Definition of a global plan

Therefore, this is how a world evangelization plan is defined:

1. A documented, christocentric plan, proposal, purpose, program, scenario, or something of a similar variety, that presupposes or starts from one or more of 10 central biblical themes (see No. 1 under criteria for inclusion above);
2. Which then articulates concern for the world's entire population;
3. And demonstrates this concern in a call or appeal to Christians to implement or envision a plan with a number of concrete elements;
4. Which plan has adequate global significance, by virtue of either its timing, or context, or novelty, or appeal, or persuasiveness, or impact, or uniqueness of any of its parts;
5. Or, by virtue of its global extent, in cases where

its sponsoring organization has work in over 50 nations of the world, or sends out over 5,000 foreign missionaries.

### Summary of types of plan

This 11-fold typology of 67 varieties of plans listed above is then used to code the table of 1,500 plans in Tables 27-19 and 27-21. The coded data can be seen in its column 6. A global analysis of the data by this typology is then given in Table 27-2.

Rearranged alphabetically, the above varieties of plans can be abbreviated to the following list of 66 types of plan:

| | | |
|---|---|---|
| Aims | Enterprises | Proposals |
| Announcements | Events | Publications |
| Appeals | Formulations | Reports |
| Articles | Goals | Resolutions |
| Assessments | Groups | Scenarios |
| Attempts | Intents | Schedules |
| Blueprints | Letters | Schemas |
| Boards | Methods | Schemes |
| Books | Mottoes | Sermons |
| Calls | Movements | Slogans |
| Campaigns | Networks | Societies |
| Challenges | Organizations | Statements |
| Charges | Outlines | Strategies |
| Committees | Panoramas | Structures |
| Conferences | Periodicals | Surveys |
| Councils | Plans | Tactics |
| Declarations | Pledges | Timetables |
| Designs | Procedures | Treatises |
| Documents | Processes | Undertakings |
| Drives | Programs | Views |
| Edicts | Projects | Visions |
| Encyclicals | Promises | Ways |

### Summarizing the 1,500 plans

Using the 13 criteria above for inclusion, in Table 27-21 each plan is described, using 15 variables. The whole corpus of plans is described, characterized, and classified by these 15 variables. In addition, estimates are given for the number of other plans generated by the six major ecclesiastical blocs from 1990-2000 in Table 27-19. These are then broken down by the various codes mentioned above. Table 27-19 gives the ecclesiastical origins of these 650 other plans.

The 90 largest of these plans are listed below in Table 27-1. These megaplans have the largest resource base and today are being massively implemented. For the most part, these 1,500 plans have been and are concerned with getting out the amazing news of Jesus Christ as Savior and Lord to all the peoples of the entire world.

### GOD'S GLOBAL PLAN IN BIBLICAL TIMES

In the beginning, God created the heavens and the earth. By bringing into being this cosmos out of chaos, God showed that he is a God of order, of planning, of strategy. God has a plan for his world, a global plan into which all of us fit one way or another.

The secret of successful living is to find out about God's plan for the world and to make ourselves useful enough to fit into it.

The first foreshadowing of what in the New Testament came to be called the Great Commission was the commission given by God to man in Genesis 1:28: 'Be fruitful and multiply, and fill the earth.'

Elaborations of this commission occur throughout Genesis and the rest of the Pentateuch and on into the historical books. After the biblical Flood about BC 4000 came a second foreshadowing of the later Great Commission. After the Flood receded, God commissioned Noah: 'Be fruitful and multiply, and fill the earth' (Gen. 9:1, RSV).

### Four Great Commissions

The biblical mandate for world evangelization arises from the beginning of Holy Scripture and works itself out in various ways in the Old Testament before becoming more explicit in the New. The mandate rests ultimately on four 'great commissions': (1) The commission to Abraham (Gen. 12:1-3, 'leave . . . go'); (2) The Great Commission for Israel (Psalm 96:3, 'Declare my glory among the nations'); (3) The Great Commission of Jesus to the Twelve (Matt. 28:19, 20, 'Go . . . and make disciples of all nations'); (4) The commission to the apostle Paul (Rom. 1:5, 'Bring about obedience to the faith among all nations').

He made his plan clear first to Abraham and then to the nation of Israel. From the beginning, however, God was not a narrow, nationalistic God. He revealed that he would not only make of Abraham a great nation, but that through him 'all peoples on earth' would be blessed (Gen. 12:3; 18:18; 22:18; 26:4; 28:14).

Essentially, God's Old Testament missionary plan rested with Abraham and Israel. The Old Testament makes two things clear: God did have a special relationship with Israel. He chose this people in a unique way to be his own people. However, equally important, none of the nations of the world escape his authority. In distinctive ways, he also uses them to accomplish his purposes.

Israel was never isolated from the flesh and blood world of politics, economics, and sociology. Her people suffered in the warp and woof of the ancient Middle East. At the same time, they enjoyed the exalted privilege of knowing and serving the one true and living God.

With that privilege came the awesome duty of bearing light to the holiness, truthfulness, and

---

## Table 27-1. The top 90 current ongoing global megaplans, with the top 31 current gigaplans, AD 2000.

This survey enumerates and lists 1,500 global plans. Of these 1,500, 90 are here termed **megaplans** defined as the largest currently-expanding organized global plans expending massive organized resources (shown as codes 5 and 6 in column 13, 'Resources', in Table 27-21), which were still in AD 2000 alive and being massively implemented across the world (shown as code 9 in column 16, 'Status', in Table 27-21). A megaplan is thus a hundred-million-dollar plan, or project (spending more than US$100 million over, on average, one decade, or since origin). Of these 90 megaplans (which are those listed in this table below), 31 are here also termed **gigaplans** (shown below in boldface type). A gigaplan is defined as a current billion-dollar plan or project or megaplan or megaproject (spending around a billion dollars or more over one decade, or since origin; shown as code 6 in column 13, 'Resources', in Table 27-21).

Note that these plans are not all completely distinct and separate from each other. Several have close links among themselves, and a handful are different plans put forward at different times by the same organization (See Table 27-21 under specific years for explanations of individual cases).

The table below sets out the 90 megaplans and 31 gigaplans in reverse chronological order by year of origin (year of initial implementation), using exact brief names as listed in Table 27-21. For further data on any specific plan or megaplan or gigaplans, consult both Table 27-21 and Table 27-22 under its stated year of origin.

The end column at the right below gives the deadline or year of final closure, if announced in this megaplan (as given in column 13, Table 27-21).

| Origin | Brief name of megaplan | Deadline | Origin | Brief name of megaplan | Deadline |
|---|---|---|---|---|---|
| 1998 | Confronting the Queen of Heaven | 2000 | 1934 | Two Thousand Tongues To Go | — |
| 1994 | **Unreached Peoples Prayer Profiles** | 2000 | 1934 | Youth for Christ International | — |
| 1993 | *Operation world* | 2000 | 1931 | Laudetur Jesus Christus (Radio Vatican) | — |
| 1991 | 7th Assembly, World Council of Churches | — | 1930 | Voice of Prophecy | — |
| 1991 | *Redemptoris Missio* | 2000 | 1930 | Bringing Christ to the Nations (The Lutheran Hour) | — |
| 1988 | Evangelistic mass campaigns: Christ for All Nations | — | 1928 | **Opus Dei** | — |
| 1988 | March for Jesus | 2000 | 1924 | United Pentecostal Church International | — |
| 1987 | **New Life 2000: A Revolutionary Plan (Here's Life World)** | 2000 | 1921 | **Legion of Mary** | — |
| 1986 | 2nd International Conference for Itinerant Evangelists | — | 1918 | Worldwide Evangelism | — |
| 1985 | God's Global Envoys: Nonresidential Missionaries | 2000 | 1917 | **Interdenominational Foreign Mission Association** | — |
| 1985 | **Integrity Keepers Conventions** | 1995 | 1913 | Christ's Etceteras (Worldwide Evangelization Crusade) | — |
| 1985 | International Catholic Programme of Evangelization | — | 1910 | Church of God (Cleveland) World Missions | — |
| 1985 | The World by 2000 | 2000 | 1899 | Gideons International | — |
| 1983 | Christian broadcasting worldwide | — | 1895 | Association of Pentecostal Churches in America (Nazarene) | — |
| 1982 | Global papal apostolic travels | — | 1893 | Africa Industrial Mission/SIM International | — |
| 1979 | **The Jesus Project ('Jesus' Film)** | 2000 | 1890 | Scandinavian/Evangelical Alliance Mission | — |
| 1977 | Focus on the Family | — | 1887 | Christian & Missionary Alliance | — |
| 1975 | World Evangelical Fellowship Missions Commission | — | 1882 | **Knights of Columbus** | — |
| 1974 | Lausanne Committee for World Evangelization | — | 1875 | Verbites: 'Evangelizzazione dei Popoli' | — |
| 1974 | **3rd Synod of Bishops: 'The Evangelization of the Modern World'** | — | 1872 | Salesian Sisters: evangelization by works of charity | — |
| 1973 | **Trinity Broadcasting Network** | — | 1870 | **Watch Tower Bible & Tract Society** | 1874 |
| 1972 | **International Catholic Charismatic Renewal** | — | 1865 | Christian Revival Association | — |
| 1972 | **Marian Movement of Priests** | — | 1863 | **New Apostolic Church** | — |
| 1969 | 'Peace on Earth' International Assemblies | 1975 | 1862 | Scheutists: 'Evangelizzazione dei popoli' | — |
| 1969 | **Jimmy Swaggart Ministries** | — | 1859 | Salesians: Christian education of youth across world | — |
| 1968 | African Independent Churches Service | — | 1845 | **Southern Baptist Convention** | — |
| 1967 | **Sacred Congregation for the Evangelization of Peoples** | — | 1844 | **Seventh-day Adventists** | 1844 |
| 1961 | Commission on World Mission and Evangelism | — | 1844 | World Alliance of YMCAs/World YWCA | — |
| 1961 | **Christian Broadcasting Network/CBN World Outreach** | — | 1831 | Presbyterian Church in the United States | — |
| 1960 | Baptist International Missions | — | 1830 | **Church of Jesus Christ of Latter-day Saints** | — |
| 1960 | **Youth With A Mission** | — | 1824 | Interdenominational citywide cooperative evangelism | — |
| 1957 | Operation Mobilization/Send The Light | — | 1819 | **Missionary Society of the Methodist Episcopal Church** | — |
| 1956 | Charismatic Movement (Second Wave, Renewal in the Holy Spirit) | — | 1810 | American Board of Commissioners for Foreign Missions | — |
| 1950 | Baptist Bible Fellowship International | — | 1804 | Foreign-language Bible Societies: BFBS, ABS, et alia | — |
| 1950 | Billy Graham Evangelistic Association | — | 1703 | Spiritans: 'Evangelizzazione degli infedeli' | — |
| 1950 | Full Gospel Businessmen's Fellowship International | — | 1680 | Christian Brothers: evangelization by schools | — |
| 1950 | Missionaries of Charity | — | 1622 | **Propaganda Fide: Spreading the Faith to the World** | — |
| 1950 | **World Vision International** | — | 1588 | **Consistorial Congregation (Sacred Congregation for Bishops)** | — |
| 1948 | World Council of Churches, 7th Function | — | 1580 | Discalced Carmelite Sisters: evangelization by prayer | — |
| 1947 | **Oral Roberts Evangelistic Association** | — | 1523 | **Conversion of Islam and the Whole World to Christ (Jesuits)** | — |
| 1946 | **United Bible Societies** | — | 1500 | Saints and martyrs as evangelizing witnesses | — |
| 1945 | **Evangelical Foreign Missions Association** | — | 1450 | Dissemination of Scriptures by typography and printing | — |
| 1943 | Conservative Baptist Foreign Mission Society | — | 1260 | Religious art: painting, stained glass, sculpture | — |
| 1943 | National Religious Broadcasters | — | 1215 | **Order of Preachers: 'Propagation of the Faith through Preaching'** | — |
| 1942 | New Tribes Mission | — | 1209 | **Order of Friars: mendicant orders of travelling preachers** | |

supreme authority of God Almighty, the one who spoke to Moses and the prophets. Amid gross immorality, injustice, oppression, and corrupt religion, Israel was called not only to be holy, but to be a 'light to the nations' (Isa. 42:6).

God wanted his salvation to 'reach to the end of the earth' (Isa. 49:6). But Israel somehow never learned how to preserve inward integrity and outward witness at the same time. In fact, nationalist emotions, political intrigue, and international double-dealing often aroused the fiercest calls for God's judgment on her enemies.

Nevertheless, God brought strangers to Israel who enjoyed his favor. King Solomon prayed magnanimously for their welfare (2 Chron. 6:32-33). He seemed to have caught God's missionary heart at that moment. The basis of his petition was that 'all the peoples of the earth may come to know thy name and fear thee.'

The prophets spoke of that spectacular time when the tide of the nations would flow toward Jerusalem. Isaiah cried out, 'Turn to me and be saved, all the ends of the earth!' (45:22).

Generally, however, God's Old Testament global plan of witness and salvation fell victim to perversity, disobedience, and idolatry, for which his special people were severely judged. The 70-year captivity in Babylon produced startling changes. Israel not only lost her desire to play the harlot with foreign gods, she also became missionary. Scattered far and near, Israelites became proselytizers for their faith.

Although despised by the Romans, to all who would listen the Jews brought hope for a coming Messiah, a moral lifestyle, a written Scripture, and places of learning and worship. They stood out faithfully against oppressive paganism and moral disarray. But when Messiah came, they missed him.

Careful reading and study of the Old Testament show that God did not quit on the world, despite the failure of his chosen missionary instruments. He still plans for the day when 'the earth will be filled with the knowledge of the glory of the Lord, as the waters cover the sea' (Hab. 2:14).

The Old Testament closes with that fervent hope firmly fixed. Hundreds of years later God acted again, choosing a people—the church of Jesus Christ—to be his missionary vessel.

***God's plan in Christ***

God's plan of world redemption called for the incarnation. Jesus Christ the eternal Word became flesh. Those who believed in him became members of a universal body, the church. With faith came allegiance to his purpose.

Christians caught the spirit of Jesus' commission and fanned throughout the Roman Empire with the good news of forgiveness and salvation. Instinctively, it seemed, they knew what to do when Jesus told them to 'go and make disciples of all nations.' Filled with the Holy Spirit, they were his 'witnesses in Jerusalem, and in all Judea and Samaria, and to the ends of the earth' (Acts 1:8).

Remarkably, the missionary vision was carried out not just by professionals, so to speak, but by the entire church body. What we call laymen or laypersons or laity were not excluded. The dynamic of the Holy Spirit controlled and impelled the body.

Nor were there any organized missionary boards or societies as we know them today. Even the historian Will Durant observed that 'Nearly every convert, with the ardor of a revolutionary, made himself an office of propaganda.'

The church shattered narrow racial and nationalistic concerns. Paul accepted God's direction to take the message to the Gentiles. Peter, after a dramatic vision, saw that Gentiles were included in God's saving purposes.

Missions overrode social and class distinctions as well. Slaves and freemen alike, poor and rich, educated and uneducated, men and women, cultured and uncultured—they all found a place in the scope of world evangelization.

***God's master plan***

The *locus classicus* of God's master plan for the universe is found in Ephesians 1-3. Note the following:

'God has allowed us to know the secret of his plan, a plan for the fullness of time, to unite all things in him, things in heaven and things on earth' (1:9, 10, NTME, RSV).

We were chosen in Christ, 'having been predestined according to the plan of him who works out everything in conformity with the purposes of his will' (1:11, IV).

This was part of God's secret plan from the very beginning (3:9).

According to God's wisdom, his plan is being worked out through the church (3:10).

His plan centers in Jesus Christ our Lord. He deserves honor, glory, praise, and dominion 'because of his master plan of salvation for the church' (3:21, LB).

God's own master plan for the world is to sum up all things in Christ. It is a great privilege to be summoned to participate in his magnificent plan.

## *THREE PLAUSIBLE GLOBAL PLANS*

***Jesus rejects three tempting plans, AD 30***

'All authority in heaven and on earth has been given to me,' Jesus told his disciples before sending them to make disciples in all nations. But before he arrived at that plan for world evangelization, he had grappled with several plausible alternatives. These plans for world conquest came from none other than the devil himself.

The first scheme was a precursor of many plans today: offer the world physical and material prosperity. 'Command these stones to become bread,' the tempter said (Matt. 4:3; Luke 4:3).

In effect, Satan proposed an economic miracle. Satisfy man's immediate needs, provide food out of rocks—especially appropriate in Palestine where only one-fifth of the land was arable. 'Become an economic Messiah and you will win the world,' Satan was saying.

What an enticing possibility, one that typifies the best of man's economic and political thinking today. Offer the masses a higher standard of living and you can win votes, power, and control, whether by Marxism or capitalism. Tragically, churches and Christian institutions can slide into this method of world evangelization, even from the best of motives.

Jesus dismissed the thought out of hand, desperately hungry though he was, having fasted 40 days in the wilderness. But Satan attacked again, offering another quite plausible plan: be a miracle worker. 'Throw yourself down (from the pinnacle),' Satan urged him (Matt. 4:6; Luke 4:9).

According to this plan, you give the world a convincing sign, a spectacular miracle, some cheap thrills. You appeal to human desires to transcend the limits of their mortality. Of course, Satan implied, you claim divine protection and compel God to prove your Messianic claims by saving you.

Some modern plans border on this approach. They rest on miracles, so to speak, to validate their authenticity. They also promise various kinds of deliverances from apparently hopeless situations. They might well deserve Karl Marx's dictum that religion is the opiate of the people. But Jesus once again rejected this plausible plan. He reminded Satan that it was wrong to tempt God this way.

The adversary of men's souls launched a final plan at Jesus: worship me and all the world will be yours (Matt. 4:9; Luke 4:7). Political power plays are not new. How attractive they are, but at what a price—selling out to the devil. But if you do, according to this plan, you can produce a political miracle. For example, Jesus could unite six million Jews against their Roman overlords. Jesus could use secular power to enforce his moral demands.

This plan appeals to the universal desire for power. It satisfies patriotic passions. It wins the world by force, not by faith. In effect, Jesus would become a political Messiah.

Jesus stormed back at Satan and reaffirmed allegiance to God alone. No, plausible as the political plan sounded, it was not worth the price. Yet, the temptation remains to use power plays even for worthwhile missionary purposes. But the world will not be won that way.

When one contemplates global plans, one can expect to be hit by what Dostoyevski's Grand Inquisitor called the temptations of Jesus: 'universal temptations.' Christians drawing up global plans over the past 1,970 years have constantly been assaulted by the devil's quite plausible plans. The following analysis of the data shows that many plans have collapsed and some have been coopted by the devil.

Malcolm Muggeridge in his famous lectures on *Christ and the media* portrays what he calls Jesus's fourth temptation: Satan offers him prime time on Rome television to preach his gospel to the entire world. Jesus refuses. But this possible scenario warns us that the devil cleverly changes tactics according to the prevailing culture. All of our plans are subject to subversion.

It's quite easy, of course, to look at the temptations of Jesus as purely personal. Obviously, Satan intended to divert him from obedience to his Father's will. The Father's will was a plan for Jesus to accomplish the world's salvation through pain and agony. So, it is quite fair to say that God's worldwide redemptive plan was at stake in the temptation.

Satan truly offered the King of Kings and Lord of Lords three alternatives to God's plan, any one of which would have been fatal. We can well imagine that Jesus reflected long and hard on what course to follow. Here was a case in which one person's obedience or disobedience meant choosing God's plan or one of the devil's.

Luke shows us that the devil never let up on Jesus (4:13). In Gethsemane, Jesus faced the issue in a final encounter. Did God's saving plan really require his humiliation, suffering, rejection, and abandonment? At that moment could Jesus have reflected back on one of the devil's earlier offers?

To sum up, Satan tempted Jesus to follow three cunningly concocted global plans for world conquest. In a word, they were (1) become an economic Messiah; (2) become a miraculous Messiah; and (3) become a political Messiah. Jesus rejected them all.

The main reason that so many of the grandiose schemes have come to naught is that global plans originate with ordinary Christians who are sinful, fallible, biased, proud, and even bigoted. They have been subject to the same temptations as Jesus. Unlike him, however, they have fallen.

The 1,500 plans have all suffered their share of temptations. Many have not just fallen; they have fallen openly, brazenly, grossly, and, in some cases, scandalously. Christians working for world evangelization need, therefore, to pray, 'Lead us not into temptation.'

As defined here, global plans are plans about how to follow Jesus, how to enroll disciples, how to herald the kingdom of God, and how to promote God's plan for the world.

In today's euphoric missionary triumphalism, we need to reflect again on the roots of our plans in the obedient suffering of Jesus Christ. The survey and analysis that follow cannot be read like the telephone book. They call us to critical self-analysis of our motives and our methods. Whose are they? Christ's or Satan's?

## *OBEYING THE GREAT COMMISSION*

***An analysis of 1,500 global plans, proposals, and scenarios, from AD 30-AD 2000***

It was noted earlier that the 1,500 global plans exist in 67 varieties and fall into 11 major groups or types.

Table 27–21 lists the 1,500 plans in the same order and describes each of them on a single line, using 16 columns. Of these 16 variables, or descriptors, the first is a reference number to help the reader count. Two are dates (years). Five are names or initials. Six are digits whose codes 0-14 have standard meanings. Two are numerical. Table 27–19 shows the same data, though in a different format.

***The tip of the iceberg***

The list of 1,500 plans is not exhaustive. They are, in fact, only the tip of the iceberg. Probably scores of plans have been drawn up but lost without historical records. Today, plans appear to proliferate like rabbits, but they disappear just as rapidly.

Several plans announced in the 1990s have already fizzled or collapsed. Some plans announced very recently, with great fanfare, have already collapsed because of internal disagreements. One or two were publicly disclaimed within a few days of their being announced.

***Reference number***

The numbers in the first column in Table 27–21 enumerate the total situation. Using the definition of a

**Global plans to evangelize the world** (read clockwise from top left): (1) **AD 30.** 'The Kingdom of God has arrived.' (Japanese print); (2) **AD 65.** Worldwide proclamation by three angels (John on Patmos). (3) **AD 197.** The blood of the martyrs is the seed.' (4) **AD 510.** Celtic peregrini and the Book of Kells. (5) **AD 635.** Nestorian world missions. (6) **AD 1209.** Order of Friars Minor. (7) **AD 1523.** Conversion of Islam and the whole world (Ignatius Loyola). (8) **AD 1792.** William Carey's *Enquiry*. (9) **AD 1885.** D.L. Moody's 'An Appeal to Disciples Everywhere.' (10) **AD 1910.** World Missionary Congress, Edinburgh, Scotland. (11) **AD 1934.** W. Cameron Townsend: Summer Institute of Linguistics. (12) **AD 1948.** Logo, World Council of Churches. (13) **AD 1958.** Greek Orthodox Missiological quarterly *Porefthendes.* and its editor Abp Yannoulatos. (14) **AD 1979.** Jesus Film shown to millions. (15) **AD 1995.** Billy Graham preaches to over 2 billion in Global Mission.

global plan (see above), this column gives an overview of a major finding, which is that over 20 centuries of Christian history, at least 1,500 global plans have been put forward. This is a staggering number. They are listed by number just so readers can keep track of them and see them in relation to history. The reference numbers facilitate further investigation and analysis.

### Type of plan
The number of plans that can be described under each of the 11 major groups, or types, are shown in Table 27–2.

Of the 1,500 plans, then, 631 (or 42%, being codes 7-10) are organized, formal plans, that is, plans properly so called. Of these, 120 are or were massively-detailed blueprints. Perhaps the largest of these before our present generation was the Interchurch World Movement in 1918 with its massive 2-volume *World survey*.

Another 691 (or 46%) can, more correctly perhaps, be called semi-plans; they have the essentials of plans, but are not fully organized as such. And 188 (or 12.5%) claim to be seeing or presenting not human plans but God's own plan for the End-times and the fate of the world.

### Ministry
Table 27–3 analyzes the main types of outreach ministry or method set forth, proposed, emphasized, or envisaged, if any, or on which the plans center. The 15 types are arranged as responses to the 7 constituent Mandates (in bold capitals) of the Great Commission, each of which is followed below by the generic name for such ministry to non-Christian and unevangelized populations.

### Printed documentation
Documentation by, of, and about global plans is important in ensuring their viability, influence and durability. Table 27–4 analyzes printed descriptions of each plan and the significance of literature about it.

## DISOBEYING THE GREAT COMMISSION

### Year of origin of plan
When did all these plans arise? A quick glance at Table 27–21 shows how they are spread out over the centuries and over recent years. A number of interesting patterns and trends can be discussed from such an analysis.

Of the 1,500 plans, 100 (7%) arose before the Protestant Reformation and 256 (17%) arose before AD 1900. One-third of them (500) occurred before 1967 and the other two-thirds since then. By 1984, one new plan a month was appearing; by 1985, one every two weeks. By 1990 one a week, which is over 50 a year, or over 1,500 a generation.

## A CATALOGUE OF WOES

### 340 reasons for 665 failed global plans
Like a sudden thunderstorm crashing on the annual church picnic, failure drenches the record of 1,500 global evangelization plans. Over the last 2,000 years, 665 plans have failed. Not only that, but 585 current plans are in danger of collapse. Why this abysmal record? What can be learned from this sad process?

The chronology of all global plans in Table 27–21 gives many reasons, but one example is a dramatic, captivating plan of 100 years ago with striking parallels today. On August 14, 1885, evangelist Dwight L. Moody and six leaders of the Northfield, Massachusetts, Convention produced 'An Appeal to Disciples Everywhere,' which urged Christians to evangelize the world by 1900. It said:

> If but ten million, out of 400 million nominal Christians, would undertake such systematic labor as that each one of that number should, in the course of the next 15 years, reach 100 other souls with the gospel message, the whole present population of the globe would have the good tidings by the year 1900!

This was a serious call and global plan, typical of hundreds of others. It was earnest, prayerful, determined. Yet within 10 years of its being proposed it was dead, its sponsors admitting that it no longer stood any chance of being achieved.

This heroic challenge to world evangelization did not find the response it sought. The reasons were many, but perhaps the key one was that it was a movement conceived only from the Western church. It did not come from the universal church. Nor did it sufficiently comprehend the obstacle of culture and political and language barriers. Nor did it work out exactly how each of the 10 million zealots were to locate his or her own group of 100 unevangelized souls.

Moving back to the larger puzzle of 665 failed plans, the temptation of Jesus provides some clues.

### Bad and good plans
Jesus faced three types of potential global plans: (1) Be an economic Messiah; (2) Be a miraculous Messiah; (3) Be a political Messiah. But Jesus instead crafted a global plan, with 7 mandates: Receive! Go! Witness! Proclaim! Disciple! Baptize! Train! Throughout his ministry, he fought the battle of good and bad plans.

When the 665 failed plans are examined, certain major groups of reasons emerge for their demise. These constitute a catalogue of woes. They are organized in Table 27–5 under the three-fold schema of Christ's temptations.

First are failures that center on insufficient resources. Jesus warned his disciples about the folly of building a tower without first collecting the necessary manpower, money, and materials (Luke 14:28-30). 'This man began to build, and was not able to finish,' he said.

Second are failures related to signs, wonders, miracles, healings, personalities, and personal inadequacies.

Third are failures related to politics, power, and empire building.

Table 27–5 classifies reasons and causes put forward by historians and other observers. Obviously, these are condensed and combined because many reasons are very similar. The three-fold typology corresponding to the temptations of Jesus is suggestive only. It does not imply that all causes can be forced into such a mold. Further, many reasons overlap the three major categories.

The 53 items in boldface type are reasons or causes external to the churches and beyond their control. All the rest of the items, 287 in number, shown in medium type, relate to internal problems within the church and the Christian world. This makes it clear that Christians cannot blame external circumstances for their 1,970-year failure to obey their Lord's commission.

## SEVENTY COUNTRIES, FIFTY TRADITIONS

### Country of origin
Global evangelization plans have originated in virtually all parts of the world. Table 27–7 gives the precise information. Names of countries are used as they were when the plans originated, not as they are now.

To AD 500, all plans originated in countries bordering the Mediterranean Sea, mainly in the Middle East. From then until 1700, plans came almost entirely from Europe and Asia, from Ireland to China. Exceptions were plans from Mexico in 1523, from North America in 1725, and from the Caribbean in 1783.

Then the United States of America began to generate plans, totaling 45 from 1800 to 1900. The center of gravity shifted from Europe to North America. Since 1900 the United States has produced some 300 plans.

But since 1950 another massive shift has taken place, this time from the North (the industrialized, affluent Western nations) to the South (the underdeveloped and developing countries known as the Third World). Since 1980 in fact, 300 global plans have originated in Third World countries.

To summarize, in AD 2000 there are 238 countries in the world. Of these, 60 are Developed nations, 130 are Less-developed nations, and 48 are Least-developed countries, sovereign and nonsovereign. Global evangelization plans have arisen in 77 countries: 27 Developed, 37 Less-developed, and 13 Least-developed.

### The contribution of Europe
This research overturns stereotypes, one of which is that Europe has become post-Christian, if not outright pagan. Admittedly Europe has great spiritual needs, but Europe has responded to the Great Commission by initiating 300 global plans, most of them in the 20th century. In fact, Europe is producing more plans than the United States.

### The contribution of the Third World
When the first list of global plans was published in May, 1987, Pedro Arana-Quiroz from Peru wrote: 'Really, it is an impressive list, but all the examples belong to North American organizations... Has the Korean church planned for world evangelization?'

As a result specific inquiries about plans originating in Third World countries were made. The results were surprising. Global evangelization plans have been produced by Christians in more countries of the Developing World (50) than in the Developed World (27).

Despite the dominance of European and North American influence in world missions, Third World Christians are making a strong contribution. They have produced 40 percent of all plans.

### A global evangelization movement
Therefore, it is safe to conclude that throughout 20 centuries of Christian history, the movement to evangelize the world has sprung from every continent and corner of the globe. This extraordinary devel-

---

**Table 27–2. 1,500 global plans arranged by 11 types.**

*(Source: Table 27–19, and column 6 of 27–21)*

| Code 1 | Type 2 | Plans 3 | % 4 | Sub-totals 5 |
|---|---|---|---|---|
| 0 | Vision or scenario | 188 | 12.5 | God's plan: |
| 1 | Call, appeal, slogan | 132 | 8.7 | 188 (12.5%) |
| 2 | Sermon, encyclical | 68 | 4.5 | |
| 3 | Document, report, book | 200 | 13.3 | Semi-plans: |
| 4 | Promise, intent, resolution | 124 | 8.2 | 691 (45.8%) |
| 5 | Unorganized attempt, movement | 66 | 4.4 | |
| 6 | Statement by organized body | 101 | 6.7 | |
| 7 | Plan announced but outline only | 143 | 9.5 | Organized |
| 8 | Serious plan with some details | 229 | 15.2 | formal plans: |
| 9 | Strategy with considerable detail | 139 | 9.2 | 631 (41.8%) |
| 10 | Massively detailed blueprint | 120 | 8.0 | |
| | **TOTAL** | **1,510** | **100.0** | |

---

**Table 27–3. 1,500 global plans arranged by 15 types of primary outreach ministry.**

*(Source: Table 27–19, and column 7 of 27–21)*

| Code 1 | Outreach ministry — Mandate 2 3 / Generic outreach 4 | Plans 5 | % 6 |
|---|---|---|---|
| | **RECEIVE! PRAYER EVANGELISM** | | |
| 0 | No human missionary activity | 52 | 3.4 |
| 1 | No activity except repentance | 62 | 4.1 |
| 2 | Intercession, prayer, prayer survey | 111 | 7.4 |
| | **GO! PRE-EVANGELISM** | | |
| 3 | Survey, research, strategy | 159 | 10.5 |
| 4 | Development, dialogue, apologetics | 57 | 3.8 |
| | **WITNESS! PERSONAL EVANGELISM** | | |
| 5 | Presence, witness, seed-sowing | 89 | 5.9 |
| 6 | Broadcasting, radio, TV, film, video | 95 | 6.3 |
| | **PROCLAIM! PREACHING EVANGELISM** | | |
| 7 | Preaching, evangelism, proclamation | 264 | 17.5 |
| 8 | Power evangelism, power healing | 142 | 9.4 |
| | **DISCIPLE! PERSUASION EVANGELISM** | | |
| 9 | Converting, discipling, winning | 93 | 6.2 |
| | **BAPTIZE! PLANTING EVANGELISM** | | |
| 10 | Church planting, baptizing | 117 | 7.8 |
| 11 | Enforced baptism and church rule | 11 | 0.7 |
| 12 | Military conquest, forced baptism | 10 | 0.7 |
| | **TRAIN! PASTORAL EVANGELISM** | | |
| 13 | Training, leadership, networking | 156 | 10.3 |
| 14 | Literature, scripture distribution | 92 | 6.1 |
| | **TOTAL PLANS** | **1,510** | **100.0** |

---

**Table 27–4. 1,500 global plans arranged by documentation.**

*(Source: Table 27–19, and column 11 of 27–21)*

| Code 1 | Documentation 2 | Plans 3 | % 4 |
|---|---|---|---|
| 0 | Nothing written except incidental reference | 52 | 3.4 |
| 1 | Briefly written up in published form | 237 | 15.7 |
| 2 | Published article, message | 334 | 22.1 |
| 3 | Published book or books | 503 | 33.3 |
| 4 | Printed publicity materials | 185 | 12.3 |
| 5 | Detailed plans for private use | 155 | 10.3 |
| 6 | Detailed logistics published as book | 44 | 2.9 |
| | **Total** | **1,510** | **100.0** |

## Table 27–5.  340 reasons and causes explaining the failure of 665 global plans which promised to evangelize the entire world.

This table classifies reasons and causes put forward by historians and other observers for the failures of 665 global plans down the ages. Shorthand terminology is used; this means that several reasons have terminological similarities with other reasons. All reasons are here placed in a 3-fold schema corresponding to the 3 global plans, or Temptations, put forward to Jesus by Satan. Clearly this typology is suggestive only and is not meant to imply that all causes can be forced into such a mold. Many reasons and causes could equally well relate to 2 of the 3 categories, or even to all 3.

The 53 items in boldface type are reasons or causes external to the churches and outside their control. All other items, shown in medium type, relate to internal problems within the Christian world.

### I.  JESUS REJECTS SATAN'S 1ST PLAN FOR AN ECONOMIC MESSIAH

1.  *Reasons and causes for failure related to resources, needs, surveys, finances, personnel, planning, logistics, administration (listed below: 124 reasons)*

absence of followup
absence of forethought
absence of laborers
absence of strategy
absence of tactics
administrative fiascos
appealing to human sensuality
avoidance of monitoring actual progress
**bank collapses**
believing own unfounded progress reports
big-business mentality
bottlenecks in flow of resources
**burgeoning materialism**
cash prizes or rewards
collapses of funding
committee-oriented mind-set
conference-oriented mentality
constant redefinitions of the task
corruption
**crash of global economy**
**currency controls and prohibitions**
**deliberately deceptive disinformation**
depersonalizing the gospel
duplication and waste
ecclesiastical crime
ecclesiastical gangsterism
embezzlements
escalating cost of missions
ethnocentrism
excessive fund-raising appeals
expediency
exploitation of natural calamities
facile eschatology
failure to assess time and energy required
failure to commission essential research
failure to complete research goals
failure to grasp true magnitude of the world
failure to network
failure to understand population explosion
failure to visualize the finished plan
failures of communication
false optimism
false reports of success
falsified balance sheets
fear of implications of research
financial mismanagement
financial scandals
free offers
giving false assurances
giving free Bibles, TV sets, buildings
ignorance of logistical realities
ignorance of any other global plans
inadequate attention to detail
inadequate giving
inadequate logistics
inadequate outlays of men and money
inadequate planning
inadequate publicity
inadequate use of traditional media
inadequate use of visual media
incorrect computations
**insoluble complexities of world's 13,000 languages**
lack of support from sister agencies
lay resistance to regimentation
letting windows of opportunity close shut
logistical snags
making things appear too easy
management fiascos
**massive currency inflation**
misinformation
mismanagement
**muddling through**
**natural disasters**
nonexistent or inadequate research
nonexistent planning
objections to segmentization
offering tempting inducements
ongoing massive gaps in coverage
opposition to master global planning
opposition to surveys, data, computers
organizational isolation
overambitious goals and deadlines
overemphasis on verbal gospel
overintellectual approach
over-reliance on technology
parochial mindset
placing all eggs in one basket
poor administration
**population explosion**
procrastination
protracted delays
rash decision-making
refusal to employ comity or networking
regional mind-set in lieu of global thinking
reluctance to heed secular research
reluctance to share lucrative resources
satisfying immediate needs
**secularism**
**secular urbanization**
setting artificial deadlines
shortages of resources
shortfalls in personnel
sloganeering without logistics
solving transient dilemmas at expense of ultimate goal
standalone use of computers and all resources

state prohibitions on personal mobility and travel
swallowing own propaganda
teaching a Prosperity Gospel
thefts of resources
ultrabroad definition of 'evangelization'
underestimating complexity of the task
undue economic involvement
undue material involvement
unexpected attrition of resources
**unexpected deaths of key administrators**
unrealistic expectations
unrelated economic inducements
unwillingness to adopt new strategies
unwillingness to take unpopular decisions
unwise business methods
unwise deadline-setting
use of tainted or laundered money
wrong factual information for planners
wrong mathematics

### II.  JESUS REJECTS SATAN'S 2ND PLAN FOR A MIRACULOUS MESSIAH

2.  *Reasons and causes for failure related to signs, wonders, and miracles, healings, discipleship, personalities, leadership (listed below: 106 reasons).*

absence of commitment
absence of risk-taking
absence of sacrifice
advertising mode
affluent life-styles of leadership
altered states of consciousness
anti-intellectualism
apathy and complacency in the churches
appealing to human sense of wonder
appointing uncommitted persons to key posts
assorted scandals and outcries
attrition among foreign missionaries
avoidance of risk and insecure situations
bogus signs and wonders
**breakdown of sociosphere**
**breakdowns in health care**
cheap grace
cheap healings
cheap marvels shown on TV
comfortable lifestyles
cronyism in key appointments
defections of key executives
**demonic activity**
**disease: malaria, smallpox, plague, epidemics, AIDS**
dislike of criticism
domineering by inflexible executives
downplaying cost of discipleship
drug addiction
excessive publicity
false claims of healings
false healers
false or unjustified optimism
false predictions and alarms
false prophets
faltering zeal for missions
fear of failure
fickleness of Christians
guaranteeing salvation
hesitation
hoaxes and swindles
hostility to impartial advice
hostility towards charismata
human failings
hypocritical or untrue claims of progress
ignorance, indifference, and apathy
ignoring of prophets and prophecies
ill-advised date-setting
illnesses of key workers
inclusivistic expansion away from original goal
incompetent administrators
indecision by top leadership
insufficient vision
intolerance of parallel authority
jurisdictional disputes
lack of response to alleged miracles
lack of spiritual fervor
lavish life-style of leaders
legalism
letting major events and opportunities go into oblivion
loss of nerve
low levels of discipleship
**Murphy's Law: 'If things can go wrong, they will'**
overblown claims
overemphasis on healings
overemphasis on signs and wonders
overrating own ability to impact world
pandering to the fear of death
paying lip-service to the Great Commission
permitting free rides in top level posts
personal aggrandisement
personal bigotry
personal moral lapses
personal nest-feathering by officials involved
personal rivalries and jealousies
personality clashes
personality shortcomings
premature claims of success
proclamation of grandiose schemes and goals
**public apathy**
public-relations mentality and approach
questionable miracles reported or shown on TV
refusal to heed warnings
reluctance to accept research findings
resistance to megaministry as depersonalizing
rigid church/mission structures

salvation by committee
sex scandals
spiritual flabbiness
spurious miracles
structural rigidities
success-story mind-set
syncretistic tendencies
'the wicked selfishness of Christians'
tinkering with inefficient machinery
top leaders ceasing to believe in original goal
trances, ecstasies, dreams
underestimating human frailty and failings
underrating real miracles required to impact world
undue emphasis on miracles
**unexpected deaths of key healers**
unexpected prophets and seers
universalism
unrealistic rhetoric
unrelated inter-agency squabbles
unwillingness to listen to researchers
wrong theology

### III  JESUS REJECTS SATAN'S 3RD PLAN FOR A POLITICAL MESSIAH

3.  *Reasons and causes for failure related to politics, power, and empire-building (listed below: 110 reasons)*

**antichristian infiltration**
appeal to latent racism
appealing to human pride and authority
appealing to patriotic bigotry
**assassinations of key mission strategizers**
autocratic methods
becoming upstaged by subsequent global plans
bureaucratic obduracy
bureaucratization
buried by masses of minutiae
changing agendas
**church/state clashes**
**closing doors**
collapse of education for global mission
**collapses of infrastructures**
collective arrogance
compelling cooperation and response
competition and rivalry
confessional disagreements
corporate ambition
**cultural barriers to the gospel**
**deliberate political attempts at subversion**
desire for fame
denominational narrowmindedness
denominational rivalries
**difficulties and dangers**
**disillusionment after massive wars and epidemics**
disrespect for human freedom of choice
domino effect among agencies
do-it-alone mentality
drastic midpoint alterations of course
ecclesiastical schisms and secessions
empire-building by officials
enforcement of reforms and decisions
entrenched bureaucracies
event-orientation instead of process-orientation
excessive committee procedures
excessive dominance of Western churches
excommunications of key leaders
failure to reach initial goals
fear of own constituencies
**forged anti-evangelization documents**
fragmentation into 33,000 denominations
**global religious persecution**
go-it-alone mindset
gradual decline or petering out
**hostile political regimes**
**hostile religious systems**
imperialism
inflexible mission agency structures
isolated responses
jockeying for power and position
lack of global vision
legalism
losing interest in primary goal
losing original vision
**mass religious espionage**
megalomania
maligning other traditions
**military coups d'etat**
**mob violence and rule**
**narrow nationalism**
organizational isolation
other agendas
other interests
overloading agenda with secular concerns
partial obedience to Commission
passage of time seen as inevitable progress to goal
paternalism
personal dictatorships
personal glory sought by officials
**political bans and prohibitions**
**political hostility**
**political instability**
**political interference**
**political pressures**
**popular hostility to Christianity**
power hunger
power struggles
**premature martyrdoms**
prevailing 'Build your own empire' mentality
pride in all its forms and ramifications
proselytism
racism

*Continued opposite*

Table 27–5 concluded

| | | |
|---|---|---|
| raw power plays | structures of sin | uncontrolled wars and warfare |
| regionalist planning versus globalist planning | sudden replacements of executives | underestimating opposition and obstacles |
| **religious intransigence** | **terrorism** | undue political involvement |
| **resurgence of non-Christian religions** | theological disarray | **unexpected deaths of key strategists** |
| search for glory | theological squabbles | use of force, coercion, weapons |
| secularizing of original objectives | **total state opposition** | vested interests |
| **shattering of postmillennial optimism** | **totalitarianism** | **violent revolutions** |
| short-term ministries seen as quick solutions | **tribalism** | widespread defeatism in the churches |
| standalone convictions, policy, or paranoia | unannounced abandonment of original goal | wrong religious geopolitics |

opment is not purely a Western phenomenon. From the beginning it has been genuinely international.

### Ecclesiastical tradition
Global evangelization plans have arisen from throughout Christendom, representing more than 40 major traditions, confessions, and families. Under these larger groups—especially Evangelical, Conservative Evangelical, Orthodox, Catholic, and Roman Catholic, for example—there are a range of smaller ecclesiastical traditions.

Altogether, including these smaller families, there are some 300 distinct church families or traditions. Almost all of them have produced global plans of one kind or another. These major categories are shown in Table 27–9.

The terms in Table 27–9 are the best, or first, or primary single adjective by which authors or sponsors would describe themselves or their plans. For this categorization, they are mutually exclusive, but of course some plans could be described by more than one label. For example, Lumen 2000 (1983) is Roman Catholic, but it is also Charismatic. Charismatic plans usually are Ecumenical. Conservative Evangelical plans are also Evangelical. This means that the actual involvement in several ecclesiastical traditions is somewhat wider than Table 27–9 appears to indicate.

Because the adjectives describing the primary ecclesiastical origin of plans overlap to some extent, they can be combined in several ways to achieve additional insights. Table 27–10 shows how they can be categorized into Early Church (the first millennium) and Later Church (the second millennium). Within each, ecclesiastical traditions are listed in order of the number of plans.

Table 27–10 also sheds further light on what has been happening. The main difference between the Early Church period and the Later Church period (AD 1000-2000) is quite obvious. Although in the first millennium global plans came from various traditions, since AD 1000 interest has diversified, following the proliferation of Christian confessions and traditions. Protestants lead with 670 plans, followed by Roman Catholics with 250. Evangelicals, a subdivision of Protestants, have produced 220. Pentecostals-Charismatics, who are represented in Protestant, Evangelical, and Roman Catholic traditions, have begun 150 plans, almost all of them since 1901.

Some 100 plans have been nondenominational (separate from any denominational control) and 70 have been interdenominational (controlled by several denominations). Among the Protestant confessions, Baptists lead the non-Pentecostals with 50 plans.

### NUMBER THE PEOPLES

#### 159 survey plans across 66 generations
From Table 27–3, it can be observed that some 159 global plans have as their primary outreach ministry and method the subjects of survey, research, strategy, and the like. In terms of the Great Commission, they are obeying the second mandate, Go! This is the category of generic outreach called Pre-evangelism, or Preparatory Evangelization. Obviously one should not start on a difficult journey before consulting maps and guide books—or, if none exist, before attempting to compile the information oneself.

The subject of counting and numbering commands a healthy respect throughout the Bible. One book of the Bible is called Numbers (in the Greek Septuagint, *arithmoi*). This is because of its emphasis on censuses and enumeration. As one example, we read: 'The Lord spoke to Moses: "Take a census of the people of Israel. Number the whole community by families. Make a detailed list of them by their tribal hosts."' (Num. 1:1-2, RSV, NEB). Often the explanation for enumeration is the need to implement God's global plan whereby the 70 Gentile nations of Genesis 10, as the harvest field, could be matched up with the 70 laborers or harvesters, symbolic of the People of Israel.

No one can accuse the church of failing to continue this biblical tradition across the centuries. This survey of global plans has turned up 159 such surveys, but because of the rather restricted definition of global plans, this is just the tip of the iceberg.

Only those global plans that have as their outreach ministry and method the subjects of survey, research, strategy, and the like are included.

Additional Protestant surveys, not included in this list of 1,500 plans, were published in 1818, 1823, 1836, 1854, 1888, 1896, and 1900. More comprehensive global surveys followed with H. P. Beach's *A geography and atlas of Protestant missions* (1906), and further detailed missions atlases in 1910, 1925, and 1938.

On the Roman Catholic side, K. Streit's statistical surveys and atlases of 1906, 1913, and 1929 were the pioneers. Subsequent Catholic atlases have been published, as *Atlas hierarchicus*, in 1968, 1976, and 1992. Most of these do not meet the definition of a survey global plan and are not included in Table 27–21.

#### Promoting the unfinished task
No one can accuse the church, either, of failing to publicize the magnitude of the unfinished task of evangelizing the globe. Over the last 200 years a fair number of surveys have been published with some variation of this title: 'The Unfinished Task of World Evangelization.' Table 27–13 lists major survey plans that have delineated this unfinished task and have included new data, in most cases with massive detail.

Table 27–13 consists of a brief selection of 46 out of the 159 survey plans, using the exact titles in Table 27–21, column 3. Included here is one more very detailed survey plan that is not coded in column 7 as a survey plan, but with the code 2, because it is primarily a prayer survey: *Operation World*, a unique work compiled to stimulate worldwide intercession for global evangelization.

Table 27–13 is not just a bibliography, but a list of items that on other grounds qualify for inclusion in the basic list of 1,500 global plans. Admittedly, these surveys are difficult to sort out among the scores of sermons, articles, books, rehashes, and outright plagiarisms. The lower end of the spectrum of types of plan (codes 0-3 in Table 27–2) is very broad, but only unique surveys or surveys of major significance are included.

Twenty-one of the 46 titles, shown in boldface type, contain the prefix 'un-'. They refer to the unfinished task, unoccupied fields, unevangelized fields, unreached people, and so on. This list proves that missionary researchers have tried to keep to subject constantly before the church.

However, it appears quite absurd—after you stand back and reflect on the list—to have surveys like these

---

### Table 27–6. A checkup scale for assessing present obstacles and future prospects of any current global plans.

Here's how to use this scale: take a pencil or yellow marker. Make a photocopy of the long list of causes of failure in Table 27–5. Concentrate on thinking about the present circumstances of one global plan you are interested in. Then read through the 340 reasons and causes for failure listed in Table 27–5. Whenever you think a particular line describes something that might in any way be present today to affect or hinder this global plan, check it or mark it. Then, when you reach the last line of the table, add up all those you have checked.

Next, find which figure in the lefthand column below represents your total of current possible obstacles or causes of eventual failure. The 2 sentences to its right then estimate your plan's present status and its probable future fate.

| OBSTACLES | PRESENT STATUS | FUTURE PROSPECTS |
|---|---|---|
| Current Total | Your global plan... | By AD 2025 your plan... |
| Under 5 | ...is in good shape | ...will have achieved its goals |
| 5-9 | ...has problems | ...will have fallen far short |
| 10-19 | ...is in serious trouble | ...will be fizzling out |
| 20-50 | ...faces insurmountable difficulties | ...will have collapsed. |

---

### Table 27–7. 1,500 global plans arranged by country and world of origin.

Country names below are contemporary but cover any former names used in Table 27–21, column 8. The analysis into the 3 worlds used by the United Nations is given to illustrate where plans have come from. Source: Tables 27-19 and 27-21.

| Ref | Country | Plans | Developed | Less-developed | Least-developed | Ref | Country | Plans | Developed | Less-developed | Least-developed |
|---|---|---|---|---|---|---|---|---|---|---|---|
| 1 | 2 | 3 | 4 | 5 | 6 | 1 | 2 | 3 | 4 | 5 | 6 |
| 1 | Algeria | 2 | | 2 | | 36 | Malta | 1 | 1 | | |
| 2 | Argentina | 2 | | 2 | | 37 | Mexico | 3 | | 3 | |
| 3 | Australia | 6 | 6 | | | 38 | Mongolia | 1 | | 1 | |
| 4 | Belgium | 5 | 5 | | | 39 | Myanmar | 1 | | | 1 |
| 5 | Bolivia | 1 | | 1 | | 40 | Netherlands | 13 | 13 | | |
| 6 | Brazil | 8 | | 8 | | 41 | New Caledonia | 1 | | 1 | |
| 7 | Britain | 101 | 101 | | | 42 | New Zealand | 1 | 1 | | |
| 8 | Bulgaria | 1 | 1 | | | 43 | Nicaragua | 1 | | 1 | |
| 9 | Cameroon | 1 | | 1 | | 44 | Nigeria | 9 | | 9 | |
| 10 | Canada | 11 | 11 | | | 45 | Norway | 6 | 6 | | |
| 11 | China | 8 | | 8 | | 46 | Palestine | 1 | | 1 | |
| 12 | Costa Rica | 2 | | 2 | | 47 | Peru | 3 | | 3 | |
| 13 | Cyprus | 1 | | 1 | | 48 | Philippines | 6 | | 6 | |
| 14 | Czech Republic | 3 | 3 | | | 49 | Romania | 1 | 1 | | |
| 15 | Denmark | 2 | 2 | | | 50 | Russia | 3 | 3 | | |
| 16 | Ecuador | 1 | | 1 | | 51 | Samoa | 1 | | | 1 |
| 17 | Egypt | 9 | | 9 | | 52 | Saudi Arabia | 1 | | 1 | |
| 18 | Ethiopia | 1 | | | 1 | 53 | Singapore | 12 | | 12 | |
| 19 | France | 19 | 19 | | | 54 | South Africa | 1 | | 1 | |
| 20 | Germany | 31 | 31 | | | 55 | South Korea | 20 | | 20 | |
| 21 | Greece | 8 | 8 | | | 56 | Spain | 11 | 11 | | |
| 22 | Holy See | 37 | 37 | | | 57 | Sweden | 5 | 5 | | |
| 23 | Hungary | 1 | 1 | | | 58 | Switzerland | 21 | 21 | | |
| 24 | India | 16 | | 16 | | 59 | Syria | 6 | | 6 | |
| 25 | Indonesia | 3 | | 3 | | 60 | Taiwan | 1 | | 1 | |
| 26 | Iran | 2 | | 2 | | 61 | Thailand | 4 | | 4 | |
| 27 | Ireland | 8 | 8 | | | 62 | Tunisia | 2 | | 2 | |
| 28 | Israel | 30 | | 30 | | 63 | Turkey | 6 | | 6 | |
| 29 | Italy | 39 | 39 | | | 64 | USA | 334 | 334 | | |
| 30 | Jamaica | 2 | | 2 | | 65 | Venezuela | 3 | | 3 | |
| 31 | Japan | 6 | 6 | | | 66 | Yugoslavia | 1 | 1 | | |
| 32 | Jordan | 1 | | 1 | | 67 | Zimbabwe | 1 | | 1 | |
| 33 | Kenya | 8 | | 8 | | 68 | other plans | 650 | 239 | 314 | 97 |
| 34 | Latvia | 1 | 1 | | | | **TOTAL** | **1,510** | **915** | **495** | **100** |
| 35 | Malaysia | 2 | | 2 | | | | | | | |

**Table 27–8.  1,500 global plans arranged by developmental world of origin.**

Enumerated into the 3 worlds recognized by the United Nations.

| World 1 | Countries in world 2 | Countries with plans 3 | Plans 4 | % 5 |
|---|---|---|---|---|
| Developed world | 60 | 27 | 915 | 60.6 |
| Less-developed world | 130 | 37 | 495 | 32.8 |
| Least-developed world | 48 | 13 | 100 | 6.6 |
| WORLD TOTAL, AD 33-2000 | 238 | 77 | 1,510 | 100.0 |

**Table 27–9.  1,500 global plans arranged by primary ecclesiastical origin.**

*(Source: Table 27–19, and column 9 of 27–21)*

| Ref 1 | Tradition 2 | Plans 3 | % 4 |
|---|---|---|---|
| 1 | Pre-Pentecost | 5 | 0.3 |
| 2 | Adventist | 5 | 0.3 |
| 3 | Anabaptist | 4 | 0.3 |
| 4 | Anglican | 57 | 3.8 |
| 5 | Apostolic | 14 | 0.9 |
| 6 | Baptist | 35 | 2.3 |
| 7 | Brethren | 2 | 0.1 |
| 8 | Catholic | 22 | 1.5 |
| 9 | Catholic Apostolic | 2 | 0.1 |
| 10 | Celtic | 1 | 0.1 |
| 11 | Charismatic | 25 | 1.7 |
| 12 | Christadelphian | 1 | 0.1 |
| 13 | Congregationalist | 11 | 0.7 |
| 14 | Conservative Evangelical | 49 | 3.3 |
| 15 | Disciples | 2 | 0.1 |
| 16 | Eastern Orthodox | 10 | 0.7 |
| 17 | Ecumenical | 82 | 5.4 |
| 18 | Evangelical | 68 | 4.5 |
| 19 | Evangelical/Charismatic | 6 | 0.4 |
| 20 | Evangelical/Ecumenical | 2 | 0.1 |
| 21 | Fundamentalist | 13 | 0.9 |
| 22 | Holiness | 7 | 0.5 |
| 23 | Hussite | 1 | 0.1 |
| 24 | Independent | 410 | 27.2 |
| 25 | Interdenominational | 54 | 3.6 |
| 26 | Lutheran | 17 | 1.1 |
| 27 | Mennonite | 1 | 0.1 |
| 28 | Messianic Jewish | 2 | 0.1 |
| 29 | Methodist | 22 | 1.5 |
| 30 | Montanist | 2 | 0.1 |
| 31 | Moravian | 1 | 0.1 |
| 32 | Mormon | 2 | 0.1 |
| 33 | Nestorian | 6 | 0.4 |
| 34 | Nondenominational | 93 | 6.2 |
| 35 | Old Catholic | 2 | 0.1 |
| 36 | Oriental Orthodox | 1 | 0.0 |
| 37 | Orthodox | 37 | 2.5 |
| 38 | Pan-Christian | 1 | 0.1 |
| 39 | Pentecostal | 42 | 2.8 |
| 40 | Pentecostal/Charismatic | 13 | 0.9 |
| 41 | Presbyterian | 19 | 1.3 |
| 42 | Protestant | 151 | 10.0 |
| 43 | Quaker | 2 | 0.1 |
| 44 | Reformed | 11 | 0.7 |
| 45 | Roman Catholic | 182 | 12.1 |
| 46 | Salvationist | 1 | 0.1 |
| 47 | Southern Baptist | 1 | 0.1 |
| 48 | Witnesses/Marginal | 13 | 0.9 |
| | **WORLD TOTAL, AD 33–AD 2000** | **1,510** | **100.0** |

put out at the rate of eight or 10 every generation. Throughout the last 100 years the number of unreached people has grown to over 1.6 billion. What has been the point of all these survey plans?

*Ignoring the surveys*

The astonishing fact is that most of the executives and administrators of our 20th-century global evangelization plans have been or are ignorant of these survey global plans. This was discovered by interviewing a number of church and mission executives. None of them knew about all the survey plans in Table 27–13. None of them had studied the materials in more than 10 percent of the survey plans of the last 30 years.

Most of them were unable to describe or articulate the particular values of any of these materials. Most of them acknowledged the importance of these survey plans, but regarded studying them as something for their subordinates to do. 'I don't have time to get involved in such details,' one of them said. On the other hand, none of them knew which of his subordinates, if any, had actually studied the plans.

Might this well be a case of the blind leading the blind? Of course, some mission executives could very well question this indictment. If so, they could photocopy Table 27–13 and check or highlight any of the 46 survey plans they have actually seen. Then highlight in a different color any of them that they would be prepared to describe and speak about for one minute before an audience of fellow executives.

One thing is for sure: these survey plans burn into our consciences like a branding iron the dilemma of the unevangelized world. Nobody can argue with the facts. They won't go away even if we ignore them. They remain to plague us year after year until we do something.

*Current status*

Any outsider looking at the data amassed here should ask one obvious question, 'With all these plans, why haven't we done better?' Tragically, it is because a vast number of them simply collapsed, fizzled out, or were never implemented. Table 27–11 tells the story.

Table 27–11 shows that 665 plans (44%) of all 1,500 plans have already failed for one reason or another, or they have been abandoned, superseded, or just forgotten. Launched full of hope, they are now defunct. Like damp fireworks after a rain, they sputtered for awhile and then fizzled out, hardly lamented by anyone. In view of the colossal magnitude of the resources expended on them, this is a record of shocking waste, of a catastrophe of enormous proportions.

Another 585 plans (39%) are clearly in the decaying process, although their sponsors may refuse to admit it. Altogether, some 845 plans (56%) are still alive in varying degrees of activity. But only 260 (17%) of the plans are vibrantly alive today and making any clear, measurable progress toward their professed goal of world evangelization.

*Silver and gold have I none?*

'Silver and gold have I none,' said the Apostle Peter at the Temple gate in Jerusalem, 'but such as I have I give you. In the name of Jesus Christ of Nazareth, rise up and walk!' (Acts 3:6).

Throughout the history of the 59 neglected generations, Christians have complained that they did not have adequate resources to obey the Great Commission. To hear some missions protagonists, one would think that the church has lived in a state of abject poverty.

However, this is utter nonsense. The latest acquisitions made by Christians since 1980 are 332 million computers. Their capital value today is no less than $900 billion. And they are backed up by a new kind of Christian army—200 million Christian computer specialists (50 million computer professionals, 150 million other computer literates).

The fact is that the church has always had enormous resources of both money and people, more than enough to evangelize the world many times over.

Neither are the churches short of reliable, regular income. In AD 2000, for example, Christian laypersons are giving at the rate of $270 billion a year to operate organized global Christianity. The problem arises at management levels.

To see how mismanagement by a few can destroy even the most massive global plan, turn to Table 27–21 for the year 1918. In this case, $336 million was raised and then the plan was destroyed within a week. This story, of the massive Interchurch World Movement, has been thoroughly documented in the literature.

For a more current example, turn to 1969 and see how a gigaplan that raised $150 million a year virtually collapsed on one day in 1988 in a management scandal involving the top evangelist.

*Summarizing resources*

To understand this summary, this is how the most important categories are defined:

1. 'Sizeable' resources refers to plans on each of which Christians have expended over 1,000 worker-years, or over $100,000 a year, for an average of 10 years. Some 246 plans have been in this category. The minimum total in this category would be 120,000 worker years, or $12 million.

2. 'Massive' resources refers to plans each with over 10,000 worker-years, or over $10 million a year, for an average of 10 years. Some 210 plans are in this category, 59 of which are termed megaplans because they are massive but are also being massively implemented and expanding across the world (code 9 in column 16 of Table 27–21). The minimum total of all expended resources in this category would be 1,500,000 worker-years, or $1,500 million.

3. 'Gigantic' resources refers to plans each with over 100,000 worker-years, or over $100 million a year, or a total of $1 billion over the years of the plan's life. The biggest current gigaplan is spending over $550 million a year on its own standalone world mission plan. Together, the 57 gigaplans have expended, are expending, and will expend well over $40 billion.

Therefore, it's safe to assume that the 1,500 global plans have already expended some four million worker-years and $50 billion.

### GOD'S GLOBAL ENVOYS

*The role of nonresidential missionaries*

There are types of full-time ministry open to foreigners seeking to reach people in closed countries. Two of them are legal, in the sense of abiding by anti-religious laws in those countries. Of those two, the traditional one is the residential missionary. Many people still see this as the only Great Commission alternative.

**Table 27–10.  1,500 global plans under various ecclesiastical cover names from AD 33–AD 2000.**

Note: Because the categories and their totals below overlap and are not mutually exclusive, numbers of plans in this table should not be added to get further subtotals.

| Period Ecclesiastical term 1 2 | Plans 3 | % 4 |
|---|---|---|
| **1st Millennium: Early Church:** | **64** | **4.2** |
| Catholic | 22 | 1.5 |
| Orthodox | 14 | 0.9 |
| Apostolic | 14 | 0.9 |
| Nestorian | 5 | 0.3 |
| Pre-Pentecost AD 33 | 5 | 0.3 |
| Montanist | 2 | 0.1 |
| Celtic | 1 | 0.1 |
| Anglican | 1 | 0.1 |
| **2nd Millennium: Later Church:** | **1,446** | **95.8** |
| Protestant | 300 | 19.9 |
| Roman Catholic | 250 | 16.6 |
| Evangelical | 150 | 9.9 |
| Pentecostal/Charismatic | 100 | 6.6 |
| Independent | 500 | 33.1 |
| Nondenominational | 100 | 6.6 |
| Ecumenical | 100 | 6.6 |
| Interdenominational | 70 | 4.6 |
| Conservative Evangelical | 70 | 4.6 |
| Anglican | 60 | 4.0 |
| Baptist | 50 | 3.3 |
| Presbyterian/Reformed | 40 | 2.6 |
| Methodist | 25 | 1.7 |
| Lutheran | 20 | 1.3 |
| Fundamentalist | 20 | 1.3 |
| Orthodox | 40 | 2.6 |
| Congregationalist | 15 | 1.0 |
| Marginal | 20 | 1.3 |
| **WORLD TOTAL, AD 33-2000** | **1,510** | **100.0** |

**Table 27–11.  1,500 global plans arranged by current status.**

*(Source: Table 27–19, and column 16 of 27–21)*

| Code 1 | Status 2 | Plans 3 | % 4 | Sub-totals 5 |
|---|---|---|---|---|
| 0 | Fizzled out, dead, forgotten | 362 | 24.0 | 24% fizzled |
| 1 | Defunct because no interest | 125 | 8.3 | out, dead |
| 2 | Defunct because completion claimed | 40 | 2.7 | |
| 3 | Implemented but not achieved | 138 | 9.1 | |
| 4 | Alive but fizzling out | 80 | 5.3 | 59% fizzling |
| 5 | Alive but in decline | 158 | 10.5 | out, dying |
| 6 | Alive but static | 205 | 13.6 | |
| 7 | Alive but redefined | 142 | 9.4 | 17% alive |
| 8 | Alive and making progress | 160 | 10.6 | and making |
| 9 | Alive and massively implemented | 100 | 6.6 | progress |
| | **TOTAL** | **1,510** | **100.0** | |

**Table 27–12.  1,500 global plans arranged by magnitude of resources expended.**

*(Source: Table 27–19, and column 13 of 27–21)*

| Code 1 | Resources 2 | Plans 3 | % 4 |
|---|---|---|---|
| 0 | Negligible | 171 | 11.3 |
| 1 | Minimal | 295 | 19.5 |
| 2 | Limited | 235 | 15.6 |
| 3 | Modest | 296 | 19.6 |
| 4 | Sizeable | 246 | 16.3 |
| 5 | Massive | 210 | 13.9 |
| 6 | Gigantic | 57 | 3.8 |
| | **Total** | **1,510** | **100.0** |

However, because residential foreign missionaries are being banned in country after country—at the rate of around three new countries per year—an alternative must be found. There is a major alternative: the nonresidential missionary.

To review, any world evangelization approach must be based on thorough studies and surveys of all of the world's unevangelized population segments. Without this, any strategy is useless. Briefly, there are 4,000 or so ethnolinguistic peoples and groups that are largely unevangelized. Or, 1,000 large cities. Or, around 30 countries that are to a high degree inaccessible to cross-cultural mission.

For these situations nonresidential missions is proposed as perhaps a valuable approach, or, in some cases, an invaluable approach. Where several approaches are possible, this might be the most appropriate. In a number of hard-core situations, it is the only approach possible.

Using data now available, missions strategists can rank peoples, cities, and countries according to their priorities. Then they can match their priorities with the most appropriate approach.

*Four vital core elements*
First, however, some clarification is needed. This concept of the nonresidential missionary includes four vital core elements:

1. Full-time, professional mission through missionaries recruited, appointed, sent, and supported by their own mission boards, societies, or agencies, of any citizenship and sent from any country in the world.

2. The unhindered pursuit of the evangelization of each missionary's single, clearly defined target population segment through residence in a convenient open city anywhere in the world (a world class city, or at least one with good telecommunication and networking facilities, with total freedom of activity and freedom from surveillance).

3. Not attempting to evangelize one's segment alone, but strategizing for the segment's evangelization in co-operation with all other involved or concerned Great Commission Christians who want to target that same segment.

4. Setting as a goal, or overarching objective, the full evangelization of the segment—with all persons having heard the gospel and having had the opportunity to respond—by a target year such as AD 2025.

*Nonresidential mission*
The following definition, from the World Evangelization Database, is not simply an exercise in semantics. It defines a concept designed to reach the vast unevangelized world. It includes scores of ideas from missionaries, mission executives, and the whole context of Christian missions. Therefore, the exact wording is important and none of the elements should be omitted when disseminating the whole idea.

A nonresidential missionary is a full-time, appointed, salaried or supported professional career missionary of any nationality, who is assigned by his or her board or agency in any country—through a matching process designed to concentrate on the priorities of first-time evangelization and to avoid gaps or inadvertent duplications with other agencies—to a ministry to one single unevangelized population segment of the unevangelized world (one metropolis, one people, or one country).

If married, with his or her spouse as co-worker, he resides with his family outside that segment or its country (either because legal residence as a missionary is prohibited or otherwise impossible, or because for other reasons it is inadvisable or unnecessary) and is based in an open city with good international communications facilities.

He then networks with all other concerned Great Commission Christians, local and otherwise, denominations and agencies, who are targeting, or want to target, the same segment, with the overarching objective of seeing to it that all persons in his population segment become evangelized by AD 2025 (which means their having had the opportunity to hear and respond to the gospel), and that at least a hundred new converts be made (by all parties) and a beachhead church be planted (at least 4 or 5 local groups, or churches, or organized church fellowships) in that segment by that time.

The essential elements of his task include the following:

1. Accept as his personal vocation a full-time ministry concentrating on strategizing for the evangelization of his segment in cooperation with other Great Commission parties.

2.. Research and survey the whole secular, religious, and Christian situation of that single segment, thus becoming expert on the subject within his first six months.

3. Learn and become proficient in that segment's main language and culture (market fluency, that is the ability to get around), thus gaining an entree and providing credibility among all specialists in the subject of that population segment.

4. Draw up and help to see implemented a wide range of ministry and megaministry options directed toward that segment.

5. Report briefly on a monthly standard form or short telecommunication to his board, outlining progress with that segment, to enable adequate monitoring and assistance to proceed.

6. Relate throughout (entirely voluntarily, of course, and either directly or through his board) in a two-way relationship to the World Evangelization Database and its associated global network of infobases (using optional laptop computer), which in turn will answer his information requests and will regularly update him with new information, contacts, and suggestions.

7. Become an advocate or lobby at home and abroad, among his own constituency and wider, for his segment's legitimate rights to mission, evangelization, and all necessary resources.

8. Relate as part of a global team to his board's other nonresidential missionaries, each of whom has been assigned to a different segment, possibly with small clusters of two to six couples and singles assigned to widely separated segments, but all sharing accommodation in major world-class cities.

*A summary description*
The key words and ideas in this concept can be summarized as follows, with the ten major ones in boldface type: restricted-access world; global **segmentization**; **unevangelized population segments**; **engagement**; one people, metropolis, or country per missionary; **nonresidential missionary; matching up; networking**; **Great Commission Christians;** research; survey, language; **ministry options**; infobasing; databasing; monthly monitoring; **megaministry; advocacy**; overarching objective; AD 2025 and Beyond.

Another way to present this concept is to set out as a series of descriptive nouns and adjectives, as is done in Table 27–14. These describe the special dimensions, emphases, steps, activities, and stages characterizing the nonresidential missionary.

He or she is not expected to do all of this alone. In fact, he or she may never preach in the streets, translate the Bible, broadcast, or do house-to-house visiting. His or her job simply is to see to it that somebody does each of these things as and when and where possible. In other words, he or she accepts responsibility for seeing to it that, through the Great Commission network anything that needs to be done actually gets done by somebody, towards the AD 2025 goal.

## MATCHING UP NEEDS AND EVANGELIZERS

*How to begin a nonresidential ministry*
An essential element in the new concept of nonresidential mission is that very detailed and accurate matching procedures need to be made available to those missionaries and agencies who want to utilize their resources to fill this approach.

Exact and detailed surveys of unevangelized population segments have long existed, for over 200 years in fact. The new feature today is that current survey data on the unreached and unevangelized worlds are computerized and instantly accessible. This means that any agency, or any potential missionary, of any nationality whatever, in any country of the world, and from any telephone number in the world, can immediately find out how to match up his or her own vocation, interests and skills with a genuinely unevangelized population segment.

There are a number of different published surveys of unreached peoples available today. A few are linked to computer infobases and databases.

---

**Table 27–13. Major survey plans delineating the unfinished task of world evangelization, AD 1792-AD 2000.**

1. This is a listing of surveys and survey plans which in their own day offered new, hard data on the unfinished task, usually incorporating new and original ideals, suggestions, or survey plans as to what to do to remedy the situation.
2. The year given below is not date of publication in print, but year of related global plan, although in most cases it is also year of print publication; for details of any, see Table 27–21 under the year stated.
3. All titles listed below are the titles of global plans exactly word for word as listed in Table 27–21, column 3. Items in italics refer to survey plans published as books or journals, items in quotes to plans published as articles or reports.
4. All items deal with the problem and the extent of the unfinished task. Items in boldface type, however, are those which actually use in their titles the world 'Unfinished' or a close synonym.
*(Source: Table 27–21, columns 2, 3 and 7.)*

| Year | Title of survey plan (brief name as listed in Table 27–21, column 3) | Year | Title of survey plan (brief name as listed in Table 27–21, column 3) |
|---|---|---|---|
| 1792 | *Obligations of Christians for Conversion of the Heathens* | 1949 | *World Christian handbook (1949, 1952, 1957, 1962, 1968)* |
| 1880 | *"A plan to evangelize the World", The missionary review* | 1955 | *Survey of world missions* |
| 1884 | *"No conversion of Nations without adequate outlay"* | 1956 | *Mission fields today: a brief world survey* |
| 1891 | *The encyclopedia of missions: historical, statistical* | 1957 | *World evangelism today* |
| 1894 | *Methods of the evangelization of the non-Christian world* | 1957 | ***The unfinished task*** |
| 1900 | *The evangelization of the world in this generation* | 1958 | *Bilan du monde: encyclopédie catholique du monde chrétien* |
| 1902 | *Centennial survey of foreign missions* | 1960 | ***Facing the unfinished task*** |
| 1906 | *World mission atlases and surveys* | 1961 | **2nd World Survey: "19 Point Program to Reach the Unreached"** |
| 1908 | ***The unfinished task of the Christian church*** | 1967 | *Encyclopedia of modern Christian missions* |
| 1910 | *"Unoccupied sections of the world"/Edinburgh Conference* | 1974 | *Operation World: a guide to praying for the world* |
| 1910 | *God's missionary plan for the world* | 1974 | ***Reaching the unreached*** |
| 1911 | **Unoccupied mission field** | 1979 | *"The unfinished task of world mission"* |
| 1912 | *International review of missions* | 1979 | **Conference on Unreached Peoples** |
| 1916 | **World Dominion Movement: surveys of unevangelized regions** | 1979 | ***Unreached Peoples series*** |
| 1918 | Interchurch World Movement of North America, *World survey* | 1981 | **"Reaching Unreached Peoples"** |
| 1925 | *World missionary atlas* | 1982 | **"The Unevangelized", *World Christian encyclopedia, 1900-2000*** |
| 1926 | ***The unfinished task of foreign missions*** | 1984 | ***The unfinished task*** |
| 1928 | ***The unfinished evangelistic task*** | 1988 | *"Great Commission Deadline: the Year 2000"* |
| 1936 | *Awaiting the light: unevangelised areas of the world* | 1990 | *Our globe and how to reach it* |
| 1938 | *"Unoccupied fields", Interpretative statistical survey* | 1993 | *Operation world* |
| 1939 | **"The Unfinished Evangelistic Task"** | 1994 | **Unreached Peoples Prayer Profiles** |
| 1942 | **1st World Survey of Unreached Areas: "Black Spots Survey"** | 1997 | *World Churches handbook* |
| 1948 | *Set a watchman: a world survey* | 2000 | *World Christian encyclopedia, second edition* |

### The role of sending agencies

The aim of this is to move through a relatively short process in which every unevangelized population segment in the world becomes matched up with at least one missionary or couple, of any nationality, as soon as possible. The process, in any single case, can be surprisingly rapid. Actual cases that we have implemented in the last year or two have involved interviews ranging from a few days to less than two hours.

Note first of all that responsible agencies act autonomously throughout. There need be no attempt at central control. Any agencies anywhere in the world are free to make a commitment to evangelizing any segments they choose. But wasteful overlay or duplication has to be avoided. Likewise, all the segments should be covered. The scandal of unevangelized gaps decade after decade must be ended. For this reason, the segmentization and matching-up processes need to be carefully monitored and reported back to all groups and agencies participating in them.

Second, because sensitive ministries operate in sensitive parts of the world, privacy and confidentiality are vital. Hence, there must be clear understanding and details carefully worked out with all involved regarding the limits to publicity regarding any and all parts of the segmentization and matching-up process, as well as the ongoing evangelization in the nonresidential mode.

When an agency has understood and accepted the basic proposal to engage in nonresidential mission and ministry, a detailed listing of the procedures to implement it could look somewhat as follows:

1. *Segmentization.* All concerned need to familiarize themselves in detail with the extent of the global unfinished task and exactly how it can be broken down into segments (cities and peoples) or 'bite-sized chunks,' that is, pieces each capable of being undertaken by one missionary or couple.

2. *Definitions.* Agreements should be reached on tentative definitions concerning acceptable levels of evangelization and discipling for these segments in order to reach the overarching objective by AD 2025; the levels decided on will determine the exact number of global segments that this scheme has to deal with; it is likely to be around 5,000.

3. *Personnel.* The number of missionary personnel to be committed can be estimated at 5,000 at a minimum, or 8,000 including spouses. This is at the initial level of one person or couple per segment, to ensure speediest possible coverage of the entire list of segments. Each person or couple would undertake to see to it that his/her or their segment becomes evangelized by AD 2025 as a result of coordinating of all resources available to Great Commission Christians.

4. *Distinctives.* Some of the distinctives which this corps of personnel would need or require, and which their agencies would need to implement, can be elaborated as follows:
   —New patterns of recruitment.
   —Implications of mobility of residence, as contrasted with stable long-term residence in country of service.
   —Ability to strategize and make decisions within a network.
   —Clear understanding and articulation of the segmented approach, and the reasons for the principle of one ministry or couple per segment.
   —Briefing sessions for potential recruits in adequately-equipped strategy centers.
   —Target selection by personal vocation and agency approval.
   —Specialized training weeks at selected colleges and centers.
   —Self-guided training for 6-12 months (language, research, surveys, diasporas, other Christians).
   —Low-key relation to home church and agencies.
   —Protection of confidential aspects from press and publicity.
   —Higher than usual mobility, travel, courses, books, maps, telephone, computer, other expenses.
   —Ways and means of making contact with local Christians in target country and cooperating with all other interested Christian bodies.
   —Ability to decide when to have other types of workers or resources invited in.
   —Instant staff attention to appeals or requests from missionaries on field (e.g. 'Please contact this broadcasting agency...', 'Please send 10 Tibetan Bibles to this address...').
   —Brief monthly standardized reports to agency on progress (one written sheet, or one e-mail monthly, with appropriate precautions).
   —Security procedures overseas including for emergency messages.
   —Priority concentration on AD 2025 goal without major digression to other types of comprehensive mission.

5. *Home staff support.* Staff in agencies' offices handling nonresidential missionaries should be fully committed to the distinctives and free of all prior obligations so that they can concentrate on the delicate and sensitive touch required throughout, and apply the distinctives uniformly to all missionaries and to all outside agencies.

6. *Online model.* Such offices could operate an 'expert system' that is a computerized model, continuously updated, giving daily status and monitoring of this entire world evangelization ministry and its progress.

7. *Logistics.* Researchers at the agencies could rapidly produce all necessary research and logistics needed by the scheme (e.g. bibliographies, maps, contacts, ethnics in Western countries, lists of all agencies at work, resources available through home mission agencies, where one can learn each language involved, local research or study centers, availability of resources in Europe, Asia, Africa, Latin America, etc).

8. *Briefing sheets.* They would also prepare confidential one-page descriptions of each and every segment (people, city, country) of the unfinished task, put together as (a) one large loose-leaf folder, (b) a user-friendly computer program, (c) a set of maps and graphics, and (d) a standard strategy room presentation of these data primarily to orient and brief (i) cooperating agencies and their executives, and (ii) accepted recruits and volunteers, and to assist nonresidential missionaries in each finding the one target of his choice with immediate removal of each segment from (a) to (d) once its match with personnel is agreed on.

9. *Monitoring system.* They could further prepare a computerized information flow system capable of handling the entire scheme including regular feedback from missionaries on the field, with the capability of showing the exact status of any and all aspects of progress with the scheme at any moment.

10. *No-publicity zones.* Agencies would need to delineate confidential no-publicity zones into which part of the scheme's activities would need to be placed, covering assignments to especially sensitive areas or cities or countries.

11. *Orientation courses.* Briefing and orientation courses could be prepared for the large number of applicants from agencies that the scheme is certain to engender.

12. *Recruiting.* Recruitment patterns need to be set in motion among (a) present foreign missionary personnel, (b) home missions personnel in sending countries, (c) seminaries, and (d) likely or potential recruits in churches themselves. Clear statements and recruitment profiles and guidelines for agencies can also be prepared immediately.

13. *Publicity.* A last feature would be to regularly review, monitor and control information flow concerning the whole scheme and all its involved personnel to press and publicity outlets, on the basis that this should be kept to as low a level as is reasonable.

### How the nonresidential missionary begins work

After the matching-up operation is completed, the new nonresidential missionary will immediately find plenty to do. The nonresidential missionary could make a beginning as follows:
   —Begin reading everything available on your target population.
   —Begin study of the major home language involved.
   —Begin a standardized survey of this population, local/national Christians, all other Christian bodies or agencies present or interested, scripture and broadcasting situations.
   —Contact and befriend diaspora individuals or groups in North America, Europe, Australasia, Latin America, and elsewhere.
   —Discuss strategies with friends, colleagues, staff, other nonresidential missionaries, also with selected outside contacts.
   —Plan and evaluate myriad ministry options—varieties of outreach ministries and evangelistic approaches that can be suggested to persons and agencies in the network.
   —Continuously probe for further ministry options and new evangelistic openings, with due regard for sensitivity of the target's situation.
   —Avoid all public reference to your own exact target population or other people's; use instead a more general or vague geographic term.
   —Understand the need for sensitivity and confidentiality of sources, contacts, and cooperating persons and agencies.
   —In due course leave home in your sending country and establish your residence (with family if married) in a strategic city abroad (preferably an open world-class city or large metropolis), or wherever would be most effective for this ministry; be prepared to relocate as needed. The important feature of a city of residence is that (a) it must have good telecommunication facilities with the rest of the world (e.g. electronic mail), and (b) it must be an open city permitting the surveillance-free and uncontrolled use of networking, information, libraries, contact-making, conferencing, travel, telephone, teleconferencing, facilities, photocopying, printing, etc.
   —Understand the importance of your brief monthly standardized report to your own agency and staff.

This is a large enough agenda to keep any professional missionary satisfied.

## CLOSURE, DEADLINES, AND COUNTDOWN THINKING

### 90 current megaplans including 31 gigaplans

The end of the Second Millennium of the Christian era on 31 December 2000 (or, in popular usage 31 December 1999) has long been the focus of study by professional futurists and secular planners. The secular literature on the subject is enormous. Among Christians the subject has taken off in a large way since around 1970, and in a massive way since 1980.

It would be wrong, however, to think of the ideas of closure and deadlines as only a 20th-century phenomenon in Christian history. These ideas have been present from the very beginning, often associated with anticipated dates and years for the second advent of Christ.

### Deadlines

Three related subjects are involved at this point: closure, deadlines, and countdown thinking. Several megaplans utilize this terminology. Closure involves ideas of how God might intend to wind down the historical process and complete world evangelization; also about how Christians can get their act together and meet whatever conditions God may require in respect of this subject. Deadlines refer to actual dates actually quoted as goals of plans for fulfillment of world evangelization and usually (but not necessarily) also the End-times. Countdown thinking refers to how missiologists and missions protagonists are systematizing the passing years and months as a deadline approaches.

Deadlines for the completion of world evangelization have, however, been relatively rare in history's 1,500 global plans. These may be examined in Table 27-21, column 12. Most plans have not specified a deadline. Only recently have plans publicized exact dates in the future. Of these, most had the exact year AD 2000 as their closure date. The earliest AD 2000 schemas before the year 1970 were those in AD 85, 1139, 1350, 1547, 1770, 1884, 1960, 1966, and one in 1970 itself. But from 1970 onwards—exactly one 30-year generation before AD 2000—people's imagination was suddenly caught and AD 2000 global plans began to mushroom.

## Table 27–14. Twelve dimensions and 84 characteristics of nonresidential missionaries.

Don't be put off by this catalog below! It's not a definition of a supermissionary of superhuman abilities. Regard it as you would a new city road map, or a new telephone directory, or a new college text book. It's a careful definition of, or guide to, a new concept: the nonresidential missionary. He or she is simply a committed Christian worker or couple who want to serve an unevangelized population segment in a restricted-access part of the world. This therefore is a list of emphases or aspects or steps or stages or activities which should characterize him or them. Any ordinary missionary or couple, from any country, of any nationality, are capable of filling this bill. He or she doesn't have to engage in all possible evangelistic activities directly—merely check that somebody does. It is a fact a list of a number of steps he or she should take, or aspects of mission that he or she should embrace.

The list of emphases or aspects is divided into 12 major categories or dimensions (in boldface capital type on the left). The list then gives in its second column 84 characteristics or descriptors (descriptive nouns or verbs or adjectives describing who the missionary is or what he or she does). Each is then expanded and explained in the one-sentence comment that follows.

While most of the 12 major dimensions below describe a life's ministry over the years AD 2000 and beyond, all of them could be begun and be well under way within 12 months of him first hearing the call. The research and survey side could easily be completed within 6 months, though it would be updated continuously thereafter.

The nonresidential missionary can be described here as:

| Ref | DIMENSION / Characteristic | One-sentence or explanation |
|---|---|---|
| | **CALLED** | |
| 1 | called | He or she is **called** to follow Christ across today's world. |
| 2 | missionary | He is a **missionary** working within the Christian world mission. |
| 3 | foreign | Most of the time he crosses political frontiers as an alien or **foreigner.** |
| 4 | cross-cultural | His ministry is **cross-cultural**, from his own culture to a different culture. |
| 5 | evangelizer | His primary role is as **evangelizer**, among unevangelized populations. |
| 6 | global | **Globally** oriented, he combs the world for other Great Commission cooperators. |
| 7 | professional | He and his spouse are **professional** foreign missionaries. |
| 8 | career | Being a missionary is his **career**, possibly or probably for life. |
| 9 | monovocational | Though he may have secular skills, mission or ministry is his **overarching vocation.** |
| 10 | full-time | He undertakes it as a **full-time** job, not a part-time interest. |
| 11 | legal | In whichever country he visits, he **obeys the laws** concerning overt evangelism. |
| 12 | nonpolitical | He is **apolitical** and secure from future state hostility, evictions or bannings. |
| 13 | nontraditional | As traditional residential mission is impossible, he becomes **nontraditional.** |
| 14 | nonresidential | Unable to reside in his target segment, he becomes **nonresidential.** |
| 15 | mobile | Resident with his family 70% of the time, he remains **mobile** and flexible. |
| | **APPOINTED** | |
| 16 | recruited | He is **recruited** by a foreign mission board or agency or church or support body. |
| 17 | selected | They test his vocation and qualifications and then **select** him for service. |
| 18 | trained | In missionary learning centers, he becomes **trained** in missions and missiology. |
| 19 | appointed | He is **appointed** by his board as one of their recognized missionaries. |
| 20 | sent | He is employed and **sent** by his board or sending body out on mission. |
| 21 | supported | He is subsequently **supported** by his board regularly (money, aid, prayer, travel). |
| | **MATCHED-UP** | |
| 22 | targeting | He holds discussions to locate a **target** population (people, city, or country). |
| 23 | matched-up | His talents and vocation are now **matched up** with possible segments. |
| 24 | focused | He finally **focuses** in on one single unevangelized population segment. |
| 25 | concentrated | It becomes a **concentrated** evangelizing ministry avoiding diversions. |
| 26 | commissioned | His board agrees to engage this segment and **commissions** him to his new ministry. |
| | **RESEARCHING** | |
| 27 | language-learning | He learns the **language** (market fluency) and thereby wins wide credibility. |
| 28 | studying | He masters his segment: **studies** maps, books, bibliographies, reports, tapes. |
| 29 | consulting | He compiles a list of **consultants** and centers expert on his segment. |
| 30 | researching | He **researches** (makes new discoveries about) his target population. |
| 31 | specializing | He takes vernacular newspapers and journals, and joins **specialist** societies. |
| | **NETWORKING** | |
| 32 | surveying | He **surveys** the entire spectrum of Great Commission activities within his segment. |
| 33 | recognizing | He **recognizes,** and aligns himself with, all involved Great Commission Christians. |
| 34 | cooperating | He actively **cooperates** with them, and gets them to cooperate with each other. |
| 35 | networking | He documents the existing **network,** becomes a major node, makes it a team. |
| 36 | team-player | He forges a de facto **Great Commission team** out of all working for his segment. |
| 37 | informing | He develops a wide-ranging **information** network and keeps the team informed. |
| 38 | catalyzing | Where necessary, as a **catalyzer** he urges new work and new approaches. |
| 39 | contextualizing | He helps the network honor the **global context** of all segments and their interests. |
| | **STRATEGIZING** | |
| 40 | biblical | He studies and emulates **biblical** strategic roles (Apostle Paul, et alii). |
| 41 | discerning | He analyses and **discerns** bridges and barriers to the gospel in his segment. |
| 42 | strategizing | He works out, privately and through the network, an overall **strategy.** |
| 43 | coordinating | He **coordinates** any other approaches or ministries when necessary. |
| 44 | integrating | He supports holistic ministry by helping to **integrate** evangelism and social concern. |
| 45 | communicating | Even when isolated, he **communicates** continually via phone, modem, electronic mail. |
| 46 | translating | He circulates strategic concepts **translated** into the language. |
| 47 | prioritizing | He assists the network to **prioritize** its Great Commission activities. |
| 48 | telecommunicating | If he has become a laptop computer user, he **telecommunicates** discreetly. |
| 49 | databasing | He utilizes multilingual infobases and **databases,** keeps up to date. |
| 50 | updated | He receives monthly computerized **updates** on his segment: literature, data, contacts. |
| 51 | reporting | He **reports** monthly to his agency on one short standard form or computer screen. |
| 52 | updating | He provides fuller **updating** status material, as available, regularly to his base. |
| 53 | monitoring | He tracks and **monitors** his segment's unevangelized status continually. |
| 54 | calendaring | He **calendars** (keeps track of future dates) and ensures items occur on schedule. |
| | **INTERCEDING** | |
| 55 | praying | He gets the network **praying** that the AD 2025 overarching objective may be met. |
| 56 | prayer-mobilizing | He **mobilizes prayer partners** in any country where this is possible. |
| 57 | interceding | He develops a ministry of informed **intercession** by home churches and agencies. |
| | **EVANGELIZING** | |
| 58 | evangelizing | His main task is **evangelizing**, in its 200 or so distinct dimensions and methods. |
| 59 | goal-oriented | His **goal** is that everyone in his segment become evangelized by AD 2025. |
| 60 | responsible | He accepts **responsibility** to see to it that the whole network achieves this goal. |
| 61 | future-oriented | He orients his ministry to **'AD 2025 and Beyond'**. |
| 62 | teaching | His main **teaching** is, informally, on how the network can achieve this goal. |
| | **MINISTERING** | |
| 63 | ministering | He continually draws up new **ministry options** and gets the team implementing them. |
| 64 | megaministering | He plans for **megaministry** approaches to his segment. |
| 65 | proclaiming | He sees to it that by all methods a continuous **proclamation** of Christ goes on. |
| 66 | seed-sowing | His goal is: to see adequate scripture distribution, **broadcasting**, literature, etc. |
| 67 | disciple-making | His goal is: at least 100 new **disciples made** in this segment by AD 2025. |
| 68 | church-planting | His goal is: 4 or 5 new beachhead **churches planted** and leaders trained by AD 2025. |
| 69 | indigenizing | He encourages emergence of new **indigenous** expressions of Christianity in his segment. |
| | **IMPLEMENTING** | |
| 70 | visiting | He **visits** his target as a tourist or for secular events (conferences, etc). |
| 71 | entrepreneurial | Creative and versatile, he exploits **opportunities** as and when they occur. |
| 72 | facilitating | As a **facilitator**, he actively assists others to get their roles performed. |
| 73 | locating | He advises on possible **location** of tentmakers or others resident in the segment. |
| 74 | mobilizing | As a **mobilizer**, he locates new resources, finds additional personnel. |
| 75 | implementing | As an **implementer**, he ensures all agreed steps actually get implemented. |
| 76 | conflict-avoiding | He **avoids conflict** between his segment's interests and outside Christian work. |
| | **ADVOCATING** | |
| 77 | relating | He maintains **good relations** with secular, religious and Christian authorities. |
| 78 | advocating | He serves as **advocate**, anywhere, for his segment and their evangelization. |
| 79 | lobbying | When necessary he **lobbies** energetically on behalf of his segment. |
| 80 | low-key | Aware of the dangers of publicity, he keeps a **low profile.** |
| 81 | sensitizing | He alerts and **sensitizes** the network to needs for confidentiality and security. |
| | **TRAINING** | |
| 82 | equipping | He sees to it that indigenous leadership emerges **equipped** for ministry. |
| 83 | training | He assists with **training** seminars for new nonresidential missionaries anywhere. |
| 84 | recruiting | He keeps alert to **recruit** nonresidential missionaries for segments elsewhere. |

### *Megaplans and gigaplans*

The major proponents of closure and the AD 2000 deadline were, interestingly enough, the most massive of all the recently-launched global plans. Virtually all of them latched onto the millennial date, as can been seen from the last column in Table 27–1.

Table 27–1 sets out the situation today with regard to the 90 largest global plans out of the 1,500 total, which are so enormous they are called by the new term megaplans. These are current, ongoing, global plans, each of which is in process of spending hundreds of millions of dollars to achieve its goal of world evangelization.

Of these the 31 biggest plans, ones which we are terming the Top 31, are megaplans that are termed gigaplans. These are plans each of which is in process of spending over one billion dollars to achieve its goal.

Note again in particular the final column, 'Deadline'. Until 1976 no megaplan incorporated the AD 2000 theme. Then came the first AD 2000 megaplan properly so called: the Southern Baptist gigaplan, Bold Mission Thrust, calling its 12 million baptized members (24 million adherents) to the clearly-stated overarching objective: 'That Southern Baptists understand, accept, and become involved in the mission to enable every person in the world to have opportunity to hear and to respond to the gospel of Christ by the year 2000" (1978 Southern Baptist Convention Annual, page 47). Halfway on its course to 2000, this plan was again formally reaffirmed by the SBC Foreign Mission Board in a 1988 resolution using exactly the same terminology.

Over the succeeding years since 1976, every single successive new megaplan followed suit and focused on a deadline date, in almost every case AD 2000.

## *REACHING THE WORLD BY AD 2000?*

Where do we stand today with regard to global evangelization plans and the AD 2000 deadline? The answer is simple. Although something like one third of the Top 31 (11 current gigaplans) espoused the AD 2000 motif, they were unable to meet their goals.

Missions writer Jim Reapsome wrote extensively on current barriers to world evangelization. In 6 analytical articles published in 1988 he located 40 different major stumbling blocks or hurdles. He discussed them under five headings: (1) the church's lagging commitment; (2) strategic roadblocks; (3) problems with mission agencies; (4) religious and political opposition; (5) rising costs.

A survey of 10 missions experts revealed some formidable hazards. Things like the church's lagging commitment to world missions, problems within our missions organizations and with our strategies, religious and political opposition, and the mounting costs of missions. To these must be added the exploding world population, rapid urbanization, language barriers, and religious syncretism.

### *The church's lagging commitment*

Patrick Johnstone, International Research Secretary of WEC International and compiler of *Operation World*, believes that the world will not be won to Christ so long as the church's structure, terminology, and theological education have a 'built-in bias to produce static hierarchies, buildings, and a comfortable lifestyle for its members.'

Richard Sollis, head of the Research and Planning Department of New Tribes Mission, claimed that relatively few churches make world evangelization their priority. He thinks that 'insufficient vision, discipleship, and obedience' have bottle-necked the flow of personnel and resources needed to finish the task.

### *Strategic roadblocks*

Among the strategic barriers to world evangelization cited were:

1. A poor grasp of communications principles. Missiologist Ralph Covell questioned whether missionaries have learned how to make the gospel intelligible to people with radically different world views.
2. The lack of data. The hurdle of identifying the people who need to be reached must be overcome. 'Without hard data, the dream of reaching the world for Christ becomes nothing more

than that—a dream,' said Jim Montgomery, president of Dawn Ministries. For example, when Presbyterians in Ghana found out that in one area there were 167 villages with no churches, they put into action a plan to change that in the next five years. Related to lack of data is confusion about how to use what is available. Various agencies compile their own target lists according to their specific goals, such as broadcasting, translation, gospel records, homes to visit, or literature to distribute.

3. Language barriers. Millions of people are denied access to the knowledge of Jesus Christ because the gospel has never been made known to them in a language that they can grasp.
4. Lack of unified church-planting goals. Western agencies find it hard to work out these goals in cooperation and planning with existing churches in Africa, Asia, Europe, and Latin America.
5. Improper allocation of personnel. Some agencies pack too many missionaries in some places and neglect other areas.
6. Western quick-response evangelism. Some evangelization methods call for people to make commitments without proper understanding of essential biblical truths.
7. Shallow approaches. Some missionaries fail to see the difference between people's felt needs and their primary spiritual needs.
8. Pioneer evangelism not a high priority. With many demands and competing interests, some agencies do not make pioneer church planting their number one priority.

### Problems within mission agencies
One would think that with the growth of management skills and maturity, mission agencies by this time would have overcome some inherent roadblocks to world evangelization. But a number of pesky problems persist. Among them:

1. Dependence on Western mission structures, which stymies development of partnerships with mission agencies and churches in other countries.
2. Continued competition with other mission agencies and denominations.
3. Management fears change. This leads to an unwillingness to look at new strategies and to make hard decisions in the home office as well as overseas.
4. Waste and duplication, caused by organizational isolationism, empire building, jockeying for power and position, and jealous guarding of funding structures and supporting constituencies.

### Religious and political opposition
This survey found that religious and political opposition did not rank at the top of the list of barriers to world evangelization. Apparently problems are more internal than external.

However, missiologist David Hesselgrave summed up this barrier: 'Totalitarianism, anti-conversion efforts, closed and partially closed countries, martyrdoms, the resurgence of non-Christian religions and world views, and demonic activity' all stand in the way of reaching the world.

### Rising costs
Hesselgrave also observed that 'affluence has a way of numbing mission concern.' Therefore, when it comes to rising costs of world evangelization, he wondered if 'more attention and funding devoted to keeping missionaries equipped and well cared for' will have a damaging effect on the effort to reach the unreached.

### Why the special AD 2000 plans?
In view of the foregoing, was it not foolish to project the completion of the task by AD 2000? This survey said no. Both churches and mission agencies need a stiff shot in the arm. 'Unless we have something to aim at, we won't hit it,' said Ian Hay, general director of SIM International. 'Our forebears sought to reach the world in their generation. Did they do it? No, but they certainly stimulated an army of missionaries,' Hay said.

## A HARD LOOK AT SOME AD 2000 GOALS

### The Millennial year
Professional futurists first began to speculate in earnest about the world in AD 2000 some 40 years beforehand in 1960. In the 1970s, scores of conferences of secular scholars were held to think about the end of the century. Books, articles, and journals all mushroomed. By 1976, Christian global megaplans began to announce AD 2000 as their deadline. By 1988 churches and agencies of all kinds were following suit.

Note again that the first day of the 21st century was not 1 January 2000 (January 1, 2000), but 1 January 2001 (January 1, 2001). This is the correct, logical, strict usage, but there is also a widespread popular usage in which this first day of the 21st century is regarded as 1 January 2000.

Note also that secular futurists are now calling for the abandonment of the Gregorian Calendar and the global introduction, on that very day, of the new Constant Calendar in which dates always fall on the same day of the week. AD 2000 is being seen as a magnetic turning-point in God's dealings with man. Over the last 700 years, in fact, so many predictions have been made about this date that we should pause to examine some of them, to construct our own forecast, and to show how alternate scenarios can be drawn up.

### Assessing 15 major goals
By 1990 several hundred goals had been announced by Christian mission agencies and denominations. A collection of 15 of the most significant of these is assembled below in Table 27–15. Each of these goals was repeatedly brought before the Christian public throughout the Decade of Evangelization, 1990-2000. In every case, Christian leaders emphasized the fact that these goals could be reached by AD 2000.

For each of the 15 goals listed in Table 27–15, an assessment is made of progress by AD 2000. These assessments clearly show how far short of the stated goals agencies and churches fell. Although no one would deny that the Decade of Evangelization represented significant activity related to world evangelization, apparently this activity was startlingly short of what was actually needed to achieve these goals. Agencies and churches presumably vastly underestimated what was required to reach their own goals.

### Some things are just not possible
One can move then from the larger goals of Christian missions to examining the AD 2000 goals of 6 of the larger current plans. One asks: Why were they unable to meet these goals? Hundreds of global plans in the past have obtained from the Christian public large amounts of money, manpower, resources, enthusiasm, and prayer support, only to collapse without reaching their goals.

As noted earlier, the year AD 2000 had long been considered the most likely *terminus ad quem* of God's plans for the world. Of history's 1,500 distinct plans to complete world evangelization, those referring to AD 2000 have numbered at least 200. One thinks of the Protestant radio plan, 'The World by 2000' (sponsored by the 4 international broadcasting agencies TWR, FEBC, HCJB, and ELWA), with its aim 'to provide every man, woman and child on earth the opportunity to turn on their radio and hear the gospel of Jesus Christ in a language they can understand...by the year 2000.

Its Catholic counterpart, Lumen 2000, aimed (through worldwide evangelistic TV coverage using direct broadcast satellites) 'to preach the gospel of Jesus to the uttermost parts of the Earth, spreading the love of Jesus around the globe' (based in Dallas, Texas [USA], with Vatican Television in Rome). World Literature Crusade (Every Home for Christ) had a plan called 'Into every home by 2000,' which aimed to place two pieces of Christian literature in every home on Earth by AD 2000. The Catholic Charismatic office in the Vatican evolved as its plan 'Evangelization 2000.' Its published goal was 'To give Jesus Christ the 2,000th birthday gift of a world more Christian than not' (usually abbreviated as 51% Christian), or 'To give Jesus a 2,000th birthday present of a billion new believers.'

A similar goal was announced by the worldwide Charismatic Renewal in the Mainline Churches, as emblazoned on the top of the cover of their official journal, *AD 2000 Together*: 'To bring the majority of

---

**Table 27–15.  Assessing 15 major AD 2000 global goals related to numerous global plans addressing the unfinished task of world evangelization.**

This is a listing of 15 global goals, related to numerous global plans, pledging to complete world evangelization by the year 2000. Most of these were announced around or before 1990 with 10 or more years remaining before AD 2000. At least 1,000 mission agencies and churches were directly involved in promoting and attempting to achieve these goals. Nearly all of these published brochures and/or other literature detailing their involvement in reaching these goals.

Further documentation for these goals can be found in Table 27–21 or in Part 2 "CosmoChronology". A list of 186 goals was presented in 1990 in *Our globe and how to reach it* (New Hope Press).

In each case an assessment of the goal's progress by AD 2000 is made. The statement relating to what progress had been achieved by AD 2000 is backed up by evidence in both this volume and *World Christian encyclopedia*.

One can immediately see that agencies and churches fell far short of these key 15 goals. In many cases, very little progress was made. This is especially true in the deployment of personnel and other resources to World A. In the case of foreign missionaries and scripture distribution, World A continues to receive only a small portion of what is required for goal #8 to be fulfilled.

Note that goals that refer to World A refered to World A

countries. When these goals were stated the countries making up World A were different than the current list of 38 reported in this volume. As an example, the country of China was considered a World A country when these goals were announced. Thus, in reporting progress, the original list of 30 countries, including China, is used to evaluate a given goal.

| No. | Goal to be reached by AD 2000 | Actual progress by AD 2000 |
|---|---|---|
| 1. | Enroll 200 million Christians in a world prayer force praying daily for closure in world evangelization. | 200 million Christians praying daily for world evangelization. |
| 2. | Increase the proportion of Christian annual finance expended on World A, from 0.5% to 4%. | 0.4% of Christian annual finance expended on World A. |
| 3. | Feed and nourish the world's 600 million persons on the verge of starvation. | 500 million persons on the verge of starvation. |
| 4. | Evangelize World A's 4,850 peoples, metropolises, and countries. | 5,538 peoples, metropolises, and countries in World A. |
| 5. | Record and make available a gospel message in every language on Earth. | 5,600 out of 13,500 languages have a gospel message. |
| 6. | Increase World A's share of Christian broadcast hours from 0.01% to 20%. | 0.3% of Christian broadcast hours directed to World A. |
| 7. | Prepare and show to everyone gospel films, specifically the 'Jesus' film, in 500 languages. | 'Jesus' film in 600 languages shown to 4 billion people (with duplications). |
| 8. | Present the gospel message to all 6.1 billion people. | 4.5 billion (73.1%) have heard; 1.6 billion have not. |
| 9. | Enable 300,000 itinerant charismatic evangelists to target World A. | 50,000 itinerant charismatic evangelists actively evangelizing. |
| 10. | Bring a majority of the human race to Jesus Christ by AD 2000. | 33.0% of the world's population professes Jesus Christ. |
| 11. | Establish a church-planting movement in every people on Earth. | 14,000 minipeoples have such a movement, 10,000 do not. |
| 12. | Increase World A's share of full-time Christian workers from 0.7% to 5% by 2000. | 2.3% of full-time Christian workers minister in World A. |
| 13. | Increase World A's share of foreign missionaries received from today's 1.1% to 40% by AD 2000. | World A's share: 4%. |
| 14. | Increase World A's share of annual scripture distribution from 1% to 25% by AD 2000. | Only 1% of annual scripture distribution targeted on World A. |
| 15. | Distribute a Scripture selection to every soul on Earth in his or her own language. | 2.4 billion people (40% of world) have no scripture selections. |

the human race to Jesus Christ by the end of the century.' The goal of its 1987 North American General Congress on the Holy Spirit and World Evangelization, held in New Orleans (USA) in July, was stated as '1.5 billion new Christians' between 1987 and 2000.

The most formidably organized of all these plans has been the USA Southern Baptists' 1976 plan 'Bold Mission Thrust.' Its overarching objective, first published in 1976, was 'that every person in the world shall have the opportunity to hear the gospel of Christ in the next 25 years,' also phrased as 'to preach the gospel to all the people in the world by 2000.'

Why did all of these plans fail to reach their stated goals by AD 2000? What is the forecast, today, as to when these projects are likely to reach their goals?

## *AD 2000 AND BEYOND*

### *More new plans arise*

By the year 2000 the rate of creation of new global plans had risen to around one new plan every nine days, or 50 a year. There is every indication that this rate will increase rapidly over the next 5 or 10 years. Instead of being caught napping, the Christian world might well try to evolve a mechanism for fitting such new plans into a wider strategy as each of them emerges.

## *THE CONCLUSION OF YEAR 2000 PLANS*

No irony can be lost on the fact that as the year 2000 came to a close, one of the largest of the global plans collapsed. Over 1,600 leaders from 110 nations were expected to gather in Jerusalem for the Celebrate Messiah 2000 conference (expected to meet from 27 December 2000 until 2 January 2001). This conference, organized as the last major event of the AD 2000 and Beyond Movement, was to feature plenary sessions on topics ranging from women in world evangelization to the current status of world evangelization goals. An all night prayer meeting was scheduled to bring in the new millennium. Due to political unrest in Jerusalem, the meeting was canceled with less than two weeks to go. Organizers offered sincere apologies, and as planned, its offices in Colorado Springs shut down a few weeks later.

This story mirrors that of dozens of other large plans and hundreds of smaller ones. Goals for evangelizing the world by AD 2000 simply were not met. Many AD 2000 focused plans were forced to redirect effort elsewhere. Others simply collapsed. Some are continuing on without reference to the year 2000 as a goal. But in every case, the goal of evangelizing the world by AD 2000 was not realized.

An analysis of the reasons why these plans failed reveals an interesting variety of root problems. The following is a list of the major difficulties.

1. The global nature of the plans dissipated resources. Many organizations working in 100 or less countries announced global plans that implicitly assumed that all 238 countries would be legitimate targets. This had the unintended consequence of agencies deploying personnel and resources in heavily-Christian countries where they previously had no work.
2. Many agencies embarked on their plans with a lack of understanding of the limited nature of their own resources. In other words, they made plans that continued to deploy personnel in more heavily-Christian places without fully realizing how this led to neglecting the least evangelized. Most agencies resisted strategic planning processes that pointed this out.

**Table 27–16. 1,500 global plans arranged by cooperation with other traditions.**

(Source: Table 27–19 and 27-21, column 10).

| Code<br>1 | Plans<br>2 | %<br>3 | Cooperation<br>4 | Sub-totals<br>5 |
|---|---|---|---|---|
| 0 | 311 | 20.6 | None | |
| 1 | 356 | 23.6 | Minimal | 66% non-cooperating |
| 2 | 331 | 21.9 | Partial | or partially cooperating |
| 3 | 317 | 21.0 | General | |
| 4 | 126 | 8.3 | Essential | 95% ignoring non-like- |
| 5 | 69 | 4.6 | Total | minded plans |
| **Total** | **1,510** | **100.0** | | |

3. Some agencies and churches could not resist a continual process of reinvention of their plans. A plan was announced, implemented for a few years, seen to fall short of its goals, abandoned, and then reworked with a new name with similar goals. This process produced a phenomenal number of slogans and catch-phrases.
4. Almost all of the plans vastly underestimated the complexity of the world's peoples and languages in monitoring its goals. India, with its vast number of castes and languages was declared nearly 'reached' on a number of occasions, yet in AD 2000 over 90% of all Christian workers, both foreign and national, were completely out of touch with Hindus and Muslims.
5. Many plans, in the end, insisted that the limited progress that was made justified their setting of goals in the first place. While it can be conceded that much progress was made in world evangelization in the 1990s, the expectations raised by overarching plans and commitments has been shown to have a negative effect on the overall task. Of particular concern was the tendency to overstate progress in world evangelization, leaving the impression that very little was left to be done. This trend intensified as the year 2000 grew closer.
6. There yet remains much confusion over who the least evangelized actually are. The underlying confusion seems to issue from the fact that many agencies and churches insist on calling heavily-Christian or heavily-evangelized peoples 'unreached'. A fundamental misunderstanding of the nature of evangelization and conversion is at the heart of the problem. Even where clarity was brought through documentation such as *Redemptoris Missio* or the Manila Manifesto, strategists insisted on broadening their interpretation. For example, Roman Catholics, in response to the need for new evangelization, sent missionaries to Norway, a predominantly Protestant land.
7. Over the past three decades, published lists of unreached peoples have consistently depicted heavily-Christian peoples as unreached. The problem seems to be at the level of methodology—how lists are drawn up. Most are primarily the opinions of individual missionaries and agencies as to what groups are unreached. Thus heavily-Methodist groups are often considered by Baptists as unreached and vice versa. Given the fragmentation of the Christian church and the vast number of denominations (33,800), it is no wonder that nearly every people in the world is considered 'unreached' by someone else.
8. Personnel under the auspices of these global plans are expected to receive a divine call before they target the least evangelized. Although divine guidance is essential to the missionary task, many plans did not take into account strategic implications of the biblical basis of mission. The clearly implied priority of the least evangelized in Great Commission accounts in the Scriptures was often overruled by personal preferences under the guise of personal divine guidance.
9. Persons sent out under these global plans go mainly where invited. Exacerbating the deployment imbalance is the fact that most deployment begins with some kind of invitation. Since Christians normally do the inviting, non-Christian situations are not fairly represented in this process. Many plans stated their preference for the unevangelized but utilized invitations to deploy their resources. As a result, the vast majority of their resources ended up in already-Christian contexts.
10. Many global plans adopted the strategy of going to 'harvestable' fields first. This usually meant a nominally Christian situation open to saturation evangelism from other Christian traditions. Thus Roman Catholic Argentina was considered a great harvest field by Evangelical Protestants. However, evidence seems to point in the opposite direction: the least evangelized appear, for the most part, to be the most responsive (See evidence people by people in Table 8-2 , column 36 in *WCE* Part 8 "Ethnosphere"). This means that plans focused on the harvest will need to reconsider targets in the 21st century.
11. The least evangelized are often called resistant. This statement overlooks the important fact that peoples who have received little attention cannot be labeled 'resistant'. Resistance can only be measured when there has been significant effort. Consequently, terms such as 'overlooked', 'ignored', and 'neglected' are usually more appropriate.

## *NETWORKING FOR WORLD EVANGELIZATION*

### *It is easier not to cooperate*

Managing this huge apparatus of the Christian world mission today are some 4,000 foreign mission agencies. Influencing them are 2 contrasting varieties of leadership: (a) hierarchies operating organizations or bureaucracies, and (b) networks. Every organization has a hierarchy, or chain of command, which can be envisaged as a vertical line downwards from president or chairman to executive secretary to directors to typists and messengers. By contrast, a network links together horizontally (as equals, without executive authority) a variety of interested parties in different agencies and organizations: executives in unrelated bodies, information people, researchers, scholars, ideas people, secular contacts, and so on. The term network refers to all types of associations spontaneously created to address problems and offer possibilities primarily outside of established institutions.

Many persons concerned for world mission labor under the delusion that these 4,000 agencies all cooperate together as a single gigantic network. There is, however, a peculiar difficulty in that what has grown up over the years is not a network but a vast number of isolated standalone global plans.

A single, specific, finely-honed question illustrates this: How much actual cooperation has there been between global plans, and especially global megaplans and global gigaplans? The straight answer to the straight question is startling indeed.

### *Cooperation*

To answer this question, one must examine how global Christianity's 300 distinct ecclesiastical traditions have cooperated when they have produced global plans. The picture is frightening (Table 27–16). The reader can see fuller definitions of the 6 terms used to describe 'Attitude to cooperation' below found in the codebook for column 10 at the beginning of Table 27–21.

What this means is that some 1,000 or two thirds (66%) of all these global plans have been launched in some degree as standalone, self-sufficient plans, either with no reference to other like-minded traditions, or merely nominal reference, or inviting other like-minded parties to sign up under their leadership. Any supposed network simply does not exist. Each global plan has, in varying degrees, viewed itself, or its sponsor, as at the center of world evangelization. Strangely enough, this situation can be interpreted in 2 diametrically opposite ways, one bad, the other good.

The first interpretation is that this is a bad situation, a grim one, a lamentable one. It ascribes the standalone mode as due to incurable tunnel vision—this ignorance of the vast extent of other Christians committed to Christ's Great Commission, this cavalier attitude to the rest of the Christian world—which is, in one word, pathetic. This may well be true. This absence of any network is catastrophic. It is probably the major single cause of the fiasco of today's unevangelized world of 1.6 billion persons largely untouched from one year to the next by either the 1,500 global plans or the top 300 plans still being actively implemented today.

For these reasons, many Christians regard the 1,000 standalone global plans (codes 0,1,2 in Table 27–16) as intrinsically bad, evil, even diabolical. They see them as the modern-day counterpart to the 3 satanic global plans that Jesus rejected at his Temptation. These 1,000 plans, they say, have taken the easy way out, each trying to do it all unilaterally, avoiding Christ's categorical desire and prayer, 'That they may all be one' (John 17:11,21,22, RSV).

Among those decrying the resultant waste and duplication are Tokunboh Adeyemo of the Association of Evangelicals of Africa and Madagascar, in Kenya, chairman of the World Evangelical Fellowship, who wrote on the need for Evangelical cooperation: 'Rep-

## Table 27–17.  90 major currently-existing global strategy committees concerned to implement world evangelization.

Note: This is not an approved list of recommended committees, but a descriptive list of the diversity that exists today. Several marginal churches, often termed quasi-Christian or pseudo-Christian, also claim to be implementing Christ's Great Commission. Entries in bold type are gigaplans (each spending $1 billion on its plan).

| Origin | Name of ongoing committee | Sponsors |
|---|---|---|
| 1209 | **Order of Friars: mendicant orders of travelling preachers** | OFM |
| 1215 | **Order of Preachers: 'Propagation of the Faith through Preaching'** | OP |
| 1523 | **Conversion of Islam and the Whole World to Christ (Jesuits)** | SJ |
| 1580 | Discalced Carmelite Sisters: evangelization by prayer | – |
| 1588 | **Consistorial Congregation (Sacred Congregation for Bishops)** | – |
| 1622 | **Propaganda Fide: Spreading the Faith to the World** | – |
| 1680 | Christian Brothers: evangelization by schools | FSC |
| 1703 | Spiritans: *'Evangelizzazione degli infedeli'* | CSSp |
| 1804 | Foreign-language Bible Societies: BFBS, ABS, et alia | BFBS |
| 1819 | **Missionary Society of the Methodist Episcopal Church** | BGM |
| 1830 | **Church of Jesus Christ of Latter-day Saints** | CJCLdS |
| 1844 | **Seventh-day Adventists** | SDA |
| 1845 | **Southern Baptist Convention** | SBC-FMB |
| 1859 | Salesians: Christian education of youth across world | SDB |
| 1862 | Scheutists: *'Evangelizzazione dei popoli'* | CICM |
| 1863 | **New Apostolic Church** | NAK(NAC) |
| 1865 | Christian Revival Association | SA |
| 1870 | **Watch Tower Bible & Tract Society** | WTBTS-IBSA |
| 1872 | Salesian Sisters: evangelization by works of charity | FMA |
| 1875 | Verbites: *'Evangelizzazione dei Popoli'* | SVD |
| 1882 | **Knights of Columbus** | K of C |
| 1887 | Christian & Missionary Alliance | C&MA |
| 1890 | Scandinavian/Evangelical Alliance Mission | TEAM |
| 1893 | Africa Industrial Mission/SIM International | SIM |
| 1895 | Association of Pentecostal Churches in America (Nazarene) | APCA-CoN |
| 1899 | Gideons International | – |
| 1910 | Church of God (Cleveland) World Missions | CoGWM |
| 1913 | Christ's Etceteras (Worldwide Evangelization Crusade) | WEC |
| 1917 | **Interdenominational Foreign Mission Association** | IFMA |
| 1918 | Worldwide Evangelism | ICFG |
| 1921 | **Legion of Mary** | – |
| 1924 | United Pentecostal Church International | UPCI-FMD |
| 1928 | **Opus Dei** | O.D. |
| 1930 | Voice of Prophecy | SDA |
| 1930 | Bringing Christ to the Nations (The Lutheran Hour) | LCMS |
| 1931 | Laudetur Jesus Christus (Radio Vatican) | SJ |
| 1934 | Two Thousand Tongues To Go | WBT-SIL |
| 1934 | Youth for Christ International | YFCI |
| 1942 | New Tribes Mission | NTM |
| 1943 | Conservative Baptist Foreign Mission Society | CBFMS |
| 1945 | **Evangelical Foreign Missions Association** | EFMA/NAE |
| 1946 | **United Bible Societies** | UBS/BFBS |
| 1947 | **Oral Roberts Evangelistic Association** | OREA/ORU/CBM |
| 1948 | World Council of Churches, 7th Function | WCC |
| 1950 | Billy Graham Evangelistic Association | BGEA |
| 1950 | **World Vision International** | WV-WVI |
| 1950 | Full Gospel Businessmen's Fellowship International | FGBFI |
| 1950 | Missionaries of Charity | MC |
| 1957 | Operation Mobilization/Send The Light | OM-STL |
| 1960 | **Youth With A Mission** | YWAM/AoG |
| 1961 | Commission on World Mission and Evangelism | DWME-CWME |
| 1961 | **Christian Broadcasting Network/CBN World Outreach** | WYAH(CBN) |
| 1967 | **Sacred Congregation for the Evangelization of Peoples** | SCEP-RCC |
| 1969 | **Jimmy Swaggart Ministries** | JSM-AoG |
| 1972 | Marian | |
| 1972 | **International Catholic Charismatic Renewal** | ICCRO |
| 1973 | **Trinity Broadcasting Network** | TBN |
| 1974 | Lausanne Committee for World Evangelization | ICOWE-LCWE |
| 1974 | **3rd Synod of Bishops: 'The Evangelization of the Modern World'** | SB-RCC |
| 1975 | World Evangelical Fellowship Missions Commission | MC-WEF |
| 1976 | **Bold Mission Thrust** | BMT-SBC |
| 1977 | Focus on the Family | – |
| 1979 | **The 'Jesus' Film Project** | CCCI |
| 1982 | **Project 223** | YWAM |
| 1983 | Third World mission societies: The last age of missions | OCM/TWMA |
| 1985 | Korean Churches' Plan for Entering Every Country | – |
| 1985 | **Integrity Keepers Conventions** | IBSA-JWs |
| 1985 | **Global Strategy Committee, Seventh-day Adventists** | GSC-SDA |
| 1985 | The World by 2000 | TWR/FEBC/HCJB |
| 1986 | Reaching the World's Cities by AD 2000 | AoG(USA)-DFM |
| 1986 | 'Renew the Church—Reach the World' | WEF |
| 1987 | **Evangelization 2000/New Evangelization 2000** | E-2000 |
| 1987 | AD 2000 Together | NARSC |
| 1987 | **New Life 2000: A Revolutionary Plan (Here's Life World)** | CCCI |
| 1987 | **Decade of Harvest** | AoG(USA) |
| 1987 | COMIBAM '87/Ibero-American Missions Congress | COMIBAM |
| 1987 | World Evangelism World Plan 1987-1991 | WE-WMC |
| 1988 | Charismatics United for World Evangelization | CUWE/CCC/NARSC |
| 1988 | Third World Missions Advance | TWMA/AMA/PI |
| 1988 | March for Jesus | MFJ |
| 1989 | International Bishops' Retreat 2000 | E-2000 |
| 1990 | **Decade of Universal Evangelization** | E-2000 |
| 1990 | EXPLO '90 Worldwide Satellite Strategy | CCCI-HLW |
| 1991 | **Global Congress of Charismatic Leaders for World Evangelization** | CUWE/ICCRO |
| 1991 | Redemptoris Missio | RM |
| 1993 | Praying through the Window | PTW |
| 1998 | Confronting the Queen of Heaven | – |
| 1999 | AD 2000 Jubilee Year | RCC |

etition or duplication should be avoided at all cost. We should call an international consultation of the major groups interested in the subject-matter to pray and plan on how to synchronize our effort.'

*The standalone mode*
But there is a second interpretation. Networks, like committees, often have no executive clout and accomplish nothing. On this interpretation, the standalone mode is the only one with any chance of succeeding and actually accomplishing the goal's overarching objective. In this mode, the sponsor publicly announces and accepts total responsibility for the completion of the entire task, whether other agencies provide support or not.

It is easy to see the attractiveness of this mode. By contrast, consider its opposite—the comity approach, characterized by 'Let's all of us agencies agree to work together and to divide up the task, each accepting responsibility for completing only 'our appropriate part.'' This is, frankly, a let-out, a cop-out, a loophole, a black hole of gigantic proportions. The church can never fulfill the Great Commission as long as its different component parts each assign themselves a modest, manageable, easy-to-work, piece of the total responsibility. Too many gaps and unclaimed tasks result. The harvest force is then a chain only as strong as its weakest link. If one agency fails to evangelize its agreed share of the world, then the overarching goal of the entire plan has failed.

What is needed, therefore, is for all the component parts to each embrace responsibility for the whole, whether the other parts fail or not. In other words, only the standalone mode has any chance of ultimately reaching the goal. But, paradoxically, it can never reach that goal unless it networks with other Great Commission Christians.

Another, more serious, problem results from the fact that 95% of all global plans (codes 0-4 in Table 18) ignore or write off all other Christian traditions which are not 'like-minded.' This term 'like-minded' is a composite of denominational jingoism, past historical antagonisms, ecclesiastical tradition, preference, ethnocentrism, racism, cultural imperialism, ignorance, arrogance, and a host of other factors.

Only 4.6% of all plans build on networking between the entire spectrum of all Christians of all traditions.

*A network of standalone plans*
What is needed therefore is to combine network and hierarchy—ideas and executive clout. The ideal might, therefore, well be to encourage a network of standalone plans each characterized by (a) a standalone acceptance of total responsibility, together with (b) a recognition of the essential value of the rest of the network, resulting in (c) recognition of, acceptance of, and cooperation with, all other global plans espoused by Great Commission Christians.

### THE TOP NINE MAINLINE GREAT COMMISSION GLOBAL MEGANETWORKS

*Computer giganetworking as the acid test*
The greatest challenge of all facing global Christianity today is this: Can all who profess to be Great Commission Christians be persuaded at the very least to acknowledge each other's existence and to use today's massive resources for some kind of agreed Great Commission objectives, perhaps in major problem areas such as closed countries or unreached peoples.

The fact of the matter is that mainline global Christianity today and its global mission can be classified into nine distinct, huge, global meganetworks. In addition to these nine mainline Christian networks, there are also three marginal or quasi-Christian networks whose existence cannot be ignored. The whole situation is set out in Table 27–18.

The new urgency about the existence of tunnel vision today is that all these Great Commission Christians and their meganetworks—mainline and marginal—have now got hold of, own, and operate the staggering figure of some 332 million computers and, largely separately in stand-alone modes, are expending billions a year supposedly on global plans to evangelize the world.

*A new definition of networking*
The concept of networking is now so broadly used, understood, and misunderstood in Christian circles that it means little more than 'us Christians talking to other like-minded Christians.' If talking to 20 colleagues in 20 offices is called networking, the word is debased. If corresponding by mail with 20 of your buddies is called networking, the word is squandered. If everybody is networking, nobody is networking. If everything is networking, nothing is networking. The word has lost any cutting edge, any boundaries, and hence any value to clarify today's

situation.

This difficulty can be overcome by always using the adjective 'human' for this sort of networking. A human network is obviously valuable and commendable.

In the context of global mission, the simple term *network* should be restricted to mean solely and exclusively electronic networking, and in particular, computer networking, or networking that involves the regular use of several computers. Likewise, a network for purposes of the following discussion means at least three computers linked together electronically in some recognizably regular form.

In fact, a quick assessment would be that so far as expediting the world mission of the Christian church is concerned, most of its networks are luxuries or palliatives serving very limited or restricted purposes among groupings of like-minded offices and the harried executives who occupy them. At best, they serve the interests of home mission by denominations in strongly christianized countries. They are hardly yet in any sense a major force for furthering foreign or world mission.

### Elements of a computer network
The following 23 features are found in computer networks. At least one of these must be present and in regular use before the term network can correctly be applied. Hundreds of such secular global networks now exist. One such is the Internet, now with 300 million users in virtually every country of the world. Scores of other networks are vast, global meganetworks.

1. Electronic mail: regular sending and receiving of messages.
2. News services: the regular electronic dissemination of bulletins, releases, updates.
3. World Wide Web pages, home pages, bulletin boards, computer conferencing, 3-month conferences, instantaneous committee meetings.
4. Telephones: computerized calling, automated calling and answering, conferencing, freeze-frame visual talks, videophone.
5. Cable/telegram/telex: sending cables world-wide direct from your screen.
6. Fax/multifax: sending pages of digitized pictures and text via telephone.
7. Text-processing: word-processing of same document by several editors at once.
8. Large-scale data-gathering: regular electronic amassing of large volumes of original grassroots data.
9. Statistical analysis: ongoing examination and analysis (using spreadsheets, SPSS, et alia).
10. Color graphics, diagrams, charts, maps.
11. Display: online projection to very large wall screens, animated graphics, video mixes, etc.
12. Publishing: writing, production, and electronic dissemination of jointly-produced literature, status reports, et alia.
13. Desktop publishing.
14. Broadcasting: electronic media, radio, television, cable TV, use of commercial networks by Christians.
15. Datacasting: regular broadcasting of large volumes of updated computerized data.
16. Teleporting: sending huge packets of computerized data through land and satellite routes.
17. Voice: recognition, production, voice-activated computer systems, automatic language translation.
18. Image: scanning, digitized imaging, image-processing, computer-aided design.
19. Future scenarios, futuristics, futurological analyzes, futures research.
20. Infobases, methods of handling infoglut (information overload).
21. Databases: relational databasing, databased automated decision-making, videotext.
22. Knowledge bases, knowledge systems, knowledge engineering.
23. Expert systems: synergetics, self-replicating systems, robotics, artificial intelligence.

Every one of the above features has immediate value and relevance to Christian mission. But how many Christian networks today incorporate them?

### Four categories of network
Christians concerned with obedience to the Great Commission can discern four distinct categories of network, based on increasing degrees of complexity.

1. A *Great Commission network* today is defined here as any agency, or organization or aggregate of contacts which (1) frequently articulates or refers back to the Commission; (2) centers on obedience to it; (3) utilizes a number of computers to make the network function every day, initially utilizing electronic mail; and (4) results in some kind of missionary sending endeavor. There are several thousand such networks in agencies functioning today.

Every Christian agency has its own human network (reverting for a moment to the wider, generalized use of the term) consisting of personnel, executives, constituency, libraries, advisers, consultants, secular contacts, and so on.

2. A *Great Commission global network* today is a computerized Great Commission network as defined above which, in addition, has global significance, articulates the global mandate, demonstrates a global concern, has some kind of global agenda, and undertakes concrete activities for the implementation of world evangelization. Usually, it would consist of either (a) a grouping of smaller organizations that are themselves Great Commission networks, or (b) a single standalone Great Commission network that is sufficiently large and global by itself to be so described. One criterion for a global network could be: an annual budget of over $10 million, or employing over 1,000 full-time Christian workers.

There are several highly-publicized global networks of this kind in the world today. In most cases each global network imagines that it is the world's major one, or the best developed one, or the most sophisticated one, or the most significant one, or even the only one. In fact, there are at least 90 of them, 56 being mainline.

3. A *Great Commission global meganetwork* is a global network as defined above but of larger scope and size, which links together a number of like-minded but distinct and separate global networks with similar ecclesiastical stance, utilizing computer networking and involving electronic mail, news services, faxing, bulletin boards, and infobasing.

4. A *Great Commission global giganetwork* (a concept which does not at present exist in practice) would be defined as a network linking all (or at least a majority) of global Christianity's meganetworks in one single, immense, worldwide, loose, voluntary network involving at the very least electronic mail, news, faxing, multifaxing, bulletin boards, infobasing, and databasing, without infringing on local autonomy.

### Global meganetworks
The actual situation in the Decade of Evangelism (1990-2000) looked like this: 332 million computers—93% being microcomputers—are owned or operated by Christians or their churches and agencies. The vast majority (96%) are used as stand-alone systems—used only in offices, or to serve or entertain only the individuals or families who own personal or home computers. Only 4% (13 million) take part in any computer networking activity.

These networks and their computers as viewed from the beginning of the Decade of Evangelism can be classified into nine de facto global meganetworks as shown in Table 27–18. These are arranged in chronological order of emergence on the Christian scene (in every case long before the emergence of computers, in eras when networking simply meant talking to each other across hierarchical organizational lines). Note that six of them are mutually exclusive (Nos. 1, 2, 3, 4, 5, 6), i.e. their totals of computers, or plans, or Christians (with small adjustments for doubly-affiliated Christians or plans or computers) add up to the global totals for mainline meganetworks on the last line of the table. The other three meganetworks (Nos. 7, 8, 9) overlap entirely with varying parts of the main six. To assist the reader by providing information on other apparently similar massive meganetworks, the table divides networks into two categories: mainline Christian networks, and marginal or quasi-Christian networks.

### Mainline Christian networks and meganetworks
1. *Orthodox* (dating from AD 33). Originating in Jerusalem at Pentecost, the church of the eastern part of the Roman empire has now become the world of Orthodoxy and embraces 215 million Christians in 135 countries. After centuries of persecution under Islam and Communism, it has become a massive, tightly-knit, largely private and clandestine human network that is now in process of rediscovering and reaffirming the centrality of the Great Commission. Computers are relatively rare and new on the scene, used as yet only in its Western branches (Western Europe, Americas, Australasia).

2. *Catholic.* The Roman Catholic world of the first millennium expanded across the world under the three great missionary global human networks—Franciscans (1209), Dominicans (1215), and Jesuits (1523). Foreign missions have been organized under Propaganda Fide since 1622 (in 1967 renamed Sacred Congregation for the Evangelization of Peoples). This huge contemporary global meganetwork—composed of scores of smaller global networks—now serves 1,057 million church members in 235 countries.

3. *Anglican.* Dating from 1st-century Britain, Anglicanism became globally organized in 1867 and now serves 80 million baptized Anglicans in 166 countries. Strongest in Britain, North America, and Australasia, it has the second highest per capita income of any meganetwork.

4. *Protestant.* The organized Protestant world dates from the 7th century and as the fourth largest global meganetwork it serves 342 million Christians through over 100 large global networks including 43 world confessional councils (the first being the Alliance of Reformed Churches, 1875). All have their world headquarters in Europe or the USA, and have massive computerized networks. The largest single denomination with the most highly-organized computer network is that of the Southern Baptist Convention, whose members own and operate 12 million computers with extensive global networking.

5. *Third-World indigenous.* This vast aggregate of 11,000 denominations indigenous to Third-World peoples begun independently of Western missions, dates from the 16th century and now embraces 386 million Christians in 221 countries (reclassified as Independents, including white-led movements). Since the year 1900 a vast human network of indigenous Christian councils, federations, and fellowships with no affiliation to Europe or America has arisen. In Africa alone these number 100 councils covering 50 countries. (Their story is documented in Barrett, *Rise up and walk! Conciliarism in the African Indigenous Churches*, Oxford University Press, 1988). Computer usage is confined mainly to stand-alone systems in a handful of the economically better-off churches.

6. *Old/Reformed Catholic.* Smallest of the global meganetworks is the Old Catholic/Reformed Catholic family of churches with 3.7 million members. Its major global network, the International Old Catholic Bishops' Conference, represents 7.5 million Christians because it includes several large churches classified here under No. 5 (Third-World indigenous churches). Computer usage is small and computer networking has barely begun.

7. *Evangelical.* The Evangelical world is usually dated as emerging from the Evangelical Revival in Britain from 1738. With its 210 million Evangelicals (Conservative, Conciliar, or Fundamentalist) this world has arisen largely as a subdivision within Protestantism. It has huge financial resources and over 40 million computers owned within several major global networks (overlapping almost completely with those in meganetworks Nos. 3, 4, and 5). Interagency networking between the 11 major Evangelical global networks (listed in Table 27–18 under No. 7) is, however, still confined to occasional electronic mail between closely related networks only.

8. *Pentecostal/Charismatic.* The movement termed the Renewal in the Holy Spirit began in 1783 among Blacks in Northern America and the Caribbean. It has now grown to become a global meganetwork embracing 524 million church members in 237 countries (these statistics overlap 50% with those of meganetworks Nos. 2, 3, 4, 5, 7 and 9).

**Table 27–18.** **The world's top 80 current mainline Great Commission global networks and the top nine mainline global meganetworks, in relation to plans, megaplans, gigaplans, and a possible giganetwork; with three marginal global meganetworks.**

The table sets out the current global meganetworks and a selection of each's component global networks as they appeared at the beginning of the Decade of Evangelism. Note that network totals (e.g. of computers) do not add up to meganetwork totals because the networks listed are only a selection of all existing networks, and because of widespread overlapping.

This table describes, not prescribes, nor evaluates, nor endorses, nor approves, nor disapproves. Most networks are good, some are bad. Some are transparently Christian, some less so, some scarcely at all. some succeed, at least partially, in obedience to the Great Commission. Others clearly fail. This table is a first attempt at objective scrutiny.

*Meanings of columns:*
2. *Begun.* Year each network as existing today can be said to have originated as a human network.
3. *GLOBAL MEGANETWORK.* Short adjectival form of name for each, whether organized consortium or unorganized sphere of interest.
4. *Global network.* This table gives only a selection of the component global networks (being in some cases mininetworks). Those with asterisk * also belong to a second chronologically-earlier meganetwork, or to 2 or even to 3 earlier meganetworks, and some overlap significantly with further global networks as well. Several others without asterisks may also thus overlap. Several Protestant bodies would regard themselves also as part of the Evangelical, Charismatic, and Ecumenical meganetworks, though this is not evident in the table.
5. *Christians.* World total of constituency, i.e. affiliated church members (in millions, in 1988) represented by, or related to, each network. Note network totals for columns 5-8, 10, do not add up to meganetwork totals because former are only a selection from the latter, or networks with asterisk * overlap significantly with other global networks.
6-8. *Related plans.* Totals of global plans for world evangelization (past and present, over period AD 30-1991 but only counting plans since human network was first organized in early stages) sponsored by or directly related to each network, of 3 varieties: column 6, *global plans* large and small, past and present; column 7, *global megaplans* (over $100 million each); column 8, *global gigaplans* ($1 billion or more each). Note that column 7 includes the figures in 8, and column 6 includes those in both 7 and 8.
9. *Resources.* General order of magnitude of total current 10-year resources of personnel and finances actually deployed today to operate each of the 70 networks and 12 meganetworks set out in the table. This includes resources of all agencies involved in, or represented in, each network. This covers (a) Christian workers or personnel, and (b) budget or expenditures of network or meganetwork over 10-year period. (This variable is similar to, but not defined identically with, column 13 in Table 27–21, which relates to global plans themselves).

*Code*
| | | |
|---|---|---|
| 0 | = | negligible: less than 1 worker-year (negligible expenditures) |
| 1 | = | minimal: 1-10 worker-years (a few individuals, minimal expenditures) |
| 2 | = | limited: 10-100 worker-years (a small team, limited finance or under US$10,000 a year) |
| 3 | = | modest (or, adequate): 100-1,000 worker-years (10-100 workers, or $10,000-100,000 a year) |
| 4 | = | sizeable: 1,000-10,000 worker-years (100-1,000 workers, or $100,000-$10 million a year, or under $100 million in a decade) |
| 5 | = | massive: over 10,000 worker-years (over 1,000 workers, or $10 million-$100 million a year, or over $100 million in a decade) |
| 6 | = | gigantic: over 50,000 worker-years (over 5,000 workers, or $100 million a year, or over $1 billion in a decade) |
| 7 | = | mammoth: over 1 million worker-years (over 100,000 workers, or $500 million a year, or over $5 billion in a decade) |

10. *Computers.* Estimate in millions of the numbers of distinct computers (mainframes, minis, micros, word-processors) owned and operated by Christians, churches and agencies in or related to each grouping shown (1988).
11. *Computer networking.* Based on current usage of the 42 million computers now owned and operated within global Christianity, this variable describes the size and significance of current intranetwork use (use within each network) of computer networking (electronic mail, news servicing, bulletin boarding, faxing, text, voice, imaging, infobasing, databasing, expert systems), as contrasted with standalone (one-agency) systems. The code is:
| | | |
|---|---|---|
| 0 | = | no organized network, only a few standalone computers |
| 1 | = | occasional networking, many standalone computers |
| 2 | = | rudimentary electronic mail/news/text partial global mininetwork |
| 3 | = | global mail/news/bulletin board/fax/text/infobase network |
| 4 | = | massive global mail/news/bulletin board/fax/text/voice and image digitization/infobase/database/expert systems network |

12. *Giganetworking (actual).* Columns 12 and 13 code the current situation with regard to giganetworking, defined as actual (column 12) and potential (column 13) computer networking between the global meganetworks, as existing in 1988. For any one global meganetwork (or each of its constituent global networks), this variable is the total of the other global meganetworks with which (column 12) it is involved in some degree of computer networking for world evangelization, or (column 13) it is prepared to begin such networking in the future. Both columns use the following codes divided into 5 stages (A,B,C,D,E) of current involvement in or interest in the concept of one, single, worldwide, Great-Commission-centered, world-evangelization-centered, global giganetwork open to "all", or "most" other global networks and meganetworks. The code is:
| | | |
|---|---|---|
| | | A. NO INTEREST IN GIGANETWORKING WITH ANYONE |
| 0 | = | nothing happening at all, or total rejection of idea |
| | | B. LITTLE INTEREST IN GIGANETWORKING |
| 1 | = | networking with one other meganetwork, despite internal opposition |
| 2 | = | networking with 2 other meganetworks, despite disinterest |
| 3 | = | networking with 3 other meganetworks, but hostility to more |
| | | C. SOME INTEREST IN GIGANETWORKING |
| 4 | = | networking with 4 other meganetworks, and interest in more |
| 5 | = | networking with 5 other meganetworks, and open to more |
| | | D. ACCEPTANCE OF GIGANETWORKING IN GENERAL |
| 6 | = | networking with 6 other meganetworks, with rapid expansion |
| 7 | = | networking with 7 other meganetworks, and mutual respect |
| | | E. TOTAL COMMITMENT TO GIGANETWORKING |
| 8 | = | committed in theory to networking with most Great Commission Christians |
| 9 | = | fully committed to networking with all Great Commission Christians |
| 10 | = | now practicing full networking with all Great Commission Christians |

13. *Giganetworking (potential).* Potential computer networking for world evangelization between meganetworks. This column is a measure of a network's attitude to the subject as just described above. The codes are the same as for column 12.

| Ref | Begun | GLOBAL MEGANETWORK global network | Christians millions | Related plans | | | Resources | Comp m | Net | Giganet | |
|---|---|---|---|---|---|---|---|---|---|---|---|
| | | | | global | mega | giga | | | | Act | Pct |
| 1 | 2 | 3 4 | 5 | 6 | 7 | 8 | 9 | 10 | 11 | 12 | 13 |
| | | **A. MAINLINE CHRISTIAN NETWORKS AND MEGANETWORKS** | | | | | | | | | |
| 1. | AD 33 | **ORTHODOX** | 175.4 | 28 | 0 | 0 | 5 | 0.7 | 1 | 0 | 5 |
| | 1855 | Pan-Orthodox world missions | 30.0 | 7 | 0 | 0 | 5 | 0.4 | 0 | 0 | 4 |
| | 1961 | Great & Holy Council of the Orthodox Church | 137.5 | 27 | 0 | 0 | 4 | 0.6 | 1 | 0 | 5 |
| | 1965 | Oriental Orthodox Churches Conference | 31.5 | 1 | 0 | 0 | 3 | 0.1 | 0 | 0 | 3 |
| 2. | AD 50 | **ROMAN CATHOLIC** | 926.4 | 117 | 17 | 8 | 7 | 15.2 | 2 | 2 | 7 |
| | 1209 | Franciscans (OFM) | 200.0 | 4 | 1 | 1 | 6 | 2.0 | 2 | 0 | 6 |
| | 1215 | Dominicans (OP) | 150.0 | 3 | 1 | 1 | 6 | 1.6 | 2 | 0 | 6 |
| | 1523 | Society of Jesus (SJ) | 250.0 | 5 | 1 | 1 | 6 | 2.0 | 2 | 0 | 7 |
| | 1588 | Sacred Congregation for Bishops | 794.0 | 35 | 2 | 2 | 6 | 12.0 | 2 | 1 | 5 |
| | 1622 | SC for Evangelization of Peoples | 108.3 | 20 | 1 | 1 | 6 | 3.0 | 2 | 1 | 5 |
| | 1920 | Catholic multinationals | 300.0 | 30 | 15 | 8 | 6 | 8.0 | 3 | 3 | 6 |
| | 1967 | Synod of Bishops/*Synodus Episcoporum* | 926.4 | 60 | 3 | 3 | 7 | 15.1 | 2 | 1 | 5 |
| 3. | AD 61 | **ANGLICAN** | 52.4 | 32 | 0 | 0 | 5 | 4.9 | 2 | 2 | 8 |
| | 1867 | Lambeth Conference of Bishops | 51.6 | 4 | 0 | 0 | 5 | 4.8 | 1 | 0 | 8 |
| | 1910 | Episcopal Church in the USA | 2.7 | 2 | 0 | 0 | 4 | 1.2 | 2 | 0 | 7 |
| | 1968 | Anglican Consultative Council | 51.6 | 1 | 0 | 0 | 4 | 4.8 | 1 | 0 | 7 |
| | 1970 | Anglican multinationals | 50.0 | 2 | 0 | 0 | 4 | 2.0 | 2 | 4 | 6 |
| 4. | AD 690 | **PROTESTANT** | 311.9 | 490 | 44 | 16 | 7 | 16.4 | 2 | 2 | 7 |
| | 1810 | Protestant multinationals | 500.0 | 70 | 40 | 15 | 6 | 10.0 | 3 | 4 | 7 |
| | 1819 | United Methodist Church (UMC) | 19.0 | 8 | 2 | 1 | 6 | 3.1 | 3 | 1 | 7 |
| | 1844 | Seventh-day Adventists (SDA) | 15.0 | 4 | 2 | 1 | 6 | 0.6 | 3 | 0 | 0 |
| | 1845 | Southern Baptist Convention (FMB) | 28.0 | 10 | 3 | 2 | 6 | 4.2 | 4 | 3 | 3 |
| | 1865 | Salvation Army (Salvationists) | 4.5 | 1 | 1 | 0 | 5 | 0.4 | 1 | 1 | 4 |
| | 1875 | 40 Protestant confessional councils | 220.0 | 20 | 10 | 1 | 6 | 3.0 | 1 | 1 | 6 |
| | 1875 | World Alliance of Reformed Churches (WARC) | 55.0 | 25 | 0 | 0 | 5 | 4.0 | 1 | 1 | 5 |
| | 1876 | World Methodist Council (WMC) | 40.5 | 12 | 1 | 0 | 5 | 3.5 | 2 | 0 | 5 |
| | 1905 | Baptist World Alliance (BWA) | 45.0 | 15 | 0 | 0 | 4 | 5.0 | 1 | 1 | 7 |
| | 1925 | Mennonite World Conference (MWC) | 1.3 | 1 | 0 | 0 | 4 | 0.2 | 1 | 1 | 5 |
| | 1947 | Lutheran World Federation (LWF) | 75.0 | 10 | 1 | 0 | 4 | 3.0 | 2 | 2 | 7 |
| | 1957 | Conference of Christian World Communions* | 1,385.7 | 1 | 0 | 0 | 6 | 30.0 | 1 | 0 | 7 |
| 5. | 1549 | **THIRD-WORLD INDIGENOUS** | 131.8 | 3 | 0 | 0 | 4 | 0.7 | 1 | 0 | 7 |
| | 1741 | Non-White indigenous churches | 120.0 | 1 | 0 | 0 | 3 | 0.6 | 1 | 0 | 6 |
| | 1978 | Organization of African Instituted Churches | 10.0 | 2 | 0 | 0 | 2 | 0.0 | 0 | 0 | 7 |
| 6. | 1724 | **OLD/REFORMED CATHOLIC** | 3.7 | 4 | 1 | 1 | 6 | 0.3 | 1 | 0 | 5 |
| | 1832 | Catholic Apostolic Church (CAC) | 0.1 | 1 | 0 | 0 | 3 | 0.0 | 0 | 0 | 0 |
| | 1863 | New Apostolic Church (NAC) | 1.7 | 1 | 1 | 1 | 6 | 0.1 | 2 | 0 | 0 |
| | 1871 | Old Catholic Bishops Conference (IOCBC)* | 7.5 | 2 | 0 | 0 | 4 | 0.2 | 0 | 0 | 5 |
| 7. | 1738 | **EVANGELICAL** | 220.0 | 111 | 45 | 15 | 7 | 12.3 | 1 | 1 | 4 |
| | 1846 | World Evangelical Fellowship (WEF) | 100.0 | 5 | 1 | 0 | 5 | 1.5 | 2 | 0 | 3 |
| | 1900 | Independent Evangelicals/Fundamentalists | 70.0 | 30 | 6 | 4 | 6 | 6.0 | 1 | 0 | 0 |
| | 1917 | IFMA/EFMA | 29.0 | 21 | 5 | 2 | 6 | 1.0 | 2 | 1 | 2 |
| | 1948 | International Council of Christian Churches | 4.7 | 4 | 0 | 0 | 5 | 0.1 | 0 | 0 | 0 |
| | 1951 | Campus Crusade for Christ International | 10.0 | 15 | 3 | 2 | 6 | 1.6 | 3 | 0 | 1 |

*Continued opposite*

Table 27–18 concluded

| Ref 1 | Begun 2 | GLOBAL MEGANETWORK<br>global network<br>3 4 | Christians<br>millions<br>5 | Related plans<br>global 6 | mega 7 | giga 8 | Resources<br>9 | Comp<br>m<br>10 | Net<br>11 | Giganet<br>Act 12 | Pct 13 |
|---|---|---|---|---|---|---|---|---|---|---|---|
| | 1951 | Evangelical multinationals (WVI,TWR,&c) | 23.0 | 40 | 22 | 10 | 6 | 3.0 | 3 | 1 | 3 |
| | 1974 | Lausanne Committee for World Evangelization | 2.5 | 19 | 1 | 0 | 5 | 0.2 | 1 | 0 | 4 |
| | 1976 | Chinese Coordination Centre of World Evangelism | 6.0 | 3 | 0 | 0 | 3 | 0.1 | 2 | 1 | 3 |
| | 1987 | International Conference of Evangelical Bible Societies | 30.0 | 1 | 0 | 0 | 4 | 2.0 | 2 | 0 | 0 |
| | 1987 | COMIBAM/Ibero-American Missions Congress | 34.0 | 2 | 1 | 0 | 5 | 0.2 | 2 | 1 | 3 |
| | 1988 | Third World Missions Advance (TWMA) | 45.0 | 4 | 2 | 0 | 5 | 0.2 | 2 | 2 | 3 |
| 8. | 1783 | **PENTECOSTAL/CHARISMATIC** | 332.6 | 89 | 20 | 10 | 7 | 9.6 | 1 | 1 | 8 |
| | 1913 | Assemblies of God* | 23.9 | 6 | 3 | 2 | 5 | 3.1 | 2 | 0 | 3 |
| | 1947 | World Conference of Pentecostal Churches* | 52.5 | 30 | 7 | 3 | 3 | 5.0 | 0 | 0 | 1 |
| | 1950 | Pentecostal/charismatic multinationals | 60.0 | 35 | 20 | 8 | 6 | 4.0 | 2 | 0 | 1 |
| | 1972 | Catholic Charismatic Renewal (ICCRO)* | 63.5 | 2 | 2 | 2 | 6 | 2.0 | 2 | 1 | 3 |
| | 1979 | Sharing of Ministries Abroad (SOMA)* | 1.9 | 1 | 0 | 0 | 4 | 0.2 | 1 | 0 | 5 |
| | 1987 | Evangelization 2000/New Evangelization 2000* | 926.4 | 10 | 5 | 4 | 6 | 15.0 | 2 | 1 | 5 |
| | 1987 | AD 2000 Together* | 210.0 | 10 | 4 | 3 | 5 | 5.0 | 1 | 1 | 5 |
| | 1987 | Charismatics United for World Evangelization* | 270.0 | 1 | 1 | 0 | 5 | 6.0 | 1 | 0 | 5 |
| 9. | 1855 | **ECUMENICAL/CONCILIAR** | 420.0 | 80 | 2 | 1 | 6 | 9.3 | 2 | 2 | 8 |
| | 1855 | World Alliance of YMCAs/World YWCA* | 11.5 | 6 | 1 | 0 | 5 | 0.8 | 1 | 2 | 7 |
| | 1895 | World Student Christian Federation (WSCF)* | 3.5 | 10 | 1 | 0 | 4 | 0.2 | 1 | 2 | 7 |
| | 1946 | United Bible Societies (UBS)* | 1,450.0 | 6 | 2 | 1 | 5 | 8.0 | 3 | 4 | 8 |
| | 1946 | Ecumenical multinationals | 950.0 | 10 | 2 | 1 | 6 | 4.0 | 3 | 4 | 8 |
| | 1948 | World Council of Churches (WCC)* | 398.0 | 12 | 2 | 0 | 5 | 9.0 | 2 | 2 | 8 |
| | 1961 | Commission on World Mission and Evangelism* | 120.0 | 6 | 1 | 0 | 5 | 3.0 | 2 | 2 | 7 |
| | | **GLOBAL TOTALS FOR 9 MAINLINE MEGANETWORKS** | 1,487.6 | 780 | 75 | 30 | 7 | 37.6 | 44% | 8% | 49% |
| | | **B. MARGINAL OR QUASI-CHRISTIAN NETWORKS AND MEGANETWORKS** | | | | | | | | | |
| 10. | 1566 | **MARGINAL CHRISTIAN** | 3.6 | 2 | 0 | 0 | 6 | 1.4 | 1 | 0 | 0 |
| | 1778 | Unitarian Universalist Association (UUA) | 0.3 | 0 | 0 | 0 | 4 | 0.1 | 1 | 0 | 0 |
| | 1879 | Church of Christ, Scientist | 1.4 | 0 | 0 | 0 | 5 | 0.5 | 3 | 0 | 0 |
| | 1887 | Unity School of Christianity | 0.2 | 0 | 0 | 0 | 4 | 0.1 | 2 | 0 | 0 |
| | 1900 | International Association for Liberal Christianity | 1.3 | 0 | 0 | 0 | 5 | 0.3 | 2 | 0 | 0 |
| | 1914 | International New Thought Alliance (INTA) | 0.2 | 0 | 0 | 0 | 4 | 0.1 | 1 | 0 | 0 |
| | 1930 | Worldwide Church of God | 0.4 | 0 | 0 | 0 | 5 | 0.2 | 3 | 0 | 0 |
| | 1948 | International Association of Religious Science Churches | 0.1 | 0 | 0 | 0 | 4 | 0.0 | 0 | 0 | 0 |
| | 1954 | Unification Church International | 0.6 | 1 | 0 | 0 | 5 | 0.2 | 0 | 0 | 0 |
| 11. | 1830 | **MORMON** | 6.9 | 2 | 1 | 1 | 7 | 1.9 | 4 | 0 | 0 |
| | 1830 | Church of Jesus Christ of Latter-day Saints | 6.2 | 1 | 1 | 1 | 6 | 1.8 | 4 | 0 | 0 |
| | 1831 | 90 Mormon schismatic denominations | 0.7 | 0 | 0 | 0 | 3 | 0.1 | 1 | 0 | 0 |
| | 1850 | Mormon multinationals | 2.0 | 1 | 1 | 1 | 6 | 1.0 | 4 | 0 | 0 |
| | 1860 | Reorganized Church of Jesus Christ of LDS | 0.3 | 1 | 0 | 0 | 4 | 0.1 | 1 | 0 | 0 |
| 12. | 1870 | **WITNESSES** | 11.9 | 4 | 2 | 2 | 7 | 1.1 | 3 | 0 | 0 |
| | 1870 | Watch Tower Bible and Tract Society (WTBTS) | 11.5 | 4 | 2 | 2 | 6 | 1.1 | 3 | 0 | 0 |
| | 1900 | 30 Witnesses schismatic denominations | 0.4 | 0 | 0 | 0 | 3 | 0.0 | 0 | 0 | 0 |
| | 1930 | Jehovah's Christian Witnesses multinationals | 2.0 | 4 | 2 | 2 | 6 | 0.5 | 3 | 0 | 0 |
| | 1986 | Integrity Keepers Conventions (IBSA) | 11.5 | 1 | 1 | 1 | 6 | 1.1 | 3 | 0 | 0 |
| | | **GLOBAL TOTALS FOR ALL 12 MEGANETWORKS** | 1,510.0 | 788 | 78 | 33 | 7 | 42.0 | 44% | 8% | 49% |

Its members probably communicate more with each other in close interpersonal relationships in and across their constituent global networks than do those of any other meganetwork or their constituent networks. The Pentecostal-Charismatic meganetwork receives personal incomes totaling $880 billion a year.

9. *Ecumenical.* Dating from 1855, this is the most recent of the mainline meganetworks, though of course its roots go back several centuries into Protestant history. The best known of its component global networks is the World Council of Churches with 500 million church members. Altogether, the Ecumenical meganetwork has some 600 million member Christians. The Catholic meganetwork (No. 2) cooperates with the Ecumenical meganetwork, but is not part of it (it is not a member of the WCC nor of the United Bible Societies and other major Ecumenical agencies). Computer usage is surprisingly small; both standalone and networking use have lagged far behind those in several of its largest constituent members.

### Marginal or quasi-Christian networks and meganetworks

These are networks which are usually understood by mainline Christian traditions to be only marginally Christian, or quasi-Christian, or pseudo-Christian. This category, however, excludes clearly non-Christian bodies, syncretistic religions, interfaith or New Age bodies, as well as Islam, Hinduism, Buddhism, Baha'i, and other world religions.

The following points should be noted: (1) The 16 marginal networks listed insist that they are Christians, whatever the mainline Christian world may say. (2) They profess to follow Jesus Christ as Lord and Savior (but, usually, not as God). (3) The Bible as the Word of God plays a major role; for the great majority of languages, mainline Christian Bible translations are purchased, distributed, and utilized. (4) These networks profess allegiance to Christ's Great Commission and frequently refer to it. (5) Most go

much further and articulate as central concerns all or most of the 10 biblical themes enumerated earlier. The fact that their interpretations (eg. of the time of the Second Advent) may be wildly arbitrary is not the issue here.

In this category, there are three global meganetworks and at least 16 global networks, as follows:

10. *Marginal Christian.* The Protestant Reformation and Counter-Reformation in Europe over the centuries have spawned a vast number of Western heterodox movements, deviant churches, and parachristian or quasi-Christian denominations. These usually claim a second or supplementary or ongoing source of divine revelation in addition to the Bible (a new Book, angels, visions), but nevertheless include Jesus Christ, the Cross, the Resurrection, the Great Commission, and other central Christian features. Best-known are Unitarians, begun in 1566 in Romania and Hungary, also called Free Christians, Liberal Christians, Universalists, Non-Trinitarians. Others include: British-Israelites, Christian Science, Metaphysical, New Thought, Religious Science, Spiritists, Swedenborgians, Unity, etc.

All of these have been widely studied by Protestant and Catholic scholars and written up in the literature. The category here omits the two largest marginal bodies (Mormons and Witnesses) which are so huge that they are treated in the table as separate meganetworks.

Although this marginal meganetwork is over four centuries old, it is the least-developed of them all, the smallest, the least enthusiastic, and has produced the fewest global plans. (See Table 27–11 at the year 1600 for Bruno's Magico-Religious System for an exception.) Their technical networking is also the least developed. They recognize nobody outside, and are dismissed as cults by all the other Christian meganetworks.

11. *Mormon.* The Church of Jesus Christ of Latter-day Saints (LDS) and its 90 split-off schismatic denominations, with 6.9 million Mormons, do not recognize or cooperate with any other Christian

church. They regard all other churches as apostate. In turn, all other churches regard them as heretical. Despite this, Evangelical analysts can state of the Mormons: 'Their discipline, ingenuity, persistence, and dedication to the task of world evangelization is a challenge that we cannot ignore.' (M. Albrecht & P. Rogers, *Hidden in plain sight: an examination of Mormon mission strategy*, 1987, page 2).

The LDS global commitment to Christ's Great Commission has resulted by 1988 in an annual foreign missions expenditure estimated at $550 million—the world's largest by a single agency. The LDS global network of 1.9 million computers is global Christianity's largest and most sophisticated single global network, involving electronic mail, news service, text-processing, broadcasting, multifaxing, imaging, infobasing, and databasing. Its most striking event was the creation by Mormons in 1981 of the world's largest television network using satellites, with over 700 receiving stations.

12. *Witnesses.* The Watch Tower Bible and Tract Society began in 1870. Later it was renamed International Bible Students Association, and in 1931 Jehovah's Christian Witnesses. It now numbers 11.9 million witnesses in 208 countries. It baptizes 200,000 new members every year, but a million members defected and left between 1973 and 1983. It regards the rest of global Christianity as apostate, and all other Christian churches and agencies in turn deny it is a Christian body. The paradox is that this last sentence is true, but that it is also true that Witnesses claim passionately to be followers of Jesus Christ as Lord, appealing to the Great Commission.

Jehovah's Witnesses have given ample evidence of being Jehovah's integrity keepers. Included especially in their mark of integrity is their faithfully keeping Jesus' command: 'Go . . . and make disciples of people of all the nations, baptizing them' (Matt. 28:19). (*1986 Yearbook of Jehovah's Witnesses*, page 253.)

Watch Tower operates what is clearly the largest global meganetwork of all, if one includes personnel and products as well as computers and money. It fields (excluding its 30 schismatic neo-Protestant offshoot denominations) over 100,000 full-time workers and over three million door-to-door member evangelists/witnesses. Its computer network (estimated at over a million systems) produces 550 million high-quality magazines in 100 languages every year for worldwide distribution.

### The problem of unorthodoxy

Why should mainline networks bother to consider relating seriously to what are usually called cults or cult groups—specifically, Nos. 10, 11, and 12, which are the Marginal Christian, Mormon, and Witnesses meganetworks? These three meganetworks all claim to accept Jesus as Savior and Lord and claim to be Great Commission Christians; and all are big enough to warrant being taken seriously. In this analysis, theological criteria—dogmas or doctrines, christologies, ecclesiologies, church polities, church union, mission methods, etc are not being investigated.

### A global giganetwork

To what extent, if any, do the nine mainline Great Commission global meganetworks cooperate across meganetwork lines to form a Great Commission giganetwork?

Examining data in Table 27–18, one must be careful not to count as trans-meganetwork cooperation the 14 global networks shown with asterisks (*) which means they also belong to, or exist within, another meganetwork. Thus, the members of Charismatics United for World Evangelization (CUWE) belong to meganetworks Nos. 2, 3, 4, 7, 8, and 9. Obviously, their presence in two distinct meganetworks does not of itself necessarily imply that any significant giganetworking is going on.

Other networks, not asterisked here, are counted by two meganetworks. For instance, the Southern Baptist Convention is part of No. 4, Protestant, and a member of the Baptist World Alliance; but it is also part of No. 7, Evangelical.

The answer to the question above is—they hardly cooperate at all. Column 12 in Table 27–18 shows how little computer giganetworking there actually is at present. Of the nine mainline global meganetworks, three have nothing to do with any other meganetworks, nor they them.

Columns 12 (the actual situation) and 13 (the potential or future situation) show that there is little interest yet in giganetworking. Adding the nine total figures for mainline meganetworks only, column 12 yields a total of 10 out of a maximum possible of 90 (11%). In other words, two-thirds of a people generation after the introduction of microcomputers in 1971, only 11% of the Christian world's mainline meganetworks are networking with any other outside Great Commission agency. And column 13 with its total for meganetworks of 59 out of the maximum possible of 90 (65%) shows that, one decade after the mass availability of computers across the world began in 1978, over one third (35%) of the Christian world's mainline meganetworks have little or no interest in such Great Commission giganetworking now or in the future.

At the same time, note the extraordinary fact that, like it or not, all the essential elements of such a Great Commission global giganetwork are already in place: 332 million computers owned and operated by Christians, 100 million other screens or terminals, 4,000 Great Commission computer networks 56 global networks, nine meganetworks, and vast armies of 50 million Christians who are expert operators, programmers, or systems analysts. Giganetworking could begin tomorrow if Christians wanted to.

### Summary

At the outset of The Decade of Evangelism there were 36 possible giganetworking relationships involving 72 one-way attitudes between the nine mainline Great Commission global meganetworks. At most, only 50% of all networks had any dealings at all with the other half. Defined as actual, concrete, computer networking, this drops to only 8%.

And only 65% have any interest in doing this in the future. Here we have, perhaps, the heart of the dilemma—the ultimate reason for failure to obey the Great Commission. Christians want to obey it only in standalone modes, in the company of their immediate circles of like-minded colleagues, but without the correctives supplied by being part of wider networks. They do not see the possible benefits of learning from other Great Commission Christians. They prefer the comfortable circle of their own kind to the stimulation, encouragement, and instruction of those engaged in the same task of world evangelization.

## STRATEGY, TACTICS, AND CHAINS OF COMMAND

The problem can be reduced to its starkest terms when one considers the subject of strategy for world evangelization. And the starkest of the issues is: Do Christians stand any chance of winning their war if they continue insisting on using multiple strategies under multiple chains of command, or is some single strategy required or even indispensable? That is, is strategy, or are strategies needed?

### A chaos of multiple chains of command

Most of the large networks, and all of the largest ones sponsoring megaplans or gigaplans, have final-authority type, high-command type, global strategy committees.

Table 27–17 is a brief selection of currently-existing global strategy committees, arranged by year of origin. The list is not complete or exhaustive. Also, some may not appear directly comparable, but all are executive committees, or have executive committees or steering committees. Most use the actual word *strategy*. Almost all are standalone, unrelated to any other such committees, though a handful of individuals sit on two of the committees. Those of a single denomination (mainly the Roman Catholic ones) are of course related, but in most cases are startlingly unrelated when one examines their actual deliberations on strategic matters.

Note again that this list is not an approved list of recommended committees. It is a purely descriptive list of what is actually out there and what ordinary Christians are likely to come across sooner or later.

Surprisingly, the four earliest in this listing are over a century old but are still intact, meeting regularly, producing minutes and decisions on strategy, and so on. Mainline Protestants have been far less organized until the last three decades or so. (There were many Protestant strategy committees over the period 1700-1960, but none of them are still alive today). The story of Protestantism in this respect seems to be one of constantly starting top-level strategy committees only to see them disappear after 5 or 10 years.

Another interesting facet is the earlier emphasis on full-time key personnel as strategists. After the Day of Pentecost in AD 33, the Twelve Apostles did not primarily serve as local pastors, nor local administrators, nor bishops, nor missionaries, nor evangelists. They were the founder members of the Church, and so served primarily as strategists in evangelism, eventually as global strategists in evangelization. In the 11th century 'cardinals' were 'hinge

| | Anglican | Independent | Marginal | Orthodox | Protestant | Roman Catholic | Total | %of Total |
|---|---|---|---|---|---|---|---|---|
| | 1 | 2 | 3 | 4 | 5 | 6 | 7 | 8 | 9 |

Table 27–19. **650 other global plans by six major ecclesiastical megablocs, AD 1900–2000.**

| | Anglican 1 | Independent 2 | Marginal 3 | Orthodox 4 | Protestant 5 | Roman Catholic 6 | Total 7 | %of Total 8 | 9 |
|---|---|---|---|---|---|---|---|---|---|
| **Total** | **20** | **400** | **10** | **20** | **150** | **50** | **650** | **100.0** | |
| Type 0 | 2 | 80 | 1 | 4 | 20 | 5 | 112 | 17.2 | |
| 1 | 1 | 50 | 1 | 3 | 15 | 10 | 80 | 12.3 | |
| 2 | 1 | 20 | 1 | 2 | 10 | 5 | 39 | 6.0 | |
| 3 | 4 | 40 | 2 | 2 | 15 | 3 | 66 | 10.2 | |
| 4 | 3 | 20 | 1 | 0 | 5 | 2 | 31 | 4.8 | |
| 5 | 1 | 20 | 0 | 0 | 5 | 0 | 26 | 4.0 | |
| 6 | 1 | 20 | 1 | 2 | 10 | 3 | 37 | 5.7 | |
| 7 | 1 | 55 | 1 | 2 | 10 | 4 | 73 | 11.2 | |
| 8 | 3 | 70 | 1 | 3 | 30 | 10 | 117 | 18.0 | |
| 9 | 2 | 15 | 1 | 2 | 20 | 7 | 47 | 7.2 | |
| 10 | 1 | 10 | 0 | 0 | 10 | 1 | 22 | 3.4 | |
| Ministry 0 | 0 | 15 | 0 | 0 | 5 | 0 | 20 | 3.1 | |
| 1 | 1 | 20 | 0 | 1 | 5 | 2 | 29 | 4.5 | |
| 2 | 1 | 40 | 1 | 2 | 10 | 5 | 59 | 9.1 | |
| 3 | 1 | 30 | 2 | 2 | 10 | 5 | 50 | 7.7 | |
| 4 | 2 | 10 | 0 | 0 | 5 | 5 | 22 | 3.4 | |
| 5 | 1 | 30 | 1 | 2 | 5 | 2 | 41 | 6.3 | |
| 6 | 1 | 40 | 1 | 0 | 5 | 2 | 49 | 7.5 | |
| 7 | 1 | 30 | 2 | 2 | 10 | 3 | 48 | 7.4 | |
| 8 | 4 | 50 | 0 | 1 | 5 | 2 | 62 | 9.5 | |
| 9 | 3 | 30 | 2 | 3 | 20 | 4 | 62 | 9.5 | |
| 10 | 1 | 50 | 1 | 4 | 30 | 5 | 91 | 14.0 | |
| 11 | 0 | 5 | 0 | 0 | 0 | 0 | 5 | 0.8 | |
| 12 | 0 | 0 | 0 | 0 | 0 | 0 | 0 | 0.0 | |
| 13 | 2 | 30 | 0 | 2 | 30 | 10 | 74 | 11.4 | |
| 14 | 2 | 20 | 0 | 1 | 10 | 5 | 38 | 5.8 | |
| Cooperation 0 | 4 | 90 | 9 | 10 | 10 | 10 | 133 | 20.5 | |
| 1 | 5 | 120 | 1 | 5 | 50 | 15 | 196 | 30.2 | |
| 2 | 5 | 70 | 0 | 5 | 40 | 15 | 135 | 20.8 | |
| 3 | 3 | 60 | 0 | 0 | 20 | 5 | 88 | 13.5 | |
| 4 | 2 | 40 | 0 | 0 | 20 | 5 | 67 | 10.3 | |
| 5 | 1 | 20 | 0 | 0 | 10 | 0 | 31 | 4.8 | |
| Print 0 | 1 | 15 | 0 | 2 | 10 | 3 | 31 | 4.8 | |
| 1 | 3 | 80 | 1 | 2 | 30 | 10 | 126 | 19.4 | |
| 2 | 8 | 150 | 1 | 5 | 40 | 17 | 221 | 34.0 | |
| 3 | 5 | 120 | 3 | 6 | 40 | 10 | 184 | 28.3 | |
| 4 | 1 | 20 | 2 | 3 | 15 | 5 | 46 | 7.1 | |
| 5 | 1 | 10 | 2 | 2 | 10 | 4 | 29 | 4.5 | |
| 6 | 1 | 5 | 1 | 0 | 5 | 1 | 13 | 2.0 | |
| Deadline | 10 | 250 | 4 | 10 | 60 | 20 | 354 | 54.5 | |
| 2000 | 5 | 100 | 4 | 6 | 50 | 20 | 185 | 28.5 | |
| 2025 | 5 | 50 | 2 | 4 | 40 | 10 | 111 | 17.1 | |
| Resources 0 | 3 | 90 | 0 | 2 | 5 | 0 | 100 | 15.4 | |
| 1 | 5 | 150 | 2 | 6 | 15 | 5 | 183 | 28.2 | |
| 2 | 4 | 50 | 3 | 4 | 20 | 10 | 91 | 14.0 | |
| 3 | 3 | 50 | 2 | 4 | 60 | 20 | 139 | 21.4 | |
| 4 | 2 | 30 | 2 | 2 | 30 | 10 | 76 | 11.7 | |
| 5 | 2 | 20 | 1 | 2 | 15 | 4 | 44 | 6.8 | |
| 6 | 1 | 10 | 0 | 0 | 5 | 1 | 17 | 2.6 | |
| Status 0 | 0 | 10 | 0 | 2 | 0 | 1 | 13 | 2.0 | |
| 1 | 2 | 50 | 0 | 2 | 5 | 3 | 62 | 9.5 | |
| 2 | 2 | 10 | 0 | 4 | 5 | 3 | 24 | 3.7 | |
| 3 | 3 | 50 | 0 | 2 | 10 | 5 | 70 | 10.8 | |
| 4 | 2 | 30 | 0 | 2 | 10 | 5 | 49 | 7.5 | |
| 5 | 3 | 80 | 2 | 2 | 20 | 5 | 112 | 17.2 | |
| 6 | 3 | 100 | 3 | 2 | 50 | 10 | 168 | 25.8 | |
| 7 | 3 | 40 | 2 | 2 | 30 | 10 | 87 | 13.4 | |
| 8 | 2 | 25 | 2 | 2 | 15 | 5 | 51 | 7.8 | |
| 9 | 0 | 5 | 2 | 1 | 0 | 5 | 14 | 2.2 | |
| Developed World | 8 | 150 | 3 | 8 | 50 | 20 | 239 | 36.8 | |
| Less-developed World | 10 | 200 | 5 | 9 | 70 | 20 | 314 | 48.3 | |
| Least-developed World | 2 | 50 | 2 | 3 | 30 | 10 | 97 | 14.9 | |

**Table 27–20. 650 other global plans arranged by primary ecclesiastical origin.**

| Ref 1 | Tradition 2 | Plans 3 | % 4 |
|---|---|---|---|
| 1 | Adventist | 4 | 0.6 |
| 2 | Anabaptist | 3 | 0.5 |
| 3 | Anglican | 20 | 3.1 |
| 4 | Baptist | 25 | 3.8 |
| 5 | Brethren | 1 | 0.2 |
| 6 | Catholic Apostolic | 1 | 0.2 |
| 7 | Charismatic | 55 | 8.5 |
| 8 | Congregational | 5 | 0.8 |
| 9 | Conservative Evangelical | 40 | 6.2 |
| 10 | Disciples | 5 | 0.8 |
| 11 | Eastern Orthodox | 15 | 2.3 |
| 12 | Ecumenical | 39 | 6.0 |
| 13 | Evangelical | 30 | 4.6 |
| 14 | Evangelical/Charismatic | 45 | 6.9 |
| 15 | Evangelical/Ecumenical | 20 | 3.1 |
| 16 | Fundamentalist | 25 | 3.8 |
| 17 | Holiness | 5 | 0.8 |
| 18 | Interdenominational | 50 | 7.7 |
| 19 | Lutheran | 10 | 1.5 |
| 20 | Mennonite | 1 | 0.2 |
| 21 | Messianic Jewish | 3 | 0.5 |
| 22 | Methodist | 15 | 2.3 |
| 23 | Moravian | 1 | 0.2 |
| 24 | Mormon | 5 | 0.8 |
| 25 | Nondenominational | 100 | 15.4 |
| 26 | Old Catholic | 1 | 0.2 |
| 27 | Orthodox | 5 | 0.8 |
| 28 | Pentecostal | 40 | 6.2 |
| 29 | Pentecostal/Charismatic | 15 | 2.3 |
| 30 | Presbyterian | 15 | 2.3 |
| 31 | Quaker | 1 | 0.2 |
| 32 | Reformed | 5 | 0.8 |
| 33 | Roman Catholic | 40 | 6.2 |
| 34 | Witnesses | 5 | 0.8 |
| | **Total** | **650** | **100.0** |

persons' (from the Latin *cardo*, hinge), hence considered essential in strategic thinking. The title 'Apostles' has fared likewise: hundreds of denominations today have recognized or appointed living apostles to govern the church as the original Twelve Apostles did. At the present time there are thousands of leaders around the world designated apostles by their churches—especially in Pentecostalism, African indigenous churches, independent charismatic churches, and varieties of sects and fringe bodies. Most exist to handle strategy. Thus an apostle in the Church of Jesus Christ of Latter-day Saints is one of 12 traveling global counselors and strategists for the church. In fact, their Quorum of the Twelve Apostles is a permanently traveling body that administers and regulates strategy worldwide.

All of these committees represent large, influential organizations, or consortia of agencies, wielding massive budgets. Behind them stand 70 global networks spending $45 billion on their separate plans to evangelize the world. And all have separate, powerful chains of command.

The startling fact is that, if you examine the ongoing minutes of each of these committees, you will find that in almost all cases none of them either mentions, or has any relationship to, any of the other committees. Each wields its own chain of command; other chains of command, although on the identical subject, are either impostors or an embarrassment.

### *Multiple tactics, not multiple strategies*

This confusion seems to be mainly due to confusing strategy with tactics. The latter word comes from the classical Greek word *taktika* (arrangement). Tactics, in military usage, means:

> 1. the science of arranging and maneuvering military and naval forces in action or before the enemy, especially (as distinguished from strategy) with reference to short-range objectives. 2. skillful methods or procedures. (Webster's *New World dictionary of the American language,* 1984). In other words, strategy deals with the overall plan for winning the war; tactics deal with methods and procedures for winning individual battles or engagements at different times and places in that war.

In Christian terms, these multifold committees under multifold chains of command would bring significant clarification if they described their committees as concerned with tactics rather than strategy.

### *Strategy as a single, unified plan*

Further clarification on this dilemma comes from a return to basic semantics. *Stratos* was the classical Greek word for 'army'; *strategia* meant 'generalship,' and *strategos* was the 'general.' Today, the English word strategy, in military usage, means:

> 1. (a) the science of planning and directing large-scale military operations, specifically (as distinguished from tactics) of maneuvering forces into the most advantageous position prior to actual engagement with the enemy, (b) a plan or action based on this; 2. skill in managing or planning. (Webster's *New World dictionary of the American language, 1984*). In warfare, an army determined to win the war has one general who works with one chain of command to pursue one strategy out of a number of possible strategies. Any army with rival generals and multiple chains of command all pursuing multiple strategies and operating incommunicado would surely be routed in the first major engagement.

The question, therefore, is: Can Christians win this particular battle—for world evangelization—with multiple strategies that do not relate to each other's strategies, multiple higher commands that do not speak to each other, let alone network, and multiple final authorities that do not even know of each other's existence?

## *BIBLIOGRAPHY*


'Administrating ministry: the use of strategic planning and management in a ministry setting.' P. A. Metzler. D.Min. thesis, Concordia Seminary, 211p.

*An enquiry into the obligation of Christians to use means for the conversion of the heathen.* W. Carey. Leicester, UK: Ann Ireland, 1792. 87p.

*Atlas of global strategy.* L. Freedman. New York: Facts on File, 1985. 192p.

*Church and ministry strategic planning: from concept to success.* R. H. Migliore, R. E. Stevens & D. L. Loudon. *Haworth marketing and resources.* New York: Haworth Press, 1994. 172p.

*Core competency–based strategy.* A. Campbell & K. S. Luchs (ed). *Smart strategies series.* London: International Thompson Business Press, 1997. 333p.

*Corporate planning for nonprofit organizations.* J. M. Hardy. New York: National YMCA Program Materials, 1973. 119p.

*Corporate planning: guide to strategic management.* D. E. Hussey. 4th ed. Oxford, UK and New York: Pergamon Press, 1991. 263p.

*Corporate strategy: resources and the scope of the firm.* D. J. Collis & C. A. Montgomery. Chicago: Irwin Professional, 1997. 794p.

*DAWN 2000: 7 million churches to go: the personal story of the DAWN strategy for world evangelism.* J. Montgomery. Pasadena, CA: William Carey Library, 1989. 239p.

*Discerning your congregation's future: a strategic and spiritual approach.* R. M. Oswald & R. E. Friedrich Jr. Bethesda, MD: Alban Institute, 1996. 191p.

*Essays on strategy.* Washington, DC: National Defense University Press, annual. (Winning student essays from the Senior Services Colleges in the Joint Chiefs of Staff Strategy Essay Competition).

*Essentials of strategic management.* J. D. Hunger & T. L. Wheelen. Reading, MA: Addison–Wesley, 1997. 224p.

*Ethics through corporate strategy.* D. R. Gilbert. New York: Oxford University Press, 1992. 264p.

*From management goal to organizational results: transforming strategies into action.* K. Curtis. Westport, CT: Quorum Books, 1994. 222p.

*Fundamental issues in strategy: a research agenda.* R. R. Rumelt et al (ed). Boston: Harvard Business School Press, 1994. 650p.

*Futuropting: how churches can do multiple scenario planning.* R. L. Perry. Richmond, VA: Organizational Health Associates, 1995. 92p.

*Global strategic management: the essential.* H. Vernon-Wortzel & L. H. Wortzel. 2nd ed. New York: John Wiley, 1990. 558p. (Revised edition of *Strategic management of multinational corporations*, 1985).

*Grand strategies in war and peace.* P. Kennedy (ed). New Haven, CT: Yale University Press, 1991. 238p.

*Handbook of business strategy.* W. D. Guth (ed). Boston: Warren, Gorham & Lamont, 1985–. (Annual).

*History of the art of war within the framework of political history.* H. Delbrück. Trans., W. J. Renfroe Jr. Westport, CT: Greenwood Press, 1975–85. 4 vols. (Translation of *Geschichte der Kriegskunst im Rahmen der politischen Geschichte*, 1920).

*Il pensiero strategico (Strategic thought).* C. Jean (ed). Milan: Franco Angeli, 1985.

*Introduction à la stratégie.* A. Beaufre. Paris: Librarie Armand Colin, 1963.

*Introduction to the theory of games.* J. C. C. McKinsey. *The Rand series.* New York: McGraw-Hill, 1952. 381p. (On developing strategic thinking).

*Keyguide to information sources in strategic studies.* K. Booth & E. Herring. London and New York: Mansell, 1994. 255p.

*Makers of modern strategy: from Machiavelli to the nuclear age.* P. Paret et al (ed). Princeton, NJ: Princeton University Press, 1986. 947p. (Updates volume of same name by E. M. Earle, 1943).

*Mission critical: the 7 strategic traps that derail even the smartest companies.* J. C. Picken & G. G. Dess. Chicago: Irwin Professional, 1997. 264p.

*National military strategy of the United States.* Washington, DC: Joint Chiefs of Staff, 1992. 29p.

*Naval strategy: compared and contrasted with the principles and practice of military operations on land.* A. T. Mahan. Boston: Little, Brown, 1911.

*On war.* C. von Clausewitz. Trans. and ed., M. Howard & P. Paret. 1833; reprint, Princeton, NJ: Princeton University Press, 1976. 3 vols.

*Quality–centered strategic planning: a step–by–step guide.* J. R. Dew. New York: Quality Resources, 1997. 238p.

*Research in strategic management and information technology.* Greenwich, CT: JAI Press, 1994–. (Annual).

*Results–oriented government: a guide to strategic planning and performance measurement in the public sector.* Research Triangle Park, NC: Southern Growth Policies Board, 1996. 24p. (Prepared by the Southern Growth Policies Board and the Southern Consortium of University Public Service Organizations).

*Soviet military strategy.* V. D. Sokolovskiy (Marshall of the Soviet Union). Ed., H. F. Scott. 3rd ed. New York: Crane, Russka & Co., 1975. (*Voyennaya stratagiya*, 1968).

*Stratagem and the vocabulary of military trickery.* E. L. Wheeler. Leiden and New York: E. J. Brill, 1988. 139p.

*Stratageme.* H. von Senger. Bern, Switzerland: Scherz Verlag, 1988. (English edition published as *The book of stratagems: tactics for triumph and survival.* Trans. and ed., M. B. Gubitz. New York: Viking Press, 1991. 411p.).

*Strategic management in public and nonprofit organizations: managing public concerns in an era of limits.* J. Koteen. 2nd ed. Westport, CT: Praeger, 1997. 368p.

*Strategic management in the global economy.* H. Vernon–Wertzel & L. H. Wortzel. 3rd ed. New York: John Wiley, 1997. 591p.

*Strategic planning and strategic management for church organizations.* Chicago: Center for Parish Development, 1992. 26p.

*Strategic planning for church organizations.* R. R. Broholm. Valley Forge, PA: Judson Press, 1969. 32p.

*Strategic planning for public and nonprofit organizations: a guide to strengthening and sustaining organizational achievement.* J. M. Bryson. Rev. ed. San Francisco: Jossey–Bass, 1995. 347p.

*Strategic power: military capabilities and political utility.* E. N. Luttwak. *The Washington papers*, IV, 38. Beverly Hills, CA: Sage Publications; Washington, DC: Georgetown University, The Center for Strategic and International Studies, 1976. 70p.

*Strategy and history: collected essays, vol. 2.* E. N. Luttwak. New Brunswick, NJ: Transaction Books, 1985. 265p.

*Strategy and politics: collected essays, vol 1.* E. N. Luttwak. New Brunswick, NJ: Transaction Books, 1980. 336p.

*Strategy for defeat: the Luftwaffe, 1933–1945.* W. Murray. Maxwell, AL: Air University Press, 1983.

*Strategy: the logic of war and peace.* E. N. Luttwak. Cambridge, MA: Belknap Press, 1987. 295p.

*The board member's guide to strategic planning: a practical approach to strengthening nonprofit organizations.* F. Howe. *The Jossey-Bass nonprofit sector series.* San Francisco: Jossey-Bass, 1997. 135p.

*The earliest Christian mission to 'all nations': in the light of Matthew's gospel.* J. LeGrand. Atlanta: Scholar's Press, 1995. 301p.

*The evangelization of the world in this generation.* J. R. Mott. New York: Student Volunteer Movement for Foreign Missions, 1900. 253p.

*The grand strategy of the Roman Empire: from the first century to the third.* E. N. Luttwak. Baltimore, MD and London: The Johns Hopkins University Press, 1976. 269p. (5th printing, 1990).

*The grand strategy of the Soviet Union.* E. N. Luttwak. New York: St. Martin's Press, 1983.

*The Great Commission handbook.* Evanston, IL: Center for Information on Christian Student Opportunities, annual.

*The Leader of the future: new visions, strategies, and practices for the next era.* F. Hesselbein, M. Goldsmith & R. Beckhard (ed). *The Drucker Foundation future series.* San Francisco: Jossey-Bass, 1996. 344p.

*The making of strategy.* W. Murray, M. Knox & A. Bernstein (eds). New York and Cambridge, UK: Cambridge University Press, 1996. 704p.

*The maritime strategy.* J. Watkins et al. Annapolis, MD: U. S. Naval Institute, 1986.

*The strategy of conflict.* T. C. Schelling. 2nd ed. Cambridge, MA: Harvard University Press, 1980.

*The strategy of deception: a study in world–wide communist tactics.* J. J. Kirkpatrick (ed). New York: Farrar, Straus, 1963. 469p.

*The strategy process.* H. Mintzberg & J. B. Quinn. 3rd ed. Upper Saddle River, NJ: Prentice Hall, 1996.

*The way of strategy.* W. A. Levinson. Milwaukee, WI: ASQC Quality Press, 1994. 279p.

*Thinking strategically: the competitive edge in business, politics, and everyday life.* A. K. Dixit & B. J. Nalebuff. New York: W. W. Norton, 1991. 407p.

## Table 27–21. 1,500 global plans to evangelize the world, AD 30-AD 2000, with future scenarios.

This table enumerates and evaluates 1,500 plans, proposals, visions, goals, methods, schemes, schemas, programs, structures, groups, organizations, promises, pledges, calls, appeals, slogans, mottos, documents, reports, publications, events, conferences, resolutions, statements, intents, or attempts, all related specifically or clearly to implementing world evangelization.

This table sets out, in chronological order, the great majority of the known publicly-announced significant plans and proposals put forward by the broad spectrum of Christians of all kinds over the last 2,000 years for undertaking and completing the task of world evangelization. Most acknowledge, or quote, or start from, Christ's Great Commission with its 6 New Testament accounts. Titles in italics refer to published books, or to journals. These plans are global in the sense that they encompass or envisage or refer to or in principle imply mission to the entire world. The definition covers only those which are explicitly worldwide or global in scope, or which relate to work in 50 or more countries, or which expound methods proposed for worldwide mission; it excludes plans or attempts clearly nonglobal because restricted to a single field, a single country, or a handful of countries, or a single region, or a single continent only, or a limited selection of all these.

Each of the global plans listed in the present table may be seen described in further detail, in historical context, in Table 27–22. Additional data on the context of these plans may also be found in Part 2 "CosmoChronology".

In a sense, this listing and total 1,500 is only symbolic. Other plans exist, unknown and unheralded. New plans are surfacing weekly.

The meanings of the 16 columns below, describing all global plans, are as follows. Note again that the evaluations shown by code values chosen for particular plans are not evaluations of the sponsoring bodies or events themselves, but are evaluations of the relevance and significance of the plans vis-a-vis world evangelization.

A further point of explanation is that the code values of 6 variables (Nos 6,7,10,11,13,16) begin at zero (0) in order to signify nil or nothing respectively, no human plan (6), no human activity (7), no cooperation (10), nothing in print (11), negligible resources (13), no current existence (16).

### Column

1. *No:* Reference number in this listing.
2. *Year* of origin of plan—year proposed, year announced, year begun, year of initial implementation (for details of each case, see Table 27–21 under this same year).
3. *Brief name* for this plan.
4. *Author:* Name of author, originator, sponsor, chairman, executive, implementer, or most prominent individual.
5. *Initials* or acronym for plan, if used, or for its originating church, agency, or organization (parentheses give alternate or additional names; hyphens elaborate entities within wider organizations; slashes separate cooperating agencies or organizations).
6. *Type* of plan, using the following code graduating from the absence of human plans (0) to massively-detailed master plans (10):
   - 0 = a vision or view or scenario of the End-time with God's plan for world evangelization
   - 1 = a one-time call, appeal, slogan, motto, challenge to Christians to evangelize the world
   - 2 = a call embodied in a published sermon, edict, encyclical, charge, or letter
   - 3 = a call embodied in a printed document, report, book, treatise, article, analysis, survey, assessment, periodical, or publication
   - 4 = a promise, pledge, intent, proposal, declaration, conference resolution
   - 5 = an unorganized attempt, undertaking, movement, campaign, event, drive, enterprise, network
   - 6 = a statement of basic purpose by an ongoing organization, group, structure, committee, council, board, or society
   - 7 = announcement of a plan, or its outline only with no details worked out; a project, aim, goal
   - 8 = a serious plan with some details, a design, method, way, procedure, process, formulation, tactics
   - 9 = a well worked-out scheme or schema with considerable detail, a strategy, a program
   - 10 = a massively-detailed plan or master blueprint detailing logistics, personnel, finances, timetables, schedules
7. *Ministry:* Main type of outreach ministry of method set forth, proposed, emphasized, or envisaged, if any, or claimed by the sponsor of the plan, or on which this plan centers. This is a broad spectrum survey in which we report how sponsors see themselves relating to the Great Commission. The 15 types below are arranged as responses under the 7 constituent Mandates of the Great Commission, each of which is followed below by (also in bold capitals) the generic name for such ministry to non-Christian and unevangelized populations.

   **RECEIVE!**              **PRAYER EVANGELISM**
   - 0 = no human missionary activity proposed or required, as God will do it by supernatural means
   - 1 = no human missionary activity proposed or required, except repentance and nurture of one's personal life
   - 2 = prayer, intercession, prayer mobilization, prayer survey, worship, monastic life, revival, revivals

   **GO!**              **PRE-EVANGELISM**
   - 3 = survey, information, scholarship, research, strategy, study, communication
   - 4 = relief, charity, development, liberation, conscientization, dialogue, apologetics

   **WITNESS!**              **PERSONAL EVANGELISM**
   - 5 = presence, lifestyle, witness and/or martyrdom on the part of believers, lay apostolate, sowing, seed-sowing
   - 6 = broadcasting: radio, television, film, video, audio, hi-tech

   **PROCLAIM!**              **PREACHING EVANGELISM**
   - 7 = preaching, proclamation, evangelism, mission
   - 8 = power evangelism with signs and wonders, power healing, miracles

   **DISCIPLE!**              **PERSUASION EVANGELISM**
   - 9 = winning, persuading, converting, reaping, harvesting,, discipling

   **BAPTIZE!**              **PLANTING EVANGELISM**
   - 10 = church planting, baptizing
   - 11 = forcible or enforced baptism and church rule
   - 12 = military conquest with forcible baptism and church rule

   **TRAIN!**              **PASTORAL EVANGELISM**
   - 13 = training, education, leadership, conferences, networking, coordination, pastoralia, administration
   - 14 = literature, scripture distribution, literacy, art

8. *Country of origin:* Where this plan originated or was implemented; the country most associated with this plan. Note that the name given is that of the country at the time of origin, which in several early cases differs from its current name.
9. *Ecclesiastical tradition* or confession or family related to this plan, or that of author. This is the best or first single adjective by which the plan and its sponsors would primarily describe its affiliation or stance. Note a distinction between 2 often-confused terms: 'Nondenominational' refers to plans developed independently of existing major denominations or traditions, outside their control, and not accountable to them; whereas 'Interdenominational' is reserved for those plans in whose evolution a number of denominations have been involved, over which plans they exercise collectively a measure of control and receive a degree of accountability. By contrast, a denominational label ('Methodist', 'Lutheran', etc) usually implies a firmer degree of control and accountability.
10. *Cooperation:* Original plan's degree of cooperation with, or recognition of, or control or influence by, other ecclesiastical traditions, other Christians, other agencies, or (in the most advanced case) with the entire spectrum of all traditions, Christians and agencies:
    - 0 = none: a standalone, self-sufficient plan, viewing its sponsor as at the center of world evangelization, with little or no reference to other traditions
    - 1 = minimal: nominal reference to other like-minded traditions or bodies
    - 2 = partial: other like-minded traditions or bodies may participate if they wish
    - 3 = general: cooperation of all like-minded traditions and churches and agencies needed, wanted, and assumed
    - 4 = essential: cooperation of other like-minded traditions and bodies indispensable
    - 5 = total: plan envisages cooperation of entire spectrum of all Christians of all traditions, like-minded and otherwise
11. *Print:* Is there any printed description of this plan? How significant is literature concerning it?
    - 0 = nothing written except incidental reference
    - 1 = briefly written up in published form
    - 2 = based on published article or articles, encyclical, message
    - 3 = based on published book or books
    - 4 = printed publicity materials
    - 5 = detailed plans and logistics printed for private use
    - 6 = detailed plans and logistics published as a book or books
12. *Resources:* General order of magnitude of total resources of mission-related personnel and finances actually employed or expended, or actually made available for implementing this plan during its lifetime, or during its heyday, or (in current plans) potential future lifetime. This variable differs from No. 6 ('Type', which deals with the plan's original intent or expectation), in that No. 13 'Resources' deals with actual mission-related resources subsequently deployed. This covers Christian workers or personnel involved, either at origin, or at peak, or today; and (b) budget or budgets or cost represented by this plan, or if this plan were implemented; or, annual budget of sponsoring body and related bodies over 5 or 10-year period, or period envisaged.

    The term 'worker-year' is similar to 'man-hour' or 'man-year' and gives a rough estimate of the scale of work and resources involved, assuming on average a plan lasts 10 years. The code 4 indicates a sizeable global plan with expenditure of the order of $1 million or more, over a 10-year period. The code 5 indicates what we here are terming a megaplan, for cases where the plan is still being massively implemented (which means code 9 in column 16). The code 6 here indicates in all cases what we are terming a gigaplan (billion-dollar plan).
    - 0 = negligible: less than 1 worker-year (one individual's work only, negligible expenditures)
    - 1 = minimal: 1-10 worker-years (a few individuals, minimal expenditures)
    - 2 = limited: 10-100 worker-years (e.g. a small team, with limited finance or under $10,000 a year)
    - 3 = modest (or, adequate): 100-1,000 worker-years (e.g. from 10-100 workers, or from $10,000-100,000 a year)
    - 4 = sizeable: 1,000-10,000 worker-years (e.g. from 100-1,000 workers, or from $100,000 to $10 million a year)
    - 5 = massive: over 10,000 worker-years (e.g. over 1,000 workers, or from $10 million to $100 million a year)
    - 6 = gigantic: over 50,000 worker-years (e.g. over 5,000 workers, or over $100 million a year or $1 billion over one decade)
13. *Deadline:* Year of final closure, if announced in this plan, or date when Endtime envisaged (a dash, -, means no such date proposed).
14. *Unevangelized:* Percentage of the world's population, at year of plan's origin, which was unevangelized (unaware of Christianity, Christ or the gospel). This variable is equal to 100 minus % evangelized (column 16) from Table 2-1. Its derivation is described in Part 19 "Macroevangelistics". It is given here as a measure of the extent of the unfinished task of world evangelization.
15. *Unevangelized per Christian:* Total unevangelized persons in world divided by total Christians in world, at year of plan's origin = (100 minus column 16 divided by column 7, both from Table 2-1. This ratio is a measure of the relative difficulty of the unfinished task at the time the plan was first put forward.
16. *Current status:* Present status of plan as a global plan to implement world evangelization. Note that this variable refers to the current status of the plan, which is not necessarily the same as the current status of its sponsor.
    - 0 = fizzled out, collapsed, dropped, abandoned, forgotten, superseded, without reaching stated goal; self-imposed deadline now passed
    - 1 = defunct, because little or insufficient interest shown
    - 2 = defunct, because completion of task claimed
    - 3 = implemented but overarching goal not or not yet achieved
    - 4 = still alive, but plan clearly fizzling out
    - 5 = still alive, but plan in decline
    - 6 = still alive, but static
    - 7 = still alive, but with original evangelization goals abandoned, scaled down, redefined, given up, or otherwise ignored
    - 8 = alive and making progress toward original goals
    - 9 = alive and being massively implemented

*Continued opposite*

*Table 27–21 continued*

| *No.* *1* | *Year* *2* | *Name* *3* | *Author* *4* | *Initials* *5* | *Type* *6* | *Min* *7* | *Origin* *8* | *Tradition* *9* | *Coop* *10* | *Pr* *11* | *Res* *12* | *Dline* *13* | *Unev* *14* | *Ratio* *15* | *Stat* *16* |
|---|---|---|---|---|---|---|---|---|---|---|---|---|---|---|---|
| 1 | AD 30 | 'The Kingdom of God has arrived' | Jesus of Nazareth | – | 1 | 8 | Palestine | Pre-Pentecost | 5 | 3 | 4 | – | 99.9 | – | 9 |
| 2 | 31 | The Twelve Apostles as personal evangelists | Jesus the Rabbi | – | 8 | 8 | Palestine | Pre-Pentecost | 5 | 3 | 2 | – | 99.9 | – | 3 |
| 3 | 31 | Mission to Israel | Jesus the Messiah | – | 8 | 8 | Palestine | Pre-Pentecost | 5 | 3 | 2 | – | 99.9 | – | 1 |
| 4 | 31 | Mission of the Seventy | Jesus the Son of Man | – | 8 | 8 | Palestine | Pre-Pentecost | 5 | 3 | 3 | – | 99.9 | – | 1 |
| 5 | 32 | Lightning spread to all nations | Jesus the Returning Judge | – | 0 | 8 | Palestine | Pre-Pentecost | 5 | 3 | 3 | – | 99.9 | – | 1 |
| 6 | 33 | Great Commission-1 | The Risen Lord | – | 1 | 8 | Palestine | Apostolic | 5 | 3 | 4 | – | 99.8 | 42550.0 | 9 |
| 7 | 33 | Great Commission-2 | The Ascended King | – | 1 | 8 | Palestine | Apostolic | 5 | 3 | 4 | – | 99.8 | 42550.0 | 9 |
| 8 | 34 | Mission of the Twelve to the Jewish Diaspora | The Twelve Apostles | – | 5 | 8 | Palestine | Apostolic | 5 | 3 | 3 | 70 | 99.4 | 17020.0 | 1 |
| 9 | 35 | Power Evangelism, with Signs and Wonders | The Twelve Apostles | – | 7 | 8 | Palestine | Apostolic | 5 | 3 | 2 | – | 99.0 | 6481.0 | 3 |
| 10 | 36 | Martyrdom: witness unto death | Stephen the Protomartyr | – | 0 | 5 | Palestine | Apostolic | 5 | 3 | 1 | – | 98.6 | 5594.0 | 3 |
| 11 | 38 | Evangelization of the first Gentiles | The Twelve Apostles | – | 5 | 8 | Palestine | Apostolic | 5 | 3 | 2 | – | 97.7 | 4157.0 | 3 |
| 12 | 38 | Peter's mission to the Gentiles | Apostle Peter | – | 5 | 8 | Palestine | Apostolic | 5 | 3 | 1 | – | 97.7 | 4157.0 | 3 |
| 13 | c38 | Worldwide witness of the Twelve | The Twelve Apostles | – | 5 | 5 | Palestine | Apostolic | 5 | 3 | 2 | – | 97.7 | 4157.0 | 1 |
| 14 | 46 | Paul's urban mission from city to city | Apostle Paul | – | 8 | 8 | Syria | Apostolic | 5 | 3 | 1 | – | 94.4 | 944.0 | 3 |
| 15 | 61 | Preaching to all Creation | Apostle Paul | – | 6 | 8 | Greece | Apostolic | 5 | 3 | 2 | – | 88.2 | 294.0 | 2 |
| 16 | 65 | Worldwide Proclamation by Three Angels | John the Divine | – | 0 | 0 | Asia Minor | Apostolic | 5 | 3 | 0 | – | 86.5 | 288.3 | 9 |
| 17 | 66 | A History of the Great Commission (Luke-Acts) | Luke the Physician | – | 3 | 8 | Italy | Apostolic | 5 | 3 | 3 | – | 86.1 | 287.0 | 2 |
| 18 | c85 | *Epistle of Barnabas* | Barnabas | – | 3 | 1 | Cyprus | Apostolic | 3 | 2 | 0 | 2000 | 78.2 | 156.4 | 0 |
| 19 | 94 | 'Entire Roman Empire has been evangelized' | Clement of Rome | – | 3 | 8 | Italy | Catholic | 3 | 2 | 1 | – | 74.5 | 149.0 | 2 |
| 20 | 96 | Foreordained martyrdom | John the Divine | – | 0 | 5 | Asia Minor | Apostolic | 5 | 3 | 3 | – | 73.7 | 122.8 | 9 |
| 21 | c100 | Evangelization via cities and trade routes | Ignatius of Antioch | – | 5 | 9 | Syria | Catholic | 3 | 1 | 3 | – | 72.0 | 120.0 | 8 |
| 22 | c130 | Church-planting and conversions through casual contacts | Telesphorus | – | 5 | 10 | Italy | Catholic | 3 | 1 | 2 | – | 70.8 | 47.2 | 8 |
| 23 | c140 | *Shepherd of Hermas* | Hermas | – | 3 | 7 | Italy | Catholic | 3 | 2 | 3 | – | 70.4 | 39.1 | 2 |
| 24 | c150 | Disciple-training school proclaiming Christ to every race | Justin Martyr | – | 7 | 13 | Italy | Catholic | 3 | 3 | 3 | – | 70.0 | 35.0 | 2 |
| 25 | 156 | New Age of the Holy Spirit | Montanus | – | 0 | 1 | Asia Minor | Montanist | 0 | 2 | 0 | – | 69.8 | 31.7 | 0 |
| 26 | c180 | Antichrist, Christ, and Millennium | Irenaeus of Lyons | – | 0 | 0 | France | Catholic | 0 | 2 | 0 | – | 68.8 | 23.7 | 0 |
| 27 | 197 | 'The blood of the martyrs is seed' | Tertullian | – | 0 | 5 | Tunisia | Montanist | 1 | 3 | 1 | – | 68.1 | 20.0 | 2 |
| 28 | c205 | Apologetics relating gospel to pagan philosophy and culture | Clement of Alexandria | – | 7 | 3 | Egypt | Orthodox | 3 | 3 | 1 | – | 67.9 | 17.9 | 2 |
| 29 | c220 | Reaching unreached populations throughout the Oikumene | Origen | – | 2 | 7 | Egypt | Orthodox | 3 | 3 | 3 | – | 67.4 | 13.8 | 9 |
| 30 | 249 | Missionary bishops strategically located across world | Cornelius of Rome | – | 9 | 10 | France | Catholic | 0 | 3 | 5 | – | 66.5 | 9.6 | 0 |
| 31 | c270 | Eremitical monasticism challenging lifestyle of the rich | Anthony | – | 5 | 2 | Egypt | Orthodox | 2 | 3 | 4 | – | 65.9 | 7.9 | 8 |
| 32 | 303 | Witness under total persecution | Peter I Seal of Martyrs | – | 0 | 5 | Egypt | Orthodox | 5 | 3 | 5 | – | 64.9 | 6.1 | 8 |
| 33 | 308 | Church of the Martyrs | Meletius of Lycopolis | – | 0 | 5 | Egypt | Orthodox | 0 | 3 | 5 | – | 64.7 | 5.8 | 0 |
| 34 | c310 | *Demonstratio Evangelica* | Eusebius of Caesarea | – | 3 | 1 | Palestine | Orthodox | 3 | 3 | 2 | – | 64.6 | 5.8 | 2 |
| 35 | 313 | State establishment of Christianity as outreach plan | Constantine | – | 10 | 12 | Byzantium | Orthodox | 0 | 3 | 5 | – | 64.5 | 5.6 | 0 |
| 36 | c320 | Itinerant evangelization by Cenobitic monasticism | Pachomius | – | 8 | 2 | Egypt | Orthodox | 2 | 3 | 5 | – | 64.2 | 5.4 | 8 |
| 37 | 325 | Ecumenical councils plan Christian presence | Eusebius of Caesarea | – | 10 | 13 | Palestine | Orthodox | 5 | 3 | 5 | – | 64.0 | 5.1 | 0 |
| 38 | 347 | 'Antichrist will persecute Christians' | Cyril of Jerusalem | – | 0 | 5 | Palestine | Orthodox | 0 | 2 | 0 | – | 63.1 | 4.4 | 0 |
| 39 | c360 | *Apostolic Constitutions* | Dionysius Exiguus | – | 3 | 7 | Syria | Orthodox | 2 | 3 | 1 | – | 62.6 | 4.1 | 0 |
| 40 | 374 | Signs, Healings, and Glossolalia | Ambrose of Milan | – | 2 | 8 | Italy | Catholic | 1 | 2 | 1 | – | 62.0 | 3.8 | 0 |
| 41 | 378 | Signs, Wonders, and Martyrs | Jerome | – | 0 | 5 | Palestine | Catholic | 1 | 3 | 5 | – | 61.9 | 3.7 | 2 |
| 42 | 378 | 'Antichrist has been born' | Martin of Tours | – | 0 | 1 | France | Catholic | 0 | 2 | 0 | – | 61.9 | 3.7 | 0 |
| 43 | 392 | Western monasticism with itinerant evangelization | John Cassian | – | 5 | 2 | Palestine | Catholic | 2 | 3 | 5 | – | 61.3 | 3.4 | 8 |
| 44 | 398 | Constantinople School of Evangelists for Great Commission | John Chrysostom | – | 8 | 13 | Byzantium | Orthodox | 3 | 3 | 3 | 430 | 61.1 | 3.3 | 0 |
| 45 | c410 | Universal episcopate as plan for world mission | Innocent I | – | 10 | 10 | Algeria | Catholic | 0 | 5 | 5 | – | 60.7 | 3.2 | 8 |
| 46 | 417 | *Historia Adversus Paganos* | Paulus Orosius | – | 0 | 1 | Spain | Catholic | 3 | 3 | 0 | – | 60.5 | 3.2 | 0 |
| 47 | 426 | *The City of God* | Augustine of Hippo | – | 3 | 8 | Tunisia | Catholic | 4 | 3 | 1 | – | 60.2 | 3.1 | 0 |
| 48 | 428 | *De Vocatione Omnium Gentium* | Prosper Tiro | – | 0 | 7 | France | Catholic | 3 | 3 | 0 | – | 60.2 | 3.1 | 0 |
| 49 | 499 | Cultural translation of Jesus' message | Symmachus | – | 5 | 14 | Greece | Orthodox | 3 | 3 | 4 | – | 58.0 | 2.6 | 3 |
| 50 | c510 | Irish Peregrini: Missionary Pilgrims for Christ | Columbanus | – | 5 | 8 | Ireland | Celtic | 2 | 1 | 4 | – | 58.3 | 2.6 | 0 |
| 51 | 535 | *Topographia Christiana* | Cosmas Indicopleustes | – | 3 | 3 | Egypt | Nestorian | 1 | 3 | 2 | – | 59.0 | 2.6 | 0 |
| 52 | c550 | Nestorian monasticism sends mission across Asia | Abraham of Kashkar | – | 5 | 2 | Persia | Nestorian | 0 | 1 | 5 | – | 59.5 | 2.6 | 0 |
| 53 | 594 | 'The Last Judgment demands missions to all heathen' | Gregory the Great | – | 2 | 7 | Italy | Catholic | 0 | 3 | 1 | – | 60.8 | 2.5 | 0 |
| 54 | 635 | Nestorian world missions | Alopen | – | 9 | 7 | Syria | Nestorian | 0 | 1 | 5 | – | 62.4 | 2.6 | 0 |
| 55 | c700 | Patristic Age: Greek and Latin Fathers expound *euangelizo* | Theodotus of Ancyra | – | 3 | 3 | Greece | Orthodox | 2 | 3 | 4 | – | 65.0 | 2.7 | 0 |
| 56 | 720 | Fall of Colosseum, Rome, and the World | Bede | – | 0 | 0 | England | Anglican | 2 | 3 | 0 | – | 65.8 | 2.8 | 0 |
| 57 | 780 | Nestorian strategy of metropolitan sees worldwide | Timothy I | – | 10 | 10 | Persia | Nestorian | 0 | 3 | 5 | – | 68.2 | 3.0 | 0 |
| 58 | c780 | Forcible baptism of whole races begun | Charlemagne | – | 8 | 11 | France | Catholic | 0 | 1 | 5 | – | 68.2 | 3.0 | 0 |
| 59 | 960 | Imminent End of the World | Bernard of Thuringia | – | 0 | 0 | Germany | Catholic | 0 | 2 | 0 | 992 | 74.2 | 3.7 | 0 |
| 60 | 962 | Holy Roman Empire as Rule of Christ on Earth | John XII | – | 10 | 11 | Germany | Catholic | 0 | 3 | 5 | – | 74.2 | 3.7 | 0 |
| 61 | 992 | Coming of Antichrist into World | Adso of Montier-en-Der | – | 0 | 0 | France | Catholic | 0 | 3 | 0 | 1000 | 74.8 | 4.0 | 0 |
| 62 | 999 | Advent travel to Jerusalem | Gregory V | – | 5 | 5 | Palestine | Catholic | 0 | 1 | 2 | 1000 | 75.0 | 4.0 | 0 |
| 63 | 1000 | Mass millennial pilgrimage to await Advent | Sylvester II | – | 5 | 5 | Palestine | Catholic | 1 | 1 | 3 | 1000 | 75.0 | 4.0 | 0 |
| 64 | 1000 | Global spread of Catholic Apostolic Church of the East | Ishoyabh IV | – | 10 | 10 | Syria | Nestorian | 0 | 3 | 5 | – | 75.0 | 4.0 | 0 |
| 65 | 1090 | College of Cardinals to expand Rule of Christ | Urban II | – | 6 | 13 | Vatican | Roman Catholic | 0 | 5 | 2 | – | 74.6 | 4.0 | 8 |
| 66 | 1095 | Crusades for the Defense of Christianity | Urban II | – | 10 | 12 | Italy | Roman Catholic | 0 | 5 | 5 | – | 74.5 | 4.0 | 0 |
| 67 | 1113 | Knights of Malta | Brother Gerard | – | 8 | 5 | Palestine | Roman Catholic | 1 | 3 | 4 | – | 74.4 | 4.0 | 7 |
| 68 | 1139 | *Prophecy of the Popes* | Malachy O'Morgain | – | 0 | 0 | Ireland | Roman Catholic | 0 | 3 | 1 | 2000 | 74.3 | 3.9 | 0 |
| 69 | 1179 | Imminent major catastrophe in AD 1186 | John of Toledo | – | 0 | 0 | Spain | Roman Catholic | 0 | 1 | 0 | 1186 | 74.1 | 3.8 | 0 |
| 70 | c1180 | Final Age of the Spirit | Joachim of Fiore | – | 0 | 0 | Italy | Roman Catholic | 0 | 3 | 0 | 1260 | 74.1 | 3.8 | 0 |
| 71 | c1190 | Vernacular scriptures: *Historia Scholastica* | Petrus Comestor | – | 5 | 14 | France | Roman Catholic | 1 | 3 | 2 | – | 74.1 | 3.8 | 9 |
| 72 | 1201 | Knights of the Sword | Bishop Albert I of Riga | – | 8 | 12 | Latvia | Roman Catholic | 1 | 3 | 3 | – | 74.0 | 3.8 | 0 |
| 73 | 1209 | Order of Friars: mendicant orders of travelling preachers | Francis of Assisi | OFM | 10 | 8 | Italy | Roman Catholic | 1 | 5 | 6 | – | 73.9 | 3.7 | 9 |
| 74 | 1215 | Order of Preachers: 'Propagation of the Faith through Preaching' | Dominic | OP | 10 | 7 | France | Roman Catholic | 0 | 5 | 6 | – | 73.9 | 3.7 | 9 |
| 75 | 1221 | Bull 'Ne Si Secus' to the 13 Catholic Metropolitans | Honorius III | – | 2 | 13 | Vatican | Roman Catholic | 0 | 2 | 2 | – | 73.8 | 3.6 | 3 |
| 76 | c1250 | Church's temporal power as God's instrument for mission | Innocent IV | – | 10 | 11 | Italy | Roman Catholic | 0 | 3 | 5 | – | 73.5 | 3.4 | 5 |
| 77 | c1250 | Popular preachers warn of Coming of Antichrist | Berthold von Regensburg | OFM | 0 | 0 | Germany | Roman Catholic | 1 | 1 | 2 | – | 73.5 | 3.4 | 0 |
| 78 | 1254 | Imminent Third Age of the Holy Spirit | Gerard of Borgo San Donnino | – | 0 | 1 | Italy | Roman Catholic | 1 | 3 | 0 | 1260 | 73.5 | 3.4 | 0 |
| 79 | c1260 | Religious art: painting, stained glass, sculpture | Duccio de Buoninsegna | – | 0 | 14 | Italy | Roman Catholic | 1 | 3 | 5 | – | 73.4 | 3.3 | 8 |
| 80 | 1266 | 'Send me 100 men' | Kublai Khan | – | 1 | 9 | Mongolia | Roman Catholic | 0 | 1 | 2 | – | 73.3 | 3.3 | 0 |
| 81 | c1280 | Congregation of Friars Pilgrims for Christ Among the Gentiles | William of Tripoli | OP | 8 | 7 | France | Roman Catholic | 0 | 2 | 4 | – | 73.2 | 3.2 | 0 |
| 82 | 1288 | *Notitia Seculi* | Alexander of Roes | – | 0 | 1 | Germany | Roman Catholic | 0 | 2 | 0 | 1500 | 73.1 | 3.1 | 0 |
| 83 | 1290 | *The Coming of Antichrist* | Arnold of Villanova | – | 0 | 0 | Spain | Roman Catholic | 0 | 3 | 0 | – | 73.1 | 3.1 | 0 |
| 84 | 1315 | Liber de Fine: Preaching plus Military Force | Ramon Lull | OFM | 1 | 12 | Algeria | Roman Catholic | 0 | 3 | 1 | – | 72.7 | 3.0 | 0 |
| 85 | 1315 | The Final Coming of Antichrist | Hugh of Newcastle | OFM | 0 | 0 | France | Roman Catholic | 0 | 2 | 0 | – | 72.7 | 3.0 | 0 |
| 86 | 1349 | East Syrian/Nestorian apogee | Yabalaha III | – | 10 | 10 | Syria | Nestorian | 0 | 3 | 5 | – | 72.0 | 3.0 | 0 |
| 87 | c1350 | Revelation of Antichrist in AD 2000 | St John of the Cleft Rock | – | 0 | 1 | Italy | Roman Catholic | 0 | 0 | 0 | 2000 | 72.0 | 3.0 | 0 |
| 88 | 1399 | Wandering preachers proliferate across world | Vincent Ferrer | OP | 2 | 8 | Spain | Roman Catholic | 0 | 1 | 3 | 3936 | 73.0 | 3.0 | 9 |
| 89 | c1400 | Societas Peregrinantium pro Christo | William of Casale | OFM | 8 | 7 | Italy | Roman Catholic | 0 | 2 | 4 | – | 73.0 | 3.0 | 0 |
| 90 | 1420 | Taborite Kingdom of God | Nicholas of Pelhrimov | – | 9 | 12 | Bohemia | Hussite | 0 | 1 | 5 | – | 74.2 | 3.2 | 0 |
| 91 | 1431 | Council of Basle orders non-Christians to attend sermons | Eugenius IV | – | 2 | 11 | Switzerland | Roman Catholic | 1 | 3 | 3 | – | 74.9 | 3.3 | 0 |
| 92 | 1450 | Dissemination of Scriptures by typography and printing | Johannes Gutenberg | – | 9 | 14 | Germany | Roman Catholic | 1 | 5 | 5 | – | 76.0 | 3.5 | 9 |
| 93 | 1455 | *The Imitation of Christ* | Thomas a Kempis | – | 3 | 5 | Germany | Roman Catholic | 1 | 3 | 1 | – | 76.3 | 3.6 | 7 |
| 94 | 1490 | Reforming beggar-monks itinerate evangelizing | Wolfgang Capito | – | 5 | 7 | Germany | Roman Catholic | 0 | 1 | 3 | – | 78.4 | 4.0 | 0 |
| 95 | 1493 | 'Inter Caetera' | Alexander VI | – | 2 | 11 | Vatican | Roman Catholic | 0 | 3 | 1 | – | 78.6 | 4.1 | 0 |
| 96 | 1499 | 3-storey Rhine ark | Johannes Stoeffler | – | 0 | 1 | Germany | Roman Catholic | 0 | 1 | 0 | 1524 | 78.9 | 4.1 | 0 |
| 97 | 1500 | World missions via Spanish/Portuguese imperialism | Alexander VI | – | 10 | 11 | Vatican | Roman Catholic | 0 | 5 | 5 | – | 79.0 | 4.2 | 0 |
| 98 | 1500 | End-time predictions | Bartolomeo di Saluzzo | – | 0 | 0 | Italy | Roman Catholic | 0 | 1 | 1 | – | 79.0 | 4.2 | 0 |
| 99 | 1500 | Saints and martyrs as evangelizing witnesses | George Novi of Sophia | – | 5 | 5 | Italy | Roman Catholic | 1 | 3 | 5 | – | 79.0 | 4.2 | 8 |
| 100 | 1517 | 'Visions of the End of the World' | Leonardo da Vinci | – | 0 | 14 | Italy | Roman Catholic | 2 | 3 | 1 | – | 78.7 | 4.1 | 6 |
| 101 | c1520 | Completion of the Task by the Twelve Apostles | Martin Luther | – | 0 | 0 | Germany | Lutheran | 2 | 3 | 0 | 1558 | 78.6 | 4.1 | 2 |
| 102 | 1523 | Conquistadores enforce mass baptism across New World | Charles V | – | 10 | 12 | Mexico | Roman Catholic | 0 | 3 | 5 | – | 78.5 | 4.1 | 0 |
| 103 | 1523 | Conversion of Islam and the Whole World to Christ (Jesuits) | Ignatius Loyola | SJ | 10 | 9 | Palestine | Roman Catholic | 0 | 6 | 6 | – | 78.5 | 4.1 | 9 |
| 104 | 1523 | Astrologers' prediction of End of World in 1524 | Paracelsus (von Hohenheim) | – | 0 | 1 | Switzerland | Roman Catholic | 0 | 1 | 1 | 1524 | 78.5 | 4.1 | 0 |
| 105 | 1528 | Berne Disputation and its Ten Theses | Ulrich Zwingli | – | 2 | 7 | Switzerland | Reformed | 2 | 1 | 4 | – | 78.4 | 4.1 | 0 |
| 106 | 1530 | Melchiorites and the New Jerusalem | Melchior Hofmann | – | 9 | 12 | Netherlands | Anabaptist | 0 | 1 | 5 | 1533 | 78.4 | 4.1 | 0 |
| 107 | 1530 | Cessation of Apostolic Commission | John Calvin | – | 0 | 0 | Switzerland | Reformed | 2 | 1 | 0 | – | 78.4 | 4.1 | 2 |
| 108 | 1534 | New Zion and the Kingdom of a Thousand Years | John of Leiden | – | 9 | 12 | Germany | Anabaptist | 0 | 1 | 5 | – | 78.3 | 4.1 | 0 |
| 109 | 1536 | 'The Last Judgment' inspired by hymn 'Dies Irae' | Michelangelo Buonarroti | – | 0 | 14 | Italy | Roman Catholic | 2 | 3 | 2 | – | 78.3 | 4.1 | 7 |
| 110 | 1536 | The Only Way to Draw All Peoples to the True Religion | Bartolome de Las Casas | OP | 2 | 7 | Spain | Roman Catholic | 1 | 2 | 3 | – | 78.3 | 4.1 | 3 |
| 111 | 1547 | *The Centuries* with detailed future prophecies | Michel de Nostradamus | – | 0 | 1 | France | Roman Catholic | 0 | 3 | 4 | 2000 | 78.1 | 4.1 | 9 |
| 112 | c1547 | Anabaptist view of the Great Commission | Michael Sattler | – | 1 | 7 | Germany | Anabaptist | 0 | 1 | 3 | – | 78.1 | 4.1 | 9 |
| 113 | c1550 | Numerology of Apocalypse and End of World in 1666 | J.H. Bullinger | – | 0 | 0 | Switzerland | Reformed | 2 | 1 | 1 | 1666 | 78.0 | 4.1 | 0 |
| 114 | 1559 | Hutterian Brethren's itinerant evangelism | Jakob Hutter | – | 5 | 8 | Moravia | Anabaptist | 0 | 1 | 3 | – | 77.8 | 4.1 | 9 |
| 115 | 1568 | Commission of Cardinals begun for foreign missions | Pius V | – | 6 | 13 | Vatican | Roman Catholic | 0 | 5 | 2 | – | 77.6 | 4.1 | 0 |
| 116 | 1573 | Congregation for Conversion of Infidels | Gregory XIII | – | 6 | 13 | Vatican | Roman Catholic | 0 | 3 | 2 | – | 77.5 | 4.1 | 0 |
| 117 | 1580 | Discalced Carmelite Sisters: evangelization by prayer | Theresa of Avila | – | 10 | 2 | Spain | Roman Catholic | 0 | 5 | 5 | – | 77.4 | 4.1 | 9 |
| 118 | 1584 | Evangelistic military conquest | Alonso Sanchez | SJ | 9 | 12 | Spain | Roman Catholic | 0 | 3 | 0 | – | 77.3 | 4.1 | 0 |
| 119 | 1588 | Binding validity of Great Commission | Hadrian Saravia | – | 2 | 7 | England | Anglican | 3 | 2 | 1 | – | 77.2 | 4.1 | 0 |
| 120 | 1588 | Consistorial Congregation (Sacred Congregation for Bishops) | Sixtus V | – | 10 | 13 | Vatican | Roman Catholic | 0 | 5 | 6 | – | 77.2 | 4.1 | 9 |
| 121 | 1589 | Russian Orthodox state-supported missions | Peter the Great | ROC | 10 | 10 | Russia | Eastern Orthodox | 0 | 5 | 4 | – | 77.2 | 4.1 | 0 |
| 122 | 1594 | Logarithms and the Apocalypse, and Number of the Beast | John Napier | – | 0 | 0 | Scotland | Presbyterian | 1 | 3 | 1 | – | 77.1 | 4.1 | 0 |
| 123 | 1600 | Bruno's Magico-Religious System | Giordano Bruno | – | 0 | 1 | Italy | Roman Catholic | 0 | 3 | 1 | – | 77.0 | 4.1 | 0 |
| 124 | c1600 | Episcopi Vagantes with plans for Reunion of Christendom | Julius Ferrette | – | 5 | 2 | Italy | Old Catholic | 0 | 3 | 4 | – | 77.0 | 4.1 | 5 |

*Continued overleaf*

*Table 27–21 continued*

| *No.* 1 | *Year* 2 | *Name* 3 | *Author* 4 | *Initials* 5 | *Type* 6 | *Min* 7 | *Origin* 8 | *Tradition* 9 | *Coop* 10 | *Pr* 11 | *Res* 12 | *Dline* 13 | *Unev* 14 | *Ratio* 15 | *Stat* 16 |
|---|---|---|---|---|---|---|---|---|---|---|---|---|---|---|---|
| 125 | 1600 | *L'Histoire* | G. P. Maffei | – | 3 | 10 | Italy | Roman Catholic | 0 | 3 | 4 | – | 77.0 | 4.1 | 3 |
| 126 | 1610 | The Coming of Antichrist | Tomas Malvenda | OP | 0 | 0 | Italy | Roman Catholic | 0 | 1 | 1 | – | 76.7 | 4.0 | 0 |
| 127 | 1613 | *De Procuranda Salute Omnium Gentium* | Thomas a Jesu | – | 3 | 9 | Spain | Roman Catholic | 0 | 3 | 1 | – | 76.6 | 3.9 | 0 |
| 128 | 1620 | Mission preaching restricted to Twelve Apostles | Johann Gerhard | – | 0 | 1 | Germany | Lutheran | 0 | 3 | 0 | – | 76.3 | 3.9 | 2 |
| 129 | 1622 | Propaganda Fide: Spreading the Faith to the World | Gregory XV | – | 10 | 7 | Vatican | Roman Catholic | 0 | 6 | 6 | – | 76.3 | 3.8 | 9 |
| 130 | 1627 | Progressive Millennialism before Return of Christ | Joseph Mede | – | 0 | 1 | England | Anglican | 2 | 3 | 1 | – | 76.1 | 3.8 | 4 |
| 131 | 1630 | *Report on the Four Parts of the World* | F. Ingoli | – | 9 | 10 | Vatican | Roman Catholic | 1 | 6 | 5 | – | 76.1 | 3.8 | 8 |
| 132 | 1648 | Eleven Million Martyrs | Ildefonso de Flores | SJ | 0 | 5 | Spain | Roman Catholic | 1 | 3 | 5 | – | 75.4 | 3.6 | 8 |
| 133 | 1656 | Return of the Jews | Oliver Cromwell | – | 0 | 1 | England | Anglican | 0 | 1 | 0 | – | 75.2 | 3.5 | 0 |
| 134 | 1657 | Fifth Monarchy Men | Thomas Venner | – | 0 | 0 | England | Anglican | 0 | 1 | 2 | c1660 | 75.2 | 3.5 | 0 |
| 135 | 1658 | Antichrist as Parody of Christ | Bartholomaus Holtzhauser | – | 0 | 0 | Germany | Roman Catholic | 0 | 0 | 0 | – | 75.2 | 3.5 | 0 |
| 136 | c1660 | Millennium centered on church in Peru | G. Tenorio | OFM | 0 | 1 | Peru | Roman Catholic | 0 | 3 | 0 | – | 75.2 | 3.5 | 0 |
| 137 | 1663 | Missionary Work among Unevangelized Peoples | Justinian von Welz | – | 3 | 7 | Germany | Lutheran | 2 | 3 | 2 | – | 75.2 | 3.5 | 1 |
| 138 | 1667 | 'To Evangelize the Nations' (*Paradise Lost*) | John Milton | – | 2 | 7 | Britain | Anglican | 3 | 3 | 1 | – | 75.1 | 3.5 | 5 |
| 139 | 1680 | Christian Brothers: evangelization by schools | J.-B. de La Salle | FSC | 10 | 13 | France | Roman Catholic | 0 | 5 | 5 | – | 75.0 | 3.4 | 9 |
| 140 | 1693 | Knights of the Apocalypse | Innocent XII | – | 7 | 12 | Italy | Roman Catholic | 0 | 1 | 2 | – | 74.9 | 3.4 | 0 |
| 141 | 1698 | Society for Promoting Christian Knowledge | Thomas Bray | SPCK/SPG | 9 | 9 | Britain | Anglican | 2 | 5 | 4 | – | 74.8 | 3.4 | 7 |
| 142 | 1699 | *Observations on Daniel & the Apocalypse* | Isaac Newton | – | 3 | 3 | Britain | Anglican | 3 | 3 | 0 | 2000 | 74.8 | 3.4 | 0 |
| 143 | 1700 | Missions to Jews | E.C.H. von Hochenau | – | 7 | 7 | Germany | Lutheran | 0 | 0 | 1 | – | 74.8 | 3.4 | 1 |
| 144 | 1703 | Spiritans: 'Evangelizzazione degli infedeli' | C.F. Poullart des Places | CSSp | 10 | 7 | France | Roman Catholic | 0 | 5 | 5 | – | 74.8 | 3.4 | 9 |
| 145 | 1705 | Danish-Halle Mission | B. Ziegenbalg | – | 10 | 7 | Denmark | Lutheran | 2 | 5 | 4 | – | 74.7 | 3.3 | 7 |
| 146 | 1710 | Canstein Bible Society | K.H. von Canstein | – | 9 | 14 | Germany | Lutheran | 2 | 3 | 4 | – | 74.7 | 3.3 | 3 |
| 147 | 1725 | Great Awakening and Progressive Millennialism | Jonathan Edwards | – | 8 | 1 | North America | Congregationalist | 2 | 3 | 3 | 1990 | 74.5 | 3.4 | 0 |
| 148 | 1730 | End of the World by Deluge | William Whiston | – | 0 | 0 | Britain | Anglican | 0 | 1 | 0 | 1736 | 74.4 | 3.4 | 0 |
| 149 | 1732 | Society for Propagating the Gospel among the Heathen | N.L. von Zinzendorf | – | 9 | 8 | Germany | Moravian | 2 | 5 | 4 | – | 74.4 | 3.4 | 8 |
| 150 | 1770 | Tribulation and Antichrist in AD 2000 | Jeanne Le Rocher | – | 0 | 0 | France | Roman Catholic | 0 | 0 | 0 | 2000 | 73.6 | 3.3 | 0 |
| 151 | 1774 | United Society of Believers in Christ's Second Appearing | Ann Lee | – | 0 | 0 | Britain | Quaker | 0 | 1 | 2 | – | 73.5 | 3.3 | 0 |
| 152 | 1780 | Christendom Society and Basel Mission | C.G. Blumhardt | DCG/EMB | 9 | 7 | Germany | Evangelical | 2 | 5 | 4 | – | 73.4 | 3.2 | 7 |
| 153 | 1782 | Concerts of Prayer (for revival and world mission) | Jonathan Edwards | – | 9 | 2 | Britain | Evangelical | 2 | 5 | 3 | – | 73.3 | 3.2 | 3 |
| 154 | 1783 | Revival pentecostalism among Black slaves | George Lisle | – | 5 | 8 | Jamaica | Baptist | 0 | 1 | 3 | – | 73.3 | 3.2 | 9 |
| 155 | 1785 | Evangelical awakenings throughout Wales | Howel Harris | – | 5 | 8 | Wales | Anglican | 2 | 1 | 3 | – | 73.2 | 3.2 | 9 |
| 156 | 1787 | *The Gospel of Christ Worthy of All Acceptation* | Andrew Fuller | – | 3 | 7 | Britain | Baptist | 2 | 3 | 0 | – | 73.2 | 3.2 | 1 |
| 157 | 1792 | *Obligations of Christians for Conversion of the Heathens* | William Carey | BMS | 3 | 3 | Britain | Baptist | 2 | 3 | 0 | – | 73.0 | 3.2 | 5 |
| 158 | 1795 | London Missionary Society | William Ellis | LMS | 9 | 9 | Britain | Congregationalist | 2 | 2 | 4 | – | 72.9 | 3.2 | 7 |
| 159 | 1800 | Revival camp meetings sweep across large populations | James McGready | – | 5 | 8 | USA | Methodist | 1 | 1 | 4 | – | 72.8 | 3.1 | 4 |
| 160 | 1802 | Massachusetts Baptist Mission Society | Hezekiah Smith | MBMS | 7 | 7 | USA | Baptist | 1 | 1 | 2 | – | 72.4 | 3.1 | 1 |
| 161 | 1804 | Foreign-language Bible Societies: BFBS, ABS, et alia | Thomas Charles | BFBS | 10 | 14 | Britain | Interdenominational | 2 | 5 | 5 | – | 72.0 | 3.1 | 9 |
| 162 | 1805 | *Le dernier homme*: first modern End-of-the-World novel | J.-B. Cousin de Grainville | – | 0 | 1 | France | Roman Catholic | 0 | 3 | 1 | – | 71.8 | 3.1 | 0 |
| 163 | 1806 | Society of Inquiry on the Subject of Missions | Adoniram Judson | – | 1 | 2 | USA | Baptist | 2 | 2 | 2 | – | 71.6 | 3.1 | 0 |
| 164 | 1810 | Ecumenical missionary conferences | William Carey | BMS | 8 | 13 | India | Baptist | 3 | 1 | 0 | – | 70.8 | 3.1 | 1 |
| 165 | 1810 | American Board of Commissioners for Foreign Missions | S. Newell | ABCFM(UCBWM) | 10 | 9 | USA | Congregationalist | 2 | 5 | 5 | – | 70.7 | 3.0 | 7 |
| 166 | 1811 | *Dissertation on Antichrist* | Ethan Smith | – | 0 | 0 | USA | Evangelical | 0 | 2 | 1 | 1866 | 70.6 | 3.0 | 0 |
| 167 | 1814 | Reestablished Jesuit missions | Pius VII | SJ | 10 | 4 | Italy | Roman Catholic | 0 | 5 | 4 | – | 69.9 | 3.0 | 9 |
| 168 | 1815 | 'The Duty and Reward of Evangelizing the Heathen' | H. Bardwell | – | 2 | 7 | USA | Evangelical | 1 | 3 | 0 | – | 69.7 | 3.0 | 0 |
| 169 | 1815 | Missions of the Most Precious Blood | Caspar Del Bufalo | – | 9 | 4 | Italy | Roman Catholic | 0 | 5 | 4 | – | 69.7 | 3.0 | 8 |
| 170 | 1815 | *The Spirit of British missions* | Josiah Pratt | CMS | 2 | 7 | Britain | Anglican | 2 | 3 | 0 | – | 69.7 | 3.0 | 1 |
| 171 | 1818 | *The Conversion of the World: or the Claims of 600 Millions* | G. Hall & S. Newell | ABCFM | 3 | 9 | India | Congregationalist | 2 | 3 | 1 | – | 69.1 | 2.9 | 0 |
| 172 | 1819 | Missionary Society of the Methodist Episcopal Church | N. Bangs | BGM | 10 | 7 | USA | Methodist | 1 | 5 | 6 | – | 68.9 | 2.9 | 9 |
| 173 | c1820 | Lucifer Unchained by 1940 | Catherine Emmerich | – | 0 | 0 | Germany | Roman Catholic | 0 | 1 | 0 | c1980 | 68.7 | 2.9 | 0 |
| 174 | 1823 | 'The Conversion of the World' | Josiah Pratt | CMS | 2 | 9 | Britain | Anglican | 2 | 2 | 0 | – | 68.1 | 2.8 | 0 |
| 175 | 1824 | Interdenominational citywide cooperative evangelism | A.F. Schauffler | – | 10 | 7 | USA | Interdenominational | 2 | 3 | 5 | – | 67.9 | 2.8 | 8 |
| 176 | 1825 | Bombay Missionary Union | William Carey | BMU | 6 | 7 | India | Interdenominational | 3 | 1 | 3 | – | 67.6 | 2.8 | 0 |
| 177 | 1826 | Glasgow City Mission and 200 other city missions | David Nasmiths | LCM/NYCM/&c | 9 | 7 | Britain | Nondenominational | 2 | 3 | 4 | – | 67.4 | 2.8 | 5 |
| 178 | 1827 | Premillennial apostasy of Christendom: Dispensationalism | J.N. Darby | – | 0 | 0 | Ireland | Brethren | 0 | 3 | 1 | – | 67.2 | 2.7 | 0 |
| 179 | 1828 | Evangelizing in One Generation through Native Evangelists | Karl F.A. Gutzlaff | – | 8 | 7 | China | Lutheran | 2 | 1 | 4 | – | 67.0 | 2.7 | 0 |
| 180 | 1829 | Christian Brethren (Christian Missions in Many Lands) | A.N. Groves | CMML | 5 | 5 | Britain | Brethren | 0 | 3 | 4 | – | 66.8 | 2.7 | 8 |
| 181 | 1830 | Evangelistic campaigns through professional evangelists | Evangelist Andrew | – | 9 | 7 | USA | Interdenominational | 1 | 1 | 5 | – | 66.6 | 2.7 | 3 |
| 182 | 1830 | Church of Jesus Christ of Latter-day Saints | Joseph Smith | CJCLdS | 10 | 5 | USA | Mormon | 0 | 5 | 6 | – | 66.6 | 2.7 | 9 |
| 183 | 1831 | Presbyterian Church in the United States | J.H. Rice | PCUS | 10 | 7 | USA | Presbyterian | 1 | 5 | 5 | – | 66.4 | 2.7 | 7 |
| 184 | 1832 | Catholic Apostolic Church | Edward Irving | CAC | 0 | 0 | Britain | Catholic Apostolic | 0 | 2 | 4 | c1840 | 66.1 | 2.6 | 0 |
| 185 | 1833 | A Bible for Every Family | W. S. Plummer | ABS | 3 | 14 | USA | Ecumenical | 3 | 2 | 3 | 1853 | 65.9 | 2.6 | 0 |
| 186 | 1836 | Appeal from Missionaries at the Sandwich Islands | William Richards | ABCFM | 2 | 7 | Hawaii | Congregationalist | 2 | 2 | 1 | – | 65.2 | 2.5 | 0 |
| 187 | 1836 | *Thoughts on evangelizing the World* | T.S. Skinner | – | 3 | 7 | USA | Evangelical | 2 | 3 | 0 | – | 65.2 | 2.5 | 0 |
| 188 | 1837 | Board of Foreign Missions, Presbyterian Church in the USA | J.C. Lowrie | BFM(COEMAR) | 10 | 7 | USA | Presbyterian | 1 | 5 | 5 | – | 65.0 | 2.5 | 7 |
| 189 | 1837 | *The Time for the World's Conversion Come* | Rufus Anderson | ABCFM | 2 | 9 | USA | Congregationalist | 3 | 3 | 1 | – | 65.0 | 2.5 | 0 |
| 190 | 1841 | Church growth statistics: monitoring world evangelization | Henry Venn | CMS | 8 | 10 | Britain | Anglican | 2 | 5 | 3 | – | 64.1 | 2.4 | 8 |
| 191 | 1842 | Predictions of the End of the World | John Dee | – | 0 | 0 | Britain | Anglican | 0 | 1 | 0 | 1842 | 63.8 | 2.4 | 0 |
| 192 | 1843 | The Past and Prospective Extension of the Gospel | Anthony Grant | – | 3 | 9 | Britain | Anglican | 3 | 3 | 3 | – | 63.6 | 2.4 | 1 |
| 193 | 1844 | Seventh-day Adventists | William Miller | SDA | 0 | 1 | USA | Adventist | 0 | 5 | 6 | 1844 | 63.4 | 2.4 | 9 |
| 194 | 1844 | Christadelphians (Brothers of Christ) | John Thomas | – | 0 | 0 | USA | Christadelphian | 0 | 3 | 2 | – | 63.4 | 2.4 | 4 |
| 195 | 1844 | World Alliance of YMCAs/World YWCA | George Williams | YMCA/YWCA | 6 | 13 | Switzerland | Evangelical | 3 | 3 | 5 | – | 63.4 | 2.4 | 7 |
| 196 | 1845 | Southern Baptist Convention | James B. Taylor | SBC-FMB | 10 | 7 | USA | Baptist | 1 | 5 | 6 | – | 63.1 | 2.4 | 9 |
| 197 | 1846 | Evangelical Alliance and world conciliarism | P. Schaff | EA | 9 | 13 | Germany | Reformed | 2 | 3 | 5 | – | 62.9 | 2.3 | 8 |
| 198 | 1850 | Pyramidology and the future of Christianity | John Taylor | – | 0 | 0 | Britain | Anglican | 0 | 3 | 2 | 2001 | 61.9 | 2.3 | 1 |
| 199 | 1850 | 'Antichrist will not delay his coming' | Bertine Bouquillon | – | 0 | 1 | France | Roman Catholic | 0 | 0 | 0 | – | 61.9 | 2.3 | 0 |
| 200 | 1850 | Millionaire philanthropist-strategists | Robert Arthington | – | 9 | 7 | Britain | Quaker | 0 | 3 | 4 | – | 61.9 | 2.3 | 3 |
| 201 | 1854 | First Union Missionary Convention | Alexander Duff | – | 4 | 13 | Britain | Presbyterian | 2 | 2 | 2 | – | 61.3 | 2.2 | 0 |
| 202 | 1854 | Foreign Mission Committee, Canada Presbyterian Synod | J. Geddie | CPS/BWM-UCC | 9 | 7 | Canada | Presbyterian | 1 | 5 | 4 | – | 61.3 | 2.2 | 7 |
| 203 | c1855 | Russian Orthodox scientific basis for missions | N.I. Ilminsky | ROC | 3 | 10 | Russia | Eastern Orthodox | 0 | 3 | 0 | – | 61.2 | 2.2 | 0 |
| 204 | 1857 | Organized large-scale lay-centered mass evangelism | D.L. Moody | – | 10 | 7 | USA | Congregationalist | 2 | 4 | 5 | – | 60.9 | 2.2 | 8 |
| 205 | 1858 | 'The Duty of the present generation to evangelize the World' | J. Parker | – | 2 | 7 | USA | Evangelical | 3 | 1 | 0 | – | 60.8 | 2.1 | 0 |
| 206 | 1859 | Salesians: Christian education of youth across world | John Bosco | SDB | 10 | 13 | Italy | Roman Catholic | 0 | 5 | 5 | – | 60.6 | 2.1 | 9 |
| 207 | 1860 | Liverpool Conference on Missions | Earl of Shaftesbury | – | 4 | 7 | Britain | Anglican | 3 | 3 | 0 | – | 60.5 | 2.1 | 0 |
| 208 | 1860 | Reorganized Church of Jesus Christ of Latter Day Saints | Joseph Smith II | RCJCLDS | 6 | 7 | USA | Mormon | 0 | 3 | 4 | – | 60.5 | 2.1 | 8 |
| 209 | 1861 | Women's mission societies | Francis Mason | WUMSA | 9 | 7 | USA | Congregationalist | 2 | 5 | 5 | – | 60.3 | 2.1 | 4 |
| 210 | 1862 | Scheutists: 'Evangelizzazione dei popoli' | Theophile Verbist | CICM | 10 | 7 | Belgium | Roman Catholic | 0 | 5 | 5 | – | 60.2 | 2.1 | 9 |
| 211 | 1863 | New Apostolic Church | H. Geyer | NAK(NAC) | 0 | 1 | Germany | Catholic Apostolic | 0 | 5 | 6 | – | 60.1 | 2.1 | 9 |
| 212 | 1865 | Christian Revival Association | William Booth | SA | 9 | 8 | Britain | Salvationist | 0 | 3 | 5 | – | 59.8 | 2.0 | 9 |
| 213 | 1866 | 'The Duty of the Church to evangelize the World' | C. Dickson | PCUSA | 2 | 7 | USA | Presbyterian | 3 | 1 | 0 | – | 59.6 | 2.0 | 0 |
| 214 | 1867 | Confessional conciliarism: Lambeth Conference of Bishops | C.T. Longley | CofE | 9 | 13 | Britain | Anglican | 3 | 3 | 5 | – | 59.5 | 2.0 | 8 |
| 215 | 1867 | Combonians: 'Evangelizzazione dei popoli' | Daniele Comboni | MCCI/FSCI/MFSC | 10 | 7 | Italy | Roman Catholic | 0 | 5 | 5 | – | 59.5 | 2.0 | 8 |
| 216 | 1869 | Aryan Race as God's Chosen Evangelizers | F.W. Farrar | – | 2 | 7 | Britain | Anglican | 1 | 0 | 0 | – | 59.2 | 2.0 | 0 |
| 217 | 1870 | Megaministries (each reaching 1% of the world per year) | Charles Jackson | BFBS/ABS/NBS | 10 | 14 | Britain | Interdenominational | 3 | 6 | 5 | – | 59.0 | 2.0 | 8 |
| 218 | 1870 | Pan-Orthodox world missions | I. Veniaminov | ROC/OMS | 9 | 10 | Russia | Eastern Orthodox | 1 | 3 | 5 | – | 59.0 | 2.0 | 7 |
| 219 | 1870 | Churches of Christ (Non-Instrumental) | A. Campbell | CC | 10 | 9 | USA | Disciples | 1 | 3 | 5 | – | 59.0 | 2.0 | 7 |
| 220 | 1870 | Watch Tower Bible & Tract Society | Charles T. Russell | WTBTS-IBSA | 10 | 5 | USA | Witnesses | 0 | 6 | 6 | 1874 | 59.0 | 2.0 | 9 |
| 221 | 1871 | 'Apostolic Missions: the Gospel for Every Creature' | Joseph Angus | BMS | 2 | 7 | Britain | Baptist | 1 | 2 | 0 | – | 58.9 | 2.0 | 0 |
| 222 | 1872 | Salesian Sisters: evangelization by works of charity | John Bosco | FMA | 10 | 4 | Italy | Roman Catholic | 0 | 5 | 5 | – | 58.7 | 1.9 | 9 |
| 223 | 1873 | Regions Beyond Missionary Union | H.G. Guinness | RBMU | 8 | 7 | Britain | Nondenominational | 0 | 5 | 4 | – | 58.6 | 1.9 | 8 |
| 224 | 1874 | *Signs of the Times* | James White | SDA | 8 | 1 | USA | Adventist | 0 | 3 | 4 | – | 58.4 | 1.9 | 8 |
| 225 | 1875 | Verbites: 'Evangelizzazione dei Popoli' | Arnold Janssen | SVD | 10 | 7 | Netherlands | Roman Catholic | 0 | 5 | 5 | – | 58.3 | 1.9 | 9 |
| 226 | 1876 | Watchcry | A.T. Pierson | PCUSA | 1 | 3 | USA | Presbyterian | 3 | 3 | 1 | – | 58.1 | 1.9 | 0 |
| 227 | 1877 | Shanghai Watchword | A.T. Pierson | – | 4 | 7 | China | Interdenominational | 3 | 2 | 2 | – | 58.0 | 1.9 | 0 |
| 228 | 1877 | *Missionary Review of the World* | Royal Wilder | MRW | 9 | 9 | USA | Interdenominational | 4 | 6 | 5 | – | 58.0 | 1.9 | 3 |
| 229 | 1880 | 'A plan to evangelize the World', *The missionary review* | A.T. Pierson | – | 3 | 3 | USA | Presbyterian | 3 | 2 | 1 | – | 57.5 | 1.8 | 0 |
| 230 | 1881 | World's Christian Endeavor Union | Francis E. Clark | USCE | 9 | 13 | USA | Interdenominational | 2 | 3 | 5 | – | 57.4 | 1.8 | 5 |
| 231 | 1882 | Knights of Columbus | Rev. Micheal J. McGivney | K of C | 10 | 5 | USA | Roman Catholic | 1 | 6 | 6 | – | 57.2 | 1.8 | 9 |
| 232 | 1884 | *The Christian Century* | C.C. Morrison | – | 3 | 14 | USA | Nondenominational | 3 | 3 | 3 | 2000 | 56.9 | 1.8 | 5 |
| 233 | 1884 | 'No conversion of Nations without adequate outlay' | A.O. Van Lennep | – | 3 | 3 | USA | Ecumenical | 3 | 3 | 1 | – | 56.9 | 1.8 | 0 |
| 234 | 1885 | Ecumenical Council: 'An Appeal to Disciples Everywhere' | D.L. Moody | – | 2 | 3 | USA | Congregationalist | 3 | 2 | 2 | 1900 | 56.7 | 1.8 | 0 |
| 235 | 1886 | 1st International Christian Student Conference | D.L. Moody | – | 4 | 13 | USA | Interdenominational | 3 | 3 | 2 | 1900 | 56.6 | 1.8 | 0 |
| 236 | 1887 | Christian & Missionary Alliance | A.B. Simpson | C&MA | 9 | 7 | USA | Holiness | 2 | 3 | 5 | – | 56.4 | 1.7 | 9 |
| 237 | 1888 | Student Volunteer Movement for Foreign Missions | R.P. Wilder | SVMFM/SVMU | 9 | 13 | USA | Interdenominational | 3 | 5 | 5 | 1900 | 56.3 | 1.7 | 0 |
| 238 | 1888 | The Great Controversy | Ellen G. White | SDA | 3 | 1 | USA | Adventist | 0 | 3 | 0 | – | 56.3 | 1.7 | 9 |
| 239 | 1888 | One By One Band: *God's plan for soul winning* | T. Hogben | – | 8 | 5 | Britain | Nondenominational | 1 | 3 | 3 | – | 56.3 | 1.7 | 0 |
| 240 | 1889 | Make Jesus King | R.P. Wilder | – | 1 | 7 | Japan | Interdenominational | 3 | 1 | 2 | 1900 | 51.6 | 1.7 | 0 |
| 241 | 1889 | SVMFM closure prediction: World Evangelization by 1900 | John R. Mott | SVMFM | 0 | 7 | USA | Methodist | 3 | 1 | 0 | 1900 | 51.6 | 1.7 | 1 |
| 242 | 1890 | Scandinavian/Evangelical Alliance Mission | F. Franson | TEAM | 9 | 9 | USA | Nondenominational | 2 | 4 | 5 | – | 55.9 | 1.7 | 9 |
| 243 | 1890 | The Gospel Can and Ought to be Preached to the Whole Heathen | J.L. Stevens | – | 3 | 9 | USA | Presbyterian | 3 | 2 | 2 | 1900 | 55.9 | 1.7 | 0 |
| 244 | 1891 | *The encyclopedia of missions: historical, statistical* | H.O. Dwight | – | 3 | 3 | USA | Ecumenical | 3 | 3 | 3 | – | 55.8 | 1.7 | 3 |
| 245 | 1893 | Africa Industrial Mission/SIM International | Walter Gowans | SIM | 8 | 7 | Canada | Nondenominational | 2 | 5 | 5 | – | 55.5 | 1.7 | 9 |
| 246 | 1894 | *Methods of the evangelization of the non-Christian world* | R.N. Cust | BFBS | 3 | 3 | Britain | Anglican | 3 | 3 | 1 | – | 55.3 | 1.6 | 0 |
| 247 | 1895 | *Make Colleges in all lands centers of evangelization* | L.D. Wishard | – | 3 | 13 | USA | Ecumenical | 3 | 3 | 1 | – | 55.1 | 1.6 | 0 |
| 248 | 1895 | Association of Pentecostal Churches in America (Nazarene) | P.F. Bresee | APCA-CoN | 6 | 8 | USA | Holiness | 1 | 3 | 5 | – | 55.1 | 1.6 | 9 |

*Continued opposite*

*Table 27–21 continued*

| *No.* 1 | *Year* 2 | *Name* 3 | *Author* 4 | *Initials* 5 | *Type* 6 | *Min* 7 | *Origin* 8 | *Tradition* 9 | *Coop* 10 | *Pr* 11 | *Res* 12 | *Dline* 13 | *Unev* 14 | *Ratio* 15 | *Stat* 16 |
|---|---|---|---|---|---|---|---|---|---|---|---|---|---|---|---|
| 249 | 1895 | World Student Christian Federation | John R. Mott | WSCF | 8 | 13 | Sweden | Ecumenical | 3 | 6 | 5 | – | 55.1 | 1.6 | 7 |
| 250 | 1896 | Liverpool Students Conference | R.P. Wilder | – | 4 | 13 | Britain | Interdenominational | 3 | 3 | 2 | – | 55.0 | 1.6 | 0 |
| 251 | 1897 | 4th Lambeth Conference: resolution on Great Commission | Frederick Temple | – | 4 | 13 | Britain | Anglican | 3 | 3 | 3 | – | 54.8 | 1.6 | 0 |
| 252 | 1897 | Canterbury House of Laymen: resolution on Great Commission | Eugene Stock | CMS | 4 | 13 | Britain | Anglican | 3 | 3 | 3 | – | 54.8 | 1.6 | 0 |
| 253 | 1897 | 'Selfishness of Christians is the only hindrance' | S.M. Zwemer | RCA | 1 | 5 | Arabia | Reformed | 3 | 1 | 0 | – | 54.8 | 1.6 | 0 |
| 254 | 1897 | Encyclical 'On the Holy Spirit' | Leo XIII | – | 2 | 2 | Vatican | Roman Catholic | 0 | 2 | 1 | – | 54.8 | 1.6 | 3 |
| 255 | 1899 | Gideons International | J. Nicholson | – | 9 | 14 | USA | Nondenominational | 1 | 5 | 5 | – | 54.5 | 1.6 | 9 |
| 256 | 1899 | Golden Age of Jewish Missions | Leopold Cohn | – | 5 | 7 | Germany | Interdenominational | 2 | 3 | 4 | – | 54.5 | 1.6 | 8 |
| 257 | 1900 | New York Ecumenical Missionary Conference | J.S. Dennis | – | 4 | 7 | USA | Ecumenical | 3 | 3 | 4 | – | 54.3 | 1.6 | 0 |
| 258 | 1900 | *The evangelization of the world in this generation* | John R. Mott | SVMFM | 3 | 3 | USA | Ecumenical | 4 | 3 | 1 | 1925 | 54.3 | 1.6 | 0 |
| 259 | 1900 | Pentecostalism (First Wave, Renewal in the Holy Spirit) | C.F. Parham | – | 5 | 8 | USA | Pentecostal | 0 | 3 | 5 | – | 54.3 | 1.6 | 8 |
| 260 | 1900 | Spread of denominationalism across world | Cosmo Gordon Lang | – | 5 | 10 | USA | Interdenominational | 1 | 3 | 5 | – | 54.3 | 1.6 | 3 |
| 261 | 1901 | Latter Rain restoration | D.W. Myland | – | 7 | 8 | USA | Pentecostal | 0 | 1 | 5 | – | 54.1 | 1.6 | 8 |
| 262 | 1901 | Consolata Fathers: 'Evangelizzazione degli infedeli' | G. Allamano | IMC | 10 | 7 | Italy | Roman Catholic | 0 | 5 | 5 | – | 54.1 | 1.6 | 8 |
| 263 | 1902 | Missionary Education Movement | C.G. Trumbull | MEM | 10 | 13 | USA | Interdenominational | 3 | 4 | 5 | – | 53.8 | 1.6 | 0 |
| 264 | 1902 | Centennial survey of foreign missions | J.S. Dennis | APM | 3 | 3 | USA | Presbyterian | 3 | 6 | 3 | – | 53.8 | 1.6 | 0 |
| 265 | 1902 | *World-wide evangelization the urgent business of the Church* | T. Jays | SVMFM | 4 | 7 | Canada | Interdenominational | 4 | 3 | 4 | – | 53.8 | 1.6 | 0 |
| 266 | 1903 | All Nations Flag Church/Church of God of Prophecy | A.J. Tomlinson | CGP | 9 | 8 | USA | Pentecostal | 0 | 3 | 4 | – | 53.6 | 1.6 | 8 |
| 267 | 1904 | Welsh Revival | Evan Roberts | – | 5 | 8 | Wales | Methodist | 2 | 3 | 4 | – | 53.3 | 1.5 | 0 |
| 268 | 1904 | Premillennialism's theory that world is already evangelized | W.E. Blackstone | – | 0 | 1 | USA | Fundamentalist | 0 | 3 | 2 | – | 53.3 | 1.5 | 2 |
| 269 | 1905 | National conciliarism as basis for world mission | John R. Mott | – | 6 | 13 | France | Reformed | 3 | 3 | 5 | – | 53.1 | 1.5 | 8 |
| 270 | 1906 | World mission atlases and surveys | H.P. Beach | – | 3 | 3 | USA | Ecumenical | 4 | 3 | 2 | – | 52.8 | 1.5 | 6 |
| 271 | 1906 | Glossolalia to accomplish world evangelization | C.F. Parham | – | 0 | 1 | USA | Pentecostal | 0 | 1 | 2 | – | 52.8 | 1.5 | 0 |
| 272 | 1906 | Ist General Conference of Missionaries to the World of Islam | S.M. Zwemer | RCA | 4 | 7 | Egypt | Reformed | 3 | 3 | 3 | – | 52.8 | 1.5 | 0 |
| 273 | 1906 | Laymen's Missionary Movement | J.B. Sleman | LMM | 10 | 5 | USA | Interdenominational | 3 | 4 | 5 | – | 52.8 | 1.5 | 0 |
| 274 | 1907 | *Lord of the World* | R.H. Benson | – | 3 | 1 | Britain | Roman Catholic | 0 | 3 | 1 | c2020 | 52.6 | 1.5 | 0 |
| 275 | 1907 | Laymen's Missionary Movement of Southern Baptists | Joshua Levering | LMMSB/SBC | 8 | 13 | USA | Baptist | 1 | 5 | 4 | – | 52.6 | 1.5 | 8 |
| 276 | 1908 | *The unfinished task of the Christian church* | J.L. Barton | – | 3 | 3 | Britain | Ecumenical | 4 | 3 | 1 | – | 52.3 | 1.5 | 0 |
| 277 | 1908 | Quiet talks with world winners | S.D. Gordon | – | 3 | 9 | USA | Independent | 3 | 3 | 3 | – | 52.3 | 1.5 | 0 |
| 278 | 1910 | 'Unoccupied sections of the world'/World Missionary Conference | John R. Mott | WMC | 3 | 3 | Britain | Ecumenical | 4 | 3 | 3 | – | 51.8 | 1.5 | 3 |
| 279 | 1910 | Reunion of Christendom (Episcopal Church in the USA) | C.H. Brent | – | 8 | 13 | USA | Anglican | 4 | 3 | 4 | – | 51.8 | 1.5 | 4 |
| 280 | 1910 | Vision of coming of Antichrist | Pius X | OFM | 0 | 1 | Vatican | Roman Catholic | 0 | 2 | 1 | – | 51.8 | 1.5 | 0 |
| 281 | 1910 | *Can the world be won for Christ?* | N. Maclean | – | 3 | 9 | Britain | Ecumenical | 4 | 3 | 1 | – | 51.8 | 1.5 | 0 |
| 282 | 1910 | Men and Religion Forward Movement | John R. Mott | MRFM | 10 | 13 | USA | Interdenominational | 3 | 4 | 5 | – | 51.8 | 1.5 | 0 |
| 283 | 1910 | Church of God (Cleveland) World Missions | R.M. Evans | CoGWM | 10 | 8 | USA | Pentecostal | 0 | 5 | 5 | – | 51.8 | 1.5 | 9 |
| 284 | 1910 | *God's missionary plan for the world* | J.W. Bashford | – | 3 | 3 | Britain | Ecumenical | 3 | 3 | 1 | – | 51.8 | 1.5 | 0 |
| 285 | 1911 | *Unoccupied mission fields* | S.M. Zwemer | RCA | 3 | 3 | USA | Reformed | 3 | 3 | 1 | – | 51.6 | 1.5 | 0 |
| 286 | 1912 | *International review of missions* | J.H. Oldham | IRM | 3 | 3 | Britain | Ecumenical | 4 | 3 | 3 | – | 51.3 | 1.5 | 7 |
| 287 | 1912 | Reaching Every Home | C.E. Cowman | OMS | 8 | 7 | Japan | Holiness | 2 | 2 | 3 | – | 51.3 | 1.5 | 3 |
| 288 | 1913 | Christ's Etceteras (Worldwide Evangelization Crusade) | C.T. Studd | WEC | 9 | 7 | Britain | Nondenominational | 0 | 5 | 5 | – | 51.0 | 1.5 | 9 |
| 289 | 1913 | United Missionary Campaigns | John R. Mott | LMM/FMCNA/HMC | 10 | 7 | USA | Ecumenical | 3 | 4 | 4 | – | 51.0 | 1.5 | 0 |
| 290 | 1914 | Encyclical concerning the Last Age | Benedict XV | – | 0 | 2 | Vatican | Roman Catholic | 0 | 2 | 1 | 1914 | 50.8 | 1.5 | 0 |
| 291 | 1914 | Church Peace Union | John R. Mott | CPU/WAIF | 7 | 4 | USA | Ecumenical | 2 | 2 | 2 | – | 50.8 | 1.5 | 0 |
| 292 | 1914 | Inauguration of Kingdom of God on Earth | Charles T. Russell | WTBTS-IBSA | 10 | 5 | USA | Witnesses | 0 | 6 | 5 | 1914 | 50.8 | 1.5 | 0 |
| 293 | 1915 | Elim Foursquare Gospel Alliance | G. Jeffreys | – | 8 | 8 | Britain | Pentecostal | 0 | 2 | 3 | – | 50.6 | 1.5 | 5 |
| 294 | 1916 | World Dominion Movement: surveys of unevangelized regions | S.J.W. Clark | SAT(WDM) | 9 | 3 | Britain | Ecumenical | 3 | 5 | 3 | – | 50.5 | 1.5 | 0 |
| 295 | 1916 | *The world and the gospel* | J.H. Oldham | IRM/IMC | 3 | 4 | Britain | Ecumenical | 4 | 3 | 1 | – | 50.5 | 1.5 | 0 |
| 296 | 1917 | True Jesus Church | Paul Wei | TJC | 9 | 8 | China | Pentecostal | 0 | 5 | 4 | – | 50.3 | 1.5 | 9 |
| 297 | 1917 | Interdenominational Foreign Mission Association | H.W. Frost | IFMA | 10 | 13 | USA | Fundamentalist | 2 | 5 | 6 | – | 50.3 | 1.5 | 9 |
| 298 | 1918 | Worldwide Evangelism | Aimee S. McPherson | ICFG | 10 | 8 | USA | Pentecostal | 0 | 3 | 5 | – | 50.2 | 1.5 | 9 |
| 299 | 1918 | Christian Crusade for World Democracy | John R. Mott | CCWD | 9 | 4 | USA | Methodist | 1 | 3 | 2 | – | 50.2 | 1.5 | 0 |
| 300 | 1918 | United Drive for World Evangelism | R.E. Speer | – | 7 | 7 | USA | Presbyterian | 1 | 0 | 0 | – | 50.2 | 1.5 | 1 |
| 301 | 1918 | Interchurch World Movement of North America, World Survey | S.E. Taylor | IWM(IWMNA) | 10 | 13 | USA | Ecumenical | 3 | 6 | 5 | 1922 | 50.2 | 1.5 | 0 |
| 302 | 1919 | International Missionary Council | A.L. Warnshuis | IMC | 9 | 13 | Switzerland | Ecumenical | 3 | 3 | 4 | – | 50.0 | 1.4 | 0 |
| 303 | 1920 | League of Denominations | S.E. Taylor | IWM (IWMNA) | 7 | 13 | USA | Ecumenical | 4 | 2 | 0 | – | 49.9 | 1.4 | 1 |
| 304 | 1920 | League of Churches of Christ | Meletios IV Metaxakis | – | 7 | 13 | Turkey | Eastern Orthodox | 4 | 2 | 0 | – | 49.9 | 1.4 | 1 |
| 305 | 1920 | Planting of church in all cultures | P. Charles | – | 8 | 10 | Belgium | Roman Catholic | 1 | 3 | 5 | – | 49.9 | 1.4 | 3 |
| 306 | 1920 | Mennonite Central Committee | J.A. Lapp | MCC | 8 | 4 | USA | Mennonite | 1 | 2 | 4 | – | 49.9 | 1.4 | 8 |
| 307 | 1920 | General Council of Co-operating Baptist Missions | W.C. Haas | BMM | 8 | 7 | USA | Baptist | 0 | 5 | 5 | – | 49.9 | 1.4 | 6 |
| 308 | 1921 | Institute of Social and Religious Research | John R. Mott | – | 8 | 3 | USA | Ecumenical | 3 | 3 | 3 | – | 49.7 | 1.4 | 0 |
| 309 | 1921 | Oxford Group (Moral Re-Armament) | F.N.D. Buchman | MRA | 5 | 5 | Britain | Interdenominational | 2 | 3 | 5 | – | 49.7 | 1.4 | 4 |
| 310 | 1921 | Ecumenical Union of Pentecostal Believers | F.A. Hale | AoG-USA | 7 | 13 | USA | Pentecostal | 2 | 0 | 0 | – | 49.7 | 1.4 | 1 |
| 311 | 1921 | Electric or electronic church | Aimee S. McPherson | ICFG | 10 | 6 | USA | Pentecostal | 1 | 6 | 5 | – | 49.7 | 1.4 | 8 |
| 312 | 1921 | Legion of Mary | – | – | 9 | 5 | Ireland | Roman Catholic | 1 | 6 | 6 | – | 49.7 | 1.4 | 9 |
| 313 | 1922 | 1st International Missionary Congress | Benedict XV | IMC | 4 | 7 | Netherlands | Roman Catholic | 1 | 3 | 3 | – | 49.6 | 1.4 | 0 |
| 314 | 1922 | 'Miserimus Redemptor' | Pius XI | – | 2 | 1 | Vatican | Roman Catholic | 0 | 2 | 1 | c1930 | 49.6 | 1.4 | 0 |
| 315 | 1922 | Catholic Action: 'Ubi arcano' | Pius XI | – | 2 | 5 | Italy | Roman Catholic | 0 | 5 | 5 | – | 49.6 | 1.4 | 5 |
| 316 | 1923 | Daily radio and television church services | George V | BBC(UK) | 10 | 6 | Britain | Nondenominational | 2 | 6 | 5 | – | 49.4 | 1.4 | 6 |
| 317 | 1923 | *Evangelism in the modern world* | E.A. French | – | 3 | 7 | Britain | Methodist | 2 | 3 | 2 | – | 49.4 | 1.4 | 0 |
| 318 | c1923 | Million Testaments Campaigns | G.T.B. Davis | – | 8 | 14 | USA | Nondenominational | 1 | 3 | 3 | – | 49.4 | 1.4 | 0 |
| 319 | 1924 | Global White leadership in world evangelization | R.E. McAlister | PAW/PCI | 7 | 13 | USA | Pentecostal | 0 | 0 | 3 | – | 49.3 | 1.4 | 0 |
| 320 | 1924 | United Pentecostal Church International | J.G. Scheppe | UPCI-FMD | 10 | 8 | USA | Pentecostal | 0 | 5 | 5 | – | 49.3 | 1.4 | 9 |
| 321 | 1925 | Universal Christian Conference on Life and Work | N. Soderblom | – | 4 | 4 | Sweden | Ecumenical | 4 | 3 | 4 | – | 49.1 | 1.4 | 0 |
| 322 | 1925 | *World missionary atlas* | H.P. Beach | ISRR/IMC | 3 | 3 | USA | Ecumenical | 3 | 3 | 3 | – | 49.1 | 1.4 | 0 |
| 323 | 1926 | *The unfinished task of foreign missions* | R.E. Speer | – | 3 | 3 | USA | Presbyterian | 4 | 3 | 1 | – | 49.0 | 1.4 | 0 |
| 324 | 1926 | Lighthouse of International Foursquare Evangelism | Aimee S. McPherson | LIFE-ICFG | 8 | 13 | USA | Pentecostal | 0 | 3 | 4 | – | 49.0 | 1.4 | 8 |
| 325 | 1927 | 1st World Conference on Faith and Order | V.S. Azariah | – | 4 | 4 | Switzerland | Ecumenical | 4 | 3 | 4 | – | 48.8 | 1.4 | 0 |
| 326 | 1927 | Association of Baptists for World Evangelism | R.C. Thomas | ABWE | 9 | 7 | USA | Baptist | 0 | 3 | 4 | – | 48.8 | 1.4 | 8 |
| 327 | 1927 | *The future of Christianity* | G.H. Williams | – | 3 | 3 | Britain | Anglican | 3 | 2 | 1 | – | 48.8 | 1.4 | 0 |
| 328 | 1928 | *The unfinished evangelistic task* | C.H. Fahs | IMC | 3 | 3 | Britain | Ecumenical | 4 | 3 | 1 | – | 48.7 | 1.4 | 0 |
| 329 | 1928 | World Fundamental Baptist Missionary Fellowship | J.F. Norris | WFBMF(WBFM) | 8 | 10 | USA | Fundamentalist | 0 | 4 | 4 | – | 48.7 | 1.4 | 9 |
| 330 | 1928 | Opus Dei | J.E. De Balaguer y Albas | O.D. | 10 | 5 | Spain | Roman Catholic | 1 | 6 | 6 | – | 48.7 | 1.4 | 9 |
| 331 | 1929 | Each One Teach One | F.C. Laubach | – | 9 | 14 | Philippines | Congregationalist | 4 | 3 | 5 | – | 48.5 | 1.4 | 0 |
| 332 | 1930 | Movement for World Evangelization/Christian Holiday Crusade | Thomas Cochrane | MWE-CHC | 8 | 7 | Britain | Nondenominational | 1 | 4 | 3 | – | 48.3 | 1.4 | 5 |
| 333 | 1930 | World Council for Life and Work | William Temple | – | 4 | 4 | Britain | Ecumenical | 4 | 3 | 4 | – | 48.3 | 1.4 | 0 |
| 334 | 1930 | Voice of Prophecy | H.M.S. Richards | SDA | 0 | 6 | USA | Adventist | 0 | 5 | 5 | – | 48.3 | 1.4 | 9 |
| 335 | 1930 | Bringing Christ to the Nations (The Lutheran Hour) | W.A. Maier | LCMS | 10 | 6 | USA | Lutheran | 2 | 5 | 5 | – | 48.3 | 1.4 | 9 |
| 336 | 1930 | International Missions | B. Davidson | IM | 9 | 10 | USA | Nondenominational | 0 | 5 | 4 | – | 48.3 | 1.4 | 8 |
| 337 | 1930 | Association of Camps Farthest Out | Glenn Clark | CFO | 8 | 2 | USA | Charismatic | 2 | 4 | 4 | – | 48.3 | 1.4 | 8 |
| 338 | 1931 | Unevangelized Fields Mission | E.J. Pudney | UFM | 9 | 7 | Britain | Interdenominational | 0 | 5 | 4 | – | 48.2 | 1.4 | 9 |
| 339 | 1931 | Laudetur Jesus Christus (Radio Vatican) | Pius XI | SJ | 10 | 6 | Vatican | Roman Catholic | 0 | 5 | 5 | – | 48.2 | 1.4 | 9 |
| 340 | 1931 | World-Wide Prayer & Missionary Union | D. Dimlich | WWPMU | 8 | 2 | USA | Interdenominational | 2 | 4 | 4 | – | 48.2 | 1.4 | 5 |
| 341 | 1932 | Conference of Bible Societies | Eric M. North | ABS/BFBS | 4 | 14 | Britain | Ecumenical | 4 | 3 | 4 | – | 48.0 | 1.4 | 3 |
| 342 | 1933 | Laodicean Church Age with Millennium in 1977 | W.M. Branham | – | 0 | 0 | USA | Pentecostal | 0 | 4 | 4 | 1977 | 47.9 | 1.4 | 0 |
| 343 | 1933 | The Navigators | Dawson Trotman | – | 9 | 9 | USA | Nondenominational | 2 | 4 | 4 | – | 47.9 | 1.4 | 8 |
| 344 | 1934 | *Jesus Christ and world evangelization* | Alexander McLeish | WDM | 3 | 3 | Britain | Ecumenical | 3 | 3 | 1 | – | 47.7 | 1.4 | 0 |
| 345 | 1934 | Evangelize to a Finish to Bring Back the King | A.B. Buxton | IVMF-IVF | 4 | 7 | Britain | Interdenominational | 2 | 3 | 3 | – | 47.7 | 1.4 | 0 |
| 346 | 1934 | Biblical Research Society | D.L. Cooper | BRS | 0 | 14 | USA | Messianic Jewish | 0 | 3 | 2 | – | 47.7 | 1.4 | 0 |
| 347 | 1934 | Two Thousand Tongues To Go | W.C. Townsend | WBT-SIL | 10 | 14 | USA | Interdenominational | 1 | 5 | 5 | – | 47.7 | 1.4 | 9 |
| 348 | 1934 | Youth for Christ International | Torrey Johnson | YFCI | 9 | 7 | Canada | Interdenominational | 0 | 5 | 5 | – | 47.7 | 1.4 | 9 |
| 349 | 1935 | World Revival Crusade | G. Jeffreys | WRC | 5 | 8 | Britain | Pentecostal | 0 | 3 | 3 | – | 47.6 | 1.4 | 5 |
| 350 | c1935 | World Intercessors | Alice Huff | OMS(IAMS) | 8 | 2 | USA | Holiness | 1 | 2 | 4 | – | 47.6 | 1.4 | 8 |
| 351 | 1936 | Student Foreign Missions Fellowship | R.C. McQuilkin | SFMF-IVCF | 9 | 13 | USA | Interdenominational | 2 | 3 | 5 | – | 47.4 | 1.4 | 0 |
| 352 | 1936 | *Awaiting the light: unevangelised areas of the world* | J.G.K. Harman | IVMF | 3 | 3 | Britain | Interdenominational | 2 | 3 | 1 | – | 47.4 | 1.4 | 0 |
| 353 | 1936 | Holy Spirit Association for Unification of World Christianity | Sun Myung Moon | HSAUWC | 10 | 13 | Korea | Presbyterian | 0 | 5 | 5 | – | 47.4 | 1.4 | 7 |
| 354 | 1937 | Child Evangelism Fellowship | J.I. Overholtzer | CEF | 9 | 7 | USA | Nondenominational | 1 | 4 | 4 | – | 47.2 | 1.4 | 8 |
| 355 | 1938 | *Evangelism for the world today (125 opinions)* | John R. Mott | IMC | 3 | 3 | USA | Ecumenical | 3 | 3 | 3 | – | 47.1 | 1.4 | 3 |
| 356 | 1938 | 'Unoccupied fields', *Interpretative statistical survey* | J.I. Parker | IMC | 3 | 3 | Britain | Ecumenical | 3 | 2 | 1 | – | 47.1 | 1.4 | 0 |
| 357 | 1938 | 4th World Missionary Conference | William Paton | IMC | 4 | 7 | India | Ecumenical | 3 | 3 | 3 | – | 47.1 | 1.4 | 0 |
| 358 | 1938 | Gospel Recordings International | Joy Ridderhof | GRI | 9 | 6 | USA | Nondenominational | 0 | 5 | 3 | – | 47.1 | 1.4 | 8 |
| 359 | 1938 | World Home Bible League | W.A. Chapman | WHBL | 8 | 14 | USA | Nondenominational | 2 | 4 | 4 | – | 47.1 | 1.4 | 8 |
| 360 | 1939 | World Council of Bible Societies | Hendrik Kraemer | BFBS/ABS/NBS | 4 | 14 | Netherlands | Ecumenical | 4 | 3 | 4 | – | 46.9 | 1.4 | 0 |
| 361 | 1939 | 'The Unfinished Evangelistic Task' | Alexander McLeish | IMC/WDM | 3 | 3 | India | Ecumenical | 3 | 2 | 1 | – | 46.9 | 1.4 | 0 |
| 362 | 1939 | 'Sunday schools and world evangelism' | A. Black | IRM | 3 | 14 | Britain | Ecumenical | 3 | 2 | 0 | – | 46.9 | 1.4 | 0 |
| 363 | 1939 | World-Wide Signs Following Evangelism | L.R.M. Kopp | UFC | 7 | 8 | USA | Messianic Jewish | 0 | 2 | 2 | – | 46.9 | 1.4 | 0 |
| 364 | 1941 | Base ecclesial communities | Helder Camara | CEBEs(BECs) | 8 | 4 | Brazil | Roman Catholic | 1 | 5 | 4 | – | 46.6 | 1.4 | 9 |
| 365 | 1941 | *The battle of world evangelisation* | A.T. Houghton | IVF/BCMS | 3 | 7 | Burma | Anglican | 2 | 3 | 1 | – | 46.6 | 1.4 | 0 |
| 366 | 1941 | International multilingual Bible correspondence courses | Oswald J. Smith | EBS-BCC | 9 | 14 | Canada | Nondenominational | 2 | 5 | 4 | – | 46.6 | 1.4 | 9 |
| 367 | 1942 | 1st World Survey of Unreached Areas: 'The Black Spots Survey' | L.G. Brierley | WEC | 3 | 3 | Britain | Nondenominational | 0 | 5 | 2 | – | 46.4 | 1.4 | 1 |
| 368 | 1942 | Ling Liang World-Wide Evangelistic Mission | T.S.K. Dzao | – | 8 | 7 | China | Nondenominational | 0 | 3 | 3 | – | 46.4 | 1.4 | 5 |
| 369 | 1942 | New Tribes Mission | P.W. Fleming | NTM | 9 | 7 | USA | Fundamentalist | 1 | 4 | 5 | – | 46.4 | 1.4 | 9 |
| 370 | 1942 | Committee on World Literacy & Christian Literature (Lit-Lit) | F.C. Laubach | FMCNA | 8 | 14 | USA | Ecumenical | 3 | 3 | 2 | – | 46.4 | 1.4 | 0 |
| 371 | 1943 | National Religious Broadcasters | W.W. Ayer | NRB | 10 | 6 | USA | Nondenominational | 2 | 5 | 5 | – | 46.3 | 1.4 | 7 |
| 372 | 1943 | *'Into all the world': the Great Commission* | S.M. Zwemer | – | 3 | 3 | USA | Reformed | 2 | 3 | 1 | – | 46.3 | 1.4 | 0 |

*Continued overleaf*

*Table 27–21 continued*

| *No.* 1 | *Year* 2 | *Name* 3 | *Author* 4 | *Initials* 5 | *Type* 6 | *Min* 7 | *Origin* 8 | *Tradition* 9 | *Coop* 10 | *Pr* 11 | *Res* 12 | *Dline* 13 | *Unev* 14 | *Ratio* 15 | *Stat* 16 |
|---|---|---|---|---|---|---|---|---|---|---|---|---|---|---|---|
| 373 | 1943 | Global Outreach Mission | J.O. Blackwood | GOM | 8 | 7 | USA | Nondenominational | 1 | 3 | 4 | – | 46.3 | 1.4 | 5 |
| 374 | 1943 | Conservative Baptist Foreign Mission Society | Vincent Brushwyler | CBFMS | 7 | 10 | USA | Baptist | 1 | 4 | 5 | – | 46.3 | 1.4 | 9 |
| 375 | 1943 | Focolare Movement | Chiara Lubich | – | 8 | 2 | Italy | Roman Catholic | 2 | 6 | 4 | – | 46.3 | 1.4 | 8 |
| 376 | 1944 | Third-World missionaries begin international evangelizing | John Sung | AEC | 5 | 8 | Indonesia | Interdenominational | 2 | 1 | 5 | – | 46.1 | 1.4 | 8 |
| 377 | 1945 | Evangelical Foreign Missions Association | Clyde W. Taylor | EFMA/NAE | 8 | 13 | USA | Interdenominational | 2 | 4 | 6 | – | 46.0 | 1.3 | 9 |
| 378 | 1945 | Parachurch agencies support Great Commission ministries | Herman C. Rutgers | NBS/ABS | 10 | 13 | Netherlands | Interdenominational | 2 | 5 | 5 | – | 46.0 | 1.3 | 8 |
| 379 | 1945 | International Institute of Scientific Missionary Research | O.G. Myklebust | IISMR | 8 | 3 | Norway | Lutheran | 4 | 1 | 0 | – | 46.0 | 1.3 | 1 |
| 380 | 1945 | Foreign Missions Conference | – | FMCNA | 4 | 7 | USA | Protestant | 3 | 3 | 4 | – | 46.0 | 1.3 | 0 |
| 381 | 1946 | 'Complete Christ's Commission' and IVSFM conferences | Clyde W. Taylor | IVSFM/SFMF | 9 | 13 | USA | Interdenominational | 2 | 3 | 4 | – | 45.8 | 1.3 | 0 |
| 382 | 1946 | United Bible Societies | J.R. Temple | UBS/BFBS | 10 | 14 | Britain | Ecumenical | 4 | 5 | 6 | – | 45.8 | 1.3 | 9 |
| 383 | 1946 | World Literature Crusade | J. McAlister | WLC-EHC | 10 | 14 | Canada | Nondenominational | 2 | 5 | 4 | 1970 | 45.8 | 1.3 | 0 |
| 384 | 1946 | *Into all the world: a statement on evangelism* | V.C. Alexander | – | 3 | 7 | Scotland | Presbyterian | 1 | 3 | 2 | – | 45.8 | 1.3 | 0 |
| 385 | 1946 | Egede Institute of Missionary Study and Research | O.G. Myklebust | EIMSR | 8 | 3 | Norway | Lutheran | 3 | 3 | 2 | – | 45.8 | 1.3 | 5 |
| 386 | 1946 | Asociación Misionera Evangélica a las Naciones | Obed Alvarez | AMEN | 8 | 7 | Peru | Methodist | 2 | 3 | 4 | – | 45.8 | 1.3 | 8 |
| 387 | 1946 | Prayer: the Mightiest Force in the World | F.C. Laubach | – | 3 | 2 | USA | Ecumenical | 3 | 3 | 3 | – | 45.8 | 1.3 | 6 |
| 388 | 1947 | Whitby IMC Meeting: 'Expectant Evangelism' | C.W. Ranson | IMC | 4 | 7 | Britain | Ecumenical | 4 | 3 | 2 | – | 45.6 | 1.3 | 0 |
| 389 | 1947 | Commission on World Missions, Lutheran World Federation | Hanns Lilje | CWM-LWF | 4 | 7 | Sweden | Lutheran | 2 | 3 | 4 | – | 45.6 | 1.3 | 7 |
| 390 | 1947 | *Euntes Docete* | J. Saraiva Martins | PUU | 3 | 14 | Vatican | Roman Catholic | 1 | 2 | 2 | – | 45.6 | 1.3 | 6 |
| 391 | 1947 | *We can if we will: the challenge of world evangelism* | R.V. DeLong | – | 3 | 14 | USA | Holiness | 2 | 3 | 1 | – | 45.6 | 1.3 | 0 |
| 392 | 1947 | Fuller Theological Seminary | C.E. Fuller | – | 1 | 13 | USA | Conservative Evangelical | 2 | 5 | 4 | – | 45.6 | 1.3 | 8 |
| 393 | 1947 | World Revival Prayer League | Margaret K. Ross | – | 6 | 2 | Japan | Nondenominational | 2 | 1 | 1 | – | 45.6 | 1.3 | 0 |
| 394 | 1947 | Oral Roberts Evangelistic Association | Oral Roberts | OREA/ORU/CBM | 9 | 8 | USA | Pentecostal | 1 | 4 | 6 | – | 45.6 | 1.3 | 9 |
| 395 | 1948 | 10 World Congresses on World Evangelization | Torrey Johnson | YFCI | 4 | 7 | Switzerland | Nondenominational | 2 | 3 | 4 | – | 45.5 | 1.3 | 0 |
| 396 | 1948 | World Council of Churches, 7th Function | W.A. Visser t' Hooft | WCC | 6 | 4 | Netherlands | Ecumenical | 3 | 6 | 5 | – | 45.5 | 1.3 | 9 |
| 397 | 1948 | International Council of Christian Churches | C. McIntire | ICCC | 6 | 13 | USA | Fundamentalist | 0 | 5 | 5 | – | 45.5 | 1.3 | 5 |
| 398 | 1948 | Christian Crusade/ICCC Bible Balloon Project | B.J. Hargis | CENM/ICCC | 7 | 7 | USA | Fundamentalist | 0 | 4 | 3 | – | 45.5 | 1.3 | 0 |
| 399 | 1948 | *Set a watchman: a world survey* | F.C. Maddox | IVF | 3 | 3 | China | Interdenominational | 2 | 3 | 1 | – | 45.5 | 1.3 | 0 |
| 400 | 1948 | New Order of the Latter Rain: Global Missions Broadcast | George Hawtin | NOLR | 5 | 8 | Canada | Pentecostal | 0 | 3 | 4 | – | 45.5 | 1.3 | 3 |
| 401 | 1949 | WCC Study 'The Evangelization of Man in Modern Mass Society' | J.C. Hoekendijk | WCC | 3 | 3 | Switzerland | Ecumenical | 4 | 3 | 2 | – | 45.3 | 1.3 | 0 |
| 402 | 1949 | Association for Native Evangelism | T.L. Osborn | – | 8 | 8 | USA | Pentecostal | 0 | 4 | 4 | – | 45.3 | 1.3 | 8 |
| 403 | 1949 | World Gospel Crusades/Every Creature Crusade | C.E. Cowman | WGC/OMS | 9 | 14 | USA | Holiness | 1 | 3 | 3 | – | 45.3 | 1.3 | 4 |
| 404 | 1949 | *World Christian handbook* (1949, 1952, 1957, 1962, 1968) | K.G. Grubb | WCH/WDM | 3 | 3 | Britain | Ecumenical | 4 | 3 | 2 | – | 45.3 | 1.3 | 0 |
| 405 | 1949 | Cursillos de Cristianidad | J. Hervas | – | 8 | 13 | Spain | Roman Catholic | 1 | 5 | 4 | – | 45.3 | 1.3 | 7 |
| 406 | 1950 | Billy Graham Evangelistic Association | Billy Graham | BGEA | 10 | 7 | USA | Nondenominational | 2 | 6 | 5 | – | 45.1 | 1.3 | 9 |
| 407 | 1950 | Help Open Paths to Evangelize (HOPE) | G.F. Gudladt | HOPE | 7 | 7 | USA | Fundamentalist | 0 | 2 | 2 | – | 45.1 | 1.3 | 0 |
| 408 | 1950 | World Vision International | Bob Pierce | WV-WVI | 8 | 4 | USA | Nondenominational | 1 | 4 | 6 | – | 45.1 | 1.3 | 9 |
| 409 | 1950 | *Literacy as evangelism*/World Literacy Evangelism | F.C. Laubach | WLE | 3 | 14 | Philippines | Ecumenical | 4 | 3 | 3 | – | 45.1 | 1.3 | 3 |
| 410 | 1950 | Evangelistic broadcasting/Cathedral of Tomorrow | Rex Humbard | – | 1 | 6 | USA | Pentecostal | 0 | 4 | 5 | – | 45.1 | 1.3 | 8 |
| 411 | 1950 | Hour of Decision | Billy Graham | BGEA | 7 | 6 | USA | Baptist | 1 | 5 | 4 | – | 45.1 | 1.3 | 8 |
| 412 | 1950 | Full Gospel Businessmen's Fellowship International | D. Shakarian | FGBFI | 1 | 13 | USA | Pentecostal | 2 | 5 | 5 | – | 45.1 | 1.3 | 9 |
| 413 | 1950 | Baptist Bible Fellowship International | F. Donnelson | BBFI | 6 | 7 | USA | Baptist | 0 | 3 | 5 | – | 45.1 | 1.3 | 8 |
| 414 | 1950 | Missionaries of Charity | Mother Teresa | MC | 6 | 4 | India | Roman Catholic | 2 | 3 | 5 | – | 45.1 | 1.3 | 9 |
| 415 | 1950 | World-Wide Missions International | Basil Miller | WWM | 6 | 7 | Nigeria | Fundamentalist | 0 | 1 | 4 | – | 45.1 | 1.3 | 5 |
| 416 | 1951 | 1st World Congress of the Lay Apostolate | Pius XII | – | 1 | 5 | Italy | Roman Catholic | 0 | 3 | 3 | – | 45.0 | 1.3 | 3 |
| 417 | 1952 | *Christ's hope of the Kingdom* | Alexander McLeish | WDM | 3 | 3 | Britain | Ecumenical | 3 | 3 | 1 | – | 44.9 | 1.3 | 0 |
| 418 | 1952 | 'Trends in world evangelism' | E.J. Homrighausen | WCH-SAT | 3 | 3 | Britain | Ecumenical | 3 | 2 | 0 | – | 44.9 | 1.3 | 0 |
| 419 | 1952 | 'The Great Commission for Anabaptists' | F.H. Littell | – | 3 | 7 | USA | Methodist | 3 | 3 | 1 | – | 44.9 | 1.3 | 0 |
| 420 | 1952 | Worldwide Revival Movement | W.E. Allen | – | 3 | 2 | Ireland | Nondenominational | 0 | 3 | 2 | – | 44.9 | 1.3 | 0 |
| 421 | 1952 | World Wide Pictures | Billy Graham | WWP-BGEA | 10 | 6 | USA | Evangelical | 3 | 5 | 4 | – | 44.9 | 1.3 | 9 |
| 422 | 1953 | Indonesian Missionary Fellowship | Petrus Octavianus | WEC/IMF | 8 | 7 | Indonesia | Nondenominational | 0 | 5 | 4 | – | 44.8 | 1.3 | 8 |
| 423 | 1953 | World Committee for Christian Broadcasting | Edwin Robertson | WCCB/BBC/ICCB | 1 | 6 | Britain | Ecumenical | 2 | 1 | 2 | – | 44.8 | 1.3 | 0 |
| 424 | 1953 | 'World Evangelization in Our Time' | D.B. Barrett | CMS/BFBS | 3 | 3 | Britain | Anglican | 5 | 2 | 0 | – | 44.8 | 1.3 | 1 |
| 425 | 1953 | Congress of Catholic Action: Liberation Theology | G. Gutierrez | CA/CEBes | 4 | 4 | Peru | Roman Catholic | 1 | 5 | 5 | – | 44.8 | 1.3 | 8 |
| 426 | 1954 | 'Christ the Hope of the World' | W.A. Visser t' Hooft | WCC | 4 | 13 | USA | Ecumenical | 4 | 6 | 4 | – | 44.7 | 1.3 | 3 |
| 427 | 1954 | WCC Survey 'Evangelism: the mission of the Church' | J.C. Hoekendijk | WCC | 3 | 3 | Switzerland | Ecumenical | 4 | 3 | 3 | – | 44.7 | 1.3 | 0 |
| 428 | 1954 | MAP International | L.E. Dixon | MAP | 6 | 4 | USA | Nondenominational | 2 | 2 | 5 | – | 44.7 | 1.3 | 6 |
| 429 | 1954 | Schemes for future evangelization | J.E. Rattenbury | MCGB | 3 | 3 | Britain | Methodist | 1 | 3 | 0 | – | 44.7 | 1.3 | 0 |
| 430 | 1954 | *The Bible in world evangelism* | A.M. Chirgwin | UBS/BFBS | 3 | 14 | Britain | Ecumenical | 4 | 3 | 1 | – | 44.7 | 1.3 | 0 |
| 431 | 1954 | World Missionary Evangelism | J.E. Douglas | WME | 6 | 7 | USA | Nondenominational | 1 | 1 | 3 | – | 44.7 | 1.3 | 5 |
| 432 | 1954 | New Life League World Missionary Society | F.D. Jarvis | NLL | 6 | 14 | USA | Baptist | 0 | 4 | 4 | – | 44.7 | 1.3 | 8 |
| 433 | 1955 | World Conference on Missionary Radio | C.W. Jones | WCMR | 4 | 6 | USA | Nondenominational | 1 | 1 | 2 | – | 44.6 | 1.3 | 0 |
| 434 | 1955 | Midnight Call Missionary Work | W. Malgo | – | 7 | 7 | Switzerland | Evangelical | 1 | 2 | 3 | – | 44.6 | 1.3 | 0 |
| 435 | 1955 | *A survey of world missions* | J.C. Thiessen | – | 3 | 3 | USA | Conservative Evangelical | 2 | 3 | 2 | – | 44.6 | 1.3 | 0 |
| 436 | 1956 | Charismatic Movement (Second Wave, Renewal in the Holy Spirit) | R. Winkler | – | 5 | 2 | USA | Charismatic | 3 | 5 | 5 | – | 44.5 | 1.3 | 8 |
| 437 | 1956 | *A monthly letter about evangelism* | D.T. Niles | DWME-WCC | 3 | 14 | Switzerland | Ecumenical | 4 | 2 | 3 | – | 44.5 | 1.3 | 7 |
| 438 | 1956 | *The gospel to every creature* | L.-J. Suenens | – | 3 | 14 | Belgium | Roman Catholic | 4 | 3 | 1 | – | 44.5 | 1.3 | 0 |
| 439 | 1956 | *Mission fields today: a brief world survey* | A.J. Dain | IVF | 3 | 3 | Britain | Anglican | 3 | 3 | 2 | – | 44.5 | 1.3 | 0 |
| 440 | 1957 | *World evangelism today* | D.T. Niles | WCC | 3 | 3 | Switzerland | Ecumenical | 4 | 3 | 2 | – | 44.4 | 1.3 | 0 |
| 441 | 1957 | Global Conquest | J.P. Hogan | AoG(USA) | 8 | 8 | USA | Pentecostal | 0 | 3 | 4 | 1960 | 44.4 | 1.3 | 0 |
| 442 | 1957 | Nights of Prayer for World-wide Revival | George S. Ingram | CMS | 7 | 2 | India | Anglican | 2 | 0 | 1 | – | 44.4 | 1.3 | 0 |
| 443 | 1957 | Easter Day Encyclical | Pius XII | – | 0 | 1 | Vatican | Roman Catholic | 1 | 2 | 1 | c1965 | 44.4 | 1.3 | 0 |
| 444 | 1957 | *The unfinished task* | S.C. Neill | WCC/CMS | 3 | 3 | Ireland | Anglican | 4 | 3 | 1 | – | 44.4 | 1.3 | 0 |
| 445 | 1957 | Operation Mobilization/Send The Light | George Verwer | OM-STL | 10 | 5 | USA | Nondenominational | 2 | 5 | 5 | – | 44.4 | 1.3 | 9 |
| 446 | 1957 | Conference of World Confessional Groups | B.B. Beach | WCFs/CWCs | 6 | 13 | Switzerland | Ecumenical | 4 | 1 | 1 | – | 44.4 | 1.3 | 5 |
| 447 | 1958 | Ecumenical Mission to the World | Alan Walker | ACC | 2 | 7 | Australia | Methodist | 3 | 0 | 1 | – | 44.3 | 1.3 | 0 |
| 448 | 1958 | *Porefthendes* (Go Ye) | A. Yannoulatos | SYNDESMOS | 4 | 14 | Greece | Eastern Orthodox | 1 | 4 | 2 | – | 44.3 | 1.3 | 0 |
| 449 | 1958 | Bibles For The World | Rochunga Pudaite | BFTW | 8 | 14 | India | Conservative Evangelical | 2 | 4 | 3 | – | 44.3 | 1.3 | 6 |
| 450 | 1958 | *Bilan du monde: encyclopédie catholique du monde chrétien* | Jean Frisque | FERES | 3 | 3 | Belgium | Roman Catholic | 2 | 3 | 2 | – | 44.3 | 1.3 | 0 |
| 451 | 1959 | Sharing Christ with the Whole World | Baker J. Cauthen | SBC | 6 | 7 | USA | Baptist | 0 | 1 | 5 | – | 44.2 | 1.3 | 3 |
| 452 | 1959 | Evangelism-in-Depth | R.K. Strachan | EiD | 10 | 5 | Nicaragua | Interdenominational | 3 | 3 | 5 | – | 44.2 | 1.3 | 6 |
| 453 | 1959 | Prophecies of the final Antichrist | P.I. Rissaut | – | 0 | 0 | Palestine | Roman Catholic | 0 | 1 | 0 | 2004 | 44.2 | 1.3 | 0 |
| 454 | 1959 | Worldwide Missionary Society | David Tsutada | – | 7 | 7 | Japan | Nondenominational | 1 | 1 | 2 | – | 44.2 | 1.3 | 0 |
| 455 | 1960 | *Facing the unfinished task* | J.O. Percy | IFMA | 4 | 7 | USA | Fundamentalist | 0 | 4 | 2 | – | 44.2 | 1.3 | 0 |
| 456 | 1960 | Baptist International Missions | D. Sisk | BIM | 6 | 7 | USA | Baptist | 0 | 4 | 5 | – | 44.2 | 1.3 | 8 |
| 457 | 1960 | World MAP (World Missionary Assistance Plan) | R. Mahoney | WMAP | 8 | 13 | USA | Pentecostal | 3 | 4 | 3 | 2000 | 44.2 | 1.3 | 5 |
| 458 | 1960 | *The Gospel Blimp:* 'One Billion Unreached' | Joseph T. Bayly | IVCF-IVP | 3 | 14 | USA | Nondenominational | 2 | 3 | 1 | – | 44.2 | 1.3 | 0 |
| 459 | 1960 | Youth With A Mission | Loren Cunningham | YWAM/AoG | 10 | 8 | USA | Pentecostal | 3 | 5 | 6 | – | 44.2 | 1.3 | 9 |
| 460 | c1960 | National Evangelization Movement | Shin Hyun Gyoon | NEM | 6 | 7 | Korea | Independent | 2 | 2 | 4 | – | 44.2 | 1.3 | 8 |
| 461 | 1961 | World Missionary Press | W. Goodman | WMP | 8 | 14 | USA | Nondenominational | 1 | 1 | 3 | – | 44.2 | 1.3 | 0 |
| 462 | 1961 | 2nd World Survey: '19 Point Programme to Reach the Unreached' | L.G. Brierley | WEC | 9 | 7 | Britain | Nondenominational | 0 | 5 | 2 | – | 44.2 | 1.3 | 1 |
| 463 | 1961 | 1st Pan-Orthodox Conference | Athenagoras I | – | 6 | 5 | Greece | Eastern Orthodox | 2 | 3 | 3 | – | 44.2 | 1.3 | 8 |
| 464 | 1961 | World Evangelism | Morris Cerullo | WE(MCWE) | 7 | 8 | USA | Pentecostal | 1 | 1 | 3 | – | 44.2 | 1.3 | 5 |
| 465 | 1961 | Commission on World Mission and Evangelism | D.T. Niles | DWME-CWME | 7 | 7 | India | Ecumenical | 3 | 3 | 5 | – | 44.2 | 1.3 | 9 |
| 466 | 1961 | Joint Action for Mission | Lesslie Newbigin | JAM-WCC | 7 | 4 | Switzerland | Ecumenical | 3 | 2 | 2 | – | 44.2 | 1.3 | 0 |
| 467 | 1961 | Christian Broadcasting Network/CBN World Outreach | M.G. Robertson | WYAH(CBN) | 6 | 6 | USA | Charismatic | 1 | 5 | 6 | – | 44.2 | 1.3 | 9 |
| 468 | 1961 | 6th International Student Missionary Convention | Clyde W. Taylor | IVCF-SFMF | 4 | 13 | USA | Interdenominational | 2 | 3 | 2 | 1971 | 44.2 | 1.3 | 0 |
| 469 | 1961 | World Association for Christian Broadcasting | Edwin Robertson | WACB/WCCB/BBC | 6 | 6 | Kenya | Ecumenical | 2 | 1 | 2 | – | 44.2 | 1.3 | 0 |
| 470 | 1961 | World Radio Missionary Fellowship: HCJB-TV | C.W. Jones | HCJB-TV/WRMF | 9 | 6 | Ecuador | Nondenominational | 1 | 4 | 4 | – | 44.2 | 1.3 | 8 |
| 471 | 1961 | Theological centrality of the Great Commission | Karl Barth | – | 1 | 3 | Switzerland | Reformed | 3 | 1 | 0 | – | 44.2 | 1.3 | 1 |
| 472 | 1961 | Third World Missions Federation | Elam Angali | TWMF | 7 | 7 | Kenya | Lutheran | 2 | 0 | 1 | – | 44.2 | 1.3 | 4 |
| 473 | 1962 | Vatican Council II (21st Ecumenical Council) | John XXIII | – | 10 | 7 | Vatican | Roman Catholic | 2 | 6 | 5 | – | 44.2 | 1.3 | 3 |
| 474 | 1962 | Presence evangelization: *The missionary nature of the church* | J. Blauw | NMC | 3 | 5 | Netherlands | Ecumenical | 3 | 3 | 0 | – | 44.2 | 1.3 | 0 |
| 475 | 1962 | Haggai Institute for Advanced Leadership Training | John Haggai | HIALT | 8 | 13 | Singapore | Nondenominational | 3 | 4 | 4 | – | 44.2 | 1.3 | 6 |
| 476 | 1962 | Catholic prophecies of Antichrist | G. Barberin | – | 0 | 0 | Palestine | Roman Catholic | 0 | 3 | 3 | – | 44.2 | 1.3 | 0 |
| 477 | 1963 | Witness in Six Continents | Lesslie Newbigin | CWME-WCC | 7 | 5 | Mexico | Ecumenical | 3 | 3 | 4 | – | 44.2 | 1.3 | 0 |
| 478 | 1963 | International Christian Broadcasters | C.W. Jones | ICB | 7 | 6 | USA | Nondenominational | 2 | 1 | 2 | – | 44.2 | 1.3 | 0 |
| 479 | 1963 | 'Pacem in Terris' | John XXIII | – | 3 | 14 | Vatican | Roman Catholic | 1 | 2 | 2 | – | 44.2 | 1.3 | 0 |
| 480 | 1963 | 'God's Word for a New Age' | Olivier Beguin | UBS | 9 | 14 | Japan | Ecumenical | 3 | 2 | 5 | – | 44.2 | 1.3 | 0 |
| 481 | 1963 | New Life For All | W. Bellamy | NLFA | 9 | 9 | Nigeria | Interdenominational | 3 | 3 | 5 | – | 44.2 | 1.3 | 4 |
| 482 | 1963 | Jesus' strategy for the world: *The master plan of evangelism* | Robert E. Coleman | – | 9 | 5 | USA | Methodist | 3 | 3 | 2 | – | 44.2 | 1.3 | 3 |
| 483 | 1964 | 'Lumen Gentium' and 'Ad Gentes' | Paul VI | – | 3 | 7 | Vatican | Roman Catholic | 2 | 3 | 4 | – | 44.2 | 1.3 | 7 |
| 484 | 1964 | Each One Teach and Win One | F.C. Laubach | – | 8 | 14 | USA | Congregationalist | 3 | 3 | 3 | – | 44.2 | 1.3 | 4 |
| 485 | 1964 | *Global church growth* | D.A. McGavran | ICG-SWM | 8 | 10 | USA | Interdenominational | 2 | 2 | 2 | – | 44.2 | 1.3 | 5 |
| 486 | 1964 | Secretariat for Non-Christians | Sergio Pignedoli | – | 6 | 4 | Vatican | Roman Catholic | 1 | 3 | 3 | – | 44.2 | 1.3 | 6 |
| 487 | 1964 | *Evangelical missions quarterly* | James W. Reapsome | EMQ/EMIS | 3 | 3 | USA | Evangelical | 3 | 2 | 3 | – | 44.2 | 1.3 | 8 |
| 488 | 1965 | Oriental Orthodox Churches Conference | Kyrillos VI | OOCC | 6 | 5 | Ethiopia | Oriental Orthodox | 2 | 3 | 3 | – | 44.2 | 1.3 | 7 |
| 489 | 1965 | World Evangelization Research Centre | D.B. Barrett | WERC/CSWE | 8 | 3 | Kenya | Anglican | 3 | 2 | 1 | – | 44.2 | 1.3 | 6 |
| 490 | 1965 | Unreached Peoples emphasis | V.E.W. Hayward | IRM/AACC/WERC | 8 | 3 | Cameroon | Ecumenical | 3 | 3 | 2 | – | 44.2 | 1.3 | 8 |
| 491 | 1965 | Secretariat for Non-Believers | Franz König | – | 6 | 4 | Vatican | Roman Catholic | 1 | 3 | 3 | – | 44.2 | 1.3 | 6 |
| 492 | 1965 | 'Decree on the Apostolate of the Laity' | Paul VI | – | 3 | 5 | Vatican | Roman Catholic | 5 | 3 | 4 | – | 44.2 | 1.3 | 8 |
| 493 | 1966 | Wheaton Declaration: 'The Church's Worldwide Mission' | Clyde W. Taylor | EFMA/IFMA | 4 | 7 | USA | Conservative Evangelical | 3 | 3 | 2 | – | 44.3 | 1.3 | 0 |
| 494 | 1966 | World Congress on Evangelism | Billy Graham | BGEA/CT | 7 | 7 | Germany | Interdenominational | 3 | 3 | 3 | – | 44.3 | 1.3 | 0 |
| 495 | 1966 | Pacific Conference of Churches: 'Go Ye...' | Baiteke Nabetari | PCC | 7 | 7 | New Caledonia | Ecumenical | 3 | 1 | 2 | – | 44.3 | 1.3 | 0 |
| 496 | 1966 | Missions Advanced Research and Communication Center | E.R. Dayton | MARC-WVI | 8 | 3 | USA | Nondenominational | 2 | 4 | 4 | 2000 | 44.3 | 1.3 | 5 |

*Continued opposite*

*Table 27-21 continued*

| No. 1 | Year 2 | Name 3 | Author 4 | Initials 5 | Type 6 | Min 7 | Origin 8 | Tradition 9 | Coop 10 | Pr 11 | Res 12 | Dline 13 | Unev 14 | Ratio 15 | Stat 16 |
|---|---|---|---|---|---|---|---|---|---|---|---|---|---|---|---|
| 497 | 1966 | Release the World for Christ | C. Panos | GOC | 1 | 7 | Greece | Eastern Orthodox | 1 | 1 | 2 | – | 44.3 | 1.3 | 4 |
| 498 | 1967 | Sacred Congregation for the Evangelization of Peoples | Sergio Pignedoli | SCEP-RCC | 10 | 7 | Vatican | Roman Catholic | 2 | 6 | 6 | – | 44.3 | 1.3 | 9 |
| 499 | 1967 | International Correspondence Institute | G. Flattery | AoG(USA)-ICI | 9 | 14 | Belgium | Pentecostal | 1 | 6 | 4 | – | 44.3 | 1.3 | 8 |
| 500 | 1967 | Crusade for World Revival | P. Yonggi Cho | CWR | 1 | 7 | Korea | Pentecostal | 2 | 1 | 3 | – | 44.3 | 1.3 | 0 |
| 501 | 1967 | Council of the Laity (Pontificium Consilium pro Laicis) | Maurice Roy | – | 6 | 5 | Vatican | Roman Catholic | 1 | 4 | 5 | – | 44.3 | 1.3 | 6 |
| 502 | 1967 | *Encyclopedia of modern Christian missions* | B.L. Goddard | – | 3 | 3 | USA | Nondenominational | 4 | 3 | 2 | – | 44.3 | 1.3 | 2 |
| 503 | 1967 | Christ for the Nations | Gordon Lindsey | CFN | 6 | 7 | USA | Independent | 2 | 3 | 4 | – | 44.3 | 1.3 | 8 |
| 504 | 1968 | 'Behold I make all things new' | N. Goodall | WCC | 5 | 7 | Sweden | Ecumenical | 3 | 3 | 3 | – | 44.3 | 1.3 | 0 |
| 505 | 1968 | Total World Evangelization | J.F. Shepherd | – | 3 | 7 | USA | Evangelical | 2 | 2 | 0 | – | 44.3 | 1.3 | 0 |
| 506 | 1968 | World Association for Christian Communication | Edwin Robertson | WACC/WACB | 6 | 6 | Britain | Ecumenical | 3 | 6 | 4 | – | 44.3 | 1.3 | 3 |
| 507 | 1968 | Anglican Consultative Council | J.W.A. Howe | ACC | 6 | 13 | Britain | Anglican | 2 | 3 | 4 | – | 44.3 | 1.3 | 7 |
| 508 | 1968 | 'A strategy for world evangelism' | E.L. Copeland | SBC-FMB | 3 | 3 | USA | Baptist | 2 | 2 | 0 | – | 44.3 | 1.3 | 0 |
| 509 | 1968 | Association for World Evangelism | F. Reddington | AWE | 7 | 7 | USA | Nondenominational | 2 | 0 | 1 | – | 44.3 | 1.3 | 0 |
| 510 | 1968 | African Independent Churches Service | D.B. Barrett | AICS/CMS/COC | 9 | 13 | Kenya | Ecumenical | 5 | 5 | 5 | – | 44.3 | 1.3 | 7 |
| 511 | 1969 | Jimmy Swaggart Ministries | Jimmy L. Swaggart | JSM-AoG | 10 | 6 | USA | Pentecostal | 0 | 4 | 6 | – | 44.4 | 1.3 | 7 |
| 512 | 1969 | 'Peace on Earth' International Assemblies | Nathan H. Knorr | IBSA-JWs | 10 | 5 | Denmark | Witnesses | 0 | 6 | 5 | 1975 | 44.4 | 1.3 | 8 |
| 513 | 1969 | World Evangelism Foundation | W.H. Jackson | WEF/FMB-SBC | 9 | 7 | USA | Baptist | 0 | 4 | 4 | – | 44.4 | 1.3 | 8 |
| 514 | 1970 | Commission on Church Cooperation | J.A. Scherer | CCC-LWF | 6 | 4 | France | Lutheran | 2 | 2 | 3 | – | 44.4 | 1.3 | 6 |
| 515 | 1970 | 9th International Student Missionary Convention | Clyde W. Taylor | – | 1 | 13 | USA | Interdenominational | 2 | 4 | 3 | – | 44.4 | 1.3 | 0 |
| 516 | 1970 | *The late great planet Earth* | H. Lindsay | – | 0 | 1 | USA | Fundamentalist | 0 | 3 | 2 | – | 44.4 | 1.3 | 8 |
| 517 | 1970 | 'AD 2000: 350 million Christians in Africa' | D.B. Barrett | IRM/CMS/SWM | 8 | 3 | Kenya | Anglican | 5 | 5 | 0 | 2000 | 44.4 | 1.3 | 7 |
| 518 | 1970 | Frankfurt Declaration on Mission | P. Beyerhaus | – | 4 | 7 | Germany | Conservative Evangelical | 2 | 1 | 1 | – | 44.4 | 1.3 | 0 |
| 519 | 1970 | World Mission of Reconciliation through Jesus Christ | Robert S. Denny | BWA | 8 | 7 | USA | Baptist | 1 | 3 | 2 | – | 44.4 | 1.3 | 0 |
| 520 | 1970 | 'Strategy for world evangelism: are we too late?' | C.F.H. Henry | CT/WVI | 3 | 3 | USA | Conservative Evangelical | 3 | 2 | 0 | – | 44.4 | 1.3 | 0 |
| 521 | 1970 | Missionary Message to the World | Paul VI | – | 1 | 7 | Samoa | Roman Catholic | 2 | 2 | 2 | – | 44.4 | 1.3 | 0 |
| 522 | 1970 | *Saturation evangelism* | G.W. Peters | – | 3 | 7 | USA | Conservative Evangelical | 3 | 3 | 1 | – | 44.4 | 1.3 | 0 |
| 523 | 1970 | m.v. Logos and literature evangelism | George Miley | OM | 9 | 14 | Britain | Nondenominational | 0 | 5 | 4 | – | 44.4 | 1.3 | 4 |
| 524 | 1970 | The Late, Great Planet Earth | Hal Lindsey | – | 0 | 1 | USA | Independent | 1 | 3 | 5 | 2000 | 44.4 | 1.3 | 6 |
| 525 | 1971 | 'Issues in World Evangelism' | J.R.W. Stott | IVP | 3 | 7 | Britain | Anglican | 3 | 3 | 0 | – | 44.0 | 1.3 | 0 |
| 526 | 1971 | Final Advance of Scripture Translation | A. Bergstedt | FAST/SIL | 8 | 14 | USA | Nondenominational | 1 | 1 | 2 | – | 44.0 | 1.3 | 0 |
| 527 | 1971 | International Crusades | B.W. Mieth | IC | 7 | 7 | USA | Baptist | 1 | 4 | 4 | 2000 | 44.0 | 1.3 | 5 |
| 528 | 1971 | Conference on Church-Mission Relationships | James W. Reapsome | EMIS | 4 | 7 | USA | Conservative Evangelical | 3 | 3 | 2 | – | 44.0 | 1.3 | 0 |
| 529 | 1971 | World Evangelization Strategy Consultation | P. Rees | – | 4 | 3 | USA | Nondenominational | 2 | 0 | 1 | – | 44.0 | 1.3 | 0 |
| 530 | 1971 | Evangelical Alliance Commission on World Mission | A.M. Derham | EAGB | 3 | 7 | Britain | Evangelical | 3 | 3 | 2 | – | 44.0 | 1.3 | 0 |
| 531 | 1972 | International Catholic Charismatic Renewal | Ralph Martin | ICCRO | 5 | 2 | USA | Roman Catholic | 2 | 3 | 6 | – | 43.6 | 1.3 | 9 |
| 532 | 1972 | 'World evangelisation'/*World Pentecost* | Donald Gee | WPC | 2 | 8 | Britain | Pentecostal | 1 | 2 | 1 | – | 43.6 | 1.3 | 0 |
| 533 | 1972 | Consultation on the Gospel and Frontier Peoples | R. Pierce Beaver | – | 4 | 3 | USA | Interdenominational | 3 | 3 | 3 | – | 43.6 | 1.3 | 0 |
| 534 | 1972 | *The Explo story: a plan to change the world* | P. Eshleman | CCCI | 3 | 7 | USA | Nondenominational | 2 | 3 | 1 | – | 43.6 | 1.3 | 0 |
| 535 | 1972 | MIAMSI (Rome) | G. Benelli | MIAMSI | 6 | 5 | Italy | Roman Catholic | 1 | 1 | 2 | – | 43.6 | 1.3 | 0 |
| 536 | 1972 | *Koinonia/Look/The Frontiersman* | L.G. Brierley | WEC-IRO | 3 | 14 | Brazil | Nondenominational | 2 | 2 | 2 | – | 43.6 | 1.3 | 8 |
| 537 | 1972 | Great Commission Prayer Crusade | Vonette Bright | GCPC-CCCI | 4 | 2 | USA | Nondenominational | 3 | 4 | 3 | 1980 | 43.6 | 1.3 | 5 |
| 538 | 1972 | Salvation Today | John G. Gatu | CWME-WCC | 4 | 4 | Thailand | Ecumenical | 3 | 2 | 1 | – | 43.6 | 1.3 | 0 |
| 539 | 1972 | Marian Movement of Priests | Fr Stephano Gobbi | MMP | 8 | 2 | Italy | Roman Catholic | 1 | 3 | 6 | – | 43.6 | 1.3 | 8 |
| 540 | 1973 | Mission to The World | Paul E. McKaughan | PCA-MTW | 9 | 10 | USA | Presbyterian | 2 | 4 | 4 | – | 43.2 | 1.3 | 8 |
| 541 | 1973 | Summer Institute of World Mission | P. Yonggi Cho | SIWM | 8 | 7 | Korea | Presbyterian | 2 | 3 | 4 | – | 43.2 | 1.3 | 8 |
| 542 | 1973 | Globe Missionary Evangelism | K. Sumrall | GME | 8 | 8 | USA | Charismatic | 1 | 1 | 4 | – | 43.2 | 1.3 | 6 |
| 543 | 1973 | Seoul Declaration on Christian Mission | David J. Cho | AMA | 4 | 7 | Korea | Evangelical | 3 | 4 | 2 | – | 43.2 | 1.3 | 0 |
| 544 | 1973 | 10th Inter-Varsity Missionary Convention | J.E. Kyle | IVCF-SFMF | 1 | 7 | USA | Interdenominational | 3 | 3 | 2 | – | 43.2 | 1.3 | 0 |
| 545 | 1973 | Trinity Broadcasting Network | Paul F. Crouch | TBN | 7 | 6 | USA | Pentecostal | 1 | 4 | 6 | – | 43.2 | 1.3 | 9 |
| 546 | 1973 | World Film Crusade/Winning the World for Christ | Brother John | WFC-WTF-WMC | 7 | 6 | USA | Nondenominational | 3 | 4 | 2 | – | 43.2 | 1.3 | 4 |
| 547 | 1973 | Ephesian Method: *Breaking the stained-glass barrier* | David A. Womack | AoG | 9 | 8 | USA | Pentecostal | 2 | 3 | 2 | – | 43.2 | 1.3 | 3 |
| 548 | 1974 | Confessing Christ Today | A. Yannoulatos | – | 6 | 7 | Romania | Eastern Orthodox | 1 | 3 | 5 | – | 42.7 | 1.3 | 0 |
| 549 | 1974 | *Operation World: a guide to praying for the world* | Patrick J. Johnstone | DM/STL/OM | 3 | 2 | Zimbabwe | Conservative Evangelical | 2 | 3 | 2 | – | 42.7 | 1.3 | 3 |
| 550 | 1974 | Lausanne Committee for World Evangelization | G. Osei-Mensah | ICOWE-LCWE | 6 | 13 | Switzerland | Conservative Evangelical | 3 | 5 | 5 | – | 42.7 | 1.3 | 7 |
| 551 | 1974 | EXPLO-74 (2nd Training Conference on Evangelism) | Joon Gon Kim | CCCI | 8 | 13 | Korea | Nondenominational | 2 | 3 | 4 | – | 42.7 | 1.3 | 0 |
| 552 | 1974 | Holy Year Jubilee | Paul VI | – | 1 | 7 | Vatican | Roman Catholic | 0 | 3 | 5 | – | 42.7 | 1.3 | 0 |
| 553 | 1974 | Sharing Christ's Bold Mission | Baker J. Cauthen | FMB-SBC | 8 | 7 | USA | Baptist | 0 | 3 | 5 | – | 42.7 | 1.3 | 0 |
| 554 | 1974 | 3rd Synod of Bishops: 'The Evangelization of the Modern World' | Wladyslaw Rubin | SB-RCC | 4 | 4 | Vatican | Roman Catholic | 1 | 3 | 6 | – | 42.7 | 1.3 | 9 |
| 555 | 1974 | World Mission 1975 (World Methodist Mission) | Alan Walker | WMC | 8 | 7 | Israel | Methodist | 1 | 1 | 4 | – | 42.7 | 1.3 | 0 |
| 556 | 1974 | Mission Renewal Teams | B. Goheen | IVCF | 7 | 7 | USA | Nondenominational | 2 | 0 | 3 | – | 42.7 | 1.3 | 0 |
| 557 | 1974 | *Reaching the unreached* | E.C. Pentecost | MARC-WVI | 7 | 3 | USA | Conservative Evangelical | 2 | 3 | 1 | – | 42.7 | 1.3 | 0 |
| 558 | 1974 | Discipling A Whole Nation | J. Montgomery | DAWN | 9 | 9 | Philippines | Nondenominational | 3 | 4 | 3 | – | 42.7 | 1.3 | 9 |
| 559 | 1974 | *Religious and the evangelization of the world* | J. Cloutier | CRC-CCC | 7 | 2 | Canada | Roman Catholic | 1 | 3 | 2 | – | 42.7 | 1.3 | 0 |
| 560 | 1974 | *World evangelism and the Word of God* | A.P. Johnston | – | 3 | 7 | USA | Fundamentalist | 2 | 3 | 1 | – | 42.7 | 1.3 | 0 |
| 561 | 1974 | Presbyterian Order for World Evangelism | Roberta Winter | POWE | 6 | 3 | USA | Presbyterian | 2 | 2 | 1 | – | 42.7 | 1.3 | 4 |
| 562 | c1974 | Missão Antioquia | Jonatan Santos | MA/WEC | 8 | 7 | Brazil | Nondenominational | 0 | 1 | 3 | – | 42.7 | 1.3 | 8 |
| 563 | 1975 | Full Gospel World Mission Association | P. Yonggi Cho | FGWMA/AoG | 8 | 8 | Korea | Pentecostal | 0 | 3 | 4 | – | 42.2 | 1.3 | 9 |
| 564 | 1975 | World Conference on the Holy Spirit | M. Benhayim | – | 1 | 2 | Israel | Pentecostal | 1 | 4 | 2 | – | 42.2 | 1.3 | 0 |
| 565 | 1975 | 'Jesus Christ Frees and Unites' | Philip Potter | WCC | 4 | 4 | Kenya | Ecumenical | 3 | 4 | 5 | – | 42.2 | 1.3 | 3 |
| 566 | 1975 | 'New People for a New World--Through Christ' | Robert S. Denny | BWA | 1 | 7 | Sweden | Baptist | 1 | 3 | 5 | – | 42.2 | 1.3 | 0 |
| 567 | 1975 | World evangelization communication strategy | J.F. Engel | – | 3 | 3 | USA | Anglican | 2 | 3 | 2 | – | 42.2 | 1.3 | 0 |
| 568 | 1975 | Total Missions Thrust: Global Discipleship | Baker J. Cauthen | FMB-SBC | 9 | 9 | USA | Baptist | 0 | 6 | 5 | – | 42.2 | 1.3 | 0 |
| 569 | 1975 | Project Look Up | J. Wiebe | PLU/ICB | 8 | 6 | USA | Evangelical | 1 | 4 | 3 | – | 42.2 | 1.3 | 0 |
| 570 | 1975 | Associates for World Evangelization | Bruce Graham | AWE | 4 | 7 | USA | Evangelical | 2 | 0 | 1 | – | 42.2 | 1.3 | 0 |
| 571 | 1975 | International Missionary Congress | Agnelo Rossi | IMC-RCC | 4 | 3 | Italy | Roman Catholic | 1 | 3 | 3 | – | 42.2 | 1.3 | 0 |
| 572 | 1975 | *Evangelii Nuntiandi* | Paul VI | – | 3 | 7 | Vatican | Roman Catholic | 3 | 3 | 3 | – | 42.2 | 1.3 | 3 |
| 573 | 1975 | Total World Evangelization Vision | L. Southwick | NLI-TWEV | 6 | 14 | USA | Charismatic | 1 | 4 | 2 | – | 42.2 | 1.3 | 5 |
| 574 | 1975 | Genesis Project: New Media Bible | J. Heyman | NMB-GP/CCCI | 8 | 6 | USA | Nondenominational | 1 | 4 | 4 | – | 42.2 | 1.3 | 5 |
| 575 | 1975 | World Evangelical Fellowship Missions Commission | Theodore Williams | MC-WEF | 8 | 13 | Korea | Conservative Evangelical | 2 | 3 | 5 | – | 42.2 | 1.3 | 8 |
| 576 | 1976 | Bold Mission Thrust | W. Hultgren | BMT-SBC | 10 | 7 | USA | Baptist | 1 | 6 | 6 | 2000 | 41.7 | 1.3 | 0 |
| 577 | 1976 | Gabriel Olasoji World Evangelism | Gabriel K. Olasoji | GOWE | 8 | 8 | Nigeria | Pentecostal | 3 | 4 | 3 | – | 41.7 | 1.3 | 8 |
| 578 | 1976 | US Center for World Mission | R.D. Winter | USCWM | 10 | 7 | USA | Conservative Evangelical | 2 | 4 | 4 | 2000 | 41.7 | 1.3 | 7 |
| 579 | 1976 | Lausanne Strategy Working Group | C.P. Wagner | SWG-LCWE | 8 | 3 | USA | Conservative Evangelical | 2 | 4 | 3 | – | 41.7 | 1.3 | 0 |
| 580 | 1976 | Congress on World Missions and Evangelism | A.J. Dain | – | 1 | 7 | Australia | Evangelical | 3 | 4 | 1 | – | 41.7 | 1.3 | 0 |
| 581 | 1976 | American Military Evangelizing Nations | Ira North | AMEN-CCCC | 7 | 7 | USA | Disciples | 1 | 1 | 3 | – | 41.7 | 1.3 | 4 |
| 582 | 1976 | Church Growth International Seminars | P. Yonggi Cho | AoG | 5 | 10 | Korea | Pentecostal | 2 | 4 | 4 | 2000 | 41.7 | 1.3 | 0 |
| 583 | 1976 | 1st Chinese Congress on World Evangelization | Thomas Wang | CCOWE | 4 | 7 | Hong Kong | Evangelical | 3 | 4 | 2 | – | 41.7 | 1.3 | 8 |
| 584 | 1976 | EFMA People Groups Tally | Wade Coggins | EFMA | 3 | 3 | USA | Conservative Evangelical | 3 | 1 | 2 | 1990 | 41.7 | 1.3 | 0 |
| 585 | 1976 | Lausanne Intercession Advisory Group | Vonette Bright | LCWE/CCCI | 7 | 2 | USA | Nondenominational | 3 | 4 | 3 | – | 41.7 | 1.3 | 5 |
| 586 | 1976 | Habitat for Humanity International | M.D. Fuller | HHI | 8 | 4 | USA | Evangelical | 1 | 4 | 3 | – | 41.7 | 1.3 | 6 |
| 587 | 1976 | Fellowship of World Christians | Bruce Graham | FOW/AWE/USCWM | 1 | 7 | USA | Evangelical | 2 | 1 | 2 | – | 41.7 | 1.3 | 0 |
| 588 | 1977 | Charismatic Renewal in the Christian Churches | K. Ranaghan | – | 1 | 7 | USA | Pentecostal/Charismatic | 3 | 3 | 3 | – | 41.1 | 1.2 | 7 |
| 589 | 1977 | 'Catechetics in our time' | Paul VI | – | 3 | 13 | Vatican | Roman Catholic | 1 | 3 | 3 | – | 41.1 | 1.2 | 3 |
| 590 | 1977 | World Conference on Audio-Visuals and Evangelization | C. Hemelink | – | 4 | 6 | Germany | Ecumenical | 3 | 2 | 3 | – | 41.1 | 1.2 | 0 |
| 591 | 1977 | Here's Life, World | Bill Bright | CCCI-HLW | 10 | 7 | USA | Nondenominational | 2 | 5 | 5 | 1980 | 41.1 | 1.2 | 0 |
| 592 | 1977 | Focus on the Family | J. Dobson | – | 8 | 9 | USA | Evangelical | 3 | 4 | 5 | – | 41.1 | 1.2 | 9 |
| 593 | 1978 | World Mission 1978-1981 | Alan Walker | WMC | 9 | 7 | Australia | Methodist | 1 | 2 | 5 | 1981 | 40.5 | 1.2 | 0 |
| 594 | 1978 | International Conference on the Catholic Charismatic Renewal | L.-J. Suenens | ICCRO | 4 | 2 | Ireland | Roman Catholic | 2 | 2 | 3 | – | 40.5 | 1.2 | 0 |
| 595 | 1978 | Danvik National Conferences on World Evangelization | Sigurd Aske | – | 1 | 7 | Norway | Evangelical | 3 | 3 | 2 | – | 40.5 | 1.2 | 0 |
| 596 | 1978 | Maryknoll 'Statement of Mission Vision' | Raymond A. Hill | MM | 4 | 4 | USA | Roman Catholic | 1 | 5 | 2 | – | 40.5 | 1.2 | 3 |
| 597 | 1978 | *The battle for world evangelism* | A.P. Johnston | – | 3 | 7 | USA | Fundamentalist | 2 | 3 | 1 | – | 40.5 | 1.2 | 0 |
| 598 | 1978 | Systems, Hardware & Research for Evangelization (SHARE) | S. Wilson | SHARE-MARC-WVI | 9 | 3 | USA | Nondenominational | 3 | 4 | 3 | – | 40.5 | 1.2 | 0 |
| 599 | 1978 | Great Commission Strategy Resource Network | Larry Poland | GCSRN-CCCI | 9 | 3 | USA | Nondenominational | 2 | 5 | 3 | 1980 | 40.5 | 1.2 | 0 |
| 600 | 1979 | 'The unfinished task of world mission' | J. Verkuyl | – | 3 | 3 | Costa Rica | Reformed | 3 | 2 | 1 | – | 39.9 | 1.2 | 0 |
| 601 | 1979 | Sharing of Ministries Abroad (SOMA) | Michael C. Harper | SOMA | 9 | 8 | Britain | Anglican | 3 | 4 | 4 | – | 39.9 | 1.2 | 5 |
| 602 | 1979 | Conference on Unreached Peoples | H. Marquardt | WEF | 4 | 3 | Germany | Conservative Evangelical | 3 | 1 | 2 | – | 39.9 | 1.2 | 0 |
| 603 | 1979 | National Missionary Congress: 'A New Missionary Era' | Dermot J. Ryan | IMU | 1 | 4 | Ireland | Roman Catholic | 1 | 2 | 3 | – | 39.9 | 1.2 | 0 |
| 604 | 1979 | Pan-Orthodox Consultation on Monastic Life & Witness | Shenouda III | GOC/ROC/COC/&c | 4 | 2 | Egypt | Orthodox | 1 | 2 | 3 | – | 39.9 | 1.2 | 8 |
| 605 | 1979 | Foursquare Missions International | L. Edwards | ICFG-FMI | 8 | 8 | USA | Pentecostal | 1 | 5 | 3 | – | 39.9 | 1.2 | 9 |
| 606 | 1979 | International Charismatic Pilgrimage to Lourdes | L.-J. Suenens | ICCRO | 5 | 2 | France | Roman Catholic | 1 | 3 | 4 | – | 39.9 | 1.2 | 0 |
| 607 | 1979 | 12th Pentecostal World Conference | E. Dando | PWC | 1 | 8 | Canada | Pentecostal | 2 | 3 | 2 | – | 39.9 | 1.2 | 0 |
| 608 | 1979 | Canadian Congress on World Evangelization | L.F.S. Ford | CCWE | 1 | 7 | Canada | Evangelical | 3 | 2 | 2 | – | 39.9 | 1.2 | 0 |
| 609 | 1979 | 'Towards a New Age in Mission' | Jaime L. Sin | FABC | 1 | 4 | Philippines | Roman Catholic | 1 | 4 | 3 | – | 39.9 | 1.2 | 0 |
| 610 | 1979 | The Jesus Project ('Jesus' Film) | P. Eshleman | CCCI | 10 | 6 | Israel | Nondenominational | 3 | 5 | 6 | 2000 | 39.9 | 1.2 | 9 |
| 611 | 1979 | '120,000 Missionaries by the Year 2000' | Billy Graham | BGEA/IVCF | 1 | 7 | USA | Evangelical | 3 | 2 | 1 | 2000 | 39.9 | 1.2 | 0 |
| 612 | 1979 | Angel-I/Angel-II/Angel-III Project | B. Armstrong | NRB/WEF | 8 | 6 | USA | Nondenominational | 3 | 3 | 1 | – | 39.9 | 1.2 | 0 |
| 613 | 1979 | PTL Ministries | J. Bakker | PTL/AoG | 4 | 6 | USA | Pentecostal | 1 | 4 | 5 | – | 39.9 | 1.2 | 0 |
| 614 | 1979 | *World Christian* magazine | G. Aeschliman | ISLCFM | 6 | 14 | USA | Evangelical | 3 | 2 | 2 | – | 39.9 | 1.2 | 4 |
| 615 | 1979 | Lutherans for World Evangelization | B. Day | LWE | 6 | 3 | USA | Lutheran | 1 | 4 | 1 | – | 39.9 | 1.2 | 4 |
| 616 | 1979 | Caleb Project/Joshua Project teams | S. Hawthorne | USCWM | 9 | 3 | USA | Evangelical | 2 | 4 | 3 | – | 39.9 | 1.2 | 6 |
| 617 | 1979 | *Unreached Peoples* series | C.P. Wagner | LCWE/MARC | 5 | 3 | USA | Evangelical | 3 | 3 | 3 | – | 39.9 | 1.2 | 6 |
| 618 | 1979 | 'World evangelism by 2000 AD: can it be done?' | R.D. Winter | USCWM | 3 | 10 | USA | Conservative Evangelical | 2 | 2 | 0 | 2000 | 39.9 | 1.2 | 1 |
| 619 | 1979 | What it will take to change the world | D.Eastman | – | 3 | 2 | USA | Nondenominational | 3 | 3 | 4 | 2000 | 39.9 | 1.2 | 5 |
| 620 | 1980 | Global papal apostolic travels | John Paul II | – | 10 | 7 | Vatican | Roman Catholic | 2 | 5 | 5 | – | 39.3 | 1.2 | 7 |

*Continued overleaf*

*Table 27–21 continued*

| No. 1 | Year 2 | Name 3 | Author 4 | Initials 5 | Type 6 | Min 7 | Origin 8 | Tradition 9 | Coop 10 | Pr 11 | Res 12 | Dline 13 | Unev 14 | Ratio 15 | Stat 16 |
|---|---|---|---|---|---|---|---|---|---|---|---|---|---|---|---|
| 621 | 1980 | International Consultation on Simple Life-Style | Harvie Conn | LCWE | 1 | 5 | Britain | Evangelical | 3 | 3 | 3 | – | 39.3 | 1.2 | 1 |
| 622 | 1980 | Stuttgart Congress on World Evangelization | P. Beyerhaus | – | 1 | 7 | Germany | Evangelical | 3 | 4 | 2 | – | 39.3 | 1.2 | 0 |
| 623 | 1980 | Operation World Begin From Here | Peter P.O. Alliu | WECCM | 6 | 8 | Nigeria | Charismatic | 1 | 0 | 1 | – | 39.3 | 1.2 | 4 |
| 624 | 1980 | 'Your Kingdom Come' | Emilio Castro | CWME-WCC | 4 | 4 | Australia | Ecumenical | 3 | 4 | 4 | – | 39.3 | 1.2 | 3 |
| 625 | 1980 | Consultation on World Evangelization | G. Osei-Mensah | COWE-LCWE | 4 | 7 | Thailand | Conservative Evangelical | 3 | 4 | 3 | – | 39.3 | 1.2 | 0 |
| 626 | 1980 | 'World Evangelization Today' | G.H. Anderson | ASM | 3 | 3 | USA | Nondenominational | 2 | 2 | 1 | – | 39.3 | 1.2 | 0 |
| 627 | 1980 | 10th United Bible Societies Council Meeting | Ulrich Fick | UBS | 10 | 14 | Thailand | Ecumenical | 4 | 3 | 3 | 1990 | 39.3 | 1.2 | 1 |
| 628 | 1980 | World Evangelization Crusade | P. Yonggi Cho | CCCI | 1 | 8 | Korea | Evangelical/Charismatic | 2 | 4 | 5 | – | 39.3 | 1.2 | 0 |
| 629 | 1980 | US Festival of World Evangelization | Billy Graham | – | 1 | 7 | USA | Interdenominational | 3 | 4 | 4 | – | 39.3 | 1.2 | 0 |
| 630 | 1980 | Pan-Orthodox Consultation on Preaching & Teaching Today | A. Yannoulatos | GOC/ROC/COC/&c | 4 | 7 | Yugoslavia | Orthodox | 1 | 2 | 5 | – | 39.3 | 1.2 | 5 |
| 631 | 1980 | International Congress on Evangelization and Atheism | Karl Rahner | PUU/SJ | 4 | 4 | Italy | Roman Catholic | 1 | 3 | 4 | – | 39.3 | 1.2 | 0 |
| 632 | 1980 | 'A Church for Every People by the Year 2000' (Edinburgh 1980) | R.D. Winter | USCWM | 1 | 10 | Britain | Conservative Evangelical | 3 | 5 | 4 | 2000 | 39.3 | 1.2 | 5 |
| 633 | 1980 | *Planning strategies for world evangelization* | D.A. Fraser | MARC-WVI | 8 | 3 | USA | Conservative Evangelical | 3 | 3 | 1 | – | 39.3 | 1.2 | 0 |
| 634 | c1980 | Christ For All Nations | Reinhard Bonnke | CfAN | 8 | 7 | South Africa | Independent | 2 | 4 | 4 | – | 39.3 | 1.2 | 8 |
| 635 | 1981 | Christian broadcasting worldwide | Paul Freed | – | 10 | 6 | Netherlands | Nondenominational | 2 | 5 | 5 | – | 38.7 | 1.2 | 8 |
| 636 | 1981 | Charismatic TV evangelists | Oral Roberts | CBN/PTL/&c | 1 | 6 | USA | Pentecostal/Charismatic | 1 | 5 | 5 | – | 38.7 | 1.2 | 5 |
| 637 | 1981 | *It is Harvest Time* | P. Beyerhaus | – | 3 | 3 | Germany | Conservative Evangelical | 3 | 3 | 1 | – | 38.7 | 1.2 | 0 |
| 638 | 1981 | Evangelize the World by Computer Dialing | Bill Bright | CCCI | 7 | 6 | USA | Nondenominational | 0 | 0 | 0 | – | 38.7 | 1.2 | 0 |
| 639 | 1981 | 2nd Chinese Congress on World Evangelization | Thomas Wang | CCCOWE | 4 | 7 | Singapore | Evangelical | 3 | 3 | 2 | – | 38.7 | 1.2 | 8 |
| 640 | 1981 | World Evangelization Strategy Work Group | Imotemjen Aier | BWA | 6 | 3 | USA | Baptist | 1 | 2 | 2 | – | 38.7 | 1.2 | 4 |
| 641 | 1981 | Decade of Evangelism, World Evangelism Committee | Alan Walker | WE-WMC | 10 | 7 | USA | Methodist | 1 | 2 | 5 | 1990 | 38.7 | 1.2 | 0 |
| 642 | 1981 | *World evangelization and the simple life-style* | Harvie Conn | – | 3 | 5 | USA | Presbyterian | 3 | 3 | 2 | – | 38.7 | 1.2 | 1 |
| 643 | 1981 | 'Reaching Unreached Peoples' | Patrick J. Johnstone | EMA/WEC | 4 | 3 | Britain | Evangelical | 3 | 2 | 2 | – | 38.7 | 1.2 | 0 |
| 644 | 1981 | Mission to Unreached Peoples (Gooddeeds) | D.D. Martin | MUP | 6 | 9 | USA | Nondenominational | 1 | 4 | 2 | – | 38.7 | 1.2 | 5 |
| 645 | 1981 | Dominion Network/Video Satellite | R.W. Johnson | DVS-DBS | 10 | 6 | USA | Charismatic | 3 | 5 | 4 | – | 38.7 | 1.2 | 0 |
| 646 | 1982 | Project 223 | Floyd McClung | YWAM | 10 | 8 | USA | Charismatic | 2 | 5 | 6 | 2011 | 38.0 | 1.1 | 2 |
| 647 | 1982 | Harvest Vision: 1990 | L. Edwards | ICFG-FMI | 9 | 8 | USA | Pentecostal | 1 | 5 | 4 | 1990 | 38.0 | 1.1 | 1 |
| 648 | 1982 | International Association for Mission Studies | F. Verstraelen | IAMS | 6 | 13 | India | Nondenominational | 2 | 3 | 4 | – | 38.0 | 1.1 | 1 |
| 649 | 1982 | 'The Unevangelized', *World Christian encyclopedia, AD 1900-2000* | D.B. Barrett | WERC/CMS | 3 | 3 | Kenya | Ecumenical | 5 | 5 | 2 | 2000 | 38.0 | 1.1 | 1 |
| 650 | 1982 | Beachhead Peoples and Bridge People Groups | R.D. Winter | LCWE/USCWM | 8 | 3 | USA | Conservative Evangelical | 3 | 2 | 3 | 2000 | 38.0 | 1.1 | 5 |
| 651 | 1982 | World Satellite Evangelism | P.I. McClendon | WSE/WSC/ORU | 8 | 6 | USA | Charismatic | 2 | 5 | 4 | – | 38.0 | 1.1 | 4 |
| 652 | 1982 | 1st Korean World Mission Congress | Yong Chik Han | – | 8 | 8 | Korea | Evangelical | 2 | 4 | 4 | – | 38.0 | 1.1 | 8 |
| 653 | 1982 | *Mission and evangelism: an ecumenical affirmation* | Emilio Castro | CWME-WCC | 3 | 7 | Switzerland | Ecumenical | 3 | 3 | 4 | – | 38.0 | 1.1 | 6 |
| 654 | 1982 | Institute for World Evangelism | George Morris | IWE-WMC | 9 | 7 | USA | Methodist | 1 | 3 | 4 | 1991 | 38.0 | 1.1 | 8 |
| 655 | 1982 | *Panta ta ethni* (To All Peoples) | A. Yannoulatos | GOC-AD | 3 | 14 | Greece | Eastern Orthodox | 1 | 2 | 2 | – | 38.0 | 1.1 | 4 |
| 656 | 1982 | Frontier Peoples Committee | Larry Allman | IFMA-FPC | 7 | 3 | USA | Fundamentalist | 2 | 1 | 2 | – | 38.0 | 1.1 | 4 |
| 657 | 1982 | 'The Challenge of Our Task' | Wade Coggins | EFMA | 4 | 3 | USA | Conservative Evangelical | 4 | 3 | 2 | 2000 | 38.0 | 1.1 | 1 |
| 658 | 1983 | World Baptist Congress on Urban Evangelism | Nilson Fanini | BWA | 4 | 7 | Brazil | Baptist | 1 | 3 | 2 | – | 37.3 | 1.1 | 0 |
| 659 | 1983 | 'A global strategy for world evangelization: l05 steps' | D.B. Barrett | WERC-CSWE | 9 | 3 | Kenya | Anglican | 5 | 5 | 1 | 2000 | 37.3 | 1.1 | 0 |
| 660 | 1983 | 1st International Conference for Itinerant Evangelists | Werner Burklin | BGEA | 3 | 7 | Netherlands | Conservative Evangelical | 3 | 4 | 4 | – | 37.3 | 1.1 | 3 |
| 661 | 1983 | 'Jesus Christ the Life of the World' | Ted Scott | WCC | 10 | 4 | Canada | Ecumenical | 4 | 3 | 5 | – | 37.3 | 1.1 | 3 |
| 662 | 1983 | Global Mapping Project | R.H. Waymire | GMP | 6 | 3 | USA | Conservative Evangelical | 2 | 4 | 2 | – | 37.3 | 1.1 | 4 |
| 663 | 1983 | Lumen 2000 | Bobby Cavnar | L-2000/CTV | 9 | 6 | USA | Roman Catholic | 1 | 5 | 4 | 2000 | 37.3 | 1.1 | 4 |
| 664 | 1983 | Committee on the Holy Spirit and Frontier Missions | G. Adkins | CHSFM/USCWM | 7 | 3 | USA | Charismatic | 2 | 2 | 1 | – | 37.3 | 1.1 | 1 |
| 665 | 1983 | Third World mission societies: *The last age of missions* | Larry D. Pate | OCM/TWMA | 5 | 8 | Brazil | Evangelical | 3 | 3 | 5 | 2000 | 37.3 | 1.1 | 1 |
| 666 | 1983 | New Focus | R.K. Drollinger | – | 7 | 6 | USA | Nondenominational | 3 | 5 | 4 | 2000 | 37.3 | 1.1 | 7 |
| 667 | 1984 | Worldwide Priests Retreat | Tom Forrest | ICCRO | 4 | 2 | Vatican | Roman Catholic | 2 | 4 | 4 | 2000 | 36.7 | 1.1 | 3 |
| 668 | 1984 | International Prayer Assembly for World Evangelization | Vonette Bright | LCWE/CCCI | 8 | 2 | Korea | Evangelical | 3 | 3 | 4 | – | 36.7 | 1.1 | 0 |
| 669 | 1984 | Ethnic Chinese Congress on World Evangelization | Thomas Wang | ECCOWE | 4 | 7 | USA | Evangelical | 3 | 4 | 2 | – | 36.7 | 1.1 | 3 |
| 670 | 1984 | *International journal of frontier missions* | G. Aeschliman | IJFM | 3 | 3 | USA | Conservative Evangelical | 3 | 2 | 2 | 2000 | 36.7 | 1.1 | 5 |
| 671 | 1984 | National and Regional LCWE Conferences | L.F.S. Ford | ICOWE-2 | 8 | 13 | USA | Conservative Evangelical | 3 | 1 | 4 | – | 36.7 | 1.1 | 6 |
| 672 | 1984 | 'In Christ--Hope for the World' | Zoltan Kaldy | LWF | 1 | 4 | Hungary | Lutheran | 2 | 3 | 3 | – | 36.7 | 1.1 | 1 |
| 673 | 1984 | STEP Programme (Strategy to Every People) | Patrick J. Johnstone | STEP-WEC | 10 | 9 | Britain | Nondenominational | 1 | 5 | 4 | 1990 | 36.7 | 1.1 | 7 |
| 674 | 1984 | World Catholic Federation for the Biblical Apostolate | Alberto Ablondi | WCFBA | 1 | 14 | India | Roman Catholic | 2 | 3 | 3 | – | 36.7 | 1.1 | 8 |
| 675 | 1984 | Baptist World Discipleship Movement | F. Aular | – | 7 | 9 | Venezuela | Baptist | 1 | 1 | 2 | – | 36.7 | 1.1 | 1 |
| 676 | 1984 | *The unfinished task* | J.E. Kyle | IVCF | 3 | 3 | USA | Nondenominational | 3 | 3 | 1 | – | 36.7 | 1.1 | 1 |
| 677 | 1984 | Twenty-one Strategies for Lausanne | Bradford Smith | SWG-LCWE | 8 | 13 | USA | Conservative Evangelical | 2 | 0 | 2 | – | 36.7 | 1.1 | 1 |
| 678 | 1984 | 'Unidos en Cristo Evangelizando las Naciones' | R.H. Sperger | FEDEMEC/WEGO | 8 | 9 | Costa Rica | Evangelical | 2 | 1 | 3 | – | 36.7 | 1.1 | 6 |
| 679 | 1985 | Mission 2000 | D.A. McGavran | SWM/USCWM | 7 | 10 | USA | Conservative Evangelical | 3 | 4 | 3 | 2000 | 36.0 | 1.1 | 0 |
| 680 | 1985 | International Missionary Congress: 'Bringing Christ to Man' | R. Pellegrino | PUU | 1 | 4 | Italy | Roman Catholic | 1 | 3 | 4 | – | 36.0 | 1.1 | 0 |
| 681 | 1985 | Korean Churches' Plan for Entering Every Country | Han Ki Man | – | 10 | 8 | Korea | Interdenominational | 3 | 1 | 5 | 2000 | 36.0 | 1.1 | 0 |
| 682 | 1985 | Youth Congress on World Evangelization | H. Marquardt | – | 1 | 5 | Germany | Evangelical | 3 | 1 | 3 | – | 36.0 | 1.1 | 0 |
| 683 | 1985 | Future Trends in Christian World Mission | W. Knipe | MM(CFMSA)/ASM | 3 | 3 | USA | Roman Catholic | 2 | 4 | 2 | – | 36.0 | 1.1 | 0 |
| 684 | 1985 | *God the Evangelist* | David F. Wells | LCWE/WEF | 4 | 8 | Norway | Evangelical/Charismatic | 2 | 3 | 1 | – | 36.0 | 1.1 | 3 |
| 685 | 1985 | Integrity Keepers Conventions | F.W. Franz | IBSA-JWs | 10 | 5 | USA | Witnesses | 0 | 6 | 6 | 1995 | 36.0 | 1.1 | 9 |
| 686 | 1985 | Global Evangelization Strategy Consultation | R.K. Parks | FMB-SBC | 6 | 3 | USA | Baptist | 1 | 3 | 3 | 2000 | 36.0 | 1.1 | 0 |
| 687 | 1985 | World Conference of Baptist Evangelists | Perry Ellis | BWA/SBC | 1 | 7 | USA | Baptist | 1 | 1 | 2 | – | 36.0 | 1.1 | 0 |
| 688 | 1985 | 'God calls: choose life: the hour is late!' | Pimen I | ACPA/CPC | 1 | 13 | Czechoslovakia | Ecumenical | 4 | 2 | 2 | – | 36.0 | 1.1 | 5 |
| 689 | 1985 | 5th West Malaysia Chinese Congress on World Evangelization | Gideon Chong | CCCOWE | 1 | 7 | Malaysia | Evangelical | 3 | 3 | 3 | – | 36.0 | 1.1 | 0 |
| 690 | 1985 | 'Mobilizing Indigenous Missions for the Final Harvest'/ICOM | Panya Baba | NEMA/ECWA/SIM | 7 | 7 | Nigeria | Evangelical | 2 | 2 | 4 | 2000 | 36.0 | 1.1 | 2 |
| 691 | 1985 | Global Simultaneous Evangelistic Missions | Alan Walker | WMC | 10 | 7 | Indonesia | Methodist | 2 | 1 | 5 | – | 36.0 | 1.1 | 4 |
| 692 | 1985 | Asia Committee for World Evangelization | Fred Magbanua | LCWE | 4 | 13 | Hong Kong | Evangelical | 3 | 1 | 2 | – | 36.0 | 1.1 | 8 |
| 693 | 1985 | Global Strategy Committee, Seventh-day Adventists | Neal C. Wilson | GSC-SDA | 10 | 7 | USA | Adventist | 1 | 5 | 6 | 2000 | 36.0 | 1.1 | 0 |
| 694 | 1985 | God's Global Envoys: Nonresidential Missionaries | D.B. Barrett | WERC/FMB | 8 | 3 | USA | Interdenominational | 5 | 6 | 5 | 2000 | 36.0 | 1.1 | 7 |
| 695 | 1985 | International Catholic Programme of Evangelization | Mario Capello | ICPE | 8 | 7 | Malta | Roman Catholic | 0 | 2 | 5 | – | 36.0 | 1.1 | 8 |
| 696 | 1985 | The World by 2000 | Paul E. Freed | TWR/FEBC/HCJB | 9 | 6 | USA | Nondenominational | 1 | 5 | 5 | 2000 | 36.0 | 1.1 | 7 |
| 697 | 1985 | World Ambassadors | Mark A. Kyle | MCMI | 7 | 8 | USA | Charismatic | 1 | 4 | 3 | – | 36.0 | 1.1 | 6 |
| 698 | 1985 | World Consultation on Evangelism | Dwight Loder | WE-WMC | 4 | 7 | USA | Methodist | 1 | 5 | 2 | 1991 | 36.0 | 1.1 | 0 |
| 699 | 1985 | 1st Venezuelan Congress of World Missions | Calixto Patricio | – | 7 | 7 | Venezuela | Evangelical | 3 | 1 | 3 | 2000 | 36.0 | 1.1 | 4 |
| 700 | 1985 | CWME Orthodox Advisory Group | A. Yannoulatos | CWME-WCC | 4 | 7 | Bulgaria | Orthodox | 1 | 3 | 4 | – | 36.0 | 1.1 | 7 |
| 701 | 1985 | Global Network of Centers for World Mission | Darrell Dorr | USCWM | 9 | 7 | USA | Nondenominational | 3 | 5 | 3 | 2000 | 36.0 | 1.1 | 4 |
| 702 | 1985 | Amsterdam Prayer Conference for World Evangelization | David Bryant | LCWE/YWAM | 8 | 2 | Netherlands | Evangelical/Charismatic | 3 | 4 | 4 | – | 36.0 | 1.1 | 3 |
| 703 | 1985 | EXPLO-85 Global Christian Training Teleconference | Bailey Marks | CCCI | 10 | 13 | USA | Evangelical/Charismatic | 3 | 5 | 5 | – | 36.0 | 1.1 | 3 |
| 704 | 1985 | Association of International Mission Services | Howard Foltz | AIMS | 8 | 13 | USA | Charismatic | 3 | 4 | 3 | 2000 | 36.0 | 1.1 | 1 |
| 705 | 1985 | 'Emergency call for United Global Evangelism' | D.A. McGavran | SWM/CGI | 1 | 10 | Korea | Interdenominational | 3 | 2 | 0 | – | 36.0 | 1.1 | 1 |
| 706 | 1985 | *Power evangelism; Power healing;* and *Power encounters* | John Wimber | – | 7 | 8 | USA | Charismatic | 2 | 3 | 2 | – | 36.0 | 1.1 | 8 |
| 707 | 1986 | Reaching the World's Cities by AD 2000 | J.P. Hogan | AoG(USA)-DFM | 9 | 8 | USA | Pentecostal | 1 | 4 | 5 | 2000 | 35.2 | 1.1 | 0 |
| 708 | 1986 | Consultation on Evangelizing World-Class Cities | R. Bakke | MBI | 4 | 7 | USA | Conservative Evangelical | 1 | 3 | 2 | – | 35.2 | 1.1 | 4 |
| 709 | 1986 | *Touch the world through prayer* | W.L. Duewel | OMS | 8 | 2 | USA | Holiness | 2 | 3 | 1 | – | 35.2 | 1.1 | 6 |
| 710 | 1986 | Worldwide Student NetWork | David English | WSNW/CCCI | 9 | 7 | USA | Evangelical | 2 | 5 | 2 | 2000 | 35.2 | 1.1 | 6 |
| 711 | 1986 | International Prophetic Ministry Convention | B. Maoz | – | 4 | 1 | Israel | Pentecostal/Charismatic | 1 | 4 | 2 | – | 35.2 | 1.1 | 1 |
| 712 | 1986 | Latin American Evangelical Confraternity | M. Ortiz | CONELA | 7 | 7 | Venezuela | Conservative Evangelical | 1 | 4 | 3 | – | 35.2 | 1.1 | 1 |
| 713 | 1986 | International Conference for Equipping Evangelists | Terry Edwards | CEI | 7 | 13 | USA | Charismatic | 2 | 4 | 3 | – | 35.2 | 1.1 | 5 |
| 714 | 1986 | 'Renew the Church--Reach the World' | David M. Howard | WEF | 6 | 13 | Singapore | Conservative Evangelical | 3 | 5 | 5 | 2000 | 35.2 | 1.1 | 1 |
| 715 | 1986 | 2nd International Conference for Itinerant Evangelists | Werner Burklin | ICIE/BGEA | 4 | 7 | Netherlands | Evangelical | 3 | 4 | 5 | – | 35.2 | 1.1 | 8 |
| 716 | 1986 | 3rd Chinese Congress on World Evangelization | Thomas Wang | CCCOWE | 4 | 13 | Taiwan | Evangelical | 3 | 5 | 2 | – | 35.2 | 1.1 | 3 |
| 717 | 1986 | 24th International Old Catholic Congress | G.A. van Kleef | IOCBC | 6 | 13 | Germany | Old Catholic | 1 | 2 | 4 | – | 35.2 | 1.1 | 0 |
| 718 | 1986 | Asia Missions Association: 'Thy Will be Done on Earth' | David J. Cho | AMA/KIM | 6 | 13 | Korea | Evangelical | 3 | 4 | 3 | – | 35.2 | 1.1 | 0 |
| 719 | 1986 | Good News World/Mass Scripture Distribution | J. Godwin | BSSB-SBC | 7 | 14 | USA | Baptist | 0 | 0 | 1 | 1995 | 35.2 | 1.1 | 1 |
| 720 | 1986 | 'Toward 2000' (Issachar Frontier Missions Research) | G.K. Otis III | IFMR | 8 | 7 | USA | Conservative Evangelical | 1 | 5 | 3 | 2000 | 35.2 | 1.1 | 1 |
| 721 | 1986 | *To the ends of the Earth* | Joseph L. Bernadin | NCCB/USCMA | 7 | 7 | USA | Roman Catholic | 2 | 3 | 3 | – | 35.2 | 1.1 | 9 |
| 722 | 1986 | Mandate '86 | J.E. Kyle | IVCF | 7 | 13 | USA | Evangelical | 3 | 4 | 3 | – | 35.2 | 1.1 | 7 |
| 723 | 1986 | Presbyterian Decade of Evangelism | C. Kirkpatrick | PC(USA) | 7 | 7 | USA | Presbyterian | 1 | 4 | 4 | 2000 | 35.2 | 1.1 | 0 |
| 724 | 1986 | Leaders' Congress on the Holy Spirit & World Evangelization | H. Vinson Synan | NARSC | 7 | 8 | USA | Pentecostal/Charismatic | 3 | 4 | 4 | – | 35.2 | 1.1 | 3 |
| 725 | 1986 | Society for Frontier Missiology | R.D. Winter | USSFM-SFM | 6 | 3 | USA | Conservative Evangelical | 2 | 2 | 2 | 2000 | 35.2 | 1.1 | 6 |
| 726 | 1986 | Intercontinental Broadcasting Network | J. Martin | IBN | 7 | 6 | Norway | Charismatic | 1 | 4 | 2 | – | 35.2 | 1.1 | 4 |
| 727 | 1986 | Global Strategy Group | R.K. Parks | FMB-GSG | 6 | 9 | USA | Baptist | 2 | 1 | 3 | 2000 | 35.2 | 1.1 | 0 |
| 728 | 1986 | One Million Native Missionaries | K.P. Yohannan | GFA | 9 | 7 | India | Nondenominational | 1 | 3 | 4 | – | 35.2 | 1.1 | 8 |
| 729 | 1986 | *Wanted: World Christians* | J.H. Kane | – | 3 | 3 | USA | Conservative Evangelical | 2 | 3 | 1 | – | 35.2 | 1.1 | 6 |
| 730 | 1986 | Televised Evangelism for All | N. Van Hamm | CBN | 9 | 6 | USA | Charismatic | 0 | 0 | 3 | – | 35.2 | 1.1 | 6 |
| 731 | 1987 | Evangelization 2000/New Evangelization 2000 | Tom Forrest | E-2000 | 10 | 9 | Vatican | Roman Catholic | 3 | 4 | 6 | 2000 | 34.3 | 1.0 | 0 |
| 732 | 1987 | 'Communicating Christ to the Nations' | Robert A. Cook | NRB | 1 | 6 | USA | Conservative Evangelical | 1 | 1 | 1 | – | 34.3 | 1.0 | 1 |
| 733 | 1987 | Consultation on World Evangelization | Larry Christenson | CCC/NARSC/SOMA | 6 | 8 | Singapore | Pentecostal/Charismatic | 4 | 1 | 3 | 2000 | 34.3 | 1.0 | 0 |
| 734 | 1987 | International Conference of Evangelical Bible Societies | J.R. Powell | ICEBS/IBS | 8 | 14 | USA | Nondenominational | 2 | 4 | 4 | – | 34.3 | 1.0 | 1 |
| 735 | 1987 | 'By the Year 2000: Is God telling us something?' | Thomas Wang | LCWE | 3 | 13 | Singapore | Interdenominational | 4 | 2 | 1 | 2000 | 34.3 | 1.0 | 0 |
| 736 | 1987 | World Evangelization Strategy Committee | Gary Clark | WESC-NARSC | 9 | 3 | Britain | Pentecostal/Charismatic | 5 | 3 | 1 | 2000 | 34.3 | 1.0 | 0 |
| 737 | 1987 | Every Nation by 2000--Every Home for Christ | D.W. Kietzman | WLC-EHC | 8 | 14 | USA | Conservative Evangelical | 1 | 4 | 4 | 2000 | 34.3 | 1.0 | 7 |
| 738 | 1987 | 'Countdown to the Year 2000' | R.D. Winter | USCWM | 7 | 9 | USA | Conservative Evangelical | 3 | 1 | 2 | 2000 | 34.3 | 1.0 | 0 |
| 739 | 1987 | Global-Village Evangelism | Rochunga Pudaite | BFTW-GVE | 7 | 14 | India | Conservative Evangelical | 0 | 4 | 3 | – | 34.3 | 1.0 | 3 |
| 740 | 1987 | LCWE Younger Leaders' Conference/Singapore '87 | B. Stiller | LCWE | 4 | 13 | Singapore | Evangelical | 3 | 4 | 3 | – | 34.3 | 1.0 | 3 |
| 741 | 1987 | Global Rosary for World Peace | John Paul II | L-2000/CTV | 8 | 2 | Vatican | Roman Catholic | 1 | 1 | 4 | – | 34.3 | 1.0 | 9 |
| 742 | 1987 | *AD 2000 Together* | H. Vinson Synan | NARSC | 8 | 8 | USA | Pentecostal/Charismatic | 4 | 4 | 5 | 2000 | 34.3 | 1.0 | 0 |
| 743 | 1987 | Community Satellite Corporation | R.W. Johnson | CSC/DBS | 9 | 6 | USA | Charismatic | 1 | 4 | 4 | – | 34.3 | 1.0 | 4 |
| 744 | 1987 | Global Share Network | R.H. Waymire | GMI | 4 | 6 | USA | Nondenominational | 3 | 4 | 1 | – | 34.3 | 1.0 | 1 |

*Continued opposite*

*Table 27–21 concluded*

| *No.* 1 | *Year* 2 | *Name* 3 | *Author* 4 | *Initials* 5 | *Type* 6 | *Min* 7 | *Origin* 8 | *Tradition* 9 | *Coop* 10 | *Pr* 11 | *Res* 12 | *Dline* 13 | *Unev* 14 | *Ratio* 15 | *Stat* 16 |
|---|---|---|---|---|---|---|---|---|---|---|---|---|---|---|---|
| 745 | 1987 | God's 100,000 New Envoys | T. Yamamori | FFH | 3 | 5 | USA | Evangelical | 3 | 3 | 2 | – | 34.3 | 1.0 | 7 |
| 746 | 1987 | The Future of the Christian World Mission | D.B. Barrett | FCWM/ASM | 0 | 3 | Britain | Anglican | 5 | 2 | 1 | – | 34.3 | 1.0 | 6 |
| 747 | 1987 | Mission World '89 (International Satellite Mission) | Billy Graham | BGEA | 7 | 7 | USA | Evangelical | 3 | 4 | 4 | – | 34.3 | 1.0 | 0 |
| 748 | 1987 | Global Broadcasting System (Top Hat platform network) | Paul F. Crouch | GBS | 8 | 6 | USA | Evangelical/Charismatic | 0 | 5 | 3 | – | 34.3 | 1.0 | 1 |
| 749 | 1987 | Adopt-a-People | W. Tullis | USCWM | 9 | 13 | USA | Conservative Evangelical | 2 | 4 | 3 | – | 34.3 | 1.0 | 6 |
| 750 | 1987 | Christian Communication Technology | J.O. Crawford | CCT-AVCAPI | 8 | 14 | USA | Evangelical | 2 | 4 | 3 | 2000 | 34.3 | 1.0 | 6 |
| 751 | 1987 | Worldwide Prayer Crusade | Sheila Beatty | E-2000/CTV | 7 | 2 | Vatican | Roman Catholic | 4 | 4 | 2 | 2000 | 34.3 | 1.0 | 0 |
| 752 | 1987 | Project 2000: Helping Nationals focus on the Unreached | A. Finley | CNEC-PI | 8 | 7 | USA | Conservative Evangelical | 2 | 4 | 4 | 2000 | 34.3 | 1.0 | 6 |
| 753 | 1987 | Destiny '87: Here's Life, Black America | Crawford Loritts | CCCI/IVCF | 6 | 7 | USA | Evangelical | 1 | 4 | 2 | – | 34.3 | 1.0 | 1 |
| 754 | 1987 | New Life 2000: A Revolutionary Plan (Here's Life World) | C. Osterberg | CCCI | 10 | 7 | USA | Nondenominational | 2 | 5 | 6 | 2000 | 34.3 | 1.0 | 7 |
| 755 | 1987 | *Towards 2000: Reaching the world's billions* | Benjamin George | CFC/YFC | 3 | 5 | Malaysia | Conservative Evangelical | 3 | 3 | 0 | 2000 | 34.3 | 1.0 | 0 |
| 756 | 1987 | Interdenominational Global Missions Conferences | R.K. Parks | – | 4 | 13 | USA | Interdenominational | 3 | 1 | 3 | – | 34.3 | 1.0 | 5 |
| 757 | 1987 | *Status Report on the Great Commission* | C.D. Hutchins | WMT(WMC) | 9 | 6 | USA | Nondenominational | 5 | 6 | 2 | 2000 | 34.3 | 1.0 | 0 |
| 758 | 1987 | Decade of Harvest | J.P. Hogan | AoG(USA) | 10 | 8 | USA | Pentecostal | 1 | 4 | 6 | 2000 | 34.3 | 1.0 | 3 |
| 759 | 1987 | Ibadan Declaration on Holistic Evangelization of the World | S. Akande | AABF/BWA | 4 | 13 | Nigeria | Baptist | 1 | 2 | 2 | – | 34.3 | 1.0 | 1 |
| 760 | 1987 | 2nd Asia Leadership Congress on World Evangelization | John Cho | ALCOWE II | 4 | 13 | Singapore | Evangelical | 3 | 4 | 3 | – | 34.3 | 1.0 | 0 |
| 761 | 1987 | COMIBAM '87/Ibero-American Missions Congress | Luis Bush | COMIBAM | 4 | 8 | Brazil | Evangelical/Charismatic | 3 | 4 | 5 | 2000 | 34.3 | 1.0 | 3 |
| 762 | 1987 | Decade of Destiny for Church of God World Missions | C. Moree | CoGWM | 8 | 8 | USA | Pentecostal | 0 | 4 | 4 | 2000 | 34.3 | 1.0 | 7 |
| 763 | 1987 | Advance Ministries: Reaching the Unreached | Steve Shank | – | 6 | 8 | USA | Charismatic | 3 | 1 | 3 | – | 34.3 | 1.0 | 0 |
| 764 | 1987 | 'The Missing Key to World Evangelization' | D. Shibley | – | 3 | 2 | USA | Charismatic | 2 | 3 | 2 | – | 34.3 | 1.0 | 8 |
| 765 | 1987 | World Evangelism World Plan 1987-1991 | Maxie D. Dunnam | WE-WMC | 10 | 7 | Jamaica | Methodist | 1 | 3 | 5 | 1991 | 34.3 | 1.0 | 0 |
| 766 | 1988 | 5,300 conferences on evangelization | G.H. Anderson | OMSC/WCC/&c | 4 | 13 | Switzerland | Interdenominational | 3 | 2 | 5 | – | 33.5 | 1.0 | 4 |
| 767 | 1988 | 'Great Commission Deadline: the Year 2000' | James W. Reapsome | CT/EMIS/EMQ | 3 | 3 | USA | Evangelical | 3 | 2 | 1 | 2000 | 33.5 | 1.0 | 1 |
| 768 | 1988 | *The Church Triumphant at the End of the Age* | Nate Krupp | – | 3 | 3 | USA | Nondenominational | 2 | 3 | 1 | c2000 | 33.5 | 1.0 | 0 |
| 769 | 1988 | Churches of the Poor | Julio de Santo Ano | – | 5 | 5 | Mexico | Interdenominational | 1 | 1 | 5 | – | 33.5 | 1.0 | 8 |
| 770 | 1988 | 2nd All-India Congress on Missions & Evangelism | Ebenezer Sunder Raj | AICOME/IMA/EFI | 8 | 7 | India | Nondenominational | 3 | 5 | 3 | – | 33.5 | 1.0 | 8 |
| 771 | 1988 | World Evangelization Expert System/Database | D.B. Barrett | WEES/WED/WERC | 9 | 3 | USA | Interdenominational | 5 | 5 | 3 | 2000 | 33.5 | 1.0 | 1 |
| 772 | 1988 | 10,000 new books/articles a year on mission & evangelization | W. Henkel | BM | 3 | 3 | Germany | Nondenominational | 2 | 2 | 5 | – | 33.5 | 1.0 | 8 |
| 773 | 1988 | World Prayer Force (to enroll 165 million Christians) | John Gibson | WPF-WMT(WTF) | 7 | 2 | USA | Nondenominational | 5 | 4 | 2 | 2000 | 33.5 | 1.0 | 0 |
| 774 | 1988 | Inter-Agency Consultation on Reaching the Unreached | E.R. Dayton | FMB/WVI/&c | 8 | 3 | USA | Interdenominational | 3 | 1 | 1 | 2000 | 33.5 | 1.0 | 0 |
| 775 | 1988 | Evangelistic mass campaigns: Christ For All Nations | Reinhard Bonnke | CFAN/LPEA/&c | 10 | 7 | Argentina | Interdenominational | 2 | 4 | 5 | – | 33.5 | 1.0 | 8 |
| 776 | 1988 | Charismatics United for World Evangelization | Larry Christenson | CUWE/CCC/NARSC | 8 | 8 | Singapore | Pentecostal/Charismatic | 4 | 5 | 5 | 2000 | 33.5 | 1.0 | 0 |
| 777 | 1988 | Christian prophetic utterances | A. Woldben | – | 1 | 1 | Israel | Interdenominational | 0 | 3 | 0 | – | 33.5 | 1.0 | 6 |
| 778 | 1988 | Third World Missions Advance | David J. Cho | TWMA/AMA/PI | 4 | 7 | Brazil | Conservative Evangelical | 4 | 1 | 5 | 2000 | 33.5 | 1.0 | 0 |
| 779 | 1988 | Video churches and missions | K. Chareonwongsak | CSM | 5 | 6 | Thailand | Charismatic | 2 | 1 | 5 | 2000 | 33.5 | 1.0 | 0 |
| 780 | 1988 | Leadership '88: LCWE emerging leaders conference | Glandion Carney | LCWE | 4 | 13 | USA | Evangelical | 3 | 4 | 3 | – | 33.5 | 1.0 | 7 |
| 781 | 1988 | North American African World Missions Congress | Ekpo Ekpo | NACAC | 4 | 7 | Nigeria | Conservative Evangelical | 3 | 4 | 3 | – | 33.5 | 1.0 | 0 |
| 782 | 1988 | International Association for Mission Studies | J. Wietzke | IAMS | 4 | 3 | Italy | Nondenominational | 2 | 3 | 4 | 2000 | 33.5 | 1.0 | 3 |
| 783 | 1988 | International Evangelical Bible Consultation | Billy Graham | BGEA/LCWE | 1 | 13 | Jordan | Conservative Evangelical | 2 | 1 | 2 | – | 33.5 | 1.0 | 3 |
| 784 | 1988 | World Wesleyan Conference on Witness & Evangelism | Maxie D. Dunnam | WMC | 4 | 7 | Britain | Methodist | 1 | 4 | 3 | 1991 | 33.5 | 1.0 | 3 |
| 785 | 1988 | '88 World Evangelization Crusade | P. Yonggi Cho | – | 7 | 8 | Korea | Charismatic | 3 | 4 | 3 | 2000 | 33.5 | 1.0 | 3 |
| 786 | 1988 | March for Jesus | Graham Kendrick | MFJ | 6 | 2 | Britain | Charismatic | 4 | 4 | 5 | 2000 | 33.5 | 1.0 | 7 |
| 787 | 1988 | *World Christian news* | P. Filidis | WCN | 3 | 3 | Netherlands | Ecumenical | 4 | 3 | 4 | 2000 | 33.5 | 1.0 | 7 |
| 788 | 1989 | Global Consultation on AD 2000 and Beyond | Thomas Wang | LCWE/TWMA/FMB | 9 | 13 | Singapore | Evangelical/Ecumenical | 5 | 5 | 3 | 2000 | 32.6 | 1.0 | 3 |
| 789 | 1989 | 2nd World Consultation on Frontier Missions | L. Chen | WCFM | 4 | 7 | USA | Conservative Evangelical | 2 | 2 | 2 | 2000 | 32.6 | 1.0 | 0 |
| 790 | 1989 | 2nd World Conference on Mission & Evangelism | Eugene Stockwell | CWME-WCC | 4 | 7 | Switzerland | Ecumenical | 3 | 4 | 4 | – | 32.6 | 1.0 | 6 |
| 791 | 1989 | International Bishops' Retreat 2000 | Tom Forrest | E-2000 | 4 | 2 | Vatican | Roman Catholic | 1 | 5 | 5 | 2000 | 32.6 | 1.0 | 1 |
| 792 | 1989 | World Evangelization Conference on Liberation Theology | Maxie D. Dunnam | WMC | 4 | 4 | Brazil | Methodist | 1 | 4 | 3 | – | 32.6 | 1.0 | 0 |
| 793 | 1989 | 2nd International Congress on World Evangelization | Thomas Wang | ICOWE II | 9 | 8 | Singapore | Interdenominational | 3 | 4 | 4 | 2000 | 32.6 | 1.0 | 0 |
| 794 | 1989 | 15th Pentecostal World Conference | Jakob Zopfi | PWC/AoG | 4 | 8 | Singapore | Pentecostal | 2 | 4 | 4 | 2000 | 32.6 | 1.0 | 0 |
| 795 | 1989 | Consultation on Dimensions of Christian Martyrdom | K.H. Ting | – | 4 | 5 | Korea | Nondenominational | 3 | 5 | 1 | – | 32.6 | 1.0 | 7 |
| 796 | 1989 | Jerusalem Charismatic Leaders Meeting | Michael C. Harper | – | 7 | 8 | Israel | Charismatic | 4 | 1 | 2 | – | 32.6 | 1.0 | 3 |
| 797 | 1989 | Proposal for a Joint Worldwide Movement | Robert N. Myers | – | 1 | 13 | USA | Ecumenical | 5 | 1 | 0 | 2000 | 32.6 | 1.0 | 0 |
| 798 | 1990 | Proliferation of denominational/agency AD 2000 plans | Paul E. McKaughan | GEM/LCWE | 7 | 7 | USA | Interdenominational | 2 | 4 | 4 | 2000 | 31.6 | 1.0 | 5 |
| 799 | 1990 | Decade of Universal Evangelization | John Paul II | E-2000 | 10 | 7 | Vatican | Roman Catholic | 2 | 5 | 6 | 2000 | 31.6 | 1.0 | 3 |
| 800 | 1990 | Round the World Prayer Event | Maxie D. Dunnam | WE-WMC | 8 | 2 | Britain | Methodist | 2 | 4 | 2 | – | 31.6 | 1.0 | 1 |
| 801 | 1990 | Peace Council/Convocation of Christians | Emilio Castro | JPIC-WCC/RCC | 6 | 4 | Australia | Ecumenical | 3 | 4 | 4 | – | 31.6 | 1.0 | 5 |
| 802 | 1990 | Joint IFMA/EFMA Conference on Countdown Thinking | Wade Coggins | IFMA/EFMA | 4 | 7 | USA | Conservative Evangelical | 3 | 4 | 3 | 2000 | 31.6 | 1.0 | 0 |
| 803 | 1990 | World Congress on the Holy Spirit & World Evangelization | H. Vinson Synan | – | 6 | 8 | USA | Pentecostal/Charismatic | 4 | 5 | 5 | 2000 | 31.6 | 1.0 | 0 |
| 804 | 1990 | EXPLO '90 Worldwide Satellite Strategy | Bill Bright | CCCI-HLW | 9 | 6 | USA | Nondenominational | 1 | 5 | 5 | 2000 | 31.6 | 1.0 | 0 |
| 805 | 1990 | Asia Regional Missions Congress on AD 2000 | David J. Cho | AMA/TWMA | 4 | 7 | Korea | Evangelical | 3 | 4 | 4 | 2000 | 31.6 | 1.0 | 0 |
| 806 | 1990 | Africa Regional Missions Congress on AD 2000 | Panya Baba | LCWE/EMS/&c | 4 | 7 | Nigeria | Evangelical | 3 | 4 | 4 | 2000 | 31.6 | 1.0 | 1 |
| 807 | 1990 | AD 2000 National Consultations | Luis Bush | LCWE/TWMA | 4 | 7 | Argentina | Evangelical | 3 | 2 | 4 | 2000 | 31.6 | 1.0 | 3 |
| 808 | 1990 | National Evangelistic Crusade | Charles & Frances Hunter | NEC | 8 | 7 | USA | Charismatic | 2 | 4 | 4 | 2000 | 31.6 | 1.0 | 3 |
| 809 | 1990 | Churches Uniting in Global Mission | Robert Schuller | CUGM | 6 | 10 | USA | Nondenominational | 2 | 2 | 3 | 2000 | 31.6 | 1.0 | 1 |
| 810 | 1990 | Division for Global Mission of the ELCA | – | DGM/ELCA | 6 | 7 | USA | Lutheran | 2 | 1 | 2 | – | 31.6 | 1.0 | 5 |
| 811 | 1990 | Church Growth International | P. Yonggi Cho | CGI | 6 | 8 | Korea | Independent | 2 | 3 | 4 | – | 31.6 | 1.0 | 8 |
| 812 | 1990 | Come Down Dark Prince | Dick Bernal | – | 0 | 2 | USA | Independent | 1 | 2 | 3 | – | 31.6 | 1.0 | 8 |
| 813 | c1990 | Unveiling of His Glory | Pastor Ramon Orosa | – | 0 | 2 | Philippines | Independent | 1 | 2 | 3 | – | 31.6 | 1.0 | 8 |
| 814 | 1990 | *Our globe and how to reach it* | D. B. Barrett/T. Johnson | – | 3 | 3 | USA | Ecumenical | 5 | 3 | 6 | 2000 | 31.6 | 1.0 | 3 |
| 815 | 1991 | Global Congress of Charismatic Leaders for World Evangelization | Michael C. Harper | CUWE/ICCRO | 6 | 8 | Britain | Pentecostal/Charismatic | 4 | 4 | 6 | 2000 | 31.3 | 0.9 | 1 |
| 816 | 1991 | 7th Assembly, World Council of Churches | Emilio Castro | WCC | 4 | 4 | Australia | Ecumenical | 3 | 4 | 5 | – | 31.3 | 0.9 | 8 |
| 817 | 1991 | 4th Chinese Congress on World Evangelization | Hay-Him Chan | CCCOWE | 4 | 7 | Hong Kong | Evangelical | 3 | 4 | 3 | – | 31.3 | 0.9 | 8 |
| 818 | 1991 | Charismatic youth churches | Benson Idahosa | – | 5 | 5 | Nigeria | Charismatic | 2 | 1 | 4 | – | 31.3 | 0.9 | 8 |
| 819 | 1991 | WMC Conference on World Evangelization | Joe Hale | WE-WMC | 4 | 7 | Singapore | Methodist | 1 | 3 | 3 | – | 31.3 | 0.9 | 5 |
| 820 | 1991 | AD 2000 Regional Consultations | Luis Bush | LCWE/TWMA | 8 | 7 | Philippines | Evangelical | 4 | 5 | 4 | 2000 | 31.3 | 0.9 | 0 |
| 821 | 1991 | Great & Holy Council of the Orthodox Church | Demetrios I | EPC | 6 | 5 | Greece | Eastern Orthodox | 2 | 5 | 4 | – | 31.3 | 0.9 | 3 |
| 822 | 1991 | Third Congress on Evangelism | – | – | 4 | 7 | Japan | Evangelical | 2 | 2 | 3 | 2000 | 31.3 | 0.9 | 7 |
| 823 | 1991 | Redemptoris Missio | John Paul II | RM | 2 | 7 | Vatican | Roman Catholic | 2 | 2 | 5 | 2000 | 31.3 | 0.9 | 7 |
| 824 | 1991 | Reaching the Unreached | Baptist General Conference | BGC | 3 | 10 | USA | Baptist | 2 | 4 | 3 | 2000 | 31.3 | 0.9 | 1 |
| 825 | 1991 | *Churchless Christianity* | H. E. Hoefer | – | 3 | 9 | India | Lutheran | 5 | 3 | 3 | – | 31.3 | 0.9 | 8 |
| 826 | 1992 | Ethnoscan | D. B. Barrett | – | 3 | 3 | USA | Ecumenical | 4 | 2 | 2 | 2000 | 30.9 | 0.9 | 1 |
| 827 | 1992 | Festival of Good News AD2000 | K.C. George | – | 7 | 7 | India | Independent | 3 | 1 | 1 | 2000 | 30.9 | 0.9 | 0 |
| 828 | 1993 | AD 2000 Cities Network | Viv Gregg | – | 3 | 3 | New Zealand | Conservative Evangelical | 2 | 2 | 2 | 2000 | 30.5 | 0.9 | 1 |
| 829 | 1993 | Praying through the Window | L. Bush | PTW | 8 | 2 | USA | Evangelical | 3 | 4 | 5 | 2000 | 30.5 | 0.9 | 3 |
| 830 | 1993 | *Operation world* | P. Johnstone | OP | 3 | 2 | Britain | Evangelical | 4 | 3 | 5 | 2000 | 30.5 | 0.9 | 7 |
| 831 | 1994 | The Last Frontier | A. Willis | IMB/SBC | 7 | 7 | USA | Southern Baptist | 2 | 4 | 4 | 2000 | 30.1 | 0.9 | 3 |
| 832 | 1994 | *The Star of 2000* | J. Gary | – | 3 | 2 | USA | Ecumenical | 4 | 3 | 3 | 2000 | 30.1 | 0.9 | 1 |
| 833 | 1994 | Unreached Peoples Prayer Profiles | L. Stockstill | UPPP | 3 | 3 | USA | Interdenominational | 4 | 3 | 6 | 2000 | 30.1 | 0.9 | 7 |
| 834 | 1995 | World Christian Congress on AD 2000 and Beyond | T. Wang | LCWE/TWMA/&c | 9 | 8 | South Korea | Evangelical/Ecumenical | 3 | 1 | 5 | 2000 | 29.6 | 0.9 | 1 |
| 835 | 1995 | 3rd World Consultation on Frontier Missions | – | – | 4 | 7 | Britain | Conservative Evangelical | 3 | 1 | 2 | 2000 | 29.6 | 0.9 | 1 |
| 836 | 1995 | AD 2025 Global Monitor | T. M. Johnson | AD2025GM | 3 | 3 | USA | Ecumenical | 4 | 2 | 2 | 2025 | 29.6 | 0.9 | 6 |
| 837 | 1995 | Mobilizing New Missionaries Network | G. Verwer | – | 2 | 9 | Britain | Evangelical | 3 | 4 | 3 | 2000 | 29.6 | 0.9 | 5 |
| 838 | 1995 | CBN World Reach | E. Watt | CBN | 10 | 6 | USA | Pentecostal/Charismatic | 3 | 5 | 6 | 2000 | 29.6 | 0.9 | 5 |
| 839 | 1995 | Joshua Project 2000 | L. Bush | JP 2000 | 9 | 7 | USA | Evangelical | 3 | 4 | 3 | 2000 | 29.6 | 0.9 | 3 |
| 840 | 1997 | Joshua Harvest: All Peoples, All Persons | L. Bush | – | 7 | 7 | USA | Evangelical | 3 | 1 | 2 | – | 28.6 | 0.9 | 7 |
| 841 | 1997 | Let There Be Light | – | IBS | 7 | 14 | USA | Nondenominational | 3 | 1 | 3 | – | 28.6 | 0.9 | 8 |
| 842 | 1997 | Mission to All the World 2000 | M. Cerullo | – | 8 | 2 | USA | Pentecostal/Charismatic | 3 | 4 | 4 | 2000 | 28.6 | 0.9 | 3 |
| 843 | 1997 | Plan of 1000 Days | R. Justiniano | – | 7 | 6 | Bolivia | Nondenominational | 3 | 4 | 4 | 2000 | 28.6 | 0.9 | 3 |
| 844 | 1997 | *World churches handbook* | P. Brierley | WCH | 3 | 3 | Britain | Evangelical | 3 | 3 | 5 | – | 28.6 | 0.9 | 5 |
| 845 | 1998 | Confronting the Queen of Heaven | C. P. Wagner | – | 3 | 2 | USA | Independent | 3 | 3 | 5 | 2000 | 28.1 | 0.8 | 8 |
| 846 | 1998 | Accelerating World Evangelization | J. Rankin | SBC/IMB | 4 | 7 | USA | Baptist | 3 | 2 | 4 | – | 28.1 | 0.8 | 7 |
| 847 | 1998 | Network for Strategic Missions | E. Watt | NSM | 8 | 7 | USA | Nondenominational | 4 | 2 | 3 | – | 28.1 | 0.8 | 8 |
| 848 | 1998 | World Harvest Information Database | E. Watt | WHID | 7 | 3 | USA | Nondenominational | 3 | 1 | 1 | 2000 | 28.1 | 0.8 | 0 |
| 849 | 1998 | Completing the Commission | D. Eastman | | 9 | 2 | USA | Nondenominational | 3 | 5 | 4 | 2000 | 28.1 | 0.8 | 7 |
| 850 | 1998 | Celebrate Messiah 2000 | L. Bush | – | 8 | 2 | Israel | Evangelical | 3 | 4 | 3 | 2000 | 28.1 | 0.8 | 0 |
| 851 | 1998 | World Prayer Center | T. Haggard | WPC | 10 | 2 | USA | Pentecostal/Charismatic | 3 | 4 | 4 | – | 28.1 | 0.8 | 8 |
| 852 | 1998 | *Atlas of world Christianity* | P. Brierley/H. Wraight | AWC | 3 | 3 | Britain | Evangelical | 3 | 3 | 4 | – | 28.1 | 0.8 | 7 |
| 853 | 1999 | AD 2000 Jubilee Year | John Paul II | RCC | 10 | 13 | Vatican | Roman Catholic | 3 | 2 | 5 | 2000 | 27.5 | 0.8 | 3 |
| 854 | 1999 | Day One 2000 | J. McDowell | – | 1 | 7 | USA | Nondenominational | 3 | 1 | 4 | 2000 | 27.5 | 0.8 | 7 |
| 855 | 1999 | New Hope for the Third Millennium | H. Kamel | ACC | 2 | 6 | USA | Nondenominational | 3 | 1 | 3 | 2000 | 27.5 | 0.8 | 6 |
| 856 | 1999 | Jericho Center | D. Eastman | JC | 10 | 2 | USA | Nondenominational | 3 | 4 | 4 | – | 27.5 | 0.8 | 8 |
| 857 | 1999 | Global Evangelization Forum | T. Wang | GEF | 6 | 7 | Norway | Evangelical | 4 | 1 | 4 | – | 27.5 | 0.8 | 7 |
| 858 | 2000 | Amsterdam 2000 | B. Graham | – | 6 | 7 | Netherlands | Nondenominational | 3 | 4 | 4 | – | 26.9 | 0.8 | 8 |
| 859 | 2000 | *World Christian Encyclopedia*, second edition | D. B. Barrett/et. al. | WCE2 | 9 | 3 | USA | Ecumenical | 5 | 6 | 4 | 2025 | 26.9 | 0.8 | 8 |
| 860 | 2001 | *World Christian Trends* | D. B. Barrett/et. al. | WCT | 9 | 3 | USA | Ecumenical | 5 | 6 | 4 | 2025 | 26.9 | 0.8 | 8 |

Total of all global plans, including 650 other plans tabulated in Table 27–19: 1,510. For complete data consult CD, *World Christian database, AD 33-AD 2200*.

## Table 27–22. Evolution of a global evangelization movement: details of the 1,500 global plans in chronological sequence, with future scenarios.

This table is a historical chronology which provides one chronological entry, in standardized format, for each and every global plan listed as a single line in Table 27–21. (In a handful of cases, 2 or even 3 related plans may be described together in a single chronological entry). Each entry briefly places the plan or proposal in its historical context and gives a few further basic details. The element common to all entries is a stated intent either 'to evangelize the world', 'to reach all people', 'to disciple the nations', 'to take our part in Christ's world mission', or similar terminology; however, in the interests of brevity these standardized statements (which justify their inclusion in this catalogue of global plans) are in most cases not repeated here from one entry to another. Their presence can therefore be assumed.

AD 30 Jesus begins public ministry, starts on his immediate plan to win the world, proclaims nearness and imminence of rule of God: 'The Kingdom of God is at hand' (Mark 1:15, RSV)/'near' (NIV)/'has arrived' (NTME).

31 Jesus chooses Twelve Apostles including 4 of his first cousins and 2 zealots (Patriots or Essenes), unfolds his master plan of personal evangelism, gives them power and authority, commissions them to go initially only to Israelites (Matthew 10:1-6); later commissions Mission of the 70 disciples to evangelize the 70 Gentile nations (Luke 10:1).

32 Jesus envisages lightning spread of the gospel to all nations within one single generation: 'This Good News of the Kingdom will be proclaimed to the whole oikumene as a witness to all nations. And then the end will come' (Matthew 24:14, Jerusalem Bible).

33 Jesus' Great Commission given by the Risen Lord as his final plan and as spiritual counterpart of Genesis 1:28 with 2 components of evangelizing and discipling. 'Go forth to every part of the world (in Greek, *Cosmos*), and proclaim the Good News to the whole creation' (Mark 16:15, NEB); 'Go to all peoples everywhere and make them my disciples' (Matthew 28:19, GNB).

Jesus as Risen Lord and later Ascended King gives Great Commission in a number of different forms at different times during the 40 days to different groups, including individuals, emphasizing the 7 mandates: Receive! Go! Witness! Proclaim! Disciple! Baptize! Train!

34 Apostles (the Twelve plus others) begin evangelizing Jews widely; several remain in Jerusalem for a decade or two, several travel outside, but most continue to evangelize only Jews until AD 38 (Peter), 43 (Paul), and after AD 50 (others).

35 Proliferation of 'signs and wonders' among early believers (listed 9 times in Acts); miracles and healings at this time an everyday occurrence and an essential part of proclamation of the gospel; 'power evangelism' thus one of the normal kinds of evangelism in the Early Church.

36 Martyrdom of Stephen the protomartyr; Jewish persecution of Early Church, especially of Hellenistic Christians; gospel spreads rapidly through persecution and martyrdom.

38 After 5-year period of hesitation and partial obedience to Christ's Great Commission, first Gentiles are deliberately evangelized by the Twelve Apostles.

Commission to evangelize pagan Gentiles as Gentiles first forced on consciousness of Jewish church, through baptism by Peter of Cornelius, a God-fearer but not a Jewish proselyte (Acts 10:1-48).

c38 Twelve Apostles, after 5 years' uncertainty, scatter across globe spreading the gospel, from Ethiopia (Matthew), to Armenia (Bartholomew) to India (Thomas); all martyred over subsequent 60 years.

46 Paul's 1st missionary journey (45-48), with Barnabas; Antioch, Cyprus, Pamphilia, Pisidia, Lycaonia; develops strategy of urban evangelization and urban ministry, moving from city to city or town to town.

61 Paul writes: 'The Good News which has reached you is spreading all over the world' (Colossians 1:6, Jerusalem Bible); 'The Good News, which you have heard, has been preached to the whole human race' (Colossians 1:23; Greek 'to all creation under the sky').

65 Prophecies of John the Divine: 'I saw another angel flying high in the air, with an eternal message of Good News to announce to the peoples of the earth, to every race, tribe, language and nation' (Revelation 14:6-11, GNB).

66 Evangelist Luke concludes his 2-volume narrative (Luke-Acts): The worlds of empire and Judaism have now been evangelized, the Gospel is now known to all peoples throughout them, and the Great Commission there largely completed.

c85 Epistle of Barnabas predicts end of world: 'In six days, that is in 6,000 years, the Universe will come to an end.'

94 Clement bishop of Rome maintains that under apostle Paul the entire Roman empire became evangelized.

96 Last judgement and final retribution will not come until foreordained number of the martyrs has been completed (Revelation 6:11).

c100 Christianity predominantly urban, based on Roman cities, spreading from city to city along trade routes; later missions to Armenia, Ethiopia, China (under Nestorians) all center on capital cities.

c130 Christianity spreads principally and normally, though not exclusively, through (as prevailing strategy) the planting of churches which then serve as missionary communities to evangelize their areas by continuing to attract and enlist converts; most converts are reached through casual contacts, witnessing a martyrdom, hospitality and care of strangers, et alia.

c140 Hermas writes: 'The Son of God...has been preached to the ends of the earth' (*Shepherd of Hermas*).

c150 Justin Martyr (c100-165) founds disciple-training school over a house in Rome, documents current 'signs and wonders' (exorcisms, healings and prophesyings), and writes: 'The first Apostles, twelve in number, in the power of God went out and proclaimed Christ to every race of men'; and 'There is not one single race of men, wheather barbarians, or Greeks, or whatever they may be called, nomads, or vagrants, or herdsmen dwelling in tents, among whom prayers and giving of thanks are not offered through the name of the Crucified Jesus'; teaches that all orthodox Christians believe in a resurrection of the flesh and in a millennial reign in the New Jerusalem; martyred at Rome.

156 Phrygia; rise of Montanism under new convert Montanus (c120-c175), a puritanical, prophetic, charismatic, millennial, apocalyptic movement claiming to be a new age of the Holy Spirit; 206, Tertullian joins; 230, movement excommunicated by Synod of Iconium; continues underground until c880.

c180 Irenaeus bishop of Lyons (c120-203) documents recent charismata (exorcisms, visions, prophecies), and teaches that Antichrist will be a Jew of the tribe of Dan, also Christ will inaugurate a literal millennium of 1,000 years.

197 Tertullian (c160-222) documents recent healings and exorcisms, also writes: 'Christ commanded them to go and teach all nations. Immediately, therefore, so did the apostles'; 'The blood of the martyrs is seed'; and 'There is no nation indeed which is not Christian'; 206, joins Montanist movement.

c205 First known Christian scholar and apologist Clement of Alexandria (c155-215) deals with problem of how to relate Christian faith to Greek philosophy and culture, writes: 'The whole world, with Athens and Greece, has already become the domain of the Word'.

c220 Origen (c185-254) writes: 'The gospel of Jesus Christ has been preached in all creation under heaven, to Greeks and barbarians, to wise and foolish... It is impossible to see any race of men which has avoided accepting the teaching of Jesus'; 'The divine goodness of Our Lord and Saviour is equally diffused among the Britons, the Africans, and other nations of the world'; and 'The preaching of the gospel through the Whole Oikumene shows that the church is receiving divine support'; but also 'Many people, not only barbarians, but even in the Empire, have not yet heard the word of Christ'; and 'The gospel has not yet been preached to all nations, since it has not reached the Chinese or the Ethiopians beyond the river, and only small parts of the more remote and barbarous tribes'; 248, in *Contra Celsum* foresees possibility of conversion of entire world.

249 Seven missionary bishops sent to peoples of Gaul by Cornelius of Rome: Gatien (Tours), Trophime (Arles), Paul (Narbonne), Saturnin (Toulouse), Denis (Paris), Martial (Limoges), Austremoine (Clermont); many others also strategically located and sent in all directions.

c270 Rise of monasticism in Egypt, as direct challenge to lifestyle of the rich: (1) eremitical (Anthony of Egypt, c251-356), (2) cenobitic (Pachomius, c287-346); widespread over next 2 centuries, with many documented healings, exorcisms, miracles, signs and wonders; Egyptian monks travel widely, evangelizing in Europe, Britain, Ireland et alia.

303 10th and last imperial Roman persecution, under Diocletian; aimed at clergy and bishops, with substantial defections; destruction of all church buildings and Scriptures ordered; 500,000 Christians killed or executed in witness under total persecution.

308 Church of the Martyrs with 29 bishops in Egypt organized by bishop Meletius (died 325) of Lycopolis, in opposition to leniency towards *lapsi* favored by Peter I Ieromartyros (Seal of Martyrs) patriarch of Alexandria who is himself martyred in 311; ideal of martyrdom as major factor in evangelizing the world spreads; Meletian sect is approved by Arians, lasts until c520.

c310 Eusebius of Caesarea (c265-339) writes apologetic works: *Praeparatio evangelica* (refuting paganism), *Demonstratio evangelica* (fulfilment of Hebrew prophecy in Christ); 314, completes his *Ecclesiastical History,* and *Martyrs of Palestine*; writes 'The doctrine of the Saviour has irradiated the whole Oikumene (whole inhabited earth)', 325, at Council of Nicea expounds Matthew 28:19.

313 Constantine at Milan issues Edict of Toleration legalizing Christianity throughout Roman empire; 323, becomes sole emperor, attempts to spread gospel by law and authority.

325 Council of Nicea I (1st Ecumenical Council): council makes political province the basic unit for church's larger divisions, brings church's jurisdictional areas into line with secular dioceses and provinces of Roman empire, in order better to witness.

347 Cyril bishop of Jerusalem (310-386) teaches that Antichrist will be a magician who takes over Roman empire, claims to be Christ, deceives Jews by rebuilding Temple, persecutes Christians, then is slain at Second Advent by the Son of God.

c360 8-volume *Apostolic Constitutions*, a Syrian collection of ecclesiastical law, makes frequent allusions to Great Commission of Jesus in Matthew 28:19-20.

374 A layman, Ambrose of Milan (c339-397) acclaimed bishop by crowds; in his writings, documents current healings and glossolalia; later teaches Second Coming of Christ will be preceded by destruction of Rome and appearance of Antichrist on Earth.

378 Jerome (c345-419) writes: 'From India to Britain, all nations resound with the death and resurrection of Christ'; estimates 1.9 million Christians to have been martyred since AD 33 (out of 120 million Christians, i.e. 1.6% or 1 in 60); documents numerous current 'signs and wonders' (healings, exorcisms, miracles).

Ambrose identifies Goths with Ezekiel's Gog, proclaims imminent end of world; Martin to Tours writes 'There is no doubt that the Antichrist has already been born'.

392 Ascetic writer John Cassian (c360-435) enters Bethlehem monastery; 415, founds monastery in Marseilles; promotes spread of monasticism in West; much evangelization due to these itinerant evangelistic monks.

398 John Chrysostom (c344-407) appointed patriarch of Constantinople, founds training school for native Gothic evangelists; writes "Go and make disciples of all nations" was not said for the Apostles only, but for us also'; teaches that final Antichrist under direct inspiration of Satan will appear immediately before Second Advent of Christ in AD 430.

c410 Episcopate in Proconsular Africa, Numidia and Mauretania expands to 768 bishops; total episcopate across North Africa, including Egypt and Donatists, numbers 1,200 bishops; Honoratus at Lerins monastery trains succession of notable missionary bishops, sent across world for Christ.

417 Paulus Orosius, young Spanish priest, encouraged by Augustine to write *Historia adversus paganos,* holding Rome will survive until the coming of Antichrist.

426 Augustine (354-430) bishop of Hippo completes in 13 years his treatise *The City of God* (De Civitate Dei), against background of Visigoth invasion of Rome; propounds allegorical millennialism, but also teaches that future final Antichrist will arise as Nero Redivivus; opposes emerging theory of cessation of charismatic gifts, as overreaction to excesses of Montanism et alia with the teaching that miracles and charismata ended with the Apostolic age; documents numerous recent miracles, exorcisms, healings and resuscitations.

428 French apologist Prosper Tiro (c390-463 defends Augustine of Hippo, writes treatise *De Vocatione Omnium Gentium* envisaging Conversion of all barbarians to Christ, whose grace extends everywhere: 'Nulla pars mundi ab Evangelio vacat Christi.'

499 Task of translating Jesus' message into Greek and Latin cultures virtually completed, after 16 generations.

c510 Irish Peregrini or Exultantes Christi (unorganized wandering hermits and preachers using *pugilatores scotorum* [Irish writing-tablets] as their major piece of equipment) embark on *peregrinatio pro Christi amore* as missionary pilgrims for Christ, begin to migrate across Europe for next 400 years, to the Alps, Germany, Danube, Italy, also to Orkneys, Faeroes, Iceland, converting much of Europe in one of great missionary feats of all time.

535 Cosmas Indicopleustes, Nestorian merchant missionary over most of world, retires to monastery and in 547 completes his global survey *Topographia Christiana* in 12 Books.

c550 Nestorian monasticism organized and reformed by Abraham of Kashkar (501-586); numerous monasteries and missions begun, with special concern for physical and spiritual needs of people; through persecution, spreads across Asia to Yemen, South India, Ceylon, Samarkand, China.

594 Roman pope Gregory the Great (540-604) publishes *Dialogues* describing contemporary Christian miracles, visions, prophecies, supernatural awareness, and other spiritual gifts; places detailed planning of organized missions to all heathen among his major objectives, in view of imminence of Last Judgment.

635 China (then richest and most civilized nation on Earth): first missionary (Alopen, a Nestorian bishop from Syria) reaches Thailand and then Tang Chinese capital Chang-an (Hsian), translates Scriptures for emperor Tai-tsung; Nestorianism influential till suppressed for a time in 845.

c700 End of Patristic Age, during which Greek Fathers and Latin Fathers have all expounded the words *euangelizo, euangelizesthai, euangelismos, evangelizare, evangelizatio, evangelizator,* et alia.

720 Anglo-Saxon translations of John's Gospel by historian and theologian Bede (Baeda, c673-735), monk

Continued opposite

*Table 27–22 continued*

at Jarrow on Tyne; Bede predicts fall of Colosseum will be followed by that of Rome and then also of the whole world.

780 East Syrian bishop of Bait Baghash becomes Nestorian catholicos as Timothy I (728-823) patriarch of the East; develops global missionary strategy through mobile married monks as traders 'carrying only a stick and a bag', creates metropolitan sees in India and Central Asia (including Tibet in 797), and 80 new bishoprics.

c780 Forced baptism of Saxon race by Charlemagne; 4,500 executed in one day for resisting, thousands more deported.

960 Bernard of Thuringia predicts imminent end of world in AD 992; great alarm throughout Europe.

962 Holy Roman Empire founded by Otto I (912-973), king of Germany, crowned by pope John XII; seen as embodiment of rule of Christ on Earth; 10 million by AD 1000, 16 million by AD 1200, 29 million by 1800; finally abolished in 1806.

992 Death of abbot Adso of Montier-en-Der (of Dijon, France), whose writings describe future coming of Antichrist into world.

999 Multitudes journey to Jerusalem to await Second Coming of Christ in AD 1000, as believed prophesied in Apocrypha.

1000 Millennial year preceded by widespread terrors; followed by 150 years of vast increase in pilgrimages to Holy Land, with widespread continuing belief in imminent end of world with final king of the Franks leading all faithful to Jerusalem to await Second Coming of Christ.

Catholic Apostolic Church of the East (East Syrian or Nestorian church) is by now the most extensive in world, with 250 dioceses across Asia and 12 million adherents; expansion of Nestorianism in Tenduc, country of Keraits with Karakorum as capital, home of legendary ruler Prester John.

1090 College of Cardinals established in Rome by reforms of pope Urban II (c1042-1099), to expand rule of Christ across the Earth.

1095 Military expeditions by Western Christians against Muslim powers to liberate Holy Land, launched by pope Urban II, known as Crusades: 1st 1095-99 (People's Crusade); 2nd 1147-49; 3rd 1189-93 (Richard the Lion-Heart) 4th 1202-04; 5th 1212-21 (Children's Crusade); 6th 1228-29; 7th 1248-54; 8th 1270-72 (Prince Edward of England).

1113 Roman Catholic religious and knightly order founded by brother Gerard in Palestine to operate hospitals in the Holy Land for the care of pilgrims. Originally known as Sovereign Military Order of the Hospital of St. John of Jerusalem, later as Knights of Rhodes, then as Knights of Malta.

1139 Gaelic church reformer, abbot, archbishop and prophet, Malachy O'Morgain (c1094-1148) compiles 'Prophecy of the Popes', foretells identities, mottoes and characteristics of 122 RC popes from Celestine II (1143) to end of 20th century with final Pope of the Apocalypse (Peter the Roman), with conversion of the Jews to Christ prophesied under last pope but one.

1179 Astronomer John of Toledo Calculates major catastrophe coming in AD 1186; widespread panic follows.

c1180 Joachim of Fiore (c1130-1202), Italian Cistercian abbot and mystic, divides all history into three 40-generation ages or periods (Old Testament, New Testament, future age), writes *Vaticini del Vangelo Eterno* (Prophecies of the Eternal Gospel) and *Expositio in Apocalypsim* describing imminent crisis of evil, apocalyptic symbols of Antichrist, and his 3rd or Final Age of the Spirit (Love) coming by 1260 after Age of the Father (Law), and Age of the Son (Grace), for spiritual men through pilgrimage and great tribulation in a spiritualized Johannine Church replacing carnal Petrine Church; Joachimism spreads widely over next 3 centuries.

c1190 Rise of demand for vernacular versions of Scriptures, illustrated by *Historia Scholastica*, a narrative of biblical history, by 12th-century scholar Petrus Comestor (c1100-1180); poetical and prose versions now available in Old French (Provençal, Vaudois), Italian, Spanish.

1201 Bishop Albert I of Riga founds Knights of the Sword (also known as Brothers of the Sword, Livonian Knights, Brothers of the Militia of Christ), a Roman Catholic military order assigned the rule of the Knights Templar. Their purpose is to convert the heathen and protect missionaries in the Baltic. Later merged with Teutonic Knights.

1209 Francis of Assisi (1182-1226) founds traveling preachers (Franciscans), largest of the mendicant orders (OFM); widespread healings, signs and miracles reported; 1270, missionaries in almost every part of the known world; by 1400, missions from Lapland to Congo and Azores to China; soon reaches a medieval peak of 60,000 Franciscans by 1400, 77,000 by 1768, falling to 14,000 by 1900, rising to 40,000 by 1970.

1215 Dominic (1170-1221) founds Order of Preachers (OP, Dominicans) in southern France for 'Propagation of the Faith through Preaching', 'accepting our Lord's command, Go ye into all the world', soon reaches a peak of 12,000 Dominicans, falling to 7,055 by 1983; other orders of mendicant friars arise including in 1256 Augustinians (OSA).

1221 First of many papal mission encyclicals on foreign missionary affairs: Bull of Honorius III, 'Ne si secus' to the 13 metropolitans of the Catholic church, asking them to send out missionaries.

c1250 Height of the Catholic church's political power in Europe, taken for granted by most Christians as God's instrument for spreading the rule of Christ around the world.

Popular preachers spread warnings of coming of Antichrist; Roman popes Boniface VIII (1234-1303) and John XXII (1249-1334) inter alios each widely regarded as Antichrist.

1254 Sensational *Introduction to the Eternal Gospel* of abbot Joachim issued by ardent Spiritual, Gerard of Borgo San Donnino, claiming its prophecies have been fulfilled by Franciscan order, and insisting Age of the Spirit will begin in 1260.

c1260 Italy and Europe: greatest period of religious art begins, and lasts 400 years, with as central theme Christ's passion and crucifixion; all art—paintings, drawings, tapestries, stained-glass windows, sculpture, architecture—now regarded as major method of teaching and evangelizing illiterate populations.

1266 Mongol ruler Kublai Khan (1215-1294) requests Roman pope: 'Send me 100 men skilled in your religion... and so I shall be baptized, and then all my barons and great men, and then their subjects. And so there will be more Christians here than there are in your parts'; 2 Dominicans sent, but turn back; then 1278, pope sends 5 Franciscans; greatest missed opportunity in Christian history.

c1280 Societas Fratrum Peregrinantium Propter Christum Inter Gentes (Congregation of Friars Pilgrims for Christ Among the Gentiles) founded as Dominican foreign mission body; 1300, founds residences from Constantinople to Black Sea into India; ends 1456.

1288 German canon Alexander of Roes (in Cologne) predicts, in *Notitia Seculi*, end of world at AD 1500, being 6,000 years from foundation of world.

1290 Arnold of Villanova (c1240-1311), leading alchemist and physician of his day, writes 70 scientific works and other theological works including on the coming of Antichrist.

1315 Ramon Lull (c1232-1316), Franciscan theologian writing in Arabic and Catalan, proposes campaign of informed preaching plus military force against Muslims *(Liber de fine)*; stoned to death at Bugia (Algeria) by Muslims.

Franciscan theologian Hugh of Newcastle (c1280-1322), doctor scholasticus, teaches in Paris, writes on coming of Antichrist.

1349 Apogee of East Syrian or Nestorian expansion across Asia, geographically more extensive and more prosperous than ever before or since; 25 metropolitans (each with 6-12 suffragan bishops) in 250 dioceses in China, India, Kashgar, Samarkand, Turkestan, et alia, with total of over 15 million Christians; a mighty organization with missionary enterprise unsurpassed in Christian history.

c1350 St. John of the Cleft Rock writes: 'It is said that 20 centuries after the Incarnation of the Word, the Beast in its turn shall become a man. About the year AD 2000, Antichrist will reveal himself to the world.'

1399 Catalan Dominican wandering preacher Vincent Ferrer (c1350-1419) reevangelizes and transforms Christendom throughout Europe; brings Jews to dialogues, converts 25,000 across Europe; preaches 6,000 apocalyptic sermons each 3 hours long, with glossolalia, healings, miracles widely reported; writes of future coming of Antichrist, predicts world will end after 2,537 more years in AD 3936 (based on number of verses in Book of Psalms).

c1400 Societas Peregrinantium pro Christo founded by Franciscans.

1420 Taborites, extreme militant wing of Bohemian Hussites at Tabor south of Prague, founded as strict biblicists under their bishop Nicholas of Pelhrimov, seek to establish Kingdom of God by force of arms and military campaigns including destruction of churches; finally defeated at Lipany in 1434, Tabor captured 1452.

1431 Council of Basle (17th Ecumenical Council): question of papal supremacy, and the Hussite heresy; edict orders all Jews to attend Christian sermons.

1450 Invention of printing (typography and the printing press) by Johannes Gutenberg (c1395-1468) at Mainz, Germany, in order to disseminate the Holy Scriptures across the world; 1455, inventor ruined financially by lawsuit; in 6 languages by 1478; by 1500, more than 100 printed editions of the Bible produced.

1455 German mystic Thomas a Kempis (c1380-1471) writes *The Imitation of Christ*; a major influence on evangelization.

1490 Large numbers of reform-minded beggar monks and priests itinerate preaching and witnessing, including Wolfgang Capito (1478-1541), Paul Speratus (1484-1551) bishop of Pomerania, Gabriel Zwilling (1487-1558), Johannes Brenz (1499-1570) and many others.

1493 Pope issues Demarcation Bull 'Inter Caetera', giving Portugal authority over Africa, much of Asia and later Brazil; Spain given authority over rest of world west of a north-south line 345 miles west of the Azores.

1499 German astrologer Johannes Stoeffler (1452-1531) predicts end of world by deluge on 20 February 1524; thousands then jam boats and 3-storey ark on river Rhine.

1500 Worldwide expansion of Christianity commences again, mainly through Spanish and Portuguese Catholics.

Countless predictions made during period 1500-1700 by churchmen and scholars about exact time of End of the World.

Total of saints and martyrs who are known by name, formally recognized or canonized by the churches, now numbers over 10,000; from 1500-1903, Rome recognizes 113 further canonizations and 547 beatifications; total by 1985, known by name, for all confessions: 50,000 (0.1% of grand total all martyrs by 1985, known and unknown); total effect on world evangelization has been incalculable.

1517 Leonardo da Vinci (1452-1519), greatest genius ever, artist, scientist, engineer, inventor (submarine, tanks, aircraft, parachute, helicopter, anatomy, 'Last Supper', etc), produces 'Visions of the End of the World' or 'Deluge', depicting with overpowering pictorial imagination the primal forces that rule nature.

c1520 Martin Luther (1483-1546) writes: 'The gospel will always be preached... It has gone out throughout the length and the breadth of the world... It is made known farther and farther, to those who have not heard it before', and 'The gospel preached by the Apostles in various languages, sounds forth even now till the end of time'; teaches that institution of papacy, and hence every pope (without singling individuals out), is Antichrist; expects Advent of Christ in 1558.

1523 Spanish monarch orders Cortes to enforce mass conversion of Amerindians across New World; in Mexico, Franciscans baptize over a million in 7 years, with at times 14,000 a day; by 1536, 6 million Amerindians baptized in 17 years in Mexico alone; c1550, 800,000 Peruvian Amerindians confirmed by one archbishop of Lima.

Ignatius Loyola (1491-1556) works in Palestine for conversion of Muslims; 1534, founds Society of Jesus, with missions around world (Japan by 1549); 1556, Society becomes leading missionary order with 1,000 Jesuits; peaks at 36,038 by 1965, falls to 25,550 in 1983 in 200 countries; official scope 'Defense and Propagation of the Faith through Preaching'.

Group of astrologers announce end of world will begin with destruction of London on 1 February 1524; 20,000 gather outside city on high ground; similar views widely held by alchemists and intellectuals; Paracelsus (1493-1541) expounds influences of stars and planets on man.

1528 Berne Disputation, with its 10 Theses, brings Reformation to city of Berne; Anabaptists insist that Great Commission applies to everyone who confesses Christ's name.

1530 Anabaptist leader Melchior Hofmann (1495-1543) predicts imminent end of world in AD 1533 with Strasbourg to be the New Jerusalem; followers (Melchiorites) sell all their possessions.

Luther and Calvin teach that Great Commission (Mark 16:15) was work of 1st-century Apostles only and expired with them.

1534 Anabaptist refugees from persecution seize city of Münster, found Kingdom of A Thousand Years, eject unbelievers, establish New Jerusalem; 1534 city captured, king John of Leiden executed; the major 16th-century millenarian outburst.

1536 Sculptor and painter Michelangelo Buonarroti (1475-1564) completes vast painting 'The Last Judgement' in Sistine Chapel, Vatican, a powerful fresco of the Day of Wrath inspired by Dante and medieval hymn 'Dies irae'.

*On The Only Way to Draw all Peoples to the True Religion* (De Unico *Vocationis Modo*, written by Bartolomé de Las Casas (1474-1566); 1544 as bishop of Chiapas, he implements strategy in Guatemala, but in rebellion 2 missionaries killed (one sacrificed to idol) with 30 native Christians.

1547 Nostradamus (Michel de Notredame, 1503-1566), astrologer and physician, makes extensive prophecies from 1547, first published as *The Centuries* in 1555; condemned by Roman Index in 1781; the most widely read seer of the Renaissance, in print continuously ever since, with vast literature of commentaries; end of world predicted for either 1666, or 1734, 1886, 1943, 2000, 2038 or 3797.

c1547 Anabaptists view Great Commission as binding on all church members.

c1550 Swiss theologian and Reformed bishop J. H. Bullinger (1504-1575) interprets numerology of Book of Revelation to show world will end in 1666.

1559 Anabaptists the only Reformed grouping to deliberately work for and obey Jesus' Great Commission, especially through Hutterian Brethren's itinerant evangelism.

1568 Commission of cardinals instituted in Rome by Pius V for foreign missions in East Indies, for Italo-Greeks, and for Protestant lands of Europe; 1573, congregation for conversion of infidels formed.

1580 Discalced (Reformed) Carmelite Sisters become a separate order; by 1983, 11,649 cloistered contemplative nuns in 727 monasteries; serving evangelization of the world in name of Christ by prayer and works of charity.

1584 Jesuit priest Alonso Sanchez drafts evangelistic scheme for invasion and military conquest of China; others plan for forcible baptism of all peoples of the world.

1588 Anglican parish priest Hadrian Saravia (1531-1613) becomes one of first non-Roman advocates of foreign missions, stressing binding validity of Matthew

*Continued overleaf*

*Table 27–22 continued*

28:19: 'The command to preach the gospel to the Gentiles pertained not only to the age of the apostles, but to all future times to the end of the world.' Consistorial Congregation erected in Rome, responsible for all matters concerning all Catholic bishops and dioceses across world except Eastern-rite and missionary jurisdictions; includes Pontifical Commission for Migration and Tourism; 1967, renamed Sacred Congregation for Bishops.

1589    Russian Orthodox patriarchate instituted ('The Third Rome'); 1700, Peter the Great orders christianization of Siberia, 1721 abolishes patriarchate, rules church directly; as state church, its missions expand across Europe, Central Asia, Persia, Siberia, 1685 China, 1743 Kamchatka, 1784 Alaska, 1861 Mongolia, 1861 Japan, 1898 Korea, by means of traders, merchants, colonists, soldiers, diplomats, exiles, settlers (1 million Russians in Siberia from 1700-1783), monks, bishops, missionaries; 1826, best epoch of Russian Orthodox missions begins; 1870, Orthodox Missionary Society founded by metropolitan of Moscow, I. Veniaminov (1797-1879), in 55 Russian dioceses; whole mission enterprise destroyed in 1917 Revolution.

1594    Scottish mathematician John Napier (1550-1617) invents logarithms in order to speed up his calculations of the number of the Beast (in Revelation 13:18); writes *Plaine Discovery of the Whole Revelation of Saint John* (1594).

1600    Italian occultist-philosopher Giordano Bruno (1548-1600) proposes Christ as great magician in a magico-religious system to replace contemporary organized Christianity; holds there are an infinity of worlds in Universe, many inhabited; burnt at stake by Inquisition.

c1600   Jesuit historian Gian Pietro Maffei publishes his massive history of Portuguese expansion in Asia, *L'Histoire*. In the preface he links global exploration, international trade and world evangelization.

c1600   Episcopi Vagantes (Wandering Bishops, or Bishops-at-Large, in 15 disputed or contested lines of apostolic succession) begin to multiply across Europe; 1866, Julius Ferrette as bishop of Iona begins their modern era; by 1975, 760 bishops-at-large lead 280 distinct autocephalous Catholic churches/denominations with 10,285,000 adherents in 80 countries; each proposes grandiose plan for reunion of Christendom and conversion of world, calling on Rome, Constantinople, Canterbury and Geneva to abandon their global pretensions and join each's new ecclesiastical body.

c1610   Dominican historian Tomas Malvenda (1566-1628) translates Hebrew Old Testament into Latin, writes treatise on coming of Antichrist.

1613    Major missionary work by Discalced Carmelite monk of Spain, Thomas a Jesu (1564-1627), *De procuranda salute omnium gentium*, urges and envisages conversion of entire world to Christ.

1620    Johann Gerhard (1582-1637), theologian of Lutheran orthodoxy, holds task of mission preaching was essentially completed by the New Testament Apostles.

1622    Sacred Congregations for the Propagation of the Faith (Propaganda, meaning dissemination or progressive plantation) founded by pope Gregory XV (1554-1623); 1967, renamed by pope Paul VI as SC for the Evangelization of Peoples.

1627    English biblical scholar Joseph Mede (1586-1638), a premillennialist, writes *Apocalyptica: Key of the Revelation*, formulates theory of progressive millennialism (later termed postmillennialism): Christ will only return at close of man-made millennium on Earth.

1630    F. Ingoli (1578-1649) publishes *Report on the Four Parts of the World* in Rome describing the work of the Propaganda Fide Congregation giving detailed strategies for the evangelization of the peoples of Africa, Asia and America.

1648    Spanish Jesuit Ildefonso de Flores (1590-1660) calculates total Christian martyrs of all epochs to date at 11 million; major impact of martyrdom on world evangelization recognized; his estimate agrees closely with later survey done in 1980-1990.

1656    Calvinist and Puritan statesman Oliver Cromwell (1599-1658), protector of Commonwealth of England, Scotland, and Ireland from 1653-1658, allows Jews prohibited since 1290 to return to England, in order to hasten Christ's Second Coming.

1657    Quint (Fifth) Monarchy Men (named from Daniel 2:44; after empires of Assyria, Persia, Greece, Rome, the Fifth is at hand as the Millennium), a Puritan sect, propose abolishing established church in England to bring about Parousia; 1657 and 1661, rise in armed revolt against Cromwell, but crushed.

1658    Death of Bartholomaus Holtzhauser after predicting Antichrist would reveal himself at age of 55 years; others assert he would do so at 30 years, thus parodying Jesus the Christ.

c1660   Peruvian Franciscan theologian G. Tenorio (1602-1682) publishes treatise extolling Peruvian Indian culture and predicting Millennium will be in Peru as center of the world church.

1663    Justinian von Weltz (1621-1668) writes treatises to challenge German churches, students and Pietists to missionary work among unevangelized peoples.

1667    English poet John Milton (1608-1674) in his *Paradise Lost* draws attention to the Christian goal 'To Evangelize the Nations'.

1680    Founding in Rheims of Christian Brothers (FSC) to teach Christian doctrine to the poor and working

---

classes across the world; by 1976, 12,641 lay brothers; by 1983, declines to 9.348.

1693    Italy: secret society Knights of the Apocalypse founded to defend church against the Antichrist.

1698    First 2 non-Roman missionary societies formed, by Church of England: Society for Promoting Christian Knowledge (SPCK), and (1701) Society for the Propagation of the Gospel in Foreign Parts (SPG); goal of world evangelization claimed, but in practice they work largely in British sphere of influence.

1699    Isaac Newton (164301727) publishes Observations upon the Prophecies of Daniel and The Apocalypse of St. John; calculates fall of apocalyptic beast for 1867 and the Millennium for the year AD 2000.

1700    Evangelistic campaigns in Germany of Ernst Christoph Hochmann von Hochenau (1670-1721), major separatist Pietist/Lutheran mystic of his time, converted 1693: 'Regarding the conversion of the Jews as the sign of Christ's impending return, he engaged briefly in Jewish missionary work.'

1703    Spiritans (CSSp, Holy Ghost Fathers) founded for 'Evangelizzazione degli infedeli'; by 1983, 857 houses with 3,671 missionaries.

1705    Origin of Danish-Halle Mission (Lutheran), forerunner of Protestant missionary societies; first workers include Protestant pioneers to Tranquebar (India): Barthlomew Ziegenbalg (1682-1719), Heinrich Plutschau (1677-1747) and Christian Schwartz (1726-1798).

1710    Canstein House printing press, Halle (Germany) with first Bible society (Cansteinische Bibelanstalt) founded by count Karl von Canstein: 3 million Bibles and NTs printed in 80 years.

1725    The Great Awakening, revival in New England (USA) spreading throughout the Thirteen Colonies; begun under T. J. Frelinghuysen in New Jersey; mass conversions of dechristianized European populations in North America, led by revivalist Jonathan Edwards (1703-1758), who expounds progressive millennialism (later called postmillennialism), envisaging establishment of Christ's millennial kingdom on Earth around year 1990, with Second Advent at close of millennium; Edwards calls for 'concerts of prayer' for world revival; Awakening lasts until 1770.

1730    Anglican priest, mathematician and divine William Whiston (1667-1752) announces imminent end of world by deluge with destruction of London on 13 October 1736; panic-stricken crowds rush for high ground.

1732    Moravian missions land in St. Thomas, West Indies; 1733, Greenland; 1736, among Samoyeds of Archangelsk; 1787, Society of the United Brethren for Propagating the Gospel among the Heathen, formed in Pennsylvania, USA; 1732-1862, Moravians send abroad 2,000 missionaries.

1770    French nun Jeanne Le Royer (1732-1798) predicts tribulation, coming of Antichrist, end of papacy, and end of world in AD 2000.

1774    United Society of Believers in Christ's Second Appearing (Shakers) founded in Niskeyuna, NY (USA) by Ann Lee and pilgrims from England as millennial messianic sect in New World, based on celibacy.

1780    Deutsche Christentumsgesellschaft (Christendom Society) begun in Germany to build kingdom of God on an ecumenical basis; 1815, members found Evangelische Missionsgesellschaft in Basel (Basel Mission).

1782    Concerts of Prayer (for revival and world mission), as envisaged by Jonathan Edwards, begin and spread in Britain, then from 1790 in USA; basis for subsequent worldwide missionary advance.

1783    Native Baptist Church, first Jamaican Afro-Christian movement, begun by ex-slave, George Lisle; plays a significant political role 80 years later; precursor of later End-time pentecostal renewal across world.

1785    Evangelical awakenings (revivals) throughout Wales under Howel Harris (1714-1773) and others; 1785 Brynengan, 1786 Trecastle, 1791 Bala, 1805 Aberystwyth, 1810 Llangeitho, 1817 Beddgelert, 1821 Denbighshire, 1822 Anglesey, 1828 Carmarthenshire, 1832 Caernarvonshire, 1840 Merionethshire, 1849 South Wales, et alia.

1787    English Baptist minister Andrew Fuller (1754-1815) writes *The Gospel of Christ Worthy of All Acceptation* and over 128 other titles, urges obedience to the Great Commission.

1792    William Carey (1761-1834) publishes first statistical global survey of Christian world mission: *An Enquiry Into the Obligations of Christians, to Use Means for the Conversion of the Heathens*, accurately enumerating populations and Christians on all continents in world's first statistical survey (world population 731 million; 57% pagan/Hindu/Buddhist, 18% Muslim, 14% RC, 6% Protestant, 4% Orthodox, 1% Jewish); 1793, sails for India under Particular Baptist Society for Propagating the Gospel Among the Heathen (formed 1792); at Serampore, initiates modern era of Protestant world missions, serves without home leave for 41 years in Bengal, translates and prints Bible in 35 languages.

1795    London Missionary Society begun; founders' 'vision of a world covered by missionary centers that would reach out and link up until there was no place where the gospel was not preached'.

1800    Widespread evangelistic camp meetings begin in USA; Kentucky Revival awakening, with crowds of up to 25,000, sweeps over Kentucky, Tennessee and the Carolinas.

1802    Massachusetts Baptist Mission Society formed 'for the

---

evangelization of frontier communities'.

1804    British & Foreign Bible Society (BFBS) founded, in London, with vision of providing Scriptures to whole world.

1805    First modern end-of-the-world novel: *Le dernier homme*, by French Catholic priest J.-B. Cousin de Grainville; over next 2 centuries, several hundred more such scenarios published.

1806    USA: Haystack Prayer Meeting at Williams College, Massachusetts, launches North America foreign missions, to preach the gospel to all nations; 1810, these students form Society of Inquiry on the Subject of Missions; soon after, ABCFM is formed.

1810    W. Carey conceives idea of regional ecumenical missionary conferences around globe; nothing results until 1825 Bombay and 1854 New York.
     Congregationalists in Massachusetts, USA, organize American Board of Commissioners for Foreign Missions (ABCFM) 'to devise, adopt and prosecute ways and means for propagating the gospel among those who are destitute of the knowledge of Christianity'; by 1880, 1,200 missionaries overseas; 1961, renamed United Church Board for World Ministries, 'to serve Christ in the world'; 1985, 229 foreign missionaries in 54 countries.

1811    American clergyman Ethan Smith of Vermont writes *Dissertation on the Prophecies Related to Antichrist and the Last Times*, concludes world will end in 1866.

1814    Society of Jesus reestablished by pope Pius VII (1742-1823) after 40 years' ban, with renewed interest in global mission and evangelization.

1815    H. Bardwell publishes sermon 'The duty and reward of evangelizing the heathen', preached in Newburyport, USA.
     Italian priest Caspar Del Bufalo (1786-1837) founds Missioners of the Most Precious Blood, with as 'his goal for his missioners the evangelization of the world' through charitable works.
     *The Spirit of British Missions* (London: by an Anglican clergyman of the Church Missionary Society) appeals for workers: 'The supply of Labourers in the great work of evangelizing the world is a most important topic.'

1818    *The Conversion of the World: or the Claims of 600 Millions, and the Ability and Duty of the Churches Respecting Them:* book by G. Hall & S. Newell (ABCFM, India); proposal to convert heathen millions across world by sending 30,000 Protestant missionaries from USA and Europe in 21 years, at cost of US$4 from each Protestant and Anglican communicant in Christendom.

1819    Missionary Society of Methodist Episcopal Church organized; 1939 constitution states 'The supreme aim of missions is to make the Lord Jesus Christ known to all peoples in all lands as their divine Saviour'; 1940, 1964, reorganized as Board of Global Ministries, United Methodist Church; 1974, 839 foreign missionaries (9.5% non-USA); 1985, 516 foreign missionaries in 50 countries.

c1820   Augustinian nun, mystic and seer Catherine Emmerich (1774-1824) of Westphalia has vision of Lucifer being unchained about 1940 and Antichrist working from 1960 onwards.

1823    Josiah Pratt's annual Survey of the World (CMS, London) headed 'The Conversion of the World dependent on the more abundant influence of the Holy Spirit'.

1824    USA: beginnings of interdenominational city-wide cooperative evangelism; spreads to cities across world.

1825    Bombay Missionary Union (Anglicans, Congregationalists, Presbyterians, et alii) formed; first interdenominational regional conferences of missionaries c1855 in India, 1872 Japan, 1873 first all-India decennial conference, 1877 China, c1885 Mexico, et alia.

1826    Glasgow City Mission founded by David Nasmiths, secretary of 23 Christian societies, first of 50 city missions begun in Britain's largest cities (Bristol, Chester, Edinburgh, Glasgow, Leeds, Liverpool, 1832 London, York, et alia); also 1833 New York City Mission, Boston, Brooklyn, etc; also 1848 Hamburg, 1874 Berlin, and 70 other German cities by 1899.

1827    J. N. Darby (1800-1882), Anglican clergyman, joins Christian Brethren movement in Dublin; propounds dogma of total premillennial apostasy and ruin of Christendom (the major churches); later develops 'dispensationalism', a new variety of futurist premillennialism, dividing biblical and later history into 7 eras or dispensations.

1828    Karl Gutzlaff (1803-1851), a Lutheran, begins work in Indonesia, Siam, southern China, Hong Kong; 1844, attempts to evangelize China in one generation through 300 evangelists.

1829    Christian Brethren begin foreign missions as A.N. Groves and party go out to Baghdad, then later to India; much later, loosely organized as Christian Missions in Many Lands; by 1965, 1,200 foreign missionaries in 55 countries.

1830    USA: widespread campaigns through professional evangelists Andrew, Barnes, Burchard, Baker, Caughey, Griffith, Inskip, Knapp, Maffit, Swan.
     Joseph Smith (1805-1844) at Fayette, NY (USA), has visions of incurable corruption of Christendom, and of divine restoration of Christ's church, which lead to establishment of Church of Jesus Christ of Latter-day Saints (Mormons); 1844, murdered by mob; movement migrates to Utah as headquarters of the coming millennial kingdom; subsequently evolves

*Continued opposite*

*Table 27–22 continued*

into massive heterodox organization unrelated to the rest of global Christianity, governed since 1844 by a Council of the Twelve Apostles; by 1988, its world mission includes 34,750 foreign missionaries (1-or 2-year termers) working in over 82 countries with annual mission budget of over US$550 million.

1831 Seminary president J.H. Rice calls Presbyterian Church in the US 'a Missionary Society, the object of which is to aid in the conversion of the world'.

1832 Catholic Apostolic Church founded in London, through work of Presbyterian Edward Irving; 1836, its Twelve Apostles, claiming to be the Restored Apostolate, in England address memorandum to all rulers of Europe warning them of imminent Second Advent of Christ, but are met with total apathy; by 1988, church is almost extinct.

1833 Dr. W.S. Plummer of Virginia convinces The American Bible Society (ABS) to cooperate with other societies to put a Bible in the hands of every family in the world within twenty years. One year later they drop phrase 'within twenty years' and plan collapses.

1836 Booklet produced by ABCFM: 'The Duty of the Present Generation to Evangelize the World: An Appeal from the Missionaries at the Sandwich Islands to their Friends in the United States'.

T.S. Skinner publishes *Thoughts on evangelizing the world* (New York).

1837 Board of Foreign Missions, Presbyterian Church in the USA established 'to aid in the conversion of the world... every member of this church is a member for life of said society and bound to do all in his power for the accomplishment of this object'; 1958, becomes Commission on Ecumenical Mission and Relations, for which 'The supreme and controlling aim of the Christian Mission to the world is to make the Lord Jesus Christ known to all men... in which Christians of all lands share in evangelizing the world and permeating all of life with the spirit and truth of Christ.'

ABCFM mission strategist Rufus Anderson (1796-1880) restores apostolic model for mission; in essay 'The Time for the World's Conversion Come', first published in 1837 journal, argues that the churches are now, for the first time ever in history (as a result of rise of voluntary mission societies), adequately organized to complete the conversion of the world.

1841 CMS general secretary Henry Venn (1796-1873) requires all missionaries to complete annual questionnaires recording church growth statistics, as a means of monitoring progress in world evangelization; propounds 'three-self' goal of mission that local churches must become self-supporting, self-governing, self-propagating.

1842 Date for end of Europe by deluge as predicted by Elizabethan astrologer John Dee (1527-1608); mobs take to boats to escape.

1843 *The Past and Prospective Extension of the Gospel by Missions to the Heathen*, written by British Anglican, Anthony Grant.

1844 Date for Second Advent of Christ as predicted in 1818 by Baptist prophet William Miller (1782-1849) in USA; afterwards, Seventh-day Adventist denomination emerges, interprets date as return of Christ to Earth for 'cleansing of the sanctuary'; 1860, General Conference of Seventh-day Adventists formed in USA 'committed to the task of giving to all nations God's last invitation to prepare for the Second Advent of Christ', and envisioning 'a world-wide proclamation of the gospel to every nation and kindred and tongue and people (Revelation 14:6)'; by 1985, in 210 countries (68 countries being served by 1,052 USA foreign missionaries).

Christadelphians (Brothers of Christ) founded in USA; pacifist, adventist, premillennialist, unitarian, congregational (1,530 churches called ecclesias), no clergy; holding conditional immortality, and an imminent Millennium with Jesus reigning in Jerusalem; 90,600 adherents in 1985.

First Young Men's Christian Association (YMCA) founded, by Evangelicals in London; 1855, World Alliance of YMCAs founded in Paris (France), with headquarters in Geneva, emphasizing 'extension of His Kingdom'; world vision, lay witness to Christ, global missionary thrust; 1894, World YWCA for women; subsequently, concerns broaden; 1988, 6.5 million men members in 74 National YMCA Movements and in 16 other countries; and 5 million women members.

1845 Southern Baptist Convention, largest USA Baptist denomination, comes into being in reaction against ABFMS refusing to accept slave-owners as missionaries; based from its origin on global mission, it founds Board of Domestic Missions (later, Home Mission Board) and Foreign Mission Board, beginning work in China, then 1846 Liberia and 1850 Nigeria; by 1988, has 7,000 full-time professional missionaries at home and abroad.

1846 Beginnings of world conciliarism: Evangelical Alliance formed in London by 800 Christians representing 52 confessions, to further unity among Evangelicals worldwide; national alliances then formed in Britain and Canada (1846), Sweden and Germany (1847), India (1849), Turkey (1855), USA (1867); and international conferences held in London 1851, Paris 1855, Berlin 1857, Geneva 1861, Amsterdam 1867, New York 1873, Basel 1879, Copenhagen 1884, Florence 1891, London 1896 and the final one in 1907; 1912, title officially changed to World's Evangelical Alliance (WEA).

1850 English mathematician John Taylor demonstrates Great Pyramid of Cheops contains divine prophecy covering all history; 1865, pyramidologist Robert Menzies shows internal passages form a chronological outline.

Death of French nurse and nun Bertine Bouquillon from St. Omer (France) after predicting: 'The end of time is near and Antichrist will not delay his coming.'

British Quaker millionaire and missions philanthropist Robert Arthington (1823-1900) donates millions to missionary societies and accumulates vast store of information on frontier evangelization of all peoples in world; 1900, his will expounds global strategy of (a) do a world survey of unreached peoples, (b) supply these peoples with translations of Luke, John and Acts, (c) teach 10 people in each tribe to read the gospel, (d) visit each tribe until a church emerges, (e) that tribe evangelizes the next, while (f) missionaries move on to regions beyond; Arthington is later followed by long series of eccentric millionaire philanthropist-strategists in Europe and USA.

1854 First Union Missionary Convention, in New York, USA, guided by Alexander Duff (1806-1878): 'To what extent are we authorized by the Word of God to expect the conversion of the world to Christ?'; similar conference held in London, England; 1867, Duff appointed to first chair of evangelism and evangelical theology at New College, Edinburgh.

Foreign Mission Committee, Canada Presbyterian Synod, inaugurated; 1962, becomes Board of World Mission, United Church of Canada, 'committed by its very nature to a global mission'.

c1855 Russian surge of world mission: Orthodox missiologist N.I. Ilminsky (1821-1891) works out scientific basis for missionary work; vast missionary expansion; 1870-1917, Orthodox Missionary Society organized (St. Petersburg, Russia); 1917, its world mission is destroyed by Bolshevik Revolution.

1857 USA: evangelist D.L. Moody (1837-1899), a Congregationalist, evolves organized mass evangelism in Chicago; during his lifetime estimated to have had individual evangelistic personal dealings with 750,000 persons; perfects methods of preparation and publicity in cooperative city campaigns, use of theaters and tents, finance committees; other evangelists R.A. Torrey (1856-1928), Billy Sunday (1862-1925), Robert P. Wilder (1863-1938); beginnings of large-scale lay-centered evangelism.

1858 Sermons on evangelization increase: 1858 J. Parker publishes 'The duty of the present generation of Christians to evangelize the world', New York; 1866 C. Dickson publishes 'The duty of the Church to evangelize the World', Presbyterian Church of the USA, New York.

1859 Founding of Society of St. Francis de Sales (Salesians of Don Bosco, SDB), a religious congregation dedicated to Christian education of youth across world; by 1975, 18426 men in 1,524 houses; by 1983, 16,982 in 1,466 houses; also 17,269 Salesian Sisters (FMA).

1860 Earl of Shaftesbury, British evangelical social reformer (A.A. Cooper, 1801-1885), states: 'Those who hold the truth have the means enough, knowledge enough, and opportunity enough, to evangelize the globe fifty times over'.

Reorganized Church of Jesus Christ of Latter Day Saints begun in schism by LDS founder's son, operating through a rival Council of the Twelve Apostles; 1954, publishes *Into all the world: Council of Twelve missionary report;* 1975, branches in 28 nations (HQ Independence, MO), 1986 in 37 countries.

1861 USA: Woman's Union Missionary Society of America for Heathen Lands (WUMSA) formed in New York as pioneer women's sending society, with 40 other women's societies arising later.

1862 Founding of Congregation of Immaculate Heart of Mary (Scheutists, CICM) with as goal 'Evangelizzazione dei popoli'; by 1983, 1,507 members in 53 houses; over the years many Scheutist missionaries have been martyred.

1863 Universal Catholic Church (later renamed New Apostolic Church) founded in Germany by excommunicated German prophet H. Geyer of Catholic Apostolic Church (UK), emphasizing a successional apostolate subject to a chief apostle with quasi-papal powers, and the gifts of the Holy Spirit including prophecy, tongues, miraculous healing, sacraments, hierarchy of 48 living Apostles; by 1988, has 1.7 million members worldwide (mainly Germans) in 45 countries; cooperates with no other church.

1865 Christian Revival Association (1878, renamed Salvation Army) founded by Methodist evangelist William Booth in England for urban social outreach and street evangelism; 1985, 4,226,900 Salvationists in 75 countries, with vast social service and evangelistic activities and institutions; overriding first agenda defined in 1987 by SA general as 'To emphasize the supremacy of evangelism in fulfilling of the Lord's great commission... To work to the end that every man and woman and child has the opportunity to hear the good news of the gospel'.

1867 Beginnings of confessional conciliarism: archbishop of Canterbury C.T. Longley (1794-1868) convenes first decennial Lambeth Conference of all bishops of Anglican Communion (London), with 76 bishops present; 1875, origin of World Alliance of Reformed Churches and 1876 World Methodist Council; by 1983, grand total of 45 world confessional councils are in existence, representing all major Christian traditions, and all with own approaches to world mission.

Founding of Combonians (MCCI/FSCI/MFSC) with as goal 'Evangelizzazione dei popoli, non ancora o non sufficientemente evangelizzati', by 1983, 1,938 missionaries.

1869 Anglican Broad Church Evangelical, F.W. Farrar, later dean of Canterbury, describes Europeans as God's chosen evangelizers: 'The Aryan should advance farther and farther to... the evangelization of the whole habitable globe.'

1870 Rise of first megaministry (reaching over 1% of world per annum, i.e. 14 million people a year): BFBS, ABS and other Bible societies' distribution reaches 38,000 scriptures a day.

Pan-Orthodox world missions emerge: Orthodox Missionary Society organized in Russia by metropolitan of Moscow, I. Veniaminov (1797-1879); branches in 55 Russian dioceses; rapid missionary expansion; by 1900, Russians form largest single Christian ethnolinguistic people in whole world; 1917, Bolsheviks destroy Russian world missions; 1959, Pan-Orthodox world mission reorganized based on Athens (Greece).

Churches of Christ (Non-Instrumental), schism from Disciples of Christ, organize in USA; by 1985, they send out 982 foreign missionaries in 74 countries, with related churches in total of 141 countries.

Watch Tower Bible and Tract Society begun in USA through Charles T. Russell (1852-1916), who predicts Second Advent for 1874, later for 1914; 1879 launches magazine *Zion's Watchtower and Herald of Christ's Presence;* publishes classic, *Divine Plan of the Ages;* known at first as Russellites or Millennial Dawnists, later it becomes International Bible Students Association, then in 1931 Jehovah's Christian Witnesses (or Jehovah's Witnesses); by 1986, world's largest single missionary agency.

1871 Sermon before Baptist Missionary Society (London) by former BMS secretary Joseph Angus, entitled 'Apostolic Missions: the Gospel for Every Creature', claims gospel could be preached to every creature on Earth by 1886 or 1891 at latest; his sermon later read by USA Presbyterian theologian, Bible expositor and dispensationalist A.T. Pierson (1837-1911), who by 1876 conceives idea of a Watchcry (Watchword), supported by 1877 Shanghai missions conference, and in 1877 begins public addresses on a concrete plan for evangelizing the world.

1872 Salesian Sisters (FMA) founded, in Italy, for world mission by prayer and works of charity; by 1983, 17,269 nuns, in 60 countries.

1873 East London Institute for Home and Foreign Missions formed (UK); 1900, renamed Regions Beyond Missionary Union invoking Apostle Paul's' world vision (2 Corinthians 10:16); by 1985, 103 North American missionaries in 5 countries, 58 British in 5 countries, with total 200 missionaries of all nationalities.

1874 *Signs of the Times* magazine (originally begun in 1842 as an End-Times newspaper) reorganized as denominational organ by USA Seventh-day Adventists; by 1988, in many languages, with 300,000 monthly distribution in English alone.

1875 Founding of Society of the Divine Word (Verbites, SVD), in Steyl (Netherlands), with as goal 'Evangelizzazione dei Popoli'; by 1983, 5,413 members in 280 houses on all continents.

1876 Watchcry (Watchword) conceived by A.T. Pierson.

1877 Shanghai, China: 1st General Foreign Missions Conference, with 473 missionaries from 20 Protestant societies; states 'We want China emancipated from the thraldom of sin in this generation'; probable origin, among field missionaries, of Watchword 'The Evangelization of the World in This Generation'; similar conferences in 1890 and 1907.

*Missionary Review of the World* periodical published in USA by Royal Wilder.

1880 Circulation of Watchcry (Watchword) on various Protestant mission fields becomes crystallized in 1885 article by A.T. Pierson entitled 'A plan to evangelize the world', published in his journal *The missionary review of the world* after 20 years of reflection; Pierson calls for 'an ecumenical council solely to plan a world-wide campaign and proclaim the good tidings to every living soul in the shortest time'.

1881 United Society of Christian Endeavor formed in USA; 1895, World's Christian Endeavor Union organized (38,000 societies across world, with 2,225,000 members); 1927, International Society of Christian Endeavor; by 1965, 3 million members in 85 Protestant denominations in 80 countries; by 1987, 2 million in 78 nations.

1882 Knights of Columbus (K of C) founded by Rev. Michael J. McGivney in New Haven, Connecticut, USA. Members promote the instruction of the Catholic faith and are active in religious and charitable projects.

1884 Founding in USA of magazine 'the Christian Century' dedicated to proposition that the Kingdom of Christ will dominate the world at end of 20th century by AD 2000.

A.O. Van Lennep publishes statistical survey *The Growth of Christianity during Nineteen Centuries* (New York), blaming inadequate growth on lack of giving (in USA, annual per capita expenditure on alcohol is $49.70 but on foreign missions only $0.05);

*Continued overleaf*

*Table 27–22 continued*

concludes 'When Christ's Church shall be as lavish in its outlay of men and money as the world is, the conversion of Nations will not long be postponed'.

1885 At D.L. Moody's Northfield Convention for lay workers, A.T. Pierson chairs committee to 'divide the world according to a comity agreement' and then pursue 'the immediate occupation and evangelization of every destitute district of the earth's population', so that 'the entire current population of the earth would hear the gospel by the year 1900'; Moody prepares in 3 days 'An Appeal to Disciples Everywhere', claiming task could be completed even if only 10 million active Christians participated.

1886 1st International Christian Student Conference, Mount Hermon, Massachusetts, addressed by D.L. Moody, A.T. Pierson, et alii; 251 attenders.

1887 Christian and Missionary Alliance organized in USA; 1975, Alliance World Fellowship founded, in 51 nations; by 1985, 874 USA foreign missionaries in 50 countries.

1888 Student Volunteer Movement for Foreign Missions organized with 2,200 initial volunteers, based on Watchword 'The Evangelization of the World in This Generation'; 1892, Student Volunteer Missionary Union (SVMU) begun in Britain; by 1945, as a result of SVM, a total of 25,000 university graduates have gone overseas as foreign missionaries.

Seventh-day Adventist prophet since 1855, Ellen G. White (1827-1915), publishes *The Great Controversy* on Jehovah's cosmic dispute, writes 44 other major books and over 4,000 articles.

One By One Band started in London by T. Hogben as 'a worldwide fellowship devoted wholly to winning men to Christ', based on Hogben's book *God's plan for soul winning.*

1889 Japan: 500 Japanese students at Student Conference send telegram to SVM Conference, Northfield (USA), urging 'Make Jesus King'.

SVM chairman John R. Mott writes to sister Hattie that the task of world evangelization will be accomplished by the dawn of the 20th century.

1890 Scandinavian Alliance Mission of North America founded for world-wide evangelism and church planting; 1949, renamed TEAM (The Evangelical Alliance Mission); 1985, 929 USA missionaries in 25 countries.

'The Gospel Can and Ought to be Preached to the Whole Heathen, Jewish, and Mohammedan World in the Next Ten Years' circulated by USA Presbyterian J.L. Stevens.

1891 *The encyclopedia of missions: descriptive, historical, biographical, statistical,* edited H.O. Dwight et al (Bureau of Missions, New York, 851 pages), with massive details and articles on missions in all countries, peoples, languages, and in 5,000 cities, towns, and villages (data on all places in non-Christian lands).

1893 Sudan Interior Mission begun as Africa Industrial Mission in order to evangelize the world's largest single totally unevangelized area with no resident missionary among 90 million people (Africa's 4,000-mile Sahel and Soudan); 1982, renamed SIM International, expands to Latin America; 1985, 654 missionaries in 15 countries.

1894 *Essay on the prevailing methods of the evangelization of the non-Christian world* written by R.N. Cust, a critical survey of methods of missionary societies.

1895 L.D. Wishard writes *A new programme of missions: a movement to make the colleges in all lands centers of evangelization.*

Association of Pentecostal Churches in America (1919, renamed Church of the Nazarene) formed, 1897 begins foreign missions; by 1987, World Mission Division has 617 foreign missionaries in 84 countries, with two AD 2000 programs: Thrust to the Cities ('maximizing holiness evangelism in key cities') and Two Million Adherents by 1995.

World Student Christian Association/Federation (WSCF) emerges from Vadstena Castle meeting, Sweden, begun by SCMs around world whose 'aim was to claim students—the future leaders of their nations—for Christ and for the evangelization of the world'; after 1914, non-evangelistic interests predominate (leadership, social issues, universities, Christian presence, etc); 1987, over 3 million members and participants.

1896 'Make Jesus King'; International Students Missionary Conference, Liverpool; 800 students from 24 nations.

1897 4th Lambeth Conference; 194 Anglican bishops present; first of 14 resolutions on foreign missions passed: 'We recommend that prompt and continuous efforts be made to arouse the Church to... the fulfilment of our Lord's great commission to evangelize all nations'.

House of Laymen, Province of Canterbury (Church of England) resolves: 'In view of the Great Commission to evangelize the world, its long and serious neglect... the whole Church needs rousing on this question'.

Encyclical letter 'On the Holy Spirit' issued by pope Leo XIII, directing attention to the 7-fold gifts of the Spirit (Isaiah 11) and promoting universal novena (9-day cycle of prayer) to Holy Spirit before Pentecost Sunday each year; millions influenced.

Arabia, and the world, 'could easily be evangelized within the next 30 years if it were not for the wicked selfishness of Christians'—Samuel Zwemer, Apostle to Islam (1867-1952).

1899 Gideons International begun, for free distribution of Bibles; by 1965, active in 75 countries rising to 133 by 1985 and 137 by 1988, with 30,000 overseas members; 1987, 24 million Bibles distributed, with grand total 400 million placed over 89 years.

At end of 'Golden Age of Jewish Missions' (=19th century), over 200,000 Jews have been baptized as Protestants, and similar numbers as Roman Catholics; 650 Protestant missionaries minister to Jews at 213 mission stations across world; many believe future conversion of the Jews could ensure completion of world evangelization.

1900 New York Ecumenical Missionary Conference: 2,500 members, 200,000 attenders; delegates from 162 mission boards; 500 speakers, huge public meetings; formation of an international missionary committee (to complete world missionary task) canvassed, urged, then unanimously adopted only to fizzle out soon after.

Methodist layman John R. Mott publishes classic, *The evangelization of the world in this generation;* many Christian strategists envisage winning of entire world to Christ during 20th century, then seen as certain to be 'the Christian century'.

Origins of Pentecostalism in USA: British-Israelite holiness preacher Charles F. Parham (1873-1929, Methodist) opens Bethel Bible School near Topeka, Kansas, with 40 students; 1901, they receive baptism of Holy Spirit; 1903 revival spreads through Kansas, 1905 Houston, 1906 to Los Angeles and thence across world (1906 Norway, 1907 Chile, 1908 China, 1909 Korea, 1910 Brazil, and so on).

Total of all Christian denominations begins to rise steeply as Christianity spreads across world, from only 92 in AD 1000, to 150 in AD 1500, to 510 in AD 1800, to 1,900 by AD 1900; then by 1985 to 22,000; proliferation seen by many in 1900 as a sure guarantee that world will soon become evangelized.

1901 Latter-Rain teaching: after 1,800 years of apparent cessation of large-scale charismata and 100 years of expectancy and teaching in USA on gifts of the Spirit, 'restoration of all things' begins with Spirit-baptism and glossolalia, as pentecostal power is restored to the church; thousands of seekers travel to revival centers in USA, Europe, Asia, South America; expounded in D.W. Myland, *The Latter Rain Pentecost* (1910).

Founding of Consolata Missionary Fathers (IMC), in Turin, specifically for 'Evangelizzazione degli infedeli'; by 1983, 1,008 foreign missionaries in 248 houses.

1902 Young People's Missionary Education Movement (1911, title shortened to MEM) founded by 15 USA denominational boards, YMCA and SVMU, to enlist missionaries outside college world.

*Centennial survey of foreign missions* (New York) published by J.S. Dennis, covering statistics of all Protestant missions worldwide.

4th International Convention, Student Volunteer Movement for Foreign Missions, in Toronto, Canada, produces 691-page report *Worldwide evangelization, the urgent business of the Church.*

1903 All Nations Flag Church (Church of God of Prophecy) founded, 1911 begins work overseas (Bahamas); by 1985, links with 69 countries.

1904 Welsh revival through ministry of Evan Roberts (1878-1951) in Glamorganshire, Anglesey, Caernarvonshire, with 100,000 converts in Wales in 6 months; short-lived (1904-1906), but literally sweeps the world; worldwide publicity from the press; leads into worldwide Pentecostal movement including 1905 Switzerland and Germany, 1907 England.

Premillennialist theologian W.E. Blackstone (1841-1935) writes *The Millennium,* teaches world has already been evangelized (cities Acts 2:5, 8:4, Mark 16:20, Colossians 1:23).

1905 National conciliarism begins: 1905 Fédération Protestante de France, 1908 Federal Council of the Churches of Christ in North America (1950 NCCCUSA), 1922 National Christian Council of China, 1922 Aliança Evangélica de Angola, et alia, up to 550 nationwide councils by 1983, all in theory committed to world mission.

1906 Proliferation of world mission atlases, both Protestant (1906, 1910, 1925, 1938) and RC (1906, 1913, 1929), with statistics listed by mission societies or RC dioceses rather than by denominations and countries.

C.F. Parham teaches that missionaries need only to receive the baptism with the Holy Ghost and can then, through the gift of glossolalia, be immediately understood in native languages to the farthest corners of the world; but Pentecostal missionaries abroad try this only to report failure.

1st General Conference of Missionaries to the World of Islam, convened through Reformed missionary S.M. Zwemer, held in Cairo, Egypt.

Laymen's Missionary Movement (LMM) launched as foreign missions auxiliary agency via SVM and 17 major North American Protestant denominations; uses large city-wide conferences, crusade dinners, business methods, publicity etc; by 1916, one million men have attended its 3,000 conferences, quadrupling USA Protestant mission giving.

1907 R.H. Benson writes novel *Lord of the World,* about final struggle between Antichrist and Christ, with Armageddon and Advent, in 21st century, with Catholicism as only surviving form of religion in an atheistic world state; over period 1800-1988, numerous other science fiction authors incorporate same theme in published books and articles.

Laymen's Missionary Movement of Southern Baptists formed by 200 laymen 'for mobilized laymen to evangelize our world in our lifetime', asserting that 'Southern Baptists are able financially and otherwise to conquer the world for Christ'; 1927, renamed Baptist Brotherhood of the South; 1938, goal of 'A Million Men for Christ'; 1950, Brotherhood Commission of SBC; 1987, enrollment 572,987 including 235,687 boys under 18 years.

1908 J.L. Barton publishes *The unfinished task of the Christian church: introductory studies in the problem of the world's evangelization* (CVMU, London): 'Some have taken it to mean the complete christianization of all races and peoples on earth; others, giving every person on earth an opportunity to hear at least one address or sermon.'

S.D. Gordon publishes *Quiet talks with world winners* outlining a plan to evangelize the whole world by prayer, renewal, evangelism, and financial support.

1910 World Missionary Conference, Edinburgh, Scotland (previously called 3rd Ecumenical Missionary Conference until 1908 change); 1,355 delegates; beginning of 20th-century ecumenical movement; report of Commission I is entitled *Carrying the Gospel to all the non-Christian world,* stating 'The Church is confronted today with a literally world-wide opportunity to make Christ known', and including survey 'Unoccupied sections of the world'.

Reunion of Christendom through organic union of denominations set forth as goal by bishop C.H. Brent (1862-1929) of Protestant Episcopal Church in the USA, as essential stage to conversion of world.

Pope Pius X (1835-1914) at General Chapter of the Franciscans has vision in public of future destruction of Vatican; teaches that Anti-christ has already arrived in atheistic and pagan society of his day; condemns modernism and modernist scholarship.

N. Maclean writes *Can the world be won for Christ?* (London).

Men and Religion Forward Movement (MRFM, 1910-12) advances LMM concerns into a global social gospel organization, but includes nationwide evangelism, social-evangelism crusades, home and foreign missions, business ethics, detailed research on 70 cities, and every kind of Christian endeavor; reaches 1,492,646 persons in 60 USA towns through 7,062 meetings; 1913, carried worldwide by touring party.

Church of God (Cleveland) 'initiates efforts at world evangelism', begins World Missions in Bahamas, Egypt and Cuba; by 1985, 109 foreign missionaries with churches in 98 countries; 1987, elaborate plan Decade of Destiny announced for every year 1988-1999.

J.W. Bashford writes *God's missionary plan for the world* (London).

1911 S.M. Zwemer publishes *Unoccupied mission fields of Africa and Asia.*

1912 *International review of missions begins publications;* editor J.H. Oldham (1874-1969).

First attempt by a mission body to reach systematically every home in an entire nation: 1912-17 in Japan, Oriental Missionary Society reaches its 10,300,000 homes; later extended to other countries, then to world.

1913 English missionary C.T. Studd (1862-1931), deeply impressed by report *Carrying the Gospel,* founds Christ's Etceteras (later renamed Worldwide Evangelization Crusade) to focus on evangelizing 'the remaining unevangelized parts (peoples) of the world'.

United Missionary Campaigns across USA under LMM, Foreign Missions Conference of North America, and Home Missions Council of USA; 695 Protestant interdenominational conferences held by 1916.

1914 Newly-elected pope Benedict XV (1854-1922) issues encyclical declaring World War I to be beginning of the Last Age: 'It seems as if the days foretold by Christ had indeed come: "You shall hear of wars and rumours of wars. For nation shall rise against nation, and kingdom against kingdom" (Mt 24.6-7)'.

USA Protestantism attempts to defuse militarism by forming Church Peace Union, also World Alliance for International Friendship (Constance, Germany, on day World War I begins); based on conviction that worldwide Christian forces could 'mobilize for a warless world'; USA's militaristic cause identified with Christ's Great Commission; 1919, Life and Work Committee formed independent of World Alliance, convenes conference 1920 at Geneva.

Date of inauguration of Kingdom of God on Earth by Jehovah (with invisible Second Coming of Christ), as predicted by Watch Tower Bible and Tract Society; subsequent dates announced for Armageddon: 1925, 1941, 1975.

1915 Elim Foursquare Gospel Alliance and Revival Party begun in Britain by Pentecostal healer G. Jeffreys (1889-1962); 1935, founds World Revival Crusade.

1916 World Dominion Movement founded in Britain (1924, Survey Application Trust), publishes long series of detailed surveys of missions by countries by Anglican lay leader Kenneth G. Grubb (1900-1980) and others; formally closed in 1968.

J.H. Oldham publishes *The world and the gospel,* contending that the evangelization of the world depends on spiritual authority and power rather than on resources of men and money.

1917 True Jesus Church (Chen Ye-Su Chiao Hui) begun in Peking, a charismatic schism ex Apostolic Faith

*Continued opposite*

*Table 27-22 continued*

Movement; by 1975, a Chinese world mission with missionaries serving in Hong Kong, India, Indonesia, Japan, Korea, Malaysia, Singapore and USA.

Interdenominational Foreign Mission Association of North America (IFMA) founded 'to make possible a united testimony concerning the existing need for a speedy and complete evangelization of the world', organized by SAGM, CIM, CAM, AIM, SIM, SAIM, WUMSA and later other Protestant missions of fundamentalist stance: 1967, 44 member missions with 8,500 missionaries in over 100 countries; 1979, 49 agencies with over 9,000 in over 115 countries; 1985, 103 nondenominational agencies in USA and Canada with over 11,000 foreign missionaries (over 8,000 from North America).

1918 Worldwide Evangelism, a vision of Pentecostal evangelist Aimee S. McPherson (1890-1944), who then in 1922 broadcasts first radio sermon, and in 1923 founds Angelus Temple, Los Angeles, and the International Church of the Foursquare Gospel.

USA Methodists launch Christian Crusade for World Democracy, to further Protestant missionary expansion.

USA Presbyterian executives believe the War experience justifies 'Protestant Christianity in launching a united drive for world evangelism'.

Interchurch World Movement of North America (IWM) launched to seek 'complete evangelization of all life' and 'conquest of the world for Christ' in one massive 'forward movement'; vast support from entire range of 34 major USA denominations and 85% all USA Protestant missions; 1919, motto 'The giving of the whole Gospel to the whole world by the whole church'; aims to include virtually all church-related activity; 1920, World Survey Conference, Atlantic City (NJ) with 1,700 church leaders produces massive 2-volume World Survey books, with plan proposing evangelization of world within 3 years; 1920, member denominations raise its $336,777,572 budget but refuse to release it; in 7-day period, IWM collapses in financial fiasco and bankruptcy.

1919 International Missionary Council (IMC) launched (directly succeeding Continuation Committee of 1910 World Missionary Conference, Edinburgh) with preliminary conference in Crans, Switzerland, then in 1921 (1-6 October) formally constituted and founded at Lake Mohonk, NY (USA); 2nd meeting in Oxford, England, in 1923.

1920 Interchurch World Movement, before its own disintegration, proposes (1) a federal 'United Churches of Christ in America', and (2) a global 'League of Denominations' (parallel to League of Nations); both proposals fizzle out.

Ecumenical Patriarchate of Constantinople issues encyclical addressed to 'all the Churches of Christ' calling for formation of a 'League of Churches'.

Catholic missiologist P. Charles (1883-1954) of Louvain identifies goal of mission as the founding or planting of the visible church in all lands and in all cultural groups (Charles, *Etudes missiologiques,* 1956).

Mennonite Central Committee begun in Akron, PA (USA); many varieties of development services; by 1985, 527 foreign missionaries in 50 countries, based on long Anabaptist/Mennonite centrality of the Great Commission.

General Council of Cooperating Baptist Missions of North America organized; first vision to evangelize Africa extended in 1924 to Venezuela, then to worldwide outreach; 1953, renamed Baptist Mid-Missions; 1965, 725 USA missionaries in 27 countries; 1985, 636 missionaries in 32 countries.

1921 Institute of Social and Religious Research, New York, organized under J.R. Mott to carry on IWM's socioreligious scientific surveys; lasts until 1934.

Oxford Group formed in Britain (1921-38), later renamed Moral Re-Armament (MRA); as evangelical renewal centering on personal devotion to Christ, the 4 Absolutes, personal evangelism, and 'drawing-room evangelism', spreads rapidly through major denominations and across world; by 1950 no longer solely christocentric, embracing renewal among Buddhists, Hindus, et alii.

General Council of the Assemblies of God USA appoints committee on worldwide cooperation for 'the calling of a conference for the formation of an ecumenical union of Pentecostal believers for the more perfect and rapid evangelization of the world'; committee proves unable to meet and the effort collapses by 1923.

Origins of global electronic church; first broadcast of a church worship service (Calvary Episcopal Church, Pittsburgh, USA), first Baptist broadcast, 1922; first Pentecostal broadcast (Aimee S. McPherson); by 1988, regular listeners/viewers for Christian programs numbers 1.2 billion (24% of the world).

Roman Catholic organization Legion of Mary organized by small group of laypeople in Dublin, Ireland. Members required to lead an exemplary Christian life, attend weekly prayer meetings, and spend two hours a week in apostolic work; by AD 2000, mainly charismatics with 10 million lay RCs involved, mainly in Africa and Asia.

1922 First International Missionary Congress, at Utrecht (Roman Catholic), accession of pope Pius XI (1857-1939), who issues encyclical 'Miserimus Redemptor' stating: 'These are really the signs of the last age as was announced by Our Lord'; in further encyclical 'Ubi arcano', defines Catholic Action (long-existing organizations in Latin Europe for lay witness to Christ in everyday life) as 'participation of laymen in the hierarchical apostolate'.

1923 BBC (Britain) commences radio broadcasting, including daily Christian programmes; in USA, 10 churches now operate radio stations; by 1928, 60 stations, failing by 1933 to 30; in 1936, BBC commences religious television.

*Evangelism in the modern world* (London) written by Methodist minister, E.A. French and 9 other scholars, using definition 'Evangelism is the proclamation of good news.'

c1923 Million Testaments Campaigns founded in Philadelphia, USA, by journalist G.T.B. Davis, for scripture distribution in needy areas including China, Latin America, and the Jewish world.

1924 USA: White ministers all withdraw from interracial Pentecostal Assemblies of the World (Unitarian Pentecostals) to form a separate white denomination, explaining that 'the mixture of races prevents the effective evangelization of the world'; becomes The Pentecostal Church, Incorporated.

United Pentecostal Church International begun in USA; by 1985, Foreign Missions Division has 212 foreign missionaries in 50 countries.

1925 Universal Christian Conference on Life and Work, Stockholm (Sweden), on economics, industry, social and international problems; 600 official church delegates from 37 countries.

*World missionary atlas* produced by H.P. Beach & C.H. Fahs (New York); largest missions atlas to date.

1926 R.E. Speer writes *The unfinished task of foreign missions.*

Lighthouse of International Foursquare Evangelism (LIFE Bible College) begun by Aimee S. McPherson in Los Angeles, USA, for training in world mission and evangelism.

1927 1st World Conference on Faith and Order, Lausanne; over 400 delegates from 90 churches (Roman Catholics being forbidden by pope).

Association of Baptists for Evangelism in the Orient (ABEO) formed; 1939, name changed to ABWE (WE=World Evangelism); 1985, 462 missionaries in 21 countries.

G.H. Williams writes 'The evangelization of the world', in J. Marchant (ed), *The future of Christianity.*

1928 IMC researcher C.H. Fahs publishes exceptionally detailed world survey volume, *The unfinished evangelistic task* (London) for 1928 IMC Jerusalem Meeting 'to call attention primarily to unreached non-Christians', and to elaborate on 'the missionary obligation to extend the Christian witness over the whole surface of the globe'.

World Fundamental Baptist Missionary Fellowship (later, World Baptist Fellowship Mission) founded in Texas; its 'purpose is to help to fulfill the Great Commission by the evangelization of the world' through indigenous Baptist churches; 1985, 126 missionaries in 23 countries.

Roman Catholic organization Opus Dei (Latin: 'God's work') founded in Spain by Josemaria Esriva de Balaguer y Albas, a priest with legal and journalistic training. Members pledge to seek personal Christian perfection and strive to implement Christian ideals in their chosen occupations.

1929 Congregationalist missionary Frank C. Laubach (1884-1970) begins 'Each one teach one' method in Philippines, develops literacy primers for 300 languages worldwide; 1950, publishes *Literacy as evangelism.*

1930 Movement for World Evangelization (Mildmay Movement) begun in London to generate converts worldwide as 'God's key representatives' in the entire global range of secular worlds, leading to world evangelization within one generation; begins with world survey, with on-the-spot surveys of every mission field on Earth, publishes *World dominion;* 1955, begins annual Christian Holiday Crusade at Filey (UK); gradually abandons original global plan in order to supply evangelists and ministerial conferences for Britain, later for Portugal, Spain, India, Australia, New Zealand, et alia.

Formation of World Council for Life and Work, replacing Continuation Committee of 1925 Stockholm Conference.

Voice of Prophecy radio broadcasts begun by USA Seventh-day Adventists; by 1982, heard on 1,900 radio stations worldwide, in 57 languages; total all SDA broadcasts 4,646 weekly radio and TV, in 80 languages; 1986, related Bible correspondence schools around world number 180 in 77 languages with 520,167 annual enrollments (20,419 in English in USA) with 281,345 graduating.

'The Lutheran Hour' broadcast over station WHK in Cleveland, Ohio, begun by LCMS; 1931, heard by 5 million a week, 1943 15 million, 1965 30 million in 120 countries over more than 1,000 radio stations; 1940, foreign broadcasting now named Bringing Christ to the Nations; 1945, worldwide to 20 million a week; 1975, broadcast in over 50 languages, heard by 22 million a week; 1987, 40 million regular listeners in 34 languages around world.

International Missions (originally The India Mission) founded in USA, by B. Davidson, 'dedicated to the propagation of the gospel in obedience to the Great Commission, the ultimate goal being the establishing of self-supporting and self-propagating New Testament churches in all fields'; 1985, 159 missionaries in 12 countries.

Foundation Farthest Out begun as 'a world-belt of prayer around the world'; renamed Association of Campus Farthest Out (CFO International, USA) as 'one of the vital instruments that God is using to establish the Kingdom of God on the Earth'; 1988, prayer camps in 85 countries.

1931 Unevangelized Fields Mission (UFM) founded in London, UK; 1980, renamed UFM International; 1985, 338 missionaries in 12 countries.

Radio Vatican inaugurated in Rome by Pius XI (1857-1939); entrusted to Jesuits; daily announcement motto 'Laudetur Jesus Christus' (Praised be Jesus Christ); 1975, broadcasts to 157 countries in 32 languages for 16 hours a day; 1982, John Paul II inaugurates Vatican Television; 1987, in 35 languages.

World-Wide Prayer & Missionary Union founded (Chicago), serving 50 evangelical missions agencies.

1932 Conference of Bible Societies, London, discusses ways and means of international cooperation to bring the Scriptures to the whole world.

1933 Pentecostal preacher W.M. Branham (1909-1965) offends mainline Pentecostal denominations by prophesying that 1906-1977 is the Laodicean Church Age, followed immediately by mass apostasy, Second Advent of Christ, and the Millennium in 1977; Branhamites (followers) claim him as Last Prophet with messianic attributes.

Origin of the Navigators, a one-by-one disciple-making agency based on multiplication theory/process 'to contribute to the fulfilment of the Great Commission'; 1985, 191 overseas personnel in 30 countries.

1934 *Jesus Christ and world evangelization* published by Alexander McLeish (World Dominion Press): 'Evangelization is not civilization or Christianization'.

Britain: Inter-Varsity Missionary Fellowship, meeting in Fountains Abbey, announces its new variant of SVMU Watchword: 'Evangelize to a finish to bring back the King'.

Biblical Research Society publishes a 7-volume Messianic Series by D.L. Cooper, printing 6 million copies, distributed through 150 branches to Jews worldwide: 'These books will remain behind after the Rapture and will be read during the Tribulation by the 144,000 Jewish evangelists of Revelation 7 who will then produce worldwide revival.'

W. Cameron Townsend begins Wycliffe Bible Translators for scripture translation by professional linguists, with overseas work under name Summer Institute of Linguistics (SIL); 1959, slogan 'Two Thousand Tongues To Go' coined; by 1985, 3,022 translators serving overseas in 55 countries, aiming to translate Scriptures into every remaining tribal language on Earth.

First Youth for Christ rally in Brantford, Ontario, under Paul Guiness; 1944, YFC International begun, first in USA cities, as a worldwide evangelistic movement 'specializing in aggressive teen-age evangelism'; 1948, first of 12 annual world congresses of evangelism (Switzerland, Tokyo, Caracas, Mexico City, São Paulo, et alia); in 95 nations by 1987, now attempting to identify 600 Pacesetters to raise up a worldwide youth prayer movement.

1935 World Revival Crusade founded by Pentecostal leader G. Jeffreys.

World Intercessors (Prayer Circle Department of Oriental Missionary Society) begun as worldwide prayer movement for world evangelization; over 2,000 prayer groups by 1968; 1987, over 40,000 participants (600 groups in USA alone); World Intercession School of Prayer (6 lessons); prayer seminars; 90,000 receive magazine *Prayer and Praise Guide.*

1936 Student Foreign Missions Fellowship (SFMF) begun by IVCF (USA); 1946, begins triennial mass conventions with 'Complete Christ's Commission' and 1948 Urbana series with over 17,000 attenders each time.

J.G.K. Harman publishes *Awaiting the light: a survey of the unevangelised areas of the world* (London: Inter-Varsity Missionary Papers).

Vision received by Korean Presbyterian youth Sun Myung Moon to begin Holy Spirit Association for Unification of World Christianity (T'ongil Kyohoe); 1954, begins Unification Church as indigenous church movement in Korea; by 1970, movement has become heterodox in its stance of superseding Christianity as the latter supersedes Judaism.

1937 Child Evangelism Fellowship founded, based on belief that 'Before Christ's return a mighty work among children will encircle the globe', by 1985, 160 foreign missionaries in 60 countries.

1938 John R. Mott publishes *Evangelism for the world today,* surveying methods, usages and views of 125 Christian leaders across the world.

A. McLeish writes 'Unoccupied fields' in the *Interpretative statistical survey of the world mission of the Christian church* (IMC).

4th World Missionary Conference/Meeting of International Missionary Council, Tambaram, Madras, India; 471 delegates from 69 countries; report states: 'We summon the Churches to unite in the supreme work of world evangelization until the kingdoms of this world become the Kingdom of our Lord.'

Gospel Recordings (Language Recordings International) founded: 'The aim of the work is to produce gospel records in every known language and dialect' in order to spread the gospel throughout the world; by 1967, recordings made in 3,400 languages

*Continued overleaf*

*Table 27-22 continued*

and dialects, rising by 1988 to over 4,300.

World Home Bible League founded in Chicago with as objective 'the placement of a Bible in every Bibleless home, so that people can be won for Jesus Christ'; 1965, in 30 countries with over 4 million scriptures distributed; 1985, in over 70 countries.

1939 Conference of Bible Societies, Woudschoten (Netherlands), proposes a World Council of Bible Societies.

Essay on 'The unfinished evangelistic task' published in IMC Tambaram report.

World-wide Signs Following Evangelism, Inc. begun under United Fundamentalist Church (Los Angeles, USA).

1941 Brazil: emergence, as a new theory of evangelization, of idea of grassroots or base ecclesial communities (comunidades eclesiais de base, BECs or CEBes); 1963 formally established, with the Catholic Church standing with the poor; fully developed after 1968 Medellín and 1979 Puebla conferences.

Anglican missionary bishop-designate of Rangoon in Burma A.T. Houghton writes *The battle of world evangelisation:* 'Christ has the master plan.'

Origin of large-scale international multilingual Bible correspondence course organizations: Emmaus Bible School founded in Toronto, Canada; by 1966, courses mushroom worldwide, especially in closed countries (Morocco 110,000 enrollments).

1942 WEC missionary L.G. Brierley begins world survey research to document and reach unreached peoples, resulting in 1st World Survey of Unreached Areas (also titled *Thy Kingdom come,* or 'The Black Spots Survey') describing untouched or unoccupied areas across globe with no Christian presence or influence; survey completed 1945, parts published in WEC journal *World Conquest.*

Ling Liang World-Wide Evangelistic Mission founded in Shanghai, China 'to send Chinese missionaries to the uttermost part of the world'; 1965, in 10 countries.

New Tribes Mission begun in USA to evangelize unreached tribes across the world; by 1985, 1,438 USA missionaries in 18 countries; 1988, 2,500 missionaries working in 160 tribes, 'with 2,500 tribes still to be reached'.

Committee on World Literacy and Christian Literature (Lit-Lit) organized by F.C. Laubach's World Literacy Committee, and Committee for Christian Literature, Foreign Missions Conference of North America (25 major boards and agencies); work in over 60 countries.

1943 USA: National Religious Broadcasters of North America formed, as official broadcasting arm of National Association of Evangelicals, with 50 organizations growing by 1979 to over 800; by 1986, annual convention attracts 4,000.

S.M. Zwemer publishes '*Into all the world'; the Great Commission, a vindication and an interpretation* Zondervan).

Global Outreach Mission founded (Buffalo, NY); by 1985, 114 foreign missionaries in 13 countries.

Conservative Baptist Foreign Mission Society formed in Wheaton, IL (USA); by 1985, 525 missionaries in 25 countries, based on Great Commission imperative.

Chiara Lubich founds Focolare Movement (It. hearth, furnace, hotbed) later known as GEN (New Generation) in Trent, Italy. Members join in gospel adherence in daily life (in accord with John 17:23). Non-Christians are considered friends of the movement.

1944 Dutch East Indies sees rise of Third-World missionaries: Chinese evangelist John Sung trains 5,000 3-man evangelistic teams who make major impact across country; 1969, Japanese and Pakistani evangelistic teams; 1975, Asian Evangelists Commission (AEC) conducts crusades in Palembang, Medan and other cities.

1945 Evangelical Foreign Missions Association organized in USA: 'We recognize our responsibility under the Great Commission to give all men everywhere the privilege of hearing and receiving the message of salvation... present an urgent call to more effectively evangelize the unreached of our generation'; by 1987, 83 member agencies sending out 13,343 missionaries (11,593 from North America, 1,726 being 1-2 year short-termers).

Massive surge of new Christian parachurch agencies or multinationals independent of the churches, increasing by 1980 to 17,500 distinct and separate agencies, with multifold ministries; great majority articulate commitment to Great Commission.

Norwegian missiologist O.G. Myklebust proposes creation of an International Institute of Scientific Missionary Research, with an association and conferences devoted to global mission; ignored until IAMS formed in 1970.

Foreign Missions Conference (NCCCUSA), representing 62 leading Protestant communions in USA and Canada, announces new global plan to reach the world through sending out new wave of 200,000 foreign missionaries from North America based on budget of $2.5 billion ($25 from every church member).

1946 Series of massive student conferences in North America; 1st IVSFM Conference, Toronto, on 'Complete Christ's Commission' with 575 participants; 1948, 1st Urbana Conference, 1,400 students; steady rise in numbers to 17,112 by 1976 ('Declare His Glory among the Nations'), and 18,145 by 1984 ('Faithful in Christ Jesus').

Conference of Bible Societies, Haywards Heath (UK), creates United Bible Societies (UBS) as federation and fellowship of 13 autonomous Bible societies from Europe and North America; expands rapidly by 1986 to 70 member societies and 30 national offices, working in 180 countries; UBS becomes 'a worldwide fellowship whose aim is to reach every person with the Bible or some part of it in a language he can understand and at a price he can afford'.

World Literature Crusade (WLC) begins in Canada for radio outreach, then expands to systematic tract distribution through Every Home Crusades in 103 countries, with goal of reaching every home on Earth by 1970; results by 1985 in 1.42 billion gospel messages handed out producing 14.5 million documented written responses for Christ.

Church of Scotland publishes *Into all the world: a statement on evangelism* (Glasgow: Joint Committee on Evangelism).

Egede Institute of Missionary Study & Research, in Oslo, founded to promote scholarly research in the world mission of the church.

Asociación Misionera Evangélica Nacional (AMEN, National Evangelical Missionary Association) begun as home mission in Peru; 1979, reorganized (with Methodist personnel) as a Third-World home and foreign missionary society with a global vision, renamed Asociación Misionera Evangélica a las Naciones; thousands of young Peruvians trained; missions in 20 countries including UK, France and Spanish North Africa (Melilla).

*Prayer: the mightiest force in the world* published by Frank C. Laubach as a global plan to evangelize the world by mobilizing 10 million intercessors.

1947 5th Meeting of International Missionary Council, Whitby, Toronto, Canada; 112 delegates from 40 countries; upholds 'the evangelization of the world in this generation', coins term 'expectant evangelism'.

Lutheran World Federation (LWF) founded, with first purpose stated as 'To bear united witness before the world to the Gospel of Jesus Christ as the power of God for salvation'; 1st Assembly, at Lund, Sweden; 1949, LWF Commission on World Missions formed, meets at Oxford (UK).

Roman Catholic missiological journal begun, *Euntes docete* ('Go and teach', Matthew 28:18).

Nazarene writer R.V. DeLong writes *We can if we will: the challenge of world evangelism* (Kansas City).

Fuller Theological Seminary founded by C.E. Fuller in Pasadena, CA (USA), as part of his expressed desire 'to see the world evangelized in this generation'.

World Revival Prayer League (National Christian Women's Prayer League) founded, based on Tokyo, Japan.

Oral Roberts Evangelistic Association founded (Tulsa, OK, USA), with own foreign missions program; 1953, begins Pentecostal television preaching; becomes massive ministry with worldwide healing crusades, Oral Roberts University, City of Faith, Charismatic Bible Ministries.

1948 1st World Congress on World Evangelization (also termed 1st World Congress on Evangelism) convened by YFCI (with Billy Graham) in Beatenberg, Switzerland (August), first of long annual series; 1949, 2nd World Congress in Cannes, Frances; 1950, 3rd in Brussels; 1951, 4th in Winona Lake, Indiana (USA); 1952, 5th in Belfast; 1953, 6th in tokyo (1,200 delegates from 24 countries; workshops, crusades, teams into 43 of Japan's 44 prefectures, 4,000 commitments to Christ); 1955 São Paulo (Brazil), 1956 Caracas (Venezuela), 1957 Copenhagen; 1959 Madras (India), also Tokyo, also Mexico City, 1960 Bristol (UK), then series discontinued; culminating in 1966 Berlin Congress.

World Council of Churches (WCC) inaugurated in 1st Assembly at Amsterdam by 147 churches from 44 countries; theme 'Man's disorder and God's design'; 351 delegates and 238 alternates, but no RC observers: 'We intend to stay together' (22 August-4 September): 7th function of WCC is stated as 'To support the churches in their task of evangelisation'.

International Council of Christian Churches (ICCC) founded (anti-ecumenical, fundamentalist); 1st Congress at Amsterdam as rival to WCC; 150 persons from 29 countries (August); later plenary congresses every 3 or 4 years; 1948-1984, 98 major ICCC conferences held; 1983 plenary with 4,000 delegates from 93 nations and 399 denominations with (1988) 4.7 million members.

Christian Crusade (Christian Echoes National Ministry, USA) organized as anticommunist mission, moves to Tulsa, Oklahoma; heard over 400 radio stations, 10 TV stations; 1953, launches ICCC Bible Balloon project, sending over 1 million Scripture portions into communist Eastern Europe by means of hydrogen-filled balloons; also other missions across world.

China missionary doctor F.C. Maddox writes *Set a watchman: a world survey* (London).

Latter Rain Revival (New Order of the Latter Rain) erupts among classical Pentecostals in Saskatchewan, Canada, spreads rapidly to Europe, USA, and across world; emphasis on laying on of hands with prophecy, government by order of living apostles; begins Global Missions Broadcast; from 1965, merges into Charismatic Movement.

1949 WCC study 'The Evangelization of Man in Modern Mass Society'; surveys done in Ceylon, Finland, France, Germany, Holland, India, Latin America, Scotland, USA; publication series announced but never implemented.

T.L. Osborn Evangelistic Association established (also termed Association for Native Evangelism), for mass evangelism utilizing citizen Christian workers in overseas countries; 1965, in over 40 countries, having reached over 20,000 unevangelized areas.

World Gospel Crusades (Every Creature Crusade) founded with as its purpose 'the evangelization of the world through the mass media of communication—literature distribution. Scripture distribution, correspondence courses, radio, TV, united evangelistic campaigns' by 1965, in 60 nations: by 1986, only 4 overseas workers left, in 2 countries.

Survey Application Trust (London) produces 5-yearly survey, *World Christian handbook* (1949, 1952, 1957, 1962, 1968) edited by K.G. Grubb (1900-1980), with church membership statistics compiled and totaled for first time by denomination and country.

Cursillos de Cristianidad (short courses) movement begun in Spain by RC bishop J. Hervas; short 3-day retreats to renew personal faith of Catholics; 1950s spreads to Latin America, then to USA, 1961 Britain, then globally; many leaders later become first Catholic charismatics.

1950 USA: beginnings of evangelistic association evangelism (Billy Graham Evangelistic Association, et alia); by 1976 Billy Graham has preached face-to-face to 50,780,505 across world, in 229 crusades, with 1,526,729 inquirers (decisions or converts: 3.0 percent of attenders), and to 104,390,133 by end of 1984.

Help Open Paths to Evangelize (HOPE Bible Mission) founded in USA 'to take the gospel to unevangelized areas'; bimonthly news sheet *His Millions.*

World Vision founded (Monrovia, CA, USA) for relief and development, emergency aid, pastors' conferences; emphasis on using research, new technology, new systems, new tools, new media, 'using a computer to help evangelize the world' 'to reach the world for Christ in this generation' (vice president T.W. Engstrom, 1966 Berlin Congress on Evangelism); 1988, works in over 80 countries with over 4,400 staff (mainly nationals) on 4,254 projects.

F.C. Laubach publishes *Literacy as evangelism* (New York, Foreign Missions Conference); 1962, organizes a training agency, World Literacy Evangelism, which lasts for 4 years.

USA: evangelistic broadcasting spreads: 1950, Billy Graham begins on ABC radio, and 1951 on TV; 1953, Rex Humbard telecasts weekly, 1958 opens 5,000-seat Cathedral of Tomorrow (Akron, Ohio).

'Hour of Decision' radio program with Billy Graham begins over 150 stations; 1951, 20 million listeners (200,000 letters received per year); by 1978, 900 radio/TV stations worldwide, and a million letters per year (with 70 million viewers in USA).

Full Gospel Business Men's Fellowship International (FGBMFI) founded in USA as an end-time ministry by dairy magnate D. Shakarian after a vision of the people of every continent; preachers and women excluded; grows rapidly by 1970 to 300,000 members in 700 chapters worldwide, and by 1986 to 700,000 regular attenders worldwide in 3,000 chapters (1,715 in USA) in 95 countries including USSR, Czechoslovakia, Saudi Arabia and other closed countries.

Baptist Bible Fellowship International founded as fundamentalist mission, with (by 1985) 620 foreign missionaries in 58 countries.

Missionaries of Charity (1950 Sisters, 1963 Brothers) begun in Calcutta by Mother Teresa, one of world's greatest Catholic evangelists, to minister in the name of Jesus to the poor, destitute, sick and dying; by 1986, 2,500 sisters, 600 novices, and 344 religious houses in 77 countries including Cuba, Nicaragua, and most closed countries, with attempts to open in China and USSR; global aim 'worldwide evangelization bringing Jesus to the poorest of the poor'.

World-Wide Missions International organized by 35 churches in Nigeria; 1965, 1,100 workers in over 70 nations, with magazine circulation *(World-Wide Missions)* of 800,000; 1985, decline to 15 USA missionaries in 31 countries.

1951 1st World Congress of the Lay Apostolate, in Rome, aiming to mobilize laity (99.8% of all Christians) for outreach to the world; subsequent congresses in rome in 1957, 1967, 1975.

1952 *Christ's hope of the Kingdom* published by A. McLeish, expounding theory that Jesus envisaged lightning spread of gospel to all nations within one generation.

E.J. Homrighausen writes 'Trends in world evangelism', in *World Christian handbook, 1952* (London).

'The Great Commission for Anabaptists' written by F.H. Littell.

Worldwide Revival Movement inaugurated in Ireland by W.E. Allen and Revival Publishing Company (Lisburn) to promote theme 'Revival is the key to world evangelization.'

World Wide Pictures established by BGEA; 1953, classic movie *Mr. Texas;* by 1984, over 100 films produced and distributed, with 28,000 showings a year; viewed by over 50 million persons with 1.5 million decisions for Christ; some dubbed in 17 languages (100 prints circulate in Japan in Japanese).

*Continued opposite*

*Table 27–22 continued*

1953 Worldwide Evangelization Crusade begins work on Java, founds Batu Bible School, results in indigenous Indonesian Missionary Fellowship (organized 1961), with its own plan for world evangelization with 206 personnel by 1980.

World Committee for Christian Broadcasting (WCCB) constituted in Britain, then International Committee for Christian Broadcasting (ICCB); 1961, founds World Association for Christian Broadcasting (WACB), 1968 merges with Coordinating Committee for Christian Broadcasting (CCCB) to form World Association for Christian Communication (WACC).

Article proposing 'World Evangelization in Our Time' circulated by seminarian D.B. Barrett, illustrated by graphs of world population explosion.

Congress of Catholic Action, in Chimbote (Peru), one of roots of liberation theology; this new approach to man and God, primarily from Latin America, leads to mushrooming of BECs (base ecclesial communities), new ministries, and above all to new approaches to evangelization.

1954 2nd Assembly of World Council of Churches, in Evanston, USA: 'Christ the Hope of the World'; 502 delegates; report states 'To evangelize is to participate in Christ's life and ministry to the world'.

WCC official survey, *Evangelism: the mission of the Church to those outside her life,* notes 'an almost chaotic confusion as to the meaning and scope of evangelism'; surveys the future and suggests: 'The drama of missions and evangelism may, indeed, under God's rule over time and history be only in its infancy.'

MAP International begun in Brunswick, GA (USA), as interdenominational evangelical service agency providing medical assistance to 82 countries by 1985.

Methodist evangelist J.E. Rattenbury publishes *Evangelism and pagan England,* warns 'Schemes for future evangelization would indeed be futile dreams if the tragedy of human sin were ignored'.

*The Bible in world evangelism* published in English and French by UBS research secretary A.M. Chirgwin, a colportage specialist, emphasizing primary and indispensable role of Bible in strategy for evangelization of non-Christians.

World Missionary Evangelism begun as nondenominational service agency (Dallas, Texas), in 14 countries.

New Life League World Missionary Society begun (Waco, TX, USA), 'winning the world for Christ through the published word'; Restoration Baptist; missionary printing presses, radio, mass media, literature, in 50 countries (including printing Bibles for China).

1955 World Conference on Missionary Radio (WCMR) begun in USA; 1963, joins with National Religious Broadcasters of North America (NRB) to form International Christian Broadcasters (ICB), which disbands in 1968.

Midnight Call Missionary Work (L'Appel de Minuit) founded in Zurich, Switzerland, 'to extend the redemptive message of the gospel into unreached parts of the world'.

Missiologist J.C. Thiessen writes *A survey of world missions* (Chicago) beginning from the Great Commission.

1956 USA: charismatic (neo-pentecostal) renewal begins among Episcopal and Protestant churches, first being at Trinity Episcopal Church, Wheaton, Illinois; rapidly increases to 10% of all clergy and 1 million laity by 1970, and to 1.6 million active Spirit-baptized charismatics by 1980; over these decades, vast new proliferation of 'signs, wonders and healings' arises worldwide, accompanying expansion of charismatic movement.

DWME of WCC begins publication of regular series, *A monthly letter about evangelism;* in subsequent 33 years covers every conceivable aspect of evangelism and world evangelization

Catholic bishop L.-J. Suenens publishes *The gospel to every creature;* considerable influence on Vatican Council II.

*Mission fields today: a brief world survey* published by IVF (London, 127 pages detailing evangelization in all countries of world) edited by A.J. Dain; closing sentence 'Great indeed is the unfinished task!'

1957 WCC series of booklets published, *World evangelism today;* discontinued after only 4 titles.

Global Conquest program (Assemblies of God USA) prepared as a 'new strategy for world evangelization', for 'the rapid evangelization of the world before the return of Christ', with detailed 3-year goals especially focusing on large cities; name changed in 1967 to Good News Crusades; 1968, Council on Evangelism with its Statement of Purpose makes major impact.

Nights of Prayer for World-Wide Revival (NPWR) launched in London by Anglican layman and CMS missionary to India, G.S. Ingram (c1881-1969); continues till his death.

Pope Pius XII ends Easter Day encyclical with words 'Come, Lord Jesus, there are signs that your coming is not very far off!'

Missions scholar S.C. Neill publishes *The unfinished task* (London).

Send the Light (later termed Operation Mobilization) incorporated in USA, Mexico, then in over 50 countries; an interdenominational youth agency sending short-term mission workers abroad for evangelism and literature distribution.

Conference of World Confessional Groups founded, in Geneva, supported by 7 WCFs: BWA, FWCC, ICC, LWF, WCCC, WMC, WPA (WARC); 1968, RCC joins; 1968, name changed to Conference of World Confessional Families; 1979, renamed Conference of Christian World Communions; 1985, 29th Conference meets in Windsor, UK, with 20 WCFs/CWCs; now meeting annually; agreed positions on world mission emerge.

1958 Australian evangelist Alan Walker proposes an 'Ecumenical Mission to the World'; adopted by Australian Council of Churches, but at 1961 New Delhi Assembly proposal is rejected by WCC.

4th General Assembly of Syndesmos (international Orthodox youth organization), in Salonica, establishes major missionary activity including Pan-Orthodox Missionary Society, to be ratified by the coming Great & Holy Council of the Orthodox Church; Church of Greece's missionary institute begins missiological quarterly in Greek and English, *Porefthendes* (Go Ye), until it ceases publication in 1966; 1982, Apostoliki Diakonia begins new publication *Panta ta Ethni* (To All Peoples).

Bibles For The World (BFTW) begun by Hmar believer from Northwest India in order 'to mail a Bible to every telephone subscriber in the world by 1985" BFTW is 'committed to mail one billion Bibles to one billion families on planet earth', by 1986 'It is the stated goal of BFTW to mail a book-size copy of the New Testament, in the language of the people, to a billion homes' using telephone directories; NTs mailed 1971-1982 total to 6,444,628; 1987, averages 1,500,000 a year.

Publication of *Bilan du monde; encyclopédie catholique du monde chrétien* by Catholic researches of FERES and Eglise Vivante (Louvain, Belgium), documenting status of world mission in all countries.

1959 Southern Baptists in USA develop long-term emphasis on 'Sharing Christ around the World'/'Sharing Christ with the Whole World' (Baptist Jubilee Advance, 1959-1964, jointly with 20 other USA Baptist groups); 1970 SB Convention approves concept and phrase 'Bold Mission', and Home Mission Board develops it in 1974 'Sharing Christ's Bold Mission'; 1974 SB Convention in Dallas authorizes Foreign Mission Board and Home Mission Board to plan 'Bold new strategies' for 25 years of century; 1976 FMB develops 'Total Missions Thrust: Global Discipleship: Foreign Missions looks toward AD 2000' and 1976 'Bold New Thrusts in Foreign Missions 1976-2000'; 1976 'Bold Mission Thrust—Acts 1.8', 1977 'by the year 2000' added; 1977 BMT adopted by many state conventions and associations.

First nationwide Evangelism-in-Depth campaign organized, in Nicaragua (125 local churches, 65,000 homes visited, 126,000 attenders in 14 local crusades, 2,604 professions of faith, 500 prayer cells formed); on successful conclusion, Latin America Mission sponsors similar campaigns in 11 other Latin American countries by 1971 (1961 Costa Rica, 1962 Guatemala, 1964 Venezuela, 1965 Bolivia and Dominican Republic, 1967 Peru, 1968 Colombia, 1970 Ecuador and Haiti, 1971 Mexico and Paraguay); spreads to other parts of world, including Tokyo 1980 and Mexico 1986 (Evangelismo a Fondo); but after 1975 fades out as a movement because largely accepted and incorporated into church programs.

Death of pope Pius XII; comet heralds birth of Antichrist in Palestine (according to prophetologist P.I. Rissaut in 1948 book), 1980 career as ultimate Antichrist begins, by 2000 accepted as universal monarch; Rome destroyed; 2004, death of Antichrist.

Worldwide Missionary Society (Sekai Senkyo Kyokai) founded in Yokohama, Japan, to send Japanese missionaries to all foreign countries; mainly in India.

1960 IFMA Congress on World Missions, Chicago; closing statement reads: 'We declare the need for a total mobilization of all the resources... so that the total evangelization of the world may be achieved in this generation'; resurgence among Conservative Evangelicals of the Watchword 'The Evangelization of the World in this Generation'; congress report by J.O. Percy entitled *Facing the unfinished task.*

Baptist International Missions founded as fundamentalist missions body, with (by 1985) 593 foreign missionaries in 53 countries.

World Missionary Assistance Plan (World MAP) founded (California, USA) as interdenominational, evangelical, charismatic service agency; inaugurates Leadership Spiritual Renewal Seminars 'to create spiritual renewal among all the world's church leadership to bring change within all nations, hence worldwide evangelization, to be completed by the year 2000'; by 1987, claims 60% of that goal has been completed.

IVP editor/director J.T. Bayly writes satirical novel *The Gospel Blimp,* about an agency International Gospel Blimps Inc. who operate an airship towing sign 'One Billion Unreached'; ends in disaster; archetype of attempts to evangelize by depersonalized technology without personal contact with unevangelized populations.

Youth With A Mission (YWAM) begins as evangelical-charismatic sending agency, expanding as outgrowth of the Jesus Movement in USA; at first, little church consciousness; 1977, outfits 10,000-ton evangelistic ship m.v. Anastasis for discipleship and mercy ministries; by 1983, the world's largest evangelistic agency with 14,000 short-term young people sent overseas each year, in 56 countries; by 1987, 50,000; goal to field 100,000 a year by AD 2000.

1961 World Missionary Press begun (New Paris, IN, USA) as nondenominational agency distributing scripture booklets in 214 languages in 179 countries.

2nd World Survey of Unreached Areas (Areas of the World Unreached by the Gospel); L.G. Brierley publishes section 4, *The challenge of the unachieved,* and other WEC survey volumes describing 'The 19 Point Programme to Reach the Unreached'; also survey articles in WEC's magazine *World Wide;* in introduction quoting WEC founder C.T. Studd, Brierley states: 'Unless some new heroic effort is made by God's people entailing great sacrifices, great faith and desperate courage, the evangelization of the whole world in this and several future generations is a patent impossibility'.

1st Pan-Orthodox Conference, Rhodes (Greece); agreement to move towards a future Great & Holy Council of the Orthodox Church; subsequent conferences 1963, 1964, 1968, 1976.

World Evangelism founded in USA by Pentecostal evangelist Morris Cerullo; 1967, World Evangelism Society of Great Britain.

3rd Assembly of WCC, in New Delhi, India; Russian and other Orthodox Churches join WCC; integration of WCC and IMC, latter emerging as Division of World Mission and Evangelism (DWME and CWME) whose report states 'Two-thirds of the human race are without the knowledge of Christ as the light of the world'; report on 'Christian witness' states 'All disciples stand under the Great Commission of the One Lord'.

Joint Action for Mission (JAM) promulgated by International Missionary Council, then by DWME/WCC as 'a plan of ecumenical mission', local or global, 'recommended by CWME to be followed in all six continents'; but meets resistance from confessional and institutional structures of churches and missionary agencies, and soon peters out.

First religious TV station opened, in USA: WYAH (M.G. Robertson, in Tidewater, Virginia) later Christian Broadcasting Network; by 1980, almost every major metropolitan center in USA has its own religious TV station; by 1987 CBN World Outreach involves 'sharing the love of Jesus in more than 85 nations'.

6th International Student Missionary Convention, Urbana, Illinois, USA; 5,027 attenders; 'The world must be evangelized in one decade' (Billy Graham), 'We can evangelize the world in this decade. It is possible' (Clyde Taylor, NAE).

World Association for Christian Broadcasting (WACB) founded, becoming by 1968 the WACC.

World Radio Missionary Fellowship inaugurates HCJB-TV (Quito, Ecuador) as pioneer missionary telecaster; 1985, 218 overseas personnel in 8 countries.

Swiss Protestant scholar Karl Barth (1886-1968) writes: 'The Great Commission is truly the most genuine utterance of the risen Jesus'; widespread resurgence of interest by theologians in Commission's significance and interpretation.

African/Independent Lutheran Church (Loyalist Religion) founded in Maragoli (Kenya) as Luhya indigenous body; c1980, renamed Third World Missions Federation, with aim to promote world evangelization by Third-Worlders

1962 Vatican Council II (21st Ecumenical Council, for Roman Catholics) meets in Rome, 1962-65; 2,540 attending RC bishops, 93 non-RC observers; issues 4 constitutions, 9 decrees, 3 declarations.

Missiologist J. Blauw writes *The missionary nature of the church;* expounds presence evangelization.

Haggai Institute for Advanced Leadership Training begins courses in Singapore as a service agency training Christian leaders in national and world evangelization, with 5,100 Third-World alumni in 99 nations by 1987, and a goal of 10,000 by AD 2000.

Alleged date of birth (5 February) of future Aquarian messiah at start of Aquarian Age (all 8 planets in sign of Aquarius for first time for 2,160 years); 1962 date accepted by many Roman Catholic seers as year of birth of Antichrist; according to Jewish tradition, Antichrist will be born of the tribe of Dan, in Chorazin, north of Sea of Galilee (Israel).

1963 2nd Meeting of Commission on World Mission and Evangelism (CWME/WCC), Mexico City, on theme 'God's Mission and Our Task', modified to 'Witness in Six Continents'; 200 delegates; report holds that mission and evangelism both take place on all continents (December).

International Christian Broadcasters (ICB) formed by USA Evangelicals; 1967, meets in Concordia, Milwaukee; but fades out by 1968, displaced by NRB (USA).

Pope John XXIII promulgates 'Pacem in Terris', one of the most brilliant papal documents in history.

7th UBS Council Meeting, Hakone (Japan), with 27 member societies, launches plan 'God's Word for a New Age', agrees to publish Bible selections, sets global goal of scripture distribution; a Bible in every literate Christian home, an NT for every literate Christian, a portion for every literate adult, scripture outreach to every nonliterate, and a selection for every soul on Earth.

New Life For All (NLFA) begins as 10-year campaign in Nigeria, spreads across African countries.

*Continued overleaf*

*Table 27-22 continued*

Methodist professor of evangelism R.E. Coleman writes a classic, *The Master Plan of Evangelism*, expounding evangelistic message and methodology of Jesus, God's strategy of world conquest, long-range goals, based on training Twelve Apostles 'to go with the Gospel to the whole world', 'to win the world for Christ'.

1964 Vatican II publishes *Lumen Gentium,* 'Dogmatic Constitution on the Church'; obedience to Christ's 'solemn command' is 'the work of evangelization'; and *Ad Gentes,* 'Decree on the Church's Missionary Activity' (promulgated by Vatican II on its final day, 7 December 1965) with passages on 'the evangelization of the world'.

F.C. Laubach publishes major work, *How to teach one and win one for Christ: Christ's plan for winning the world: each one teach and win one* (Zondervan).

Missiologist D.A. McGavran begins *Church growth bulletin;* 1979, renamed *Global church growth,* stated to be 'The only worldwide missiological magazine dedicated exclusively to the Great Commission Mission', whose purpose 'is to report from the Church Growth perspective, what God is doing in world evangelization and to share effective strategies, insights and resources'.

Secretariat for Non-Christians (Secretariatus pro Non Christianis) formed in Rome by Paul VI for dialogue with adherents of all non-Christian religions throughout world.

*Evangelical missions quarterly* (EMQ) founded by IFMA/EFMA, operated by EMIS, 'dedicated in obedience to the command of Jesus Christ to the proclamation of the gospel of the Son of God to the whole world'; over next 25 years, all material relates directly or indirectly to world evangelization.

1965 Oriental Orthodox Churches Conference, in Addis Ababa: first conference of heads of Armenian, Coptic, Ethiopian, Syrian, and Malabar churches; 'The Church's role is to convey the message of salvation to the world... Christ's command "Go into all the world and preach the Gospel"... should be its central concern, its main preoccupation.'

World Evangelization Research Centre begun in Nairobi, Kenya, by CMS missionary D.B. Barrett for ecumenical-interdenominational-scholarly research; also termed CSWE (Centre for the Study of World Evangelization).

Emphasis on evangelizing tribes and peoples leads to 7-year DWME/AACC Unreached Peoples research project throughout Africa sponsored by 1965 consultation on 'The Evangelisation of West Africa Today' at Yaoundé, Cameroon.

Secretariat for Non-Believers (Secretariatus pro Non Credentibus) created in Rome by Paul VI to pursue dialogue with world's atheists, agnostics, nonreligious, nonbelievers; working by 1973 through 21 national secretariats, 2 regional bodies, and a large number of correspondents.

'Decree on the Apostolate of the Laity' promulgated by Paul VI (18 November), on the role of laypersons in the Mystical Body of Christ, 'that through them the whole world might enter into a relationship with Christ' as a result of 'their activity directed to the evangelization and sanctification of men', 'working to make the divine message of salvation known and accepted by all men throughout the world', with laity trained 'to engage in conversation with others, believers or non-believers, in order to manifest Christ's message to all men'.

1966 Evangelical Congress on 'The Church's Worldwide Mission', Wheaton, IL, USA, sponsored by both IFMA and EFMA; 938 delegates from 71 countries agree to Wheaton Declaration, holding local church chiefly responsible for ongoing mission and evangelism: 'We covenant together... for the evangelization of the world in this generation, so help us God!'

World Congress on Evangelism, Berlin: 'One race, one gospel, one task'; 1,200 delegates from over 100 countries; from now on, strategic plans and conferences for countrywide and world evangelization proliferate; closing Statement states 'Evangelism is the proclamation of the Gospel'.

1st Assembly of Pacific Conference of Churches, in Lifou, Loyalty Islands (New Caledonia), on theme 'Go Ye...'

Missions Advanced Research and Communications Center (MARC) founded by World Vision (E.R. Dayton) in Los Angeles with the express goal of 'making available and understandable the tools of technology which can aid the Church in giving every man an opportunity to say yes to Jesus Christ'.

Release the World for Christ begun as Greek Orthodox agency based in Houston, Texas, holding evangelistic crusades overseas (India, Thailand).

1967 SC Propaganda (Rome) renamed Sacred Congregation for the Evangelization of Peoples; by 1980s responsible for over 110 million Catholics in over 1,000 jurisdictions.

International Correspondence Institute founded by Assemblies of God USA as Bible courses arm of Good News Crusades, with accumulative enrollment of 5,077,014 in 164 nations by 1987, with 280,810 recorded decisions for Christ (5.5%).

South Korea: massive evangelistic campaigns held: 1965, 17-denomination 80th anniversary of Protestantism (20,000 professions of faith); 1967, Crusade for World Revival (30,000 attenders a night), linked with organization CWR begun in 1965 in Britain; 1973, Seoul crusade (3,210,000 attenders, 275,000 enquirers); 1974, EXPLO 74 training conference on evangelism and discipleship (323,419 workers from 78 countries); 1977, National Evangelization Crusade; 1978 Here's Life Korea; 1980, 16.5 million attend 4-day World Evangelization Crusade, in Seoul; et alia.

Council of the Laity (Pontificium Consilium pro Laicis) established by Paul VI to promote development of the lay apostolate and mission throughout the world by means of 600 million lay Catholics.

*Encyclopedia of modern Christian missions* published, edited by B.L. Goddard (USA); first such survey since 1891 *Encyclopedia;* documents world mission of the church, expanded Christian witness, changing Great Commission activities and plans, with details on 1,437 agencies.

1968 4th Assembly of WCC, in Uppsala, Sweden: 'Behold, I make all things new'; 2,741 participants (704 delegates, 750 press); report states 'Our part in evangelism might be described as bringing about the occasions for men's response to Jesus Christ', but also there is 'widespread defeatism in the churches about the work of evangelism and world mission' (D.T. Niles).

Evangelical theologian J.F. Shepherd writes article 'The missionary objective: total world evangelization'.

World Association for Christian Communication (WACC) founded as merger of WCCB, WACB, and CCCB; works in 60 countries.

Anglican Consultative Council begun by Lambeth Conference of Bishops, with world mission prominent; ACC-1 meets in Limuru (Kenya) in 1971; ACC-2 1973 Dublin; then 1976 Trinidad; 1979 London, Ontario; 1981 Newcastle (UK); 1984 Nigeria, 1987 Singapore (ACC-7).

Southern Baptist missiologist Luther Copeland writes 'A strategy for world evangelism' *(The Commission).*

Association for World Evangelism (AWE) founded in Portland, Oregon (USA); nondenominational; 1985, 8 workers in France and Switzerland.

African Independent Churches Service (AICS) proposed by D.B. Barrett as service agency to assist Africa's 5,000 indigenous denominations in order to help them to mobilize the world's 85 million Non-White indigenous Christians in 7,000 denominations in a global plan to evangelize the world; 1976, Egyptian Orthodox bishop A. Markos launches scheme (Organization of African Instituted (Indigenous) Churches, OAIC) based in Nairobi, Kenya, with vast activities, conferences, TEE, et alia; by 1987 a major force but with its global goal abandoned.

1969 Pentecostal evangelist Jimmy L. Swaggart begins USA radio ministry 'Camp Meeting Hour', then in 1972 television ministry; by 1987, Jimmy Swaggart Ministries air telecasts over 3,200 TV stations in 15 languages viewed by 510 million in 145 countries weekly, raising donations of $150 million a year, and claim 'The medium of television is the most expedient method of spreading the gospel the world has ever known. It is God's directive that the Great Commission be carried out by this means'; 1988, partial collapse due to sex scandal.

Jehovah's Witnesses hold series of 5-day 'Peace on Earth' International Assemblies in 13 cities (Denmark, France, Germany, Italy, UK, USA) with 840,572 attenders (25% non-JWs) and 27,442 publicly baptized; arrival of Christ's Millennial Kingdom expected in 1975; 1973, massive Assemblies across world on theme 'Divine Victory' (including Dusseldorf with 67,950 attenders, Munich with 78,792); 1976, Governing Body of Jehovah's Witnesses reorganized with 18 members (each with over 35 years of full-time witnessing); 1978 international convention series produces 100 'Victorious Faith' assemblies in 45 countries, averaging 25,000 attenders at each.

World Evangelism Foundation founded (Texas, USA) by Baptist missionaries to mobilize Southern Baptist laypersons to spread Partnership Evangelism; by 1988, over 7,000 persons from USA have held 200 major evangelistic campaigns in 40 countries, with 200,000 decisions for Christ; extensive plans for 1989, 1990, in Japan inter alia.

1970 5th Assembly, Lutheran World Federation (LWF), Evian (France), on theme 'Sent into the World'; new Commission on Church Cooperation (CCC) formed centered on evangelism, meets 1971 Tokyo, 1972 Kecskemet (Hungary), 1973 Santiago (Chile), 1974 Lund, 1975 Adelaide, 1976 Saskatoon, 1978 Montreaux, 1979 Singapore, 1981 Chicago, 1982 Stavanger.

9th International Student Missionary Convention, Urbana, USA, on theme 'World Evangelism: Why? How? Who?'; 12,304 attenders.

Popular books on premillennial eschatology (an interpretation held by 41% of all Evangelicals, and countless others) sell 31 million copies over 15 years, especially H. Lindsay's 9-title series beginning with *The late great planet Earth;* these however all dismiss human responsibility for global mission and world evangelization after only miniscule passing mention (less than 1% of text).

'AD 2000: 350 million Christians in Africa' published in IRM by D.B. Barrett, on Third-World progress towards world evangelization.

Frankfurt Declaration on Mission, promulgated by 14 Conservative Evangelical Lutheran theologians in Germany.

12th Baptist World Congress, Tokyo, launches 5-year evangelistic program 'World Mission of Reconciliation Through Jesus Christ'; officially gets under way in 1973, with campaigns across world.

*Christianity Today's* founding editor C.F.H. Henry writes 'Strategy for world evangelism: are we too late?'

From Samoa, Paul VI sends out Missionary Message to the World, urging spreading of the gospel.

Conservative Evangelical theologian G.W. Peters writes *Saturation evangelism,* on how Evangelism-in-Depth is spreading over the entire world.

OM purchases 2,500-ton evangelistic ship m.v. Logos for UK£80,000 to visit large-city ports in difficult countries around world, with literature evangelism, book sales, missionary conferences; 110 crew, total 1,500 crew from 1970-88; 20 million persons exposed to gospel through related shore teams, 7 million visitors abroad buying literature in 107 different countries; 1988, ship (then valued at £1 million) runs aground and is lost off Tierra del Fuego; 1977, sister ship m.v. Doulos (6,000 tons) begins travels, reaching 600 visitors per conference.

1971 Anglican theologian J.R.W. Stott edits 6 essays on 'Issues in World Evangelism' in his book *Christ the Liberator* (IVP).

SIL cooperation as computerized closure vision to finally complete remaining task of translating Bible into every language; main purpose to galvanize denominational Bible translating agencies (Baptist, Pentecostal, Catholic, et alia), but finally terminates in 1983 despite over 5,000 languages still remaining untranslated.

International Crusades begun in Dallas, Texas, as agency coordinating Southern Baptist 2-week Partnership Crusades overseas; goal 'To see one million people pray to receive Christ by the turn of the century using partnership evangelism'.

Conference on Church-Mission Relationships in Creative Tension, held at Green Lake, WI (USA), with 400 attenders, under aegis of EMIS and sponsored by IFMA/EFMA: 'We affirm the continuing worldwide mandate upon the worldwide church to fulfill the Great Commission of Jesus Christ.'

World Evangelization Strategy Consultation, White Sulphur Springs, Georgia, USA (December).

Chapter 'The Great Commission', in *One world, one task: report of the Evangelical Alliance Commission on World Mission* (London: Scripture Union).

1972 International Catholic Charismatic Renewal Office (ICCRO) founded as International Communications Office in Ann Arbor (USA); first 2 International Leaders' Conferences (1973, 1975) held there; 1976, office transferred to Brussels; 1981 relocates as ICCRO in Rome, organizes 5 worldwide leaders' conferences (4 in Rome, 1 in Dublin), 1985 relocates in Vatican 'moving to the heart of the Church', by 1988 representing 63.5 million Catholic pentecostals in over 160 countries.

Marian Movement of Priests founded by Fr. Stephano Gobbi, a Roman Catholic Italian priest from Milan. Its essential characteristics are consecration to the Immaculate Heart of Mary and fervent prayer. By AD 2000, 100,000 priests are involved.

*World Pentecost* editor Donald Gee writes article 'World evangelisation'; widely quoted throughout Pentecostal movement.

Consultation on the Gospel and Frontier Peoples, Chicago (December), sponsored by NCCCUSA and North American boards; detailed survey presented by D.B. Barrett entitled 'Frontier situations for evangelisation in Africa, 1972: a survey report', tabulating data, documenting and mapping situation of 213 Muslim peoples, 411 peoples responsive to Christianity, and 236 unevangelized peoples.

P. Eshleman writes *The Explo story: a plan to change the world.*

Mouvement International d'Apostolat des Mileux Sociaux Indépendants (MIAMISI) founded by RCs in Rome, dedicated to 'the evangelization of the middle and upper classes'.

Missions news periodical *Koinonia,* dealing with reaching beyond frontiers of the unevangelized world, founded in Brazil by L.G. Brierley; 1974 name changed to *Look,* in Britain, then *The Wider Look*; 1983 The Frontiersman's Fellowship.

Great Commission Prayer Crusade launched by Campus Crusade for Christ International; leadership by women; a few conferences held (Dallas 1976, 1984 International Prayer Assembly, Seoul).

World Conference and Assembly of CWME/WCC, Bangkok, Thailand (3rd Meeting of CWME): 'Salvation Today'; moratorium on foreign missions and missionaries proposed by younger churches, widely accepted 1972-80; report states 'Each generation must evangelize its own generation' (29 December 1972-8 January 1973).

1973 Mission to the World (agency of Presbyterian Church in America) launched; 1987, 500 missionaries in 40 countries, church planting in 12 countries; stress on taking its appropriate part in Great Commission; goals include evangelizing 25 world-class cities by 1993.

Korea: 1st Annual Summer Institute of World Mission (SIWM) in Seoul; by 14th Institute in 1986, some 1,000 students have been trained at East-West Center for overseas service, with goal of 10,000 Asian foreign missionaries by AD 2000.

Globe Missionary Evangelism begun (Pensacola,

*Continued opposite*

*Table 27–22 continued*

Florida), with 65 foreign missionaries in 15 countries (by 1985).

All-Asia Missions Consultation, Seoul, Korea; formation of Asia Missions Association (AMA); 1975 Inaugural Convention publishes 'Seoul Declaration on Christian Mission'.

Urbana 73: 10th Inter-Varsity Missionary Convention, Urbana, on theme 'Jesus Christ: Lord of the Universe, Hope of the World'; 14,158 attend (December); similar number each successive year up to Urbana 87 and Urbana 90 in 1990.

Trinity Broadcasting Network launched, in southern California, as Pentecostal television station 'to get the gospel to every living human being on planet Earth' before Jesus comes; by 1986, TBN owns 55 TV stations in USA with 26 affiliates, also stations in Guatemala, St. Kitts-Nevis, Italy, Ciskei.

World Film Crusade founded in Florida, USA (later known as World Thrust Films, or World Mission Crusade); 1985, Brother John publishes *Winning the World: a proposal on how to win the world for Christ now... in our generation;* 1987, further plan announced under name World Mission Teams.

Pentecostal missions executive D.A. Womack writes *Breaking the stained-glass barrier* urging church 'to abandon its sanctuaries of security and return to the evangelistic strategy of the Apostle Paul (the Ephesian Method of spontaneous lay evangelism)'; proposes mathematical formula measuring evangelization.

1974 Pan-Orthodox Consultation on 'Confessing Christ Today', Cernica, Bucharest (June); report states 'Evangelistic witness is understood to be restricted to the communication of Christ to those who do not consider themselves Christian'; 1975 (September), 'Confessing Christ through the liturgical life of the Church today', at Echmiadzin, Armenia (USSR), whose report states 'Christ said: Go ye therefore and make disciples of all nations', and calls attention to 'The fields where no one ever preached the Gospel'.

*Operation World,* a prayer survey, published by P.J. Johnstone (Dorothea Mission, and WEC); subsequent editions 1978, 1980, 1986), emphasizing world evangelization through daily intercession, centrality of local churches, and the call to 'mobilize the churches of the whole world to finish the task'.

International Congress on World Evangelization (ICOWE), Lausanne, Switzerland, on 'Let the Earth hear His Voice'; 2,700 delegates, from 150 countries, 4,000 total (50% from Third World); produces Lausanne Covenant stating: 'Evangelism itself is the proclamation of the historical, biblical Christ' (July); results by 1980 in vast, amorphous, network known as Lausanne Movement directed by LCWE (Lausanne Committee for World Evangelization).

EXPLO-74 in Seoul, Korea: 2nd Training Congress on Evangelism (Campus Crusade for Christ); 323,419 residents for one week, evening meetings 800,000 daily, with one rally drawing a new world record of 1.5 million (90% responding to invitation to commitment to Christ); biggest Christian conference in history to date (August).

Holy Year Jubilee for Roman Catholics: Paul VI proclaims 'a new period of evangelization', with full organic unity of all Christians an essential prerequisite: 'Before all men can be restored to the grace of God, communion must be reestablished between those who by faith have acknowledged and accepted Jesus Christ as the Lord of mercy who sets men free'; Holy Year in dioceses across world in 1974, in Rome in 1975.

'Sharing Christ's Bold Mission', theme developed by Southern Baptist Home Mission Board, extended to worldwide application.

3rd Ordinary Synod of Bishops (begun in 1967 with 1st, and 2nd in 1971) in Rome, on 'The Evangelization of the Modern World'; states that 'the promotion of human development forms an integral part of evangelization', closes with statement: 'We wish to confirm once more that the task of evangelizing all people constitutes the essential mission of the Church'.

World Mission 1975 (World Methodist Mission), a one-year program of worldwide witness 'offering men and women Christ', launched at Shepherds Field, Bethlehem, by World Methodist Council (decision of 12th World Methodist Conference, Denver, Colorado, USA) with 55 constituent nationwide Methodist churches (22 November).

Mission Renewal Teams begun (by D. Bryant, B. Goheen; and Fuller Theological Seminary, Pasadena) as seminarian teams teaching local churches through book *Ten Steps for World Evangelization;* wound down by 1979.

E.C. Pentecost publishes *Reaching the unreached: an introductory study on developing an overall strategy for world evangelization* (William Carey Library).

Philippines: DAWN (Discipling A Whole Nation) conference; 75 leaders of 4,000 Evangelical churches plan to have 50,000 churches planted by AD 2000, one in every barrio in the country (November); 1985, National Church Growth Strategy Congress with 300 leaders of 12,000 Evangelical churches reaffirms this goal (19-22 February); after 1981 it becomes a world plan, with motto '389 People can change the World: you can be one of them', involving 25 countries by 1987, with goal to begin by AD 2000 a DAWN project in every country of the world, with

slogan '7 Million More Churches by 2000 AD'.

*Religious and the evangelization of the world* published in Ottawa by Canadian Religious Conference, in English and French editions.

A.P. Johnston writes *World evangelism and the Word of God* (Minneapolis, MN: Bethany Fellowship); 1978, writes *The battle for world evangelism* (Wheaton, IL: Tyndale House).

Presbyterian Order for World Evangelism begun (later under USCWM, Pasadena, CA), as denominational support agency.

1975 Full Gospel World Mission Association established (1 April) in Seoul, Korea, as sending body supporting 8 overseas churches and 22 Korean missionaries; by 1985, 143 missionaries in 21 countries.

World Conference on the Holy Spirit and Holy Land Pilgrimage, Jerusalem (October).

5th Assembly of WCC, in Nairobi, Kenya: 'Jesus Christ frees and unites', 2,085 participants (850 delegates, 600 press); report on 'Confessing Christ today' states 'We are commissioned to proclaim the Gospel of Christ to the ends of the Earth'.

13th Baptist World Congress (BWA), Stockholm, on theme 'New People for a New World—Through Christ'; 9,936 delegates from 92 countries.

Communicators J.F. Engel and H.W. Norton write *What's gone wrong with the harvest? a communication strategy for the Church and world evangelization* (Zondervan).

'Total Missions Thrust: Global Discipleship' plan published by Southern Baptist Foreign Mission Board.

Project Look Up (PLU) begun by International Christian Broadcasters (USA), planning to reach world via NASA's ATS-6 geostationary satellite to beam TV seminary teaching and lay institutes across world; 1977, begins broadcasts to Puerto Rico; satellite suddenly withdrawn by NASA; 1979, PLU fizzles out due to inadequate funding, though committees go on meeting until after 1988.

Associates for World Evangelization (AWE) begun for students associated with USCWM.

International Missionary Congress on 'Evangelization and Cultures', sponsored by Pontifical Urbanian University, Rome; 600 attenders (5-12 October).

Paul VI's Apostolic Exhortation *Evangelii Nuntiandi* published (8 December) as the major Catholic statement on evangelization: 'To evangelize is first of all to bear witness'; world evangelization expounded in detail.

New Life International begun as evangelical charismatic service agency involved in TEE, literature, research; 1984, renamed Total World Evangelization Vision (Fresno, California), in 8 countries.

Genesis Project is begun to produce whole Bible on film, word for word; 33-year project envisaged, covering OT/NT with 300 films as the *New Media Bible,* to be dubbed in 27 languages; by 1986, 33 films emerge, but only Genesis and Luke completed; major achievement the 'Jesus' film with CCCI.

World Evangelical Fellowship Missions Commission inaugurated in Seoul, Korea, dedicated to development of the non-Western missionary movement (Third World missions), utilizing a network of agencies and Evangelical fellowships across the world.

1976 Southern Baptist Convention USA, meeting in Norfolk, VA, adopts resolution and plan for remainder of century to implement world evangelization through strategy Bold Mission Thrust: 'To enable every person in the world to have opportunity to hear and to respond to the gospel of Christ by the year 2000'; at 1988 midpoint, Foreign Mission Board reaffirms this intention.

Gabriel Olasoji World Evangelism (GOWE) founded in Ibadan (Nigeria) with motto 'Reaching the Unreached' based on Mark 16:15; by 1988, power evangelism and mass crusades in 25 nations.

Pasadena, USA; founding of US Center for World Mission, restricted to Conservative Evangelicals.

LCWE Strategy Working Group (SWG) formed; meets every year of two, works on plural strategies and tactics rather than any single overall strategy.

Australia: Congress on World Missions and Evangelism (May).

AMEN (American Military Evangelizing Nations) formed, by USA denomination Churches of Christ, for lay evangelism by US armed forces around world.

Church Growth International Seminars begun in Seoul by P. Yonggi Cho; by 1986, 70,000 pastors and leaders from 30 countries have attended; at 10th Seminar in 1986, goal of world evangelization announced with specific plan to win 10 million Japanese to Christ by AD 2000.

1st Chinese Congress on World Evangelization (CCOWE), Hong Kong, on 'Vision and Mission', with 1,600 participants from over 20 countries (August); CCCOWE (Chinese Coordination Centre of World Evangelism) set up in Hong Kong (October).

EFMA mission executives meet and tally the number of people groups in the unreached category which their agencies alone are in touch with, or are planning to reach by 1990; total estimated at 6,000 people groups.

Lausanne Intercession Advisory Group formed after ICOWE I; organizes conferences, annual day of prayer for world evangelization (Pentecost Sunday).

Habitat for Humanity International founded (USA) 'to eliminate poverty housing throughout the world in the name of Jesus Christ, seeking to glorify Him and

to spread His Gospel throughout the earth'; 1988, builds 2,000 houses in 300 cities; goal by 1996, to build in 2,000 North American cities and in 60 other countries.

Fellowship of World Christians (FOW) begun by USCWM for students (mostly ex-AWE) concerned for world evangelization; rallies; defunct by 1978; 1985, name taken over by different group (World Literature Crusade) offering 100 people a year two-week mission encounters in Mexico, Haiti, et alia.

1977 1st Conference on the Charismatic Renewal in the Christian Churches; ecumenical, at last embracing all pentecostal traditions; on theme 'Jesus is Lord'; in Kansas City, USA; 59,000 present (July); but after this ecumenical climax, charismatic conferences revert to monodenominational or monoconfessional status (15,000 Lutheran charismatics each year in Minneapolis, 10,000 RCs in Notre Dame, et alii).

4th Ordinary Synod of Bishops in Rome, on 'Catechetics in Our Time', dealing with evangelization of children and youth (September).

World Conference on Audio-Visuals and Evangelization, Munich (November).

J. Dobson founds Focus on the Family in California, USA which seeks to preserve traditional values and the institution of the family. Its purpose statement begins 'Focus on the Family exists to spread the Good News of Christ to those who do not know Him.'

Here's Life, World (saturation and total mobilization evangelization campaign), organized by Campus Crusade for Christ, bankrolled by History's Hundred (100 USA billionaires), launched in 100 countries, on every continent, with announced goal 'to fulfill the Great Commission in the whole world by the end of 1980'.

1978 World Mission 1978-1981 begun as World Methodist Council's 4-year plan of global evangelism.

International Conference on the Charismatic Renewal in the Catholic Church, in Dublin: 'You shall be My Witnesses'; 15,000 participants, led by L.-J. Suenens cardinal primate of Belgium (June).

1st Norwegian Congress on World Evangelization (related to LCWE), followed about every 2 years by Danvik National Conferences on Evangelization, with 140 church leaders, held in Drammen (Norway) in 1980, 1981, 1982, 1984, 1986.

7th General Chapter, Catholic Foreign Mission Society of America (Maryknoll) issues 'Statement of Mission Vision': 'Our particular task gives special emphasis to the evangelization of the poor, of cultures and of structures'.

Attempt by MARC (USA) to set up an information network for world evangelization entitled SHARE (Systems, Hardware and Research for Evangelization); scheme founders by 1985 due to inability to obtain original field data.

Great Commission Strategy Resource Network (GC-SRN) launched by CCCI 'to finish the task of reaching by 1980 those who have not yet heard the gospel', based on 5 functions: (1) information gathering and distribution, (2) resource reference, (3) research, (4) vision rooms, (5) international communication system; but peters out until by 1987 is reduced to computer hardware maintenance.

1979 Dutch missiologist J. Verkuyl writes 'The unfinished task of world mission' (Occasional essays, San José, Costa Rica).

D. Eastman reissues S.D. Gordon's *Quiet talks with world winners* (1908) as *What it will take to change the world* with updated statistics and commentary calling for world evangelization as soon as possible.

Anglican renewal agency SOMA (Sharing of Ministries Abroad) founded, 'dedicated to fostering Renewal in the Holy Spirit world wide so as to enable and equip the Church to fulfill the Great Commission of Jesus Christ, to proclaim the Kingdom of God and minister in the power of the Holy Spirit'; holds international conferences 1981 Singapore, 1983 Nairobi, 1984 Fiji, by 1987, its work in 50 countries covers 26 of the 31 Anglican Provinces worldwide.

West Germany: Conference on 'Unreached Peoples', sponsored by World Evangelical Fellowship, at Bad Liebenzell (January).

National Missionary Congress, Irish Missionary Union, at Knock, with nearly 400 Catholic missioners from every continent; theme 'A New Missionary Era' emerges (April).

Pan-Orthodox Consultation on 'The place of the monastic life within the witness of the Church today' at Amba Bishoy monastery, Egypt, seeking to rediscover past leading roles of monks and nuns in world evangelization (April-May).

Foursquare Missions International announces plan to begin work among 100 unreached peoples; by 1985, has 83 foreign missionaries with related churches in 47 countries (International Church of the Foursquare Gospel).

Over 10,000 pilgrims attend International Charismatic Pilgrimage to Lourdes on shrine's 100th anniversary (July).

12th Pentecostal World Conference, in Vancouver, Canada: 'The Holy Spirit in the Last Days' (October).

Canadian Congress on World Evangelization.

International Mission Congress (FABC and SC Propaganda), in Manila, on 'Towards a New Age in Mission: the Good News of the Kingdom to the Peoples of Asia' (2-7 December).

*Continued overleaf*

*Table 27–22 continued*

'Jesus' film produced by The Jesus Project, Campus Crusade for Christ, filmed in Palestine in 1979; by 1986, is circulating dubbed in 106 languages; annual viewers then total 275 million, decisions for Christ reach 33 million (12%); 1988, goal announced for 5,000 teams with copies dubbed in 271 languages of over a million speakers each by 1993 plus 1,000 other strategic languages and dialects by 1998 with 5 million viewers a night; also that, by AD 2000, 6 billion people shall have seen it of whom 600 to 1,500 million pray to receive Christ.

Evangelist Billy Graham (at IVCF urbana conference) and USA Evangelical foreign mission leaders issue call for '120,000 missionaries by the year 2000' in order to reach unreached peoples and establish 'A church for every people by AD 2000'.

USA: Angel-I/Angel-II/Angel-III Project to blanket Earth with gospel broadcasts proposed by NRB and WEF; 3 satellites in geostationary orbit filling roles of 3 angels of Revelation 14:6-11, each covering a third of Earth's surface, fulfilling Matthew 24:14 'for a witness unto all nations'; by 1983, author realizes project has been 'committed to death', so proposal passes into oblivion, though use of satellites for USA Christian TV grows.

TV evangelist J. Bakker of PTL Ministries announces plan to start PTL missions throughout the world; funds raised but plan fizzles out within a year; 1987, ministries collapse in financial and sex scandal.

*World Christian* magazine founded (California), focusing on young adults and world evangelization.

Lutherans for World Evangelization begun in Pasadena, CA (USA), as research and information service.

Caleb Project begun by USCWM to tap potential of students and young adults committed to world mission, undertaking field research among unreached peoples; 1986, merges with Joshua Project.

*Unreached Peoples* series of volumes published by LCWE/MARC in 1979, 1980, 1981, 1983, 1987, the latter 'Clarifying the Task' by clearly differentiating between (a) unreached ethnolinguistic peoples (each with no organized church; totalling 2,000 peoples across the world), and (b) social people groups (defined functionally; useful for deriving ministry options; totalling several million groupings).

Article 'World evangelism by 2000 AD: can it be done?' (*Moody monthly*, 80,4) written by R.D. Winter.

1980 Pope John Paul II undertakes global apostolic travels, to present the gospel to the world: over last 2 years visits Mexico, Poland, Ireland, USA, Africa, Brazil et alia; by February 1986, makes 29 official foreign pilgrimages as Catholic church's chief evangelizer.

LCWE International Consultation on Simple Life-Style, Hoddesden, UK (March), on how adoption of biblical lifestyles could accomplish world mission.

Stuttgart Congress on World evangelization, Germany (April).

A large African indigenous charismatic church, World Evangelical Crusaders in Christ Ministries (Benin City, Nigeria), begins Operation World begin From Here; other AIC denominations across Africa also advance similar global plans.

1st World Missionary Conference on Mission and Evangelism (4th Meeting of CWME/WCC), in Melbourne, Australia, with title 'Your Kingdom come' and theme 'Good News to the Poor'; 650 delegates representing 300 churches from 100 countries; 'The proclamation of the Gospel to the whole world remains an urgent obligation of all Christians' (12-24 May).

LCWE Consultation on World Evangelization (COWE) in Pattaya, Bangkok: 'How shall they hear?'; 875 delegates from 87 countries; 17 miniconsultations (16-27 June).

USA: 8th Annual Meeting, American Society of Missiology (ASM), in Wheaton (IL), on theme 'World Evangelization Today: Convergence or Divergence' (22-24 August).

10th United Bible Societies Council Meeting, Chiang Mai (Thailand), with 68 member societies, on theme 'God's Word: open for all' (September); over last 80 years, annual circulation of complete Bibles in all languages has risen from 5.4 million in 1900 to 36.8 million by 1980; UBS plan for decade to provide by 1990 common Bible translations in every language with over 1 million literates.

World Evangelization Crusade (Here's Life, Korea), Seoul; 16,500,000 attendance, including largest single meeting in Christian history to date (2.7 million).

United States Festival of World Evangelization; 50,000 participants (September).

Pan-Orthodox Consultation, organized through CWME, on 'Preaching and Teaching the Christian Faith Today' at Zica monastery, Yugoslavia; on regaining Orthodox role of proclamation in world evangelistic witness (September).

International Congress on Evangelization and Atheism, Pontifical Urbanian University, Rome (October).

1st World Consultation on Frontier Missions (WCFM), Edinburgh, organized by US Center for World Mission: 'A Church for every People by the Year 2000', 270 delegates (October).

Third Wave of 20th-century Renewal in the Holy Spirit begins in 40 major Evangelical churches, emphasizing power evangelism, power encounters, power healing, et alia.

E.R. Dayton & D.A. Fraser publish *Planning strategies*

*for world evangelization.*

1981 Christian broadcasting expands from origin in 1921 to global force heard or seen regularly by 23% of world's population.

USA: new generation of charismatic TV evangelists arises, including Oral Roberts (who began Pentecostal TV preaching in 1953) and son Richard, Pat Robertson, Rex Humbard, Jimmy Swaggart, Kenneth Copeland, Paul Crouch, Jim Bakker, et alii.

German Evangelical theologian P. Beyerhaus publishes *It is harvest time* (a textbook on world evangelization).

Evangelize the World by Computer Dialing: a scheme, proposed by several agencies, involving continuous automatic dialing through world's telephone directories and giving recorded messages to whomever replies.

2nd Chinese Congress on World Evangelization (CCOWE), on 'Life and Ministry', with over 1,500 church leaders, Singapore (June).

Baptist World Alliance; numerous meetings, papers; publishes *World Evangelization Now!* presses idea of a Baptist Fund for World Evangelization (to support Third-World missionaries); 1988, BWA General Council announces 'Vision 2000: Jesus Christ for All People' as 'a vision for encouraging world evangelization by the year 2000 AD'.

14th World Methodist Conference meets in Hawaii, endorses WMC's World Evangelism Committee's Continuing Plan for the Mission to the 80s (Decade of Evangelism), also known since 1971 inception as World Evangelism.

Missiologist H. Conn writes *Bible studies on world evangelization and the simple life-style*, with thesis that the goal can only be reached through the latter.

UK: Evangelical Missionary Alliance sponsors conference on 'Reaching Unreached Peoples: breaking new ground in areas of neglect', at High Leigh, Hertford (November).

Mission to Unreached Peoples (USA) begun under original name Gooddeeds.

Dominion Video Satellite (Dominion Network) incorporated in Florida (USA) to provide Christian radio/TV programs over DBS system (direct broadcast satellites), based on Great Commission, DBS as the angel of Revelation 14:6, 30-inch portable dish receivers, and bypassing of secular control over TV.

1982 Project 223 begun by YWAM, 'to establish a vital permanent ministry in every country on Earth', in 2 stages: (1) *trailblazing*, sending teams on evangelistic trips, one team to each of the world's 223 countries, involving initially 15,000 short-termers (2 weeks to 1 year) each year; completed in 1988 with No. 222 (Pitcairn Islands) and No. 223 (Svalbard & Jan Mayen Islands); also Project 300 to reach the 300 world-class megacities, with YWAM presence in 69 by 1988; and (2) *pioneering* (permanent residence) in 90 countries by 1988; with AD 2000 goal of 100,000 workers, aiming to fulfill the Great Commission in 25 years by AD 2011; 1988, among many new Projects introduced is Target 2000; Great Commission Torch Run, begun in Jerusalem on Easter Sunday, to involve 1 million runners.

1st ICFG Global Leadership Conference (Los Angeles) launches 'Harvest Vision: 1990', a plan produced by Foursquare Missions International to reach 160 hidden people groups, enter 76 new countries, and total 2.1 million ICFG members, all by 1990.

5th Conference, International Association for Mission Studies (IAMS), Bangalore, India, on theme 'Christ's Mission to the Multitudes: Salvation, Suffering and Struggle' (4-9 January); IAMS exists 'for the scholarly study of Christian witness and its impact in the world'.

Publication of *World Christian encyclopedia: a comparative survey of churches and religions in the modern world, AD 1900-2000*, designed deliberately as global survey to document world evangelization, the unfinished task, and rise of a global evangelization movement.

LCWE Chicago Consultation on Terminology concerning Unreached Peoples; subsequently, clear distinction drawn between (a) 'ethnolinguistic peoples' (being legitimate targets of church-planting efforts to establish beachheads with as goal in each a viable organized church fellowship able to evangelize its own culture, and (b) 'bridges' or 'bridge people groups' (smaller social or functional groupings affording opportunities for evangelism without church planting) (25-26 March).

World Satellite Evangelism (motto 'Using Mass Media to Reach the Unreached of the World for Christ') begun in Tulsa, OK, 'mobilizing media to reach every person in every home with the gospel' especially in closed countries; forms a global media task force in 50 nations, starting Christian universities and other centers.

1st Korean World Mission Congress, in Pasadena, CA (USA), with 300 delegates from Korean churches on 5 continents, 'to unite Koreans worldwide for the Great Commission of Christ' and 'to establish a Korean World Mission Coordinating Center' (17-30 May).

Major document *Mission and evangelism: an ecumenical affirmation* produced in Geneva by CWME and officially promulgated by Central Committee of WCC (July).

Institute for World Evangelism established in Atlanta, GA (USA), as major long-range achievement of World Evangelism Committee, World Methodist Council; its 1987 3rd biennial International Seminar, Atlanta, on theme 'The Holy Spirit and World Evangelization' draws over 100 delegates from 33 countries; authentic Wesleyan evangelism, with 2-fold witness to personal salvation and social redemption, given a new credibility and acceptance in Methodism worldwide.

*Panta to Ethni* (To All Peoples) begins publication under Apostoliki Diakonia (Church of Greece).

IFMA Frontier Peoples Committee formed; attempts to survey constituency of 96 IFMA member mission agencies in USA and Canada, but little substantial results; 1988, 71st IFMA Annual Meeting in Hamilton (Ontario) takes as its theme 'Countdown 2000' (12-15 September).

EFMA Missions Consultation on 'The Challenge of Our Task', in Colorado Springs, USA (27-30 September), based on *World Christian encyclopedia*; 1989, EFMA Mission Executives Retreat on 'Evangelizing the World by AD 2000', in Colorado Springs (25-28 September).

1983 World Baptist Congress on Urban Evangelism, in Niteroi, Brazil (26 June-3 July).

Lengthy document 'A global strategy for world evangelization by AD 2000: list of 105 steps or stages or aspects' produced for Southern Baptist Foreign Mission Board by WERC (Nairobi).

1st International Conference for Itinerant Evangelists, Amsterdam; theme 'Do the Work of an Evangelist'; 3,800 evangelists from 132 nations (July).

6th Assembly of WCC in Vancouver, Canada, on theme 'Jesus Christ the Life of the World'; 900 delegates (300 being women) from 310 member denominations, 850 journalists, 15,000 attenders at opening service (24 July-10 August).

Global Mapping Project started on USCWM campus, to assist churches with data and maps, with as objective 'Visualizing the Task of World Evangelization'.

Lumen 2000 launched as Catholic global television evangelism agency, based in Dallas (USA) and Vatican City, 'to preach the gospel of Jesus to the uttermost parts of the Earth, spreading the love of Jesus around the globe'; 1986, in 50 countries.

Committee on the Holy Spirit & Frontier Missions (CHSFM) begun in conjunction with USCWM to involve charismatics in frontier missions among hidden peoples; defunct by 1985.

L.E. Keyes writes *The last age of missions: a survey of Third World mission societies*, describing world evangelization by 15,000 missionaries in over 400 Third-World locally-supported societies and boards (especially from Brazil); since 1940, movement has mushroomed, with AD 2000 projection of 100,000 non-Western missionaries from 1,000 non-Western mission agencies.

New Focus Incorporated founded (San Bernardino, CA) as 'a Great Commission ministry committed to sports media strategies to reach the whole world with the gospel by the year 2000'; geared especially to TV specials at Olympics in 1988 in Korea, 1992 in Barcelona (Spain), 1996, and 2000.

1984 5th International Leaders Conference, Catholic Charismatic Renewal, in Rome attended by pope John Paul II (May); also ICCRO Worldwide Priests Retreat, in Vatican attended by 6,000 priests and 80 bishops and cardinals (October); 1990, 2nd Worldwide Priests Retreat, in Rome (14-18 September).

LCWE International Prayer Assembly for World Evangelization, Seoul, Korea (June); title, 'Seeking God's Face for a Movement of Prayer for the World'; 3,200 participants from 69 nations.

Ethnic Chinese Congress on World Evangelization (ECCOWE), in Honolulu, with 144 delegates (5-12 July).

*International journal of frontier missions* (Pasadena, USA) begun to further goal of reaching world's unreached peoples; 1988, circulation 500.

Over 30 national and 8 regional LCWE conferences on world evangelization, plus intensive prayer, commitment and planning, are organized for 5-year period leading into 1989 ICOWE II.

7th Assembly, Lutheran World Federation (LWF) in Budapest, Hungary, on 'In Christ—hope for the world'; 12,000 attenders (22 July-5 August).

STEP (Strategy to Every People) Programme introduced by WEC International, calling for '800 for the 80s' (800 new WEC workers for the 1980s), evangelizing 45 new peoples through resident teams; original name 'Worldwide Evangelization Crusade' now changed to 'Worldwide Evangelization for Christ' because 90% of new goals are among Muslim peoples.

3rd Plenary Assembly, World Catholic Federation for the Biblical Apostolate, in Bangalore, India, on theme 'Would that all of God's People were Prophets'; 120 delegates from 55 countries, representing WCFBA's 61 member Bible organizations (full members) and 125 associate member organizations (12-25 August); 1988 theme 'The Bible and the New Evangelization'.

Venezuelan Baptist Convention launches plan named Baptist World Discipleship Movement.

IVCF missions director J.E. Kyle edits volume of essays, *The unfinished task* (Regal).

Report 'Twenty-one Strategies for Lausanne' produced

*Continued opposite*

*Table 27–22 continued*

by LCWE Strategy Working Group.

Costa Rica: interdenominational missions society begun by 14 denominations, 1986 formalized as Federación Misionera Evangélica Costarricense (FEDEMEC), launches campaign 'Unidos en Cristo Evangelizando las Naciones' specifically 'From Costa Rica to the Uttermost Parts of the Earth', aiming to mobilize 10,000 world prayer missionaries and to send out 500 missionaries to 25 unreached peoples by AD 2000.

1985 'Mission 2000' scheme proposed by missiologists D.A. McGavran and R.D. Winter, aiming to plant a church in each of world's unreached peoples by AD 2000 through formation of 100,000 local church mission fellowships in Western countries.

International Missionary Congress, on theme 'Bringing Christ to Man', sponsored by Pontifical Urbanian University, Rome (18-21 February).

Korea: massive increase in number of Protestant and Catholic Korean missionaries sent abroad since first Protestant in 1912; by 1973 620 serving abroad in 30 countries (270 Protestants, 250 Korean indigenous, 90 Roman Catholics), rising by 1987 to 511 Protestants in 89 Korean mission agencies (increased from 47 agencies in 1982) in 47 nations; 1985, Protestant churches announce world evangelization plans calling for 10,000 Korean missionaries abroad by AD 2000 with at least one working in every country of the world.

Youth Congress on World Evangelization, Stuttgart, Germany (February).

Interchurch Consultation on Future Trends in Christian World Mission, Maryknoll, New York, on research methodology, sociopolitical issues, and unfinished tasks of world evangelization (15-17 February).

ICWE/WEF Consultation on the Work of the Holy Spirit and Evangelization, in Oslo, Norway; over 70 participants from 30 countries (May); results in published book *God the Evangelist.*

Integrity Keepers Conventions (persons 'Keeping integrity to Jehovah') held in 851 locations around world (averaging 6,700 attenders each), with total attenders 5,688,335 and 75,606 new baptisms; by 1986, Jehovah's Witnesses have become a vast global organization deploying more massive global resources for world conversion than any other single missionary agency: 3,229,022 publishers (active door-to-door member/evangelists, 'In harmony with Jesus' command 'Go... declare abroad the kingdom of God' in 100 languages in 208 countries, 52,177 congregations, 2,726,252 Bible study meetings a year, 8,160,597 annual Memorial (of Crucifixion) attenders, 2,762 foreign missionaries, 13,351 special pioneers, 8,920 foreign mission volunteers, and over 100,000 other full-time workers; vast annual magazine output totals 550 million (with 3,781,000 subscribers to *Watchtower* and *Awake!* in 33 language editions), and 44 million Bibles and books a year; Battle of Armageddon anticipated within 10 years, with 2 billion people killed, 144,000 Witnesses going to heaven with Christ, rest of Witnesses remaining on Earth during Millennium and then on into eternity.

1st Global Evangelization Strategy Consultation, Ridgecrest, NC (USA), with 70 participants from Baptist churches across world associated with Southern Baptist Convention; results inter alia in publication of 'The AD 2000 Series' (25-28 June).

World Conference of Baptist Evangelists, Bolivar, Missouri (USA): 'Strategies of evangelism to win world cities' (July).

6th All-Christian Peace Assembly (ACPA), convened by Christian Peace Conference (CPC), in Prague, on theme 'God calls: choose life; the hour is late!'; 800 participants from 90 countries (2-9 July).

5th West Malaysia Chinese Congress on World Evangelization, sponsored by CCCOWE, in Port Dickson (5-9 August).

International Consultation on Missions (ICOM) convened in Jos, Nigeria, by NEMA (Nigeria Evangelical Missions Association) and WEF, on theme 'Mobilizing Indigenous Missions for the Final Harvest'; 83 mission executives, mainly Nigerians (11 August).

Global Simultaneous Evangelistic Missions launched in Indonesia, Nigeria and other countries by World Methodist Council; thousands of local mission outreach campaigns planned across world.

Asia Committee for World Evangelization, Hong Kong (3-6 September).

Global Strategy Committee created by General Conference of Seventh-day Adventists, at 5-yearly meeting in New Orleans, USA (next being in 1990 in Indianapolis); Committee composed of 60 officials (3 members from each of the 11 divisions of the world, plus 30 from World Division in Washington, DC); prepares strategy for 15 million Adventists in 210 countries; at 1988 meeting in Georgia (USA), launches plan based on segmentization document 'SDA Global Strategy: The People of the World divided into approximately 5,000 population segments averaging one million'.

God's Global Envoys—Nonresidential Missionaries for World Evangelization, an overall plan evolved by WERC/FMB, Richmond, USA, envisaging cooperation of entire spectrum of all Christians of all traditions whether like-minded or not; based on 3 elements: (a) segmentization of unevangelized world into 3,000 distinct segments (peoples, cities, countries), (b) matching-up of segments with one professional missionary each, and (c) nonresidential mission and ministry through computerized research and networking; 1985, first descriptions published in print (May).

International Catholic Programme of Evangelization (ICPE) begins functioning, based on Malta, first with School of Evangelization in Valletta, then others in Rome, New Zealand, et alia; 1988, 2nd Meeting of Association of Coordinators of Catholic Schools of Evangelization, in Rome (13-16 June).

Project 'The World by 2000' announced by 3 major Christian broadcasting agencies, FEBC, HCJB/World Radio Missionary Fellowship, TWR (and later ELWA-SIM): to complete by AD 2000 giving everyone on Earth the opportunity to hear the gospel of Christ by radio (September); 1987, target modified to be (1) all major trade languages with over 1 million speakers each by AD 2000, then (2) all minor trade languages, then later (3) the world's 6,500 'heart' languages.

World Ambassadors, a plan of Maranatha Christian Ministries to evangelize the world through conversions among the 200,000 international non-Christian students from 170 nations (65 closed to missionaries) who are resident in the USA; slogan 'Reaching international students to reach the world' by returning home to plant churches; goal to train 15,000 such leaders each year.

World Consultation on Evangelism, Lake Junaluska (USA), sponsored by World Evangelism (World Methodist Council) (September); 5-year evangelism plan for 1987-1991 adopted.

1st Venezuelan Congress of World Missions, Maracay, aiming to appoint 500 missionaries by 1987 (15-19 October).

CWME Orthodox Advisory Group meets in Sofia (Bulgaria) on 1,100th anniversary of death of Methodius, issues call to rectify Orthodoxy's failure to fulfill Jesus' Great Commission and 'to reach out to the unreached' (21-26 October).

Global Network of Centers for World Mission formed, based on 30 research and study centers; 1986, issues Singapore Statement (27 June); 1988, holds its 1st World Meeting, in Singapore (1-9 November).

Amsterdam Prayer Conference for World Evangelization, sponsored by LCWE, YWAM, et alia (November).

EXPLO-85 global Christian training teleconference organized in 95 locations in 55 countries simultaneously by Campus Crusade for Christ (CCCI), using satellite video relays (6 uplinks, several thousand downlinks), training 550,000 Christian workers from 100 countries worldwide in prayer, evangelism and discipleship, with 4 telecasts reaching 60 million (27-31 December).

Association of International Mission Services (AIMS) begun, to serve Charismatic Renewal, with slogan 'Unity in the Spirit for World Evangelization'; 75 member agencies with 3,000 career missionaries; 1988, announces new global plan 'Operation Unreached'.

Church growth specialist D.A. McGavran publishes 'Emergency call for United Global Evangelism' (*Church growth,* Seoul, Korea) defining God's call as 'Evangelize, baptize, multiply churches at home and abroad', concentrating on ripe, receptive, harvest fields.

Third-wave/charismatic leader John Wimber writes *Power evangelism: signs and wonders today,* followed in 1987 by *Power healing,* also in 1988 *Power encounters among Christians in the Western world.*

1986 'Reaching the World's Cities by AD 2000', a plan of Assemblies of God (USA), Division of Foreign Missions, with 'declared objective to help evangelize every city on the face of the earth'.

Consultation on Evangelizing World Class Cities, Moody Bible Institute, Chicago (14-17 March).

OMS mission executive Wesley L. Duewel writes *Touch the world through prayer* (Zondervan).

Worldwide Student NetWork launched by CCCI (USA) with goal of evangelizing by AD 2000 all the world's 30,000 tertiary-level universities and colleges (3,000 top universities, 8,000 university colleges, 19,000 vocational or professional colleges) with 60 million students, generating parallel surge from the campus to the entire world.

International Prophetic Ministry Convention, Mount Carmel (Israel) and Jerusalem; 30 modern prophets and 5,000 attenders, at Easter (Christians of all confessions).

1st General Assembly, Latin American Evangelical Confraternity (CONELA, founded 1982, with 225 member denominations, councils, associations and agencies), in Maracaibo, Venezuela; topic, challenge to evangelize latin America and the world, with 'millions of Latin American missionaries sent to the Muslim world and other regions where they are needed' (M. Ortiz, president); 95 delegates and over 1,000 attenders (22-25 April).

USA: International Conference for Equipping Evangelists (charismatic) in Sacramento (CA), 'training thousands of evangelists to equip millions of Christians to reach billions of unbelievers' (5-9 May).

8th General Assembly, World Evangelical Fellowship, in Singapore, on 'Renew the Church—Reach the World', with 250 delegates from 50 WEF member alliances and fellowships (22-27 June).

2nd International Conference for Itinerant Evangelists (ICIE), Amsterdam; 8,000 evangelists from 150 countries (12-21 July).

3rd Chinese Congress on World Evangelization (CCOWE '86) sponsored by CCCOWE, held in Taipei (Taiwan), theme 'Renewal, Breakthrough and Growth'; 1,900 Chinese church leaders from over 20 countries (6-13 August); CCCOWE produces 6-volume survey in Chinese (2 volumes in English) of whole Chinese diaspora across world.

24th International Old Catholic Congress (International Old Catholic Bishops Conference) in Münster, Germany, on 'Witness and Service in the World' (26-30 August).

4th Triennial Convention, Asia Missions Association (AMA), in Pasadena, USA, on 'Thy Will be done on Earth' (6-12 October): Asians abroad as foreign missionaries reported as 10,210 with AD 2000 total expected to be 67,000.

Good News World (Operation World/Mass Scripture Distribution), a global plan announced by Southern Baptist Sunday School Board, Nashville (TN), as: 'Purpose: To place Scriptures in the hands of everyone in the world in 1994 to prepare for worldwide revival in 1995'.

'Toward 2000', a program of Issachar Frontier Missions Research (Seattle, USA), specializing in witness in closed countries; publishes *Strategic Times journal.*

U.S. Catholic Bishops publish NCCB pastoral statement on world mission, *To the ends of the Earth.*

Mandate '86, 1st Annual Mid-West Student Missions Conference, 'to reach the world's unreached', organized in Illinois (USA) with 800 students by IVCF-related students, supported by CCCI, AoG, SBC, IVCF et alia, with 9 related regional meetings; also Mission Advance 86 (Hamilton, Canada, 850 students); 1987, numerous student-run conferences—Mandate '87 (in Muncie, IN; 1,200 students, 23-25 January), Harvest (in Minneapolis, 6-8 February), Vision, Proclaim, Go (Global Outreach), GAP (Global Awareness Project).

USA: Presbyterian Church announces Decade of Evangelism for 1990-2000.

North American Leaders Congress on the Holy Spirit and World Evangelization (RC/Protestant charismatic renewal), New Orleans, with over 7,500 pastors and leaders, also 4,000 other attenders (October); vast numbers of regional and denominational conferences and seminars proliferate.

US Society for Frontier Missiology founded in Colorado Springs; 1987, 2nd Annual Meeting in Orlando, Florida (USA) discusses AD 2000 closure and countdown thinking; 86 mission leaders from 46 North American agencies (25-26 September).

Intercontinental Broadcasting Network (IBN) begun in Virginia Beach, USA, by independent charismatics linking up with European counterparts.

Global Strategy Group formed to coordinate planning for Southern Baptist Foreign Mission Board (December).

K.P. Yohannan (founder, Gospel for Asia) writes *The coming revolution in world missions,* describing a coming Third Wave of mission, namely a massive movement producing one million evangelists from thousands of native missionary movements in India, Asia, and across the world.

Missiologist J.H. Kane writes *Wanted: World Christians* (these being essential for world evangelization), holding as key 'A World Christian is one who recognizes his own personal responsibility for world missions.'

Televised Evangelism for All, a project proposed by Christian Broadcasting Network vice-president N. Van Hamm; 6 million 10-inch flat liquid-screen printed-circuit solar-cell television units, costing $1 each, dumped out of aircraft across world, glide to Earth over unevangelized peoples, pretuned to 18-language transmissions over 3 or 4 geostationary satellites.

1987 John Paul II announces new Office in Rome, 'Evangelization 2000', initially confined to Catholics, with news service *New Evangelization 2000,* and later to lead into ecumenical 1990-2000 Decade of Evangelization; comprising retreats, biggest public rally ever, 3-satellite global telecasts, global homilies, conscientization teams, mass video cassette distribution, with as aim to win 1.5 billion new Christians 'as a present for Jesus on his 2,000th birthday'.

44th Annual Convention & Exposition, National Religious Broadcasters (USA), Washington, with over 4,000 broadcasters, on theme 'Communicating Christ to the Nations' (31 January-4 February).

Consultation on World Evangelization, Singapore, with 31 global charismatic renewal leaders (RC/Lutheran/SOMA-Anglican, et alii) (9-12 February).

International Conference of Evangelical Bible Societies (ICEBS) founded 'to evangelize and disciple all nations through the placement of God's word', with 10 member agencies: ASGM, BLI, EHC, IBS, LBI, OD, PTL, WGC, WHBL, WMP.

T.Y.H. Wang in Singapore issues LCWE call with article 'By the Year 2000—Is God telling us something?'; many responses from across world.

National Charismatic Leaders' Conference (North American Renewal Service Committee, NARSC), related to global Charismatic Renewal in mainline denominations (300 million Christians, field 74,000 foreign missionaries), meets in Glencoe, MO (USA),

*Continued overleaf*

*Table 27–22 continued*

appoints World Evangelization Strategy Committee with AD 2000 goal in mind (4-8 May).

World Literature Crusade changes name to Every Home for Christ, proclaims goal 'to systematically place 2 gospel booklets in every home in the world, one country at a time, by AD 2000'; 40% of world's homes reached since 1946; 1986, 21,969,676 pieces of literature distributed, producing 178-509 written responses (0.8%); 1957-86, tracts distributed total 1,462,406,418, with 14,605,937 responses (1.0%).

Proposal 'Countdown to the Year 2000' circulated by USCWM founder R.D. Winter, with statistics and graphics urging the engaging (entering) and reaching (discipling) by mission agencies of 1,500 new unreached peoples every year until 17,000 have been reached by AD 2000.

Global-Village Evangelism (based on Marshall McLuhan's description of the world as now a 'global village') launched by Bibles for the World as 'a revolutionary new concept in missions' which places the local church in the center of the world mission program.

Singapore '87 LCWE International Younger Leaders' Conference on world evangelization; 300 younger Evangelical leaders from 67 countries (1-10 June).

Global Rosary for World Peace and world evangelization prayed by John Paul II in St. Peter's basilica, Vatican, and by 16 Marian shrines across the world linked by 18 satellites and 75 TV cameras, with TV audience of 1.5 billion in over 30 countries in 35 languages; most complex and ambitious television program of all time.

North American General Congress on the Holy Spirit and World Evangelization, in New Orleans (successor to 1977 Kansas City ecumenical charismatic rally); over 50,000 participants (RC/Protestant charismatic renewal), 51% RCs; theme 'Power Evangelism' (22-26 July); launches magazine *AD 2000 Together* with front page motto 'To Bring the Majority of the Human Race to Jesus Christ by the End of the Century'.

Dominion Network (satellites to homes) launched into orbit by Community Satellite Corporation, USA, utilizing DBS (direct broadcast satellites).

Global Share Network announced by Global Mapping International (USA) as a missions mapping database.

T. Yamamori writes *God's new envoys; a bold strategy for penetrating closed countries,* presenting a detailed plan describing the strategic work Christian lay tentmakers in secular work can perform in world evangelization; chapter 6 entitled 'The Basic Battle Plan' calls for 100,000 such persons in 77 closed countries.

Research project 'The Future of the Christian World Mission' begun under auspices of American Society of Missiology, majoring on scenarios for the future of world evangelization.

Mission World '89 (International Satellite Mission) announced by Billy Graham Evangelistic Association, to originate from a major global city (Seoul) and to be beamed by satellite to hundreds of other cities across the world; but whole plan suddenly cancelled 5 months later and replaced by scaled-down London crusade in 1989 with relays across England only.

Global Broadcasting System (GBS) launched for Christian radio and TV broadcasting to any place on Earth through 'Top Hat' system of super-pressure platform network of 800 high-tech balloons at 120,000 feet altitude covering whole world.

Adopt-a-People, a proposal to link North American churches and mission agencies with specific unreached people groups, begun by USCWM.

Christian Communication Technology (CCT) formed to develop AVCAPI (computer/laser reading system for illiterates) with goal: 'By the year 2000, CCT will teach every capable and willing man, woman and child on earth to read the Bible in their own language.'

Worldwide Prayer Crusade launched from Vatican City By Evangelization 2000 office, geared to Decade of Universal Evangelization 1990-2000; sudden, unexpected, and massive enthusiastic response from contemplatives, convents, and monasteries worldwide.

Project 2000 begun by Partnership International, formerly Christian Nationals Evangelism Commission (CNEC, begun 1943), now in 50 countries; project pledges 'to help establish an evangelistic growing church in each of the 17,000 unreached people groups of the world by the year 2000', 'to help strengthen 400 ministries under 80 different indigenous national organizations'.

Destiny '87 Conference (Here's Life, Black America); 1,700 Black Americans gather in Atlanta, GA, to affirm 'a growing number of black Christians believe it is their destiny to play a major role in world evangelization'.

New Life 2000 announced as closure project by Campus Crusade for Christ/Here's Life World—'the comprehensive global strategy to take the gospel to every culture on every continent by the year 2000; to present the gospel message to 6.5 billion people; to see 1 billion people receive Jesus Christ as Lord and Savior; to establish 10,000 New Life Bible study groups; to establish 1 million new churches; to provide 5,000 teams showing the 'Jesus' film 100 times

a year to 1,000 people per night (yielding 10% to 25% salvation decisions a night); to establish 15,000 prayer movements by 1995, in every city over 50,000 and all university campuses'.

*Towards 2000: Reaching the world's billions,* written by physician Benjamin George, Campaign for Christ (YFC), Malaysia; plan calls only for lifestyle evangelism (daily personal witnessing).

Interdenominational Global Missions Conference (Dallas I) convened (17-18 September) by Southern Baptist FMB president R.K. Parks, with 20 mission agencies present; agreement on (1) prayer and fasting every Pentecost weekend up to AD 2000 as 'focused intercession for global evangelization', and (2) sharing data, plans and strategies; 1988, Dallas II (February), followed by teleconferences.

*Status Report on the Great Commission* published by World Mission Teams (formerly World Mission Crusade), Florida, as open letter addressed 'To All Pastors of All Christian Churches' setting out logistics and finances of how to evangelize the world by means of 'the fourth dimension in evangelism' (1st=personal witness, 2nd=printing, 3rd=broadcasting, 4th=motion picture evangelism).

Decade of Harvest inaugurated by Assemblies of God (USA), as denominational program to reach all persons on Earth by AD 2000; coordination by Total Church Evangelism Strategy Committee, renamed in 1987 Harvest Task Force (for work within USA); 1988 (July), world conference of AoG-related churches overseas to plan strategy.

Ibadan, Nigeria: Consultation between All Africa Baptist Fellowship and Overseas Mission Bodies (October); produces Ibadan Declaration, on Great Commission and 'mutual sharing in the holistic evangelisation of the world'.

2nd Asia Leadership Congress on World Evangelization (ALCOWE or ALCOE II), under LCWE/ALCOWE auspices, in Singapore, on theme 'Witnessing for Christ through the Local Church' (20-28 October).

1st Ibero-American Missions Congress (Congreso Misionero Ibero-Americano, COMIBAM '87), in São Paulo (Brazil), with 3,500 Evangelical representatives (70% pentecostal/charismatic) from across Latin America, and preceded by series of national missions consultations in 23 countries; goal of world evangelization, with 10,000 new Latin American foreign missionary vocations generated (23-28 November).

Church of God (Cleveland, TN), with work in 98 countries, launches 'Decade of Destiny for Church of God World Missions', with a different continent targeted for each year from 1990 to 2000.

Advance Ministries: Reaching the Unreached, a mission-sending agency serving the USA's 60,000 independent charismatic churches, begun with Mennonite support.

World Evangelism World Plan 1987-1991 launched at Jamaica meeting after 15th World Methodist Conference (Nairobi, July 1986, 3,000 delegates) on theme 'Christ Jesus: God's 'Yes' for the World': 1988 Aldersgate year, Open-Air Preachings, 1989 World Conference on Physical & Spiritual Poverty, 1990 4th International Christian Youth Conference, 1991 Conference on World Evangelization followed by 16th World Methodist Conference in Singapore.

Charismatic pastor D. Shibley writes *Let's Pray in the harvest* on how to 'Discover the Missing Key to World Evangelization'.

1988    Conferences on evangelization: since 1945, some 5,510 conferences on mission and evangelism (at international, continental, regional or national level) have been held, via 5 groupings: 1,050 by Roman Catholic agencies; 1,100 by Ecumenical Movement agencies; 2,100 by Protestant and Anglican mission agencies; 840 by Evangelical mission agencies; and 420 by Charismatic Renewal agencies.

Missions journalist J.W. Reapsome polls agencies and executives, publishes analysis and assessment 'Great Commission deadline: is the year 2000 a reasonable goal or an improbable dream?' (*Christianity Today*, 15 January), followed by 5-part series in *Evangelical missions quarterly*.

Evangelist N. Krupp writes large volume *The Church Triumphant at the End of the Age, characterized by revival, restoration, unity, world evangelization, and persecution;* holds Great Commission will only be fulfilled by supernatural means of a global End-time revival.

Churches of the poor spread gospel, unorganized and unplanned, in almost every corner of Earth.

2nd All-India Congress on Missions and Evangelism (AICOME '88), sponsored by indigenous-mission body India Missions Association, IMA (with 300 member agencies), in Pune, India; 350 participants (4-8 January); global total of organized Third-World mission agencies now 500.

World Evangelization Database (segmentizing world into 250 countries, 11,000 ethnolinguistic peoples, 15,000 languages, 3,300 metropolises, et alia), first begun in 1962 as computer knowledge base, is finally brought online globally by WERC/FMB to assist mission agencies to match up nonresidential missionaries with entire unevangelized world; operated by massive computerized AI network, the World Evangelization Expert System (WEES), itself part of Great Commission Expert Systems (GCES).

Literature on evangelization: on narrower definition,

titles strictly on 'evangelize', 'evangelism' or 'evangelization' total 400 new books and articles every year; on broader definition, titles on evangelization and synonyms total 10,000 a year.

World Prayer Force inaugurated in Saint Petersburg, FL (USA), aiming to enroll 165 million Christians (10% of world total) promising to pray daily for world evangelization.

Inter-Agency Consultation for Resources and Information on Reaching the Unreached (Dallas II), held in Irving, TX (USA), by 28 denominations and agencies (9-11 February); followed by sharing of online databases and a series of Great Commission electronic teleconferences, with all mission executives and leaders participating from own headquarters.

Evangelistic citywide mass campaigns: several hundred organized multidenominational campaigns (under Billy Graham, Luis Palau, et alii), and some 3,000 denominational campaigns, are held in 1,300 metropolises and cities across the world each year; also hundreds of megameetings (over 100,000 attenders) under Christ for All Nations and numerous other charismatic agencies, using slogan 'The Great Commission to Each Generation'.

Singapore II Consultation on World Evangelization, with 65 global charismatic renewal leaders organized as CUWE, Charismatics United for World Evangelization with the new watchword 'The whole church, bringing a whole Christ, to the whole world!', 'to consider the distinctive contribution that the charismatic renewal could make in spreading the Christian gospel in the years leading up to AD 2000' (February).

Christian prophecy: millions of predictions, prophecies and proposed scenarios have been made throughout history; Catholic prophecy alone, not officially acknowledge by Rome, has produced over the centuries several thousand collected prophecies about End of World and the Antichrist, some by laypersons, some by clergy, some by monks and nuns, some by bishops, and some by popes.

Consultation to inaugurate Third World Missions Advance (TWMA), convened by AMA/IMF/EMS/COMIBAM; 35 Third-World leaders meet in Portland, OR (9-13 May); International Mutual Fund created; TWMA aims to represent the hundreds of new missions agencies, with potential of fielding 100,000 Third-World missionaries by AD 2000.

Explosive growth of charismatic, evangelical and fundamentalist 'video churches', video denominations and video mission agencies; vast rash of house-church networks begins to spread in all countries with large denominations.

Leadership '88, an LCWE conference in Washington, DC for 2,200 emerging leaders, to 'equip them to take aggressive action to fulfill the Great Commission', to 'strategize to join together for world evangelization' and 'to form new networks for completing the task of world evangelization' (27 June-1 July).

North American African World Missions Congress (initiative '88) to implement global evangelization, organized by Nigerians after 1986 formation of North American Commission of African Christians; theme 'African Initiatives in World Missions" a Strategic Gathering for a New Decade'; 1,500 Africans from over 30 African counties, living in North America, present in Chicago (13-17 July).

7th General Congress, International Association for Mission Studies (IAMS), in Rome, on theme 'Christian Mission towards the Third Millennium: the Gospel of Hope' (29 June-5 July).

International Evangelical Bible Consultation/Conference (sponsored by LCWE, BGEA et al), in Amman, Jordan, stressing biblical position on justice and human rights.

World Wesleyan Conference on Witness and Evangelism, sponsored by World Methodist Council, on 250th anniversary of John Wesley's conversion.

'88 World Evangelization Crusade, Korea, led by charismatics (Methodists, Presbyterians) and pentecostals.

March for Jesus begun in Britain by charismatic Graham Kendrick.

1989    Global Consultation on World Evangelization by AD 2000 and Beyond, convened in Singapore by a group including LCWE/COMIBAM/FMB-SBC/YWAM, inviting 2 representatives of each of the 78 major current megaplans for world evangelization, 'open to all leaders of Great Commission groups within the worldwide body of Christ' (5-8 January).

2nd World Consultation on Frontier Missions (WCFM).

2nd World Conference on Mission and Evangelism (5th Meeting of CWME/WCC, Commission on World Mission and Evangelism), San Antonio, TX (USA); 600 attenders, mostly church nominees; theme 'Your Will be Done: Mission in Christ's Way'; distributes pan-Orthodox missionary icon widely (22 May-1 June).

International Bishops' Retreat 2000 for world's 3,500 Roman Catholic bishops (October, in Rome), on theme 'Called to Evangelize', to inaugurate decade of evangelization 1990-2000; also, separately, and on same theme, Worldwide Priests' Retreat (7,000 in Rome, 14-18 September 1990) and Worldwide Theologians' Retreat (4,000 in Rome, October 1991).

World Evangelization Conference on Liberation The-

*Continued opposite*

*Table 27–22 concluded*

ology and Personal Salvation (sponsored by World Methodist Council), in Latin America.

Lausanne II, or 2nd International Congress on World Evangelization (ICOWE II) convened by Lausanne Committee (LCWE), in Manila; congress theme, 'Proclaim Christ Until He Comes', attended by 6,000 evangelizers (11-20 July).

15th Pentecostal World Conference, in Singapore, on theme 'Behold the Glory of the Lord'; over 6,000 delegates from 100 countries, 30,000 attenders (27 September-1 October).

Consultation on Dimensions of Christian Martyrdom, dealing with effects of martyrdom on upbuilding and evangelistic growth of whole church; total martyrs since AD 33 estimated at 40,500,000 (0.5% of all Christians ever), with current rate of 320,000 each year.

Jerusalem Charismatic Leaders Meeting (Pentecost 89) convened for 120 Renewal leaders worldwide, dealing with power intercession, power evangelism, world evangelization; in Jerusalem over Pentecost weekend (7-14 May).

'Proposal for a Joint Worldwide Movement', an elaborate global plan circulated by USA ecumenist R.N. Myers.

1990 Vast increases in all types of evangelization and of evangelistic activity: virtually all major Christian denominations and agencies announce programs leading up to AD 2000.

Decade of Universal Evangelization (also termed Worldwide Decade of Evangelization) inaugurated by John Paul II and other world Christian leaders, calling all Christians to a decade of mission, with as aims (a) to unite all Christians and all churches by AD 2000, and (b) to bring the total of Christ's disciples to over 50% of world (3.1 billion) by AD 2000.

Round the World Prayer Event, organized by World Evangelism (World Methodist Council), to inaugurate evangelism in decade of 1990s.

Peace Council/Convocation of Christians: World Convocation on Justice, Peace, and the Integrity of Creation (JPIC), a worldwide ecumenical event, convened by RCC, WCC et alia, to oppose injustice, war and environmental destruction.

USA: Joint IFMA/EFMA Conference convenes, after 1988 IFMA conference on 'Countdown 2000' and 1989 EFMA conference on 'Evangelizing the World by AD 2000'; approves specific allotments for 1995 schedule for reaching all peoples on Earth with gospel.

World Congress on the Holy Spirit and World Evangelization, in Indianapolis, on 'Power Evangelism'; over 60,000 attenders (Catholic/Protestant charismatic renewal).

EXPLO '90 global Christian 5-day training teleconference organized in all major countries by Campus Crusade for Christ (expanded version of EXPLO-85); also their 'Jesus' film becomes after 10 years translated into world's 280 languages each with over 1 million mother-tongue speakers, and is being shown to 10 million persons every night, of whom 2 million become converts or enquirers each night.

Asia Regional Missions Congress on AD 2000 and Beyond (LCWE/TWMA/AMA/et alia).

Africa Regional Missions Congress on AD 2000 and Beyond (LCWE/TWMA/EMS/et alia).

AD 2000 National Consultations proliferate, planned each for one country during the period 1990-1999 by LCWE/TWMA/et alia.

National Evangelistic Census, organized by Charismatic evangelists Charles & Frances Hunter.

1991 Global Congress of Charismatic Leaders for World Evangelization, in Brighton (UK), to usher in decade of evangelization before AD 2000; 10,000 renewal leaders (8-14 July).

7th Assembly, World Council of Churches (WCC), in Canberra, Australia, with delegates from 350 member denominations; call to global commitment; ongoing programs include the Ecumenical Decade (1988-1998) for Churches in Solidarity with Women (launched at Easter 1988).

4th Chinese Congress on World Evangelization, CCCOWE '91 (sponsored by CCCOWE/LCWE), in Hong Kong.

Sudden growth and mushrooming worldwide of youth churches completely outside control by denominations; loosely-organized churches begun and run by charismatic under-25s, meeting at lunch times in hotels, theaters, cinemas, shops, warehouses, anywhere; huge growth of converts.

Conference on World Evangelization organized in Singapore by World Methodist Council.

AD 2000 Regional Consultations sponsored by LCWE/TWMA/et alia begin in earnest: 1991 North America; 1991 Europe; 1991 Middle East & North Africa; 1993 Asia; 1993 Latin America; 1993 Africa.

After 30 years' preparation since 1961 1st Pan-Orthodox Conference (on island of Rhodes), Great & Holy Council of the Orthodox Church convenes in Greece as first fully-recognized ecumenical council of the entire church since 7th Ecumenical Council (Council of Nicaea II, last one recognized by Eastern Orthodox) in AD 787; statement promulgated on Orthodoxy's mission to the world; mission icon distributed.

1992 Festival of Good News AD 2000 launched by K.C. George and T. Valsom Abraham with major evangelistic conference in Trivandrum, Kerala, India, December 2-6. Stated goal is 'World Evangelization by AD 2000.'

1993 L. Bush and AD 2000 Movement, Inc. launch Praying Through The Window I targeting for prayer the 62 countries of the 10/40 window. 21 million intercessors participate during the month of October. PTWII in Oct 1995 mobilizes 36 million to pray for cities. PTWIII in Oct 1997 mobilized over 40 million to pray for unreached peoples.

1994 Final decade of 20th century proves to be greatest decade in Christian history for signs and wonders, miracles, conversions, evangelism and evangelization: greatest sign or wonder being Christians loving one another and gathering in unity everywhere.

New global plan 'The Last Frontier' targeting World A peoples via ISPD (Integrated Strategic Planning Database) launched by SBC Foreign Mission Board, replacing failed 1976 plan Bold Mission Thrust.

*The Star of 2000* published by J. Gary as call to mobilize Evangelicals for world evangelization.

1995 L. Bush announces Joshua Project 2000, a plan to plant a church among every one of 1,739 peoples listed by name (over 10,000 in population and <5% Christians). Plan is revised and renamed in 1997: Joshua Harvest to include peoples less than 10,000 in population.

World Christian Congress on AD 2000 and Beyond (LCWE/TWMA/COMIBAM/AMA/EMS/etc) held in South Korea.

3rd World Consultation on Frontier Missions (WCFM), specifically for mission executives planned but canceled due to lack of interest.

G. Verwer announces Mobilizing New Missionaries Network, calling for 200,000 new missionaries by AD 2000, half of them from the USA.

WorldReach launched by CBN (Virginia Beach, USA) on Oct. 1 with goal of proclaiming the gospel, primarily by television, to 3 billion people by AD 2000.

*AD 2025 Global Monitor*, edited by T.M. Johnson, a bimonthly tracking world evangelization plans and progresses.

1997 Two thousand participants at COLCOM '97 (Sept, Quito, Ecuador) launch Plan of 1000 Days led by Bolivian R. Justiniano. The plan calls for the mobilization of the Ibero-American church to aid in completing world evangelization by AD 2000.

M. Cerullo launches Mission to All the World 2000, a plan to mobilize millions of believers to pray for the completion of The Great Commission by the end of AD 2000.

International Bible society (IBS) announces the start of a global plan to distribute Scripture. 'Let There Be Light', which involves increased translation, creation of audience-specific evangelism tools, and Scripture publishing.

1998 World Harvest Information Database (WHID) announced at AD 2000 Track Leader meeting by E. Watt. Comprehensive tracking system abandoned within one year due to lack of funds, personnel, and support from mission agencies.

D. Eastman of Every Home for Christ (EHC) announces 10 year plan Completing the Commission with detailed goals related to prayer, training, and literature distribution.

C.P. Wagner publishes *Confronting the Queen of Heaven* contending that spiritual forces of darkness are delaying closure in world evangelization. A rally of 4,000 intercessors is planned for the following October 1 in Ephesus, Turkey to defeat the Queen of Heaven.

J. Rankin, president of the International Mission Board (IMB) of the Southern Baptist convention (SBC) announces plan "Accelerating World Evangelization" which consists of three meetings of researchers and executives identifying obstacles to closure.

T. Haggard and C.P. Wagner dedicate $36 million World Prayer Center in Colorado Springs, USA. The Center acts as an international switchboard for 50 million intercessors in 120 nations.

Celebrate Messiah 2000 conference announced by AD 2000 & Beyond Movement to be held in Jerusalem 27 Dec 2000 - 2 Jan 2001 celebrating mission accomplishment among every people. Due to political unrest in Jerusalem, meeting is canceled less than 2 weeks before it was to begin.

1999 Catholics begin preparations to celebrate Jubilee Year of AD 2000, in the Holy Year series, with pope to telecast on 25 December 2000 to billions of viewers via network of satellites.

H. Kamel, founder of Arabic Communication Center (ACC) announces "New Hope for the Third Millennium" plan aimed mainly at 220 million Arabic speakers but states "it is the time when every one in the world gets the opportunity to hear about the love of Jesus Christ."

Representatives of major Evangelical networks meet in Norway (March 21-25) to develop a new framework for cooperation into the new millennium. T. Wany appointed Chairman of the newly-formed Global Evangelization Forum.

D. Eastman of Every Home for Christ (EHC) breaks ground on new $6 million Jericho Center in Colorado Springs, USA as nerve center for 24-hour prayer and praise and a place where ministry leaders from around the world can gather together to pray and strategize for the completion of the Great Commission.

2000 B. Graham convenes Amsterdam 2000, a meeting of 10,000 evangelists, strategists, theologians, and church leaders to be held in Amsterdam, July 29 - Aug 6, 2000.

At the stroke of midnight on New Year's Eve 1999 Evangelist J. McDowell encourages 300,000 students in Day One 2000 to look forward to return of Christ and to participate in world missions.

D. B. Barrett, G. T. Kurian & T. M. Johnson publish *World Christian Encyclopedia* 2nd edition, providing detailed statistics and strategies to evangelize the world by AD 2025.

2001 D. B. Barrett & T. M. Johnson publish *World Christian Trends*, analyzing past and current attempts to evangelize the world.

2025 Respect for Christ: person of Christ now widely known and respected throughout world, by all world religions, even among atheists and agnostics; also his teachings and his gospel (but not his church) are understood and valued, though not accepted or implemented, almost universally.

Entire world finally reached with Christian gospel for first time in history, in the sense that everyone everywhere has heard or hears the gospel in depth with understanding and has access to Scripture, churches, missions, Christians, Christian broadcasting, movies, literature and other means of grace.

Global church-planting goal completed; at least one fellowship or church or congregation or nucleus of disciples has been planted as an ongoing indigenous witness in each of the world's 12,600 ethnolinguistic peoples and 4,000 metropolises of over 100,000 population.

# II. A WORLD CHRISTIAN GLOBAL ACTION PLAN (WCGAP)

1. This is a plan to bring Christians together to evangelize the world. It proposes bringing together all kinds of Christians—Catholics, Charismatics, Conciliars, Evangelicals, Fundamentalists, Independents, Neo-Apostolics, Orthodox, Pentecostals, Post-denominationalists, and Protestants—and Christians from every continent, country, people, language, and place where they live on Earth. This is a plan for world evangelization, for obedience to the Great Commission of Jesus Christ, for every person on earth to hear the gospel in a way they can understand and have a valid opportunity to become a Christian. Then the benefits of Christ's salvation and the Christian faith will be brought to all persons on Earth. Pray that this would happen soon, whether through this plan or another.

2. The World Christian Global Action Plan (WCGAP) is a response to the reality of a global evangelization movement. It does not seek to raise such a movement—a movement already exists. A multitude of Christians, churches, denominations, confessions, councils, organizations, institutions, orders, mission agencies, and plans in nearly every country, from all points in the ecclesiastical spectrum, are praying, thinking, discussing, planning and working on world evangelization—not merely local evangelization, but the evangelization of the entire world. Many Christians and many organizations, in many places, often completely unaware of each other, are dreaming the same dreams and working toward the same global goals. This plan is about how much more they could do if they were brought together and assisted in a few vital ways.

3. Some of this document is original. Some of the ideas presented here have never before been proposed, though many of them have. This plan includes ideas, elements, statements, and proposals that various Christian and mission leaders have been advocating for a long time.

Many times this plan travels into uncharted territory and explores new areas, issues, ideas, concepts, methods, and agenda items. Most of these touch on problem areas, barriers, obstacles, and sticking points around which the best intentions of all Christians could come to grief in the future as they have in the past. The WCGAP's proposed action points are designed to help Christians definitively overcome crucial problems which have extinguished many world evangelization plans in the past. This plan can be called a master plan in that it aims to master once and for all the many intractable problems or sticking points that are holding up world evangelization. It is emphatically not a 'master' in the sense of barking out orders to people. It accepts and respects the autonomy of all Christian workers, agencies, and organizations. As for its relationship with all Great Commission Christians, it remains not a master but a servant, a suggested course of action, something to offer help.

**On oversimplification**

For this plan, a large and complex document is needed. Every field of serious, organized human endeavor in the modern world is informed and guided by its own body of technical literature–books, journals, databases, complex documents, and detailed reports that organize and present relevant facts. In the Christian world mission, though we are led by the Spirit and the Word, we are not above benefiting also from facts and information. Simplicity is a Christian virtue, but oversimplicity is foolish.

In the same way, it is a mistake to proclaim one single factor to be the key, or the sole, sticking point in world evangelization. Some say the key is revival. Others say the key is prayer. Still others say the key is unity. The truth is that there is no one key. Evangelization is a complex, multi-faceted task being advanced by a complex, diverse church in a complex, multi-national, multi-cultural, multi-lingual, and multi-religious world. Even revival, in itself, does not ensure the completion of the task of world evangelization. God's people need to also understand, in great detail, the world they seek to evangelize. There are many factors that can prevent the reaching of World A, the unevangelized world, even if there is a massive revival in World C, the Christian world.

Some protest that complex databases, lists of peoples, lists of languages, lists of cities, lists of religions, and the like are not needed. But this plan is predicated on our ability to carefully assess status and monitor progress. The needs of World A cannot be rightly addressed without professional, detailed lists that have measurable variables. The large and complex task of finishing world evangelization requires large and complex planning and strategizing. To some, the WCGAP may seem complex and even unwieldy. Yet most Christians have not yet seriously grappled with the complexity and immensity of the task remaining. As a result, major progress eludes us. The solution is definitive, massive, informed, cooperative action focused on the unevangelized world, action guided by documents and data that will at times have to be detailed, complex, and large.

4. One of the most difficult, and most essential, aspects of this plan is cooperation across the boundaries of major Christian traditions. Implementation of this plan will begin with those Christians willing to cooperate in evangelization with others of different denominations, churches, communions, and confessions. The first to implement this plan will be those Evangelicals who are willing to work with Roman Catholics, those Orthodox and Conciliar Protestants willing to work with Pentecostals, those Roman Catholics willing to work with Non-White indigenous Christians, and so on. As an alternative, some have proposed separate, parallel global plans among the major disconnected blocs of Christianity, with quiet, low-key, unpublicized communication and coordination at the center.

5. This plan takes its stand firmly on all past accomplishments. Theologically, it is rooted in and centered on the life, death, and resurrection of Jesus Christ, his ascension, the coming of the Holy Spirit, the Holy Scriptures, and the church. It focuses on the lordship of Christ, the Great Commission, and worldwide mission. The plan therefore assumes the background theological stances found in the Holy Scriptures themselves, in The Apostles' Creed, in various confessions of faith over the last 5 centuries, and in the numerous pronouncements of the great missionary conferences of the last 150 years. It bases itself, in particular, on the theological positions of the 3 great 'convergent' documents on world evangelization: the Lausanne Covenant (1974; 3,400 words), Evangelii Nuntiandi (1975; 27,500 words), and Mission and Evangelism: an Ecumenical Affirmation (1982; 10,500 words).

6. This plan takes for granted, and so does not reiterate in detail, the many, vital things Christians know to be necessary in mission. These include:

- fervent, concerted, extensive prayer and intercession
- zealous Christian personal witness
- public proclamation of the kerygma
- centrality of the Bible as the Word of God
- centrality of mission from Genesis to Revelation
- God's sovereignty in world mission
- evangelizing as the church's overarching task
- central role of the local church
- exemplary, holy, godly Christian living and lifestyle
- obedience to the Great Commandment (Matthew 22:38)
- compassion for the poor and needy
- God's preferential option for the poor
- conscientization (consciousness-raising)
- liberation
- social witness and justice, social agendas
- holistic evangelism
- integrated rural development ministries
- urban-industrial mission and ministries
- healing ministries, faith healing
- material aid: food, shelter, medicine
- disaster and famine relief
- full involvement of all peoples, cultures, and languages
- leadership by Christians from all nations, races, ages, and both genders
- global leadership by youth, women, minorities
- need for training, orientation, information
- involvement of children and families
- vital need for spiritual revival and renewal
- organized cross-cultural evangelistic outreach
- discipling, church-planting, and church growth
- multiplication of churches
- partnership between agencies and churches
- whole-church, whole-world, whole-person ministry

... and so on.

All of these things have been emphasized in global plans for hundreds of years. Most are understood or presupposed in the seminal convergent documents mentioned earlier, as well as the January 1989 GCOWE 2000 'Great Commission Manifesto', the July 1989 'Manila Manifesto' of LCWE, the U. S. Catholic bishops' encyclical 'To the Ends of the Earth', the 1989 report of the CWME in San Antonio, the 1991 encyclical 'Redemptoris Missio', as well as in most other similar documents in the history of missions conferences. As a big-picture global action plan, this plan presupposes all of these items and those like them.

7. Some may be unhappy that this document is so long. To this there are two answers: (1) If world evangelization is, as we are claiming, the Christian world's single most complex and intractable problem, then a long document is appropriate; and (2) Those wanting a shorter treatment will find in the following appendix a Short Version that distills the most important points of the full WCGAP.

8. Many may be uncomfortable with the very idea of a big-picture, master global plan like this. To some, it is simply unfamiliar—they have never seen anything like it before. To others, it may not fit with how they have understood and carried out the holy ministry of evangelization. To still others, it may appear so different in nature from the ministry of Jesus and the apostles that they cannot imagine how it relates to those models.

In the work of evangelization, some things, the most important things, remain the same since ancient Christianity. Other things change as the gospel advances into the diverse languages, cultures, nations, and eras of humanity. The WCGAP is a response to the globalization of Christianity and to the comprehensiveness of the Great Commission. It takes hold of certain tools present in our era, accepts them as gifts from God, and employs them for holy purposes. The Foundational Concepts of this plan come from Scripture, from informed observation of the ways of God's church and of the complex world of our day, and from knowledge and right reason.

A global plan allows for coordination that can erase the massive waste and duplication in world missions today. A global plan allows all evangelizers to see their own work as a part of a larger whole, thus giving greater significance and greater motivation. A global plan allows larger teams to work together, thus making larger achievements possible. It allows special gifts, special resources, special expertise, special knowledge, special tools, and special victories to benefit the widest possible circle of God's workers and make the widest possible impact in God's world.

This plan calls Christians of all kinds to work together, but it is not a plan for Christian organizational mergers, or denominational mergers, or union. It focuses on world evangelization, but does not thereby devalue or criticize any other avenue of Christian ministry, worship, service, or obedience. It anticipates drawing together very large numbers of Christian workers, but only for practical purposes related to the Kingdom of God, not for the glory of any person or organization—except Jesus Christ and his church. This is a new plan, but it does not call for the abandonment of any other global evangelization plan. Some such plans will gain new energy and strength, some will expand, and many will adjust to support this plan more directly.

9. Some may be unhappy to see that this plan calls for a large organization requiring substantial resources (though still far smaller than thousands of current Christian organizations, institutions, agencies, networks, and plans). This is only a practical reality required by the nature of the plan itself. A global plan requires global goals. The monitoring of global goals requires a large research effort. The global dis-

semination of research findings requires a large communications effort, as does the global mobilization required by a global plan. Soon funds are required, and staff, and offices. The point is not to build an organization but to perform certain tasks. If these tasks require an organization, to argue against an organization is to deny the tasks and kill the plan. The WCGAP organization will have to be somewhat large if this is in fact to be a global plan, and not merely restricted to a thin slice of the global Christian family.

10. This plan is unique and unprecedented in that it draws upon, is informed by, and is motivated by a huge volume of new global data and information. These are the data presented in this *WCT*, the *World Christian encyclopedia* (*WCE*) and its related CD version, the *World Christian database AD 30–AD 2200*. These present an extensive global collection of professionally-researched statistical information on Christianity and religion, covering a vast range of factors. It is therefore not a plan built on dreams, wishes, or a general understanding of the world and the church. It is a plan built on facts. The glossary of the *WCE* serves as the glossary for this plan. The reader wanting to know the precise meaning of any terms, words, or phrases in this plan can therefore refer to that glossary and to pertinent other sections of the *WCE* that expound, explain, describe, and elucidate key terms, their definitions, their quantification, and the methodologies behind their quantification.

11. This present plan draws most extensively from the Kaleidoscopic Global Action Plan (KGAP) of 1989/1990, whose full title was *Two thousand plans toward AD 2000: a kaleidoscopic global action plan to see the world evangelized by AD 2000 and beyond*. The KGAP was compiled from the writings, statements, positions, conversations, discussions, suggestions, proposals, ideas, and interactions of the members of a working group that was formally commissioned by those who organized the Global Consultation on World Evangelization by the Year 2000 and Beyond (GCOWE I) in September 1988. This working group's mass of materials, together with a volume of other documents and comments, was collated from June 1988 onwards and then circulated to GCOWE participants. The revised document was discussed in 20 working groups for the 3 days of the Consultation from 5-8 January 1989–resulting in 300 written pages of contributions from the participants. All of this input was welcomed, studied, and incorporated. Then from January 1989 to April 1990, further discussions, correspondence, and revisions continued, leading to the version published in *Our globe and how to reach it* (1990). That final version of the KGAP drew also upon the findings of the 10-year research enquiry that produced the book *Seven hundred plans to evangelize the world: the rise of a global evangelization movement* (1988).

12. This plan, like the KGAP, is unlike other stand-alone global plans for world evangelization. The WCGAP recognizes and builds upon the already-existing macrocomplex of over 845 current global plans to evangelize the world with the over 1,600 nonglobal local, national, or regional plans. This vast complex of 2,500 plans is already in place, carrying on its work, supported by myriads of Great Commission Christians and workers in all countries of the world. They are committed to obeying the last commission of Jesus Christ the Lord and Savior, but the present modus operandi is too unstructured and too uncoordinated for these plans to succeed in achieving the common goal. To break this impasse, somebody must do something new and dramatic.

This is therefore a plan of plans, and thus something new in the history of world evangelization.

---

**On the lack of progress in world evangelization**

The total number of unevangelized persons, unaware of Christianity, Christ, and the gospel, has been more than one billion for all of the 20th century. By the last decade of the century this number had risen to 1.6 billion. Most of these live in material poverty, in contrast to the affluence of many Christians and their churches. Our current estimate is that 314,000 of these persons are evangelized for the first time every day. But this global numerical progress is cancelled out by the world's inexorable population increase of 340,000 new persons born each day. (See Global Diagram 41 in Part 1 "GeoStatus"). For a long time, therefore, with regard to reaching the goal of world evangelization, Christians have been in a state of uncertainty or stalemate, hiatus or marking time. Multitudes are converting to Christianity every day but real progress still eludes us. Christians are waiting for a completely new initiative to arise that would adequately address the daily population explosion. This situation of stalemate needs to be acknowledged in a public statement and widely recognized within Christianity.

---

## A WORLD CHRISTIAN MANIFESTO

Jesus came to seek and to save the lost (Luke 19:10). Jesus came to proclaim the good news of the kingdom of God (Luke 8:1). Jesus came, with the Spirit upon him, to preach good news to the poor, to proclaim freedom for the prisoners and recovery of sight for the blind, to release the oppressed, and to proclaim the year of the Lord's favor (Luke 4:18-19). As the Father sent Jesus, so Jesus is sending us (John 20:21).

God now commands all people everywhere to repent (Acts 17:30). Jesus commissioned his disciples to go and make disciples of all nations (Matthew 28:19), and to go into all the world and preach the good news to all creation (Mark 16:15). Jesus proclaimed that repentance and forgiveness of sins would be preached in his name to all nations (Luke 24:47), and that the gospel of the Kingdom would be preached in the whole world as a testimony to all nations (Matthew 24:14). The Great Commission calls for proclamation of the gospel to all nations, all the world, all creation, everyone, everywhere. This is a task that can and must be completed by God's people. As in the apostolic pattern, this can be pursued in a deliberate, organized way: 'This went on for two years, so that all the Jews and Greeks who lived in the province of Asia heard the word of the Lord' (Acts 19:10).

**So today**: let us proclaim the gospel to every person, in every place, in all the world; and let us do so in a deliberate, organized way to insure that all who live on earth will hear the word of the Lord.

From one man God made every nation of men, that they should inhabit the whole earth; and determined the times set for them and the exact places where they should live. God did this so that men would seek him (Acts 17:26-27). When the day of Pentecost came, there were staying in Jerusalem God-fearing Jews from every nation under heaven. Each one heard the apostles declaring the wonders of God in their own language (Acts 2:1, 5, 11). The Lamb was slain, and with his blood he purchased men for God from every tribe and language and people and nation (Revelation 5:9).

**So today**: let us proclaim the gospel among every nation God has made, among every country, every people, every tribe, and every language, in every place where God has set them. Let us proclaim the gospel to all of humanity in all of its complexity, and let us bring the Word of God to every language.

Christians are to stand firm in one spirit, contending as one for the faith of the gospel without being frightened in any way by those who oppose (Philippians 1:27-28). Jesus prayed that all of those who would believe in him through the message of the apostles would be one, so that the world might believe that Jesus was from God. Jesus prayed that all who believed in him would be brought to complete unity to let the world know that God loves them even as he loved his Son (John 17:20-23).

**So today:** let us all—Catholics, Charismatics, Conciliars, Evangelicals, Fundamentalists, Independents, Neo-Apostolics, Orthodox, Pentecostals, Postdenominationalists, and Protestants—all Christians everywhere—let us all come together to evangelize the world.

It was always the ambition of the apostle Paul to preach the gospel where Christ was not known, so that he would not be building on someone else's foundation. Rather, as it is written, 'Those who were not told about him will see, and those who have not heard will understand' (Romans 15:20-21).

**So today:** let us proclaim the gospel where Christ is not known, among those who have not heard, in the places and among the people where there are no Christians.

---

## FOUNDATIONAL CONCEPTS

The first 6 Foundational Concepts are essential to this plan. Their exact wording is negotiable, but if any of them are removed or changed in basic content, this would no longer be the WCGAP. It would become something different, smaller, weaker, less unified, and less compelling. This plan would then no longer stand as viable, coherent, and realistic.

### 1. Evangelization
Every person on earth has the unequivocal right to hear the gospel in a way she or he can understand, and to be given a valid opportunity to become a Christian. This is not the only task for the church in the world, but it is a primary, essential, and foundational task. Only when it is completed will this terrible tragedy end: that people die and face eternity without ever hearing the gospel of Jesus Christ, God's provision for salvation. The WCGAP is centered on the priority task of world evangelization.

The goal of world evangelization is not that all will believe, but that all will hear. Tragically, many will refuse God's gift of life, even to the end.

The mission of the church involves much more than the task of proclamation and evangelization. This plan makes no claim to be comprehensive for all of Christian mission. It is restricted to world evangelization and a small set of very closely related goals. No apology is made for this, since world evangelization is itself so vital, so central, and so crucial to God's will for his church in the world. Much remains to be done.

### 2. Cooperation
Christians of all countries, cultures, languages, classes, churches, denominations, confessions, ages, and both genders should work together in a coordinated way to complete the task of world evangelization. Only then can the waste of duplication and the enmity of competition be avoided. Only then can the unique, God-given gifts of each be put to greatest effect. Only then can the larger, global task be accomplished. This plan is for those Christians who are willing to work cooperatively in mission with other Christians different from themselves. Let us do together what we cannot do separately.

### 3. World A
The global church should deploy missionaries, funds, prayer, attention, education, and all resources with a priority on World A, on unevangelized individuals, and on the least-evangelized countries, cities, peoples, religions, and languages of earth. Only then will there be accelerated progress in world evangelization. Only then will those who have not heard, hear. Only then will the scandal be erased of constant re-evangelization of the already-evangelized while the unevangelized remain. The WCGAP constantly asks,

"Where is the need the greatest?" and encourages resources in that direction. This plan advocates a massive and rapid shift of Christian resources from World C and World B to World A.

## 4. AD 2025

Global goals in any important human enterprise can and should be set under the disciplines of a timetable and a date. Only then can forces and resources be best organized and mobilized. Only then can the empowerment that comes from planning be released. Only then can proper evaluation and accountability, crucial to integrity and essential to righteousness in stewardship, take place. This plan has in view those aspects of world evangelization that can and should be completed by AD 2025.

## 5. Quantification

For world evangelization, statistical research is not only helpful but essential. The church needs statistical information about the status of Christianity, religion, and evangelization in the vast diversity of humanity. The work of statistical record keeping, reporting, compiling, analyzing, publishing, teaching, explaining, and applying must be done. Only then can the truth be known. Only then can this plan, or any plan, rise above the level of mere slogans and worthy desires. Only then can closure be effectively approached and achieved. This plan urges all Christian leaders and workers to be informed and numerate to the level appropriate for their responsibilities in organized Christianity.

## 6. Segmentization

The larger task should be divided into meaningful segments that can then be assessed, assigned, engaged, and monitored one at a time: by countries, cities, peoples, languages, provinces, and other units. Only then will the larger task be approachable. Only then will there be meaningful and comprehensive coordination among the vast diversity of the world's Great Commission Christians. Only then can accurate, measurable progress toward the larger goals be reported and mid-course corrections be made. The WCGAP segments the enormous task of world evangelization into pieces that can be assigned, and thus into sub-tasks that can be achieved one by one. A simple outline of the principle of segmentization is as follows:
1. Segmentize the world.
2. Assess the status of evangelization of each segment.
3. Identify the unevangelized segments.
4. Insure that someone is evangelizing each.
5. Monitor progress and re-assign as needed.
6. Continue discovering and assigning segments.

## 7. Wholism

Evangelization requires word, sign, and deed, inseparably linked. World Christians should live and proclaim a full gospel, not a partial gospel, and should live and proclaim a full obedience to the Lordship of Christ, not a partial one. Evangelization includes a response in justice, peace, and responsibility toward creation, bringing the truth of the gospel into all areas of human experience on earth. The WCGAP assumes and affirms an understanding of the work of mission as a seamless whole.

## 8. Empowerment

All is dependent upon God. This is not a plan that can be achieved by human power and devices alone. All is dependent upon prayer. This is not a plan that can be achieved without Divine intervention. All is dependent upon holiness. This is not a plan that can be achieved by worldly Christians. All is dependent upon the Holy Spirit. This is not a plan that can be achieved by carnal Christians. All is dependent upon love. This is not a plan that can be achieved by people caught in selfish ambition.

## 9. Multi-channeling

No significant population segment should be approached by only one evangelizing method or team. Each needs many workers, many teams, many methods, and many approaches, from many sources and many directions. The WCGAP affirms the wisdom and efficacy of a multi-channeled approach to evangelization, and to tasks related to evangelization, including the communication and dissemination of this plan itself.

Although we would not think it desirable to create thousands of unconnected, disparate, and independent world evangelization plans, we cannot prevent their existence; instead, we can perceive that, in the providence of God, they provide multiple parallel channels. If one hundred of initiatives fizzle out, collapse, or are destroyed by hostile forces, hundreds of others will get through to their goals.

An analogy from computer development may help. For decades most computers tackled problems serially or linearly, that is, with one CPU (central processing unit) undertaking one single line of programming, containing a vast number of sequential steps taken one after the other. Fifth-generation computers use parallel processing, where many processors split up the problem to be solved into multiple tasks and move ahead with them all at the same time. If one processor stops or is held up, other processors take over and carry on. In a similar way, the global evangelization movement today has resulted in hundreds and even thousands of separate tracks, plans, programs, and activities, each driven by a different agency's separate processing ability. Each confession, denomination, mission, country, region, or continent has already responded to the goal of world evangelization, each on the basis of its own context, charisms, call, and character. This has resulted in something over 10,000 separate but roughly parallel tracks. Instead of attempting to change this situation, this big-picture global plan accepts it and endeavors to provide strategic guidance at certain points, vision, some coordination, monitoring, information, and the concept of common goals. This is done particularly to avoid duplication, waste, gaps in coverage, sticking points, and the like.

## 10. Mobilization

Every sector of the Body of Christ should be stirred to action. All Christians should be informed of, and motivated to participate in, world evangelization. Christians of all countries, cultures, languages, classes, churches, denominations, confessions, ages, and both genders should be mobilized. Only then will the new efforts, new initiatives, new ideas, new energy, and new resources required come together. This plan respects the work of sending as much as the work of going.

## 11. Responsibility

Two things are required for evangelization: the initiative of God and the obedience of God's people. The WCGAP is confident of the adequacy of God's initiative, but concerned over the inadequacy of Christians' obedience. Therefore it seeks to increase and direct the Spirit-empowered work of Christians. This plan contains no announcement that God is about to do a new, mighty work. It is instead a call to new and greater obedience—under the confidence that God is poised to indeed do a new, mighty work in response to, and in harmony with, the obedience of his people.

## 12. Closure

There are important, measurable tasks within the whole of Great Commission obedience that can and should be accomplished for the entire world. Closure is possible, measurable, and imperative. Many Great Commission tasks will continue even after some are completed. Even when the pioneering task of establishing a church for every people is completed, the discipling tasks will continue. Even when all have been evangelized, evangelization will be required for each new generation. Closure does not mean the end of Christian mission, but it does mean the end of some key aspects of it. This plan is directed toward closure on several of them.

## A WORLD CHRISTIAN AGENDA: THE 8 GLOBAL GOALS

Each of the following 8 goals are specific, measurable, quantifiable, realistic, attainable, and yet challenging. For each goal, a baseline assessment of the status in AD 2000 is given, drawing upon the research data in the *World Christian Encyclopedia*, and a specific, quantified AD 2025 goal is presented. Each item serves both as a goal and as a monitoring point. WCGAP research will report on most of these items annually, and on all of them at 5-year intervals. Those reports will include details by region, country, city, church or denomination, population segment, people, or language, as appropriate. WCGAP databases will show the exact segments needing new missionary effort or attention. It will then be possible to form and engage mid-course corrections, adjustments, deployments, new strategies, new emphases, new programs, and new plans. All of these goals relate closely to, support, and help insure the fulfillment of the first goal, that of finishing the task of world evangelization.

### 1. For everyone on earth to be evangelized.

*Global % Evangelized*
AD 2000: 73.1% - AD 2025 goal: 100.0%

For the precise meaning of this goal, see Part 23 "Evangelization".

### 2. For the world to be 40% Christian.

*Global % Christian*
AD 2000: 33.0% - AD 2025 goal: 40%

For the precise meaning of this goal, see Part 14 "Missiometrics".

### 3. For the world to be 20% Great Commission Christians.

*Global %Great Commission Christians*
AD 2000: 10.7 - AD 2025 goal: 20.0%

For the precise meaning of this goal, see Part 21 "GeoPersonnel".

### 4. For every 2,000 Christians to send at least one cross-cultural missionary.

*Global cross-cultural missionary sending ratio*
AD 2000: 3,000/1 - AD 2025 goal: 2,000/1

The ratio is of the number of affiliated church members per cross-cultural missionary sent. Most cross-cultural missionaries are also foreign missionaries, serving not only in cultures foreign to their native culture, but also in countries foreign to their native country. Most of them, but certainly not all. Much of the remaining work of evangelizing World A peoples will likely be done by cross-cultural missionaries working within their own countries, notably in India, China, Indonesia, and many African countries. Thus this goal is framed in terms of cross-cultural missionaries rather than foreign missionaries, though closure will at the same time require a tremendous increase in the number of foreign missionaries sent.

For the evangelization of the neglected peoples of World A, it would seem right to set a goal for deployment of cross-cultural missionaries specifically to that sector. But such a goal, like: '50% of all foreign missionaries to be in World A in AD 2025', makes no sense if World A will disappear by that date. There will need to be a structure of interim goals on this point, as also for deployment of other Christian resources to World A.

### 5. For Christians to give 3% of their income to Christian causes.

*Global giving to Christian causes -*
AD 2000: 1.8% - AD 2025 goal: 3.0%

The above numbers represent giving to Christian causes as a percentage of total income of Christians. For the precise meaning of this goal, see Part 20 "Finance". Note that this still falls far short of the biblical standard of 10%, the tithe. This goal, like the others, is written to be challenging, realistic and attainable, not ideal or to fulfill what is ultimately desired.

### 6. For there to be a church in every city.

*The number of cities without a church*
AD 2000: 116 - AD 2025 goal: 0.

Specifically, no city with a population of 50,000 or more without an active, organized Christian church or congregation where percent Christian is less than 0.02%, (open or clandestine), and (for the small countries of the world) no city that is the leading city of its country without such a church or congregation. See *WCE* Part 10 "MetroScan".

### 7. For there to be a church for every people.

*The number of peoples without a church*
AD 2000: 1236 - AD 2025 goal: 0

Specifically, for there to be no ethnolinguistic people (by country) on earth less than 0.05% Christian. See *WCE* Part 8 "Ethnosphere". A corrolary goal is the more difficult task of penetrating 10,000 unreached minipeoples with a viable indigenous church.

### 8. For there to be scriptures available in every language.

*The number of languages without scriptures*
AD 2000: 6800 - AD 2025 goal: 0

Specifically, for scriptures to be translated, printed, and distributed in every viable, living language on earth. See Part 19 "GeoScriptures".

The 8 global goals can quickly be sub-divided into goals of smaller scope by continent, region, country, province, city, district, town, denomination, denominational diocese or sub-unit, even neighborhood, village, or local church, for immediate application, deployment, and fulfillment.

## CATEGORIES OF INVOLVEMENT IN THE WCGAP

In order for any start to be made on the ambitious overarching global goals discussed above, it is necessary to propose the opening of a working office dedicated wholly to this concern. Obviously, it must have a name, so for the purposes of this plan's presentation it will here be called the International Office of the WCGAP. This International Office will maintain lists of those individuals and organizations around the world that fit with each of the following categories of involvement. Differing packages of information and services will be directed to each.

### 1. Members.
Full, official Members of the WCGAP may be individual Christians or Christian churches, denominations, networks or associations of churches, councils, organizations, institutions, orders, mission agencies, or plans. They may be formal (legally registered) or informal entities. Requirements of membership will include:
  a. Members must agree with and support the Foundational Concepts and the Global Goals.
  b. Members must help promote the WCGAP and seek to enlist other members.
  c. Members must, in their own spheres of work and ministry, seek for the fulfillment of at least one of the Global Goals.
  d. Members must contribute an initial membership donation, and annual dues, appropriate to their means, and (for organizations) size.
Privileges of WCGAP membership will include:
  a. Members will receive a monthly global WCGAP newsletter, in print or electronic form.
  b. Members will be invited to certain national, regional, or global WCGAP events.

  c. Members will receive many publications each year, including an annually-updated priority list of least-evangelized population segments, globally.
  d. Members will be able to call upon certain services from the WCGAP International Office, including information services and the services of consultants.
  e. Members will be able to call upon the services of speakers and teachers from the WCGAP leadership and its team of itinerant world evangelization instructors, speakers, professors, evangelizers, missionaries, and researchers.
  f. Members will have access to WCGAP proprietary electronic forums.
There will be procedures for admission to membership and for removal from membership.

### 2. Supporters.
Supporters of the WCGAP uphold or promote the cause of the plan in some way. This category will include all financial donors and prayer partners. As with Members, Supporters can be individual Christians or Christian organizations of any kind. None can be listed as Supporters until the International Office is informed of their interest. All Members will also be counted as Supporters.

### 3. Participants.
Participants in the WCGAP will be those who are aware of the plan, positive toward it, and working in some way for the fulfillment of any of the Global Goals. Participants will be kept informed of WCGAP and world evangelization progress. This category will allow all to recognize the very wide circle of Great

Commission Christians who are not Members or Supporters but still are positive toward, and contributing to, the goals of the WCGAP in meaningful ways. Any Participants who contact the International Office can immediately be upgraded to Supporters. All Members and Supporters will also be counted as Participants. Note that there will also be a vast circle of passive participants–Great Commission Christians and Great Commission agencies who are entirely unaware of the WCGAP but working toward the fulfillment of one or more of the 8 Global Goals.

### 4. Observers.
Observers of the WCGAP will be those non-Christian individuals or organizations who are interested in the plan and who ask to be kept informed of it. Note that only Christians can be Members, Supporters, or Participants and receive the benefits, publications, or services the WCGAP will assign to those categories of involvement.

### 5. Opponents.
The International Office will make note of those Christians and Christian organizations of any kind that make themselves prominent in opposing the WCGAP. There are many reasons why Christians are likely to oppose this plan. Opponents will be a help to the WCGAP in their own way. They can point out weaknesses, flaws, or opportunities for improvement in the plan. WCGAP leaders will listen to opponents in a spirit of humility and Christian love, and will seek to learn from them. They will also initiate careful but deliberate efforts directed to winning the favor of opponents.

---

## TASKS

---

### A. FOR THE WCGAP INTERNATIONAL OFFICE.

1. Implement a system to match-up needs with resources. Find a worker or workers for every unevangelized country, city, people, language, or population segment. This apparently simple task could, in itself, be a powerful force toward the fulfillment of the Global Goals, and is at the heart of the implementation of this plan. See to it that someone has drawn up concrete plans to provide adequate scripture, broadcasting, literature, preaching, resources, ministries, and churches among every unevangelized segment on Earth–and that these plans are being implemented. Specifically:

a. Insure coverage of all least-evangelized population segments for church-planting evangelization (Global Goals 1, 2, 6, and 7).

b. Insure coverage of all closed or inaccessible segments by nonresidential missionaries.

c. Insure coverage of all of World C for Great Commission mobilization (Global Goals 3, 4, and 5).

d. Insure coverage of all languages without the Bible for Bible translation (Global Goal 8).

2. Encourage, organize, guide, and monitor twinning of unevangelized population segments with evangelized segments of recognizably-similar makeup, background, and situation. One way to get the entire laity involved in the evangelization process would be to attempt to match up, in pairs, evangelized cities in World C with unevangelized cities in World A. Numerous varieties of secular links already exist between many such pairs of cities, based on professional skills, trade, commerce, sport, music (orchestras), academic interests, and so on. All that is now needed is to document these pairs and to encourage the emergence of a carefully-implemented evangelistic link.

3. Systematically urge all 300 newly-formed or recently-organized mission-sending agencies (Western, Third-World, charismatic, et alia) to refuse the easy path of sending missionaries to work with Christians (whether non-practicing or practicing) in World C and instead to commission their personnel entirely to World A. Many could well become nonresidential missionaries. Since Third-World countries and churches have a superabundance of young, committed evangelizers able and willing to proclaim Christ anywhere in the world, the older churches in the Western world need a concerted effort to supply the necessary logistical power.

4. Encourage, guide, and monitor all participating Great Commission churches, denominations, councils, organizations, institutions, orders, mission agencies, and plans in establishing at their headquarters a permanently-manned global desk as part of a global network of such desks. This desk would:
a. be staffed by an executive familiar with world mission, evangelization, and the WCGAP;
b. be the agency's key node in electronic contact with the wider Great Commission global network in 200 countries, and also with a specialized Global Desk Network in 100 countries;
c. provide information to the world of GCCs on its own agency's Great Commission plans, activi-

---

---

ties and progress;
d. protect the agency's global goals from being displaced or diluted by the agency's own continental, regional, national, or area goals.
e. serve as a key contact person between the agency and the WCGAP.

5. Encourage, assist, and monitor the emergence of national task forces to develop global plans for world evangelization. The Great Commission will be best served by multidenominational or multiconfessional obedience. National task forces could affirm the following emphases: spiritual motivation in prayer, indigenous leadership, interdenominational cooperation, research, working consultation, goals, corporate programs, participation by all strata, and communication with other task forces.

6. Introduce or disseminate innovations or new elements for collective implementation. Positive elements from any global plan need to be reported and spread immediately. Instead of relating solely to one agency's single global plan (as most of us do at present), we must now think: How can this new idea, new program, new resource, new technology, or new discovery relate to the total, collective, corporate implementation of the Great Commission? This big-picture plan's overall new strategy must therefore include new and recent concepts and elements such as the following:

a. Engagement with closed, closing, and difficult-access countries.
b. Segmentization and targeting as a means of global planning.
c. Reaching unreached peoples through nonresidential missionaries.
d. Continuously-itinerating Spirit-filled evangelists.
e. Cooperative, well-planned, multi-agency, multi-channeled outreach to particularly difficult unreached populations.
f. Inter-organizational and inter-confessional computer network creation and participation.
g. Tentmakers and tentmaking facilitation agencies.
h. Networking with agencies beyond one's traditionally acceptable circle.

7. Conduct a global, multi-channeled membership drive from the bottom up. Seek millions of members from among the ordinary Christian populations of every country and all major languages and peoples on earth. Seek members from the widest possible range of churches, denominations, confessions, organizations, institutions, orders and mission agencies possible. Use a wide range of communications media and channels, including personal contact, small group meetings, large group events, networking, the Internet, the World Wide Web, phone, mail, fax, literature, press releases, radio, television, videotapes, and audiotapes.

8. Conduct a global, multi-channeled membership drive from the top down. Seek thousands of members from among the formal organizations of global Christianity: churches, denominations, confessions, councils, organizations, institutions, orders, mission agencies, and plans. Begin with the largest and most significant organizations, with tailor-made strategies to seek the allegiance and membership of each. Work in a well-researched priority order, drawing upon the descriptive and statistical information of the *World Christian Encyclopedia* (Second Edition) and the *World Christian Database*.

9. Recruit and mobilize a global network of national, provincial, city-wide, and local committees, mostly of volunteers, who will receive transferable training in world evangelization and the WCGAP and will fan out throughout the Christian world, in all of its denominational and confessional diversity, to explain, and seek members for the WCGAP.

10. Seek, find, and implement creative, engaging, persuasive, and appropriate ways to communicate and promote this Plan among the millions of Christians

---

globally who, for cultural, educational, and communicative reasons, will have a natural tendency to ignore or dismiss this plan as it is written in its present form. Identify those Christians by denomination, confession, organization, culture, language, and country. With diligence and creativity, seek and enlist a maximum number of WCGAP members from among them.

11. Involve Great Commission agencies that initially reject membership. Show them research results that directly affect their work. Send to their leadership reports that show the deployment of their workers. Make recommendations (even unsolicited) as to how they could change and thus make a more strategic contribution. Recommend specific least-evangelized peoples or cities to them, making clear the needs and that their own failure to act would likely leave this segment unevangelized. In these and other ways, seek to draw them in.

12. In the global educational campaign about world mission and the WCGAP, teach about the world Christian history of plans and surveys in order to make all churches and agencies aware that (a) this is not a new fad but a long-standing concern of mission that goes back to the first recorded enumerations of unreached peoples in Genesis 10 (The Table of Nations) and in Acts 2:5-21 (Peter's sermon at Pentecost); (b) this is not a brand-new discovery to be credited to the present generation of researchers from 1965 onwards (as is at present widely believed and publicized); and (c) the churches have over the years and decades had ample notice, data, information, research, surveys, publications, warnings, and exhortations but have so far failed to act on them as seriously as they could have.

13. Continue to amend, modify, sharpen, and expand the various facets of this big-picture global plan as feedback comes in from GCCs in hundreds of other languages, and as implementation of the plan expands in countless contexts. Publish a new edition of the Plan every 5 years, with an extensive translation and distribution program.

14. Divide the 8 Global Goals into smaller units by space and time. Set sub-goals by region or country, and sub-goals by 1-year, 2-year, or 5-year blocks. For mobilization and monitoring, don't simply announce what should be accomplished in the world by AD 2025; announce what should be accomplished in East Asia by AD 2025, or what should be accomplished in North Africa by AD 2010, and so on.

15. From the initial team, map out the logistics that will be required both for the overall WCGAP, and for this International Office itself. Beginning with the Global Goals and the Tasks of this plan, calculate the staff, facilities, equipment, and budgets needed, according to a timetable stretching to AD 2025. With the help of qualified professionals in the field, compose a detailed logistical plan for the work and for the fund-raising of this Office. Map out the tasks, departments, and staff assignments both initially and for the needed growth of the organization.

16. Establish the 5 WCGAP-related World Christian offices described below.

*World Christian Prayer Office*

17. Establish a World Christian Prayer Office. Its staff of intercessors will pray over all matters related to the plan, and will stimulate, encourage, guide, and monitor informed, fervent prayer among and for all WCGAP members and all Christians. From this Office, organize a massive, global, multi-lingual prayer campaign for World A. It will be at the heart of a larger Global Prayer Strategy that recognizes and unites the 50 or so current worldwide intercessory networks.

*World Christian Research Office*

18. Initiate and facilitate global statistical research to monitor the progress of all WCGAP goals. Establish a World Christian Research Office staffed by qualified professionals who understand well the history and methods of global missions research, who have the appropriate gifts and skills, and who know the dynamics of cross-cultural, international missionary ministry from first-hand experience.

19. Keep Great Commission Christians alert and expectant over the 25-year period of this plan by commissioning an ongoing, frequent series of new studies and publications on world evangelization in a careful selection of key languages. These would include: (a) research documents, statistics, maps, graphics, bibliographies; (b) more popular versions of the same; and (c) computer versions of the same (disks, files, databases, knowledge bases, expert systems).

20. Each year publish a list of the top-priority least-evangelized segments of the global population, especially the least-evangelized peoples, cities, and languages. For each, report on their status according to the 8 Global Goals. Promote them for adoption and engagement by any Great Commission Christians, churches, organizations, orders, or mission agencies. Report on actions taken and progress made in the segments listed in the prior years' lists.

21. Every 5 years research and publish a book on the sending and receiving of Christian workers. Assess every country in the world, and for large countries assess them by region or province if there are significant imbalances. Show which countries need more missionaries. Show which do not. Show which countries are sending more missionaries, and which could send more. Form and recommend action plans accordingly. Make similar assessments for the global distribution of Christian finances, education, and other resources.

22. Research and publish an *Atlas of world evangelization*, thoroughly updated with a new edition every 5 years. Publish it in two formats: a smaller, simpler, less expensive one intended for the ordinary Christian, and a larger, more complete one for Christian leaders, for strategy, and for training purposes. Design it around the Global Goals.

23. Investigate and spotlight hindrances, duplication, overlap, waste, omissions, unnecessary elements, or endeavors or programs or allocations of resources with a view to their elimination. This must be done in a spirit of Christian humility and kindness, with wisdom and tact.

24. Offer, for purely optional use, an objective big-picture global plan cachet, a seal certifying commendable achievements (like the secular "Good Housekeeping" seal of approval or the ECFA membership seal of the Evangelical Council for Financial Accountability) as proof of meeting certain specified Great Commission standards and demonstrating accountability to the wider Christian public who pay for these plans.

*World Christian Office of Plan Consultants*

25. Establish a World Christian Office of Plan Consultants that will serve all functioning world evangelization plans through publications, personal consulting services, and events. Staff this office with a team of international, itinerant plan consultants–experienced missionaries, mission executives, and Christian leaders who understand well the WCGAP, world evangelization, and Great Commission statistics, and who are professionals in the fields of organizational planning, strategy, and leadership.

26. Research and publish regular information and news on the progress of all global plans, the emergence of new plans, and the demise of old ones.

27. Host meetings of major plan CEOs for them to learn from, and give help to, each other. Present research findings and instruction to help insure the success of their agencies' plans and the achievement of the Global Goals.

28. Appraise current global plans and offer consultant services where helpful and welcome. Assess the significance of any particular Great Commission global plan by several objective criteria or tests, including asking how many other different global plans are named in its documents or publicity. Estimate the present obstacles and future prospects facing any current global plan by using 'A Checkup Scale' (see Table 27–6). Plans will be assessed according to the disciplines of quantification–plan consultants will not be content with mere slogans or directions of ministry emphasis. These have their place, but they are not plans. At their worst, they are only fancy forms of wishful thinking–and hollow.

29. Give personalized, direct, on-site consultant services. We cannot assume that even the large, successful plans are running forward at full pace, without encumbrances, or even running in the right direction, toward the finish line. Without wise, objective guidance it is unlikely that most or even any of these plans will achieve their ambitious goals. From the wider perspective of this big-picture global plan, consultants can spot existing shortcomings and overlooked elements in plans, whether large or small, and can assist their sponsors to valuable mid-course corrections.

30. Foster coordination. Consultants can conduct widespread discussions as to the exact ways in which all the existing 2,500 major evangelization plans can or should mesh. Many of these plans are on completely separate tracks, move in totally different directions, or even contradict each other. There are yawning gaps and wasteful duplications.

31. Encourage Great Commission agencies without global plans to make them, to make plans of world-class quality, and to make plans that coordinate with the WCGAP.

32. Encourage all 585 declining or failing or collapsing global plans to each take a fresh look at their own plan, to revitalize it where possible, or to combine forces with another similar plan that is currently making progress. They could be invited to join coalitions with other global plans with similar goals, ministries, or methods.

33. Identify, and concentrate special attention and coordination on, the 10 or 20 most viable global plans,

which are likely together to move the Great Commission world 80% of the way to closure. All plans are important and should be respected and encouraged, but a small number of them, because of their size, resources, or response, deserve more action.

*World Christian Communications Office*

34. Translate and publish both the short version and the full version of this big-picture global plan from English into the 5 other major languages of the Christian world: French, German, Italian, Portuguese, and Spanish. Next, publish both versions in the world's top 21 major Christian languages (each with over 10 million church members). Then challenge Christians in each of the 100 megalanguages (those with over a million mother-tongue church members each) to translate at least the short version into those languages also. With each translation launch an extensive publication, distribution, and mobilization program.

35. Publish a monthly newsletter in the top 21 Christian languages. It should give authoritative, updated information, data, and standardized monthly indicators on all aspects of the WCGAP and the Global Goals. It should include: (a) new global evangelization plans announced since the last issue, (b) concise, concrete, significant news on any aspect of world evangelization, (c) progress reports from cooperating Great Commission agencies, (d) an overall progress report on world evangelization, (e) progress reports on WCGAP goals, (f) progress reports on specific segments (e.g. Africa, Indonesia, Uzbeks, Teheran), or on specific mission agencies, or on specific plans. This will be coordinated closely with a World Christian News Service (see 38 below) in an interchange of fast-breaking news and information. This newsletter will be offered in print, posted on the Web, offered by fax, by e-mail, and by other communications media.

36. Prepare a weekly, monthly, and quarterly version of a WCGAP Page that can be translated and reproduced in thousands of Christian newsletters, magazines, journals, and other periodicals around the world. It will present, explain, and promote the plan, list items for prayer, report on progress, and seek specific help. Pursue a massive, global, multi-lingual campaign to get this page into all significant Christian periodicals in the world.

828 PART 27—GEOSTRATEGIES

**On comity**

Prior to, but especially following the World Missionary Conference (Edinburgh, 1910), many Protestant world mission leaders worked together to establish comity agreements that parceled out regions of the world for exclusive work by selected mission organizations. Some of this is still reflected today in the strength of Lutherans in one country, the strength of Methodists in another country, and the strength of Presbyterians in yet another. What was intended to be a plan to insure the entire world was evangelized became an irritating hindrance. Some missions produced many churches while others produced few or none—sometimes because of differing receptivity, but just as often because of differing gifts, differing levels of consecration, and differing methods. Comity was in some ways helpful, but also a problem. Because of comity agreements, mission agencies were forbidden to work in certain areas where they might have otherwise carried on extremely fruitful work, planting many churches and bringing multitudes to faith in Christ.

The WCGAP is not a comity plan. No one will be hindered from working anywhere, certainly not anywhere in World A. The WCGAP strategy of segmentization seeks to take from comity what was good, and leave what was bad. The least-evangelized segments of the world's population will be identified. Churches, denominations, organizations, orders, and mission agencies will be informed and urged to send missionaries. New missionary presence will be monitored and noted so that the list of least-evangelized segments will then be affected.

37. Create and popularize a whole series of new graphics and maps illustrating world evangelization and the WCGAP, employing professional methods and produced to professional standards. Publish them in a wide range of languages and formats, some suited to the poorer churches of the world. Commission a variety of simple educational and mobilizational tools for Christians at the grass-roots level without computer access. Use such low-tech tools as pictures, comics, cartoons, blown-up photographs, wall charts, prayer guides, overhead transparencies, slides, tapes, drama scripts, puppet scripts, simulation games, missionary quiz shows, culture games, linguistic exercises, international menus, communication games, case studies, writers' workshops, et alia.

38. Initiate and implement, as a service to the entire Great Commission world with its 650 million active Christians, a multilingual World Christian News Service operated internationally and to professional standards. This news and information service should apply a unified approach to the collecting and disseminating of information vital to energizing the Great Commission world. The service can begin in the English, French, and Spanish languages, but should soon expand to the 20 major megalanguages of international telecommunications.

39. Establish a Translation Service to watch the flow of WCGAP publications and communications, insuring always that the major languages of global Christianity, and, when appropriate, the minor languages also, are served. Acknowledge the multiracial, multiethnic character of the total global Great Commission force for evangelization, and the need to serve it through multilingual mobilization. Interest, concern, writing, publications, and publicity about obeying the Great Commission are at present all heavily anglophone (tied to the English language) and anglophile (favoring the English language) with smaller amounts in Spanish, German, French, Italian, and Portuguese. But Great Commission Christians today are found in some 9,000 different ethnolinguistic peoples, especially in the Third World (the so-called Two-Thirds World). At least a million Great Commission Christian mother-tongue speakers function in each of 100 different languages. A determined effort must therefore be made to mobilize at least these 100 largest segments of the global Great Commission force in their 100 mother tongues.

40. Translate WCGAP literature, releases, and resources into: (a) the Christian world's 6 largest languages (in order of size of Christian mother-tongue speakers: Spanish, English, Portuguese, German, French, Italian); (b) the Christian world's 21 major languages, each spoken as mother tongue by over 10 million church members (the 6 listed in (a) above plus, in order of size: Chinese, Russian, Polish, Ukrainian, Dutch, Romanian, Quechua, Cebuano, Serbo-Croatian, Hungarian, Provençal, Tagalog, Greek, Korean, and Arabic); and, for the most important items, also into (c) the Christian world's 100 megalanguages (the 100 languages that each have at least a million church members). Even beyond these, the WCGAP Translation Service should develop ways to get translations into smaller minority languages, especially being alert to requests, needs, and opportunities that arise.

41. Be aware of, and sensitive to, the serious problem of infoglut in the developed world. Be careful to not merely add to the problem with a new layer of newsletters, journals, magazines, broadcasts, Web pages, cassettes, and the like. Develop a set of infoglut response actions that will guide publication and communication.

*World Christian Futures Office*

42. Establish a World Christian Futures Office where professional Christian futurists draw up and circulate for awareness and discussion a series of possible alternate scenarios for the future of Christianity and the prospects for world evangelization. Plans often fail because of leaders' inability to visualize what the world would be like with the task accomplished. What would an evangelized world look like? This office will study and report on all areas of futures research as they have bearing on the unfolding task of world evangelization and the Global Goals. Spot, discover, and report on nascent trends, both positive and negative.

43. Keep informed of new technologies that may be helpful tools in the task of world evangelization. Creatively explore possibilities as to their application. Communicate findings with GCCs worldwide.

### B. FOR GLOBAL ECUMENICAL AND CONFESSIONAL BODIES

44. Compile and publish concrete, specific, successful ideas for evangelization from the churches in your confession. Success stories not only call people to rejoice, but also show people the ideas, strategies, methods, techniques, and programs the Lord of the harvest is choosing to bless. Present case studies that are brief enough to be readable but detailed enough to be replicated.

45. With the help of, and in coordination with, WCGAP plan consultants, assess and monitor global plans, national plans, and denominational plans for evangelization within your confession. Offer seminars on planning for world evangelization and the WCGAP in various places around the world, in various languages. Help the development, refinement, and mid-course improvement of plans.

46. Commission, guide, and publish tactical and strategic practical studies that support the fulfillment of the 10 Global Goals. Enlist senior missionaries, mission and evangelism professors, and the like from among your churches and training institutions to study and write in ways that will fit with your history, distinctives, and commitments, and that will communicate well among your churches.

47. Establish global desks within all meaningful organizational units of your structure or association (cf. point 4 above).

48. Distribute information about, and encourage action toward, the least-evangelized segments of human population, as reported in WCGAP research publications.

### C. FOR CHRISTIAN CHURCHES AND DENOMINATIONS

49. Loan and finance key personnel for the WCGAP International Office and the other World Christian offices.

50. Establish a global desk (cf. point 4 above).

51. Establish or renew missionary sending agencies with fierce priority on church-planting evangelizing in World A.

52. Establish or renew extensive, vigorous programs to promote Great Commission activism in World C, to increase the proportion of GCCs in your church or denomination, to increase giving to Christian causes, and to boost frontier missionary sending.

53. Foster spiritual growth and renewal in laypeople and clergy. Mobilize clergy into frontier missionary service, and laypeople into full-time ministry and frontier missionary service. Plan and work for a large and rapid increase in the number of missionaries sent.

54. Initiate and join in the inauguration of a new, international, multidenominational, and multicultural order of full-time, itinerant, Spirit-led evangelists and evangelistic teams to take the gospel primarily to countries, cities, and peoples where no church or witness yet exists. Continuously-itinerant spontaneous ministry stands in clear contrast to organized residential and nonresidential ministry. No one denies that the following items are widely necessary and valuable to Christian ministry: residence-based ministries, organization, offices, office equipment, telephones, fax, planning, strategy, administration, correspondence, calendars, timetables, appointments, publications, and the whole vast humanly-administered machinery characterizing much of the Christian world mission today (as described in this document). Much of all this is clearly providentially-supplied, God-given. One can almost say: In countries where Christians are free to organize and plan, they must do so. But in much of today's world, anti-Christian hostility renders evangelistic organization and planning impossible. This is exactly where spontaneous, unorganized, Spirit-led, non-residence-based, itinerant, local evangelists can make a profound impact.

International momentum is therefore building to create a new and dynamic interdenominational order of itinerant, Spirit-led evangelists called the Order of Philip the Evangelizer. This is based on the unplanned, unorganized, spontaneous, sudden, go-anywhere-at-a-moment's-notice-into-untouched-territory ministry, with signs and wonders following, that characterized Philip the Deacon/Evangelist as a Christian version of an Old Testament prophet (Acts 8:4-40). This Order is beginning to be formed as separate orders in the major Christian confessions and denominations and could result in a single global federation of numerous denominational Orders of continuously-itinerating, charismatic evangelists (laity or ministers or clergy of any nationality especially Third-World and especially made up of youths and young people), operating spontaneously under the immediate impulse of the Spirit, targeting hitherto

**On human responsibility and divine initiative**

World evangelization, like all holy ministry, involves both divine initiative and human responsibility. It is the work of God, and it is the work of humans. This plan rests on the faith that there is no lack in divine initiative. God has never wavered in his holy desire, 'not wanting anyone to perish, but everyone to come to repentance' (2 Peter 3:9). God has never been stingy with empowerment; Jesus said, 'How much more will your Father in heaven give the Holy Spirit to those who ask him?' (Luke 11:13). World evangelization remains an unfinished task not because of any unfaithfulness of God, but because of the unfaithfulness of his people. We will not proclaim, 'It can happen if God works a miracle!' as if his initiative is lacking. Instead we will proclaim, 'It can happen if God's people arise and work in his power!'

Because our global plans depend on human responsibility in world evangelization, failure is a definite possibility. Christians could fail to rise to this challenge, as they did 100 years ago in the quest to evangelize the world by AD 1900. If the possibility of failure again looms large, many Christians will likely shift the rhetoric again from the human responsibility side of the equation to the divine initiative side. Many Christians will likely call for increased prayer, will call for or predict miracles, or will cry out for revival – an unusual work of God. Success or failure in reaching any or all of the 8 Global Goals depends on human obedience—that is, on whether or not Christians obey the Great Commission.

unevangelized regions. Once this is begun, training and orientation programs would become a priority.

### D. FOR MISSION ORGANIZATIONS

55. Loan and finance key personnel for the WCGAP International Office and the other World Christian Offices.

56. Encourage twinning or adoption of unevangelized population segments with evangelized segments of recognizably-similar makeup, background, and situation. On one side, draw upon WCGAP research on least-evangelized segments; on the other side, con-

---

**Every individual?**

The first global goal is about bringing the gospel to everyone, everywhere on Earth, by penetrating every segment, nation, country, race, people, language, population, community, place, or grouping with the proclamation of the gospel. In this context, the phrases 'to every last individual on Earth' or 'to every single man, woman, and child' should be avoided for 2 reasons. (a) The first has to do with scriptural authority. The older view was based on Mark 16:15, KJV/AV: 'Preach the gospel to every creature.' All recent translations follow the Greek more exactly and render the last 3 words by 'to all creation' (RSV, NIV) or 'to all mankind' (GNB/TEV). The mandate is a corporate one, not an individual one, to the whole world, to whole peoples or populations. It is to *panta ta ethne*, not to all persons as individuals. (b) Second, as a goal 'every last individual' in practice would absolve Christians of their obligation because it is physically impossible to achieve. It would commit the Christian harvest force to trying to keep track of the exact whereabouts of the 124 million new persons who will appear at random across the face of the Earth each year between now and AD 2025. They would soon discover this to be impossible. The fact is that during 2005, 2006, 2007 ... 2022, 2023, 2024, etc., new individuals will be appearing unpredictably and at random in all countries of the world at the rate of 340,000 every day (236 every minute). Since no person and no computer could possibly pinpoint their locations, they obviously can't be evangelized as individuals. But that does not mean there is no way to measure and monitor the goal of world evangelization. See Global Diagram 41 in Part 1 "GeoStatus".

---

nect with your circles of donors, supporters, and sending churches.

57. Prepare and maintain a detailed inventory of all ethno-linguistic peoples and languages in which you work. Coordinate with the peoples research and the languages research of the WCGAP Research Office.

58. Consider that the correct, ideal, or optimal role for most foreign missionaries is to serve non-Christian populations in non-Christian countries. With that, consider a new policy of redeployment of foreign missionary personnel now employed in home mission, domestic mission, or home mission abroad. Help them move out of ministry to heavily-Christian peoples in Christian lands and into ministry to non-Christian peoples in Christian lands. An analysis of the world's 845 current global plans shows that the great majority of them are targeted, de facto, on existing Christian populations, hoping to motivate the latter to make the actual contact with non-Christians. Until such plans incorporate the responsibility for making this contact directly, little progress is likely. Having said this, everybody recognizes the enormous difficulties of rapid redeployment of any kind. The planning horizon in missions is at least 5 years (from recruiting missionaries to getting them on the field cross-culturally). Nevertheless, progress will continue to be seriously hindered without a determined attempt to accelerate the process. A range of pastoral and personal concerns will come into play, and this should be done sensitively, but still with determination and a definite sense of direction and purpose.

59. Accept, pray for, and press toward the goal that the bulk of all Western foreign missionaries now working with Christian populations (whether practicing or non-practicing) in Christian environments in World C be redeployed to World A. So long as Western mission agencies continue to send 80% of their foreign missionaries (335,000) to work with heavily-christianized populations in predominantly-

Christian lands (such as the USA sending 3,000 to Brazil today), only 16% will be available for World B and 4% for World A where they are needed far more. Along with redeployment of present missionaries, deploy the upcoming missionary force of new Western candidates and recruits especially to World A.

60. Similarly, for non-Western agencies, accept, pray for, and press toward the goal that the bulk of all Third-World foreign missionaries now working with Christian populations (whether practicing or non-practicing) in Christian environments in World C be redeployed to World A. So long as Third-World mission agencies continue to send 97% of all their missionaries to work with heavily-christianized populations in predominantly-Christian lands (such as Brazil sending out 3,000 missionaries to 45 other countries over 70% Christian; or 2,200 Third-World missionaries serving in the USA), only 3% will be available for Worlds A and B where they are most needed. Along with redeployment of present missionaries, deploy the upcoming missionary force of new non-Western candidates and recruits especially to World A.

61. Adopt a multi-channeled approach to the evangelization of the unevangelized peoples or cities among which you work. Seek to enlist other organizations, other institutions, other orders, and other mission agencies to join in the work, especially with large segments. Consider the many avenues of ministry and communication that could be applied. Seek out new relationships with other Great Commission agencies and networks, especially those in other countries or in distant parts of the world. This is not about harmonizing or coming to terms with other doctrines, dogmas, modes of baptism, theologies, methodologies, missiologies, eschatologies, ecclesiologies, nor mergers, nor organic church union. This is about Great Commission solidarity in all its forms. This is about cooperating in obedience to the Great Commission and its 7 mandates.

62. In all promotional publications make clear that your work is part of a larger whole, part of a large, big-picture, cooperative global plan. Make clear that your work fits together in harmony with the contributions of a vast company of GCC effort all over the world, for the elimination of duplication and waste, and to the end that comprehensive, global goals in world evangelization will be achieved.

63. Establish a global desk (cf. point 4 above).

64. Work together with other missionary-sending agencies, of many countries, to solve the problem of currency restrictions. Most governments or regimes in the Third World restrict or prohibit the export of currency or funds, thus making the sending and supporting of foreign missionaries extremely difficult. Solve the problem so missionaries can be sent, and supported, from any country on earth. Such a solution could function in the same way that the parallel problem with scripture distribution has been solved. The United Bible Societies operates a World Service Budget of $40 million a year, administered from London and New York, into which all 180 countries served by Bible societies pay a quota annually, as they are able to and allowed to. This is then disbursed strictly in accordance with need for subsidies to the whole range of countries. Thus, a country whose regime prohibits the export of foreign currency may pay nothing to the budget for several years but might well be allocated huge sums annually for new translation projects. This deals effectively with the original danger of missionary paternalism in funding.

65. Appoint nonresidential missionaries to closed target populations until all unevangelized population segments have each at least one full-time Christian worker working to see it become fully evangelized by the year 2025. This will necessitate close monitoring of the overall situation and linking of unreached populations with agencies until every such segment in the world is covered. Distribute materials explaining the nonresidential missionary concept and how agencies are already making it work. Networking this sort of information will be important in further recruiting of such personnel. Work together with

other mission agencies to provide for all nonresidential missionaries a network of specialized, inter-mission assistance of every kind, in addition to the regular support and backup provided by their own mission agencies. In particular, help them to investigate, suggest, draw up, and selectively help to implement wide-ranging lists of imaginative ministry options for their own target populations, with overarching objectives drawn from the Global Goals. These will be specific ministries on which Great Commission Christians of one sort or another, including local churches, could easily embark if properly informed and challenged.

### E. FOR SEMINARIES, THEOLOGICAL COLLEGES, BIBLE COLLEGES, AND TRAINING INSTITUTES

66. Establish a global desk (cf. point 4 above).

67. Research, reflect, and publish new work on the Great Commission and on the mission of the church in the world. Support and critique the WCGAP from the basis of Biblical theology. Find new ways to mobilize the church to Great Commission obedience–ways that are clear, unambiguous, new (not just a repeat of earlier catchwords), striking, agreed, and capable of immediately being identified with by all the great Christian communions whose fraternal cooperation the plan hopes to enlist.

68. Prepare curricula and textbooks on the theology of mission, harvest, world evangelization, and the WCGAP to be used for training purposes (1) in training institutions and (2) with currently-active ministers and pastors. This could then lead into the more significant aspects of training: training of trainers, reevaluation of pedagogies, development of character, balance between formal and informal instruction, on-the-job training, reduced emphasis on paper qualifications alone, cultural aspects, and the like.

69. With prayer, engage in a fundamental evaluation and change process that explores how you should serve not only God's church but God's world. Consider how your resources could be applied to the fulfillment of the Global Goals, especially the evangelization of World A.

---

**If current trends continue**

It is not likely that the goals listed above will be achieved if global evangelization only continues at the present pace, by the present methods, under the present structures, and by the present trends. Without change, even serious change, there will be a shortfall. If there is no WCGAP or some similar new initiative, the following projections can be expected:

1. Global % Evangelized
   AD 2025 goal:          100.0%
   AD2025 projected:   77.0%
   Likely shortfall:       23% will remain unevangelized.
2. Global % Christian
   AD 2025 goal:          44%
   AD 2025 projected:   33.4%
   Likely shortfall:       6.6%
3. Global % Great Commission Christians
   AD 2025 goal:          20%
   AD 2025 projected:   11.3%
   Likely shortfall:       8.7%
4. Global cross-cultural missionary sending ratio
   AD 2025 goal:          2,000:1
   AD 2025 projected:   2,800:1
   Likely shortfall:       800
5. Global giving to Christian causes, as a percentage of total income of Christians
   AD 2025 goal:          3.0%
   AD 2025 projected:   2.0%
   Likely shortfall:       1.0%
6. The number of cities without a church
   AD 2025 goal:          0
   AD 2025 projected:   80
   Likely shortfall:       80
7. The number of peoples without a church
   AD 2025 goal:          0
   AD 2025 projected:   500
   Likely shortfall:       500
8. The number of languages without a Bible
   AD 2025 goal:          0
   AD 2025 projected:   4,000
   Likely shortfall:       4,000

## F. FOR LOCAL CHURCHES OR CONGREGATIONS

70. Appoint one of your leaders to serve as the WCGAP contact person and advocate.

71. Adopt a least-evangelized people or city. Travel to them, learn about them, pray for them, support Christian work among them, send missionaries to them—take responsibility for their evangelization.

72. From your church missions budget, from a special missions giving program, or from special fundraising activities, contribute to the WCGAP International Office and its staff, programs, publications, events, and related World Christian Offices.

73. Encourage and participate in the organization of a global network of 7-day or 2-week Schools of Evangelization, initiated, organized, and implemented by local churches. These would concentrate on practical aspects of evangelism, methods, hands-on experience on the streets, literature available, and the like.

74. Serve as a WCGAP advocate and resources center for your city, town, or area. Provide a base for WCGAP instruction and mobilization. Map out and pursue a strategy to enlist Supporters and Members from the churches of your area, in all their ecclesiastical, racial, class, ethic, or linguistic diversity.

## G. FOR MISSIONARIES

75. Translate this plan into the language or languages in which you have attained fluency, or commission and supervise its translation by qualified nationals where you serve. Publish and promote the plan among the speakers of these languages. Keep the WCGAP International Office informed of your efforts. Offer your services to them.

76. From your area of contact and expertise, supply needed information to the WCGAP Research Office. Gather and maintain, from the best sources, the statistical and descriptive information needed to support assessment and monitoring of the Global Goals.

77. Assess the ministry of your own missionary team against the Global Goals, and especially against the first goal. With prayer, consider re-deployment to World A. With prayer, encourage your missionary colleagues to consider the same.

78. Become a Great Commission mobilizer among all the churches you have contact with, both in your sending country and in the country where you serve. Encourage churches, Christian organizations, and ordinary Christians to become GCCs and Members of the WCGAP.

## H. FOR CHRISTIANS

79. Understand that you, as a child of God the Father, as a baptized disciple of Jesus Christ, as a temple of the Holy Spirit—you have a very important part to play in the work of God on earth. You can play an important role in the WCGAP. Begin with prayer.

80. Consider what God has given you—in experience, in knowledge, in possessions, in wisdom, in skills, in relationships—and offer all that you have to God for the evangelization of the world. Carefully read and pray over this plan and seek for ways you can help. Offer your support and services to GCC agencies that are Members of this plan.

81. Learn a language that will allow you to communicate directly with World A individuals. Recommended languages that are taught widely around the world and that are at least the trade language for many World A peoples include: French, Arabic, Turkish, Russian, Farsi, Pushtu, Urdu, Hindi, Bengali, Mandarin Chinese, Indonesian, and Korean.

82. Travel to World A, or help another Christian friend to do so. Become a World A advocate and mobilizer from that experience.

83. Serve as a volunteer worker for the WCGAP promotional, educational, or mobilizing activities in your area.

84. Pray for and contribute to the International Office.

85. Contribute knowledge, information, volunteer work, and funds to the World Christian Research Office or other Offices.

86. Join in the global prayer movement for World Evangelization assisted by the World Christian Prayer Office.

87. Contribute to an effective global plan focused on World A.

## IMPLEMENTATION

The first question in implementation: should it be pursued from the bottom up, or from the top down? Can implementation begin with a group of ordinary, grass-roots Christians who understand and believe in the WCGAP but who in themselves have no great influence, power, or resources? Or must implementation begin with the leaders of organized Christianity, with the heads of larger denominations and churches, the leaders of important councils and associations, the heads of significant organizations, institutions, and orders, the directors of major mission agencies, and the leaders of large global plans—thus seeking representation that will quickly connect with thousands, millions, and tens of millions of active Great Commission Christians, and with vast resources of all kinds?

The answer: both. A grass-roots organization can begin immediately, the moment any Christian reads this document. Ordinary Christians of any church, denomination, confession, country, people, language, class, age, or sex can have a meaningful role from the very start. And the leadership of organized Christianity in all its divisions, forms, and bodies should be approached, informed, and encouraged to join in, both formally, by official representation, adoption, and endorsement, and informally, in their private capacities.

### 1. Register your interest today.
Anyone reading this plan can take a personal, immediate step of implementation. Pray about this. Any Christian, church, denomination, organization, institution, order, or mission agency interested in this plan can contact:
  WCGAP Desk
  P.O. Box 6628
  Richmond, VA 23230
  U.S.A.
  fax: 804-355-2016
  e-mail: GEM@xc.org
The World Evangelization Research Center (WERC), an inter-denominational, ecumenical, inter-mission global missions research organization, is responsible both for the production of the *World Christian Encyclopedia* and for the initial authorship of this plan. Its WCGAP desk will pray, will maintain a database of all interested in the WCGAP, and will connect them with each other so the next, more serious steps of implementation can be taken together. WERC has no ambitions of carrying a central role in implementation beyond helping with this initial, simple step.

### 2. Participate in on-going discussion.
Through mail, telephone, e-mail, Web pages, small informal meetings, large informal meetings, and other means discuss the WCGAP. Pray over it, and over the discussion process. Draw Christians from 100 or even 200 countries into the discussion. Draw in the young and the old, men and women, rich and poor, educated and not, respected and ordinary, leaders and grass-roots Christians. Discuss all sections, points, and ideas of this plan. Listen to each other. Let ideas arise that prove themselves through the course of the discussion to be the best, the most widely accepted, the most convincing, and the wisest. Let the circle of discussion around the world grow and grow. Pray at every point in the process. Watch for those who, by their zeal for the plan and their set of experiences, training, gifts, and abilities, show themselves to be good candidates for the initial committee.

### 3. Form an initial committee.
From the very start, much prayer and attention will need to be given to the question of leadership. World-

class Christian leaders will need to come forward, bearing spiritual influence and worthy of respect, who can attract trust, cooperation, and even sacrifice for common goals—from a very diverse global Christian family. A primary task of this committee will be to call for and organize the initial conference.

### 4. Convene an initial conference.
This will be an international conference of those who to this point have shown greatest interest in, enthusiasm for, and action on behalf of, the WCGAP. Before, during, and following the conference there will be much prayer. A key result of the conference will be the appointment of the initial staff for the nascent International Office. Much work will be done even before this conference to make that possible. Specific potential staff members will be approached, for example, and funding enlisted beforehand.

### 5. Establish the initial International Office.
At the start, the office may have as few as 10 staff. Even at that, leaders will keep in view the goal that the staff represent the Body of Christ globally–rich and poor, old and young, men and women, from many different Christian confessions, from many cultures, fluent in many languages. The office will immediately give serious attention to the 6 factors most likely to scuttle or stifle the WCGAP:

a. Inter-confessional cooperation: too great a percentage of the Christian world may stumble over the idea of joining in any working relationship with Christians from different denominations, churches, confessions, or traditions that they have historically ignored or counted as enemies.
b. Lack of key leadership: a world-class movement will require world-class leadership very early in the process, leadership that will have or gain the respect and favor of many Christians from many traditions.
c. The accusation of duplication: Christians may complain that the WCGAP is a duplication of the WCC, or the LCWE, or the WEF, or the AD2000 and Beyond Movement, or a host of other cooperative or conciliar organizations.
d. Absence of key agencies: implementation of the plan could be halted, or severely hindered, if too many of the Christian world's largest and most significant churches, confessions, organizations, orders, and mission agencies reject, oppose, or ignore it.
e. Lack of grassroots involvement: a huge force of active, informed lay volunteers will be required, globally.
f. Lack of money.

### 6. Publish, disseminate and refine the Plan.
This present publication is not the final version of the WCGAP. It establishes a few key points that are non-negotiable, especially the first 6 Foundational Principles, and it shows what a final WCGAP could look like. The final version will come as a result of extensive global consultation and prayer. People tend to be unwilling to commit themselves fully to a plan they had no role in forming or praying over.

As soon as the International Office is established, a primary task will be to pray and to translate and disseminate the plan throughout the entire Great Commission Christian world, both to promote it and to improve it. This will be an open process, seeking advice, ideas, improvements, corrections, additions, and better terminology, phraseology, and tone. All major Christian churches, denominations, confessions, councils, organizations, institutions, orders, mission agencies, plans, and leaders, in every country of the world, will be contacted formally and informally. A vast number of ordinary Christians, all over the world, will be informed and consulted. All will join together in prayer concerning this plan, cooperation, and world evangelization. The International Office will need to insist: "Though you may find here things you very much dislike, we still are eager to hear from you!" The news of this plan will be spread in many ways and in many languages, through all kinds of communication forms, from the simplest and most inexpensive to the most technologically sophisticated.

The International Office will convene a series of week-long consultations in various regions of the world where Christian leaders come together to pray over and discuss the plan, moving toward a final version.

The WCGAP will be prayerfully modified, expanded, and improved, and thus made more acceptable to a wider circle of Christians–but within certain limits. Certain parts will be non-negotiable, especially the first 6 Foundational Concepts. Still, a large percentage of the world's Christians will know of, interact with, pray for, and join as Members in this Plan in the process.

### 7. Organize an initial global conference.
Ideally, this will fall before AD 2005. At this, the WCGAP will be formally launched, although already by this time there will be a large company of Members, Supporters, and Active Participants. Much fervent prayer will be offered up before, during, and following this conference.

### 8. Hold global conferences every 5 years.
These will fall in the years 2005, 2010, 2015, 2020, and 2025. Each will be a large-scale, fully international, fully multi-lingual, fully inter-confessional action consultation. Comprehensive and up-to-date monitoring reports and statistics, in simple outline and in massive detail, will be presented. Many prayers will be offered. Mid-course corrections will be proposed and adopted. New groups of younger leaders will be fully integrated into the process at each interval. The conference in 2020 will, with prayer, launch the process for preparing a new WCGAP for the period 2025-2050. The conference in 2025 will present a comprehensive review of the WCGAP global experience of 2000-2025, with appropriate rejoicing, confession, celebration, or repentance. That event will also, with humble prayers to the Triune God, launch the new WCGAP for 2025-2050 (which will likely have an entirely new name, tone, and theme), addressing the most crucial aspects of the continuing work of world evangelization and world mission.

---

## A SHORT VERSION OF THE WCGAP

### Introduction
This is a plan to bring Christians together to evangelize the world. It proposes bringing together all kinds of Christians–Catholics, Charismatics, Ecumenists, Evangelicals, Fundamentalists, Independents, Neo-Apostolics, Orthodox, Pentecostals, Postdenominationalists, and Protestants–and Christians from every continent, country, people, language, and place where they live on Earth. This is a plan for world evangelization, for obedience to the Great Commission of Jesus Christ, for every person on earth to hear the gospel in a way they can understand and have a valid opportunity to become a Christian.

In the work of evangelization, some things, the most important things, remain the same since ancient Christianity. Other things change as the gospel advances into the diverse languages, cultures, nations, and eras of humanity. The WCGAP is a response to the globalization of Christianity and to the comprehensiveness of the Great Commission. It takes hold of certain tools present in our era, accepts them as gifts from God, and employs them for holy purposes.

This plan is unique and unprecedented in that it draws upon, is informed by, and is motivated by a huge volume of new global data and information. These are the data presented here in the present *WCT, World Christian encyclopedia* and the CD, the *World Christian database*. These present an extensive global collection of professionally-researched statistical information on Christianity and religion, covering a vast range of factors. It is therefore not a plan built on dreams, wishes, or a mere general understanding of the world and the church. It is a plan built on facts.

### A World Christian Manifesto
Jesus came to seek and to save the lost (Luke 19:10). Jesus came to proclaim the good news of the kingdom of God (Luke 8:1). As the Father sent Jesus, so Jesus is sending us (John 20:21).

God now commands all people everywhere to repent (Acts 17:30). Jesus commissioned his disciples to go and make disciples of all nations (Matthew 28:19), and to go into all the world and preach the good news to all creation (Mark 16:15). Jesus proclaimed that repentance and forgiveness of sins would be preached in his name to all nations (Luke 24:47), and that the gospel of the Kingdom would be preached in the whole world as a testimony to all nations (Matthew 24:14). The Great Commission calls for proclamation of the gospel to all nations, all the world, all creation, everyone, everywhere. As in the apostolic pattern, this can be pursued in a deliberate, organized way (Acts 19:10). So today: let us proclaim the gospel to every person, in every place, in all the world; and let us do so in a deliberate, organized way to insure that all who live on earth will hear the word of the Lord.

From one man God made every nation of men, that they should inhabit the whole earth; and determined the times set for them and the exact places where they should live. God did this so that men would seek him (Acts 17:26-27). The Lamb was slain, and with his blood he purchased men for God from every tribe and language and people and nation (Revelation 5:9). So today: let us proclaim the gospel among every nation God has made, among every country, every people, every tribe, and every language, in every place where God has set them.

Christians are to stand firm in one spirit, contending as one for the faith of the gospel without being frightened in any way by those who oppose (Philippians 1:27-28). Jesus prayed that all of those who would believe in him through the message of the apostles would be one, so that the world might believe that Jesus was from God. (John 17:20-23). So today: let us all–Catholics, Charismatics, Conciliars, Evangelicals, Fundamentalists, Independents, Neo-Apostolics, Orthodox, Pentecostals, Postdenominationalists, and Protestants—all Christians everywhere—let us all come together to evangelize the world.

It was always the ambition of the Apostle Paul to preach the gospel where Christ was not known, so that he would not be building on someone else's foundation. Rather, as it is written, 'Those who were not told about him will see, and those who have not heard will understand' (Romans 15:20-21). So today: let us proclaim the gospel where Christ is not known,

among those who have not heard, in the places and among the people where there are no Christians.

*Foundational Concepts*
1. Evangelization: Every person on earth has the unequivocal right to hear the gospel in a way she or he can understand, and to be given a valid opportunity to become a Christian. The goal of world evangelization is not that all will believe, but that all will hear.
2. Cooperation: This plan is for those Christians who are willing to work cooperatively in mission with other Christians different from themselves. Let us do together what we cannot do separately.
3. World A: The WCGAP constantly asks, 'Where is the need the greatest?' and encourages resources in that direction.
4. AD 2025: This plan has in view those aspects of world evangelization that can and should be completed by AD 2025.
5. Quantification: For world evangelization, statistical research is not only helpful but essential.
6. Segmentation: The larger task should be divided into meaningful segments that can then be assessed, assigned, engaged, and monitored one at a time: by countries, cities, peoples, languages, provinces, and other units. The WCGAP segments the enormous task of world evangelization into pieces that can be assigned, and thus into sub-tasks that can be achieved one by one.

### A WORLD CHRISTIAN AGENDA: THE 8 GLOBAL GOALS

1. For everyone on earth to be evangelized.
2. For the world to be 40% Christian.
3. For the world to be 20% Great Commission Christians.
4. For every 2,000 Christians to send at least one cross-cultural missionary.
5. For Christians to give 3% of their income to Christian causes.
6. For there to be a church in every city.
7. For there to be a church for every people.
8. For there to be a Bible in every language.

*Tasks*
The full version of the WCGAP includes a list of 87 distinct, challenging, yet achievable tasks directed specifically to the achievement of the 8 Global Goals

by AD2025. Specific tasks are appointed for the WCGAP International Office (including its prayer office, research office, office of plan consultants, communications office, and futures office), for global ecumenical and confessional bodies, for Christian churches and denominations, for mission organizations, for seminaries, (theological colleges, Bible colleges, and training institutes), for local churches, for missionaries, and for individual Christians.

*Implementation*
A grass-roots organization can begin immediately, the moment any Christian reads this document. Ordinary Christians of any church, denomination, confession, country, people, language, class, age, or sex can have a meaningful role from the very start. And the leadership of organized Christianity in all its divisions, forms, and bodies should be approached, informed, and encouraged to join in, both formally, by official representation, adoption, and endorsement, and informally, in their private capacities.

1. Register your interest today. Contact:
   WCGAP Desk
   P.O. Box 6628
   Richmond, VA 23230
   U.S.A.
   fax: 804-355-2016
   e-mail: GEM@xc.org
2. Participate in on-going discussion. Through mail, telephone, e-mail, Web pages, small informal meetings, large informal meetings, and other means discuss the WCGAP. Pray over it, and over the discussion process. Watch for those who, by their zeal for the plan and their set of experiences, training, gifts, and abilities, show themselves to be good candidates for the initial committee.
3. Form an initial committee.
4. Convene an initial conference.
   This will be an international conference of those who to this point have shown greatest interest in, enthusiasm for, and action on behalf of, the WCGAP.
5. Establish the initial International Office.
6. Publish, disseminate and refine the Plan.
7. Organize an initial global conference. Ideally, this will fall before AD 2005. At this, the WCGAP will be formally launched. Much fervent prayer will be offered up before, during, and following this conference.

Part 28

# GEOTARGETING

Global and local sharing to benefit peoples and religions

*I have always tried to preach where people have never heard about Christ.*
—Apostle Paul, Romans 15:20, Contemporary English Version

*Arabia could easily be evangelized within the next thirty years if it were not for the wicked selfishness of Christians.*
—S. M. Zwemer in John R. Mott 1900: 145

*Advance into the unoccupied fields of the world is the highest form of missionary strategy.*
—Samuel Marinus Zwemer, Apostle to Islam, 1911

Targeting is a sophisticated procedure adopted by the United Nations and countless other non-military organizations for reaching their non-military, nonviolent, and non-coercive goals. Here we give it a pacifist meaning: planned global and local sharing to directly benefit peoples and religions. Two complementary but quite different approaches are here described.

Firstly, Part 28 sets out a precise scale for assessing who and where populations are who most need the myriad benefits of Christianity, Christ, and the gospel. This results in a precise instrument measuring any people's situation on a 10-point scale, extendible to a more-detailed 34-point scale. This leads to the listing of the 3,638 most unreached (least reached) peoples noted in Table 28–5, which is based on the targeting value of every people in all countries as listed in *WCE* Part 8 "Ethno-Sphere", column 37.

Secondly, a quite different approach sees the globe's populations divided up by its 9,900 distinct and separate religions. This is as set out in Part 17 "Religiometrics" and its Tables 17-5 and 17-6. In these tables their column 9 with its 6-point scale 'Contact' provides a listing of 354 religions and their followers having no contact at all with organized Christianity. Global totals are shown in Table 28–6. All these religionists could be beneficiaries of planned targeting for a determined attempt to open contact with a view to sharing the benefits of Christianity, Christ, and the gospel.

# Global and local sharing to benefit peoples and religions

## EVANGELISTIC TARGETABILITY

The words 'target', 'targeting', and 'targetability' as used here have no military or hostile or weapons-related connotations at all. They have the strictly biblical meaning of persons and peoples with whom Christians share, or ought to share, all the rich benefits of Christianity, Christ, and the gospel. Our main meaning and synonyms for 'target' are 'beneficiary' or 'sharer'. When referring to any people as a target, therefore, we imply only that the people either are at present beneficiaries of the gospel, or deserve to be, or ought to be, and that Christians have a responsibility in the sharing process.

With this understanding, the term 'targets' continues in use here because it is too concise and precise to be abandoned.

### Priority or primacy for targeting: the T-scale
The evangelism variable e (offers per capita per year) derived at the end of Part 24 "Microevangelistics" has a range of possible values from 0 (zero) to a theoretical maximum of 912.5 offers per capita per year. The variable can be categorized and coded into a simpler scale T with 10 levels of evangelistic provision or 30 levels of evangelistic targetability. This variable has several meanings, of ascending complexity: (1) its original meaning of T = current level of evangelism-hours per capita per year; (2) its associated meaning of T = current level of offers received per capita per year; (3) T = resulting level of sparseness or superfluity of evangelism among a specific population; (4) T = adequacy of present rate of provision of evangelism; (5) T = a scale of priority, priorities, or prioritizing, with T =1 signifying top or first priority for mission agencies; and (6) T = a detailed scale of targetability, or current target-worthiness. This ranges from populations which are or should be the most deserving No. 1 prime targets (T = 1) located in World A, the unevangelized world, all the way to those for which additional evangelism directed at them is unnecessary and even wasteful or counterproductive, from the standpoint of any global mission strategy, and so should have the lowest priority (T = 10). These latter peoples are located in heavily-christianized areas in our World C, the Christian world.

The scale is set out in Graphic 28-1 and in Table 28–1 as follows, under 2 different standpoints: (a) Evangelistic Provision, composed of current status of world mission, evangelization, mission activity, and current failure in evangelism; and (b) Evangelistic Targetability, with proposed retargeting, with scales T-1 to T-10, as a means of future prioritizing. Scale (a) is listed in order of increasing evangelism. In scale (b) the codes still have the same meaning but the order of the 10 code lines is reversed in order to create a list of increasing *absence* of evangelism and hence a scale of increasing targetability. So on both scales code 1 means 'Peoples with this code should be regarded as Target No. 1, the first or primary targets of mission, the top priorities for missions'.

---

**Graphic 28–1. Geotargeting: how to share the benefits of Christianity with the most strategic targets and avoid 6 levels of pseudo-targets in world evangelization.**

This graphic analyzes the data required to prioritize targets in world mission. A more elaborate diagram, comparing the present situation with 2 other earlier global parallels, is shown as Global Diagram 63 in Part 1 "GeoStatus". The Christian parallel to secular counterparts is the church's foreign missionary force of 420,000 career professionals from 200 countries. They are the church's intercontinental elite, carefully trained to hit crossculturally the longest-distance targets. The church's dynamic for world mission begins in the lowest of the 3 levels of World C (shown shaded), initiated by Great Commission Christians (the source is shown below by *). They attempt to aim upwards at the non-Christian world (Worlds A and B). By contrast with secular strategies, however, the Christian mission has allowed 91% of these forces to then be diverted (see black arrows) to plum targets—close, relatively easy, glittering targets entirely within World C—15% on the home base (Target 10) where a third of all foreign missionaries are always on leave, and 76% working among inactive Christians abroad (Targets 9 and 8). As a result, only 8.7% of all Christian personnel, outreach and evangelism ever gets through to World B, and only 0.3% to World A.
We ask therefore—How can we stop allowing these inactive Christian levels to thus obstruct and dissipate mission to the non-Christian world? One answer is—study closely history's lessons for successful strategy in Graphics 1 and 2 of Global Diagram 63.

| Current status of world mission | | | | | | Current mission activity | | | | Current failure to evangelize | | Proposed retargeting | |
|---|---|---|---|---|---|---|---|---|---|---|---|---|---|
| World<br><br>column 1 | Level<br><br>2 | Evangelism<br>(e p.a.p.c.)<br>3 | Persons<br><br>4 | Population<br>(m=millions)<br>5 | Evangelization<br>(E)<br>6 | Missions<br>(7 arrows)<br>7 | Targets<br>(10 squares)<br>8 | Activity<br>(10 tactics)<br>9 | % used of all<br>resources<br>10 | Offers a day<br><br>11 | Time to<br>evangelize all<br>12 | Target<br><br>13 | Peoples<br><br>14 |
| **World A**<br>(unevangelized persons) | 1.<br><br>e=0 | | Untargeted | 145m | Nothing | 1 | | Warfare | 0.00% | 2,000 offers a day | over 100 years | T-1 | 818 |
| | 2.<br><br>e=0.1 | | Uncontacted | 276m | Scarcity | 2 | | Hostilities | 0.01% | 24,000 offers a day | 30 years | T-2 | 705 |
| | 3.<br><br>e=1 | | Unreached | 523m | Infrequency | 3 | | Marauding | 0.1% | 0.5 million offers a day | 3 years | T-3 | 762 |
| | 4. | | Barely reached | 1,271m | Inadequacy | | 4 | Skirmishing | 0.2% | 15 million offers a day | 3 months | T-4 | 1,353 |
| **World B**<br>(evangelized non-Christians) | e=10<br>5.<br><br>e=40 | | Partially evangelized non-Christians | 1,480m | Subsistence | | 5 | Policing | 0.7% | 87 million offers a day | 1 month | T-5 | 1,106 |
| | 6.<br><br>e=100 | | Moderately evangelized non-Christians | 207m | Adequacy | | 6 | Advising | 1% | 35 million offers a day | 1 week | T-6 | 893 |
| | 7. | | Heavily evangelized non-Christians | 210m | Sufficiency | | 7 | Building | 7% | 87 million offers a day | 2 days | T-7 | 950 |
| **World C**<br>(Christians) | e=200<br>8.<br><br>e=300 | | Nominal Christians | 94m | Superfluity | | 8 | Mopping-up | 26% | 67 million offers a day | 1 day | T-8 | 1,224 |
| | 9.<br><br>e=400 | | Non-practicing church members | 600m | Saturation | | 9 | Looting | 50% | 580 million offers a day | 15 hours | T-9 | 1,532 |
| | 10. | | Great Commission Christians, and others practicing | 1,248m | Oversaturation | | 10 | Home-basing | 15% | 1,800 million offers a day | 8 hours | T-10 | 3,240 |
| | | | **TOTAL** | **6,055m** | | | | | **TOTAL 100%** | **2,700 million** | | | **12,583** |

Graphic 3. WORLD EVANGELIZATION, 2000-2025.
Targeting with the gospel and world mission resources
✳ = source of missionary personnel

Notes: "e"= average evangelism-hours (offers) received per year per capita

⊡ = glittering pseudo-targets   □ = legitimate targets

**Table 28–1. Criteria for the T-scale, measuring evangelistic provision and targetability.**

a) EVANGELISTIC PROVISION

| T-code | Evangelism experienced by individuals | Criteria | Present offers per capita | World |
|---|---|---|---|---|
| | INADEQUATE PROVISION—PRIME TARGET | | | |
| 1 | No ongoing evangelism | e=0 (or e<0.01) | None in a century | A |
| 2 | Scarce evangelism | 0.1>e>0.01 | Under 1 in a decade | A |
| 3 | Infrequent evangelism | 1>e>0.1 | From 1 a year to 1 a decade | A |
| 4 | Inadequate ongoing evangelism | 10>e>1 | From 1 a month to 1 a year | A |
| | ADEQUATE PROVISION—OCCASIONAL TARGET | | | |
| 5 | Subsistence-level evangelism | 40>e>10 | From 1 a week to 1 a month | B |
| 6 | Adequate ongoing evangelism | 100>e>40 | From 2 a week to 1 a week | B |
| 7 | Sufficient evangelism | 200>e>100 | From 4 a week to 2 a week | B |
| | EXCESSIVE PROVISION—UNNECESSARY TARGET | | | |
| 8 | Superfluous evangelism | 300>e>200 | From 6 a week to 4 a week | C |
| 9 | Saturated evangelism | 400>e>300 | Around once daily | C |
| 10 | Oversaturated evangelism | e>400 | Well over once daily | C |

b) EVANGELISTIC TARGETABILITY: the Targeting Factor, T

| T-code | Population | Criteria | Present offers per capita | World |
|---|---|---|---|---|
| | CHRISTIANS | | | |
| 10 | Great Commission Christians | e>400 | Well over once daily | C |
| 9 | Non-practicing church members | 400>e>300 | Around once daily | C |
| 8 | Unaffiliated Christians | 300>e>200 | From 6 a week to 4 a week | C |
| | EVANGELIZED NON-CHRISTIANS | | | |
| 7 | Heavily-evangelized non-Christians | 200>e>100 | From 4 a week to 2 a week | B |
| 6 | Moderately-evangelized non-Christians | 100>e>40 | From 2 a week to 1 a week | B |
| 5 | Partially-evangelized non-Christians | 40>e>10 | From 1 a week to 1 a month | B |
| | UNEVANGELIZED NON-CHRISTIANS | | | |
| 4 | Barely reached non-Christians | 10>e>1 | From 1 a month to 1 a year | A |
| 3 | Unreached non-Christians | 1>e>0.1 | From 1 a year to 1 a decade | A |
| 2 | Uncontacted non-Christians | 0.1>e>0.01 | Under 1 in a decade | A |
| 1 | Untargeted non-Christians | e<0.01 | None in a century | A |

### *Targeting by absence of basic ministries*

A refinement of the above scales provides a much more detailed scale of targetability based on the presence or absence of 24 basic ministries among the listing of 45 ministries under which the concept of evangelism has been defined, analyzed, and enumerated in Part 22 "Evangelism". This enables us to list and rank all 12,600 peoples of the world, ranking them by priority or urgency where sharing the benefits of the Christian gospel is concerned.

### *24 basic ministries or entry points*

As shown in the second scale (b) above, Target 1 (Untargeted non-Christians) is defined as the situation of a people with the criterion e<0.01. In practice, this often also implies one, 2, or 3 additional criteria: D=0, mi=0, AC<0.1 (for meanings see Table 28–2 below). In addition to these 4 major basic ministries, absence of which is deprivation of a people's rights to the benefits of Christianity, there are 20 other basic ministries—or entry points for gospel and mission—in the complete absence of which a people or population is seriously deprived. These 24 basic ministries are listed in Table 28–2.

A people may, however, correctly be termed 'untargeted'—having no denominations, no mission agencies, virtually no evangelism, and virtually no Christians in their midst—but still at the same time have a number of lesser or incidental ministries, or spinoffs from ministries to related peoples elsewhere. These could serve as entry points for gospel and missions in the future. Note therefore in Table 28–2 the definition of 'Presence' or 'Absence' in these 24 ministries, arranged here in the same order as they are shown in the columns of *WCE* Part 8 "EthnoSphere".

### *Measuring absence of basic ministries/entry points*

In addition to the above T-scale's numerical code from 1 to 10, 2 decimal points are now added to the code for all untargeted peoples (already coded '1') to signify the presence or absence of these additional influences (incipient ministries, incidental ministries, or spinoff entry points for the gospel and hence for missions). This produces the 24 additional targetability codes shown in Table 28–3. Note that this is not an additional, separate scale but is an integral continuation of the single T-scale given in 2 forms in Table 28–1.

### *Enumerating the global targeting situation*

Using this expanded scale, Table 28–4 summarizes every ethnolinguistic people by the targeting variable first given in WCE Part 4 "Ethnosphere", column 37. Table 28–4 columns 2 and 3 show that T-1 peoples with access to over 15 ministries achieve the level of evangelistic offers which takes them to the T-2 level, hence there are no peoples with codes 1.16 to 1.23. Columns 4 and 5 enumerate an alternative World A, B, C classification based on e as described in Part 25 "Macroevangelistics". Column 8 shows that T-1 to T-3 peoples receive on average less than one evangelistic offer per capita per year, while total offers per day (column 11) amount to 2,000 of the 2.7 billion offers given worldwide.

This global empirical overview shows the depth of the remaining task. For all T-1 peoples, the time it would take the current level of ministries to evangelize the whole population is longer than a lifetime, whereas people oversaturated with evangelism can expect to hear the gospel daily.

### *Summary: 'untargeted' means deprived of the 24 basic ministries*

So the worst-case hard core of totally unevangelized and unreached peoples consists of those peoples who have less than 16, and down to *none at all*, of these 24 basic ministries or points of entry for the gospel. This hard core consists of all those peoples who are coded '1' on this variable.

Thus the term 'untargeted' is seen as a subset of the flexible concept of 'unreached people'. As a strictly-defined technical term 'unreached' stands here for World A peoples with infrequent or negligible ongoing evangelism (1>e). But because of the widespread use of 'unreached' in a more popularized sense, we could also define it as covering all World A peoples, who are then arranged under the 4 layers of inadequate evangelistic provision—inadequacy, infrequency, scarcity, and virtually nothing. The last of these (the untargeted) is in turn then arranged under 24 levels of progressive evangelistic deprivation.

Unreached peoples in its strictest sense can thus be seen to be best defined as all those peoples who receive less than one evangelistic offer per year, while 'untargeted' peoples have been, and remain, deprived of the basic ministries through which the benefits of Christianity are usually mediated.

### *A whole range of usages of 'an unreached people'*

However, this analysis is quick to state that almost

**Table 28–2. Definitions of presence or absence of 24 basic ministries/entry points.**

The numbers under the column headed "EthnoSphere" below inform the reader under which column in *WCE* Part 8 "EthnoSphere" he or she may find the values of any ministry, for every ethnolinguistic people. The two end columns below then give the codes of those data in EthnoSphere which thereby define 'presence' or 'absence'. The latter can be shown by either a zero (0), or a period (.), or in 4 cases a minuscule level (0.01%, or 0.1, or 1).

Note that any people can be, and have been, evangelized with only a small selection of these ministries present. And although this list gives 24 varieties of ministry, in practice the maximum that it is possible to have is only 19 since p, n, and b are only useful if there are no P, N, or B; and of the 3 second-language scriptures, only 1 is counted by the present method.

| Code | | Basic ministries/entry points | EthnoSphere | Presence | Absence |
|---|---|---|---|---|---|
| AC | = | local affiliated Christians or church members, % | 11 | >0.1 | <0.1 |
| Jf | = | "Jesus" Film in mother tongue or related language | 13 | 1-4 | 0 |
| au | = | audio scriptures | 14 | c-B | . |
| nr | = | New Reader Portions (NRP) or Scriptures (NRS) | 15 | s | . |
| br | = | scriptures available in Braille | 16 | u | . |
| hi | = | scriptures available in signed language | 17 | h | . |
| d | = | personal evangelism by Great Commission Christians | 18 | 2-10 | 0 or 1 |
| wa | = | work among | 19 | 1-10 | 0 |
| xc | = | cross-cultural mission | 20 | 1-60 | 0 |
| me | = | mass evangelism | 21 | 1-5 | 0 |
| mi | = | mission agencies at work | 22 | 1-5 | 0 |
| P | = | portion/gospel only published in mother tongue | 24 | P | . . . |
| p | = | near-portion/gospel (in related language within cluster) | 24 | p | . . . |
| N | = | New Testament published in mother tongue | 25 | N | . . |
| n | = | near-NT (in related language within cluster) | 25 | n | . . |
| B | = | Bible published in mother tongue | 26 | B | . |
| b | = | near-Bible (in related language within cluster) | 26 | b | . |
| sp | = | portion/gospel available via a majority's second language | 27 | p | . |
| sn | = | NT available via a majority's second language | 27 | n | . |
| sb | = | Bible available via a majority's second language | 27 | b | . |
| D | = | denominations present | 28 | 1-5 | 0 |
| aC | = | alien Christians resident with 1 or more churches | 29 | 2-10 | 0 or 1 |
| ra | = | countries transmitting Christian radio | 30 | c-8 | 0 |
| e | = | evangelism-hours per capita per year | 34 | >0.01 | <0.01 |

**Table 28–3. Twenty-four targetability codes for untargeted peoples lacking the 24 basic ministries/entry points.**

These codes form the conclusion of the T-scale set out in Table 28–1. The codes are arranged in numerical order from 1.00 to 1.23, but in reverse order in order to create a scale of increasing absence of ministries and therefore a scale of increasing targetability. T=1.00 at the bottom thus represents the most targetable code of all—the one it makes most sense for Christian missions to take seriously as their biggest challenge.

Note that by definition the ministry of evangelism e is always absent for all these 24 codes, since the untargeted category T=1 is defined by e<0.01.

| T-code | Increasing absence of ministries | Criteria | |
|---|---|---|---|
| 1.23 | Absence of 1 basic ministry | 23 | basic ministries present |
| 1.22 | Absence of 2 basic ministries | 22 | basic ministries present |
| 1.21 | Absence of 3 basic ministries | 21 | basic ministries present |
| 1.20 | Absence of 4 major ministries | 20 | basic ministries present |
| 1.19 | Absence of 5 basic ministries | 19 | basic ministries present |
| 1.18 | Absence of 6 basic ministries | 18 | basic ministries present |
| 1.17 | Absence of 7 basic ministries | 17 | basic ministries present |
| 1.16 | Absence of 8 basic ministries | 16 | basic ministries present |
| 1.15 | Absence of 9 basic ministries | 15 | basic ministries present |
| 1.14 | Absence of 10 basic ministries | 14 | basic ministries present |
| 1.13 | Absence of 11 basic ministries | 13 | basic ministries present |
| 1.12 | Absence of 12 basic ministries | 12 | basic ministries present |
| 1.11 | Absence of 13 basic ministries | 11 | basic ministries present |
| 1.10 | Absence of 14 basic ministries | 10 | basic ministries present |
| 1.09 | Absence of 15 basic ministries | 9 | basic ministries present |
| 1.08 | Absence of 16 basic ministries | 8 | basic ministries present |
| 1.07 | Absence of 17 basic ministries | 7 | basic ministries present |
| 1.06 | Absence of 18 basic ministries | 6 | basic ministries present |
| 1.05 | Absence of 19 basic ministries | 5 | basic ministries present |
| 1.04 | Absence of 20 basic ministries | 4 | basic ministries present |
| 1.03 | Absence of 21 basic ministries | 3 | basic ministries present |
| 1.02 | Absence of 22 basic ministries | 2 | basic ministries present |
| 1.01 | Absence of 23 basic ministries | 1 | basic ministry present |
| 1.00 | Absence of all 24 basic ministries | No | basic ministry present |

## Table 28–4. The world's 12,600 ethnolinguistic peoples enumerated by 34 targetability factors.

| EVANGELISTIC TARGETABILITY | | | | | | | | | | |
|---|---|---|---|---|---|---|---|---|---|---|
| T-code | Peoples | Population | Description of peoples | World | Ministries per people | Current evangelism | e | Offers per capita | Time to evangelize all | Offers per day |
| 1 | 2 | 3 | 4 | 5 | 6 | 7 | 8 | 9 | 10 | 11 |
| | | | **World A** (Defined as e<10) | | | | | | | |
| | | | UNEVANGELIZED NON-CHRISTIANS | | | | | | | |
| 1.00 | 3 | 20,000 | Untargeted | A | 0 | None of any kind | 0.0004 | None | never | 0 |
| 1.01 | 21 | 237,000 | Untargeted | A | 1 | None | 0.0004 | None | 2000 years | 0 |
| 1.02 | 46 | 895,000 | Untargeted | A | 2 | None | 0.0011 | None | 1000 years | 3 |
| 1.03 | 67 | 2,386,000 | Untargeted | A | 3 | None | 0.0023 | None | 400 years | 15 |
| 1.04 | 73 | 5,846,000 | Untargeted | A | 4 | None | 0.0023 | None | 400 years | 37 |
| 1.05 | 50 | 10,238,000 | Untargeted | A | 5 | None | 0.0037 | None | 300 years | 105 |
| 1.06 | 57 | 8,922,000 | Untargeted | A | 6 | Negligible | 0.0044 | Negligible | 200 years | 109 |
| 1.07 | 74 | 14,197,000 | Untargeted | A | 7 | Negligible | 0.0058 | Negligible | 200 years | 224 |
| 1.08 | 93 | 13,541,000 | Untargeted | A | 8 | Negligible | 0.0057 | Negligible | 200 years | 211 |
| 1.09 | 64 | 15,377,000 | Untargeted | A | 9 | Negligible | 0.0057 | Negligible | 200 years | 238 |
| 1.10 | 51 | 3,624,000 | Untargeted | A | 10 | Negligible | 0.0053 | Negligible | 200 years | 53 |
| 1.11 | 56 | 7,617,000 | Untargeted | A | 11 | Negligible | 0.0054 | Negligible | 200 years | 112 |
| 1.12 | 62 | 11,855,000 | Untargeted | A | 12 | Negligible | 0.0047 | Negligible | 200 years | 154 |
| 1.13 | 75 | 25,999,000 | Untargeted | A | 13 | Negligible | 0.0057 | Negligible | 200 years | 409 |
| 1.14 | 23 | 24,111,000 | Untargeted | A | 14 | Negligible | 0.0073 | Negligible | 100 years | 481 |
| 1.15 | 3 | 67,000 | Untargeted | A | 15 | Negligible | 0.0090 | Negligible | 100 years | 2 |
| 1.16 | 0 | 0 | Untargeted | A | 16 | Negligible | — | Negligible | 100 years | — |
| 1.17 | 0 | 0 | Untargeted | A | 17 | Negligible | — | Negligible | 100 years | — |
| 1.18 | 0 | 0 | Untargeted | A | 18 | Negligible | — | Negligible | 100 years | — |
| 1.19 | 0 | 0 | Untargeted | A | 19 | Negligible | — | Negligible | 100 years | — |
| 1.20 | 0 | 0 | Untargeted | A | 20 | Negligible | — | Negligible | 100 years | — |
| 1.21 | 0 | 0 | Untargeted | A | 21 | Negligible | — | Negligible | 100 years | — |
| 1.22 | 0 | 0 | Untargeted | A | 22 | Negligible | — | Negligible | 100 years | — |
| 1.23 | 0 | 0 | Untargeted | A | 23 | Negligible | — | None in a century | 100 years | — |
| 1 | 818 | 144,932,000 | Untargeted | A | 20 | No ongoing evangelism | 0.01 | None in a century | 200 years | 2,151 |
| 2 | 705 | 276,428,000 | Uncontacted | A | 21 | Scarce evangelism | 0.03 | Under 1 in a decade | 30 years | 23,890 |
| 3 | 762 | 522,759,000 | Unreached | A | 22 | Infrequent evangelism | 0.33 | From 1 a year to 1 a decade | 3 years | 475,000 |
| 4 | 1,353 | 1,270,694,000 | Barely reached | A | 22 | Inadequate ongoing evangelism | 4.38 | From 1 a month to 1 a year | 3 months | 15,261,000 |
| | | | **World B** (Defined as 200>e>10) | | | | | | | |
| | | | EVANGELIZED NON-CHRISTIANS | | | | | | | |
| 5 | 1,106 | 1,480,161,000 | Partially-evangelized | B | 23 | Subsistence-level evangelism | 21 | From 1 a week to 1 a month | 1 months | 87,068,000 |
| 6 | 893 | 207,045,000 | Moderately-evangelized | B | 23 | Adequate ongoing evangelism | 61 | From 2 a week to 1 a week | 1 week | 34,674,000 |
| 7 | 950 | 210,462,000 | Heavily-evangelized | B | 23 | Sufficient evangelism | 151 | From 4 a week to 2 a week | 2 days | 86,848,000 |
| | | | **World C** (Defined as e>200) | | | | | | | |
| | | | CHRISTIANS | | | | | | | |
| 8 | 1,224 | 94,165,000 | Unaffiliated Christians | C | 24 | Superfluous evangelism | 259 | From 6 a week to 4 a week | 17 hours | 66,719,000 |
| 9 | 1,532 | 600,393,000 | Nonpracticing church members | C | 24 | Saturated evangelism | 354 | Around once daily | 12 hours | 581,866,000 |
| 10 | 3,240 | 1,248,011,000 | Great Commission Christians | C | 24 | Oversaturated evangelism | 536 | Well over once daily | 8 hours | 1,833,822,000 |
| **Globe** | **12,583** | **6,055,050,000** | | | | | **163** | | | **2,706,758,000** |

all other precise definitions of unreached people are valid, and most in fact have wide current usage. Since the term 'unreached people' has been used in this variety of divergent meanings and definitions, the present analysis ends by giving the numerical values associated with some of these divergent usages. The reader can then select the definition that best suits his or her immediate purpose.

These 11 different definitions are summarized in Table 28–5.

### The value of nonconfessional definitions
In addition to the varieties of definition of unreached peoples listed in Table 28–5 there is a large number of others that are favored by, and restricted to, one single Christian confession or ecclesiastical family—Roman Catholic, Catholic Charismatic, Evangelical, Anglican Evangelical, Conservative Evangelical, Southern Baptist, Joshua Project, and so on. The whole field is immensely complicated by this plethora of divergent definitions. What the present survey attempts to do, therefore, is to set forth a handful of definitions broadly acceptable to all Great Commission Christians.

### Strategic planning
The whole targeting scale or its alternatives can thus be seen to provide an objective starting-point for missionary planning in a complex and bewildering world of thousands of potential targets clamoring for attention, resources, and personnel. On the reasonable premise that top priority in distributing the benefits of Christianity should be assigned to those who at present have none of them, the top priority of the Christian world mission should therefore be those peoples coded here as 1.00, followed by those coded 1.01, then 1.02, 1.03, 1.04, and so on.

## Table 28–5. 11 differing definitions of the concept 'an unreached people' with each's current global enumeration.

The concept 'an unreached people' is in practice widely but loosely used. It can mean any of the following definitions, numbered 1 to 11, or any grouping or range of them.

| Terminology and definition | Peoples | AD 2000 population |
|---|---|---|
| 1 | 2 | 3 |
| UNTARGETED PEOPLES (T=1) | | |
| 1. A people without any of the 24 basic ministries. | 3 | 20,000 |
| 2. A people with only one of the 24 basic ministries. | 21 | 237,000 |
| 3. A people with anywhere from 2 to 19 of these basic ministries. | 794 | 144,675,000 |
| UNCONTACTED PEOPLES (T=2) | | |
| 4. A people with e, evangelistic offers per capita p.a., defined as 0.1>e>0.01. | 705 | 276,428,000 |
| UNREACHED PEOPLES on Targeting Scale (T=3) | | |
| 5. A people with e defined by 1>e>0.1 | 762 | 522,759,000 |
| 6. All peoples with Targeting variable 3 or less (T=3, 2, or 1), i.e. e<1. | 2,285 | 944,119,000 |
| BARELY REACHED PEOPLES on Targeting Scale (T = 4) | | |
| 7. A people inadequately reached (10>e>1) | 1,353 | 1,270,894,000 |
| UNEVANGELIZED PEOPLES | | |
| 8. All peoples with e defined by e<10, that is T=4, 3, 2, or 1. | 3,638 | 2,214,813,000 |
| 9. All peoples clearly designated as World A peoples, defined as E<50%. | 3,833 | 1,106,766,000 |
| 10. All peoples with few Christians (AC<5%) resident in World A countries. | 1,012 | 589,044,000 |
| 11. The entire population of all peoples in all World A countries. | 1,448 | 605,304,000 |

### Postscript: pioneering through intercession
One of the basic ministries listed in Part 22 "Evangelism" (see Table 22–3) and in Part 24 "Microevangelistics" (Table 24–9) is intercessory prayer for a specific named people or other population segment. It is not listed in the T-scale because it is a hidden ministry. It is therefore basically impossible to say with any certainty at any point in time 'Nobody anywhere is praying for this people.' Also, from the people's own standpoint, all the 24 ministries on the T-scale are not hidden from them but are visible, audible, and tangible for the people themselves.

Christians should however be made aware that if they want to make an immediate start on reaching the totally unreached, they could begin the ministry of intercessory prayer for any people coded here as 1 and particularly 1.00 to 1.02. Their hidden ministry would thus be the first known ministry among that particular people.

## TARGETING RELIGIOUS SYSTEMS

### An alternative way of sharing benefits

A quite different approach for enumerating the unfinished task of world evangelization is to analyze contact between organized Christianity as a religion and each of the non-Christian religions. Those with no contact should therefore, logically, be the first to be targeted with any new efforts to share the benefits of the gospel.

Data on all 9,900 distinct and separate religions is set out in Part 17 "Religiometrics", Tables 17-5 and 17-6. The degree of contact (using the 6-point scale given below in Table 28–6 columns 1 and 2) is shown in Table 17-5 column 9. Results of the analysis are given in Table 28–6 below.

The overall situation is best explained in column 11 of Table 28–6. There, the 9,900 religions are broken down into the 6 levels of contact set out in column 2 and coded in column 1. From the targeting point of view, 3,980 religions (with contact from codes 4 and 5) already have virtually complete contact with organized Christian churches, missions, institutions, and agencies. They do not need more contact. What resources for contact exist—church workers, publications, broadcasting, finance—are needed primarily by the 353 religions currently with no contact at all with churches or agencies (code 0) and so continue to remain involuntarily unaware of Christianity, Christ, and the gospel.

The names of these 353 uncontacted religions can be seen from Table 17-5 or 17-6 by running one's eye down column 9 looking for the digit 0. The number of each's adherents can also be seen there. Note that many religionists (adherents of a particular religion) overlap with other religions; for example, 'Sunnis', 'Shias', 'Sufis', 'Hanafites', 'Zaydis', and 'Ahmadis' overlap somewhat with each other and also all overlap 100 per cent with 'Muslims'). But the situation is clear enough to justify a mission board or agency to make a sizable dent in the situation by assigning 2 persons to work with any one of the 353.

---

## BIBLIOGRAPHY

The United Nations publication *Review of recent national demographic target setting* (1st edition 1989) deals exhaustively with the whole subject of targeting. It includes copious data on particular countries' attempts at targeting, and the attempts of the UN and its members to force reluctant nations to exchange vague platitudes ('Our target is 100% literacy and zero infant mortality') for firm targets and publicized final completion dates. The book ends with a wide-ranging bibliography of some 120 items, many describing, and being published by, one particular country.

**Table 28–6.** The current status of contact between (a) organized Christianity and (b) each of the globe's 9,900 religions, producing a scale for targeting the sharing of the benefits of Christianity, Christ, and the gospel.

| Code | Contact with Christianity | LISTED RELIGIONS (named in Table 17-5) | | UNLISTED RELIGIONS (not named in Table 17-5) | | | | | | ALL RELIGIONS | | | |
| | | | | Lesser ethnoreligions | | Peripheral religions | | Hidden religions | | | | | |
| | | Religions | Adherents | Religions | Adherents | Religions | Adherents | Religions | Adherents | Religions | % | Adherents | % |
| 1 | 2 | 3 | 4 | 5 | 6 | 7 | 8 | 9 | 10 | 11 | 12 | 13 | 14 |
| 0 | No contact | 184 | 578,027,000 | 169 | 1,871,000 | | | | | 353 | 4 | 579,898,000 | 1 |
| 1 | Sparse or occasional contact | 377 | 3,189,565,000 | 1,170 | 15,073,000 | | | 500 | 1,000,000 | 2,047 | 21 | 3,205,638,000 | 6 |
| 2 | Limited contact | 387 | 12,877,563,000 | 296 | 4,595,000 | 2,000 | 20,000,000 | | | 2,683 | 27 | 12,902,158,000 | 26 |
| 3 | Moderate contact | 326 | 3,345,922,000 | 502 | 6,049,000 | | | | | 828 | 8 | 3,351,971,000 | 7 |
| 4 | Extensive contact | 123 | 1,348,263,000 | 267 | 2,946,000 | | | | | 390 | 4 | 1,351,209,000 | 3 |
| 5 | Universal or total contact | 1,444 | 27,962,721,000 | 2,146 | 14,680,000 | | | | | 3,590 | 36 | 27,977,401,000 | 57 |
| | Totals of lines above | 2,841 | 49,302,061,000 | 4,550 | 45,214,000 | 2,000 | 20,000,000 | 500 | 1,000,000 | 9,891 | 100 | 49,368,275,000 | 100 |
| | Multi-counted adherents | — | — | — | — | — | — | — | — | — | — | -43,313,224,000 | — |
| | **Global population** | — | — | — | — | — | — | — | — | — | — | 6,055,049,000 | — |

Part 29

# FUTURESCAN

Futuristics in the analysis of Christianity and religion, AD 2001-AD 2200

*Seal up the vision, for it concerns the distant future. I, Daniel, was exhausted and lay ill for several days.*
—Daniel 8:26-27, New International Version

*The Spirit makes us sure about what we will be in the future.*
—Romans 8:33, Contemporary English Version

*The future is as bright as the promises of God.*
—Adoniram Judson, Baptist pioneer in Burma (1788-1850)

*The further back you look, the further ahead you can see.*
—Winston Churchill, 1960

At this point the science of mission invokes the even newer science of futuristics, the scientific study of the future. Part 2 "CosmoChronology" has already documented over a thousand entries describing possible alternate future scenarios for the followers of Christianity. Now Part 29 covers the range of secular and religious variables. Tables 29-1 and 29-6 set out most likely numerical values for more than 300 global variables at the key turning points AD 1900, AD 2000, AD 2025, AD 2050, AD 2100, and AD 2200.

# Futuristics in the analysis of Christianity and religion, AD 2001-AD 2200

## CHRONOLOGY OF FUTURISM AND THE FUTURE

### How to understand the future in CosmoChronology

Part 2 "CosmoChronology" can be divided into two major parts by the divide between the years before and after 2000. The first half, dealing with past and present up to 2000, delineates the phenomenon and the phenomena of *futurism*. The last half, dealing with *the future* itself, as we today see it, describes possible or probable events and scenarios relating to AD 2000 onwards into the distant future.

### Part I: Futurism (BC 47,000-AD 2000)

About 800 entries in this part of the chronology deal with the past and present of futurism. This term covers the study and practice of the future, also termed futurology, futuristics, or futures studies.

Most of these entries are derived from the extensive literature on the subject. Items in Table 29–5, '470 leading futurist books and futurists since BC 1760' are also included in this chronology.

Futurism itself is analyzed here under 7 chronological eras or layers, or genres of writing, or categories, best referred to as the *dimensions* of futurism. These 7 dimensions are described in Table 29–2.Each generates a vast annual literature today.

### Futurists in 100 professions

Futurists in history and down to the present day are found in all the disciplines, all the sciences, all the professions, and in virtually every walk of life. Table 29–3 lists the 59 most significant of those professions.

### 18 types of futurism entry

The chronology contains the following varieties of entries depicting futurism:

- bibliographical evolution of futurism
- conferences and meetings
- eschatological developments
- evolution of the 7 dimensions of futurism
- false/failed predictions throughout history
- famous futurists
- founding of futurist organizations
- futurist centers and movements
- inventions/discoveries about futurism
- major personalities of historical significance
- millennial false alarms of the past
- notable futurist books and authors
- numerology and numeracy
- past and present methodologies
- past predictions by eminent persons
- scholarship and interpretation
- seminal science fiction past and present
- watershed historical events

### The problem of selection

A vast number of other possible entries have been excluded because too numerous. It is necessary for such a chronology to restrict itself to clear boundaries and firm principles of inclusion, so inevitably many contenders get excluded. Here is a typical borderline case that didn't get in: Heidegger. One of the main exponents of Existentialism, German philosopher Martin Heidegger (1889-1976) is not usually considered a futurist although he did in fact explore definitively certain aspects of futurism. Our boundaries are therefore inevitably somewhat arbitrary.

### Part II: The Future (AD 2001 onwards)

Entries after AD 2000 in the chronology focus especially on the predictive endeavors of futurism. Most of these entries also are derived from the literature. Each future entry is in fact a miniscenario, expanded somewhere else as a full-blown future scenario, in a book, appendix, chapter or paragraph.

### 18 types of futures entry

Entries are of many varieties, of which the following form a partial summary:

- astronomers' predictions
- computerization forecasts
- cosmological futures
- demographic futures
- economic forecasts
- future catastrophes
- future geopolitics
- future inventions
- future methodologies
- futures of religions
- infotech forecasts
- medical forecasts
- military prognoses
- miniscenarios from science fiction
- miniscenarios predicted by current science
- possible/probable/preferable events
- space travel scenarios
- widely-believed possible Ends of the World

The reader will notice that no attempt is made here to bring all of these entries into a single, consistent whole. Since the chronology is built on a multitude of contributions and contributors, a number of entries are contradictory and should be left as such. They can thus be called alternate futures, or different scenarios on the same subject.

---

## THE WIDER SECULAR GLOBAL CONTEXT

Detailed statistical projections estimating the size of major categories for future years are essential to any long-term global program. This is particularly true where human populations are involved. From the founding of the United Nations in 1945, that organization and numerous collaborating agencies and bodies have spearheaded this task by compiling and regularly publishing every two years global statistics of the future. From 1950 the end target date for its computerized databases was AD 2000; more recently this has been advanced to AD 2025, then to AD 2050, and now to AD 2200.

The table at right, 'Global statistics of the future' describes the global situation in past, present, and future by giving, for 20 major subject spheres, comparative statistics for the whole world in four columns representing four points in time: in AD 1900, in mid-1995, in AD 2025, and in the year AD 2200.

### Demographics, 1950-2025

The base demographic statistics come from two United Nations publications. The first is *World population prospects: the 1998 revision* (New York: United Nations, 1999). This is a printout from the UN's computerized database which is updated continuously and published every two years as a large book, and also on disk or tape for computer users. Its future projections to AD 2025 are given under four alternate scenarios. These are labeled Medium-Variant projections, High-Variant projections, Low-Variant projections, and Constant Fertility Variant Projections. Figures are

### Table 29–1. Global statistics of the past and the future, AD 1900-AD 2200.

| YEAR: | 1900 | 1995 | AD 2025 | AD 2200 |
|---|---|---|---|---|
| **GLOBAL POPULATION** | | | | |
| World | 1,620 million | 5,759 million | 8,472 million | 11,600 million |
|   Males | 818 million | 2,900 million | 4,256 million | 5,810 million |
|   Females | 802 million | 2,859 million | 4,217 million | 5,790 million |
| Ratio males to females | 1.020 | 1.014 | 1.009 | 1.003 |
| Population density, per sq. km. | 12 | 42 | 62 | 85 |
| Age distribution, as % of world: | | | | |
|   Infants, ages 0-4 | 12.0 | 11.5 | 8.4 | 5.0 |
|   Children, ages 5-14 | 18.0 | 20.4 | 16.5 | 12.7 |
|   Children under 15 | 30.0 | 31.9 | 24.9 | 17.7 |
|   Youths, ages 15-24 | 25.0 | 17.9 | 15.9 | 13.0 |
|   Seniors, ages 60 or over | 2.5 | 9.5 | 14.1 | 30.0 |
|   Elderly, ages 65 or over | 1.3 | 6.5 | 9.7 | 24.6 |
|   Aged, ages 80 or over | 0.2 | 1.0 | 1.6 | 10.6 |
|   School-age children (6-11) | 10.0 | 12.4 | 9.9 | 6.0 |
|   School-age children (12-14) | 4.0 | 5.8 | 4.9 | 3.0 |
|   School-age children 15-17) | 5.0 | 5.4 | 4.9 | 3.0 |
|   Student-age youths (18-23) | 13.0 | 10.8 | 9.5 | 7.0 |
| Median age, years | 15.0 | 25.1 | 31.0 | 42.7 |
| **VITAL STATISTICS** | | | | |
| Population increase p.a. | 14.6 million | 93.3 million | 84.5 million | 2.3 million |
|   Births p.a. | 58.3 million | 144.8 million | 147.9 million | 141.5 million |
|   Deaths p.a. | 43.7 million | 51.5 million | 63.4 million | 139.2 million |
| Natural increase, % p.a. | 0.90 | 1.63 | 1.02 | 0.02 |
|   Birth rate % p.a. | 3.60 | 2.51 | 1.79 | 1.22 |
|   Death rate % p.a. | 2.70 | 0.89 | 0.77 | 1.20 |
| Life expectancy, years | 36.2 | 65.4 | 72.5 | 84.9 |
|   Males | 34.0 | 63.4 | 70.2 | 82.5 |
|   Females | 39.0 | 67.5 | 75.0 | 87.5 |
| **CITIES WORLDWIDE** | | | | |
| Metropolises (over 100,000 population) | 300 | 3,780 | 6,800 | 65,000 |
| Megacities (over 1 million population) | 20 | 380 | 650 | 3,050 |
| Urbanites (urban dwellers) | 233 million | 2,603 million | 5,185 million | 10,440 million |
| Ruralites (rural dwellers) | 1,387 million | 3,156 million | 3,287 million | 1,160 million |

*Continued overleaf*

given for every country, region, continent, and the whole world, at 16 points in time every five years over the period AD 1950-2025. This is done systematically for each of 26 basic demographic variables.

### Demographics to AD 2200

Secondly, in 1992 the United Nations published *Long-range world population projections: two centuries of population growth, 1950-2150*, followed by an updated edition in 1999. This makes demographic projections through the near-term future (up to 5 years ahead), through the middle-range future (5 to 30 years ahead, i.e. up to AD 2025), then through the long-range future (30 to 100 years ahead, i.e. up to AD 2100), and finally into the distant future (100 to 1,000 years ahead) culminating in figures for AD 2200. Statistics are provided for seven alternate scenarios: a Medium-Fertility extension, High-Fertility, Medium/High-Fertility, Low-Fertility, Medium/Low-Fertility, Constant-Fertility, and Instant-Replacement-Fertility extensions. Our table utilizes throughout only the most likely of the seven, namely the Medium-Variant and Medium-Fertility extension.

### Demographics for AD 1900

Comprehensive demographics for the year 1900 were collected in national population censuses by all countries of the world at that time. These have been compiled comparatively in *WCE* Part 4 "Countries" for each of the world's 238 countries.

### Non-demographic statistical categories

The table's numerous non-demographic categories build on these demographic past compilations and future projections. Past and present figures for a vast number of categories are given in B. R. Mitchell, *International historical statistics, 1750-1988* (Macmillan/UK, 1990, 3 volumes). Future figures shown here for the years 2025 and 2200 have been published, with tables, graphics, explanation, and commentary, in the *AD 2000 Global Monitor*, issues numbers 23-27 (September 1992-January 1993). A large number of other topics are examined and enumerated in a handbook of global statistics entitled *Our globe and how to reach it* (New Hope, 1990). Other categories have been computed primarily for the table below. A handful of lines are repeated under a second heading to improve comprehensiveness.

Note that the number of zeroes and other digits in a particular statistic indicate what precision each statistic claims. Many zeroes indicate a rounded number and hence an approximation or rough estimate. By contrast, a figure given to the last digit is likely to be an exact count. Likewise, use of the words 'million' or 'billion' implies approximation or estimation. Thus '1 billion' is more approximate than '1.0 billion', which in turn is more approximate than '1,002 million', which is more approximate than '1,002,350,000'.

### Future and far-future projections

The two columns for the years 2025 and 2200 should not be considered as concrete predictions for those years. They give only the figures considered most likely in the present investigation, or by authorities in their fields, based on present knowledge and current trends. In fact a wide range of alternate scenarios exists, similar to the UN's seven-fold range described above.

### The meaning of zero categories

A brief word of interpretation can be given here on some of the more surprising aspects of this table. One is the numerous appearances of '0' (zero) in the first column, for over 30 categories. These simply mean that in the year 1900 they did not exist or had not yet started. Radio and television, for instance, had not yet been invented. The AIDS epidemic had not begun.

Another surprising aspect is the string of 46 zeroes in the last column representing the most likely situation in AD 2200. Zeroes there are not, as might appear at first glance, due to naive utopianism. Rather, many of the zeroes represent a considered and realistic assessment of what would appear very probable after 250 years of determined, informed, aggressive, democratic activism concerning all aspects of human rights by many millions of advocates. Many futurists see various diseases or social disorders as certain to be eliminated once and for all by advances in medical expertise. On such scenarios, it is likely that new democratics, new social programs, new science, new technology, new medicine and other future

*Table 29–1–continued*

| | YEAR: | 1900 | 1995 | AD 2025 | AD 2200 |
|---|---|---|---|---|---|
| Urbanites, % of world | | 14.4 | 45.2 | 61.2 | 90.0 |
| Ruralites, % of world | | 85.6 | 54.8 | 38.8 | 10.0 |
| Urban poor | | 100 million | 1,640 million | 3,050 million | 100 million |
| Urban slum dwellers | | 20 million | 810 million | 2,100 million | 50 million |
| **STATUS OF WOMEN** | | | | | |
| Global female population | | 802 million | 2,859 million | 4,217 million | 5,790 million |
| % literates among women | | 15 | 56 | 70 | 85 |
| Female life expectancy, years | | 39.0 | 67.5 | 75.0 | 87.5 |
| Women denied full rights or equality | | 750 million | 2,500 million | 1,800 million | 100 million |
| % world income received by women | | 1 | 10 | 20 | 40 |
| % world property owned by women | | 0 | 1 | 3 | 20 |
| Women as % of all poor | | 80 | 70 | 60 | 55 |
| Women as % of all illiterates | | 80 | 66 | 55 | 52 |
| Women as % of all refugees | | 65 | 80 | 70 | 60 |
| Women as % of all ill/sick | | 60 | 75 | 57 | 52 |
| Female urban poor | | 20 million | 700 million | 1,400 million | 80 million |
| Female urban slumdwellers | | 2 million | 320 million | 980 million | 40 million |
| **MOTHERHOOD** | | | | | |
| Women of childbearing age (15-49) | | 389 million | 1,341 million | 2,041 million | 2,320 million |
| Ditto, % of world population | | 24.0 | 25.3 | 24.7 | 20.0 |
| Fertility rate (births per woman) | | 4.0 | 3.17 | 2.36 | 2.06 |
| Gross reproduction rate, per woman | | 2.0 | 1.55 | 1.15 | 0.7 |
| Net reproduction rate, per woman | | 1.8 | 1.36 | 1.08 | 0.6 |
| Contraceptive prevalence rate, % | | 5 | 56 | 75 | 95 |
| Birth rate, % p.a. (males, females) | | 3.60 | 2.51 | 1.79 | 1.22 |
| Births p.a. (males, females) | | 58.3 million | 144.8 million | 147.9 million | 141.5 million |
| Induced abortions, p.a. | | 5 million | 60 million | 130 million | 500 million |
| Maternal mortality, p.a. total | | 550,000 | 500,000 | 400,000 | 80,000 |
| Ditto due to abortion | | 210,000 | 200,000 | 150,000 | 30,000 |
| **FAMILIES** | | | | | |
| Families/homes/households | | 324 million | 1,339 million | 2,118 million | 3,135 million |
| Household size, persons | | 5.0 | 4.3 | 4.0 | 3.7 |
| Households headed by women, % | | 3 | 33 | 55 | 70 |
| New families each year | | 12 million | 34 million | 38 million | 39 million |
| % women 15-19 already married | | 15 | 23 | 25 | 35 |
| Dependency ratio, % | | 70.0 | 62.6 | 52.1 | 45.0 |
| Marriage rate per 1000 population p.a. | | 3 | 4 | 5 | 6 |
| Divorce rate per 1000 population p.a. | | 0.05 | 0.4 | 1 | 3 |
| Battered women | | 95 million | 200 million | 500 million | 100 million |
| Women raped p.a. | | 10 million | 15 million | 25 million | 5 million |
| Child-abuse incidents p.a. | | 15 million | 90 million | 70 million | 30 million |
| **CHILDREN** | | | | | |
| Infants (0-4 years) | | 194 million | 662 million | 712 million | 580 million |
| Children (5-14) | | 292 million | 1,175 million | 1,398 million | 1,473 million |
| School-age children (6-14) | | 227 million | 1,048 million | 1,254 million | 1,044 million |
| Babies born malnourished, p.a. | | 8 million | 10 million | 25 million | 1 million |
| Sick/ill children | | 300 million | 600 million | 1,000 million | 200 million |
| Exploited child labor | | 30 million | 50 million | 200 million | 20 million |
| Orphans | | 150 million | 450 million | 1,000 million | 1,500 million |
| Abandoned children and infants | | 140 million | 60 million | 260 million | 500 million |
| Homeless/family-less children | | 250 million | 300 million | 700 million | 1,000 million |
| Megacity street children | | 1 million | 100 million | 300 million | 800 million |
| Infant mortality (under 1), % p.a. | | 9.0 | 5.9 | 3.1 | 0.5 |
| Toddler mortality (1-4 years), % p.a. | | 3.0 | 1.0 | 0.7 | 0.1 |
| **EDUCATION** | | | | | |
| Primary schools | | 300,000 | 3.2 million | 4 million | 5 million |
| Pupils in school | | 35 million | 980 million | 1.5 billion | 1.3 billion |
| Adults, primary-educated | | 100 million | 1.2 billion | 3.3 billion | 7.5 billion |
| Adults without primary education | | 926 million | 2.7 billion | 3.1 billion | 2.0 billion |
| School teachers | | 2 million | 39 million | 50 million | 100 million |
| University campuses | | 500 | 20,000 | 30,000 | 100,000 |
| College students | | 2 million | 65 million | 120 million | 500 million |
| Foreign students | | 20,000 | 3 million | 15 million | 100 million |
| **ILLNESS AND DISEASE** | | | | | |
| Sufferers from disease or illness | | 420 million | 1,152 million | 1,395 million | 15 million |
| Sufferers experiencing chronic pain | | 350 million | 900 million | 1,400 million | 14 million |
| Nonsighted (totally blind) | | 9 million | 28 million | 35 million | 50 million |
| Hearing-impaired (deaf) | | 90 million | 320 million | 500 million | 700 million |
| Leprosy sufferers (lepers) | | 5 million | 13 million | 1 million | 0 |
| New malaria cases p.a. | | 100 million | 400 million | 30 million | 0 |
| Psychotics | | 10 million | 51 million | 10 million | 0 |
| Schizophrenics | | 2 million | 10 million | 0 | 0 |
| Psychoneurotics | | 150 million | 950 million | 1.1 billion | 1.5 billion |
| Suicides p.a. | | 300,000 | 410,000 | 500,000 | 1 million |
| Disabled (handicapped) | | 400 million | 1.6 billion | 1.8 billion | 2 billion |
| Handicapped children | | 100 million | 340 million | 500 million | 700 million |
| Severely mentally-retarded | | 40 million | 130 million | 50 million | 0 |
| Arthritics | | 80 million | 300 million | 50 million | 0 |
| Persons not immunized | | 1.4 billion | 4 billion | 100 million | 0 |
| Diarrheal deaths of under-5s,p.a. | | 2 million | 5 million | 700,000 | 0 |
| AIDS carriers | | 0 | 70 million | 400 million | 0 |
| AIDS-related deaths p.a. | | 0 | 500,000 | 10 million | 0 |
| Tobacco smokers | | 42 million | 650 million | 20 million | 0 |
| Tobacco-related deaths p.a. | | 150,000 | 2.6 million | 5 million | 0 |
| Drug addicts (illicit drug users) | | 1 million | 65 million | 100 million | 0 |
| **HEALTH CARE** | | | | | |
| Persons in good health | | 300 million | 1.1 billion | 2.4 | 7 billion |
| Physicians | | 1 million | 5.2 million | 7.9 million | 13 million |
| Nurses and midwives | | 2 million | 7.7 million | 10.5 million | 16 million |
| Dentists | | 100,000 | 500,000 | 800,000 | 1,400,000 |
| Pharmacists | | 50,000 | 520,000 | 1 billion | 1.6 billion |
| World pharmaceutical market, $ p.a. | | 200 million | 130 billion | 400 billion | 2 trillion |
| Hospitals | | 60,000 | 240,000 | 300,000 | 500,000 |
| Hospital beds | | 4 million | 18.2 million | 23 million | 35 million |
| Mental institutions | | 20,000 | 150,000 | 200,000 | 1,000 |
| Health care costs, $ p.a. | | 10 billion | 2,500 billion | 4 trillion | 10 trillion |
| Population per doctor | | 9,500 | 3,780 | 2,500 | 500 |
| **HUMAN RIGHTS AND ABUSES** | | | | | |
| The poor (living in poverty) | | 1.2 billion | 2.4 billion | 3.3 billion | 100 million |

*Continued opposite*

breakthroughs will virtually eliminate disease and poverty and other social misfortunes. Also total electronic monitoring may well eliminate crime, fraud and an extensive array of other anti-social behavior patterns.

Where this seems to be the most likely future development, zeroes occur in the table. At the same time, it should be noted that a specific zero should not be interpreted as meaning 'absolutely nobody, or nothing'. Rather, it means that the general order of magnitude of the category, as indicated by its 1995 and 2025 figures, is likely to fall to negligible proportions by 2200.

A number of other categories which can be seen to fall off and decline dramatically in numbers have similar explanations. It means that the world's activists are dealing with the intolerable situation of earlier years.

### Additional data on statistical futures

For further explanation and illustration of particular statistical situations, with the relevant context, the reader is referred to Part 2 "CosmoChronology". Inter alia, this lists a whole variety of new scientific and medical discoveries and the future dates when current analysts expect them to surface.

### THE FUTURE OF CHRISTIANITY

1. *Immediate prospects* (during the 1990's). This decade has witnessed a dramatic change in the fortunes of all branches of Christianity. After gradual decline from 1900-1970, the years 1980-1994 have seen a radical reversal related to the three major geographical areas of anti-Christian hostility across the world. (a) From 1987-1990 the final collapse of all Eastern Europe's Communist regimes took place. (b) From 1988-1991 a similar collapse of the USSR saw 30 millions of 1988's 60 million professed atheists move decisively to open profession of allegiance to Christ and Christianity. As one illustration, in these three years the professional movie 'Jesus' (Luke's Gospel, 2 hours 5 minutes) was seen by 85% of all Russians. And (c) although mainland China remained rigidly Communist, its churches grew from 1.5 million members in 1970 to 78 million members by 1995.

This decade has been marked by growing good relations and mutual respect between Christianity and the other great world religions—Islam, Hinduism, Buddhism, Judaism, et alia. All participated in the 1993 World Parliament of Religions in Chicago, which produced strong affirmations on global ethics as well as hundreds of collaborative projects.

2. *Short-term trends* (up to AD 2025). From 2000-2025 the total of all Christians is likely to increase 31% to 2,617 million (33.4% of the world). Of these, 888 million are expected to be practicing Christians. 812 millions will be Pentecostals/Charismatics; 80% of them will be non-whites in Third-World countries. 80% of all Christians will be urbanites. By 2025 the continent with the second largest number of Christians is likely to be Africa with 634 millions. Other predictions for 2025: 8 million full-time workers, 1.5 billion general-purpose computers owned or operated by Christians or churches. Projected annual income and expenditures in 2025 are as follows: Personal income of all Christians: $44.2 trillion. Churches' income: $870 billion. Ecclesiastical crime: $65 billion. Foreign missions: $60 billion.

An indicator of the future vitality of Christianity can be seen in the following projections concerning Christian literature by AD 2025. New commercially-sold Christian book titles per year: an increase from 25,000 in AD 2000 to 70,000 in 2025. Christian periodicals: a rise from 35,000 to 100,000. Demand for Christian scriptures is likewise expected to mushroom by 2025, with these annual sales expected: 180 million Bibles, 250 million New Testaments, 8 billion Gospels. All of these, produced in 5,000 major languages, are expected to be in crystal clear idiomatic form, and in many formats including print, audio, video, disc, comics, Braille, signed, and interactive versions.

Christianity's expertise in modern communication techniques developed extensively since the 1950s. It will be further evident in future global broadcasting. Current projections are for an increase from 4,000 Christian radio/TV stations with 2,150 million monthly listeners/viewers across the world, to (in 2025) 5,400 stations with 3,800 million regular listen-

*Table 29-1-continued*

| YEAR: | 1900 | 1995 | AD 2025 | AD 2200 |
|---|---|---|---|---|
| Absolutely poor (in absolute poverty) | 900 million | 960 million | 700 million | 0 |
| Undernourished | 1.2 billion | 1.8 billion | 500 million | 0 |
| Hungry | 700 million | 950 million | 400 million | 0 |
| Severely malnourished | 500 million | 550 million | 300 million | 0 |
| On verge of starvation | 200 million | 400 million | 200 million | 0 |
| Starvation-related deaths p.a. | 20 million | 20 million | 10 million | 0 |
| Without safe drinking water | 1.4 billion | 1.3 billion | 1 billion | 0 |
| With unsafe water and bad sanitation | 1.5 billion | 3.0 billion | 1 billion | 30 million |
| Killed by dirty water, per day | 20,000 | 25,000 | 10,000 | 0 |
| With no access to electricity, % | 86 | 41 | 30 | 0 |
| With no access to radio or TV, % | 100 | 67 | 20 | 0 |
| Without adequate shelter | 200 million | 1.1 billion | 700 million | 10 million |
| With no shelter whatsoever | 50 million | 100 million | 30 million | 0 |
| No access to schools | 1.2 billion | 1 billion | 500 million | 0 |
| Without money to buy food | 500 million | 1.1 billion | 700 million | 0 |
| With no access to medical care | 1.1 billion | 1.5 billion | 700 million | 0 |
| Cave-dwellers | 200 million | 50 million | 10 million | 0 |
| Stateless (with no nationality) | 1 million | 10 million | 5 million | 0 |
| Prisoners | 5 million | 100 million | 50 million | 10 million |
| Prisoners being tortured | 500,000 | 100,000 | 0 | 0 |
| Disenfranchised (no control by vote) | 1.2 billion | 2.1 billion | 100 million | 0 |
| Non-readers (orate, illiterate adults) | 739 million | 1,392 million | 1,171 million | 382 million |
| Permanently unsettled refugees | 50 million | 14 million | 10 million | 0 |
| Persons abused in childhood | 400 million | 300 million | 350 million | 0 |
| Persons with human rights violated | 1.4 billion | 2,590 million | 1.7 billion | 30 million |
| **COMMUNICATION** | | | | |
| Languages | 11,600 | 13,500 | 11,000 | 2,000 |
| Trade languages | 200 | 700 | 800 | 2,000 |
| Official state languages | 25 | 95 | 150 | 500 |
| Countries with own radio services | 0 | 270 | 300 | 100 |
| Countries with own TV services | 0 | 150 | 250 | 100 |
| Radio sets in use | 0 | 1.8 billion | 5 billion | 9 billion |
| Radio hours broadcast p.a. | 0 | 24 million | 60 million | 1 billion |
| Television sets | 0 | 850 million | 5 billion | 10 billion |
| TV hours broadcast p.a. | 0 | 21 million | 70 million | 1 billion |
| Ham radio operators | 0 | 1.2 million | 2 million | 30 million |
| Daily newspapers | 750 | 8,300 | 7,000 | 20,000 |
| Newspaper circulation | 70 million | 590 million | 1 billion | 3 billion |
| Newsprint per global inhabitant, lbs p.a. | 0.1 | 12 | 10 | 10 |
| Mail, pieces p.a. | 1 billion | 280 billion | 450 billion | 2 trillion |
| Electronic mail messages p.a. | 0 | 6 billion | 50 billion | 1 trillion |
| Telephones | 3 million | 750 million | 1.1 billion | 4 billion |
| Direct-dial telephones | 0 | 710 million | 1.1 billion | 4 billion |
| Telephone calls made, p.a. | 150 million | 120 billion | 300 billion | 1 trillion |
| Fax machines | 0 | 35 million | 350 million | 10 billion |
| Videocassette recorders (VCRs) | 0 | 500 million | 2 billion | 10 billion |
| Cinemas | 100 | 250,000 | 400,000 | 2 billion |
| Cinema seats | 5,000 | 75 million | 200 million | 1 billion |
| Cinema attenders p.a. | 200,000 | 15 billion | 30 billion | 1 trillion |
| General-purpose computers | 0 | 150 million | 850 million | 700 billion |
| Computer sales p.a. | 0 | 35 million | 380 million | 3 billion |
| Computer power, MIPS (world total) | 0 | 1 million | 1,500 million | 25 trillion |
| Electronic bulletin boards (BSS) | 0 | 100,000 | 1 million | 100 million |
| Internet computer users | 0 | 28 million | 2,080 million | 3 billion |
| **TRANSPORTATION** | | | | |
| Roads, length in miles | 1 million | 17 million | 25 million | 40 million |
| Bicycles | 10,000 | 850 million | 1.7 billion | 2 billion |
| Commercial vehicles | 0 | 120 million | 250 million | 300 million |
| Passenger cars | 30,000 | 410 million | 500 million | 700 million |
| Cars produced p.a. | 3,000 | 45 million | 40 million | 50 million |
| Railway track, length in miles | 454,730 | 880,000 | 1.5 million | 5 million |
| Rail passenger-miles p.a. | 10 billion | 1,100 billion | 2 trillion | 3 trillion |
| Air traffic, passenger-miles p.a. | 0 | 950 billion | 3 trillion | 10 trillion |
| Airport and airfields | 0 | 67,000 | 100,000 | 500,000 |
| Sea traffic: merchant ships | 2,000 | 75,300 | 100,000 | 300,000 |
| Sea freight, tonnes p.a. | 10 million | 3.6 billion | 10 billion | 100 billion |
| Sea (merchant seafarers) | 300,000 | 10 million | 15 million | 10 million |
| **INDUSTRIALIZATION** | | | | |
| Economically active persons | 300 million | 2.4 billion | 3 billion | 5 billion |
| Labor force, persons | 100 million | 1.9 billion | 2.5 billion | 4 billion |
| Unemployed | 10 million | 100 million | 200 million | 500 million |
| Underemployed | 30 million | 600 million | 1 billion | 2 billion |
| Beggars | 10 million | 80 million | 150 million | 300 million |
| Scientists and engineers | 1 million | 38 million | 60 million | 100 million |
| Pure scientists | 10,000 | 1 million | 1.3 million | 2 million |
| Scientific research, $ p.a. | 100 million | 125 billion | 200 billion | 400 billion |
| Industrial robots | 0 | 14 million | 25 million | 100 million |
| Known chemicals | 5,000 | 7 million | 10 million | 20 million |
| New chemicals created p.a. | 200 | 10,000 | 50,000 | 60,000 |
| Police officers | 400,000 | 5.1 million | 6 million | 7 million |
| Professional firefighters | 100,000 | 2 million | 2.5 million | 3 million |
| Lawyers | 300,000 | 6 million | 8 million | 9 million |
| Labor migrants | 2 million | 150 million | 300 million | 500 million |
| **ENERGY PRODUCTION** | | | | |
| Primary energy, quads BTU p.a. | 10 billion | 3.2 quadrillion | 9 quadrillion | 10 quintillion |
| Coal, known reserves, metric tons | 50 million | 7,600 billion | 8 trillion | 4 trillion |
| Coal, kg mined per capita p.a. | 1,000 | 1,870 | 2,000 | 2,500 |
| Electricity, kwh p.a. | 100 million | 9.7 trillion | 100 trillion | 1 quadrillion |
| Petroleum, known reserves, metric tons | 0 | 91 billion | 100 billion | 1 billion |
| Oil, total recoverable reserves, barrels | 1 billion | 1,635 billion | 2 trillion | 0 |
| Oil, output in barrels p.a. | 1 million | 19.8 billion | 30 billion | 1 billion |
| Nuclear power produced, kwh p.a. | 0 | 630 million | 1 trillion | 100 trillion |
| Natural gas, known reserves, cubic meters | 100 billion | 86 trillion | 100 trillion | 200 trillion |
| **TOURISM** | | | | |
| Foreign tourists p.a. | 1 million | 350 million | 600 million | 2 billion |
| Domestic tourists p.a. | 5 million | 3.7 billion | 4.5 billion | 5 billion |
| Registered hotel beds | 500,000 | 15.0 million | 30 million | 100 million |
| Religious pilgrims p.a. | 2 million | 350 million | 800 million | 1.5 billion |
| **FINANCE AND TRADE** | | | | |
| Gross world product, $ p.a. | 200 billion | 18 trillion | 30 trillion | 300 trillion |
| World imports, $ p.a. | 30 billion | 2,200 billion | 4 trillion | 25 trillion |

*Continued overleaf*

ers/viewers.
xcb

3. *Long-term futures* (after AD 2025). Most churches will continue to be heavily involved in the whole range of human and societal problems and issues. All denominations will increasingly mold their lifestyles and programs to the Bible's challengingly high standards. Examination of the large number of detailed projections and miniscenarios (see Part 2 "CosmoChronology") will also show the definitive ending of five centuries of conflict between science and religion.

On the most likely scenario, the number of Christians by AD 2200 will rise to 4,347 millions, or 38.8% of the globe.

Although firmly anchored in the world and its troubles, organized religions will continue to demonstrate their other-worldly aspect. In AD 2000, 78% of the world's populations—members of virtually all of the world's religions—expected the imminent return of the Christ, or (Islam) of the Mahdi, or (Buddhism) of Maitreya, or (Judaism) of the Messiah, and so on. Christians have always been futurists, expecting the Second Advent. (Example: In the USA in 1993, 72% of national samples replied Yes to the question 'Do you believe Jesus Christ will return to earth one day?'). In 1993, books in print in English included 2,000 serious titles dealing with Christian eschatology. Up to the 1900s, 80% of all serious or professional futurists were committed Christians, with many luminaries such as Isaac Newton (who compiled biblical commentaries on the Books of Daniel and Revelation) and mathematician John Napier (who invented logarithms to speed up his calculations on the Number of the Beast in Revelation). By 2000 that percentage had dropped to 50%. By 2025, it is likely to have risen again somewhat to 60%.

The enormous wealth of new knowledge concerning futurism and the future (documented in detail in Part 2 "CosmoChronology") suggests that major rapprochements between conflicting religious ideologies are likely as long-term prospects for the globe.

Table 29-1–concluded

| | YEAR: | 1900 | 1995 | AD 2025 | AD 2200 |
|---|---|---|---|---|---|
| World exports, $ p.a. | | 25 billion | 2,100 billion | 3 trillion | 20 trillion |
| Balance of trade, $ | | 5 billion | 100 billion | 1 trillion | 5 trillion |
| Gold reserves, kg | | 2 million | 32 million | 50 million | 1 billion |
| Foreign economic aid, $ p.a. | | 50 million | 60 billion | 200 billion | 2 trillion |
| Average income per person, $ p.a. | | 125 | 3,120 | 3,540 | 25,860 |
| Average family income, $ p.a. | | 625 | 13,440 | 14,160 | 95,700 |
| Transnationals (TNCs, multinationals) | | 400 | 10,800 | 20,000 | 300,000 |
| Nongovernmental organizations (NGOs) | | 50 | 3,500 | 10,000 | 100,000 |
| Millionaires (each worth over $1 million) | | 20,000 | 2.5 million | 6 million | 300 million |
| Billionaires (each worth over $1 billion) | | 10 | 400 | 600 | 10,000 |
| Cost of advertising, $ p.a. | | 300 million | 120 billion | 300 billion | 2 trillion |
| Betting and gambling, $ p.a. | | 1 billion | 700 billion | 1,500 billion | 3 trillion |
| Business failures (bankruptcies) p.a. | | 5,000 | 250,000 | 300,000 | 100,000 |
| **MILITARIZATION** | | | | | |
| Military expenditures, $ p.a. | | 500 million | 950 billion | 100 billion | 20 billion |
| Troops in regular armed forces | | 5 million | 25 million | 15 million | 2 million |
| Paramilitary troops | | 2 million | 280 million | 5 million | 1 million |
| Military supply personnel | | 200,000 | 52 million | 20 million | 30 million |
| Combat aircraft | | 0 | 60,000 | 20,000 | 2,000 |
| Nuclear warheads | | 0 | 65,000 | 1,000 | 0 |
| Submarine-borne SLBMs | | 0 | 9,200 | 500 | 0 |
| Chemical weapons, tons | | 1,000 | 300,000 | 10,000 | 0 |
| International arms trade, % p.a. | | 5 million | 42 billion | 20 billion | 0 |
| Handguns (personal firearms) | | 1 million | 600 million | 100 million | 0 |
| **CRIME** | | | | | |
| Crimes (registered) p.a. | | 5 million | 500 million | 400 million | 10 million |
| Property crimes p.a. | | 2 million | 100 million | 50 million | 1 million |
| Violent crimes p.a. | | 2 million | 27 million | 30 million | 1 million |
| Criminals | | 4 million | 550 million | 350 million | 15 million |
| Murders p.a. | | 500,000 | 950,000 | 800,000 | 10,000 |
| Terrorist incidents p.a. | | 100 | 4,000 | 2,000 | 200 |
| Cost of all varieties of crimes, $ p.a. | | 750 million | 3,300 billion | 2 trillion | 10 billion |
| White-collar crime, $ p.a. | | 200 million | 1,000 billion | 500 billion | 1 billion |
| Financial fraud, $ p.a. | | 150 million | 900 billion | 400 billion | 1 billion |
| Organized crime, $ p.a. | | 100 million | 600 billion | 1 trillion | 2 billion |
| Credit card fraud, $ p.a. | | 0 | 550 billion | 200 billion | 1 billion |
| Alcohol/liquor expenditures, $ p.a. | | 50 million | 380 billion | 50 billion | 0 |
| World purchases of cigarettes, $ p.a. | | 30 million | 290 billion | 10 billion | 0 |
| Illegal drug traffic, $ p.a. | | 20 million | 150 billion | 10 billion | 0 |
| Shoplifting, $ p.a. | | 20 million | 95 billion | 5 billion | 0 |
| Computer crime, $ p.a. | | 0 | 60 billion | 10 billion | 1 billion |
| Major art thefts, $ p.a. | | 100 million | 25 billion | 1 billion | 0 |
| Pornography, $ p.a. | | 20 million | 20 billion | 1 billion | 0 |
| Automobile thefts, $ p.a. | | 0 | 20 billion | 1 billion | 0 |
| **LITERATURE** | | | | | |
| Adult population (over 15) | | 1,026 million | 3,937 million | 6,421 million | 9,547 million |
| Literates | | 287 million | 2,545 million | 5,250 million | 9,165 million |
| Nonliterates | | 739 million | 1,392 million | 1,171 million | 382 million |
| Literates, % of adults | | 27.9 | 54.7 | 81.8 | 96.0 |
| Nonliterates, % of adults | | 72.1 | 45.3 | 18.2 | 4.0 |
| New book titles p.a. | | 40,000 | 880,000 | 950,000 | 3 million |
| Books printed p.a. | | 900 million | 30 billion | 50 billion | 100 million |
| Scientific journals | | 15,000 | 350,000 | 450,000 | 2 million |
| Scientific articles published p.a. | | 60,000 | 2 million | 3 million | 10 million |
| Periodicals | | 9,000 | 130,000 | 180,000 | 500,000 |
| Magazines | | 40,000 | 500,000 | 700,000 | 3 million |
| Encyclopedias | | 100 | 500 | 1,000 | 3,000 |
| General encyclopedias | | 20 | 70 | 200 | 500 |
| Subject encyclopedias | | 80 | 430 | 800 | 2,500 |
| Bookshops | | 65,000 | 600,000 | 1 million | 10 million |
| Public libraries | | 30,000 | 270,000 | 500,000 | 2 million |
| Library volumes (books) | | 70 million | 3.7 billion | 10 billion | 100 billion |

**RELIGION:** see Table 29–6

## LEADING FUTURISTS SINCE BC 1760

The next section of this survey will now draw up, in Table 29–5, a selective listing of the major or most interesting futurists and futurist books over the last 4 millennia (4,000 years). A main criterion in selection is that each title must be explicitly futurist, which means it should contain either the words 'future', 'futurists', or cognates, or one or other of the words 'predict', 'forecast', or a reference to the 21st century, Third Millennium or even further in the future.

The value of the resulting list will be evident if the reader thinks about each title and then attempts to create applications or parallel approaches that could be used to further understanding of problems in the analysis of global Christianity in its context of the world's religions.

A 'futurist book' in this survey is defined as (1) a published work which is (2) mainly or entirely concerned with the future and what may happen in the days or months or years ahead, and (3) which contributes definitively or substantially to human knowledge about the future—either with regard to thought, or understanding, or practice about some area or aspect of the future. Each book's author is thus correctly termed a 'futurist', although he or she may be better known under another profession or discipline, such as a philosopher (Plato, Jaspers), or a socialist (Marx), historian (Didsbury, Wagar), theologian (Augustine, Cullman, Schweitzer, Tillich, Kung), orator (Cicero), mathematician (Napier, Newton), astronomer (Ptolemy, Kepler, Berry, Sagan), sociologist (Bell), engineer (Fuller), biblical exegete (Bultmann), statesman (Wang, More), politician (Lamm, Gore), or physicist (Dyson, O'Neill, Hawking). In this sense the end 3 columns of Table 29–5 code the listing of some 470 futurist books by 560 leading futurists. Most are, or were in their own day, leading scholars in their own disciplines as well.

Although during compilation the listing attempted to restrict authors' writings to one book each, over 30 authors had to be included more than once in order to cover truly significant titles. Note that, as arguably among the most influential futurists of all time, 4 authors—H. G. Wells, I. F. Clarke, A. C. Clarke, W. W. Wagar—each have more than 2 of their books listed. Note also in passing that our list follows the practice in English of capitalizing most of the words in titles before 1860 but thereafter changes to the modern practice of capitalizing only proper names.

Futurism goes back in time some 50,000 years to the origin of Homo Sapiens itself. Historian Wagar identifies 5 chronological layers or overlapping eras of futurism: divination, revelation, progressivism, historicism, social science. Today we need to subdivide to produce two further distinct categories: science fiction, and issues. The latter category is directly relevant to present-day needs and problems, hence forms the largest category here with 26% of all the works studied.

This means therefore that futurism can be described as consisting of 7 dimensions, defined as follows and shown in Tables 29-2 and 29-5. Note also that all 7 are still widely practiced today, with extensive literatures.

In chronological order, these 7 layers or genres of writing or categories, best referred to as dimensions, have been:

1. divination (including oracles, astrology, numerology, augury, palmistry, magic, occultism, tarot, dreams, haruspicy, horoscopes, soothsaying, clairvoyance, mysticism, New Age thinking); beginning around BC 47,000, with a first major literature recorded here by BC 1760 and BC 1141;
2. revelation (biblical prophecy, adventism in all religions, messianism, apocalypticism, millennialism, eschatology); beginning BC 4000, with extensive literature from BC 700 onward;
3. progressivism (inevitable progress, evolution, Enlightenment, golden ages, utopias, optimism); beginning some 4 centuries before Christ, with classics from BC 360 on;
4. historicism (histories, critiques, criticism, historiography, historical analyses, diachronic explanation, historical novels, dystopias, failed utopias, predictive drama, devolution, pessimism); beginning in the Middle Ages, with notable classics from AD 1609 on;
5. science fiction (future fiction, scenarios); beginning several centuries ago, crystallizing into classics at least by AD 1771;
6. sciences: hard and soft sciences, including the social sciences (sociology, anthropology, economics, political science, social analysis, military analysis); physics, chemistry, biology; also Earth

sciences, astronomy, astrophysics, cosmology; under way some hundreds of years ago, exemplified here in 1897 literature, followed by the serious or formal beginning in 1902 of futurism as a social scientific approach or discipline;

7. issues (specific current concerns, technology, single topics, world problems, present surveys, trends, values, applications, methodologies, computer modeling, forecasting, technological forecasting, scientific predicting, resources, polls, planning, strategizing, management); with professional analysis under way by 1936 and then begun in earnest in 1968.

Dimensions 1, 2, and 3 explain the 21 earliest entries in Table 29–5 below. The other 4 levels then classify the wide range of future interests later covered.

It is interesting to observe that writers in any of these 7 layers or genres—whether ardent protagonists or impartial analysts—tend to think their level or genre is the only real or correct or proper or significant interpretation of futurism. As a result they also tend to ignore, downplay, minimize, or even attack the role of the other 6 levels. Thus issues writers frequently deny science fiction any value or usefulness to futurism; historicists criticize progressivist utopias as naive and outmoded; social scientists and planners get irritated at the intrusion of religion; and writers on Christianity are opposed to occultism and other aspects of New Age metaphysics. Whether we like these 7 levels or not, however, they all exist and all are widely propagated today as serious enquiry into the future.

How many people in today's world are interested in the future? More than you might expect. Persons across the world involved with astrology or other aspects of divination are thought to number well over one billion. And religious persons expecting the future supernatural coming of a Messiah (in 20 major world religions) number a massive 78% of the world.

As we view the total sphere of futurist literature, it is wise therefore to acknowledge the existence (and significance) of both popular futurism as well as academic futurism, amateur futurism as well as professional futurism, and even bad futurism as well as good futurism. This listing attempts to survey the second halves of these 3 dichotomies.

With several tens of thousands of professional thinkers, writers, scholars, speakers, teachers, engineers, and practitioners of the future known today, one could produce a whole range of such lists as one's '10 Leading Futurists', depending on one's exact criteria, one's preferences, one's levels, and one's broadness of reading. The list given here is one possible list based on significant contributions to futurism, futuristics, futurology or futures study—the art or science of the future, or its understanding, or practice, or research, or teaching, and any or all other varieties of study of the future.

The year before each title refers the reader in most cases to each book's entry (date of publication) in Part 2 "CosmoChronology" in this book. This enables the reader to examine the context from which the titles have emerged.

We move now to give codes through which this listing can be analyzed. At the end of the listing itself will be found a brief statistical summary of some aspects.

### Codes for Table 29–5
Each futurist book and its futurist author in this listing are here given, in columns 4-6, a single code made up of the following 3 elements separated by 2 hyphens. The first element (column 4) assigns the item

to one or other of the 7 eras or layers or dimensions of futurism as described above; the second element (column 5) gives the author's main profession; and the third element (column 6) describes how far into the future this particular book's treatment extends.

### Table 29–2. Seven dimensions of futurism.

| Layer | Code | Dimension | Begun | Books | % |
|---|---|---|---|---|---|
| 1 | D | Divination | BC 47,000 | 29 | 6.1 |
| 2 | R | Revelation | BC 4000 | 111 | 23.5 |
| 3 | P | Progressivism | BC 360 | 28 | 5.9 |
| 4 | H | Historicism | AD 1609 | 35 | 7.4 |
| 5 | F | Science fiction | AD 1771 | 26 | 5.5 |
| 6 | S | Sciences | AD 1897 | 90 | 19.0 |
| 7 | I | Issues | AD 1936 | 154 | 32.6 |
| | | | Totals | 473 | 100 |

### Table 29–3. Professions of futurist authors.

| Code | Profession | Books | % |
|---|---|---|---|
| a1 | Anthropologist | 6 | 1.2 |
| a2 | Apologist | 1 | 0.2 |
| a3 | Archeologist | 1 | 0.2 |
| a4 | Artist | 3 | 0.6 |
| a5 | Astrologer | 5 | 1.1 |
| a6 | Astronomer | 5 | 1.1 |
| a7 | Astrophysicist | 1 | 0.2 |
| b1 | Biblical scholar | 14 | 3.0 |
| b2 | Bibliographer | 5 | 1.1 |
| b3 | Biologist | 2 | 0.4 |
| b4 | Businessman | 4 | 0.8 |
| c1 | Chemist | 2 | 0.4 |
| c2 | Computer scientist | 6 | 1.3 |
| c3 | Cosmologist | 2 | 0.4 |
| d1 | Demographer | 2 | 0.4 |
| d2 | Dramatist | 2 | 0.4 |
| e1 | Ecclesiastic | 18 | 3.8 |
| e2 | Ecologist | 7 | 1.5 |
| e3 | Economist | 28 | 5.9 |
| e4 | Educator | 6 | 1.2 |
| e5 | Engineer | 26 | 5.5 |
| e6 | Environmentalist | 8 | 1.7 |
| e7 | Ethnographer | 1 | 0.2 |
| f1 | Forecaster | 13 | 2.7 |
| g1 | Geographer | 0 | 0 |
| g2 | Geologist | 2 | 0.4 |
| h1 | Historian | 34 | 7.2 |
| i1 | Industrialist | 1 | 0.2 |
| j1 | Journalist | 12 | 2.5 |
| l1 | Lawyer | 6 | 1.2 |
| l2 | Librarian | 1 | 0.2 |
| l3 | Linguist | 1 | 0.2 |
| m1 | Mathematician | 8 | 1.7 |
| m2 | Methodologist | 0 | 0 |
| m3 | Military analyst | 1 | 0.2 |
| m4 | Missiologist | 7 | 1.5 |
| m5 | Mystic | 1 | 0.2 |
| n1 | Novelist | 20 | 4.2 |
| o1 | Orator | 1 | 0.2 |
| p1 | Philosopher | 15 | 3.2 |
| p2 | Physician | 2 | 0.4 |
| p3 | Physicist | 15 | 3.2 |
| p4 | Planner | 17 | 3.6 |
| p5 | Political scientist | 19 | 4.0 |
| p6 | Politician | 3 | 0.6 |
| p7 | Pollster | 0 | 0 |
| p8 | Prophet | 3 | 0.6 |
| p9 | Psychologist | 9 | 1.9 |
| r1 | Religion scholar | 13 | 2.7 |
| r2 | Revolutionary | 1 | 0.2 |
| s1 | Sociologist | 26 | 5.5 |
| s2 | Statesman | 4 | 0.8 |
| s3 | Strategist | 4 | 0.8 |
| s4 | Surgeon | 1 | 0.2 |
| t1 | Theologian | 22 | 4.7 |
| t2 | Trend analyst | 6 | 1.2 |
| u1 | Urbanologist | 7 | 1.5 |
| w1 | Writer | 41 | 8.7 |
| z1 | Zoologist | 2 | 0.4 |
| | Total | 473 | 100.0 |

### Column 4: Seven dimensions of futurism
This variable with its code, a single capital letter, answers the question:

Under which layer or genre or dimension of futurism can this book best be described?

The first subcolumn in Table 29–2 here lists these 7 dimensions; the second subcolumn gives the single-capital code as used in Table 29–5; the third gives its name; the fourth describes the year, approximately, when the era can be said to have begun, in a major or significant or organized form; the fifth gives the number of futurist books in Table 29–5 on each dimension; and the sixth the number as a percentage of the total.

### Column 5: Professions of futurist authors
This variable with its code (a letter and a number) answers the question:

Under what main ongoing profession or discipline can this author best be described? The question refers to the author's (or first author's) major training and occupation and does not refer to the particular book concerned. Note that an author with 2 books listed may have, and be listed as having, 2 different professions at different stages in his or her career.

Table 29–3 set out these 59 professions with their related totals. On a separate aspect, note that the proportion of these futurists who are women is exactly 10%.

### Table 29–4. Nine periods of the future.

| Code | Range | Books | % |
|---|---|---|---|
| | SHORT-TERM FUTURES | | |
| 1. | The immediate future (to 1 year ahead) | 8 | 1.7 |
| 2. | The near-term future (1-5 years ahead) | 23 | 4.9 |
| 3. | The middle-range future (5-30 years ahead). | 117 | 24.7 |
| | LONG-TERM FUTURES | | |
| 4. | The long-range future (30-100 years ahead, i.e. up to AD 2100) | 208 | 44.0 |
| 5. | The distant future (100-1,000 years ahead, i.e. AD 2100-3000) | 77 | 16.3 |
| 6. | The far distant future (over 1,000 years hence, i.e. after AD 3000) | 16 | 3.4 |
| 7. | The megafuture (after AD 1 million, up to end of Solar System) | 8 | 1.7 |
| 8. | The gigafuture (after AD 1 billion, up to death of stars) | 7 | 1.5 |
| 9. | The eschatofuture (after AD 1 trillion, on to $10^{100}$ years) | 9 | 1.9 |
| | Total | 473 | 100.0 |

### Column 6: Nine basic periods of the future
This variable delineates 9 basic periods into which the future can be divided, for purposes of analysis. The exact question that this coding answers for each of the futurist books and their futurist authors in this present listing below is, not which period does it concentrate on, but:

Up to how far into the future does this book extend, envisage, predict, or describe? How far ahead is the author thinking of?

Table 29–4 elaborates on the 9 periods involved. The terminal dates AD 2025 and 2100 in codes 3-5 of Table 29–4 are the end-point as envisaged only by recent entries published after 1965. Before that, the code means only the first half of the parenthesis ('5-30 years ahead', or '30-100 years ahead').

## Table 29–5.  470 leading futurist books written by 560 futurists from BC 1760 up to AD 2000 today.

| Year<br>1 | Book title<br>2 | Author/futurist<br>3 | Code<br>4 5 6 |
|---|---|---|---|
| BC 1760 | The Book of Celestial Omens (Enuma Anu Enlil) | Hammurabi | D-s2-2 |
| 1141 | The Book of Changes (I Ching) | Wen Wang | D-s2-2 |
| 700 | The Book of Isaiah (The Vision of Isaiah) | Isaiah the Prophet | R-p8-4 |
| 360 | The Republic (Politeia) | Plato | P-p1-3 |
| 45 | On Divination (De Divinatione I-II) | Cicero | D-o1-2 |
| AD c90 | On the Failure of the Oracles (De Oraculorum Defectu) | Plutarch | D-w1-1 |
| 96 | The Book of Revelation (Apokalypsis Ioannou) | John the Divine | R-p8-3 |
| c140 | Tetrabiblos: Work on Astrology (Quadripartitum) | Ptolemy | D-m1-2 |
| c230 | Treatise on Christ and the Antichrist | Hippolytus | R-e1-4 |
| 313 | The 7th Book of Divine Precepts (Divinae Institutiones) | Lactantius | R-p1-4 |
| 426 | The City of God (De Civitate Dei) | Augustine of Hippo | R-e1-5 |
| c850 | Great Introduction to the Science of Astrology | Abu Mashar | D-a5-3 |
| 950 | Letter on the Origin and Time of the Antichrist. | Adso of Montier-en-Der | R-e1-4 |
| 1139 | The Prophecy of the Popes | Malachy O'Morgain | R-e1-5 |
| 1180 | Exposition on the Apocalypse | Joachim of Fiore | R-m5-4 |
| 1272 | On the Eternity of the World (De Aeternitate Mundi) | Thomas Aquinas | R-t1-5 |
| 1495 | The Compendium of Revelations | Girolamo Savonarola | R-p8-4 |
| 1516 | Utopia | Thomas More | P-s2-4 |
| 1555 | Centuries | Nostradamus | D-p2-6 |
| 1594 | Plaine Discovery of the Whole Revelation of Saint John | John Napier | R-m1-5 |
| 1602 | The City of the Sun (Civitas Solis) | Tommaso Campanella | P-p1-2 |
| 1609 | Somnium, or the Astronomy of the Moon | Johannes Kepler | H-a6-4 |
| 1619 | Christianopolis | Johann V. Andreae | P-e1-4 |
| 1624 | New Atlantis | Francis Bacon | P-s2-4 |
| 1627 | Apocalyptica:  Key of the Revelation | Joseph Mede | R-b1-5 |
| 1638 | The Man in the Moon | Francis Godwin | P-e1-4 |
| 1699 | Observations upon the Prophesies of Daniel and the Apocalypse of St John | Isaac Newton | R-m1-5 |
| 1771 | Memoirs of the Year 2500 (L'an 2440) | Louis-S. Mercier | F-n1-5 |
| 1793 | Sketch for a Historical Picture of the Progress of the Human Mind | Marquis de Condorcet | P-p1-5 |
| 1798 | An Essay on the Principle of Population as it affects the Future Improvement of Society | Thomas R. Malthus | H-e1-4 |
| 1798 | The Last Man: or, Omegarus and Syderia, a Romance in Futurity (Le dernier homme) | J.-B. Cousin de Grainville | H-e1-5 |
| 1826 | The Last Man | Mary W. Shelley | H-w1-5 |
| 1834 | The Romance of the Future (Le Roman de l'Avenir) | Felix Bodin | F-w1-3 |
| 1836 | Three Hundred Years Hence | Mary Griffith | P-n1-5 |
| 1848 | The Communist Manifesto | Karl Marx & F. Engels | P-r2-4 |
| 1851 | System of Positive Polity (Systeme de politique positive) | Auguste Comte | P-s1-4 |
| 1864 | From the Earth to the Moon | Jules Verne | F-n1-4 |
| 1872 | The novel of the next Century (A jovo szazad regenye) | Mor Jokai | F-w1-4 |
| 1878 | Jesus is coming: God's hope for a restless world | William E. Blackstone | R-t1-3 |
| 1885 | After London: or, Wild England | J. Richard Jefferies | H-n1-4 |
| 1888 | Looking backward: 2000-1887 | Edward Bellamy | P-j1-5 |
| 1890 | News from Nowhere: an epoch of rest | William Morris | P-a4-3 |
| 1890 | AD 2000 | Alvarado M. Fuller | P-n1-5 |
| 1893 | The religion of the future | J.T. Gracey | R-m4-4 |
| 1895 | The time machine | H.G. Wells | F-n1-7 |
| 1897 | The non-religion of the future: a sociological study | J.M. Guyau | S-s1-4 |
| 1897 | Forecasts of the coming century | Edward Carpenter | P-w1-4 |
| 1898 | Astrological geomancy in Africa | J.A. Abayomi Cole | D-a1-1 |
| 1899 | Eschatology: the doctrine of a future life in Israel, Judaism and Christianity | R.H. Charles | R-b1-5 |
| 1901 | Anticipations of scientific progress upon human life and thought | H.G. Wells | S-p1-2 |
| 1901 | The mystery of the Kingdom of God | Albert Schweitzer | R-p1-5 |
| 1904 | The Millennium | William E. Blackstone | R-t1-5 |
| 1908 | Avesta eschatology: compared with the Books of Daniel and Revelation | Lawrence H. Mills | R-r1-5 |
| 1908 | The doctrine of the Last Things: Jewish and Christian | W.O.E. Oesterley | R-r1-5 |
| 1912 | Astrology and religion among the Greeks and Romans | Franz Cumont | D-a3-2 |
| 1920 | Beyond the Planet Earth | K.E. Tsiolkovsky | S-e5-4 |
| 1922 | Back to Methuselah | George Bernard Shaw | P-d2-6 |
| 1924 | We | E. Zamiatin | H-e5-3 |
| 1924 | Daedalus, or science and the future | J.B.S. Haldane | S-b3-4 |
| 1927 | The future of Christianity | James Marchant | R-h1-3 |
| 1930 | The present and future of religion | C.E.M. Joad | R-p1-5 |
| 1930 | Last and first Men | Olaf Stapledon | F-h1-8 |
| 1931 | Brave new world | Aldous Huxley | H-n1-5 |
| 1933 | The shape of things to come | H.G. Wells | P-n1-5 |
| 1936 | The next hundred years:  the unfinished business of science | Clifford C. Furnas | S-c1-4 |
| 1936 | The future of marriage in Western civilization | Edward A. Westermarck | I-s1-3 |
| 1937 | Witchcraft, oracles, and magic among the Azande | E.E. Evans-Pritchard | D-a1-1 |
| 1937 | The Star Maker | Olaf Stapledon | F-p1-8 |
| 1938 | Prophecy and divination among the Hebrews and other Semites | Alfred Guillaume | R-r1-1 |
| 1938 | Out of the Silent Planet | C.S. Lewis | R-a2-4 |
| 1941 | Religion and the world of tomorrow | W. W. Van Kirk | R-w1-3 |
| 1942 | The Foundation trilogy | Isaac Asimov | F-n1-6 |
| 1942 | The future of industrial man | Peter F. Drucker | S-p4-4 |
| 1943 | Science, religion and the future | Charles E. Raven | R-h1-4 |
| 1944 | The Church looks forward | William Temple | R-e1-3 |
| 1946 | The Christian future: or the modern mind outrun | E. Rosenstock-Huessy | R-w1-4 |
| 1946 | The Beginning and the End (Essai de metaphysique eschatologique) | Nikolay A. Berdyayev | R-p1-4 |
| 1946 | Christ and time (Christus und die Zeit) | Oscar Cullman | R-t1-4 |
| 1947 | World Christianity: yesterday, today, tomorrow | Henry P. Van Dusen | R-t1-4 |
| 1949 | The prospect for Christianity | K.S. Latourette | R-h1-4 |
| 1949 | Cosmos and history: the myth of the eternal return | Mircea Eliade | S-r1-4 |
| 1949 | Nineteen Eighty-Four | George Orwell | H-j1-4 |
| 1950 | Eschatology and ethics in the teaching of Jesus | Amos N. Wilder | R-b1-4 |
| 1953 | The next million years | Charles G. Darwin | S-p3-6 |
| 1953 | The future of cities and urban redevelopment | Catherine Bauer et al | I-u1-4 |
| 1954 | Tomorrow is already here:  scenes from a man-made world | Robert Jungk | I-p4-1 |
| 1954 | The Christian hope and the Second Coming | P.S. Minear | R-b1-5 |
| 1954 | The challenge of man's future | Harrison S. Brown | S-c1-4 |
| 1954 | Jesus and the future | George R. Beasley-Murray | R-t1-4 |
| 1955 | Cities in flight | James Blish | F-n1-6 |
| 1955 | The foreseeable future | George Thomson | S-p3-3 |
| 1956 | The coming world civilization | William E. Hocking | P-p1-4 |
| 1957 | History and eschatology: the presence of eternity | Rudolf K. Bultmann | R-b1-6 |
| 1957 | The pursuit of the Millennium: revolutionary messianism in Medieval and Reformation Europe | Norman R.C. Cohn | R-h1-5 |
| 1958 | The future of mankind (Die Atombombe und die Zukunft des Menschen) | Karl T. Jaspers | H-p1-4 |
| 1959 | The future of man (L'avenir de l'homme) | Pierre Teilhard de Chardin | R-g2-7 |
| 1959 | The Childe Cycle: the final Encyclopedia | Gordon R. Dickson | F-n1-6 |
| 1959 | The future as history | Robert L. Heilbroner | S-e3-4 |
| 1960 | Social intelligence for America's future | Bertram Gross | S-p5-4 |
| 1961 | The tale of the future: an annotated bibliography | Ian F. Clarke | H-h1-5 |
| 1961 | Ndembu divination: its symbolism and techniques | Victor W. Turner | D-a1-1 |
| 1963 | Profiles of the future: an inquiry into the limits of the possible | Arthur C. Clarke | S-p3-5 |
| 1963 | The Last Judgment in Protestant theology from orthodoxy to Ritschl | James P. Martin | R-t1-5 |

*Continued opposite*

Table 29–5—continued

| Year | Title | Author | Code |
|---|---|---|---|
| 1963 | The City of Man: prophecies of a world civilization in 20th-century thought | W. Warren Wagar | H–h1–4 |
| 1964 | The art of conjecture | Bertrand de Jouvenel | S–e3–3 |
| 1964 | Inventing the future | Dennis Gabor | S–p3–4 |
| 1965 | The coming of the Third Church: an analysis of the present and future of the church | Walbert Buhlmann | R–m4–4 |
| 1965 | The Christian of the future | Karl Rahner | R–t1–4 |
| 1965 | The future | Theodore J. Gordon | S–e5–3 |
| 1965 | The Church of the 21st century: prospects and proposals | R.E. Sommerfeld | R–t1–4 |
| 1966 | The future of religions | Paul Tillich | R–t1–5 |
| 1966 | Voices prophesying war, 1763–1984 | Ian F. Clarke | H–h1–5 |
| 1966 | Arab divination | Toufic Fahd | D–a1–1 |
| 1967 | A torrent of faces | James Blish & N.L. Knight | F–n1–6 |
| 1967 | Toward the year 2000: work in progress | Daniel Bell | S–s1–4 |
| 1967 | The Year 2000: a framework for speculation on the next 33 years | Herman Kahn & A.J. Wiener | S–p5–4 |
| 1967 | The next 500 years: scientific predictions of major social trends | Burnham P. Beckwith | S–f1–5 |
| 1968 | Yesterday's tomorrows: a historical survey of future societies | W.H.G. Armytage | H–h1–4 |
| 1968 | God and the future of man | Edward Schillebeeckx | R–t1–4 |
| 1968 | 2001: a space odyssey | Arthur C. Clarke | F–n1–4 |
| 1968 | The trumpet shall sound: a study of 'Cargo' cults in Melanesia | Peter Worsley | R–s1–2 |
| 1968 | Technological forecasting for industry and government | James R. Bright | I–e5–2 |
| 1969 | Mankind 2000 | Robert Jungk & Johan Galtung | S–p4–4 |
| 1969 | Religion in the year 2000 | Andrew Greeley | R–s1–4 |
| 1969 | Religion, revolution and the future | Jurgen Moltmann | R–t1–4 |
| 1969 | Ifa divination | William R. Bascom | D–a1–1 |
| 1969 | The future of the future | John McHale | S–s1–5 |
| 1970 | The church at the end of the 20th century | Francis A. Schaeffer | R–p1–4 |
| 1970 | The future of the Christian church | A.M. Ramsey & L.-J. Suenens | R–e1–3 |
| 1970 | Futurology: the struggle over the future | Ossip K. Flechtheim | S–p5–4 |
| 1970 | An alternative future for America's Third Century | Robert Theobald | S–e3–4 |
| 1970 | Future shock | Alvin Toffler | I–t2–3 |
| 1970 | The late great Planet Earth | Hal Lindsey & C.C. Carlson | R–b1–2 |
| 1971 | Islam the religion of the future | Sayyid Kutb | R–e4–3 |
| 1971 | Prognostics: a science in the making surveys and creates the future | F.L. Polak | S–s1–3 |
| 1971 | The future of cities and the future of Man | Griscom Morgan & Arthur Morgan | I–u1–4 |
| 1971 | The future of the Christian world mission | W.J. Danker & W.J. Kang | R–m4–3 |
| 1971 | Surviving the future | Arnold Toynbee | H–h1–4 |
| 1972 | The future executive | Harlan Cleveland | I–p5–2 |
| 1972 | Buddhism, Christianity, and the future of man | Douglas A. Fox | R–r1–4 |
| 1972 | The shape of the church to come | Karl Rahner | R–t1–3 |
| 1972 | The futurists | Alvin Toffler | I–t2–3 |
| 1972 | The limits to growth | Donella H. & Dennis L. Meadows et al | S–e5–4 |
| 1972 | Technological forecasting for decision making | Joseph P. Martino | I–e5–3 |
| 1973 | World dynamics | Jay W. Forrester | S–e5–3 |
| 1973 | Encyclopedia of biblical prophecy: the complete guide to scriptural predictions and their fulfilment | J. Barton Payne | R–b1–4 |
| 1973 | Trillion year spree: the history of science fiction | Brian W. Aldiss | F–w1–9 |
| 1973 | The historical Jesus and the Kingdom of God: present and future in message and ministry | Richard H. Hiers | R–b1–3 |
| 1973 | The future of planning | Peter Cowan | I–p4–3 |
| 1974 | The Sibylline Oracles of Egyptian Judaism | John J. Collins | D–b1–2 |
| 1974 | The next ten thousand years: a vision of man's future in the Universe | Adrian Berry | S–a6–6 |
| 1974 | The future of technological civilization | Victor C. Ferkiss | I–e3–4 |
| 1974 | The future of the church: the theology of renewal of Willem A. Visser't Hooft | Francois C. Gerard | R–t1–3 |
| 1975 | Ecotopia | Ernest Callenbach | P–e2–3 |
| 1975 | Mystical dimensions of Islam | Annemarie Schimmel | D–r1–3 |
| 1975 | A study of future worlds | Richard A. Falk | S–l1–4 |
| 1975 | The Delphi Method | Harold A. Linstone | I–p4–3 |
| 1975 | Planning alternative world futures: values, methods, and models | L.R. Beres & H.R. Targ | I–p5–4 |
| 1975 | Religion 2101 A.D.: who or what will be God? | H. H. Ward. | R–w1–5 |
| 1976 | Freud and future religious experience | A.J. De Luca | S–p9–3 |
| 1976 | Eschatus: future prophecies from Nostradamus' ancient writings | Bruce Pennington | D–a4–6 |
| 1976 | Millennium: a novel about people and politics in the year 1999 | Ben Bova | F–n1–3 |
| 1976 | Future facts: a forecast of the world before the end of the century | Stephen Rosen | I–w1–3 |
| 1976 | An incomplete guide to the future | Willis W. Harman | S–e5–4 |
| 1976 | The next 200 years: a scenario for America and the world | Herman Kahn, Leon C. Martel, W. Morrow | S–p5–5 |
| 1976 | The future of the multinational enterprise | Peter J. Buckley & Mark Casson | I–e3–3 |
| 1976 | Future energy production systems: heat and mass transfer processes | Jesse C. Denton & N.H. Afgan | I–e5–4 |
| 1976 | The coming of post-industrial society: a venture in social forecasting | Daniel Bell | S–s1–4 |
| 1977 | The study of the future: understanding and shaping tomorrow's world | Edward S. Cornish | S–j1–4 |
| 1977 | The high frontier: human colonies in space | Gerard K. O'Neill | S–p3–4 |
| 1977 | The oracle of geomancy: techniques of earth divination | Stephen Skinner | D–a5–3 |
| 1977 | Futurology: promise, performance, prospects | Victor C. Ferkiss | S–e3–4 |
| 1978 | Forecasting: an appraisal for policymakers and planners | William L. Ascher | I–p5–3 |
| 1978 | Utopian literature: a bibliography | G.R. Negley | P–b2–4 |
| 1978 | Creating alternative futures: the end of economics | Hazel Henderson | S–e3–4 |
| 1978 | The encyclopedia of prophecy | Omar V. Garrison | R–w1–3 |
| 1978 | The Delphic Oracle: its responses and operations | Joseph Fontenrose | D–h1–4 |
| 1978 | Long range forecasting: from crystal ball to computer | J. Scott Armstrong | I–f1–4 |
| 1978 | Handbook of futures research | Jib Fowles | S–m1–4 |
| 1978 | Forecasting in sociology: some paradigms | Igor V. Bestuzhev-Lada | I–s1–3 |
| 1978 | The future of industrial societies: problems, prospects, solutions | Wolfgang Michalski | I–e3–4 |
| 1979 | The Bible and the future | A. Hoekema | R–t1–5 |
| 1979 | Uncertain futures: challenges for decision-makers | Robert U. Ayres | I–p3–3 |
| 1979 | Apocalyptic spirituality: treatises and letters | Bernard McGinn | R–h1–4 |
| 1979 | Future survey annual (yearly, 1979-1993) | Michael Marien | I–b2–3 |
| 1979 | The pattern of expectation, 1644-2001 | Ian F. Clarke | H–h1–5 |
| 1979 | The encyclopedia of science fiction: an illustrated A-Z | Peter Nicholls | F–w1–7 |
| 1979 | The future: a guide to information sources | World Future Society | I–p4–3 |
| 1979 | Living in the shadow of the Second Coming: American Premillennialism, 1875-1982 | Timothy P. Weber | R–h1–2 |
| 1979 | The challenge of the future: visions and versions | William A. Conboy | I–e4–4 |
| 1980 | Future man | Chris Morgan | S–e3–5 |
| 1980 | Islamic Messianism: the idea of the Mahdi in Twelver Shi'ism | A.A. Sachedina | R–h1–3 |
| 1980 | The Aquarian Conspiracy: personal and social transformation in the 1980s | Marilyn Ferguson | D–w1–4 |
| 1981 | Future life (L'Avenir de la vie) | Michel Salomon | I–b3–4 |
| 1981 | Judging the future | James A. Dator & Clement Bezold | S–p5–4 |
| 1981 | Future females: a critical anthology | Marleen S. Barr | F–w1–6 |
| 1981 | 2081: a hopeful view of the human future | Gerard K. O'Neill | S–p3–4 |
| 1981 | After Man: a zoology of the future | Dougal Dixon | S–z1–7 |
| 1981 | The Islamic understanding of death and resurrection | Jane I. Smith & Yvonne Y. Haddad | R–r1–3 |
| 1981 | One hundred pages for the future: reflections of the President of the Club of Rome | Aurelio Peccei | S–i1–4 |
| 1982 | Terminal visions: the literature of Last Things | W. Warren Wagar | H–h1–7 |
| 1982 | The Omni Future almanac | Robert Weil | I–w1–4 |
| 1982 | Cities in the 21st century | Gary M. Gappert & R.V. Knight | I–u1–4 |
| 1982 | The evolutionary journey: a personal guide to a positive future | Barbara Marx Hubbard | D–p5–5 |
| 1982 | A history of the end of the world: an invisible book | Yuri Rubinsky & Ian Wiseman | H–h1–8 |
| 1982 | The science in science fiction: does science fiction foretell the future? | Peter Nicholls | H–j1–8 |
| 1982 | The future role of the World Bank | Robert S. McNamara | I–p6–3 |
| 1983 | The ultimate fate of the Universe | Jumal N. Islam | S–c3–9 |
| 1983 | Business planning for an uncertain future | Roy Amara & A.J. Lipinski | I–p4–2 |
| 1983 | Looking forward: a guide to futures research | Olaf Helmer | S–m1–3 |
| 1983 | Visions of desirable societies | Eleonora B. Masini | S–l1–4 |
| 1983 | Prophecy in early Christianity and the ancient Mediterranean world | David E. Aune | R–b1–3 |

*Continued overleaf*

*Table 29–5–continued*

| Year | Title | Author | Code |
|---|---|---|---|
| 1983 | The future of electronic learning | Mary A. White | I-e4-3 |
| 1984 | Future man: brave new world or genetic nightmare? | Brian M. Stableford | S-s1-5 |
| 1984 | Making the future work | John Diebold | I-b4-3 |
| 1984 | The encyclopedia of science fiction movies | Phil Hardy | H-w1-7 |
| 1984 | The future of Anglican theology | M. Darrol Bryant | R-t1-3 |
| 1984 | Marriage and the family in the year 2020 | Lester A. Kirkendall & Arthur E. Gravatt | I-s1-4 |
| 1985 | Islamic futures: the shape of ideas to come | Ziauddin Sardar | R-w1-5 |
| 1985 | Megatraumas: America at the Year 2000 | Richard D. Lamm | I-p6-3 |
| 1985 | Contact: a novel | Carl Sagan | F-a6-3 |
| 1985 | Visions of apocalypse: end or rebirth? | Saul Friedlander et al | S-h1-8 |
| 1985 | The extraterrestrial encyclopedia: our search for life in outer space | Joseph A. Angelo Jr | S-e5-4 |
| 1985 | World futures: a critical analysis of alternatives | Barry B. Hughes | S-p4-4 |
| 1985 | The Third Millennium: a history of the world, AD 2000-3000 | Brian M. Stableford & D. Langford | S-s1-5 |
| 1985 | Silico Sapiens: the fundamentals and future of robots | Joseph G. Deken | I-c2-4 |
| 1985 | The future of religion: secularization, revival, and cult formation | Rodney Stark & W. Bainbridge | R-s1-3 |
| 1986 | Arthur C. Clarke's July 20, 2019 | Arthur C. Clarke | F-n1-4 |
| 1986 | Issues management: how you can plan, organize and manage for the future | Joseph F. Coates et al | I-p4-2 |
| 1986 | The future of the metropolis: Berlin, London, Paris, New York: economic aspects | Hans-Jurgen Ewers | I-e3-4 |
| 1986 | Ancient Hindu astrology for the modern Western astrologer | James T. Braha | D-a5-2 |
| 1986 | The church of the future: a model for the year 2001 | Walbert Buhlmann | R-m4-3 |
| 1986 | The future of technics and civilization | Lewis Mumford | I-ul-4 |
| 1987 | Omni's Future medical almanac | Dick Teresi & Patrice G. Adcroft | I-j1-4 |
| 1987 | Cosmos, chaos, and gospel: a chronology of world evangelization from Creation to New Creation | David B. Barrett | R-m4-9 |
| 1987 | 100 predictions for the Baby Boom: the next 50 years | Cheryl Russell | I-f1-4 |
| 1987 | Nostradamus and the Millennium: predictions of the future | John Hogue | D-w1-6 |
| 1987 | 2061: Odyssey Three | Arthur C. Clarke | F-n1-4 |
| 1987 | The future of biblical studies: the Hebrew Scriptures | Richard E. Friedman & Hugh G. Williamson | R-b1-3 |
| 1987 | Apocalypse 2000: economic breakdown and the suicide of democracy, 1989-2000 | Peter Jay & Michael Stewart | F-e3-3 |
| 1987 | Theology for the Third Millennium: an ecumenical view | Hans Kung | R-t1-5 |
| 1987 | Utopia and Anti-Utopia in modern times | J. Krishan Kumar | H-s1-4 |
| 1987 | A brief history of time: from the Big Bang to black holes | Stephen W. Hawking | S-p3-9 |
| 1987 | The future of astrology | A. Tad Mann | D-a5-4 |
| 1987 | The future of urbanization: facing the ecological and economic constraints | Lester R. Brown & Jodi L. Jacobson | I-e2-3 |
| 1987 | The future of Christian ethics | Ronald H. Preston | R-t1-4 |
| 1987 | The future of new religious movements | David G. Bromley & Phillip E. Hammond | R-s1-3 |
| 1987 | Our common future | Jim MacNeill | I-e3-3 |
| 1987 | Futures of Christianity: historical, contemporary and future trends within the worldwide church | David L. Edwards | R-e1-4 |
| 1987 | Space: the next twenty-five years | Thomas R. McDonough | I-e5-3 |
| 1987 | The future of Muslim civilization | Ziauddin Sardar | R-w1-5 |
| 1988 | The Gaia peace atlas: survival into the Third Millennium | Frank Barnaby | I-p3-4 |
| 1988 | Maitreya, the future Buddha | Alan Sponberg & Helen Hardacre | R-r1-6 |
| 1988 | Apocalypse when? Cosmic catastrophe and the fate of the universe | Frank E. Close | S-p3-9 |
| 1988 | Global mind change: the promise of the last years of the Twentieth Century | Willis W. Harman | S-e5-3 |
| 1988 | The future of liberation theology: essays in honor of Gustavo Gutierrez | Marc H. Ellis & Otto Maduro | R-s1-3 |
| 1988 | The future of sociology | Edgar F. Borgatta & Karen S. Cook | S-s1-4 |
| 1988 | The future of the international system: the United States and the world political economy | Theodore Geiger | I-e3-4 |
| 1988 | Future cities and information technology | Eskil Block & Tibor C. Hottovy | I-ul-3 |
| 1988 | Infinite in all directions | Freeman J. Dyson | S-p3-9 |
| 1989 | Megamistakes: forecasting and the myth of rapid technological change | Steven P. Schnaars | I-f1-3 |
| 1989 | The future: opportunity not destiny | Howard F. Didsbury Jr | I-h1-4 |
| 1989 | Future directions for psychiatry | John A. Talbott | S-p9-3 |
| 1989 | Future mind: artificial intelligence, merging the mystical and the technological in the 21st century | Jerome C. Glenn | D-s3-4 |
| 1989 | What futurists believe | Joseph F. Coates & Jennifer Jarratt | I-p4-3 |
| 1989 | The future of literary theory | Ralph Cohen | S-h1-3 |
| 1989 | A short history of the future | W. Warren Wagar | H-h1-5 |
| 1989 | Mass dreams of the future: the coming apocalyptic New Age | Chet B. Snow & Helen Wambach | D-p9-5 |
| 1989 | History of the future: a chronology | Peter Lorie & Sidd Murray-Clark | D-j1-5 |
| 1989 | Building a world community: humanism in the 21st century | Paul W. Kurtz | I-p1-4 |
| 1989 | The future of psychiatry as a medical specialty | Joel Yager | S-p9-3 |
| 1990 | The next one hundred years: shaping the fate of our living Earth | Jonathan Weiner | I-j1-4 |
| 1990 | The population explosion | Paul R. & Anne H. Ehrlich | I-e2-4 |
| 1990 | One Earth, one future: our changing global environment | Cheryl S. Silver & Ruth S. DeFries | I-e6-4 |
| 1990 | Future wealth: a new economics for the 21st century | James H. Robertson | I-e3-3 |
| 1990 | Forecasting, planning, and strategy for the 21st century | Spyros G. Makridakis | I-s3-4 |
| 1990 | Man after Man: an anthropology of the future | Dougal Dixon | S-z1-7 |
| 1990 | Evil and evolutionary eschatology | Julian Casserley | R-t1-5 |
| 1990 | The Gaia atlas of future worlds: challenge and opportunity in an age of change | Norman Myers | S-e3-4 |
| 1990 | First contact: the search for extraterrestrial intelligence | Ben Bova & Byron Preiss | H-j1-5 |
| 1990 | Century's end: a cultural history of the fin de siecle from the 990s through the 1990s | Hillel Schwartz | H-h1-4 |
| 1990 | Earth | David Brin | F-a7-4 |
| 1990 | Theology of hope: a contemporary Christian eschatology | Jurgen Moltmann | R-t1-4 |
| 1990 | Millennium: winners and losers in the coming world order | Jacques Attali | I-e3-4 |
| 1990 | Megatrends 2000: ten new directions for the 1990s | John Naisbitt & Patricia Aburdene | I-t2-3 |
| 1990 | Time travel: a guide to journeys in the fourth dimension | John W. Macvey | S-a6-8 |
| 1990 | The future of the Jews | David Vital | I-h1-4 |
| 1990 | Future crime | Ben Bova | I-n1-4 |
| 1990 | The future of satellite communications | George A. Codding | I-e5-4 |
| 1990 | The future of Antarctica: exploitation versus preservation | Grahame Cook | I-e2-4 |
| 1990 | Predicting the future: an illustrated history and guide to the techniques | Albert S. Lyons | D-s4-3 |
| 1990 | The Gaia atlas of first peoples: a future for the indigenous world | Julian Burger | S-e7-4 |
| 1991 | The plot of the future: utopia and dystopia in modern drama | Dragan Klaic | H-d2-4 |
| 1991 | Leadership for the 21st century | Joseph C. Rost | I-e4-3 |
| 1991 | Cities of the 21st century: new technologies and spatial systems | John Brotchie et al | I-ul-4 |
| 1991 | World travel and tourism review: indicators, trends and forecasts | Donald E. Hawkins & J.R. Brent Ritchie | I-f1-3 |
| 1991 | The futures of culture | Eleonora B. Masini | I-l1-4 |
| 1991 | Studies for the 21st century | Martha J. Garrett et al | I-p4-4 |
| 1991 | A brief history of eternity | R. Peacock | S-c3-9 |
| 1991 | The future of Early Christianity | Birgir A. Pearson | R-b1-3 |
| 1991 | Mapping the next millennium: the discovery of new geographies | Stephen S. Hall | I-w1-5 |
| 1991 | Technology 2001: the future of computing and communications | Derek Leebaert | I-c2-3 |
| 1991 | The art of the long view: planning for the future in an uncertain world | Peter Schwartz | I-p4-4 |
| 1991 | Target Earth! Asteroid collisions past and future | Jon Erickson | S-g2-4 |
| 1991 | The hope of the Early Church: a handbook of Patristic eschatology | Brian E. Daley | R-h1-3 |
| 1991 | Unbounding the future: the nanotechnology revolution | K. Eric Drexler & Chris Peterson | S-p3-4 |
| 1991 | The futures research directory: individuals 1991-92 | World Future Society | I-p4-3 |
| 1991 | Crystal globe: the haves and have-nots of the New World Order | Marvin Cetron & Owen Davies | I-f1-3 |
| 1991 | Future air traffic control and navigation systems | James E. French | I-e5-4 |
| 1991 | Future directions in artificial intelligence | Peter A. Flach & R.A. Meersman | I-c2-4 |
| 1991 | The evolution of the future | F. W. Elwell | P-w1-4 |
| 1991 | The future of banking | James L. Pierce | I-e3-4 |
| 1991 | The shape of the future: the post-Cold-War world | Donald M. Snow | S-p5-3 |
| 1991 | Once upon a future time: studies in a Buddhist prophecy of decline | Jan Nattier | R-r1-6 |
| 1991 | Into the 21st century: a handbook for a sustainable future | Brian Burrows et al | I-e6-4 |
| 1991 | The next three futures: paradigms of things to come | W. Warren Wagar | H-h1-5 |
| 1991 | The futures of development: 10th World Conference, World Futures Studies Federation | Eleonora Masini, J.A. Dator, & Sharon Rodgers | I-l1-4 |
| 1991 | The march of the millennia: a key to looking at history | Isaac Asimov & Frank White | H-n1-5 |
| 1991 | Saving the planet: how to shape an environmentally sustainable global economy | Lester R. Brown, C. Flavin, Sandra Postel | I-e2-3 |
| 1991 | FutureSpeak: a fan's guide to the language of science fiction | Roberta Rogow | F-w1-8 |
| 1992 | Beyond the limits: confronting global collapse, envisioning a sustainable future | Donella H. & Dennis L. Meadows, J. Randers | S-e5-4 |

*Continued opposite*

Table 29–5–continued

| 1992 | Voices prophesying war: future wars 1763-3749 | Ian F. Clarke | H-h1-6 |
|------|-----------------------------------------------|---------------|--------|
| 1992 | When time shall be no more: prophecy belief in modern American culture | Paul Boyer | R-h1-2 |
| 1992 | Predictions: society's telltale signature reveals the past and forecasts the future | Theodore Modis | I-m1-4 |
| 1992 | Earth in the balance: ecology and the human spirit | Albert Gore | I-p6-3 |
| 1992 | Millennialism: an international bibliography | Theodore T. Daniels | R-b2-4 |
| 1992 | Long-range world population projections, 1950-2150 | United Nations | S-d1-5 |
| 1992 | Cosmography: a posthumous scenario for the future of humanity | R. Buckminster Fuller | P-e5-4 |
| 1992 | Megatrends for women | Patricia Aburdene & John Naisbitt | I-t2-3 |
| 1992 | Living at the end of the ages: apocalyptic expectation in the Radical Reformation | Walter Klaassen | R-h1-2 |
| 1992 | The heavens are falling: the scientific prediction of catastrophes in our time | Walter J. Karplus | S-c2-5 |
| 1992 | The global partnership for environment and development: a guide to Agenda 21 | UNCED | I-e6-4 |
| 1992 | Visions of the future: art, technology, and computing in the 21st century | Clifford A. Pickover | I-c2-4 |
| 1992 | FutureCrime: an anthology of the shape of crimes to come | Cynthia Manson & Charles Ardai | I-w1-4 |
| 1992 | Managing for the future: the 1990s and beyond | Peter F. Drucker | I-p4-3 |
| 1992 | A glimpse of the future: technology forecasts for global strategists | McKinley Conway | I-e5-4 |
| 1992 | Visions for the 21st century | Sheila Moorcroft | I-e3-4 |
| 1992 | Vital signs: the trends that are shaping our future | Lester R. Brown | I-e2-3 |
| 1992 | Future wars: the world's most dangerous flashpoints | Trevor N. Dupuy | S-m3-2 |
| 1992 | Long-term prospects for the world economy | OECD | I-e3-3 |
| 1992 | Technology and the future of work | Paul S. Adler | I-p4-3 |
| 1992 | Mythical past, elusive future: history and society in an anxious age | Frank Furedi | H-h1-3 |
| 1992 | The white hole in time: our future evolution and the meaning of now | Peter Russell | P-w1-5 |
| 1992 | Future databases: proceedings of the 2nd Far-East Workshop | Q.M. Chen et al | I-c2-4 |
| 1992 | The future of international telecommunications: the legal regime | Umberto Leanza et al | I-l1-4 |
| 1992 | The future of the world trading system | John Walley | I-e3-4 |
| 1992 | Earth Summit: Agenda 21: the United Nations programme of action from Rio | United Nations | I-e6-3 |
| 1993 | Agenda 21: the Earth Summit strategy to save our planet | Daniel Sitarz | I-l1-3 |
| 1993 | Jesus and the Last Days: the interpretation of the Olivet discourse | George R. Beasley-Murray | R-t1-4 |
| 1993 | Cosmos, chaos, and the world to come: the ancient roots of apocalyptic faith | Norman R.C. Cohn | R-h1-5 |
| 1993 | Predicting the future | Leo Howe & Alan Wain | I-a1-9 |
| 1993 | World population prospects: the 1992 revision (also 1994, 1996, 1998) | United Nations | S-d1-4 |
| 1993 | Christianity in the 21st century: reflections on the challenges ahead | Robert Wuthnow | R-s1-4 |
| 1993 | Preparing for the 21st century | Paul Kennedy | I-h1-4 |
| 1993 | A global agenda: issues before the 48th General Assembly of the United Nations | John Tessitore & Susan Woolfson | I-p5-2 |
| 1993 | The years ahead: perils, problems, and promises | Howard F. Didsbury Jr | I-h1-4 |
| 1993 | Doomsday: the end of the world, a view through time | Russell Chandler | R-j1-4 |
| 1993 | Apocalypticism in the Western tradition | Bernard McGinn | R-h1-4 |
| 1993 | The history of the future: images of the 21st century | Christophe Canto & Odile Faliu | F-a4-5 |
| 1993 | Toward the 21st century in Christian mission | James M. Phillips & Robert T. Coote | R-m4-3 |
| 1993 | Airport cities 21: the new global transport centers of the 21st century | McKinley Conway | I-e5-4 |
| 1993 | Resources for the future: an international annotated bibliography | Alan J. Mayne | I-b2-5 |
| 1993 | The knowledge base of futures studies | Richard A. Slaughter | I-e4-4 |
| 1993 | New Testament eschatology: historical and cultural background | George W. Buchanan | R-b1-4 |
| 1993 | The futures research directory: organizations and periodicals, 1993-94 | Lane Jennings | I-j1-5 |
| 1993 | Future trends in telecommunications | R.J. Horrocks & R.W.A. Scarr | I-e5-3 |
| 1993 | International futures: choices in the creation of a new world order | Barry B. Hughes | I-p4-4 |
| 1993 | Critical juncture: the future of peacekeeping | Michael Renner | I-w1-3 |
| 1993 | Waiting for the Millennium: the United Nations and the future of world order | J. Martin Rochester | I-p5-3 |
| 1993 | The encyclopedia of science fiction, 2nd edition | John Clute & Peter Nicholls | F-w1-7 |
| 1993 | Utopias and the Millennium | J. Krishan Kumar & Stephen Bann | H-s1-5 |
| 1993 | A brief history of the future | Allan E. Goodman | I-p5-4 |
| 1993 | Looking forward: the next forty years | John M. Templeton | I-b4-4 |
| 1993 | The evolving self: a psychology for the third millennium | Mihaly Csikszentmihalyi | S-p9-5 |
| 1993 | Future systems: the story of tomorrow | Martin Pawley | I-e5-3 |
| 1993 | Temples of tomorrow: world religions and the future | Richard Kirby & Earl D. C. Brewer | R-s1-3 |
| 1993 | Visions of the future: art, technology, and computing | Clifford A. Pickover | P-m1-4 |
| 1993 | Airport cities 21: the new global transport centers | McKinley Conway | I-e5-4 |
| 1994 | Faith and the future: studies in Christian eschatology | Raymond E. Brown et al | R-b1-3 |
| 1994 | Encyclopedia of the future | George T. Kurian & Graham T.T. Molitor | S-w1-9 |
| 1994 | On the coming of the Third Millennium (Tertio Millennio Adveniente) | John Paul II | R-e1-5 |
| 1994 | The road to 2015: profiles of the future | John L. Peterson | I-w1-3 |
| 1994 | Vision 2020: reordering chaos for global survival | Ervin Laszlo | I-p1-3 |
| 1995 | World futures and the United Nations: an annotated guide to 250 recent books and publications | Michael Marien | I-b2-3 |
| 1995 | Terrorism 2000: the future face of terrorism | Marvin J. Cetron | I-f1-3 |
| 1995 | The next 500 years: life in the coming millennium | Adrian Berry | S-a6-5 |
| 1995 | Divining the future: prognostication from astrology to zoomancy | Eva Shaw | D-w1-4 |
| 1995 | Future health: computers and medicine in the 21st century | Clifford A. Pickover | I-m1-4 |
| 1995 | Small is powerful: the future as if people really mattered | John Papworth | P-w1-5 |
| 1995 | The end of the future: the waning of the high-tech world | Jean Gimpel | H-w1-3 |
| 1995 | The hope at hand: revival for the 21st century | David Bryant | R-e1-4 |
| 1995 | Future libraries | R. Howard Bloch & Carla A. Hesse | I-l2-4 |
| 1995 | Fire from heaven: the rise of pentecostal spirituality and reshaping of religion in the 21st century | Harvey Cox. | R-t1-4 |
| 1995 | Futuropting: how churches can do multiple scenario planning | R. L. Perry | R-p4-3 |
| 1995 | Restoration and renewal: the church in the Third Millennium | J. F. Eagan | R-e1-4 |
| 1996 | The future of the book | Geoffrey Nunberg | I-l3-3 |
| 1996 | The future of the city in post-industrial societies | Joseph F. Coates | I-f1-4 |
| 1996 | 2025: scenarios of US and global society reshaped by science and technology | Joseph F. Coates, John B. Mahaffie, Andy Hines | S-f1-3 |
| 1996 | Nanotechnology: molecular speculations of global abundance | B. C. Crandell | S-p3-4 |
| 1996 | Fractal horizons: the future use of fractals | Clifford A. Pickover | S-m1-4 |
| 1996 | The future of the newspaper industry: how electronic newspapers will outrun their competition | Kenton W. Elderkin | I-j1-3 |
| 1996 | Cyberfutures: culture and politics on the information superhighway | Ziauddin Sardar & Jerome R. Ravetz | I-p5-3 |
| 1996 | Welcome to the next church | Charles Trueheart | R-j1-2 |
| 1996 | The futures of women: scenarios for the 21st century | Pamela McCorduck & Nancy Ramsey | I-w1-4 |
| 1996 | Millennium III, century XXI: a retrospective on the future | Peter N. Stearns | I-h1-4 |
| 1996 | Predictions for a new millennium | Noel Tyl | D-a5-5 |
| 1996 | Growth triumphant: the twenty-first century in historical perspective | Richard A. Easterlin | H-e3-4 |
| 1996 | Impact and future challenges of new communication technologies | FUTURESCO | S-w1-5 |
| 1996 | Water 2010: four scenarios for 21st century water systems | Richard Pinkham and Scott Chaplin | I-e6-4 |
| 1996 | The human genome project and the future of health care | Thomas H. Murray, Mark A. Rothstein, et al | S-p2-4 |
| 1996 | Digital money: the new era of Internet commerce | Daniel C. Lynch & Leslie Lundquist | I-e3-3 |
| 1996 | The future is ours: foreseeing, managing and creating the future | Graham H. May | P-w1-4 |
| 1996 | Foundations of futures studies: human science for a new era | Wendell Bell | I-s1-4 |
| 1996 | The future of law: facing the challenges of information technology | Richard Susskind | I-l1-3 |
| 1996 | Vision bearers: evangelism in the 21st century | Richard Kew & Cyril Okorocha | R-e1-4 |
| 1996 | The coming of the millennium: good news for the whole human race | Darrell Fasching | R-w1-5 |
| 1996 | Internet dreams: archetypes, myths, and metaphors | Mark Stefik & Vinton G. Cerf | S-c2-4 |
| 1996 | Vital signs 1996: the trends that are shaping our future | L. R. Brown, C. Flavin & H. Kane | I-e6-3 |
| 1996 | Cardinals for the Third Millennium (Cardinali del terzo millennio) | G. Galazka | R-e1-3 |
| 1997 | 3001: the final odyssey | Arthur C. Clarke | F-n1-5 |
| 1997 | Cities in our future: growth and form, environmental health and social equity | Robert Geddes | I-u1-5 |
| 1997 | Probable tomorrows: how science and technology will transform our lives in the next twenty years | Marvin J. Cetron | S-f1-3 |
| 1997 | 50 great investments for the 21st century | Diego J. Veitia | I-e3-4 |
| 1997 | Workforce 2020: work and workers in the 21st century | Leslie Lenkowsky | I-s1-4 |
| 1997 | The future of the global environment: a model-based analysis | Jan Bakkes & Jaap van Woerden | S-e6-4 |
| 1997 | The long boom: a history of the future 1980-2020 | Peter Schwartz & Peter Leyden | H-e3-3 |
| 1997 | Insider's guide to the future: the powerful forces shaping our future...and how to profit from them | Edith Weiner & Arnold Brown | H-f1-3 |
| 1997 | The organization of the future | Frances Hesselbein | I-t2-3 |
| 1997 | Emerging technologies: what's ahead for 2001-2030 | William E. Halal, Michael D. Kull, Ann Leffman | S-e3-3 |
| 1997 | Development highlights of the twentieth century: with lessons for century 21 | McKinley Conway | P-e5-4 |

Continued overleaf

*Table 29–5–concluded*

| | | | |
|---|---|---|---|
| 1997 | Visions: how science will revolutionize the 21st century | Michio Kaku | S-p3-4 |
| 1997 | The quest for alien planets: exploring worlds outside the solar system | Paul Halpern | S-p3-4 |
| 1997 | After contact: the human response to extraterrestrial life | Albert A. Harrison | S-p9-4 |
| 1997 | Predicting the future: from Jules Verne to Bill Gates | John Malone | I-w1-5 |
| 1997 | The future of ethnicity, race, and nationality | Walter L. Wallace | H-s1-6 |
| 1997 | The future of the self: inventing the postmodern person | Walter Truett Anderson | P-p9-4 |
| 1997 | The next twenty years of your life: a personal guide into the year 2017 | Richard Worzel | I-w1-3 |
| 1997 | The world in 2020: towards a new global age | OECD | I-e3-3 |
| 1997 | Chaotics: an agenda for business and society in the 21st century | Georges Anderla, Anthony Dunning, S. Forge | I-b4-4 |
| 1997 | Made to measure: new materials for the 21st century | Philip Ball | S-e5-4 |
| 1997 | The end of Christendom and the future of Christianity | Douglas John Hall | R-r1-4 |
| 1997 | The year 2000: essays on the end | Charles B. Strozier & Michael Flynn | R-r1-2 |
| 1997 | Anticipating the future: twenty millennia of human progress | Barry Buzan & Gerald Segal | P-w1-5 |
| 1997 | Mind and brain sciences in the 21st century | Robert L. Solso | S-p9-4 |
| 1997 | Beyond calculation: the next fifty years of computing | Peter J. Denning & Robert M. Metcalfe | S-c2-4 |
| 1998 | The fortune sellers: the big business of buying and selling predictions | William A. Sherden | I-f1-4 |
| 1998 | A global ethic for global politics and economics | Hans Küng | R-t1-3 |
| 1998 | International rights and responsibilities for the future | Kenneth W. Hunter & Timothy C. Mack | I-w1-4 |
| 1998 | Global trends 2005: the challenge of a new millennium | Michael J. Mazarr | P-p5-2 |
| 1998 | Lifestyles of the new millennium: 65 forecasts | Marian Salzman | S-w1-5 |
| 1998 | The community of the future | Frances Hesselbein, Marshall Goldsmith, & et al | I-t2-4 |
| 1998 | Which world? scenarios for the 21st century | Allen Hammond | I-f1-4 |
| 1998 | The future of food: long-term prospects for the agro-food sector | OECD Forum for the Future | I-e3-3 |
| 1998 | Millennial perspectives: strengths and limitations of long-term forecasts | Graham T.T. Molitor | I-t2-5 |
| 1998 | Utopistics: or, historical choices of the twenty-first century | Immanuel Wallerstein | H-p5-4 |
| 1998 | The future of the electronic marketplace | Derek Leebaert | I-e3-4 |
| 1998 | The university—alternative futures | Sohail Inayatullah & Jenny Gidley | I-e4-4 |
| 1998 | The prospering parachurch: enlarging the boundaries of God's kingdom | Wesley K. Willmer & J. David Schmidt | R-w1-3 |
| 1998 | Culture: beacon of the future | D. Paul Schafer | I-s1-4 |
| 1998 | Caring for future generations: Jewish, Christian and Islamic perspectives | Emmanuel Agius & Lionel Chircop | R-r1-4 |
| 1998 | Predicting the future: an introduction to the theory of forecasting | Nicholas Rescher | I-t2-4 |
| 1998 | Christianity for the 21st century | Philip F. Esler | R-e1-4 |
| 1998 | Remember the poor: the challenge to theology in the twenty-first century | Joery Rieger | R-w1-4 |
| 1998 | The future of Islam and the west: clash of civilizations or peaceful coexistence? | Shireen T. Hunter | R-r1-4 |
| 1998 | The future of the United Nations system: potential for the 21st century | Chadwick F. Alger | I-p5-4 |
| 1998 | Harnessing light: optical science and engineering for the 21st century | National Research Council, USA | S-e5-4 |
| 1998 | The Macmillan atlas of the future | Ian Pearson | I-s3-5 |
| 1999 | Navigating the future: a personal guide to success in the New Millennium | Mikela Tarlow & Philip Tarlow | I-p9-5 |
| 1999 | The shape of things to come: seven imperatives for winning in the new world of business | Richard W. Oliver | I-b4-4 |
| 1999 | The shape of the future: world politics in a new century | Donald M. Snow | I-p5-4 |
| 1999 | Rescuing all our futures: the future of futures studies | Ziauddin Sardar | I-w1-5 |

## *RELIGION AND FUTURISM*

The last section of this Part 29 "FutureScan" will review the literature and the whole subject in broadest perspective.

In the past one hundred years the study of the future has emerged as a professional enterprise with leading scientists, economists, astronauts, physicists, politicians, educators, and clergy making significant contributions. Within this now well-developed discipline of futurology is the subdiscipline of the study of the future of religion. At first glance this might appear to be a minor area but in the context of human history the literature is formidable.

The role of religion, at the heart of human values and behavior, in international human development is well known through the writings of anthropologists, historians, sociologists, and other scholars. Consequently, its role in the future holds promise for charting the future development of humanity. Nonetheless, writing about the future of religion has always been somewhat of a hazardous business. It would seen that those brave enough to venture into this realm are drawn inexorably to two extreme visions of the religious future of mankind—from fanciful predictions of religious utopia on the one side to inexorable decline and collapse on the other. Perhaps this is due to the strong feelings and opinions of those who write about the future of religion—mainly devout religionists or ultra-secularists.

Most of this kind of writing is ultimately based on impressions, presuppositions, and qualitative hunches. Consequently, much of the literature is vague, unhelpful, and essentially, personal opinion. Thus, the wide range of predictions in the literature appears to be mainly the result of the breadth of philosophical perspective of those offering opinions, not the result of any objective analysis. This fact prompts prominent futurist Warren Wagar to admit 'As futurists, we are really out of our depth in trying to chart the far future of religion' (*The next three futures:* 140).

The absence of quantitative data for the future of religion is at least partially by design. The tools for a preliminary study have been available for some time. However, a bias against religion from leading futurists ('Religion—it's hard to kill.' *What futurists believe:* 83) and an apparent omission of quantitative analysis by theologians have obscured the need for such a study. As long as there is little or no data to examine, readers will have no quantitative recourse for testing hypotheses when faced with a broad range of scenarios—collapse, religious utopia, or any scenario between these two extremes. Thus, it is apparent that the only way to rectify this situation is to provide both data and a methodology for the quantitative analysis of future of religion. Students of the future of religion will then possess an objective tool for evaluating subjective opinions of both futurists and theologians—or anyone else brave enough to venture an opinion.

Furthermore, it will provide a platform for completely new commentary and analysis. A method for analyzing the quantitative future of religion could be used by scholars in many disciplines—anthropologists, futurists, historians, religionists, sociologists, theologians, and so on. The wide range of opinions presented by these and others could be evaluated by anyone with the proper quantitative tools. Such a set of readily available tools will encourage more accountability for those writing on the future of religion. This includes those who write with conviction about both extremes of the future of religion.

The same tools could be used by anyone wanting to test the impact of their own assumptions about religion, the nonreligious, and atheism. They could calculate numeric values to match their assumptions and apply these to the appropriate demographic data to produce their own statistical scenarios for the future. The result of their calculations would be tied to their assumptions and the defense of these same assumptions.

This methodology would also provide important context in the integrated field of international human development. Books and studies on this subject are full of quantitative data on a wide range of human activities. but one is hard pressed to find serious studies linking religion, demography, and human development. Yet no one would argue that these three separately all play no crucial role in the future of humanity. As we shall see, the synergy created when these four (religion, demography, development, and the future) are brought together can be remarkable.

## *REVIEW OF THE LITERATURE*

A brief overview of literature on the future of religion yields a wide range of personal opinions about what is likely to happen. Some views are based on strong philosophical or theological points of view. Others seem to be the result of either ignorance or indifference toward religion.

An analysis of books and articles on the future shows a consistent bias against the staying-power of religion into the future. In *What futurists believe*, the two authors demonstrate that most futurists do not take religion seriously or are interested in only its aberrations or extremes (e.g. fanaticism, fundamentalism). They conclude that 'Religious belief as a motivator of human action and a source of values is mentioned by several of the futurist panel, most frequently in the context of fundamentalism. However its influence over the long term is assumed to be in decline (p. 25).' This assumption is consistently made by futurists with little awareness of or regard for quantitative evidence. They generally do not investigate data on the very subject for which they offer such confident opinions and advice.

Equally prolific are the writers expounding a future where religion (in its various forms) is central to the destiny of mankind. This ranges from pseudo-humanistic utopias (still based on religion) to Christian, Muslim, or Buddhist eschatological visions to New Age cosmic consciousness sans organized religion. These writers also offer little quantitative evidence for their views.

### *Non-quantitative views of the future of religion*

Catholic sociologist Andrew M. Greeley wrote in 1969, 'As Peter Berger has pointed out, there is very little in the current literature of the future of religion, mostly because the futurists assume that religion either will not play much part in the future, or is irrelevant to human behavior (an assumption which, by the way, is implicit, so that no data are advanced to establish it)' (p. 4-5). It is true that since the founding of the World Future Society (1965) most futurists have been concerned about economics, science, business, the environment, and other 'secular' concerns (these are the main topics in the WFS's magazine *The futurist*.) It should be noted however that the best-selling futurist work in this same period was Hal Lindsey's *Late great planet earth* (1976) with 25 million copies in print and still selling strong in the 1990s. Furthermore a study of the history of futurist publications from the earliest times shows a solid 40% from religious sources with the most widely read in history being The Revelation of John (c. AD 90), which has been translated into over 1,000 languages. Nonetheless, the bulk of futurist writings has been in the 20th century, and we now turn to a quick overview of some of this literature.

### *Predicting the demise or collapse of religion*

Social scientists continue to predict a decline in the prevalence of religion. 'Many of the classical theorists who laid the foundations for the discipline of sociology were altogether convinced that religion had reached the pinnacle of its influence in the early modern period and could no longer be regarded as a formative institution for giving definition to late-modern patterns of development. The participation of major religious communities during the last decade in the world's trouble spots—for example, Northern Ireland, the Middle East, Latin America and so forth—

can even be dismissed as a last ditch effort by fundamentalists of one stripe or another to forestall the inevitable eclipse of religious hegemony in a world already well on the way toward deep structural secularization' (*Religion and global order*). This basic assumption about the declining role of religion in the future profoundly affects not only the discipline of sociology but many interrelated fields.

Much of this is due to observations of the rise of the nonreligious in the Western world. Most scientists assume that this trend is a global one. The reasons for such trends are well-documented. The influences of secularism, materialism, and agnosticism chip away at religion. The problem comes in extrapolating these trends into the future. Physicist Gerald O'Neill observes that 'most prophets overestimated how much the world would be transformed by social and political change and underestimated how much the world would be transformed by social and political change and underestimated the forces of technological change' (*2081: a hopeful view*). This observation reinforces the need for quantitative tools for examining the future of religion, since there appears to be a bias towards building into future scenarios major social and political changes while not anticipating technological changes. This is encountered throughout this overview of literature on the future of religion.

Futurist H. Gerjouy acknowledges the problem of bias in the extrapolation of trends into the future when he writes 'What I foresee seems very sensitive to what I have most recently experienced... the future is chaotically dependent on the present... the future may vary discontinuously as a function of the present. Even tiny changes in the present may generate enormous changes in the future, provided we look far enough ahead' (1992:5).

There are all sorts of ways to forecast the future. One newly published method is that of S curves (Modis 1992). The author asserts that the growth of any type of population might display the S-shaped pattern characteristic of natural growth. When this the case then you can look for missing data—either in the future as forecasting or in the past as backcasting. His one case study on religion examines the canonization of Christian saints. According to missing data from the future, Christianity should prepare for some kind of cataclysmic shakeup around the turn of the millennium. Modis' S curve analysis is too inflexible for most quantitative analysis of the future since it requires enough data to generate a long-term pattern. It is not strictly a method of extrapolation but is more useful for examining patterns after the fact.

Yet most people interested in the future of religion feel the need for objectivity that comes with quantitative analysis. Duke and Johnson, picking up many clues for the resiliency of religion in the face of secularization, conclude their study of Barrett's *World Christian encyclopedia* data with the appeal, 'It is time to reassess the relatively weak empirical foundations of secularization theory and move on to more empirically based explanations of religious change' (1989:96). Here again is an appeal for quantitative tools (and their application to religion).

Others have gone down in history hoping for or predicting the utter collapse of religion in general or of a specific religion. In summing up the attack Karl Marx leveled on organized religion, Richard Tarnas writes, 'To transform the world, to realize the ideals of human justice and community, man must rid himself of the religious delusion' (1991:315-316). H.G. Wells (1933) predicted that before 1960, all the world's national governments would collapse, paving the way for a World State based on worldwide air transport. By 1977, this State would suppress all religions. 'From Voltaire to Marx every Enlightenment thinker thought that religion would disappear in the 20th century because religion was fetishism, animistic superstition,' says Harvard's professor emeritus Daniel Bell' (*Megatrends 2000:* 295). English philosopher Bertrand Russell was quite clear in his lecture 'Has religion made useful contributions to civilization?' (first published in 1930) on his desire for the future of religion. He concluded 'It is possible that mankind is on the threshold of a golden age but, if so, it will be necessary first to slay the dragon that guards the door, and that dragon is religion'.

Today many scientists, educators, philosophers, and even religionists uncritically accept this assumption. One constantly comes across predictions of the decline of religion. The fourth major trend in social scientist Burnham Beckwith's *The next 500 years* is 'The decline of religion and superstition'. Beckwith puts this in a list of 31 major trends he believes will shape the next few centuries.

### *Religion in the short-range 'trends analysis' future*

Books based on trends analysis written on the short-range future for businessmen and politicians have mixed things to say about religion. Some are virtually silent on the subject such as Marvin Cetron and Owen Davies' book *Crystal globe: the haves and have nots of the new world order* (1991) where in the Appendix A '90 Major Trends Now Changing Our World' religion is not even mentioned. Others, like John Naisbitt and Patricia Aburdene, are more interested in the future of religion. In their *Megatrends 2000* (1990), a whole chapter is devoted to the subject. Their conclusion, after a flurry of disjointed statistics on various religions, is that mankind is becoming more spiritual than organized religion can handle. This is essentially a variation on the theory of the decline of organized religion in favor of individual spirituality espoused by most New Age thinkers.

Futurist Alvin Toffler writes 'The emerging global power game in the decades ahead cannot be understood without taking into account the rising power of Islam, Catholicism, and other religions—or of global conflicts and holy wars among them' (1990:458) but his vision sees religion in a confrontational role with human society. In fact, religion is highly integrated in human society and is far more prevalent in the lives of the majority of mankind than most futurists care to admit.

In a related vein, the future itself contains a constant reference point which is religious in nature. In *Futures: human and divine*, Lutheran professor Ted Peters sets forth his purpose 'First, to show that future consciousness itself is an intensely religious phenomenon; and second, to present one view of Christian eschatology that securely anchors a holistic value system in the future of God' (1997:14). He argues that a valid concern for the future constantly puts one in touch with ultimate values which are intrinsically religious. Thus, most futurists are not concerned with trivial matters but whether or not humanity will survive. Peters argues that values such as these are at the heart of religion and that without them humanism is an empty shell. When the questions we ask about the future become more important we are inexorably drawn into deeper values.

### *The environment and religion*

A few others see religion taking a central role in the future of humanity and the preservation of the planet. Paul and Anne Ehrlich (1990) are concerned that religious leaders help their constituencies understand the effects of population growth on the earth's ability to support life. Many environmentalists now see the leaders of the world's religions as vital players in a sustainable long-term development plan for our planet. Most global issues impacting the future are now in the boardrooms and committees of major world religious traditions. The future of religion is therefore related to the future of humanity.

In Laszlo's enumeration of the goals of mankind (1977) he recognizes the crucial role of world religions in not only the implementation of those goals but the setting of them as well. 'Apart from the complex theologies of the world religions, the forms of allegiance and value they inspire constitute a major force in the world' (p. 369). What follows is a lengthy discussion on how religions can contribute to world solidarity and the achievement of mankind's goals for the future.

### *The influence of technology*

Neil Postman adds another influence he calls 'technopoly' defined as the 'the deification of technology, which means that culture seeks its authorization in technology. The term is aptly used for a culture whose available theories do not offer guidance about what is acceptable information in the moral domain' (1992:70,79). Many see in the inevitable progress caused by advances in science and technology, the decline of religion. 'Not only do technologies determine how we interact—even providing surrogate intimacy—they also threaten to replace God as an object of worship' (Chandler 1992:307). Gulzar Haider expresses some of the fears that religionists often voice about the use of technology in his short reflection 'An 'Islamic future' Without a Name' (1991:311-316). Upon arriving in Arafat, Saudi Arabia in the year 2020 he is continually confronted by Muslims enamored with technology including the use of strategic mapping and computers for redrawing the global Muslim empire and preaching. He is saddened to see that his fellow Muslims are more enamored with the latest technology than with Allah.

In some future religions or sects, computers or artificial intelligences will be worshiped. 'Idol worship will become popular again, as humans find in artificial intelligences idols that have eyes that see, ears that hear, mouths that talk, etc. Adding to the mystique of robots will be their thoroughly immaculate incarnation, free from whatever taints might be thought to derive from a sexual origin' (Gerjouy 1992:12). Whether or not such things come to pass depends on how far people are willing to go in their relationship with technology. 'The process of metaphorical deification will continue—and continue to be denied in the name of common sense or as a form of idolatry' (Hardison, Jr. 1989:341).

But science and technology are not inherently opposed to religion. Gerjouy predicts that in the future 'the distinction between religion and science will be lost in the increasing complexity and ambiguity of both'. Science will eventually learn to recognize and value mystical, subjective, and aesthetic criteria.

### *Worship of the future as religion*

One interesting and ironic possibility for the future of religion is that the future may itself become a basis for a family of religions. 'A main tenet of these religions will be that adherents will attain physical immortality through future technology operated by triumphant future adherents of the sect, who will reward their dead spiritual ancestors by restoring them to life in the material paradise the triumphant sect will create. In other sects, salvation will be anticipated, not be means of some remote future revival, but soon, when the sect's (often superhuman) descendants will reach back in time to reward its early adherents. Such religions will resemble cargo cults in their expectation of benefits to come from contact with our prosperous children's children' (Gerjouy 1992:12). A growing awareness of time and its effect on humanity, as well as the possibility of time travel, or at least, sending messages backwards in time, increases the likelihood of the scenario outlined by Gerjouy.

### *A history of the future and religion*

State University of New York historian Warren Wagar's brilliant *A short history of the future* (1989) has a strong secularist base. Nevertheless, Wagar's three scenarios, developed chronologically from the 1990s to 2200, chronicle the rise and fall of various *new* religions.

The first is the Church of the Purification, a popular anti-modernist religious sect founded in 2038. It represents a return to primitive Christianity and in the context of the collapse of Earth, Inc. and the rise of the Commonwealth, produces thousands of martyrs each year. The Church is opposed by the rising World party, which eventually suppresses all religious expression.

Second, when the Commonwealth is well established, 'The secular pieties of substantialism in many ways took the place of religious feeling. Absorbed in the myriad tasks of postwar reconstruction and social transformation, most people deserted the old faiths'. Though religious freedom is guaranteed under the laws of the Commonwealth, society is so thoroughly secularized that religion does not (and is not allowed to) make an impact on government. This is true in the case of the Islamic lands in particular where fewer than half the population are orthodox Muslims (note the massive decline from today's 90%). They are simply not allowed to build an Islamic civilization though they can practice their faith—a contradiction in Islam.

Third, the Commonwealth declines as ethnic and religious groups demand the right to live under their own laws. 'If observant Muslims wished to set up a society governed by the shari'a, then they should be free to do so. If Hindus living among them objected, then the Hindus should be free to leave and form their own societies'. The result is the House of Earth, which by 2157 is 41,525 autonomous communities spread all over Earth and in space. One of these is 250 self-styled Apocalyptic Bible Baptists in Mississippi, USA. Orthodox Muslims can govern themselves by shari'a, but erosion of religious conviction leads to the establishment of only a few of these globally. Most political parties then disband but 'the only parties that survived belonged to evangelical faiths, for whom world conversion was a duty enjoined by their respective gods. But as major forces in world politics they had no future. World politics itself had ceased, for all practical purposes, to exist'. The 23rd century then opens with the rise of Absolute Relativism, which assumes that all truth claims are true until and unless proven false.

All of these views are consistent with Wagar's philosophical starting point. 'The secular religion of "the service of the being" sketched in my *Building the city of man* and *A short history of the future*, is the only faith that makes any sense to me' (Wagar 1991:140). In Warren Wagar's *The next three futures* only 3 pages are dedicated to the future of religion. Here he asks the question 'What is the likelihood that any religion or religious philosophy, from Christianity and Islam to humanism, will sharply increase its sphere of followers in the world as a whole in the next century of serve as the matrix of a majoritarian world culture? The answer is, very little likelihood'. 'Some may grow or decline in relation to others, and all will make some contribution, positive or negative, to whatever majoritarian world culture emerges (if any). But the days of mass conversion are long past. Just as there are no more empty or sparsely settled lands available for colonizing, so there are no more pagans or infidels waiting to receive the Word' (140).

***Other secular futures***

Sociologist Brian Stableford and weapons physicist David Langford also see religion on the decline. In their masterful *The third millennium: a history of the world; AD 2000-3000*, by the middle of the 21st century, the last great 'religion,' Marxism, is on the decline. The world's old faiths have all but disappeared. What we do see in the future is the Solar Army from 2012 (purist antinuclear movement based on Inca sungod), ecological mysticism in the 2200 (the glorification of Nature), the new monasticism in 2250 (retreat from communication networks), Archaic Catholics in 2400 (opposing birth control), James Elvey and followers in late 25th century (American Black Baptist who saves Christianity from extinction by preaching against evils of the cities), and NeoStoicism in the 28th century (a movement among rejuvenates reacting to the hedonism of the day). Yet each of these was a minority movement with little or no staying power. The vast majority of men and women in the future appear to be nonreligious.

***Religion in science fiction***

While most futurists treat religion as in long-term decline, many future scenarios in the genre of science fiction depict religion either as nonexistent or in a fanatical, fundamentalist light. There is discontinuity. New religions rise up in place of old with the worship of technology or science as central theme. Here again, this is a strange polarization. In many of the alternate futures portrayed by science fiction writers, religion as we know it today has all but vanished and been replaced by the worship of computers or technology in general.

It is important to remember that science fiction is written from the standpoint of current trends and practices. 'We give our readers the experience of living in futures that are the consequences of certain choices. Choices we're making right now. this makes science fiction potentially the realest of realistic storytelling. We don't just tell you how things *are*. We can show you how things might end up *because* of the way things are' (*Future on fire*, Italics his). Science fiction then is not immune to current trends and attitudes. In fact, it is so deeply colored by them that the projection methodology (albeit a qualitative one) inherent in the scenario writing is severely flawed. The creative edge in science fiction is created not so much by an author's realistic portrayal of the future but in his ability to deal with the complexities of human society set in another context. This, the strength of the genre, explains the diverse treatment religion receives. All the scenario writers cannot be right but their views of religion in the future should not be treated as what is likely to happen so much as commentary on the human condition in the present projected into the future.

***In the near future—religion plays a role***

Exceptions to the strange treatment of religion in the distant future are found in many stories and scenarios set in the near future. Works on the future often include religious characters in their stories. One such unusually sane religious fundamentalist is Palmer Joss in Carl Sagan's *Contact: A novel*. When a message is received from another star Joss as spokesman for the religious community, states that 'Representatives of the major faiths ought to be a part of the process of decoding'). Subsequently Joss plays an important role in humanity's interpretation of the message.

The central character of Ben Bova's *Mars* in Native American Jamie Waterman whose faith is instrumental in the first successful manned landing on Mars. The parallel strands of the Red Planet and Jamie's southwestern United States homeland are woven together throughout the work. 'Jamie stood in the brightly warm sunlight of New Mexico even though the sky was a delicate Martian pink. He slid his helmet visor up, knowing he no longer needed his hard suit to protect him. He was coming home, his true home, where two worlds met and blended in the unity and balance that he had unconsciously sought since childhood. For the first time in his life Jamie felt in harmony with the world, with both his worlds, with all worlds.' (458). Waterman is the key to the discovery of life on Mars and his personal religion guides and directs him throughout the expedition.

The sensitive portrayal of the devout Catholic Michael O'Toole and the African tribal religionist roots of Nicole des Jardins in the Rama series (*Rama II*, 1989 and *The garden of Rama*, 1991 both by Arthur C. Clarke and Gentry Lee) is rare indeed. Here O'Toole struggles with the meaning of contact with an alien race, the issue of abortion, and practicing his faith. Jardins draws strength from her religious roots to face many challenges far from Earth. All characters in the series must face up to religion, reconciling their actions with their faith.

***The more distant future—humanity in space***

Religion in the distant future is less recognizable. In essence, the farther one extrapolates into the future the farther one gets from 'predictable' and familiar territory. The 14 books of the Galactic empire of Isaac Asimov (including the *Foundation* series and the Robot novels), written from 1942 to 1988, contain little reference to religion—except where it is used to anesthetize rival civilizations. Perhaps this is not surprising in light of Asimov's commitment to nonreligious humanism. A universe with 40 billion humans thousands of years into the future shows mankind in control of his own destiny. The gods of organized and unorganized religion have long since receded into oblivion.

Conversely, in Gordon R. Dickson's *The Childe cycle* series (12 vols., 1959-present), one of science fiction's most popular future histories, religion plays a central role. Of the three Splinter Cultures developed through space colonization, two are clearly religious in orientation. The Friendlies are faith-holders whose roots are in Christianity. The Exotics are mystics with roots in Eastern religion. The third culture is one of professional soldiers, the Dorsai. The hero, Hal Mayne, is a product of all three cultures and draws on all three to save humanity in the 24th century (see *The Final Encyclopedia*, 1984 or *The Chantry Guild*, 1988). A satan-figure, Bleys Ahrens, battles Mayne to lull all human cultures into stasis (see *Young Bleys*, 1992).

***The resiliency of religion***

For the past two centuries, certain influential writers (some already alluded to) have predicted the death of religion as the inevitable consequence of science, education, and modern economics. Rodney Stark and William Sims Bainbridge begin their book *The future of religion* with the following observation, 'At least since the Enlightenment, most Western intellectuals have anticipated the death of religion as eagerly as ancient Israel awaited the messiah. Social scientists have particularly excelled in predicting the impending triumph of reason over "superstition". The most illustrious figures in sociology, anthropology, and psychology have unanimously expressed confidence that their children, or surely their grandchildren, would live to see the dawn of a new era in which, to paraphrase Freud, the infantile illusions of religion would be outgrown'. The authors, however, go on to argue that 'the vision of a religionless future is but illusion'. They recognize that secularization is a powerful trend in the present but that it is not a new phenomenon. Religious economies have always had to deal with secularizing influences but along with secularization comes two counterbalancing factors: revival and religious innovation. Thus, while society is all the time exercising a secularizing influence, breakaway protest groups form to give a more virile otherworldliness to mainstream faith and new religious traditions are formed to wrest dominant market positions from older faiths. But for all the evidence offered by Stark and Bainbridge for the enduring strength of religion (primarily as the result of the relentless infusion of life by new religious movements), they offer no statistical or numerical guidelines for the future of religion.

Careful thinking by futurists often results in a more considered prediction about religions in the future. Futurist H. Gerjouy in 'The most significant events of the next thousand years' (1992) counters pessimistic views of the future by stating that 'There will be radiation and proliferation of religions, and new important religions will spring up that will attract many adherents. Some religions and philosophies will focus on returning human beings to their irrational, even animal, roots. Others will aim at transformation into superior or radically different beings'. Unfortunately such thinking is rare among Gerjouy's contemporaries. However, even Gerjouy would benefit from quantitative evidence for his statements because it would provide guidelines for him to estimate the impact that such new religions might have on the future. He recognizes their likelihood of development but not the scope of their influence.

Thomas Hine recognized this in his evaluation of religious expectations of the end of the world. He writes, 'Up to now, those who have expected the imminent end of the world have been disappointed while whose who have reverently engaged the challenges of their times have very likely found greater satisfaction. In any event, it is surely possible that the coming of the third millennium will lead to an upsurge in religious faith—both new and traditional—which would change current attitudes toward the future'. Hine, like Gerjouy, might have a better idea of how widespread this trend could be if he had access to quantitative tools to analyze the future of religion.

Historically, however, many books on the future treat religion as a central tenet. One such work is Edward Bellamy's *Looking backward, 2000-1887* which was published in 1887. In ten years it had sold nearly one million copies in England and America, and had been translated into German, French, Russian, Italian, Arabic, Bulgarian, and several other languages. Bellamy was the son of a Baptist clergyman and one of his paternal ancestors was Dr. Joseph Bellamy, a distinguished theologian of revolutionary days, and a friend of Jonathan Edwards. Thus his social views were strongly anti-materialistic and spiritual.

His *Looking backward* grew out of his conviction that a true Christian response to the commands of Christ would best be worked out in a socialist fashion. This is reflected in the following passage where the host Dr. Leete explains to the visitor to the year 2000 from 1887, Mr. West, how all people are cared for by a benevolent government. 'As soon as the nation became the sole producer of all sorts of commodities, there was no need of exchanges between individuals that they might get what they required. Everything was procurable from one source, and nothing could be procured anywhere else. A system of direct distribution from the national storehouses took the place of trade, and for this money was unnecessary'. Later, when listening to a sermon over the 'air waves', West is stunned to hear that man's response to God has lifted the human race from wars, inequality, and a litany of human woes.

Bellamy's future then is one in which religion—specifically Christianity—has transformed mankind into a benevolent global community. Bellamy was criticized for talking in terms of only 50 years to accomplish this great feat. One reviewer suggested the figure should have been 75 centuries! Bellamy answered the review in 1888 with the following words 'True and humane man and women, of every degree, are in a mood of exasperation, verging on absolute revolt, against social conditions that reduce life to a brutal struggle for existence, mock every dictate of ethics and religion, and render well-nigh futile the efforts of philanthropy...Our children will surely see it, and we, too, are already men and women, if we deserve it by our faith and by our works' (Letter to the editor, *Boston transcript*, 1988).

The weakness of Bellamy's scenario is best described by O'Neill (1981), who saw the tendency in most future scenario writing to overestimate social changes while underestimating technological ones. Bellamy defends a rather simple socialist transition of mankind into global benevolence while describing technological changes at most a decade or two in the future (from the vantage point of 1887). This weakness is almost universal and is at the heart of most utopian visions, whether they are religious or humanist in perspective.

Hiley H. Ward set out a scenario of religion in the 22nd century in his 1975 work *Religion 2101 A.D.* Ward, sets forth the premise that 'Christianity is likely to be around for a long time to come in some form.' He then surveys the current literature on futurism drawing out its implications for religion in the future with such interesting applications as telepathic sermons, God as supermachine, and pluralistic Christianity. But even Ward cannot resist the temptation to mutate the Christianity of the future so badly as to be unrecognizable within a little over a century. 'Pewsitters' (20th century style mainline Christians) are old-fashioned simpletons, replaced by the Church of the Celebration of the Holy World Cosmos, a synthesis of Christianity, pantheism, Hinduism, and technology. After 2000 years of unbroken orthodox use, the Lord's Prayer becomes 'Our Fathers which are in heavens, hallowed be thy names. Thy kingdoms come, Thy wills be done in earths, as they are in heavens. Give us these days our daily breads. And forgive us our debts, as we forgive our debtors. And lead us not into temptations, but deliver us from evils, For thine are the kingdoms, and the powers and the glories, eon unto eon.' Ward's point is that we never can be too sure about what forms religion will take in the future.

L.E. Browne, writing in the *International review of missions* in 1949, ventured his opinion under the title 'The religion of the world in AD 3000'. Browne predicts the extinction of not only polytheism (including Hinduism) but of all major religions except Christianity. He goes on to say the only competitor to Christianity will be materialism, which is essentially a belief that man doesn't need God or ethics. Browne did not utilize any quantitative methods to produce this scenario. It represents more of a quantum leap in envisioning the future of religion. Even so, if he had thought through the quantitative implications of the disappearance of Islam, Hinduism, Buddhism, and Judaism over time he might have been more cautious in his predictions. Using the year 3000 for his commentary absolved him of some of this responsibility—anything can happen in 1050 years.

## *THE MANY FUTURES OF CHRISTIANITY*

If anyone should have something to say about the future it should be Christians. 'Christianity is a religion turned towards the future, moving towards the parousia, towards the final meeting with the Lord' (Ramsey and Suenens 1970:17). Christians ought to have a great deal to say about not only the future of Christianity, but the future of mankind. Unfortunately, the vast majority of Christian books on the future only use the future as a literary tool to focus attention on the present situation and what must be done.

Most books on the future of Christianity are written by theologians. These usually involve a look forward from some pivotal moment in Christian history, such as Karl Rahner's look forward from Vatican II in *The Christian of the future*. Rahner describes changes that can be expected in theological emphases and structure in Catholicism. Though he describes the Christian of the future as one who 'will not anxiously scan statistics to see whether the Church is really the biggest ideological organization or not, or whether it is growing proportionately quicker or slower than world population,' Rahner delves into some impressions of the relative percentages of Christians in the world. He evidently feels that it is important to understand the situation but not so important to quantify it.

Perhaps the theologian to write most seriously and consistently on the future is German Catholic Hans Küng. His major treatise *Theology for the Third Millennium* deals with a paradigm shift which represents a narrowing of the perceived chasm between the various Christian traditions (particularly Catholicism, Orthodoxy, and Protestantism). Christianity in the future need not be polarized as differences in theology are often artificially accentuated by the political and structural context. The new paradigm is an ecumenical one, but without sacrificing distinctives of faith and tradition.

Though Kenneth Cragg strongly disagreed that 'the secular impact will soon rob creed and worship of all but antiquarian interest before the march of secularized technology' (1968:65) he nonetheless saw Christianity in decline. 'In so far as religions have their relative importance determined by numbers, Christianity is rapidly losing ground, dwindling from perhaps a third of humanity in the nineteen-fifties to less than a fifth three decades hence when the millennium turns'.

### *The minority view*

A common view of the future of Christianity is that of a small minority in an ocean of humanity. Catholic missiologist Louis Luzbetak states 'The signs of the times tell us that no matter how great the effort made to evangelize the world—and evangelization must continue—Christians will, according to God's own design, always remain but a "little flock"' (1987:132). Rahner states, 'At that future date there will be Christian or Catholic communities all over the world, though not evenly distributed. Everywhere they will be a little flock, because mankind grows quicker than Christendom...the Christians will form only a relatively small minority...that future Christian will be living as a member of a little flock in an immeasurably vast world of non-Christians' (1967:85, 78-79, 82). Note also Wilbert R. Shenk's assertion (1987) that 'The church of the future will be a minority church in most parts of the world.' David Bosch (1980) noted that the world was 36% Christian in 1900, had dropped off th 26 percent in 1980, and would decline to 16% by AD 2000. Bosch and some of the others mentioned above overestimated the influence of secularization or had different interpretations of how Christians should be counted. The methodology developed and applied in this study intends to overcome these pitfalls by using a consistent definition of Christianity and by using more recent data on the impact of secularization.

### *Prophecy and eschatology*

Another important subject within the broader rubric of the future of Christianity is that of eschatology—the study of the last things. Since the beginnings of Christianity many Christians have made predictions of one kind or another. 'Out of the Old Testament's 23,210 verses, 6,641 verses contain prophetic information about the future. That means more than 28 percent of the entire Old Testament is concerned with prophecy. In the New Testament there are 7,914 verses, and 1,711 of them also contain predictive material. So, for the entire Bible's 31,124 verses, 8,352 of them contain prophecy' (Ankerberg and Weldon 1991:13). In Acts 11:28 a prophet named Agabus accurately predicted that a severe famine would spread over the entire Roman world. But a whole string of others have seen a different future: the apocalypse, the end of the world, the final judgment—and have boldly set dates for them. While many of these took place in Christian history, a significant number of these have taken place in the last two or three decades. William Alnor carefully chronicles these in *Soothsayers of the Second Advent* 1990.)

A more substantial study is that of Paul Boyer, *When time shall be no more: prophecy belief in modern American culture* (1992). Boyer thoroughly researches the origins of prophecy in antiquity, particularly early Jewish and Christian apocalyptic writings. the development and interpretation of these is then traced up through the modern period. The bulk of Boyer's emphasis is on American culture and the effect that belief in prophecy has had on the Cold War. But he cites much evidence in the continuing belief in prophecy in the post-Cold War era. This aspect of future thinking among Christians remains strong.

In addition, Tom Sine (1987) offers compelling evidence that American Christians in particular often have a 'seriously schizophrenic vision of the future'. On one side, there is biblically-based pessimism about where the world is headed with the hope that the Lord will deliver souls in the end. On the other hand, these same Christians live in hope of the American dream—of financial success and material prosperity.

A far more prolific genre of prophecy goes beyond date setting to that of describing the future. The Book of Isaiah from the Old Testament and The Revelation of John both fit this category. They describe a future scenario and give clues as to when it might occur but no specific dates are set. Using a play on George Orwell's *1984*, Larry Poland chooses the year 2084 to describe in detail the millennial kingdom of God (1991). Three people from the present are transported to this future where they observe both kingdoms and are faced with which they will choose. This type of literature in Christianity is very common.

There are many appeals from theologians and missiologists for a fresh dose of eschatological urgency to better equip Christians for the future. For a recent example see Scherer (1991) where he pleads with Ecumenicals and Evangelicals alike to reemphasize eschatology to give church union and world mission new vigor. Evangelical theologian Peter Beyerhaus (1992) asserts that 'the future is a central perspective in the biblical message.' He is particularly concerned though how the future should be viewed from a theologically orthodox view of God's kingdom. He offers an in-depth analysis of how many different Christians currently view the future in their understanding of God's kingdom.

### *The Year 2000*

In *The coming-of-age of Christianity* (Marchant 1950) two top Christian scholars venture into our subject. Kenneth Scott Latourette, Yale historian, asked the question, Will Christianity win all men? Will it ultimately prevail? Latourette, as historian, reviews the waxing and waning of the world Christian movement and concludes with 'If in the brief nineteen and a half centuries since his birth Jesus Christ has had such a growing influence upon mankind, we might expect that in the course of another ten or twenty-five or hundred thousands years, still brief as compared with the total span of human life on this planet, all mankind will become not only professedly Christian but actually attain to 'the fullness of the stature of Christ'' (p. 132). But Latourette is cautious in this precise meaning because at some point human history will end as we know it and a new heaven and a new earth will descend. The big question is how much will be accomplished before that happens. We cannot know, says Latourette, but whether we experience recession or advance the net effect always takes us forward.

Ecumenical leader Henry Pitney Van Dusen (ibid) saw two possibilities for the future of Christianity—most specifically possible by the year 2000. First, the proclamation of the gospel to every living creature. Second, the union of all the churches, excepting Roman Catholicism.

In a festschrift in honor of R. Pierce Beaver twenty years later, W. Richey Hogg sounds very much like Van Dusen. Hogg outlines the symbiotic nature of the Ecumenical movement and the world mission movement. He sees the 30 years leading up to the year 2000 as a prime opportunity for church union and world evangelization (Danker and Kang 1971).

### *Summary*

In conclusion, the reader of literature on the future of religion is confronted with a dizzying range of opinions on what might be expected. Writing from a wide range of disciplines, scholars, as well as economists, environmentalists, science fiction writers and others, paint a future for religion ranging from its extinction to it central role for human survival. Everyone can't be right and yet no quantitative tools have yet been utilized to further narrow down the options or to evaluate existing opinions.

In the midst of this confusion, it would seem natural that Christian scholars, theologians, and authors should be able to shed light on the future—which plays a central role in the Christian faith. But eschatological and non-eschatological views put forth by Christians nearly match the range of opinions offered by secular or non-Christian authors. Thus, a quantitative methodology would be equally helpful to Christians interested in the future of Christianity and world religions.

## *STATISTICAL PROJECTIONS OF RELIGIONS*

The opportunity to project the future of religious affiliation has presented itself for the first time with the recent availability of four publications and two databases. Foundational demographic data for every country in the world are available for the years 1950-2050 through the United Nations Demographic Database (see United Nations, 1999). Data on religions and Christianity for every country are available through the World Evangelization Database. Data beyond 2050 for the world's nine major continental areas are available for the first time in the UN's publication *Long-range world population projections: two centuries of population growth, 1950-2150* (1992).

### *Stage One*

Christian data are more complete globally than data on other religions. This data is presented in Country

Tables 2 in *WCE* Part 4 "Countries" for each of the world's 238 countries. Statistics on the world's 33,000 denominations are given for 1970 and 1995 (and projected to AD 2025 on *WCD*).

### Stage Two

But Christian data must be presented in the total context of other religions and demographic data. This is done in Tables 1 for each country in *WCE* Part 4 "Countries". Here one finds a breakdown of the population into all of its constituent pieces–religious and nonreligious for the years 1900, 1970, 1990, 1995, 2000 and 2025 (2050 is added on *WCD*). The growth rates from 1990-2000 of all categories are presented here as well. This gives one the basis for future projections. Thus, if evidence exists that the Christian church is in decline in a particular country, then the percentage to be matched to that country at a future date will be lowered to an appropriate level. With adjustments made to religious and nonreligious populations in each country a second stage of analysis is added. Now one can view the effects demographic change and change in religious adherence. The results of this method are shown below in Table 29–6.

### Stage Three

Our summary table includes all religions by country and is thus suited perfectly for demographic manipulation. Analysis of the country tables begins by using the AD 2000 figures as a base from which to project all future tables (to 2200) using only demographic tools.

Thus, the country and regional totals reflect United Nations projections while all religious percentages within a country region remain unchanged. This allows us to examine how demographic growth or decline alone within a particular country or region affects the global total. This yields remarkable insights into what we can expect from the most consistent source of growth and decline of religious and nonreligious adherence—births and deaths. The results are shown below for columns labeled 'Demographic from 2000' for the years 2025, 2050, 2100, and 2200. This amounts to our third stage of analysis of the future of religion.

### Stage Four

The fourth stage allows us to use results from our country-by-country analysis to update the trends to 2200. From this base, more reasonable future projections for religions can be made. The results are presented below in columns labeled 'Adjusted from 2000 or 2050'. The adjustments yield what could be considered our most likely scenario.

### Stage Five

Using either the demographic projections or the adjusted scenarios, one can now introduce explicit assumptions to produce alternative scenarios. Two such scenarios are presented below, both starting from the 2050 'adjusted' figures. First the 'Muslim revival' scenario assumes that in the six regions of the world Muslims gain 10% of the population by 2100 and 10% more by 2200. The losers in each case are the major-

ity religions (or nonreligious). Under this scenario, Muslims would grow to over 4.2 billion or 38% of the world's population by AD 2200.

Second, the 'nonreligious' scenario assumes that secularization hits the world's two largest religions, Christianity and Islam, very hard. By 2100 10% of Christians and 10% of Muslims have defected. Another 10% defect by AD 2200. From a high of 60% in AD 2050, these two religions plummet to only 43% of the world's population by 2200.

The table below illustrates how a quantitative methodology for projecting the future of religion can produce multiple scenarios. In each case the assumptions are explicit and can be examined at the level of 238 countries (1900-2050) or 6 major regions (2050-2200). UN projections are updated every two years and numerous studies on religious affiliation are published every year. The method described here is flexible enough to utilize new demographic and religious information. Projections five years from now could look quite different.

### Summary

A secondary side effect of this study is the evidence it provides for the quantitative resiliency of religion over the next two hundred years. Purely demographic changes do not show a massive decline in religious adherence. The onus would be on the person putting forth such a statement to prove that massive defections from religious adherence represent a plausible assumption. At present they do not.

### Table 29–6. Scenarios for adherents of world religions, AD 1900-AD 2200.

| | 1900 | % | 1950 | % | 1970 | % | 1990 | % | 2000 | % |
|---|---|---|---|---|---|---|---|---|---|---|
| Christians | 558,131,000 | 34.5% | 849,352,000 | 33.7% | 1,236,314,000 | 33.4% | 1,747,462,000 | 33.2% | 1,999,564,000 | 33.0% |
| Muslims | 199,941,000 | 12.3% | 349,295,000 | 13.9% | 553,568,000 | 15.0% | 962,357,000 | 18.3% | 1,188,243,000 | 19.6% |
| Nonreligious | 3,024,000 | 0.2% | 332,170,000 | 13.2% | 532,116,000 | 14.4% | 707,118,000 | 13.4% | 768,159,000 | 15.0% |
| Hindus | 203,003,000 | 12.5% | 314,269,000 | 12.5% | 462,598,000 | 12.5% | 685,999,000 | 13.0% | 811,336,000 | 13.4% |
| Chinese folk-religionists | 380,006,000 | 23.5% | 208,865,000 | 8.3% | 231,865,000 | 6.3% | 347,651,000 | 6.6% | 384,807,000 | 6.4% |
| Buddhists | 127,077,000 | 7.8% | 171,118,000 | 6.8% | 233,424,000 | 6.3% | 323,107,000 | 6.1% | 359,982,000 | 5.9% |
| Ethnoreligionists | 117,559,000 | 6.6% | 138,229,000 | 5.5% | 160,278,000 | 4.3% | 200,035,000 | 3.8% | 228,367,000 | 3.8% |
| Atheists | 226,000 | 0.0% | 99,658,000 | 4.0% | 165,400,000 | 4.5% | 145,719,000 | 2.8% | 150,090,000 | 2.5% |
| New-Religionists | 5,910,000 | 0.4% | 27,379,000 | 1.1% | 77,762,000 | 2.1% | 92,396,000 | 1.8% | 102,356,000 | 1.7% |
| Sikhs | 2,962,000 | 0.2% | 6,515,000 | 0.3% | 10,618,000 | 0.3% | 19,332,000 | 0.4% | 23,258,000 | 0.4% |
| Jews | 12,292,000 | 0.8% | 11,641,000 | 0.5% | 14,763,000 | 0.4% | 13,189,000 | 0.3% | 14,434,000 | 0.2% |
| Spiritists | 269,000 | 0.7% | 3,558,000 | 0.1% | 4,603,000 | 0.1% | 10,155,000 | 0.2% | 12,334,000 | 0.2% |
| Baha'is | 10,000 | 0.0% | 251,000 | 0.0% | 2,657,000 | 0.1% | 5,672,000 | 0.1% | 7,106,000 | 0.1% |
| Confucians | 640,000 | 0.0% | 1,752,000 | 0.1% | 4,759,000 | 0.1% | 5,856,000 | 0.1% | 6,299,000 | 0.1% |
| Jains | 1,323,000 | 0.1% | 1,871,000 | 0.1% | 2,618,000 | 0.1% | 3,868,000 | 0.1% | 4,218,000 | 0.1% |
| Shintoists | 6,720,000 | 0.4% | 3,519,000 | 0.1% | 4,175,000 | 0.1% | 3,082,000 | 0.1% | 2,762,000 | 0.1% |
| Other religionists | 533,000 | 0.1% | 2,053,000 | 0.1% | 2,630,000 | 0.1% | 5,323,000 | 0.1% | 6,264,000 | 0.1% |
| **Total population** | **1,619,626,000** | **100.0%** | **2,516,443,000** | **100.0%** | **3,696,148,000** | **100.0%** | **5,266,442,000** | **100.0%** | **6,055,049,000** | **100.0%** |

| | Demographic from 2000 | | Adjusted from 2000 | | Demographic from 2000 | | Adjusted from 2000 | | Demographic from 2000 | |
|---|---|---|---|---|---|---|---|---|---|---|
| | 2025 | % | 2025 | % | 2050 | % | 2050 | % | 2100 | % |
| Christians | 2,535,806,000 | 32.4% | 2,616,670,000 | 33.4% | 2,894,874,000 | 32.5% | 3,051,564,000 | 34.3% | 3,379,108,000 | 32.4% |
| Muslims | 1,768,059,000 | 22.6% | 1,784,876,000 | 22.8% | 2,211,838,000 | 24.8% | 2,229,282,000 | 25.0% | 2,649,967,000 | 25.4% |
| Nonreligious | 878,359,000 | 11.2% | 875,121,000 | 11.2% | 881,809,000 | 9.9% | 887,995,000 | 10.0% | 960,518,000 | 9.2% |
| Hindus | 1,071,613,000 | 13.7% | 1,049,231,000 | 13.4% | 1,237,325,000 | 13.9% | 1,175,298,000 | 13.2% | 1,313,176,000 | 12.6% |
| Chinese folk-religionists | 447,832,000 | 5.7% | 448,843,000 | 5.7% | 449,872,000 | 5.1% | 454,333,000 | 5.1% | 484,685,000 | 4.7% |
| Buddhists | 425,502,000 | 5.4% | 418,345,000 | 5.3% | 444,091,000 | 5.0% | 424,607,000 | 4.8% | 610,625,000 | 5.9% |
| Ethnoreligionists | 327,782,000 | 4.2% | 277,247,000 | 3.5% | 404,707,000 | 4.5% | 303,599,000 | 3.4% | 527,625,000 | 5.0% |
| Atheists | 170,982,000 | 2.2% | 159,544,000 | 2.0% | 171,199,000 | 1.9% | 169,150,000 | 1.9% | 188,692,000 | 1.8% |
| New-Religionists | 119,929,000 | 1.5% | 114,720,000 | 1.5% | 126,686,000 | 1.4% | 118,845,000 | 1.3% | 195,395,000 | 1.9% |
| Sikhs | 30,450,000 | 0.4% | 31,378,000 | 0.4% | 34,948,000 | 0.4% | 37,059,000 | 0.4% | 36,924,000 | 0.4% |
| Jews | 17,484,000 | 0.2% | 16,053,000 | 0.2% | 19,057,000 | 0.2% | 16,695,000 | 0.2% | 21,141,000 | 0.2% |
| Spiritists | 15,474,000 | 0.2% | 16,212,000 | 0.2% | 17,126,000 | 0.2% | 20,709,000 | 0.2% | 20,939,000 | 0.2% |
| Baha'is | 9,911,000 | 0.1% | 12,062,000 | 0.2% | 12,062,000 | 0.1% | 18,001,000 | 0.2% | 14,747,000 | 0.1% |
| Confucians | 7,152,000 | 0.1% | 6,818,000 | 0.1% | 7,104,000 | 0.1% | 6,953,000 | 0.1% | 12,069,000 | 0.1% |
| Jains | 5,561,000 | 0.1% | 6,116,000 | 0.1% | 6,400,000 | 0.1% | 6,733,000 | 0.1% | 6,846,000 | 0.1% |
| Shintoists | 2,654,000 | 0.0% | 3,066,000 | 0.1% | 2,315,000 | 0.0% | 1,655,000 | 0.0% | 5,264,000 | 0.1% |
| Other religionists | 7,900,000 | 0.1% | 7,900,000 | 0.1% | 9,500,000 | 0.1% | 9,500,000 | 0.1% | 1,401,000 | 0.0% |
| **Total population** | **7,823,703,000** | **100.0%** | **7,823,703,000** | **100.0%** | **8,909,095,000** | **100.0%** | **8,909,095,000** | **100.0%** | **10,414,000,000** | **100.0%** |

| | Adjusted from 2050 | | Demographic from 2000 | | Adjusted from 2050 | | Muslim revival | | Nonreligious | |
|---|---|---|---|---|---|---|---|---|---|---|
| | 2100 | % | 2200 | % | 2200 | % | 2200 | % | 2200 | % |
| Christians | 3,800,099,000 | 36.5% | 3,611,370,000 | 32.2% | 4,347,378,000 | 38.8% | 3,456,912,000 | 30.9% | 2,852,314,000 | 25.5% |
| Muslims | 2,874,540,000 | 27.6% | 2,876,182,000 | 25.7% | 3,065,179,000 | 27.4% | 4,241,533,000 | 37.9% | 2,011,064,000 | 18.0% |
| Nonreligious | 959,818,000 | 9.2% | 1,030,937,000 | 9.2% | 1,212,302,000 | 10.8% | 1,154,091,000 | 10.3% | 3,761,050,000 | 33.6% |
| Hindus | 1,153,978,000 | 11.1% | 1,398,740,000 | 12.5% | 952,234,000 | 8.5% | 776,437,000 | 6.9% | 952,234,000 | 8.5% |
| Chinese folk-religionists | 475,183,000 | 4.6% | 522,974,000 | 4.7% | 442,190,000 | 4.0% | 442,190,000 | 4.0% | 442,190,000 | 4.0% |
| Buddhists | 397,100,000 | 3.8% | 659,806,000 | 5.9% | 344,080,000 | 3.1% | 294,080,000 | 2.6% | 344,080,000 | 3.1% |
| Ethnoreligionists | 323,995,000 | 3.1% | 573,836,000 | 5.1% | 369,920,000 | 3.3% | 369,920,000 | 3.3% | 369,920,000 | 3.3% |
| Atheists | 190,527,000 | 1.8% | 202,668,000 | 1.8% | 206,000,000 | 1.8% | 206,000,000 | 1.8% | 206,000,000 | 1.8% |
| New-Religionists | 106,911,000 | 1.0% | 211,315,000 | 1.9% | 67,336,000 | 0.6% | 67,336,000 | 0.6% | 67,336,000 | 0.6% |
| Sikhs | 40,414,000 | 0.4% | 39,273,000 | 0.4% | 42,496,000 | 0.4% | 42,496,000 | 0.4% | 42,496,000 | 0.4% |
| Jews | 15,828,000 | 0.2% | 22,456,000 | 0.2% | 11,673,000 | 0.1% | 11,673,000 | 0.1% | 11,673,000 | 0.1% |
| Spiritists | 27,435,000 | 0.3% | 21,997,000 | 0.2% | 40,059,000 | 0.4% | 40,059,000 | 0.4% | 40,059,000 | 0.4% |
| Baha'is | 33,091,000 | 0.3% | 15,892,000 | 0.1% | 81,538,000 | 0.7% | 81,538,000 | 0.7% | 81,538,000 | 0.7% |
| Confucians | 6,039,000 | 0.1% | 13,056,000 | 0.1% | 3,495,000 | 0.0% | 3,495,000 | 0.0% | 3,495,000 | 0.0% |
| Jains | 6,658,000 | 0.1% | 7,290,000 | 0.1% | 8,345,000 | 0.1% | 8,345,000 | 0.1% | 8,345,000 | 0.1% |
| Shintoists | 890,000 | 0.0% | 5,692,000 | 0.1% | 388,000 | 0.0% | 388,000 | 0.0% | 388,000 | 0.0% |
| Other religionists | 2,809,000 | 0.0% | 1,478,000 | 0.0% | 5,481,000 | 0.1% | 5,481,000 | 0.1% | 5,481,000 | 0.1% |
| **Total population** | **10,414,000,000** | **100.0%** | **11,200,000,000** | **100.0%** | **11,200,000,000** | **100.0%** | **11,200,000,000** | **100.0%** | **11,200,000,000** | **100.0%** |

Part 30

# GLOSSARY

Quick-reference definitions of key variables, technical terms, and neologisms

*Glossary: a list of difficult, technical, or foreign terms with definitions or translations.*
—Webster's New World dictionary of the American language, 1984

Being defined as a collection of 'unusual terms', 'technical terms', 'terms limited to special areas of knowledge', or a list of 'difficult words requiring explanation' (*Webster's Third new international dictionary*), this glossary is designed to offer brief, definitive definitions of all such terms, especially of neologisms and new usages occurring throughout this volume. Although all are terms in English usage, their counterparts at least in the world's 400 major lingua francas have to be continuously borne in mind.

# Quick-reference definitions of key variables, technical terms, and neologisms

## NEW AND UNUSUAL TERMS AND CONCEPTS EVOLVED IN THIS VOLUME

*Words in italics refer to each's own entry alphabetically (also shown by 'qv' or 'q.v.', quod vide, 'which see'). For a more detailed listing, see WCE Part 12 "Dictionary". Almost all these are English terms; for parallels in other languages, this survey defers to the World Bank of International Terms, WBIT (International Organization for Unification of Terminological Neologisms, IOUTN). See Z. Stoberski, The road to transnationalization of terminology, Warsaw (Poland), 1989. These specialists estimate that, largely due to advances in science and technology and to the world's 70,000 periodicals, there are now 2.7 million technical terms in use in the world's developed countries; and every month 300 more neologisms are created.*

---

**access.** This variable measures the degree to which speakers of a language can read the Scriptures in a language they understand. There are 2 varieties: (1) *direct* access to Scripture is available when a translation has been made into a people's mother tongue; and (2) *indirect* access to Scripture is available when *near-scripture* (near-Bible, near-NT, etc) exists (translation in a language within the same cluster/outer language as the people's mother tongue).

**action point.** A sticking point or aspect holding up world evangelization which requires definite, specific action in order to overcome it.

**adequacy.** The quality or state of sufficiency of resources or activities to meet prior standards or promises, with special reference to meeting stated goals published by religious bodies.

**adherents.** *Followers*, supporters, members, believers, devotees of a religion.

**adult.** A person who is 15 years old or above.

**advocacy.** The process of championing a particular *unevangelized* population *segment*, especially if voiceless or neglected, and continually seeking opportunities to present its case for a larger share of Christian resources.

**affiliated.** *Followers* of a religion enrolled and known to its leadership, usually with names written on rolls.

**affiliated Christians.** Church members: all persons belonging to or connected with organized churches, whose names are inscribed, written or entered on the churches' books, records, or rolls.

**agencies-in-peoples.** A measure of the widespread distribution of mission agencies across the world which quantifies one agency working in 50 peoples as 50 of these units.

**agnostics.** Persons who have no religion or do not believe in God but not militantly so.

**alien Christian scale.** Referring to a a specific people or other segment, this is a computed scale from 0-10 measuring culturally alien (non-indigenous) Christian and evangelistic influence on the people by estimating the number of Christians from other cultures who reside on its territory.

**alien Christians.** Christians who reside in or work on the territory of a different culture.

**alternate future.** A range of 2 or more future *scenarios* depicting possible future developments by means of trends and *statistics*, ranging from optimistic to pessimistic and covering all possible eventualities.

**apostle.** A Christian worker sent out on a special, primary, or initiatory mission among non-Christians.

**apostolate.** The office, duties, or period of activity of an apostle, or apostles, or of the whole body of the church in its mission to the world.

**Apostolatus Copiae.** (Latin: official translation into English: *Workforce for the Apostolate*). In Roman Catholic usage, the main statistical category for counting personnel (bishops, priests, deacons, monks, nuns, sisters, layworkers, catechists).

**artificial languages.** International languages created by linguists: Volapuk, Esperanto, Ido, Occidental, Novial, Interlingua. None have caught on.

**astrology.** A pseudo-science claiming to foretell the future by studying supposed influence of moon, planets, and stars on human affairs.

**atheists.** Militantly anti-religious or anti-Christian agnostics, secularists, or marxists.

**audio gospel.** A cassette or tape or recording of a complete Gospel.

**audio scriptures.** *Portions* (gospels) or *selections* (verses) on cassette, tape, or recording.

**autoglossonym.** Name for a people's own language as used by the people themselves in their own language; often with prefix or suffix meaning 'the language of'.

**autonym.** Indigenous or own name for a language; *autoglossonym*.

**baptized, the.** *Followers* of Christianity who have undergone the formality or ceremony of baptism.

**beachhead.** The initial planting of indigenous fellowships in an otherwise *unreached* people or *unevangelized* population segment.

**believers.** Term in wide use in secularized or nonreligious societies or regimes for describing *followers* of religion.

**Bible.** This term is always used to describe only the whole or complete Bible of 66 Books (sometimes plus Apocrypha).

**Bibles in use.** Number of Bibles in place in a country or population, allowing for the constant loss of copies due to wear and tear or other forms of attrition.

**biblioglossonym.** The name chosen by a Bible society by which a translation of the Bible, or part of it, is formally known; often the anglicized form (e.g. French, German, Russian), often the speakers' own *autoglossonym* (français, deutsch, russki).

**bibliometrics.** The science of measurement of books, libraries, cataloguing, publishing, use of books, analysis, future usage.

**bilinguals.** Persons speaking or understanding a second language in addition to their own mother tongue.

**billion.** 1,000 millions (American usage; British, French, and German usage is a million millions).

**billionaire.** An individual (or occasionally a family) worth one *billion* USA dollars or over.

**bishop.** Christian clergyman having authority over a wide geographic area.

**bite-sized piece.** Colloquial term for manageable population *segments* which, because of either their homogeneity or their moderate size, are capable of being monitored by a single nonresidential missionary or couple.

**bivocational.** Adjective describing a tentmaker or missionary with the dual vocation of (a) a secular profession in a restricted-access country, undertaken in order to exercise (b) part-time Christian *witness* or service or church planting.

**black money.** Banked profits directly from criminal enterprise, unlaundered or only partially-laundered.

**Book.** Any one of the 39 distinct books constituting the Christian Bible, or any set of them, which has been translated whole (at least one complete book), published, and distributed in a language; also termed a *scripture*, or a *portion* or a *gospel*; capitalized with a 'B' to distinguish it from other varieties of book, and as a parallel to 'Bible', 'Testament'.

**book titles.** Term used to refer to distinct and separate books, as in a library or bookstore, to avoid misunderstanding with copies or print runs of the same book.

**bridge people.** A variety of *people group* that can be regarded as a bridge for evangelistic ministry toward an otherwise unreachable or inaccessible target segment.

**brother.** A lay member of a men's religious order; or more loosely, a male coreligionist.

**cargo cults.** Religious movements in Oceania based on prophecies that if appropriate religious rites are performed, God will send ships and aircraft filled with cargo and goods.

**catechist.** A church worker who instructs catechumens in the fundamentals of the Christian faith before baptism.

**catechumen.** A non-member of a church receiving instruction in Christian doctrine, ethics, and morality, prior to admission into the church through baptism.

**Catholic Charismatics.** Roman Catholics who have come into an experience of baptism or renewal in the Holy Spirit.

**Catholic Evangelicals.** Roman Catholics who call themselves also by the term *Evangelicals*, and regard themselves as in the national or global community of Evangelicals and their alliances and fellowships.

**catholicos.** Leading *bishop* or *patriarch* of an Orthodox church or denomination.

**census.** A large-scale formal act of counting or evaluating of people and property.

**chain.** A second layer of close language relationships in the *linguasphere*.

**chances.** Used in the numerical analysis of distinct occasions or opportunities for persons to become disciples of Christ; synonymous with offers, invitations.

**charismatic.** A religious person or group or movement stressing direct divine inspiration, glossolalia, faith healing and similar ministries.

**Charismatic.** Used here to refer to the organized Charismatic Renewal within the nonpentecostal mainline denominations.

**Charismatics.** Baptized members affiliated to nonpentecostal denominations who have entered into the experience of being filled with the Holy Spirit; the Second Wave of the Pentecostal/Charismatic/Neocharismatic Renewal.

**children.** Term describing all persons under 15 years old, though often a distinction is made between infants (0-5 years old) and children proper, 5-14 years old.

**Christian.** Followers of Jesus Christ as Lord, of all kinds, all traditions and confessions, and all degrees of commitment.

**Christian safety index.** An index, 0-100, with 100 as the safest, measuring the relative safety of Christians living in a particular country. The index measures a country's human suffering, murder rate, and religious liberty.

**Christian World.** In the *3-tier schema*, this is *World C*, consisting of all who individually are *Christians*.

**Christian world communion.** Formerly termed a world confessional family, now a standard term for any *communion* of Christian denominations.

**Christians ever.** Total number of Christians who have ever lived, computed as (a) live Christians (those alive today), plus (b) dead Christians who lived at earlier times.

**Christopagans.** Roman Catholics of Latin background, chiefly in Latin America, who combine traditional pre-Columbian ethnoreligion with popular Roman Catholic religiosity (images, shamans, incense, idols, nomenclature).

**clandestine religion.** See *hidden religion*.

**Classical Pentecostals.** Denominational Pentecostals of North American or European origin founded before the year 1945, of 2 types: Baptistic Pentecostals, and Holiness Pentecostals, both being Trinitarian.

**clergy.** *Followers* of a religion who become ordained for religious services; ministers, pastors, priests, rabbis, bishops, et alii.

**clerical order.** A large-order/congregation/institute/society of full-time ordained workers (clergy, monks, brothers, nuns), often functioning as itself a separate autonomous religion.

**closed country.** A country whose government or regime has closed it to some major form or forms of Christian ministry from outside, usually resident foreign missionaries, visiting evangelists, or freely distributed *scriptures*, Christian literature, tapes or videos or films, or other Christian influences from outside.

**closed-country ministry.** Legal or illegal modes of Christian mission and ministry, resident or *itinerant*, full-time or part-time, in countries otherwise closed to Christian activity.

**closing country.** A country still open to outside Christian influences but whose increasing restrictions suggest it may become closed within a few months or years.

**closure.** The concept that the mandate of the church for world mission can be completed in a measurable way by evangelizing or reaching all peoples on Earth; not effectively invoked unless attached to some sort of deadline, the usual one in the 1980s and 1990s being AD 2000.

**cluster.** *Language cluster* (qv). In religion, a grouping or family of related religions. *Culture cluster* is a synonym for *ethnocultural family*.

**colporteur.** An itinerant evangelist whose main function is the sale and dissemination of scripture copies; usually in the employ of a Bible society.

**communion.** A family of religions or denominations with many common ties and features; often called a confession, or world confessional family.

**comparative demographic evangelization.** An index of the extent of evangelization among a population or population *segment*, as measured by a scale of 270 variables or indicators, and summed up as *E%*, the percentage of persons who have become evangelized.

**complete Bibles.** Copies of the whole Bible with 66 Books (sometimes plus Apocrypha).

**Conciliar Evangelicals.** *Evangelicals* who are members of non-Evangelical denominations or churches that have extensive conciliar relationships.

**confession.** In ecclesiastical demography, any large communion or ecclesiastical tradition tracing its origins to a formal event, historic creed or confession.

**congregation.** (1) A local church or grouping of worshipers. (2) A religious order, society, or institute (mainly Roman Catholic usage).

**contact.** The degree of contact between (a) a religion and (b) organized Christianity and its world mission.

**continent.** Defined by United Nations as one of 6 Major Areas/Regions/Macroregions.

**continental area.** UN definition of continent, now renamed *major area*.

**convergency.** A concept describing the unstructured way in which the *world evangelization* thrusts of 7 major ecclesiastical traditions (Roman Catholic, Orthodox, Ecumenical, Evangelical, Catholic Charismatic, Pentecostal/Charismatic, and Fundamentalist) have converged since 1970 in stated aims, goals, terminology, theology, missiology, publications, periodicals, activities, cooperation, and programs, as a result of lay pressures and initiatives, and in many cases despite opposition from their own leaders.

**conversion.**  A change in a person's allegiance or membership in one religion to allegiance or membership in another.

**converts.**  Persons who have become *followers* of a religion, leaving their former religion or nonreligion.

**cosmoreligion.**  A universal (non-local) religion open to all, with over 200 million adherents.

**cost-effectiveness.**  As a comparative measure, the total cost, to Christians in a country, of baptizing one person.

**country.**  A term covering both (a) sovereign nations, and (b) nonsovereign territories (dependencies or colonies) which are not integral parts of larger parent nations.

**countrytrends.**  A shorthand term for all instruments, measuring devices, and measurements, country by country, of all varieties of variables and changes measured by churches and agencies in the pursuit of their global mission.

**covert evangelizers.**  Active Christians working anonymously or secretly.

**creole.**  A hybrid or *pijin* language which has now consolidated into a language with its own mother tongue speakers.

**cross-cultural missions scale.**  A computed scale from 0-16 measuring the influence of cross-cultural missionary presence and activity within a people or other *segment*.

**crypto-Christians.**  Secret believers, hidden Christians, usually known to churches but not to state or secular or non-Christian religious society.

**culture.**  A grouping of identical peoples in different countries all with the same total pattern of human behavior and its products.

**culture cluster.**  Termed here an *ethnocultural family*.

**culture net.**  Termed here a *local race*.

**culture world.**  Major 7-part culture classification variously defined as culture civilization, with its own characteristic culture worldview, and culture lifestyle, particularly noted for its stylized skin color or pigmentation, biogenetic pool, color pool.

**Cursillistas.**  Roman Catholics since 1949, and Protestants since 1970, who have attended and completed a short course or retreat under the movement Cursillos de Cristianidad; including many early leaders of the Catholic Charismatic Renewal.

**databasing.**  Use of a large collection of data (facts or figures) in a computer, organized so that it can be expanded, updated, and retrieved rapidly.

**datacasting.**  The regular broadcasting of large quantities of computerized data over the airwaves for automatic reception and use by computer users, mainly with microcomputers.

**denomination.**  Any agency consisting of a number of congregations or churches voluntarily aligning themselves with it. As a statistical unit in this survey, a 'denomination' always refers to one single country. Thus the Roman Catholic Church, although a single organization, is described here as consisting of 236 denominations in the world's 238 countries.

**Denominational Pentecostals.**  Church members belonging to *Pentecostal* denominations dating mainly from the first 2 decades of the 20th century and no later than 1945; also termed *First-Wavers*, or *Classical Pentecostals*.

**denominationalism.**  The promoting of centralized agencies exercising control or oversight over their recognized congregations.

**denominationalist.**  A person, executive, board, or committee who actively or aggressively promote denominationalism.

**density.**  The quantity or number of copies of the Christian Scriptures physically present in an area or population at a specified time; and its relationship to Christian definitions of *adequacy* and sufficiency.

**descriptor.**  Any describable property of a religious entity, characteristic, property, or data.

**dimension.**  Empirical characteristic of a measurement, size, magnitude, activity, quality, extent, scope, often assuming an explanatory function.

**direct access.**  *Access* (qv) to Scripture in one's own mother tongue.

**dirty money.**  Underground money, criminal profits, undeclared, unrecorded, untaxed, illegal monies of all kinds.

**disaffiliated.**  One-time church members who later repudiate that membership, and in countries allowing it, obtain legal separation from their church.

**disciple.**  A follower, learner, or adherent of a religious leader; especially of followers with personal, devoted relationship with Jesus Christ.

**disciple-opportunities.**  Chances or opportunities for individuals or groups to accept Christ as Savior and Lord.

**disciples.**  Followers, adherents attached to Jesus or another prominent leader.

**discipleship scale.**  A computed scale from 0-10 measuring the evangelistic influence of Christian discipleship in a population *segment* by estimating the number of disciples.

**distribution.**  In Bible society usage, term for measuring annual circulation or sale of scripture copies.

**distribution goal.**  Any announced deadline some years into the future for reaching a firm numerical goal or objective.

**doubly-affiliated Christians.**  Persons who are baptized members of 2 or more denominations at the same time.

**doubly-counted Catholics.**  Catholics counted as members of an older diocese or jurisdiction who also get counted again as members of a newer diocese when it is divided off from its parent diocese.

**doubly-counted religionists.**  Persons counted as belonging to 2 or more religions, hence counted twice in censuses.

**E.**  A computed estimate of the percentage of persons in a

particular population *segment* (world, country, people, city) who have become evangelized, by or at a particular date.

**e-mail.**  Electronic mail (qv).

**ecclesiastical crime.**  Criminal activity on the part of church officials; restricted in scope here to embezzlements of church funds by their top custodians (treasurers, presidents, et alii).

**ecclesiastical tradition.**  See *tradition*.

**education rate.**  Percentage of the school-age population (aged 5-24) who are enrolled in schools.

**electronic mail (e-mail).**  The regular sending and receiving of mail, letters, memos, and reports, over a computer network locally or worldwide.

**embezzlement.**  The stealing or taking by fraud of monies entrusted to one's care; in the present survey, specifically used for very large sums stolen by fraud by top custodians or treasurers.

**engagement.**  An initial stage or first step in the process of a foreign mission agency formally beginning or taking responsibility for ministry in a foreign country where hitherto it has had no work; often focused on a particular people group or other *segment*.

**enrolment.**  A formal procedure in which new church members have their names written on the church's membership rolls.

**enumeration.**  The process of listing all relevant items or names or, if very numerous, of counting them.

**ethnic non-users.**  Members of an ethnic group who do not use or understand its own mother-tongue language, preferring instead to learn and use a lingua franca.

**ethnocultural family.**  A larger cover name for a cultural collectivity, also termed a microrace, culture cluster, culture complex, ethnic family, single breeding population, culture family, a large grouping of specific cultures.

**ethnocultural people.**  A single people in a single country, being an ethnic or racial population or people group defined by its ethnic and cultural behavior and features.

**ethnolinguistic people.**  A distinct homogeneous ethnic or racial group within a single country, speaking its own language (one single mother tongue). A large people spread across 2, 3, 4, or several countries is treated here as being 2, 3, 4, or several distinct ethnolinguistic peoples.

**ethnolinguistics.**  The study of relations between ethnic terms and terminology and their language or linguistic usages.

**ethnometrics.**  The scientific measurement and study of the whole world of ethnicity and specific ethnic peoples.

**ethnoreligionists.**  Followers of a non-Christian or preChristian religion tied closely to a specific ethnic group, with membership restricted to that group; usually animists, polytheists, or shamanists. Older terminology: pagans, heathens, tribal religionists, traditional religionists.

**ethnosphere.**  The world with its populations and cultures seen in terms of its ethnicity.

**euangelizo (Greek).**  This central biblical concept has 140 synonyms in biblical Greek and 700 meanings in current English centered around the English transliteration *evangelize*.

**Evangelical Catholics.**  Baptized Roman Catholics who are also affiliated to, or attenders at, or members of, churches that the state (in Latin countries) in its censuses terms Evangelicos, Evangéliques, Evangelicals (but in English usage called Protestants)..

**evangelicals.**  Church members of evangelical conviction, involved in Christ's mission on Earth; synonymous with Great Commission Christians.

**Evangelicals.**  A subdivision mainly of Protestants consisting of all affiliated church members calling themselves Evangelicals, or all persons belonging to Evangelical congregations, churches or denominations; characterized by commitment to personal religion.

**evangelism.**  The church's organized activity of spreading the gospel, in circumstances it can control, in contrast to *witness* which is the normal term for the informal, spontaneous, unorganized sharing of their faith by individual Christians in circumstances they do not control.

**evangelism-hours.**  Amount of time in hours spent by evangelists among a specific population.

**evangelistics.**  The science of, or the scientific study of, the growth and expansion of Christianity.

**evangelization.**  (a) The whole process of spreading the good news of the Kingdom of God; (b) the extent to which the good news has been spread; (c) the extent of awareness of Christianity, Christ, and the gospel.

**evangelize.**  To spread the good news of Christ, with signs following, in both supernatural power and compassionate deed, to preach, to persuade, to call to faith in Christ; and 700 other meanings in English.

**Evangelized Non-Christian World.**  In the *3-tier schema*, this is *World B* which consists of all non-Christians who have nevertheless become evangelized.

**evangelized person.**  An individual who has had adequate opportunity or opportunities to hear the gospel and to respond to it, whether he responds positively or negatively.

**evangelizer.**  A Christian who is active regularly in *witness*, *evangelism*, and winning others to Christ.

**expert system.**  A computer software program that encapsulates the expertise of a recognized human expert in some domain of knowledge; consisting of a knowledge base (facts and heuristics or rules of thumb), an inference engine or reasoning system, and a natural-language user interface.

**exposure.**  Used as a measure of evangelism by numerous agencies (e.g. Campus Crusade for Christ): workers fill in statistical reports stating how many persons they have exposed to the gospel in a presentation over the last month or year.

**externally evangelized.**  Those persons in a people or population who have become evangelized as a result of persons or agencies or programs from outside their own

people or population.

**faithful, the.**  Term in wide use in Orthodox church circles to describe total membership or constituency.

**fax.**  Facsimile transmission of digitized pictures or text over telephone lines.

**First World.**  In the post World War II terminology originated with Charles de Gaulle, the Western world (Europe, Northern America) in contrast to the communist world and the *Third World*.

**First-Wavers.**  Denominational Pentecostals (Classical Pentecostals), members of mainline USA churches and their worldwide constituencies.

**folk-religionists.**  Adherents of local cults or religions, often rural, in which elements of major world religions are blended with folk beliefs and customs.

**follower.**  A *believer* in a particular religion, also synonymously termed an *adherent, practitioner, disciple, religionist*. In Christianity, follower is the preferred translation used by the Contemporary English Version for the NT Greek word *mathetes* (Latin, *discipulus*), synonym for 'disciple'; an adherent with a personal, devoted relationship to Christ.

**followers.**  Persons following a great leader's religious teachings; adherents, disciples, members, et alia.

**force for evangelism.**  The effective evangelizing nucleus in the church, made up of active *Great Commission Christians* who are engaged in some form of regular evangelizing.

**force for evangelization.**  The total of all practicing church members, whose practice has various direct and indirect influences on *evangelization*.

**foreign missionary.**  A full-time Christian worker who works in a country in which he or she is not a citizen but an alien.

**foreign missions.**  Christian outreach carried out in any other countries than where a sending church or mission is based.

**frontier missionary.**  A full-time foreign or cross-cultural missionary who works among an *unreached people*, an *unevangelized* population *segment* or in *World A*.

**frontier missions.**  Missionary work among the unreached or unevangelized peoples of the world, i.e. World A.

**frontier people.**  An alternate term for an *unreached* minipeople.

**futures.**  Futurists usually speak of possible futures in the plural when discussing the future of a particular entity or concept, posing a range of 2 or 3 *scenarios* of the future instead of a more risky single future prediction.

**futurescan.**  A wide-ranging glance or survey of possible or alternate future scenarios, from the Christian standpoint.

**futuristics (or, futurology).**  The professional study of the future employing a wide range of analytical tools and scientific procedures.

**generation.**  The average period (about 30 years) between the birth of one generational group on Earth, and that of the next; a 30-year period.

**geoatlas.**  A compilation or compendium of global maps highlighting Christian or religious variables

**geocodebook.**  Systematic presentation of all variables, abbreviations, and codes used in presentation and analysis of large volumes of Christian data.

**geocommission.**  A synonym for Christ's *Great Commission* to evangelize the world.

**geographic race.**  Subdivision of the 5 races of humankind, with each of the 13 geographic races being based on one continent or part thereof; also termed continental race, or regional race.

**geolinguistics.**  The new science of the spatial study of language use and distribution.

**geopersonnel.**  The status, study, and analysis of Christian workers of all kinds, at the global level.

**georenewal.**  Any religious or Christian renewal or revival movement that is significant at the global level.

**georeligion.**  A worldwide religion, or segment of a larger religion, that is global, universal, non-local, open to all as members.

**geoscriptures.**  Distribution and density of the Christian Scriptures at the global level.

**geostatistics.**  Statistics of the whole globe and its population, from the Christian viewpoint.

**geostatus.**  The overall situation and status of the globe's whole population, in particular from the religious and Christian standpoints.

**geostrategies.**  Concrete plans, usually publicized, to effect the evangelization of the world.

**geotrend.**  A long-term or short-term change in the global situation, demographic or religious.

**giganetwork.**  An electronic network linking a vast number of computers, around one billion or more. The number of general-purpose computers in the world reached 509 million by AD 2000 and will pass one billion by AD 2004. The number of Christian-owned and operated general-purpose computers is likely to reach one billion by AD 2008.

**global codes.**  Codes used in the analysis of Christianity and mission which have the same meaning across the whole area of statistical analysis.

**global desk.**  A central office within a *Great Commission agency* charged with keeping the agency accountable to its global goals as they relate to the unevangelized world, networking with other *Great Commission Christians*, and maintaining a deliberate and regular electronic link with other global desks in other agencies across the world.

**global diagram.**  A single-page analysis of a mission situation, concept, or term bringing together all relevant data, tables, graphics, diagrams, photographs.

**global evangelization movement.**  A term describing the vast number of distinct agencies and plans directed towards *world evangelization* which have proliferated across the world since the year 1900.

**global meganetwork.**  A *Great Commission* global *meganetwork* .

**global mission.**  The mission of Jesus Christ as it involves the entire world.

**global missions.** Mission agencies with work in over 50 nations of the world or sending out over 5,000 foreign missionary personnel.

**global network.** A *Great Commission* global network.

**global plans.** A documented, christocentric plan, proposal, or program that starts with the Great Commission and articulates concern for evangelizing the world's entire population.

**global religion.** A *universal religion* with adherents from 10 million to 200 million.

**global statistics.** Numbers, series of figures, and other varieties of *statistics* describing any aspect of the entire world, the Earth, our globe, its populations, its problems, its past, its present, and its future.

**globalist.** A specialist in *globalistics*, one who consistently takes the global view and emphasizes the big-picture approach to researching and understanding world problems.

**globalistics.** The professional study of the world in its entirety, with all its peoples, groupings, problems, and possibilities; together with detailed statistical enumeration.

**globalized evangelization.** An organized pseudo-global attempt by a church or mission agency to reach the world by taking a successful local program of mission and *evangelism*, adding to it simply a veneer of global terminology, and then regarding it as certain to *evangelize* the whole world.

**globalized mission.** Pseudo-global missions, as initiated by mission agencies which profess to work for *global mission*, which propound a veneer of global or pseudo-global terminology, but which operate in budget-program isolation from other missions.

**globalized missions.** An impressionistic term for mission agencies whose publicity and propaganda continuously employs global mission terminology but whose actions in practice remain parochial.

**globe.** A term referring here to the entire population of Earth, used instead of 'world' to distinguish it from the usage *World A, World B, World C.*

**glossozone (zone).** One of 100 linguistic areas describing the whole world of 13,500 languages.

**goals.** An aim or set of objectives to accomplish a purpose, here relating to world evangelization, usually in a specified time or by a certain date.

**gospel.** (1) The Good News about God, Jesus Christ, salvation and discipleship. (2) When capitalized, one of the 4 Gospels (Matthew, Mark, Luke, John). (3) Not capitalized, a printed copy of one of the Gospels for mass distribution.

**graph.** A diagram with 2 axes, horizontal and vertical, with changes in variables represented by lines or curves.

**graphic.** A visual or pictorial form of transmitting complex data or information; a line diagram.

**gray money.** Dirty money or criminal profits laundered by banks.

**Great Commission.** The final commandment of Jesus Christ on Earth, to his disciples before his Ascension, ordering the evangelizing, discipling, baptizing, and training of all peoples as his followers.

**Great Commission (used as an adjective).** A descriptive term for persons or organizations or plans or activities of any nationality, denomination, or confession which are based on Christ's Great Commission and which are actively working to obey it, personally and corporately.

**Great Commission agency.** A church or parachurch or service agency which publicizes its raison d'dtre as obedience to Christ's Great Commission.

**Great Commission Christians.** Believers in Jesus Christ who are aware of the implications of Christ's Great Commission, who have accepted its personal challenge in their lives and ministries, are attempting to obey his commands and mandates, and who are seeking to influence the body of Christ to implement it.

**Great Commission instrument panel.** A standard panel of 6 *instruments* employed here in every country's descriptive article in *WCE* Part 4 to indicate the status of religion, mission, and evangelization in that country.

**Great Commission network.** A Great Commission network is defined as any agency or organization or aggregate of contacts which (1) frequently articulates or refers back to the Commission, (2) centers on obedience to it, (3) utilizes a number of computers to make the network function every day, initially utilizing electronic mail, and (4) results in some kind of missionary sending endeavor.

**harvest force.** The cutting edge of all frontier use of Christian resources in mission to non-Christians—personnel, organizations, agencies deployed for *global mission*; also termed *Great Commission Christians* and groupings.

**hearers.** Persons understanding a language at a lower level than native speakers, understanding it but not competent at conversing in it.

**hearing impaired persons.** Deaf and partially-deaf persons, able to converse by signing (use of a signed language).

**heuristic.** The use of empirical knowledge and rules of thumb in problem-solving by an expert or an *expert system*.

**hidden Buddhist believers in Christ.** NBBC (q.v.).
**hidden Hindu believers in Christ.** NBBC (q.v.).
**hidden Muslim believers in Christ.** NBBC (q.v.).
**hidden people.** An alternate term for an *unreached minipeople*.

**hidden religion.** A minor religious system that operates in a clandestine, often subversive or illegal mode.

**home missionary.** A full-time missionary worker assigned to work in the country where he or she is a citizen.

**household size.** Standard size, for statistical purposes, of a family, composed of 2 spouses, 2 children (under 15), and one adult (15 or over).

**human network.** The linking together of people as nodes horizontally (as equals, without hierarchy or executive au-

thority); the linking of numbers of individuals or organizations to address common interests or problems.

**human rights.** The whole range of the rights of individuals, families, communities, religious persons, as set out in the UN's 1948 Universal Declaration on Human Rights (especially the detailing of religious freedoms).

**idiom.** A language whose speech community regards it and its autoglossonym as their mother tongue and which shares less than 95% common vocabulary with any other idiom.

**independency.** The ecclesiastical position rejecting control of churches by centralized denominationalist headquarters; organizing churches and missions independent of historic Christianity.

**Independents.** One of Christianity's 6 ecclesiastico-cultural megablocs, separated from, uninterested in, and independent of historic denominationalist Christianity (the other 5 megablocs).

**indicator.** Any descriptive property or variable, a measuring device.

**indirect access.** *Access* (qv) to Scripture but only through a near-scripture in a language in the same *cluster*.

**infants.** Children or babies under 5 years old; the preschool population.

**infobasing.** Use of a large collection of useful, understandable, and easily retrieved information stored in a computer. Information is more useful than raw data (facts and figures) but less organized than knowledge (understanding, learning) or wisdom (superior understanding).

**inner language.** Alternative term for a *language* (qv) as utilized in this *WCE/WCT/WCD* survey.

**inner lingua franca.** A common language with over 100,000 non-native speakers, and strictly defined as a *language* (inner language) in the World Language Classification.

**instrument.** Any measuring device (Websters); in missiological usage, any of the 2,056 means or methods employed by churches and missions to record the progress and status of Christianity,and so recorded and described in the present *WCE/WCT/WCD.*

**instrument panel.** Juxtaposition of the main basic instruments (in aviation, the conventional 6 flight instruments) essential for pilot or driver to control his mode of transportation.

**instrumentation.** The developing and use of scientific measuring devices used by churches and agencies to document or record progress or change.

**instruments.** As described here, these are measuring devices or gauges or documents (e.g. questionnaires) used by churches and missions to document or record progress or lack of it.

**intercessors.** Christians undertaking to pray daily for unreached peoples, for World A, for non-Christians; often in institutions (monasteries, converts, ashrams) or in other structured situations (prayerwalking, Praying through the Window).

**interdenominational.** Occurring between or among or common to several or many different denominations; accountable to several denominations, or partially or completely controlled by them.

**internally evangelized.** Those persons in a people or population who have become evangelized as a result of persons or agencies of their own people or population.

**internationals.** (1) Persons living abroad; workers, laborers, businessman, entrepreneurs, students, and many other categories of persons who live, reside, and work in a foreign country; excluding tourists or other transients. (2) Professionals working for United Nations-related agencies or parallel global organizations (as contrasted with national or regional bodies).

**Internet.** A network of computer networks which allows users to communicate using electronic mail, to retrieve data stored in databases, and to access websites and the World Wide Web.

**invitations.** Clearcut opportunities for hearers to accept Christ and become disciples; synonymous with offers, chances.

**isolated radio believers.** Persons in isolated areas with no churches or missions who have become Christians through radio programs.

**itinerant.** Adjective describing an evangelist, missionary, or other church worker whose ministry involves being continually on the move from one city or people or country to the next.

**kaleidoscopic.** Multifaceted, many-featured, constantly changing, applying here to the complex components of global mission.

**keyword.** In library cataloguing (OCLC and Library of Congress coding), the main word or words describing the contents of a book.

**knowledge base.** A collection of data, rules, inferences, and procedures in a specific field of interest, organized to form the basis for an intelligent computer *expert system*.

**language.** A grouping of *idioms* or dialects whose speech communities share 85% or more common vocabulary.

**language cluster.** Also termed outer language, a grouping of languages which shares 80% or more lexical similarity (shared words, the basic vocabulary of human experience).

**language net.** A grouping of languages sharing 70% or more common vocabulary.

**language set.** A grouping of *languages* sharing 30% common vocabulary.

**language user.** Speakers of a specific language who can understand or use other languages within a cluster through sharing 80% common vocabulary.

**language, inner.** Technical name for the popularly used simplification *'language'.*

**language, outer.** Synonym for *language cluster*.

**latent Christians.** Christians, both church members and unaffiliated, who do not involve themselves in Christ's mis-

sion on Earth (and so are not counted here as *Great Commission Christians*).

**lexicostatistics.** The study of languages by comparing lexicons (word lists) and finding how many words, and what percentages of a standard word-list, are shared in common by 2 or more languages.

**limited-access country.** A country whose government or regime limits access by alien foreign missionaries wishing to reside, usually by small or decreasing quotas or progressively shorter residence permits; see *closing country*.

**lingua franca.** Or, 'common language'. Originally a hybrid language (Italian/Spanish/French/Greek/Arabic/Turkish elements) used in Mediterranean ports; now any language with a large number of *non-native speakers* (defined in this survey as over 100,000), e.g. state official languages, national languages, trade languages, broadcasting languages, and all languages of wider communication.

**lingua franca, inner.** See *inner lingua franca*.
**lingua franca, outer.** See *outer lingua franca*.

**lingua francas.** Common languages with over 100,000 non-native speakers each, of 2 main kinds: (a) outer lingua francas are each a *language cluster* (outer language), and (b) inner lingua francas are each a *language* (inner language), as defined in the World Language Classification.

**linguametrics.** The scientific measurement and study of the whole world of languages (as distinct from linguistics).

**linguasphere.** The global continuum of languages, extended by humankind around the world since the onset of speech; the multilingual structure of human communication; the continuum of all spoken conventions through space and time—lexical, phonological, and grammatical.

**listing.** A series of items or measurements of religious variables ranked by size; often limited to The Top Ten (countries, populations, etc).

**literates.** Adults over 15 years old who have learned how to read and write in a language, either their mother-tongue or lingua franca or other second language.

**live Christians.** Christians actually alive and living, at the date indicated; by contrast, *Christians ever* includes all who have died in previous years. Likewise with population, evangelized, charismatics, and any other long-term categories.

**local race.** Demographic unit variously defined as culture province, culture net, culture area, culture sphere, nation, national race, local breeding population, reproductive isolate, genetically distinct population.

**local religion.** A single ethnoreligion or tribal religion restricted to a local tribe's, or people's, population.

**macro region.** United Nations' definition of continent, dividing the world into 6 such regions; previously named *continental area* now replaced by *major area*.

**macro segment.** A major population subgrouping which occupies a primary or significant place in a global taxonomy of populations, and which is used in detailing the remaining *unfinished task*.

**macrodenomination.** A Christian denomination in a country whose affiliated members number 10 million or more.

**macroevangelistics.** The scientific study of the propagation of Christianity at the macroscopic or global level.

**macroreligion.** A global or worldwide religion or family of religions, usually with from 20 to 100 million adherents.

**macrozone.** One of 10 global zones used in language classification.

**mainline Christianity.** A term for *mainstream Christianity*.

**mainstream Christianity.** Denominations, churches, agencies, and Christians who adhere to and proclaim the central verities of the Christian faith: God the Creator, the Fall, original sin, historicity of Jesus, deity of Christ, deity of the Holy Spirit, the Resurrection, Ascension, Pentecost, Atonement, salvation, inspiration of the Bible, discipleship, sanctification, Second Advent of Christ.

**major area.** UN term used in statistical enumerations instead of the looser term 'continent'.

**major civil division (MCD).** United Nations' term for the next level of administrative or political subdivision in a country immediately below nationwide level.

**Mandates.** Seven basic commands, known collectively as the Great Commission, given by Christ to his disciples, namely the imperatives Receive! Go! Witness! Proclaim! Disciple! Baptize! Train!

**marginal Christians.** Members affiliated to bodies holding most mainstream Christian doctrines except on the nature of Christ, and existence of the Trinity; also professing a second source of revelation in addition to the Bible.

**martyr.** A Christian martyr is a believer in Christ who loses his or her life, prematurely, in a situation of *witness*, as a result of human hostility.

**martyrdom situation.** Any description of mass or multiple martyrdoms at one point in Christian history.

**martyrdom, intensity of.** Christian martyrdom measured by the ratio of martyrs to local Christians in a given martyrdom situation.

**martyrdom, magnitude of.** Christian martyrdom measured by the sheer number of martyrs in a given martyrdom situation.

**martyrology.** The study of the phenomenon of martyrdom with particular reference to its demography.

**matching up or matching.** The process of linking or linking up a particular *unreached people* or *unevangelized population segment* with a specific ministry or mission agency or missionary; in particular, with a nonresidential missionary whose vocation it would be to see that the segment becomes evangelized.

**maternal mortality rate.** The annual number of deaths of women from pregnancy-related causes per 100,000 live births.

**measure.** Extent, size, capacity, or dimensions as determined by a standard; any attempt to compare anything with a standard.

**megabloc.** One of 6 major ecclesiastico-cultural subdivi-

sions of affiliated Christians and their churches.
**megacensus.** Used here to refer to the totality of the churches' and their agencies' annual censuses of their adherents, activities, personnel, finances, ministries, and all aspects of their mission in the world; these 50,000 or so separate and distinct annual censuses are not centrally coordinated but are nevertheless reported and analyzed here as a single megaphenomenon.
**megachurch.** A very large local congregation or church, with membership in the range 1,000 to 1 million.
**megacity.** A *metropolis* or other city with a population of over one million persons.
**megacommunion.** A worldwide communion, world confessional family, or family of megatraditions, usually with over 10 million adherents.
**megadenomination.** A Christian denomination whose affiliated members in a country number one million or more.
**megametrodwellers.** Persons residing in cities with populations greater than a million.
**megaministry.** A specific global or other large-scale ministry reaching or evangelizing over one million persons a day, or (in earlier years) over 1% of the world's population every year.
**megamissionary.** A term coined for a missionary who is engaged in or working with a *megaministry.*
**meganetwork.** An electronic network linking a very large number of computers, around one million or more.
**megapeople.** An *ethnolinguistic people* speaking a single mother tongue whose population numbers over one million.
**megareligion.** A world religion or family of religions, usually with from one to 20 million adherents.
**megarich.** All *millionaires* of all kinds.
**megatrend.** A particularly vast, large, or significant *trend* affecting large populations.
**megatypology.** A global typology illustrating and explaining any vast worldwide religious movement or phenomenon.
**members.** Affiliated (which usually means enrolled with names recorded) church members.
**Messianic Jews.** Jewish believers in Christ as Messiah who opt not to join mainline churches but form independent churches retaining much Hebrew terminology and Jewish traditions and customs.
**Metaphysical churches.** Term describing churches or religious bodies which, dating back to the 19th-century New Thought movement in the USA, includes spiritism, Theosophy, religious science, et alia.
**metrodweller.** A person residing in a city with a population greater than 50,000.
**metropeople.** An *ethnolinguistic people* or *sociopeople* resident in a *metropolis*, and forming a distinct homogenous group within it.
**metropolis.** The central city of a country or region or area, whether large or small (from the Greek for 'mother city').
**metropolitan.** For Roman Catholics, an archbishop with authority over bishops of a church province; for Eastern Orthodox, a bishop ranking just below patriarch.
**metroscan.** A statistical analysis of the world's metropolises, especially analyzing the presence or absence of Christians and evangelization.
**micro segment.** A minor population subgrouping which occupies only a minor or secondary place in a global taxonomy of populations, and which is used for local targeting in *evangelization.*
**microevangelistics.** The scientific study of the propagation of Christianity at the microscopic level of individuals, then of churches, peoples, countries.
**micropeople.** A small close-knit homogenous population *segment.*
**microreligion.** A minuscule organized local religion with under 1,000 adherents.
**millionaire.** An individual (or occasionally a family) worth one million USA dollars or over.
**minipeople.** The largest *people group* within which the gospel can spread as a church-planting movement without encountering barriers of understanding or acceptance.
**ministry option.** One of a list of possible or potential ministries or missionary or evangelistic approaches that a nonresidential missionary draws up, which he considers could be undertaken by a large variety of agents and agencies on behalf on his target segment.
**minor religions.** Peripheral, marginal, or hidden groupings on the periphery of this survey's definition of a religion.
**missiological breakthrough.** A term employed as a synonym to minimum mission achievement, which in turn rests on the basic, essential need for a *people movement* to Christ in a given culture.
**missiology.** Academic discipline or professional study of the church's task of spreading the Christian faith among nations of the world.
**missiometrics.** The science of mission with special reference to measurement, statistics, and analysis.
**mission.** The task, obligation, or commission adopted by the church to share and spread the Christian faith and all its benefits to all peoples throughout the world.
**monitoring.** The process of regularly tracking and recording the progress of *evangelization* in a particular *unreached people* or *unevangelized* population *segment* with special reference to measuring the impact of all *Great Commission* activities and influences.
**monodenomination.** A large Christian *denomination* of over 1 million affiliated members, which therefore functions as a Christian religion in its own right.
**monolinguals.** Persons speaking or understanding only one language, namely their mother tongue.
**monoreligion.** An ethnoreligion restricted in membership to one culture or people.
**monovocational.** In contrast to *bivocational* persons, monovocational persons describes missionaries whose main or only vocation and profession is full-time Christian service with particular emphasis on the ministry of evangelization and evangelism that results in churches.
**moribund microreligion.** A very small organized local religion, rapidly declining, with under 100 adherents.
**mother tongue.** Main language of a person's home or childhood; the first language spoken in an individual's home in his early or earliest childhood; one's first language or native language.
**multichanneling.** A mode of operation which accepts the present unsatisfactory multiplicity of *global plans* on the part of hundreds of mission agencies, recognizing that their *standalone* nature at least serves as insurance against multiple or overall failure.
**multi-counted.** Religionists who are counted as adherents by several separate religions, requiring care to avoid overestimation in statistical totals.
**multilinguals.** Persons speaking or using or understanding, or fluent in, more than 2 distinct languages.
**multiple-counted religionists.** Persons counted as belonging to , or part of, or regarded as in, more than 2 distinct religions.
**multimillionaire.** An individual worth many tens of millions of USA dollars.
**name for God.** In any people's Christian scriptures, the major name used for God, the Supreme Being.
**nation.** A politically-organized nationality with independent, self-governing, autonomous existence as a sovereign *country* or nation-state, hence eligible for membership in the United Nations.
**native language.** Mother tongue (qv).
**natural increase.** Births in a population minus deaths within a fixed period, usually one year. Sometimes a figure for net immigration is added.
**near-Bible.** A Bible translation in a language in the same cluster as languages without translations but sufficiently close for speakers of the latter to utilize it.
**near-gospel.** A gospel translation in a language within the same cluster as several languages without, but which can use it because they share 80% common vocabulary.
**near-NT.** For a language without its own translation of the New Testament, any translation in a related-language within its cluster can be understood and used.
**near-scriptures.** Scriptures which can benefit a scriptureless language because the 2 languages concerned are within the same cluster.
**Neo-Apostolic Reformation.** Self-appellation of *Postdenominationalists/Independents.*
**neocharismatic.** A religious person or movement similar to a charismatic but unconnected with mainline pentecostal or nonpentecostal denominations.
**Neocharismatic.** An adherent of the Third Wave of the Pentecostal/Charismatic Renewal in the Holy Spirit.
**Neocharismatics.** Members of the Third Wave of the Pentecostal/Charismatic Renewal characterized by the adjectives Independent, Postdenominationalist, and Neo-Apostolic.
**neolinguasphere.** The *linguasphere* since the invention of electronic communication.
**neologism.** Any new word, or new meaning for an established word, with particular reference to explanation of religion, religions, and religious phenomena.
**Neopagans.** New 20th-century attempts to revive longdead traditional pre-Christian religion and beliefs.
**net.** See *language net, culture net.*
**networking.** A term so widely used for any type of non-hierarchical communication that its value is best preserved by: (a) restricting it to mean computer networking or electronic networking involving the regular linking of 3 or more computers; and (b) using the term 'human networking' when all other kinds of non-electronic communication are meant.
**new Christians.** Totals of all who become Christians for the first time are larger than annual church growth because they equal annual increase in number of Christians plus annual deaths of Christians.
**New Reader Scriptures.** 1-, 2-, 4-, or 8- page Selections of texts, or whole Book translations of a gospel (New Reader Portions) prepared for newly literate readers, always illustrated.
**New-Religionists.** Adherents of Hindu or Buddhist sects or offshoots, or new syncretistic religious combining Christianity with Eastern religions, mostly in Asia.
**newly baptized.** Believers baptized within the last oneyear period.
**nomenklatura** (Russian). Privileged bureaucratic elites in Communist or formerly-Communist countries.
**non-baptized believers in Christ (NBBCs).** Members of non-Christian religions who become converted to faith in Christ as Lord but choose not to join Christian denominations but to remain in their religions as witnesses there to Christ.
**Non-Christians.** Generic term for describing all persons in the world who are not Christians.
**non-native language.** Any language understood by a people although not their mother tongue.
**non-native speakers.** Speakers of a language as a second or third or other language.
**Non-White indigenous Christians.** Independent believers, on every continent, who form their own autonomous churches, mostly pentecostal or charismatic in emphasis.
**nondenominational.** Of a parachurch agency, unrelated to any denomination or denominations, not accountable to any, outside their control.
**nonreligion.** Absence of religion, replaced by either nonmilitant agnosticism or militant atheism.
**nonreligious.** Persons professing no religion, no interest in religion; secularists, materialists; agnostics, but not militantly antireligious or atheists.
**nonreligionists.** Term encompassing the 2 varieties of unbeliever: (a) *agnostics* or secularists or materialists, who are *nonreligious* but not hostile to religion, and (b) *atheists* or anti-religious/anti-religionists militantly opposed or hostile to religion.
**nonresidential missionary.** A fulltime foreign missionary committed to evangelizing an ethnolinguistic people living in a country or countries where foreign missionaries are prohibited; and conducting his or her ministry from an open city in another country permitting full freedom of missionary action.
**nonsovereign country.** A political entity or country which is not free of external control, hence not a nation but a colony or other dependent territory.
**nonsighted persons.** The blind.
**Occultist churches.** Bodies, often claiming the title Christian, who invoke the mysterious, secret, supernatural, esoteric in religion and magic.
**offers.** A scientific count producing numbers of concrete *disciple-opportunities*, invitations, chances to hear the gospel and become disciples of Christ.
**Oneness Pentecostals.** Denominational Pentecostals originating in the USA from 1910 onwards, now widespread worldwide, who emphasize baptism in the name of 'Jesus Only' and who oppose the doctrine of the Trinity.
**online.** Connecting through a network, modem, or highspeed cable to a computer service, usually accessing email or the World Wide Web.
**order.** See *clerical order.*
**outer language.** Alternative term for a *language cluster* (qv).
**outer lingua franca.** A common language with over 100,000 *non-native speakers*, and strictly defined as a language cluster (outer language) in World Language Classification; a *lingua franca* identical to a *language cluster* or outer language, with all component languages sharing 80% basic vocabulary of common human experience.
**outreach.** The churches' organized mission of reaching out with the Good News to persons outside their fellowship, especially to Non-Christians in Worlds A and B.
**overt evangelizers.** Evangelizing Christians who work openly without having to fear government spies or religious police in hostile lands.
**p.a.** Per annum, per year, each year, every year, annual, yearly, over the previous 12 months.
**p.d.** Per diem, per day, daily.
**parachurch.** Almost a church, partly a church, usually a service agency of the churches, but offering alternate or rival Sunday worship services unrelated to existing churches.
**paradenomination.** A recent network of churches that is becoming a new denomination but resisting denominationalist shortcomings.
**parareligionists.** Members of a body that is almost a religion, partly a religion, often self-identifying as such.
**party.** A politico-religious grouping of religionists with its major function as a political one.
**pedigree.** A religion's coded family tree or lineage, relationship to existing religions, ancestry, line of descent.
**pentecostal.** A general descriptive noun or adjective for any person or group or movement stressing direct divine inspiration by the Holy Spirit and exhibiting glossalia, faith healing, and parallel phenomena
**Pentecostal.** A church member, or church, or organization affiliated to a *Classical Pentecostal* denomination.
**people movement.** The spread of the gospel among a people in such a way that all individuals in that group are presented with an opportunity to know Christ; usually accompanied by significant response.
**people, people group.** A grouping of individuals who perceive themselves to have a common affinity for one another because of their shared language, religion, ethnicity, residence, occupation, class or caste, situation, etc. or combination of these. The statistical unit 'people' in this survey always refers to a people, or part thereof, in one single country.
**peripheral religion.** A religion on the periphery of this survey's definition of religion.
**persecution.** Persecution of believers specifically on religious grounds, though this is often denied.
**pijin, pidgin.** A hybrid contact language used for communication between groups having different native languages; when a pidgin becomes the mother tongue of a community it is customarily called a *creole.*
**pluridenominational.** A country's situation where denominations number over 1,000.
**polytheists.** Ethnoreligionists (q.v.) who worship several or many gods and deities.
**popular-religionists.** Practitioners of popularized versions of Christianity often combined with non-Christian features or superstitions.
**Portions.** Copies of a complete Book of the Bible, usually one of the 4 Gospels.
**Postcharismatics.** Formerly active Charismatics in mainline nonpentecostal denominations who still regard themselves as Charismatics though active in other different areas of church life.
**postdenominationalism.** Viewpoint rejecting close control of local churches or congregations by centralized denominations.
**Postdenominationalists.** Independents and others who have replaced historic denominationalism by non-centralized lifestyle and church order.
**Postpentecostals.** Former members of classical Pentecostal denominations who leave to join nonpentecostal mainline churches but still regard themselves as Pentecostals.
**practice, religious.** Minimum attendance at church service on major festivals (Christmas, Easter, Pentecost).
**practitioners.** In a religion, its practicing members, followers, adherents, who actively follow religious precepts and standards.
**priest.** A pastor, minister, presbyter, elder, clergyman, authorized (in hierarchical denominations) to administer the

sacraments.
**Prepentecostals.** Believers experiencing or manifesting marks of baptism in the Holy Spirit (glossolalia, healings) before the arrival of Denominational Pentecostalism.
**prioritization.** The science of setting priorities, especially as it relates the world's least evangelized population segments, e.g. peoples.
**professing Christians.** Persons publicly professing, confessing, declaring, stating, self-identifying themselves as followers of Christ, usually in censuses or public-opinion polls.
**Quasi-Christians.** Seemingly, partly, almost in some sense, to be Christians.
**quasireligion.** Seemingly or partially a religion; or a secular movement which is partly or virtually a religion, but is also either antireligious or nonreligious or pseudo-religious.
**quasipentecostal.** Nonpentecostal or noncharismatic church members or churches which nevertheless are apparently/seemingly/largely pentecostal or semipentecostal in practice; especially strong in Third-World countries;not usually counted in Renewal enumerations.
**R&D.** Research and development, usually a budget item with a fixed percentage (1-10%) of a nation's or a large organization's annual income.
**race.** Biological grouping or stock, inherited at birth.
**reached.** Having heard the gospel, understanding it, and having had the opportunity to respond by joining an indigenous church or fellowship of one's own culture.
**reached minipeople.** A *minipeople* with a *viable indigenous church* capable of evangelizing the whole group, that is, with the resources and vision to reach out to the whole people.
**reached people.** An *ethnolinguistic people* with a *viable indigenous church* with the resources and vision to *evangelize* the whole people.
**reached person.** An individual who has had an adequate opportunity to hear the gospel and to respond to it, and also to contact a church of his own culture and to meet and join in fellowship with other believers.
**region.** UN term for statistical enumeration referring to a subdivision of a major area (continent).
**relational database.** A collection of data items organized as a set of formally-described tables from which data can be accessed or reassembled.
**religiocluster.** A council or association of dissimilar religions which functions as its own religion.
**religiometrics.** The scientific measurement and analysis of religions and adherents, with special reference to description, analysis, trends.
**religion.** A religion is a grouping of persons with beliefs about God or gods, and defined by its adherents' loyalty to it, by their acceptance of it as unique and superior to all other religions, and by its relative autonomy.
**religionists.** Persons professing adherence to any religion, as contrasted with atheists or nonreligious persons.
**religious.** A noun in Roman Catholic usage describing all clergy, monks, and nuns belonging to a community, order, institute, congregation, monastery, or convent.
**religious liberty.** Freedom to practice one's religion with the full range of religious rights specified in the UN's 1948 *Universal Declaration of Human Rights.*
**religious libraries.** A large library (over 100,000 volumes) specializing mainly in the study of religion.
**Renewal.** (1) Generic term for over 100 different current movements of revival or awakening or new spiritual life across the whole spectrum of global Christianity, involving 1,100 million Christians (68% of all affiliated church members). (2) Shorthand term for the entire Pentecostal/ Charismatic/Neocharismatic Renewal in the Holy Spirit.
**Renewalists.** Shorthand term for followers of the Pentecostal/Charismatic/Neocharismatic Renewal in the Holy Spirit.
**response.** In religious usage, the measurable number of persons accepting an evangelistic invitation of any kind, making decisions, joining catechumenate classes, becoming baptized or otherwise joining the church.
**responsiveness** of a population, R, a measure quantified as new church members baptized per year, per million evangelism-hours expended per year. Higher values indicate greater responsiveness to evangelism, lowest values signify small or even zero response.
**restricted-access country.** A country whose government or regime restricts access by foreign missionaries wishing to reside, foreign Christians wishing to visit, or foreign Christian literature, or broadcasting, or other Christian ministries or influences.
**ruralites.** Rural dweller, person residing in the countryside rather than in an urban area.
**scenario.** A description of one possible future situation with regard to a church or agency or person or population or country, developed by detailed compilation of likely trends and statistics. The study of the future of any such situation is best conducted by drawing up a range of 2 or 3 such scenarios, termed possible *alternate futures,* ranging from optimistic to pessimistic and covering all possible eventualities, good or bad.
**Scripture (with capital 'S').** Holy Scripture, the Christian Scriptures, the Bible.
**scripture (with small 's').** Printed copy or copies of the Bible, New Testament, Gospel, Portion, New Reader Portion, or any other Book (all the foregoing being capitalized to distinguish them from less specialized varieties of book or publication); or selection of Scripture texts.
**Scripture language.** A language in which some Scripture activity exists, either distribution of complete *scriptures* (complete *Books* of the Bible) in print, radio, audio, or video versions; or partial scriptures (ongoing translation and preparation of complete scriptures, or use of selections of texts in print, radio, or audio versions).
**scripture translation status.** A language's status with regard to translation, publication, provision and availability of its own Bible, New Testament, Portion (gospel), and Selection.
**Second World.** Formerly used of the Communist world, and still used now of the Communist/ex-Communist world.
**second-language scriptures.** Copies of Scripture used by persons without mother-tongue scriptures; usually in lingua francas.
**Second-Wavers.** Charismatics in the Renewal within mainline nonpentecostal churches.
**segment.** Any homogeneous subdivision of the world's population, made for purposes of understanding and analysis; the most generalized English translation of the biblical Greek word *ethnos* (usually translated 'people').
**segmentization.** The process of dividing the world's population into meaningful small *segments,* usually countries, peoples, or cities in order to assist toward their *targeting* and *evangelization.*
**Selections.** 1-, 2-, 4-, or 8-page leaflets or booklets of Scripture texts on a topical theme, used in mass-distribute campaigns by Bible societies and churches in many lands.
**Self-Religionists.** Followers of varieties of religion centering on benefiting followers personally and helping them live prosperous lives.
**semilogarithmic.** A graph with usually a linear axis horizontally but a logarithmic scale on the vertical axis, permitting the inclusion on the same graph of small numbers together with very large numbers several orders of magnitude greater.
**service agency.** Major national, international or country-wide bodies, parachurch organizations and agencies which assist or serve the churches but are not themselves denominations or church-planting missions.
**shamanists.** Ethnoreligionists with a hierarchy of shamans and healers.
**short-term (short-service) missionary.** Persons serving abroad as foreign missionary personnel under a recognized mission agency for a single period of from 3 to 24 months only.
**slumdwellers.** Persons residing in make-shift dwellings on the streets of the world's cities.
**sociolect.** An *idiom* or dialect differing from a standard only in pronunciation, accent, or special vocabulary.
**sociopeople.** A *people* or population group defined primarily by some sociological category such as class, caste, occupation, age, abode, for which a specific evangelistic strategy may be developed; sometimes regarded as a *bridge people* useful for initiating evangelism.
**sovereign country.** A *nation,* being an autonomous independent country free of external control.
**speadsheet.** Computer software that organizes numerical data into rows and columns for computing, analyzing, and charting utilizing formulas and other techniques.
**speakers.** Users of a language capable of conversing in it.
**Spiritist churches.** Those claiming the title Christian but believing in the action or agency of spirits of the dead, producing mediumistic phenomena.
**standalone.** This adjective as used here does not refer to individuals but to agencies or *global plans* which operate organizationally unrelated to the rest of the *Great Commission* world, i.e. with budget and program unrelated to those of other agencies; also used of a computer or network which serves only its immediate user without being linked or networked to other computers or other networks.
**standard evangelistic unit** (SEU). A standardized measure of the volume of evangelism, so that 1 SEU=one million evangelistic *offers* (disciple opportunities).
**statistics.** Facts or data of a numerical kind assembled, classified, and tabulated so as to present significant information about a given subject; the science of this process. Statistics are the shortest and most compact form of factual description with regard to a population or situation.
**strategy coordinator.** See nonresidential missionary.
**structures of sin.** The superstructure of organized human activity based on selfishness, greed, sin, evil, that keeps half the world's population in degrading poverty.
**stylized color.** A typology of race included in *culture world.*
**subsidiary georeligion.** A large megabloc or other segment of a universal georeligion.
**supercity.** A city with over 4 million inhabitants.
**supergiant.** A city with over 10 million inhabitants.
**target people.** An ethnolinguistic people which is the evangelistic focus of a Christian worker, missionary, couple, or small team seeking to benefit that people in measurable ways.
**targeting.** In religious and missionary usage, the establishing of goals followed by implementation of ministries and resources directly intending to benefit non-Christian populations.
**targeting variable.** Term from United Nations' usage denoting priority of measurable benefits: literacy, health care, famine or disaster relief (1-10, with 1=top priority).
**teleporting.** The transmission of very large quantities of digitized data by telecommunication round through teleports (specialized ground stations handling huge volumes daily).
**Third World.** Developing nations not politically aligned with either the Western (Capitalist) world (the First World) or the Communist/Marxist-related world (the Second World). The term is purely chronological (like 'third child') and has never carried connotations of inferiority (as 'third-rate' does). It is the standard term to use for the nonaligned world and should be used instead of popularized alternatives like 'Two-Thirds World', a noncomparative term based only on population size.
**Third-Wavers.** Believers who have experienced baptism in the Holy Spirit but who do not affiliate with First-Wavers or Second-Wavers but instead join Neocharismatic/Post-denominational congregations.
**three (3) tier schema.** A stylized schematic representation in which, to enhance the understanding of *world evangelization,* the globe is divided into 3 slices or tiers or worlds, and given the names *World A,* the *Unevangelized World; World B,* the *Evangelized Non-Christian World*; and *World C,* the *Christian World.*
**tradition.** An ecclesiastical family or type of denominations sharing historical and/or many common features.
**transbloc grouping.** A large grouping of Christians sharing certain common central beliefs that transcend historic confessional bounds.
**translinguals.** Persons able to navigate with reasonable competence between 2 or more languages within their own language cluster (or, a wider definition, within their own language net).
**transient (noun).** A person who is present in a country or area temporarily before moving on; usually a visitor, tourist, person on business, military personnel, refugee, displaced person.
**trend.** A tendency, change, rate of change in a religious population, event, condition, or property, which can then be measured; usually expressed per diem (day), per year, per decade, per century, or per millennium, etc.
**tribal religionists.** *Ethnoreligionists* (qv).
**Trinitarianism.** The Christian doctrine of the triune nature of the Godhead (Father, Son, and Holy Spirit). In the 20th century, this has become the major non-negotiable dogma of mainstream Christianity.
**triumphalism.** In Christian parlance, either (1) inordinate pride in publicizing huge memberships or rapid church growth, or (2) self-praise or publicized self-congratulation over an agency's achievements.
**typology.** The study of types, symbols, symbolism, especially those describing religion or religious properties or phenomena, in order to make sense of vast masses of intractable data.
**U.** A computed estimate of the percentage of peoples in a particular population *segment* (world, country, person, city) who are unevangelized; equivalent to 100-E, as %.
**unaffiliated Christians.** Persons professing allegiance and commitment to Christ but who have no church affiliation.
**unevangelized.** Never having heard the Good News of Jesus Christ.
**unevangelized persons.** Individuals who have had no adequate opportunity to hear the gospel or respond to it; persons who are unaware of Christianity, Christ, and the gospel; those who have never heard the name of Jesus.
**unevangelized World.** In the *3-tier schema,* this is *World A,* consisting of all non-Christians who have not been evangelized.
**unfinished task.** The remaining task of evangelization, as the task of the Christian church on Earth, viewed as the church's responsibility usually viewed as completing the fulfillment of Christ's Great Commission,
**unimax people.** An alternate term for *minipeople* emphasizing the maximum size of people in which the gospel can spread before encountering barriers.
**universal georeligion.** A large non-local religion making membership open to all of any race, language, or background.
**unreached.** Never having heard the gospel nor having had the opportunity to contact an indigenous church or fellowship of one's own culture.
**unreached minipeople.** A *minipeople* with no *viable indigenous church.*
**unreached people.** An *ethnolinguistic people* which does not have its own *viable indigenous church.*
**unreached person.** Individuals who have, or have had, no adequate opportunity to hear the gospel, or to respond to it, or to meet and have fellowship with other believers.
**urban dweller.** *urbanites* (qv).
**urbanites.** Urban dwellers, persons residing in a city, town, or recognized urban area.
**users of a language.** All persons in a country who can understand a language since it belongs to a language cluster containing their own.
**variable.** Any quality or phenomenon or aspect of religion that varies or changes and then can be measured by an instrument or measuring device.
**vehicular megalanguage.** A language with a million or more speakers which acts a a trade language or lingua franca.
**viable indigenous church.** Within an *ethnolinguistic people* or *minipeople,* an indigenous community of believing Christians with adequate numbers and resources to evangelize their own *people group* without needing outside cross-cultural assistance.
**visual gospel.** (1) A film or movie of the life of Christ, either via video, or in an 8mm or 16mm presentation; or (2) a film strip based on a gospel, or (3) an art exhibit illustrating the Good News by works of art (paintings) or photographs.
**volume of evangelism.** A scientifically-derived computed estimate of the percentage of persons in a country or other population *segment* who have become influenced by evangelism to awareness of Christianity, Christ, and the gospel.
**witness.** The normal term used for the informal, spontaneous, unorganized sharing of their faith, by presence, word, or deed, by individual Christians in circumstances they do not control; as contrasted with organized *evangelism.*
**workforce.** Collective term for the whole body of all Christian workers, clergy, and other personnel.
**Workforce for the Apostolate.** *Apostolatus Copiae* (qv).
**World A.** In the *3-tier schema* or representation of the Earth, the *Unevangelized World,* i.e. the world of all unevangelized individuals.
**World A countries.** Countries in which evangelized individuals number under 50% of the population.
**World A individuals.** All unevangelized individuals unaware of Christianity, Christ, or the gospel.

**World A peoples.**   Ethnolinguistic peoples each with over 50% of population unevangelized.

**World B.**   In the *3-tier schema* or representation of the Earth, the *Evangelized Non-Christian World*, i.e. all non-Christians who have nevertheless become evangelized.

**World B countries.**   Countries in which evangelized persons number over 50% but Christians number less than 60%.

**World B individuals.**   Non-Christians who have nevertheless become evangelized.

**World B peoples.**   Ethnolinguistic peoples among whom evangelized persons number over 50% but Christians under 60%.

**World C.**   In the *3-tier schema* or representation of the Earth, the *Christian World*, i.e. the world of all who individually are Christians.

**World C countries.**   Countries in which Christians number 60% or more of the population.

**World C individuals.**   Persons who are Christians.

**World C peoples.**   Ethnolinguistic peoples among whom 60% or more of the population are Christian.

**world evangelization.**   The term used for the goal of reaching the entire world with the gospel of Christ, or of giving every *people* and population on Earth the opportunity to hear the gospel with understanding and to become disciples of Christ.

**world religion.**   A worldwide universal religion with from 1 million to 10 million adherents.

**World Wide Web.**   A hypermedia-based system for browsing Internet sites, housing millions of home pages, including most Christian organizations.

**worship center.**   A church building or congregation's premises or other place for regular weekly services of Christian worship.

**zone.**   In linguistic classification, a *glossozone* (qv), numbering 100 across the world.

Part 31

# BIBLIOGRAPHY

Trends in world bibliography of Christianity and religions, with 148 keywords

*There are also many other things which Jesus did; were every one of them to be written,*
*I suppose that the world itself could not contain the books that would be written.*

—John 21:25, Revised Standard Version

*Men of learning–whether you be theologians, exegetes or historians–*
*the work of evangelization needs your tireless work of research.*

—Paul VI, *Evangelii Nuntiandi*, 1975

Bibliometrics is the science of measuring or counting books, authoring, publishing, librarianship, cataloging, distribution, usages, and the like. Part 31 utilizes this approach to generate its own statistical variables. These include the total books available today on any country's Christian and religious situations, the total such new books published or newly discovered and catalogued each year, and the global totals of books available on a range of 148 major Christian and religious subjects or keywords (with 30 being on related secular subjects). This *WCT-WCE-WCD* project also contains its own bibliographies listing 9,000 different titles. Here, Part 31 ends with a Selective World Bibliography with 1,380 titles, mainly works in English, over half being on Christianity.

Two instruments, or 2 vast collections of instruments enabling this analysis are (1) the *Library of Congress subject headings* (24th edition, 5 volumes, 2001) which is updated annually and which describes subjects for all books worldwide by its coding system (250,000 subject headings, 37,200 geographic headings, etc.); and (2) the Online Computer Library Catalogue, which holds these data on 45 million book titles via the world's 50,000 largest libraries.

# Trends in world bibliography of Christianity and religions, with 148 keywords

The Fourth Evangelist, John, was so impressed by the magnitude of Jesus' impact on the world that he ended his narrative by saying:

> Jesus did many other things. If they were all written in books, I don't suppose there would be room enough in the whole world for all the books. (John 21:25, Contemporary English Version).

Today's facts and figures on the subject support John's vision.

To illustrate: the name of Jesus Christ is very widely known across the whole literate world and its cultures. Table 31–1 reveals that libraries contain over 174,000 distinct books whose main subject is Jesus and his significance. No one else has ever generated such an enormous and powerful impact on the human mind.

It is the same when the literature generated by the Christian religion that Jesus created is examined. Table 31–2 shows how numerous books are on a whole range of terms mostly arising from Jesus' ministry.

The location of this vast amount of material is also worldwide. The literature described in these tables is found in libraries in every country of the world—even in countries hostile to the contemporary Christian enterprise. The whole phenomenon can best be studied in any of the world's largest libraries, all open to the public. Table 31–3 lists 130 of the largest specifically Christian libraries each of which has over 120,000 titles on its shelves and in its computerized catalogs. And Table 13-4 lists the total number of books describing empirical Christianity and religion in each country of today's world, together with totals in the bibliographies on every country in *WCE* Part 4 "Countries".

## 5 MILLION BOOKS ABOUT CHRISTIANITY

Christian literature worldwide—books, encyclopedias, atlases, dictionaries, reports, surveys, articles, devotional material, and so forth—is vast and grow-

### Table 31–1. Book titles with Jesus Christ as main subject.

*a. Total titles ever with these 3 terms as subject heading*

| Language | Jesus Christ | Jesus | Christ |
|---|---|---|---|
| English | 170,500 | 174,925 | 80,327 |
| German | 6,613 | 6,681 | 6,783 |
| French | 3,348 | 3,636 | 3,395 |
| Spanish | 2,434 | 3,400 | 3,395 |
| Italian | 1,261 | 1,295 | 1,272 |
| Dutch | 700 | 718 | 706 |
| Portuguese | 397 | 481 | 416 |
| Korean | 262 | 263 | 26 |
| Chinese | 242 | 245 | 245 |
| Polish | 215 | 225 | 217 |
| Arabic | 195 | 195 | 197 |
| Russian | 189 | 197 | 191 |
| Japanese | 112 | 245 | 245 |

*b. Books with name in title*

| | Jesus Christ | Jesus | Christ |
|---|---|---|---|
| All languages | 16,912 | 55,587 | 63,076 |

ing rapidly. A few examples will suffice to demonstrate this fact. The largest Christian library in the world is the Vatican Library (Biblioteca Apostolica Vaticana) in Vatican City, Rome. It contains 32% of the whole world's different books on Christianity—1,600,000 printed books, 150,000 manuscript volumes, 8,300 incunabula (ancient manuscripts), and also a database of 773,470 records accessible anywhere in the world via Telnet. Next come major theological libraries at universities and divinity schools. The largest in America is that of Union Theological Seminary, New York, with 700,000 books. The Regenstein Library at the University of Chicago has 600,000 in its theological holdings; Harvard University's Andover-Harvard Divinity Library holds 500,000 items; and Yale University's Divinity Library over 400,000 items. The holdings of several major free-standing seminary libraries approach similar levels: Princeton Theological Seminary's Speer Library holds 475,000 items, Union Theological Seminary (Richmond) and Presbyterian School of Christian Education's Morton Library 295,000 items, and Fuller Theological Seminary's McAlister Library has 220,000 items. This present survey estimates the grand total of all books primarily on Christianity and religion to have now reached 5,030,000 distinct and different titles in some 2,000 different languages. Each year sees an additional 95,000 new titles published. From all these, this *WCE/WCT/WCD* project has selected and included here the bibliographical details listing the 8,500 most significant books for the main purpose of describing the whole phenomenon of empirical global Christianity.

Almost any attempt to grasp the full scope of this vast corpus of literature is bound to be incomplete, even if the attempt is simply to count titles. The researcher who sets out to accomplish even this most basic task quickly runs into at least 3 major obstacles. First, there exists to date no truly universal, international, comprehensive bibliographic database or catalogue on all subjects. Several very large computer databases do exist. Globally, the major one covering the sum total of all human knowledge on all subjects is OCLC (Online Computer Library Catalog or Center). Its Online Union Catalog lists 40 million titles growing by 2 million more each year. Begun in 1971, it now has 26,249 participating libraries in 64 countries around the world. It lists the physical locations of 652 million copies of books; and it has handled 79 million interlibrary loan requests. In addition to OCLC, several large universities run parallel but much smaller catalogues majoring on literature in either French, German, Spanish, Russian, Chinese, or Japanese.

While the number of titles immediately available through all of these is breathtaking, none encom-

**World's largest Christian library.** The Vatican Apostolic Library, in Rome, holds 1.6 million books (32% of all 5 million extant titles). *Top.* Main hall. *Left.* Reading room at related missions library. *Right.* Missions librarian Willi Henkel explains a research procedure to pope John Paul II.

passes all the literature in all the world on every subject. Moreover, they overlap to some extent, leaving the researcher the daunting task of correlating titles from the different major databases.

A second barrier to any attempt at a complete enumeration of world Christian literature is precisely this explosion of Christian literature around the world. In the past few decades Christian literature of all types—never in short supply—has begun to increase at a formidable rate, as indicated by title counts for all major Christian and religious themes in Table 31–3. It is reported that in the USA, in addition to the current 50,000 publishing houses utilizing the ISBN cataloging system, some 7,000 new publishers receive ISBN numbers each year. Of the books all these organizations publish, religious books form the single largest bloc with 11.3% of the total in 1997. Efforts have been made to track systematically the growth of this literature, though none is complete. The American Theological Library Association (ATLA) maintains a comprehensive bibliographic database, available in print and in electronic versions. The print versions appear as *Religion Index One: periodicals*, and *Religion Index Two: multi-author works*. The electronic version appears as *ATLA religion database on CD-ROM*. In addition, ATLA, through a consortium of member libraries, has compiled a two-volume index of non-Western Christian literature in North American libraries, the *International Christian literature documentation project*. This index, however, does not index literature in libraries in non-Western countries. Recently a group of ATLA member librarians has begun to explore the possibility of creating a more inclusive database of world Christian literature, to include literature from libraries outside North America. Meanwhile, the literature continues to outpace one's ability to track it. However, even the ATLA databases concentrate on academic works, leaving much devotional and evangelistic material unsurveyed and hence unquantified.

A third major problem, which would exist even if the first two could be overcome, is that a fair amount of Christian literature is published in some 5,000 languages remote from Western scholarship. Remote also from Western library networks, this vast literature is in the main locally catalogued but remains unknown in Europe and America. From tracts to translations, much literature for emerging Christian groups either does not find its way into libraries with wider circulation channels or it finds its way only into small libraries whose collections do not participate in larger cataloguing endeavors. In either case a sizable segment of the literature remains unreachable to all but the most persistent global bibliographer.

## *OVERVIEW OF BIBLIOGRAPHIES IN WCE and WCT*

That said, it still remains possible to produce a meaningful overview of world Christian literature. In the present volume and *WCE*, 5 types of literature selections are provided, as follows.

### *1. Global counts of titles*

The first level of description is a simple count of titles. The figures in Tables 31-1, 31-3, and 31-4 provide this, derived from searches of the OCLC database. By entering discrete search terms from the Library of Congress subject index, exact indicators of the current scope of the literature emerged. The results of this inquiry, found in these 2 largest tables, contain many surprises. Important caveats remain, since OCLC does not yet catalog the contents of many major libraries outside the United States of America, especially those in the non-English speaking world. Nonetheless, it does provide a general idea of the immensity of Christian literature worldwide.

### *2. Country bibliographies*

The second major description of world Christian literature lies in the bibliographies that follow all of the country surveys in *WCE* Part 4 "Countries". Here the truly global nature of Christianity is illustrated through literature on Christianity and religion in every nation on the face of the globe.The grand total of all books in this category—those describing Christianity each in one single country—is 380,300. In the case of larger countries and countries whose populations are at least historically Christian, the literature dramatically outnumbers the space available for an adequate listing. Instead of attempting a complete cataloging, a selection of the most significant of the vast literature describing Christianity and religion in each country is provided here. In the case of smaller countries or those in which Christianity represents a small minority of the population, the bibliographies are more comprehensive, and in some cases are virtually complete. Indeed, there exists little or no Chris-

**Table 31–2. 130 of the world's largest Christian and/or theological libraries with over 120,000 books each, AD 2000.**

Below are listed 130 of the world's largest Christian, theological, and/or religious libraries, ranked by size (number of bound or print volumes). The location of each within its country is either indicated by its city name being included in its title, or by adding the city or state name, anglicized, after the library's name, and a comma.

| *Name* | *Country* | *Volumes* |
|---|---|---|
| Biblioteca Apostolica Vaticana | Holy See | 1,600,000 |
| Katholische Universitat Eichstatt | Germany | 1,200,000 |
| Trinity College/University of Dublin | Ireland | 1,100,000 |
| Urbe (Roman Network of Libraries), Rome | Italy | 1,100,000 |
| Katholieke Universiteit Leuven | Belgium | 920,000 |
| Tübingen University | Germany | 900,000 |
| Institut Catholique de Paris | France | 810,000 |
| Pontificia Universita Gregoriana, Vatican City | Holy See | 780,000 |
| Ludwig-Maximilians-Universitat, Munich | Germany | 750,000 |
| University of St Andrews (Church of Scotland) | Britain | 720,000 |
| Union Theological Seminary, New York | USA | 710,000 |
| Catholic University of Gottingen | Germany | 650,000 |
| Regenstein Library, University of Chicago | USA | 600,000 |
| Pontificia Universita Salesiana, Rome | Italy | 510,000 |
| Calvin Theological Seminary, Grand Rapids | USA | 503,780 |
| Université Catholique de Louvain | Belgium | 500,000 |
| San Francisco de Borja Facultad Teologica, Barcelona | Spain | 500,000 |
| S. J. Saint-Albert, Louvain | Belgium | 500,000 |
| Andover-Harvard Theological Library, Cambridge, MA | USA | 500,000 |
| Pitts Theology Library, Emory University, Atlanta | USA | 485,000 |
| Bibliotheek Canisianum (Jesuit), Maastricht | Netherlands | 477,000 |
| Princeton Theological Seminary | USA | 475,000 |
| Theologische Hogeschool (Jesuit), Amsterdam | Netherlands | 460,000 |
| Pontificia Universita Lateranense, Vatican City | Holy See | 450,000 |
| Sint Jan Berchmanscollege, Heverlee | Belgium | 450,000 |
| Drew University Theological School, Madison, NJ | USA | 449,280 |
| Jesuit-Krauss-McCormick Library, Chicago | USA | 430,000 |
| Southwestern Baptist Theological Seminary, Fort Worth | USA | 420,010 |
| Yale University Divinity School, New Haven | USA | 415,810 |
| Facultés Dominicaines, Soissy-sur-Seine | France | 400,000 |
| Pontificia Universita S Tommaso d'Aquino (Dominican), Rome | Italy | 395,000 |
| ITC Atlanta University Center | USA | 384,350 |
| Graduate Theological Union, Berkeley | USA | 382,530 |
| Pontificio Ateneo Antonianum (OFM), Rome | Italy | 380,000 |
| US Library of Congress (religion holdings), Washington, DC | USA | 370,000 |
| Southern Baptist Theological Seminary, Louisville | USA | 361,710 |
| St Johns University School of Theology, Collegeville | USA | 359,710 |
| Bischofliche-Theologische Hochschule, Eichstatt | Germany | 350,000 |
| Institut Catholique de Toulouse | France | 350,000 |
| Pontificia Universita Urbaniana, Vatican City | Holy See | 350,000 |
| Andrews University (SDA), Berrian Springs, MI | USA | 340,000 |
| Erzbischofliche Akademische, Paderborn | Germany | 320,000 |
| Duke University Divinity School, Durham, NC | USA | 308,030 |
| Catholic University of America, Washington, DC | USA | 307,220 |
| Garrett Evangelical/Seabury/United Library, Evanston | USA | 303,410 |
| Bollandists Library (saints, martyrs), Brussels | Belgium | 300,000 |
| Union Theological Seminary, Richmond, VA | USA | 295,630 |
| Bischofliches Priesterseminars Mainz | Germany | 290,000 |
| Colgate Rochester Divinity School, Rochester | USA | 283,490 |
| Jesuit Faculté de Théologie, Lyon | France | 280,000 |
| St Vincent College, Latrobe, PA | USA | 280,000 |
| San Francisco Theological Seminary (PCUSA) | USA | 280,000 |
| Episcopal Divinity/Weston Jesuit Sch of Theology, Cambridge, MA | USA | 277,174 |
| University of Notre Dame, IN | USA | 273,907 |
| Perkins School of Theology, Dallas | USA | 270,900 |
| Erzbischofliche Diozesan-Bibliothek, Cologne | Germany | 270,000 |
| Facultés Catholiques de Lyon | France | 270,000 |
| Pacific School of Religion, Berkeley, CA | USA | 265,000 |
| Groot Seminarie 's-Hertogenbosch | Netherlands | 250,000 |
| Theologische Fakultat Trier | Germany | 250,000 |
| The Evangelical Library, London | Britain | 250,000 |

| *Name* | *Country* | *Volumes* |
|---|---|---|
| Pittsburgh Theological Seminary | USA | 245,540 |
| Reformed Academy of Theology, Budapest | Hungary | 240,000 |
| Kirchlichen Hochschule Berlin | Germany | 240,000 |
| Moravian Theological Seminary, Bethlehem, PA | USA | 237,128 |
| Trinity Evangelical Divinity School, Deerfield, IL | USA | 235,130 |
| New Orleans Baptist Theological Seminary | USA | 234,597 |
| General Theological Seminary, New York | USA | 234,510 |
| North Park Theological Seminary, Chicago | USA | 229,685 |
| Congregational Library, Boston | USA | 225,275 |
| Luther Seminary Library, St. Paul, MN | USA | 221,569 |
| Free University of the Netherlands, Amsterdam | Netherlands | 220,000 |
| Fuller Theological Seminary (McAlister), Pasadena, CA | USA | 220,000 |
| St Patrick's College, Maynooth | Ireland | 220,000 |
| Pontifical University of Santo Tomas, Manila | Philippines | 220,000 |
| Bethel Theological Seminary, St Paul, MN | USA | 215,000 |
| Concordia Seminary Library, St. Louis | USA | 213,840 |
| Asbury Theological Seminary, Wilmore, KY | USA | 204,598 |
| Caritasbibliothek, Freiburg im Breisgau | Germany | 200,000 |
| Groot Seminarie Mechelen-Brussel | Belgium | 200,000 |
| H. Orton Wiley (Nazarene) Library, Point Loma, CA | USA | 200,000 |
| Jesuitenkollegs, Innsbruck | Austria | 200,000 |
| Sion College (Anglican), London | Britain | 200,000 |
| Erskine College & Theological Seminary, Due West, SC | USA | 199,487 |
| Anderson University, Anderson, IN | USA | 197,752 |
| Evangelical Lutheran Library, Budapest | Hungary | 190,000 |
| David Lipscomb University, Nashville, TN | USA | 184,506 |
| Reformed Theological Seminary, Jackson, MS | USA | 181,964 |
| Iliff School of Theology, Denver, CO | USA | 181,457 |
| Biola/Talbot Theological Seminary, La Mirada, CA | USA | 180,000 |
| Diozesanbibliothek Aachen | Germany | 180,000 |
| Makerere University, Kampala | Uganda | 180,000 |
| Universidad Javeriana-Facultades Eclesiaticas, Bogota | Colombia | 180,000 |
| Vanderbilt University Divinity School, Nashville | USA | 168,729 |
| Claremont School of Theology, Claremont, CA | USA | 167,726 |
| Grand Seminaire de Montreal | Canada | 165,000 |
| Pontificia Facolta Teologica Marianum, Rome | Italy | 165,000 |
| Gordon-Conwell Theological Seminary, South Hamilton, MA | USA | 163,588 |
| Seminario Vescovile di Novara | Italy | 160,000 |
| Society of Friends Library, London | Britain | 160,000 |
| Chung Chi College, Shatin, Hong Kong | China | 160,000 |
| Dallas Theological Seminary, Texas | USA | 158,023 |
| Christian Theological Seminary, Indianapolis | USA | 151,126 |
| Austin Presbyterian Theological Seminary, Austin, TX | USA | 150,114 |
| Grand Seminaire de Nancy | France | 150,000 |
| Concordia Theological Seminary, Fort Wayne, IN | USA | 149,769 |
| Denver Conservative Baptist Seminary | USA | 140,875 |
| Humboldt-Universitat Theologischer Institut, Berlin | Germany | 140,000 |
| Dr Williams' Library (Nonconformity), London | Britain | 140,000 |
| Christ the King Seminary, East Aurora, NY | USA | 138,997 |
| Collegio Alberoni (Vincentians), Piacenza | Italy | 138,000 |
| Moore Theological College Library, Sydney | Australia | 135,700 |
| Joint Theological Library, Parkville | Australia | 135,000 |
| Boston University School of Theology | USA | 131,000 |
| Tokyo Union Theological Seminary | Japan | 131,000 |
| Doshisha University, Nishijin, Kyoto | Japan | 130,000 |
| Columbia Theological Seminary, Decatur, GA | USA | 126,293 |
| Oral Roberts University, Tulsa, OK | USA | 120,111 |
| Total USA & Canada libraries with over 50,000 volumes | | 135 |
| **Global total all Christian libraries with over 50,000 volumes** | | **400** |

## Table 31–3. Book titles on 148 major Christian and religious subjects and keywords, measured in the years 1998 and 2001.

The world's major English-language monitoring system for cataloguing, listing, locating, providing, and loaning the world's 40 million distinct and different book titles held in public and private libraries is termed OCLC (Online Computer Library Catalog). Although it specializes in English-language books, its libraries include books in 360 other languages also. The table below accesses this Catalog to determine the magnitude of the world's current literature on Christianity in the context of a few major secular or non-Christian terms. The latter are shown below in italics. All in medium type are Christian terms, or in practice are mainly Christian subjects. This survey was done in October 1998, then repeated in April 2001.

**Column 1** lists terms by which the US Library of Congress classifies the main subject, keyword or keywords of each book; note that terms ending in a hyphen cover all subjects containing that root (thus 'martyr-' includes 'martyrs', 'martyrdom', 'martyred', etc). **Columns 2 and 6** enumerate the worldwide total of different titles on that subject, copies of which still exist today on Earth and therefore can, normally, for any enquirer anywhere on Earth, be seen on his screen, have its details printed out, or be loaned by mail for 2-3 weeks. **Columns 3 and 7** reduce each total to include only books published since 1970.

**Columns 4 and 8** provide an estimate of the number of new titles on each subject being published every year in AD 1998 and 2001. **Column 5 and 9** enumerate all books which actually include the exact keyword (column 1) in their titles. Some of these may be larger than column 2 or 6 when their main subject is more inclusive than column 1's term. **Column 10.** Annual growth in number of titles in 2.5 years since 1998, due to new publication but also new libraries joining OCLC. **Global grand total.** Total of all titles whose main subject is Christianity or some aspect of it, excluding secular and non-Christian terms.

| Search term(s) | 1998 Total titles ever | 1998 Titles since 1970 | 1998 New per year | 1998 With term in title | 2001 Total titles ever | 2001 Titles since 1970 | 2001 New per year | 2001 With term in title | rate percent p.a. |
|---|---|---|---|---|---|---|---|---|---|
| 1 | 2 | 3 | 4 | 5 | 6 | 7 | 8 | 9 | 10 |
| Advent | 7,127 | 2,483 | 92 | 4,578 | 13,897 | 5,826 | 194 | 4,857 | 30.6 |
| Anglican- | 10,422 | 4,561 | 169 | 6,201 | 18,393 | 7,582 | 253 | 6,641 | 25.5 |
| *animism* | 500 | 200 | 7 | 100 | 558 | 288 | 10 | 138 | 4.5 |
| apostasy | 452 | 181 | 7 | 439 | 929 | 398 | 13 | 481 | 33.4 |
| apostle- | 12,670 | 4,260 | 158 | 10,081 | 25,272 | 8,173 | 272 | 10,880 | 31.8 |
| apostolic- | 2,609 | 757 | 28 | 8,905 | 15,053 | 3,507 | 117 | 9,318 | 101.6 |
| architecture, religio- | 516 | 369 | 14 | 226 | 2,035 | 1,366 | 46 | 240 | 73.1 |
| *art, religio-* | 4,460 | 2,566 | 95 | 1,738 | 11,411 | 6,967 | 232 | 1,745 | 45.6 |
| art, Christian | 10,284 | 5,751 | 213 | 33 | 13,978 | 8,388 | 280 | 503 | 13.1 |
| *astrophysics* | 4,601 | 3,400 | 126 | 3,500 | 7,548 | 5,743 | 191 | 1,756 | 21.9 |
| *atheis-* | 3,226 | 1,444 | 53 | 2,217 | 6,223 | 2,389 | 80 | 2,685 | 30.1 |
| *Baha'i* | 1,095 | 797 | 30 | 678 | 2,137 | 1,463 | 49 | 882 | 30.7 |
| bapti- | 66,163 | 26,129 | 968 | 55,253 | 78,945 | 31,573 | 1,052 | 65,000 | 7.3 |
| baptism | 10,883 | 2,931 | 109 | 10,463 | 16,623 | 5,204 | 173 | 11,000 | 18.5 |
| Bible | 261,303 | 103,592 | 3,837 | 145,868 | 448,729 | 186,520 | 6,217 | 155,952 | 24.1 |
| biblical | 45,218 | 24,051 | 891 | 17,475 | 87,430 | 50,705 | 1,690 | 18,317 | 30.2 |
| *broadcasting* | 638 | 398 | 15 | 113 | 49,020 | 35,738 | 1,191 | 8,438 | 467.8 |
| *Buddh-* | 46,096 | 29,283 | 1,085 | 14,942 | 63,885 | 45,216 | 1,507 | 16,000 | 13.9 |
| *Buddhism* | 4,772 | 2,711 | 100 | 4,772 | 46,610 | 32,830 | 1,094 | 6,167 | 148.8 |
| catechist, -m. | 15,061 | 1,958 | 73 | 16,234 | 17,171 | 2,613 | 87 | 17,500 | 5.4 |
| Catholic- | 198,678 | 76,293 | 2,826 | 54,383 | 226,155 | 81,354 | 2,712 | 60,000 | 5.3 |
| Charismatic | 1,000 | 900 | 33 | 500 | 2,160 | 2,046 | 68 | 1,391 | 36.1 |
| Christ | 80,327 | 31,172 | 1,155 | 63,076 | 185,171 | 73,480 | 2,449 | 79,924 | 39.7 |
| Christian | 192,339 | 105,301 | 3,900 | 111,318 | 409,963 | 219,405 | 7,314 | 125,961 | 35.4 |
| Christian- | 308,087 | 178,371 | 6,606 | 164,582 | 427,321 | 226,782 | 7,559 | 139,713 | 14.0 |
| Christianity | 105,554 | 67,578 | 2,503 | 21,414 | 167,461 | 103,644 | 3,455 | 24,530 | 20.3 |
| church | 563,393 | 210,816 | 7,808 | 273,284 | 915,252 | 361,816 | 12,061 | 300,702 | 21.4 |
| church & state | 30,100 | 9,130 | 338 | 6,099 | 32,477 | 10,000 | 333 | 7,698 | 3.1 |
| church, growth | 4,982 | 4,729 | 175 | 3,314 | 9,201 | 7,613 | 254 | 3,562 | 27.8 |
| church, renewal | 2,957 | 2,424 | 90 | 866 | 5,684 | 4,689 | 156 | 956 | 29.9 |
| *cities* | 58,067 | 39,614 | 1,467 | 44,210 | 121,998 | 74,303 | 2,477 | 46,011 | 34.6 |
| *city* | 174,511 | 110,712 | 4,100 | 312,804 | 744,614 | 421,966 | 14,066 | 340,035 | 78.7 |
| clergy | 46,129 | 20,693 | 766 | 9,444 | 62,239 | 27,076 | 903 | 10,411 | 12.7 |
| *Communism, -t.* | 68,496 | 45,000 | 1,667 | 23,856 | 127,000 | 67,609 | 2,254 | 26,239 | 28.0 |
| confession, Christian | 3,899 | 1,251 | 46 | 18,000 | 2,157 | 820 | 27 | 511 | -21.1 |
| conversion | 13,171 | 7,420 | 275 | 18,981 | 41,346 | 27,001 | 900 | 19,400 | 58.0 |
| *cosmology* | 8,618 | 7,500 | 278 | 4,000 | 10,375 | 7,124 | 237 | 1,773 | 7.7 |
| *Creation (of universe).* | 13,272 | 8,000 | 296 | 7,500 | 16,000 | 9,000 | 300 | 8,000 | 7.8 |
| creeds | 9,975 | 3,100 | 115 | 4,771 | 9,482 | 1,757 | 59 | 1,029 | -2.0 |
| Crucifixion | 2,356 | 1,199 | 44 | 1,136 | 4,999 | 2,549 | 85 | 1,210 | 35.1 |
| *cults* | 3,891 | 2,821 | 104 | 1,375 | 6,701 | 5,033 | 168 | 1,548 | 24.3 |
| *culture(s)* | 85,624 | 60,000 | 2,222 | 70,000 | 255,047 | 172,110 | 5,737 | 84,540 | 54.7 |
| *culture, religion* | 1,534 | 1,259 | 47 | 1,648 | 8,650 | 6,518 | 217 | 1,173 | 99.7 |
| denomination- | 6116 | 2030 | 75 | 4,296 | 7,756 | 2,158 | 72 | 5,141 | 10.0 |
| drama, religio- | 2,448 | 1,093 | 40 | 569 | 4,751 | 2,538 | 85 | 494 | 30.4 |
| education, Christian | 21,894 | 14,233 | 527 | 5,454 | 37,206 | 22,480 | 749 | 5,359 | 23.6 |
| education, religious | 24,244 | 11,597 | 430 | 7,017 | 36,823 | 18,498 | 617 | 5,381 | 18.2 |
| *Enlightenment* | 3,139 | 1,100 | 41 | 2,732 | 7,683 | 3,202 | 107 | 3,172 | 43.1 |
| eschatolog- | 6,583 | 3,032 | 112 | 1,972 | 9,698 | 5,259 | 175 | 2,384 | 16.8 |
| *ethnic-* | 34,568 | 31,142 | 1,153 | 20,104 | 70,397 | 62,603 | 2,087 | 21,894 | 32.9 |
| Evangelical | 8,079 | 2,668 | 99 | 12,623 | 29,924 | 15,415 | 514 | 12,840 | 68.8 |
| Evangelicalism | 3,001 | 2,179 | 81 | 360 | 4,324 | 3,036 | 101 | 436 | 15.7 |
| evangelism | 1,069 | 834 | 31 | 5,411 | 9,060 | 6,346 | 212 | 6,157 | 135.1 |
| evangelist, -s | 2,556 | 1,411 | 52 | 3,800 | 8,369 | 3,327 | 111 | 3,775 | 60.7 |
| evangelistic work | 12,881 | 8,716 | 323 | 152 | 16,372 | 11,377 | 379 | 104 | 10.1 |
| faith- | 15,941 | 8,538 | 316 | 54,845 | 18,615 | 10,551 | 352 | 58,611 | 6.4 |
| *finance* | 253,139 | 163,542 | 6,057 | 66,611 | 346,881 | 229,707 | 7,657 | 47,561 | 13.4 |
| finance/Christ-/church | 5,042 | 2,305 | 85 | 681 | 5,704 | 2,532 | 84 | 270 | 5.1 |
| Fundamentalism, -t | 3,895 | 3,248 | 120 | 2,588 | 4,773 | 3,677 | 123 | 2,024 | 8.5 |
| *futur-* | 150,000 | 130,000 | 4,815 | 100,000 | 186,583 | 142,195 | 4,740 | 121,934 | 9.1 |
| futur-, Christian- | 667 | 346 | 13 | 699 | 3,051 | 1,958 | 65 | 609 | 83.7 |
| Genesis, Book of | 1,000 | 400 | 15 | 500 | 1,272 | 453 | 15 | 600 | 10.1 |
| *geograph-* | 110,317 | 54,752 | 2,028 | 107,992 | 130,389 | 68,211 | 2,274 | 110,000 | 6.9 |
| *geolog-* | 183,824 | 106,607 | 3,948 | 208,569 | 206,806 | 122,471 | 4,082 | 215,000 | 4.8 |
| *geometr-* | 31,236 | 13,587 | 503 | 39,907 | 34,903 | 14,360 | 479 | 45,000 | 4.5 |
| God | 33,387 | 16,493 | 611 | 78,197 | 183,320 | 101,648 | 3,388 | 99,323 | 97.6 |
| gospel- | 36,903 | 23,642 | 876 | 42,849 | 97,389 | 48,494 | 1,616 | 48,720 | 47.4 |
| *Hindu-* | 27,873 | 16,545 | 613 | 8,788 | 35,180 | 20,580 | 686 | 6,796 | 9.8 |
| *Hinduism* | 8,851 | 5,444 | 202 | 1,285 | 12,828 | 8,427 | 281 | 1,663 | 16.0 |
| holiness | 3,154 | 1,123 | 42 | 3,976 | 8,054 | 3,584 | 119 | 8,000 | 45.5 |
| Holy Spirit | 8,875 | 4,503 | 167 | 5,761 | 13,527 | 7,707 | 257 | 5,539 | 18.4 |
| *human rights* | 37,016 | 28,000 | 1,037 | 26,000 | 38,753 | 33,989 | 1,133 | 16,624 | 1.9 |
| independent church- | 1,396 | 599 | 22 | 2,328 | 4,254 | 1,479 | 49 | 1,581 | 56.2 |
| *Islam* | 40,435 | 29,846 | 1,105 | 16,741 | 76,655 | 56,938 | 1,898 | 26,440 | 29.2 |
| *instrument* | 150,000 | 95,000 | 3,519 | 38,000 | 160,018 | 104,623 | 3,487 | 47,762 | 2.6 |
| *instrumentation* | 21,000 | 13,000 | 481 | 6,000 | 24,036 | 15,072 | 502 | 8,044 | 5.5 |
| *Jainism* | 1,395 | 760 | 28 | 218 | 2,054 | 1,220 | 41 | 278 | 16.7 |
| Jesus | 68,391 | 26,647 | 987 | 55,587 | 174,925 | 87,614 | 2,920 | 71,671 | 45.6 |

| Search term(s) | 1998 Total titles ever | 1998 Titles since 1970 | 1998 New per year | 1998 With term in title | 2001 Total titles ever | 2001 Titles since 1970 | 2001 New per year | 2001 With term in title | rate percent p.a. |
|---|---|---|---|---|---|---|---|---|---|
| 1 | 2 | 3 | 4 | 5 | 6 | 7 | 8 | 9 | 10 |
| *Judaism* | 45,217 | 23,570 | 873 | 5,295 | 64,796 | 37,809 | 1,260 | 5,834 | 15.5 |
| *language-* | 780,544 | 470,346 | 17,420 | 161,950 | 1,053,434 | 663,619 | 22,121 | 156,776 | 12.7 |
| *language & culture* | 3,111 | 2,800 | 104 | 2,890 | 13,524 | 10,495 | 350 | 10,000 | 80.0 |
| *linguistic-* | 24,707 | 20,205 | 748 | 27,960 | 54,959 | 43,088 | 1,436 | 14,837 | 37.7 |
| *literacy* | 13,879 | 12,623 | 468 | 15,444 | 32,327 | 30,150 | 1,005 | 15,723 | 40.2 |
| Lutheran | 39,303 | 13,125 | 486 | 17,533 | 54,754 | 22,993 | 766 | 16,623 | 14.2 |
| martyr- | 4,849 | 1,448 | 54 | 11,843 | 14,104 | 4,349 | 145 | 7,966 | 53.3 |
| martyr-, Christian | 1,903 | 829 | 31 | 713 | 3,071 | 1,370 | 46 | 301 | 21.1 |
| martyrdom | 381 | 234 | 9 | 1,432 | 2,705 | 947 | 32 | 1,573 | 119.0 |
| media, Christian- | 335 | 274 | 10 | 128 | 1,117 | 892 | 30 | 300 | 61.9 |
| measuring Christianity | 750 | 400 | 15 | 120 | 807 | 473 | 16 | 160 | 3.0 |
| messianism | 305 | 195 | 7 | 106 | 596 | 421 | 14 | 138 | 30.7 |
| Methodism, -t | 46,486 | 15,670 | 580 | 36,982 | 39,465 | 26,933 | 898 | 35,235 | -6.3 |
| missio- | 93,431 | 1,264 | 47 | 83,976 | 120,200 | 45,132 | 1,504 | 90,000 | 10.6 |
| missio-, Christian | 7,588 | 4,416 | 164 | 4,056 | 5,706 | 3,260 | 109 | 4,000 | -10.8 |
| *missio-, Islam* | 628 | 376 | 14 | 134 | 798 | 499 | 17 | 200 | 10.1 |
| missionary, -ies | 19,468 | 8,533 | 316 | 25,560 | 55,303 | 18,928 | 631 | 28,326 | 51.8 |
| missions | 80,576 | 25,451 | 943 | 18,988 | 111,490 | 39,113 | 1,304 | 19,695 | 13.9 |
| missions, theory | 2,000 | 1,286 | 48 | 35 | 2,492 | 1,667 | 56 | 36 | 9.2 |
| *money* | 29,353 | 13,016 | 482 | 40,802 | 94,385 | 55,220 | 1,841 | 43,944 | 59.6 |
| money/finance, church | 3,881 | 1,398 | 52 | 458 | 6,079 | 2,569 | 86 | 452 | 19.7 |
| Mormon, -s. | 19,789 | 5,996 | 222 | 9,783 | 27,763 | 13,925 | 464 | 8,063 | 14.5 |
| *Muhammad* | 16,219 | 8,800 | 326 | 8,006 | 27,993 | 18,853 | 628 | 8,339 | 24.4 |
| Museums, religio- | 2,000 | 1,000 | 37 | 150 | 2,101 | 1,093 | 36 | 169 | 2.0 |
| *Muslim- (Moslem-)* | 15,164 | 11,415 | 423 | 6,683 | 29,657 | 22,850 | 762 | 8,952 | 30.8 |
| New Testament | 1,827 | 998 | 37 | 25,666 | 44,140 | 15,036 | 501 | 27,098 | 257.5 |
| *occultism* | 9,290 | 5,998 | 222 | 499 | 12,128 | 8,343 | 278 | 563 | 11.3 |
| Old Testament | 2,413 | 1,282 | 47 | 16,057 | 23,444 | 10,012 | 334 | 14,423 | 148.3 |
| Orthodox- | 18,261 | 9,596 | 355 | 8,486 | 33,856 | 18,216 | 607 | 10,005 | 28.0 |
| Pentecostal- | 4,551 | 3,164 | 117 | 1,953 | 6,769 | 5,107 | 170 | 2,310 | 17.2 |
| *persecution* | 10,138 | 8,200 | 304 | 6,000 | 17,149 | 9,885 | 330 | 3,886 | 23.4 |
| pilgrim- | 7,935 | 3,967 | 147 | 15,687 | 24,984 | 11,132 | 371 | 11,933 | 58.2 |
| pilgrim-, Christian- | 1,703 | 1,253 | 46 | 455 | 4,023 | 2,703 | 90 | 339 | 41.0 |
| pilgrimage | 4,875 | 3,022 | 112 | 4,833 | 8,026 | 3,728 | 124 | 5,259 | 22.1 |
| *polytheism* | 160 | 65 | 2 | 30 | 174 | 75 | 3 | 47 | 3.4 |
| pope- | 21,228 | 6,227 | 231 | 14,683 | 37,860 | 11,945 | 398 | 12,001 | 26.0 |
| pope or papacy | 25,298 | 7,179 | 266 | 15,501 | 35,252 | 11,734 | 391 | 10,602 | 14.2 |
| *postmodernism, -t* | 3,165 | 3,158 | 117 | 965 | 5,249 | 5,209 | 174 | 1,050 | 22.4 |
| pray- | 50,312 | 20,668 | 765 | 49,118 | 59,719 | 26,507 | 884 | 55,000 | 7.1 |
| preach- | 11,545 | 5,993 | 222 | 57,664 | 85,955 | 18,816 | 627 | 66,620 | 123.2 |
| prophet, -ecy | 15,697 | 7,299 | 270 | 17,836 | 30,596 | 15,809 | 527 | 14,888 | 30.6 |
| Protestant- | 20,647 | 5,510 | 204 | 30,861 | 46,288 | 12,653 | 422 | 24,033 | 38.1 |
| *race(s)* | 90,280 | 65,000 | 2,407 | 60,000 | 94,308 | 64,908 | 2,164 | 30,068 | 1.8 |
| *read-* | 214,192 | 144,689 | 5,359 | 284,364 | 248,042 | 174,208 | 5,807 | 120,000 | 6.0 |
| *reading* | 113,347 | 88,896 | 3,292 | 130,074 | 259,988 | 176,673 | 5,889 | 112,283 | 39.4 |
| Reformation | 14,533 | 3,565 | 132 | 15,919 | 32,435 | 9,254 | 308 | 16,028 | 37.9 |
| Reformed | 14,664 | 4,357 | 161 | 10,915 | 26,298 | 9,209 | 307 | 10,586 | 26.3 |
| religious awakening | 250 | 160 | 6 | 30 | 279 | 184 | 6 | 39 | 4.5 |
| *religion* | 114,658 | 56,434 | 2,090 | 72,466 | 239,007 | 115,540 | 3,851 | 81,227 | 34.2 |
| religion & state | 4,766 | 2,496 | 92 | 1,792 | 6,000 | 4,000 | 133 | 2,100 | 9.6 |
| *religions* | 17,569 | 8,968 | 332 | 9,929 | 41,092 | 19,412 | 647 | 10,261 | 40.5 |
| *research-* | 237,623 | 182,254 | 6,750 | 610,953 | 285,470 | 213,244 | 7,108 | 286,755 | 7.6 |
| *science* | 359,531 | 177,850 | 6,587 | 458,073 | 827,161 | 557,638 | 18,588 | 210,073 | 39.6 |
| *science and religion* | 10,764 | 5,300 | 196 | 7,000 | 17,111 | 6,785 | 226 | 2,953 | 20.4 |
| Scripture | 41,000 | 10,000 | 370 | 20,000 | 43,279 | 13,913 | 464 | 29,016 | 2.2 |
| *sect-* | 21,651 | 13,952 | 517 | 139,794 | 21,041 | 11,866 | 396 | 3,072 | -1.1 |
| sect-, Christian | 1,679 | 987 | 37 | 734 | 2,602 | 1,366 | 46 | 26 | 19.2 |
| *shamanism* | 1,436 | 1,253 | 46 | 369 | 2,462 | 2,209 | 74 | 547 | 24.1 |
| *Sikhism* | 1,043 | 780 | 29 | 223 | 1,758 | 1,295 | 43 | 301 | 23.2 |
| *Taoism* | 2,531 | 1,579 | 58 | 336 | 4,301 | 3,031 | 101 | 444 | 23.6 |
| *trend* | 60,000 | 40,000 | 1,481 | 30000 | 73,984 | 56,757 | 1,892 | 51,625 | 8.7 |
| Trinity | 8,346 | 3,332 | 123 | 11,462 | 30,240 | 14,945 | 498 | 14,067 | 67.4 |
| union, Christian | 7,894 | 2,674 | 99 | 1,445 | 8,388 | 2,871 | 96 | 575 | 2.5 |
| *urban-* | 83,356 | 69,137 | 2,561 | 137,913 | 100,922 | 84,479 | 2,816 | 150,000 | 7.9 |
| Vatican | 6,338 | 2,620 | 97 | 9,866 | 14,865 | 5,748 | 192 | 5,507 | 40.6 |
| world, Christian- | 6,582 | 1,738 | 64 | 5,180 | 7,000 | 2,000 | 67 | 6,000 | 2.5 |
| worship | 11,662 | 6,421 | 238 | 19,299 | 43,009 | 20,610 | 687 | 24,562 | 68.5 |
| worship, Christian | 990 | 768 | 28 | 2,523 | 7,913 | 4,253 | 142 | 3,121 | 129.7 |
| *writing* | 38,362 | 29,404 | 1,089 | 52,843 | 125,321 | 91,963 | 3,065 | 59,143 | 60.6 |
| Zoroastrianism | 430 | 200 | 7 | 210 | 455 | 224 | 7 | 240 | 2.3 |
| other Christian items | 300,000 | 160,000 | 6,000 | 50,000 | 200,000 | 120,000 | 4,000 | 60,000 | -15.0 |
| total Christian | 3,202,000 | 1,390,000 | 51,000 | 1,937,000 | 5,230,000 | 2,378,000 | 88,000 | 2,056,000 | 21.7 |
| less duplicates | -630,000 | -290,000 | -11,000 | -537,000 | -1,000,000 | -500,000 | -19,000 | -800,000 | 20.3 |
| uncatalogued | 1,500,000 | 900,000 | 33,000 | 500,000 | 800,000 | 700,000 | 26,000 | 900,000 | -22.2 |
| **Global grand total** | 4,072,000 | 2,000,000 | 74,000 | 1,900,000 | 5,030,000 | 2,578,000 | 95,000 | 2,156,000 | 8.8 |

tian literature for several areas of the world, a clue to the still-great need for such descriptive writing.

Two aspects of the country bibliographies bear highlighting. First, the size of the bibliographic selection for each country corresponds very approximately to the population of the country, at least up to a point. A rule of thumb has been used of a minimum of one entry per 500,000 population, and/or its Christian population, resulting in a maximum for most countries of around 50 entries. Some countries have warranted exceptions to these rules. The bibliographies for many small countries, such as Brunei, with a population of about 285,000, exceed the minimum number of entries, since slavish adherence to the rule of thumb would result in unnecessarily brief bibliographies. Conversely, the bibliographies of many larger countries, in particular China and the United States of America, exceed the usual maximum since their literature is so vast. The second notable aspect of these bibliographies is that most contain works about the religious situation in general as well as about Christianity in each country, with emphasis on descriptive works. Here one finds studies utilizing history, sociology, anthropology, statistics, and other descriptive methodologies that provide a starting point for in depth study of the situation facing the church as it seeks to live out its calling.

### *3. Topical bibliographies*

The third major type of selection of world Christian literature lies in the bibliographies that follow 9 of the 15 distinct Parts in *WCE* and 22 Parts of the 31 in *WCT*. These bibliographies all deal with different areas of Christian activity and point the careful reader to other sources of similar information or to sources of methodology used in the sections. They help to substantiate both the present methodologies and the conclusions of this research.

**Table 31–4. Bibliographical sources and resources by country: the number of significant books each describing a single country's empirical state of Christianity and related religion, for the world's 238 countries, measured in October 1998 and in April 2001.**

Among the main sources for the data on all countries in the *WCT-WCE-WCD* project are the 5 million books on Christianity and related religion enumerated in Table 31–3 and the 380,300 books on Christianity and related religion in individual single countries enumerated below. The meanings of the columns are as follows. ***Column 1.*** Name of country. ***Column 2.*** Total of all books (including, occasionally, reports, manuscripts, dissertations, major articles, audio and video materials) whose main subject as assessed by the US Library of Congress is *Christianity* (including *church-* and related religious elements) *within the country* shown, this column's count being done in October 1998. ***Column 3.*** Similar data from second count done in April 2001 (30 months later). ***Column 4.*** Annual rate of increase, % p.a., in book totals for 1998-2001. ***Column 5.*** Total bibliographical items listed country by country in *WCE* Part 4 "Countries", being a small selection of the most significant books describing the broader subject of *Christianity, religion, and religions* in the *country* indicated, i.e. the role and place of Christianity and religion, or one of its components, in the country's history and present situation. These titles' names are given in full in each country's bibliography after its text in the standardized articles in *WCE* Part 4 "Countries". Those bibliographies also contain a small number of journal articles. The reader wishing to consult the full bibliography on Christianity in a particular country (here enumerated in Column 3) can call up the complete titles on screen or in printout at any of the 28,000 OCLC-equipped major libraries across the world, using as here the search indicators 'country name' followed by 'Christian-' and/or 'church-'.

| Country 1 | 1998 Books 2 | 2001 Books 3 | Rate 4 | Part 12 5 |
|---|---|---|---|---|
| Afghanistan | 20 | 59 | 54.1 | 17 |
| Albania | 72 | 113 | 19.8 | 18 |
| Algeria | 470 | 485 | 1.3 | 22 |
| American Samoa | 10 | 12 | 7.6 | 5 |
| Andorra | 9 | 15 | 22.7 | 6 |
| Angola | 122 | 188 | 18.9 | 32 |
| Anguilla | 4 | 5 | 9.3 | 2 |
| Antarctica | 15 | 20 | 12.2 | 17 |
| Antigua | 10 | 12 | 7.6 | 9 |
| Argentina | 1,001 | 1,491 | 17.3 | 46 |
| Armenia | 501 | 750 | 17.5 | 31 |
| Aruba | 6 | 7 | 6.4 | 5 |
| Australia | 3,195 | 4,045 | 9.9 | 61 |
| Austria | 2,185 | 2,617 | 7.5 | 25 |
| Azerbaijan | 18 | 49 | 49.3 | 6 |
| Bahamas | 45 | 81 | 26.5 | 17 |
| Bahrain | 10 | 17 | 23.6 | 7 |
| Bangladesh | 68 | 146 | 35.7 | 40 |
| Barbados | 62 | 114 | 27.6 | 21 |
| Belgium | 1,594 | 2,040 | 10.4 | 17 |
| Belize | 27 | 55 | 32.9 | 20 |
| Belorussia | 97 | 110 | 5.2 | 10 |
| Benin | 60 | 165 | 49.9 | 17 |
| Bermuda | 43 | 79 | 27.5 | 3 |
| Bhutan | 20 | 25 | 9.3 | 16 |
| Bolivia | 392 | 649 | 22.3 | 32 |
| Bosnia-Herzegovina | 50 | 55 | 3.9 | 37 |
| Botswana | 52 | 68 | 11.3 | 34 |
| Bougainville | 5 | 8 | 20.7 | 7 |
| Brazil | 3,280 | 4,222 | 10.6 | 57 |
| Britain | 18,527 | 23,816 | 10.6 | 88 |
| British Indian Ocean Terr | 3 | 3 | 0.0 | 2 |
| British Virgin Islands | 12 | 12 | 0.0 | 9 |
| Brunei | 12 | 13 | 3.3 | 10 |
| Bulgaria | 768 | 905 | 6.8 | 25 |
| Burkina Faso | 41 | 86 | 34.5 | 35 |
| Burundi | 55 | 80 | 16.2 | 23 |
| Cambodia | 29 | 59 | 32.9 | 12 |
| Cameroon | 291 | 406 | 14.2 | 47 |
| Canada | 5,856 | 11,245 | 29.8 | 56 |
| Cape Verde | 28 | 35 | 9.3 | 15 |
| Cayman Islands | 5 | 6 | 7.6 | 4 |
| Central African Republic | 40 | 55 | 13.6 | 14 |
| Chad | 24 | 152 | 109.2 | 8 |
| Channel Islands | 30 | 42 | 14.4 | 2 |
| Chile | 1,160 | 1,592 | 13.5 | 40 |
| China | 4,645 | 7,956 | 24.0 | 148 |
| Christmas Island | 2 | 2 | 0.0 | 2 |
| Cocos (Keeling) Is | 5 | 5 | 0.0 | 3 |
| Colombia | 910 | 1,286 | 14.8 | 44 |
| Comoros | 10 | 11 | 3.9 | 7 |
| Congo-Brazzaville | 34 | 60 | 25.5 | 18 |
| Congo-Zaire | 1,011 | 1,100 | 3.4 | 52 |
| Cook Islands | 9 | 16 | 25.9 | 7 |
| Costa Rica | 223 | 355 | 20.4 | 24 |
| Croatia | 512 | 619 | 7.9 | 41 |
| Cuba | 441 | 818 | 28.0 | 34 |
| Cyprus | 212 | 299 | 14.7 | 19 |
| Czech Republic | 708 | 940 | 12.0 | 31 |
| Denmark | 1,773 | 2,137 | 7.8 | 24 |
| Djibouti | 10 | 11 | 3.9 | 8 |
| Dominica | 14 | 26 | 28.1 | 6 |
| Dominican Republic | 253 | 305 | 7.8 | 34 |
| Ecuador | 1,021 | 1,242 | 8.2 | 22 |
| Egypt | 1,211 | 3,590 | 54.4 | 51 |
| El Salvador | 430 | 554 | 10.7 | 22 |
| Equatorial Guinea | 20 | 21 | 2.0 | 18 |
| Eritrea | 10 | 24 | 41.9 | 9 |
| Estonia | 105 | 156 | 17.2 | 21 |
| Ethiopia | 553 | 774 | 14.4 | 43 |
| Faeroe Islands | 20 | 22 | 3.9 | 14 |
| Falkland Islands | 16 | 20 | 9.3 | 12 |
| Fiji | 83 | 155 | 28.4 | 40 |
| Finland | 662 | 859 | 11.0 | 32 |
| France | 19,811 | 25,230 | 10.2 | 47 |
| French Guiana | 10 | 15 | 17.6 | 4 |
| French Polynesia | 33 | 43 | 11.2 | 17 |
| Gabon | 38 | 67 | 25.5 | 27 |
| Gambia | 18 | 32 | 25.9 | 14 |
| Georgia | 11 | 15 | 13.2 | 9 |

| Country 1 | 1998 Books 2 | 2001 Books 3 | Rate 4 | Part 12 5 |
|---|---|---|---|---|
| Germany | 20,911 | 25,416 | 8.1 | 41 |
| Ghana | 373 | 577 | 19.1 | 57 |
| Gibraltar | 12 | 39 | 60.2 | 10 |
| Greece | 3,186 | 5,513 | 24.5 | 25 |
| Greenland | 103 | 167 | 21.3 | 23 |
| Grenada | 20 | 29 | 16.0 | 13 |
| Guadeloupe | 29 | 37 | 10.2 | 10 |
| Guam | 12 | 30 | 44.3 | 5 |
| Guatemala | 628 | 1,359 | 36.2 | 50 |
| Guinea | 561 | 869 | 19.1 | 7 |
| Guinea-Bissau | 40 | 45 | 4.8 | 20 |
| Guyana | 63 | 119 | 29.0 | 16 |
| Haiti | 325 | 524 | 21.1 | 37 |
| Holy See | 31,636 | 35,000 | 4.1 | 16 |
| Honduras | 177 | 258 | 16.3 | 16 |
| Hungary | 1,551 | 1,831 | 6.9 | 39 |
| Iceland | 141 | 214 | 18.2 | 17 |
| India | 5,141 | 10,364 | 32.4 | 121 |
| Indonesia | 1,262 | 2,638 | 34.3 | 73 |
| Iran | 212 | 745 | 65.3 | 40 |
| Iraq | 271 | 280 | 1.3 | 24 |
| Ireland | 6,604 | 9,172 | 14.0 | 35 |
| Isle of Man | 30 | 74 | 43.5 | 12 |
| Israel | 4,100 | 5,200 | 10.0 | 38 |
| Italy | 16,618 | 19,829 | 7.3 | 25 |
| Ivory Coast | 40 | 45 | 4.8 | 25 |
| Jamaica | 276 | 580 | 34.6 | 36 |
| Japan | 3,157 | 6,151 | 30.6 | 72 |
| Jordan | 138 | 656 | 86.6 | 8 |
| Kazakhstan | 20 | 43 | 35.8 | 9 |
| Kenya | 651 | 954 | 16.5 | 49 |
| Kirghizia | 10 | 11 | 3.9 | 7 |
| Kiribati | 12 | 17 | 14.9 | 10 |
| Kuwait | 20 | 23 | 5.7 | 12 |
| Laos | 36 | 91 | 44.9 | 27 |
| Latvia | 130 | 198 | 18.3 | 18 |
| Lebanon | 560 | 916 | 21.8 | 41 |
| Lesotho | 72 | 101 | 14.5 | 22 |
| Liberia | 248 | 329 | 12.0 | 24 |
| Libya | 11 | 28 | 45.3 | 14 |
| Liechtenstein | 6 | 28 | 85.2 | 5 |
| Lithuania | 355 | 477 | 12.5 | 22 |
| Luxembourg | 71 | 179 | 44.8 | 8 |
| Macedonia | 218 | 342 | 19.7 | 34 |
| Madagascar | 212 | 364 | 24.1 | 36 |
| Malawi | 192 | 256 | 12.2 | 31 |
| Malaysia | 218 | 412 | 29.0 | 58 |
| Maldives | 8 | 9 | 4.8 | 7 |
| Mali | 20 | 94 | 85.7 | 18 |
| Malta | 137 | 227 | 22.4 | 16 |
| Marshall Islands | 15 | 35 | 40.3 | 7 |
| Martinique | 18 | 27 | 17.6 | 10 |
| Mauritania | 17 | 18 | 2.3 | 14 |
| Mauritius | 58 | 95 | 21.8 | 26 |
| Mayotte | 7 | 7 | 0.0 | 6 |
| Mexico | 6,891 | 10,611 | 18.8 | 54 |
| Micronesia | 43 | 58 | 12.7 | 17 |
| Moldavia | 45 | 59 | 11.4 | 3 |
| Monaco | 15 | 49 | 60.6 | 12 |
| Mongolia | 29 | 92 | 58.7 | 25 |
| Montserrat | 15 | 55 | 68.2 | 10 |
| Morocco | 43 | 274 | 109.8 | 40 |
| Mozambique | 164 | 197 | 7.6 | 30 |
| Myanmar | 241 | 479 | 31.6 | 48 |
| Namibia | 195 | 245 | 9.6 | 27 |
| Nauru | 3 | 3 | 0.0 | 3 |
| Nepal | 45 | 171 | 70.6 | 70 |
| Netherlands | 3,973 | 5,998 | 17.9 | 39 |
| Netherlands Antilles | 17 | 23 | 12.9 | 14 |
| New Caledonia | 30 | 39 | 11.1 | 16 |
| New Zealand | 658 | 1,135 | 24.4 | 35 |
| Nicaragua | 578 | 672 | 6.2 | 35 |
| Niger | 32 | 94 | 53.9 | 19 |
| Nigeria | 1,403 | 2,341 | 22.7 | 85 |
| Niue Island | 11 | 12 | 3.5 | 10 |
| Norfolk Island | 8 | 8 | 0.0 | 7 |
| North Korea | 150 | 160 | 2.6 | 19 |
| Northern Cyprus | 10 | 11 | 3.9 | 5 |
| Northern Mariana Is | 2 | 3 | 17.6 | 1 |
| Norway | 1,213 | 1,523 | 9.5 | 34 |

| Country 1 | 1998 Books 2 | 2001 Books 3 | Rate 4 | Part 12 5 |
|---|---|---|---|---|
| Oman | 24 | 52 | 36.2 | 21 |
| Pakistan | 258 | 444 | 24.3 | 54 |
| Palau | 22 | 25 | 5.2 | 5 |
| Palestine | 2,700 | 2,900 | 2.9 | 17 |
| Panama | 139 | 254 | 27.3 | 10 |
| Papua New Guinea | 356 | 506 | 15.1 | 57 |
| Paraguay | 249 | 324 | 11.1 | 19 |
| Peru | 1,039 | 1,962 | 29.0 | 42 |
| Philippines | 1,692 | 2,235 | 11.8 | 53 |
| Pitcairn Islands | 12 | 12 | 0.0 | 8 |
| Poland | 3,716 | 4,381 | 6.8 | 57 |
| Portugal | 1,151 | 1,562 | 13.0 | 29 |
| Puerto Rico | 381 | 570 | 17.5 | 40 |
| Qatar | 10 | 11 | 3.9 | 7 |
| Reunion | 18 | 25 | 14.0 | 14 |
| Romania | 1,622 | 1,800 | 4.3 | 39 |
| Russia | 3,421 | 5,809 | 23.6 | 83 |
| Rwanda | 120 | 180 | 17.6 | 40 |
| Sahara | 12 | 57 | 86.5 | 11 |
| St Helena | 25 | 26 | 1.6 | 3 |
| St Kitts & Nevis | 15 | 18 | 7.6 | 10 |
| St Lucia | 13 | 15 | 5.9 | 12 |
| St Pierre & Miquelon | 2 | 2 | 0.0 | 1 |
| St Vincent & Grenadines | 10 | 11 | 3.9 | 8 |
| Samoa | 54 | 110 | 32.9 | 20 |
| San Marino | 13 | 71 | 97.2 | 2 |
| Sao Tome & Principe | 11 | 12 | 3.5 | 9 |
| Saudi Arabia | 28 | 68 | 42.6 | 26 |
| Senegal | 44 | 86 | 30.7 | 38 |
| Seychelles | 12 | 13 | 3.3 | 9 |
| Sierra Leone | 122 | 198 | 21.4 | 33 |
| Singapore | 180 | 342 | 29.3 | 49 |
| Slovakia | 227 | 301 | 11.9 | 33 |
| Slovenia | 267 | 300 | 4.8 | 36 |
| Solomon Islands | 103 | 136 | 11.8 | 27 |
| Somalia | 20 | 28 | 14.4 | 17 |
| Somaliland | 6 | 10 | 22.7 | 8 |
| South Africa | 2,626 | 3,135 | 7.3 | 91 |
| South Korea | 845 | 1,100 | 11.1 | 51 |
| Spain | 7,716 | 9,533 | 8.8 | 51 |
| Spanish North Africa | 5 | 6 | 7.6 | 4 |
| Sri Lanka | 249 | 466 | 28.5 | 45 |
| Sudan | 230 | 386 | 23.0 | 49 |
| Suriname | 25 | 113 | 82.8 | 24 |
| Svalbard & Jan Mayen Is | 2 | 2 | 0.0 | 2 |
| Swaziland | 53 | 71 | 12.4 | 22 |
| Sweden | 2,025 | 2,503 | 8.8 | 24 |
| Switzerland | 2,738 | 4,645 | 23.5 | 33 |
| Syria | 340 | 640 | 28.8 | 29 |
| Taiwan | 404 | 768 | 29.3 | 46 |
| Tajikistan | 8 | 10 | 9.3 | 7 |
| Tanzania | 341 | 521 | 18.5 | 43 |
| Thailand | 283 | 523 | 27.8 | 57 |
| Timor | 29 | 55 | 29.2 | 27 |
| Togo | 41 | 104 | 45.1 | 22 |
| Tokelau Islands | 8 | 9 | 4.8 | 7 |
| Tonga | 121 | 142 | 6.6 | 22 |
| Trinidad & Tobago | 49 | 97 | 31.4 | 39 |
| Tunisia | 65 | 94 | 15.9 | 27 |
| Turkey | 1,338 | 1,908 | 15.3 | 37 |
| Turkmenistan | 15 | 21 | 14.4 | 14 |
| Turks & Caicos Islands | 2 | 3 | 17.6 | 2 |
| Tuvalu | 10 | 11 | 3.9 | 9 |
| Uganda | 357 | 472 | 11.8 | 51 |
| Ukraine | 1,360 | 1,719 | 9.8 | 43 |
| United Arab Emirates | 18 | 30 | 22.7 | 15 |
| USA | 41,948 | 60,877 | 16.1 | 119 |
| Uruguay | 219 | 316 | 15.8 | 22 |
| Uzbekistan | 15 | 29 | 30.2 | 14 |
| Vanuatu | 90 | 114 | 9.9 | 22 |
| Venezuela | 498 | 687 | 13.7 | 34 |
| Viet Nam | 110 | 130 | 6.9 | 35 |
| Virgin Islands of the US | 17 | 20 | 6.7 | 16 |
| Wallis & Futuna Islands | 8 | 9 | 4.8 | 1 |
| Yemen | 26 | 27 | 1.5 | 24 |
| Yugoslavia | 769 | 1,123 | 16.4 | 38 |
| Zambia | 198 | 275 | 14.0 | 44 |
| Zimbabwe | 310 | 470 | 18.1 | 46 |
| ***Total for all countries*** | 275,506 | 380,348 | 13.8 | 6,286 |

### 4. *A world bibliography of Christian directories*

This 500-title listing, in *WCE* Part 14 "Directory", lists the various types of directories available to assist readers to navigate this immense resource.

### 5. *A world bibliography of Christianity and religion*

The last major type of selection of world Christian literature is the *Selective world bibliography of Christianity and religion* that immediately follows this essay. In this more comprehensive bibliography an attempt has been made to provide the reader with listings of significant works on several major areas of study of Christianity and religion. This bibliography consists, in the main, of multi-volume works such as commentaries, reference works, and so forth. In some cases single-volume works are listed, including dictionaries, lexicons, etymologies, biographies, chronologies, bibliographies, bibliographies of bibliographies, and other works that are both highly comprehensive and widely acclaimed as standard works in their field.

## DESCRIBING THE WORLD BIBLIOGRAPHY

This largest bibliography of the 4 varieties of bibliographies is here divided into 3 main sections, as follows.

*A. Christianity and Christian literature.* The first main section of the world bibliography deals exclusively with Christianity and its literature. It is divided into 10 smaller lists. The first list includes works detailing the contemporary status of Christianity around the world. Here one will find works on topics such as major confessional groups, ethnolinguistics, and other areas that describe the state of Christianity today. These titles should guide the careful reader to consider the prospects and possibilities the church faces as it seeks to carry out its mission.

The second list includes major works in the field of biblical studies. Major commentaries, dictionaries, encyclopedias, and bibliographies make up the works here. Attention should be drawn to the vast resources devoted to serious research with regard to the Bible.

The third list includes major collections, encyclopedias, and dictionaries in church history. It includes studies and reference works in the field of church history, but not works that are themselves the subject of historical study.

The fourth list focuses on the history of doctrine. This list is distinct from the previous one in that it focuses on classical sources, rather than studies based on source materials The reader will find major works from the history of Christianity that have had the most significant impact on the development of Christian doctrine over the centuries through the post-World War II period. The placement of a number of 20th century works here does not imply that these works are out of date; rather, it represents a judgment that they are works of such enduring importance that theologians will have to take account of them for decades, perhaps even for centuries to come.

The fifth list includes major reference works and collections dealing with contemporary theology. Works included in this list concentrate on the major works in areas of theological work from approximately the past 30 to 40 years. Included in this list are works that could constitute a wide variety of bibliographies. Indeed, one would rarely expect to find

Carl Henry's *God, revelation, and authority* on the same list as Rosemary Radford Reuther's *Sexism and God–talk*. However, to split this particular list into its half-dozen or so possible sub-lists would have been pedantic.

The sixth list highlights theological ethics. The seventh list deals with works related to the study of mission, missions, missiology, and mission work. Works here focus on major histories of mission, methodologies, and reference works. The eighth list treats ecumenism. This list includes the major documents of ecumenical movements in the last hundred or so years, major studies of these movements, and reference works that focus on ecumenism.

The ninth list is perhaps the broadest in scope. It deals with major reference works related to Christianity and art, architecture, spirituality, liturgy, and so forth. This list focuses on what could be called the esthetic or experiential elements of Christianity. The tenth list of this Part deals with the relationship of science and religion, and in particular, of science and Christianity. This is a major development and a most illuminating one. Lastly, the eleventh list deals with all world religions including Christianity.

*B. The non-Christian religious context.* The second main section of the world bibliography highlights the non-Christian religious context in which Christianity is situated. This section is divided into 6 lists. Lists 1 through 4 deal with 4 other world religions: Islam, Hinduism, Buddhism, and also Judaism as the closest to Christianity through the shared Old Testament.

List 5 deals with other religions, and List 6 with interfaith dialogue. The aim here is to provide reading lists for non-specialists who wish to find definitive sources of information on religions with which Christianity interacts. In each list one will find not only major reference works about each religion, but also major works from within those religions, including historical and theological works by authors who practice them. The present attempt is to point the reader not only to descriptive works, but also to places where one may encounter devoted practitioners of these religions, and thus meet the religions on their own terms.

*C. Approaches to the study of religion.* The third main section of the world bibliography briefly examines a variety of methodological approaches to the study of religion and religions, including Christianity. Here the reader will find works describing or outlining methodologies used to study religion in general and Christianity in particular. This section attempts to provide a sense of the variety of methodological tools available to contemporary researchers and scholars. Inclusion of sources and methodologies does not imply either endorsement or indictment, but rather is an indication of the variety of tools that currently exists to study religion and religious phenomena, as well as the serious attention that religion receives. The range of approaches to the study of religion indicates, among other things, that the study of religion is not limited to one or two highly specialized disciplines, but can be profitably approached by almost any field of research. This range of approaches also points to the fact that religion can be— and is—studied from both the 'outside' as well as from 'within'. That is, some approaches lend themselves to a view of religion that does not assume the truth of any particular religion's claims. Other approaches, meanwhile, assume that the researcher believes the claims of the religion studied. Indeed, debate among scholars rages over the relationship between religious studies, as it exists primarily in Western colleges and universities, and theological studies. In general, religious studies indicate approaches that seek to apply scientific and social scientific methods to the study of religion as a phenomenon, while theological studies indicate approaches that seek to explicate the faith itself. Even this distinction does not do justice to the reality of the situation, however, for a number of prominent scholars disagree on the precise difference between the two. Suffice it to say that concern with methodology has occupied, and is likely to occupy for some time, the attention of serious students of religion and religions.

While a complete taxonomy of approaches to the study of religion is not necessary for this encyclopedia's purposes, some of the major contemporary and

historic approaches to the study of religion have been placed in context. Here we give 8 more lists. List 1 presents general works on methodology. Often these are general reference works or major textbooks that seek to orient students to the study of religion. List 2 presents works on the philosophy of religion. List 3 contains works that study religion from a historical perspective; List 4 highlights works in the sociology of religion; List 5 the anthropology of religion, List 6 the psychology of religion; and List 7 presents works that study religious ethics. Lastly, List 8 presents works that study other approaches to the study of religions and religious phenomena.

The last 2 sections of this world bibliography contain invaluable tools. First is a list that includes major resources found in electronic media, such as CD-ROM and online resources. This is perhaps the least definitive list of all, for not only is the number of resources on electronic media growing rapidly but also the variety of electronic media continues to proliferate. It is entirely possible that between the time the present work goes to press and its actual appearance in print, quite new media will have come to market. Given these possibilities, the purpose in this list is not to be even remotely complete, but simply to point the reader to a rapidly growing area of publication that will increasingly affect the study of Christianity and religion.

The final list here is a bibliography of bibliographies that touch on the previous 4 major listings. It is a formidable tool indeed.

## THE IMPACT OF THESE MATERIALS

Doubtless many will be surprised at the findings of this bibliographical investigation. Agnostics or others who remain skeptical of the Christian movement—its size, its impact, its claims—will find it difficult to believe that such a 'minor' or 'outdated' religious movement could generate so many titles, let alone so much serious attention. And even if skeptics accept the size of the literature, they will question its quality and its scholarship. To these, the bibliographies in this *WCE-WCT-WCD* project are an invitation to explore the world of Christian literature before attempting overall or definitive judgments. Even if unconvinced by the normative claims of Christianity, one can at least begin to appreciate both the seriousness with which Christians approach the faith, as well as the quality of much of the work that grows out of it.

Others will no doubt simply feel overwhelmed by the extent of the literature. Even those who are already widely read may feel that they have barely touched upon the wealth of information on Christianity. To these, the bibliographies in the Encyclopedia are both a challenge and an aid. They challenge Christians to discover for themselves the rich variety of Christian literature beyond the comfortable limits of their accustomed reading. They aid Christians by providing some sense of how this vast collection may be organized and by pointing to some of the major works in the various fields. Hopefully readers of various stripes will think twice before dismissing persons and movements whose approaches and commitments are different from their own.

Still others may simply abandon any such efforts to expand their knowledge. Seeing that one person cannot possibly master even a portion of the works that may be relevant to their fields, they may deem it a waste of time to wade through the literature. Regrettably this is precisely the reaction that decision-makers are most likely to have. Christian mission executives are no exception at this point. Overwhelmed with the demands on their time, often lacking adequate human and financial resources, and facing a massive undertaking with endless deadlines, they simply do not have the time (so they would say) to engage all the literature relevant to the missionary enterprise. The unfortunate result is poorly focused efforts that waste valuable resources. To these, the bibliographies in *WCE/WCT/WCD* are likewise a challenge. They challenge leaders to face boldly the vast horizons of Christian scholarship and to utilize the mass of research to provide them with invaluable guidance in fulfilling the Great Commission. Too much is at stake and too many resources are available to waste.

The problem, then, is how to make sense of the mass of resources available. Therein lies the key to understanding the purpose of these bibliographies in this work. In a word, they attempt to create order out of chaos.

### ORGANIZING PRINCIPLES EMPLOYED

As has been mentioned, these bibliographies do not claim to be exhaustive. Nor do they claim to cover all the most important literature in its entirety. As bibliographies, they are selective. They are meant, above all, to be illustrative. That is, they seek to highlight the vastness of world Christian literature. Their purpose is to point the careful reader to other sources of similar information. They also serve to document and substantiate the data, events, statements, measurements, analysis, concepts, findings, conclusions, and claims described in this project's 48 Parts and especially in its country articles in *WCE* Part 4.

Any single bibliographical entry in an English-language bibliography of books consists of up to 16 standard components: its title; a subtitle if present; sometimes a translation into English if a non-English title; additional explanatory title of any series or event or collection that explains the main title; names of authors, editors, and translators; year of publication; edition (if second, third, etc. is significant); number of volumes if more than one; titles and other details of component volumes; main title's number of pages if useful to substantiate length; name of publisher; city or place of publication, with country if necessary for clarity; and lastly, brief note or annotation in parentheses in cases where there is additional valuable information relevant for the purposes of the listing.

There are a number of different purposes varying from one type of bibliography to another. They can be organized on any one of the different components based on which of them the author wants to put first.

The most common order used in presenting information begins with the author's name, organized alphabetically by surname and initials. This is useful for shorter bibliographies or for audiences who know the names of many or most of the significant authors on the subject. This method is less helpful in larger bibliographies or for those where most readers would not be familiar with authors' names or significance. Other recognized forms are organized chronologically by year of publication, or by author with his or her works arranged chronologically. This is most helpful when most authors listed have multiple entries.

Another popular form is not to organize the entries into a list by any single component, but instead to write a reasonably short bibliographical essay mentioning the 10, 20, 30, or 40 major books on the subject being considered.

The procedure followed here is different in that most readers will not be familiar with authors' names, so lengthy listings of works by author mean little or nothing. For such readers, the most important component is the title, so it helps them most to make this the first item in every entry. This Encyclopedia therefore follows, in all its bibliographies, the practice of listing works alphabetically by title. Since these listings are computerized and automated, alphabetization follows strict rules including recognition of the definite and indefinite articles (The, A, An). Thus, *A Baptist bibliography* precedes *Acta sanctorum quotquot toto orbe coluntur*.

Another rule followed here throughout in English titles is to abandon the long-standing and widespread practice of artificially capitalizing all, or most, of the words in titles. Instead, we capitalize only names, titles, proper nouns, or adjectives referring to organizations. The most immediate beneficiary of this policy is the clearing up of ambiguities surrounding key words like 'church', 'gospel', 'evangelical', 'charismatic', and so on, which can employ either initial capitals or initial lowercase letters and thereby convey different meanings.

### SUMMARY

These bibliographies, then, both complement and extend further the rest of the research in the *WCE/WCT/WCD* project. They complement the other materials by providing the reader with further sources of information for verification and ongoing study. They extend the research to the extent that they represent a part of the data on world Christianity. In fact, they point beyond themselves to incredible wealth of accumulated knowledge on Christianity and religion in a whole variety of aspects. One can find other, more comprehensive bibliographies on almost any topic in *WCE/WCT/WCD*; many of them are listed here. The overall bibliographies given here are unique in the range of topics covered under one cover. They aim to leave the reader without excuse for willful ignorance of the resources available for understanding the Christian phenomenon or the place of Christianity in the world. One need not become familiar with all of the 8,500 or so titles here to make good use of the knowledge they contain. Indeed, no one can. However, judicious use of these bibliographies can pay enormous dividends in terms of knowledge, as well as in terms of a more effective stewardship of resources in Christian mission and ministry. To the extent that these bibliographies assist the reader in developing greater understanding of Christianity in its world context, they achieve their purpose.

### SELECTIVE WORLD BIBLIOGRAPHY OF CHRISTIANITY AND RELIGION

Some 1,380 titles on this subject are shown on the following 12 pages, beginning opposite.

# I. CHRISTIANITY

## 1. CONTEMPORARY STATUS OF CHRISTIANITY

*A critical guide to Catholic reference books.* J. P. McCabe. 3rd ed. Englewood, CO: Libraries Unlimited, 1989. 337p.

*A dictionary of Greek Orthodoxy.* N. D. Patrinacos. Pleasantville, NY: Hellenic Heritage Publications, 1984. 391p.

*A guide to the study of the Pentecostal movement.* C. E. Jones. ATLA Bibliographic Series, 6. Metuchen, NJ and London: American Theological Library Association and Scarecrow Press, 1983. 1,245p in 2 vols. (Dated, but an important bibliography of the Pentecostal movement.)

*An international directory of theological schools 1997.* A. Gilmore (ed). London: SCM Press; Geneva: WCC Publications, 1996. 512p.

*Annuario pontificio 1997.* Vatican City: Libreria Editrice Vaticana, 1997. 2,490p.

*Annuarium statisticum ecclesiae 1994 (Statistical yearbook of the church 1994).* Vatican City: Secretaria Status, 1994. 449p.

*Atlas hierarchicus: descriptio geographica et statistica ecclesiae catholicae tum occidentis tum orientis.* H. Emmerich. Mödling, Austria: St Gabriel–Verlag, 1968 (76p.), 1976, (107p. plus maps.); 5th edition 1992 (118p. plus maps. ed. Z. Stezycki) 1976. 107p. (Contemporary survey of all Roman Catholic jurisdictions; in French, English, German, Italian, and Spanish).

*Atlas of religious change in America, 1952–1990.* P. L. Halvorson & W. M. Newman. Atlanta: Glenmary Research Center, 1994. 236p.

*Atlas zur Kirchengeschichte: Die Christlichen in Geschichte und Gegenwart.* H. Jedin, K. S. Latourette & J. Martin (eds). Freiburg im Breisgau: Herder, 1987. 190p.

*Bilan du monde: encyclopédie catholique du monde chrétien.* J. Frisque et al. (eds). 2nd ed. Louvain: Casterman, 1964. 2 vols.

*Catholic encyclopedia.* New York: McGraw-Hill, 1967–1989. 18 vols. (International reference work on the constitution, doctrine, discipline and history of the Catholic church).

*Charismatic Christianity as a global culture.* K. Poewe (ed). Studies in comparative religion. Columbia, SC: University of South Carolina Press, 1994. 316p.

*Chinese churches handbook.* G. Law. Hong Kong: Chinese Coordination Centre of World Evangelism, 1982. 378p.

*Christianity and democracy: a theology for a just world order.* J. W. de Gruchy. Cambridge studies in ideology and religion, 7. New York and Cambridge, UK: Cambridge University Press, 1995. 308p.

*Constitutions of the countries of the world.* A. P. Blaustein & G. H. Flanz. Dobbs Ferry, NY: Oceana Publications, 1971–. 17 vols; (Updated texts, chronologies, bibliographies; deals with constitutional status of Christianity and religion).

*Corpus dictionary of Western Churches.* T. C. O'Brien (ed). Washington, DC: Corpus Publications, 1970. 820p. (Primarily Roman Catholic).

*Death of the church.* M. Regele. Grand Rapids, MI: Zondervan, 1995.

*Defenders of God: the fundamentalist revolt against the modern age.* B. B. Lawrence. San Francisco: Harper & Row, 1989. 318p. (Fundamentalist movements in several religions, including Christianity, Judaism, and Islam.).

*Enciclopedia cattolica.* Città del Vaticano: Enciclopedia Cattolica, 1948–54. 12 vols.

*Enciclopedia ecclesiastica.* A. Bernareggi. Milan: F. Vallardi, 1942–63. 7 vols.

*Encyclopedia of Methodism.* M. Simpson. New York: Gordon Press, 1977. 2 vols.

*Encyclopedia of modern Christian missions: the agencies.* B. L. Goddard (ed). Camden, NJ: T. Nelson, 1967. 762p.

*Encyclopedia of Southern Baptists.* Nashville, TN: Broadman, 1958. 2 vols. (All Baptist denominations and movements).

*Encyclopedia of the Lutheran Church.* J. Bodensieck (ed). Minneapolis, MN: Augsburg, 1965. 3 vols.

*Encyclopedia of the Reformed faith.* D. F. McKim & D. F. Wright (eds). Louisville, KY: Westminster John Knox; Edinburgh: Saint Andrew, 1992. 438p.

*Encyclopedia of world Methodism.* N. B. Harmon (ed). Nashville, TN: United Methodist Publishing House, 1974. 2 vols.

*Encyclopedic dictionary of religion.* C. M. Aherne, T. C. O'Brien & P. K. Meagher (eds). Palatine, IL: Corpus, 1977. 3 vols. (Primarily Roman Catholic).

*Encyclopédie du protestantisme.* P. Gisel (ed). Paris: Cerf; Geneva: Labor et Fides, 1995. 1,700p.

*Encyklopedia katolicka.* F. Gryglewicz, R. Lukaszyk & Z. Sulowski (eds). Lublin, Poland: Catholic University, 1973–. (Polish; multivolume).

*Ethnologue: languages of the world.* B. F. Grimes (ed). 13th ed. Dallas: Summer Institute of Linguistics, 1996. 1,391p in 3 vols. (Current data on 6,703 languages, including status of scripture translation. Vols. 2 and 3 are indexes of language names and language families).

*Fire from heaven: the rise of Pentecostal spirituality and the reshaping of religion in the twenty–first century.* H. Cox. Reading, MA: Addison–Wesley, 1995. 339p.

*Guida delle missioni cattoliche.* Vatican City: SC Propaganda, 1975. 1,628p. (Earlier editions 1934, 1946, 1950, 1970).

*Handbook of denominations in America.* F. S. Mead & S. S. Hill. 10th ed. Nashville, TN: Abingdon, 1995. 352p.

*Handbuch der Ostkirchenkunde.* E. von Ivánka, J. Tyciak & P. Wiertz (eds). 2nd ed. Düsseldorf: Patmos, 1990–93. 3 vols. (Best overall reference work on Eastern churches.)

*Handbuch der Pfingstbewegung.* W. J. Hollenweger. Geneva, 1965–67. 10 vols. (Duplicated; University Microfilms and ATLA Microtext Project).

*Iglesias de Oriente (Churches of the East).* A. S. Hernández. Santander: Editorial Sal Terrae, 1959–63. 2 vols. (Includes annotated bibliography of 2,250 items).

*Kleines Wörterbuch des christlichen Orients.* J. Assfalg & P. Krüger. Wiesbaden: Harrassowitz, 1975. 493p. (Translated into French as *Petit dictionnaire de l'Orient chrétien.* Turnhout: Brepols, 1991).

*Les Ordres religieux: Guide historique.* G. Duchet-Sachaux & M. Duchet-Sachaux. Paris: Flammarion, 1993. 320p.

*Les Ordres religieux: La Vie et l'art.* G. Le Bras (ed). Paris: Flammarion, 1979–80. 1,525p. in 2 vols.

*Let the earth hear his voice: a comprehensive reference volume on world evangelization.* J. D. Douglas. Minneapolis, MN: World Wide Publications, 1975. 1,471p. (International Congress on World Evangelization, Lausanne 1974).

*Lexikon der christlicher Kirchen und Sekten.* J. Gründler. Vienna: Herder, 1961. 2 vols. (History and description of all denominations).

*Lexikon für Theologie und Kirche.* W. Kasper (ed). 3rd ed. Freiburg: Herder, 1993–. 4 vols.; in progress to 10 vols.

*Lutheran cyclopedia.* E. L. Lueker (ed). St. Louis, MO: Concordia, 1954. 1,160p.

*Modern American religion.* M. E. Marty. Chicago: University of Chicago Press, 1986–1996. 3 vols.

*New Catholic encyclopedia.* Washington, DC: Catholic University of America, 1967. 15 vols.

*Operation world: a handbook for world intercession.* P. J. Johnstone. Grand Rapids, MI: Zondervan, 1993. 666p. (1st edition 1974, 208p).

*Opus Dei: who, how, why.* G. Romano. Trans., E. C. Lane. New York: Alba House, 1995. 207p.

*Oriente cattolico: cenni storici e statistiche.* 4th ed. Vatican City: S. C. per le Chiese Orientali, 1974. 857p.

*Pentecostalism: origins and developments worldwide.* W. J. Hollenweger. Peabody, USA: Hendrickson, 1997. 495p.

*Prime–time religion: an encyclopedia of religious broadcasting.* J. G. Melton, P. C. Lucas & J. R. Stone. Phoenix, AZ: Oryx, 1997. 432p.

*Profiles in belief: the religious bodies of the United States and Canada.* A. C. Piepkorn. New York: Harper & Row, 1977–79. 4 vols in 3.

*Puebla and beyond: documentation and commentary.* J. Eagleson & P. Scharper (eds). Trans., J. Drury. Maryknoll, NY: Orbis Books, 1979. 383p.

*Reimagining denominationalism: interpretive essays.* R. B. Mullin & R. E. Richey (eds). Religion in America series. New York: Oxford University Press, 1994. 336p.

'Religion,' in *Propaedia of New Encyclopaedia Britannica.* p.498–559. Chicago: Encyclopaedia Britannica, 1975.

*Scriptures of the world: a compilation of the 2,018 languages in which at least one book of the Bible has been published since the Bible was first printed by Johann Gutenberg.* L. Lupas & E. F. Rhodes (eds). New York and Reading, UK: United Bible Societies, 1992. 145p.

*Sekai kirisuto–kyo hyakka–jiten (Encyclopedia of world Christianity).* M. Takenaka et al. (eds). Tokyo: Kyobunkwan, 1986. (Japanese translation of the first edition of the *World Christian encyclopedia*).

*Selective bibliography on evangelism and evangelization.* D. B. Barrett. Nairobi: Centre for the Study of World Evangelization, 1980. (1,400 items).

*Seventh–day Adventist encyclopedia.* D. F. Neufeld (ed). Washington, DC: Review & Herald, 1966–76. 10 vols.

*Six hundred ecumenical consultations 1948–1982.* A. J. van der Bent. Geneva: World Council of Churches, 1983. 254p.

'The Anglican world in figures,' D. B. Barrett & T. de Bordenave III, London: Anglican Frontier Missions, 1998. 4p. (Prepared for Lambeth Conference 1998).

*The book of a thousand tongues.* E. A. Nida (ed). 2nd ed. London: United Bible Societies, 1972. 536p. (Catalogue of 1,399 languages with printed scriptures, giving a scripture passage for each).

*The challenge of basic Christian communities.* S. Torres & J. Eagleson (eds). Maryknoll, NY: Orbis, 1982.

*The charismatic movement: a guide to the study of neo–pentecostalism with emphasis on Anglo–American sources.* C. E. Jones. ATLA Bibliographic Series, 30. Metuchen, NJ and London: American Theological Library Association and Scarecrow Press, 1995. 1,266p in 2 vols. (A major bibliography of the charismatic movement).

*The Christian churches of the East.* D. Attwater. London: Geoffrey Chapman, 1961. 2 vols.

*The Christian conspiracy: how the teachings of Christ have been altered by Christians.* L. D. Moore. Atlanta: Pendulum Plus Press, 1994. 357p.

*The Eastern Christian churches: a brief survey.* R. G. Roberson. 3rd ed. Rome: Pontificum Studiorum Orientalium, 1990. 129p.

*The fundamentalism project.* M. E. Marty & R. S. Appleby (eds). Chicago: University of Chicago Press, 1991–96. 5 vols. (Vol. 1: *Fundamentalisms observed*; vol. 2: *Fundamentalisms and the state*; vol. 3: *Fundamentalisms and society*; vol. 4: *Accounting for fundamentalisms*; vol. 5: *Fundamentalisms comprehended*. A cross–religious study).

*The gospel in a pluralist society.* L. Newbigin. Grand Rapids, MI: Eerdmans, 1989.

*The HarperCollins encyclopedia of Catholicism.* R. P. McBrien (ed). San Francisco: Harper, 1995. 1,387p.

*The index of leading spiritual indicators: trends in morality, beliefs, lifestyles, religious and spiritual thought, behavior, and church involvement.* G. Barna. Dallas: Word, 1996. 160p.

*The Latvian Orthodox church.* Protopresbyter Alexander Cherney. Welshpool, Wales, UK: Stylite Publishing, 1985. 143p.

*The Mennonite encyclopedia: a comprehensive reference work on the Anabaptist–Mennonite movement.* Scottdale, PA: Mennonite Publishing House, 1955–59. 4 vols.

*The modern Catholic encyclopedia.* M. Glazier & M. Hellwig (eds). London: Gill & Macmillan; Collegeville, MN: Liturgical Press, 1994. 958p.

*The new Catholic encyclopedia.* W. J. McDonald (ed). New York: McGraw-Hill, 1967. 15 vols.

*The Orthodox Church.* T. Ware. 2nd ed. London: Penguin, 1983. 352p.

*The Orthodox Church in the Ecumenical Movement: documents and statements 1902–1975.* C. G. Patelos (ed). Geneva: World Council of Churches, 1978. 360p.

*The revenge of God: the resurgence of Islam, Christianity and Judaism in the modern world.* G. Kepel. University Park, PA: Pennsylvania State University Press, 1994. 215p. (Translated by A. Braley from *La Revanche de Dieu*).

*The sociology of Protestantism.* R. Mehl. Trans., J. H. Farley. London: SCM Press, 1970. 336p.

*The world year book of religion: the religious situation.* D. R. Cutler (ed). London: Evans Brothers, 1968–69.

*Théo: L'Encyclopédie catholique pour tous.* M. Dubost (ed). Paris: Droguet–Ardant/Fayard, 1993.

*Turning over a new leaf: Protestant missions and the Orthodox churches of the Middle East: the final report of a multi–mission study group on Orthodoxy.* London: Interserve, 1992. 134p. (Promotes Protestant and Orthodox cooperation).

*Twentieth–century religious thought: the frontiers of philosophy and theology, 1900–1960.* J. Macquarrie. New York: Harper & Row, 1963. 415p.

*Weltkirchenlexikon.* F. H. Littell & H. H. Walz (eds). *Handbuch der Ökumene im Auftrag des Deutschen Evangelischen.* Stuttgart: Kreuz–Verlag, 1960.

*World Christian encyclopedia: a comparative survey of churches and religions in the modern world, AD 1900–2000.* D. B. Barrett (ed). Nairobi: Oxford University Press, 1982. 1,025p.

*World Christian handbook.* E. J. Bingle, K. G. Grubb & H. W. Coxill (eds). 5th ed. London: Lutterworth, 1967. (Statistics).

*Yearbook of the Orthodox Church, 1978.* Munich: Verlag Alex Proc, 1978. 309p. (Annual on Eastern Orthodox jurisdictions worldwide, alternately published in English, French, and German).

## 2. BIBLICAL STUDIES

*A bibliography of New Testament bibliographies.* J. C. Hurd. New York: Seabury, 1966. (1,300 articles and books).

*A concordance to the Greek Testament.* W. F. Moulton & A. S. Geden. 5th ed. Edinburgh: T. & T. Clark, 1978. 1,126p.

*A decade of Bible bibliography.* Oxford, UK: Blackwell, 1967. (Covers 1957–66).

*A dictionary of Biblical interpretation.* R. J. Coggins & J. L. Houlden (eds). London: SCM; New York: Trinity Press International, 1990. 765p.

*A dictionary of Biblical tradition in English literature.* D. L. Jeffrey (ed). Grand Rapids, MI: Eerdmans, 1992. 992p.

*A dictionary of the Bible.* W. R. F. Browning. Oxford, UK and New York: Oxford University Press, 1996. 438p.

*A Greek–English lexicon of the New Testament and other early Christian literature.* W. Bauer, W. F. Arndt, F. W. Gingrich. 2nd ed. Chicago: University of Chicago Press, 1979. 940p.

*Almanac of the Bible.* G. Wigoder, S. M. Paul & B. T. Vivian (eds). Jerusalem: Jerusalem Publishing House; New York: Henry Holt, 1991. 448p.

*An introduction to New Testament Christology.* R. E. Brown. New York: Paulist Press, 1994. 238p.

*Analytical concordance to the Bible.* R. Young. 22nd ed. 1881; New York: Funk & Wagnalls, 1955. 1,257p. (Coded to dictionary of original Hebrew/Greek terms; 311,000 references).

*Atlas of the Bible.* L. H. Grollenberg. Trans., J. M. H. Reid & H. H. Rowley. New York and London: Nelson, 1956. 166p. (Originally published as *Atlas van de Bijbel*, Amsterdam: Elsevier).

*Austieg und Niedergang der römischen Welt: Geschichte Roms im Spiegel der neueren Forschung. II. Principat.* W. Haase & H. Temporini (eds). Berlin and New York: de Gruyter, 1982–1988. 4,794p. (Vols. 25.1 through 25.6 of 80 volumes).

*Baker encyclopedia of Bible places.* J. Bimson (ed). Grand Rapids, MI: Baker, 1995.

*Bible bibliography, 1967–73.* P. R. Ackroyd (ed). Oxford, UK: Blackwell, 1975. (Works in nearly 20 languages).

*Biblia Patristica: index des citations et allusions bibliques dans la littérature patristique.* Paris: CNRS, 1975–80. 3 vols. (27,000 references; computerized).

*Biblical resources for ministry: a bibliography of works in biblical studies.* D. R. Bauer. 2nd ed. Nappanee, IN: Evangel, 1995. 144p.

*Biblical theology of the Old and New Testaments.* B. Childs. Minneapolis, MN: Fortress, 1992.

*Bibliographie de la Septante: (1970–1993). (Bibliography of the Septuagint).* C. Dogniez. Supplements to Vetus Testamentum, 60. Leiden and New York: E. J. Brill, 1995. 361p.

*Bibliographies for biblical research.* W. E. Mills (ed). Lewiston, NY: E. Mellen Press, 1993–1996. 6 vols.

*Bibliography of literature on First Peter.* A. Casurella. New Testament tools and studies, 23. Leiden and New York: E. J. Brill, 1996. 178p.

*Bibliography of New Testament literature, 1900–1950.* T. Akaishi (ed). San Anselmo, CA: Seminary Cooperative Store, 1953. 312p. (2,400 annotated items).

*Catalogue of English Bible translations: a classified bibliography of versions and editions including books, parts, and Old and New Testament Apocrypha and Apocryphal books.* W. J. Chamberlin. Bibliographies and indexes in religious studies, 21. New York: Greenwood, 1991. 946p. (The best and most complete for its listing of English Bible translations, 9,000 titles and editions).

*Comentario biblico de Collegeville.* Collegeville, MN: The Liturgical Press.

*Commentaries.* J. Calvin. Grand Rapids, MI: Baker. 22 vols.

*Das Alte Testament Deutsch.* G. von Rad et al. (eds). Göttingen: Vandenhoeck & Ruprecht, 1949–66. 25 vols.

*Das Neue Testament Deutsch.* G. Friedrich (ed). Göttingen: Vandenhoeck & Ruprecht, 1960–68. 4 vols.

*Dictionary of Christ and the Gospels.* J. Hastings. New York: Scribner, 1906–1908. 2 vols.

*Dictionary of Jesus and the Gospels.* J. B. Green & S. McKnight (eds). Downers Grove, IL and Leicester, UK: InterVarsity, 1992. 959p.

*Dictionary of Paul and his letters.* G. Hawthorne & R. P. Martin (eds). Downers Grove, IL and Leicester, UK: InterVarsity, 1993. 1,067p.

*Dictionary of the Bible.* F. C. Grant & H. H. Rowley (eds). New York: Scribner, 1963. 1,059p.
*Dictionary of the Bible.* J. Hastings. Edinburgh: T. & T. Clark, 1898–1904. 5 vols.
*Dictionnaire de la Bible: supplément.* L. Pirot (ed). Paris: Letouzey et Ané, 1928–. 12 vols. to date.
*Elenchus bibliographicus biblicus.* P. Nober. Rome: Biblical Institute, 1970. (Annual).
*Eleven years of Bible bibliography: the book lists of the Society for Old Testament study, 1946–56.* H. H. Rowley (ed). Indian Hill, CO: Falcon's Wing, 1957. 804p.
*Encyclopaedia biblica: thesaurus rerum biblicarum alphabetico ordine digestus.* Hierosolymis: Instituti Bialik, 1950–.
*Encyclopaedia of biblical theology.* J. B. Bauer. London: Sheed & Ward, 1970. 3 vols. (Translation of 1959 *Bibeltheologisches Wörterbuch*).
*Encyclopedia biblica.* T. K. Cheyne & J. S. Black. New York: Gordon Press Publications, 1977. 4 vols.
*Encyclopedia of archaeological excavations in the Holy Land.* Stern. N.p., 1995. 4 vols.
*Encyclopedia of Bible difficulties.* G. J. Archer Jr. Grand Rapids, MI: Zondervan, 1982. 352p.
*Encyclopedia of Biblical errancy.* C. D. McKinsey. Buffalo, NY: Prometheus Books, 1995. 553p.
*Encyclopedia of biblical interpretation: a millenial anthology.* M. M. Kasher & H. Freedman (eds). New York: American Biblical Encyclopedia Society, 1953–79. 9 vols. (Jewish biblical interpretations from Talmudic–Midrashic literature).
*Encyclopedia of Biblical personalities: Ishei haTanach.* Y. Chasidah. Brooklyn, NY: Mesorah Publications, 1994.
*Encyclopedia of Biblical prophecy: the complete guide to scriptural predictions and their fulfillment.* J. B. Payne. Grand Rapids, MI: Baker, 1996. 779p.
*Encyclopedic dictionary of the Bible.* L. F. Hartman (ed). New York: McGraw–Hill, 1963. 2,600p.
*Etudes bibliques.* Paris: Lethielleux. (Commentary series).
*Evangelical dictionary of biblical theology.* W. A. Elwell (ed). Grand Rapids, MI: Baker, 1996.
*Exhaustive concordance of the Bible.* J. Strong. London: Hodder, 1894. 1,807p. (Every work of KJ (AV), RV Bibles).
*Handbook of Biblical criticism.* R. N. Soulen. 2nd ed. Atlanta: John Knox, 1981. 239p.
*Harper's Bible commentary.* J. L. Mays (ed). San Francisco: Harper, 1988. 1,344p. (2nd ed. in preparation).
*Hermeneia: a critical and historical commentary on the Bible.* Minneapolis, MN: Fortress Press. (Aims to present most complete surveys of research on each book of the Bible).
*Hermeneutika BibleWorks 3.5 on CD–ROM.*
*Historical catalogue of printed editions of the English Bible, 1525–1961.* A. S. Herbert. London: BFBS, 1968. (Lists 2,525 distinct editions of the Bible or parts of it).
*Illustrated dictionary and concordance of the Bible.* G. Wigoder (ed). Jerusalem: Jerusalem Publishing House; New York: Macmillan, 1986. 1,070p.
*Index of articles on the New Testament and the early church.* B. M. Metzger. Philadelphia: Society of Biblical Literature, 1951. 182p. (Indexes 2,350 articles).
*International critical commentary on the Holy Scriptures.* S. R. Driver, A. Plummer & C. A. Briggs (eds). Edinburgh: T. & T. Clark, 1896–1937. 45 vols. (Commentary series).
*Internationale Zeitschriftenschau für Bibelwissenschaft und Grenzgebiete.* Stuttgart: Verlag Katholisches Bibelwerk, biennial since 1952. (Mostly German abstracts).
*Interpretation: a Bible commentary for teaching and preaching.* J. L. Mays et al. (eds). Louisville, KY: Westminster John Knox, 1986–. 36 vols. to date. (A series designed to bring scholarly work to bear on practical tasks of ministry).
*Journal for the study of the Old Testament supplement series.* Sheffield, UK: JSOT Press. 269 vols. to date.
*Konkordanz zum hebräischen Alten Testament.* G. Lisowsky. Stuttgart: Privilegierte Württembergische Bibelanstalt, 1958. 1,672p.
*Kritisch–Exegetischer Kommentar über das Neue Testament.* H. A. W. Meyer. Göttingen: Vandenhoeck & Ruprecht, 1856–1859. 7 vols.
*La concordance de la Bible: concordantia polyglotta.* Turnhout, Belgium: Brepols, 1980. 5 vols. (First complete Bible concordance in French with Hebrew, Greek, Latin, and English parallels).
*Life applications Bible commentary.* Wheaton, IL: Tyndale House.
*Literary currents in Biblical interpretation.* D. Fewell & D. M. Gunn (eds). Louisville, KY: Westminster John Knox, 1990–1995. 14 vols.
*Mercer dictionary of the Bible.* W. E. Mills (ed). Macon, GA: Mercer University Press, 1990. 1,023p. (Published in Britain as *The Lutterworth Dictionary of the Bible.* Cambridge, UK: Lutterworth, 1990).
*Models for interpretation of scripture.* J. Goldingay. Grand Rapids, MI: Eerdmans; Carlisle PA: Paternoster Press, 1995. 338p.
*Modern New Testament concordance.* M. Darton (ed). London: Darton, Longman & Todd, 1976. (Words and 341 themes, for all modern English versions).
*Moffatt New Testament commentary.* J. Moffatt (ed). New York: Harper, 1927–50. 17 vols.
*Moody Gospel commentary.* Chicago: Moody Press.
*Multipurpose tools for Bible study.* F. W. Danker. 4th ed. Minneapolis, MN: Fortress, 1993.
*Nelson's complete concordance of the Revised Standard Version.* J. W. Ellison (ed). New York: Thomas Nelson, 1957.
*New American commentary.* Nashville, TN: Broadman & Holman.
*New Bible commentary: 21st century edition.* D. A. Carson et al. (eds). 4th ed. Leicester, UK and Downers Grove, IL: InterVarsity, 1994. 1,468p.
*New Bible dictionary.* D. R. W. Wood (ed). 3rd ed. Downers Grove, IL: InterVarsity, 1996. 1,318p.
*New international dictionary of New Testament theology.* C. Brown (ed). Grand Rapids, MI: Zondervan, 1975–78. 3 vols. (Articles on NT Greek words).
*New Testament abstracts.* Weston, MA: Theological Faculty, Weston College, 1956–. (Issued 3 times a year; abstracts in English from articles in many languages).
*New Testament tools and studies.* B. M. Metzger (ed). Leiden: E. J. Brill, 1966–80. Vol I: *Index to periodical literature on the Apostle Paul.* Vol VI: *Index to periodical literature on Christ and the Gospels* (10,090 entries). Vol VII: *A classified bibligraphy of literature on the Acts of the Apostles* (6,645 entries). Vol X: *Philological, versional and patristic.*
*NIV application commentary.* Grand Rapids, MI: Zondervan.
*Old testament abstracts on CD–ROM.* Washington, DC: The Catholic Biblical Association; Evanston, IL: American Theological Library Association, annual since 1995.
*Orbis biblicus et orientalis.* Göttingen: Vandenhoeck & Ruprecht. 158 vols. to date.
*Society of Biblical Literature dissertation series.* Atlanta: Scholar's Press. 161 vols. to date.
*Society of Biblical Literature monograph series.* Atlanta: Scholar's Press. 49 vols. to date.
*Society of Biblical Literature writings from the ancient world series.* Atlanta: Scholar's Press. 5 vols. to date.
*Soncino books of the Bible.* London and New York: Soncino Press, 1945–51. 13 vols.
*Supplements to "Vetus testamentum".* Leiden: E. J. Brill. 70 vols. to date.
*Table pastorale de la Bible.* G. Passelecq & F. Poswick (eds). Paris: Lethielleux, 1974. 1,214p. (Over 9,000 articles on words and themes).
*Thayer's Greek–English lexicon of the New Testament: a dictionary numerically coded to Strong's exhaustive concordance.* J. H. Thayer. Nashville, TN: Broadman, 1977. 752p.
*The Anchor Bible.* Garden City, NY: Doubleday, 1964–. In progress to 38 vols. (Commentary series).
*The Anchor Bible dictionary.* D. N. Freedman et al. (eds). New York: Doubleday, 1992. 6 vols.
*The Bible book: resources for reading the New Testament.* E. Hort. New York: Crossroad, 1983. (A somewhat dated layperson's guide to the tools for biblical studies).
*The book of Ephesians: an annotated bibliography.* W. W. Klein. *Books of the Bible, 8; Garland reference library of the humanities,* 1,466. New York: Garland, 1996. 335p.
*The book of Jeremiah: an annotated bibliography.* H. O. Thompson. *ATLA bibliography series,* 41. Lanham, MD: Scarecrow Press, 1996. 777p.
*The book of Psalms: an annotated bibliography.* T. Wittstruck. *Books of the Bible, 5; Garland reference library of the humanities,* 1,413. New York: Garland, 1994. 2 vols.
*The book of Revelation: an annotated bibliography.* R. L. Muse. *Books of the Bible, 2; Garland reference library of the humanities,* 1,387. New York: Garland, 1996. 388p.
*The books of the Bible.* B. W. Anderson (ed). New York: Scribner, 1989. 2 vols., 879p.
*The Cambridge companion to the Bible.* H. C. Kee et al. Cambridge, UK: Cambridge University Press, 1997. 624p.
*The Cambridge history of the Bible.* P. R. Ackroyd and C. F. Evans (vol. 1), G. W. Lampe (vol. 2), S. L. Greenslade (vol. 3) (eds). Cambridge, UK: Cambridge University Press, 1963–70. 3 vols.
*The computer Bible.* J. A. Baird & D. N. Freedman (eds). Wooster, OH: Biblical Research Associates, Vols I–XV, 1975–78. (Word frequencies, concordances, indexes, using KWIC; computerization to make immediately available massive amounts of critical data).
*The dictionary of Bible and religion.* W. H. Gentz (ed). Nashville, TN: Abingdon Press, 1986. 1,147p.
*The early versions of the New Testament.* B. M. Metzger. Oxford, UK: Oxford University Press, 1977. (Origin, transmission, manuscripts, printed editions, for all versions up to AD 1000).
*The Eerdmans Bible dictionary.* A. C. Myers (ed). Grand Rapids, MI: Eerdmans, 1987. 1,103p. (Translated and updated from *Bijbelse encyclopedie.* W. H. Gispen (ed). Kampen: Kok, 1975).
*The Englishman's Greek concordance of the New Testament numerically coded to Strong's exhaustive concordance.* G. V. Wigram. Nashville, TN: Broadman, 1979. 1,174p.
*The HarperCollins Bible dictionary.* P. J. Achtemeier et al. (eds). 2nd ed. San Francisco: Harper, 1996. 1,280p.
*The international standard Bible encyclopedia.* G. W. Bromiley (ed). 3rd ed. Grand Rapids, MI: Eerdmans, 1979–1988. 4 vols., 4,466p.
*The interpreter's Bible.* G. A. Buttrick (ed). New York: Abingdon, 1951–57. 12 vols. (Exegesis and exposition of entire Bible).
*The interpreter's dictionary of the Bible: an illustrated encyclopedia.* G. A. Buttrick (ed). New York: Abingdon, 1962. 4 vols., with 1976 supplementary volume.
*The IVP New Testament commentary series.* Downers Grove, IL: InterVarsity.
*The new international commentary on the New Testament.* Grand Rapids, MI: Eerdmans, 1953–. 27 vols. to date.
*The new international commentary on the Old Testament.* Grand Rapids, MI: Eerdmans, 1965–. 15 vols. to date.
*The new interpreter's Bible.* Nashville, TN: Abingdon Press, 1994–. 6 vols. to date.
*The new Jerome Biblical commentary.* R. E. Brown S.S., J. A. Fitzmyer S.J. & R. E. Murphy O.Carm (eds). Englewood Cliffs, NJ: Prentice-Hall, 1990; London: Geoffrey Chapman, 1989; paperback, 1993.
*The Old Testament library.* P. R. Ackroyd et al. (eds). Louisville, KY: Westminster John Knox, 1961–. 48 vols.
*The Oxford companion to the Bible.* B. M. Metzger & M. D. Coogan (eds). New York and Oxford, UK: Oxford University Press, 1993. 933p.
*The Schocken Bible, Vol. I: The five books of Moses.* E. Fox. New York: Schocken, 1995. 1,056p.
*Theological dictionary of the New Testament.* G. Kittel et al. (eds). Trans., G. W. Bromiley. Grand Rapids, MI: Eerdmans, 1963–74. 9 vols. (Translation from German, *Theologisches Wörterbuch zum Neuen Testament*).
*Theological dictionary of the New Testament: abridged in one volume.* G. Kittel & G. Friedrich (eds). Trans., G. Bromiley. Grand Rapids, MI: Eerdmans; Devon, UK: Paternoster Press, 1985. 1392p.
*Theologisches Wörterbuch zum Alten Testament.* G. J. Botterweck & H. Ringgren. Stuttgart: W. Kohlhammer. (English edition by Eerdmans).
*Tyndale Old Testament Commentaries.* D. J. Wiseman (ed). Leicester, UK and Downers Grove, IL: InterVarsity, 1964–. 26 vols.
*Understanding the Old Testament.* B. W. Anderson. 4th ed. Englewood Cliffs, NJ: Prentice–Hall, 1986.
*Westminster Bible companion.* P. D. Miller & D. L. Bartlett (eds). Louisville, KY: Westminster John Knox, 1995–. 13 vols. to date. (A commentary for lay persons, designed as a replacement series to *The laymen's Bible commentary*).
*What is postmodern biblical criticism?* A. K. M. Adam. *Guides to biblical scholarship, New Testament series.* Minneapolis, MN: Fortress, 1995. 95p.
*Who's who in the New Testament.* R. Brownrigg. 1971; reprint, New York: Oxford University Press, 1993. 448p.
*Who's who in the Old Testament together with Apocrypha.* J. Comay. 1971; reprint, New York: Oxford University Press, 1993. 448p.
*Word Biblical commentaries.* D. A. Hubbard & G. W. Barker (eds). Waco, TX: Word, 1982–. 52 vols.


### 3. CHURCH HISTORY


*A Baptist bibliography: being a register of printed material by and about Baptists, including works written against the Baptists.* E. C. Starr. Rochester, NY: American Baptist Historical Society, 1947–76. 25 vols.
*A dictionary of Christian biography.* H. Wace & W. C. Piercy (eds). 1911; reprint, Peabody, MA: Hendrickson, 1994. 1,040p.
*A documentary history of religion in America.* E. S. Gaustad. Grand Rapids, MI: Eerdmans, 1982–83. 2 vols.
*A history of Black Baptists.* L. Fitts. Nashville, TN: Broadman, 1985. 368p.
*A history of Christianity.* K. S. Latourette. London: Eyre & Spottiswode; New York: Harper & Row, 1953. 2 vols., 1,544p. (A classic of missions history.).
*A history of Christianity in Asia.* S. H. Moffett. New York: HarperCollins, 1991–. 2 vols. (Vol. 2 expected, 1999).
*A history of the expansion of Christianity.* K. S. Latourette. New York: Harper, 1937–45. 7 vols.
*A religious history of the American people.* S. E. Ahlstrom. New Haven, CT: Yale University Press, 1972. 1,174p. (A classic text on the history of Christianity and other religions in the United States).
*A violent evangelism: the political and religious conquest of the Americas.* L. N. Rivera. Louisville, KY: Westminster John Knox, 1992.
*Acta sanctorum quotquot toto orbe coluntur.* Paris: Palmé, 1863–1940. 85 vols. (The indispensable research work on the lives of the saints).
*American Christianity: an historical interpretation with representative documents.* H. S. Smith, R. T. Handy & L. A. Loetscher. New York: Scribner, 1960–63. 2 vols.
*Analecta Bollandiana.* Brussels: Société des Bollandistes, 1882–. (Quarterly; current bibliography on lives of saints).
*Archiv für Reformationsgeschichte.* N.p., 1903–.
*Atlas of the crusades.* J. Riley–Smith (ed). New York: Facts on File, 1990.
*Atlas of the early Christian world.* F. van der Meer & C. Mohrmann. Trans. and ed., M. F. Hedlund & H. H. Rowley. London: T. Nelson, 1958. 216p. (620 plates, 42 maps; first 6 centuries AD).
*Backgrounds of early Christianity.* E. Ferguson. 2nd ed. Grand Rapids, MI: Eerdmans, 1993. 631p.
*Bibliographie de cartographie ecclésiastique.* J. N. B. van den Brink et al. (eds). Leiden: E. J. Brill, Commission International d'Histoire Ecclésiastique Comparée, 1968–.
*Bibliographie de la Réforme, 1450–1648.* J. N. B. van den Brink et al. (eds). Leiden: E. J. Brill, 1958–70. 7 vols. (Covers 17 European countries plus U.S.).
*Bibliography of published articles on American Presbyterianism, 1901–1980.* H. M. Parker. *Bibliographies and indexes in religious studies,* 4. Westport, CT: Greenwood, 1985. 272p.
*Bibliotheca Sanctorum.* Rome: Città Nuova, 1987–91. 13 vols. (Dictionary of saints; originally published 1961–70).
*Bishops at large: some autocephalous churches of the past hundred years and their founders.* P. F. Anson. London: Faber and Faber, 1964. 593p.
*Black evangelists: the spread of Christianity in Uganda, 1891–1914.* M. L. Pirouet. London: Rex Collings, 1978. 269p.
*Black religions in the New World.* G. E. Simpson. New York: Columbia University Press, 1978. 429p.
*Butler's lives of patron saints.* M. Walsh (ed). San Francisco: Harper & Row, 1987. 492p.
*Butler's lives of the saints: complete edition.* H. Thurston S.J. [1856–1939] & D. Attwater [1892–1977] (eds). London: Burns & Oates; Westminster, MD: Christian Classics, 1956; reprint, 1966. 2,900p.
*Catholisme: hier—aujord'hui—demain.* G. Jacquemet, G. Mathon & G. Baudry (eds). Paris: Letouzey & Ané, 1948–. 14 vols., 2 fasc. to date; in process to 15 vols. (Covers European Catholicism).
*Christendom: the Christian churches, their doctrines, constitutional forms and ways of worship.* E. Molland. London: A. R. Mowbray, 1959. 432p.
*Christianity: the first two thousand years.* D. L. Edwards. Maryknoll, NY: Orbis Books, 1997.
*Church history: an introduction to research, reference works, and methods.* J. E. Bradley & R. A. Muller. Grand Rapids, MI: Eerdmans, 1995. 252p.
*Civilization of the ancient Mediterranean: Greece and Rome.*

M. Grant & R. Kitzinger (eds). New York: Scribner, 1988. 3 vols.
*Coptic Egypt.* B. Watterson. Edinburgh: Scotish Academy Press, 1988. 197p.
*Cross and sword: an eyewitness history of Christianity in Latin America.* H. M. Goodpasture (ed). Maryknoll, NY: Orbis, 1989.
*Diccionario de historia eclesiástica.* Madrid: Instituto Superior de Investigaciones Cientificas. 4 vols.
*Dictionary of Catholic biography.* J. J. Delaney & J. E. Tobin. Garden City, NY: Doubleday, 1961. 1,245p. (Biographies of 15,000 Catholics from beginning to 1961).
*Dictionary of Christian biography, literature, sects, and doctrines.* W. Smith & H. Wace. London: Murray, 1877–87. 4 vols. (Especially English, Scottish, and Irish church history; subjects to the end of the 8th century AD).
*Dictionary of pentecostal and charismatic movements.* S. M. Burgess & G. B. McGee (eds). Grand Rapids, MI: Zondervan, 1988. 927p. (A new edition, *The new international dictionary of Pentecostal and Charismatic movements*, Stanley Burgess, ed., forthcoming in AD 2000).
*Dictionary of the Apostolic church.* J. Hastings. New York: Scribner, 1916. 2 vols.
*Dictionary of the Middle Ages.* J. R. Strayer (ed). New York: Scribner, 1982–1989. 13 vols.
*Dictionnaire de droit canonique, contant tous les termes du droit canonique.* R. Nez (ed). Paris: Letouzey & Ané, 1935–65. 7 vols. (Canon law in the Catholic church).
*Dictionnaire des ordres religieux.* P. Hélyot. Paris: Migne, 1859–63. 4 vols.
*Dictionnaire des philosophes antiques.* R. Goulet (ed). Paris: CNRS, 1989–. 841p. in 1 vol. to date; in progress to 10 vols.
*Dictionnaire d'histoire et de géographie ecclésiastiques.* A. Baudrillart & R. Aubert (eds). Paris: Letouzey & Ané, 1912–. 24 vols. to date; fasc. 150, 1995.
*Dictionnaire historique de la papauté.* P. Levillain (ed). Paris: Fayard, 1994. 1,776p.
*Die Religionen in Geschichte und Gegenwart: Handwörterbuch für Theologie und Religionswissenschaft.* K. Galling (ed). 3rd ed. Tübingen: J. B. C. Mohr, 1986. 7 vols.
*Dizionario patristico e di antichità cristiane.* A. di Bernardino (ed). Casale Monferrato: Marietti, 1983. 2,320p. in 3 vols. (English and French translations appear under the respective titles, *Encyclopedia of the early church* and *Dictionnaire encyclopédique du christianisme ancien*).
*Documents illustrative of the history of the church.* B. J. Kidd. London: SPCK; New York: Macmillan, 1920–41. 3 vols. (From apostolic times to AD 1500).
*Encyclopedia of African American religions.* L. G. Murphy, J. G. Melton & G. L. Ward (eds). New York: Garland, 1993. 1,002p.
*Encyclopedia of American Catholic history.* M. Glazier. Ed., T. Shelly. Collegeville, MN: Liturgical Press, 1997.
*Encyclopedia of American religions.* J. G. Melton. 5th ed. Detroit, MI: Gale Research, 1996.
*Encyclopedia of early Christianity.* E. Ferguson (ed). 2nd ed. *Garland reference library of the humanities.* New York: Garland, 1997. 1,240p. in 2 vols.
*Encyclopedia of German resistance to the Nazi movement.* W. Benz & W. H. Pehle (eds). Del Mar, CA: Continuum, 1996. 360p.
*Encyclopedia of heresies and heretics.* C. S. Clifton. Santa Barbara, CA: ABC-CLIO, 1992.
*Encyclopedia of the American religious experience.* C. H. Lippy & P. W. Williams (eds). New York: Scribner, 1987. 1,888p. in 3 vols.
*From federation to communion: the history of the Lutheran World Federation.* J. H. Schørring et al. Minneapolis, MN: Fortress Press, 1997. 576p.
*Fruit of the vine: a history of the Brethren, 1708–1995.* D. F. Durnbaugh. N.p., 1996. 400p.
*Great leaders of the Christian church.* J. D. Woodbridge (ed). Chicago: Moody Press, 1988. 384p.
*Handbook of denominations in America.* F. S. Mead & S. S. Hill. 10th ed. Nashville, TN: Abingdon, 1995. 352p.
*Histoire de l'Eglise depuis les origines jusqu'a nos jours.* J. B. Duroselle & E. Jarry (eds). Paris: Bloud & Gay. 26 vols.
*Histoire du Christianisme des origines à nos jours.* J. M. Mayeur, L. Pietri, A. Vauchez & M. Venard. Paris: Desclée, 1995. 14 vols.
*Historians of the Christian tradition: their methodology and influence on Western thought.* M. Bauman & M. I. Klauber. Nashville, TN: Broadman & Holman, 1995. 637p.
*Historical dictionary of Methodism.* C. Yrigoyen Jr. & S. Warrick (eds). *Religions, philosophies, and movements series*, 8. N.p., 1996. 328p.
*Historical dictionary of the Orthodox Church.* M. Prokurat, A. Golitzin & M. D. Peterson. *Religions, philosophies, and movements series*, 9. N.p., 1996. 738p.
*History of the Christian church.* P. Schaff. New York: Scribner, 1889–1910. 7 vols.
*Jehova's Witnesses: proclaimers of God's Kingdom.* Brooklyn, NY: Watchtower Bible and Tract Society of New York and the International Bible Students Association, 1993. 750p.
*Jesuiten–Lexikon: die Gesellschaft Jesu einst und jetzt.* L. Koch S.J. (ed). 1934; Löwen: Bibliothek SJ, 1963. 939p.
*Lexikon des Mittelalters.* Munich and Zürich: Artemis, 1980–. 8 vols. to date; in progress to 10 vols.
*Modern American Protestantism and its world.* M. E. Marty (ed). Munich and New York: K. G. Sauer, 1992–1993. 14 vols.
*New 20th–century encyclopedia of religious knowledge.* J. D. Douglas (ed). Grand Rapids, MI: Baker, 1991. 912p.
*Nouvelle histoire de l'Eglise.* L. J. Rogier, R. Aubert & M. D. Knowles. Paris: Le Seuil, 1963–74. 5 vols.
*Ostkirchliche Studien.* Würzburg: Augustinus-Verlag, 1952–. (Quarterly. The best bibliographical source on the Eastern churches, with about 90 pages of bibliography each year).
*Reallexikon für Antike und Christentum: Sachwörterbuch zur Auseinandersetzung des Christentums mit der antiken Welt.* T. Klauser, E. Dassmann et al. (eds). Stuttgart: Hiersmann, 1941–. 17 vols. to date; in progress to 30 vols. (Relationship of the ancient world to Christianity to 6th century AD).
*Revue d'histoire ecclésiastique.* Louvain-la-Neuve: Université Catholique de Louvain. 1900-72, Vols 1-67; in progress.
*Schaff–Herzog encyclopedia.* S. M. Jackson. New York: Funk & Wagnalls, 1908 and 1912. 12 vols and index.
*Taking the Word to the world: fifty years of the United Bible Societies.* E. H. Robertson. Nashville, TN: T. Nelson, 1996. 350p.
*The Archbishop Iakovos library of ecclesiastical and historical sources.* Brookline, MA: Hellenic College Press.
*The Blackwell dictionary of evangelical biography: 1730–1860.* D. M. Lewis (ed). Oxford, UK and Cambridge, MA: Blackwell Reference, 1995. 2 vols., 1314p.
*The Byzantine legacy in the Orthodox church.* J. Meyendorff. Crestwood, NY: St. Vladimir's Seminary Press, 1982. 268p.
*The Cambridge history of the Bible.* P. R. Ackroyd and C. F. Evans (vol. 1), G. W. Lampe (vol. 2), S. L. Greenslade (vol. 3) (eds). Cambridge, UK: Cambridge University Press, 1963–70. 3 vols.
*The concise dictionary of early Christianity.* J. F. Kelly. Collegeville, MN: The Liturgical, 1992. 203p.
*The concise dictionary of the Christian tradition: doctrine, liturgy, history.* J. D. Douglas, W. A. Elwell & P. Toon (eds). Grand Rapids, MI: Zondervan, 1989. 419p.
*The early church: an annotated bibliography of literature in English.* T. A. Robinson & B. Shaw. *ATLA bibliography series*, 33. Metuchen, NJ: Scarecrow Press, 1993. 522p.
*The encyclopedia of American religious history.* E. Queen, S. R. Prothero & G. H. Shattuck. New York: Facts on File, 1996.
*The encyclopedia of missions: descriptive, historical, biographical, statistical.* O. Dwight, H. A. Tupper & E. M. Bliss (eds). 2nd ed. New York and London: Funk & Wagnalls, 1904; reprint, Detroit, MI: Gale Research, 1975. 865p.
*The English Bible from KJV to NIV: a history and evaluation.* J. P. Lewis. 2nd ed. Grand Rapids, MI: Baker, 1991. 512p.
*The history of the popes, from the close of the Middle Ages.* L. Pastor. Trans., F. I. Anthrobus et al. London: Hodges, 1891–1953. 40 vols. (Covers the period 1305–1799).
*The Macmillan atlas history of Christianity.* F. H. Littell. New York: Macmillan; London: Collier Macmillan, 1976. 196p.
*The modern encyclopedia of religion in Russia and the Soviet Union.* P. D. Steeves (ed). Gulf Breeze, FL: Academic International Press, 1988–. 5 vols.; in progress to 25 vols.
*The new Cambridge medieval history.* R. McKitterick (ed). Cambridge, UK: Cambridge University Press. 2 vols.
*The new international dictionary of the Christian Church.* J. D. Douglas (ed). Exeter, UK: Paternoster Press, 1978. 1,200p.; 5,000 articles.
*The Oxford dictionary of Byzantium.* A. P. Kashdan (ed). New York: Oxford University Press, 1991. 3 vols.
*The Oxford dictionary of the Christian church.* F. L. Cross & E. A. Livingstone (eds). 3rd ed. London: Oxford University Press, 1997. 1,823p. (Earlier editions, 1957, 1974, 1983; also an abridged version, *The Concise Oxford dictionary of the Christian Church*).
*The Oxford dictionary of the Popes.* J. N. D. Kelly. New York and Oxford, UK: Oxford University Press, 1986; paperback 1988. 361p.
*The Oxford encyclopedia of the Reformation.* H. J. Hillerbrand (ed). New York and Oxford, UK: Oxford University Press, 1996. 4 vols., 1,965p.
*The Oxford illustrated history of Christianity.* J. McManners (ed). Oxford, UK and New York: Oxford University Press, 1991; paperback, 1993. 736p.
*The presence of God: a history of Western Christian mysticism.* B. McGinn. New York: Crossroad, 1992–. 2 vols. to date; in planning to 4 vols.
*The Westminster dictionary of church history.* J. C. Brauer (ed). Philadelphia: Westminster Press, 1971. 899p.
*Thriskeutiki kai Ithiki Egyklopaidia (Religious and ethical encyclopedia).* Athens: A. Martinos, 1962–68. 12 vols. (Greece and Greek Orthodoxy).
*Twentieth–century shapers of American popular religion.* C. H. Lippy (ed). New York: Greenwood Press, 1989. 519p.

## 4. HISTORY OF DOCTRINE

*A history of Christian doctrine.* D. K. Bernard. Hazelwood, MO: Word Aflame Press, 1995–. 1 vol. to date. (Written from a Pentecostal perspective).
*An essay on the development of Christian doctrine.* John Henry Cardinal Newman. 6th ed. 1845; Notre Dame, IN: University of Notre Dame Press, 1989. 473p.
*Ancient Christian writers: the works of the Fathers in translation.* J. Quasten & W. J. Burghardt (eds). London: Longmans, Green, 1946–63. 31 vols.
*Annotated bibliography of Luther studies, 1977–1983.* K. Hagen. *Sixteenth century bibliography*, 24. St. Louis, MO: Center for Reformation Research, 1985. 91p.
*Anselm of Canturbury.* J. Hopkins & H. Richardson (eds). Toronto and New York: E. Mellen Press, 1974–76. 4 vols.
*Ante–Nicene Fathers: translations of the writings of the Fathers down to AD 325.* A. Roberts & J. Donaldson (eds). 1896–97; reprint, Grand Rapids: Eerdmans, 1956. 10 vols.
*Archiv für Katholisches Kirchenrecht.* 1857–1941; reprint, Leiden: E. J. Brill, 1973–75. 121 vols. (Germany, Austria, and Switzerland).
*Archiv für Reformationsgeschichte.* N.p., 1903–.
*Augustinus–Lexikon.* C. Mayer (ed). Basel: Schwabe, 1986–. 1 vol. to date; in progress to 7 vols. (Articles in German, French, and English discuss the life and thought of Augustine).
*Bibliographia Calviniana, 1532–1899.* D. A. Erichson. Nieuwkoop: De Graaf, 1950.
*Bibliographia Patristica.* W. Schneemelcher. Berlin: de Gruyter, 1959–65. 10 vols.
*Brief introduction to the study of theology with reference to the scientific standpoint and the Catholic system (Kurze Einleitung in das Studium der Theologie).* J. S. Drey. Trans., M. J. Himes. 1819; Notre Dame, IN: University of Notre Dame Press, 1994. 220p.
*Brief outline of the study of theology (Kurze Darstellung des theologischen Studiums).* Friedrich Schleiermacher. 1811, 1830; Lewiston, NY: E. Mellen Press, 1990. 252p.
*Bulletin de théologie ancienne et médiévale.* Louvain: Abbey Mont César. in progress.
*Calvin–Bibliographie, 1901–1959.* W. Niesel. Munich: C. Kaiser, 1961. (Continuation of *Bibliographia Calviniana*).
*Confessions.* St. Augustine. Trans., H. Chadwick. Oxford, UK: Oxford University Press, 1991. 339p.
*Creeds of the churches: a reader in Christian doctrine from the Bible to the present.* J. H. Leith (ed). 3rd ed. Atlanta: John Knox Press, 1982. 746p.
*De doctrina Christiana.* St. Augustine. Trans. and ed., R. P. H. Greene. *Oxford early Christian texts.* Oxford, UK and New York: Clarendon, 1995.
*Dialogues concerning natural religion.* David Hume. *The Hafner library of classics.* 1779; New York: Hafner, Macmillan; London: Collier Macmillan, 1948. 113p.
*Dictionnaire de théologie catholique.* B. Loth & A. Michel (eds). Begun by Vacant & Mangenot, now E. Amann, 1909-50, 15 vols. Paris: Letouzey, 1951–72. 3 vols.
*Dictionnaire de théologie catholique.* A. Vacant, E. Mangenot & É. Amann (eds). Paris: Letouzey & Ané, 1909–50. 30 parts, 15 vols.
*Dispensationalism.* C. C. Ryrie. Rev. ed. 1965; Chicago: Moody, 1995. 224p.
*Emil Brunner: a bibliography.* M. G. McKim. *ATLA bibliographies*, 40. Lanham, MD: Scarecrow Press, 1996. 105p.
*Encyclopaedia of religion and ethics.* J. Hastings (ed). Edinburgh: T. & T. Clark; New York: Scribner, 1908–27. 12 vols.
*Encyclopedia of heresies and heretics.* C. S. Clifton. Santa Barbara, CA: ABC-CLIO, 1992.
*Encyklopädie der katholischen Theologie und ihrer Hülfswissenschaften.* H. J. Wertzer. Ed., F. Kaulen. Freiburg im Breisgau: Herder, 1882–1901. 12 vols. and index.
*Fear and trembling; and sickness unto death.* Søren Kierkegaard. Trans., W. Lowrie. 1843, 1849; Princeton, NJ: Princeton University Press, 1941, 1968. 278p.
*Four anti-Pelagian writings: on nature and grace; on the proceedings of Pelagius; on the predestination of the saints; on the gift of perseverence.* St. Augustine. Trans., J. A. Mourant & W. J. Collinge. *The fathers of the church*, 86. Washington, DC: Catholic University Press, 1992. 370p.
*God was in Christ: an essay on incarnation and atonement.* D. M. Baillie. New York: Scribner, 1948. 230p.
*Historians of the Christian tradition: their methodology and influence on Western thought.* M. Bauman & M. I. Klauber. Nashville, TN: Broadman & Holman, 1995. 637p.
*Institutes of the Christian religion.* J. Calvin. Trans., F. L. Battles. *Library of Christian classics*, 20–21. Philadelphia: Westminster, 1960. 2 vols. (Annotated translation of the 1559 edition).
*Library of early Christianity.* W. A. Meeks (ed). Louisville, KY: Westminster John Knox, 1985–1987. 8 vols.
*Loeb classical library.* London: Heinemann, 1912–89. 488 vols. (Contains Greek and Latin texts and English translations on facing pages of the Greek and Latin classics).
*Luther's works.* J. Pelikan & H. T. Lehmann (eds). Philadelphia: Muhlenburg; St. Louis, MO: Concordia, 1971–. 56 vols. to date.
*Medieval philosophers.* J. Hackett (ed). Detroit, MI: Gale Research, 1992. 479p.
*On religion: speeches to its cultured despisers.* Friedrich Schleiermacher. Trans., R. Crouter. *Texts in German philosophy.* 1799; Cambridge, UK: Cambridge University Press, 1988. 243p. (Translation of *Über die Religion*).
*On the unity of Christ.* Saint Cyril, Patriarch of Alexandria. Trans., J. A. McGuckin. Crestwood, NY: St. Vladimir's Seminary Press, 1995.
*On virginity.* St. Ambrose. Toronto: Peregrinn, 1991. 65p.
*Oxford early Christian texts.* Oxford, UK and New York: Clarendon Press.
*Patrologiae cursus completus, seu biblioteca universalis.* J. P. Migne. Paris: Migne, 1844–80. 221 vols. (Latin and Greek fathers).
*Protestant thought in the nineteenth century.* C. Welch. New Haven, CT: Yale University Press, 1972–1985. 2 vols.
*Realencyklopädie für protestantische Theologie und Kirche.* J. J. Herzog. Leipzig, Hinrichs: Albert Hauck, 1896–1913. 24 vols.
*Reformed dogmatics.* L. Berkhof. Grand Rapids, MI: Eerdmans, 1932–37. 4 vols.
*Religion within the limits of reason alone (Der Religion innerhalb der Grenzen der bloßen Vernunft).* Immanuel Kant. Trans., T. M. Greene & H. H. Hudson. 1793; New York: Harper Torchbooks, 1960. 345p.
*Saint Ambrose: theological and dogmatic works.* St. Ambrose. Trans., R. J. Deferrari. *The fathers of the church*, 44. Washington, DC: Catholic University Press, 1963. 366p.
*Sancti Ambrosii opera.* St. Ambrose. Vindobonae, Pragae: F. Tempsky, 1897–1990. 7 vols in 11 to date.
*Select library of Nicene and post–Nicene Fathers of the Christian church.* P. Schaff (ed). New York: Christian Literature Co., 1886–1900. 28 vols.
*Sources chrétiennes.* Paris: Éditions de Cerf, 1990–. 431 vols to date.
*Systematic theology.* L. Berkhof. 2nd ed. Grand Rapids, MI: Eerdmans, 1941. 759p.
*Systematic theology.* L. S. Chafer. Dallas, TX: Dallas Seminary Press, 1947–48. 8 vols.
*The Christian faith (Glaubenslehre).* Friedrich Schleiermacher. Ed., H. R. Mackintosh & J. S. Stewart. 1830; Edinburgh: T & T Clark, 1989. 772p.
*The Christian tradition: a history of the development of doctrine.* J. Pelikan. Chicago: University of Chicago Press, 1971–1989. 5 vols.
*The complete works of John Wesley.* T. Jackson (ed). Nashville, TN: Abingdon, 1856–62. 15 vols.

*The creeds of Christendom: with a history and critical notes.* 6th rev. ed. New York, London: Harper, 1919. 3 vols.

*The fathers of the church.* Washington, DC: Catholic University of America Press, 1947–. 96 vols to date.

*The fundamentals: a testimony to the truth.* A. C. Dixon, L. Meyer & R. A. Torrey (eds). Chicago: Testimony Publishing. 12 vols. of 128p. each. (These 12 little volumes were published as a reaction against the perceived threat of higher biblical criticism, and are the source of the term, "Fundamentalism").

*The library of Christian classics.* J. Baillie, J. T. McNeil & H. P. Van Dusen (eds). London: SCM Press; Philadelphia: Westminster, 1954–57. 26 vols. (A selection of important Christian treatises written before AD 1600).

*The origins and development of African theology.* G. H. Muzorewa. Maryknoll, NY: Orbis, 1985. 146p.

*The summa theologica of St. Thomas Aquinas.* London: Burns, Oates & Washbourne, 1964–72. 32 vols.

*The works of Saint Augustine.* St. Augustine. Ed., J. E. Rotelle. Brooklyn, NY: New City Press, 1990–. 16 vols to date.

*What is Christianity?* Adolph von Harnack. Trans., T. B. Saunders. *Fortress texts in modern theology.* 1900; Philadelphia: Fortress, 1957. 319p. (Translation of *Das Wesen des Christentums*).

*Who's who in theology: from the first century to the present.* J. Bowden. London: SCM Press, 1990; New York: Crossroad, 1992. 160p.

*Women and religion: the original sourcebook of women in Christian thought.* E. A. Clark & H. Richardson (eds). San Francisco: Harper, 1996. 399p.

**5. THEOLOGY**

*A basic Christian theology.* A. J. Conyers. Nashville, TN: Broadman & Holman, 1995.

*A bibliography.* K. Baago. *Library of Christian theology.* Madras: The Christian Literature Society, 1969. 110p. (A bibliography of theological works by Indian authors.).

*A Black theology of liberation.* J. Cone. 20th anniv. ed. 1970; Maryknoll, NY: Orbis, 1986, 1990. 236p.

*A brief theology of revelation.* C. Gunton. Edinburgh: T. & T. Clark, 1995. 144p.

*A Catholic dictionary of theology.* H. F. Davis et al. (eds). London: T. Nelson, 1962–1971. 3 vols. (A 4th volume was never published).

*A handbook of Christian theologians.* M. E. Marty & D. G. Peerman (eds). 2nd ed. Nashville: Abingdon, 1984. 735p.

*A handbook of theological terms.* V. A. Harvey. New York: Macmillan; London: Collier Macmillan, 1964. 253p.

*A new handbook of Christian theology.* D. W. Musser & J. L. Price (eds). Nashville, TN: Abingdon, 1992. 525p.

*A preface to theology.* W. C. Gilpin. Chicago: University of Chicago Press, 1996. 236p.

*A theological book list.* London: Theological Education Fund, 1960, 1965, 1968. (Comprehensive bibliographies on all subjects, with emphasis on works available for seminaries in developing countries; 3,000 entries).

*A theology of liberation: history, politics and salvation.* G. Gutiérrez. Trans. and ed., C. Inda & J. Eagleson. 15th anniv. ed. 1973; Maryknoll, NY: Orbis, 1988. 312p.

*A theology of the Jewish–Christian reality.* P. M. van Buren. 1980-87; Lanham, MD: University Press of America, 1995. 3 vols.

*A theology primer.* R. Neville. Albany, NY: State University of New York Press, 1991.

*American religious creeds: an essential compendium of more than 450 statements of belief and doctrine.* J. G. Melton (ed). 1988; New York: Triumph Books, 1991. 3 vols. (Texts of doctrinal documents of a wide variety of Christian and non–Christian religious groups in the U.S.).

*Assurance of things hoped for: a theology of Christian faith.* A. Dulles. New York: Oxford University Press, 1994.

*Basic Christian doctrine.* J. H. Leith. Louisville, KY: Westminster John Knox, 1993.

*Beyond liberalism and fundamentalism: how modern and postmodern philosophy set the theological agenda.* N. Murphy. Valley Forge, PA: Trinity Press International, 1996. 172p.

*Bible doctrines: a Pentecostal perspective.* W. W. Menzies & S. M. Horton. Springfield, MO: Logion Press, 1993.

*Bibliography in contextual theology in Africa.* J. R. Cochrane, I. W. Henderson & G. O. West (eds). Pietermaritzburg, South Africa: Cluster Publications, 1993–. 1 vol. to date.

*Bilanz der Theology im 20 Jahrhundert.* H. Vorgrimler & R. Van der Gucht (eds). Freiburg im Breisgau: Herder, 1970. 3 vols.

*Blessed rage for order.* D. Tracy. 1975; Chicago: University of Chicago Press, 1996.

*Catholicism.* R. McBrien. Rev. ed. Oak Grove, MN: Winston Press, 1994.

*Christian doctrine.* S. Guthrie. Rev. ed. Louisville, KY: Westminster John Knox, 1994. 448p.

*Christian dogmatics.* C. Braaten & R. Jenson (eds). Philadelphia: Fortress, 1984. 2 vols.

*Christian faith: an introduction to the study of faith.* H. Berkhof. Trans., S. Woudstra. Rev. ed. Grand Rapids, MI: Eerdmans, 1986.

*Christian foundations.* D. Bloesch. Downer's Gove, IL: InterVarsity, 1992–. 2 vols. to date; in progress to 7 vols.

*Christian systematic theology in a world context.* N. Smart & S. Konstantine. Minneapolis, MN: Fortress, 1991.

*Christian theology.* M. J. Erickson. Grand Rapids, MI: Eerdmans, 1983–85. 3 vols.

*Christian theology: an eschatological approach.* T. Finger. Scottdale, PA: Herald Press, 1985–87. 2 vols.

*Christian theology: an introduction.* A. McGrath. Oxford, UK: Basil Blackwell, 1993.

*Christian theology: an introduction to its traditions and tasks.* P. C. Hodgson & R. H. King (eds). 2nd ed. Minneapolis, MN: Fortress, 1994.

*Christianity: essence, history, and future.* H. Küng. New York: Continuum, 1995. 962p.

*Christliche Philosophie im katholischen Denken des 19. und 20. Jahrhunderts.* E. Coreth, W. M. Neidl & Pfligersdorfer (eds). Graz, Vienna, and Cologne: Styria Verlag, 1987–1989. 3 vols., 2,591p.

*Christology: a Biblical, historical, and systematic study of Jesus.* G. O'Collins S.J. Oxford, UK: Oxford University Press, 1995. 345p.

*Church dogmatics (Die kirchliche Dogmatik).* Karl Barth. Trans., G. T. Thompson. Edinburgh: T & T Clark, 1936–1968, 13 vols. in 4 parts.

*Companion encyclopedia of theology.* P. Byrne & L. Houlden (eds). London and New York: Routledge, 1995. 1,116p.

*Concilium Vaticanum II: concordance, index verborum, liste de fréquence, tables comparatives.* P. Delhaye, M. Gueret & P. Tombeur (eds). Leuven: CETEDOC, 1974. 978p.

*Contours of Christian theology.* Downers Grove, IL: InterVarsity, 1993–. 3 vols. to date.

*Credible Christianity: the Gospel in contemporary society.* H. Montefiore. Grand Rapids, MI: Eerdmans.

*Dictionary of Christian theology.* P. A. Angeles. San Francisco: Harper & Row, 1985. 221p.

*Dictionary of ethics, theology, and society.* P. B. Clarke & A. Linzey (eds). London and New York: Routledge, 1996. 960p.

*Dictionary of feminist theologies.* L. M. Russell & J. S. Clarkson (eds). Louisville, KY: Westminster John Knox, 1996.

*Dietrich Bonhoeffer works.* W. W. Floyd (ed). Minneapolis, MN: Fortress. 3 vols. to date; in progress to 17 vols.

*Dizionario di teologia fondamentale (Dictionary of fundamental theology).* R. Latourelle S.J. & R. Fisichelle (eds). Assissi: Cittadella, 1990. (Published in English, New York: Crossroad, 1994).

*Doctrines of the Christian religion.* W. W. Stevens. Nashville, TN: Broadman, 1967.

*Doxology.* G. Wainwright. Oxford, UK: Oxford University Press, 1980.

*Ecclesia: a theological encyclopedia of the church.* C. O'Donnell. Collegeville, MN: Liturgical Press, 1996. 542p.

*Enciclopedia del pensiero sociale cristiano.* R. Spiazzi (ed). Bologna: Edizioni Studio Dominicano, 1992.

*Essentials of evangelical theology.* D. Bloesch. San Francisco: Harper & Row, 1978–79. 2 vols.

*Evangelical dictionary of theology.* W. A. Elwell (ed). Grand Rapids, MI: Baker, 1984; Basingstoke, UK: Marshall–Pickering, 1985. 1,226p. (Also in a shorter version, *Concise evangelical dictionary of theology*).

*Evangelical theology: a survey and review.* R. Lightner. Grand Rapids, MI: Baker, 1990.

*Evangelisches Kirchenlexikon: Internationale theologische Enzyklopädie.* E. Fahlbusch et al. (eds). 3rd ed. Göttingen: Vandenhoeck & Ruprecht, 1986–. 3 vols., in progress to 4 vols.

*Evangelisches Kirchenlexikon: kirchlich–theologisches Handwörterbuch.* H. Brunotte & O. Weber (eds). Göttingen: Vandenhoeck & Ruprecht, 1955–61. 4 vols.

*Faith seeking understanding: an introduction to systematic theology.* D. Migliore. Grand Rapids, MI: Eerdmans, 1991.

*Foundations of Christian faith: an introduction to the idea of Christianity.* K. Rahner. New York: Seabury Press, 1978.

*Foundations of dogmatics (Grundlagen der Dogmatik).* O. Weber. Trans., D. L. Guder. Grand Rapids, MI: Eerdmans, 1981–83. 2 vols.

*God Christ church: a practical guide to process theology.* M. H. Suchocki. New York: Crossroad, 1982.

*God, creation, and revelation: a neo–evangelical theology.* P. Jewett. Grand Rapids, MI: Eerdmans, 1991. 554p. (Originally intended as the first of a multi–volume work before the author's death).

*God encountered.* F. J. van Beeck. Vol. I: New York: Harper & Row, 1988; vol. II: Collegeville, MN: Liturgical Press, 1993. 2 vols.

*God, revelation, and authority.* C. F. H. Henry. Waco, TX: Word, 1976–83. 6 vols.

*God–walk: liberation shaping dogmatics.* F. Herzog. Maryknoll, NY: Orbis, 1988.

*God—the world's future: systematic theology for a postmodern era.* T. Peters. Minneapolis, MN: Fortress, 1992.

*Handbook of evangelical theologians.* W. A. Elwell (ed). Grand Rapids, MI: Baker, 1993.

*Handbuch der Pastoraltheologie.* F. X. Arnold, K. Rahner et al. (eds). Freiburg im Breisgau: Herder. 1964–72, 6 vols.

*Handwörterbuch religiöser Gegenwartsfragen.* U. Ruh, D. Seeber & R. Walter (eds). Frieburg, Basel, and Vienna: Herder, 1986.

*History and the theology of liberation: a Latin American perspective.* E. Dussel. Maryknoll, NY: Orbis, 1976.

*Images of Jesus.* C. W. du Toit (ed). Pretoria, South Africa: University of South Africa, 1997.

*In the face of mystery: a constructive theology.* G. Kaufman. Cambridge, MA: Harvard University Press, 1993.

*Integrative theology.* G. R. Lewis & B. A. Demarest. Grand Rapids, MI: Zondervan, 1987–95. 3 vols.

*Introduction to theology.* O. Thomas. Cambridge, MA: Greeno, Hadden and Co., 1973.

*Kleines Theologisches Wörterbuch.* K. Rahner & H. Vorgrimler. 7th ed. Freiburg im Breisgau: Herder, 1969.

*Lexikon der katholischen Dogmatik.* W. Beinert (ed). Freiburg: Herder, 1987. (An English translation appears as *Handbook of Catholic theology.* W. Beinert and F. Schüssler Fiorenza (eds). New York: Crossroad, 1995).

*Lexikon für Theologie und Kirche.* J. Höfer & K. Rahner (eds). Freiburg: Herder, 1957–65. 10 vols; 3 vols on Vatican Council plus index (1967).

*Lift every voice: constructing Christian theologies from the underside.* S. B. Thistlewaite & M. P. Engel (eds). San Francisco: Harper & Row, 1990.

*Message and existence.* L. Gilkey. New York: Seabury, 1979.

*Messianic theology.* J. Moltmann. San Francisco: Harper, 1981–92. 5 vols.

*Mysterium salutis.* Dogmatic catholique de l'histoire du salut. J. Feiner and M. Löhrer (Ed). Paris: Le Cerf. 1969-. 12 vols. to date; in progress to 16 vols.

*New dictionary of theology.* S. B. Ferguson & D. F. Wright (eds). Downers Grove, IL and Leicester, UK: InterVarsity, 1988. 757p.

*Not every spirit: a dogmatics of Christian unbelief.* C. Morse. Valley Forge, PA: Trinity Press International, 1994.

*One Christ—many religions: toward a revised christology.* S. J. Samartha. *Faith meets faith series.* Maryknoll, NY: Orbis, 1991. 206p.

*Orthodox dogmatic theology.* M. Pomazansky. Trans., S. Rose. Wichita, KS: Eighth Day Books, 1994.

*Orthodoxy and heterodoxy.* J. Metz & E. Schillebeeckx (eds). Edinburgh: T. & T. Clark, 1987. 155p.

*Principles of Christian theology.* J. Macquarrie. 2nd ed. New York: Scribner, 1977. 557p.

*Reconstructing Christian theology.* R. S. Chopp & M. L. Taylor. Minneapolis, MN: Fortress, 1994.

*Reformational theology: a new paradigm for doing theology.* G. Spykman. Grand Rapids, MI: Eerdmans, 1992.

*Religious and theological abstracts.* Meyerstown, PA, 1958–. 41 vols. to date. (Quarterly).

*Re–membering and Re–Imagining.* N. J. Berneking & P. C. Jo-ern. Cleveland, OH: Pilgrim Press, 1995. 263p. (Documents from the Re-Imagining conference, 1993).

*Responsible faith: Christian theology in light of twentieth century questions.* H. Schwarz. Minneapolis, MN: Augsburg, 1986.

*Revisioning evangelical theology: a fresh agenda.* S. J. Grenz. Downers Grove, IL: InterVarsity, 1993. 208p.

*Sacramentum mundi: an encyclopedia of theology.* K. Rahner et al. (eds). London: Burns & Oates, 1968–70. 6 vols.

*Sexism and God–talk.* R. R. Ruether. Boston: Beacon Press, 1983.

*Studies in dogmatics.* G. C. Berkouwer. Trans. and ed., G. W. Bromiley. Grand Rapids, MI: Eerdmans, 1962–76.

*Systematic theology.* J. W. McClendon. Nashville, TN: Abingdon Press, 1986. 2 vols.

*Systematic theology.* W. Pannenberg. Trans., G. Bromiley. Grand Rapids, MI: Eerdmans, 1991.

*Systematic theology.* R. J. Rushdoony. Vallecito, CA: Ross House, 1994. 2 vols.

*Systematic theology.* O. Thomas. San Francisco: Harper, 1987–92. 3 vols.

*Systematic theology.* P. Tillich. Chicago: University of Chicago Press, 1951–63. 3 vols.

*Systematic theology: a historicist perspective.* G. Kaufman. New York: Scribner, 1969. 565p.

*Systematic theology: a modern Protestant approach.* K. Cauthen. Lewistown, NY: E. Mellen Press, 1986.

*Systematic theology: an introduction to biblical doctrine.* W. Grudem. Grand Rapids, MI: Harper/Zondervan, 1994.

*Systematic theology: biblical, historical, and systematic.* J. L. Garrett Jr. Grand Rapids, MI: Eerdmans, 1990–95. 2 vols.

*Systematic theology from a Charismatic perspective.* W. Rodman. Grand Rapids, MI: Zondervan, 1988–92. 3 vols.

*Systematic theology: Roman Catholic perspectives.* F. S. Fiorenza & J. Galvin (eds). Minneapolis, MN: Fortress, 1991. 2 vols.

*The Blackwell encyclopedia of modern Christian thought.* A. E. McGrath (ed). Oxford, UK and Cambridge, MA: Blackwell Reference, 1993. 714p.

*The challenge of basic Christian communities.* S. Torres & J. Eagleson (eds). Maryknoll, NY: Orbis, 1982.

*The Christian doctrine of God: one being, three persons.* T. F. Torrance. Edinburgh: T. & T. Clark, 1996. 272p.

*The Christian story.* G. Fackre. Grand Rapids, MI: Eerdmans, 1978–87. 2 vols.

*The cry of my people: out of captivity in Latin America.* M. Arias & E. Arias. New York: Friendship Press, 1980.

*The evangelical faith.* H. Thielicke. Grand Rapids, MI: Eerdmans, 1974–82. 3 vols.

*The faith we confess: an ecumenical dogmatics.* J. M. Lochman. Trans., D. Lewis. Philadelphia: Fortress, 1984.

*The Father's spirit of sonship: reconceiving the Trinity.* T. G. Weinandy. Edinburgh: T. & T. Clark, 1995. 159p.

*The Göttingen dogmatics: introduction to the Christian religion.* K. Barth. Trans., G. W. Bromiley & H. R. ed. Grand Rapids, MI: Eerdmans, 1991.

*The melody of theology: a philosophical dictionary.* J. Pelikan. Cambridge, MA: Harvard University Press, 1988. 284p.

*The modern theologians: an introduction to Christian theology in the twentieth century.* D. F. Ford (ed). Oxford, UK and New York: Blackwell Reference, 1989. 2 vols., 699p.

*The new dictionary of Catholic social thought.* J. Dwyer (ed). Collegeville, MN: Liturgical Press, 1994. 1,050p.

*The origins and development of African theology.* G. H. Muzorewa. Maryknoll, NY: Orbis, 1985. 146p.

*The reign of God: an introduction to Christian theology from a Seventh–day Adventist perspective.* R. Rice. Berrien Springs, MI: Andrews University Press, 1985.

*The Westminster dictionary of theological terms.* D. K. McKim (ed). Louisville, KY: Westminster John Knox, 1996. (Contains over 5,000 theological terms.).

*The word of truth: a summary of Christian doctrine based on biblical revelation.* D. Moody. Grand Rapids, MI: Eerdmans, 1981. 640p.

*Theological dictionary.* K. Rahner & H. Vorgrimler. Trans., R. Strachan, ed., C. Ernst. New York: Seabury, 1965. 493p.

*Theological questions: analysis and argument.* O. Thomas. Wilton, CT: Morehouse–Barlow, 1983.

*Theologische realenzyklopädie.* G. Müller (ed). Berlin: de Gruyter, 1974–. 24 vols. and 20,000p to date.

*Theology for the community of God.* S. Grenz. Nashville, TN: Broadman & Holman, 1994.

*Theology for the third millenium: an ecumenical view.* H. Küng. Trans., P. Heinegg. New York: Doubleday, 1988. 324p.

*Thinking about God: an introduction to theology.* D. Soelle. London: SCM Press; Philadelphia: Trinity Press International, 1990.

*Thinking the faith: Christian theology in a North American context; professing the faith: Christian theology in a North Amer-*

*ican context; confessing the faith: Christian theology in a North American context.* D. J. Hall. Minneapolis, MN: Augsburg Fortress, 1989–96. 3 vols.

*Tracking the maze: finding our way through modern theology from an evangelical perspective.* C. H. Pinnock. San Francisco: Harper & Row, 1990.

*Trinitas: a theological encyclopedia of the Holy Trinity.* M. O. O'Carroll. Wilmington, DE: Michael Glazier, 1987; Collegeville, MI: Michael Glazier/Liturgical, 1993.

*Twentieth–century religious thought.* J. Macquarrie. London: SCM Press; Philadelphia: Trinity Press International, 1988. 486p.

*We have been believers: an African American systematic theology.* J. H. Evans. Minneapolis, MN: Fortress, 1992.

*What Christians believe: a biblical and historical summary.* A. F. Johnson & R. E. Webber. Grand Rapids, MI: Zondervan, 1989.

*Winds of the Spirit: a constructive Christian theology.* P. C. Hodgson. Louisville, KY: Westminster John Knox, 1994.

*Wörterbuch des Christentums.* V. Drehsen et al. (eds). Gütersloh: Gerd Mohn, 1988. 1439p.

## 6. THEOLOGICAL ETHICS

*A passion for the possible: a message to U.S. churches.* W. S. Coffin. Louisville, KY: Westminster John Knox, 1993. 88p.

*After virtue: a study in moral theory.* A. MacIntyre. Notre Dame, IN: University of Notre Dame Press, 1981.

*An interpretation of Christian ethics.* R. Niebuhr. 1935; San Francisco: Harper & Row, 1963. 158p.

*Authentic transformation: a new vision of Christ and culture.* G. H. Stassen, D. M. Yeager & J. H. Yoder. Nashville, TN: Abingdon, 1996. 299p.

*Beyond integrity: a Judeo–Christian approach to business ethics.* S. B. Rae & K. L. Wong. Grand Rapids, MI: Zondervan, 1996. 656p.

*Changing witness: Catholic bishops and public policy, 1917–1994.* M. Warner. Grand Rapids, MI: Eerdmans, 1995. 220p.

*Christ and Culture.* H. R. Niebuhr. New York: Harper & Row, 1951. 217p.

*Christian ethics.* R. E. O. White. Macon, GA: Mercer University Press, 1994. 698p.

*Competing gospels: public theology and economic theory.* R. G. Simons. Alexandria, Australia: Dwyer, 1995. 253p.

*Confusions in Christian social ethics: problems for Geneva and Rome.* R. H. Preston. Grand Rapids, MI: Eerdmans, 1995. 215p.

*Dictionary of ethics, theology, and society.* P. B. Clarke & A. Linzey (eds). London and New York: Routledge, 1996. 960p.

*Economic justice for all: pastoral letter on Catholic social teaching and the U.S. economy.* Washington, DC: United States Catholic Conference, National Conference of Catholic Bishops, 1986.

*Encyclopedia of ethics.* L. C. Becker & C. Becker. New York: Garland, 1992. 2 vols, 1,462p.

*Encyclopedia of morals.* V. T. Ferm (ed). Repr. ed. Westport, CT: Greenwood, 1969. 682p.

*Encyclopedia of war and ethics.* D. A. Wells (ed). Westport, CT: Greenwood, 1996. 568p.

*Ethics.* D. Bonhoeffer. Ed., E. Bethge. 1949; New York: Collier/Macmillan, 1986. 382p. (Bonhoeffer, hanged in a Nazi concentration camp in 1945, never finished his *Ethics.* This volume is a compilation of early drafts and fragments written from 1940–1943).

*Ethics from a theocentric perspective; vol. 1, theology and ethics; vol. 2, ethics and theology.* J. Gustafson. Chicago: University of Chicago Press, 1981–84, 2 vols.

*For the nations: evangelical and public.* J. H. Yoder. Grand Rapids, MI: Eerdmans, 1997. 257p.

*Ideology in America: challenges to faith.* A. Geyer. Louisville, KY: Westminster John Knox, 1997. 149p.

*In praise of virtue: an exploration of the biblical virtues in a Christian context.* B. W. Farley. Grand Rapids, MI: Eerdmans, 1995. 191p.

*Library of theological ethics.* R. Lovin et al. (eds). Louisville, KY: Westminster John Knox, 1992–. 15 vols. to date. (Reprints, usually facsimile, of important older texts).

*Postmodern times: a Christian guide to contemporary thought and culture.* G. E. Veith Jr. Wheaton, IL: Crossway, 1994. 256p.

*Protestant and Roman Catholic ethics.* J. Gustafson. Chicago: University of Chicago Press, 1978. 204p.

*Public theology and political economy: Christian stewardship in modern society.* M. L. Stackhouse. 1987; Lanham, MD: University Press of America, 1991. 191p.

*Religion and human rights.* J. Kelsay & S. B. Twiss (eds). New York: The Project on Religion and Human Rights, 1994. 135p.

*Religion in public life: a dilemma for democracy.* R. E. Thiemann. Washington, DC: Georgetown University Press, 1996. 186p.

*Religious human rights in global perspective: religious perspectives and legal perspectives.* J. Witte Jr. & J. D. van der Vyer (eds). The Hague and Boston: M. Nijhoff, 1996. 2 vols.

*Resident aliens: life in the Christian colony.* S. Hauerwas & W. H. Willimon. Nashville, TN: Abingdon, 1989. 175p. (Written for laypersons by a pair of Duke University professors, this short book has been influential in promoting Christian communitarianism).

*Sexual ethics: an evangelical perspective.* S. J. Grenz. Louisville, KY: Westminster John Knox, 1997. 311p.

*The encyclopedia of religion and ethics.* J. Hastings (ed). Edinburgh: T. & T. Clark, 1926. 13 vols.

*The ethical demand.* K. E. Løgstrup. Ed., H. Fink & A. MacIntyre. Rev. ed. 1971; Notre Dame, IN: University of Notre Dame Press, 1997. 331p.

*The family in theological perspective.* S. C. Barton (ed). Edinburgh: T & T Clark, 1996. 367p.

*The moral quest: foundations of Christian ethics.* S. J. Grenz. Downers Grove, IL: InterVarsity, 1997. 379p.

*The politics of Jesus.* J. H. Yoder. Grand Rapids, MI: Eerdmans, 1972. 260p.

*The sources of Christian ethics.* S. Pinckaers. Trans., M. T. Noble. Washington, DC: Catholic University of America, 1995. 510p.

*The Westminster dictionary of Christian ethics.* J. Childress & J. Macquarrie (eds). 2nd ed. Philadelphia: Westminster, 1986. 687p. (Published in Britain as *A new dictionary of Christian ethics.* London: SCM Press, 1986, 1993).

*Theology and biotechnology: implications for a new science.* C. Deane–Drummond. London: Geoffrey Chapman, 1998.

*Threskeutike kai ethike enkyklopaideia (Religious and ethical encyclopedia).* Athens: Martinos, 1962–68. 12 vols.

## 7. MISSIOLOGY

*A Church for all peoples: missionary issues in a world Church.* E. LaVerdiere (ed). Collegeville, MN: Liturgical Press, 1993. 104p.

*A history of the expansion of Christianity.* K. S. Latourette. New York: Harper, 1937–45. 7 vols.

*Anglican cycle of prayer: praying together for persons and places around the world—1996.* London: Church House Publishing; Cincinnati, OH: Forward Movement Publications, 1995. 160p. (Annual publication of the Anglican Communion designed to focus attention on the world of Anglican missions worldwide).

*Ateismo e dialogo: bolletino del Segretariato per i Non–Credenti.* Rome, 1966–. (Christian dialogue with atheism and Marxism).

*Atlas du monde chrétien: l'expansion du Christianisme à travers les siècles.* A. Freitag et al. Paris and Brussels: Elsevier, 1959. 215p. (Maps and photographs. English edition under title, *The twentieth century atlas of the Christian world: the expansion of Christianity through the centuries.* New York: Hawthorn, 1964).

*Believing in the future: toward a missiology of Western culture.* D. J. Bosch. *Christian mission and modern culture.* Valley Forge, PA: Trinity Press International, 1995. 79p.

*Bibliographia missionaria.* 1935–74; Rome: Pontificia Università do Propagande Fide, 1986–. 50 vols. to date. (Annual review of previous year's literature; until 1971, some overlap with *Bibliotheca missionum,* but has now superseded it for current literature).

'Bibliography on world mission and evangelism,' *International review of mission,* (At end of all issues).

*Bibliotheca missionum.* R. Streit. Freiburg: Herder, 1916–71. 28 vols. (The major complete and retrospective Catholic bibliography of missions; discontinued 1971 and superseded by *Bibliographia missionaria*).

*Called and empowered: global mission in Pentecostal perspective.* M. Dempster, B. D. Klaus & D. Petersen (eds). Peabody, MA: Hendrickson, 1991.

*Carrying the gospel to all the non-Christian world.* Edinburgh: Oliphant/Revell, 1910. (World Missionary Conference, Report of Commission I).

*Catholic mission history.* J. Schmidlin. Techny, IL: Mission Press, 1933. 878p. (Translated from the German).

*Catholic mission theory.* J. Schmidlin. Techny, IL: Mission Press, 1931. 559p. (Translation of *Katolische Missionslehre im Grundriss*).

*Christian mission in the twentieth century.* T. Yates. Cambridge, UK: Cambridge University Press, 1994. 291p.

*Christianity and missions, 1450–1800.* J. S. Cummins (ed). *An expanding world: the European impact on world history, 1450–1800,* 28. Brookfield, VT: Ashgate, 1997. 350p.

*Christianity and the religions: a biblical theology of world religions.* E. Rommen & H. Netland (eds). *Evangelical Missiological Society series,* 2. Pasadena, CA: William Carey Library, 1995. 274p.

*Classic texts in mission and world Christianity.* N. E. Thomas (ed). *American Society of Missiology series,* 20. Maryknoll, NY: Orbis, 1995. 366p.

*Concise dictionary of the Christian world mission.* S. Neill, G. H. Anderson & J. Goodwin (eds). London: Lutterworth, 1970. 704p.

*Contemporary missiology: an introduction.* J. Verkuyl. Trans. & ed., D. Cooper. Grand Rapids, MI: Eerdmans, 1978. 428p.

*Critical bibliography of missiology.* L. Vriens. Nijmegen: VSKB Publ, 1960.

*Dictionary catalog of the Missionary Research Library, New York.* Boston: G.K. Hall, 1967. 17 vols., 13,039p. (273,000 entries).

*Dictionary of mission: theology, history, perspectives.* K. Müller et al. (eds). *American Society of Missiology series,* 24. Maryknoll, NY: Orbis, 1997. 544p.

*Encyclopedia of missions: descriptive, historical, biographical, statistical.* H. O. Dwight et al. (eds). 1904. Repr. ed. Detroit, MI: Omnigraphics, 1975.

*Encyclopedia of modern Christian missions: the agencies.* B. L. Goddard (ed). Camden, NJ: T. Nelson, 1967. 762p.

*Errand to the world: American Protestant thought and foreign missions.* W. R. Hutchison. Chicago: University of Chicago Press, 1987. 239p.

*God's call to mission.* D. W. Shenk. Scottdale, PA: Herald Press, 1994. 229p.

*Gospel and mission in the writings of Paul: an exegetical and theological analysis.* P. T. O'Brien. Grand Rapids, MI: Baker, 1993. 175p.

*Histoire universelle des missions catholiques.* S. Delacroix. Paris: Librarie Grund, 1956–58. 4 vols. (Profuse illustrations and maps).

*International review of missions: index 1912–1966.* O. G. Myklebust. Geneva: IRM, 1968. (Bibliography of 1,900 articles).

*Lexikon missionstheologischer grundbegriffe.* K. Müller & T. Sundermeier (eds). Berlin: Dietrich Reiner, 1987.

*Media in church and mission: communicating the gospel.* V. Søgaard. Pasadena, CA: William Carey Library, 1993. 301p.

*Missiological abstracts, 25 years, 1966–1991.* G. R. Grimes (ed). Rev. ed. Pasadena, CA: Fuller Theological Seminary, 1991. 336p. (Abstracts of 720 dissertations, theses, and projects produced at the School of World Mission at Fuller Theological Seminary).

*Missiology: an ecumenical introduction: texts and contexts of global Christianity.* F. J. Verstraelen (ed). Grand Rapids, MI: Eerdmans, 1995. 505p.

*Mission trends.* G. H. Anderson & T. F. Stransky C.S.P. (eds). New York: Paulist Press; Grand Rapids, MI: Eerdmans. 5 vols.

*New directions in mission and evangelization; vol. 1: basic statements 1974–1991; vol. 2: theological foundations.* J. A. Scherer & S. B. Bevans (eds). Maryknoll, NY: Orbis, 1992. 2 vols.

*On the way to fuller koinonia.* T. F. Best & G. Gassmann (eds). *Faith and Order paper,* 166. Geneva: World Council of Churches, 1994. 348p.

*Pentecost, mission and ecumenism: essays on intercultural theology.* J. A. B. Jongeneel et al. (eds). *Studies in the intercultural history of Christianity,* 75. Frankfurt am Main: Peter Lang, 1992. 386p.

*Philosophy, science and theology of mission in the 19th and 20th centuries: a missiological encyclopedia.* J. A. B. Jongeneel (ed). *Studies in the intercultural history of Christianity,* 92, 106. Frankfurt am Main: P. Lang, 1995–1997. 2 vols.

*Portugal em Africa. Revista de Cultura Missionária.* Lisbon: Editorial LIAM, 1894–1971. (Bi-monthly).

*Re–visioning mission: the Catholic Church and culture in postmodern America.* R. G. Cote. *Isaac Hecker studies in religion and American culture.* Mahwah, NJ: Paulist, 1996. 197p.

*Roots of the great debate in mission: mission in historical and theological perspective.* R. E. Hedlund. *Theological issues series,* 3. Bangalore, India: Theological Book Trust, 1993. 529p.

*Sacrae Congregationis de Propaganda Fide Memoria Rerum.* J. Metzler et al. (eds). Freiburg: Herder, 1972–76. 3 vols., 4,500p. (History of Catholic missions, 1622–1972).

*Scripture and strategy: the use of the Bible in postmodern church and mission.* D. J. Hesselgrave. *Evangelical Missiological Society series,* 1. Pasadena, CA: William Carey Library, 1994. 192p.

*Spiritual power and missions: raising the issues.* E. Rommen (ed). *Evangelical Missiological Society series,* 3. Pasadena, CA: William Carey Library, 1995. 163p.

*Studies in missions: an index of theses on missions.* Monrovia, CA: MARC, 1974. 73p. (200 theses and dissertations).

*The Christian-Marxist dialogue: an annotated bibliography, 1959–1969.* A. J. van der Bent. Geneva: World Council of Churches, 1969. 90p. (1,200 titles in 5 languages).

*The evangelization of the world in this generation.* J. R. Mott. New York: Student Volunteer Movement for Foreign Missions, 1900. 253p.

*The good news of the kingdom: mission theology for the third millennium.* C. Van Engen, D. S. Gilliland & P. Pierson (eds). Maryknoll, NY: Orbis Books, 1993. 336p.

*The gospel and frontier peoples: a report of a consultation, December 1972.* R. P. Beaver (ed). Pasadena, CA: William Carey Library, 1972. 413p.

*The recovery of mission: beyond the pluralist paradigm.* V. Ramachandra. Grand Rapids, MI: Eerdmans, 1996. 305p.

*Transforming mission: paradigm shifts in theology of mission.* D. J. Bosch. *American Society of Missiology series,* 16. Maryknoll, NY: Orbis, 1991. 597p.

*Wichtige daten der Missionsgeschichte.* T. Ohm. Münster: Aschendorffsche Verlagsbuchhandlung, 1956. (French: *Les principaux faits de l'histoire des missions,* 1961. 162p).

*Write the vision: the Church renewed.* W. R. Shenk. *Christian mission and modern culture.* Valley Forge, PA: Trinity Press International, 1995. 127p.

## 8. ECUMENISM

*A history of the ecumenical movement, 1517–1948 (Vol 1).* R. Rouse & S. C. Neill. London: SPCK; Philadelphia: Westminster, 1954. 822p.

*Bibliografia tes Oikoumenikes Kineseos, 1960–1970 (Bibliography of the ecumenical movement).* V. T. Istavridis. Athens: Theologia, 1978. 78p. (Orthodoxy and ecumenism; 1,500 titles).

*Classified catalog of the Ecumenical Movement, World Council of Churches, Geneva.* Boston: G. K. Hall, 1972. 2 vols., 967p. (20,300 entries).

*Commentary of the documents of Vatican II.* H. Vorgrimler (ed). New York: Herder & Herder, 1967–72. 5 vols.

*Dictionary of the ecumenical movement.* N. Lossky et al. (eds). Geneva: WCC Publications and Grand Rapids, MI: Eerdmans, 1991. 1,212p.

*Documents on Christian unity.* G. K. A. Bell. London and New York: Oxford University Press, 1929–58. 4 vols. (Illustrates the growth of the world ecumenical movement).

*Ecumenical terminology.* Geneva: World Council of Churches, 1975. 564p. (4 languages, 1,335 words, titles).

*Ecumenism around the world: a directory of ecumenical institutes, centers, and organizations.* 2nd ed. Rome: Centro pro Unione (Friars of the Atonement), 1974. 169p.

*Forging a common future: Catholic, Judaic, and Protestant relations for a new millenium.* A. Greeley et al. Ed., J. Neusner. Cleveland, OH: Pilgrim Press, 1997. 122p.

*Historical dictionary of ecumenical Christianity.* A. J. van der Bent. *Historical dictionaries of religions, philosophies, and movements,* 3. Metuchen, NJ and London: Scarecrow Press, 1994. 626p.

*Internationale Ökumenische Bibliographie/International Ecumenical Bibliography/Bibliographie Oecuménique Internationale/Bibliografí Ecuménica Internacional.* C. Graves et al. (eds). München: Chr Kaiser Verlag, 1962–75. 10 vols. (In English, French, German, and Spanish. 55,000 titles, over half articles, on contemporary dialogue between churches and with other religions).

*Liberation and orthodoxy: the promise and failures of intecon-*

*fessional dialogue.* Y. Tesfai. Maryknoll, NY: Orbis, 1996. 208p.
*Mission and evangelism: an ecumenical affirmation.* E. Castro (ed). Geneva: CWME, 1982.
*Oecumene* 1 (1977) and 2 (1978). Strasbourg: CERDIC, 1977–78. (Ecumenical bibliography; abstracts of over 1,000 journals).
*Ökumene Lexikon: Kirchen, Religionen, Bewegunen.* H. Krüger, W. Löser & W. Müller-Römheld (eds). Frankfurt am Main: Verlag Otto Lembeck and Verlag Josef Knecht, 1983. 673p.
*Reclaiming the great tradition: evangelicals, Catholics and Orthodox in dialogue.* J. S. Custinger. Downers Grove, IL: InterVaristy, 1997. 214p.
'Selective bibliography of significant current ecumenical books and pamphlets,' *The ecumenical review*, (quarterly).
*Sharing in one hope: Bangalore 1978, reports and documents from the meeting of the Faith and Order Commission. Faith and Order paper*, 92. Geneva: World Council of Churches, Commission on Faith and Order, 1978. 304p.
*Six hundred ecumenical consultations 1948–1982.* A. J. van der Bent. Geneva: World Council of Churches, 1983. 254p.
*The ecumenical advance: a history of the ecumenical movement, 1948–1968.* H. E. Fey (ed). London: SPCK, 1970. 525p.
*The ecumenical movement: an anthology of key texts and voices.* M. Kinnamon & B. Cope (eds). Grand Rapids, MI: Eerdmans; Geneva: WCC Publications, 1996. 564p.
*The Orthodox Church in the Ecumenical Movement: documents and statements 1902–1975.* C. G. Patelos (ed). Geneva: World Council of Churches, 1978. 360p.
*The reconciliation of peoples: challenge to the churches.* G. Brown & H. Wells (eds). Geneva: WCC Publications; Maryknoll, NY: Orbis, 1997. 199p.
*Toward a Christian theology of religious pluralism.* J. Dupuis. Maryknoll, NY: Orbis, 1997. 447p.

## 9. ESTHETICS

*20 centuries of great preaching: an encyclopedia of preaching.* C. E. Fant Jr & W. M. Pinson Jr (eds). Waco, TX: Word, 1971. 13 vols.
*A bibliography of Christian worship.* B. Thompson (ed). *ATLA bibliography series*, 25. Philadelphia: American Theological Library Association; Metuchen, NJ, Scarecrow Press. 828p.
*A bibliography of sources in Christianity and the arts.* D. M. Kari. *Studies in art and religious interpretation*, 16. Lewiston, NY: E. Mellen Press, 1995. 774p.
*A dictionary of hymnology.* J. Julian (ed). 1907; New York: Dover, 1957. 2 vols.
*A dictionary of liturgical terms.* P. H. Pfatteicher. Philadelphia: Trinity Press International, 1991. 143p.
*A dictionary of liturgy and worship.* J. G. Davies (ed). London: SCM, 1972. 385p.
*A feast of Anglican spirituality.* R. Backhouse. Norwich, UK: Canterbury Press, 1998.
*A pastoral liturgy bibliography.* 2nd rev. ed. Notre Dame, IN: Notre Dame Center for Pastoral Liturgy, 1981. 28p.
*A treasury of Russian spirituality.* G. P. Fedotov (ed). London: Sheed & Ward, 1950. 501p.
*Art and the Reformation: an annotated bibliography.* L. B. Parshall & P. W. Parshall. *A Reference publication in art history.* Boston, MA: G. K. Hall, 1986. 328p.
*Art in the Armenian Church: origins and teaching.* G. Kochakian. New York: St. Vartan Press, 1995.
*Art of the Christian world, A.D. 200–1500: a handbook of styles and forms.* Y. Christe et al. New York: Rizzoli International Publications, 1982. 504p.
*Asceticism.* V. L. Wimbaugh & R. Valantasis (eds). New York: Oxford University Press, 1955.
*Bibliographia internationalis spiritualitatis.* Roma: Pontifical Institute of Spirituality, 1966–68. 3 vols. (6,487 titles in vol. 3).
*Bulgarian monasteries: monuments of history, culture, and art.* G. Chavrukov. Sofia: Naouka i Izkoustvo, 1974. 371p. (Photographic collection).
*Christian art in Asia.* M. Takenaka. Tokyo: Kyo Bun Kwan, 1975. 171p.
*Christian art in India.* J. F. Butler. Madras: Christian Literature Society, 1986. 199p.
*Christian art of the 4th to 12th centuries.* F. Abbate (ed). Trans., P. Swinglehurst. Milan: Fratelli Fabbri Editore; London and New York: Octopus Books, 1972. 158p.
*Christian spirituality: the essential guide to the most influential spiritual writings of the Christian tradition.* F. N. Magill & I. P. McGreal (eds). San Francisco: Harper & Row, 1988. 713p.
*Christian symbols in a world community.* D. J. Fleming. New York: Friendship Press, 1940. 160p.
*Christianity,* section 24 in *Iconography of religions.* Leiden: E. J. Brill, 1979-. 4 vols. to date.
*Christianity and the arts in Russia.* W. C. Brumfield & M. Velimirovich (eds). Cambridge, UK: Cambridge University Press, 1991. 172p.
*Concise encyclopedia of preaching.* W. H. Willimon & R. Lischer (eds). Louisville, KY: Westminster John Knox, 1995. 540p.
*Dictionary of Catholic devotions.* M. Walsh. London: Burnes & Oates; San Francisco: Harper, 1993. 366p.
*Dictionnaire d'archéologie chrétienne et de liturgie.* F. Cabrol, H. Leclerq & H. Marrou (eds). Paris: Letouzey & Ané, 1903–53. 30 parts, 15 vols.
*Dictionnaire de la vie spirituelle.* S. de Fiores & T. Goffi (eds). Paris: Le Cerf, 1987. 1,268p. (Adapted from the Italian, *Nuovo Dizionario di spiritualità.* Rome: Edizioni Paoline, 1983).
*Dictionnaire de spiritualité, ascétique et mystique.* M. Viller S.J. et al. (eds). Paris: Beachesne, 1937–1994. 20 vols.
*Dictionnaire des église de France, Belgique, Luxembourg, Suisse.* J. Brosse et al (eds). Paris: Robert Laffont, 1971. 5 vols. (History and architecture of church buildings).
*Dictionnaire encyclopédique de la liturgie.* D. Sartore & A. M. Triacca (eds). Turnhout: Brepols, 1992–. 1 vol.; in planning to 2 vols.
*Dizionario francescano: Spiritualità.* E. Caroli (ed). Padua: Edizioni Messagero, 1983.
*Encyclopedia of medieval church art.* E. G. Tasker and J. Beaumont. London: B. T. Batsford, 1993. 320p.
*Encyclopédie des musiques sacrées.* J. Porte (ed). Tours, France: Labergerie–Mame, 1968–71. 4 vols. (Vol. 4 consists of records).
*Façades and festivals of Antigua: a guide to church fronts and celebrations.* D. L. Jickling & E. Elliott. Antigua, Guatemala: Casa del Sol, 1989. 75p.
*Historic churches of Barbados.* B. Hill. Bridgetown, Barbados: Art Heritage Publications, 1984. 128p.
*Iconography of Christian art.* G. Schiller. New York: NY Graphic Society, 1971. 2 vols. (3 vols in German edition).
*Icons: windows on eternity: theology and spirituality in colour.* G. Limouris. *Faith and Order paper*, 147. Geneva: WCC Publications, 1990. 238p.
*Images of religion in Australian art.* R. Crumlin. Kensington, NSW: Bay Books, 1988. 204p.
*Kirkjuboarstólarir og Kirkjubøur: brot úr søgu føroyska biskupssætisins.* K. J. Krogh. Tórshavn: E. Thomsen, 1988. 133p. (Treats the history and art of the church on the Faeroe Islands).
*La Bible et les saints: Guide iconographique.* G. Duchet-Suchaux & M. Pastoreau. Paris: Flammarion, 1990. 319p. (English edition, *The Bible and the saints: Flammarion iconographic guides.* Paris and New York: Flammarion, 1994).
*Lexikon der Christlichen Ikonographie.* E. Kirschbaum et al. (eds). Freiburg im Breisgau: Herder, 1968–76. 8 vols.
*Monasteries in Bulgaria.* L. Prashkov, E. Bakalova & S. Boyadjiev. Sofia: Spectrum, 1990. 286p.
*Orthodox saints: spiritual profiles for modern man.* G. Poulos. 4th ed. Brookline, MA: Holy Cross Orthodox Press, 1990–1992. 4 vols.
*Outward signs: the language of Christian symbolism.* E. N. West. New York: Walker, 1989. 254p.
*Reallexikon zur byzantinischen Kunst.* K. Wessel & M. Restle (eds). Stuttgart: Hierseman, 1963–. 4 vols. (Explores interrelation of religion and art in Eastern Christianity).
*Repertorium hymnologicum.* C. U. J. Chevalier. Louvain and Brussels: Société des Bollandistes, 1892–1920. 6 vols.
*Saints of the Roman calendar including feasts proper to the English–speaking world.* E. Lodi. New York: Alba House, 1992. 444p.
*Serima: towards an African expression of Christian belief = Ein Versuch in afrikanisch–christlicher Kunst.* A. B. Plangger & M. Diethelm. Gwelo, Rhodesia: Mambo Press, 1974. 76p.
*Shaker architecture.* H. F. Schiffer. Exton, PA: Schiffer, 1979.
*Spirituality and the secular quest.* P. H. Van Ness (ed). *World spirituality: an encyclopedic history of the religious quest*, 26. New York: Crossroad, 1996.
'St. Lucian carnival: a Caribbean art form.' R. D. Dunstan. Ph.D. dissertation, State University of New York at Stony Brook, Stony Brook, NY, 1978. 373p. (A study of the preparations for and celebration of carnival, the pre–Lenten celebration. Includes consideration of the religious implications of carnival in St. Lucia).
*The American Shakers and their furniture.* J. G. Shea. New York: Van Nostrand, 1971.
*The Bible in 20th century art.* N. Usherwood & P. Holberton (eds). London: Pagoda Books, 1987. 111p.
*The Bible through Asian eyes.* M. Takenaka & R. O'Grady. Aukland, NZ: Pace Publishing, 1991. 199p.
*The Christian oriental carpet: a presentation of its development, iconologically and iconographically, from its beginnings to the 18th century.* V. Gantzhorn. Trans., C. Madsen. Köln: Benedikt Taschen, 1991. 532p. (A translation of the author's doctoral dissertation at the Eberhard-Karls-Univesität, Tübingen).
*The dictionary of art.* J. Turner (ed). New York: Grove, 1996. 34 vols.
*"The habitation of thy house, Lord, I have loved well ...": Reformed ecclesiastical art in Hungary.* J. Hapák & B. Takács. Budapest: Officina Nova, 1991. 79p.
*The icon handbook: a guide to understanding icons and the liturgy, symbols and practices of the Russian Orthodox Church.* D. Coomler. Springfield, IL: Templegate, 1995. 319p.
*The liturgical dictionary of Eastern Christianity.* P. D. Day. London: Burns & Oates; Collegeville, MN: Liturgical Press, 1993. 343p.
*The new dictionary of sacramental worship.* P. E. Fink S.J. (ed). Collegeville, MN: Liturgical Press, 1990. 1352p.
*The new Westminster dictionary of liturgy and worship.* J. G. Davies (ed). 2nd ed. Philadelphia: Westminster, 1986. 570p. (Published in Britain as *A new dictionary of liturgy and worship.* London: SCM Press, 1986, 1989).
*The Oxford companion to Christian art and architecture.* P. Murray & L. Murray. Oxford, UK and New York: Oxford University Press, 1996. 608p.
*The painted churches of Cyprus: treasures of Byzantine art.* A. Stylianou & J. Stylianou. London: Trigraph for the A. G. Leventis Foundation, 1985. 518p.
*The painted churches of Romania: a visitor's impressions.* J. Fletcher. London: New Knowledge Books, 1971. 103p.
*The presense of God: a history of Western Christian mysticism.* B. McGinn. New York: Crossroad, 1992–. 2 vols. to date; in planning to 4 vols.
*The Sistine Chapel.* F. Papava (ed). Vatican City: Monumenti, 1992.
*The study of spirituality.* C. Jones, G. Wainwright & E. Yarnold SJ (eds). New York and Oxford, UK: Oxford University Press, 1986.
*The Westminster dictionary of Christian education.* K. B. Cully (ed). Philadelphia: Westminster, 1962. 812p. (A second edition was published by Harper, *Harper's encyclopedia of religious knowledge.* San Francisco: Harper, 1990. 739p).
*The Westminster dictionary of Christian spirituality.* G. S. Wakefield (ed). Philadelphia: Westminster, 1983. 416p. (Published in Britain as *A dictionary of Christian spirituality.* London: SCM Press, 1983, 1988).
*Vies des saints et des bienheureux selon l'ordre du calendrier, avec l'historique des fêtes.* J. Baudot [1857-1929], L. Chaussin [1891–1945] & Bénédictins de Paris [to 1959] (eds). Paris: Letouzey et Ané, 1935–1959. 7,500p.
*Zimbabwe Christian art: the first collected exhibition 28th November–13th December held at the Anglican Cathedral, Harare opened by H.E. the Rev Canaan Banana, president of the Republic of Zimbabwe.* Harare: Anglican Cathedral, 1986. 24p.

## 10. SCIENCE AND RELIGION

*A Christian view of modern science.* R. L. Raymond. Nutley, NJ: Presbyterian and Reformed, 1977.
*Belief in God in an age of science.* J. Polkinghorne. New Haven: Yale University Press, 1999. 160p.
*Beyond the cosmos: what recent discoveries in astronomy and physics reveal about the nature of God.* H. Ross. Colorado Springs, CO: NavPress, 1996. 236p.
*Chance and providence: God's action in a world governed by scientific law.* W. Pollard. London: Faber, 1958.
*Chaos and complexity: scientific perspectives on divine action.* R. J. Russell, N. Murphy, and A. Peacocke, editors. Vatican City: Vatican Observatory Publications, 1995. 418p.
*Creation and the world of science.* A. Peacocke. Oxford: Clarendon Press, 1979.
*Evolution and the Bible.* E. G. Conklin. Chicago: American Institute of Sacred Literature, 1922. (Modernist defense of teaching evolution).
*Faith and the physical world.* D. Dye. Grand Rapids, MI: Eerdmans, 1966.
*God and creation.* P. J. Flamming. Nashville, TN: Broadman Press, 1984. 164p.
*God and the astronomers.* R. Jastrow. New York: W.W. Norton, 1992. 156p. (Evidence for the Big Bang).
*God and the new physics.* P. Davies. New York: Simon & Schuster, 1983.
*In the beginning God: modern science and the Christian doctrine of creation.* J.D. Weaver. Oxford: Regent's Park College, 1994. 218p.
*Intelligent design: the bridge between science & theology.* W. A. Dembski. Downers Grove, IL: InterVarsity Press, 1999. 242p.
*Modern cosmology and the Christian idea of God.* E.A. Milne. Oxford: Clarendon Press, 1952.
*On the moral nature of the universe: theology, cosmology, and ethics.* N. Murphy and G. F. R. Ellis. Minneapolis: Fortress Press, 1996. 270p.
*Quantum cosmology and the laws of nature: scientific perspectives on divine action.* R. J. Russell, N. Murphy, and C. J. Isham. Vatican City: Vatican Observatory Publications, 1993.
*Quarks, chaos & Christianity.* J. Polkinghorne. New York: Crossroad, 1995. 123p.
*Religion and scientific naturalism: overcoming the conflicts.* D. R. Griffen. State University of New York Press, 2000. 345p. (Draws on philosophy of A. N. Whitehead).
*Religion in an age of science.* I. Barbour. San Francisco: HarperSanFrancisco, 1990.
*Science and creation: the search for understanding.* J. Polkinghorne. London: SPCK, 1988.
*Science and its limits: the natural sciences in Christian perspective.* D. Ratzsch. Downers Grove, IL: InterVarsity Press, 2000. 192p.
*Science and providence: God's interaction with the world.* J. Polkinghorne. London: SPCK, 1989.
*Science and religion: a critical survey.* H. Rolston III. New York: Random House, 1987.
*Science and the Christian experiment.* A. Peacocke. London: Oxford University Press, 1971.
*Science and theology: an introduction.* J. Polkinghorne. Philadelphia: Fortress Press, 1999. 176p.
*Stages of thought: the co-evolution of religious thought and science.* M. H. Barnes. New York: Oxford University Press, 2000. 334p. (Utilizes cognitive theories of Piaget).
*Summer for the gods: the Scopes trial and America's continuing debate over science and religion.* E. J. Larson. New York: Basic Books, 1997. 318p.
*The Christian view of science and scripture.* B. Ramm. London: Paternoster, 1955.
*The creator and the cosmos: how the greatest scientific discoveries of the century reveal God.* H. Ross. Colorado Springs, CO: NavPress, 1993. 186p.
*The creationists: the evolution of scientific creationism.* R.L. Numbers. New York: Knopf, 1992.
*The end of the world and the ends of God: science and theology on eschatology.* J. Polkinghorne and M. Welker, editors. Trinity Press International, 2000.
*The mind of God: science and the search for ultimate meaning.* P. Davies. New York: Simon & Schuster, 1992.
*The new consciousness in science and religion.* H.K. Schilling. London: SCM Press, 1973.
*The new faith-science debate.* J.M. Magnum, editor. Minneapolis: Fortress Press, 1989.
*The sciences and theology in the twentieth century.* A. Peacocke, editor. Notre Dame, IN: University of Notre Dame Press, 1981.
*Theology for a scientific age: being and becoming—natural, divine, and human.* A. Peacocke. Minneapolis: Fortress Press, 1993. 438p.
*Theology in the age of scientific reasoning.* N. Murphy. Ithaca, NY: Cornell University Press, 1990. 218p. (Draws on new historicist accounts of science, particularly Imre Lakatos).

## 11. WORLD RELIGIONS (including Christianity)

*A dictionary of non-Christian religions.* G. Parrinder. Philadelphia, PA: Westminster, 1971. 320p.
*A handbook of living religions.* J. R. Hinnells (ed). London and

New York: Viking, 1984; London: Penguin, 1991. 528p.
*A reader's guide to the great religions.* C. J. Adams (ed). 2nd ed. New York: Free Press; London: Collier Macmillan, 1977. 539p.
*A sourcebook for earth's community of religions.* J. D. Beversluis (ed). Rev. ed. Grand Rapids, MI: CoNexus Press—Sourcebook Project; New York: Global Education Associates, 1995. 376p. (Contains statements from the Parliament of the World's Religions, Chicago, 1993).
*Atlas of the world's religions.* N.Smart (ed). New York: Oxford University Press, 1999. 240p.
*Christian faith amidst religious pluralism: an introductory bibliography.* D. G. Dawe et al. Richmond, VA: Union Theological Seminary in Virginia, 1980. 115p.
*Christianity and the New Age religion: a bridge toward mutual understanding.* L. D. Moore. Atlanta: Pendulum Plus Press, 1993. 244p.
*Companions in consciousness: the Bible and the New Age movement.* R. Quillo. Liguori, MO: Triumph Books, 1995. 191p.
*Concise dictionary of religion.* I. Hexham. Downers Grove, IL: InterVarsity Press, 1993. 245p.
*Contemporary religions: a world guide.* I. Harris et al (eds). Harlow, UK: Longman, 1992. 511p.
*Defenders of God: the fundamentalist revolt against the modern age.* B. B. Lawrence. San Francisco: Harper & Row, 1989. 318p. (An examination of fundamentalist movements in several religions, including Christianity, Judaism, and Islam.).
*Dictionary of cults, sects, religions and the occult.* G. A. Mather & L. A. Nichols. Grand Rapids, MI: Zondervan, 1993. 384p.
*Dictionary of religion and philosophy.* G. MacGregor. New York: Paragon House, 1989; paperback, 1991. 696p. (Published in Britain under the title, *The everyman dictionary of religion and philosophy,* London: Dent, 1990.).
*Dictionnaire des religions.* P. Poupard (ed). 3rd ed. Paris: Presses Universitaires de France, 1993. 2,218p in 2 vols.
*Encyclopaedia of religion and ethics.* J. Hastings (ed). Edinburgh: T. & T. Clark; New York: Scribner, 1908–27. 12 vols.
*Geography of religions.* D. E. Sopher. *Foundations of cultural geography series.* Englewood Cliffs, NJ: Prentice-Hall, 1967. 128p.
*Great religions of the world.* M. Severy (ed). *The Story of Man Library.* Washington, DC: National Geographic Society. 420p. (Examines Hinduism, Buddhism, Judaism, Islam, and Christianity).
*Histoire des religions.* H. Puech (ed). Paris: Gallimard, 1970–1976. 3 vols.
*Historical atlas of the religions of the world.* I. R. al Faruqi & D. E. Sopher (eds). New York: Macmillan; London: Collier Macmillan, 1974. 368p.
*Interfaith directory.* F. Clark (ed). New York: International Religious Foundation, 1987. 194p.
*International directory of the world's religions.* J. G. Melton et al (eds). Santa Barbara, CA: ABC CLIO, 2000. (Multivolume).
*International directory of the world's religions.* G. Ward. Carmel, CA: Apogee Press, 1991.
*Japanese religion.* H. Ichiro et al (eds). Tokyo: Kodensha, 1972. 272p.
*Keyguide to information sources on world religions.* J. Holm. London: Mansell Publishing, 1991. 271p.
*Le grand atlas des religions.* C. Baladier (ed). Paris: Encyclopaedia Universalis, 1990. 413p.
*Longman guide to living religions.* I. Harris et al. (eds). London: Longman Current Affairs, 1994. 294p.
*New dictionary of religions.* J. R. Hinnells (ed). Oxford, UK and Cambridge, MA: Blackwell Reference, 1995. 760p. (Enlarged edition of two earlier titles, *The Penguin dictionary of religions,* New York: Viking, 1984; and *The facts on file dictionary of religions,* New York and London: Facts on File, 1984.).
*Our religions.* A. Sharma (ed). San Francisco: Harper, 1993. 547p.
*Religion in Europe: contemporary perspectives.* S. Gill et al. (eds). Kampen, Netherlands: Kok Pharos Publishing, 1994.
*Religions of America: ferment and faith in an age of crisis.* L. Rosten (ed). Rev. ed. New York: Simon & Schuster, 1975. 672p.
*Religions of Asia.* J. Y. Fenton et al. 2nd ed. New York: St. Martin's Press, 1988. 336p.
*Religions of the world.* L. M. Hopfe, L. R. Hopfe & L. M. H. Hopfe (eds). 6th ed. Englewood Cliffs, NJ: Prentice-Hall, 1994. 454p.
*Religious information sources: a worldwide guide.* J. G. Melton & M. A. Köszegi. New York: Garland, 1992. 581p.
*Religious traditions of the world: a journey through Africa, Mesoamerica, North America, Judaism, Christianity, Islam, Hinduism, Buddhism, China, and Japan.* H. B. Earhart (ed). San Francisco: Harper, 1993. 1,224p.
*Sacred worlds: an introduction to geography and religion.* C. C. Park. London and New York: Routledge, 1994. 346p.
*The concise encyclopedia of living faiths.* R. C. Zaehner (ed). New York: Hawthorn Books, 1959. 431p.
*The Continuum dictionary of religion.* M. Pye (ed). New York: Crossroad/Continuum, 1994. 332p. (Published in Britain as *The Macmillan dictionary of religion.*).
*The Eliade guide to world religions.* M. Eliade, I. P. Couliano & H. S. Wiesner. San Francisco: Harper, 1991. 313p. (Later issued as *HarperCollins concise guide to world religions.* 2000. 320p).
*The encyclopedia of religion.* M. Eliade et al. (eds). 1986; New York: Macmillan, 1993. 16 vols.
*The encyclopedia of world faiths: an illustrated survey of the world's living religions.* P. Bishop & M. Darton (eds). New York: Facts on File, 1987. 352p.
*The HarperCollins dictionary of religion.* J. Z. Smith (ed). San Francisco: HarperCollins, 1995. 184p.
*The Oxford dictionary of world religions.* J. Bowker. Oxford: Oxford University Press, 1996. 1,111p.
*The Penguin dictionary of religions.* J. R. Hinnells (ed). New York and London: Penguin Books, 1984. 550p. (Includes brief articles on 1,150 terms, as well as an extensive section of bibliographies).
*The perennial dictionary of world religions.* K. Crim (ed). San Francisco: Harper & Row, 1989. 830p. (A reprint of *The Abingdon dictionary of living religions,* Nashville, TN: Abingdon, 1981).
*The world's religions.* N. Smart. New York: Cambridge University Press, 1995. 576p.
*The world's religions.* S. Sutherland et al. (eds). London: Routledge; Boston: G. K. Hall, 1988. 1,009p.
*The world's religions: understanding the living faiths.* P. B. Clarke (ed). Pleasantville, NY and London: Reader's Digest and Marshall Editions, 1993. 220p.
*Twentieth century encyclopedia of religious knowledge.* L. A. Loetscher (ed). Grand Rapids, MI: Baker, 1955. 2 vols.
*Who's who of world religions.* J. R. Hinnells (ed). New York: Simon & Schuster, 1992. 576p.
*World religions: a sourcebook for students of Christian theology.* R. Viladesau & M. Massa (eds). Mahwah, NJ: Paulist, 1994. 285p. (An anthology of selections from sacred texts of non-Christian world religions).
*World religions and human liberation.* D. Cohn-Sherbok. *Faith meets faith series.* Maryknoll, NY: Orbis, 1992. 151p.
*World religions: the great faiths explored and explained.* J. Bowker. London: DK Limited, 1997. 200p.

## II. NON-CHRISTIAN CONTEXT

### 1. ISLAM

*A bibliography of Islamic law, 1980–1993.* L. Al-Zwaini & R. Peters. *Handbuch der Orientalistik. Erste Abteilung, der Nahe und Mittlere Osten (Handbook of Oriental studies, Near and Middle East),* 19. Leiden and New York: E. J. Brill, 1994. 248p.
*A commentary on the Qur'an.* R. Bell. Manchester, UK: University of Manchester Press, 1991. 630p. in 2 vols. (From a draft written by Richard Bell and edited by C. E. Bosworth and M. E. J. Richardson).
*A concordance of the Qur'an.* H. E. Kassis. Berkeley, CA: University of California Press, 1983. 1,483p.
*A popular dictionary of Islam.* I. R. Netton. London: Curzon, 1992. 279p. (For beginning students of Islam).
*A reader on classical Islam.* F. E. Peters. Princeton, NJ: Princeton University Press, 1994. 440.
*An introduction to Islam.* D. Waines. New York: Cambridge University Press, 1995. 344p.
*Annuaire du monde musulman.* L. Massignon. Paris: Presses Universitaires de France, 1954 (4th edition). 428p.
*Deciphering the signs of God: a phenomenological approach to Islam.* A. Scimmel. Albany, NY: State University of New York Press, 1994. 319p.
*Der Koran: Kommentar und Konkordanz.* R. Paret. 5th ed. Stuttgart: Kohlhammer, 1994. 555p.
*Dictionnaire des symboles musulmans: ristes, mystique et civilisation.* M. Chebel. Paris: Albin Michel, 1995. 501p.
*Encyclopedia Iranica.* E. Yarshater (ed). London and New York: Routledge & Kegan Paul, 1985–90 (vols. 1–4); Costa Mesa, CA: Mazda Publishing, 1992– (vols. 5–7). 7 vols. to date; in progress to at least 15 vols.
*Encyclopédie philosophique universelle.* A. Jacob (ed). Paris: Presses Universitaires de France, 1989–92. 5 vols. in 3. (51 articles on a variety of topics concerning Islam are scattered throughout).
*Everyday life in the Muslim Middle East.* D. L. Bowen & E. A. Early (eds). Bloomington, IN: Indiana University Press, 1993. (Describes life in World A).
*Higher learning in Islam: the classical period 700 AD to 1300 AD.* C. M. Stanton. Savage, MD: Rowman & Littlefield, 1990. 225p. (Scholarly look at the Golden Age of Islam).
*Index Islamicus 1906–1955: a catalogue of articles on Islamic subjects in periodicals and other collective publications.* J. D. Pearson et al. Cambridge, UK: Heffer, 1958. 807p. (Supplemental vols published in 1962, 1967, 1972, 1977).
*Islam,* section 22 in *Iconography of religions.* Leiden: E. J. Brill, 1974–. 3 vols. to date. (2 volumes on Muslim architecture and one volume on India and Pakistan).
*Islam and Islamic groups: a worldwide reference guide.* F. Shaikh (ed). Harlow, Essex, UK: Longman Group, 1992. 326p. (A political guide to Islam).
*Islam in North America: a sourcebook.* M. A. Köszegi & J. G. Melton (eds). New York: Garland, 1992. 392p.
*Islam in tribal societies: from the Atlas to the Indus.* A. S. Ahmed & D. M. Hart. London: Routledge & Kegan Paul, 1984. 350p.
*Islamic Da'wah in the West: Muslim missionary activity and the dynamics of conversion to Islam.* L. Poston. Oxford, UK: Oxford University Press, 1992. 224p.
*Islamologie.* F. M. Pareja (ed). Beyrouth: Imprimerie Catholique, 1957–64. 1,149p. (Though dated, still an excellent resource.).
*Judaism, Christianity, and Islam: the classical texts and their interpretation.* F. E. Peters. Princeton, NJ: Princeton University Press, 1990. 1248.
*Lexikon religiöser Grundbegriffe: Judentum, Christentum, Islam.* A. T. Khoury (ed). Graz: Styria, 1987. 637p. (A comparison of Judaism, Christianity, and Islam).
*Muhammad and Jesus: a comparison of the prophets and their teachings.* W. E. Phipps. New York: Continuum, 1996. 316p.
*Muslim minorities in the West.* S. Z. Abedin & Z. Sardar (eds). *Studies of Muslim minorities.* London: Grey Seal, 1995. 222p.
*Muslim peoples: a world ethnographic survey.* R. V. Weekes (ed). 2nd ed. Westport, CT: Greenwood, 1984. 2 vols.
*Muslim women throughout the world: a bibliography.* M. Kimball & B. R. von Schlegell. Sterling, VA: Lynne Reiner, 1997. 285p.
*Piety and power: Muslims and Christians in West Africa.* L. Sanneh. Maryknoll, NY: Orbis Books, 1996.
*Political Islam: religion and politics in the Arab world.* N. N. Ayubi. London: Routledge, 1991. 302p.
*Qur'anic Christians: an analysis of classical and modern exegesis.* J. D. McAuliffe. Cambridge, UK and New York: Cambridge University Press, 1991. 352p. (Examines the Islamic understanding of Christians. Studies passages in the Qur'an that make ostensibly positive remarks about Christians).
*Religion and tradition in Islamic Central Asia.* M. B. Olcott. Armonk, NY: M. E. Sharpe, 1992.
*Shi'a Islam: from religion to revolution.* H. Halm. 176p.
'The black Muslims as a new religious movement: their evolution and implications for the study of religion in a pluralistic context,' L. H. Mamiya, in *Conflict and cooperation between contemporary religious groups.* Chuo Academic Research Group. Tokyo: Nakamura, 1988.
*The Cambridge history of Islam.* P. M. Holt, A. K. S. Lambton & B. Lewis (eds). London: Cambridge University Press, 1970. 4 vols.
*The Cambridge illustrated history of the Islamic world.* F. Robinson (ed). Cambridge, UK: Cambridge University Press, 1996. 352p.
*The concise encyclopedia of Islam.* C. Glassé. San Francisco: Harper, 1989; paperback, 1991. 472p.
*The contemporary Islamic revival: a critical survey and bibliography.* Y. Y. Haddad, J. O. Voll & J. L. Esposito. Westport, CT: Greenwood, 1991. 230p.
*The cultural atlas of Islam.* I. R. al Faruqi & L. L. al Faruqi. New York: Macmillan, 1986. 528p. (Not a true atlas, this work examines a wide variety of aspects of Islam from the perspective of two devoted followers).
*The encyclopædia of Islam.* J. M. J. van Lent. 2nd ed. Leiden: E. J. Brill, 1997.
*The encyclopedia of Islam: new edition.* H. A. R. Gibb [1895–1971] and C. E. Bosworth et al. (eds). Leiden: E. J. Brill, 1960–. 9,000p. in 8 vols to date.
*The hajj: the Muslim pilgrimage to Mecca and the holy places.* F. E. Peters. Princeton, NJ: Princeton University Press, 1994. 452.
*The influence of Islam upon Africa.* J. S. Trimingham. 1968; London: Librairie du Liban, 1980. 182p.
*The Iranians: Persia, Islam and the soul of a nation.* S. Mackey. New York: Dutton, 1996. 448p.
*The Islamic revival since 1988: a critical survey and bibliography.* Y. Y. Haddad & J. L. Esposito. *Bibliographies and indexes in religious studies,* 45. Westport, CT: Greenwood, 1997. 317p.
*The Isma'ilis: their history and doctrines.* F. Daftary. Cambridge, UK: Cambridge University Press, 1990. 822p.
*The Jews of Islam.* B. Lewis. Princeton, NJ: Princeton University Press, 1984. 257p.
*The lawful and the prohibited in Islam.* Y. Al-Qaradawi. 20th ed. Plainfield, IN: American Trust, 1994.
*The Muslim almanac.* A. Nanji (ed). Detroit, MI: Gale Research, 1995.
*The Oxford encyclopedia of the modern Islamic world.* J. L. Esposito (ed). New York and Oxford, UK: Oxford University Press, 1995. 1,920p. in 4 vols.
*The Prophet and the Pharoah: Muslim extremism in Egypt.* G. Kepel. Trans., J. Rothschild. London: Al Saqi, 1985. 251p. (Translated from the French, *Le prophète et Pharaon.* Paris: La Découverte, 1984.).
*The quarterly index Islamicus: current books, articles and papers on Islamic studies.* J. D. Pearson (ed). London: Mansell, 1977–91; Bowker–Saur, 1992–93.
*The revenge of God: the resurgence of Islam, Christianity and Judaism in the modern world.* G. Kepel. University Park, PA: Pennsylvania State University Press, 1994. 215p. (Translated by A. Braley from *La Revanche de Dieu*).
*The rumbling volcano: Islamic fundamentalism in Egypt.* N. Jabbour. Pasadena, CA: Mandate Press, 1993. 311p.
*The Shiites: ritual and popular piety in a Muslim community.* D. Pinault. New York: St. Martin's Press, 1992. 240p.
*The Sufis.* I. Shah. New York: Doubleday, 1964. 429p.
*The veil and the male elite: a feminist interpretation of women's rights in Islam.* F. Mernissi. Reading, MA: Addison-Wesley, 1991. 240p.

### 2. JUDAISM

*A book of Jewish concepts.* P. Birnbaum. 2nd ed. New York: Hebrew Publishing, 1988. 732p.
*Atlas of modern Jewish history.* E. Friesel. New York: Oxford University Press, 1990. 159p.
*Contemporary Jewish religious thought: original essays on critical concepts, movements and beliefs.* A. A. Cohen & P. Mendes–Flohr (eds). New York: Scribner, 1987. 1,183p.
*Encyclopaedia Judaica: das Judentum in Geschichte und Gegenwart.* Berlin: Verlag Esckol, 1928–34. 10 vols.
*Encyclopedia Judaica.* C. Roth & G. Wigoder (eds). Jerusalem: Keter Publishing House, 1972. 16 vols.
*Encyclopedia of Hasidism.* T. M. Rabinowicz (ed). Northvale, NJ: Jason Aronson, 1996.
*Encyclopedia of Jewish history: events and eras of the Jewish people.* J. Alpher (ed). New York: Facts on File, 1986. 288p.
*Encyclopedia of Jewish prayer: Ashkenazic and Sephardic rites.* M. Nulman. 1993; Arcade, NY: C. N. Aronson, 1996. 464p.
*Encyclopedia of Talmudic sages.* G. Bader. Arcade, NY: C. N. Aronson, 1993. 888p.
*Encyclopedia of the holocaust.* I. Guttman (ed). New York and London: Macmillan, 1990. 4 vols.
*Encyclopedia of the Jewish religion.* Z. Werblosky & G. Wigoder (eds). Bellmore, NY: Modan/Adama Books, 1986. 478p.
*Encyclopedia Talmudica: a digest of Halachic Literature and Jewish law from the Tannaitic period to the present time alphabetically arranged.* Rabbi Meyer Berlin. Jerusalem: Talmudic Encyclopedia Institute, 1969–. 2,900p. in 4 vols. to date. (Translated from the 18 vol. Hebrew edition).

*Events and movements in modern Judaism.* R. Patai & E. Goldsmith (eds). New York: Paragon House, 1995. 316p.
*Holocaust literature: a handbook of critical, historical and literary writings.* S. S. Friedman (ed). Westport, CT and London: Greenwood, 1994. 707p. (An essential handbook for anyone studying holocaust literature).
*Jewish Encyclopedia.* C. Adler et al. (eds). New York: Funk & Wagnalls, 1901–06. 12 vols. Rev. ed. I. Singer (ed), New York: Katy Publishers, 1964. 12 vols.
*Jewish literacy: the most important things to know about the Jewish religion, its people and its history.* Rabbi Joseph Telushkin. New York: Morrow, 1991. 688p.
*Jewish–American history and culture: an encyclopedia.* J. Fischel & S. Pinsker. New York: Garland, 1991.
*Jews and Christians: a troubled family.* W. Harrelson & R. M. Falk. Nashville, TN: Abingdon, 1990. 208p.
*Judaism,* section 23 in *Iconography of religions.* Leiden: E. J. Brill, 1975–. 4 vols. to date. (Covers Jewish sanctuary, Jewish year, Jewish life cycle, and Samaritans).
*Judaism and Christianity: a guide to the reference literature.* E. D. Starkey. *Reference sources in the humanities series.* Englewood, CO: Libraries Unlimited, 1991. 270p.
*Judaism: between yesterday and tomorrow.* H. Küng. New York: Continuum, 1992. 775p.
*Judaism, Christianity, and Islam: the classical texts and their interpretation.* F. E. Peters. Princeton, NJ: Princeton University Press, 1990. 1248.
*Lexikon religiöser Grundbegriffe: Judentum, Christentum, Islam.* A. T. Khoury (ed). Graz: Styria, 1987. 637p. (A comparison of Judaism, Christianity, and Islam).
*Neues Lexikon des Judentums.* J. H. Schoeps (ed). Frankfurt: Bertelsman, 1992.
*New encyclopedia of Zionism and Israel.* G. Wigoder (ed). 2nd ed. London and Toronto: Associated University Presses, 1994.
*Perpetual dilemma: Jewish religion in the Jewish state.* S. Z. Abramov. Cranbury, NJ: Associated University Presses, 1976. 432p.
*Response to modernity: a history of the Reform Movement in Judaism.* M. A. Meyere. New York: Oxford University Press, 1988.
*The Blackwell dictionary of Judaica.* D. Cohn–Sherbok. Oxford, UK and Cambridge, MA: Blackwell Reference, 1992. 642p.
*The encyclopedia of Jewish symbols.* E. Frankel & B. P. Teutsch. 1992; Arcade, NY: C. N. Aronson, 1995. 256p.
*The encyclopedia of Judaism.* G. Wigoder (ed). Jerusalem: Jerusalem Publishing House; New York: Macmillan, 1989. 800p.
*The Jews of Islam.* B. Lewis. Princeton, NJ: Princeton University Press, 1984. 257p.
*The joys of Hebrew.* L. Glinert. New York and Oxford, UK: Oxford University Press, 1992. 304p. (Explains the usage of more than six hundred (transliterated) Hebrew terms of particular importance to Jewish life).
*The other Jews: the Sephardim today.* D. J. Elazar. New York: Basic Books, 1989. 248p.
*The Oxford dictionary of the Jewish religion.* R. J. Z. Werblowsky & G. Wigoder (eds). New York and London: Oxford University Press, 1996. (An updated edition of *The encyclopedia of the Jewish religion.* Jerusalem: Masada, 1965; New York: Holt, Rinehart & Winston, 1966).
*The revenge of God: the resurgence of Islam, Christianity and Judaism in the modern world.* G. Kepel. University Park, PA: Pennsylvania State University Press, 1994. 215p. (Translated by A. Braley from *La Revanche de Dieu*).
*The timetables of Jewish history: a chronology of the most important people and events in Jewish history.* J. Gribetz et al. New York: Simon & Schuster, 1993. 752p.
*The vocabulary of Jewish life.* A. M. Heller. 2nd ed. New York: Hebrew Publishing, 1967. 367p.
*Tradition, innovation, conflict: Jewishness and Judaism in contemporary Israel.* Z. Sobel & B. Beit-Hallahmi (eds). *SUNY series in Israeli studies.* Albany, NY: State University of New York Press, 1991. 304p.
*Vanishing diaspora: the Jews in Europe since 1945.* B. Wasserstein. Cambridge, MA: Harvard University Press, 1996. 352p.

## 3. HINDUISM

*A classical dictionary of Hindu mythology and religion, geography, history, and literature.* J. Dowson. First edition 1879; 8th edition, London: Routledge & Kegen Paul, 1953. 411p.
*A dictionary of Hinduism: its mythology, folklore and development, 1500 BC—AD 1500.* M. Stutley & J. Stutley. London: Routledge & Kegan Paul, 1977. 390p. (Published in the U.S. as *Harper's dictionary of Hinduism: its mythology, folklore, philosophy, literature and history.*).
*A primer of Hinduism.* J. N. Farquhar. N.p., 1993. 208p.
*A survey of Hinduism.* K. R. Klostermeier. 2nd ed. Albany, NY: State University of New York Press, 1994. 734p.
*An introduction to Hinduism.* G. Flood. New York: Cambridge University Press, 1996. 350p.
*Encyclopaedia of Puranic beliefs and practices.* S. A. Dange. New Dehli: Narraing, 1986–90. 5 vols.
*Encyclopaedia of Sikh religion and culture.* R. C. Dogra & G. S. Mansukhani. Columbia, MO: South Asia Books, 1995.
*Encyclopaedia of the Hindu world.* G. R. Garg (ed). New Delhi: Concept Publishing, 1992–. 9 vols to date; in progress to 100 vols.
*Encyclopaedia of Vedanta.* R. M. Sharma. Columbia, MO: South Asia Books, 1993.
*Encyclopedia of Sikhism.* H. Singh (ed). Patiala, India: Punjabi University.
*Historical dictionary of Sikhism.* W. H. McLeod. *Religions, philosophies, and movements series,* 5. Metuchen, NJ: Scarecrow Press, 1995. 338p.
*Sikhism and the Sikhs: an annotated bibliography.* P. M. Rai. *Bibliographies and indexes in religious studies,* 13. New York: Greenwood, 1989. 272p.
*The camphor flame: popular Hinduism and society in India.* C. J. Fuller. Princeton, NJ: Princeton University Press, 1992. 328p.
*The crown of Hinduism.* J. N. Farquhar. 1913; reprint, 1971. 458p.
*The Sikh diaspora: migration and the experience beyond Punjab.* N. G. Barrier & V. A. Dusenbery (eds). Delhi: Chanakya Publications, 1989. 362p.
*The Sikhs.* No. 16 in section 13, *Indian religions,* in *Iconography of religions.* G. R. Thursby. Leiden: E. J. Brill, 1992. 42p.

## 4. BUDDHISM

*A concise history of Buddhism.* A. Skilton. 2nd ed. Birmingham, UK: Windhorse, 1997. 269p.
*An encyclopedia of Buddhist deities.* F. W. Bunce. New Delhi: D. K. Printworld, 1994.
*An introduction to Buddhism.* P. Harvey. New York: Cambridge University Press, 1990. 396p.
*An introduction to Tantric Buddhism.* S. B. Dargyay. Berkeley, CA: Shambhala, 1974. 211p.
*Bibliographie bouddhique.* Paris: Librarie d'Amérique et d'Orient, 1930–61 (fasc. 1–31). (Annual).
*Bibliography on Buddhism.* S. Hanayama. Tokyo: Hokuseido Press, 1961. 869p. (15,073 numbered entries).
*Buddhism: art and faith.* W. Zwalf (ed). London: British Museum Publications, 1985. 300p.
*Buddhism in Afghanistan and Central Asia.* No. 14 in section 13, *Indian religions,* in *Iconography of religions,* S. Gaulier, R. Jera-Bezard & M. Maillard. Leiden: E. J. Brill, 1976. 2 vols.
*Buddhism of Tibet.* Tenzin Gyatso, Fourteenth Dalai Lama. Trans. and ed., J. Hopkins. Ithaca, NY: Snow Lion, 1987. 219p.
*Buddhism's contribution to the world culture and civilization.* A. W. P. Guruge & D. C. Ahir (eds). New Delhi: Maha Bodhi Society of India, 1977. 219p. (Conference papers).
*Buddhist iconography.* L. Chandra. 3rd ed. New Delhi: Aditya Prakashan, 1988. 2 vols.
*Buddhist spirituality: India, Southeast Asia, Tibet, China.* T. Yoshinori. New York: Crossroad, 1993. 500p.
*Cent Clés pour comprendre le zen.* C. Durix. 2nd ed. 1976; Paris: Courrier du Livre, 1991. 367p.
*Encyclopaedia of Buddhism.* G. P. Malalasekera et al. (eds). Colombo, Sri Lanka: Government of Sri Lanka, 1961–. 5 vols. to date; in progress to 11 vols.
*Encyclopaedia of Buddhist deities, demigods, godlings, saints and demons: with special focus on iconographic attributes.* F. W. Bunce (ed). Columbia, MO: South Asia Books, 1994.
*Handbook of Tibetan culture.* G. Coleman (ed). London: Rider, 1993; Boston: Shambhala, 1994. 430p.
*Historical dictionary of Buddhism.* C. S. Prebish. *Religions, philosophies, and movements series,* 1. Metuchen, NJ and London: Scarecrow Press, 1993. 425p.
*Les Dieux du bouddhisme: guide iconographique.* L. Fréderic. Paris: Flammarion, 1992. 360p. (English translation, *Buddhism: Flammarion iconographic guides*).
*Présence du bouddhisme.* R. de Berval (ed). 2nd ed. Saigon: France–Asie, 1959; Paris: Gallimard, 1987. 816p.
*The Buddhist handbook: a complete guide to Buddhist teaching, practice, history and schools.* J. Snelling. Rochester, VT: Inner Traditions; London: Rider, 1992. 377p.
*The Buddhist world of Southeat Asia.* D. K. Swearer. *SUNY Series in religion.* Albany, NY: State University of New York Press, 1995. 272p.
*The history of Buddhism in India and Tibet.* Bu-ston. Trans., E. Obermiller. *Bibliotheca Indo-Buddhica,* 26. Delhi: Sri Satguru, 1986. 231p.
*The iconography of Chinese Buddhism in traditional China.* No. 5 of section 12, *East and Central Asia,* of *Iconography of religions.* H. A. van Oort. Leiden: E. J. Brill, 1986. 2 vols.
*The iconography of Korean Buddhist painting.* No. 9 of section 12, *East and Central Asia,* of *Iconography of religions.* H. H. Sorensen. Leiden: E. J. Brill, 1988. 21p.
*The world of Buddhism: Buddhist monks and nuns in society.* H. Bechert & R. Gombrich. London: Thames & Hudson, 1984. 198p. (Highly illustrated coffee-table style book).

## 5. OTHER RELIGIONS

*A dictionary of comparative religion.* S. G. F. Brandon (ed). London: Weidenfeld & Nicolson, 1970.
*A dictionary of non–Christian religions.* G. Parrinder. Amersham: Hulton; Philadelphia: Westminster, 1971; reprint, Hulton, 1981. 320p.
*A dictionary of religious and spiritual quotations.* G. Parrinder. London: Routledge; New York: Simon & Schuster, 1989. 228p.
*America's alternative religions.* T. Miller (ed). *SUNY series in religious studies.* Albany, NY: State University of New York Press, 1995. 484p. (Includes some Christian denominations and sects).
*An introduction to Taiwanese folk religions.* G. P. Kramer & G. Wu. Taipei, 1970. 89p.
*Anthroposophy: a fragment.* R. Steiner. Trans., C. E. Creeger. *Classics in anthroposophy.* Hudson, NY: Anthroposophic Press, 1996.
*Approaches to Jaina studies: philosophy, logic, rituals and symbols.* O. Qvarnström & N. K. Wagle (eds). Toronto: University of Toronto, Centre for South Asian Studies, 1997.
*Atheism and theism.* J. J. C. Smart. *Great debates in philosophy.* Oxford, UK and Cambridge, MA: Blackwell, 1996. 240p.
*Bibliography of new religious movements in primal societies.* H. W. Turner. Boston and New York: G. K. Hall, 1977–92. 6 vols.
*Botswana handbook of churches: a handbook of churches, ecumenical organisations, theological institutions and other world religions in Botswana.* J. N. Amanze. Gaborone, Botswana: Pula Press, 1994. 327p.
*Defining Jainism: reform in the Jain tradition.* J. E. Cort. Toronto: University of Toronto, Centre for South Asian Studies, 1995.
*Dictionary of Celtic mythology.* P. B. Ellis. New York: Oxford University Press, 1992; paperback, 1994. 232p.
*Dictionary of cults, sects, religions and the occult.* G. A. Mather & L. A. Nichols. Grand Rapids, MI: Zondervan, 1993. 396p.
*Dictionary of deities and demons in the Bible.* K. van der Toorn, B. Becking & P. van der Horst (eds). Leiden, Cologne, and New York: E. J. Brill, 1995. 923p.
*Dictionary of Native American mythology.* S. D. Gill & I. F. Sullivan (eds). Santa Barbara, CA: ABC-CLIO, 1992; New York: Oxford University Press, 1994. 455p.
*Dictionary of Polynesian mythology.* R. D. Craig. New York: Greenwood, 1989. 465p.
*Dieux d'hommes: Dictionnaire des messianismes et millénarismes de l'Ere chrétienne.* H. Desroche et al. Paris and The Hague: Mouton, 1969. 281p.
*Encyclopaedia of occultism.* L. Spence. 1960; New York: Carol Publishing, 1984. 464p.
*Encyclopaedia of eastern philosophy and religion.* S. Schumacher & G. Woerner (eds). Boston: Shambhala, 1994. 482p.
*Encyclopedia of gods: over 2,500 deities of the world.* M. Jordan. New York: Facts on File, 1993. 351p.
*Encyclopedia of Indian philosophies.* K. H. Potter (ed). Delhi: Motilal Banarsidass; Princeton, NJ: Princeton University Press, 1970–1990. 5 vols.
*Encyclopedia of Mormonism.* D. H. Ludlow. New York: Macmillan, 1992. 5 vols.
*Encyclopedia of mythology.* A. Cotterell. Oxford, UK and New York: Oxford University Press, 1986.
*Encyclopedia of mythology.* E. Flaum. Philadelphia: Courage Books, 1993.
*Encyclopedia of myths and legends.* S. Gordon. North Pomfret, VT: Trafalgar, 1994. 799p.
*Encyclopedia of Native American religions.* A. Hirschfelder & P. Molin (eds). Reprint. 1996. 384p.
*Encyclopedia of palmistry.* E. O. Campbell. New York: Berkley Publishing, 1996. 320p.
*Encyclopedia of parapsychology and psychical research.* A. S. Berger & J. Berger. Champaign, IL: Marlowe, 1994. 554p.
*Encyclopedia of signs, omens, and superstitions.* Zolar. New York: Carol Publishing Group, 1995. 400p.
*Encyclopedia of superstitions, folklore and the occult sciences of the world.* C. L. Daniels & C. M. Stevans (eds). Repr. ed. Detroit, MI: Omnigraphics, 1997. 3 vols.
*Encyclopedia of Tarot.* S. R. Kaplan. Stamford, CT: US Games Systems, 1978–1990. 3 vols.
*Encyclopedia of traditional epics.* G. M. Jackson. Santa Barbara, CA: ABC-CLIO, 1994. 750p.
*Encyclopedia of witchcraft and demonology.* R. H. Robbins. New York: Random House, 1988.
*Encyclopedia of witches and witchcraft.* R. E. Guiley. New York: Facts on File, 1990. 432p.
*Encyclopedia of women in world religions.* Englewood Cliffs, NJ: Prentice-Hall, 1996.
*Extraordinary groups: an examination of unconventional life–styles.* W. M. Kephart & W. W. Zellner. 5th ed. New York: St. Martin's, 1994. 334p.
*Fundamentalism as an ecumenical challenge.* H. Küng & J. Moltmann (eds). London: SCM Press, 1992. 144p.
*Goddesses in world mythology.* M. Ann & D. M. Imel. Santa Barbara, CA: ABC-CLIO, 1993. 675p.
*Guide to the gods.* M. Leach. Santa Barbara, CA: ABC-CLIO, 1992. 1,007p.
*Jain directory of North America.* Boston: Jain Center of Greater Boston, 1992.
*La voie Jaina: histoire, spiritualité, vie des ascètes pèlerines de l'Inde.* N. Shântâ. Paris: O.E.I.L., 1985. 615p.
*Lexikon der Götter und Dämonen.* M. Lurker. Stuttgart: A. Krämer, 1984. 451p. (English edition, *Dictionary of gods and goddesses, devils and demons.* London and New York: Routledge, 1987–88).
*Lexikon der östlichen Weisheitslehren.* S. Shumacher & G. Woerner (eds). Bern and Munich: Otto Barth, 1986. (English translation, *The encyclopedia of Eastern philosophy and religion: Buddhism, Hinduism, Taoism, Zen*).
*Lexikon der religionen: phänomene—geschichte—ideen.* H. Waldenfels (ed). Freiburg: Herder, 1987; paperback, 1992. 751p.
*Living without religion: eupraxophy.* P. Kurtz. Amherst, NY: Prometheus, 1994. 159p. (Coins the term 'eupraxophy,' meaning 'good conduct and wisdom in living.' Advocates moral life apart from religion).
*Money and power in the new religions.* J. T. Richardson (ed). Lewiston, NY: E. Mellen Press, 1988.
*Mythes et croyances du monde entier.* A. Akoun (ed). Paris: Lidis-Brepols, 1985. 5 vols.
*Mythologies.* Y. Bonnefoy. Chicago: University of Chicago Press, 1991. 2 vols, 1,305p. (Translated and restructed under the direction of Wendy Doniger from the French, *Dictionnaire des mythologies et des religions, des sociétés traditionelles et du monde antique,* 1981. Translated by Gerald Honnigsblum, et al. A paperback edition in 4 vols. appeared in 1992.).
*Myths, gods and fantasy.* P. Allardica. Santa Barbara, CA: ABC-CLIO, 1991. 232p.
*Myths of the world: a thematic encyclopedia.* M. Jordan. London: Kyle Cathie, 1993. 319p.
*New religions and the new Europe.* R. Towler (ed). Aarhus, Denmark: Aarhus University Press, 1995. 246p.
*New religions as global cultures.* I. Hexham & K. Poewe. Boulder, CO: Westview Press.
*New religious movements and the churches.* A. R. Brockway & J. P. Rajashekar (eds). Geneva: WCC Publications, 1987. 221p. (Report of a consultation sponsored by the Lutheran World Federation and the World Council of Churches held in Amsterdam, 1986).
*New religious movements in the United States and Canada: a critical assessment and annotated bibliography.* D. Choquette. *Bibliographies and indexes in religious studies,* 5. Westport, CT: Greenwood, 1985. 235p.
*Pacific mythology: an encyclopedia of myth and legend.* J. Knappert. London: Aquarian; San Francisco: Thorsons, 1992.

334p.
*Puranic encyclopaedia: a comprehensive dictionary with special reference to the Epic and Puranic literature.* V. Mani. 4th English ed. Delhi: Motilal Banarsidass, 1975. 930p.
*Riches and renunciation: religion, economy, and society among the Jains.* J. Laidlaw. Oxford, UK: Oxford University Press, 1995. 446p.
*Scripture and community: collected essays on the Jains.* K. W. Folkert. Ed., J. E. Cort. Atlanta: Scholars Press, 1993. 468p.
*South Asian religions in the Americas: an annotated bibliography of immigrant religious traditions.* J. Y. Fenton. *Bibliographies and indexes in religious studies.* Westport, CT: Greenwood.
*Taoist ritual and popular cults of Southeast China.* K. Dean. Princeton, NJ: Princeton University Press, 1993. 320p.
*The advent of Sun Myung Moon: the origins, beliefs, and practices of the Unification Church.* G. D. Chryssides. New York: St. Martin's, 1991. 242p.
*The Aquarian guide to African mythology.* J. Knappert. Wellingborough: Aquarian, 1990. 272p.
*The Children of God/Family of Love: an annotated bibliography.* W. D. Pritchett. *Sects and cults in America. Bibliographical guides*, 5; *Garland reference library of social science*, 209. New York: Garland, 1985. 209p.
*The clever adulteress and other stories: a treasury of Jain literature.* P. Grandoff (ed). London: Mosaic Press, 1990. 290p.
*The dictionary of religious terms.* D. T. Kauffman. London: Marshall, Morgan & Scott, 1967. 455p. (11,000 definitions).
*The encyclopaedia of Middle Eastern mythology and religion.* J. Knappert. Shaftesbury, UK, and Rockport, MA: Element, 1993. 309p.
*The encyclopedia of native American religion: an introduction.* A. Hirschfelder & P. Molin (eds). New York and Oxford, UK: Facts on File, 1992. 379p.
*The Encyclopedia of unbelief.* G. Stein (ed). Buffalo, NY: Prometheus, 1985. 835p.
*The Facts on File encyclopedia of world mythology and legend.* A. S. Mercatante. New York: Facts on File, 1988. 825p.
*The fundamentalism project.* M. E. Marty & R. S. Appleby (eds). Chicago: University of Chicago Press, 1991–96. 5 vols. (Vol. 1: *Fundamentalisms observed*; vol. 2: *Fundamentalisms and the state*; vol. 3: *Fundamentalisms and society*; vol. 4: *Accounting for fundamentalisms*; vol. 5: *Fundamentalisms comprehended.* A cross–religious study).
*The future of religion: secularization, revival, and cult formation.* R. Stark & W. Bainbridge. Berkeley, CA: University of California Press, 1985. 579p.
*The Jaina path of purification.* P. S. Jaini. Berkeley, CA: University of California Press, 1979.
*The New Age movement in American culture.* R. Kyle. Lanham, MD: University Press of America, 1995. 289p.
*The new religions of Japan: a spotlight on the most significant development in postwar Japan.* H. Thomsen. Rutland, VT and Tokyo: Tuttle, 1963. 269p.
*The religions of the oppressed: a study of modern messianic cults.* V. Lanternari. New York: Mentor, 1963. 286p. (Translated by L. Sergio from the Italian, *Movimenti religiosi di libertà e di salvezzi dei popoli oppressi*).
'The rise of Spiritism in North America,' M. Ortiz, *Urban mission*, 5, 4 (March 1988), 11–17.
*The social dimensions of sectarianism: sects and new religious movements in contemporary society.* B. R. Wilson. Oxford, UK and New York: Clarendon, 1992. 311p.
*The social impact of new religious movements.* B. R. Wilson (ed). *Conference series*, 9. Barrytown, NY: The Unification Theological Seminary, 1991. 256p. (A collection of essays by a diverse group of sociologists, including J. D. Hunter, examining the rise of the Unification Church.).
*The way of heaven: an introduction to the Confucian religious life.* No. 3 of section 12, *East and Central Asia*, of *Iconography of religions.* R. L. Taylor. Leiden: E. J. Brill, 1986. 37p.
*The Zoroastrian faith: tradition and modern research.* S. A. Nigosian. Cheektowaga, NY: McGill-Queen's University Press, 1993.
*Trattato di antropologia del sacro.* J. Ries (ed). Milan: Jaca Book, 1989–. 5 vols; in progress to 7 vols.
*Wörterbuch der Mythologie.* H. W. Haussig (ed). Stuttgart: Klett-Cotta, 1965–1984. 5 vols.
*Zoroastrians: their religious beliefs and practices.* M. Boyce. London and Boston: Routledge & Kegan Paul, 1979. 374p.

### 6. INTERFAITH DIALOGUE

*A bibliography of interchurch and interconfessional theological dialogues.* J. F. Puglisi & S. J. Voicu. Rome: Centro pro unione, 1984. 260p.
*A bridge to Buddhist–Christian dialogue.* S. Yagi & L. Swidler. Mahwah, NJ: Paulist, 1990. 162p.
*A sourcebook for earth's community of religions.* J. D. Beversluis (ed). Rev. ed. Grand Rapids, MI: CoNexus Press—Sourcebook Project; New York: Global Education Associates, 1995. 376p. (Contains statements from the Parliament of the World's Religions, Chicago, 1993).
*A wider vision: a history of the World Congress of Faiths 1936–1996.* M. Braybrooke. Oxford, UK: Oneworld, 1996. 192p.
*Ateismo e dialogo: bolletino del Segretariato per i Non–Credenti.* Rome, 1966–. (Christian dialogue with atheism and Marxism).
*Atlas of the crusades.* J. Riley–Smith (ed). New York: Facts on File, 1990.
*Christ in Islam and Christianity.* N. Robinson. Albany, NY: State University of New York Press, 1991. 246p.
*Christianity and the encounter of the world religions.* P. Tillich. New York and London: Columbia University Press, 1963. 107p. (1961 Bampton lectures at Columbia University).
*Christianity and the world religions: paths to dialogue with Islam, Hinduism, and Buddhism.* H. Küng et al. Garden City, NY: Doubleday, 1986. 480p.
*Disinheriting the Jews: Abraham in early Christian controversy.* J. S. Siker. Louisville, KY: Westminster John Knox, 1991. 296p.
*Faith meets faith series.* Maryknoll, NY: Orbis, 1990.
*Hinduism and Christianity.* J. L. Brockington. New York: St. Martin's Press, 1992. 229p. (Delineates contacts since the 3rd century).
*Hindus and Christians: a century of Protestant ecumenical thought.* S. W. Ariarajah. *Currents of encounter*, 5. Amsterdam: Editions Rodopi; Grand Rapids, MI: Eerdmans, 1991. 254p.
*Interfaith directory.* F. Clark (ed). New York: International Religious Foundation, 1987. 194p.
*Jerusalem blessed, Jerusalem cursed: Jews, Christians, and Muslims in the Holy City from David's time to our own.* T. A. Idinopulos. Chicago: Ivan R. Dee, 1991. 343p.
*Jewish perspectives on Christianity: Leo Baeck, Martin Buber, Franz Rosenzweig, Will Herberg, and Abraham J. Heschel.* F. A. Rothschild (ed). New York: Crossroad, 1990. 373p.
*Jews and Christians: a troubled family.* W. Harrelson & R. M. Falk. Nashville, TN: Abingdon, 1990. 208p.
*Muhammad and Jesus: a comparison of the prophets and their teachings.* W. E. Phipps. New York: Continuum, 1996. 316p.
*Neely's history of the Parliament of Religions and Religious Congresses at the World's Columbian Exposition.* W. R. Houghton. Chicago: Neely, 1893.
*One Christ—many religions: toward a revised christology.* S. J. Samartha. *Faith meets faith series.* Maryknoll, NY: Orbis, 1991. 206p.
*One earth many religions: multifaith dialogue and global responsibility.* P. F. Knitter. Maryknoll, NY: Orbis, 1995. 232p.
*Piety and power: Muslims and Christians in West Africa.* L. Sanneh. Maryknoll, NY: Orbis Books, 1996.
*Qur'anic Christians: an analysis of classical and modern exegesis.* J. D. McAuliffe. Cambridge, UK and New York: Cambridge University Press, 1991. 352p. (Islamic understanding of Christians. Studies passages in the Qur'an that make ostensibly positive remarks about Christians).
*Religion in the Middle East: three religions in concord and conflict.* A. J. Arberry. Cambridge, UK: Cambridge University Press, 1969. 2 vols. (Vol. 1: *Judaism and Christianity*; vol. 2: *Islam*, and *Concord and Conflict*).
*The Christ and the faiths.* K. Cragg. London: SCM; Philadelphia: Westminster, 1986. 372p.
*The integration of Islam and Hinduism in Western Europe.* W. A. R. Shadid & P. S. van Koningsveld. Kampen, Netherlands: Kok Pharos, 1991. 264p.
*The Jews of Islam.* B. Lewis. Princeton, NJ: Princeton University Press, 1984. 257p.
*The World's Parliament of Religions.* J. H. Barrows. Chicago: Parliament Publishing Company, 1893.
*The World's Parliament of Religions: the east/west encounter, Chicago, 1893.* R. H. Seager. *Religion in North America series.* Bloomington, IN: Indiana University Press, 1995. 239p.
*World fellowship: addresses and messages by leading spokesmen of all faiths, races and countries.* C. F. Weller (ed). New York: Liveright Publishing, 1935. 1,004p. (A collection of addresses of leaders of a number of faiths for the First International Congress of the World Fellowship of Faiths, held in Chicago in 1934).

## III. APPROACHES TO THE STUDY OF RELIGION

### 1. GENERAL METHODOLOGIES

*Dictionary of religion and philosophy.* G. MacGregor. New York: Paragon House, 1989; paperback, 1991. 696p. (Published in Britain under the title, *The everyman dictionary of religion and philosophy*, London: Dent, 1990.).
*Encyclopedia of contemporary literary theory: approaches, scholars, terms.* I. R. Makaryk (ed). Toronto: University of Toronto Press, 1993. 576p.
*Encyclopedia of the Enlightenment.* P. H. Reill & E. J. Wilson. New York: Facts on File, 1996. 464p.
*Encyclopédie des sciences religieuses.* (A major French Catholic collection composed of 6 series).
*Guides to theological inquiry.* P. Lakeland & K. Tanner (eds). Minneapolis, MN: Fortress. 4 vols. to date; 4 more vols.).
*Handbuch der Religionspädagogik.* E. Feifel (ed). 1973–75, 3 vols.
*Handbuch religionswissenschaftlicher grundbegriffe.* H. Cancik, B. Gladigow & M. Laubscher (eds). Stuttgart: Kohlhammer, 1988–. 3 vols., 2 forthcoming.
*Method and theory in the study and interpretation of religion.* New York: Mouton.
*Philosophical foundations of the social sciences: analyzing controversies in social research.* H. Kincaid. Cambridge, UK, and New York: Cambridge University Press, 1996.
*Social research methods and statistics.* W. S. Bainbridge. Belmont, CA: Wadsworth, 1992.
*Social scientific studies of religion.* M. I. Berkowitz & J. Johnson. Pittsburgh: University of Pittsburgh Press, 1967.
*The scientific study of religion.* J. M. Yinger. New York: Macmillan, 1970.
*Toronto studies in religion.* D. Wiebe. New York: Peter Lang. 20 vols. to date.

### 2. PHILOSOPHY OF RELIGION

*A companion to philosophy of religion.* P. L. Quinn & C. Taliaferro (eds). *Blackwell companions to philosophy*, 8. Cambridge, MA: Blackwell, 1997. 655p. (A guide for nonspecialists).
*A dictionary of philosophy.* T. Mautner. Cambridge, MA: Blackwell, 1995.
*Catalog of the Hoose Library of Philosophy, University of Southern California (Los Angeles).* Boston: G. K. Hall, 1968. 6 vols. (96,000 entries, 4,577 pages).
*Divine discourse: philosophical reflections on the claim that God speaks.* N. Wolterstorff. Cambridge, UK and New York: Cambridge University Press, 1995. 336p.
*Encyclopedia of philosophy.* D. M. Borchert (ed). New York: Simon & Schuster, 1996.
*Encyclopedia of philosophy.* P. Edwards (ed). New York: Collier-Macmillan, 1967. 8 vols.
*Encyclopedia of the philosophical sciences in outline.* G. W. F. Hegel. Ed., E. Behler. Del Mar, CA: Continuum, 1990. 24 vols.
*God, reason, and religions: new essays in the philosophy of religion.* E. T. Long (ed). *Studies in philosophy and religion*, 18. Boston: Kluwer, 1996.
*Ontological arguments and belief in God.* G. Oppy. Cambridge, UK: Cambridge University Press, 1996. 394p.
*Philosophy as a way of life: spiritual exercises from Socrates to Foucault.* P. Hadot. Trans., M. Chase. Oxford, UK: Blackwell, 1995. 319p.
*Philosophy in the 20th century: Catholic and Christian.* G. McLean. Vol. I: *An annotated bibliography of philosophy in Catholic thought, 1900–64.* Vol. II: *A bibliography of Christian philosophy and contemporary issues.* New York: Ungar, 1967.
*Philosophy of religion.* J. Hick. Englewood Cliffs, NJ: Preutice-Hall, 1963.
*Prolegomena to religious pluralism: reference and realism in religion.* P. Byrne. New York: St. Martin's, 1995. 255p.
*Répetoire bibliographique de la philosophie.* Louvain: Editions de l'Institut Supérieure de Philosophie, 1948–70.
*The beginning and the end of "religion".* N. Lash. Cambridge, UK: Cambridge University Press, 1996. 296p.
*The Blackwell companion to philosophy.* N. Bunnin & E. P. Tsui-james (eds). Cambridge, MA: Blackwell, 1995.
*The essence of Christianity (Das Wesen des Christentums).* Ludwig Feuerbach. Trans., G. Eliot. 1841; New York: Harper, 1957. 383p.
*The handbook of Western philosophy.* G. H. R. Parkinson (ed). London and New York: Macmillan, 1988. 935p.
*The naturalness of religious ideas: a cognitive theory of religion.* P. Boyer. Berkeley, CA: University of California Press, 1994.
*The Oxford dictionary of philosophy.* S. Blackburn. Oxford, UK and New York: Oxford University Press, 1994. 416p.
*Voprosy nauchnogo ateizma (Questions of scientific atheism).* Moscow: Mysl. 1966–75
*World philosophies: an historical introduction.* D. E. Cooper. Oxford, UK and Cambridge, MA: Blackwell, 1996.

### 3. HISTORY OF RELIGION

*Church history: an introduction to research, reference works, and methods.* J. E. Bradley & R. A. Muller. Grand Rapids, MI: Eerdmans, 1995. 252p.
*Essays in the history of religions.* J. Kitagawa & G. Alles (eds). New York: Macmillan, 1988.
*Handbuch der Religionsgeschichte.* J. P. Asmussen, J. Laessoe & C. Colpe. Göttingen: Vandenhoeck & Ruprecht, 1971–72. 3 vols.
*Histoire des religions.* H. Puech (ed). Paris: Gallimard, 1970–1976. 3 vols.
*Historians of the Christian tradition: their methodology and influence on Western thought.* M. Bauman & M. I. Klauber. Nashville, TN: Broadman & Holman, 1995. 637p.
*The history of religions: essays in methodology.* M. Eliade & J. Kitagawa (eds). Chicago: University of Chicago Press, 1959.
*The history of religions: essays on the problem of understanding.* J. Kitagawa (ed). Chicago: University of Chicago Press, 1967.
*The modern researcher.* J. Barzun & H. F. Graff. 4th ed. New York: Harcourt Brace Jovanovich, 1985. 476p.
*World historians and their goals: twentieth–century answers to modernism.* P. Costello. DeKalb, IL: Northern Illinois University Press, 1993. 325p.

### 4. SOCIOLOGY OF RELIGION

*Atlas narodov mira (Atlas of the peoples of the world).* Moscow: Akademii Nauk SSSR, 1964. 184p. (Not concerned with religion per se, but its ethnic maps locate ethnic minorities of religious importance).
*Dieux d'hommes: Dictionnaire des messianismes et millénarismes de l'Ere chrétienne.* H. Desroche et al. Paris and The Hague: Mouton, 1969. 281p.
*Encyclopedia of sociology.* E. F. Borgatta & M. L. Borgatta (eds). New York: Macmillan, 1991. 4 vols.
*Habits of the heart: individualism and commitment in American life.* R. N. Bellah et al. Berkeley, CA: University of California Press, 1985. (An influential study of the loss of the 'second language' of piety in American culture).
*Human values in a changing world: a dialogue on the social role of religion.* B. Wilson & D. Ikeda. London: Macdonald, 1984; Secaucus, NJ: Lyle Stewart, 1987. 364p.
*International bibliography of sociology of religion*, in *Social compass* (International review of socio-religious studies), Louvain, 1958–1972.
*International encyclopedia of the social sciences.* D. L. Sills (ed). New York: Collier-Macmillan. 1968, 17 vols. (Reprinted, 1972, in 8 vols).
*L'État des religions dans le monde.* M. Clévenot (ed). Paris: La Découverte/Le Cerf, 1987. 640p.
'Marxist analysis and sociology of religions: an outline of international bibliography up to 1975,' O. Maduro, *Social compass*, XXII, 3–4 (1975), 401–479. (Lists 1,215 books, 730 articles, in 7 Western languages).
*Millhands and preachers.* L. Pope. New Haven, CT: Yale University Press, 1942.
*Protestant, Catholic, Jew.* W. Herberg. Garden City, NY: Doubleday, 1955.
*Public religions in the modern world.* J. Casanova. Chicago: University of Chicago Press, 1994. 330p.

*Religion and the individual.* C. D. Baatson, P. Schoenrade & W. L. Ventis. New York: Oxford University Press, 1993.

*Religion in politics: a world guide.* S. Mews (ed). Chicago and London: World Guide, 1989. 342p. (Examines religious political parties in over 200 countries).

*Religion in sociological perspective: essays in the empirical study of religion.* C. Y. Glock. *The Wadsworth series in sociology.* Belmont, CA: Wadsworth, 1973. 325p.

*Religion: the social context.* M. B. McGuire. Belmont, CA: Wadsworth, 1992.

*Religious diversity and social change.* K. J. Christiano. New York: Cambridge University Press, 1987.

*Religious sects.* B. R. Wilson. New York: McGraw–Hill, 1970.

*Sects and society.* B. R. Wilson. Berkeley, CA: University of California Press, 1961.

*Sociology of Christianity: an international bibliography.* H. Carrier & E. Pin (eds). Rome: Gregorian University Press, 1964. 313p.

*Tables, signalétiques, Archives de sociologie des religions.* Paris: CNRS, 1972. 300p. (Now *Archives des sciences sociales des religions:* reviews and abstracts of journal from 1956–70).

*The churching of America 1776–1990.* R. Fink & R. Stark. New Brunswick, NJ, 1992.

*The good society.* R. N. Bellah et al. New York: Knopf, 1991.

*The Protestant ethic and the spirit of capitalism.* M. Weber. Trans., T. Parsons. New York: Scribner, 1958. 313p.

*The sacred canopy: elements of a sociological theory of religion.* P. Berger. Garden City, NY: Anchor Books, Doubleday, 1967, 1969. 239p.

*The social construction of reality: a treatise in the sociology of knowledge.* P. Berger & T. Luckman. Garden City, NY: Doubleday, 1966. 231p.

*The social impact of new religious movements.* B. R. Wilson (ed). New York: Rose of Sharon Press, 1981.

*The social impact of new religious movements.* B. R. Wilson (ed). *Conference series,* 9. Barrytown, NY: The Unification Theological Seminary, 1991. 256p. (A collection of essays by a diverse and respected group of sociologists, including James Davison Hunter and others, examining the rise of the Unification Church.).

*The social sources of denominationalism.* H. R. Niebuhr. New York: Holt, 1929.

*The social teaching of the Christian churches.* E. Troeltsch. Trans., O. Wyon. *Library of theological ethics.* 1911; New York: Harper, 1960; Louisville, KY: Westminster John Knox Press, 1992. 2 vols.

*The sociological study of religion.* B. R. Scharf. New York: Harper, 1970. 190p.

'The sociology of conversion,' W. S. Bainbridge, in *Handbook of religious conversion,* p.178–91. H. N. Maloney & S. Southard (ed). Birmingham, AL: Religious Education Press, 1992.

*The sociology of religion.* T. F. O'Dea. Englewood Cliffs, NJ: Prentice–Hall, 1966.

*The sociology of religious movements.* W. S. Bainbridge. New York and London: Routlegde, 1997. 480p.

*Wondrous events: foundations of religious belief.* J. McClenon. Philadelphia: University of Pennsylvania Press, 1994.

#### 5. ANTHROPOLOGY OF RELIGION

*Anthropological studies of religion: an introductory text.* B. Morris. Cambridge, UK and New York: Cambridge University Press, 1987, 1989. 379p.

*Conceptualizing religion: immanent anthropologists, transcendent natives, and unbound categories.* B. Saler. Leiden: E. J. Brill, 1993.

*Religion: an anthropological view.* A. F. C. Wallace. New York: Random House, 1966.

*Religion, deviance, and social control.* R. Stark & W. S. Bainbridge. New York: Routledge, 1997. 204p.

*The pursuit of certainty: religious and cultural formulations.* W. James (ed). London: Routledge, 1995. 328p.

#### 6. PSYCHOLOGY OF RELIGION

*Annotated bibliography in religion and psychology.* W. W. Meissner. N.p.: Academy of Religion and Health, 1961.

*Baker encyclopedia of psychology.* D. G. Benner (ed). Grand Rapids, MI: Baker, 1985. 1246p.

*Encyclopedia of psychiatry, psychology, and psychoanalysis.* B. Wolman. New York: Henry Holt, 1996. 1,200p.

*Encyclopedia of psychology.* R. J. Corsini (ed). 2nd ed. New York: Wiley, 1994. 4 vols; 2,464p.

*Encyclopedia of psychology.* H. J. Eysenck, W. Arnold & R. Meili (eds). London: Search Press. 1972, 3 vols.

*Handbook of religious experience.* R. W. Hood Jr (ed). Birmingham, AL: Religious Education Press, 1995. 661p.

*Is religion good for your health?* H. G. Koenig. Binghamton, NY: Hayworth, 1997. 147p. (Examines empirical evidence and suggests religion's beneficial role in mental health).

*Psychoanalytic studies in religion: a critical assessment and annotated bibliography.* B. Beit-Hallahmi. *Bibliographies and indexes in religious studies.* Westport, CT: Greenwood.

*Psychology of religion: classic and contemporary.* D. M. Wulff. 2nd ed. New York: Wiley, 1997. 781p.

*The collected works of C. G. Jung.* H. Read, M. Fordham & G. Adler et al (eds). *Bollingen Series.* Princeton, NJ: Princeton University Press, 1953—72. 17 vols. (Vol 11: *Psychology and religion: east and west,* 1958).

*The handbook of social psychology.* G. Lindzey & E. Aronson (eds). 2nd ed. Reading, MA: Addison-Wesley, 1968-69. 5 vols. (Psychology of religion: vol 5, p. 602-659).

*The innate capacity: mysticism, psychology, and philosophy.* R. K. C. Forman (ed). New York: Oxford Univerity Press.

*The psychology of religion: theoretical approaches.* B. Spilka & D. N. McIntosh (eds). Boulder, CO: Westview Press, 1996.

*The varieties of religious experience: a study in human nature.* W. James. 1902; Cambridge, MA: Harvard University Press, 1985. 770p. (One of the classics in this field. Originally the Gifford Lectures on Natural Religion, 1901–02).

*Young man Luther: a study in psychoanalysis and history.* E. Erickson. New York: Norton. 288p.

#### 7. RELIGIOUS ETHICS

*After virtue: a study in moral theory.* A. MacIntyre. Notre Dame, IN: University of Notre Dame Press, 1981.

*Beyond integrity: a Judeo–Christian approach to business ethics.* S. B. Rae & K. L. Wong. Grand Rapids, MI: Zondervan, 1996. 656p.

*Competing gospels: public theology and economic theory.* R. G. Simons. Alexandria, Australia: Dwyer, 1995. 253p.

*Dictionary of ethics, theology, and society.* P. B. Clarke & A. Linzey (eds). London and New York: Routledge, 1996. 960p.

*Encyclopedia of ethics.* L. C. Becker & C. Becker. New York: Garland, 1992. 2 vols, 1,462p.

*Encyclopedia of morals.* V. T. Ferm (ed). Repr. ed. Westport, CT: Greenwood, 1969. 682p.

*Encyclopedia of war and ethics.* D. A. Wells (ed). Westport, CT: Greenwood, 1996. 568p.

*Religion and human rights.* J. Kelsay & S. B. Twiss (eds). New York: The Project on Religion and Human Rights, 1994. 135p.

*Religion in public life: a dilemma for democracy.* R. E. Thiemann. Washington, DC: Georgetown University Press, 1996. 186p.

*Religious human rights in global perspective: religious perspectives and legal perspectives.* J. Witte Jr. & J. D. van der Vyer (eds). The Hague and Boston: M. Nijhoff, 1996. 2 vols.

*The encyclopedia of religion and ethics.* J. Hastings (ed). Edinburgh: T. & T. Clark, 1926. 13 vols.

*The ethical demand.* K. E. Løgstrup. Ed., H. Fink & A. MacIntyre. Rev. ed. 1971; Notre Dame, IN: University of Notre Dame Press, 1997. 331p.

#### 8. OTHER APPROACHES

*Biblical numerology: a basic study of the use of numbers in the Bible.* J. J. Davis. Grand Rapids, MI: Baker, 1968. 174p.

*Concise dictionary of religious quotations.* W. Neill (ed). London: Mowbray, 1975. 224p. (2,500 quotations by topic; Christian, Muslim, Hindu, et al).

*Cultures in conflict: a global survey of ethnic, racial, linguistic, religious and nationalist factors.* E. M. Rhoodie. Jefferson, NC: McFarland, 1993. 976p.

*Encyclopedia of cosmology: historical philosophical, and scientific foundations of modern cosmology.* N. S. Hetherington (ed). Text ed. New York: Garland, 1993. 704p.

*Encyclopedia of creation myths.* D. A. Leeming & M. A. Leeming. Santa Barbara, CA: ABC-CLIO, 1994. 330p.

*Mythologies.* Y. Bonnefoy. Chicago: University of Chicago Press, 1991. 2 vols, 1,305p. (Translated and restructed under the direction of Wendy Doniger from the French, *Dictionnaire des mythologies et des religions, des sociétés traditionelles et du monde antique,* 1981. Translated by Gerald Honnigsblum, et al. A paperback edition in 4 vols. appeared in 1992.).

*Number in Scripture: its supernatural design and spiritual significance.* E. W. Bullinger. Grand Rapids, MI: Kregel Publications, 1967. 311p.

*Religious and social ritual: interdisciplinary explorations.* M. B. Aune & V. DeMarinis. Albany, NY: State University of New York Press, 1996.

*Sacred worlds: an introduction to geography and religion.* C. C. Park. London and New York: Routledge, 1994. 346p.

*The philosophy of religious language: sign, symbol, and story.* D. R. Stiver. Cambridge, MA: Blackwell, 1996.

*The world treasury of religious quotations.* R. L. Woods (ed). New York: Hawthorn Books, 1966. (15,000 quotations, arranged by subject).

## IV. ELECTRONIC MEDIA

*Academic index.* Information Access Co., Foster City, CA. (Covers 950 scholarly journals; is available online and in CD-ROM).

*Biblia Patristica: index des citations et allusions bibliques dans la littérature patristique.* Paris: CNRS, 1975–80. 3 vols. (27,000 references; computerized).

*Britannica online.* Chicago: Encyclopaedia Britannica, 1994–. 44,000,000+ words.

*CD–ROMs in print, 1996: an international guide to CD–ROM, CD–I, 3DO, MMDC, CD32, multimedia and electronic book products.* M. Desmarais. New York: Gale Research, 1996. 1,243p.

*Directory of electronic journals, newsletters, and scholarly discussion lists.* Association of Research Libraries. Washington, DC: Association of Research Libraries, 1991. 173p.

*Directory of online databases.* New York. Cuadra/Elsevier Science Publishing Co., Inc.,

*Directory of portable databases.* New York. Cuadra/Elsevier Science Publishing.

*Earthquest.* Palo Alto, CA. Earthquest, Inc., (Hypercard stack which focuses upon global ecological, environmental, and historical issues).

*Ethnic NewsWatch.* Stamford, CT. SoftLine Information Company, (Selected articles from 100 top North American newspapers and magazines.)

*Hermeneutika BibleWorks 3.5 on CD–ROM.*

*Judaism and Christianity: a guide to the reference literature.* E. D. Starkey. *Reference sources in the humanities series.* Englewood, CO: Libraries Unlimited, 1991. 270p.

*Old testament abstracts on CD–ROM.* Washington, DC: The Catholic Biblical Association; Evanston, IL: American Theological Library Association, annual since 1995.

*RIC: Répetoire bibliographique des institutiones chrétiennes.* R. Metz & J. Schlick (eds). Strasbourg: Centre de Recherche et Documentation des Institutions Chrétiennes (CERDIC), annual since 1968. (Computer-produced indexes of Christian publications during the year; in 5 languages. 6,400 entries a year, increasing. Also RIC supplément, *Bibliographies thématiques*).

*South African theological bibliography on CD–ROM.* Pretroria: Research Institute for Theology and Religion, University of South Africa; Evanston, IL: American Theological Library Association, annual since 1995.

*Statbase locator on disk: UNSTAT's guide to international computerized statistical databases.* New York. United Nations Publications,

*The Catholic periodical and literature index on CD–ROM.* Catholic Library Association; Evanston, IL: American Theological Library Association, annual since 1996.

*The CD–ROM directory.* M. Finlay & J. Mitchell. 7th ed. Detroit, MI: Omnigraphics, 1992. 750p.

*The computer Bible.* J. A. Baird & D. N. Freedman (eds). Wooster, OH: Biblical Research Associates, Vols I–XV, 1975–78. (Word frequencies, concordances, indexes, using KWIC; computerization to make immediately available massive amounts of critical data).

*The Sage digital library (CD-ROM).* Albany, OR: Sage Software. Contains 220 books.

## V. BIBLIOGRAPHIES

*A biblical law bibliography: arranged by subject and by author.* J. W. Welch. *Toronto studies in theology,* 51. Lewiston, NY: E. Mellen Press, 1990. 339p.

*A bibliography.* K. Baago. *Library of Christian theology.* Madras: The Christian Literature Society, 1969. 110p. (A bibliography of theological works by Indian authors.).

*A bibliography of bibliographies in religion.* J. G. Barrow. Ann Arbor, MI: Edwards Bros, 1930, 5th edition 1955. 489p. (1,945 titles with short evaluations).

*A bibliography of Christian worship.* B. Thompson (ed). *ATLA bibliography series,* 25. Philadelphia: American Theological Library Association; Metuchen, NJ, Scarecrow Press. 828p.

*A bibliography of Greek New Testament manuscripts.* J. K. Elliott. *Monographic series, Society for New Testament Studies,* 62. Cambridge, UK and New York: Cambridge University Press, 1988. 231p.

*A bibliography of interchurch and interconfessional theological dialogues.* J. F. Puglisi & S. J. Voicu. Rome: Centro pro unione, 1984. 260p.

*A bibliography of Islamic law, 1980–1993.* L. Al-Zwaini & R. Peters. *Handbuch der Orientalistik. Erste Abteilung, der Nahe und Mittlere Osten (Handbook of Oriental studies, Near and Middle East),* 19. Leiden and New York: E. J. Brill, 1994. 248p.

*A bibliography of modern African religious movements.* R. C. Mitchel & H. W. Turner. Evanston, IL: Northwestern University Press, 1966. 132p. (1,300 items; updated annually in *Journal of religion in Africa*).

*A bibliography of New Testament bibliographies.* J. C. Hurd. New York: Seabury, 1966. (1,300 articles and books).

*A bibliography of Oman, 1900–1950.* R. King & J. H. Stevens. *Occasional paper series,* 2. Durham, UK: University of Durham, Centre for Middle Eastern and Islamic Studies, 1973. 141p.

*A bibliography of Salvation Army literature in English (1865–1987).* R. G. Moyles. *Texts and studies in religion,* 38. Lewiston, NY: E. Mellen Press, 1988. 217p.

*A bibliography of sources in Christianity and the arts.* D. M. Kari. *Studies in art and religious interpretation,* 16. Lewiston, NY: E. Mellen Press, 1995. 774p.

*A bibliography of the periodical literature on the Acts of the Apostles, 1962–1984.* W. E. Mills. *Supplements to Novum Testamentum,* 58. Leiden: E. J. Brill, 1986. 145p.

*A bibliography of the Samaritans.* A. D. Crown. 2nd ed. *ATLA bibliography series,* 32. Philadelphia: American Theological Library Association; Metuchen, NJ: Scarecrow Press, 1993. 393p.

*A bibliography on temples of the ancient Near East and Mediterranean world: arranged by subject and by author.* D. W. Parry, S. D. Ricks & J. W. Welch. *Ancient Near Eastern texts and studies,* 9. Lewiston NY: E. Mellen Press, 1991. 320p.

*A critical bibliography of writings on Judaism.* D. B. Griffiths. *Jewish studies,* 2. Lewiston, NY: E. Mellen Press, 1988. 2 vols.

*A critical guide to Catholic reference books.* J. P. McCabe. 3rd ed. Englewood, CO: Libraries Unlimited, 1989. 337p.

*A decade of Bible bibliography.* Oxford, UK: Blackwell, 1967. (Covers 1957–66).

*A guide to films about the Pacific islands.* J. D. Hamnett. Honolulu, HI: University of Hawaii, Pacific Islands Studies Program, 1986. 148p.

*A guide to the study of the Pentecostal movement.* C. E. Jones. *ATLA Bibliographic Series,* 6. Metuchen, NJ and London: American Theological Library Association and Scarecrow Press, 1983. 1,245p in 2 vols. (Though dated, remains an important bibliography of the Pentecostal movement).

*A pastoral liturgy bibliography.* 2nd rev. ed. Notre Dame, IN: Notre Dame Center for Pastoral Liturgy, 1981. 28p.

*A theological book list.* London: Theological Education Fund, 1960, 1965, 1968. (Comprehensive bibliographies on all subjects, with emphasis on works available for seminaries in developing countries; 3,000 entries).

*African theology: a critical analysis and annotated bibliography.* J. U. Young III. *Bibliographies and indexes in religious studies,* 26. Westport, CT: Greenwood, 1993. 269p.

*AIDS—issues in religion, ethics, and care: a Park Ridge Center bibliography.* K. A. Cahalan. Park Ridge, IL: Park Ridge Cente, 1988. 130p.

*American Puritan studies: an annotated bibliography of dissertations, 1882–1981.* M. S. Montgomery. *Bibliographies and indexes in American history,* 1. Westport, CT: Greenwood, 1984. 451p.

*An annotated and classified bibliography of English literature pertaining to the Ethiopian Orthodox Church.* J. Bonk. *ATLA bibliography series*, 11. Metuchen, NJ: American Theological Library Association and Scarecrow Press, 1984. 127p.

*An annotated critical bibliography of feminist criticism.* M. Humm. *Harvester annotated critical bibliographies.* Boston, MA: G. K. Hall, 1987. 251p.

*An Aramaic bibliography.* J. A. Fitzmyer et al. *Publications of the Comprehensive Aramaic Lexicon Project.* Baltimore, MD: Johns Hopkins University Press, 1992.

*An introductory bibliography for the study of Scripture.* J. A. Fitzmyer. 3rd ed. *Subsidia Biblica*, 3. Rome: Editrice pontificio istituto biblico, 1990. 231p. (Revised edition of *An introductory bibliography for the study of Scripture,* G. S. Glanzman).

*Analytical guide to the bibliographies on the Arabian Peninsula.* C. L. Geddes. *Bibliographic series*, 4. Denver, CO: American Institute of Islamic Studies, 1974.

*Annotated bibliography in religion and psychology.* W. W. Meissner. N.p.: Academy of Religion and Health, 1961.

*Annotated bibliography of Luther studies, 1977–1983.* K. Hagen. *Sixteenth century bibliography*, 24. St. Louis, MO: Center for Reformation Research, 1985. 91p.

*Annotated bibliography of Mennonite writings on war and peace, 1930–1980.* W. M. Swartley & C. J. Dyck (eds). Scottdale, PA: Herald, 1987. 740p. (Prepared by the Institute of Mennonite Studies, Elkhart, IN).

*Apartheid: a selective annotated bibliography,1979–1987.* S. E. Pyatt. *Garland reference library of social science*, 587. New York: Garland, 1990. 188p.

*Art and the Reformation: an annotated bibliography.* L. B. Parshall & P. W. Parshall. *A Reference publication in art history.* Boston, MA: G. K. Hall, 1986. 328p.

*Augustine's De civitate Dei: an annotated bibliography of modern criticism, 1960–1990.* D. F. Donnelly & M. A. Sherman. New York: P. Lang, 1991. 119p.

*Bible bibliography, 1967–73.* P. R. Ackroyd (ed). Oxford, UK: Blackwell, 1975. (Works in nearly 20 languages).

*Biblia Patristica: index des citations et allusions bibliques dans la littérature patristique.* Paris: CNRS, 1975–80. 3 vols. (27,000 references; computerized).

*Biblical resources for ministry: a bibliography.* D. R. Bauer (ed). Wilmore, KY: Division of Biblical Studies, Asbury Theological Seminary, 1990. 95p.

*Biblical resources for ministry: a bibliography of works in biblical studies.* D. R. Bauer. 2nd ed. Nappanee, IN: Evangel, 1995. 144p.

*Bibliografia tes Oikoumenikes Kineseos, 1960–1970 (Bibliography of the ecumenical movement).* V. T. Istravridis. Athens: Theologia, 1978. 78p. (Orthodoxy and ecumenism; 1,500 titles).

*Bibliographia Calviniana, 1532–1899.* D. A. Erichson. Nieuwkoop: De Graaf, 1950.

*Bibliographia internationalis spiritualitatis.* Roma: Pontifical Institute of Spirituality, 1966–68. 3 vols. (6,487 titles in v.3).

*Bibliographia missionaria.* 1935–74; Rome: Pontificia Università de Propagande Fide, 1986–. 50 vols. to date. (Annual review of previous year's literature; until 1971, some overlap with *Bibliotheca missionum,* but has now superseded it for current literature).

*Bibliographia Patristica.* W. Schneemelcher. Berlin: de Gruyter, 1959–65. 10 vols.

*Bibliographie bouddhique.* Paris: Librarie d'Amérique et d'Orient, 1930–61 (fasc. 1–31). (Annual).

*Bibliographie de cartographie ecclésiastique.* J. N. B. van den Brink et al. (eds). Leiden: E. J. Brill, Commission International d'Histoire Ecclésiastique Comparée, 1968–.

*Bibliographie de la Réforme, 1450–1648.* J. N. B. van den Brink et al. (eds). Leiden: E. J. Brill, 1958–70. 7 vols. (Covers 17 European countries plus U.S.).

*Bibliographie de la Septante: (1970–1993). (Bibliography of the Septuagint).* C. Dogniez. *Supplements to Vetus Testamentum*, 60. Leiden and New York: E. J. Brill, 1995.

*Bibliographies for biblical research.* W. E. Mills (ed). Lewiston, NY: E. Mellen Press, 1993–1996. 6 vols.

*Bibliography in contextual theology in Africa.* J. R. Cochrane, I. W. Henderson & G. O. West (eds). Pietermaritzburg, South Africa: Cluster Publications, 1993–. 1 vol. to date.

*Bibliography of British theological literature, 1850–1940.* D. Y. Hadidian. *Bibliographia tripotamopolitana*, 12. Pittsburgh, PA: Barbour Library, Pittsburgh Theological Seminary, 1985. 485p.

*Bibliography of literature on First Peter.* A. Casurella. *New Testament tools and studies*, 23. Leiden and New York: E. J. Brill, 1996. 178p.

*Bibliography of new religions: movements in primal societies.* H. W. Turner. Boston: G. K. Hall. Vol 2, Black Africa, 1977 (278, 1,900 entries); Vol 2, North America (280); Vols. 3-4, Latin America & Caribbean, Asia with Oceania.

*Bibliography of new religious movements in primal societies.* H. W. Turner. Boston and New York: G. K. Hall, 1977–92. 6 vols.

*Bibliography of New Testament literature, 1900–1950.* T. Akaishi (ed). San Anselmo, CA: Seminary Cooperative Store, 1953. 312p. (2,400 annotated items).

'Bibliography of original Christian writings in India in Tamil.' J. G. Muthuraj. Manuscript, Tamilnadu Theological Seminary, 161p.

*Bibliography of published articles on American Presbyterianism, 1901–1980.* H. M. Parker. *Bibliographies and indexes in religious studies*, 4. Westport, CT: Greenwood, 1985. 272p.

*Bibliography of religion in the South.* C. H. Lippy. Macon, GA: Mercer University Press, 1985. 514p.

*Bibliography on Buddhism.* S. Hanayama. Tokyo: Hokuseido Press, 1961. 869p. (15,073 numbered entries).

'Bibliography on world mission and evangelism,' *International review of mission.* (At end of all issues).

*Bibliotheca missionum.* R. Streit. Freiburg: Herder, 1916–71. 28 vols. (The major complete and retrospective Catholic bibliography of missions; discontinued 1971 and superseded by *Bibliographia missionaria*).

*Black theology: a critical assessment and annotated bibliography.* J. H. Evans. *Bibliographies and indexes in religious studies*, 10. New York: Greenwood, 1987. 217p.

*Bonhoeffer bibliography: primary sources and secondary literature in English.* W. W. Floyd & C. J. Green. Evanston, IL: American Theological Library Association, 1992. 159p.

*Buletin signalétique: sciences religieuses.* Paris: Centre de Documentation Sciences Humaines. 1947-74, vols 1-28; (8,000 periodical article abstracts a year).

*Calvin bibliography 1991.* P. De Klerk. p.389-411.

*Calvin–Bibliographie, 1901–1959.* W. Niesel. Munich: C. Kaiser, 1961. (Continuation of *Bibliographia Calviniana*).

*Catalog of the Hoose Library of Philosophy, University of Southern California (Los Angeles).* Boston: G. K. Hall, 1968. 6 vols. (96,000 entries, 4,577 pages).

*Catalogue of English Bible translations: a classified bibliography of versions and editions including books, parts, and Old and New Testament Apocrypha and Apocryphal books.* W. J. Chamberlin. *Bibliographies and indexes in religious studies*, 21. New York: Greenwood, 1991. 946p. (The best and most complete for its listing of English Bible translations, 9,000 titles and editions).

*Catholic periodical and literature index.* Haverford, PA: Catholic Library Association, 1930–72. vols 1-17.

*Charismatic religion in modern research: a bibliography.* W. E. Mills. *NABPR bibliographic series*, 1. Macon, GA: Mercer University Press, 1985. 17p

*Chaucer and the Bible: a critical review of research, indexes, and bibliography.* L. L. Besserman. *Garland reference library of the humanities*, 839. New York: Garland, 1988.

*China bibliography: a research guide to reference works about China past and present.* H. T. Zurndorfer. *Handbuch der Orientalistik*, Vierte Abteilung, China, 1. Leiden and New York: E. J. Brill, 1995. 394p.

*Christian faith amidst religious pluralism: an introductory bibliography.* D. G. Dawe et al. Richmond, VA: Union Theological Seminary in Virginia, 1980. 115p.

*Christian periodical index.* Buffalo, NY: Christian Librarians' Fellowship, Quarterly. (Covers a relatively small but important number of conservative Protestant periodicals from 1956 to the present).

*Christian spirituality: the essential guide to the most influential spiritual writings of the Christian tradition.* F. N. Magill & I. P. McGreal (eds). San Francisco: Harper & Row, 1988.

*Christianity and Marxism worldwide: an annotated bibliography.* M. R. Elliott (ed). Wheaton, IL: Institute for the Study of Christianity and Marxism, Wheaton College, 1988.

*Cities and churches: an international bibliography.* L. H. Hartley. *ATLA bibliography series*, 31. Metuchen, NJ: Scarecrow Press, 1992. 3 vols.

*Cultural anthropology of the Middle East: a bibliography.* R. Strijp. *Handbuch der Orientalistik. Erste Abteilung, Der Nahe und der Mittlere Osten*, 10. Leiden and New York: E. J. Brill, 1992–. 2 vols. to date.

*Current bibliography on African affairs.* P. Boesch (ed). Farmingdale, NY: Baywood Publishing Company, 1962–67. N.s. 1968—.

*Das Evangelische Schrifttum.* Gesamtausgabe 1975. Stuttgart: Vereinigung Evangelischer Buchhändler. 448p. (Protestant literature: 9,760 titles).

*Der Katholische Schrifttum (Gesamtausgabe 1975).* Stuttgart: Verbannd Katholischer Verleger & Buchhändler. 288p. (Catholic literature: 5,760 titles).

*Dissertation Abstracts International:* (1) *Comprehensive dissertation index, 1861–1975,* on all subjects, and (2) *Datrix II* computer retrieval system, by keywords in title, of over 500,000 North American and European university doctoral dissertations (300,000 on humanities and social sciences; about 8,000 on religion and Christianity; 950 with 'Catholic' in title, 490 with 'Protestant', 1,160 with 'Christian', 1,780 with 'church', 490 with 'God', 1,200 with 'theology' or 'theological', 2,400 with 'religion', etc). Annual and monthly editions and supplements, in volumes, printout or microfiche.

*Elenchus bibliographicus biblicus.* P. Nober. Rome: Biblical Institute, 1970. (Annual).

*Eleven years of Bible bibliography: the book lists of the Society for Old Testament study, 1946–56.* H. H. Rowley (ed). Indian Hill, CO: Falcon's Wing, 1957. 804p. (Annotated).

*Emil Brunner: a bibliography.* M. G. McKim. *ATLA bibliographies*, 40. Lanham, MD: Scarecrow Press, 1996. 105p.

*Encyclopedia of library and information science.* Kent. New York: Dekker, 1968–1996. 58 vols.

*English religion, 1500–1540: a bibliography.* D. D. Smeeton. *NABPR bibliographic series*, 2. Macon, GA: Mercer University Press, 1988. 114p.

*Ethnographic bibliography of North America, 4th edition. Supplement 1973–1987.* M. M. Martin & T. J. O'Leary. New Haven, CT: Human Relations Area Files Press, 1990. 3 vols. (Previously published as *Ethnographic bibliography of North America.* G. P. Murdock, 1960, 1975.).

*Evangelical secularism in the Russian Empire and the USSR: a bibliographic guide.* A. W. Wardin Jr. *ATLA bibliography series*, 36. Metuchen, NJ: Scarecrow Press, 1995. 906p.

*Feminist spirituality and the feminine divine: an annotated bibliography.* A. Carson. *The Crossing Press feminist series.* Trumansburg, NY: Crossing Press, 1986. 139p.

*Glossolalia: a bibliography.* W. E. Mills. *Studies in the Bible and early Christianity*, 6. New York: E. Mellen Press, 1985. 129p.

*Guide to atlases: world, regional, national, thematic.* G. L. Alexander. Metuchen, NJ: Scarecrow Press, 1971. (Listing of atlases published since 1950. 54 are listed under 'Bible and Christian history').

*Guide to Catholic literature, 1888–1940.* Detroit: Romig, 1940.

*Guide to religious periodicals.* (Provides an index to denominational publications, mainly American, post-1964).

*Holiness works: a bibliography.* W. C. Miller (ed). Kansas City, MO: Printed for Nazarene Theological Seminary by Nazarene Publishing House, 1986. 120p. (Revised edition of *The master bibliography of Holiness Works,* Beacon Hill Press, 1965).

*Holocaust literature: a handbook of critical, historical and literary writings.* S. S. Friedman (ed). Westport, CT and London: Greenwood, 1994. 707p. (An essential handbook for anyone studying holocaust literature).

*Index Islamicus 1906–1955: a catalogue of articles on Islamic subjects in periodicals and other collective publications.* J. D. Pearson et al. Cambridge, UK: Heffer, 1958. 807p. (Supplements published in 1962, 1967, 1972, 1977).

*Index of articles on the New Testament and the early church.* B. M. Metzger. Philadelphia: Society of Biblical Literature, 1951. 182p. (Indexes 2,350 articles).

*Interfaith dialogue: an annotated bibliography.* J. H. Berthrong. Wofford Heights, CA: Multifaith Resources, 1993. 32p.

*International bibliography of sociology of religion,* in *Social compass* (Intenational review of socio-religious studies), Louvain, 1958–1972.

*International Christian literature documentation project.* D. W. Geyer. Evanston, IL: American Theological Library Association, 1993. 2 vols, 1,730p. (Indexes nonwestern Christian literature in North American libraries.).

*Irregular serials and annuals: an international directory.* E. Koltay (ed). 1st ed. New York: R.R. Bowker, 1967. (350 items on religion out of 14,500).

*Jerusalem, the Holy City: a bibliography.* J. D. Purvis. *ATLA bibliography series*, 20. St. Meinrad, IN: American Theological Library Association; Metuchen, NJ: Scarecrow Press, 1988–1991. 2 vols.

*Jesus the Christ: a bibliography.* L. J. White. *Theological and Biblical resources*, 4. Wilmington, DE: Michael Glazier, 1988. 157p.

*Jewish Christians in the United States: a bibliography.* K. Pruter. *Sects and cults in America, Bibliographical guides*, 7; *Garland reference library of social science*, 306. New York: Garland, 1987. 203p.

*Jewish–Christian relations: an annotated bibliography and resource guide.* M. Shermis. Bloomington, IN: Indiana University Press, 1988. 306p.

*Johannine bibliography, 1966–1985: a cumulative bibliography on the Fourth gospel.* G. van Belle. *Bibliotheca Ephemeridum theologicarum Lovaniensium*, 82. Leuven: Leuven University Press, 1988. 580p. (Variant title: *Cumulative bibliography on the Fourth gospel.* Also published in series *Collectanea biblica et religiosa antiqua*).

*John and Charles Wesley: a bibliography.* B. Jarboe. *ATLA bibliography series*, 22. Metuchen, NJ: Scarecrow Press, 1987. 419p.

*Jonathan Edwards: an annotated bibliography,1979–1993.* M. X. Lesser. *Bibliographies and indexes in religious studies*, 30. Westport, CT: Greenwood, 1994. 220p.

*Judaism and Christianity: a guide to the reference literature.* E. D. Starkey. *Reference sources in the humanities series.* Englewood, CO: Libraries Unlimited, 1991. 270p.

*Katholische Zeitungen und Zeitschriften,* in Streit-Dindinger, *Biblioteca missionum (Africa, vol XX,* p.716–742; India, vol XXVIII, p.484–506; China, vol XIV, p.378–408; Oceania, vol XXI, p.711–717).

*Literary–critical approaches to the Bible: an annotated bibliography.* M. Minor. West Cornwall, CT: Locust Hill, 1992. 551p.

*Malcolm X: a comprehensive annotated bibliography.* T. V. Johnson. *Garland reference library of social science*, 288. New York: Garland, 1986. 201p.

*Martin Luther King, Jr.: an annotated bibliography.* S. E. Pyatt. *Bibliographies and indexes in Afro-American and African studies*, 12. New York: Greenwood, 1986. 168p.

'Marxist analysis and sociology of religions: an outline of international bibliography up to 1975,' O. Maduro, *Social compass*, XXII, 3–4 (1975), 401–479. (Lists 1,215 books, 730 articles, in 7 Western languages).

*Matrology: a bibliography of writings by Christian women from the first to the fifteenth centuries.* A. Kadel. New York: Continuum, 1995. 191p.

*Missiological abstracts, 25 years, 1966–1991.* G. R. Grimes (ed). Rev. ed. Pasadena, CA: Fuller Theological Seminary, 1991. 336p. (Abstracts of 720 dissertations, theses, and projects produced at the School of World Mission at Fuller Theological Seminary).

*Missions and evangelism: a bibliography selected from the ATLA religion database, January, 1985.* A. E. Hurd & P. D. Petersen (eds). Rev. ed. Chicago: American Theological Library Association, Religion Indexes, 1985. 788p.

*Modern American popular religion: a critical assessment and annotated bibliography.* C. H. Lippy. *Bibliographies and indexes in religious studies*, 37. Westport, CT: Greenwood, 1996. 264p.

*Muslim women throughout the world: a bibliography.* M. Kimball & B. R. von Schlegell. Sterling, VA: Lynne Reiner, 1997. 285p.

*Muslims in India: a bibliography of their religious, socio–economic and political literature.* Satyaprakash. Haryana, India: Indian Documenation Service, 1985. 299p.

*New Eden and new Babylon: religious thoughts of American authors: a bibliography.* N. R. Burr. 11 vols.

*New religious movements in the United States and Canada: a critical assessment and annotated bibliography.* D. Choquette. *Bibliographies and indexes in religious studies*, 5. Westport, CT: Greenwood, 1985. 235p.

*New Testament abstracts.* Weston, MA: Theological Faculty, Weston College, 1956–. (Issued 3 times a year; abstracts in English from articles in many languages).

*New Testament Christology: a critical assessment and annotated bibliography.* A. J. Hultgren. *Bibliographies and indexes in religious studies*, 12. New York: Greenwood, 1988. 499p.

*New Testament tools and studies.* B. M. Metzger (ed). Leiden: E. J. Brill, 1966–80. Vol I: *Index to periodical literature on the Apostle Paul.* Vol VI: *Index to periodical literature on Christ and the Gospels* (10,090 entries). Vol VII: *A classified bibliography of literature on the Acts of the Apostles* (6,645 entries). Vol X: *Philological, versional and patristic.*

*Old testament abstracts on CD–ROM.* Washington, DC: The Catholic Biblical Association; Evanston, IL: American Theological Library Association, annual since 1995.

*Oman and southeastern Arabia: a bibliographic survey.* M. O. Shannon. Boston: G. K. Hall, 1978. 165p.

*Ostkirchliche Studien.* Würzburg: Augustinus-Verlag, 1952–. (Quarterly. The best bibliographical source on the Eastern churches, with about 90 pages of bibliography each year).

*P. T. Forsyth bibliography and index.* R. Benedetto. *Bibliographies and indexes in religious studies*, 27. Westport, CT: Greenwood, 1993. 187p.

*Paul and his interpreters: an annotated bibliography.* G. L. Borchert. *TSF-IBR bibliographic study guides.* Madison, WI: Theological Students Fellowship, 1985. 129p.

*Peace, disarmament and war: a bibliography selected from the ATLA religion database.* A. E. Hurd (ed). Rev. ed. Chicago: American Theological Library Association, 1985. 464p.

*Periodicals from Africa: a bibliography and union list of periodicals published in Africa.* C. Travis & M. Alman. *Bibliographies and guides in African studies.* Boston, MA: G. K. Hall, 1977. 619p.

*Philo of Alexandria: an annotated bibliography, 1937–1986.* R. Radice & D. T. Runia. *Supplements to Vigiliae Christianae*, 8. Leiden and New York: E. J. Brill, 1988. 510p.

*Philosophy in the 20th century: Catholic and Christian.* G. McLean. Vol. I: A*n annotated bibliography of philosophy in Catholic thought, 1900–64.* Vol. II: *A bibliography of Christian philosophy and contemporary issues.* New York: Ungar, 1967.

*Protestant theological education in America: a bibliography.* H. F. Day. *ATLA bibliography series*, 15. Chicago: American Theological Library Association; Metuchen, NJ: Scarecrow Press, 1985. 521p.

*Psychoanalytic studies in religion: a critical assessment and annotated bibliography.* B. Beit-Hallahmi. *Bibliographies and indexes in religious studies.* Westport, CT: Greenwood.

*Recent reference books in religion: a guide for students, scholars, researchers, buyers and readers.* W. M. Johnston. Downers Grove, IL: InterVarsity, 1996. 318p. (Contains annotations on 318 major reference books on religion. The majority of books annotated are on Christianity, but it also contains other major religions.).

*Religion and the American experience, the twentieth century: a bibliography of doctoral dissertations.* A. P. Young & E. J. Holley. *Bibliographies and indexes in religious studies*, 31. Westport, CT: Greenwood, 1994. 426p.

'Religion', in *Guide to reference books,* 9th Edition, E. P. Sheehy (Chicago: American Library Association, 1976), p.252-283. (Details of 410 dictionaries, encyclopedias, directories, manuals, in English and other languages; 322 on Christianity).

*Religion index one: periodicals* (formerly *Index to religious periodical literature*), and *Religion index two: multi-author works* (essays, conferences, etc). Ed., G. F. Dickerson. Chicago: American Theological Library Association. 12 vols, 1949–77. (Vol 9, 1969–70, comprised 227p plus 75p of book reviews; since 1975, all articles are abstracted).

'Religions and theology' in *Ulrich's international periodicals directory*, Vol II (New York, London: R.R. Bowker, 14th edition, 1971), p.873–902. (Of the 35,000 periodicals currently published throughout the world, 1,000 deal with religion and theology).

*Religious and theological abstracts.* Meyerstown, PA, 1958–. 41 vols. to date. (Quarterly).

*Religious books and serials in print, 1978–1979.* New York: Bowker, 1978 (1st Edition). 1,259p. (Over 47,400 entries for titles available from 1,700 publishers, under 4,600 subject headings; classified by subject, author, title).

*Religious books for children: an annotated bibliography.* P. P. Dole. 3rd ed. *A CSLA bibliography.* Portland, OR: Church and Synagogue Library Association, 1993. 39p.

*Religious books in print, 1974.* Religious Books Publishers Group. London: Whitaker, 1975. (Nearly 10,000 titles under 18 headings).

*Religious colleges and universities in America: a selected bibliography.* T. C. Hunt & J. C. Carper. *Garland reference library of social science*, 422. New York: Garland, 1988. 374p.

*Religious conflict in America: a bibliography.* A. J. Menendez. *Garland reference library of social science*, 262. New York: Garland, 1985. 140p.

*Religious schools in America: a selected bibliography.* T. C. Hunt, J. C. Carper & C. R. Kniker. *Garland reference library of social science*, 338. New York: Garland, 1986. 402p.

*Religious seminaries in America: a selected bibliography.* T. C. Hunt & J. C. Carper. *Garland reference library of social science*, 539. New York: Garland, 1989. 240p.

*Research in ritual studies: a programmatic essay and bibliography.* R. L. Grimes. *ATLA bibliography series*, 14. Chicago: American Theological Library Association and Metuchen, NJ: Scarecrow Press, 1985. 174p.

*Research on religion and aging: an annotated bibliography.* H. G. Koenig. *Bibliographies and indexes in gerontology*, 27. Westport, CT: Greenwood, 1995. 190p.

*Resources for Buddhist–Christian encounter: an annotated bibliography.* H. L. Wells. Wofford Heights, CA: Multifaith Resources, 1993. 30p. (Prepared by the Educational Resources Committee of the Society for Buddhist-Christian Studies).

*Resources in sacred dance: annotated bibliography: books, booklets and pamphlets, articles and publications, organizations, non–print, and general dance resources.* K. Troxell (ed). Peterborough, NH: Sacred Dance Guild, 1986. 40p.

*Rhetorical criticism of the Bible: a comprehensive bibliography with notes on history and method.* D. F. Watson & A. J. Hauser. *Biblical interpretation series*, 4. Leiden and New York: E. J. Brill, 1994. 226p.

*RIC: Répetoire bibliographique des institutiones chrétiennes.* R. Metz & J. Schlick (eds). Strasbourg: Centre de Recherche et Documentation des Institutions Chrétiennes (CERDIC), annual since 1968. (Computer-produced indexes of Christian publications during the year; in 5 languages. 6,400 entries a year, increasing. Also RIC supplément, *Bibliographies thématiques*).

*School prayer and other religious issues in American public education: a bibliography.* A. J. Menendez. *Garland reference library of social science*, 291. New York: Garland, 1985. 178p.

*Selective bibliography on evangelism and evangelization.* D. B. Barrett. Nairobi: Centre for the Study of World Evangelization, 1980. (1,400 items).

*Seventh-day Adventist (SDA) periodical index.* Riverside, CA: Loma Linda University Libraries, 1971—. (4,000 articles, book reviews, editorials from over 40 SDA periodicals).

*Shelf list of the Union Theological Seminary Library, New York.* Boston: G. K. Hall, 1960. 10 vols.

*Sikhism and the Sikhs: an annotated bibliography.* P. M. Rai. *Bibliographies and indexes in religious studies*, 13. New York: Greenwood, 1989. 272p.

*Social scientific criticism of the New Testament: a bibliography.* D. M. May. *NABPR bibliographic series*, 4. Macon, GA: Mercer University Press, 1991. 106p.

*Sociology of Christianity: an international bibliography.* H. Carrier & E. Pin (eds). Rome: Gregorian University Press, 1964. 313p.

*Source book on Arabian Gulf States, Arabian Gulf in general, Kuwait, Bahrain, Qatar and Oman.* S. Kabeel. Kuwait: Kuwait University, Libraries Department, 1975. 427p. (With over 3,000 item bibliography).

*South African theological bibliography on CD–ROM.* Pretroria: Research Institute for Theology and Religion, University of South Africa; Evanston, IL: American Theological Library Association, annual since 1995.

*South Asian religions in the Americas: an annotated bibliography of immigrant religious traditions.* J. Y. Fenton. *Bibliographies and indexes in religious studies.* Westport, CT: Greenwood.

*The Bible and modern literary criticism: a critical assessment and annotated bibliography.* M. A. Powell. *Bibliographies and indexes in religious studies*, 22. New York: Greenwood, 1992. 484p.

*The book of Daniel: an annotated bibliography.* H. O. Thompson. *Garland reference library of the humanities, 1,310; Books of the Bible*, 1. New York: Garland, 1993. 588p.

*The book of Ephesians: an annotated bibliography.* W. W. Klein. *Books of the Bible, 8; Garland reference library of the humanities*, 1,466. New York: Garland, 1996. 335p.

*The book of Jeremiah: an annotated bibliography.* H. O. Thompson. *ATLA bibliography series*, 41. Lanham, MD: Scarecrow Press, 1996. 777p.

*The book of Psalms: an annotated bibliography.* T. Wittstruck. *Books of the Bible, 5; Garland reference library of the humanities*, 1,413. New York: Garland, 1994. 2 vols.

*The book of Revelation: an annotated bibliography.* R. L. Muse. *Books of the Bible, 2; Garland reference library of the humanities*, 1,387. New York: Garland, 1996. 388p.

*The book of Ruth: an annotated bibliography.* M. Caspi. *Books of the Bible, 7; Garland reference library of the humanities*, 1,410. New York: Garland, 1994. 147p.

*The Books of Chronicles: a classified bibliography.* I. Kalimi. *Simor Bible bibliographies.* Jerusalem: Simor, 1990. 246p. (Entries in English, Hebrew, German, and French).

*The Catholic novel: an annotated bibliography.* A. J. Menendez. *Garland reference library of the humanities*, 690. New York: Garland, 1988. 342p.

*The Catholic periodical and literature index on CD–ROM.* N.p.: Catholic Library Association; Evanston, IL: American Theological Library Association, annual since 1996.

*The charismatic movement: a guide to the study of neo–pentecostalism with emphasis on Anglo–American sources.* C. E. Jones. *ATLA Bibliographic Series*, 30. Metuchen, NJ and London: American Theological Library Association and Scarecrow Press, 1995. 1,266p in 2 vols. (A major bibliography of the charismatic movement).

*The Children of God/Family of Love: an annotated bibliography.* W. D. Pritchett. *Sects and cults in America. Bibliographical guides*, 5; *Garland reference library of social science*, 209. New York: Garland, 1985. 209p.

*The church: a bibliography.* A. R. Dulles & P. Granfield. Wilmington, DE: Michael Glazier, 1985. 166p.

*The Churches of God, Seventh-day: a bibliography.* J. Bjorling. *Bibliographies on sects and cults in America*, 8; *Garland reference library of the humanities*, 362. New York: Garland, 1987. 315p.

*The contemporary Islamic revival: a critical survey and bibliography.* Y. Y. Haddad, J. O. Voll & J. L. Esposito. Westport, CT: Greenwood, 1991. 230p.

*The Disciples and American culture: a bibliography of works by Disciples of Christ members, 1866–1984.* L. R. Galbraith & H. F. Day. *ATLA bibliography series*, 26. Metuchen, NJ: Scarecrow Press, 1990. 390p.

*The doctrine of the Holy Spirit: a bibliography showing its chronological development.* E. D. Schandorff. *ATLA bibliography series*, 28. Lanham, MD: American Theological Library Association and Scarecrow Press, 1995. 2 vols.

*The early church: an annotated bibliography of literature in English.* T. A. Robinson & B. D. Shaw. *ATLA bibliography series*, 23. Philadelphia: American Theological Library Association; Metuchen, NJ: Scarecrow Press, 1993. 518p.

*The early church: an annotated bibliography of literature in English.* T. A. Robinson & B. Shaw. *ATLA bibliography series*, 33. Metuchen, NJ: Scarecrow Press, 1993. 522p.

*The Gospel of Luke: a cumulative bibliography 1973–1988.* F. van Segbroeck. *Bibliotheca Ephemeridum theologicarum Lovaniensium*, 88. Louvain: Leuven University Press, 1989. 243p.

*The Gospel of Mark: a cumulative bibliography1950–1990.* F. Neirynck. *Bibliotheca Ephemeridum theologicarum Lovaniensium*, 102. Leuven: Leuven University Press, 1992. 729p.

*The Holy Spirit: a bibliography.* W. E. Mills. Peabody, MA: Hendrickson Publishers, 1988. 181p.

*The Islamic revival since 1988: a critical survey and bibliography.* Y. Y. Haddad & J. L. Esposito. *Bibliographies and indexes in religious studies*, 45. Westport, CT: Greenwood, 1997. 317p.

*The literary lives of Jesus: an international bibliography of poetry, drama, fiction, and criticism.* A. L. Birney. *Garland reference library of the humanities*, 735. New York: Garland, 1989. 212p.

*The lives of Jesus: a history and bibliography.* W. S. Kissinger. *Garland reference library of the humanities*, 452. New York: Garland, 1985. 243p.

*The New Testament: a bibliography.* D. J. Harrington. *Theological and biblical resources*, 2. Wilmington, DE: Michael Glazier, 1985. 242p.

*The Oxford movement and its leaders: a bibliography of secondary and lesser primary sources.* L. N. Crumb. *ATLA bibliography series*, 24. Metuchen, NJ: American Theological Library Association and Scarecrow Press, 1988. 737p.

*The Oxford movement and its leaders: a bibliography of secondary and lesser primary sources, supplement.* L. N. Crumb. *ATLA bibliography series*, 24. Metuchen, NJ: Scarecrow Press, 1993. 312p.

*The peace tradition in the Catholic Church: an annotated bibliography.* R. G. Musto. *Garland reference library of social science*, 339. New York: Garland, 1987. 619p. (Companion volume to *The Catholic peace tradition*).

*The quarterly index Islamicus: current books, articles and papers on Islamic studies.* J. D. Pearson (ed). London: Mansell, 1977–91; Bowker–Saur, 1992–93.

*The Society for Old Testament Studies book list 1995.* L. L. Grabbe (ed). Atlanta: Scholar's Press, 1995. 203p. (Reviews of more than 500 titles).

*The sociology of religion: an organizational bibliography.* A. J. Blasi & M. W. Cuneo. *Garland library of sociology*, 18; *Garland reference library of social science*, 612. New York: Garland, 1990. 488p.

*The synoptic problem: a bibliography, 1716–1988.* T. R. W. Longstaff & P. A. Thomas (eds). *New gospel studies*, 4. Macon, GA: Mercer University Press, 1988. 263p.

*The Unification Church in America: a bibliography and research guide.* M. L. Mickler. *Sects and cults in America. Bibliographical guides*, 9; *Garland reference library of social science*, 211. New York: Garland, 1987. 238p.

*The Yogacara school of Buddhism: a bibliography.* J. Powers. *ATLA bibliography series*, 27. Philadelphia: American Theological Library Association; Metuchen, NJ: Scarecrow Press, 1991. 257p.

*Theodicy: an annotated bibliography on the problem of evil, 1960–1990.* B. L. Whitney. *Garland reference library of the humanities*, 1,111. New York: Garland, 1993. 659p.

*Theodicy, suffering, and good and evil: a bibliography selected from the ATLA religion database.* T. J. Davis (ed). Chicago: American Theological Library Association, 1987. 297p.

*Theological education in Africa: an annotated bibliography.* G. Lund. Wheaton, IL: Billy Graham Center, 1992. 48p.

'Theology and religion', in M. M. Reynolds, *A guide to theses and dissertations: an annotated, international bibliography of bibliographies* (Detroit, MI: Gale Research Company, 1975), p.499–511. (54 out of 2,200 bibliographies).

*Tropical Africa and the Old Testament: a select and annotated bibliography.* K. Holter. *Bibliography series, University of Oslo, Faculty of Theology*, 6. Oslo, Norway: University of Oslo, Faculty of Theology, 1996. 106p.

*Western language literature on pre–Islamic central Arabia: an annotated bibliography.* S. D. Ricks. *Bibliographic series, American Institute of Islamic Studies*, 10. Denver, CO: American Institute of Islamic Studies, 1991. 169p.

*Women and religion in Britain and Ireland: an annotated bibliography from the Reformation to 1993.* D. A. Johnson. *ATLA bibliography series*, 39. Lanham, MD: Scarecrow Press, 1995. 304p.

*Women and religion in India: an annotated bibliography of sources in English, 1975–92.* N. A. Falk. Kalamazoo, MI: New Issues Press, College of Arts and Sciences, Western Michigan University, 1994. 241p.

*Women and women's issues in North American Lutheranism: a bibliography.* B. A. DeBerg & E. Sherman. Minneapolis, MN: Augsburg Fortress, 1992. 52p. (Produced under the sponsorship of the Commission for Women of the ELCA).

*Women in American religious history: an annotated bibliography and guide to sources.* D. C. Bass & S. H. Boyd. *G. K. Hall women's studies publications.* Boston, MA: G. K. Hall, 1986. 169p.

*Women in Christian history: a bibliography.* C. D. Blevins. Macon, GA: Mercer University Press, 1995. 122p.

*Women in the New Testament: a select bibliography.* I. M. Lindboe. *Bibliography series*, no. 1. Oslo: University of Oslo, Faculty of Theology, 1990. 90p.

*World guide to libraries/Internationales Biblioteks–handbuch.* 4th ed. New York: Bowker. 1974, 2 vols. (Survey of 36,932 libraries in 157 countries, each with over 30,000 volumes; total religious and theological libraries, 2,100).

Part 32

# INDEXES

Country names, abbreviations, acronyms,
initials, photographs, topics

*The end of the survey is the beginning of action.*
—Samuel Marinus Zwemer, Apostle to Islam (1867-1952)

These indexes to *World Christian trends* assist the reader to navigate in situations of poor information visibility and to find whatever instrumentation or measurement or trend is needed at the moment.

# Table 32–1. Polyglot glossary of religious terminology.

The Christian world worships, preaches, teaches, communicates, and functions in more than 10,000 languages, large and small, around the globe. Christians of 6,700 different languages have at least portions of Scripture they can understand. All of this requires the use of very important theological, ecclesiastical, liturgical, religious, and missiological terms. As Christian faith has spread from language to language through 2 millennia, missionaries have faced the challenge of what words to use in each new language to convey Christian truth or to employ in Christian life, service, and worship. Should one (1) find a word that already exists in the new language and put it to new use, or (2) introduce a foreign word as a new term in the new language, or (3) invent a new word by taking one from another language and changing the sounds or orthography to make it fit comfortably in the new language? Each approach has been used many times, and important debates in mission theology have centered on this process, the most notable being the choice of the word for 'God' in Chinese. Some terms have migrated from the words used by the prophets, the apostles, and Jesus himself into thousands of present-day languages. Other terms have been transformed through long chains of transliteration to hundreds of similar, but different, forms.

This list demonstrates the results of this process for 8 of the world's greatest Christian languages. Note that none of these terms began in any of these languages, but in the Greek, Aramaic, and Hebrew of biblical times. This list provides a resource that may help the reader understand many of the non-English names and terms that appear throughout WCE/WCT/WCD. It stands as a reminder that the training of missionaries and world Christian workers of all kinds requires instruction in key Christian terms among many languages. Finally, it is a helpful tool for the large number of international and intercultural Christian churches, denominations, and ministries that must function in many languages.

| English | Chinese | French | German | Italian | Portuguese | Russian | Spanish |
|---|---|---|---|---|---|---|---|
| apostle | shitu | apôtre | Apostel | apostolo | apóstolo | apostol | apóstol |
| baptism | jinli | baptême | Taufe | battesimo | baptismo | kreshchenie | bautismo |
| baptize, to | shoujin | baptizer | taufen | battezzare | baptizar | krestit | bautizar |
| Bible | Shengjing | Bible | Bibel | Bibbia | Bíblia | Biblia | Biblia |
| bishop | zhujiao | evêque | Bischof | vescovo | bispo | episkop | obispo |
| blessing | zhufu | bénédiction | Segen | benedizione | bênção | blagoslovenie | bendición |
| Christ | Jidu | Christ | Christus | Cristo | Cristo | Khristos | Cristo |
| Christian | jidujiaotu | Chrétien/Chrétienne | Christ/Christin | Cristiano | Cristão | khristianin | Cristiano |
| Christianity | Jidujiao | Christianisme | Christentum | Cristianesimo | Cristianismo | Khristianstvo | Cristianismo |
| church | jiaotang | église | Kirche | chiesa | igreja | tserkov | iglesia |
| commandment | jielü | commandement | Gebot | comandamento | mandamento | zapoved | mandamiento |
| communion | shengcan | communion | Kommunion | communione | comunhão | prichastie | comunión |
| community | shequ | communauté | Gemeinschaft | comunità | comunidad | soobshchestvo | comunidad |
| confession | renzui | confession | Bekenntnis | confessione | confissão | ispoved | confesión |
| congregation | huizhong | congrégation | Kongregation | congregazione | congregação | sobranie | congregación |
| conversion | zhuanbian | conversion | Bekehrung | conversione | conversação | obrashchenie | conversión |
| council | juhui | conseil | Rat | concilio | concelho | soviet | consejo |
| cross | shizijia | croix | Kreuz | croce | cruz | krest | cruz |
| denomination | jiaopai | dénomination | Denomination | denominazione | denominação | veroispovedanie | denominación |
| devil | mogui | diable | Teufel | diavolo | diablo | dyavol | diablo |
| evangelist | chuanjiaoshi | évangéliste | evangelist | evangelista | evangelista | evangelist | evangelista |
| faith | xinxin | foi | Glaube | fede | religião | vera | fe |
| fasting | zhaijie | jeûne | Fasten | digiuno | jejum | post | vigilia |
| fellowship | zhunei | communauté | Gemeinschaft | compagnia | comunhão | bratstvo | comunidad |
| God | Shen | Dieu | Gott | Dio | Deus | Bog | Dios |
| gospel | fuyin | évangile | Evangelium | Vangelo | evangelho | evangelie | evangelio |
| grace | renci | grâce | Gnade | grazia | graça | milost | gracia |
| heaven | tiantang | ciel | Himmel | cielo | céu | nebesa | cielo |
| hell | diyu | enfer | Hölle | inferno | inferno | ad | infierno |
| Holy Spirit | shengling | Saint-Esprit | Heilige Geist | Spirito Santo | Espírito Santo | svyatoy dukh | Santo Espíritu |
| hymn | zanmeishi | hymne | Hymne | inno | hino | tserkovny gimn | himno |
| independent | zizhude | indépendant | selbstandig | indipendente | independente | nezavisimy | indipendiente |
| Jesus | Yesu | Jésus | Jesus | Gesù | Jesus | Iisus | Jesús |
| Lord | Zhu | Seigneur | der Herr | Signore | Senhor | Gospod | Señor |
| love | ci ai | aimer | Liebe | amore | amor | lyubov | amor |
| man/men | ren | homme/hommes | Mann | uomo/uomini | homen | chelovek | hombre |
| minister, a | mushi | pasteur | Pfarrer | pastore | pastor | svyashchennik | pastor |
| missionary | chuanjiaoshi | missionnaire | Missionar | missionario | missionário | missioner | misionario |
| New Testament | Xinyuequanshu | Nouveau Testament | Neue Testament | Nuovo Testamento | Novo Testamento | Novy Zavet | Nuevo Testamento |
| offering | fengxian | offrande | Opfer | offerta | offrenda | pozhertvovanie | oblación |
| Old Testament | Jiuyuequanshu | Ancien Testament | Alte Testament | Antico Testamento | Antigo Testamento | Vetkhy Zavet | Antiguo Testamento |
| prayer | daogao | prière | Gebet | preghiera | oração | molitva | rezo |
| preacher | mushi | prédicateur | Prediger | predicatore | pregador | propovednik | predicador |
| preaching | jiangdao | prédication | Predigt | predicatione | pregar | propovedovanie | predicación |
| priest | shenfu | prêtre | Priester | prete | sacerdote | svyashchennik | sacerdote |
| prophet | xianzhi | prophète | Prophet | profeta | profeta | prorok | profeta |
| religion | zongjiao | religion | Religion | religione | religião | religia | religión |
| repentance | chanhui | repentir | Reue | pentimento | arrependimento | raskayanie | arrepentimiento |
| resurrection | fuhuo | résurrection | Auferstehung | risurrezione | ressurreição | voskresenie | resurrección |
| sacrament | shengcan | sacrement | Sakrament | sacramento | sacramento | prichastie | sacramento |
| sacrifice | xisheng | sacrifice | Opfer | sacrificio | sacrifício | zhertva | sacrificio |
| saint | shengren | saint | Sankt | santo | santo | svatoy | santo |
| salvation | jiushi | salut | Heil | salvazione | salvação | spacenie | salvación |
| sermon | jiangdao | sermon | Predigt | predica | sermão | propved | sermón |
| service (worship) | zhurichongbai | office divin | Gottsdienst | servizio | cerimonia | sluzhba | servicio |
| sin | zui-e | péché | Sünde | peccato | pecado | grekh | pecado |
| soul | linghun | âme | Seele | anima | alma | dusha | alma |
| spirit | shengling | esprit | Geist | spirito | espírito | dukh | espíritu |
| testimony | jiansheng | témoignage | Zeugnis | attestazione | testemunho | svidetelstvo | testimonio |
| traditions | chuantong | traditions | Traditions | tradizioni | tradição | traditsii | tradicións |
| Trinity | Sanweiyiti | Trinité | Dreieinigkeit | Trinità | Trindade | Troitsa | Trinidad |
| witness, a | jianzhengren | témoin | Zeuge | teste | testamunha | svidetel | testigo |
| worship | chongbai | adoration | Anbeten | adorare | adoração | poklonenie | adorar |

## Table 32–2.  Names of countries in 6 major languages.

Hundreds of millions of Christian workers have to live their lives and do their work, including their Christian service, in multilingual situations. Tens of thousands of Christian denominations, churches, organizations, missions, and orders must communicate and function in many languages. They all must remember that the names of countries change from language to language. This list presents standard short names of all the countries of the world in 6 major Christian languages. Not all of the official UN languages are here (Russian, Chinese, and Arabic are excluded). German, for example, is not an official language for the UN, though it is for the WCC, a fact that shows its special importance in international Christian communication. This entire WCE/WCT/WCD project seeks to present Christianity in the global, international context, though it must be written in one language. With this list, those many Christians interested and involved in the global context will be able to refer to the nations of the world in more than one language, which can prove not only useful but important.

| English | French | German | Italian | Portuguese | Spanish |
|---|---|---|---|---|---|
| Afghanistan | Afghanistan | Afghanistan | Afghanistan | Afeganistão | Afganistán |
| Albania | Albanie | Albanien | Albania | Albania | Albania |
| Algeria | Algéria | Algerian | Algeria | Algélia | Argelia |
| American Samoa | Samoa Américaine | Amerikanisch-Samoa | Samoa Americane | Samoa Americana | Samoa Americana |
| Andorra | Andorre | Andorra | Andorra | Andorra | Andorra |
| Angola | Angola | Angolo | Angola | Angola | Angola |
| Anguilla | Anguilla | Anguilla | Anguilla | Anguilla | Anguila |
| Antarctica | Antarctique | Antarkis | Anartide | Antártico | Antártico |
| Antigua & Barbuda | Antigua | Antigua | Antigua | Antigua | Antigua |
| Argentina | Argentine | Argentinien | Argentina | Argentina | Argentina |
| Armenia | Arménie | Armenian | Armenia | Armenia | Armenia |
| Aruba | Aruba | Aruba | Aruba | Aruba | Aruba |
| Australia | Australie | Australien | Australia | Austrâlia | Australia |
| Austria | Autriche | Osterreich | Austria | Austria | Austria |
| Azerbaijan | Azerbaïdjan | Azerbaijien | Azerbaijan | Azerbaijan | Azerbaiyan |
| Bahamas | Bahamas | Bahamainsein | Bahama | Baamas | Bahamas |
| Bahrain | Bahrein | Bahrein | Bahrein | Barhein | Bahrain |
| Bangladesh | Bangladesh | Bangladesch | Bangladesh | Bangladesh | Bangladesh |
| Barbados | Barbade | Barbados | Barbados | Barbados | Barbados |
| Belgium | Belgique | Belgien | Belgio | Bélgica | Bélgica |
| Belize | Belize | Belize | Belize | Blize | Belice |
| Belorussia | Bélarus | Belarußland | Belarus | Belarús | Belarús |
| Benin | Bénin | Benin | Benin | Benin | Benin |
| Bermuda | Bermudes | Bermudsinsein | Bermuda | Bermudas | Bermudas |
| Bhutan | Bhoutan | Bhutan | Bhutan | Bhutan | Bután (Bhután) |
| Bolivia | Bolivie | Bolivien | Bolivia | Bolívia | Bolivia |
| Bosnia-Herzegovina | Bosnie-Herzégovine | Bosnien-Hertzegovinien | Bosnia-Herzegovina | Bosnia-Herzegovina | Bosnia-Herzegovina |
| Botswana | Botswana | Botswana | Botswana | Botswana | Botswana |
| Bougainville | Bougainville | Bougainville | Bougainville | Bougainville | Bougainville |
| Brazil | Brésil | Brasilien | Brasile | Brasil | Brasil |
| Britain (UK of GB & NI) | Royaume Uni (Grande-Brétagne) | Grossbritannien | Regno Unita (Gran Bretagna) | Reino Unido | Reino Unido |
| British Indian OceanTerritory | Territoire Britannique de l'Océan Indien | Britisches Indischer Ozean Territorium | Territorio Britannico dell'Oceano Indiano | Território Britânico do Oceano Indico | Territorio Británico del Océano Indico |
| British Virgin Islands | Iles Vierges Britanniques | Britisch Jungferninseln | Vergini Isole (GB) | Ilhas Virgens Britânicas | Islas Virgenes Británicas |
| Brunei | Brunéi | Brunei | Brunei | Brunei | Brunei |
| Bulgaria | Bulgarie | Bulgarien | Bulgaria | Bulgaria | Bulgaria |
| Burkina Faso | Burkina Faso | Burkina Faso | Burkina Faso | Burkina Faso | Burkina Faso |
| Burundi | Burundi | Burundi | Burundi | Burundi | Burundi |
| Cambodia | Cambodge | Kambodscha | Cambodia | Comboja | Camboya |
| Cameroon | Cameroun | Kamerun | Camerun | Camarões | Camerú |
| Canada | Canada | Kanada | Canadà | Canadá | Canadá |
| Cape Verde | Cap-Vert | Kap-verdische Inseln | Isole del Capo Verde | Cabo Verde | Cabo Verde |
| Cayman Islands | Iles Caimanes | Kaiman Inseln | Isole Caiman | Ilhas Caiman | Islas Caimán |
| Central African Republic | République Centrafricaine | Zentralafrikanisches Republik | Repubblica Centrafricana | República Centro-Africana | República Centroafricana |
| Chad | Tchad | Tschad | Ciad | Chade | Chad |
| Channel Islands | Iles Anglo-Normandes | Kanal Inseln | Isole del Canel | Ilhas Canal | Islas del Canal |
| Chile | Chili | Chile | Cile | Chile | Chile |
| China | Chine | China | Cina | China | China |
| Christmas Island | Ile Christmas | Weihnachtinsel | Isola Christmas | Ilha Natal | Isla Christmas |
| Cocos (Keeling) Islands | Iles des Cocos (Keeling) | Kokos-Inseln | Isole Cocos (Keeling) | Ilhas Cocos (Keeling) | Islas Cocos (Keeling) |
| Colombia | Colombie | Kolombien | Colombia | Colômbia | Colombia |
| Comoros | Comores | Komoren | Comore | Comores | Comores |
| Congo-Brazzaville | Congo Brazzaville | Congo Brazzaville | Kongo Brazzaville | Congo Brazzaville | Congo Brazzaville |
| Congo-Zaire | Congo-Zaïre | Congo-Zaire | Kongo Zaire | Congo-Zaire | Congo-Zaire |
| Cook Islands | Iles Cook | Cook-Inseln | Isole Cook | Ilhas Cook | Islas Cook |
| Costa Rica | Costa Rica | Costerica | Costa Rica | Costa Rica | Costa Rica |
| Croatia | Croatie | Croatien | Croatia | Croacia | Croacia |
| Cuba | Cuba | Cuba | Cuba | Cuba | Cuba |
| Cyprus | Chypre | Zypern | Cipro | Chipre | Chipre |
| Czech Republic | République tchèque | Tschechisch Republik | Repubblica Ceca | República Checa | República Checa |
| Denmark | Danemark | Dänemark | Danimarca | Danamarca | Dinamarca |
| Djibouti | Djibouti | Dschibuti | Djibouti | Djibouti | Djibouti |
| Dominica | Dominique | Dominica | Dominica | Dominica | Dominica |
| Dominican Republic | République Dominicaine | Dominikanische Republik | Repubblica Dominicana | República Dominicana | República Dominicana |
| Ecuador | Equateur | Equador | Ecuador | Equador | Ecuador |
| Egypt | Egypte | Agypten | Egitto | Egito | Egipto |
| El Salvador | El Salvador | El Salvador | El Salvador | El Salvador | El Salvador |
| Equatorial Guinea | Guinée Equatoriale | Aquatorial-Guinea | Guinea Equatoriale | Guiné Equatorial | Guinea Ecuatorial |
| Eritrea | Erythrée | Eritreien | Eritrea | Eritrea | Eritrea |
| Estonia | Estonie | Estonien | Estonia | Estonia | Estonia |
| Ethiopia | Ethiopie | Athiopien | Etiopia | Etiopia | Etiopía |
| Faeroe Islands | Iles Féroé | Fäöer Inseln | Isole Faroë | Ilhas Feroe | Islas Feroe |
| Falkland Islands | Iles Falkland | Falklandinseln | Isole Falkland | Ilhas Malvinas | Islas Malvinas |
| Fiji | Fidji | Fidschi | Figi | Fiji | Fiji |
| Finland | Finlande | Finnland | Finlandia | Finlândia | Finlandia |
| France | France | Frankreich | Francia | França | Francia |
| French Guiana | Guyane Française | Französisch-Guyana | Guyana Francese | Guyana Francesa | Guayana Francesa |
| French Polynesia | Polynésie Française | Französisch-Polynesien | Polinesia Francese | Polinésia Francesa | Polinesia Francesa |
| Gabon | Gabon | Gabun | Gabon | Gabão | Gabón |
| Gambia | Gambie | Gambia | Gambia | Gambia | Gambia |
| Germany | Allemagne | Deutschland | Germania | Alemanha | Alemania |
| Ghana | Ghana | Ghana | Ghana | Gana | Ghana |
| Gibraltar | Gibraltar | Gibraltar | Giliterra | Gibraltar | Gibraltar |
| Greece | Grèce | Griechenland | Grecia | Grécia | Grecia |
| Greenland | Groenland | Grönland | Groenlandia | Gronelândia | Groenlandia |
| Grenada | Grenade | Grenada | Grenada | Grenada | Granada |
| Guadeloupe | Guadeloupe | Guadeloupe | Guadalupa | Guadalupe | Guadalupe |
| Guam | Guam | Guam | Guam | Guam | Guam |
| Guatemala | Guatemala | Guatemala | Guatemala | Guatemala | Guatemala |
| Guinea | Guinée | Guinea | Guinea | Guiné | Guinea |
| Guinea-Bissau | Guinée-Bissau | Guinea-Bissau | Guinea-Bissau | Guiné-Bissau | Guinea-Bissau |
| Guyana | Guyane | Guayana | Guyana | Guiana | Guayana |
| Haiti | Haïti | Haiti | Haiti | Haití | Haití |
| Holy See | Saint-Siège | Heilige Stuhl | Santa Sede | Santa Sé | Santa Sede |
| Honduras | Honduras | Honduras | Honduras | Honduras | Honduras |
| Hungary | Hongrie | Ungarn | Ungheria | Hungria | Hungría |
| Iceland | Islande | Island | Islanda | Islândia | Islandia |
| India | Inde | Indien | India | India | India |
| Indonesia | Indonésie | Indonesien | Indonesia | Indonésia | Indonesia |
| Iran | Iran | Iran | Iran | Irã | Irán |
| Iraq | Irak | Irak | Iraq | Iraque | Iraq |
| Ireland | Irlande | Irland | Irlanda | Irlanda | Irlanda |
| Isle of Man | Ile de Man | Insel Man | Isola Man | Ilha de Man | Isla de Man |
| Israel | Israël | Israel | Israele | Israel | Israel |
| Italy | Italie | Italien | Italia | Itália | Italia |
| Ivory Coast | Côte d'Ivoire | Elfenbeinküste | Costa d'Avorio | Costa do Marfim | Costa de Marfil |
| Jamaica | Jamaïque | Jamaika | Giamaica | Jamaica | Jamaica |
| Japan | Japon | Japan | Giappone | Japão | Japón |
| Jordan | Jordanie | Jordanien | Giordania | Jordania | Jordania |
| Kazakhstan | Kazakstan | Kazakstan | Kazakstan | Kazajstán | Kazajstán |
| Kenya | Kenya | Kenia | Kenya | Quênia | Kenia (Kenya) |
| Kirghizia | Kirghizistan | Kirgiztan | Kirgiztan | Kirgistán | Kirguistán |
| Kiribati | Iles Gilbert | Gilbert Inseln | Isole Gilbert | Ilhas Gilbert | Islas Gilbert |

## Table 32–3. Index of Christian and religious abbreviations, acronyms, and initials, listed alphabetically by initials.

Some 8,000 sets of initials, most being abbreviations of the names of organizations, are widely used by Christians around the world, or are used in their extensive literature across the 20th century. This index lists, alphabetically by initials, a representative selection of some 2,570 of them. First are all recognized and widely-used abbreviations used in this volume and in the whole *WCE/WCT/WCD* project (excluding codes designed only for this volume, which are given in Part 16 "GeoCodebook"); second are acronyms (names as words formed from the initial letters of other words); third are initials of Christian and religious bodies in widespread or international use; fourth are a select few other abbreviations, not of organizations, but commonly used by Christians (e.g. KJV). The vast majority relate to Christian and religious organizations, with a few widely-used secular abbreviations.

As this is a simple quick-reference tool, translations into other languages are not usually given, nor additional identification, description, or explanation. Most bodies may be identified further from various other resources in *WCT* Part 17 or *WCE* Part 14 "Directory". In some cases, the initials do not match the name given, because the commonly-used initials come from one language while the commonly-used name comes from another. This is especially true for Roman Catholic religious orders and congregations, whose initials are usually taken from Latin. Although this index deals predominantly with the abbreviations of names and titles in the main European language they are used in, in a number of cases their counterpart initials in other international languages are also given, with equivalents (e.g. WCC=COE=OKR). In cases where the same initials are used by 2 different bodies, both usages are given. Most of the organizations listed here are still in existence under the names shown, but a small proportion no longer exist or have changed their names; they are given here for historical interest and ease of identification. In many cases, both older and newer names are given (e.g. CIM and OMF, same body, name changed 50 years ago).

An interesting trend of recent decades is that many mission organizations have jettisoned outdated names without departing from well-known initials, resulting in new names that are curious cross-breeds of form. Thus, e.g. Bible Churchmen's Missionary Society became BCMS Crosslinks, Central American Mission became CAM International, Overseas Crusades became OC International, Oriental Missionary Society became OMS International, Regions Beyond Missionary Union became RBMU International (now World Team), Sudan Interior Mission became SIM International, Unevangelized Fields Mission became UFM International, Worldwide Evangelization Crusade became WEC International, and the Conservative Baptist Foreign Mission Society became CBInternational. These new names are, in fact, names, and not still acronyms—the organizations have deliberately departed from earlier implied geographical restrictions or unpleasant terms (e.g. 'crusade'). That they have deliberately adopted new names with such awkward forms shows the power and importance of initials and acronyms.

Many thousands of initials and abbreviations used in the Christian world are not included here. This listing emphasizes global organizations and organizations of international influence, thus excluding (1) initials of churches and denominations within a country, except major plurinational or global ones, (2) most organizations at the subnational level, and (3) a number at the national level, too. For these, see the individual country articles and tables in *WCE* Part 4 "Countries". National denominations and organizations whose influence spreads over many nations are more likely to be included.

Note the following abbreviations in some names: Ev (Evangelical), Ch or Chs (church,-es), Egl (Eglise), Ig or Igl (Iglesia).

# A

| | |
|---|---|
| AA | apostolic administration |
| AA | Assumptionists (Augustinians of the Assumption) |
| AABF | All Africa Baptist Fellowship |
| AACC | All Africa Conference of Churches |
| AACJM | African Apostolic Church of Johane Maranke |
| AAM | American Advent Mission |
| AAPC | Adopt-a-People Clearinghouse |
| AB | Augsburg Bekenntnis/Confession |
| ABC | African Brotherhood Church |
| ABCFM | American Board of Commissioners for Foreign Missions |
| ABCIM | American Baptist Churches in the USA, International Ministries |
| ABCUSA | American Baptist Churches in the USA |
| ABFMS | American Baptist Foreign Mission Society |
| ABHMS | American Baptist Home Mission Societies |
| ABM | Australian Board of Missions |
| ABMS | Australian Baptist Missionary Society |
| ABOSG | Association of Believers in One Supreme God |
| ABS | American Bible Society |
| ABWE | Association of Baptists for World Evangelism |
| AC | Apostolic Church (Great Britain) |
| ACAC | American Christian Action Council |
| ACBC | Australian Catholic Bishops' Conference |
| ACC | Advent Christian Church |
| ACC | Anglican Consultative Council |
| ACC | Anguilla Christian Council |
| ACC | Australian Council of Churches |
| ACCC | American Council of Christian Churches |
| ACCC | Australian Consultative Council of ICCC |
| ACE | Action Catholique de l'Enfance |
| ACE | Ayuda Cristiana Evangélica (Christian Aid) |
| ACEACCAM | Association des Conférences Episcopales de l'Afrique Centrale et du Cameroun |
| ACECCT | Association des Conférences Episcopales du Congo/RCA/Tchad |
| ACERAC | Association des Conferences Episcopales de la Region de Afrique Centrale |
| ACF | Action Catholique Familiale |
| ACF | Asociación Cristiana Femenina (YWCA) |
| ACGF | Action Catholique Générale des Femmes |
| ACGH | Action Catholique Générale des Hommes |
| ACI | Action Catholique des Milieux Indépendants |
| ACIERA | Argentine Alliance of Evangelical Churches |
| ACIERU | Asociacion Cristiana de Iglesias Ev de Uruguay |
| ACISJF | Association Catholique Internationale des Services de la Jeunesse Féminine |
| ACJ | Asociación Cristiana de Jovenes (YMCA) |
| ACKD | Arbeitsgemeinschaft Christlicher Kirchen in der BRD |
| ACKDDR | Arbeitsgemeinschaft Christlicher Kirchen in der DDR |
| ACKS | Arbeitsgemeinschaft Christlicher Kirchen in der Schweiz |
| ACKS | Swiss Christian Council of Churches |
| ACM | Alliance Chrétienne Missionnaire |
| ACMC | Advancing Churches in Missions Commitment |
| ACMC | Association of Church Missions Committees |
| ACMM | Apostolic Church Missionary Movement |
| ACNAC | Anglican Council of North America & the Caribbean |
| ACO | Action Catholique Ouvrière |
| ACP | Apostolic Church of Pentecost |
| ACROSS | Africa Committee for the Rehabilitation of the Southern Sudan |
| ACTS | Asia Center for Theological Studies and Mission |
| ACU | Action Catholique Universitaire |
| AD | Anno Domini (In the Year of Our Lord) |
| AD | archdiocese |
| AdD | Asambleas de Dios |
| AdD | Assemblées de Dieu |
| ADEOPA | Association des Eglises et Oeuvres Protestants en Algérie |
| ADIL | Angkatan Democratic Liberal Sabah |
| AE | African Enterprise |
| AEA | Albanian Evangelical Alliance |
| AEA | Association of Evangelicals of Africa |
| AEA | Australian Evangelical Alliance |
| AEAM | Association of Evangelicals of Africa and Madagascar |
| AEBET | Asociación Evangélica Boliviana de Educación Teológica |
| AEBG | Asociación Evangelistica de Billy Graham |
| AEC | Alianza Evangélica Costarricense |
| AEC | Antilles Episcopal Conference |
| AEC | Association des Eglises Chrétiennes |
| AECB | All-India Ecumenical Coordinating Body |
| AECEWA | Association of Episcopal Conferences of English-speaking West Africa |
| AECSVG | Association of Ev Chs of St Vincent & the Grenadines |
| AECT | Association des Eglises Chretiennes du Togo |
| AEE | African Evangelistic Enterprise |
| AEE | Alianza Evangelica Espanola |
| AEEC | Association des Eglises Evangéliques Centrafricaines |
| AEET | Asociación Evangélica de Educación Teológica |
| AEF | Africa Evangelical Fellowship |
| AEF | Alliance Evangelique Francaise |
| AEF | Asia Evangelistic Fellowship |
| AEG | Alianza Evangélica de Guatemala |
| AEGM | Anglican Evangelical Group Movement |
| AEH | Alianza Evangélica Hondureña |
| AEI | Alleanza Evangelica Italiana |
| AEL | Association of Evangelicals of Liberia |
| AELC | Association of Evangelical Lutheran Churches |
| AEM | Arbeitsgemeinschaft Evangelikaler Missionen |
| AEM | Associacao Ev de Mocambique |
| AEP | Aliança Evangélica Portuguesa |
| AEP | Alianza Evangélica de Panamá |
| AEPB | Alliance des Eglises Protestantes du Burundi |
| AERDO | Association of Evangelical Relief and Development Organizations |
| AETTE | Associação Evangélica Teológica para Treinamonto por Extensão |
| AEV | Alianza de Evangelicos |
| AEZ | Alliance Evangelique du Zaire |
| AFI | Auxiliaires Féminines Internationales |
| AFIC | Australian Federation of Islamic Councils |
| AFIPM | Asoc Fraternal de Igls Pentecostales |
| AFM | Anglican Frontier Missions |
| AFM | Apostolic Faith Mission |
| AFMSA | Apostolic Faith Mission of South Africa |
| AFPRO | Action for Food Production Office |
| AFREC | Africa Regional Center, UBS |
| AGC | Associated Gospel Churches |
| AGEMPEM | Association des Egl et Missions Protestants du Mali |
| AHDM | Al Hidayah Dawa Movement |
| AI | artificial intelligence |
| AIC | Africa Inland Church |
| AIC | Association of Independent Churches |
| AICA | African Independent Churches Association |
| AICA | Agencia Informativa Católica Argentina |
| AICC | Aboriginal and Islander Catholic Council |
| AICC | African Independent Churches' Conference |
| AICM | African Independent Churches Movement |
| AICN | African Israel Church Nineveh |
| AICOME | All-India Congress on Missions & Evangelism |
| AICS | African Independent Churches Service |
| AICs | African Indigenous/Independent Churches |
| AIDS | acquired immune deficiency syndrome |
| AIEC | Association of Evangelical Churches of Colombia |
| AIFNC | All-India Federation of National Churches |
| AIL/LIA | Association Interconfessionale du Luxembourg |
| AIM | Africa Inland Mission |
| AIMI | Africa Inland Mission International |
| AIMS | Accelerating International Mission Strategies |
| AIMS | Association of International Mission Services |
| AIPF | All-India Pentecostal Fellowship |
| AIPREM | Alianza de Iglesias Presb y Ref de Mexico |
| AJI | Amar Jyoti India |
| AKC | Arbeitskreis Kritisches Christentum |
| ALC | American Lutheran Church |
| ALCOE | Asian Leadership Conference on Evangelism |
| ALER | Asociación Latinoamericana de Educación Radiofónica |
| ALET | Asociación Latinoamericana de Escuelas Teológicas |
| ALFALIT | Alfabetización y Literatura |
| AM | Antioch Mission |
| AM | audio modulation, amplitude modulation |
| AMA | Asia Missions Association |
| AMAA | Armenian Missionary Association of America |
| AMAC | Medical Aid to Central Africa |
| AMDAC | Aid to Maternity Dispensaries of Central Africa |
| AMEC | African Methodist Episcopal Church |
| AMECEA | Association of Member Episcopal Conferences in Eastern Africa |
| AMEN | American Military Evangelizing Nations |
| AMEN | Asociacíón Misionera Evangélica a Las Naciones |
| AMEZC | African Methodist Episcopal Zion Church |
| AMG | American Mission to Greeks |
| AMORC | Ancient Mystical Order Rosae Crucis |
| AMREC | Americas Regional Center, UBS |
| AMSS | Association of Muslims of Southern Sudan |
| AMTB | Associaçao de Missoes Transculturais Brazileiras |
| AN | abbey nullius |
| ANDEB | Asociación Nacional de Evangélicos de Bolivia |
| AO | autonomous oblast |
| AOC | African Orthodox Church |
| AOCTS | Assemblea degli Ordinari Cattolici di Terra Santa |
| AoG | Assemblies of God |
| AOI | Asian Outreach International |
| AP | Annuario Pontificio |
| APCA | Association of Pentecostal Churches in America |
| APCM | Asia Pacific Christian Mission |
| APCTE | Association for the Promotion of Chinese Theological Education |
| ARCIC | Anglican/Roman Catholic International Commission |
| ARE | Assoc for Research & Enlightenment |
| ARENSA | Asociación Regional Episcopal del Norte del Sud América |
| ARIF | Arakan Rohingya Islamic Front |
| ARM | Anglican Renewal Ministries |
| ARMS | Amateur Radio Missionary Service |
| ARPC | Associate Reformed Presbyterian Church |
| ARZA | Association of Reform Zionists of America |
| ASGM | American Scripture Gift Mission |
| ASIT | Asociación Sudamericana de Instituciones Teológicas |
| ASO | Apostolado Seglar Organizado |
| ASPREC | Asia Pacific Regional Center, UBS |
| ASSR | Autonomous Soviet Socialist Republic |
| ASTE | Associação de Seminarios Teológicos Evangélicos |
| ASV | American Standard Version (of the Bible) |
| ATENE | Association for Theological Education in the Near East |
| AUCECB | All-Union Council of Evangelical Christians-Baptists |
| AV | Augsburg Confession |
| AV | Authorized Version (of the Bible) |
| AVC | Association of Vineyard Churches |
| AWCF | Apostolic World Christian Fellowship |
| AWE | Associates for World Evangelization |
| AWE | Association for World Evangelism |
| AWF | Alliance World Fellowship |
| AWM | Arab World Ministries |
| AZASA | Assembly of Zionist & Apostolic Churches of South Africa |

# B

| | |
|---|---|
| B | Barnabites (Clerics Regular of St Paul) |
| BAM | Brazilian Association of Missions |
| BAVACO | Broadcasting and Audio-Visual Aids Committee |
| BB | Boys' Brigade |
| BB | Bush Brotherhood |
| BBC | British Broadcasting Corporation |
| BBFI | Baptist Bible Fellowship International |
| BBS | bulletin board system |
| BC | Before Christ |
| BCAS | Bush Church Aid Society |
| BCC | Belize Christian Council |
| BCC | Bible correspondence course |
| BCC | Botswana Christian Council |

| | |
|---|---|
| BCC | British Council of Churches |
| BCE | Before Christian Era, or Before Common Era |
| BCEC | Barbados Council of Evangelical Churches |
| BCEOM | Bureau Central d'Etude pour les Equipements d'Outre Mer |
| BCF | Bangladesh Christian Fellowship |
| BCMC | Belgian Christian Missionary Church |
| BCMS | BCMS Crosslinks |
| BCMS | Bible Churchmen's Missionary Society |
| BCOQ | Baptist Churches of Ontario and Quebec |
| BCPCU | Bishops' Commission for Promoting Christian Unity |
| BCS | Bishops' Conference of Scotland |
| BCSC | Belize Christian Social Council |
| BCSL | Bishops' Conference of Sri Lanka |
| BCU | Bible Christian Union |
| BCWM | Brethren in Christ World Missions |
| BD | bachelor of divinity |
| BDKJ | Bund der Deutschen Katholischen Jugend |
| BEC | British Evangelical Council |
| BECs | basic ecclesial communities |
| BEM | Belgian Evangelical Mission |
| BEM | Borneo Evangelical Mission |
| BERRS | Bangladesh Ecumenical Relief & Rehabilitation Service |
| BFBS | British & Foreign Bible Society |
| BFM | Bethany Fellowship Missions |
| BFM | Board of Foreign Missions |
| BFTW | Bibles For The World |
| BGC | Baptist General Conference |
| BGEA | Billy Graham Evangelistic Association |
| BGM | Board of Global Ministries |
| BiCC | Brethren in Christ Church |
| BICE | Bureau International Catholique de l'Enfance |
| BIM | Baptist International Missions |
| BIM | Bureau d'Information Missionnaire |
| BIP | Bureau d'Information Protestant |
| BJP | Bharata Janata Parishad |
| BKBIH | Episcopal Conference of Bosnia-Herzegovina |
| BKED | Bund Katholischer Erzieher Deutschlands |
| BLASC | Bureau de Liaison d'Action Sociale et Caritative |
| BLI | Bible Literature International |
| BLIROI | Bureau de Liaison de l'Information Religieuse dans l'Océan Indien |
| BLUCE | Bible Lands Union for Christian Education |
| BM | Basel Mission |
| BM | Bibliografia Missionaria |
| BMAA | Baptist Missionary Association of America |
| BMC | Bible Missionary Church |
| BML | Bangladesh Muslim League |
| BMM | Baptist Mid-Missions |
| BMMF | Bible and Medical Missionary Fellowship |
| BMS | Baptist Missionary Society |
| BMT | Bold Mission Thrust |
| BNCC | Bangladesh National Council of Churches |
| BP | boîte postale/post box |
| BPS | Buddhist Publication Society |
| BPT | Bethel Pentecostal Temple |
| BRAVS | Broadcasting and Audio-Visual Services |
| BRF | Bible Reading Fellowship |
| BRS | Biblical Research Society |
| BS | Bible School |
| BUGBI | Baptist Union of GB & Ireland |
| BVM | Bibeltrogner Vänner (Bible True Friends) |
| BWA | Baptist World Alliance |
| BWM | Board of World Ministries |
| BWY | British Wheel of Yoga |
| BYM | Blessing Youth Mission |

## C

| | |
|---|---|
| C | catholicate, diocese of catholicos |
| C | central |
| c | circa (approximately) |
| C&S | Cherubim & Seraphim |
| CA | Catholic Action |
| CA | Church Army |
| CAAC | Council of African & Allied Churches in the UK |
| CAC | Catholic Apostolic Church |
| CAC | Christ Apostolic Church |
| CACC | Central Africa Christian Council |
| CACE | Confederación Argentina Católica de Educadores |
| CADEC | Christian Action for Development in the Caribbean |
| CAF | Church of the Apostolic Faith |
| CAFOD | Catholic Fund for Overseas Development |
| CAHP | Co-ordinating Agency for Health and Planning |
| CAJ | Christliche Arbeitjugen |
| CALA | Consejo Anglicano Latinoamericano |
| CALM | Centro Assistenza Laici Missionari |
| CAM | Central American Mission |
| CAMEO | Committee to Assist Missionary Education Overseas |
| CAMI | CAM International |
| CAN | Christian Association of Nigeria |
| CAPA | Council of Anglican Provinces of Africa |
| CAR | Conferencia Argentina de Religiosos |
| CARA | Christian Action by Radio in Africa |
| CARAVS | Christian Association for Radio Audio-Visual Services |
| CARE | Catholic Action for Racial Education |
| CARE | Citizen's Association for Racial Equality |
| CARF | Christian Amateur Radio Fellowship |
| CARITAS | Catholic Relief Services |
| CARP | Caisse Auxiliaire de Retraites des Ministres du Culte Protestant |
| CASA | Christian Agency for Social Action, Relief and Development |
| CASA | Consejo Anglicano Sud Americano |
| CASC | Confederación Autonoma de Sindicatos Cristianos |
| CATA | Comité Acesor de Textos Autodidacticos |
| CATF | Catholic African Teachers' Federation of South Africa |
| CAVE | Centro Audio-Visual Evangélico |
| CAVEA | Centro Audio-Visual Evangélico de la Argentina |
| CAVISAT | Centre for Audio-Visual Instruction via Satellite |
| CAWD | Churches' Action for World Development |
| CB | citizens band (radio) |
| CBA | Catholic Biblical Association |
| CBA | Catholic Broadcasting Association |
| CBAI | Catholic Biblical Association of India |
| CBCB | Catholic Bishops' Conference of Bangladesh |
| CBCI | Catholic Bishops' Conference of India |
| CBCJ | Catholic Bishops' Conference of Japan |
| CBCK | Catholic Bishops' Conference of Korea |
| CBCP | Catholic Bishops' Conference of the Philippines |
| CBCPNGSI | Catholic Bishops' Conference of PNG & SI |
| CBF | Cooperative Baptist Fellowship |
| CBFMS | Conservative Baptist Foreign Mission Society |
| CBHMS | Conservative Baptist Home Mission Society |
| CBI | CBInternational (Conservative Baptist) |
| CBIM | Canadian Baptist International Ministries |
| CBK | Czech Bishops' Conference |
| CBM | Christadelphian Bible Mission |
| CBMEC | Comité Belge de Mission Evangélique au Congo |
| CBN | Christian Broadcasting Network |
| CBOMB | Canadian Baptist Overseas Mission Board |
| CBS | Christian Broadcasting System |
| CC | Churches of Christ |
| CCA | Christian Conference of Asia |
| CCAC | Comité de Coordination des Mouvements des Jeunes |
| CCAI | Comisión Católica Argentina de Immigración |
| CCANZ | Conference of Churches in Aotearoa/New Zealand |
| CCAP | Church of Central Africa Presbyterian |
| CCB | Christian Congregation of Brazil |
| CCB | Christian Council of Botswana |
| CCBI-LR | Conference of Catholic Bishops of India/Latin Rite |
| CCC | Canadian Catholic Conference/Conférence Catholique Canadienne |
| CCC | Canadian Council of Churches |
| CCC | Caribbean Conference of Churches |
| CCC | Centro Cattolico Cinematografico |
| CCC | Charismatic Concerns Committee |
| CCC | China Christian Council |
| CCC | Christian Catholic Church |
| CCC | Commission on Church Cooperation |
| CCC | Congregational Christian Churches |
| CCCA | Catholic Civics Clubs of America |
| CCCB | Coordinating Committee for Christian Broadcasting |
| CCCC | Caribbean Council of Christian Churches |
| CCCC | Christian Churches & Churches of Christ |
| CCCC | Confederación Colegios Cubanos Católicos |
| CCCE | Council for Co-operation of Churches in Ethiopia |
| CCCG | Council of Christian Churches in Germany |
| CCCI | Campus Crusade for Christ International |
| CCCI | Council of Christian Churches in India |
| CCCS | Committee of Christian Churches in Suriname |
| CCCS | Commonwealth and Continental Church Society |
| CCE | Conseil Canadien des Eglises |
| CCEA | Christian Churches' Educational Association |
| CCEA | Council of the Church in East Asia |
| CCECB | Council of Churches of Evangelical Christians-Baptists |
| CCEE | Consilium Conferentiarum Episcopalium Europae |
| CCEM | Comisión Católica Española de Migración |
| CCEM | Conseil Chretien des Eglises a Madagascar |
| CCEP | Comisión Coordinadora Evangélica de Paraguay |
| CCF | Catholic Communications Foundation |
| CCF | Centro da Cultura Filmica |
| CCF | Christian Children's Fund |
| CCFD | Comité Catholique National contra la Faim et pour le Développement |
| CCG | Christian Council of Ghana |
| CCH | Collegium Catholicum Holmiense |
| CCH/CHC | Czechoslovak Hussite Church |
| CCI | Confraternidad Cristiana de Iglesias |
| CCIA | Commission of the Churches on International Affairs |
| CCIC | Catholic Charismatic Information Center |
| CCID | Center Catholique d'Information Discographique |
| CCII | Catholic Communications Institute of Ireland |
| CCJCA | Caribbean Committee for Joint Christian Action |
| CCJP | Consultation of the Church and the Jewish People |
| CCK | Council of Churches in Kuwait |
| CCL | Christian Council of Lesotho |
| CCM | Christian Council of Malawi |
| CCM | Conselho Cristão de Moçambique |
| CCM | Council of Churches of Malaysia |
| CCMA | Catholic Campus Ministry Association |
| CCMIE | Comité Catholique pour les Migrations Intra-Européennes de la CICM |
| CCN | Christian Council of Nigeria |
| CCN | Council of Churches in the Netherlands |
| CCNA | Christian Church of North America |
| CCOC | Centro Católico de Orientación Cinematográfica |
| CCODP | Canadian Catholic Organization for Development and Peace |
| CCOWE | Chinese Congress on World Evangelization |
| CCOWE | Chinese Coordination Center of World Evangelism |
| CCPD | Commission on the Churches' Participation in Development |
| CCPM | Comisión Católica Peruana de Migración |
| CCR | Catholic Charismatic Renewal |
| CCR | Centro Cattolico Radiofonico |
| CCR | Christian Council of Rhodesia |
| CCRT | Centre Catholique de Radio et Télévision |
| CCS | Church of Christ, Scientist |
| CCSA | Christian Committee for Service in Algeria |
| CCSEA | Council of the Church in South East Asia |
| CCSM | Confédération Chrétienne des Syndicats Malgaches |
| CCSV | Christian Council of St Vincent |
| CCT | Centro Cattolico Teatrale |
| CCT | Christian Council of Tanzania |
| CCT | Council of the Church of Christ in Thailand |
| CCTD | Catholic Council of Thailand for Development |
| CCTM | Centro Collegamenti Tecnici per la Missioni |
| CCTT | Christian Council of Trinidad & Tobago |
| CCTV | Centro Cattolico Televisivo |
| CCUA | Catholic Central Union of America |
| CCVM | Comisión Católica Venezolana de Migración |
| CCW | Caribbean Church Women |
| CCW | Council of Churches for Wales |
| CCWD | Christian Crusade for World Democracy |
| CCWE | Canadian Congress on World Evangelization |
| CCWL | Catholic Council on Working Life |
| CCWM | Congregational Council for World Mission |
| CCYUA | Catholic Central Youth Union of America |
| CCZ | Christian Council of Zambia |
| CDG | Community Development Group |
| CDTCG | Centrale Démocratique des Travailleurs Chrétiens de Guadeloupe |
| CDUCE | Christian Democratic Union of Central Europe |
| CE | Christian Education |
| CE | Christian Era (similar to AD, but used by Jehovah's Witnesses and non-Christians) |
| CE | Common Era (secular replacement for AD) |
| CEA | Confederación Espiritista Argentina |
| CEA | Conferencia Episcopal Argentina |
| CEAP | Catholic Educational Association of the Philippines |
| CEAST | Confèrencia Episcopal de Angola e São Tomé |
| CEB | Confederação Evangélica do Brasil |
| CEB | Conference Episcopale du Benin |
| CEB | Conferencia Episcopal de Bolivia |
| CEBes | comunidades de base |
| CEBFN | Conference des Eveques de Burkina Faso |
| CEC | Centro de Estudios Cristianos |
| CEC | Comisión Episcopal del Clero |
| CEC | Concilio Evangélico de Chile |
| CEC | Confederacion Evangelica de Colombia |
| CEC | Conference Episcopale du Congo |
| CEC | Conference of European Churches |
| CEC | Conferencia Episcopal de Colombia |
| CEC | Conferencia Episcopal de Cuba |
| CEC | Confraternidad Evangelica de Chile |
| CEC | Cruzada Estudiantil para Cristo (Campus Crusade) |
| CECA | Conference Episcopale Centrafricaine |
| CECAB | Conference des Eveques Catholiques du Burundi |
| CECC | Conference des Eveques Catholiques du Canada |
| CECH | Conferencia Episcopal de Chile |
| CECI | Centre d'Etudes et de Coopération International |
| CECI | Comite Espanol de Cooperacion Entre Iglesias |
| CECI | Conference Episcopale de la Cote d'Ivoire |
| CECOR | Conferencia Episcopal de Costa Rica |
| CECOSNE | Centro Educativo de Comunicacões do Nordeste |
| CECOWE | Centrum voor Communicatiewetenschappen |
| CECVN | Confédération des Etudiants Catholiques du Vietnam |
| CED | Conferencia del Episcopado Dominicano |
| CEDA | Centre d'Edition et Diffusion Africaine |
| CEDEC | Confederación Evangélica de Colombia |
| CEDES | Conferencia Episcopal de El Salvador |
| CEDIMA | Centrale d'Editions et de Diffusion de Matériel Audio-Visuel |
| CEDOC | Confederación Ecuatoriana de Organizaciones Sindicales Cristianas |
| CEDOI | Conference Episcopale de l'Ocean Indien |
| CEDUCI | Centro de Educación Cinematograáfica |
| CEE | Conferencia Episcopal Española |
| CEE | Confraternidad Evangélica Ecuatoriana |
| CEE | Consejo Evangélico Español |
| CEEC | Commission Episcopale pour l'Ecole Catholique |
| CEECA | Conférence des Evêques de l'Empire Centrafricaine |
| CEEEFE | Commission des Eglises Evangéliques d'Expression Française a l'Extérieur |
| CEEH | Conseil des Eglises Evangéliques d'Haiti |
| CEEP | Comité Central Evangélico en el Paraguay |
| CEF | Child Evangelism Fellowship |
| CEF | Conference des Eveques de France |
| CEF | Conférence Episcopale de France |
| CEFOD | Centre d'Etudes et de Formation pour le Développement |
| CEG | Conference Episcopale de la Guinee |
| CEG | Conference Episcopale du Gabon |
| CEG | Conferencia Episcopal de Guatemala |
| CEG | Conferentia Episcopolis Graeciae |
| CEGE | Conference Episcopal de Guinea Ecuatorial |
| CEH | Conférence Episcopale d'Haiti |
| CEH | Conferencia Episcopal de Honduras |
| CEH | Confraternidad Ev de Honduras |
| CEHVN | Conférence Episcopale de Haute-Volta et Niger |
| CEI | Centro Ecuménico de Informaçoes |
| CEI | Christian Equippers International |
| CEI | Conferenza Episcopale Italiana |
| CEIAL | Movimento Laici per l'America Latina |
| CEL | Conferentia Episcopalis Lettoniae |
| CEL | Conferentia Episcopalis Lituaniae |

| | |
|---|---|
| CELA | Catholics for Latin America |
| CELA | Conferencia Evangélica Latinoamericana |
| CELAC | Conférence Episcopale du Laos et Cambodge |
| CELADEC | Comisión Evangélica Latinoamericana de Educación Cristiana |
| CELAM | Consejo Episcopal Latinoamericano |
| CELIM | Centro Laici Italiani per le Missioni |
| CELRA | Conférence des Evêques Latins dans les Régions Arabes |
| CEM | Centro Educazione Missionario |
| CEM | Confederación Evangélico Mundial |
| CEM | Conference Episcopale de Madagascar |
| CEM | Conference Episcopale du Mali |
| CEM | Conferencia del Episcopado Mexicano |
| CEM | Conferência Episcopal de Moçambique |
| CEME | Comité Episcopal des Missions à l'Extérieur |
| CEMJ | Centre d'Enseignement des Monitrices de la Jeunesse |
| CEMS | Church of England Men's Society |
| CEN | Conferencia Episcopal de Nicaragua |
| CENAMI | Centro Nacional de Ayuda a las Misiones Indigenas |
| CENC | Conference Episcopale Nationale du Cameroun |
| CENCOS | Centro Nacional de Comunicación Social |
| CENDAC | Centro d'Azione Culturale |
| CENFO | Centre de Formation Socio-Pastorale |
| CENM | Christian Echoes National Ministry |
| CENPRO | Centro de Producción y Formación |
| CEOC | Centro de Orientación Cinematográfica |
| CEOSS | Coptic Evangelical Organization for Social Services |
| CEP | Centre d'Etudes Pastorales |
| CEP | Conferencia Episcopal de Panamá |
| CEP | Conferencia Episcopal Paraguaya |
| CEP | Conferencia Episcopal Peruana |
| CEP | Conferencia Episcopal Puertorriqueña |
| CEP | Congregation for the Evangelization of Peoples |
| CEPA | Comité Evangélico Permanente Ayuda |
| CEPAC | Conférence des Evêques du Pacifique |
| CEPAD | Comité Evangélico pro Ayuda al Desarrollo |
| CEPM | Conférencia Episcopal Portuguese da Metrópole |
| CEPR | Concilio Evangélico de Puerto Rico |
| CEPRHU | Centro de Promoción Humana del Nordeste |
| CEPZA | Conseil des Eglises Protestantes du Zaire |
| CEQ | Corporation des Enseignants du Québec |
| CER | Conference Episcopale du Rwanda |
| CER | Conferencia Ecuatoriana de Religiosos |
| CER | Romanian Catholic Episcopal Conference |
| CERAO | Conférence Episcopale Régionale de l'Afrique Occidentale Francophone |
| CERCA | Conférence des Evêques de la RCA |
| CERJ | Centro de Ecumenismo do Rio de Janeiro |
| CERNA | Conference Episcopal Regional du Nord de l'Afrique |
| CES | Conference des Eveques Suisses |
| CES | Conferentia Episcopalis Scandiae |
| CES | Confraternidad Evangelica Salvadorena |
| CESI | Centro Editoriale Studi |
| CESM | Conférence Episcopale de Sénégal—Mauritanie |
| CESSAC | Church of England Soldiers', Sailors' & Airmens' Clubs |
| CET | Conference Episcopale du Tchad |
| CET | Conference Episcopale du Togo |
| CETA | Conférence des Eglises de Toute l'Afrique (AACC) |
| CETAD | Centre d'Enseignement Théologique à Distance |
| CETE | Centro Experimental de TV Educación |
| CETEDI | Centre des Techniques de Diffusion et Relations Publiques |
| CETMI | Comité des Eglises auprès des Travailleurs Migrants |
| CEU | Conferencia Episcopal del Uruguay |
| CEU | Conferenza Episcopale Ucraina |
| CEV | Conferencia Episcopal Venezolana |
| CEV | Consejo Evangélico de Venezuela |
| CEV | Contemporary English Version (of the Bible) |
| CEVAA | Communauté Evangélique d'Action Apostolique |
| CEVN | Conference Episcopale du Viet Nam |
| CEYA | Caribbean Ecumenical Youth Action |
| CEZ | Conférence Episcopale du Congo-Zaire |
| CFA | Congregation of Alexian Brothers |
| CFAN | Christ For All Nations |
| CFC | Campaign for Christ |
| CFC | Council of Free Churches |
| CFC | Fratelli Cristiani |
| CFCCCF | Catholic Fraternity of Charismatic Covenant Communities and Fellowships |
| CFCCF | Council of Free Christians & Churches in Finland |
| CFCH | Council of Free Churches in Hungary |
| CFCJ | Conselho da Fraternidade Cristà-Judaica |
| CFD | Christlicher Friedensdienst |
| CFEC | Confederacion Fundamentalista de Igl Ev de Chile |
| CFGC | Chaplaincy of Full Gospel Churches |
| CFIM | Christ for India Movement |
| CFMMA | Fratelli della Misericordia di Santa Maria Ausiliatrice |
| CFMSA | Catholic Foreign Mission Society of America |
| CFO | Camps Farthest Out |
| CFP | Fratelli Poveri di San Francesco Serafico |
| CFS | Congregation of the Priestly Fraternity |
| CFSM | Christian Family and Social Movement |
| CFTC | Confédération Française des Travailleurs Chrétiens |
| CFX | Brothers of St Francis Xavier |
| CGAL | Conseil Général de l'Apostolat des Laïcs |
| CGBD | Christlicher Gewerkschaftsbund Deutschlands |
| CGEA | Church of God in East Africa |
| CGH | Church of God Holiness |
| CGI | Church Growth International |
| CGM | Church Growth Movement |
| CGNA | Churches of God in North America (General Eldership) |
| CGP | Church of God of Prophecy |
| CHA | Catholic Hospital Association |
| CHA | Christian Holiness Association |
| CHAG | Christian Hospital Association of Ghana |
| CHC | Calvary Holiness Church |
| CHC | Christian Holiday Crusade |
| CHFD | Commission Haitienne des Eglises pour le Développement |
| CHIEF | Christian Hope Indian Eskimo Fellowship |
| CHR | Conférence Haitienne des Religieux |
| CHSFM | Committee on the Holy Spirit and Frontier Missions |
| CIA | China Islamic Association |
| CIAC | Centro Italiano Addestramento Cinematografico |
| CIAE | Conselho das Igrejas Angolanas Evangélicas |
| CIC | Centrum Informationis Catholicum |
| CIC | Christian Information Center |
| CIC | Consejo de Iglesias de Cuba |
| CICC | Christian Interconfessional Consultative Committee |
| CICC | Cook Islands Christian Church |
| CICM | Commission Internationale Catholique pour les Migrations |
| CICM | Missionaries of Scheut (Immaculate Heart of Mary Mission Society) (Scheutists) |
| CICOP | Catholic Inter-American Cooperation Program |
| CIDAL | Centre International de Documentation Audio-Visuelle |
| CIDER | Centro Italiano Documentari Educativi Religiosi |
| CIDEV | Centre d'Information sur le Développement |
| CIDSE | Coopération Internationale pour le Développement Socio Economique |
| CIEC | Confederación Interamericana de Educación Catótica |
| CIEF | Centro de Investigaciones y Estudios Familiares |
| CIEF | Confederação das Igrejas Evangélicas Fundamentalistas |
| CIEFB | Confederation of Fundamental Ev Chs of Bolivia |
| CIEGE | Council of Ev Chs in Equatorial Guinea |
| CIEMAL | Council of Evangelical Methodist Churches in Latin America |
| CIIC | Concilio Internacional de Iglesias Cristianas (ICCC) |
| CIIR | Catholic Institute for International Relations |
| CIM | China Inland Mission |
| CIM | Comité des Instituts Missionnaires |
| CIMADE | Comité Inter-Mouvements auprès des Evacués |
| CIMIADE | Commission des Institutions et Mouvements Internationaux Apostoliques des Enfants |
| CIMS | Consociatio Internationalis Musicae Sacrae |
| CIO | Centro de Información y Orientación |
| CIO | Church Information Office |
| CIOEW | Catholic Information Office for England and Wales |
| CIP | Centre d'Information de Presse |
| CIPBC | Church of India, Pakistan, Burma, and Ceylon |
| CIPL | Commission Interdiocésaine de Pastorale Liturgique |
| CIRH | Conferencia de Institutos Religiosos de Honduras |
| CIRIC | Centre International de Reportages et d'Information Culturelle |
| CIRMA | Conferencia de Institutos Religiosos de México |
| CIS | Catholic Immigrant Service |
| CISL | Confederazione Italiana Sindacati Lavoratori |
| CISM | Conferenza Italiana dei Superiori Maggiori |
| CISR | Conférence Internationale de Sociologie Religieuse |
| CITA | Communications Institute of the Americas |
| CITC | Christian Industrial Training Center |
| CITC | Christian International Travel Club |
| CJ | Josephite Fathers (Congregation of St Joseph) |
| CJA | Christlich-Judische Arbeitsgemeinschaft in der Schweiz |
| CJC | Conseil de la Jeunesse Catholique |
| CJCLdS | Church of Jesus Christ of Latter-day Saints (Mormons) |
| CJM | Eudists (Congregation of Jesus and Mary) |
| CJPM | Central Japan Pioneer Mission |
| CJSS | Conference on Jewish Social Studies |
| CLA | Church of the Lord Aladura |
| CLADE | Congreso Latinoamericano de Evangelización |
| CLAF | Comité Latinoamericano de la Fé |
| CLAI | Concilio Latinoamericano de Iglesias |
| CLAIM | Christian Literature Association in Malawi |
| CLAL | Coopération des Laiques en Amérique Latine |
| CLAME | Comunidad Latinoamericana de Ministerios Evangélicos |
| CLAR | Confederación Latino Americana de Religiosos |
| CLAST | Latin American Federation of Christian Trade Unions |
| CLAT | Latin American Federation of Workers |
| CLATT | Comité Latinoamericano de Textos Teológicos |
| CLB | Church of the Lutheran Brethren |
| CLC | Christian Literature Crusade/Crociata del Libro Cristiano |
| CLIM | Centro Laici Italiani per le Missioni |
| CLS | Christian Literature Society |
| CLSA | Canon Law Society of America |
| CLSA | Christian Literature Service Association |
| CM | Calvary Ministries (Nigeria) |
| CM | Lazzarists (Congregation of the Mission), Vincentians |
| CMA | Christian and Missionary Alliance |
| CMA | Church Music Association |
| CMC | Catholic Media Council |
| CMC | Central Missions Commissariat |
| CMC | Christian Medical Commission |
| CMCC | Council of Muslim Communities of Canada |
| CMCSS | Council of Managers of Catholic Secondary Schools |
| CMCW | Christian Mission to the Communist World |
| CMEC | Christian Methodist Episcopal Church |
| CMF | Christian Family Movement |
| CMF | Christian Missionary Fellowship |
| CMF | Christian Missionary Foundation (Nigeria) |
| CMF | Claretians (Missionary Sons of the Immaculate Heart of Mary) |
| CMF | Franciscan Clarissians |
| CMI | Carmeliani della BV Maria Immacolata |
| CMI | Consejo Mundial de Iglesias (WCC) |
| CMJ | Church's Ministry among the Jews |
| CMM | Congregation of Mariannhill Missionaries |
| CMML | Christian Missions in Many Lands |
| CMN | Conseil Missionnaire National |
| CMRSWI | Conference of Major Religious Superiors of Women's Institutes |
| CMS | Catholic Mission Society |
| CMS | Christian Medical Society |
| CMS | Church Missionary Society (Church Mission Society) |
| CMSF | Missionary Congregation of St Francis of Assisi |
| CMSM | Conference of Major Superiors of Men's Institutes |
| CMT | Confédération Mondiale du Travail |
| CMWF | Christian Medical Workers' Fellowship |
| CNBB | Conferência Nacional dos Bispos do Brasil |
| CNEB | Conseil National des Eglises du Burundi |
| CNEC | Christian Nationals Evangelism Commission |
| CNEP | Concilio Nacional Evangélico del Peru |
| CNEP | Confederación Nacional Escuelas Particulares |
| CNEWA | Catholic Near East Welfare Association |
| CNG | Christlich Nationaler Gewerkschaftsbund der Schweiz |
| CNI | Catholic News Service of India |
| CNI | Church of North India |
| CNIR | Conferencia Nacional dos Institutos Religiosos |
| CNM | Conseil National Missionnaire |
| CNPC | Centre National de Presse Catholique |
| CNPL | Centre National de Pastorale Liturgique |
| CNSP | Catholic News Service of Pakistan |
| CoB | Church of the Brethren |
| COC | Centro de Orientación Cinematográfica |
| CoC | Church of Christ |
| COC | Coptic Orthodox Church |
| COCC | Confederación de Obreros y Campesinos Cristianos |
| COCC | Conference de Obispos Catolicos de Cuba |
| COCDYC | Conservative & Christian Democratic Youth Community |
| COCU | Church of Christ Uniting |
| COCU | Consultation on Church Union |
| COCU | Council on Christian Unity |
| CODEL | Cooperation in Development |
| CODEPA | Centro de Orieniação e Documentação do Ensino Particular |
| CODIAM | Committee for the Development of Intellectual Investments in Africa & Madagascar |
| COE | Conseil Oecuménique des Eglises (WCC) |
| COEM | Comité Oecuménique d'Entr'aide au Maroc |
| COEMAR | Commission on Ecumenical Mission and Relations |
| COEMAS | Congress on Evangelism for Malaysia and Singapore |
| COFAE | Co-ordinating Office for Asian Evangelism |
| CofE | Church of England |
| CoG | Church of God |
| CoGiC | Church of God in Christ |
| CoGWM | Church of God World Missions |
| COJO | World Conference of Jewish Organizations |
| COLJCB | Church of Our Lord Jesus Christ (Bickertonites) |
| COM | Centro de Orientacáo Missionária |
| COMBASE | Comisión Bolivianā do Acción Social Evangélica |
| COMIBAM | Ibero-American Missions Committee |
| COMIBAM | Ibero-American Missions Congress |
| COMINA | Conselho Missionário Nacional |
| CoN | Church of the Nazarene |
| CONCUR | Confederación Cubana de Religiosos |
| CONDOR | Confederación Dominicana de Religiosos |
| CONELA | Confraternidad Evangélica Latinoamericana |
| CONELCO | Conseil des Eglises Libres du Congo |
| CONEMEX | Confraternidad Evangelica Mexicana |
| Conf | conference |
| CONFER | Conferencia Argentina de Religiosas |
| CONFER | Conferencia de Religiosos |
| CONFER | Conferencia Española de Religiosos |
| CONFER | Conferencia Nacional Nicaraguense de Institutos Religiosos |
| CONFERRE | Conferencia de Religiosos de Chile |
| CONFREGUA | Conferencia de Religiosos y Religiosas de Guatemala |
| CONFRES | Confederación de Religiosos de El Salvador |
| CONIC | Conselho Nacional de Ig Cristas do Brasil |
| CONVER | Conferencia Venezolana de Religiosos |
| COp | Calasantini (Congregation of St Joseph Calasanctius for Christian Works) |
| COPAL | Collège pour l'Amérique Latine |
| COPE | Cadena de Ondas Populares Españolas |
| COPIC | Conselho Português de Igrejas Cristãs |
| CORDAC | Central Africa Broadcasting Company |
| CORE | Committee for Overseas Relief |
| COREB | Conférence des Ordinaires du Rwanda et du Burundi |
| CORPORI | Conferencia de Religiosas de Puerto Rico |
| CORR | Christian Organization for Relief and Rehabilitation |
| CORSO | Council of Organizations for Relief Services Over- |

EPF    European Pentecostal Fellowship
EPIS    Enseignement par l'Image et par le Son
EPS    Ecumenical Press Service
ERA    Educational (Renewal) Agency
ERBOL    Escuelas Radiofónicas de Bolivia
ERF    Educational Renewal Fund
ERV    English Revised Version (of the Bible)
ESA    Evangelization Society of Australia
ESCEAL    Estudios Sociológicos dul Cristianismo Evangélico en America Latina
ESG    Evangelische Studentengemeinde in Osterreich
ESII    Ecumenical Social & Industrial Institute
ESP    Ecumenical Sharing of Personnel
esp    especially
ESP    extra-sensory perception (telepathy)
ESYSME    Ecumenical Secretariat for Youth and Students of the Middle East
et al    & others
et alia    & other things
et alii    & other people
ETS    Evangelical Theological Society
EUB    Evangelical United Brethren
EUREC    Europe Regional Center, UBS
EUSA    Evangelical Union of South America
eV    eingetragener Verein (registered society) (Germany)
Ev-l    Evangelisch-lutherische
Ev-L    Evanglelisch-lutherische
EVAF    Evangelismo a Fondo (Evangelism-in-Depth)
EWIBM    East & West Indies Bible Mission
ex    out of, from (used in this Encyclopedia exclusively of schisms or secessions)
EYCE    Ecumenical Youth Council in Europe
EYS    Ecumenical Youth Service
EZA    Evangelische Alliantie (Netherlands)
EZE    Evangelische Zentralstelle für Entwicklungshilfe

# F

FABC    Federation of Asian Bishops' Conferences
FAIE    Federación Argentina de Iglesias Evangélicas
FAIS    Federation des Associations Islamiques du Senegal
FALMI    Francescane Ausiliarie Laiche Missionairie Immacolata
FAO    Food and Agriculture Organization
FASE    Federação de Orgãos para Assistencia Social e Educacional
FAST    Association for Final Advance of Scripture Translation
FBC    Freewill Baptist Church
FBF    see OH
FBM    French Bible Mission
FBT    Federation of Buddhists of Thailand
FC    Figli della Carità
FCA    Fellowship of Christian Athletes
FCAC    Federal Council of African Churches
FCAM    Followers of Christ Association of Malawi
FCBCO    Federation of Catholic Bishops' Conferences of Oceania
FCC    Fiji Council of Churches
FCCS    Fellowship of Christian Churches in Samoa
FCEI    Federazione delle Chiese Evangeliche in Italia
FCFC    Free Church Federal Council
FCI    Fellowship of Christ in India
FCIC    Federal Catholic Immigration Committee
FCME    Federación Católica de los Maestros Españoles
FdCC    Canossians (Congregation of Sons of Charity)
FDM    Brothers of Mercy
FDP    Brothers of Divine Providence
FDPMM    Father Divine Peace Mission Movement
FEAM    Far East Apostolic Mission
FEB    Fédèração Espírita Brasileira
FEBA    Far East Broadcasting Association
FEBC    Far East Broadcasting Company
FEBC    Fellowship of Evangelical Baptist Churches
FEBEC    Federación Boliviana de Educación Católica
FEC    Fédération des Enseignements Catholiques
FEC    Finnish Ecumenical Council
FECC    Fédération des Eglises Chrétiennes du Congo
FECCC    Far Eastern Council of Christian Churches
FECI    Fédération Evangélique de Côte d'Ivoire
FECI    Federation Evangelique de la Cote d'Ivoire
FECI    Federation of Evangelical Churches of India
FECOR    Federación Costarricense de Religiosos
FECUN    Federación Española Comunidades Universitarias
FEDAAS    Federación Española de Asociaciones de Asistentes Sociales
FEDAE    Federazione Istituti Dipendenti dalla Autorita Ecclesiastica
FEDEMEC    Federación Misionera Evangélica Costarricense
FEDEPAR    Federación de Religiosos y Religiosas de Panamá
FEE    Fellowship of Evangelicals in Egypt
FEECA    Europäische Foderation für Katholische Erwachsensbildung
FEET    Fédération des Eglises Evangéliques du Tchad
FEGC    Far Eastern Gospel Crusade
FELCSA    Federation of Evangelical Lutheran Churches in Southern Africa
FEM    Federación Evangélica de México
FEME    Fédération des Eglises et Missions Evangéliques en Haute-Volta
FEMEBF    Federation des Egl et Missions Ev du Burkina Faso
FEMEC    Fédération des Eglises et Missions Evangéliques du Cameroun
FENEC    Federación Nicaraguense Educación Católica

FEPS    Fédération des Eglises Protestantes de la Suisse
FERE    Federación Española de Religiosos de Enseñanza
FEREC    Federación de Religiosas de Costa Rica
FERELPAR    Federación de Religiosos del Paraguay
FERES    Fédération Internationale des Instituts de Recherches Socio-Religieuses
FERVE    Federación de Religiosas de Venezuela
FES    Fraternité Evangélique du Sénégal
FFF    Free Farmers' Federation
FFFM    Finnish Free Foreign Mission
FFKM    Fédération Chrétien de Madagascar
FFKMMT    Federation des Egllises Independents de Madagascar
FFM    Fellowship of Faith for the Muslim
FFNI    Fellowship for Neighbors India
FFPM    Christian Council of Madagascar
FFSC    Fratelli Francescani della Santa Croce (Treviri)
FFSI    Fratelli Figli di San Giuseppe del Rwanda (Bayozefiti)
FFW    Federation of Free Workers
FGBMFI    Full Gospel Business Men's Fellowship International
FGC    Friends General Conference
FGER    Federación Guatemalteca de Escuelas Radiofónicas
FHSC    Fédération Haitienne des Syndicats Chrétiens
FIAC    Fédération Internationale des Agences Catholiques de Presse
FIAMC    International Federation of Associations of Catholic Doctors
FIANZ    Federation of Islamic Associations of New Zealand
FIC    Brothers of the Immaculate Conception (Fratelli dell' Immacolata Concezione di Maastricht)
FIC    Fédération des Instituteurs Chrétiens de Belgique
FICEP    Fédération Internationale Catholique d'Education Physique et Sportive
FICIR    Federazione Italiana Centre e Instituts per la Riabilitazione
FICP    Institute of Brothers of Christian Instruction of Ploërmel
FIDJC    Fédération Internationale des Directeurs de Journaux Catholiques
FIDJC    Fédération Internationale des Journalistes Catholiques
FIEC    Fellowship of Independent Evangelical Churches
FIEU    Federación de Iglesias Evangélicas del Uruguay
FIGS    Federation of Islamic Communities of Surinam
FIH    Fédération des Institutions Hospitalières
FIHC    Fédération Internationale des Hommes Catholiques
FIMCAP    Fédération Internationale des Communautés de Jeunesse Catholique Paroissiales
FIPC    Fédération Internationale des Pharmaciens Catholiques
FIRAS    Federazione Italiana Religiose Asistenza Sociale
FIS    Front Islamique du Salut
FIUC    Fédération Internationale des Universités Catholiques
FKG    Frikyrkliga Gymnasistrorelsen
FLOD    Society for Liturgy and Drama
FM    France Mission Trust
FM    frequency modulation
FMA    Foreign Missions Association
FMB    Foreign Mission Board
FMB-SBC    Foreign Mission Board-Southern Baptist
FMC    Free Methodist Church
FMI    Foursquare Missions International
FMI    Sons of Mary Immaculate (Chavagne Fathers)
FMICAB    Federation of Mosques in Belgium
FMJC    Fédération Mondiale de Jeunesse Catholique
FMJFC    Federación Mundial de la Juventud Femenina Católica
FML    Fiji Muslim League
FMM    Franciscan Missionaries of Mary
FMM    Fratelli della Misericordia
FMON    Federation of Muslim Organizations in the Netherlands
FMPB    Friends Missionary Prayer Band
FMS    Finnish Missionary Society
FMS    Marist Brothers
FMS    Sons of Mary, Health of the Sick
FMSI    Figli di Santa Maria Immacolata
FNIRF    Federação Nacional dos Institutos Religiosos Femininos
FNMF    Federation Nationale des Musulmans de France
FNP    Fédération Nationale des Patros Masculins de Belgique
FNPF    Fédération Nationale des Patros de Jeunes Filles
FOCSIV    Federazione Organizzazioni Cristiane di Servizio Internazionale Volontano
FOCUS    Fellowship of Christian Unions
FOI    Formation Oecuménique Interconfessionnelle
FOM    Fellowship of Missions
FONCABA    Fondation Catholique des Bourses pour Etudiants Africains
FOR    Fellowship of Reconciliation
FPC    Free Protestant Church
FPCGI    Fellowship of the Pentecostal Churches of God in India
FPF    Fédération Protestante de France
FR    Freiburger Rundbrief
FRU    Federación de Religiosos del Uruguay
FS    Fathers of Sion
FSA    Family and Social Action
FSC    Brothers of Christian Schools (de la Salle Brothers)
FSC    Fédération des Scouts Catholiques

FSCI    Figli del Sacro Cuore di Gesu
FSCJ    Verona Fathers, Combonians (Sons of the Sacred Heart)
FSF    Brothers of the Holy Family of Belley
FSG    Brothers of St Gabriel
FSJU    Fonds Social Jurf Unifié
FSMI    Congregation of Sons of Mary Immaculate
FSMS    Fédération des Services Médico-Sociaux
FUACE    Fédération Universelle des Associations Chrétiennes d'Etudiants
FUCI    Federazione Universitaria Cattolica Italiana
FUM    Friends United Mission
FWCC    Friends World Committee for Consultation

# G

GAM    Gruppi Appoggio Missionario
GAP    Global Action Plan
GARB    General Association of Regular Baptists
GB    Great Britain
GBC    Ghana Bishops' Conference
GBU    Gruppi Biblici Universitari (IFES)
GBUAF    Groupes Bibliques Universitaires d'Afrique Francophone
GCC    Gambia Christian Council
GCC    Great Commission Christian
GCC    Guyana Council of Churches
GCF    Graduates Christian Fellowship
GCIP    Great Commission Instrument Panel
GCOWE    Global Consultation on World Evangelization by AD 2000 & Beyond
GCP    Guild of Catholic Psychiatrists
GCPC    Great Commission Prayer Crusade
GCUC    Ghana Church Union Committee
GCUC    Ghana Council of United Churches
GEF    Ghana Evangelical Fellowship
GELC    Gossner Evangelical Lutheran Church
GEM    Global Evangelization Movement
GEM    Gospel Extension Ministry
GEM    Greater Europe Mission
GEM    Group on Education for Mission
GEMS    Gospel Echoing Missionary Society
GF    Graduates' Fellowship
GFA    Gospel For Asia
GFF    Gospel Furthering Fellowship
GFS    Girls Friendly Society
GGMS    Gospel Gypsy Missionary Society
GHM    German Hermannsburg Mission
GIPC    Gilbert Islands Protestant Church
GISC    Confédération Internationale du Guidisme
GKN    Gereformeerde Kerken in Nederland
GLAM    Gruppo Laici Attività Missionaria
GmbH    Gesellschaft mit beschränkter Haftung (= Limited, Incorporated) (Germany)
GME    Globe Missionary Evangelism
GMF    German Missionary Fellowship
GMI    Global Mapping International
GMP    Global Mapping Project
GMU    Gospel Missionary Union
GMWA    Gospel Multimedia Workers Association
GNB    Good News Bible
GOC    Greek Orthodox Church
GOM    Global Outreach Mission
GOP    Groupe Oecuménique de Pastorale
GOWE    Gabriel Olasoji World Evangelism
GPC    Ghana Pentecostal Council
GR    Gospel Recordings
GRI    Gospel Recordings International
GVE    Global Village Evangelism

# H

HAESA    Haimanote Abew Ethiopian Students Association
HANSEA    Student Christian Movement of Ethiopia
HB    Helvetische Bekenntnis/Confession
HBK    Croatian Episcopal Conference
HCJB    Heralding Christ Jesus' Blessings
HCMS    Hibernian Church Missionary Society
HEKS    Hilfswerk der Evangelischen Kirchen der Schweiz
HELVETIAS    Associazione Svizzera di Asistenza Tecnica
HHI    Habitat for Humanity International
HIALT    Haggai Institute for Advanced Leadership Training
HKACM    Hong Kong Association of Christian Missions
HKBP    Batak Protestant Christian Church
HKCC    Hong Kong Christian Council
HKCCCU    Hong Kong Chinese Christian Churches Union
HKCEC    Hong Kong Catholic Education Council
HKFCS    Hong Kong Federation of Catholic Students
HLW    Here's Life World
HOACF    Herrnandad Obrero de Acción Católica Femenina
HOACM    Herrnandad Obrero de Acción Católica Masculina
HOPE    Help Open Paths to Evangelize
HOREMCO    Hokkaido Radio Evangelism Mass Communications
HPK    Himpunan Penghayat Kepercayaan
HQ    headquarters
HSAUWC    Holy Spirit Association for Unification of World Christianity

# I

IAD    Institut des Arts et Diffusion
IAHR    International Association for the History of Reli-

gions
IALC International Association for Liberal Christianity and Religious Freedom
IAM International Afghan Mission
IAML International Association of Music Libraries
IAMS Inter-American Missionary Society
IAMS International Association for Mission Studies
IARF International Association for Religious Freedom
IARSC International Association of Religious Science Churches
IASOT International Association for the Study of the Old Testament
IBCC India Bible Christian Council
IBETE Instituto Batista de Educaçaão Teológica por Extensão
IBMR International Bulletin of Missionary Research
IBO Associazione Internazionale dei Soci Costruttori
IBPFM Independent Board for Presbyterian Foreign Missions
IBPM Indo-Burma Pioneer Mission
IBRA International Bible Reading Association
IBRA International Broadcasting Association
IBS International Bible Society
IBSA International Bible Students Association
IBT Institute for Bible Translation (Sweden)
IC International Crusades
IC Rosminians (Institute of Charity)
ICA Inter-Church Aid
ICAB Igreja Católica Apostólica Brasileira
ICB International Christian Broadcasters
ICC International Congregational Council
ICC Iran Council of Churches
ICC Irish Council of Churches
ICCB Centre Islamique et Culturel de Belgique
ICCB International Committee for Christian Broadcasting
ICCC International Communion of Charismatic Churches
ICCC International Confederation of Catholic Charities (Caritas)
ICCC International Council of Christian Churches
ICCEC International Communion of the Charismatic Episcopal Church
ICCFM International Confederation of Christian Family Movements
ICCJ International Council of Christians & Jews
ICCOWE International Charismatic Consultation on World Evangelization
ICCP International Congress of Christian Physicians
ICCRO International Catholic Charismatic Renewal Office
ICCRS International Catholic Charismatic Renewal Services
ICEBS International Conference of Evangelical Bible Societies
ICFG International Church of the Foursquare Gospel
ICG Institute of Church Growth
ICI Interamerican Cooperative Institute
ICI Interkerkelijk Contact Israel
ICI International Correspondence Institute
ICIA Información Católica Ibero-americana
ICIE International Conference for Itinerant Evangelists
ICJ Internationaler Christlicher Jugendaustausch
ICLM International Christian Leadership Movement
ICM Instituto de Capacitación Misionera
ICM Sisters of the Immaculate Heart of Mary
ICMA International Christian Maritime Association
ICMC International Catholic Migration Commission
ICMICA International Catholic Movement for Intellectual and Cultural Affairs (Pax Romana)
ICO International Communications Office
ICODES Instituto Colombiano de Desarrollo Social
ICOM International Consultation on Missions
ICOWE International Congress on World Evangelization
ICPE International Catholic Programme of Evangelization
ICRA International Catholic Rural Association
ICS Intercontinental Church Society
ICSA Islamic Council of South Africa
ICSF Islamic Council of the South Pacific
ICU International Christian University
ICUI Instituto Católico Uruguayo de Immigración
ICUIS Institute on the Church in Urban-Industrial Society
ICUSR Interchurch Committee on Urban Squatter Resettlement
ICVA International Council of Voluntary Agencies
ICYE International Christian Youth Exchange
IDAC International Development Assistance Commission
IDER Instituto de Educación Rural
IDESAC Instituto para el Desarrollo Económico Social de América Central
IDI Instituto de Desenvolvimento Integral
IDOC International Documentation on the Contemporary Church
IDUM Interdenominational Directors of Urban Missions
IEB Irish Evangelistic Band
IEF Gypsy Pentecostal Churches
IEM Indian Evangelical Mission
IEME Instituto Español de San Francisco Javier para Misiones Extranjeras (Burgos Foreign Mission Society)
IER Instituto de Educación Rural
IET Indian Evangelical Team
IFCC International Fellowship of Charismatic Churches
IFCO Inter-Religious Foundation for Community Organization
IFES International Fellowship of Evangelical Students
IFFEC International Federation of Free Evangelical Churches
IFI/PIC Philippine Independent Church
IFMA Interdenominational Foreign Mission Association
IFMR Issachar Frontier Missions Research
IFOR International Fellowship of Reconciliation
IFOTES International Federation for Services of Emergency Telephonic Help
IFR instrument flight rules (blind flying)
IFT International Federation of Translators
IGL International Gospel League
IGO intergovernmental organization
IHCA International Hebrew Christian Alliance
IHCF International Hospital Christian Fellowship
IHECS Institut des Hautes Etudes des Communications Sociales
IHEU International Humanist & Ethical Union
IHM International Holiness Mission
IJA Institute of Jewish Affairs
IJFM International Journal of Frontier Missions
IKOR Interkerkelijk Overlag in Radio Aangelegenheden
IKUE International Union of Catholic Esperantists
ILAFO International League for Apostolic Faith & Order
ILC International Lutheran Council
ILM Institute of Labor and Management
ILP Instituto Latinoamericano de Liturgia Pastoral
IM Inlandische Mission
IM instant messaging
IM International Missions
IMA India Missions Association
IMB International Mission Board
IMBISA Interterritorial Meeting of Bishops in Southern Africa
IMC Consolata Fathers (Consolata Society for Foreign Missions)
IMC International Missionary Congress
IMC International Missionary Council
IMCA Indo-Maurician Catholic Association
IMCS International Movement of Catholic Students (Pax Romana)
IME Institut Médical Evangélique
IMF Indonesia Missionary Fellowship
IMHEKD Innere Mission und Hilfswek der EKD
IMI International Missions
IMPL Infdormations Missionnaires pour Laics
IMRA International Mission Radio Association
IMS Icelandic Missionary Society
IMS Indian Missionary Society
IMU Irish Missionary Union
INADES Institut Africain pour le Développement Economique et Social
INAP Instituto Nacional de Acción Poblacional
INC Iglesia ni Cristo (Manalista)
Inc Incorporated (USA, UK, et al)
INCAMI Instituto Católico Chileno de Migración
INCUPO Instituto de Cultura Popular
INEB International Network of Engaged Buddhists
INEL Instituto Nacional de Estudios Litúrgicos
INF International Nepal Fellowship
INODEP Institut Oecuménique au Service du Développement des Peuples
INTA International New Thought Alliance
INTA International New Thought Association
INTERFILM International Inter-Church Film Centre
INVICTA Instituto de Vivienda Caritas
IOCBC International Old Catholic Bishops Conference
IOM India Outreach Missions
IoMCC Isle of Man Council of Churches
IOUTN International Organization for Unification of Terminological Neologisms
IPA International Pentecostal Assemblies
IPAS Instituto di Patronato per l'Assistenza Sociale
IPCG India Pentecostal Church of God
IPHC International Pentecostal Holiness Church
IPLAJ Instituto de Pastoral Latinoamericano de la Juventud
IPRU Instituto de Promoción Economico-Social de Uruguay
IRAM Institut de Recherche et d'Application des Méthodes de Développement
IRAM International Reformed Agency for Migration
IRETI Interdiocesan Religious Education Training Institute
IRFED Institut International de Recherches et de Formation en vue du Développement
IRGC Pasdaran
IRM International Review of Mission(s)
IRO Inter-Religious Organization of Trinidad and Tobago
IRO International Research Office
IROTT Inter-Religious Organization of Trinidad & Tobago
ISAC Institute for Social Action in China
ISAL Iglesia y Sociedad en América Latina
ISAV Instituto de Sistemas Audiovisuales
ISBC International Society of Bible Collectors
ISCF Inter-Schools Christian Fellowship
ISCO Institut Supérieur de Culture Ouvriére
ISF International Spiritualist Federation
ISFM International Society of Frontier Missiology
ISI International Students, Inc.
ISNA Islamic Society of North America
ISO Institute of Social Order
ISO International Standardization Organization
ISPANG Islamic Society of Papua New Guinea
ISRR Institute of Social and Religious Research
ISTEP Instituto Superior de Teologia Pastoral
IT information technology
IT International Teams
ITCA Independent Television Companies Association
ITECIC Instituto de Teologia e de Ciencias de Comportamento Humano
ITECO Coopération Technique Internationale
ITER Instituto de Teología de Recife
IUAM Islamic Union of Afghan Mujaheddin
IUGM International Union of Gospel Missions
IULCW International Union of Liberal Christian Women
IURD Igreja Universal do Reino de Deus
IVCF Inter-Varsity Christian Fellowship
IVF Inter-Varsity Fellowship
IVMF Inter-Varsity Missionary Fellowship
IVP Inter-Varsity Press
IWM Interchurch World Movement
IZA Institut für Internationale Zusammenarbeit

## J

J jurisdiction
JAARS Jungle Aviation and Radio Service
JAC Juventud Agrária Católica
JAC/F Jeunesse Agricole Chrétienne/Files
JAD Jeunesse Agricole pour le Développement
JAEC Jamaica Association of Evangelical Churches
JAM Joint Action for Mission
JBU Jamaica Baptist Union
JC Jesus Christ, Jésus-Christ, Jesu Cristo
JCA Joint Church Aid
JCC Jamaica Council of Churches
JCC Jersey Council of Churches
JCEA Jamaica Catholic Education Association
JCM Standing Conference of Jews, Christian and Muslims in Europe
JCMC Japan Catholic Migration Commission
JEA Japan Evangelical Association
JEB Japan Evangelistic Band
JEC Juventud Estudiantil Católica
JEC/F Jeunesse Etudiante Chrétienne/Filles
JEF Japan Evangelical Fellowship
JEM Jerusalem and the East Mission
JEMA Japan Evangelical Missionary Association
JESCOM International Jesuit Centre for Social Communication
JESSYC Junta Evangélica de Servicio Social y Cultural
JEW Jewish Evangelical Witness
JFJ Jews for Jesus
JIB Jamaat-i Islami of Bangladesh
JIC/F Jeunesse Indépendante Chrétienne/Filles
JICI Jeunesse Indépendante Catholique Internationale
JILF Jesus is Lord Fellowship
JK Jesus Kristus (German)
JKPS Jatiyo Kristiyo Prochar Samity
JOC Juventud Obrera Cristiana
JOC/F Jeunesse Ouvrière Chrétienne/Filles
JOCI Jeunesse Ouvrière Internationale
JPC Japan Protestant Council
JPIC Justice, Peace & the Integrity of Creation
JRSK Joint Refugee Services of Kenya
JS Jehovah Shammah
JSAC Joint Strategy and Action Committee
JSM Jimmy Swaggart Ministries
JTC Juventud Travajadora Colombiana
JUC Jeunesse Universitaire Catholique
JUC Juventud Universitaria Cristiana
JUDCA Christian Democratic Youth of Latin America
JUI Jamiat ul-Ulama-i Islam
JUM Joint Urban Ministry
JUMP Joint Urban Mission Program
JWs Jehovah's Witnesses

## K

K&S Kerubu ati (&) Serafu
KAATS Korean Association of Accredited Theological Schools
KAB Katholische Arbeiter und Angestellten-bewegung
KAB Katholische Arbeiterbewegung
KAB Katholische Arbeitnehmer-Bewegung
KALM Kenya Association for Liturgical Music
KAVA Korean Association of voluntary Agencies
KBS Katholieke Bijbelstichting
KCBAC Kenya Christian Broadcasting Advisory Committee
KCES Katholieke Centrale Emigratiestichting
KCF Korean Christian Federation
KCMC Korean Catholic Migration Commission
KCMS Kenya Church Music Society
KCTPF Kenya Christian Teachers' Prayer Fellowship
KCWM Korea Catholic Workers Movement
KDSE Katholische Deutsche Studenten-Einigung
KEC Kenya Episcopal Conference
KEF Himalaya Evangelical Fellowship
KEK Konferenz Europäischer Kirchen
KEP Polish Episcopal Conference
KESPEKRI Indonesian Federation of Christian Workers' Associations
KFD Katholische Fernseharbeit in Deutschland
KGAP Kaleidoscopic Global Action Plan
KHCF Kenya Hospitals Christian Fellowship
KHJO Katholische Hochschuljugend Osterreichs
KIM Korean International Mission
KIPA Katholische Internationale Press-Agentur
KJR Katholische Jeugdraad
KJV King James Version (of the Bible)
KLJB Katholische Landjugendbewegung
KLO Katholische Lehrerschaft Osterreichs
KLS Katholischer Lehrerverein der Schweiz
KLS Katholischer Sudtiroler Lehrerbund

NHA National Holiness Association
NHK Netherlands Reformed Church (Nederduits Hervormde Kerk)
NIV New International Version (of the Bible)
NKJV New King James Version (of the Bible)
NKV Nederlandse Christlijke Bond van Overheidspersoneel
NLFA New Life for All
NLI New Life International
NLL New Life League
NLM Norwegian Lutheran Mission
NMA Norwegian Missionary Alliance
NMC National Missionary Council
NMM Native Missionary Movement
NMR Nederlandse Missieraad
NMS National Missionary Society
NMS Norwegian Missionary Society
NMZ Nordelbisches Zentrum für Weltmission und Kirchlichen Weltdienst
NNAE National Negro Evangelical Association
NOBC National Office for Black Catholics
NOOR National Organization for Ophthalmic Rehabilitation
NOW National Organization for Women
NPY Norwegian Pentecostal Mission
NRB National Religious Broadcasters
NRC Netherlands Reformed Church
NRGP Nationaale Raad voor Gezinspastoraal
NRP New Reader Scripture Portions
NRS New Reader Scripture Selections
NRSV New Revised Standard Version (of the Bible)
NS Nossa Senhora, Nuestra Señora
NSFC National Sister Formation Conference
NSS Navjeevan Susamachar Samiti
NSVC National Sisters Vocation Conference
NT New Testament
NTM New Tribes Mission
NTME New Testament in Modern English
NTMU New Testament Missionary Union
NW northwest, northwestern
NWEF North West Frontier Fellowship
NYBA National Young Buddhist Association
NYLC National Young Life Campaign
NZBFMS New Zealand Baptist Foreign Mission Society
NZCCC NZ Consultative Co of ICCC
NZEC New Zealand Episcopal Conference
NZG Netherlands Missionary Society (Nederlandsch Zendeling-Genootschap)

## O

O ordinariate
OAIC Organization of African Instituted (Independent) Churches
OAR Order of Recollect Augustinians
OBC Order of Buddhist Contemplatives
OBNOVA Federation of Associations of Ukrainian Catholic Students
OBPC Brazil for Christ Ev Pentecostal Church
OBSC Open Bible Standard Churches
OC Carmelites (Order of Our Lady of Mt Carmel)
OCart Carthusian Order
OCASEI Obra Católica de Asistencia a Estudiantes Iberoamericano
OCASHA Obra de Cooperación Apostólica Seglar Hispano-Americana
OCD Order of Discalced Carmelites
OCEC Oficio Central de Educación Católica
OCES Office Chrétien de l'Enregistrement Sonore
OCFC Office Catholique Français du Cinéma
OCFRT Office Catholique Francais de Radio-Télévision
OCI OC International (formerly Overseas Crusades)
OCIC Office Catholique International Cinéma
OCIPE Office Catholique d'Information sur les Problèmes Européens
OCist Cistercians
OCL Office Chrétien du Livre
OCM Grupe d'Organismes de Coopération Missionnaire
OCMCS Oficina Coordinadora de los Medios de Comunicación Social
OCR Cistercian Order, Reformed (Trappists)
OCSHA Obra de Cooperación Sacerdotal Hispanoamericana
OCSO Trappists (Order of Cistercians of the Strict Observance)
OCU Officers Christian Union
OCYAK Orthodox Christian Youth Association of Kenya
OD Open Doors with Brother Andrew
OdeM Mercedarians (Order of Our Lady of Mercy for the Ransom of Captives)
ODUCAL Organización de Universidades Católicas de América Latina
OESA Hermit Augustinians (Order of Hermits of St Augustine)
OFM Franciscan (Order of Friars Minor)
OFMCap Capuchins (Order of Friars Minor Capuchin)
OFMConv Conventuals (Order of Friars Minor Conventual)
OH Order of Brothers Hospitallers of St John of God
OHC Order of the Holy Cross
OIC Organisations Internationales Catholiques
OIC Organization of the Islamic Conference
OIEC Office International de l'Enseignement Catholique
OJD Okumenscher Jugenddienste
OJRiO Okumenischer Jugendrat in Osterreich
OKB Osterreichische Katholische Bibelwerk
OKR Okumenischer Rat der Kirchen (WCC)
OM Minim Hermits of St Francis of Paola
OM Operation Mobilization

OMECO Oficina Nacional de Medios de Communicación Social
OMF Overseas Missionary Fellowship
OMI Missionaries Oblates of Mary Immaculate
OMS Oriental Missionary Society
OMSC Overseas Ministries Study Center
OMSI OMS International
OMV Oblates of the Blessed Virgin Mary
ONCS Office National des Communications Sociales
OOCC Oriental Orthodox Churches Conference
OP Dominicans (Order of Preachers)
OPC Orthodox Presbyterian Church
OPraem Premonstratensians, or Norbertines (Canons Regular of Prémontré)
ORSA Recollect Augustinians (Order of Augustinian Recollects)
ORU Oral Roberts University
OSA Augustinian Friars (Order of St Augustine)
OSB Confederate Benedictines (Order of St Benedict)
OSBM Basilians (Order of St Basil the Great)
OSC Crosier Fathers (Canons Regular of the Order of the Holy Cross)
OSC Orthodox Syrian Church
OSCam Camillians (Ministers of the Sick, Clerics Regular)
OSCE Orthodox Syrian Catholicossate of the East
OSCO Overseas Students Coordination
OSFO Osborn Foundation International
OSFS Oblates of St Francis de Sales
OSLAM Organización de Seminanos Latinoamericanos
OSM Servites (Order of the Servants of Mary)
OSsT Trinitarian Fathers (Order of the Most Holy Trinity)
OSU Ursuline Sisters of the Roman Union
OT Old Testament
OUP Oxford University Press
OW Operation World
OYM Orthodox Youth Movement

## P

p number of pages in book, article, or periodical
P patriarchate, patriarchal diocese
p.a. per annum/year
p.d. per diem/daily
PA Patres Albi, Pères d'Afrique (WF)
PA prefecture apostolic
PABATS Philippine Association of Bible and Theological Schools
PACLA Pan-African Christian Leadership Assembly
PACTEE Pakistan Committee on Theological Education by Extension
PAFES Pan African Fellowship of Evangelical Students
PAFTEE Philippine Committee on Theological Education by Extension
PAG Pentecostal Assemblies of God
PAG Pentecostal Association of Ghana
PALMS Paulian Association Lay Missionary Secretariat
PAO Professional Athletes Outreach
PAoC Pentecostal Assemblies of Canada
PAoW Pentecostal Assemblies of the World
PAoWI Pentecostal Assemblies of the West Indies
PAS Pan-Malaysian Islamic Party
PAS Pater Ahlbrinckstrichting
PATS Philippines Association of Theological Schools
PAVLA Papal Volunteers for Latin America
PAW Pentecostal Assemblies of the World
PBCS Pakistan Bible Correspondence School
PCA Presbyterian Church in America
PCA Presbyterian Church of Australia
PCC Pacific Conference of Churches
PCC Pentecostal Church of Christ
PCCC Pakistan Council of Christian Churches
PCCNA Pentecostal/Charismatic Chs of North America
PCE Presbyterian Church of England
PCEA Presbyterian Church of East Africa
PCEC Philippine Council of Evangelical Churches
PCFEC Philippine Council of Fundamental Ev Chs
PCG Pentecostal Church of God
PCI Pentecostal Church Incorporated
PCJ Prètres du Sacré-Coeur de Jésus de Bétharram
PCMA Protestant Churches Medical Association
PCR Programme to Combat Racism
PCSA Presbyterian Church of South Africa
PCTK Protestant Churches in Tuvalu & Kiribati
PCUS Presbyterian Church in the US
PCUSA Presbyterian Church of the USA
PCW Presbyterian Church of Wales
PDC Partido Democrata Cristiano
PDG Pastoral Development Group
PE patriarchal exarchate
PEA Panhellenic Evangelical Alliance
PEC Pakistan Episcopal Conference
PECC Protestant Evangelical Council in Croatia
PECUSA Protestant Episcopal Church in the USA
PEFA Pentecostal Evangelical Fellowship of Africa
PEMS Paris Evangelical Missionary Society
PERKIM All-Malaysia Muslim Welfare Association
PERSETHIA Association of Theological Schools in Indonesia
PFES Pakistan Fellowship of Evangelical Students
PFI Prison Fellowship International
PFM Marist Brothers (Little Brothers of Mary)
PFNA Pentecostal Fellowship of North America
PFZ Pentecostal Fellowship of Zimbabwe
PHAM Private Hospital Association of Malawi
PHC Pentecostal Holiness Church
PhD doctor of philosophy
PI Partners International (Christian Nationals Evangelism Commission)

PI Programmed Instruction
PICEC Pacific Islands Christian Education Council
PII Association of Ev Churches of Indonesia
PIME Pontifical Institute for Foreign Missions (Pontificio Istituto Missioni Estere)
PISA Priests' Institute for Social Action
PJM Philippines for Jesus Movement
PKE Priesterkreise fur Konziliare Erneuerung
PLK Church of Perfect Liberty
PMCA Pentecostal Mission Churches Association
PME Foreign Missions Society, Province of Quebec
PMF Philippine Missionary Fellowship
PMU Pontifical Missionary Union
PMV Pro Mundi Vita
PMW Pontifical Missionary Works
PN prelature (prelacy) nullius
PNCC Polish National Catholic Church
PNCEA Paulist National Catholic Evangelization Association
PPC Propaganda Popular Católica
PPP Discoteca Pax, Centro Propaganda Popular Católica
PRE Polish Ecumenical Council
PSA Paraboles et Symbôles pour Aujourd'hui
PSS Sulpicians (Society of the Priests of St Sulpice)
PSSC Missionari di San Carlo (Scalabrinians)
PTFWR Philadelphia Task Force on Women in Religion
PTL Pocket Testament League
PTS Protestant Truth Society
PUCRGS Pontificia Universidade Católica do Rio Grande do Sul
PUCRJ Pontificia Universidade Católica do Rio de Janeiro
PUCSP Pontificia Universidade Católica de São Paulo
PUU Pontifical Urbanian University
PWC Pentecostal World Conference

## Q

QIF Qua Iboe Fellowship
qv quod vide (which see; i.e. refer to previous item)

## R

R&D research and development
RADIUS Religious Drama Society of Great Britain
RBMU Regions Beyond Missionary Union
RC Reformed Church
RC Roman Catholic
RCA Reformed Church in America
RCBC Rhodesia Catholic Bishops' Conference
RCC Rhodesia Christian Conference
RCC Roman Catholic Church
RCCCC Republic of China Council of Christian Chs
RCI Congregation of Rogationist Fathers of the Heart of Jesus
RCJCLdS Reorganized Church of Jesus Christ of Latter-day Saints
RCL Religion in Communist Lands
RCMS Church Missionary Society (Rwanda Mission)
REA Romanian Evangelical Alliance
REB Revised English Bible
REC Reformed Episcopal Church
REP Religious Education Press
RES Reformed Ecumenical Synod
RGG Religion in Geschichte und Gegenwart
RICA Reformed Independent Churches Association
RICB Radio-Télévision Catholique Belge
RIDCSEAP Regional Islamic Dawa Council SE
RKPN Rooms Katholiek Partij Nederland
RKZ Romisch-Katholische Zentralkonferenz der Landeskirchen
RM Rhenish Mission
RN priory nullius
RNA Religious Newswriters Association
RNMDSF Royal National Mission to Deep Sea Fishermen
ROC Russian Orthodox Church
ROCOR Russian Orthodox Church Outside of Russia
ROEG Rassemblement Oecuménique des Eglises de Genève
RPCES Reformed Presbyterian Church, Evangelical Synod
RPCNA Reformed Presbyterian Church of North America
RPS Reformed Press Service
RSAK Religious Superiors' Association of Kenya
RSB Radio School of the Bible
RSCM Royal Society for Church Music
RSMT Red Sea Mission Team
RSP Rashtriya Susamachar Parishad
RSS Rashtriya Swayamsevak Sangh
RSV Religiosi di San Vicenzo de' Paoli, Padri e Fratelli
RSV Revised Standard Version (of the Bible)
RUCOM Rural Consultation Mission
RV Revised Version (of the Bible)
RVat Radio Vatican
RVOG Radio Voice of the Gospel

## S

S south, southern
SA Franciscan Friars of the Atonement (Graymoor)
SA Salvation Army
SA Soeurs d'Afrique (White Sisters)
SABA Sino-American Buddhist Association
SABMS South African Baptist Missionary Society
SABS Sisters of Adoration

| | |
|---|---|
| SAC | Pallottines (Society of the Catholic Apostolate) |
| SAC | Social Action Center |
| SACBC | Southern Africa Catholic Bishops' Conference |
| SACC | South African Council of Churches |
| SACCC | South African Council of Christian Churches |
| SACLA | South Africa Christian Leadership Assembly |
| SACP | Southern African Council of Priests |
| SAGM | South Africa General Mission |
| SAIM | South America Indian Mission |
| SAIRI | Sup As for Islamic Revolution in Iraq |
| SAM | South America Mission |
| SAM | Swedish Alliance Mission |
| SAMS | South American Missionary Society |
| SASRA | Soldiers' and Airmen's Scripture Readers' Association |
| SAVI | Service d'Accueil aux Voyageurs et aux Immigrants |
| SB | Synod of Bishops |
| SBC | Southern Baptist Convention |
| SBF | Southern Baptist Foundation |
| SBI | Society of Biblical Literature |
| SBLE | Society of Biblical Literature and Exegesis |
| SBU | Sociedades Biblicas Unidas (UBS) |
| SC | Brothers of the Sacred Heart (Fratelli del Sacro Cuore) |
| SC | Sacré-Coeur |
| SC | Sacred Congregation (in Rome) |
| SCA | Student Christian Association |
| SCAD | Société Civile et Agricole de Dzoghégan |
| SCC | Scottish Churches Council |
| SCC | Sudan Council of Churches |
| SCC | Swaziland Conference of Churches |
| SCCC | Singapore Council of Christian Churches |
| SCEM | Singapore Center for Evangelism and Missions |
| SCEP | Sacred Congregation for the Evangelization of Peoples |
| SCJ | Congregation of the Priests of the Sacred Heart |
| SCJ | Priests of the Sacred Heart (Betharram) |
| SCJ | Society of the Sacred Heart of the Infant Jesus |
| SCLC | Southern Christian Leadership Conference |
| SCM | Student Christian Movement |
| SCOBA | Standing Conference of Canonical Orthodox Bishops in the Americas |
| SCS | Social Communications Service |
| SDA | Seventh-day Adventists |
| SDB | Salesians of St John Bosco (Society of St Francis de Sales) |
| SDB | Seventh Day Baptists |
| SDBC | Seventh Day Baptist Church |
| SDF | Scouts de France |
| SDS | Salvatorians (Society of the Divine Saviour) |
| SDV | Società Divine Vocazioni (Padri Vocazionisti) |
| SE | southeast, southeastern |
| SEA | Schweizerische Evangelische Allianz |
| SEA | Swedish Evangelical Alliance |
| SEAN | Seminario por Extension a las Naciones |
| SEAR | Société d'Exportation d' Art Religieux |
| SEARSOLIN | South East Asian Rural Social Leadership Institute |
| SEARV | South East Asia Radio Voice |
| SEC | Sudan Episcopal Conference |
| SEC | Swedish Ecumenical Council |
| SECAM | Symposium of Episcopal Conferences of Africa and Madagascar |
| SEDAC | Secretariado Episcopal de América Central y Panamá |
| SEDECOS | Secretariado de Communicación Social |
| SEFAI | Schweizerische Evangelische Freundeskreis für die Araber in Israel |
| SEI | Servicio Evangélico de Información |
| sek | Sekretär, sekretariat (German) |
| SEKURF | Swedish Ecumenical Committee for Development |
| SEMA | Société pour l'Evangélisation par des Moyens Audio-Visuels |
| SEMINCI | Semaña Internacional de Cine Religioso y de Valores Humanos |
| SEMR | Schweizérischer Evangelischer Missionsrat |
| SEMS | Swedish Evangelical Missionary Society |
| SEN | Servicio Evangélico Nacional |
| SEND | SEND International |
| SENDA | Servicio Evangélico Noticioso do América |
| SER | Sistema Educativo Radiofónico de México |
| SERB | Sistema Educativo Radiofónico de Bragança |
| SERCAP | Secretariado para Religiosos de Centroamérica y Panamá |
| SERCOS | Servicio de Communicación Social |
| SERPAL | Servicio Radifónico para Latina América |
| SESOMEX | Secretariado Social Mexicano |
| SEUL | Servicio Europeo de Universitarios Latinoamericanos |
| SF | Figli della Sacra Famiglia |
| SFB | Sisters of the Holy Family of Bordeaux |
| SFCC | Swedish Free Church Council |
| SFM | Scarboro Foreign Mission Society |
| SFM | Swedish Free Mission |
| SFMF | Student Foreign Missions Fellowship |
| SG | Gabriallists |
| SGA | Slavic Gospel Association |
| SGM | Scripture Gift Mission |
| SHARE | Systems, Hardware & Research for Evangelization |
| SHCJ | Sisters of the Holy Child Jesus |
| SHPF | Société de l'Histoire du Protestantisme Français |
| SIAC | International Secretariat of Catholic Artists |
| SIAMA | Society for the Interests of Active Missionaries in Asia |
| SICA | Service d'Images Chrétiennes Africaines |
| SICA | Solomon Islands Christian Association |
| SICO | Servizio Informazioni per la Chiese Orientali |
| SIDIC | International Information Service for Jewish-Christian Relations |
| SIEIC | Secrétariat International des Elèves Ingénieurs Catholiques |
| SIESC | Secrétariat International des Enseignants Secondaires Catholiques |
| SIF | Service Incroyance-Foi |
| SIL | Summer Institute of Linguistics |
| SIM | Sudan Interior Mission (SIM International) |
| SIPE | Servicio de Información Prensa y Espetáculos |
| SIRC | Servizio Informazioni Romano Cattolico |
| SISC | Supreme Islamic Shii Council |
| SJ | Jesuits (Society of Jesus) |
| SKAF | Schweizerische Katholische Arbeitsgemeinschaft für Fremdarbeiter |
| SKLW | Schweizerisches Katholisches Laienhelferwerk |
| SLEF | Sierra Leone Evangelical Fellowship |
| SLM | Swedish Lutheran Mission |
| SLMC | Sierra Leone Muslim Congress |
| SLMC | Sri Lanka Muslim Congress |
| SM | Swiss Mission |
| SM(1) | Marianist Fathers (Society of Mary) |
| SM(2) | Marist Fathers (Society of Mary) |
| SMA | Société des Missions Africaines (African Missions Society of Lyons) |
| SMB | Swiss Bethlehem Fathers (Missionary Society of Bethlehem in Switzerland) |
| SMI | Spanish Missionaries of Burgos (Spanish Institute of St Francis Xavier for the Foreign Missions) |
| SMM | Montfort Fathers (Company of Mary) |
| SMP | Portuguese Society for Foreign Missions/Portuguese Missionary Society |
| SMST | Società Missioni di San Tomaso Apostolo di Palai |
| SNC | Secretariat for Non-Christians |
| SNE | Service National d'Emigration |
| SNEC | Secrétariat National de l'Enseignement Catholique |
| SNPS | Secretariado Nacional de Pastoral Social |
| SNTS | Studiorum Nove Testamenti Societas |
| SNU | Spiritualists National Union |
| SO | Acoemetae |
| SOC | Cistercian Order of the Common Observance |
| SODEPAX | Committee on Society, Development and Peace |
| SOJEMO | Ecumenical Office for Students and Youth in the Middle East |
| SOMA | Sharing of Ministries Abroad |
| SORPE | Servico de Orientação Rural de Pernambuco |
| SP | Piarists (Poor Clerics Regular of the Mother of the Pious Schools) |
| SP | Scolopians |
| SP | Servants of the Holy Paraclete |
| SPAC | South Pacific Anglican Council |
| SPATS | South Pacific Association of Theological Schools |
| SPCA | Secrétariat Permanent du Clergé Africain |
| SPCK | Society for Promoting Christian Knowledge |
| SPG | Society for the Propagation of the Gospel |
| SPM | Swiss Pentecostal Mission |
| SPRE-E | Spiritual Re-emphasis |
| SPROCAS | Study Project on Christianity in Apartheid Society |
| SPS | Kiltegan Fathers (Society of St Patrick for Foreign Missions) |
| SPS | Society for Pentecostal Studies |
| SRAM | Secrétariat Régional pour l'Afrique et Madagascar |
| SRF | Self-Realization Fellowship |
| SSB | Sunday School Board (Southern Baptist) |
| SSC | Maynooth (Missionary Society of St Columban) |
| SSC | Società Sacerdoti di San Giuseppe Benedetto Cottolengo |
| SSCC | Picpus Fathers (Congregation of the Sacred Hearts of Jesus and Mary) |
| SSE | Fathers of St Edmund |
| SSEM | South Sea Evangelical Mission |
| SSF | Society of St Francis |
| SSI | Missionari di San Giuseppe nel Messico |
| SSID | Servicio Social de Iglesias Dominicanas |
| SSJ | Society of St Joseph of the Sacred Heart |
| SSJE | Society of St John the Evangelist |
| SSK | Slovenia Bishops' Conference |
| SSM | Society of the Sacred Mission |
| SSND | School Sisters of Notre Dame |
| SSP | Pauline Fathers (Society of St Paul for the Apostolate of Communications) |
| SSpS | Missionary Sisters Servants of the Holy Spirit |
| SSS | Congregation of Blessed Sacrament Fathers |
| ST | Missionari Servi della Santissima Trinità |
| STAG | Student Technical Assistance Group |
| STAM | Società Tecnica Aiuto Missioni |
| STAR | Service Technique Africain de Radiodiffusion |
| STB | bachelor of sacred theology |
| STD | doctor of sacred theology |
| STE | Service Technique pour l'Education |
| STEP | Strategy to Every People |
| STM | master of sacred theology |
| SU | Scripture Union |
| SUM | Sudan United Mission |
| SUM | SUM Fellowship |
| SUN | Spiritual Unity of Nations |
| SUPKEM | Supreme Council of Kenya Muslims |
| SVD | Verbites, Missionaries of Steyl (Society of the Divine Word) |
| SVEA | Schweizerische Verband Evangelischer Arbeiter und Angestellter |
| SVM | Student Volunteer Movement |
| SVMFM | Student Volunteer Movement for Foreign Missions |
| SVMU | Student Volunteer Missionary Union |
| SW | short-wave |
| SW | southwest, southwestern |
| SWG | Strategy Working Group |
| SWM | School of World Mission |
| SX | Society of St Francis Xavier for Foreign Missions (Parma) |
| SYNDESMOS | World Fellowship of Orthodox Youth Organizations |
| SZM | Schweizerische Zigeuner-Mission |

## T

| | |
|---|---|
| TAFTEE | Association for Theological Education by Extension |
| TAM-ICCC | The Associated Missions, International Council of Christian Churches |
| TAP | Theological Assistance Program |
| TAVES | Tamilnadu Audio-Visual Education Service |
| TBL | The Bible League |
| TBN | Trinity Broadcasting Network |
| TCC | Tonga Council of Churches |
| TCICC | Turks & Caicos Inter-Church Committee |
| TEAM | The Evangelical Alliance Mission |
| TEAM | Training for Ecumenical Action in Mission |
| TEC | Tanzania Episcopal Conference |
| TEE | Theological Education by Extension |
| TEF | Theological Education Fund |
| TELL | The Evangelical Latin League |
| TEMA | The European Missionary Association |
| TEPA | Tele-Escuela Popular Americana |
| TEV | Today's English Version (same as GNB) |
| TF | Trinity Fellowship |
| TFLOPS | trillion floating point operations per second |
| TFP | Sociedade Brasileira de Defesa da Tradição, Familia e Propriedade |
| ThD | doctor of theology |
| TIFC | Transmitting Internationally for Christ |
| TJC | True Jesus Church |
| TLM | The Leprosy Mission |
| TM | Transcendental Meditation |
| TMI | Teen Missions International |
| TNBCLC | Tamil Nadu Biblical, Catechetical and Liturgical Center |
| TOB | Traduction Oecuménique de la Bible |
| TOCD | Tertiary of the Order of Discalced Carmelites |
| TOMS | Thailand Overseas Missionary Society |
| TOR | Third Order Regular of St Francis |
| TOSD | Tertiary of the Order of St Dominic |
| TOSF | Tertiary of the Order of St Francis |
| TPM | The Pentecostal Mission |
| TTCEC | Trinidad & Tobago Council of Evangelical Churches |
| TV | television |
| TVC | Tecnici Volontari Cristiani |
| TWMA | Third World Missions Association |
| TWMF | Third World Missions Federation |
| TWO | Teen World Outreach |
| TWR | Trans World Radio |

## U

| | |
|---|---|
| UACPB | Union Apostolique et Culturelle des Prietres Burundais |
| UAE | Uganda Association of Evangelicals |
| UAE | United Arab Emirates |
| UAHC | Union of American Hebrew Congregations |
| UAICC | Uniting Aboriginal and Islander Christian Congress |
| UAIM | United Andean Indian Mission |
| UB | United Brethren |
| UBC | United Brethren Church |
| UBC | United Brethren in Christ |
| UBRAJE | União Brasileira de Juventudes Ecuménicas |
| UBS | United Bible Societies |
| UC | Union Conference (Seventh-day Adventist) |
| UCADE | Unión Cristiana Americana de Educadores |
| UCASI | Unione Cattolica Assistenti Sociali Italiane |
| UCBWM | United Church Board for World Ministries |
| UCC | United Church of Christ |
| UCCan | United Church of Canada |
| UCCI | United Christian Council in Israel |
| UCCP | United Christian Council in Palestine |
| UCCP | United Church of Christ in the Philippines |
| UCCSL | United Christian Council of Sierra Leone |
| UCEC | Union Camerounaise des Etudiants Catholiques |
| UCEI | Ufficio Centrale per l'Emigrazione Italiana |
| UCF | Unions Chrétiennes Féminines |
| UCIP | Union Catholique Internationale de la Pressa |
| UCISS | Union Catholique Internationale de Service Social |
| UCJF | Union Chrétienne de Jeunes Filles |
| UCJG | Union Chrétienne de Jeunes Gens |
| UCL | Université Catholique de Louvain |
| UCLAP | Latin American Union of the Catholic Press |
| UCM | University Christian Movement |
| UCMS | United Christian Missionary Society |
| UCNI | United Church of North India |
| UCP | Unione Cattolica Pubblicità |
| UCSEI | Ufficio Centrale Studenti Esteri in Italia |
| UCSI | Unione Cattolica della Stampa Italiana |
| UD | united diocese |
| UDAL | Union Dahoméenne d'Apostolat des Laïcs |
| UDs | united dioceses |
| UDTC | Union des Congrégations (Féminines) en Tunisie |
| UEAAB | United Ev Association of Antigua-Barbuda |
| UEC | Uganda Episcopal Conference |
| UEC | Union of Evangelical Churches |
| UECA | Union des Etudiants Catholiques Africains |
| UEDNOP | União das Escolas Dominicais do Norte de Por- |

| | |
|---|---|
| | tugal |
| UEO | United Ecumenical Organization |
| UESI | Union of Evangelical Students of India |
| UFFMS | Union Fédérale Française de Musique Sacrée |
| UFM | Unevangelized Fields Mission (UFM International) |
| UHF | ultra high frequency |
| UIM | Urban Industrial Mission |
| UISG | Unione Internazionale delle Superiore Generali |
| UJCC | Uganda Joint Christian Council |
| ULAJE | Unión Latinoamericana de Juventud Evangélica |
| UM | Union Mission (Seventh-day Adventist) |
| UM | Utrecht Mission |
| UMAWATA | Association of Diocesan Priests of Tanzania |
| UMC | United Methodist Church |
| UMCA | United Missionary Church of Africa |
| UMCA | Universities Mission to Central Africa |
| UMCOR | United Methodist Commission for Overseas Relief |
| UMCS | United Muslim Community of Sweden |
| UMMI | Unione Medici Missionaria Italiana |
| UMMON | Union of Moroccan Muslim Organizations in the Netherlands |
| UMN | United Mission to Nepal |
| UMOFC | Unión Mundial de Organizaciones Femeninas Católicas |
| UMPL | Union de Misiones Pentecostales Libres |
| UMS | United Missionary Society |
| UN | United Nations |
| UNAEDE | Union Nationale des Assistants et Educateurs de l'Enfance |
| UNAS | Unión Nacional de Apostolado Seglar |
| UNCAHS | Union Nationale des Congrégations d'Action Hospitalière et Sociale |
| UNCC | Unión Nacional de Colegios Católicos |
| UNCLAP | Unión Latinoamericana de Prènsa Católica |
| UNDA | International Catholic Association for Radio and Television (Latin, wave) |
| UNEC | Unión Nacional Educación Católica |
| UNEC | Union Nationale des Etablissements Catholiques |
| UNELAM | Movimiento pro Unidad Evangélica Latinoamericana |
| UNIAPAC | Union Internationale Chrétienne des Dirigeants d'Entreprise |
| UNICO | Unión de Instituciones Biblicas de la Gran Colombia |
| UNIFE | Universidad Femenina Sagrado Corazón |
| UoB | Unity of Brethren, Unity of the Brethren |
| UOIF | Union des Organisations Islamiques de France |
| UOSR | Union des Oeuvres Sociales Réunionnaises |
| UPC | United Pentecostal Church |
| UPCI | United Pentecostal Church International |
| UPCUSA | United Presbyterian Church in the USA |
| UPFGCI | United Pentecostal Full Gospel Churches of Indonesia |
| UPG | Universal Prayer Group |
| UPUSA | United Presbyterian Church in the USA |
| URG | Union des Religieux de Grèce |
| URI | Union des Religieuses d'Israel |
| URM | Union des Religieuses de Madagascar |
| USCC | United States Catholic Conference |
| USCE | United Society of Christian Endeavor |
| USCL | United Society for Christian Literature |
| USCMA | US Catholic Mission Association |
| USCWM | U.S. Center for World Mission |
| USG | Unione dei Superiori Generali |
| USICOP | United States Interreligious Committee on Peace |
| USMDC | Union des Supérieures Majeures et Déléguées du Cameroun |
| USMI | Unione Superiore Maggiori d'Italia |
| USMM | Union des Supérieurs Majeurs de Madagascar |
| USMSR | Union des Supérieures Majeures de Suisse Romande |
| USPG | United Society for the Propagation of the Gospel |
| USTC | Union Seychelloise des Travailleurs Chrétiens |
| USUMA | Union des Supérieures Majeures du Zaïre |
| UTJ | United Torah Judaism |
| UUA | Unitarian Universalist Association |
| UUSC | Unitarian Universalist Service Committee |
| UVA | Una Voce Helvetica |

| | |
|---|---|
| UWM | United World Mission |

# V

| | |
|---|---|
| V | vicariate |
| VA | vicariate apostolic |
| VBE | Verband Bildung und Erziehung |
| VBS | Vacation Bible Schools |
| VCAMS | Voice of China and Asia Missionary Society |
| VCC | Vanuatu Christian Council |
| VDO | Vereinigung Deutscher Ordensoberen |
| VELKD | Vereinigte Ev-Lutherische Kirche Deutschlands |
| VERTA | Visayan Educational Radio and TV Association |
| VFKO | Vereinigung der Frauenorden und Kongregationen Österreichs |
| VFR | visual flight rules (contact flying) |
| VHF | very high frequency |
| VHOB | Vereinigung Höherer Ordensoberen der Bruderorden und Kongregationen Deutschlands |
| VHOD | Vereinigung Höherer Ordensoberienen Deutschlands |
| VHP | Vishwa Hindu Parishad |
| VICS | Volunteer International Christian Service |
| VIICC | St Thomas Inter-Church Council |
| VISA | Volunteers in Service Abroad |
| VKDL | Verein Katholischer Deutscher Lehrerinen |
| VKLS | Verein Katholischer Lehrerinnen der Schweiz |
| VKW | Verbond van Christelijke Werkgevers |
| VMM | Volunteer Missionary Movement |
| VOP | Voice of Prophecy |
| VP | patriarchal vicariate |

# W

| | |
|---|---|
| W | west, western |
| WACB | World Association for Christian Broadcasting |
| WACC | World Association for Christian Communication |
| WACCC | West Africa Council of Christian Churches |
| WAGF | World Assemblies of God Fellowship |
| WAMRAC | World Association of Methodist Radio Amateurs & Clubs |
| WARC | World Alliance of Reformed Churches (Presbyterian and Congregational) |
| WBFM | World Baptist Fellowship Mission |
| WBIT | World Bank of Information Terms |
| WBSC | World Buddhist Sangha Council |
| WBTI | Wycliffe Bible Translators International |
| WC | Wesleyan Church |
| WCBC | World Council of Biblical Churches |
| WCC | World Council of Churches |
| WCCC | World Convention of Churches of Christ |
| WCCE | World Council of Christian Education |
| WCCP | World Conference of Christians for Palestine |
| WCD | World Christian Database |
| WCE | World Christian Encyclopedia |
| WCEU | World Christian Endeavor Union |
| WCF | Workers' Christian Fellowship |
| WCF | World Congress of Faiths |
| WCFBA | World Catholic Federation for the Biblical Apostolate |
| WCFI | World Congress of Friday Imams |
| WCFs | World Confessional Families |
| WCG | Worldwide Church of God |
| WCGAP | World Christian Global Action Plan |
| WCH | World Christian Handbook |
| WCL | William Carey Library |
| WCMR | World Conference on Missionary Radio |
| WCPC | World Conference of Pentecostal Churches |
| WCT | World Christian Trends |
| WEC | Worldwide Evangelization Crusade (WEC International) |
| WEF | World Evangelical Fellowship |
| WEGO | World Encounter Gospel Organization |
| WELG | Women's Ecumenical Liaison Group |
| WERC | World Evangelization Research Center |
| WF | White Fathers (Society of Missionaries of Africa) |
| WF(PB) | White Fathers |
| WFB | World Fellowship of Buddhists |

| | |
|---|---|
| WFBMF | World Fundamental Baptist Missionary Fellowship |
| WFC | World Film Crusade |
| WFMW | World Federation of Methodist Women |
| WFR | World Fellowship of Religions |
| WFS | World Future Society |
| WGC | World Gospel Crusades |
| WGM | World Gospel Mission |
| WH | World Horizons |
| WHBL | World Home Bible League |
| WHC | World Hindu Conference |
| WIC | World Islamic Congress |
| WICS | World Islamic Call Society |
| WIM | West Indies Mission |
| WLC | World Literature Crusade |
| WLE | World Literacy Evangelism |
| WLSM | World Library of Sacred Music |
| WMC | World Methodist Council |
| WMC | World Missionary Conference |
| WMC | World Muslim Congress |
| WME | World Missionary Evangelism |
| WMMS | Wesleyan Methodist Missionary Society |
| WMPL | World Mission Prayer League |
| WMU | Woman's Missionary Union |
| WNWDAL | Webster's New World Dictionary of the American Language |
| WPM | World Presbyterian Mission |
| WRC | World Relief Commission |
| WRC | World Revival Crusade |
| WRMF | World Radio Missionary Fellowship |
| WSC | World Spiritual Council |
| WSCF | World Student Christian Federation |
| WT | World Team |
| WTBTS | Watch Tower Bible & Tract Society |
| WTF | World Thrust Films |
| WTNIDEL | Webster's Third New International Dictionary of the English Language |
| WU | World Union |
| WUCT | World Union of Catholic Teachers |
| WV | Weisse Vater (WF) |
| WVI | World Vision International |
| WWCTU | World Women's Christian Temperance Union |
| WWM | World-Wide Missions |
| WWP | World Wide Pictures |
| WWPMU | World-Wide Prayer & Missionary Union |
| WYD | World Youth Day |
| WYP | World Youth Project |

# Y

| | |
|---|---|
| YBC | Yugoslav Bishops' Conference |
| YCGS | Young Catholic Girl Students |
| YCS | Young Catholic Students |
| YCS | Young Christian Socialists |
| YCW | Young Catholic Workers |
| YCW | Young Christian Workers |
| YFC | Youth for Christ |
| YFCI | Youth for Christ International |
| YIC | Yugoslav Islamic Community |
| YM | Yearly Meeting (Friends) |
| YMBA | Young Men's Buddhist Association |
| YMCA | Young Men's Christian Association |
| YUGO | Youth Unlimited Gospel Outreach |
| YWAM | Youth With A Mission |
| YWCA | Young Women's Christian Association |

# Z

| | |
|---|---|
| ZAC | Zambia Anglican Council |
| ZCBC | Zimbabwe Catholic Bishops' Conference |
| ZCC | Zion Christian Church |
| ZCCD | Zambia Christian Commission for Development |
| ZEC | Zambia Episcopal Conference |
| ZEM | Zaire Evangelistic Mission |
| ZZG | Zeist Mission Society (Zeister Zendingsgenootschap) |

## Table 32–4. Photographic index.

Listed here are all subjects and topics illustrated in the photographs contained in this volume, or described in their accompanying captions. In particular, the index lists their countries, places, occasions, events, persons, peoples, languages, cultures, ethnolinguistic groups, religions, types of Christian, ecclesiastical blocs and traditions, types of denomination, types of Christian organization, councils, activities, evangelism, religious practices, resources, buildings, projects, rituals, liturgies, uniforms, vestments, robes, representations (images, icons, paintings, statues, art), and the range of phenomena of religion and Christianity in general. It also lists illustrations of the methods of description, enumeration and analysis evolved in this volume. On the other hand, the index does not record the smaller details of all photographs. In general, it omits names of small towns and villages, also names of smaller denominations and individual churches or congregations.

The index omits certain widely-applicable terms that would otherwise occur too frequently. 'Roman Catholics' and 'Protestants', for instance, occur in every other illustration.

Terms thus omitted include: cathedrals, Christian, Christians, church, churches, church buildings, Protestants, Roman Catholics, Catholics, Evangelicals (partially included), priests, ministers, clergy, preachers.

Christianity is noted in greater detail than other religions. For 'processions', for example, the listing is of Christian processions, even though processions of other religions may appear in the volume. So also with many other listings.

## Table 32–5. Standard and definitive locations index.

This is primarily an index of general subjects, major categories of data, and types of information.

KEY
1. Numbers standing alone (1–999) = page numbers of major or definitive locations, always preceded by Part number.
2. Entries without page numbers = standard locations, repeated for all countries.
3. The world 'total' = global total of category shown.

There is no need in this volume for a general subject index

because (a) most significant material has already been presented throughout under several alphabetical listings (countries, denominations, service agencies, directory entries), and (b) most specific categories of data or information are placed in standardized locations within the overall framework. As a result, comparative data from one country to the next can rapidly be found. This final index attempts to facilitate the whole process of locating specific types of data.

There are 2 types of entry below: those with page numbers, and those with Part numbers. These will now be described in further detail.

All numbers (1–999) standing alone below are *page num-*

*bers* unless otherwise clearly stated. These, located by preceding Part number, give the definitive or major or unique location or locations of specific categories—items of data or information or definition, or directory of names; they also indicate pages with global maps where relevant. Hence, if you wish to find the total number of Methodists, or Maronites, in the world for a particular year, this index refers you to its definitive location. Sometimes 2 or more locations are given, placing the required total in different contexts. This represents the quickest way of finding herein an exact total or figure or definition that you require for any clearly-defined category.

---

### INDEX TO MAJOR SUBJECTS IN THE 33 PARTS

atlas, Part 33
Bible distribution, Part 19
bibliography, Part 31
Christian finances, Part 20
Christianity, global status of, Part 1
chronology, Part 2
church growth, Part 26
codebook, Part 16
countries, statistics of, Part 12
cultures, Part 18
evangelism, Part 22
evangelization, Parts 23-25
evangelization, global status of, Part 1
finances, Christian, Part 20
future, Parts 2, 29
global statistics, Parts 9,10
glossary, Part 30
Great Commission, Part 3
history, Part 2
independency, Part 6
indexes, Part 32
instrumentation, Part 15
leaders, Part 8
lists, Top 10, Part 11
maps, Part 33
martyrdom, Part 4
methodology, Parts 14, 24
missiometrics, Part 14
monitoring, Part 13
peoples, Part 18
personnel, Part 21
plans, global, Part 27
postdenominationalism, Part 6
religions, Part 17
renewal, Part 5
response, Part 26
scriptures, Part 19
statistics, Parts 9,10
statistics, by country, Part 12
strategies, Parts 27-28
targeting, Part 28
Top 10 lists, Part 11
trends, Part 7
Who's Who, Part 8
workers, Christian, Part 21
World Christian Global Action Plan, Part 27
Worlds A, B, C, Part 25

---

10/40 Window, map, Part 33, Global Map 4
24 hour worldwide statistical changes, Part 1, Table 1-4
600 books classified by 4 codes, Part 14, Table 14-6
600 classics impinging on missiometrics, Part 14, Table 14-7

## A

abbreviations, Christian, Part 32, Table 32-3
absolute poverty, Part 20, 653
absolute poverty, Christians living in, Part 20, 653
acronyms, Christian, Part 32, Table 32-3
activities, global Christian, Part 12, Table 12-1
AD 2000 & goals, Part 27, 792f
AD2025 (WCGAP), Part 27, 827
adequacy of Christian work and resources, Part 24, Table 24-10
adequacy, established levels of, Part 24, Table 24-9
adequacy, inadequacy, superfluity of Christian resources, Part 24, Table 24-10
adherents of all religions by continents, Part 10, Table 10-6
adherents of all religions, global, Part 1, Table 1-2
adult Christians, world totals, Part 10, Table 10-12
adult church members, total, Part 10, Table 10-9
adult literates, Part 10, Table 10-12
adults, world totals, Part 10, Table 10-12
Adventists, global statistics, Part 10, Table 10-9
affiliated Christians, total, Part 1, Table 1-2
affiliation, church, definition, Part 14, 473f
affluence, Part 1, GD 18
Afghanistan, Part 12, Table 12-1
Africa, adherents of all religions in, Part 10, Table 10-6
African Independent Christians/churches, global statistics, Part 10, Table 10-9
Africans, total, Part 10, Table 10-6
Afro-American spiritists, total, Part 1, Table 1-2
Afro-Brazilian cultists, total, Part 1, Table 1-2
Afro-Caribbean religionists, total, Part 1, Table 1-2
agency evangelism, Part 24, Table 24-8

agnostics, total, Part 1, Table 1-2
agriculture, Part 1, GD 21
Ahmadis, total, Part 1, Table 1-2
Alawites, total, Part 1, Table 1-2
Albania, Part 12, Table 12-1
Algeria, Part 12, Table 12-1
alien Christians among a people, Part 24, Table 24-12
aliens received from abroad as missionaries, Part 12, Table 12-1, columns 111-112
American Samoa, Part 12, Table 12-1
Anabaptists/Mennonites, global statistics, Part 10, Table 10-9
Andorra, Part 12, Table 12-1
Anglican Charismatics, Part 5, Table 5-8
Anglican denominations, fastest-growing (Top 10), Part 11, 403
Anglican denominations, largest (Top 10), Part 11, 403
Anglican Evangelicals, Part 5, Graphic 5-3
Anglican Evangelicals, global statistics, Part 10, Table 10-9
Anglican growth rate, countries with highest (Top 10), Part 11, 402
Anglican national/plurinational churches, Part 5, Table 5-3
Anglican World in Figures 2000, Part 5, 271-273
Anglicanism, bibliography, Part 5, 273-274
Anglicans, by continent, AD 1900-AD 2025, Part 10, Table 10-6
Anglicans, by continent, AD1900-AD 2000, Part 5, Global Map 5-1
Anglicans, by country, AD1900-AD 2000, Part 5, Table 5-4
Anglicans, church & global statistics, Part 5, Table 5-3, Part 10, Table 10-9
Anglicans, countries with most (Top 10), Part 11, 401
Anglicans, global minisurvey, Part 5, 271-274
Anglicans, High Church, global statistics, Part 10, Table 10-9
Anglicans, Low Church, global statistics, Part 10, Table 10-9
Anglicans, total, Part 1, Table 1-2
Anglo-Catholics, global statistics, Part 10, Table 10-9
Angola, Part 12, Table 12-1
Anguilla, Part 12, Table 12-1
animists, total, Part 1, Table 1-2
annual rate of increase, all religions, Part 1, Table 1-2
Annual reports, 1952-2001., Part 1, Table AA
Antarctica, Part 12, Table 12-1
Antigua, Part 12, Table 12-1
Apostles, martyrdom of, Part 4, Table 4-2
apostolate to the world, Part 1, GD 15
apostolate, persons dedicated to the, Part 21
Apostolic Age, Part 2
apostolic force, Part 21
Apostolic Pentecostals, global statistics, Part 10, Table 10-9
Arabic-speaking Orthodox, global statistics, Part 10, Table 10-9
Argentina, Part 12, Table 12-1
Armenia, Part 12, Table 12-1
Armenian Apostolics, total, Part 10, Table 10-9
Armenian Orthodox, global statistics, Part 10, Table 10-9
Aruba, Part 12, Table 12-1
Ashkenazis, total, Part 1, Table 1-2
Asian Indigenous churches, total, Part 10, Table 10-9
Asians, total, Part 10, Table 10-6
atheist growth rate, countries with highest (Top 10), Part 11, 401
atheistic countries, Part 10, Table 10-13
atheistic states, Part 12, Table 12-1, columns 60-63
atheists, by continent, AD 1900-AD 2025, Part 10, Table 10-6
atheists, countries with most (Top 10), Part 11, 400
atheists, peoples with most (Top 10), Part 11, 403
atheists, total, Part 1, Table 1-2
atlas, Part 33
atlases, Part 31
attendance, church, enumeration, Part 14, 474
audiences, radio/TV, Part 12, Table 12-1, columns 147-149
audio scriptures, evangelism by, Part 22, 685
audiovisual ministries, evangelism by, Part 22, 684
Australia, Part 12, Table 12-1
Austria, Part 12, Table 12-1
autocephalous episcopal churches, Part 6, Table 6-10
availability of scriptures, in all countries, Part 12, Table 12-1
Azerbaijan, Part 12, Table 12-1

## B

background martyrdom, varieties of, Part 4, Table 4-9
Baha'is, by continent, AD 1900-AD 2025, Part 10, Table 10-6

Baha'is, peoples with most (Top 10), Part 11, 404
Baha'is, total, Part 1, Table 1-2, Part 17
Bahamas, Part 12, Table 12-1
Bahrain, Part 12, Table 12-1
Bangladesh, Part 12, Table 12-1
baptisms, total annual, Part 1, GD 41
Baptistic-Pentecostals, global statistics, Part 10, Table 10-9
Baptists, global statistics, Part 10, Table 10-9
Barbados, Part 12, Table 12-1
barriers to world evangelization, Part 27, 791
Belgium, Part 12, Table 12-1
belief, enumeration of , Part 14, 474
Belize, Part 12, Table 12-1
Belorussia, Part 12, Table 12-1
Belorussian Orthodox, global statistics, Part 10, Table 10-9
Benin, Part 12, Table 12-1
Bermuda, Part 12, Table 12-1
Bhutan, Part 12, Table 12-1
Bible (translation, versions, distribution), bibliography, Part 19, 645
Bible distribution, by country, Part 12, Table 12-1, 420-425
Bible, largest peoples without their own (Top 10), Part 11, 404
Bibles distributed, for all countries, Part 12, Table 12-1, columns 120-125
Bibles needed & distributed, AD 400-AD 2025, Part 19, Table 19-2
Bibles, evangelism by, Part 22, 690
biblical imperatives of missiometrics, Part 14, Table 14-1
biblical imperatives of missiometrics, full listing of English, Part 14, Table 14-2
biblical origins of missiometrics, Part 14, 447
biblical studies, bibliography, Part 31, 871-872
biblical theology of mission, Part 3, 213-216
bibliographic resources, by country, Part 31, Table 31-4
bibliographical listing of 600 missiometric classics, Part 14, Table 14-7
bibliographies in this volume, Part 31, 866f
bibliography on trends, Part 7, 334
bibliography, Part 31
bibliography, Anglicanism, Part 5, 273-274
bibliography, Bible (translation, versions, distribution), Part 19, 645
bibliography, Biblical studies, Part 31, 871-872
bibliography, bibliographies, Part 31, 880f
bibliography, Buddhism, Part 31, 878
bibliography, Catholic Charismatic Renewal, Part 5, 278
bibliography, Christianity & religions, Part 31
bibliography, Christianity, contemporary status, Part 31, 871
bibliography, church history, Part 31, 872-873
bibliography, ecumenism, Part 31, 875-876
bibliography, electronic media, Part 31, 880
bibliography, esthetics (Christian), Part 31, 876
bibliography, evangelism, Part 22, 691-693
bibliography, finance, Christian, Part 20, 663-664
bibliography, future, Part 29, 846-850; Part 29, Table 29-5
bibliography, global plans, Part 27, 799
bibliography, Great Commission, Part 3, 224
bibliography, Hinduism, Part 31, 878
bibliography, history of doctrine, Part 31, 873-874
bibliography, history, Part 2, 100
bibliography, independency, Part 6, 301
bibliography, interfaith dialogue, Part 31, 879
bibliography, Islam, Part 31, 877
bibliography, Judaism, Part 31, 877-878
bibliography, macroevangelistics, Part 25, 769
bibliography, major subjects in, Part 31, Table 31-5
bibliography, martyrdom, Part 4, 235-237
bibliography, missiology, Part 31, 875
bibliography, non-Christian religions, Part 31, 877f
bibliography, peoples, Part 18, 633-638
bibliography, postdenominationalism, Part 6, 301
bibliography, religion, study of, Part 31, 879f
bibliography, renewal, Part 5, 290
bibliography, scriptures, Part 19, 645
bibliography, statistics, Part 9, 360
bibliography, theological ethics, Part 31, 875
bibliography, theology, Part 31, 874
Black Muslims, total, Part 1, Table 1-2
blind persons, countries with most (top 10), Part 11, 399
Bolivia, Part 12, Table 12-1
book titles on Christian & religious subjects, Part 31, Table 31-3
book titles with 'Jesus Christ', by language, Part 31, Table 31-1
books about Christianity, Part 31, 865f
books, Christian, evangelism by, Part 22, 690
books, futurist, Part 29, Table 29-5
Bosnia-Herzegovina, Part 12, Table 12-1
Botswana, Part 12, Table 12-1

# Acknowledgements

The authors and editors wish to acknowledge their indebtedness not only to the contributors, collaborators, and consultants listed at the beginning of the First and Second Editions of WCE/WCT/WCD, but also to the very large number of other persons and organizations who supplied information each about their own activities. Many of the denominations listed in each country, and many other agencies and bodies mentioned or described, supplied this information to us either directly by mail, e-mail, or in person in interviews.

We also express gratitude to a number of church-related organizations which contributed grants towards the compiling either of one of the two Editions or of both. Grants and assistance small or large were received from the following: Adveniat (Germany), American Baptist Churches, Anglican Church of Canada, Anglican Consultative Council (UK), Anglican Frontier Missions, Apostolic Nunciature of Kenya, Bethany World Prayer Center, Bishops' Conference of Germany, William R. Bright, Campus Crusade for Christ International, Caleb Project, CBInternational, Christian Church (Disciples of Christ), Church Missionary Society (UK), Church of the Province of Kenya, Church of the Savior Philadelphia, John & Pam Cobb, Commission on World Mission and Evangelism/WCC, Cooperative Baptist Fellowship, Crowell Trust, Des Plaines Trust, Division of Overseas Ministries/NCCCUSA, Mark & Beth Dubis, Dunwoody Foundation, Episcopal Church in the USA, FERES (Belgium), Field Ministry Internships, First Foursquare Church on the Way Los Angeles, Global Center Samford University, Global Strategy Mission Association, Humanum (Germany), the 'Jesus' Film Project, Kempsville Presbyterian Church Virginia Beach, John & Beth Labonty, Lausanne Committee for World Evangelization, Lonnie & Ramona Long, Lutheran Church Missouri Synod, Lutheran World Federation, Maryknoll Mission, Missio (Germany), Mission Training and Resource Center (Pasadena), Missions Advanced Research and Communication Center (Monrovia, USA), National Council of Churches of Christ in the USA, The Navigators, Network of Strategic Missions, William R. O'Brien, Operation World, Jerry & Deana Parker, Charles Price, Sacred Congregation for the Evangelization of Peoples, Short-term Evangelical Mission, Southern Baptist Convention, St. Giles Endowment Fund, St. Giles Presbyterian Church Richmond, Strang Communications, Survey Application Trust (Grubb Institute for World Studies, UK), Vinson Synan, Third Presbyterian Church Richmond, United Bible Societies, United Church of Christ (USA), United Methodist Church (World Division, Board of Global Ministries), United Presbyterian Church in the USA, Virginia Baptist Resource Center, World Council of Churches, World Mission Prayer League, World Reach, World Vision International. Among donors of smaller grants were: Abbaye d'Orval (Belgium), American Baptist Foreign Missionary Society, Assemblies of God (USA), Christian Reformed Church, Conservative Baptist Association of America, Department of Philosophy & Religious Studies/University of Nairobi, Lutheran Church in America, The Navigators, Netherlands Reformed Church, Reformed Church in America, Sudan Interior Mission, United Church Board for World Mission, United Reformed Church (UK), US Center for World Mission, West Indies Mission, Westminster Presbyterian Church (Richmond), World Radio Missionary Fellowship, et alia.

**Maps**
The authors are grateful also to Oxford Cartographers for designing and producing the 16 Global Maps in Part 33 "GeoAtlas", and also to Oxford University Press who permitted us to reproduce in our Part 33 their 18 Human Environment maps from the Oxford World Atlas/Penguin World Atlas, suitably updated by Oxford Cartographers.

**Photographs**
We further acknowledge with gratitude the assistance of a number of photographic libraries and agencies, as well as individual experts and specialists, in the assembling of a collection of illustrations which would do justice to the complexity of contemporary global Christianity and its context in the modern world. Half of the photographs in the First Edition were the editor's own. Half in the 2001 editions WCE/WCT were taken and supplied by Maurice Harvey, photojournalist of the United Bible Societies for many years. The other photographs in both Editions were supplied by the organizations and persons listed alphabetically below (with individuals included alphabetically by surname), whose cooperation and permission to reproduce has been much appreciated. In a number of cases, the denominations illustrated in photographs sent us copies waiving credit or charges. Their illustrations have made our survey that much more complete. Lastly, a few professional photographic libraries searched their collections for our more unusual categories.

Every effort has been made to trace and contact copyright owners. If there are any inadvertent omissions in these acknowledgements, we apologize to those concerned and will remedy this when possible.

**Photo credits**
Joy Adamson, Aegte Foto, Africapix, Agenzia Informazioni Missionarie, Hamilton Aikin, Air France, AMECEA, American Bible Society, Anglican Consultative Council, AREPI, Argus Group, Asia Theological Association, Associated Newspapers Ltd, Associated Press Ltd, Association Culturelle Orthodoxe Russe, Association of Evangelicals of Africa & Madagascar, Audiovisie NZR Baarn, Australian Inland Mission, Dr K. Baago, L. Balterman, Baptist Missionary Society, Carlo Bavagnoli, BBC Photographic Library, Bernhard Johnson, British & Foreign Bible Society, British Airways, British Museum, Brunner & C., Camera Hawaii, Camera Press Ltd, Camerapix, Campus Crusade for Christ, Candida Photos, Central Office of Information, Central Press Photos Ltd, Ceylon Pictorials, Christian Mission to the Communist World, Christian Weekly Newspapers Ltd, Christianity Today, Church Information Office, Church Missionary Society, Church Times, Church of Jesus Christ of Latter-day Saints, Church World Service, Collection Iris, Council for World Mission, Create International, Gerald Cubitt, Dagen, Daily News, M. L. Daneel, P. V. de Decker, Die Burger, Jesper Dijohn, Gregory Duriniak, East African Standard, East African Venture Co, Editions de Luxe Estel Lavelle, Editions Greff, Editions Hoa-qui, Editions Jaeger, Edizioni Angeli Terni, Evangelical Union of South America, Eveche de Basse-Terre, Fides-Foto, Foto Felici, Foto Simon, Gibraltar Tourist Office, Dr Roswith Gerloff, Lydon Giles, V. G. Greisen, Hal Herman, Dr Norman Horner, Iglesia Anglicana en el Norte Argentina, Indonesia Council of Churches, Info (Botswana), International Baha'i Audio-Visual Center, Michael Irwin, Carl Iwasaki, Harold D. Jantz, Jeremy Grayson, Jersey Evening Post, John Piercy Ltd, D. Kalaba, Otis Keener, Keston College, Leon V. Kofod, Edouard Kutter Jr, Hans Lachmann, RWJV, Lamontfoto, Lausanne Committee for World Evangelization, Life Picture Service, Logos Ministry for Orthodox Renewal, London Daily Mail, Luis Palau Evangelistic Team Inc, K. Lyons, L'Osservatore Romano, Michael McCann, D. A. McGavran, Kalevi A. Mäkinen, Malaysian Airline System, Malaysian Information Service, Ted Marriott, K. Martens, Maryknoll, Dr John Mbiti, Methodist Church in Tonga, Methodist Church Nigeria, Methodist Missionary Society, Methodist Missions, Methodist Prints, Robert Miles, Missionary Aviation Fellowship, Missions to Seamen, J. H. Moore, Nationfoto, New Covenant Magazine, Newsweek International, Nordisk Pressefoto, Operation Mobilization, T. J. Padwick, Paris-Match, May Park, C. D. Paulme, Photo Almassy, Photo COE, Photo Lamont, Pilgrim Films, Paul Popper Ltd, Porter's Photo News, Press Association Ltd, Pressefoto, Johann Gürer, Pressfoto, Pretoria News, Qantas, Radio Times Hulton Picture Library, M. T. Ramakatane, Revista Mundo, Rex Studio Garbis Semerdjian, Ross Photo, Royal Norwegian Ministry of Foreign Affairs, Salvation Army Information, Ernest Satow, Frank Scherschel, Walter Scott, Max Seifert, Seventh-day Adventists, Calvin Shenk, SIM Publications, S. Skulina, Sky-foto Möller, Lester Sloan, Peter Solbjerghoj, South American Missionary Society, Southern Baptist Convention, Sport & General Press Agency, State Museum Berlin, Swazi Times, Sygma, George Talanos, John Taylor, The News/New York, Pat Thomas, Time, Inc, Trans World Radio, Dr Gary Trompf, Y. Tourigny, Dr Harold W. Turner, UNESCO, Unification Church, United Bible Societies, United Church of Canada/Berkeley Studio, Unitedf Methodist Communications, United Methodist Global Ministries, United Methodist Missions, United Nations, United Press International, United Society for the Propagation of the Gospel, Rein Välme, J.-F. Vincent, Vivante Afrique, Harold Wenger, West Indies Mission, Wide World Photos Inc, World Council of Churches, World Outlook, World Pentecost Magazine, World Vision International, Worldwide Evangelization Crusade

**Technical description**
The authors and editors also acknowledge their indebtedness to the large number of persons and organizations who supplied information, data, and programs about their own activities in electronic form.

Computers played an essential role in the formation and presentation of this work. The following lists the major areas of development, the programs and the equipment used.

The GEM file server/workstation was custom built from Tailored Data Solutions in Chester, Virginia. It is a dual Pentium™ 350 MHz with 256 MB of RAM running Windows NT™ 4.0 SP4 with two 10 GB Quantum™ hard drives. The 'Great Commission Instrument Panel' graphics were developed using Microsoft Visual FoxPro™ 5.0 and Macromedia Freehand 9.0, Microsoft Excel™ 97 with SP2, and Corel Draw™ 7. Databases were developed on Microsoft Visual FoxPro™ 5.0 and Microsoft Access™ 97 with SP2.

The bulk of data entry was undertaken on five machines: an Apple Macintosh PowerPC™ 6100/60AV with a Sonnett Crescendo™ G3 NuBus card, 40 MB RAM and 250 MB hard drive; two Apple Power Macintosh™ G3 233 MHz with 96 MB RAM and a 4 GB hard drive; an Apple iMac™ 233 MHz with 64 MB of RAM and a 4 GB hard drive; a Dell Dimension XPS™ P133c Pentium 133 MHz, 32 MB RAM, and a 3 GB hard drive; and a Compaq Presario™ 4712 Pentium 166 MHz with 72 MB RAM and a 3 GB hard drive.

Desktop publishing was handled on an Apple Power Macintosh™ G3 233 MHz with 96 MB RAM, 4 GB hard drive, and an Apple 17 inch screen and an Apple 466 MHz G4 Titanium tower with a 30 GB hard drive, 256 MB of SDRAM, CD-RW, and a Hitachi SuperScan™ Pro 21 inch screen. The manuscript was published using QuarkXPress™ 4.1 with Em Software XData™ 4.1 and MarkzWare MarkzTools™ III 8.07. Photos were produced using an HP 5370C scanner with tranparancy adapter, HP Precision-Scan Pro software, and Adobe Photoshop™ 4.0.1. Graphics were developed using Macromedia Freehand 9 and Ready, Set, Go™. Prepress preparations were processed with MarkzWare Flightcheck™ 3.84, and Adobe Acrobat™ 4.05a.

The manuscript was printed on an Apple LaserWriter™ 8500 with 48 MB of RAM.

Part 33

# GEOATLAS

A mini-atlas of human environment, Christianity,
and ministries in the global context

*The light of Christ illuminates the whole world.*
—Liturgy of the Presanctified, Byzantine rite, AD 692

CONTENTS OF PART 33 "GEOATLAS"

This mini-atlas is divided into 2 sections: an 8-page section with 16 global religious trend maps, and a 16-page section with 18 secular politico-geographical human environment maps.

Certain limitations of these maps arise because they are designed to have 4 mulitple uses,

as follows. (1) The usual service is visually to readers as they turn over page by page. For such, all 34 maps may appear overcrowded, with too much detail and with many names and sentences in very small type. This however is normal in world atlases. (2) The PDF disk in the sleeve inside the rear cover of this volume en-

ables the reader to rapidly search for any name or word in the entire volume, and to magnify on screen or to print out any part of any map. (3) Electronic versions (WCD) expand these functions. (4) All 34 color maps, as well as 74 Global Diagrams and any related data, can be made available as full-size color wall charts.

## A. Trends in global Christianity and world evangelization

The data on which Global Maps 1-16 are based come from WCT's first 32 Parts and also WCE's Part 4 "Countries", Country Tables 1 and 2. Taken in conjunction with Maps 1-18 below, they contribute to the subject known as the geography of religion, and in particular the geography of Christianity, and the geography of missions. Every Global Map locates on it the names of the UN-termed 7 continents (major areas, shown in capital letters in double-line window boxes) and 20 regions (shown in up-

per/lowercase type in thin rectangular window boxes. All these names are set out in detail on Table 7-2, or in Part 12 "CountryTrends", column 3). Note however that the Global Maps are meant to illustrate only the subjects in the titles; to keep them uncluttered, no names of countries are added except the Top Ten in Global Map 15. For any country's secular details, the reader should consult Maps 1-18. Note also that the unit used throughout these first 16 Global Maps is the country—every

country is given a single color in each Global Map, corresponding to its value of the variable being depicted. Note carefully too that the situation of many countries is fluid, often very fluid, which means that some countries slip into or out of the colored categories, or their exact numerical state, as the months go by. This means that the Global Maps and their colors should be viewed as visual aids, an impressionistic portrait in oils rather than a precise photograph.

*Page*

## B. The modern secular world: human environment and activity

The 18 maps in this section describe the modern secular world which forms the context for global Christianity and religion. They are intended to illustrate the country data in WCT Part 12 "CountryTrends" as well as in each country's article and text in WCE Part 4 "Countries". They are arranged not geographically but chronologically, in approximately the order of the worldwide expansion of Christianity by continents and regions, beginning with the cradle region of the Middle East. All countries are shown except the smaller Pacific islands. In the listing below, after each region a typical or representative country is named for

illustrative purposes, followed by the date of the definitive coming of Christianity (as documented here in WCT Part 2 "CosmoChronology").

### Key to human environment maps
These maps portray the secular context for the study of religion. For each country the following 22 subject areas have been quantified and/or depicted (see each map's small key for more detail):
topographical features (heights in meters), political boundaries (state and internal), vegetation (forest to desert), land usage (farming,

paddy, irrigation), rural population density (4 levels of brown shading), metropolises and cities (each with impressionistic yellow population blocs), motorways, railways, shipping routes, ports, shipping (5 sizes, largest over 70 million tonnage p.a.), airports, air traffic (10 levels, with highest level 10 = over 1.5 million incoming flights p.a.), hydro-electric power stations (HEP), dams, canals, and mining (extraction of 14 major minerals). These and other variables on the maps are explained in the small box on each map which is reproduced here in the box below.

POPULATION & CITIES / LAND USE key box:
per sq. kilometre: 100, 10, 1, under 1; coniferous forest, mixed forest, deciduous forest, tropical forest; 1 million, 100,000, others; farming; motorways, main roads, railways; paddy, other irrigation; shipping, air traffic; savanna; HEP station, iron mining etc; desert, sand, other, marsh or bog; heights in metres

## Additional secular and religious country variables .

A large number of additional variables describing countries can be found in 2 parallel atlases. For religious data, *The state of religion atlas* (J. O'Brien, M. Palmer, D. B. Barrett, 1993)

contains 34 world maps depicting world religions with a wide range of 100 newly–quantified variables. For secular data, *The new state of the world atlas* (M. Kidron, D. Smith, 6th edi-

tion 1999) has 50 world maps with a wealth of data on over 100 recently quantified variables (e.g. Map 27 'Human rights').

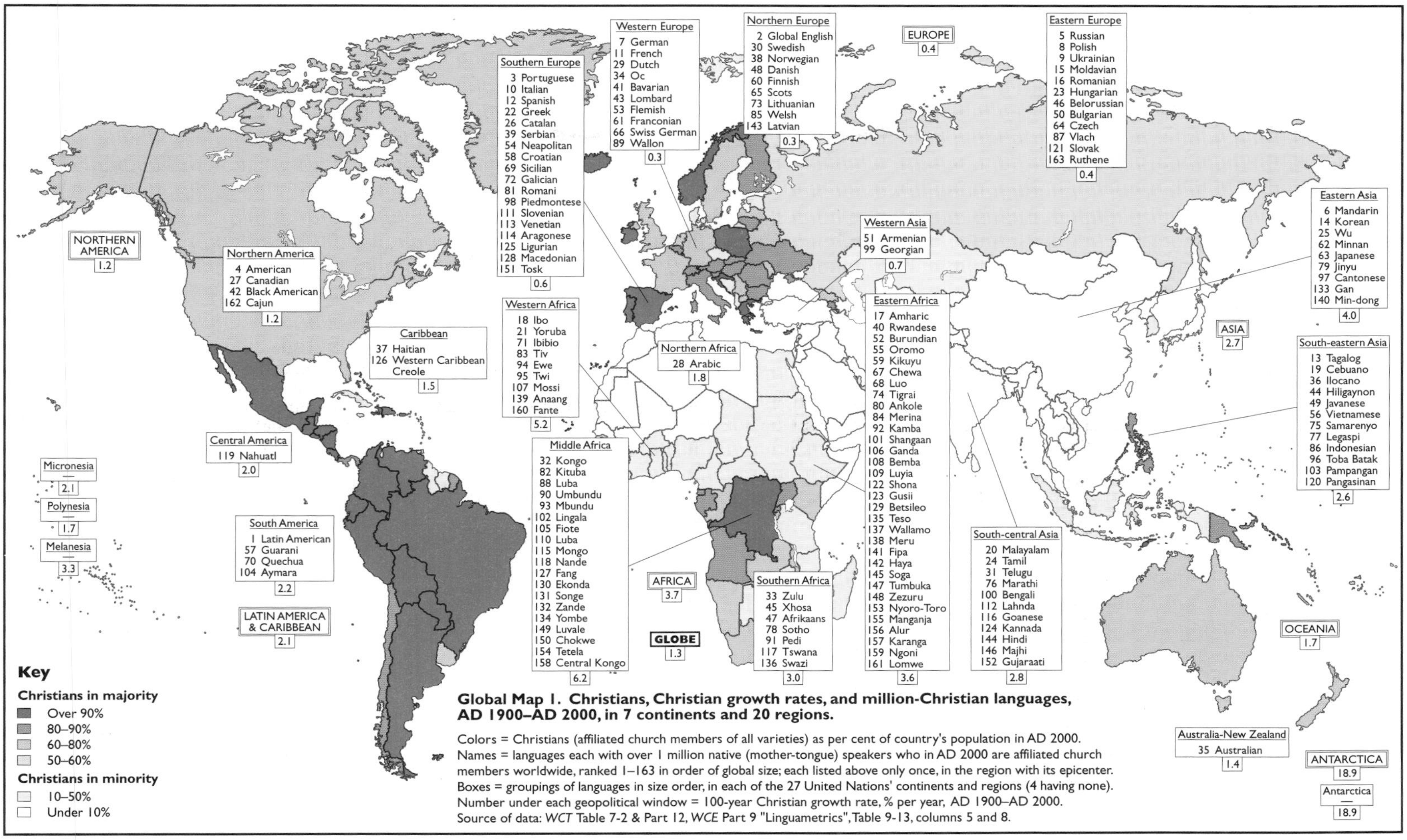

## Global Map 1.

**EUROPE** 0.4

**Western Europe**
7 German
11 French
29 Dutch
34 Oc
41 Bavarian
43 Lombard
53 Flemish
61 Franconian
66 Swiss German
89 Wallon
0.3

**Northern Europe**
2 Global English
30 Swedish
38 Norwegian
48 Danish
60 Finnish
65 Scots
73 Lithuanian
85 Welsh
143 Latvian
0.3

**Eastern Europe**
5 Russian
8 Polish
9 Ukrainian
15 Moldavian
16 Romanian
23 Hungarian
46 Belorussian
50 Bulgarian
64 Czech
87 Vlach
121 Slovak
163 Ruthene
0.4

**Southern Europe**
3 Portuguese
10 Italian
12 Spanish
22 Greek
26 Catalan
39 Serbian
54 Neapolitan
58 Croatian
69 Sicilian
72 Galician
81 Romani
98 Piedmontese
111 Slovenian
113 Venetian
114 Aragonese
125 Ligurian
128 Macedonian
151 Tosk
0.6

**NORTHERN AMERICA** 1.2

**Northern America**
4 American
27 Canadian
42 Black American
162 Cajun
1.2

**Caribbean**
37 Haitian
126 Western Caribbean Creole
1.5

**Central America**
119 Nahuatl
2.0

**South America**
1 Latin American
57 Guarani
70 Quechua
104 Aymara
2.2

**LATIN AMERICA & CARIBBEAN** 2.1

**Micronesia** 2.1
**Polynesia** 1.7
**Melanesia** 3.3

**Western Africa**
18 Ibo
21 Yoruba
71 Ibibio
83 Tiv
94 Ewe
95 Twi
107 Mossi
139 Anaang
160 Fante
5.2

**Northern Africa**
28 Arabic
1.8

**Middle Africa**
32 Kongo
82 Kituba
88 Luba
90 Umbundu
93 Mbundu
102 Lingala
105 Fiote
110 Luba
118 Mongo
127 Nande
130 Ekonda
131 Songe
132 Zande
134 Yombe
149 Luvale
150 Chokwe
154 Tetela
158 Central Kongo
6.2

**AFRICA** 3.7

**GLOBE** 1.3

**Southern Africa**
33 Zulu
45 Xhosa
47 Afrikaans
78 Sotho
91 Pedi
117 Tswana
136 Swazi
3.0

**Western Asia**
51 Armenian
99 Georgian
0.7

**Eastern Africa**
17 Amharic
40 Rwandese
52 Burundian
55 Oromo
59 Kikuyu
67 Chewa
68 Luo
74 Tigrai
80 Ankole
84 Merina
92 Kamba
101 Shangaan
106 Ganda
108 Bemba
109 Luyia
122 Shona
123 Gusii
129 Betsileo
135 Teso
137 Wallamo
138 Meru
141 Fipa
142 Haya
145 Soga
147 Tumbuka
148 Zezuru
153 Nyoro-Toro
155 Manganja
156 Alur
157 Karanga
159 Ngoni
161 Lomwe
3.6

**ASIA** 2.7

**Eastern Asia**
6 Mandarin
14 Korean
25 Wu
62 Minnan
63 Japanese
79 Jinyu
133 Gan
140 Min-dong
4.0

**South-eastern Asia**
13 Tagalog
19 Cebuano
36 Ilocano
44 Hiligaynon
49 Javanese
56 Vietnamese
75 Samarenyo
77 Legaspi
86 Indonesian
96 Toba Batak
103 Pampangan
120 Pangasinan
2.6

**South-central Asia**
20 Malayalam
24 Tamil
31 Telugu
76 Marathi
100 Bengali
112 Lahnda
116 Goanese
124 Kannada
144 Hindi
146 Majhi
152 Gujaraati
2.8

**OCEANIA** 1.7

**Australia-New Zealand**
35 Australian
1.4

**ANTARCTICA** 18.9

**Antarctica** 18.9

**Key**

**Christians in majority**
Over 90%
80–90%
60–80%
50–60%

**Christians in minority**
10–50%
Under 10%

**Global Map 1. Christians, Christian growth rates, and million-Christian languages, AD 1900–AD 2000, in 7 continents and 20 regions.**

Colors = Christians (affiliated church members of all varieties) as per cent of country's population in AD 2000.
Names = languages each with over 1 million native (mother-tongue) speakers who in AD 2000 are affiliated church members worldwide, ranked 1–163 in order of global size; each listed above only once, in the region with its epicenter.
Boxes = groupings of languages in size order, in each of the 27 United Nations' continents and regions (4 having none).
Number under each geopolitical window = 100-year Christian growth rate, % per year, AD 1900–AD 2000.
Source of data: WCT Table 7-2 & Part 12, WCE Part 9 "Linguametrics", Table 9-13, columns 5 and 8.

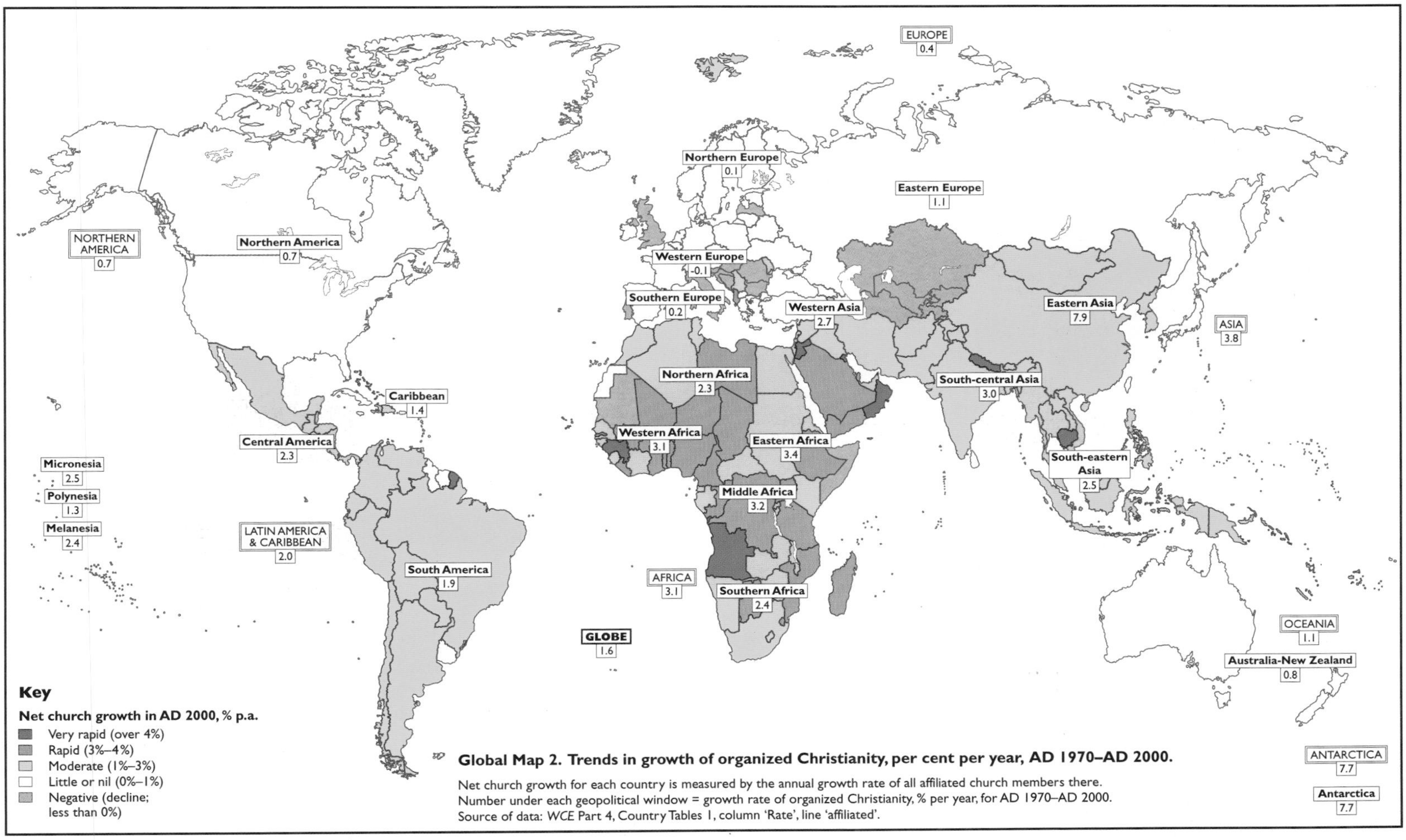

---

**EUROPE** 0.4

**Northern Europe** 0.1
**Eastern Europe** 1.1
**Western Europe** -0.1
**Southern Europe** 0.2
**Western Asia** 2.7
**Eastern Asia** 7.9
**ASIA** 3.8

**NORTHERN AMERICA** 0.7
**Northern America** 0.7

**Northern Africa** 2.3
**South-central Asia** 3.0

**Caribbean** 1.4
**Central America** 2.3

**Western Africa** 3.1
**Eastern Africa** 3.4
**South-eastern Asia** 2.5

**Micronesia** 2.5
**Polynesia** 1.3
**Melanesia** 2.4

**Middle Africa** 3.2

**LATIN AMERICA & CARIBBEAN** 2.0

**South America** 1.9

**AFRICA** 3.1
**Southern Africa** 2.4

**GLOBE** 1.6

**OCEANIA**
**Australia-New Zealand** 0.8

**ANTARCTICA** 7.7
**Antarctica** 7.7

**Key**

**Net church growth in AD 2000, % p.a.**
Very rapid (over 4%)
Rapid (3%–4%)
Moderate (1%–3%)
Little or nil (0%–1%)
Negative (decline; less than 0%)

**Global Map 2. Trends in growth of organized Christianity, per cent per year, AD 1970–AD 2000.**

Net church growth for each country is measured by the annual growth rate of all affiliated church members there.
Number under each geopolitical window = growth rate of organized Christianity, % per year, for AD 1970–AD 2000.
Source of data: WCE Part 4, Country Tables 1, column 'Rate', line 'affiliated'.

**Key**

World A = the unevangelized world in 1900
(countries with evangelized persons E<50%)

World B = the evangelized non-Christian world in 1900
(countries with E>=50% but Christians AC<60%)

World C = the Christian world in 1900
(countries with AC>=60%)

**Global Map 3. Trends in evangelization and christianization in Worlds A, B, and C countries, AD 1900.**

Number under each geopolitical window = growth rate of evangelized persons, % per year, throughout the century AD 1800–AD 1900.
Source of data: *WCE* Country Tables 1, column 'AD 1900'.

**Key**

World A = the unevangelized world in 2000
(countries with evangelized persons E<50%)

World B = the evangelized non-Christian world in 2000
(countries with E>=50% but Christians AC<60%)

World C = the Christian world in 2000
(countries with AC>=60%)

**Global Map 4. Trends in evangelization and christianization in Worlds A, B, and C countries, AD 2000.**

The 10/40 Window is a popularized version of World A not amenable to statistical data-gathering or analysis.
Number under each geopolitical window = growth rate of evangelized persons, % per year, throughout the century AD 1900–AD 2000.
Source of data: *WCE* Country Tables 1, column 'AD 2000'.

**Global Map 5. Trends in evangelization and christianization in Worlds A, B, and C countries, AD 2025.**

Number under each geopolitical window = growth rate of evangelized persons, % per year, throughout AD 2000–AD 2025.
Source of data: WCE Country Tables 1, column 'AD 2025', based on the assumption that current trends continue.

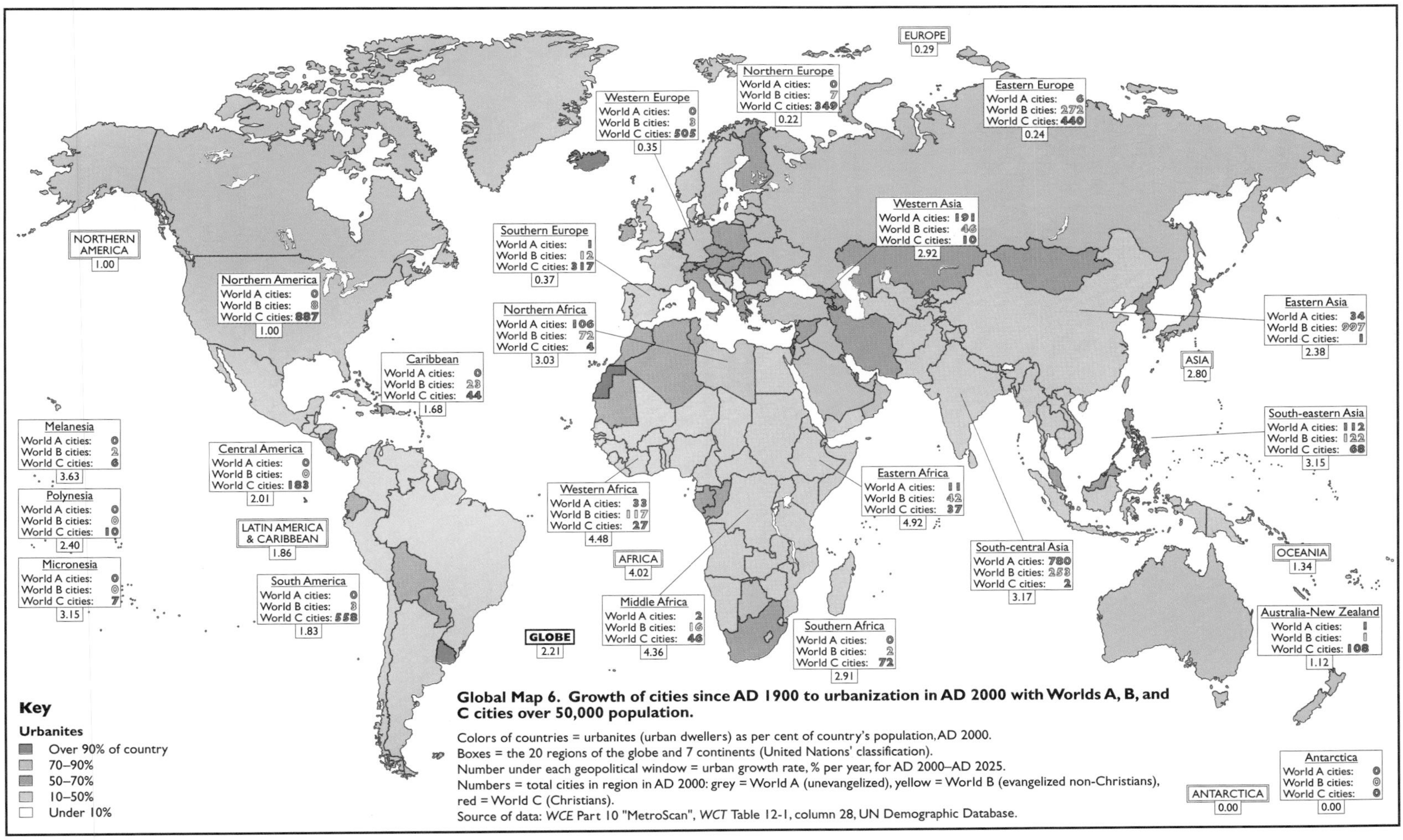

**Key**

- World A = the unevangelized world in 2025 (countries with evangelized persons E<50%)
- World B = the evangelized non-Christian world in 2025 (countries with E>=50% but Christians AC<60%)
- World C = the Christian world in 2025 (countries with AC>=60%)

Map 5 labels:
EUROPE -0.1; Northern Europe 0.0; Eastern Europe -0.2; Western Europe 0.0; Southern Europe -0.3; Western Asia 2.2; Eastern Asia 0.9; ASIA 1.3; NORTHERN AMERICA 0.6; Northern America 0.6; Caribbean 0.9; Central America 1.3; Northern Africa 1.8; South-central Asia 1.7; Micronesia 2.3; Polynesia 1.5; Melanesia 1.8; Western Africa 2.5; Eastern Africa 2.3; South-eastern Asia 1.5; Middle Africa 2.7; LATIN AMERICA & CARIBBEAN 1.2; South America 1.2; AFRICA 2.2; Southern Africa 0.7; GLOBE 1.2; OCEANIA 1.1; Australia-New Zealand 0.8; ANTARCTICA 3.3; Antarctica 3.3

**Global Map 6. Growth of cities since AD 1900 to urbanization in AD 2000 with Worlds A, B, and C cities over 50,000 population.**

Colors of countries = urbanites (urban dwellers) as per cent of country's population, AD 2000.
Boxes = the 20 regions of the globe and 7 continents (United Nations' classification).
Number under each geopolitical window = urban growth rate, % per year, for AD 2000–AD 2025.
Numbers = total cities in region in AD 2000: grey = World A (unevangelized), yellow = World B (evangelized non-Christians), red = World C (Christians).
Source of data: WCE Part 10 "MetroScan", WCT Table 12-1, column 28, UN Demographic Database.

**Key**

**Urbanites**
- Over 90% of country
- 70–90%
- 50–70%
- 10–50%
- Under 10%

Map 6 labels:
EUROPE 0.29; Northern Europe — World A cities: 0, World B cities: 7, World C cities: 349 — 0.22; Western Europe — World A cities: 1, World B cities: 3, World C cities: 505 — 0.35; Eastern Europe — World A cities: 6, World B cities: 272, World C cities: 440 — 0.24; Western Asia — World A cities: 191, World B cities: 46, World C cities: 10 — 2.92; Eastern Asia — World A cities: 34, World B cities: 997, World C cities: 1 — 2.38; ASIA 2.80; Southern Europe — World A cities: 1, World B cities: 12, World C cities: 317 — 0.37; Northern Africa — World A cities: 106, World B cities: 72, World C cities: 4 — 3.03; NORTHERN AMERICA 1.00; Northern America — World A cities: 0, World B cities: 8, World C cities: 887 — 1.00; Caribbean — World A cities: 0, World B cities: 23, World C cities: 44 — 1.68; Central America — World A cities: 0, World B cities: 0, World C cities: 183 — 2.01; Western Africa — World A cities: 33, World B cities: 117, World C cities: 27 — 4.48; Eastern Africa — World A cities: 11, World B cities: 42, World C cities: 37 — 4.92; South-central Asia — World A cities: 780, World B cities: 283, World C cities: 2 — 3.17; South-eastern Asia — World A cities: 112, World B cities: 122, World C cities: 68 — 3.15; Melanesia — World A cities: 0, World B cities: 2, World C cities: 6 — 3.63; Polynesia — World A cities: 0, World B cities: 0, World C cities: 10 — 2.40; Micronesia — World A cities: 0, World B cities: 0, World C cities: 7 — 3.15; LATIN AMERICA & CARIBBEAN 1.86; South America — World A cities: 0, World B cities: 3, World C cities: 558 — 1.83; AFRICA 4.02; Middle Africa — World A cities: 2, World B cities: 16, World C cities: 48 — 4.36; Southern Africa — World A cities: 0, World B cities: 2, World C cities: 72 — 2.91; GLOBE 2.21; OCEANIA 1.34; Australia-New Zealand — World A cities: 1, World B cities: 1, World C cities: 108 — 1.12; ANTARCTICA — World A cities: 0, World B cities: 0, World C cities: 0 — 0.00; Antarctica — World A cities: 0, World B cities: 0, World C cities: 0 — 0.00

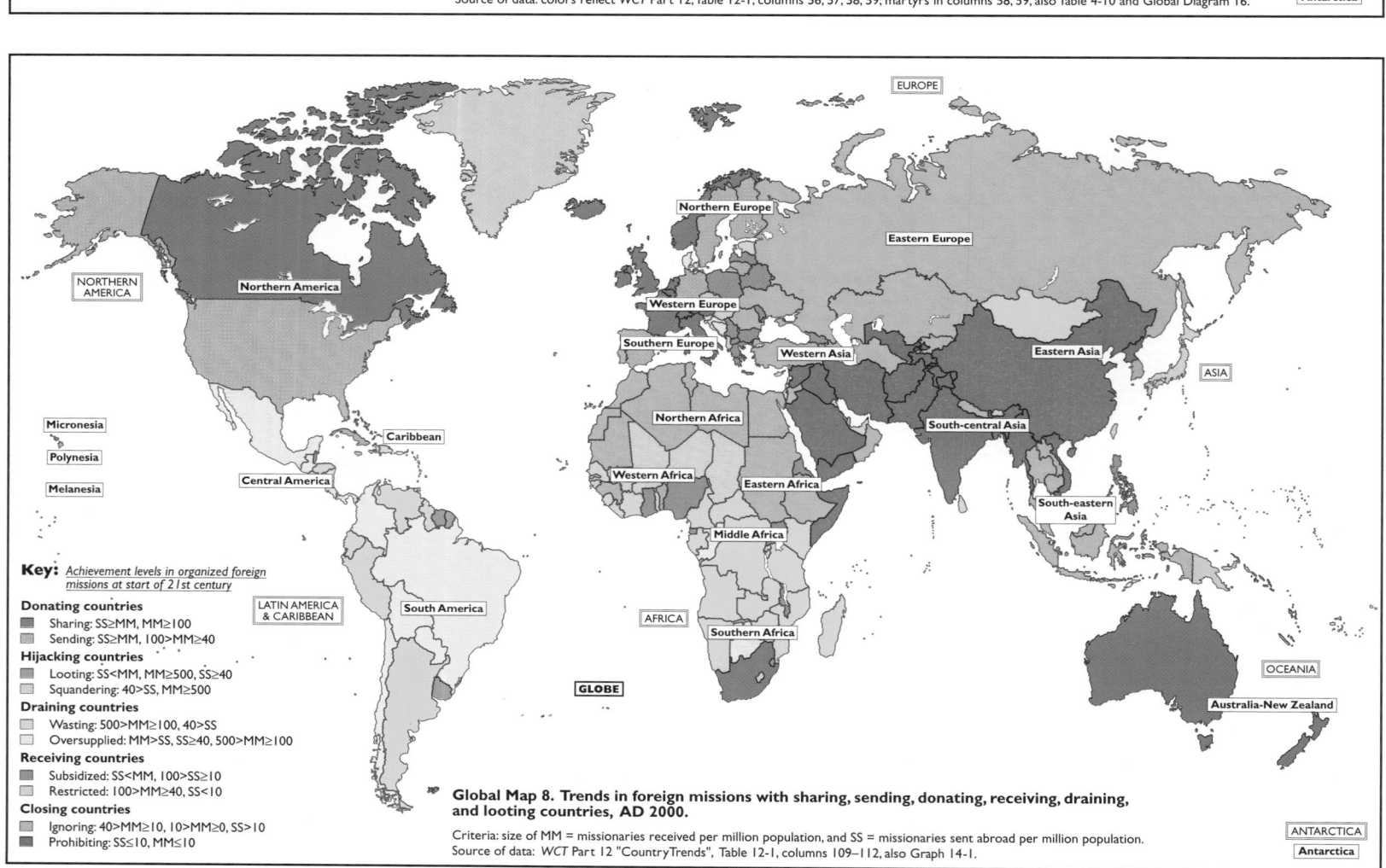

**Key:** _Achievement levels in religious liberty at start of 21st century_

**Religious liberty achieved**
- Very safe (CSI>85%)
- Safe (CSI 80–85%)
- Marginally safe (CSI 70–79%)

**Religious persecution present**
- Some obstruction, harassment (CSI 60–69%)
- Some persecution (CSI 50–59%)

**Martyrdom situations predominant**
- Dangerous (CSI 40–49%)
- Highly dangerous (CSI under 40%)

**Global Map 7. Trends in religious liberty, safety or persecution, and martyrdom in 150 countries, AD 1900–AD 2000.**

Color depicts the level of CSI (Christian Safety Index); additional data depicts extremes of danger in martyrdoms.
+ = major 20th-century martyrdom situation with over 100,000 Christians killed.
O = 20th-century martyrdom situation with 10,000–100,000 Christians killed.
Source of data: colors reflect WCT Part 12, Table 12-1, columns 56, 57, 58, 59; martyrs in columns 58, 59, also Table 4-10 and Global Diagram 16.

**Key:** _Achievement levels in organized foreign missions at start of 21st century_

**Donating countries**
- Sharing: SS≥MM, MM≥100
- Sending: SS≥MM, 100>MM≥40

**Hijacking countries**
- Looting: SS<MM, MM≥500, SS≥40
- Squandering: 40>SS, MM≥500

**Draining countries**
- Wasting: 500>MM≥100, 40>SS
- Oversupplied: MM>SS, SS≥40, 500>MM≥100

**Receiving countries**
- Subsidized: SS<MM, 100>SS≥10
- Restricted: 100>MM≥40, SS<10

**Closing countries**
- Ignoring: 40>MM≥10, 10>MM≥0, SS>10
- Prohibiting: SS≤10, MM≤10

**Global Map 8. Trends in foreign missions with sharing, sending, donating, receiving, draining, and looting countries, AD 2000.**

Criteria: size of MM = missionaries received per million population, and SS = missionaries sent abroad per million population.
Source of data: WCT Part 12 "CountryTrends", Table 12-1, columns 109–112, also Graph 14-1.

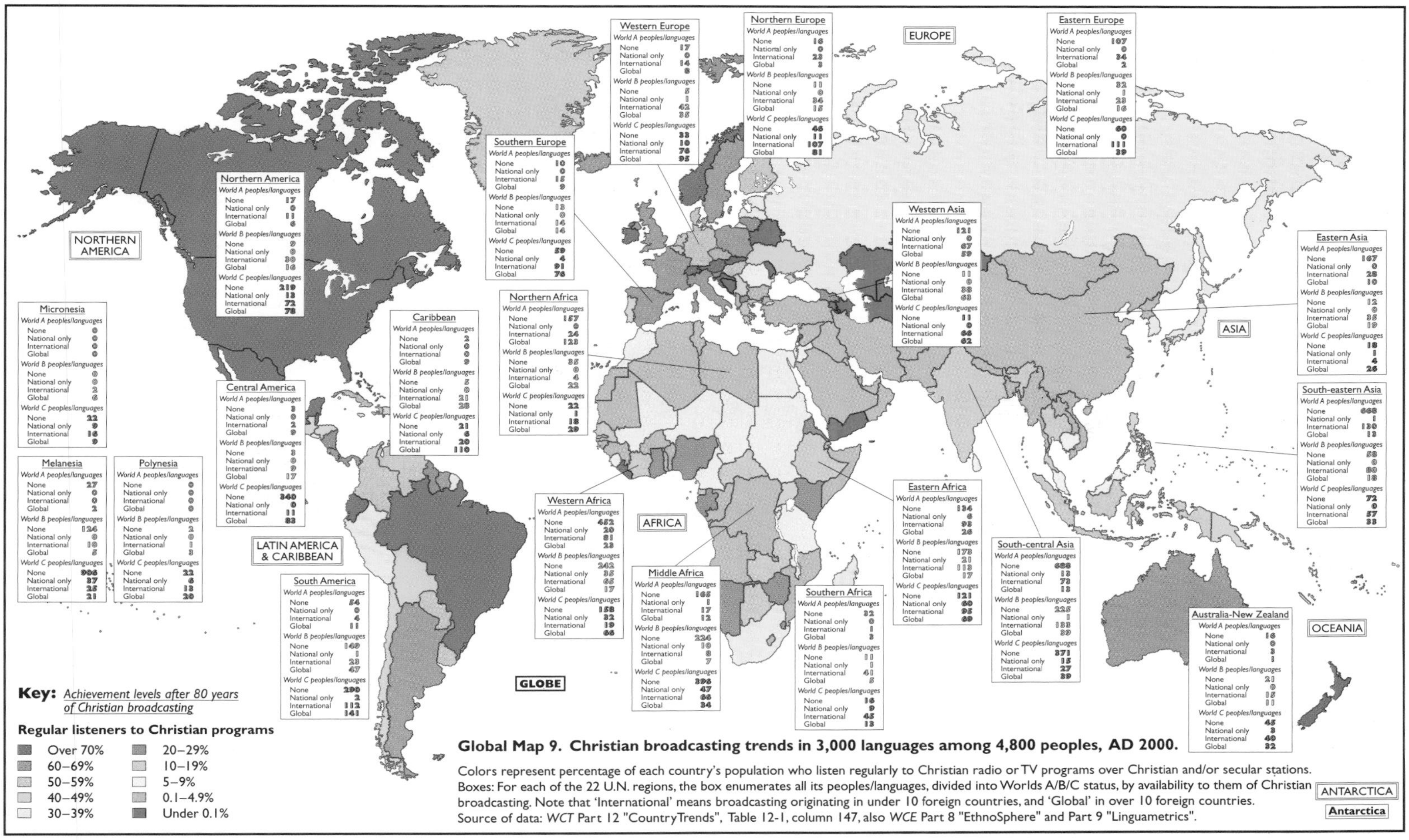

**Key:** *Achievement levels after 80 years of Christian broadcasting*

**Regular listeners to Christian programs**

| | |
|---|---|
| Over 70% | 20–29% |
| 60–69% | 10–19% |
| 50–59% | 5–9% |
| 40–49% | 0.1–4.9% |
| 30–39% | Under 0.1% |

**Global Map 9. Christian broadcasting trends in 3,000 languages among 4,800 peoples, AD 2000.**

Colors represent percentage of each country's population who listen regularly to Christian radio or TV programs over Christian and/or secular stations. Boxes: For each of the 22 U.N. regions, the box enumerates all its peoples/languages, divided into Worlds A/B/C status, by availability to them of Christian broadcasting. Note that 'International' means broadcasting originating in under 10 foreign countries, and 'Global' in over 10 foreign countries. Source of data: *WCT* Part 12 "CountryTrends", Table 12-1, column 147, also *WCE* Part 8 "EthnoSphere" and Part 9 "Linguametrics".

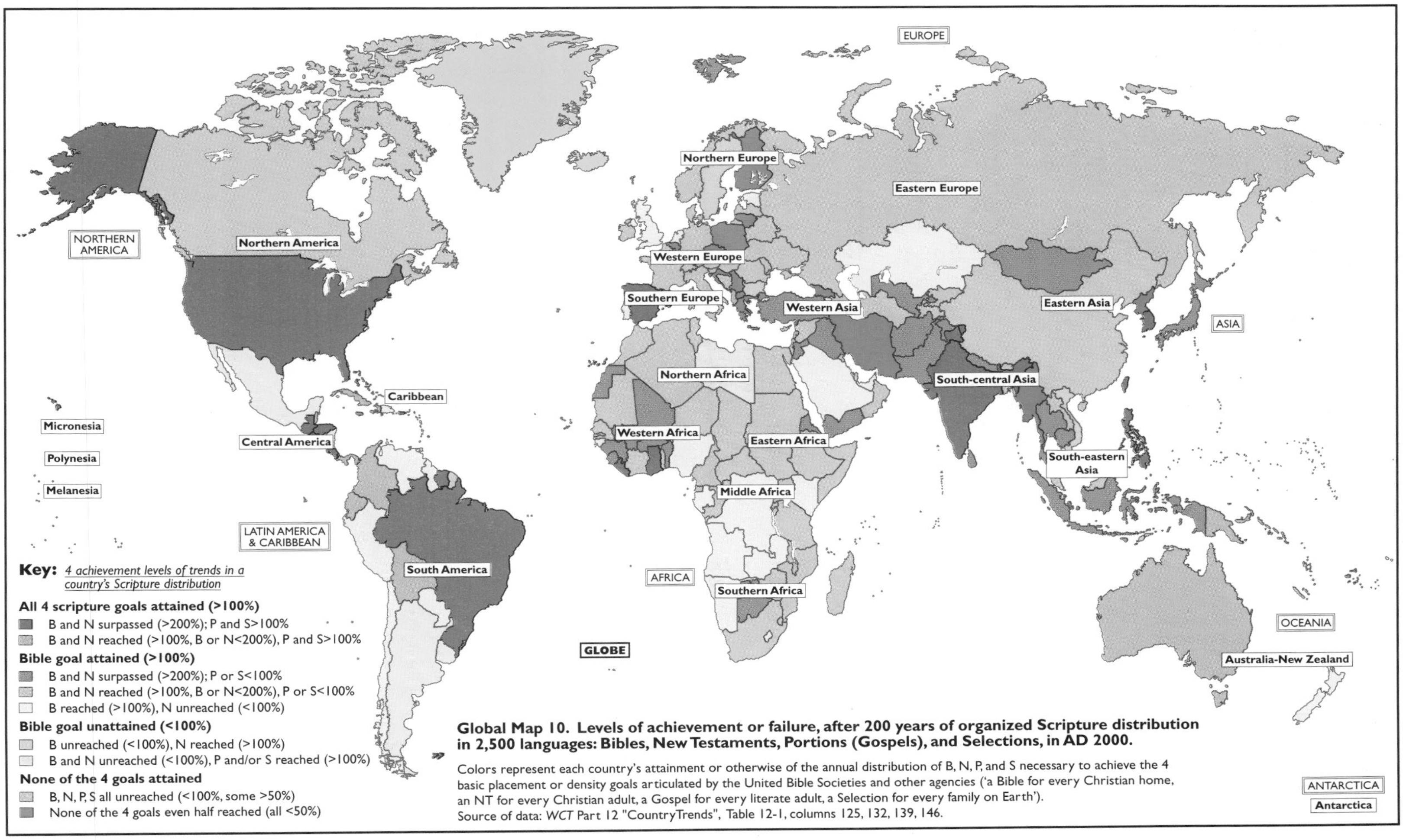

**Key:** *4 achievement levels of trends in a country's Scripture distribution*

**All 4 scripture goals attained (>100%)**
- B and N surpassed (>200%); P and S>100%
- B and N reached (>100%, B or N<200%), P and S>100%

**Bible goal attained (>100%)**
- B and N surpassed (>200%); P or S<100%
- B and N reached (>100%, B or N<200%), P or S<100%
- B reached (>100%), N unreached (<100%)

**Bible goal unattained (<100%)**
- B unreached (<100%), N reached (>100%)
- B and N unreached (<100%), P and/or S reached (>100%)

**None of the 4 goals attained**
- B, N, P, S all unreached (<100%, some >50%)
- None of the 4 goals even half reached (all <50%)

**Global Map 10. Levels of achievement or failure, after 200 years of organized Scripture distribution in 2,500 languages: Bibles, New Testaments, Portions (Gospels), and Selections, in AD 2000.**

Colors represent each country's attainment or otherwise of the annual distribution of B, N, P, and S necessary to achieve the 4 basic placement or density goals articulated by the United Bible Societies and other agencies ('a Bible for every Christian home, an NT for every Christian adult, a Gospel for every literate adult, a Selection for every family on Earth'). Source of data: *WCT* Part 12 "CountryTrends", Table 12-1, columns 125, 132, 139, 146.

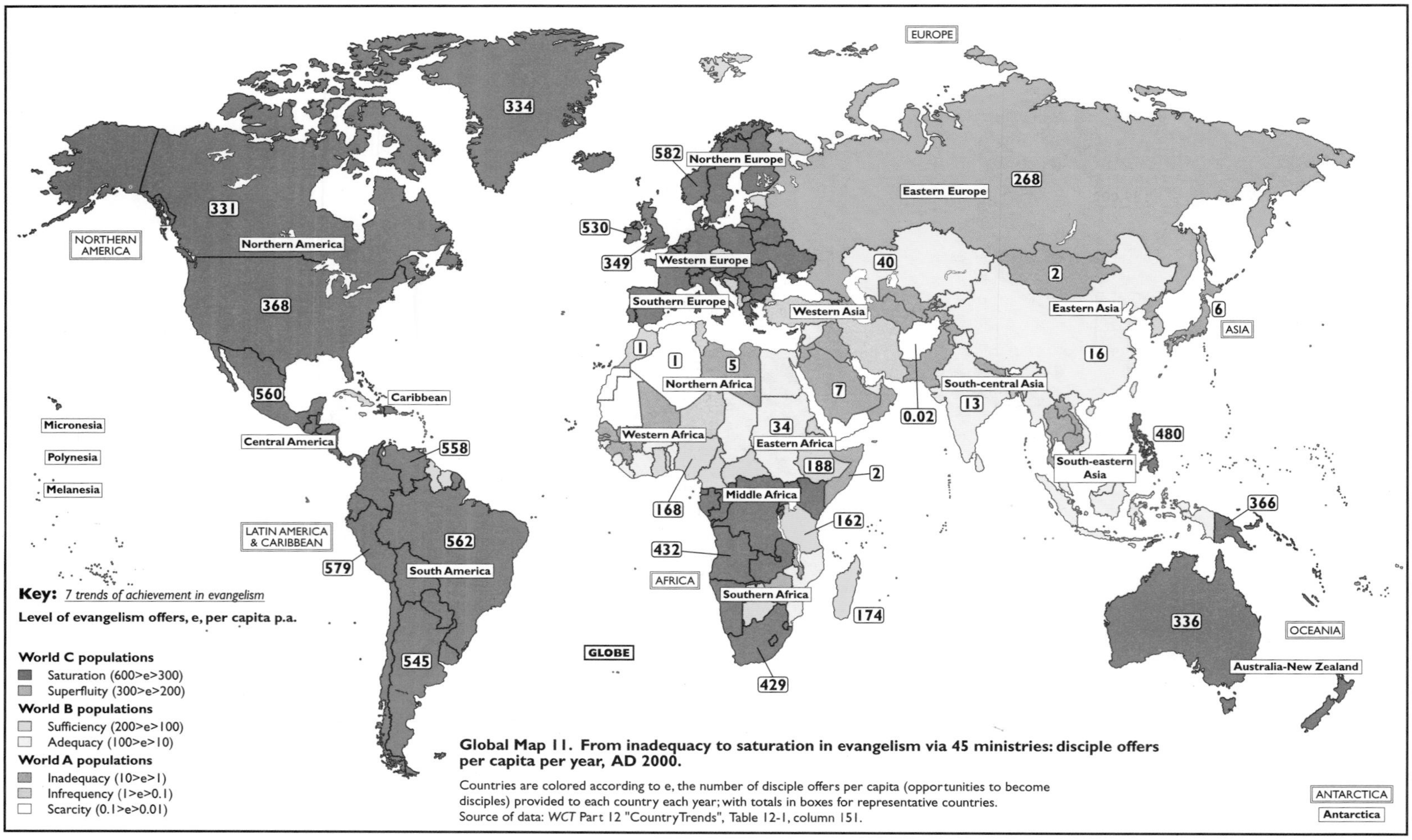

EUROPE

334

582  Northern Europe

268  Eastern Europe

530

331

349  Western Europe

NORTHERN
AMERICA

Northern America

40

2  Eastern Asia

6

ASIA

368

Southern Europe

Western Asia

South-central Asia

560

1

1

5

0.02

13

16

480

Caribbean

Northern Africa

7

Central America

558

34  Eastern Africa

South-eastern
Asia

Micronesia

Western Africa

188

2

366

Polynesia

168

Middle Africa

162

Melanesia

LATIN AMERICA
& CARIBBEAN

562

432

579

South America

174

336

545

**Key:** _7 trends of achievement in evangelism_

Southern Africa

429

GLOBE

AFRICA

OCEANIA

Australia-New Zealand

Level of evangelism offers, e, per capita p.a.

**World C populations**
- ⬛ Saturation (600>e>300)
- ⬛ Superfluity (300>e>200)

**World B populations**
- ⬜ Sufficiency (200>e>100)
- ⬜ Adequacy (100>e>10)

**World A populations**
- ⬛ Inadequacy (10>e>1)
- ⬜ Infrequency (1>e>0.1)
- ⬜ Scarcity (0.1>e>0.01)

**Global Map 11. From inadequacy to saturation in evangelism via 45 ministries: disciple offers
per capita per year, AD 2000.**

Countries are colored according to e, the number of disciple offers per capita (opportunities to become
disciples) provided to each country each year; with totals in boxes for representative countries.
Source of data: _WCT_ Part 12 "CountryTrends", Table 12-1, column 151.

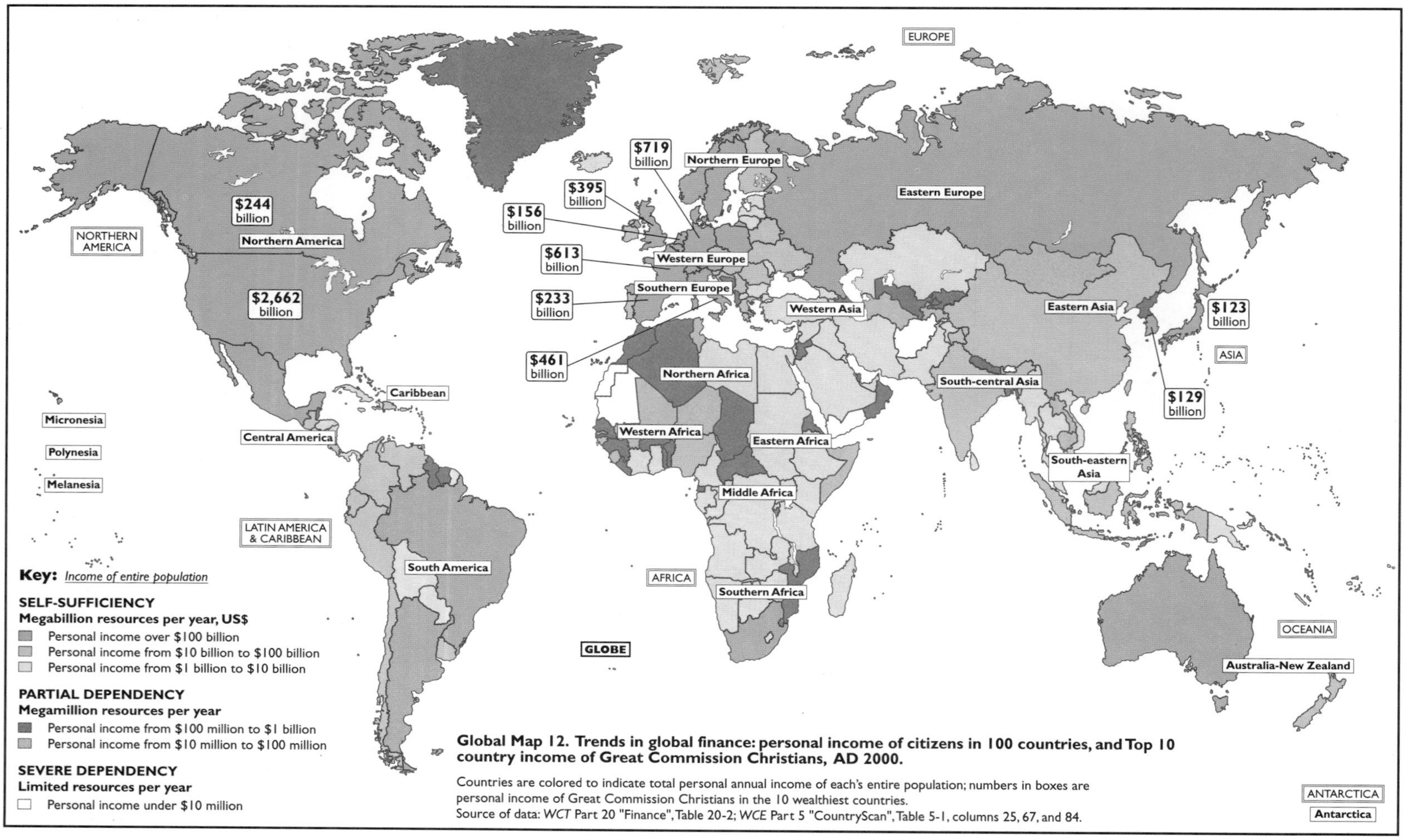

ANTARCTICA

Antarctica

---

EUROPE

$719
billion  Northern Europe

Eastern Europe

$395
billion

$156
billion

$613
billion  Western Europe

NORTHERN
AMERICA

Northern America

$233
billion  Southern Europe

Western Asia

Eastern Asia

$123
billion

$2,662
billion

$461
billion

ASIA

$129
billion

Caribbean

Northern Africa

South-central Asia

Micronesia

Central America

Western Africa

Eastern Africa

Polynesia

South-eastern
Asia

Melanesia

Middle Africa

LATIN AMERICA
& CARIBBEAN

South America

AFRICA

GLOBE

Southern Africa

OCEANIA

Australia-New Zealand

**Key:** _Income of entire population_

**SELF-SUFFICIENCY**
Megabillion resources per year, US$
- ⬛ Personal income over $100 billion
- ⬛ Personal income from $10 billion to $100 billion
- ⬜ Personal income from $1 billion to $10 billion

**PARTIAL DEPENDENCY**
Megamillion resources per year
- ⬛ Personal income from $100 million to $1 billion
- ⬛ Personal income from $10 million to $100 million

**SEVERE DEPENDENCY**
Limited resources per year
- ⬜ Personal income under $10 million

**Global Map 12. Trends in global finance: personal income of citizens in 100 countries, and Top 10
country income of Great Commission Christians, AD 2000.**

Countries are colored to indicate total personal annual income of each's entire population; numbers in boxes are
personal income of Great Commission Christians in the 10 wealthiest countries.
Source of data: _WCT_ Part 20 "Finance", Table 20-2; _WCE_ Part 5 "CountryScan", Table 5-1, columns 25, 67, and 84.

ANTARCTICA

Antarctica

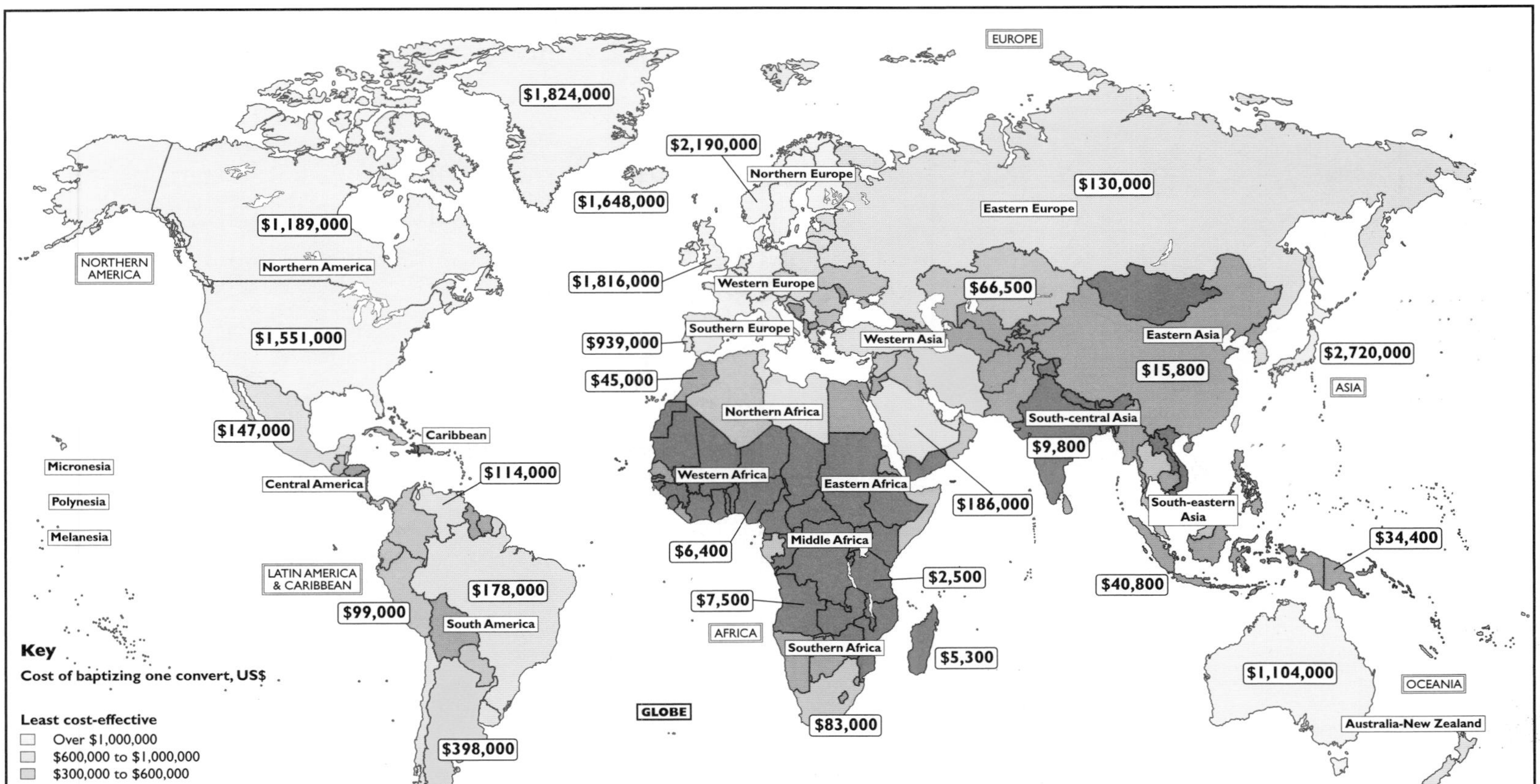

## Global Map 13

$1,824,000

EUROPE

$2,190,000

Northern Europe

$130,000

Eastern Europe

$1,648,000

NORTHERN
AMERICA

Northern America

$1,189,000

$1,816,000   Western Europe

$66,500

Eastern Asia

$1,551,000

$939,000   Southern Europe     Western Asia

$45,000

ASIA

$2,720,000

$15,800

$147,000

Caribbean

Northern Africa

South-central Asia

Micronesia

Central America

$114,000

$9,800

Polynesia

$186,000

South-eastern
Asia

Melanesia

Western Africa     Eastern Africa

$34,400

LATIN AMERICA
& CARIBBEAN

Middle Africa

$6,400

$40,800

$99,000

$178,000

$7,500

$2,500

South America

AFRICA

$83,000

Southern Africa

$5,300

GLOBE

$1,104,000

OCEANIA

$398,000

Australia-New Zealand

### Key

**Cost of baptizing one convert, US$**

**Least cost-effective**
- ☐ Over $1,000,000
- ☐ $600,000 to $1,000,000
- ☐ $300,000 to $600,000

**More cost-effective**
- ☐ $100,000 to $300,000
- ☐ $50,000 to $100,000
- ☐ $10,000 to $50,000

**Most cost-effective**
- ☐ Under $10,000

**Global Map 13. Cost-effectiveness of world mission: cost of baptizing each new convert, AD 2000.**

Colors indicate the relative expensiveness of baptism when the total cost and expenses of the Christian community and outreach in a country are assessed.

Boxes give cost for each of 27 typical countries. As well as time contrasts, trends can provide geographic contrast: consider an India-based foreign mission attempting to win converts in Japan (280 times as expensive as in India).

Source of data: WCT Part 12 "CountryTrends", Table 12-1, column 100.

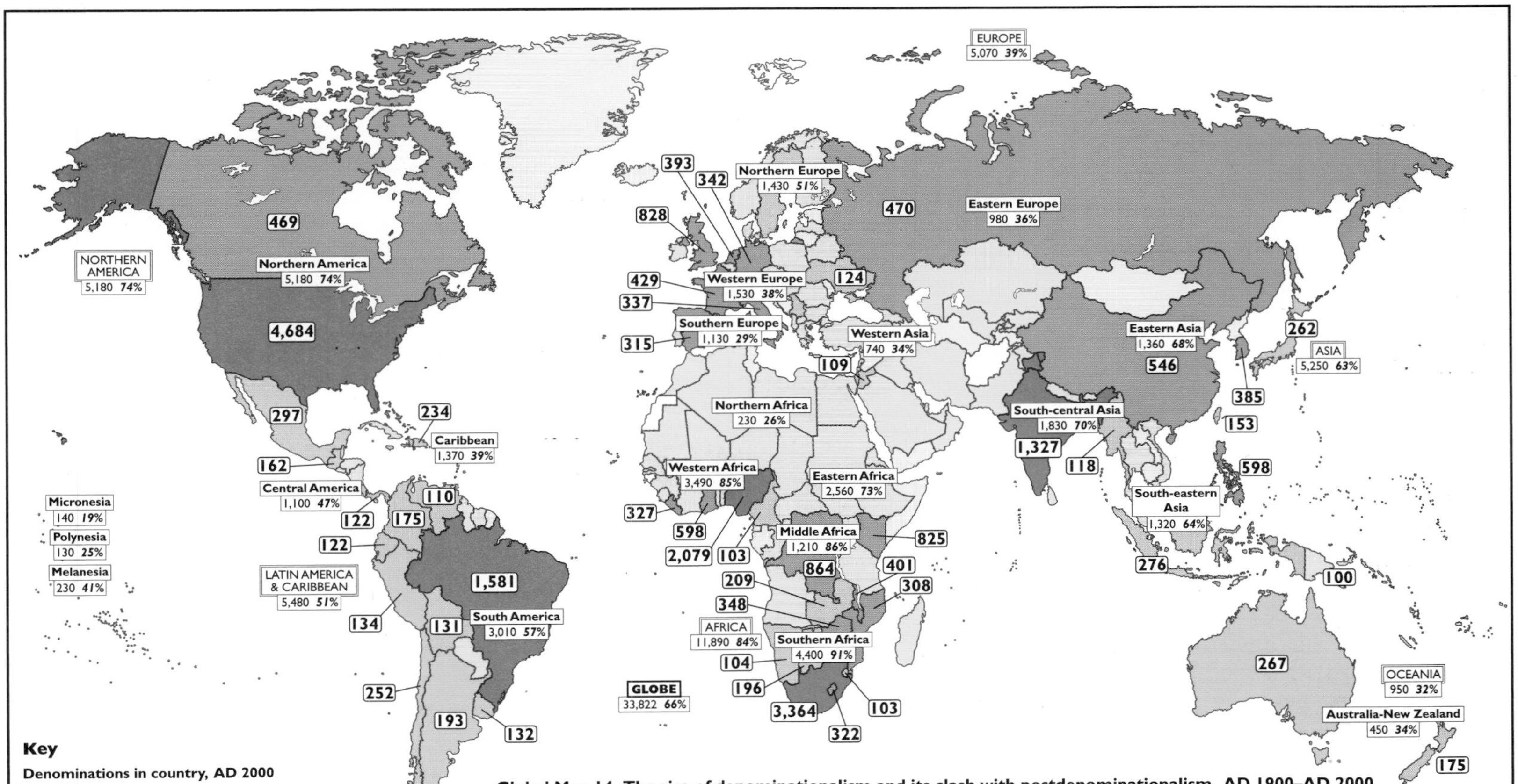

ANTARCTICA

Antarctica

## Global Map 14

EUROPE
5,070 39%

393   342   Northern Europe
1,430 51%

828   470   Eastern Europe
980 36%

469

NORTHERN
AMERICA
5,180 74%

Northern America
5,180 74%

429   Western Europe
1,530 38%

124

4,684

337   Southern Europe
1,130 29%

Western Asia
740 34%

Eastern Asia
1,360 68%

262

ASIA
5,250 63%

315   109   546   385

297   234   153

162   Caribbean
1,370 39%

Northern Africa
230 26%

South-central Asia
1,830 70%

Micronesia
140 19%

Central America
1,100 47%

110   1,327   118   598

Polynesia
130 25%

122   175   Western Africa
3,490 85%

Eastern Africa
2,560 73%

South-eastern
Asia
1,320 64%

Melanesia
230 41%

122   327   598   Middle Africa
1,210 86%

825   276   100

LATIN AMERICA
& CARIBBEAN
5,480 51%

2,079   103   209   864   401

134   131   South America
3,010 57%

348   308

1,581   AFRICA
11,890 84%

Southern Africa
4,400 91%

252   193   132   GLOBE
33,822 66%

104

267   OCEANIA
950 32%

196

3,364   103   Australia-New Zealand
450 34%

322

175

### Key

**Denominations in country, AD 2000**
- ■ 1,000 or over
- ■ 300 to 1,000
- ■ 100 to 300
- ☐ 30 to 100
- ☐ 10 to 30
- ☐ Under 10

**Global Map 14. The rise of denominationalism and its clash with postdenominationalism, AD 1900–AD 2000.**

Every Christian confession and denomination regards itself as in some sense a renewal of apostolic Christianity with the duty to multiply globally.

Numbers in country boxes = total denominations in every country with 100 or more.

Under each geopolitical window are 2 numbers: total denominations, and (in bold italics) % of them which are postdenominationalist (Independent rejecting denominationalism).

Source of data: WCT Part 12 "CountryTrends", Table 12-1, column 80; WCE Part 4, Country Tables 2 (final 6 lines); also WCT Global Diagram 17.

ANTARCTICA
2 0%

Antarctica
2 0%

## Global Map 15

EUROPE
5.3 0.9

Northern Europe
3.9 1.0

Eastern Europe
5.3 0.8

NORTHERN
AMERICA
4.1 1.3

Northern America
4.1 1.3

Western Europe
5.5 1.2

Southern Europe
9.1 0.7

Western Asia
10.3 2.7

Eastern Asia
15.3 1.9

ASIA
9.0 1.9

2. USA
75,156,000

9. Mexico
13,050,000

Caribbean
6.1 1.5

Northern Africa
9.3 3.0

3. China
54,275,000

South-central Asia
9.7 2.1

5. India
33,530,000

7. Philippines
20,050,000

Central America
8.4 1.8

Western Africa
7.6 2.4

Eastern Africa
8.8 2.7

Micronesia
8.2 3.0

10. Colombia
12,585,000

South-eastern
Asia
5.3 1.7

Polynesia
7.8 2.1

4. Nigeria
35,885,000

Middle Africa
5.1 3.2

Melanesia
7.1 2.4

1. Brazil
79,950,000

8. Congo–Zaire
17,750,000

LATIN AMERICA
& CARIBBEAN
8.4 1.4

South America
8.5 1.4

AFRICA
6.6 2.4

Southern Africa
5.8 0.9

OCEANIA
10.1 1.7

GLOBE
6.6 2.4

6. South Africa
21,200,000

Australia–New Zealand
12.7 1.4

### Key

**Renewal members as % of country's population, AD 2000**

- Members exceed 20%
- Members number from 10% to 20%
- Members number from 5% to 10%
- Members number from 2% to 5%
- Members number from 1% to 2%
- Members number under 1%
- The 10 largest countries (>10 million each)
- Countries with 5–10 million

ANTARCTICA
7.6 2.4

Antarctica
7.6 2.4

**Global Map 15. Trends in the Pentecostal/Charismatic/Neocharismatic Renewal in the Holy Spirit, AD 1970–AD 2025.**

Large red dots represent countries with the 10 largest numbers of members (over 10 million each, shown with their numbers in italics), ranked 1–10; and small red dots represent 8 countries with 5–10 million each, in AD 2000.
Though distinct ecclesiastically, the 3 Waves of the Renewal share the same pentecostal-charismatic experience in the Holy Spirit.
The 2 numbers under each geopolitical window = growth rates p. a. of the Renewal (a) from AD 1970–AD 2000, followed by (b) from AD 2000–AD 2025.
Source of data: WCT Part 12 "CountryTrends", Table 12-1, columns 77, 78, 79; WCE Part 4, Country Tables 1, column 'AD 2000'; Part 1, Tables 1–6a, 1–6b.

## Global Map 16

EUROPE
0.0

Northern Europe
0.0

Eastern Europe
0.2

NORTHERN
AMERICA
0.4

Northern America
0.4

Western Europe
-0.1

Southern Europe
-0.3

Western Asia
1.4

Eastern Asia
1.5

ASIA
1.6

Caribbean
1.0

Northern Africa
1.5

South-central Asia
1.8

Central America
1.3

Western Africa
2.3

Eastern Africa
2.4

Micronesia
2.2

South-eastern
Asia
1.6

Polynesia
1.4

Middle Africa
2.8

Melanesia
1.8

LATIN AMERICA
& CARIBBEAN
1.2

South America
1.1

AFRICA
2.3

Southern Africa
0.7

OCEANIA
1.0

GLOBE
1.1

Australia–New Zealand
0.6

### Key

**Prospects in the 21st century**

- Bright
- Fair
- Static
- Dull
- Bleak

ANTARCTICA
3.5

Antarctica
3.5

**Global Map 16. 20th-century trends and 21st-century future prospects for Christianity, for each of 7 continents and 20 regions.**

The future is here viewed from the standpoint of religious liberty, human rights, safety from harassment or persecution, surviving the murder rate, church growth, and flourishing of Christian outreach; all with the assumption that present trends continue.
Numbers under each geopolitical window = growth rate, % per year, of Christians during AD 2000–AD 2025.
Source of data: WCT Part 12 "CountryTrends", Table 12-1, columns 166, 167; also WCE Part 4 "Countries", text paragraphs 'Future trends and prospects' in each country.